CONCISE
DICTIONARY
OF
AMERICAN
BIOGRAPHY

American Council of Learned Societies

The American Council of Learned Societies, organized in 1919 for the purpose of advancing the study of the humanities and of the humanistic aspects of the social sciences, is a nonprofit federation comprising fifty-one national scholarly groups. The Council represents the humanities in the United States in the International Union of Academies, provides fellowships and grants-in-aid, supports research-and-planning conferences and symposia, and sponsors special projects and scholarly publications.

MEMBER ORGANIZATIONS

AMERICAN PHILOSOPHICAL SOCIETY, 1743

AMERICAN ACADEMY OF ARTS AND SCIENCES, 1780

AMERICAN ANTIQUARIAN SOCIETY, 1812

AMERICAN ORIENTAL SOCIETY, 1842

AMERICAN NUMISMATIC SOCIETY, 1858

AMERICAN PHILOLOGICAL ASSOCIATION, 1869

ARCHAEOLOGICAL INSTITUTE OF AMERICA, 1879

SOCIETY OF BIBLICAL LITERATURE, 1880

MODERN LANGUAGE ASSOCIATION OF AMERICA, 1883

AMERICAN HISTORICAL ASSOCIATION, 1884

AMERICAN ECONOMIC ASSOCIATION, 1885

AMERICAN FOLKLORE SOCIETY, 1888

AMERICAN DIALECT SOCIETY, 1889

AMERICAN PSYCHOLOGICAL ASSOCIATION, 1892

ASSOCIATION OF AMERICAN LAW SCHOOLS, 1900

AMERICAN PHILOSOPHICAL ASSOCIATION, 1901

AMERICAN ANTHROPOLOGICAL ASSOCIATION, 1902

AMERICAN POLITICAL SCIENCE ASSOCIATION, 1903

BIBLIOGRAPHICAL SOCIETY OF AMERICA, 1904

ASSOCIATION OF AMERICAN GEOGRAPHERS, 1904

HISPANIC SOCIETY OF AMERICA, 1904

AMERICAN SOCIOLOGICAL ASSOCIATION, 1905

AMERICAN SOCIETY OF INTERNATIONAL LAW, 1906

ORGANIZATION OF AMERICAN HISTORIANS, 1907

AMERICAN ACADEMY OF RELIGION, 1909

COLLEGE ART ASSOCIATION, 1912

HISTORY OF SCIENCE SOCIETY, 1924

LINGUISTIC SOCIETY OF AMERICA, 1924

MEDIEVAL ACADEMY OF AMERICA, 1925

AMERICAN MUSICOLOGICAL SOCIETY, 1934

SOCIETY OF ARCHITECTURAL HISTORIANS, 1940

ECONOMIC HISTORY ASSOCIATION, 1940

ASSOCIATION FOR ASIAN STUDIES, 1941

AMERICAN SOCIETY FOR AESTHETICS, 1942

AMERICAN ASSOCIATION FOR THE ADVANCEMENT OF SLAVIC STUDIES, 1948

AMERICAN STUDIES ASSOCIATION, 1950

METAPHYSICAL SOCIETY OF AMERICA, 1950

NORTH AMERICAN CONFERENCE ON BRITISH STUDIES, 1950

RENAISSANCE SOCIETY OF AMERICA, 1954

SOCIETY FOR ETHNOMUSICOLOGY, 1955

AMERICAN SOCIETY FOR LEGAL HISTORY, 1956

AMERICAN SOCIETY FOR THEATRE RESEARCH, 1956

AFRICAN STUDIES ASSOCIATION, 1957

SOCIETY FOR THE HISTORY OF TECHNOLOGY, 1958

SOCIETY FOR CINEMA STUDIES, 1959

AMERICAN COMPARATIVE LITERATURE ASSOCIATION, 1960

MIDDLE EAST STUDIES ASSOCIATION OF NORTH AMERICA, 1966

LATIN AMERICAN STUDIES ASSOCIATION, 1966

AMERICAN SOCIETY FOR EIGHTEENTH-CENTURY STUDIES, 1969

ASSOCIATION FOR JEWISH STUDIES, 1969

SIXTEENTH CENTURY STUDIES CONFERENCE, 1970

CONCISE
DICTIONARY
OF
AMERICAN
BIOGRAPHY

FOURTH EDITION
COMPLETE TO 1970

CHARLES SCRIBNER'S SONS
NEW YORK

COLLIER MACMILLAN CANADA
TORONTO

MAXWELL MACMILLAN INTERNATIONAL
NEW YORK   OXFORD   SINGAPORE   SYDNEY

Copyright © 1964, 1977, 1980, 1990 Charles Scribner's Sons

Library of Congress Cataloging in Publication Data

Concise Dictionary of American biography.—4th ed. complete to 1970.
    p.   cm.
    "American Council of Learned Societies"—P.
    Includes index.
    ISBN 0-684-19188-1
    1. United States—Biography—Dictionaries.   I. American Council
of Learned Societies.
E176.D564   1990
920.073—dc20   90-8951
                                                    CIP

IMPRESSION
1 2 3 4 5 6 7 8 9 10

Charles Scribner's Sons   Collier Macmillan Canada, Inc.
Macmillan Publishing Company   1200 Eglington Ave. East
866 Third Ave.   Suite 200
New York, New York 10022   Don Mills, Ontario M3C 3N1

American Council of Learned Societies Committee on the

DICTIONARY OF AMERICAN BIOGRAPHY

Editorial Staff

Project Editor
ANN B. TOBACK

Biography Editors

JEFFREY L. BENEKE   MARY K. DEEGAN

MELISSA DOBSON   LOUISE B. KETZ   EMILY WRIGHT

Proofreaders

JONATHAN G. ARETAKIS   W. CUNNINGHAM BISSELL   KATHLEEN DERZIPILSKI

JERILYN FAMIGHETTI   GRETCHEN GORDON   CAROL HOLMES

LELAND S. LOWTHER   IRINA RYBACEK   DANA M. SCHWARTZ

RUTH VISCOUNT   STEPHEN WAGLEY

Director of Production
MATTHEW M. KARDOVICH

Senior Editor
JOHN FITZPATRICK

Publisher
KAREN DAY

Contents

Preface

The plan of the Fourth Edition of the *Concise Dictionary of American Biography* generally follows that of the earlier editions. (The reprinted "Preface to the First Edition" follows.) All of the condensed biographies published in previous editions are included here, this time in a single alphabetical sequence. With the addition of newly condensed biographies from Supplements 7 (1981) and 8 (1988), the *Concise Dictionary of American Biography* now includes entries on all 18,110 persons treated in the parent set and its supplements. The coverage of the work is thereby extended to include all outstanding Americans who died prior to 1 January 1971.

While the population of the United States has increased greatly each decade, the number of subjects deemed worthy of inclusion in the *Dictionary of American Biography* has remained relatively constant. Indeed some entries in the *Dictionary* might even be considered marginal when compared with the more illustrious figures with whom they share space. For the most part, however, the men and women considered here had careers that were of national and even international importance.

As with the Third Edition, it has been found that newly condensed biographies of twentieth-century Americans have tended to run, on average, somewhat longer than the typical entries of the First Edition. Technological advances and social changes have altered the makeup of American civilization at speeds unimaginable to our ancestors, and many fields of endeavor in which modern Americans have distinguished themselves either did not exist in the past (*e.g.*, professional athletics, broadcasting) or else have become vastly more complex than before (*e.g.*, science and technology). Some additional words of explanation have often been necessary to define a field as well as a person's contribution to it.

Although the old biographies have not been substantially revised since their initial publication, some alterations have been made in consideration of modern sensibilities. For example, the new text usually reads "black" instead of "Negro." Some antiquated terminology, such as "mental defective," has been replaced by modern usage.

This is the first edition to include an Occupations Index, which identifies the 1,156 fields in which the biographees earned distinction. We hope that this feature will increase the usefulness of the work and suggest new research opportunities.

Preface to the First Edition

The *Dictionary of American Biography*—the distinguished parent of the present book—is a multi-volume standard reference work to be found today in every general library here and abroad. Sponsored by the American Council of Learned Societies and edited under its supervision, the *Dictionary* contains 14,870 biographies of Americans who have made memorable contributions to our national life. Each of these biographies is a "book in little"—each is the work of a specialist, written with authority and scupulous scholarship. No living person is included. In order to maintain the standards of scholarship and objectivity instituted by the original projectors of the work, an interval of at least ten years is allowed to elapse between the death of any potential subject and his consideration for inclusion by the Editorial Committee.

This plan and philosophy of the parent work should be borne in mind by users of the *Concise Dictionary of American Biography*. It makes no attempt to exceed the scope of its original, whose coverage at present does not extend to any subject whose death took place later than December 31, 1940.

The *Concise Dictionary* provides the essential facts of each biography in the larger work for ready reference by students, research workers, journalists, and indeed anyone who wishes to inform himself quickly about the dates of birth and death, ancestry, education, thought and accomplishments of notable Americans—minor figures and major alike. Every biography contained in the parent work has been summarized; none has been omitted. As in the original work, the order of the entries is alphabetical by the last name of the subject. Entries from the supplementary volumes have been introduced at their appropriate positions in a single alphabet and noted so as to facilitate further reference to the multi-volume *Dictionary*. As the arrangement of articles is alphabetical, and as most users of the *Concise Dictionary* will refer to it for information about a person whose last name at least they already know, an Index was considered unnecessary.

A maximum of 1,300 pages in clear, well-spaced type was set as a reasonable physical limit for the *Concise Dictionary of American Biography*. The number of words allotted to each subject by the original editors of the large *Dictionary* determined the length of each concise entry. The scale of reduction to be employed was fixed at approximately 1–14. It was understood from the start, however, that no strictly mathematical rule of reduction could be applied and the scale has been varied liberally in the interest of clarity. Often a comparatively unimportant subject required rather full treatment because his single achievement, to be comprehensible, had to be explained in detail. On the other hand, outstanding men and women whose contribution to society was general rather than specific could often be dealt with in three or four lines. Inventors and technicians, for example, tended to fall in the first category; naval officers, proceeding in the course of exemplary service careers from one command to another without any obvious high point of drama, are typical of the second, as are many clergymen and educators.

Generally speaking, the *Concise Dictionary of American Biography* contains three types of entries:

1. *Minimal*, giving (a) the places and dates of the subject's birth and death, (b) his occupation, (c) a reference to his genealogy *if he were related to any person or persons also cited in the work*, (d) his education *if it played a significant role in his career*, (e) the date of his arrival in the United States *if he were an immigrant*, and (f) a brief statement of his outstanding achievements.

2. *Median*, in which all the information provided in a minimal entry is given, plus critical comment on the subject's achievements and a brief appraisal of his character and influence. If an author, the titles and dates of publication of his principal works are cited; if a soldier, the campaigns and battles in which he distinguished himself; if a jurist, his leading opinions.

3. *Extended entries*, in which the content, style and spirit of the original biographies have been preserved as fully as possible.

In the shorter entries, the facts of the subject's career have been the principal concern; the editors have tried to present those facts and characteristics upon which the original biographers appeared to lay most stress. They have attempted no interpretations or additions of their own.

In composing many of the minimal entries considerations of space dictated the use of an elliptical style, much like that used in similar entries in the *Concise Dictionary of National Biography*—the linking of dissociated facts in a sequence separated by semi-colons. Consideration of space also forbade any extended explanation in shorter articles of the historical processes with which the subjects were concerned. Participation in a treaty negotiation, for example, is merely stated; the reader must look elsewhere for a full account of the details and significance of the treaty in question.

Some of the articles have been amended to include new information which recent scholarship has brought to light. The editors presently engaged in preparing the monumental editions of the papers of Benjamin Franklin and Alexander Hamilton, for example, were generous with advice. The extended article on Thomas Jefferson was revised by the author of the original biography, Mr. Dumas Malone. In a few instances, where the original biography contained serious errors, an entirely new treatment has been provided. All errata presently cited at the head of Volume I of the parent work have been included in the *Concise* versions.

A

AANDAHL, FRED GEORGE (b. Litchville, Barnes County, N.Dak., 1897; d. Fargo, N.Dak., 1966), congressman and governor of North Dakota. Elected to the state senate in 1930 and reelected in 1938. To break the authority exercised by the Nonpartisan League in the Republican party, he and others formed the Republican Organizing Committee (ROC) in 1943. Became the first ROC governor in 1944, and his reelections in 1946 and 1948 marked the decline of the Nonpartisan League. As governor, followed his conservative bent, insisting upon legislative restraint and vetoing some appropriations endorsed by ROC legislations. In 1950 won a seat in the U.S. House of Representatives. Was appointed assistant secretary of the interior for water and power development (1953) and held the post until the end of the Eisenhower administration.

ABBE, CLEVELAND (b. New York, N.Y., 1838; d. 1916), astronomer, meteorologist. Issued pioneer weather forecasts based on telegraphic reports, 1869; with U.S. Weather Service, 1871–1916.

ABBETT, LEON (b. Philadelphia, Pa., 1836; d. Jersey City, N.J., 1894), lawyer. As Democratic governor of New Jersey, 1883–86, imposed equitable taxes on railroad and other corporations.

ABBEY, EDWIN AUSTIN (b. Philadelphia, Pa., 1852; d. London, England, 1911), illustrator, mural painter. Studied at Pennsylvania Academy; joined staff of illustrators, Harper's Weekly, 1871, resigning in 1874 to free-lance. Concentrating on faithful re-creation of 17th- and 18th-century modes and manners in pen and water-color, he developed a charming, original style. Commissioned to sketch in England in 1878, he remained there save for brief visits to America. His best work is found in Selections from the Poetry of Robert Herrick (1882), Goldsmith's She Stoops to Conquer (1886), Old Songs (1889); as muralist, he won fame for designs in the Boston Public Library and the Pennsylvania state capitol.

ABBEY, HENRY (b. Rondout, N.Y., 1842; d. Tenafly, N.J., 1911), minor poet.

ABBEY, HENRY EUGENE (b. Akron, Ohio, 1846; d. 1896), theatrical and operatic manager. Presented finest European talents in "road" tours of smaller American cities.

ABBOT, BENJAMIN (b. Andover, Mass., 1762; d. Exeter, N.H., 1849), educator. Graduated Harvard, 1788. Principal of Phillips Exeter Academy, a position he held with great influence, 1788–1838.

ABBOT, EZRA (b. Jackson, Maine, 1819; d. 1884), biblical scholar, librarian, teacher, editor. In his generation, the greatest American critic of the New Testament text.

ABBOT, FRANCIS ELLINGWOOD (b. Boston, Mass., 1836; d. 1903), Unitarian clergyman, philosopher. Rejected contemporary Unitarianism for what he termed "Free Religion." His subtle criticism of the then dominant idealism in philosophy was premature and without immediate influence.

ABBOT, GORHAM DUMMER (b. Brunswick, Maine, 1807; d. South Natick, Mass., 1874), Presbyterian clergyman, educator. Active in higher education for women; established Spingler Institute in New York City; influenced Matthew Vassar to devote his wealth to education.

ABBOT, HENRY LARCOM (b. Beverly, Mass., 1831; d. 1927), army engineer. Graduated West Point, 1854. Assisted Capt. A. A. Humphreys's investigation of channel improvement along lower Mississippi and with him advocated use of levees in flood control. After serving in Civil War, developed the army's Engineer School of Application, making it a research center for problems of military engineering. Promoted to brigadier general upon retirement in 1895. Acted as consulting engineer to French and American Panama Canal companies; the decision to build a lock-canal rather than a sea-level canal was based on his report. Professor of hydraulic engineering, George Washington University, 1905–10.

ABBOT, JOEL (b. Westford, Mass., 1793; d. Hong Kong, China, 1855), naval officer. Distinguished service, War of 1812; commanded frigate in Perry's Japanese expedition, 1852–54.

ABBOT, WILLIS JOHN (b. New Haven, Conn., 1863; d. Brookline, Mass., 1934), journalist, author. Editor, Christian Science Monitor, 1921–27; promoted Monitor peace plan; actively interested in international adjudication and peace organizations.

ABBOTT, AUSTIN (b. Boston, Mass., 1831; d. New York, N.Y., 1896), lawyer. Brother of Benjamin V. Abbott, Edward Abbott, and Lyman Abbott. Author of Trial Evidence (1880); counsel for defense in Tilton v. Beecher. Dean of Law School, New York University, 1891–96.

ABBOTT, BENJAMIN (b. 1732; d. Salem, N.J., 1796), religious enthusiast. Methodist circuit preacher in southern New Jersey.

ABBOTT, BENJAMIN VAUGHAN (b. Boston, Mass., 1830; d. Brooklyn, N.Y., 1890), lawyer, author. Collaborated with brother Austin Abbott in writing treatises, digests, reports, and briefs. Son of Jacob Abbott.

ABBOTT, CHARLES CONRAD (b. Trenton, N.J., 1843; d. Bristol, Pa., 1919), naturalist, archaeologist. Wrote semi-popular accounts of nature study along the Delaware. Student of American Indian culture.

ABBOTT, EDITH (b. Grand Island, Nebr., 1876; d. Grand Island, 1957), social worker, educator, author. Studied at the University of Nebraska, University of Chicago (Ph.D., 1905), and at the London School of Economics. Abbott was a pioneer in the new field of social work, joining Sophonisba Breckinridge on the staff of the Chicago School of Civics and Philanthropy; in 1920, after residing at Hull House, Abbott and Breckinridge incorporated their school into the University of Chicago as the School of Social Service Administration. Abbot taught there until her retirement; she was dean from 1924 to 1942. She served two terms as president of the National Association of Social Workers and edited the *Social Review*, which she founded in 1927.

ABBOTT, EDWARD (*b. Farmington, Maine, 1841; d. 1908*), Congregational and Episcopal clergyman, author. Editor *Literary World*, 1878–88, 1895–1903; rector, St. James's Episcopal Church, North Cambridge, Mass. Brother of Austin, Benjamin V., and Lyman Abbott.

ABBOTT, ELEANOR HALLOWELL (*b. Cambridge, Mass., 1872; d. Portsmouth, N.H., 1958*), novelist, short story writer. Studied at Radcliffe College. Wrote several novels and short stories, many concerning invalids. Her best-known works include the novel *Molly Make-Believe* (1910) and *Being Little in Cambridge When Everyone Else Was Big* (1936). Her many short stories were published in leading magazines.

ABBOTT, EMMA (*b. Chicago, Ill., 1850; d. Salt Lake City, Utah, 1891*), dramatic soprano. Formed Abbott English Opera Co., popularizing opera in America, 1878–91.

ABBOTT, FRANK (*b. Shapleigh, Maine, 1836; d. 1897*), dentist. Invented operative instruments for almost every phase of dental work. Dean, New York College of Dentistry, 1869–97.

ABBOTT, FRANK FROST (*b. Redding, Conn., 1860; d. Montreux, Switzerland, 1924*), classical scholar. Professor of Latin, University of Chicago, 1891–1908; Princeton, 1908–24. Specialist in Roman social and political life.

ABBOTT, GRACE (*b. Grand Island, Nebr., 1878; d. Chicago, Ill., 1939*), social worker, administrator of the first Child Labor Act; chief, federal Children's Bureau, 1921–34.

ABBOTT, HORACE (*b. Sudbury, Mass., 1806; d. Baltimore, Md., 1887*), iron manufacturer. Produced armor plates for the original *Monitor* and vessels of her class. Leader in Baltimore business and financial circles.

ABBOTT, JACOB (*b. Hallowell, Maine, 1803; d. Farmington, Maine, 1879*), Congregational clergyman, educator, writer of children's books. Author of the famous *Rollo* series, which combined simple stories with instruction in ethics, religion, science, and history. Brother of Gorham D. and John S. C. Abbott; father of Austin, Benjamin V., and Lyman Abbott.

ABBOTT, JOHN STEVENS CABOT (*b. Brunswick, Maine, 1805; d. Fair Haven, Conn., 1877*), Congregational clergyman. Brother of Gorham D. Abbot and Jacob Abbott; author of a popular eulogistic *History of Napoleon Bonaparte* (1855).

ABBOTT, JOSEPH CARTER (*b. Concord, N.H., 1825; d. Wilmington, N.C., 1881*), journalist, politician. Active Republican leader in reconstruction of North Carolina, 1866–71.

ABBOTT, LYMAN (*b. Roxbury, Mass., 1835; d. 1922*), Congregational clergyman, author. Son of Jacob Abbott; brother of Austin and Benjamin V. Abbott. During Civil War held pastorate at Terre Haute, Indiana; resigned at end of war to join commission of laymen and ministers dedicated to aid Southern reconstruction. Appointed editor, *The Illustrated Christian Weekly*, 1870; left in 1876 to become associated with Henry Ward Beecher in editorship of *Christian Union*; at Beecher's removal became editor in chief and so continued after paper was renamed *Outlook*, 1893. Succeeded Beecher as pastor of Plymouth Congregational Church,

Brooklyn, N.Y., 1890–99. Supported important reform movements and made *Outlook* a powerful exponent of progressive Christianity. Influential works: *The Life and Literature of the Ancient Hebrews* (1901), *Theology of an Evolutionist* (1897).

ABBOTT, ROBERT SENGSTACKE (*b. St. Simon's Island, Ga., 1868; d. Chicago, Ill., 1940*), newspaper editor. Founder (1905) and publisher of the *Chicago Defender*.

ABBOTT, SAMUEL WARREN (*b. Woburn, Mass., 1837; d. 1904*), physician, statistician. M.D., Harvard, 1862. Civil War surgeon; pioneer leader of public health movement in America; early student of demography.

ABBOTT, WILLIAM HAWKINS (*b. Middlebury, Conn., 1819; d. 1901*), petroleum producer and refiner. Constructed first oil refinery at Titusville, Pa., 1861; promoted business and civic development of that city.

ABEEL, DAVID (*b. New Brunswick, N.J., 1804; d. Albany, N.Y., 1846*), missionary of Dutch Reformed Church in Far East *post* 1830.

ABEL, JOHN JACOB (*b. near Cleveland, Ohio, 1857; d. Baltimore, Md., 1938*), pharmacologist and biological chemist. Director of laboratory for endocrine research at Johns Hopkins medical school.

ABEL-HENDERSON, ANNIE HELOISE (*b. Fernhurst, Sussex, England, 1873; d. Aberdeen, Wash., 1947*), teacher, historian. Came to America, 1885; raised in Kansas. Graduated University of Kansas, 1898; M.A., 1900; Ph.D., Yale, 1905. Taught at Goucher College, 1906–15, rising to professor and head of history department; professor of history at Smith College, 1916–22. After an unsuccessful marriage and some years of independent research, she was appointed professor of history at University of Kansas, retiring in 1930 but continuing to do research, lecture, and write. She was early recognized as a painstaking scholar, specializing at first in the documentary study of the Indian tribes west of the Mississippi. Three-volume *The Slaveholding Indians* (1915–25) considered her most important book, but she rendered her greatest service in editing and publishing masses of original documents relative to both American and British policies toward native peoples. Co-editor of the Lewis Tappan Papers, 1927.

ABELL, ARUNAH SHEPHERDSON (*b. East Providence, R.I., 1806; d. Baltimore, Md., 1888*), journalist. With W. M. Swain and A. H. Simmons, began Philadelphia "penny paper," the *Public Ledger*, 1836. This successful venture resulted in the same partners' foundation of a second paper under Abell's sole management, the *Baltimore Sun*, 1837. Moving to Baltimore, he built the *Sun* into an accurate, impartial, and independent journal. He was a pioneer in modern impersonal journalism; in the classification and systematic gathering of local news; and in the development of speedy general news service using pony express, carrier pigeons, and Morse's recently invented telegraph.

ABERCROMBY, JAMES (*b. Glassaugh, Banffshire, Scotland, 1706; d. 1781*), British general. Given full command of British forces in America, spring 1758; met bloody and total defeat at Ticonderoga; recalled to England, fall 1758.

ABERNETHY, GEORGE (*b. New York, N.Y., 1807; d. Portland, Oreg., 1877*), merchant, churchman, administrator. Pioneer businessman in Oregon; associate of Rev. Jason Lee; provisional governor, 1845 and 1847.

ABERT, JOHN JAMES (*b. Shepherdstown[?], Va., 1788; d. Washington, D.C., 1863*), topographical engineer. Attended West Point, 1808–11. Practiced law in Washington, D.C., and

Ohio. After serving as a volunteer in the War of 1812, he was appointed major in the Topographical Engineers. Assisted Ferdinand Rudolph Hassler in making geodetic surveys along the Atlantic Coast and topographical surveys in the eastern United States; was chief of the Topographical Bureau from 1834 to 1861, and responsible for the extensive surveys of the West made during this period.

ABORN, MILTON (*b. Marysville, Calif., 1864; d. New York, N.Y., 1933*), operatic impresario.

ABRAMS, ALBERT (*b. San Francisco, Calif., 1863; d. 1924*), physician. Founder of "E.R.A." system of universal diagnosis and treatment of disease, based on changes of electrical potential in the skin.

ABT, ISAAC ARTHUR (*b. Wilmington, Ill., 1867; d. Chicago, Ill., 1955*), pediatrician. Received M.D. from the Chicago Medical College (now Northwestern University Medical School) in 1891. A pioneer in American pediatrics, Abt founded Sarah Morris Children's Hospital, Chicago's first children's hospital, 1909. Editor and founder of many pediatric journals and leader of many medical societies, Abt remained the leading figure in his field until his death.

ACCAU (ACCAULT). *See* ACO, MICHEL.

ACHESON, EDWARD GOODRICH (*b. Washington, Pa., 1856; d. New York, N.Y., 1931*), inventor, pioneer of electrothermal industry. After only a few years' schooling, he became a timekeeper at a blast furnace; in 1873 patented a rock-boring machine to be used in coal mines; in 1880 worked as a draftsman for Thomas A. Edison at Menlo Park; thereafter, spent several years in Europe helping to install lighting plants. On returning to America he set up his own laboratory and sold rights for an anti-induction telephone wire. His interest in abrasives led to the development of an electric furnace, a procedure for making artificial graphite, and the discovery of carborundum. Founded at least five companies dependent on the electrothermal process.

ACKER, CHARLES ERNEST (*b. Bourbon, Ind., 1868; d. Ossining, N.Y., 1920*), inventor, manufacturer. Perfected process for producing caustic soda and chlorine by electrolysis of molten salt; held over forty electrochemical patents.

ACO, MICHEL (*fl. 1680–1702*), French explorer. Sent by La Salle to explore upper Mississippi, 1680. Business partner of La Salle's associates, Tonty and La Forest, 1693.

ACOSTA, BERTRAM BLANCHARD ("BERT") (*b. San Diego, Calif., 1895; d. Denver, Colo., 1954*), aviator, aeronautical engineer. Studied at Throop Polytechnic Institute (now California Institute of Technology). Helped train pilots in World War I and became engineering consultant to the Bureau of Aircraft Production. Was a crew member of the *America*, commanded by Richard E. Byrd, which was forced down off the Normandy coast in its attempted flight to Paris in June 1927. Though following Lindbergh's flight by a month, the crew of the *America* received heroes' welcomes in Paris and New York.

ACRELIUS, ISRAEL (*b. Öster-Åker, Sweden, 1714; d. 1800*), Lutheran clergyman, author. Pastor at Christina (Wilmington, Del.), 1749–56; wrote *History of New Sweden* (1759), describing region under Swedish, Dutch, and English rule.

ADAIR, JAMES (*b. Ireland, ca. 1709; d. ca. 1783*), Indian trader, author. His *History of the American Indians* (1775) is an eyewitness record of aboriginal manners, customs, and languages.

ADAIR, JOHN (*b. Chester Co., S.C., 1757; d. Mercer Co., Ky., 1840*), soldier, politician, Indian fighter. Nine times elected to Kentucky legislature; governor of Kentucky, 1820–24; representative in Congress, 1831–33. Partisan of the common people and "relief" leader.

ADAMIC, LOUIS (*b. Blato, Austria [now Yugoslavia], 1899; d. near Rigelsville, N.J., 1951*), journalist, novelist. Immigrated to the U.S. in 1913. Author of several articles on social issues, Adamic became known for his books about the difficulties of American immigrants; in 1934 he published *The Native's Return*, an account of his travels to his native Yugoslavia, followed by the novels *Grandsons* (1935) and *Cradle of Life* (1936). *My Native Land* (1943), his most influential book, explained the crisis in Yugoslavia and was pro-Tito. Adamic was criticized by the Catholic Church as being pro-Communist and subversive, even though he supported Tito's break with Russia in 1948 and became an outspoken critic of Soviet Communism. *Dinner at the White House* (1946) was an account of a dinner he and Churchill attended as guests of Roosevelt in 1942. Adamic died mysteriously in 1951; though the police termed his death a suicide, there was speculation that he was murdered by Soviet agents who wanted to silence his pro-Tito writings.

ADAMS, ABIGAIL (*b. Weymouth, Mass., 1744; d. Quincy, Mass., 1818*), wife of Pres. John Adams. Wrote distinguished letters containing vivid pictures of the times.

ADAMS, ABIJAH (*b. Boston, Mass., ca. 1754; d. Boston, 1816*), journalist. Edited Boston *Independent Chronicle*, chief supporter of Jeffersonian principles in New England, 1800–16.

ADAMS, ALVA (*b. Iowa Co., Wis., 1850; d. 1922*), businessman. Democratic governor of Colorado, 1886–88, 1896–98. Developed the state's school and prison systems; reelected 1904 but was disqualified.

ADAMS, ALVIN (*b. Andover, Vt., 1804; d. 1877*), pioneer in express business. Founded Adams Express Co., 1840.

ADAMS, ANDREW (*b. Stratford, Conn., 1736; d. 1797*), Revolutionary patriot, Connecticut legislator, and jurist.

ADAMS, ANDY (*b. Whitley Co., Ind., 1859; d. Colorado Springs, Colo., 1935*), cowboy, author. Gained knowledge for his *Log of a Cowboy* (1903) "from the hurricane deck of a Texas horse."

ADAMS, ANNETTE ABBOTT (*b. Prattville, Calif., 1877; d. Sacramento, Calif., 1956*), attorney, judge. Received doctorate in jurisprudence from the University of California in 1912. The first woman assistant attorney general, 1920–21; appointed special assistant counsel to the U.S. attorney general by President Roosevelt in 1935. In 1942, she was appointed presiding judge of the Court of Appeals for the Third District of California in Sacramento. Served (1942–52) as judge on California appellate court.

ADAMS, BROOKS (*b. Quincy, Mass., 1848; d. Boston, Mass, 1927*), historian. Brother of Charles Francis Adams (1835–1915) and Henry B. Adams. His first work, *The Emancipation of Massachusetts* (1887), attracted attention by its vigorous assault upon the traditional approach to early New England history. Studying trade routes and their influence upon history, he next published *Law of Civilization and Decay* (1895), attempting to prove that human societies were differentiated because of unequal natural endowment of energy. In subsequent volumes he extended this "law" into modern times, hoping to forecast the direction of social movement. Although his books were based on sound research they are permeated by strong prejudices which dominate and sometimes distort their conclusions.

ADAMS, CHARLES (*b. Pomerania, Germany, 1845[?]; d. Denver, Colo., 1895*), soldier, diplomat. Indian fighter; agent to the Utes, 1872–74; minister to Bolivia, 1880–82; post-office inspector, 1881–85.

ADAMS, CHARLES BAKER (*b. Dorchester, Mass., 1814; d. St. Thomas, Virgin Islands, 1853*), naturalist. His *Contributions to Conchology* (1849–52) and *Catalogue of Shells Collected at Panama* (1852) are still standard manuals.

ADAMS, CHARLES FOLLEN (*b. Dorchester, Mass., 1842; d. 1918*), poet. *Leedle Yawcob Strauss, and Other Poems* (1877) represents his skill and originality in German dialect verse.

ADAMS, CHARLES FRANCIS (*b. Boston, Mass., 1807; d. Boston, 1886*), diplomat, son of John Quincy Adams. Graduated Harvard, 1825; practiced law. Elected to Massachusetts legislature as a Whig, 1840; served three years in the House and two in the state senate. Elected to Congress as a Republican, 1858, he gained recognition for his moderate views. Appointed minister to England, 1861. For seven years he stayed at that post, utilizing all his personal and intellectual powers in the *Trent* affair, the *Alabama* case, and other matters involving the neutrality of England and the rivalry between Union and Confederate representatives seeking European recognition. In an England that tended to favor the Confederacy he enhanced the Northern position without resorting to humiliating compromises or war. As biographer and editor of the works of his grandfather, Pres. John Adams, he worked with care and discretion.

ADAMS, CHARLES FRANCIS (*b. Boston, Mass., 1835; d. Washington, D.C., 1915*), railroad expert, civic leader, historian. Son of the preceding; brother of Brooks Adams and Henry B. Adams. Graduated Harvard, 1856; practiced law. Served as cavalry officer during Civil War; mustered out as brevet brigadier general, 1865. Exposed criminal actions of railroad speculators in *Chapters of Erie* (1871); headed Massachusetts Board of Railroad Commissioners, 1872; made chairman of the government directors of Union Pacific Railroad, 1878, he became president of that road in 1884. His participation in Quincy city government resulted in important educational reforms there and in his subsequent appointment to a park commission for Boston and vicinity. He was author of a number of papers and several books on topics in New England history and a biography of his father.

ADAMS, CHARLES FRANCIS (*b. Quincy, Mass., 1866; d. Boston, Mass., 1954*), financier, statesman, yachtsman, philanthropist. Graduated from Harvard (B.A., 1888), Harvard Law School, 1892. As treasurer of the Corporation of Harvard College (1898–1929) he increased endowments from $15 million to $120 million. In 1920 Adams piloted the sloop *Resolute* to a very close victory over Sir Thomas Lipton's challenger *Shamrock IV*, becoming the first amateur ever to defend the *America's* Cup. In 1917 Adams received more votes than any other candidate for delegate-at-large to the Massachusetts constitutional convention. Three years later the state Democratic party put his name forward as a presidential elector without consulting him, and he shifted his support to the Republicans. As Secretary of the Navy (1929–33), he resigned all his business interests and soon won the respect of both President Hoover and the navy. The revival of Japanese militancy became his chief concern. Served as key American delegate at London naval conference in 1930.

ADAMS, CHARLES KENDALL (*b. Derby, Vt., 1835; d. Redlands, Calif., 1902*), historian. President of Cornell University, 1885–92, and of University of Wisconsin, 1892–1901; author of *Democracy and Monarchy in France* (1874).

ADAMS, CHARLES R. (*b. Charlestown, Mass., 1834; d. West Harwich, Mass., 1900*), opera singer. Greatest American tenor of his time; teacher of Hiltz, Melba, and Eames.

ADAMS, CYRUS CORNELIUS (*b. Naperville, Ill., 1849; d. New York, N.Y., 1928*), geographical writer, editor. Helped establish study of geography as an American university subject.

ADAMS, DANIEL (*b. Townsend, Mass., 1773; d. Keene, N.H., 1864*), physician, educator. Author of two once widely used school texts, *The Scholar's Arithmetic* (1801) and *The Understanding Reader* (*ca.* 1803).

ADAMS, DANIEL WEISSIGER (*b. Frankfort, Ky., 1820; d. New Orleans, La., 1872*), lawyer, Confederate brigadier general. Brother of William Wirt Adams.

ADAMS, DUDLEY W. (*b. Winchendon, Mass., 1831; d. 1897*), horticulturist. Established Iron Clad Nursery at Waukon, Iowa, 1856; promoter of National Grange; was elected its Master, 1873. Framed proposals for railroad-freight legislation which were introduced into Congress, 1873–74; although no federal legislation was secured at that time, his suggestions for fixed rates and the abolition of discriminatory practices were later incorporated into national and state regulations governing railroads. Moved to Florida in 1875, planted extensive orange and other fruit orchards, and did much to develop horticultural industry there.

ADAMS, EBENEZER (*b. New Ispwich, N.H., 1765; d. 1841*), educator. Graduated Dartmouth, 1791. Professor at Dartmouth, 1809–33; a factor in the celebrated "Dartmouth College Case."

ADAMS, EDWARD DEAN (*b. Boston, Mass., 1846; d. 1931*), banker, industrialist. Leader in utilizing Niagara Falls for electrical power production; reorganizer and director of many railroads; art connoisseur.

ADAMS, EDWIN (*b. Medford, Mass., 1834; d. 1877*), actor. Considered one of America's best light comedians, he supported Edwin Booth, and had his greatest success in the role of "Enoch Arden," 1869.

ADAMS, ELIPHALET (*b. Dedham, Mass., 1677; d. New London, Conn., 1753*), clergyman. Pastor at New London, 1708/9–52; trustee of Yale College, 1720–38.

ADAMS, EPHRAIM DOUGLASS (*b. Decorah, Iowa, 1865; d. 1930*), historian, teacher. Author of *Great Britain and the American Civil War* (1925); directed assembling of materials for the Hoover War Library.

ADAMS, FRANK RAMSAY (*b. Morrison, Ill., 1883; d. Whitehall, Mich., 1963*), lyricist, journalist, novelist, screenwriter. With Will M. Hough and Joseph Edgar ("Joe") Howard, wrote and produced musicals that dominated the Chicago stage for almost a decade in the early 1900's, contributing lyrics for over 200 songs. After working as a reporter, turned to fiction and produced numerous light-hearted romances. Also worked as a staff scenario writer and screenwriter in Hollywood, collaborating on scripts for some twenty-five movies.

ADAMS, FRANKLIN PIERCE (*b. Chicago, Ill., 1881; d. New York City, 1960*), journalist, radio personality. Studied briefly at the University of Michigan. Wrote humorous and literary columns for the *New York Evening Mail* (1904–13), the *New York Tribune* (1913–22), the *New York World* (1922–31), the *New York Herald-Tribune* (1931–37), and the *New York Post* (1937–41). From 1938 to 1948, he was the literary expert on the radio program "Information Please." Adams was known for his acerbic wit; recognition in his column "The Conning Tower" was a much sought-after honor.

ADAMS, FREDERICK UPHAM (*b. Boston, Mass., 1859; d. Larchmont, N.Y., 1921*), inventor, author. Improved electric lighting and railway equipment.

ADAMS, GEORGE BURTON (*b. Fairfield*, Vt., *1851; d. 1925*), historian. Professor of history at Yale, 1888–1925; authoritative writer on medieval subjects and on English constitutional history.

ADAMS, HANNAH (*b. Medfield, Mass., 1755; d. Boston, Mass., 1831*), compiler of historical information. Probably the first professional female writer in America.

ADAMS, HENRY BROOKS (*b. Boston, Mass., 1838; d. Washington, D.C., 1918*), historian. Great-grandson of John Adams, grandson of John Quincy Adams, son of Charles Francis Adams (1807–1886); brother of Brooks Adams and Charles Francis Adams (1835–1915). Graduated Harvard, 1858. Studied civil law at Berlin and Dresden, 1859–60, but made little progress. In Washington, D.C., as secretary to father, 1860–61; despite wish to serve in Union army, he went with father to London and continued to act as secretary during father's eventful term as United States minister to Court of St. James, 1861–68. On return to America, was at once fascinated and repelled by the crudeness and strength of American life, and its contrasts with the cultivated society of Europe. Accepted appointment as assistant professor of history at Harvard, 1870. His instinct for perfection made him rate his academic work as a failure, but he introduced the seminar system of study and trained some brilliant students. Married Marian Hooper, 1872. In 1877, left Harvard and made his home in Washington, D.C., regarding his "function in life to be stable-companion to statesmen." His fastidious response to the knavery of political life at that time was expressed in an anonymous novel, *Democracy* (1880). Abandoning hopes of a political career, he became a scholarly and disillusioned observer, withdrawn among a small circle of intimates such as John Hay, statesman, Clarence King, geologist and traveler, and John LaFarge, artist. After the death of his wife in 1885, he traveled in the Orient and returned to continue his research into the beginnings of our national government, producing his *History of the United States* (1889–91), a masterly study of the administrations of Jefferson and Madison. After further travel to the South Seas, Mexico, the Far West, and Europe, the direction of his interests shifted from early American history to the study of the resolution of spiritual and material forces in medieval Europe and the exposition of a personal philosophy of history in *Mont-St.-Michel and Chartres* (1904; 1913), the enigmatic *Education of Henry Adams* (1907; 1918), and *A Letter to American Teachers of History* (1910). Among his other books are *Documents Relating to New England Federalism* (1877), *The Life of Albert Gallatin* (1879), and *Esther* (1884).

ADAMS, HENRY CARTER (*b. Davenport, Iowa, 1851; d. 1921*), economist, statistician. Early opponent of *laissez-faire* economics; student of American financial and administrative problems.

ADAMS, HENRY CULLEN (*b. Oneida Co., N.Y., 1850; d. 1906*), congressman from Wisconsin, 1902–06. Supported dual statehood for New Mexico, Arizona; active in passage of the Meat Inspection Law, the National Food and Drug Act, and the Adams Act, providing agricultural research funds.

ADAMS, HERBERT BAXTER (*b. Shutesbury, Mass., 1850; d. 1901*), historian. Instrumental in development of the study of political science and history at Johns Hopkins University; active with Moses C. Tyler and Charles K. Adams in organization of American Historical Association, 1884.

ADAMS, HERBERT SAMUEL (*b. West Concord, Vt., 1858; d. New York, N.Y., 1945*), sculptor. Studied at Massachusetts Normal Art School, Boston, and in Paris, 1885–90, where he established a studio. Returned to America, 1890, and taught at Pratt Institute, 1890–98. Member of the art colony at Cornish, N.H., where he was associate of Augustus Saint-Gaudens and Daniel Chester French. His portrait busts of women were his most notable works, distinguished by delicate modeling and sensitive use of ornament and costume; in later work, he provided color by use of tinting and other materials such as woods, metals, and semiprecious stones. Also celebrated for portrait statues (W. C. Bryant, Bryant Park, New York City; Joseph Henry, Library of Congress), and bronze doors for churches and public buildings (St. Bartholomew's Church, New York City; Library of Congress).

ADAMS, ISAAC (*b. Rochester, N.H., 1802; d. 1883*), inventor. Devised "Adams Power Press" in 1827, a machine widely used in book printing prior to introduction of modern cylinder press.

ADAMS, JAMES HOPKINS (*b. Richmond Co., S.C., 1812; d. 1861*), politician, planter. Strong advocate of states' rights. During governorship of South Carolina, 1854–58, proposed reopening of African slave trade.

ADAMS, JAMES TRUSLOW (*b. Brooklyn, N.Y. 1878; d. Southport, Conn., 1949*), historian. A.B., Brooklyn Polytechnic Institute, 1898; M.A., Yale, 1900. Retired from business as a stockbroker, 1912, and devoted himself to the study and writing of Long Island local history, demonstrating sufficient ability as scholar and writer to be named a member of "The Inquiry" which assembled data for use by the U.S. delegation to the Paris Peace Conference, which he attended as cartographer. After World War I, he published four works which gave him national reputation as a writer: *The Founding of New England* (1921, Pulitzer Prize in history); *Revolutionary New England, 1691–1776* (1923); *New England in the Republic* (1926); and *Provincial Society, 1690–1763* (1927). More a popularizer of ideas than an original thinker, Adams succeeded through literary quality, a capacity for telling generalizations, and the expression of attitudes and concepts that commanded respect among intellectuals of the 1920's. He was also successful as a writer of articles on contemporary issues for many of the leading newspapers and magazines. His most popular book, *The Epic of America* (1931), was a broad survey of what he called "the American dream."

ADAMS, JASPER (*b. East Medway, Mass., 1793; d. 1841*), Episcopal clergyman. President of Charleston College, Charleston, S.C., 1824–26, 1828–36; first president of Hobart College, 1826–28.

ADAMS, JOHN (*b. Braintree, Mass., 1735; d. Quincy, Mass., 1826*), president of the United States. Graduated Harvard, 1755. Taught school at Worcester, Mass.; studied law and was admitted to Boston bar, 1758. Married Abigail Smith, 1764. Was early identified with the cause of American independence by his association with Gridley and Otis in their presentation of Boston's memorial against the closing of the courts and by his legal opposition to Stamp Act and other British measures for taxation of the colonies. Elected to General Court as representative of Boston, 1770, he served a one-year term. His condemnation of the Boston Port Act brought him back into public life, and he was chosen in 1774 to act as one of the delegates representing Massachusetts in the first Continental Congress. In the second Congress, 1775–77, he was active in persuading the hesitant Congress to declare its independence from English rule, seconding Richard Henry Lee's motion for independence, foreign alliances and confederacy, and working on the Declaration of Independence itself although his contributions to the text of that document were negligible. When the Declaration was brought before the Congress he was, as Jefferson wrote, "its ablest advocate and defender against the multifarious assaults it encountered."

He served on a number of congressional committees and on the newly created Board of War. From 1778 to 1788 he acted in diplomatic capacities in France, Holland, and England; with John

Jay and Benjamin Franklin he settled the provisional articles of the Treaty of Peace with Great Britain. After serving three years as first envoy to the Court of St. James's, he returned to America in 1788.

When Washington was unanimously chosen president under the new Constitution, Adams received enough of the scattered votes to be made vice president. Reelected in 1792, he aided Hamilton's financial measures but was never fully able to gain his complete confidence. Hamilton intervened in the election of 1796, hoping to keep Adams in the vice presidency; the plan failed in that Adams was chosen president, but it drew enough votes to mortify him and make Jefferson his vice president. His administration faced two serious problems: abroad, relations with the revolutionary government of France had deteriorated to a dangerous degree; at home, he was surrounded by antagonistic Jeffersonians and a cabinet who looked to Hamilton and not to the president as the party leader. John Marshall, C. C. Pinckney, and Elbridge Gerry were commissioned to renew diplomatic relations with France, but they were rebuffed. Adams, prepared for this failure, had to face the possibility of war with the French Republic. Congress, under Hamilton's influence, passed the Alien and Sedition Acts, 1798, and planned a large provisional army with Washington at its head to defend America against French invasion; a navy department was also created. Gerry, who stayed on in France after his fellow commissioners departed, landed at Boston in the fall of 1798 with news of a French desire to renew negotiations. Adams did not exclude the possibility of a peaceful solution if American envoys were accorded proper treatment; however, Hamilton was urging war with France, an attack on Spanish America, and the creation of a large standing army. On his own initiative, Adams appointed W. Vans Murray as minister to the French Republic and proposed the choice of a special peace commission. Congress was outraged, but his bold act was acclaimed by the popular press, and neither Hamilton nor Congress could thwart it. Adams's disloyal cabinet, believing Bourbon restoration was at hand, opposed the president's policy and frustrated it at first. Adams, however, completed instructions for the mission and authorized its departure by Nov. 1, 1799. (Peace was concluded on Sept. 30, 1800, at Morfontaine.) He had surprised and angered his advisers and antagonized Hamilton, but he had prevented a war with France and honorably preserved the neutrality of the United States. The price was his own political career. Federalist leaders regarded him as a traitor to the party and did their best thenceforward to discredit him. Adams ousted Hamilton's friends Pickering and McHenry from his cabinet and replaced them with Samuel Dexter and John Marshall, yet the unsuspected Wolcott remained to act as informer to the opposition. Facing the election of 1800 without party backing and with the added disadvantage of Hamilton's recently published attack, *Letter Concerning the Public Conduct and Character of John Adams*, he lost the presidency to Thomas Jefferson. In closing his controversial presidential career he created a large number of life appointments to federal posts and by so doing increased the enmity of Jefferson.

He then retired to Quincy, where he was completely isolated from national affairs except for his interest in the *Chesapeake* incident and in the career of his son, John Quincy Adams. If party success were the only criterion in judgment of a man of politics, John Adams would be ranked as a failure, for the Federalists lost their influence as a party during his time in office. But he was never a partisan. Loyalty to his country and devotion to the office of the presidency were not to be sacrificed in the choice of a politically expedient solution. Disinterested, careful of his independence and jealous of others, he stood alone, and so largely lost the benefit he might have gained from consultation and mutual action.

ADAMS, JOHN (*b. Canterbury, Conn., 1772; d. 1863*), educator. Fourth principal of Phillips Academy, Andover, Mass., 1810–32.

ADAMS, JOHN (*b. Nashville, Tenn., 1825; d. 1864*), Confederate soldier. Graduated West Point, 1846. Served in 1st Dragoons, 1846–60, rising to captain. As Confederate brigadier general, killed at battle of Franklin.

ADAMS, JOHN COLEMAN (*b. Malden, Mass., 1849; d. Hartford, Conn., 1922*), Universalist clergyman.

ADAMS, JOHN QUINCY (*b. Braintree, Mass., 1767; d. Washington, D.C., 1848*), president of the United States. Eldest son of John (1735–1826) and Abigail (Smith) Adams. Attended several European universities and academies; acted as secretary to Francis Dana, American minister to Russia, 1781–83, and as secretary to John Adams during peace negotiations, 1783. Returned to America and graduated Harvard, 1787. Entered legal profession, 1790. Commissioned by Washington as minister to the Netherlands, 1794; married Louisa Catherine Johnson, 1797; served as minister to Berlin. Resumed Boston law practice, 1801. Elected to U.S. Senate, 1803. Believing that the current bill for the possession of Louisiana was a violation of the Constitution, he introduced several aimed at its correction. His report on Senator John Smith, his attitude on the impeachment of Judge Pickering, his apparent support of the administration in the *Chesapeake* affair, and his votes in favor of the Embargo of 1807 were all in opposition to the Federalist party's views. A special senatorial election was called, and he was forced to resign in 1808. The Federalist tendency to placate the English forced him at times into the Republican camp, but he remained an independent, suspected by both parties. Appointed minister to Russia by Madison, 1809, he was nominated and confirmed to the Supreme Court of U.S., 1811, but declined and remained at St. Petersburg, where he was able to conclude favorable trade agreements. Russia, invaded by Napoleon, joined forces with Great Britain against France; meanwhile America had declared war on the English. Finding his allies in opposing camps, the Tsar offered to mediate between the two countries. Adams, James A. Bayard, and Albert Gallatin were dispatched to represent American interests, 1813. This first peace mission proved to be premature. A second one, including the aforementioned along with Jonathan Russell and Henry Clay, was successful at Ghent, 1814, owing mainly to Adams and Gallatin, who managed to work in concert. Clay and Adams differed on important issues, particularly over Clay's wish to prolong the war.

Appointed secretary of state by Monroe in 1817, Adams's previous experience was invaluable, but his blunt, direct methods made him unpopular in the cabinet, and he was soon to learn that the "era of good feeling" was more apparent than real. Many men were contending for the presidency; Clay was in opposition; and the revolting Spanish colonies in America brought many serious problems before the new secretary of state. The Floridas, still Spanish possessions, were a refuge for hostile Indians and malefactors who raided bordering states at will. When Andrew Jackson campaigned against these raiders and pursued them into Spanish territory, Adams defended the trespass on the grounds that Americans were obliged to act in self-defense since Spain had proved incapable of policing her territories; thus Jackson's conduct was justified, and British and Spanish protests were silenced. In 1819 Adams completed the treaty whereby the United States obtained the Floridas; to accomplish this it was necessary to give up claims on Texas. He also reached an agreement with Great Britain postponing the Oregon question by permitting a ten-year joint occupation of that territory.

In 1822 Monroe formally recognized the independence of the Spanish colonies in America. Adams urged the president to formulate his opposition to the forceful interference of European powers in South America into an American policy. The president's message embodying this principle is known as the Monroe Doctrine, with credit for it equally divided between him and Adams.

The presidential election of 1824 gave none of the four candidates a majority of the votes. Jackson received 99; Adams, 84; Crawford, 41; and Clay, 37. Disliking Jackson, Clay gave his support to Adams, who later made him his secretary of state after Adams's choice as president by the House of Representatives. The defeated Jackson claimed mistakenly that Adams and Clay had entered into a corrupt bargain in order to bring themselves into power. In his inaugural address, President Adams outlined a broad plan for internal improvements. Northern strict constructionists were astonished to learn that he proposed extension of federal powers; Southerners feared that slavery might be abolished in the course of the "improvements;" therefore, a congressional opposition formed at the very beginning of the administration, and Adams's program met with bitter opposition.

Defeated by Jackson in his bid for re-election in 1828, he retired to his farm and books. Elected to Congress in 1831 as an independent, he represented his district in eight successive Congresses, for a period of almost 17 fruitful years. After 1835 he was consistently opposed to slavery and its extension into recently acquired territories. Adams made the then (1836) revolutionary suggestion that in case of "civil, servile, or foreign" war in the South, slavery might be abolished by military authority; that is, the president or commander could rightly order universal emancipation. He debated and acted with complete independence. Even as chairman of the Committee on Foreign Affairs he figured prominently in questions of slavery; his position in the case of slaves who gained their freedom by capturing the vessel *Creole* caused the resignation of all of the Southern committee members. In the case of a revolt of slaves on another ship, the *Amistad*, Adams appeared before the Supreme Court, 1841, and argued in behalf of their freedom.

Interested in science, he prepared a report on the standardization of weights and measures, urged the government to establish an astronomical observatory, and was chairman of the committee responsible for the proper usage of the funds made available for the construction of the Smithsonian Institution. The best summary of his remarkable congressional years is to be found in his *Address of John Quincy Adams in his Constituents of the Twelfth Congressional District* (1842), which embodied his conception of what the South and the slave power had done or wished to do, and how far their policy had been aided by a sacrifice of principle by the North.

A student of political institutions often deeply engrossed by immediate problems, a man who voted and spoke without the party discipline that made others more prudent or silent, his individual course appeared to be an erratic one but it was guided by his unquestioned patriotism, his belief in natural law and rights, and his passion for the freedom of all men, including slaves. His *Memoirs* (ed. C. F. Adams, 1874–77) and *Life in a New England Town* (ed. C. F. Adams, Jr., 1903) are sources of important autobiographical and historical material.

ADAMS, JOSEPH ALEXANDER (*b. New Germantown, N.J., 1803; d. New Jersey, 1880*), wood engraver. Protégé of Alexander Anderson; his principal work, the sixteen hundred illustrations for Harper's *Illuminated Bible* (1843).

ADAMS, JOSEPH QUINCY (*b. Greenville, S.C., 1881; d. Washington, D.C., 1946*), educator, Shakespeare scholar. A.B., Wake Forest College, 1900; M.A., 1901; Ph.D., Cornell University, 1906; studied also at University of Chicago and University of London. Taught at Cornell, 1905–31, becoming professor in 1919. Supervisor of research, Folger Shakespeare Library (Wash-

ington, D.C.), 1931–34; director, *post* 1934. Extended scope and collections of the library. Four books gave him an international scholarly reputation: *Shakespeare Playhouses* (1917), *The Dramatic Records of Sir Henry Herbert* (1917), *Life of William Shakespeare* (1923), and *Chief Pre-Shakespearian Dramas* (1924).

ADAMS, MAUDE (*b. Salt Lake City, Utah, 1872; d. Tannersville, N.Y., 1953*), actress. Known for her roles in the plays of Clyde Fitch and James Barrie. Her greatest success was the title role of Barrie's *Peter Pan* (1905). Also appeared in Shakespearean roles, giving her last performance in 1934. She was the supervisor of an acting school at Stephens College, Mo., 1937–50.

ADAMS, NEHEMIAH (*b. Salem, Mass., 1806; d. 1878*), Congregational clergyman. During the Unitarian controversy he published many pamphlets and books in defense of orthodoxy.

ADAMS, RANDOLPH GREENFIELD (*b. Philadelphia, Pa., 1892; d. Ann Arbor, Mich., 1951*), historian, librarian. Received Ph.D., from University of Pennsylvania in 1920; custodian of the Wm. L. Clements Library of American History at the University of Michigan from 1923 until his death. Adams introduced the concept of the rare-book library for research in the Midwest and served on the advisory council for *The Dictionary of American History*. Advisor in 1940 for the establishment of the Franklin D. Roosevelt Library at Hyde Park, New York.

ADAMS, ROBERT (*b. Philadelphia, Pa., 1846; d. 1906*), lawyer, legislator. Republican congressman from Pennsylvania, 1893–1906; drafted, introduced, and forced passage of resolution declaring war against Spain, 1898.

ADAMS, SAMUEL (*b. Boston, Mass., 1722; d. Boston, 1803*), Revolutionary statesman. Second cousin of John Adams, second president of the United States. Graduated Harvard, 1740; studied law; failed in various business enterprises. Acted as tax collector of the Town of Boston, 1756–64. Married Elizabeth Checkley, 1749 (d. 1757); Elizabeth Wells, 1764.

Although unable to manage his own affairs, he showed an early talent for local politics, founding a political club and contributing articles to its newspaper, the *Independent Advertiser*. Associated with a popular party hostile to the wealthy minority who held political power in Massachusetts, he personally disliked the outstanding member of this "aristocracy," Thomas Hutchinson, lieutenant-governor, member of the Council, and chief justice. In 1764 the Sugar and Stamp acts brought Adams and his party into prominence; they denounced the conservative Hutchinson and accused him of sympathizing with oppressive British measures. Elected to the Massachusetts House of Representatives, 1765, Adams acted with colleagues in the Caucus Club and the Sons of Liberty to secure a majority of radicals in the House and excluded five conservative members from the Council, including Hutchinson. Reelected in 1766 and gaining radical party leadership, he opposed Governor Bernard and Lieutenant-Governor Hutchinson, fought enforcement of the Townshend Acts by various Commissioners of Customs, drafted the famous "Circular Letter" to the assemblies of other provinces and that for the "Convention" of the patriot party held in Boston in 1768, and stirred up a popular hatred for British garrison troops which climaxed in the Boston Massacre of 1770. Effective as a polemical writer, he wrote many letters to prominent persons in England and America, contributed articles to the *Boston Gazette* and other journals, and drafted most of the official papers of the House. He formulated basic premises as early as 1765 from which could be deduced the conclusions reached in the Declaration of Independence; e.g., that taxation without representation was unconstitutional and that colonial legislatures were "subordinate" but not "subject" to Parliament. His political theories gave him an intercolonial reputation and were influential in the later establishment of state legislatures limited by a "fixed" constitution. After repeal of the Townshend duties, 1770, hostility against Great Britain tended to subside, but Adams worked to renew it by writing some forty bitter articles to Boston newspapers protesting the removal of the General Court from Boston to Cambridge, criticizing the independent tenure of judges and the fact that Governor Hutchinson received his salary from the Crown and not from the General Court. Not content with mere verbal action, he moved Boston Town Meeting to appoint in 1772 a committee of correspondence which would state the rights and grievances of the Colonies "to the several towns and to the world." This action may be regarded as the origin of revolutionary government in Massachusetts. As a member of the committee, he drafted a declaration of rights stressing America's legislative independence of Parliament; the alarmed Governor Hutchinson prepared a carefully worded reply that temporarily checked formation of correspondence committees. Adams countered by publishing some of Hutchinson's private letters which set forth views hostile to the radical faction. Realizing that the arrival of tea ships, cleared under North's Tea Act, might be used to precipitate a crisis, Adams drafted a resolution adopted by Boston Town Meeting declaring all who aided in the landing or selling of tea shipped by the East India Company to be enemies of America and moved, during a mass meeting at Faneuil Hall, that the tea "shall be returned to the place from which it came at all events." On Dec. 16, 1773, the day on which a lately arrived tea cargo had to be entered or confiscated, learning that Hutchinson had refused clearance for the return of the tea ships, he gave the signal which sent the "Mohawks" down to the wharf, where they threw the tea into the harbor.

With the enactment of the Coercive Acts Adams took a lead in organizing resistance, strongly supporting the creation of an intercolonial congress. Appointed delegate to the first Continental Congress, 1774, he was instrumental in organizing the convention that adopted the famous "Suffolk Resolves," virtually placing Massachusetts in a state of rebellion. Elected to the second Congress, 1775, he favored immediate independence, supported the resolution for the formation of independent state governments, proposed a confederation of such colonies as were ready for independence, and voted for and signed the Declaration of Independence. Essentially a revolutionary agitator, he possessed little talent as a constructive statesman. His influence and popularity declined after the final breach with Great Britain. He served in Congress until 1781, when he returned to Boston. He was defeated in a bid for Congress, 1788; was elected lieutenant-governor of Massachusetts, 1789–93, and subsequently governor, 1794–97.

ADAMS, SAMUEL HOPKINS (*b. Dunkirk, N.Y., 1871; d. Beaufort, S.C., 1958*), author, journalist. Studied at Hamilton College. Began his career at *McClure's Magazine* and *Collier's Weekly*, writing a series of articles exposing the patent medicine industry; the series was later published as *The Great American Fraud* (1906). Novels include *Flaming Youth* (1923) and *Revelry* (1926), a fictionalized account of Harding's presidency. He also wrote a serious account of that administration, *Incredible Era* (1939). Screenplays include *It Happened One Night* and *The Harvey Girls* (1942). Published *Grandfather Stories* (1955), a series of *New Yorker* essays.

ADAMS, THOMAS SEWALL (*b. Baltimore, Md., 1873; d. 1933*), economist, professor at University of Wisconsin, Cornell, and Yale. Expert on taxation.

ADAMS, WALTER SYDNEY (*b. Kessab, Syria, 1876; d. Pasadena, Calif., 1956*), astronomer. Studied at Dartmouth College and Yerkes Observatory at the University of Chicago, where he was an assistant to George E. Hale (1900–04). In that year, he

traveled with Hale to establish the Mount Wilson Solar Observatory in California; became acting director (1910) and director (1923–46). An expert in spectroscopy, Adams discovered major spectral differences in the sun and the luminosities of stars. Produced one of the most valuable empirical techniques for determining stellar luminosities, and hence distances—the method of spectroscopic parallaxes.

ADAMS, WILLIAM (*b. Colchester, Conn., 1807; d. 1880*), Presbyterian clergyman. Graduated from Yale, 1827. A founder of Union Theological Seminary, 1836, and its president, 1874–80.

ADAMS, WILLIAM LYSANDER (*b. Painesville, Ohio, 1821; d. Hood River, Oreg., 1906*), Campbellite preacher, physician. Editor *Oregon City Argus*; one of the founders of the Republican party in Oregon.

ADAMS, WILLIAM TAYLOR (*b. Bellingham, Mass., 1822; d. Boston, Mass., 1897*), writer of juvenile stories under the name "Oliver Optic." His first attempt at writing a book for boys, *The Boat Club* (1855), was a great popular success; he wrote five more volumes in the *Boat Club* series and other series, including *Great Western, Lake Shore, Onward and Upward, Yacht Club, Riverdale Story Books*, and *Woodville Stories*. Extended travels through Europe, Asia, and Africa furnished material for the *Young American Abroad* and *All Over the World* series; the Civil War forms the background of the *Army and Navy* and *Blue and Gray* series. In all, he wrote 126 books and about a thousand short tales for periodicals which he edited.

ADAMS, WILLIAM WIRT (*b. Frankfort, Ky., 1819; d. Jackson, Miss., 1888*), Confederate soldier, brother of Daniel W. Adams. Raised and commanded the 1st Mississippi Cavalry; promoted to brigadier general, 1863.

ADDAMS, JANE (*b. Cedarville, Ill., 1860; d. 1935*), social reformer, founder of Hull-House settlement in Chicago. Graduated from Rockford College; went on to Woman's Medical College in Philadelphia, where her health broke in 1882. During invalidism in Europe, studied settlement work. Opened Hull-House in a needy Chicago section in 1889. Her tact in handling people, affection for children, and impulse to help attracted love and disarmed criticism. By 1905 she had financed and built the finest plant devoted to working-class recreation and education in the United States. Her supreme practical achievement was to recruit and hold many able women who acknowledged her leadership. Artists and educators also brought to Hull-House a cultural program which included a music school, a labor museum, and the Hull-House Players. She brought her work to public attention by her many books, of which *Twenty Years at Hull-House* (1910) was outstanding. From 1915 to 1934 she opposed war as the supreme social evil.

ADDICKS, JOHN EDWARD O'SULLIVAN (*b. Philadelphia, Pa., 1841; d. New York, N.Y., 1919*), promoter. Promoted and speculated in securities of gas companies on the East Coast; organized the Gas Trust in Chicago; was unsuccessful in a unique seventeen-year fight to become U.S. senator from Delaware.

ADE, GEORGE (*b. Kentland, Ind., 1866; d. Brook, Ind., 1944*), author, playwright. Graduated Purdue University, B.S., 1887. Studied law briefly; worked as advertising writer and reporter for Indiana newspapers and Chicago *Morning News* (later *Record*). Wrote daily column of stories and sketches which provided material for first book. *Artie* (1896), and for *Pink Marsh* (1897) and *Doc' Horne* (1899). Used current idiom and catch phrases in a series of *Record* sketches, published in book form as *Fables in Slang* (1899) and very successful as imaginative, satirical comments on country ignorance and city pretension. Other collections of "fables" followed in 1901, 1902, and 1903. Between 1900 and 1910, Ade devoted his energies to writing for the stage, producing a number of hit musicals and comedies: *The Sultan of Sulu*, 1902; *The County Chairman*, 1903; and his best-known work, *The College Widow*, 1904. *Post* 1910, he spent his time in travel, entertaining friends at his estate in Indiana, and political and philanthropic activities. One of his last books, *The Old-Time Saloon* (1931), expressed his distaste for prohibition.

ADEE, ALVEY AUGUSTUS (*b. Astoria, Oreg., 1842; d. 1924*), diplomat. Held various foreign and domestic posts in the State Department, 1869-1924; expert drafter of diplomatic messages, treaties, and other state papers.

ADGATE, ANDREW (*d. Philadelphia, Pa., 1793*), musician. An early promoter of musical education in Philadelphia.

ADIE, DAVID CRAIG (*b. Hamilton, Scotland, 1888; d. Albany, N.Y., 1943*), social worker. Trained as a book-binder, served as labor organizer; came to America, 1913. Worked in Minneapolis, Minn., as labor-relations adviser. During World War I, served Minnesota Public Safety Commission as adviser on factory labor recruitment; served as associate secretary of national War Labor Policies Board. Impartial chairman of arbitration board for men's clothing industry, New York, N.Y., 1919–21; general secretary, Charity Organization Society, Buffalo, N.Y., 1921–32; New York State Commissioner of Social Welfare, *post* 1932. Favored broadening of federal social insurance; implementation of rehabilitation services; creation of federal welfare program which through grants-in-aid to the states would establish nationwide standards of eligibility and maximum and minimum allowances.

ADKINS, HOMER BURTON (*b. near Newport, Ohio, 1892; d. Madison, Wis., 1949*), chemist. B.S., Denison University, 1915; M.S., Ohio State, 1916; Ph.D., Ohio State, 1918. A leader in research and teaching of organic chemistry at University of Wisconsin, 1919–49. Early in his career, Adkins undertook the study of catalytic reactions, particularly those involving hydrogenation of organic compounds; later he studied the reactions of organic compounds with carbon monoxide under high pressure in the presence of catalysts. Between 1940 and 1946, he and his staff at Wisconsin were deeply concerned with military research programs.

ADLER, CYRUS (*b. Van Buren, Ark., 1863; d. Philadelphia, Pa., 1940*), orientalist, educational administrator, Jewish leader. A graduate of the University of Pennsylvania and Johns Hopkins, Adler became president of Dropsie College in 1908, after teaching and administrative posts at Johns Hopkins, the U.S. National Museum, and the Smithsonian Institution. A leader of American Judaism, Adler opposed Zionism but cooperated with Zionist leaders after the Balfour Declaration. He became president of the Jewish Theological Seminary in 1924, of the American Jewish Committee in 1929. He founded the American Jewish Historical Society, 1888, and edited the *Jewish Quarterly Review*, 1910–40.

ADLER, ELMER (*b. Rochester, N.Y., 1884; d. San Juan, Puerto Rico, 1962*), collector, printer, publisher, and bibliophile. A lifelong collector of books and fine prints, was considered an authority on the printed word. Founded Pynson Printers in 1922, where, in 1938, he established a permanent exhibit and center for study of the history of the printed word. In 1927 was a cofounder of Random House publishers. Was chief editor, designer, and producer of *Colophon* (1930–40) and *New Colophon* (1948–50). Established a department of graphic arts at Princeton University, where he was named assistant professor and curator in 1946. Retired from Princeton in 1952, and in 1956 became curator of La Casa del Libro, a museum and design center in Puerto Rico.

ADLER, FELIX (*b. Alzey, Germany, 1851; d. 1933*), religious leader, educator. Came to America as a child; A.B., Columbia (N.Y.), 1870; Ph.D., Heidelberg, 1873. In 1876 he founded the Society for Ethical Culture, a movement which became the central activity of his life. His philosophical position is found in two of his books, *An Ethical Philosophy of Life* (1918) and *The Reconstruction of the Spiritual Ideal* (1924). His appeal lay in a combination of moral insight, intellectual range, and a dedication to the ethical motive as a way of deepening and extending beneficent relations between the individual and the group.

ADLER, FELIX (*b. Clinton, Iowa, 1897; d. New York, N.Y., 1960*). A famous clown with the Ringling Brothers and Barnum and Bailey Circus (1910–59), remembered for his baby pig acts. Adler also performed at the White House.

ADLER, GEORGE J. (*b. Leipzig, Germany, 1821; d. New York, N.Y., 1868*), philologist. Professor of modern languages at New York University, 1846–53. Compiled *Dictionary of the German and English Languages* (1849).

ADLER, POLLY (*b. Ivanovo, White Russia, 1900; d. Hollywood, Calif., 1962*), madam and author. Born Pearl Adler, she immigrated to the U.S. in 1912 and became a citizen in 1929. In 1920 she established a Manhattan house of prostitution, where she also sold liquor. Her "house" became a "salon" for powerful politicians whose renown seems to have been partly responsible for the fact that she was able to remain in business despite numerous arrests and despite the notoriety that resulted from her involvement in the Seabury Committee investigation of the early 1930's. Her connections with gangland figures were also a factor. In 1943 she retired and moved to Los Angeles, where she wrote her best-selling autobiography *A House Is Not a Home* (1953).

ADLER, SAMUEL (*b. Worms, Germany, 1809; d. 1891*), rabbi of Temple Emanu-El, New York City, *post* 1857. Prominent in the foundation of Reform Judaism. Father of Felix Adler.

ADLER, SARA (*b. Odessa, Russia, 1858; d. New York, N.Y., 1953*), actress. Immigrated to the U.S. in 1884. With her husband, Jacob Adler, she was instrumental in transforming the Yiddish stage from primarily vaudeville and music hall platform to that of serious classical theater of the highest artistic standards. Also performed in translations of Shakespeare, Ibsen, and Tolstoy. Her greatest role was that of Katusha Maslova in an adaptation of Tolstoy's *Resurrection*.

ADLUM, JOHN (*b. York, Pa., 1759; d. Georgetown, D.C., 1836*), pioneer in viticulture. Cultivated, studied, and improved American grapes, popularizing the Catawba variety.

ADRAIN, ROBERT (*b. Carrickfergus, Ireland, 1775; d. 1843*), mathematician. Taught at Pennsylvania, Rutgers, and Columbia universities, 1809–34; did original work on the exponential law of error.

ADRIAN, GILBERT (*b. Naugatuck, Conn., 1903; d. Hollywood, Calif., 1959*), costume and dress designer. Studied at the New York School of Fine and Applied Arts and in Paris. After designing costumes for three *Music Box* revues for Irving Berlin in New York, Adrian went to Hollywood to design the costumes for the film *Eagle* starring Rudolph Valentino (1925). Subsequent films include *Daddy Long Legs* (1930), *The Women*, *The Wizard of Oz*, *The Philadelphia Story*, and *Woman of the Year*. In 1941, he established his own couture house; he was awarded the Coty American Fashion Critics Award in 1945.

AFFLECK, THOMAS (*b. Dumfries, Scotland, 1812; d. 1868*), agricultural writer. Came to America, 1832. Advanced agriculture in the South through his writings and the example of his successful undertakings in Mississippi and Texas. An early advocate of diversified farming.

AGASSIZ, ALEXANDER (b. Neuchâtel, Switzerland, 1835; d. 1910), zoologist, oceanographer, mine operator, son of Jean Louis Agassiz. Came to America, 1849; studied mining, engineering, chemistry, and natural history at Harvard; received A.B., 1855, B.S. in engineering, 1857. Superintendent at copper mines, Calumet, Mich., 1867–69; greatly improved output and working conditions. Began issuing the most important work of his scientific career, *Revision of the Echini*, in 1872. Curator of Harvard University Museum, 1874. Developing a new interest in marine biology, he began a series of cruises exploring the Gulf Stream, West Indies, Bahamas, Hawaiian Islands, and Pacific aboard the government-owned *Blake* and *Albatross*, and private vessels, 1877–1904; published extensive reports on expeditions. Although he did little classroom teaching, his generosity toward young scientists and his interest in their work gave him an influence which transcended classroom instruction.

AGASSIZ, ELIZABETH CABOT CARY (b. Boston, Mass., 1822; d. Arlington Heights, Mass., 1907), educator. One of the founders of Radcliffe College; author of a life of her husband, Jean Louis Agassiz.

AGASSIZ, JEAN LOUIS RODOLPHE (b. Motier-en-Vuly, Switzerland, 1807; d. Cambridge, Mass., 1873), naturalist. Studied medicine, 1824–30, at Universities of Zurich and Heidelberg, and at University of Munich with the embryologist Döllinger. In 1829, published *The Fishes of Brazil*, one of the most important accounts of a local fish fauna presented to that time. Met the master comparative anatomist Cuvier in Paris, 1831; continued his researches on fossil fish by utilizing the collections available at the Jardin des Plantes. Influenced by Cuvier's attempts to found a classification of animals on a structural basis, he wrote *Recherches sur les Poissons fossiles* (1833–44), a pioneer work on the fish fauna of the primitive seas. Through the intervention of the distinguished explorer Humboldt, he had obtained a post as professor of natural history at Neuchâtel, 1832. His teaching years were not devoid of zoological research; he gained European fame through the publication of: *History of the Fresh Water Fishes of Central Europe* (1839–42), *Études critiques sur les Mollusques fossiles* (1840–45), *Nomenclator Zoologicus* (1842–46), and *Monograph on the Fossil Fishes of the Old Red or Devonian of the British Isles and Russia* (1844–45). Learning of de Charpentier and Venetz's recently expounded theory of local glacial action, he extended it to include large portions of Europe and explained present geological formations and land contours in terms of the glacial movements of an earlier epoch, the Ice Age. After eight years of studying existing glaciers he wrote *Études sur les Glaciers* (1840), to be followed by *Système Glaciaire* (1846) and *Nouvelles études et expériences sur les Glaciers actuels* (1847). Visiting America in 1846, Agassiz stayed and made several trips on Coast Survey steamers as a guest of the government at Harvard University, 1848. He led a group exploring the northern and eastern shores of Lake Superior, 1848, and a ten weeks' exploration of the Florida Reefs, 1851. Began ca. 1856 assembling material for his ten-volume *Contributions to the Natural History of the United States*; four of the projected ten volumes were published. The first volume, containing the *Essay on Classification* (1857), was considered to be his greatest contribution to natural history during his life in America. In the *Essay* he developed Cuvier's ideas, attempting to relate embryonic changes to the succession of geological ages; it was his extension of Cuvier's work plus his own idealism that led him to oppose the Darwinian theory of evolution by natural selection. Abroad in summer of 1859, he returned to Cambridge, raised funds through public and private appropriations, and began construction of a museum of

comparative zoology. Made extensive explorations of Brazil, 1865; studied glacial phenomena in the Rocky Mountains, 1868. In 1869 he lectured at Cornell, participated in Coast Survey dredging operations near Cuba, and presented an exhaustive memoir of the life and work of Humboldt. The strain of this heavy work schedule caused an attack of apoplexy which prevented his return to the Museum until November 1870. Aboard the Coast Survey vessel *Hassler*, on her 1871 trip to California, he was unable to do any effective deep-sea dredging, as he had planned, but he saw new evidence for his glacier theory around the Magellan Straits and the Chiloê Islands. Shortly prior to his death he founded the Anderson School of Natural History, a summer school where teachers could study science by directly observing the natural life available in their immediate surroundings. In October 1873 he gave his final course of lectures at the Museum and then wrote what was to be his last article, "Evolution and Permanence of Type," a justification of his attitude toward current trends in biology.

His influence on American thought was twofold: first, his prestige, enthusiasm, and teaching methods greatly accelerated the serious study of natural history; and secondly, his criticisms of current educational practices, especially rote memorization and classical studies, resulted in a new emphasis on advanced and original work as factors in mental training.

AGATE, ALFRED T. (b. Sparta, N.Y., 1812; d. Washington, D.C., 1846), illustrator, painter of miniatures. Botanical artist on the Wilkes Exploring Expedition, 1838–42.

AGATE, FREDERICK STYLES (b. Sparta, N.Y., 1803; d. Sparta, 1844), painter, brother of Alfred T. Agate. Historical and portrait painter; a founder of the National Academy of Design.

AGEE, JAMES RUFUS (b. Knoxville, Tenn., 1909; d. New York, N.Y., 1955), novelist, poet, critic, screenwriter. Graduated from Harvard, 1932. As a reporter for *Fortune*, 1932–39, Agee covered various social crises of the Great Depression. In 1936, the magazine commissioned him and photographer Walker Evans to report on conditions of tenant farmers in the South. The resulting book, *Let Us Now Praise Famous Men* (1941), became Agee's most famous work and was critically if not commercially successful.

Film critic for *Time* and *The Nation* (1941–1948) and author of screenplays including *The African Queen* (1951) and *The Night of the Hunter* (1955).

His posthumously published novel, *A Death in the Family* (1957), is autobiographical and centers on his father's death in Knoxville before World War I. It won the Pulitzer Prize and was later adapted for the stage and cinema under the title *All the Way Home*.

AGGREY, JAMES EMMAN KWEGYIR (b. Anamabu, West Africa, 1875; d. New York, N.Y., 1927), African educator.

AGNEW, CORNELIUS REA (b. New York, N.Y., 1830; d. 1888), ophthalmologist. Graduated Columbia College, 1849; M.D., College of Physicians and Surgeons, New York, 1852; studied abroad, 1855. Surgeon general of New York state militia, 1858; medical director of the New York State Hospital for Volunteers, 1861; an organizer of the U.S. Sanitary Commission. With Drs. Van Buren and Gibbs prepared plans for Judiciary Square Hospital at Washington, model for the pavilion system of hospitals. Active in foundation of Columbia School of Mines, in an ophthalmic clinic at College of Physicians and Surgeons, and in both the Brooklyn and Manhattan Eye and Ear Hospitals. Professor of eye and ear diseases at College of Physicians and Surgeons, 1869–88.

AGNEW, DAVID HAYES (*b. Lancaster Co., Pa., 1818; d. 1892*), surgeon, teacher of anatomy and surgery. Graduated medical department, University of Pennsylvania, 1838. Bought, 1852, and revived Philadelphia School of Anatomy where he acquired the reputation of being an extremely able lecturer and demonstrator. Served during the Civil War as surgeon in government hospitals and became an expert in gun-shot wounds. In 1870 he was appointed professor of clinical surgery, and in the following year professor of surgery at the University of Pennsylvania, retiring as professor emeritus in 1889. Noted as a consultant and author of *Treatise on the Principles and Practice of Surgery* (1878, 1881, 1883).

AGNEW, ELIZA (*b. New York, N.Y., 1807; d. Oodooville, Ceylon, 1883*), missionary to Ceylon, 1840–83, for American Board of Commissioners for Foreign Missions; pioneer in education of Ceylonese women.

AGNUS, FELIX (*b. Lyons, France, 1839; d. 1925*), Union soldier, newspaperman. Came to America, 1860; won Civil War brevet of brigadier general. Managed and published *Baltimore American*, 1869–1920.

AGRAMONTE Y SIMONI, ARISTIDES (*b. Camaguey, Cuba, 1868; d. New Orleans, La., 1931*), pathologist, expert in tropical medicine. Took a conspicuous part in the work of the Reed Yellow Fever Board.

AIKEN, CHARLES AUGUSTUS (*b. Manchester, Vt., 1827; d. Princeton, N.J., 1892*), educator. Professor of Latin at Dartmouth, 1859–66, and Princeton, 1866–69; president of Union College, Schenectady, N.Y., 1869–71; professor of Christian ethics and apologetics, Princeton, 1871–92.

AIKEN, DAVID WYATT (*b. Winnsboro, S.C., 1828; d. 1887*), Confederate soldier, agricultural editor. Democratic congressman from South Carolina, 1876–86; spokesman for militant agrarian interests.

AIKEN, GEORGE L. (*b. Boston, Mass., 1830; d. Jersey City, N.J., 1876*), actor and playwright. Wrote the original successful dramatization of Harriet Beecher Stowe's novel *Uncle Tom's Cabin* (1852).

AIKEN, WILLIAM (*b. Charleston, S.C., 1806; d. Flat Rock, N.C., 1887*), planter, statesman, philanthropist. Governor of South Carolina, 1844–46; representative in Congress, 1851–57; influenced important legislation through his position on leading committees and his acceptability to all Democratic factions.

AIKENS, ANDREW JACKSON (*b. Barnard, Vt., 1830; d. 1909*), editor, publisher. A founder of the Chicago and New York Newspaper Unions, ancestors of the Western Newspaper Union.

AIME, VALCOUR (*b. St. Charles, La., 1798; d. St. James Parish, La., 1867*), sugar planter. Sugar was refined for the first time in the United States at his refinery in St. James Parish. In 1829, Aime applied steam power to his machinery; he accepted new and superior processes as they appeared and was the leading advocate of the Rillieux apparatus. He experimented with cane planted at varying distances, early adopted fertilizers, used peas and clover on his land, and urged Southern planters to diversify their crops to the point of complete self-sufficiency. Successful in overcoming losses suffered in the Civil War, in later years he donated large sums of money to religious and educational institutions.

AINSLIE, HEW (*b. Bargeny Mains, Ayrshire, Scotland, 1792; d. Louisville, Ky., 1878*), poet. Came to America, 1822. Published *Scottish Songs, Ballads, and Poems* (1855).

AINSLIE, PETER (*b. Dunnsville, Va., 1867; d. Baltimore, Md., 1934*), Disciples of Christ minister; advocate of Christian unity.

AINSWORTH, FREDERICK CRAYTON (*b. Woodstock, Vt., 1852; d. Washington, D.C., 1934*), army officer. Chief of Record and Pension Office, War Department, 1892–1904; adjutant general until 1912.

AITKEN, ROBERT (*b. Dalkeith, Scotland, 1734; d. 1802*), printer, publisher, engraver. Issued at Philadelphia *Aitken's General American Register* (1773); published the *Pennsylvania Magazine* (1775–76), to which Thomas Paine, Francis Hopkinson, and John Witherspoon were contributors. When the outbreak of the Revolution stopped the importation of English-printed Bibles, he undertook his greatest publishing enterprise, the first complete English Bible printed in America (1782). This venture was a financial failure despite congressional authorization and the support of religious organizations.

AITKIN, ROBERT GRANT (*b. Jackson, Calif., 1864; d. Berkeley, Calif., 1951*), astronomer. After graduating from Williams College (B.A., 1883), taught mathematics and astronomy at the University of the Pacific in California. In 1895, became assistant astronomer at Lick Observatory, Mount Hamilton, Calif., and retired as director in 1935. An expert in the new field of double-star observation and theories, he undertook the systematic measurement of double stars discovered by S. W. Burnham. From 1896 to 1915, with W. J. Hussey, he surveyed all stars to the ninth magnitude observable from Lick, which included 100,000 stars. Published a report of this work, *The Binary Stars* (1918) and *New General Catalogue of Double Stars Within 120° of the North Pole* (1932). President, American Astronomical Society, 1937–40.

AKELEY, CARL ETHAN (*b. Clarendon, N.Y., 1864; d. Africa, 1926*), taxidermist, inventor, naturalist, explorer. Developed techniques for construction of habitat groups; collected specimens and made groups for the Field Museum and the American Museum of Natural History; invented the Akeley Cement Gun and a motion-picture camera.

AKELEY, MARY LEONORE (*b. Mary Leonore Jobe, Tappan, Ohio, 1878; d. Stonington, Conn., 1966*), explorer, author, and educator. Ph.B. (1897), Scio (Ohio) College; graduate studies at Bryn Mawr (1901–03); M.A. (1909), Columbia University. While teaching at Hunter College, New York City (1907–16), conducted major explorations of the Canadian Northwest. Was active in the Camp Fire Girls and operated Camp Mystic in Mystic, Conn., for affluent urban girls (1916–30). Married explorer Carl Ethan Akeley (1924) and in 1926–27 accompanied him on an African expedition. When he died in Africa, she took on the direction of the safari, and upon returning to the U.S. devoted herself to his work. Known as the woman who "brought the jungle to Central Park West," she was special adviser and assistant for the African Hall in the American Museum of Natural History and dedicated the Akeley African Hall when it opened in 1936. Lectured extensively about her African experience and wrote seven books, all on Africa. Was active in the establishment of a system of nature reserves throughout Africa.

AKERMAN, AMOS TAPPAN (*b. Portsmouth, N.H., 1821; d. Cartersville, Ga., 1880*), lawyer, public official. Conservative Republican in postwar Georgia; member of Georgia state constitutional convention, 1868; U.S. attorney general, 1870–71.

AKERS, BENJAMIN PAUL (*b. Saccarappa, Maine, 1825; d. Philadelphia, Pa., 1861*), neo-classic sculptor. His best-known works are *Una and the Lion*, *St. Elizabeth of Hungary*, and *The Dead Pearl Diver*.

AKERS, ELIZABETH CHASE (*b. Strong, Maine, 1832; d. Tuckahoe, N.Y., 1911*), writer. Wife of Benjamin P. Akers; author of "Rock Me to Sleep" (1860) and other minor verse.

AKINS, ZOË (*b. Humansville, Mo., 1886; d. Pasadena, Calif., 1958*), playwright, poet, screenwriter. Studied at Monticello Seminary and Hosmer Hall, in St. Louis. Akins wrote poetry before turning to plays with *The Magical City* (1916), produced by the Washington Square Players. Her first success was *Déclassée* (1919), a starring vehicle for Ethel Barrymore; other plays include *Daddy's Gone-A-Hunting* (1921) and *The Greeks Had a Word For It* (1930), which became the basis for the film *How to Marry A Millionaire*. Wrote the scripts for *Morning Glory* (1933), *Outcast Lady* (1934), *Camille* (1937), and *Zaza* (1939). Awarded the Pulitzer Prize (1935) for her adaptation of Edith Wharton's *The Old Maid*.

AKO, MICHEL. *See* ACO, MICHEL.

ALARCÓN, HERNANDO DE (*fl. 1540*), Spanish explorer. When Coronado departed on his overland expedition in search of the Seven Cities of Cíbola, Alarcón was sent along the Mexican coast to provide sea support. He entered the Gulf of California and proceeded up the Colorado River attempting to establish contact with Coronado; failing, he returned to the Gulf. A second attempt took him up the Colorado to a point not far from the beginning of the Grand Canyon. A substantial achievement of Alarcón's expedition was a map of the Gulf of California drawn (1541) by his pilot. On this map the Gulf was shown to be a true one and not a passage; therefore California was not an island as had been suspected.

ALBEE, EDWARD FRANKLIN (*b. Machias, Maine, 1857; d. Palm Beach, Fla., 1930*), theater manager and builder. Along with B. F. Keith, founded a vaudeville circuit and raised standards of popular entertainment.

ALBEE, ERNEST (*b. Langdon, N.H., 1865; d. 1927*), philosopher. Instructor and professor of philosophy, Cornell University, 1892–1927; author of *The History of English Utilitarianism* (1902).

ALBRIGHT, JACOB (*b. Pottstown, Pa., 1759; d. 1808*), Methodist religious leader. Traveled through Pennsylvania, Maryland, and Virginia, 1796–1808, preaching to German settlers.

ALBRO, LEWIS COLT (*b. Pittsfield, Mass., 1876; d. 1924*), architect. One of the best modern American domestic designers.

ALCORN, JAMES LUSK (*b. near Golconda, Ill., 1816; d. 1894*), lawyer. Raised in Kentucky. Served as Whig member of Mississippi senate, 1848–56; as representative, 1846, 1856, 1865; was author and foremost champion of the legislation establishing the levee system along the Mississippi River. Delegate to Mississippi secession convention, 1861. After the Civil War he entered the Republican party hoping to utilize the black vote in the best interests of the state. Elected governor of Mississippi, 1869; resigned two years later to enter U.S. Senate. As a senator, 1871–77, he urged the removal of the political disabilities of former secessionists, resisted all efforts to enforce social equality by legislation, denounced the federal cotton tax, and defended separate schools for both races in Mississippi.

ALCOTT, AMOS BRONSON (*b. near Wolcott, Conn., 1799; d. 1888*), educator, author, mystic. Held various teaching positions, 1823–33; although an able teacher, he was unsuccessful because of his advanced educational and religious views. Opened a school in Boston, 1834; rightly suspected of encouraging independent thinking in religious matters, he lost pupils and the school failed. Moved to Concord, Mass., 1840; founded Fruitlands, a short-lived Utopian community, 1844–45. Appointed superintendent of Concord schools, 1859, he introduced some of his best educational innovations, which included singing, calisthenics, study of physiology, and a parent-teacher club. A writer of both verse and prose, he is best remembered for his association with Hawthorne, Emerson, and Thoreau and for the extreme form of transcendental idealism which he cultivated and used as a guide for his own actions.

ALCOTT, LOUISA MAY (*b. Germantown, Pa., 1832; d. Boston, Mass., 1888*), author, daughter of Amos Bronson Alcott and Abigail (May) Alcott. She showed an early talent for literature, writing poems, plays, and short stories; by 1860 her work began to be published in the *Atlantic Monthly*. Served as a hospital nurse during the Civil War. Visited Europe, 1865, and then returned to America, where she became editor of a children's magazine, *Merry's Museum*, 1867. Her novel *Little Women* (1868, 1869), based on her own family life, brought great personal success, established her as a writer of books for children and enabled her to make her family financially independent. Among her other works are *Hospital Sketches* (1863), *An Old Fashioned Girl* (1870), and *Little Men* (1871).

ALCOTT, WILLIAM ANDRUS (*b. Wolcott, Conn., 1798; d. Newton, Mass., 1859*), educator, physician, pioneer in physical education. A cousin of Amos Bronson Alcott; wrote numerous works on educational reform and healthful living.

ALDEN, CYNTHIA MAY WESTOVER (*b. Afton, Iowa, 1862; d. 1931*), philanthropic promoter; founder and president of the International Sunshine Society.

ALDEN, EBENEZER (*b. Randolph, Mass., 1788; d. Randolph, 1881*), medical historian, bibliophile, and genealogist. Author of a history of the Massachusetts Medical Society (1838).

ALDEN, HENRY MILLS (*b. Mt. Tabor, Vt., 1836; d. New York, N.Y., 1919*), editor, author. Under his editorship, 1869–1919, *Harper's Magazine* became the most widely circulated American periodical of its type.

ALDEN, ICHABOD (*b. Duxbury, Mass., 1739; d. Cherry Valley, N.Y., 1778*), Revolutionary soldier. Appointed to command at Cherry Valley, he disregarded advance warnings and was killed in the Nov. 11, 1778 massacre by Tories and Indians under Walter Butler and Brant.

ALDEN, ISABELLA MACDONALD (*b. Rochester, N.Y., 1841; d. Palo Alto, Calif, 1930*), author. Editor and writer for Sunday-school periodicals; author of the "Pansy" books for young people.

ALDEN, JAMES (*b. Portland, Maine, 1810; d. San Francisco, Calif., 1877*), naval officer. Served in Wilkes Exploring Expedition, 1838–42. As captain of USS *Brooklyn* at Mobile Bay, his hesitation drew forth Farragut's famous "Damn the torpedoes!" remark.

ALDEN, JOHN (*b. ca. 1599; d. Duxbury, Mass., 1687*), one of the *Mayflower* Pilgrims; signer of the *Mayflower* Compact. Removed from Plymouth to Duxbury, *ca.* 1627. He held various public offices, including surveyor of highways; member of local committee for raising a force against the Indians; deputy from Duxbury, *ca.* 1641 to 1649; member of local council of war, 1675; member of colony's council of war in 1646, 1653, 1658, and 1667; treasurer, 1656–58; governor's assistant, Jan. 1, 1632–33 through 1640–41, and again in 1650–86. He was "deputy governor" in 1664–65, also in 1677 following King Philip's War. Married Priscilla Mullens (or Molines). The famous story used by

Longfellow in *The Courtship of Miles Standish* is without foundation.

ALDEN, JOHN FERRIS (*b. Cohoes, N.Y., 1852; d. 1917*), civil engineer. Directed Rochester Bridge & Iron Works, 1885–1901; built many railroad bridges in United States and Canada.

ALDEN, JOSEPH (*b. Cairo, N.Y., 1807; d. 1885*), educator. Taught at Williams College, 1835–52; at Lafayette College, 1852–57. President of Jefferson College, 1857–62; principal of State Normal School, Albany, 1867–82.

ALDEN, RAYMOND MACDONALD (*b. New Hartford, N.Y., 1873; d. Philadelphia, Pa., 1924*), philologist. Edited variorum edition of *The Sonnets of Shakespeare* (1916).

ALDEN, TIMOTHY (*b. Yarmouth, Mass., 1771; d. Pittsburgh, Pa., 1839*), Congregational clergyman, college president, antiquarian. Graduated Harvard, 1794; founded Allegheny College, 1817. Author of *A Collection of American Epitaphs* (1814).

ALDEN, WILLIAM LIVINGSTON (*b. Williamstown, Mass., 1837; d. Buffalo, N.Y., 1908*), journalist. Introduced the sport of canoeing to America.

ALDERMAN, EDWIN ANDERSON (*b. Wilmington, N.C., 1861; d. 1931*), educator and orator. Leader in the field of popular education; outstanding president of University of Virginia, 1904–31.

ALDRICH, BESS GENEVRA STREETER (*b. Cedar Falls, Iowa, 1881; d. Elmwood, Nebr., 1954*), novelist, short story writer. Although never critically acclaimed, Aldrich published 168 short stories in popular magazines and thirteen novels dealing with pioneer life in the Midwest; the best-known are *A Lantern in Her Hand* (1928), *A White Bird Flying* (1931), and *The Lieutenant's Lady* (1942).

ALDRICH, CHARLES ANDERSON (*b. Plymouth, Mass., 1888; d. Rochester, Minn., 1949*), pediatrician, educator. Graduated Northwestern, 1914; M.D., Northwestern, 1915. Began general practice in Winnetka. After graduate training at New York Nursery and Children's Hospital, and at Children's Hospital and Massachusetts General Hospital, Boston, he began a busy pediatric practice in the Chicago area, 1921. A staff member at several hospitals, he became professor of pediatrics at Northwestern Medical School, 1941, having taught there since 1934. From 1944 until his death, he was director of the Rochester Child Health Institute of the Mayo Clinic. Author of a number of publications, notably on nephritis, he developed tests for measurement of edema and for degree of hearing in the newborn. His major contribution lay in bringing child development studies into pediatric thought, causing a shift away from the rigid, arbitrary child-rearing practices (especially in feeding) that had evolved apace with expanding scientific knowledge. With his wife he wrote the widely read *Babies Are Human Beings* (1938), a masterly presentation in layman's terms of data to support the thesis that child-rearing should be collaboration with growth, a series of sensible compromises between the baby's needs and desires and the expectations of society.

ALDRICH, CHESTER HOLMES (*b. Providence, R.I., 1871; d. Rome, Italy, 1940*), architect. Partner in Delano & Aldrich; director, American Academy in Rome, 1935–40.

ALDRICH, EDGAR (*b. Pittsburg, N.H., 1848; d. 1921*), jurist, U.S. district judge of New Hampshire, 1891–1921; appointed master in the litigation involving Mary Baker Eddy, 1907.

ALDRICH, LOUIS (*b. Ohio, 1843; d. Kennebunkport, Maine, 1901*), actor. Versatile in support of Edwin Forrest, Edwin Booth,

and Charlotte Cushman, he had his greatest success as Joe Saunders in Bartley Campbell's *My Partner*, 1879–85.

ALDRICH, NELSON WILMARTH (*b. Foster, R.I., 1841; d. 1915*), statesman, financier. Achieved early success in business; married Abby Chapman, 1866. Elected to Congress, 1878, 1880; made an independent campaign for the Rhode Island seat left vacant by death of General Burnside and entered the U.S. Senate, 1881. Soon became identified with a small group of Republican senatorial leaders who, like himself, could act independently without fear of losing their constituencies. A protectionist and spokesman for business, he challenged the Mills Bill and brought forward a counter-proposal, 1888; in 1890 he was concerned with the Silver Purchase Act, the Anti-Trust Act, the Force Act, and the McKinley Tariff. In 1892, a time of great Democratic victories, he and a few other successful Republican senators obtained control of their party's power in the upper house. Four years later, when the Republican party regained strength, the coterie—called the "Big Four" and composed of Aldrich, Allison of Iowa, Platt of Connecticut, and Spooner of Wisconsin—acting with almost complete unanimity dominated the Senate until Platt's death in 1905. Aldrich's association with the Dingley Tariff of 1897 gave him a popular reputation as the protectionist senator *par excellence*; however, his true aims were the maintenance of the *status quo*, the unification of his party and the preparation of important legislation necessary to resolve impending monetary problems. The following year, the "Four" struggled hard to prevent war with Spain, reluctantly accepted McKinley's reversal of policy, and then gave obligatory support to the war. Theodore Roosevelt's accession to the presidency did not alter the influence of the "Four" who supported his program in Congress and advised him on matters regarding Cuba. In 1902 Aldrich and his group met with Roosevelt and determined the official position of the party in the approaching elections; yet, within two years, Roosevelt's defiance of the Senate transformed Aldrich into the leader of the opposition. The Aldrich-Roosevelt political duel centered about Roosevelt's attempts to control foreign policy without seeking the Senate's advice and his approval of the Hepburn Rate Bill (1906), a bill giving extensive railway rate-fixing powers to the Interstate Commerce Commission.

In 1908, after contributing to Taft's nomination, Aldrich went abroad to make a thorough study of modern banking as chairman of the National Monetary Commission, which had been established by the Aldrich-Vreeland Act, an emergency measure made necessary by the panic of 1907. He returned to America determined to introduce important and extensive changes in the existing banking system; instead he faced another tariff battle in Congress. Certain Western Republicans, including La Follette, formed a bloc whose aim was not a reduction of the tariff but a rearrangement of rates which would favor their sectional interests. Eastern senators opposed these insurgents; their differences were forcibly resolved in the Payne-Aldrich Tariff, 1909. His dominant position challenged and rendered untenable by the Republican insurgents, Aldrich ended his senatorial career in 1911. The Aldrich Plan, a scheme for banking reform, was the principal interest of his remaining years. Possessed of great skill as a parliamentarian, Aldrich was a superb judge of human nature in individual instances but defective in assessing mass psychology.

ALDRICH, RICHARD (*b. Providence, R.I., 1863; d. Rome, Italy, 1937*), principal music critic of the *New York Times*, 1902–23.

ALDRICH, THOMAS BAILEY (*b. Portsmouth, N.H., 1836; d. 1907*), poet, writer of fiction, editor. Held numerous editorial positions in New York, 1856–61; was a war correspondent, 1861–62; moved to Boston, 1865, as editor of *Every Saturday*;

made the acquaintance of Longfellow, Lowell, Holmes, Hawthorne, and Whittier. Editor of the *Atlantic Monthly* , 1881–90. His best prose work is *The Story of a Bad Boy* (1870). His short stories, notably *Marjorie Daw* (1873), are superior to his longer fiction. Aldrich's poetry is marked by technical skill and polish but is minor in range.

ALDRIDGE, IRA FREDERICK (*b. New York, N.Y.*[?], *1807; d. Lodz, Poland, 1867*), tragedian. A black, and a protégé of Edmund Kean, he was considered one of the ablest interpreters of Shakespeare of his day both in England and on the Continent.

ALEMANY, JOSÉ SADOC (*b. Vich, Spain, 1814; d. Spain, 1888*), Roman Catholic clergyman, Dominican missionary. Came to America, 1841; consecrated bishop of Monterey, 1850. Was exemplary bishop and archbishop of San Francisco, 1853–84.

ALEXANDER, ABRAHAM (*b. 1717; d. 1786*), Revolutionary patriot. As member of the Committee for Safety, Mecklenburg Co., N.C., he presided over the meeting at Charlotte, May 31, 1775, whose resolutions called for creation of a county government independent of England.

ALEXANDER, ARCHIBALD (*b. Lexington, Va., 1772; d. 1851*), Presbyterian clergyman, educator, author. First professor at theological seminary in Princeton; held chair of theology, 1812–51.

ALEXANDER, BARTON STONE (*b. Nicholas Co., Ky., 1819; d. 1878*), Union soldier, engineer. Graduated West Point, 1842; a principal agent in planning and constructing defenses of Washington, 1861–65.

ALEXANDER, DE ALVA STANWOOD (*b. Richmond, Maine, 1845; d. 1925*), Republican representative from New York, historian. Author of *Political History of the State of New York* (1906, 1909, 1923).

ALEXANDER, EDWARD PORTER (*b. Washington, Ga., 1835; d. 1910*), Confederate artillerist, author, railroad executive. Graduated West Point, 1857. As army engineer, aided in development of the breech-loading rifle and the "wig-wag" signaling system. At Georgia's secession he resigned his commission and served in Confederate signal service and ordnance. Appointed November 1862 to command of a battalion of artillery in Longstreet's corps, he participated in battles of Fredericksburg, Chancellorsville, and Gettysburg. Accompanied Longstreet to Georgia, then to Knoxville and the Tennessee mountains; made brigadier general, 1864, and served with Lee's army until surrender, 1865. After the war Alexander held important positions in the railroad industry. His comprehensive and important *Military Memoirs of a Confederate* appeared in 1907.

ALEXANDER, FRANCIS (*b. Killingly, Conn., 1800; d. Florence, Italy*[?], *ca. 1881*), painter, lithographer. A popular portraitist in Boston, 1832–1860.

ALEXANDER, FRANZ GABRIEL (*b. Budapest, Austria-Hungary, 1891; d. Palm Springs, Calif., 1964*), psychoanalyst. M.D. (1913), University of Budapest. Became the first training candidate accepted by the Institute for Psychoanalysis in Berlin, where he was considered one of Freud's best pupils and was appointed assistant in 1921. In 1930 became professor of psychoanalysis at the University of Chicago, and in 1932 founded the Chicago Institute for Psychoanalysis, where he remained director for twenty-five years, working with numerous distinguished psychoanalysts and studying the relationship between specific psychic conflicts and psychosomatic dysfunction. Became citizen in 1938. In 1956 became director of psychiatric and psychosomatic research at Mt. Sinai Hospital in Los Angeles, where his principle research involved patient-therapist interaction. From 1957 to 1963 was clinical professor of psychiatry at the University of Southern California School of Medicine. A leader in the field of psychoanalysis, he was noted for his ability to remain above factionalism and for his anti-authoritarianism.

ALEXANDER, GROSS (*b. Scottsville, Ky., 1852; d. Long Beach, Calif., 1915*), Methodist clergyman. Professor of Greek, Vanderbilt University, 1884–1902; editor of Methodist publications.

ALEXANDER, GROVER CLEVELAND (*b. Elba, Howard Co., Nebr., 1887; d. St. Paul, Nebr., 1950*), baseball player. Entered organized baseball, 1909, as pitcher with Galesburg, Ill., club; then to Indianapolis club of the American Association, to Syracuse of the New York State League (for which he won twenty-nine games in 1910), and to the Philadelphia club of the National League for the 1911 season. His twenty-eight victories that season set a record for a first-year pitcher in the majors. Traded to the Chicago Cubs in 1917. Served in France in World War I. When discharged in 1919 returned to the Cubs. By 1926, his disregard of training rules had made him a problem, and he was traded to the St. Louis Cardinals on a waiver. Was a vital factor in securing the 1926 world championship for the Cardinals. He did well in 1927 and 1928, but in 1929, because of his drinking, he was sent home before the end of the season and traded that winter to Philadelphia. Released in mid-season, 1930, he drifted into the minors and semi-professional outfits, and at last into menial odd jobs. Pitched 440 complete games, winning 373, of which 90 were shutouts. His lifetime average of runs earned against him (2.56) set the major-league record.

ALEXANDER, HARTLEY BURR (*b. Lincoln, Nebr., 1873; d. Claremont, Calif., 1939*), philosopher, anthropologist; special interest in mythology of the American Indian. Taught at University of Nebraska and Scripps College.

ALEXANDER, JAMES (*b. Scotland, 1691; d. Albany, N.Y., 1756*), lawyer, politician, statesman. Fled to America in consequence of involvement with the Rebellion of 1715; studied and practiced law. Made a member of the New York Council, 1721, and in 1973, of the New Jersey Council; attorney general of New Jersey, 1723–27. An active opponent of Governor Cosby's arbitrary rule, he was dismissed from the Council of New York, 1732, and in 1735 removed from the Council of New Jersey. His greatest prominence was attained in 1735, when he, with William Smith, volunteered to serve as counsel to the printer and publisher John Peter Zenger. In the course of Zenger's trial, both were declared in contempt and stricken from the roll of attorneys. Reinstated as a member of the bar, Alexander was recalled to both Councils on Cosby's death, and from 1736–56 was active in both capacities. He died at Albany while opposing legislation he considered oppressive to the people of the colony.

ALEXANDER, JOHN HENRY (*b. Annapolis, Md., 1812; d. 1867*), geologist, coal-mining executive. Author of *A Universal Dictionary of Weights and Measures, Ancient and Modern* (1850).

ALEXANDER, JOHN WHITE (*b. Allegheny, Pa., 1856; d. 1915*), painter. Began his career as an illustrator for *Harper's*, 1874; studied in France, Germany, and Italy. Primarily a portraitist; his output was distinguished and prodigious. He also painted landscapes and was chosen to paint the murals around the grand staircase of the Carnegie Institute, Pittsburgh. He gave long and devoted service as an officer in art societies both at home and abroad.

ALEXANDER, JOSEPH ADDISON (*b. Philadelphia, Pa., 1809; d. 1860*), educator, linguist, author. Son of Archibald Alexander (1772–1851). Instructor and professor of Biblical language and literature, Princeton Seminary, 1834–60; editor of *Biblical Repertory* and author of several Biblical commentaries.

ALEXANDER, SAMUEL DAVIES (*b. Princeton, N.J., 1819; d. New York, N.Y., 1894*), Presbyterian clergyman, author. Son of Archibald Alexander (1772–1851). Graduated Princeton Seminary, 1847; pastor of Fifteenth Street Church of New York, 1856–89.

ALEXANDER, STEPHEN (*b. Schenectady, N.Y., 1806; d. 1883*), astronomer. Associated with Joseph Henry, 1830–32; professor of astronomy at Princeton, 1834–77, and author of astronomical works.

ALEXANDER, WILL WINTON (*b. near Morrisville, Mo., 1884; d. Chapel Hill, N.C., 1956*), authority on race relations. Studied at Scarritt-Morrisville College and Vanderbilt University. Alexander was a Methodist pastor from 1911 to 1917, when he joined the YMCA War Work Council in Georgia. In 1919, he helped found the Commission on Interracial Cooperation in Atlanta, serving as director for the next twenty-five years. In 1935, he became an assistant and later administrator of the Resettlement Administration in Washington; when that agency was succeeded by the Farm Security Administration in 1937, Alexander became its head, serving until 1940. From 1940 to 1948, he was vice president of the Rosenwald Fund and served as advisor to various federal agencies, especially on the problems of minorities.

ALEXANDER, WILLIAM (*b. New York, N.Y., 1726; d. 1783*), Revolutionary soldier, better known as Lord Stirling; son of James Alexander (1691–1756). Wealthy and socially prominent, he was surveyor general of New Jersey, member of the Council, and assistant to the governor. Active in the popular cause, on the outbreak of Revolution he was commissioned brigadier general with chief command of New York City and directed building of defensive fortifications. Commended for brave leadership during the battle of Long Island, Aug. 27, 1776, he participated in the battle of Trenton and was promoted to major general early in 1777. He led a division at Brandywine and held his last important battle command at Monmouth. His talent for organization and his energetic yet prudent character made him highly esteemed in the Continental army.

ALEXANDER, WILLIAM DEWITT (*b. Honolulu, Hawaii, 1833; d. Honolulu, 1913*), historian, geographer. Graduated Yale University, 1855. One of Hawaii's ablest scholars, he wrote *Brief History of the Hawaiian People* (1891) and a history of the revolution of 1893.

ALFONCE (ALFONSE), JEAN. *See* ALLEFONSCE, JEAN.

ALFORD, LEON PRATT (*b. Simsbury, Conn., 1877; d. New York, N.Y., 1942*), publicist of industrial management. Graduated Worcester (Mass.) Polytechnic, B.S. in electrical engineering, 1896; M.E., 1905. Worked in production and plant design for United Shoe Machinery Co. Went to New York, N.Y., 1907, as associate editor of *American Machinist*; served as editor in chief, 1911–17. He was subsequently editor of *Industrial Management* and other journals, in which he publicized the ideas of Frederick W. Taylor and Henry L. Gantt, and advanced the programs of the movement they began. He was author of *Principles of Industrial Management* (1940) and several earlier, authoritative works in this field. He served also as an officer of the Ronald Press Company and as head of the manufacturing costs unit of the Federal Communications Commission; *post* 1937, he was chairman of the department of industrial engineering, New York University.

ALGER, CYRUS (*b. Bridgewater, Mass., 1781; d. 1856*), ironmaster, inventor. Established an iron foundry in South Boston, 1809; achieved financial success through government ammunition contracts during War of 1812 and through bold real-estate speculation, especially in development of South Boston. By 1827 his was the largest and best-equipped iron works in the United States. Widely known as an inventor, he designed the first cylinder stoves in 1822, held several patents for cast-iron articles and produced the first rifled gun in 1834. He perfected a process for strengthening cast-iron, improved reverberatory furnace and turned out the first perfect brass cannon ever made for the American government. Active in Boston politics, he was a member of the Common Council, 1822, and served as alderman, 1824, 1827.

ALGER, HORATIO (*b. Revere, Mass., 1832; d. Natick, Mass., 1899*), successful writer of boys' stories. Graduated Harvard Divinity School, 1860. Accepted post as minister but resigned in 1866 and moved to New York to establish a literary career. Through his charitable interest in the Newsboys' Lodging House, he obtained a detailed knowledge of the life of street urchins and then sentimentalized and idealized that life in his very popular novels, *Ragged Dick* (1867), *Luck and Pluck* (1869), *Tattered Tom* (1871), and many others. His books, preaching the philosophy that virtue is always rewarded with wealth, have left a deeper mark on the American character than the works of many a greater mind.

ALGER, RUSSELL ALEXANDER (*b. Ohio, 1836; d. 1907*), lumber dealer, Union soldier. Elected Republican governor of Michigan, 1884; chosen commander of the Grand Army of the Republic, 1889. Served as secretary of war, March 1897 to July 1899, and resigned at McKinley's request after a tenure marked by mismanagement.

ALGER, WILLIAM ROUNSEVILLE (*b. Freetown, Mass., 1822; d. 1905*), Unitarian clergyman. Graduated Harvard Divinity School, 1847. Wrote *Critical History of the Doctrine of a Future Life* (1864) and other books.

ALISON, FRANCIS (*b. Leck, Ireland, 1705; d. Philadelphia, Pa., 1779*), Presbyterian clergyman, educator. Immigrated to America, 1735. Taught at Philadelphia Latin Academy, 1752–79; regarded by contemporaries as America's greatest classical scholar.

ALLAIRE, JAMES PETER (*b. New Rochelle, N.Y., 1785; d. 1858*), master mechanic, engine builder. Founded first steam-engine works in New York City, 1816; leading manufacturer of steam-boat engines.

ALLAN, JOHN (*b. Edinburgh Castle, Scotland, 1746/7; d. Lubec Mills, Maine, 1805*), Revolutionary soldier. Member of provincial Assembly, Nova Scotia, 1770–76. Forced to leave Nova Scotia because of his opposition to British government, he settled in Machias, Maine. In 1777, the Continental Congress appointed him agent to the Eastern Indians, whose friendship he secured for the American cause.

ALLEFONSCE, JEAN (*b. Saintonge, France, ca. 1482; d. ca. 1557*), French navigator, chief pilot of Roberval's expedition, 1542. In search of a western passage to Cathay, he may have ascended the St. Lawrence River to the Saguenay.

ALLEN, ALEXANDER VIETS GRISWOLD (*b. Otis, Mass., 1841; d. Cambridge, Mass., 1908*), Episcopal clergyman. His *Continuity of Christian Thought* (1884) emphasized the contributions of the Greek theologians.

ALLEN, ANDREW (*b. Philadelphia, Pa., 1740; d. London, England, 1825*), lawyer, Pennsylvania official, Loyalist. Son of William Allen (1704–1780).

ALLEN, ANTHONY BENEZET (*b. Hampshire Co., Mass., 1802; d. Flushing, N.Y., 1892*), farmer, writer, manufacturer of and dealer in farm machinery. Founded the *American Agriculturist*, 1842; made and popularized improved mowers, plows, and reapers.

ALLEN, ARTHUR AUGUSTUS (*b. Buffalo, N.Y., 1885; d. Ithaca, N.Y., 1964*), ornithologist. Received his Ph.D. (1911) from Cornell, where he later became professor of ornithology. A popular and influential teacher, he created the first American course in wildlife conservation, created an ornithology laboratory at Cornell, and was active in producing the first recordings of singing wild birds. His *Laboratory Notebook* (1927) and his textbook, *The Book of Bird Life* (1930), were widely read, as were his *American Bird Biographies* (1934) and *The Golden Plover and Other Birds* (1939).

ALLEN, CHARLES (*b. Greenfield, Mass., 1827; d. Boston, Mass., 1913*), jurist. Attorney general of Massachusetts, 1867–72; associate justice of supreme court, Massachusetts, 1882–98.

ALLEN, DAVID OLIVER (*b. Barre, Mass., 1799; d. Lowell, Mass., 1863*), Congregational missionary to India, 1827–53; worked on a translation of the Scriptures into the Marathi language.

ALLEN, EDGAR (*b. Canyon City, Colo., 1892; d. in U.S. service at sea, 1943*), physiologist, anatomist. Raised in Providence, R.I. Graduated Brown University, Ph.B., 1915; M.A., 1916; Ph.D., 1921. Taught anatomy. Washington University, St. Louis, Mo., 1919–23; professor of anatomy, medical school, University of Missouri, 1923–33 (dean, 1930–33); professor of anatomy, medical school, Yale, *post* 1933. Collaborated with E. A. Doisy in research in the physiology of reproduction and ovarian physiology and endocrinology; he was interested also in the relation of sex hormones to cancer.

ALLEN, EDWARD ELLIS (*b. West Newton, Mass., 1861; d. Plainfield, N.J., 1950*), educator of the blind. Graduated Harvard, 1884. After a year at Harvard Medical School, he taught at Royal Normal College, London, 1886–8, returning to be headmaster of the boys' school of the Perkins Institution for the Blind, Boston. Principal, Pennsylvania Institution for the Blind, Philadelphia, 1890–1907. Stressed music, nature study, athletics, and reading, and initiated a program to help graduates find employment and self-sufficiency. Succeeded Michael Anagnos as director of the Perkins Institution, 1907, and moved the school to a suburban estate, re-establishing it on the "cottage-family" plan. Sponsored scientific research in the psychology of blindness, and also the development of tests and measurements for use in the education of blind students. Did much to raise the teaching of the blind to a professional level. Retired from Perkins in 1931, but continued efforts in behalf of the blind until his death.

ALLEN, EDWARD TYSON (*b. New Haven, Conn., 1875; d. Portland, Oreg., 1942*), forester. Raised in southern California and on a Washington State homestead; tutored by his father, who had taught metallurgy and chemistry at Yale. Appointed forest ranger for Pacific Northwest reserves, 1898, he joined the U.S. Department of Agriculture's Bureau of Forestry (later U.S. Forest Service), 1899. Close associate of Gifford Pinchot. Helped determine national forest boundaries throughout vast regions of the West, and in 1906–9 was in charge of national forests in Washington, Oregon, and Alaska. Author of the model contract for sale of standing timber in the national forests and the first authoritative manual on administration of national forest reserves. Served as manager of the Western Forestry and Conservation Association, 1909–32, acquiring expert knowledge of forest economics and taxation, and acted frequently as mediator in disputes between the federal government and the lumber industry. A strong believer in intelligent cooperation between timber owners and the federal authorities, he helped draft the Clarke-McNary Act of 1924.

ALLEN, ELISHA HUNT (*b. 1804; d. Washington, D.C., 1883*), Whig representative from Maine, diplomat. American consul at Honolulu; held important cabinet posts in the Hawaiian government, 1857–76.

ALLEN, ELIZABETH CHASE AKERS. *See* AKERS, ELIZABETH CHASE.

ALLEN, ETHAN (*b. Litchfield, Conn., 1737/8; d. Burlington, Vt., 1789*), Revolutionary soldier, author. Residing, 1769, in the New Hampshire Grants (the present state of Vermont), he became involved in the dispute between New York and New Hampshire for its control and commanded the Green Mountain Boys, 1770–75. Aided in the capture of Fort Ticonderoga, 1775, and was imprisoned by the British when taken during the 1775 expedition against Canada. Upon his release, 1778, he was active in local affairs in Vermont and unsuccessfully presented its claim for separate status to the Continental Congress. Together with his brothers Ira and Levi Allen, he was implicated in a 1780–83 attempt to negotiate a separate treaty with Britain, favorable to Vermont. Allen was author of a narrative of his captivity (1779), several pamphlets on Vermont's claims, and a defense of freethinking in religion.

ALLEN, FLORENCE ELLINWOOD (*b. Salt Lake City, Utah, 1884; d. Waite Hill, Ohio, 1966*), jurist and feminist. B.A. (1904) and M.A. (1908), College for Women of Western Reserve University; LL.B. cum laude (1913), New York University. An active worker for women's rights, especially woman's suffrage, she was the first woman in the nation to be elected judge of the Court of Common Pleas of Cuyahoga County (1920) and to the Ohio Supreme Court (1922) and 1928). In 1934 was appointed to the Court of Appeals for the Sixth Circuit, encompassing Ohio, Michigan, Kentucky, and Tennessee, and served for twenty-five years, writing numerous important decisions. Became the first woman to serve as a chief judge of a federal appellate court (1958). After World War II worked extensively for human rights and world peace and was the first female recipient of the Albert Gallatin Medal, given by New York University for service to humanity (1960).

ALLEN, FRED (*b. Cambridge, Mass., 1894; d. New York, N.Y., 1956*), comedian. Born John Sullivan, Allen entered vaudeville in 1911 and achieved fame around 1916 for his comedy routines. Began on radio in 1932 and, with his wife, Portland Hoffa, appeared continuously until 1949.

ALLEN, FREDERIC DE FOREST (*b. Oberlin, Ohio, 1844; d. 1897*), classical scholar. Professor of classical philology, Harvard, 1880–97; director of American School of Classical Studies at Athens, 1885–86; author of *Remnants of Early Latin* (1880).

ALLEN, FREDERICK LEWIS (*b. Boston, Mass., 1890; d. New York, N.Y., 1954*), magazine editor, social historian. After receiving M.A. from Harvard, 1914, was assistant to the editor of the *Atlantic* and in 1917 became director of publicity for the Council of National Defense in Washington. In 1923, he joined the staff of *Harper's Magazine*; was editor in chief, 1941–54. His books include *Only Yesterday* (1931), an account of the 1920's, *The Lords of Creation* (1935), and *The Big Change* (1952), a survey of postwar social, political, and technological changes in the U.S.

ALLEN, GEORGE (*b. Milton, Vt., 1808; d. Philadelphia, Pa., 1876*), educator, Episcopal clergyman, author. Professor of languages, Delaware College, 1837–45; professor of Latin and Greek, University of Pennsylvania, 1845–76.

ALLEN, GEORGE VENABLE (*b. Durham, N.C., 1903; d. Bahama, N.C., 1970*), diplomat and federal administrator. Entered the U.S. Foreign Service in 1930 and served in a wide variety of diplomatic positions before assuming his most significant role: director (1957–60) of the U.S. Information Agency (USIA). At the time the USIA was obliged to counteract the spectacular success of the Soviet Union's orbiting satellite, *Sputnik*, which had dealt a blow to the American image abroad. He eschewed strident propaganda and favored a subtle approach; under his leadership more English was taught overseas, more English broadcasting was carried over the Voice of America, and more attention was paid to American participation in trade fairs. For the USIA his tenure marked an improvement in congressional relations, an increase in cultural operations, and a move in the direction of greater professionalism. President Lyndon Johnson called him out of diplomatic retirement in 1966, naming him Career Ambassador (one of sixteen then to hold that honorific title) and appointing him to head the Foreign Service Institute. He retired again in 1969.

ALLEN, GLOVER MORRILL (*b. Walpole, N.H., 1879; d. Cambridge, Mass., 1942*), naturalist. Nephew of James Schouler. Raised in Newton, Mass. Graduated Harvard, 1901; Ph.D., biology, 1904. Held posts at the Boston Society of Natural History and at the Harvard Museum of Comparative Zoology; at the latter, he had virtual charge of the mammal collections *post* 1907 although he was not named formally as curator until 1925. Appointed lecturer in zoology at Harvard, 1924; associate professor, 1928; professor, 1938. Had great ability both as a field naturalist and as a taxonomist; he made a number of important collecting trips. Most noteworthy scientific writings were *The Mammals of China and Mongolia* (1938–40) and *Bats* (1939), the most detailed, accurate, and readable general account in the field.

ALLEN, GRACIE (*b. Grace Ethel Cecile Rosalie Allen, San Francisco, Calif., 1905; d. Los Angeles, Calif., 1964*), entertainer. With her partner and husband George Burns (m. 1926), reached top billing in vaudeville in the 1920's, and in the 1930's their radio show, the "Burns and Allen Comedy Show," was ranked as one of the top three shows in the U.S. The two starred in a number of feature films and from 1950 to 1958 were popular on television. Was one of America's favorite female entertainers, pioneering, with Burns, in the development of the domestic situation comedy.

ALLEN, HARRISON (*b. Philadelphia, Pa., 1841; d. 1897*), anatomist, physician. A pioneer American laryngologist; his most original contributions were made to the study of comparative anatomy. He held professorships at the University of Pennsylvania medical school *post* 1865.

ALLEN, HENRY JUSTIN (*b. Pittsfield, Pa., 1868; d. Wichita, Kans., 1950*), newspaper publisher, politician. Raised on a farm in Clay Co., Kans. Attended Baker University for two years. Went to work for the *Salina Daily Republican* in 1892, soon becoming chief editorial writer and advertising manager. Acquired interests in a number of papers; sold them all in 1907 and bought the *Wichita Beacon*, which he held until 1928. A crusading journalist, he used the *Beacon* to expose corruption and advance reform. A one-time foe of the Populists and staunch Republican, he supported Theodore Roosevelt in 1912, but with the decline of the Progressive party he returned to the Republican fold in 1916. While on duty with the Red Cross and the Y.M.C.A. in France, he was nominated by the Republicans for governor of Kansas, 1918. Elected by a record vote. Reelected, 1920, but was unable to

get his liberal reform bills past the legislature and is perhaps best known for the controversial Kansas Industrial Act of 1920. U.S. senator, 1929–30, filling out the unexpired term of Charles Curtis. Editor and part owner of the *Topeka State Journal*, 1935–40.

ALLEN, HENRY TUREMAN (*b. Sharpsburg, Ky., 1859; d. Buena Vista Spring, Pa., 1930*), soldier. Organized and led the Philippine Constabulary; tactful and brilliant commander of American occupation forces in Germany, 1919–23.

ALLEN, HENRY WATKINS (*b. Prince Edward Co., Va., 1820; d. Mexico City, Mexico, 1866*), Confederate soldier, lawyer, sugar planter. Raised in Missouri, he volunteered for the Texas army, 1842, settling thereafter in Mississippi and Louisiana as a lawyer and planter. As colonel of the 4th Louisiana, he distinguished himself at Shiloh and in defense of Vicksburg, and was incapacitated for field duty by wounds received at Baton Rouge. Elected governor of Louisiana, 1864, he established a system of state stores, factories, and foundries and restored the state's fallen industry and commerce. After Lee's surrender he saved Louisiana from invasion by negotiating the surrender of the strong Confederate forces west of the Mississippi. Allen was the single great administrator produced by the Confederacy.

ALLEN, HERVEY (*b. Pittsburgh, Pa., 1889; d. Miami, Fla., 1949*), biographer, novelist, poet, teacher. Attended U.S. Naval Academy, 1909–11; B.S., University of Pittsburgh, 1915. Served with National Guard on Mexican border, and as infantry officer in France during World War I. His war diary, *Toward the Flame* (1926; rev., 1934), is considered among the best books of its kind. After the war, and a brief period of graduate study at Harvard, taught English in a Charleston, S.C., high school, Columbia University (1925–26), Vassar College (1926–27), and for a number of years *post* 1929 lectured on poetry at the Bread Loaf Writers' Conference. Considerable reputation during the 1920's for his poetry (eight volumes in all were published), which has not endured. Principally remembered for his impressive, extremely detailed biography *Israfel: The Life and Times of Edgar Allan Poe* (1926), and for his novel *Anthony Adverse* (1933), a story in the picaresque tradition which dealt with the adventures of a romantic hero in the era of Napoleon. It was extraordinarily successful and began a trend toward the writing of very long, adventure-packed novels on historical subjects. Among his other novels were *Action at Aquila* (1938), a Civil War story, and three out of a projected five tales which dealt with the western frontier of colonial Pennsylvania (*The Forest and the Fort*, 1943; *Bedford Village*, 1944; and *Toward the Morning*, 1948).

ALLEN, HORATIO (*b. Schenectady, N.Y., 1802; d. near South Orange, N.J., 1899*), civil engineer, inventor. Graduated Columbia College, 1823. While resident engineer to the Delaware and Hudson canal company, 1828, he was sent to England to purchase the first steam locomotives to be used in America (Honesdale, Pa., 1829). As chief engineer, South Carolina Railroad Co., he directed construction of "Best Friend," the first locomotive built for sale in the United States. Appointed assistant principal engineer of the Croton Aqueduct, 1838, he was also consulting engineer to the New York & Erie Railroad Co. and a proprietor of Stillman, Allen & Co., specializing in building marine engines. He retired in 1870 but was consulted in the planning of the Brooklyn Bridge and the Panama Railroad.

ALLEN, IRA (*b. Cornwall, Conn., 1751; d. Philadelphia, Pa., 1814*), political leader, brother of Ethan Allen. Delegate to Windsor Convention and aided in drafting constitution of Vermont, 1777; served as secretary of the Council of Safety, member of Governor's Council, first state treasurer and as representative in negotiations for Vermont's independence. Hoping to force the Continental Congress to recognize Vermont, he joined his brothers in moves to effect separate peace with Britain, 1780–83.

ALLEN, JAMES LANE (*b. near Lexington, Ky., 1849; d. 1925*), novelist, short-story writer. Popularized Blue Grass region of Kentucky in *Flute and Violin* (1891), A *Kentucky Cardinal* (1894), *Aftermath* (1895), and other works.

ALLEN, JEREMIAH MERVIN (*b. Enfield, Conn., 1833; d. Hartford, Conn., 1903*), engineer, pioneer in steam-boiler insurance. Managed, 1867–1903, the first company organized to inspect steam-boilers and insure their owners against explosion damage.

ALLEN, JOEL ASAPH (*b. near Springfield, Mass., 1838; d. 1921*), zoologist, author. Curator of birds, Harvard Museum of Comparative Zoology, 1867–85; headed department of birds and mammals, American Museum of Natural History, 1885–1921.

ALLEN, JOHN (*b. Broome Co., N.Y., 1810; d. Plainfield, N.J., 1892*), dentist. Invented a superior artificial denture, the "continuous gum" type, patented 1851.

ALLEN, JOHN F. (*b. England, 1829; d. New York, N.Y., 1900*), engineer, inventor. Came to America as a boy. Aided in development of the Porter-Allen engine, a pioneer high-speed steam engine, and of pneumatic riveting devices.

ALLEN, JOHN JAMES (*b. Woodstock, Va., 1797; d. Botetourt Co., Va., 1871*), jurist. Judge of Virginia court of appeals, 1840–65.

ALLEN, JOSEPH HENRY (*b. Northboro, Mass., 1820; d. Cambridge, Mass., 1898*), Unitarian clergyman. Author (with J. B. Greenough) of several popular Latin manuals.

ALLEN, KELCEY (*b. Brooklyn, N.Y., 1875; d. New York, N.Y., 1951*), drama critic. Achieved fame as a phrasemaker and wit through his job as drama critic for *Women's Wear Daily*, a position he created in 1915 and held until his death. A founder and treasurer of the Drama Critics Circle.

ALLEN, LEWIS FALLEY (*b. Westfield, Mass., 1800; d. Buffalo, N.Y., 1890*), stock breeder, farm writer. Founder and editor of *American Shorthorn Herdbook*.

ALLEN, NATHAN (*b. Princeton, Mass., 1813; d. Lowell, Mass., 1889*), physician. Attempted to establish a general law of propagation applicable to all organic life.

ALLEN, NATHAN H. (*b. Marion, Mass., 1848; d. 1925*), musician, composer. Organist at First Church, Hartford, Conn., 1883–1906; composer of songs, cantatas, and organ works.

ALLEN, PAUL (*b. Providence, R.I., 1775; d. Baltimore, Md., 1826*), editor, poet. Published *Original Poems, Serious and Entertaining* (1801); editor (with Nicholas Biddle) of *History of the Expedition under the Command of Captains Lewis and Clark* (1814).

ALLEN, PHILIP (*b. Providence, R.I., 1785; d. 1865*), textile manufacturer. Governor of Rhode Island, 1851–53, he gained control of the state Democratic party machinery after a struggle with Thomas Dorr. He served as U.S. senator, 1853–59.

ALLEN, RICHARD (*b. Philadelphia, Pa., 1760; d. 1831*), founder and first bishop, 1816, of African Methodist Episcopal Church.

ALLEN, RICHARD LAMB (*b. Westfield, Mass., 1803; d. Stockholm, Sweden, 1869*), agriculturist, editor, manufacturer.

Brother of Anthony B. and Lewis F. Allen. Co-founder of *American Agriculturist*, 1842; manufacturer of agricultural implements and author of agricultural handbooks.

ALLEN, ROBERT (*b. Ohio, 1812; d. Geneva, Switzerland, 1886*), Union soldier. Graduated West Point, 1836; able and honest chief quartermaster for the armies in the West, 1861–65.

ALLEN, THOMAS (*b. Pittsfield, Mass., 1813; d. Washington, D.C., 1882*), railroad builder. A prime mover in the National Railroad Convention at St. Louis, Mo., 1849, and in the initiation of the policy of state loans to railroads. President, Pacific Railroad, 1851–54. As partner in Allen, Copp and Nisbet, financed early railroads in Missouri and Illinois.

ALLEN, THOMAS M. (*b. Shenandoah [now Warren] Co., Va., 1797; d. 1871*), pioneer minister of Disciples of Christ in Kentucky and Missouri.

ALLEN, TIMOTHY FIELD (*b. Westminster, Vt., 1837; d. New York, N.Y., 1902*), physician, botanist. His practice and writings contributed largely to the establishment of homeopathic medicine; dean of New York Homeopathic Medical College, 1882–93.

ALLEN, VIOLA EMILY (*b. Huntsville, Ala., 1867; d. New York, N.Y., 1948*), actress. Raised in Boston Mass., the child of acting parents, and in New York City. Professional debut at Madison Square Theater, New York City, July 4, 1882, in *Esmeralda*, taking the title role. Played Shakespearean and classic repertory roles, 1883–84, supporting John McCullough; then as leading lady on tour with, among others, Lawrence Barrett and Tomasso Salvini. Between 1888 and 1893, increased her reputation as an actress of intelligence, beauty, and romantic charm in both classic and modern plays. Leading lady at Charles Frohman's Empire Theater, New York, 1893–98, but left the Frohman company to achieve stardom under George Tyler's management in *The Christian* (1898). Series of Shakespearean revivals between 1903 and 1907 took her on tour as Viola in *Twelfth Night*, Hermione and Perdita in *The Winter's Tale*, Rosalind in *As You Like It*, and Imogen in *Cymbeline*. During the next decade, appeared in a number of successes, but her 1916 revivals of *The Merry Wives of Windsor* and *Macbeth* were badly received and she virtually retired from the stage.

ALLEN, WILLIAM (*b. Philadelphia, Pa., 1704; d. 1780*), merchant, jurist. Chief justice of Pennsylvania, 1750–74; benefactor of educational and civic enterprises in Pennsylvania; founder of Allentown. Retired to England on the failure of his plan for reconciliation, 1774.

ALLEN, WILLIAM (*b. Pittsfield, Mass., 1784; d. 1868*), Congregationalist clergyman, educator, author. Compiled *American Biographical and Historical Dictionary* (1809), the earliest of its kind; president of Bowdoin College, 1819–31, 1833–38.

ALLEN, WILLIAM (*b. Edenton, N.C., 1803; d. near Chillicothe, Ohio, 1879*), lawyer. An ardent expansionist Democrat, he served in Congress from Ohio, 1833–35, 1837–49, and was Democratic governor of Ohio, 1874–76.

ALLEN, WILLIAM FRANCIS (*b. Northboro, Mass., 1830; d. 1889*), classical scholar. Professor of ancient languages and history, University of Wisconsin, 1867–89; author of *Short History of the Roman People* (1890) and co-author with his brother Joseph H. Allen of the "Allen and Greenough" Latin text series.

ALLEN, WILLIAM FREDERICK (*b. Bordentown, N.J., 1846; d. 1915*), railroad expert. His most important work was in the adoption of standard time for railways. Acting as secretary and treasurer of the General Time Convention and later the American Railway Association, 1875–1915, he devised a plan for reduction of the fifty existing time standards to four time zones which was officially recognized on Nov. 18, 1883.

ALLEN, WILIAM HENRY (*b. Providence, R.I., 1784; d. 1813*), naval officer. Served on the frigates *Chesapeake* and *United States*, 1807–12; received command of the sloop-of-war *Argus*, 1813; killed in action with HMS *Pelican*.

ALLEN, WILLIAM HENRY (*b. Manchester, Maine, 1808; d. 1882*), educator. Graduated Bowdoin, 1833; professor, Dickinson College, 1836–46; president of Girard College, 1849–62, 1867–82, and of Pennsylvania Agricultural College, 1865–67.

ALLEN, WILLIAM JOSHUA (*b. Wilson Co., Tenn., 1829; d. Hot Springs, Ark., 1901*), jurist, lawyer. Moved to Illinois, 1830; active in the movement to separate southern Illinois from the Union in 1862. U.S. district judge for southern Illinois, 1887–1901.

ALLEN, WILLIAM VINCENT (*b. Midway, Ohio, 1847; d. Madison, Nebr., 1924*), lawyer. Acclaimed "the intellectual giant of Populism," he served as U.S. senator from Nebraska, 1893–1901.

ALLEN, YOUNG JOHN (*b. Burke Co., Ga., 1836; d. Shanghai, China, 1907*), Methodist missionary to China, 1859–1907.

ALLEN, ZACHARIAH (*b. Providence, R.I., 1795; d. Providence, 1882*), inventor, author, reformer. Invented the centrifugal ball governor for steam engines, 1834, and many other devices, including leather-belt power transmission and central heating by hot air. Promoted free education for working people and wrote numerous popular scientific works.

ALLERTON, ISAAC (*b. England, ca. 1586; d. New Haven, Conn., 1658/9*), Pilgrim father, trader. Arrived in Plymouth on the *Mayflower*, 1620; served as assistant to Governor Bradford, 1621–24, and in 1625 was requested to negotiate with merchant-financiers who no longer wished to support the colony. In successive trips to England, he reached a settlement, 1626, for repayment of the original expense of equipping the colony; borrowed money to purchase much-needed supplies; arranged for the emigration of the remainder of the Leyden congregation, 1629; interested a new group of English merchants in the venture, and secured the Patent of 1630, which at last gave the Pilgrims a title to their lands and property. He then purchased a large consignment of trading goods without the colony's authorization, doubled their indebtedness, and lost his position as agent, 1631. After he left Plymouth, his private trading ventures with Virginia, the West Indies, and Manhattan made him a wealthy man.

ALLERTON, SAMUEL WATERS (*b. Amenia Union, N.Y., 1828; d. South Pasadena, Calif., 1914*), capitalist. Engaged in small livestock ventures, 1852–59, in 1860 he moved to Chicago, Ill., and made his formal and profitable entrance into the business world by cornering the pork market. Considered one of the founders of modern Chicago, he was the chief factor in organizing the First National Bank of Chicago, 1863; began the movement for the successful establishment of a union stockyard, 1865–66; and brought about the adoption of the street-railway cable car, 1880–82. Founder and president of the Allerton Packing Co., he invested his rapidly growing fortune in the stockyards of Pittsburgh, Baltimore, and Jersey City, and in large tracts of Western farmlands.

ALLIBONE, SAMUEL AUSTIN (*b. Philadelphia, Pa., 1816; d. Lucerne, Switzerland, 1889*), lexicographer, librarian. Author of *A Critical Dictionary of English Literature* (1858, 1871); cataloguer of the Lenox Library, New York City.

ALLINE, HENRY (*b. Newport, R.I., 1748; d. North Hampton, N.H., 1784*), revivalist. Migrated to Nova Scotia, 1760. A self-taught itinerant preacher, he has been called "the Whitefield of Nova Scotia."

ALLINSON, ANNE CROSBY EMERY (*b. Ellsworth, Maine, 1871; d. Hancock Point, Maine, 1932*), educator and writer. Classicist; dean of women at Wisconsin and Brown universities.

ALLINSON, FRANCIS GREENLEAF (*b. Burlington, N.J., 1856; d. Hancock Point, Maine, 1931*), classicist. Professor of Greek at Brown University; translator of Menander. Husband of Anne Crosby Emery Allinson.

ALLIS, EDWARD PHELPS (*b. Cazenovia, N.Y., 1824; d. 1889*), manufacturer. Established the Reliance Iron Works in Milwaukee, Wis., 1861, later the Allis Co., manufacturers of heavy machinery and steam engines.

ALLISON, NATHANIEL (*b. Webster Co., Mo., 1876; d. La Jolla, Calif., 1932*), orthopedic surgeon, professor of surgery. Devised standard splints and dressings for the army, 1917.

ALLISON, RICHARD (*b. Orange Co., N.Y., 1757; d. Cincinnati, Ohio, 1816*), army medical officer. Head of the army medical service in the 1790's; leading practitioner in Cincinnati, Ohio, *post* 1805.

ALLISON, SAMUEL KING (*b. Chicago, Ill., 1900; d. Oxford, England, 1965*), physicist. Ph.D. (1923), University of Chicago. After his early work on X-ray research, developed the first laboratory for nuclear physics in the University of Chicago physics department and later became active in work on the atomic bomb, working with Enrico Fermi's group, becoming overall coordinator of all scientific work at Arthur H. Compton's "metallurgical laboratory" at the University of Chicago, and acting as chairman of the Technical and Scheduling Committee that brought work on the atomic bomb to a successful conclusion at Los Alamos, N.M.

ALLISON, WILLIAM BOYD (*b. Perry Township, Ohio, 1829; d. 1908*), Republican political leader. Moved to Dubuque, Iowa, *ca.* 1857, and entered practice of law there. Congressman from Iowa, 1862–70, when his views on the currency issue and the wool and iron tariff schedules marked him as a moderationist who could balance both party and sectional loyalties. His entanglement with J. G. Blaine in railroad construction jobbery did him no permanent political harm. Capable of uniting opposing groups, he served in the U.S. Senate, 1872–1908, holding the chairmanship of Appropriations, 1881–1908, and of the caucus, 1897–1908. His associate Nelson Aldrich described his special ability in calling him "a master of the arts of conciliation and construction." As a senior senator he declined cabinet offers and worked to strengthen his own political influence as a party harmonizer and manipulator.

ALLOEZ (ALLOUES), CLAUDE JEAN. *See* ALLOUEZ, CLAUDE JEAN.

ALLOUEZ, CLAUDE JEAN (*b. Saint-Didier, Haute Loire, France, 1622; d. near the present Niles, Mich., 1689*), Jesuit missionary. Ordained a priest, 1655; in 1658 went to Canada. Appointed vicar general, 1663, for all traders and natives of the Northwest, he visited tribes in that territory, regulated the relations of traders with natives and opened new missions. He traveled extensively among the Indians of the Lakes Superior and Nipigon regions, 1665–67. On the other Western journeys he visited Green Bay, Lake Winnebago, and the site of present Oshkosh; he founded a mission at De Pere (Wis.) in 1671. Upon Marquette's death in 1675, Allouez was ordered to continue his work among the Illinois; except for one trip to Green Bay, he spent the remainder of his life in Illinois country.

ALLPORT, GORDON WILLARD (*b. Montezuma, Ind., 1897; d. Cambridge, Mass., 1967*), social psychologist. B.A. (1919), M.A. (1921), Ph.D. (1922), Harvard. Taught psychology at Harvard from 1930 on, becoming the first Cabot Professor of Social Ethics in 1966. His most influential book was *Personality: A Psychological Interpretation* (1937), revised as *Patterns and Growth in Personality* in 1961. One of his most original contributions was *The Use of Personal Documents in Psychological Science* (1942), in which he analyzed the use of personal writings and artistic creations as ways of understanding an individual. Was elected president of the American Psychological Association (1939) and of the Society for the Psychological Study of Social Issues (1944). Gave Lowell Lectures in Boston, Terry Lectures at Yale, and the Hoernle Lecture in South Africa. Received the Gold Medal of the American Psychological Foundation (1963). Because his global but imprecise approach ran counter to the trend toward diminutive theories implemented with precision, he is little known to graduate students today.

ALLSTON, ROBERT FRANCIS WITHERS (*b. All Saints' Parish, S.C., 1801; d. 1864*), South Carolina planter. Graduated West Point, 1821. Served as state senator, 1833–56, and as governor, 1856–58; outstanding as a scientific agriculturist.

ALLSTON, WASHINGTON (*b. South Carolina, 1779; d. Cambridge, Mass., 1843*), artist, author. Studied painting under Benjamin West, Royal Academy, London, 1801–03; went on an artistic tour of the Continent, 1803–08, and while in Italy established friendships with Coleridge and Washington Irving. After a short return trip to America, 1808–10, he settled in England, where he produced his greatest painting, "Dead Man Revived by Touching the Bones of the Prophet Elisha." His career interrupted by illness, he issued a volume of verse, *The Sylphs of the Seasons* (1813), painted Coleridge's portrait, and resumed artistic productivity with "Uriel in the Sun" and "Jacob's Ladder." In 1818 financial reverses forced a return to America, where his artistic career terminated abruptly despite the efforts of friends who commissioned a vast "Belshazzar's Feast," still uncompleted at his death.

ALLYN, ROBERT (*b. Ledyard, Conn., 1817; d. 1894*), educator. Held numerous educational posts, including the presidency of Wesleyan Female Academy, McKendree College, and Southern Illinois State University.

ALMY, JOHN JAY (*b. Newport, R.I., 1815; d. Washington, D.C., 1895*), naval officer. During Civil War, commanded cruiser blockading Confederate ports; retired in 1877 after performing the longest service at sea of any officer since the founding of the navy.

ALOES (ALOUES), CLAUDE JEAN. *See* ALLOUEZ, CLAUDE JEAN.

ALPHONCE (ALPHONSE), JEAN. *See* ALLEFONSCE, JEAN.

ALPHONSA, MOTHER (*b. Lenox, Mass., 1851; d. 1926*), philanthropist, religious superior. Born Rose Hawthorne, youngest daughter of Nathaniel Hawthorne; married G. P. Lathrop, 1871; converted to the Roman Catholic faith, 1891. Inheriting rich literary and cultural traditions from her parents, she published some verse, several short sketches, and *Memories of Hawthorne* (1897). Post 1896, she devoted her life to the care of cancer patients, founding the order of nuns known as the Servants of Relief for Incurable Cancer.

ALSOP, GEORGE (*b. England, 1638*). Author of *A Character of the Province of Mary-Land* (London, 1666), an enthusiastic and exaggerated account of that colony.

ALSOP, RICHARD (*b. Middletown, Conn., 1761; d. Flatbush, N.Y., 1815*), satirist, poet. One of the "Hartford Wits," best known for his anti-Republican political satires *The Echo* (1791–1805, 1807) and *The Political Greenhouse* (1799).

ALSTON, JOSEPH (*b. All Saints' Parish, S.C., ca. 1779; d. 1816*), lawyer, planter, legislator. Married Theodosia Burr, 1801, and was involved in the Burr Conspiracy, 1806. Governor of South Carolina, 1812–14.

ALSTON, THEODOSIA (BURR). *See* BURR, THEODOSIA.

ALTER, DAVID (*b. Westmoreland Co., Pa., 1807; d. 1881*), physician, physicist. Among his many minor inventions and discoveries were a successful electric clock, a method of purifying bromine, and a model electric locomotive. Of greater importance were his deflecting-needle electric telegraph, 1836, and his method of obtaining coal-oil from coal. His most important work was done in connection with spectrum analysis. Independently and almost simultaneously he and Ångstrom published what has come to be known as Kirchhoff's Second Law. Alter's discovery, appearing in an American journal, did not receive full recognition, but there is no evidence for those who charge Kirchhoff with theft of Alter's ideas.

ALTGELD, JOHN PETER (*b. Nieder Selters, Germany, 1847; d. 1902*), lawyer, political leader, reformer. Brought to the United States in infancy. Elected to superior court, Cook Co. (Chicago), Ill., 1886, resigned as chief justice, 1891; elected Democratic governor of Illinois, 1892. In 1893, after studying the appeals of four men under conviction of complicity in the murders during the Chicago Haymarket Riot of 1886, he issued pardons on the grounds of a miscarriage of justice in the original trial. He protested federal military intervention in the Pullman strike of 1894, and in 1896, accepting the doctrine of free silver, influenced acceptance by the Democrats of a 16:1 plank in the national election platform. He was renominated, 1896, but lost the election to John R. Tanner.

ALTHAM, JOHN (*b. 1589; d. St. Mary's Co., Md., 1640*), Jesuit missionary. Joined the initial group of Maryland settlers, 1633; explored the Potomac River with Calvert and conducted missions to the Indians.

ALTMAN, BENJAMIN (*b. New York, N.Y., 1840; d. New York, 1913*), merchant, philanthropist, art patron. Founder of B. Altman & Co., New York City department store.

ALTSHELER, JOSEPH ALEXANDER (*b. Three Springs, Ky., 1862; d. 1919*), editor, author. Using American history as his theme, he wrote six popular series of novels for boys (1897–1919).

ALVARADO, JUAN BAUTISTA (*b. Monterey, Calif., 1809; d. 1882*), governor of Mexican California. Assumed the governorship, 1836, in a move for local control; organized his department into districts and subdistricts, overcame personal jealousies of rivals, and made unsuccessful attempts to resuscitate the secularized missions and to establish a superior court. Illness forced him to surrender his office to General Manuel Micheltorena, 1841.

ALVEY, RICHARD HENRY (*b. St. Mary's Co., Md., 1826; d. Hagerstown, Md., 1906*), jurist. Sponsored the "Alvey Resolution" favoring secession, 1861; held important judicial posts in Maryland and the District of Columbia, 1867–1904.

ALVORD, BENJAMIN (*b. Rutland, Vt., 1813; d. 1884*), Union soldier. Graduated West Point, 1833; during the Civil War commanded in Oregon Territory and successfully opposed secessionist sympathies there.

ALVORD, CLARENCE WALWORTH (*b. Greenfield, Mass., 1868; d. 1929*), historian. Instructor and professor of history, University of Illinois, 1901–20; influential in the development of the Mississippi Valley Historical Association; general editor of *Illinois Historical Collections*; author of *Mississippi Valley in British Politics* (1917).

ALVORD, CORYDON ALEXIS (*b. Winchester, Conn., 1813; d. 1874*), printer. A specialist in antiquarian printing jobs; superintendent for the Tweed-controlled New York Printing Co.

ALVORD, HENRY ELIJAH (*b. Greenfield, Mass., 1844; d. 1904*), educator, specialist in dairy husbandry. Pioneer leader in the establishment of the cooperative creamery system; held numerous agricultural teaching posts in land-grant colleges.

AMADAS, PHILIP (*fl. 1584–85*), English navigator. Commanded ships in Raleigh's expeditions to America, 1584, 1585.

AMATEIS, LOUIS (*b. Turin, Italy, 1855; d. 1913*), sculptor. Best-known works are bronze doors made for west entrance of Capitol, Washington, D.C., and numerous monuments in Texas.

AMBLER, JAMES MARKHAM MARSHALL (*b. Markham, Va., 1848; d. Siberia, 1881*), military surgeon, explorer. Surgeon aboard the *Jeannette* during its disastrous voyage to Arctic regions, 1879–81.

AMENT, WILLIAM SCOTT (*b. Owosso, Mich., 1851; d. China, 1909*), Congregational clergyman. Missionary to China, 1877–85, 1888–1909; exhibited great courage in aiding Christian converts during Boxer Rebellion.

AMERINGER, OSCAR (*b. Achstetten, near Ulm, Württemberg, Germany, 1870; d. Oklahoma City, Okla., 1943*), labor organizer, Socialist editor and pamphleteer. Son of a cabinetmaker, he apprenticed in his father's shop; immigrated to Cincinnati, Ohio, to avoid military service before his sixteenth birthday; educated himself by extensive reading; worked at odd jobs and had success as a portrait painter. Studied art at Munich, 1891–96; returning to America, he tramped over the Midwest and Southwest, teaching music and directing local bands. Settled for a time in Columbus, Ohio, as life insurance salesman. Ran for mayor of Columbus on Socialist ticket, 1903, and also started a newspaper (*Labor World*) in support of industrial unions. Removed to Oklahoma City, Okla., 1907, as field organizer for Socialist party and was author of a number of pamphlets which put the party's message in pithy, down-to-earth prose. In Milwaukee, Wis., 1910–14, he helped elect Victor Berger to Congress and continued work as organizer. Founded *Oklahoma Leader*, 1914. Opposed U.S. entry in World War I. After the war, he remained active in Oklahoma politics and served as editor and publisher of the *Illinois Miner*, 1922–31, in which his "Adam Coaldigger" column won him recognition. *Post* 1931, he edited and published the *Oklahoma Leader*, renamed the *American Guardian* in 1931.

AMES, ADELBERT (*b. Rockland, Maine, 1835; d. 1933*), Union soldier. Graduated West Point, 1861. After brilliant Civil War service, was Reconstruction senator and governor of Mississippi. He was compelled to resign as governor, 1876.

AMES, CHARLES GORDON (*b. Dorchester, Mass., 1828; d. Boston, Mass., 1912*), Baptist and Unitarian clergyman, editor.

AMES, EDWARD RAYMOND (*b. Adams Co., Ohio, 1806; d. Baltimore, Md., 1897*), Methodist bishop.

AMES, EDWARD SCRIBNER (*b. Eau Claire, Wis., 1870; d. Chicago, Ill., 1958*), philosopher, clergyman. Studied at Drake University, the Yale Divinity School, and University of Chicago (Ph.D., 1895). Professor of philosophy (1900–35) at the University of Chicago; dean of the Disciples Divinity House (1937–45); editor of the religious publication *The Scroll* (1903–51). His major works include *The Psychology of Religious Experience* (1910) and *Religion* (1929). Deeply influenced by the philosophy of William James. A leading spokesman of liberal religion in America, Ames combined the critical, adventurous spirit of science with the idealistic and inspirational life of religion.

AMES, EZRA (*b. Framingham, Mass., 1768; d. Albany, N.Y., 1836*), portrait painter. Painted miniatures and oils of celebrated New Yorkers during residence at Albany, N.Y., 1795–1836.

AMES, FISHER (*b. Dedham, Mass., 1758; d. Dedham, 1808*), statesman, publicist. Graduated Harvard, 1774. Congressman from Massachusetts, 1789–97; highest-minded of the Federalists, he was unselfish in his belief that the ideals of the Roman republic could be realized in the United States by the rule of an aristocracy of talent. An outstanding parliamentary orator, his greatest speech was made, 1796, in defense of Jay's Treaty. He was suspicious of democracy, and events of the French Revolution inspired him with a passionate fear of Jacobinism which colored all his later thinking and writing. Son of Nathaniel Ames (1708–1764).

AMES, FREDERICK LOTHROP (*b. North Easton, Mass., 1835; d. 1893*), philanthropist, capitalist. Son of Oliver Ames (1807–77); active in his family's manifold business concerns.

AMES, HERMAN VANDENBURG (*b. Lancaster, Mass., 1865; d. Philadelphia, Pa., 1935*), historian, dean of graduate school, University of Pennsylvania. Inspired and directed preservation of the state archives.

AMES, JAMES BARR (*b. Boston, Mass., 1846; d. 1910*), educator, legal writer. Successfully furthered C. C. Langdell's system of teaching law by the study of reported cases; professor at Harvard Law School *post* 1877; dean, *post* 1895.

AMES, JAMES TYLER (*b. Lowell, Mass., 1810; d. 1883*), mechanic, manufacturer. From 1847 to 1874 he headed the Ames Manufacturing Co., one of America's largest producers of tools, textile machinery, and munitions.

AMES, JOSEPH ALEXANDER (*b. Roxbury, Mass., 1816; d. New York, N.Y., 1872*), portrait painter.

AMES, JOSEPH SWEETMAN (*b. Manchester, Vt., 1864; d. Baltimore, Md., 1943*), physicist, educator. Raised in Niles, Mich. Graduated Johns Hopkins, 1886; worked in Helmholtz's laboratory in Berlin; did spectrographic research at Johns Hopkins *post* 1887, receiving a Ph.D., 1890. Taught physics at Johns Hopkins; appointed professor, 1898. Author of several textbooks and *The Constitution of Matter* (1913). As director of the Johns Hopkins physical laboratory *post* 1901, Ames showed great administrative talents. Held various university offices, including dean of the college faculty and provost, and guided the university ably through the worst of the Depression as president, 1929–35. A member or leader of several scientific boards and commissions, he did outstanding work *post* 1915 with the National Advisory Committee for Aeronautics (predecessor of NASA), instituting new lines of research, heading the annual conference with industry engineers, and keeping Congress and the public informed of the Committee's work.

AMES, MARY CLEMNER. *See* CLEMNER, MARY.

AMES, NATHAN PEABODY (*b. Chelmsford, Mass., 1803; d. 1847*), metal-worker, manufacturer. With his brother James Tyler Ames, he developed a family cutlery business into the Ames Manufacturing Co. at Chicopee, Mass., a principal factor in the industrial development of western Massachusetts.

AMES, NATHANIEL (*b. Bridgewater, Mass., 1708; d. Dedham, Mass., 1764*), almanac-maker, physician. Founder and editor, 1725–64, of an almanac which was a household word in New England.

AMES, OAKES (*b. Easton, Mass., 1804; d. North Easton, Mass., 1873*), manufacturer, capitalist, politician. In 1844 he became a partner with his brother Oliver (1807–77) in Oliver Ames and Sons, the family shovel-making business; great prosperity came with agricultural development of the West and the Civil War. From 1862–73 Oakes Ames served as Republican congressman from Massachusetts. Both he and his brother were drawn, 1865, into the Crédit Mobilier scheme for building the Union Pacific Railroad; fearing legislative investigation of the scheme, early in 1868 he distributed shares of stock in the Crédit Mobilier to fellow congressmen in the hope of influencing them in the company's favor. Revelation of this during the presidential campaign of 1872 brought Ames a censure by resolution of the House of Representatives.

AMES, OAKES (*b. North Easton, Mass., 1874; d. Ormond, Fla., 1950*), botanist. Son of Oliver Ames (1831–1895); grandson of Oakes Ames (1804–1873). Graduated Harvard, 1898; M.A., 1899. Joined Harvard faculty as assistant in botany, 1898, rising to professor in 1926. Appointed Arnold professor of botany, 1932; served as research professor of botany, 1935–41. Also held a number of administrative posts at Harvard. He was director of the Botanical Garden, 1909–22, and when he succeeded as director of the Botanical Museum (1937–45) he made it one of the world's foremost research centers in paleobotany, orchidology, and economic botany. A gifted administrator and fund-raiser, while supervisor of the Arnold Arboretum (1927–35) Ames doubled its endowment and broadened its research activities to include work in forest pathology, genetics, and plant ecology. His chief personal interest was orchids. He wrote the section on orchids for the seventh edition of Gray's *Botany*, 1908, and collected on a wide scale; he was equally celebrated as a pioneer in the field of economic botany. His *Economic Annuals and Human Cultures* (1939) is a classic.

AMES, OLIVER (*b. West Bridgewater, Mass., 1779; d. North Easton, Mass., 1863*), pioneer manufacturer. Father of Oliver (1807–77) and Oakes Ames; founder of the Ames shovel factories.

AMES, OLIVER (*b. Plymouth, Mass., 1807; d. North Easton, Mass., 1877*), manufacturer, railroad promoter. Brother of Oakes Ames, whom he joined in building the Easton Branch Railroad and then in the financing and building of the Union Pacific Railroad. Served as president of the Union Pacific, 1866–71. On his brother's death in 1873, he successfully reorganized the family business, Oliver Ames and Sons, and restored its prosperity.

AMES, OLIVER (*b. North Easton, Mass., 1831; d. 1895*), capitalist, philanthropist. Son of Oakes Ames. Became the dominant figure in Oliver Ames and Sons on the death of his uncle (Oliver Ames, 1807–77), with whom he had worked to restore the firm. A fortunate and far-seeing financier, he was director of many

banks, railroads, and land companies. Served ably as Republican governor of Massachusetts, 1886–90, and retired to give his time to business, travel, cultural interests, and charities.

AMES, SAMUEL (*b. Providence, R.I., 1806; d. Providence, 1865*), jurist.

AMES, WINTHROP (*b. North Easton, Mass., 1870; d. Boston, Mass., 1937*), theatrical manager and producer. Noted for impeccable taste and high standards; active in the New York theater, 1908–29.

AMHERST, JEFFREY (*b. Riverhead, Kent, England, 1717; d. 1797*), British soldier. After serving in several important continental campaigns, he was ordered to North America in 1758. The French stronghold of Louisburg, Cape Breton Island, Canada, fell to his army and a supporting fleet under Boscawen on July 27. This was the first British victory in the Seven Years' War, and towns in several New England states were named Amherst in his honor. As commander in chief in North America, Amherst was to support Wolfe in the Quebec campaign of 1759, but was delayed by the need to capture Ticonderoga and Crown Point on his way northward from winter quarters at Albany. After Wolfe's sole success at Quebec, Amherst directed the capture of Montreal in 1760, and made Canada a part of the British empire. Amherst had been appointed governor of Virginia, but did not reside there and was superseded. Returning to England in the winter of 1763–64, he served thereafter as a military adviser to the cabinet until 1778, when he was made commander in chief of British forces in England. He was made Baron Amherst in 1776, and in 1796 given the rank of field marshal.

AMIDON, CHARLES FREMONT (*b. Chautauqua Co., N.Y., 1856; d. Tucson, Ariz., 1937*), jurist. U.S. district judge for North Dakota, 1896–1928, whose progressive opinions had national influence.

AMMANN, OTHMAR HERMANN (*b. Schaffhausen, Switzerland, 1879; d. Rye, N.Y., 1965*), civil engineer. Graduated from the Swiss Federal Polytechnic Institute in Zurich in 1902. Moved to America in 1904 and became a U.S. citizen in 1924. Was a pioneer in the building of bridges that were marvels of functional engineering and were characterized by grace and classic beauty as well. Secured his place as a leading designer of bridges through his work on the George Washington Bridge over the Hudson River; some of his most famous projects include the Kill Van Kull Bridge, the Triborough and Bronx-Whitestone bridges, and the Verazano-Narrows Bridge.

AMMEN, DANIEL (*b. Ohio, 1819; d. near Washington, D.C., 1898*), naval officer. A distinguished ship commander in Civil War; retired as rear admiral, 1878.

AMMEN, JACOB (*b. Fincastle, Va., 1807; d. Lockland, Ohio, 1894*), Union soldier. Brother of Daniel Ammen; capable administrator of the East Tennessee district, 1864–65.

AMMONS, ELIAS MILTON (*b. Macon Co., N.C., 1860; d. 1925*), ranchman. Went with family to Colorado, 1871; entered cattle business, 1886, and throughout life retained an interest in all forms of agriculture. Held several state offices as a Republican; in 1896 became a "Silver Republican" and accepted Democratic nominations in 1904 and 1906, winning election in 1912 as governor. During the great strike in the Colorado coal fields, 1913–14, he was accused of favoring the mine-owners. In 1915, after expiration of his term in office, he returned to business and civic enterprises.

AMORY, THOMAS (*b. Limerick, Ireland, 1682; d. Boston, Mass., 1728*), merchant. Settled in Boston, 1720; developed an extensive trade both inland and abroad.

ANAGNOS, MICHAEL (*b. Papingo, Greece, 1837; d. 1906*), Greek patriot, American educator of the blind. Director of Perkins Institution for blind, 1876–1906; founded first kindergarten for blind children.

ANDERSON, ALEXANDER (*b. New York, N.Y., 1775; d. Jersey City, N.J., 1870*), engraver. A self-taught engraver at 12 years of age, he entered medical studies, 1789, but continued engraving on type metal and made illustrations for *The Pilgrim's Progress, Tom Thumb's Folio, Dilworth's Spelling Book,* and *Webster's Spelling Book.* In 1794, after seeing some Bewick illustrations, he undertook wood engraving, becoming America's first worker in that medium and a most prolific one to the end of his life. A faithful student of Bewick's method, he redrew and engraved 300 illustrations for the first American edition of Bewick's *General History of Quadrupeds* (1804).

ANDERSON, BENJAMIN MCALESTER (*b. Columbia, Mo., 1886; d. Santa Monica, Calif., 1949*), economist. Graduated University of Missouri, 1906; M.A., University of Illinois, 1910; Ph.D., Columbia University, 1911. Author of *Social Value* (1911), *The Value of Money* (1917), and other books. Taught economics at Columbia and Harvard. As economic adviser to Chase National Bank, 1920–39, wrote and edited the *Chase Economic Bulletin.* Professor of economics and banking, University of California at Los Angeles, 1939–49. Criticized quantity theory of money as set forth by Irving Fisher; strong advocate of gold standard and equally strong opponent of Keynesian ideas; favored free markets and reduction of trade barriers; blamed cheap money, deficit financing, and the substitution of bank credit for savings as the bases for economic maladjustment and inflation.

ANDERSON, DAVID LAWRENCE (*b. Summerhill, S.C., 1850; d. China, 1911*), Methodist missionary, educator. Founder and first president of Soochow University, 1901–10.

ANDERSON, EDWIN HATFIELD (*b. Zionsville, Ind., 1861; d. Evanston, Ill., 1947*), librarian. Raised in Kansas. Graduated Wabash College, 1883. Read law; tried newspaper work and teaching. Attended the New York State Library School, Albany, N.Y., 1890–91; cataloguer at the Newberry Library, Chicago, 1891–92. Librarian, Carnegie Free Library, Braddock, Pa., 1892–95; Carnegie Library, Pittsburgh, Pa., 1895–1904, where he did innovative work and established a training school for children's librarians. After a brief trial of other work, he returned to the library field in 1906, succeeding Melvil Dewey as director of the New York State Library and Library School. In 1908, he moved to New York City as assistant director of the New York Public Library, becoming director in 1913 and serving until 1934. Gave much time to developing the branch system, introduced a number of new departments, and started a library school in 1911 which later (1926) became a constituent of the School of Library Service, Columbia University.

ANDERSON, ELIZABETH MILBANK (*b. New York, N.Y., 1850; d. 1921*), philanthropist. Contributed liberally to Barnard College, the Children's Aid Society of New York, and to many social welfare agencies; established the Milbank Memorial Fund.

ANDERSON, GALUSHA (*b. Clarendon, N.Y., 1832; d. 1918*), Baptist clergyman. Active abolitionist; president of the (old) University of Chicago, 1878–85, and of Denison University, 1887–90.

ANDERSON, GEORGE THOMAS (*b. Georgia, 1824; d. Anniston, Ala., 1901*), Confederate brigadier general. Served principally with R. E. Lee's army; distinguished himself at Antietam and Gettysburg.

ANDERSON, HENRY TOMPKINS (*b. Caroline Co., Va., 1812; d. Washington, D.C., 1872*), Disciples of Christ clergyman, scholar. Translator of New Testament (1864).

ANDERSON, JAMES PATTON (*b. Franklin Co., Tenn., 1822; d. 1872*), Confederate soldier. Colonel, 1st Florida Regiment; commissioned brigadier, 1862, and major general, 1864.

ANDERSON, JOHN ALEXANDER (*b. Washington Co., Pa., 1834; d. Liverpool, England, 1892*), Presbyterian clergyman. President of Kansas State Agricultural College, 1873–78; member of Congress from Kansas, 1878–91; appointed consul general to Cairo, Egypt, 1891.

ANDERSON, JOSEPH (*b. White Marsh, Pa., 1757; d. 1837*), jurist. U.S. senator from Tennessee, 1797–1815; comptroller of U.S. Treasury, 1815–1836.

ANDERSON, JOSEPH REID (*b. near Fincastle, Va., 1813; d. Isles of Shoals, N.H., 1892*), Confederate soldier, manufacturer. Graduated West Point, 1836; resigned from army, 1837. In 1843 he leased the Tredegar Iron Co., Richmond, Va.; in 1848 he became its owner and developed it into a leading producer of locomotives, munitions, and naval machinery. A secessionist, he supplied cannon and ammunition to the Southern states, entered the Confederate army, and was commissioned brigadier general, 1861. The Tredegar Works became the sole Confederate source of heavy guns, 1861–63, the laboratory for Confederate ordnance experiment, and an active producer of projectiles, iron-clad plates, railroad rolling-stock, and furnace machinery.

ANDERSON, MARTIN BREWER (*b. Brunswick, Maine, 1815; d. Lake Helen, Fla., 1890*), educator. President of the University of Rochester, 1853–88; an editor of *Johnson's Cyclopaedia*; president of the American Baptist Missionary Union.

ANDERSON, MARY (*b. Sacramento, Calif., 1859; d. Worcestershire, England, 1940*), actress. Acclaimed for her beauty and talent in classical roles; retired to England in 1889.

ANDERSON, MARY (*b. Lidköping, Sweden, 1872; d. Washington, D.C., 1965*), labor organizer and public official. Immigrated to the U.S. at the age of sixteen and became a citizen in 1915. Active in trade unions—first in the Chicago area, then nationally and internationally—she emphasized equal pay for equal work for women. Headed the newly created Women's Bureau of the United States Department of Labor (1920–44). Wrote *Woman at Work: The Autobiography of Mary Anderson As Told to Mary N. Winslow* (1951).

ANDERSON, MAXWELL (*b. Atlantic, Pa., 1888; d. Stamford, Conn., 1959*), playwright. Studied at the University of North Dakota and Stanford (M.A., 1913). Served on the editorial staff of the *New Republic* (1918–24). The first of his thirty-three plays, *White Death,* a verse tragedy, was written in 1923; he then collaborated with Laurence Stallings on *What Price Glory?* (1924), a realistic war play. Anderson's great love for romantic verse tragedy led to *Elizabeth the Queen* (1930) and *Winterset* (1935). *Winterset* and *High Tor* (1937) both won the New York Drama Critics Circle Award. Was awarded the Pulitzer Prize for *Both Your Houses* (1933). Other major plays include *Saturday's Children* (1927), *Wingless Victory* (1936), *Key Largo* (1939), *Anne of the Thousand Days* (1948), *Barefoot in Athens* (1951), and *The Bad Seed* (1954). Other collaborations include *Knickerbocker*

Holiday (1938) and *Lost in the Stars* (1949), both with music by Kurt Weill.

ANDERSON, PAUL YEWELL (*b. Knox Co., Tenn., 1893; d. Washington, D.C., 1938*), journalist. Pulitzer Prize–winning Washington correspondent for the *St. Louis Post-Dispatch.*

ANDERSON, RICHARD CLOUGH (*b. Hanover Co., Va., 1750; d. near Louisville, Ky., 1826*), Revolutionary soldier. As surveyor general of Virginia's western lands, settled in Kentucky *post* 1783.

ANDERSON, RICHARD HERON (*b. Statesburg, S.C., 1821; d. 1879*), Confederate soldier. Graduated West Point, 1842; served on the Western frontier and saw action during the Mexican War. Commissioned brigadier general, Confederate army, 1861, he assisted Bragg at Pensacola and was sent to Virginia to command a brigade in Longstreet's division. Commissioned major general, 1862, and given a divisional command, he participated in the second battle of Bull Run, and was wounded at Antietam. He served under Lee's direct command during the battle of Chancellorsville, 1863, and played a vital role at Gettysburg. Replacing the badly wounded Longstreet as corps commander in the Wilderness Campaign, 1864, he captured Spotsylvania; after Longstreet's return to duty, Anderson accepted divisional commands during the remainder of the war.

ANDERSON, ROBERT (*b. near Louisville, Ky., 1805; d. Nice, France, 1871*), Union soldier. Son of Richard C. Anderson (1750–1826). Graduated West Point, 1825; served in Scott's campaign against City of Mexico, 1847; promoted to major, 1857. When secession became imminent, he was sent to command the forts in Charleston Harbor, S.C. On Dec. 20, 1860, South Carolina passed an ordinance of secession; six days later Anderson spiked the guns at Fort Moultrie and moved the garrison to Fort Sumter, which he surrendered after a siege on Apr. 13, 1861. Promoted to brigadier general, May 1861, he helped save Kentucky for the Union.

ANDERSON, SHERWOOD (*b. Camden, Ohio, 1876; d. Colón, Panama Canal Zone, 1941*), author. Raised in a number of small Ohio towns; helped support family by working at odd jobs while completing grammar school and nine months of high school; later stated that his unfortunate, hard-working mother "first awoke [his] hunger to see beneath the surface of lives." Removed to Chicago, 1896; worked in a produce warehouse; served with National Guard in Spanish-American War; attended Wittenberg Academy in Springfield, Ohio, 1899–1900. Between June 1900 and 1922, he had considerable success in the advertising and mail-order business, but subsequent to 1909 (when he began writing fiction), and especially after 1912, when he had an attack of amnesia, he found himself more and more repelled by business and by the standard American concept of success. Meanwhile he had published *Windy McPherson's Son* (1916), a novel about a man's rise in and rejection of business; *Marching Men* (1917); and a collection of free-verse poems entitled *Mid-American Chants* (1918). In 1919, his masterpiece, *Winesburg, Ohio*, was published. This series of brooding Midwest tales, plotless but carefully formed, dealt with the thwarted lives of ordinary people from which the protagonist learns self-understanding and achieves his own emotional maturity. In 1920 he published his best novel, *Poor White*; in 1921, some of his best stories were collected in *The Triumph of the Egg*. Many of his tales expressed his dislike of sexual repression, middle-class conventions, business ethics, and machine civilization.

In 1922, he made a final break with dependency on daily work and business, and was fortunate in receiving financial support from various admirers who supplemented the meager returns brought him by his books. His *A Story Teller's Story* (1924) was a fanciful autobiography in which he described his life as representative of the life of the artist in America. *Dark Laughter* (1925), his only financially successful novel, ended the most creative period of his life.

Post 1926, despite continued wanderings in the United States and abroad, he made his home in the mountains near Marion, Va., and for a short time edited weekly newspapers there. Highly regarded by contemporary writers during the 1920's, he received the first *Dial* award in 1921. Troubled by recurring depression, and difficulties with a succession of wives, he began to find writing increasingly hard; his work between 1926 and the end of his life lacked quality and his reputation among fellow writers declined. During the 1930's, he became interested in the condition of labor in the South, and he traveled about the United States and wrote a number of articles sensitively observant of Depression life, collected in *Puzzled America* (1935). His last novel was *Kit Brandon* (1936). Anderson's importance lay in his breaking down of formula approaches to writing, especially in his stories, and in his influence on other writers.

ANDERSON, VICTOR VANCE (*b. Barbourville, Ky., 1879; d. Staatsburg, N.Y., 1960*), psychiatrist, author, educator, physician. Studied at Union College in Kentucky and the University of Louisville. In New York, Anderson founded America's first child guidance clinics; from 1919 to 1924 was medical director of the federal government's National Committee for Mental Hygiene. Founded American Orthopsychiatric Association, 1924. Founder of the Anderson School in Staatsburg, N.Y. (director, 1924–60).

ANDERSON, WILLIAM (*b. Accomac Co., Va., 1762; d. Chester, Pa., 1829*), soldier, legislator. Served in the U.S. House of Representatives as a member from Pennsylvania, 1808–18, supporting Jefferson's policies; judge, Delaware Co. court, Pennsylvania, 1826–29.

ANDRÉ, LOUIS (*b. St. Rémy, France, 1623 or 1631; d. Quebec, Canada, 1715*), Jesuit missionary, Indian linguist. Preached to Indians in northern Wisconsin and Canada.

ANDREIS, ANDREW JAMES FELIX BARTHOLOMEW DE (*b. Piedmont, Italy, 1778; d. St. Louis, Mo., 1820*), Vincentian priest. Volunteered, 1815, to assist Bishop Louis Du Bourg on his American mission; worked in Kentucky and Missouri.

ANDREW, ABRAM PIATT (*b. La Porte, Ind., 1873; d. Gloucester, Mass., 1936*), economist. Professor of economics, Harvard, 1903–09; government adviser on banking reform ("Aldrich Plan"); Republican representative from Massachusetts, 1921–36.

ANDREW, JAMES OSGOOD (*b. Wilkes Co., Ga., 1794; d. Mobile, Ala., 1871*), Elected bishop by General Conference of Methodist Church, 1832. Although he renounced all rights and control over slaves owned by his wife, the General Conference ruled in 1844 that he should forgo his episcopal office until his connection with slave-ownership should cease. Southern delegates challenged this ruling, and a "Plan of Separation" and division of the church was drawn up, making the Methodist church in the South independent and self-governing. Bishop Andrew then served as a bishop of the Methodist Episcopal Church, South, until his retirement in 1866.

ANDREW, JOHN ALBION (*b. Windham, Maine, 1818; d. Boston, Mass., 1867*), governor of Massachusetts. Graduated Bowdoin, 1837; admitted to the bar, 1840. Achieved Republican leadership upon election to the state legislature, 1857. After John Brown's raid he solicited funds for him and his family and became so widely identified with the incident that he was cited to appear before a senatorial committee investigating it, and was chosen chairman of the state delegation to the 1860 Republican National Convention. A leader of anti-slavery opinion in Massachusetts, he was elected governor, 1860. He sent the state militia to aid in the defense of Washington; mobilized all the resources of his state in support of the Union; joined other Northern governors at the 1862 Altoona conference; and urged the organization of separate corps and regiments for black soldiers. Reelected governor, 1864, he retired, 1866, the embodiment of the patriotic spirit of his state.

ANDREW, SAMUEL (*b. Cambridge, Mass., 1656; d. Milford, Conn., 1738*), Congregational clergyman, one of the founders of Yale College, and from 1707 to 1719 its acting rector.

ANDREWS, ALEXANDER BOYD (*b. near Franklinton, N.C., 1841; d. 1915*), railroad promoter. Conspicuous among the men who rebuilt the South in the half-century following the Civil War.

ANDREWS, BERT (*b. Colorado Springs, Colo., 1901; d. Denver, Colo., 1953*), newspaper correspondent. Studied at Stanford University. On staff of the *New York Herald-Tribune* 1937–53; head of its Washington bureau, 1941–53. Covered most of the important events of World War II, the U.N. Conference in San Francisco, and the Yalta Conference in 1945. Received the Pulitzer Prize in 1947 for articles critical of the abuses of the anti-Communist forces in Washington and published *Washington Witch Hunt* in 1948. Working with Richard Nixon, he was instrumental in obtaining the conviction of Alger Hiss.

ANDREWS, CHARLES (*b. New York Mills, N.Y., 1827; d. Syracuse, N.Y., 1918*), jurist. Judge, New York court of appeals, 1870–1897; chief justice, 1881–82, 1892–97.

ANDREWS, CHARLES BARTLETT (*b. N. Sunderland, Mass., 1836; d. 1902*), jurist. Governor of Connecticut, 1879–81; outstanding judge of the superior court, *post* 1881.

ANDREWS, CHARLES MCLEAN (*b. Wethersfield, Conn., 1863; d. New Haven, Conn., 1943*), historian. Son of William W. Andrews; nephew of Israel W. and Samuel J. Andrews. Graduated Trinity College (Hartford, Conn.), 1884; Ph.D., Johns Hopkins, 1889. Influenced at Hopkins by Herbert B. Adams; took F. W. Maitland and Leopold von Ranke as his models in scholarship. Taught at Bryn Mawr, 1889–1907; Johns Hopkins, 1907–10; and Yale (Farnam professor), 1910–31. Felt that American colonies could be correctly understood only if studied as ongoing colonies of the mother country, not as embryonic states of a future independent nation. Set forth this view (then unorthodox) in a paper read before the American Historical Association in 1898. Regarded his co-editorship of the Carnegie Institution's guide to documents pertaining to American colonial history in English archives (three volumes, 1908–14) as his most important contribution to historical scholarship. In *The Colonial Background of the American Revolution* (1924), he advanced the view that the Revolution was an inevitable clash between a short-sighted and too rigid British colonial policy and a new spirit in the colonies engendered by an extended period of social, political, and economic development. After retirement he devoted himself to *The Colonial Period of American History* (four volumes published of a projected seven, 1934–38), which brought him wide acclaim. First volume awarded Pulitzer Prize in history, 1935.

ANDREWS, CHAUNCEY HUMMASON (*b. Vienna, Ohio, 1823; d. 1893*), mine operator, railroad builder, manufacturer. Developed the coal industry and short-line railroads in Ohio and western Pennsylvania.

ANDREWS, CHRISTOPHER COLUMBUS (*b. Hillsboro, N.H., 1829; d. St. Paul, Minn., 1922*), lawyer, author. Immigrated to Kansas, 1854; to Minnesota, 1857. Served with distinction as Union soldier. U.S. minister to Norway and Sweden, 1869–77; consul general to Brazil, 1882–85; pioneer forest conservationist.

ANDREWS, EDWARD GAYER (*b. New Hartford, N.Y., 1825; d. Brooklyn, N.Y., 1907*), Methodist bishop. Principal of Cazenovia Seminary, 1855–64; reorganized Methodist churches in Europe and India.

ANDREWS, ELISHA BENJAMIN (*b. Hinsdale, N.H., 1844; d. Interlachen, Fla., 1917*), college president. Graduated Brown University, 1870; studied at Newton Theological Institution, 1872–74; president and professor of philosophy, Denison University, 1875–79; professor of history, Brown, 1883–88; president of Brown, 1889–98. The modern period in Brown's history begins with Andrews's accession. He greatly increased student enrollment and the size of the faculty; founded the Women's College; created important new departments; and provided strong, personal leadership in meeting administrative problems. Resigned, 1897, because his right to express his views on the silver question was challenged by the corporation; withdrew resignation after influential educators and alumni petitioned the university. Served as vigorous and effective chancellor, University of Nebraska, 1900–08.

ANDREWS, FRANK MAXWELL (*b. Nashville, Tenn., 1884; d. Iceland, 1943*), Army Air Corps officer. Graduated West Point, 1906; commissioned in cavalry. Assigned to Air Section of Signal Corps, 1917. After flight training, as lieutenant colonel held several supervisory posts and became chief of the inspection division in Washington, D.C. Served briefly in the War Plans Division of the General Staff and in 1920–23 was Air Service officer of the Army of Occupation in Germany. Commanded advanced flying school, Kelly Field, 1925–27. Spent most of 1927–33 in the Army's advanced command and tactical schools; served in the office of the chief of the Air Corps, 1929–32. During the mid-1930's set several speed and long-distance records. During 1934 and 1935, took part in the final phases of Air Corps reorganization and strongly supported the plan for a central striking force under the top command of the Army; in 1935 was placed in command of the new organization and promoted to major general (temporary). Developed a small but efficient fighting force, agitating constantly and aggressively for more heavy, long-range bombers. Completed tour of duty in 1939, and reverted to permanent rank of colonel. Assigned to a minor post.

Recalled to the General Staff by General George C. Marshall, new chief of staff. In swift succession, promoted to lieutenant general and given charge of the Caribbean Defense Command. Took command of U.S. forces in the Middle East in 1942 and early in 1943 succeeded General Dwight D. Eisenhower in command of all U.S. forces in the European Theater of Operations. Died in an air crash.

ANDREWS, GARNETT (*b. Georgia, 1837; d. Chattanooga, Tenn., 1903*), lawyer, Confederate soldier. Organized a regiment of foreigners drawn from ranks of federal prisoners, the "Galvanized Yankees."

ANDREWS, GEORGE LEONARD (*b. Bridgewater, Mass., 1828; d. Brookline, Mass., 1899*), Union soler. In command of territorial district about Baton Rouge; organized and trained black troops, 1862–65. Professor of modern languages, West Point, 1871–92.

ANDREWS, GEORGE PIERCE (*b. Bridgton, Maine, 1835; d. 1902*), jurist. Prosecutor in the Gordon case (a slaver arrested for piracy), 1862; New York supreme court justice, 1883–1902.

ANDREWS, ISRAEL DEWOLF (*b. Campobello, New Brunswick, or Eastport, Maine*, ca. *1813–1820; d. Boston, Mass., 1871*), consul, lobbyist. Chief promoter of the Canadian-American trade reciprocity treaty of 1854.

ANDREWS, ISRAEL WARD (*b. Danbury, Conn., 1815; d. Hartford, Conn., 1888*), educator. President of Marietta College, Ohio, 1855–85.

ANDREWS, JOHN (*b. Cecil Co., Md., 1746; d. 1813*), Episcopal clergyman, educator.

ANDREWS, JOHN BERTRAM (*b. South Wayne, Lafayette Co., Wis., 1880; d. New York, N.Y., 1943*), economist, social reformer, labor expert. Graduated University of Wisconsin, 1904; Ph.D., 1908, under John R. Commons, with whom he collaborated on several books, including *Principles of Labor Legislation* (1916). Served as executive secretary of the American Association for Labor Legislation and edited its *Review*, 1911–43; worked to establish compensation laws for industrial accidents; to promote industrial safety (particularly in the match industry); and to institute unemployment, old age, and health insurance programs on a basis of voluntarism rather than under government control. His model federal unemployment insurance plan and bill became part of the Social Security Act of 1935.

ANDREWS, JOSEPH (*b. Massachusetts*, ca. *1805; d. Boston or Hingham, Mass., 1873*), engraver. One of America's best line engravers; excelled in portrait work.

ANDREWS, LORIN (*b. Ashland, Ohio, 1819; d. Gambier, Ohio, 1861*), educator. President of Kenyon College, 1853–61.

ANDREWS, LORRIN (*b. East Windsor [now Vernon], Conn., 1795; d. Honolulu, Hawaii, 1868*), missionary, educator. As a missionary to Hawaii, 1828–41, he established a teacher training school and the first newspaper; he held important offices in Hawaiian government, 1845–59.

ANDREWS, ROY CHAPMAN (*b. Beloit, Wis., 1884; d. Carmel, Calif., 1960*), explorer, zoologist, author. Studied at Beloit College and Columbia (M.S., 1913). Associated with the American Museum of Natural History in New York from 1906, he became vice-director, 1931–34, and director, 1935–42. A leading authority on whales, Andrews went on many expeditions collecting specimens for the museum. Led five major Central Asiatic expeditions (1922–30), which brought together representatives from half a dozen scientific disciplines. These trips yielded many specimens of early mammals and dinosaurs, including the largest carnivore, named the *Andrewsarches* in honor of its discoverer; and two dozen perfectly preserved dinosaur eggs found in the Gobi Desert in 1928, which made Andrews world famous. Significant both for his won findings and the attention he drew to the value of the explorer-naturalist and large-scale scientific exploration. Major works include *On the Trail of Ancient Man* (1926) and *This Amazing Planet* (1940).

ANDREWS, SAMUEL JAMES (*b. Danbury, Conn., 1817; d. 1906*), clergyman, author. An early supporter and pastor of the Catholic Apostolic Church; younger brother of William W. Andrews.

ANDREWS, SHERLOCK JAMES (*b. Wallingford, Conn., 1801; d. 1880*), lawyer, jurist, Whig congressman from Ohio, 1840–42. Prominent in early development of Cleveland, Ohio. A member of the Ohio constitutional convention, 1850–51, he supported black rights at a critical time.

ANDREWS, SIDNEY (*b. Sheffield, Mass., 1835; d. 1880*), journalist. Traveled through Carolina and Georgia as a special correspondent for Northern newspapers, 1864–69.

ANDREWS, STEPHEN PEARL (*b. Templeton, Mass., 1812; d. New York, N.Y., 1886*), abolitionist, reformer, eccentric philosopher. Spelling reform and shorthand enthusiast; established "universology," a deductive science of the universe.

ANDREWS, WILLIAM LORING (*b. New York, N.Y., 1837; d. 1920*), bibliophile. A founder of the Grolier Club and the Society of Iconophiles, New York City.

ANDREWS, WILLIAM WATSON (*b. Windham, Conn., 1810; d. 1897*), clergyman. Traveling evangelist of the Catholic Apostolic Church (Irvingites); brother of Samuel J. Andrews.

ANDROS, EDMUND (*b. London, England, 1637; d. London, 1714*), baronet, soldier, colonial governor. Governor of New York, 1674–81; recalled to England; knighted, ca. *1681*. James II, wishing to consolidate the individualistic New England colonies into one royal province, formed the Dominion of New England with Andros as governor, 1686. The new government, administered by royal appointees, conflicted with the claims and interests of the colonists; at the instigation of Increase and Cotton Mather they rose in revolt against Andros in 1689, imprisoning him along with other Dominion officials. His reputation undamaged by his New England experience, he was appointed governor of Virginia, 1692, and retired to England in 1697.

ANDRUS, ETHEL PERCY (*b. San Francisco, Calif., 1884; d. Long Beach, Calif., 1967*), educator and founder of retired persons organizations. Ph.B. (1903), University of Chicago; B.S. (1918), Lewis Institute (later the Illinois Institute of Technology; M.A. (1928) and Ph.D. (1930), University of Southern California. Was principal of Abraham Lincoln High School in Los Angeles (1916–44); as the first woman high school principal in California, she established the Opportunity School for Adults in the evenings and worked successfully to reduce the rate of juvenile delinquency in the neighborhood. In retirement, she founded and became president of the National Retired Teachers Association (1947) and also founded the American Association of Retired Persons (1958).

ANGEL, BENJAMIN FRANKLIN (*b. Burlington, N.Y., 1815; d. Geneseo, N.Y., 1894*), lawyer, diplomat. Held diplomatic posts in Hawaii, China, Norway, and Sweden.

ANGELA, MOTHER (*b. near Brownsville, Pa., 1824; d. 1887*), educator. Born Eliza Maria Gillespie. Served almost 30 years as superior of the Sisters of the Holy Cross in the United States; supervised Civil War nursing work of her nuns; founded St. Mary's, Notre Dame, Ind.

ANGELL, GEORGE THORNDIKE (*b. Southbridge, Mass., 1823; d. Boston, Mass., 1909*), reformer. With Mrs. William Appleton, founded Massachusetts Society for the Prevention of Cruelty to Animals.

ANGELL, ISRAEL (*b. Providence, R.I., 1740; d. Smithfield, R.I., 1832*), Revolutionary soldier. Served at siege of Boston and at battles of Brandywine, Red Bank, Monmouth, and, notably, Springfield, N.J.

ANGELL, JAMES BURRILL (*b. near Scituate, R.I., 1829; d. Ann Arbor, Mich., 1916*), journalist, college president, diplomat. Graduated Brown University, 1849; studied in Europe, 1851–52; returned to take chair of modern languages at Brown, 1853. In 1858 he began contributing leading articles to the *Providence Journal*, giving particular attention to European and international politics; he resigned his chair at Brown, 1860, in order to assume the editorship of the newspaper. Under his direction the *Journal* endorsed Lincoln as the Republican candidate, at first dismissed Southern threats of secession, and consistently supported the government during the Civil War. After unsuccessfully attempting to purchase the paper from its owner, Henry B. Anthony, Angell accepted presidency of the University of Vermont, 1866. The university, chartered by the legislature in 1791, received no state support and was in poor financial condition. The new president was forced to speak before public meetings in several New England states, soliciting contributions for the school. As a result of this canvass, $100,000 was raised, new buildings were constructed on the campus, and the people of the state were brought to regard the university as an integral and necessary part of public education. The University of Michigan in 1871 was one of the largest American educational institutions of that time. Its curriculum was liberal and its faculty relatively large and well selected, yet, due to the state's policy of financial support, its equipment and salary scale were inadequate. Angell, elected to the presidency of Michigan, proposed for the state "the higher positive office of promoting by all means the intellectual and moral growth of the citizens." His achievements as president, 1871–1909, were of a dual nature: first, his personal influence as a teacher and administrator who interested himself in his students; second, his organizational and educational innovations—broadening of the curriculum to include those who had not had classical preparation; establishment of first permanent system of admission requirements for medical schools, 1874; creation of the first professorship in the science and art of teaching, 1879; and institution of comprehensive examinations as part of the requirements for a bachelor's degree, 1877. He supplemented the duties of president by undertaking occasional but important national diplomatic missions. In 1880, as minister to China, he concluded a treaty whereby the United States might "regulate, limit, or suspend" but not "absolutely prohibit" the entry and residence of Chinese laborers; at the same time a commercial treaty governing the opium trade was signed. He was minister to Turkey during the Spanish-American War, 1897–98. Angell was a regent of the Smithsonian Institution, one of the founders of the American Historical Association, 1884, and its president, 1893–94.

ANGELL, JAMES ROWLAND (*b. Burlington, Vt., 1869; d. Hamden, Conn., 1949*), psychologist, university president. Son of James Burrill Angell; raised in Ann Arbor, Mich. Graduated University of Michigan, 1890; M.A., 1891. Strongly influenced by John Dewey. Studied at Harvard, 1891–92, under Josiah Royce and William James, whom he served as research assistant. Spent a year in Europe, studying at Berlin under Ebbinghaus and Paulsen, and at Halle under Erdmann and Vaihinger. Instructor, University of Minnesota, 1893; assistant professor of philosophy, University of Chicago, 1894–1901; professor, 1904; chairman, department of psychology, 1905. Promoted the Chicago school of psychology known as "functionalism." *Psychology* (1904) promoted the viewpoint of James; *Chapters from Modern Psychology* (1912) surveyed the entire field of academic psychology. Strongly positivist, he rejected Freudianism and behaviorism and in time parted company with much of James's thinking; his scientific rationalism was closer to the mood of John Dewey. Dean of the senior college at University of Chicago, 1908, dean of the faculties, 1911. Served on committees in Washington during World War I, returning as acting president of Chicago, in 1918. Became chairman of the National Research Council; moved to New York City, 1920, to head the Carnegie Corporation. President of Yale University, 1921–1937. Power at Yale had long resided in an oligarchy of senior professors; the presidency was weak. Increased Yale endowment more than four-fold. Founded the School of Nursing and the Institute of Human Relations (originally called Institute of Psychology), strengthened the professional schools and the graduate school of arts and sciences, and stressed appointment of professors on a more scholarly basis. Adopted a residential college plan, the result of a gift by Edward S. Harkness, even though Angell and Harkness were personally at odds. After retirement was educational consultant for the National Broadcasting Company.

ANGELL, JOSEPH KINNICUTT (*b. Providence, R.I., 1794; d. Boston, Mass., 1857*), lawyer. Author of several authoritative legal treatises, including *The Law of Private Corporations Aggregate* (1832).

ANGELL, WILLIAM GORHAM (*b. Providence, R.I., 1811; d. 1870*), inventor. Improved screw-making machinery; president, American Screw Co.

ANGLIN, MARGARET MARY (*b. Ottawa, Ont., 1876; d. Toronto, Canada, 1958*), actress. Studied at the Empire Dramatic School in New York and was apprentice with the Charles Frohman and James O'Neill companies. Had a major success in William Vaughan Moody's modern play *The Great Divide*, 1906. Turned from tragedy to comedy in 1911, eventually playing in *The Importance of Being Ernest* and *Lady Windermere's Fan*. Produced a series of Greek plays at the Greek Theatre of the University of California at Berkeley, 1915; in 1921, she repeated the role of Clytemnestra in *Iphigenia in Aulis* at the Manhattan Opera House, with Walter Damrosch conducting a musical accompaniment he had composed for the play. Last appeared in a 1943 road production of Lillian Hellman's *Watch on the Rhine*.

ANNEKE, MATHILDE FRANZISKA. *See* GIESLER-ANNEKE, MATHILDE FRANZISKA.

ANNENBERG, MOSES LOUIS (*b. Kalwischen, East Prussia, 1878; d. Rochester, Minn., 1942*), newspaper publisher, racing-news entrepreneur. Came to America as a child; raised in Chicago, Ill. After numerous odd jobs, was employed by W. R. Hearst's *Evening American* as subscription solicitor; became circulation manager of the *Examiner*, 1904, and supervised a vicious battle for control of choice street-sale positions. Removed to Milwaukee, Wis., ca. 1907, started a successful newspaper distribution agency, and made profitable investments in real estate. Appointed publisher of the *Wisconsin News*, 1917; tripled its circulation. Became circulation director for all Hearst newspapers and magazines, 1920, retaining control of all his personal businesses, to which he added the *Daily Racing Form* in 1922. Resigned from Hearst organization, 1926; acquired among other racing papers the N.Y. *Morning Telegraph*. Beginning in 1927, began to acquire control of racing wire services, establishing a virtual monopoly of the supply of instant racetrack information to bookmakers by 1930. Founder and publisher of the *Miami Tribune* (1934–37); staked his claim to journalistic respectability in Philadelphia, purchasing the *Inquirer* in 1936 and reviving it; also engaged in Republican organization politics. In 1939, his wire services were dissolved under federal pressure; indicted for income tax evasion and sentenced to three years in prison.

ANSHUTZ, THOMAS POLLOCK (*b. Newport, Ky., 1851; d. Fort Washington, Pa., 1912*), painter, teacher at Pennsylvania Academy of Fine Arts; among other eminent painters, his pupils included Robert Henri, John Sloan, George Luks, and William Glackens.

ANSON, ADRIAN CONSTANTINE (*b. Marshalltown, Iowa, 1852; d. 1922*), baseball player. Batted an average of .331 over 22 seasons, 1876–97, as first baseman, captain, and manager of the Chicago club, National League.

ANTES, HENRY (*b. Freinsheim, Germany, 1701; d. Frederick, Pa., 1755*), religious leader. Came to America, *ca.* 1720; associated with Moravians, 1741–55.

ANTHON, CHARLES (*b. New York, N.Y., 1797; d. New York, N.Y., 1867*), classical scholar. Graduated Columbia College, 1815. Chosen adjunct professor of Greek and Latin, Columbia, 1820; in 1830 made Jay professor of Greek language and literature and put in charge of Columbia Grammar School. During the middle of the 19th century his influence upon the study of classics in the United States was probably greater than that of any other one man. He was one of those who introduced the results of foreign (mainly German) scholarship into the United States. His *Horatii Poemata* (1830) was the first American critical and exegetical edition of a classical author. For thirty years he edited annually at least one volume of a classical text for school and college use.

ANTHON, CHARLES EDWARD (*b. New York, N.Y., 1823; d. Bremen, Germany, 1883*), educator, numismatist. Son of John Anthon.

ANTHON, JOHN (*b. Detroit, Mich., 1784; d. 1863*), lawyer. Brother of Charles Anthon. Assisted in founding New York Law Institute; elected its president, 1852–63.

ANTHONY, ANDREW VARICK STOUT (*b. New York, N.Y., 1835; d. West Newton, Mass., 1906*), wood engraver. Superintended production of fine illustrated editions for Ticknor and Fields and successor firms, 1866–89.

ANTHONY, GEORGE TOBEY (*b. near Mayfield, N.Y., 1824; d. 1896*), businessman, Union soldier. Removed to Leavenworth, Kans., 1865; influenced agricultural methods as editor of the *Kansas Farmer;* effective and honest Republican governor of Kansas, 1876–80.

ANTHONY, HENRY BOWEN (*b. Coventry, R.I., 1815; d. 1884*), journalist, politician. Proprietor, *Providence Journal;* governor of Rhode Island, 1849–1850; U.S. senator, conservative Republican, 1858–1884.

ANTHONY, JOHN GOULD (*b. Providence, R.I., 1804; d. 1877*), zoologist. Collected and studied freshwater mollusks; scientific associate of Louis Agassiz.

ANTHONY, JOHN J. (*b. Lester Kroll, New York, N.Y., 1898; d. San Francisco, Calif., 1970*), radio personality and human-relations adviser. After serving a jail sentence for nonpayment of alimony to the wife he had divorced in 1929, he founded the Marital Relations Institute and made himself director, providing counseling and information for seekers of marital advice and submitting reports to the New York State legislature calling for changes in New York marriage and divorce laws. In 1930 started being heard on the New York radio station WMCA, offering advice on marriage and domestic life; in 1937 WMCA began airing his show "The Goodwill Hour." Although it drew considerable criticism from psychiatrists, the show was extremely successful with Sunday-night listeners. His book *Marriage and Family Problems and How to Solve Them* (1939) sold well. His show lost its network distribution in 1953, and he moved to Los Angeles, at which point his career took a downturn. Was among the first and most successful of America's many media psychologists.

ANTHONY, KATHARINE SUSAN (*b. Roseville, Ark., 1877; d. New York, N.Y., 1965*), writer, biographer, and women's rights advocate. Deeply interested in women's issues and the women's movement, she wrote *Mothers Who Must Earn* (1914), *Feminism in Germany and Scandinavia* (1915), and *Labor Laws of New York: A Handbook* (1917). From the 1920's through the 1950's she wrote articles for women's magazines and biographies of women such as Margaret Fuller, Catherine the Great, Queen Elizabeth, Marie Antoinette, Louisa May Alcott, Dolly Madison, and Susan B. Anthony, many of whom she treated from a Freudian perspective.

ANTHONY, SISTER (*b. Limerick, Ireland, 1814; d. 1897*), nurse. Born Mary O'Connell; educated by Ursulines, Charlestown, Mass.; entered American Sisters of Charity, 1835. Worked in hospitals, Cincinnati, Ohio, 1837–80. With other members of her community, she won special commendation for field and hospital work during the Civil War.

ANTHONY, SUSAN BROWNELL (*b. Adams, Mass., 1820; d. Rochester, N.Y., 1906*), reformer. Prevented from speaking at a temperance meeting because of her sex, she and others formed in 1852 the Woman's State Temperance Society of New York. Convinced that women could work effectively for social betterment only if they had rights and privileges held by men, she spent her life in lecture tours and campaigns through various states in the interest of woman suffrage. She supported black suffrage for male and female, took a radical abolitionist stand prior to the Civil War, and was instrumental in formation of the National Woman Suffrage Association. In 1892, after merger of the organization with a rival group, she was elected president of the combined societies and served until 1900.

ANTHONY, WILLIAM ARNOLD (*b. Coventry, R.I., 1835; d. New York, N.Y., 1908*), physicist, pioneer in teaching of electrical engineering. Contributed to development of gas-filled lamp.

ANTIN, MARY (*b. Polotsk, Russia, 1881; d. Suffern, N.Y., 1949*), author, social worker. Came to America with her family, 1894; raised in Boston, Mass. Attended Teachers College, Columbia, and Barnard College, New York City. Married Amadeus W. Grabau, 1901. Her autobiography, *The Promised Land* (1912), which covered her memories of childhood in Russia and in the Boston slums, won her high place as a commentator on Jewish immigrant life in America and as a strong proponent of the success of the "melting-pot" concept.

ANTOINE, PÈRE (*b. Sedella, Spain, 1748; d. New Orleans, La., 1829*), Capuchin friar. Parish priest in New Orleans, 1785–90,; 1795–1805; 1819–29. A complex and controversial figure.

ANZA, JUAN BAUTISTA DE (*b. Sonora, Mexico, 1735*), Spanish explorer. Hoping to anticipate possible occupation by the Russians or the English, Spain planned to occupy the Pacific Coast of North America as far as the bay of Monterey and beyond. Anza, with a group of soldiers, set forth from his presidio of Tubac to establish an overland supply route from Sonora to Monterey, 1774. He proved the practicability of such a route and was rewarded with the rank of lieutenant-colonel. On his second California expedition, 1775, he explored the land about San Francisco Bay, ascended the San Joaquin River for a short distance, and chose a site for the San Francisco presidio. He served as governor of New Mexico, 1777–88.

APES, WILLIAM (*b. Near Colrain, Mass., 1798*), Pequot Indian missionary and author.

APPENZELLER, HENRY GERHARD (*b. Suderton, Pa., 1858; d. near Kunsan, Korea, 1902*), Methodist missionary. Established a Methodist printing house in Korea, edited *Korean Review*, and established Pai Chai School for boys in Seoul.

APPLE, THOMAS GILMORE (*b. Easton, Pa., 1829; d. 1898*), theologian, educator. President of Mercersburg College,

1865–71; president, Franklin and Marshall College, 1877; identified with the so-called "Mercersburg Theology" system.

APPLEBY, JOHN FRANICS (*b. Westmoreland, N.Y., 1840; d. 1917*), inventor. Removed to Wisconsin as a child. At eighteen he conceived the idea of a machine that would bind reaped sheaves of grain; lack of funds prevented its development. In 1867, he displayed his first complete binder at Mazomanie, Wis.; in 1878 he was granted patents for a perfected twine binder. Manufacture of the "Appleby Knotter" on a large scale was begun by Gammon and Deering in 1878. Other manufacturers of harvesters procured rights and it became the most popular binding machine.

APPLEGATE, JESSE (*b. Kentucky, 1811; d. 1888*), surveyor, legislator, publicist. Joined the 1843 immigration to Oregon and settled in the Willamette Valley; was leader of the party which opened a southern road into Oregon in 1845. A member of the legislative committee of the Provisional Government, he secured the adherence to it of the managers of the British Hudson's Bay Co., thus politically unifying the Oregon settlement for the first time. Active in state constitutional convention, 1857, he was also influential in securing Lincoln's election and maintaining the national cause during the Civil War. In 1849 he settled on a large ranch in the Umpqua Valley and raised beef cattle. Author of *A Day With the Cow Column in 1843*.

APPLETON, DANIEL (*b. Haverhill, Mass., 1785; d. New York, N.Y., 1849*), publisher. With his son, William Henry Appleton, founded the firm of D. Appleton & Co., 1838.

APPLETON, JAMES (*b. Ipswich, Mass., 1785; d. 1862*), reformer, one of the first (1832) to propose state prohibition as a remedy for intemperance.

APPLETON, JESSE (*b. New Ipswich, N.H., 1772; d. Brunswick, Maine, 1819*), theologian, educator. President of Bowdoin College, 1807–19.

APPLETON, JOHN (*b. New Ipswich, N.H., 1804; d. 1891*), legal reformer and theorist. Associate justice, 1852–62, chief justice, 1862–83, of Maine supreme judicial court; author of *The Rules of Evidence* (1860).

APPLETON, JOHN (*b. Beverly, Mass., 1815; d. Portland, Maine, 1864*), lawyer, Maine congressman, diplomat. Assistant secretary of state, 1857–60; minister to Russia, 1860–61.

APPLETON, NATHAN (*b. New Ipswich, N.H., 1779; d. Boston, Mass., 1861*), manufacturer, banker. Brother of Samuel Appleton. Invested in Francis Lowell's power mill for making cotton cloth at Waltham, Mass., 1813; there, with his associates, established the principles of the American textile industry—power machinery with cheap female labor, and a separate selling organization. Successful at Waltham, they founded the industrial city of Lowell and built manufacturing centers at Manchester, N.H., and Lawrence, Mass. Elected to Congress, 1830, Appleton assisted in framing and defending the protective tariff of 1832 and supported Biddle and Clay against Jackson in the Bank of the U.S. controversy. He was an organizer of the Boston Athenaeum and its treasurer, 1816–27.

APPLETON, NATHANIEL WALKER (*b. Boston, Mass., 1775; d. 1795*), physician. Incorporator of the Massachusetts Medical Society, 1781, and its recording secretary for the first ten years of its existence.

APPLETON, SAMUEL (*b. New Ipswich, N.H., 1766; d. Boston, Mass., 1853*), merchant. Brother of Nathan Appleton; trader and investor in New England real estate and industry; retired at sixty to devote his income to philanthropy.

APPLETON, THOMAS GOLD (*b. Boston, Mass., 1812; d. 1884*), essayist, poet, and artist; a witty member of the literary coterie which made Boston famous in the middle of the 19th century.

APPLETON, WILLIAM HENRY (*b. Haverhill, Mass., 1814; d. New York, N.Y., 1899*), publisher. Joined his father, Daniel Appleton, in the firm of D. Appleton & Co., 1838.

APPLETON, WILLIAM SUMNER (*b. Boston, Mass., 1874; d. Boston, 1947*), antiquarian. Grandson of Nathan Appleton. Graduated Harvard, 1896. Prevented by poor health from following a business or professional career, he devoted his time, talents, and money to the work of the Society for the Preservation of New England Antiquities, which he founded in 1910 for the purpose of acquiring, restoring, and preserving historic buildings.

APPLETON, WILLIAM WORTHEN (*b. Brooklyn, N.Y., 1845; d. New York, N.Y., 1924*), publisher. Son of William H. Appleton.

APTHORP, WILLIAM FOSTER (*b. Boston, Mass., 1848; d. Vevey, Switzerland, 1913*), music critic. Music editor, *Atlantic Monthly*, and dramatic and music critic for several Boston newspapers.

ARBUCKLE, JOHN (*b. Pittsburgh, Pa., 1839; d. Brooklyn, N.Y., 1912*), merchant. Leading coffee importer and ship owner; inventor of machinery used in food packaging and ship salvage.

ARCHBOLD, JOHN DUSTIN (*b. Leesburg, Ohio, 1848; d. 1916*), capitalist. Speculator in Pennsylvania oil fields, 1866. When the South Improvement Co., whose membership included John D. Rockefeller, blocked the advance of Pennsylvania oil producers by obtaining railroad freight rebates, Archbold united the leading men of the Titusville region and defeated this strong Cleveland group. He then joined the Cleveland combination in working out a national organization to control the oil industry; from 1882 until his death he was dominant in Standard Oil Co. policy, acted as spokesman for the company, and improved the product and its distribution. In 1911, at the dissolution of the original company, he became president of Standard Oil (N.J.).

ARCHDALE, JOHN (*b. England, ca. 1642; d. England, ca. 1717*), colonial governor. Agent for Gorges claims in Maine, 1664–65; governor of Carolina, 1694; passed colony's first recorded liquor law.

ARCHER, BRANCH TANNER (*b. Virginia, 1790; d. 1856*), political leader in Texas. A commissioner to the United States, 1836; member of first Texas Congress; secretary of war in cabinet of President Lamar.

ARCHER, FREDERIC (*b. Oxford, England, 1838; d. Pittsburgh, Pa., 1901*), organist. One of the first players to popularize the organ recital in America; director of music, Carnegie Institute, Pittsburgh, Pa., 1895–1901.

ARCHER, JAMES J. (*b. Stafford, Md., 1817; d. 1864*), Confederate soldier. Commissioned brigadier general, 1862; fought in the battles of Seven Days, Cedar Mountain, Second Manassas, Antietam, Fredericksburg, Chancellorsville.

ARCHER, JOHN (*b. Churchville, Md., 1741; d. Harford Co., Md., 1810*), physician, medical teacher. Received the first medical degree (B.M., Philadelphia College of Medicine, 1768) ever earned in this country.

ARCHER, SAMUEL (*b. near Columbus, N.J., 1771; d. Philadelphia, Pa., 1839*), merchant, philanthropist. Engaged in importing from India and China, and from Europe; first merchant to export American cotton goods to Asia on a large scale; an original manager of the Philadelphia Saving Fund Society, 1816.

ARCHER, STEVENSON (*b. Harford Co., Md., 1786; d. Harford Co., 1848*), jurist. Judge, Maryland court of appeals, 1824–48.

ARCHER, WILLIAM SEGAR (*b. Amelia Co., Va., 1789; d. Amelia Co., 1855*), Congressman, Whig, from Virginia, 1820–35; U.S. senator from Virginia, 1841–47; advocated annexation of Texas.

ARCHIPENKO, ALEXANDER (*b. Kiev, Ukraine [now Soviet Union], 1887; d. New York, N.Y., 1964*), sculptor, painter, and graphic artist. Belonged to the cubist-abstract movement in Paris around 1910. Opened an art school in Paris in 1912 and another in Berlin (1921–23). Immigrated to New York City in 1923 and became a citizen in 1929. Opened three art schools in the U.S. and taught at some eleven American colleges. Developed a technique of mobile sculpture-painting that anticipated later kinetic sculpture and was also involved in graphic art throughout his life.

ARDEN, EDWIN HUNTER PENDLETON (*b. St. Louis, Mo., 1864; d. 1918*), actor, manager, playwright. Starred in a series of his own plays, 1883–92; noted for his appearance with Maude Adams in Rostand's *L'Aiglon*, 1900.

ARDEN, ELIZABETH (*b. Florence Nightingale Graham, Woodbridge, Canada, 1878; d. New York, N.Y., 1966*), beautician and cosmetics manufacturer. Became U.S. citizen, 1915. After learning how to give facial massages while working for Eleanor Adair, in 1909 she opened a salon with Elizabeth Hubbard on Fifth Avenue; when the women parted in 1910, she kept the salon and adopted the name Elizabeth Arden. Using a scientific approach new to cosmetics, she perfected a facial and the popular cleansing cream Amoretta. In 1914 opened her first branch salon in Washington, D.C., and in the years that followed opened more branches. Her company eventually boasted 300 products sold in forty-four countries. Introduced eye shadow and mascara to the U.S. in 1917, and in 1932 began a line of lipsticks and other makeup to match the user's clothes. Also made the first record on how to do exercises and opened the first exercise room associated with a beauty salon. Established the restorative beauty treatment centers: Maine Chance Farm (1934) and Arizona Maine Chance Farm (1947). In 1943 started a fashion business; Oscar de la Renta was among her designers. In the 1950's she opened the first men's boutique attached to a beauty salon; earlier she had been the first manufacturer of women's cosmetics to put out a line for men. Upon her death, her company was sold to Eli Lilly and Company.

ARENSBERG, WALTER CONRAD (*b. Pittsburgh, Pa., 1878; d. Hollywood, Calif., 1954*), art collector, poet, Baconian. Graduated from Harvard, 1900. Known for his influence on the modern art movement in the U.S., Arensberg was a friend and publicizer of such artists as Marcel Duchamp, Jean Arp, Alfred Stieglitz, and the poet Wallace Stevens. A believer that Bacon wrote most of Shakespeare's works, he published *The Cryptography of Shakespeare* (1922) and *The Shakespearean Mystery* (1928).

ARENTS, ALBERT (*b. Clausthal, Germany, 1840; d. Alameda, Calif., 1914*), metallurgist. Immigrated to America, 1865; his siphon lead-well was a revolutionary step in lead-silver smelting.

ARGALL, PHILIP (*b. Newtownards, Ireland, 1854; d. 1922*), engineer, metallurgist. Came to the United States in 1887; applied the new cyanide process for gold extraction in Colorado mines, 1895; consulting engineer to British and American mining firms.

ARGALL, SAMUEL (*fl. 1609–24*), baronet, adventurer, deputy governor of Virginia. Pioneered direct trans-Atlantic route from England to Virginia, 1609. Accompanied Lord Delaware to Virginia, 1610; went to Cape Cod to secure fish for starving Virginia colonists. Subsequent trading trips northward resulted in his appointment to expel encroaching French in the Mt. Desert area, 1613; he later forced the Dutch settlement on the Hudson to declare allegiance to England. Deputy governor of Virginia, 1617–19. At end of his administration most of the public property was wasted and the colony was poverty-stricken.

ARLEN, MICHAEL (*b. Ruse, Bulgaria, 1895; d. New York, N.Y., 1956*), novelist, short story writer. Born Dikran Kouyoumdjian, the son of Armenian immigrants, Arlen published his first work, *The London Venture*, in 1919. His best-known work, *The Green Hat* (1924), was made into the successful film *A Woman of Affairs* (1928), starring Greta Garbo. The work established Arlen as a writer of popular, titillating, and slightly indecent novels. Other works include *Man's Mortality* (1933), a serious political work; and *The Flying Dutchman* (1939), his last novel.

ARLISS, GEORGE (*b. London, England, 1868; d. London, 1946*), actor, playwright. Stage name of George Augustus Andrews. Son of a convivial London printer. Arliss was stage-struck from boyhood. Even as an amateur and as a player in second-rate provincial and touring companies, he recognized that character parts best suited his talents and devoted great effort to refinement of his skill in such parts. He never ceased praising the value of the training received in playing stock company repertory. His first big step up was in the touring company of Pinero's *The Notorious Mrs. Ebbsmith*; his first important London West End engagement came in 1898 in *On and Off*. After two years in this play, he joined Mrs. Patrick Campbell's company at the Royalty Theater, supporting her in (again) *The Notorious Mrs. Ebbsmith* and Pinero's *The Second Mrs. Tanqueray* (1900–01). He and his actress wife Florence Montgomery accompanied Mrs. Campbell to America in 1901, where she toured with the two Pinero plays and where reviewers were enthusiastic over Arliss's performances. David Belasco signed him to play in *The Darling of the Gods*, starring Blanche Bates, in which again he won praise (1902–03). With this began a pattern for the Arlisses that was to continue with slight variation throughout his career: autumn to spring, acting in America; summer vacations in England.

Arliss joined Mrs. Fiske's company in 1904, playing important supporting roles such as the Marquis of Steyne in *Becky Sharp* and Judge Brack in *Hedda Gabler*; he also appeared with Mrs. Fiske in *The New York Idea* (1906), *Tess of the D'Urbervilles* (1907), and *Rosmersholm* (1907), and on tour, 1907–08. In 1908, he played the lead in Molnár's *The Devil*. He became a celebrity in Louis Parker's play *Disraeli*, written at Arliss's suggestion and a sensation of the 1911 season; he played the lead for four more seasons. He had further successes in a number of plays between 1915 and 1920. William Archer's *The Green Goddess* (New York, 1921–23; London, 1924) and John Galsworthy's *Old English* (1924; on tour, 1925–27) provided him with two of his most popular roles, which he later recreated in films. His last stage appearance was as Shylock in *The Merchant of Venice* (1928; on tour, 1928–29). Thereafter, he became a major motion picture star, making over twenty films, which included, in addition to *Disraeli* (1929), *The Millionaire* (1931), *Voltaire* (1933), *The House of Rothschild* (1934; perhaps his best), *The Iron Duke* (1935), and *Richelieu* (1935). The subtlety and apparent effortlessness of his work masked his painstaking devotion to the techniques of acting.

ARMISTEAD, GEORGE (*b. New Market, Va., 1780; d. Baltimore, Md., 1818*), soldier. Commanded at Fort McHenry during the famous defense against the British attack in 1814.

ARMISTEAD, LEWIS ADDISON (*b. Newbern, N.C., 1817; d. Gettysburg, Pa., 1863*), Confederate soldier. Distinguished in the Mexican War. Appointed brigadier general, 1862; killed leading a brigade in Pickett's charge.

ARMOUR, PHILIP DANFORTH (*b. Stockbridge, N.Y., 1832; d. Chicago, Ill., 1901*), meat packer. Entered meat packing trade with John Plankinton, Milwaukee, Wis., 1863; first great success in business was a speculation in pork, 1865. Added a pork packaging plant to his brother's grain business, 1868. By 1875, the expanding Armour interests were concentrated in Chicago, Ill. One of the earliest Chicago packers, Armour introduced economies by improving slaughtering techniques and finding uses for waste; he adopted modern refrigeration methods, purchased his own railroad cars, and established Eastern distribution centers. About 1880, he began preparation of canned meats on a large scale and the shipment of his products abroad. Much of his wealth was expended for philanthropic purposes.

ARMOUR, THOMAS DICKSON ("TOMMY") (*b. Edinburgh, Scotland, 1895; d. Larchmont, N.Y., 1968*), professional golfer. After World War I competed in British amateur golf tournaments and rose immediately to the forefront of the amateur ranks. Immigrated to the U.S. in 1921 and became a citizen in 1924. Turned professional in 1924, and during the next eleven years won fourteen major titles. After his competitive years, established a reputation as one of the most successful teachers of golf; Bobby Jones was one of his students. Also wrote three well-received books on golf. Was elected to the Professional Golfers Association Hall of Fame in 1940.

ARMSBY, HENRY PRENTISS (*b. Northbridge, Mass., 1853; d. 1921*), agricultural chemist. Professor of agricultural chemistry, University of Wisconsin, 1879–86; organized the Pennsylvania Agricultural Station and served as its director, 1887–1907; dean of the Pennsylvania School of Agriculture, 1890–1902; after 1907 did research at the Pennsylvania Institute of Animal Nutrition. His influential treatise *A Manual of Cattle Feeding* (1880) was the first of his classic researches into the fundamental physiological laws governing animal nutrition. He developed a respiration calorimeter for farm animals, demonstrated the validity of the principle of conservation energy in cattle, and studied the efficiency of different types and ages of animals as converters of "waste" into animal food.

ARMSTRONG, DAVID MAITLAND (*b. near Newburgh, N.Y., 1836; d. New York, N.Y., 1918*), painter, worker in stained glass. Painted frescoes for Chicago World's Fair, 1893; made stained-glass windows for St. Paul's Chapel, Columbia University.

ARMSTRONG, EDWARD COOKE (*b. Winchester, Va., 1871; d. Princeton, N.J., 1944*), Romance philologist, educator. Graduated Randolph-Macon, 1890; Ph.D., Johns Hopkins, 1897. Taught at Johns Hopkins, 1897–1917; chairman of Romance languages department *post* 1910. Professor of French, Princeton, 1917–39, where he organized a group of scholars to study the Alexander cycle of Old French poems. An outstanding scholar and trainer of scholars, Armstrong was a leader in the work of the Modern Language Association, and in the founding and policy-making of the American Council of Learned Societies.

ARMSTRONG, EDWIN HOWARD (*b. New York, N.Y., 1890; d. New York, 1954*), electrical engineer, inventor. Before graduating from Columbia School of Engineering in 1913, Armstrong devised the regenerative circuit, the key to the continuous-wave transmitter. During service in World War I, he invented the superheterodyne circuit, which became the basic circuit used in radio and television receivers. Returning to Columbia, he continued his research, selling various patents to the radio industry. In 1933, he brought forth the wide-band frequency modulation (FM) system that became the basis of high-fidelity broadcasting, microwave relay links, and space communications.

ARMSTRONG, FRANK C. (*b. Choctaw Agency, Indian Territory, 1835; d. Bar Harbor, Maine, 1909*), Confederate soldier. Held numerous cavalry commands in the Western campaigns; commissioned brigadier general, 1863.

ARMSTRONG, GEORGE BUCHANAN (*b. County Armagh, Ireland, 1882; d. Chicago, Ill., 1871*). Came to America in 1830. Suggested sorting of mail on trains, 1864; instituted and developed the railway mail service.

ARMSTRONG, GEORGE DOD (*b. Mendham, N.J., 1813; d. Norfolk, Va., 1899*), Presbyterian clergyman and controversial writer. Author of *The Christian Doctrine of Slavery* (1857).

ARMSTRONG, GEORGE WASHINGTON (*b. Boston, Mass., 1836; d. 1901*). Founded the Armstrong Transfer Co., a transfer, news, and restaurant service on New England railways.

ARMSTRONG, HENRY WORTHINGTON ("HARRY") (*b. Somerville Mass., 1879; d. New York, N.Y., 1951*), composer, vaudeville performer, pianist. Armstrong wrote many popular songs at the turn of the century, the best-known of which was "Sweet Adeline."

ARMSTRONG, JOHN (*b. Brookborough Parish, Ireland, 1717; d. Carlisle, Pa., 1795*), Pennsylvania soldier, politician. Captured Indian headquarters at Kittanning, Pa., 1756; held several commands during the Revolution; commissioned major general, 1777.

ARMSTRONG, JOHN (*b. New Jersey, 1755; d. Armstrong's Station, Ind., 1816*), soldier, explorer. After serving as an officer in the Revolution he undertook duties on the Ohio frontier, becoming one of the best-known woodsmen, explorers, and military characters of the early West. Commandant at Fort Pitt, 1785–86. In 1790, acting under secret government orders, he explored Spanish territory, proceeding up the Missouri some distance above St. Louis; intertribal Indian wars ended this one-man forerunner of the Lewis and Clark expedition. Resigning from the army, 1793, he served as treasurer of the Northwest Territory and held local offices.

ARMSTRONG, JOHN (*b. Carlisle, Pa., 1758; d. Red Hook, N.Y., 1843*), soldier, diplomat. Son of John Armstrong (1717–95). Served as an officer during the Revolution; composed the notorious "Newburgh Letters" (1783) suggesting that the army should take matters into its own hands if Congress failed to meet its demands for arrears of pay. Originally a Federalist, his marriage to Alida Livingston in 1789 brought him Republican political preferment; he served as U.S. senator from New York, 1800–02, 1803–04, resigning to become minister to France. Little glory could be won by an American minister at Napoleon's court during Armstrong's residence there, 1804–10, but it is to his credit that he objected to the subservient attitude of the American administration. Anxious to retire in triumph, he accepted the 1810 note in which the French sought to convince the Americans that Napoleon had revoked the Berlin and Milan decrees. This note, with its apparent yielding to the United States, was accepted without any probing into the true meaning of the new French policy; thus Armstrong must accept part of the responsibility for the break with England and the War of 1812. Appointed secretary of war by President Madison in 1813, his one notable achievement—the advancement of Generals Andrew Jackson, Jacob Brown, and Winfield Scott—is overshadowed by many mistakes and failures which culminated in losses on the Northern frontier and the capture of Washington by the British, 1814. He resigned from his secretaryship and political life in 1814 and retired to a life as a gentleman farmer.

ARMSTRONG, PAUL (*b. Kidder, Mo., 1869; d. New York, N.Y., 1915*), playwright. A writer of melodramas; author of *Alias Jimmy Valentine* (1909).

ARMSTRONG, ROBERT (*b. Abingdon, Va., 1792; d. 1854*), soldier. Brigadier general during the second Seminole War; unsuccessful Tennessee gubernatorial candidate, 1837.

ARMSTRONG, SAMUEL CHAPMAN (*b. Maui, Hawaii, 1839; d. 1893*), educator. Attended Williams College, 1861. Volunteered for Civil War and was commissioned colonel of Ninth Regiment, U.S. black troops, 1864; at end of war received brevet rank of brigadier general. Because of his conspicuous success in working with black soldiers he was appointed an agent of the Freedmen's Bureau, in charge of a camp of emancipated slaves near Hampton, Va. Realizing the need of industrial education for the freedman, he brought about the founding of Hampton Normal and Industrial Institute, 1868.

ARMSTRONG, SAMUEL TURELI (*b. Dorchester, Mass., 1784; d. 1850*), publisher, banker, Massachusetts Whig politician.

ARNO, PETER (*b. Curtis Arnoux Peters, Jr., New York, N.Y., 1904; d. Harrison, N.Y., 1968*), cartoonist. His work appeared regularly in the *New Yorker* from 1925 until his death and helped to establish the magazine's distinctive voice and style. Was one of the first cartoonists to use the one-line caption consistently, so that it became his trademark. Over the course of his career, his cartoons became increasingly economical, both verbally and visually; his favorite subjects were old roues, generously proportioned dowagers, curvaceous showgirls, haughty maître d's, and brainless ingenues, all of whom he depicted with powerful black lines and crisp silhouettes.

ARNOLD, AZA (*b. Smithfield, R.I., 1788; d. Washington, D.C., 1865*), inventor. Made valuable improvements in cotton-roving machines, increasing both the quantity and quality of the product.

ARNOLD, BENEDICT (*b. Norwich, Conn., 1741; d. London, England, 1801*), Revolutionary patriot and traitor. Arnold joined colonial troops in the French and Indian War, 1755; saw service on Lakes George and Champlain. Moved to New Haven, 1762; became a prosperous trader, and captain in the Connecticut militia. At outbreak of the Revolution he formed a plan to obtain military supplies for the Committee of Safety of Massachusetts by capturing Fort Ticonderoga; while en route to Ticonderoga he met Ethan Allen heading a similar expedition. After some difficulties the rival leaders agreed to issue joint commands; on May 10, 1775, they captured the fort. Arnold then sailed to the northern end of Lake Champlain and captured the fort at St. Johns. He returned to Connecticut when further conflict regarding jurisdiction resulted in his being "investigated" and superseded. General Washington, approving Arnold's project of an attack on Canada, sent Schuyler to capture Montreal while Arnold was ordered to Quebec by a new way across Maine. With forces decimated by disease, fatigue, and starvation, Arnold joined Montgomery (who replaced Schuyler) in an unsuccessful attack on Quebec, Dec. 31, 1775. Arnold, though badly wounded in the assault, blockaded the city until spring, when British reinforcements arrived. Foreseeing a contest

for the Lakes, he hastily assembled a "fleet" and met Carleton's British war vessels on Champlain, Oct. 11, 1776; the American "fleet" was defeated, but Arnold's fierce resistance upset British plans to capture Ticonderoga. He returned to New England to learn that Congress had failed to give him a deserved promotion to major general; angry at the slight, he was dissuaded from resigning by Washington's personal plea. When the British attacked Connecticut in 1777, he defeated their superior force and was promoted to major general, but not retroactively. Later that year his enemies in Congress attempted to investigate his conduct in Canada; he offered his resignation and once more Washington intervened, this time stating that Arnold's services were needed to halt Burgoyne's southern advance from Canada. Arnold raised the siege of crucial Fort Stanwix, rejoined the main army under Gates, and with him defeated Burgoyne at Saratoga, Sept.–Oct., 1777. Named commander at Philadelphia, June, 1778, and marrying into Philadelphia society, he began his betrayal of the American cause. His motives were fourfold: anger at repeated slights of Congress; need for ready money to maintain his social position; resentment at the Pennsylvania authorities; indignation of a Protestant at an alliance with the Catholic French. He regularly sent important military information to Sir Henry Clinton, 1779–80, and, when assigned to command of the strategic post at West Point, offered to surrender the garrison to him. The price of betrayal was set, and Arnold met the British spy André to arrange the surrender in September 1780; shortly thereafter André was captured, and Arnold fled to the British. He led marauding expeditions into Virginia and Connecticut, and in 1781 sailed with his family to an unhappy life in England, where he received no further rewards for his past services to the Crown.

ARNOLD, EDWARD (*b. New York, N.Y., 1890; d. Encino, Calif., 1956*), actor. Born Guenther Edward Schneider, he entered the theater at age fifteen and played juvenile roles with the Ethel Barrymore and Frohman companies. Appeared in the film *Sunrise-A Song of Two Humans* (1927) and with the Theatre Guild in *A Month in the Country* (1930) and *Miracle at Verdun* (1931). Played in more than ninety films, including *Rasputin and the Empress* (1932), *Whistling in the Dark* (1933), *Diamond Jim* (1935), *Idiot's Delight* (1939), *Dear Ruth* (1947), *You Can't Take It With You, Meet John Doe,* and *The Devil and Daniel Webster.* Also appeared in radio series "Mr. President."

ARNOLD, GEORGE (*b. New York, N.Y., 1834; d. Monmouth Co., N.J., 1865*), poet. Associated with the New York "Bohemian" group which met at Pfaff's beer cellar; author of light verse and short stories.

ARNOLD, HAROLD DeFOREST (*b. Woodstock, Conn., 1883; d. Summit, N.J., 1933*), scientist. Joined the Western Electric Co. in 1911, when industrial research was in its infancy. Developed a mercury arc amplifier and directed improvements in the 3-electrode vacuum tube which led to transcontinental telephony in 1914 and intercontinental radio telephony in 1915. As director of research at Western Electric Co. and later at the Bell Telephone Laboratories, he inaugurated physical and chemical investigations which have been applied in radio, motion pictures, transoceanic cables, and high-fidelity phonographs as well as the telephone.

ARNOLD, HENRY HARLEY (*b. Gladwyne, Pa., 1886; d. near Sonoma, Calif., 1950*), Air Force officer. Nicknamed "Hap" for "Happy." Graduated West Point, 1907. Commissioned in the infantry, served in the Philippines and on Governor's Island, New York. Volunteered for flight training in the Aviation Section of the Signal Corps, 1911, and after two months' course at the Wright Brothers' School in Dayton, Ohio, became an instructor at the Signal Corps School, College Park, Md. A skillful and daring pilot, Arnold in 1912 won the Mackay Trophy. Again with the infantry in the Philippines, 1913–16, he returned to the Aviation Section as a captain and was assigned early in 1917 to organize the 7th Aero squadron for defense of the Canal Zone. On U.S. entry into World War I, he was recalled to Washington, where he served in administrative capacities and rose to be assistant director of military aeronautics. In the fight for an independent air force, he sympathized with his friend General William Mitchell and testified in his favor at Mitchell's court-martial, but did not so engage himself as to injure his own career. After duty at Fort Riley, Kans., attendance (1928–29) at the Command and General Staff School, and commands at Fairfield and Wright Field, Ohio, he was promoted to lieutenant colonel in 1931 and sent to transform March Field, Riverside, Calif., from a primary training school into an operational base housing bomber and pursuit units. Made commander of the 1st Fighter Wing, 1933, Arnold took on the additional duty of commanding thirty C.C.C. camps in the West. In March 1935, as temporary brigadier general, he was given command of the 1st Wing of the General Headquarters Air Force; in January 1936, he returned to Washington as assistant chief of the Army Air Corps; in September 1938, now a major general, he became its chief.

With the aid of Harry Hopkins, he encouraged President Franklin D. Roosevelt to expand vastly the basic elements of U.S. air power. On his own initiative, he persuaded the aircraft industry to begin the radical changes needed for high future production goals; likewise, before funds were appropriated, he talked private flying schools into expensive preparations to serve as contract schools for primary pilot training. As events worsened, he was responsible for allocation of aircraft production to army, navy, and World War II allies, a difficult task. On establishment of the Army Air Forces in 1941, he was made chief; as lieutenant general, he was the air member of the U.S. Joint Chiefs of Staff; he was responsible, therefore, for building the air arm, and also for helping formulate policy and strategy for conduct of the war. Soon, the Army Air Forces achieved a quasi-independence. Arnold was promoted to general in March 1943, and to the new rank of general of the army in December 1944. He attended all the conferences of the Combined Chiefs of Staff which charted the course of the war, and in 1944, 1945, and part of 1946 was commanding general of the Twentieth Air Force, whose B-29 bombers were to hasten the defeat of Japan (issuing his orders via radio from the Pentagon). He applied to be relieved early in 1946 because of heart trouble and retired to a small ranch he had bought near Sonoma, Calif. Of his many honors, he was most pleased with his final promotion (May 1949) to permanent general of the Air Force, which symbolized the creation of an independent Air Force. His greatest achievement was his building-up of the greatest air force the world had seen.

ARNOLD, ISAAC NEWTON (*b. Hartwick, N.Y., 1815; d. 1884*), lawyer, historian. Republican Congressman from Illinois, 1860–64; introduced important legislation prohibiting slavery. A founder of the Chicago Historical Society.

ARNOLD, JONATHAN (*b. Providence, R.I., 1741; d. St. Johnsbury, Vt., 1793*), Revolutionary patriot. Drafted the 1776 law repealing the Rhode Island oath of allegiance to England; leading founder of St. Johnsbury, Vt.

ARNOLD, LAUREN BRIGGS (*b. Fairfield, N.Y., 1814; d. 1888*), dairy husbandman. Spent his life in the discovery and teaching of better methods of dairy practice; especially noted for his improvements in the manufacture of cheese.

ARNOLD, LESLIE PHILIP (*b. New Haven, Conn., 1893; d. Leonia, N.J., 1961*), pioneer aviator and airline executive. While enlisted with the Army Air Service, participated in several record-breaking flight experiments with his copilot Lowell H. Smith. After leaving the Air Service in 1928, he was an airline executive for several airlines, his longest affiliation being with Eastern Airlines.

ARNOLD, LEWIS GOLDING (*b. New Jersey, 1817; d. 1871*), Union general. Graduated West Point, 1837. Organized the defense of strategic Fort Jefferson in the Dry Tortugas, 1861.

ARNOLD, RICHARD (*b. Providence, R.I., 1828; d. Governor's Island, N.Y., 1882*), Union soldier, artillerist. Graduated West Point, 1850.

ARNOLD, RICHARD DENNIS (*b. Savannah, Ga., 1808; d. Savannah, 1876*), physician, politician. A founder of the American Medical Association, 1846.

ARNOLD, SAMUEL. *See* BOOTH, JOHN WILKES.

ARNOLD, SAMUEL GREENE (*b. Providence, R.I., 1821; d. Middletown, R.I., 1880*), historian. Author of *History of Rhode Island and Providence Plantation* (1859).

ARNOLD, THURMAN WESLEY (*b. Laramie, Wyo., 1891; d. Alexandria, Va., 1969*), lawyer, educator, social analyst, and government official. B.A. (1911), Princeton; LL.D. (1914), Harvard Law School. In 1930 began teaching at Yale, then the center of legal realism and innovative legal education. Became noted for his attacks on traditional legal theory and his efforts to bring social scientific and psychological insights into legal study and training. In *The Symbols of Government* (1935) and *The Folklore of Capitalism* (1937), he exposed the myths surrounding established institutions. As assistant attorney general in charge of antitrust enforcement (1938–43), became known as the New Deal's "trustbuster in chief." As an appellate judge for the U.S. Court of Appeals for the District of Columbia (1943–45), wrote several important opinions. Later, as senior member of the Washington firm of Arnold, Fortas, and Porter, became one of the nation's preeminent practitioners of corporate law and representation. Was a staunch defender of civil liberties during the McCarthy era.

ARRINGTON, ALFRED W. (*b. Iredell Co., N.C., 1810; d. Chicago, Ill., 1867*), lawyer, poet. Practiced law in Arkansas, Texas, and Illinois. Author of novels, newspaper sketches, and *Poems* (1869).

ARTHUR, CHESTER ALAN (*b. Fairfield, Vt., 1830; d. New York, N.Y., 1886*), president of the United States. Graduated Union College, 1848; practiced law in New York City. Closely associated with New York's Republican governor, Edwin D. Morgan, he served as quartermaster general of the state of New York, 1861–62. In 1871 President Grant recognized his active participation in Republican party affairs by making him collector of the Port of New York. Trained in the school of practical politics, he viewed the Custom House as a branch of Senator Roscoe Conkling's political machine; even though his administration was an honest one, the Custom House was overstaffed with clerks and laborers who recognized their obligations on election days. In 1876, on the election of President Hayes, reforms were ordered in the operation of the New York Custom House; Arthur opposed them and was ousted. Considered a martyr to party devotion, he was nominated vice president at the 1880 Republican Convention in order to pacify Grant's supporters; when the incoming President Garfield was assassinated in 1881, Arthur assumed the presidency. He surprised political friends and enemies by conducting his administration with independence and integrity. He supported a proposed reform of the civil service and attempted a revision of the tariff, but his efforts were not enough to stem the popular trend toward the Democratic party. The professional Republican politicians were alienated by his nonpartisan zeal for effective administration, and he was refused renomination in 1884.

ARTHUR, JOSEPH CHARLES (*b. Lowville, N.Y., 1850; d. Brook, Ind., 1942*), botanist. Raised near Charles City, Iowa. Graduated Iowa State College, Ames, 1872; M.S., 1877. After teaching at the universities of Wisconsin and Minnesota, appointed botanist at the Geneva, N.Y., Agricultural Experiment Station, 1884. Began research at Cornell University in plant pathology and mycology; received the Sc.D. in 1886. At Purdue University, 1887–1915, where he founded and headed the department of botany and plant pathology. Major contribution was in mycology, particularly the understanding of the life cycles, distribution, and classification of North American rust fungi; also carried out work of both scientific and economic importance on pear blight, cereal smuts, diseases of sugar beets, and potato scab.

ARTHUR, PETER M. (*b. Scotland, 1831; d. Winnipeg, Canada, 1903*), labor leader. Arrived in America, 1842. Associated with the Brotherhood of Locomotive Engineers, 1863–1903, he made it into one of the strongest and most conservative of labor unions.

ARTHUR, TIMOTHY SHAY (*b. near Newburgh, N.Y., 1809; d. Philadelphia, Pa., 1885*), editor, author. After serving as a watchmaker's apprentice and clerk, he chose a career in writing and held editorial positions on five Baltimore journals. He soon found a steady market in *Godey's Lady's Book* and other magazines for his moralistic stories. His first important book was a group of temperance tales (1842), but his greatest success was achieved in 1854 with *Ten Nights in a Barroom*, a temperance novel whose contemporary sale was second only to that of *Uncle Tom's Cabin*.

ARTHUR, WILLIAM (*b. near Ballymena, Ireland, 1797; d. Newtonville, N.Y., 1875*), Baptist clergyman, antiquarian. Held pastorates in Vermont and New York; father of Chester A. Arthur.

ARTZYBASHEFF, BORIS (*b. Kharkov, Ukraine [now Soviet Union], 1899; d. Old-Lyme, Conn., 1965*), artist, illustrator, and author. Immigrated to U.S. in 1919 and became a citizen in 1926. Worked as an illustrator for *New York World* before gaining the attention of E. P. Dutton publishing house, which subsequently commissioned him to illustrate Mamin Siberiak's *Verotchka's Tales* (1922). Thereafter was in demand as an illustrator of children's books with foreign settings. Created some of his best illustrative work during the 1930's, including his first book of prose and his only original story, *Shaydullah* (1931). Began his long association with Time Inc. in 1934, drawing statistical charts, maps, and graphs for *Fortune*, and in 1941 began his series of illustrations for *Life*, depicting war machines with human attributes. In 1941 began creating cover portraits for *Time*, producing 219 such portraits over the next 24 years.

ARVIN, NEWTON (*b. Valparaiso, Ind., 1900; d. Northampton, Mass., 1963*), literary critic and teacher. B.A., summa cum laude (1921), Harvard; taught at Smith College throughout his teaching career. His early reviews and essays—chiefly about American writers—were published in the *Freeman* as well as the *New York Herald Tribune*, the *Independent*, and the *Atlantic Monthly*. During the Depression became increasingly concerned with social and political questions and published essays on literature and politics. In 1932 he pledged to vote Communist and in 1954 was accused of "un-American activities." As of 1930 he began a long association with Yaddo, the writer's colony near Saratoga Springs, N.Y., and became elected to the board of directors in 1939. His reviews and essays appeared frequently in the *New Republic*, the *Nation*, and the *Partisan Review*. Edmund Wilson described him as "one of the two or three best contemporary writers on American classical literature." His scholarly works include *Hawthorne* (1929), *Whitman* (1938), *Moby Dick* (1948), *Herman Melville* (1950), and *Longfellow: His Life and Work* (1963).

ASBOTH, ALEXANDER SÁNDOR (*b. Keszthely, Hungary, 1811; d. Buenos Aires, Argentina, 1868*), Union soldier. Came to the United States with Kossuth. Won brevet as major general of volunteers, 1865; died soon after appointment as U.S. minister to Uruguay and Argentina.

ASBURY, FRANCIS (*b. Birmingham, England, 1845; d. Virginia, 1816*), pioneer Methodist preacher and bishop. Converted to Methodism through the influence of his emotional and devout mother, he volunteered to go with Richard Wright as a missionary to America, 1771. In America he joined Richard Boardman on his preaching circuit but soon left him and preached in the villages of Westchester Co., N.Y.; appointed superintendent of Methodists in America, Oct. 1772, he was relieved of the post, June 1773. He quarreled with his successor, Thomas Rankin, and was ordered to return to England in 1775. At this critical moment he determined to stay on, await the eventual departure of Rankin, and obtain a unique place in an independent American Methodist organization. During the Revolution the Methodists were suspected of Loyalist sympathies, but Asbury, although he refused to take the Maryland oath of allegiance, became convinced of eventual American victory and became a citizen of Delaware. Controversy involving the Northern and Southern Methodist ministers was resolved by him at a conference that was a complete victory for the Northern party and a personal triumph for Asbury. By 1782 Asbury was the virtual head of the Methodist organization in America. When Wesley sent Thomas Coke in 1784 to act jointly with him in superintending the Methodist societies, Asbury insisted that the appointment be made by a regular conference; chosen as joint superintendent, he assumed the title of bishop and gained practical control of the Methodist organization. Although in theory a servant of the Methodist conference, he was an autocratic ruler who appointed preachers as he chose and accepted but subdued the associate bishop elected to aid him. He traveled widely through all of the colonies and was the planner of those far-flung preaching campaigns which made the circuit-rider a familiar frontier figure. As an organizer and administrator, Francis Asbury holds a primacy in the annals of his sect.

ASBURY, HERBERT (*b. Farmington, Mo., 1891; d. New York, N.Y., 1963*), newspaperman and historian. Worked on various newspapers in Illinois, Georgia, and New York through 1928. Became nationally known in 1926 when H.L. Mencken published his article about a prostitute, "Hatrack," for which Mencken was arrested on obscenity charges. Thereafter his writing provoked comment and controversy, both for the subject matter—histories of vice, crime, and self-indulgence—and for his uninvolved, nonjudgmental attitude toward what he portrayed. His articles appeared in the *New Yorker*, *Cosmopolitan*, and other magazines, and his books include his autobiographical *Up From Methodism* (1926), *The Gangs of New York* (1928), *The Barbary Coast: An Informal History of the San Francisco Underworld* (1933), *Sucker's Progress: An Informal History of Gambling in America* (1938), and *The Great Illusion: An Informal History of Prohibition* (1950).

ASCH, MORRIS JOSEPH (*b. Philadelphia, Pa., 1833; d. 1902*), laryngologist, soldier. Saw extensive medical service during the Civil War and in the West; practiced thereafter in New York City. Deviser of the "Asch operation" for deviation of the nasal septum.

ASHBURNER, CHARLES ALBERT (*b. Philadelphia, Pa., 1854; d. 1889*), geologist. Surveyed Pennsylvania iron and oil districts; organized and headed a survey of the anthracite field, 1880–86.

ASHBY, TURNER (*b. near Markham, Va., 1828; d. near Harrisonburg, Va., 1862*), Confederate soldier. Distinguished in the Valley campaign, 1862.

ASHE, JOHN (*b. Grovely, N.C.[?], ca. 1720; d. Sampson Co., N.C., 1781*), soldier, politician. His defeat at Briar Creek in 1778 resulted in the British capture of Georgia.

ASHE, JOHN BAPTISTA (*b. Rocky Point, N.C., 1748; d. Halifax, N.C.,)*, member of the Continental Congress, 1787–88; U.S. representative from North Carolina, 1789–93; governor, 1802.

ASHE, SAMUEL (*b. near Beaufort, N.C., 1725; d. Rocky Point, N.C., 1813*), jurist, Revolutionary patriot. Presiding judge of the first North Carolina supreme court; governor of North Carolina, 1795–98.

ASHE, THOMAS SAMUEL (*b. Orange Co., N.C., 1812; d. 1887*), legislator. Served in the Confederate Congress; elected to the U.S. Congress, 1872; state supreme court judge, 1878–87.

ASHE, WILLIAM SHEPPARD (*b. Rocky Point, N.C., 1814; d. Rocky Point, 1862*), planter, lawyer. Grandson of Samuel Ashe. Democratic Congressman from North Carolina, 1849–52; president, Wilmington & Weldon Railroad; directed Confederate government transportation, New Orleans to Richmond.

ASHER, JOSEPH MAYOR (*b. Manchester, England, 1872; d. New York, N.Y., 1909*), rabbi. Professor of homiletics, Jewish Theological Seminary of America, 1902–09; served several New York congregations as an eloquent preacher.

ASHFORD, BAILEY KELLY (*b. Washington, D.C., 1873; d. San Juan, P.R., 1934*), physician, research worker in tropical medicine. His discovery that the hookworm was the cause of tropical anemia and his successful campaign against the disease in Puerto Rico led to a later world-wide campaign by the Rockefeller Institute.

ASHHURST, JOHN (*b. Philadelphia, Pa., 1839; d. 1900*), surgeon, author. Professor of surgery, University of Pennsylvania; author of *Principles and Practise of Surgery* (1871) and editor of *International Encyclopedia of Surgery* (1881–86).

ASHLEY, JAMES MITCHELL (*b. Allegheny Co., Pa., 1824; d. 1896*), congressman. Originally a Democrat, his intense antagonism to slavery swept him into the Republican camp in 1854. While a U.S. representative from Ohio, 1859–69, he sponsored the first bill to introduce minority representation in the territorial governments, prepared the first measure for the reconstruction of the Southern states presented to Congress, and with Lot M. Morrill drew up the 1862 bill to abolish slavery in the District of Columbia. He considered his greatest achievement to be his successful introduction of the first proposition to abolish slavery by a constitutional amendment. Andrew Johnson's impeachment was initiated by him, and the president's acquittal brought Ashley's defeat in 1868. Appointed governor of Montana in 1869, he later served as president of the Toledo, Ann Arbor and Northern Michigan Railroad.

ASHLEY, WILLIAM HENRY (*b. Powhatan Co., Va., ca. 1778; d. Cooper Co., Mo., 1838*), fur trader, explorer, congressman. Settled in Missouri between 1803 and 1805 and engaged in the manufacture of gunpowder and the mining of saltpeter and lead; was elected lieutenant governor of Missouri, 1820. In 1822–23 he and Andrew Henry turned to fur trading and dispatched expeditions up the Missouri to the Yellowstone and

across South Pass into the Green River valley. A year later Ashley abandoned the fixed trading method of operation, substituting for it an annual rendezvous of trappers and traders conducted at any convenient and accessible place. The first of these was held at the confluence of Henry's Fork and the Green River. Between 1824 and 1826, Ashley and his men covered a great range of territory in present-day Nebraska, Colorado, Wyoming, and Utah as they carried supplies to the "mountain men" at the rendezvous and brought the furs back to St. Louis. He was congressman from Missouri on an anti-Jackson ticket, 1831–37, and championed Western interests.

ASHMEAD, ISAAC (*b. Germantown, Pa., 1790; d. 1870*), printer. Introduced the composition roller, and the hydraulic press for smooth-pressing wet sheets; printer to the American Sunday School Union.

ASHMEAD, WILLIAM HARRIS (*b. Philadelphia, Pa., 1855; d. 1908*), entomologist. Author of important papers on the taxonomy of insect pests.

ASHMORE, WILLIAM (*b. Putnam, Ohio, 1824; d. Wallaston, Mass., 1909*), Baptist missionary to China, 1850–1903.

ASHMUN, GEORGE (*b. Blandford, Mass., 1804; d. Springfield, Mass., 1870*), lawyer, legislator. Whig Congressman from Massachusetts, 1845–51; opposed the Mexican War. Served as chairman of the 1860 Republican Convention in Chicago and was an adviser to President Lincoln.

ASHMUN, JEHUDI (*b. Champlain, N.Y., 1794; d. New Haven, Conn., 1828*), colonial agent. Graduated University of Vermont, 1816; entered Congregational ministry. While editor of the *Theological Repertory* he became interested in the work of the American Colonization Society and was appointed a special U.S. government representative to Liberia in 1822. With 37 new colonists he sailed to Africa and found the settlement in a desperate situation; most of the settlers were ill, supplies were exhausted, and a large native force threatened to attack. Assuming leadership, he built defenses and repulsed the enemy. In May 1823, he was superseded by a new agent, who soon returned to America. Shortly thereafter, Ashmun was fully authorized as agent and headed the enterprise until 1828.

ASHURST, HENRY FOUNTAIN (*b. Winnemucca, Nev., 1874; d. Washington, D.C., 1962*), U.S. senator. Although raised in Arizona, graduated from Stockton Business College in California (1896) and completed his formal education at the University of Michigan Law School (1904). In 1896 was elected as a Democrat to the Territorial House of Representatives and was reelected to a second term. Was elected to the Territorial Senate in 1902, serving one term. Was district attorney of Coconino County (1904–08). As U.S. senator (1912–40), he was a devoted Wilsonian and during the 1920's was a consistent critic of the Republican administrations. Chaired the Indian Affairs Committee (1914–21), and in 1933 became chair of the Judiciary Committee, a post he filled for the remainder of his career in the Senate. He attacked the Ku Klux Klan at the height of its power in the 1920's, and possibly the highlight of his Senate career was his attack on Huey Long in 1935. However, his name is associated with no significant measure or cause; he gained a wide reputation for his sartorial splendor, eloquent oratory, and inconsistency (for example, he voted both for the Eighteenth Amendment and its repeal). His diary, edited by George F. Sparks and entitled *A Many Colored Toga*, was published in 1962.

ASPINWALL, WILLIAM (*b. Brookline, Mass., 1743; d. 1823*), physician. Military surgeon in the Revolution; opened an inoculation hospital for smallpox in 1783, the second of its kind in America.

ASPINWALL, WILLIAM HENRY (*b. New York, N.Y., 1807; d. 1875*), merchant. Succeeded his uncles in the management of the great G. G. and S. Howland trading firm, 1837. In 1850 he resigned active leadership in Howland and Aspinwall, entered the Pacific Railroad & Panama Steamship Co., and directed the building of a railroad across the isthmus of Panama. The railroad in conjunction with his Pacific Mail Steamship Co. gave the Aspinwall interest a monopoly on the best passenger and trade route to California during the gold-rush years. After the Civil War he retired from active business and interested himself in the social, civic, and artistic life of New York City.

ASTOR, JOHN JACOB (*b. Waldorf, Germany, 1763; d. New York, N.Y., 1848*), fur trader, capitalist. While en route to America in 1784 he met a fellow immigrant who had successfully traded for furs with the Indians, and decided to enter this business; by 1786 he was established in his own shop on Water St., New York City, and made frequent trips to Canada in connection with his fur-trading ventures. By 1800 he had amassed a fortune of $250,000, was acknowledged the leading factor in the trade, and began to make large purchases of New York real estate. The Louisiana Purchase opened new trading vistas to him. In 1808 he consolidated his holdings in the American Fur Co. and made plans to circumvent the St. Louis control of the fur trade in the Far West by planting a central depot at the mouth of the Columbia River through which furs collected in the interior would be shipped most efficiently to Chinese markets. The vessels would then load merchandise for European trading, complete the European circuit, and reload with items for American markets. Astoria was founded as the exchange center in 1811, and a vessel carrying men and supplies was dispatched to the Oregon territory. A series of disasters and the coming of the War of 1812 ended this enterprise; in 1813 the British took possession of Astor's establishment at the mouth of the Columbia. Astoria was a victim of the war, but its owner was repaid by lending money at a ruinous rate of interest to the U.S. government. At the signing of the peace he attempted once again to monopolize fur trading in the trans-Mississippi region, but Western opposition was strong, and the returns of his bold campaigns were diminished by losses to the Indians and a decline in fur value. In 1834 he sold all his fur interests and retired to the administration of his twenty-million-dollar fortune. Founded Astor Library, New York City.

ASTOR, JOHN JACOB (*b. New York, N.Y., 1822; d. New York, 1890*), capitalist. Son of William Backhouse Astor; administered the family estate and expanded the facilities of the Astor Library.

ASTOR, JOHN JACOB (*b. Rhinebeck, N.Y., 1864; d. 1912*), capitalist, inventor. Great-grandson of John Jacob Astor (1763–1848). Managed family estate; died in *Titanic* disaster.

ASTOR, WILLIAM BACKHOUSE (*b. New York, N.Y., 1792; d. New York, 1875*), capitalist. Son of John Jacob Astor (1763–1848). Continued his father's policy of investing in New York real estate.

ASTOR, WILLIAM VINCENT (*b. New York, N.Y., 1891; d. New York, 1959*), financier, navy officer, sportsman, public benefactor. Attended Harvard briefly before entering the family business at age twenty. Served in the navy during World War I and World War II, achieving the rank of naval reserve captain. Astor divested himself of the family's real estate holdings in New York City and expanded his financial enterprises. He helped to found *Today* magazine in 1933 and was owner and chairman of the board until his death. A close friend of Franklin D. Roosevelt, he was an early supporter of the New Deal. Founded the Vincent Astor Foundation (1948); trustee of the Astor Library in New York.

ASTOR, WILLIAM WALDORF (*b. New York, N.Y., 1848; d. Brighton, England, 1919*), capitalist. Son of John Jacob Astor (1822–90). Moved to England, 1890, becoming a British subject, 1899, and was raised to the peerage as Viscount Astor, 1917.

ATCHISON, DAVID RICE (*b. Frogtown, Ky., 1807; d. Gower, Mo., 1886*), lawyer, senator. Removed to Missouri, 1830; U.S. senator, Democrat, from Missouri, 1843–55. He was chairman of the important Committee on Indian Affairs, promoted land-grant legislation to aid Missouri railroads, and was elected president *pro tempore* of the Senate 16 times. Associated with the pro-slavery faction, and an opponent of Thomas H. Benton, he worked for the repeal of the Missouri Compromise and influenced passage of the Kansas-Nebraska Bill. After losing the election of 1855 he lapsed into obscurity.

ATHERTON, CHARLES GORDON (*b. Amherst, N.H., 1804; d. 1853*), lawyer, politician. Democratic congressman from New Hampshire, 1836–43; U.S. senator, 1843–49. Introduced the 1838 "gag resolutions" forbidding the introduction of memorials on slavery.

ATHERTON, GEORGE WASHINGTON (*b. Boxford Mass., 1837; d. 1906*), college president. Championed land-grant colleges; became president of Pennsylvania State College, 1882, and can be considered its real founder.

ATHERTON, GERTRUDE FRANKLIN HORN (*b. San Francisco, Calif., 1857; d. San Francisco, 1948*), novelist. Attended schools in California and Kentucky. Turned to writing as an escape from an unsatisfactory marriage to a wealthy Californian. Her first novel, *The Randolphs of Redwoods*, serialized in the San Francisco *Argonaut*, derived from a contemporary local scandal and infuriated her family and society generally. When her husband died in 1887, she came to New York, where she published *What Dreams May Come* (1888) and *Hermia Suydam* (1889), distinguished by liberated female characters, sexual candor, and romantic melodrama. In 1895, she went to England, where her books were welcomed as revelations of the American character, although Henry James found both her and her books vulgar. Practically every one of her stories centered upon a woman who claims the right to think and act for herself. A second principal theme in her work was Spanish life in old California, typified in *The Californians* (1898) and *The Splendid Idle Forties* (1902). Her most ambitious and successful books were fictionalized biographies: *The Conqueror*, about Alexander Hamilton (1902); *Rezanov*, about N. P. Rezanov (1906); and *The Immortal Marriage*, about Pericles and Aspasia (1927). After undergoing Steinach's rejuvenation therapy, she wrote *Black Oxen* (1923), which popularized the treatment in the United States. She was also the author of a lively autobiography, *Adventures of a Novelist* (1932).

ATHERTON, JOSHUA (*b. Harvard, Mass., 1737; d. Amherst, N.H., 1809*), lawyer, Loyalist during the Revolution, early antislavery leader.

ATKINS, JEARUM (*b. Vermont; fl. 1840–80*), inventor. Devised an automatic mechanism to rake severed grain from a reaper platform, 1852.

ATKINSON, EDWARD (*b. Brookline, Mass., 1827; d. 1905*), industrialist, economist. Helped establish and later headed the Boston Manufacturers Mutual Insurance Co.; improved industrial architecture by insisting on safe construction of factories.

ATKINSON, GEORGE FRANCIS (*b. Raisinville, Mich., 1854; d. Tacoma, Wash., 1918*), botanist. First president of the

American Botanical Society; an outstanding mycologist and the author of *Studies of American Fungi* (1900).

ATKINSON, GEORGE HENRY (*b. Newburyport, Mass., 1819; d. 1889*), Congregational clergyman, educator, community builder. As missionary in Oregon, he fostered public education there and became an enthusiastic propagandist for settling and farming the Pacific Northwest.

ATKINSON, GEORGE WESLEY (*b. Kanawha Co., Va., 1845; d. 1925*), author, lecturer, jurist. Republican governor of West Virginia, 1896; judge of the U.S. Court of Claims, 1905–16.

ATKINSON, HENRY (*b. North Carolina, 1782; d. Jefferson Barracks, Mo., 1842*), soldier. Entered the regular army, 1808; promoted colonel, 1815; assigned command of the 1819 "Yellowstone Expedition," an unsuccessful project aimed at warning Indians and British fur traders by sending American soldiers to the mouth of the Yellowstone River. In 1825 he commanded another expedition to the upper Missouri, reached the Yellowstone mouth, held treaty councils with a number of Indian tribes, and on his return to St. Louis selected the site for the historic post Jefferson Barracks. He was in general command of troops in the Black Hawk War, 1832, and supervised the removal of the Winnebagos from Wisconsin, 1840.

ATKINSON, HENRY AVERY (*b. Merced, Calif., 1877; d. Baltimore, Md., 1960*), clergyman, foundation executive. Studied at Pacific Methodist College and Garrett Bible Institute. As general secretary of the Church Peace Union (1918–55), he became an ardent internationalist, espousing the cause of peace through the churches of the world. Campaigned for U.S. entry into the League of Nations and was an unofficial consultant at the U.N. conference in San Francisco in 1945. General secretary of the Universal Christian Conference on Life and Work (1920–32) and founder of the World Council of Churches (1948).

ATKINSON, JOHN (*b. Deerfield, N.Y., 1835; d. Haverstraw, N.Y., 1897*), Methodist clergyman. Author of several important histories of American Methodism and of the hymn "Shall We Meet Beyond the River?"

ATKINSON, THOMAS (*b. Dinwiddie Co., Va., 1807; d. Wilmington, N.C., 1881*), Episcopal bishop of North Carolina, 1853–81; aided the establishment of the University of the South; supported the Confederate cause.

ATKINSON, WILLIAM BIDDLE (*b. Haverford, Pa., 1832; d. 1909*), obstetrician. Author of a valuable reference work on American medical biography, *The Physicians and Surgeons of the United States* (1878).

ATKINSON, WILLIAM YATES (*b. Oakland, Ga., 1854; d. Newnan, Ga., 1899*), lawyer. Governor of Georgia, 1894–98.

ATKINSON, WILMER (*b. Bucks Co., Pa., 1840; d. 1920*), journalist. Founded and edited the *Farm Journal*, 1877–1917.

ATLEE, JOHN LIGHT (*b. Lancaster, Pa., 1799; d. Lancaster, 1885*), physician. Expert in obstetrical surgery.

ATLEE, WASHINGTON LEMUEL (*b. Lancaster, Pa., 1808; d. 1878*), surgeon. Brother of John L. Atlee, and with him an early proponent of ovariotomy.

ATTERBURY, GROSVENOR (*b. Detroit, Mich., 1869; d. Southampton, N.Y., 1956*), architect, town planner. Studied at Yale, Columbia University School of Architecture, and the École des Beaux Arts in Paris. The architect and planner for the model town of Forest Hills in New York City (1909), Atterbury introduced the earliest practical examples of prefabrication in the country. His work in the use of precast concrete as a mass building material was funded mainly by the Russell Sage Foundation. Was architect of private homes and estates and the American Wing of the Metropolitan Museum of Art in New York (1922–24). Instrumental in founding the National Housing Association (1910).

ATTERBURY, WILLIAM WALLACE (*b. New Albany, Ind., 1866; d. 1935*), railroad president. Converted the Pennsylvania R.R. line from New York to Washington to electric operation; director general of transportation, American Expeditionary Forces in World War I.

ATTUCKS, CRISPUS (*b. ca. 1723; d. Boston, Mass., 1770*), American patriot. Leader of the mob which precipitated the Boston Massacre, he lost his life in the affray. Considered the first casualty of the American Revolution. A black, he was a runaway slave.

ATWATER, CALEB (*b. North Adams, Mass., 1778; d. Circleville, Ohio, 1867*), pioneer, author. Settled in Ohio, 1815, where he practiced law; elected to Ohio legislature, 1821; supported the construction of highways and canals and the provision of popular education. He was one of three commissioners appointed by President Jackson to treat with the Indians at Prairie du Chien, 1829; in 1838 he published *A History of the State of Ohio, Natural and Civil*. Atwater was a social and intellectual pioneer of the Middle West, and perhaps the first advocate of forest conservation; he was one of the first to predict the success of the railway, the first historian of his state, and the founder of its school system.

ATWATER, LYMAN HOTCHKISS (*b. New Haven, Conn., 1813; d. Princeton, N.J., 1883*), Congregational clergyman, educator. Professor of philosophy, Princeton, 1854–83; prolific writer in defense of old-school Calvinism.

ATWATER, WILBUR OLIN (*b. Johnsburg, N.Y., 1844; d. 1907*), pioneer in agricultural chemistry. Studied chemistry at Yale University and at Leipzig and Berlin; professor of chemistry, Wesleyan University, Middletown, Conn., 1873–1907. Aided in the establishment of the first state agricultural station in the United States (Middletown, Conn., 1875). Through Atwater's efforts Congress made funds available to every state for at least one such station, 1887. As a chemist, he discovered that free atmospheric nitrogen is assimilated by leguminous plants, 1881. With E. B. Rosa he built the Atwater-Rosa calorimeter, 1892–97; he thereafter demonstrated that the law of conservation of energy is valid for human beings and prepared an elaborate table giving the calorific value of various foodstuffs.

ATWOOD, CHARLES B. (*b. Charlestown, Mass., 1849; d. 1895*), architect. Designed the twin Vanderbilt houses, Fifth Avenue, New York City; served as designer in chief of the Chicago World's Fair, 1893.

ATWOOD, DAVID (*b. Bedford, N.H., 1815; d. Madison, Wis., 1889*), editor, politician. Founded the politically influential *Wisconsin State Journal*, 1852.

ATWOOD, LEWIS JOHN (*b. Goshen, Conn., 1827; d. Waterbury, Conn., 1909*), inventor, manufacturer. With Hiram W. Hayden he invented sheet-brass lampburners for use with petroleum, 1855; he also devised a scrap-metal press.

ATWOOD, WALLACE WALTER (*b. Chicago, Ill., 1872; d. Annisquam, Mass., 1949*), geologist, geographer, educator. Graduated University of Chicago, 1897; Ph.D., 1903. Taught geology at Chicago *post* 1902, becoming associate professor, but left Chicago to be professor of physiography (geomorphology) at

Harvard, 1913. Appointed geologist in the U.S. Geological Survey in 1909, he held that rank until his death. His principal scientific contributions derived from his fieldwork. One of the last to work in the empirical tradition of the 19th-century topographical surveys of the West, he chose the Rockies, and in particular the San Juan Mountains in southwestern Colorado, as his principal area of investigation. Between 1909 and 1948, he spent over twenty-five seasons there, exploring, studying, and recording the region's geological and geographical characteristics. From 1920 to 1946, he was president of Clark University, Worcester, Mass. Principal contributions were the establishment of the outstanding Graduate School of Geography at Clark; co-authorship of a series of textbooks for elementary and junior high school students which exemplified new concepts; and his popularization of science, as in his book *The Rocky Mountains* (1945).

ATZERODT, GEORGE A.   *See* BOOTH, JOHN WILKES.

AUCHMUTY, RICHARD TYLDEN   (*b. New York, N.Y., 1831; d. Lenox, Mass., 1893*), architect. Founded the New York Trade School in 1881, one of the earliest institutions to combine theoretical instruction and shop practice.

AUCHMUTY, ROBERT   (*b. Scotland; d. Roxbury, Mass., 1750*), colonial jurist. Judge of Admiralty, Massachusetts, 1733–41.

AUCHMUTY, ROBERT   (*b. Boston, Mass.; d. England, 1788*), colonial jurist. Son of Robert Auchmuty (d. 1750); served with John Adams as counsel to Capt. Preston in the Boston Massacre case, 1770; removed to England, 1776.

AUCHMUTY, SAMUEL   (*b. Boston, Mass., 1722; d. New York, N.Y., 1777*), Anglican minister, Loyalist. Brother of Robert Auchmuty (d. 1788); rector of Trinity Church, New York City, 1764–77.

AUDSLEY, GEORGE ASHDOWN   (*b. Elgin, Scotland, 1838; d. 1925*), architect, organ designer. Worked in America, 1892–1925; author of many books on ornament, in particular *The Ornamental Arts of Japan* (1884).

AUDUBON, JOHN JAMES   (*b. Les Cayes, Santo Domingo, 1785; d. New York, N.Y., 1851*), artist, ornithologist. Natural son of Jean Audubon, a French sea captain, trader, and planter, and a Creole mistress, John James Audubon was taken to France in 1789 and formally adopted by his father and his father's legal wife. At the age of fifteen, he began a collection of original drawings of French birds; in 1802–03 he studied drawing in Paris under David. Early in 1804 he took up residence in America on an estate his father owned near Philadelphia; there, he made the first "banding" experiment ever made on the young of an American wild bird. In 1805 he went back to France; in the following year, having formed a partnership with Ferdinand Rozier, he returned to American and opened (with Rozier) a general store in Louisville, Ky. He married Lucy Bakewell in 1808.

Audubon roamed the country in eager pursuit of rare birds to study and sketch while his partner "kept store"; in the spring of 1810 the store was moved down the Ohio to Henderson, Ky., but it was not a success at either location. A series of other business enterprises ended in 1819 with Audubon's bankruptcy.

While he was attempting to support his family by sketching portraits, and as a tutor and drawing master, he determined to publish his bird drawings. In Philadelphia, where he had gone seeking a publisher, he was advised to offer his work in Europe, where interest in the subject would be greater and where skilled engravers could be found. Accordingly he sailed in 1826, and was successful in finding subscribers for his work in Liverpool, Edinburgh, and London; he was also fortunate in securing the

services of Robert Havell, Jr., as engraver for the project. *The Birds of America* in large folio size began to appear in 1827 and was published in parts, the final part appearing in 1838. *The Ornithological Biography*, a text commentary on the hand-colored plates in *The Birds*, was published between 1831 and 1839; in this work he had the help of William MacGillivray, who also assisted in the methodical catalogue entitled *Synopsis of the Birds of North America* (1839).

Audubon returned to the United States in 1831 with a European reputation as naturalist and artist. He continued his explorations and sketching in Texas, Florida, and Labrador until 1834, when he went back to Edinburgh. He came home once again, 1839, and began preparation of an octavo edition of *The Birds* (New York and Philadelphia, 1840–44). He also undertook with John Bachman a work on *The Viviparous Quadrupeds of North America* (plates, 1842–45; text, 1846–54).

Despite criticism of his work, both as art and as science, Audubon remains at the head of early American ornithologists. His only rival, Alexander Wilson, produced work which was more original and more steadily scientific, but it lacked the scope, magnificence, and general usefulness of *The Birds of America*.

AUER, JOHN   (*b. Rochester, N.Y., 1875; d. 1948*), pharmacologist, physiologist. Graduated University of Michigan, 1898; M.D., John Hopkins, 1902. Associated with the Rockefeller Institute for Medical Research, 1904–20, as assistant and close colleague of Samuel J. Meltzer, collaborating with him on a number of papers dealing with the anesthetic and relaxative effects of magnesium sulphate administered intravenously, with findings of great value in treatment of tetanus, eclampsia, and other spasmodic conditions. They also devised a means of ventilating the lungs in surgery by a stream of air blown into them through the trachea, thus aerating the blood without breathing movements of the chest. By including an anesthetic vapor in the air stream, a patient could be kept under surgical anesthesia even after the chest was opened. This invention found worldwide use in thoracic surgery. In 1906, Auer's first independent publication described hitherto unnoticed inclusions (Auer bodies) in the large lymphocytes in acute leukemia. With a junior colleague, he supplied the data that led Meltzer to propose the now accepted hypothesis that bronchial asthma results from anaphylactic sensitivity to foreign proteins. *Post* 1920, he devoted most of his time to teaching, as professor of pharmacology at the St. Louis University School of Medicine.

AUGUR, CHRISTOPHER COLUMBUS   (*b. Kendall, N.Y., 1821; d. Georgetown, D.C., 1898*), Union soldier. Graduated West Point, 1843. Served in the Mexican War; in Oregon, 1852–56; and with distinction in several theaters of the Civil War. Promoted brigadier general, regular army, 1869, he retired in 1885.

AUGUR, HEZEKIAH   (*b. New Haven, Conn., 1791; d. 1858*), sculptor. Overcame paternal objections and financial difficulties to become an interesting precursor in American sculpture.

AUGUSTUS, JOHN   (*b. 1785; d. Boston, Mass., 1859*), philanthropist. From 1841 to 1859, served without pay as a pioneer probation officer and friend to the unfortunate of Boston.

AUSTELL, ALFRED   (*b. near Dandridge, Tenn., 1814; d. Atlanta, Ga., 1881*), financier. Removed to Campbellton, Ga. 1836; in 1858, foreseeing the future importance of Atlanta, he settled there as a merchant. At the end of the Civil War he organized the Atlanta National Bank, the first Southern bank to be chartered under the Act of 1863, and made it an outstanding factor in the economic development of Georgia and the rebuilding of the

South. He was also active and successful in railroad enterprises and in cotton brokerage.

AUSTEN, (ELIZABETH) ALICE (*b.* Staten Island, N.Y., 1866; *d.* Staten Island, 1951), photographer. Austen's work is remembered chiefly for her pictures of the emancipated woman of her day, which often depict a defiant and almost satiric stand against the sexual mores of the time. Most of her work was completed by the end of World War I. In 1951, she was discovered by Oliver Jensen, who was doing research for his book, *Revolt of American Women*. After that, her work appeared in *Life*, *Holiday*, and *Pageant*, and a special exhibition of her work was given in Richmondtown, Staten Island.

AUSTEN, PETER TOWNSEND (*b.* Clifton, N.Y., 1852; *d.* 1907), chemist. Professor of chemistry, Rutgers, 1878–91; thereafter a consultant and inventor of dyeing and bleaching processes.

AUSTIN, BENJAMIN (*b.* Boston, Mass., 1752; *d.* 1820), political leader. A successful merchant, he succeeded Samuel Adams as leader of the more radical Boston Republicans (Democrats) during the troubled years 1789–96. Author of *Constitutional Republicanism, in Opposition to Fallacious Federalism* (1803).

AUSTIN, DAVID (*b.* New Haven, Conn., 1759; *d.* Bozrah, Conn., 1831), Congregational clergyman. Widely known in his day for his preachings and writings on the millennium.

AUSTIN, HENRY (*b.* Mt. Carmel, Conn., 1804; *d.* New Haven, Conn., 1891), architect. Trained in the office of Ithiel Town; designed many private and public buildings in New Haven, including a library for Yale (1842).

AUSTIN, JAMES TRECOTHICK (*b.* Boston, Mass., 1784; *d.* Boston, 1870), lawyer. Son of Jonathan L. Austin. Attorney general of Massachusetts, 1832–43; a foe of abolitionism.

AUSTIN, JANE GOODWIN (*b.* Worcester, Mass., 1831; *d.* 1894), author. Her novels of early New England were based on careful research and include *Standish of Standish* (1889) and *Betty Alden* (1891).

AUSTIN, JONATHAN LORING (*b.* Boston, Mass., 1748; *d.* Boston, 1826), brother and partner of Benjamin Austin; served as confidential messenger and secretary for the American commissioners to France, 1777–79.

AUSTIN, MARY (*b.* Carlinville, Ill., 1868; *d.* Santa Fe, N.Mex., 1934), author, feminist. Her best work is nature writing in the tradition of John Muir and Henry David Thoreau. Among her more important books are: *The Land of Little Rain* (1903) and *A Woman of Genius* (1912).

AUSTIN, MOSES (*b.* Durham, Conn., 1761; *d.* 1821), merchant. First interested in lead mining during the Revolution, he worked a mine in southwestern Virginia between 1789 and 1798, moving in the latter year to Missouri; there he reopened the old Mine à Burton and founded the town of Potosi. His fortune lost in the collapse of the Bank of St. Louis and the depression of 1819, he applied in December 1820 to the Spanish authorities for a permit to settle 300 families in Texas. The permit was granted in January 1821; but Austin died before making the move, and his son Stephen F. Austin carried out the proposed colonization.

AUSTIN, SAMUEL (*b.* New Haven, Conn., 1760; *d.* 1830), Congregational clergyman. Pastor of the First Church in Worcester, Mass., 1790–1815; a firm opponent of Unitarianism. President of the University of Vermont, 1815–21.

AUSTIN, STEPHEN FULLER (*b.* Wythe Co., Va., 1793; *d.* Tex., 1836), founder of Texas. Son of Moses Austin, he was

successively a storekeeper, the manager of the family lead mines in Missouri, adjutant of the militia, and a member of the Missouri territorial legislature, 1814–20, before the collapse of the family fortunes (*see* Moses Austin). He moved to Arkansas and then to Louisiana, where he studied law and assisted on the staff of the *Louisiana Advertiser*. This training, added to an intimate understanding of frontier life, fitted him to be founder and ruler of a wilderness commonwealth.

Skeptical at first of his father's scheme for settling 300 families in Texas, he soon dedicated himself to the task. He visited Texas in 1821, and in January 1822 planted the first legal settlement of Anglo-Americans there on a fertile, well-watered site bordering the Gulf of Mexico. A question of right arising, Austin secured ratification by the new independent Mexican government of the grant made to his father by the dispossessed Spanish authorities.

Until 1828, Austin acted as executive, lawmaker, chief judge, and military commander within his grant. Even after the organization of a constitutional local government, his influence continued to be great, and he directed the colony in effect until 1832. Under laws passed in 1825 by the Mexican federal government he was able to extend his grant, and was the most successful of all the *empresarios*, as those who contracted to settle colonists were called. During the early years, his labors were enormous. He fixed and administered the land system, pushed back the Indians, mapped the province and charted its rivers and bays, brought in many new immigrants, fostered the commerce of the colony, and provided for the establishment of schools. He was largely responsible for the enactment of liberal laws with respect to colonization, debt, and criminal process; he was also responsible for a law permitting the continued introduction of slaves in the form of indentured servants.

Austin, loyal to Mexico, counseled aloofness from the party struggles which were racking the republic. He felt that Texas would develop best as a state of Mexico, and favored complete independence over any annexation by the United States. In April 1833, however, relations between the settlers and the Mexican government reached a critical stage; although Austin considered it inexpedient, a convention was held and a petition written requesting separation of Texas from the state of Coahuila and the creation of an independent state government. Sent to Mexico City to secure approval of this, Austin was jailed on the charge that he was plotting to annex Texas to the United States. Released without trial in July 1835, he returned to Texas and was soon engaged in the Texas Revolution, serving first as commander of the volunteer army and then as a commissioner to the United States in an effort to secure aid and sympathy. Partially successful in this mission, he and his colleagues came home in June 1836; in September, Sam Houston defeated him in the election for the presidency of the Republic of Texas. He served as secretary of state under Houston until December, when he died.

AUSTIN, WARREN ROBINSON (*b.* Highgate Center, Vt., 1877; *d.* Burlington, Vt., 1962), U.S. senator and ambassador to the United Nations. Admitted to the Vermont bar in 1902, he served as state's attorney from 1904 to 1906. The Second Circuit of the U.S. Court admitted him to practice in 1906, and in 1907 he was named a U.S. commissioner. Was elected mayor of St. Albans, Vt., in 1909 and was admitted to practice before the Supreme Court in 1914. In 1931, he won a seat in the Senate. His fifteen-year senatorial career was characterized by an anti-New Deal stance in domestic affairs and a bipartisan, internationalist position in foreign relations. Was most noticeable as one of a tiny minority of internationalist Republicans, a stance for which, in 1942, his party purged him from the informal assistant minority leader's position he had held since 1933 and that prevented him from receiving the Senate Foreign Relations Committee assignment he wished until 1944. In 1946 he became first U.S.

ambassador to the U.N., where he was a valued American spokesman who provided an important link between the U.S. and the U.N., though he had little effect on policy decisions. The latter phase of his career was characterized by an increasingly anti-Communist stance.

AUSTIN, WILLIAM (*b. Lunenburg, Mass., 1778; d. Charlestown, Mass., 1841*), author. His short story "Peter Rugg, the Missing Man" (1824) is perhaps the most original and imaginative American tale before Hawthorne and Poe.

AVERELL, WILLIAM WOODS (*b. Cameron, N.Y., 1832; d. Bath, N.Y., 1900*), Union soldier. Graduated West Point, 1855. An outstanding cavalryman, he commanded the 2nd Cavalry Division in action at Kelly's Ford, 1863.

AVERY, BENJAMIN PARKE (*b. New York, N.Y., 1828; d. Peking, China, 1875*), journalist, diplomat. Editor of the San Francisco *Bulletin*, 1863–73; appointed minister to China, 1874.

AVERY, ISAAC WHEELER (*b. St. Augustine, Fla., 1837; d. 1897*), Confederate soldier. Active in the politics and journalism of the Reconstruction era in Georgia.

AVERY, JOHN (*b. Conway, Mass., 1837; d. North Bridgeton, Maine, 1887*), linguist. His scholarly interests were concerned chiefly with the languages and literature of India.

AVERY, MILTON CLARK (*b. Altmar, N.Y., 1893; d. New York, N.Y., 1965*), artist. Was primarily a painter of nature. His landscapes and seascapes, in which he verged closest to the frontier of abstraction, exerted a special fascination for such artists as Mark Rothko and Adolph Gottlieb, who painted nonobjectively. His color sense and attitude toward art were closer to that of Henri Matisse than those of any other American artist of his time. Many of his best works date from his later years, and acknowledgement of his achievement has continued to grow in New York City since his death.

AVERY, OSWALD THEODORE (*b. Halifax, Nova Scotia, 1877; d. Nashville, Tenn., 1955*), bacteriologist, immunologist. Studied at Colgate and Columbia University College of Physicians and Surgeons (M.D., 1904). On staff of Rockefeller Institute Hospital, 1913–43; emeritus, 1943–48. Conducted research on bacterial nutrition, the host-parasite relation, and bacterial transformation. The last of these questioned the assumption that the specificity of the hereditary material was carried by proteins, a concept that became a foundation of modern molecular biology and that won Avery consideration for the Nobel Prize.

AVERY, SAMUEL PUTNAM (*b. New York, N.Y., 1822; d. 1904*), art connoisseur, philanthropist. An art dealer whose advice was valued by the principal American collectors of his time.

AVERY, SEWELL LEE (*b. Saginaw, Mich., 1874; d. Chicago, Ill., 1960*), business executive. Studied at the University of Michigan (LL.B., 1894). Affiliated with the U.S. Gypsum Company from 1901; president, 1905–37; chairman, 1937–51. Successfully guided the company through the Great Depression, earning a reputation for business acumen and for conservative labor practices. In 1931, became chief executive of Montgomery Ward and Co. and saved that company from financial collapse through hard business practices. During World War II, gained fame as an opponent of the War Labor Board; in 1943, he resisted a takeover by the federal government under the Smith-Connally Act and was forcibly removed from the company's offices. After World War II, Avery failed to save Ward from financial difficulties; and he was forced to resign in 1955. The company later became a subsidiary of the Mobil Corporation.

AVERY, WILLIAM WAIGSTILL (*b. Burke Co., N.C., 1816; d. Morganton, N.C., 1864*), lawyer, member of the Confederate Provisional Congress.

AWL, WILLIAM MACLAY (*b. Harrisburg, Pa., 1799; d. 1876*), alienist. Promoted a bill founding the first Ohio "State Hospital" for the insane, and appointed its superintendent, 1838; helped establish the Ohio State Medical Society.

AXTELL, SAMUEL BEACH (*b. Franklin Co., Ohio, 1819; d. Morristown, N.J., 1891*), lawyer, politician, jurist. Governor of Utah, 1874, and of New Mexico. 1875–78; chief justice, supreme court of New Mexico, 1882–85.

AYALA, JUAN MANUEL DE (*fl. 1775*), Spanish navigator. Explored and charted San Francisco Bay, 1775.

AYCOCK, CHARLES BRANTLEY (*b. Wayne Co., N.C., 1859; d. 1912*), governor of North Carolina, 1901–05, Democrat. Led successful campaigns for improvement of public educational work.

AYDELOTTE, FRANK (*b. Sullivan, Ind., 1880; d. Princeton, N.J., 1956*), college president, foundation officer. Studied at the University of Indiana, Harvard, and at Oxford (B.Litt., 1908) as a Rhodes Scholar. Professor of English at M.I.T., from 1915 to 1921; from 1914 to 1921 was editor of the *American Oxonian*. In 1917, he became American secretary of the Rhodes Trust. As president of Swarthmore College (1921–40) he transformed it into one of the nation's finest small colleges. Second director of the Institute for Advanced Study in Princeton (1940–47).

AYER, EDWARD EVERETT (*b. Kenosha, Wis., 1841; d. Pasadena, Calif., 1927*), railway lumberman, bibliophile, collector. A founder of the Field Museum of Natural History. Chicago, and its president, 1893–98; a trustee of the Newberry Library, 1892–1911.

AYER, FRANCIS WAYLAND (*b. Lee, Mass., 1848; d. 1923*), advertising agent. Started the advertising firm of N. W. Ayer & son in Philadelphia, Pa., 1869; published the well-known *American Newspaper Annual and Directory*. Ayer introduced the "open-contract" plan, whereby the agent made strict accounting of his use of client's money; he also developed use of trademarks, slogans, pictorial displays, and all the usual devices of present-day advertising. An honorable man, he did much to raise ethical standards of American advertising.

AYER, JAMES COOK (*b. Ledyard, Conn., 1818; d. Winchendon, Mass., 1878*), physician. Proprietor of "Cherry Pectoral" and other patent medicines; promoter of textile and mining enterprises.

AYLLÓN, LUCAS VÁSQUEZ DE (*b. Toledo, Spain, ca. 1475; d. 1526*), Spanish explorer. A judge of the supreme court of Hispaniola (Santo Domingo), he fitted out an expedition in 1520 to search for a fabled land of great wealth supposed to lie to the north and west. In June 1521, his captains reached the mouth of a large river on the coast of what is now the Carolinas; the Indians whom they met called the land "Chicora." Soon after the return of the expedition, Ayllón went to Spain and was granted the new-found region by Charles V. Ayllón, who did not make a voyage there until 1526, but ships sent by him took possession of the land in the name of the Spanish king and cruised for some 250 leagues along the coast. In June or July 1526, Ayllón sailed from Santo Domingo with five or six hundred settlers and landed at what is thought to have been the mouth of the Cape Fear River; he then sailed in an uncertain direction to another river mouth (the Peedee, the Santee, and the James have all been suggested), where he founded a colony called San Miguel de Gualdape. Many of the colonists sickened and died; Ayllón died in October. The survivors abandoned the colony and returned to Santo Domingo.

AYLWIN, JOHN CUSHING (*b. Quebec, Canada, ca. 1780; d. 1813*), naval officer. Sailing master of the USS *Constitution*; killed in action with the *Java*.

AYRES, ANNE (*b. London, England, 1816; d. New York, N.Y., 1896*), original member of the Sisterhood of the Holy Communion. She was the first woman in the United States to become a Protestant nun.

AYRES, BROWN (*b. Memphis, Tenn., 1856; d. 1919*), engineer, educator. President of the University of Tennessee, 1904–19; responsible for its expansion and reorganization.

AYRES, LEONARD PORTER (*b. Niantic, Conn., 1879; d. Cleveland, Ohio, 1946*), economist, statistician. Ph.B., Boston University, 1902. Taught school in Puerto Rico, 1902–07, rising to the general superintendency of the island's schools and organizing the Insular Bureau of Statistics. M.A. (1909) and Ph.D. (1910) Boston University. On the staff of the Russell Sage Foundation, 1908–17; won reputation as an innovator in research administration and the application of statistical methods to educational and social research. Between 1917 and 1920, applied the techniques of social research to national defense, war, and the making of peace, holding a number of important public offices. Chief statistical officer to the American Peace Commission. *Post* 1920, chief economist of the Cleveland Trust Company, in charge of statistics and editor of its *Business Bulletin*, which was widely read; author of a number of books and articles. One of the few economists to foresee the Great Depression, throughout the 1930's he criticized the inhibiting tendencies of the NRA, favored public regulation of banking, and minimized the influence on recovery of abandoning the gold standard.

AYRES, ROMEYN BECK (*b. Montgomery Co., N.Y., 1825; d. Fort Hamilton, N.Y., 1888*), Union soldier. Graduated West Point, 1847. Chief of artillery and infantry commander in the Army of the Potomac.

AYRES, WILLIAM AUGUSTUS (*b. Elizabethtown, Ill., 1867; d. Washington, D.C., 1952*), congressman, federal trade commissioner. Studied at Friends' University. Elected to Congress in 1914, he was often the only Democrat from Kansas during his nine terms. A supporter of Franklin D. Roosevelt, he served on the Federal Trade Commission from 1934 to 1952, achieving little publicity during his tenure.

AZARIAS, BROTHER (*b. near Killenaule, Ireland, 1847; d. 1893*), educator, author. Born Patrick Mullany; entered Brothers of the Christian Schools, 1862. Author of a remarkable *Essay Contributing to a Philosophy of Literature* (1874) and other books.

B

BAADE, WILHELM HEINRICH WALTER (b. Scröttinghausen, Germany, 1893; d. Göttingen, Germany, 1960), astronomer. Studied at the universities of Münster and Göttingen (Ph.D., 1919). From 1919 to 1931, assistant and observer at the Bergedorf observatory of the University of Hamburg. Staff of the Mount Wilson Observatory in California (1931–58). After studying the components of the elliptical and spiral galaxies and globular clusters, Baade was able to classify two discrete populations, Type I and Type II. Using stellar populations as a guide, he predicted the presence of cluster-type variable stars in parts of the Andromeda nebula, but they were too faint to be resolved with the 100-inch reflector; when the 200-inch reflector at Palomar was installed in 1948, Baade resumed his research but soon realized the cluster-type variables were still beyond his reach. This fact could be reconciled with other data only by recalibrating the scale of absolute luminosities of the cluster-type and Cepheid variable stars, a step that virtually doubled the distance of all galaxies. Announced in 1952, the discovery climaxed Baade's studies on the contents of stellar systems.

BABBITT, BENJAMIN TALBOT (b. Westmoreland, N.Y., 1809; d. 1889), inventor, manufacturer of baking-powder and "Babbitt's Best Soap"; held numerous chemical and mechanical patents.

BABBITT, IRVING (b. Dayton, Ohio, 1865; d. Cambridge, Mass., 1933), teacher and author, neo-humanist. After graduating from Harvard in 1889 he returned in 1894 to begin a brilliant teaching career there and at many other universities as guest lecturer. His six major books treat the problem of modern culture in the light of the humanism established in ancient Greece, China, and the Renaissance: Literature and the American College (1908); The New Laokoon (1910), The Masters of Modern French Criticism (1912), Rousseau and Romanticism (1919), Democracy and Leadership (1924) and On Being Creative (1932). The problem as he saw it was to reestablish critical standards which had been undermined by romanticism and naturalism.

BABBITT, ISAAC (b. Taunton, Mass., 1799; d. Somerville, Mass., 1862), Invented a superior journal-box and its alloy lining; a widely used bearing-metal was named for him.

BABCOCK, GEORGE HERMAN (b. near Otsego, N.Y., 1832; d. 1893), engineer, inventor. With his father in 1854, Babcock invented the first polychromatic printing-press and a commercially successful job printing-press. While employed at Hope Iron Works, Providence, R.I., he and Stephen Wilcox invented and brought out the Babcock and Wilcox steam-engine, an early automatic cut-off engine of excellent design. The two inventors formed a partnership and secured a patent in 1867 for a water-tube high-pressure boiler; in 1868 they moved to New York to manufacture the boiler; in 1881 the highly successful firm was incorporated with Babcock as president.

BABCOCK, HOWARD EDWARD (b. near Gilbertsville, N.Y., 1889; d. New York, N.Y., 1950), farm cooperative leader, agricultural educator. B.A., Syracuse University 1911. Taught vocational agriculture in high schools, 1911–13; county agent for Cattaraugus and Tompkins counties (N.Y.), 1913, assistant state leader of county agents, 1914, and state leader, 1916–20. From 1918 to 1920, was secretary of the New York Conference Board of Farm Organizations and was instrumental in having the Board sponsor the founding of the G.L.F. (Cooperative Grange League Federation Exchange), 1920. He was one of the original directors of this statewide cooperative purchasing organization, and when it began to falter in 1922 through inept management, Babcock took over as general manager (1922–32 and 1935–37) and made it the best regional purchasing cooperative in the nation. He also taught marketing at Cornell University and ran his own progressive farm near Ithaca, N.Y. He helped found (and served as director, 1940–43) the G.L.F. School of Cooperative Administration. A trustee of Cornell post 1930, he was instrumental in founding the Cornell schools of Nutrition, Business Administration, and Labor Relations. Federal adviser, notably for help in putting the Farm Credit Administration on a sound operating basis.

BABCOCK, JAMES FRANCIS (b. Boston, Mass., 1844; d. 1897), chemist. Massachusetts state assayer of alcoholic beverages, 1875–85; as Boston inspector of milk he rigidly enforced laws against adulteration.

BABCOCK, JAMES WOOD (b. Chester, S.C., 1856; d. 1922), psychiatrist. Investigated or stimulated the investigation of many important problems in psychiatry and the care of the insane; published (1908) the first comprehensive American account of pellagra.

BABCOCK, JOSEPH WEEKS (b. Swanton, Vt., 1850; d. Washington, D.C., 1909). Representative in Congress from Wisconsin, 1892–1906; chairman of Republican Congressional Campaign Committee, 1894–1904.

BABCOCK, MALTBIE DAVENPORT (b. Syracuse, N.Y., 1858; d. Naples, Italy, 1901), Presbyterian clergyman, author. Pastor, Brown Memorial Church, Baltimore, 1887–99, and Brick Presbyterian Church, New York City, 1899–1901.

BABCOCK, ORVILLE E. (b. Franklin, Vt., 1835; d. Mosquito Inlet, Fla., 1884), engineer, soldier. Graduated West Point, 1861. Private secretary to President Grant who defended him when accused of complicity in the "Whisky Ring" frauds, 1869–75.

BABCOCK, STEPHEN MOULTON (b. Bridgewater, N.Y., 1843; d. Madison, Wis., 1931), agricultural chemist. Made many valuable contributions to agriculture; best known for invention of the milk-fat test which bears his name.

BABCOCK, WASHINGTON IRVING (b. Stonington, Conn., 1858; d. New York, N.Y., 1917), naval architect. Introduced the mould system of ship construction and designed the first large ships specially built for traffic on the Great Lakes.

BABSON, ROGER WARD (*b. Gloucester, Mass., 1875; d. Lake Wales, Fla., 1967*), business forecaster, statistician, and author. In 1904 established the Business Statistical Organization, Inc. (later Babson Statistical Organization, Inc.) and began to issue *Composite Circular*, which provided information on bond offerings. In 1907 launched his *Babsonchart*, which advised clients on when to buy and sell stocks, bonds, and commodities, and the *Supervised List*, which suggested what to buy and sell. In 1919 established the Babson Institute (later Babson College), then the only undergraduate business school in the U.S. Also established Webber College in 1927 to train women for business. Published thirty-nine books by 1935, when his autobiography came out.

BACCALONI, SALVATORE (*b. Rome, Italy, 1900; d. New York, N.Y., 1969*), opera singer. In the 1930's and 1940's achieved international renown for his sharply defined characterizations and comedic talent as well as for his vocalism. First appeared with the Metropolitan Opera in 1940, and for more than two decades was the principal basso buffo; was heard 297 times in New York City and 146 times on tour, in fifteen roles. Also appeared in non-singing character roles in films.

BACHE, ALEXANDER DALLAS (*b. Philadelphia, Pa., 1806; d. 1867*), physicist. Great-grandson of Benjamin Franklin. Professor of natural philosophy and chemistry, University of Pennsylvania, 1828–1836. In 1836 he was appointed first president of Girard College; because of delay in opening Girard he spent three years in reorganizing the Philadelphia public schools and then resumed his professorship. On Dec. 12, 1843, he was made superintendent of the U.S. Coast Survey, a position he held until his death. Throughout his career he kept up his interest in scientific research, especially in terrestrial magnetism; he founded the first magnetic observatory in America and made magnetic work an important part of the regular operations of the Coast Survey. He was a regent of the Smithsonian Institution and the first president of the National Academy of Sciences.

BACHE, BENJAMIN FRANKLIN (*b. Philadelphia, Pa., 1769; d. Philadelphia, 1798*), journalist. Grandson of Benjamin Franklin; founder of the Philadelphia *General Advertiser*, better known as the *Aurora*, a journal supporting the Democratic-Republican party. The paper contained extended accounts of European and domestic affairs but was notorious for virulent abuse of public figures; Washington was accused of overdrawing his salary, and forged letters attributed to him were reprinted by the *Aurora* in 1796. Bache made public the text of the secret Jay treaty in 1795; opened his columns to the French minister Adet in 1796 and published a particularly abusive "valedictory" at Washington's retirement in 1797. In June 1998, Bache was arrested under the Sedition Act for libeling President Adams.

BACHE, FRANKLIN (*b. Philadelphia, Pa., 1792; d. 1864*), teacher, chemist, physician. Son of Benjamin Franklin Bache; made important early contributions to development of chemical theory.

BACHE, JULES SIMON (*b. New York, N.Y., 1861; d. Palm Beach, Fla., 1944*), financier, art collector. Began business in father's mirror and glass firm; became cashier of an uncle's brokerage firm, 1880, and was admitted to partnership, 1886. In 1892, he became head of the firm, thereafter known as J. S. Bache and Company, which prospered as financial agent for a number of "trusts" and other enterprises. Bache also expanded his brokerage business, setting up profitable branch offices linked by an extensive wire system. Guided by Joseph Duveen, Bache acquired between 1919 and 1929 a notable collection of paintings, sculpture, and other art objects, now at the Metropolitan Museum of Art, New York.

BACHE, RICHARD (*b. Settle, England, 1737; d. 1811*), merchant. Immigrated to New York City in 1765. Successful trader and issuer of private insurance policies; succeeded his father-in-law, Benjamin Franklin, as postmaster general.

BACHE, THEOPHYLACT (*b. Settle, England, 1734/35; d. New York, N.Y., 1807*), merchant, Loyalist. Brother and partner of Richard Bache; immigrated to New York City in 1751; president of New York Chamber of Commerce, 1773.

BACHELDER, JOHN (*b. Weare, N.H., 1817; d. Houghton, Mich., 1906*), inventor, manufacturer. Improved the Howe sewing machine by developing the continuous feed, the vertical needle, and the horizontal table.

BACHELLER, IRVING (*b. Pierrepont, N.Y., 1859; d. White Plains, N.Y., 1950*), novelist. B.S., St. Lawrence University, 1882. After a short time on staff of a Brooklyn, N.Y., newspaper, he was cofounder in 1884 of the New York Press Syndicate (the first such enterprise in metropolitan journalism) which, within a decade, was distributing fiction and feature stories to the leading newspapers in the nation. The syndicate serialized Crane's *The Red Badge of Courage* in 1893, and was responsible for introducing to its subscribers the work of Conan Doyle, Kipling, Hope, and other leading contemporary writers. In 1896, Bacheller sold the Syndicate and resumed efforts at making a writing career of his own, which up to then had not been very successful. The result was a romantic novel about pioneers in the St. Lawrence valley, *Eben Holden* (1900), a critical success and an immediate best-seller (about 750,000 copies). His next novel, *D'ri and I* (1901), was also a success, blending patriotism, humor, Yankee character, and romance as did *Eben Holden*. Bacheller continued to write for the next forty years, publishing more than thirty novels and numerous short stories, essays, and poems.

BACHER, OTTO HENRY (*b. Cleveland, Ohio, 1856; d. Bronxville, N.Y., 1909*), etcher. Worked with Duveneck and Whistler in Venice; a leading pen-and-ink illustrator in the 1890's.

BACHMAN, JOHN (*b. Rhinebeck, N.Y., 1790; d. Columbia, S.C., 1874*), naturalist, Lutheran clergyman. Best known for collaboration with J. J. Audubon upon *The Viviparous Quadrupeds of North America*.

BACHMANN, WERNER EMMANUEL (*b. Detroit, Mich., 1901; d. Ann Arbor, Mich., 1951*), organic chemist. Ph.D., University of Michigan, 1926. Bachmann's earliest work, in collaboration with Moses Gomberg of Michigan, concerned the coupling of benzene rings to establish a diphenyl linkage—the Gomberg-Bachmann reaction (1924). His most outstanding contribution was his work with steroid hormones; in 1939, he synthesized equilenin, the first synthesis of a sex hormone. His work later led to the development of methods of synthesis of the related estrogenic hormones, estrone and androsterone. During World War II, developed new procedures for the manufacture of the high explosive RDX.

BACHRACH, LOUIS FABIAN (*b. Baltimore, Md., 1881; d. Boston, Mass., 1963*), portrait photographer, essayist, and connoisseur. After apprenticing with his father, the pioneering photographer David Bachrach, Jr., he worked with his brother Walter and, later, his two sons, Bradford Keyser and Louis Fabian, Jr., to run a successful chain of studios, at one point prior to the Depression owning some forty-eight studios and owning nine upon his retirement in 1955. Was noted for his devotion to high standards of portraiture and his persistent application of sound business principles to the operation of portrait studios. Contributed to magazines and newspapers on a variety of subjects and was a connoisseur and collector of art and historic objects.

BACKUS, AZEL (*b. Norwich, Conn., 1765; d. Clinton, N.Y., 1816*), Congregational clergyman; first president of Hamilton College, 1812–16.

BACKUS, ISAAC (*b. Norwich, Conn., 1724; d. Middleborough, Mass., 1806*), Separatist and Baptist minister, historian. A Norwich Separatist from Congregationalism in 1746, he served as a New Light minister, 1748–56; converted to Baptist principles, he organized a Baptist church at Middleborough, Mass., in 1756 and served it as pastor until his death. A tireless itinerant preacher, his influence was wide and always on the side of independence and democratic control of each local church; he was a champion of religion against civil control—the greatest since Roger Williams. His *History of New England, with Particular Reference to the Denomination of Christians Called Baptists* (1777–96) is a primary source for students of colonial religious problems.

BACKUS, TRUMAN JAY (*b. Milan, N.Y., 1842; d. Brooklyn, N.Y., 1908*), educator. President, Packer Collegiate Institute, Brooklyn, 1883–1908.

BACON, ALICE MABEL (*b. New Haven, Conn., 1858; d. 1918*), writer, teacher, lecturer. Taught at Hampton Institute, 1883–88, 1889–99, and at schools in Japan.

BACON, AUGUSTUS OCTAVIUS (*b. Bryan Co., Ga., 1839; d. Washington, D.C., 1914*), lawyer. U.S. senator, Democrat, from Georgia, 1894–1914; introduced resolution opposing acquisition of the Philippines.

BACON, BENJAMIN WISNER (*b. Litchfield, Conn., 1860; d. 1932*), clergyman, teacher, writer. Known for his free and suggestive application of higher criticism to the origin and nature of the four Gospels.

BACON, DAVID (*b. Woodstock, Conn., 1771; d. Hartford, Conn., 1817*), Congregational clergyman. Missionary to Indians in Lake Erie and Mackinac Islands region; founded Tallmadge, Ohio, 1807.

BACON, DELIA SALTER (*b. Tallmadge, Ohio, 1811; d. 1859*), author. In *Philosophy of the Plays of Shakspere Unfolded* (1857), she maintained that the plays were really the work of Raleigh, Spenser, and Sir Francis Bacon.

BACON, EDWARD PAYSON (*b. Reading, N.Y., 1834; d. Daytona, Fla., 1916*). Organized E. P. Bacon & Co., a leading grain trading firm in Chicago and Milwaukee, and was influential in formulating the Interstate Commerce Law of 1906.

BACON, EDWIN MUNROE (*b. Providence, R.I., 1844; d. Cambridge, Mass., 1916*), journalist. Editor, *Boston Globe*, 1873–78; *Daily Advertiser*, 1883–86; *Boston Post*, 1886–91. Author of books descriptive of Boston and New England.

BACON, FRANK (*b. Marysville, Calif., 1864; d. Chicago, Ill., 1922*), actor, playwright. With Winchell Smith, wrote the long-run play *Lightnin'* (1918).

BACON, HENRY (*b. Watseka, Ill., 1866; d. 1924*), architect. Trained in office of McKim, Mead and White, he worked in partnership (1887 to 1902) with James Brite; thereafter on his own. A devoted adherent of the theory of Greek architecture, he became interested in monumental work and the design of pedestals and architectural settings for statues and worked jointly on many occasions with Saint-Gaudens and D. C. French. In 1923 he was awarded the gold medal of the American Institute of Architects for his greatest achievement, the Lincoln Memorial in Washington, D.C.

BACON, JOHN (*b. Canterbury, Conn., 1738; d. Stockbridge, Mass., 1820*), Congregational clergyman, legislator. A leading Jeffersonian Democrat of western Massachusetts.

BACON, LEONARD (*b. Detroit, Mich., 1802; d. New Haven, Conn., 1881*), Congregational clergyman. Son of Rev. David Bacon. Graduated Yale, 1820, and Andover Theological Seminary; minister to the First Church of New Haven, Conn., 1825–66; acting professor of revealed theology, 1866–71, and lecturer on church polity and American church history, 1871–81, Yale Divinity School. As a speaker and as editor of the *Christian Spectator* and the *New Englander*, he influenced Congregationalism by arousing pride in its traditions and its polity; he was also author of *The Genesis of the New England Churches* (1874), a history of Congregationalism. An early leader in the antislavery cause, he had no sympathy with extreme abolitionists; he organized a society for the improvement of New Haven Negroes and was a founder and chief editor of the free-soil paper the *Independent*.

BACON, LEONARD (*b. Solvay, N.Y., 1887; d. Peace Dale, R.I., 1954*), poet and critic. Graduated Yale, 1909. After several editions and translations of other works including *The Cid* (1919), in 1923, he published his first major work, *Ulug Beg*, a mock epic; in 1939, he wrote his most well-received piece, *The Furioso*, a mock epic on Gabriele D'Annunzio. He received the Pulitzer Prize in 1940 for his book *Sunderland, Capture, and Other Poems*.

BACON, LEONARD WOOLSEY (*b. New Haven, Conn., 1830; d. 1907*), Congregational clergyman. Son of Reverend Leonard Bacon. Author of a number of forceful polemical works.

BACON, NATHANIEL (*b. Suffolk, England, 1647; d. Gloucester Co., Va., 1676*), colonial leader. An emigrant to Virginia, with powerful relatives in England, he settled at Curl's Neck on James River. Leader of an unauthorized, popular expedition against the Indians in 1676, he dispersed the enemy and then forced Governor Berkeley to a call a new Assembly at which he meant to introduce changes in the law of the colony. After arrest by Berkeley, pardon, and release, he led his followers to Jamestown and extorted from the governor a formal commission to march against the Indians. Thereafter, on news that the governor had proclaimed him a rebel, he turned his force against Jamestown, burnt it, and compelled all citizens within his power to swear fealty to himself. Just as he was about to introduce an alleged program of reforms he died, and the rebellion collapsed.

BACON, ROBERT (*b. Jamaica Plain, Mass., 1860; d. 1919*), banker, diplomat, soldier. Partner in J. P. Morgan & Co.; assistant secretary of state, 1905–09; an advocate of American entry into World War I, in which he served with distinction.

BACON, THOMAS (*b. Isle of Man, England, ca. 1700; d. Frederick, Md., 1768*), clergyman of the Church of England in Maryland, 1744/5–68; editor, *Laws of Maryland at Large* (1765), an important work.

BADÈ, WILLIAM FREDERIC (*b. Carver, Minn., 1871; d. Berkeley, Calif., 1936*), archeologist. Excavated Tell en-Nasbeh, Palestine; professor of Semitic languages and Old Testament literature, Pacific School of Religion, 1902–36.

BADEAU, ADAM (*b. New York, N.Y., 1831; d. Ridgewood, N.J., 1895*), author, soldier, diplomat. Closely associated in military and civilian life with the subject, he wrote *Military*

History of Ulysses S. Grant (1868, 1881) and helped Grant write his *Memoirs.*

BADGER, CHARLES JOHNSTON (*b. Rockville, Md., 1853; d. Blue Ridge Summit, Md., 1932*), naval officer. Head of the General Board of the Navy, 1917–21.

BADGER, GEORGE EDMUND (*b. New Bern, N.C., 1795; d. 1866*), jurist, secretary of the navy. U.S. senator, Whig, from North Carolina, 1846–55; as a lawyer he ranked before the U.S. Supreme Court with Webster, Crittenden, Berrien, and Cushing.

BADGER, JOSEPH (*b. Charlestown, Mass., 1708; d. Boston, Mass., 1765*), artist. The principal portrait painter in Boston from about 1748 to 1760.

BADGER, JOSEPH (*b. Wilbraham, Mass., 1757; d. Perrysburg, Ohio, 1846*), Congregational clergyman. Founded first church in the Western Reserve at Austinburg, Ohio; served as missionary in Ohio, 1800–35.

BADGER, OSCAR CHARLES (*b. Mansfield, Conn., 1823; d. 1899*), naval officer. An authority on ordnance, he served with distinction along the Atlantic Coast during the Civil War.

BADIN, STEPHEN THEODORE (*b. Orléans, France, 1768; d. Cincinnati, Ohio, 1853*), missionary. Fled from the revolutionary fury in France to Baltimore, Md., 1792, where he continued studies for the priesthood; was ordained by Bishop Carroll in 1793, the first Roman Catholic priest ordained in the United States. Assigned to Kentucky, he rode horseback all along the frontier, visiting isolated communities and setting up log chapels; by 1800 he was vicar general for Kentucky. Retiring to France in 1819, he returned to America in 1828. He served briefly as pastor of a parish at Monroe, Mich., and then as a missionary to the Potawatomi Indians in western Michigan. About 1832 he acquired by either grant or purchase the land on which the University of Notre Dame is presently located.

BAEKLAND, LEO HENDRIK (*b. St. Martens-Latem, near Ghent, Belgium, 1863; d. Beacon, N.Y., 1944*), industrial chemist, inventor of Velox paper for photographic prints and of Bakelite. Apprenticed as a boy to a shoemaker, he managed by scholarships and through the interested aid of others to attend the University of Ghent, earning a doctorate of science, *maxima cum laude,* in 1884. After a few years in academic life, he questioned his choice of a profession and looked about to find some means of combining academic skills and contacts with industrial research. Meanwhile, he had obtained a Belgian patent on a photographic dry plate which he had devised (1887); it carried its own developer in an inactive form. A company founded to produce and market the plate did not succeed; moreover, the time he spent on the company's problems affected his performance as a teacher. His quest for work in industry brought him ultimately to New York City, where in 1891 he became chemist for E. and H. T. Anthony, producers of dry plates and print papers for the photographic trade. Two years later, he set up as a private consultant and concentrated his efforts on the invention of a photographic print paper that could be developed by artificial light whose intensity, unlike sunlight, could be controlled. The result was a paper utilizing silver chloride, to which he gave the trade name "Velox." The production and marketing firm which he formed with a partner to sell Velox was successful; in 1899 he sold it to the Eastman Kodak Company.

Losing his interest in business, he turned his attention to laboratory work on problems that interested him, among them the electrolysis of common salt and the production of synthetic resins. Employed as consultant by Elon H. Hooker in the development of C. P. Townsend's cell for the production of sodium hydroxide and chlorine by electrolysis of brine, Baekland suggested improve-

ments which were basic to the success of the enterprise. After a careful study of European work on phenolic resins, he began experiments in his own laboratory on the reaction of phenol and formaldehyde; by 1907, he was able to control the reaction so as to produce a resin which (unlike celluloid and others) when heated became permanently solid. The product, which was named "Bakelite," was an electrical insulator, inert to heat, and resistant to most chemicals; it could also be fabricated by molding into intricate shapes. Bakelite was an almost instant success; when the inventor made his first public report on the product (1909), he had already explored its applicability in forty industries. In 1910, he organized the General Bakelite Company for its production and sale; after absorbing several competitors, it became the Bakelite Corporation in 1924.

BAER, GEORGE FREDERICK (*b. near Lavansville, Pa., 1842; d. 1914*), lawyer. After success in bringing several damage suits against the Philadelphia & Reading Railway Co., he was employed by that company as counsel, 1870. A director of the Reading, he opposed company plans to invade the railway territory of his friend J. P. Morgan and resigned; Morgan gained control of the Reading, reorganized it, and made Baer president. In 1902, year of the great anthracite coal strike, he became the leader of forces resisting the strike and gained nation-wide fame by publication of a letter in which he implied that God had given the propertied interests control over laboring men.

BAER, WILLIAM STEVENSON (*b. Baltimore, Md., 1872; d. Baltimore, 1931*), orthopedic surgeon. Rediscoverer of cure for osteomyelitis; operated to restore motion in fused joints by introduction of animal membranes.

BAERMANN, CARL (*b. Munich, Germany, 1839; d. Newton, Mass., 1913*), teacher of music, pianist. Student of Liszt; settled in Boston, Mass., 1881, where he taught a number of distinguished students.

BAETJER, FREDERICK HENRY (*b. Baltimore, Md., 1874; d. Catonsville, Md., 1933*), physician, pioneer roentgenologist. Advanced the use of X rays by great personal sacrifice.

BAGBY, ARTHUR PENDLETON (*b. Louisa Co., Va., 1794; d. Mobile, Ala., 1858*). Removed to Alabama, 1818. Governor of Alabama, Democrat, 1837–41; U.S. senator, 1841–48; opposed Tyler's nomination for presidency, rewarded with U.S. ministry to Russia, 1848–49.

BAGBY, GEORGE WILLIAM (*b. Buckingham Co., Va., 1828; d. Richmond, Va., 1883*), editor, popular lecturer, and humorist; his representative works to be found in *The Old Virginia Gentleman, etc.* (1910).

BAGLEY, WILLIAM CHANDLER (*b. Detroit, Mich., 1874; d. New York, N.Y., 1946*), educator. Graduated Michigan Agricultural College, 1895. After teaching two years in a lumbering town in Michigan's Upper Peninsula, he went to study at University of Wisconsin, receiving the M.S. in 1898. Ph.D. in psychology and education, Cornell, 1900. Principal of an elementary school in St. Louis, Mo., for a year, and then professor of psychology and pedagogy at Montana State Normal College, 1902–06, serving also as superintendent of the public schools of the town of Dillon. Taught at State Normal School, Oswego, N.Y., 1906–08. Professor of education at University of Illinois, 1908, becoming director of the School of Education in 1909. Leaving Illinois, 1917, he held a professorship at Teachers College, Columbia University, until retirement in 1939.

Bagley was concerned to define a general theory of education and to professionalize teacher training. He was at first confident that psychological and biological research would discover and verify fundamental principles on which a science of education could be built. This view was reflected in his *The Educative Process* (1905) and *Classroom Management* (1907). By 1911, when he published *Educational Values*, he had begun to lose faith in psychology; and by 1918, he had concluded that teaching was not an applied science, but an art. Much of Bagley's career was devoted to improving the professional preparation of public school teachers; he was author, or coauthor, of a number of books aimed at upgrading the profession, such as *Craftsmanship in Teaching* (1911). He also collaborated on several grade school textbooks, among them A *History of the American People*, written with Charles A. Beard. When he retired from teaching, he helped organize the Society for the Advancement of Education, and was editor until his death of *School and Society*, its journal.

Fundamental to Bagley's thought was his emphasis on the collective social good as opposed to the satisfaction of individual desires, a concern which contributed to his critical attitude toward progressive education. Deplored proneness of progressives to overvalue every scientific and philosophical innovation and to substitute fads and panaceas for sound, continuing practices.

BAILEY, ANN (*b. Liverpool, England, 1742; d. Gallia Co., Ohio, 1825*), pioneer. Came to America, 1761. Served as a scout and messenger on the Virginia border, 1774–92.

BAILEY, ANNA WARNER (*b. Groton, Conn., 1758; d. 1851*), heroine at battle of Groton Heights, 1781; contributed her flannel petticoat for cartridge wadding, Groton, Conn., 1813.

BAILEY, EBENEZER (*b. 1795; d. Lynn, Mass., 1839*), educator. Principal of first high school for girls in Massachusetts, 1826.

BAILEY, FLORENCE AUGUSTA MERRIAM (*b. Locust Grove, near Port Leyden, N.Y., 1863; d. Washington, D.C., 1948*), ornithologist, writer, teacher. Sister of Clinton H. Merriam. Attended Smith College as a special student, 1882–86; helped found one of the first chapters of the Audubon Society. Her early essays on bird life were collected and augmented in *Birds Through an Opera Glass* (1889). Stricken with tuberculosis, she went West in 1893. Recovered her health and extended the range of her studies of wild nature. In 1899, she married Vernon Bailey of the U.S. Biological Survey; she often shared in his field trips and they assisted each other in authorship. Among Mrs. Bailey's many books, two were major achievements: *Handbook of Birds of the Western United States* (1902) and *Birds of New Mexico* (1928).

BAILEY, FRANCIS (*b. Lancaster Co., Pa., ca. 1735; d. 1815*), printer, journalist. Published *Lancaster Almanac*; edited *The Freeman's Journal, post* 1781. Official printer for Congress and the state of Pennsylvania.

BAILEY, FRANK HARVEY (*b. Cranesville, Pa., 1851; d. Arizona, 1921*), engineer, naval officer, Designed the *Columbia* and *Minneapolis*, two of the fastest large vessels of their day, 1890–1900.

BAILEY, GAMALIEL (*b. Mount Holly, N.J., 1807; d. 1859*), physician, journalist, antislavery agitator. In 1837 he became sole editor and proprietor of the *Cincinnati Philanthropist*, the first antislavery newspaper in the West, which he issued in spite of mob opposition; he also founded a daily, the *Herald*. In 1847 he moved to Washington, D.C., as editor in chief of the *National Era*, sponsored by the American and Foreign Anti-Slavery Society. For the next 12 years he exerted a wide moral and political influence; although the *Era* had many distinguished contributors (John G. Whittier, Theodore Parker, and Harriet Beecher Stowe, for example), Bailey's wise and fair direction was responsible for its success.

BAILEY, (IRENE) TEMPLE (*b. Petersburg, Va., 1880[?]; d. Washington, D.C., 1953*), novelist and short story writer. A popular writer who achieved little critical acclaim but great commercial success, Bailey published dozens of short stories in magazines; her many novels, some of which were serialized by leading literary magazines, were widely read. *The Tin Soldier* (1919), *The Dim Lantern* (1923), and *The Blue Cloak* (1941) became best sellers.

BAILEY, JACOB (*b. Rowley, Mass., 1731; d. Annapolis, Nova Scotia, 1818*), pioneer missionary of the Church of England in Maine, 1760–79; Loyalist.

BAILEY, JACOB WHITMAN (*b. Ward [now Auburn], Mass., 1811; d. 1857*), botanist, chemist, geologist. Graduated West Point, 1832, where he taught chemistry, mineralogy and geology, 1834–57. Distinguished for research among minor algae, and a pioneer American microscopist.

BAILEY, JAMES ANTHONY (*b. Detroit, Mich., 1847; d. Mount Vernon, N.Y., 1906*), showman. A founder of Cooper & Bailey circus, 1872; united with P. T. Barnum, 1881, as Barnum & Bailey show.

BAILEY, JAMES MONTGOMERY (*b. Albany, N.Y., 1841; d. Danbury, Conn., 1894*), journalist, the "Danbury News Man."

BAILEY, JOSEPH (*b. Pennsville, Ohio, 1825; d. near Nevada, Mo., 1867*), Union soldier, engineer. Rendered outstanding service in the Red River campaign, 1864, by devising means for the fleet to return downstream in low water.

BAILEY, JOSEPH WELDON (*b. Crystal Springs, Miss., 1863; d. Sherman, Tex., 1929*), lawyer. U.S. senator from Texas, Democrat, 1901–13. Helped pass Hepburn Rate Bill, 1906; center of so-called "Bailey Controversy," 1907.

BAILEY, JOSIAH WILLIAM (*b. Warrenton, N.C., 1873; d. Raleigh, N.C., 1946*), lawyer, journalist, politician. B.A., Wake Forest College, 1893. Assumed editorship of father's newspaper, the *Biblical Recorder*, 1893. His advocacy of improvement of North Carolina public schools drew him into politics. His support of Furnifold Simmons in 1898 was rewarded when Simmons saw to it that Bailey's educational proposals were enacted by the legislature in 1899. Resigned as editor of the *Recorder* in 1907, and began law practice in Raleigh and increased his political activity. Although associated with the Simmons Democratic party machine, he was reputed a progressive because he urged reform in state elections, helped establish a commission form of government for Raleigh, and worked to improve the law limiting child labor. Appointed collector of internal revenue for the eastern district of North Carolina (*post* 1919 for the entire state) by President Wilson, he served with marked efficiency, 1913–21. In 1924, he failed in an independent bid for the gubernatorial nomination. When Simmons bolted the Democratic party and backed Herbert Hoover in the 1928 campaign for the presidency, Bailey supported Alfred E. Smith; two years later, he ran against Simmons in the primary on that issue, and won nomination and election to the U.S. Senate, where he remained until his death. An early supporter of the New Deal, he came to fear its trend to centralization and became a spokesman for a bipartisan group of senators who opposed administration policies. He supported Franklin D. Roosevelt's bids for reelection. He also supported the administration's foreign policy and wartime programs, and as chairman of the Senate Commerce Committee played an important part in determining national maritime policy and in procuring merchant vessels for defense purposes. Championed the establishment of the United Nations. A rather solemn, dignified man of strict principles, he was dubbed "Holy Joe" by the press.

BAILEY, LIBERTY HYDE (*b. Van Buren County, Mich., 1858; d. Ithaca, N.Y., 1954*), horticulturist, botanist, and educator. M.S., Michigan Agricultural College (now Michigan State) in 1885. Known mainly as a pioneer in the field of scientific agriculture, Bailey worked ceaselessly to develop horticulture into a recognized science. Instrumental in establishing the State College of Agriculture at Cornell in 1904, serving as its dean until 1913. In 1908, President Theodore Roosevelt appointed him chairman of the Commission on Country Life; in 1935, the Bailey Hortorium was established at Cornell, and Bailey served as its unpaid director until 1951.

BAILEY, LYDIA R. (*b. 1779; d. Philadelphia, Pa., 1869*), printer. Worked successfully in Philadelphia, 1808–61.

BAILEY, MILDRED (*b. Tekoa, Wash., 1907; d. Poughkeepsie, N.Y., 1951*), jazz singer. Considered one of the finest jazz stylists of her time, Bailey began with Paul Whiteman during the 1930's, and along with her husband, Red Norvo, became known as "Mr. and Mrs. Swing" from a radio program they shared. Her most famous recording was "Rockin' Chair."

BAILEY, RUFUS WILLIAM (*b. North Yarmouth, Maine, 1793; d. Tex., 1863*), Congregational clergyman. After a long career of teaching and preaching in South Carolina, North Carolina, and Virginia, served as president of Austin College, Texas, 1858–63.

BAILEY, SOLON IRVING (*b. Lisbon, N.H., 1854; d. 1931*), astronomer. Pioneer in the photography and discovery of distant galaxies; first detected small variations in stars closely paced in the globular clusters.

BAILEY, THEODORUS (*b. Chateaugay, N.Y., 1805; d. Washington, D.C., 1877*), naval officer. Second in command under Farragut in the attack on New Orleans, 1862; retired 1866 as rear admiral.

BAILLY, JOSEPH ALEXIS (*b. Paris, France, 1825; d. Philadelphia, Pa., 1883*), sculptor. Came to America, *post* 1848. Attained considerable reputation in Philadelphia.

BAIN, GEORGE LUKE SCOBIE (*b. Stirling, Scotland, 1836; d. 1891*), merchant-miller. Pioneered in developing the direct exportation of flour from St. Louis, Mo., to foreign countries.

BAINBRIDGE, WILLIAM (*b. Princeton, N.J., 1774; d. Philadelphia, Pa., 1833*), naval officer. Commanded merchant vessels in the European trade, 1793–98. When French aggressions and the depredations of the Barbary States awoke the American navy to new life, he received command of the 14-gun *Retaliation* with rank of lieutenant commandant. Cruising in the West Indies, fall of 1798, he was captured by two French frigates but saved his consorts, the *Montezuma* and *Norfolk*, by convincing the French commander of their superior firepower; after imprisonment in Guadeloupe, he returned to America, was promoted to master commandant and given command of the *Norfolk*. Bainbridge's account of the indignities suffered by Americans at Guadeloupe was partly responsible for the prompt passing by Congress of the Retaliation Act. After numerous successes in the West Indies he was ordered to cruise off Havana, and rendered excellent service in convoying and blockading enemy privateers; on May 2, 1800, he was promoted to captain, the highest naval rank at that time. In the same month he was given command of the 24-gun *George Washington* and ordered to bear America's tribute to the powerful Dey of Algiers; he performed this humiliating task in a diplomatic manner. Given command of the frigate *Philadelphia*, with orders to join Preble's squadron operating against the Barbary States, he

proceeded to Tripoli, inadvertently grounded his ship in the harbor, and was imprisoned with his crew, October 1803. Released from imprisonment, 1805, he returned to America. For the next seven years he saw some merchant service and held several naval commands; in February 1812, he joined Commodore Charles Stewart in protesting the government's proposal to lay up all naval vessels lest they be captured by the powerful British fleet. Succeeding Isaac Hull in command of the *Constitution*, he sailed for the South Atlantic where he attacked and captured a British frigate; he returned to Boston, February 1813. During the rest of the war, he oversaw construction of the 74-gun *Independence*, thereafter taking her to the Mediterranean where he succeeded Commodore Decatur in command. His last service afloat was aboard the *Columbus* in 1820.

BAIRD, ABSALOM (*b. Washington, Pa., 1824; d. near Relay, Md., 1905*), Union soldier. Graduated West Point, 1849. Outstanding division commander at Chickamauga; accompanied Sherman on march through Georgia; brevetted major general, 1864.

BAIRD, CHARLES WASHINGTON (*b. Princeton, N.J., 1828; d. Rye, N.Y., 1887*), Presbyterian clergyman, historian. Author of *The Chronicle of a Border Town: A History of Rye, 1660–1870* (1871) and *The History of the Huguenot Emigration to America* (1885).

BAIRD, HENRY CAREY (*b. Bridesburg, Pa., 1825; d. Wayne, Pa., 1912*), publisher, economic writer. Established Henry Carey Baird & Co. in 1849, the first publishing company in America to specialize in books on technical and industrial subjects. He is best known as an expositor and popularizer of the teachings of the "Pennsylvania School" of "national economists" of which his uncle Henry Carey and grandfather Mathew Carey were founders.

BAIRD, HENRY MARTYN (*b. Philadelphia, Pa., 1832; d. Yonkers, N.Y., 1906*), Presbyterian clergyman, historian. Professor of Greek, New York University, 1860–1902; like his brother Charles W. Baird, wrote extensively on the history of the Huguenots.

BAIRD, MATTHEW (*b. near Londonderry, Ireland, 1817; d. 1877*), locomotive builder. Came to America, 1821. Purchased interest in Baldwin's locomotive works at Philadelphia, Pa., 1854; became sole proprietor in 1866.

BAIRD, ROBERT (*b. near Pittsburgh, Pa., 1798; d. 1863*), Presbyterian clergyman. Father of Charles W. and Henry M. Baird. Influenced passage of legislation establishing public school system in New Jersey.

BAIRD, SAMUEL JOHN (*b. Newark, Ohio, 1817; d. West Clifton Forge, Va., 1893*), Presbyterian clergyman, author. Edited *Collection of the Arts, Deliverances and Testimonies . . . of the Presbyterian Church . . .* (1854), a codification of the decisions of the General Assembly.

BAIRD, SPENCER FULLERTON (*b. Reading, Pa., 1823; d. Woods Hole, Mass., 1887*), zoologist. Graduated Dickinson College, 1840; appointed professor of natural history there, 1846. At Dickinson he inaugurated the method of field study of botany and zoology so successfully used by Agassiz and expanded the fish and reptile collections of the college museum; became also professor of chemistry, 1848. Two years later he went to the Smithsonian Institution, Washington, as assistant secretary to the director, Joseph Henry; upon Henry's death, 1878, he was elected to the secretaryship. He developed a huge network of agencies, both private and governmental, to gather material for the Smithsonian collections; in 1879 Congress authorized a building to house these collections. For nearly twenty years Baird was a prolific writer on ornithology and zoology, publishing *Catalogue of North American Birds* (1858); *Review of American Birds* (1864–66); *A History of North American Birds* (1874), with T. M. Brewer and R. Ridgway; *North American Reptiles* (1853) with C. Girard; and *Catalogue of North American Mammals* (1857). It was as an accurate observer and reporter, not as a theorist, that he influenced ornithology and founded the "Baird School," so ably represented by E. Coues, J. A. Allen, R. Ridgway, J. Cassin, and T. M. Brewer. The third stage in Baird's career dates from the foundation of the U.S. Commission of Fish and Fisheries, 1871, when President Grant requested him to head the new organization. The work of the commission comprised all forms of ichthyological knowledge and fish protection. Thorough studies of the life histories of American fish were instituted; the deep waters of the Atlantic and Pacific were explored; numerous fish hatcheries increased the abundance of local fishes and introduced foreign species. The principal headquarters for investigation were at Woods Hole, Mass., now one of the world's great marine laboratories.

BAKER, BENJAMIN A. (*b. New York, N.Y., 1818; d. New York, 1890*), playwright, actor, manager. Introduced local conditions as background of melodrama; in *A Glance at New York in 1848* and *New York As It Is* (1848) portrayed "Mose, the Bowery Boy."

BAKER, BENJAMIN FRANKLIN (*b. Wenham, Mass., 1811; d. 1889*), musician, teacher, composer. Established Boston Music School, 1857–68; published songs, vocal quartets, cantatas, and musical theory textbooks.

BAKER, DANIEL (*b. Midway, Ga., 1791; d. Austin, Tex., 1857*), Presbyterian clergyman, educator. While missionary to Texas in 1840, participated in organization of the first presbytery there; was president of Austin College, 1853–57.

BAKER, DOROTHY DODDS (*b. Missoula, Mont., 1907; d. Springville, Calif., 1968*), novelist. Her major work was *Young Man With A Horn* (1938), a sensitive, expert novel about jazz music and musicians. The book was a best seller and was turned into a popular motion picture in 1950. Also wrote *Trio* (1943), about a mature woman's mental and sexual control over a female student. She and her husband wrote a play of the same title, based on the novel, and they also wrote a television play called "The Ninth Day." Also wrote *Our Gifted Son* (1948) and *Cassandra at the Wedding* (1962). Contributed short stories to a variety of periodicals and lectured about writing at colleges.

BAKER, EDWARD DICKINSON (*b. London, England, 1811; d. 1861*), lawyer. Came to America as a child. Practiced in Springfield, Ill., *post* 1835, and was Lincoln's successful opponent for Whig congressional nomination, 1844. Served as Illinois congressman, 1845–47, 1849–51; as U.S. senator, Republican, from Oregon, 1860–61; killed in action with Union army at Ball's Bluff, Va.

BAKER, FRANK (*b. Pulaski, N.Y., 1841; d. Washington, D.C., 1918*), anatomist, historian of medicine. Professor of anatomy, Georgetown University, 1883–1918.

BAKER, GEORGE AUGUSTUS (*b. New York, N.Y., 1821; d. 1880*), portrait painter, miniaturist.

BAKER, GEORGE FISHER (*b. 1840; d. 1931*), banker, philanthropist. Director of many corporations; principal association with the First National Bank of New York.

BAKER, GEORGE PIERCE (*b. Providence, R.I., 1866; d. New York, N.Y., 1935*), instructor in playwriting. Graduated Harvard, 1887; became an instructor there the following year. Experimented in 1905 with a course in practical playwriting, something never done before in American colleges; founded the famous course "English 47" in 1906 at Harvard. The "47 Workshop" followed which included non-student workers and an audience who wrote criticisms after each performance. Students included Eugene O'Neill, Sidney Howard, and George Abbott. Baker moved the Workshop to Yale in 1925 where he remained until retirement in 1933. He secured academic respect for the theatre arts, influenced both amateur and professional stages, and raised the standard of playwriting in America.

BAKER, HARVY HUMPHREY (*b. Brookline, Mass., 1869; d. Brookline, 1915*), first judge of the juvenile court of Boston, appointed 1906.

BAKER, HUGH POTTER (*b. St. Croix Falls, Wis., 1878; d. Orlando, Fla., 1950*), forester, educator. Brother of Ray Stannard Baker, B.S., Michigan Agricultural College, 1901; master of forestry degree, Yale, 1904; doctor of economics, University of Munich, 1910. Worked part-time in the federal Bureau of Forestry headed by Gifford Pinchot (1901–07), assistant professor of forestry at Iowa State College, Ames (1904–07). As professor of forestry at Pennsylvania State College, 1907–12, he raised that department to major status within the college of agriculture. As first dean of the N.Y. State College of Forestry at Syracuse University, 1912–20, he brought it to top academic rank and embodied in it a school for training men in one- and two-year courses as rangers, guards, tree-planters, and nursery foremen, the first such technical institute in the United States. Between 1920 and 1930, he was engaged in several business activities, returning to his former post as dean of the N.Y. State College of Forestry in 1930. Became president of Massachusetts State College in Amherst, 1933, supervised its expansion of programs and facilities until his retirement in 1947.

BAKER, JAMES (*b. Belleville, Ill., 1818; d. Little Snake River valley, Wyo., 1898*), trapper, guide, pioneer settler. Chief of scouts for General W. S. Harney, 1855–58.

BAKER, JAMES HEATON (*b. Monroe, Ohio, 1829; d. 1913*), politician, soldier, journalist. Secretary of state, Ohio, 1855–57, and Minnesota territory, 1859–61; federal commissioner of pensions, 1871–75; surveyor general of Minnesota, 1875–79.

BAKER, JAMES HUTCHINS (*b. near Harmony, Maine, 1848; d. Denver, Colo., 1925*), educator. Principal of Denver High School, 1874–91; president of University of Colorado, 1892–1914.

BAKER, JEHU (*b. Fayette Co., Ky., 1822; d. 1903*), lawyer, editor, radical Republican congressman from Illinois.

BAKER, JOHN FRANKLIN (*b. Trappe, Md., 1886; d. Trappe, Md., 1963*), baseball player best known as "Home Run" Baker. Third baseman for the Philadelphia Athletics (1909–14), he was one of the leading power hitters in the "dead-ball" era. While playing for Philadelphia, he average more than 100 runs batted in, leading the American League in 1912 and 1913. He also led the league in home runs for four years (1911–14), with twelve his highest total. In four consecutive World Series (1910–14), he batted .378, one of the highest World Series averages ever achieved. Played less illustriously for the New York Yankees (1916–19 and 1921–22), after which he retired. Was elected to the Baseball Hall of Fame in 1955.

BAKER, LA FAYETTE CURRY (*b. Stafford, N.Y., 1826; d. Philadelphia, Pa., 1868*), detective, Civil War chief of U.S.

Secret Service. Planned and directed expedition that captured John Wilkes Booth and D. C. Herold.

BAKER, LAURENCE SIMMONS (*b. Coles Hill, N.C., 1830; d. Suffolk, Va., 1907*), Confederate soldier. Cavalry officer actively engaged in all operations of Lee's army, 1862–63; held commands in North and South Carolina, 1864–65.

BAKER, LORENZO DOW (*b. Wellfleet, Mass, 1840; d. 1908*), sea captain, planter, merchant. First importer of Jamaican bananas; managing director, Jamaica division, United Fruit Co., 1897–1908.

BAKER, MARCUS (*b. Kalamazoo, Mich., 1849; d. Washington, D.C., 1903*), geographer. *Post* 1886, a member of the U.S. Geological Survey, he directed the topographic work of the northeastern division; was a founder of the National Geographic Society.

BAKER, NEWTON DIEHL (*b. Martinsburg, W. Va., 1871; d. Shaker Heights, Ohio, 1937*), lawyer, mayor of Cleveland, secretary of war. Graduated Johns Hopkins, 1892; obtained law degree from Washington and Lee, 1894. Practiced law briefly in Martinsburg, served for a year as secretary to Postmaster General William L. Wilson, then joined a Cleveland, Ohio, law firm. Married Elizabeth Leopold, 1902. Baker soon attracted the attention of Tom Loftin Johnson, reform mayor of Cleveland. As assistant director of the city's law department, then as city solicitor, Baker wholeheartedly supported Johnson's program of sound municipal government. Active in tax-reform plans, he played a major role in obtaining a 3-cent fare on the city transport lines. Johnson was defeated in 1909, but Baker was returned as city solicitor. Elected mayor in 1911 and reelected in 1913, Baker obtained a new "home rule" charter for the city, built a municipal power plant, and provided many other basic services.

A supporter of Woodrow Wilson in 1912, Baker became Wilson's secretary of war in March 1916, playing a rather static role during his first year in office. After April 1917, however, he showed good sense and vigor in administering the wartime conscription act, reorganizing the War Department and supporting General Pershing. Baker was criticized by professional soldiers, by publicists like Oswald Garrison Villard, and by members of both political parties for his conduct of his duties. He was hampered by many factors beyond his control, but if he was not a great secretary of war he did satisfy his president and became one of Wilson's most trusted confidants.

After the war Baker returned to Cleveland and the practice of law. As counsel for many large companies he became increasingly conservative, breaking with President Franklin D. Roosevelt over the constitutionality of the Tennessee Valley Authority. The year before his death he was mentioned as a vice presidential candidate on a coalition ticket of Republicans and conservative Democrats.

BAKER, OLIVER EDWIN (*b. Tiffin, Ohio, 1883; d. College Park, Md., 1949*), agricultural and economic geographer. A.B., Heidelberg (Tiffin, Ohio), 1903; M.A., 1904; M.A., Columbia University, 1905, studied forestry at Yale, 1907–08; Ph.D. in economics, University of Wisconsin, 1921. Baker also studied agriculture at Wisconsin, specializing in soils and doing research on the effects of climate on Wisconsin agriculture. Worked in the Office of Farm Management, U.S. Department of Agriculture, 1912–20, on long-term projects, delineating agricultural regions and mapping the physical basis of agricultural production and trade. Staff, Bureau of Agricultural Economics, 1922–42, working on studies of land utilization and population problems and the enhancement of rural life. Professor at the University of Maryland *post* 1942; created and developed the department of geography.

BAKER, OSMON CLEANDER (*b. Marlow, N.H., 1812; d. Concord, N.H., 1871*), Methodist bishop. Organizer of Newbury Seminary; professor of homiletics, Methodist General Biblical Institute; authority on Methodist law and discipline.

BAKER, PETER CARPENTER (*b. North Hempstead, N.Y., 1822; d. 1889*), printer, publisher. Founder of the New York Typothetae, a printing trade organization; partner in Baker, Voorhis and Co., law book publishers.

BAKER, RAY STANNARD (*b. Lansing, Mich., 1870; d. Amherst, Mass., 1946*), journalist, author. Brother of Hugh Potter Baker. Raised in St. Croix Falls, Wis., in a bookish, Presbyterian family; father an agent for the land interests of Caleb Cushing, and constantly at war with predatory lumber interests. Graduated from Michigan Agricultural College, B.S., 1889. After trying business and the law, he went to Chicago in 1892, determined to find literary work. As a reporter on the *Chicago News-Record*, 1892–98, he awoke to social realities and the need for reforms through experiences with urban poverty, Coxey's Army, and the Pullman Strike. Between 1898 and 1906, he was on the staff of *McClure's Magazine*. At first, a supporter of American imperialism and an optimistic admirer of the expanding economy, he wrote glowing accounts of these and of such contemporary heroes as Theodore Roosevelt and J. P. Morgan. He became a "muckraker" only later, joining Ida Tarbell and others on *McClure's* in the magazine's crusade against corruption and lawlessness. In 1906, he and several associates left *McClure's* and bought the *American Magazine* which they sought to make an organ of optimism and constructive reporting. For this magazine, Baker wrote a series of essays under the pseudonym "David Grayson" which were later published as *Adventures in Contentment* and had extraordinary success. The imaginary Grayson, a gentleman farmer, held forth on the joys of country life and preached a cosmic idealism, Emersonian in tone. Eventually nine volumes of these essays were published between 1907 and 1942.

In 1908, Baker published *Following the Color Line*, a pioneer field report on race relations, liberal by the standards of the day. His enthusiastic reports on political insurgency between 1909 and 1912 helped mobilize public opinion behind insurgents in both parties. Resenting Theodore Roosevelt's attitude toward Robert La Follette's candidacy, Baker supported Woodrow Wilson in 1912 and soon became a confirmed Wilsonian. After World War I, Baker served as director of the press bureau for the American delegation at the Peace Conference and strongly supported Wilson in the fight over the Versailles Treaty. Designated by Wilson as his authorized biographer, Baker devoted many years to his eight-volume *Woodrow Wilson: Life and Letters* (1927–39), awarded the Pulitzer Prize in 1940. He was author also of two volumes of autobiography: *Native American* (1941) and *American Chronicle* (1945).

BAKER, REMEMBER (*b. Woodbury, Conn., 1737; d. St. Johns, Canada, 1775*), soldier. Settled in what is now Vermont, 1764; commanded a company of Green Mountain Boys; associate of Ethan Allen.

BAKER, SARA JOSEPHINE (*b. Poughkeepsie, N.Y., 1873; d. New York, N.Y., 1945*), physician, public health administrator. Graduated Women's Medical College of the New York Infirmary, 1898. Began practice in New York City, 1900. Appointed medical inspector in the city health department, 1901, she soon gained first-hand knowledge of tenement life and the medical problems resulting from poverty and ignorance. Promoted assistant to the commissioner of health, she carried out a number of assignments and concluded through experience that the control of childhood disease should be a matter of prevention rather than cure. In the summer of 1908, working on the Lower East Side of New York with a staff of nurses, she demonstrated that prompt instruction of the mothers and newborn children in the baby's proper care resulted in a dramatic lowering of infant mortality. This led to the creation of a Bureau of Child Hygiene which she headed, the first official bureau of its kind. The Bureau instituted strict licensing of midwives, encouraged the foster mother system for foundlings, and gave impetus to the school lunch movement. When she retired in 1923, every state had a bureau of child hygiene, and infant mortality in New York City had dropped to 66 deaths per thousand.

BAKER, WALTER RANSOM GAIL (*b. Lockport, N.Y., 1892; d. Syracuse, N.Y., 1960*), electrical engineer. Studied at Union College (M.E.E., 1919). Employed by General Electric (1916–29; 1935–57). From 1929 to 1935, he managed the production of radio apparatus for the Radio Corporation of America in Camden, N.J. Vice president of G.E. from 1941. Baker played a major role in the advent of commercial television, serving as chairman of the National Television System Committee responsible for standardization of the industry. Although the beginnings of television were delayed by World War II, Baker's contributions were instrumental in launching the industry after the war, when he served as chairman of a second NTSC committee on color television. Advocated educational television.

BAKER, WILLIAM MUMFORD (*b. Washington, D.C., 1825; d. Boston, Mass., 1883*), Presbyterian clergyman. Held pastorates in Arkansas and Texas, 1850–65; author of *Inside: A Chronicle of Secession* (1866) under pseudonym of George F. Harrington.

BALBACH, EDWARD (*b. Karlsruhe, Germany, 1839; d. 1910*), metallurgist. Immigrated to New Jersey, 1850; with father, introduced European processes of smelting silver-lead ores.

BALCH, EMILY GREENE (*b. Jamaica Plain, Mass., 1867; d. Cambridge, Mass., 1961*), social worker and peace activist. Taught courses on the labor movement, socialism, and immigration at Wellesley College from the late 1890's to 1918. Was active in many social and political causes, perhaps her most notable achievements being her participation in the founding of the Women's Trade Union League (1903); her attendance at the International Congress of Women at The Hague (1915); and her position as secretary-treasurer of the Women's International League for Peace and Freedom (1919–22 and 1934–35). In addition to a volume of poetry and a volume of prose, she published several works on social and political issues, including *Our Slavic Fellow Citizens* (1910), one of the more frequently cited books on histories of immigration. In 1946 was joint recipient of the Nobel Peace Prize.

BALCH, GEORGE BEALL (*b. Shelbyville, Tenn., 1821; d. Raleigh, N.C., 1908*), naval officer. Held responsible commands in Mexican and Civil wars; promoted rear admiral, 1878; superintendent of U.S. Naval Academy, 1879–81.

BALCH, THOMAS WILLING (*b. Wiesbaden, Germany, 1866; d. Atlantic City, N.J., 1927*), lawyer. A man of wealth, he practiced law in Philadelphia and published numerous books on special interests, notably genealogy and international arbitration.

BALDWIN, ABRAHAM (*b. North Guilford, Conn., 1754; d. Washington, D.C., 1807*), statesman. Graduated Yale, 1772; served as chaplain during Revolutionary War; removed to Georgia, 1784. Author of Georgia charter providing for a complete state educational system, he was also titular president of the projected state university and organizer of Franklin College, now University of Georgia. Ablest Georgia delegate to the Federal Convention,

1787, he served as congressman, Democratic-Republican, 1789–99, and as U.S. senator, 1799–1807.

BALDWIN, EDWARD ROBINSON (*b. Bethel, Conn., 1864; d. Saranac Lake, N.Y., 1947*), physician, pioneer in tuberculosis research. M.D., Yale Medical School, 1890. Soon after starting practice in Cromwell, Conn., contracted pulmonary tuberculosis. Went for cure in 1892 to the sanatorium of Dr. Edward L. Trudeau in the Adirondacks. While under treatment, he engaged part-time in laboratory duties and gave particular attention to research into the problems of native and acquired resistance to the disease. By 1908, had become recognized as a leader in the field of tuberculosis research and at an international congress in Washington, D.C. presented a paper emphasizing the role played by mild infection or even inoculation with dead tubercle bacilli in stimulating a strong resistance to more serious infection. He developed this theme extensively in later years, and epitomized his views in *Tuberculosis: Bacteriology, Pathology, and Laboratory Diagnosis* (1927), written with two of his laboratory associates. Published more than a hundred papers on his subject. Director of the Saranac Lake laboratory until 1926.

BALDWIN, ELIHU WHITTLESEY (*b. Durham, N.Y., 1789; d. 1840*), Presbyterian clergyman, educator. First president of Wabash College, Crawfordville, Ind., 1836–40.

BALDWIN, EVELYN BRIGGS (*b. Springfield, Mo., 1862; d. Washington, D.C., 1933*), Arctic explorer. Made unsuccessful dash to the North Pole in 1902.

BALDWIN, FRANK STEPHEN (*b. New Hartford, Conn., 1838; d. 1925*), inventor. In 1874, designed one of the first adding machines ever to be sold in the United States; in 1902, invented a calculator which, in association with J. R. Monroe, he successfully marketed as the Monroe Calculating Machine.

BALDWIN, HENRY (*b. New Haven, Conn., 1780; d. Philadelphia, Pa., 1844*), jurist. Half-brother of Abraham Baldwin. Graduated Yale, 1797, studied law with Alexander J. Dallas, and practiced in western Pennsylvania. Appointed by Andrew Jackson an associate justice of the U.S. Supreme Court, 1830.

BALDWIN, HENRY PERRINE (*b. Lahaina, Maui, Hawaii, 1842; d. Makawao, 1911*), sugar planter, capitalist. Influential in Hawaiian affairs, 1887–1904.

BALDWIN, HENRY PORTER (*b. Coventry, R.I., 1814; d. 1892*), businessman, politician. Settled in Detroit, Mich., 1838. President of Detroit National Bank, 1863–87; Republican governor of Michigan, 1869–73.

BALDWIN, JAMES MARK (*b. Columbia, S.C., 1861; d. Paris, France, 1934*), psychologist. Cofounder and editor, *Psychological Review*, 1894–1909; his most valuable work was in child and social psychology.

BALDWIN, JOHN (*b. North Branford, Conn., 1799; d. Baldwin, La., 1884*), grindstone manufacturer. Founder of Baldwin-Wallace College, Berea, Ohio, 1845; Baker University, Kansas, 1859; Baldwin Public School, Louisiana, 1867.

BALDWIN, JOHN BROWN (*b. Staunton, Va., 1820; d. 1873*), lawyer, politician. Devised a code of procedural rules still in use in Virginia House of Delegates.

BALDWIN, JOHN DENISON (*b. North Stonington, Conn., 1809; d. Worcester, Mass., 1883*), journalist. Owner and editor of the *Worcester Spy*, 1859–83.

BALDWIN, JOSEPH (*b. Newcastle, Pa., 1827; d. 1899*), educator. Founder of normal school system in Missouri; first professor of pedagogy at University of Texas, 1891.

BALDWIN, JOSEPH GLOVER (*b. near Winchester, Va., 1815; d. 1864*), jurist, author. Removed to Southwest, 1836, after self-education in law; practiced in both Mississippi and Alabama. In 1853 he published *The Flush Times of Alabama and Mississippi*, a lively and satiric interpretative study of backwoods society, and in 1855 a serious volume of essays on American political figures entitled *Party Leaders*. He settled in California in 1854, becoming an associate justice of the state supreme court in 1858 and returning to private practice in 1862.

BALDWIN, LOAMMI (*b. North Woburn, Mass., 1744/5; d. North Woburn, 1807*), civil engineer, soldier. Leading projector and chief engineer of the Middlesex Canal, a means of connecting the Charles and Merrimac rivers; this work, authorized by the Massachusetts legislature in 1793, was not completed until 1803. While surveying for the canal, he found an apple tree with superior fruit, cut scions for grafting, and produced the "Baldwin," a winter apple of eastern America.

BALDWIN, LOAMMI (*b. North Woburn, Mass., 1780; d. 1838*), civil engineer, lawyer. son of the preceding. Constructed Fort Strong, Boston Harbor, 1814; in 1819 was made engineer of improvements in Boston. Between 1817 and 1820 he was engaged on public works in Virginia; in 1821 he began work as engineer of the Union Canal (extending from Reading to Middletown, Pa.), one of the outstanding projects of the time. After a year in Europe, 1824–25, he determined the correct proportions for the Bunker Hill Monument and surveyed the route for a proposed canal to link Boston Harbor with the Hudson River and the Erie Canal. He also designed and built large naval dry docks at Charlestown, Mass., and Norfolk, Va.

BALDWIN, MATTHIAS WILLIAM (*b. Elizabethtown, N.J., 1795; d. Frankford, Pa., 1866*), manufacturer, philanthropist. In partnership with David Mason, 1825–27, he manufactured hydraulic presses, textile printing machinery, and stationary steam engines. *Post* 1831, he built for Phila. and Germantown R.R. "Old Ironsides," one of the first American locomotives to be actually employed in transportation. Subsequent to 1841, he manufactured only locomotives at his Philadelphia shops, and at the time of his death (since 1854 in partnership with Matthew Baird) the Baldwin Locomotive Works had turned out more than 1,500. Baldwin's charities were extensive.

BALDWIN, ROGER SHERMAN (*b. New Haven, Conn., 1793; d. 1863*), lawyer. Son of Simeon Baldwin, grandson of Roger Sherman. U.S. senator, Whig, from Connecticut, 1847–51; defense counsel in *Amistad* case (decided 1841).

BALDWIN, SIMEON (*b. Norwich, Conn., 1761; d. 1851*), jurist. Representative in Congress, Federalist, from Connecticut, 1803–05; judge, supreme court of errors, Connecticut, 1806–18.

BALDWIN, SIMEON EBEN (*b. New Haven, Conn., 1840; d. 1927*), jurist. Son of Roger S. Baldwin. Graduated Yale, 1861; admitted to the bar, 1863. A founder and president of the American Bar Association, professor in the Yale Law School, 1869–1919, and chief justice of the Connecticut supreme court, retiring in 1910. Never a professional politician, he early became identified with Connecticut political life; he served as governor (Democrat), 1910–14, but was defeated in a bid for the U.S. Senate, 1915. He was named to various state commissions of legal reform and was a U.S. delegate to International Prison Congresses, 1899 and 1905. He was a member of many historical, philosophical, scientific, and artistic societies.

BALDWIN, THERON (*b. Goshen, Conn., 1801; d. Orange, N.J., 1870*), Congregational clergyman, pioneer missionary in Illinois.

BALDWIN, WILLIAM (*b. Newlin, Pa., 1779; d. Franklin, Mo., 1819*), physician. Botanist on Major Stephen Long's expedition to the Rocky Mountains, 1819.

BALDWIN, WILLIAM HENRY (*b. Boston, Mass., 1863; d. 1905*), railroad executive. Served with Union Pacific, 1886–91; vice president, Père Marquette, 1891–94; vice president, Southern, 1894–96; president, Long Island Railroad, 1896–1905.

BALESTIER, CHARLES WOLCOTT (*b. Rochester, N.Y., 1861; d. Dresden, Germany, 1891*), author. American publisher and friend of Rudyard Kipling; collaborated with him in *The Naulahka* (1892).

BALL, ALBERT (*b. Boylston, Mass., 1835; d. Claremont, N.H., 1927*), engineer, inventor. Chief mechanical engineer, Sullivan Machine Co., 1868–1914; designer of the diamond-core drill and other mining and quarrying tools.

BALL, EPHRAIM (*b. Lake Township, Ohio, 1812; d. 1872*), manufacturer, inventor. Formed a company to manufacture threshers, 1840; designed the very popular "Blue Plough" and manufactured the "Hussey Reaper." A series of experiments resulted in Ball's principal contribution to the development of agricultural machinery, the "Ohio Mower," patented in 1857; this was the first of the two-wheeled flexible or hinged bar mowers to gain a wide reputation.

BALL, FRANK CLAYTON (*b. Greensburg, Ohio, 1857; d. Muncie, Ind., 1943*), industrialist, philanthropist. Raised in western New York State. After several false starts, he and his brothers were successful in the business of manufacturing and selling tin and glass containers for oils and varnishes. In 1885, the firm (Ball Brothers Company), discovering that the patent covering the "Mason Jar" had expired, began producing glass fruit jars and caps. In 1887, seeking to cut costs by use of natural gas rather than coal, the firm moved from Buffalo, N.Y., to a new factory in Muncie, Ind. Ball Brothers enjoyed phenomenal growth, through inventions of their own and by buying exclusive rights to inventions of others, a practice which gave the firm a dominant position in the industry. Frank Ball was president of the company from its start until his death. He and his brothers worked closely and harmoniously together, both in business and in philanthropy. Their benefactions, totaling more than seven million dollars, were distributed principally to institutions in Muncie and in the state of Indiana, and it was their practice to make each gift contingent on a similar or larger contribution by the public.

BALL, GEORGE ALEXANDER (*b. Trumbull County, Ohio, 1862; d. Muncie, Ind., 1955*), manufacturer. The youngest of five brothers, Ball was the driving force in the family whose glass jar enterprise became the world's largest. Transformed the home canning of food. The company was the subject of criticism in the famous sociological studies *Middletown* and *Middletown in Transition*.

BALL, THOMAS (*b. Charlestown, Mass., 1819; d. Montclair, N.J., 1911*), sculptor. A self-trained painter and engraver, his greatest work, an equestrian statue of Washington, was erected in the Boston Public Garden in 1869. His most significant pieces include: "St. John the Evangelist," 1875 (Forest Hills Cemetery); "Emancipation," showing Lincoln and a kneeling slave, 1875 (Washington, D.C.); and statues of Webster (Central Park, New York City), Josiah Quincy (Boston City Hall), and Charles Sumner (Public Garden, Boston).

BALLANTINE, ARTHUR ATWOOD (*b. Oberlin, Ohio, 1883; d. New York, N.Y., 1960*), corporate lawyer and Treasury official. Studied at Harvard University (LL.D., 1907). Assistant secretary and undersecretary of the Treasury (1931–33) under President Herbert Hoover. Helped organize and was one of the first directors of the Reconstruction Finance Corporation. Ballantine continued to serve as an advisor to Franklin D. Roosevelt and was instrumental in convincing the president to close the banks in 1933; he also devised the plan for reopening the nation's banks before returning to private practice in New York City.

BALLARD, BLAND WILLIAMS (*b. near Fredericksburg, Va., 1759; d. Shelby Co., Ky., 1853*), pioneer. Settled in Kentucky, 1780, and was active in frontier Indian wars until 1795; served five terms in Kentucky legislature.

BALLINGER, RICHARD ACHILLES (*b. Boonesboro, Iowa, 1858; d. Seattle, Wash., 1922*), lawyer. Graduated Williams, 1884. Removed to Washington Territory *post* 1886; served as reform mayor of Seattle, 1904–06. Appointed by President Taft to succeed J. R. Garfield as secretary of the interior, 1909, Ballinger was accused of failure to support the policies of public-land conservation instituted by the preceding president, Theodore Roosevelt. The controversy that followed was damaging to the Taft administration, and Ballinger resigned his post in 1911.

BALLOU, ADIN (*b. Cumberland, R.I., 1803; d. 1890*), Universalist clergyman, reformer. Editor of the *Independent Messenger*, 1831–39; founder of the utopian Hopedale Community at Milford, Mass., 1841–68.

BALLOU, HOSEA (*b. Richmond, N.H., 1771; d. Boston, Mass., 1852*), Universalist clergyman. Missionary and leader in the Universalist Church; editor of *Universalist Magazine*, 1819–28, and *Universalist Expositor*, 1830–44.

BALLOU, HOSEA (*b. Guilford, Vt., 1796; d. 1861*), Universalist clergyman. Grandnephew of the preceding. Author of *Ancient History of Universalism* (1829); first president of Tufts College, 1854–61.

BALLOU, MATURIN MURRAY (*b. Boston, Mass., 1820; d. Cairo, Egypt, 1895*), journalist, traveler, author. Son of Hosea Ballou (1771–1852). Edited, 1851–59, *Gleason's Pictorial*, later called *Ballou's Pictorial*, an early American illustrated paper; editor, *Boston Daily Globe*, 1872–74.

BALTIMORE, CHARLES CALVERT, THIRD LORD. *See* CALVERT, CHARLES.

BALTIMORE, GEORGE CALVERT, FIRST LORD. *See* CALVERT, GEORGE.

BAMBERGER, LOUIS (*b. Baltimore, Md., 1855; d. South Orange, N.J., 1944*), merchant, philanthropist. Entered business at fourteen, as clerk in dry goods store owned by his mother's brothers (Hutzler Brothers); joined father in wholesale notions trade, 1871; worked as a buyer in New York City, 1887–92, while looking for chance to establish his own business. Purchasing a bankrupt dry goods house in Newark, N.J., 1892, he and partners built it up as L. Bamberger and Company into one of the nation's largest department stores and pioneered in many modern retailing techniques. In 1922, Bamberger established WOR, one of the first commercial radio broadcasting stations; he was also responsible for a most enlightened labor policy for employees. After making extensive donations of a conventional nature to public philanthropies, he endowed the Institute for Advanced Study in Princeton, N.J., 1930, to which he and his sister gave approximately eighteen million dollars. He also left collections of art and Americana to the Newark Museum (which he had built) and the New Jersey Historical Society.

BANCROFT, AARON (*b. Reading, Mass., 1755; d. Worcester, Mass., 1839*), clergyman, author. Father of George Bancroft; a founder and first president of the American Unitarian Association, 1825–36.

BANCROFT, CECIL FRANKLIN PATCH (*b. New Ipswich, N.H., 1839; d. Andover, Mass., 1901*), educator. Graduated Dartmouth, 1860; Andover Theological Seminary, 1867. Appointed principal of Phillips Academy, Andover, Mass., in 1873, he found the Academy at a critical moment in its history. During the 28 years of his administration he transformed Andover both materially and scholastically; he replaced the three-year program with a four-year one, increased the endowments, and strengthened the faculty.

BANCROFT, EDGAR ADDISON (*b. Galesburg, Ill., 1857; d. Karuizawa, Japan, 1925*), lawyer, orator, diplomat. Counsel to several railroads, and to the International Harvester Co., 1907–20; ambassador to Japan, 1924–25.

BANCROFT, EDWARD (*b. Westfield, Mass., 1744; d. Margate, England, 1821*), writer, inventor. Acted as a double spy for England and America, 1776–83.

BANCROFT, FREDERIC (*b. Galesburg, Ill., 1860; d. Washington, D.C., 1945*), historian, philanthropist. Graduated Amherst, 1882; Ph.D., Columbia University, 1885; studied also at University of Berlin. Librarian, U.S. Department of State, 1888–92; thereafter devoted himself to research and writing, principally on various phases of the history of the South. He was author of a life of William H. Seward and edited the papers of Carl Schurz (published 1913). His estate, nearly two million dollars, was left to Columbia University for the purchase of books on American history and for the annual award of prizes in American history and biography.

BANCROFT, GEORGE (*b. Worcester, Mass., 1800; d. Washington, D.C., 1891*), historian, diplomat. Son of Aaron Bancroft. Graduated Harvard, 1817; took doctorate at University of Göttingen, 1820. After a tour on the Continent he returned to Harvard where he taught for one year as a tutor in Greek; his foreign social and educational views irritated both the students and the authorities. Two more unsuccessful ventures followed: the publication of a volume of poems in 1823, and an attempt to establish a superior boys' school, based on European models, at Round Hill, Northampton, Mass. After quitting the school in 1831, he began preparation of his famous *History of the United States*. The first volume was published in 1834; the second, with a second edition of the first, appeared in 1837; the third in 1840. At this point, Bancroft had completed his survey of the period of colonization. The success of the work was gratifying and immediate, although some perceptive critics noted a marked political bias in favor of Jacksonian democracy. The Democrats had few intellectual supporters in Whiggish New England, hence Bancroft rose rapidly in his party's councils; as a delegate to the National Democratic Convention in 1844 he played an important part in the nomination of James K. Polk for the presidency and was rewarded with the secretaryship of the navy in Polk's cabinet. During a short term of 18 months, he established the Naval Academy at Annapolis, aided the work of the Naval Observatory, and was a faithful supporter of his chief's policies. In 1846 he went to London as U.S. minister to Great Britain; in addition to fulfilling the demands of his post he undertook extensive researches into French and English documentary sources and amassed material for the continuation of his great historical project.

On his return to America in 1849 he devoted himself primarily to his historical work, issuing six volumes between 1852 and 1866 in which the story of the American Revolution was told. At first considering President Lincoln quite inadequate for the tasks confronting him in the Civil War, Bancroft early recognized Lincoln's quality and gave him support with voice and pen. He was close to President Andrew Johnson and received from him an appointment as U.S. minister to Berlin in 1867; there, until 1874, he showed himself an able diplomat, moved in the best social and academic circles, and engaged in the research for the tenth and final volume of the *History*, which was published in 1874. In 1876 he brought out a "thoroughly revised" edition of the entire work in six volumes; in 1882, a *History of the Formation of the Constitution of the United States*; and in 1883–85 a final revision of the *History* in which he corrected errors and toned down the floridity of his earlier style.

Bancroft wrote always with the strong bias of an ardent believer in democratic government, and his style of expression is tinged with the enthusiasm of the old-style patriotic orator, yet his title "Father of American History" is a just one.

BANCROFT, HUBERT HOWE (*b. Granville, Ohio, 1832; d. 1918*), historian. Went to California in 1852; prospered as a merchant and publisher in San Francisco. Out of an interest in collecting books on Pacific Coast history, evolved the project of a vast history of the coast and Rocky Mountain region, extending also to Alaska, and to Mexico and Central America. With H. L. Oak as assistant, Bancroft organized a force of archivists, copyists, and reporters who sought out source data wherever it was to be found; in many instances, surviving pioneers were interviewed and their recollections noted. After organization and editing, five volumes on the native races of the area, 28 volumes of history, and six volumes of "essays" were published between 1875 and 1800.

BANCROFT, WILDER DWIGHT (*b. Middletown, R.I., 1867; d. Ithaca, N.Y., 1953*), chemist. Studied at Harvard and Leipzig (Ph.D., 1892). Professor, Cornell (1895–1937). Bancroft became the leading proponent of teaching physical chemistry in the U.S. Specializing in the field of colloid chemistry, he published *Applied Colloid Chemistry* in 1921. Founded the *Journal of Physical Chemistry* in 1896.

BANDELIER, ADOLPH FRANCIS ALPHONSE (*b. Berne, Switzerland, 1840; d. Seville, Spain, 1914*), historian, explorer, anthropologist. Came to America, 1848; educated at home (Highland, Ill.) and at the University of Berne where he studied geology. His earliest scholarly contributions dealt with the society of the ancient Mexicans (1877–79); in 1880 he was engaged by the Archaeological Institute of America to conduct researches in New Mexico where he was active until 1889. After publication of studies on the Indians and history of the Southwest, he worked from 1892 to 1902 on archaeological and archival research in Peru and Bolivia. His devotion to original sources resulted in the discrediting of the romantic school of American aboriginal history.

BANGS, FRANCIS NEHEMIAH (*b. New York, N.Y., 1828; d. Ocala, Fla., 1885*), lawyer. Active in removal of corrupt New York judges after "Tweed Ring" exposure, 1871.

BANGS, FRANK C. (*b. Alexandria, Va., 1833; d. 1908*), actor. Supported Forrest, Hackett, Booth, and others, 1851–72.

BANGS, JOHN KENDRICK (*b. Yonkers, N.Y., 1862; d. 1922*), humorist, editor, lecturer. Best known for *Three Weeks in Politics* (1894) and *A Houseboat on the Styx* (1895).

BANGS, NATHAN (*b. Stratford, Conn., 1778; d. 1862*), Methodist clergyman. Editor of the Methodist Book Concern, New York; founder of the Methodist Missionary Society; acting president of Wesleyan University, 1841–43.

BANISTER, JOHN (*b. Twigworth, England, 1650; d. Virginia, 1692*), botanist. Author of catalogues of Virginia plants in John Ray's *Historia Plantarum* and of unfinished "Natural History of Virginia."

BANISTER, JOHN (*b. Bristol Parish, Va., 1734; d. 1788*), Revolutionary patriot. Member of Virginia Convention, 1776, Virginia House of Burgesses, 1777; a delegate to the Continental Congress, 1778–79; a framer and signer of the Articles of Confederation.

BANISTER, ZILPAH POLLY GRANT (*b. Norfolk, Conn., 1794; d. 1874*), educator. Associate of Mary Lyon in schools at Derry, N.H., and Ipswich, Mass.

BANKHEAD, JOHN HOLLIS (*b. Moscow, Ala., 1842; d. 1920*), U.S. senator from Alabama, Democrat, 1907–20. Promoted federal aid for improvement of roads, 1916.

BANKHEAD, JOHN HOLLIS (*b. Moscow, Ala., 1872; d. Bethesda, Md., 1946*), lawyer, politician. Son of John Hollis Bankhead (1842–1920); brother of William B. Bankhead. Graduated University of Alabama, 1891; LL.B., Georgetown University Law School, 1893. Built up good practice in Jasper, Ala. As U.S. senator from Alabama, Democrat, 1931–46, he was advocate of agricultural interests and a strong supporter of the early New Deal, seeking to benefit the tenant farmers and sharecroppers as well as the large commercial producers. To this end, he was influential in establishing the Resettlement Administration, later the Farm Security Administration. He attacked wartime efforts to hold down farm prices (1941–45) and disliked the growing influence of labor in the Democratic party. He opposed President Harry Truman's domestic program.

BANKHEAD, TALLULAH (*b. Huntsville, Ala., 1902; d. New York, N.Y., 1968*), actress. At fifteen she won a magazine contest that landed her a role in a film; although she continued in films off and on, with the exception of her performance in Alfred Hitchcock's *Lifeboat* (1944), her film career was undistinguished. She appeared in several shows on Broadway around 1920 and then moved to England, where she soon became the object of a Tallulah craze; for many her beauty, seductively husky voice, intelligence, wit, and outrageousness personified the exuberance of the 1920's. She did sixteen plays during her eight years in England, most notably Noel Coward's *Fallen Angels* (1925), Michael Arlen's *The Green Hat* (1925), and Sidney Howard's *They Knew What They Wanted* (1926). In the 1930's she established herself as one of Broadway's leading ladies and remained busy in the theater during the 1940's and 1950's. Some of her most widely hailed performances were in *The Little Foxes* (1939) and *The Skin of Our Teeth* (1942), and she enjoyed a long run in *Private Lives* (1948). She also hosted "The Big Show" (1950–52) on radio.

BANKHEAD, WILLIAM BROCKMAN (*b. Moscow, Ala., 1874; d. Bethesda, Md., 1940*), Democratic congressman from Alabama, 1916–40. Speaker of the House of Representatives, 1936–40; son and brother of Senators John H. Bankhead I and II; father of actress Tallulah Bankhead.

BANKS, CHARLES EDWARD (*b. Portland, Maine, 1854; d. Hartford, Conn., 1931*), public health official, historian, and genealogist. Wrote important studies of Plymouth Colony settlers and New England towns.

BANKS, NATHANIEL PRENTISS (*b. Waltham, Mass., 1816; d. Waltham, 1894*), Union soldier, Massachusetts legislator. Congressman, Democrat and "Know-Nothing," from Massachusetts,

1853–57; his election as Speaker of the House, 1856, was hailed as an antislavery victory. He sought and won the governorship of Massachusetts as a Republican, 1858–60. Commissioned major general of volunteers in 1861, he began a military career marked by courage if not always by the greatest tactical skill; he fought in Shenandoah Valley, 1862, received thanks of Congress for his 1863 capture of Port Hudson, and headed the disastrous 1864 Red River Expedition. Returned to Congress as a Republican, 1865–73; as a Democrat, 1875–77; again as a Republican, 1878–79 and 1889–90.

BANNER, PETER (*b. Boston, Mass., 1794–1828*), architect. Designed Eben Crafts House, Roxbury, Mass., and Park Street Church, Boston.

BANNISTER, NATHANIEL HARRINGTON (*b. 1813; d. 1847*), playwright, actor. Popular actor in South and West; author of *Putnam* (1844) and other melodramas; one of the most prolific of early American dramatists.

BANVARD, JOHN (*b. New York, N.Y., 1815; d. Watertown, S.Dak., 1891*), painter, writer. Painted (*post* 1840) and exhibited a huge, crude panorama of the Mississippi River.

BANVARD, JOSEPH (*b. New York, N.Y., 1810; d. Neponset, Mass., 1887*), author, Baptist clergyman. Held several New England pastorates; wrote a number of moralizing works on American history.

BAPST, JOHN (*b. La Roche, Switzerland, 1815; d. Mount Hope, Md., 1887*), Jesuit priest, educator. Missionary in Maine, 1848–59; first rector of Boston College, 1860–69.

BARA, THEDA (*b. Cincinnati, Ohio, 1885[?]; d. Los Angeles, Calif., 1955*), actress. Studied at the University of Cincinnati. Theda Bara achieved fame with her film *A Fool There Was* (1914) made by the Fox Film Co. In it she played a vampire, establishing her image as a sinful woman and introducing the word *vamp* into the language. She appeared in films until 1919, the most famous of which was *Cleopatra* (1917), and which helped establish the Fox Film Co. as a giant in the film industry. After an unsuccessful attempt as a stage actress, she retired to married life in California.

BARAGA, FREDERIC (*b. near Döbernig, Austria, 1797; d. Marquette, Mich., 1868*), Roman Catholic priest. Missionary to Indians of Lake Superior region; wrote important grammar (1850) and dictionary (1853) of the Chippewa language; consecrated bishop of Sault Ste. Marie, 1853, and of Marquette, 1865.

BARANOV, ALEXANDER ANDREEVICH (*b. 1746; d. 1819*), fur trader. Directed affairs of the Russian American Company in Alaska, 1790–1818.

BARBER, AMZI LORENZO (*b. Saxton's River, Vt., 1843; d. 1909*), capitalist. First to exploit the so-called pitch lake on the Island of Trinidad, using its asphalt for street paving.

BARBER, DONN (*b. Washington, D.C., 1871; d. 1925*), architect. Trained in office of Carrère and Hastings and at the Beaux Arts in Paris; his buildings include the Connecticut Supreme Court and State Library in Hartford, Conn., and the Department of Justice building, Washington, D.C.

BARBER, EDWIN ATLEE (*b. Baltimore, Md., 1851; d. 1916*), archaeologist. A leading authority on ceramic art in all its branches.

BARBER, FRANCIS (*b. Princeton, N.J., 1751; d. Newburgh, N.Y., 1783*), soldier. After distinguished service, 1776–81, was sent by Washington to quell mutiny of New Jersey and Pennsylvania troops in the latter year.

BARBER, JOHN WARNER (*b. East Windsor, Conn., 1798; d. New Haven, Conn., 1885*), engraver, historian. With Henry Howe, produced a series of illustrated books on antiquities and local history of the states of the Union.

BARBER, OHIO COLUMBUS (*b. Middlebury, Ohio, 1841; d. Akron, Ohio, 1920*), manufacturer. Founded the Diamond Match Co., 1881; active in industrial development of the Akron area.

BARBEY, DANIEL EDWARD (*b. Portland, Oreg., 1889; d. Bremerton, Wash., 1969*), naval officer. Graduated U.S. Naval Academy (1912). Appointed head of the new amphibious-warfare section at the Navy Department (1942), he oversaw the development and tactical employment of specialized assault craft and tackled the problems of offloading transports and supply ships at beachheads. During World War II he organized the VII Amphibious Force in the Southwest Pacific theater; by the time of Japan's surrender the force had put ashore more than one million men in fifty-six landings over a two-year period. Was commander of the Seventh Fleet (1945), the Atlantic Fleet's amphibious forces (1946), and the Fourth Fleet (1946); was made chairman of the Joint Military Board to study America's strategic requirements in the Far East (1947); and served in the dual role of commandant of the Tenth Naval District and Caribbean Sea Frontier (1947–50) and the Thirteenth Naval District (1950–51). Retired with the rank of vice admiral in 1951 and published his wartime memoirs, *MacArthur's Amphibious Navy* (1969).

BARBOUR, CLARENCE AUGUSTUS (*b. Hartford, Conn., 1867; d. Providence, R.I., 1937*), Baptist clergyman; president, Colgate Rochester Divinity School, 1928–29; president, Brown University, 1929–37.

BARBOUR, HENRY CLAY (*b. Hartford, Conn., 1886; d. New Haven, Conn., 1943*), pharmacologist. A.B., Trinity College, 1906; M.D., Johns Hopkins, 1910; studied abroad in Freiburg, Vienna (with Hans Horst Meyer), and London, 1911–12. Assistant professor of pharmacology and toxicology, Yale, 1912–21. He then taught at McGill University and the University of Louisville, returning to Yale as associate professor, 1931, and rising to professor in 1940. Principally interested in the study of heat regulation in the animal body, he investigated the physiology of heat production and heat loss, the regulation of body temperature by the central and peripheral nervous systems and by hormones, and the production and relief of fever. Particularly important were his demonstrations of water exchange in the animal body and its function in controlling temperature; for this study, he devised (with W. F. Hamilton) the falling-drop method for measuring the specific gravity of fluids. *Post* 1932, he published eighteen papers on the biological properties of heavy water. Author of the textbook *Experimental Pharmacology and Toxicology* (1932).

BARBOUR, JAMES (*b. Barboursville, Va., 1775; d. Barboursville, 1842*), statesman. Governor of Virginia, 1812–15; U.S. senator, 1815–25; secretary of war, 1825–28. Originally a Jeffersonian Democrat, he became a strong supporter of John Q. Adams and eventually a Whig.

BARBOUR, JOHN STRODE, JR. (*b. Culpeper Co., Va., 1820; d. 1892*), lawyer, financier. President of Orange and Alexandria Railroad, 1852–85. Revived Democratic party in Virginia, 1883–89, breaking control of William Mahone.

BARBOUR, OLIVER LORENZO (*b. Cambridge, N.Y., 1811; d. Saratoga Springs, N.Y., 1889*), lawyer. Nephew and confidential clerk of Reuben H. Walworth; a prolific writer on chancery and equity practice; editor of reports on N.Y. supreme court decisions, 1848–78.

BARBOUR, PHILIP PENDLETON (*b. Barboursville, Va.,* *1783; d. Orange Co., Va., 1841*), lawyer, statesman. Brother of James Barbour. Congressman from Virginia, Democrat, 1814–25; 1827–30. President, Virginia constitutional convention, 1829–30; counsel for the state in the case of *Cohens* v. *Virginia;* federal judge, 1830–36; supreme court justice, 1836–41. An uncompromising advocate of states' rights.

BARBOUR, THOMAS (*b. Martha's Vineyard, Mass., 1884; d. Boston, Mass., 1946*), naturalist, herpetologist, museum director. A.B., Harvard, 1906; Ph.D., 1910. Associated with the Harvard Museum of Comparative Zoology *post* 1910 (director, 1927–46), he rejuvenated it, improving the order of the collections, encouraging research by its staff, and extending its activities to include fieldwork in Florida and elsewhere. He interested himself also in development of the Atkins Garden in Cuba and the Barro Colorado tropical station in the Canal Zone. His own work lay mainly in systematic zoology, especially herpetology; a major contribution was his co-authorship of *A Check List of North American Amphibians and Reptiles* (1917).

BARCLAY, THOMAS (*b. New York, N.Y., 1753; d. New York, 1830*), Loyalist.

BARD, JOHN (*b. Burlington, N.J., 1716; d. Hyde Park, N.Y., 1799*), physician. Apprenticed in medicine to John Kearsly in Philadelphia and practiced there until 1746. At his friend Benjamin Franklin's urging, he moved then to New York where he built up a large practice; in 1759 he instituted a quarantine system for the port of New York, and as early as 1750 participated in the first recorded dissection of a body for the purpose of instructing medical students. He was chosen first president of the Medical Society of the State of New York, 1788.

BARD, SAMUEL (*b. Philadelphia, Pa., 1742; d. Hyde Park, N.Y., 1821*), physician. Son of John Bard. Graduated King's College (Columbia), 1760; studied medicine at London and took the M.D. degree at Edinburgh, 1765. Practiced in New York with his father, specializing in obstetrics on which he later (1807) wrote a textbook. A Loyalist during the Revolution, Bard practiced during the British occupation of New York but lost no credit thereby with the Americans. Owing in part to his efforts, New York Hospital was opened, 1791. In 1792, when the medical school in New York (in which he had taught theory and practice of medicine *post* 1768) was united with Columbia College, he became dean; in 1811 he was elected president of the original College of Physicians and Surgeons.

BARD, WILLIAM (*b. Philadelphia, Pa., 1778; d. Staten Island, N.Y., 1853*). Son of Samuel Bard; founded New York Life Insurance and Trust Co. (chartered 1830), the first firm to make life insurance a specialty.

BARDEEN, CHARLES WILLIAM (*b. Groton, Mass., 1847; d. Syracuse, N.Y., 1924*), publisher. Editor of the *School Bulletin,* 1874–1924.

BARDEN, GRAHAM ARTHUR (*b. Sampson County, N.C., 1896; d. New Bern, N.C., 1967*), attorney and U.S. Congressman. Law degree, University of North Carolina (1920). In the U.S. Congress (1934–61), he served as a member of the Rivers and Harbors, Education and Labor, and Library committees. Was instrumental in passing the Vocational Rehabilitation Act and the Vocational Education Act, and secured passage of the Library Service Act. Broke with the Roosevelt administration in 1944, thereafter generally voting with the right wing of the Republican party, opposing most administration bills. These included such social reform measures as fair employment practices and federal aid to education. In 1956 cosigned the "Southern Manifesto,"

which denounced the Supreme Court's 1954 school-desegregation decision.

BARKER, ALBERT SMITH (*b. Hanson, Mass., 1843; d. 1916*), naval officer. Graduated U.S. Naval Academy, 1863; promoted rear admiral, 1905, after holding many important commands.

BARKER, BENJAMIN FORDYCE (*b. Wilton, Maine, 1818; d. 1891*), physician. Graduated Bowdoin, 1837; M.D., Bowdoin, 1841; studied also at Paris. Came to New York in 1849 at suggestion of Willard Parker to take chair of obstetrics at New York Medical College; in 1861 obtained charter for the Bellevue Hospital Medical School, which he served as professor of obstetrics and gynecology until 1891. He is said to have introduced the use of the hypodermic syringe into American medicine.

BARKER, GEORGE FREDERICK (*b. Charlestown, Mass., 1835; d. 1910*), chemist, physicist. Graduated Yale, 1858. Professor of physics, University of Pennsylvania, 1873–1900; was also distinguished as a consultant, an editor of scientific periodicals, and an early writer on radioactivity.

BARKER, JACOB (*b. Swan Island, Maine, 1779; d. Philadelphia, Pa., 1871*), merchant, lawyer, financier. Barker's eventful career was marked by alternate successes and reverses on a grand scale; he is credited with providing financial support for the government in 1812–15.

BARKER, JAMES NELSON (*b. Philadelphia, Pa., 1784; d. Washington, D.C., 1858*), dramatist. His *The Indian Princess* (produced 1808) was the first acted play by an American on an Indian theme, the first to deal with Pocahontas, and the first to be acted in England after its American production. He served as comptroller of the treasury, 1838–41, and thereafter in various treasury posts.

BARKER, JAMES WILLIAM (*b. White Plains, N.Y., 1815; d. Rahway, N.J., 1869*), merchant. Active in New York and national politics; Know-Nothing party candidate for mayor of New York City, 1854.

BARKER, JEREMIAH (*b. Scituate, Mass., 1752; d. Gorham, Maine, 1835*), physician, medical theorist.

BARKER, JOSIAH (*b. Marshfield, Mass., 1763; d. Charlestown, Mass., 1847*), shipbuilder. Built the men-of-war *Virginia, Vermont,* and *Cumberland;* master carpenter on the *Independence;* rebuilt USS *Constitution,* 1834.

BARKER, WHARTON (*b. Philadelphia, Pa., 1846; d. 1921*), financier, publicist. Active in Philadelphia banking firms; presidential candidate of "middle of the road" Populists, 1900.

BARKLEY, ALBEN WILLIAM (*b. Lowes, Ky., 1877; d. Lexington, Va., 1956*), U.S. representative, senator, and vice president. Studied at Marvin College (B.A., 1897), Emory College (1897–98), and the University of Virginia Law School (Summer, 1902). After serving as a county judge in Kentucky, he was elected to the House of Representatives as a Democrat (1912–1923). A representative of the rural progressive wing of the Democratic party, Barkley was a supporter of Wilson and an ardent internationalist. A popular liberal orator, he was elected to the Senate in 1926, serving until 1948 and again from 1954 until his death. In the Senate, Barkley established himself as a prominent supporter of the New Deal. He was majority leader from 1937 until 1946, when he became minority leader. In the Senate, Barkley was known as a compromiser between the Congress and the White House, and though he was involved in all major pieces of legislation, no bills bore his name. In 1944, after some important differences with Roosevelt, he resigned as majority leader but was reelected immediately by fellow Democrats. Nominated to run with Harry S. Truman in 1948, he served until 1953 as vice president. An effective administration publicist and purveyor of goodwill, he was universally known as the "Veep," a term coined by his grandson. Reelected to the Senate in 1954, he served until his death.

BARKSDALE, WILLIAM (*b. Rutherford Co., Tenn., 1821; d. Gettysburg, Pa., 1863*), Confederate soldier. Congressman, Democrat, from Mississippi, 1853–61; appointed brigadier general, 1862; killed in action.

BARLOW, FRANCIS CHANNING (*b. Brooklyn, N.Y., 1834; d. New York, N.Y., 1896*), Union soldier. Held brigade commands at Antietam and Gettysburg; promoted major general, 1865. After the war practiced law and was effective as a reforming public official.

BARLOW, JOEL (*b. Redding, Conn., 1754; d. near Cracow, Poland, 1812*), poet, statesman. Graduated Yale, 1778. Versatile, ambitious, he early projected an epic on glories of America, served as chaplain of 4th Massachusetts brigade, helped edit a periodical, engaged in business, and joined with the "Hartford Wits" in writing the *Annarchiad* (1786–87). The first version of his epic appeared in 1787; entitled *The Vision of Columbus*, its stately, inflated couplets brought him immediate recognition. Admitted to the bar in 1786, he associated himself with the Scioto Company, a land speculation, and went to France in 1788 as the company's agent. His own inexperience and the dishonesty of several of his associates caused the firm to fail; from 1790 to 1792 he lived in London, supporting himself by his pen and becoming identified with the most advanced radical thinkers of the time. His political prose works belong to this period: *A Letter to the National Convention of France* (1792), *Advice to the Privileged Orders* (1792), and also the verse philippic *The Conspiracy of Kings* (1792). Proscribed by the British government, he went to Paris; by 1794, through speculation in French bonds, he was a rich man.

Returning to America in 1805, after a decade of activity abroad during which he served as American consul to Algiers, he settled on an estate named "Kalorama" near Washington, D.C. He published *The Columbiad* in 1807, a reworking of the epic theme of *The Vision of Columbus*; he also projected a great national institution for research and study of the arts and sciences. Appointed minister to France in 1811 by President Madison, he hoped to persuade Napoleon to give American commerce more generous treatment; after a year of diplomatic evasion he was informed that Napoleon would discuss terms of a treaty with him at Vilna, Poland. The French defeat in Russia ended all hopes of the conference and Barlow left Vilna for Paris. Taken seriously ill between Warsaw and Cracow, he died at the village of Zarnowiec. His epic efforts are rarely read; he is remembered best for a humorous poem, *Hasty Pudding*, written in 1793 and published in 1796.

BARLOW, JOHN WHITNEY (*b. Perry, N.Y., 1838; d. Jerusalem, 1914*), army engineer. Graduated West Point, 1861. Commanded engineer detachment on first government exploration of Yellowstone region, 1871, and on the Muscle Shoals project, 1886–90.

BARLOW, SAMUEL LATHAM MITCHILL (*b. Granville, Mass., 1826; d. Glen Cove, N.Y., 1889*), lawyer, bibliophile. Successful specialist in large corporation practice.

BARNABEE, HENRY CLAY (*b. Portsmouth, N.H., 1833; d. 1917*), actor, singer. Comedian, associated with light opera in Boston; starred in DeKoven's *Robin Hood* as the sheriff of Nottingham.

BARNARD, CHARLES (*b. Boston, Mass., 1838; d. Pasadena, Calif., 1920*), writer on gardening; minor playwright.

BARNARD, CHARLES FRANCIS (*b. Boston, Mass., 1808; d. Somerville, Mass., 1884*), Unitarian clergyman, philanthropist. Founder of Warren Street Chapel, Boston; devoted himself to care and education of waifs.

BARNARD, CHESTER IRVING (*b. Malden, Mass., 1886; d. New York, N.Y., 1961*), telephone executive and foundation trustee. President of the New Jersey Bell Telephone Company (1927–48). Wrote *The Functions of the Executive* (1938) and the less well-known *Organization and Management* (1948). Served on numerous civic and welfare boards at the local, state, and national levels. Received the Presidential Medal for Merit in 1946 for his work as president of the United Service Organizations for National Defense (1942–45) and his directorship of the National War Fund (1943–46). He was a representative on the United Nations Atomic Energy Committee after World War II.

BARNARD, DANIEL DEWEY (*b. Sheffield, Mass., 1796; d. Albany, N.Y., 1861*), lawyer. Congressman, Whig, from New York, 1827–29, 1839–45. Served as U.S. minister to Prussia, 1850–53.

BARNARD, EDWARD EMERSON (*b. Nashville, Tenn., 1857; d. 1923*), astronomer. Pioneer in astronomical photography.

BARNARD, FREDERICK AUGUSTUS PORTER (*b. Sheffield, Mass., 1809; d. New York, N.Y., 1889*), college president. Graduated Yale, 1828. Active in education in Alabama and Mississippi, 1837–61; president of Columbia University, 1864–89. Encouraged elective system of studies and from 1879 to his death urged the admission of women to the university on equal basis with men. Barnard College, a result of his efforts, was opened six months after his death.

BARNARD, GEORGE GREY (*b. Bellefonte, Pa., 1863; d. New York, N.Y., 1938*), sculptor. Studied at the Chicago Art Institute and the École des Beaux Arts in Paris. Exhibiting at the Beaux-Arts Salon in 1894, he won quick acclaim. Chief among his many important commissions were sculptures for the State Capitol, Harrisburg, Pa. His collection of Gothic and Romanesque sculpture formed the nucleus of the Metropolitan Museum's collection at The Cloisters in New York's Fort Tryon Park. Barnard usually carved his monumental realistic figures directly in stone, in contrast with many of his contemporaries who thought and worked only in clay.

BARNARD, HENRY (*b. Hartford, Conn., 1811; d. Hartford, 1900*), educator. Shares with Horace Mann the credit for stimulating and directing the movement for free public education. Graduated Yale, 1830. As secretary of Connecticut board of commissioners for education, 1838–42, he woke the state from its apathy but was legislated out of office. From 1843 until 1849, he revolutionized the public schools of Rhode Island. Returning to Connecticut in 1849 as superintendent of common schools, and also as principal of a normal school, he continued his work until 1855 when he resigned to undertake publication at his own expense of the *American Journal of Education* (1855–82), an encyclopedic survey of educational literature. His example in Connecticut and Rhode Island, and the information which he made available to those in charge of schools, have had a lasting effect on the American public school system.

BARNARD, JOHN (*b. Boston, Mass., 1681; d. Marblehead, Mass., 1770*), Congregational clergyman. Graduated Harvard, 1700. A mathematician and scholar, he was largely responsible for the prosperity of Marblehead, where he served as minister, 1716–70.

BARNARD, JOHN GROSS (*b. Sheffield, Mass., 1815; d. 1882*), Union soldier. Brother of F. A. P. Barnard; graduated West Point, 1833. Fortifications expert; engineer on major river and harbor improvements; chief engineer on defenses of Washington, D.C., in the Civil War; chief engineer on the staffs of generals McClellan and Grant.

BARNES, ALBERT (*b. Rome, N.Y., d. Philadelphia, Pa., 1870*), Presbyterian clergyman. A prominent figure in the division between the Old and New schools of American Presbyterianism, 1837.

BARNES, ALBERT COOMBS (*b. Philadelphia, Pa., 1872; d. Chester County, Pa., 1951*), art collector, pharmacologist. M.D., University of Pennsylvania, 1892. After practicing medicine in Philadelphia, his interests turned to pharmacology. In 1902 he founded a company to sell his invention of the antiseptic Argyrol. Barnes turned to art collecting and aesthetics while his firm made him rich. By 1915, he had published articles on aesthetics and had collected what is considered one of the world's finest collections of French nineteenth- and twentieth-century art. A friend and colleague of John Dewey, he founded the Barnes Foundation (1922), an institution for the study of art and aesthetics, with a twenty-six room gallery to house the collection. Dewey was named education director.

BARNES, CHARLES REID (*b. Madison, Ind., 1858; d. Chicago, Ill., 1910*), botanist. Taught at universities of Wisconsin and Chicago, 1887–1910; with J. M. Coulter and others, prepared textbooks stressing experimental and morphological method of botanical instruction.

BARNES, CHARLOTTE MARY SANFORD (*b. New York, N.Y., 1818; d. 1863*), actress. Author of *Octavia Bragaldi* (produced 1837), a romantic tragedy on the Beauchamp murder case in Kentucky, and other plays.

BARNES, JAMES (*b. Boston, Mass., 1801; d. Springfield, Mass., 1869*), Union soldier, engineer. Graduated West Point, 1829. Resigned commission, 1836, and became engineer and superintendent in railroad construction. Appointed colonel of 18th Massachusetts, 1861; held brigade and divisional commands; received brevet as major general, 1864.

BARNES, JOSEPH K. (*b. Philadelphia, Pa., 1817; d. Washington, D.C., 1833*), military surgeon. Served in Seminole, Mexican, and Civil wars; appointed surgeon general of the army, 1864. Attended both Lincoln and Garfield on their deathbeds.

BARNES, JULIUS HOWARD (*b. Little Rock, Ark., 1873; d. Duluth, Minn., 1959*), industrialist and government advisor. Self-educated, Barnes became president and owner of the Barnes-Ames Company (1910), one of the nation's largest exporters of wheat. During World War I, he served on the Food Administration under Herbert Hoover; after the war, he continued as president of the U.S. Grain Corporation which served as purchasing agent for the American Relief Administration. From 1929 to 1931, he headed President Hoover's National Business Survey Conference, attempting to restore confidence in the nation's economy. He was an ardent backer of the construction of the Saint Lawrence Seaway. President of the U.S. Chamber of Commerce, 1922–24, board of directors until 1931. Bad investments, philanthropies, and money spent in the seaway campaign had depleted his fortune to $52,000 at his death.

BARNES, MARY DOWNING SHELDON (*b. Oswego, N.Y., 1850; d. London, England, 1898*), educator. Daughter of Edward A. Sheldon. Graduated University of Michigan, 1874; taught at Wellesley and Stanford University.

BARNETT, GEORGE ERNEST (*b. Cambridge, Md., 1873; d. Baltimore, Md., 1938*), economist. Johns Hopkins University faculty, 1901–38; specialist in labor economics.

BARNEY, JOSHUA (*b. Baltimore Co., Md., 1759; d. Pittsburgh, Pa., 1818*), naval officer. Distinguished as navy and privateer captain, 1775–1815. In action between the *Hyder-Ally* and the British *General Monk*, 1782, he fought brilliantly; his management of his flotilla in defense of Washington, D.C., 1814, and his conduct at the battle of Bladensburg were outstanding events of the War of 1812.

BARNUM, FRANCES COURTENAY BAYLOR. *See* BAYLOR, FRANCES COURTENAY.

BARNUM, HENRY A. (*b. Jamesville, N.Y., 1833; d. New York, N.Y., 1892*), Union soldier. Commissioned colonel, 1862, after gallant action at Malvern Hill; brigadier general, 1865.

BARNUM, PHINEAS TAYLOR (*b. Bethel, Conn., 1810; d. Bridgeport, Conn., 1891*), showman. Celebrated for his practical exposition of the philosophy of humbug, Barnum made his first trial of public credulity in 1835 with Joice Heth, an ancient crone alleged to have been George Washington's nurse. His American Museum in New York was opened in 1842; along with legitimate curios and a menagerie, it featured a succession of ingenious and humorous shows including the woolly horse, the Feejee mermaid, the bearded lady, the "Egress," General Tom Thumb the dwarf, and many others. Barnum's genius for advertising and his acute measurement of how much the public would take brought him fame and fortune. On sheer nerve, he promoted Jenny Lind's concert tour in America (1850) into a financial and personal triumph. His last speculation, a circus billed as the "Greatest Show on Earth," opened in Brooklyn, N.Y., 1871. Ten years later, Barnum joined forces with the keenest of his competitors, and the circus was thereafter presented as Barnum and Bailey's. For years, one of its main attractions was the elephant Jumbo who was described by the master of publicity as "the only mastodon left on earth."

BARNUM, ZENUS (*b. near Wilkes-Barre, Pa., 1810; d. Baltimore, Md., 1865*), hotel-keeper, capitalist. Proprietor of Barnum's Hotel, Baltimore; a pioneer in the telegraph and railroad industries.

BARNWELL, JOHN (*b. Ireland, ca. 1671; d. 1724*), colonial agent. Immigrated to South Carolina, 1701; became a colonial official and led punitive expedition against the Tuscarora Indians, 1711–12.

BARNWELL, ROBERT WOODWARD (*b. near Beaufort, S.C., 1801; d. Columbia, S.C., 1882*), educator, statesman. Graduated Harvard, 1821. While congressman from South Carolina, 1829–33, signed the ordinance of nullification; was president of South Carolina College, 1835–41. During a six-month term in the U.S. Senate, 1850, as Calhoun's successor, he was an active but moderate defender of the Southern view; in 1861 he was temporary chairman of the Southern Congress in Montgomery and a signer of the Confederate constitution. Confederate senator from South Carolina, 1861–65, he served as chairman of the faculty, University of South Carolina, 1865–73.

BARR, AMELIA EDITH HUDDLESTON (*b. Ulverston, England, 1831; d. 1919*), author. Came to America, 1853, resided New York City *post* 1868. Among her eighty books, *A Bow of Orange Ribbon* (1886) is notable.

BARR, CHARLES (*b. Gourock, Scotland, 1864; d. Southampton, England, 1911*), sea captain. From 1884, when he came to America, until his death he was an outstanding skipper of racing yachts.

BARRADALL, EDWARD (*b. England, 1704; d. Williamsburg, Va., 1743*), lawyer. Attorney general of Virginia, 1737–43; wrote *Cases Adjudged in the General Court of Virginia from April 1733 to October 1741*, a valuable source.

BARRELL, JOSEPH (*b. New Providence, N.J., 1869; d. 1919*), geologist, engineer. Professor of geology, Yale, 1903–19. His investigations of magmatic stoping, in connection with a Montana mine, resulted in a classic paper in the literature covering igneous intrusions. Regional geology, evolution, genesis of the earth, and especially isostasy (the problem of the stability of the earth's crust under changing conditions of erosion and sedimentation) were all subjects of papers published by Barrell. Of equal importance and magnitude were his writings on rhythms in geological processes and measurements of geological time.

BARRÈRE, GEORGES (*b. Bordeaux, France, 1876; d. Kingston, N.Y., 1944*), musician. Raised in Paris. Studied at the Conservatoire de Musique, specializing in flute; won first prize, 1895. After army service, gave private lessons and played with Schola Cantorum, the Colonne Orchestra, and at the Paris opera. Invited by Walter Damrosch to be first flute in the New York Symphony Orchestra, 1905, he remained with it (except for the season of 1918) until its merger with the New York Philharmonic (1928), and then continued with that organization. He taught at the Institute of Musical Art (New York), 1905–30, and thereafter at the Juilliard School. In addition to his orchestral and teaching duties, he founded several chamber music groups; in 1914, one of these was expanded into the Barrère Little Symphony, which, like the earlier chamber music ensembles, toured the United States with great success.

BARRETT, ALBERT MOORE (*b. Austin, Ill., 1871; d. Ann Arbor, Mich., 1936*), psychiatrist, neuropathologist. First director, Michigan State Psychopathic Hospital, 1906–36; professor of psychiatry, University of Michigan, 1907–36.

BARRETT, BENJAMIN FISKE (*b. Dresden, Maine, 1808; d. Philadelphia, Pa., 1892*), preacher and writer of the New Church. Held ministries in New York City, Cincinnati, and Philadelphia; a founder of the Swedenborg Publishing Association.

BARRETT, CHARLES SIMON (*b. Pike Co., Ga., 1866; d. Union City, Ga., 1935*), president of the Farmers' Union, 1906–28.

BARRETT, FRANK ALOYSIUS (*b. near Omaha, Nebr., 1892; d. Cheyenne, Wyo., 1962*), Wyoming congressman, governor, and U.S. senator. After establishing a thriving legal practice in Lusk, Wyo., he held a variety of civic and political positions in the state. A Republican, he was elected to the House of Representatives in 1942 and served for eight years there as a leader of western interests, demanding greater local control over grazing and mineral rights on the public domain. A conservative, he voted in favor of the Taft-Hartley Act and supported the House Un-American Activities Committee and the Mundt-Nixon Communist-control bill of 1948. Became governor of Wyoming in 1950 and served as U.S. senator from 1952 until 1958; in this capacity, he again reflected the West's hunger for economic development, frequently through federal stimulation, and simultaneously its hostility to federal control and regulation.

BARRETT, GEORGE HORTON (*b. Exeter, England, 1794; d. New York, N.Y., 1860*), actor, theater manager.

BARRETT, JANIE PORTER (*b. Athens, Ga., 1865; d. Hampton, Va., 1948*), social worker, educator. Graduated Hampton Institute, 1884. Taught at a Georgia rural school for two terms, at Hampton Institute (1886–87), and at Haines Normal and Industrial School (Augusta). Married Harris Barrett in 1889 and settled in Hampton, Va. Soon began informal day care center for children in her neighborhood, and at her own expense founded the Locust Street Social Settlement, the first of its kind for blacks. Girls were taught domestic arts; mothers were taught child care; health clubs, reading clubs, and classes in sewing, flower raising, homemaking, poultry raising, all contributed to improvement in personal and community life. In this work, she received aid from students and staff at Hampton Institute, and from white philanthropists. She also gave vigorous support to the juvenile court movement. A prime mover in organizing the Virginia State Federation of Colored Womens's Clubs (1908), she mobilized its forces to finance an industrial home school for delinquent girls, which opened at Peake, Va., in 1915. Conducted on humane and sensible lines under her direction, 1915–40, the school was rated among the best of its kind in the United States.

BARRETT, JOHN (*b. Grafton, Vt., 1866; d. Bellows Falls, Vt., 1938*), diplomat, publicist. Director general of the Pan-American Union, 1907–20.

BARRETT, KATE WALLER (*b. Clifton, Va., 1858; d. Alexandria, Va., 1925*), philanthropic worker. Identified with the National Florence Crittenton Mission for wayward girls; vice president and general superintendent in 1897; president, 1909–25.

BARRETT, LAWRENCE (*b. Paterson, N.J., 1838; d. New York, N.Y., 1891*), actor. After touring in supporting roles, 1853–57, he played briefly in New York with Edwin Booth who was henceforward to be his friend and frequent professional associate; during 1858–60 he played with several Boston companies. Save for war service, 1861–62, all his study and energies were devoted to the stage; he was a player and a manager in New York, Philadelphia, New Orleans, Cincinnati, and San Francisco. He is remembered today especially for his roles in support of Booth, and in particular "Cassius" in *Julius Caesar*. His energy, capacity for study, and diligence won him high place among actors of the 19th century.

BARRINGER, DANIEL MOREAU (*b. near Concord, N.C., 1896; d. White Sulphur Springs, W.Va., 1873*), lawyer, diplomat. Congressman, Whig, from North Carolina, 1843–49; minister to Spain, 1849–53.

BARRINGER, RUFUS (*b. near Concord, N.C., 1821; d. 1895*), lawyer, Confederate soldier. An able cavalry officer; appointed brigadier general, 1864. Brother of Daniel M. Barringer.

BARRON, CLARENCE WALKER (*b. Boston, Mass., 1855; d. 1928*), financial editor. Founder of *Barron's*, president of Dow, Jones & Co.

BARRON, JAMES (*b. 1768; d. Norfolk, Va., 1851*), naval officer. Commissioned lieutenant, U.S. Navy, 1798; captain, 1799. Commanded the *Essex* and the *President*, and was active in Mediterranean operations until 1805. In 1807, as commodore aboard the ill-prepared *Chesapeake* he bore the brunt of blame for her disgrace in an engagement with H.M.S. *Leopard* and was sentenced by court-martial to suspension without pay for five years. Restored to duty in 1813, he was refused active service at sea; convinced that he was victim of a plot of fellow officers he challenged and killed Stephen Decatur in a duel, 1820.

BARRON, SAMUEL d *b. Hampton, Va., 1809; d. 1888*), Confederate naval officer. Captain in the Confederate States

Navy; took a leading part in distribution of ordnance, organization of coastal defense, and procurement of commerce raiders abroad.

BARROW, EDWARD GRANT (*b. Springfield, Ill., 1868; d. Rye, N.Y., 1953*), baseball executive. Managed the Boston Red Sox, 1917–19, where he converted Babe Ruth from a star pitcher into a slugging outfielder. In 1921, he followed Ruth to the New York Yankees, as general manager of the team un 1945; as president, 1939–45; and chairman of the board, 1945–47. He was elected to the National Baseball Hall of Fame in 1953.

BARROW, WASHINGTON (*b. Davidson Co., Tenn., 1817; d. St. Louis, Mo., 1866*). Whig politician; editor of Nashville *Republican Banner, post* 1844.

BARROWS, ALICE PRENTICE (*b. Lowell, Mass., 1877; d. New York, 1954*), teacher and school building specialist. Graduated Vassar, 1900, and studied at Columbia University. After teaching briefly at Vassar and working in the educational field in New York City, Barrows joined the U.S. Office of Education as a specialist in school buildings, become an innovator in the field of education environments.

BARROWS, DAVID PRESCOTT (*b. Ravenswood, Ill., 1873; d. Orinda, Calif., 1954*), anthropologist, political scientist, university president, and journalist. Studied at Pomona College, University of California, Columbia University, and the University of Chicago (Ph.D., 1897). Barrows was superintendent and later director of schools under the American colonial government in the Philippines (1900–09). Returning to the U.S., he taught at Berkeley until World War I. In 1916, he worked with Herbert Hoover for Belgian Relief. From 1919 to 1923, he was president of the University of California, but resigned over differences with the regents. Later joined the political science department (1924–43). During World War II, he was active in the relocation of Japanese Americans in California. A right-wing Republican, Barrows worked as a radio commentator (1943–44) and then as a columnist for the International News Service. He accused Roosevelt of "appeasement," considered Truman a "disaster," and charged the State Department with being "sympathetic to the communist movement" in China.

BARROWS, JOHN HENRY (*b. near Medina, Mich., 1847; d. 1902*), Congregational clergyman. Supervised "Parliament of Religious" at World's Columbian Exposition, 1893; president, Oberlin College, 1898–1902.

BARROWS, SAMUEL JUNE (*b. New York, N.Y., 1845; d. 1909*), Unitarian clergyman, prison reformer. Secured passage of New York's first probation law; largely instrumental in enactment of the federal parole law; editor, the *Christian Register*, 1880–96.

BARRY, JOHN (*b. Tacumshane, Ireland, 1745; d. 1803*), naval officer. Settled in Philadelphia, Pa., 1760. The *Lexington*, under his command in 1776, was the first regularly commissioned American cruiser to capture a British warship; he later commanded the *Effingham*, the *Raleigh*, and, in 1781–82, the *Alliance*. He was named senior captain in 1794 and given command of the *United States*; four years later he took charge of all naval forces in West Indian waters. After escorting the American envoys to France in 1799, he commanded the Guadeloupe station, 1799–1801. He died at the head of the navy.

BARRY, JOHN STEWART (*b. Amherst, N.H., 1802; d. Constantine, Mich., 1870*), governor of Michigan, Democrat, 1842–46, 1849–51. Stabilized state finances after collapse of the 1835–41 boom in finance and internal improvements.

BARRY, PATRICK (*b. near Belfast, Ireland, 1816; d. Rochester, N.Y., 1890*), horticulturist. Pioneer fruit-grower in western New York; wrote (1851) *The Fruit Garden* (later called *Barry's Fruit Garden*).

BARRY, PHILIP JAMES QUINN (*b. Rochester, N.Y., 1896; d. New York, N.Y., 1949*), playwright. Graduated Yale, 1919, after World War I service with State Department; attended G. P. Baker's "47 Workshop" at Harvard. Although distinguished as a writer of high comedy, he continued throughout his career to experiment, exhibiting a sense of the ultimate sadness of life and the endless assault of evil upon good. Work ranged through almost every form of drama from farce through fantasy and satire to tragedy and included *You and I* (1923) and *The Youngest* (1924), both comedies of character; *White Wings* (1926), a satirical fantasy; *Paris Bound* (1927) and *Holiday* (1928), comedies; *Hotel Universe* (1930), a poetic fantasy; *Tomorrow and Tomorrow* (1931), a serious drama; *The Animal Kingdom* (1932), a comedy; *Here Come the Clowns* (1938), a serious drama of good and evil; and *The Philadelphia Story* (1939), a high comedy and Barry's biggest hit. During the 1940's, he wrote three plays reflecting his concern with the war then in progress. His final play, *Second Threshold*, was completed by Robert E. Sherwood from a first draft.

BARRY, WILLIAM FARQUHAR (*b. New York, N.Y., 1818; d. Fort McHenry, Md., 1879*), Union soldier. Graduated West Point, 1838. Chief of artillery, Army of the Potomac; also on Grant's and Sherman's staffs in the same capacity.

BARRY, WILLIAM TAYLOR (*b. Lunenburg, Va., 1785; d. Liverpool, England, 1835*), lawyer, statesman. From early boyhood a resident of Lexington, Ky., Barry became a leader in the Democratic party in that state. Elected lieutenant-governor in 1821, he supported the "relief" measures instituted to rescue the people from the effects of bank failures and general depression that had followed the prosperity and speculative optimism of the years 1815–19. His support of Andrew Jackson in 1828 won him appointment as postmaster general; in 1834–35, he denounced a congressional investigation of his department as a piece of partisan spite and resigned. Jackson immediately appointed him minister to Spain, but he died on his way to his post.

BARRY, WILLIAM TAYLOR SULLIVAN (*b. Columbus, Miss., 1821; d. Columbus, 1868*), Confederate statesman and soldier. A leader in the disunionist wing of the Democratic party in Mississippi; member of the Confederate Congress, 1861–62; colonel, 35th Mississippi Infantry, 1862–65.

BARRYMORE, ETHEL (*b. Philadelphia, Pa., 1879; d. Hollywood, Calif., 1959*), actress. A member of the Barrymore acting dynasty, Ethel Barrymore began acting in 1894 and gave her last performance in 1956 in the film *Johnny Trouble*. Her first leading role in New York was in Clyde Fitch's *Captain Jinks of the Horse Marines* (1901). Other roles included Nora in Ibsen's *A Doll's House* (1905), the leads in Maugham's *Lady Frederick* (1908) and *The Constant Wife* (1926), and Gerhart Hauptmann's *Rose Bernd* (1922). Films include *The Corn Is Green* (1940); *None but the Lonely Heart* (1944), for which she won the Academy Award; *Portrait of Jennie* (1949); *Pinky* (1949); *Kind Lady* (1951); and *Young at Heart* (1954). Famous for her rich, vibrant voice and classical beauty, Barrymore retained both throughout her career.

BARRYMORE, GEORGIANA EMMA DREW (*b. 1856; d. Santa Barbara, Calif., 1893*), actress. Daughter of John Drew (1827–1862) and Louisa Lane Drew. Distinguished in light witty roles; mother of Ethel, Lionel, and John Barrymore.

BARRYMORE, JOHN (*b. Philadelphia, Pa., 1882; d. Hollywood, Calif., 1942*), actor. Son of Maurice and Georgiana Barrymore; brother of Ethel and Lionel Barrymore. Heir to an acting heritage that reached back four generations, he received a bizarre formal education which included art study in London and New York. His principal talent during adolescence appeared to be for bohemian antics and semi-serious scrapes. Turning to the theater, he made his first professional appearance in Chicago, Oct. 31, 1903, playing Max in Sudermann's *Magda*. Two months later, he made his New York debut in Clyde Fitch's *Glad of It*. On tour for several years with William Collier in *The Dictator*, he learned his craft thoroughly. After playing the title role in *The Fortune Hunter* (opening in New York, Sept. 4, 1909), he became over the next five years the idol of feminine theatergoers. Influenced by his friend Edward Sheldon, he sought for roles of more depth; after playing with success William Falder in Galsworthy's *Justice* (1916), he gave a hint of his great abilities in *Peter Ibbetson* (1917). After success in widely differing character roles in Tolstoy's *Redemption* (1918) and *The Jest* (1919), he reached the fullness of art in the 1920 production at New York's Plymouth Theater of Shakespeare's *Richard III*. After twenty-seven performances, he collapsed from exhaustion. He gave his most memorable performance in *Hamlet*, which opened in New York on Nov. 16, 1922. Impatient with the repetition of the role, he closed the play in February 1923. Revived *Hamlet* again in New York that November and took the production briefly on tour. In the spring of 1925, he played Hamlet in London to great success.

Meanwhile, he had established himself as a motion-picture star. He had first appeared in *The Dictator* in 1912, and over the next nine years had made fourteen pictures. Only *Dr. Jekyll and Mr. Hyde* (1920) was worthy of his abilities. With *The Sea Beast* and *Don Juan* (both 1926), "the great profile," as he became known, began to be paid huge sums for his work and the same homage that he had received as a theater matinee idol. Talking films ruined many careers but enhanced Barrymore's. By the time he joined his brother Lionel at the Metro-Goldwyn-Mayer studios in 1932, he was receiving $150,000 a picture. His most memorable films date from this period: *Grand Hotel* (1932), *Rasputin and the Empress* (1932), *Reunion in Vienna* (1933), *Dinner at Eight* (1933), and *Topaze* (1933). The Barrymore legend grew while his health declined. Living on a lavish scale, he became more and more subject to fits of anger and depression over his personal life which led him to excessive drinking. In the fall of 1933, he experienced for the first time a lapse of memory which seemed to him anticipatory of the fate of his father who had had such a symptom before his mental breakdown and death. Although ill and despondent, he made one of his finest appearances in *Twentieth Century* (1934). Thereafter the trail ran steadily down. Deep in debt, he made movies and did radio work to avoid bankruptcy. He toured in a trivial comedy, *My Dear Children* (1939), in which his inability to remember his lines was compensated by extemporized clowning.

Barrymore was married four times: to Katherine Harris in 1910; to Blanche Oelrichs Thomas (Michael Strange) in 1920; to Dolores Costello in 1928; and to Elaine Barrie in 1936.

BARRYMORE, LIONEL (*b. Philadelphia, Pa., 1878; d. Van Nuys, Calif., 1954*), actor. Member of the famous Barrymore family of actors, Lionel was most successful in character parts. From 1909 to 1912, he worked in silent films with W. D. Griffith and the Metro Film company in Hollywood. He nevertheless continued to work on the stage, excelling in *Peter Ibbetson*, *The Copperhead*, and *The Jest*. In 1925 he left the theater for good. Major films include *Mata Hari*, *Grand Hotel*, *Dinner at Eight*, *Treasure Island*, *David Copperfield*, *Ah! Wilderness*, and *Captains Courageous*. Barrymore also played Dr. Gillespie in the *Dr. Kildare* series and was an amateur composer, artist, and novelist. In 1931, he won an Academy Award for his performance in *A Free Soul*. Barrymore was also a famous radio personality, as "The Mayor of the Town" and as Scrooge in Dickens' *A Christmas Carol*, which he repeated every Christmas for twenty years.

BARRYMORE, MAURICE (*b. Fort Agra, India, 1847; d. 1905*), actor. Born Herbert Blythe, he chose Barrymore as a professional name when he went on the stage in 1872; came to America three years later. Notable in supporting roles with such actors as Jefferson, Fanny Davenport, Modjeska, and Mrs. Fiske, his many attempts to star by himself were unsuccessful. He married Georgiana Drew, 1876.

BARSOTTI, CHARLES (*b. Bagni di San Giuliano, Italy, 1850; d. Coytesville, N.J., 1927*), publisher. Came to America, 1872. Founded *Il Progresso* (New York, 1880), first Italian daily newspaper in the United States.

BARSTOW, WILLIAM AUGUSTUS (*b. Connecticut, 1813; d. 1865*), politician. Settled in Wisconsin, 1839; Democratic governor of Wisconsin, 1853–56; later engaged in banking, milling, and railroad development.

BARTH, CARL GEORG LANGE (*b. Christiania [Oslo], Norway, 1860; d. Philadelphia, Pa., 1939*), mechanical engineer. Pioneer (with Frederick W. Taylor) of scientific management for industry.

BARTHELMESS, RICHARD (*b. New York, N.Y., 1895; d. Southampton, N.Y., 1963*), motion picture actor. During three decades in motion pictures, he appeared in seventy-six films. His career was launched with *Broken Blossoms* (1919), in which he starred with Lillian Gish. Formed Inspiration Pictures in the early 1920's but terminated his financial interest in the company in 1926 in order to accept a three-film-per-year contract with First National Pictures (now Warner Brothers). Was one of the founders of the Academy of Motion Picture Arts and Sciences. His first talkie was *Weary River* (1929), and his last motion picture performance was in *The Spoilers* (1942).

BARTHOLDT, RICHARD (*b. Schleiz, Germany, 1855; d. St. Louis, Mo., 1932*). Came to America, 1872. Editor of *St. Louis Tribune*; congressman, Republican, from Missouri, 1892–1915. Took a leading part in all peace movements before the outbreak of World War I.

BARTHOLOMEW, EDWARD SHEFFIELD (*b. Colchester, Conn., 1822; d. Naples, Italy, 1858*), sculptor in neo-classic style.

BARTHOLOW, ROBERTS (*b. New Windsor, Md., 1831; d. Philadelphia, Pa., 1904*), physician. Army surgeon, 1855–64; thereafter taught and practiced in Cincinnati and Philadelphia. A voluminous writer on medical subjects.

BARTLETT, EDWARD LEWIS ("BOB") (*b. Seattle, Wash., 1904; d. Cleveland, Ohio, 1968*), U.S. Senator. Grew up in Fairbanks, Alaska. As Alaska's delegate to the U.S. Congress (1945–59), lobbied effectively to obtain federal monies for the territory and labored tirelessly to gain statehood for Alaska. When Alaska became a state in 1959, became senior senator from Alaska (reelected 1960 and 1966). Was a loyal Democrat who largely supported the programs of Presidents Kennedy and Johnson. As a member of the Senate Commerce Committee, advocated federal appropriations for the fishing and maritime industries. Was largely responsible for the passage of the Radiation Control for Health and Safety Act (1968). Was one of the first senators to call for a negotiated settlement in Vietnam.

BARTLETT, ELISHA (*b. Smithfield, R.I., 1804; d. Smithfield, 1855*), physician. Taught medicine, 1832–55, at Berkshire Medical Institution, Transylvania University, Maryland, New York University, Louisville, and College of Physicians and Surgeons (New York). Author of *The Fevers in the United States* (1842) and a classic *Essay on the Philosophy of Medicine* (1844).

BARTLETT, FRANCIS ALONZO (*b. Belchertown, Mass., 1882; d. Stamford, Conn., 1963*), tree-care expert. Founded the Bartlett Shade Tree Experts Company, started the Bartlett School of Tree Surgery, formed the Barlett Tree Research Laboratories, and initiated the National Shade Tree Conference, later renamed the International Shade Tree Conference. Conducted important research into shade trees, attempted to educate the public about caring for shade trees, was instrumental in saving the chestnut tree from extinction in the United States, and helped to slow down the transmission of the Dutch elm disease.

BARTLETT, HOMER NEWTON (*b. Olive, N.Y., 1845; d. Hoboken, N.J., 1920*), musical composer. Organist at several New York churches, 1862–1912; wrote 269 compositions including "Grand Polka de Concert" (1867).

BARTLETT, ICHABOD (*b. Salisbury, N.H., 1786; d. Portsmouth, N.H., 1853*), lawyer, politician. One of counsel in Dartmouth College Case, 1817; a leader of the New Hampshire bar; congressman, National Republican, from New Hampshire, 1822–29.

BARTLETT, JOHN (*b. Plymouth, Mass., 1820; d. Cambridge, Mass., 1905*), editor, publisher. Partner in Little, Brown & Co.; edited *Familiar Quotations* (first ed., 1855).

BARTLETT, JOHN RUSSELL (*b. Providence, R.I., 1805; d. Providence, 1886*), bibliographer, author. A New York bookseller, 1836–50, active in the New-York Historical Society; served as U.S. commissioner to run boundary line between Texas and Mexico, 1850–53; secretary of state of Rhode Island, 1855–72. Was associated with John Carter Brown in building his American library at Providence, 1856–86. Author of *Dictionary of Americanisms* (1848); *Personal Narrative of Explorations . . . with United States and Mexican Boundary Commission* (1854). Edited *Records of the Colony of Rhode Island: 1636–1792* and the *John Carter Brown Catalogue* (1865–82), a pioneer descriptive bibliography.

BARTLETT, JOHN SHERREN (*b. Dorsetshire, England, 1790; d. 1863*), physician, journalist. Established the *Albion* (New York, 1822–48), a newspaper for British residents of the United States.

BARTLETT, JOSEPH (*b. Plymouth, Mass., 1762; d. 1827*), lawyer, politician, eccentric. Graduated Harvard, 1782. Practiced law in Massachusetts, Maine, and New Hampshire. Author of a remarkable volume of original aphorisms (Portsmouth, N.H., 1810).

BARTLETT, JOSIAH (*b. Amesbury, Mass., 1729; d. Kingston, N.H., 1795*), physician. Signer of the Declaration of Independence from New Hampshire; member of Continental Congress, 1774; 1775–76; 1778–79; chief justice, New Hampshire court of common pleas, 1779–82. Justice, state superior court, 1782–88; chief justice, 1788–90. President (governor) of New Hampshire, 1790–92; first governor, 1793–94.

BARTLETT, PAUL WAYLAND (*b. New Haven, Conn., 1865; d. Paris, France, 1925*), sculptor. Studied in Paris. Won early recognition for studies of animals; his later work featured romantic portrait statues of heroic size and concept, also allegorical subjects. Best known for the bronze Columbus and the Michelangelo in the Library of Congress, the sculptures on the pediment of the House wing of the Capitol, Washington, D.C., and the bronze equestrian Lafayette in the court of the Louvre, Paris.

BARTLETT, SAMUEL COLCORD (*b. Salisbury, N.H., 1817; d. Hanover, N.H., 1898*), Congregational clergyman. Professor of biblical literature, Chicago Theological Seminary, 1858–77; president, Dartmouth College, 1877–92.

BARTLETT, WILLIAM (*b. Newburyport, Mass., 1748; d. Newburyport, 1841*), merchant. Generous benefactor of Andover Theological Seminary.

BARTLETT, WILLIAM HOLMES CHAMBERS (*b. Lancaster Co., Pa., 1804; d. Yonkers, N.Y., 1893*), mathematician. Best known for his *Elements of Analytical Mechanics* (1853), the first work of its kind published in the United States.

BARTLEY, MORDECAI (*b. Fayette Co., Pa., 1783; d. Mansfield, Ohio, 1870*), farmer, merchant. Settled in Ohio, 1809. As congressman, National Republican, from Ohio, 1823–31, was first to propose use of land grants in that state for support of public schools. Served as Whig governor, 1844–46.

BARTOL, CYRUS AUGUSTUS (*b. Freeport, Maine, 1813; d. Boston, Mass., 1900*), Unitarian clergyman. Pastor, West Church, Boston, 1837–89; pastor emeritus until death. A follower of Ralph Waldo Emerson.

BARTON, BENJAMIN SMITH (*b. Lancaster, Pa., 1766; d. Philadelphia, Pa., 1815*), physician, naturalist. Studied at Edinburgh, London, and Göttingen (M.D., 1789); practiced in Philadelphia, and taught at University of Pennsylvania, 1791–1815. Author of *Collections for an Essay Towards a Materia Medica of the United States* (1798, 1804) and *Elements of Botany* (1803), the first textbook on botany written by an American.

BARTON, BRUCE FAIRCHILD (*b. Robbins, Tenn., 1886; d. New York, N.Y., 1967*), advertising executive, author, and U.S. Congressman. Wrote sunny, uplifting essays for magazines, collected in *More Power to You* (1917), *It's a Good Old World* (1920), *Better Days,* (1927), and *On the Up and Up* (1929). His *The Man Nobody Knows* (1925), in which he portrayed Jesus Christ as the first great businessman, was a huge success. In 1928, with Roy Durstine, Alex Osborn, and George Batten, formed Batten, Barton, Durstine, and Osborn, later one of the largest advertising agencies in the U.S. Among his advertising successes was the creation of the character Betty Crocker. Ran successfully for Congress in 1936, and for two terms represented Manhattan's affluent "silk-stocking district." A conservative Republican, he staunchly opposed the New Deal and Roosevelt.

BARTON, CLARA (*b. Oxford, Mass., 1821; d. Glen Echo, near Washington, D.C., 1912*), organizer of the American Red Cross. As a successful schoolteacher, 1836–54, she displayed her basic characteristics of quick, practical response to an immediate need, delight in difficulties, aggressive independence, and extraordinary nervous energy. While working in the Patent Office, Washington, D.C., 1861, she met the tragic lack of supplies for the Civil War wounded by organizing a distributing agency for contributions to the soldiers' welfare and by personally delivering what was needed at the very point of action; she later acted as superintendent of nurses with the Army of the James, and for four years after the war superintended a search for missing soldiers. Abroad for her health in 1869–70, she distributed relief in Strasbourg, Paris, Lyons, and other cities in association with the International Red Cross of Geneva (consequent on the Franco-Prussian War); she returned to America, 1873. In 1877, approved by the authorities at Geneva, she revived an earlier effort to associate the United States with the International Red Cross; in 1881 the National Society of the Red Cross was organized and incorporated, with Clara Barton as president; in 1882, the U.S. Senate approved adoption of the Geneva Convention as a result of her continuous effort and pressure.

From 1882 to 1904, Clara Barton directed the activities of the American Red Cross; the founder's refusal to delegate responsibility, however, and her proneness to arbitrary action resulted in a loss of public confidence. In 1900 the society was reincorporated with a new charter, but continuing dissensions over the founder's policies ended in 1904 with a investigation by a special committee. No report was ever presented by the committee, but Clara Barton resigned in June 1904, and the society was completely reorganized.

BARTON, DAVID (*b. near Greenville, Tenn., 1783; d. near Boonville, Mo., 1837*), statesman. First U.S. senator from Missouri, 1821–31; foe of Thomas Hart Benton, and center of violent political battles.

BARTON, GEORGE AARON (*b. East Farnham, Quebec, Canada, 1859; d. Weston, Mass., 1942*), orientalist, biblical scholar. Graduated Haverford College, 1882. Born of Quaker parents; joined the Episcopal Church and was ordained to the priesthood, 1919. After a trial of business and teaching, began graduate study at Harvard in 1889; received the first Ph.D. awarded by Harvard in Semitics, 1891. Professor of biblical literature and Semitic languages, Bryn Mawr, 1891–1922; professor of Semitic languages and history of religion, University of Pennsylvania, 1922–32. Taught also at the Divinity School of the Protestant Episcopal Church in Philadelphia, and was director of the American School of Oriental Research in Baghdad. His major contribution to scholarly literature was *A Sketch of Semitic Origins* (1902), which he replaced with an entirely new work, *Semitic and Hamitic Origins* (1934). He was author also of *Archaeology and the Bible* (1916), of the commentary on Ecclesiastes (1908) in the International Critical Commentary series, and of a number of popular and semipopular works on religious subjects.

BARTON, JAMES EDWARD (*b. Gloucester, N.Y., 1890; d. Mineola, N.Y., 1962*), comedian, dancer, and singer. Began his career at the age of two and worked in stock companies and vaudeville shows as a young man. Achieved acclaim for his dancing in *The Passing Show of 1919* (1919), and over the next fifteen years became known as a top hoofer on the stage. Turning to acting in 1934, he achieved acclaim for his performance in the role of Jeeter Lester in the play *Tobacco Road*. Over the next five years he performed that role 1,899 times, and his success with the play led to motion picture contracts. For the remainder of his career he alternated between stage and screen, and his last screen appearance was in *The Misfits* (1961).

BARTON, JAMES LEVI (*b. Charlotte, Vt., 1855; d. Brookline, Mass., 1936*), Congregational clergyman. Missionary at Harpoot, Turkey, 1885–94; foreign secretary of American Board of Commissioners for Foreign Missions, 1894–1927.

BARTON, JOHN RHEA (*b. Lancaster, Pa., 1794; d. Philadelphia, Pa., 1871*), surgeon. Nephew of Benjamin S. Barton. Pioneer in orthopedic procedures; deviser of "Barton's bandage" for jaw fractures.

BARTON, ROBERT THOMAS (*b. Winchester, Va., 1842; d. 1917*), lawyer. Authority on Chancery practice; editor, *Virginia Colonial Decisions . . . General Court of Virginia, 1728–1741* (1909).

BARTON, SETH MAXWELL (*b. Fredericksburg, Va., 1829; d. Washington, D.C., 1900*), Confederate soldier. Graduated West Point, 1849. Acted as Jackson's chief engineer, 1861–62; relieved of brigade command on charges, 1864, but restored that same year.

BARTON, THOMAS PENNANT (*b. Philadelphia. Pa., 1803; d. 1869*), bibliophile. Son of Benjamin S. Barton; son-in-law of Edward Livingston. His notable collection of rare books went to Boston Public Library.

BARTON, WILLIAM (*b. Warren, R.I., 1748; d. Providence, R.I., 1831*), Revolutionary soldier. Made daring capture of British General Prescott at Rhode Island, July 1777.

BARTON, WILLIAM ELEAZAR (*b. Sublette, Ill., 1861; d. Brooklyn, N.Y., 1930*), Congregationalist clergyman of wide influence; author of many books about Abraham Lincoln.

BARTON, WILLIAM PAUL CRILLON (*b. Philadelphia, Pa., 1786; d. Philadelphia, 1856*), botanist, surgeon. Nephew of Benjamin S. Barton whom he succeeded as professor of botany, University of Pennsylvania, 1815. Appointed U.S. Navy surgeon, 1809; first chief of Navy Bureau of Medicine and Surgery, 1842–44. Author of *Vegetable Materia Medica of the United States* (1817–19) and other works.

BARTRAM, JOHB (*b. Marple, Pa., 1699; d. 1777*), first native American botanist. His early interest in plants was encouraged probably by James Logan (1674–1751); in 1728 he laid out a botanic garden on land he had bought at Kingsessing on the Schuylkill and began what were probably the first hybridizing experiments in America. He began a correspondence and exchange of specimens with Peter Collinson, the English plantsman, *ca.* 1733; through Collinson, Bartram's American plants were distributed abroad and he became internationally celebrated. Linnaeus called him the greatest "natural botanist" then in the world. Bartram made many journeys at his own expense to the frontiers in order to gather seeds and bulbs for transplanting: in 1738 to western Virginia and the Blue Ridge, in 1755 through the Catskills, in 1760 to the Carolinas. In 1765, as Royal Botanist, he journeyed from Charleston, S.C., to St. Augustine, Fla., and explored the St. John's River by canoe; on this trip he observed all forms of life, examined mineral resources, and prepared a map of the river.

Bartram's ideas were anticipatory of modern thinking, particularly in geology. His suggestion of a great survey trip westward, made to Benjamin Franklin, bears strong resemblance to Jefferson's later instructions given to Lewis and Clark. His botanic garden, enlarged by his son William, still survives as part of Philadelphia's park system.

He was author of *Observations on the Inhabitants, Climate, Soil, etc. . . . made by John Bartram in his travels from Pensilvania to Lake Ontario* (1751); his explorations in Georgia and Florida are in Stork's *Description of East Florida, with a Journal by John Bartram* (London, 1769).

BARTRAM, WILLIAM (*b. Kingsessing, [now Philadelphia], Pa., 1739; d. Kingsessing, 1823*), traveler and naturalist. Son of John Bartram, whom he accompanied on Florida journey, 1765–66. On behalf of British botanist John Fothergill, William Bartram explored southeastern part of what is now United States, 1773–77, sending his patron colored botanical drawings, journals, seeds, and specimens. Subsequent to his father's death in 1777, he became a partner in the family botanic garden with his brother John. His *Travels through North and South Carolina, Georgia, East and West Florida, the Cherokee Country, etc.* (Philadelphia, 1791) is the chief cause of his fame; a literary as well as a scientific triumph, it was translated into several languages and influenced among others Chateaubriand, Coleridge, and Wordsworth. Most of the plates in Benjamin S. Barton's *Elements of Botany* (1803) were engraved after drawings by Bartram. Alexander Wilson was inspired by him to produce his *American Ornithology*.

BARUCH, BERNARD MANNES (*b. Camden, S.C., 1870; New York, N.Y., 1965*), financier and public adviser. Personal speculations on the stock market made him a millionaire by the age of thirty. In the years prior to World War I he began to put his wealth to use in politics and public affairs and became a friend and admirer of Woodrow Wilson. A preparedness advocate, in 1917 he was appointed chairman of the newly formed War Industries Board and member of the president's war council. After the war, he took part in the postwar peace conference, an experience he recorded in *The Making of the Reparation and Economic Sections of the Treaty* (1920), written with fellow delegate John Foster Dulles. In his postwar activities he propounded the Wilsonian view that social stability and economic prosperity in the postwar world required new forms of cooperative institutions among business, labor, and agriculture, and between business and the government. During the interwar period, he campaigned for industrial preparedness, preaching a message of total mobilization of population and resources through comprehensive price and wage controls in the event of war. By the late 1930's Roosevelt had come to consult him frequently and publicly on defense matters, but during World War II he preferred political influence over administrative power, exercising that influence through friendships with key war administrators, to whom he consistently advised one-man administrative control. By the end of World War II he had become firmly established as an American folk hero, and President Truman appointed him ambassador to the United Nations Atomic Energy Commission in 1946; this constituted his last opportunity to directly influence the nature of major government policy during the Truman administration, for he differed from Truman on several important aspects of postwar policy. His life is recorded in Margaret L. Coit's biography *Mr. Baruch* (1957) and in his autobiographies *Baruch: My Own Story* (1957) and *Baruch: The Public Years* (1960).

BARUCH, SIMON (*b. Schwersen, Germany, 1840; d. 1921*), physician. Immigrated as a youth and received professional training in Charleston, S.C., and at Medical College of Virginia; served 1862–65 as surgeon, Confederate Army. Practiced in Camden, S.C., 1865–81, and then removed to New York City where he became known as a leading exponent of hydrotherapy and a public-health advocate.

BARUS, CARL (*b. Cincinnati, Ohio, 1856; d. Providence, R.I., 1935*), physicist. Professor, and Dean of Graduate School, Brown University. Made important contributions to geophysics. Inventor of the displacement interferometer.

BARZYŃSKI, VINCENT (*b. Sulislawice, Poland, 1838; d. Chicago, Ill., 1899*), Roman Catholic priest. Served in Texas, 1866–74. Thereafter, as pastor of St. Stanislaus Kostka Church, Chicago, he was a notable force in improving the spiritual and material condition of Polish immigrants.

BASCOM, FLORENCE (*b. Williamstown, Mass., 1862; D. Northampton, Mass., 1945*), geologist. Daughter of John Bascom. A.B. and B.L., 1882; B.S., 1884; A.M., 1887—all from University of Wisconsin. After teaching science for a time at Rockford Seminary, she resumed study at Johns Hopkins, taking as her field the Piedmont area of Maryland, and later of Pennsylvania, on which she became the authority. She was awarded the Ph.D. in 1893, the first woman to win that degree at Johns Hopkins, and the first woman in the United States to earn a doctorate in geology. She taught two years at Ohio State, and then at Bryn Mawr, 1895–1928, becoming professor in 1906. She was associated with the U.S. Geological Survey, 1896–1938, and produced several area survey folios. She also took a keen interest in geomorphology and crystallography.

BASCOM, HENRY BIDLEMAN (*b. Hancock, N.Y., 1796; d. Louisville, Ky., 1850*), Methodist clergyman. Removed as a child to Maysville, Ky., later to Brown Co., Ohio. Circuit rider *post* 1813; chaplain to Congress, 1823. President, Transylvania University, 1842–49; elected bishop, Methodist Episcopal Church South, 1850.

BASCOM, JOHN (*b. Genoa, N.Y., 1827; d. Williamstown, Mass., 1911*), philosopher, educator. Graduated Williams College, 1849; influenced by teaching of Laurens Hickok while attending Auburn Seminary. Taught at Williams, 1852–74, 1891–1903; president, University of Wisconsin, 1874–87.

BASHFORD, COLES (*b. New York State, 1816; d. Prescott, Ariz., 1878*), politician. Controversial Republican governor of Wisconsin, 1856; active in early territorial government of Arizona.

BASHFORD, JAMES WHITFORD (*b. Fayette, Wis., 1849; d. Pasadena, Calif., 1919*), Methodist clergyman. President, Ohio Wesleyan University, 1889–1904; missionary bishop, China area, 1904–15.

BASKERVILLE, CHARLES (*b. Deer Brook, Miss., 1870; d. New York, N.Y., 1922*), chemist. Director, chemical laboratories, College of the City of New York, 1904–22; an effective teacher and able industrial consultant.

BASS, EDWARD (*b. Dorchester, Mass., 1726; d. Newburyport, Mass., 1803*), Episcopal clergyman. Graduated Harvard, 1744; ordained in London, 1752. Rector, St. Paul's Newburyport, 1752–1803; consecrated first bishop of Massachusetts, 1797.

BASS, SAM (*b. near Mitchell, Ind. 1851; d. Round Rock, Tex., 1878*), bandit, train-robber, killed in an attempt to rob the Round Rock bank.

BASS, WILLIAM CAPERS (*b. Augusta, Ga., 1831; d. Macon, Ga., 1894*), Methodist clergyman. President, Methodist Wesleyan Female College, Macon, 1874–94.

BASSE, JEREMIAH (*d. Burlington, N.J., 1725*), colonial official. Commissioned governor of East and West Jersey, 1697; favored anti-proprietary party, and was superseded, 1699. Secretary of the royal government of New Jersey, 1702–14.

BASSETT, EDWARD MURRAY (*b. Brooklyn, N.Y., 1863; d. Brooklyn, 1948*), lawyer, city planner. Raised in Watertown, N.Y. Graduated Amherst, 1884; Columbia University Law School, 1886. Specialized in bankruptcy and real estate law, which, together with a civic concern, made him aware of the need to protect New York City from unrestricted growth and exploitation by builders. Served as chairman of the commission which drew up New York's zoning ordinance of 1916, the first comprehensive zoning law in the United States. The law, a disappointment to many reformers, reflected Bassett's view of zoning as a means of improving the quality of urban life rather than as an instrument of social change. Continued advocacy of zoning through writing, lecturing, and service on consulting boards and commissions throughout his active life. He was author of, among other works, *The Master Plan* (1938).

BASSETT, JAMES (*b. Mundus, Canada, 1834; d. Los Angeles, Calif., 1906*), Presbyterian clergyman. Missionary to Persia, 1871–84; thereafter in pastoral work in United States.

BASSETT, JOHN SPENCER (*b. Tarboro, N.C., 1867; d. Washington, D.C., 1928*), historian. Graduated Trinity (Duke), 1888; Ph.D., Johns Hopkins, 1894. Taught at Duke, 1894–1906; professor, Smith College, 1906–28. Author, among others, of *Regulators of North Carolina* (1895); *The Federalist System* (1906);

Life of Andrew Jackson (1911). Editor of a number of valuable primary historical sources.

BASSETT, RICHARD (*b. Cecil Co., Md., 1745; d. Bohemia Manor, Md., 1815*), statesman. U.S. senator, Federalist, from Delaware, 1789–93; governor of Delaware, 1799–1801.

BASSETT, WILLIAM HASTINGS (*b. New Bedford, Mass., 1868; d. Cheshire, Conn., 1934*), metallurgical engineer. Pioneer in the microscopic examination of copper alloys and the manufacture of brass goods of standard quality.

BASSO, (JOSEPH) HAMILTON (*b. New Orleans, La., 1904; d. New Haven, Conn., 1964*), novelist and journalist. As a beginning writer, he worked as a reporter for several New Orleans newspapers and contributed to the *Double-Dealer*. Later he worked as associate editor of the *New Republic* (1935–37), contributing editor for *Time* magazine (1942–43), and associate editor of the *New Yorker* (1944–62), to which he also regularly contributed short pieces. He began his novelistic career in 1929 with the autobiographical *Relics and Angels*, and of his eleven novels, the most successful was *The View from Pompey's Head* (1954), a best-seller made into a major motion picture.

BATCHELDER, JOHN PUTNAM (*b. Wilton, N.H., 1784; d. New York, N.Y., 1868*), surgeon. Innovator in operating techniques for eye and facial surgery; an inventor and improver of surgical instruments.

BATCHELDER, SAMUEL (*b. Jaffrey, N.H., 1784; d. Cambridge, Mass., 1879*), cotton manufacturer. Invented, among other mill devices, a dynamometer for measuring power of belt-driven machinery.

BATCHELLER, GEORGE SHERMAN (*b. Batchellerville, N.Y., 1837; d. Paris, France, 1908*), Union soldier, statesman, lawyer. U.S. judge, International Tribunal in Egypt, 1876–85, 1898–1908.

BATCHELOR, GEORGE (*b. Southbury, Conn., 1836; d. 1923*), Unitarian clergyman. Editor, *Christian Register*, 1898–1911.

BATE, WILLIAM BRIMAGE (*b. Bledsoe's Lick, Tenn., 1826; d. Washington, D.C., 1905*), politician. Served in Mexican War; rose from private to major general in Confederate Army, and distinguished himself at Shiloh, Murfreesboro, Chattanooga, and in the Atlanta and Tennessee campaigns. Active in opposition to Brownlow's postwar government. Served as Democratic governor of Tennessee, 1882–86; as U.S. senator, 1886–1905.

BATEMAN, HARRY (*b. Manchester, England, 1882; d. Utah, 1946*), mathematician, expert in mathematical physics. B.A., Cambridge University, 1903, with highest honors; became a fellow of Trinity College, 1904; studied in Paris and Göttingen, 1905–06. Taught at Liverpool and Manchester universities. Came to America, 1910, as lecturer at Bryn Mawr; was associated with Johns Hopkins, 1912–17, where he received the Ph.D. degree in 1913. *Post* 1917, professor of theoretical physics and aeronautics at California Institute of Technology. His first mathematical papers were in geometry and algebraic geometry; he specialized, however, in mathematical physics, electro-, hydro-, and aerodynamics. His principal published contributions are *The Mathematical Analysis of Electrical and Optical Wave Motion on the Basis of Maxwell's Equation* (1915); his report on hydrodynamics contained in a 1932 *Bulletin* of the National Research Council (the most erudite of his works); and his monograph, *Partial Differential Equations of Mathematical Physics* (1932), which is his finest large-scale work. Edited technical journals and was a

cofounder of the *Quarterly of Applied Mathematics*. Died en route by train to New York City.

BATEMAN, KATE JOSEPHINE *b. 1843; d. London, England, 1917*), actress. Appeared 1846–54 as child prodigy with sister Ellen; as mature player won success in *Leah the Forsaken* (1863) and in support of Henry Irving at the Lyceum, London.

BATEMAN, NEWTON (*b. Fairton, N.J., 1822; d. Galesburg, Ill., 1897*), educator. Removed to Illinois, 1833; was a leader in building up common schools, serving as superintendent of public instruction, 1859–63, 1865–75. A friend of Abraham Lincoln. President, Knox College, 1874–92; emeritus, 1892–97.

BATEMAN, SIDNEY FRANCS COWELL (*b. New York, N.Y.[?], 1823; d. London, England, 1881*), actress, playwright, manager. Mother of Kate and Ellen Bateman. Managed Lyceum Theatre, London, 1871–78; Sadler's Wells, 1878–81.

BATES, ARLO (*b. East Machias, Maine, 1850; d. Boston, Mass., 1918*), educator, author. Graduated Bowdoin, 1876. Editor, *Boston Sunday Courier*, 1880–93; author during this time of fiction and verse. Professor of English, Massachusetts Institute of Technology, *post* 1893.

BATES, BARNABAS (*b. Edmonton, England, 1785; d. Boston, Mass., 1853*), clergyman. Came to America as a child. *Post* 1839, agitated for postal reform and a reduction of rates.

BATES, BLANCHE (*b. Portland, Oreg., 1873; d. San Francisco, Calif., 1941*), actress. Born of theatrical parents; debut with L. R. Stockwell's company, San Francisco, 1893; toured with T. D. Frawley's company, 1894–98; played secondary roles in Augustin Daly's company, 1898–99. Although her occasional appearances in plays by Shakespeare and Ibsen gave evidence of artistic talent, she made her way to stardom in a series of successful (and rather shoddy) plays either written by David Belasco or produced by him. These included *Madame Butterfly* (1900); *Under Two Flags* (1901); *The Darling of the Gods* (1902), which ran for almost three years; and *The Girl of the Golden West* (1905), in which she gave her best performance. In 1912, she married George Creel. Associated thereafter with Charles Frohman, she sought for roles of more depth but with no great success except for the lead in *The Famous Mrs. Fair* (1919). After retiring from the stage in 1926, she appeared briefly in the part of Lena Surrege in the New York production of *The Lake* (1933).

BATES, DANIEL MOORE (*b. Laurel, Del., 1821; d. Richmond, Va., 1879*), jurist. Chancellor of Delaware, 1865–73. Editor, *Reports of Cases . . . Court of Chancery of Delaware* (1876, 1878).

BATES, EDWARD (*b. Goochland Co., Va., 1793; d. St. Louis, Mo., 1869*), statesman. Brother of Frederick Bates, at whose suggestion he removed to St. Louis, 1814, and began practice of law, 1816. Congressman, Whig, from Missouri, 1827–29, he thereafter held local office until his speech at the 1847 River and Harbor Improvement Convention, Chicago, made him nationally prominent. He opposed repeal of the Missouri Compromise and the admission of Kansas under the Lecompton Constitution, thus drawing closer to the nascent Republican party although he presided over the Whig National Convention at Baltimore, 1856. Border state leaders favored him as Republican nominee for the presidency in 1860. His choice as Lincoln's attorney general made him the first cabinet officer to be chosen from west of the Mississippi; he served 1861–64, resigning over abuses he attributed to Seward, Chase, and Stanton. Thereafter he fought the policies of the Radical Republicans in Missouri and elsewhere as a conspiracy against all government by law.

BATES, FREDERICK (*b. Goochland Co., Va., 1777; d. near Chesterfield, Mo., 1825*), lawyer. Brother of Edward Bates. Removed to Detroit, Mich., 1797, where he prospered as a merchant until 1805. Appointed secretary of Louisiana Territory, 1806, and served until 1812 when he became secretary of Missouri Territory. He was elected governor of the state of Missouri, 1824.

BATES, GEORGE HANDY (*b. Dover, Del., 1845; d. 1916*), lawyer. Son of Daniel M. Bates. Influential in Democratic politics; author of a report on Samoan affairs, 1886, and one of U.S. commissioners at conference on Samoa, Berlin, 1889.

BATES, JAMES (*b. Greene, Maine, 1789; d. 1882*), physician, surgeon, congressman.

BATES, JOHN COALTER (*b. St. Charles Co., Mo., 1842; d. San Diego, Calif., 1919*), soldier. Son of Edward Bates. Remained in the army after Civil War service. Prominent in assault on El Caney, 1898, and in the Philippine insurrection. Commissioned lieutenant general on becoming chief of staff, 1906.

BATES, JOSHUA (*b. Weymouth, Mass., 1788; d. 1864*), financier, philanthropist. Removed to England, 1816, as general agent for Boston merchant William Gray; became partner in great banking firm of Baring Brothers, 1828, and eventually senior partner. Largest contributor to founding of the Boston Public Library.

BATES, KATHERINE LEE (*b. Falmouth, Mass., 1859; d. 1929*), educator, poet, author of "America the Beautiful."

BATES, ONWARD (*b. St. Charles Co., Mo., 1850; d. Augusta, Ga., 1936*), civil engineer, specialist in railroad bridges.

BATES, SAMUEL PENNIMAN (*b. Mendon, Mass., 1827; d. 1902*), educator. Graduated Brown University, 1851; active in Pennsylvania public school work.

BATES, WALTER (*b. Darien, Conn., 1760; d. 1842*), Loyalist. Removed in 1783 to Nova Scotia, where he served for many years as sheriff of King's Co. Author of *Kinston and the Loyalists . . . of 1783* (1889) and *The Mysterious Stranger* (1816)

BATTERSON, JAMES GOODWIN (*b. Wintonbury, Conn., 1823; d. Hartford, Conn., 1901*), businessman. After successful operation of New England Granite Works, he founded the Travelers Insurance Co., 1863.

BATTEY, ROBERT (*b. Augusta, Ga., 1828; d. Rome, Ga., 1895*), physician, surgeon. Studied privately and at University of Pennsylvania; M.D., Jefferson Medical College, Phila., 1857. Served in Confederate medical corps as field surgeon and hospital director, 1861–65; practiced thereafter in Rome, Ga. Celebrated since 1858 for his work with hernias and fistulas, he opened up an important field of surgery in 1872 with "Battey's Operation" for the removal of human ovaries by abdominal, and later by vaginal, section.

BATTLE, BURRELL BUNN (*b. Hinds Co., Miss., 1838; d. Little Rock, Ark., 1917*), jurist. Began practice of law at Lewisville, Ark., 1858. After service in Confederate Army, 1861–65, was a leader in opposition to governors Clayton and Hadley. Justice, Arkansas supreme court, 1885–1911.

BATTLE, CULLEN ANDREWS (*b. Powelton, Ga., 1829; d. Greensboro, N.C., 1905*), politician. Removed to Eufaula, Ala., as a child; admitted to Alabama bar, 1852. An uncompromising secessionist, he served with distinction in the Confederate Army, 1861–65; after the war he returned to practice in Tuskegee, Ala., removing to Newbern, N.C., in 1880.

BATTLE, KEMP PLUMMER (*b. Franklin Co., N.C., 1831; d. 1919*), educator. Son of William H. Battle. President, University of North Carolina, 1876–91; professor of history, 1891–1907; emeritus thereafter. Author of *History of the University of North Carolina* (1907, 1912).

BATTLE, WILLIAM HORN (*b. Edgecombe Co., N.C., 1802; d. Chapel Hill N.C., 1879*), lawyer, jurist. Professor of law, University of North Carolina, 1845–68; justice, state supreme court, 1852–68; revised North Carolina statutes, 1833–37, and again in 1873.

BATTS, ROBERT LYNN (*b. Bastrop, Tex., 1864; d. Austin, Texas, 1935*), lawyer, judge. Outstanding in fostering the growth of the University of Texas.

BAUER, HAROLD VICTOR (*b. New Malden, England, 1873; d. Miami, Fla., 1951*), pianist, music educator. After beginning a career as a violinist and studying with Adolf Pollitzer in London, Bauer abandoned that instrument for a career as a concert pianist. Although not a student of Paderewski, he did work with him briefly in Paris. Made American debut in 1900 with the Boston Symphony. Concertized extensively around the world to critical acclaim until World War I, when he settled in New York. In 1917 helped organize the Manhattan School of Music and in 1919 the Beethoven Association. A well-known performer on radio, Bauer also was widely known as a recording artist, making over 200 records. His specialties were Beethoven, Schumann, Brahms, Franck, Debussy, and Saint-Saëns.

BAUER, LOUIS AGRICOLA (*b. Cincinnati, Ohio, 1865; d. 1932*), physicist and magnetician. Conducted world magnetic survey; studied magnetic effect directly attributable to solar activity.

BAUGHER, HENRY LOUIS (*b. Abbottstown, Pa., 1804; d. Gettysburg, Pa., 1868*), Lutheran clergyman. Professor of Greek and rhetoric, Gettysburg College, 1831–50; president, 1850–68.

BAUM, HEDWIG ("VICKI") (*b. Vienna, Austria, 1888; d. Hollywood, Calif., 1960*), novelist. Trained as a musician, Baum wrote several popular novels in German. She is remembered mainly as the author of the novel *Menschen im Hotel* (1929), which was translated as *Grand Hotel* in English, and which became the source of a successful Broadway play (1930) and film starring Greta Garbo, Joan Crawford, Wallace Beery, and John and Lionel Barrymore (1932). Baum immigrated to the U.S. in the 1930's. She chiefly wrote screenplays in Hollywood until her death.

BAUM, LYMAN FRANK (*b. Chittenango, N.Y., 1856; d. Hollywood, Calif., 1919*), author. Followed success of *The Wonderful Wizard of Oz* (1900, with artist W. W. Denslow) with thirteen further *Oz* stories and numerous works for children issued over such pen-names as "Schuyler Staunton," "Floyd Akers," and "Edith Van Dyne."

BAUSCH, EDWARD (*b. Rochester, N.Y., 1854; d. Rochester, 1944*), industrialist, inventor. Son of a German immigrant optician and lens grinder who, with a partner, manufactured hard-rubber parts for optical instruments as the Bausch & Lomb Optical Company. Edward Bausch attended local schools and studied engineering at Cornell University, 1871–74. He then joined his father in business, and developed the design and production of microscopes by the firm, concentrating on the production of high-quality, moderately priced instruments. Endorsement by Dr. Oliver Wendell Holmes and others followed and the firm prospered. In 1882, Bausch received his first patent for the Trichinoscope, designed for the detection of contamination in meat. Becoming interested in photography, he took charge of production of photographic lenses at Bausch & Lomb (1883), collaborating with George Eastman for whose expanding Kodak business he supplied lenses *post* 1888 and also iris diaphragm shutters, for which Bausch received the patent in 1891. After 1893, Bausch & Lomb held exclusive American rights for manufacture of Zeiss anastigmatic lenses, binoculars, and range finders. Edward Bausch became president of the firm on his father's death in 1926, and chairman of the board in 1935. He gave generously to Rochester charities and public institutions.

BAUSMAN, BENJAMIN (*b. near Lancaster, Pa., 1824; d. Reading, Pa., 1909*), clergyman of the German Reformed Church. Pastor, St. Paul's Reading, Pa., 1863–1909.

BAXLEY, HENRY WILLIS (*b. Baltimore, Md., 1803; d. 1876*), physician, surgeon. Graduated in medicine, University of Maryland, 1824. Cofounded (1839) the Baltimore College of Dental Surgery, the first to be organized formally either here or abroad; endowed the chair of pathology, Johns Hopkins Medical School.

BAXTER, ELISHA (*b. Rutherford Co., N.C., 1827; d. Batesville, Ark., 1899*), lawyer. Removed to Arkansas, 1852. An opponent of secession; raised and commanded Arkansas Unionist troops in Civil War. During Reconstruction period, Baxter headed reform elements in Republican party in Arkansas, contesting governorship with Joseph Brooks, 1873–74.

BAXTER, HENRY (*b. Sidney Plains, N.Y., 1821; d. Jonesville, Mich., 1873*), Union soldier. Entered Civil War as captain of Michigan volunteers; after service in Army of the Potomac, 1861–65, was mustered out as brevet major general.

BAXTER, JOHN (*b. Rutherford Co., N.C., 1819; d. 1886*), lawyer. Brother of Elisha Baxter. Removed to Knoxville, Tenn., 1857, after success at North Carolina bar. A leading Tennessee Unionist, he became a political follower of William G. Brownlow *post* 1872 and was appointed U.S. circuit judge, 1877.

BAXTER, WILLIAM (*b. Leeds, England, 1820; d. New Castle, Pa., 1880*), clergyman of the Christian (Disciples) Church. Immigrated to America as a child. His book *Pea Ridge and Prairie Grove* (1864) is an authentic record of his experiences as a Union sympathizer in Arkansas, 1860–63.

BAYARD, JAMES ASH(E)TON (*b. Philadelphia, Pa., 1767; d. Wilmington, Del., 1815*), statesman, diplomat. Graduated Princeton, 1784. Studied law with Joseph Reed and Jared Ingersoll; admitted to bar at New Castle and Philadelphia, 1787; began practice at Wilmington, Del., 1787. Married Ann, daughter of Richard Bassett, chief justice of Delaware, 1795. Congressman, Federalist, from Delaware, 1797–1803; U.S. senator, 1805–13. As congressman, Bayard played a decisive role in the choice of Thomas Jefferson for president of the United States over Aaron Burr by the House of Representatives, 1800–01. Sane and moderate in his views, he exerted himself to prevent war, 1809–12, advising Federalist support of all acts which would improve the nation's defensive strength. Served with John Q. Adams and Albert Gallatin as United States representative at Ghent, 1813–14, and was chosen to serve as member of commission to negotiate commercial treaty with Great Britain, 1814–15. His health failing, he sailed from England, June 1815, and died at his home six days after arrival in the United States.

BAYARD, JAMES ASHETON (*b. Wilmington, Del., 1799; d. Wilmington, 1880*), lawyer. Son of James A. Bayard (1767–1815). Graduated Union College, 1818; admitted to Delaware bar, 1822; counsel in many important cases. U.S. senator, Democrat, from Delaware, 1851–64, 1867–69. A

conservative Unionist from a border state, Bayard became a Republican *post* 1857 but returned to the Democratic party after Lincoln's death. Even as a Republican, he opposed most antislavery measures as invasions of property rights; he resigned from the Senate, 1864, in protest against the test oath for office-holders.

BAYARD, JOHN BUBENHEIM (*b. Bohemia Manor, Md., 1738; d. New Brunswick, N.J., 1807*), merchant, Revolutionary patriot. Uncle of James A. Bayard (1767–1815). Active in protests against British rule, 1766–76; major and colonel, Philadelphia Associators, and commended for gallantry at Princeton; speaker, Pennsylvania Assembly, 1777–78. A leader among the Federalists.

BAYARD, NICHOLAS (*b. Alphen, Holland, 1644; d. New York, N.Y., 1707*), colonial official. Brought to New Amsterdam, 1647; nephew of Peter Stuyvesant. Clerk to the Dutch secretary of the province, he succeeded him in office after 1664 and was later appointed surveyor of customs. Imprisoned under the English Governor Andros, he was favored by Governor Dongan, serving as a councillor and as mayor of New York, 1685–87; he was imprisoned again during Jacob Leisler's usurpation and had further difficulties with Governor Bellomont, 1697–1701.

BAYARD, RICHARD HENRY (*b. Wilmington, Del., 1796; d. Philadelphia, Pa., 1868*), lawyer. Son of James A. Bayard (1767–1815). Mayor of Wilmington, 1832–35; U.S. senator, Democrat, from Delaware, 1836–39, 1840–45.

BAYARD, SAMUEL (*b. Philadelphia, Pa., 1767; d. Princeton, N.J., 1840*), jurist. Son of John B. Bayard. Agent for American claims before British admiralty courts, 1795–99; *post* 1806, served as presiding judge, court of common pleas, Somerset Co., N.J., and was identified with New Jersey civic and educational affairs.

BAYARD, THOMAS FRANCIS (*b. Wilmington, Del., 1828; d. Dedham, Mass., 1898*), statesman. Son of James A. Bayard (1799–1880). Admitted to the bar 1851, he practiced with great success in his native city. As U.S. senator, Democrat, from Delaware, 1869–85, he opposed expansion of federal power and class legislation of every kind; he felt that lawmaking should be restricted to necessary measures only and that administration should be honest and frugal above all else. He received considerable support for the presidential nomination in 1880 and again in 1884, and was appointed secretary of state by Grover Cleveland in 1885. His policies were consistently on the side of peace and arbitration, but the three major diplomatic issues of his term were unsolved when he left office: the North Atlantic Fisheries question; the Bering Sea sealing dispute; the adjustment of conflicting interests in Samoa. Appointed ambassador to Great Britain, 1893, he served until 1897, refusing to be stampeded into unfriendly speech or action during the Venezuela dispute of 1895–96. He was throughout his life a man of high ideals and exalted patriotism.

BAYARD, WILLIAM (*b. New York, N.Y., 1761; d. New York, 1826*), merchant. Partner in LeRoy, Bayard & Co., 1786–1826, a leading commercial house and shipping concern.

BAYLES, JAMES COPPER (*b. New York, N.Y., 1845; d. 1913*), editor of the *Iron Age*, 1869–89; distinguished as a writer on engineering subjects.

BAYLEY, JAMES ROOSEVELT (*b. Rye, N.Y., 1814, d. Newark, N.J., 1877*), Roman Catholic clergyman. Grandson of Richard Bayley; nephew of Elizabeth A. B. Seton. Ordained in the Episcopal ministry, 1835, he resigned in 1841 on appearance of Newman's *Tract XC* and became a Catholic in Rome, April 1842. After study at St. Sulpice in Paris, he was ordained by Archbishop

Hughes of New York in 1844; he served as the archbishop's secretary, 1848–53. Consecrated first bishop of Newark, N.J., 1853, he was promoted to the archiepiscopal see of Baltimore, 1872. An able administrator, he was also author of *A Brief Sketch of the Early History of the Catholic Church on the Island of New York* (1853, 1874) and *Memoirs of the Rt. Rev. Simon Brute* (1855, 1876).

BAYLEY, RICHARD (*b. Fairfield, Conn., 1745; d. New York, N.Y., 1801*), physician. Studied with John Charlton in New York and with William Hunter in London. His pathological studies during a fatal croup epidemic, 1774, helped him cut the mortality of the disease almost in half. In 1792 he became professor of anatomy, and later in surgery, on the medical faculty of Columbia College, New York City. As a practicing physician and as health physician to the port of New York, he did heroic service during the yellow fever epidemics *post* 1795. He was author of *An Account of the Epidemic Fever . . . of 1795* (1796) and *Letters from the Health Office Submitted to the New York Common Council*; he also helped in the early formulation of both the federal and state quarantine laws.

BAYLIES, FRANCIS (*b. Taunton, Mass., 1783; d. 1852*), lawyer. As acting minister to Buenos Aires, 1832, broke off treaty talks in dispute over Falkland Islands fisheries.

BAYLOR, FRANCES COURTENAY (*b. Fort Smith, Ark., 1848; d. Winchester, Va., 1920*), novelist and miscellaneous writer. Author of, among others, *Juan and Juanita* (1888).

BAYLOR, GEORGE (*b. Caroline Co., Va., 1752; d. Bridgetown, Barbados, 1784*), aide-de-camp to Washington in Revolutionary War; his dragoon detachment slaughtered in British surprise at Old Tappan, 1778.

BAYLOR, ROBERT EMMET BLEDSOE (*b. Kentucky, 1793[?]; d. Washington Co., Tex., 1873*), jurist, Baptist preacher. Removed to Alabama, 1820; to Texas, 1839, where he served as a judge until the Civil War. Cofounder of Baylor University.

BAYLY, THOMAS HENRY (*b. near Accomac, Va., 1810; d. 1856*), lawyer, planter. Congressman, Democrat, from Virginia, 1844–56; influential in carrying through the compromises of 1850.

BAYMA, JOSEPH (*b. Cirie, Italy, 1816; d. Santa Clara, Calif., 1892*), Jesuit priest, mathematician, physicist. Ordained, 1847; was professor of philosophy at Stonyhurst College, England, 1858–69. Assigned to California, he served as president (1869–72) and as professor of higher mathematics (1872–80) at St. Ignatius College, San Francisco. His chief scientific work was his innovating *Elements of Molecular Mechanics* (1866).

BAYNHAM, WILLIAM (*b. South Carolina[?], 1749; d. Virginia[?], 1814*), physician, surgeon. Credited with performance of the first successful operation for extra-uterine pregnancy, he practiced *post* 1785 in Essex, Va.

BAZETT, HENRY CUTHBERT (*b. Gravesend, England, 1885; d. at sea, 1950*), physiologist. Graduated Wadham College, Oxford, 1908 (received M.S., 1913, and M.D., 1919); received clinical training at St. Thomas's Hospital, and was qualified in 1910. Serving with high distinction with the Royal Army Medical Corps in France during World War I, he became much interested in wound shock as well as in the sensation and effects of cold. After the war, he taught clinical pathology at Oxford, and came to America in 1921 to accept the professorship of physiology at the University of Pennsylvania, a post he retained until his death. His research work embraced the study of nervous system function, circulation, blood volume, temperature sense, and body temperature regulation. He made a major contribution to the discovery of "counter current" effects, studied acclimatization in man, and was the first to establish clearly that an increase in blood volume occurs in adaptation to a hot environment. Many of his experiments were performed rather drastically on himself. During World War II, his advice was sought continually both here and in England; from 1941 to 1943, he headed the Canadian research program in aviation medicine, and he also served with the U.S. Office of Scientific Research and Development.

BAZIOTES, WILLIAM (*b. Pittsburgh, Pa., 1912; d. New York, N.Y., 1963*), artist. Over the course of his career he developed a mature style that showed a variety of influences: surrealism, classicism, and primitivism were coupled with a regard for science, mysticism, and poetry. He taught at various schools in the New York City area, helped found the Subject of the Artist art school in New York City, and was an associate professor of art at Hunter College (1952–63). The Art Institute of Chicago awarded him the Walter M. Campana Memorial Purchase Prize for his painting *Cyclops* (1947) and the Frank Logan Medal for *The Sea* (1961).

BEACH, ALFRED ELY (*b. Springfield, Mass., 1826; d. 1896*), inventor, editor. Son of Moses Y. Beach. Partner in *Scientific American*, 1846–96; also editor. Inventor of pneumatic carrier systems, an improved tunneling shield, and a typewriter (1847).

BEACH, AMY MARCY CHENEY (*b. Henniker, N.H., 1867; d. New York, N.Y., 1944*), composer, pianist. Raised in Boston, Mass. Began formal piano study at age six; continued study (1876–82) with J. E. Perabo, Carl Baermann, and others; made professional debut at Boston Music Hall, Oct. 24, 1883, and first appearance with Boston Symphony, March 28, 1885 (playing Chopin's F Minor Concerto). After marriage late in 1885 to Dr. H. H. A. Beach, she was encouraged by him to concentrate on composition rather than public performances. Largely self-taught in musical theory, and writing in the musical idiom of the late 19th-century romantics, she published more than 150 works which were well received both in America and Europe. Between 1910 and 1914, she lived abroad; resuming concert work, she gave many performances, chiefly of her own works, in Berlin and other German cities. Returning home, she continued her career until shortly before her death. Among her works were songs set to lyrics by Shakespeare, Browning, and other poets, English, French, and German; a Mass in E Flat (1892), her first major work; a Gaelic Symphony (1896); much church music; and examples of almost every musical genre. Her "Canticle of the Sun," a cantata, composed in 1925, was first performed at the Worcester, Mass., Music Festival in 1931, conducted by Albert Stoessel.

BEACH, FREDERICK CONVERSE (*b. Brooklyn, N.Y., 1848; d. 1918*), patent solicitor. Succeeded his father, Alfred E. Beach, as a director of the Scientific American Co.

BEACH, HARLAN PAGE (*b. Essex Co., N.J., 1854; d. Winter Park, Fla., 1933*), missionary to China. Professor of missions at Yale University, 1906–21.

BEACH, MOSES SPERRY (*b. Springfield, Mass., 1822; d. Peekskill, N.Y., 1892*), journalist. Son of Moses Y. Beach. Proprietor of the *New York Sun*, 1848–68.

BEACH, MOSES YALE (*b. Wallingford, Conn., 1800; d. Wallingford, 1868*), journalist, inventor. Worked at his trade as a cabinet-maker and experimented unsuccessfully with mechanical devices until his invention of a rag-cutting machine for use in paper mills secured him an interest in a mill at Saugerties, N.Y., 1829. This enterprise failing, he became manager of the mechanical department of the *New York Sun*; he bought out the founder, Benjamin H. Day, in 1838. On his retirement in 1848, the *Sun* was considered the leading penny newspaper; its circulation was about 50,000 and it claimed the largest cash advertising patronage in the nation. Beach was also a founder of the New York Associated Press and is credited with inventing the syndicated news article (1841).

BEACH, REX (b. *Atwood, Mich., 1877; d. Sebring, Fla., 1949*), novelist, scenarist. After prospecting and mining in Alaska, 1897–1902, without much success, he was inspired by Jack London's use of personal experiences to attempt similar fiction of his own. He became a frequent contributor to magazines; his first book, *Pardners* (1905), was a collection of ten stories about life in Alaska and the West. His novel, *The Spoilers* (1906), a runaway best-seller, was also about Alaska, as was his second novel, *The Barrier* (1907). He continued to turn out successful fiction well into the 1940's; all his stories were written in a romantic vein with careful attention to background, and illustrated the virtues of courage, hard work, and personal integrity. By reserving movie rights in his book contracts, he made a great deal of money in successive sales of his works to Hollywood. He was very successful also in commercial growing of flowers and vegetables, and in raising cattle.

BEACH, SYLVIA WOODBRIDGE (b. *Nancy Woodbridge Beach, Baltimore, Md., 1887; d. Paris, France, 1962*), bookseller and publisher. In 1919 opened an English-language bookshop in Paris, Shakespeare and Company, which became the most important center in Paris for disseminating literature in the English language. Among her regular patrons were André Gide and Valéry and the expatriot American writers then living in Paris. Although devoted to the classics, Beach above all promoted the new writing that was being published by small presses and magazines, and she courageously published James Joyce's *Ulysses* in 1922, despite charges of obscenity and limited financial means. Her shop was closed by the Germans during World War II, and she was unable to reopen it after the war.

BEACH, WILLIAM AUGUSTUS (b. *Saratoga Springs, N.Y., 1809; d. 1884*), lawyer. After successful practice at Saratoga and Troy, N.Y., 1833–70, Beach moved to New York City as attorney for Vanderbilt interests. He appeared in many leading cases, 1870–84, including the Barnard impeachment and the Beecher-Tilton trial.

BEACH, WOOSTER (b. *Trumbull, Conn., 1794; d. 1868*), physician. Author of *The American Practice of Medicine* (1833) and other unconventional medical works; founder of the *Eclectic Medical Journal*, 1836; president, National Eclectic Medical Association, 1855.

BEADLE, ERASTUS FLAVEL (b. *Otsego Co., N.Y., 1821; d. Cooperstown, N.Y., 1894*), printer, originator of the "dime novel."

BEADLE, WILLIAM HENRY HARRISON (b. *Parke Co., Ind., 1838; d. San Francisco, Calif., 1915*), educator. As surveyor general and, later, superintendent of public instruction, Dakota Territory (1869–89), Beadle fought for the principle that school lands should never be sold for less than ten dollars an acre; this principle was written into the constitutions of several Western states.

BEAL, WILLIAM JAMES (b. *Adrian, Mich., 1833; d. Amherst, Mass., 1924*), teacher, pioneer in the "new botany." Pupil of Agassiz and Asa Gray, he taught at Michigan Agricultural College, 1871–1910. His efforts resulted in establishment of the state Forestry Commission, 1887.

BEALE, EDWARD FITZGERALD (b. *Washington, D.C., 1822; d. Washington, 1893*), explorer. As young naval officer, served under Stockton in California, 1846, and with Kit Carson distinguished himself as messenger from General Kearny after battle of San Pasqual. Thereafter as dispatch bearer traveled to Washington, February–June 1847, and in July–September 1848 made another transcontinental journey carrying first official news of California gold. In all, before resignation from service, 1851, he made six journeys from ocean to ocean. Subsequently he acted as Indian agent for California and Nevada, and with G. H. Heap made survey, 1853, for a railroad route from Missouri frontier through southern Colorado and Utah to Los Angeles. He also made several Western road surveys, 1857–59.

BEALE, JOSEPH HENRY (b. *Dorchester, Mass., 1861; d. Cambridge, Mass., 1943*), professor of law. Graduated Harvard, 1882; Harvard Law School, 1887. Taught many branches of law as a member of the Harvard Law School faculty, 1890–1938; founder of law school at University of Chicago while on leave from Harvard, 1902–04. A dynamic teacher, Beale was author of numerous articles for law reviews and twenty-seven books, including a number of case books and the three-volume *A Treatise on the Conflict of Laws* (1935). He was a founder of the American Legal History Society in 1933, and its first president.

BEALE, RICHARD LEE TURBERVILLE (b. *Westmoreland Co., Va., 1819; d. Hague, Va., 1893*), lawyer, politician. Served in Confederate cavalry, 1861–65.

BEALL, JOHN YATES (b. *Jefferson Co., Va., 1835; d. Governors Island, N.Y., 1865*), Confederate soldier. Arrested, December 1864, for sabotage and other activities on Canadian border; executed as spy.

BEALL, SAMUEL WOOTTON (b. *Montgomery Co., Md., 1807; d. Helena, Mont., 1868*), public official, politician. Active in fight for Wisconsin's statehood, 1840–48. Led exploration to Pikes Peak, 1859; helped found city of Denver, Colo.

BEALS, RALPH ALBERT (b. *Deming, N.M., 1899; d. Boston, Mass., 1954*), educator and librarian. Studied at University of California, Harvard (M.A., 1925). Instructor, Harvard, 1925–28; New York University, 1928–1933; assistant to the director of American Association of Adult Education, 1933–38. After studying library science at the University of Chicago Graduate Library School, he became assistant librarian at the Washington, D.C., Public Library, 1940–42. Served as library director and professor at the University of Chicago, 1942–45; dean of the Graduate Library School, 1945–46. In 1946 Beals became director of the New York City Public Library; while there he successfully obtained the first state aid for the system and greatly improved its financial standing.

BEAMAN, CHARLES COTESWORTH (b. *Houlton, Maine, 1840; d. New York, N.Y., 1900*), lawyer. Graduated Harvard, 1861. Acted for United States in controversy with England over Alabama Claims, 1871–76; partner in Evarts, Southmayd, and Choate.

BEAN, LEON LENWOOD (b. *Greenwood, Maine, 1872; d. Miami Shores, Fla., 1967*), businessman. An avid outdoorsman, in 1911 he designed the "Maine Hunting Shoe" and began selling them in 1912. In 1917 he opened a factory in Freeport, and by 1924 was producing outdoor and casual clothing and footwear; outdoor-sports equipment; canoeing gear; and camp furnishings. His goods were advertsied through the L. L. Bean Catalog, and mail orders provided most of his business. L. L. Bean, Inc., became a flourishing business and has continued as a family business since his death. Wrote the popular *Hunting, Fishing,* *and Camping* (1942) as well as *My Store: The Autobiography of a Down-East Merchant* (1960).

BEAN, TARLETON HOFFMAN (*b. Bainbridge, Pa., 1846; d. 1916*), ichthyologist. Fish culturist and authority on fresh-water fish in America; initiated national movement for preservation of native fish.

BEARD, CHARLES AUSTIN (*b. near Knightstown, Ind., 1874; d. New Haven, Conn., 1948*), historian, political scientist. Son of a well-to-do farmer and businessman. Ph.B., De Pauw University, 1898. Studied at Oxford University; concerned himself with labor politics, and aided in founding Ruskin Hall at Oxford. Married Mary Ritter, 1900. His first book, *The Industrial Revolution* (1901), struck a dominant chord of his thinking: the central theme of history is man's increasing assertion of his right and power to determine his own religion and politics, and corporately to control every form of his material environment. A.M. (1903) and Ph.D. (1904), Columbia University. A teacher of history at Columbia, 1904–07, he moved to the department of public law and became professor of politics in 1915. He collaborated with James Harvey Robinson on *The Development of Modern Europe* (1907–08); author of *American Government and Politics* (1910), a pioneering textbook. In 1913, he published *An Economic Interpretation of the Constitution of the United States* which asserted that the framers of that document were actuated more by concern for the property rights of their friends and themselves than by principles of political science, or by zeal for the public good. As this doctrine accorded with current Progressive prejudices, the book was widely read and approved. Later scholarship has called its methodology and conclusions in question. Beard applied an economic interpretation to later periods of American history in subsequent books, particularly in *The Rise of American Civilization* (1927), written in collaboration with his wife.

In 1917, resigned his professorship when Columbia denied reappointment to several faculty members because of their criticism of U.S. intervention in World War I. Thereafter, he held no regular academic appointment but remained active as writer and public figure. A founder of the New School for Social Research (1919), the Workers' Education Bureau (1921), and advisor to members of Congress and government officials.

During the last two decades of his life was increasingly concerned with foreign affairs and American neutrality. The depression of the 1930's caused him to revise his economic interpretation of politics, his belief in objective scholarship and "scientific" history, and his concern for a balance of power in Europe. He believed in a collectivist democracy, rooted in a relatively self-sufficient and nationally planned economy, disentangled from imperial ambitions and European alliances. His *Devil Theory of War* (1936) denounced the idea of wicked warmakers as a fiction, and asserted that President Woodrow Wilson had been pressured into World War I by bankers. Opposed naval expansion, lend-lease, universal military training, and prophesied that President Franklin D. Roosevelt would use some incident in the Pacific as an excuse for supporting Allied imperialism. In *President Roosevelt and the Coming of the War* (1948), he argued that Japan had been deliberately maneuvered into attacking the United States. *The Republic* (1943) was a revision of his views on the Founding Fathers; he now saw them as men with a deep sense of social responsibility for national unity and constitutional government. His career was characterized by a mordant sense of historical fate coupled with an indignant idealism.

BEARD, DANIEL CARTER (*b. Cincinnati, Ohio, 1850; d. Suffern, N.Y., 1941*), illustrator, author, youth leader. Son of James Henry Beard; brother of James C. Beard and Thomas F. Beard.

Studied civil engineering at Worrall's Academy (Covington, Ky.), graduating in 1869; worked four years as a surveyor, and then as a maker of insurance company maps. In New York City, 1878, studied illustration at the Art Students League, supporting himself by hack design work. Contributed sketches and articles to *St. Nicholas Magazine*. *What to Do and How to Do It: The American Boy's Handy Book* (1882), a juvenile classic, was followed by fifteen additional handicraft books over the next half-century. His illustrations for Mark Twain's *A Connecticut Yankee* (1889) were mordant and delighted the author but aroused much controversy because of their propagandistic fervor for the single-tax movement. Became editor of *Recreation*, a sportsmen's magazine, 1905; advocated wildlife conservation. To promote circulation, organized a boys' club dedicated to conservation, outdoor life, and the pioneer spirit; similar organization founded in connection with *Pictorial Review*. Both programs influenced formation of the Boy Scouts. Beard held office in the new movement and designed the hat, shirt, and neckerchief.

BEARD, GEORGE MILLER (*b. Montville, Conn., 1839; d. 1883*), physician. Graduated Yale, 1862; College of Physicians and Surgeons, New York, 1866. Pioneer in neurology in America; known internationally for research on electrotherapeutics.

BEARD, JAMES CARTER (*b. Cincinnati, Ohio, 1837; d. New Orleans, La., 1913*), illustrator. Son of James H. Beard. Celebrated for drawings and articles on plant and animal life.

BEARD, JAMES HENRY (*b. Buffalo, N.Y., 1812; d. Flushing, N.Y., 1893*), artist. Itinerant portrait painter, 1830–45; settled in New York City, 1846; specialized in painting domestic animals.

BEARD, MARY (*b. Dover, N.H., 1876; d. New York, N.Y., 1946*), administrator and educator in nursing and public health. Graduated New York Hospital School of Nursing, 1903; worked as a visiting nurse, 1904–09. Returned to public health nursing after two years in laboratory work, and as director of the Boston Instructive District Nursing Association, 1912–22, and of the Community Health Association, 1922–24, worked to achieve efficient, joint planning by voluntary and official preventive health services. Between 1924 and 1938, holding various posts with the Rockefeller Foundation, she was responsible for a number of projects to advance nursing education and public health service in the United States and abroad. As director of the nursing service of the American Red Cross, 1938–44, she supervised a massive wartime recruitment program, advocating policies which would meet military needs without depriving the civilian population of adequate nursing or the nursing schools of capable instructors.

BEARD, MARY RITTER (*b. Indianapolis, Ind., 1876; d. Scottsdale, Ariz., 1958*), historian and author. Studied at DePauw and Columbia. Remembered for her ardent work in the feminist movement and as a collaborator with her historian husband, Charles Beard, Mary Beard's works include *Woman's Work in Municipalities* (1915) and *Woman as Force in History* (1946), her most famous work. Collaborations with her husband include *The Rise of American Civilization* (1927) and *The Basic History of the United States* (1944).

BEARD, RICHARD (*b. Sumner Co., Tenn., 1799; d. 1880*), Cumberland Presbyterian clergyman. President, Cumberland College, Kentucky, 1843–54; professor of theology, Cumberland University, Tennessee, *post* 1854.

BEARD, THOMAS FRANCIS (*b. Cincinnati, Ohio, 1842; d. 1905*), illustrator, cartoonist. Son of James H. Beard.

BEARD, WILLIAM HOLBROOK (*b. Painesville, Ohio, 1824; d. New York, N.Y., 1900*), artist. Brother of James H. Beard. Known especially for humorous story-pictures of animals in human roles.

BEARDSHEAR, WILLIAM MILLER (*b. Ohio, 1850; d. Iowa, 1902*), United Brethren clergyman. President, Western College, Toledo, Iowa, 1881–89; Iowa State College of Agriculture, 1891–1902.

BEARDSLEY, EBEN EDWARDS (*b. Stepney, Conn., 1808; d. New Haven, Conn., 1891*), Episcopal clergyman. Rector, St. Thomas's Church, New Haven, 1848–91. Author of lives of Samuel Johnson, D.D., and Bishop Samuel Seabury, and *History of the Episcopal Church in Connecticut* (1865, 1868).

BEARDSLEY, SAMUEL (*b. Hoosick, N.Y., 1790; d. Utica, N.Y., 1860*), jurist, congressman. Attorney general of New York, 1836–39; justice, New York supreme court, 1844–47; chief justice, 1847.

BEARY, DONALD BRADFORD (*b. Helena, Mont., 1888; d. San Diego, Calif., 1966*), naval officer. Completed studies at the U.S. Naval Academy (1910); M.S. in electrical engineering, Columbia (1917). During World War I patrolled North Atlantic waters and was awarded the Navy Cross for his wartime activities. Thereafter he worked in a variety of positions at sea, in Washington, D.C., and at Annapolis. During World War II he received the Distinguished Service Medal for his performance as commander of the Fleet Operational Training Command, Atlantic Fleet, an assignment that put him in charge of some eighteen sound schools and antisubmarine training and refresher centers. After reporting for duty with the Pacific Fleet in 1944, assisted with the organization of the Service Squadron 6, whose highly mobile vessels brought fuel, arms, and provisions to fleets at sea. He was awarded the Legion of Merit with a Gold star for his actions during the period January–September 1945. Retired at the rank of vice admiral in 1950.

BEASLEY, FREDERICK (*b. near Edenton, N.C., 1777; d. Elizabethtown, N.J., 1845*), Episcopal clergyman. Professor of philosophy, University of Pennsylvania, 1813–28. Author of *A Search of Truth* (1822), defending Locke.

BEASLEY, MERCER (*b. Philadelphia, Pa., 1815; d. Trenton, N.J., 1897*), jurist. Son of Frederick Beasley. Distinguished chief justice, New Jersey, 1864–97.

BEATTIE, FRANCIS ROBERT (*b. Guelph, Canada, 1848; d. Louisville, Ky., 1906*), Presbyterian clergyman. Professor of theology, Presbyterian Seminary, Louisville, Ky., 1893–1906. Author of *Apologetics* (1903).

BEATTY, ADAM (*b. Hagerstown, Md., 1777; d. Mason Co., Ky., 1858*), lawyer, agricultural writer. Author of *Essays on Practical Agriculture* (1844).

BEATTY, CHARLES CLINTON (*b. Co. Antrim, Ireland, ca. 1715; d. Barbados, 1772*), Presbyterian clergyman. Came to America, 1729. Attended the Log College under William Tennant; was popular preacher and frontier missionary in Pennsylvania, Virginia, and North Carolina.

BEATTY, CLYDE RAYMOND (*b. near Chillicothe, Ohio, 1903; d. Ventura, Calif., 1965*), wild animal trainer. Over a forty-year period, he reigned virtually unchallenged as the foremost American handler of big cats. He trained some 2,000 lions and tigers as well as several bears, leopards, pumas, and jaguars. He always preferred the mixture of lions and tigers, whose hostility to each other he used for his own protection; at one time he worked with forty of these big cats in the giant center stage. Started his own circus in 1935 and made vaudeville, radio, and movie appearances as well as producing several books, including *The Big Cage* (1933) written with Edward Anthony.

BEATTY, JOHN (*b. Neshaminy, Pa., 1749; d. near Princeton, N.J., 1826*), Revolutionary soldier, politician, physician. Son of Charles C. Beatty. Secretary of state of New Jersey, 1795–1805.

BEATTY, JOHN (*b. near Sandusky, Ohio, 1828; d. 1914*), soldier, legislator, banker. Partner with brother in private bank, Cardington, Ohio; rose to brigade command in Union Army; congressman, Republican, from Ohio, 1868–73. Organized Citizens Savings Bank, Columbus, Ohio, and served as president, 1873–1903.

BEATTY, WILLARD WALCOTT (*b. Berkeley, Calif., 1891; d. Washington, D.C., 1961*), educator. Upon the success of his and Carleton Washburne's child-centered "Winnetka Technique," in 1926 he was appointed superintendent of the school system of Bronxville, N.Y., where his progressive reforms became known as the "Bronxville experiment." In the 1930's was a leader in progressive education and was president of the Progressive Educational Association (1933–37). As director of education in the Bureau of Indian Affairs (1936–51), he acted as a significant transition figure in the evolution of a contemporary, more sensitive approach to the educational needs of American Indians.

BEATTY, WILLIAM HENRY (*b. Monclova, Ohio, 1838; d. San Francisco, Calif., 1914*), jurist. Removed to California, 1853; district judge in Nevada, 1864–75; justice, supreme court of Nevada, 1875–80; chief justice of California, 1888–1914.

BEATY, AMOS LEONIDAS (*b. Red River Co., Tex., 1870; d. New York, N.Y., 1939*), lawyer, oil executive. President of Texas Co., 1920–26, and American Petroleum Institute.

BEAUCHAMP, WILLIAM (*b. Kent Co., Del., 1772; d. Paoli, Ind., 1824*), Methodist clergyman. Itinerant preacher, 1794–1815; editor, *Western Christian Monitor*, 1816; served thereafter in Illinois, Missouri, and Indiana.

BEAUCHAMP, WILLIAM MARTIN (*b. Coldenham, N.Y., 1830; d. 1925*), Episcopal clergyman, historian. Authority on history of the Iroquois; archaeologist, New York State Museum.

BEAUMONT, JOHN COLT (*b. Wilkes-Barre, Pa., 1821; d. Durham, N.H., 1882*), naval officer. Served in Mexican War; commanded U.S.S. *Miantonomoh*, first monitor to cross the Atlantic, 1866.

BEAUMONT, WILLIAM (*b. Lebanon, Conn., 1785; d. St. Louis, Mo., 1853*), surgeon. Son of a Connecticut farmer, Beaumont is believed to have had only a common-school education. Apprenticed, 1810, to Dr. Benjamin Chandler in St. Albans, Vt., he was licensed to practice medicine in Vermont, June 1812, and was commissioned surgeon's mate to the 6th Infantry at Plattsburg, N.Y., in the same year. Resigning from the army in 1815, he began private practice at Plattsburg; he enlisted again in 1820 and was sent as post surgeon to Fort Mackinac.

Alexis St. Martin, a young Canadian laborer, was accidentally shot in the stomach on June 6, 1822. Beaumont found him with an open wound "more than the size of the palm of a man's hand" and parts of the lung and punctured stomach protruding from it. Although he thought it impossible the man could survive, Beaumont had St. Martin placed in the military hospital, where he dressed the wound daily for about a year. The stomach adhered to the intercostal muscles and did not drop back into the abdominal cavity. Ultimately a flap of skin covered the opening in the organ, but it could be pushed back so as to expose the interior of the stomach. After a year St. Martin was judged a pauper and ordered returned to Lower Canada, though Beaumont pleaded the trip would kill him. His pleas unheeded, he took the patient into his own home to care for him.

About 1825 Beaumont formed the idea of using his patient for pioneer studies in the processes of digestion. Not long after his experiments had begun, St. Martin ran away. Beaumont published his preliminary findings in which he showed that gastric juice, when removed from the stomach and placed in bottles, digests food the same way but more slowly than under natural conditions. His observations were sufficient to overthrow many prevalent theories on digestion.

While stationed at other army posts, Beaumont continued to search for St. Martin, finally locating him in Lower Canada where he had married. The man and his family were transported to Fort Crawford at Beaumont's expense in August 1829, and the experiments were continued for two years. Patient and family then went back to Canada, agreeing to return when requested. St. Martin kept his promise, and Beaumont worked with him again from November 1832 to March 1834; in 1833, he published his *Experiments and Observations on the Gastric Juice and the Physiology of Digestion*, the greatest contribution ever made to the knowledge of gastric digestion and physiology of the stomach. Beaumont had conferred with many chemists in his endeavor to secure a precise analysis of the gastric juice; Prof. Robley Dunglison of the University of Virginia found that it contained free hydrochloric acid and a second digestive factor which later research proved to be pepsin. The 238 experiments detailed in the book established the relative digestibility of many articles of diet. Beaumont's discoveries began a new era in the study of the stomach and its functions.

St. Martin returned to Canada in 1834, and Beaumont was unsuccessful in attempts to bring him back. In 1838, after disagreements with the newly appointed surgeon general, Beumont resigned from the army and entered private practice in St. Louis.

BEAUPRÉ, ARTHUR MATTHIAS) *b. Oswego Township, Ill., 1853; d. Chicago, Ill., 1919*), lawyer, diplomat. Consul and minister to Colombia, 1899–1903; handled details of Hay-Herrán Treaty. Minister also to the Argentine, the Netherlands, and Cuba.

BEAUREGARD, PIERRE GUSTAVE TOUTANT (*b. near New Orleans, La., 1818; d. New Orleans, 1893*), Confederate soldier. Graduated West Point, 1838. Engineer officer on Scott's staff in Mexican War; chief engineer for draining operations, New Orleans, 1858–61. As Confederate brigadier, commanded forces around Charleston, S.C., 1861. Although junior to Joseph E. Johnston, issued orders for first battle of Bull Run and was promoted to full general. Succeeded A. S. Johnston in command at Shiloh, 1862; soon thereafter his illness caused his replacement in Western theater by Braxton Bragg. Defended the South Carolina and Georgia coasts, 1863–64; soundly defeated Butler at Drewry's Bluff, May 1864, and foiled Union drive on Richmond. After administrative command in West, he returned to fight in Carolina campaign under J. E. Johnston. Post war he held various civil positions including managership of Louisiana Lottery. As a commander he was courageous and skilled in fortification but weak in strategy and method.

BEAUX, CECILIA (*b. Philadelphia, Pa., 1855; d. Gloucester, Mass., 1942*), portrait painter. Began studies in the studio of cousin, Catherine Ann Janvier; also received instruction from William Sartain. Her first important painting was a portrait of her sister and nephew, done in 1883–84, which won a prize at the Pennsylvania Academy exhibition in 1885, and was shown in the Paris Salon, 1886. Going to Paris, 1888, she worked at the Académie Julian with the leading teachers of that day, none of whom had any appreciable influence on her style, which had the breadth, insight, and fluency of her contemporary John Singer Sargent, but not quite the same brilliance. Began successful career as portrait painter in Philadelphia, and after 1900 in New York City. Six of her portraits were hung as a group in the 1896 Paris Salon. Her sitters numbered many famous people, but her most pleasing pictures are informal ones of her family and friends such as "Ernesta" (1914), at the Metropolitan Museum of Art, and "The Dancing Lesson" (1899–1900), at the Art Institute of Chicago.

BEAVER, JAMES ADDAMS (*b. Millerstown, Pa., 1837; d. 1914*), Union soldier, lawyer. Governor of Pennsylvania, Republican, 1887–91; judge, Pennsylvania superior court, 1895–1914.

BEAVERS, LOUISE (*b. Cincinnati, Ohio, 1902; d. Los Angeles, Calif., 1962*), film actress. Her thirty-year film career began with her appearance in *Uncle Tom's Cabin* (1927), after which she played numerous roles as a fat and happy domestic to such stars as Mae West and Jean Harlow. Although she won an Oscar nomination for her role as Aunt Delilah in *Imitation of Life* (1934), thus becoming the first black to achieve stardom in Hollywood, she continued to be cast as a maid. However, she did have an important feature role in *Rainbow on the River* (1936), and her fine performance in *The Jackie Robinson Story* (1950) was another departure from the usual stereotype. During the 1950's she launched her television career, starring in "Beulah" and appearing in other shows.

BECHET, SIDNEY (*b. New Orleans, La., 1897; d. Paris, France, 1959*), musician. Considered one of the greatest jazz clarinetists and saxophonists, Bechet, who was self-taught and never learned to read music, began his career in New Orleans performing with such notable bands as Joe "King" Oliver. Left New Orleans in 1917. In Europe (1919–21) he purportedly performed before King George V and in concert at the Royal Philharmonic Hall. Worked with Duke Ellington, Ford Dabney, and singer Mamie Smith. In France and Germany (1925–29), he worked with Josephine Baker in "La Revue Nègre." In the U.S., during World War II, he played at Eddie Condon's wartime concerts at Town Hall. Returned to France where he became the most popular jazz musician and where he lived until his death.

BECK, CARL (*b. Neckargemünd, Germany, 1856; d. Pelham, N.Y., 1911*), surgeon. Graduated, M.D., Jena, 1879. Came to America, 1881; pioneer in application of X ray to medicine and surgery.

BECK, CHARLES (*b. Heidelberg, Germany, 1798; d. Cambridge, Mass., 1866*), classical scholar. Ph.D. Tübingen, 1823; came to America, 1824. Professor of Latin, Harvard, 1832–50; helped introduce German scholarship into the United States.

BECK, JAMES MONTGOMERY (*b. Philadelphia, Pa., 1861; d. Washington, D.C., 1936*), corporation lawyer. Admitted to Philadelphia bar, 1884; assistant U.S. attorney general, 1900–03. A leading Republican critic of Woodrow Wilson's war policies, Beck welcomed Harding's election as a triumph for conservatism. Appointed solicitor general, 1921, he resigned in 1925; served as congressman from Pennsylvania, 1927–34. Author of *The Constitution of the United States* (1922) and *The Vanishing Rights of the States* (1926).

BECK, JOHANN HEINRICH (*b. Cleveland, Ohio, 1856; d. Cleveland, 1924*), conductor, composer. Director, Cleveland "Pop" Orchestra, 1901–12.

BECK, JOHN BRODHEAD (*b. Schenectady, N.Y., 1794; d. Rhinebeck, N.Y., 1851*), physician. M.D., 1817, College of

Physicians and Surgeons, New York. Collaborated with brother Theodric R. Beck in treatise on medical jurisprudence.

BECK, LEWIS CALEB (*b. Schenectady, N.Y., 1798; d. Albany, N.Y., 1853*), physician, naturalist, chemist. Brother of John B. Beck and Theodric R. Beck. Professor of chemistry, Albany Medical College and Rutgers. Author of works on botany, chemistry, and food adulteration.

BECK, MARTIN (*b. Liptó Szent Miklos, Hungary, 1867; d. New York, N.Y., 1940*), vaudeville impresario (Orpheum Vaudeville Circuit, Palace Theater) and theatrical manager.

BECK, THEODORIC ROMEYN (*b. Schenectady, N.Y., 1791; d. Utica, N.Y., 1855*), physician, philanthropist. Author of *Elements of Medical Jurisprudence* (1823), first authoritative book on subject published in the United States. Brother of John B. and Lewis C. Beck.

BECKER, CARL LOTUS (*b. Black Hawk County, Iowa, 1873; d. Ithaca, N.Y., 1945*), historian. Graduated University of Wisconsin, 1896. Influenced by Frederick J. Turner and Charles H. Haskins, he chose history as his profession. Graduate study at Wisconsin and Columbia University. Taught at Pennsylvania State College and Dartmouth; assistant professor, University of Kansas, 1902. Ph.D., Wisconsin, 1907. In 1916, he left Kansas for the University of Minnesota; in 1917, he joined the history department at Cornell University where he taught until his retirement in 1941. Reputation rests in the main on his gracefully written publications, principally in the field of American history (yet his most famous book was *The Heavenly City of the 18th Century Philosophers* [1932]).

His pioneering *History of Political Parties in the Province of New York* (1909) emphasized the importance of property distinctions in the democratization of New York politics. His next major works were *The Eve of the Revolution* (1918) and *The Declaration of Independence* (1922). Becker's abiding interest lay in the history of ideas, especially of those ideas which had helped bring about the revolutions in the 18th century. He never took seriously the economic interpretation of the history of ideas. He was far from sharing the opinion held by his friends among the "New Historians" that the study of history could contribute directly to the cure of society's ills. Advanced the concept of historical relativism, aimed at exposing what he regarded as the limits of historical knowledge. His views were widely criticized. Following retirement, he continued to write and became known to a more general readership through such books as *How New Will the Better World Be?* (1944) and *Freedom and Responsibility in the American Way of Life* (1945).

BECKER, GEORGE FERDINAND (*b. New York, N.Y., 1847; d. Washington, D.C. 1919*), geologist, mathematician, physicist. Graduated Harvard, 1868; Ph.D., Heidelberg, 1869; Berlin Academy of Mines, 1871. Taught mining and metallurgy, University of California, Berkeley, 1874–79. Served on King survey of the 40th Parallel. His *Geology of the Comstock Lode* (1882) marked a new era in geological investigations in America. Becker also studied quicksilver deposits of Pacific Coast and made investigations abroad. His valuable contributions were in abstruse chemico-physical problems and methods of solving them. Carnegie Geophysical Laboratory was largely an outgrowth of his work.

BECKET, FREDERICK MARK (*b. Montreal, Canada 1875; d. New York, N.Y., 1942*), metallurgist. B.S. in electrical engineering, McGill University, 1895. Made advanced studies at Columbia University in physical chemistry and metallurgy. Employed by several firms in the electrochemical field, he organized his own research laboratory (1903) in which he worked out the silicon reduction process for producing low-carbon ferrolloys in an electric furnace. Work laid the foundation for production of low-carbon ferroachrome and stainless steels. He also experimented successfully with production of silicon alloys. As chief metallurgist for a predecessor of Union Carbide Corporation, and with that firm after its incorporation until retirement in 1940, he continued experimentation, producing results which made possible the manufacture of the ferrozirconium and ferrovanadium alloys used for armor plate. As head of Union Carbide's research laboratories, he inspired and developed a notable staff of assistants and successors.

BECKNELL, WILLIAM (*b. Amherst Co., Va., ca. 1796; d. 1865*), explorer, trader, pioneer in Santa Fe trade. Took pack train via upper Arkansas to Santa Fe and Taos, 1821; took wagon train via Cimarron to San Miguel, 1822, establishing new route. Removed to Texas, 1834.

BECKWITH, CLARENCE AUGUSTINE (*b. Charlemont, Mass., 1849; d. Bangor, Maine, 1931*), Congregational clergyman, educator. Professor of theology, Bangor Seminary, 1893–1905; Chicago Seminary, 1905–26.

BECKWITH, JAMES CAROLL (*b. Hannibal, Mo., 1852; d. New York, N.Y., 1917*), painter. Studied Chicago Academy, 1868–71; New York National Academy, 1871–73; and in Paris with Yvon and Duran; a friend of J. S. Sargent. Returned to America, 1878, and was successful as portrait painter and in genre work. Breaking with the conservatives, Beckwith and other young artists formed the Society of American Artists and also organized Art Students League, at which he was an influential teacher.

BECKWOURTH, JAMES P. (*b. Virginia, 1798; d. ca. 1867*). His roving exploits as hunter and squaw man are described in T. D. Bonner's *Life and Adventures of J. P. Beckworth* (1856).

BEDAUX, CHARLES EUGENE (*b. Charenton-le-Pont, France, 1886; d. Miami, Fla., 1944*), efficiency expert, Nazi collaborator. Came to America, 1906; became a citizen, 1917. Setting up as a "management consultant," he devised a rival system to that of Frederick W. Taylor, which was essentially a simple speed-up disguised in pseudo-scientific jargon. His system had remarkable success, since it did not require any major restructuring of management, as Taylor's system did: it was adopted by some of the world's largest corporations, and Bedaux was able to live luxuriously in France. Ambitious for social acceptance and for a role in world affairs, he cultivated celebrities, and in particular the leaders of Nazi Germany. *Post* 1940, he was an economic adviser to the Nazi rulers of occupied France, and to the government at Vichy. Captured in Algeria in November 1942, he was returned to the United States. He committed suicide while in custody.

BEDFORD, GUNNING (*b. 1742; d. 1797*), Revolutionary soldier, politician. Cousin of Gunning Bedford (1747–1812). Governor of Delaware, 1796–97.

BEDFORD, GUNNING (*b. Philadelphia, Pa., 1747; d. Wilmington, Del., 1812*), Revolutionary statesman. Champion of rights of small states in Federal Convention, 1787; federal judge, 1789–1812.

BEDINGER, GEORGE MICHAEL (*b. York Co., Pa., 1756; d. near Blue Licks, Ky., 1843*), Revolutionary soldier. Early Kentucky settler and opponent of slavery.

BEE, BARNARD ELLIOTT (*b. Charleston, S.C., 1824; d. Bull Run, Va., 1861*), Confederate soldier. Raised in Texas; graduated West Point, 1845; meritorious service in Mexican War and on frontier. As Confederate brigadier, commanded key point at first battle of Bull Run, where he was killed. His reference to T. J. Jackson's brigade "standing like a stone wall" was origin of Jackson's nickname "Stonewall."

BEE, HAMILTON PRIOLEAU (*b. Charleston, S.C., 1822; d. San Antonio, Tex., 1897*), Confederate soldier. Brother of Barnard E. Bee. Commanded at Brownsville, Texas, and expedited importation of munitions across Mexican border.

BEEBE, (CHARLES) WILLIAM (*b. Brooklyn, N.Y., 1877; d. Simla, Trinidad, 1962*), naturalist and oceanographer. After studying zoology at Columbia University and working briefly as a curator for the New York Zoological Society, as of 1900 he began traveling widely to conduct field research. In 1928, he set up the tropical research unit of the New York Zoological Society on the Bermudan island of Nonsuch, where he made numerous descents in the bathysphere with Otis Barton, who developed the spherical diving device. In 1949 he established a research station on land he had bought at Simla, in Trinidad, which he later presented to the Zoological Society and where he continued working until his death. His major contributions lay in the breadth and detail of his field observations, his emphasis upon the interrelationships of living forms, his abiding concern with conservation, and the felicity with which he expressed himself in some 800 articles and in the twenty-four books he produced between 1905 and 1955.

BEECHER, CATHARINE ESTHER (*b. East Hampton, N.Y., 1800; d. 1878*), educator, reformer. Daughter of Lyman Beecher.

BEECHER, CHARLES (*b. Litchfield, Conn. 1815; d. Georgetown, Mass., 1900*), Congregational clergyman. Son of Lyman Beecher. Pastor, First Congregational Church, Georgetown, Mass., 1857–81, and held other pastorates. Shared family propensity for reform.

BEECHER, CHARLES EMERSON (*b. Dunkirk, N.Y., 1856; d. New Haven, Conn., 1904*), paleontologist. Curator, Yale geological collections, 1888–1904.

BEECHER, EDWARD (*b. East Hampton, N.Y., 1803; d. Brooklyn, N.Y., 1895*), Congregational clergyman. President, Illinois College, 1830–44; held pastorates in Boston, Galesburg, Ill., and Brooklyn, N.Y.; active in antislavery work. Son of Lyman Beecher.

BEECHER, HENRY WARD (*b. Litchfield, Conn., 1813; d. Brooklyn, N.Y., 1887*), clergyman, publicist. Son of Lyman Beecher and Roxana (Foote) Beecher. Graduated Amherst, 1834; studied at Lane Theological Seminary, Cincinnati. Licensed to preach, 1837, but was refused ordination by Old School Presbytery in Indiana to which a local church had called him. Married Eunice White Bullard, 1837. Ordained by Cincinnati New School Presbytery, 1838, he was for eight years pastor of Second Presbyterian Church, Indianapolis. Unconventional in dress and manner, he believed that a sermon was effective only when it altered the moral character of the listeners; he strove deliberately for emotional response. His direct, pithy style, touches of humor, and flights of imagination made him a popular preacher; the same qualities in his writing won him a wide audience in periodicals. In 1847, his growing fame brought him to the pastorate of Plymouth Church, Brooklyn, N.Y. (Congregationalist). Few American clergymen have attained the influence and public position which soon became his. His theatrical techniques of expression, his bold and often wise pronouncements on public questions such as slavery and municipal reform, his very genuine sympathy with and understanding of human difficulties, all combined to fascinate his generation. Believing that slavery was fundamentally wrong, he held that the Constitution forbade interference with it in the slave states; left to itself it would wither. Meanwhile, all means should be employed to prevent its spread to the new Territories. He campaigned for Frémont in 1856, and for Lincoln, and was a strong supporter of the Civil War.

After the war, he supported President Johnson's policy of re-admitting the seceded states and withdrawing military government from them. Not a brilliant or original thinker, his genius lay in the practical use of other men's ideas and their propagation by means of his overflowing energy and oratorical talents. Freedom was a passion with him, and he had singularly little prejudice. His latter years were disturbed by accusations of sexual immorality made, 1872, by a member of his church. A subsequent civil suit for damages brought about a sensational trial at which the jury failed to agree. His popularity, though diminished, was not destroyed; a council of Congregational churches examined the evidence and exonerated him. He continued his work on the lecture platform and at Plymouth Church until his death.

BEECHER, LYMAN (*b. New Haven, Conn., 1775; d. Brooklyn, N.Y., 1863*), Presbyterian clergyman. Father of Catharine E., Charles, Edward, Henry Ward, Thomas K. Beecher, and Harriet Beecher Stowe. Graduated Yale, 1797; ordained 1799. Pastor, Presbyterian Church, East Hampton, N.Y., 1799–1810; Litchfield, Conn., 1810–26; Hanover Street Church, Boston, 1826–32, where he conducted a continuous revival which resulted in a growth in intolerance. First president, Lane Theological Seminary, Cincinnati, 1832–50, and center of much theological controversy and opposition from conservative Presbyterians.

BEECHER, THOMAS KINNICUT (*b. Litchfield, Conn., 1824; d. Elmira, N.Y., 1900*), Congregational clergyman. Pastor, Congregational Church, Elmira, N.Y., 1854–1900. Pioneer in church social work. Son of Lyman Beecher.

BEER, GEORGE LOUIS (*b. Staten Island, N.Y., 1872; d. 1920*), historian. Graduated Columbia, 1892. Retiring from business, 1903, he began research along economic lines which resulted in the three major works: *British Colonial Policy, 1754–65* (1907); *The Origins of the British Colonial System, 1578–1660* (1908); and *The Old Colonial System: Part I* (1912). These did much to correct long prevalent errors in American thinking on the subject. Beer served with ability as chief of the colonial division, American delegation to Paris Peace Conference, helping to draft mandates for administration of former German colonies.

BEER, THOMAS (*b. Council Bluffs, Iowa, 1889; d. New York, N.Y., 1940*), writer. Author, among other, of *Stephen Crane* (1923) and *The Mauve Decade* (1926).

BEER, WILLIAM (*b. Plymouth, England, 1849; d. New Orleans, La., 1927*), librarian, Howard Memorial Library, New Orleans, 1891–1927; was a prominent figure in social and literary life of that city.

BEERS, CLIFFORD WHITTINGHAM (*b. New Haven, Conn., 1876; d. Providence, R.I., 1943*), founder of the mental hygiene movement. A graduate of Yale's Sheffield Scientific School, Beers spent three years (1900–03) in mental hospitals and on his release was determined to effect their reform. His book *A Mind That Found Itself* (1908) set forth his program for the transformation of mental hospitals from custodial institutions into therapeutic ones. Gifted as an organizer and fund-raiser, and with the support of leading physicians and men of science, he founded the National Committee for Mental Hygiene (1909) and made it for several decades the leader in practically every aspect of the mental health movement. *Post* 1922, he extended his work on an international scale.

BEERS, ETHEL LYNN (*b. Goshen, N.Y., 1827; d. New York, N.Y., 1879*), poet. Published *All Quiet Along the Potomac, and Other Poems* (1879); the title-poem first appeared, 1861, as "The Picket Guard."

BEERS, HENRY AUGUSTIN (*b. Buffalo, N.Y., 1847; d. 1926*), author, educator. Graduated Yale, 1869; taught English literature there, 1871–1916; professor emeritus, 1916–26. Author of studies on romanticism.

BEERY, WALLACE FITZGERALD (*b. Kansas City, Mo., 1885; d. Beverly Hills, Calif., 1949*), actor. School dropout, railroad section hand, and elephant trainer with Ringling Brothers circus, Beery became a musical comedy chorus man in 1904; his first break came in 1907, when he replaced Raymond Hitchcock briefly in *A Yankee Tourist*. He left the stage in 1913 to work in screen comedies for the Essanay Company; in 1916–18, he worked as actor and director for Universal and Keystone studios in Hollywood. Turning from comedy, became for a few years a leading screen villain. Between 1925 and 1929, under contract to Paramount Pictures, he made among other films a series of comedies with Raymond Hatton. Paramount lacked confidence in his ability to succeed in sound pictures and dropped him in 1929. Metro-Goldwyn-Mayer took him on and developed him into one of the studio's principal box-office attractions in such pictures as *The Champ* (1931), *Viva Villa!* (1934), *Grand Hotel* (1932), and *Treasure Island* (1934), and as a costar with Marie Dressler (*Tugboat Annie*, 1933). He is said to have earned M-G-M an estimated fifty million dollars.

BEESON, CHARLES HENRY (*b. Columbia City, Ind., 1870; d. Chicago, Ill., 1949*), classical scholar, medievalist, paleographer. B.A., Indiana University, 1893; M.A., 1895. Graduate study at University of Chicago with William G. Hale; Ph.D., University of Munich, 1907, where he worked with Ludwig Traube. Joining the faculty of University of Chicago as instructor in Latin, he became professor in 1918 and retired in 1935. During World War I, his skill as a textual critic was employed in code and cipher work. His achievements in scholarship may be epitomized by citation of four of his books: his definitive edition of Hegemonius published by the Prussian Academy (1906); *Isidor-Studien* (1913), on Isidore of Seville; *A Primer of Mediaeval Latin* (1925), whose introduction is a magisterial summary of differences between classical and medieval Latin; and *Lupus of Ferrières as Scribe and Text Critic* (1930).

BEGLEY, EDWARD JAMES ("ED") (*b. Hartford, Conn., 1901; d. Van Nuys, Calif., 1970*), actor. After being an announcer, actor, writer, producer, and disc jockey for WTIC in Hartford, in 1943 moved to network radio and became one of radio's busiest actors. First appeared on Broadway in *Land of Fame* (1943), though his breakthrough play was Arthur Miller's *All My Sons* (1947). Thereafter his Broadway performances included *Inherit the Wind* (1955), in which he played Matthew Harrison Brady and for which he received the Donaldson, Variety, and Tony awards; *Look Homeward, Angel* (1958); and *Advise and Consent* (1960). Between 1948 and 1952 he worked primarily in films and then was prominent in the so-called golden age of television drama, appearing on most of the new medium's major drama anthologies. Won an Academy Award as best supporting actor for his role in the film *Sweet Bird of Youth* (1962). In the 1960's remained active in television and films.

BEHAN, WILLIAM JAMES (*b. New Orleans, La., 1840; d. New Orleans, 1928*), sugar planter, political leader. Mayor, New Orleans, 1882–84; later turned Republican in protest against Democratic plan to cut sugar tariff.

BEHN, SOSTHENES (*b. St. Thomas, Virgin Islands, 1882; d. New York, N.Y., 1957*), businessman. Studied at Ste. Barbe College, Paris. Immigrated to the U.S. in 1898. Founder and president of International Telephone and Telegraph Corporation (I.T.&T.) in 1920; chairman of the board, 1948–56. Behn, along with his brother, Hernand, built I.T.&T. into the world's largest international communications conglomerate, acquiring the International Western Electric Company in 1925 and establishing the International Telecommunications Laboratories in 1945. In spite of severe setbacks and losses in Spain, Latin America, Nazi Germany, and the communist nations of eastern Europe, Behn was able to keep I.T.&T. a leader in international conglomerates and international corporations by never subordinating the company's concerns to those of any nation. At Behn's death in 1957, the firm was a $760 million worldwide communications empire.

BEHREND, BERNARD ARTHUR (*b. Villeneuve, Switzerland, 1875; d. 1932*), electrical engineer. Designer of turbo-electric machinery.

BEHRENDS, ADOLPHUS JULIUS FREDERICK (*b. Nymwegen, Holland, 1839; d. Brooklyn, N.Y., 1900*), clergyman. Brought to America as a child. Originally a Baptist, he won reputation as pastor of Central Congregational Church, Brooklyn, 1883–1900.

BEHRENDT, WALTER CURT (*b. Metz, Lorraine, 1884; d. Norwich, Vt., 1945*), architect, regional planner. Doctorate in engineering, Technische Hochschule, Dresden, 1911. Served in the Prussian Ministry of Public Works, Army private in World War I, and thereafter played a leading part in postwar housing and industrial programs. Also won fame as an architectural historian and critic, and was a sympathetic but discriminating advocate of the new trends in architecture and decoration represented by the Weimar and Bauhaus groups. Of Jewish descent, he left Germany in 1934 to become a lecturer at Dartmouth, and technical director (1937–41) of the Buffalo, N.Y., City Planning Association. In 1941, returned to Dartmouth as professor of city planning and housing and became U.S. citizen. Wrote, among other works, *Modern Building* (1937), probably the best critical and historical summation of the modern (post eclectic) movement in architecture.

BEHRENS, HENRY (*b. Munstadt, Germany, 1815; d. 1895*), Jesuit priest. Superior of Buffalo (N.Y.) Mission, 1872–78, 1886–92. Established St. Ignatius College (now John Carroll University), Cleveland, Ohio, 1886.

BEISSEL, JOHANN CONRAD (*b. Eberbach, Germany, 1690; d. 1768*), hymn writer, founder of Solitary Brethren of the Community of Seventh Day Baptists at Ephrata, Lancaster Co., Pa., 1732.

BELASCO, DAVID (*b. San Francisco, Calif., 1853; d. 1931*), actor, dramatist, producer. As a boy, recited ballads in public for pennies and wrote plays based on dime novels. After acting and directing in San Francisco, 1871–79, went to New York as hack dramatist and stage manager. Achieved financial independence in 1895 with *The Heart of Maryland*. *Madame Butterfly* (1900) and other successes followed. His ability to create illusion of reality and atmosphere and his painstaking perfectionism set a new standard of technical excellence in the American theater.

BELCHER, JONATHAN (*b. Cambridge, Mass., 1681/2; d. Elizabethtown, N.J., 1757*), merchant. Graduated Harvard, 1699; traveled extensively in Europe; returning to Boston, he became successful in trade. Elected to Massachusetts Council, 1718, he was reelected seven times. Appointed governor of Massachusetts and New Hampshire, 1729/30, he failed in efforts to please both colonial and royal interests, and was dismissed from both governorships in 1741. After rehabilitating himself with the government in England, he was appointed governor of New Jersey, 1746, where he was active in founding the College of New Jersey (Princeton).

BELCOURT, GEORGE ANTOINE (*b. Bay du Febvre, Canada, 1803; d. Shediac, New Brunswick, 1874*), Roman Catholic priest. Pioneer missionary in western Canada and North Dakota; student of the Saulteux (Chippewa) language.

BELDEN, JOSIAH (*b. Cromwell, Conn., 1815; d. New York, N.Y., 1892*), California pioneer, member of Bartleson-Bidwell party from Independence, Mo., to the Pacific, 1841. Later rancher, storekeeper, first mayor of San Jose.

BELKNAP, GEORGE EUGENE (*b. Newport, N.H., 1832; d. Key West, Fla., 1903*), naval officer.

BELKNAP, JEREMY (*b. Boston, Mass., 1744; d. Boston, 1798*), Congregational clergyman, historian. Graduated Harvard, 1762; pastor at Dover, N.H., 1766–86; at Federal Street Church, Boston, 1787, until his death. Author of outstanding three-volume *History of New Hampshire* (1784, 1791, 1792); *The Foresters* (1792); *American Biography* (1794, 1798); and other works. In 1790–91 he helped form an antiquarian society which in 1794 became the Massachusetts Historical Society, first of its kind in the United States.

BELKNAP, WILLIAM WORTH (*b. Newburgh, N.Y., 1829; d. Washington, D.C., 1890*), lawyer, Union soldier. Secretary of war, 1869–76; resigned in face of charges of malfeasance in office.

BELL, ALEXANDER GRAHAM (*b. Edinburgh, Scotland, 1847; d. Cape Breton, Nova Scotia, 1922*), inventor of telephone, leader in education of the deaf. Son of Alexander Melville Bell, scientist and author in the field of vocal physiology and elocution, and grandson of Alexander Bell, a professor of elocution in London. Alexander Graham Bell went to London *ca.* 1868 as professional assistant to his father, who had taken over the grandfather's work there; he assumed complete charge while his father was on a lecture tour in America in 1868 and worked with him until the family moved to Canada in 1870. While in London he took courses in anatomy and physiology at University College. His work for the deaf began in this period. His father had invented "Visible Speech," a system of symbols indicating the position of the vocal organs in speaking; the younger Bell adapted this system for use in teaching the deaf to talk.

After the family came to Canada, Bell went to Boston in 1871 to train the teachers at a special day school for the deaf, the first of its kind anywhere, which had been started by the Boston School Board and began a private class for teachers of the deaf, 1872. Appointed professor of vocal physiology and the mechanics of speech at Boston University, 1873, he instituted a similar class there, started a series of conventions for teachers of speech to the deaf and took private pupils as well.

Bell did his first original scientific study in 1865 on the resonance pitches of the mouth cavities during utterance of vowel sounds. Amid his other activities, 1873–76, he was experimenting with a phonautograph, a multiple telegraph, and an electric speaking telegraph or telephone. He conceived the theory of the telephone in 1874; a year later, encouraged by Prof. Joseph Henry and while experimenting on the multiple telegraph, he finally hit upon the practical solution to the problem of reproducing the human voice electrically. Experiments to improve quality continued; in 1876 the first complete intelligible sentence was transmitted. The following year a conversation between Boston and New York was conducted. Patents were issued to Bell in 1876 and 1877, but many claimants contested his rights. After extensive litigation, the U.S. Supreme Court upheld all of Bell's claims. The first organization for commercial development of the invention, the Bell Telephone Co., was formed in 1877. That same year Bell married Mabel G. Hubbard, who had been deaf from early childhood. After traveling with her in Europe to introduce the telephone to England and France, he returned to Washington, D.C., in 1878, where he continued inventive activity in fields

related to the telephone. He became a citizen of the United States in 1882. At the Volta Laboratory, which he financed, he and two associates worked on numerous projects including Bell's photophone, the induction balance, and the audiometer; they also invented and patented several improvements on Edison's phonograph. Bell was president of the National Geographic Society, 1896–1904, and did much to forward the success of the Society and its magazine.

Aviation was Bell's primary interest after 1897. He encouraged the work of Samuel P. Langley, invented the tetrahedral kite, and in 1907 founded the Aerial Experiment Association, under whose auspices the first public flight of a heavier-than-air machine was made in 1908.

BELL, ALEXANDER MELVILLE (*b. Edinburgh, Scotland, 1819; d. 1905*), educator. Father of Alexander G. Bell. Author of *Visible Speech* (1867).

BELL, BERNARD IDDINGS (*b. Dayton, Ohio, 1886; d. Chicago, Ill., 1958*), clergyman, educator, and author. Studied at the University of Chicago (B.A., 1907) and the Western Theological Seminary. Dean of St. Paul's Cathedral Church in Fond du Lac, Wis., 1913–19; warden of St. Stephen's College (now Bard College), 1919–30; canon at St. John's Cathedral in Providence, R.I., 1933–46. An Episcopalian conservative, Bell wrote many works against secularism and the rule of the masses. His works include *Affirmations* (1938), *A Catholic Looks at His World* (1936), and *Crowd Culture* (1952).

BELL, CHARLES HENRY (*b. Chester, N.H., 1823; d. Exeter, N.H., 1893*), lawyer, politician. Author of *The Bench and Bar of New Hampshire* (1894) and other works on history of that state.

BELL, CLARK (*b. Whitesville, N.Y., 1832; d. New York, N.Y., 1918*), lawyer, expert in medical jurisprudence.

BELL, DE BENNEVILLE ("BERT") (*b. Philadelphia, Pa., 1894; d. Philadelphia, 1959*), sports figure. Studied at the University of Pennsylvania. After playing football with his college team, Bell coached college teams in the Philadelphia area until 1933 when he became part owner of the future Philadelphia Eagles, and, from 1936 to 1940, full owner. From 1940 to 1946, he was part owner of the Pittsburgh Steelers. In 1946, Bell became commissioner of the National Football League, a position he held until his death. Under his tenure, professional football became one of the biggest sports businesses in the nation. He died while watching a game between the Eagles and the Steelers.

BELL, ERIC TEMPLE (*b. Aberdeen, Scotland, 1883; d. Watsonville, Calif., 1960*), mathematician, author, and educator. Immigrated to the U.S. in 1902; studied at Stanford, the University of Washington, and at Columbia (Ph.D., 1912). As well as teaching at the University of Washington, Chicago, Harvard, and the California Institute of Technology (1926–53), Bell was a popularizer of mathematics; his books include *The Development of Mathematics* (1940) and *Men of Mathematics* (1937). Sometimes using the name John Tain, Bell published seventeen science-fiction novels, including *Before the Dawn* (1934) and *The Time Stream* (1946).

BELL, FREDERIC SOMERS (*b. Webster City, Iowa, 1859; d. Winona, Minn., 1938*), lumberman. President, Weyerhaeuser Timber Co., 1928–34.

BELL, HENRY HAYWOOD (*b. North Carolina, 1808; d. near Osaka, Japan, 1868*), naval officer. Served as chief of staff to Farragut, 1862; commanded West Gulf Squadron, 1863; in Asiatic waters, 1865 and after.

BELL, ISAAC (*b. New York, N.Y., 1846; d. 1889*), cotton merchant, politician. Established one of first brokerage firms to unite operations in the cotton region with Northern speculative market.

BELL, JACOB (*b. Middlesex [now Darien], Conn., 1792; d. 1852*), shipbuilder. His New York shipyard built sailing packets for the Collins Line, the *Trade Wind* and other well-known clipper ships, and the first ocean steamships launched in New York (1840).

BELL, JAMES FORD (*b. Philadelphia, Pa., 1879; d. Minneapolis, Minn., 1961*), industrialist and first president of General Mills. After becoming president of Washburn Crosby, a merchant-milling firm headed by his father, he organized the consolidation of a number of milling companies to form General Mills Company in 1928. Under his leadership, first as president and after 1934 as chairman of the board, General Mills met the problems facing the flour-milling industry in the late 1920's, and by the late 1940's grew to be twice as large as its nearest competitor, Pillsbury Flour Mills.

BELL, JAMES FRANKLIN (*b. near Shelbyville, Ky., 1856; d. 1919*), army officer. Graduated West Point, 1878. Served in West, 1878–98, and with special distinction in the Philippine insurrection; promoted major general, 1907; chief of staff of the army, 1906–11.

BELL, JAMES MADISON (*b. Gallipolis, Ohio, 1826; d. 1902*), black poet, lecturer. Friend of John Brown; worked against slavery; resident *post* 1865 in Toledo, Ohio. Author of *Poetical Works* (1901).

BELL, JAMES STROUD (*b. Philadelphia, Pa., 1847; d. 1915*), merchant miller. Reorganizer, 1888, and president of the Washburn-Crosby Co., 1889–1915; innovator in promoting cereal sales by packaging and advertising.

BELL, JOHN (*b. near Nashville, Tenn., 1797; d. Stewart Co., Tenn., 1869*), Southern statesman. Graduated Cumberland College, 1814; began practice of law at Franklin, Tenn., later removing to Nashville, where he led the bar. As congressman, Democrat, 1827–41, Bell was at first a supporter of Jackson but became ultimately the leader of the Whig party in Tennessee and accepted cabinet post of secretary of war from President W. H. Harrison, 1841. In opposition to President Tyler, he resigned in the same year.

After six years' retirement, Bell was elected to the U.S. Senate in 1847, continuing to serve until 1859. During this period of increasing bitterness between North and South, Bell distinguished himself as one of the most consistently conservative and nationally minded Southerners. Although a slave owner, he never became an apostle of slavery, and was opposed to extremism on either side. As a member of the lower house he had supported John Quincy Adams in defense of the right of petition, opposing those who sought to prevent reception or consideration of antislavery petitions. In the Senate, when controversy arose over the question of slavery in the territories the United States had acquired from Mexico, Bell affirmed the constitutionality of congressional prohibition of slavery in the territories, although he did not agree with the policy. He supported President Taylor's plan of admitting the territories to statehood even if the exclusion of slavery should result. In 1854 he broke with other Southerners and opposed reopening the bitter controversy over slavery by passage of the Kansas-Nebraska Act; four years later he defied instructions from the Tennessee legislature to support the admission of Kansas under the Lecompton constitution, believing it wrong to force slavery upon an unwilling people. Bitterly denounced in the South for his moderate attitude, he gained respect in the North.

By 1858 the Whig party was dead. Bell supported the short-lived Native Americans and also considered uniting former Southern Whigs with moderate Republicans. But by this time moderation was not popular. In 1860 a group of moderates, most of them former Whigs, supported Bell for president and Edward Everett for vice president on the ticket of the Constitutional Union party. Bell received the electoral votes of Tennessee, Kentucky, and Virginia. His campaign had been a plea for preservation of the Union. He and his followers opposed secession, and he sought to promote compromise even after Lincoln's administration began. Yet when Fort Sumter was fired upon and Lincoln called for troops, Bell advised Tennessee to enter into "alliance" with the seceded states if the federal government attempted their coercion. This ended his career. He spent his remaining years lamenting the war and what it had brought both to the South and to the nation.

BELL, LAWRENCE DALE (*b. Mentone, Ind., 1894; d. Buffalo, N.Y., 1956*), aerospace pioneer and entrepreneur. Founded the Bell Aircraft Corporation in Buffalo in 1935. A leader in aircraft design during World War II, Bell produced the P-39 and P-63. Supervised production of a B-29 bomber a day at Marietta, Ga. After the war, he concentrated on helicopters and guided missiles. The Bell Model 47 became the most widely used helicopter in the world. Bell retired as president of the company in 1956, but remained chairman of the board until his death.

BELL, LOUIS (*b. New Hampshire, 1864; d. 1923*), physicist, engineer. Graduated Dartmouth, 1884; began serious work in physics and chemistry at Johns Hopkins, his most important work there being determination of wave-length of D_1 line in spectrum of sodium. Appointed chief engineer in power transmission department of General Electric, 1893, he became authority of polyphase transmission. After 1895, as consulting engineer in Boston, did "diagnostic work on sick electric railways." Coauthor of *The Electric Railway* (1892); author, *Power transmission for Electric Railroads* (1896), *The Art of Illumination* (1902), and *The Telescope* (1922). Over forty patents testify to his originality.

BELL, LUTHER VOSE (*b. Francestown, N.H., 1806; d. Budd's Ferry, Md., 1862*), physician, politician. Son of Samuel Bell. Superintendent, McLean Hospital for Insane, Charlestown, Mass., 1836–56. Described a form of insanity (1848) thereafter known as Bell's Disease or Bell's Mania.

BELL, PETER HANSBOROUGH (*b. near Fredericksburg, Va., 1808; d. Warren Co., N.C., 1898*), soldier. Fought at San Jacinto and as Texas Ranger in Mexican War; governor of Texas, 1849–52; congressman, Democrat, from Texas, 1853–57.

BELL, ROBERT (*b. Glasgow, Scotland, ca. 1732; d. Richmond, Va., 1784*), bookseller. Came to America *ca.* 1766; famous for wit and drollery. Published at Philadelphia the first edition of Paine's *Common Sense* (1776), the first American edition of Blackstone's *Commentaries*, and other notable works.

BELL, SAMUEL (*b. Londonderry, N.H., 1770; d. Chester, N.H., 1850*), lawyer. Graduated Dartmouth, 1793. Democratic-Republican governor of New Hampshire, 1819–23, U.S. senator, 1823–35. The rise of Jacksonian democracy caused his retirement from Congress.

BELLAMY, EDWARD (*b. Chicopee Falls, Mass., 1850; d. Chicopee Falls, 1898*), author, utopian socialist. Studied law; with brother Charles founded Springfield *Daily News*, 1880; contributed to magazines. Becoming more seriously concerned with social questions, devoted himself exclusively to them. Author of *The Duke of Stockbridge* (1879, newspaper publication; 1900, book form); *Looking Backward* (1888), a famous utopian romance; *Equality* (1897); and other books.

BELLAMY, ELIZABETH WHITFIELD CROOM (*b. near Quincy, Fla., 1837; d. Mobile, Ala., 1900*), teacher, author of romantic novels of life in the South.

BELLAMY, JOSEPH (*b. Cheshire, Conn., 1719; d. Bethlehem, Conn., 1790*), theologian. Graduated Yale, 1735. Follower of Jonathan Edwards; wrote on New Light theology; pastor at Bethlehem, Conn., 1738–90.

BELLANCA, DOROTHY JACOBS (*b. Zemel, Latvia, 1894; d. New York, N.Y., 1946*), labor leader, social reformer. Came to Baltimore, Md., 1900, with her Jewish immigrant parents; left public school at thirteen to work as a buttonhole maker. Led strike of Baltimore buttonhole makers, 1912; delegate to founding convention of Amalgamated Clothing Workers of America, 1914. She became a member of that union's executive board, 1916, and as organizer of female workers participated in organizing campaigns in Chicago, Philadelphia, and New York City. Married August Bellanca, a fellow board member, in 1918. Soon resuming union activity, she worked to organize shops which had moved out of cities to escape the union; this work was intensified in the 1930's. Took part in the 1934 general strike in the textile industry and in 1937–38 was a special organizer for the CIO. Textile Workers in the South. She was also active in politics and an appointed member of numerous public committees concerned with labor matters.

BELLANCA, GIUSEPPE MARIO (*b. Sciacca, Sicily, 1886; d. New York, N.Y., 1960*), aeronautical designer and manufacturer. Designer of a successful early monoplane, the CF, first flown in 1922, and of the famous *Columbia*, which was flown nonstop across the Atlantic two weeks after Lindbergh's flight. Bellanca remained an innovative designer but never became a major manufacturer of aircraft.

BELLEW, FRANK HENRY TEMPLE (*b. Cawnpore, India, 1828; d. 1888*), illustrator. Came to America, 1850. Worked for leading magazines as comic artist and caricaturist.

BELLINGHAM, RICHARD (*b. Boston, England, ca. 1592; d. 1672*), lawyer. Came to Boston, New England, 1634. Held various posts, 1635–65; was governor of Massachusetts, 1641, 1654, 1665–72. Espoused popular cause against Winthrop.

BELLOMONT, EARL OF. *See* COOTE, RICHARD.

BELLOWS, ALBERT FITCH (*b. Milford, Mass., 1829; d. 1883*), landscape painter, etcher. A painstaking depicter of rural scenes.

BELLOWS, GEORGE WESLEY (*b. Columbus, Ohio, 1882; d. New York, N.Y., 1925*), painter, lithographer, illustrator. Studied under Robert Henri and was influenced by theories of Jay Hambidge and by example of Goya and Daumier; interested especially in everyday subjects and city street life. Taught at Art Students League, New York City, and Art Institute, Chicago. By 1915 he expanded his interests to include country subjects and the horrors of war; his pictures of events in World War I are among his best. *Post* 1916 he gave particular attention to lithography and undertook book illustration. Bellows's works in all types were stamped with his own personality and rank with the best art of this period.

BELLOWS, HENRY WHITNEY (*b. Boston, Mass., 1814; d. New York, N.Y., 1882*), Unitarian clergyman. Graduated Harvard, 1832; Harvard Divinity School, 1837. Pastor, First Unitarian Church (later, Church of All Souls), New York City, 1839–82. Founder and president, U.S. Sanitary Commission in the Civil War; editor, *Christian Examiner*, 1866–77.

BELMONT, ALVA ERTSKIN SMITH VANDERBILT (*b. Mobile, Ala., 1853; d. Paris, France, 1933*), social leader, suffragette.

BELMONT, AUGUST (*b. Alzei, Germany, 1816; d. New York, N.Y., 1890*), capitalist. Trained in Rothschilds' office, Frankfurt, he managed branch offices of the firm and profited by the panic of 1837 to begin banking business in New York, establishing what became Belmont and Co., and acting as agent for the Rothschilds. Soon a leading banker, he became a U.S. citizen, married a daughter of Matthew C. Perry, and was active in the Democratic party. Served as minister to Netherlands, 1853–57. In the Civil War, he aided Union cause by his influence in European political and financial circles.

BELO, ALFRED HORATIO (*b. Salem, N.C., 1839; d. 1901*), Confederate soldier, journalist. A publisher of *Galveston News*, 1866–1901; established *Dallas News*, 1885; an incorporator of Associated Press.

BEMAN, NATHAN SIDNEY SMITH (*b. New Lebanon, N.Y., 1785; d. 1871*), Presbyterian clergyman. Pastor, First Presbyterian Church, Troy, N.Y., 1823–63. Head of New School movement; author of *Letters to Rev. John Hughes* (1851). President, Rensselaer Polytechnic Institute, 1845–65.

BEMELMANS, LUDWIG (*b. Meran, Austrian Tyrol [now Merano, Italy], 1898; d. New York, N.Y., 1962*), writer and artist. Immigrated to the U.S. in 1914 and became a citizen in 1918. Launched his literary career in 1934 with *Hansi*, an illustrated juvenile book. A comic writer, his works include *My War with the United States* (1937) and *Yolande and the Thief* (1945). After 1953 he produced some of his best work, particularly *Are You Hungry, Are You Cold* (1960), and during this period he also began to paint seriously; the characteristic works reproduced in *My Life in Art* (1958) are reminiscent of Chagall in mood and of the fauvists in method.

BEMENT, CALEB N. (*b. New York, 1790; d. Poughkeepsie, N.Y., 1868*), agriculturalist, inventor, publicist. Author of *American Poulterer's Companion* (1844); a strong influence in his time towards improvement of American agriculture.

BEMENT, CLARENCE SWEET (*b. Mishawaka, Ind., 1843; d. 1923*), machine-tool manufacturer, collector of books, coins, and minerals.

BEMIS, GEORGE (*b. Waltham, Mass., 1815; d. Nice, France, 1878*), lawyer. Graduated Harvard, 1835; Harvard Law School, 1839. Practiced criminal law in Boston; acted in Webster-Parkman case and in Alabama Claims cases.

BEMIS, HAROLD EDWARD (*b. Cawker City, Kans., 1883; d. 1931*), veterinarian, soldier, educator. As head of department at Iowa State College, 1909–27, made substantial contributions to study of veterinary surgery.

BENAVIDES, ALONZO DE (*fl. 1600–64*), Franciscan friar. Arrived in New Mexico, 1622, to work among Apaches; set up missions at Picuries, Taos, Acoma, and other places, converting more than 16,000 tribesmen. His *Memorial* to the king of Spain (presented 1630, revised 1634) gives history of the missions and description of physical aspects of the country. Assigned to Goa, India, 1634, he became Archbishop of that place.

BENBRIDGE, HENRY (*b. Philadelphia, Pa., 1744; d. 1812*), portrait painter. Possibly trained by Wallaston; studied in Italy; encouraged by Benjamin West. Returned to America, 1770; practiced in Philadelphia, Charleston, S.C., and Norfolk, Va.

BENCHLEY, ROBERT CHARLES (*b. Worcester, Mass., 1889; d. New York, N.Y., 1945*), author, critic, actor. Graduated from Harvard, 1913, where he was president of the *Lampoon*. After a succession of tedious jobs in Boston and New York, including reporting, public relations, and editing, he became managing editor of *Vanity Fair* in May 1919. He resigned early in 1920 in sympathy with his colleague Dorothy Parker who had been dismissed, and for about a year wrote a book column for the *New York World*. His first collection of humorous articles, *Of All Things*, was published in 1921. He was drama critic for *Life* magazine, 1920–29. His first contribution to the *New Yorker* appeared in December 1925; by 1927, he was writing a regular feature for it, "The Wayward Press," and he was the magazine's drama critic, 1929–40. Ten collections of his writings were published between 1921 and 1938. Benchley's wit was moderate, reasonable, and good-humored; like his criticism, it reflected the outlook of the sensible, educated everyman. His literary career was paralleled by his role as popular comic actor on stage, screen, and radio. His monologue "The Treasurer's Report" was first presented professionally in *The Music Box Revue* of 1923, then in vaudeville, and in 1928 as his first motion-picture "short." Other short films included "The Sex Life of the Polyp" and "How to Sleep" (1936), which won an Academy Award. He also appeared in a number of feature-length pictures.

BENDER, CHARLES ALBERT ("CHIEF") (*b. Brainerd, Minn., 1883; d. 1954*), baseball pitcher. A Chippewa, Bender studied at the Carlisle Indian School and at Dickinson College. Pitcher with the Philadelphia Athletics, 1903–14; scout and pitching coach, 1939–54; Philadelphia Phillies, 1915–17. From 1917 to 1939, coached in the minor leagues and the U.S. Naval Academy. Elected to the National Baseball Hall of Fame, 1953.

BENDER, GEORGE HARRISON (*b. Cleveland, Ohio, 1896; d. Chagrin Falls, Ohio, 1961*), U.S. congressman and senator. Served in the U.S. House of Representatives from 1938 until 1954, with the exception of a defeat in 1948. In Congress he vigorously criticized the foreign and domestic policies of President Franklin D. Roosevelt and wrote *The Challenge of 1940* (1940) as an indictment of the administration. After World War II he championed measures to abolish poll taxes and denounced the Truman Doctrine and the Marshall Plan. While serving in the U.S. Senate (1953–55), he reversed his early isolationist views and gave solid support to the Eisenhower program. His last government post was as special assistant to the secretary of the interior (1957–58), after which his association with the Teamsters Union caused a decline in his political career.

BENDIX, VINCENT (*b. Moline, Ill., 1881; d. New York, N.Y., 1945*), inventor, industrialist. A self-taught mechanical technologist, Bendix patented the first dependable starting mechanism for automobiles in 1914 and successfully licensed its manufacture; in 1924, he was equally successful in promoting the four-wheel brake linkage system and the internal-expanding brake shoe invented by Henri Perrot. Through his own inventions, or through licenses on the patents of others, he acquired for his Bendix Corporation a near monopoly on critical automobile components. He followed the same course after entering the aviation industry in 1927–29, producing, through companies controlled by him, magnetos, instruments, electrical equipment, and other essential components. After 1937, although he remained president of the corporation, his importance in its affairs diminished, and he resigned in 1942. Founded home appliance corporation in 1937. By 1939, heavy financial losses incident to his investments in Chicago real estate had forced him into bankruptcy. Established Transcontinental Air Race and was the donor of the Bendix Trophy.

BENEDICT, DAVID (*b. Norwalk, Conn., 1779; d. 1874*), Baptist clergyman, historian. Author of pioneer studies in history of his church.

BENEDICT, ERASTUS CORNELIUS (*b. Branford, Conn., 1800; d. New York, N.Y., 1880*), lawyer. Specialist in admiralty cases; a prime factor, 1840–80, in New York's educational progress and in founding College of the City of New York.

BENEDICT, RUTH FULTON (*b. New York, N.Y., 1887; d. New York, 1948*), anthropologist. Raised on a farm near Norwich, N.Y., in St. Joseph, Mo., Owatonna, Minn., and Buffalo, N.Y. Graduated Vassar, 1909; traveled in Europe; did charity work in Buffalo; taught school in California; married S. R. Benedict, 1914. Dissatisfied with marriage and attempts at writing, she tried social work again, modern dancing, and finally anthropology. Began study at Columbia University with Franz Boas, 1921; Ph.D., 1923, with a dissertation on the "guardian spirit concept" in American Indian religion. Lecturer in anthropology at Columbia, 1923–31; did fieldwork in California and the Southwest, producing volumes on Cochiti and Zuni myths. In *Patterns of Culture* (1934), she saw cultures as "personality writ large," and argued that each one selected and elaborated a "certain segment of the great arc of potential human purposes and motivations." Psychological normality was thus culturally defined, and the misfit is the person whose disposition is not capitalized by his culture. Separating from her husband in 1931, she served as assistant and later associate professor at Columbia until 1943. She assumed many of Boas's teaching and other responsibilities, and in effect headed the anthropology department, 1936–39. Left Columbia in 1943 to work for Office of War Information, heading a section that applied anthropological methods to the production of "national character studies" of complex societies. *The Chrysanthemum and the Sword* (1946), an account of Japanese culture, was one result of this work. Returning to Columbia in 1946, she became a director of a government-funded project for Research in Contemporary Cultures and was promoted to a full professorship shortly before her death. Taken as a whole, her work provided much of the foundation of the modern culture and personality movement and was an expression of anthropology's fundamental humanistic strain.

BENEDICT, STANLEY ROSSITER (*b. Cincinnati, Ohio, 1884; d. Elmsford, N.Y. 1936*), biological chemist. Graduated University of Cincinnati, 1906; Ph.D. Yale, 1908. Professor of chemistry, Cornell University Medical College, 1931–36. Married Ruth Fulton, 1913, who, as Ruth Benedict, became a well-known anthropologist. Benedict's major contributions were in the area of analytical biochemistry; he originated Benedict's solution, a universally used reagent for testing sugar in the urine, and with associates made many fruitful studies in quantitative blood chemistry and metabolism.

BENÉT, STEPHEN VINCENT (*b. Bethlehem, Pa., 1898; d. New York, N.Y., 1943*), poet, novelist, short-story writer. Brother of William R. Benét. Raised in military family. By 1913, he had published verses in *St. Nicholas* magazine; first book, *Five Men and Pompey*, was published at his brother's expense, 1915, the year he entered Yale. While still an undergraduate, he published two more volumes of poems: *The Drug-Shop* (1917) and *Young Adventure* (1918). Entered graduate school at Yale on a fellowship, 1919. His master's thesis, a manuscript of verse, was published as *Heavens and Earth* (1920) and shared 1921 Poetry Society of America award with Carl Sandburg. First novel, *The Beginning of Wisdom* (1921), was followed by *Young People's Pride* (1922) and *Jean Huguenot* (1923). He now concentrated on writing formula short stories for popular magazines as a means of making a living, reserving his artistic ambitions for his poetry, of which a selection, *Tiger Joy* (1925), appeared to critical applause. He published *Spanish Bayonet*, a serious, romantic historical novel, in 1926. Tiring of the popular fiction he was grinding out, he experimented with the use of materials out of the American past, employing fantasy in treatment and giving them the color of folklore ("The Devil and Daniel Webster," for example, and "Johnny Pye and the Fool-Killer"); these had both commercial and critical success. In 1928, his narrative Civil War poem *John Brown's Body* was a book club choice, a best-seller in its own right, and winner of the Pulitzer Prize for poetry in 1929, although certain critics sneered at the work as lacking "the higher virtues" of poetry.

Losses in the stock market crash of 1929 forced Benét into a return to hackwork, but he still found time for poetry. In collaboration with his wife, he bought out the charming *Book of Americans* (1933); in 1936, he published *Burning City*, in which he expressed the stresses of a "decade of tension." Wrote effective propaganda for the Office of War Information during World War II. A fragment of an epic poem about the westward movement of America, on which he had been working for fifteen years, was published posthumously as *Western Star* (1943) and a won a Pulitzer Prize.

BENÉT, WILLIAM ROSE (*b. Fort Hamilton, N.Y., 1886; d. New York, N.Y., 1950*), poet, editor. Brother of Stephen Vincent Benét. Graduated Sheffield Scientific School, Yale, 1907. After rising to assistant editor of the *Century* magazine, he served in the army during World War I. Returning to editorial work, he was associated principally with the *Saturday Review of Literature* whose predecessor, the *Literary Review*, he had helped found. His books of poems include *Merchants from Cathay* (1913); *Perpetual Light* (1919); and *The Dust Which Is God*, an autobiography in verse which won the Pulitzer Prize for 1941. His poetry has been described as like the man himself, "generous, sometimes too lavish, overflowing with . . . brotherly good will."

BENEZET, ANTHONY (*b. San Quentin, France, 1713; d. Philadelphia, Pa., 1784*), philanthropist, teacher. Became Quaker convert, and removed to Philadelphia, 1731. Author of *A Caution and Warning to Great Britain and Her Colonies on the Calamitous State of the Enslaved Negroes* (1766) and *Historical Account of Guinea* (1771).

BENHAM, HENRY WASHINGTON (*b. Quebec, Canada, 1813; d. 1884*), engineer, soldier. Graduated West Point, 1837. Served as engineer in Mexican and Civil wars; in charge of New York and Boston harbor defenses, 1865–82.

BENJAMIN, ASHER (*b. Greenfield, Mass., 1773; d. Springfield, Mass., 1845*), architect. Designed many houses and churches in Windsor, Vt., Boston, Springfield, Mass., and other places in New England. His importance lies primarily in his writings on architecture, which include *The Country Builder's Assistant* (1797), *The American Builder's Companion* (1806), *The Rudiments of Architecture* (1814), and *The Practical House Carpenter* (1830). Through these tasteful books, late colonial details and designs won wide influence among builders.

BENJAMIN, GEORGE HILLARD (*b. New York, N.Y., 1852; d. 1927*), lawyer, engineer, patent expert, inventor. Son of Park Benjamin (1809–64).

BENJAMIN, JUDAH PHILIP (*b. St. Thomas, British West Indies, 1811; d. Paris, France, 1884*), lawyer, statesman. Son of Philip Benjamin, an English Jew, and Rebecca de Mendes, of a Portuguese Jewish family. Taken to Charleston, S.C., as a child; studied at Fayetteville Academy, North Carolina; briefly at Yale. *Post* 1828 worked in New Orleans and studied law; with Thomas Slidell, issued a *Digest of the Reported Decisions of the Superior Court of Louisiana* (1834). Became nationally known through participation in case of brig *Creole*; acquired sugar plantation. Failure of a friend whom he had endorsed cost him his plantation

and threw him back upon law practice.

Served as Whig in state legislature; as U.S. senator from Louisiana, 1852–61. Sharing the general Southern belief that the upsetting of sectional balance in Compromise of 1850 demanded some foreign expansion for redress, he began to favor a "Southern party." In 1856 he declared himself a Democrat, supported Buchanan, and was returned to the Senate as a Democrat, 1858. One of the earliest Southern senators to advocate secession, he resigned his seat, 1861. Three weeks later Jefferson Davis appointed him attorney general of the Confederacy. In September 1861 he was made head of Confederate War Department, whose position, not generally known in South, was already critical because of poor credit and inadequate supplies. Blamed for the loss of Roanoke Island, 1862, though it appears now there was little ground for holding him responsible, he was widely attacked, but Davis stood behind him; on resignation of R. M. T. Hunter as secretary of state, Davis appointed Benjamin to the post while investigation of the Roanoke Island affair was still under way. Bitter attacks continued, the appointment being described as "reckless defiance of popular sentiment." Benjamin, however, maintained his calm, was mainstay of the oversensitive Davis. More realistic in viewing the Confederacy's desperate position than many Southerners, he began to develop a plan for using slaves as soldiers on assumption they would then receive their freedom. This possibility terrified more conventional Southerners. The Confederate Congress defeated the recommendation and provided, for slave soldiers but not for emancipation.

When the Northern armies in 1865 finally shattered all hopes, Benjamin calmly made his last recommendations in connection with the terms of J. E. Johnston's surrender, then escaped via the West Indies to England, 1866. There, he built a new career at the English bar. His standing in the legal world received unique recognition when he was admitted to the bar after five months as a student. He joined the northern circuit, which included Liverpool, where his professional skill was already known. His *Treatise on the Law of Sale of Personal Property* (1868) showed remarkable familiarity with English and civil law and immediately became a standard work. Rapidly establishing himself as without a superior in appeal cases, he was in such demand he finally declined to appear before any court other than the House of Lords or the Judicial Committee of the Privy Council without a special fee. Between 1872 and 1882 he appeared in no less than 136 reported cases before these tribunals, all involving questions of great legal significance or affecting large financial interests. His capacity for logical analysis, remarkable facility with language, and his profound legal knowledge combined to make him preeminent in many fields of law.

BENJAMIN, NATHAN (*b. Catskill, N.Y., 1811; d. Constantinople, Turkey, 1855*), Congregational clergyman. Missionary to Greece and Armenia, 1836–52.

BENJAMIN, PARK (*b. Demerara, British Guiana, 1809; d. New York, N.Y., 1864*), editor. Came to Norwich, Conn., as a child. Graduated Trinity College, Hartford, 1829. Restless and temperamental, he abandoned law practice for journalism *post* 1834 and was associated among others with the *New England Magazine*, Horace Greeley's *New Yorker*, the *New World*, and the New York *Evening Signal*. Benjamin was known for the caustic quality of his critical writing and as the author of much minor verse.

BENJAMIN, PARK (*b. New York, N.Y., 1849; d. 1922*), author, patent lawyer. Son of Park Benjamin (1809–64). Graduated Annapolis, 1867; admitted to bar, 1870. Wrote extensively on scientific subjects.

BENJAMIN, SAMUEL GREENE WHEELER (*b. Argos, Greece, 1837; d. Burlington, Vt., 1914*), author, painter, diplomat. Son of Nathan Benjamin. Graduated Williams, 1859; first American minister to Persia, 1883–85.

BENNER, PHILIP (*b. Chester Co., Pa., 1762; d. Bellefonte, Pa., 1832*), merchant, leading ironmaster in Centre Co., Pa., for forty years.

BENNET, SANFORD FILLMORE (*b. Eden, N.Y., 1836; d. 1898*), physician. Author of songs and hymns, including "The Sweet By and By." Practiced medicine in Illinois and Wisconsin, *post* 1865.

BENNETT, CALEB PREW (*b. Kennett Township, Pa., 1758; d. Wilmington, Del., 1836*), Revolutionary soldier. Moved to Delaware as a child. First Democratic governor of Delaware, 1833–36.

BENNETT, CHARLES EDWIN (*b. Providence, R.I., 1858; d. 1921*), classical scholar. Graduated Brown, 1878; additional studies, Harvard, Leipzig, Berlin, Heidelberg. Professor of Latin, Cornell, 1892–1921. Author among many other books of *A Latin Grammar* (1895) and scholarly texts of the Latin classics.

BENNETT, CONSTANCE CAMPBELL (*b. New York, N.Y., 1904; d. Fort Dix, N.J., 1965*), actress. Starred in a series of popular Hollywood movies in the period around 1930. *Common Clay* (1930) established her screen image as that of a woman of easy virtue, tempted by the fast life of the idle rich, who ultimately finds redemption in a good marriage to a man with more stable values. This formula made her one of the highest-paid stars in Hollywood. Her best known and most respected film of the period of her popularity was George Cukor's *What Price Hollywood* (1932), refilmed three times as *A Star Is Born*. After this, her film career took a downturn, though she continued to appear in films and on stage, radio, and television.

BENNETT, DE ROBIGNE MORTIMER (*b. near Otsego Lake, N.Y., 1818; d. New York, N.Y., 1882*), freethinker. Published the *Truthseeker, post* 1873.

BENNETT, EDMUND HATCH (*b. Manchester, Vt., 1824; d. 1898*), jurist, legal writer. Dean, Boston University Law School, 1876–98.

BENNETT, EMERSON (*b. Monson, Mass., 1822; d. Philadelphia, Pa., 1905*), author. A busy contributor of fiction to popular journals and newspapers. Among his romantic melodramas are *The League of the Miami* (1845), *The Bandits of the Osage* (1847), *Mike Fink* (1848), and *The Prairie Flower* (1849), all of which are in the dime-novel class.

BENNETT, FLOYD (*b. near Warrensburg, N.Y., 1890; d. Quebec, Canada, 1928*), aviator. Navy pilot; friend and associate of Admiral R. E. Byrd on polar explorations *post* 1925.

BENNETT, HENRY GARLAND (*b. Nevada Co., Ark., 1886; d. near Teheran, Iran, 1951*), college president, assistant secretary of state, administrator of the Technical Cooperation Administration (Point Four Program). Studied at Ouachita College, University of Oklahoma, and Columbia University. Made Oklahoma A. and M. into the second largest agricultural college in the United States. During the Great Depression, he utilized many New Deal programs to support his program of reconstruction; gained national recognition for his knowledge of agricultural education. Delegate to the International Food and Agricultural Organization Conference on European rehabilitation, 1945; advised Emperor Haile Selassie on the organization of an agricultural training center in Ethiopia, 1950. Appointed assistant secretary of state to serve as head of the Point Four Program, 1950, designed to combat the spread of communism through dissemination of technical skills in underdeveloped countries.

BENNETT, HUGH HAMMOND (*b. Wadesboro, N.C., 1881; d. Falls Church, Va., 1960*), soil conservationist. Studied at the University of North Carolina. Bennett was a leading pioneer in the field of soil conservation for the Bureau of Soils at the Department of Agriculture from 1903; director of the Soil Erosion Service (1933) and of the Soil Conservation Service (1935). His efforts led to the passage of the first soil conservation act (1935).

BENNETT, JAMES GORDON (*b. Keith, Scotland, 1795; d. New York, N.Y., 1872*), editor, publisher. Attended a Catholic seminary at Aberdeen for a few years; immigrated 1819 to Halifax, N.S., thence to Portland, Maine, and Boston, Mass., where he worked as a copyboy and as clerk in a bookstore. After a year of various employments in New York (1822) and some months in South Carolina on the staff of the *Charleston Courier*, he settled in New York and became by 1826 a regular contributor to several newspapers including the *New York Courier*. His attacks on sharpers and speculators won him a local reputation and aroused considerable resentment. He was on the staff of the *New York Enquirer* during 1827–28, reporting from both New York and Washington, and winning national attention for a series of bold, personal sketches of leading men in the capital. At his suggestion, J. W. Webb, proprietor of the *Courier*, purchased the *Enquirer*, the first issue of the combined papers appearing in May 1829. That fall, Bennett became associate editor of the *Courier and Enquirer* and made it a forceful organ of Jacksonian democracy. On Webb's sudden espousal of the Whig cause in 1832, Bennett resigned.

Resolving to begin operations on his own, and with the recent success of the penny *New York Sun* as an encouraging example, Bennett began publication of the penny *New York Herald* in May 1835. He had little capital and no party support, yet the *Herald* was an immediate success because of its comprehensive and piquant coverage of local news, its reports on the stock and money markets, and its highly independent editorials on all manner of subjects. Viciously attacked by other journals for the *Herald*'s flippancy and sensationalism, Bennett saw the circulation rise in proportion to the attacks, and by 1842 the *Herald* occupied its own building with facilities for printing some fifty thousand copies daily. To his political feuds with Van Buren and Seward, he now added personal disputes with Daniel O'Connell, the Irish liberator, and Archbishop Hughes of New York.

After 1844, Bennett's life was comparatively uneventful, being identified with the steady rise of the *Herald* to preeminence as a news-gathering sheet through the efforts of an unrivaled corps of European and American correspondents. The *Herald* was the first paper to make lavish use of the telegraph. For the most part, it supported the Democrats in politics, and Bennett was accused of favoring the Southern point of view in the great controversies of the 1850's. In 1856, however, Bennett supported Frémont, reverting in 1860 to Douglas. After some hesitation, Bennett supported Lincoln in 1864. Although he retired in 1867, he continued to direct the policies of the paper and to write for it. At the time of his retirement, the *Herald* had a daily circulation of ninety thousand, its advertising revenue was surpassed only by the London *Times*, and its annual profits approached $400,000.

BENNETT, JAMES GORDON (*b. New York, N.Y., 1841; d. Beaulieu, France, 1918*), editor, capitalist. Son of James Gordon Bennett (1795–1872); educated mainly in Europe; served as lieutenant, U.S. Navy, during Civil War. As managing editor and director of the *New York Herald*, 1867–1918, he was explosive, erratic, and domineering, although up to 1877 he showed a capacity for gathering men of ability about him. Stanley's famous search for Dr. Livingstone, 1870–71, was inspired by him. After 1877 he was a virtual expatriate in France, managing his newspaper properties by cable and refusing to delegate adequate authority to his home staff. By the 1890's the *Herald*'s once-commanding position was slowly being lost. He was widely known as a sportsman. The James Gordon Bennett trophies for automobile driving, balloon racing, and aviation were donated by him.

BENNETT, NATHANIEL (*b. Clinton, N.Y., 1818; d. San Francisco, Calif., 1886*), lawyer, jurist. Immigrated to California, 1849; practiced law in San Francisco. Reported early decisions of California supreme court (1852); became leader of state bar.

BENNETT, RICHARD (*b. Deacons Mills, Ind., 1870; d. Los Angeles, Calif., 1944*), actor. Father of actresses Constance and Joan Bennett. After a roving period that included work as a Great Lakes sailor, professional boxer, and medicine show assistant, Bennett made his professional debut in *The Limited Mail* (1891). Engagements with road companies followed, mainly in the Midwest. Appeared in New York in *The Proper Caper* (1897) and became a matinee idol in a series of hits. In 1905, he rose on the scale, playing Hector Malone in Shaw's *Man and Superman*; in 1908, he supported Maude Adams as John Shand in Barrie's *What Every Woman Knows*. Produced and starred in Brieux's *Damaged Goods* (1913). Played the lead in Eugene O'Neill's *Beyond the Horizon* (1920), for whose production he was largely responsible; O'Neill said that Bennett's extensive cutting and rewriting had been for him "a liberal education." Other of Bennett's outstanding performances were in *He Who Gets Slapped* (1922) and *They Knew What They Wanted* (1924). Developed into consummate character actor. Appeared on the West Coast in plays and films but returned to Broadway (1935) as Judge Gaunt in *Winterset*. Helped found the Bucks County Playhouse, New Hope, Pa.

BENNING, HENRY LEWIS (*b. Columbia Co., Ga., 1814; d. Columbus, Ga., 1875*), jurist, statesman, Confederate soldier. An ardent secessionist, he favored withdrawal from Union in 1850 crisis; as justice of Georgia supreme court, 1853–59, delivered opinion that a state supreme court is not bound to U.S. Supreme Court on constitutional questions, the two being "coordinate and co-equal." Had distinguished record in Civil War.

BENSLEY, ROBERT RUSSELL (*b. near Hamilton, Ont., 1867; d. Chicago, Ill., 1956*), anatomist. Studied at the University of Toronto (M.D., 1892). Taught at Toronto (1892–01) and Chicago (1901–33). Director of the Hull Laboratory of Anatomy from 1905. Developed the techniques of centrifugation and freeze-drying for anatomical research. President of the American Association of Anatomists, 1918.

BENSON, EGBERT (*b. New York, N.Y., 1746; d. Jamaica, N.Y., 1833*), Revolutionary leader, New York legislator and jurist. A Federalist, he was considered second only to Alexander Hamilton in legal learning.

BENSON, EUGENE (*b. Hyde Park, N.Y., 1839; d. Venice, Italy, 1908*), painter.

BENSON, FRANK WESTON (*b. Salem, Mass., 1862; d. Salem, 1951*), painter and etcher. Studied at the Museum of Fine Arts in Boston (1880–83); then taught there (1889–1912). Studied at the Académie Julien, Paris (1883–85). His painting, *The Sisters*, was shown at the 1900 Paris exposition; *The Three Graces* and *The Four Seasons* are panels in the Library of Congress. Known mainly for his naturalistic renderings of wildlife, particularly birds.

BENSON, OSCAR HERMAN (*b. Delhi, Iowa, 1875; d. Gettysburg, Pa., 1951*), educator and organizer of youth groups. Studied at Iowa State Teachers' College, Iowa State University, and the University of Chicago. Known mainly for founding the 4-H Clubs of America, around 1905. Staff of the Boy Scouts of America, 1926–40, as director of rural scouting services.

BENSON, WILLIAM SHEPHERD (*b. Bibb Co., Ga., 1855; d. Washington, D.C., 1932*), naval officer. From 1877, on graduation from Annapolis, until World War I, Admiral Benson served in many capacities ashore and afloat. Made chief of Naval Operations in 1915, he organized this new office and prepared the navy for war. Postwar Chairman of the U.S. Shipping Board, he served as a member of the Board until 1928.

BENT, CHARLES (*b. Charleston, Va., now W. Va., 1799; d. Taos, N.Mex., 1847*), frontier trader. Raised in Ohio and Missouri and trained in fur trade; with brother William and Ceran St. Vrain built stockade on upper Arkansas, 1824. In 1828 they began building the famous trading post Bent's Fort, 80 miles northeast of Taos, completing it in 1832. Charles led trade caravans from American frontier to Santa Fe in 1829, 1832, and 1833. Appointed civil governor of New Mexico, 1846. After American conquest, he was killed in the 1847 uprising at Taos.

BENT, JOSIAH (*b. Milton, Mass., 1771; d. 1836*), manufacturer of first water crackers produced in America.

BENT, SILAS (*b. South St. Louis, Mo., 1820; d. Shelter Island, N.Y., 1887*), naval officer, oceanographer. Brother of Charles and William Bent. Carried out surveys in Japanese waters on Perry expedition, 1852–54, including study of Kuro Siwo current in Pacific.

BENT, SILAS (*b. Millersburg, Ky., 1882; d. Stamford, Conn., 1945*), journalist, author. Graduated Ogden College, 1902. After twenty years in newspapers, magazine editing, political and economic public relations, and education for journalism, Bent turned to a career of free-lance writing and lecturing as a critic of the policies and practices of the American press. His caustic revelations were published in *Atlantic Monthly*, *Collier's*, *New Republic*, and other magazines, and in nine books, including *Ballyhoo: The Voice of the Press* (1927) and *Newspaper Crusaders: A Neglected Story* (1939). Highly critical of "big industry" journalism unduly influenced by profit-motivated advertisers. Also wrote a novel and biographies of Oliver Wendell Holmes and Zachary Taylor.

BENT, WILLIAM (*b. St. Louis, Mo., 1809; d, Boggsville, Colo., 1869*), frontiersman, trader, first permanent white settler in Colorado. Brother of Charles and Silas Bent. Directed building of Bent's Fort, 1828–32; managed if for many years. *Post* 1849 built trading post, later known as Fort Lyon; settled, 1859, near mouth of the Purgatoire as rancher.

BENTLEY, ARTHUR FISHER (*b. Freeport, Ill., 1870; d. Paoli, Ind., 1957*), political scientist, philosopher, and sociologist. Studied at Johns Hopkins (Ph.D., 1895). He published a classic study of pressure groups, *The Process of Government*, in 1908. In *Relativity in Man and Society* (1926), he advocated adoption by sociologists of Einstein's method of viewing space and time as dimensions or integral phases of the events they describe. He developed this theme further in *Behavior, Knowledge, Fact* (1935). His works strongly influenced John Dewey, with whom he collaborated on *Knowing and the Known* (1949).

BENTLEY, ELIZABETH TERRILL (*b. New Milford, Conn., 1908; d. New Haven, Conn., 1963*), Soviet agent and FBI informer. Joined the Communist party in 1935. Allegedly became a member of a secret Communist underground led by Jacob Golos in New York, acting as courier between him and a group of Communist agents employed in the federal bureaucracy in Washington. Claimed that after Golos' death in 1943 she took a larger role in espionage and Communist party work, but her autobiography casts doubt on this contention. In 1945 told her story to the FBI and served the FBI as its agent within the Communist party until the last weeks of 1946. In 1948 testified before the House of Representatives Committee on Un-American Activities, though none of the over three dozen people she named was ever indicted for espionage. Her testimony at the two trials of William W. Remington helped convict him of perjury and Morton Sobell and Julius and Ethel Rosenberg of spying for the Soviet Union.

BENTLEY, WILLIAM (*b. Boston, Mass., 1759; d. Salem, Mass., 1819*), Unitarian clergyman, author. Graduated Harvard, 1777. Pastor, East Church, Salem, 1783–1819. A pioneer in Unitarianism when New England was still Calvinistic, he was, unlike most of the clergy, a Jeffersonian Republican, and his church became a center of liberalism. He was noted for his regular contributions to the *Salem Register*; his diary of the years 1784–1819 (published 1905–14) gives a unique picture of a New England seaport in early years of the new nation.

BENTLEY, WILSON ALWYN (*b. Jericho, Vt., 1865; d. Jericho, 1931*), meteorologist. Photographer of snow crystals.

BENTON, ALLEN RICHARDSON (*b. Ira, N.Y., 1822; d. Lincoln, Nebr., 1914*), educator. Organized University of Nebraska, 1871.

BENTON, JAMES GILCHRIST (*b. Lebanon, N.H., 1820; d. Springfield, Mass., 1881*), ordnance expert. Graduated West Point, 1842. Commanded Springfield Armory, 1866–81; invented numerous improvements for Springfield rifle.

BENTON, JOEL (*b. Amenia, N.Y., 1832; d. Poughkeepsie, N.Y., 1911*), journalist.

BENTON, JOSIAH HENRY (*b. Addison, Vt., 1843; d. Boston, Mass., 1917*), railroad lawyer.

BENTON, THOMAS HART (*b. Hillsboro, N.C., 1782; d. Washington, D.C., 1858*), statesman. In early youth, supervised widowed mother's large farm near Nashville, Tenn., admitted to bar, 1811; served in War of 1812. Removed to St. Louis, Mo., 1815, where he edited the *Missouri Enquirer* and enjoyed a lucrative law practice. Elected to the U.S. Senate in 1820, in 1821 he began a career of 30 years in that body and became involved in his life-long interest, defense of sound money. He favored settlers, opposed land speculation, promoted navigation of the Mississippi, and was in all things a champion of the West. Estranged from Jackson as a result of an incident during the War of 1812, he renewed friendship, worked for him in campaign of 1828 and became administration spokesman in the Senate. His views on slavery changed materially at this time. Opposed in 1820 to all slavery restriction in Missouri, by 1828 he favored gradual abolition. Slavery was hindering settlement, and to a Westerner and expansionist this was a serious indictment.

Senate floor leader in the fight against the National Bank, his speeches won a popular support which enabled Jackson to veto recharter in 1836. As champion of hard money, Benton caused ratio between gold and silver to be changed from 15 to 1 to 16 to 1 and returned gold to circulation. The stipulation that public lands be paid for in hard money, sponsored by Benton and carried through by Jackson, also supported this movement. Such profound changes in the nation's financial structure hastened the panic of 1837, but Benton unfairly attributed the panic to the Bank's activities. The fight for specie divided the Democratic party into the "Hard" and "Soft" factions and won Benton the nickname "Old Bullion."

Holding strong views on distribution of public lands, Benton took a democratic position, favoring lower cash prices and the grant of free homesteads of 160 acres based on five years' settlement and improvement.

A Van Buren supporter in 1840, Benton took sides with Tyler against the Whigs. He was opposed to the acquisition of Texas, also to the extremist position on the Oregon question, preferring compromise to war. However, he upheld the government in the subsequent war with Mexico.

Essentially moderate, he remained so on the slavery question, difficult though this was. Opposing both extension and abolition, he wished only for peace and the maintenance of the Union. In 1847 he refused to follow instructions from the Missouri legislature on the Calhoun Resolutions, believing them subversive of the Union. During the debate on the Compromise of 1850 he opposed too generous concessions to secessionists; sensing that they would be unsatisfied with anything but complete control, he felt the compromise was a sham. His attitude offended his constituents. Although he had championed essential Western interests, such as the pony express, the telegraph, and the railroad, they could not forgive him, and in 1850 Missouri elected a Whig. Benton then sought election to the House where he fought vainly against the Missouri Compromise repeal. In a brief period of retirement before his death, he wrote *Thirty Years' View* (1854–56), one of the outstanding political autobiographies, and completed an *Abridgement of the Debates of Congress from 1789 to 1856* (1857–61).

BENTON, THOMAS HART (*b. Williamson Co., Tenn., 1816; d. St. Louis, Mo., 1879*), educator. Nephew of Thomas H. Benton (1782–1858). Secured legislation which was basis for public school system of Iowa; was Iowa superintendent of public instruction, 1848–54.

BERENSON, BERNARD (*b. Biturmansk, Lithuania, 1865; d. near Florence, Italy, 1959*), art historian and connoisseur, was born Bernard Valvrojenski. Studied at Harvard University. Perhaps the greatest connoisseur of Italian art of his time, Berenson developed a systematic, almost scientific method of telling the authentic from the fake imitative work of art. He established a reputation through his books, which include *The Study and Criticism of Italian Art* (1902) and his greatest scholarly work, *Drawings of the Florentine Painters* (1903). Employed as a collector, authenticator, and advisor by wealthy art lovers, he amassed a fortune which enabled him to buy the Villa I Tatti near Florence. At his death, he bequeathed the house, library, and collections to Harvard University. I Tatti is now the Harvard Center for Italian Renaissance Studies in Florence.

BERENSON, SENDA (*b. Biturmansk, Lithuania, 1868; d. Santa Barbara, Calif., 1954*), sportswoman and physical educator, was born Senda Valvrojenski. Immigrated to the U.S. in 1875. Studied at the Boston Normal School of Gymnastics. Taught physical training at Smith College, 1892–1911. Known chiefly for introducing women's basketball to the world. Helped develop and edit the "official rules" for the game, which were used until the 1960's. Sister of Bernard Berenson.

BERG, GERTRUDE EDELSTEIN (*b. New York, N.Y., 1899; d. New York, N.Y., 1966*), actress, author, and producer. In 1929 her radio show "The Rise of the Goldbergs" premiered on NBC; she played the main role of Molly. By 1931 the program, later renamed "The Goldbergs," was broadcast nationally five evenings a week and was second in popularity only to the radio series "Amos 'n' Andy." As Molly Goldberg, she became the operational definition of the Jewish mother, warm, nurturing, omnicompetent, but nagging. The series went off the air in 1935 but returned on CBS (1936–45, 1949–51). In 1948 she wrote and starred in a stage version of "The Goldbergs," *Me and Molly*, which was successful on Broadway. With N. Richard Nash she wrote the screenplay for the film *Molly* (1951), in which she starred. "The Goldbergs" also appeared on television (1949–51).

BERG, JOSEPH FREDERIC (*b. Antigua, B.W.I., 1812; d. 1871*), Dutch Reformed clergyman. Withdrew from German Reformed Church to Dutch, 1852; held pastorates in Pennsylvania.

BERGER, DANIEL (*b. near Reading, Pa., 1832; d. 1920*), United Brethren clergyman.

BERGER, MEYER (*b. New York, N.Y., 1889; d. New York, 1959*), reporter, columnist, author. A self-educated columnist for the *New York Times*, (1928–59), Berger covered many New York City events, in particular the organized-crime trials during Prohibition. His daily column, "About New York," with the by-line Mike Berger, first appeared in 1939. He was awarded the Pulitzer Prize in 1950 for his coverage of the killing of thirteen people in New Jersey. Books include *The Story of the New York Times* (1951).

BERGER, VICTOR LOUIS (*b. Nieder-Rehbach, Austria, 1860; d. 1929*), socialist, journalist. Came to America, 1878; settled in Milwaukee, Wis. Founded the *Wisconsin Vorwärts*, 1892, and devoted himself to socialist journalism and politics. With Debs and Seymour Stedman, founded the Socialist Democratic party which, with the Socialist Labor party, became the Socialist party in 1901. Served as congressman from Wisconsin, 1911–1913, first Socialist elected to Congress. Indicted, 1918, under Espionage Act after publication of articles opposing entry of the United States into World War I; re-elected to Congress, 1918 and 1919, but was denied seat because of anti-war position. When the Supreme Court reversed the lower court's decision, he returned to Congress, 1923, and remained until 1928. Berger's career is largely the story of socialist political development in America.

BERGH, CHRISTIAN (*b. near Rhinebeck, N.Y., 1763; d. New York, N.Y., 1843*), shipbuilder. Father of Henry Bergh. Built frigate *President* and many sailing packets.

BERGH, HENRY (*b. New York, N.Y., 1811; d. New York, 1888*), founder, 1866, and first president of American Society for the Prevention of Cruelty to Animals.

BERGMANN, CARL (*b. Ebersbach, Germany, 1821; d. New York, N.Y., 1876*), orchestral conductor. Came to America, 1849. Conducted New York Philharmonic Society, 1858–76; introduced many works by romantic school to the United States.

BERGMANN, MAX (*b. Fürth, Germany, 1886; d. New York, N.Y., 1944*), biochemist. Graduated University of Munich, 1907; Ph. D., University of Berlin, 1911. Associated with Emil Fischer in research on amino acids, carbohydrates, and tannins, 1911–19; professor at Technische Hochschule, Dresden, and engaged in research for the leather industry, 1921–33. Came to United States, 1933. Associated with the Rockefeller Institute for Medical Research *post* 1934; directed the work of his laboratory along two lines: applying the "carbobenzoxy" method for synthesis of peptides (which he and an associate had devised in 1932) so as to produce synthetic peptide substrates for protein-splitting enzymes; and developing new methods for the quantitative analysis of the amino acid composition of proteins.

BERKELEY, JOHN (*b. England; d. Virginia, 1622*), English ironmaster. Came to America, 1621. Built first ironworks in British America near Richmond, Va., 1622.

BERKELEY, NORBONNE. *See* BOTETOURT, NORBORNE BERKELEY, BARON DE.

BERKELEY, WILLIAM (*b. Somersetshire, England, 1606; d. England, 1677*), baronet, colonial governor. Courtier and playwright, in 1642 he assumed governorship of Virginia and helped quiet faction-torn colony. Encouraged diversification of crops; promoted exploration to find easiest route through mountains; led defense against the Indians, 1644. Deposed by Commonwealth *post* 1648, he returned to office at Restoration. Thereafter he gave colonists little voice even in local affairs. His course of executions and confiscations after Bacon's rebellion, 1676, brought investigation by England, resulting in appointment of successor to whom Berkeley at first refused to yield.

BERKENMEYER, WILHELM CHRISTOPH (*b. Bodenteich, Germany, 1686; d. Athens, N.Y., 1751*), Lutheran clergyman. Came to New York, 1725. For many years only regularly ordained Lutheran minister in Upper New York State.

BERKMAN, ALEXANDER (*b. Vilna, Russia, 1870; d. Nice, France, 1936*), anarchist, author. Immigrated to America, 1887; imprisoned 14 years for attempt to assassinate Henry Frick; deported, 1919, with Emma Goldman.

BERKOWITZ, HENRY (*b. Pittsburgh, Pa., 1857; d. 1924*), rabbi. Graduated University of Cincinnati, 1881, and Hebrew Union College. One of first four rabbis ordained in the United States (1883). After early pastorates in South and West, became rabbi of Rodeph Scholem Synagogue, Philadelphia, 1892–1922. Founded Jewish Chautauqua Society, 1893.

BERLINER, EMILE (*b. Hanover, Germany, 1851; d. Washington, D.C., 1929*), inventor. Educated in Germany; came to Washington, D.C., 1870. Discovered that variations in battery current through a telegraph key could be produced by variations in contact pressure; this led to his invention of the microphone, 1877. In 1887, he invented the "Gramophone," which recorded and reproduced sounds on a disc rather than on a cylinder, the basis of the modern phonographic industry. Under his direction, 1919, his son Henry devised a working helicopter.

BERMUDEZ, EDOUARD EDMOND (*b. New Orleans, La., 1832; d. New Orleans, 1892*), lawyer, Confederate soldier. Judge, Louisiana supreme court, 1880–92.

BERNARD, BAYLE. *See* BERNARD, WILLIAM BAYLE.

BERNARD, FRANCIS (*b. England, 1712; d. Aylesbury, England, 1779*), baronet, barrister, colonial governor. Appointed governor of New Jersey, 1758; governor of Massachusetts, 1760. He ruled for nine turbulent years, which included period of Sugar Act, Writs of Assistance, Stamp Act, quartering of troops in Boston. More understanding of colonial viewpoint than many, he tried to have sugar duty lowered, thought Stamp Act inexpedient. Later, he strongly opposed political desires of colonists; letters from him to officials in England were published, 1769, in Boston and caused removal from post in that year.

BERNARD, JOHN (*b. Portsmouth, England, 1756; d. England, 1828*), actor, theatrical manager. Came to America, 1797; managed companies in Boston and Albany; excelled as comedian.

BERNARD, SIMON (*b. Dôle, France, 1779; d. France, 1839*), French military engineer. After Napoleon's fall, acted as virtual chief of engineers, U.S. Army, in planning coast defenses. Returned to France, 1830.

BERNARD, WILLIAM BAYLE (*b. Boston, Mass., 1807; d. England, 1875*), dramatist. Son of John Bernard. Removed to England, 1819, where he became successful minor playwright and editor of father's *Retrospections of the Stage* (1830) and other works.

BERNAYS, AUGUSTUS CHARLES (*b. Highland, Ill., 1854; d. 1907*), surgeon. M.D., Heidelberg, 1876; studied also in Berlin and Vienna. Taught and practiced in St. Louis, Mo.; pioneer in antiseptic and aseptic surgery.

BERNET, JOHN JOSEPH (*b. Brant, N.Y., 1868; d. Cleveland, Ohio, 1935*), railroad executive. President of New York, Chicago, and St. Louis; the Erie; the Chesapeake and Ohio; and other railroads.

BERNSTEIN, ALINE (*b. New York, N.Y., 1882; d. New York, 1955*), scenic and costume designer. Studied at Hunter College and the New York School for Applied Design. First woman member of the United Scenic Art Union of the AFL. Worked in New York with the Neighborhood Playhouse, the Theatre Guild, and the Civic Repertory Theatre; achieved great success with her designs for Lillian Hellman's *The Children's Hour, The Little Foxes,* and *Days to Come.* Cofounder and director of the Museum of Costume Art (1937), later the Costume Institute of the Metropolitan Museum. In 1949, awarded the Antoinette Perry Award for her design for *Regina,* an operatic adaptation of *The Little Foxes.* Author of several books, including the novel *Miss Condon,* which was a best-seller. Bernstein was also known for her stormy five-year affair with novelist Thomas Wolfe, who dedicated *Look Homeward, Angel* to "A.B."

BERNSTEIN, HERMAN (*b. Neustadt-Scherwindt, Russia, 1876; d. Sheffield, Mass., 1935*), journalist, diplomat. Immigrated to America, 1893. Translator of Chekhov, Gorki, Andreyev, and other Russian writers, his "scoop" story of the *Potemkin* revolt (1905) caused a sensation. Until the outbreak of World War I he reported from Europe the inner workings of the Russian government for the *New York Times;* his interviews with famous Europeans were widely read. Returning to Russia in 1917, he came upon and published the famous "Willy-Nicky" correspondence and exposed the forged *Protocols of the Wise Men of Zion.* Founded *The Day,* 1914; edited the *Jewish Tribune,* 1925–29; served as an interpreter of Jewish life and ideals. Minister to Albania, 1930–33.

BERRIEN, JOHN MACPHERSON (*b. New Jersey, 1781; d. Savannah, Ga., 1856*), jurist, politician. Raised in Georgia, graduated Princeton, 1796. Studied law in Savannah, Ga.; admitted to bar there, 1799; judge of eastern circuit, 1810–21. U.S. senator, Democrat, 1824–29. Became Jackson's attorney general, 1829; resigned over Eaton affair, 1831. Returned to Senate as Whig, served 1841–52 and became a leader of his party, supporting Whigs on Bank question, protective tariffs, compromise of slavery issue. *Post* 1850, he changed position and opposed Clay's compromise, admission of California, abolition of slave trade in District of Columbia. Convinced the Whigs would not protect Southern interests, he withdrew from party, 1850. Later joined Know-Nothing party.

BERRY, EDWARD WILBER (*b. Newark, N.J., 1875; d. Stonington, Conn., 1945*), paleobotanist, educator. Educated at Passaic (N.J.) High School; worked as office boy, salesman, and newspaper editor and publisher, 1890–1905, while pursuing studies in geology and botany which resulted in influential, published research papers. Invited by William B. Clark to assist him at Johns Hopkins University, Berry spent a year there in special study, thereafter rising from instructor, 1907–10, to professor, 1917–42. He served also as dean of the college, 1929–42, and as provost of the university, 1935–42. Appointed to the U.S. Geological Survey, 1910, he served as senior geologist, 1917–42; during the latter period he was assistant state geologist of Maryland. Concentrated on taxonomic paleobotany; pioneered in the paleobotany of South America. Textbooks *Tree Ancestors* (1923) and *Paleontology* (1929) had considerable success.

BERRY, GEORGE LEONARD (*b. Lee Valley, Tenn., 1882; d. Rogersville, Tenn., 1948*), labor leader. An orphan, Berry was raised in Mississippi where he learned the printing trade. By 1907, he had become superintendent of a large printing plant in San Francisco, Calif. Active in trade union work *post* 1899, he was elected president of the Pressmen's Union in 1907 and held the position until his death. Moving the union's national headquarters to Rogersville, Tenn., he established there a retirement home, a tuberculosis sanatorium, and a trade school; he also inaugurated a pension fund and reformed the union's election procedures. A believer in conciliation, he loathed strikes and secured nationwide arbitration agreements with employers. Criticized for his high-handed dealings with union funds, he never lost the loyal support of the union's members. Appointed to fill out an unexpired term in the U.S. Senate, serving in 1937–38. In 1936, helped organize Labor's Non-Partisan League and was chosen its first president. Convicted and fined for income tax evasion and investigated by Congress (posthumously) for "misuse" of union funds.

BERRY, HIRAM GREGORY (*b. Thomaston, Maine, 1824; d. Chancellorsville, Va., 1863*), businessman, Union soldier. Colonel of Maine militia, rose to major general, distinguishing himself at Fair Oaks and Fredericksburg.

BERRY, JAMES HENDERSON (*b. Jackson Co., Ala., 1841; d. 1913*), lawyer, Confederate soldier. Democratic governor of Arkansas, 1882–84; U.S. senator, 1885–1907.

BERRY, MARTHA MCCHESNEY (*b. near Rome, Ga., 1866; d. Atlanta, Ga., 1942*), educator. Privately educated. Daughter of a wealthy planter and cotton broker, she assisted in the management of the plantation *post* 1887 and became interested in the religious education of the children of nearby mountain people. This led to her determination (about 1896) to devote her entire time and means to teaching boys of the highlands "the way to help themselves." From a one-room day school, she soon progressed to a year-round boarding establishment where manual crafts were taught as well as academic subjects, and a work-study plan instituted. The school flourished, and similar district agricultural and mechanical schools, modeled on hers, were instituted by Georgia and other states. In 1909, she extended her work to education of mountain girls in the "Berry way" of self-help, plain living, close ties to the native culture, and all forms of training necessary for decent rural living. Expanding her facilities with the aid of a number of interested philanthropists, she added a grammar school in 1916 and in 1926 a junior college, which became a senior college in 1930.

BERRY, NATHANIEL SPRINGER (*b. Bath, Maine, 1796; d. Bristol, N.H., 1894*), businessman, politician. Extreme abolitionist; Republican governor of New Hampshire, 1861–63; ranked high among Civil War governors.

BERRYMAN, CLIFFORD KENNEDY (*b. near Versailles, Ky., 1869; d. Washington, D.C., 1949*), editorial cartoonist. Self-taught and worked for a time as a draftsman in the U.S. Patent Office. In 1889, began contributing sketches to the *Washington Post;* became the *Post's* editorial cartoonist in 1896. His 1902 cartoon of Theodore Roosevelt refusing to shoot a bear cub was responsible for the "Teddy Bear" vogue and won him national fame, although he got none of the profits. In 1907, he left the *Post* to become editorial cartoonist for the *Washington Star* and remained with that paper until his death. His work was as a rule whimsical and gentle. In 1943, his "But Where Is the Boat Going," critical of administration manpower policies, won the Pulitzer Prize.

BERTRAM, JOHN (*b. Isle of Jersey, England, 1796; d. 1882*), sea captain, merchant. Came to America, 1807. Identified with trade out of Salem, *post* 1812, especially to Zanzibar; made fortune in Pacific trade *post* 1848.

BERWIND, EDWARD JULIUS (*b. Philadelphia, Pa., 1848; d. New York, N.Y., 1936*), business executive and capitalist. President, 1886–1930, Berwind-White Coal Co., reputedly the world's largest owner of coal-mining properties.

BESSE, ARTHUR LYMAN (*b. Bridgeport, Conn., 1887; d. New York, N.Y., 1951*), businessman and trade association executive. B.A., Harvard, 1909. President (1933–51), National Association of Wool Manufacturers. Advised the government on defense problems related to the wool industry during World War II.

BESSEY, CHARLES EDWIN (*b. Wayne Co., Ohio, 1845; d. 1915*), botanist. Graduated Michigan Agricultural College, 1869; studied under Asa Gray. Professor of agriculture and botany, dean and chancellor, University of Nebraska, 1884–1915.

BESTOR, ARTHUR EUGENE (*b. Dixon, Ill., 1879; d. New York, N.Y., 1944*), educator. Graduated University of Chicago, 1901; taught history and political science at Franklin College, and in extension division of University of Chicago. Active throughout his life in the field of adult education, he was identified with the Chautauqua movement *post* 1905, serving as assistant director, director, and president. Principally responsible for Chautauqua's specialization after World War I in professional study for teachers, advanced musical training, and general cultural courses; also for securing degree credit for its offerings.

BETHUNE, GEORGE WASHINGTON (*b. New York, N.Y., 1805; d. Florence, Italy, 1862*), Dutch Reformed clergyman, author. Distinguished pastor, Utica, Brooklyn, and New York, N.Y.; also Philadelphia, Pa. Edited first American edition of Walton's *Angler*.

BETHUNE, MARY MCLEOD (*b. Mayesville, S.C., 1875; d. Daytona Beach, Fla., 1955*), college president and government official. Studied at Scotia Seminary (now Barber-Scotia College) and at Moody Bible Institute. In 1904, she founded the Daytona Normal and Industrial Institute, an elementary and secondary school for blacks, which in 1929 became Bethune-Cookman College, now a four-year liberal arts college. President, National Association of Colored Women (1924–28); vice president of the National Association for the Advancement of Colored People (1940–55) and of the National Urban League. In 1935, she founded and served as president of the National Council of Negro Women. A friend of Eleanor Roosevelt, Bethune was appointed by Franklin D. Roosevelt as a member of the National Youth Administration (1935) and as an advisor to the president on minority affairs.

BETTENDORF, WILLIAM PETER (*b. Mendota, Ill., 1857; d. 1910*), manufacturer. Invented Bettendorf Metal Wheel for wagons, and machinery for its manufacture; also widely used railroad car equipment.

BETTMAN, ALFRED (*b. Cincinnati, Ohio, 1873; d. Altoona, Pa., 1945*), lawyer, city planner. A.B., Harvard, 1894; graduated Harvard Law School, 1898. Practiced successfully in Cincinnati and held several public appointments; special assistant to the U.S. attorney general during World War I, responsible for drafting many wartime restraints, notably those dealing with aliens, al-though himself deeply concerned with protection of personal liberties. Active in exposing the lax and often corrupt administration of criminal law. Joined United City Planning Committee, 1917; author of Ohio statutes giving cities the right to create planning boards and to regulate subdivisions within three miles of their boundaries. Wrote U.S. Department of Commerce Standard State Zoning Enabling Act (1924) and its Standard City Enabling Act (1927). His most important contribution was his successful argument before the Supreme Court on the constitutionality of zoning.

BETTS, SAMUEL ROSSITER (*b. Richmond, Mass., 1786; d. 1868*), jurist. Admitted to bar, 1809; appointed, 1823, circuit judge, supreme court of New York; served, 1826–67, as federal judge, New York southern district; outstanding in admiralty law.

BEVAN, ARTHUR DEAN (*b. Chicago, Ill., 1861; d. Lake Forest, Ill., 1943*), surgeon. M.D., Rush Medical College, 1883. Associated with Rush Medical College, 1887–1934; professor of anatomy and surgery and chairman of the department of surgery, *post* 1902. Specialized in surgery of the stomach and breast tumors and developed a number of surgical procedures. Celebrated for his efforts to improve standards of medical education as chairman of the American Medical Association's committee on that topic, 1902–16, 1920–28; campaign led directly to the famous Flexner Report (1910). With Dean Lewis edited the translation of Erich Lexer's textbook, which appeared as *General Surgery* (1908).

BEVERIDGE, ALBERT JEREMIAH (*b. Highland Co., Ohio, 1862; d. 1927*), politician, historian, orator. Raised on an Illinois farm. Graduated DePauw (then Asbury College), 1885; practiced law in Indianapolis, Ind. An outstanding Republican campaigner, he served as U.S. senator from Indiana, 1899–1911. He was one of the "insurgents" who formed the Progressive party, 1912. Supporting Theodore Roosevelt, he favored prevention of trust abuses, opposed injurious child labor, desired non-partisan tariff commission. A distinguished writer of history, his principal work is *The Life of John Marshall* (1916, 1919). His biography of Lincoln remained unfinished at his death.

BEVERLEY, ROBERT (*b. Middlesex Co., Va., ca. 1673; d. Beverly Park, Va., 1722*), colonial official, planter, historian. Educated in England; held important posts in provincial government. Author of *History and Present State of Virginia* (1705, revised 1722).

BEVIER, ISABEL (*b. near Plymouth, Ohio, 1860; d. Urbana, Ill., 1942*), home economist. Graduated College of Wooster, 1885; studied also at Case School of Applied Science, Harvard, Wesleyan University, Western Reserve, and Massachusetts Institute of Technology. Taught science at Pennsylvania College for Women, 1888–97, and chemistry at Lake Erie College, 1898–1900. Professor of household science at University of Illinois, 1900–21; built department of national prominence. Insisted on entrance requirements that met those of other departments and discouraged any narrowly utilitarian approach to study of household economy. Chairman of the home economics department at University of California at Los Angeles, 1921–23, returning to the University of Illinois to join the staff of the extension service, 1928–30.

BEWLEY, ANTHONY (*b. Tennessee, 1804; d. Fort Worth, Texas, 1860*), Methodist clergyman, missionary to Arkansas and Texas. Murdered by mob for his antislavery views.

BIARD, PIERRE (*b. Grenoble, France, ca. 1567; d. Avignon, France, 1622*), Jesuit missionary. Entered Society of Jesus, 1583; came to Canada, 1611; kidnapped from settlement in present

Maine by Samuel Argall, 1613. Author of a *Relation* of his experiences (1616).

BIBB, GEORGE MORTIMER (*b. Prince Edward Co., Va., 1776; d. Georgetown, D.C., 1859*), lawyer. "War Hawk" senator from Kentucky, 1811–14; Democratic senator, 1829–35; Kentucky jurist, 1835–44; U.S. secretary of treasury, 1844–45.

BIBB, WILLIAM WYATT (*b. Amelia Co., Ga., 1781; d. Autauga Co., Ala., 1820*), physician, politician. Removed to Georgia, 1801; congressman, Democrat, 1805–13; U.S. senator, 1813–16. Governor of Alabama territory (and later state), 1817–20.

BICKEL, LUKE WASHINGTON (*b. Cincinnati, Ohio, 1866; d. 1917*), sea captain. Baptist missionary to islands in Inland Sea of Japan.

BICKERDYKE, MARY ANN BALL (*b. Knox Co., Ohio, 1817; d. Bunker Hill, Kans., 1901*), nurse. Known as "Mother Bickerdyke," aided sick and wounded in Civil War; agent, U.S. Sanitary Commission.

BICKETT, THOMAS WALTER (*b. Monroe, N.C., 1869; d. 1921*), lawyer, politician. Attorney general, North Carolina, 1908–16; as Democratic governor, 1916–20, pressed measures for tax reform, increased teacher salaries, broader agricultural education.

BICKMORE, ALBERT SMITH (*b. Tenant's Harbor, Maine, 1839; d. Nonquitt, Mass., 1914*), educator, naturalist. Dominant factor in founding American Museum of Natural History, New York City; was its superintendent, 1869–84, and its curator of public instruction, 1884–1904.

BIDDLE, ANTHONY JOSEPH DREXEL, JR. (*b. Philadelphia, Pa., 1896; d. Washington, D.C., 1961*), diplomat. From 1935 until 1941 served in various diplomatic positions in Norway, Poland, and France. From 1941 until 1944 served, chiefly in London, as the U.S. ambassador extraordinary and minister plenipotentiary to various refugee European governments and was also minister to Luxembourg. In 1944, went on active duty with the army, where his work as foreign liaison officer in the Department of the Army brought him the rank of brigadier general in 1951. Went on inactive army status in 1955, and in 1961 was promoted to lieutenant general in the Pennsylvania National Guard, his highest rank. Returning to diplomacy in 1961, he was ambassador to Spain until his death.

BIDDLE, CLEMENT (*b. Philadelphia, Pa., 1740; d. Philadelphia, 1814*), Revolutionary soldier, merchant. An aide and friend of Greene and Washington.

BIDDLE, FRANCIS BEVERLEY (*b. Paris, France, 1886; d. Cape Cod, Mass., 1968*), lawyer, judge, and U.S. attorney general. B.A. cum laude (1909), LL.B. cum laude (1911), Harvard. As personal secretary of Associate Justice Oliver Wendell Holmes (1911–12), was deeply influenced by Holmes's brand of liberalism and later wrote two biographies of his mentor. Worked for two decades in the law firm of Barnes, Biddle, and Myers. Increasingly disaffected with the Republican party, he supported Franklin D. Roosevelt's campaign for presidency, and in 1934 Roosevelt named him chairman of the newly created National Labor Relations Board, where he worked to give a new deal to organized labor. In 1938 helped refute all charges of corrupt practices made against the Tennessee Valley Authority. Appointed U.S. solicitor general in 1940, he argued and won fifteen major government cases testing the constitutionality of New Deal legislation. Was attorney general (1941–45) and chief U.S. representative at the Nuremberg trials. Wrote *The Fear of Freedom* (1951), an attack on McCarthyism, and a candid two-volume autobiography, as well as one novel, *Llanfear Pattern* (1927).

BIDDLE, HORACE P. (*b. Fairfield Co., Ohio, 1811; d. 1900*), Indiana jurist.

BIDDLE, JAMES (*b. Philadelphia, Pa., 1783; d. Philadelphia, 1848*), naval officer. Became midshipman, 1800; thereafter served in campaigns against Tripoli; obtained first independent command, 1810, sloop-of-war *Syren*. In War of 1812, as first lieutenant of *Wasp*, led boarding party which took H.M.S. *Frolic*; commanding sloop-of-war *Hornet*, took British brig *Penguin*. Afterward Biddle held many important commands at sea; negotiated first treaty between United States and China, 1846.

BIDDLE, NICHOLAS (*b. Philadelphia, Pa., 1750; d. off Charleston, S.C., 1778*), naval officer. Trained in merchant service; entered British Navy, 1772; shipped as coxswain on Royal Geographical Society polar expedition, 1773, in company with Horatio Nelson. Resigned commission on return from Arctic; offered services to Congress. Commanded brig *Andrea Doria*, 1775–76, making numerous captures of British vessels in North Atlantic. In command of the *Randolph*, after a successful West Indian cruise, he engaged H.M.S. *Yarmouth* off Charleston, S.C., March 1778, in which action his ship blew up.

BIDDLE, NICHOLAS (*b. Philadelphia, Pa., 1786; d. Philadelphia, 1844*), scholar, statesman, financier. Brother of James Biddle; nephew of Nicholas Biddle (1750–1778). Studied at University of Pennsylvania; graduated College of New Jersey (Princeton), 1801. Traveled over much of Europe, 1804–07, serving as secretary to John Armstrong in U.S. mission to France, and as secretary of the legation at London under James Monroe.

Returning from abroad, Biddle was admitted to the bar, 1809; in the same year he became a member of the "Tuesday Club" established by Joseph Dennie to encourage contributions to the *Port Folio* magazine. Primarily a man of letters, 1809–14, Biddle served in the Pennsylvania legislature, 1810–11.

Requested in 1810 by William Clark to write a narrative of his Louisiana expedition with Meriwether Lewis, Biddle worked (1810–12) at weaving notes, journals, and Clark's oral statements into a cohesive narrative. It was published in 1814 as *History of the Expedition of Captains Lewis and Clark* after being seen through the press by journalist Paul Allen. Meanwhile Biddle had become increasingly active in editorial management of the *Port Folio*; when Dennie died in 1812, Biddle became editor of what was then the leading literary periodical in America.

Drawn from scholarly life by pressures of the War of 1812, Biddle aided in getting loans for the War Department, entered state senate, 1814, and initiated measures for protection of Philadelphia. Invited by President Monroe to become one of the five government directors of the (second) Bank of the United States, he threw himself into the study of banking and soon became one of the best informed and most efficient members of the board. He served as president of the Bank, 1823–39, engaging in a celebrated controversy with President Jackson (1823–33) over the Bank's right to a national charter.

After his resignation, he retired to "Andalusia," his country place on the Delaware. There he entertained distinguished guests, maintained his interest in literature, architecture, and education, and wrote numerous papers and addresses on economic and literary subjects.

BIDLACK, BENJAMIN ALDEN (*b. Paris, N.Y., 1804; d. 1849*), lawyer, diplomat. Negotiated Treaty of 1846 (ratified 1848) between the United States and New Granada, giving right-of-way across Isthmus of Panama.

BIDWELL, BARNABAS (*b. Tyringham, Mass., 1763; d. 1833*), lawyer. Graduated Yale, 1785. Prominent in Massachusetts politics, 1791–1810; absconded to Canada after shortage in accounts. Author of a tragedy, *The Mercenary Match* (1785).

BIDWELL, JOHN (*b. Chautauqua Co., N.Y., 1819; d. California, 1900*), pioneer, politician. Raised in Ohio; removed to Missouri frontier, 1839. Left Independence, Mo., 1841, with the Bartleson party, the first emigrant train to make the journey to California from Missouri. Naturalized a Californian, 1844, at outbreak of 1844 revolt against Micheltorena he and Sutter were imprisoned, but soon made peace with the rebels. On July 4, 1846, Bidwell was one of those who drew up the resolution of independence from Mexico. Made a second lieutenant of the California battalion after accompanying Frémont to Monterey, he became magistrate of San Luis Rey district and served as major in reconquest of Los Angeles. Prospected on Feather River, first to find gold there. Acquired Rancho Chico, north of Sacramento, 1849, and developed it for the rest of his life, becoming most noted agriculturalist in state.

BIDWELL, MARSHALL SPRING (*b. Stockbridge, Mass., 1799; d. New York, N.Y., 1872*), lawyer, Canadian politician. Son of Barnabas Bidwell. Forced to leave Canada for political reasons, 1837, he practiced law with great success in New York.

BIDWELL, WALTER HILLIARD (*b. Farmington, Conn., 1798; d. Saratoga Springs, N.Y., 1881*), editor, publisher. Graduated Yale, 1827; Yale Divinity School, 1833. *Post* 1841 edited numerous religious publications, including *Eclectic Magazine* which he owned, 1846–81.

BIEN, JULIUS (*b. Naumburg, Germany, 1826; d. 1909*), lithographer, map engraver. Studied graphic arts at Cassel and Frankfurt. Came to America, 1849; started lithographic business in New York City. Observing low standard of maps produced here, after interview with Secretary of War Jefferson Davis, he undertook engraving of maps for Pacific Railroad surveys, *post* 1855, one of which became standard map of the West for over 25 years. Thereafter he engraved and printed maps for most major government geographical and geological publications. During his career he did more than any other person to create and establish scientific standards for American cartography.

BIENVILLE, JEAN BAPTISTE LE MOYNE, SIEUR DE (*b. Longueuil, Canada, 1680; d. France, 1767*), pioneer, explorer, founder of Mobile and New Orleans. Brother of Pierre Le Moyne, Sieur d'Iberville, with whom he served in naval battles in North Atlantic and Hudson Bay, 1695–98. He accompanied Iberville on an expedition to rediscover the mouth of the Mississippi to form a French colony there, landing off what is now Biloxi, Miss., late in 1698, and making the first settlement on the coast at Old Biloxi. In 1699, Bienville explored the lower reaches of the Mississippi; in 1700 he explored the Red River as far as Natchitoches; in 1701 he succeeded to full command over the colony. Resolving in 1702 to move to a better site, he built Fort Louis on Mobile Bay which was removed in 1710 to the present site of Mobile, Ala. He was dismissed as governor of Louisiana after the colony was granted to Crozat's company in 1712 and served as second in command during Cadillac's administration, 1713–16. When John Law's colonization company took over Louisiana in 1717, Bienville was restored to command of the province; realizing the importance of changing its base to the Mississippi, he had New Orleans laid out in 1718 although it did not become the capital until 1722. Lack of support by the controlling Company of the Indies and increasing difficulties with the Natchez Indians brought about Bienville's recall to France in 1725. Despite a notable defense of his administration, he was deprived of all his offices and lived quietly in Paris

until 1732 when he was reinstated as governor, returning to the colony in 1733. After a decade of struggle against the Indians which resulted in an indecisive peace, he offered his resignation and left Louisiana in May 1743, never to return. His maintenance of Louisiana for so many years with such meagre resources is proof of his abilities.

BIERCE, AMBROSE GWINETT (*b. Meigs Co., Ohio, 1842; d. Mexico, 1914[?]*), journalist, author. Pseudonym, "Dod Grile." Raised on farm; had no formal education. Served with Indiana infantry in Civil War; severely wounded at Kenesaw Mountain. Settling in San Francisco *post* 1866, he won recognition for caustic wit in contributions to weekly journals, especially the *Argonaut* and the *News Letter* of which he became editor. His first fiction was published in the *Overland Monthly*, 1871. Worked in England as a journalist, 1872–76; returning to San Francisco, he wrote for the *Wasp* and the *Argonaut* and conducted a column in Hearst's *Examiner*, 1887–96. In 1897 he became Washington correspondent of the *New York American*. Disillusioned, and no longer effective in his creative work, he disappeared into Mexico, 1913. He was author of *The Fiend's Delight* (1872), *Nuggets and Dust* (1872), *Cobwebs from an Empty Skull* (1874), *Tales of Soldiers and Civilians* (1891), *The Monk and the Hangman's Daughter* (1892, with G. A. Danziger), *Can Such Things Be?* (1893), and *The Devil's Dictionary* (1906). He had a masterly touch with unusual and abnormal fictional plots and a fine compression of style.

BIERSTADT, ALBERT (*b. Solingen, Germany, 1830; d. 1902*), landscape painter. Came to America in infancy; raised in New Bedford, Mass. Studied at Düsseldorf and Rome, 1853–57. Returning home, he joined General Lander's 1858 surveying expedition for an overland wagon route and made sketches of Far West which were basis for heroic canvases painted later, including *Laramie Peak, In the Rocky Mountains*, and many others.

BIFFLE, LESLIE (*b. Boydsville, Ark., 1889; d. Washington, D.C., 1966*), secretary of the U.S. Senate. Minority assistant secretary of the Senate 1925–33, majority secretary 1933–45. Earned a lasting reputation as a shrewd nose counter, skilled parliamentarian, and discreet confidant; won respect from both parties and often interceded to smooth relations between competing personalities. In 1935 befriended freshman Democratic senator Harry Truman, with whom he developed a close personal relationship. In 1945 was unanimously elected secretary of the Senate and retained that position until 1953, except for a two-year period (1947–49) when he served as executive director of the Democratic Policy Committee during a Republican takeover of the Senate. When Truman became president in 1945, he emerged as the Senate's chief liaison with the White House. Retired in 1953 but remained in the capital as a consultant.

BIGELOW, ERASTUS BRIGHAM (*b. West Boylston, Mass., 1814; d. Boston, Mass., 1879*), inventor, economist. Invented a power loom, 1837, for production of coach lace, and formed the Clinton Co., 1838, to build and operate the looms. He is remembered principally as the inventor and perfecter of power looms for producing carpets.

BIGELOW, FRANK HAGAR (*b. Concord, Mass., 1851; d. Vienna, Austria, 1924*), meteorologist, Episcopal clergyman. Demonstrated, 1896–1901, that centers of extra-tropical cyclones occur on line of separation between warm and cold air masses.

BIGELOW, HARRY AUGUSTUS (*b. Norwood, Mass., 1874; d. Chicago, Ill., 1950*), law educator. Graduated Harvard, 1896; Harvard Law School, 1899. After practicing in Honolulu, Hawaii, 1900–04, he aided in establishing the law school of the University of Chicago. Became professor of law, 1909; dean of the law school, 1929–39. An authority on the law of real and personal property, he was author of widely used casebooks and the innovative *Introduction to the Law of Real Property* (1919).

BIGELOW, HENRY BRYANT (*b. Boston, Mass., 1879; d. Concord, Mass., 1967*), oceanographer. B.A. (1901) and Ph.D. (1906), Harvard. Became curator of coelenterates at the Harvard Museum of Comparative Zoology (1913), then lecturer at the college (1921), associate professor and curator of oceanography (1927), and professor (1931). Conducted many cruises to study the oceanography of the Gulf of Maine (1912–28). When the National Academy of Sciences established a Committee on Oceanography in 1927, he was appointed secretary, and his 1928 report on the role of the U.S. in worldwide oceanography led to the establishment of the Woods Hole Oceanographic Institution in Massachusetts, of which he was director (1930–40). Published extensively on fish, especially sharks and related species.

BIGELOW, HENRY JACOB (*b. Boston, Mass., 1818; d. 1890*), surgeon. Son of Jacob Bigelow. Graduated Harvard, 1837; studied medicine with father, at medical schools of Dartmouth and Harvard, and in Paris, France. Received M.D., Harvard, 1841; practiced in Boston after 1844. Was associated with discovery of surgical anaesthesia, 1846, when, probably through his influence, ether was administered by W. T. G. Morton in an operation at Massachusetts General Hospital. For almost forty years the dominating figure in New England surgery, Bigelow also taught and made important surgical contributions. He improved an instrument for crushing bladder stones and perfected an evacuator to remove the fragments, designating the operation "litholapaxy." His *Manual of Orthopedic Surgery* (1844) directed attention to a field previously neglected in America.

BIGELOW, JACOB (*b. Sudbury, Mass., 1787; d. Boston, Mass., 1879*), botanist, physician. Graduated Harvard, 1806; M.D., University of Pennsylvania, 1810, where he studied under Dr. B. S. Barton. Practiced in Boston as successor to James Jackson; lectured on botany. Professor of materia medica, Harvard Medical School, 1815–55. Bigelow's *Florula Bostoniensis* (1814) was standard work in New England botany until Gray's *Manual* appeared, 1848. His principal work was *American Medical Botany* (1817, 1818, 1820), and he had an important share in editing the first *American Pharmacopaeia* (1820). His *Discourse on Self-limited Diseases* (1835) was said by Holmes to have exerted more influence on medical practice in America than any other work that had ever been published in this country.

BIGELOW, JOHN (*b. Bristol, N.Y., 1817; d. 1911*), editor, diplomat, author. Graduated Union College, 1835. Admitted to New York bar, 1838. Shared in owning and editing New York *Evening Post*, 1848–61; was outspoken against slavery and for free trade. Appointed consul general at Paris, 1861, minister to France, 1865, his diplomatic work during Civil War ranks second in importance only to that of Charles Francis Adams at London. Editor of Franklin's *Autobiography* (1868) and *The Complete Works of Benjamin Franklin* (1887–88); author of lives of Franklin, Samuel J. Tilden, and others.

BIGELOW, MELVILLE MADISON (*b. near Eaton Rapids, Mich., 1846; d. Boston, Mass., 1921*), educator, legal writer. University of Michigan, A.B. 1866, LL.B. 1868; Harvard, Ph.D. 1879. Admitted to Tennessee bar, 1868. Interested in historical development of law, he went to Boston, 1870, to undertake research and remained there to practice and as faculty member and dean of Boston University Law School, 1872–1921. Among his many scholarly works were *The Law of Estoppel and its Application in Practice* (1872) which established his reputation,

Elements of the Law of Torts (1878) which became a standard textbook, and *The Law of Fraud on its Civil Side* (1888–90).

BIGELOW, WILLIAM STURGIS (*b. 1850; d. 1926*), physician, orientalist. Son of Henry J. Bigelow. Authority on Japanese language, religion, and philosophy; made collections of Japanese art now in Boston Art Museum.

BIGGERS, EARL DERR (*b. Warren, Ohio, 1884,; d. Pasadena, Calif., 1933*), novelist, dramatist. Creator of the fictional detective Charlie Chan.

BIGGS, ASA (*b. Williamston, N.C., 1811; d. Norfolk, Va., 1878*), jurist, politician. Joint codifier of North Carolina laws, 1851–55; district judge, 1858–65.

BIGGS, HERMANN MICHAEL (*b. Trumansburg, N.Y., 1859; d. 1923*), pioneer in preventive medicine. Professor, Bellevue Medical College, New York, *post* 1886; health official in New York City and State, 1892–1923. Introduced use of diphtheria antitoxin in United States, 1894, and was active in fight against tuberculosis.

BIGLER, JOHN (*b. near Carlisle, Pa., 1805; d. 1871*), lawyer, pioneer. Removed to Illinois, then overland to California, 1849. His wife was the first white woman to make a home in Sacramento. Elected to first state legislature, San Jose, 1849; elected Democratic governor, 1851; re-elected 1853. Effective minister to Chile, 1857–61. On return to California he practiced law and was active in Democratic politics.

BIGLER, WILLIAM (*b. Shermansburg, Pa., 1814; d. 1880*), printer, lumberman, railroad promoter. Democratic governor of Pennsylvania, 1851–54; U.S. senator, 1856–62.

BILBO, THEODORE GILMORE (*b. Juniper Grove, Poplarville, Pearl River County, Miss., 1877; d. New Orleans, La., 1947*), lawyer, politician. Attended Peabody Normal College, 1897–1900; taught school in Mississippi; studied law at Vanderbilt University, 1905–07, and briefly at University of Michigan. Beginning practice in Mississippi, he entered politics and developed a colorful, sometimes bawdy, style of oratory. A state senator, 1908–12, he was a supporter of James K. Vardaman. Accused of accepting a bribe and asked to resign, he held himself out as a persecuted champion of the poor, ran for lieutenant governor, and was elected, serving from 1912 to 1916. Tried and acquitted on another bribery charge (1914), he ran for governor, was elected, and served until 1920. As governor, he brought the state a number of important reforms, notably a tax equalization law. Unable to succeed himself as governor, he sought a seat in Congress but lost the primary; in 1923, he lost his bid for a second term as governor. Returned to the governorship in 1927, but was involved in scandals and discredited. By 1934, he was back on the political scene and won election to the U.S. Senate. Until the late 1930's, he served unobtrusively, supporting the New Deal and working hard for his constituents. He then came forward as an extreme racist, denouncing blacks, immigrants, and labor unions, and opposing all legislation in their favor. He was reelected in 1940, and again in 1946. He died while under investigation, and facing a possible refusal by the Senate to seat him.

BILLIKOPF, JACOB (*b. Vilna, Russia, 1883; d. Philadelphia, Pa., 1950*), social worker, labor arbitrator. Came to America, with parents, at age thirteen; grew up in Richmond, Va. Attended Richmond College; received bachelor of philanthropy from University of Chicago, 1903; graduate study at Chicago and New York School of Philanthropy. Served as superintendent of a Jewish settlement house in Cincinnati (1904–05), superintendent of Jewish charities in Milwaukee (1905–07), and superintendent of

United Jewish Charities in Kansas City, Mo. (1907–18). Led in establishing the pioneering Kansas City Board of Public Welfare. Between 1918 and 1920, he was in New York City, heading a national campaign to raise money for relief of Jewish victims of World War I. *Post* 1920, he was executive director of the Federation of Jewish Charities, and served as arbitrator of labor disputes and on many public boards and commissions relative to relief and welfare.

BILLINGS, ASA WHITE KENNEY (*b. Omaha, Nebr., 1876; d. La Jolla, Calif., 1949*), civil and electrical engineer. Graduated Harvard, 1895, majoring in physics; took master's degree in 1896. Worked on street railway and power plant construction in Pittsburgh, and Havana, Cuba. *Post* 1911, supervised dam construction in Texas and Spain. In 1922, joined Canadian corporation, known as "The Light," which operated the principal electric company in Brazil. Retired as its president in 1946. Created hydroelectric plants which added millions of kilowatts to Brazil's power supply and aided in flood control, irrigation, water supply, and fish culture. Contributed greatly to the industrial development of São Paulo.

BILLINGS, CHARLES ETHAN (*b. Wethersfield, Vt., 1835; d. 1920*), manufacturer, tool-maker. Developed (*post* 1862) treatment process for drop-forgings that made possible machine production of pistol frames and other articles previously fabricated by hand.

BILLINGS, FRANK (*b. Highland, Wis., 1854; d. Chicago, Ill., 1932*), physician. Demonstrated the causal relation of focal infections to systematic disease; associated with development of Chicago medical schools and societies.

BILLINGS, FREDERICK (*b. Royalton, Vt., 1823; d. 1890*), lawyer, railroad executive, philanthropist. Graduated University of Vermont, 1844. Removed to California, 1849, and opened a law office which developed into the leading San Francisco law firm of its time. An original partner in the Northern Pacific Railroad, Billings organized its land department and conducted it with great success, keeping prices low and advertising extensively. After reorganizing the road subsequent to the panic of 1873, he became its president in 1879 and financed completion of its trackage from Dakota to the Columbia. Forced out by Henry Villard in 1881, he became an active promoter of the Nicaraguan canal project and a benefactor of the University of Vermont, Amherst College, and other institutions. The town of Billings, Mont., is named for him.

BILLINGS, JOHN SHAW (*b. Switzerland Co., Ind., 1838; d. 1913*), librarian, surgeon. Graduated Miami University, 1857; M.D., Medical College of Ohio, 1860. Union medical officer, 1862–64; with surgeon general's office, 1864–94. Published, with Dr. Robert Fletcher, an *Index Catalogue* (1880–95) of the library of the surgeon general's department, a most important contribution to American medicine. Billings planned John Hopkins Hospital and was a pioneer in preventive medicine. His last seventeen years were spent in New York. Called there to consolidate the Astor, Lenox, and Tilden libraries into New York Public Library, he was really its creator.

BILLINGS, JOSH. *See* SHAW, HENRY WHEELER.

BILLINGS, WILLIAM (*b. Boston, Mass., 1746; d. 1800*), early singing-master, composer. A tanner by trade, he was a choir singer, interested in music and weary of the then poor state of church music. With more enthusiasm than knowledge, he wrote hymn tunes, became a singing teacher, trained choirs at several Boston churches. He introduced the pitchpipe in churches; impressed by counterpoint, he composed in this manner, and his efforts met with success despite their crudeness. Author of *The*

New England Psalm-Singer (1770), *The Singing Master's Assistant or Key to Practical Music* (1778), *The Suffolk Harmony* (1786), and other books.

BILLINGSLEY, JOHN SHERMAN (*b. North Enid, Okla., 1900; d. New York, N.Y., 1966*), nightclub owner. In 1929 opened a speakeasy in New York City called the Stork Club, which was closed by Prohibition agents. In 1932 a second version was opened, and with the repeal of Prohibition in 1933 the club moved to its last location, 3 East 53rd Street. Capitalizing shewdly upon the new chic of "café society," which in the 1930's and 1940's was characterized by a mingling of society figures and entertainers, he soon made the club "the New Yorkiest place in town," as Walter Winchell put it. In the 1950's a long decline set in, beginning in 1951 when Josephine Baker, the black entertainer, entered a charge of discrimination against the club (an investigation did not support the charges). By the 1960's the discothèque had become the popular kind of nightclub, and the club closed on 5 October 1965.

BILLY THE KID (*b. New York, N.Y., 1859; d. Fort Sumner, N.Mex., 1881*), desperado. True name, William H. Bonney.

BIMELER, JOSEPH MICHAEL (*b. Germany, ca. 1778; d. Tuscarawas Co., Ohio, 1853*), founder of communal Society of Zoar in Ohio. Came to America, 1817.

BINFORD, JESSIE FLORENCE (*b. Marshalltown, Iowa, 1876; d. Marshalltown, Iowa, 1966*), social worker. After meeting Jane Addams and visiting her famous settlement, Hull House, became a permanent resident (1905–63). Made her most significant contributions to social work as superintendent (1916–52) of the Juvenile Protective Association (JPA), a voluntary child-welfare organization formed in 1906 as the Juvenile Protective League (its name was changed in 1909) and based at Hull House. She fought against the drug and liquor traffic aimed at juveniles, fought the black market in babies, advocated local censorship of movies, attacked gamblers, and pressured the police and the courts into doing a better job of law enforcement. Sometimes called "the conscience of Chicago," she has been credited with diverting as many as 75,000 youngsters from lives of crime and poverty.

BINGA, JESSE (*b. Detroit, Mich., 1865; d. Chicago, Ill., 1950*), banker, realtor. After completing two years of high school, he worked for a time for an attorney; between 1885 and 1893, he traveled over a great part of the West as an itinerant barber, railroad porter, and successful dealer in land. In 1898, he set up a real estate office on South State Street in Chicago and was active in opening up good quality housing on the south side of the city for his fellow blacks. In 1908, he started the Binga Bank, the first to be owned, managed, directed, or controlled by blacks in the North. With the great migration of blacks to Chicago that started during World War I, he grew successful and rich; he owned much property, and his bank (chartered by the state in 1921) was flourishing. His name had become synonymous with black progress and business achievement. Unhappily, the onset of the Depression forced down the value of south side real estate, deposits declined, and despite Binga's efforts to save it, the bank closed in July 1930. Its failure cost him his own personal fortune and swallowed up the savings of many small depositors. Served three years in prison for embezzlement and fraud.

BINGAY, MALCOLM WALLACE (*b. Sandwich, Ont., 1884; d. Detroit, Mich., 1953*), newspaper editor. Colorful managing editor of the *Detroit News* (1914–28) and of the *Detroit Free Press* (1930–53). He coordinated a story on an American Legion parade in 1931 that won five *Free Press* reporters a Pulitzer Prize. Famous for an editorial announcing Thomas E. Dewey's election to the presidency in 1948. His flamboyant and highly personal style coupled with his conservative politics often alienated both the public and his colleagues.

BINGHAM, AMELIA (*b. Hicksville, Ohio, 1869; d. New York, N.Y., 1927*), actress. One of the most popular of American road attractions; had great success in Clyde Fitch's *The Climbers* (1901).

BINGHAM, ANNE WILLING (*b. Philadelphia, Pa., 1764; d. Bermuda, 1801*), society leader, *saloniste*. Beautiful and witty wife of William Bingham; reigned over the "Republican Court" in Philadelphia, 1789–99.

BINGHAM, CALEB (*b. Salisbury, Conn., 1757; d. Boston, Mass., 1817*), bookseller, pioneer writer of textbooks. Graduated Dartmouth, 1782. Prominent advocate of free public schools; edited *The Columbia Orator* (1797).

BINGHAM, GEORGE CALEB (*b. Augusta Co., Va., 1811; d. Kansas City, Mo., 1879*), portrait and genre painter. Began early to copy engravings and to paint; by 1834 had made art his vocation. Studied briefly at Pennsylvania Academy of Fine Arts, lived in Washington, D.C., 1840–44, and in Europe 1856–58, but spent most of his life in Missouri where his family had settled in 1819. His first genre painting to receive much attention was "Jolly Flatboatmen," selected by the American Art Union for annual engraving, 1846. Interested in politics, he held state offices; many of his pictures are on political subjects ("Canvassing for a Vote," "Stump Speaking"). His genre work has preserved with realism and humor characteristic scenes from old-time Missouri life.

BINGHAM, HARRY (*b. Concord, Vt., 1821; d. 1900*), New Hampshire lawyer and Democratic legislator.

BINGHAM, HIRAM (*b. Bennington, Vt., 1789; d. New Haven, Conn., 1869*), Congregational clergyman. Sandwich Islands missionary, 1820–40; devised alphabet for language; with associates translated Bible into Hawaiian.

BINGHAM, HIRAM (*b. Honolulu, Hawaii, 1831; d. Baltimore, Md., 1908*), Congregational clergyman. Son of Hiram Bingham (1789–1869). Missionary to Micronesia.

BINGHAM, HIRAM (*b. Honolulu, Hawaii, 1875; d. Washington, D.C., 1956*), explorer and U.S. Senator. Studied at Yale, the University of California, and Harvard, where he received a Ph.D. in South American history. Bingham taught at Yale from 1907 to 1924; during this period he conducted many explorations of Latin America, discovering the Inca cities of Vitcos and Machu Picchu in 1911. His books include *Across South America* (1911) and *Lost City of the Incas* (1948). A conservative Republican, Bingham's first elected office was as lieutenant governor of Connecticut, 1922–24; he was elected governor in 1924, but was nominated to fill a vacant seat in the Senate, where he served from 1924 to 1932. In the Senate, Bingham was active on the President's Aircraft Board and drafted the first attempt at federal regulation of civil aviation, the Air Commerce Act of 1926. Censured by the Senate (1929) for admitting a lobbyist to closed sessions of the Finance Committee. President, National Aeronautic Association (1928–34). Headed the Loyalty Review Board of the Civil Service Commission (1951–53), under President Harry S. Truman. His actions led to the dismissal of many employees from government service on charges of "reasonable doubt" of "loyalty."

BINGHAM, JOHN ARMOR (*b. Mercer, Pa., 1815; d. Cadiz, Ohio, 1900*), lawyer, Ohio politician. As congressman, Whig and Republican, 1855–73 (except for 38th Congress), played a leading role in trial of Lincoln's assassins, also in impeachment trial of President Johnson.

BINGHAM, ROBERT WORTH (*b. Orange Co., N.C., 1871; d. Baltimore, Md., 1937*), lawyer, newspaper proprietor, diplomat. LL.B., University of Louisville, 1897. In 1918 acquired control of the Louisville *Courier-Journal* and *Louisville Times*. An independent Democrat, interested especially in agricultural progress, his newspapers in 1932 supported Roosevelt, who appointed Bingham ambassador to the Court of St. James, a post he held until his death.

BINGHAM, WALTER VAN DYKE (*b. Swan Lake, Iowa, 1880; d. Washington, D.C., 1952*), psychologist. Studied at the University of Kansas, Beloit College, Chicago (Ph.D., 1905), and Harvard (M.A., 1907). After teaching at Columbia and Dartmouth, Bingham joined the faculty of the Carnegie Institute of Technology and founded the first department of applied psychology in the U.S. During World War I, helped devise the first intelligence tests used by the army in the classification of personnel. During World War II, served as chief psychologist to the adjutant general of the U.S. Department of War. Post 1949 was consultant to the Secretary of Defense.

BINGHAM, WILLIAM (*b. Philadelphia, Pa., 1752; d. 1804*), trader, privateer owner. Founder and director, Bank of North America, 1781; successful land speculator and turnpike promoter; U.S. senator from Pennsylvania. 1795–1801.

BINGHAM, WILLIAM (*b. North Carolina, 1835; d. Orange Co., N.C., 1873*), educator.

BINKLEY, ROBERT CEDRIC (*b. Mannheim, Pa., 1897; d. Cleveland, Ohio, 1940*), historian. Librarian, Hoover Library, Stanford University, 1922–27; authority on the reproduction and preservation of research materials.

BINKLEY, WILFRED ELLSWORTH (*b. Lafayette, Ohio, 1883; d. Ada, Ohio, 1965*), educator and author. In 1921 he began his long association with Ohio Northern University, earning his M.A. (1926) and Ph.D. (1936) there and remaining as assistant professor of political science and history until his death. His two most important books, *President and Congress* (1943) and *American Political Parties* (1949), were characterized by a consistent concern for analysis shaped by the force of historical events. A historian and political scientist, he thus wed political analysis and historical causation. His other books included *The Man in the White House* (1959) and *A Grammar of American Politics* (1949).

BINNEY, AMOS (*b. Boston, Mass., 1803; d. 1847*), zoologist. Graduated Brown, 1821; M.D., Harvard, 1826. Won an international reputation for his *Terrestrial Air-Breathing Mollusks*, published posthumously (1851).

BINNEY, HORACE (*b. Philadelphia, Pa., 1780; d. Philadelphia, 1875*), lawyer. Graduated Harvard, 1797. Studied law in office of Jared Ingersoll; admitted to bar, 1800. By 1809, when he issued the first volume of his *Reports of Cases Adjudged in the Supreme Court of Pennsylvania* (six volumes in all, covering cases to 1814), he was in successful practice as an expert in marine cases and had represented the United States Bank before the Supreme Court. He occupied a leading position at the bar, 1816–37, when he virtually retired from court work and confined himself to giving opinions particularly on land titles. An anti-Jackson man, he served a single term in Congress, 1833–35. Sincere, devoted to principle, he gave notable service to his city and state; subsequent to his retirement from practice in 1850 he gave much time to writing on constitutional questions. His reputation rests on two great cases in which he appeared: *Lyle* v. *Richards*, 1823, and the Girard trust case of 1844 (*Vidal et al.* v. *Philadelphia et al.*).

BINNS, JOHN (*b. Dublin, Ireland, 1772; d. 1860*), journalist, politician, author. Associate of William Godwin and English radicals; immigrated to Pennsylvania, 1801. Published the outspoken, radical *Democratic Press* (Philadelphia, 1807–29).

BINNS, JOHN ALEXANDER (*b. Loudoun Co., Va.*, ca. *1761; d. 1813*), Virginia farmer, soil conservationist. Applied gypsum to his crops as fertilizer, 1784; increased yields encouraged further experiments on clover, grass, grains. His ideas on agricultural improvements were published in *A Treatise on Practical Farming* (1803). The "Loudoun System" of planting and plowing thus became widely known and practiced in Maryland and Virginia.

BIRCH, REGINALD BATHURST (*b. London, England, 1856; d. New York, N.Y., 1943*), artist. Immigrated to San Francisco, Calif., with parents, 1870. Studied at Royal Academy in Munich, and published drawings in Vienna, Paris, and Rome publications, 1873–81. Settled in New York City; did pen-and-ink illustrations for *St. Nicholas, Century, Youth's Companion*, and other magazines. He made his first and greatest success as illustrator of Frances H. Burnett's *Little Lord Fauntleroy* (1886). Thereafter, he was one of the leading illustrators of books and magazine stories until about 1914, when artistic fashion changed and his work ceased to be sought. He emerged from obscurity in 1933 and illustrated some twenty books before failing eyesight forced a halt in 1941.

BIRCH, THOMAS (*b. England, 1779; d. 1851*), pioneer landscape and marine painter. Son of William R. Birch. Came to America, 1794. Celebrated for paintings of sea battles in War of 1812; also painted views of historic buildings around Philadelphia.

BIRCH, WILLIAM RUSSELL (*b. Warwickshire, England, 1755; d. 1834*), painter, engraver. Came to America, 1794. Won high reputation for miniatures on enamel.

BIRCHALL, FREDERICK THOMAS (*b. Warrington, England, 1868; d. Bridgewater, Nova Scotia, 1955*), journalist. Immigrated to the U.S. in 1893. Acting managing editor (1926–31) and director of European news service (1931–41) of the *New York Times*. Birchall won the Pulitzer Prize for his coverage of the rise of Hitler and Nazism. In 1940, he published *The Storm Breaks: Panorama of Europe and the Forces That Have Wrecked Its Peace*.

BIRD, ARTHUR (*b. Cambridge, Mass., 1856; d. 1923*), composer. Spent most of life abroad, principally in Berlin. Prolific composer in almost all forms; winner of Paderewski prize, 1901.

BIRD, FREDERIC MAYER (*b. Philadelphia, Pa., 1838; d. South Bethlehem, Pa., 1908*), Lutheran and Episcopal clergyman, hymnologist, editor. Son of Robert M. Bird.

BIRD, ROBERT MONTGOMERY (*b. New Castle, Del., 1806; d. Philadelphia, Pa., 1854*), physician, playwright, novelist. His romantic tragedies *The Gladiator* (produced New York, 1831) and *Oralloossa* (produced Philadelphia, 1832), the domestic tragedy *The Broker of Bogota* (produced New York, 1834), and other plays were written for Edwin Forrest, with whom Bird had a disagreement over money owed him. Turning to the novel, Bird published *Calavar* (1834); *The Infidel* (1835); *The Hawks of Hawk Hollow* (1835); his best work, *Nick of the Woods* (1837); and several minor works.

BIRD WOMAN.   *See* SACAGAWEA.

BIRDSEYE, CLARENCE (*b. Brooklyn, N.Y., 1886; d. New York, N.Y., 1956*), scientist and inventor. Studied briefly at Amherst College. Inventor of process for quick-freezing foods in convenient packages. Birdseye's inventions and business acumen (he held over 300 patents) revolutionized the food industry and brought widespread changes to agriculture. The firm eventually became the General Foods Corporation, which retained Birdseye's name on its frozen-food products.

BIRGE, EDWARD ASAHEL (*b. Troy, N.Y., 1851; d. Madison, Wis., 1950*), limnologist, educator. A.B., Williams College, 1873; Ph.D., Harvard, 1878. An instructor in natural philosophy at University of Wisconsin, 1876–79, he was made professor of zoology there in 1879. He spent a year (1880–81) studying histology and physiology in Leipzig, and then returned to Wisconsin. Instituted laboratory courses in bacteriology and physiology and established (1887) the first premedical course given at Wisconsin. Birge continued his earlier research on *Cladocera* and became an authority on their taxonomy, but he is chiefly famous as a pioneer limnologist. Director, Wisconsin Geological and Natural History Survey (1897–1919); supervised a variety of projects and carried on his own classic studies of Wisconsin lakes as individual, integrated entities. About 1905, began long collaboration with Chancey Juday. President of Wisconsin from 1918 until his retirement in 1925.

After retirement, Birge continued his research and established (with Juday) the Trout Lake Limnological Laboratory near Minocqua, Wis., where he did probably his most important investigation on the penetration of light into lake water.

BIRGE, HENRY WARNER (*b. Hartford, Conn., 1825; d. New York, N.Y., 1888*), Union soldier, merchant. Brigade and division commander in New Orleans and Port Hudson campaigns, and later in Red River campaign.

BIRKBECK, MORRIS (*b. Settle, England, 1764; d. Fox River, Ill., 1825*), pioneer, publicist. Immigrated to Illinois, 1817; an associate of George Flower. Author of *Notes on a Journey in America* (1817) and *Letters from Illinois* (1818).

BIRKHOFF, GEORGE DAVID (*b. Overisel, near Holland, Mich., 1884; d. Cambridge, Mass., 1944*), mathematician. Raised in Chicago, Ill. A.B., Harvard, 1905; A.M., 1906; Ph.D., University of Chicago, 1907. Taught at University of Wisconsin, 1907–09; professor at Princeton, 1909–12; professor of mathematics at Harvard *post* 1912. At Princeton, developed interest in dynamical systems and associated problems in the theory of differential equations, winning recognition as a master in this field. Solved a geometrical problem that had defied the efforts at solution of Henri Poincaré. Problem had an important bearing on the presence of periodic orbits in a dynamical system, and his solution (1913) won worldwide acclaim. His creative powers reached full development at Harvard and were displayed in brilliant papers on differential and difference equations, and dynamical systems; his lectures delivered before the American Mathematical Society were developed into his book *Dynamical Systems* (1927). Of all Birkhoff's profound results, however, his ergodic theorem of 1931 was probably the most fruitful in its consequences in dynamics, probability theory, group theory, and functional analysis. He wrote also on relativity and on quantitative bases for canons of beauty in music, art, and poetry.

BIRNEY, DAVID BELL (*b. Huntsville, Ala., 1825; d. Philadelphia, Pa., 1864*), Union soldier. Son of James G. Birney. Fought with Army of the Potomac; commanded 10th Army Corps under Grant.

BIRNEY, JAMES (*b. Danville, Ky., 1817; d. Bay City, Mich., 1888*), lawyer, diplomat. Son of James G. Birney. Established Bay City *Chronicle*, 1871. U.S. minister to The Hague, 1876–82.

BIRNEY, JAMES GILLESPIE (*b. Danville, Ky., 1792; d. Eagleswood, N.J., 1857*), antislavery leader. Graduated Princeton, 1810; admitted to bar, 1814; practiced in Danville. Removed to Alabama, 1818. *Post* 1826, was interested in African colonization movement and restriction of slavery and domestic slave trade. Returned in 1832 to Danville and grew more aggressive in antislavery activities; issued first number of the *Philanthropist* in Ohio, 1836, removing the publication to New York in 1837. In it he attacked Democrats and Whigs, and urged necessity of political action on abolitionists as against the policies urged by W. L. Garrison. Birney was antislavery presidential candidate in 1840 and 1844 (Liberty party). He occupied a peculiar position in the American antislavery movement, passing as he did from belief in amelioration and gradual emancipation to abolition by constitutional and peaceful means.

BIRNEY, WILLIAM (*b. Madison Co., Ala., 1819; d. Washington, D.C., 1907*), Union soldier, lawyer. Son and biographer of James G. Birney.

BISHOP, ABRAHAM (*b. New Haven, Conn., 1763; d. New Haven, 1844*), Jeffersonian politician. Delivered noteworthy addresses against conservatives and Federalists; collector of the port of New Haven, 1803–29.

BISHOP, CHARLES REED (*b. Glens Falls, N.Y., 1822; d. California, 1915*), banker in Hawaii, philanthropist. Benefactor of Hawaiian schools.

BISHOP, JOEL PRENTISS (*b. Volney, N.Y., 1814; d. Cambridge, Mass., 1901*), lawyer. Wrote treatises on legal subjects, including *Commentaries on Marriage, Divorce and Separation* (1852) and *Criminal Law* (1856–58), which became classics.

BISHOP, JOHN PEALE (*b. Charles Town, Jefferson County. W. Va., 1892; d. Hyannis, Mass., 1944*), author. Graduated Princeton, 1917, where he drew attention as a writer of poetry and associated with F. Scott Fitzgerald and Edmund Wilson. His first book of verse, *Green Fruit*, was published in 1917. After World War I army service, he was managing editor (1920–22) of *Vanity Fair* magazine; in 1922, with Wilson, he published *The Undertaker's Garland*, a collection of verse and prose. Resident mainly in France, 1922–33, Bishop was acquainted with the expatriate writers of the period but produced little work of his own; in 1931, he published a collection of stories, *Many Thousands Gone*. After returning to America in 1933, he settled eventually at South Chatham, Mass., on Cape Cod. He published a collection of poems, *Now With His Love* (1933), and in 1935 a novel, *Act of Darkness*, and *Minute Particulars*, further poems. Between 1933 and 1940, he wrote a number of perceptive critical essays and reviews of books. The bulk of his writing, marked by a commitment to disciplined artistry, was an elaboration of one idea: the need for, and the consequences of a lack of, tradition in modern society.

BISHOP, NATHAN (*b. Vernon, N.Y., 1808; d. Saratoga Springs, N.Y., 1880*), educator, philanthropist.

BISHOP, ROBERT HAMILTON (*b. Whitburn, Scotland, 1777; d. Pleasant Hill, Ohio, 1855*), pioneer Presbyterian minister in Kentucky and Ohio. Came to America, 1802; president, Miami University, 1824–41; antislavery advocate.

BISHOP, ROBERT ROBERTS (*b. Medfield, Mass., 1834; d. Newton, Mass., 1909*), lawyer. Associate justice, Massachusetts superior court, 1888–1909.

BISHOP, SETH SCOTT (*b. Fond du Lac, Wis., 1852; d. 1923*), Chicago laryngologist. Author of *Diseases of the Ear, Nose and Throat* (1897), and *The Ear and Its Diseases* (1906).

BISHOP, WILLIAM DARIUS (*b. Bloomfield, N.J., 1827; d. 1904*), railway official. President, New York and New Haven Railroad, 1866–79.

BISPHAM, DAVID SCULL (*b. Philadelphia, Pa., 1857; d. 1921*), baritone. Sang opera at Covent Garden and Metropolitan; helped establish high standards in American song recitals. Wrote *A Quaker Singer's Recollections* (1920).

BISSELL, EDWIN CONE (*b. Schoharie, N.Y., 1832; d. Chicago, Ill., 1894*), Congregational clergyman, Hebrew scholar. Author of *The Pentateuch, Its Origin and Structure* (1885).

BISSELL, GEORGE EDWIN (*b. New Preston, Conn., 1839; d. Mt. Vernon, N.Y., 1920*), sculptor.

BISSELL, GEORGE HENRY (*b. Hanover, N.H., 1821; d. 1884*), promoter of petroleum industry. Graduated Dartmouth, 1845. After work in journalism and education in the South, he began law practice with J. G. Eveleth in New York, 1853. On a visit to Dartmouth, he became interested in petroleum samples from Oil Creek region of Pennsylvania. After investigation, he and Eveleth leased lands, organized the Pennsylvania Rock Oil Co., 1854, first U.S. oil company. Boring for oil in manner of artesian wells, an important innovation, was first suggested by Bissell.

BISSELL, WILLIAM HENRY (*b. Yates Co., N.Y., 1811; d. 1860*), physician, lawyer. Removed to Illinois, 1834. Congressman, Democrat and Independent, 1848–54; Republican governor, 1856–60.

BISSELL, WILSON SHANNON (*b. Oneida Co., N.Y., 1847; d. Buffalo, N.Y., 1903*), lawyer. Associated in law firm with Grover Cleveland; postmaster general, 1893–94.

BITTER, KARL THEODORE FRANCIS (*b. Vienna, Austria, 1867; d. New York, N.Y., 1915*), sculptor. Trained as a decorative modeler in Vienna. Came to New York in 1889 and found work with firm of architectural modelers; became protégé of architect Richard M. Hunt; won competition for one of bronze gates of Trinity Church, 1891. His exterior and interior decorations were in great demand, but *post* 1900 he refused "commercial" orders and limited himself to work of a more idealistic character. His enormous production included civic monuments, historical figures, portraits, and memorials.

BITZER, GEORGE WILLIAM (*b. Roxbury, Mass., 1872; d. Los Angeles, Calif., 1944*), pioneer motion-picture cameraman; known as "Billy." Moved to New York City at uncertain date; attended Cooper Union at night; worked as an electrician. Joined Biograph Company, 1896, as cameraman and projectionist; *post* 1900, was principal cameraman for the company. Between 1908 and 1929 (when he was blacklisted by the industry for trade union activity), Bitzer was the close collaborator of David Wark Griffith in innovative film work. He was cameraman for all the classic Griffith pictures. Many technical contributions once attributed to Griffith were developed prior to their collaboration in films photographed by Bitzer. He made his principal contribution to technique in the development of the iris, a process for focusing attention and for fading in and out of a scene.

BIXBY, HORACE EZRA (*b. Geneseo, N.Y., 1826; d. Maplewood, Mo., 1912*), Mississippi pilot. Mark Twain's instructor and partner on the river.

BIXBY, JAMES THOMPSON (*b. Barre, Mass., 1843; d. Yonkers, N.Y., 1921*), Unitarian clergyman. Leader in Liberal Ministers' Association.

BJERREGAARD, CARL HENRIK ANDREAS (*b. Fredericia, Denmark, 1845; d. 1922*), mystical philosopher, librarian. Worked at

Astor Library and its successor, New York Public Library, 1879–1922.

BLACK, EUGENE ROBERT (*b. Atlanta, Ga., 1873; d. Atlanta, 1934*), banker. Governor of Federal Reserve Board in the critical period, 1933–34.

BLACK, FRANK SWETT (*b. Limington, Maine, 1853; d. 1913*), lawyer. Republican governor of New York, 1897–99.

BLACK, GREENE VARDIMAN (*b. near Winchester, Ill., 1836; d. 1915*), dentist. Began practice in Winchester, 1857. Taught at dental colleges in Missouri, Iowa, and Chicago, 1870–91; from 1891 until his death he was a professor at Northwestern University Dental School, becoming dean in 1897. His first important publication of original research appeared in 1869 and dealt with the causes of the loss of workability by cohesive gold when stored. Other important papers by him presented new views on diseases of the periodontal membrane, the extension of cavities in order to prevent further decay, the falsity of the theory that the density of a tooth had anything to do with its proneness to decay, and the preparation of stable amalgam alloys. His several books included *Dental Anatomy* (1891), a standard text in its field.

BLACK HAWK (*b. Sauk village on Rock River, Ill., 1767; d. Iowa, 1838*), Sauk war chief, protagonist of the "Black Hawk War." Resentful of Americans and disavowing Sauk cession of ancestral lands by treaty of 1804, Black Hawk helped British in War of 1812 and was a leader under Tecumseh. In late spring, 1832, in an effort to repossess Sauk lands in Illinois from white settlers, he was opposed by troops under General Henry Atkinson and by Illinois volunteers and defeated at battle of Bad Axe. Taken east, he met President Jackson and was returned to Iowa after brief confinement. The *Autobiography of Black Hawk* (1833) is an American classic.

BLACK, JAMES (*b. Lewisburg, Pa., 1823; d. 1893*), lawyer. Founder of the National Prohibition Party. Active in temperance movement from 1840 to death; first Prohibition candidate for presidency, 1872.

BLACK, JEREMIAH SULLIVAN (*b. near Stony Creek, Pa., 1810; d. York, Pa., 1883*), lawyer, statesman. Educated at local schools; studied law with Chauncey Forward in Somerset, Pa., admitted to bar, 1830. Gained experience as deputy attorney general for his county; was active in politics as a Jacksonian Democrat. Judge of court of common pleas, 16th district, 1842–51; justice of supreme court of Pennsylvania, 1851–57. Appointed U.S. attorney general by President Buchanan, 1857, he served until December, 1860. Temperamental, stubborn, absent-minded, Black held strong opinions on many issues. His most important service as attorney general concerned California land titles; with assistance of Edwin M. Stanton and others, he uncovered a system of fraud in district court decisions. Resolute in enforcing the law, even when unpopular, he defended Buchanan's administration policy, attacked Stephen Douglas's "squatter sovereignty," and upheld Kansas' Lecompton Constitution.

In secession crisis, he argued that while Executive might not coerce a seceding state, he was duty bound to enforce the laws and protect federal property. Buchanan failed to take the advice which Black urged on him until it was too late. On resignation of Lewis Cass as secretary of state, Black took his post in December, 1860, and served in the difficult days preceding Lincoln's inauguration. Physically ill and in financial difficulties, Black restored his fortunes as an expert in litigation over California land titles. He opposed secession, gave tacit approval to the prosecution of the Civil War, but was a sharp critic of the administration's arbitrary actions, confiscation policy, and disregard of civil rights. He later counseled President Andrew Johnson, defended Samuel J. Tilden before the Electoral Commission, championed unpopular causes. He helped revise the Pennsylvania constitution, 1873.

BLACK, JOHN CHARLES (*b. Lexington, Miss., 1839; d. 1915*), lawyer, Union soldier. Raised in Illinois where he practiced law; active Democrat; member, and for nine years president, U.S. Civil Service Commission, 1903–13.

BLACK, WILLIAM MURRAY (*b. Lancaster, Pa., 1855; d. 1933*), army officer and engineer. Graduated West Point, 1877; chief of Army Engineers, 1916–19.

BLACKBURN, GIDEON (*b. Augusta Co., Va., 1772; d. 1838*), Presbyterian clergyman, educator. Missionary to Cherokee Indians.

BLACKBURN, JOSEPH (*fl. 1753–63 in Boston, Mass., and Portsmouth, N.H.*), colonial portrait painter.

BLACKBURN, JOSEPH CLAY STYLES (*b. Woodford Co., Ky., 1838; d. 1918*), lawyer, Confederate soldier. Congressman, Democrat, from Kentucky, 1875–85; U.S. senator, 1885–97, 1901–07. Active in unearthing scandals of Grant administration.

BLACKBURN, LUKE PRYOR (*b. Fayette Co., Ky., 1816; d. Frankfort, Ky., 1887*), physician, Democratic governor of Kentucky, 1879–83. Fought yellow fever epidemics in several states; induced federal government to aid in control of the disease.

BLACKBURN, WILLIAM MAXWELL (*b. Carlisle, Ind., 1828; d. Pierre, S.Dak., 1898*), Presbyterian clergyman. Professor of biblical history, Northwest Seminary, Chicago, Ill., 1868–81; president, Pierre University (later Huron College), 1885–98.

BLACKFAN, KENNETH DANIEL (*b. Cambridge, N.Y., 1883; d. Louisville, Ky., 1941*), pediatrician. M.D., Albany (N.Y.) Medical College, 1905. After a year as laboratory assistant to Richard M. Pearce, Blackfan was in general practice until 1909, when he began a series of residencies in pediatrics in Philadelphia, St. Louis, Mo., and Baltimore, Md. Assistant to John Howland at Johns Hopkins, he taught pediatrics there, 1913–20, and made important contributions in research, one of which was a classical study of hydrocephalus with Walter E. Dandy. As professor of pediatrics and chief of the Children's Hospital at University of Cincinnati, 1920–23, and at Harvard Medical School, 1923–41, he proved himself an excellent administrator, physician, and teacher, raising his department to top rank. Made valuable studies in hematology.

BLACKFORD, CHARLES MINOR (*b. Fredericksburg, Va., 1833; d. Lynchburg, Va., 1903*), lawyer, Confederate soldier.

BLACKMUR, RICHARD PALMER (*b. Springfield, Mass., 1904; d. Princeton, N.J., 1965*), literary critic, author, and teacher. In the late 1920's he established his reputation as one of the foremost American critics with his essays for the little magazine *Hound and Horn*. Twelve critical essays, mostly on modern poets, were published in 1935 as *The Double Agent*, and with this book, said Allen Tate, Blackmur "invented" New Criticism, which called for close scrutiny of texts with little reference to biographical and cultural considerations. Few critics have examined their material so acutely as Blackmur in this collection or in *The Expense of Greatness* (1940). In 1937 he produced his first book of poetry, *From Jordan's Delight*. During the 1930's, his chief labor was his projected life of Henry Adams, which he never finished but which, at his death, stood as a satisfying, complete work. In 1940 he accepted an appointment at Princeton University, where he remained for the rest of his life and became a powerful presence in the American literary establishment, partly because he directed the Christian Gauss Seminars in Criticism, beginning in 1956. After his appointment to Princeton, his poetic inspiration dried up, and his criticism became increasingly abstract. The major work of his life was *Language As Gesture* (1952), arguably the finest criticism ever published in America.

BLACKSTONE, HARRY (*b. Henry Boughton, Chicago, Ill., 1885; d. Hollywood, Calif., 1965*), magician. In 1904 he began his career with his brother Peter, doing many performances in vaudeville with a show that included musical numbers and magic tricks involving animals as well as people. Was an expert at sleight of hand and card tricks and wrote popular how-to books on magic. Performed at the White House for President Calvin Coolidge and during World War II entertained throughout the country with the USO. The late 1940's was a time of great success for his *Show of 1001 Wonders*. He also had a radio series, and after he stopped giving stage shows in 1955, he continued to make television appearances.

BLACKSTONE, WILLIAM (*b. near Salisbury, England, 1595; d. near present Pawtucket, R.I., 1675*), New England colonist. Came to Massachusetts, ca. 1623, first settler in what is now Boston; moved after disagreements with Puritans, 1634.

BLACKTON, JAMES STUART (*b. Sheffield, England, 1875; d. Los Angeles, Calif., 1941*), motion picture pioneer. Came to America with parents, 1886; worked as a carpenter, newspaper reporter, illustrator. Soon after Edison's first public showing of motion pictures, Blackton and an associate bought a projecting Kinetoscope from Edison and began to make and exhibit films (*The Burglar on the Roof*, 1897; *Tearing Down the Spanish Flag*, 1898). On a trip to Cuba to photograph the Spanish-American War at first hand, Blackton was first to employ the "close-up" shot. In 1900, he and his associates incorporated their enterprise as the Vitagraph Company; as it grew in scope, he began to relinquish direction of some films to others and became a "producer" or supervisor. Among innovations credited to him are the first animated cartoon and the first use of dialogue in subtitles; in 1909, he produced the first films of feature length (*Les Miserables* and *The Life of Moses*) which were shown as serials; in 1910, he founded the first "fan" magazine. Resigning from Vitagraph in 1917, he worked as producer-director with other studios in the United States and England; he returned to Vitagraph, 1923–25. Bad investments resulted in his bankruptcy, 1931.

BLACKWELL, ALICE STONE (*b. Orange, N.J., 1857; d. Cambridge, Mass., 1950*), women's rights editor, humanitarian. Daughter of Henry Browne Blackwell and Lucy Stone; niece of Elizabeth Blackwell. Graduated Boston University, 1881. Editor of *Woman's Journal*, 1881–1916; also edited *Woman's Column*, a bulletin of suffrage news sent out to newspapers. Author of *Lucy Stone: Pioneer of Woman's Rights* (1930). A Unitarian in religion, she was active in many societies for the furthering of humanitarian causes.

BLACKWELL, ANTOINETTE LOUISA BROWN (*b. Henrietta, N.Y., 1825; d. 1921*), reformer, Congregational pastor. Eloquent speaker and writer, active for abolition, women's rights, prohibition.

BLACKWELL, ELIZABETH (*b. Bristol, England, 1821; d. Hastings, England, 1910*), first woman medical doctor of modern times. Came to America, 1832. Taught school; began reading medicine in 1845. Admitted after great difficulties to Geneva Medical School of Western New York, she received much-publicized M.D., 1849. Studied and practiced in Paris and London; opened with sister Emily a private dispensary in New York which later (1857) became incorporated into New York Infirmary and College for Women. Active during Civil War in organizing field nurses, in 1869 she settled permanently in England.

BLACKWELL, HENRY BROWN (*b. Bristol, England, 1825; d. Dorchester, Mass., 1909*), editor. Brother of Elizabeth Blackwell. Early advocate of woman suffrage, other liberal movements. Married to Lucy Stone.

BLACKWELL, LUCY STONE. *See* STONE, LUCY.

BLADEN, WILLIAM (*b. Hemsworth, England, 1673; d Maryland, 1718*), publisher. Came to Maryland, 1690. Active in public affairs, he held many official posts; as clerk of Assembly, supervised printing of colony laws *post* 1700.

BLAIKIE, WILLIAM (*b. New York, N.Y., 1843; d. 1904*), lawyer, athlete, promoter of physical training. Published popular *How to Get Strong and How to Stay So*, 1879.

BLAINE, ANITA (EUGENIE) MCCORMICK (*b. Manchester, Vt., 1866; d. 1954*), philanthropist. The daughter of Cyrus Hall McCormick, Blaine gave away over $10 million in her lifetime to various charities and foundations, including the Francis W. Parker School in Chicago; the McCormick Theological Seminary; and the Foundation for World Peace. At her death, she left over $20 million to be distributed to various institutions under the auspices of the New World Foundation, which she endowed.

BLAINE, JAMES GILLESPIE (*b. West Brownsville, Pa., 1830; d. Washington, D.C., 1893*), statesman. Graduated Washington College, Pa. Began to teach in Kentucky, but not liking the South, took a teaching position at the Pennsylvania Institute for the Blind, Philadelphia, 1852–54, studying law while in that city. Married Harriet Stanwood, 1850. Her family were settled in Augusta, Maine, and Blaine entered journalism there, 1854, purchasing an interest in the *Kennebec Journal*. He was identified with Maine thereafter.

In his first year of editorship he abandoned his formal Whig allegiance and was instrumental in giving the name "Republican" currency in the East. A delegate to the fist Republican convention, 1856, he was one of that party's founders, and expected it to carry on Whig measures as well as to oppose slavery. An orator of thrilling power, with talent for interpreting election returns and for remembering names and faces, he became chairman of the Maine Republican committee, 1859, holding the post until 1881 and becoming accepted party dictator in the state. Elected to the Maine legislature, 1858, and twice re-elected, he was speaker in his last two terms. Entering Congress in 1863, he served in the House until 1876; as speaker, 1869–75. He was U.S. senator, 1876–81.

Firm in support of Lincoln, he was less radical and vindictive in the Reconstruction period than many of his fellow Republicans. Favoring black suffrage, he helped pass an amendment to Thaddeus Stevens' military government bill which insisted on what Radicals called "universal suffrage and universal amnesty" as basis for Reconstruction. This was a notable victory for a young congressman. Coming through this period with the reputation of a level-headed liberal who could nevertheless be trusted even by the Grand Army, he built up popularity in the West. Associated with James A. Garfield and W. B. Allison, he made one lasting enemy, Roscoe Conkling of New York. Conkling became a leading Grant supporter, or "Stalwart," Blaine head of the opposition within the party, the "Half-Breeds." His chance for presidential nomination in 1876 seemed good, but charges brought against him by a Democratic committee investigating railroad graft were imperfectly refuted by Blaine, the "Stalwarts" opposed him, and the nomination went to Rutherford B. Hayes. Blaine worked to build up his position in preparation for the 1880 campaign, meanwhile supporting Hayes's administration against attacks by Conkling.

Garfield, however, was nominated. As before, Blaine took it with good grace, worked with Garfield in the campaign and became his secretary of state, resigning in 1881 after Garfield was shot. Finally in 1884, though the Republicans were still divided, Blaine was nominated for the presidency on the first ballot. Defection of "Mugwump" Republicans because of the railroad graft affair, apprehension over his foreign policy and the Burchard incident in New York lost him key states. Grover Cleveland won the election.

Still the most powerful Republican, Blaine was expected to be renominated in 1888, but refused a candidacy and was influential in the nomination of Benjamin Harrison. He became secretary of state under Harrison, serving 1889–92.

Blaine's permanent influence was through his foreign policy. Known as a politician, he was generally expected to emphasize political aspects of the office, but shattered this expectation by his genuine interest in building a constructive policy which would be adjusted to changing conditions. Despite shortcomings, common to his generation, of lack of training in international law or diplomatic history, he was a forerunner of American world interest and much in advance of his time.

Active in formulating an Isthmian canal policy and in securing treaties for protection of migratory animal life, his most constructive work had to do with South America. Since the Civil War, relations between Latin America and Great Britain had been growing more intimate at the expense of the United States; this had important economic aspects. Dissatisfied with the negative aspects of the Monroe Doctrine, Blaine in his first period as secretary of state evolved a policy which would unite the American nations into a real system, use good offices of the United States to maintain peace, and have joint conferences to plan measures of mutual advantage. His whole policy of Pan-Americanism was dropped when he resigned in 1881, but he continued to urge his views in magazine articles and through friends in Congress and implemented them in his later term of office. In October 1889, when the Pan-American Congress met in Washington, Blaine was influential in drawing up recommendations and laid foundation of the Bureau of American Republics at Washington. He also worked to promote reciprocity treaties and increase trade with Latin American countries, and is conspicuous as the only outstanding public figure between Seward and Hay who was genuinely interested in foreign affairs.

BLAINE, JOHN JAMES (*b. near Castle Rock, Wis., 1875; d. Wisconsin, 1934*), lawyer, politician. Progressive Republican governor of Wisconsin, 1921–27; U.S. senator, 1927–32.

BLAIR, AUSTIN (*b. Caroline, N.Y., 1818; d. 1894*), lawyer. Removed to Michigan, 1841. Energetic Republican governor of that state, 1860–65.

BLAIR, EMILY NEWELL (*b. Joplin, Mo., 1877; d. Alexandria, Va., 1951*), writer and politician. Studied at Goucher College. An active suffragist, Blair helped found the League of Women Voters in 1920; in 1921, she was elected to the Democratic National Committee from Missouri and served as first vice-chairman from 1924 to 1928. She was an associate editor of *Good Housekeeping* and wrote a monthly column from 1925 to 1933. In 1933, she was appointed to the Consumer's Advisory Board; chairman, 1935. She was the only woman on the Advisory Council of the National Recovery Administration. Blair at first advocated that women not become "women voters" but simply voters and politicians. She later reversed this position and called for a revival of feminism and for "women politicians" elected by a female constituency.

BLAIR, FRANCIS PRESTON (*b. Abingdon, Va., 1791; d. 1876*), journalist, politician. Graduated Transylvania University, 1811. Served briefly in War of 1812. Returning to Kentucky home, he actively fought "Old Court" party as assistant on *Argus of Western America*. Soon joined Jacksonians; wrote in favor of lower tariff, cheap land, direct election of president; opposed Bank of the United States. Jackson called him to Washington where he established administration organ, the *Globe*, 1830, continuing as editor until 1845. In these years Blair exerted much power, was member of Jackson's Kitchen Cabinet. He later turned to Republicans, supported Lincoln in 1860, and backed Lincoln's Reconstruction program but was driven back to Democratic party by extremists.

BLAIR, FRANCIS PRESTON (*b. Lexington Ky., 1821; d. St. Louis, Mo., 1875*), Union soldier, statesman. Son of Francis P. Blair (1791–1876). Graduated Princeton, 1841. Admitted to bar, and practiced in St. Louis, Mo., *post* 1842. Fought in Mexican War. Organized Free-Soil party in Missouri, opposed slave interest on moral and economic grounds. As congressman, Free-Soil, 1856–58, Republican, 1860–62, was a leader in saving Missouri for Union and rose to major general in active Civil War service. Recalled to Congress, 1864, he backed Lincoln's policy on Reconstruction, was later involved in Missouri controversy between Radical Republicans and moderates like himself. Reverting to Democratic party, he cooperated with Liberal Republicans, was elected to Missouri legislature, and was chosen U.S. senator by that body, 1871–73.

BLAIR, HENRY WILLIAM (*b. Campton, N.H., 1834; d. 1920*), lawyer, Union soldier. Congressman, Republican, from New Hampshire, 1875–79; U.S. senator, 1879–91. Proponent of federal aid to public schools, woman suffrage, labor legislation.

BLAIR, JAMES (*b. Scotland, 1655; d. Virginia, 1743*), founder and first president, William and Mary College. Came to Virginia as missionary, 1685. Appointed Bishop of London's commissary, 1689, he urged establishment of a college which was chartered 1693. Blair was named president. Minister at Jamestown, later Williamsburg, he managed, despite opposition, indifference, and a disastrous fire, to see the college well established before he died.

BLAIR, JOHN (*b. probably Virginia, 1687; d. 1771*), acting governor of Virginia, 1758 and 1768. Nephew of James Blair.

BLAIR, JOHN (*b. Williamsburg, Va., 1732; d. Williamsburg, 1800*), jurist. Son of John Blair (1687–1771). Patriot, Virginia judge, delegate to constitutional convention. Associate justice, U.S. Supreme Court, 1789–96.

BLAIR, JOHN INSLEY (*b. near Belvidere, N.J., 1802; d. 1899*), capitalist, philanthropist. Began as storekeeper and miller; expanding interest to mining, he participated, 1846, in founding Lackawanna Coal and Iron Co. and was one of largest stockholders in Delaware, Lackawanna, and Western Railroad. Interested in development of Western railroads, he joined in getting charter of Union Pacific, was at one time president of 16 roads, and laid out sites for over 80 towns in the West. Benefactor of Princeton, Blair Academy, Presbyterian church.

BLAIR, MONTGOMERY (*b. Franklin Co., Ky., 1813; d. 1883*), lawyer, statesman. Son of Francis P. Blair (1791–1876). Graduated West Point, 1835; resigned commission, 1836, to study law. Settled in St. Louis, 1837. Protégé of Thomas Hart Benton; practiced law, served as mayor and judge. Moving to Maryland, 1853, practiced chiefly before U.S. Supreme Court. A border man, he believed slavery question could be settled peaceably; was counsel for Dred Scott. A Democrat turned moderate Republican, he was postmaster general under Lincoln, organized army postal system, introduced compulsory payment of postage, other improvements. Forced by Radicals to resign, 1864, he continued loyal to Lincoln and his Reconstruction plan, but eventually drifted back to Democrats, supporting Seymour in 1868 and acting as Samuel J. Tilden's counsel before Electoral Commission.

BLAIR, SAMUEL (*b. Ulster, Ireland, 1712; d. Chester Co., Pa., 1751*), Presbyterian clergyman.

BLAIR, WILLIAM RICHARDS (*b. Coleraine, County Derry, Ireland, 1874; d. Fair Haven, N.J., 1962*), physicist and inventor. Immigrated to the U.S. in 1884. Ph.D. (1906), University of Chicago. Began his career as a meteorologist, but after joining the army turned his attention to developing the pulse-echo radar, which he advocated over thermal or sound detection. By 1937 he was able to demonstrate SCR-268, a short-range radio locator. All further development—such as radar countermeasures, airborne radar, and microwave early warning—were based on the SCR-268, which was the backbone of the military detection as late as 1944. Despite considerable evidence that his claim to this invention was legitimate and despite the patent he received for it in 1945, many have refused to recognize him as the inventor of the pulse-echo system.

BLAKE, ELI WHITNEY (*b. Westborough, Mass., 1795; d. New Haven, Conn., 1886*), inventor, manufacturer. Best known for stone-crushing machine, patented 1858.

BLAKE, FRANCIS (*b. Needham, Mass., 1850; d. 1913*), inventor, physicist. Patented telephone transmitter, 1878, the mechanical features of which made practical the fundamental principles of Berliner microphone.

BLAKE, FRANCIS GILMAN (*b. Mansfield Valley, Pa., 1887; d. Washington, D.C., 1952*), physician. Studied at Dartmouth (B.A., 1908) and Harvard Medical School (M.D., 1913). Associate in medicine at the hospital of the Rockefeller Institute, 1919–21, where he began work with viruses, assisted by J. D. Trask. These studies, published in 1921, proved conclusively that measles is caused by a virus. Professor at Yale Medical School, 1921–52, serving as dean, 1940–47. Blake continued his work with infectious diseases, in particular pneumonia and influenza.

BLAKE, HOMER CRANE (*b. Dutchess Co., N.Y., 1822; d. 1880*), naval officer.

BLAKE, JOHN LAURIS (*b. Northwood, N.H., 1788; d. Orange, N.J., 1857*), Episcopal clergyman, author of popular encyclopedias.

BLAKE, LILLIE DEVEREUX (*b. Raleigh, N.C., 1835; d. New York, N.Y., 1913*), author, reformer. Championed woman suffrage, economic reforms for women. Wrote stories, novels, including *Fettered for Life* (1874).

BLAKE, LYMAN REED (*b. South Abington, Mass., 1835; d. 1883*), inventor. Conceived idea of a machine which could sew soles of shoes to uppers. First designed a shoe that could be sewed, essentially the present-day shoe, then made and patented (1858) a machine which would sew it. Sold patent to Gordon McKay; later worked with him to promote and improve machine which came into almost universal use.

BLAKE, MARY ELIZABETH MCGRATH (*b. Dungarven, Ireland, 1840; d. Boston, Mass., 1907*), author of *Poems* (1882) and numerous other ephemeral works.

BLAKE, WILLIAM PHIPPS (*b. New York, N.Y., 1825; d. 1910*), geologist, mining engineer, teacher.

BLAKE, WILLIAM RUFUS (*b. Halifax, N.S., 1805; d. Boston, Mass., 1863*), actor. Popular comedian, made American debut in New York, 1824; managed theatres in New York, Philadelphia,

Boston; a member of Burton's, Laura Keene's and Wallack's stock companies.

BLAKELEY, GEORGE HENRY (*b. on a farm between Hanover and Livingston, N.J., 1865; d. Newport, R.I., 1942*), engineer, steel executive. B.S., Rutgers, 1884; trained through practical experience as apprentice and draftsman. Chief engineer of Passaic Rolling Mill Co., 1890–1906, he designed and built (among others) the 155th Street bridge over the Harlem River, New York City. Credited with the successful introduction of the thin-web, wide-flange girders, beams, and H-columns, made under a rolling process devised by Henry Grey, for use in building. Later called "Bethlehem sections," they were a factor in making the Bethlehem Steel Company one of the largest producers of commercial steel.

BLAKELOCK, RALPH ALBERT (*b. New York, N.Y., 1847; d. New York State, 1919*), landscape painter. Self-taught but influenced by rich colors and enamel-like technique of A. P. Ryder. Suffering a mental breakdown *ca.* 1899, he was elected to National Academy, 1913, while in an asylum. His works, essentially romantic mood pictures, recall 18th-century Dutch and English landscapes influenced by Rembrandt.

BLAKELY, JOHNSTON (*b. Seaford, Ireland, 1781; d. at sea, 1814*), naval officer. Came to America as a child. Became midshipman in navy, 1800; served in Mediterranean. Commanding brig *Enterprise*, 1811–13, and sloop-of-war *Wasp*, 1814, won several engagements with British. After engagement with British brig *Atlanta* in September 1814, east of Madeira, the *Wasp* is known to have sailed farther south, but nothing more was ever heard from her.

BLAKESLEE, ERASTUS (*b. Plymouth, Conn., 1838; d. Brookline, Mass., 1908*), Congregational clergyman. Organized Bible Study Union, Boston, 1892, which published lessons for all grades, widely used in Protestant churches.

BLAKESLEE, HOWARD WALTER (*b. New Dungeness, Wash., 1880; d. Port Washington, N.Y., 1952*), science writer and editor. Studied at the University of Michigan. Science editor and reporter for the Associated Press from 1928 until his death. Pulitzer Prize, 1937. From 1945 on, his speciality was reporting the development and testing of the atomic bomb. Despite his lack of formal scientific education, Blakeslee educated himself sufficiently to cover and make comprehensible to the general reader important scientific events. He was instrumental in making the reporting of science an important aspect of modern journalism.

BLALOCK, ALFRED (*b. Culloden, Ga., 1899; d. Baltimore, Md., 1964*), surgeon and educator. M.D. (1924), Johns Hopkins School of Medicine. In 1925 became chief resident in surgery at the school of medicine at Vanderbilt University, where he began his work on shock, gathering overwhelming evidence that shock was caused by decrease in blood volume; his recognition of the need for volume replacement was corroborated during World War II, when many lives were saved by the use of blood, blood substitutes, and volume expanders. In 1941 became professor of surgery at the Johns Hopkins School of Medicine and surgeon in chief of Johns Hopkins Hospital. There he collaborated with others in performing, for the first time, total removal of the thymus gland in patients with myasthenia gravis, an operation still utilized in the treatment of this disease. He also devised subclavian-pulmonary artery anastomosis, an operation for improving pulmonary circulation in children with pulmonic stenosis; he performed the first successful operation of this procedure on a patient with the tetralogy of Fallot ("blue baby" syndrome in children), a monumental achievement that brought fame to him and Helen B.

Taussig, a pediatric cardiologist who had suggested the procedure to him.

BLALOCK, NELSON GALES (*b. Mitchell Co., N.C., 1836; d. Walla Walla, Wash., 1913*), physician, agriculturist.

BLANC, ANTOINE (*b. Sury, France, 1792; d. New Orleans, La., 1860*), Roman Catholic clergyman. Came to America, 1817. Consecrated bishop of New Orleans, 1835; raised to archbishop, 1851.

BLANCHARD, JONATHAN (*b. Rockingham, Vt., 1811; d. 1892*), Presbyterian clergyman. Graduated Middlebury, 1832. President, Knox College, Galesburg, Ill., 1845–57; Wheaton College, Ill., 1860–82, and emeritus to 1892.

BLANCHARD, NEWTON CRAIN (*b. Rapides Parish, La., 1849; d. 1922*), lawyer. Congressman, Democrat, from Louisiana, 1881–93; U.S. senator, 1893–97; governor of Louisiana, 1904–08.

BLANCHARD, THOMAS (*b. Sutton, Mass., 1788; d. 1864*), inventor. While working on problem of turning gunstocks at the Springfield Arsenal, he developed the whole principle of turning irregular forms from a pattern. His machine, declared by Congress to stand among the chief American inventions, consisted of a friction wheel touching the pattern and a cutting wheel secured to the same shaft. Many machine tools and woodworking machines depend on this principle. Continuing to invent, he patented a steam carriage (1825) and designed and built stern-wheel steamboats for use on shallow rivers.

BLANCHET, FRANÇOIS NORBERT (*b. Quebec Prov., Canada, 1795; d. Portland, Oreg., 1883*), Catholic missionary. Ordained in Quebec, 1819. Worked as a missionary to Indians in New Brunswick and at parish in Montreal. Responding to need for priests among trappers, traders, and Iroquois of Oregon region, he went west and was highly successful, establishing missions in Walla Walla, Vancouver, Astoria and elsewhere in northwest. Made bishop, 1843, and in 1846 archbishop of newly established see of Oregon City, he traveled in Europe and South America to collect money and enlist priests and nuns for service in Oregon. Despite many difficulties; he built up his see, removing it to Portland, 1862.

BLAND, RICHARD (*b. Virginia, 1710; d. 1776*), statesman. Son of Virginia planter, educated at William and Mary. Member of House of Burgesses, 1742–75. Became champion of public rights as early as 1753; opposed clergy, helped draw up 1764 resolution respecting taxation imposed on Virginia from outside. Author of *An Inquiry into the Rights of the British Colonies* (1766), earliest published defense of colonial attitude on taxation. Hopeful for peace, he opposed Patrick Henry's plan for arming of colony, 1775. Member of revolutionary conventions of March 1775, July 1775, May 1776, and the first two Continental Congresses. Learned and able, he preserved many valuable historical documents and records.

BLAND, RICHARD PARKS (*b. near Hartford, Ky., 1835; d. 1899*), lawyer, congressional leader of "Free Silver" movement. Congressman, Democrat, from Missouri, 1872–95, 1897–99. As chairman of Committee on Mines and Mining, 1875–77, led fight for free silver coinage; became a national figure with passage of Bland-Allison Act over Hayes's veto, 1878. Opposed Sherman Silver Purchase Act, led Free Silver wing of Democratic party. Urged advantages of Free Silver to "producing classes" in general, not only agrarian group. Strongly opposed monopolies, protective tariff, imperialism.

BLAND, THEODORICK (*b. Prince George Co., Va., 1742; d. 1790*), planter, physician, Revolutionary soldier.

BLAND, THOMAS (*b. Newark, England, 1809; d. 1885*), naturalist. Settled in New York, 1852. Became authority on North American mollusks. Coauthor, Part I, "Land and Fresh-water Shells of North America," in *Smithsonian Collections* (1869).

BLANDY, WILLIAM HENRY PURNELL (*b. New York, N.Y., 1890; d. St. Albans, N.Y., 1954*), naval officer. Studied at Delaware College and the U.S. Naval Academy, graduating first in his class (1913). After serving aboard several ships and at various shore facilities, Blandy received his first command only in 1934. He was promoted to rear admiral and became chief of the naval Bureau of Ordnance in 1941. In 1943, he assumed a flag command under the Fifth Amphibious Force of the Pacific Fleet and commanded all preinvasion activities for the attacks on Iwo Jima and Okinawa in 1945. After the war, Blandy, a vice admiral, was made Deputy Chief of Naval Operations for Special Weapons. Headed a task force to assess the effectiveness of atomic weapons at the Bikini Atoll in 1946. Promoted to four-star admiral, 1947, and named to command the Atlantic Fleet. Bypassed for Chief of Naval Operations. A member of the so-called admirals' revolt against the decision not to build a supercarrier, Blandy testified before Congress on the issue. Retired in 1950.

BLANKENBURG, RUDOLPH (*b. Barntrup, Germany, 1843; d. 1918*), merchant. Reform mayor of Philadelphia, 1911–15. Author of the phrase "the powers that prey."

BLASDEL, HENRY GOODE (*b. Dearborn Co., Ind., 1825; d. 1900*), merchant, miner. Governor of Nevada, Republican, 1864–70.

BLASHFIELD, EDWIN HOWLAND (*b. New York, N.Y., 1848; d. South Dennis, Mass., 1936*), mural painter. Left engineering school to study figure painting with Léon Bonnat in Paris. Success of mural commission for Chicago World's Fair, 1893, led to many major assignments, including murals for the Library of Congress and the state capitols of Minnesota, Iowa, South Dakota, and Wisconsin, as well as many private commissions. Blashfield was a founder of the Municipal Art Society, New York City, and president of the National Academy of Design, 1920–26.

BLATCH, HARRIOT EATON STANTON (*b. Seneca Falls, N.Y., 1856; d. Greenwich, Conn., 1940*), social reformer. Daughter of Henry Brewster and Elizabeth Cady Stanton. Founder, 1907, Equality League of Self-Supporting Women; writer on woman suffrage and peace.

BLATCHFORD, RICHARD MILFORD (*b. Stratford, Conn., 1798; d. Newport, R.I., 1875*), lawyer. Counsel, *post* 1826, for Bank of United States, also for Bank of England in the United States. Commissioner of New York Central Park, 1859–70.

BLATCHFORD, SAMUEL (*b. New York, N.Y., 1820; d. Newport, R.I., 1893*), lawyer, jurist. Son of Richard M. Blatchford. Specialist in maritime and patent law. Associate justice, U.S. Supreme Court, 1882–93.

BLAUSTEIN, DAVID (*b. Lida, Russian Poland, 1866; d. 1912*), rabbi, educator. Came to America, 1886. Graduated Harvard, 1893. First of trained Jewish social workers. Superintendent, Educational Alliance, New York, which set example for Jewish settlements elsewhere.

BLAVATSKY, HELENA PETROVNA HAHN (*b. Ekaterinoslav, Russia, 1831; d. London, England, 1891*), founder of Theosophical movement. Resided in New York, N.Y., 1873–78.

BLEASE, COLEMAN LIVINGSTON (*b. near Newberry Courthouse, S.C., 1868; d. Columbia, S.C., 1942*), lawyer politician. Attended Newberry College; LL.B., Georgetown University, 1889; began successful practice in Newberry and neighborhood. As member of South Carolina legislature, he was a follower of Benjamin R. Tillman in the early 1890's. Elected to the state senate, 1904. Elected governor, 1910, campaigning as the champion of the poor white farmer and textile worker. Engendered bitter factionalism and brought needed social reform to a standstill. Opposed child labor laws, factory inspection laws, and compulsory school attendance, and denounced corporations, aristocrats, critical newspapers, and blacks. Reelected governor in 1912, but defeated for U.S. Senate in 1914, and for the governorship in 1916. His attacks on President Woodrow Wilson cost him a Senate seat in 1918, but he was successful in 1924. Opposed liberal legislation and delivered harangues in defense of lynching. Defeated for reelection in 1930 but retained substantial support.

BLECKLEY, LOGAN EDWING (*b. Rabun Co., Ga., 1827; d. 1907*), jurist. Associate justice, Georgia supreme court, 1875–80; chief justice, 1887–94. Decisions widely quoted because of witty style, faculty for simple statement of complex matters.

BLEDSOE, ALBERT TAYLOR (*b. Kentucky, 1809; d. Alexandria, Va., 1877*), Confederate official, lawyer, educator. Edited *Southern Review*, 1867–77, representing attitude of unreconstructed Southerners on Civil War, industrialism, evolution, democracy.

BLEECKER, ANN ELIZA (*b. New York, N.Y., 1752; d. Tomhanick, N.Y., 1783*), poet. Her lyrics and prose were published in *Posthumous Works* (New York, 1793).

BLENK, JAMES HUBERT (*b. Neustadt, Bavaria, 1856; d. New Orleans, La., 1917*), Roman Catholic clergyman. Came to America in infancy. A Marist, he became bishop of Puerto Rico, 1899, and archbishop of New Orleans, 1906.

BLENNERHASSETT, HARMAN (*b. Hampshire, England, 1765; d. Isle of Guernsey, England, 1831*), associate of Aaron Burr. Educated at Trinity College, Dublin; admitted to Irish bar, 1790. Came to America, 1796; settled on island in Ohio River, establishing elaborate home there. Met Aaron Burr, 1805. His apparent means and enthusiasm attracted Burr; the island became a center for Burr's separatist activities in the West. Blennerhassett helped make first payment on Bastrop Purchase. Suspicious Virginia militia raided and looted the island, Dec 11, 1806. Blennerhassett had left the night before; joined Burr at mouth of Cumberland. Later arrested and brought to trial, Blennerhassett went free when Burr failed to be convicted.

BLEYER, WILLARD GROSVENOR (*b. Milwaukee, Wis., 1873; d. 1935*), professor of journalism, University of Wisconsin, 1905–35. Author of pioneer textbooks in the field; standardized teaching of journalism on a national scale.

BLICHFELDT, HANS FREDERIK (*b. Iller, Jutland, Denmark, 1873; d. Palo Alto, Calif., 1945*), mathematician. Immigrated to the United States, 1888. Although he had qualified for entrance to the University of Copenhagen, worked as a manual laborer, 1888–92. While working as a draftsman for the engineering department of Whatcom County, Wash. (1892–94), he was urged by admirers of his unusual mathematical abilities to apply for admission as a special student to Stanford University. He took his A.B. in mathematics, 1896, and his A.M., 1897. Working under Sophus Lie at the University of Leipzig (1897–98), he received the Ph.D. *summa cum laude* in 1898. Thereafter, he taught mathematics at Stanford, *post* 1913 as professor. Made important contributions to the theory of groups and the geometry of numbers. In addition to some two dozen research papers of importance, he was author of the second part of *Theory and Application of Finite Groups* (1916) and of *Finite Collineation Groups* (1917).

BLINN, HOLBROOK (*b. San Francisco, Calif., 1872; d. Croton, N.Y., 1928*), actor. Popular in England and America. Organized Princess Theatre, New York, 1913.

BLISS, AARON THOMAS (*b. Peterboro, N.Y., 1837; d. 1906*), lumberman. Removed to Saginaw, Mich., 1865. Republican governor of Michigan, 1900–04; progressive and able.

BLISS, CORNELIUS NEWTON (*b. Fall River, Mass., 1833; d. 1911*), textile merchant, politician. Conservative Republican, active in New York City and national politics; U.S. secretary of interior, 1896–98.

BLISS, CORNELIUS NEWTON (*b. New York, N.Y., 1874; d. New York, 1949*), philanthropist, businessman. Son of Cornelius N. Bliss (1833–1911); brother of Lizzie P. Bliss. Graduated Harvard, 1897. A partner in family business, Bliss Fabyan and Co., 1899–1940; active also in Republican politics, national and state. Divided his concerns between practical relief of the poor and encouragement of the arts. Board member and chairman of the Metropolitan Opera, and trustee of the Metropolitan Museum of Art and the Museum of Modern Art. He was also active in the American Red Cross.

BLISS, DANIEL (*b. Georgia, Vt., 1823; d. 1916*), Congregational clergyman, missionary. Founder, first president, Syrian Protestant College (now American University), Beirut, 1866–1902.

BLISS, EDWIN ELISHA (*b. Putney, Vt., 1817; d. 1892*), Congregational clergyman. Missionary to Armenia and Turkey, 1843–92.

BLISS, EDWIN MUNSELL (*b. Erzerum, Turkey, 1848; d. Washington, D.C., 1919*), Congregational clergyman. Bible Society agent in Levant. Edited *Encyclopaedia of Missions*, 1889–91.

BLISS, ELIPHALET WILLIAMS (*b. Fly Creek, N.Y., 1836; d. Brooklyn, N.Y., 1903*), manufacturer. Founded E. W. Bliss Co., 1867, whose machine shops made tools and dies for sheet metal work, torpedoes, shells for navy.

BLISS, FREDERICK JONES (*b. Suq al-Gharb, Syria, 1859; d. White Plains, N.Y., 1937*), archeologist. Son of Daniel Bliss. Graduated Amherst, 1880. Active, 1891–1901, in Palestinian excavations, excelling at chronological determinations.

BLISS, GEORGE (*b. Northampton, Mass., 1816; d. 1896*), merchant, banker. Settled in New York, N.Y., 1844. Made fortune in dry goods by foreseeing Civil War price rise. Partner of Levi P. Morton in banking firm.

BLISS, GEORGE (*b. Springfield, Mass., 1830; d. Wakefield, R.I., 1897*), lawyer. Graduated Harvard, 1851; admitted to New York bar, 1857. A skilled legislative draftsman, he drew up, among many other laws, the 1873 charter of New York City and its first Tenement House Act. In 1882, he was special prosecutor in the "Star Route" cases.

BLISS, GILBERT AMES (*b. Chicago, Ill., 1876; d. Harvey, Ill., 1951*), mathematician and educator. Studied at the University of Chicago (Ph.D., 1900) and the University of Göttingen. Faculty, Chicago, 1908–41; chairman of the mathematics department, 1927–41. Specialist in the calculus of variations, Bliss served on the board of the National Research Council (1924–36). In 1946, he published his monumental *Lectures on the Calculus of Variations*.

BLISS, HOWARD SWEETSER (*b. Suq al-Gharb, Syria, 1860; d. Saranac Lake, N.Y., 1920*), Congregational clergyman, missionary educator. President, Syrian Protestant College, succeeding father, Daniel Bliss, in 1903.

BLISS, JONATHAN (*b. Springfield, Mass., 1742; d. Fredericton, Canada, 1822*), jurist. Graduated Harvard, 1763. As member of General Court *post* 1768, he was a consistent Tory and removed to England, 1775. Returning in 1785 to New Brunswick, he served as attorney general and chief justice.

BLISS, PHILEMON (*b. North Canton, Conn., 1814; d. St. Paul, Minn., 1889*), Ohio congressman, Missouri jurist. Dean, University of Missouri school of law, 1872–89.

BLISS, PHILIP PAUL (*b. Clearfield Co., Pa., 1838; d. Ashtabula, Ohio, 1876*), singing evangelist. Co-author with Ira Sankey of *Gospel Songs* (1874) containing "Hold the Fort" and other popular hymns.

BLISS, PORTER CORNELIUS (*b. Cattaraugus Reservation, N.Y., 1838; d. New York, N.Y., 1885*), traveler, explorer, journalist. Expert on Latin America; an editor of *New York Herald*.

BLISS, ROBERT WOODS (*b. St. Louis, Mo., 1875; d. Washington, D.C., 1962*), diplomat. Entered the diplomatic service in 1900 and served in various capacities at various cities in South America and Europe before being named ambassador to Argentina in 1927. Retired in 1933 but after U.S. entry into World War II was called out of retirement to serve in advisory capacities in Washington, D.C., retiring again in 1945. A collector of pre-Columbian, medieval, and Byzantine art, he and his wife donated their collection, along with their Washington, D.C., estate, Dumbarton Oaks, to Harvard, and he wrote *The Indigenous Art of the Americas* (1947; reissued as *Pre-Columbian Art* in 1957).

BLISS, TASKER HOWARD (*b. Lewisburg, Pa., 1853; d. 1930*), soldier, scholar, diplomat. Graduated West Point, 1876. Assigned to the artillery, he was recalled to West Point to teach under Major General J. M. Schofield, then superintendent. When General Schofield succeeded General Sheridan as commanding general of the army in 1888, he chose Bliss as his aide. When war broke out in 1898, Bliss was made a major and took part in the Puerto Rican campaign. Was chief of Cuban customs houses during the occupation and later negotiated the Cuban reciprocity treaty. Was made brigadier general by President McKinley and became founding president of the new Army War College. In 1905 he was sent to the Philippines to command the Department of Luzon, then Mindanao, and finally the Philippine Division. Returning to Washington, 1909, he became assistant chief of staff; was acting chief of staff soon after World War I broke out, and chief of staff, September 1917. In October, Bliss went to Europe as military aide under Edward M. House to effect better coordination of the Allied effort, and on his return presented an exhaustive report urging the importance of prompt and unified action. He returned to Europe as military representative on the Supreme War Council where, in President Wilson's absence, Bliss had a statesman's role. His letters to Newton D. Baker reveal how the Allied leaders early sought to circumvent the President's Fourteen Points and his plans for a League of Nations. He was for a unified field command and supported General Pershing's insistence that American troops should not be infiltrated into Allied armies. He was for unconditional surrender of the German army and, farsightedly, for the support of the German Republic to ensure its endurance. Chosen delegate to the Peace Conference, he opposed granting a mandate over Shantung to Japan. He was relieved as chief of staff

in 1918. In his declining years his great interest was in advocating the entry of the United States into the World Court, and peace through reduction of armaments.

BLISS, WILLIAM DWIGHT PORTER (*b. Constantinople, Turkey, 1856; d. New York, N.Y., 1926*), Congregationalist, later Episcopal clergyman. Son of Edwin E. Bliss. Organized first Christian Socialist Society in United States, 1889.

BLITZ, ANTONIO (*b. England [?], 1810; d. Philadelphia, Pa., 1877*), magician. Varied talents included sleight-of-hand and ventriloquism.

BLITZSTEIN, MARC (*b. Philadelphia, Pa., 1905; d. Fort-de-France, Martinique, 1964*), composer and playwright. After beginning his career in scholastic competition, by the late 1920's he turned toward the musical theater and political commentary. His first important work was *The Cradle Will Rock* (1936), which the authorities unsuccessfully attempted to suppress. A member of the Communist party (1938–49), his political beliefs—particularly his antagonism to fascism—are reflected in such works as *I've Got the Tune* (1937), *No for an Answer* 1941, *The Spanish Earth* (1937), *Freedom Morning* (1943), and *Airborne Symphony* (completed 1946), his most famous work for the concert stage. Possibly his major achievement was *Regina* (1949), an operatic treatment of Lillian Hellman's *The Little Foxes*. Although not considered innovative in purely musicological terms, he made considerable and underrated contributions to the ongoing search for new ways to blend music and drama and to break down the subtle barriers between the "classical" and the "popular."

BLOCH, CLAUDE CHARLES (*b. Woodbury, Ky., 1878; d. Washington, D.C., 1967*), naval officer. Graduated U.S. Naval Academy (1899). Held a variety of important positions at the prestigious Bureau of Ordnance (1905–11), later becoming chief (1923–27) of the Bureau of Ordnance. In the 1930's became a major figure in the navy, arguing so forcibly for preparedness that the press dubbed him the "Jack Dempsey of the Navy." As commandant of the Fourteenth Naval District based at Pearl Harbor, was one of the few senior officers not criticized during subsequent investigations of the disaster, since he had tried to strengthen Hawaii's defenses. Retired in 1942 with the rank of full admiral.

BLOCH, ERNEST (*b. Geneva, Switzerland, 1880; d. Portland, Oreg., 1959*), composer. After academic training at the *collège* in Geneva, studied at the Royal Conservatory in Brussels and privately in Munich and Frankfurt. Lived in Paris, where his opera, *Macbeth*, received its premiere at the Opéra Comique. Failing to establish himself in the musical world, he returned to Geneva to join his father's business. Rescued by the French musicologist Romain Rolland, he taught at the Geneva Conservatory from 1911 to 1915. He then turned from the post-Romantic style of his earlier compositions to concentrate on a more ethnic style, using his own Jewish background and Hebraic intervallic and rhythmic patterns. Immigrated to the U.S. in 1916, where he conducted for a touring dance company. Teacher at the Mannes School of Music (1917–20). Director, Cleveland Institute of Music (1920–25) and the San Francisco Conservatory (1925–30). Through largesse of a patron, settled in Italy and devoted himself to composing (1930–38). Returned to U.S. and settled in Portland, Ore. Major works include *Suite symphonique* (1944), String Quartet no. 3 (1952), and Concerto Grosso no. 2 (1952)—all of which received the New York Music Critics Circle award.

BLOCK, ADRIAEN (*fl. 1610–24*), Dutch mariner, explorer. First detailed map of southern New England coast (1616) drawn as far as Cape Ann from his data. Block Island named for him.

BLOCK, PAUL (*b. Elmira, N.Y., 1877; d. New York, N.Y., 1941*), newspaper publisher and advertising executive. Went to work, 1893, as an advertising solicitor for a local newspaper; founded Paul Block Associates in New York City, 1897, as a national agency to solicit advertising for daily newspapers. *Post* 1916, held varying degrees of ownership or control over a number of newspapers, merging them and managing them with an alert eye to the business office and setting policy on national issues, but allowing his editors much latitude otherwise. At his death, he retained only the *Toledo Blade, Toledo Times,* and *Pittsburgh Post-Gazette.* He was for many years a friend and business associate of William Randolph Hearst.

BLODGET, LORIN (*b. near Jamestown, N.Y., 1823; d. 1901*), statistician, climatologist, publicist. Associated with Smithsonian Institution; wrote *Climatology of the United States,* (1857), first important American work on subject.

BLODGET, SAMUEL (*b. Woburn, Mass., 1724; d. Derryfield, Mass., 1807*), merchant, manufacturer. Planned and built, 1794–1807, canal around Amoskeag Falls on Merrimac.

BLODGET, SAMUEL (*b. Goffstown, N.H., 1757; d. Baltimore, Md., 1814*), merchant, economist, architect. Son of Samuel Blodget (1724–1807). Made fortune in East India trade. Moved to Philadelphia, 1789, became a director of Insurance Company of North America. Designed building for first Bank of the United States, Philadelphia. Began buying Washington, D.C., real estate, 1792; was active in promoting city's development. Submitted plan in competition for U.S. Capitol design, suggested founding a national university at Washington.

BLODGETT, BENJAMIN COLMAN (*b. Boston, Mass., 1838; d. Seattle, Wash., 1925*), pianist, organist, music teacher, composer. Director, Smith College School of Music, 1880–1903.

BLODGETT, HENRY WILLIAMS (*b. Amherst, Mass., 1821; d. 1905*), lawyer. Raised in Illinois. U.S. district judge in Illinois, 1869–92.

BLODGETT, JOHN WOOD (*b. Hersey, Mich., 1860; d. Grand Rapids, Mich., 1951*), lumberman, civic leader, philanthropist. Creator of a vast logging and milling conglomerate, Blodgett was active in national politics and served on the Republican National Committee from 1900 to 1912. His philanthropy supported many charitable causes, including the foundation of the Blodgett Memorial Hospital in Grand Rapids.

BLOEDE, GERTRUDE (*b. Dresden. Germany, 1845; d. Baldwin, N.Y., 1905*), poet. Came to America as a child. Published several volumes of verse under pseudonym of Stuart Sterne.

BLOOD, BENJAMIN PAUL (*b. Amsterdam, N.Y., 1832; d. 1919*), philosopher, mystic, poet.

BLOODGOOD, JOSEPH COLT (*b. Milwaukee, Wis., 1867; d. 1935*), surgeon, surgical pathologist. Professor of surgery, Johns Hopkins, 1895–1935; a leading authority on cancer.

BLOODWORTH, TIMOTHY (*b. New Hanover Co., N.C., 1736; d. Washington, N.C., 1814*), politician, radical antifederalist. U.S. senator from North Carolina, 1795–1807.

BLOOM, SOL (*b. Pekin, Ill., 1870; d. Bethesda, Md., 1949*), businessman, politician. Raised in San Francisco, Calif., child of poor Jewish immigrant parents, he went to work at seven years of age in a brush factory. At fifteen, he was assistant treasurer of the Alcazar Theater; before he was twenty, he was a theatrical entrepreneur. In 1893, he supervised the amusement section of Chicago's World's Columbian Exposition. Remaining in Chicago, he engaged in music publishing, selling music and instruments by

mail, and developing a chain of music departments in stores. He moved to New York City, 1903, where he was, among other things, the national distributor of Victor talking machines. By 1910, he had withdrawn from the music business to concentrate with success on real estate operations in midtown Manhattan. Well-to-do, and anxious to "do something noble," he ran for Congress in 1923 as a Democrat in the normally Republican 19th N.Y. Congressional District (later the 20th). Victor in a hard-fought contest, he served in the House of Representatives until his death. Until 1939, his career in Congress was comparatively routine, although he effectively managed the celebration of the George Washington bicentennial, and the sesquicentennial of the U.S. Constitution, with much of his old theatrical flair. Becoming by seniority head of the crucial Foreign Affairs Committee of the House in 1939, he soon dispelled any doubts of his capacity for the task. He proved a superb strategist in securing legislation to implement President Roosevelt's policies, including Lend-Lease, extension of the draft, and the arming of merchant ships. He was later a strong supporter of the United Nations and the sponsor of legislation supporting the United Nations Relief and Rehabilitation Administration; he represented the United States on the UNRRA committee. In the postwar years, he secured aid for the state of Israel, favored the "Truman Doctrine," and backed the Marshall Plan.

BLOOMER, AMELIA JENKS (*b. Homer, N.Y., 1818; d. Council Bluffs, Iowa, 1894*), reformer. Attended first meeting on women's rights, Seneca Falls, N.Y., 1848, but only as spectator, her earliest reform activity being in the temperance movement. Founded the *Lily,* 1849, one of first papers published by a woman, and wrote on unjust marriage laws, suffrage, education. She was thus one of the pioneers in the women's rights movement, but through publicity and ridicule her name is associated primarily with dress reform and the "Bloomer costume."

BLOOMFIELD, JOSEPH (*b. Woodbridge, N.J., 1753; d. Burlington, N.J., 1823*), lawyer, Revolutionary soldier. Democratic-Republican governor of New Jersey, 1801, 1803–12.

BLOOMFIELD, LEONARD (*b. Chicago, Ill., 1887; d. New Haven, Conn., 1949*), linguist. Nephew of Maurice Bloomfield and Fannie Bloomfield Zeisler. B.A., Harvard, 1906; Ph.D., University of Chicago, 1909. Taught at a number of universities in the Midwest; Sterling professor of linguistics at Yale, 1940–46. Labored to establish linguistics as an empirical science, and as a means for understanding human conduct and man's place in nature. Author of *Language* (1933).

BLOOMFIELD, MAURICE (*b. Bielitz, Austria, 1855; d. San Francisco, Calif., 1928*), orientalist, philologist. Came to America as a child. Educated at Furman, Yale, Johns Hopkins. Chief work was the editing, translating, interpreting of sacred texts of the Vedas.

BLOOMFIELD, MEYER (*b. Bucharest, Rumania, 1878; d. New York, N.Y., 1938*), social worker, lawyer. Came to New York as a child. Graduated College of City of New York, 1899; Harvard, 1901. Pioneer in vocational guidance and personnel management.

BLOOMFIELD-ZEISLER, FANNIE. *See* ZEISLER, FANNIE BLOOMFIELD.

BLOOMGARDEN, SOLOMON (*b. Wertzblowo, Lithuania, 1870; d. 1927*), writer. Came to America, 1890. Wrote extensively under pen name "Yehoash," mainly in Yiddish; translated Jewish Bible into Yiddish.

BLOOR, ELLA REEVE (*b. Staten Island, N.Y., 1862; d. Richlandtown, Pa., 1951*), feminist, labor agitator, Socialist and Communist leader. Bloor, who was known as "Mother Bloor," was the first woman to run for elective office in Connecticut (1908); in 1918, she ran for lieutenant governor in New York; in 1938, she ran for governor of Pennsylvania. By the 1920's, Bloor had switched party affiliation from the Socialist Labor to the Communist Party; in 1921–22, she attended the First and Second Red International of Labor Unions in Moscow. She helped to organize party units throughout the country, attempting to organize the status of women within the Communist Party. From 1941–1947, she headed the Communist Party of Pennsylvania. Considered the "foremost American women communist."

BLOUNT, JAMES HENDERSON (*b. Jones Co., Ga., 1837; d. Macon, Ga., 1903*), lawyer, congressman, diplomatic envoy. Special commissioner to Hawaii, 1893. His criticism of American involvement in revolution against Liliuokalani determined policy against annexation.

BLOUNT, THOMAS (*b. Edgecombe Co., N.C., 1759; d. Washington, D.C., 1812*), Revolutionary soldier, merchant, Democratic-Republican politician. Congressman from North Carolina, 1793–99, 1805–09, 1811–12.

BLOUNT, WILLIAM (*b. Edgecombe Co., N.C., 1749; d. Knoxville, Tenn., 1800*), politician. Brother of Thomas Blount; half-brother of Willie Blount. After Revolutionary War service, was four times in North Carolina House of Commons, twice in state Senate; he was later a delegate to Congress, 1782–83, 1786–87, and a member of the federal constitutional convention, 1787. Considered plain, honest, and sincere by contemporaries, he became governor of Tennessee territory, 1790, and concurrently superintendent of Indian Affairs, Southern Department. Popular and sympathetic with settlers, he was elected U.S. senator in 1796 when the territory became a state. In financial difficulties over speculations in land, he became involved in a scheme to transfer control of Spanish Florida and Louisiana to Great Britain and was expelled from the Senate, 1797; his impeachment was later dismissed. Returning to Tennessee, he served in the state senate as speaker until death.

BLOUNT, WILLIE (*b. North Carolina, 1768; d. Montgomery Co., Tenn., 1835*), planter, jurist. Half-brother of Thomas and William Blount. Democratic-Republican governor of Tennessee, 1809–15.

BLOW, HENRY TAYLOR (*b. Virginia, 1817; d. 1875*), capitalist, diplomat. Removed to St. Louis, Mo., *ca.* 1830. A pioneer in lead and lead-products business, he was instrumental in developing lead mines of southwestern Missouri and transforming St. Louis into a commercial center. Opposing extension of slavery, he became a Free-Soiler and helped organize Republican party in state. Elected to Congress, 1862 and 1864, he served on joint committee on Reconstruction. Appointed minister to Brazil, 1869–71, he helped bring closer relations with that country.

BLOW, SUSAN ELIZABETH (*b. St. Louis, Mo., 1843; d. New York, N.Y., 1916*). Daughter of Henry T. Blow. Trained by follower of Froebel. Opened first American public kindergarten, St. Louis, 1873; also training school, 1874.

BLOWERS, SAMPSON SALTER (*b. Boston, Mass., 1742; d. Halifax, N.S., 1842*), jurist. Graduated Harvard, 1763. Loyalist, settled in Nova Scotia after Revolution; chief justice there, 1797–1833.

BLOXHAM, WILLIAM DUNNINGTON (*b. Tallahassee, Fla., 1835; d. Tallahassee, 1911*), planter, public servant. Governor of Florida, 1881–85, 1897–1901; a conservative Democrat, his highly successful administrations improved the state's financial condition.

BLUE, GERALD MONTGOMERY ("MONTY") (*b. Indianapolis, Ind., 1877[?]; d. Milwaukee, Wis., 1963*), motion picture actor. Played supporting roles in a variety of pictures before attracting attention in *The Affairs of Anatol* (1921), after which he was popular in leading roles throughout the 1920's. When sound was introduced to the movie industry, he was reduced to bit parts, but by 1940 had established himself as one of Hollywood's more capable character actors, and appeared in a wide variety of films, many of them Westerns. In the 1950's he appeared in supporting roles in a number of filmed television series.

BLUE, VICTOR (*b. Richmond Co., N.C., 1865; d. 1928*), naval officer. Graduated Annapolis, 1887. Established presence of Cervera's squadron in Santiago harbor, June 1898.

BLUEMNER, OSCAR FLORIANS (*b. Hanover, Germany, 1867; d. South Braintree, Mass., 1938*), architect, experimental painter. Came to America, 1892. Sought to establish analogies between music and painting.

BLUM, ROBERT FREDERICK (*b. Cincinnati, Ohio, 1857; d. New York, N.Y., 1903*), painter. Apprentice in lithographic firm; fellow-student with Kenyon Cox in Cincinnati and Philadelphia; went to New York, 1878, and worked as illustrator in style of Fortuny. In 1889 he made a long-deferred trip to Japan; his two-year stay produced much outstanding work. Moved to Greenwich Village soon after returning, a pioneer in migration of artists there. Distinguished in many mediums.

BLUNT, EDMUND MARCH (*b. Portsmouth, N.H., 1770; d. Sing Sing, N.Y., 1862*), hydrographer. Publisher and bookseller in Newburyport, Mass. Published *American Coast Pilot* (ed. Furlong), 1796; also brought out *New Practical Navigator* (1799) and *Bowditch's New American Practical Navigator* (1801). These, with preparation of charts, made Blunt's shop the center of American nautical publications. Removing to New York, *post* 1805, Blunt continued his business; among his later publications was *Stranger's Guide to the City of New York* (1817).

BLUNT, GEORGE WILLIAM (*b. Newburyport, Mass., 1802; d. New York, N.Y., 1878*), hydrographer. Son of Edmund M. Blunt. Associated with father and brother Edmund in making charts and nautical instruments. Editor, among other works, of *The Young Sea Officer's Sheet Anchor* (1843).

BLUNT, JAMES GILLPATRICK (*b. Trenton, Maine, 1826; d. Washington, D.C., 1881*), physician, Union soldier. Kansas associate of John Brown.

BLY, NELLIE. *See* SEAMAN, ELIZABETH COCHRANE.

BLYTHE, HERBERT. *See* BARRYMORE, MAURICE.

BOARDMAN, MABEL THORP (*b. Cleveland, Ohio, 1860; d. Washington, D.C., 1946*), Red Cross leader. A dominant figure in the Red Cross after the retirement of Clara Barton (1904) and the reorganization of the association under government auspices, she won public confidence, vastly extended services, and raised a permanent endowment fund. Unable to delegate responsibility, she handled matters down to the finest detail. Removed from control during World War I, she returned as national secretary, 1921, and took a strong stand against the trend toward professional leadership and the view that the association should engage in social welfare work in the intervals between emergencies. Overruled, she carried her conviction of the importance of volunteer leadership into a new project, the Red Cross Volunteer Service, which she served as director, 1923–40. Continuing as national secretary, she directed relief projects during World War II until her retirement in December 1944.

BOARDMAN, THOMAS DANFORTH (*b. Litchfield, Conn., 1784; d. Hartford, Conn., 1873*), pewterer. Last pure representative of ancient tradition in pewter-making; pioneered in manufacture of britannia-ware, block tin.

BOAS, EMIL LEOPOLD (*b. Goerlitz, Germany, 1854; d. Greenwich, Conn., 1912*). General manager, later sole American director, Hamburg–American line, 1892–1912.

BOAS, FRANZ (*b. Minden, Westphalia, Germany, 1858; d. New York, N.Y., 1942*), anthropologist. Born of Jewish parents who had kept only "an emotional affection for the ceremonial" of their tradition. The father was a prosperous merchant; the mother was a sister-in-law of Abraham Jacobi and devoted to science. Studied successively at Heidelberg, Bonn, and Kiel, 1877–81, and later described his university studies as a compromise between the purely intellectual impulse that led him first to physics, and the intense, emotional interest in the phenomena of the world that led him to shift to the study of geography. He also awoke to a recognition that there are "domains of our experience" where the quantitative, mechanistic assumptions of the physicist are not applicable, and resolved to develop a program of research on the interrelationship of the objective and the subjective worlds; this was to lead him eventually from physics to anthropology. This program began to take more definite form during the winter of 1882–83, which he spent in Berlin, coming in contact with Rudolf Virchow and Adolf Bastian. Proposing to study the reaction of the human mind to natural environment by investigating the interrelationship of migration routes, native geographical knowledge, and actual physical geography among the Eskimo, he went to Baffin Land in June 1883. After spending more than a year near Cumberland Sound in geographic and ehtnographic researches, he spent the winter of 1884–85 in the United States. His stay among the Eskimo had profoundly affected him. Already alienated from a Germany which seemed devoted to crass materialism, imperial ambitions, and a rising anti-Semitism which threatened to bar him from an academic career, he found the simple, shared routines of existence in Baffin Land to have a strong appeal. He left with a conviction of the relativity of the idea of a cultured individual; also, his scholarly interest had shifted from migration routes to a desire to understand what determined the behavior of human beings—in particular, to study the psychological origin of implicit belief in the authority of tradition.

Returning to Germany under pressure from his parents and his university mentor, Theobald Fischer, Boas spent the next year working under Bastian at the Royal Ethnographic Museum in Berlin and awaiting his habilitation as privatdocent at the University of Berlin. He offered as his thesis the geographical results of his Baffin Land researches. Apparently at this time, under the influence of Bastian and Virchow, and while he was writing up the ethnographic results of his trip (*The Central Eskimo*, 1888), he came finally to reject geographical determinism and to develop his characteristic anthropological viewpoint. At the same time, he developed plans for a second field trip—to the area that was to be the focus of his anthropological interests for the rest of his life; the Indians of the Northwest Coast of Canada. Although he finally qualified as docent in physical geography in the late spring of 1886, Boas had barely given his inaugural lecture before he was off to America.

As it turned out, his departure was permanent. After a three-month stay in the Northwest, during which he made a general ethnographic reconnaissance of the area, Boas went to New York, where he accepted a position as geographical editor of *Science*. On Mar. 10, 1887, he married Marie A. E. Krackowizer.

During the spring of 1887 he made two important statements of his basic scientific viewpoint. In the first, "The Study of Geography," he argued that there were two equally valid approaches to scientific "truth"—the "physical" method and the "historical" method. In the second statement, "The Occurrence of Similar Inventions in Areas Widely Apart," Boas confronted certain basic assumptions of the dominant evolutionary viewpoint in American cultural anthropology, and in effect subordinated the "physical" to the "historical" method as far as anthropology was concerned.

From 1887 to 1894 Boas carried out five field trips on the Northwest Coast, collecting data on the physical, linguistic, and cultural characteristics of a large number of Northwest Coast tribes, in the process accomplishing his "self-professionalization" in each of these major areas of anthropological inquiry. His primary focus was the Kwakiutl and his primary interest was the collection of accurate folktale texts that would serve as the basis for linguistic analysis and historical reconstruction.

In the fall of 1887 he tried unsuccessfully to organize an ethnological society in New York. Early the next year he established a lifelong tie to the Boston-based American Folklore Society (whose *Journal* he edited from 1908 to 1925). In the fall of 1889 he became a docent in anthropology at Clark University and there in 1892 produced the first American Ph.D. in anthropology. Boas' job at Clark ended with the financial crisis and faculty revolt of that same year. Boas spent the next two years as Frederic Ward Putnam's chief assistant at the World's Columbian Exposition in Chicago. His hopes for a permanent position there at the newly founded Field Museum were frustrated by what Boas regarded as the machinations of members of the Bureau of Ethnology. After more than a year of unemployment he established what was to become a permanent institutional affiliation. In December 1895 he again joined Putnam as assistant curator of the department of anthropology at the American Museum of Natural History in New York, and early the following year he became lecturer in physical anthropology at Columbia University. In 1899 he was promoted to a full professorship. Boas then attempted to redefine the profession of anthropology. His researches on the distribution of folklore elements, employing a quasi-statistical method derived in 1888 from E. B. Taylor, became by 1896 a fully elaborated critique of the comparative method of anthropology. His field work had produced *The Social Organization and the Secret Societies of the Kwakiutl Indians* (1897), the first of a long series of ethnographic volumes on that tribe (which was supplemented by the work of George Hunt, a half-Indian whom Boas trained and supervised as an ethnographer). In 1897, Boas conceived and directed a long-running program of field research to investigate the historical relations of the aboriginal tribes of Northwestern America and the Asian continent. In 1901 he was appointed honorary philologist at the Bureau of Ethnology and a full curator at the Museum. Boas helped found the American Anthropological Association in 1902. In 1905 he resigned from the Museum in a bitter dispute over what he regarded as the subordination of the Museum's research to public entertainment.

In 1911 appeared the initial volume of the *Handbook of American Indian Languages*, a decade-long cooperative effort. Boas' second major work of 1911 was his report for the United States Immigration Commission on *Changes in Bodily Form of Descendants of Immigrants*. The third and most important work of 1911 was *The Mind of Primitive Man*, which drew on various writings of the previous seventeen years to confront the widely current stereotype of the mentally inferior and dark-skinned savage.

Boas was to make a total of eight more trips to the field and almost every year until his death saw the publication of one or more pieces of scholarly work. The last thirty years of his life are best viewed in terms of his institutional and pedagogical activities, his public role as advocate of the anthropological viewpoint, and a series of political issues relating to his own somewhat ambiguous cultural identity. He had become an American citizen in 1891, but remained in a deep sense culturally German and made more than a dozen trips back after his emigration.

Between 1910 and 1912 Boas was in Mexico at the short-lived International School of American Archaeology and Ethnology, which he had helped to found, and at which he did his only important archaeological work. He was outspoken in his opposition to American entry into World War I and in 1929 he publicly accused four unnamed anthropologists of prostituting their scientific integrity by spying for the United States government in Mexico. As a result, the American Anthropological Association censured and almost expelled him. Within a few years, however, Boas and his students dominated American anthropology.

Boas was extremely active from 1920 to 1928 in the Emergency Society for German and Austrian Science and Art. With the rise of Nazism, however, his relationship to Germany underwent a further evolution. From about 1900, Boas was much concerned with attitudes on issues of race. From the mid-1920's, he was instrumental in stimulating a wide range of research in this area. After 1933 the pace of these activities heightened despite his age and recurrent illness, working first through the American Jewish Committee for Democracy and Intellectual Freedom. He died of a heart attack in the middle of his eighty-fifth year while he was speaking on racism.

The general course of American anthropology until after 1940 may be seen as the working out of various aspects of Boas' own thinking. Until about 1920 the major preoccupation was the critique of evolutionism; the 1920's saw the dominance of diffusionary studies of culture areas; the 1930's, of studies of acculturation, culture patterns, and of culture and personality—all of which may be interpreted as deriving directly from Boas.

In the 1950's and 1960's, Boas came under sharp criticism from anthropologists who were concerned with the systematic study of social structure, or who turned once again to the study of the evolution of human culture in a deterministic framework. More generally, there was a widespread feeling that his anthropological contribution was negative rather than constructive, and there is no doubt that, as he conceived them, the methods of history and of science tended to be mutually inhibitive and to discourage generalization.

BÔCHER, MAXIME (*b. Boston, Mass., 1867; d. 1918*), mathematician. Graduated Harvard, 1888; Ph.D., Göttingen, 1891. Successful teacher at Harvard, 1891–1918.

BOCOCK, THOMAS STANLEY (*b. Buckingham Co., Va., 1815; d. near Appomattox Court House, Va., 1891*), lawyer. Congressman, Democrat, from Virginia, 1847–61. Speaker, Confederate House of Representatives, in both First and Second Congresses.

BODANZKY, ARTUR (*b. Vienna, Austria, 1877; d. New York, 1939*), opera and orchestra conductor. Came to America, 1915. With Metropolitan Opera, 1915–39; Society of the Friends of Music, 1920–31.

BODE, BOYD HENRY (*b. Ridott, Ill., 1873; d. Gainesville., Fla., 1953*), philosopher and educator. Studied at the University of Michigan (B.A., 1897) and at Cornell (Ph.D., 1900). Professor of education at Ohio State University, 1921–1944. Influenced by the progressive theories of John Dewey, Bode sought to guide American education away from the dualities inherent in the mind/spirit separation to that of a unified education based on pursuit of creative freedom and scientific inquiry. His books include *Fundamentals of Education* (1921), *Modern Educational Theories* (1927), and *How We Learn* (1940).

BODENHEIM, MAXWELL (*b. Hermanville, Miss., 1892; d. New York, N.Y., 1954*), author and poet. No formal education after expulsion from Hyde Park, Ill., High School in 1908. Member of the Chicago literary circle which included Sherwood Anderson, Theodore Dreiser, and Carl Sandburg; Bodenheim removed to New York in 1915 and published the first of his eleven volumes of poetry, *Minna and Myself*, in 1918. Other volumes of poetry include *Introducing Irony* (1922), *Against This Age* (1923), and *Returning to Emotion* (1927). Some of his novels include *Crazy Man* (1924) and *Replenishing Jessica* (1925), which was branded indecent. As an editor of the poetry magazine *Others* (1916), Bodenheim discovered Hart Crane. His last book of poetry, *Selected Poems* (1946), showed his solid accomplishment in poetry, but Bodenheim's career was destroyed by scandalous behavior and alcoholism. He was murdered in New York City in 1954.

BOEHLER, PETER (*b. Frankfurt-am-Main, Germany, 1712; d. England, 1775*), bishop in Moravian Church. Started mission in Savannah, 1738; helped found Moravian settlement, Bethlehem, Pa. Later vice-superintendent, American Province.

BOEHM, HENRY (*b. Lancaster Co., Pa., 1775; d. 1875*), Methodist itinerant preacher. Son of Martin Boehm. Preached in English and German, superintended translation of Methodist doctrine into German. Traveled circuits in many states, 1800–64.

BOEHM, JOHN PHILIP (*b. Hochstadt, Germany, 1683; d. Hellertown, Pa., 1749*), German Reformed clergyman. Came to America, 1720. Founder of German Reformed Church in Pennsylvania.

BOEHM, MARTIN (*b. Conestoga Township, Pa., 1725; d. 1812*), Mennonite bishop, United Brethren bishop. Expelled by Mennonites for lack of orthodoxy, helped found United Brethren in Christ; also affiliated with Methodists.

BOEING, WILLIAM EDWARD (*b. Detroit, Mich., 1881; d. on Puget Sound, Wash., 1956*), aviation pioneer and business executive. Studied briefly at Yale University. Founder of the Boeing Aircraft Company in 1916; later the company expanded, encompassing many aviation concerns to become United Aircraft and Transport in 1928; in 1934, following a government order, the company was divided into Boeing Aircraft, United Aircraft, and United Airlines. A pioneer in air transportation, Boeing successfully built many planes that competed in the rising airmail service during the 1930's. Introduced the first genuinely modern transport plane, the twin-engine 247, in 1933. He retired from the aviation industry in 1934, embittered by government rulings.

BOELEN, JACOB (*b. Netherlands, ca. 1654; d. New York, N.Y., 1729*), silversmith. Came to America as a child. Ranks among best silverworkers in early New York.

BOGAN, LOUISE MARIE (*b. Livermore Falls, Maine, 1897; d. New York, N.Y., 1970*), poet, short-story writer, and critic. Her first book, *Body of This Death* (1923), established her as one of the foremost lyric poets of her generation. Her next volumes of poetry were *Dark Summer* (1929) and *The Sleeping Fury* (1937). In the late 1930's became a vigorous and outspoken opponent of political cant, and the light verse of *Poems and New Poems* (1941) took a satiric view of the current scene. Also wrote reviews for the *New Yorker* (1931–1969) and published a brief critical history, *Achievement in American Poetry, 1900–1950* (1951), *Collected Poems, 1923–1953* (1954); and *Selected Criticism: Poetry and Prose* (1955). Her final collected edition was *The Blue Estuaries: Poems 1923–1968* (1968), and her criticism is collected in *A Poet's Alphabet* (1970). She is often placed in the tradition of 17th-century metaphysical verse.

BOGARDUS, EVERARDUS (*b. Woerden, Netherlands, 1607; d. off Welsh coast, 1647*), second minister of New Netherland, 1633–47. Involved in much controversy with colonial officials.

BOGARDUS, JAMES (*b. Catskill, N.Y., 1800; d. New York, N.Y., 1874*), inventor. Apprenticed early to watchmaker; specialized in engraving and die-sinking. Patented "ring flyer," 1830, used in cotton-spinning machinery for over fifty years. Other inventions include eccentric sugar-grinding mill, gas meter, engraving machine for watch dials, a rice-grinder, a dynamometer, and many others. Probably his greatest contribution was introduction of cast iron in building construction, used for his own factory building, erected 1850. Later he erected many other iron buildings including Public Ledger Building in Philadelphia, Birch Building in Chicago, Baltimore *Sun* offices.

BOGART, HUMPHREY DEFOREST (*b. New York, N.Y., 1889; d. Beverly Hills, Calif., 1957*), actor. Studied briefly at Phillips Andover Academy. Bogart worked in a few Broadway plays before signing with Fox Studios in 1930. In the Broadway production of *The Petrified Forest*, he was spotted by Warner Brothers and later appeared in the movie version, which made him a star. Other films include *Dark Victory* (1940), *The Maltese Falcon* (1941), *Casablanca* (1942), *To Have and Have Not* (1944), *The Treasure of the Sierra Madre* (1948), *The African Queen* (1951), *The Caine Mutiny* (1954), *Sabrina* (1954), *The Desperate Hours* (1955), and *We're No Angels* (1955). Remembered for his portrayals of criminals and tough guys with a heart and unquestionable integrity, Bogart has become one the most famous of film actors.

BOGART, JOHN (*b. Albany, N.Y., 1836; d. 1920*), engineer. Graduated Rutgers, 1853. Worked for New York Central Railroad, served as engineer in Civil War. Showing great versatility, he was best known for work in park planning and improvement in New York and other cities, and for work on hydroelectric development in United States and Canada. He had great influence in decision as to system adopted at Niagara and was chief engineer of 60,000 horsepower plant project in Tennessee River near Chattanooga. Also prepared plans for first subway system in New York and for tunnels under the Hudson to Jersey City and Hoboken.

BOGGS, CHARLES STUART (*b. New Brunswick, N.J., 1811; d. 1888*), naval officer. Served conspicuously in Mexican and Civil wars; commanded *Varuna*, first vessel to pass Confederate guns below New Orleans, 1862. Became rear admiral, 1870.

BOGGS, LILLBURN W. (*b. Lexington, Ky., 1792; d. Napa Valley, Calif., 1860*), storekeeper, merchant. Removed to St. Louis, Mo., 1816. Democratic governor of Missouri, 1836–40. Removed to California, 1846, where he served as *alcalde* of northern part until start of state government.

BOGUE, VIRGIL GAY (*b. Norfolk, N.Y., 1846; d. at sea, 1916*), civil engineer. Worked chiefly with railroads, first in South America, later for various railways in West; expert on railroad economics.

BOGY, LEWIS VITAL (*b. Sainte Genevieve, Mo., 1813; d. 1877*), lawyer. Leader in reconstruction of Democratic party in Missouri after Civil War; U.S. senator, 1872–1877.

BOHM, MAX (*b. Cleveland, Ohio, 1861; d. Provincetown, Mass., 1923*), painter. Studied at Cleveland Art School and in Paris. His early marines and later subject pieces were essentially romantic and idealistic.

BOHUNE, LAWRENCE (*d. West Indies, 1621*), first physician general of London Co. in Virginia, appointed 1620. Transported 300 colonists.

BOIES, HENRY MARTYN (*b. Lee, Mass., 1837; d. 1903*), capitalist. President of powder manufacturing firm in Scranton, Pa.; later of Dickson Manufacturing Co., which gained international position in manufacture of engines, machinery.

BOIES, HORACE (*b. Erie Co., N.Y., 1827; d. 1923*), lawyer. Settled in Waterloo, Iowa, 1867. Democratic governor of Iowa, 1889–93.

BOISE, REUBEN PATRICK (*b. Blandford, Mass., 1819; d. 1907*), jurist. Removed to Portland, Oreg., 1850. Active in formulating Oregon's constitution, 1857; judge, Oregon supreme and district courts.

BOISEN, ANTON THEOPHILUS (*b. Bloomington, Ind., 1876; d. Elgin, Ill., 1965*), theologian, psychologist, and founder of the movement for clinical pastoral education. Ordained in the Presbyterian Church (1911), he studied in several theological seminaries and did pastoral work at several psychological hospitals. In 1925 he offered his first summer program of "clinical experience" for seminarians at Worcester (Mass.) State Hospital; his program was incorporated in 1930 as the Council for the Clinical Training of Theological Students. He suffered numerous breakdowns and psychotic episodes that he chronicled in "My Own Case Record" (1928), later revised and published as *Out of the Depths: An Autobiographical Study of Mental Disorder and Religious Experience* (1960). He also published other books and many articles on the relationship between mental disorder and religious experience.

BOISSEVAIN, INEZ MILHOLLAND (*b. New York, N.Y., 1886; d. 1916*), reformer. Graduated Vassar, 1909. Worked for women's rights in fields of education, working conditions, suffrage. Active in National Woman's Party campaign, 1916.

BOK, EDWARD WILLIAM (*b. den Helder, Netherlands, 1863; d. Lake Wales, Fla., 1930*), editor, author, philanthropist, peace advocate. Immigrated to New York, 1870; until 1889 tried his hand at stenography, the stock market, editorial work, advertising, and supplying his own newspaper syndicate with a "woman's page." Became editor of the *Ladies' Home Journal*, 1889. His innovations not only outsold competitors but effected many reforms including passage of conservation laws and the Food and Drug Acts of 1906. Author of 1921 Pulitzer Prize autobiography, *The Americanization of Edward Bok* (1920). A generous and civic-minded benefactor of the arts and education.

BOKER, GEORGE HENRY (*b. Philadelphia, Pa., 1823; d. Philadelphia, 1890*), poet, playwright, diplomat. Graduated College of New Jersey (Princeton), 1842. His blank verse tragedy *Calaynos* (1848) was produced first in London, 1849, and not until 1851 in Philadelphia. After writing five more plays, several of which were produced, he brought out his dramatic masterpiece, *Francesca da Rimini* (produced New York, 1855; revived 1882, 1901), but grew dissatisfied with what he considered lack of recognition. He published his lyric poems, notably his sonnets, together with his verse plays in *Plays and Poems* (1856). During the Civil War, in addition to writing and publishing *Poems of the War* (1864), he was active in founding and managing the Union League in Philadelphia, first in the country; after the war he continued to publish poetry and to give effective, quiet encouragement to other writers, particularly to William G. Simms and Paul H. Hayne. His diplomatic service was as minister to Turkey, 1871–75, and to Russia, 1875–78.

BOLDT, GEORGE C. (*b. Island of Rügen, Germany, 1851; d. 1916*), hotelman. Came to America, 1864. Projected and managed New York's Waldorf-Astoria Hotel and Philadelphia's Belle-vue-Stratford. Raised standards of American hotelkeeping.

BOLL, JACOB (*b. Bremgarten, Switzerland, 1828; d. Tex., 1880*), geologist, naturalist. Collected and worked in Texas *post* 1869; discovered many new fossil species.

BOLLAN, WILLIAM (*b. England, ca. 1710; d. ca. 1782*), lawyer. Colonial agent of Massachusetts, 1745–62.

BOLLER, ALFRED PANCOAST (*b. Philadelphia, Pa., 1840; d. 1912*), civil engineer. Graduated Rensselaer Polytechnic, 1861. Expert on foundations and bridges, particularly draw-spans.

BOLLES, FRANK (*b. Winchester, Mass., 1856; d. 1894*), nature writer. Secretary of Harvard University, 1887–94; built his office into one of wide influence. Founded Harvard Cooperative Society.

BOLLMAN, JUSTUS ERICH (*b. Hoya, Hanover, Germany, 1769; d. Jamaica, West Indies, 1821*), physician. Aided in escape of Lafayette from Olmütz; came to America, 1796. As agent of Aaron Burr, delivered Burr's cipher letter to General Wilkinson, 1806. Refused pardon offered if he gave testimony on Burr's plans.

BOLM, ADOLPH RUDOLPHOVITCH (*b. St. Petersburg, Russia, 1884; d. Los Angeles, Calif., 1951*), dancer and choreographer. Studied at the Imperial Ballet School; dancer with the Maryinsky Company (1903–11), where he danced with Anna Pavlova. Joined Diaghilev's Ballets Russes, 1911. Toured the U.S. and codirector with Nijinsky in 1917, when he was seriously injured in an onstage accident. Choreographer for the Metropolitan Opera Ballet (1917–24); ballet master for the Chicago Civic Opera (1920); ballet master for the San Francisco Opera (1932). Bolm's own company, the Ballet Intime (later the Adolph Bolm Ballet), toured the U.S. many times, in 1928 with Agnes De Mille. Bolm returned to New York in 1939 to participate in the first Ballet Theatre season and in 1942–43 he was Ballet Theatre's ballet master and *regisseur general*. Bolm's principal dance roles included *Prince Igor* (Chief Warrior), *Carnival* (Pierrot), *Petrouchka* (the Moor), and *Le Coq d'Or* (King Dodon).

BOLTON, HENRY CARRINGTON (*b. New York, N.Y., 1843; d. Washington, D.C., 1903*), chemist, bibliographer of chemistry.

BOLTON, HERBERT EUGENE (*b. near Tomah, Wis., 1870; d. Berkeley, Calif., 1953*), historian. Studied at Wisconsin and Pennsylvania (Ph.D., 1899). Professor (1911–45) and chairman (1919–40) of the department of history at California. Bolton, regarded as one of the giants among American historians, was a leading expert in the history of the Spanish settlement of the Southwest. Major works include *The Colonization of North America, 1492–1783* (1920), written with T. M. Marshall, and *The Spanish Borderlands* (1921). President, American Historical Association (1932).

BOLTON, SARAH KNOWLES (*b. Farmington, Conn., 1841; d. 1916*), author, reformer. Active in temperance movement; interested also in education for women.

BOLTON, SARAH TITTLE BARRETT (*b. Newport, Ky., 1814; d. 1893*), poet. Author of the popular "Paddle Your Own Canoe."

BOLTWOOD, BERTRAM BORDEN (*b. Amherst, Mass., 1870; d. Maine, 1927*), chemist, physicist. Graduated Yale, 1892. Studied in Munich and Leipzig, then taught at Yale; received Ph.D. there, 1897. Professor of radio-chemistry Yale, 1910–27. Devoted much time to building of Sloane Physics Laboratory, later to construction of Sterling Chemical Laboratory. Made many basic contributions to knowledge of radioactivity, including the proof that radium is a disintegration product of uranium; the discovery of ionium; the experimental work on which the science of isotopy is based; and a method of calculating age of uranium minerals, used in geology. Also did first investigation in this country of radioactivity of natural waters.

BOLTZIUS, JOHANN MARTIN (*b. Germany, 1703; d. 1765*), Lutheran clergyman. Came to America, 1734, as pastor of Salzburger immigrants; helped establish and was spiritual and business leader of colony at Ebenezer, Ga., 1734–65.

BOLZA, OSKAR (*b. Bergzabern, Rhenish Palatinate, Germany, 1857; d. Freiburg im Breisgau, Germany, 1942*), mathematician. Deciding in 1878 to concentrate on mathematics, he spent the years 1878–81 in study with E. B. Christoffel and Theodor Reye at Strasbourg, Hermann A. Schwarz at Göttingen, and Karl Weierstrass at University of Berlin. After a year of teaching at the Freiburg Gymnasium, he returned to his studies. His solution of the determination of hyperelliptic integrals which are reducible to elliptic integrals by a transformation of the fourth degree and subsequent developments formed the basis for his doctoral dissertation (under Felix Klein), and he received the degree from Göttingen in 1886. He taught briefly at Johns Hopkins, at Clark University, 1889–92, and at the University of Chicago, 1893–1910. He then returned to Freiburg. After 1917, he interested himself principally in religious psychology and language study. Bolza made many contributions to the calculus of variations, which was his main interest after 1901 and on which he published a classic treatise in 1908–09.

BOMBERGER, JOHN HENRY AUGUSTUS (*b. Lancaster, Pa., 1817; d. 1890*), German Reformed clergyman. A founder and first president (1869–90) of Ursinus College.

BOMFORD, GEORGE (*b. New York, N.Y., 1782; d. Boston, Mass., 1848*), soldier. Greatest ordnance expert of his time; chief of U.S. Army ordnance, *post* 1832. Invented Columbiad howitzer.

BONAPARTE, CHARLES JOSEPH (*b. Baltimore, Md., 1851; d. near Baltimore, 1921*), lawyer, municipal and civil service reformer. Grandson of Jerome Bonaparte and Elizabeth P. Bonaparte. Graduated Harvard, 1872; Harvard Law School, 1874. Practicing in Baltimore, he helped found Baltimore Reform League and National Civil Service Reform League; interest in civil service reform brought him in contact with Theodore Roosevelt. He served as U.S. secretary of the navy, 1905–06, and as attorney general, 1906–09; strongly antitrust, his most notable achievement was dissolution of the American Tobacco Co.

BONAPARTE, ELIZABETH PATTERSON (*b. Baltimore, Md., 1785; d. Baltimore, 1879*), wife of Jerome Bonaparte, brother of Emperor Napoleon I; married in Baltimore, 1803. Napoleon refused to recognize the marriage. Jerome returned to France in 1805 to negotiate a reconciliation but was unsuccessful and the marriage was declared null by French council of state. Elizabeth received 60,000 francs annually on condition she stay in America, renounce Bonaparte name. She later secured an American divorce and went to Europe where she received much attention in society. Her son's legitimacy was recognized by Napoleon III, but right to succession disallowed.

BONAPARTE, JEROME NAPOLEON (*b. Baltimore, Md., 1830; d. Pride's Crossing, Mass., 1893*), soldier. Grandson of Jerome Bonaparte and Elizabeth P. Bonaparte. Graduated West Point, 1852; resigned from U.S. Army and served with French Army from Crimean War until 1870.

BONARD, LOUIS (*b. Rouen, France, 1809; d. New York, N.Y., 1871*), businessman, inventor. Left all his property to American Society for Prevention of Cruelty to Animals.

BOND, CARRIE JACOBS (*b. Janesville, Wis., 1862; d. Hollywood, Calif., 1946*), songwriter. Author of about 170 published songs, including "I Love You Truly" and "The End of a Perfect Day."

BOND, ELIZABETH POWELL (*b. Dutchess Co., N.Y., 1841; d. 1926*), educator, author. Dean of Swarthmore College, 1890–1906.

BOND, GEORGE PHILLIPS (*b. Dorchester, Mass., 1825; d. 1865*), astronomer. Son of William C. Bond. Director, Harvard College Observatory, 1859–65. Credited with discovery of Hyperion; founder of photographic astronomy.

BOND, HUGH LENNOX (*b. Baltimore, Md., 1828; d. 1893*), jurist. Maryland criminal court judge, 1860–67; judge of fourth U.S. circuit court, 1870–93. Broke Ku Klux Klan reign of terror in South Carolina; gave decision which made Hayes president.

BOND, SHADRACH (*b. Baltimore Co., Md., ca. 1773; d. Kaskaskia, Ill. 1832*). Held several offices in Illinois territory; first delegate to Congress, 1812–14; first governor of state of Illinois, 1818–22.

BOND, THOMAS (*b. Calvert Co., Md., 1712; d. 1784*), physician. Studied first with Dr. Alexander Hamilton in Annapolis, completed medical education in Europe. Began practicing in Philadelphia about 1734. Interested in hygiene and epidemiology, he was also a skilled surgeon and a leader in founding the Pennsylvania Hospital. Conceived of by Bond, promoted by Benjamin Franklin, the hospital opened in 1752, Bond and others giving services free. Bond there began (1766) first course of clinical lectures given in United States.

BOND, WILLIAM CRANCH (*b. Falmouth, Maine, 1789; d. 1859*), clockmaker, instrument-maker, astronomer. Gathered data in Europe for proposed Harvard College Observatory; its first director, 1839–59.

BONER, JOHN HENRY (*b. Salem, N.C., 1845; d. Washington, D.C., 1903*), editor, poet.

BONFILS, FREDERICK GILMER (*b. Lincoln Co., Mo., 1860; d. Denver, Colo., 1933*) and HARRY HEYE TAMMEN (*b. Baltimore, Md., 1856; d. Denver, Colo., 1924*), newspaper publishers. Bonfils, having made money operating a lottery in Kansas City, was persuaded to invest $12,500 in the Denver *Evening Post* by Tammen, a former bartender and dabbler in journalism. Naming the paper the *Denver Post*, the partners, by unconventional methods, screaming headlines, attacks on public officials, and support of progressive causes, pushed the weekday circulation to 150,000. The *Post* became hated and feared. Their sensational operations became a national issue in the Teapot Dome scandal, when the *Post's* attacks were associated with a suit against Harry F. Sinclair.

BONHAM, MILLEDGE LUKE (*b. Red Bank, S.C., 1813; d. 1890*), lawyer, Confederate soldier. Graduated South Carolina College, 1834. Served in Seminole War, and with distinction in Mexican War. Congressman, Democrat, 1857–60; Confederate brigadier; governor of South Carolina, 1862–65.

BONNER, JOHN (*b. London, England[?], ca. 1643; d. Boston, Mass., 1725/26*), mariner, map-maker. Came to Boston *ca.* 1670. Shipowner, skilled pilot, shipbuilder. Published a celebrated map of Boston (1722).

BONNER, ROBERT (*b. near Londonderry, Ireland, 1824; d. 1899*), newspaper editor, turfman. Came to America, 1839; learned printing trade. Published *New York Ledger, post* 1851, which by advertising and lavish spending for "family" fiction reached almost half-million circulation.

BONNEVILLE, BENJAMIN LOUIS EULALIE DE (*b. near Paris, France, 1796; d. Fort Smith, Ark., 1878*), soldier. Came to America as a child. Graduated West Point, 1815; served in various capacities until 1866. He is remembered for his fur-hunting expedition of 1832–35, a controversial episode in which Washington Irving was his partisan.

BONNEY, CHARLES CARROLL (*b. Hamilton, N.Y., 1831; d. Chicago, Ill., 1903*), lawyer, educationist, reformer. Advocated international court of justice, legal and constitutional reforms. Prominent in planning 1893 World's Fair congresses.

BONNEY, WILLIAM H. *See* BILLY THE KID.

BONSAL, STEPHEN (*b. Baltimore, Md., 1865; d. Washington, D.C., 1951*), journalist, author, diplomat. Studied at the universities of Heidelberg and Vienna. Correspondent for the *New York Herald*, 1887–93. Entered the diplomatic corps and became secretary and chargé d'affaires in Madrid, Tokyo, Peking, and Korea, 1893–97; secretary to the governor general of the Philippines, 1913. President Wilson's interpreter at the Versailles Peace Conference, 1919, and also served as consultant on Balkan affairs. After the conference, he joined the Inter-Allied Mission to Austria-Hungary and the Balkan states.

In the early 1930's, returned to journalism and writing, traveling widely in the U.S.S.R., China, and Manchuria. His book on the Versailles conference, *Unfinished Business* (1945), attempted to inform the world facing the peace conferences at the end of World War II of the mistakes of the 1919 conference.

BONSTELLE, JESSIE (*b. Greece, N.Y., 1872; d. 1932*), actress, producer, stock company manager. Leader in the community theater movement; discovered many well-known players.

BONWILL, WILLIAM GIBSON ARLINGTON (*b. Camden, Del., 1833; d. 1899*), dentist. Inventor of electromagnetic mallet (patented 1873), the automatic engine-mallet, and many other dental instruments and processes. He was the first to devise an anatomical articulator.

BONZANO, ADOLPHUS (*b. Ehingen, Germany, 1830; d. 1913*), engineer, inventor. Came to America, 1850. A leader in American bridge construction, 1865–98. Chief among his many inventions is the rail joint which bears his name.

BOOLE, ELLA ALEXANDER (*b. Van Wert, Ohio, 1858; d. 1952*), temperance leader. Received M.A., College of Wooster, 1878. President of the Women's Christian Temperance Union, 1925; treasurer of the World WCTU, 1920–25; president, 1931–47. Intransigent and inflexible in her views, she was the implacable enemy of any liberalization of the Volstead Act. Author of *Give Prohibition Its Chance* (1929).

BOONE, DANIEL (*b. near Reading, Pa., 1734; d. Missouri, 1820*), pioneer, Indian fighter. Of Quaker stock; became a hunter of game and furs at twelve years of age. Started off with his family for North Carolina, 1750; spent about a year in Shenandoah valley before settling at Buffalo Lick on north fork of the Yadkin, 1751. Daniel accompanied a North Carolina contingent as a teamster in Braddock's campaign, 1755, thereby meeting John Finley, a hunter, who told him stories of the Kentucky wilderness. Returning to his father's farm, he married Rebeccah Bryan, 1756. In 1765, after visiting Florida, he proposed to settle in Pensacola; his wife objected to the plan and Boone gave it up.

Still interested in Kentucky, he journeyed to a point in present Floyd Co., 1767, returning home in the spring of 1768. With Finley and several others he went westward again in 1769, traversed Cumberland Gap and set up a camp at Station Camp Creek; he returned home, 1771. As agent for Colonel Richard Henderson of the Transylvania Co., he led out the first division of settlers to Kentucky in March 1775. In April he reached the place which was to become Boonesborough and began erection of a fort. That fall, he journeyed back to North Carolina and returned with his own family and twenty recruits for the settlement.

Hunting, surveying, and Indian fighting occupied him for the next two years. Captured by the Shawnees, 1778, he escaped and in September of that year helped in the defense of Boonesborough. After a trip east, he returned in October 1779, with a new party of settlers. The repudiation of Henderson's land titles by Virginia sent him east again in the spring of 1780 with $20,000 collected from settlers for purchase of land warrants; on the way he was robbed of the entire amount, and on his return moved to Boone's Station. He was made lieutenant colonel of Fayette Co. when Kentucky was divided into three counties; later he served in other offices and in the legislature. Although he had taken up many tracts of land, all had been improperly entered; in 1785, the first of a series of ejectment suits by which he was to lose all his holdings was begun. In 1786, he moved to Maysville.

Boone left Kentucky in the fall of 1788 for Point Pleasant, at the mouth of the Great Kanawha in what is now West Virginia. He was appointed lieutenant colonel of Kanawha Co., 1789, and in 1791 was chosen its legislative delegate. Sometime in 1798 or 1799, deprived of his last Kentucky holding, he moved to what is now Missouri, obtaining a grant of land at the mouth of Femme Osage Creek. He was appointed magistrate of this district, 1800, holding the post until the territory was ceded to the United States, 1804. Once again his land title was voided by the U.S. land commissioners, but was confirmed by Congress after many delays in February 1814. His wife died, 1813; his remaining years were spent mostly at the home of his son Nathan, where he died.

Modern criticism has dealt harshly with the Boone legend. He first came into general notice through his so-called autobiography in John Filson, *The Discovery, Settlement, and Present State of Kentucke* (1784), which was known in Europe through its reprinting in later editions of Gilbert Imlay's *Topographical Description of the Western Territory of North America*. The stanzas devoted to Boone in the eighth canto of Byron's *Don Juan* gave him worldwide celebrity and he gradually became the one overshadowing frontier heroic figure. He was acclaimed as the discoverer of Kentucky, its first explorer, its first settler, even "the First White Man of the West," although none of these distinctions was his by right. His true titles to fame were in his character; he had the frontier virtues of courage, endurance, a mastery of woodcraft, and expertness with a rifle. Although almost illiterate, he had strong native intelligence; his counsel was eagerly sought. Modest, loyal, and honest, he never harbored resentment, even when wronged.

BOORMAN, JAMES (*b. Kent, England, 1783; d. 1866*), New York merchant. Came to America, 1795. Originator of Hudson River Railroad; a founder of Bank of Commerce.

BOOTH, AGNES (*b. Sydney, Australia, 1846; d. 1910*), actress. Born Marian Agnes Rookes. Wife of Junius Brutus Booth the younger.

BOOTH, ALBERT JAMES, JR. ("ALBIE") (*b. New Haven, Conn., 1908; d. New York, N.Y., 1959*), athlete, coach, referee, businessman. Studied at Yale University, where he achieved national fame as a star halfback and baseball player. Booth, who was the real-life embodiment of Frank Merriwell, single-handedly defeated archrival Harvard in both football and baseball. After his playing career was ended by illness, he coached at Yale and New York University and also refereed briefly. *Post* 1932 was successful executive with the Sealtest Corporation.

BOOTH, BALLINGTON (*b. Brighouse, England, 1857; d. Blue Point, N.Y., 1940*). Founder, 1896, of Volunteers of America, a religious and social-welfare organization. Son of William Booth, who founded the Salvation Army.

BOOTH, EDWIN THOMAS (*b. near Bel Air, Md., 1833; d. New York, N.Y., 1893*), actor. Son of Junius Brutus Booth. At an early age began to accompany his talented, erratic father on theatrical tours. Made debut in a minor role in *Richard III*, Boston, 1849. Played occasional juvenile parts in support of father but had no success in longer roles. Between 1852 and 1856, trouped with varying success in California, Australia, Hawaii; first took public's fancy as stock-company leading man in Sacramento, 1856. Now an accomplished actor, his style modeled on his father's and the tradition of Edmund Kean, but with a sustained power and intellectual quality which were all his own, he went East, played in Baltimore and the South, and made triumphant appearances in Boston and New York, 1857, rising almost at once to the top of his profession. He married Mary Devlin, an actress, 1860. After engagements in London, Liverpool, and Manchester, he was seen at the New York Winter Garden, 1862–63, retiring temporarily from the stage when his wife died in February 1863. He then undertook management of the Winter Garden, also purchasing a theater in Philadelphia with John S. Clarke. In 1864–65 he played *Hamlet* for a famous run of a hundred nights in New York. After his brother John Wilkes Booth assassinated President Lincoln, he went into brief retirement although he had been entirely loyal to the Union. When he returned to the stage in 1866 his audience showed itself equally loyal to him. Managing the Winter Garden, he put on a series of the most lavishly staged performances in America, terminated by a disastrous fire, March 1867, which destroyed scenery, costumes, and a library. Almost immediately he started plans for Booth's Theatre, which opened February 1869. The seasons of 1869–74 at the new theater marked an epoch in the history of the American stage. Booth performed in Shakespearean and other roles supported by many leading stars of the day. The theater failed financially during the panic of 1873–74 and Booth went into bankruptcy. He carried on gallantly for almost twenty years, touring with the great success in America, in the British Isles, and on the Continent. He remained to the end one of the greatest actors of his time, in spite of gradually declining powers. His last performance was in *Hamlet* at Brooklyn, N.Y., 1891.

BOOTH, EVANGELINE CORY (*b. Hackney, London, England, 1865; d. Hartsdale, N.Y., 1950*), general of the Salvation Army. Daughter of the Army's founders, William and Catherine Booth. Active in Army service from childhood, she became American commander in chief, 1904. She increased the independence of the American branch, greatly extended its services, and built orphanages, rescue missions, shelters for the homeless and the aged, and hospitals. She personally supervised relief work of the Army after the San Francisco earthquake in 1906. Under her command, the American Army became a highly popular philanthropy supported by a national fund-raising apparatus. Elected general in 1934, she returned to England and was an effective, dedicated supervisor of the Army's global operations until her retirement in 1939.

BOOTH, JAMES CURTIS (*b. Philadelphia, Pa., 1810; d. 1888*), chemist. An outstanding teacher and expert in analysis. Melter and refiner at Philadelphia mint, 1849–88.

BOOTH, JOHN WILKES (*b. near Bel Air, Md., 1838; d. 1865*), actor, assassin of President Lincoln. Son of Junius Brutus Booth; brother of Edwin Booth. Made his debut at St. Charles Theatre, Baltimore, 1855. Acted in Philadelphia, 1857–58; played leading Shakespearean roles in a Richmond stock company, 1859; later toured with notable success in South, Southwest, and North. His acting was marked more by inspiration and daring innovation than by finish. His charm and handsome appearance also gained him popularity. In 1863 illness brought temporary retirement from the stage, although he gave two notable performances in 1864–65. Unlike the rest of his family, he sympathized with the South, regarding slavery as a God-given blessing and becoming gradually more fanatical in his views. In 1859 he had been a member of Virginia militia company which took part in the arrest and execution of John Brown. As early as the fall of 1864 he formed a plan to abduct Lincoln, hoping to end the war or at least secure an exchange of Southern prisoners; to this end, he gathered a band of associates which included Samuel Arnold, Michael O'Laughlin, John H. Surratt, David Herold, George Atzerodt, and Lewis Powell (Payne). He and his accomplices lay in wait for Lincoln on the outskirts of Washington, Mar. 20, 1865, but the president failed to appear. Soon afterward Richmond was captured, Lee surrendered, and the plot came to naught.

It was probably after Lincoln's speech on April 11, advocating limited black suffrage, that Booth decided upon assassination. The details were not arranged until April 14, when Booth learned that Lincoln was to attend Laura Keene's performance of *Our American Cousin* at Ford's Theatre that night. Atzerodt, deputed to murder Vice President Andrew Johnson, did nothing, but Payne seriously wounded Secretary of State W. H. Seward. Booth, after shooting Lincoln, fell as he leaped from the theater box to the stage and broke his leg, but managed to flee on his horse. Herold, who had accompanied Payne, joined Booth in Maryland. The two went to the home of Dr. Samuel Mudd, who set Booth's leg. Thus delayed, they hid in the woods nearly a week before they could cross the Potomac to Virginia. Then they proceeded to the house of Richard H. Garrett, in whose barn they were apprehended on April 26. It has never been established whether Booth shot himself or was killed by Boston Corbett, a fanatical soldier who disobeyed orders and fired. Although it was quite certain from his behavior and from the objects found on the body that the man thus slain was indeed Booth, and although the body was identified by several persons including a doctor and a dentist, a legend arose that Booth escaped alive. He was reported seen in many places in America and abroad. Booth's various accomplices were tried before a military commission in one of the most irregular trials in history.

BOOTH, JUNIUS BRUTUS (*b. London, England, 1796; d. en route to Cincinnati, Ohio, 1852*), actor. Brilliant, erratic father of John W. and Edwin Booth. Came to America, 1821. Foremost tragedian of his day in America.

BOOTH, MARY LOUISE (*b. Yaphank, N.Y., 1831; d. 1889*), author, translator. Edited *Harper's Bazaar*, 1867–89. Author of *History of the City of New York* (1859) and other works.

BOOTH, NEWTON (*b. Salem, Ind., 1825; d. Sacramento, Calif., 1892*), lawyer, merchant, Republican governor of California, 1871–75. As U.S. senator, 1875–81, was active for adoption of the silver certificate, settlement of land titles.

BOOTH-TUCKER, EMMA MOSS (*b. Gateshead, England, 1860; d. near Dean Lake, Mo., 1903*), Consul of Salvation Army. Worked in India; in America, 1896–1903.

BOOTT, KIRK (*b. Boston, Mass., 1790; d. Lowell, Mass., 1837*), manufacturer. Active in establishment of mill village which became Lowell. A pioneer of industrial feudalism, his management of Lowell determined character of many American industrial communities.

BORAH, WILLIAM EDGAR (*b. Jasper Township, Ill., 1865; d. Washington, D.C., 1940*), U.S. senator from Idaho. Son of a stern Presbyterian minister who intended him for the ministry, he attended the University of Kansas, 1885–87, was called to the Kansas bar, and moved west in 1890 to practice law in Boise, Idaho. Soon active in politics, he became chairman of the Republican State Central Committee in 1892, and ran unsuccessfully for Congress on a Silver Republican ticket in 1896. In 1895 he married Mary O'Connell, daughter of Idaho's governor. Running successfully as a Roosevelt supporter in 1906, he was sent, January 1907, to the U.S. Senate, where he served without interruption until his death. Though he had been a corporation lawyer and had won national prominence as prosecutor of the I.W.W. leader William Dudley Haywood, Borah sponsored bills to create the Department of Labor and the Children's Bureau, led the fight in the Senate for the income tax, and uncompromisingly opposed the trusts. A Jeffersonian Democrat in his political philosophy, Borah stressed equality of opportunity; his interest in social reform, however, was tempered by a dislike of federal centralization and a devotion to states' rights. He was a political maverick, inconsistent in his voting record. Opposing most of the progressive legislation of the Wilson administration, Borah was the leader of the bitter-end irreconcilables opposing the League of Nations. In favor of international action so long as political decisions and military sanctions were not required, he helped bring about the Washington disarmament conference of 1921 and the (Kellogg-Briand) Pact of Paris. He hoped to achieve world peace by extending the rule of law, and favored an international court with compulsory jurisdiction but no sanctions other than of public opinion. As chairman of the Senate Committee on Foreign Relations (from 1924), Borah was the most powerful force in foreign affairs in the country.

Borah enthusiastically supported Herbert Hoover in 1928 but soon resumed his familiar role of the Great Opposer. He felt Hoover was not doing enough to relieve the Depression and later supported much New Deal legislation, though not the NRA or the Supreme Court bill. A magnificent orator, a constitutionalist with a concept of society often irrelevant to 20th-century America, Borah had few equals in his ability to rouse the country on public questions and was often mentioned as a possible presidential candidate.

BORCHARD, EDWIN MONTEFIORE (*b. New York, N.Y., 1884; d. Hamden, Conn., 1951*), professor in international law. Studied at City College of New York, New York Law School (LL.B., 1905), and Columbia University (B.A., 1908; Ph.D., 1913). After a meteoric career, which included acting as adviser to American delegations at the Hague, law librarian of Congress, and assistant solicitor for the State Department, Borchard became professor of law at Yale University in 1919. He remained at that post until 1950. A specialist in international law, particularly diplomatic protection of alien citizens and property. Sought obligatory submission of foreign claims to international tribunals. From 1919 to 1939 became a prominent spokesman for traditional neutrality. Unlike the isolationists, however, he believed that international law could preserve neutrality. Served on the national committee of the American Civil Liberties Union and was a one-man lobbyist for passage of a bill providing relief to individuals wrongly convicted of a crime. Opposed the Nuremburg Trials and the Potsdam Agreement as acts of vengeance. His *Diplomatic Protection of Citizens Abroad* (1915) remains a classic.

BORDEN, GAIL (*b. Norwich, N.Y., 1801; d. Borden, Tex., 1874*), surveyor, inventor. Raised as farm boy in Kentucky and

Indiana, learned surveying from his father. Taught in backwoods schools of Indiana territory, also in Mississippi where he was U.S. deputy surveyor. Farmed and raised stock at Stephen Austin's colony in Texas; superintended official surveys; laid out city of Galveston; and was agent for Galveston City Co., 1839–51. Concerned with pioneers' hardships, he began work on idea for preparing concentrated food. After failure with a "meat biscuit," he patented a process for evaporating milk, 1856; during Civil War its use spread rapidly as soldiers introduced it to the civilian population.

BORDEN, LIZZIE ANDREW (b. Fall River, Mass., 1860; d. 1927), alleged murderess in a case widely publicized.

BORDEN, RICHARD (b. Freetown, Mass., 1795; d. 1874), manufacturer, executive. Helped form Fall River Iron Works; was treasurer and agent, 1821–74. Prominent also in cotton milling, railroad building, steamship transportation.

BORDEN, SIMEON (b. Fall River, Mass., 1798; d. 1856), skilled mechanic, civil engineer. An outstanding surveyor, he constructed base bar for Massachusetts town survey, 1830, the most accurate instrument of its kind at that time in the United States.

BORDLEY, JOHN BEALE (b. Annapolis, Md., 1727; d. 1804), lawyer, agriculturalist. Farmed on large scale on island at mouth of Wye River, post 1770. Experimented with crop rotation, grew wheat in place of tobacco, also hemp, flax, other products. Brought about formation of Philadelphia Society for Promoting Agriculture, 1785. Results of his farm operations and experiments were published as Essays and Notes on Husbandry and Rural Affairs (1799, 1801).

BORÉ, JEAN ÉTIENNE (b. Louisiana, 1741; d. near New Orleans, La., 1820), sugar planter. Generally credited with having established the sugar industry in Louisiana, 1795.

BOREMAN, ARTHUR INGRAM (b. Waynesburg, Pa., 1823; d. 1896), lawyer. Active in preventing secession of western Virginia. Governor of West Virginia, 1863–68; U.S. senator, Republican, 1869–75.

BORG, GEORGE WILLIAM (b. West Burlington, Iowa, 1887; d. Janesville, Wis., 1960), inventor and businessman. Attended Augustana College. Founded a company for manufacturing an automobile disk clutch in Moline, Ill.; merged with the Warner Gear Company and other companies to become the Borg-Warner Corporation in 1928. In 1940 established the George W. Borg Corporation and withdrew from the direction of Borg-Warner. Originally a manufacturer of clocks for automobiles, the company moved into the textile field and was highly successful.

BORGLUM, JOHN GUTZON DE LA MOTHE (b. near Bear Lake, Idaho Territory, 1867; d. Chicago, Ill., 1941), sculptor, painter. Known as Gutzon Borglum; brother of Solon H. Borglum. Raised in Ogden, Utah, St. Louis, Mo., and Fremont, Nebr. Moved with family to California, 1884. Determined to become an artist, he apprenticed himself to a Los Angeles engraver and lithographer, then studied painting in San Francisco under Virgil Williams and was influenced by the landscape work of William Keith. Patronized by Jessie Benton Frémont, he worked at painting until 1890 when he left for further study in Paris. He studied for a year at the Académie Julian and at the École des Beaux Arts, forming a lasting friendship with Auguste Rodin; he then spent a year in Spain. Returning to California, 1893, he lived and worked in the Sierra Madre and aided in the campaign for preservation of the Mission buildings. Believing that conditions were more favorable for an artist in England, he lived there, 1896–1901, gaining some

reputation for his portraits and busts of children. He returned to establish a studio in New York City, 1901, and concentrated on sculpture; his Mares of Diomedes won a gold medal at the St. Louis Exposition, 1904. By 1915, he was firmly established as a sculptor and had executed a number of important commissions. In that year, he undertook to create a colossal Confederate memorial on the face of Stone Mountain, near Atlanta, Ga., the central figures to be equestrian figures of R. E. Lee, Jefferson Davis, and Stonewall Jackson. Begun in 1916, the work was finished in part by January 1924, but a disagreement over funds brought about his discharge from the project early in 1925 and he destroyed his models to prevent their use by his successor. Meanwhile, in 1924 he had been invited to initiate a similar project in the Black Hills of South Dakota and chose the face of Mount Rushmore for a "shrine of democracy." Work was begun in 1927; Congress authorized funds for it in 1929; the first section (the head of George Washington) was unveiled in 1930, with similar colossal portraits of Jefferson, Lincoln, and Theodore Roosevelt to follow. Despite bickering between the domineering, single-minded sculptor and the National Park Service, Borglum virtually finished all the figures before his death. Among his other notable sculptures were the Altgeld Memorial (1915) in Chicago, the North Carolina War Memorial (1929) at Gettysburg, and the Trail Drivers Memorial (1940) in San Antonio.

Borglum was a man of strong opinions, highly articulate, and much more of a public figure than most artists. He was deeply patriotic and felt it his duty to be involved in politics and civic affairs. He was also interested in aviation, and a vigorous participant in sports.

BORGLUM, SOLON HANNIBAL (b. Ogden, Utah, 1868; d. 1922), sculptor. Brother of Gutzon Borglum. Particularly effective in studies of animals and in depicting American frontier life.

BORI, LUCREZIA (b. Gandia, Spain, 1887; d. New York, N.Y., 1960), operatic soprano. Studied at the Valencia Conservatory. Bori debuted at the Metropolitan Opera in 1912 in the title role of Puccini's Manon Lescaut; her last performance was given in 1936. In all she sang 606 performances in twenty-nine roles which included La Bohème, La Traviata, and Mignon. One of the great sopranos of the century, she was acclaimed for her musicianship, beauty of voice, and stage presence. In 1942, she became the first singer to serve on the board of directors of the Metropolitan Opera. She became an American citizen in 1943.

BORIE, ADOLPH EDWARD (b. Philadelphia, Pa., 1809; d. Philadelphia, 1880), merchant, financier.

BORIE, ADOLPHE (b. Philadelphia, Pa., 1877; d. 1934), portrait painter.

BORING, EDWIN GARRIGUES (b. Philadelphia, Pa., 1886; d. Cambridge, Mass., 1968), psychologist and teacher. M.A. (1912) and Ph.D. (1914), Cornell. Directed the psychological laboratory at Harvard (1924–49), becoming full professor in 1928 and chairman of the newly established Department of Psychology in 1934. Was coeditor of the American Journal of Psychology (1925–46) and editor of Contemporary Psychology (1956–61). His first and most important book was A History of Experimental Psychology (1929; revised and enlarged in 1950), after which he wrote several other works on psychology and a brief autobiography, Psychologist at Large (1961). Described as a "universalist," he was less interested in research than in writing about the history of psychology, editing professional journals, and guiding the psychology department at Harvard.

BORING, WILLIAM ALCIPHRON (b. Carlinville, Ill., 1859; d. New York, N.Y., 1937), architect. First dean, 1931–34, School of Architecture, Columbia University.

BORLAND, SOLON (*b. near Suffolk, Va., 1808; d. in or near Houston, Tex., 1864*), physician, diplomat. U.S. senator from Arkansas, 1848–53; minister to Nicaragua, 1853. Brigadier general in Confederate Army.

BORZAGE, FRANK (*b. Salt Lake City, Utah, 1893; d. Los Angeles, Calif., 1962*), motion picture director and producer. After winning Academy Awards for his direction of *Seventh Heaven* (1927) and *Bad Girl* (1931), he directed many melodramatic romantic classics in the 1930's, the most productive and artistically important decade of his career. Among his most acclaimed films were *A Farewell to Arms* (1932), *Man's Castle* (1933), *Little Man, What Now?* (1934), *Desire* (1936), *History Is Made at Night* (1937), and *Three Comrades* (1938). He became heavily involved with production in the 1940's. His last film was *The Big Fisherman* (1959).

BOSS, LEWIS (*b. Providence, R.I., 1846; d. 1912*), astronomer. Authority on star positions; published *The Preliminary General Catalogue of 6188 Stars for the Epoch 1900* (Carnegie Institution, 1910).

BOSTON, CHARLES ANDERSON (*b. Baltimore, Md., 1863; d. New York, N.Y., 1935*), lawyer and legal scholar. Active in movements for reform of judicial and professional ethics.

BOSTWICK, ARTHUR ELMORE (*b. Litchfield, Conn., 1860; d. Oak Grove, Mo., 1942*), librarian. A.B., Yale, 1881; Ph.D., 1883. Engaged in editing reference works, 1886–95; science editor of the *Literary Digest*, 1891–1933. Entered library work as librarian of New York Free Circulating Library, 1895; convinced that public libraries were primarily instruments of popular education, not merely for reference by scholars, he instituted an open-shelf policy and developed branches. He continued to hold and act on this philosophy in successive posts at Brooklyn Public Library (1899–1901), New York Public Library (1901–09), and St. Louis Public Library (1909–38). He was author of *The American Public Library* (1910).

BOSWORTH, EDWARD INCREASE (*b. Elgin, Ill., 1861; d. 1927*), Congregational clergyman, educator. Long associated with Oberlin College and Theological Seminary.

BOSWORTH, FRANCKE HUNTINGTON (*b. Marietta, Ohio, 1843; d. 1925*), laryngologist. Graduated Yale, 1862. After service in Civil War, settled in New York; graduated M.D. from Bellevue Hospital and Medical College, 1868, and taught there *post* 1873. Published *Handbook upon Diseases of the Throat and Nose* (1879) and a celebrated *Manual of the Diseases of the Throat and Nose* (1881). Most extensive work was *A Treatise on Diseases of the Nose and Throat* (1889, 1892). His contributions to the subject, together with those of J. Solis-Cohen and Sir Morrell MacKenzie, may be said to have created science of laryngology; he was also important in developing science of rhinology.

BOTELER, ALEXANDER ROBINSON (*b. Virginia, 1815; d. Shepherdstown, W.Va., 1892*), U.S. and Confederate congressman. Served as aide on staffs of T. J. Jackson and J. E. B. Stuart.

BOTETOURT, NORBORNE BERKELEY, BARON DE (*b. England, ca. 1718; d. Williamsburg, Va., 1770*), colonial governor of Virginia, 1768–70. Able, well-intentioned, he was powerless to halt the drift toward rebellion.

BOTSFORD, GEORGE WILLIS (*b. West Union, Iowa, 1862; d. New York, N.Y., 1917*), historian. Taught ancient history at Harvard, and at Columbia University, 1902–17.

BOTTA, ANNE CHARLOTTE LYNCH (*b. Bennington, Vt., 1815; d. New York, N.Y., 1891*), educator, author. Presided at her New York home, *post* 1845, over first important salon in history of American letters; friend of Poe, Greeley, Margaret Fuller, and many others.

BOTTA, VINCENZO (*b. Cavallermaggiore, Italy, 1818; d. New York, N.Y., 1894*), scholar. Husband of Anne C. L. Botta. Came to America, 1853. Taught Italian at new York University; author of a study on Dante and other works.

BOTTINEAU, PIERRE (*b. Minnesota, ca. 1817; d. 1895*), half-Chippewa guide, called "Kit Carson of the Northwest." He guided many expeditions, 1850–70, including I. I. Stevens' railroad survey, 1853, the Fisk expedition, 1862, and General Sibley's Sioux campaign, 1863.

BOTTOME, MARGARET MCDONALD (*b. New York, N.Y., 1827; d. 1906*), writer. Organizer (1886) of International Order of the King's Daughters and Sons.

BOTTS, CHARLES TYLER (*b. Virginia, 1809; d. Oakland, Calif., 1884*), lawyer, editor. Brother of John M. Botts. Established popular agricultural journal, the *Southern Planter*, 1841. Removed to California, 1848.

BOTTS, JOHN MINOR (*b. Dumfries, Va., 1802; d. 1869*), lawyer, author. Virginia legislator, Whig, 1833–39; congressman, 1839–43, 1847–49. Vocal and aggressive foe of the Democrats, he opposed annexation of Texas, the Mexican War and President Tyler's bank and tariff vetoes. Played vital part in passage of 1850 Compromise. Convinced that Democrats were engaged in a conspiracy to provoke secession by any means, he struggled to hold Virginia in Union. At outbreak of Civil War, he withdrew to his farm near Richmond; imprisoned by Confederates, 1862, he later settled in Culpeper Co. He led conservative wing of Virginia Unionists *post* 1865, but accepted radical position and lost influence.

BOUCHÉ, RENÉ ROBERT (*b. Prague, Austria-Hungary, 1905; d. East Grinsted, Sussex, England, 1963*), fashion and advertising illustrator and painter. By the late 1930's had established himself as an art director and advertising and fashion illustrator in Paris. During World War II he immigrated to the U.S., becoming a citizen in the mid–1940's. Maintained a strong relationship with *Vogue* enterprises throughout his life and also made advertising sketches for Saks Fifth Avenue and handled most of Elizabeth Arden's advertising campaigns. In the 1950's he continued his advertising illustrations but began a project to restore portraiture to its pride of place in art and produced a volume of exceptional portrait drawings.

BOUCHER, HORACE EDWARD (*b. Italy, 1873; d. 1935*), ship modeler and naval architect.

BOUCHER, JONATHAN (*b. Blencogo, England, 1737/38; d. England, 1804*), Loyalist, Anglican clergyman. Tutor, schoolmaster, and rector in Virginia and Maryland, 1759–75; preached against colonial resistance. Author of *A View of the Causes and Consequences of the American Revolution* (1797).

BOUCICAULT, DION (*b. Dublin, Ireland, 1820; d. New York, N.Y., 1890*), dramatist, actor. Acted in provincial theaters in England, and in London; wrote and adapted many plays for English stage, including the well-known *London Assurance* (produced 1841). Came to America, 1853. Toured as actor; wrote topical melodramas; opened theater in Washington, 1858; directed New York's Winter Garden, 1859. In this same year he wrote *The Octoroon*, a play about slavery which was a great success; in 1860, his *The Colleen Bawn* was first of a long series of Irish dramas, including *Arrah-na-Pogue* (1864) and *The Shaughraun* (1874). In London 1862–72, he then returned to America. Boucicault wrote or adapted in all 132 plays. He inaugurated the "long run" system, and did much to keep American drama lively in the mid-19th century.

BOUCK, WILLIAM C. (*b. Schoharie Co., N.Y., 1786; d. Schoharie Co., 1859*), farmer, politician. New York canal commissioner, 1821–40; superintended part of Erie Canal construction. Democratic governor of New York, 1843–44.

BOUDIN, LOUIS BOUDINOV (*b. Ukraine, 1874; d. New York, N.Y., 1952*), lawyer and author. Immigrated to the U.S. in 1891. Studied at New York University (LL.B., 1896; LL.M., 1897). A major Marxist apologist, Boudin wrote *The Theoretical Systems of Karl Marx in the Light of Recent Criticism* (1907). From the 1920's through the 1940's he was a leading labor lawyer, resisting all attempts to curb union organizers through injunctions. His best known book, *Government by Judiciary* (1932), is an elaborate and combative historical survey of judicial review in the United States.

BOUDINOT, ELIAS (*b. Philadelphia, Pa., 1740; d. Burlington, N.J., 1821*), lawyer, Revolutionary statesman. Close associate of Washington. Commissary general of prisoners; member of Continental Congress, 1777–84, and president of Congress, 1782; secretary of foreign affairs, 1783–84. Federalist congressman from New Jersey, 1789–95. Director of U.S. Mint, 1795–1805.

BOUDINOT, ELIAS (*b. Georgia, ca. 1803; d. Indian Territory, 1839*), Indian editor. Edited *Cherokee Phoenix*, 1824–35. Murdered for his part in agreeing to removal of Cherokee to West.

BOUDINOT, ELIAS CORNELIUS (*b. near present Rome, Ga., 1835; d. Indian Territory, 1890*), lawyer. Son of Elias Boudinot (1803–1839). Cherokee delegate from Indian Territory to Confederate Congress. After Civil War, helped restore peaceful relations between Cherokee and United States.

BOULIGNY, DOMINIQUE (*b. New Orleans, La., ca. 1771; d. New Orleans, 1833*), legislator. Prominent in Louisiana politics in early 19th century, U.S. senator from Louisiana, 1824–29.

BOUNETHEAU, HENRY BRINTNELL (*b. Charleston, S.C., 1797; d. Charleston, 1877*), miniature painter. Primarily a businessman; worked in manner of Charles Fraser.

BOUQUET, HENRY (*b. Rolle, Switzerland, 1719; d. Pensacola, Fla., 1765*), soldier. Entered service of Holland as cadet, 1736; rose to lieutenant colonel. Accepted lieutenant colonelcy of first battalion, Royal American Regiment of British Army, 1755; went to America, 1756. Promoted colonel, 1758, he served as second under General John Forbes in expedition against Fort Duquesne. Gaining much experience along frontier, he adapted discipline of European armies to exigencies of wilderness warfare and was far in advance of military practice of the day. In Pontiac's conspiracy he proved worth of his methods at Edgehill and Bushy Run, 1763. In 1764 he brought about surrender of all prisoners in Indian hands and concluded a general peace.

BOUQUILLON, THOMAS JOSEPH (*b. Warneton, Belgium, 1840; d. Brussels, Belgium, 1902*), Roman Catholic clergyman, theologian. Studied at Menin, Roulers, Bruges, Gregorian University at Rome. Ordained, Rome, 1865; D.D., 1867. Professor of moral theology, Bruges, 1867–77; professor of theology, University of Lille, 1877–85. Accepted chair of moral theology at new Catholic University, Washington, D.C., 1889; taught there until his death. Bouquillon's chief contribution to Catholic thought lay in his effort to restore to moral theology the scientific and historical prestige with which St. Thomas and other early thinkers had invested it; his major work on this subject is *Theologia Moralis Fundamentalis* (3rd edition, Bruges, 1903). Influential in development of Catholic University, he was also active in Catholic controversy on education, 1891–92.

BOURGMONT, ÉTIENNE VENYARD, SIEUR DE (*b. France, ca. 1680; d. ca. 1730*), French adventurer. Explored extensively up Missouri River *ante* 1717; built Fort Orléans, 1723. Undertook expedition, 1724, penetrating to western border of what became Kansas.

BOURKE, JOHN GREGORY (*b. Philadelphia, Pa., 1846; d. 1896*), soldier, ethnologist. Served in Civil War; graduated West Point, 1869, and was assigned to frontier duty with 3rd Cavalry. Author of valuable first-hand studies of Plains and Southwest Indian tribes.

BOURNE, BENJAMIN (*b. Bristol, R.I., 1755; d. 1808*), Revolutionary soldier, jurist. Active for ratification of Constitution in Rhode Island; served in first four U.S. congresses; judge, U.S. district court in Rhode Island, *post* 1801.

BOURNE, EDWARD GAYLORD (*b. Strykersville, N.Y., 1860; d. New Haven, Conn., 1908*), historian. Graduated Yale, 1883; Ph.D., 1892. Professor of history at Yale, *post* 1895. Author of *Essays in Historical Criticism* (1901), *Spain in America* (1904), and other works.

BOURNE, GEORGE (*b. Westbury, England, 1780; d. New York, N.Y., 1845*), Presbyterian and Dutch Reformed clergyman, abolitionist, journalist. Fanatical opponent of slavery, women's rights, and the Catholic Church. Author of *Lorette* (1834) and other works.

BOURNE, JONATHAN (*b. New Bedford, Mass., 1855; d. Washington, D.C., 1940*), U.S. senator, Republican, from Oregon, 1906–12. The first senator to be elected by direct primary.

BOURNE, NEHEMIAH (*b. London, England, ca. 1611; d. England, 1691*), shipbuilder, British rear admiral. Built ships in Boston, 1638–ca. 1642, including Gov. Winthrop's *Trial*, first vessel of any size laid down at Boston. Prominent in the navy of the Commonwealth, 1650–60.

BOURNE, RANDOLPH SILLIMAN (*b. Bloomfield, N.J., 1886; d. New York, N.Y., 1918*), essayist. Graduated Columbia, 1913. Author of *Youth and Life* (1913); *The Gary Schools* (1916); *Education and Living* (1917); and *The History of a Literary Radical* (1920).

BOUTELL, HENRY SHERMAN (*b. Boston, Mass., 1856; d. San Remo, Italy, 1926*), lawyer, diplomat. Prominent Chicago attorney; congressman, Republican, from Illinois, 1897–1911; envoy to Switzerland, 1911–13. Taught international and constitutional law at Georgetown University, 1914–23.

BOUTELLE, CHARLES ADDISON (*b. Damariscotta, Maine, 1839; d. 1901*), journalist. Served in U.S. Navy in Civil War. Editor, *Whig and Courier*, Bangor, Maine, *post* 1870; congressman, Republican, from Maine, 1882–1901. Championed modern strong navy.

BOUTON, JOHN BELL (*b. Concord, N.H., 1830; d. 1902*), author. Son of Nathaniel Bouton. Editor, *Cleveland Plain-Dealer*, 1851–57; later with *Journal of Commerce*, *Appleton's Annual Cyclopedia*.

BOUTON, NATHANIEL (*b. Norwalk, Conn., 1799; d. Concord, N.H., 1878*), Congregational clergyman. State historian of New Hampshire, whose documentary history he edited and published, 1867–77.

BOUTWELL, GEORGE SEWALL (*b. Brookline, Mass., 1818; d. 1905*), politician, lawyer. Free-soil and Democratic governor of Massachusetts, 1851–52; an organizer of Republican party in that state. Congressman, radical Republican, 1863–69; a leader in movement to impeach President Johnson. Secretary of treasury, 1869–73; U.S. senator from Massachusetts, 1873–77.

BOUVET, MARIE MARGUERITE (*b. New Orleans, La., 1865; d. Reading, Pa., 1915*), linguist, writer of books for young people.

BOUVIER, JOHN (*b. Condognan, France, 1787; d. 1851*), judge, legal writer. Came to America, *ca.* 1801. Practiced in Philadelphia *post* 1823. Author of a celebrated *Law Dictionary* (first edition, 1839).

BOVARD, OLIVER KIRBY (*b. Jacksonville, Ill., 1872; d. St. Louis, Mo., 1945*), newspaper editor. Left public school at fourteen; worked as clerk and as reporter for *St. Louis Star*; joined staff of *St. Louis Post-Dispatch*, 1898, and became city editor, 1900. He improved quality of local reporting, started crusades against traction and utility frauds, and supported efforts of city reformers. After ten months (1909) on the *New York World*, he returned to the *Post-Dispatch* as managing editor and held that position until his resignation in 1938. He exercised full control over all news departments, continuing a policy of investigative reporting, insisting on accuracy, and developing a brilliant staff which included four future Pulitzer Prize winners; in 1918, distrusting the wire services, he established his own Washington bureau. Believing that the chief problem of American society was unequal distribution of wealth, and that the New Deal had not gone far enough in its moves toward a middle ground between capitalism and pure socialism, he found himself in conflict with Joseph Pulitzer, Jr., the politically moderate editor and publisher of the *Post-Dispatch*. Their differences over the paper's policies led to Bovard's resignation.

BOVIE, WILLIAM T. (*b. Augusta, Mich., 1882; d. Fairfield, Maine, 1958*), inventor and biophysicist. Studied at Albion College, the University of Michigan (B.A., 1905), the University of Missouri, (M.A., 1910), and Harvard (Ph.D., 1914). Remembered for his work on the effects of ultraviolet light on plants and protoplasm, Bovie was the first American to put radium into a usable solution for the treatment of cancer. Assistant professor of biophysics at Harvard (1920–27) and chairman of the department at Northwestern (1927–29). From 1939 until 1948 he was at Colby College. The 1930's were spent at his private research laboratory in Bar Harbor, Me. Invented the Bovie unit, an electrosurgical knife, in 1926.

BOW, CLARA GORDON (*b. Brooklyn, N.Y., 1905; d. Culver City, Calif., 1965*), actress. Throughout the 1920's she played a series of unexceptional roles, gaining recognition as a vivacious little redheaded flapper with wide brown eyes. After her appearance in *The Plastic Age* (1925), about youth and morality in the Jazz Age, she was touted as "the hottest jazz baby in films." Her reputation as the "It Girl" began in 1927, when she played the lead in *It*; "it" was supposedly the quality possessed by rare individuals to attract members of the opposite sex, and she became the personification of that quality. Her career declined rapidly after the 1920's.

BOWDEN, JOHN (*b. Ireland, 1751; d. Ballston Spa, N.Y., 1817*), Anglican clergyman. Studied at Princeton; graduated King's College (Columbia), N.Y., 1772; ordained 1774. Held rectorates in Connecticut; first principal of Episcopal Academy at Cheshire, 1796–1802. Professor of philosophy, logic, at Columbia, 1802–17.

BOWDITCH, CHARLES PICKERING (*b. 1842; d. 1921*), archaeologist. Graduated Harvard, 1863. Grandson of Nathaniel Bowditch. Scholar of Maya hieroglyphics, published *Numeration, Calendar Systems and Astronomical Knowledge of the Mayas* (1910). Harvard's Peabody Museum received his collections and valuable library.

BOWDITCH, HENRY INGERSOLL (*b. Salem, Mass., 1808; d. 1892*), physician, abolitionist. Son of Nathaniel Bowditch. Graduated Harvard, 1828; M.D., Harvard Medical School, 1832. After two years' study in Paris, returned to Boston to practice. Became follower of W. L. Garrison, assisted runaway slaves, actively fostered antislavery cause in North. Associated with Massachusetts General Hospital, 1838–92; professor, Harvard Medical School, 1859–67. Contributions to medicine include studies of tuberculosis, popularizing of procedure for removal of pleural effusions, and, most important, his influence in stimulating public health movement in Massachusetts and the nation. Published *Public Hygiene in America* (1877).

BOWDITCH, HENRY PICKERING (*b. Boston, Mass., 1840; d. 1911*), physiologist. Grandson of Nathaniel Bowditch. Graduated Harvard, 1861; served in Civil War; studied comparative anatomy at Lawrence Scientific School; M.D., Harvard Medical School, 1868. Studied in Paris, and at Leipzig under Carl Ludwig, 1869–71. Established at Harvard Medical School, 1871, first physiological laboratory in United States, remaining there as professor until retirement, 1906, and serving as dean, Medical School, 1883–93. Versatile, inventive, he also did important studies of growth rates in schoolchildren. Foremost American physiologist after Beaumont, Bowditch made findings which are classical on the *Treppe* or "All or None" principle of cardiac muscle behavior (Leipzig, 1871), and on the indefatigability of nerve fiber (1885).

BOWDITCH, NATHANIEL (*b. Salem, Mass., 1773; d. Boston, Mass., 1838*), astronomer, mathematician. Son of a shipmaster and cooper, he left school to help his father, 1783, became a clerk or apprentice in a ship-chandlery at twelve years of age, and continued there until his first sea voyage, 1795. During these years he read voraciously, and with his retentive memory acquired information on many subjects; he constructed an almanac, studied French and Euclid, learned Latin in order to read Newton. Between 1795 and 1803 he made five voyages, the last as master and supercargo. At the suggestion of a publisher in Newburyport, he checked accuracy of a popular English work, *The Practical Navigator* by J. H. Moore, and made revisions published in an American edition (1799), with his brother William collaborating. More revisions and additions were made, so many that the third edition, printed 1801, was issued in 1802, titled *The New American Practical Navigator*. Ten editions were published in Bowditch's lifetime; many more have appeared since. Bowditch was elected a Fellow of the American Academy of Arts and Sciences, 1799; in 1802 he received an honorary Master of Arts degree from Harvard. Appointed president of the Essex Fire and Marine Insurance Co., 1804, he held office until 1823 when he became actuary of the Massachusetts Hospital Life Insurance Co. in Boston.

Bowditch did most of his scientific work during his years in Salem. In addition to the work already mentioned, he made a chart of the harbors of Salem, Beverly, and Manchester (published 1896; second edition, 1834), and also proposed and solved a dozen problems in Adrain's *Analyst* (1808, 1814). Far more important, however, were papers published in the American Academy's *Memoirs* (1804–20), and the preparation of the translation, with much of the commentary, of the first four volumes of Laplace's *Mécanique céleste*. This translation was done before 1818, but was not published until 1829–39. So elaborate were the notes, in elucidation and in attempting to bring the subjects up-to-date, that the translated work was more than double the size of the original. It has been described as marking "an epoch in American science by bringing the great work of Laplace down to the reach of the best American students of his time." Not a genius or discoverer, but rather an exceptionally able critic, Bowditch accomplished much scientific work and won a prominent place among early American intellectuals even though most of his time was devoted to other affairs.

BOWDOIN, JAMES (*b. Boston, Mass., 1726; d. Boston, 1790*), Revolutionary statesman, merchant. Married, 1748, Elizabeth Erving, daughter of another prosperous Boston merchant. He met serious losses in the Revolutionary period, but remained wealthy because of large holdings in Boston real estate and Maine lands.

Bowdoin's political career began in 1753 with his election to the General Court. Serving three terms in the lower house, he was chosen a member of the Council, 1757. This body had generally favored the British viewpoint; Bowdoin's influence was important in aligning it with colonial interests. He stressed particularly the economic aspects of the dispute with England. In 1774 General Gage negatived Bowdoin's election to the Council. The General Court elected him delegate to the Continental Congress, but failure of his own health and his wife's forced him to decline. John Hancock took his place. In August 1775 the Provincial Congress appointed him first member of its executive council; he resigned in 1777 for reasons of health. Elected to the state constitutional convention, 1779, he was chosen president of the convention, and chairman of the subcommittee which drafted the instrument. John Adams wrote most of the final document, but Bowdoin exercised much influence.

After Hancock retired as governor, 1785, it was apparent that serious economic and social troubles threatened the new Commonwealth of Massachusetts. Bowdoin ran for the office against the candidate of the "popular" interest, Thomas Cushing, and won after the election was thrown into the legislature, which was dominated by commercial and property interests. He was reelected in 1786. During his administration occurred the crisis of 1786–87 known as "Shays's Rebellion." Although greater statesmanship might have averted insurrection, Bowdoin's handling of the actual crisis was prompt and vigorous, and helped to stabilize both the state and ultimately the new nation by insistence on the paramount importance of law and order. He had previously shown vision in urging increased federal powers to permit control of commerce which he believed essential to economic stabilization, thus taking as early part in the movement for a Federal Constitution. Although Bowdoin's suppression of the insurgent debtors by force was widely approved outside Massachusetts, there his prestige suffered; many citizens believed that needed reforms had been too slow in forthcoming. Bowdoin retired from the governorship in April 1787. His last public service came in January 1788 when he was a delegate to the Massachusetts convention to pass on adoption of the Federal Constitution.

Bowdoin was also interested in science and literature. First president of the American Academy of Arts and Sciences, he was especially interested in physics and astronomy and wrote many papers for the Academy's *Transactions*. His chief memorial, appropriately, is the college named for him which was chartered in Maine four years after his death.

BOWDOIN, JAMES (*b. Boston, Mass., 1752; d. Naushon Island, Mass., 1811*), merchant, diplomat. Son of James Bowdoin (1726–1790). Appointed minister to Spain by Jefferson, he participated (1804–08) in unsuccessful negotiations regarding Florida. Benefactor, Bowdoin College.

BOWEN, ABEL (*b. Greenbush, N.Y., 1790; d. 1850*), wood engraver, publisher. Removed to Boston, Mass., 1811. Designer-engraver of *The Naval Monument* (1816), *Picture of Boston* (1828), and other works.

BOWEN, FRANCIS (*b. Charlestown, Mass., 1811; d. 1890*), philosopher. Graduated Harvard,, 1833. Taught philosophy and political economy at Harvard, *post* 1835; editor, *North American Review*, 1843–53. Author of *Modern Philosophy from Descartes to Schopenhauer and Hartmann* (1877) and many other works.

BOWEN, GEORGE (*b. Middlebury, Vt., 1816; d. Bombay, India, 1888*), missionary. Preached in Bombay, 1848–88; *post* 1873 was a Methodist. Edited *Bombay Guardian*, 1854–88.

BOWEN, HENRY CHANDLER (*b. Woodstock, Conn., 1813; d. Brooklyn, N.Y., 1896*), merchant. A founder, and later publisher and proprietor, of Congregationalist *Independent*. Associate of Henry W. Beecher and Theodore Tilton.

BOWEN, HERBERT WOLCOTT (*b. Brooklyn, N.Y., 1856; d. 1927*), lawyer, diplomat. Son of Henry C. Bowen. Graduated Yale, 1878. Consul general in Spain, Persia; minister to Venezuela in crisis of 1902. Dismissed from diplomatic service, 1905, after difficulties with Theodore Roosevelt.

BOWEN, LOUISE DE KOVEN (*b. Chicago., Ill., 1859; d. Chicago., 1953*), philanthropist and social worker. Studied at Dearborn Seminary. Associated with Chicago's Hull House from 1893 until her death in 1953. Bowen contributed money and effort to Hull House, working closely with Jane Addams. In 1899, she organized the first juvenile court in the U.S. After Addams' death in 1935, she became treasurer and then president of the settlement house.

BOWEN, NORMAN LEVI (*b. Kingston, Ontario., 1887; d. Washington, D.C., 1956*), geologist and petrologist. Studied at Queens University (M.A., 1907; B.S., 1909) and the Massachusetts Institute of Technology (Ph.D., 1912). His entire professional life spent with the Geophysical Laboratory of the Carnegie Institution in Washington; established the phase diagrams for the principal components of igneous rocks and applied them to develop the modern magmatic theory of petrogenesis. In doing so he made Washington, with the Carnegie Institution and the U.S. Geological Survey, the world center of experimental petrology.

BOWEN, THOMAS MEADE (*b. near Burlington, Iowa, 1835; d. Pueblo, Colo., 1906*), miner, lawyer, politician. U.S. senator, Republican, from Colorado, 1883–89.

BOWERS, CLAUDE GERNADE (*b. Westfield, Ind., 1878; d. New York, N.Y., 1958*), journalist, orator, historian, diplomat. Self-educated. After an early career on Indiana newspapers, he became secretary to Senate majority leader John W. Kern. Editor, *New York Evening World* (1923–31) and *New York Journal* (1931–33). An ardent Democrat and popular orator, he was the keynote speaker at the 1928 convention. Invited to nominate Roosevelt at the 1932 convention, he declined owing to pressure from Hearst. Still friendly with the president, however, he was appointed ambassador to Spain (1933–39), serving during that country's turbulent civil war, and to Chile (1939–53). Books include *Jefferson and Hamilton* (1925), which was influential in the Jefferson revival; *My Mission to Spain* (1954) and *Chile Through Embassy Windows* (1958).

BOWERS, ELIZABETH CROCKER (*b. Ridgefield, Conn., 1830; d. Washington, D.C., 1895*), actress. Played leading roles in America and England, 1846–94, and in support of Edwin Booth, Lawrence Barrett, and many others.

BOWERS, LLOYD WHEATON (*b. Springfield, Mass., 1859; d. 1910*), lawyer. General counsel, Chicago and North Western Railroad; played conspicuous part in litigation over government control of railroads. Effective U.S. solicitor general, 1909–10.

BOWERS, THEODORE SHELTON (*b. Hummelstown, Pa., 1832; d. Garrison, N.Y., 1866*), Union soldier. Faithful aide to General U. S. Grant, 1862–66.

BOWES, EDWARD J. (*b. San Francisco, Calif, 1874; d. Rumson, N.J., 1946*), businessman, theater owner, radio personality. Left school at age thirteen to work as office boy in a real estate firm; by 1904, had a flourishing real estate business of his own, and was a friend and colleague in municipal reform of Fremont Older. Soon recouping losses he suffered in the 1906 San Francisco earthquake, he shifted his business activities to the theater and became a partner in buying and operating the Cort Theater in New York City and the Park Square Theater in Boston. In 1918, he was a partner in the construction of New York's Capitol Theater, one of the first movie palaces, and became its managing director. He was also a vice president of Goldwyn Pictures, and later of Metro-Goldwyn-Mayer. In 1925, he took over the weekly radio program which had been broadcast from the Capitol by "Roxy [S. L. Rothafel] and His Gang" since 1922, retaining the basic format of variety and audience participation and adding his own running commentary. In 1934, after becoming manager of WHN, a radio station owned by Metro-Goldwyn-Mayer, he started "Major Bowes Amateur Hour," which proved a great success both as a feature on network radio and as a source of profitable touring companies. He retired in 1945.

BOWIE, JAMES (*b. Logan Co., Ky., 1796; d. San Antonio, Tex., 1836*), Texas soldier. Spent most of childhood in Catahoula Parish, La. Little is known of his earliest exploits. About 1828, he went to Texas, settling in San Antonio, acquiring land and becoming a Mexican citizen in 1830. As tension grew between Americans and the Mexican government, Bowie was usually on side of resistance and was a captain in the fight at Nacogdoches, 1832. He played a leading part when hostilities broke out in 1835; as colonel of the revolutionary forces, he was important in campaign which cleared Texas of the Mexican Army. When Santa Anna returned in 1836, Bowie was among the Americans who made the famous stand at the Alamo, where all were killed. Bowie was reputedly inventor of the "bowie knife."

BOWIE, ODEN (*b. Prince Georges Co., Md., 1826; d. Prince Georges Co., 1894*), businessman, turf patron. President, Baltimore and Potomac Railroad, 1860–94. Democratic governor of Maryland, 1867–72; *de facto,* 1869–72.

BOWIE, RICHARD JOHNS (*b. Georgetown, D.C., 1807; d. Montgomery Co., Md., 1881*), lawyer, politician. Congressman, Whig, from Maryland, 1849–53. Outstanding chief justice, Maryland court of appeals, 1861–81.

BOWIE, ROBERT (*b. near Nottingham, Md., 1750; d. Nottingham, 1818*), Revolutionary soldier, politician. Democratic-Republican governor of Maryland, 1803–07; 1811–12.

BOWIE, WILLIAM (*b. Anne Arundel Co., Md., 1872; d. Washington, D.C., 1940*), geodesist. Chief, Division of Geodesy, U.S. Coast and Geodetic Survey, 1909–36.

BOWKER, RICHARD ROGERS (*b. Salem, Mass., 1848; d. Stockbridge, Mass., 1933*), editor, publisher, bibliographer, author, library promoter. Graduated from City College of New York, 1868. Held posts on several New York papers. In 1879, purchased *Publishers' Weekly,* which he edited from 1884 until his death, and took over issuance of the *American Catalog,* listing all books in print in the United States. With Leypoldt and Dewey, founded the *Library Journal* and arranged the organization meeting of the American Library Association. He was an able business executive in many fields. An independent Republican, he attacked bossism, drafted the original national civil-service-reform plank, drew up a postal code, and at almost 85 was attracted to the New Deal.

BOWLER, METCALF (*b. London, England, 1726; d. 1789*), Rhode Island patriot, businessman. Came to America, ca. 1743. Prospered in trade at Newport, R.I., but was virtually ruined by the Revolution.

BOWLES, SAMUEL (*b. Hartford, Conn., 1797; d. Springfield, Mass., 1851*), printer, newspaper editor. Formed partnership with John Francis, 1819, in publishing *Hartford Times.* This having failed, he moved to Springfield, Mass., 1824, to establish a new weekly there. First issue of *Springfield Republican* appeared Sept. 8, 1824. It grew steadily owing to editorial independence and outstanding local coverage. The daily *Republican* first appeared Mar. 27, 1844. Bowles's chief contribution was in establishing firmly the paper which his son made nationally famous.

BOWLES, SAMUEL (*b. Springfield, Mass., 1826; d. Springfield, 1878*), editor. Son of Samuel Bowles (1797–1851). Joined *Springfield Republican,* 1843, as general helper. Within a year he assumed most of the extra work incident to issue of a daily edition. His health broke down in the winter of 1844–45. After recuperating in Louisiana, he continued his work on the daily with such energy that it was soon established on a permanent basis. In 1848 the paper absorbed the *Springfield Gazette,* and established its supremacy in western Massachusetts. Telegraphic news was rapidly developed; many new features were instituted; pithy and pungent editorials began to displace the longer articles on the editorial page.

In 1851, when his father died, the younger Bowles was able to take complete control of the paper. Its political course had not yet developed firmly. In 1848 it stated, "Our motto is NO COMPROMISE, NO MORE SLAVE TERRITORY." But it wavered in 1850 and supported Clay's compromise plan. Early in 1851 Bowles announced that the paper was still Whig although the Whig party was clearly on the wane. In the early fifties, still conservative on slavery, the paper attacked the abolitionists and supported the Fugitive Slave Act, but with the Kansas-Nebraska struggle a new aggressive policy developed. Bowles declared the Kansas-Nebraska bill "a huge stride backward." By 1854 he had repudiated the Whigs. Scorning the pretensions of the Native American party, he kept urging establishment of a new party of freedom. One of the earliest editors to advocate nomination of Frémont, Bowles worked indefatigably for his election. With its espousal of the Republican party, the *Springfield Republican* entered the flood-tide of its success. Its circulation rose rapidly; it was hailed by the *New York Tribune* as "the best and ablest country journal ever published on this continent." Well edited, offering leadership in its editorial views, it had circulation and influence throughout all the free states and territories.

At this time Bowles, although he had previously refused a position on the *New York Tribune* as well as editorship of a projected new daily in Philadelphia, resigned editorship of the *Republican* and assumed that of a new Boston newspaper, the *Traveller.* It was to be Republican, independent, and progressive, and take the lead among Boston papers. Its backers, however, were not united, nor was it as strong financially as it had appeared. Thwarted in all his efforts, Bowles resigned after four months, returning to the *Republican* in which he had retained controlling ownership. Throughout the pre–Civil War years he increased the power of the paper, primarily through the weekly edition which dealt in national rather than local news. Bowles drove himself and his staff incessantly, producing a paper with high standards in both news and editorials. He denounced the execution of John Brown, supported Lincoln, but did not agree with radicals who urged harsh measures against all rebels. Criticizing Lincoln for wartime infringements on civil rights, he supported his renomination and his Reconstruction policies.

The political and financial corruption of the seventies found in Bowles a strong assailant. He denounced James Fisk, provoking a libel suit which was not pressed. He also exposed D. D. Field, the counsel for Fisk, Gould, and Tweed. Shocked by the Crédit Mobilier and other scandals, he joined in the Liberal Republican movement of 1872, working for nomination of Charles Francis Adams. Disappointed at Greeley's nomination, he supported him nevertheless.

Bowles's last twenty years were marked by ill health. The *Republican's* prosperity had made possible an enlarged staff, and he was able to take frequent vacations, but when at work he continued at his usual intense pace. Erratic, impulsive, devoted to the *Republican* above all else, he was at times ruthless, alienating others by his tactless actions. Dissatisfied with the methods of his younger brother, Benjamin Franklin Bowles, long in charge of paper's counting room, he dismissed him by letter in 1875.

A pioneer in establishment of independent journalism, Bowles gave the nation its first demonstration of what a provincial newspaper might accomplish. For a quarter-century he was a real leader of American opinion.

BOWLES, SAMUEL   (*b. Springfield, Mass., 1851; d. 1915*), editor. Son of Samuel Bowles (1826–1878). Early trained by his father to take charge of the *Springfield Republican*, he undertook business management of the newspaper, 1875. His father's illness threw more responsibility on him; at the elder Bowles's death he assumed full charge. Editor, publisher, and treasurer for nearly forty years, he maintained the *Republican's* high standards and continued its editorial independence, supporting Cleveland, opposing Bryan and waging war on jingoism and imperialism.

BOWLES, WILLIAM AUGUSTUS   (*b. Frederick Co., Md., 1763; d. Havana, Cuba, 1805*), adventurer. Incited Creek Indians against Spain in three Florida filibustering expeditions, 1788, 1791–92, 1799.

BOWMAN, ISAIAH   (*b. Waterloo, Ontario, Canada, 1878; d. Baltimore, Md., 1950*), geographer, educator. Raised near Brown City, Mich. After teaching in rural schools, and attendance at Ferris Institute and the Normal College in Ypsilanti (where he studied under M. S. W. Jefferson), he was a student and assistant of William Morris Davis at Harvard. After graduation in 1905, he taught geographical subjects at Yale in the department of geology until 1915. During this time, he made studies for the U.S. and Indiana state geological surveys, led two expeditions to South America and participated in a third, wrote a textbook, *Forest Physiography* (1911, the first thorough treatment of the landforms of the United States), and completed his Ph.D. dissertation, "The Geography of the Central Andes." Appointed director of the American Geographical Society in 1915, he improved the style and scope of its publications and threw the support of the society behind the work of geographers and explorers the world over. During World War I, he placed the institution's facilities, including its large collection of maps, at the disposal of the government. When accurate data were needed for the redrawing of European boundaries at the projected Peace Conference in Paris, the American Geographical Society became host to the "Inquiry," the body of experts assembled to prepare the materials. Bowman also served as chief territorial specialist for the U.S. delegation at the Conference, and on a number of commissions. He was author of many articles and seventeen books, including: *The New World, Problems*

in Political Geography (1921); *The Pioneer Fringe* (1931), a study of the "science of settlement"; and *Geography in Relation to the Social Sciences* (1934).

Bowman was president of Johns Hopkins University, 1935–48, lifting the institution out of debt and helping to deploy its resources for service in World War II. Personally, he served as special advisor to the secretary of state, as a member of the State Department's political and policy committee, and as chairman of its territorial committee. He was a member of the U.S. delegation to the Dumbarton Oaks Conference, and chairman of the advisors to the U.S. delegation at the San Francisco Conference in 1945. Following his retirement, he gave much of his time to the Economic Cooperation Administration.

BOWMAN, JOHN BRYAN   (*b. Mercer Co., Ky., 1824; d. 1891*), founder of Kentucky University, of which he was regent, 1865–74.

BOWMAN, THOMAS   (*b. Berwick, Pa., 1817; d. 1914*), Methodist clergyman, educator. Graduated Dickinson College, 1837. President Asbury (later DePauw) University, 1858–72; elected bishop, 1872.

BOWNE, BORDEN PARKER   (*b. Leonardville, N.J., 1847; d. 1910*), Methodist clergyman, philosopher. Headed department of philosophy, Boston University, 1876–1910; was also dean of the graduate school there. Opposed mechanistic determinism, developed philosophy of Personalism.

BOWNE, JOHN   (*b. Matlock, England, 1627/28; d. Flushing, N.Y., 1695*), Quaker leader. Came to America, 1649; settled in Flushing, 1653. His banishment for conducting meetings at his house brought establishment, 1663, of religious liberty in New Netherland.

BOYCE, JAMES PETIGRU   (*b. Charleston, S.C., 1827; d. Pau, France, 1888*), Baptist minister, educator. Active in founding Southern Baptist Theological Seminary, Greenville, S.C., 1859.

BOYD, BELLE   (*b. Martinsburg, Va., 1844; d. Kilbourne, Wis., 1900*), Confederate spy, actress. Published account of activities in *Belle Boyd in Camp and Prison* (London, 1865); lectured on her exploits.

BOYD, DAVID FRENCH   (*b. Wytheville, Va., 1834; d. Baton Rouge, La., 1899*), educator, Confederate soldier. Graduated University of Virginia, 1856. Important in development of Louisiana State University and its president, 1865–80. Dismissed for political reasons, he was recalled in 1884 but soon resigned.

BOYD, HARRIET ANN.   *See* HAWES, HARRIET ANN BOYD.

BOYD, JAMES   (*b. Harrisburg, Pa., 1888; d. Princeton, N.J., 1944*), novelist. Graduated Princeton, 1910; studied literature at Trinity College, Cambridge, and taught English and French in Harrisburg before illness forced him to give up teaching, 1914. After long convalescence, he served in the U.S. Army Ambulance Service, 1917–19. Settling after World War I on a farm near Southern Pines, N.C., he found materials in the region for much of the writing which was to occupy him thereafter. His reputation as a writer rests chiefly on a series of historical novels, distinguished by accuracy, formal grace and style, and fidelity to the psychology and manners of the periods of which they treat. They included *Drums* (1925), *Marching On* (1927), *Long Hunt* (1930), *Roll River* (1935), and *Bitter Creek* (1939).

BOYD, JOHN PARKER   (*b. Newburyport, Mass., 1764; d. 1830*), soldier. After service at end of Revolution, was in India, 1789–1808, as a mercenary. Re-entering U.S. Army, he fought at

Tippecanoe; made poor showing as brigadier general, War of 1812.

BOYD, LYNN (*b. Nashville, Tenn., 1800; d. 1859*), lawyer. Raised in Christian Co., Ky. Congressman, Democrat, from Kentucky, 1835–37; 1839–55. Speaker of the House, 1851–55. Led fight in House for passage of 1850 Compromise.

BOYD, RICHARD HENRY (*b. Noxubee Co., Miss., 1843; d. 1922*), Baptist clergyman. Leader among black Baptists in Texas. Organized National Baptist Publishing Board, 1897.

BOYD, THOMAS ALEXANDER (*b. Defiance, Ohio, 1898; d. 1935*), novelist and biographer.

BOYD, THOMAS DUCKETT (*b. Wytheville, Va., 1854; d. 1932*), Southern educator; influential president of Louisiana State University, 1896–1927.

BOYD, WILLIAM KENNETH (*b. Curryville, Mo., 1879; d. Durham, N.C., 1938*), historian. Graduated Trinity College (Duke), 1897; Ph.D., Columbia, 1906. Taught at Duke, *post* 1906. Specialist in social and economic history of the South.

BOYDEN, ROLAND WILLIAM (*b. Beverly, Mass., 1863; d. Beverly, 1931*), lawyer, statesman. Advocated "ability to pay" policy in dealing with German reparations; member of reparations commissions, and Permanent Court of Arbitration *post* World War I.

BOYDEN, SETH (*b. Foxborough, Mass., 1788; d. Hilton, N.J., 1870*), inventor, manufacturer. Brother of Uriah A. Boyden. His many inventions include the first American "patent" leather process and a process for making malleable cast iron (patented 1831). He made the first application of cut-off governing to stationary steam engines and developed the Wetherill grate for making oxide of zinc.

BOYDEN, URIAH ATHERTON (*b. Foxborough, Mass., 1804; d., Boston, Mass., 1879*), engineer, inventor. Worked for brother, Seth Boyden, and afterwards in railroad and mill construction. Self-taught, he became engineer for Amoskeag Manufacturing Co. and designed hydraulic works at Manchester, N.H.; he also designed highly efficient turbine waterwheel, 1844, for Appleton mills at Lowell, Mass., improving on design of Fourneyron. The Boyden water wheel was soon adopted in many mills and power plants.

BOYÉ, MARTIN HANS (*b. Copenhagen, Denmark, 1812; d. Coopersburg, Pa., 1909*), research chemist, physicist, geologist. Came to America, 1836. M.D., University of Pennsylvania, 1844. Associated in research with James C. Booth and others. Refined cottonseed oil, 1845.

BOYESEN, HJALMAR HJORTH (*b. Frederiksvärn, Norway, 1848; d. 1895*), author, educator. Came to America, 1869. A protégé of W. D. Howells, his novel *Gunnar* (1874) established him. Taught German at Cornell, 1874–80; at Columbia, 1881–95. A prolific writer of fiction and literary criticism.

BOYLE, JEREMIAH TILFORD (*b. Kentucky, 1818; d. 1871*), lawyer, Union soldier. Son of John Boyle. Controversial military commander of Kentucky, 1862–64; took severe measures against noncombatants suspected of favoring Confederacy.

BOYLE, JOHN (*b. near Tazewell, Va., 1774; d. near Danville, Ky., 1835*), judge. Congressman, Democratic-Republican, from Kentucky, 1803–09. Conservative, highly regarded chief justice, Kentucky court of appeals, 1810–26; later U.S. district judge for Kentucky.

BOYLE, JOHN J. (*b. New York, N.Y., 1851; d. New York, 1917*), sculptor. Studied with Thomas Eakins at Pennsylvania Academy and at the Beaux Arts, Paris. Celebrated for heroic groups, massive in design, and for masculine vigor in portraits such as his Franklin (Philadelphia) and John Barry (Washington, D.C.).

BOYLE, MICHAEL J. (*b. Woodland, Minn., 1879; d. Miami, Fla., 1958*), labor leader. Member of the International Brotherhood of Electrical Workers from 1904; served on the national executive board from 1914. "Umbrella Mike" Boyle, business agent for Local 134, was a colorful labor figure on the Chicago labor scene until his death. Twice sentenced to jail for misdoings, but emerged as a respected leader, successfully guiding his union through the Depression. He maintained the loyalty of the rank and file, whom he represented tirelessly in negotiations, always putting their interests first. He also made a fortune on his own.

BOYLE, THOMAS (*b. Marblehead, Mass., 1776[?]; d. at sea, 1825[?]*), merchant mariner. Outstanding privateer captain of War of 1812. In *Comet* and *Chasseur*, took some eighty prizes; instituted a burlesque one-ship blockade of the British Isles, 1814.

BOYLSTON, ZABDIEL (*b. Muddy River, now Brookline, Mass., 1679; d. Brookline, 1766*), physician, first to introduce practice of smallpox inoculation in America. On outbreak of smallpox in Boston, 1721, Cotton Mather, having learned of inoculation of slaves in Africa, urged the practice on Boston physicians. Boylston began inoculating in June. He and Mather were attacked physically and in the press; feeling became so intense that they wrote several pamphlets defending the practice and themselves. By the following February, Boylston had inoculated 241 persons, of whom only six died. His results were published in his *Historical Account of the Smallpox* (London, 1726), a masterly clinical presentation and the first of its kind from an American physician.

BOYNTON, CHARLES BRANDON (*b. West Stockbridge, Mass., 1806; d. Cincinnati, Ohio, 1883*), Presbyterian and Congregational clergyman. Served long pastorates at Vine Street Church, Cincinnati. Author of *A Journey Through Kansas* (1855) and other works on world politics and naval affairs.

BOYNTON, EDWARD CARLISLE (*b. Windsor, Vt., 1824; d. Newburgh, N.Y., 1893*), soldier. Graduated West Point, 1846. Author of *History of West Point*.

BOZEMAN, JOHN M. (*b. Georgia, 1835; d. at Yellowstone Crossing, Mont., 1867*), trailmaker. Opened Bozeman Trail to Virginia City, Mont. 1863–65.

BOZEMAN, NATHAN (*b. Butler Co., Ala., 1825; d. 1905*), surgeon. Improved on J. Marion Sims's method for treating vesico-vaginal fistula; introduced operation of kolpokleisis, 1859. Practiced in New York City *post* 1865.

BOZMAN, JOHN LEEDS (*b. Oxford Neck, Md., 1757; d. 1823*), lawyer. Author of *History of Maryland, from its First Settlement . . . to the Restoration* (published 1837).

BRACE, CHARLES (*b. Litchfield, Conn., 1826; d. Campfer, Switzerland, 1890*), philanthropist. Influential in founding Children's Aid Society, 1853. Pioneer in modern philanthropic methods based on self-help. Author of *The Dangerous Classes of New York* (1872) and other works.

BRACE, CHARLES LORING (*b. Hastings-on-Hudson, N.Y., 1855; d. Santa Barbara, Calif., 1938*), social welfare worker. Son of Charles L. Brace (1826–1890). Secretary, Children's Aid Society, 1890–1928.

BRACE, DEWITT BRISTOL (*b. Wilson, N.Y., 1859; d. 1905*), physicist. Graduated Boston University, 1881; Ph.D., Berlin, 1885. Headed physics department, University of Nebraska, 1888–1905. Optics specialist concerned with velocity of propagation of light; constructed Brace spectrophotometer and other devices.

BRACE, DONALD CLIFFORD (*b. West Winfield, N.Y., 1881; d. New York, N.Y., 1955*), publisher. Studied at Columbia University (B.A., 1904). Founder, with Alfred Harcourt and Will D. Howe, of Harcourt, Brace and Howe in 1919. The firm became known as Harcout Brace in 1921. Publishers of some of the century's most famous writers, including Sinclair Lewis, John Maynard Keynes, Virginia Woolf, Clive Bell, T. S. Eliot, Carl Sandburg, and Louis Untermeyer. Brace was vice president and treasurer of the company, 1919–42; president, 1942–48, chairman of the board, 1949.

BRACE, JOHN PIERCE (*b. Litchfield, Conn., 1793; d. Litchfield, 1872*), educator, author. Graduated Williams, 1812. Principal, Hartford Female Seminary, 1832–47. Editor, *Hartford Courant*, 1849–63.

BRACHVOGEL, UDO (*b. Herrengrebin, German Poland, 1835; d. New York, N.Y., 1913*), author. Came to America, 1866. Editor of several German–language journals; his *Gedichte* (Leipzig and New York, 1912) is a collection of his best poems and translations.

BRACKENRIDGE, HENRY MARIE (*b. Pittsburgh, Pa., 1786; d. near Pittsburgh, 1871*), lawyer, author. Son of Hugh H. Brackenridge. Varied career included law practice in Baltimore and elsewhere, service in Maryland legislature, extensive travel in the West and Southwest, and residence as an official in Florida, 1821–32. His pamphlet *South America: A Letter . . . to James Monroe* (1817) urged recognition of South American nations and a policy like that later defined in Monroe Doctrine; he became secretary of commission sent to study situation in South America. Among his books are *Views of Louisiana* (1814); *History of the Late War* (1816); *Voyage to South America* (1819); *Recollections of Persons and Places in the West* (1834); and *History of the Insurrection in Western Pennsylvania* (1859).

BRACKENRIDGE, HUGH HENRY (*b. near Campbeltown, Scotland, 1748; d. Carlisle, Pa., 1816*), jurist, author. Came to York Co., Pa., as small child. Graduated Princeton, 1771 (M.A., 1774). Taught school; studied divinity; wrote in support of Revolution and served as chaplain. After studying law with Samuel Chase in Annapolis, Brackenridge removed to Pittsburgh, Pa., 1781; there, he practiced, helped establish first newspaper (*Pittsburgh Gazette*, 1786), engaged in politics. An active Democratic-Republican, he served *post* 1799 as judge of the Pennsylvania supreme court. His picaresque novel *Modern Chivalry* (in parts, 1792–1815), a satire on democratic excesses, is important in American literature and the first literary work of the West. Among his other works are *The Rising Glory of America* (with Philip Freneau, 1772); *The Battle of Bunker's Hill* (1776); *The Death of General Montgomery* (1777); *Six Political Discourses* (1788); and *Law Miscellanies* (1814).

BRACKENRIDGE, WILLIAM D. (*b. Ayr, Scotland, 1810; d. Baltimore, Md., 1893*), botanist. Came to America, *ca.* 1837. Served on Wilkes's exploring expedition in Pacific, 1838–42; wrote the report on ferns (1854; Vol. XVI of the expedition's reports).

BRACKETT, ANNA CALLENDER (*b. Boston, Mass., 1836; d. 1911*), educator. First woman to head a normal school in United States (St. Louis, Mo.), *ca.* 1862; conducted girls' school in New York City, 1870–95.

BRACKETT, CHARLES WILLIAM (*b. Saratoga Springs, N.Y., 1892; d. Bel Air, Calif., 1969*), writer and motion picture director. Is best known for his fourteen-year, thirteen-film collaboration with Billy Wilder, with whom he became one of the most famous screen-writing teams in Hollywood. Beginning with *Five Graves to Cairo* (1943), they became a writing-directing-producing team; both wrote, Wilder directed, and he produced. Their two most famous films were *The Lost Weekend* (1945) and their last collaboration, *Sunset Boulevard* (1950). Continued as a writer and producer for Twentieth-Century Fox in the 1950's. Was president of the Screen Writers' Guild (1938–39) and of the Academy of Motion Picture Arts and Sciences (1949–55). Was given a special Oscar for outstanding service to the academy in 1957.

BRACKETT, EDWARD AUGUSTUS (*b. Vassalboro, Maine, 1818; d. 1908*), sculptor, pisciculturist. Chairman, Massachusetts Fish Commission; inventor of the hatching-trap presently in use.

BRACKETT, JEFFREY RICHARDSON (*b. Quincy, Mass., 1860; d. Charleston, S.C., 1949*), social work educator. A.B., Harvard, 1883; Ph.D., Johns Hopkins, 1889. As a member and officer of the Charity Organization Society of Baltimore, Md., *ca.* 1891–1904, and chairman of several city relief committees, he concluded that closer cooperation between public and private charities was needed, and that individual casework alone would not get at the roots of poverty, which were to be found in the "social economy of the time, in industrial conditions, lack of vocational training, social barriers, and public apathy." His recommendations for reform resulted in creation of a Board of Supervisors of City Charities, of which he was chairman; he was also named head of the Department of Charities and Correction. A consistent advocate of formal, professional training for social workers, he was equally insistent that such training must be based on a broad academic program. In 1904, he organized the Boston School of Social Work under joint sponsorship of Harvard University and Simmons College, which offered full–time training combining academic and field work. He served as director until retirement in 1920. He was active also as adviser to the Massachusetts Board of Public Welfare, and to other charitable and social service institutions.

BRADBURY, JAMES WARE (*b. Parsonsfield, Maine, 1802; d. 1901*), lawyer, leader among Maine Democrats. U.S. senator, 1846–52. Union supporter, he led split when Democratic state convention denounced Civil War, 1861.

BRADBURY, THEOPHILUS (*b. Newbury, Mass., 1739; d. Newburyport, Mass., 1803*), lawyer. Justice, supreme judicial court of Massachusetts, 1797–1803.

BRADBURY, WILLIAM BATCHELDER (*b. York, Maine, 1816; d. Montclair, N.J., 1868*), music teacher, piano manufacturer. Pupil of Lowell Mason; compiled over fifty singing books for church choirs.

BRADDOCK, EDWARD (*b. Scotland, 1695; d. near Great Meadows, Pa., 1755*), British general. Ensign, Coldstream Guards, 1710; rose to major general, 1754. Chosen to command all British forces in North America in campaign against French on the Ohio, Braddock landed in Virginia, February 1755. His task made more difficult by inadequate preparation in England, intercolonial jealousies, and his own disdain of provincial troops and their methods, he began operations against Fort Duquesne (present site of Pittsburgh, Pa.) by cutting a road westward from the frontier settlements in Pennsylvania, the first road across the

Alleghenies. Ambushed by French and Indians as he was nearing Fort Duquesne, July 9, 1755, Braddock lost over half his army and was himself mortally wounded, dying four days later.

BRADFORD, ALDEN (*b. Duxbury, Mass., 1765; d. 1843*), politician, editor. His *Massachusetts State Papers* (1815) and *Life of Jonathan Mayhew* (1838) are still of value for the original historical documents they contain.

BRADFORD, ALEXANDER WARFIELD (*b. Albany, N.Y., 1815; d. New York, N.Y., 1867*), lawyer. Able New York City surrogate, 1848–58. Highly successful in private practice, expert in civil and canon law.

BRADFORD, AMORY HOME (*b. Granby, N.Y., 1846; d. 1911*), Congregational minister, author. Pastor, Montclair, N.J., 1870–1911.

BRADFORD, ANDREW (*b. Pennsylvania, 1686; d. Philadelphia, Pa., 1742*), pioneer printer. Son of William Bradford (1663–1752). Issued *American Weekly Mercury*, 1719, first newspaper in Pennsylvania, third in United States; also published *American Magazine*, 1741.

BRADFORD, AUGUSTUS WILLIAMSON (*b. Bel Air, Md., 1806; d. Baltimore, Md., 1881*), lawyer. Practiced in Bel Air and Baltimore; settled permanently in Baltimore, 1838. Prominent in Whig party. Elected Unionist governor of Maryland, 1861, he strongly but unsuccessfully urged Lincoln to prevent interference by federal army in 1863 election, at which he was reelected. The state convention of 1864, which adopted constitution abolishing slavery in Maryland, was called by him.

BRADFORD, EDWARD GREEN (*b. Bohemia Manor, Md., 1819; d. Wilmington, Del., 1884*), jurist. U.S. district attorney for Delaware, 1861–66; federal district judge for Delaware, *post* 1871.

BRADFORD, EDWARD HICKLING (*b. Roxbury, Mass., 1848; d. 1926*), orthopedic surgeon. Graduated Harvard, 1869; M.D., Harvard, 1873. Associated with Boston Children's Hospital; professor and dean at Harvard Medical School. Founded first school for handicapped children in America, Boston, 1893.

BRADFORD, GAMALIEL (*b. Boston, Mass., 1831; d. Boston, 1911*), banker, publicist. Advocate of civil service and other reforms.

BRADFORD, GAMALIEL (*b. Boston, Mass., 1863; d. Wellesley Hills, Mass., 1832*), biographer, critic. Exponent of "psychographic" method of biography in *Lee the American* (1912), *A Naturalist of Souls* (1917), and others.

BRADFORD, JOHN (*b. Prince William Co., Va., 1749; d. Lexington, Ky., 1830*), pioneer printer of Kentucky. Brought out first number of *Kentucke Gazette* (spelling changed, March 1789) on Aug. 11, 1787; also issued *Kentucke Almanac*, pioneer pamphlet of the West, 1788. Published acts of first Kentucky legislature, 1792; this was the first book printed there.

BRADFORD, JOSEPH (*b. near Nashville, Tenn., 1843; d. 1886*), actor, journalist, poet, playwright. Christened William Randolph Hunter.

BRADFORD, ROARK WHITNEY WICKLIFFE (*b. Lauderdale Co., Tenn., 1896; d. New Orleans, La., 1948*), novelist, short story writer, journalist. Raised on his father's cotton plantation, he was early acquainted with the songs, stories, and general culture of the black families who worked on it. After service with the Army in World War I, he worked for newspapers in Georgia and Louisiana, but decided in 1926 to become a free-lance writer. His first

attempts to write stories dealt with black life and were successful; one of them won first prize in the O. Henry Memorial competition for 1927. A volume of stories, which were essentially adaptations of accounts from the Bible as told by blacks, appeared in 1928 as *Ol' Man Adam an' His Chillun*. A dramatic version of this work by Marc Connelly entitled *The Green Pastures* (1930), was a theatrical triumph and won a joint award of the Pulitzer Prize. Thereafter, Bradford was a widely admired and popular writer, focusing his stories and novels principally on the sentimental-comic aspects of the black experience. He died as a result of an infection contracted while serving with the U.S. Navy in World War II.

BRADFORD, THOMAS (*b. Philadelphia, Pa., 1745; d. Philadelphia, 1838*), printer and publisher. Son of William Bradford (1721/2–1791). Started *Merchants' Daily Advertiser*, Philadelphia, 1797. Financial and book pages of modern newspaper go back to innovations made by him.

BRADFORD, WILLIAM (*b. Austerfield, England, 1589/90; d. Plymouth, Mass., 1657*), Pilgrim Father. As a boy, he began to read the Bible and to attend sermons of noted nonconformist, Rev. Richard Clyfton, at Babworth. Soon he joined the group which met at William Brewster's house in Scrooby, which became a separatist church in 1606; he accompanied the group to Holland, 1609. Bradford became a tradesman and citizen of Leyden; in this period (1609–20) he must have acquired the wide theological and general knowledge to which his writings attest. He was much influenced by the liberal spirit of John Robinson and William Brewster.

Bradford took a responsible part in the preparations for moving to the New World. From the sailing of the *Speedwell* from Delfshaven (*ca.* Aug. 1, 1620), his life is inseparable from the history of the Pilgrim colony. He signed the Mayflower Compact; shared all the experiences of the landing and the settlement at Plymouth; was ill the first winter, but recovered. In April 1621, on the death of John Carver, he was elected governor of the colony.

By the time Bradford took office, the great sickness had taken 13 of the 24 heads of families, all but four of their wives, and all but six of the unattached men. The *Mayflower* had returned to England, provisions were low, and no harvest would come for four months. In like circumstances other colonies had perished. But a combination of good fortune (which Bradford attributed to the guiding hand of God), his own leadership, and the aid of men like Brewster, Winslow, and Standish, on whom he leaned, helped Plymouth to survive.

Bradford was reelected governor thirty times between 1622 and 1656. His difficulties in the early days were augmented by the presence of persons engaged as servants or attached to the colony by the London merchants who had financed the venture. Some pulled their weight, but others started factions, cheated the Pilgrims, and armed the Indians. Bradford dealt with them ably, as a Christian and as a consummate politician. When the original "merchant adventurers" or stockholders were bought out in 1627 by Bradford and the leading Pilgrims, it was decided that all in the colony should share in the land, houses, tools, and cattle acquired. This placed the colony on a sound economic basis, and assimilated the outsiders to Pilgrim ideals. When the "Warwick patent" in 1630 made Bradford proprietor of jurisdiction and soil, he at once shared his right with the "Old Comers." In all his business management, he kept in mind that the colony would not prosper unless its members had a stake in its prosperity.

In his first 15 years in office, Bradford had more plenary authority than any other English colonial governor between 1619 and 1685. Until 1636, when laws were drafted placing the government on a quasi-constitutional basis, he was principal judge and treasurer. Even after this he acted with great independence. Democracy has been read into the Pilgrim government by later historians; it is not found in the records, but Bradford's ability and discretion, both in internal matters and in relations with other colonies, maintained him in office with only one recorded incident of discontent with his rule.

Bradford began writing his *History of Plimmoth Plantation* about 1630, completing it in 1651. Probably intended to be handed down in his family, it was not printed in full until 1856, although historians had used the manuscript earlier. The work of an educated man, well versed in the Geneva version of the Bible, it tells a worthy story well, but is equally valuable for what it reflects of the simplicity and sincerity of the author's character. It has been largely responsible for giving the Pilgrims and their colony the prominent place they occupy in American history and popular tradition.

BRADFORD, WILLIAM (*b. Barnwell, England, 1663; d. New York, N.Y., 1752*), pioneer printer of the English middle colonies. Set up press in Pennsylvania, 1685. Harassed and disappointed, he went back to England, 1689. Persuaded to return by promise of greater encouragement, he became involved in the turbulence over the schism led by George Keith. His press was seized and he was arrested, but freed after jury disagreed. Made official printer to the Crown in New York, 1693, he removed there and served until retirement, 1742. Among his imprints are many public documents, including "Votes" of the assembly and collections of New York laws. Bradford printed the first New York paper currency, 1709; the first American Book of Common Prayer, 1710; the first history of New York, 1727. He also issued New York's first newspaper, *New-York Gazette*, 1725.

BRADFORD, WILLIAM (*b. New York, N.Y., 1721/2; d. Philadelphia, Pa., 1791*), "patriot-printer of 1776." Grandson of William Bradford (1663–1752); nephew of Andrew Bradford, who was his master in the trade. Began business in Philadelphia, 1742, at "The Sign of the Bible." Issued first number of *Weekly Advertiser*, 1742; widely circulated, it continued almost uninterrupted until 1793. Published *American Magazine and Monthly Chronicle*, 1757–58; also *American Magazine, or General Repository*, 1769. Opponent of the Stamp Act and early advocate of a continental congress; made printer to Congress, 1775. He fought with the Pennsylvania militia and was severely wounded at Princeton; his health and fortune suffered severely thereby.

BRADFORD, WILLIAM (*b. Philadelphia, Pa., 1755; d. 1795*), Revolutionary soldier, jurist. Son of William Bradford (1721/2–1791). U.S. attorney general, 1794–95.

BRADFORD, WILLIAM (*b. Fairhaven, Mass., 1823; d. 1892*), marine painter. His careful, realistic views of ships and coastlines from New England to the Arctic were popular here and abroad.

BRADISH, LUTHER (*b. Cummington, Mass., 1783; d. Newport, R.I., 1863*), diplomat, lawyer, statesman. U.S. agent to government of Turkey, 1820; traveled in Europe until 1826. Thereafter active as a Whig in New York State politics, and in philanthropic work.

BRADLEY, CHARLES HENRY (*b. Johnson, Vt., 1860; d. 1922*). Headed Farm and Trades School, Boston, 1888–1922. His innovations and improvements gave it a national reputation.

BRADLEY, CHARLES WILLIAM (*b. New Haven, Conn., 1807; d. New Haven, 1865*), Episcopal clergyman, diplomat, Sinologist. U.S. consul in China and Malaya, 1849–60; bequeathed library to American Oriental Society.

BRADLEY, DENIS MARY (*b. Ireland, 1846; d. 1903*), Roman Catholic clergyman. Came to America as a child. Consecrated first bishop of Manchester, N.H., 1884, and served until his death.

BRADLEY, FRANK HOWE (*b. New Haven, Conn., 1838; d. near Nacoochee, Ga., 1879*), geologist. Participated in state surveys of Illinois, Indiana, Idaho. Taught at University of Tennessee, 1869–75.

BRADLEY, FREDERICK WORTHEN (*b. Nevada Co., Calif., 1863; d. Alta, Calif., 1933*), mining engineer.

BRADLEY, JOHN EDWIN (*b. Lee, Mass., 1839; d. Randolph, Mass., 1912*), educator. Outstanding as principal, Albany, N.Y., Free Academy, 1868–86. President, Illinois College, 1892–1900. Superintendent of schools, Minneapolis, Minn., and Randolph, Mass.

BRADLEY, JOSEPH P. (*b. Berne, N.Y., 1813; d. 1892*), lawyer, Supreme Court justice. Graduated Rutgers, 1836. Admitted to New Jersey bar, 1839; specialized in patent, commercial, corporation cases. Originally a Whig, he became strong Unionist after attack on Fort Sumter. Named to U.S. Supreme Court, 1870. Influenced by John Marshall and strongly conservative, Bradley wrote many notable opinions: his concurring opinion in *Knox* v. *Lee* invokes, obviously for the first time in a Supreme Court decision, the doctrine that the national government possesses certain inherent powers; his dissent in Slaughter House Cases anticipates later interpretations of the Fourteenth Amendment. Bradley also contributed in drawing line between "exclusive" power of Congress over interstate commerce and the taxing powers of the states and made important rulings in *Boyd* v. *U.S.*, *ex parte Siebold* and *Hans* v. *Louisiana*.

BRADLEY, LYDIA MOSS (*b. Vevay, Ind., 1816; d. 1908*), philanthropist. Successful business woman, benefactor of many institutions in Peoria, Ill.; founded Bradley Polytechnic Institute.

BRADLEY, MILTON (*b. Vienna, Maine, 1836; d. 1911*), pioneer American game manufacturer. Promoted interest in kindergartens in America; published children's books and manufactured kindergarten materials.

BRADLEY, STEPHEN ROW (*b. Wallingford, Conn., 1754; d. 1830*), Revolutionary soldier, jurist. Judge of Vermont supreme court; U.S. senator, (Democrat) Republican, 1791–94 and 1801–13.

BRADLEY, WILLIAM CZAR (*b. Westminster, Vt., 1782; d. 1867*), lawyer, Son of Stephen R. Bradley. Congressman, Democrat, from Vermont, 1813–15, 1823–27. Leader of Jacksonian Democrats in Vermont, he was later a Free-Soiler and a Republican.

BRADLEY, WILLIAM O'CONNELL (*b. near Lancaster, Ky., 1847; d. Washington, D.C., 1914*), lawyer. A Republican leader in Kentucky and governor of the state, 1896–1900; U.S. senator, 1908–14.

BRADSTREET, ANNE (*b. Northampton[?], England, ca. 1612; d. N. Andover, Mass., 1672*), poet. Came to Massachusetts Bay, 1630, with Winthrop's party, which included her husband, Simon Bradstreet, and her father, Thomas Dudley. Settling at Ipswich, the Bradstreets moved to North Andover about 1644. Author of *The Tenth Muse* (London, 1650), the first book of poems by an Englishwoman in America.

BRADSTREET, JOHN (*b. Nova Scotia[?], ca. 1711; d. New York, 1774*), soldier. Served with British and colonial forces, 1735–74; distinguished at the capture of Fort Frontenac, 1758.

BRADSTREET, SIMON (*b. England, 1603; d. Salem, Mass., 1697*), colonial statesman. Came to Massachusetts, 1630; held many public offices, including secretary of the colony, assistant; was governor, 1679–86, 1689–92. Commissioner, New England Confederation, 1644–77.

BRADWELL, JAMES BOLESWORTH (*b. Loughborough, England, 1828; d. Chicago, Ill., 1907*), lawyer, jurist. Practiced in Chicago, 1855–1903; expert on probate law. Prepared *Illinois Appellate Court Reports*.

BRADWELL, MYRA (*b. Manchester, Vt., 1831; d. Chicago, Ill., 1894*), lawyer, editor. Wife of James B. Bradwell. Established *Chicago Legal News*, 1868. Fought for legislation allowing women free choice of profession; active in Suffrage movement.

BRADY, ALICE (*b. New York, N.Y., 1892; d. Hollywood, Calif., 1939*), stage and screen actress. Daughter of actor-producer William A. Brady.

BRADY, ANTHONY NICHOLAS (*b. Lille, France, 1843; d. 1913*), businessman. Came to America as a child. Raised in Troy, N.Y. Prospered as tea-store owner and general contractor, later as promoter of public utilities and municipal traction lines.

BRADY, CYRUS TOWNSEND (*b. Allegheny, Pa., 1861; d. Yonkers, N.Y., 1920*), Episcopal clergyman, novelist.

BRADY, JAMES TOPHAM (*b. New York, N.Y., 1815; d. New York, 1869*), lawyer. Leader at New York bar, *post* 1840.

BRADY, JOHN GREEN (*b. New York, N.Y., 1848; d. Sitka, Alaska, 1918*), governor of Alaska, 1897–1906. Did much to inform the American public of Alaska's resources and needs.

BRADY, MATHEW B. (*b. Warren Co., N.Y., ca. 1823; d. New York, N.Y., 1896*), photographer. Already celebrated as a daguerreotypist *post* 1842, he turned to the photographic process, 1855. Famous for his *Gallery of Illustrious Americans* (1850) and for his monumental photographic coverage of the Civil War.

BRADY, MILDRED ALICE EDIE (*b. Little Rock, Ark., 1906; d. Harrison, N.Y., 1965*), reporter, editor, and consumer advocate. With her husband, Robert Alexander Brady (m. 1956), established the Western Consumers Union in Berkeley, Calif. (1938). When the Union closed in 1940, she returned to New York City and edited the periodical *Bread and Butter* for Consumers Union. She worked as a specialist on consumer education for the Consumer Division of the Office of Price Administration in Washington, D.C. (1942–44), and in 1950 began writing and editing a column for *Consumer Reports* called "Economics for Consumers." She was editorial director of *Consumer Reports* (1958–64) when she became senior editor. During her career, she also worked as an editor, writer, and reporter for a variety of publications.

BRADY, WILLIAM ALOYSIUS (*b. San Francisco, Calif., 1863; d. New York, N.Y., 1950*), theatrical manager and producer. Raised in New York City, he worked as a newsboy and shined shoes, early abandoning school to haunt the theaters. About 1879, he returned to San Francisco, where he ran a newsstand until he was hired as call boy with Bartley Campbell's production of *The White Slave*, 1882. After some years of barnstorming in the West as an actor, he opened at the People's Theater in New York City's Bowery in his own production of Boucicault's melodrama *After Dark*, April 1889. Successful in this, he turned to sports promotion, acting as manager for prizefight champion James J. Corbett and writing *Gentleman Jack* (1892) in which the champion appeared. Co-producer with Florenz Ziegfeld of *Way Down East* (1898), Brady reaped a fortune after Ziegfeld withdrew from the undertaking; the play toured successfully for more than twenty years and was filmed by D. W. Griffith. After marriage to Grace George in 1899, he starred her in a number of plays by Sardou, Shaw, and others; he also helped many actors and actresses to stardom, including David Warfield, Douglas Fairbanks, Helen Hayes, Katharine Cornell, and his daughter (by his first wife, Marie René), Alice Brady. Among his more than 250 productions, the one to run longest on Broadway was Elmer Rice's *Street Scene* (1929).

BRAGDON, CLAUDE FAYETTE (*b. Oberlin, Ohio, 1866; d. New York, N.Y., 1946*), architect, author. Raised in New York State. Trained as a draftsman in a Rochester, N.Y., office. After some years of wandering, he achieved success as an architect in Rochester and upper New York after 1901, but rebelled at having to please the materialistic taste of his clients. An admirer of Louis Sullivan, he edited a collection of Sullivan's essays and wrote a preface to *The Autobiography of an Idea* (1924). Much of his thinking was colored by his faith in theosophy. In 1923, he gave up his architectural practice and moved to New York City where he practiced stage design, in particular for the productions of Walter Hampden.

BRAGG, BRAXTON (*b. Warrenton, N.C., 1817; d. Galveston, Tex., 1876*), Confederate soldier. Graduated West Point, 1837; distinguished in Mexican War; brevetted lieutenant colonel for extraordinary work at Buena Vista. Resigned from army, 1856; settled in Louisiana as planter; as commissioner of public works, he designed state drainage and levee systems. Commissioned Confederate brigadier general, 1861, he was effective in command of right wing on first day of Shiloh. Promoted full general, he relieved Beauregard in command of Army of Tennessee, June 1862. At Perryville and Stone River his withdrawals after initial success caused dissatisfaction, but he retained command by favor of Jefferson Davis. Victorious at Chickamauga, September 1863, he laid siege to Federals in Chattanooga but they attacked in November and forced Bragg to retreat into Georgia. He surrendered command to J. E. Johnston in December, and served in Richmond during 1864, nominally commander in chief. After the war he practiced as a civil engineer in Alabama and Texas.

BRAGG, EDWARD STUYVESANT (*b. Unadilla, N.Y., 1827; d. Fond du Lac, Wis., 1912*), Union soldier, lawyer. Removed to Wisconsin, 1850, settling at Fond du Lac. Commissioned captain in 6th Wisconsin Infantry, he rose by the end of the Civil War to brigadier general on merit alone. Congressman, Democrat, from Wisconsin, 1877–83, 1885–87; author of epigram in defense of Grover Cleveland, "We love him for the enemies he has made." A leading "Gold Democrat," *post* 1896.

BRAGG, THOMAS (*b. Warrenton, N.C., 1810; d. 1872*), lawyer, Confederate statesman. Brother of Braxton Bragg. Democratic governor of North Carolina, 1855–59; U.S. senator, 1859–61. Confederate attorney general, 1861–March 1862.

BRAINARD, DANIEL (*b. Oneida Co., N.Y., 1812; d. Chicago, Ill., 1866*), surgeon, pioneer in medical education. Settled in Chicago, 1836. Dominating figure at Rush Medical College from its founding, 1843, to his death. Author of a classic essay on treatment of fractures (1854) and other works.

BRAINARD, JOHN GARDINER CALKINS (*b. New London, Conn., 1796; d. New London, 1828*), poet. Author of *Occasional Pieces of Poetry* (1825) and *Fugitive Tales* (1830). Praised by Whittier, damned by Poe.

BRAINERD, DAVID (*b. Haddam, Conn., 1718; d. Northampton, Mass., 1747*), missionary to the Indians in western Massachusetts, New York, and New Jersey. Author of a celebrated spiritual journal, published 1746 and 1749.

BRAINERD, ERASTUS (*b. Middletown, Conn., 1855; d. Seattle, Wash., 1922*), editor. Served on newspapers in several eastern cities; removed to Seattle, 1890; edited *Seattle Post-Intelligencer*, 1904–11. Publicized Seattle as starting point for Yukon gold rushers, 1897.

BRAINERD, EZRA (*b. St. Albans, Vt., 1844; d. 1924*), botanist, geologist, educator. Worked many years on hybridism in violets. President, Middlebury College, 1885–1906.

BRAINERD, JOHN (*b. Haddam, Conn., 1720; d. Deerfield, N.J., 1781*), missionary to the Indians. Brother of David Brainerd, whose work he continued.

BRAINERD, LAWRENCE (*b. East Hartford, Conn., 1794; d. 1870*), merchant, farmer, banker in Vermont. Active in steamboat and railroad development. U.S. senator, Free-Soiler, from Vermont, 1854.

BRAINERD, THOMAS (*b. Leyden, N.Y., 1804; d. Scranton, Pa., 1866*), Presbyterian clergyman, editor. Associate of Lyman Beecher in Cincinnati, Ohio; later pastor (1837–66) at Third Church, Philadelphia. Author of *Life of John Brainerd* (1865).

BRAMLETTE, THOMAS E. (*b. Cumberland Co., Ky., 1817; d. Louisville, Ky., 1875*), lawyer, jurist. Union Democrat, governor of Kentucky, 1863–67; gradually became bitter critic of Lincoln.

BRANCH, JOHN (*b. Halifax, N.C., 1782; d. Enfield, N.C., 1863*), planter, politician. Democratic governor of North Carolina, 1817–20; strongly advocated state aid to education, abolition of imprisonment for debt, internal improvements. U.S. senator, 1823–29; secretary of navy, 1829–31, forced to resign because of involvement in Eaton affair. Elected to Congress, 1831, he retired after one term; his last public service was as governor of Florida, 1843–45.

BRANCH, LAWRENCE O'BRYAN (*b. Enfield, N.C., 1820; d. Sharpsburg, Md., 1862*), lawyer, Confederate soldier. Nephew of John Branch. Congressman, Democrat, from North Carolina, 1855–61. Killed in action.

BRAND, MAX. *See* FAUST, FREDERICK SHILLER.

BRANDEGEE, FRANK BOSWORTH (*b. New London, Conn., 1864; d. Washington, D.C., 1924*), lawyer, politician. Congressman, Republican, from Connecticut, 1902–05; U.S. senator, 1905–24. Opposed League of Nations, income tax, childlabor legislation, direct election of senators. Delighted in obstruction.

BRANDEGEE, TOWNSHEND STITH (*b. Berlin, Conn., 1843; d. Berkeley, Calif., 1925*), botanist. A pioneer collector in the West and authority on plants of California region. Author of *Plantae Mexicanae Purpusianae* (1909–24).

BRANDEIS, LOUIS DEMBITZ (*b. Louisville, Ky., 1856; d. Washington, D.C., 1941*), lawyer, jurist. Born of Jewish parents who had emigrated from what is today Czechoslovakia, subsequent to the failure of the 1848 revolutions. He first attended public schools and then spent the years 1873–75 at the Annen Realschule in Dresden. He then entered Harvard Law School. An outstanding student, he was influenced by James Bradley Thayer, whose doctrine of judicial self-restraint in the review of acts of legislatures was to be a powerful theme in Brandeis' own concept of the judicial office. He received his law degree in 1877, but spent the next year in graduate work at Harvard where he had come to know the leading academic figures through the friendship of

Nathaniel S. Shaler. After a brief interval of practice in St. Louis, Mo., he welcomed an offer of partnership in Boston with a classmate, Samuel D. Warren, Jr., and the firm of Warren and Brandeis was established in 1879. Association with Warren extended Brandeis' social and professional relationships; he served Justice Horace Gray as a part-time law clerk for two years, and made the acquaintance of Oliver Wendell Holmes, Jr. By 1890, the practice of the firm was flourishing and Brandeis was earning about $50,000 a year. He was active also on behalf of Harvard Law School, organizing a national association of alumni in 1886 and serving as its first secretary, and endowing a professorship.

Financial independence enabled Brandeis to devote himself to public causes. He was much affected by the violence of the Homestead steel strike (1892) and the writings of Henry George and Henry Demarest Lloyd, but the influence of Tractarians upon him was probably due to an innate affinity.

His diverse achievements at the bar display a striking and instinctive harmony of theme. In an early article, "The Right to Privacy," Brandeis argued that "the right to be let alone" ought to be secured against invasion except for some compelling reason of public welfare.

Brandeis helped found the Public Franchise League in Boston in 1900 and was its moving force in resisting long-term exclusive franchises for the Boston Elevated Railway Company and other public utilities. As unpaid counsel for the League and the State Board of Trade, he addressed himself to the problem of rates and service in the gas industry in Boston. He successfully urged adoption (1906) of the London sliding-scale plan, under which dividends might be increased as rates were reduced. Whether his espousal of such measures marked him as a conservative, progressive, or radical was of no moment to him, though in later years he said that he had always considered himself a conservative. He regarded as doctrinaire those proposals of reform that neglected to assess the capabilities, limitations, and accountability of men.

Brandeis regarded his plan for savings-bank insurance for the workingman as his most significant achievement. In a series of articles entitled "Breaking the Money Trust," he furnished documentation and analysis for the Progressive movement. His views were given new vitality in early New Deal legislation for the protection of investors and consumers.

In 1910 Brandeis came into sharp collision with the Taft administration, in an investigation of its practices concerning conservation of mineral lands in Alaska. A young employee in the Interior Department had appealed directly to the President and thus lost his job. Brandeis represented him. Although the President was supported by a vote of the investigations committee, on party lines, Secretary of the Interior Ballinger resigned shortly thereafter and his successor promulgated policies for the conservation of Alaskan resources substantially in accord with recommendations formulated by Brandeis. Conservation was for him only one of the great themes of the inquiry. In his closing argument he said, "We are not dealing here with a question of the conservation of natural resources merely; it is the conservation and development of the individual . . . With this great government building up, . . . the one thing we need is men in subordinate places who will think for themselves and who will think and act in full recognition of the obligations as a part of the governing body."

Brandeis' most important contribution as an advocate in constitutional litigation was what came to be known as the "Brandeis brief."

In the field of labor relations Brandeis put his emphasis on regularity of employment and a sharing of responsibility between management and workers. He opposed the closed shop as he did other forms of monopoly.

His mediation in the garment workers' strike in 1910 was one of two events that led Brandeis, in middle life, to a rediscovery of his

Jewish origins and an active dedication to Zionism. In 1914, the headquarters of the World Zionist Organization were moved to the United States and Brandeis became chairman of the operating committee. Through his friendship with President Wilson he was able to gain important support for the Balfour Declaration of 1917 and a British mandate with adequate boundaries. He visited Palestine in 1919. Following a rift between himself and Chaim Weizmann, Brandeis withdrew from any position of responsibility. His ardent support of the cause, however, did not abate, even after he became a member of the Supreme Court.

Brandeis' immersion in public causes was abetted by his wife, Alice Goldmark, his second cousin, whom he married on Mar. 23, 1891.

In politics Brandeis was an independent. He bolted the Republican party to support Cleveland in 1884, but reverted to the Republicans to vote for Taft in 1908. For a time he was an enthusiastic Progressive, but after the party split he gave his support to Woodrow Wilson in preference to Theodore Roosevelt. After Wilson's election there was reason to expect that Brandeis would be named to the cabinet as attorney general or secretary of commerce. The president-elect did make detailed inquiries to that end, but apparently was dissuaded by hostile judgments of Brandeis as a dangerous radical who would be a divisive element in the administration.

Brandeis was an influential adviser in the early years of the Wilson administration. When a sharp conflict arose within Democratic ranks in 1913 over the structure and control of the proposed Federal Reserve system, Wilson called on him for guidance. Brandeis gave strong support to the position of William Jennings Bryan and the Progressives, and the law as enacted reflected his counsel.

In 1913–14 he applied himself, with his friend George Rublee, to drafting the bill that became the Federal Trade Commission Act of 1914. On Jan. 28, 1916, Wilson nominated Brandeis for the Supreme Court. For four months there was bitter controversy over the nomination in the Senate Judiciary Committee and in the country. Brandeis himself did not appear before the committee; not until 1939 was the practice of inviting a nominee instituted. Seven former presidents of the American Bar Association urged rejection. Brandeis ascribed the opposition to the fact that he was a Jew, the first to be nominated to the Court, and to the impression that he was a radical. The nomination was confirmed by the Senate on June 1, 1916, 47 to 22.

On the court, Brandeis was generally aligned with Justice Holmes, frequently in dissent, in support of the validity of state or federal social and economic legislation. His philosophy allowed for latitude in social experimentation and judicial self-restraint. He spoke of the dangers involved when judges sought to arrest the process of experimentation, as promising for the social sciences as it was fruitful for the natural sciences. When Congress limited the President's removal power over executive appointees, as it had been exercised by President Wilson, he did not hesitate to write one of his most powerful opinions in vindication of Congress and against the chief executive who had appointed him. In a series of cases involving the duty of a state court to give full faith and credit to the judgments of other states, he took positions rejecting, literally, the claims of a widow, an orphan, and a workingman.

Those who saw Brandeis as a sentimental reformer were no less mistaken than those who regarded him as a dangerous radical. He took a restrictive view of the standing of litigants to challenge the constitutional validity of legislation and applied this canon even when a majority of the Court reached a decision on the constitutional merits that was congenial to him. Believing that the limits of capacity in even the best of men are soon reached, he distrusted centralization of governmental power equally with bigness in industry, valued the federal system as a means for the sharing of

power and responsibility, and so was disposed to sustain the authority of the states until Congress had unmistakably preempted the field.

In one area—freedom of speech, press, and assembly—Brandeis was vigilant to strike down state or federal controls unless they were justified by a clear and present danger of serious public harm. He also condemned wiretapping by federal officers in violation of state law. His dissenting views, generally, later became the law of the land.

Brandeis was an admirer of Franklin D. Roosevelt but not an uncritical enthusiast of the New Deal. He joined in the decision holding the National Industrial Recovery Act unconstitutional, but dissented from the decision overturning the Agricultural Adjustment Act. The second phase of the New Deal, directed to more far-reaching economic reform, was more congenial to him.

President Roosevelt's attempt in 1937 to enlarge the Supreme Court was a painful experience for Brandeis. Strongly as he disapproved of most of the judicial votes of the period, he was even more concerned for the independence of the judiciary. He scrupulously refrained from any public utterance on the subject and rejected an invitation from Senator Burton K. Wheeler that he approach Chief Justice Hughes. In a letter Hughes refuted charges that the Court required additional members to keep abreast of business, and stated that he had the concurrence of the two senior justices, Brandeis and Willis Van Devanter. The letter contributed importantly to the defeat of the bill.

Brandeis' distinctive eminence in the history of American law rests on an extraordinary fusion of prophetic vision, moral intensity, and grasp of practical affairs.

BRANDON, GERARD CHITTOCQUE (*b. near Natchez, Miss., 1788; d. near Fort Adams, Miss., 1850*), lawyer, planter. Governor of Mississippi, 1827–32, the first native Mississippian to hold the office.

BRANIFF, THOMAS ELMER (*b. Salina, Kans., 1883; d. near Shreveport, La., 1954*), airline executive. Founder of Braniff International, the only major airline carrying the name of an individual.

BRANN, WILLIAM COWPER (*b. Humboldt, Ill., 1855; d. Waco, Tex., 1898*), journalist, editor of the successful Waco *Iconoclast*. His career of bitter invective and wide-ranging antipathies climaxed in his death in a gun battle.

BRANNAN, JOHN MILTON (*b. near Washington, D.C., 1819; d. New York, N.Y., 1892*), Union soldier. Graduated West Point, 1841. Artillery specialist, distinguished in Mexican and Civil Wars; brevetted major general, 1865.

BRANNAN, SAMUEL (*b. Saco, Maine, 1819; d. Escondido, Calif., 1889*), California pioneer. Moved to Ohio, 1833; learned printing, visited most of states as journeyman printer. Became Mormon, 1842; published papers in New York for Mormon church. Led Mormon group from New York to California by sea, arriving July 1846, first Anglo-American settlers to arrive after California's capture by United States. Brannan was soon a leader in San Francisco. He is said to have been the first to bring news of the gold strike at Sutter's Mill to the town. He also issued the first number of the *California Star*, San Francisco's first newspaper, January 1847; served on first city council and helped organize Society of California Pioneers. The San Francisco Committee of Vigilance of 1851 was formed in his office. Investing in real estate, he became one of the wealthiest men in California, but later lost his fortune.

BRANNER, JOHN CASPER (*b. New Market, Tenn., 1850; d. Stanford, Calif., 1922*), geologist. Surveyed in Brazil, compiled geological map of that country. Professor at Stanford, 1891–1916; president, 1913–16.

BRANNON, HENRY (*b. Winchester, Va., 1837; d. 1914*), jurist. Justice, supreme court of appeals of West Virginia, 1888–1912. Had preponderant share in shaping law of state in its early days.

BRANT, JOSEPH (*b. 1742; d. 1807*), Mohawk chief. Indian name, Thayendanegea. Accompanied Sir William Johnson in campaign of 1755; in school at Lebanon, Conn., 1761–63; fought against Pontiac. Worked to bring Iroquois to aid of British in Revolution. Commissioned captain, he visited England, where he was "lionized" in society; returning to America he commanded Indian partisans, terrorizing Mohawk Valley region, directing Cherry Valley massacre, 1778. After the war, Brant induced Governor Haldimand of Canada to assign land to Mohawks. In England, 1785, he procured funds to indemnify Iroquois for losses and for purchase of new lands. Later he opposed attempts of speculators to take Mohawk lands.

BRANTLEY, THEODORE (*b. Wilson Co., Tenn., 1851; d. 1922*), jurist. Chief justice, Montana supreme court, 1898–1922. His decisions on water rights and other local issues brought about a reformed constitution and a new state system of law.

BRASHEAR, JOHN ALFRED (*b. Brownsville, Pa., 1840; d. Pittsburgh, Pa., 1920*), maker of astronomical lenses and precision instruments.

BRASLAU, SOPHIE (*b. New York, N.Y., 1892; d. New York, 1935*), operatic contralto; with Metropolitan Opera Co., 1913–20.

BRATTLE, THOMAS (*b. Boston, Mass., 1658; d. Boston, 1713*), merchant. Organized Brattle Street Church, 1698. As treasurer, Harvard College, 1693–1713, almost tripled its resources.

BRATTLE, WILLIAM (*b. Boston, Mass., 1662; d. 1716/7*), Congregational clergyman, educator. Brother of Thomas Brattle. Pastor of the church in Cambridge, Mass., *post* 1696; Harvard tutor.

BRATTON, JOHN (*b. Winnsboro, S.C., 1831; d. Winnsboro, 1898*), physician, Confederate soldier.

BRAWLEY, WILLIAM HIRAM (*b. Chester, S.C., 1841; d. Charleston, S.C., 1916*), jurist, Confederate soldier. Congressman, Democrat, from South Carolina, 1890–94; opponent of Free Silver. U.S. district judge for South Carolina, *post* 1894.

BRAXTON, CARTER (*b. Newington, Va., 1736; d. Richmond, Va., 1797*), Revolutionary statesman. Member, House of Burgesses, 1761–75; served in Revolutionary conventions, 1774–76, and in Continental Congress, 1776. Signer of the Declaration of Independence. Served as Virginia legislator, 1776–97.

BRAY, THOMAS (*b. Marton, England, 1656; d. London, England, 1729/30*), Anglican clergyman. As bishop of London's commissary for Maryland, was largely responsible for establishment of Church of England in that colony, 1696–1702. To support dissemination of books among colonial clergy and, later, clergy at home, he founded Society for Promoting Christian Knowledge (1699) and strongly promoted Society for the Propagation of the Gospel (1701). His interest in the colonies continued until his death.

BRAYMAN, MASON (*b. Buffalo, N.Y., 1813; d. Kansas City, Mo., 1895*), lawyer, editor, Union soldier. Practiced law in Illinois, *post* 1842; rose to major general in Civil War; led wandering life thereafter as journalist. Appointed territorial governor of Idaho, 1876, he served a single controversial term.

BRAYTON, CHARLES RAY (*b. Apponaug, R.I., 1840; d. Providence, R.I., 1910*), politician, Union soldier. Agent for Republican senators H. B. Anthony and N. W. Aldrich in corrupt management of state politics, *ca.* 1870–1906.

BRAZER, JOHN (*b. Worcester, Mass., 1789; d. Salem, Mass., 1846*), Unitarian clergyman. Graduated Harvard, 1813; professor of Latin there, 1817–20. Pastor, North Church, Salem, 1820–46. His thought is an anticipation of Transcendentalism and Emerson's later doctrines.

BREARLY, DAVID (*b. Spring Grove, N.J., 1745; d. 1790*), jurist. As chief justice of New Jersey supreme court, gave opinion in *Holmes* v. *Walton* (1780), in which was asserted the principle of judicial power over unconstitutional legislation.

BREASTED, JAMES HENRY (*b. Rockford, Ill., 1865; d. New York, N.Y., 1935*), Egyptologist, archaeologist, and historian. Graduated A.M., Yale, 1892; Ph.D., 1894, University of Berlin. At University of Chicago became first teacher of Egyptology in America. Published A *History of Egypt* (1905), a collation and translation of *Ancient Records of Egypt* (1906–07), and, in collaboration, many excellent textbooks. Presented a new chapter in the history of human thought in *Development of Religion and Thought in Ancient Egypt* (1912). Founded Oriental Institute, University of Chicago, 1919.

BREAUX, JOSEPH ARSENNE (*b. Iberville Parish, La., 1838; d. 1926*), jurist. Reformed Louisiana public school laws and practice, 1888; chief justice, state supreme court, 1904–14.

BRECK, GEORGE WILLIAM (*b. Washington, D.C., 1863; d. Flushing, N.Y., 1920*), mural painter. Director, American Academy of Fine Arts, Rome, 1904–09.

BRECK, JAMES LLOYD (*b. near Philadelphia, Pa., 1818; d. Benicia, Calif., 1876*), Episcopal clergyman. Missionary in Wisconsin and Minnesota, 1841–67; founder of Seabury Divinity School, Faribault, Minn.

BRECK, SAMUEL (*b. Boston, Mass., 1771; d. 1862*), merchant. Removed to Philadelphia, 1792, and took a leading social and political position there. Wrote *Recollections* (published 1877), a valuable source volume.

BRECKENRIDGE, JAMES (*b. Botetourt Co., Va. 1763; d. Botetourt Co., 1833*), Revolutionary soldier, lawyer. Congressman, Federalist, from Virginia, 1809–17; a leader of his party in that state. Brother of John Breckinridge (1760–1806).

BRECKINRIDGE, AIDA DE ACOSTA (*b. Elberon, N.J., 1884; d. Bedford, N.Y., 1962*), organization executive and philanthropist. Her career interests spanned the fields of child health, welfare, and aid to the handicapped. Her major public activity was her work in aiding the blind. After losing most of her eyesight due to glaucoma, she raised more than $5 million to establish the Wilmer Ophthalmological Institute at Johns Hopkins in 1929. In the 1940's she raised $50,000 to establish The Eye Bank for Sight Restoration, which was incorporated in 1945, and served as executive director during the first ten years of the Eye Bank's operation. She received the Migel Medal, the highest award of the American Foundation for the Blind, in 1956.

BRECKINRIDGE, DESHA (*b. Lexington, Ky., 1867; d. Lexington, 1935*), editor, publisher, civic leader, horseman. Under his management the *Lexington Herald* earned a national reputation.

BRECKINRIDGE, HENRY SKILLMAN (*b. Chicago, Ill., 1886; d. New York, N.Y., 1960*), lawyer and government official. Studied at Princeton (B.A., 1907) and Harvard Law School (LL.B., 1910). Assistant secretary of war under Woodrow Wilson, 1913–16. An advocate of American preparedness for war, Breckinridge resigned because of Wilson's reluctance to build up the nation's defenses. In 1936, he opposed Franklin D. Roosevelt in the primaries. Championed American intervention on behalf of European allies.

BRECKINRDIGE, JOHN (*b. near Staunton, Va., 1760; d. near Lexington, Ky., 1806*), lawyer, statesman. Brother of James Breckenridge. Moved to Kentucky, 1792. Served as state attorney general, 1795–96; in state legislature, 1797–1801 (speaker, in second term); in U.S. Senate, 1801–05. Appointed U.S. attorney general, 1805. An outstanding Democratic-Republican spokesman for the new West, he assisted Jefferson on the Kentucky Resolutions, 1798, reformed Kentucky penal code, and was influential in formation of the state's second constitution.

BRECKINRIDGE, JOHN (*b. near Lexington, Ky., 1797; d. near Lexington, 1841*), Presbyterian clergyman. Son of John Breckinridge (1760–1806). Graduated Princeton, 1818; Princeton Seminary, 1820–21; ordained 1823. An aggressive champion of the Old School theology, he engaged Rev. John Hughes in public debate, 1833 and 1835–36, on the issue of Protestantism *vs.* Catholicism.

BRECKINRIDGE, JOHN CABELL (*b. near Lexington, Ky., 1821; d. Lexington, 1875*), statesman, soldier. Grandson of John Breckinridge (1760–1806). Graduated Centre College, 1839; continued studies at College of New Jersey and Transylvania College. Practiced law at Lexington beginning 1845; served briefly in war with Mexico. Entered state legislature, 1849; won election as congressman, 1851, Democrat, from one of Henry Clay's strongest Whig districts, and was reelected, 1853. Established as one of the most popular men in his section, he was nominated for vice presidency, 1856; served ably with Buchanan. When Southern delegates quit Democratic convention at Charleston, 1860, and held own convention at Baltimore, Breckinridge was nominated by them for the presidency on a platform reaffirming extreme Southern view of slavery; during campaign that followed he defended himself against charge of encouraging disunion, received 72 electoral votes at the election but did not carry his own state. As vice president during rest of term, he advocated Crittenden Compromise; in his view, the Constitution did not give the federal government power to coerce any state. He returned to Kentucky after Lincoln's inauguration; when that state abandoned its first position of neutrality and welcomed Union troops he fled to escape arrest and joined army of the Confederacy.

Despite lack of experience, he served ably at battles of Shiloh, Vicksburg, Baton Rouge, Port Hudson, and Murfreesboro, rising to divisional command and the rank of major general. In May 1863, attached to General J. E. Johnston's army, he was present at battle of Jackson, Miss.; later, he commanded a division of the Army of Tennessee at Chickamauga and Missionary Ridge. Called by Lee to the Shenandoah valley, he then commanded a division at Cold Harbor and participated in the raids on Washington, D.C., July 1864; he was appointed Confederate secretary of war, Feb. 1865.

After Lee's surrender he fled the country, remaining in Europe and Canada until permitted to return to Lexington, 1869, where he resumed his law practice and took a prominent part in the development of railroads in his state.

BRECKINRIDGE, ROBERT JEFFERSON (*b. near Lexington, Ky., 1800; d. Danville, Ky., 1871*), lawyer, Presbyterian clergyman. Son of John Breckinridge (1760–1806). Chiefly responsible for the "Act and Testimony" of 1834 that led to split of "Old" and "New" Schools in Presbyterianism; reformer of state public schools, 1847–51; professor at Danville Theological Seminary, 1851–69; bitter opponent of slavery, Catholicism, Universalism.

BRECKINRIDGE, SOPHONISBA PRESTON (*b. Lexington, Ky., 1866; d. Chicago, Ill., 1948*), social worker. Daughter of William C. P. Breckinridge. Graduated Wellesley, 1888; admitted to Kentucky bar, 1895; Ph.D., University of Chicago, 1901; J.D., University of Chicago Law School, 1904. Taught political science at University of Chicago; worked part-time at Hull House, 1907–21; began to teach at Chicago School of Civics and Philanthropy, 1907. She became dean of the school and director of research, and in 1920 was responsible for its incorporation into the University of Chicago as the Graduate School of Social Service Administration. With Edith Abbott, she made the school one of the nation's leading institutions, retiring in 1942. She was coauthor of *The Delinquent Child and the Home* (1912), *Truancy and Non–Attendance in the Chicago Schools* (1917), and *The Tenements of Chicago* (1936). Her lifelong concern with the role of women in American society was reflected in articles and in *Marriage and the Civic Rights of Women* (1931) and *Women in the Twentieth Century* (1933). Pursuit of her research drew her into participation in many reform movements. In 1912, she helped draft the platform of the Progressive party. She was author also of books on housing, public welfare administration, and the family and the state.

BRECKINRIDGE, WILLIAM CAMPBELL PRESTON (*b. Baltimore, Md., 1837; d. Lexington, Ky., 1904*), lawyer, editor. Son of Robert J. Breckinridge. Served with Confederate forces, 1862–65. Editor, *Lexington Observer and Reporter*, 1866–68; chief editorial writer, *Lexington Morning Herald*, 1897–1904.

BREED, EBENEZER (*b. Lynn, Mass., 1766; d. Lynn, 1839*), wholesale shoe merchant. Instrumental in passage of tariff act, 1789, which protected domestic shoe manufacturers.

BREEN, JOSEPH IGNATIUS (*b. Philadelphia, Pa., 1890; d. Hollywood, Calif., 1965*), Hollywood film censor. As head of the Production Code Administration (1934–54), he implemented and enforced the 1930 production code, which was largely a response to a drive by Roman Catholics for higher moral standards in movies than those resulting from the less stringent, less strictly enforced code exercised by Will Hays in the 1920's. In this capacity he censored some political material and watched out for religioethnic stereotyping but concerned himself mainly with sex and obscenity and required producers to receive the Breen "Purity Seal" before releasing their films. He received a special Oscar from the Motion Picture Academy in 1953.

BREEN, PATRICK (*b. Ireland; d. San Juan Bautista, Calif., 1868*), diarist of the ill-fated Donner party of California emigrants (1846).

BREESE, KIDDER RANDOLPH (*b. Philadelphia, Pa., 1831; d. 1881*), naval officer. Fleet captain under Adm. D. D. Porter, 1864–65; commandant of midshipmen, U.S. Naval Academy, 1873.

BREESE, SIDNEY (*b. Whitesboro, N.Y., 1800; d. 1878*), jurist, politician. Graduated Union College, 1818. Removed to Kaskaskia, Ill.; was admitted to bar, 1820; became active Democratic politician; served as U.S. senator from Illinois, 1843–49. Elected justice of state supreme court, 1857, he served with great ability until his death. His most famous decision was in the case of *Munn* v. *Illinois* (1876), when he upheld the doctrine of the regulative power of the state over corporations in whose business the public interest is involved.

BRENNAN, FRANCIS JAMES (*b. Shenandoah, Pa., 1894; d. Philadelphia, Pa., 1968*), Roman Catholic canon lawyer, jurist, and cardinal. D.D. (1920), Pontifical Roman Seminary; received doctorate in civil and canon law (1924), Juridical Seminary of St. Apollinare in Rome. In 1940 became the first American appointed an auditor (judge) of the Rota, the Vatican court of appeals from diocesan tribunals. In 1967 was nominated to the College of Cardinals, and thereafter worked in the Curia, the collective title given to the administrative, judicial, and legislative bodies that govern the Roman Catholic church. Rose higher in the ranks of the Roman Curia than any American before him.

BRENNEMANN, JOSEPH (*b. near Peru, Ill., 1872; d. Reading, Vt., 1944*), pediatrician. Ph.B., University of Michigan, 1895; M.D., Northwestern, 1900. In general practice on the South Side of Chicago until 1910. After a year's postgraduate study in Germany and Austria, he specialized in pediatrics, serving on dispensary and hospital staffs and teaching that subject at Northwestern, the University of Chicago, and the University of Southern California. Author of a major contribution to the subject of rheumatism and rheumatic heart disease in children (1914) and editor of *The Practice of Pediatrics* (1936).

BRENNER, VICTOR DAVID (*b. Shavli, Russia, 1871; d. New York, N.Y., 1924*), sculptor, medalist. Designer of the Lincoln cent (1909).

BRENON, HERBERT (*b. Dublin, Ireland, 1880; d. Los Angeles, Calif., 1958*), motion picture producer and director. Studied at the University of London. Immigrated to the U.S. in 1896. One of the leading directors of silent films. Brenon began his cinema career in 1909 with Carl Laemmle; his first major film was *Neptune's Daughter* (1914), starring Annette Kellerman. Brenon's films made for William Fox include *The Two Orphans* (1915), starring Theda Bara, and *A Daughter of the Gods*, with Kellerman. Between 1923 and 1927, he directed for Famous Players-Lasky. Films included *Peter Pan* (1924) and *A Kiss for Cinderella* (1925), by James M. Barrie, and *Beau Geste*, starring Ronald Colman. His sound films included *The Lummox* (1930), *The Girl of the Rio* (1932), and *The Flying Squad* (1940), his last film. Frequently grouped with DeMille and Griffith as the "Big Three" during the silent era.

BRENT, CHARLES HENRY (*b. Newcastle, Ontario, Canada, 1862; d. Lausanne, Switzerland, 1929*), Protestant Episcopal clergyman. Graduated Trinity College, Toronto, 1884; was ordained priest in 1887. In 1901 elected first Episcopal missionary bishop to the Philippines, he began a lifelong battle against the opium trade. When the United States entered World War I, he went to France as a chaplain of the Young Men's Christian Association and was soon made chaplain at general headquarters by General Pershing. His greatest work was done after the war in the field of Christian unity.

BRENT, MARGARET (*b. Gloucester, England, 1600; d. 1670/ 71*), America's first feminist. Migrated to St. Mary's, Md., with sister and two brothers, 1638. Family relationships and political affiliations secured to them large land grants and high offices. The first woman of Maryland to hold land in her own right, she aided Governor Calvert in suppressing the Claiborne Rebellion, 1646. In 1648, she appealed to Assembly for two votes in their proceedings, one for herself as landowner and the other as attorney for Lord Baltimore. On denial of her plea, in resentment she moved to Virginia, 1650.

BRENTANO, LORENZ (*b. Mannheim, Germany, 1813; d. Chicago, Ill., 1891*), statesman, journalist. Immigrated to America, 1850. Developed *Illinois Staatszeitung* into influential Chicago daily and leading German Republican paper in Northwest.

BRERETON, JOHN. *See* BRIERTON, JOHN.

BRERETON, LEWIS HYDE (*b. Pittsburgh, Pa., 1890; d. Washington, D.C., 1967*), military aviator. After graduating from the U.S. Naval Academy (1911), transferred to the aviation section of the army. An energetic and generally successful army air leader during both world wars, he was almost unique in commanding air power in all three theaters of World War II, an experience he recorded in *The Brereton Diaries* (1946). As commander of the Far Eastern Air Force under General Douglas MacArthur at Manila, is considered partially to blame for the destruction of B-17 bombers by Japanese planes at Clark Field. Commanded the U.S. Middle East Air Force, soon redesignated the Ninth Air Force, and then all U.S. Army forces in the Middle East; his greatest achievement was the great bombing raid on the Axis oil refineries at Ploesti, Romania. Continued to head the Ninth Air Force in the European Theater of Operations, and in 1944 assumed command of the First Allied Airborne Army. Retired at the rank of lieutenant general in 1948.

BRETT, GEORGE PLATT (*b. London, England, 1858; d. Fairfield, Conn., 1936*), publisher. Came to America, 1869. President, Macmillan Co. (1896–1931).

BRETT, WILLIAM HOWARD (*b. Braceville, Ohio, 1846; d. 1918*), librarian. Built Cleveland Public Library into great city-wide system, 1884–1918. Organized (1894) and headed Library School of Western Reserve University.

BREVOORT, JAMES RENWICK (*b. Yonkers, N.Y., 1832; d. Yonkers, 1918*), landscape painter.

BREWER, CHARLES (*b. Boston, Mass., 1804; d. Jamaica Plain, Mass., 1885*), sea captain, merchant. Headed prosperous Honolulu trading firm, C. Brewer & Co.

BREWER, DAVID JOSIAH (*b. Smyrna, Asia Minor, 1837; d. Washington, D.C., 1910*), jurist. Graduated Yale, 1856; read law with uncle, David Dudley Field, and graduated Albany Law School, 1858. Resided Leavenworth, Kans., 1858–90, serving as justice of state supreme court, 1870–84. Named federal justice for 8th circuit, 1884, he was appointed in 1889 to the U.S. Supreme Court by President Harrison, serving until death. A moderate conservative, he resisted the drift toward federal centralization of power and was stern in defense of personal liberty and property rights. In 1895–97 he was president of commission appointed by Congress to investigate Venezuela–British Guiana boundary dispute.

BREWER, MARK SPENCER (*b. Oakland Co., Mich., 1837; d. Washington, D.C., 1901*), Congressman, Republican, from Michigan, 1876–80; 1887–91; member of Civil Service Commission, 1898–1901.

BREWER, THOMAS MAYO (*b. Boston, Mass., 1814; d. 1880*), ornithologist, oölogist. Author of *North American Oölogy* (1857), and of biographies in Baird, Brewer, and Ridgway's *History of North American Birds* (1875).

BREWER, WILLIAM HENRY (*b. Poughkeepsie, N.Y., 1828; d. 1910*), botanist, geologist, agriculturist. Assisted J. D. Whitney in geological survey of California, 1860–64; established first American agricultural experiment station. Professor of agriculture, Sheffield Scientific School, Yale, 1864–1903.

BREWSTER, BENJAMIN HARRIS (*b. Salem Co., N.J., 1816; d. Philadelphia, Pa., 1888*), attorney general of the United States. Prosecuted Star Route frauds in Post Office Department, 1881–84.

BREWSTER, FREDERICK CARROLL (*b. Philadelphia, Pa., 1825; d. Salisbury, N.C., 1898*), lawyer, jurist. Brother of Benjamin H. Brewster. A leader of the Pennsylvania bar.

BREWSTER, JAMES (*b. Preston, Conn., 1788; d. New Haven, Conn., 1866*), carriage-builder, railway-promoter, philanthropist. Developed the "Brewster wagon" and set a new standard for American vehicles of all types.

BREWSTER, OSMYN (*b. Worthington, Mass., 1797; d. 1889*), printer. Partner in Crocker & Brewster, publishers of religious books, 1825–76.

BREWSTER, RALPH OWEN (*b. Dexter, Maine, 1888; d. Brookline, Mass., 1961*), lawyer, governor of Maine, and U.S. senator. After serving as a Republican in the Maine legislature, he was elected governor of Maine in 1924 and 1926. Served in the U.S. House of Representatives (1934–40) and in the U.S. Senate (1940–52). He opposed most of Franklin D. Roosevelt's New Deal, particularly the Supreme Court "packing" plan and the bill to abolish public-utility holding companies. Was a member of the Senate Naval Affairs Committee, was named to the War Investigating Committee during World War II, and in 1946 served on the Joint Congressional Committee of Inquiry formed to investigate the attack on Pearl Harbor.

BREWSTER, WILLIAM (*b. England, 1567; d. Plymouth, Mass., 1644*), Pilgrim Father, Elder of the church at Plymouth. Spent his childhood in Scrooby, Nottinghamshire, where his father was bailiff and postmaster; attended Peterhouse, Cambridge, for a brief period where he first acquired Separatist ideas. A trusted aid in the foreign service, 1583–89, he returned to Scrooby and assumed father's positions, 1589. Became leading member of Puritan group at Scrooby, immigrating with them to Holland, 1608, and moving with them to Leyden, 1609, where he became elder and teacher of the new church and a printer of Puritan books. Served as principal agent in 1617 negotiations with Virginia Company over a land grant and permission to colonize; thereafter took a minor part in settling details of immigration. Sailed aboard *Mayflower*, 1620. Although not "called" as a minister, he was the real religious leader in Plymouth colony and was second only to Bradford in administrative decisions.

BREWSTER, WILLIAM (*b. Wakefield, Mass., 1851; d. 1919*), ornithologist. His collection of North American birds (now in Museum of Comparative Zoology, Cambridge, Mass.) was the finest of its time.

BRICE, CALVIN STEWART (*b. Denmark, Ohio, 1845; d. New York, N.Y., 1898*), railroad builder, lawyer. Graduated Miami University, 1863; rose to rank of lieutenant colonel in Civil War. Gained distinction as corporation lawyer. In 1870 became projector and manager of railroad enterprises, outlining plan for a road to link Toledo and Ohio coal fields. President of Lake Erie and Western RR. *post* 1887; active in many other American railroads, as well as a project for exclusive right of way between Canton and Hankow in China. National Democratic chairman, 1889; U.S. senator from Ohio, 1891–96.

BRICE, FANNY (*b. New York, N.Y., 1891; d. Beverly Hills, Calif., 1951*), comedienne and singer. Brice achieved fame in Florenz Ziegfeld's *Follies of 1910*, and was featured in seven *Follies* from 1910 to 1923, and again in 1934. After many vaudeville tours, plays, and movies, she began her radio series,

Baby Snooks, with CBS in 1944. Brice was the inspiration for the Broadway musical *Funny Girl* in 1964, which was filmed in 1968.

BRICKELL, HENRY HERSCHEL (*b. Senatobia, Miss., 1889; d. Branchville, Conn., 1952*), editor and writer. Studied at the University of Mississippi. Editor for Henry Holt and Co. (1928–33) and for Doubleday, Doran and Co. (1940) in New York. At Doubleday, he assumed the editorship of the annual O. Henry Memorial Award Prize Stories. During the 1930's and 1940's, he was a leading literary critic and reviewer for major newspapers and magazines. Brickell also translated many works from Spanish to English, and English to Spanish. In 1941, he was appointed to the Foreign Service Auxiliary in Bogotá, Columbia, where he established one of the first U.S. cultural centers. In 1946, he was chief of the Division of International Exchange of Persons.

BRICKELL, ROBERT COMAN (*b. Tuscumbia, Ala., 1824; d. Huntsville, Ala., 1900*), jurist. Chief justice, Alabama supreme court, 1874–84.

BRIDGER, JAMES (*b. Richmond, Va., 1804; d. near Kansas City, Mo., 1881*), fur trader, frontiersman, scout. Removed with family to St. Louis, Mo., about 1812; orphaned at age 13; in 1822 joined Ashley's fur-trapping venture to the sources of Missouri River. Connected with northwest fur companies, 1822–42; first white man to visit Great Salt Lake, 1824. Established Fort Bridger, a way station in southwestern Wyoming, 1843; was a friend of notable figures in westward movement. Driven out by Mormons, 1853, he returned as guide to General A. S. Johnston's Utah invasion, 1857–58. Served also as guide to Raynolds Yellowstone expedition, 1859–60, Berthoud's engineering party, 1861, and Powder River expeditions, 1865–66; retired 1868.

BRIDGERS, ROBERT RUFUS (*b. Edgecombe Co., N.C., 1819; d. Columbia, S.C., 1888*), Confederate congressman, industrialist. President, Wilmington & Weldon and Columbia & Augusta railroads, 1865–88.

BRIDGES, CALVIN BLACKMAN (*b. Schuyler Falls, N.Y., 1889; d. Los Angeles, Calif., 1938*), geneticist. Graduated Columbia University, B.S., 1912, Ph.D., 1916, where he worked, 1910–28, with the zoologist Thomas Hunt Morgan. With Morgan, A. H. Sturtevant and H. J. Muller, Bridges did pioneering studies of the genetics of the fruit fly *Drosophila*. Bridges' researches were especially concerned with proving the chromosome theory of heredity, and culminated in the formulation of the theory of "genic balance." Moving with Morgan to the California Institute of Technology in 1928, Bridges' later work was notable for investigations of the giant chromosomes in larval salivary glands, affording a new approach to the study of gene mutations.

BRIDGES, (HENRY) STYLES (*b. West Pembroke, Maine, 1898; d. Concord, N.H., 1961*), governor of New Hampshire and U.S. senator. A Republican, he was elected governor of New Hampshire in 1934, at thirty-six the youngest chief executive in the history of New Hampshire and the youngest in the nation at that time. Served in the U.S. Senate from 1936 until his death. During the long years of Democratic control of the Congress, he consistently criticized Democratic acts and administration policies and was consistently anti–New Deal, anti–Communist, and fiscally and politically conservative.

BRIDGES, ROBERT (*d. 1656*), magistrate of Lynn, Mass. Instrumental in establishment of Saugus Iron Works, 1643, first in the colonies.

BRIDGES, ROBERT (*b. Philadelphia, Pa., 1806; d. 1882*), physician, botanist. Professor of chemistry, Philadelphia College of Pharmacy, 1842–79.

BRIDGES, THOMAS JEFFERSON DAVIS ("TOMMY") (*b. Gordonsville, Tenn., 1906; d. Nashville, Tenn., 1968*), major-league baseball pitcher. A right-handed pitcher and batter, he spent his entire major-league career with the Detroit Tigers (1930–46), winning 194 games, including 33 shutouts, and losing 138. His career earned-run average was 3.57. The sharp-breaking curve became his forte, but he also had a very good fastball. He led the American League in strikeouts in 1935 (163), and in 1936 in both strikeouts (175) and victories (23). He pitched in four World Series (1934, 1935, 1940, and 1945). Was selected for the all-star game for a number of years and was credited with winning the 1939 game. After his release from the Tigers, pitched in the minor-league for Portland, Seattle, and San Francisco (1946–50), worked as a coach for the Toledo Mud Hens (1951), and as a scout for the Tigers (1958–60) and the New York Mets (1963–68).

BRIDGMAN, ELIJAH COLEMAN (*b. Belchertown, Mass., 1801; d. China, 1861*). Missionary to China for the American Board, 1830–61. Edited *Chinese Repository,* 1832–47. Published *Chinese Chrestomathy* (1841), a practical manual of the Cantonese dialect.

BRIDGMAN, FREDERIC ARTHUR (*b. Tuskegee, Ala., 1847; d. Rouen, France, 1927*), painter. Pupil of Gérôme; painted oriental and archaeological subjects.

BRIDGMAN, HERBERT LAWRENCE (*b. Amherst, Mass., 1844; d. 1924*), newspaper publisher, explorer.

BRIDGMAN, LAURA DEWEY (*b. Hanover, N.H., 1829; d. Boston, Mass., 1889*), pupil of S. G. Howe at Perkins Institution, 1837; the first blind deaf-mute to be systematically educated.

BRIDGMAN, PERCY WILLIAMS (*b. Cambridge, Mass., 1882; d. Randolph, N.H., 1961*), physicist and philosopher of science. B.A. (1904), M.A. (1905), and Ph.D. (1908), Harvard. Taught at Harvard, 1910–54. Improved methods of measuring high pressures, making it possible to subject test materials to much higher pressures than had previously been possible and thus breaking new ground in the study of mechanical, electrical, and thermal properties of materials under high pressure. He also evolved the influential "operational" perspective on science, particularly physics, in which he attempted to eradicate meaningless concepts that might be inhibiting the growth of science by insisting that all physical and mental concepts be definable in terms of actual, explicit operations. Wrote *The Physics of High Pressure* (1931), *The Logic of Modern Physics* (1927), and *The Intelligent Individual and Society* (1938). Received the 1946 Nobel Prize for physics.

BRIERTON, JOHN (*b. Norwich, England, 1572; d. post 1619*), author of *A Briefe and True Relation of the Discoverie of the North Part of Virginia* (1602), the earliest English work about New England.

BRIGGS, CHARLES AUGUSTUS (*b. New York, N.Y., 1841; d. New York, 1913*), Presbyterian, later Episcopal, clergyman. Professor at Union Theological Seminary, 1874–1913. Tried for heresy, 1892, because of views on Biblical criticism. Edited *International Critical Commentary, International Theological Library.*

BRIGGS, CHARLES FREDERICK (*b. Nantucket, Mass., 1804; d. Brooklyn, N.Y., 1877*), journalist. Founded *Broadway Journal,* 1844; an editor, *Putnam's Magazine,* the *New York Times,* and *The Independent;* author of *The Adventures of Harry Franco* (1839) and other books.

BRIGGS, CLARE A. (*b. Reedsburg, Wis., 1875; d. New York, N.Y., 1930*), graphic humorist whose versatile output included "Mr. and Mrs." and "When a Feller Needs a Friend."

BRIGGS, GEORGE NIXON (*b. Adams, Mass., 1796; d. 1861*), lawyer, statesman. Congressman, Whig, from Massachusetts, 1831–43; governor of Massachusetts, 1844–51; a consistent opponent of slavery.

BRIGGS, LEBARON RUSSELL (*b. Salem, Mass., 1855; d. Milwaukee, Wis., 1934*), educator. Professor and dean, Harvard University, 1878–1925; president, Radcliffe College, 1903–23. Author of *School, College, and Character* (1901) and *Routine and Ideals* (1904).

BRIGGS, LLOYD VERNON (*b. Boston, Mass., 1863; d. Tucson, Ariz., 1941*), psychiatrist. Briggs passed the entrance examinations for Harvard Medical School at age fifteen. Refused admission because of his youth, he was allowed to attend lectures through influence of Henry I. Bowditch. Ill health delayed his M.D. (Medical College of Virginia) until 1899. After practicing psychiatry in Boston, and a year's study abroad under Kraepelin and Carl Jung, he devoted himself after 1906 to improving the treatment of the insane and the delinquent. Before and after his appointment as secretary to the Massachusetts State Board of Insanity, he was responsible for broad reforms in the management and supervision of institutions, and for creation of a state department of mental health. He also sponsored a state law, passed in 1921, which required a psychological evaluation before trial of persons indicted for capital crimes. In U.S. Army service during World War I, he established neuropsychiatric services for victims of shell shock. In his last published work, argued against capital punishment as a deterrent to crime.

BRIGGS, LYMAN JAMES (*b. Assyria, Mich., 1874; d. Washington, D.C., 1963*), physicist. Ph.D. (1901), Johns Hopkins. Worked for the U.S. Department of Agriculture (1896–1920), where he established the science of soil physics. After 1920 he was chief of the Mechanics and Sound Division of the National Bureau of Standards, where he and Paul Heyl invented the earth inductor compass and he and Hugh L. Dryden made pioneer measurements of flow around airfoils. Served as director of the Bureau from 1932 until the end of World War II. In 1939 he became chair of the first government committee to investigate possible military use of atomic energy, and in 1948 was awarded the Medal of Merit for his work relating to atomic fission.

BRIGHAM, ALBERT PERRY (*b. Perry, N.Y., 1855; d. 1932*), geographer, university professor. Made notable contributions to the geographic interpretation of history; active in Association of American Geographers.

BRIGHAM, AMARIAH (*b. New Marlboro, Mass., 1798; d. 1849*), physician. Founded *American Journal of Insanity,* 1844; wrote on mental health.

BRIGHAM, JOSEPH HENRY (*b. Lodi, Ohio, 1838; d. 1904*), agriculturist. Master, National Grange, for four terms from 1889.

BRIGHAM, MARY ANN (*b. Westboro, Mass., 1829; d. 1889*), educator. Associate principal, Brooklyn Heights Seminary, 1863–89; chosen first president of Mount Holyoke College, but died before taking office.

BRIGHT, EDWARD (*b. Kingston, England, 1808; d. 1894*). Immigrated as a child to Utica, N.Y. Editor of the *Examiner,* leading Baptist newspaper, *post* 1855.

BRIGHT, JAMES WILSON (*b. Aaronsburg, Pa., 1852; d. 1926*), philologist. Professor of English, Johns Hopkins, 1893–1925. Editor, *Modern Language Notes*, 1886–1915; editor in chief, 1916–25.

BRIGHT, JESSE DAVID (*b. Norwich, N.Y., 1812; d. Baltimore, Md., 1875*), politician. Led pro-slavery wing of Indiana Democratic party; U.S. senator from Indiana, 1845–62. Expelled from Senate, 1862, for treason.

BRIGHT EYES (*b. Omaha Reservation, Nebr., 1854; d. near Bancroft, Nebr., 1903*), advocate of Indian rights. Named Susette La Flesche; made protest tour in East, 1879, against arbitrary removals of tribes.

BRIGHTLY, FREDERICK CHARLES (*b. Bungay, England, 1812; d. Germantown, Pa., 1888*), lawyer. Immigrated to America, 1831; author of valuable digests of early laws.

BRIGHTMAN, EDGAR SHEFFIELD (*b. Holbrook, Mass., 1884; d. Newton, Mass., 1953*), philosopher and educator. Studied at Brown University (B.A., 1906; M.A., 1908), Boston University School of Theology (S.T.B., 1910), Boston University (Ph.D., 1912). He also studied at the universities of Marburg and Berlin. Taught at Boston, 1919; chairman of the philosophy department, 1925. He published fourteen books, including *Religious Values* (1925), *The Problem of God* (1930), and *Moral Laws* (1933). Although a strong Methodist, his approach to religious issues was philosophical. An inspiring teacher, he greatly influenced many of his students, including Martin Luther King, Jr.

BRILL, ABRAHAM ARDEN (*b. Kanczuga, Galicia, Austria-Hungary, 1874; d. New York, N.Y., 1948*), psychoanalyst. Immigrated to New York City at age fifteen; worked in clothing trade. Attended public schools and City College of New York; Ph.B., New York University, 1901; M.D., College of Physicians and Surgeons, Columbia University; 1903. Began practice of psychiatry at N.Y. State Hospital, Central Islip. Going abroad for further study (1907–08), he discovered his lifework in the hospital at Zurich where Freud's theories were being tested. He visited Freud in Vienna, and returned to New York with permission to translate a work by Carl Jung and all of Freud's works. Became the first practicing psychoanalyst in America. By his articles, translations, and personal proselytizing, he carried the Freudian message to the American medical profession and public and was in great part responsible for its acceptance and success. On the other hand, he tended to oversimplify in his writing and sometimes to mistranslate; also, his preoccupation with the grossly sexual and his insensitivity to intellectual subtleties gave much of American psychoanalysis both a sensational and simplistic tendency for some years.

BRILL, NATHAN EDWIN (*b. New York, N.Y., 1859; d. New York, 1925*), physician. Attending physician, Mt. Sinai Hospital, 1893–1923; outstanding diagnostician and clinician.

BRINCKLÉ, WILLIAM DRAPER (*b. St. Jones' Neck, Del., 1798; d. Groveville, N.J., 1862*), physician, pomologist.

BRINKERHOFF, JACOB (*b. Niles, N.Y., 1810; d. 1880*), jurist, legislator. Congressman, Democrat, from Ohio, 1843–47; became Free-Soiler and Republican. Justice, Ohio supreme court, 1856–71. Claimed authorship of Wilmot Proviso.

BRINKERHOFF, ROELIFF (*b. Cayuga Co., N.Y., 1828; d. Mansfield, Ohio, 1911*), lawyer, penologist.

BRINKLEY, JOHN RICHARD (*b. Jackson Co., N.C., 1885; d. San Antonio, Tex., 1942*), medical charlatan. Orphaned at age ten, he had a haphazard elementary school education; between 1908 and 1913, he worked in various Southern towns as a railroad telegraph operator, and attended an eclectic medical school in Chicago without completing the course. On the strength of credentials from a "diploma mill" in Kansas City, he was licensed to practice in Arkansas (1913–16), and through reciprocal agreements then in effect obtained licensure in several other states. Settling in Milford, Kans., he began (in 1917) to practice a sexual rejuvenation therapy through transplant of goat glands. Financially successful, he founded in 1923 the first radio broadcasting station in Kansas, KFKB, as a means of advertising his business; he diagnosed the ailments of listeners (developing a thriving trade in mail-order drugs) between programs of country music, fundamentalist theology, market news, and speeches by state political figures. Under attack by medical authorities and others, he was denied renewal of KFKB's license in 1930; his Kansas license to practice medicine was also revoked. Undaunted, he set up a powerful broadcast station (XER) in Mexico, just across the Rio Grande from Del Rio, Texas, and continued to prosper as before, shifting his practice to prostate gland surgery and amassing a very large fortune. Denounced as a quack, he sued for libel but lost the suit in 1939. Malpractice suits multiplied; the federal government claimed payment of back income taxes; and in 1941, the Mexican government closed down the "radio doctor's" station. He managed through transfer of assets, and a bankruptcy, to salvage a large part of his fortune but his career in "medicine" was over.

BRINTON, CLARENCE CRANE (*b. Winsted, Conn., 1898; d. Cambridge, Mass., 1968*), historian and teacher. B.A. (1919), Harvard; Ph.D., New College, Oxford. Taught at Harvard after 1923, becoming full professor by 1942 and being named McLean Professor of Ancient and Modern History in 1946. Influenced by the thinking of physiologist Lawrence J. Henderson and Italian sociologist Vilfredo Pareto, he was also drawn to the "new history" of James Harvey Robinson, which substituted the analysis of social and cultural development for the narrative of politics and war. The books that established him as an authority on modern European history include *The Jacobins: A Study in the New History* (1930), *English Political Thought in the Nineteenth Century* (1933), *A Decade of Revolution, 1789–1799* (1934), and *The Anatomy of Revolution* (1938). After World War II he became a recognized expert on "intellectual history," a term he was among the first to employ, with such books as *Ideas and Men: The Story of Western Thought* (1950), *The Portable Age of Reason Reader* (1956), and *A History of Western Morals* (1959).

BRINTON, DANIEL GARRISON (*b. Thornbury, Pa., 1837; d. 1899*), pioneer anthropologist. Graduated Yale, 1858; M.D., Jefferson Medical College, 1861; served as military surgeon, 1862–65. Editor, *Medical and Surgical Reporter*, 1874–87, retiring to give full time to anthropology. Never a field-worker, his researches were of great and lasting value. Of particular merit were *Notes on the Floridian Peninsula* (1859) and *The American Race* (1891). His *Library of Aboriginal American Literature* (v.d.), an editing and translation of texts, included the Maya Chronicles (1882).

BRINTON, JOHN HILL (*b. Philadelphia, Pa., 1832; d. Philadelphia, 1907*), surgeon. Lecturer in and professor of surgery, Jefferson Medical College, 1855–1906; helped prepare *Medical and Surgical History of the War of the Rebellion* (1870–88), in which he had served with distinction.

BRISBANE, ALBERT (*b. Batavia, N.Y., 1809; d. Richmond, Va., 1890*), Utopian social reformer. Educated privately; studied in Paris with Cousin and Guizot, and in Berlin with Hegel. Strongly influenced by Fourier's theory of association. Brisbane spent two years in study with Fourier and returned to America,

1834, to propagate the doctrine. Was encouraged by Horace Greeley, but public interest was not caught for long. Author of *Social Destiny of Man* (1840), *Association* (1843), and *General Introduction to Social Sciences* (1876).

BRISBANE, ARTHUR (*b. Buffalo, N.Y., 1864; d. New York, N.Y., 1936*), newspaper editor and writer. Son of the social reformer Albert Brisbane, after European schooling he became a reporter on the *New York Sun*, 1885. In 1890 he joined Joseph Pulitzer's *New York World*; six years later, as editor of the *Sunday World*, he engaged in a sensational circulation battle with the *Journal* of William Randolph Hearst. Brisbane joined Hearst in 1897 and provided the sensational appeal to mass tastes, the jingoistic propaganda, the surface learning, and adjustable conscience that the ambitious publisher wanted in his editor. Brisbane remained with Hearst until his death, editing the *Journal* and other papers, and writing a widely syndicated column, "Today."

BRISTED, CHARLES ASTOR (*b. New York, N.Y., 1820; d. 1874*), author. Great-grandson of John Jacob Astor. Graduated Yale, 1839; graduated Trinity College, Cambridge, 1845. Wrote studies in philology and somewhat acid sketches of American society.

BRISTED, JOHN (*b. Sherborne, England, 1778; d. Bristol, R.I., 1855*), Episcopal clergyman. Came to America as lawyer, 1806; ordained *ca.* 1828. Father of C. A. Bristed.

BRISTOL, JOHN BUNYAN (*b. Hillsdale, N.Y., 1826; d. New York, N.Y., 1909*), landscape painter.

BRISTOL, MARK LAMBERT (*b. Glassboro, N.J., 1868; d. Washington, D.C., 1939*), naval officer and diplomat. High commissioner to Turkey, 1919–27.

BRISTOL, WILLIAM HENRY (*b. Waterbury, Conn., 1859; d. New Haven, Conn., 1930*), mechanical engineer, university professor, inventor, and pioneer manufacturer of recording instruments. Graduated M.E. from Stevens Institute of Technology, 1884; returned two years later to teach until 1907. While at Stevens he patented a steel fastener for joining leather belts, and with his brother Franklin B. Bristol organized the Bristol Co. in 1889 to manufacture them. Perfected devices for measuring pressure and temperature that were accepted throughout industry as the standard of accuracy. Invented the Bristolphone for synchronized recording of sound and action.

BRISTOW, BENJAMIN HELM (*b. Elkton, Ky., 1832; d. New York, N.Y., 1896*), lawyer, statesman. Graduated Jefferson College, Pennsylvania, 1851; admitted to bar 1853; fought in Civil War as ardent Unionist. Served in Kentucky senate, 1863–65; fought for ratification of 13th Amendment and Lincoln's reelection. U.S. attorney for Kentucky, 1866–70. Appointed solicitor general, 1870, and secretary of treasury, 1874; in latter office broke up Whiskey Ring. Resignation forced by President Grant, 1876, on ground that Bristow was scheming for presidential nomination. Removed to New York City, 1878, where he became a leader of the bar.

BRISTOW, GEORGE FREDERICK (*b. Brooklyn, N.Y., 1825; d. 1898*), composer, violinist, teacher.

BRISTOW, JOSEPH LITTLE (*b. near Hazel Green, Wolfe Co., Ky., 1861; d. near Annandale, Va., 1944*), lawyer, politician. Settled permanently in Kansas, 1879. Graduated Baker University, 1886. While clerk of the district court of Douglas County, 1886–90, he read law; in 1890, he bought the first of a series of Kansas newspapers which he was to own throughout his political career (notably the *Salina Evening Journal*). An ardent anti-Populist, he rose in the state Republican organization and served

as private secretary to Governor Edmund N. Morrill, 1895–97. Appointed assistant postmaster general by President McKinley, he moved vigorously against corruption in the postal system; his implication of several prominent Republican legislators brought about his forced resignation, 1905. Manifesting progressive tendencies, he supported adoption of a direct primary in Kansas for nomination to the U.S. Senate, a measure passed in 1908. That same year, after a campaign managed by William Allen White, Bristow won the primary and was elected to the Senate by the state legislature in January 1909. He was effective as a speaker because of his earnestness and uncompromising respect for facts. He allied himself with the insurgents, led by Robert M. La Follette, in opposing much of President Taft's program; his most important contribution was his authorship of the resolution that (after some modification) became the 17th Amendment to the U.S. Constitution, providing for direct election of senators. He supported La Follette for the Republican presidential nomination in 1912, and after the party split supported Theodore Roosevelt. His refusal to join the Progressive party, however, cost him the backing of Kansas Progressives and he lost his bid for reelection in 1914. After another failure to regain his Senate seat in 1918, he removed to Virginia to develop property he had purchased there.

BRITTON, NATHANIEL LORD (*b. Staten Island, N.Y., 1859; d. 1934*), botanist and author. Organized and directed the New York Botanical Garden, 1896–1929.

BROADHEAD, GARLAND CARR (*b. near Charlottesville, Va., 1827; d. 1912*), geologist, engineer. Differentiated coal measures of Missouri and Kansas; established Ozarkian Series.

BROADHEAD, JAMES OVERTON (*b. near Charlottesville, Va., 1819; d. 1898*), outstanding Missouri lawyer. Brother of Garland C. Broadhead. Special commissioner to France, 1885, on spoliation claims.

BROADUS, JOHN ALBERT (*b. western Virginia, 1827; d. 1895*), Baptist clergyman. Professor, Southern Baptist Seminary, Greenville, S.C., 1858; later its president at Louisville, Ky., 1889–95.

BROCKETT, LINUS PIERPONT (*b. Canton, Conn., 1820; d. Brooklyn, N.Y., 1893*), author, physician.

BROCKMEYER, HENRY C. *See* BROKMEYER, HENRY C.

BROCKWAY, ZEBULON REED (*b. Lyme, Conn., 1827; d. 1920*), penologist. Superintendent, House of Correction, Detroit, 1861–72; superintendent, Elmira State Reformatory, 1876–1900.

BRÖDEL, MAX (*b. Leipzig, Germany, 1870; d. Baltimore, Md., 1941*), anatomist, medical illustrator. Attended public schools; studied at Leipzig Academy of Fine Arts, 1885–90. His work as illustrator for medical research in progress at the University of Leipzig impressed William H. Welch and Franklin P. Mall, who brought him to the United States in 1894 to make drawings of operative procedures and pathological specimens for Howard A. Kelly at Johns Hopkins. His illustrations for Kelly's *Operative Gynecology* (1898) and T. S. Cullen's *Cancer of the Uterus* (1900) brought him recognition as the foremost in his field in the United States. From 1911 to his retirement in 1940 he directed at Johns Hopkins a "Department of Art as Applied to Medicine," for training of medical artists. To improve his skill, he studied anatomy and physiology, carrying out laboratory research of his own in order to gain a clearer idea of what he had to portray. These investigations led to his discovery of "Brödel's line"; he also devised a suture to repair a prolapsed kidney.

BRODERICK, DAVID COLBRETH (*b. Washington, D.C., 1820; d. California, 1859*), politician. Moved to New York City, 1834; father's death in 1837 left him to support mother and younger brother. Active in Tammany politics, 1840–48, he owned a saloon and prospered. Moved to California, 1849, and engaged again in politics; by 1854 was a power in the local Democratic party and president of the state senate. Chosen U.S. senator in 1857, he traded off the seat to William M. Gwin in return for a promise of federal patronage that was not honored. Hostile to the pro-slavery elements in his party, he lost his life in a duel with David S. Terry, one of the pro-slavery leaders.

BRODHEAD, DANIEL (*b. Albany, N.Y., 1736; d. Milford, Pa., 1809*), soldier. Moved to Reading, Pa., 1773; commanded Pennsylvania troops in Revolution; subdued Indians along Allegheny River, 1779 and 1781.

BRODHEAD, JOHN ROMEYN (*b. Philadelphia, Pa., 1814; d. New York, N.Y., 1873*), historian, archivist. Author of classic *History of the State of New York* (1853, 1871).

BROKENSHIRE, NORMAN ERNEST (*b. Murcheson, Ontario, Canada, 1898; d. Smithtown, N.Y., 1965*), radio announcer, commentator, and newspaper editor. In the 1920's he became one of radio's first personalities because of his ad-lib skills and rolling, resonant, and deliberate voice. In the 1930's was the announcer for several highly popular radio programs and became one of radio's highest-paid personalities. After a downturn in his career due to alcoholism, he made a comeback in the 1940's. In the 1950's he left big-time radio but continued to host programs on stations on Long Island, including "The Brokenshire Show" on WKIT after 1957. He was also editor of the *Port Jefferson Record* (1958–61).

BROKMEYER, HENRY C. (*b. near Minden, Prussia, 1828; d. 1906*), philosopher. Came to America, 1844. Translated Hegel's *Larger Logic*, and initiated the "St. Louis Movement" of German (Hegelian) idealism.

BROMFIELD, JOHN (*b. Newburyport, Mass., 1779; d. Boston, Mass., 1849*), philanthropist, China merchant. Benefactor to Boston charities and institutions.

BROMFIELD, LOUIS (*b. Mansfield, Ohio, 1896; d. Columbus, Ohio, 1956*), novelist and experimental farmer. Studied at Cornell and at Columbia. A popular novelist through the twenties, Bromfield is remembered for his novels concerning his native Ohio, dislike of industrialism, and Jeffersonian convictions. Works include *The Green Bay Tree* (1924), *Possession* (1925), and *Early Autumn* (1926), for which he received the Pulitzer Prize, *The Rains Came* (1937), and *Night in Bombay* (1940). He lived in France until 1938, when he returned to Ohio and devoted his life to restoring his holdings in rural Ohio, the famous Malabar Farm. Later works include *Pleasant Valley* (1945), *Malabar Farm* (1948), *From My Experience* (1955), and *Animals and Other People* (1955).

BROMLEY, ISAAC HILL (*b. Norwich, Conn., 1833; d. Norwich, 1898*), journalist. Editorial staff, *New York Tribune*, 1873–82; 1891–98.

BRONDEL, JOHN BAPTIST (*b. Bruges, Belgium, 1842; d. Helena, Mont., 1903*), Roman Catholic clergyman. Missionary in the Northwest *post* 1864; bishop of Vancouver, 1879–84, and of Helena, Mont., thereafter.

BRONSON, HENRY (*b. Waterbury, Conn. 1804; d. New Haven, Conn., 1893*), physician, historian. Professor, Yale Medical School, 1842–60; author of *History of Waterbury* (1858).

BRONSON, WALTER COCHRANE (*b. Roxbury, Mass., 1862; d. Oxford, England, 1928*), educator, anthropologist, editor. Professor of English literature, Brown University, 1905–27.

BROOKE, CHARLES FREDERICK TUCKER (*b. Morgantown, W.Va., 1883; d. New Haven, Conn., 1946*), scholar, educator. B.A., West Virginia University, 1901; M.A., 1902; did graduate work in German at University of Chicago, 1901–04. On a Rhodes scholarship to St. John's College, Oxford, he changed his field and took the B.A. and B.Litt. (1907) in English literature. After a year as instructor at Cornell, he moved to Yale in 1909 where he spent the rest of his life. In 1921, he was made full professor of English; in 1931, he was appointed Sterling professor. His published works were numerous and included *The Tudor Drama* (1911), *Essays on Shakespeare and Other Elizabethans* (1948), and a text and a life of Christopher Marlowe; best known as a Shakespeare editor and scholar and served as general editor of the Yale edition of Shakespeare. His seminar in Shakespeare was one of the most popular courses for graduate students at Yale. Pioneered the modern study of Neo-Latin poetry.

BROOKE, FRANCIS TALIAFERRO (*b. Smithfield, Va., 1763; d. 1851*), Revolutionary soldier. Judge, Virginia supreme court of appeals, 1811–51.

BROOKE, JOHN MERCER (*b. near Tampa, Fla., 1826; d. Lexington, Ky., 1906*), naval officer, scientist. Midshipman, U.S. Navy, 1841; graduated Annapolis, 1847; with Coast Survey, 1849–50. At Naval Observatory, 1851–53; invented deep-sea sounding apparatus, which made possible mapping topography of ocean bottom; explored North Pacific and prepared charts, 1854; surveyed Japanese east coast, 1858–60. Entered Confederate States navy, 1861. Planned reconstruction of *Merrimack*; developed "Brooke" gun; was chief of Bureau of Ordnance and Hydrography. Professor of physics and astronomy, Virginia Military Institute, 1866–99.

BROOKE, JOHN RUTTER (*b. Montgomery Co., Pa., 1838; d. Philadelphia, Pa., 1926*), Union soldier. Distinguished at Gettysburg. As major general, commanded 1st Corps, 1898.

BROOKER, CHARLES FREDERICK (*b. Litchfield, Conn., 1847; d. Daytona, Fla., 1926*), manufacturer, financier. Formed American Brass Co., 1899; was its president, 1900–20.

BROOKHART, SMITH WILDMAN (*b. near Arbela, Mo., 1869; d. Whipple, Ariz., 1944*), lawyer, politician. Raised in Iowa. Graduated Southern Iowa Normal and Scientific Institute, 1889. Taught school in Keosauqua, Iowa; read law, and began practice in Washington Township, 1892. Entering politics as a vigorous opponent of railroads, corporate interests, and Eastern financiers, he aligned himself with the progressive wing of the Republican party, supporting Theodore Roosevelt in 1912. After returning from World War I service, he challenged the Republican organization, and over its opposition was elected to fill out an unexpired term in the U.S. Senate, 1922. Failed of reelection in 1924 but was successful in 1926. Speaking for the farmers and organized labor, he was one of the farm bloc group who were dubbed "Sons of the Wild Jackass," a continuous and caustic critic of Republican administration policies. Among other measures which he favored were federal control of stock speculation, government ownership of railroads, and abolition of the gold standard. As an alternative to competitive economics, he proposed producers' and consumers' cooperatives, based on the Rochdale system. Defeated in the 1932 primary and again in 1936.

BROOKINGS, ROBERT SOMERS (*b. Cecil Co., Md., 1850; d. Washington, D.C., 1932*), business executive, philanthropist, educator. With little more than elementary school education, became virtual head of the Cupples woodenware company, St. Louis, at 22. Built Cupples Station, 1895, a railroad terminal that revolutionized the distribution of goods in St. Louis and served as a model for other cities. Retired from business in 1896 and devoted himself to higher education. Developed Washington University, St. Louis, especially the medical school. From his 1917 experience as chairman of the price-fixing committee came his interest in public affairs, which resulted in the establishment of the Brookings Institution, 1928.

BROOKS, ALFRED HULSE (*b. Ann Arbor, Mich., 1871; d. 1924*), geologist, geographer. Headed Alaskan division, U.S. Geological Survey, 1902–24; author of *Geography and Geology of Alaska* (1906).

BROOKS, BYRON ALDEN (*b. Theresa, N.Y., 1845; d. Brooklyn, N.Y., 1911*), teacher, inventor. Improved typewriter, 1878, by putting both capital and small letters on same striking lever, with a key to shift position.

BROOKS, CHARLES (*b. Medford, Mass., 1795; d. Medford, 1872*), Unitarian clergyman. Wrote *Family Prayer Book*, 1821. Influential in normal-school movement, 1835–39.

BROOKS, CHARLES TIMOTHY (*b. Salem, Mass., 1813; d. Newport, R.I., 1883*), Unitarian clergyman, poet. Pastor, Unitarian Church, Newport, 1837–71. Able translator of German literature.

BROOKS, ELBRIDGE STREETER (*b. Lowell, Mass., 1846; d. Somerville, Mass., 1902*). Editor, D. Lothrop & Co., 1887–1902; author of historical sketches for children.

BROOKS, ERASTUS (*b. Portland, Maine, 1815; d. Staten Island, N.Y., 1886*), journalist, politician. Editor, *New York Express*, 1844–77; active in Know-Nothing party. Brother of James Brooks.

BROOKS, GEORGE WASHINGTON (*b. Elizabeth City, N.C., 1821; d. 1882*), lawyer. Southern Unionist; U.S. judge, district of North Carolina, 1865–82.

BROOKS, JAMES (*b. Portland, Maine, 1810; d. 1873*), journalist. Brother of Erastus Brooks. Noted correspondent in Washington; publisher, *New York Express*, 1836–73. Received Crédit Mobilier bribe, 1868, while a government director of the Union Pacific.

BROOKS, JAMES GORDON (*b. Red Hook, N.Y., 1801; d. Albany, N.Y., 1841*), editor, poet. Author, with wife, of *The Rivals of Este* (1829).

BROOKS, JOHN (*b. Medford, Mass., 1752; d. Medford, 1825*), physician, Revolutionary soldier. On "Newburgh Address" committee, 1783. Federalist governor of Massachusetts, 1816–22.

BROOKS, JOHN GRAHAM (*b. Acworth, N.H., 1846; d. Cambridge, Mass., 1938*), sociologist and reformer. Left the Unitarian ministry, 1891, to devote his career to analyzing and writing about labor-employer relationships.

BROOKS, MARIA GOWEN (*b. Medford, Mass., ca. 1794; d. Cuba, 1845*), poet. Pen name, "Maria del Occidente." Works include *Zóphiël* (1833), prose tale *Idomen* (1843).

BROOKS, MARY ELIZABETH AIKEN. *See* BROOKS, JAMES GORDON.

BROOKS, NOAH (*b. Castine, Maine, 1830; d. Pasadena, Calif., 1903*), journalist. Close friend of Lincoln. Editor, *New York Tribune*, 1871–76, *New York Times*, 1876–84, and other newspapers in both East and West; author of *The Boy Emigrants* (1876).

BROOKS, OVERTON (*b. East Baton Rouge Parish, La., 1897; d. Bethesda, Md., 1961*), congressman. A Democrat, he was elected to the U.S. Senate in 1936 and served there for twenty-six years. Decidedly antilabor and a staunch advocate of federal assistance to farmers. Toward the end of his career became one of the leading proponents of an enlarged space program and a manned space satellite and was also involved in the development of the nation's water resources. However, was best known for his interest in military reserve affairs. His first assignment was to the House Military Affairs Committee (later the Armed Services Committee), on which he served for the rest of his life and in which capacity he was involved in the development and regulation of military reserve forces.

BROOKS, PETER CHARDON (*b. North Yarmouth, Maine, 1767; d. Boston, Mass., 1849*), Boston merchant and insurance broker, 1789–1803. Reputed the wealthiest man in New England.

BROOKS, PHILLIPS (*b. Boston, Mass., 1835; d. Boston, 1893*), Episcopal clergyman. Graduated Harvard, 1855; entered seminary at Alexandria, Va., and was ordained, 1859. His sermon at Independence Hall, Philadelphia, 1865, over Lincoln's body received nationwide attention; also his sermon at 1865 Harvard commemoration of Civil War dead. Wrote "O Little Town of Bethlehem" for Sunday school, 1868. Rector of Trinity Church, Boston, 1869–91; delivered *Lectures on Preaching*, Yale Divinity School, 1877; bishop of Massachusetts, 1891–93. Outstanding as pulpit orator and pastor; a "broad" churchman.

BROOKS, PRESTON SMITH (*b. Edgefield, S.C., 1819; d. Washington, D.C., 1857*), Attacked Charles Sumner of Massachusetts, 1856, for slur on uncle, Senator A. P. Butler of South Carolina. Congressman, Democrat, from South Carolina, 1853–57.

BROOKS, RICHARD EDWIN (*b. Braintree, Mass., 1865; d. Washington, D.C., 1919*), sculptor and portrait medalist.

BROOKS, THOMAS BENTON (*b. Monroe, N.Y., 1836; d. 1900*), geologist, mining engineer. Attended Union College School of Engineering, 1856–58; rose to brevet colonel in Civil War. General manager of Iron Cliff mine in Marquette District, Mich., *post* 1865; directed economic division, state geological survey of Upper Peninsula, 1869–73. His report was a full manual of every phase of mining and smelting iron ores of Lake Superior region.

BROOKS, VAN WYCK (*b. Plainfield, N.J., 1886; d. Bridgewater, Conn., 1963*), critic, biographer, and literary historian. With *America's Coming-of-Age* (1915), in which he called attention to the weakness of America's classics, he obtained a prominent position in the vanguard of the American literary establishment, which he retained throughout the 1920's. Introducing the terms "highbrow" and "lowbrow" into American discourse, he railed against American society for being so consumed by acquisitiveness that it holds all other energies and values in contempt. In *The Ordeal of Mark Twain* (1920), a pioneer effort in psychobiography, he presented Twain as a case study of an American writer compromised by rewards and riches won for submission to philistine rule. (He later repudiated central aspects of this work's thesis.) The second phase of his career began with *The Flowering of New England, 1815–1865* (1936), first of five volumes collectively called *Makers and Finders*. Having earlier demonstrated the ulcerous effects of America on the creative spirit, in the volumes of *Makers and Finders* he discovered a "usable" past in national life and letters and a fertile American "collective literary mind." Criticized for reversing his earlier opinions and for his traditionalist, antimodernist stance in literary matters, he lost standing among literary intellectuals in the postwar era, but published many more books and articles before his death.

BROOKS, WILLIAM KEITH (*b. Cleveland, Ohio, 1848; d. 1908*), zoologist. Founded Chesapeake Zoological Laboratory, 1878. Taught morphology and biology, Johns Hopkins, 1876–1908. Author of *Law of Heredity* (1883), *Foundations of Zoology* (1899).

BROOKS, WILLIAM ROBERT (*b. Maidstone, England, 1844; d. Geneva, N.Y., 1921*), astronomer. Came to America, 1857. A pioneer in application of photography to celestial observation; discoverer of twenty-seven comets; professor of astronomy, Hobart College.

BROOKS, WILLIAM THOMAS HARBAUGH (*b. New Lisbon, Ohio, 1821; d. Huntsville, Ala., 1870*), Union soldier. Graduated West Point, 1841. Served in Mexican War and on frontier; rose to division commander in Civil War.

BROPHY, JOHN (*b. St. Helens, Lancanshire, England, 1883; d. Falls Church, Va., 1963*), labor leader. Immigrated to the U.S. in 1892, joined the United Mine Workers Union (UMW) in 1899, and was elected to union offices in Pennsylvania. Strongly opposed John L. Lewis, national president of the UMW, disagreeing with Lewis on matters such as relations with nonunion members and nationalization of the mines. However, in 1933 Lewis invited him to help in organization of the union, and when Lewis formed the Committee for Industrial Organization (CIO) he became director of the organization, playing a crucial role in the organizing drives that tripled the size of the labor movement in the 1930's. In the late 1930's Lewis attempted to oust him from the CIO, but when Philip Murray took over the CIO presidency, he was made director of industrial union councils. During the war he devoted much of his time to service on the War Labor Board, and after the war he became a key figure in the fight against Communists in the CIO.

BROPHY, THOMAS D'ARCY (*b. Butte, Mont., 1893; d. Poughkeepsie, N.Y., 1967*), advertising executive. Was vice president (1933), president (1937), and chairman (1949) of the advertising firm of Kenyon and Eckhardt in New York City. Initiated the use of well-known personalities to deliver ads. Helped establish the Advertising Council, a public-relations group for advertising agencies (1940). Believing in the use of advertising to promote public welfare, ran a highly successful campaign for funds for the United Service Organization (1941). Was elected chairman of the American Association of Advertising Agencies (1947) and formed the American Heritage Foundation (1947). Received the first Distinguished Service Award of the Advertising Federation of America (1959).

BROPHY, TRUMAN WILLIAM (*b. Goodings Grove, Ill., 1848; d. 1928*), oral surgeon. Originated successful operation to correct cleft palate and harelip. Wrote *Oral Surgery* (1915) and *Cleft Lip and Palate* (1923).

BROSS, WILLIAM (*b. Sussex Co., N.J., 1813; d. Chicago, Ill., 1890*), journalist. Established Chicago *Democratic Press*, 1852; combined it with the *Tribune*, 1857; thereafter the *Tribune* prospered with the rise of Chicago.

BROUGH, CHARLES HILLMAN (*b. Clinton, Miss., 1876; d. Washington, D.C., 1935*), educator, lecturer, public servant. Governor of Arkansas, 1916–18.

BROUGH, JOHN (*b. Marietta, Ohio, 1811; d. 1865*). Editor, *Cincinnati Enquirer*; successful railroad executive. Republican governor of Ohio, 1864–65.

BROUGHAM, JOHN (*b. Dublin, Ireland, 1810; d. New York, N.Y., 1880*), actor, playwright. Began American career in New York, N.Y., 1842. Excelled in comic writing and impersonations.

BROUN, HEYWOOD CAMPBELL (*b. Brooklyn, N.Y., 1888; d. New York, N.Y., 1939*), newspaper columnist, author, organizer of the American Newspaper Guild, 1933. Attended Harvard, 1906–10. Reporter, sportswriter, drama and literary critic, and war correspondent for the *New York Tribune*, 1912–21. Joined the *New York World*, 1921, as a columnist; disagreements resulting from his views on the Sacco-Vanzetti case led to his dismissal in 1928. While a columnist for the *New York Telegram* and *World-Telegram*, 1928–July 1939, Broun published his own literary and humorous weekly and presided over the union he had helped to organize. His syndicated column, often in disagreement with the policies of the newspapers in which it appeared and expressive of his own views and personality, set a new pattern in American journalism.

BROWARD, NAPOLEON BONAPARTE (*b. Duval Co., Fla., 1857; d. 1910*). Governor of Florida, Democrat, 1905–10; promoted drainage of Everglades.

BROWER, JACOB VRADENBERG (*b. York, Mich., 1844; d. 1905*), explorer, archaeologist. Located aboriginal mounds at Mile Lac, Minn., also at the site of Quivira in Kansas.

BROWERE, JOHN HENRI ISAAC (*b. New York, N.Y., 1792; d. New York, 1834*), sculptor. Created series of life masks of great Americans, perfected by a process now unknown.

BROWN, AARON VENABLE (*b. Brunswick Co., Va., 1795; d. 1859*), lawyer. Democratic Congressman from Tennessee, 1839–45; a champion of Oregon occupation and Texas annexation. Governor of Tennessee, 1845–47; postmaster general in Buchanan cabinet (1857–59).

BROWN, ADDISON (*b. West Newbury, Mass., 1830; d. New York, N.Y., 1913*), lawyer. Federal judge, southern district of New York, 1881–1901. Coauthor of *Illustrated Flora of the Northern United States* (1896–98).

BROWN, ALBERT GALLATIN (*b. Chester District, S.C., 1813; d. near Terry, Miss., 1880*), lawyer, politician. Moved to Mississippi, 1823. Congressman, Democrat, 1839–41; 1848–61. Able governor of Mississippi, 1844–48. Confederate senator, 1862–65.

BROWN, ALEXANDER (*b. Co. Antrim, Ireland, 1764; d. Baltimore, Md., 1834*), one of the foremost mercantile figures of his time. Came to America, 1800, and opened a linen shop in Baltimore. The business expanded into worldwide trading and shipping activities; branches were managed by sons (Brown Brothers & Co., in New York and Philadelphia; Brown, Shipley & Co., Liverpool, etc.). Extensive commercial ties abroad encouraged the change of a mercantile business into a merchant banking house; its greatest period of growth was between 1824 and 1834. Brown and his sons were among the founders of the Baltimore and Ohio Railroad and were active in many other civic and commercial movements.

BROWN, ALEXANDER (*b. Glenmore, Va., 1843; d. 1906*), historian. Active in revision of old concepts of Virginia's colonial history; author of *The Genesis of the United States* (1890) and other carefully researched works.

BROWN, ALEXANDER EPHRAIM (*b. Cleveland, Ohio, 1852; d. Cleveland, 1911*), engineer, manufacturer. Inventor of the Brown hoisting and conveying machine (1879) for handling coal and ores.

BROWN, ANTOINETTE.   *See* BLACKWELL, ANTOINETTE LOUISA BROWN.

BROWN, BEDFORD (*b. Caswell Co., N.C., 1792; d. 1870*), North Carolina legislator. U.S. senator, 1829–40; supporter of Andrew Jackson's policies.

BROWN, BENJAMIN GRATZ (*b. Lexington, Ky., 1826; d. 1885*), lawyer, statesman. Graduated Yale, 1847; admitted to Kentucky bar; moved to St. Louis, Mo., 1849. Served in lower branch of Missouri legislature, 1852–59; his 1857 speech against a joint resolution that declared abolition of slavery impracticable is regarded as start of Free-Soil movement in Missouri. Defeated in 1857 as Free-Soil Democrat candidate for governorship, he was active in formation of Republican party in the state, was a delegate to the 1860 Chicago convention, and cooperated with his cousin Frank P. Blair, Jr., and with General Lyon in opposing the Missouri secessionists. As U.S. senator, 1863–67, he spoke for universal suffrage, for government ownership and operation of telegraph lines, and for the merit system in civil service; as Liberal Republican governor of Missouri, 1871–73, he opposed radical reconstruction policy. In 1872, he ran for vice president of the United States on the Liberal Republican ticket headed by Horace Greeley; after his defeat he resumed his law practice.

BROWN, CARLETON (*b. Oberlin, Ohio, 1869; d. Glen Ridge, N.J., 1941*), philologist, educator. B.A., Carleton College, 1888; attended Andover Theological Seminary, 1890–93, and was ordained a Unitarian minister, 1894. Gave up the ministry for graduate study in English at Harvard and received Ph.D. in 1903. Taught at Harvard, Bryn Mawr, University of Minnesota; professor at New York University, 1927–39. Devoted his principal research to Middle English texts; coauthor of *The Index of Middle English Verse* (1943). Did outstanding work as secretary of Modern Language Association, 1920–34, and editor of *PMLA*.

BROWN, CHARLES BROCKDEN (*b. Philadelphia, Pa., 1771; d. Philadelphia, 1810*), novelist, journalist, the first American to make authorship his principal profession. A romantic revolutionary and a writer of somber intensity, he was strongly influenced by the work of William Godwin. Author of *Alcuin: A Dialogue* (1798), *Wieland* (1798), *Arthur Mervyn* (1799, 1800), *Ormond* (1799), *Edgar Huntly* (1799), *Clara Howard* (1801), *Jane Talbot* (1801), and various pamphlets and translations. He also edited *The Monthly Magazine and American Review* (N.Y., 1799–1800), *The Literary Magazine and American Register* (Phila., 1803–07), and *The American Register or General Repository, etc.* (Phila., 1807–11).

BROWN, CHARLES REYNOLDS (*b. near Bethany, W.Va., 1862; d. New Haven, Conn., 1950*), Congregational clergyman, educator. Raised in Washington County, Iowa. Graduated University of Iowa, 1883. After considering study of law, he decided on the ministry and took the degree of S.T.B. at Boston University School of Theology, 1889. Minister of a Methodist church in Cincinnati, Ohio, for three years; then, on becoming a Congregationalist, he held pastorates in Charlestown, Mass., and from 1896 to 1911 in Oakland, Calif., where he expressed his social concern by involvement with the labor movement. As dean of the Divinity School, Yale University, 1911–28, he brought new life to it, but he was perhaps best known as a gifted preacher. Author of *The Social Message of the Modern Pulpit* (1906) and *The Art of Preaching* (1922).

BROWN, CHARLES RUFUS (*b. East Kingston, N.H., 1849; d. Stoneham, Mass., 1914*), Baptist clergyman. Taught Old Testament studies at Newton Theological Institution, 1883–1914.

BROWN, CHARLOTTE EMERSON (*b. Andover, Mass., 1838; d. East Orange, N.J., 1895*). An organizer, and first president (1890), of the General Federation of Women's Clubs.

BROWN, CHARLOTTE HAWKINS (*b. Henderson, N.C., 1883; d. Greensboro, N.C., 1961*), educator. Studied at State Normal School in Salem, Mass.; in 1901 accepted a teaching position offered her by the American Missionary Association to teach in a one-room schoolhouse in Sedalia, N.C.; and in 1902 raised funds to found the Palmer Memorial Institute in Sedalia. Modeled after Hampton and Tuskegee, the school became a leader among the fifteen private educational enterprises for blacks that emerged in North Carolina between 1871 and 1910. In addition to directing the Palmer Institute, she worked for social reform and civil rights in North Carolina. Retired as director of Palmer in 1952 but remained director of finance until 1955.

BROWN, CLARENCE JAMES (*b. Blanchester, Ohio, 1893; d. Bethesda, Md., 1965*), congressman. A Republican, he served in the House of Representatives from the Seventh Ohio Congressional District (1938–64). Was a defender of civil rights, voting for the abolition of poll taxes. On domestic issues was conservative: opposed New Deal job creation programs; was a consistent opponent of what he deemed labor's excesses; and in the postwar period favored a creation of a permanent House Un-American Activities Committee. Served for many years on the House Rules Committee, which was often regarded as a bottleneck for progressive legislation.

BROWN, DAVID PAUL (*b. Philadelphia, Pa., 1795; d. Philadelphia, 1872*), lawyer, orator. Author of *Sertorius*, a tragedy (produced 1830), a vehicle for Junius Brutus Booth, and other plays.

BROWN, EBENEZER (*b. probably Chesterfield, Mass., 1795; d. Baltimore, Md., 1889*), Methodist clergyman. Served in New Orleans, 1819, as first missionary sent out by Methodist Board; in 1829, manufactured first detachable collars at Troy, N.Y.

BROWN, ELMER ELLSWORTH (*b. Kiantone, N.Y., 1861; d. 1934*), chancellor of New York University. During his term, 1911–1933, the university became one of the largest in the United States.

BROWN, ERNEST WILLIAM (*b. Hull, England, 1866; d. New Haven, Conn., 1938*), mathematician, student of celestial mechanics. Attended Cambridge University, B.A., 1887, M.A., 1891. Came to America to teach at Haverford College, 1891–1907; professor of mathematics at Yale, 1907–32. Brown's interest in the moon's motion led to his *An Introductory Treatise on the Lunar Theory* (1896). He then constructed a new lunar theory, based on researches of George William Hill. Brown's monumental *Tables of the Motion of the Moon* (1919) immediately established the superiority of his theory. His explanation of the observed fluctuations of the moon as being due to irregular changes in the earth's rate of rotation was fully confirmed in 1939. He also contributed to planetary theory.

BROWN, ETHAN ALLEN (*b. Darien, Conn., 1766; d. Indianapolis, Ind., 1852*), politician. Established a law practice at Cincinnati, Ohio, 1804. Democratic governor of Ohio, 1818–22; U.S. senator, 1822–25. Promoted canals and internal improvements.

BROWN, FAYETTE (*b. North Bloomfield, Ohio, 1823; d. Cleveland, Ohio, 1910*), banker, iron manufacturer. Patented improvements in blast furnace design and charging hoists; a pioneer in water transport of ore on Great Lakes; promoted loading inventions of son, Alexander Ephraim Brown.

BROWN, FRANCIS (*b. Chester, N.H., 1784; d. Hanover, N.H., 1820*). President of Dartmouth College, 1815–20; Congregational clergyman.

BROWN, FRANCIS (*b. Hanover, N.H., 1849; d. New York, N.Y., 1916*), professor of theology. Son of Samuel Gilman Brown. Graduated Dartmouth, 1870; Union Theological Seminary, 1877; was a disciple of Charles A. Briggs and his successor in 1890 as professor of Old Testament languages at Union. Editor of *Hebrew and English Lexicon of the Old Testament* (completed 1906); president of Union Theological Seminary, 1908–16.

BROWN, FREDERIC TILDEN (*b. New York, N.Y., 1853; d. Bethel, Maine, 1910*), surgeon. Developed improved instruments for use in his genito-urinary specialty.

BROWN, GEORGE (*b. Ballymena, Ireland, 1787; d. Baltimore, Md., 1859*), banker. Son of Alexander Brown (1764–1834). A projector and first treasurer of the Baltimore and Ohio railroad.

BROWN, GEORGE (*b. Wilton, N.H., 1823; d. Barre, Mass., 1892*), physician. Improved techniques for instruction of the mentally retarded at Elm Hill School, Barre, Mass., 1850–92.

BROWN, GEORGE PLINY (*b. Lenox Township, Ohio, 1836; d. Bloomington, Ill., 1910*), educator. President, Indiana State Normal School, Terre Haute, 1879–86; editor, *School and Home Education*, 1888–1910.

BROWN, GEORGE WILLIAM (*b. Baltimore, Md., 1812; d. 1890*), lawyer. As Baltimore mayor, 1859–61, broke grip of Know-Nothing party on city; imprisoned for short period at start of Civil War on suspicion of Southern sympathies, he served as judge, supreme bench of Baltimore, 1872–88.

BROWN, GERTRUDE FOSTER (*b. Morrison, Ill., 1867; d. Westport, Conn., 1956*), suffragist and musician. Studied at the New England Conservatory of Music. For a time a concert pianist, Brown became interested in woman's suffrage in 1910; by 1913, she was president of the N.Y. Woman Suffrage Association; later she became vice president of the N.Y. State Woman's Suffrage Party, and, in 1917, vice president of the national organization. She was director of Women's Overseas Hospitals in France during World War I and helped found the National League of Women Voters.

BROWN, GOOLD (*b. Providence, R.I., 1791; d. Lynn, Mass., 1857*), grammarian. Author of *Institutes of English Grammar* (1823), for many years a popular text.

BROWN, HENRY BILLINGS (*b. South Lee, Mass., 1836; d. Bronxville, N.Y., 1913*), jurist. Authority on admiralty law; associate justice, U.S. Supreme Court, 1890–1906.

BROWN, HENRY CORDIS (*b. near St. Clairsville, Ohio, 1820; d. San Diego, Calif., 1906*), capitalist. Prospered in Denver, Colo., real estate, 1860–93; builder of Brown Palace Hotel, Denver, 1889.

BROWN, HENRY KIRKE (*b. Leyden, Mass., 1814; d. Newburgh, N.Y., 1886*), sculptor. Teacher of J. Q. A. Ward; executed equestrian statue of Washington, Union Square, New York City, and other works.

BROWN, ISAAC VAN ARSDALE (*b. Pluckemin, N.J., 1784; d. 1861*), Presbyterian clergyman. Founded Lawrenceville School, 1810; served as its principal until 1833.

BROWN, JACOB JENNINGS (*b. Bucks Co., Pa., 1775; d. 1828*), soldier. After teaching school, and surveying in Ohio, promoted a settlement at Brownsville, N.Y., near Watertown, 1799, and prospered in farming and land operations. Active in the militia *post* 1809, he successfully defended Sackett's Harbor, 1813. In 1814, appointed major general commanding in western New York, he began an invasion of Canada that was successful at the ably fought battles of Chippewa and Niagara (or Lundy's Lane) but met ultimate failure for lack of naval support. He commanded the army of the United States, 1821–28.

BROWN, JAMES (*b. near Staunton, Va., 1766; d. Philadelphia, Pa., 1835*), lawyer. U.S. senator, Democrat, from Louisiana, 1813–17 and 1819–23; U.S. minister to France, 1823–29.

BROWN, JAMES (*b. Ireland, 1791; d. New York, N.Y., 1877*), banker. Son of Alexander Brown. Founded Brown Brothers and Co., New York branch of his father's Baltimore firm.

BROWN, JAMES (*b. Acton, Mass., 1800; d. 1855*), bookseller, publisher. With C. C. Little, founded Boston publishing firm of Little, Brown & Co., 1837.

BROWN, JAMES SALISBURY (*b. Pawtucket, R.I., 1802; d. Pawtucket, 1879*), inventor, head of the Brown Machine Works. Introduced many improvements in cotton machinery; devised a variety of special tools.

BROWN, JOHN (*b. Providence, R.I., 1736; d. Providence, 1803*), merchant. Brother of Nicholas (1729–91), Joseph, and Moses (1738–1836) Brown. At first their partner, he withdrew *ca.* 1770 from the family business to trade on his own account. Headed raiding party against British vessel *Gaspee*, 1772; employed his ships and trade connections in service of Congress during Revolutionary War. Brown and Francis, his firm, sent out the first Providence vessel to engage in the East India and China trade, 1787. He served for twenty years as treasurer of Brown University (Rhode Island College).

BROWN, JOHN (*b. Haverhill, Mass., 1744; d. near Stone Arabia, N.Y., 1780*), lawyer, soldier. Gathered Canadian intelligence for General Schuyler, 1775; with Ethan Allen attacked Montreal; with Montgomery and Arnold before Quebec, Dec. 1775. Captured Fort George, N.Y., 1777; killed in expedition against Tories and Mohawks.

BROWN, JOHN (*b. Staunton, Va., 1757; d. Frankfort, Ky., 1837*), statesman. Removed to Kentucky, 1782; first U.S. senator from that state, 1792–1805; an outstanding spokesman for the West.

BROWN, JOHN (*b. Torrington, Conn., 1800; d. Charlestown, W.Va., 1859*), "Brown of Osawatomie." Child of a roving father and a mother who died insane (her family had a history of mental instability); spent boyhood in Hudson, Ohio; was by turns a drover, a tanner, a land speculator, and a dealer in sheep. Brown's career before 1855 was a record of bankruptcies, lawsuits, and drifting from place to place. Always an abolitionist, the idea that slaves must be freed by force became obsessive in his mind about the time of the free-soil *vs.* slave-interest fight for Kansas, 1855. From a free-soil settlement they had established on the Osawatomie there, he and his sons led a murderous guerrilla attack on a pro-slave settlement in reprisal for the sack of Lawrence, Kans., during May 1856. Driven from Kansas, Brown returned East to become the idol of the abolition party; he was encouraged by Gerrit Smith and others in a plan to establish a free state for escaped slaves and free blacks in the mountains of Maryland and Virginia, wherefrom active hostility against slave owners could be directed. After a brief 1858 skirmish on the Kansas-Missouri border, Brown fixed on Harper's Ferry, Va., as a base for the future operations; in midsummer, 1859, his "army" of twenty-one men assembled at a farm nearby; on the night of Oct. 16 he raided Harper's Ferry, seizing on the U.S. armory there and securing the bridges. Local militia and a company of U.S. marines under Colonel R. E. Lee penned Brown and his followers in the engine house of the armory; following his refusal to surrender, the soldiers took the place by storm. After a trial for treason he was sentenced to death and was hanged.

BROWN, JOHN A. (*b. Ireland, 1788; d. 1872*), banker. Son of Alexander Brown. Established Philadelphia branch of father's firm, 1818; it was later Brown and Bowen, and finally Brown Brothers & Co.

BROWN, JOHN APPLETON (*b. West Newbury, Mass., 1844; d. New York, N.Y., 1902*), landscape painter.

BROWN, JOHN CALVIN (*b. Giles Co., Tenn., 1827; d. Red Boiling Springs, Tenn., 1889*), lawyer, Confederate soldier. Democratic governor of Tennessee, 1870–74; supervised construction of Texas & Pacific railroad *post* 1876. Brother of Neill S. Brown.

BROWN, JOHN CARTER (*b. Providence, R.I., 1797; d. 1874*), book collector. Assembled the great library that bears his name, now at Brown University. Son of Nicholas Brown (1769–1841).

BROWN, JOHN GEORGE (*b. Durham, England, 1831; d. New York, N.Y., 1913*), painter. Came to America *ca.* 1853; specialized in popular renderings of American town and country types; was a president of the National Academy.

BROWN, JOHN MASON, JR. (*b. Louisville, Ky., 1900; d. New York, N.Y., 1969*), theater critic, writer, and lecturer. Drama critic for the *New York Evening Post* (1929–41). Taught courses on the history of the drama at the American Laboratory Theater (1925–31), and had a successful career as a lecturer. His first book, *The Modern Theatre in Revolt* (1929), anticipated his sympathetic responses to the American political plays of the 1930's. During World War II made broadcasts from the flagship *Ancon*, some of which were collected in *To All Hands* (1943). Many of his books are collections of his reviews of Broadway seasons, such as *Upstage* (1930), *Two on the Aisle* (1938), and *Broadway in Review* (1940). The essays for his column "Seeing Things" for the *Saturday Review* (1944–46) were collected in four books (published 1946–52). Among his other books, his most ambitious undertaking was a full-scale biography of playwright Robert E. Sherwood, *The Worlds of Robert E. Sherwood: Mirror to His Times, 1896–1939* (1965) and the posthumous *The Ordeal of a Playwright: Robert E. Sherwood and the Challenge of War* (1970). As a radio and TV personality (1944–49), an editor for the Book-of-the-Month Club (1956–69), and a member of the advisory committee for the Pulitzer Prize, he became a respected molder of public taste in the creative arts.

BROWN, JOHN MIFFLIN (*b. Odessa, Del., 1817; d. Washington, D.C., 1893*), bishop of the African Methodist Episcopal Church, 1868–93; principal of Union Seminary, Ohio; founder of Paul Quinn College, Waco, Texas.

BROWN, JOHN NEWTON (*b. New London, Conn., 1803; d. 1868*), Baptist clergyman. Pastor, scholar, and editor; an author of the *New Hampshire Confession of Faith* (1833).

BROWN, JOHN PORTER (*b. Chillicothe, Ohio, 1814; d. Constantinople, Turkey, 1872*), diplomat, Orientalist. Served in various capacities at the American legation, Constantinople, 1832–72.

BROWN, JOHN YOUNG (*b. Elizabethtown, Ky., 1835; d. 1904*), lawyer. Democratic governor of Kentucky, 1891–95.

BROWN, JOSEPH (*b. Providence, R.I., 1733; d. 1785*), merchant, scientist. Brother of Nicholas (1729–1791), Moses (1738–1836), and John Brown (1736–1803); withdrew from family firm to conduct experiments in electricity and mechanics.

BROWN, JOSEPH EMERSON (*b. Pickens District, S.C., 1821; d. 1894*), lawyer, statesman. Practiced law in Canton, Ga.; active in Democratic politics. Able, controversial governor of Georgia, 1857–65; active as a Republican, 1866–71; reentered Democratic party, and served as U.S. senator, 1880–91. President of Western & Atlantic Railroad.

BROWN, JOSEPH ROGERS (*b. Warren, R.I., 1810; d. Isles of Shoals, N.H., 1876*), inventor, manufacturer. Designer and builder of high-precision machine tools; head of Brown & Sharpe Manufacturing Co.

BROWN, LAWRASON (*b. Baltimore, Md., 1871; d. Saranac Lake, N.Y., 1937*), physician. Resident and consulting physician, Trudeau Sanitarium, 1900–37; a national leader in the control of tuberculosis.

BROWN, MARGARET WISE (*b. Brooklyn, N.Y., 1910; d. Nice, France, 1952*), author of children's books. Studied at Hollins College. Brown published over 100 books for children, including the series of "noisy" books, which helped children to understand the world through hearing, and the "sleepy" books, which helped children to accept the world of dreams. Her titles include *The Noisy Book* (1939), *The Dream Book* (1950), and *SHHHhhhh . . . . . . bang* (1943).

BROWN, MATHER (*b. Boston, Mass., 1761; d. London, England, 1831*), painter. Pupil of Gilbert Stuart and Benjamin West. Miniaturist in Boston until 1780 when he went abroad; thereafter painted portraits and historical subjects in London, 1784–1809, in the English provincial towns until 1824, and in London again until death.

BROWN, MORRIS (*b. Charleston, S.C., 1770; d. 1849*), bishop of the African Methodist Episcopal Church, 1828–49. Was responsible for a wide extension of the denomination during his episcopacy.

BROWN, MOSES (*b. Providence, R.I., 1738; d. Providence, 1836*), manufacturer and philanthropist. Brother of Nicholas Brown (1729–1791), John Brown (1736–1803), and Joseph Brown (1733–1785). Member of firm of Nicholas Brown & Co., 1763–73. After the Revolutionary War, he was among first cotton manufacturers in the United States, and induced Samuel Slater to set up Arkwright machines here.

BROWN, MOSES (*b. Newbury, Mass., 1742; d. Newburyport, Mass., 1827*), merchant. A benefactor and founding donor of Andover Theological Seminary.

BROWN, NEILL SMITH (*b. Giles Co., Tenn., 1810; d. Nashville, Tenn., 1886*), lawyer, politician. Brother of John Calvin Brown. Whig governor of Tennessee, 1847–49; U.S. minister to Russia, 1850–53.

BROWN, NICHOLAS (*b. Providence, R.I., 1729; d. 1791*), merchant. Brother of John Brown (1736–1803), Joseph Brown (1733–1785), and Moses Brown (1738–1836); senior partner in trading firm established by their father and known after 1762 as Nicholas Brown & Co. Before the Revolutionary War the firm's vessels ventured to all West Indian and European ports, while the brothers interested themselves in development of local industries such as whale oil, iron manufacture, and distilling. Brown and his brother Joseph were responsible for the location of Rhode Island College at Providence, 1767; in 1804, after further family benefactions, it became known as Brown University.

BROWN, NICHOLAS (*b. Providence, R.I., 1769; d. Providence, 1841*), merchant, philanthropist. Son of Nicholas Brown (1729–1791), father of John Carter Brown. Carried on firm established by father and uncles, extending its interests to the Far East, to cotton manufacture, and to western land speculation; a benefactor of Brown University.

BROWN, OBADIAH (*b. Providence, R.I., 1771; d. 1822*), merchant. Son of Moses Brown (1738–1836); joined his father as a partner in cotton manufacture, 1792.

BROWN, OLYMPIA (*b. Prairie Ronde, Mich., 1835; d. Baltimore, Md., 1926*), feminist. Ordained minister in Universalist Church, 1863, the first woman to be ordained in America to a regularly constituted religious body; after 1866, an ardent campaigner for woman suffrage.

BROWN, PERCY (*b. Cambridge, Mass., 1875; d. Egypt, near Scituate, Mass., 1950*), physician, roentgenologist. M.D., Harvard Medical School, 1900. Became interested in roentgen rays while intern at Boston Children's Hospital; started private practice, 1904. Exerted influence to establish professional standards and training for physicians practicing roentgenology (radiology); held clinical teaching appointments in that subject at Harvard, 1911–22. After service with U.S. Army Medical Corps in World War I, he gave up private practice and became associated with various large clinics as roentgenologist; he retired for reasons of health in 1934. Author of numerous articles and *American Martyrs to American Science Through the Roentgen Rays* (1935).

BROWN, PHOEBE HINSDALE (*b. Canaan, N.Y., 1783; d. Monson, Mass.[?], 1861*), hymn writer.

BROWN, RALPH HALL (*b. Ayer, Mass., 1898; d. St. Paul, Minn., 1948*), historical geographer. B.S., University of Pennsylvania, 1921; Ph.D., University of Wisconsin, 1925. Taught at University of Colorado, 1925–29; assistant, associate, and full professor of geography, University of Minnesota, 1929–48. Author of *Mirror for Americans: Likeness of the Eastern Seaboard, 1810* (1943), a synoptic, cross-sectional view of the area's systematic and regional geography as seen through the eyes of an imagined scholar-traveler. He was author also of *Historical Geography of the United States* (1948), a textbook. His work was an important antecedent of the perceptual approach to historical geography.

BROWN, SAMUEL (*b. Rockbridge Co., Va., 1769; d. near Huntsville, Ala., 1830*), physician. Brother of James Brown (1766–1835) and John Brown (1757–1837).

BROWN, SAMUEL GILMAN (*b. Hanover, N.H., 1813; d. Utica, N.Y., 1885*), educator. Professor of oratory, philosophy, political economy at Dartmouth, 1840–67; president, Hamilton College, 1867–81.

BROWN, SAMUEL ROBBINS (*b. East Windsor, Conn., 1810; d. Monson, Mass., 1880*), missionary to China and Japan for Dutch Reformed Church.

BROWN, SIMON (*b. Newburyport, Mass., 1802; d. near Concord, Mass., 1873*), editor of the *New England Farmer*, post 1858.

BROWN, SOLYMAN (*b. Litchfield, Conn., 1790; d. Dodge Center, Minn., 1876*), a pioneer in the American dental profession. Graduated Yale, 1812; with Eleazar Parmly organized first dental association, in New York, N.Y., 1834; served also as a Swedenborgian minister.

BROWN, SYLVANUS (*b. Valley Falls, R.I., 1747; d. Pawtucket, R.I., 1824*), inventor, millwright. Built the first American power spinning machine from Samuel Slater's description of the parts, 1790.

BROWN, WALTER FOLGER (*b. Massillon, Ohio, 1869; d. Toledo, Ohio, 1961*), lawyer, politician, and postmaster general. A.B. (1892), Harvard; attended Harvard Law School 1894–96. While chairman of the Ohio Republican Central Committee (1906–12), he backed the presidency of Taft. Declared himself a progressive in 1911, backed Theodore Roosevelt's unsuccessful campaign for the presidency, and as delegate to the Ohio Constitutional Convention of 1912, introduced progressive amendments to the state constitution. Returned to the Republican party in 1916 and contributed significantly to Warren G. Harding's 1920 presidential campaign. Harding appointed him chairman of the Joint Congressional Reorganization Committee, and under his leadership (1921–24) the committee recommended sweeping organizational changes. After being elected president, Herbert Hoover appointed him postmaster general; he improved the efficiency of the national post office and expanded the air transport of mail by negotiating favorable contracts with large aviation companies.

BROWN, WILLIAM (*b. Haddingtonshire, Scotland, 1752; d. Alexandria, Va., 1792*), physician. While in service with Revolutionary army, wrote the first pharmacopeia to be published in the United States (1778).

BROWN, WILLIAM ADAMS (*b. New York, N.Y., 1865; d. New York, 1943*), Presbyterian clergyman, liberal theologian, leader in the ecumenical movement. Grandson of James Brown (1791–1877), and of William Adams. B.A., Yale, 1886; M.A., 1888; Ph.D., 1901. Graduated Union Theological Seminary, 1890. During two years at University of Berlin, he was influenced strongly by Adolf Harnack. On his return from Germany, he began a long teaching career at Union Theological and was ordained in January 1893; he was professor of systematic theology, 1898–1930, and research professor in applied Christianity, 1930–36. Beyond the classroom, he was active in urban reform movements, settlement work, and home missions, acting on his conviction that the church had a duty to work as a social institution. A liberal and modernist in theology, he had two great concerns: to discern and to teach "the essence of Christianity"; and to promote church unity. He took a decisive part in the movement that culminated in the organization of the World Council of Churches, 1938. The best summary of his mature thought is his book *The Church: Catholic and Protestant* (1935).

BROWN, WILLIAM CARLOS (*b. Norway, N.Y., 1853; d. Pasadena, Calif., 1924*), railroad executive. Raised in Iowa. Rose from engine fireman to general manager of Chicago, Burlington & Quincy Railroad; president of New York Central, 1909–14.

BROWN, WILLIAM GARROTT (*b. Marion, Ala., 1868; d. New Canaan, Conn., 1913*), author of *The Lower South in American History* (1902) and lives of Andrew Jackson, Stephen Douglas, and Oliver Ellsworth.

BROWN, WILLIAM HENRY (*b. Little Britain Township, Pa., 1836; d. Belfast, Ireland, 1910*), civil engineer. Self-taught, Brown was chief engineer of the Pennsylvania Railroad,

1881–1906, and responsible for a vast amount of bridge and terminal construction.

BROWN, WILLIAM HILL (*b. Boston, Mass., 1765; d. Murfreesboro, N.C., 1793*), author of *The Power of Sympathy* (1789), considered the first American novel.

BROWN, WILLIAM HUGHEY (*b. North Huntington Township, Pa., 1815; d. Philadelphia, Pa., 1875*), coal operator. First mine operator to ship coal in towed flatboats, 1858; supplied coal for Union warships on Mississippi in Civil War.

BROWN, WILLIAM WELLS (*b. Lexington, Ky., ca. 1816; d. Chelsea, Mass., 1884*), black reformer. Escaped from slavery, 1834; was celebrated in his own time as a lecturer and historian of his race.

BROWNE, BENJAMIN FREDERICK (*b. Salem, Mass., 1793; d. Salem, 1873*), druggist. His narrative of a privateer cruise, 1812–15, was edited by Nathaniel Hawthorne as "Papers of an Old Dartmoor Prisoner" in *U.S. Magazine* (serially, through 1846) and republished with additions in 1926 as *The Yarn of a Yankee Privateer*.

BROWNE, CHARLES ALBERT (*b. North Adams, Mass., 1870; d. Washington, D.C., 1947*), chemist. B.A., Williams College, 1892. After work in a commercial analytical laboratory, as laboratory assistant at Pennsylvania State College, and as chemist at the Pennsylvania Agricultural Experiment Station, he enrolled as a student of Bernhard Tollens at the University of Göttingen, 1900; Ph.D., 1902. Employed as research chemist at the Louisiana Agricultural Experiment Station in New Orleans, he was so successful that he was appointed in 1906 the chief of the sugar division in the U.S. Department of Agriculture Bureau of Chemistry, Washington, D.C. A year later, he resigned to establish the New York Sugar Trade Laboratory, an industry quality control organization that he headed until 1923. He then returned to the Department of Agriculture as chief of the Bureau of Chemistry and served under various titles until retirement, 1940. A recognized authority on the chemistry of sugar, he was interested also in general problems of agricultural biochemistry, and in the history of chemistry. Major work was *A Source Book of Agricultural Chemistry* (1944), which combined his classical, historical, and scientific interests in a single work.

BROWNE, CHARLES FARRAR (*b. Waterford, Maine, 1834; d. Southampton, England, 1867*), "Artemus Ward," humorist. His reporting of the adventures and opinions of a traveling showman in the Cleveland *Plain Dealer*, 1858, was continued in the New York periodical *Vanity Fair* and published in book form as *Artemus Ward: His Book* (1862). Speaking in the person of his character, Browne toured the entire country as a "moral lecturer" with great success; his hilarious comments coupled with a mock-lugubrious delivery won him the admiration of Abraham Lincoln and the young Mark Twain. Returning from the West, Browne appeared in 1864 with a new "lecture," a comic panorama of life in Utah with the title "Artemus Ward Among the Mormons." A triumphant visit to England, 1866–67, crowned his career. He died of tuberculosis.

BROWNE, DANIEL JAY (*b. Fremont, N.H., 1804; no data on death*), agricultural and scientific writer.

BROWNE, FRANCIS FISHER (*b. South Halifax, Vt., 1843; d. Santa Barbara, Calif., 1913*), editor of the *Dial* (Chicago), 1880–1913, a journal of critical opinion.

BROWNE, HERBERT WHEILDON COTTON (*b. Boston, Mass., 1860; d. Boston, 1946*), architect. Studied at Boston Museum of Fine Arts School, Massachusetts Institute of Technology, and in Europe. Joined Arthur Little in the Boston firm of Little and Browne, 1890. The firm specialized in large and elegant city and country houses that were sometimes more tasteful than their owners. Browne combined a deep feeling for the New England past with an equal affection for Italian architecture of the baroque and Empire periods; he was also a skilled watercolorist. Following Little's death in 1925, he continued to practice in partnership with Lester Couch. When Couch died in 1939, Browne retired and closed the firm.

BROWNE, IRVING (*b. Marshall, N.Y., 1835; d. Buffalo, N.Y., 1899*), legal writer. Editor, *Albany Law Journal*, 1879–93; author of numerous textbooks and legal compilations.

BROWNE, JOHN (*d. Wannamoisett, R.I., 1662*), a liberal and influential magistrate of Plymouth Colony, 1635–54.

BROWNE, JOHN ROSS (*b. Dublin, Ireland, 1821; d. Oakland, Calif., 1875*), author. Came to America, 1832 or 1833; was raised in Kentucky. Traveled extensively for more than a quarter-century; was official reporter for California constitutional convention, 1849. Wrote, and illustrated, among others: *Etchings of a Whaling Cruise* (1846); *Crusoe's Island* (1864); and *Adventures in the Apache Country* (1869).

BROWNE, JUNIUS HENRI (*b. Seneca Falls, N.Y., 1833; d. New York, N.Y., 1902*), journalist. War correspondent, *New York Tribune*, 1861–63; wrote *Four Years in Secessia* (1865).

BROWNE, THOMAS (*d. St. Vincent, British West Indies, 1825*), Tory partisan commander in Georgia, 1776–82.

BROWNE, WILLIAM (*b. Salem, Mass., 1737; d. London, England, 1802*), Loyalist. Graduated Harvard, 1755. A man of property, a colonial judge, and a *mandamus* Councillor in 1774, he removed to London, 1776, after the fall of Boston. He served with great ability as governor of Bermuda, 1781–88.

BROWNE, WILLIAM HAND (*b. Baltimore, Md., 1828; d. Baltimore, 1912*), educator, author. Associated with Johns Hopkins University as librarian and professor, 1879–1912; editor, *Archives of Maryland.*

BROWNELL, HENRY HOWARD (*b. Providence, R.I., 1820; d. East Hartford, Conn., 1872*), author of *Lyrics of a Day* (1864), a notable collection of narrative poems on Civil War engagements.

BROWNELL, THOMAS CHURCH (*b. Westport, Mass., 1779; d. Hartford, Conn., 1865*), Episcopal clergyman. Consecrated bishop of Connecticut, 1819; first president of Trinity College, Hartford, 1823–31.

BROWNELL, WILLIAM CRARY (*b. New York, N.Y., 1851; d. New York, 1928*), critic. Graduated Amherst, 1871. Editor, Charles Scribner's Sons, 1888–1928; author of *French Traits* (1889); *Victorian Prose Masters* (1901); *American Prose Masters* (1909).

BROWNING, JOHN MOSES (*b. Ogden, Utah, 1855; d. near Liège, Belgium, 1926*), inventor. Designer of guns, notably the automatic pistol, the heavy machine-gun and the light automatic rifle used by the U.S. Army in the first World War.

BROWNING, ORVILLE HICKMAN (*b. Harrison Co., Ky., 1806; d. 1881*), lawyer, statesman. Settled in Quincy, Ill., 1831; active as a Whig in politics until 1856, thereafter a Republican until after the Civil War. Appointed to the U.S. Senate for sessions of 1861–62, he at first supported Lincoln's policy but opposed Emancipation Proclamation. Secretary of interior in Andrew Johnson's cabinet, he stood by the president in the impeachment crisis and left office in 1869. Elected on Democratic ticket in

Illinois constitutional convention, 1869–70. Thereafter he practiced as a railroad lawyer.

BROWNING, TOD (*b. Charles A. Browning, Louisville, Ky., 1880; d. Santa Monica, Calif., 1962*), film director, writer, and actor. His forty-eight films, preoccupied with grotesque motifs and drawn from the circus and underworld, encourage viewers almost cynically to distrust complacent, corrupt appearances, and also show a rare sympathy for characters ostracized by society and victimized by their own obsessions. He emerged as a major director with ten features with Priscilla Dean (1918–23). Between 1923 and 1929 did a series of grotesque fantasies with Lon Chaney for MGM, beginning with the popular film *The Unholy Three* (filmed 1925). After the coming of sound, *Dracula* (1931) was his most popular film, though the commercially unsuccessful *Freaks* (1932) is considered his finest work.

BROWNLEE, JAMES FORBIS (*b. Oakland, Calif., 1891; d. Greensfield Hill, Conn., 1960*), business executive. Studied at Harvard. After serving as a director of General Foods and president of Frankfort Distilleries, Brownlee entered government service, serving on the War Production Board and the War Food Administration, and in 1946, was a deputy director of the Office of Economic Stabilization. After World War II, he became chairman of the board of the Minute Maid Corporation and, in 1953, was named a trustee of the Ford Foundation.

BROWNLEE, WILLIAM CRAIG (*b. Lanarkshire, Scotland, 1784; d. 1860*), Presbyterian clergyman. Came to America, *ca.* 1808; served churches in New Jersey, Pennsylvania, and New York; a stout orthodox Calvinist and anti-Catholic.

BROWNLOW, WILLIAM GANNAWAY (*b. Wythe Co., Va., 1805; d. Knoxville, Tenn., 1877*), Methodist clergyman, journalist, politician. Taken to Tennessee as a child; served as itinerant minister, 1826–36. Edited several newspapers, 1838–49; edited *Knoxville Whig*, 1849–61, and made it an uncompromising voice against secession. After brief imprisonment by Confederates, he was driven out of Tennessee, 1862, returning the next year with the Union Army. As governor of Tennessee, 1865–69, he stood for disfranchisement of all who had fought against the Union in the Civil War.

BROWNSON, ORESTES AUGUSTUS (*b. Stockbridge, Vt., 1803; d. Detroit, Mich., 1876*), philosopher, author. After long identification with New England liberal movements, and pastorates as a Universalist and Unitarian minister, he became a Catholic, 1844. His trenchant, profoundly thought-out views on society and politics were expressed in his *Boston Quarterly Review* (1838–42) and *Brownson's Quarterly Review* (1844–65; and *post* 1872). His books include: *The Convert* (1857) and *The American Republic* (1865).

BROWNSON, WILLARD HERBERT (*b. Lyons, N.Y., 1845; d. Washington, D.C., 1935*), naval officer.

BRUCE, ANDREW ALEXANDER (*b. Nunda Drug, Madras Presidency, India, 1866; d. 1934*), professor of law at universities of Wisconsin, North Dakota, and Minnesota, and at Northwestern University.

BRUCE, ARCHIBALD (*b. New York, N.Y., 1777; d. New York, 1818*), physician, mineralogist. Graduated Columbia, A.B., 1797; M.D., Edinburgh, 1800. Discoverer of brucite; founded the *American Mineralogical Journal* (1810).

BRUCE, BLANCHE K. (*b. Farmville, Va., 1841; d. Washington, D.C., 1898*), politician, planter. A black, Bruce served as U.S. senator from Mississippi, 1875–81.

BRUCE, EDWARD BRIGHT (*b. Dover Plains, N.Y., 1879; d. Hollywood, Fla., 1943*), lawyer, businessman, painter, federal art project administrator. Graduated Columbia University, 1901; Columbia Law School, 1904. After a career in law and business in the Philippines and China, 1907–19, he revived his boyhood ambition to be a painter. Moving to Italy, 1922, he began serious work under guidance of his friend Maurice Sterne, concentrating on landscapes that were distinguished by simplicity of composition and execution, and by individual rhythms that grew naturally from the conception. His work won critical praise, and his gallery shows were very successful; one of his paintings was bought for the Luxembourg Museum. Returning to the United States, 1929, he lived and painted in Oregon and California, 1930–31. In 1932, he moved to Washington, D.C., as a lobbyist to help promote Philippine independence and became increasingly involved in New Deal politics. Organizer of the first government-sponsored arts project under the Civil Works Administration, 1933, for relief of unemployed artists, he subsequently directed the program for choice of artists by anonymous competition to execute mural paintings and sculpture for decoration of public buildings. In 1940, he was appointed to the Federal Commission of Fine Arts.

BRUCE, GEORGE (*b. Edinburgh, Scotland, 1781; d. New York, N.Y., 1866*), typefounder. Came to America, *ca.* 1796. With brother David introduced stereotype process *ca.* 1812; invented a type-casting machine.

BRUCE, LENNY (*b. Leonard Alfred Schneider, Mineola, N.Y., 1925; d. Hollywood, Calif., 1966*), comedian. Began his career in the New York area and in 1953 moved to the West Coast, where for the next five years he worked mostly as master of ceremonies and comedian for various burlesque theaters. During the years 1958–61, he gained notoriety from his appearances at the hungry i and other San Francisco bistros with skits that wove jazz idioms, Yiddish slang, and profane language into a surrealistic comic vision, much of which was improvised. Beginning in late 1961, was repeatedly arrested for giving obscene performances. Was also arrested several times for possessing narcotics. Unable to secure work, he declared bankruptcy and shortly thereafter was found dead of a narcotics overdose. His legacy includes a number of recordings of his performances, a film of a late cabaret appearance, the autobiography *How to Talk Dirty and Influence People* (1965), and a collection of his finest routines, edited by John Cohen as *The Essential Lenny Bruce* (1967). In 1974 the biographical film *Lenny* appeared, starring Dustin Hoffman in the title role.

BRUCE, PHILIP ALEXANDER (*b. Staunton Hill, Va., 1856; d. Charlottesville, Va., 1933*), historian. Chronicler of colonial Virginia; historian of the University of Virginia.

BRUCE, ROBERT (*b. Scone, Scotland, 1778; d. Pittsburgh, Pa., 1846*), Presbyterian clergyman, educator. Came to America, 1806; settled in Pittsburgh, 1808; served as pastor of First United Presbyterian church, 1808–46. Principal, Western University of Pennsylvania, 1822–43.

BRUCE, WILLIAM CABELL (*b. Staunton Hill, Charlotte County, Va., 1860; d. Ruxton, Md., 1946*), lawyer, statesman, municipal reformer. Brother of Philip A. Bruce. LL.B., University of Maryland School of Law, 1882; practiced in Baltimore, Md. A Jeffersonian Democrat, he was active in support of reform in both Baltimore city and Maryland state government. Appointed city solicitor, 1903, he drafted the acts that permitted financing of municipal improvements; he was also one of the commissioners appointed in 1909 to draft a new, more effective charter for Baltimore, and served as counsel to the Maryland Public Service Commission, 1910–22. As U.S. senator from Maryland, 1923–29, he defended individual rights and opposed lynching, the Ku Klux Klan, and the expansion of federal power. He was author of the Pulitzer Prize biography *Benjamin Franklin, Self-Revealed* (1917) and *John Randolph of Roanoke* (1922).

BRUCKER, WILBER MARION (*b. Saginaw, Mich., 1894; d. Detroit, Mich., 1968*), secretary of the army. Graduated from the University of Michigan Law School (1916). After World War I, set up law practice in Saginaw and became active in Republican affairs, holding several county and state offices (1919–30) before being elected governor of Michigan (1930). Was defeated in 1932. In 1954 was appointed general counsel for the U.S. Defense Department, where he gained national attention when he laughed aloud at Senator Joseph McCarthy for his accusation that President Eisenhower and others were conspiring to cover up military disloyalty. In 1955 was appointed secretary of the army, and in 1957 supervised the federal troops dispatched by President Eisenhower to maintain order in Little Rock, Ark. In 1960 returned to Detroit to practice law in partnership with his son.

BRÜHL, GUSTAV (*b. Herdorf, Germany, 1826; d. Cincinnati, Ohio, 1903*), physician, author. Came to America, 1848; practiced and taught medicine in Cincinnati; wrote archaeological studies and poetry.

BRULÉ, ÉTIENNE (*b. Champigny, France, ca. 1592; d. 1632*), explorer. Came to New France, 1608, with Champlain; probably the first white man to see the Great Lakes, all of which he explored with exception of Lake Michigan.

BRUMBY, RICHARD TRAPIER (*b. Sumter District, S.C., 1804; d. 1875*), educator. Graduated South Carolina College, 1824. Professor of chemistry, University of Alabama, 1834–49; prepared (1838) first systematic report of Alabama mineral resources.

BRUMIDI, CONSTANTINO (*b. Rome, Italy, 1805, d. Washington, D.C., 1880*), painter. Came to America, 1852. Designed and painted the frescoes in the U.S. Capitol.

BRUNNER, ARNOLD WILLIAM (*b. New York, N.Y., 1857; d. 1925*), architect, city planner. Graduated Massachusetts Institute of Technology, 1879; worked in office of George B. Post. Principal works are in New York City, Harrisburg, Pa., and Cleveland, Ohio.

BRUNSWICK, RUTH MACK (*b. Chicago, Ill., 1897; d. New York, N.Y., 1946*), psychoanalyst. Daughter of Julian W. Mack. Graduated Radcliffe, 1918; Tufts Medical School, 1922. Went to Vienna, 1923, to pursue interest in psychoanalysis and was patient of Freud. Divorced in 1924 from H. L. Blumgart, whom she had married while an undergraduate, she remained in Vienna until 1938, an intimate associate and disciple of Freud who chose her to continue treatment of the "Wolf-man." Married Mark Brunswick, a cousin of her first husband, 1928. Forced out of Vienna by the Nazis, 1938, she settled in New York City where she continued to practice. She was divorced again in 1945. She was author of a few excellent studies, but her greatest contribution was the example she gave other analysts as a humane and perceptive practitioner who gave unswerving adherence to the best in scientific, psychoanalytic theory.

BRUNTON, DAVID WILLIAM (*b. Ayr, Canada, 1849; d. 1927*), mining engineer, inventor. Manager of mines at Leadville and Aspen, Colo., where he developed his speciality of driving long tunnels; became technical adviser to Anaconda interests. Inventor of a mechanical ore-sampler and of the Brunton pocket-transit.

BRUSH, CHARLES FRANCIS (*b. Cuyahoga Co., Ohio, 1849; d. Cleveland, Ohio, 1929*), inventor. Graduated University of Michigan, 1869, as a mining engineer; perfected a dynamo that came into wide use. Announced invention of the Brush arc light, 1878. Other inventions related to electroplating, storage batteries, and dynamos. After his Brush Electric Co. was taken over by the General Electric Co., Brush improved on Carl Linde's process for extracting oxygen from liquid air; became founder and first president of the Linde Air Products Co.

BRUSH, EDWARD NATHANIEL (*b. Glenwood, N.Y., 1852; d. 1933*), psychiatrist. Associated editorially with *American Journal of Psychiatry*, 1878–84; 1897–1931.

BRUSH, GEORGE DE FOREST (*b. Shelbyville, Tenn., 1855; d. Hanover, N.H., 1941*), painter. Raised in Danbury, Conn. Studied at National Academy of Design, New York City, under L. E. Wilmarth, and at the École des Beaux Arts, Paris, under J. L. Gérôme. Returning from Europe, 1880, he spent several years in Wyoming and Montana, living with various Indian tribes and developing a sympathy with their culture and a concern for their decline under white encroachment. His paintings of Shoshone, Crow, and Arapaho brought him his first success; well composed, rich in color, and meticulously painted, they were more romantic tableaux than raw truth. Setting up a studio in New York City, Brush taught at the Art Students League, 1885–98; between 1898 and 1914, he spent frequent sojourns in Europe. He was made an Academician, 1908, and received many other honors. About 1890, he had shifted from poetic portrayals of Indian life to portraits, and in particular to semiclassical "mother and child" groups (e.g., the circular *Mother and Child* in Boston Museum of Fine Arts) that brought him a wide audience and financial success. A hard worker and a perfectionist, he remained a firm believer in idealism and nobility as prime themes in painting.

BRUSH, GEORGE JARVIS (*b. Brooklyn, N.Y., 1831; d. 1912*), mineralogist. Professor of mineralogy, Sheffield Scientific School, 1855–72; director, Sheffield, 1872–98. Author of *Manual of Determinative Mineralogy* (1874).

BRUTÉ DE RÉMUR, SIMON WILLIAM GABRIEL (*b. Rennes, France, 1779; d. Vincennes, Ind., 1839*), Roman Catholic clergyman. Graduated from medical school at Paris with highest prize; entered Seminary of St. Sulpice; on ordination, 1808, joined Sulpicians. Volunteered to accompany Bishop Flaget of Kentucky back to America; taught in St. Mary's Seminary, Baltimore, St. Mary's College, Emmitsburg, and was then appointed rector of Baltimore seminary. His health failing, he returned to Emmitsburg and taught there, 1818–1834. Named first bishop of Vincennes, 1834.

BRYAN, CHARLES WAYLAND (*b. Salem, Ill., 1867; d. Lincoln, Nebr., 1945*), businessman, politician. Brother of William Jennings Bryan. Moved to Nebraska, 1891; entered politics in 1896, as aide in his brother's presidential campaign. A hardworking and efficient administrator, he managed William's finances, scheduled his speaking engagements, and helped formulate campaign strategy; he ran the *Commoner*, 1901–23, serving *post* 1914 as both associate editor and publisher. As Democratic mayor of Lincoln, Nebr., 1915–17, he championed municipal ownership of utilities and expanded welfare services; elected governor, 1922, he advocated a state income tax, a reduced budget, and a rural credits program, but was blocked by the Republican-dominated legislature. Democratic candidate for the vice presidency in 1924, he failed to carry even Nebraska. Elected governor again in 1930 and 1932, he worked hard to solve Depression problems. Failing of nomination for the U.S. Senate, 1934, he served again as mayor of Lincoln, 1935–37. Like his brother, he was basically an agrarian reformer.

BRYAN, GEORGE (*b. Dublin, Ireland, 1731; d. Philadelphia, Pa., 1791*), jurist, politician. Pennsylvania assemblyman, 1764–65, 1779; instrumental in drafting 1779 act for gradual abolition of slavery; judge, Pennsylvania supreme court, 1780–91; opposed Federal Constitution.

BRYAN, JOHN STEWART (*b. Brook Hill, near Richmond, Va., 1871; d. Richmond, 1944*), newspaper publisher, college president. A.B. and A.M., University of Virginia, 1893; LL.B., Harvard, 1897. Joined father in management of *Richmond Times-Dispatch* (and later the *News Leader*, 1900; succeeded him as president of the company, 1907. Sold the *Times-Dispatch*, 1914, but reacquired it, 1940. A leader in community activities, and a moderate progressive in opinion. As president of the College of William and Mary, 1934–42, he strove to build it into a great liberal arts college by improving the quality and morale of both faculty and student body.

BRYAN, KIRK (*b. Albuquerque, N.M., 1888; d. Cody, Wyo., 1950*), geologist, geomorphologist. B.A., University of New Mexico, 1909; did graduate work at Yale, receiving Ph.d., 1920. Associated with U.S. Geological Survey, 1912–27; thereafter taught at Harvard, becoming professor of physiography, 1943. His early fieldwork, carried out in the Southwest and the Sacramento Valley of California, dealt with groundwater supplies in arid and semiarid regions; he became an authority on the geology of water conservation and dam sites. He developed a major interest in geological research as an aid to archaeological and anthropological investigation. His major contribution, however, was the training of students for careers in universities and in the Geological Survey.

BRYAN, MARY EDWARDS (*b. near Tallahassee, Fla., 1842; d. 1913*), journalist, author. Associate editor, *Sunny South*, 1874–84; wrote *Manch* (1880), *Wild Work* (1881), and many other melodramatic tales.

BRYAN, THOMAS BARBOUR (*b. Alexandria, Va., 1828; d. Washington, D.C., 1906*), lawyer. Influenced choice of Chicago as site of 1893 World's Fair; vice president of fair.

BRYAN, WILLIAM JENNINGS (*b. Salem, Ill., 1860; d. Dayton, Tenn., 1925*), political leader. Graduated Illinois College, 1881; read law at Union College of Law, Chicago, and in Lyman Trumbull's office; practiced law in Jacksonville, Ill., 1883–87. Married Mary Baird, 1884. Moved to Lincoln, Nebr., where after successful but not brilliant law career he entered politics. Elected to Congress as Democrat, 1890, in normally Republican district; reelected, 1892. He sat on Ways and Means Committee in Congress; spoke fluently on tariff; voted against repeal of silver purchase law of 1890 and attacked President Cleveland for urging unconditional repeal. His candidacy for U.S. Senate, 1894, was unsuccessful. He then worked as editor in chief of *Omaha World-Herald* and as a Chautauqua lecturer; was vigorous speaker for free silver.

In 1896, Bryan received Democratic presidential nomination on fifth ballot, after his famous "Cross of Gold" speech stampeded the Chicago convention: "You shall not press down upon the brow of labor this crown of thorns. You shall not crucify mankind upon a cross of gold." In face of abusive treatment from the press and political enemies who made fun of his youth, his oratory, and in slips of speech, he carried his ideas to the country as no other candidate since Henry Clay. Bryan campaigned with vigor and skill, stressing the social and sectional struggle between Wall Street and the "toiling masses," and the silver issue; he lost to McKinley by 600,000 votes in a total vote of 13,600,000, with electoral vote 271 to 176. After the Spanish-American War he resumed leadership of Democratic party and accepted presidential nomination in 1900 on condition that silver plank be retained but that

"expansion" would be "paramount issue." Defeated on issue of expansion by greater margin than in 1896 (electoral vote 292 to 155), he wrote for a weekly newspaper, the *Commoner*; the paper was bitterly denounced by opponents as demagogic, setting poor against rich. Eastern Democrats displaced Bryan with Alton B. Parker in 1904 convention, in belief that business would support a conservative against Theodore Roosevelt, but Parker's poor showing reestablished Bryan's position as party leader.

His third and last nomination came in 1908 on first ballot, but he received only 162 of 483 electoral votes. In the 1912 convention he helped nominate Woodrow Wilson. As secretary of state from Wilson's inauguration until June 1915, when deep pacifist convictions forced his resignation, he used influence unselfishly to carry administration reform measures through Congress. He approved the administration's Mexican policy, was in accord with decision not to continue government support to Six-Power loan to China, and opposed "dollar diplomacy" in Latin America. In his own view, his notable service was negotiation of arbitration treaties with thirty foreign states. After resignation, he refused to criticize Wilson and campaigned for him in 1916. At his last political appearance in the 1924 Democratic convention, Bryan supported W. G. McAdoo against Alfred E. Smith. Hostile to modern evolutionary theory of man, he acted for prosecution in 1925 trial of J. T. Scopes for breaking a Tennessee statute by teaching Darwinism.

BRYANT, GRIDLEY (*b. Scituate, Mass., 1789; d. Scituate, 1867*), civil engineer, inventor. Devised portable derrick, 1823; engineer of Quincy Railroad for transportation of granite, 1826, introducing iron-plated rails and the eight-wheeled car.

BRYANT, JOHN HOWARD (*b. Cummington, Mass., 1807; d. Princeton, Ill., 1902*). Pioneer settler (1832) in Bureau Co., Ill.; brother of William Cullen Bryant.

BRYANT, JOSEPH DECATUR (*b. East Troy, Wis., 1845; d. 1914*), surgeon. Graduated Bellevue Hospital Medical College, 1868. Performed operation for sarcoma on Grover Cleveland's jaw, 1893; author of *Manual of Operative Surgery* (1884); editor, *American Practice of Surgery* (1906–11).

BRYANT, LOUISE FRANCES STEVENS (*b. Paris, France, 1885; d. Bronxville, N.Y., 1959*), social researcher, medical editor. Studied at Smith College and the University of Pennsylvania (Ph.D. in medical science, 1914). From 1909 to 1911, she was educational director of the Russell Sage Foundation, where she gained a national reputation for her work in child nutrition and public school feeding. After holding various positions in social work and medical fields, Bryant became executive secretary of the National Committee on Maternal Health (1927–35). As such she was responsible for the publication of numerous works on human sexuality and birth control, subjects highly controversial in the 1930's. She retired from the committee in 1935 because of poor health.

BRYANT, RALPH CLEMENT (*b. Princeton, Ill., 1877; d. New Haven, Conn., 1939*), forester and educator. Organized and directed, 1906–39, the educational program in logging and lumbering at Yale School of Forestry.

BRYANT, WILLIAM CULLEN (*b. Cummington, Mass., 1794; d. New York, N.Y., 1878*), poet, editor. His father was a physician and surgeon, fond of music and poetry; his early education was in district schools, and he was taught by Rev. Thomas Snell and Rev. Moses Hallock. Precocious and a voracious reader, Bryant was encouraged to write verses by his father who also provided sound criticism. The natural beauty of his boyhood surroundings inspired in him an intense and lifelong love of nature. After a year (1810–11) at Williams College, he read law, 1811–14; was admitted to the bar, August 1815, and practiced until 1825. Removing to New York City in that year, he became assistant editor of the *Evening Post*, 1826. Succeeding William Coleman as editor in 1829, he held the post until his own death.

An anti-Jefferson satire *The Embargo* (1808) had appeared from his pen, but his first great poem "Thanatopsis" was not written until 1811 and remained unpublished until 1817 when an abbreviated version was printed in the September issue of the *North American Review*. Meanwhile a reading of Wordsworth's *Lyrical Ballads* dimmed the earlier influences of Pope, Kirke White, Blair, and Cowper; Bryant understood that his impulse to be a poet could best be realized in expression of the natural beauty that he felt so immediately and strongly. His poetic fame was unchallenged after he published *Poems* (1821), a small volume but important, containing an improved version of "Thanatopsis" and lyrics of genius such as "Green River," "To a Waterfowl," and "The Yellow Violet." In 1824–25, the period of his greatest productivity, he wrote "Rizpah," "Autumn Woods," and "Forest Hymn, " which rank among his finest poems.

Regarding journalism at first as a secondary interest, he hoped to live off it while devoting the major part of his time to pure literature. The *Evening Post*'s rapid decline between 1830–36, when he left its actual management in the hands of assistants, taught him a sharp lesson; he labored day and night to restore the paper and from that time gave it his first concern. By 1840, he had become one of the leading Democratic editors in the nation; he supported Jackson and Van Buren, opposed high tariffs, advocated a complete separation between government and banking, and began to take an advanced position against slavery. As a poet, he suffered from the heavy demands his work made on his time, yet he published new work in *Poems* (1832), *The Fountain, and Other Poems* (1842), and *The White-Footed Doe* (1844).

Bryant and the *Evening Post* broke sharply with the Democratic party in 1848, supporting Van Buren's Free-Soil candidacy; in 1850, he opposed Clay's Compromise, urging the free states not to yield on a single principle; by 1853, the *Post* reached a radical antislavery position. In the campaign of 1856, Bryant enthusiastically threw his influence behind Frémont and during the four years following made his paper one of the most vigorous of "Black Republican" organs. He introduced Abraham Lincoln at Cooper Union in 1860 and supported him in 1864, although assailing his policies of moderation in dealing with the South and his hesitation in proclaiming full emancipation of slaves. After the Civil War, Bryant broke away from the Radical Republicans and supported Andrew Johnson's policies. Although estranged from the Grant administration by its low moral tone, its tariff policy and its treatment of the South, he remained a Republican and kept the *Evening Post* Republican.

Untired in civic, social, and charitable endeavors, Bryant's last important literary enterprise was a translation of all Homer's works in blank verse (published 1870–72). Acknowledged great as a poet of nature, he lacked warmth of emotion in human concerns and intellectual depth; within his restricted range, however, he produced a small body of well-received poetry.

BRYCE, LLOYD STEPHENS (*b. Flushing, N.Y., 1851; d. 1917*), politician, author. Editor, *North American Review*, 1889–96.

BRYSON, LYMAN LLOYD (*b. Valentine, Nebr., 1888; d. New York, N.Y., 1959*), educator, radio broadcaster, and author. Studied at the University of Michigan. Professor of education at Teachers College, Columbia (1934–53). An advocate of adult education, Bryson was director of education for CBS from 1942. He was featured on many educational radio and television series, including "Invitation to Learning" and "Lamp Unto My Feet."

During World War II he was chief of the Bureau of Special Operations for the Office of War Information. Books include *The Next America: Prophecy and Faith* (1952) and *The Drive Toward Reason* (1954).

BUCHANAN, FRANKLIN (*b. Baltimore, Md., 1800; d. Talbot Co., Md., 1874*), naval officer. Became midshipman, 1815; promoted commander, 1841; in 1845, having submitted plan for new Naval School at Annapolis, he was appointed its first superintendent. Commanded sloop *Germantown* throughout Mexican War; commanded steam frigate *Susquehanna*, flagship of Perry's Japan squadron; promoted captain, 1855. Joined Confederate States Navy as captain, 1861. Commanded Chesapeake Bay Squadron, 1862, with flag on reconstructed *Merrimack*; surprised Union squadron in Hampton Roads, destroying *Congress* and *Cumberland*. Became admiral and ranking officer; commanded in battle of Mobile Bay, 1864.

BUCHANAN, JAMES (*b. near Mercersburg, Pa., 1791; d. near Lancaster, Pa., 1868*), president of the United States. He was descended from North-Ireland Scottish Presbyterians; his father, a successful storekeeper, came to America, 1783. James graduated Dickinson College, 1809; read law at Lancaster, Pa., and was admitted to the bar, 1812. Oratorical power and sound legal knowledge brought him professional success. Elected as a Federalist to state House of Representatives, 1814, he was reelected, 1815; retiring from politics, the death of his intended wife brought him back into the arena. He was elected to U.S. Congress as a Federalist, 1820; reelected as a Democrat, 1824.

During J. Q. Adams' administration, Buchanan made his first public statement on slavery in a debate on the Panama Mission: it was a moral and political evil; it was irremediable; it was a duty to help people of the South in the event of slave insurrections. For services in Jackson campaign of 1828, Buchanan was appointed chairman of committee on judiciary; in 1831, he accepted the ministry to Russia. On return to the United States, he was elected to the U.S. Senate to fill an unfinished term; he was reelected for a full term in 1837, and again in 1843. As senator from Pennsylvania, he opposed slavery in the abstract but recognized duty of government to protect it where it existed; he denounced abolitionists but upheld right of petition. A "favorite son" possibility for presidency in 1844, he supported James K. Polk after nomination and helped carry Pennsylvania for him. Appointed secretary of state in Polk's cabinet, Buchanan served the full term, contributing powerful aid in the settlement of the Oregon question with Great Britain and in the delicate negotiations over annexation of Texas, 1845. His delaying tactics until a revolutionary change in Mexico gave a new prospect of settlement coincided with a military skirmish on the Texas border and lent justification to Polk's message to Congress declaring that a state of war existed by Mexico's own acts. Meanwhile he had ended the dispute over Oregon by a treaty based on a compromise of territorial claims, and was responsible for Polk's restatement of the Monroe Doctrine against British ambitions in California and Central America.

After four years' retirement, Buchanan campaigned for Franklin Pierce, 1852, but was passed over for W. L. Marcy in choice of secretary of state; he accepted ministry to Great Britain. He joined in drawing up the Ostend Manifesto on the status of Cuba, 1854. Returning home in April 1856, he was more than ever a presidential possibility; by his absence he had escaped involvement in the bitter fight over the Kansas-Nebraska bill and received nomination on the 17th ballot. His platform proclaimed the finality of the Compromise of 1850 and endorsed principle of noninterference by Congress with slavery in territories. At the election, he received 1,800,000 votes; Frémont, the Republican candidate, received 1,300,000; Fillmore, the Whig-"Know-Nothing" candidate, about 900,000. His inaugural address declared for strict construction of the Constitution; as for slavery in the territories, he declared the question one for judicial decision and referred to the Dred Scott case (then pending) as destined to offer a solution to which all good citizens should submit. He divided representation in his cabinet equally between slave-holding and free states.

Reasonably successful in foreign policy, his strict constructionist views kept him from asserting any leadership in recovery from the financial panic of 1857. Accepting, as he did, the Dred Scott decision as final word on status of slavery in Kansas-Nebraska, he split the Democratic party by recommending early in 1858 the pro-slavery Lecompton constitution for Kansas. In the crisis that followed, and in the desperate months between Lincoln's election and the end of his term, Buchanan denied the right of any state to secede but confessed his helplessness in the face of actual secession; while his administration fell to pieces through resignations, he did his best to use his own personal influence for reconciliation. Early in 1861, he adopted a stiffer policy toward South Carolina and instituted legislation to broaden the president's powers. He took his part in Lincoln's inauguration and then retired to "Wheatland," his estate near Lancaster, Pa. He supported the administration throughout the Civil War as a Union Democrat.

Northern criticism that his lack of vigor encouraged secession and the formation of the Confederacy is unjustified. Primarily a constitutional lawyer, secure in the belief that legal solutions and compromises were all-sufficient, he was fitted neither by nature nor training to "ride the whirlwind" of his time.

BUCHANAN, JOHN (*b. Prince Georges Co., Md., 1772; d. 1844*), jurist. Chief justice, Maryland court of appeals, 1824–44; made important decisions in *Chesapeake & Ohio Canal Co. v. Baltimore & Ohio*, and in *Calvert v. Davis*.

BUCHANAN, JOSEPH (*b. Washington Co., Va., 1785; d. Louisville, Ky., 1829*), educator, inventor. Lecturer in medicine, Transylvania University; called "the earliest native physiological psychologist"; journalist in Kentucky; projector and builder of a steam-driven wagon, 1824–25.

BUCHANAN, JOSEPH RAY (*b. Hannibal, Mo., 1851; d. Montclair, N.J., 1924*), labor agitator. Active in western trade-union affairs, 1880–88, and in Knights of Labor; an organizer of the Populist party; in later life, labor editor of American Press Association and *New York Evening Journal*.

BUCHANAN, JOSEPH RODES (*b. Frankfort, Ky., 1814; d. San Jose, Calif., 1899*), physician, eccentric. Author of treatises on healing sciences of his own devisal, "Sarcognomy" and "Psychometry."

BUCHANAN, ROBERT CHRISTIE (*b. Baltimore, Md., 1811; d. Washington, D.C., 1878*), Union soldier. Graduated West Point, 1830. Distinguished in Black Hawk, Seminole, Mexican, and Civil wars; major general by brevet, 1865; commanded Department of Louisiana, 1868.

BUCHANAN, SCOTT MILROSS (*b. Sprague, Wash., 1895; d. Santa Barbara, Calif., 1968*), philosopher, author, and educator. B.A. (1916), Amherst; Ph.D. (1925), Harvard. Held a lifelong commitment to interdisciplinary approaches to intellectual matters and to study of the classics of art, literature, philosophy, science, and mathematics of the Western tradition. These beliefs are reflected in his numerous publications, which include *Possibility* (1927), *Poetry and Mathematics* (1929), *Symbolic Distance in Relation to Analogy and Fiction* (1932), *The Portable Plato* (editor, 1948), and *Essay in Politics* (1953). Among his many pedagogical experiences, he was assistant director of the People's Institute in New York City (1925–29), professor of philosophy at the University of Virginia (1929–36), dean of St. John's College

(1937–47), director of Liberal Arts, Inc. (1947–49), consultant, trustee, and secretary of the Foundation for World Government (1948–58), and a founder and senior fellow of the Center for the Study of Democratic Institutions (1957–68).

BUCHANAN, THOMAS (*b. Glasgow, Scotland, 1744; d. New York, N.Y., 1815*), merchant. Came to America, 1763; a partner in W. & T. Buchanan; vice president, N.Y. Chamber of Commerce, 1780–83.

BUCHANAN, WILLIAM INSCO (*b. Covington, Ohio, 1852; d. 1909*), businessman, diplomat. Promoter of "Corn Palaces," Sioux City, Iowa; chief of agriculture department, Chicago World's Fair, 1893. Served on many missions to Central and South America.

BUCHER, JOHN CONRAD (*b. Neunkirch, Switzerland, 1730; d. Annville, Pa., 1780*), soldier, German Reformed clergyman. Came to America, *post* 1755; officer in French & Indian war and Pontiac uprising. Ordained, 1767, he served frontier congregations and was first to preach in German beyond Alleghenies.

BUCHMAN, FRANK NATHAN DANIEL (*b. Pennsburg, Pa., 1878; d. Freudenstadt, Germany, 1961*), founder of the controversial religious movement known successively as the First Century Christian Fellowship (1920's), the Oxford Group (after 1928), and Moral Re-Armament (after 1938). Completed the course at the Mt. Airy Lutheran Theological Seminary and was ordained in 1902. Traveled throughout the world to advocate his movement, which sought to bring individuals to dynamic spiritual earnestness within the framework of their own religious traditions. Emphasized confession, absolute commitment to God, and regular meditation. The confessions took place at house parties, often held in luxurious settings and attended by prominent people. The movement lost momentum during World War II but rallied somewhat after the war, when he received citations for his efforts in postwar reconciliation and international goodwill and established his plush world headquarters at Caux, Switzerland.

BUCHTEL, JOHN RICHARDS (*b. Green Township, Ohio, 1820; d. Akron, Ohio, 1892*), businessman, philanthropist. Helped develop mineral resources of Hocking Valley; benefactor, Akron University.

BUCK, ALBERT HENRY (*b. New York, N.Y., 1842; d. 1922*), otologist, medical historian. Son of Gurdon Buck. College of Physicians and Surgeons, New York, M.D. 1867. Author of *Diagnosis and Treatment of Ear Diseases* (1880); also, *Growth of Medicine* (1917) and *Dawn of Modern Medicine* (1920). Coeditor, *American Practice of Surgery* (1906–11).

BUCK, DANIEL (*b. Hebron, Conn., 1753; d. Vermont, 1816*), lawyer, legislator. A first settler of Norwich, Vt. *ca.* 1784, where he afterwards practiced; congressman, Federalist, from Vermont, 1795–97.

BUCK, DUDLEY (*b. Hartford, Conn., 1839; d. Orange, N.J., 1909*), composer, organist. Studied music in his birthplace, and at Leipzig, Dresden, and Paris. After 1862, organist at churches in Hartford, Chicago, Boston, and Brooklyn, N.Y. One of the first American composers to possess solid musicianship; American organ music practically begins with his compositions for Protestant church services. Of his larger works, the most important are concert cantatas, including "Paul Revere's Ride," "The Centennial Meditation of Columbia" (1876), and "The Light of Asia" (1889).

BUCK, FRANKLYN HOWARD (*b. Gainsville, Tex., 1884; d. Houston, Tex., 1950*), showman, wild animal entrepreneur. Better known as Frank Buck. Leaving school in the seventh grade, he led a knockabout existence until 1911 when he made a considerable profit by buying and selling collections of tropical birds. Setting up headquarters in Singapore, he soon became a major supplier of Asian fauna to zoos, circuses, and exhibitors; he participated in the capture of his specimens only infrequently, buying them as a rule from other dealers. He had a notable talent for publicity. During the 1930's he parlayed what had been a colorful but hardly remarkable career into a national reputation, dramatizing himself in such books as *Bring 'em Back Alive* (1930) and lectures, radio talks, and six wild-animal movies.

BUCK, GURDON (*b. New York, N.Y., 1807; d. New York, 1877*), surgeon. College of Physicians and Surgeons, New York, M.D. 1830; studied for two years in Paris, Berlin, and Vienna; settled to practice in New York, 1837. A great surgeon of the pre-Lister period, his chief contributions were in management of fractures (Buck's Extension) and in plastic surgery.

BUCK, LEFFERT LEFFERTS (*b. Canton, N.Y., 1837; d. 1909*), civil engineer. Graduated Rensselaer Polytechnic Institute, 1868. One of the great bridge builders of his time, remembered principally for his work in bridging Niagara Falls and for the Williamsburg Bridge, New York City.

BUCK, PHILO MELVIN (*b. Corning, N.Y., 1846; d. 1924*), Methodist clergyman. Missionary to India, 1870–76; 1879–1914.

BUCKALEW, CHARLES ROLLIN (*b. Columbia Co., Pa., 1821; d. Bloomsburg, Pa., 1899*), lawyer, legislator. U.S. senator, Democrat, from Pennsylvania, 1863–69; a proponent of penal code reform and proportional representation; opposed Republican policies after Civil War.

BUCKHOUT, ISAAC CRAIG (*b. Eastchester, N.Y., 1830; d. White Plains, N.Y., 1874*), civil engineer. Designed and built old Grand Central station, the Fourth Avenue cut, and other constructions for the New York & Harlem Railroad.

BUCKINGHAM, JOSEPH TINKER (*b. Windham, Conn., 1779; d. Cambridge, Mass., 1861*), editor. An able and imaginative journalist, publisher of the *Polyanthos* (1806–07; 1812–14), the *New England Galaxy* (1817–28), the *Boston Courier* (1824–48), the *New England Magazine* (1831–34), and others. Author of two useful books of reminiscent history, *Specimens of Newspaper Literature* (1850) and *Personal Memoirs* (1852).

BUCKINGHAM, WILLIAM ALFRED (*b. Lebanon, Conn., 1804; d. 1875*), businessman, legislator. Governor of Connecticut, Republican, 1858–66; a constant and able supporter of Lincoln in the Civil War. U.S. senator from Connecticut, 1869–75.

BUCKLAND, CYRUS (*b. East Hartford, Conn., 1799; d. Springfield, Mass., 1891*), inventor. Pattern-maker and designer of machine-tools, Springfield Armory, 1828–57; his inventions include a gunstock process (1846) and a rifling machine (1855).

BUCKLAND, RALPH POMEROY (*b. Leyden, Mass., 1812; d. Fremont, Ohio, 1892*), lawyer, soldier. Commended by Sherman for work as brigade commander at Shiloh; brevet major general, 1866.

BUCKLER, THOMAS HEPBURN (*b. near Baltimore, Md., 1812; d. 1901*), physician. Prominent Baltimore practitioner, active in study of cholera and other epidemic diseases and in modern treatment of tuberculosis. Practiced in Paris, France, 1866–90.

BUCKLEY, JAMES MONROE (*b. Rahway, N.J., 1836; d. 1920*), Methodist clergyman. Editor, *Christian Advocate,* 1880–1912.

BUCKLEY, OLIVER ELLSWORTH (*b. Sloan, Iowa, 1887; d. Newark, N.J., 1959*), physicist, research engineer. Studied at Grinnell College and at Cornell (Ph.D., 1914). Researcher and executive at the Bell Telephone Laboratories; director (1933); vice president (1936); president (1940); and chairman of the board from 1950 to 1952. Inventor of the ionization manometer, a means for pressure measurements in high vacuums. Chairman of the President's Science Advisory Committee from 1950. Under Buckley, Bell Labs developed the underwater telegraph cable system, the transistor, guided missile systems, and microwave relay systems. A subsidiary, the Sandia Corporation, carried out an atomic weapons program.

BUCKLEY, SAMUEL BOTSFORD (*b. Torrey, N.Y., 1809; d. Austin, Tex., 1883*), botanist, field naturalist. Associated with geological surveys in Texas; collected specimens of plants, etc., in Alabama, Tennessee, and the Carolinas; discovered a zeuglodon skeleton, Alabama, 1842.

BUCKMINSTER, JOSEPH STEVENS (*b. Portsmouth, N.H., 1784; d. Boston, Mass., 1812*), Unitarian clergyman. Graduated Harvard, 1800; ordained and installed at Brattle Street Church, Boston, 1805. Brilliant preacher and scholar; a founder of Boston Athenaeum.

BUCKNELL, WILLIAM (*b. near Marcus Hook, Pa., 1811; d. 1890*), businessman, philanthropist. Acquiring wealth in realty speculation and public utilities, he became large contributor to Baptist missions and to University of Lewisburg, renamed Bucknell in 1887.

BUCKNER, EMORY ROY (*b. Pottawattamie Co., Iowa, 1877; d. New York, N.Y., 1941*), lawyer. Raised in Nebraska. Worked as schoolteacher in Nebraska and Oklahoma, and as a court stenographer. Graduated University of Nebraska, 1904, and was recommended to Harvard Law School by Roscoe Pound who helped raise money to send him there. Receiving the LL.B., 1907, he ranked third in his class and became friends with many fellow students, including Felix Frankfurter. Joining the staff of the U.S. Attorney's office in New York City under Henry L. Stimson, he shifted in 1910 to the office of the district attorney of New York County; he served as counsel to an investigation of police corruption, 1912–13. He then entered private practice in partnership with Elihu Root, Jr. and Grenville Clark; his skill in planning and conducting trials was a principal factor in the firm's success. As U.S. Attorney for the Southern District of New York, 1925–27, he made a gallant try at enforcing the prohibition law (of which he personally disapproved), but his most significant case was the prosecution of Harry M. Dougherty and Thomas W. Miller (former alien property custodian) on charges of bribery. Buckner is gratefully remembered for his kindness to young lawyers and law students.

BUCKNER, SIMON BOLIVAR (*b. near Munfordville, Ky., 1823; d. near Munfordville, 1914*), Confederate soldier. Graduated West Point, 1844. After gallant service in Mexican War and on frontiers, resigned from army, 1855; entered business in Chicago, Ill., where he prospered. Settled in Louisville, Ky., 1858; brought Kentucky militia to high efficiency by 1861. Identified with early effort to keep the state neutral in Civil War, Buckner joined Confederate forces as brigadier general when state legislature abandoned neutrality. Surrendered Fort Donelson to Grant, 1862; on exchange was promoted major general and, in 1864, lieutenant general, serving capably until end of war. In business, New Orleans, 1866–68; permitted to return to Kentucky in the latter year, he became editor of *Louisville Courier*. Successful in effort to recover some of his sequestrated property, he entered politics; he was Democratic governor of Kentucky, 1887–91.

BUCKNER, SIMON BOLIVAR (*b. near Munfordville, Ky., 1886; d. Okinawa, Ryukyu Islands, 1945*), soldier. Son of Simon B. Buckner (1823–1914). Graduated West Point, 1908; commissioned in infantry. Served in Philippines, on Mexican border, and in Air Service training during World War I. Attended and taught at Command and General Staff School, and at Army War College; taught at West Point, 1919–23, 1932–33. Commandant of cadets, West Point, 1933–36. Promoted colonel, 1937, he organized the Alaskan Defense Command, 1940, and commanded U.S. Army forces during the successful operations against the Japanese in the Aleutians. He was made major general in August 1941, lieutenant general in 1943. Ordered to the central Pacific in June 1944 as commander of the new Tenth Army (which included Marine Corps divisions and Navy land contingents), he prepared for and led the invasion of Okinawa, the largest amphibious operation of the Pacific war. A few days before the successful end of the campaign (June 18, 1945), he was killed at a forward observation position.

BUDD, EDWARD GOWEN (*b. Smyrna, Del., 1870; d. Germantown, Pa., 1946*), industrialist. Completed high school, 1887; worked as machinist's apprentice in Smyrna and Philadelphia, Pa.; continued engineering education in night classes and correspondence courses. After rising to position of foreman of a drafting office, in 1899 he joined the American Pulley Company as factory manager. Here, he first recognized the capabilities of press- and die-formed, light-gauge, sheet-metal stampings as an alternative to forgings and castings. Becoming general manager (1902) of the Hale and Kilburn Company, makers of railroad car seats and interior trim for Pullman and other firms, he introduced use of pressed steel parts joined by oxyacetylene welding. When his proposal for constructing all-steel automobile bodies on a commercial basis for the emergent motorcar industry was rejected, he left Hale and Kilburn (1912) and set up the Edward G. Budd Manufacturing Company. Soon, he was supplying welded, all-steel touring and roadster bodies for Oakland, Dodge, Willys-Overland, Cadillac, Studebaker, and Franklin cars. Returning to automobile work after manufacturing military equipment during World War I, he added an all-steel sedan body to his line. In the early 1920's, he conducted experiments that resulted in production of large, one-piece, steel components, such as floors, roof panels, and door panels with integral window frames; this "monopiece" construction came in time to be generally adopted by the industry. In 1919 he began making tapered steel disk wheels under license from the Michelin Company; later included production of the artillery type of steel disk wheel, made from a single stamping.

Pioneered in the fabrication of stainless steel, after his chief engineer, E. J. W. Ragsdale, devised the "Shotweld" method of controlled-resistance welding—a process that made it possible to join stainless steel without impairing its structural strength. Although the automotive industry remained the major source of income, the building of stainless steel railroad "streamliners" helped materially to restore profitability *post* 1934. During World War II, the Budd facilities were again wholly converted to production of war matériel.

BUDD, JOSEPH LANCASTER (*b. near Peekskill, N.Y., 1835; d. Phoenix, Ariz., 1904*), horticulturist. Removed to Iowa in the 1860's; was a successful nurseryman and orchardist, and professor of horticulture and forestry, Iowa Agricultural College, 1876–96. He adapted standard practices to the climate of the Northwest,

introducing hardier varieties of trees and extending successful fruit growing much further north than had been thought possible.

BUDD, RALPH (*b. Washburn, Iowa, 1879; d. Santa Barbara, Calif., 1962*), railroad executive. Became president of the Great Northern Railroad in 1919. His presidency of the Chicago, Burlington, and Quincy (1932–49) marked the culmination of his career; during the Depression he simplified the divisional structure, introduced the nation's first streamlined train to enter regular service (the *Pioneer Zephyr*, in 1934), and helped to quadruple the Burlington's transcontinental business. Also carried out a debt reduction plan that significantly reduced the Burlington's charges for fixed interest between 1940 and 1945. In 1945 introduced the dome car. Served as transportation commissioner for President Franklin D. Roosevelt (1940–41). After retirement, was chairman of the Chicago Transit Authority.

BUEHLER, HUBER GRAY (*b. Gettysburg, Pa., 1864; d. Lakeville, Conn., 1924*), educator. Headmaster, Hotchkiss School, Lakeville, 1904–24.

BUEL, JESSE (*b. Coventry, Conn., 1778; d. Danbury, Conn., 1839*), agriculturist. Printer and newspaper publisher, New York State, 1797–1820; founder of Albany, N.Y., *Argus*. From 1821 to 1839, experimented in scientific agriculture on a farm west of Albany; as a member of New York Assembly, 1823–35, Buel devoted all energies to improvement of agriculture and rural life, pressing for establishment of a state agricultural school. His writings and influence had effect long after his own time.

BUELL, ABEL (*b. Killingworth, Conn., 1741/42; d. New Haven, Conn., 1822*), silversmith, typefounder, engraver. A most ingenious, if morally unstable, craftsman, Buell designed and cast printing types in 1769, probably the first ever made by an American; his map of the United States (published March 1784) was the first map of the new nation to be engraved by one of its own citizens. For some years, he engaged in various activities in New Haven, setting up a cotton mill (1795), operating a line of packet boats, etc. In 1799, he removed to Hartford, thereafter to Stockbridge, Mass., and returned at last to New Haven where he died in the Alms House.

BUELL, DON CARLOS (*b. near Marietta, Ohio, 1818; d. Rockport, Ky., 1898*), Union soldier. Graduated West Point, 1841; served with credit in Mexican War and thereafter in adjutant general's office. Appointed brigadier general, 1861, he helped organize Army of the Potomac; in November 1861, commanding Army of the Ohio, he attempted to liberate eastern Tennessee. Buell's aid to Grant at Shiloh was decisive in that battle. Promoted major general, March 1862, he was discharged in 1864 after a lengthy investigation of his conduct after battle of Perryville, October 1862.

BUFFALO BILL. *See* CODY, WILLIAM FREDERICK.

BUFFUM, ARNOLD (*b. Smithfield, R.I., 1782; d. Perth Amboy, N.J., 1859*), antislavery lecturer. A Quaker and a maker of hats, Buffum was president of New England Anti-Slavery Society, 1832, and its lecturing agent in Pennsylvania, Ohio, and Indiana; his daughter was Elizabeth Chace.

BUFORD, ABRAHAM (*b. Culpeper Co., Va., 1749; d. near Georgetown, Ky., 1833*), Revolutionary soldier. Defeated by Tarleton, 1780, in the no-quarter engagement of the Waxhaws.

BUFORD, ABRAHAM (*b. Woodford Co., Ky., 1820; d. Danville, Ind., 1884*), Confederate soldier. Graduated West Point, 1841; served in Mexican War and on the frontiers as cavalry officer. Resigned from army, 1854, and bred horses and cattle in Kentucky. Appointed brigadier general by Confederates, 1862;

served under Bragg, Loring, and Forrest. Resumed stock breeding after Civil War.

BUFORD, JOHN (*b. Woodford Co., Ky., 1826; d. Washington, D.C., 1863*), Union soldier. Graduated West Point, 1848; served with cavalry in Texas, New Mexico, Nebraska, and in the Mormon expedition, 1857–58. After minor service in Washington, 1861, Buford was appointed brigadier general, July 1862; he was severely wounded at Lewis Ford in August, returning to duty as chief of cavalry, Army of the Potomac in September. Early in 1863, he took command of the reserve cavalry and distinguished himself in covering Hooker's retreat after Chancellorsville; he commanded a division with great credit at Gettysburg. On leave of absence because of failing health, he was commissioned major general in December 1863, just before his death.

BUFORD, NAPOLEON BONAPARTE (*b. Woodford Co., Ky., 1807; d. Chicago, Ill., 1883*), Union soldier. Half-brother of John Buford; graduated West Point, 1827; resigned from army, 1835, and settled in Rock Island, Ill., 1842, as a businessman, railroad promoter, and banker. Colonel of 27th Illinois volunteers, 1861, he fought in the Western campaigns; he was promoted brigadier general, April 1862, and did his best work as commander of the East Arkansas District, 1863–65. Mustering out as brevet major general, he returned to business in Colorado and Chicago.

BULEY, ROSCOE CARLYLE (*b. Georgetown, Ind., 1893; d. Indianapolis, Ind., 1968*), historian. B.A. (1914) and M.A. (1916), Indiana University; Ph.D. (1925), University of Wisconsin. Taught history at Indiana University (1925–64). A leading authority on the states of the Old Northwest, especially Indiana, he published articles in the *Mississippi Valley Historical Review* and wrote *The Midwest Pioneer: His Ills, Cures, and Doctors* (1945), with Madge E. Pickard; the two-volume *The Old Northwest: Pioneer Period, 1815–1840* (1951); and four histories of insurance groups. His works, though weak on analysis, provide valuable and detailed information in a readable form.

BULFINCH, CHARLES (*b. Boston, Mass., 1763; d. Boston, 1844*), architect. Son of a wealthy and cultivated Boston family; graduated Harvard, 1781; interest in architecture stimulated by European tour, 1785–87; Jefferson's classical tendency also influenced him. Designed churches in Boston, Taunton, and Pittsfield, Mass.; classical interest seen in his Beacon monument (1789) and triumphal arch for Washington's Boston reception (1789); designed State House at Hartford, Conn., begun in 1792. His public work of this first period was crowned by Massachusetts State House on Beacon Hill, completed 1800. He exerted also at this time important influence upon New England domestic architecture, introducing delicate detail in the Adam style, oval parlors, and the use for the first time in New England of curved staircases. Franklin Crescent, Boston, the first attempt in America to erect a row of houses in a coherent design, was begun by him in 1793.

Elected to board of selectmen of Boston, 1791, he served, with one interval, for 26 years. Financial depression in 1795 left him bankrupt; his architectural talents, hitherto generously exercised for others, now became the basis for a professional practice. The years of his chairmanship of the board of selectmen, 1799–1817, were those of the great development of old Boston, for which his dual capacity as official and architect was in great part responsible. He turned the neglected Common into a park and fronted it on three sides with buildings of uniform character; he laid out the lands on Boston Neck, in South Boston, and on site of the Mill Pond; he designed India Wharf, the Almshouse, two schools, the enlargement of Faneuil Hall, the Boylston Market, and the Court House. During this period he did public buildings elsewhere in Massachusetts, the State Prison at Charlestown, the Massachusetts General Hospital, banks, churches, and private homes. Of the churches the most notable were the Cathedral of the Holy Cross and the New South Church, both in Boston, and Christ Church in Lancaster.

At resignation of Latrobe, architect of the Capitol, in 1817, President Monroe offered the post to Bulfinch, who removed to Washington, D.C., with his family. Called on to complete the wings and construct the central part along lines already established by earlier architects, his own chief contribution was the detailed form of the western front. Returning to Boston, 1830, he lived in retirement until death. He exercised a wide influence on New England architecture where his version of the Adam style became characteristic of the early Republican period, remaining dominant until advent *ca.* 1820 of the Greek revival.

BULFINCH, THOMAS (*b. Newton, Mass., 1796; d. Boston, Mass., 1867*), author. Son of Charles Bulfinch; graduated Harvard, 1814. Unsuccessful in business, he took a clerkship in the Merchants' Bank, Boston, which he held from 1837 to his death; he devoted his leisure to study of literature and natural history, and to writing. Among his books, the best known are two highly successful attempts to retell classic and other myths in popular form: *The Age of Fable* (1855) and *The Age of Chivalry* (1858).

BULKELEY, MORGAN GARDNER (*b. East Haddam, Conn., 1837; d. 1922*), businessman, politician. President, Aetna Life Insurance Co., 1879–1922; a director of many other corporations. Mayor, Hartford, Conn., 1880–88; governor of Connecticut, Republican, 1888–92; U.S. senator from Connecticut, 1905–11.

BULKELEY, PETER (*b. Odell, England, 1582/3; d. Concord, Mass., 1658/9*), Puritan clergyman. Immigrated to Massachusetts, 1636; a founder and the first minister of Concord.

BULKLEY, JOHN WILLIAMS (*b. Fairfield, Conn., 1802; d. 1888*), educator. Superintendent of schools, Brooklyn, N.Y.; first president of New York state teachers' association (1845) and a founder of the National Teachers' Association (now National Education Association).

BULKLEY, LUCIUS DUNCAN (*b. New York, N.Y., 1845; d. 1928*), physician, dermatologist. Founded New York Skin and Cancer Hospital, 1882; advocated nonsurgical treatment of cancer; author of *Manual of Diseases of the Skin* (1882).

BULL, EPHRAIM WALES (*b. Boston, Mass., 1806; d. 1895*), horticulturist. Developed the Concord grape, first exhibited 1853.

BULL, WILLIAM (*b. South Carolina, 1683; d. 1755*), lieutenant governor of South Carolina, 1738–55. During his administration, constitutional reforms included governor's exclusion from Council's legislative sessions, Commons House control of money bills.

BULL, WILLIAM (*b. Ashley Hall, S.C., 1710; d. London, England, 1791*), colonial governor of South Carolina. Son of William Bull (1683–1755). Studied medicine at Leyden; was first native-born American to receive M.D. degree, but devoted himself to agriculture and politics. Member of Commons House, 1736–49; speaker in 1740–42 and 1744–49. Appointed to the Council, 1748, he served ably until he became lieutenant governor, 1759; acting as governor for some eight years between 1760 and 1775, he tried to stem revolutionary sentiment *post* 1764, but by 1774 power had passed to the Provincial Congress. Bull retained respect of people, and his estates were exempted from confiscation; he left colony with British troops, 1782, and spent remaining years in London.

BULL, WILLIAM TILLINGHAST (*b. Newport, R.I., 1849; d. New York, N.Y., 1909*), surgeon. Graduated Harvard, 1869;

M.D., College of Physicians and Surgeons, New York, 1872; made clinical studies in Europe. Professor of surgery, College of Physicians and Surgeons, 1889–1904. Specialized in surgery of abdomen, contributing procedures for treatment of gunshot wounds of abdomen; wrote on hernia for medical textbooks; published noteworthy paper on cancer of the breast (1894). Influenced by work of Lister, he was one of first American surgeons to adopt antisepsis.

BULLARD, HENRY ADAMS (*b. Pepperell, Mass., 1788; d. New Orleans, La., 1851*), jurist. Judge, Louisiana supreme court, 1834–46; congressman from Louisiana, Whig, 1830–34, 1950–51. Founder, Louisiana Historical Society, 1836.

BULLARD, ROBERT LEE (*b. near Opelika, Ala., 1861; d. Governors Island, New York, N.Y., 1947*), soldier. Graduated West Point, 1885. Commissioned in the infantry, he served in the Southwest, in the Philippines, in the provisional government of Cuba, and on the Mexican border, rising to colonel's rank and winning reputation as an excellent field commander with a thorough knowledge of military theory and practice. Promoted to brigadier general in June 1917, he accompanied the 1st Division, American Expeditionary Forces, to France; in August, promoted to major general, he was made commandant of the infantry officer specialist schools; in December, he was given command of the 1st Division and assembled an exceptional group of officers around him, including three future chiefs of staff. After the successful attack of the 1st Division on Cantigny (May 1918), he was given command of the III Corps, which fought with credit in the Aisne-Marne and Meuse-Argonne offensives. Promoted to lieutenant general, he took charge of the Second Army shortly before the Armistice. After the war, he commanded the II Corps Area until retirement in 1925.

BULLARD, WILLIAM HANNUM GRUBB (*b. Media, Pa., 1866; d. 1927*), naval officer. Graduated U.S. Naval Academy, 1886. Reorganized electrical engineering department of Naval Academy, 1907–11; superintendent of naval radio service, 1912–16; commanded battleship *Arkansas*, 1916–18; director of communications, Navy Department, 1919–21; promoted rear admiral, 1919. Has been called "the father of American radio." Prevented foreign acquisition of patent rights in Alexanderson alternator and counseled formation of what developed into Radio Corporation of America.

BULLITT, ALEXANDER SCOTT (*b. Dumfries, Va., 1762; d. Jefferson Co., Ky., 1816*), planter, Kentucky legislator. Lieutenant governor of Kentucky, 1800–04.

BULLITT, HENRY MASSIE (*b. Shelby County, Ky., 1817; d. Louisville, Ky., 1880*), physician, teacher. Founded Kentucky School of Medicine, 1850, and Louisville Medical College, 1868.

BULLITT, WILLIAM CHRISTIAN (*b. Philadelphia, Pa., 1891; d. Neuilly, France, 1967*), diplomat. After working as a European correspondent for the *Philadelphia Public Ledger*, was appointed chief of the Bureau of Central European Information in the State Department (1917). His testimony before the Senate Foreign Relations Committee (1919) was an important factor in the failure of the Treaty of Versailles to win ratification. In 1932 Franklin D. Roosevelt, of whom he had been an early supporter, appointed him special assistant to the secretary of state, and in 1933 he was appointed the first ambassador to Moscow; he became increasingly distrustful of Stalin and began developing a strident anti–Communism that he cultivated the rest of his life. Appointed ambassador to France in 1936, he became Roosevelt's most valuable adviser on European affairs. After the fall of Paris (1940), he returned to the U.S. and advocated all-out aid short of war to Britain and France. Was appointed ambassador-at-large on a fact-

finding mission to North Africa and the Middle East in 1941, but by the following year he and Roosevelt had had a disagreement, and he never received another appointment.

BULLOCH, ARCHIBALD (*b. Charleston, S.C., 1729/30; d. 1777*), lawyer, planter. First president of the Provincial Congress of Georgia, 1775–77; an active patriot.

BULLOCH, JAMES DUNWODY (*b. near Savannah, Ga., 1823; d. 1901*), naval officer, Confederate agent. Appointed midshipman, U.S. Navy, 1839; commanded various vessels in mail service to Gulf of Mexico, *post* 1851. Retiring from navy, he entered private mail shipping service, becoming identified with New York interests. At start of Civil War, he was named Confederate navy agent to buy or build war vessels in England; all Confederate cruisers except the *Georgia* were equipped and sent out under his instructions. *Post* March 1863, he moved his operations to Paris, France. He settled in Liverpool, England, at end of war, engaging in cotton business there.

BULLOCK, RUFUS BROWN (*b. Bethlehem, N.Y., 1834; d. Atlanta, Ga., 1907*), businessman, politician. Governor of Georgia, Republican, 1868–71; indicted and tried for embezzlement of public funds, 1876, but acquitted.

BULLOCK, WILLIAM A. (*b. Greenville, N.Y., 1813; d. 1867*), inventor, manufacturer. His Bullock Press (1865) was the first to print from a continuous roll of paper, first to cut the sheet either before or after printing, and first to print both sides of the sheet.

BUMSTEAD, FREEMAN JOSIAH (*b. Boston, Mass., 1826; d. 1879*), surgeon. Graduated Williams College, 1847; M.D., Harvard, 1851. One of first reputable practitioners to specialize in venereal diseases; author of classic *Pathology and Treatment of Venereal Diseases* (1861).

BUMSTEAD, HENRY ANDREWS (*b. Pekin, Ill., 1870; d. 1920*), Professor of physics and director of Sloane Laboratory, Yale, 1906–20. Investigated properties of delta rays emitted by metals under influence of alpha rays, 1911–20.

BUMSTEAD, HORACE (*b. Boston, Mass., 1841; d. 1919*), Congregational minister, educator. Brother of Freeman J. Bumstead. As president of Atlanta University, 1888–1907, advocated broad, liberal arts education for black leaders.

BUNCE, OLIVER BELL (*b. New York, N.Y., 1828; d. New York, 1890*), publisher. Literary manager, D. Appleton & Co.; editor, *Appleton's Journal*; a specialist in devising successful subscription sets and illustrated "gift" books.

BUNCE, WILLIAM GEDNEY (*b. Hartford, Conn., 1840; d. Hartford, 1916*), painter. An impressionist who did his principal work in Venice.

BUNDY, HARVEY HOLLISTER (*b. Grand Rapids, Mich., 1888; d. Boston, Mass., 1963*), lawyer, assistant secretary of state, assistant to the secretary of war. Law degree, Harvard, 1914. His successful legal practice, primarily as partner in the Boston firm of Choate, Hall, and Stewart, was frequently interrupted by calls to government service. Was appointed assistant to Secretary of State Henry L. Stimson in 1931 and helped organize the Foreign Bond Holders Protective Council. In 1941 again became special assistant to Stimson, now secretary of war. Helped create the new-weapons section of the General Staff, which was made independent in 1942, and became a prime mover in coordinating the rapid development of scientific projects, in particular the atom bomb.

BUNDY, JONAS MILLS (*b. Colebrook, N.H., 1835; d. Paris, France, 1891*), journalist. Founder and editor, *New York Evening Mail*; later edited *Mail and Express*. Prepared appeal to public against Tweed Ring, 1871; wrote campaign biography of James A. Garfield (1880).

BUNKER, ARTHUR HUGH (*b.* *Yonkers, N.Y., 1895; d. New York, N.Y.¢ 1964*), corporation executive and World War II mobilization administrator. Among other executive activities was president of the Radium Company of Colorado, owner of United States Vanadium, and executive vice president (later, general partner) of the Lehman Corporation. During World War II, he joined other major corporation executives who organized and administered war production, serving in various high-ranking positions with the War Production Board (WPB). In these positions he opposed liberals who wanted reconversion to begin before the war ended. In 1944 was elevated to WPB chief of staff in a reorganization that practically eliminated liberals. Resigned from the WPB in 1944 and continued his corporate activities.

BUNNER, HENRY CUYLER (*b. Oswego, N.Y., 1855; d. Nutley, N.J., 1896*), author. Staff writer and editor, *Puck*, 1877–96; suggested famous cartoon (1884) satirizing James G. Blaine as the "Tattooed Man"; contributed verse, parodies, editorials. His short fiction is distinguished by skillful construction and word economy; French influences are obvious. His works include: *Airs from Arcady* (1884); *The Midge* (1886); *The Story of a New York House* (1887); *Zadoc Pine* (1891); and *Made in France* (1893).

BURBANK, LUTHER (*b. Lancaster, Mass., 1849; d. Santa Rosa, Calif., 1926*), plant breeder. Educated in district school and at local academy; influenced by Darwin's *Variation of Animals and Plants under Domestication* and other works by Darwin. Became a market gardener, *ca.* 1870; removed to Santa Rosa, Calif., 1875, where he conducted plant breeding experiments for fifty years. Produced many better varieties of cultivated plants; implications of his work for scientific research were lost, however, as he kept no systematic collection of data observed. Burbank's genius lay in his sensitive recognition and careful selection of desirable variations; his most intensive work was done with plums, berries, and lilies.

BURBRIDGE, STEPHEN GANO (*b. Scott Co., Ky., 1831; d. Brooklyn, N.Y., 1894*), Union soldier. Commanded District of Kentucky, 1864–65; was ruthless in suppression of guerrilla warfare.

BURCHARD, SAMUEL DICKINSON (*b. Steuben, N.Y., 1812; d. Saratoga, N.Y., 1891*), Presbyterian clergyman. Memorable as author of the "Rum, Romanism and Rebellion" catchword in the presidential campaign of 1884; pastor, Houston Street Church, New York, 1839–79; president, Rutgers Female Academy.

BURCHFIELD, CHARLES EPHRAIM (*b. Ashtabula, Ohio, 1893; d. Buffalo, N.Y., 1967*), painter. Labeled himself a romantic realist, a term that reflects his fluctuation between surrealism and realism. He dated his career from 1915, when he began to paint outdoors. In works such as *Crickets in November, Noonday Heat,* and *Church Bells Ringing—Rainy Winter Night* (all 1917), he attempted to capture the emotions of nature in pictorial form with the use of symbolism and distortion, in a manner similar to that of the European expressionists. By 1920 he had become dissatisfied with his work and moved toward the realism of his middle period. Though works such as *House of Mystery* (1924) retain the brooding and anthropomorphic qualities of his early period, they also show a shift toward the subjects typical of the regionalist school. In 1943 he returned to nature paintings and attempted to synthesize the abstract and fantastic quality of his early period with the realism of his middle period, and although some critics felt that he achieved this goal, others felt that his nature fantasies of the 1940's and 1950's were overblown and too

contrived. From the 1950's until his death he continued to gain critical attention, with major exhibitions of his work staged throughout the U.S.

BURDEN, HENRY (*b. Dunblane, Scotland, 1791; d. Woodside, N.Y., 1871*), ironmaster. Immigrated to Albany, N.Y., 1819. Inventor of machines for making horseshoes (1835), hookhead railroad spikes (1836, 1840), and for rolling iron into cylindrical bars (1840). Established firm of H. Burden & Sons, 1848.

BURDETTE, ROBERT JONES (*b. Greensboro, Pa., 1844; d. 1914*), humorist, lyceum lecturer, Baptist clergyman. Won reputation as columnist on Burlington, Iowa, *Hawk-Eye,* 1874 *et seq.*; author of *The Rise and Fall of the Moustache* (1877); became pastor, Temple Baptist Church, Los Angeles, Calif., 1903.

BURDICK, EUGENE LEONARD (*b. Sheldon, Iowa, 1918; d. San Diego, Calif., 1965*), political theorist and writer. Earned undergraduate degree in psychology at Stanford in 1941, and in 1948 went to England as a Rhodes scholar, completing his Oxford D.Phil. in political science in 1950. Became assistant professor of political science at Berkeley, where he was a popular lecturer and respected political theorist. Having won a Breadloaf Writer's Fellowship for 1948 and a major short story prize while doing graduate studies at Stanford, he wrote numerous novels, most notably *The Ugly American* (1958), written with William J. Lederer, and *Fail-Safe* (1962), written with Harvey Wheeler.

BURDICK, FRANCIS MARION (*b. De Ruyter, N.Y., 1845; d. De Ruyter, 1920*), legal writer. Graduated Hamilton College, 1869; LL.B., Hamilton, 1872. Practiced law in Utica, N.Y.; reform mayor of Utica, 1882. Professor of law at Hamilton; at Cornell University, 1887–91; Dwight Professor of Law, Columbia University, 1891–1916. His works include: *Cases on Torts* (1891); *The Law of Sales of Personal Property* (1897); *The Law of Partnership* (1899); *The Law of Torts* (1905).

BURDICK, USHER LLOYD (*b. Owatonna, Minn., 1879; d. Washington, D.C., 1960*), lawyer, congressman, author. Studied at Mayville Normal School and the University of Minnesota (LL.B., 1904). Active in North Dakota politics (lieutenant governor, 1910) and elected to Congress (1934–44 and 1948–59). A Republican, Burdick was an isolationist both before and after World War II. Father of Senator Quentin Burdick, a Democrat.

BURGESS, ALEXANDER (*b. Providence, R.I., 1819; d. St. Albans, Vt., 1901*), Episcopal clergyman. First bishop of Quincy, Ill., elected and consecrated, 1878; especially skilled in canon law.

BURGESS, EDWARD (*b. West Sandwich, Mass., 1848; d. Boston, Mass., 1891*), yacht designer, entomologist. Among yachts designed by him were *Puritan, Mayflower,* and *Volunteer,* successful contenders for America's Cup, 1885–87.

BURGESS, FRANK GELETT (*b. Boston, Mass., 1866; d. Carmel, Calif., 1951*), novelist, poet, playwright, humorist, and illustrator. Graduated M.I.T., 1887. Founded the humorous magazine *The Lark* in San Francisco in 1895. The magazine achieved fame with the publication of Burgess' poem, "Purple Cow." He moved to New York City in 1897, where he became editor and contributor to many humor and literary magazines. His books include the "goop" series, intended to teach children manners, *Love in A Hurry* (1907), and the play *The Purple Cow.*

BURGESS, GEORGE (*b. Providence, R.I., 1809; d. 1866*), Episcopal clergyman. Brother of Alexander Burgess. Bishop of Maine, elected and consecrated, 1847.

BURGESS, GEORGE KIMBALL (*b. Newton, Mass., 1874; d. 1932*), physicist. Director of the National Bureau of Standards,

1923–32; known for his work in the standardization of light and temperature scales.

BURGESS, JOHN WILLIAM (*b. Giles Co., Tenn., 1844; d. Brookline, Mass., 1931*), university professor and dean, author. The son of slaveowners who upheld the Union, he served with Union Army, 1862–64. Graduated Amherst College, 1867; studied in Germany, 1871–73. At Columbia College, New York City, he organized a faculty and school of political science, 1880, the first in the United States devoted to the systematic study of politics and public law. Founded the *Political Science Quarterly*. His influence was strong in the development of Columbia as a true university. In his many books he developed a unique theory of nationalism and the state.

BURGESS, NEIL (*b. Boston, Mass., 1851[?]; d. 1910*), actor. Specialized in burlesque portrayals of elderly women; most popular performance in *The County Fair*.

BURGESS, THORNTON WALDO (*b. Sandwich, Mass., 1874; d. Hampden, Mass., 1965*), author of children's stories. After working as a writer for various magazines from 1895 to 1911, he began a long association with Little, Brown in Boston, who published his first children's stories, *Old Mother West Wind* (1910) and *Mother West Wind's Children* (1911). Little, Brown, published some fifty-four volumes of children's stories by Burgess, plus his autobiography, *Now I Remember* (1960). In addition, he marketed thirty-two books through other publishers. His writing reflected his belief that animal stories were the most effective means of instilling good moral values and a reverence for nature in children.

BURGESS, W(ILLIAM) STARLING (*b. Boston, Mass., 1878; d. Hoboken, N.J., 1947*), naval architect, airplane manufacturer. Son of Edward Burgess. Graduated Harvard, 1901. As designer and builder of yachts and commercial vessels, he displayed a flair for experimentation and produced a number of fast, impressive, class boats as well as the *Jane Palmer* (1904), the largest five-masted sailing schooner ever built. In 1910, he opened his own airplane manufacturing company at Marblehead, Mass., which he sold out to the Curtiss Company, 1916. Meanwhile, applying his knowledge of the sea to naval seaplane design, he produced (among other types) the Burgess-Dunne seaplane, which won him the 1915 Collier Trophy. After World War I, in which he served with the U.S. Navy, he returned to yacht designing, introducing innovations in hulls, rigging, and sails—notably the staysail rig, first used on the schooner *Advance*, 1924. During the 1930's, he and his associates dominated American yachting, utilizing modern aerodynamic and industrial techniques in the design of thousands of superior vessels. Among them were *Enterprise*, *Rainbow*, and *Ranger*, defenders of the America's Cup.

BURGEVINE, HENRY ANDREA (*b. New Bern or Chapel Hill, N.C., 1836; d. China, 1865*), adventurer. Took command of mercenary "Ever Victorious Army" in China, 1862; after dismissal, sided with Taiping rebels and was charged with treason.

BURGIS, WILLIAM (*fl. New York and Boston, 1718–31*), artist, engraver. His surviving works are of great antiquarian interest and include: *South Prospect of . . . New York* (1718); *South East View of . . . Boston* (1723/24); *Prospect of the Colledges in Cambridge in New England* (1726); and *View of the New Dutch Church (New York)* (1731 or 1732).

BURK, FREDERIC LISTER (*b. Blenheim, Canada, 1862; d. 1924*), educator. Graduated University of California, 1883; Ph.D., Clark University, 1898. President, State Normal School, San Francisco; proponent of a "motivated individual instruction" theory.

BURK, JOHN DALY (*b. Ireland, ca. 1775; d. Petersburg, Va., 1808*), author. Came to America, 1796. His works include *History of Virginia* (in four volumes, 1804, 1805, 1816), and the plays *Bunker Hill* (produced 1797) and *Female Patriotism* (produced 1798).

BURKE, AEDANUS (*b. Galway, Ireland, 1743; d. Charleston, S.C., 1802*), Revolutionary soldier, congressman, jurist. Appointed associate judge in South Carolina, 1778; representative in legislature, 1781–82 and 1784–89; pamphleteered for leniency in treatment of Loyalists after Revolution; attacked idea of an American aristocracy in *Considerations on the Order of the Cincinnati* (1783). Voted against adoption of Federal Constitution; attacked eligibility of president to succeed himself; in first Congress opposed excise tax and establishment of United States Bank, but favored assumption of state debt and paying Continental obligations at par; firm proponent of slavery. Served on commission to revise and digest South Carolina law, 1785–89; elected chancellor of court of equity, 1799.

BURKE, BILLIE (*b. May William Ethelbert Appleton Burke, Washington, D.C., 1886; d. Los Angeles, Calif., 1970*), stage and screen actress. After establishing herself in London as one of the great beauties of the day, she appeared in numerous plays in New York (1907–31) and was also busy in silent films (1917–21). Married Florenz Ziegfeld, Jr. (1914), with whom she had a stormy and much-publicized relationship until his death in 1932. In the early 1930's she returned to Hollywood and became reestablished in the movies, appearing in more than sixty feature films between 1933 and 1960, often as a daffy, fluttery, but always well-intentioned character. She thought her best role was Glinda, the Good Witch of the North, in *The Wizard of Oz* (1939). She also did occasional stage and television dramas, starred on "The Billie Burke Show" on radio (1944–46), and hosted "At Home with Billie Burke" on television in the early 1950's.

BURKE, CHARLES ST. THOMAS (*b. 1822; d. New York, 1854*), actor, dramatist. Specialized in comic parts with the companies of Joseph Jefferson II and W. E. Burton.

BURKE, JOHN G. *See* BOURKE, JOHN GREGORY.

BURKE, JOHN JOSEPH (*b. New York, N.Y., 1875; d. Washington, D.C., 1936*), Roman Catholic clergyman, Paulist. Editor, the *Catholic World*, 1904–22; secretary, National Catholic Welfare Conference, 1919–36.

BURKE, STEVENSON (*b. near Ogdensburg, N.Y., 1826; d. Cleveland, Ohio, 1904*), lawyer, railroad promoter. Admitted to Ohio bar, 1848. President, Cleveland & Mahoning Valley Railway, 1880–1904.

BURKE, THOMAS (*b. Co. Galway, Ireland, ca. 1747; d. Orange Co., N.C., 1783*), Revolutionary statesman. Settled in Virginia after immigration, practicing medicine and then law; removed to North Carolina, 1771, and represented Orange Co. in all provincial congresses except the first. Was aligned with radical group in framing a state government; advocated annual elections, sovereignty of the people, separation of church and state, and ratification by the people in the 1776 sessions at Halifax. Served in Continental Congress, 1776–81; governor of North Carolina, 1781–spring of 1782.

BURKE, THOMAS (*b. Clinton Co., N.Y., 1849; d. New York, N.Y., 1925*), lawyer. Admitted to Michigan bar, 1873; removed to Seattle, Wash., 1875, where he became that city's foremost citizen.

BURLEIGH, CHARLES CALISTUS (*b. Plainfield, Conn., 1810; d. Northampton, Mass., 1878*), abolitionist, associate of Samuel J. May and William Lloyd Garrison.

BURLEIGH, GEORGE SHEPARD (*b. Plainfield, Conn., 1821; d. 1903*), poet, reformer. Brother of Charles C. Burleigh.

BURLEIGH, HENRY THACKER (*b. Erie, Pa., 1866; d. Stamford, Conn., 1949*), singer, composer. As a boy, acquired familiarity with black folksongs from his maternal grandfather, who was born a slave, and was encouraged in musical study by his mother. After graduation from Erie high school, he worked as a stenographer and built up a local reputation as a singer. A student at the National Conservatory of Music, New York City, 1892–96, he studied voice with Christian Fritsch, harmony with Rubin Goldmark, and counterpoint with John White and Max Spicker. Also became friends with Anton Dvořák, who was then the director, and sang and explained black folksongs for him. From 1894 until 1946, he was baritone soloist at St. George's Church in New York City; he held the same position at New York's Temple Emanu-El. He made extensive concert tours in the United States and in Europe, and from 1911 until his death was a music editor for G. Ricordi & Co. Composer of many art songs and ballads, he made his great contribution to music with artistic settings of black spirituals for solo voice and chorus, of which "Deep River" (1916) was the first. He was most generous to struggling black musicians.

BURLEIGH, WILLIAM HENRY (*b. Woodstock, Conn., 1812; d. Brooklyn, N.Y., 1871*), journalist, reformer. Brother of Charles C. and George S. Burleigh. Editor, *Christian Freeman*, 1843; *Prohibitionist*, 1849–55. Author of *Poems* (1841); *The Rum Fiend* (1871).

BURLESON, ALBERT SIDNEY (*b. San Marcos, Tex., 1863; d. Austin, Tex., 1937*), Democratic congressman, 1899–1913; postmaster general, 1913–21. A conservative politician, criticized by both business and labor interests.

BURLESON, EDWARD (*b. Buncombe Co., N.C., 1798; d. Austin, Tex., 1851*), soldier, frontier leader. Commander at siege of San Antonio, 1835; fought at San Jacinto. Elected to first Texas senate, 1836; as Republic of Texas vice president, 1841.

BURLESON, HUGH LATIMER (*b. Northfield, Minn., 1865; d. 1933*), Episcopal clergyman. Missionary bishop of South Dakota, 1916–31; an expert on Indian problems.

BURLESON, RUFUS CLARENCE (*b. Morgan Co., Ala., 1823; d. 1901*), Baptist clergyman, educator. President, Baylor University, 1851–61; established Waco University, 1861. President of both schools when consolidated, 1886–97.

BURLIN, NATALIE CURTIS (*b. New York, N.Y., 1875; d. Paris, France, 1921*), student of Indian and black music. Published *The Indians' Book* (1907); *Hampton Series Negro Folk-Songs* (1918–19).

BURLINGAME, ANSON (*b. New Berlin, N.Y., 1820; d. St. Petersburg, Russia, 1870*), diplomat. Congressman, Free-Soil and Republican, from Massachusetts, 1855–60; minister to China, 1861–67. Head of the first diplomatic mission sent by China to foreign powers, 1867–70, which resulted in the Burlingame Treaty with the United States (July 1868) and an equivalent declaration from Great Britain acknowledging sovereignty of China.

BURLINGAME, EDWARD LIVERMORE (*b. Boston, Mass., 1848; d. 1922*), editor. Son of Anson Burlingame, and served as his secretary in China and on his special mission, 1867–70. Literary adviser, Charles Scribner's Sons, *post* 1879; editor, *Scribner's Magazine*, 1886–1914.

BURLINGHAM, CHARLES CULP (*b. Plainfield, N.J., 1858; d. New York, N.Y., 1959*), lawyer and civic leader. Studied at Harvard and Columbia (LL.B., 1881). A liberal advocate of judicial and political reforms, Burlingham was also an expert in admiralty law. He was influential in the selection of judges for the New York area, and served as advisor to many governors and presidents. President of the Bar Association of the City of New York (1929–31). He was a close advisor of Fiorello H. La Guardia. He retired from the practice of law in 1953.

BURNAM, JOHN MILLER (*b. Irvine, Ky., 1864; d. Pomona, Calif., 1921*), educator. Graduated Yale, A.B. 1884, Ph.D. 1886. Professor of Latin, University of Cincinnati; specialist in paleography.

BURNAP, GEORGE WASHINGTON (*b. Merrimac, N.H., 1802; d. Baltimore, Md., 1859*), Unitarian clergyman. Pastor, First Independent Church, Baltimore, 1828–59.

BURNET, DAVID GOUVERNEUR (*b. Newark, N.J., 1788; d. Galveston, Tex., 1870*), politician. Joined Miranda revolts in Venezuela, 1806 and 1808; in business in Ohio and Louisiana; lived for a time among Comanches on upper Colorado River. Settled in Texas, 1831; active in events that led up to Texas rebellion against Mexico; served in convention that issued Texas Declaration of Independence. President of Republic of Texas, 1836, he was succeeded in October of that year by Sam Houston whom he bitterly opposed thereafter. Son of William Burnet (1730–1791).

BURNET, JACOB (*b. Newark, N.J., 1770; d. Cincinnati, Ohio, 1853*), lawyer, politician. Brother of David G. Burnet. Settled in Cincinnati, 1796; played leading part in organization of Ohio, in passing Land Act of 1820, and in financing internal improvements. Judge of Ohio supreme court, 1821–28; U.S. senator, Federalist, from Ohio, 1828–31.

BURNET, WILLIAM (*b. The Hague, Holland, 1688; d. Boston, Mass., 1729*), colonial governor. Son of Gilbert Burnet, Bishop of Salisbury; godson of King William III of England. Appointed governor of New York and New Jersey, 1720, where his statesmanlike Indian policy won him enmity of traders and Provincial Assembly. Reassigned as governor of Massachusetts, 1728.

BURNET, WILLIAM (*b. near Newark, N.J., 1730; d. Newark, 1791*), physician. Father of David G. and Jacob Burnet. Graduated College of New Jersey (Princeton), 1749. Active in opposition to English rule; chairman, Essex Co. committee of safety, 1775–76; member of Continental Congress, 1776–77 and 1780; physician and surgeon general, Eastern District military hospitals.

BURNETT, CHARLES HENRY (*b. Philadelphia, Pa., 1842; d. Bryn Mawr, Pa., 1902*), otologist. Deviser of operations for relief of chronic catarrhal otitis; an outstanding investigator of the physiology of hearing.

BURNETT, FRANCES ELIZA HODGSON (*b. Manchester, England, 1849; d. 1924*), author. Raised in poverty, she came with her family to America, 1865, settling near Knoxville, Tenn. Her plays and her forty or more novels were very popular in their day, although marked by sentimentality and an excess of romantic imagination. She is remembered chiefly for *Little Lord Fauntleroy* (1866), *Sara Crewe* (1888), and *Little Saint Elizabeth* (1890), "fairy tales of real life" as they have been called.

BURNETT, HENRY LAWRENCE (b. Youngstown, Ohio, 1838; d. New York, N.Y., 1916), lawyer, Union soldier. Prominent in military trials, 1863–65; prepared evidence in trials of Lincoln's assassins. Practiced law in Cincinnati and New York, serving as federal district attorney, southern district of New York, 1898–1906.

BURNETT, JOSEPH (b. Southborough, Mass., 1820; d. 1894), manufacturing chemist. Founded St. Mark's School, 1865.

BURNETT, PETER HARDEMAN (b. Nashville, Tenn., 1807; d. San Francisco, Calif., 1895), pioneer. Went to Oregon in 1843; settled on farm near mouth of Willamette, later near present site of Hillsboro, Oreg. Served on Oregon legislative committee, 1844; as judge of supreme court, 1845; elected to legislature, 1848. Led company to California goldfields, 1848; appointed judge of superior court of California, August 1849; elected governor of California, November 1849, serving until January 1851. Founder and president of Pacific Bank, San Francisco.

BURNETT, SWAN MOSES (b. New Market, Tenn., 1847; d. Washington, D.C., 1906), physician. Husband of Frances Hodgson Burnett. Specialist in ophthalmology and otology.

BURNHAM, CLARA LOUISE ROOT (b. Newtown, Mass., 1854; d. Casco Bay, Maine, 1927), author of popular novels.

BURNHAM, DANIEL HUDSON (b. Henderson, N.Y., 1846; d. Heidelberg, Germany, 1912), architect. As a child, moved to Chicago, Ill.; studied architecture there and entered office of Carter, Drake and Wight, 1872. In successful partnership with John W. Root, 1873–91, employed new structural concepts and materials in skyscrapers such as the Chicago Montauk and Monadnock buildings. Burnham and Root were made supervisors in planning the 1893 World's Columbian Exposition at Chicago (Root, consulting architect; Burnham, chief of construction); owing to Root's death in 1891 the task of coordinating efforts of principal artists and architects in erecting and decorating the great series of related buildings fell on Burnham. Success of the enterprise was attributed to Burnham's energy, taste, and ability to organize. Forming a new partnership, he undertook many important commissions; in 1901 he accepted chairmanship of a commission for development of Washington, D.C. The 1902 report of this commission (which included Charles F. McKim, Augustus Saint-Gaudens, and Frederick L. Olmsted, Jr.) marks the beginning of the modern city-planning movement in the United States. Burnham also made city plans for Cleveland, Ohio, San Francisco, Calif., Manila, Philippines, and his native Chicago, which owes the development of its lakefront to the Burnham Plan. He was chairman of the National Commission of Fine Arts and a founder of the American Academy in Rome.

BURNHAM, FREDERICK RUSSELL (b. Tivoli, near Mankato, Minn., 1861; d. Santa Barbara, Calif., 1947), explorer, scout, soldier of fortune. After a youth in frontier Minnesota and Los Angeles, Calif., then a small ranching town, Burnham chose the life of a scout and systematically set about learning his craft. Beginning at age thirteen as a horseback messenger for Western Union, he spent twenty years ranging over the Southwest and Mexico, hunting, prospecting, fighting the Apache, and serving as a deputy sheriff; at the same time, he learned all he could from older scouts, studied military science, and became expert in reading the "signs of the trail." All of this served him in his remarkable career, 1893–1904, as scout and explorer for Cecil Rhodes' British South Africa Company, and as chief of scouts for the British Army during the Boer War. Returning to the United States, 1904, he engaged in prospecting and archaeological expeditions in Mexico, and was associated with John Hays Hammond in land and oil ventures in Mexico and California.

BURNHAM, SHERBURNE WESLEY (b. Thetford, Vt., 1838; d. 1921), senior astronomer, Yerkes Observatory, 1897–1914; published General Catalogue of Double Stars (1906).

BURNHAM, WILLIAM HENRY (b. Dunbarton, N.H., 1855; d. Dunbarton, 1941), educational psychologist, mental hygienist. A.B., Harvard, 1882; Ph.D., Johns Hopkins (under G. Stanley Hall), 1888. Taught at Clark University post 1890; professor of pedagogy, 1906–26. Author of more than two hundred papers on child study, the mental health of schoolchildren, and the development of the science of education; also of The Normal Mind (1924), Great Teachers and Mental Health (1926), and The Wholesome Personality (1932). Believing that the fundamental conditions of mental health are integration and adjustment, and that the basic element of integration is within an infant at birth, he held that a normal course of personality development follows a sequence of integrations at higher and higher levels, at each stage reaching tentative solutions to problems that reappear as problematical on a higher level. Education should mediate between an old conditioned response (habit) that has become inadequate and a new adaptation to the conditions of life.

BURNS, ANTHONY (b. Stafford Co., Va., 1834; d. St. Catherine's, Canada, 1862), fled north from slavery, 1854, was arrested in Boston and was center of a great public commotion there when returned as a fugitive slave. His freedom was later purchased, and he served as minister of a Baptist church.

BURNS, BOB (b. Greenwood, Ark., 1890; d. Encino, Calif., 1956), radio and film star. Studied briefly at the University of Arkansas. Inventor, in 1920, of the musical instrument called the "bazooka." Burns performed in vaudeville until 1930, when he began to make films in Hollywood which included Young as You Feel, with Will Rogers, and Rhythm on the Range (1937), with Bing Crosby and Martha Raye. His radio programs include "The Kraft Music Hall" (1935–41) and his own show, "The Arkansas Traveler" (1941–47).

BURNS, OTWAY (b. Onslow Co., N.C., 1775[?]; d. Portsmouth, N.C., 1850), privateersman, shipbuilder. As captain of the Snap-Dragon, 1812–14, preyed on British commerce from Greenland to Brazil; in a single 1813 cruise, he accounted for goods worth over $2.5 million.

BURNS, WILLIAM JOHN (b. Baltimore, Md., 1861; d. Sarasota, Fla., 1932), detective, founder of the detective agency bearing his name.

BURNSIDE, AMBROSE EVERETT (b. Liberty, Ind., 1824; d. Bristol, R.I., 1881), Union soldier. Graduated West Point, 1847; resigned commission, 1853; engaged unsuccessfully in business in Rhode Island. Appointed major general of state militia. Organized and led 1st Rhode Island regiment, 1861; fought successful campaign on North Carolina coast, January to April 1862, and was commissioned major general of volunteers; twice offered command of Army of the Potomac, which he refused. At Antietam, September 1862, poor reconnaissance by Burnside resulted in ineffective use of his corps; appointed commander of the Army of the Potomac over his own protest, he met defeat with heavy loss at Fredericksburg, December 1862. Assigned to command Department of the Ohio, March 1863, his strategic retreat to Knoxville, Tenn., helped Grant defeat Bragg at Chattanooga, November 1863. In command of 9th Corps, January to July 1864, Burnside was held responsible for loss at Petersburg crater; he resigned commission toward end of the war. Held corporate positions subsequently; was governor of Rhode Island, 1866–68, and U.S. senator from Rhode Island, 1875–81.

BURR, AARON (b. Fairfield, Conn., 1715/16; d. Princeton, N.J., 1757), Presbyterian clergyman. Pastor, First Church, Newark, N.J.; president, College of New Jersey (Princeton), 1748–57.

BURR, AARON (b. Newark, N.J., 1756; d. Port Richmond, N.Y., 1836), Revolutionary soldier, lawyer, vice president of the United States. Son of Aaron Burr (1715/16–1757) and Esther Edwards, daughter of Jonathan Edwards (1703–1758). Reared by a maternal uncle, Timothy Edwards, and tutored for a time by Tapping Reeve, young Burr graduated with distinction from the College of New Jersey, 1772. Hesitant over choice of a career, he began study of theology; he left off in 1774 to study law. After serving with credit in the American invasion of Canada, 1775–76, he joined Washington's staff in New York with rank of major; mutual antagonism caused Burr's transfer to General Israel Putnam's staff with whom he did good service at Long Island and during evacuation of New York. Appointed lieutenant colonel in the Continental Line, July 1777, ill health brought on by overexertion forced him to resign from army, March 1779. After further study of law, he was licensed in New York early in 1782 as attorney. He married Mrs. Theodosia (Bartow) Prevost, in July 1782; despite disparity in their ages and her invalidism, he was devoted to her and to their daughter, Theodosia Burr. Successful in practice of law in New York, 1783–89, he tried to increase income by extensive speculations; his generosity and self-indulgence, however, made of him an incurable spendthrift. At first balked in attempts to enter politics because Alexander Hamilton, his rival, led one New York faction, and George Clinton, leader of the opposing faction, did not seek his support, he made himself of sufficient value to Clinton to be named state attorney general by him in 1789. After participating in a questionable sale of state lands, Burr was transferred to the U.S. Senate in which he represented New York, 1791–97. Unaccepted by either major party group, and having won the enmity of Hamilton by opposing his financial policies, Burr failed of reelection to the Senate; he was chosen a state assemblyman, however, in April 1797. His connection with a bill to aid the Holland Land Co., in which he had a financial interest, and another to secure a charter for the Manhattan Co. caused his defeat in 1799. By means of the political machine that he had built up, the Democratic-Republican party won control of the New York legislature in 1800 and Burr was able to secure endorsement of himself for the vice presidency; he then secured a pledge from Democratic-Republican members of Congress to support him equally with Thomas Jefferson at the election. Owing to this agreement, he tied for the presidency but immediately disclaimed any competition for the highest office and served as vice president under Jefferson. In office, he alienated the Democratic-Republicans and was supplanted as their candidate in 1804 by George Clinton; defeated the same year by Morgan Lewis in a contest for the governorship of New York, he ended a 15-year period of patience with Hamilton's private and public invective against him by challenging Hamilton to a duel. His enemy's death, after their meeting at Weehawken, N.J., July 11, 1804, caused Burr to flee southward to escape indictment.

For some time hopeful of exploiting current difficulties with Spain to his own advantage, Burr conferred with a fellow schemer, James Wilkinson, at Philadelphia; he also approached Robert Merry, British minister, requesting financial and naval aid in bringing about the separation of the western states from the Union but it is supposed that he never intended to act on this treasonable proposal. Meanwhile he presided with great impartiality and dignity over the impeachment of Supreme Court Justice Samuel Chase, his last act as retiring vice president.

Burr persisted in his separatist schemes with Wilkinson and others; on a journey in 1805 from Pittsburgh to New Orleans he received marked attentions everywhere and there was great speculation as to what he intended. Speculation soon turned to suspicion, and a diplomatic settlement of differences between Spain and the United States having ended the chance of a legitimate reason for seizure or invasion of any of the Spanish colonies, Burr and his associates were left with only the chance of some provocative border incident setting the frontier aflame. Burr's second trip westward in August 1806 led to his arraignment twice in Kentucky before a federal grand jury and a third arraignment early in 1807 in Mississippi Territory, all of which resulted in acquittal. Fearing that his associate Wilkinson (who had betrayed him) would seize him for trial by court-martial, Burr fled toward Mobile but was apprehended near the border and brought back for trial before Chief Justice Marshall in the Virginia circuit court. This famous trial began formally on May 22, 1807, and ended in September with the jury's finding that Burr was innocent of treason as defined by the Chief Justice. A second charge of misdemeanor for organizing an invasion of Spanish territory was also dismissed.

Burr sailed abroad in June 1808. He proposed to Great Britain a scheme for revolutionizing Mexico; in 1810, he attempted to persuade Napoleon to aid in freeing the Spanish colonies and Louisiana, going so far as an offer to act as head of a conspiracy to embroil the United States in war with the English. Unsuccessful in these and other plans, he returned to the United States in May 1812 and reentered legal practice in New York. Serenely spendthrift to the end of his long life, in July 1833 he married the wealthy widow of Stephen Jumel, who sued him for divorce a year later.

BURR, ALFRED EDMUND (b. 1815; d. Hartford, Conn., 1900). Editor, Hartford *Daily Times*, 1841–1900; influenced state Democratic platforms; a pioneer in tariff-reform policy.

BURR, ENOCH FITCH (b. Greens Farms, Conn., 1818; d. Hamburg, Conn., 1907), Congregational minister. Sought scientific proofs of religion, writing *Parish Astronomy* (1867), *Pater Mundi* (1870), *Doctrine of Evolution* (1873).

BURR, GEORGE LINCOLN (b. Oramel, N.Y., 1857; d. Ithaca, N.Y., 1938), historian and librarian. Teacher of medieval history, 1881–1922, librarian 1888–1938, at Cornell University.

BURR, THEODOSIA (b. Albany, N.Y., 1783; d. 1813), daughter of Aaron Burr. Married Joseph Alston, 1801. Father's confidante and agent during exile; lost at sea.

BURR, WILLIAM HUBERT (b. Waterford, Conn., 1851; d. 1934), engineer. Professor of engineering, Columbia University, 1893–1916; served on Isthmian Canal Commissions.

BURRAGE, HENRY SWEETSER (b. Fitchburg, Mass., 1837; d. 1926), editor, historian. Edited *Zion's Advocate*, Portland, Maine, 1873–1905. Became Maine state historian, 1907. Writings include *History of Baptists of Maine* (1904).

BURRAGE, WALTER LINCOLN (b. Boston, Mass., 1860; d. Brookline, Mass., 1935), physician, gynecologist. Historian of the Massachusetts Medical Society.

BURRALL, WILLIAM PORTER (b. Canaan, Conn., 1806; d. Hartford, Conn., 1874), lawyer, railroad executive. President, Housatonic Railroad, 1839–54; Hartford and New Haven, 1867–72.

BURRELL, DAVID JAMES (b. Mount Pleasant, Pa., 1844; d. New York, N.Y., 1926), clergyman. Pastor of Presbyterian and Dutch Reformed churches; active advocate of temperance.

BURRILL, ALEXANDER MANSFIELD (*b. New York, N.Y., 1807; d. 1869*), lawyer, author. Works include *Practice of Supreme Court of New York in Personal Actions* (1840), *New Law Dictionary* (1850–51).

BURRILL, JAMES (*b. Providence, R.I., 1772; d. Washington, D.C., 1820*), lawyer, politician. Rhode Island attorney general, 1797–1813; state assemblyman, 1813–16 (speaker, 1814–16); U.S. senator, Federalist, from Rhode Island, 1817–20.

BURRILL, THOMAS JONATHAN (*b. near Pittsfield, Mass., 1839; d. 1916*), botanist, horticulturist. Removed to Illinois, 1848; graduated Illinois State Normal School, 1865. Professor of natural history, University of Illinois; also vice president of that institution, and acting president, 1891–94, 1902. A leading figure in Illinois Horticultural Society and the Society of American Bacteriologists, Burrill was among the first of modern microscopists and a pioneer in study of bacterial diseases of plants.

BURRINGTON, GEORGE (*b. England, ca. 1680; d. London, England, 1759*). As colonial governor of North Carolina, 1723–25, 1731–34, he undertook extensive public works, largely self-financed; development of Cape Fear section was owing to him.

BURRITT, ELIHU (*b. New Britain, Conn., 1810; d. New Britain, 1879*), "The Learned Blacksmith," linguist, reformer. Formed League of Universal Brotherhood, 1846; organized world peace congresses, beginning at Brussels, 1848.

BURROUGHS, BRYSON (*b. Hyde Park, Mass., 1869; d. 1934*), artist. Curator of paintings, Metropolitan Museum of Art, New York City, 1906–34.

BURROUGHS, EDGAR RICE (*b. Chicago, Ill., 1875; d. Encino, Calif., 1950*), popular novelist, creator of Tarzan. After a number of vicissitudes, Burroughs became a writer of fiction for pulp magazines; his first novel was written as a serial for *All-Story* (serialized in 1912; published as a book, *A Princess of Mars*, 1917). It was the first of some sixty-eight titles. His work falls into three long groups or series: the Martian series, which began with the story cited above; the Pellucidar series, which began in 1922 with *At the Earth's Core*; and his most famous series, begun in 1914 with *Tarzan of the Apes*. His writing was uneven and often amateurish, but possessed at best a racy, headlong power of description and narration. The character of Tarzan was exploited in comic strips and books, a radio serial, and a number of profitable motion pictures.

BURROUGHS, JOHN (*b. near Roxbury, N.Y., 1837; d. 1921*), author. Mainly self-taught, Burroughs was a schoolteacher, 1854–63, delighting in nature-study and modeling his thought and style on Emerson. From 1863 to 1873, he lived in Washington, D.C., working as a treasury department clerk and cultivating the friendship of Walt Whitman. Subsequent to 1873, he resided mainly near Esopus, N.Y., writing, on the average, a book every two years for the remainder of his long life. Distinguished in his own time as a sage and prophet, and much in the company of Theodore Roosevelt and other enthusiasts for nature, his importance today lies in his establishment of the American "nature essay" as a literary type and in the vividness and felicity of his style. His works include: *Notes on Walt Whitman as Poet and Person* (1867; 1871); *Wake-Robin* (1871); *Winter Sunshine* (1875); *Locusts and Wild Honey* (1879); *Fresh Fields* (1885); *Leaf and Tendril* (1908); *The Breath of Life* (1915).

BURROUGHS, JOHN CURTIS (*b. Stamford, N.Y., 1817; d. Chicago, Ill., 1892*), Baptist clergyman. First president of (old) University of Chicago, 1857–73.

BURROUGHS, WILLIAM SEWARD (*b. Auburn, N.Y., 1855; d. Citronelle, Ala., 1898*), inventor. Patented in 1892 a practical adding machine that recorded both the separate items and the final result.

BURROW, TRIGANT (*b. Norfolk, Va., 1875; d. Greens Farms, Conn., 1950*), psychiatrist, phylobiologist. Graduated Fordham, 1895; M.D., University of Virginia, 1899; Ph.D., Johns Hopkins, 1909. After study in Zurich with Carl Jung, he began to practice in Baltimore, Md., 1910. A Freudian purist, he left practice in 1921 to work out a new approach to cure of nervous disorders by group analysis (see *The Social Basis of Consciousness*, 1927). Believing that man collectively has power to shape his own destiny, and that the cause of neurosis generally was to be found in man's social-biological heritage, he rejected much of conventional Western culture and tradition. He reentered practice in New York, 1927, and developed his ideas through his Lifwynn Foundation and in numerous papers and books. Neglected by the psychoanalytical elite, his ideas later had influence, especially on the family analysis movement of the 1960's.

BURROWES, EDWARD THOMAS (*b. Sherbrooke, Canada, 1852; d. 1918*), window shade and screen manufacturer; holder of forty patents on such devices. Removed to Portland, Maine, as a youth and resided there all his life.

BURROWES, THOMAS HENRY (*b. Strasburg, Pa., 1805; d. 1871*), lawyer, politician. Influential in organizing Pennsylvania public school system, 1836–38.

BURROWS, JULIUS CAESAR (*b. Northeast, Pa., 1837; d. Kalamazoo, Mich., 1915*), lawyer. Removed to Ohio as a boy, and later to Michigan. Congressman, Republican, from Michigan, 1873–74, 1879–83, 1885–94; U.S. senator from Michigan, 1894–1911. Member of Monetary Commission, 1909–12.

BURROWS, WILLIAM (*b. Kinderton, Pa., 1785; d. 1813*), naval officer. Killed commanding USS *Enterprise* in victory over HMS *Boxer*, 1813.

BURSON, WILLIAM WORTH (*b. Utica, Pa., 1832; d. Rockford, Ill., 1913*), inventor, manufacturer. Patented twine and wire grain binders (1860, 1861, and later patents); also developed automatic knitting machinery.

BURT, JOHN (*b. Wales, N.Y., 1814; d. Detroit, Mich., 1886*), inventor, capitalist. Son of William A. Burt. Removed to Michigan, 1824; worked with father as surveyor of Michigan upper peninsula, 1841–51. Thereafter, located and operated mines in that region, developed and built railroads and canals. His patents included improvements in iron manufacture and a new type of canal lock.

BURT, MARY ELIZABETH (*b. Lake Geneva, Wis., 1850; d. Coytesville, N.J., 1918*), educator. Editor of numerous readers and texts for schools.

BURT, WILLIAM AUSTIN (*b. Petersham, Mass., 1792; d. 1858*), surveyor, inventor. Developed mechanical skill at early age; taught himself surveying, mathematics, mechanics while helping father on farm; worked as millwright, 1813–31. Settled near Detroit, Mich., 1824, and held many civic posts; appointed surveyor of Macomb Co., 1831, and U.S. Deputy Surveyor, 1833. Ran surveys of Michigan upper peninsula and also the course of the 5th Principal Meridian in Iowa. Discoverer of iron deposits in Marquette Co., Mich., 1844. Invented a writing machine, the "Typographer," 1829; a solar compass to offset magnetic attraction, 1836; the equatorial sextant, 1856. He was also a prime mover in construction of Sault Ste. Marie canal.

BURTON, ASA (*b. Stonington, Conn., 1752; d. Thetford, Vt., 1836*), Congregational clergyman, teacher of theology, and pastor at Thetford *post* 1779.

BURTON, CLARENCE MONROE (*b. Sierra Co., Calif., 1853; d. 1932*), historian, lawyer, founder, and donor of the Burton Historical Collection of the Detroit Public Library.

BURTON, ERNEST DE WITT (*b. Granville, Ohio, 1856; d. 1925*), Baptist clergyman. Professor of New Testament literature, University of Chicago, 1892–1923; president, University of Chicago, 1923–25. Author of *Harmony of the Gospels* (1894).

BURTON, FREDERICK RUSSELL (*b. Jonesville, Mich., 1861; d. Lake Hopatcong, N.J., 1909*), composer, author of *American Primitive Music* (1909).

BURTON, HAROLD HITZ (*b. Jamaica Plain, Mass., 1888; d. Washington, D.C., 1964*), associate justice of the Supreme Court. After graduating from Harvard Law School (1912), practiced law with a variety of firms before joining Cull, Burton, and Laughlin in Cleveland (1925). In 1929 became member of the Ohio House of Representatives and director of law for the city of Cleveland. Elected mayor of Cleveland in 1934, was reelected in 1937 and 1939. Elected in 1940 to the U.S. Senate, he established himself as a moderate Republican with a conservative but nondoctrinaire slant. In 1945 became the first Truman appointee to the Supreme Court, where he quickly joined the Frankfurter, self-restraint wing. His behavior as a justice was cautious, at times ambivalent, and generally conservative. He tended to uphold government power, especially when the issue was one of balancing individual liberty against national security. In the economic area he was concerned about the growth of union power, feeling labor had to be reined in. But he did not shrink from government regulation of business as well. In the civil rights field, he consistently voted to extend the constitutional rights of blacks. In the 1950's, as the Warren Court majority took shape, Burton found himself more and more with the conservative dissenters. Although not an outstanding Supreme Court figure, he was a unifying influence at a time when the Supreme Court was often bitterly divided. Retired in 1958.

BURTON, HUTCHINS GORDON (*b. Virginia, or Granville Co., N.C., ca. 1774; d. 1836*), lawyer. Congressman from North Carolina, 1819–24; governor of North Carolina, 1824–27.

BURTON, MARION LE ROY (*b. Brooklyn, Iowa, 1874; d. 1925*), Congregational clergyman. President of Smith College, 1910–17; of University of Minnesota, 1917–20; of University of Michigan, 1920–25; raised large endowments for each.

BURTON, NATHANIEL JUDSON (*b. Trumbull, Conn., 1824; d. 1887*), Congregational clergyman.

BURTON, RICHARD EUGENE (*b. Hartford, Conn., 1861; d. Winter Park, Fla., 1940*), poet, literary critic, lecturer. Chairman, department of English, University of Minnesota, 1898–1902; 1906–25.

BURTON, THEODORE ELIJAH (*b. Jefferson, Ohio, 1851; d. 1929*), U.S. senator and representative from Ohio. A Republican, he was the foe of "pork-barrel" legislation and was singularly independent in his legislative record.

BURTON, WARREN (*b. Wilton, N.H., 1800; d. 1866*), Unitarian and Swedenborgian clergyman. Proponent of social reform through education; an early advocate of parent-teacher associations. Author of *The District School as It Was* (1833) and *Helps to Education* (1863).

BURTON, WILLIAM (*b. Sussex Co., Del., 1789; d. 1866*), physician. Democratic governor of Delaware, 1859–63; a loyal Unionist, he opposed federal encroachments on Delaware rights.

BURTON, WILLIAM EVANS (*b. London, England, 1804; d. New York, N.Y., 1860*), actor. Came to America, 1834, and was successful in comic roles; managed Burton's Theatre, Chambers St., New York City, 1848–56, with outstanding success.

BUSCH, ADOLPHUS (*b. Mainz on the Rhine, 1839; d. near Langenschwalbach, Germany, 1913*), brewer, industrialist. Came to America, 1857. A founder of Anheuser-Busch; pioneer in mechanical refrigeration and diesel engine building; donor to many charities.

BUSH, GEORGE (*b. Norwich, Vt., 1796; d. 1859*), Presbyterian and Swedenborgian clergyman. Professor of Hebrew, New York University, 1831–47.

BUSH, LINCOLN (*b. Cook Co., Ill., 1860; d. East Orange, N.J., 1940*), civil engineer, specializing in railroad and bridge work.

BUSH-BROWN, HENRY KIRKE (*b. Ogdensburg, N.Y., 1857; d. 1935*), sculptor.

BUSHMAN, FRANCIS XAVIER (*b. Baltimore, Md., 1883; d. Pacific Palisades, Calif., 1966*), actor. Upon the release of his first film, *His Friend's Wife* (1911), he became the first great romantic lead in the history of motion-pictures. He and Beverly Bayne became the first great romantic film team, appearing together in *A Good Catch* (1912) and in *Graustark* (1915), his most popular film, and marrying in 1918 (divorced 1932). His career suffered a permanent setback in 1918, when his fans discovered the existence of his first wife and five children. Thereafter he continued to appear in films and on radio and television, but although he almost made a comeback with his role in *Ben-Hur* (1926), he never achieved stardom again.

BUSHNELL, ASA SMITH (*b. Rome, N.Y., 1834; d. Columbus, Ohio, 1904*), businessman, politician. Removed to Ohio as a child; prospered after Civil War in the manufacture of harvesters. Republican governor of Ohio, 1895–99.

BUSHNELL, DAVID (*b. Saybrook, Conn., ca. 1742; d. Warrenton, Ga., 1824*), inventor, "father of the submarine." Graduated Yale, 1775; in the same year completed a man-propelled submarine that carried outside a wooden magazine of powder and a clock mechanism for igniting it at any chosen time. "Bushnell's Turtle," as it was called, was equipped with vertical and horizontal screws; a foot-operated valve in the keel let in water for submerging, two hand-operated pumps ejected it for ascending. After unsuccessful attempts to destroy British ships with the device, 1776–77, Bushnell yielded to ridicule and gave up further experimentation.

BUSHNELL, GEORGE ENSIGN (*b. Worcester, Mass., 1853; d. 1924*), tuberculosis specialist. Headed U.S. Army tuberculosis hospital, Fort Bayard, N. Mex., 1904–17; introduced rapid methods for detection of disease; author of *Epidemiology of Tuberculosis* (1920).

BUSHNELL, HORACE (*b. Bantam, Conn., 1802; d. Hartford, Conn., 1876*), Congregational clergyman, theologian. Graduated Yale, 1827; studied law while acting as tutor in Yale College, 1828–31. While awaiting admission to bar, participation in a spiritual revival influenced by him to enter Yale Divinity School. Reacting against Nathaniel W. Taylor's defense of the Calvinist system of theology, his intuitive, imaginative mind found inspiration in S. T. Coleridge's *Aids to Reflection*, a book that had a greater influence on him than any except the Bible. Ordained pastor of North Church, Hartford, Conn., 1833, at a time when Old and New Schools of New England theology were in fierce debate, he sided with neither, attempting in his own words: "to comprehend, if possible, the truth contended for in both." Broken in health, 1845, he spent a year in European travel. In 1849, he sustained a mystical experience whose meaning he explained in his *God in Christ*; orthodox reviewers were severe with the book, and he answered their objections and redefined his views in *Christ in Theology* (1851). Increasing bronchial trouble dictated a move to California, 1856; while there he was offered presidency of what later became University of California, but declined the post.

Returning to Hartford, he published *Sermons for the New Life* (1858). Although he resigned his pastorate in 1861 for reasons of health, the vigor of his mind was unimpaired; his works in retirement include: *Christian Nurture* (1861); *Work and Play* (1864); *Christ and his Salvation* (1864); and *The Vicarious Sacrifice* (1866), which is the most permanently significant of his books and contains his concept of the atoning work of Christ, commonly known as the "moral influence" theory of the Atonement. These were followed by *Moral Uses of Dark Things* (1868); *Women's Suffrage* (1869); *Sermons on Living Subjects* (1872); and a restatement, somewhat modified, of his views on the Atonement in *Forgiveness and Law* (1874). He applied his principle of seeing truth on both sides to national questions also, opposing both the fugitive slave law and abolitionism.

The distinctive character of Bushnell's contribution to theology may be stated thus: Theologians of the 19th century were no longer comfortable with Jonathan Edwards' reshaping of Calvinist thought and its conception of human nature; yet, although they disagreed in many respects, they were as one in seeing theology as an intellectual system to be established by precise processes of logic. Bushnell, like a poet, apprehended truth by intuition; he appealed to life rather than to logic. He broke with prevailing theological views, first, in suggesting that churches turn toward giving the young an early and clearly defined doctrine of Christian growth rather than focus on conversion of adults; second, in his view of the Trinity; third, in his interpretation of the meaning of the Cross and his repudiation of the penal and governmental theories of the Atonement; fourth, in declaring that no sharp line should be drawn between natural and supernatural, reason and revelation, sacred and profane, and denying that human nature and nature itself were involved in the fall of Adam. The key to his thought, according to his best biographer, lies in his conception of God as immanent in His works.

BUSSEY, CYRUS (*b. Hubbard, Ohio, 1833; d. Washington, D.C., 1915*), Union soldier. Commanded Iowa troops in Missouri campaigns, 1861; served in West and Southwest, 1861–65.

BUTLER, ANDREW PICKENS (*b. Ninety Six District, S.C., 1796; d. Edgefield, S.C., 1857*), lawyer. A leader of the Calhoun faction; U.S. senator, Democrat, from South Carolina, 1846–57. Charles Sumner's attack on Butler in the Senate, May 1856, led to Sumner's beating by Preston Brooks.

BUTLER, BENJAMIN FRANKLIN (*b. Columbia Co., N.Y., 1795; d. Paris, France, 1858*), lawyer, politician. Admitted to New York bar, 1817; from 1817–21 in office of Martin Van Buren; district attorney, Albany Co., N.Y., 1821–24. One of commission to revise New York Statutes, 1825. U.S. attorney general, 1833–37, acting also as secretary of war from October 1836 to March 1837; U.S. attorney for southern district of New York, 1838–41 and 1845–48. Thereafter he devoted himself entirely to the law as a leader of the New York bar. Originally a

Jackson Democrat, he supported Van Buren on the Free-Soil ticket in 1848 and joined the Republican party at its inception.

BUTLER, BENJAMIN FRANKLIN (*b. Deerfield, N.H., 1818; d. Washington, D.C., 1893*), Union soldier, politician. Graduated Waterbury (now Colby) College, 1838. Admitted to Massachusetts bar, 1840, he built up an extensive and lucrative practice. Believing strongly in the Union and in his own ability, he served 1861–65 in various commands, sometimes brilliantly and always controversially. He originated the term "contraband" for slaves fleeing from their owners to the Union lines; his administration of New Orleans, 1862, won him the violent hatred of the South and the imputation of corruption in office. Originally a Democrat, at the war's end Butler was identified with the radical wing of the Republicans; as a member of Congress, 1866–75, he was prominent in the impeachment of Andrew Johnson and an advocate of harsh Reconstruction policies. Detested by all Massachusetts conservatives, he was twice defeated in campaigns for governor of that state; in 1878, he returned to Congress as an independent Greenbacker. In 1882, running as a Democrat, he was elected governor of Massachusetts, failing of reelection in 1883. His last political activity was in securing nomination for the presidency, 1884, by the Anti-Monopoly and Greenback parties; he polled a very small vote.

BUTLER, BURRIDGE DAVENAL (*b. Louisville, Ky., 1868; d. Phoenix, Ariz., 1948*), agricultural publisher. After experience in journalism with the Scripps-McRae chain and other newspapers, and as a founder of Clover Leaf Newspapers, he acquired ownership about 1909 of a farm paper, *Prairie Farmer*, and built it into a highly successful, crusading journal. He added another dimension to the paper's influence in 1928 by operating a Chicago radio station, WLS, specifically to serve and entertain farm families. In his later years, he was owner of radio stations in Phoenix and Tucson, Ariz., and of another journal, the *Arizona Farmer*. He left a great part of his estate to youth-oriented charities.

BUTLER, CHARLES (*b. Kinderhook Landing, Columbia Co., N.Y., 1802; d. New York, N.Y., 1897*), lawyer, philanthropist. Brother of Benjamin F. Butler (1795–1858). Acquired extensive holdings in Chicago property and was active in development of Midwestern railroads; in 1843 and 1846, prevented repudiation of state bonds by Indiana and Michigan. A founder, 1836, of Union Theological Seminary, New York.

BUTLER, EZRA (*b. Lancaster, Mass., 1763; d. 1838*), Baptist clergyman. Settled in Waterbury, Vt., after the Revolutionary War, in which he served. An able public servant, and Democratic governor of Vermont, 1826–27.

BUTLER, HOWARD CROSBY (*b. Croton Falls, N.Y., 1872; d. Neuilly, France, 1922*), archaeologist. Professor of art and archaeology, Princeton, 1901–22; excavator of ancient Sardis. Author of *Archaeology and Other Arts* (1903) and *Sardis* (1922).

BUTLER, JOHN (*b. New London, Conn., 1728; d. Niagara, Canada, 1796*), Loyalist, Indian agent. Commanded Indian forces on British drive down Mohawk Valley, 1777; recruited and commanded Butler's Rangers in Tory raid on Wyoming Valley, 1778; defeated by General John Sullivan at Newtown (Elmira), N.Y., 1779.

BUTLER, JOHN WESLEY (*b. Shelburn Falls, Mass., 1851; d. Mexico City, Mexico, 1918*), Methodist clergyman. Missionary in Mexico, 1874–1918.

BUTLER, MARION (*b. Sampson Co., N.C., 1863; d. Takoma Park, Md., 1938*), farm leader. President, Southern Alliance, 1894; national chairman, Populist party, 1896–1904.

BUTLER, MATTHEW CALBRAITH (*b. Greenville, S.C., 1836; d. Columbia, S.C., 1909*), Confederate soldier, politician. Nephew of Andrew Pickens Butler. Served with distinction in Confederate Army, 1861–65, rising to major general; U.S. senator, Democrat, from South Carolina, 1877–94.

BUTLER, NICHOLAS MURRAY (*b. Elizabeth, N.J., 1862; d. New York, N.Y., 1947*), educator, president of Columbia University. Graduated Columbia, 1882; M.A., 1883; Ph.D., 1884. Interested as an undergraduate in journalism, law, and politics, Murray was influenced by Frederick A. P. Barnard and John W. Burgess to enter the field of education. Became a member of the Columbia faculty as assistant in philosophy, 1885. Rose rapidly to professor of philosophy, ethics, and psychology, and lecturer in education, 1890. *Post* 1895, his title was professor of philosophy and education. He participated in the choice of a new site for Columbia on Morningside Heights and was chiefly responsible for the successful summer school that was established in 1900. He was also responsible for the organization of a degree-granting school (chartered in 1889) for professional training of public schoolteachers, known *post* 1892 as Teachers College. Resigning as its president, 1891, he remained on its board of trustees and pressed for its affiliation with Columbia, 1893.

Succeeding Seth Low as president of Columbia (installed in April, 1902), Butler turned his marked executive talents to enhancing its status as a university. He encouraged the growth of the graduate faculties, tightened the bonds of the professional schools to Columbia and directed the creation of new ones, and further centralized administration. By 1914, Columbia had the largest endowment of any American university.

From the beginning of his academic career up to his retirement as president of Columbia in 1945, Butler was engaged in public affairs. In most respects a Republican party regular, he helped draft platforms, campaigned for nominees, and influenced the policies of those elected. An early supporter and adviser of Theodore Roosevelt, Butler had virtually broken with him by 1908 over Roosevelt's urging of greater federal control over the economy. As advisor to Taft and later Republican presidents, he stood for a basic, Hamiltonian conservatism in domestic affairs and government by a trained and enlightened elite.

He was an influential figure in international affairs, often serving as an unofficial presidential envoy. In his view, lasting peace would follow from enlightened public opinion, limitation of armaments, and an independent, international judiciary. He aided Andrew Carnegie in establishing the Carnegie Endowment for International Peace (1910), and also helped found the Carnegie Foundation for the Advancement of Teaching, and the Carnegie Corporation. For his labors in the successful creation of the Kellogg-Briand Pact, and its ratification by the United States, and in general for his activity as a peacemaker, he was awarded (with Jane Addams) the Nobel Peace Prize in 1931. Through the Carnegie Endowment, Butler sponsored the 1935 Chatham House Conference in London, which suggested easing of the burdens of debtor nations and the lowering of tariffs. As events worsened, he disapproved of the U.S. neutrality acts and roundly attacked isolationism.

BUTLER, PIERCE (*b. Co. Carlow, Ireland, 1744; d. Philadelphia, Pa., 1822*), planter, politician. Settled in Prince William's Parish, S.C., *post* 1771; in state legislature, 1778–82, 1784–89, where he championed democratic reforms. Worked for strong central government in federal convention, 1787. U.S. senator, Federalist, from South Carolina, 1789–96, 1802–06.

BUTLER, PIERCE (*b. near Northfield, Minn., 1866; d. Washington, D.C., 1939*), lawyer, justice of the U.S. Supreme Court. Son of Irish immigrants, he graduated from Carleton College, 1887, was admitted to the Minnesota bar, 1888, and began practice in St. Paul. Forceful, tenacious, with an extraordinary command of facts, he became an expert in railroad rate cases, and senior partner in one of the great law firms of the Northwest. Appointed as a Democrat to the Supreme Court in 1922, his views were authoritarian and conservative. Totally opposed to the New Deal, Butler dissented in 73 cases (more than half his total dissents) in his last three terms.

BUTLER, PIERCE MASON (*b. Mount Willing, S.C., 1798; d. Churubusco, Mexico, 1847*), politician, soldier. Brother of Andrew Pickens Butler. Governor of South Carolina, 1836–38; agent to the Cherokees, 1838–46; killed in action as colonel of Palmetto Regiment.

BUTLER, RICHARD (*b. Dublin, Ireland, 1743; d. 1791*), Revolutionary soldier, Indian agent. Served in all theaters of the war *post* 1776 and was brevetted brigadier general, 1783. Appointed Indian Commissioner by Congress, he negotiated important treaties with Iroquois, Delaware, Chippewa, and Shawnee tribes, 1784–86. He was killed in the rout of General Arthur St. Clair's expedition against the Ohio tribes, 1791.

BUTLER, SIMEON (*b. West Hartford, Conn., 1770; d. Northampton, Mass., 1847*), bookseller and publisher in Northampton, *post* 1790.

BUTLER, SMEDLEY DARLINGTON (*b. West Chester, Pa., 1881; d. Philadelphia, Pa., 1940*), Marine Corps officer. "Old Gimlet Eye"; a picturesque and controversial soldier.

BUTLER, THOMAS BELDEN (*b. Wethersfield, Conn., 1806; d. Hartford, Conn., 1873*), physician, jurist. Justice of state superior court, 1855–61; of supreme court of errors, 1861–73.

BUTLER, WALTER N. (*b. near Johnstown, N.Y., date unknown; d. 1781*), Loyalist, soldier. Son of John Butler. Led Tory and Indian attack on Cherry Valley, N.Y., November 1778; killed at West Canada Creek on retreat after raid on Mohawk Valley.

BUTLER, WILLIAM (*b. Prince William Co., Va., 1759; d. Edgefield District, S.C., 1821*), Revolutionary soldier. Father of Andrew P. Butler and Pierce M. Butler. Congressman, Democratic-Republican, from South Carolina, 1800–13.

BUTLER, WILLIAM (*b. Dublin, Ireland, 1818; d. Old Orchard, Maine, 1899*), Methodist clergyman. Came to America, 1850. Father of John Wesley Butler. Headed Methodist mission in India, 1856–64; in Mexico, 1873–79.

BUTLER, WILLIAM ALLEN (*b. Albany, N.Y., 1825; d. Yonkers, N.Y., 1902*), lawyer, author. Son of Benjamin F. Butler (1795–1858); authority on admiralty law. His best-known work is the sparkling satirical poem *Nothing to Wear* (1857).

BUTLER, WILLIAM ORLANDO (*b. Jessamine Co., Ky., 1791; d. Carrollton, Ky., 1880*), soldier, lawyer, farmer, statesman. Served with great distinction in War of 1812 and Mexican War. Congressman, Democrat, from Kentucky, 1839–43; Democratic vice presidential candidate, 1848; a staunch Union Democrat during Civil War.

BUTLER, ZEBULON (*b. Ipswich, Mass., 1731; d. Wilkes-Barre, Pa., 1795*), soldier. Reared in Lyme, Conn.; led Connecticut settlers along Susquehanna in the so-called Pennamite wars with Pennsylvania, 1769–75. Unsuccessfully defended Wyoming Valley against Tory-Indian raid, 1778.

BUTTERFIELD, DANIEL (*b. Utica, N.Y., 1831; d. Cold Spring, N.Y., 1901*), Union soldier. Son of John Butterfield; graduated Union College, 1849; employed in father's express business. Entered Civil War as colonel, 12th New York Regiment, and served with great distinction, 1861–65; during the war he was chief of staff to Generals Hooker and Meade, was several times wounded, and was honored at the end by a brevet of major general of regulars. On retirement from the army in 1870, he returned to business in which he had a varied and successful career.

BUTTERFIELD, JOHN (*b. Berne, N.Y., 1801; d. Utica, N.Y., 1869*), expressman, financier. Active in western New York stage lines, steamboat operation, and railroad promotion, he was an organizer of the American Express Co., 1850. In 1857, he and associates undertook the first transcontinental stage line and Butterfield as president of the Overland Mail Co. planned and established the service.

BUTTERFIELD, KENYON LEECH (*b. Lapeer, Mich., 1868; d. 1935*), college president, rural sociologist. Leader in the country-life movement; president, Massachusetts Agricultural College, 1906–24; Michigan State College, 1924–28.

BUTTERICK, EBENEZER (*b. Sterling, Mass., 1836; d. 1903*), inventor (with wife) of standardized paper clothes patterns, first marketed commercially in 1863.

BUTTERWORTH, BENJAMIN (*b. Hamilton Township, Ohio, 1837; d. Thomasville, Ga., 1898*), lawyer, politician. Congressman, Republican, from Ohio, 1879–83, 1885–90; special counsel in South Carolina election cases, 1882–83; U.S. commissioner of patents, 1883–85, 1897–98.

BUTTERWORTH, HEZEKIAH (*b. Warren, R.I., 1839; d. 1905*), journalist. Prolific contributor to *Youth's Companion,* 1870–94.

BUTTRICK, WALLACE (*b. Potsdam, N.Y., 1853; d. Baltimore, Md., 1926*), Baptist clergyman. As secretary (1903–17), president (1917–23), and chairman (1923–26) of the Rockefeller General Education Board, he promoted progress in education, particularly in the South; he was also active in promotion of education for the professions.

BUTTS, ISAAC (*b. Dutchess Co., N.Y., 1816; d. 1874*), publisher and editor of the *Daily Advertiser,* Rochester, N.Y., and later of the Rochester *Daily Union.*

BUTTZ, HENRY ANSON (*b. Middle Smithfield, Pa., 1835; d. 1920*), Methodist clergyman. Notable president of Drew Theological Seminary, 1880–1912; emeritus, 1912–20. Learned in Greek and New Testament exegesis.

BYERLY, WILLIAM ELWOOD (*b. Philadelphia, Pa., 1849; d. Swarthmore, Pa., 1935*), mathematician. Author of textbooks on calculus; a prime factor in growth of Radcliffe College.

BYFORD, WILLIAM HEATH (*b. Eaton, Ohio, 1817; d. Chicago, Ill., 1890*), gynecologist. Professor of gynecology, Rush Medical College, 1879–90; a pioneer in his field. Author of *Treatise on the Theory and Practice of Obstetrics* (1870) and other works.

BYINGTON, CYRUS (*b. Stockbridge, Mass., 1793; d. 1868*), Congregational clergyman. Missionary to Choctaw Indians *post* 1820; author of a grammar and dictionary of the Choctaw language.

BYLES, MATHER (*b. Boston, Mass, 1706/07; d. Boston, 1788*), Congregational clergyman. Graduated Harvard, 1725; ordained minister of Hollis Street Church, Boston, 1732. Dismissed from his pulpit for Tory sympathies, 1776. Cheerful and witty, he was a correspondent of Pope and Isaac Watts; he was

author of *Poems on Several Occasions* (1744) and numerous theological works of an orthodox Calvinist character.

BYNUM, WILLIAM PRESTON (*b. Stokes Co., N.C., 1820; d. Charlotte, N.C., 1909*), jurist, Confederate soldier.

BYOIR, CARL ROBERT (*b. Des Moines, Iowa, 1888; d. New York, N.Y., 1957*), public relations counsel. Studied at the University of Iowa and at Columbia (LL.B., 1912). During World War I, served as associate chairman of the Committee on Public Information in Washington, a major propaganda effort for the war. Attended the Versailles Peace Conference as a publicist for the U.S. views on peace and was advisor for a time to Czechoslovak President Thomáš Masaryk. Founded the Carl Byoir and Associates public relations firm in 1930. The company handled many famous clients, including Cuban dictator Geraldo Machado, A&P, and the Eastern Railroad Presidents Conference.

BYRD, HARRY FLOOD (*b. Martinsburg, W.Va., 1887; d. Berryville, Va., 1966*), governor of Virginia and U.S. senator. In the Virginia state senate (1915–25), he rose to prominence as a fiscal conservative and a moderate on social issues. As governor of Virginia (1925), he is remembered as a conservative stalwart, though he was a progressive senator by the standards of his era. Although he was limited to only one four-year term as governor under the Virginia Constitution, for the next four decades he was the major force in Virginia's political affairs. Appointed to fill a vacant seat in the Senate in 1932, he remained there until his resignation in 1965 and rose to power as a leader of southern conservatives. Was chairman of the Senate Finance Committee (1955–65) and of a largely ceremonial panel called the Joint Committee on Reduction of Nonessential Federal Expenditures. Was one of the earliest Democratic critics of the New Deal, between 1933 and 1945 voting with Republicans 45 percent of the time. Despite his differences with Roosevelt over domestic policy, he generally backed the administration's foreign policy. Was a staunch opponent of civil rights reform.

BYRD, RICHARD EVELYN (*b. Winchester, Va., 1888; d. Boston, Mass., 1957*), aviator and explorer. Studied at Virginia Military Institute, the University of Virginia, and at the U.S. Naval Academy. Byrd was designated naval aviator in 1918 and made commander of the U.S. Air Forces in Canada. After the Armistice, he became assistant to the director of naval aviation and a naval liaison to Congress. Remembered as the first man to lead expeditions to the Arctic and Antarctic, Byrd first went to the polar regions in a 1925 expedition to Greenland, which he explored by air. On May 9, 1926, he successfully flew to the North Pole, accompanied by Chief Machinist's Mate Floyd Bennett. In 1929, he flew to the South Pole. For his efforts he was promoted to the rank of rear admiral and awarded the Navy Cross. Byrd made other expeditions to the Antarctic, one in 1933 and another in 1939, when he established a permanent U.S. presence on the subcontinent. In 1946, he returned to the Antarctic with over 4,000 men to map the region. In 1955, President Eisenhower appointed him officer in charge of the U.S. Antarctic programs.

BYRD, WILLIAM (*b. London, England, 1652; d. 1704*), planter, merchant, Indian trader. Came to Virginia when young; by uncle's will inherited lands at present site of Richmond, 1671. Served in House of Burgesses, 1677–82; became member of the Council of State, 1683. Took up residence at Westover, 1691. In 1703 he became president of the Council. Byrd's wealth was based on tobacco planting and export; the importation of black slaves and all manner of manufactured articles; fur trading with the Indians; land speculation.

BYRD, WILLIAM (*b. Virginia, 1674; d. Westover, Va., 1744*), planter, colonial official, author. Son of William Byrd

(1652–1704). Schooled abroad, 1684–92; studied at Middle Temple, London. Elected to House of Burgesses, 1692, on return to Virginia; in England, 1697–1704; entered Council of State, 1709. Resisted Governor Spotswood's attempts to remove supreme judicial power from Council. Lived in ease and state at Westover *post* 1720, managing with a rather lax hand the properties left him by his father. His witty, graceful writings remained unpublished until 1841; they include *The History of the Dividing Line, A Journal to the Land of Eden,* and the *Progress to the Mines.* His letters and diaries have also been published and are valuable historical sources.

BYRNE, ANDREW (*b. Navan, Ireland, 1802; d. Little Rock, Ark., 1862*), Roman Catholic clergyman. Came to America, 1820; ordained, 1827; served as pastor of churches in Charleston, S.C., and New York, N.Y. Appointed first bishop of Little Rock, 1844.

BYRNE, DONN. *See* DONN-BYRNE, BRIAN OSWALD.

BYRNE, JOHN (*b. Kilkeel, Ireland, 1825; d. Montreux, Switzerland, 1902*), physician, surgeon. M.D. Edinburgh, 1846. Came to America, 1848, and practiced in Brooklyn, N.Y. Adapted electric cautery-knife to surgery of malignant disease of uterus, *ca.* 1870.

BYRNES, THOMAS (*b. Ireland, 1842; d. 1910*), policeman, "Inspector Byrnes." Brought to America in infancy; joined New York City police force, 1863. Won fame in solving Manhattan Savings Bank case, 1878; reorganized New York detective bureau, 1880, making it highly efficient.

BYRNS, JOSEPH WELLINGTON (*b. Robertson Co., Tenn., 1869; d. Washington, D.C., 1936*). Congressman, Democrat, from Tennessee, 1909–36 (majority leader, 1932–35; speaker, 1935–36).

C

CABELL, JAMES BRANCH (b. Richmond, Va., 1879; d. Richmond, 1958), novelist, essayist, historian. Studied at the College of William and Mary. In addition to his essays and work in genealogy, Cabell is remembered as the author of the novel *Jurgen* (1919); the book was declared indecent in New York State, and its success was guaranteed. Although he was admired by Sinclair Lewis, H. L. Mencken, and Carl Van Doren, Cabell's reputation as a writer has not held up in literary circles. Other works include *It Happened in Florida*, a trilogy (1943–49), and an eighteen-volume edition of his works (1927–30).

CABELL, JAMES LAWRENCE (b. Nelson Co., Va., 1813; d. Albemarle Co., Va., 1889), physician. M.D. University of Maryland, 1834. Professor of anatomy, surgery, and physiology, University of Virginia, 1837–89; author of *Testimony of Modern Science to the Unity of Mankind* (1858).

CABELL, JOSEPH CARRINGTON (b. Amherst, now Nelson, Co., Va., 1778; d. 1856), principal coadjutor of Thomas Jefferson in founding University of Virginia. Brother of William H. Cabell. Identified by choice with Virginia affairs although fitted for national eminence. Pioneer of James River and Kanawha Canal project.

CABELL, NATHANIEL FRANCIS (b. "Warminster," Nelson Co., Va., 1807; d. 1891), author. Wrote voluminously on topics of religion, genealogy, and agricultural history of Virginia; editor, *The Lee Papers* (1858–60).

CABELL, SAMUEL JORDAN (b. Amherst, now Nelson, Co., Va., 1756; d. Nelson Co., 1818), Revolutionary soldier. Son of William Cabell. Commissioned major for bravery at Saratoga, 1777; served under Washington, 1778–79, and under General Lincoln in southern campaign. Congressman, Democratic-Republican, from Virginia, 1795–1803.

CABELL, WILLIAM (b. Virginia, 1729/30; d. Nelson Co., Va., 1798Revolutionary patriot. Member of Committee of Safety, and of committee which prepared for Declaration of Rights and a form of government for Virginia. Served in both houses of state legislature; voted against ratification of federal Constitution.

CABELL, WILLIAM H. (b. near Cartersville, Va., 1772; d. Richmond, Va., 1853), lawyer. Brother of Joseph C. Cabell. Elected governor of Virginia, 1805; served three terms. Judge of state court of appeals, 1811–51; president of the court, 1842–51.

CABELL, WILLIAM LEWIS (b. Danville, Va., 1827; d. 1911), Confederate soldier, lawyer. Graduated West Point, 1850. Resigned from army, 1861, and was thereafter on staffs of Confederate generals Beauregard and J. E. Johnston; served with distinction in trans-Mississippi department, 1862–64. Studied law after the war and removed to Dallas, Tex., 1872; mayor of Dallas, 1874–76 and 1882.

CABET, ÉTIENNE (b. Dijon, France, 1788; d. St. Louis, Mo., 1856), reformer, communist. Set forth a social doctrine in his *Voyage en Icarie* (1839) which he hoped to realize in a utopian settlement on the Red River in Texas. Failing there, his followers leased the old Mormon settlement at Nauvoo, Ill., where he presided, 1849–55.

CABLE, FRANK TAYLOR (b. New Milford, Conn., 1863; d. New London, Conn., 1945), electrical engineer. Worked on a dairy farm and as a mechanic; studied electrical engineering at night at Drexel Institute and Franklin Institute, Philadelphia. Associated with John P. Holland, 1897–1900, in early submarine construction and trial work; later worked for Electric Boat Company and subsidiaries. Received patents on a number of submarine devices. Author of *The Birth and Development of the American Submarine* (1924).

CABLE, GEORGE WASHINGTON (b. New Orleans, La., 1844; d. St. Petersburg, Fla., 1925), author. Began to write after service, 1863–65, with Confederate cavalry; became a reporter for New Orleans *Picayune*, 1869, but soon took position as clerk with a firm of cotton factors. Fascinated by stories on which he chanced in a survey of old city records, he set them down in a series of sketches which were immediately successful on publication in *Scribner's Monthly*, 1873–76. They appeared in book form as *Old Creole Days* (1879). Subsequent publication of *The Grandissimes* (1880) and *Madame Delphine* (1881) established him as a writer of sensitivity and mood who had added a new "region" to American fiction; with Bret Harte, he was a pioneer in "local color" work. Although he continued to write until his death, his later books lacked the quality of his earlier ones; he became active in movements for reform of prisons, election laws, and the condition of the black, and aroused the resentment of southerners. After 1885, he made his home in Northampton, Mass. His later books include *Dr. Sevier* (1885); *The Silent South* (1885); *The Negro Question* (1888); *John March, Southerner* (1894); *The Cavalier* (1901).

CABOT, ARTHUR TRACY (b. Boston, Mass., 1852; d. 1912), surgeon. Graduated Harvard, B.A., 1872; M.D., 1876. In London, 1877, to study surgical pathology, he heard Lister's inaugural address and was thereafter an apostle of the antiseptic system; returning to Boston, he built up a general practice, specializing in surgery *post* 1886. He served as instructor, Harvard Medical School, 1878–80 and 1885–96, and was active in public health promotion; his extensive writings appeared mainly in the *Boston Medical and Surgical Journal*.

CABOT, EDWARD CLARKE (b. Boston, Mass., 1818; d. Brookline, Mass., 1901), architect. Designer of Boston Athenaeum (1845), Boston Theater (1852–53), and Johns Hopkins University hospital (completed 1889). These and his many excellent country houses were distinguished for delicacy and restraint.

CABOT, GEORGE (*b. Salem, Mass., 1752; d. Boston, Mass., 1823*), merchant, politician. Escaped dismissal from Harvard, 1768; went to sea; was skipper of a schooner within two years. Gave up active seafaring, *ca.* 1777, and entered family shipping and trading firm. In partnership with Joseph Lee, 1785–95, he earned a "reasonable and sufficient" fortune in shipping and trading. Temperament and interest made him favor a strong central government. He was early identified with the Federalist point of view and was a trusted follower and adviser of Alexander Hamilton. As U.S. senator from Massachusetts, 1791–86, he favored the Jay Treaty and close alliance with Great Britain. On retirement from public life, he expanded his business interests and indulged a growing pessimism over the course of the nation; he opposed Jefferson and his policies, but as president of the Hartford Convention (1814) worked with Harrison G. Otis to prevent radical action by that body.

CABOT, GODFREY LOWELL (*b. Boston, Mass., 1861; d. Boston, 1962*), industrialist and philanthropist. Studied at Massachusetts Institute of Technology and Harvard (B.A. chemistry, 1882), Zurich Polytechnicum, and the University of Zurich. Originally in business with his brother Samuel, he built the Grantsville Carbon Works in West Virginia (1899) and eventually acquired eleven plants, becoming the nation's leading producer of carbon black. Through Godfrey L. Cabot, Inc., and its successor, the Cabot Corp., his industrial empire expanded to encompass gas, oil, minerals, and research. An avid pilot, he served as president of the National Aeronautic Association. His philanthropy included large gifts to MIT and Harvard. A leader of the Watch and Word Society, he helped establish Boston as the center of blue-nosed puritanism. During the McCarthy era he spoke in defense of professors and others accused of Communist sympathies.

CABOT, HUGH (*b. Beverly Farms, Mass., 1872; d. Ellsworth, Maine, 1945*), surgeon, medical educator, and reformer. Brother of Richard C. Cabot. B.A., Harvard, 1894; M.D., Harvard Medical School, 1898. Entered practice with his cousin, Arthur T. Cabot. Taught genitourinary surgery at Harvard, 1910–19, serving in France during World War I, briefly in 1916 and 1917–18. Appointed professor of surgery at University of Michigan Medical School, 1920; dean, 1921. Meeting all opposition to reform with uncompromising determination, he made enemies and was relieved as dean in 1930. He then served as professor of surgery at the University of Minnesota Graduate School of Medicine, and as consulting surgeon at the Mayo Clinic, 1930–39. He stressed the importance of behavioral studies in premedical courses and the introduction of clinical study early in the curriculum, lest students view their patients less as people than as laboratory animals. He resumed practice in Boston in 1939, and devoted himself to further medical reforms; many of his ideas were far in advance of their time, principally his attacks on the fee system and his contention that the federal government must assume the burden of medical school and hospital deficits and must underwrite proper medical care for the poor. He was also a leader in the antitrust action which prohibited professional-society reprisals against physicians who joined in group health plans or other cooperatives. A charter member of the American College of Surgeons, he was author of *Modern Urology* (1918).

CABOT, RICHARD CLARKE (*b. Brookline, Mass., 1868; d. Cambridge, Mass., 1939*), physician, medical reformer, social worker. Graduated, 1892, from Harvard Medical School, he taught there, 1899–1933, and was on the staff of Massachusetts General Hospital from 1898 to 1921, from 1912 as chief of staff. Convinced of the importance of social and psychic factors in the diagnosis and treatment of disease (especially in the case of clinic patients). Cabot inaugurated, 1905, a medical social service unit at Massachusetts General, a pioneer form of medical social work. A distinguished teacher and practitioner, he was also a productive writer—on medical subjects, social work, and social ethics. He occupied the chair of social ethics at Harvard College from 1920 to 1934.

CABRILLO, JUAN RODRIGUEZ (*d. San Miguel Island, Calif., 1543*), explorer of the coast of California, 1542.

CABRINI, FRANCES XAVIER (*b. Sant' Angelo Lodigiano, Lombardy, Italy, 1850; d. Chicago, Ill., 1917*), founder of a religious community and first citizen of the United States to be canonized by the Catholic Church. Taught school and supervised an orphanage before becoming prioress (1877) of her foundation, the Institute of the Missionary Sisters of the Sacred Heart. After founding orphanages and schools, she was sent by Pope Leo XIII to the United States to help Italian immigrants living in slums, many of whom were losing the Catholic faith. Disappointments she faced on her arrival in 1889 did not discourage her from establishing 70 hospitals and educational institutions throughout the Western Hemisphere and western Europe. Pronounced venerable in 1933, Mother Cabrini was canonized in 1946.

CADILLAC, ANTOINE DE LA MOTHE SIEUR (*b. Gascony, France, ca. 1656; d. Castle Sarrazin, Gascony, 1730*), founder of Detroit. Came to Canada, 1683; lived at Port Royal and for a brief time on his grant in what is now Maine. Through friendship of Count Frontenac, he received command of post at Mackinac, 1694, but was relieved of it in 1697. In 1699, he went to France with a scheme for protecting the French fur trade from English raids by erecting a post on Detroit River; receiving a grant of Detroit and a trade monopoly, he led a body of colonists there in 1701. Zealous, enthusiastic, covetous, and high-handed, Cadillac after many difficulties was recalled in 1711 and appointed governor of the new colony of Louisiana, where he arrived in 1713. He was soon at odds with the colonists and was superseded, 1716, returning to France.

CADMAN, CHARLES WAKEFIELD (*b. Johnstown, Pa., 1881; d. Los Angeles, Calif., 1946*), composer, pianist, organist. Made musical studies in Pittsburgh, Pa.; was a church organist in Pittsburgh and in Denver, Colo.; resided in California *post* 1917. Became interested in American Indian music by reading the ethnological studies of Alice Fletcher and Francis La Flesche; employed Indian melodies and themes in a number of songs, piano compositions, and orchestral suites, and in his operas *Daoma* (1912), *Shanewis* (1918), and *The Sunset Trail* (1922). He wrote other operas on American historical themes, but is particularly remembered for two extremely successful songs: "At Dawning" (1906) and "From the Land of the Sky-blue Water" (1908).

CADMAN, SAMUEL PARKES (*b. Wellington, England, 1864; d. Plattsburg, N.Y., 1936*), clergyman. Originally a Methodist, he became pastor of Brooklyn's Central Congregational Church, 1900–36. One of the first "radio pastors."

CADWALADER, JOHN (*b. Philadelphia, Pa., 1742; d. 1786*), Revolutionary soldier. Appointed brigadier general of Pennsylvania militia, 1776; fought at Trenton, Princeton, Brandywine, Germantown, and Monmouth. His duel with General Conway caused the collapse of the "Conway Cabal" against Washington.

CADWALADER, JOHN (*b. Philadelphia, Pa., 1805; d. Philadelphia, 1879*), jurist. Graduated University of Pennsylvania, 1821; admitted to the bar, 1825. Counsel to Bank of the United States, *post* 1830; acted in behalf of the United States in the "cloth cases" of 1839; was associated with Daniel Webster in the Girard will case. Judge of U.S. district court, eastern district of Pennsylvania, 1858–79.

CADWALADER, LAMBERT (*b. Trenton, N.J., 1743; d. "Greenwood," near Trenton, 1823*). Brother of John Cadwalader (1742–86); Revolutionary patriot and soldier.

CADWALADER, THOMAS (*b. Philadelphia, Pa., 1707 or 1708; d. Trenton, N.J., 1799*), physician. Father of John (1742–86) and Lambert Cadwalader. Studied medicine with physician uncle in England and France; had large practice in Philadelphia. Lived in Trenton, N.J., 1738–50, returning to Philadelphia. Active in civic and cultural affairs and in early stages of resistance to English rule. Performed in 1742 one of he earliest recorded autopsies in America.

CADY, DANIEL (*b. Chatham, N.Y., 1773; d. Johnstown, N.Y., 1859*), jurist. Specialist in equity and real property law; father of Elizabeth Cady Stanton.

CADY, SARAH LOUISE ENSIGN (*b. Northampton, Mass., 1829; d. New York, N.Y., 1912*), educator. Principal and proprietor, West End Institute, New Haven, Conn., 1870–99.

CAFFERY, DONELSON (*b. near Franklin, La., 1835; d. New Orleans, La., 1906*), sugar planter, statesman. U.S. senator, Democrat, from Louisiana, 1892–1901; opposed free silver, the sugar bounty, and the war with Spain.

CAFFIN, CHARLES HENRY (*b. Sittingbourne, Kent, England, 1854; d. 1918*), author. Came to America, 1892; art critic and writer of popular books on art.

CAHAN, ABRAHAM (*b. Podberezya, Russia, 1860; d. New York, N.Y., 1951*), journalist, labor leader, novelist. Immigrated to the U.S. in 1882. Studied at the Vilna Teachers Institute. One of the original editors of the *Jewish Daily Forward* (1897), Cahan became its driving force and built the paper into one of the country's largest dailies. It was the first newspaper to place novelists, including Sholem Asch and I. J. Singer, on a weekly salary. Cahan was an early labor agitator and helped organize some of the first Jewish trade unions in the 1880's. In 1890, he became an editor for the United Hebrew Trade organ, *Arbeiter Zeitung*. Cahan published his novel *Raphael Naarizoch* in the *Arbeiter Zeitung* in 1894. In 1896, he wrote *Yekl: A Tale of the New York Ghetto*, considered the first authentic immigrant novel. His best-known novel was *The Rise of David Levinsky* (1917). As an editor, Cahan was a member of the American delegation to the Paris Peace Conference.

CAHILL, HOLGER (*b. Snaefellsnessysla, Iceland, 1887; d. Stockbridge, Mass., 1960*), art authority, author, curator. Studied at New York University, Columbia, and the New School for Social Research. Assistant director of the Newark Museum (1922–32); director of exhibitions at the Museum of Modern Art in New York City (1932–35). Appointed national director of the Federal Art Project (1935–43). As director he administered the funds for public works art projects of the New Deal and compiled the *Index of American Design*. Cahill was an expert in modern art with special interest in contemporary American art. Books include *Art in America in Modern Times* (1934), with Alfred H. Barr, Jr., and a novel, *Look South to the Polar Star* (1947).

CAHN, EDMOND NATHANIEL (*b. New Orleans, La., 1906; d. New York, N.Y., 1964*), lawyer and legal philosopher. Attended Tulane (B.A., 1925; J.D., 1927), then practiced law in New York City until 1950, when he joined the faculty at the New York University School of Law. Cahn's legal philosophy dealt mainly with ethical and moral aspects of the law, especially those dealing with the rights of the individual. His first book, *The Sense of Injustice* (1949), argued that the law exists to serve the everyday needs of citizens; justice is served not by obeying natural laws or accepting legalized power, but by preventing "the sense of injustice." In *The Moral Decision* (1955), Cahn argued from Hebraic and Hellenic principles for a legal approach that was rooted in America's moral precepts. The basis for moral decisions, he argued, was in a dynamic human nature achieving active adjustment in a complex and fluid community. *The Predicament of Democratic Man* (1961) develops the biblical insight that a people is accountable for the moral quality of its law. The people, he felt, must accept responsibility for the transgressions of their government. Throughout his writings Cahn propounded "fact-skepticism," an approach developed by Jerome Frank. This led him to oppose the death penalty as an irreversible act produced by a fallible legal system. Cahn viewed his scholarly task as furnishing the theoretical underpinnings of a philosophy of action to provide a more just society. He was active in the Union for Democratic Action (forerunner to the Americans for Democratic Action), the New York League to Abolish Capital Punishment, and the American Civil Liberties Union.

CAIN, RICHARD HARVEY (*b. Greenbrier Co., Va., 1825; d. 1887*), Methodist clergyman, politician. Licensed to preach at Hannibal, Mo., 1844, he allied himself with the African Methodist Episcopal church and held pastorates in Iowa, New York, and South Carolina. As member of Congress from South Carolina during Reconstruction, he strove for clean politics; elected bishop, 1880, his last years were spent in Louisiana and Texas.

CAIN, WILLIAM (*b. Hillsboro, N.C., 1847; d. 1930*), mathematician. Professor, and head of Department of Engineering, University of North Carolina, 1888–1920; a pioneer in writing American civil engineering textbooks.

CAINES, GEORGE (*b. 1771; d. Catskill, N.Y., 1825*), lawyer. First official reporter of legal decisions, appointed by the New York Supreme Court, 1804; editor, *Caines' Cases in Error* (1805–07) and other works.

CAJORI, FLORIAN (*b. Switzerland, 1859; d. 1930*), historian of mathematics and professor, University of California, 1918–29. Author of many authoritative works, including *A History of Mathematical Notations* (1928–29).

CALDER, ALEXANDER STIRLING (*b. Philadelphia, Pa., 1870; d. New York, N.Y., 1945*), sculptor. Son of Alexander M. Calder, celebrated for his colossal bronze statue of William Penn on the dome of the Philadelphia City Hall. The younger Calder studied at Pennsylvania Academy of the Fine Arts, and in Paris with Henri Chapu and Alexandre Falguière. Returning to Philadelphia, 1892, he taught modeling at the Pennsylvania Academy, opened his own studio, and won an 1894 competition to make a portrait bust of Samuel D. Gross. The most important of his early larger sculptures are the Sun Dial in Fairmount Park, Philadelphia (1903), and the Sewell Cross (1905) in Harleigh Cemetery, Camden, N.J. Among his outstanding later works are a statue of Marcus Whitman (1909); the H. C. Lea Memorial, Laurel Hill Cemetery, Philadelphia (1912); the Fountain of Energy and other monumental works for the Panama-Pacific Exposition (1915); the Fountain of the Three Rivers, Logan Circle, Philadelphia (1924); and the memorial to Leif Ericsson, Reykjavik, Iceland (1931).

CALDWELL, ALEXANDER (*b. Drake's Ferry, Pa.; d. Leavenworth, Kans., 1917*), businessman, politician. Contractor for delivery of army stores to posts west of the Missouri, 1861; promoter of Kansas railroads, *post* 1870. Denied seat in U.S. Senate, 1871, on charge that bribery dictated his appointment.

CALDWELL, CHARLES (*b. Caswell Co., N.C., 1772; d. 1853*), physician. Pioneer medical educator in Mississippi Valley; founded and directed medical school, Transylvania (Lexington, Ky.), 1819–37; professor, Louisville Medical Institute, 1837–49.

CALDWELL, CHARLES HENRY BROMEDGE (*b. Hingham, Mass., 1823; d. 1877*), naval officer. In command of *Itasca*, April 1862, helped open passage to New Orleans for Farragut's fleet.

CALDWELL, DAVID (*b. Lancaster Co., Pa., 1725; d. North Carolina, 1824*), Presbyterian clergyman. Prominent in patriotic affairs during the Revolution; pastor at Alamance, N.C., 1768–1820.

CALDWELL, EUGENE WILSON (*b. Savannah, Mo., 1870; d. 1918*), roentgenologist. Inventor of many improvements in X-ray apparatus; died of injuries suffered in experimentation.

CALDWELL, HENRY CLAY (*b. Marshall Co., Va., 1832; d. Los Angeles, Calif., 1915*), jurist. Raised in Iowa; appointed U.S. judge for war-ravaged Arkansas district, 1864, he served until 1890 with scrupulous impartiality; presiding justice, 8th Federal District, 1890–1903.

CALDWELL, JAMES (*b. Charlotte Co., Va., 1734; d. Elizabeth, N.J., 1781*), Presbyterian clergyman, patriot. Graduated Princeton, 1759; settled as pastor, Elizabeth, N.J.; known as the "Soldier Parson" in Revolutionary War.

CALDWELL, JOSEPH (*b. Lamington, N.J., 1773; d. 1835*), mathematician, educator. Graduated Princeton, 1791. Professor of mathematics, University of North Carolina, 1796–1804 and 1812–17; its president, 1804–12 and 1817–35; a force for internal improvements and public education in North Carolina.

CALDWELL, OTIS WILLIAM (*b. Lebanon, Ind., 1869; d. New Milford, Conn., 1947*), educator, B.S., Franklin College, 1894; Ph.D., University of Chicago, 1898. A lifelong proponent of the value of science as an essential element of public school curricula, Caldwell left his post as professor of botany at the University of Chicago (where he was also head of the Department of Natural Sciences in the School of Education, and dean of the University College) in 1917 to direct the Lincoln School (1917–27), New York City. He also became a professor at Columbia Teachers College, with which the new, experimental school was affiliated. During his tenure as director he won wide reputation for the school as a successful example of progressive education on its practical side. Retired from the Teachers College faculty, 1935.

CALEF, ROBERT (*b. probably England, 1648; d. Roxbury, Mass., 1719*), merchant. His book *More Wonders of the Invisible World* (written 1697, printed in London, 1700) was a powerful indictment of the Salem witchcraft trials of 1692 and a blow at domination of New England thought by the Mather dynasty.

CALHOUN, JOHN (*b. Boston, Mass., 1806; d. St. Joseph, Mo., 1859*), politician. Settled in Springfield, Ill., 1830; helped Abraham Lincoln study surveying. Served thrice as mayor of Springfield; appointed surveyor of Kansas and Nebraska, 1854, he became involved in the alleged frauds connected with the Lecompton constitutional convention, 1857.

CALHOUN, JOHN CALDWELL (*b. Abbeville District, S.C., 1782; d. Washington, D.C., 1850*), statesman, political philosopher. Descended from Scotch-Irish pioneers who entered Pennsylvania ca. 1733. Subsequent to Braddock's defeat (1755), the family moved south and settled in the South Carolina uplands near the Savannah River. Calhoun's father, Patrick, was for many years a member of the South Carolina legislature; his death in 1796 thrust family burdens on the son and interrupted his formal

education until 1800. He then resumed school and graduated from Yale, 1804. After law studies at Tapping Reeve's school, Litchfield, Conn., and in office of Henry W. DeSaussure, Charleston, S.C., he began practice in Abbeville, S.C. Finding legal work uncongenial, he was fortunate in a marriage (1811) with Floride Bouneau, whose means, added to his own, left him financially independent.

Active from youth in politics, he was elected to the South Carolina legislature in 1808 and had a share in the revision of representation in that body whereby control of the lower house was given the upland districts and preponderance in the state senate to the lowlands. This device of mutual checks or "concurrent majorities" he was later to propose for relief of sectional differences on the national scale. Elected congressman, Democratic-Republican, in 1810, he served as acting chairman, Committee on Foreign Affairs; his report, presented June 3, 1812, recommending war on Great Britain, was written by Monroe but won popular notice for Calhoun. During the War of 1812, he was tireless in support of the war and the administration; thereafter, he distrusted efficacy of the Treaty of Ghent and was zealous in promoting national strength, urging an effective navy, an adequate standing army, a road-building policy, a system of internal revenue, a national bank, and the encouragement of native manufactures. At this period he favored a protective tariff. Appointed secretary of war in Monroe's cabinet (1817–25), he improved army organization and established the offices of surgeon general, commissary general, and quartermaster general.

Elected vice president by a large majority in 1824, he presided over the Senate with meticulous abstinence from the partisanship of the period; obviously shaping his course for the presidency, he allied himself with Andrew Jackson and was elected for a second term as vice president in 1828. Soon alienated from Jackson, Calhoun found himself in an equal quandary over protectionism. Opposition to protection was rising in the South, but his northern supporters favored it. Basing his decision on the national interest, he had voted against the woolens bill (1827); he had expressed himself in confidence as opposed to any policy which would put the geographical interests in hostile array, or would "make two of one nation." Now in 1828, fearing that the insistence of Congress on the Tariff of Abominations would force the South to a desperate reaction, he composed the "South Carolina Exposition" for issues by the state legislature; as his authorship remained a secret until 1832, its bold warning that pursuance of a protectionist program would result in the counterstroke which was to become famous as "nullification" committed him to nothing at the time. His efforts to achieve intersectional accord failing, and with President Jackson approving the systematically protective tariff of 1832, Calhoun published that August a letter to Governor Hamilton in which he gave logic and substance to the doctrine of nullification. Premising that sovereignty is in the people and that both central and state governments under the American federal system are only organs of popular power, he declared that in the event of an exceeding of power by the central government against the will of the people of any state, the people could hold a convention and declare the act of Congress null; they could also require the state government to prohibit enforcement of the obnoxious act within the limits of the state. He developed all phases of this doctrine extensively and was careful to distinguish the right of nullification from the right of secession.

President Jackson's forceful reaction to nullification having ended in a face-saving compromise, a new alignment of political forces took place and Whig was opposed to Democrat; Calhoun at first held himself aloof from both, but his dislike of Jackson and Jackson's favorites inclined him to act as a Whig auxiliary. Under Van Buren, he shifted to the Democratic side. Early in 1833, he had resigned the vice presidency and now, as senator from South

Carolina, sat in Congress, where his able attention to public business increased his following in the South and won back for him the respect of many northerners.

The rise of the abolition movement made it impossible for Calhoun to return to his earlier nationalistic position. Menaced by destruction of their capital (as represented by their slaves) and a potential social chaos, southerners looked for a strategy of defense; Calhoun came to be regarded as the main source of plans, arguments, and inspiration. Although he had shown only luke-warm acquiescence in the slave-system earlier in his career, the agitation of Garrison and others altered his mind; in 1833 he said that slavery might give the South greater reason than the tariff to cherish states' rights and by 1837 he was found asserting that slavery was a positive good. He deprecated controversy over disputes between the sections, which he considered unessential, but on vital issues he was aggressive in defense of "southern rights." Active under President Tyler, in whose cabinet he served for a time as secretary of state, he retired to private life at the outset of President Polk's term; he returned to the Senate as war threatened with Mexico, war which he vehemently opposed.

Wilmot's proposal to prohibit slavery in all areas to be acquired by the war involved Calhoun in furious controversy. He urged that all territories were an estate owned by the states of the Union in common; that the federal government administered them only as a trustee; that any citizen of any state had full right to immigrate to any territory, carrying with him whatever property he owned, and was entitled to federal protection of his property until the territory should become a state. No slaveholder, therefore, could be debarred from transport and continued use of his slaves. In effect, Congress was estopped from restricting the spread of slaveholding. As a permanent expression of his philosophy of government, he wrote his *Disquisition on Government* and his *Discourse on the Constitution and Government of the United States*; these appeared in published form after his death.

The doctrines contained in these treatises were studied with respect at home and abroad, especially his plea for adequate checks against encroachments of government and the spoliation of minorities in promotion of majority interests, and his restatement of the right of the people to challenge any assumptions of undelegated authority. As a device to perpetuate the Union and secure at the same time the tranquillity of the South, he advocated amendment of the Constitution to allow election of two chief executives, each to represent one of the great sections of the country.

Convinced as he was that the South was doomed under the existing state of party government, Calhoun summoned a meeting in January 1849 of southern statesmen to consider an address which he had written for their signature and issue to their constituents. It reviewed the history of the slavery issue, prophetically foretold the evils that were to come, and called for unity in holding southern rights paramount to party allegiance. Only a minority signed it. He then endeavored to promote a convention of the slaveholding states. Before the end of the year, California's application for statehood under a constitution excluding slavery re-opened legislative battle. Ill and old, Calhoun tottered to his place in the Senate chamber to preach resistance by the South to the point of independence if that should prove essential for its social security.

His last formal speech gave his adverse opinion of Henry Clay's omnibus bill which proposed to settle the many issues on a give-and-take basis. This was read by Senator Mason on March 14, 1850, while its author sat voiceless in his chair. Virtually his last spoken words were, "The South, the poor South."

CALHOUN, PATRICK (*b. Fort Hill, near Pendleton, S.C., 1856; d. Pasadena, Calif., 1943*), lawyer, financier. Grandson of John C. Calhoun and of Duff Green. Studied law with his grandfather Green; practiced briefly in St. Louis, Mo.; built up lucrative practice in Atlanta, Ga., *post* 1878. He engaged also in a wide range of business enterprises, including land speculation in cotton properties, oil, mining, manufacturing, and railroads. About 1894, he gave up his legal practice and devoted full time to business, dealing in street railway properties in northern cities, and developing the Euclid Heights section of Cleveland, Ohio. Removing to San Francisco, Calif., about 1900, he became president (1906) of the consolidated street railway system of that city; in 1907, he and other executives of he system were indicted for bribery but no conviction resulted. In 1913, he was forced out of his presidency of the system for improper use of company funds. Thereafter, his fortunes steadily declined.

CALHOUN, WILLIAM BARRON (*b. Boston, Mass., 1795; d. Springfield, Mass., 1865*), lawyer, politician, educator. Graduated Yale, 1814; admitted to Massachusetts bar, 1818. Held numerous public offices with credit; had a lifelong interest in teacher-training.

CALHOUN, WILLIAM JAMES (*b. Pittsburgh, Pa., 1848; d. Chicago, Ill., 1916*), diplomat. Practiced law, Danville, Ill., 1875–98; thereafter in Chicago. His reports on condition of Cuba, 1897, reconciled McKinley to intervention; he served as minister to China, 1909–13.

CALIFORNIA JOE (*b. near Stanford, Ky., 1829; d. Camp Robinson, Nebr., 1876*), army scout. Born Moses Embree Miller, he went west in 1849, served in the Civil War, and after the war as a guide and scout on the plains; he was associated with General Custer's commands, *post* 1868, and won fame in the writings of Custer and his wife.

CALKINS, EARNEST ELMO (*b. Geneseo, Ill., 1868; d. New York, N.Y., 1964*), advertising executive and author. Severely deafened in his youth, Calkins became a voracious reader and received a B.A. from Knox College (1891). Beginning with advertising jobs with newspapers and department stores in Illinois, he went on to join the Charles Austin Bates advertising agency in New York City. In 1902, with Ralph Holden, he formed the Calkins and Holden agency, which quickly prospered. In 1905 Calkins and Holden published the textbook *Modern Advertising*, and Calkins went on to write and lecture widely on business and advertising. In 1931 he resigned as president of Calkins and Holden, and in his later years devoted his energies to writing on a broad range of issues, especially on the problems of the deaf. Some fifty pieces of his appeared in the *Atlantic Monthly*.

CALKINS, GARY NATHAN (*b. Valparaiso, Ind., 1869; d. Scarsdale, N.Y., 1943*), zoologist. B.S., Massachusetts Institute of Technology, 1890; Ph.D., Columbia University, 1898. Member of the Department of Zoology at Columbia *post* 1894, he was named professor in 1904. From 1907 to 1939, he was professor of protozoology, the first such appointment in the United States; he was also associated for many years with the Marine Biological Laboratory, Woods Hole, Mass. The leading protozoologist of his generation, he was particularly noted for studies of the life cycle of *Uroleptus mobilis*. Author of a number of scientific papers and books, including *The Protozoa* (1901) and *The Biology of the Protozoa* (1926).

CALKINS, MARY WHITON (*b. Hartford, Conn., 1863; d. 1930*), the first American woman to attain eminence in the field of philosophy. Pupil of Josiah Royce, she taught psychology and philosophy at Wellesley College, 1890–1929.

CALKINS, NORMAN ALLISON (*b. Gainesville, N.Y., 1822; d. New York, N.Y., 1895*), educator. Author of *Primary Object Lessons for a Graduated Course of Development* (1861), a Pestalozzian treatise which had great influence in primary school teaching.

CALKINS, PHINEAS WOLCOTT (*b. Painted Post, now Corning, N.Y., 1831; d. 1924*), Congregational clergyman. Held many eastern and midwestern pastorates; at death, pastor emeritus of Montvale Church, Woburn, Mass.

CALKINS, WOLCOTT. *See* CALKINS, PHINEAS WOLCOTT.

CALL, RICHARD KEITH (*b. Prince George Co., Va., 1791; d. 1862*), lawyer, politician. Moved to Kentucky as a boy; schooled in Tennessee. Served under Andrew Jackson in War of 1812 and Creek campaigns; resigned army commission, 1821, and set up law practice in Pensacola, Fla. Territorial delegate from Florida, 1823–25. Built third railroad in United States (Tallahassee–St. Marks), 1832–34. Democratic governor of Florida, 1836–39; Whig governor of Florida, 1841–44. Strove to hold Florida in the Union, but went with his state on secession.

CALLAHAN, PATRICK HENRY (*b. Cleveland, Ohio, 1865; d. Louisville, Ky., 1940*), paint manufacturer, proponent of industrial partnership, crusading Catholic layman. Instituted, 1915, profit-sharing in his Louisville Varnish Co.

CALLAWAY, MORGAN (*b. Cuthbert, Ga., 1862; d. Austin, Tex., 1937*), philologist. Author of authoritative studies of Old English syntax; professor of English, University of Texas, 1890–1936.

CALLAWAY, SAMUEL RODGER (*b. Toronto, Canada, 1850; d. 1904*), railroad executive. His reorganization of Toledo, St. Louis & Kansas City line, 1887–95, led to presidency of New York Central, 1898–1901; he was first president of American Locomotive Co., 1901–04.

CALLENDER, GUY STEVENS (*b. Hartsgrove, Ohio, 1865; d. 1915*), historian, economist. Professor of political economy, Sheffield Scientific School, Yale, 1903–15. Author of masterly *Selections from the Economic History of the United States* (1909).

CALLENDER, JAMES THOMSON (*b. Scotland, 1758; d. Richmond, Va., 1803*), political writer. Came to America, *post* 1793, and was patronized by Thomas Jefferson. Author of scurrilous *History of the United States for 1796* (1797), *The Prospect Before Us* (1800–01), and other tracts.

CALLENDER, JOHN (*b. Boston, Mass., 1706; d. Newport, R.I., 1748*), Baptist clergyman. Pastor at Newport, 1731–48; author of valuable *Historical Discourse on the Civil and Religious Affairs of the Colony of Rhode Island* (1739).

CALLIMACHOS, PANOS DEMETRIOS (*b. Madytos, Dardanelles, Turkey, 1879; d. New York, N.Y., 1963*), Greek Orthodox priest, writer, and advocate of Hellenism. Studied at the University of Athens (D.D., 1902), then worked as a journalist and secretary of the patriarchate of Alexandria. His first book was *The Patriarchate of Alexandria in Abyssinia*. During the Balkan Wars (1912–13) he served as a volunteer chaplain and journalist. In 1914 he immigrated to the U.S. and quickly became a leading figure among Greek-Americans, promoting the preservation of Greek language, customs, and traditions. He served as priest of St. Constantine's Church in Brooklyn. As an editor of the Greek-language daily *National Herald*, Callimachos campaigned against assimilation and the restoration of the Greek monarchy in 1935. In 1944 he became editor of *Eleutheros Typos*, a Greek-language weekly. His last book was *How and Why Americans Succeed*.

CALVERLEY, CHARLES (*b. Albany, N.Y., 1833; d. Essex Falls, N.J., 1914*), sculptor. Pupil of Erastus D. Palmer; specialized in portrait busts and medallions.

CALVERT, CHARLES (*b. England, 1637; d. 1715*), third Lord Baltimore, son of Cecilius Calvert. Governor of Maryland, 1661–75; proprietor, 1675–1715.

CALVERT, CHARLES BENEDICT (*b. Riverdale, Md., 1808; d. Riverdale, 1864*), agriculturist. Prime mover in founding Maryland Agricultural College; as a congressman, 1861–64, active in establishing federal Bureau (now Department) of Agriculture, 1862.

CALVERT, GEORGE (*b. Kipling, Yorkshire, England, ca. 1580; d. 1632*), first Lord Baltimore, projector of Maryland. Educated at Oxford; served Sir Robert Cecil as secretary, 1606–12; knighted, 1617; secretary of state and Privy Councillor, 1619–25; created Baron Baltimore, 1625. In 1624, announced his conversion to Catholic faith and resigned offices but was retained as a Privy Councillor. Had become in 1620 proprietor by purchase of part of Newfoundland; this was erected by royal grant into province of Avalon, 1623, but the colony did not thrive. Calvert petitioned for a grant in warmer climate, 1629; in 1632, Charles I granted him territory in what is now Virginia. Opposition by Virginia settlers and the Virginia Company caused substitution of lands between 40° north latitude and Potomac River, extending westward to longitude of that river's first source. Calvert died before charter of Maryland passed the Great Seal; it was issued to his son Cecilius, first proprietor of Maryland.

CALVERT, GEORGE HENRY (*b. Riverdale, Md., 1803; d. Newport, R.I., 1889*), author. Brother of Charles B. Calvert; settled in Newport, 1843, after extensive travel abroad. Author of minor verse, studies of Goethe and the English Romantic poets, and an essay on manners, *The Gentleman* (1863).

CALVERT, LEONARD (*b. England, 1606; d. Maryland, 1647*), colonial governor. Son of George Calvert; brother of Cecilius Calvert, second Lord Baltimore. Came to Maryland with first colonists aboard the *Ark* and the *Dove*, March 1634, and set up a government at St. Mary's City. Formally commissioned governor, 1637, he served until his death in that capacity. His support of laws passed by the Assembly over his brother's veto led to the right of initiative in legislation passing to that body.

CALVERTON, VICTOR FRANCIS (*b. Baltimore, Md., 1900; d. New York, N.Y., 1840*), originally named George Goetz. Applied Marxist critical principles to the social sciences and literature.

CALVIN, SAMUEL (*b. Wigtonshire, Scotland, 1840; d. 1911*), geologist. Immigrated to America, 1851; raised in Buchanan Co., Iowa. Professor of natural history, Iowa State, *post* 1874; state geologist, 1892–1904 and 1906–11. Did valuable work on fossils of upper Mississippi Valley.

CAMBRELENG, CHURCHILL CALDOM (*b. Washington, N.C., 1786; d. West Neck, N.Y., 1862*), politician. Successful in business in New York City, 1802–21; congressman, Democrat, from New York, 1821–39, and administration leader in the House for both Jackson and Van Buren. Minister to Russia, 1840–41. Took prominent part in New York "Barnburner" movement, 1847–48.

CAMDEN, JOHNSON, NEWLON (*b. Collins Settlement, Va., 1828; d. 1908*), businessman. Pioneered in oil on the Little Kanawha, 1860; entered refinery business, Parkersburg, W.Va., 1869; promoted railroads in area and became a Standard Oil Co. director. U.S. senator, Democrat, from West Virginia, 1881–87 and 1893–95.

CAMERON, ANDREW CARR (*b. Berwick-on-Tweed, England, 1836; d. 1892*), labor leader, editor. Immigrated to America *ca.* 1851; was printer on Chicago *Courant* (later *Times* and active in typographical union. Edited *Workingman's Advocate*, 1864–80; helped organize National Labor Union, devoted to formation of an independent labor party.

CAMERON, ARCHIBALD (*b. Lochaber, Scotland, ca. 1771; d. Kentucky, 1836*), Presbyterian clergyman. Raised by an elder brother in Nelson Co., Ky. Ordained, 1796, he was leading exponent of orthodox Calvinism in Nelson, Shelby, and Jefferson counties.

CAMERON, JAMES DONALD (*b. Middletown, Pa., 1833; d. 1918*), businessman, politician. Son of Simon Cameron, whom he aided in family enterprises and in control of Republican party in Pennsylvania, succeeding to the leadership after father's retirement. President, Northern Central Railroad, 1863–74; secretary of war, 1876–77; U.S. senator from Pennsylvania, 1877–97.

CAMERON, ROBERT ALEXANDER (*b. Brooklyn, N.Y., 1828; d. Canon City, Colo., 1894*), Union soldier, colonizer. Joined with Nathan C. Meeker in post–Civil War Union Colony movement for planting farm colonies in West. Active in founding Greeley, Colo., and Colorado Springs.

CAMERON, SIMON (*b. Lancaster Co., Pa., 1799; d. 1889*), businessman, politician. Managed newspapers, 1821–26. Ownership of Harrisburg, Pa., *Republican* gave him influence in state and national politics; lucrative appointment as state printer provided means for his branching out into canal building and the creation of a network of local railroads which he later united in the Northern Central. He also engaged in banking, iron making, and insurance. Soon wealthy, he was a staunch supporter of protective tariffs. Originally a Democrat, he maneuvered his election to the U.S. Senate in 1845 by means which won him enmity of James Buchanan and regular party men; he failed of election in 1849 and again in 1855. Becoming a Republican he was returned to the Senate in 1857; thereafter he strengthened his position as dictator of Pennsylvania politics. Support of Lincoln in 1860 won him post of secretary of war; his corrupt conduct of office caused his removal, 1862, by appointment as minister to Russia. Returning home, 1863, he ran unsuccessfully for the Senate; in 1867 he was elected and served as senator until 1877 when he forced the subservient Pennsylvania legislature to accept his son, James Donald Cameron, as his successor. His iron control of his state was based on patronage and shrewd manipulation of men.

CAMERON, WILLIAM EVELYN (*b. Petersburg, Va., 1842; d. 1927*), newspaper editor. Joined "Readjuster" faction of Virginia Democrats, 1879; served as governor of the state, 1882–86. Editor, *Norfolk Virginian* (1908–15) and *Virginian-Pilot* (1915–19).

CAMM, JOHN (*b. Hornsea, England, 1718; d. 1778*), Anglican clergyman. Appointed minister, Newport Parish, Va., 1745; professor of divinity, College of William and Mary, 1749. Leader of clergy in assailing Two Penny Acts, 1755 and 1758. President, William and Mary, 1771–77.

CAMMERHOFF, JOHN CHRISTOPHER FREDERICK (*b. Hillersleben, Germany, 1721; d. Pennsylvania, 1751*), Moravian missionary to Pennsylvania and New York settlers, and to the Iroquois, 1746–51.

CAMP, DAVID NELSON (*b. Durham, Conn., 1820; d. 1916*), educator. Professor and principal, Connecticut Normal School, 1849–66; associate of Henry Barnard; principal, New Britain (Conn.) Seminary.

CAMP, HIRAM (*b. Plymouth, Conn., 1811; d. New Haven, Conn., 1893*), clock manufacturer, philanthropist. President, New Haven Clock Co., 1853–92. A founder of Mount Hermon School and Northfield Seminary.

CAMP, JOHN LAFAYETTE (*b. near Birmingham, Ala., 1828; d. San Antonio, Tex., 1891*), lawyer, planter. Moved to Gilmer, Tex., 1849; served with distinction in Civil War as colonel, 14th Texas Cavalry. Active in local politics; helped prepare Texas Constitution of 1876; served on state bench, 1878–84.

CAMP, JOHN LAFAYETTE (*b. Gilmer, Tex., 1855; d. San Antonio, Tex., 1918*), jurist. Son of the preceding. State district judge, 1897–1914; federal attorney, western Texas district, 1914–18. Instrumental in preserving the Alamo.

CAMP, WALTER CHAUNCEY (*b. New Britain, Conn., 1859; d. New York, N.Y., 1925*), promoter of American football. Graduated Yale, 1880; attended Yale Medical School. Associated 1883–1925 with New Haven Clock Co.; *post* 1888, became athletic director and head advisory football coach at Yale. Many of the rules of the game as now played were suggested by Camp; he developed its strategy, and raised its level of sportsmanship. He originated the All-American selections, 1889, and the "daily dozen" exercises for keeping physically fit.

CAMPANIUS, JOHN (*b. Stockholm, Sweden, 1601; d. Sweden, 1683*), Lutheran clergyman, missionary. Accompanied Governor Printz to Swedish colony on Delaware; chaplain to settlers at Fort Christina (now Wilmington, Del.), 1643–48. His efforts to convert the Delaware Indians to Christianity were reasonably successful; he studied their folkways and language and translated Luther's *Shorter Catechism* into Delaware (printed 1696). His grandson, Thomas Campanius "Homiensis," incorporated John's account of his voyage to America in his *Description of the Province of New Sweden*.

CAMPAU, JOSEPH (*b. Detroit, Mich., 1769; d. Detroit, 1863*), trader. Invested profits from Indian trading in purchase of real estate which growth of Detroit made increasingly valuable; was considered Michigan's wealthiest citizen.

CAMPBELL, ALEXANDER (*b. Co. Antrim, Ireland, 1788; d. Bethany, W.Va., 1866*), one of the founders of the Disciples of Christ. Immigrated to America, 1809. Succeeded his father as pastor of an independent church at Brush Run, Pa., 1813; affiliated with Baptists; lectured and wrote in the *Christian Baptist*, 1823 and after, with hope of promulgating his own opinions, but was forced into a separate denomination. Author of an English translation of the Bible (1827) and other works; founder of Bethany College, 1840.

CAMPBELL, ALLAN (*b. Albany, N.Y., 1815; d. New York, N.Y., 1894*), civil engineer. Helped construct railroads in Georgia, New York, and the Republic of Chile; chief engineer and later president of the Harlem Railroad. Active in New York civic work.

CAMPBELL, ANDREW (*b. near Trenton, N.J., 1821; d. 1890*), inventor, manufacturer. As foreman in shop of A. B. Taylor & Co., developed paper-feed mechanisms and automatic features for printing presses, 1853–58. Invented and manufactured the Campbell Country Press, 1861–66; a two-revolution picture press, 1867; and others.

CAMPBELL, BARTLEY (*b. Pittsburgh, Pa., 1843; d. Middletown, N.Y., 1888*), playwright. Shares with Augustin Daly and Bronson Howard the honor of establishing in America the profession of the playwright on a firm basis. Author of *The Virginian* (produced 1873); *My Partner* (his best, produced 1879); and *The White Slave* (produced 1882), which contains the immortal line "Rags are royal raiment when worn for virtue's sake."

CAMPBELL, CHARLES (*b. Petersburg, Va., 1807; d. 1876*), historian. Author of *An Introduction to the History of the Colony and Ancient Dominion of Virginia* (1847; new edition, 1860), a work which established him as a local historian; he was also editor of the *Bland Papers* (1840–43).

CAMPBELL, CHARLES MACFIE (*b. Edinburgh, Scotland, 1876; d. Cambridge, Mass., 1943*), psychiatrist. M.A., Edinburgh University, 1897; M.B. and Ch.B., 1902; M.D., 1911. After study in France and Germany, and a year's residency at the Royal Infirmary in Edinburgh under Alexander Bruce, he came to New York City in 1904 and worked until 1911 under Adolf Meyer on the staff of the Psychiatric Institute, Ward's Island. He then served on the staff of Bloomingdale Hospital, White Plains, N.Y., 1911–13; between 1913 and 1920, he was associate director of Phipps Psychiatric Clinic at Johns Hopkins Hospital, also teaching at Johns Hopkins Medical School. *Post* 1920, he was professor of psychiatry at Harvard Medical School and medical director of Boston Psychopathic Hospital. A brilliant teacher, he was primarily a clinician rather than a theorist; his chief contribution to the understanding of emotional disorders was his conviction that mental illness is not an entity but the product of maladjustment to a total life situation.

CAMPBELL, DOUGLAS HOUGHTON (*b. Detroit, Mich., 1859; d. Palo Alto, Calif., 1953*), botanist. Received Ph.D. from the University of Michigan in 1886. Chairman of the botany department at Stanford (1891–1925). Campbell's work concerned the relation between the life cycles of higher and lower plants.

CAMPBELL, FRANCIS JOSEPH (*b. Winchester, Tenn., 1832; d. 1914*), educator of the blind. Sightless from the age of four, he became a teacher of music at Perkins Institution, Boston, and cofounder of Royal Academy of Music for the Blind, London.

CAMPBELL, GEORGE WASHINGTON (*b. Tongue, Scotland, 1769; d. Nashville, Tenn., 1848*), lawyer, diplomat. Brought to North Carolina as a child; graduated Princeton, 1794. Removed to Knoxville, Tenn., and practiced law. Congressman, Democratic-Republican, 1803–09; elected U.S. senator, 1811; entered cabinet as secretary of treasury, 1814, but soon resigned and returned to Senate. Minister to Russia, 1818–20, after which he retired to private life.

CAMPBELL, GEORGE WASHINGTON (*b. Cherry Valley, N.Y., 1817; d. 1898*), horticulturist. Celebrated as a grape-breeder; developer of the Campbell Early variety.

CAMPBELL, HENRY FRASER (*b. Augusta, Ga., 1824; d. 1891*), physician. Graduated M.D., University of Georgia, 1842. Held various professorates at Medical College of Georgia, 1854–66, 1868–91; made original studies on nature of autonomic nervous system. A pioneer in preventive medicine.

CAMPBELL, JAMES (*b. Southwark, Pa., 1812; d. 1893*), lawyer, Pennsylvania jurist. As U.S. postmaster general, 1853–57, tried earnestly to improve the efficiency of the department.

CAMPBELL, JAMES HEPBURN (*b. Williamsport, Pa., 1820; d. near Wayne, Pa., 1895*), lawyer. Congressman, Whig, from Pennsylvania, 1845–56; elected as Republican, 1858–62; chairman of special committee on Pacific Railroad; ardent protectionist.

CAMPBELL, JAMES VALENTINE (*b. Buffalo, N.Y., 1823; d. 1890*), jurist. Moved as a child to Detroit, Mich. Justice, Michigan Supreme Court, 1858–90; law professor, University of Michigan, 1859–85.

CAMPBELL, JOHN. *See* LOUDOUN, JOHN CAMPBELL, FOURTH EARL OF.

CAMPBELL, JOHN (*b. Scotland, 1653; d. Boston, Mass., 1727/8*), journalist. Postmaster at Boston, 1702–18; published *Boston News-Letter*, 1704–22, the first established and continuously published American newspaper.

CAMPBELL, JOHN ARCHIBALD (*b. Washington, Ga., 1811; d. 1889*), jurist. Graduated Franklin College (University of Georgia), 1825; attended West Point; studied law, and was admitted to practice by special act of Georgia legislature, 1829. Removed first to Montgomery, then to Mobile, Ala. Rose rapidly in profession; served as delegate to Nashville Convention, 1850. Appointed justice of U.S. Supreme Court, 1853. Of great ability and integrity, he cared little for public opinion; he opposed monopolies and upheld strict construction of the Constitution; he was denounced in his own section for severity to Latin American filibusters and by abolitionists for his opinion in the Dred Scott case. Opposed to secession, he was suspected by Confederates for his part in Seward's scheme to relieve Fort Sumter; yet he resigned his judicial position, followed his state, and served as assistant secretary of war in Confederate government, 1862–65. On postwar return to practice in New Orleans, he appeared in many important actions, including the "Slaughterhouse Cases" and *New York and New Hampshire* v. *Louisiana*.

CAMPBELL, JOHN WILSON (*b. Augusta Co., Va., 1782; d. Ohio, 1833*), jurist. Congressman, Democrat, from Ohio, 1817–27; U.S. district judge, 1829–33.

CAMPBELL, JOSIAH A. PATTERSON (*b. Waxhaw Settlement, S.C., 1830; d. 1917*), jurist. Practiced law in Mississippi, *post* 1847; served in Confederate army, 1862–65. Justice of Mississippi Supreme Court, 1876–94.

CAMPBELL, LEWIS DAVIS (*b. Franklin, Ohio, 1811; d. 1882*), editor, diplomat, lawyer. Congressman, Whig, from Ohio, 1848–58. Appointed minister to Mexico, 1866, he failed badly in an attempt to mediate in the Maximilian-Juarez conflict and was superseded.

CAMPBELL, LORD WILLIAM (*b. Southampton, England, 1778*), colonial governor of South Carolina. Arrived at Charleston, June 1775. After ineffectual efforts to rally Tories and Indians in support of royal cause, fled to HMS *Tamar*; served as volunteer in British attack on Charleston, 1776.

CAMPBELL, MARIUS ROBINSON (*b. Garden grove, Iowa, 1858; d. Pinellas Park, Fla., 1940*), geologist and physiographer. With U.S. Geological Survey, 1888–1932; made geologic studies of national coal resources.

CAMPBELL, PRINCE LUCIEN (*b. Newmarket, Mo., 1861; d. 1925*), president of University of Oregon, 1902–25.

CAMPBELL, ROBERT (*b. Aughlane, Ireland, 1804; d. St. Louis, Mo., 1879*), fur trapper, capitalist. Came to America, *ca.* 1824; went out with Ashley's second fur expedition, 1825, thereafter personally engaging in northern region fur trade until 1835. Partner in Sublette & Campbell, 1832–42. Prospered as merchant and banker in St. Louis.

CAMPBELL, THOMAS (*b. Ireland, 1763; d. Bethany, W.Va., 1854*), clergyman. Came to America, 1807. With his son, Alexander Campbell, a founder of the Disciples of Christ.

CAMPBELL, THOMAS JOSEPH (*b. New York, N.Y., 1848; d. Monroe, N.Y., 1925*), Jesuit priest. Ordained 1880. President, St. John's College (Fordham), 1885–88 and 1896–1900. Editor,

America, 1910–14; author, *The Jesuits: 1534–1921* (1921), and many other works.

CAMPBELL, WILLIAM (*b. Augusta Co., Va., 1745; d. Rocky Mills, Va., 1781*), Revolutionary soldier. Settled near Abingdon, Va.; brother-in-law of Patrick Henry. Active in Indian border wars; colonel of Virginia militia, and distinguished at battles of King's Mountain, 1780, and Guilford, 1781.

CAMPBELL, WILLIAM (*b. Gateshead-on-Tyne, England, 1876; d. New York, N.Y., 1936*), metallurgist. Teacher of geology and metallurgy, Columbia University, 1903–36.

CAMPBELL, WILLIAM BOWEN (*b. Sumner Co., Tenn., 1807; d. 1867*), lawyer, politician. Congressman, Whig, from Tennessee, 1837–43; Unionist, 1865–67. Elected governor of Tennessee, 1851, after distinguished service in Mexican War. Strong antisecessionist.

CAMPBELL, WILLIAM EDWARD MARCH (*b. Mobile, Ala., 1893; d. New Orleans, La., 1954*), novelist, short-story writer. Studied at Valparaiso University and the University of Alabama. Campbell signed all of his fiction with the name William March. The author of many short stories, March is best remembered for his novel *Company K* (1935), which tells of experiences as a marine in World War I, and *The Bad Seed* (1954), which Maxwell Anderson adapted for the stage; the play was made into a successful film in 1956.

CAMPBELL, WILLIAM HENRY (*b. Baltimore, Md., 1808; d. New Brunswick, N.J., 1890*), Reformed Church clergyman. President, Rutgers College, 1863–82.

CAMPBELL, WILLIAM W. (*b. Cherry Valley, N.Y., 1806; d. 1881*), jurist, historian. Congressman, Know-Nothing party, from New York, 1845–47; justice of superior court, New York City, 1849–55; justice of state supreme court, 1857–65. Author of *Annals of Tryon County* (1831).

CAMPBELL, WILLIAM WALLACE (*b. Hancock Co., Ohio, 1862; d. San Francisco, Calif., 1938*), astronomer. Graduated University of Michigan, 1886. From 1890 to 1923 he was at Lick Observatory, Mount Hamilton, Calif., becoming director in 1901. His work with the Mills spectrograph, which he designed, helped lay the foundations for the new science of astrophysics. His interest in spectrographic measurement of stellar radial velocities to determine the sun's motion through the stars led to the publication (1928) of a definitive catalogue by Campbell and Joseph H. Moore. He was president of the University of California, 1923–30.

CANAGA, ALFRED BRUCE (*b. Scio, Ohio, 1850; d. Boston, Mass., 1806*), naval engineer. Chief designer of propulsion and other machinery for U.S. Navy under Admiral George W. Melville.

CANBY, EDWARD RICHARD SPRIGG (*b. Kentucky, 1817; d. California, 1873*), Union soldier. Graduated West Point, 1839; served in Florida War and was twice brevetted for gallantry in Mexican War. Commanded Department of New Mexico during Civil War, frustrating Confederate plan to seize California, 1861–62; served thereafter in Washington and New York, and as commander of Division of West Mississippi. Captured Mobile, Ala., April 1865; in May received surrender of last Confederate armies in field. Appointed brigadier general, regular army, 1866, he served with great ability in the South and was assigned to command on Pacific Coast, 1870. He was killed on a peace mission to the Modoc tribe in northern California.

CANBY, HENRY SEIDEL (*b. Wilmington, Del., 1878; d. Ossining, N.Y., 1961*), editor, literary critic, and educator. Raised as a Quaker, Canby attended Yale (Ph.D. English, 1905). He taught at Yale (1900–16), during which time he published *The Short Story* (1902), *The Short Story in English* (1909), *A Study of the Short Story* (1913), and *College Sons and College Fathers* (1915). From 1911 to 1920 he was an assistant editor on the newly founded *Yale Review*. He wrote of his World War I experiences in Britain in *Education by Violence* (1919) and published his only novel, *Our House*, that same year. He returned to Yale after the war and then became the first editor of the *Literary Review* in 1920. His views on literary journalism were explained in *Everyday Americans* (1920), and he published *Better Writing* in 1926. In 1924 Canby helped found the *Saturday Review of Literature*, which he edited until 1936. From 1926–55, Canby served on the board of judges of the Book-of-the-Month Club. Other writings include *Definitions* (1922, 1924), *American Estimates* (1929), *Classic Americans* (1931), *The Age of Confidence* (1934), *Alma Mater* (1936), *Seven Years' Harvest* (1936), *Thoreau* (1939), and *Walt Whitman* (1943). With Robert Spiller, Canby produced *A Literary History of America* (1948). His final work was *Turn West, Turn East* (1951) a study of Mark Twain and Henry James. Canby typified the American intellectual of the post–World War I era who sought to adjust the values on nineteenth-century liberalism to twentieth-century realities.

CANDEE, LEVERETT (*b. Oxford, Conn., 1795; d. 1863*), pioneer rubber manufacturer under Goodyear patent, 1842; made overshoes at Hamden, Conn.

CANDLER, ALLEN DANIEL (*b. Lumpkin Co., Ga., 1834; d. 1910*), educator, businessman. After Confederate war service, taught in Georgia schools. Moved to Gainesville, Ga., 1870, and entered contracting business; president of Gainesville, Jefferson & Southern Railroad, 1879–92. Congressman, Democrat, 1882–90; governor of Georgia, 1898–1902.

CANDLER, ASA GRIGGS (*b. near Villa Rica, Ga., 1851; d. 1929*), manufacturer, philanthropist. Trained as a pharmacist; bought Coca-Cola formula, 1887. Developed the enterprise and sold it, 1919, for $25 million; prospered also in Atlanta, Ga., real estate. Generous in gifts for public improvements in that city, he was also a principal benefactor of Emory University.

CANDLER, WARREN AKIN (*b. near Villa Rica, Carroll County, Ga., 1857; d. Atlanta, Ga., 1941*), Methodist clergyman, educator. Brother of Asa G. Candler. Graduated Emory College, 1875. After serving various Georgia pastorates, and winning reputation as a revival preacher, he improved the financial and academic standing of Emory College as its president, 1888–98. As a bishop of the Methodist Episcopal Church, South, 1898–1934, he stood for a strong episcopacy, activity in foreign missions, and strictly orthodox belief. He led the fight to keep Vanderbilt University under denominational control, in the takeover of Southern Methodist University from the Texas Conference, and in the establishment of Emory University, Atlanta.

CANFIELD, JAMES HULME (*b. Delaware, Ohio, 1847; d. New York, N.Y., 1909*), educator. Graduated Williams, 1868; practiced law at St. Joseph, Mich., 1872–77. Professor, University of Kansas, 1877–91; chancellor, University of Nebraska, 1891–95; president, Ohio State University, 1895–99; librarian, Columbia University, 1899–1909. An able and tactful administrator.

CANFIELD, RICHARD A. (*b. New Bedford, Mass., 1855; d. 1914*), gambler, art collector. Proprietor of gambling houses in Providence and Newport, R.I., New York City, and elsewhere; collector of furniture, ceramics, and the work of J. A. M. Whistler.

CANNON, ANNIE JUMP (*b. Dover, Del., 1863; d. Cambridge, Mass., 1941*), astronomer. Graduated Wellesley, 1884; made special studies in astronomy at Radcliffe. Associated with the Harvard Observatory, 1896–1940, she devised the classification system for spectra in use at all observatories; she was also author of the Henry Draper Catalogue of stellar spectra (1918–24) and its extensions (1925 and 1949). She also published catalogues of variable stars in 1903 and 1907. Among her many honors was the first doctorate of science granted by Oxford University to a woman (1925).

CANNON, CHARLES JAMES (*b. New York, N.Y., 1800; d. 1860*), author of minor periodical verse and fiction, and of several plays; *The Oath of Office* (produced 1850, published 1854) is his best drama.

CANNON, CLARENCE (*b. Elsberry, Mo., 1879; d. Washington, D.C., 1964*), congressman. Studied at William Jewell College (B.A., 1903; M.A., 1904) and received a law degree from the University of Missouri (1908). Taught at Stephens College (1904–08), then practiced law for three years. Upon moving to Washington, D.C., he worked for his congressman, Champ Clark, and in 1920 was appointed parliamentarian of the Democratic National Convention, a post he held until 1960. Cannon published several books and articles on parliamentary law and the procedures and rules of the House. In 1922 he was elected to the House of Representatives, beginning a career that lasted more than forty years. In 1941 he became chairman of the House Committee on Appropriations. Cannon was stubborn and combative and clashed frequently with fellow politicians. He considered his committee to be the guardian of the national treasury and came to criticize foreign aid and the program to land a man on the moon.

CANNON, GEORGE QUAYLE (*b. Liverpool, England, 1827; d. 1901*), Mormon leader. Migrated to Nauvoo, Ill., 1842; to Salt Lake valley, 1847. Missionary in California and in Hawaii; private secretary to Brigham Young. Utah delegate to Congress, 1872–82. Chosen an apostle in Church of Latter-day Saints, 1859.

CANNON, HARRIET STARR (*b. Charleston, S.C., 1823; d. Peekskill, N.Y., 1896*), founder and first mother superior of the Episcopal Sisterhood of St. Mary, 1865–96.

CANNON, JAMES (*b. Salisbury, Md., 1864; d. Chicago, Ill., 1944*), Methodist clergyman, temperance reformer. Nephew of William Cannon. B.A., Randolph-Macon College, 1884; B.D., Princeton Theological Seminary, 1888; M.A., Princeton, 1890. Keen of mind, strong of will, and combative, Cannon succeeded as pastor, educator, and sectarian editor; by 1909, he was recognized as the dominant figure in the Virginia Conference of the Methodist Episcopal Church, South. Elected a bishop, 1918, he took on added responsibilities for foreign mission supervision, continued active in the Federal Council of Churches, and was a leader in he movement for Methodist unification. He was best known, however, as a temperance reformer, the most effective lobbyist of the Anti-Saloon League during and after the campaign for passage of the 18th Amendment. In 1928, he exerted all his influence against the "wet" Democratic candidate for the presidency, Alfred E. Smith. Beginning in 1929, he was the object of investigations by Congress and by his church into alleged misconduct; although he was officially cleared, he never recovered his former position of power. He retired in 1938.

CANNON, JAMES GRAHAM (*b. Delhi, N.Y., 1858; d. 1916*), banker. Associated *ca.* 1876–1914 with Fourth National Bank, New York City; president, 1910–14. Authority on credit analysis and clearinghouse practice.

CANNON, JOSEPH GURNERY (*b. New Garden, N.C., 1836; d. 1926*), politician. Raised in Indiana, "Uncle Joe" Cannon studied law and began practice at Shelbyville, Ill., 1858; later he removed to Danville, his home for the rest of his life. Congressman, Republican, from Illinois, 1873–91, 1893–1913, 1915–23. Coarse, unprogressive, yet by reason of his long membership in the House of Representatives rising to important committee posts, he served as Speaker, 1903–11; his arbitrary, partisan control of procedure in that post became known as Cannonism.

CANNON, NEWTON (*b. Guilford Co., N.C., 1781; d. 1841*), planter, politician. Removed with parents to frontier settlement of Cumberland, Tenn., 1790. Congressman from Tennessee, 1814–23 (save for one term); first Whig governor of Tennessee, 1835–39.

CANNON, WALTER BRADFORD (*b. Prairie du Chien, Wis., 1871; d. near Franklin, N.H., 1945*), physiologist. Graduated Harvard, 1896; M.A., 1897; M.D., Harvard Medical School, 1900. Beginning as instructor in physiology at Harvard Medical School, he succeeded Henry P. Bowditch as George Higginson professor of physiology in 1906 and served until 1942. Among his contributions to the study of the physiology of digestion were his basic technique (announced in 1897) for securing satisfactory X-ray pictures of the soft organs of the alimentary canal by feeding the patient a meal mixed with bismuth subnitrate or barium sulphate; his demonstration by experiment (1911) of the mechanical factors of digestion, with an accompanying theory of the local causes of hunger and thirst. From early observation of the effect of psychic disturbance on digestion, he was led to a concentrated study (1911–17) of the physiology of emotions (*Bodily Changes in Pain, Hunger, Fear and Rage* [1915]; rev. ed., 1929). Neglecting to follow up on his observation of a "mysterious factor" operating in the transmission of nerve impulses, which earned the Nobel Prize for others, he engaged in the research that established the theory of homeostasis (*Wisdom of the Body*, 1932).

CANNON, WILLIAM (*b. Bridgeville, Del., 1809; d. 1865*), vigorous supporter of the federal government as Union governor of Delaware, 1863–65.

CANONCHET (*d. Stonington, Conn., 1676*), chief sachem of the Narragansett, defeated in the "Great Swamp Fight," near present South Kingston, R.I., 1675.

CANONGE, LOUIS PLACIDE (*b. New Orleans, La., 1822; d. 1893*), journalist. Contributor to *L'Abeille* and other French journals; author of a number of plays produced in French at New Orleans, 1840–56; excelled as a writer of feuilletons.

CANONICUS (*b. ca. 1565; d. 1647*), Narragansett chief. Granted Rhode Island to Roger Williams.

CANTOR, EDDIE (*b. New York, N.Y., 1892; d. Hollywood, Calif., 1964*), comedian. Raised by his grandmother, he never finished elementary school. Cantor began in vaudeville in 1907, soon joining a touring company and assuming the blackface role he became associated with. He began a close, lifelong friendship with George Jessel in *Kid Kabaret* (1912–14). The producer Florenz Ziegfeld put him in *Midnight Frolic* (1917) and *Ziegfeld's Follies* (1917–19). He starred in the musical comedies *Kid Boots* (1923) and *Whoopee* (1928–30) and films such as *Palmy Days* (1931), *The Kid from Spain* (1932), *Roman Scandals* (1933), *Kid Millions* (1934), *Strike Me Pink* (1936), and *Forty Little Mothers* (1940). Cantor enjoyed a successful twenty-year career in radio and appeared in several comedy and variety shows on television. His last movie was a brief appearance in *The Eddie Cantor Story* (1953).

CANTRIL, ALBERT HADLEY (b. Hyrum, Utah, 1906; d. Princeton, N.J., 1969), social psychologist and public-opinion analyst. Graduate of Dartmouth (1928) and Harvard (Ph.D., 1931), also studied at the universities of Munich and Berlin. Taught at Dartmouth, Harvard (1932–35), Columbia University Teachers College (1936), and Princeton (1936–55). He became head of the Institute for International Social Research in 1955 where, with associate Lloyd Free, he researched the relation between public opinion and governmental policy. In Princeton, Cantril collaborated with George Gallup, adding psychological insight to Gallup's polling techniques. He pioneered in correlating polling results with policy formation. His books include *The Psychology of Radio* (1935, with Gordon W. Allport), *The Invasion from Mars* (1940), *The Psychology of Social Movements* (1941), *Gauging Public Opinion* (1944), *Understanding Man's Social Behavior: Preliminary Notes* (1947), *The Psychology of Ego-Involvements* (1947, with Muzafer Sherif), *The "Why" of Man's Experience* (1950), *Tensions That Cause Wars* (1950), *How Nations See Each Other* (1953, with William Buchanan), *The Politics of Despair* (1958), *Soviet Leaders and Mastery Over Man* (1960), *Reflections on the Human Venture* (1960, coedited with Charles H. Bumstead), *Human Nature and Political Systems* (1961), *The Pattern of Human Concerns* (1965), *The Political Beliefs of Americans* (1967, with Lloyd Free), and *The Human Dimension* (1967).

CAPEN, ELMER HEWITT (b. Stoughton, Mass., 1838; d. 1905), Universalist clergyman. Ordained 1865, he held pastorates in Gloucester, Mass.; St. Paul, Minn.; and Providence, R.I. President, Tufts College, *post* 1875.

CAPEN, NAHUM (b. Canton, Mass., 1804; d. 1886), miscellaneous writer. As postmaster of Boston, Mass., 1857–61, he is said to have introduced street letterboxes.

CAPEN, SAMUEL BILLINGS (b. Boston, Mass., 1842; d. Shanghai, China, 1914), merchant. Active in civic affairs, and in Congregational church work; president, American Board of Commissioners for Foreign Missions. 1899–1914; trustee of Wellesley College.

CAPEN, SAMUEL PAUL (b. Somerville, Mass., 1878; d. Buffalo, N.Y., 1956), educator. Studied at Tufts College, Harvard, and the University of Pennsylvania (Ph.D., 1902). Taught at Clark College (1911–14). From 1914 to 1919, specialist for the U.S. Bureau of Education; from 1919 to 1922, director of the American Council on Education. Served as chancellor of Buffalo University (1922–50) until his retirement.

CAPERS, ELLISON (b. Charleston, S.C., 1837; d. Columbia, S.C., 1908), Confederate soldier, Episcopal clergyman. Entered ministry after rising to rank of brigadier general in Civil War; held pastorates in Alabama and South Carolina; consecrated assistant bishop of South Carolina, 1893.

CAPERS, WILLIAM (b. St. Thomas' Parish, S.C., 1790; d. near Anderson Court House, S.C., 1855), Methodist clergyman. Bishop, Methodist Church South, 1846–55. Father of Ellison Capers. Ordained elder in South Carolina Conference, 1812, he became the most popular Methodist preacher in the South; he worked extensively among Creek Indians and plantation slaves.

CAPONE, ALPHONSE (b. Brooklyn, N.Y., 1899; d. Miami, Fla., 1947), bootlegger. A school dropout, street gangster, bartender, and bouncer, he rose to prominence in Chicago *post* 1920. A member of the staff of John Torrio, a manager of vice resorts who became successful in the bootlegging industry that had been spawned by the 18th (Prohibition) Amendment, Capone soon moved into a position of leadership in the organization. When Torrio was shot by rival gangsters in 1925 and departed for an extended "vacation" in Europe, Capone took over as leader of the coalition of criminals, known as the "syndicate," which extended its control over the beer and liquor trade, gambling, and vice in the Chicago area. Through corruption of politicians and law enforcement officers, and a remorseless elimination of competition by murder, the syndicate flourished. By 1928, it was moving into the field of labor racketeering. Federal action resulted in the conviction of several Capone partners for income tax evasion, and in 1931 Capone himself was sentenced to eleven years in prison for income-tax fraud and conspiracy. Suffering from advanced syphilis which affected his brain, he was released from Alcatraz penitentiary in 1939.

CAPPER, ARTHUR (b. Garnett, Kans., 1865; d. Topeka, Kans., 1951), publisher, politician. Owner of a newspaper empire, Capper's possessions included the *Topeka Daily Capital*, *Kansas City Kansan*, and *Capper's Weekly*. In 1914, he was elected Republican governor of Kansas; in 1918, to the U.S. Senate, serving five consecutive terms. Capper was an isolationist and, though a Republican, a supporter of the New Deal. His years as governor brought no profound changes to Kansas. In the Senate his voice was rarely heard, although for a while he served as leader of the Farm Bloc.

CAPPS, EDWARD (b. Jacksonville, Ill., 1866; d. Princeton, N.J., 1950), classicist. Graduated Illinois College, 1887; Ph.D., Yale, 1891. Principal research in Greek drama and theater. Taught Greek at University of Chicago, 1892–1907; professor of Greek, Princeton, 1907–36. In 1914, he turned from creative scholarship to administrative work. He became an American editor of the Loeb Classical Library; in 1920–21, he served as his friend President Wilson's envoy extraordinary to Greece and Montenegro. A founder and first president of the American Association of University Professors (1920). As chairman of the managing committee of the American School of Classical Studies at Athens (1919–39), he vastly increased its endowment and won for it in 1928 the privilege of excavating the Agora at Athens.

CAPPS, WASHINGTON LEE (b. Portsmouth, Va., 1864; d. Washington, D.C., 1935), naval officer. Chief of U.S. Navy Bureau of Construction. 1903–10; devised skeleton mast and the "all big gun" ship.

CAPRON, HORACE (b. Attleboro, Mass., 1804; d. Washington, D.C., 1885), agriculturist. Began large-scale, scientific farming while in charge of a cotton factory in Laurel, Md. Removed to Illinois, 1854, and continued farming until appointment as U.S. commissioner of agriculture, 1867. Revolutionized Japanese farming methods while adviser in development of Hokkaido island, 1871–75.

CAPTAIN JACK (b. ca. 1837; d. Fort Klamath, Oreg., 1873), Indian name, Kientpoos; led hostiles in Modoc War, 1872–73. Taken after stubborn defense of the lava beds south of Tule Lake, Calif., Jack was hanged for murder of peace commissioners Gen. E. R. S. Canby and Rev. Eleazer Thomas.

CARAWAY, HATTIE OPHELIA WYATT b. near Bakerville, Tenn., 1878; d. Falls Church, Va., 1950), U.S. senator. Married Thaddeus H. Caraway, 1902. Appointed in November 1931 to her late husband's post as U.S. senator, Democrat, from Arkansas, she won a special election in January 1932 for the remainder of the term, thus becoming the first woman ever elected to the Senate. She was reelected to a full term in November 1932, and again in 1938, but was unsuccessful in 1944. She was a consistent supporter of the New Deal. Although never a feminist, she no doubt was influenced by her political success. In 1943 she cosponsored the equal rights amendment.

CARAWAY, THADDEUS HORATIUS b. Spring Hill, Mo., 1871; d. Little Rock, Ark., 1931), U.S. senator from Arkansas, 1920–31; liberal Democrat and reformer.

CARBUTT, JOHN (b. Sheffield, England, 1832; d. Philadelphia, Pa., 1905), photographic innovator. Immigrated to America, 1853, and settled in Chicago. Successfully used gelatine in preparation of dry plates as early as 1868, producing a plate which did not require development for months after the image was taken; marketed the first American gelatine dry plates, 1879; made notable contributions to color photography.

CÁRDENAS, GARCÍ LÓPEZ DE (fl. 1540), explorer. Discovered the Grand Canyon of the Colorado while a member of the Coronado expedition, 1540–42.

CARDOZO, BENJAMIN NATHAN (b. New York, N.Y., 1870; d. Port Chester, N.Y., 1938), lawyer, jurist, justice of the U.S. Supreme Court. Graduated from Columbia University, B.A., 1889, and M.A., 1890, and was admitted to the New York bar in 1891. For the next 22 years he practiced law, principally as counsel for other lawyers, at times as referee in complex commercial cases. In 1913 he was elected to the Supreme Court of New York, but within six weeks he received a temporary appointment to the Court of Appeals, the state's highest court. In 1917 he was elected to the latter court for a 14-year term; in 1926 he was chosen chief judge. As he had been a lawyers' lawyer, so Cardozo became a judges' judge. His legal mastery, conveyed with great felicity, gave unusual distinction to the New York Reports. His philosophic temper of mind was reflected not only in his legal opinions but also in four volumes of essays written during this period: *The Nature of the Judicial Process* (1921), *The Growth of the Law* (1924), *The Paradoxes of Legal Science* (1928), and *Law and Literature* (1931).

In 1932 President Hoover, upon the resignation of Justice Oliver Wendell Holmes, appointed Cardozo to the U.S. Supreme Court. With great rapidity Cardozo made the adjustment from preoccupation with the comparatively restricted problems of private litigation to the exacting demands of legal statesmanship. He regarded his role as that of "historian and prophet all in one," and like his master, Holmes, he made of the judicial process a blend of continuity and creativeness. His few short years on the Supreme Court coincided with one of the most tempestuous periods in the Court's history—the years of its invalidation of much of the New Deal legislation and the consequent proposal of President Roosevelt for reconstruction of the Court. Cardozo faced courageously the application of the Constitution to a rapidly changing world. With Justices Stone and Brandeis he joined in a series of dissents which charted the course for a later broader interpretation of federal powers. Shy and sensitive, immensely learned yet natively humble, Cardozo transcended the heated controversies of his day to take his place as one of the dozen or so truly great judges in the Court's history.

CARDOZO, JACOB NEWTON (b. Savannah, Ga., 1786; d. Savannah, 1873), economist. Edited *Southern Patriot*, Charleston, S.C., 1817–45; drew up first petition from the South on behalf of free trade, ca. 1827. Author of *Notes on Political Economy* (1826), advancing doctrine later developed by Henry C. Carey and the American national school.

CAREY, HENRY CHARLES (b. Philadelphia, Pa., 1793; d. 1879), economist. Son of Mathew Carey. His numerous works, influential here and abroad, took issue with the English classical school of economists and interpreted in an optimistic spirit the rapid expansion of American economic life during his time. A stout believer in laissez-faire, about 1844 he was "converted" to protectionism. He and his followers constitute what has been called the American national school of political economy. The evolution of his thought may be traced in *Essay on the Rate of Wages* (1835); *Principles of Political Economy* (1837, 1838, 1840); *Past, Present and Future* (1848); *Harmony of Interests* (1851); *The Principles of Social Science* (1858, 1859); and *The Unity of Law* (1872).

CAREY, JOSEPH MAULL (b. Milton, Del., 1845; d. 1924), lawyer. Served as justice of Supreme Court of Wyoming, 1872–76, and thrice as territorial delegate to Congress; introduced bill for Wyoming admission as state, 1890. First U.S. senator from Wyoming, Republican, 1890–96; Democratic governor, 1911–15.

CAREY, MATHEW (b. Dublin, Ireland, 1760; d. Philadelphia, Pa., 1839), publisher, economist. Father of Henry C. Carey, who developed his economic ideas. Came to America, 1784, after involvement in Irish revolutionary activity; set up as a publisher-bookseller in Philadelphia with aid from Lafayette. Published the *Pennsylvania Herald* (starting January 1785); also the eclectic periodical *The American Museum*, 1787–92, in which much valuable material was reprinted. His book-publishing activities prospered and his firm became a leader in the period 1795–1835. *Post* 1815 he became an active exponent of protectionism, in support of which he wrote many tracts and essays. Among his books are *The Olive Branch* (1814) and *Vindiciae Hibernicae* (1819), which defended the Irish character.

CARLETON, HENRY (b. Virginia, ca. 1785; d. 1863), Louisiana jurist. Translator (with Louis M. Lislet) of *Las Siete Partidas* (1820), the principal Spanish law code long enforced in Louisiana.

CARLETON, HENRY GUY (b. Fort Union, N.Mex., 1856; d. Atlantic City, N.J., 1910), playwright. Author of *The Gilded Fool* (1892), *Butterflies* (1894), and other plays.

CARLETON, WILL (b. near Hudson, Mich., 1845; d. Brooklyn, N.Y., 1912), poet. Author of many ballads of simple life, notably "Betsy and I Are Out" (1871), "Over the Hill to the Poor House, " and others which appeared in his book *Farm Ballads* (1873). He was author also of *Farm Legends* (1875), *Farm Festivals* (1881), and *City Ballads* (1885), and was one of the first poets to give public readings from his own works.

CARLILE, JOHN SNYDER) b. Winchester, Va., 1817; d. Clarksburg, W.Va., 1878), lawyer. Drafted Unionist address to people of western Virginia, 1861; mismanaged bill erecting new state of West Virginia.

CARLISLE, FLOYD LESLIE (b. Watertown, N.Y., 1881; d. Locust Valley, L.I., N.Y., 1942), financier, public utility executive. President, Northern New York Trust Company, 1910–22; president, St. Regis Paper Company, 1916–34. Organized in association with the younger J. P. Morgan the Niagara Hudson Power Company, 1929, of which he became board chairman. Also reorganized New York City utilities into Consolidated Edison Company, and was director of other Morgan holding companies for power and light enterprises.

CARLISLE, JAMES MANDEVILLE (b. Alexandria, Va., 1814; d. Washington, D.C., 1877), lawyer. Specialist in international cases; served as counsel for Spain, Great Britain, Colombia, and Costa Rica.

CARLISLE, JOHN GRIFFIN (b. Campbell, now Kenton, Co., Ky., 1835; d. 1910), lawyer, statesman. Admitted to the bar, 1858, began practice in Covington, Ky.; was neutral during Civil War. Served in state legislature, and was elected lieutenant governor, 1871. Congressman, Democrat, 1877–90 (outstanding Speaker of the House, 1883–90), he resigned to accept appointment as U.S. senator. Active in tariff reform movement and rebuilding of U.S. merchant marine, he left Senate to be secretary of treasury, 1893–96; his support of "sound money" principles then, and in campaign of 1896, brought him virtual banishment from Kentucky. He removed to New York City, where he resumed legal practice.

CARLL, JOHN FRANKLIN (*b. Bushwick, N.Y., 1828; d. Waldron, Ark., 1904*), civil engineer, geologist. His work with Pennsylvania Geological Survey, 1874–85, was basic in establishing geology of petroleum along scientific lines.

CARLSON, ANTON JULIUS (*b. Svarteborg, Sweden, 1875; d. Chicago, Ill., 1956*), physiologist. Immigrated to the U.S. in 1891. Studied at Augustana College and at Stanford, Ph.D., 1902. Taught at the University of Chicago from 1904 to 1940. His early research was on elucidating the mechanism of the propagation of nerve impulses and he later became interested in the comparative physiology of the thyroid and parathyroid. His last years were occupied with the social responsibilities of scientists.

CARLSON, CHESTER FLOYD (*b. Seattle, Wash., 1906; d. New York, N.Y., 1968*), inventor and patent lawyer. Studied physics at the California Institute of Technology (B.S., 1930) and graduated from the New York Law School. Perceived the need for an office copying machine while heading the patent department of P. R. Mallory and Company. By 1937 he arrived at the basic concept of electrophotography (later called xerography), for which he was issued a patent in 1942. Working with the Battelle Memorial Institute of Columbus, Ohio, a nonprofit research organization, and the Haloid Company of Rochester, N.Y., a manufacturer of photographic paper, Carlson helped bring about the introduction of the first commercial copier in 1950. With the Xerox 914, introduced in 1959 as a convenient and simple office copier, the significance of Carlson's invention became fully evident. Haloid changed its name to Haloid Xerox in 1958 and to Xerox in 1961. Carlson became a multimillionaire from royalties and stock from Xerox.

CARLSON, EVANS FORDYCE (*b. Sidney, N.Y., 1896; d. Portland, Oreg., 1947*), soldier. Joined U.S. Army, 1912; rose to rank of captain in World War I; worked briefly postwar as a salesman; entered U.S. Marine Corps as a private, 1922, and was commissioned, 1923. Served with distinction in China and Nicaragua; made acquaintance of Franklin D. Roosevelt, whom he served as a private intelligence source in China *post* 1937. The first foreign military observer to see at first hand the operations of the Chinese Red Army, he gave high praise to the Communist military and political activity, apparently under the impression that they were egalitarian democrats. Resigning from the Marine Corps, 1939, "to be free to speak and write," he returned in 1941 and was promoted lieutenant colonel, 1942. As commander of a Marine battalion called "Carlson's Raiders," he received much publicity for the capture of Makin Island, August 1942. After another successful campaign on Guadalcanal, late in 1942, he was withdrawn from combat for duties as official observer. He retired in July 1946 with the rank of brigadier general. Carlson spent the last year of his life as an associate of groups opposing U.S. cold war policy. Supported Henry Wallace's Progressive party candidacy for the presidency and called for cessation of aid to Chiang Kai-shek until the latter formed a coalition government with the Communists.

CARMACK, EDWARD WARD (*b. Sumner Co., Tenn., 1858; d. Nashville, Tenn., 1908*), editor, prohibitionist. As editor of *Columbia Herald*, *Nashville American*, and *Memphis Commercial Appeal*, and also as congressman and U.S. senator from Tennessee, an influential and militant crusader for good government and prohibition of the liquor traffic.

CARMICHAEL, OLIVER CROMWELL (*b. near Good Water, Clay County, Ala., 1891; d. Asheville, N.C., 1966*), educator. Studied at the University of Alabama (B.A., 1911; M.A., 1914) and was a Rhodes Scholar at Oxford (1913–17), earning a B.S. and a diploma in anthropology. Taught at the University of Alabama (1911–12) and Florence Normal School in Birmingham (1912–13), served in both the British and U.S. armies in World War I, after which he was a high school and grammar school educator. In 1922 he became dean and assistant to the president of Alabama State College for Women, then became its president (1926–35). At Vanderbilt University he was a dean (1935), vice-chancellor (1936), and chancellor (1937–46), and helped expand the curriculum and facilities. Carmichael was president of the Carnegie Foundation for the Advancement of Teaching (1946–53), chairman of the board of trustees of the New York State university system (1948–53), and president of the University of Alabama in Tuscaloosa (1953–57). He then became a consultant to the Fund for the Advancement of Education. His books include *The Changing Role of Higher Education* (1949), *Universities, Commonwealth and American* (1959), and *Graduate Education* (1961).

CARMICHAEL, WILLIAM (*b. Queen Annes Co., Md.; d. Madrid, Spain, 1795*), diplomat. Secretary to Franklin, Silas Deane, and Arthur Lee during their commission to enlist France in aid of the revolting colonies; individually responsible for Lafayette's coming to America. Secretary to John Jay during Spanish mission, 1780–82, thereafter acting as chargé d'affaires at Madrid, 1782–92, and as commissioner with William Short to secure a treaty with Spain, 1792–94.

CARNAHAN, JAMES (*b. Cumberland Co., Pa., 1775; d. 1859*), Presbyterian clergyman. President of Princeton University, 1823–54.

CARNAP, RUDOLF (*b. Ronsdorf, near Barmen, Germany, 1891; d. Santa Monica, Calif., 1970*), philosopher and educator. Studied at the universities of Jena and Freiburg in Breisgau (1910–14) and received a doctorate at Jena (1921). Taught at the University of Vienna (1926–31) and the German University in Prague (1931–35) before immigrating to the U.S. Became a professor of philosophy at the University of Chicago (1936). Carnap was at Harvard (1940–41), then lived near Santa Fe, N.M., on a Rockefeller Foundation Research grant (1942–44). He returned to the University of Chicago in 1944 where he remained until 1952, except for a semester in 1950 at the University of Illinois in Urbana. He was at the Institute for Advanced Study in Princeton (1952–54), then taught at the University of California at Los Angeles (1954–61). His writings include *The Logical Structure of the World* (1928), *Pseudo Problems in Philosophy* (1928), *The Logical Syntax of Language* 1934), *Philosophy and Logical Syntax* (1935), *Foundations of Logic and Mathematics* (1939), *Introduction to Semantics* (1942), *Formalization of Logic* (1943), *Meaning and Necessity* (1947), *Logical Foundations of Probability* (1950), and *The Continuum of Inductive Methods* (1952).

CARNEGIE, ANDREW (*b. Dunfermline, Scotland, 1835; d. Shadowbrook, Mass., 1919*), manufacturer, self-styled "distributor of wealth for the improvement of mankind." Son of a handloom weaver active in Chartist and anti–Corn Law agitation; grandson of Thomas Morrison, a well-informed and irrepressible Scottish agitator for social and political reform. Early inspired by an uncle with a romantic love of Scottish history and poetry. Carnegie came, 1848, with his family to Allegheny, Pa., where he went to work as bobbin boy in a cotton factory. His spare time was spent in self-education by reading; at the age of sixteen he was contributing letters to the *New York Tribune*. Employed as messenger in a Pittsburgh telegraph office, he taught himself to distinguish the letters by sound and became an operator; Thomas A. Scott of the Pennsylvania Railroad employed him as personal telegrapher and private secretary. While with the railroad, 1853–65, he introduced use of Pullman sleeping cars, acquiring one-eighth interest in the Woodruff Co., original holder of the Pullman patents; he was also active in the transportation of troops during the Civil War and organized the military telegraph department.

Resigning from the railroad in 1865, he turned all his energies to the iron industry, which had received a great impetus during the war; his Keystone Bridge Co. succeeded largely through his own gifts as a salesman. By 1873, after success in oil operations and in the sale of railroad securities abroad, he committed all his profits to what was then a new American industry—steel. He declared policy of "putting all his eggs in one basket, and then watching the basket" was brilliantly successful. By 1889, American steel production had passed Great Britain's and stood first in the world. Carnegie believed his success was due to organization. He once suggested as his epitaph "Here lies the man who was able to surround himself with men far cleverer than himself," for his associates included Capt. "Bill" Jones, Henry Clay Frick, and Charles M. Schwab. His company, until shortly before its absorption by U.S. Steel (1901), was never a corporation; it was a limited partnership, every share being held by working associates. Carnegie always held a majority interest, and the remainder was distributed on the basis of each man's record, thus driving his associates to put forth their best efforts. He was a successful innovator, insisting upon up-to-date machinery, for which he made immense outlays during times of depression, when costs were low; his competitors meanwhile would face returning prosperity with outdated equipment, thus giving him a competitive advantage.

Throughout his later life Carnegie maintained many friendships in the literary and political world; with Matthew Arnold, Herbert Spencer ("the man to whom I owe most"), William E. Gladstone, James Bryce, James G. Blaine, Theodore Roosevelt, Mark Twain, and Elihu Root. His volume *Triumphant Democracy* (1886) contained a glowing account of American progress. From 1883 to 1919 his closest friend was the scholar John Morley.

In possession of a vast fortune through his daring and efficient operations, he set forth in an article entitled "Wealth" (*North American Review*, 1889) his concept of stewardship, or the responsibility of rich men to regard surplus wealth as held in trust for the public benefit. Since the accumulator of great wealth was prima facie an exceptional person, it was his duty to employ the talents which had made the fortune in its distribution for the "improvement of mankind." By 1900 he was ready to put his theory into practice, and in 1901 he sold the Carnegie Co. to the newly formed U.S. Steel Corporation for $250 million. Thereafter, through the Carnegie Corporation of New York and other agencies, he disposed of some $350 million in many public benefactions, which included support of scientific research, erection of public library buildings, the advancement of teaching, the furthering of international peace, and the reward of heroic acts.

CARNEGIE, DALE (*b. Maryville, Mo., 1888; d. Forest Hills, N.Y., 1955*), author, public speaker. Studied at State Teachers College, Warrensburg, Mo. After a brief and unsuccessful career in selling, Carnegie went to New York City in 1912 where he began lecturing on public speaking at the YMCA. By 1915, he had published his first book, *The Art of Public Speaking*. He befriended Lowell Thomas, who hired him as a business manager for his tour

of Great Britain. His most famous book, *How to Win Friends and Influence People* (1926), sold almost five million copies.

CARNEGIE, HATTIE (*b. Vienna, Austria, 1886; d. New York, N.Y., 1956*), fashion designer, retailer. Owner of couture stores in New York from 1909, Carnegie became famous for her imports of Parisian designs and for her own work; received the American Fashion Critics' Award in 1948.

CARNEGIE, MARY CROWNINSHIELD ENDICOTT CHAMBERLAIN (*b. Salem, Mass., 1864; d. London, England, 1957*), hostess. Wife of Joseph Chamberlain and stepmother to Austen, a future foreign secretary, and Neville, a future prime minister. Married the Reverend William Hartley Carnegie (1916). A noted hostess in London until her death.

CARNEY, THOMAS (*b. Delaware Co., Ohio, 1824; d. 1888*), businessman. Prospered in wholesale trade in Cincinnati; removed to Leavenworth, Kans., 1858 or 1859. Republican governor of Kansas, 1862–64.

CARNOCHAN, JOHN MURRAY (*b. Savannah, Ga., 1817; d. 1887*), surgeon. Graduated College of Physicians and Surgeons, New York, 1836; did graduate work in Paris and London. A brilliant pioneer in many fields; author of *Contributions to Operative Surgery* (first series 1858, second series 1877–78).

CARONDELET, FRANCISCO LUIS HECTOR, BARON DE (*b. Noyelles, Flanders, ca. 1748; d. Quito, Ecuador, 1807*), Spanish governor of Louisiana and West Florida, 1791–97. Devoted to public works, he built a canal to link New Orleans with the Gulf of Mexico via Lake Pontchartrain, reformed the police, instituted a street-lighting system. His attempts to extend Spanish rule over all the Mississippi Valley, to protect Louisiana commerce and to hold off encroaching American frontiersmen were unfortunate and embarrassed his home government; his domestic policy alienated the Creoles.

CAROTHERS, WALLACE HUME (*b. Burlington, Iowa, 1896; d. Philadelphia, Pa., 1937*), chemist, inventor of nylon. Graduated from Tarkio (Mo.) College, B.S., 1920, and the University of Illinois, M.S., 1921, and Ph.D., 1924. After teaching at Illinois and Harvard he joined E. I. du Pont de Nemours Co. in 1928 to direct a new fundamental research program in organic chemistry. He initiated investigations of vinylacetylene, which led to the commercial development of the synthetic rubber neoprene. From 1929 to 1937 Carothers and his associates made comprehensive studies of the synthesis of polymers of high molecular weight. These researches provided a general theory of polymerization processes, culminating in 1939 in the commercial production of nylon fiber and laying the basis for other synthetic fibers.

CARPENTER, CYRUS CLAY (*b. Harford, Pa., 1829; d. 1898*), Republican governor of Iowa, 1871–75. The "Granger Law" regulating railroads in Iowa was passed during his administration.

CARPENTER, EDMUND JANES (*b. North Attleboro, Mass., 1845; d. Milton, Mass., 1924*), journalist. On staff of Boston *Globe, Advertiser*, and *Transcript*; author of A *Woman of Shawmut* (1891).

CARPENTER, FRANCIS BICKNELL (*b. Homer, N.Y., 1830; d. New York, N.Y., 1900*), portrait painter. The painting of Lincoln reading the Emancipation Proclamation to his cabinet which hangs in the Capitol is his; he was author of *Six Months at the White House* (1866), a firsthand study of the president.

CARPENTER, FRANK GEORGE (*b. Mansfield, Ohio, 1855; d. Nanking, China, 1924*), author of syndicated letters, books, and several series of geographical *Readers*, the fruit of 36 years of travel.

CARPENTER, FRANKLIN REUBEN (*b. Parkersburg, W.Va., 1848; d. Denver, Colo., 1910*), mining engineer. Expert in processes for smelting and treating metals.

CARPENTER, GEORGE RICE (*b. Eskimo River, Labrador, now Canada, 1863; d. 1909*), educator, author. Professor of rhetoric, Columbia University, 1893–1909; author of a number of literary textbooks and lives of Whittier and Whitman.

CARPENTER, JOHN ALDEN (*b. Park Ridge, Ill., 1876; d. Chicago, Ill., 1951*), business executive, composer. Studied at Harvard (M.A., 1922). While serving as vice president of his family's company, Carpenter pursued his interests in composition, studying in Italy with English composer Edward Elgar. His major works were influenced by the French composers, rather than the German, and impressionism profoundly shaped his thinking, as did American jazz. Major works include a suite for orchestra, *Adventures in a Perambulator* (1915), and *Krazy Kat*, a jazz ballet based on a comic strip character and performed in New York in 1922 with choreography by Adolph Bolm. *Skyscrapers*, another ballet depicting work and play in an industrial environment and again choreographed by Bolm, had a successful production at the Metropolitan Opera House in 1926. Carpenter is also remembered for his many fine art songs.

CARPENTER, MATTHEW HALE (*b. Moretown, Vt., 1824; d. 1881*), lawyer. Removed to Wisconsin, 1848; U.S. senator, Republican, from Wisconsin, 1869–75 and 1879–81. Counsel for W. W. Belknap at impeachment trial and for Samuel J. Tilden before electoral commission.

CARPENTER, STEPHEN CULLEN (*b. Ireland; d. Washington, D.C., ca. 1820*), journalist. Came to America, *ca.* 1802, and established Federalist *Courier* at Charleston, S.C., 1803. Moved to New York and edited anti-French *Peoples' Friend*, 1806–07; edited *Mirror of Taste and Dramatic Censor* at Philadelphia, 1810–11. Author of *Memoirs of Jefferson* (1809).

CARPENTER, STEPHEN HASKINS (*b. Little Falls, N.Y., 1831; d. Geneva, N.Y., 1878*), educator. Professor of English, University of Wisconsin, 1868–78; author of *Introduction to the Study of the Anglo-Saxon Language* (1875).

CARR, BENJAMIN (*b. England, 1769; d. Philadelphia, Pa., 1831*), musician. Came to Philadelphia, 1793; established first music store there and became famous as singer, organist, and promoter of music. His works include a *Federal Overture* (1796), an opera *The Archers* (produced in New York, 1796), a volume of *Masses, Vespers and Litanies* (1805), and other.

CARR, CHARLOTTE ELIZABETH (*b. Dayton, Ohio, 1890; d. New York, N.Y., 1956*), social worker. Studied at Vassar College. Served as assistant secretary and later as secretary of labor and industry of Pennsylvania (1931–34). Director of Emergency Relief Bureau in New York City (1935–37). Succeeded Jane Addams as head of Chicago's Hull House (1937–42). From 1945 to 1953 she was the head of the Citizens' Committee on Children of New York City.

CARR, DABNEY (*b. Virginia, 1773; d. Richmond, Va., 1837*), jurist. Justice of Virginia Supreme Court of Appeals, 1824–37.

CARR, DABNEY SMITHY (*b. Albemarle Co., Va., 1802; d. Charlottesville, Va., 1854*), diplomat, journalist. Founded pro-Jackson *Baltimore Republican and Commercial Advertiser*, 1827. Naval officer of Baltimore, Md., port, 1829–43; minister to Turkey, 1843–50.

CARR, ELIAS (*b. near Tarboro, N.C., 1839; d. near Tarboro, 1900*), agriculturist. President, state Farmers' Alliance, 1891;

Democratic governor of North Carolina, 1893–97. An able administrator and proponent of public education.

CARR, EUGENE ASA (*b. Concord, N.Y., 1830; d. Washington, D.C., 1910*), Union soldier. Graduated West Point, 1850. Won Medal of Honor for gallantry as division commander, Pea Ridge, 1862. Highly reputed as Indian fighter on the frontier, 1868–91.

CARR, JOSEPH BRADFORD (*b. Albany, N.Y., 1828; d. Troy, N.Y., 1895*), Union brigadier general, Republican politician, businessman.

CARR, MATTHEW. *See* CARR, THOMAS MATTHEW.

CARR, THOMAS MATTHEW (*b. probably Galway, Ireland, 1750; d. Philadelphia, Pa., 1820*), Augustinian friar. Came to America, 1796; founded the first establishment of his order in the United States, St. Augustine's Church, Philadelphia, 1796.

CARR, WILBUR JOHN (*b. near Taylorsville, Ohio, 1870; d. Baltimore, Md., 1942*), U.S. State Department official. Graduated Commercial College of University of Kentucky, 1889; LL.B., Georgetown University, 1894; LL.M., George Washington University, 1899. Entered the State Department as a clerk, 1892; became chief of the Consular Bureau, 1902, and chief clerk of the State Department, 1907, with responsibility for the Consular Service, of which he was made director in 1909. In 1924, he became head of the newly created Foreign Service, with title of assistant secretary of state, retaining the post until 1937. He served as U.S. minister to Czechoslovakia, 1937–39. Throughout his career, he strove to keep the service as professional and nonpartisan as possible.

CARREL, ALEXIS (*b. Sainte-Foy-les-Lyon, France, 1873; d. Paris, France, 1944*), surgeon, experimental biologist. Took baccalaureate in letters at Lyons, 1890; in science at Dijon, 1891. Studied medicine at University of Lyons, where he held title of prosector, 1899–1902; he received the formal M.D. degree in 1900. Worked out a successful technique for suturing wounds of arteries and veins and for restoring the flow of blood through completely severed vessels (first reported, 1902). His intellectual independence and open criticism of local medical politics and prejudices cost him a university career in France and he went to the University of Chicago, as a guest in the Department of Physiology, 1904–06. His articles and lectures on further experiments in blood-vessel surgery and organ transplants won him appointment to the staff of the Rockefeller Institute, New York City, where he remained, 1906–38. He was awarded the Nobel Prize in 1912 for his work, on which rest all subsequent advances in surgery of the heart and transplantation of organs. Created a whole new art of tissue culture, thinking that human tissues and even whole organs might be cultivated artificially for substitution of diseased parts of the body; work contributed greatly to knowledge of normal cell life and of malignant growths, and more recently to the understanding of viruses and the preparation of vaccines. After World War I service with the French army, he returned to the Rockefeller Institute and launched an investigation of the causes of cancer which came to nothing; *post* 1930, he returned to the laboratory cultivation of whole organs. These experiments had no practical application in surgery, but were useful to subsequent workers in development of heart-lung machines and other technical aids to vascular surgery and physiology. He published *Man, the Unknown*, a speculative essay in the possibilities of scientific achievement (1935). Returned to France after the fall of Paris in World War II as member of a mission to investigate the nutritional needs of children in wartime. Remained there with the visionary intention of directing an institute for the study of human problems, which would guide the recovery of France and foil Hitler's scheme to subjugate the nation. The government at Vichy gave his institute a charter and a large subvention, and he brought together a group of young scientists and others to work on subjects relevant to the project. Vichy's support and his own outspoken opinion of the prewar French politicians caused him unfairly to be branded a collaborationist.

CARRÈRE, JOHN MERVEN (*b. Rio de Janeiro, Brazil, 1858; d. New York, N.Y., 1911*), architect. Graduated École des Beaux-Arts, Paris, 1882; entered office of McKim, Mead and White; formed partnership with Thomas Hastings. Earliest commissions of firm executed in modified Spanish Renaissance style, mainly at St. Augustine, Fla., 1887–90. Carrère and Hastings designed many public and commercial buildings as well as elaborate country houses in French Renaissance style; their chief works were the U.S. Senate and House Office Buildings, Washington, D.C. (1905 and 1906), the New Theater, New York City (1906–09), and the New York Public Library, completed in 1911.

CARRICK, SAMUEL (*b. York Co., Pa., 1760; d. Knoxville, Tenn., 1809*), Presbyterian clergyman. A missionary on the Tennessee frontier, he organized the first Presbyterian church in Knoxville, *ca.* 1792; in 1794 he became president of Blount College (later the University of Tennessee).

CARRIER, WILLIS HAVILAND (*b. near Angola, N.Y., 1876; d. New York, N.Y., 1950*), mechanical engineer. Graduated Cornell University, 1901. Developed and designed a radical refrigerating machine, the centrifugal compressor, which used nontoxic refrigerants. This machine opened the way to modern air-conditioning. Headed the Carrier Engineering Corporation and its successor, Carrier Corporation, 1915–48. Held more than 80 patents on air-conditioning systems.

CARRINGTON, ELAINE STERN (*b. New York, N.Y., 1891; d. New York, 1958*), magazine, radio scriptwriter. Studied at Columbia. Writer of many stories for popular magazines, Carrington is best remembered as the writer for the radio soap opera "Pepper Young's Family."

CARRINGTON, HENRY BEEBEE (*b. Wallingford, Conn., 1824; d. 1912*), lawyer, soldier. Graduated Yale, 1845; entered practice of law, Columbus, Ohio, 1848; was locally prominent in organization of Republican party. As adjutant general of Ohio militia, he put nine regiments in field, 1861, and helped save West Virginia for the Union. Active throughout Civil War in raising and training troops, he continued in army as colonel, 18th Infantry; in service against Indians, 1865–69, he built Fort Phil Kearny, served in the Red Cloud campaign, and protected the builders of the Union Pacific Railroad against Indian raids. He was author of *Battles of the American Revolution* (1876) and revised his wife's book *Ab-sa-ra-ka, Home of the Crows* (1868, and subsequent editions).

CARRINGTON, PAUL (*b. Cumberland, Co., Va., 1733; d. "Mulberry Hill," Charlotte Co., Va., 1818*), jurist. Active in the Revolution, he served as chief justice of the Virginia General Court, 1780–89, and as justice of the court of appeals, 1789–1807.

CARROLL, CHARLES (*b. Annapolis, Md., 1736; d. Baltimore, Md., 1832*), Revolutionary leader, signer of the Declaration of Independence. Son of Charles Carroll and Elizabeth Brooke; educated locally by the Society of Jesus and in their colleges at St. Omer, Flanders, Rheims, and Paris. Returned to Maryland, 1765, after further study of law in London; began development of Carrollton Manor, Frederick Co., and lived life of landed proprietor. Entered political life as opponent of David Dulany, 1773; the controversy in the *Maryland Gazette* established Carroll as a popular leader. He served on Committees of Correspondence and Safety and accompanied Benjamin Franklin and Samuel Chase on their ill-fated journey to Canada, 1776, seeking union between Canada and the revolting colonies. Member of Continental Congress, 1776–78; U.S. senator, Federalist, from Maryland, 1789–92. Active in trade and land development, he was an original director of the Baltimore & Ohio Railroad.

CARROLL, DANIEL (*b. Upper Marlboro, Md., 1730; d. Rock Creek, Md., 1796*), commissioner of the District of Columbia, 1791–95. Cousin of Charles Carroll; brother of John Carroll; U.S. senator, Federalist, from Maryland, in 1st Congress.

CARROLL, EARL (*b. Pittsburgh, Pa., 1893; d. 1948*), theatrical producer and director, songwriter. Author of some 400 lyrics for popular songs. Author, producer, and director of a series of *Earl Carroll Vanities* for the New York stage (and on the road), 1923–36. The *Vanities* were formula girls-and-music revues, gaudy and strictly commercial, which had a special appeal to popular taste in the 1920's. In 1936, he shifted his producing activities to Hollywood, Calif. He died in an air crash between San Diego and New York.

CARROLL, HOWARD (*b. Albany, N.Y., 1854; d. New York, N.Y., 1916*), journalist, businessman. Inspector general, New York State troops, 1898.

CARROLL, JAMES (*b. Woolwich, England, 1854; d. 1907*), investigator of yellow fever. Immigrated to Canada, 1869. Enlisted in U.S. Army, 1874; served nine years in infantry and as hospital steward, 1883–98. Studied medicine at University of the City of New York, 1886–87, and at University of Maryland, 1889–91; received M.D. degree from Maryland and also studied bacteriology and pathology at Johns Hopkins. Made assistant to Walter Reed at Army Medical Museum, 1895; appointed acting assistant surgeon, 1898, and to the Yellow Fever Commission, 1900. Believing with Reed that Dr. Carlos Finlay's theory of yellow fever transmission was most promising, Carroll underwent experiment of applying an infected mosquito to his arm; the resulting attack of fever proved the theory and caused Carroll a permanent heart lesion. Carroll also demonstrated that the virus of yellow fever was ultramicroscopic. In 1902, he succeeded Reed as professor of bacteriology and pathology at Columbian University, Washington, D.C., and at the Army Medical School.

CARROLL, JOHN (*b. Upper Marlboro, Md., 1735; d. Baltimore, Md., 1815*), first Roman Catholic bishop in the United States, first archbishop of Baltimore. Brother of Daniel Carroll, cousin of Charles Carroll. Educated at St. Omer's College in French Flanders; entered Society of Jesus, 1753, and studied at Watten, Bruges, and Liège; ordained at Liège, 1767 or 1769. On suppression of the Society, 1773, went to England and then returned home; lived privately in mother's house at Rock Creek, Md., serving spiritual needs of neighboring Catholic families. Accompanied Charles Carroll, Franklin, and Chase on fruitless 1776 mission to Canada. Joined in 1784 clergy petition to Rome to provide frame of government for Catholic Church in America; in 1784–85 was named superior of American missions by Pope Pius VI, and in 1790 was consecrated first bishop of American hierarchy. Became archbishop, 1808. Outstanding as administrator under difficult circumstances. Founder of Georgetown University, 1789, he established St. Mary's diocesan seminary, Baltimore, and Mt. St. Mary College, Emmitsburg, Md., and was associated with organization of Sisters of Charity by Mother Elizabeth Seton.

CARROLL, JOHN LEE (*b. "Homewood," near Baltimore, Md., 1830; d. Washington, D.C., 1911*), lawyer. Great-grandson of Charles Carroll; Democratic governor of Maryland, 1875–79.

CARROLL, SAMUEL SPRIGG (*b. Washington, D.C., 1832; d. Montgomery Co., Md., 1893*), Union soldier. Graduated West Point, 1856. Served throughout Civil War as brigade and division commander; three times wounded, retired as major general, 1869.

CARROLL, WILLIAM (*b. near Pittsburgh, Pa., 1788; d. 1844*), soldier, politician. Removed to Nashville, Tenn., *ca.* 1810; served in Creek War; succeeded Andrew Jackson as major general, Tennessee militia, and supported him in battle of New Orleans. Democratic governor of Tennessee, 1821–27 and 1829–35.

CARRORA, JOSEPH. *See* DUNDEE, JOHNNY.

CARRUTH, FRED HAYDEN (*b. Wabasha Co., Minn., 1862; d. 1932*), humorist, author. Editor, *Woman's Home Companion*, 1905–17.

CARRYL, GUY WETMORE (*b. New York, N.Y., 1873; d. New York, 1904*), author. Resided in Paris, 1896–1902; wrote mildly cynical verse, and among other prose a collection of short stories, *Zut and Other Parisians* (1903).

CARSON, CHRISTOPHER ("KIT") (*b. Madison Co., Ky., 1809; d. Fort Lyon, Colo., 1868*), trapper, guide, Indian agent, soldier. Removed with family to Boone's Lick district of Missouri, 1811. Ran away from apprenticeship to a saddler, 1826, and joined a Santa Fe expedition as "cavvy boy." Engaged in trapping party out of Taos, August 1829, he crossed Mojave Desert to California, and returned to Taos, 1831; from this he emerged an experienced trapper and Indian fighter. In the fall of 1831, he joined Thomas Fitzpatrick in a trapping venture to the north; thereafter until 1841 he trapped in the northern regions (present-day Utah, Montana, Idaho, Wyoming). Returning from a trip to St. Louis, Mo., early in 1842, he met John Charles Frémont and served as guide on Frémont's first expedition, June–October 1842; he shared honors as guide with Thomas Fitzpatrick on Frémont's second expedition, 1843–44. Present on the third expedition, he shared in the conquest of California, 1846–47, and accompanied Edward Fitzgerald Beale eastward in March, bearing dispatches to Washington.

Settling down in Taos after refusal of the Senate to confirm a commission granted him in the regular army, Carson served as agent for the Utes, 1853–61. During this time he dictated the narrative of his life and adventures which appeared in 1858, edited by DeWitt C. Peters. He resigned as agent at outbreak of Civil War and organized and led the 1st New Mexican Volunteer Infantry; he took part in the battle of Valverde, 1862, and in successful campaigns against the Mescalero Apaches and the Navajos, the Kiowas and the Comanches. He received a brevet of brigadier general, March 1865. Commanding at Fort Garland, Colo., 1866–67, his health began to fail; after a fruitless journey east in hope of medical relief, he returned to his new home in Boggsville, Colo., in April 1868. He died about six weeks later.

Plain-spoken, modest and unlettered, Carson's integrity was remarked on by all with whom he had contact.

CARSON, HAMPTON LAWRENCE (*b. Philadelphia, Pa., 1852; d. 1929*), lawyer, historian. Authority on constitutional law; book collector and benefactor of Philadelphia libraries.

CARSON, JACK (*b. Carman, Manitoba, Canada, 1910; d. Encino, Calif., 1963*), comedian and actor. Studied at Illinois College and Carleton College (1928). Began his show business career playing the midwestern vaudeville circuit. In 1936 he moved to Hollywood and studied drama at the Ben Bard School of Drama. He appeared in such films as *Destry Rides Again* (1939), *Mr. Smith Goes to Washington* (1939), *The Strawberry Blonde* (1941), *Roughly Speaking* (1945), *A Star is Born* (1954), and *Cat on a Hot Tin Roof* (1958). Carson was a popular radio performer,

serving as master of ceremonies for the NBC Pacific Coast network show "Signal Caravan," followed by national shows on CBS and NBC. In television he was one of the original hosts of NBC's "All Star Review" (1950–52), and he appeared in more than thirty television plays.

CARSON, JOHN RENSHAW (*b. Pittsburgh, Pa., 1886; d. New Hope, Pa., 1940*), electrical engineer. Graduated Princeton University, B.S., 1907; E.E., 1909; M.S., 1912. In 1914 he joined the American Telephone and Telegraph Co. Carson's mathematical analysis of the vacuum thermionic amplifier (triode) led to his greatest invention—the single-sideband carrier-suppressed method of high-frequency transmission. Another major contribution was in using operational calculus to advance the theory of transient oscillations in transmission lines and networks. From 1934 he was with the Bell Telephone Laboratories as transmission theory engineer and research mathematician. About 50 scientific papers and 25 U.S. patents evince Carson's profundity and creativeness.

CARSON, JOSEPH (*b. Philadelphia, Pa., 1808; d. 1876*), physician. Professor of materia medica and pharmacy, University of Pennsylvania, 1850–76; author of *Illustrations of Medical Botany* (1847), *History of the Medical Department of the University of Pennsylvania* (1869), and other works.

CARSON, "KIT." *See* CARSON, CHRISTOPHER ("KIT")

CARSON, RACHEL LOUISE (*b. Springdale, Pa., 1907; d. Silver Spring, Md., 1964*), marine biologist and writer. Spent her childhood on a farm near Pittsburgh, where she developed her interest in the natural environment. Graduated from Pennsylvania College for Women (now Chatham College) in 1929 and received an M.A. in zoology from Johns Hopkins (1932). She taught at the University of Maryland (1931–36) and spent several summers at the Marine Biological Laboratory, Woods Hole, Mass. During this period she wrote on science for the *Baltimore Sunday Sun*. Carson was a writer for the U.S. Bureau of Fisheries (which later became the Fish and Wildlife Service), 1936–52, becoming editor in chief in 1949. In 1941 she published *Under the Sea-Wind*, a book on the sea. *The Sea Around Us* (1951), which was serialized in the *New Yorker*, became an instant hit and remained on the *New York Times* best seller list for eighty-six weeks. Her first book was rereleased, and it too became a best seller. Carson was able to leave her government job and devote herself to writing full time. After *The Edge of the Sea* (1956), she turned her attention away from the sea and toward the dangers of pesticides and herbicides. *Silent Spring* (1962) is credited with setting in motion the modern environmental movement. Though denounced by the chemical industry, the book helped to bring about a presidential advisory committee to investigate the impact of pesticides. Eventually, many pesticides were banned or brought under stringent controls.

CARSON, SIMEON LEWIS (*b. Marion, N.C., 1882; d. Washington, D.C., 1954*), physician and surgeon. Received M.D. from the University of Michigan (1903). From 1908 to 1918 Carson was the assistant surgeon in chief at Freedmen's Hospital in Washington, D.C. One of the nation's first black surgeons, Carson opened and headed Carson's Private Hospital (1919) in Washington. This was a low-cost institution, offering first-class, personalized medical care to poor blacks. From 1929 to 1936 he was clinical professor of surgery at Howard University. The hospital operated until Carson retired in 1938.

CARTER, BOAKE (*b. Baku, Russia, 1898; d. Hollywood, Calif., 1944*), journalist, radio commentator. Christened Harold T. H. Carter; his parents were British and he was raised in England. Came to the United States, 1920. After several years of wandering, he went to work for the *Philadelphia Daily News*, eventually becoming assistant city editor. Beginning his career as radio broadcaster, 1930, he began to give regular news broadcasts for the *Daily News*, 1931, soon gaining a commercial sponsor. He won national recognition for his emotional, editorialized coverage of the Lindbergh kidnapping case and subsequent trial, 1932. As a regular evening news commentator, 1933–38, he became very popular, throve on controversy, and freely criticized the labor unions, U.S. naval policy, and the New Deal. *Post* 1938, his popularity declined as listeners came to prefer straight news reporting to dramatized comment.

CARTER, CAROLINE LOUISE DUDLEY (*b. Lexington, Ky.*[?], *1862; d. Santa Monica, Calif., 1937*), actress. Starred, as Mrs. Leslie Carter, in *The Heart of Maryland* and many other plays.

CARTER, ELIAS (*b. Ward, Mass., 1781; d. Worcester, Mass., 1864*), architect. Worked in Greek Revival style, adapting it to New England use; best examples of his skill to be found in houses at Worcester *post* 1828.

CARTER, FRANKLIN (*b. Waterbury, Conn., 1837; d. Williamstown, Mass., 1919*), educator. President, Williams College, 1881–1901, in which time he modernized the curriculum, improved the faculty, and built up the endowment.

CARTER, HENRY ALPHEUS PEIRCE (*b. Honolulu, Hawaii, 1837; d. New York, N.Y., 1891*), merchant, diplomat. Negotiated Hawaii–United States sugar reciprocity treaty, 1876; Hawaiian minister to the United States, 1883–91.

CARTER, HENRY ROSE (*b. Caroline Co., Va., 1852; d. Washington, D.C., 1925*), epidemiologist, sanitarian. Graduated University of Virginia, 1873, as civil engineer; University of Maryland, 1879, as M.D.

Entering the Marine Hospital Service, he interested himself in yellow fever research and problems of marine quarantine; represented federal government in fight against yellow fever epidemics in southern states, 1893, and 1897–98. Author of classical papers on yellow fever. In 1913 he conducted the first campaign for malaria control in the United States; in 1915, he was commissioned assistant surgeon general of the U.S. Public Health Service.

CARTER, JAMES COOLIDGE (*b. Lancaster, Mass., 1827; d. New York, N.Y., 1905*), lawyer. Graduated Harvard, 1850. Admitted to New York bar, 1853; associated with Charles O'Conor in Jumel will case and Tweed Ring cases, and with many other important cases in New York. Prominent in movements for municipal reform and leader of the fight against codification of the common law as proposed by David Dudley Field. In the last years of his practice he engaged chiefly in cases involving constitutional questions.

CARTER, JAMES GORDON (*b. Leominster, Mass., 1795; d. Chicago, Ill., 1849*), educator. Graduated Harvard, 1820. As teacher, legislator, and author of textbooks, he was in forefront of reform and improvement of New England common schools, 1821–40.

CARTER, JESSE BENEDICT (*b. New York, N.Y., 1872; d. Cervignano, Italy, 1917*), classical scholar. Graduated Princeton, 1893; Ph.D., University of Halle, 1898. Authority on Roman religion. Director, American School of Classical Studies in Rome, 1907–11; director, Classical School, American Academy in Rome, 1911–13, and of the Academy, 1913–17.

CARTER, JOHN (*b. Virginia, 1737; d. 1781*), pioneer. One of first settlers (*ca.* 1770) in western North Carolina; chairman of the commissioners of the Watauga Association; at his death, one of the largest landholders west of the Allegheny Mountains.

CARTER, JOHN (*b. Philadelphia, Pa., 1745; d. Providence, R.I., 1814*), printer. Editor-publisher of the *Providence Gazette*, 1768–1814. Great-grandfather of John Carter Brown.

CARTER, LANDON (*b. Virginia, 1760; d. Tennessee, 1800*), pioneer. Son of John Carter (1737–81). Supported the movement to erect northeast Tennessee into the independent state of Franklin; held public offices under the government of Franklin, of the Southwest Territory, and of Tennessee.

CARTER, MRS. LESLIE. See CARTER, CAROLINE LOUISE DUDLEY.

CARTER, ROBERT (*b. Lancaster Co., Va., 1663; d. Lancaster Co., 1732*), colonial official and landholder, popularly known as "King" Carter. A prominent member of the Virginia Assembly, he was Speaker in 1696 and 1699; from 1699 to 1732, a member of the Council, he was president, 1726–32. Agent for the Fairfax family, proprietors of the "Northern Neck," 1702–11 and 1722–32. At his death, one of the wealthiest men in the colonies.

CARTER, ROBERT (*b. Albany, N.Y., 1819; d. Cambridge, Mass., 1879*), author. Coeditor with James Russell Lowell of the *Pioneer* (1843); editor, among others, of the Boston *Commonwealth* and the Rochester, N.Y., *Democrat*.

CARTER, SAMUEL POWHATAN (*b. Elizabethton, Tenn., 1819; d. Washington, D.C., 1891*), naval and army officer, the only American who has ever been both rear admiral and major general. Graduated Annapolis, 1846. Organized first Union troops from Tennessee and served as brigade and division commander, 1861–65. Returned to naval duty, 1866; served at sea, and as commander of midshipmen, Annapolis, 1870–73.

CARTER, THOMAS HENRY (*b. Scioto Co., Ohio, 1854; d. 1911*), lawyer. Studied law at Burlington, Iowa; removed, 1882, to Helena, Mont. Elected territorial delegate, Republican, from Montana, 1888; first congressman, 1889; U.S. senator, 1895 and again in 1905. A strong partisan of western interests.

CARTER, WILLIAM SAMUEL (*b. Austin, Tex., 1859; d. Baltimore, Md., 1923*), trade union official. Editor, Brotherhood of Locomotive Firemen and Enginemen's magazine, 1894–1904; secretary-treasurer of the union, 1904–09; president, 1909–22.

CARTERET, PHILIP (*b. Isle of Jersey, England, 1639; d. East Jersey, 1682*), colonial official. Came to what is today Elizabethport, N.J., 1665, as first governor of New Jersey; summoned first session of New Jersey legislature, 1668. After brief period of Dutch reconquest of New Netheran, Carteret became governor of East Jersey portion of the province but his authority was challenged by Sir Edmund Andros *post* 1680. He resigned the office, 1682.

CARTWRIGHT, PETER (*b. Amherst Co., Va., 1785; d. 1872*), Methodist clergyman. Raised in Logan Co., Ky., where his father located in 1793. Converted to Methodism, 1801, and given an exhorter's license, 1802; became a traveling preacher, 1803. His early itineraries took him through Kentucky, Tennessee, Indiana, and Ohio; he became one of the most celebrated frontier preachers and was ordained elder in 1808. In 1824, because of his hatred of slavery, he had himself transferred to the Sangamon Circuit in Illinois and made his home at Pleasant Hills. Until his death he was a leader in western religious activities. Twice a member of the Illinois legislature, he was defeated for Congress by Abraham Lincoln in 1846.

CARTY, JOHN JOSEPH (*b. Cambridge, Mass., 1861; d. Baltimore, Md., 1932*), electrical engineer. Entered service of the Bell Telephone company in 1879. His early years were notable for his invention of the "common battery," which made the commercial development of telephony in metropolitan areas practical; for development of a high-resistance-bridging signal bell for substations, which permitted a widespread extension of telephone service; and for his discovery that the principal cause of cross-interference between telephone circuits was electrostatic, not electromagnetic, unbalance. As chief engineer of the American Telephone and Telegraph Co., he supervised experimentation which led to modern long-distance telephony overland and trans-oceanic radio-telephony.

CARUS, PAUL (*b. Ilsenburg, Germany, 1852; d. 1919*), rationalist philosopher, identified with the *Open Court* publications, Chicago, Ill., *post* 1887.

CARUSO, ENRICO (*b. Naples, Italy, 1873; d. Naples, 1921*), operatic tenor. Debut, November 1894, at Teatro Nuovo, Naples; won international reputation, 1898, in premiere of *Fedora* at Teatro Lirico, Milan. Opened his first season at Metropolitan Opera, New York, November 1903, in *Rigoletto*; thereafter, until failure of his health in 1920, he was the idol of American operagoers. Generous, kindly, and unspoiled by success, he sang on every occasion as if it were the high point of his career.

CARUTHERS, WILLIAM ALEXANDER (*b. Lexington, Va., 1802; d. Marietta, Ga., 1846*), physician. Author of *The Kentuckian in New York* (1834), *The Cavaliers of Virginia* (1834–35), and *The Knights of the Horse-Shoe* (1845).

CARVALHO, SOLOMON SOLIS (*b. Baltimore, Md., 1856; d. Plainfield, N.J., 1942*), newspaper executive. Raised in New York City. A.B., City College of New York, 1877. Starting as a reporter for the City News Association, then for the *New York Sun*, he became in 1887 an aide to Joseph Pulitzer on the *New York World*. Between 1892 and 1895, he had absolute power over expenditures in every department of the *World*. After a disagreement with Pulitzer, he joined the organization of William Randolph Hearst, whom he served as general manager with great intelligence, professional knowledge, and complete discretion. Retiring in 1917, he continued to work as a highly paid consultant of the Hearst publications.

CARVER, GEORGE WASHINGTON (*b. near Diamond Grove, Mo., ca. 1861; d. Tuskegee, Ala., 1843*), agricultural chemist, educator, botanist. The frail, sickly child of black slave parents, he was raised in the household of Moses Carver after his father's death and the kidnapping of his mother and sister by raiders from Arkansas. About 1875, he left the Carver family to acquire formal education; for the next few years, he worked at odd jobs and attended schools in Neosho, Mo., and several Kansas towns. Denied admission to college because of his race in 1885, he finally succeeded in winning admission to Simpson College, Indianola, Iowa, in 1890. He considered a career as an artist (for which he had talent) but decided to study agriculture as a better economic prospect. Transferred to Iowa State College at Ames, 1891; B.S., 1894; and M.S., 1896. Served for two years as assistant to Louis H. Pammell. He also had charge of the college greenhouse, conducting experiments there in cross-fertilization and propagation of plants that won the praise of James Wilson.

Soon after completing his graduate work in 1896, he accepted the invitation of Booker T. Washington to serve as director of agricultural work at Tuskegee Institute, in Alabama, a post that was broadened to include direction of the school's agricultural experiment station. There, he taught and experimented until his death.

His early years at Tuskegee were notable for the conferences and institutes he conducted to teach farmers better agricultural methods and the need for a balanced diet. His "mobile school," which carried equipment in a wagon to rural locations for demonstration of better methods of farming and improved home economics, was in his opinion one of the most important contributions to education. His work soon convinced him that the troubles of farmers in the South, both white and black, were caused mainly by lack of crop diversification, ignorance of soil conservation and plant protection, and inadequate utilization of farm products and by-products. His experiments, discoveries, and recommendations with respect to remedying these conditions brought him international fame. He urged the planting of peanuts, sweet potatoes, cowpeas, and other neglected crops in place of the ubiquitous cotton, which exhausted the soil and was prey to the boll weevil; at the same time, he conducted investigations into the diseases of peanuts and other southern crops and methods of preserving such crops through dehydration. The development of peanuts and sweet potatoes as leading crops in the South was an effect of his demonstration of their possibilities. In his laboratory at Tuskegee, he began, about 1915, to produce special exhibits of peanut products that eventually included some 325 items; his sweet potato products numbered 118. He also exhibited 75 pecan products, and many more from soybeans, cotton, cowpeas, and wild plums. Only one of his discoveries was patented; he intended them to be available for the widest possible use.

CARVER, JOHN (*b. Nottinghamshire or Derbyshire, England, ca. 1576; d. Plymouth, Mass., 1621*), first governor of Plymouth. Immigrated to Holland, 1609; joined Pilgrims at Leyden, *ca.* 1610–11. Active in Pilgrim projects for American settlement, he organized those sailing direct from England, hired the *Mayflower*, and sailed aboard her, 1620. Aside from his March 1621 treaty with Massasoit, we know nothing of his activities or policies as governor.

CARVER, JONATHAN (*b. Weymouth, Mass., 1710; d. 1780*), traveler. At instance of Maj. Robert Rogers, Carver set out westward in 1766 along the Great Lakes from Mackinac. He crossed to the Mississippi by the Green Bay–Fox–Wisconsin route, ascended the river, reached Lake Superior by the Chippewa and St. Croix rivers, and returned in the fall of 1767 to Mackinac. Disappointed in hope of publishing his narrative of travel in America, he sailed for England, 1769, residing there for the remainder of his life. His book *Travels in Interior Parts of America* (London, 1778) ran through many editions.

CARY, ALICE (*b. near Cincinnati, Ohio, 1820; d. New York, N.Y., 1871*), poet. Author (with sister Phoebe) of *Poems* (1849); author also of *Clovernook Papers* (1852) and other works. First president of the first American woman's club.

CARY, ANNIE LOUISE (*b. Wayne, Maine, 1842; d. New York, N.Y., 1921*), contralto. Operatic debut at Copenhagen, 1867–68; returned to America, 1870. Until retirement, 1882, one of the most celebrated contraltos in opera, appearing in London and St. Petersburg as well as New York.

CARY, ARCHIBALD (*b. Virginia, 1721; d. Ampthill, Va., 1787*), planter, industrialist. *Post* 1750, extended his father's manufacturing projects at Ampthill, operating a furnace and foundry and a flour mill. Representative of Chesterfield Co. in Virginia Assembly from 1756; a member of all Virginia Revolutionary conventions.

CARY, EDWARD (*b. Albany, N.Y., 1840; d. New York, N.Y., 1917*), editorial writer, *New York Times*, 1871–1917.

CARY, ELISABETH LUTHER (*b. Brooklyn, N.Y., 1867; d. Brooklyn, 1936*), art critic of the *New York Times*, 1908–36, the newspaper's first full-time specialist in this field.

CARY, LOTT (*b. Charles City Co., Va., ca. 1780; d. Liberia, 1828*), Baptist clergyman. Purchased freedom from slavery for self and family, *ca.* 1813, and received license to preach. Removed to Freetown, Liberia, 1821, as pastor of first Baptist church there; he and associates settled at Cape Montserado. Chosen vice-agent of the colony, 1826, he was killed while helping defend the colony against the Deys.

CARY, PHOEBE (*b. near Cincinnati, Ohio, 1824; d. New York, N.Y., 1871*), poet. Sister of Alice Cary; author of the hymn "One Sweetly Solemn Thought."

CASANOWICZ, IMMANUEL MOSES (*b. Zhaludok, Russia, 1853; d. Washington, D.C., 1927*), orientalist, archaeologist. Came to America, *ca.* 1882; Ph.D., Johns Hopkins, 1892. Associated with U.S. National Museum *post* 1906.

CASE, FRANCIS HIGBEE (*b. Everly, Iowa, 1896; d. Bethesda, Md., 1962*), journalist and U.S. congressman and senator. Studied at Dakota Wesleyan University and Northwestern (M.A., 1920). Served in the Marine Corps (1918) and held reserve commissions in the army (1924–31) and the marines (from 1937). After working in journalism while at Northwestern, he returned to South Dakota in 1922 to serve as editor, writer, and owner of several newspapers. While publishing the *Custer Chronicle*, Case entered public life as a state regent of education (1931–33). In 1936 he was elected to the first of seven terms in the House of Representatives as a Republican serving western South Dakota. In the House, he served on the Appropriations Committee and generally promoted an isolationist foreign policy. Case drafted a bill in 1946 that would have allowed tighter control of labor; although vetoed by President Truman, Case's proposal presaged the Taft-Hartley Act of 1947. Case was elected to the Senate in 1950 and 1956, where he served on the Armed Services and Public Works committees. He caused an uproar in 1956 when he disclosed his refusal to accept a $2,500 "campaign contribution" from a lawyer serving as an oil company lobbyist. Shortly before his death, Case was named to the Senate Committee on Preparedness. In 1962 Congress authorized the naming of a new span across Washington channel of the Potomac River in his honor. The following year the Fort Randall Reservoir in South Dakota was renamed Lake Francis Case.

CASE, JEROME INCREASE (*b. Williamstown, N.Y., 1818; d. 1891*), manufacturer and designer of improved farm machinery. Founded the J. I. Case Co. of Racine, Wis.; prominent in local politics and banking.

CASE, LEONARD (*b. Westmoreland Co., Pa., 1786; d. Cleveland, Ohio, 1864*), lawyer, land agent. Immigrated with family to Warren, Ohio, 1800; as clerk of local court began study of law and was admitted to bar, 1814. From 1816 to his death, identified with the growth of Cleveland as real estate trader, lawyer, and public official. Served as agent for the Connecticut Land Co., 1827–55.

CASE, LEONARD (*b. Cleveland, Ohio, 1820; d. Cleveland, 1880*), philanthropist. Succeeding to the large fortune of his father (Leonard Case, 1786–1864), he was a benefactor of the Cleveland Library, the Western Reserve Historical Society, and other civic and charitable activities. In 1877, he gave a large part of his property to found the Case School of Applied Science.

CASE, SHIRLEY JACKSON (*b. Hatfield Point, New Brunswick, Canada, 1872; d. Lakeland, Fla., 1847*), historian, clergyman.

B.A., Acadia University, 1893; M.A., 1896, B.D., Yale University Divinity School, 1904; Ph.D., Yale, 1906. Professor of history and philosophy of religion, Bates College, 1906–08. Taught New Testament interpretation at University of Chicago Divinity School, *post* 1908, and also early church history, *post* 1917. Named chairman of the church history department, 1923, he was designated professor of the history of early Christianity, 1925. He served as dean of the Divinity School at Chicago, 1933–38. From 1940 to 1947, he was professor of religion at Florida Southern College and dean of the Florida School of Religion. As director of church history studies at Chicago, he built up an outstanding faculty and encouraged innovative research. His major contribution, however, was in the field of historical scholarship as exponent of the sociohistorical method (the "Chicago school" method) which insists on careful review of all dimensions of a given culture (the total environment) prior to work with documents of any specific event within its context. Among many books which he wrote from his own research, the one which best exemplifies his talent and method is *Jesus: A New Biography* (1927).

CASE, WILLIAM SCOVILLE (*b. Tariffville, Conn., 1863; d. 1921*), lawyer, jurist. Graduated Yale, 1885; admitted to Connecticut bar, 1887. Judge of the common pleas, Hartford Co., 1897–1901; of the superior court, 1901–19; of the supreme court of errors thereafter.

CASEY, JOSEPH (*b. Washington Co., Md., 1814; d. 1879*), jurist. Congressman, Whig, from Pennsylvania, 1848–51; editor of *Casey's Reports*, 1856–61. Appointed justice of U.S. Court of Claims, 1861, and chief justice, 1863, he resigned in 1870.

CASEY, SILAS (*b. East Greenwich, R.I., 1807; d. Brooklyn, N.Y., 1882*), Union soldier. Graduated West Point, 1826. Served on midwestern frontier and in Seminole War; served under Scott in Mexico, 1847, and was wounded in storming of Chapultepec. Author of *Casey's Tactics* (1862), long standard. Distinguished in early campaigns of Civil War; *post* 1862, commanded part of the defenses of Washington, D.C., as major general of volunteers. Retired from active service, 1868.

CASEY, THOMAS LINCOLN (*b. Sackett's Harbor, N.Y., 1831; d. Washington, D.C., 1896*), army engineer. Specialist in fortifications; completed construction in 1884 of the Washington Monument.

CASH, WILBUR JOSEPH (*b. Gaffney, S.C., 1900; d. Mexico City, Mexico, 1941*), journalist. Graduated Wake Forest College, 1922. Author of *The Mind of the South* (1941), an analysis of the sentiments, prejudices, standards, and values common to white people in the South, which gave that region its distinctive character. The book was influential in preparing the way for improvement of race relations.

CASILEAR, JOHN WILLIAM (*b. New York, N.Y., 1811; d. Saratoga, N.Y., 1893*), engraver, painter. Apprentice of Peter Maverick, he became a banknote engraver and a partner in American Bank Note Co. *Post* 1854, he gave most of his time to landscape painting.

CASS, GEORGE WASHINGTON (*b. near Dresden, Ohio, 1810; d. 1888*), engineer. Nephew of Lewis Cass. Graduated West Point, 1832; assigned to duty with Topographical Engineers. Assisted in construction of Cumberland Road, 1832–36. Resigning commission, he entered business, organizing first steamboat line on Monongahela River. Thereafter was president of Adams Express Co.; the Pittsburgh, Fort Wayne and Chicago Railroad; and the Northern Pacific Railroad.

CASS, LEWIS (*b. Exeter, N.H., 1782; d. Detroit, Mich., 1866*), soldier, statesman. Moving west in 1799, he established a law practice at Marietta, Ohio, 1802, but soon removed to Zanesville. Elected to Ohio legislature, 1806, he opposed Aaron Burr's schemes and won Jefferson's favorable notice. During War of 1812 as colonel of the 2nd Ohio, he won distinction at Malden and at the battle of the Thames; he was appointed governor of Michigan Territory, 1813. His term (1813–31) was marked by helpful, firm, and constructive service; he was particularly effective in dealing with the Indians. Following service as secretary of war in Andrew Jackson's cabinet (1831–36), he was appointed minister to France; he resigned after a dispute with Daniel Webster which increased his national prestige. As U.S. senator, Democrat, from Michigan, 1845–48, he favored a strong attitude toward England on the Oregon question, approved the war with Mexico, and opposed the Wilmot Proviso. His views on the containment of slavery anticipated Douglas's later doctrine of "squatter sovereignty."

Nominated for the presidency, 1848, he was defeated because Van Buren divided the Democratic vote; in 1851 he was reelected to the Senate. His career reached its high point 1857–60, when as secretary of state in Buchanan's cabinet he scored diplomatic victories in disputes with Great Britain and Paraguay. Preeminently a nationalist and a Union man, he resigned in December 1860 as a protest against the decision not to reinforce the forts in Charleston Harbor. In his last public appearance, 1862, he urged enlistment in the Union army; during his retirement he resumed the scholarly and literary interests which had always served him for relaxation.

CASSATT, ALEXANDER JOHNSTON (*b. Pittsburgh, Pa., 1839; d. 1906*), civil engineer, railroad executive. Graduated Rensselaer Polytechnic Institute, 1859. Entered engineering department of the Pennsylvania Railroad, 1861; pioneered in introduction of the airbrake, and was made general superintendent, 1870. In 1873 he became general manager of lines east of Pittsburgh and was concerned in the general expansion of the system that then took place; chosen first vice president in 1880, he retired from active duty, 1882. Recalled to take the presidency of the Pennsylvania, 1899, he served until his death. As president, he improved the operating conditions of the road and nearly doubled its earnings. His "community of interest" solution of the rebate problem was an acceptable stopgap until the passage of the Hepburn Act. Another of his outstanding achievements was the construction of the Pennsylvania Terminal in New York.

CASSATT, MARY (*b. Allegheny City, Pa., 1845; d. Mesnil-Théribus, France, 1926*), artist. Sister of Alexander Johnston Cassatt. After 1874 a permanent resident of France, she became an artistic disciple of Degas; she exhibited with the impressionists, 1879–86, and gave her first independent exhibit at Paris, 1893. Original and successful in her work with pastels and in oils, she is regarded as the most distinguished etcher, excepting Whistler, that America has produced.

CASSIDY, MARSHALL WHITING (*b. Washington, D.C., 1892; d. Glen Cove, N.Y., 1968*), horseracing official. Worked as an assistant for his father, the well-known race starter Mars Cassidy, then as a starter at various tracks, 1921–34. He was steward at the Hialeah track in Florida (1930's), then N.Y. state steward. As executive secretary of the Jockey Club of New York City (1941–64), Cassidy became a leader of Thoroughbred racing in the U.S. He was vice president and director of racing for the Greater New York Racing Association, director of Thoroughbred Racing Associations, Inc., and a trustee of the Turf Foundation and the Horsemen's Benevolent and Protective Association Foundation. Cassidy also helped design several major racetracks.

CASSIDY, WILLIAM (*b. Albany, N.Y., 1815; d. Albany, 1873*), journalist. Editor of the Albany *Atlas* and, *post* 1856, of the combined *Atlas* and *Argus*; a vehement supporter of the Democratic party.

CASSIN, JOHN (*b. near Media, Pa., 1813; d. 1869*), ornithologist. As manager of Bowen's engraving and lithographing plant in Philadelphia, he produced illustrations for many government scientific publications; in his spare time, he arranged and identified the great collection of birds belonging to the Academy of Natural Sciences. In addition to contributions to government exploration reports, he wrote many papers for the Academy *Proceedings* and also *Illustrations of the Birds of California, Texas, Oregon, British and Russian America* (1856), in supplement to Audubon.

CASSODAY, JOHN BOLIVAR (*b. Fairfield, N.Y., 1830; d. 1907*), jurist. Chief justice, Supreme Court of Wisconsin, 1895–1907.

CASTLE, IRENE FOOTE (*b. New Rochelle, N.Y., 1893; d. Eureka Springs, Ark., 1969*), exhibition ballroom dancer and actress. With her first husband, Vernon, became a leader of the dance craze sparked by Irving Berlin's songs. They popularized the Castle walk, the Castle waltz, the one-step, the hesitation waltz, the tango, the maxixe, and the fox-trot. The Castle's ran a dance school, wrote the instructional book *Modern Dancing* (1914), and made a popular instructional dance film. They starred in Irving Berlin's first musical, *Watch Your Step* (1914), written especially for them, and the 1915 film *Whirl of Life*. An innovative dresser, Irene Castle was one of the most photographed women of the World War I era. Following Vernon's death in 1918 she wrote *My Husband* (1919) and went on to star in a total of seventeen silent films. In 1939 Fred Astaire and Ginger Rogers played the Castles in the film *The Story of Vernon and Irene Castle*. Her autobiography is *Castles in the Air* (1958).

CASTLE, VERNON BLYTHE (*b. Norwich, England, 1887; d. Fort Worth, Tex., 1918*), dancer. Born Vernon Blythe; assumed the name Castle in 1907. With his wife Irene (Foote) Castle, he revolutionized popular dancing in the years 1912–14, creating the one-step, turkey-trot, and many other dances. After gallant service in Royal Flying Corps, 1916–18, he crashed while instructing aviation cadets.

CASTLE, WILLIAM RICHARDS, JR. (*b. Honolulu, Hawaii, 1878; d. Washington, D.C., 1963*), diplomat and writer. Graduated from Harvard (A.B., 1900), where he served as assistant dean (1906–13) and dean (1913–15). In 1915 he became editor of *Harvard Graduates' Magazine* and two years later was appointed director of the Bureau of Communications of the National American Red Cross. During this period he published several books of fiction and nonfiction: *The Green Vase* (1912), *Hawaii, Past and Present* (1913), *The Pillar of Sand* (1914), and *Wake Up, America* (1916). Castle's State Department career began when he became special assistant (1919–21) and then chief (1921–27) attached to the Division of West European Affairs. He then became assistant secretary of state. In 1929 he was named ambassador to Japan, where he developed a sympathetic view of Japanese ambitions in the Far East. In 1931 President Hoover named Castle undersecretary of state, in which position his pro-Japanese views brought him into conflict with other diplomats, including Secretary of State Henry Stimson. An opponent of the New Deal and many foreign policy views of the Roosevelt administration, Castle left the State Department in 1933. He was a frequent speaker and author of magazine articles on current events. He served as president (1945–52) of the Garfield Memorial Hospital in Washington, D.C.

CASWELL, ALEXIS (*b. Taunton, Mass., 1799; d. 1877*), president of Brown University, 1868–72, after 35 years of service there as professor of mathematics, natural philosophy, and astronomy.

CASWELL, RICHARD (*b. Cecil Co., Md., 1729; d. Fayetteville, N.C., 1789*), Revolutionary soldier, politician. Major general, North Carolina militia; governor of North Carolina, 1776–80 and 1785–87.

CATALDO, JOSEPH MARIA (*b. Terracina, Sicily, 1837; d. St. Andrew's Mission, Pendleton, Oreg., 1928*), Jesuit missionary in the Pacific Northwest, 1866–1928; founder of Gonzaga University, Spokane, Wash., 1887.

CATCHINGS, WADDILL (*b. Sewannee, Tenn., 1879; d. Pompano Beach, Fla., 1967*), investment banker, economist, and writer. Studied at Harvard (B.A., 1901; LL.B., 1904). His success assisting firms in bankruptcy led to his becoming director of numerous corporations. During World War I he was a member of the advisory council to the U.S. secretary of labor and chaired the war committee of the U.S. Chamber of Commerce. He was with the banking firm of Goldman, Sachs, and Company (1918–30), where he became president. Catchings is best remembered for his books. With William Trufant Foster he wrote *Money* (1923), *Profits* (1925), *Business Without a Buyer* (1927), *The Road to Plenty* (1928), and *Progress and Plenty* (1930). He also wrote *Money, Men, and Machines* (1953, with Charles F. Roos), *Do Economists Understand Business?* (1955), *Bias Against Business* (1956), and *Are We Mis-managing Money?* (1960).

CATESBY, MARK (*b. Sudbury, England, ca. 1679; d. London, England, 1749*), naturalist and traveler. In Virginia, 1712–19; in South Carolina, Georgia, Florida, 1722–25/6. Wrote and illustrated *The National History of Carolina, Florida, and the Bahama Islands* (1731, 1743, 1748).

CATHCART, JAMES LEANDER (*b. Mt. Murragh, Ireland, 1767; d. Washington, D.C., 1843*), consul. Brought to America as a child; served at sea during the Revolution. Taken prisoner by Algerines, 1785, he rose high in service of the Dey. Associated with William Eaton in Tripoli adventure; later consul at Madeira and Cadiz.

CATHCART, WILLIAM (*b. Co. Londonderry, Ireland, 1826; d. 1908*), Baptist clergyman. Came to America, 1853; pastor of Second Baptist Church, Philadelphia, Pa. Best known as editor of the *Baptist Encyclopedia* (1883).

CATHER, WILLA (*b. near Winchester, Va., 1873; d. New York, N.Y., 1947*), novelist, poet. Moved with her family to Webster County, Nebr., 1883; was strongly influenced by the change in environment, the need to grapple with and understand the new land, which she later called the "happiness and curse" of her life. Educated first in Red Cloud, Nebr., she was fortunate in cultivated neighbors who introduced her to French and German culture, the classical languages, and music. The prairie life stimulated her imagination; she absorbed the stories of local immigrants from Europe in a photographic detail that she would later employ with an added lyricism in her mature work. While a student at the University of Nebraska, she worked as drama critic and columnist for Lincoln newspapers and continued this work after receiving her B.A. in 1895. In June 1896, she went to work in Pittsburgh, Pa., at first as editor on a small magazine, then as telegraph editor and reviewer on the *Daily Leader*. Already the author of published fiction and verse, and wishing more time for creative work, she turned in 1901 to high school teaching and moved into the home of a friend, Isabelle McClung, the daughter of a Pittsburgh judge. Her first book, *April Twilights* (1903), a collection of poems interesting primarily as a gloss to her fiction,

was followed by *The Troll Garden* (1905), consisting of stories about artists, a subject that never ceased to engage her. Her most ambitious fictional portrait of the artist, *The Song of the Lark* (1915), was inspired by the opera singer Olive Fremstad. The lure of New York for the title character in "Paul's Case," the best of the early stories, was also autobiographical. In 1906, S. S. McClure offered her a New York job on his muckraking magazine.

After publishing her first novel, *Alexander's Bridge* (1912), she visited the Southwest, which became symbolically significant in several novels. She returned east invigorated, ending both her journalistic career and her long literary apprenticeship with the completion of *O Pioneers!* (1913).

Influenced by Sarah Orne Jewett, Cather had made unconventional use of Nebraska material as early as 1909 in "The Enchanted Bluff." She believed in the possibility of a society aesthetically and ethically worthy of the land. Characteristically, in her frontier fiction, she located this possibility in the European immigrants, with their rich cultural traditions and love of life.

She became first increasingly elegiac in tone and then embittered as she saw the defeat of her cultural-agrarian ideal in actuality. In *My Antonia* (1918) the Bohemian heroine fulfills her vital nature on a farm in creative motherhood, but for the narrator, a New York lawyer whose story it is as much as hers, she exists finally as an image of a shared "incommunicable past." A *Lost Lady* (1923) followed a diffuse slack book, *One of Ours*, which nevertheless won the Pulitzer Prize in 1922.

The Professor's House (1925) and *My Mortal Enemy* (1926) were transitional to her discovery of the frontier spirit in history. Her Protestant (Baptist) heritage prevented conversion to Catholicism, but an instinctive sympathy for its ritual beauty and discipline informs her last important work. *Death Comes for the Archbishop* (1927) is her most artistically poised "narrative," a word she preferred for this book to "novel," *Shadows on the Rock* (1931) is permeated by a simpler, more static piety. *Obscure Destinies* (1932) is unmarred by the sentimentalism and querulous tone of some of her other late writing. Her last novel, *Sapphira and the Slave Girl* (1940), reflects the physical and creative diminishment of her last years. The title of the collection of critical essays and literary portraits which she published in 1936, *Not Under Forty*, warning off the younger generation, indicates her defensive sense of isolation, especially in the ideological 1930's. She died of a cerebral hemorrhage in New York City and at her request was buried on a hillside in Jaffrey, N.H.

CATHERWOOD, MARY HARTWELL (*b. Luray, Ohio, 1847; d. Chicago, Ill., 1902*), novelist. Author of, among others, *The Romance of Dollard* (1889); *The Story of Tonty* (1890); *Old Kaskaskia* (1893); *Mackinac and Lake Stories* (1899).

CATLETT, SIDNEY (*b. Evansville, Ind., 1910; d. Chicago, Ill., 1951*), jazz drummer. Considered one of the finest jazz drummers of the 1930's and 1940's, Catlett appeared with the leading bands of his time, including Louis Armstrong, Benny Goodman, Roy Eldridge, and Fletcher Henderson.

CATLIN, GEORGE (*b. Wilkes-Barre, Pa., 1796; d. 1872*), artist. Practiced law in western Pennsylvania until 1823, when he set up in Philadelphia as portraitist. He worked mainly in Washington, D.C., 1824–29, but visited Albany, N.Y., 1828, where he painted portraits of DeWitt Clinton and other New York notables. On seeing at Philadelphia a delegation of Indians from the Far West, he resolved "to use my art and so much of the labors of my future life as might be required in rescuing from oblivion the looks and customs of the vanishing races of native man in America." From 1829 to 1838 he painted some 600 portraits of distinguished Indians, accompanied by pictures of villages, games, religious ceremonies and occupations; he exhibited this collection here and abroad, 1837–52. His published works include *Letters and Notes on . . . North American Indians* (1841); *Catlin's North American Indian Portfolio* (1845); *Life Among the Indians* (1867).

CATON, JOHN DEAN (*b. Monroe, N.Y., 1812; d. Chicago, Ill., 1895*), jurist. Settled in Chicago, 1833, opening first law office there. Chief justice, Illinois Supreme Court, 1855–64.

CATRON, JOHN (*b. Pennsylvania, ca. 1786; d. 1865*), jurist. Raised in Virginia and Kentucky, he moved to Tennessee, 1812. Admitted to the bar, 1815, he was proficient in land law and successful; from 1824 to 1834 he served as a judge of the Supreme Court of Errors and Appeals, from 1831 to 1834 chief justice. Appointed by Andrew Jackson to the U.S. Supreme Court, 1837, he was regarded as particularly strong in dealing with cases involving the common law and equity jurisprudence. He was a strong Unionist during the Civil War.

CATT, CARRIE CLINTON LANE CHAPMAN (*b. Ripon, Wis., 1859; d. New Rochelle, N.Y., 1947*), feminist, woman suffrage leader. Raised in northern Iowa. B.S., Iowa State College, Ames, 1880. Acquired through readings in Darwin and Herbert Spencer a belief in evolutionary progress through social change which served her thereafter as a guide to interpretation of history and a philosophy of action. She read law for a year, but became principal of the Mason City, Iowa, high school. Superintendent, Mason City schools, 1883, a post necessarily, although reluctantly, surrendered two years later (Feb. 12, 1885) when she married Leo Chapman, owner and editor of the *Mason City Republican*. As assistant editor of her husband's newspaper, she attended the 1885 convention of the Iowa Suffrage Association, and readily converted to the suffrage cause.

In 1886 Chapman died in California. Stranded in San Francisco, she found work on a trade paper and saw at first hand the wretched exploitation of working women. A year later an emotional crisis precipitated by frustration and despair ended in a resolve to devote her life to the emancipation of women. Became recording secretary of the Iowa Suffrage Association and discovered her talent for organizational work.

In 1890 Carrie Chapman went to Washington, D.C., as an Iowa delegate to the historic national convention that reunited the suffrage movement as the National American Woman Suffrage Association (NAWSA). Susan B. Anthony engaged her to campaign in South Dakota for an approaching suffrage referendum. Carrie Chapman married George William Catt on June 10, 1890. He signed jointly with her a legally attested document providing that she would spend four months each year in suffrage work. At his death in 1905, he left her financially independent, able to devote the rest of her life to the woman suffrage movement.

From 1890 to 1895 Carrie Chapman Catt participated in a series of state suffrage referenda and congressional hearings on the federal suffrage amendment, under the tutelage of Anthony. At Catt's suggestion, a national organization committee was set up in 1895 to intensify efforts to mobilize widespread latent support for woman suffrage. As chairman, she was director of operations. In 1900 she succeeded Anthony as president of NAWSA.

During the four years of her presidency, Carrie Chapman Catt worked vigorously to shift NAWSA emphasis from propaganda to political action. Swinging the organization into the orbit of the progressive movement, she won allies among liberal and "social justice" reformers of both sexes. Withdrew from the presidency in 1904 because of her husband's ill health. After his death Catt divided her energies between suffrage activities in New York and international feminism. In 1908, she organized the New York Woman Suffrage party. In 1913 the council served as the nucleus of the Empire State Campaign Committee, led by Catt, which conducted the brilliant though unsuccessful referendum cam-

paign of 1915. Two years later an intensified effort by the same disciplined organization was successful in enfranchising the women of New York State.

Beginning in 1902, she had encouraged a sharper focus on woman suffrage among the affiliates of the International Council of Women, preparing the way for the establishment of the International Woman Suffrage Alliance at the Berlin Congress in 1904. Elected president, Catt was the acknowledged leader and chief fund-raiser of the IWSA until 1923, presiding over congresses in Copenhagen (1906), London (1908), Amsterdam (1909), Stockholm (1911), and Budapest (1913). Accompanied by the Dutch feminist Dr. Aletta Jacobs, she toured the world (1911–13), organizing feminists in several Asian and African countries, and increasing the affiliates of IWSA from 9 to 32. In January 1915, Catt joined Jane Addams in Organizing the Woman's Peace party to ally with a similar European coalition. This group unsuccessfully pressed for mediation to end the war through a conference of neutrals. In 1922–23 she made an organizing trip to South American countries.

Catt returned to the national presidency in December 1915. She led the opposition to Alice Paul's demand that all other efforts be abandoned in order to concentrate on the federal woman suffrage amendment. The 1914 convention formally repudiated Paul's approach and thus forced Paul and her followers to withdraw from NAWSA and thereafter go their own way as the National Woman's party.

Her judgment and tact, enhanced by the realization of the part women voters had played in his reelection and reinforced by the string of suffrage victories in 1917 and 1918, including the spectacular New York victory, won President Wilson's commitment to the suffrage amendment. In 1914 Catt was named chief legatee of Miriam Florence Folline Leslie's publishing fortune, amounting to $2 million. Nearly $1 million became available to suffrage workers in 1917 and was spent in a nationwide educational and publicity campaign, creating the momentum that carried the movement to victory. The amendment was proclaimed part of the Constitution on Aug. 26, 1920. Catt was instrumental in establishing the League of Women Voters (1920).

CATTELL, ALEXANDER GILMORE (*b. Salem, N.J., 1816; d. 1894*), banker, politician. Moved to Philadelphia, 1846; president of Corn Exchange Bank, 1858–71. U.S. senator, Republican, from Pennsylvania, 1866–72.

CATTELL, JAMES MCKEEN (*b. Easton, Pa., 1860; d. Lancaster, Pa., 1944*), psychologist, editor. Son of William C. Cattell; nephew of Alexander G. Cattell. Graduated Lafayette College, 1880. Studied at Göttingen with Lotze and at Leipzig with Wundt, for whom he served as first assistant in charge of the laboratory, 1885–86. The experiments from which he drew his doctoral dissertation centered on the reaction-time experiment; varying the method and applying it to a number of basic problems, he produced seminal studies in reading, perception, and association. He then made further studies at St. John's College, Cambridge, where he extended his experiments on association and made the acquaintance of Francis Galton and other leaders in his field. In January 1889, he returned permanently to the United States, receiving from the University of Pennsylvania appointment to the first American professorship wholly in psychology. In 1890 he first called attention to the need to make mental tests on large numbers of individuals in order to get accurate measures of the constancy of certain mental processes, and also to provide the individual with a gauge of his aptitudes and capacities. He became professor of psychology at Columbia University in 1891. During his tenure there, he made several other experimental contributions, the most important being the "order of merit" method, used in arranging judgments of value in psychophysics and aesthetics. A leading influence in making American psychology an experimental science, occupied with method, quantification of data, and the statistical treatment of results. He led also in the American reorientation of Wundt's psychology of the generalized mind into study of the range of behavior of individuals an groups under varying conditions. His chief failing was his blindness to the principles which characterize the organism functioning as a whole.

In 1894, he founded (with J. M. Baldwin) *Psychological Review*, serving as editor until 1902. Also in 1894, he bought the weekly magazine *Science*. Founded *American Men of Science* (1906), *School and Society* (1915), and *Leaders in Education* (1932). Attempted radical reform of the American scientific community. His efforts to expand the power of Columbia faculty and students resulted in his dismissal in 1917. The affair became a celebrated case of academic freedom. Thereafter concentrated on his publications and the American Association for the Advancement of Science.

CATTELL, WILLIAM CASSADAY (*b. Salem, N.J., 1827; d. 1898*), Presbyterian clergyman. President, Lafayette College, Easton, Pa., 1863–83.

CAWEIN, MADISON JULIUS (*b. Louisville, Ky., 1865; d. 1914*), poet. Author of 36 volumes of verse expressing a romantic idealism and a love of nature.

CAYTON, HORACE ROSCOE (*b. Seattle, Wash., 1903; d. Paris, France, 1970*), sociologist and writer. Studied at the University of Washington (B.A., 1931), then went to the University of Chicago on a fellowship, where he began to distinguish himself as a researcher, administrator, and writer in what would be called today "black studies." He was a special assistant to Secretary of the Interior Harold Ickes (1934–35), with the task of studying the affect of New Deal legislation on black workers. He taught at Fisk University (1935–36), then headed a research unit funded by the Works Progress Administration (1936–39) that studied the black community in Chicago. From 1939 to 1949 Cayton directed Chicago's Parkway Community House, and he wrote for the *Pittsburgh Courier* through the 1940's and early 1950's. Troubled by alcoholism, he held a variety of jobs through the 1950's and 1960's. He was a frequent lecturer at universities and cultural symposia, and at the time of his death he had begun to research a biography of his friend Richard Wright. Cayton wrote *Black Workers and the New Unions* (1939, with George S. Mitchell), *Black Metropolis* (1945, with St. Clair Drake), and his autobiography, *Long Old Road* (1965).

CAYVAN, GEORGIA (*b. Bath, Maine, 1858; d. Flushing, N.Y., 1906*), actress. Made professional debut at Boston, Mass., 1879; leading lady of the Lyceum Theatre Stock Company, New York, 1888–94.

CAZENOVE, THÉOPHILE (*b. Amsterdam, Holland, 1740; d. Paris, France, 1811*), financier. Arrived in America, 1790, as agent for Dutch speculators in U.S. state and federal securities; persuaded them to buy wild lands in western New York and Pennsylvania commonly called the "Holland Purchase" which he developed until 1799. Cazenovia, N.Y., is named for him.

CELESTIN, OSCAR "PAPA" (*b. Napoleonville, La., 1884; d. New Orleans, La., 1954*), jazz cornet and trumpet player. New Orleans based, Celestin performed with the Tuxedo Hall Band, one of the most famous in that city. At times the band included such famous trumpeters as Louis Armstrong and Joe "King" Oliver. Celestin was instrumental in the jazz revival in New Orleans after World War II, and in 1952, he played at the White House for President Eisenhower.

CÉLORON DE BLAINVILLE, PIERRE JOSEPH DE (*b. Montreal, Canada, 1693; d. 1759*), explorer. Commanded at Michilimackinac, 1734–42; at Detroit, Niagara, and Crown Point, 1742–47. In June 1749, he headed an expedition down the Ohio to expel English traders from the region and assert French claims there.

CERMAK, ANTON JOSEPH (*b. Kladno, Czechoslovakia, 1873; d. Miami, Fla., 1933*), Democratic mayor of Chicago, killed by an assassin's bullet aimed at President-elect F. D. Roosevelt.

CERRÉ, JEAN GABRIEL (*b. Montreal, Canada, 1734; d. St. Louis, Mo., 1805*), merchant, fur trader. Established at Kaskaskia, Ill., by 1755; he became one of the wealthiest men in the Illinois country. Removed to St. Louis *ante* 1780.

CESARE, OSCAR EDWARD (*b. Linköping, Ostergötland, Sweden, 1883; d. Stamford, Conn., 1948*), cartoonist, artist, journalist. Studied art in Paris; came to the United States about 1901; pursued studies in Buffalo, N.Y., then went to Chicago, Ill., as reporter and artist for several newspapers, including the *Chicago Tribune*. Influenced by Doré, Daumier, Boardman Robinson. Moved to New York, where he worked in succession on staffs of the *World*, *Sun*, and *Evening Post*; also contributed to *Outlook* and other magazines. A reader of history and a man of shrewd political insight and strong, unorthodox opinions, he was particularly effective during the World War I period. In 1920, he became a regular contributor to the *New York Times* Sunday magazine section.

CESNOLA, LUIGI PALMA DI (*b. Rivarolo, Italy, 1832; d. 1904*), soldier, archaeologist. Came to America, 1860. Appointed U.S. consul at Cyprus after distinguished service in Civil War. Between 1865 and 1876, at his own expense, he pioneered in excavating ancient sites on the island, digging up 35,573 objects. From 1879 until his death he was director of the Metropolitan Museum of Art, New York City.

CHACE, ELIZABETH BUFFUM (*b. Providence, R.I., 1806; d. Central Falls, R.I., 1899*), antislavery and woman-suffrage advocate. Daughter of Arnold Buffum.

CHADBOURNE, PAUL ANSEL (*b. North Berwick, Maine, 1823; d. New York, N.Y., 1883*), educator. President, Massachusetts Agricultural College, 1866 and 1882–83; University of Wisconsin, 1867–70; Williams College, 1872–81.

CHADWICK, FRENCH ENSOR (*b. Morgantown, W.Va., 1844; d. New York, N.Y., 1919*), naval officer. Graduated U.S. Naval Academy (Newport), 1864. Active in naval intelligence, *post* 1882; commanded USS *New York* in Spanish-American War; president, Naval War College, 1900–03; retired as rear admiral, 1903.

CHADWICK, GEORGE WHITEFIELD (*b. Lowell, Mass., 1854; d. 1931*), composer. Studied at New England Conservatory of Music, 1872–75, and in Germany, 1877–80. Teacher and later director of the New England Conservatory, 1882–1931. Belongs as a composer to the so-called New England Group, which reflected the influence of the classic-romantic German composers of the 19th century. His major works include the *Rip Van Winkle Overture*, *Melpomene*, and *Ecce Jam Noctis*.

CHADWICK, HENRY (*b. Exeter, England, 1824; d. 1908*), sportsman. Came to America, 1837. A newspaperman on New York and Brooklyn dailies, he became the first important sports writer in America, 1856–86. The rules of baseball are largely his work, and he was editor of *Spalding's Official Baseball Guide*.

CHADWICK, JAMES READ (b. *Boston, Mass., 1844; d. 1905*), physician. Graduated Harvard, 1865; Harvard Medical School, 1871. For many years a gynecologist and professor of that subject at Harvard. Established Boston Medical Library, 1875.

CHADWICK, JOHN WHITE (b. *Marblehead, Mass., 1840; d. Brooklyn, N.Y., 1904*), Unitarian clergyman. Wrote extensively in favor of Darwinism; pastor in Brooklyn, N.Y.

CHAFEE, ZECHARIAH, JR. (b. *Providence, R.I., 1885; d. Cambridge, Mass., 1957*), law professor and civil libertarian. Studied at Brown University and Harvard Law School, LL.B., 1913. Taught at Harvard Law School from 1916 to 1956. In 1918, Chafee wrote an article on freedom of speech during wartime for the *New Republic*; his book *Freedom of Speech* (1920) established Chafee as one of the nation's leading civil libertarians. He chaired the American Bar Association Commission on the Bill of Rights in 1938. During World War II, he served on the Commission on Freedom of the Press, and afterward performed similar functions for the U.N.

CHAFFEE, ADNA ROMANZA (b. *Orwell, Ohio, 1842; d. Los Angeles, Calif., 1914*), soldier. Commissioned from the ranks during Civil War; served in southwest Indian campaigns, 1867–92, with 6th and 9th Cavalry. As brigadier general, 1898, he was outstanding at battle of El Caney; he later commanded the American contingent in the Boxer uprising. Promoted major general, 1901, he commanded in the Philippines; as lieutenant general, he was chief of staff of the army, 1904–06, retiring in the latter year.

CHAFFEE, ADNA ROMANZA (b. *Junction City, Kans., 1884; d. Boston, Mass., 1941*), soldier. Son of Adna R. Chaffee (1842–1914). Graduated West Point, 1906; commissioned in cavalry; graduated cavalry school, Saumur, France, 1912. Served with distinction in World War I, thereafter holding important command positions; served with operations and training division of the General Staff, 1927–31. A leader in the development of U.S. armored forces, over much internal army opposition he planned and organized an experimental unit which would act independently of other forces and be made up of tanks, motorized guns, and motorized infantry. This led to creation of the nucleus of a mechanized force in the 1st Cavalry Regiment (Mechanized) at Fort Knox, Ky., 1931 and after. In the 1934 spring maneuvers at Fort Riley, Kans., the new unit demonstrated its superiority over horse cavalry and Chaffee returned to Washington to expand it; in 1938, promoted to brigadier general, he took command of the 7th Cavalry Brigade (Mechanized). Appointed chief of an independent Armored Force in July 1940, he set up two armored divisions by October and was promoted to major general.

CHAFFEE, JEROME B. (b. *near Lockport, N.Y., 1825; d. Westchester Co., N.Y., 1886*), banker, political leader. Raised in Adrian, Mich. Migrated to Pikes Peak region, 1860, and prospered in mining operations. A founder and president of First National Bank, Denver, Colo., 1865–80; a proponent of Colorado statehood, and first U.S. senator from Colorado, Republican, 1877–79.

CHAFFEE, ROGER BRUCE (b. *Grand Rapids, Mich., 1935; d. Cape Kennedy, Fla., 1967*), naval officer and astronaut. Studied at Purdue (B.S., 1957), then commissioned an ensign in the navy. He became an astronaut trainee with the National Aeronautics and Space Administration in 1963 and in 1966 was named to the crew of the first Apollo spacecraft to be tested in flight. He died in a fire in the Apollo capsule with Virgil Grissom and Edward White.

CHAFIN, EUGENE WILDER (b. *East Troy, Wis., 1852; d. Long Beach, Calif., 1920*), lawyer, temperance leader. Prohibition party candidate for president, 1908 and 1912.

CHAILLÉ-LONG, CHARLES (b. *Princess Anne, Md., 1842; d. 1917*), explorer, lawyer. Explored upper Nile basin, 1874, as staff officer of Egyptian army. Practiced international law in Paris. Served as U.S. consul in Egypt and Korea.

CHALKLEY, THOMAS (b. *Southwark, England, 1675; d. Tortola, V.I., 1741*), Quaker minister, merchant mariner. Author of a celebrated journal, first published in *A Collection of the Works of Thos. Chalkley* (Philadelphia, 1749). Resident in or near Philadelphia, Pa., *post* 1701, he made numerous journeys "in the ministry."

CHALMERS, JAMES RONALD (b. *Halifax Co., Va., 1831; d. Memphis, Tenn., 1898*), lawyer. Left law practice in Mississippi to serve in Confederate forces; at end of Civil War commanded 1st Division of Forrest's cavalry. An aggressive figure in Mississippi politics, 1876–86, he served as congressman. Democrat and Independent, 1877–81 and 1884–85.

CHALMERS, WILLIAM JAMES (b. *Chicago, Ill., 1852; d. Chicago, 1938*), industrialist. Executive officer of Fraser & Chalmers Co., and Allis-Chalmers Co., manufacturers of power machinery.

CHAMBERLAIN, ALEXANDER FRANCIS (b. *Kenninghall, England, 1865; d. Worcester, Mass., 1914*), anthropologist. Graduated University of Toronto, 1886; Clark University, Ph.D., 1892. A teacher of anthropology at Clark University, 1893–1914; editor, *Journal of American Folk-Lore*.

CHAMBERLAIN, CHARLES JOSEPH (b. *near Sullivan, Ohio, 1863; d. Chicago, Ill., 1943*), botanist. A.B., Oberlin College, 1888; Ph.D., University of Chicago, 1896. Taught botany at Chicago *post* 1897, rising to professor of botany, 1915–29. His major area of research was the cycads, which he studied and collected in many parts of the world. His books, which have been described as "keystones in the arch of morphological literature," include *Methods in Plant Histology* (1901); *Morphology of Gymnosperms* (1910), expanded from an earlier work in collaboration with John M. Coulter; and *The Living Cycads* (1919).

CHAMBERLAIN, DANIEL HENRY (b. *West Brookfield, Mass., 1835; d. Charlottesville, Va., 1907*), lawyer. After Civil War service, settled in South Carolina, 1866–77; Republican governor of that state, 1874–76. Thereafter, practiced law in New York.

CHAMBERLAIN, GEORGE EARLE (b. *near Natchez, Miss., 1854; d. 1928*), lawyer. Settled in Oregon, 1876. Democratic governor of Oregon, 1902–09; U.S. senator, 1909–21; sharp critic of War Department, 1917, as chairman of Senate Military Affairs Committee.

CHAMBERLAIN, HENRY RICHARDSON (b. *Peoria, Ill., 1859; d. London, 1911*), editor and foreign correspondent. Brilliant representative of *New York Sun* in London, 1892–1911.

CHAMBERLAIN, JACOB (b. *Sharon, Conn., 1835; d. 1908*), Dutch Reformed minister. Raised in Hudson, Ohio; missionary to India, 1860–1908.

CHAMBERLAIN, JOSEPH PERKINS (b. *Cleveland, Ohio, 1873; d. New York, N.Y., 1951*), lawyer. Studied at Harvard, the University of California, and Hastings Law School in San Francisco (1898). He later studied international law at the University of Paris. Chamberlain helped establish and fund the Legislative Drafting Research Fund at Columbia in 1911, director, 1918–51. As a member of Columbia's faculty, he was influential in the improvement in the writing of legislation, especially in the U.S. government; his work in Washington led to the establishment of offices of counsel for the committees of the House and Senate. In 1927, he helped draft part of the Kellogg-Briand Pact.

CHAMBERLAIN, JOSHUA LAWRENCE (*b. Brewer, Maine, 1828; d. Portland, Maine, 1914*), educator. Graduated Bowdoin, 1852. Teacher of modern languages et al., Bowdoin, 1856–62; president of Bowdoin, 1871–83. Received the Medal of Honor for gallantry at Gettysburg; promoted brigadier general on the field at Petersburg; mustered out, 1866, as brevet major general of volunteers. Republican governor of Maine, 1866–70.

CHAMBERLAIN, MELLEN (*b. Pembroke, N.H., 1821; d. 1900*), lawyer, jurist, historian. Graduated Dartmouth, 1844; Harvard Law School, 1848. Practiced law in Boston, Mass.; served in state legislature. Associate justice and chief justice, Boston municipal court, 1866–78. Librarian, Boston Public Library, 1878–90. Author of numerous studies of early U.S. history.

CHAMBERLAIN, NATHAN HENRY (*b. Sandwich, Mass.,* ca. *1828; d. Sandwich, 1901*), Episcopal clergyman. Ordained to Unitarian ministry, 1857; to Episcopal priesthood, 1864. Served as rector of churches in Connecticut, New York, Wisconsin, and Massachusetts, 1864–89.

CHAMBERLAIN, WILLIAM ISAAC (*b. Sharon, Conn., 1837; d. 1920*), agriculturist. Brother of Jacob Chamberlain. Raised in Hudson, Ohio, where he applied scientific management to farming; elected Ohio secretary of agriculture, 1880–86. President, Iowa Agricultural College, 1886–90. Author of *Tile Drainage* (1891).

CHAMBERLIN, EDWARD HASTINGS (*b. La Conner, Wash., 1899; d. Cambridge, Mass., 1967*), economist and educator. Studied at the University of Iowa (B.S., 1920), the University of Michigan (M.A., 1924), and Harvard (Ph.D., 1927). He began teaching at Harvard in 1929, where he served as chairman of the Department of History, Government, and Economics (1939–43) and David A. Wells Professor in Political Economy (1951–63). He is best known for his theory of monopolistic competition. He wrote *The Theory of Monopolistic Competition* (1933); *The Economics of the Recovery Program* (1934), with Seymour Harris, Joseph Schumpter, and Edward Mason; *The Consumer Services of the Government* (editor, 1936); *Monopoly and Competition and Their Regulation* (editor, 1954); *Towards a More General Theory of Value* (1957); and *The Economic Analysis of Labor Union Power* (1958). In 1959 he served as a consultant to the President's Council of Economic Advisers.

CHAMBERLIN, THOMAS CROWDER (*b. Mattoon, Ill., 1843; d. 1928*), geologist. Graduated Beloit College, 1866, and attended graduate school of University of Michigan. Taught at Beloit, Columbia University, and University of Chicago; assistant state geologist of Wisconsin, 1873–76, and chief, 1877–82. Founder and editor, *Journal of Geology*, 1893–1922. Regarded as the ranking geologist of America, he made a threefold contribution to science: through research in glacial phenomena, geological climates, and in cosmic geology.

CHAMBERS, CHARLES JULIUS. *See* CHAMBERS, JAMES JULIUS.

CHAMBERS, EZEKIEL FORMAN (*b. Chestertown, Md., 1788; d. 1867*), jurist. U.S. senator, Whig, from Maryland, 1826–34; district judge and judge of state court of appeals, 1834–50.

CHAMBERS, GEORGE (*b. Chambersburg, Pa., 1786; d. Chambersburg, 1866*), lawyer. Graduated Princeton, 1804. Admitted to bar, 1807, he became expert in Pennsylvania land law.

The largest landowner in Franklin Co., he devoted much time to promotion of education and agriculture there.

CHAMBERS, JAMES JULIUS (*b. Bellefontaine, Ohio, 1850; d. 1920*), journalist. Explored headwaters of Mississippi River, 1872. On staff of *New York Herald*, 1873–89; organized Paris *Herald*, 1887. Managing editor, *New York World*, 1889–91; a free-lance writer thereafter.

CHAMBERS, JOHN (*b. Bromley Bridge, N.J., 1780; d. Paris, Ky., 1852*), lawyer, politician. Removed to Washington, Ky., 1794; admitted to practice law, 1800. Congressman, Whig, from Kentucky, 1828–29 and 1835–39. Governor, Iowa Territory, 1841–45; notably successful in handling Indian affairs.

CHAMBERS, JULIUS. *See* CHAMBERS, JAMES JULIUS.

CHAMBERS, ROBERT WILLIAM (*b. Brooklyn, N.Y., 1865; d. New York, N.Y., 1933*), novelist and illustrator. Produced 72 books, of which *Cardigan* (1901) is best remembered.

CHAMBERS, TALBOT WILSON (*b. Carlisle, Pa., 1819; d. 1896*), Dutch Reformed clergyman, theologian. Pastor at Somerville, N.J., 1840–49; a minister of Collegiate Reformed Church, New York City, 1849–96; strongly conservative.

CHAMBERS, WHITTAKER (*b. Philadelphia, Pa., 1901; d. Westminster, Md., 1961*), journalist, writer, one-time Soviet agent. Born Jay Vivian Chambers, he attended Columbia (1920–23, 1924–25), where he impressed literary circles with his poetry, drama, and stories. In 1925 he joined the Communist party and began organizing and teaching for the party and writing for the *Daily Worker*. Chambers became a gifted translator of works from German and French and mastered twelve languages. He left the Communist party in 1929 and returned in 1931, becoming editor of the *New Masses*. He was tapped for underground work in 1932 and in 1934 began nurturing a group of influential Soviet agents in Washington, D.C., who passed classified government information to Moscow. Chambers organized international networks for Soviet military intelligence, traveled to Russia for training, and was decorated as an officer in the Red Army. Disillusioned with Communism, he left the underground (1938) and soon began writing for *Time* magazine, quickly rising to the post of senior editor. Appearing before the House Committee on Un-American Activities in 1948, Chambers alleged that dozens of officials in the executive branch, including Alger Hiss, were Communists or party sympathizers. His autobiography, *Witness*, was published in 1952. Chambers was an editor of William F. Buckley's *National Review*, 1957–60. He also became a confidant of Richard Nixon.

CHAMPLAIN, SAMUEL DE (*b. Brouage, France,* ca. *1567; d. Quebec, Canada, 1635*), explorer, founder of Canada. Son of a naval captain; as a young man saw service in French army and navy. Commanding ship *St. Julien* on an enforced voyage to New Spain, 1599–1601, he had an unusual opportunity to visit Spanish possessions in the West Indies, Mexico, Central America, and northern South America. His elaborate report to Henry IV of France on his observations won him a pension, a patent of nobility, and the king's encouragement to attempt foundation of a permanent colony in North America. In 1603 he made a preliminary voyage thither in company with a fur-trading expedition, exploring the St. Lawrence River as far as Lachine Rapids and publishing his observations of the country and its inhabitants on his return. Under patronage of the Sieur de Monts (who disapproved of a settlement on the St. Lawrence and directed the choice of a warmer region), Champlain sailed in 1604 and founded a colony on Douchet Island at the mouth of the St. Croix in present-day New Brunswick. As this site proved unhealthy, he moved the colony to Port Royal, Nova Scotia, in 1605, where it remained until 1607. During this time, he was the mainstay of the colony; he also made three exploring expeditions along the coast of New England, discovering and naming Mount Desert and reaching as far as Vineyard Sound to the southward.

Having persuaded the king to permit foundation of a colony on the St. Lawrence, Champlain founded and settled Quebec in 1608. While aiding Huron Indians in a war against their enemies the Iroquois in 1609, he entered on the lake which still bears his name and, by subduing the Iroquois with firearms, won their lasting enmity to France.

After a visit home in 1610 and the arrangement of a new charter for the colony (1611) under patronage of the Prince de Condé, he determined to explore westward in hope of finding a route to the western sea. He ascended the Ottawa River in 1613 as far as Morrison Island, and in 1615 went with some Hurons to their home on Georgian Bay; he was the first to describe, map, and name Lake Huron. Joining in another war party against the Iroquois that autumn, he crossed the east end of Lake Ontario and recognized it as source of the St. Lawrence; severely wounded in a fight with Iroquois in what is now Madison Co., N.Y., he returned home with the Hurons and spent the winter with them. He returned to France in 1616.

Thenceforward he devoted himself to the development of his colony; he spent the years 1620–24 in Canada. In 1625, he won Richelieu's interest in the colony which resulted in the formation (1627) of the Company of One Hundred Associates, a means for recruitment and equipping of new colonists. Taken prisoner during a 1629 raid on Quebec by English freebooters, Champlain remained out of New France until 1633. He then returned as governor and did not quit Canada for the remainder of his life. Jean Nicolet made his explorations of 1634–35 at Champlain's direction.

Champlain was author of the description of his voyage of 1603 entitled *Des Sauvages: Les Voyages du Sieur de Champlain* (Paris, 1613), which included his map of 1612; *Voyages et Descouvertes faites en la Nouvelle France* (Paris, 1619); *Les Voyages de la Nouvelle France Occidentale dicte Canada . . . 1603 jusques en l'an 1629* (Paris, 1632), which included a map of the St. Lawrence and its sources.

CHAMPLIN, JOHN DENISON (*b. 1834; d. 1915*), editor of encyclopedias and reference works, including *Cyclopedia of Painters and Paintings* (1886–87).

CHAMPLIN, JOHN WAYNE (*b. Kingston, N.Y., 1831; d. Grand Rapids, Mich., 1901*), jurist. Removed to Michigan, 1854; studied law and began practice, 1855. Elected to numerous offices in Grand Rapids, including mayor, 1867. Justice of state supreme court, 1884–90; chief justice, 1890–91.

CHAMPLIN, STEPHEN (*b. South Kingston, R.I., 1789; d. 1870*), naval officer. Cousin of Oliver H. Perry and Matthew C. Perry. Served in lake campaigns, War of 1812, including battle of Lake Erie, where he commanded the *Scorpion*; he later wrote a narrative of the battle.

CHAMPNEY, BENJAMIN (*b. New Ipswich, N.H., 1817; d. 1907*), painter. Assisted Vanderlyn on *Landing of Columbus* in the Capitol, Washington, D.C.; a follower of the Hudson River school of landscapists.

CHAMPNEY, JAMES WELLS (*b. Boston, Mass., 1843; d. 1903*), painter, illustrator. Did successful pastel portraits *post* 1885; was one of the first American painters to apply French impressionist theory of "values."

CHANCHE, JOHN MARY JOSEPH (*b. Baltimore, Md., 1795; d. Frederick City, Md., 1852*), Roman Catholic clergyman, Sulpician. Consecrated first bishop of Natchez, Miss., 1841.

CHANDLER, CHARLES FREDERICK (*b. Lancaster, Mass., 1836; d. 1925*), industrial chemist. Studied at Lawrence Scientific School, Harvard, and at Berlin and Göttingen, where he received the doctorate. Returning to America, he taught chemistry, geology, and mineralogy at Columbia University; in 1864 he was a cofounder of the Columbia School of Mines, of which he was later dean. He succeeded Charles A. Joy as head of the chemistry department at Columbia and remained in that post until 1910. His brilliant work as a teacher was only a small part of his total achievement. He was a leading authority on water supplies, sanitation, oil refining, and assaying. He gave outstanding service to New York City on its Board of Health, 1866–83, exposing food adulteration and abating nuisances. His valuable contributions to applied chemistry, in the words of a 1920 honors citation, placed the entire world in his debt.

CHANDLER, ELIZABETH MARGARET (*b. Centre, Del., 1807; d. Lenawee Co., Mich., 1834*), author. Contributor of verse and prose to the *Genius of Universal Emancipation*; author of *Essays, Philanthropic and Moral* (1836) and *Poetical Works* (edited by Benjamin Lundy, 1836), both published posthumously.

CHANDLER, HARRY (*b. Landaff, N.H., 1864; d. Los Angeles, Calif., 1944*), newspaper publisher, real estate developer. Removed permanently to Southern California for reasons of health, 1885. Beginning as a clerk in circulation department of the *Los Angeles Times*, he bought and operated several newspaper distribution routes as an independent contractor; in 1894, he married the daughter of Harrison Gray Otis (1837–1917), owner of the *Times*, and was appointed its business manager. Assuming more and more responsibility, he succeeded Otis as president and publisher, 1917. Also successfully speculated in real estate in Southern California and Mexico. Innovative and enterprising, he built his paper up to a commanding position as an advertising medium; his most important achievement as a journalist was his use of the press to boost the qualities of his city and section. A conservative Republican and a power in local politics, he fought labor unions (although himself paying wages above union scale). Apparently in response, in 1910 the *Times* building was blown up by a bomb placed beneath the floor under his desk. He also opposed public ownership of utilities, and constantly criticized the New Deal. After retirement as president and publisher in 1941, he remained active as chairman of the board of the Times-Mirror Company.

CHANDLER, JOHN (*b. Epping, N.H., 1762; d. 1841*), soldier. After service in Revolution, settled in then district of Maine, 1784. A zealous militiaman, he was commissioned brigadier general in War of 1812 and served in northern campaigns. Chosen U.S. senator, Democrat, from state of Maine, 1820–29.

CHANDLER, JOHN SCUDDER (*b. Madura, India, 1849; d. Madura, 1934*), Congregationalist missionary; editor of the *Tamil Lexicon*; aided in revising the Old and New Testaments in Tamil.

CHANDLER, JOSEPH RIPLEY (*b. Kingston, Mass., 1792; d. Philadelphia, Pa., 1880*), journalist. Editor, *Gazette of the United States* and *North American*, 1822–47; editor, *Graham's Magazine*, 1843–49. Congressman, Whig, from Pennsylvania, 1849–55. U.S. minister to Naples, 1858–61. A strong foe of religious intolerance and a prison reformer.

CHANDLER, JULIAN ALVIN CARROLL (*b. Caroline Co., Va., 1872; d. 1934*), educator, president of the College of William and Mary, 1919–34.

CHANDLER, PELEG WHITMAN (*b. New Gloucester, Maine, 1816; d. 1889*), lawyer. Prominent in Boston civic life, 1840–65, and considered the best jury pleader of his time in Massachusetts.

CHANDLER, RAYMOND THORNTON (*b. Chicago, Ill., 1888; d. La Jolla, Calif., 1959*), novelist. Author of many stories, Chandler is remembered for his mystery novels which introduced the character of Philip Marlowe to American fiction. Books include *The Big Sleep* (1939), *Farewell, My Lovely* (1940), *The Little Sister* (1949), and *The Long Goodbye* (1953). His screenplays include an adaptation of James M. Cain's *Double Indemnity* (1943), which won him an Academy Award nomination. President of the Mystery Writers of America, 1959. Chandler's works are considered by many to transcend the mystery book and become artistic studies of the criminal milieu.

CHANDLER, SETH CARLO (*b. Boston, Mass., 1846; d. Wellesley, Mass., 1913*), astronomer. Constructor of the almucantar; editor of the *Astronomical Journal*; worked for many years on demonstration of the variation of latitude.

CHANDLER, THOMAS BRADBURY (*b. Woodstock, Conn., 1726; d. Elizabethtown, N.J., 1790*), Anglican clergyman. Graduated Yale, 1745; ordained, 1751. Rector, St. John's, Elizabethtown, N.J. A leading advocate for an American episcopacy, he was a Loyalist in the Revolution; he spent the years 1775–85 in England, but returned to his parish in the latter year. He was author of several pamphlets on the episcopal question, and possibly the author of the Tory tract *What Think Ye of the Congress Now* (1775).

CHANDLER, WILLIAM EATON (*b. Concord, N.H., 1835; d. Concord, 1917*), lawyer, politician, journalist. Active in state politics, he held office in Navy and Treasury departments under Lincoln and Johnson and was a prominent Republican party strategist, *post* 1867. As secretary of the navy, 1882–85, he established program of steel warship construction but was severely criticized for its early failure in details. He was U.S. senator from New Hampshire, 1887–1901.

CHANDLER, ZACHARIAH (*b. Bedford, N.H., 1813; d. 1879*), politician. Removed to Detroit, Mich., 1833, and grew rich in trade, banking, and land speculation. At first a Whig, he was a signer of the call for the first Republican state convention at Jackson, Mich., 1854. He served as U.S. senator from Michigan, 1857–75, and again in 1879; allied with the Radical Republican and antislavery element of his party, he pressed for the fullest prosecution of the war against the seceding states and regarded the Reconstruction acts as too lax. His use of federal patronage to sustain his political power and his despotic partisan control of the Republican machine in Michigan made him for years the undisputed boss of the state. Defeated, 1874, for reelection to the Senate, he was made secretary of the interior in 1875 and reorganized the department by wholesale dismissals for alleged dishonesty or incompetence, leaving office in March 1877.

CHANEY, LON (*b. Colorado Springs, Colo., 1883; d. 1930*), screen actor, "the Man of a Thousand Faces." Distinguished by great skill as a pantomimist and makeup artist.

CHANFRAU, FRANCIS S. (*b. New York, N.Y., 1824; d. 1884*), actor. Achieved fame in 1848 as "Mose" in *A Glance at New York*; starred in *Kit, the Arkansas Traveller* for 12 seasons *post* 1872.

CHANFRAU, HENRIETTA BAKER (*b. Philadelphia, Pa., 1837; d. Burlington, N.J., 1909*), actress. Wife of Francis S. Chanfrau. Active in the theater, 1854–84; "discoverer" of Mary Anderson.

CHANG AND ENG (*b. Meklong, Siam, 1811; d. 1874*), "the Siamese Twins." Made extensive tours of the United States and Europe; settled as farmers in North Carolina. Married sisters Sarah and Adelaide Yates in 1843. Chang had ten children, Eng had nine. Eng awoke during the night of Jan. 16, 1874 to find his brother dead beside him; he himself died, perhaps from fright, a few hours later.

CHANNING, EDWARD (*b. Dorchester, Mass., 1856; d. 1931*), historian. Son of William E. Channing (1818–1901); nephew of Margaret Fuller. Stimulated at Harvard by the teaching of Henry Adams, Channing took his doctorate in 1880 and began his career as teacher of American history there in 1883. His essay of that year, "Town and County Government in the English Colonies," won a prize, was printed in the Johns Hopkins Studies series, and was the first paper delivered at the first meeting of the American Historical Association. Disliked for his personality but respected for his scholarly integrity and for the worth of what he taught, he continued to teach until 1929. Very early in his career, he had determined to write a history of the United States which should be all his own, relating what had happened, why, and what it meant, with emphasis on deflating popular myths and the social, economic, and intellectual factors. Working on a strict research regimen, he concentrated on this task, publishing the first volume (*The Planting of a New Nation in the New World: 1000–1660*) in 1905. Succeeding volumes appeared at approximately four-year intervals. *The War for Southern Independence* (1925) was the sixth volume; much of volume seven was ready for publication when he died. He was author also of several popular textbooks.

CHANNING, EDWARD TYRRELL (*b. Newport, R.I., 1790; d. Cambridge, Mass., 1856*), brother of Walter and William E. Channing (1780–1842). Boylston professor of rhetoric at Harvard, 1819–51.

CHANNING, WALTER (*b. Newport, R.I., 1786; d. 1876*), physician. Brother of Edward T. and William E. Channing (1780–1842). Dean of Harvard Medical School, 1819–47; pioneered with ether in childbirth cases.

CHANNING, WILLIAM ELLERY (*b. Newport, R.I., 1780; d. 1842*), Unitarian clergyman, was descended from old New England stock. As a student at Harvard he was described as serious, overthoughtful, and inclined to introspection, but acutely sensitive to conditions around him. After graduation, 1798, he spent a year and a half as tutor in a Richmond, Va., family. During this period he acquired habits of overwork and ascetic discipline which undermined his health. Upon his return to Newport, Channing turned to theology. He continued his studies while serving *post* 1802 as a "regent" or proctor at Harvard. Ordained and installed as minister of the Federal Street Church, Boston, in 1803, he retained his pastorate until his death. He married his cousin, Ruth Gibbs, in 1814. Channing was by nature a Broad Churchman who accepted Christianity as a way of life and was eager to persuade others to walk in it. He had no new doctrines to propose. His real contribution to theology is expressed in the inscription on his statue in the Boston Public Gardens: "He breathed into theology a humane spirit." Searching the Christian Scriptures for support of the Calvinism in which he had been reared, he found there no justification for belief in a "jealous" God, a mankind conceived in iniquity, the vicarious sacrifice of an innocent victim as atonement for "sin" in which man's will had no part, or election by grace. Instead, he preached a gospel of the goodness of God, the essential virtue and perfectability of man, and the freedom of the will, with its consequent responsibility for action. He hesitated to adopt the name Unitarian for fear that the formation of a new group with a distinctive name would soon produce a "Unitarian orthodoxy" as rigid as the old, but when he recognized that the movement had gone beyond his control, he devoted himself to it and became its leader. In 1819 he preached a sermon defining the position of the Unitarian party and defending the right of its members to Christian fellowship. In 1820 he organized the Berry Street Conference of liberal ministers, out of which developed, in 1825, the American Unitarian Association.

In 1822 poor health caused him to take a prolonged vacation in Europe; after his return Channing began to devote much of his energy to writing. His essays on Milton, Fénelon, and Napoleon had wide circulation. In *Self-Culture* (1838) Channing made a plea for adult education and advocated the policy of setting apart the funds derived from the sale of public lands to support public education. The influence of Channing on American literature was very direct. Emerson, Bryant, Longfellow, Lowell, and Holmes were all closely associated with the Unitarian movement, and acknowledged their indebtedness to Channing. In his *Remarks on American Literature* (1830), Channing urged American writers to find inspiration in what is characteristic of their own land rather than to imitate English models.

Politics was always of interest to Channing. His early associations were with the Federalists, but the trend of his own thought allied him with Jefferson rather than with Hamilton. He was conscious of tremendous revolutionary forces at work in society. Channing held slavery to be an unspeakable evil; but he considered war to be also an evil, and civil war the most dreadful of all wars to contemplate. He was attacked by both southerners and northerners for his views on the slavery question, but his addresses (e.g., *Slavery*, 1835) did much to prepare people to understand and follow Abraham Lincoln. He was also a pioneer in the modern movement against war, and the Massachusetts Peace Society was organized in his study. In his discussion of temperance, the condition of laborers, and public education, Channing was clearly in advance of his time; his views were surprisingly anticipatory of the thought of present-day social workers.

CHANNING, WILLIAM ELLERY (*b. Boston, Mass., 1818; d. 1901*), poet. Son of Walter Channing; friend of Thoreau, Emerson, Hawthorne. Wrote the first biography of Thoreau (1873).

CHANNING, WILLIAM FRANCIS (*b. Boston, Mass., 1820; d. 1901*), inventor. Son of William E. Channing (1780–1842). With Moses G. Farmer invented magnetic-electric fire-alarm telegraph from which the modern fire-alarm system has evolved.

CHANNING, WILLIAM HENRY (*b. Boston, Mass., 1810; d. London, England, 1884*), Unitarian clergyman, reformer. Nephew of William E. Channing (1780–1842), whose biography he wrote in 1848.

CHANUTE, OCTAVE (*b. Paris, France, 1832; d. 1910*), civil engineer, aerial navigator. Came to America as a child; educated in New York City. Successful in engineering career with western railroads and as private consultant, his major contribution was in aerial navigation. Studying the work of Otto and Gustav Lilienthal, Chanute made in 1896–97 probably the first scientific gliding experiments in America; he designed the Chanute biplane, upon which the Wrights largely modeled their first glider. He wrote extensively on aerial navigation and on the engineering problems of flight.

CHAPELLE, DICKEY (*b. Shorewood, Wis., 1918; d. near Chulai, Vietnam, 1965*), photojournalist and war correspondent. Born Georgette Louis Meyer, she attended Massachusetts Institute of Technology for one year, then took flying lessons and began to study photography. She worked as a free-lance photojournalist and in 1942 became a war correspondent for *Look* magazine. In 1945 she was sent to the Pacific by Fawcett Publications as a

photographer. In 1946–47 she was an associate editor of *Seventeen* magazine. During the next six years she worked with her husband, photographer Tony Chapelle, to document the war devastation in Europe and the Middle East. During the winter of 1956–57 she was sent by *Life* magazine and the International Rescue Committee to photograph Hungarian refugees; she wound up spending seven weeks in Hungarian jails. In the late 1950's she photographed military activities in Algeria, Lebanon, and Cuba. She published her autobiography, *What's a Woman Doing Here?*, in 1962. While photographing combat in Vietnam for such publications as *Reader's Digest* and *National Geographic*, she was killed in a mine explosion.

CHAPELLE, PLACIDE LOUIS (*b. Runes, France, 1842; d. New Orleans, La., 1905*), Catholic archbishop of New Orleans, 1898–1905; apostolic delegate to Cuba, Puerto Rico, and the Philippines.

CHAPIN, AARON LUCIUS (*b. Hartford, Conn., 1817; d. 1892*), Congregational clergyman. First president of Beloit College, Wisconsin, 1850–86.

CHAPIN, ALONZO BOWEN (*b. Somers, Conn., 1808; d. Hartford, Conn., 1858*), Episcopal clergyman. Wrote extensively on biblical and local history; outstanding work a *View of the Organization and Order of the Primitive Church* (1842).

CHAPIN, CALVIN (*b. Chicopee, Mass., 1763; d. 1851*), Congregational clergyman. A founder of the American Board of Foreign Missions and a pioneer in the temperance cause. Pastor, Wethersfield, Conn., 1794–1851.

CHAPIN, CHARLES VALUE (*b. Providence, R.I., 1856; d. Providence, 1941*), public health officer, epidemiologist. B.A., Brown University, 1876. Began medical study with his father and another local physician; studied also at New York College of Physicians and Surgeons, and at Bellevue Hospital Medical College, under William H. Welch, M.D., 1879. Impatient with private practice, he welcomed appointment as Providence superintendent of health, 1884–1932. He was also city registrar *post* 1888. Helped establish first (1888) municipal bacteriological laboratory in the United States and made its work the practical basis of his fight to control disease. He made careful field studies and statistical analyses of the incidence of common infectious diseases, concluding that they were spread principally by contact (*The Sources and Modes of Infection*, 1910). Providence City Hospital became a model for similar U.S. institutions, and his ideas formed much of the scientific underpinning of the modern public health movement. His *Report on State Public Health Work* (1916) had important influence in reforming public health administration and methods.

CHAPIN, CHESTER WILLIAM (*b. Ludlow, Mass., 1798; d. Springfield, Mass., 1883*), railroad promoter. Active in development of transportation in the Connecticut Valley, president of Boston and Albany Railroad, 1854–77.

CHAPIN, EDWIN HUBBELL (*b. Union Village, N.Y., 1814; d. 1880*), Universalist clergyman. Eloquent preacher and voluminous writer. The Church of the Divine Paternity, New York, N.Y., was his principal pastorate.

CHAPIN, HENRY DWIGHT (*b. Steubenville, Ohio, 1857; d. Bronxville, N.Y., 1942*), pediatrician, social reformer. Raised in Trenton, N.J., and New York City. B.S., Princeton, 1877; studied medicine with Stephen Smith and at New York College of Physicians and Surgeons, M.D., 1881. Entering practice in 1884, he began in 1885 to teach a course in disease of children at New York Post-Graduate Medical School and Hospital, and was professor of that subject there, 1886–1920. Observing the special problems of nutrition and health of poor children from the tenements, he began a social service unit at the hospital, 1890; also held that society had a duty to "strengthen the weak for more successful effort," which inspired his zeal for proper early nourishment of infants. His most significant contributions to infant nutrition were recognition of an inability to digest protein and the intestinal origin of acidosis. Advocated placement of foundlings and neglected convalescents in foster homes. He and his wife nurtured some 98 infants in their own home before adoptive parents assumed their care. This work developed into the Alice Chapin Nursery, which in 1943 was merged into the Spence-Chapin Adoption Service.

CHAPIN, JAMES PAUL (*b. New York, N.Y., 1889; d. New York, 1964*), ornithologist. Enthusiastic about natural history from his boyhood, he began studying biology at Columbia in 1906. From 1909 to 1915 he was in Africa with the American Museum of Natural History's Belgian Congo Expedition. Upon returning to New York he became an assistant in the museum's ornithology department. He returned to Columbia (B.A., 1916; M.A., 1917), then served in France during World War I. Chapin returned to the museum in 1919, serving as associate curator, 1923–48. Most of his time was devoted to studying the bird materials brought back from the Belgian Congo in 1915. He received a Ph.D. from Columbia in 1932. His four-volume *Birds of the Belgian Congo* (1932–54) was a major contribution to African ornithology.

CHAPIN, ROY DIKEMAN (*b. Lansing, Mich., 1880; d. Detroit, Mich., 1936*), automobile manufacturer. Worked for the Olds Motor Works, 1901–06. Determined to head his own company, Chapin and Howard E. Coffin secured financial backing for a car designed by Coffin, and achieved financial independence in 1910 with the acquisition of the Hudson Motor Car Co. As president, 1910–23, Chapin introduced the popular-priced Essex, popularized the closed car, and reorganized Hudson's finances; resumed presidency of the firm in 1933. He devoted much time and effort to the cause of good roads. An energetic individualist and convincing speaker, he served as U.S. secretary of commerce from July 1932 to March 1933.

CHAPLIN, JEREMIAH (*b. Rowley, Mass., 1776; d. Hamilton, N.Y., 1841*), Baptist clergyman. As president (1817–33) of Waterville College, Maine, laid foundations for later success of Colby College.

CHAPLIN, RALPH HOSEA (*b. Ames, Kans., 1887; d. Tacoma, Wash., 1961*), radical editor, poet, songwriter, and commercial artist. Worked as an apprentice commercial artist at the American Art School and studied at the Chicago Art Institute. Having become a socialist as a teenager, he became an illustrator for the *International Socialist Review* and a member of the board of directors (1908–13) of the Charles H. Kerr Publishing Company. In 1913 he joined the Industrial Workers of the World (IWW, or "Wobblies") and contributed regularly to its paper, *Solidarity*. He became a close friend of IWW leader "Big Bill" Haywood and wrote the words to the most famous American labor song, "Solidarity Forever" (1915). In 1917 he became editor of *Solidarity*, and that same year a collection of his poems about striking coal miners, *When the Leaves Come Out*, was published. With other IWW leaders, he was convicted in 1918 of conspiracy to violate the wartime espionage and sedition acts, for which he served a prison term (1921–23). A collection of his prison poems was published as *Bars and Shadows* (1922). Chaplin joined the Communist party in 1919, but broke with Communism in 1928 and became a critic of President Roosevelt and the Congress of Industrial Organizations. He became an editor for the American Federation of Labor. His

autobiography, *Wobbly: The Rough and Tumble Story of an American Radical* foreshadowed the anticommunist hysteria of the McCarthy era. In his final years he was curator at the Washington State Historical Society.

CHAPMAN, ALVAN WENTWORTH (*b. Southampton, Mass., 1809; d. Apalachicola, Fla., 1899*), physician, botanist. Leader in southern botany for fifty years; author of pioneering manual, *Flora of the Southern States* (1860).

CHAPMAN, FRANK MICHLER (*b. West Englewood, N.J., 1864; d. New York, N.Y., 1945*), ornithologist. Graduating from Englewood Academy in 1880, he worked for a bank, 1880–86, but devoted his free time to the study of birds. Employed on the staff of the American Museum of Natural History *post* 1887, he rose through the curatorial ranks to be chairman of the Department of Birds, 1920–42. Founder and editor of *Bird-Lore* magazine, 1899–1935. Major innovation was the creation of "habitat groups"—specimens mounted in natural attitudes in a lifelike reproduction of their actual habitat. Prolific author.

CHAPMAN, HENRY CADWALADER (*b. Philadelphia, Pa., 1845; d. Bar Harbor, Maine, 1909*), physician, biologist.

CHAPMAN, JOHN (*b. Massachusetts, ca. 1775; d. Allen Co., Ind., 1847*), called "Johnny Appleseed." Carried apple seed and seeds of vegetables and herbs from Pennsylvania to be planted in the Middle West; after 1810 apparently made Ashland Co., Ohio, his center of activity. Was considered a great medicine man by the Indians. During War of 1912 earned gratitude of frontier settlers by warning them of impending Indian attacks. His legendary life has inspired numerous literary works.

CHAPMAN, JOHN GADSBY (*b. Alexandria, Va., 1808; d. 1889*), painter. Studied at Pennsylvania Academy of Fine Arts, and at Rome and Florence. Taught and practiced wood-engraving, painted portraits, illustrated publications. *The American Drawing Book* (1847) by Chapman was said to be the finest drawing book ever published. An artist of great ability, his work has quality, charm, and skill. After 1848 he resided principally in Rome.

CHAPMAN, JOHN JAY (*b. New York, N.Y., 1862; d. Poughkeepsie, N.Y., 1933*), essayist, poet.

CHAPMAN, JOHN WILBUR (*b. Richmond, Ind., 1859; d. 1918*), Presbyterian evangelist.

CHAPMAN, MARIA WESTON (*b. Weymouth, Mass., 1806; d. 1885*), reformer. Active in abolitionist societies, she aided W. L. Garrison in antislavery agitation. Edited and wrote for the *Non-Resistant*, the *Liberator*, and the *Liberty Bell*.

CHAPMAN, NATHANIEL (*b. Summer Hill, Va., 1780; d. 1853*), physician. Pupil of Benjamin Rush; M.D., University of Pennsylvania, 1801; practiced and taught in Philadelphia. Founded Medical Institute of Philadelphia; was first president of American Medical Association, 1848.

CHAPMAN, REUBEN (*b. Virginia, 1802; d. Alabama, 1882*), lawyer. Congressman, Democrat, from Alabama, 1835–47; governor of Alabama, 1847–51.

CHAPMAN, VICTOR EMMANUEL (*b. New York, N.Y., 1890; d. near Douaumont, France, 1916*), first pilot of Lafayette Escadrille to be killed in action. Son of John Jay Chapman.

CHAPPELL, ABSALOM HARRIS (*b. Hancock Co., Ga., 1801; d. Columbus, Ga., 1878*), lawyer. Georgia legislator and congressman. A states' rights Whig.

CHARLES, WILLIAM (*b. Edinburgh, Scotland, 1776; d. Philadelphia, Pa., 1820*), etcher, engraver. Noted for his etched caricatures in the manner of Gillray and Rowlandson, on events of the War of 1812.

CHARLESS, JOSEPH (*b. Westmeath, Ireland, 1772; d. 1834*), Founded *Missouri Gazette* (St. Louis), in 1808; this pioneer newspaper of the West exerted wide influence in support of Henry Clay and his policies.

CHARLEVOIX, PIERRE FRANÇOIS XAVIER DE (*b. St. Quentin, France, 1682; d. La Flèche, France, 1761*), Jesuit priest, explorer, historian. Taught at Quebec, 1705–09. Returned to New France in 1720 to ascertain the boundaries of Acadia and to find a new route to the West. He traveled up the St. Lawrence and through the Great Lakes, visited the Illinois settlements, and finally reached New Orleans and Biloxi early in 1722. The record of his journey, *Journal historique*, was appended to his *Histoire de la Nouvelle France* (1744) and also published separately. It is important because of his accurate observations and because he was the only traveler in the first part of the 18th century to describe interior America. He published several other historical studies.

CHARLTON, THOMAS USHER PULASKI (*b. Camden, S.C., 1779; d. Savannah, Ga., 1835*), jurist, author. Held various public offices in Georgia; noted as compiler of the first volume of Georgia court decisions (1824).

CHASE, EDNA WOOLMAN b. *Asbury Park, N.J., 1877; d. Sarasota, Fla., 1957*), magazine editor. Chase began work for *Vogue* in 1895; by 1914 she was editor; editor in chief, 1929–52; chairman of the board, 1952–57. With *Vogue* owner Condé Montrose Nast, Chase built *Vogue* into the leading fashion magazine in the nation, with English, French, and German editions as well. She introduced the art of high-fashion photography into the magazine and, in 1914, she organized the first American fashion show. When the magazine merged with *Vanity Fair* in 1936, literary works, including those of Thomas Wolfe, were included. Chase won the Legion of Honor from France in 1935. Her autobiography, *Always in Vogue*, was published in 1954.

CHASE, GEORGE (*b. Portland, Maine, 1849; d. 1924*), law professor. Graduated Yale, 1870; Columbia Law School, 1873. Founder and dean of New York Law School *post* 1891.

CHASE, HARRY WOODBURN (*b. Groveland, Mass., 1883; d. Sarasota, Fla., 1955*), educator. Studied at Dartmouth College and Clark University (Ph.D., 1910), where he translated lectures given at the university by Sigmund Freud. Taught at University of North Carolina (1910–19); president (1919–30). While at North Carolina, Chase developed the University of North Carolina Press. From 1930 to 1933, he was president of the University of Illinois. From 1933 to 1951, he was chancellor of New York University. Under his leadership, the university became the nation's largest, adding such facilities as the New York University–Bellevue Hospital Medical Center and a new law school.

CHASE, IRAH (*b. Stratton, Vt., 1793; d. 1864*), Baptist clergyman. Professor at Newton Theological Institution, 1825–45, where he stressed scientific study of the Scriptures.

CHASE, (MARY) AGNES MERRILL (*b. Iroquois Co., Ill., 1869; d. Bethesda, Md., 1963*), systematic botanist and agrostologist. Studied at the Lewis Institute and the University of Chicago, in 1900 became assistant in botany at the Field Museum of Natural History in Chicago. She joined the U.S. Department of Agriculture (USDA) in 1903 as a botanical illustrator, rising to become assistant in systematic agrostology (1907), assistant botanist (1923), associate botanist (1925), and senior botanist in charge of all systematic agrostology for the Bureau of Plant Industry of the USDA (1936). She served as custodian of the Section of Grasses of the U.S. National Museum, later becoming research associate in the Division of Plants. With Albert S. Hitchcock, with whom she worked at the USDA, Chase published *The North American Species of Panicum* (1910), *Tropical North American Species of Panicum* (1915), and *Grasses of the West Indies* (1917). Her *First Book of Grasses, the Structure of Grasses Explained for Beginners* was published in 1922, and in 1951 she published a revised edition of Hitchcock's *Manual of Grasses of the United States*. She completely revised the annotated index to grass species of more than 80,000 cards, published in three volumes in 1962.

CHASE, PHILANDER (*b. Cornish, N.H., 1775; d. 1852*), Episcopal clergyman. Graduated Dartmouth, 1796; ordained, 1799. Served as pastor in New York; New Orleans, La.; and Hartford, Conn., before undertaking missionary activity in Ohio, 1817. Consecrated bishop of Ohio at Philadelphia, 1819. Anxious to provide a local seminary for the West, he founded it with aid from Lord Kenyon and other Englishmen, whence its name Kenyon College. He resigned his bishopric, 1831, and removed to Michigan; in 1835, the newly organized diocese of Illinois elected him to its episcopate. Champion of the "Low Church" position, he was chosen presiding bishop of the Episcopal church in 1843.

CHASE, PLINY EARLE (*b. Worcester, Mass., 1820; d. 1886*), scientist. Brother of Thomas Chase. Professor of natural sciences, Haverford College, 1871–75; of philosophy, 1875–86.

CHASE, SALMON PORTLAND (*b. Cornish, N.H., 1808; d. New York, N.Y., 1873*), statesman. Nephew of Philander Chase, Episcopal bishop of Ohio, who guided him after his father's death in 1817, and with whom he lived near Columbus. He attended Cincinnati College and was graduated from Dartmouth, 1826. He then conducted a school for boys in Washington, D.C., and read law under the nominal supervision of William Writ. Admitted to the bar in 1829, he soon settled in Cincinnati and became occupied, in addition to legal duties, with antislavery activities and various literary ventures. He compiled the *Statutes of Ohio* (1833–35), a standard work which proved most serviceable to lawyers. Despite scornful opposition Chase defended escaped slaves and was called "the attorney general for runaway blacks." In politics Chase subordinated party interests to the central issue of slavery. Originally a Whig, he joined the Liberty party in 1840 and became one of its outstanding leaders. He was active in the Free-Soil movement of 1848. In 1849 the Free-Soilers and the Democrats in the Ohio legislature elected Chase to the U.S. Senate.

Nominated in 1855 by the Republicans for governor of Ohio and elected, he was reelected in 1859. In 1856 Chase had been an avowed aspirant for the Republican presidential nomination, but his position was weaker than Frémont's; in 1860 he was again prominently mentioned for the presidency. When at the Chicago convention he polled only 49 votes on the first ballot, his friends threw their votes to Lincoln. Chosen U.S. senator again in 1860, Chase resigned to become Lincoln's secretary of the treasury.

As director of the country's finances, 1861–64, Chase shouldered a variety of heavy responsibilities. The state of public credit was poor and Chase was fortunate to have the assistance of Jay Cooke in marketing federal bonds. Chase was the originator of the national banking system, established by law in 1863. As a cabinet member Chase helped formulate policy on the major questions of the war; and in general he supported those measures which were directed toward its vigorous prosecution. In 1862 a group of radical senators attempted to force a reconstruction of the cabinet in which Chase would be the major power and Seward would be made to resign. Although this move failed, both Seward and Chase submitted their resignations, which Lincoln refused to accept. In 1864 the confidential "Pomeroy Circular" criticized Lincoln and urged Chase's nomination for president. When this paper was made public, Chase again offered to resign and Lincoln once more refused. Later in the year, after a difference of opinion over an appointment, Chase again presented his resignation and Lincoln accepted it.

In the summer of 1864 there was a movement to revive Chase's candidacy and to induce Lincoln to withdraw; the movement was unsuccessful and Chase campaigned for Lincoln. In October, Chase was appointed chief justice of the U.S. Supreme Court. Though he advocated black suffrage and favored the radical policy of Reconstruction, he became disillusioned with the corruption of the postwar years. A painful duty for Chase was that of presiding over the trial of Jefferson Davis for treason. Chase favored the quashing of the grand jury indictment. The case was appealed to the Supreme Court, but proceedings were terminated with the issuance of President Johnson's universal pardon in December 1868. Presiding over the Senate in the impeachment trial of President Johnson. Chase insisted that the Senate was a court which must follow proper procedures and he asserted his prerogatives as presiding judge. He was heavily criticized for this and accused of being a partisan of the president. Chase's presidential ambitions were again manifested in 1868 when, after being ignored in the Republican convention, he became the subject of a determined but unsuccessful boom among Democrats. In the meantime, the Supreme Court was called upon to decide a series of perplexing cases, many dealing with questions of Reconstruction, in which Chase acted with scrupulous impartiality.

CHASE, SAMUEL (*b. Somerset Co., Md., 1741; d. 1811*), lawyer, Revolutionary leader, justice of the United States Supreme Court. A delegate to the Maryland Assembly (1764–84), Chase was also an active member of the Continental Congress until 1778 when he was attacked by Hamilton for questionable business dealings. He influenced Maryland opinion in favor of independence, and signed the Declaration of Indpendence. *Post* 1788, he served as chief judge of the Baltimore criminal court and of the general court of Maryland. An opponent of the Constitution, he later became a Federalist and in 1796 a member of the U.S. Supreme Court, where his performance ranks as the most notable previous to Marshall. His high-handedness led to impeachment proceedings in 1804–05 which, despite Jefferson's pressure, ended in Chase's acquittal.

CHASE, THOMAS (*b. Worcester, Mass., 1827; d. Providence, R.I., 1892*), classical scholar. Graduated Harvard, 1848. Taught at Harvard and at Haverford College; served as president of Haverford, 1875–86.

CHASE, WILLIAM MERRITT (*b. Williamsburg, Ind., 1849; d. 1916*), artist. After studying and painting in Indianapolis, New York and St. Louis, he went to Munich in 1872 and worked under F. Wagner and Karl von Piloty. Returning to New York in 1878, he became a successful teacher and, as president of the Society of American Artists, a leader among younger painters dissatisfied with the conventions governing the National Academy. No American painter taught such large numbers of students while at the same time producing so much original work. He excelled in still lifes.

CHATARD, FRANCIS SILAS (*b. Baltimore, Md., 1834; d. Indianapolis, Ind., 1918*), physician. Roman Catholic bishop of Vincennes, 1878–98; of Indianapolis, 1898–1918. Rector, American College of Rome, 1868–78.

CHATTERTON, RUTH (*b. New York, N.Y., 1893; d. Norwalk, Conn., 1961*), actress and novelist. First appeared on the New York stage in *The Great Name* (1911), and in 1914 accepted the starring role in *Daddy Long-Legs*. She appeared in many Broadway productions through 1925, then moved to Hollywood to pursue a film career, which began with *Sins of the Father* (1928). Her first film success came the next year in *Madame X*. In 1936 she ended her American film career and moved to England, where she starred in a play and made two movies. She returned to New York in 1939, then played in road company productions for several years before returning to Broadway in 1946 in *Second Best Bed*. She last appeared on Broadway in *Idiot's Delight* (1951), and her last stage appearance was in *The Chalk Garden* (1956) in St. Louis. In 1950 Chatterton published the novel *Homeward Borne*, which became a best-seller. She also wrote *The Betrayers* (1953), *Pride of the Peacock* (1954), and *The Southern Wild* (1958).

CHAUMONOT, PIERRE JOSEPH MARIE (*b. Burgundy, France, 1611; d. Quebec, Canada, 1693*), Jesuit missionary. Worked among Indian tribes in New France, 1639–92, chiefly among the fugitive Christian Hurons.

CHAUNCEY, ISAAC (*b. Black Rock, Conn., 1772; d. Washington, D.C., 1840*), naval officer. Organized and commanded U.S. naval forces on Lakes Ontario and Erie, 1812–15; later held important administrative posts in navy.

CHAUNCY, CHARLES *b. Yardleybury, England, 1592; d. Cambridge, Mass., 1671/2*), nonconformist clergyman, second president of Harvard College (1654–71/2). Came to New England, 1638; served churches in Plymouth and Scituate, Mass., before appointment to Harvard.

CHAUNCY, CHARLES (*b. Boston, Mass., 1705; d. Boston, 1787*), clergyman. Great-grandson of Charles Chauncy (1592–1671/2). Graduated Harvard, 1721; minister of the First Church in Boston, 1727–87. Acknowledged leader of the liberals of his generation, the most influential clergyman of his time in Boston and, with the exception of Jonathan Edwards, in all New England. His numerous writings were concerned primarily with three controversies: revivalism, episcopacy, and the benevolence of God; he opposed the emotionalism of Edwards and Whitefield, the institution of an American episcopacy, and excessive rigorism.

CHAUVENET, WILLIAM (*b. Milford, Pa., 1820; d. St. Paul, Minn., 1870*), mathematician, astronomer. Graduated Yale, 1840. Appointed professor of mathematics in the navy, he became head of the Philadelphia school for midshipmen, 1842, and was largely responsible for establishing the U.S. Naval Academy on a firm, scientific basis. He was author, among other works, of classic treatises on trigonometry and astronomy which had international reputation. He served as chancellor of Washington University, St. Louis, Mo., 1862–69.

CHAVEZ, DENNIS (*b. Los Chavez, Valencia County, N.M., 1888; d. Washington, D.C., 1962*), lawyer and U.S. senator. Became a clerk in the U.S. Senate (1918–19) and attended Georgetown University Law School (LL.B., 1920). Served as a Democrat in the New Mexico House of Representatives (1923–24) before being elected to the U.S. House in 1930. In 1935 Chavez was appointed to the Senate seat of Bronson F. Cutting, who died in an airplane crash. He was elected senator in his own right in 1936, serving until his death. An advocate of the Good Neighbor Policy toward Latin America, Chavez took a special interest in Puerto Rico. As a proponent of minority's integrating into the larger society, he opposed programs to aid American Indians to restore their culture and regain their land and proposed making English the language of Puerto Rico. He led a long battle to establish a permanent Employment Practices Commission and served as chairman of the Senate Appropriations Subcommittee for Defense.

CHAVIS, JOHN (*b.* ca. *1763; d. 1838*), Presbyterian missionary, educator. Born either in the West Indies or near Oxford, N.C., Chavis was a full-blooded black. Educated under President Witherspoon of the College of New Jersey and at Washington Academy (now Washington and Lee University), he established a classical school at which many prominent North Carolinians were prepared for college, 1810–32.

CHEATHAM, BENJAMIN FRANKLIN (*b. Nashville, Tenn., 1820; d. 1886*), Confederate major general. Engaged in dispute with Hood over conduct of Spring Hill battle in Tennessee campaign, 1864.

CHECKLEY, JOHN (*b. Boston, Mass., 1680; d. 1754*), Anglican clergyman, bookseller, controversial writer.

CHEESMAN, FORMAN (*b. New York, N.Y., 1763; d. 1821*), shipbuilder, naval architect. Instrumental in promoting growth of New York shipbuilding industry, 1800–20.

CHEETHAM, JAMES (*b. Manchester[?], England, 1772; d. New York, N.Y., 1810*, journalist. Came to America, *post* 1798; edited the Republican newspaper *The American Citizen.* A bitter political enemy of Aaron Burr. Cheetham was author of *Life of Thomas Paine* (1809).

CHEEVER, EZEKIEL (*b. London, England, 1614/15; d. Boston, Mass., 1708*), educator, classicist. Came to New England, 1637. Taught at New Haven, Conn., and at Ipswich and Charlestown, Mass. Outstanding as master of Boston Latin School, 1670–1708; author of renowned *Accidence, a Short Introduction to the Latin Tongue.*

CHEEVER, GEORGE BARRELL (*b. Hallowell, Maine, 1807; d. Englewood, N.J., 1890*), Congregational clergyman, reformer.

CHEEVER, HENRY THEODORE (*b. Hallowell, Maine, 1814; d. Worcester, Mass., 1897*), Congregational clergyman, liberal theologian. Brother of George B. Cheever.

CHENEY, BENJAMIN PIERCE (*b. Hillsborough, N.H., 1815; d. 1895*), pioneer in New England express business. Founded the United States & Canada Express Co., which he later merged with the American Express Co. Active in promotion of western railroads and in banking.

CHENEY, CHARLES EDWARD (*b. Canandaigua, N.Y., 1836; d. 1916*), clergyman. After controversy with his bishop, 1869–72, over excessive evangelicalism in his Chicago parish, he helped organize the Reformed Episcopal church (1873); he served the new body as bishop and continued as pastor of Christ Church, Chicago, until his death.

CHENEY, EDNAH DOW LITTLEHALE (*b. Boston, Mass., 1824; d. 1904*), author, reformer. Wife of Seth W. Cheney. Supported antislavery cause, Freedman's Society, and woman suffrage.

CHENEY, JOHN (*b. South Manchester, Conn., 1801; d. South Manchester, 1885*), engraver. Brother of Seth W. and Ward Cheney. His small engravings, published in annuals and similar books, are unexcelled of their kind.

CHENEY, JOHN VANCE (*b. Groveland, N.Y., 1848; d. San Diego, Calif., 1922*), author. Librarian of Free Public Library, San Francisco, 1887–94; of Newberry Library, Chicago, 1894–1909.

CHENEY, OREN BURBANK (*b. Holderness, N.H., 1816; d. 1903*), Baptist clergyman. Graduated Dartmouth, 1839. Helped found Bates College, Maine, and was its first president, 1864–94; emeritus to 1903.

CHENEY, PERSON COLBY (*b. Holderness, N.H., 1828; d. 1901*), paper manufacturer. Republican governor of New Hampshire, 1875–77.

CHENEY, SETH WELLS (*b. South Manchester, Conn., 1810; d. 1856*), crayon artist, engraver. Brother of John and Ward Cheney. Successful as a crayon portrait artist in Boston, Mass., 1841–53.

CHENEY, WARD (*b. South Manchester, Conn., 1813; d. 1876*), pioneer silk manufacturer. Brother of John and Seth W. Cheney. President, Cheney Brothers Silk Manufacturing Co., 1854–76, and noted for business acumen and concern for employees.

CHENNAULT, CLAIRE LEE (*b. Commerce, Tex., 1893; d. New Orleans, La., 1958*), military leader, airline executive. Studied at Louisiana State University and at State Normal School at Natchitoches. Commissioned in the Army Air Service in 1920. From 1930 to 1937, he was stationed at Air Corps Tactical School, Langley, Va. His book on air tactics, *The Role of Defensive Pursuit* (1935), gained him a national reputation. He was forced to retire from the Army in 1937, but immediately went to China and became Chiang Kai-shek's personal advisor during the Japanese invasion. Finding support in the U.S. for his plans to build an air force in China, he was able, by 1941, to launch his American Volunteer Group consisting of private American flyers. The group gained world fame as the Flying Tigers and they were incorporated into the U.S. Army in 1942. During the war the Tigers inflicted considerable damage on the Japanese forces. Chennault was forced to retire in 1945 because of charges of insubordination brought against him by General Joseph Stilwell. In 1946, he founded an airline known as CAT, which served the Chinese Nationalists and later the CIA in the Far East.

CHERRINGTON, ERNEST HURST (*b. Hamden, Ohio, 1877; d. Worthington, Ohio, 1950*), temperance reformer, Methodist lay leader. Becoming a full-time temperance worker for the Ohio Anti-Saloon League, 1902, Cherrington rose through the effectiveness of his work to office in the national organization of the league; in 1909, he was named editor of its newspaper, the *American Issue*, and general manager of its publishing activities. During the next decade, he built up a huge enterprise producing propaganda for prohibition; he also developed the league's fund-raising program, managed its finances, organized its national speakers' bureau, and directed its international expansion. Bishop James Cannon considered Cherrington the one man most responsible for the adoption of the 18th Amendment.

CHESEBROUGH, CAROLINE (*b. Canandaigua, N.Y., 1825; d. Piermont, N.Y., 1873*), novelist.

CHESHIRE, JOSEPH BLOUNT (*b. Tarboro, N.C., 1850; d. Charlotte, N.C., 1932*), Episcopal clergyman. Bishop of North Carolina, 1893–1932.

CHESNUT, JAMES (*b. Camden, S.C., 1815; d. Saarsfield, S.C., 1885*), lawyer, planter, Confederate soldier. Graduated Princeton, 1835; practiced law in Camden, S.C. Democrat and secessionist member of South Carolina General Assembly *post* 1840; president of senate, 1856–58. Elected to U.S. Senate, 1858, he vigorously defended slavery. Resigning in 1860, he helped draft ordinance of secession in South Carolina convention. In the Provisional Congress of the Confederate States he aided in drafting the permanent constitution. After service as aide to General Beauregard and on staff of President Davis, 1861–64, he became brigadier general in command of reserve forces in South Carolina. He took an active part in opposing reconstruction of South Carolina.

CHESSMAN, CARYL WHITTIER (*b. St. Joseph, Mich., 1921; d. San Quentin, Calif., 1960*), criminal and writer. From 1937 until his death in 1960, Chessman spent only one and a half years outside of prisons; he was convicted in 1948 on seventeen counts of felony, including kidnapping, and was sentenced to die. He successfully fought the sentence for twelve years, his appeals finally reaching the Supreme Court. He was executed at San Quentin in 1960 after eight postponements. His book, *Cell 2455, Death Row* (1954) earned him money for his legal battles and made him into a cause célèbre for groups opposed to capital punishment.

CHESTER, COLBY MITCHELL (*b. Annapolis, Md., 1877; d. Greenwich, Conn., 1965*), lawyer and corporation officer. Graduate of Yale (Ph.B., 1897; B.A., 1898) and New York Law School (LL.B., 1900). He practiced law until 1904, when he became treasurer of an industrial supply firm. He resumed his law practice in 1911, specializing in corporate law, then served on active duty in the National Guard (1917–18). In 1919 Chester entered the food industry with the Postum Cereal Company of Battle Creek, Mich., becoming its president in 1924. In 1929 Postum merged with fifteen other companies to form the General Foods Corporation. Chester served as president (1929–35), became chairman of the board in 1935, then chairman of the executive committee (1943–46). He served as chairman of the board and director of many other companies and was active in civic and philanthropic affairs.

CHESTER, COLBY MITCHELL (*b. New London, Conn., 1844; d. Rye, N.Y., 1932*), naval officer. Graduated Annapolis, 1863. The "Chester claims" to trade concessions in Turkey, 1922, received wide publicity in connection with agitation against "dollar diplomacy."

CHESTER, GEORGE RANDOLPH (*b. Ohio, 1869; d. New York, N.Y., 1924*), author of *Get-Rich-Quick Wallingford* (1908) and other novels and stories.

CHESTER, JOSEPH LEMUEL (*b. Norwich, Conn., 1821; d. England, 1882*), genealogist, journalist.

CHETLAIN, AUGUSTUS LOUIS (*b. St. Louis, Mo., 1824; d. 1914*), Union soldier, banker. Organized and was president of Home National Bank, Chicago.

CHEVER, JAMES W. (*b. Salem, Mass., 1791; d. Salem, 1857*), privateersman. Captain of the successful privateer *America*, 1813–15. Later commanded Salem merchant ships.

CHEVERUS, JOHN LOUIS ANN MAGDALEN LEFEBRE DE (*b. Mayenne, France, 1768; d. Bordeaux, France, 1836*), Roman Catholic clergyman. Ordained in Paris, 1790. On refusing oath to support civil constitution of clergy was deprived of his parish and imprisoned; escaped from Cordeliers prison to London, 1972; came to Boston, 1796. Ministered to Maine Penobscots and to scattered New England congregations, earning respect and warm liking of Protestants. Assisted in founding the Boston Athenaeum, to which he left his library. Consecrated bishop of Boston with all New England as his diocese, 1810, he served until 1823 when he returned to France as bishop of Montauban. Became archbishop of Bordeaux, 1826, and was elevated to the cardinalate, 1836.

CHEVES, LANGDON (*b. Abbeville District, S.C., 1776; d. Columbia, S.C., 1857*), lawyer, financier. Admitted to bar, 1797; practiced successfully in Charleston, S.C. Held several state

offices. As congressman, Democratic-Republican, 1810–15, he was an effective debater and prominent in the group which precipitated War of 1812. As president of the Bank of the United States, 1819–22, he restored the bank to sound financial condition. Returning to South Carolina, 1829, though a strong believer in secession, he opposed separate state action. The unpopularity of his views caused him to withdraw from public life.

CHEW, BENJAMIN (*b. West River, Md., 1722; d. 1810*), lawyer. Chief justice of Pennsylvania Supreme Court, 1774–76; judge and president of High Court of Errors and Appeals, 1791–1808.

CHEYNEY, EDWARD POTTS (*b. Wallingford, Pa., 1861; d. Chester, Pa., 1947*), historian. B.A., University of Pennsylvania, 1883; bachelor of finance (Wharton School), 1884. Taught history at Pennsylvania *post* 1884, becoming professor, 1897; retired, 1934. To his early scrupulous concern for objectivity, he later added a commitment to the "New History," with its emphasis on the continuity of historical process, the broad range of man's activities and interests, and the use of social science disciplines and techniques. His books, dealing principally with English history, included a standard textbook, *A Short History of England* (1904), and his most ambitious study, *A History of England, from the Defeat of the Armada to the Death of Elizabeth* (2 vols., 1914, 1926). The latter, though largely a conventional narrative and lacking in any consideration of the science, literature, and religious concerns of the period, was based on meticulous research. Cheyney contributed to the growth of the historical profession and helped to establish the American Historical Association as an important force.

CHICKERING, JONAS (*b. Mason Village, N.H., 1798; d. 1853*), piano manufacturer. Founded firm of Stewart & Chickering in Boston, Mass., 1823, and soon assumed full control; in 1837 he built the first grand piano with full iron frame made in a single casting, and in 1843 patented a new deflection of the strings. Chickering invented the first practical method of overstringing grand pianos in 1845. He has been called the "father of American pianoforte-making."

CHIERA, EDWARD (*b. Rome, Italy, 1885; d. 1933*), orientalist. Came to America, 1907. Professor of Assyriology, University of Chicago. Editor of the *Assyrian Dictionary*, 1927–33; author of works on Sumerian texts.

CHILD, CHARLES MANNING (*b. Ypsilanti, Mich., 1869; d. Palo Alto, Calif., 1954*), zoologist. Studied at Wesleyan University, and the University of Leipzig (Ph.D., 1894). From 1895 to 1937, taught at the University of Chicago, becoming chairman of the zoology department. Lectured at Stanford University after retirement. His major work concerned the regenerative process of invertebrates, especially coelenterates and flatworms, and led to his development of the gradient theory. In 1928 Child founded the journal *Physiological Zoology*. His work is summed up in his *Patterns and Problems of Development* (1941).

CHILD, DAVID LEE (*b. West Boylston, Mass., 1794; d. Wayland, Mass., 1874*), lawyer, journalist, antislavery reformer.

CHILD, FRANCIS JAMES (*b. Boston, Mass., 1825; d. Cambridge, Mass., 1896*), philologist. Graduated Harvard, 1846; studied at Göttingen and Berlin. Returning to Harvard, he was Boylston professor of rhetoric and oratory, 1851–76; professor of English, 1876–96. The most notable philologists of the succeeding generation were trained in his classroom, and his total influence on the culture of the nation was great. His chief works include *Poetical Works of Edmund Spenser* (1855), the best text and fullest biography of Spenser available at the time; "Observations on the Language of Chaucer" (1863), which began a new era of Chaucerian scholarship; "Observations on the Language of Gower's *Confessio Amantis*" (1873); and the monumental *English and Scottish Popular Ballads* (1883–98).

CHILD, FRANK SAMUEL (*b. Exeter, N.Y., 1854; d. Fairfield, Conn., 1922*), Congregational clergyman. Pastor at Fairfield, 1888–1922; author of *The Colonial Parson of New England* (1896) and other works on colonial history.

CHILD, LYDIA MARIA FRANCIS (*b. Medford, Mass., 1802; d. 1880*), abolitionist. Author of the novels *Hobomok* (1824) and *The Rebels* (1825); wrote many other works representative of her diverse interests.

CHILD, RICHARD WASHBURN (*b. Worcester, Mass., 1881; d. New York, N.Y., 1935*), author, diplomat.

CHILD, ROBERT (*b. Northfleet, England, ca. 1613; d. Ireland, 1654*), physician, Remonstrant. Among those who petitioned the General Court, 1646, for the rights of freemen to be established in Massachusetts.

CHILDE, JOHN (*b. West Boylston, Mass., 1802; d. Springfield, Mass., 1858*), pioneer civil engineer. Graduated West Point, 1827. Solved many engineering problems in establishment of new railroad lines.

CHILDS, CEPHAS GRIER (*b. Plumstead Township, Pa., 1793; d. 1871*), engraver, editor, publisher. Pioneered in establishing lithography on a commercial basis in the United States. Edited several Philadelphia commercial periodicals.

CHILDS, GEORGE WILLIAM (*b. Baltimore, Md., 1829; d. Philadelphia, Pa., 1894*), publisher. Successful in the book trade and as proprietor of the Philadelphia *Public Ledger*, 1864–94.

CHILDS, THOMAS (*b. Pittsfield, Mass., 1796; d. Fort Brooke, Fla., 1853*), soldier. Served with distinction in War of 1812, the second Seminole War, and the Mexican War.

CHILTON, WILLIAM PARIS (*b. near Elizabethtown, Ky., 1810; d. Montgomery, Ala., 1871*), jurist. Chief justice of Alabama Supreme Court, 1852–56; influential member of both regular Confederate Congresses.

CHINI, EUSEBIO FRANCISCO. *See* KINO, EUSEBIO FRANCISCO.

CHIPMAN, DANIEL (*b. Salisbury, Conn., 1765; d. 1850*), lawyer. Active in Vermont politics; influential in five constitutional conventions. Author of *The life of Hon. Nathaniel Chipman* (1846), his brother.

CHIPMAN, NATHANIEL (*b. Salisbury, Conn., 1752; d. Tinmouth, Vt., 1843*), jurist. Graduated Yale, 1777; practiced law in Tinmouth, Vt. In 1787 became assistant justice of the Vermont Supreme Court; served as chief justice of the court at three different times. Was prominent in Bennington constitutional convention (1791) and helped to negotiate for admittance of Vermont to the Union. Served as federal judge in the district of Vermont, 1791–93; as U.S. senator, 1798–1804. As member of a committee to revise the state code, he was largely responsible for the statutes of 1797.

CHIPMAN, WARD (*b. Marblehead, Mass., 1754; d. New Brunswick, Canada, 1824*), loyalist. Served with British forces in the Revolution; removed to New Brunswick, 1784, where he practiced law and served as solicitor general and as a judge of the supreme court.

CHISHOLM, HUGH JOSEPH (*b. Niagara Falls, Canada, 1847; d. 1912*), paper manufacturer. Organized Maine paper manufacturing firms; was a founder of International Paper Co., 1898.

CHISOLM, ALEXANDER ROBERT (*b. Beaufort, S.C., 1834; d. 1910*), Confederate soldier, financier. Removed to New York City, 1869; was stockbroker and founder of *Financial and Mining Record*.

CHISOLM, JOHN JULIAN (*b. Charleston, S.C., 1830; d. Petersburg, Va., 1903*), surgeon, oculist. Author of Confederate *Manual of Military Surgery* (1861); University of Maryland professor, 1869–93; specialist in ophthalmology.

CHISUM, JOHN SIMPSON (*b. Hardeman Co., Tenn., 1824; d. Eureka Springs, Ark., 1884*). One of the first (1866) Texas cattlemen to shift his operations to the ranges of New Mexico. Despite frequent Indian raids and the depredations of white rustlers, Chisum prospered; he established himself at South Spring, N.Mex., 1873. Probably the largest individual cattle owner in the United States, for many years he was the "cattle king of America." His part, if any, in the famous Lincoln County War of 1878–79 is a matter of dispute. He later became a leader in the movement to end lawlessness in New Mexico.

CHITTENDEN, HIRAM MARTIN (*b. Yorkshire, N.Y., 1858; d. Seattle, Wash., 1917*), military engineer, historian. Graduated West Point, 1884. Engineering service in Yellowstone National Park awakened his interest in western history and topography and a desire to preserve the park area. Despite an arduous professional life he was author of important historical studies, which include *The Yellowstone National Park* (1895); *The American Fur Trade of the Far West* (1902); and *The History of Early Steamboat Navigation on the Missouri River* (1903).

CHITTENDEN, MARTIN (*b. Salisbury, Conn., 1763; d. Williston, Vt., 1840*). Son of Thomas Chittenden. Federalist governor of Vermont, 1813–15.

CHITTENDEN, RUSSELL HENRY (*b. New Haven, Conn., 1856; d. New Haven, 1943*), biochemist, Ph.B., Sheffield Scientific School, Yale, 1875; taught the first laboratory course in physiological chemistry (biochemistry) in America during his senior year and until 1878, when he studied for a year with Wilhelm Kühne at Heidelberg. Returning to Yale and continuing to teach, he was granted the Ph.D. in 1880. Appointed professor of physiological chemistry at Sheffield Scientific School, 1882. He was director of the school, 1898–1922, and treasurer *post* 1904, during which time he greatly expanded its faculty and physical facilities as an entity largely independent of Yale College. His principal research up to 1890 dealt with the chemical nature of proteins and the enzymatic digestion of starch. He proceeded then to important research on the protein requirements of man, setting forth his findings in favor of a low-protein diet in *Physiological Economy in Nutrition* (1904), and defending his position in *The Nutrition of Man* (1907). He continued to lecture until 1916, although he undertook little research of his own after 1904.

CHITTENDEN, SIMEON BALDWIN (*b. Guilford, Conn., 1814; d. Brooklyn, N.Y., 1889*), merchant. Student of economics and theorist on currency problems.

CHITTENDEN, THOMAS (*b. East Guilford, Conn., 1730; d. 1797*), politician. In 1774 received a grant of land in Williston, Vt. Was prominent in the conventions which culminated in formation of the state of Vermont; in 1777 helped draw up declaration for the new state and, with others, unsuccessfully petitioned the Continental Congress for recognition; was president of the Council of Safety. Helped Ira Allen draw up Vermont Constitution. In 1778 became first Vermont governor, an office he held, except for the year 1789–90, until 1797. Participated with Ethan Allen and others in secret negotiations with General Haldimand, commander of British forces in Canada, 1780–83.

CHIVERS, THOMAS HOLLEY (*b. near Washington, Ga., 1809; d. Decatur, Ga., 1858*), poet. Friend and rival of Edgar Allan Poe. His visionary and prolific output includes *The Lost Pleiad and Other Poems* and *Eonchs of Ruby* (1850).

CHOATE, ANNE HYDE CLARKE (*b. Cooperstown, N.Y., 1886; d. Pleasantville, N.Y., 1967*), a leader of the Girl Scout movement. Persuaded by the founder of the Girl Scouts of America, Juliette Low (a family friend), to become involved in scouting in 1915, she served as national vice president of the Girl Scouts (1916–20), 1922–37), president (1920–22), and honorary vice president (1937–57). She also served on the board of directors and the executive committee. But she concentrated on international scouting as a member of the international committee (1920–55) and as chairwoman of the Juliette Low World Friendship Committee (1927–55). Choate was also involved in historic preservation efforts.

CHOATE, JOSEPH HODGES (*b. Salem, Mass., 1832; d. New York, N.Y., 1917*), lawyer, diplomat. Graduated Harvard, 1852; Harvard Law School, 1854. Became a partner in Butler, Evarts and Southmayd, New York law firm; handled a wide variety of cases in his long and successful career. Probably his most important arguments were in the Income Tax Cases before the U.S. Supreme Court, 1895. Choate was a leader in cultural and humanitarian activities, an active Republican, a prominent "club man," and a celebrated after-dinner speaker. As ambassador to Great Britain, 1899–1905, he was noted for his success in settling Alaskan boundary question, in abrogating Clayton-Bulwer Treaty, and for goodwill he gained for the United States. He was prominent at the Second Hague Conference of 1907, where he served as head of the American delegation.

CHOATE, RUFUS (*b. Hog Island, Mass., 1799; d. Halifax, Nova Scotia, now Canada, 1859*), lawyer, statesman. Graduated Dartmouth, 1819; admitted to bar, 1822; began his law practice in Danvers, Mass. With Daniel Webster, Edward Everett, and Caleb Cushing organized Whig party in Massachusetts, and served out Webster's term in U.S. Senate, 1841–45. Defended Webster's position on the Compromise of 1850 and in 1855 denounced the Republican party as "sectional" and "anti-Union." Choate's fame rests on his oratorical skill and on his eminent leadership of the bar.

CHOPIN, KATE O'FLAHERTY (*b. St. Louis, Mo., 1851; d. 1904*), author. Noted for interpretations of the Creoles in *Bayou Folk* (1894), *The Awakening* (1899), and other books.

CHORPENNING, GEORGE (*b. Somerset, Pa., 1820; d. 1894*), pioneer western mail man. Operated mail service from Utah to the Pacific Coast, 1851–60, under conditions of great hardship.

CHOTZINOFF, SAMUEL (*b. Vitebsk, Russia, 1889; d. New York, N.Y., 1964*), pianist and music critic. Immigrated with his family to New York City in 1896 and took his first piano lessons when he was ten years old, later studying with Jeanne Franke. He made his public debut as a soloist in 1905. Chotzinoff attended Columbia (1908–11) but left without graduating to become the accompanist for the violinist Efrem Zimbalist (until 1918). During this time he also accompanied the sopranos Alma Gluck and Frieda Hempel. He was Jascha Heifetz's accompanist, 1919–20. His music criticism appeared in *Vanity Fair*, the *New York World*, and the *Evening Post*. In 1936 he became music consultant to the NBC radio network, where he assembled the NBC Symphony Orchestra and served as commentator for the orchestra's regular Saturday night broadcasts. He was appointed general music director for NBC radio and television in 1949 and organized the NBC Television Opera Theater. His last writings were *Toscanini: An Intimate Portrait* (1956) and *A Little Nightmusic* (1964).

CHOUART, MÉDART. *See* GROSEILLIERS, MÉDART CHOUART, SIEUR DE.

CHOUTEAU, AUGUSTE. *See* CHOUTEAU, RENÉ AUGUSTE.

CHOUTEAU, AUGUSTE PIERRE (*b. St. Louis, Mo., 1786; d. near Fort Gibson, Indian Territory, 1838*), fur trader, frontier soldier. Son of Jean Pierre Chouteau.

CHOUTEAU, JEAN PIERRE (*b. New Orleans, La., 1758; d. St. Louis, Mo., 1849*), fur trader. U.S. agent for the Osages, cofounder of St. Louis Missouri Fur Co., 1809, with Manuel Lisa, William Clark et al.

CHOUTEAU, PIERRE (*b. St. Louis, Mo., 1789; d. St. Louis, 1865*), merchant, fur trader, financier. Son of Jean Pierre Chouteau.

CHOUTEAU, RENÉ AUGUSTE (*b. New Orleans, La., 1749; d. St. Louis, Mo., 1829*), trader, assistant to Pierre Laclede in founding of St. Louis. Commanded party beginning construction of St. Louis, early in 1764; derived fortune from trading, especially with Osage Indians; served as territorial justice, colonel of St. Louis militia, chairman of board of trustees of town of St. Louis. Negotiated several Indian treaties as federal commissioner. Described as "a man of incorruptible integrity," he became St. Louis's wealthiest citizen and largest landholder.

CHOVET, ABRAHAM (*b. London, England, 1704; d. Philadelphia, Pa., 1790*), surgeon, anatomist. Came to Philadelphia, *ante* 1774, where he practiced successfully and taught anatomy.

CHRISTIAN, HENRY ASBURY (*b. Lynchburg, Va., 1876; d. Whitefield, N.H., 1951*), physician. Studied at Randolph-Macon College, Johns Hopkins University School of Medicine, and Harvard (A.M., 1903). Affiliated with Harvard Medical School (1903–39). Christian became an effective hospital director, specializing in diseases of the kidney and of the heart muscle. Served as chairman of the Division of Medical Sciences of the National Research Council; fellow of the American Academy of Arts and Sciences; honorary fellow of the Royal College of Physicians in London.

CHRISTIAN, WILLIAM (*b. Staunton, Va., ca. 1743; d. near Jeffersonville, Ind., 1786*), soldier, politician. Member of Virginia Committee of Safety; led punitive expeditions against the Cherokee and other Indian tribes.

CHRISTIANCY, ISAAC PECKHAM (*b. Johnstown, N.Y., 1812; d. Monroe, Mich., 1890*), lawyer. Removed to Michigan, 1836. Judge of state supreme court, 1858–74; U.S. senator, Republican, 1874–79.

CHRISTIE, JOHN WALTER (*b. River Edge, N.J., 1865; d. Falls Church, Va., 1944*), inventor. Went to work at 16 in Delamater Iron Works, New York City; attended evening classes at Cooper Union; became consulting engineer for several steamship lines. Soon after 1900, he entered the automotive field, building cars of his own design and competing with them in international test races; in 1904, he began promoting a front-wheel-drive car which he had designed. Began successful manufacture of wheeled tractors for fire-fighting equipment, 1912, and entered the field of military ordnance, 1916, with a four-wheel-drive truck. Beginning in World War I, he took an active part in the development of tanks and other armored vehicles; invented the convertible principle which permitted the vehicles to travel either with or without tracks by utilizing a single suspension system and larger, rubber-tired wheels. He also produced an amphibious gun carriage. None of his vehicles was adopted by the U.S. Army. In 1928, introduced the milestone M 1928 convertible tank chassis. The M 1928 achieved 42 miles per hour as against 18 miles per hour for existing army tanks. The Ordnance Department bought 7 and had about 25 more built under license from Christie. By 1939, the system was dropped in favor of a less expensive system.

His designs were the basis of the Soviet BT series, which evolved into the T−34, one of the most effective tanks of World War II. The British also produced a series of Christie-type cruiser tanks.

CHRISTY, DAVID (*b. 1802*), antislavery writer, geologist. As agent of American Colonization Society in Ohio, advocated black emigration to Liberia; author of the important study *Cotton Is King* (1855).

CHRISTY, EDWIN P. (*b. Philadelphia, Pa., 1815; d. New York, N.Y., 1862*), minstrel. Originated the Christy Minstrels at Buffalo, N.Y., 1842.

CHRISTY, HOWARD CHANDLER (*b. Morgan County, Ohio, 1873; d. New York, N.Y., 1952*), illustrator, portraitist, mural painter. Studied at the Art Students League and the National Academy of Design. First success was illustrating Theodore Roosevelt's "Rough Riders" in action in Cuba; created the "Christy Girl" for *Scribner's* around the turn of the century. This figure was published in many leading magazines of the time. Painted portraits of numerous notable subjects, including Benito Mussolini, President and Mrs. Coolidge, Charles Evans Hughes, and Amelia Earhart. Best-known painting is the oil "Signing the Constitution" (1940) which hangs in the U.S. Capitol. Painted the famous murals in New York's Café des Artistes.

CHRYSLER, WALTER PERCY (*b. Wamego, Kans., 1875; d. Great Neck, N.Y., 1940*), automobile manufacturer. After high school graduation, became a railroad mechanic and by 1912 was works manager of the American Locomotive Co. That same year, he joined the Buick Motor Co. as works manager at $6,000 a year. His practical talents applied to a rapidly expanding industry were spectacularly successful; he became president of Buick in 1916 at $500,000 a year. Leaving Buick in 1920, he reorganized and became president of Maxwell Motor Car Co. In 1925 Maxwell became Chrysler Corporation, purchasing Dodge Brothers in 1928. By 1935, when he retired, his company was second in the industry.

CHURCH, ALONZO (*b. near Brattleboro, Vt., 1793; d. near Athens, Ga., 1862*), educator. Graduated Middlebury College, 1816; effective president of University of Georgia, 1829–59.

CHURCH, BENJAMIN (*b. Plymouth, Mass., 1639; d. near Little Compton, R.I., 1718*), soldier. As captain of a Plymouth company, fought in King Philip's War; was wounded at the Great Swamp Fight, 1675, and ambushed Philip near Mount Hope (Bristol, R.I.), 1676. Thereafter, he served occasionally as magistrate and selectman; also, during King William's and Queen Anne's wars, as major and colonel in five raids against the French and Indians in Maine and Nova Scotia. Retired from active service in 1704.

CHURCH, BENJAMIN (*b. Newport, R.I., 1734; d. at sea, 1778 [?]*), physician, author, traitor. Grandson of Benjamin Church (1639–1718). Graduated Harvard, 1754. High in the councils of the patriots and an associate of John Adams and Joseph Warren, Church was a paid informant of the British authorities in Boston. Appointed director and chief physician of the American army hospital at Cambridge, Mass., 1775, he was detected in cipher correspondence with the enemy and was court-martialed in October of that year.

CHURCH, FREDERICK EDWIN (*b. Hartford, Conn., 1826; d. New York, N.Y., 1900*), landscape painter. A pupil of Thomas Cole. Chief among his works, *The Heart of the Andes* (exhibited 1859) and *Niagara Falls* (1857).

CHURCH, FREDERICK STUART (*b. Grand Rapids, Mich., 1842; d. 1924*), painter, illustrator.

CHURCH, GEORGE EARL (*b. New Bedford, Mass., 1835; d. London, England, 1910*), civil engineer, explorer, writer. Authority on Latin American geography and history.

CHURCH, IRVING PORTER (*b. Ansonia, Conn., 1851; d. Ithaca, N.Y., 1931*), educator. Professor of civil engineering, Cornell University, 1876–1916; author of textbooks on engineering.

CHURCH, JOHN ADAMS (*b. Rochester, N.Y., 1843; d. 1917*), metallurgist. Graduated Columbia School of Mines, 1867. Improved smelter techniques; introduced American mining methods in China.

CHURCH, PHARCELLUS (*b. Seneca, N.Y., 1801; d. 1886*), Baptist clergyman. Held pastorates in Rochester, N.Y.; Boston, Mass.; and Brooklyn, N.Y. Wrote theological works and was active in religious journalism.

CHURCH, WILLIAM CONANT (*b. Rochester, N.Y., 1836; d. 1917*), editor. Son of Pharcellus Church. Cofounder and editor of *Army and Navy Journal* (1863) and *Galaxy Magazine* (1866).

CHURCHILL, THOMAS JAMES (*b. Jefferson Co., Ky., 1824; d. 1905*), planter, lawyer, Confederate soldier. Removed to Arkansas, 1848. Directed defense of Arkansas Post, 1862; elected Democratic governor of Arkansas, 1880.

CHURCHILL, WILLIAM (*b. Brooklyn, N.Y., 1859; d. 1920*), philologist, ethnologist. Graduated Yale, 1882. Began study of Polynesian languages as consul general to Samoa, 1896–99. Author of *Polynesian Wanderings* (1910).

CHURCHILL, WINSTON (*b. St. Louis, Mo., 1871; d. Winter Park, Fla., 1847*), novelist, political reformer. Graduated U.S. Naval Academy, 1894. Resigning his commission three months after graduation, he turned to a writing career. After publishing *The Celebrity* (1898), he won national fame as author of a series of historical romances: *Richard Carvel* (1899); *The Crisis* (1901); and *The Crossing* (1904). His novel *Coniston* (1906), a study of political corruption, marked a shift in the author's interests; henceforth, influenced by Herbert Croly and Theodore Roosevelt, he set about reforming New Hampshire politics (he had been a resident of the state since 1898). As a member of the legislature, and as unsuccessful liberal Republican candidate for governor, 1906, he set forces in motion which broke corporation and lobbyist control and compelled many reforms. His later writing concerned itself with modern social problems and their solution. These novels included *A Modern Chronicle* (1910), *The Inside of the Cup* (1912), and *A Far Country* (1915). Neither his vogue as a popular novelist nor his activity in politics survived the end of the Progressive era.

CHURCHMAN, WILLIAM HENRY (*b. Baltimore, Md., 1818; d. 1882*), educator of the blind. A superior administrator, he did his best work at Indiana Institution for the Education of the Blind.

CICOTTE, EDWARD VICTOR (*b. Detroit, Mich., 1884; d. Detroit, Mich., 1969*), baseball pitcher. Signed by the Detroit Tigers in 1905, he played in the minor leagues until 1908, when he joined the Boston Red Sox. He was traded to the Chicago White Sox in 1912, and his pitching helped lead them to two American League pennants and a World Series title. Over his fourteen-year career, Cicotte compiled a 210-148 win-loss record and a 2.37 earned-run average. His involvement in the 1919 "Black Sox" scandal, in which he admitted taking money to help throw the World Series, ended his baseball career.

CILLEY, JOSEPH (*b. Nottingham, N.H., 1734; d. Nottingham, 1799*), Revolutionary soldier, judge, politician. As major general of militia, quashed New Hampshire rebellion of 1786.

CIST, CHARLES (*b. St. Petersburg, Russia, 1738; d. Bethlehem, Pa., 1805*), printer, publisher. Born Charles Thiel; changed name on immigration to Philadelphia, Pa., 1769. Published Paine's *The American Crisis* (1776) and other important works. Helped organize Lehigh Coal Mine Company, 1792.

CIST, CHARLES (*b. Philadelphia, Pa., 1792; d. College Hill, Ohio, 1868*), merchant, editor. Son of Charles Cist (1738–1805). Published statistical and historical studies of Cincinnati and Ohio.

CIST, HENRY MARTYN (*b. Cincinnati, Ohio, 1839; d. Rome, Italy, 1902*), Union soldier, lawyer, military historian. Son of Charles Cist (1792–1868). Author of *The Army of the Cumberland* (1882).

CIST, JACOB (*b. Philadelphia, Pa., 1782; d. Wilkes-Barre, Pa., 1825*), naturalist, anthracite coal pioneer, inventor. Son of Charles Cist (1738–1805). Postmaster of Wilkes-Barre; did geological and botanical studies in that area; tried unsuccessfully to promote use of anthracite coal.

CLAFLIN, HORACE BRIGHAM (*b. Milford, Mass., 1811; d. 1885*), merchant. Pioneer in manufacturing own goods for jobbing to retailers; founder of H. B. Claflin and Co., New York, N.Y., 1843.

CLAFLIN, JOHN (*b. Brooklyn, N.Y., 1850; d. Morristown, N.J., 1938*), merchant. Son of Horace B. Claflin. Headed H. B. Claflin Co., 1885–1914.

CLAFLIN, TENNESSEE. *See* WOODHULL, VICTORIA.

CLAFLIN, WILLIAM (*b. Milford, Mass., 1818; d. 1905*), shoe manufacturer. Republican governor of Massachusetts, 1869–71.

CLAGETT, WYSEMAN (*b. Bristol, England, 1721; d. Litchfield, N.H., 1784*), lawyer. Served as King's Attorney for New Hampshire, 1765–69; during the Revolution was active in provincial congresses and the Committee of Public Safety and was influential in drafting the New Hampshire Constitution. Solicitor general of New Hampshire, 1781–84.

CLAGHORN, GEORGE (*b. Chilmark, Mass., 1748; d. Seekonk, R.I., 1824*), Revolutionary soldier, shipbuilder. Built first American whaler to double Cape Horn; was naval constructor of frigate *Constitution*.

CLAIBORNE, JOHN FRANCIS HAMTRAMCK (*b. near Natchez, Miss., 1807; d. 1884*), congressman, historian. Edited Democratic newspapers in Mississippi and Louisiana. Author of *Life and Times of Sam Dale* (1860), a life of John A. Quitman, and an unfinished history of Mississippi.

CLAIBORNE, NATHANIEL HERBERT (*b. Sussex Co., Va., 1777; d. Franklin Co., Va., 1859*), politician. Congressman, Democrat, from Virginia, 1825–37; an opponent of governmental waste.

CLAIBORNE, WILLIAM (*b. Westmoreland Co., England, ca. 1587; d. ca. 1677*), colonist. Appointed surveyor for colony of Virginia, 1621; became secretary of state and a member of the council. Opposed Lord Baltimore's claims to land within the boundaries of the 1609 Virginia Company grant, and established himself as trader of Kent Island in Chesapeake Bay, 1631. Unsuccessfully resisted Lord Baltimore's claim to Kent Island. Exploiting anti-Catholic feelings in Maryland, Claiborne incited insurrection and held province from October 1644 to December 1646, and was member of a parliamentary commission for government of Chesapeake Bay plantations, 1652–57.

CLAIBORNE, WILLIAM CHARLES COLES (*b. Sussex Co., Va., 1775; d. 1817*), lawyer, statesman. Member of Tennessee constitutional convention and judge of state supreme court. Congressman, Democratic-Republican, from Tennessee, 1797–1801; governor of Mississippi Territory, 1801–03, and of Louisiana, 1804–16. Unfamiliar with local customs and sentiment, Claiborne encountered much opposition despite his evident honesty and kindness; he also had difficulty with Andrew Jackson during defense of New Orleans in War of 1812. Elected to the U.S. Senate, January 1817, he died before taking office.

CLAP, THOMAS (*b. Scituate, Mass., 1703; d. 1767*), Congregational clergyman. Graduated Harvard, 1722. A rigid Calvinist and a stern disciplinarian, he was elected president of Yale in 1739 and served until his resignation in 1766.

CLAPP, ASA (*b. Mansfield, Mass., 1762; d. Portland, Maine, 1848*), shipmaster, merchant.

CLAPP, CHARLES HORACE (*b. Boston, Mass., 1883; d. 1935*), geologist. President, Montana State University, 1921–35.

CLAPP, GEORGE ALFRED. *See* DOCKSTADER, LEW.

CLAPP, WILLIAM WARLAND (*b. Boston, Mass., 1826; d. Boston, 1891*), journalist, author. Edited *Boston Journal*; published *A Record of the Boston Stage* (1853); wrote and adapted plays.

CLAPPER, RAYMOND LEWIS (*b. Linn Co., Kans. 1892; d. Eniwetok, Marshall Islands, 1944*), newspaper columnist. Soon after his birth his family moved to the Armourdale packinghouse section of Kansas City, Kans., where the father worked in a soap factory. An avid reader who organized an extensive file of clippings, he was drawn by his admiration for the Kansas editor William Allen White to the local print shop as its "devil," moved up to apprentice, and became a union journeyman. Did not complete high school.

On Mar. 31, 1913, Clapper married Olive Vincent Ewing. That autumn they walked to Lawrence and enrolled in the University of Kansas. Clapper edited the college paper and sent campus news to the *Kansas City Star*. In 1916, he joined the United Press in Chicago.

His first national news scoop came during the Republican National Convention of 1920 when Senator Charles Curtis emerged from the celebrated "smoke-filled room" and told his fellow Kansan that the party leaders were going to try to swing the nomination to Harding. Chief political writer for the United Press in Washington (1923–28) and the bureau manager (1929–33). Covered the Scopes trial in 1925 and the London Naval Conference of 1930. The exposé *Racketeering in Washington* appeared in 1933.

In 1934, joined the *Washington Post* and began a daily interpretive column, "Between You and Me." Nine years later he was appearing in 176 papers, had an estimated 10 million readers, and had entered radio broadcasting. He reported the attack on Sicily and the bombing of Rome and late in 1943 began to write from New Britain, New Guinea, and Guadalcanal. He died at Eniwetok when his plane hit another American bomber and crashed.

CLARK, ABRAHAM (*b. near Elizabethtown, N.J., 1726; d. near Elizabethtown, 1794*), surveyor, lawyer, farmer, signer of the Declaration of Independence. Member of New Jersey provincial congress, 1775, and of Continental Congress, 1776, he was thrice rechosen as a New Jersey representative, with interim service in the state legislature. Democratic in theory and practice, he served with ability as U.S. congressman, 1791–94.

CLARK, ALVAN (*b. Ashfield, Mass., 1804; d. 1887*), portrait painter, astronomer, renowned maker of astronomical lenses.

CLARK, ALVAN GRAHAM (*b. Fall River, Mass., 1832; d. 1897*), maker of astronomical lenses, astronomer. Son of Alvan Clark. Discovered Sirius companion, produced 40–inch lenses of Yerkes telescope.

CLARK, ARTHUR HAMILTON (*b. Boston, Mass., 1841; d. Newburyport, Mass., 1922*), master mariner, historian. Sailed on every ocean. Lloyd's New York agent, 1895–1920. Author of *The Clipper Ship Era* (1910) and other authoritative works.

CLARK, BENNETT CHAMP (*b. Bowling Green, Mo., 1890; d. Gloucester, Mass., 1954*), lawyer, U.S. senator, federal judge. Studied at University of Missouri and George Washington University (LL.B., 1914). Served in France in World War I; helped found the American Legion in Paris, 1919. Practiced law in Missouri until elected to the U.S. Senate (1934–44). Basically opposed to the New Deal and an ardent isolationist. A friend and supporter of President Truman, he was appointed to the Circuit Court of Appeals for the District of Columbia (1945–53).

CLARK, BOBBY (*b. Springfield, Ohio, 1888; d. New York, N.Y., 1960*), entertainer. Working from 1905 until 1936 with a partner, Paul McCullough, Clark played first in minstrels, then circuses (Ringling Brothers, 1906–12), vaudeville (appearing in the Irving Berlin *Music Box Revue* of 1922 and 1924), and burlesque. In 1926, the team went to Hollywood, where they made over seventy shorts for major studios. After McCullough's death in 1936, Clark turned to the stage playing roles in Congreve's *Love for Love* and Sheridan's *The Rivals*. He retired in 1948.

CLARK, CHAMP. *See* CLARK, JAMES BEAUCHAMP ("CHAMP").

CLARK, CHARLES (*b. Cincinnati, Ohio, 1810; d. 1877*), planter, Confederate brigadier general. Removed to Mississippi, *ca.* 1831. Crippled in battle, 1862. Elected governor of Mississippi and served until May 1865.

CLARK, CHARLES EDGAR (*b. Bradford, Vt., 1843; d. 1922*), naval officer. Commanded USS *Oregon* on its dash around Cape Horn, 1898.

CLARK, CHARLES HEBER (*b. Berlin, Md., 1847; d. Conshohocken, Pa., 1915*), journalist, humorist. Under pseudonym "Max Adeler," wrote *Out of the Hurly Burly* (1874) and other books.

CLARK, CHARLES HOPKINS (*b. Hartford, Conn., 1848; d. Hartford, 1926*), editor. Long associated with the *Hartford Courant*; editor, 1900–26.

CLARK, DANIEL (*b. Sligo, Ireland, 1766; d. 1813*), merchant. Came to New Orleans, 1786; prospered in river and sea trade; as consul at New Orleans was associated with James Wilkinson in his intrigues. Elected delegate to Congress from Orleans Territory,

1806, he served one term. He was author of *Proofs of the Corruption of Gen. James Wilkinson* (1809).

CLARK, DANIEL (*b. Stratham, N.H., 1809; d. 1891*), politician, jurist. U.S. senator, Republican, from New Hampshire, 1857–66; vigorously opposed slavery and secession. Federal judge, district of New Hampshire, 1866–91.

CLARK, FELTON GRANDISON (*b. Baton Rouge, La., 1903; d. New Orleans, La., 1970*), educator. Studied at Beloit College (B.A., 1924) and Columbia (M.A., 1925; Ph.D., 1933). He taught at Wiley College (1925–27), Southern University (1927–30), and Howard University (1931–33) before returning to Southern in 1934 as dean. He served as president of Southern, 1938–69. Clark served on a number of national bodies and was a member of several committees in the Education Department.

CLARK, FRANCIS EDWARD (*b. Aylmer, Canada, 1851; d. 1927*), Congregational clergyman. As pastor in Portland, Maine, organized the Christian Endeavor Society, 1881.

CLARK, GEORGE ROGERS (*b. near Charlottesville, Va., 1752; d. near Louisville, Ky., 1818*), soldier. Trained as a surveyor; in 1773 explored down the Ohio River; in 1774 took part in Dunmore's War and surveyed for the Ohio Company along the Kentucky River. Active in opposition to speculators who wished to make Kentucky a proprietary colony. Commanded Kentucky militia at opening of Revolution. Made plan in 1778 to attack and take over the Illinois country; by August his little army of 175 men had captured Kaskaskia, Cahokia, and Vincennes. Clark then stopped a British counteroffensive which had reached Vincennes, and made the English force surrender. During 1779 and 1780 he consolidated his gains and prevented the English from recapturing the Illinois country, the Falls of the Ohio (Louisville), Pittsburgh, and Fort Cumberland. He also marched to the relief of St. Louis and Cahokia, and defeated a force of British and Indians at Piqua. The war in the West continued after Cornwallis' surrender, and Clark, as Virginia brigadier general, won another encounter with the Shawnee at Chillicothe in November 1782. Clark's military dominance over the Old Northwest was a prime factor in confirming its cession to the United States in the 1783 Treaty of Paris.

After the war Clark served on the Board of Commissioners to supervise land allotment in the Illinois grant to his former soldiers, and on a commission concluding a treaty with the Indians. In 1786 during an unsuccessful expedition against the Wabash tribes, Clark seized goods brought to Vincennes by Spanish traders. This act was utilized by James Wilkinson, former Continental brigadier general, to discredit Clark, who stood in Wilkinson's path toward preferment in Kentucky. Clark lost the support of Virginia and the national government. He was prevented (1793) by Washington from enlisting in an expedition on behalf of France for the conquest of Louisiana. On the failure of another (1798) military project on behalf of the French, he returned to Louisville, and in 1803 went to live at Clarksville, on the Indiana side of the Ohio River, where he spent his time supervising land apportionment and running a gristmill. After a stroke of paralysis and the loss of one leg, he returned to live with his sister at Locust Grove, near Louisville. His own account of the conquest of the Old Northwest is to be found in a *Memoir*, which he wrote in 1791.

CLARK, GEORGE WHITEFIELD (*b. South Orange, N.J., 1831; d. 1911*), Baptist clergyman. Author of *Clark's People's Commentary* on the New Testament.

CLARK, GREENLEAF (*b. Plaistow, N.H., 1835; d. Lamanda Park, Calif., 1904*), railroad lawyer, practicing in St. Paul, Minn., 1858–88.

CLARK, GRENVILLE (*b. New York, N.Y., 1882; d. Dublin, N.H., 1967*), peace advocate. Graduate of Harvard Law School (1906), then practiced law in New York City. In 1909 he set up a law firm with two college friends. In 1915 he became a founder, then secretary, of the Military Training Camps Association, a forerunner of the Reserve Officers Training Corps. In 1940 Clark became chairman of the National Emergency Committee for Selective Service, for which he wrote the Selective Service Act of that year, and he chaired the Citizens Committee for National War Service (1944–45). In 1939 he published *A Federation of Free Peoples*. Prompted by the explosion of the atom bomb in 1945 he worked for years to insure peace through law. With Louis B. Sohn he wrote *World Peace Through World Law* (1958). He was involved in the civil rights movement and sponsored a Soviet-American conference in 1960.

CLARK, HENRY JAMES (*b. Easton, Mass., 1826; d. 1873*), zoologist, botanist. Pupil of Asa Gray and Louis Agassiz; excelled in histological research. Author of *Mind in Nature* (1865), and an associate with Agassiz in *Contributions to the Natural History of the United States* (1857–62).

CLARK, HORACE FRANCIS (*b. Southbury, Conn., 1815; d. 1873*), lawyer, banker. *Post* 1857, became a heavy investor in railroads and was associated with the ventures of his father-in-law, Cornelius Vanderbilt.

CLARK, JAMES (*b. Bedford Co., Va., 1779; d. 1839*), lawyer, jurist. Removed to Kentucky when a boy. Judge, circuit court of Kentucky, 1817–24; active in Whig party, he was governor of Kentucky, 1836–39.

CLARK, JAMES BEAUCHAMP ("CHAMP") (*b. near Lawrenceburg, Ky., 1850; d. 1921*), lawyer, politician. Graduated Bethany College, 1873. Practiced law; edited local Democratic newspapers; sat in Missouri legislature, 1889–91. Congressman, Democrat, from Missouri, 1893–1921 (except for 1895–97); Speaker of the House, 1911–19. In 1912 lost Democratic presidential nomination to Woodrow Wilson after 14th ballot. Opposed Selective Draft Act of 1917; was minority leader in 1919–21 term.

CLARK, JOHN (*b. Edgecombe Co., N.C., 1766; d. St. Andrew's Bay, Fla., 1832*), soldier. Son of Elijah Clarke. Governor of Georgia, 1819–23; leader of frontier people against the Troup faction of wealthy planters.

CLARK, JOHN BATES (*b. Providence, R.I., 1847; d. New York, N.Y., 1938*), economist. Attended Brown University and Amherst College, graduating from Amherst, 1872. He had planned to enter the ministry; instead he did advanced work in economics in Germany, then taught economics at Carleton, Smith, and Amherst colleges before joining, 1895, the faculty of Columbia University, where he remained until his retirement in 1923.

Clark's first book, *The Philosophy of Wealth* (1886), reflected his concern with ethical values and contained in germinal form the principles of his formal economic analysis. These principles were definitively outlined in his most important book, *The Distribution of Wealth* (1899), which confirmed his position as the premier economic theorist of America. Clark's "marginal utility" theory was founded on the following premises: (1) a sharp distinction between economic statics and economic dynamics, the first being used as a means to the eventual goal of dynamic analysis; (2) the universal applicability of the marginal analysis to both labor and capital; (3) a distinction between capital and capital goods, capital being a fund perpetuated and made mobile by replacement of capital goods (labor being a somewhat similar mobile fund); (4) the identification of normal wages with the marginal product of labor

and normal interest with the marginal product of capital; (5) the identification of profits and losses which depart from this norm as dynamic phenomena, profit being a reward for productive improvements; (6) the basing of all these results on free and fair competition, an organic social process which, in an effort to offer the buyer more, must improve production, thus keeping the economy fluid and serving as the most powerful driving force for progress.

Other books by Clark include *The Control of Trusts* (1901), *Essentials of Economic Theory* (1907), *Social Justice Without Socialism* (1914), and *A Tender of Peace* (1935). Though a symbol of conservatism in his later years, the logic and incisiveness of his economic writings exerted a wide influence.

CLARK, JOHN MAURICE (*b. Northampton, Mass., 1884; d. Westport, Conn., 1963*), economist. Graduated from Amherst and Columbia (Ph.D., 1910), taught at Colorado College, Amherst, and the University of Chicago. He then returned to Columbia as professor (1926–53). Son of economist John Bates Clark, he helped revise his father's *The Control of Trusts* (1912) and succeeded to his father's chair at Columbia. Clark sought to maximize freedom in economic life, even at the expense of lost efficiency. He sought to minimize controls with a consistency that betrayed an emotional as well as a rational objective. Although he dealt with most aspects of the economy, he focused on the mechanics of disappearing competition. In Clark's hands economic theory became largely a description of potent institutions, or habits, that profoundly modify free conduct. His writings include *Studies in the Economics of Overhead Costs* (1923), *Social Control of Business* (1926), *Strategic Factors in Business Cycles* (1934), *The Costs of the World War to the American People* (1931), and *Alternative to Serfdom* (1947). He was president of the American Economic Association in 1935 and was awarded its Walker Medal in 1952.

CLARK, JONAS (*b. Newton, Mass., 1730/31; d. Lexington, Mass., 1805*), Congregational clergyman, patriot. Pastor at Lexington, 1755–1805; adviser of Samuel Adams and John Hancock.

CLARK, JONAS GILMAN (*b. Hubbardston, Mass., 1815; d. Worcester, Mass., 1900*), merchant. Founder of Clark University, Worcester, Mass., 1887.

CLARK, JOSEPH SYLVESTER (*b. South Plymouth, Mass., 1800; d. 1861*), Congregational clergyman. Author of *A Historical Sketch of the Congregational Churches of Massachusetts* (1858).

CLARK, JOSHUA REUBEN, JR. (*b. near Grantsville, Utah, 1871; d. Salt Lake City, Utah, 1961*), lawyer, diplomat, and churchman. Studied at the University of Utah (B.S., 1898) and Columbia Law School (LL.B., 1906). In 1906 he became assistant solicitor of the State Department, where he wrote *Judicial Determination of Questions of Citizenship*, an authoritative text for immigration cases. He was appointed solicitor of the State Department by President Taft in 1910 and prepared *Memorandum on the Right to Protect Citizens in Foreign Countries by Landing Forces*. In 1913 he opened a law office in Washington, D.C., with branches in New York and Salt Lake City. He served as a major on the Army Judge Advocate General's staff during World War I. In 1928 he was appointed undersecretary of state and he drew up the "Clark Memoradum" on the Monroe Doctrine. He was ambassador to Mexico, 1930–33, after which he began a new career as a high official in the Church of Jesus Christ of Latter-Day Saints. He served as an apostle of the church from 1934 until his death.

CLARK, LEWIS GAYLORD (*b. Otisco, N.Y., 1808; d. Piermont, N.Y., 1873*). Twin brother of Willis G. Clark. Editor of the *Knickerbocker magazine*, 1834–61; author of *Knick-Knacks from an Editor's Table* (1852).

CLARK, MYRON HOLLEY (*b. Naples, N.Y., 1806; d. 1892*), politician, businessman. Governor of New York, 1854–58; elected by a coalition of Whigs, Free-Soilers, and Prohibitionists which is said to have originated the Republican party in New York.

CLARK, SHELDON (*b. Oxford, Conn., 1785; d. Oxford, 1840*), farmer. A notable benefactor of Yale; founded Clark professorship of philosophy there.

CLARK, THOMAS MARCH (*b. Newburyport, Mass., 1812; d. Newport, R.I., 1903*), Episcopal clergyman. Graduated Yale, 1831; ordained in Episcopal Church, 1836; consecrated bishop of Rhode Island, 1854.

CLARK, WALTER (*b. Halifax Co., N.C., 1846; d. 1924*), Confederate soldier, jurist. Judge, North Carolina superior court, 1885–88; supreme court, 1889–1924, and chief justice, 1902–24.

CLARK, WALTER LEIGHTON (*b. Philadelphia, Pa., 1859; d. Stockbridge, Mass., 1935*), mechanical engineer, art patron. Founder, Grand Central Galleries, New York City.

CLARK, WILLIAM (*b. Caroline Co., Va., 1770; d. St. Louis, Mo., 1838*), explorer, Indian agent. Brother of George Rogers Clark. Moved with his family to Louisville, Ky., 1785; participated in military expeditions against marauding Indians. After St. Clair's defeat, 1791, Clark enlisted for regular service and was commissioned as lieutenant of infantry, 1792. He served under General Anthony Wayne, commanded a supply party to the Chickasaw Indians, was stationed at Vincennes and Cincinnati, participated in the battle of Fallen Timbers, and was sent on a truce mission to the Spanish forces at Natchez. He resigned from the army in 1796 and traveled widely on behalf of his brother George, whose Revolutionary accounts Virginia refused to settle. In 1803 he accepted offer of Meriwether Lewis to join in an expedition to explore the Louisiana Purchase and find a route to the Pacific Ocean. The expedition set out on May 14, 1804, up the Missouri River; wintered among the Mandan in North Dakota, and in 1805 ascended the upper Missouri, crossed the Continental Divide, and followed the Columbia to its mouth. Retracing their route overland, they discovered other mountain passes and returned to St. Louis, Sept. 23, 1806. Clark contributed to the success of the expedition his frontier experience, his map-drawing skill, and his ability to sketch birds, fish, and other animals.

Appointed brigadier general of the militia for Louisiana (later Missouri) Territory and superintendent of Indian affairs at St. Louis, Clark made his home there for the rest of his life. As governor of Missouri Territory he was in charge of Indian defense during the War of 1812; after the war he successfully reconciled the western Indians; appointed agents and factors; and, together with Governor Lewis Cass, negotiated Indian treaty of Prairie du Chien, 1825.

CLARK, WILLIAM ANDREWS (*b. Fayette Co., Pa., 1839; d. 1925*), merchant, mine operator. Removed to Iowa, 1856; worked in Colorado and Montana gold mines; operated mining-town stores. *Post* 1872, invested profits in mining claims at Butte, Mont., and built stamp mills and smelters. Represented mining interests in Montana politics and feuded with his fellow Democrat Marcus Daly. A refined but coldly practical man, he built up one of the West's greatest mining businesses and served as U.S. senator from Montana, 1901–07.

CLARK, WILLIAM BULLOCK (*b. Brattleboro, Vt., 1860; d. North Haven, Maine, 1917*), geologist. Graduated Amherst,

1884; Ph.D., Munich, 1887. Taught geology, Johns Hopkins, 1887–1917; Maryland state geologist, 1896–1917.

CLARK, WILLIAM SMITH (*b. Ashfield, Mass., 1826; d. 1886*), Union soldier, scientist. President, Massachusetts Agricultural College, 1867–79.

CLARK, WILLIAM THOMAS (*b. Norwalk, Conn., 1831; d. 1905*), Union soldier, lawyer. Practiced law, Davenport, Iowa, 1856–61; served in western theater of Civil War; congressman, Republican, from Texas, 1869–72.

CLARK, WILLIS GAYLORD (*b. Otisco, N.Y., 1808; d. Philadelphia, Pa., 1841*), poet, editor. Twin brother of Lewis G. Clark. His literary remains and poems were edited by his brother.

CLARKE, SIR CASPAR PURDON (*b. Richmond, Ireland, 1846; d. 1911*), architect, archaeologist, art connoisseur, baronet. Director, Victoria and Albert Museum, London; Metropolitan Museum of Art, New York, 1905–10.

CLARKE, ELIJAH (*b. Edgecombe Co., N.C., 1733; d. Wilkes Co., Ga., 1799*), Revolutionary soldier. A troublesome factor on the Georgia frontier, 1787–94, involved in intrigues with the Indians, the French, and the English.

CLARKE, FRANCIS DEVEREUX (*b. Raleigh, N.C., 1849; d. Flint, Mich., 1913*), educator of the deaf. Director, Arkansas Institute for the Deaf, Little Rock; State School for the Deaf, Flint, Mich., 1892–1913.

CLARKE, FRANK WIGGLESWORTH (*b. Boston, Mass., 1847; d. 1931*), geological chemist. Student of Wolcott Gibbs. Chairman of the International Committee on Atomic Weights, 1900–22; author of *The Data of Geochemistry* (1908, rev. 1924).

CLARKE, GEORGE (*b. near Bath, England, 1676; d. Cheshire, England, 1760*), colonial official. Secretary of the Province of New York, 1703–43; lieutenant governor, 1736–43.

CLARKE, HELEN ARCHIBALD (*b. Philadelphia, Pa., 1860; d. Boston, Mass., 1926*), author, editor, musician. Founder and editor of *Poet Lore*.

CLARKE, JAMES FREEMAN (*b. Hanover, N.H., 1810; d. 1888*), Unitarian clergyman. Graduated Harvard, 1829; Harvard Divinity School, 1833. As minister in Louisville, Ky., 1833–40, edited the *Western Messenger*. Pastor at Boston, Mass., of the Church of the Disciples, 1841–50, 1854 until death. He was active in behalf of temperance, woman suffrage, and abolition of slavery. A transcendentalist, his most notable characteristics were balance and wisdom.

CLARKE, JAMES PAUL (*b. Yazoo City Miss., 1854; d. Little Rock, Ark., 1916*), lawyer. Governor of Arkansas, 1893–95; U.S. senator, Democrat, from Arkansas, 1903–16.

CLARKE, JOHN (*b. Westhorpe, England, 1609; d. Newport, R.I., 1676*), Baptist clergyman, statesman. Came to Boston, 1637, but immigrated to Rhode Island, where in 1639, with William Coddington, he founded Newport. Largely instrumental in securing royal charter for Rhode Island, 1663.

CLARKE, JOHN HESSIN (*b. New Lisbon, Ohio, 1857; d. San Diego, Calif., 1945*), lawyer, U.S. Supreme Court justice. Graduated Western Reserve College, 1877; studied law with father. Admitted to Ohio bar, 1878. Practicing briefly in New Lisbon and in Youngstown, 1880–97, he prospered as a trial lawyer in corporation cases, was active in civic affairs, and entered local politics as a Democrat. Moving his practice to Cleveland, 1897, he became a specialist in all aspects of railroad law; he also became a member of the circle of reformers associated with Tom L. Johnson, who sought to aid labor, democratize government, and eliminate the abuses of bossism and big business. A friend of Newton D. Baker, he was appointed a federal district court judge in 1914; in 1916, President Wilson elevated him to the U.S. Supreme Court. Serving until 1922, he supported in his opinions a broad extension of national and state power over the economy, to aid labor, on the one hand, and, on the other, to curb business malpractices and prosecute the trusts. After retirement because of ill health, he worked on behalf of the League of Nations and later in support of the New Deal.

CLARKE, JOHN MASON (b. *Canandaigua, N.Y., 1857; d. 1925*), paleontologist. Graduated Amherst, 1877. New York state paleontologist, 1898–1925; built up New York State Museum, Albany.

CLARKE, JOHN SLEEPER (b. *Baltimore, Md., 1833; d. 1899*), distinguished comedian and manager in America and England, 1851–87. Married a daughter of Junius Brutus Booth.

CLARKE, JONAS. *See* CLARK, JONAS.

CLARKE, JOSEPH IGNATIUS CONSTANTINE (b. *Kingstown, Ireland, 1846; d. 1925*), journalist. Came to America, 1868, after involvement in Irish revolutionary activities; won high reputation as editor and writer on *New York Herald* and *Morning Journal.* Publicity director, Standard Oil Co., 1906–13.

CLARKE, MCDONALD (b. *Bath, Maine, 1798; d. Blackwells Island, N.Y., 1842*), the "Mad Poet." A New York character, 1819–41; friend of Fitz-Greene Halleck and other writers.

CLARKE, MARY BAYARD DEVEREAUX (b. *Raleigh, N.C., 1827; d. New Bern, N.C., 1886*), author.

CLARKE, MARY FRANCIS (b. *Dublin, Ireland, 1803; d. 1887*), founder, and first superior, of Sisters of Charity of the Blessed Virgin Mary at Philadelphia, 1833.

CLARKE, REBECCA SOPHIA (b. *Norridgewock, Maine, 1833; d. Norridgewock, 1906*), writer of children's books under pseudonym "Sophie May." Wrote *Little Prudy* and *Dotty Dimple* stories.

CLARKE, RICHARD (b. *Boston, Mass., 1711; d. London, England, 1795*), Boston merchant, Loyalist.

CLARKE, ROBERT (b. *Annan, Scotland, 1829; d. Glendale, Ohio, 1899*), publisher, bookseller. Operated leading western book publishing firm in Cincinnati; specialized in bibliographies of American history and archaeology.

CLARKE, THOMAS BENEDICT (b. *New York, N.Y., 1848; d. New York, 1931*), art collector.

CLARKE, THOMAS SHIELDS (b. *Pittsburgh, Pa., 1860; d. New York, N.Y., 1920*), sculptor, painter. Studied at Art Students League and in Paris under Boulanger, Gérôme, and others. Among his best works in sculpture are four caryatids on New York City Appellate Court Building.

CLARKE, WALTER (b. *Newport, R.I., ca .1638; d. Newport, 1714*), colonial official. Deputy governor of Rhode Island, 1679–86 and 1700–14; governor, 1676–77, 1686, and 1696–98; opposed Governor Andros.

CLARKE, WILLIAM NEWTON (b. *Cazenovia, N.Y., 1841; d. Deland, Fla., 1912*), Baptist clergyman, educator. Author of *An Outline of Christian Theology* (1898).

CLARKSON, COKER FIFIELD (b. *Frankfort, Maine, 1811; d. Des Moines, Iowa, 1890*), editor. Settled in Iowa, 1855; editor, *Iowa State Register,* 1870–90; a pioneer in Iowa agricultural education.

CLARKSON, JOHN GIBSON (b. *Cambridge, Mass., 1861; d. Waltham, Mass., 1909*), baseball player. Pitcher for Chicago, Boston, and Cleveland; with Mike Kelly, part of the $10,000 Battery.

CLARKSON, MATTHEW (b. *New York, N.Y., 1758; d. New York, 1825*), Revolutionary soldier. A leading citizen of his city; supported many public improvement societies.

CLAUSEN, CLAUS LAURITZ (b. *Aerö, Denmark, 1820; d. Paulsbo, Wash., 1892*), pioneer Lutheran clergyman. Pastor in Wisconsin, Iowa, and Minnesota, 1843–85; founder of St. Ansgar, Iowa.

CLAXTON, KATE (b. *Somerville, N.J., 1848; d. New York, N.Y., 1924*), actress. Made debut in Chicago, 1869; famous as Louise in *The Two Orphans.*

CLAY, ALBERT TOBIAS (b. *Hanover, Pa., 1866; d. 1925*), Lutheran clergyman, orientalist. Taught Assyriology at University of Pennsylvania and at Yale; noted editor of cuneiform texts.

CLAY, CASSIUS MARCELLUS (b. *Madison Co., Ky., 1810; d. 1903*), abolitionist. Son of Green Clay. Graduated Yale, 1832. Entered Kentucky politics as an advocate of internal improvements. Inspired by William Lloyd Garrison, he published the *True American*, an abolitionist paper, in Lexington, 1845. Evicted from there, he issued the paper from Cincinnati and from Louisville, where he called it the *Examiner.* Fought with distinction in the Mexican War. In 1849 built up emancipation party in Kentucky; supported Frémont and Lincoln; fought briefly in Civil War. U.S. minister to Russia, 1861–62 and 1863–69.

CLAY, CLEMENT CLAIBORNE (b. *near Huntsville, Ala., 1816; d. 1882*), lawyer. Son of Clement Comer Clay. U.S. senator, Democrat, from Alabama, 1853–61; sought unsuccessfully to conduct informal peace negotiations with the North in Canada, 1864.

CLAY, CLEMENT COMER (b. *Halifax Co., Va., 1789; d. Huntsville, Ala., 1866*), lawyer. Removed to Huntsville, 1811. Held numerous offices in Alabama; congressman, Democrat, 1829–35; governor, 1836–37; U.S. senator, 1837–41.

CLAY, EDWARD WILLIAMS (b. *Philadelphia, Pa., 1799; d. New York, N.Y., 1857*), etcher, engraver, caricaturist. Author of *Life in Philadelphia* (1828–29).

CLAY, GREEN (b. *Powhatan Co., Va., 1757; d. Kentucky, 1826*), soldier. Father of Cassius M. Clay. Removed to Kentucky *ca.* 1777; worked as surveyor and prospered in land purchases. Served as Virginia and Kentucky legislator; as major general, Kentucky militia, raised siege of Fort Meigs, 1813.

CLAY, HENRY (b. *Hanover Co., Va., 1777; d. Washington, D.C., 1852*), statesman. Had three years of formal schooling in a log school. When he was fourteen, his family moved to Richmond, where Henry worked in a retail store, in the office of the clerk of the High Court of Chancery, and as amanuensis for Chancellor George Wythe. Clay began study of law in the office of Attorney General Robert Brooke in 1796 and within one year secured license to practice. He moved to Lexington, Ky., 1797, where he gained an excellent reputation as a criminal lawyer. Entered politics in 1798, when he denounced the Sedition Law in a speech at Lexington. Served in Kentucky legislature, 1803–06, and showed himself typically western in his point of view. Conservative where sanctity of law and established usages were concerned, he opposed the repeal of the charter of the Kentucky Insurance Co. on the ground of the inviolability of contracts, and limited the exclusion from Kentucky courts of English precedents to the period after July 4, 1776. He agreed to defend Aaron Burr and, before leaving for Washington to fill out John Adair's term in the U.S. Senate, received Burr's written statement of innocence. After being persuaded by Jefferson of Burr's guilt, he never again spoke to Burr. During 1806–07 Senate sessions Clay supported internal improvements. After serving as Speaker of the Kentucky legislature, 1807–09, he returned to the U.S. Senate, where he introduced resolutions praising Jefferson's embargo measures. Speaking in favor of home manufactures in 1810, he laid the foundations for his "American system." He opposed the chartering of the Bank of the United States as being dangerous to democratic institutions and unconstitutional (a doctrine which he later abandoned) and upheld the Perdido River as eastern boundary of the Louisiana Purchase.

Desiring to be "an immediate representative of the people," he left the U.S. Senate for the House, was elected Speaker (1811), and became spokesman for the "war hawks," pushing Madison into war with Britain in 1812. In the 1814 peace negotiations at Ghent, he strongly opposed J. Q. Adams' recommendations to exchange the right of free navigation on the Mississippi for the Newfoundland fisheries. He reentered the House after his return from Ghent and served there until 1821 (as Speaker until 1820). Declining offers of diplomatic posts and of the secretaryship of war, Clay nursed an ambition for the presidency which haunted him to his dying day and made his life an unending series of disappointments. He became a persistent critic of national administrations and an advocate of internal improvements, rechartering of the bank, protection of American industries, and strong national defense. The Bank was rechartered and the protective principle was incorporated in the tariff of 1816, but Clay's program of internal improvements was not carried out during his lifetime. He incurred the enmity of Andrew Jackson in 1819 when he attacked him for his invasion of Florida.

In the debates on the Missouri Compromise, Clay saw the struggle as one for continuance of the Union of equal states, not for the extension or restriction of slavery. Looking on the danger of any extension of federal power as settled by the compromise, Clay returned to Kentucky to look after his private affairs. Reentering the Congress, 1823, he was again House Speaker. In 1824 he secured passage of the highest protective tariff enacted up to then. As a candidate in the disputed presidential election of 1824, he failed to receive enough support to be voted upon by the House. Instructed by the Kentucky legislature to cast his vote for Jackson, Clay ignored these instructions and voted for Adams, effecting Adams' election. When Adams appointed Clay secretary of state, Clay was accused of a "corrupt bargain," a charge which was to follow him throughout his career. Clay's four years as secretary of state proved uneventful and uninteresting. The 1828 victory of Jackson disheartened Clay, who resented seeing a military chieftain in the White House. Reelected to the U.S. Senate in 1831, a bitter adversary of Jackson, Clay found his bills for bank recharter and distribution of land sale proceeds vetoed by the president.

Defeated as anti-Jackson candidate in the presidential election of 1832, Clay, with the aid of Calhoun, solved the South Carolina nullification crisis by securing passage for his compromise tariff bill of 1833. The next year, he was instrumental in having the Senate censure Jackson for his removal of bank deposits, although in 1837 the Senate expunged the censure resolutions from the record. After Van Buren's election and the panic of 1837 Clay opposed Van Buren's subtreasury system and in so doing parted company with Calhoun. Thanks to maneuvers of Thurlow Weed,

the 1840 Whig convention threw the presidential nomination to W. H. Harrison with John Tyler as running-mate. Though enraged over Weed's trickery, Clay campaigned for the Whig ticket. He rejected the secretaryship of state for himself, and in the Senate proposed as the new administration's program the repeal of the subtreasury system, the rechartering of the Bank of the United States, the distribution among the states of proceeds from public land sales and the passage of a new tariff. When Tyler succeeded to the presidency after Harrison's death, Clay found his program rejected except for the repeal of the subtreasury system. Deeply disappointed, Clay resigned from the Senate in 1842, only to find himself nominated by several states as Whig presidential candidate for the 1844 elections. Both he and Van Buren, who expected to be the Democratic nominee, agreed to oppose the immediate annexation of Texas, but, as the Democrats were determined on expansion, Van Buren lost the nomination to Polk. Clay, who had been nominated by acclamation, then declared that slavery was not an issue in the Texas question and endorsed Texas annexation "without dishonor, without war, with the common consent of the Union, and upon just and fair terms." This maneuver lost him New York and thereby the election. He supported the war with Mexico after it was declared.

Popular enthusiasm shown him in eastern cities prompted Clay in 1848 again to announce his candidacy. But this time the Whigs, feeling that Clay could not be elected, deserted him; General Zachary Taylor was nominated and elected. Deeply worried by the rising sectional struggle, Clay returned to the Senate in 1849 and introduced his resolutions for gradual emancipation. He sought to restrain radicals of both North and South, warned the South against secession, and supported the Compromise of 1850. He spent his last years in this effort and died in the service of his country. He was buried in Lexington cemetery amid national mourning. No man in American public life ever had more ardent supporters or more bitter enemies than Clay. Kentucky absorbed his strong Unionism, but refused to adopt his plan of emancipation. Frequently tempted to seek the pleasures of private life, he could never resist the importunities of his friends and his love of debate. Enthusiasm and warmth characterized his speaking, getting the best of his reason at times and leading him into untenable positions. He lacked the profound knowledge of Webster and the philosophical powers of Calhoun, but he excelled in his understanding of human nature, in his ability to appeal to the common reason, and in his absolute fearlessness in stating his convictions.

CLAY, JOSEPH (b. Yorkshire, England, 1741; d. 1804), merchant, Revolutionary officer, member of the Continental Congress. Nephew of James Habersham. Immigrated to Georgia, 1760. Prospered as Savannah merchant and planter; a "father" of the University of Georgia.

CLAY, JOSEPH (b. Savannah, Ga., 1764; d. Boston, Mass., 1811), Baptist clergyman, lawyer, jurist. Son of Joseph Clay (1741–1804). Influential member of Georgia constitutional convention of 1795; pastor, First Baptist Church, Boston, 1807–09.

CLAY, MATTHEW (b. Halifax Co., Va., 1754; d. Halifax Court House, Va., 1815), Revolutionary soldier, planter. Congressman, Democratic-Republican, from Virginia, 1795–1813; 1815.

CLAYPOLE, EDWARD WALLER (b. Ross, England, 1835; d. Long Beach, Calif., 1901), geologist, educator. Came to America, 1872. Taught at Antioch and Buchtel colleges, Ohio; worked briefly on geological survey of Pennsylvania. Discovered fish remains in Pennsylvania Silurian rocks.

CLAYTON, AUGUSTIN SMITH (*b. Fredericksburg, Va., 1783; d. 1839*), lawyer. Removed as an infant to Georgia; practiced law in Athens. As Georgia circuit judge, in *Worcester* v. *Georgia*, Clayton overruled Worcester's contention that Georgia lacked authority to extend its jurisdiction over the Cherokee nation. When the Supreme Court declared Georgia's position unconstitutional, Clayton voiced his objections. In 1831 he entered Congress as a Democrat and became a firm advocate of state sovereignty. The only avowed nullifier among first-rank Georgia politicians, he was equally radical in his opposition to the Bank of the United States. He retired from Congress in 1835.

CLAYTON, HENRY DE LAMAR (*b. Barbour Co., Ala., 1857; d. Eufaula, Ala., 1929*), lawyer. Congressman, Democrat, from Alabama, 1896–1914; U.S. district judge, 1914–29; largely responsible for the amendment to the Sherman Antitrust Act which bears his name.

CLAYTON, JOHN (*b. Fulham, England, ca. 1685; d. 1773[?]*), botanist. Came to Virginia, 1705, and was clerk of Gloster Co. until his death. Collected Virginia plants; his researches were presented in Gronovius' *Flora Virginica* (1739, 1743, 1762).

CLAYTON, JOHN MIDDLETON (*b. Dagsborough, Del., 1796; d. Dover, Del., 1856*), farmer, lawyer, statesman. Studied at Yale and Litchfield law school; practiced law in Dover, Del., *post* 1819. A loyal Adams supporter, he entered the U.S. Senate as Delaware Whig in 1828, supported Jackson on nullification, but opposed him on the tariff and bank issues. Reelected in 1834, Clayton resigned in 1836, became chief justice of Delaware. He returned to the Senate, 1845; in 1848 he supported Zachary Taylor and was appointed secretary of state. He opened up trade relations with the Orient, and with England concluded Clayton-Bulwer Treaty, which provided for a neutralized international canal across Central America. Resigning office in 1850, he returned once more to the Senate, 1852.

CLAYTON, JOSHUA (*b. Cecil Co., Md., 1744; d. Bohemia Manor, Del., 1798*), physician, Revolutionary soldier. President (governor) of Delaware, 1789–96; U.S. senator, 1798.

CLAYTON, POWELL (*b. Bethel Co., Pa., 1833; d. Washington, D.C., 1914*), Union soldier, planter, politician. Republican boss of Arkansas after 1868; carpetbag governor of Arkansas, 1868–71; served also in Senate and as ambassador to Mexico.

CLAYTON, THOMAS (*b. Massey's Cross Roads, Md., 1777; d. New Castle, Del., 1854*), jurist. Delaware secretary of state, attorney general, and chief justice; a moderate, independent Whig, he served as U.S. senator, 1824–28 and 1837–47.

CLAYTON, WILLIAM LOCKHART (*b. near Tupelo, Miss., 1880; d. Houston, Tex., 1966*), executive and government official. A founder in 1904 of Anderson, Clayton, and Company, which became the world's largest cotton-trading firm by 1920, when he became chairman of the board. A Democrat, Clayton began in government service with the War Industries Board (1918). He reentered government service in 1940 with the Reconstruction Finance Corporation and the Export-Import Bank. As assistant secretary of commerce (1942–44), assistant secretary of state for economic affairs (1944–46), and undersecretary of state (1946–48), he became the most significant economic foreign-policy maker in the Truman administration. He headed the Reparations Committee at the Potsdam Conference (1945) and became a major proponent of American aid for the economic recovery of postwar Europe. Clayton strongly supported the aid to Greece and Turkey that comprised the Truman Doctrine, and he was instrumental in helping formulate the Marshall Plan. His last major service for the State Department was his participation in the November 1947 Havana Conference to establish the International Trade Organization. In 1948 he returned to Houston and Anderson, Clayton, and Company, where he remained until 1961.

CLEAVELAND, MOSES (*b. Canterbury, Conn., 1754; d. Canterbury, 1806*), lawyer, Revolutionary soldier. As a director of Connecticut Land Co., supervised settlement of Cleveland, Ohio, in Western Reserve, 1796.

CLEAVELAND, PARKER (*b. Byfield, Mass., 1780; d. Brunswick, Maine, 1858*), scientist. Graduated Harvard, 1799. Tutored mathematics and natural philosophy at Harvard, and taught at Bowdoin College, 1805–58. Wrote first American work on mineralogy and geology (1816).

CLEBURNE, PATRICK RONAYNE (*b. Co. Cork, Ireland, 1828; d. Franklin, Tenn., 1864*), Confederate soldier, lawyer. Came to America, 1849, and settled in Arkansas. Commended for valor at Shiloh, Chickamauga, Missionary Ridge; rose to rank of major general. Died in battle.

CLEGHORN, SARAH NORCLIFFE (*b. Norfolk, Va., 1876; d. Philadelphia, Pa., 1959*), reformer, novelist, poet. Studied at Radcliffe College. During the 1890's, she contributed poetry to *Harper's*, the *Atlantic*, and *Scribner's*. She joined the Socialist party in 1913 and was a friend of Norman Thomas. Her books include the *Spinster* (1916) and *The Seamless Robe* (1945), Cleghorn is also remembered for her protest poems, which were widely popular in her day.

CLEMENS, JEREMIAH (*b. Huntsville, Ala., 1814; d. Huntsville, 1865*), soldier, author. Served against Cherokee and in war for Texas independence and Mexican War. Author of *Bernard Lile* (1856), *The Rivals* (1860), and other historical novels. U.S. senator, Democrat, from Alabama, 1849–56; a strong Unionist.

CLEMENS, SAMUEL LANGHORNE ("MARK TWAIN") (*b. Florida, Mo., 1835; d. Redding, Conn., 1910*), humorist, novelist. Resided in Hannibal, Mo., a small town on the Mississippi River, 1839–53. On death of his father, 1847, young Clemens was apprenticed to a printer; he became expert at the trade, read widely, and began to write for his brother's newspaper, published in Hannibal, and for other papers elsewhere. In 1853–54, he worked his way as a journeyman printer to St. Louis, New York, Philadelphia, and back to Keokuk, Iowa, where he was employed by his brother, who had left Hannibal. From Keokuk, after an abortive plan to make his fortune in South America, he set out in 1857 for New Orleans, on the way apprenticing himself to a river pilot. His four years as a pilot on the Mississippi were his "university"; they gave him an epic theme, broadened his experience of human nature, and supplied him with abundant colorful material for his later work.

When the Civil War closed the river, and after a brief experience of military life, Clemens took a post in Nevada as secretary to his brother Orion, who had been appointed secretary to the territorial governor. Turning at first to prospecting and mining, Clemens became in 1862 a reporter in Virginia City, using the pseudonym "Mark Twain." Having no particular literary principles, he readily adapted himself to frontier journalism in all its boisterous and burlesque phases. His ambition broadened with the arrival in Virginia City of the humorist Artemus Ward (Charles Farrar Browne), who gave him encouragement. He left for California in 1864, worked as a reporter, met Bret Harte, and in 1865 wrote the story of the "Jumping Frog," which was promptly reprinted in newspapers the country over. A local celebrity, he made a journalistic trip to the Sandwich Islands and came east on the first leg of a similar tour around the world, commissioned by a California newspaper. Characteristically changing his plans, he stopped in New York to deliver a triumphant lecture at Cooper Union and to publish his first book (*The Celebrated Jumping Frog of Calaveras County, and Other Sketches*, 1867). He then sailed to the Holy Land with a party of excursionists aboard the *Quaker City*, a trip which he described in a book that made him a national figure, *The Innocents Abroad* (1869). Through an acquaintance made on this voyage, he met and married Olivia Langdon in 1870, a marriage whose effect on the writer's art has been the subject of controversy.

Now with his roots permanently in the East, he met a popular taste for knowledge of the Old South and the Far West with works which exploited all his knowledge of, and feeling for, these two subjects. *Roughing It* (1872) was a classic account of his days in Nevada; *The Gilded Age* (1873, written in collaboration with Charles Dudley Warner) satirized contemporary life but drew on the author's recollections of his own boyhood. His turning away from satire in his next important work, *The Adventures of Tom Sawyer* (1876), has occasioned much debate among critics, but it is fair to consider that the impulse to satirize was only a part of Clement's mental constitution. His theological, political, economic, and social opinions were rough-and-ready, not grounded in any set of principles and therefore susceptible to influence by the more intricate conditions of the settled society of the East. His immense delight in life in general and his comic energy were the determinants of what he wrote at the height of his powers (1869–89). This very robustness of his art made him an uneven writer who poured out the pages as they came and had later to decide, or have it decided for him, to what degree they required editing. The *Sketches, New and Old* (1875) and similar collections are plainly inferior to *Roughing it, The Gilded Age, Tom Sawyer, A Tramp Abroad* (1880), and *The Adventures of Huckleberry Finn* (1885), nor are these themselves of equal merit. Without much question, he touched his peak in *Huckleberry Finn* and in the first part of *Life on the Mississippi* (1883); in these works, he dealt with the river and with his own youth, two subjects about which he was preeminently well informed and which employed his superior talent for humorous autobiography. His style was largely governed by his ear; as a lecturer, he had learned to fit rhythm, diction, tempo, and pauses to listeners rather than readers; this in turn accounts for certain defects of taste in his works.

Despite his success, Clemens refused to confine himself to exploitation of his Mississippi experiences. *The Prince and the Pauper* (1882) takes place in Elizabethan England; *A Connecticut Yankee in King Arthur's Court* (1889) drew comedy from the presence of a modern utilitarian American in the world of chivalry.

After his marriage and his settlement at Hartford, Conn., in the early seventies, Clemens had written constantly, traveled as a lecturer in Europe and through much of the United States, dabbled with the stage, invested heavily and without success in a mechanical typesetter and other speculative ventures, and had become his own publisher by putting money into the firm of Charles L. Webster & Co., which prospered for a time but failed disastrously in 1894. During the nineties, his physical strength waned and his literary output was less steady and unified. The works of this period include *The American Claimant* (1892), two sequels to *Tom Sawyer*, and *The Tragedy of Pudd'nhead Wilson* (1894); all these inclined too much to melodrama. *Personal Recollections of Joan of Arc* (1896) expressed the quintessence of that tenderness which was as much a part of him as his earlier boisterousness and his later bitterness.

Personal tragedies now began to color his view of life. Following his bankruptcy in 1894, he set off on a lecture tour around the world whereby he was able to pay off his debts by 1898; his contact with the older, static societies of Asia, however, served to deepen his pessimism. This attitude is shown in the record of his lecture tour, *Following the Equator* (1897). His extension of this mood will be found in three works written in 1898: "The Man That Corrupted Hadleyburg" (1900); *What Is Man?* (privately printed, 1906); and "The Mysterious Stranger" (not published until 1916). They are in dialectic about on a level with Ingersoll's "village atheist" posturing, but are significant in showing how a representative American responded to his observations in a way diametrically opposite to the standard optimism of the period.

After the dark year of 1898 Clemens apparently grew in resignation, pitying rather than despising mankind. He remained a restless traveler, commented freely on contemporary matters, and was an untiring public lecturer. In 1907 he wrote *Christian Science*, an attack upon what he deemed a menacing new cult, and in 1904, *Is Shakespeare Dead?*, an unimportant addition to the Baconian controversy. His wife died in 1904. During his last days he received many honors, but he cherished most the Oxford degree of doctor of literature, conferred in 1907. He died at his house, "Stormfield," in Redding, Conn. While during his life Clemens could never correct the popular impression of him as chiefly a fun-maker, the posthumous publication of his later works and of his autobiography revealed his inner life of rage and contempt, of dissent and disillusion, of despair and pity.

CLEMENT, EDWARD HENRY (*b. Chelsea, Mass., 1843; d. Concord, Mass., 1920*), journalist. Associate editor, Boston *Transcript*, 1875–81; editor, 1881–1905.

CLEMENT, FRANK GOAD (*b. Dickson, Tenn., 1920; d. Nashville, Tenn., 1969*), governor of Tennessee. Attended Cumberland University and Vanderbilt Law School (LL.B., 1942). Worked as an agent for the Federal Bureau of Investigation and served as general counsel for the Tennessee Railroad and Public Utilities Commission (1946–50). Elected governor of Tennessee in 1952 at the age of thirty-two. In 1954 he won Tennessee's first constitutionally mandated four-year term. Clement delivered the keynote address at the Democratic National Convention in 1956. Forbidden by law to succeed himself, Clement won a third term as governor in 1962. As a candidate for the Senate in 1966, he was defeated by Republican Howard Baker, Jr.

CLEMENT, MARTIN WITHINGTON (*b. Sunbury, Pa., 1881; d. Rosemont, Pa., 1966*), railroad executive. Attended Trinity College (B.S., 1901), then joined the engineering staff of the Pennsylvania Railroad (PRR). He was vice president in charge of operations (1926–33), directing one of the largest capital improvement programs in railroad history—the electrification of the PRR mainline between New York and Philadelphia. Clement became PRR vice president in 1933, acting president in 1934, and president in 1935. From 1949 until his 1951 retirement he was chairman of the board. In 1938 President Roosevelt appointed Clement to the joint labor-management Committee of Six, whose recommendations contributed to the Transportation Act of 1940.

CLEMENT, RUFUS EARLY (*b. Salisbury, N.C., 1900; d. New York, N.Y., 1967*), educator and civic leader. Studied at Livingstone College (graduated 1919), Garrett Biblical Institute (B.D., 1922), and Northwestern (M.A., 1922; Ph.D., 1930). Ordained a minister in the American Methodist Episcopal Zion (AMEZ) church in 1922, he taught at Livingstone (1922–31) while conducting services in rural AMEZ congregations on weekends. He was dean of Louisville Municipal College for Negroes (1931–37), then became president of Atlanta University in 1937. During his thirty-year presidency, Clement turned Atlanta University into a major educational center. He became the first black member of the Atlanta board of education in 1953, on which he served until his death.

CLEMENTS, FREDERIC EDWARD (*b. Lincoln, Nebr., 1874; d. Santa Barbara, Calif., 1945*), botanist, pioneer ecologist. B.Sc., University of Nebraska, 1894; M.A., 1896; Ph.D., 1898. Taught botany at Nebraska, 1897–1907; headed botany department at University of Minnesota, 1907–17; research associate of Carnegie Institution of Washington; at Tucson, Ariz., 1917–25; at Santa Barbara, Calif., *post* 1925. Collaborated with Roscoe Pound in the classic study *The Phytogeography of Nebraska* (1898). One of the first (with Henry C. Cowles) to appreciate the scientific importance of ecology, he devised a precise terminology for the field, much of which remains basic; in 1916, he published his *Plant Succession*, a work of profound scholarship, in which he formalized his "Clementsian system" and set forth his theory of the development of vegetation. During the 1930's, he was a valued consultant in applied ecology, as it concerned restoration of lands in the West and land-use policy in general. Described as "the greatest individual creator of the modern science of vegetation."

CLEMENTS, JUDSON CLAUDIUS (*b. Walker Co., Ga., 1846; d. 1917*), lawyer. Congressman, Democrat, from Georgia, 1881–91; an able and respected member of Interstate Commerce Commission, 1892–1917.

CLEMENTS, WILLIAM LAWRENCE (*b. Ann Arbor, Mich., 1861; d. Bay City, Mich., 1934*), industrialist, book collector. Gave Clements Library of Americana to the University of Michigan.

CLEMMER, MARY (*b. Utica, N.Y., 1839; d. Washington, D.C. 1884*), author. Her best work took the form of Washington letters to newspapers and columns on topics of public interest.

CLEMSON, THOMAS GREEN (*b. Philadelphia, Pa., 1807; d. 1888*), mining engineer, founder of Clemson College, South Carolina. Son-in-law of John C. Calhoun.

CLERC, LAURENT (*b. La Balme, France, 1785; d. 1869*), educator of the deaf. Pupil of Abbé Sicard. With Thomas H. Gallaudet, opened first American school for the deaf at Hartford, Conn., 1817.

CLEVELAND, AARON (*b. Cambridge, Mass., 1715; d. Philadelphia, Pa., 1757*), Congregational, later Episcopal, clergyman. Graduated Harvard, 1735. Pastor to several churches in New England. After ordination by bishop of London, 1754, returned to America as missionary of Society for the Propagation of the Gospel.

CLEVELAND, BENJAMIN (*b. Prince William Co., Va., 1738; d. South Carolina, 1806*), Revolutionary soldier, frontier judge. Commanded North Carolina partisan troops.

CLEVELAND, CHAUNCEY FITCH (*b. Hampton, Conn., 1799; d. Hampton, 1887*), lawyer. Reforming Democratic governor of Connecticut, 1842–43; a war Republican, he later returned to the Democratic party.

CLEVELAND, GROVER. *See* CLEVELAND, STEPHEN GROVER.

CLEVELAND, HORACE WILLIAM SHALER (*b. Lancaster, Mass., 1814; d. Hinsdale, Ill., 1900*), landscape architect. Son of Richard J. Cleveland. Worked mainly in Midwest. Among his best-known works are the Minneapolis and Omaha park systems; Natural Bridge, Va., grounds; Sleepy Hollow Cemetery, Concord, Mass.

CLEVELAND, RICHARD JEFFRY (*b. Salem, Mass., 1773; d. Danvers, Mass., 1860*), merchant navigator. Went to sea at 18; was captain at 24. The account of his extraordinary career and his feats of navigation in small sailing vessels will be found in his *Narrative of Voyages and Commercial Enterprises* (1842), a classic work on the sea.

CLEVELAND, STEPHEN GROVER (*b. Caldwell, N.J., 1837; d. Princeton, N.J., 1908*), president of the United States. Mainly self-educated, owing to early death of his father, a Presbyterian clergyman, and his consequent responsibility to care for his brothers and mother. Resident near Buffalo, N.Y., he studied law, was admitted to the bar, 1859, and became known as a careful, dependable legal workman. A Democrat by conviction, he entered politics and served as assistant district attorney and sheriff of Erie Co., N.Y. He was elected reform mayor of Buffalo in 1881, and was nominated and elected governor of New York in 1882. Stubborn honesty and independence of political control distinguished his term in office and won him the lasting enmity of Tammany Hall, the powerful New York City Democratic organization.

In 1884, since many Republicans distrusted their candidate, James G. Blaine, and would be willing to support an "unbossed" Democrat, Cleveland was nominated for the presidency. Elected after a campaign of unusual virulence and bitterness, the first Democrat to be president since the Civil War, he showed himself adamant against graft, extravagance, and excessive tariff protection, although he was forced to temper with expediency his own instinct for reform of the civil service. Renominated, he lost the election of 1888 to Benjamin Harrison and retired to private law practice. Popular revolt against Republican tariff policies and some adroit campaigning by his friends brought Cleveland the Democratic nomination and election in 1892.

His taking office in 1893 was coincident with a great financial panic. Firmly opposed in principle to currency inflation, he forced Congress to repeal the Sherman Silver Purchase Act, thereby alienating southern and western Democrats but stabilizing the nation's money position. The treasury surplus existing at the end of his first term had dwindled away during Harrison's administration, and Cleveland was forced to use desperate but successful means of maintaining a gold balance. Labor strife accompanied the depression of business, and he employed federal troops to suppress violence. He also opposed nascent American imperialistic tendencies, refusing to permit aid to rebel movements in Hawaii and Cuba; but in a boundary dispute between England's colony of Guiana and Venezuela, he vigorously supported the Monroe Doctrine and persuaded England to arbitrate. His painstaking, highly individual style of action was too just and fair for the bulk of his party, and in 1896 the Democrats repudiated his policies by nominating William J. Bryan. Cleveland retired to private life in Princeton, N.J., serving in important business capacities and occupying a commanding elder statesman position until his death.

CLEVENGER, SHOBAL VAIL (*b. near Middletown, Ohio, 1812; d. at sea, 1843*), sculptor. Self-taught; worked in Cincinnati. His work consists almost entirely of portrait busts.

CLEVENGER, SHOBAL VAIL (*b. Florence, Italy, 1843; d. 1920*), psychiatrist. Son of Shobal V. Clevenger (1812–43). An engineer, he turned to medicine. Author of *Comparative Physiology and Psychology* (1884) and *Spinal Concussion* (1889), a neurological classic which gave him an international reputation.

CLEWELL, JOHN HENRY (*b. Salem, N.C., 1855; d. 1922*), Moravian clergyman. Principal and president, Winston-Salem Academy and College, 1888–1909; president, Moravian Seminary and College for Women, Bethlehem, Pa., 1909–22.

CLEWS, HENRY (*b. Staffordshire, England, 1834; d. 1923*), financier. During Civil War his firm, later Henry Clews & Co., ranked second to Jay Cooke & Co. in amount of government bonds sold.

CLIFFORD, JOHN HENRY (*b. Providence, R.I., 1809; d. New Bedford, Mass., 1876*), lawyer. Served as attorney general and governor of Massachusetts; president, Boston & Providence Railroad, 1867–76.

CLIFFORD, NATHAN (*b. Rumney, N.H., 1803; d. 1881*), jurist. A Jackson Democrat, he served as Speaker in the Maine Assembly, as state attorney general, and as congressman from Maine, 1838–43. In 1846 President Polk appointed him U.S. attorney general; in addition to his legal duties he was entrusted with diplomatic negotiations with Mexico. He retired to the practice of law in Portland, Maine, after his recall in 1849. In 1858 he was appointed to the U.S. Supreme Court. During his 23 years of service he wrote the Court's opinion in 398 cases and penned 8 concurring and 49 dissenting opinions. His specialties were commercial and maritime law, Mexican land grants, procedure and practice. His opinions tended to draw sharp dividing lines between federal and state authority. As senior associate justice he presided over the Hayes-Tilden Electoral Commission, 1877.

CLIFFTON, WILLIAM (*b. Philadelphia, Pa., 1772; d. Philadelphia, 1799*), poet. Author of *The Group* (1796), a satiric attack on Gallatin, and other satires; his collected poems were published at New York in 1800.

CLIFT, EDWARD MONTGOMERY (*b. Omaha, Nebr., 1920; d. New York, N.Y., 1966*), actor. Began acting when he was thirteen; first appeared on Broadway in *Fly Away Home* (1935). Clift appeared in thirteen plays in New York, including *Yr. Obedient Husband* and *Dame Nature* (1938), *There Shall Be No Night* (1940), *Out of the Frying Pan* (1941), *The Skin of Our Teeth* and *Mexican Mural* (1942), *The Searching Wind* (1944), and *You Touched Me!* and *Foxhole in the Parlor* (1945). His first film was *Red River* (1948), with John Wayne. He received his first Oscar nomination for best actor in *The Search* (1948). He was also nominated for his work in *A Place in the Sun* (1951), *From Here to Eternity* (1953), and *Judgment at Nuremberg* (1961). Clift's other films included *Raintree County* (1957), *Wild River* and *The Misfits* (1960), and *Freud* (1962).

CLIFTON, JOSEPHINE (*b. New York, N.Y., 1813; d. New Orleans, La., 1847*), actress. First American to star in England, 1834. N. P. Willis' *Bianca Visconti* was written for her, 1837.

CLINCH, CHARLES POWELL (*b. New York, N.Y., 1797; d. New York, 1880*), author. An associate and friend of F. G. Halleck and the "Knickerbocker" group.

CLINE, GENEVIEVE ROSE (*b. Warren, Ohio, 1879; d. Cleveland, Ohio, 1959*), lawyer, judge. Studied at Oberlin College and at Baldwin-Wallace College (LL.B., 1921). Cline was one of the first women to be appointed a federal judge; President Coolidge appointed her to the U.S. Customs Court in 1928; she served until 1953.

CLINGMAN, THOMAS LANIER (*b. Huntersville, N.C., 1812; d. 1897*), politician, Confederate soldier. Congressman from mountain region of North Carolina, first Whig, later Democrat, 1843–45, 1847–58; U.S. senator, 1858–61. Left Whig party, 1852, over the slavery issue.

CLINTON, DEWITT (*b. Little Britain, N.Y., 1769; d. Albany, N.Y., 1828*), statesman, philanthropist, man of letters. Son of James Clinton. Graduated Columbia, 1786. Studied law, and in 1787 published letters signed "A Countryman" in the *New York Journal* opposing the proposed U.S. Constitution. He served as secretary to his uncle George Clinton, Antifederalist New York

governor, and as secretary of the Board of Regents and of the Board of Fortification. With the fall of his party in 1795 he lost his offices and turned for the time to the study of natural science. In 1797 he was elected to the state assembly, in 1798 to the state senate, and in 1801 to the governor's Council of Appointment. There he claimed the council members' right to propose candidates for office, rather than simply to ratify or reject the governor's nominations, and proceeded to supplant Federalist appointees with Republicans.

Appointed in 1802 to the U.S. Senate, he opposed the seizure of New Orleans, and introduced the 12th Amendment. In October 1803 he resigned to accept the mayoralty of New York City, which he held from 1803 to 1815 with exception of two annual terms (1807–08 and 1810–11). No mayor has done more for the city. He was chief organizer of the Public School Society, 1805, the chief patron of the city's Orphan Asylum and of the City Hospital. He inspected markets and docks, quelled mobs, strengthened fortifications, resisted British attempts to impress sailors in New York Harbor and to blockade the Narrows, and was last mayor to preside in the mayor's court. He also served as state senator, 1806–11, and lieutenant governor, 1811–13. The state's most powerful political leader, he broke with Gov. Morgan Lewis, whom he had supported in 1804, and in 1807 supplanted him with Daniel D. Tompkins. His independence of Democratic-Republican party control won him favor with the Federalists, who considered him as a possible candidate for the presidency in 1812, although they did not formally nominate him. As he had already been nominated by the Republicans of the New York legislature, his position seemed equivocal, and he was defeated by an electoral vote of 128–89. His consorting with Federalists cost him the confidence of his own party; he was not renominated for lieutenant governor, and in 1815 was removed from his office of mayor.

Clinton now devoted himself to the promotion of a project for a state canal which would join the Great Lakes with the Hudson. On Apr. 17, 1816, the legislature accepted his plan, and he was appointed to the canal commission. When he was elected governor of New York the next year, he continued active prosecution of the canal project. Believing in constructive leadership and active government, he gained the support of many Federalists during his term but at the same time built up a strong opposition among disgruntled Tammany politicians. He won the reelection for governor by only a slight margin, and did not seek a third term in 1822. When he retired, he was the strongest man in New York's public life, but the weakest in partisan support. He returned to the governorship two years later, however, aided rather than hindered by the precipitate action of his enemies, the "Albany Regency," who, in April 1824, had removed him from his office as canal commissioner. As governor, he took a prominent part in the celebration over completion of the Erie and Champlain canals in 1825. He had been responsible for making New York rather than New Orleans the port of the Northwest.

Clinton's achievements exceed those of the mere politician and statesman. He was the foremost spokesman for public education in New York and the leading promoter of Lancasterian schools in the whole country. A naturalist of real ability, he discovered a native American wheat and a new variety of fish; he published papers on pigeons, swallows, rice, and other topics, as well as his *Introductory Discourse* (1814), an able summary and review of scientific knowledge in America. He was active in many scientific and literary societies. In 1806 he succeeded in removing the political disabilities of Roman Catholics in New York, and was admired as a man of liberal ideas and administrative competence. He was always inept at intrigue, rather overbearing in manner, and indifferent to his political supporters. Personally unpopular, he was disliked by Republicans for his aristocratic tastes and by Federalists for his democratic principles.

CLINTON, GEORGE (*b. England, ca. 1686; d. England, 1761*), colonial official. Father of Sir Henry Clinton. In 1708 entered the British navy, in which he rose to the rank of admiral of the white squadron and, in 1757, to the position of senior flag officer. From 1741 to 1753 he served as governor of New York, proving to be a weak executive, dominated successively by Chief Justice De Lancey and Senior Councillor Cadwallader Colden, and losing control of appropriations and appointment of officers to the assembly. His administration permanently weakened royal government in New York and increased popular control.

CLINTON, GEORGE (*b. Little Britain, N.Y., 1739; d. Washington, D.C., 1812*), Revolutionary soldier, statesman. Served as New York delegate to Second Continental Congress and brigadier general in Continental army. In 1777 was elected New York governor, a post which he held for six successive terms. A believer in states' rights, he vigorously opposed adoption of the Constitution and wrote the famous "Cato" letters in the *New York Journal*, 1787. In 1789 and 1793 he met increasing hostility from Federalists, and in 1795 declined to stand for reelection. The Democratic-Republican victory of 1800 brought Clinton back as governor, and 1804 and 1808 he was elected vice president of the United States.

CLINTON, GEORGE WYLIE (*b. Lancaster Co., N.C., 1859; d. 1921*), bishop of the A.M.E. Zion Church, *post* 1896. Edited *Afro-American Spokesman* and *Star of Zion.*

CLINTON, JAMES (*b. Ulster Co., N.Y., 1733; d. Little Britain, N.Y., 1812*), Revolutionary soldier. Brother of George Clinton (1739–1812); father of DeWitt Clinton. Defended Hudson highlands, 1777; with Gen. John Sullivan, destroyed power of Indians in upper New York state, 1779; commanded a brigade at Yorktown.

CLOPTON, DAVID (*b. Putnam Co., 1820; d. Montgomery, Ala., 1892*), jurist. Removed to Alabama, 1844; served in U.S. and Confederate congresses, 1859–65; judge, Alabama Supreme Court, 1884–92.

CLOPTON, JOHN (*b. New Kent Co., Va., 1756; d. 1816*), Revolutionary soldier. Congressman, Democratic-Republican, 1795–1816, excepting the 6th Congress when he was defeated by John Marshall.

CLOSSON, WILLIAM BAXTER (*b. Thetford, Vt., 1848; d. 1926*), painter, wood engraver.

CLOTHIER, WILLIAM JACKSON (*b. Sharon Hill, Pa., 1881; d. Valley Hill Farm, Pa., 1962*), coal merchant and athlete. Studied at Swarthmore and Harvard, from which he graduated in 1904. In college he played football, ice hockey, and tennis, and he went on to become a nationally ranked tennis player. He played on the American Davis Cup team (1905–06) and won the National Singles Championship (1906). He was partner in the banking house of Montgomery, Clothier, and Tyler (1907–21). In 1911 he organized the Boone County Coal Corp., and he became its president in 1915. His nearly 1,000 acre farm, Valley Hill Farm, became a spectacular recreational center where the Clothiers bred and trained horses and hounds. He was president of the International Tennis Hall of Fame in Newport, R.I. (1954–57), into which he was inducted in 1956.

CLOUD, HENRY ROE (*b. Winnebago, Nebr., 1886; d. Siletz, Oreg., 1950*), educator, federal administrator. Born of Winnebago Indian parents. B.A., Yale, 1910; M.A., 1914. B.D., Auburn Theological Seminary, 1913, and ordained in Presbyterian ministry. Early a leader in movements to improve the condition of American Indians, he founded Roe (later American) Indian Institute, Wichita, Kans., 1915, and served as its superintendent through 1930. He was a member of the staff of the Brookings Institution survey of Indian affairs, 1926–27 and 1929–30, and coauthor of the Merriam Report (1928). After two years (1931–33) in the U.S. Office of Indian Affairs, he was appointed superintendent of Haskell Institute, Lawrence, Kans., in August 1933, and served until 1936. Thereafter, he held supervisory posts in the field for the Office of Indian Affairs. Among the most eloquent and best trained of his generation of educated Indian spokesmen, Cloud believed that the assimilation of the Indians into white society was inevitable; he insisted, however, that the nature of the transition should be determined by Indian leaders and with full regard to the preservation of Indian culture.

CLOUD, NOAH BARTLETT (*b. Edgefield, S.C., 1809; d. Montgomery, Ala., 1875*), planter, politician. Removed to Alabama, 1846. Edited at Montgomery the *American Cotton Planter*, 1853–61; his work of primary importance in agricultural progress of the state.

CLOUGH, JOHN EVERETT (*b. near Frewsburg, N.Y., 1836; d. Rochester, N.Y., 1910*), Baptist clergyman. Ordained 1864, Burlington, Iowa, he worked in India as a missionary until 1905.

CLOUGH, WILLIAM PITT (*b. Freetown, N.Y., 1845; d. 1916*), lawyer. Removed to Minnesota, 1867. A close associate of James J. Hill, he was a vice president of Northern Securities Co. and the Northern Pacific Railway.

CLUETT, SANFORD LOCKWOOD (*b. Troy, N.Y., 1874; d. Palm Beach, Fla., 1968*), inventor and industrialist. A graduate of Rensselaer Polytechnic Institute (1898), he was awarded more than 200 patents. Working for a farm machinery company, he developed mowers with vertical lifts that were operable from the driver's seat. He also invented Clupak, a stretchable paper that is difficult to tear. In 1919 Cluett joined the textile firm of Cluett, Peabody, and Company, which had been started by his uncles. He became a director in 1921 and a vice president in 1927. His most significant invention was the processing of cloth to reduce shrinkage (Sanforized cloth).

CLYMAN, JAMES (*b. Fauquier Co., Va., 1792; d. Napa, Calif., 1881*), trapper, pioneer settler. Served as mounted ranger in War of 1812; in 1823 went to St. Louis and joined Ashley's second expedition to ascend the Missouri. Journeyed to Green River with Smith-Fitzpatrick party, 1824; thus was one of first whites to cross South Pass from the east. After further adventures in the West opened store at Danville, Ill., served in Black Hawk War; fought Indians on Wisconsin frontier. In 1844 traveled to Oregon and California. After return to Independence, Mo., 1846, he guided an 1848 immigrant party to California; there he married and established his own ranch. His diaries and reminiscences, edited as *James Clyman, American Frontiersman* (1928), are a rich source of early western history.

CLYMER, GEORGE (*b. Philadelphia, Pa., 1739; d. Philadelphia, 1813*), merchant, signer of Declaration of Independence and of the U.S. Constitution. As a member of Pennsylvania Council of Safety, Continental treasurer and congressman (1776–77, 1780–82), he served ably on many commissions and on the boards of war and of the treasury. His services were of particular value in financial matter. As a member of the U.S. Congress, 1789–91, he supported Washington but favored a pro-French and Jeffersonian economic policy.

CLYMER, GEORGE E. (*b. Bucks Co., Pa., 1754; d. London, England, 1834*), inventor. A carpenter and joiner, he devised a unique plow especially adapted to Pennsylvania soils, and a superior pump which was used in the construction of piers for the first permanent Schuylkill River bridge. His most important invention (1817), the "Columbian" handprinting press, the first real American invention in printing, was the result of 16 years' effort. Its price, however, prevented its ready sale in America. In 1817 Clymer took it to England, where it was widely used as it was in other countries of Europe.

COAKLEY, CORNELIUS GODFREY (*b. Brooklyn, N.Y., 1862; d. New York, N.Y., 1934*), laryngologist.

COALTER, JOHN. *See* COLTER, JOHN.

COAN, TITUS (*b. Killingworth, Conn., 1801; d. 1882*), Presbyterian clergyman. Missionary to Hawaii, 1834–82.

COATES, FLORENCE EARLE (*b. Philadelphia, Pa., 1850; d. Philadelphia, 1927*), poet.

COATES, GEORGE HENRY (*b. Windsor, Vt., 1849; d. 1921*), inventor, manufacturer. At Worcester, Mass., developed large hair-clipper manufacturing plant. Patented (1892) a flexible shaft for transmission of power to drilling and grinding machinery.

COATES, SAMUEL (*b. Philadelphia, Pa., 1748; d. Philadelphia, 1830*), merchant, philanthropist. Active benefactor of Pennsylvania Hospital, overseer of Philadelphia Quaker schools, and a director of first Bank of the United States.

COBB, ANDREW JACKSON (*b. Athens, Ga., 1857; d. 1925*), jurist, law teacher. Son of Howell Cobb. Taught at University of Georgia; was dean of Atlanta Law School. Served as associate justice of Georgia Supreme Court, 1896–1908. Gave decision in first U.S. "right of privacy" case.

COBB, DAVID (*b. Attleborough, Mass., 1748; d. Boston, Mass., 1830*), Revolutionary officer, judge, politician.

COBB, ELIJAH (*b. Brewster, Mass., 1768; d. Brewster, 1848*), sea captain. His colorful and typical career is to be found in his autobiography, *Elijah Cobb, a Cape Cod Skipper* (edited by R. D. Paine, 1925).

COBB, FRANK IRVING (*b. Shawnee Co., Kans., 1869; d. 1923*), journalist. Raised in Michigan. Editorial writer, Detroit *Evening News*, 1899–1903; adviser to Joseph Pulitzer on New York *World*, 1904–11, editor in chief, 1911–23.

COBB, HOWELL (*b. Jefferson Co., Ga., 1815; d. New York, N.Y., 1868*), lawyer, politician. Belonged to planter-class family with long record of public service. Graduated University of Georgia, 1834; admitted to bar, 1836. Congressman, Democrat, from Georgia, 1843–51, 1855–57. Supported annexation of Texas and the Mexican War; opposed Calhoun's call for a southern party, 1849. In 1850 led Union Democrats to victory in Georgia, but drew upon himself the relentless hatred of southern-rights people. His greatest victory came with his 1851 election as governor on a Unionist ticket. Read out of Georgia Democratic party, he was not reelected, but was returned to Congress. Efficient as secretary of the treasury, 1857–60. After Lincoln's election, advocated immediate secession and was chairman of Montgomery convention to organize Confederacy. After war service as Confederate major general, returned to law practice and opposed Reconstruction policies.

COBB, IRVIN SHREWSBURY (*b. Paducah, Ky., 1876; d. New York, N.Y., 1944*), newspaperman, author, humorist. Left school at 16; rose from reporter on *Paducah Daily News* to managing editor in three years. After work on a number of midwestern papers, he went to New York City in 1904, won notice for his

reporting of the Russo-Japanese peace negotiations, 1905, and was appointed staff humorist of the *New York Evening World* and the *World* Sunday edition. In 1911, he left newspaper work to become a staff contributor to the *Saturday Evening Post* (1911–22) and *Cosmopolitan* (1922–32). Meanwhile, he had been a correspondent in World War I, and *post* 1909 one of the most widely read short-story writers of the period. His stories, often set in the western Kentucky of his youth, appeared in the leading magazines and were later published in collections such as *Back Home* (1912), *Local Color* (1916), and *J. Poindexter, Colored* (1922). Many of the stories dealt with the character Judge Priest. He also wrote numerous best-selling books of humor (*Speaking of Operations*—1915), and was a successful after-dinner speaker and Chautauqua lecturer. Removing to Hollywood, Calif., 1934, he worked as a scriptwriter and actor. *Stickfuls* (1923) is his account of his experiences as a newspaperman.

COBB, JONATHAN HOLMES (*b. Sharon, Mass., 1799; d. 1882*), lawyer. Practiced in Dedham, Mass., promoted silk manufacture in Massachusetts and established, 1837, one of earliest silk mills in the United States.

COBB, LYMAN (*b. Lenox, Mass., 1800; d. Colesburg, Pa., 1864*), educator. Wrote spelling, reading, and arithmetic textbooks. A Pestalozzian, he was author of *Evil Tendencies of Corporal Punishment* (1847).

COBB, NATHAN AUGUSTUS (*b. Spencer, Mass., 1859; d. Baltimore, Md., 1932*), nematologist, agronomist.

COBB, SYLVANUS (*b. Norway, Maine, 1798; d. Boston, Mass., 1866*), Universalist clergyman. Chief missionary of Universalism in Maine; published *The Christian Freeman*, 1839–62.

COBB, SYLVANUS (*b. Waterville, Maine, 1823; d. Hyde Park, Mass., 1887*), author of melodramatic popular fiction, mainly for Bonner's *New York Ledger*.

COBB, THOMAS READE ROOTES (*b. Jefferson Co., Ga., 1823; d. Fredericksburg, Va., 1862*), lawyer, Confederate soldier. Brother of Howell Cobb. Codified Georgia laws (1851); was ardent promoter of secession; a brigadier general, he died in battle.

COBB, TYRUS RAYMOND ("TY") (*b. Narrows, Banks County, Ga., 1886; d. Atlanta, Ga., 1961*), baseball player. Generally acknowledged to have been the greatest all-around offensive baseball player, he began as a star player on a local sandlot team. In 1905 he joined the Detroit Tigers, batting only .240 in his first year. In 1906 he batted .320, the first of twenty-three straight years in which he hit .300 or better. During that period he led the league in batting twelve times, nine in a row. Three times he hit over .400 in a season, his highest average being .420 in 1911. Cobb was also a wizard on the base paths. In his career he stole 892 bases, a record that stood for half a century. His brawls with other ballplayers— and once with an umpire—were legend. In 1912 he was suspended for jumping into the bleachers to strike a heckling fan. Cobb was player-manager of the Tigers, 1920–26. He played for the Philadelphia Athletics in 1927 and 1928. His career 4,191 hits stood as a major league record until it was broken by Pete Rose in 1985. His career batting average was a record .367. Cobb was the first player elected to the Baseball Hall of Fame (1936).

COBB, WILLIAM HENRY (*b. Marion, Mass., 1846; d. Boston, Mass., 1923*), Congregational clergyman, librarian. Old Testament scholar of international standing, authority on history of Congregationalism and an editor of *Journal of Biblical Literature*.

COBBETT, WILLIAM (*b. Farnham, England, 1763; d. 1835*), journalist, pseudonym "Peter Porcupine." Living in the United States as a political refugee from 1792 to 1800 and from 1817 to 1819, he was a founder of American partisan journalism. His anti-Jacobin pamphlets include *Observations on the Emigration of Dr. Priestley* (1794), *A Bone to Gnaw for the Democrats* (1795), and *The Life and Adventures of Peter Porcupine* (1796). In his *Political Censor* and his newspaper *Porcupine's Gazette* (1797–1800), he upheld the Federalists and lambasted the Democratic-Republicans with savage sarcasm. In 1799 he was fined for libel of Dr. Benjamin Rush, and in 1800 left for England. Returning in 1817, he settled at New Hyde Park, N.Y., and devoted himself to agriculture and authorship until his return home in 1819. The major phases of his career belong to English history, in which he figures as one of the great radical pamphleteers.

COBO, ALBERT EUGENE (*b. Detroit, Mich., 1893; d. Detroit, 1957*), businessman and politician. Cobo was "lent" to the city of Detroit in 1933 by the Burroughs Adding Machine Co., where he was a sales executive, to help the city's financial department. In 1949, he ran as a non-partisan candidate for mayor of Detroit; he served until his death in 1957.

COBURN, ABNER (*b. Canaan, Maine, 1803; d. 1885*), businessman, philanthropist. He was a land and lumber dealer and president of Maine Central Railroad, and served as Republican governor of Maine, 1863–66, with a nonpartisan efficiency that cost him renomination.

COBURN, FOSTER DWIGHT (*b. Cold Springs, Wis., 1846; d. 1924*), agricultural editor, administrator. Removed to Kansas, 1867. Edited *Livestock Indicator*; served as secretary of Kansas State Board of Agriculture. Author of *Swine in America* (1909).

COCHRAN, ALEXANDER SMITH (*b. Yonkers, N.Y., d. Saranac Lake, N.Y., 1929*), manufacturer, philanthropist. Liberal president of Alexander Smith Carpet Co.; benefactor of many institutions, including the Metropolitan Museum of Art and Yale University.

COCHRAN, JOHN (*b. Sadsbury, Pa., 1730; d. Palatine, N.Y., 1807*), physician. Practiced in New Jersey; during the Revolution served with great distinction as surgeon and director general of Continental army hospitals, 1777–83.

COCHRANE, ELIZABETH. *See* SEAMAN, ELIZABETH COCHRANE.

COCHRANE, GORDON STANLEY ("MICKEY") (*b. Bridgewater, Mass., 1903; d. Lake Forest, Ill., 1962*), baseball player. Broke into professional baseball in 1923; in 1925 he began a long association with Connie Mack, owner and manager of the Philadelphia Athletics. For nine years he was Mack's regular catcher, and he hit over .300 in six seasons. He was an outstanding defensive player and had the highest fielding average of any catcher in four seasons. In 1928 and 1934 he was selected the most valuable player in the league. Cochrane became player-manager of the Detroit Tigers in 1933 and led them to the World Series in 1934 and 1935. In 1937 he suffered a career-ending skull fracture in a game. He had a lifetime batting average of .320. In 1947 Cochrane was elected to the Baseball Hall of Fame, and in 1952 he and Bill Dickey were named the best catchers of the half-century by the All-American Board of Baseball.

COCHRANE, HENRY CLAY (*b. Chester, Pa., 1842; d. 1913*), Marine Corps officer, 1861–1905. Commended for service in Egypt, the Philippines, and China.

COCHRANE, JOHN (*b. Palatine, N.Y., 1813; d. 1898*), lawyer, politician. Grandson of John Cochran. As congressman from New York, Democrat, 1857–61, he upheld Southern viewpoint, but in 1861 joined Union army. Nominated for vice president, 1864, he withdrew before election. In 1872 supported Horace Greeley.

COCKE, JOHN HARTWELL (*b. Surry Co., Va., 1780; d. 1866*), planter, publicist. Promoter of new agricultural methods in Virginia; opponent of slavery. With Jefferson and J. C. Cabell, aided founding University of Virginia.

COCKE, PHILIP ST. GEORGE (*b. Fluvanna Co., Va., 1809; d. Powhatan Co., Va., 1861*), soldier, planter. Son of John H. Cocke. Graduated West Point, 1832. Benefactor of Virginia Military Institute; brigadier general in Confederate army.

COCKE, WILLIAM (*b. Amelia Co., Va., 1748; d. 1828*), soldier, legislator, Indian agent. Removed *ca.* 1774 to the Holston Valley frontier; a leader in separatist "state of Franklin" movement; U.S. senator from Tennessee, 1796–97, 1799–1805.

COCKERELL, THEODORE DRU ALISON (*b. Norwood, London, England, 1866; d. San Diego, Calif., 1948*), naturalist. Immigrated for reasons of health to Colorado, 1887; began a comprehensive catalogue of the entire biota of the Rocky Mountain region. Apparently recovered, he returned to England for a year (1890–91) and worked at the British Museum and as assistant to Alfred Russel Wallace. After holding curatorship of a public museum in Kingston, Jamaica, 1891–93, his health failed again and he served as professor of entomology and zoology at New Mexico Agricultural College, 1893–1900. Thereafter, he was associated with faculties of other colleges in the Rocky Mountain region, and was lecturer and professor of zoology at the University of Colorado, 1904–34. A naturalist in the broad tradition of the 19th century, he was best known for his work in entomology and a recognized authority on the taxonomy of bees; he pioneered in the classification of fossil fish by their isolated scales. Author of several books and nearly 4,000 papers and notes.

COCKERILL, JOHN ALBERT (*b. Adams Co., Ohio, 1845; d. Cairo, Egypt, 1896*), journalist. Managing editor, *Cincinnati Enquirer* and *Baltimore Gazette*; aid to Joseph Pulitzer on *St. Louis Post-Dispatch* and *New York World*; died as a special correspondent for *New York Herald*.

COCKRAN, WILLIAM BOURKE (*b. Co. Sligo, Ireland, 1854; d. 1923*), lawyer, orator. Came to America, *ca.* 1871. A force in New York Democratic politics, although constantly in opposition; served in Congress, 1887–89, 1891–95, 1905–09, 1921–23.

COCKRELL, FRANCIS MARION (*b. near Columbus, Mo., 1834; d. 1915*), Confederate soldier, lawyer. U.S. senator, Democrat, from Missouri, 1875–1905.

CODDINGTON, WILLIAM (*b. Boston, England, 1601; d. Newport, R.I., 1678*), governor of Aquidneck. Came to Massachusetts, 1630. Protested treatment of Anne Hutchinson, 1637; withdrew, 1638, to Aquidneck (now Rhode Island) and in 1639 founded Newport. Reluctantly agreed to unification of Aquidneck with Providence Plantations.

CODMAN, JOHN (*b. Dorchester, Mass., 1814; d. Boston, Mass., 1900*), sea captain. Active in merchant service, 1834–65.

CODY, WILLIAM FREDERICK (*b. Scott Co., Iowa, 1846; d. Denver, Colo., 1917*), scout, showman, better known as "Buffalo Bill." As a youth worked as "cavvy boy"; as mounted messenger for Russell, Majors & Waddell; Pony Express rider; and, during Civil War, as scout and trooper. Furnished buffalo meat for food contractors to Kansas Pacific Railroad, which gave him his nickname. Was chief scout of 5th Cavalry. Played leading role, 1872–76, in Col. E. Z. C. Judson's play *Scouts of the Prairies*. During Sioux War of 1876, returned to 5th Cavalry. In partnership with Maj. Frank North, took up cattle ranching near North Platte, Nebr. In 1883 started his "Wild West" exhibition, in which he toured all over the world. *Post* 1894, he settled on a ranch in the Big Horn Basin in Wyoming.

COE, GEORGE ALBERT (*b*. Mendon, N.Y., 1862; *d*. Claremont, Calif., 1951), scholar and religious educator. Studied at the University of Rochester and the Boston University School of Theology (Ph.D., 1891). Taught at the University of Southern California (1888–93); Northwestern University (1893–1909); the Union Theological Seminary (1909–1922); and Columbia Teachers College (1922–27). One of the first pioneers in the psychology of religion, his best-known works include *Psychology of Religion* (1916) and *A Social Theory of Religious Education* (1917). One of the most influential intellectuals of American Protestantism of the early twentieth century, Coe finally rejected organized religion as ineffective in rectifying social inequality and he embraced Marxian Messianism.

COE, GEORGE SIMMONS (*b*. Newport, R.I., 1817; *d*. Englewood, N.J., 1896), banker. President of American Exchange Bank, 1860–94, and, in 1881, of American Bankers Association; helped establish New York Clearing House.

COE, ISRAEL (*b*. Goshen, Conn., 1794; *d*. Waterbury, Conn., 1891), brass manufacturer. A pioneer in brass rolling industry.

COERNE, LOUIS ADOLPHE (*b*. Newark, N.J., 1870; *d*. Boston, Mass., 1922), composer, teacher of music. His best work is the opera *Zenobia*.

COFER, MARTIN HARDIN (*b*. Elizabethtown, Ky., 1832; *d*. Frankfort, Ky., 1881), Confederate soldier, jurist. Judge, Kentucky circuit court, 1870–74; justice, state court of appeals, 1874–81; chief justice, 1881.

COFFEY, JAMES VINCENT (*b*. New York, N.Y., 1846; *d*. 1919), jurist. Practiced in California, *post* 1869. Judge of probate, San Francisco Co., for 36 years *post* 1882.

COFFIN, CHARLES ALBERT (*b*. Somerset Co., Maine, 1844; *d*. 1926), industrialist. Originally in shoe and leather business, became one of Lynn Syndicate, which established Thomson-Houston Co. at Lynn, Mass. In 1892, became president of General Electric Co., which was formed through merger of Thomson-Houston Co. with the Edison General Electric Co. of New York; was chairman of board of directors, *post* 1913. Coffin's leadership led to company's phenomenal growth.

COFFIN, CHARLES CARLETON (*b*. Boscawen, N.H., 1823; *d*. Brookline, Mass., 1896), Civil War correspondent, author. His books for boys, especially *The Boys of '76* (1876), were deservedly popular.

COFFIN, CHARLES FISHER (*b*. North Carolina, 1823; *d*. Chicago, Ill, 1916), banker, Quaker minister. Raised in Indiana and was a successful banker there. As clerk of Indiana Yearly Meeting of Friends, 1857–85, was one of America's leading Quakers.

COFFIN, HENRY SLOANE (*b*. New York, N.Y., 1877; *d*. Lakeville, Conn., 1954), clergyman, educator. Studied at Yale; New College, Edinburgh, Scotland; and Union Theological Seminary (B.D., 1900). Minister of the Madison Avenue Presbyterian Church in New York City, 1905–26. President, the Union Theological Seminary, 1926–45. From 1922 to 1945, member of the corporation of Yale. At Union, Coffin oversaw such notable

theologians as Reinhold Niebuhr and Paul Tillich. He advocated activist roles for his theologians.

COFFIN, HOWARD EARLE (*b*. near West Milton, Ohio, 1873; *d*. Sea Island, Ga., 1937), chief engineer and vice president, Hudson Motor Co., 1910–30. Contributed to technical standardization in automobile and aircraft industries.

COFFIN, SIR ISAAC (*b*. Boston, Mass., 1759; *d*. 1839), baronet, British admiral, Loyalist, philanthropist. Entered Royal Navy, 1773; promoted full admiral, 1814. Brother of John Coffin.

COFFIN, JAMES HENRY (*b*. Martha's Vineyard, Mass., 1806; *d*. 1873), mathematician, meteorologist. Graduated Amherst, 1828. After several teaching posts, served as professor of mathematics, Lafayette College, 1846 to his death. Author of *Winds of the Globe* (1875).

COFFIN, JOHN (*b*. Boston, Mass., 1756; *d*. New Brunswick, Canada, 1838), Loyalist. Fought through the Revolution with Tory units; removed after the war to New Brunswick. Brother of Sir Isaac Coffin.

COFFIN, LEVI (*b*. New Garden, N.C., 1789; *d*. 1877), leader in operations of the Underground Railroad, 1826–46; his home in Newport, Ind., was a station on the route to freedom.

COFFIN, LORENZO (*b*. near Alton, N.H., 1823; *d*. 1915), philanthropist. Was responsible for congressional legislation requiring self-couplers and airbrakes on freight trains; founded railroad workers' Temperance Association.

COFFIN, ROBERT PETER TRISTRAM (*b*. Brunswick, Maine, 1892; *d*. Portland, Maine, 1955), poet, teacher, and editor. Studied at Bowdoin College, Princeton (M.A., 1916), and was a Rhodes Scholar at Trinity College, Oxford (B.A., 1920). Taught at Wells College (1921–34); professor at Bowdoin College (1934–55). Coffin won the Pulitzer Prize for his poetry volume *Strange Holiness* in 1935. His poems dealt with the people of Maine, and he was called "the New England Carl Sandburg." Critical works include *New Poetry of New England: Frost and Robinson* (1938).

COFFIN, WILLIAM ANDERSON (*b*. Allegheny, Pa., 1855; *d*. 1925), painter, art critic. Distinguished for landscapes; wrote art criticism for the *Nation*, the New York *Evening Post*, and the *Sun*.

COFFMAN, LOTUS DELTA (*b*. near Salem, Ind., 1875; *d*. Minneapolis, Minn., 1938), educator. Dean of College of Education, 1915–20, and president, 1920–38, of University of Minnesota.

COGDELL, JOHN STEVENS (*b*. Charleston or Georgetown, S.C., 1778; *d*. Charleston, 1847), sculptor, painter, lawyer.

COGGESHALL, GEORGE (*b*. Milford, Conn., 1784; *d*. Milford, 1861), privateer, merchant mariner and captain. Author of several volumes of voyages, and *History of the American Privateers* (1856).

COGGESHALL, WILLIAM TURNER (*b*. Lewistown, Pa., 1824; *d*. near Quito, Ecuador, 1867), journalist. His outstanding work was *Poets and Poetry of the West* (1860). He was American minister to Ecuador, 1866–67.

COGHILL, GEORGE ELLETT (*b*. Beaucoup Township, Washington County, Ill., 1872; *d*. near Gainesville, Fla., 1941), biologist, anatomist. B.A., Brown University, 1896; M.S., University of New Mexico, 1899; Ph.D., Brown, 1902. Taught at a number of schools before settling as professor of histology and anatomy, University of Kansas Medical School, 1913–25. From

1925 to 1935, he was professor of comparative anatomy at the Wistar Institute, Philadelphia, Pa. Coghill's principal contribution to science, the results of a long-range program of laborious and largely single-handed research conducted under difficulties, is contained in 12 papers published between 1914 and 1936 in the *Journal of Comparative Neurology*. In these "Correlated Anatomical and Physiological Studies of the Growth of the Nervous System of Amphibia" and in other research reports, he gave experimental evidence for his challenge to the prevalent theory of the role played by reflexes in behavior. He found that movements involving the whole body occur before the sense organs develop and independently of sensory stimulus; that from the beginning, the organism exhibits a total pattern of behavior with a high degree of autonomy from the stimulating environment; and that this pattern of maturation and autonomy describes the organism's development better than does the theory of increasingly complex reflex responses.

COGHLAN, ROSE (b. *Peterborough, England, 1851; d. Harrison, N.Y., 1932*), actress. Noted for her success in artificial high comedy in Wallack's Company, 1877–88.

COGSWELL, JOSEPH GREEN (b. *Ipswich, Mass., 1786; d. Cambridge, Mass., 1871*), teacher, librarian. Graduated Harvard, 1806; studied law under Fisher Ames and Judge Prescott; engaged in mercantile ventures in southern Europe. With Edward Everett and George Ticknor, studied at Göttingen, 1817; met and later corresponded with Goethe; traveled widely in Europe. In 1820 became librarian and professor of mineralogy and geology at Harvard; in 1823, with George Bancroft, established Round Hill School at Northampton, Mass. Became John Jacob Astor's adviser in establishment of the Astor Public Library in New York; from 1848 to 1861 served as its superintendent and compiled its printed catalogues.

COGSWELL, WILLIAM BROWNE (b. *Oswego, N.Y., 1834; d. 1921*), mining engineer. Introduced Solvay process of manufacturing soda to America.

COHAN, GEORGE MICHAEL (b. *Providence, R.I., 1878; d. New York, N.Y., 1942*), actor, playwright, composer, theatrical producer. In addition to his many appearances on the stage, George M. Cohan wrote some 40 plays, collaborated in as many others, shared in the production of about 150 more, and composed more than 500 songs, including the famous "Over There" (1917). Born to parents who were vaudeville artists and always on the move, he ended his formal schooling at age eight; as an infant, he made his first appearance when carried on stage by his mother in a sketch written by his father. After about the age of ten, he toured with his family as one of the "Four Cohans"; at thirteen, he played the lead in a dramatization of *Peck's Bad Boy*. During his years with the Four Cohans (in which they attained top billing in vaudeville), George contrived the song-and-dance style that was to be a feature of his later Broadway successes.

After the failure on Broadway of two musical shows that he had written, he formed a producing partnership in 1904 with Sam H. Harris which presented many hits before dissolution in 1920. Their first production, *Little Johnny Jones* (1904), was a showcase for Cohan's own talents as a brash, fast-talking song-and-dance man and it included two long-lived popular songs, "Give My Regards to Broadway" and "Yankee Doodle Dandy"; after a lukewarm critical reception in New York, it had a successful road tour and was enthusiastically received by the public when it reopened in New York, 1905. A series of successful musicals followed which featured tuneful songs scattered through plots that combined comedy and melodrama; among them were *Forty-five Minutes from Broadway* (1906), *George Washington, Jr.* (1906), and *The Man Who Owns Broadway* (1909). He was author also of such nonmusical plays as *Get-Rich-Quick Wallingford* (1910),

Broadway Jones (1912, in which Cohan appeared in his first straight part on Broadway), *Seven Keys to Baldpate* (1913, a mystery farce), and *The Tavern* (1920, a parody of popular thrillers). After siding with the managers during the Actors Equity strike in 1919 as a matter of principle, he took Equity's victory as a personal humiliation, dissolved his partnership with Sam Harris, and vowed to leave show business. Although he continued to write and produce (but without his former success), he increasingly lost touch with the contemporary theater. In his latter years, he won a new reputation as an actor of mature skill, appearing in plays by others, such as *Ah, Wilderness!* (1933) and *I'd Rather Be Right* (1937).

COHEN, FELIX SOLOMON (b. *New York, N.Y., 1907; d. Washington, D.C., 1953*), lawyer. Studied at the City College of New York, Harvard (Ph.D., 1929) and Columbia Law School (LL.B., 1931). Solicitor in the Department of the Interior, 1933–48. A leading expert on Indian affairs, he helped draft the legislation for the Indian Reorganization Act of 1934; he was instrumental in creating the Indian Claims Commission, which allowed tribes to bring suit against the federal government. His most important publication was the *Handbook of Federal Indian Laws* (1941). In 1948, he became general counsel to the Association of American Indian Affairs.

COHEN, JACOB DA SILVA SOLIS (b. *New York, N.Y., 1838; d. 1927*), physician. Expert in use of laryngoscope; wrote book on inhalation (1867) and *Diseases of the Throat* (1872).

COHEN, JOHN SANFORD (b. *Augusta, Ga., 1870; d. 1935*), journalist. Outstanding editor of the *Atlanta Journal*, 1900–35; prominent in Democratic politics.

COHEN, MENDES (b. *Baltimore, Md., 1831; d. Baltimore, 1915*), civil engineer. Associated with Baltimore & Ohio, Hudson River, Ohio & Mississippi, and other railroads as engineer or president. Active in many civic and historical societies.

COHEN, MORRIS RAPHAEL (b. *Minsk, Russia, 1880; d. Washington, D.C., 1947*), philosopher. Born of Jewish parents who immigrated to New York City, 1892. B.S., College of the City of New York, 1900; Ph.D., Harvard, 1906. After teaching elementary school and high school classes in mathematics in New York City, he became a member of the Department of Philosophy at the College of the City of New York in 1912, where he remained until his retirement in 1938. He was also at various times visiting professor of philosophy at a number of universities, including Yale, Harvard, Columbia, and Chicago. To Cohen, philosophy was disciplined critical reflection on the interpretations which men place on the primary materials of their experience—interpretations that are codified in the propositions certified by the positive sciences, in the norms contained in moral and legal rules, or in the evaluations and standards manifested in aesthetic criticism. Philosophic reflection, as he conceived of it, should seek to make explicit the logical articulation of claims to knowledge, the grounds on which their credibility rests, and the import of their content for a coherent view of nature and humanity. His philosophy was a thoroughgoing naturalism, but informed by far-ranging studies of intellectual methods employed in the pursuit of reliably based knowledge. He was also a vigorous exponent of a liberal social philosophy that joined faith in rational analysis with willingness to use the instrumentalities of the state to achieve a more just society. He was author of *Reason and Nature: An Essay on the Meaning of Scientific Method* (1931), several volumes of essays and studies published posthumously, and an autobiography. A close student of the writings of C. S. Peirce, he published the first collection of Peirce's work in book form as *Chance, Love and Logic* (1923).

COHEN, OCTAVUS ROY (*b. Charleston, S.C., 1891; d. Los Angeles, Calif., 1959*), novelist and playwright. Studied at Clemson College. Author of over fifty-seven volumes that include short stories, plays, novels, and radio and film scripts. Created the popular Jim Hanvey detective series; wrote the play *The Crimson Alibi* (1919) and novels such as *Florian Slappey* (1938), an affectionate but condescending treatment of blacks. In 1945–46, he was a scriptwriter for the "Amos 'n' Andy" radio show. Cohen has received no serious critical treatment, but his works provide valuable insights into the popular mores of the first half of the century.

COHN, ALFRED A. (*b. Freeport, Ill., 1880; d. Los Angeles, Calif., 1951*), reporter, publicity man, writer. Author of over 100 film scripts, Cohn is best-known for the script of *The Jazz Singer* (1927), the first commercial talking motion picture. Other scripts include *The Cisco Kid* (1931) and *Mystery Ranch* (1932).

COHN, ALFRED EINSTEIN (*b. New York, N.Y., 1879; d. New Milford, Conn., 1957*), physician. Received M.D. from Columbia, 1904; further study at Freiburg, Germany, and in London. From 1909 to 1911, associated with Mount Sinai Hospital in New York; from 1911 to 1944, with the Rockefeller Institute for Medical Research in New York. Introduced the first electrocardiograph to the United States in 1909 and was responsible for its acceptance in clinical practice in this country. Cohn's interest in public health was reflected in an important study written with Claire Lingg, *The Burden of Diseases in the United States* (1950).

COHN, EDWIN JOSEPH (*b. New York, N.Y., 1892; d. Boston, Mass., 1953*), biochemist and protein chemist. Studied at Amherst College and the University of Chicago (Ph.D., 1917). Professor of physical chemistry at the Harvard Medical School (1920–1953). Cohn's specialty was protein chemistry. Before and during World War II, he worked on various albumin preparations, in particular, serum albumin, gamma globulin, and fibrin foam and film.

COHN, HARRY (*b. New York, N.Y., 1891; d. Phoenix, Ariz., 1958*), motion picture producer. Founded the C.B.C. Film Sales Corp. in 1920 which, in 1924, became Columbia Pictures; Cohn was vice president from 1924 to 1932 and president from 1932 to 1958. Cohn's main director was Frank Capra, whose films included *It Happened One Night* (1934), *Mr. Deeds Goes to Town* (1936), *Lost Horizon* (1937), and *Mr. Smith Goes to Washington* (1939). Films by other directors include *Picnic* (1956) and *The Bridge on the River Kwai* (1957).

COIT, HENRY AUGUSTUS (*b. Wilmington, Del., 1830; d. Concord, N.H., 1895*), Episcopal clergyman. First rector of St. Paul's School, Concord, N.H., 1856–95; ranked with Arnold, Fellenberg, and Muhlenberg as a master pedagogue.

COIT, HENRY LEBER (*b. Peapack, N.J., 1854; d. Newark, N.J., 1917*), physician. Led campaign, *post* 1889, for the introduction of "certified milk" to reduce infant mortality; promoted establishment of Newark's Babies' Hospital.

COIT, STANTON (*b. Columbus, Ohio, 1875; d. Birling Gap, Sussex, England, 1944*), Ethical Culture leader, founder of the first social settlement in the United States. Graduated Amherst, 1879; attended Columbia University; associated himself with Felix Adler; took Ph.D. at University of Berlin, 1885. After spending three months at Toynbee Hall, London, he returned to New York City, resumed his work with Adler, and established what he called a "Neighborhood Guild" (1886), a social settlement. An ethical socialist, he had complete faith in the ability of working people to run their own affairs, and leadership in the guild was expected to come from the community which it served.

Removing to England in 1888 as an Ethical Culture leader in London, he had little influence thereafter on the American settlement movement.

COIT, THOMAS WINTHROP (*b. New London, Conn., 1803; d. 1885*), Episcopal clergyman, educator. Author of *Puritanism, or a Churchman's Defense* (1845).

COKE, RICHARD (*b. Williamsburg, Va., 1829; d. Waco, Tex., 1897*), lawyer, Confederate soldier. Removed to Texas, 1850; Democratic governor of Texas, 1874–76; U.S. senator, 1876–94.

COKE, THOMAS (*b. Brecon, Wales, 1747; d. England, 1814*), Methodist bishop. An Anglican curate, he joined John Wesley, 1777, and assisted him as correspondent, becoming in 1782 president of Irish Methodist conference. In 1784 Wesley appointed him first superintendent of the Methodist church in America. Coke preached in Delaware, Maryland, Pennsylvania, and Virginia and presided over the 1784 general conference of the American Methodist church, where Francis Asbury's views prevailed. From 1784 to 1803 Coke made nine voyages to America, exercising only nominal control over American Methodism. As president of the Methodist missionary committee *post* 1804, Coke was conspicuously successful.

COKER, DAVID ROBERT (*b. Hartsville, S.C., 1870; d. Hartsville, 1938*), agriculturist, philanthropist. Son of James L. Coker. Bred improved strains of short-staple cotton.

COKER, JAMES LIDE (*b. near Society Hill, S.C., 1837; d. Hartsville, S.C., 1918*), manufacturer. A versatile businessman, he engaged in farming, banking, retailing, railroad building; founded Coker College for women, Hartsville, S.C.

COLBURN, DANA POND (*b. West Dedham, Mass., 1823; d. Bristol, R.I., 1859*), educator. A Pestalozzian, he employed rational, rather than memory, methods; taught at Rhode Island normal schools.

COLBURN, IRVING WIGHTMAN (*b. Fitchburg, Mass., 1861; d. 1917*), manufacturer. Inventor of machines and process for drawing continuous sheets of glass (patented 1908) which were exploited commercially by Libbey-Owens Co.

COLBURN, WARREN (*b. Dedham, Mass., 1793; d. Lowell, Mass., 1833*), teacher. His mathematics textbooks on the inductive method (1821–25) broke new ground.

COLBURN, ZERAH (*b. Cabot, Vt., 1804; d. Norwich, Vt., 1839*), mathematical prodigy. Author of an autobiography (1833).

COLBY, BAINBRIDGE (*b. St. Louis, Mo., 1869; d. Bemus Point, N.Y., 1850*), lawyer. B.A., Williams College, 1890; LL.B., New York Law School, 1892. Practiced successfully in New York City. Initially a Republican, he helped found the Progressive party in 1912, and in 1916 led a group of dissident Progressives who endorsed the reelection of Woodrow Wilson. Soon afterward he joined the Democratic party. A member of the U.S. Shipping Board, 1917–19, he was appointed U.S. secretary of state in March 1920, replacing Robert Lansing. Colby vigorously defended President Wilson's position on the League of Nations, but his uncritical loyalty to the president kept him from urging concessions to the Republican critics of the Versailles Treaty which might have effected a compromise. His most significant achievements were in improving Latin American relations by a successful program of conciliation that foreshadowed the Good Neighbor policy. Leaving office with Wilson in 1921, he was for a brief period a law partner of the former president (1921–23). Repelled by what he termed the "collectivism" of the New Deal, he supported Republican presidential candidates in 1936 and 1940.

COLBY, FRANK MOORE (*b. Washington, D.C., 1865; d. 1925*), author. Editor, *New International Year Book*, 1898–1925; contributed to many encyclopedias and periodicals. Author of brief pungent essays as in *Constrained Attitudes* (1910).

COLBY, GARDNER (*b. Bowdoinham, Maine, 1810; d. Newton, Mass., 1879*), merchant, philanthropist. Prospered in Civil War clothing contracts. President, Wisconsin Central Railroad. Helped finance school at Waterville, Maine, later Colby College.

COLBY, LUTHER (*b. Amesbury, Mass., 1814; d. 1894*), spiritualist. Editor, the *Banner of Light*, 1857–94.

COLCORD, LINCOLN ROSS (*b. at sea, off Cape Horn, 1883; d. Belfast, Maine, 1947*), journalist, maritime historian. Descendent of a seafaring family, Colcord grew up aboard ships and was educated by his parents; he attended the University of Maine intermittently, 1900–06. Settling in Searsport, Maine, 1909, he began writing magazine short stories, of which several collections were published in book form (e.g., *The Drifting Diamond*, 1912). After involvement in the movement for political reform *post* 1912 as a radical activist, he became disillusioned with politics, and indeed, with modern Americans, whom he regarded as regimented and lacking in the hardihood and character of their ancestors. Resident in Searsport *post* 1929, he devoted himself to maritime history, conversation, enjoyment of life, and the development of friendships.

COLDEN, CADWALLADER (*b. Ireland, 1688; n.s.; d. Long Island, N.Y., 1776*), Loyalist, philosopher, scientist. Came to New York, 1718; was made colony's surveyor general, 1720; in 1721 was appointed to Governor's Council; lieutenant governor of the colony, 1761–76. Published contributions to history, applied mathematics, botany, physics, medicine, and philosophy, and corresponded with eminent scientists of his day. Among his books are *The History of the Five Indian Nations* (1727) and *An Explication of the First Causes of Action in Matter* (1745, revised 1751). An honest and able public servant, he refused to go along with popular agitation subsequent to the Stamp Act and grew progressively unpopular, although he managed to keep a fair balance between radicals and conservatives until 1774.

COLDEN, CADWALLADER DAVID (*b. Flushing, N.Y., 1769; d. Jersey City, N.J., 1834*), lawyer. Grandson of Cadwallader Colden. Federalist mayor of New York, 1818–20; congressman from New York, 1821–23. Actively interested in navigation, internal improvements, and reform.

COLDEN, JANE (*b. probably New York, N.Y., 1724; d. 1766*), first woman botanist in New World. Daughter of Cadwallader Colden, she cooperated in Colden's study of the New York flora according to Linnaeus' system.

COLE, CHESTER CICERO (*b. Oxford, N.Y., 1824; d. 1913*), jurist, teacher of law. Graduated Harvard Law School, 1848. Settled in Des Moines, Iowa, 1856; judge, Iowa Supreme Court, 1864–76; taught law at Drake University.

COLE, FRANK NELSON (*b. Ashland, Mass., 1861; d. 1926*), mathematician. Graduated Harvard, 1882; Ph.D., 1886. Taught at Harvard, Michigan, Columbia; editor, American Mathematical Society *Bulletin*, 1897–1925.

COLE, GEORGE WATSON (*b. Warren, Conn., 1850; d. California, 1939*), bibliographer. First librarian, 1920–24, Henry E. Huntington Library and Art Gallery, San Marino, Calif.

COLE, JOSEPH FOXCROFT (*b. Jay, Maine, 1837; d. Winchester, Mass., 1892*), painter. A commercial lithographer, he studied art in France; painted serious, low-toned landscapes in French manner; brought French art to New England's attention.

COLE, NAT ("KING") (*b. Montgomery, Ala, 1919; d. Santa Monica, Calif., 1965*), singer and pianist. Son of a Baptist minister, began playing organ and piano in his father's church at the age of twelve. He made his first recordings, for Decca Records, with the Rogues of Rhythm when he was nineteen. Cole formed the King Cole Trio, which became popular with jazz fans, especially after recording with vibraphonist Lionel Hampton in 1940. With Capitol Records, Cole recorded nearly all his important work as a pianist between 1941 and 1947. Citing financial necessity, he then virtually abondoned piano to become a popular singer with such hits as "Get Your Kicks on Route 66," "Mona Lisa," "The Christmas Song," and "Unforgettable." He appeared in seven feature films, the last being *Cat Ballou* (1965). Cole was the first black musical artist to have a sponsored radio series and the first black to have a weekly series on national television (1956–57).

COLE, THOMAS (*b. Bolton-le-Moor, England, 1801; d. Catskill, N.Y., 1848*), artist, pioneer of the Hudson River school. Came to America, 1819. Worked as block-engraver in his father's wallpaper factory at Steubenville, Ohio, 1820–22; *post* 1824 , worked in New York, N.Y., and at Catskill. Became celebrated for his romantic landscapes, which were praised by John Trumbull, William Dunlap, and William Cullen Bryant. Visited Europe, 1829–32; after return to New York painted *The Course of Empire*, the most remarkable of his works, and *The Voyage of Life*.

COLE, TIMOTHY (*b. London, England, 1852; d. 1931*), wood-engraver. Founded the "new school" of American reproductive wood-engraving.

COLEMAN, CHARLES CARYL (*b. Buffalo, N.Y., 1840; d. Capri, Italy, 1928*), painter. Worked with William Hunt and Elihu Vedder in Rome; the subjects of his mature work were landscapes.

COLEMAN, LEIGHTON (*b. Philadelphia, Pa., 1837; d. 1907*), Episcopal bishop of Delaware, 1888–1907.

COLEMAN, LYMAN (*b. Middlefield, Mass., 1796; d. Easton, Pa., 1882*), Congregational clergyman, educator. Graduated Yale, 1817. Professor of classics at Amherst, Princeton, and Lafayette College, 1861–82.

COLEMAN, WILLIAM (*b. Boston, Mass., 1766; d. New York, N.Y., 1829*), Federalist journalist. Editor, New York *Evening Post*, 1801–29; associate and supporter of Alexander Hamilton.

COLEMAN, WILLIAM TELL (*b. near Cynthiana, Ky., 1824; d. San Francisco, Calif., 1893*), merchant. Moved to California, 1849; operated stores at Placerville, Sacramento, and San Francisco; a leader of vigilantes, 1851 and 1856.

COLES, EDWARD (*b. Albemarle Co., Va., 1786; d. Philadelphia, Pa., 1868*), abolitionist. Secretary to James Madison, 1809–15. Settled in Illinois, 1819, where he emancipated his slaves; Democratic governor of Illinois, 1822–26.

COLFAX, SCHUYLER (*b. New York, N.Y., 1823; d. Mankato, Minn., 1885*), politician. Removed to Indiana, 1836; edited principal Whig newspaper in northern Indiana; took active part in forming Republican party in that state. Congressman from Indiana, 1855–69; Speaker of the House, 1863–69; vice president of the United States, 1869–73. His implication in Crédit Mobilier scandal and others ruined him politically.

COLGATE, JAMES BOORMAN (*b. New York, N.Y., 1818; d. 1904*), stockbroker. Son of William Colgate. Benefactor of Colgate University.

COLGATE, WILLIAM (*b. Hollingbourn, England, 1783; d. New York, N.Y., 1857*), manufacturer. Came to America, 1795. Worked as a tallow chandler; in 1806 started his own firm for the manufacture of soap, which became outstanding. A Baptist, he was a generous benefactor of the schools which later became Colgate University.

COLLAMER, JACOB (*b. Troy, N.Y., 1791; d. Woodstock, Vt., 1865*), lawyer, Vermont legislator and jurist. Congressman, Whig, from Vermont, 1843–49; U.S. postmaster general, 1849–50; U.S. senator, Republican, from Vermont, 1864–65.

COLLENS, THOMAS WHARTON (*b. New Orleans, La., 1812; d. 1879*), jurist, writer. Held various posts in Louisiana judiciary, 1842–73. Wrote several tragedies locally produced.

COLLES, CHRISTOPHER (*b. Ireland, 1739; d. New York, 1816*), engineer, inventor, promoter of internal improvements. Came to America, *post* 1765. One of the first Americans to design a steam engine and probably the first (1785) to propose a canal connecting the Great Lakes with the Hudson River. Surveyed roads of New York and Pennsylvania; engaged in business, but always returned to invention of useful devices, to astronomical calculations, and to schemes for canals and roads. Held position in custom service. Author of A *Survey of the Roads of the United States* (1789).

COLLIER, BARRON GIFT (*b. Memphis, Tenn., 1873; d. New York, N.Y., 1939*), advertising promoter, developer of Florida's lower west coast properties.

COLLIER, CONSTANCE (*b. Windsor, England, 1878; d. New York, N.Y., 1955*), actress. Collier performed in many productions of Shakespeare in London and Europe, performing Cleopatra before the Kaiser in Berlin. Her American debut was in Henry Bernstein's *Samson* in New York in 1908; in 1915, she appeared in W.D. Griffith's film *Intolerance*. She moved to the U.S. in 1927. Her many plays include Ferber and Kaufman's *Dinner at Eight* (1932). Films include *Thunder in the City* (1937). An acting coach, she worked with such artists as Katharine Hepburn, Jennifer Jones, and Gene Tierney.

COLLIER, HENRY WATKINS (*b. Lunenburg Co., Va., 1801; d. Bailey Springs, Ala., 1855*), lawyer. Practiced in Alabama; chief justice of state supreme court, 1837–49; Democratic governor of Alabama, 1849–53. A middle-of-the-road conservative in national affairs.

COLLIER, HIRAM PRICE (*b. Davenport, Iowa, 1860; d. Fünen Island, Denmark, 1913*), author. Unitarian minister in Massachusetts, 1882–91. Wrote numerous books, of which *Mr. Picket Pin and His Friends* (1894) and *England and the English* (1909) are best known.

COLLIER, JOHN (*b. Atlanta, Ga., 1884; d. Taos, N.M., 1968*), community organizer and reformer. Studied at Columbia and the Collège de France. With the People's Institute in New York City (1908–14, 1915–19) he worked with immigrants and promoted cultural pluralism. He founded, and served as executive secretary (1923–33) of, the American Indian Defense Association. As commissioner of Indian affairs (1933–45), appointed by President Roosevelt, Collier became the architect of the Indian Reorganization Act of 1934. In 1940 he helped establish the Inter-American Institute of the Indian in Mexico City. In 1945 he organized, then became president of, the Institute of Ethnic Affairs; at the same time he taught at the City College of New York

(1947–54). He also taught at Knox College in Illinois (1955–56). He wrote *Indians of the Americas* (1947), *Patterns and Ceremonials of the Indians of the Southwest* (1949), *On the Gleaming Way* (1962), and *From Every Zenith* (1963).

COLLIER, PETER (*b. Chittenango, N.Y., 1835; d. Ann Arbor, Mich., 1896*), agricultural chemist. Graduated Yale, 1861, and Ph.D., 1866; M.D., University of Vermont, 1870. Chief chemist, U.S. Department of Agriculture, 1877–83. Author of *Sorghum: Its Culture and Manufacture* (1884). Director, New York Agricultural Station, Geneva, N.Y., 1887–95.

COLLIER, PETER FENELON (*b. Co. Carlow, Ireland, 1849; d. 1909*), publisher. Came to America, 1866. Founder of P. F. Collier & Co., in 1888 founded *Once a Week*, replaced in 1896 by *Collier's Weekly*.

COLLIER, PRICE. *See* COLLIER, HIRAM PRICE.

COLLINS, EDWARD KNIGHT (*b. Truro, Mass., 1802; d. New York, N.Y., 1878*), shipowner. Operator of packet lines to Veracruz and New Orleans, in 1836 he started the Dramatic Line from New York to England. Impressed with the success of the subsidized British Cunard mail steamers, Collins in 1847 obtained a contract with the U.S. postmaster general specifying the construction and subsidized operation of five mail-carrying steamships. The steamers of the Collins Line exceeded the speed of the Cunard liners, attracted the cream of the passenger trade and forced reduction of British freight rates. Disaster came with the sinking of the *Arctic*, 1854, the disappearance of the *Pacific*, 1856, and the cancellation of the congressional subsidy. In 1858 Collins had to dissolve his company.

COLLINS, EDWARD TROWBRIDGE (*b. Tarrytown, N.Y., 1887; d. Boston, Mass., 1951*), baseball player, coach, manager. Studied at Columbia. Second baseman for Philadelphia Athletics under Connie Mack (1907–15); coach (1927–1933). Joined the Chicago White Sox (1915–26). Managed the Boston Red Sox from 1933 to 1950. Elected to the National Baseball Hall of Fame in 1939.

COLLINS, FRANK SHIPLEY (*b. Boston, Mass., 1848; d. New Haven, Conn., 1920*), botanist. Earned his living as a factory manager. Became authority on American algae; author of *The Green Algae of North America* (1909).

COLLINS, GUY N. (*b. Mertensia, N.Y., 1872; d. Lanham, Md., 1938*), plant explorer, geneticist. With U.S. Department of Agriculture, 1901–38; used biometrics to plan and evaluate experiments, especially studies of maize.

COLLINS, JOHN (*b. Newport, R.I., 1717; d. 1795*), Revolutionary patriot. Governor of Rhode Island, 1786–90.

COLLINS, JOHN ANDERSON (*b. Manchester, Vt., ca. 1810; d. ca. 1879*), abolitionist, social reformer. General agent, Massachusetts Anti-Slavery Society; founded unsuccessful Fourieristic community at Skaneateles, N.Y. Last heard of in California, 1879.

COLLINS, NAPOLEON (*b. Pennsylvania, 1814; d. Callao, Peru, 1875*), naval officer. Captured Confederate raider *Florida*, 1864, at Bahia, Brazil; a rear admiral after 1874, he commanded South Pacific Squadron.

COLLINS, PATRICK ANDREW (*b. Ballinafauna, Ireland, 1844; d. Virginia Hot Springs, 1905*), politician. Came to America as a child; raised in Massachusetts and Ohio; returned to Boston, 1859. Graduated Harvard Law School, 1871. A Democrat, he served in Massachusetts General Court, in Congress, 1883–89, and as mayor of Boston, 1901–05.

COLLYER, ROBERT (*b. Keighley, England, 1823; d. 1912*), clergyman. Came to America, 1850. At first a Methodist lay preacher, he served as a Unitarian pastor in Chicago, Ill., 1859–79, and as pastor of the Church of the Messiah, New York City, *post* 1879.

COLMAN, BENJAMIN (*b. Boston, Mass., 1673; d. 1747*), clergyman. Graduated Harvard, 1692. Minister of Boston's Brattle Street Church, 1699–1747; a fellow and overseer of Harvard. He endorsed the Great Awakening.

COLMAN, HENRY (*b. Boston, Mass., 1785; d. Islington, England, 1849*), Unitarian minister, agricultural writer. Pastor of Independent Congregational Church, Salem, Mass., 1825–31; made agricultural surveys in Massachusetts, 1837–38; published report on European agriculture (1844).

COLMAN, JOHN (*b. London, England, 1670; d. ca. 1753*), merchant. Brother of Benjamin Colman. Came to Boston, Mass., as an infant. Active in local currency and banking disputes, 1714–39.

COLMAN, LUCY NEWHALL (*b. Sturbridge, Mass., 1817; d. Syracuse, N.Y., 1906*), abolitionist, antislavery lecturer.

COLMAN, NORMAN JAY (*b. near Richfield Springs, N.Y., 1827; d. 1911*), agricultural journalist, lawyer. Practiced in Indiana; removing to Missouri, he published *Colman's Rural World*, 1865–1911. First U.S. secretary of agriculture (February 1889), he had, while commissioner, written the Hatch Act (1887), which originated agricultural experiment stations.

COLMAN, RONALD CHARLES (*b. Richmond, Surrey, England, 1891; d. Santa Barbara, Calif., 1958*), actor. After performing in small parts in London and on Broadway (Colman immigrated to the U.S. in 1920), Colman turned to films, starring in *The White Sister* with Lillian Gish (1923); other silent films include *Stella Dallas* (1925) and *Beau Geste* (1926). Sound films include *Arrowsmith* (1931), *A Tale of Two Cities* (1935), *The Prisoner of Zenda* (1937), *Random Harvest* (1942), and *A Double Life* (1947), for which he won the Academy Award.

COLMAN, SAMUEL (*b. Portland, Maine, 1832; d. New York, N.Y., 1920*), landscape painter. Pupil of A. B. Durand.

COLPITTS, EDWIN HENRY (*b. Point de Bute, New Brunswick, Canada, 1872; d. Orange, N.J., 1949*), communications engineer. B.A., Mount Allison University, 1893; B.A., Harvard, 1896; M.S., Harvard, 1897. After service as assistant to the director of Harvard's Jefferson Physical Laboratory, 1897–99, he began a lifetime association with the American Bell Telephone Co., rising to a vice presidency of American Telephone and Telegraph (1924–34) and of Bell Telephone Laboratories (1934–37). He retired in 1937. A problem-solver and keen analyst, Colpitts made a number of outstanding contributions to the technology of long-distance telephony and radio. His work with loading coils helped extend the range of long-distance telephony; his studies of capacitance and other factors solved the problems of crosstalk and power-line interference. His successful adaptation of vacuum tubes for telephone use (1915) was the beginning of the electronic age in communications. He was also inventor of the Colpitts system of modulation for radiotelephony, and the Colpitts oscillatory circuit, a vital factor in development of radio circuitry.

COLQUITT, ALFRED HOLT (*b. Walton Co., Ga., 1824; d. 1894*), statesman, Confederate soldier. Son of Walter T. Colquitt. An extreme pro-Southern Democrat, he served in the Georgia legislature and as congressman, 1853–55. Subsequent to his war service, he fought the Reconstruction policies of Congress and served ably, if arbitrarily, as Democratic governor of Georgia, 1876–82; U.S. senator, 1883–94.

COLQUITT, WALTER TERRY (*b. Halifax Co., Va., 1799; d. 1855*), lawyer, statesman. Raised in Georgia. Congressman, state's rights Whig, 1838–43; U.S. senator, Democrat, 1843–48.

COLSTON, RALEIGH EDWARD (*b. Paris, France, 1825; d. Richmond, Va., 1896*), Confederate soldier. Graduated Virginia Military Institute, 1846, and taught there. After effective Civil War service, was colonel in Egyptian army, 1873–79.

COLT, LEBARON BRADFORD (*b. Dedham, Mass., 1846; d. 1924*), jurist. Graduated Yale, 1868. Began practice of law in Chicago; removed, 1875, to Bristol, R.I. Federal judge, 1881–1913; U.S. senator, Republican, from Rhode Island, 1913–24.

COLT, SAMUEL (*b. Hartford, Conn., 1814; d. 1862*), inventor, manufacturer. Between 1831 and 1833 applied for patent and constructed models of the first practical multishot pistol and rifle of the revolving barrel type, for which he received his first U.S. patent in 1836. Unsuccessful in persuading armed forces to adopt them, he lost his rights to them *post* 1842. At outbreak of Mexican War, on receipt of order for a thousand of his pistols from the government, he recaptured his patents and began to manufacture firearms. In 1848, after a year at Whitneyville, Conn., he established the business at Hartford, Conn.

COLTER, JOHN (*b. in or near Staunton, Va., ca. 1775; d. near Dundee, Mo., 1813*), trapper, explorer. Served ably on expedition of Lewis and Clark, 1803–06; then joined Manuel Lisa's trapping party and explored the Yellowstone region, 1807. Trapped along upper Missouri and Yellowstone, 1808–10.

COLTON, CALVIN (*b. Longmeadow, Mass., 1789; d. Savannah, Ga., 1857*), clergyman, journalist, politician. Official biographer of Henry Clay and editor of his works.

COLTON, ELIZABETH AVERY (*b. Indian Territory, 1872; d. 1924*), educator. Prominent in raising standards of southern colleges for women; head of English department, Meredith College, Raleigh, N.C.

COLTON, GARDNER QUINCY (*b. Georgia, Vt., 1814; d. Rotterdam, Netherlands, 1898*), anesthetist. Brother of Walter Colton. Introduced nitrous oxide as anesthetic for dental practice, 1844–63.

COLTON, GEORGE RADCLIFFE (*b. Galesburg, Ill., 1865; d. 1916*), customs expert. A Nebraska banker, he organized Philippine customs service and was governor of Puerto Rico from 1909 to 1913.

COLTON, WALTER (*b. Rutland Co., Vt., 1797; d. Philadelphia, Pa., 1851*), Congregational clergyman, journalist. A navy chaplain, 1831–51; played a notable part in conquest of California, 1846–49; author of several books, including the valuable *Three Years in California* (1850).

COLTRANE, JOHN WILLIAM (*b. Hamlet, N.C., 1926; d. New York, N.Y., 1967*), jazz musician and composer. Played alto and tenor saxophone with a number of groups before joining the legendary Miles Davis Quintet in 1955. He captured critical attention with his highly arpeggiated approach to music. Coltrane incorporated Indian musical concepts into his jazz compositions and established the soprano saxophone as a standard jazz instrument. His most famous recordings were made with his own group, the best-known version of which included McCoy Tyner, Jimmy Garrison, and Elvin Jones.

COLVER, NATHANIEL (*b. Orwell, Vt., 1794; d. 1870*), Baptist clergyman. An abolitionist, his principal pastorate was at Tremont Temple, Boston, Mass., 1839–52; he was a founder of University of Chicago Divinity School.

COLVER, WILLIAM BYRON (*b. Wellington, Ohio, 1870; d. 1926*), editor, chairman of Federal Trade Commission. Vigorous champion of public causes, he wrote for *Cleveland Plain Dealer* and *Press* and supported reforms of Tom L. Johnson; general editorial director, Scripps-Howard, 1919–24.

COLVIN, STEPHEN SHELDON (*b. Phenix, R.I., 1869; d. 1923*), educational psychologist, author. Graduated Brown, 1891; studied in Europe and under G. Stanley Hall; taught at Brown, Illinois, Columbia; wrote *The Learning Process* (1911) and other works.

COLVOCORESSES, GEORGE MUSALAS (*b. Chios, Greece, 1816; d. Bridgeport, Conn., 1872*), naval officer. Author of *Four Years in a Government Exploring Expedition* (1852).

COLWELL, STEPHEN (*b. Brooke Co., Va., 1800; d. Philadelphia, Pa., 1871*), political economist, lawyer. A protectionist of the school of Henry C. Carey, he also stressed the social implications of Christian doctrine.

COMAN, CHARLOTTE BUELL (*b. Waterville, N.Y., 1833; d. Yonkers, N.Y., 1924*), artist. Studied with James R. Brevoort, and in Europe. Painted landscapes after the manner of Corot and Daubigny.

COMBS, LESLIE (*b. Clarke Co., Ky., 1793; d. Lexington, Ky., 1881*), soldier, Unionist, legislator, and lawyer.

COMBS, MOSES NEWELL (*b. Morris Co., N.J., 1753; d. Newark, N.J., 1834*), manufacturer, philanthropist. Called "father of Newark industries," he prospered in shoe and leather business. Founded one of the first night schools at Newark, 1794.

COMER, BRAXTON BRAGG (*b. Barbour Co., Ala., 1848; d. 1927*), businessman. As governor of Alabama, 1907–11, he secured state railroad code, prohibition, and child-labor laws; obtained unprecedentedly large appropriations for colleges and schools.

COMFORT, WILL LEVINGTON (*b. Kalamazoo, Mich., 1878; d. Los Angeles, Calif., 1932*), war correspondent, novelist, occultist.

COMISKEY, GRACE ELIZABETH REIDY (*b. Chicago, Ill., 1893; d. Chicago, Ill., 1956*), baseball executive. The wife of the heir and owner of the Chicago White Sox, Grace Comiskey took over ownership of the club after her husband's death in 1939; she retained ownership until her death, passing on the club to her daughter and sons.

COMMONS, JOHN ROGERS (*b. Hollansburg, Ohio, 1862; d. Raleigh, N.C., 1945*), economist. Raised in Union City and Winchester, Ind. Graduated Oberlin, 1888; studied at Johns Hopkins with Richard T. Ely, 1888–90. Taught economics at Wesleyan, Oberlin, Indiana (1892–95), and Syracuse (1895–99). His academic career was impeded by a growing reputation for radicalism. His Presbyterian background shaped his belief that an educated elite was necessary to guide the mass of people through inevitable conflict toward social harmony. Economics could be understood only within the context of a nation's cultural development, institutional changes, and government policy—all of which had to be studied empirically through direct observation and interviews. He was influenced also by the thinking of the Austrian school of economists and by Prussian accomplishments in state efficiency. Aware of the doctrines of Marx and

Henry George, he rejected their general conclusions. Anxious early in his career to reconcile religion and social science, he came to depend on rationalism and pragmatism—instead of Christian charity—to resolve conflict.

As a teacher, he ranged broadly over questions of socialism, the family, pauperism, prisons, charity, and the state. His early works included the heterodox *Distribution of Wealth* (1893), *Proportional Representation* (1896), and a number of articles on currency, labor, and municipal reform. In such works as *Races and Immigrants in America* (1907), he examined and sought to isolate what he called racial characteristics among industrial groups, and then to evaluate their effect on the organizational life of trade unions or entire sections of the economy; in this effort, he postulated "inferiority" and "superiority" with a presumptuous dogmatism.

Commons returned to academic life in 1904 when he joined the Department of Political Economy at the University of Wisconsin, remaining there until retirement in 1932. He found the Wisconsin of Robert M. La Follette an ideal environment for combining his scholarly activities with his interest in practical reform. Assisted by students, he drafted the Wisconsin civil service law (1905), its public utility law (1907), and its workmen's compensation act (1911)—the first in the nation to withstand constitutional challenge. He also framed legislation against exploitation by loan sharks, helped initiate the first multilanguage public employment office in the country, and advised La Follette on questions of railroad regulation and taxation. On the municipal level, he organized and directed (1911–13) the Bureau of Economy and Efficiency for Milwaukee's Socialist mayor. The achievement in which Commons took greatest pride was his role in the creation of the Wisconsin Industrial Commission.

He was a founder of the American Association for Labor Legislation (1906) and served on U.S. Commission on Industrial Relations (1913–15), Russell Sage Foundation "Pittsburgh Survey" (1906–07), and editorial staff of *Survey Magazine*. Commons strongly supported America's role in World War I, endorsed Milwaukee's "Americanization" efforts, and urged employers to force their foreign-born workers to learn English, in part to reduce the threat of radicalism.

In 1923 he helped represent four western states before the Federal Trade Commission in opposition to the regional price discrimination of U.S. Steel. Argued that the goal of social insurance legislation should be the prevention of economic hardship rather than the maintenance or redistribution of income. Urged that each employer be required to set aside his own unemployment insurance reserve fund; thus, rather than see it depleted, he would conduct his business in such a way as to keep employment as high as possible. This concept found general expression in the unemployment provisions of the federal Social Security Act of 1935. Many of his programs for Wisconsin served as models for New Deal measures. Commons served (1923–35) as president of the National Consumer's League.

Principal editor of the ten-volume *Documentary History of American Industrial Society* (1910–11). The writings of Commons and his students came to constitute the Wisconsin school of labor history. That school reached its classic expression in the *History of Labor in the United States*, which reflected Commons' conviction that labor history must be viewed as an integral part of a larger economic philosophy.

Commons published only two clearly theoretical works, *Legal Foundations of Capitalism* (1924) and *Institutional Economics* (1934). Economic competition, he believed, arose out of a condition common to all societies: the necessity to protect property rights to scarce resources.

Besides law and custom, ethics was an important philosophical companion to economics. Commons refused to apply the biological principles of Darwinism to human economic behavior. The courts were the keystone of Commons' economic analysis, and he saw the U.S. Supreme Court as the nation's "supreme faculty of political economy." He hoped that American courts would facilitate the acceptance of customs of the laboring class, including minimum wages, maximum hours, and improved conditions of labor.

COMPTON, ARTHUR HOLLY (*b. Wooster, Ohio, 1892; d. Berkeley, Calif., 1962*), physicist. Studied at the College of Wooster (B.S., 1913) and Princeton (Ph.D., 1916). Utilizing O. W. Richardson's X-ray equipment, his dissertation research determined the distribution of electrons in crystals by studying the intensity of X rays reflected from them as a function of angle of reflection. As an instructor in physics at the University of Minnesota (1916–17) he studied the reflection of X rays from a magnetic crystal, work that led him to conclude in 1920 that magnetism is not an atomic effect. He worked for Westinghouse Lamp Company (1917–19), where he was involved in the development of the sodium vapor lamp. In 1919–20 he studied with Ernest Rutherford and J. J. Thomson at the Cavendish Laboratory in Cambridge, England. Compton taught at Washington University in St. Louis from 1920 to 1923, the year in which he published his discovery of the Compton effect, which provided the first conclusive experimental proof of Einstein's light quantum hypothesis. For this discovery he shared the 1927 Nobel Prize with C.T.R. Wilson. The same year he was elected to the National Academy of Sciences.

Compton taught at the University of Chicago (1923–45), where in 1930 he turned his attention to cosmological processes. With financial support from the Carnegie Institution he conducted a world survey of cosmic rays (1931–34), which proved that the cosmic-ray intensity steadily decreases as one moves from the poles to the equator. As director of the Metallurgical Laboratory of the Manhattan Project (1942–45), he brought Enrico Fermi to Chicago to help produce the atomic bomb, which Compton recommended for use against Japan. After the war he became chancellor of Washington University (1945–53), professor of natural philosophy (1954–61), and professor at large (1961). He was awarded the U.S. Government Medal for Merit in 1946.

COMPTON, KARL TAYLOR (*b. Wooster, Ohio, 1887; d. New York, N.Y., 1954*), physicist. Studied at the College of Wooster and at Princeton (Ph.D., 1912). Taught at Princeton (1915–30), becoming chairman of the physics department. In 1930, he became president of the Massachusetts Institute of Technology, remaining there until 1948. Compton transformed M.I.T. from a small undergraduate school of engineering into one of the most distinguished technical institutions in the world. Under his leadership, the M.I.T. Radiation Laboratory developed radar and for this effort he received the Order of Merit for hastening the end of the war (1946). In 1948, President Truman appointed him chairman of the Research and Development Board of the National Military Establishment.

COMSTOCK, ANTHONY (*b. New Canaan, Conn., 1844; d. 1915*), reformer. *Post* 1871, supported by the YMCA, he began a crusade, which ended only with his death, against publishers and sellers of obscene literature. He forced the adoption of postal legislation preventing mail shipment of obscene materials; was secretary of Society for Suppression of Vice and a special agent of the Post Office Department. Incorruptible and zealous, he was unable to distinguish between good art and bad, and frequently attacked works of artistic and literary value.

COMSTOCK, ELIZABETH L. (*b. Maidenhead, England, 1815; d. Union Springs, N.Y., 1891*), Quaker minister. Settled in Rollin, Mich., 1858; advocated abolition, temperance, and prison reform; during Civil War ministered to wounded and imprisoned soldiers.

COMSTOCK, GEORGE CARY (*b. Madison, Wis., 1855; d. Beloit, Wis., 1934*), astronomer. Director, Washburn Observatory, 1899–1922. Demonstrated that many stars are apparently faint because they are intrinsically of low luminosity, not because they are far away.

COMSTOCK, GEORGE FRANKLIN (*b. near Williamstown, N.Y., 1811; d. Syracuse, N.Y., 1892*), jurist. Justice, New York Court of Appeals, 1855–61; a profound equity lawyer; initiated organization of Syracuse University.

COMSTOCK, HENRY TOMPKINS PAIGE (*b. Trenton, Canada, 1820; d. near Bozeman, Mont., 1870*), trapper, prospector. Claimant of ground where Comstock lode, named for him, was found.

COMSTOCK, JOHN HENRY (*b. Janesville, Wis., 1849; d. Ithaca, N.Y., 1931*), entomologist. Professor of entomology, Cornell University, 1882–1914; his original studies in *Wings of Insects* (1918) formed the basis of the greatest advance of the period in entomology.

CONANT, ALBAN JASPER (*b. Chelsea, Vt., 1821; d. New York, N.Y., 1915*), artist, archaeologist. Settled in St. Louis, Mo., 1857; promoted artistic interest; wrote pioneer studies, *The Archaeology of Missouri* (1876) and *Footprints of Vanished Races in the Mississippi Valley* (1879).

CONANT, CHARLES ARTHUR (*b. Winchester, Mass., 1861; d. Havana, Cuba, 1915*), journalist. Washington correspondent, specializing in finance, 1889–1901; later a banker and financial expert in Philippines, Nicaragua, and elsewhere.

CONANT, HANNAH O'BRIEN CHAPLIN (*b. Danvers, Mass., 1809; d. 1865*), writer. Wife of Thomas J. Conant, whom she assisted in his theological work.

CONANT, HEZEKIAH (*b. Dudley, Mass., 1872; d. 1902*), inventor, manufacturer. Invented "gas check" for breech-loading firearms, 1856; devised and patented many improvements in the manufacture of thread.

CONANT, ROGER (*b. East Budleigh, England, ca. 1592; d. Beverly, Mass., 1679*). Colonial official. Settled at Nantasket, 1624; upon request of settlers served as governor on Cape Ann, 1625, and at new settlement at Salem, 1626.

CONANT, THOMAS JEFFERSON (*b. Brandon, Vt., 1802; d. Brooklyn, N.Y., 1891*), Baptist clergyman, philologist. Member of American Bible Revision Committee; author of a simple, forceful translation of the Bible, and other works.

CONATY, THOMAS JAMES (*b. Kilnalec, Ireland, 1847; d. Los Angeles, Calif., 1915*), Roman Catholic clergyman, educator. Graduated Holy Cross College, 1869; ordained 1872. Pastor at Worcester, Mass.; was rector of Catholic University, 1897–1903, and president of National Catholic Education Association, 1899–1903. Bishop of Monterey and Los Angeles, *post* 1903.

CONBOY, MARTIN (*b. New York, N.Y., 1878; d. New York, 1944*), lawyer, Roman Catholic lay leader. Graduated Gonzaga College, Washington, D.C., B.A., 1898; M.A., 1899. LL.B., Georgetown University, 1898. Practiced in New York City *post* 1903. An efficient director of the World War I draft in New York City, Conboy acted on numerous occasions as adviser and special counsel in public affairs, notably in the investigation of the administration of Mayor James J. Walker (1932). As U.S. attorney for the southern district of New York, 1933–34, he won test cases involving New Deal laws against gold hoarding and certain provisions of the National Industrial Recovery Act.

CONBOY, SARA AGNES MCLAUGHLIN (*b. Boston, Mass., 1870; d. 1928*), labor leader. Secretary-treasurer, United Textile Workers; first woman to wield influence in A.F. of L. councils; effective in securing labor legislation and as conciliator.

CONDIT, JOHN (*b. New Jersey, 1755; d. Orange, N.J., 1834*), surgeon. Congressman, Democratic-Republican, from New Jersey, 1799–1803, 1819–20; U.S. senator, 1803–17.

CONDON, THOMAS (*b. near Fermoy, Ireland, 1822; d. 1907*), Congregational clergyman, geologist. Came to America as a boy; served as missionary in Oregon, 1853–73; taught geology at Pacific University and University of Oregon, 1873–1905; a pioneer in local paleontology.

CONE, ETTA (*b. Baltimore, Md., 1870; d. Blowing Rock, N.C., 1949*), art collector. In association with her sister **Claribel** (*b. Jonesboro, Tenn., 1864; d. Lausanne, Switzerland, 1929*), she acquired a notable collection of modern paintings, drawings, and sculpture (including a comprehensive collection of Matisse's work), together with other art objects, which was bequeathed to the Baltimore Museum of Art. The sisters were strongly influenced by their friends Leo and Gertrude Stein.

CONE, HUTCHINSON INGHAM (*b. Brooklyn, N.Y., 1871; d. Orlando, Fla., 1941*), naval officer, shipping executive. Raised in Florida. Graduated East Florida Military and Agricultural College, 1889; U.S. Naval Academy, 1894. As fleet engineer for the Atlantic Fleet's famous round-the-world cruise, Cone performed outstanding service and was appointed by President Theodore Roosevelt in May 1909 to a four-year term as chief of the Bureau of Engineering. During his tenure, he did much to modernize the navy's engineering practices. During World War I, as head of U.S. Naval Aviation Forces, Foreign Service, he was in charge of air protection of convoys from bases which he built in Britain, France, and Italy. Despite problems of equipment and supply, he brought the naval air force to a high level of operational activity. Retiring as rear admiral, 1922, he held a number of government posts related to the merchant marine; *post* 1937, he was chairman of the board of Moore-McCormack Lines.

CONE, MOSES HERMAN (*b. Jonesboro, Tenn., 1857; d. 1908*), cotton merchant, denim manufacturer at Greensboro, N.C.

CONE, ORELLO (*b. Lincklaen, N.Y., 1835; d. 1905*), New Testament scholar. His *Gospel Criticism and Historical Christianity* (1891) was ablest American work on higher criticism; taught at St. Lawrence University, Canton, N.Y.

CONE, RUSSELL GLENN (*b. Ottumwa, Iowa 1896; d. Vallejo, Calif., 1961*), civil engineer. Received his B.S. degree in civil engineering at the University of Illinois at Urbana. Began working as a junior engineer on the construction of the Delaware River Bridge, then was promoted to resident engineer in charge of span construction. He was resident engineer on the Ambassador Bridge (1927–30), then became general manager of the Tacony-Palmyra Toll Bridge (1930). As an authority on suspension bridge construction, he became resident engineer in charge of construction on the Golden Gate Bridge (1933–37) and then engineer in charge of maintenance for the Golden Gate Bridge and Highway District (1937–41). Joining the Solas Mason Company of New York in 1941, he directed the construction of large ordnance plants during the war and then helped the firm enter the field of atomic weapons design and production. Cone served as site project manager for the atomic tests staged by the Atomic Energy Commission at Frenchman's Flat and Yucca Flats (1950–53). In 1956 he was involved in building the foundations for the Carquinez Strait Bridge at Crockett, Calif.

CONE, SPENCER HOUGHTON (*b. Princeton, N.J., 1785; d. New York, N.Y., 1855*), Baptist clergyman. Was actor, journalist, soldier. An outstanding preacher, he was a founder and head of the American and Foreign Bible Society, 1837–50, and president of American Bible Union.

CONEY, JABEZ (*b. Dedham, Mass., 1804; d. 1872*), millwright, engineer. At South Boston, 1848, built machinery for USS *Saranac*, the first steam vessel in the navy.

CONEY, JOHN (*b. Boston, Mass., 1655; d. 1722*), silversmith. A fine craftsman, he engraved plates for first Massachusetts paper money; Apollos Rivoire (father of Paul Revere) was his apprentice.

CONGDON, CHARLES TABER (*b. New Bedford, Mass., 1821; d. New York, N.Y., 1891*), journalist. As *New York Tribune* staff member, 1857–82, called "Greeley's right hand"; author of *Tribune Essays* (1869) and *Reminiscences of a Journalist* (1880).

CONGER, EDWIN HURD (*b. near Galesburg, Ill., 1843; d. 1907*), Union soldier, diplomat. A successful Iowa businessman, he served in several diplomatic posts, distinguishing himself as minister to China, 1898–1904, during Boxer Rebellion.

CONKLIN, EDWIN GRANT (*b. Waldo, Ohio, 1863; d. Princeton, N.J., 1952*), biologist, educator. Studied at Ohio Wesleyan University and at Johns Hopkins (Ph.D., 1891). A specialist in embryology and cytology and an ardent evolutionist, Conklin was one of the leading proponents of the importance of cytoplasmic localization and segregation during development. He taught at Ohio Wesleyan and at the University of Pennsylvania before he became chairman of the biology department at Princeton (1908–33). In 1915, he published the widely read *Heredity and Environment in the Development of Men*.

CONKLIN, JENNIE MARIA DRINKWATER. *See* DRINKWATER, JENNIE MARIA.

CONKLING, ALFRED (*b. Amagansett, N.Y., 1789; d. Utica, N.Y., 1874*), lawyer, jurist. Father of Roscoe Conkling. Federal judge, northern district of New York, 1825–52; U.S. minister to Mexico, 1852; author of several legal treatises.

CONKLING, ROSCOE (*b. Albany, N.Y., 1829; d. New York, N.Y., 1888*), politician, lawyer. Son of Alfred Conkling. Admitted to the bar, 1850. Skilled in "spread-eagle" oratory, he rose rapidly in Whig party councils and was mayor of Utica, N.Y., 1858. Except for the years 1863–65, he served as congressman, 1859–67, becoming a "War Republican" and an advocate of vigorous repression in Reconstruction of the South. Ambitious and able, he was elected U.S. senator from New York, 1867; from then, until his resignation from the Senate in 1881, he was Republican leader in his state and an aspirant to the presidency. A friend and supporter of Grant, Conkling was a bitter enemy of Presidents Hayes and Garfield and of James G. Blaine. He opposed civil service reform and gave up politics after an unsuccessful fight against Garfield's application of the power of appointment to federal jobs, which he considered the perquisite of the New York organization.

CONNALLY, THOMAS TERRY ("TOM") (*b. near Hewitt, McLennan County, Tex., 1877; d. Washington, D.C., 1963*), lawyer, U.S. congressman, and senator. Attended Baylor (B.A., 1896) and University of Texas Law School (LL.B., 1898). Began practicing law in Marlin (1899) and was elected to the Texas House of Representatives (1916). In the House, Connally, a Democrat, opposed Republican tariff policy and evidenced a deep concern for southern agriculture. In 1928 he was elected to the U.S. Senate. Early in the Depression he urged President Roosevelt to reduce taxes drastically and inaugurate federal borrowing for direct relief. But Connally opposed the National Recovery Act (1933) and led the fight against reorganization of the Supreme Court (1937). He directed the Senate filibuster against antilynching legislation in the 1930's and 1940's.

Connally assiduously defended his state's interests in Congress, securing assistance to ranching, cotton, and oil interests. On the Senate Foreign Relations Committee he moved closer to Roosevelt's foreign policies at the end of the 1930's. He helped repeal the arms embargo, supported the Selective Service Act (1940), and helped secure passage of the Lend-Lease Act (1941). In 1941 Connally became chairman of the Foreign Relations Committee, and he worked hard to construct a bipartisan consensus on foreign policy. A conservative on domestic issues, he was vice-chairman of the American delegation to the United Nations conference (1945) and led the Senate in ratifying the U.N. Charter and the law that authorized U.S. participation in the U.N. After losing his committee chairmanship to a brief Republican control of Congress (1946–48), Connally returned to his post to work for approval of the North Atlantic Treaty. He retired from the Senate after his fourth term to practice law in Washington and compile his memoirs.

CONNELLY, CORNELIA (*b. Philadelphia, Pa., 1809; d. 1879*), founder of the Society of the Holy Child Jesus, 1846.

CONNELLY, HENRY (*b. Nelson Co., Ky., 1800; d. Santa Fe, N.Mex., 1866*), physician, pioneer trader. As governor of New Mexico, 1861–66, he was largely responsible for New Mexico's stand against the Confederacy.

CONNELLY, PIERCE FRANCIS (*b. Grand Coteau, La., 1841*), sculptor. Son of Cornelia Connelly. Worked abroad; exhibited in America with great success in 1876.

CONNER, CHARLOTTE MARY SANFORD BARNES. *See* BARNES, CHARLOTTE MARY SANFORD.

CONNER, DAVID (*b. Harrisburg, Pa., 1792; d. Philadelphia, Pa., 1856*), naval officer. Won two Congressional Medals for service on the *Hornet*, 1811–17; during Mexican War commanded naval forces in Caribbean and Gulf.

CONNER, JAMES (*b. Charleston, S.C., 1829; d. Richmond, Va., 1883*), lawyer, Confederate soldier. South Carolina attorney general, 1876–77; established legality of Wade Hampton government.

CONNEY, JOHN. *See* CONEY, JOHN.

CONNICK, CHARLES JAY (*b. Springboro, Pa., 1875; d. Boston, Mass., 1945*), artist in stained glass. Apprenticed at first as an illustrator, and *post* 1894 in a Pittsburgh, Pa., stained-glass studio, Connick rebelled against the ordinary practice of the time which arranged heavy opaque or opalescent glass in static pictures, seeking instead to attain "the vibration of color in a constantly changing light." Removing to Boston, 1900, he became a close friend and collaborator of Ralph Adams Cram. Influenced by the English artist C. W. Whall and his own examination of medieval work, he produced a great number of masterly windows for churches throughout the United States. Author of *Adventures in Light and Color* (1937).

CONNOLLY, JOHN (*b. York Co., Pa., ca. 1743; d. Montreal, Canada, 1813*), Loyalist, agent of Lord Dunmore. After incomplete apprenticeship to a physician, served as medical officer in frontier Indian campaigns, 1762–64. Supported Dunmore in claiming for Virginia territory around Fort Pitt. Commissioned commandant at the fort by Dunmore, 1773, he halted the Pennsylvania trade with the Indians. In 1775, after winning Indian support for England, he planned with Dunmore to recapture Fort Pitt and use it as a base for a joint operation to divide the colonies. Was imprisoned, 1776–80, exchanged and recaptured at Yorktown. As lieutenant governor of Detroit, he intrigued, 1788, to win Kentucky allegiance to Britain.

CONNOLLY, JOHN (*b. Slane, Ireland, 1750; d. 1825*), Dominican priest. Consecrated second bishop of New York, 1814. Successfully overcame dangers of racial antagonism and lay trusteeism; established orphan asylum.

CONNOLLY, MAUREEN CATHERINE (*b. San Diego, Calif., 1934; d. Dallas, Tex., 1969*), tennis player and coach. Began playing professional tennis in 1949, having already won more than fifty championships and become the youngest person ever to win the national junior title. She was U.S. Singles Champion (1951–53), French Singles Champion (1953–54), Wimbledon Singles Champion (1952–54), Australian Singles Champion (1953), and U.S. Clay Court Singles Champion (1953–54). She was ranked number one in the world (1952–54). She became in 1953 the first woman to win the grand slam of tennis, and she was named female athlete of the year by the Associated Press in 1952, 1953, and 1954. An injury suffered while riding her horse in 1954 ended her playing career. She then turned to coaching youngsters.

CONNOLLY, THOMAS H. (*b. Manchester, England, 1870; d. Natick, Mass., 1961*), baseball umpire. Immigrated with his family to the U.S. when he was thirteen, settling in Natick, Mass. At fifteen he began umpiring local YMCA, school, and sandlot games. His first professional job (1894) was in the New England League. He moved to the National League in 1898 for two and a half seasons, quitting because he felt the owners did not offer enough support in disputes with players. In 1901 Connolly umpired the first game in the new American League. He also umpired the first games at Shibe Park (Philadelphia), Fenway Park (Boston), and Yankee Stadium (New York). With Hank O'Day he umpired the first modern World Series (1903). When he retired from active officiating (1931), Connolly became chief of staff of American League umpires. He retired in 1954. In 1953 he and Bill Klem were elected to the Baseball Hall of Fame, the first umpires to be so honored.

CONNOR, HENRY GROVES (*b. Wilmington, N.C., 1852; d. 1924*), jurist. Author of Connor Act, 1884; as federal district judge, 1909–24, broke postwar prejudice of North Carolina against federal courts.

CONNOR, PATRICK EDWARD (*b. Co. Kerry, Ireland, 1820; d. 1891*), pioneer, soldier, Indian fighter. Came to America as a child. Fought in Seminole and Mexican wars; removed to California, 1849. Commanded in district of Utah, 1861–64, and in Powder River campaign, 1865. Thereafter, he engaged in business and was a leader of the anti-Mormons in Utah.

CONNOR, ROBERT DIGGES WIMBERLY (*b. Wilson, N.C., 1878; d. Durham, N.C., 1950*), historian, archivist. Ph.B., University of North Carolina, 1899. As secretary of the North Carolina Historical Commission, 1903–21, he collected and organized the state's historical records and established a model historical agency. Professor of history and government at University of North Carolina, 1921–34, he was appointed the first archivist of the United States, 1934. Gathered and organized the National Archives with great tact and in line with the highest professional standards. Resigned in 1941 and returned to North Carolina as Craige professor of jurisprudence and history.

CONOVER, HARRY SAYLES (*b. Chicago, Ill., 1911; d. Elmhurst, Queens, N.Y., 1965*), founder of the Harry Conover Modeling Agency. Began working as a model in 1935 for the John Robert Powers Modeling Agency, the foremost agency of the day. Although successful as a model, Conover's interest turned to management, and he opened an office in New York City in 1939. By 1942 Harry Conover Modeling Agency was agent for about 200 models and was grossing $750,000 annually. Conover saw a need for the fresh-faced, natural look in modeling, which he provided with his "Conover Cover Girls." His models included Shelley Winters, Joan Caulfield, Nina Foch, Anita Colby, and Jinx Falkenburg. Added prestige came with the successful movie *Cover Girl* (1944) starring Rita Hayworth and Gene Kelly. Conover served as a technical adviser and provided both the name and background models. In 1949 he established a special television department, which became very successful booking models exclusively for television. As the agency's success increased, Conover indulged in wild spending to support a lavish lifestyle and the agency began to lose ground. The inability to pay child models in 1959 led to the dissolution of the Conover Modeling Agency. In 1964, dependent on the financial support of his mother, Conover was arrested for nonpayment of alimony and child support, for which he received a prison term.

CONOVER, OBADIAH MILTON (*b. Dayton, Ohio, 1825; d. London, England, 1884*), educator, lawyer. Taught classical languages and literature at University of Wisconsin; was reporter of Wisconsin Supreme Court, 1864–84, and state librarian.

CONRAD, CHARLES MAGILL (*b. Winchester, Va., 1804; d. New Orleans, La., 1878*), lawyer, statesman. A Whig, he served briefly in Louisiana legislature, as congressman and U.S. senator, as secretary of war, 1850–53, and prominently in Confederate Congress.

CONRAD, FRANK (*b. Pittsburgh, Pa., 1874; d. Miami, Fla., 1941*), electrical engineer, radio pioneer. Served apprenticeship in Westinghouse electrical manufacturing plant. Through extraordinary mechanical and inventive aptitude became engineer in charge of special development, 1904, and *post* 1921 was assistant chief engineer of the Westinghouse company. In 1897, he developed the type of watt-hour meter still in wide use; he later was responsible for design and development of an automobile electrical system, circuit breakers, mercury-vapor rectifiers, and many other devices. He is chiefly famous, however, for his work *post* 1912 in radio. During World War I, his research at Westinghouse led to the only reliable airplane radio to be widely employed. He began to broadcast recorded music from a home station in 1919; in November 1920, the first regular commercial radio broadcasts were begun at the Westinghouse Pittsburgh station. He also made notable contributions to the technology of shortwave and ultrahigh-frequency radio work.

CONRAD, HOLMES (*b. Winchester, Va., 1840; d. Winchester, 1916*), lawyer. Influential Democratic legislator and leader of Virginia bar; U.S. solicitor general, 1895–97; outstanding in appeals before U.S. Supreme Court.

CONRAD, ROBERT TAYLOR (*b. Philadelphia, Pa., 1810; d. Philadelphia, 1858*), dramatist, jurist. His first play, *Conrad, King of Naples*, was produced successfully in Philadelphia, 1832; his best-known work was produced first in 1835 as *Aylmere*, but was later rewritten; under the title *Jack Cade* it was part of the repertory of Forrest, John McCullough, and others. Conrad was a distinguished figure in Philadelphia journalism; he served also as a judge of the city criminal court and as Know-Nothing mayor of Philadelphia, 1854–56. His poems and the text of *Jack Cade* were published as *Aylmere, or the Bondman of Kent; and Other Poems* (1852).

CONRIED, HEINRICH (*b. Bielitz, Austria, 1855; d. Meran, Austria, 1909*), actor, impresario. Came to America, *ca.* 1877, to manage the German stock companies at the Thalia and Irving Place theaters, New York. His excellent productions of drama and operetta won him wide recognition. As manager of the Metropolitan Opera, 1903–08, he gave unauthorized first production of Wagner's *Parsifal*, 1903, outside of Wagner Festival at Bayreuth.

CONSIDÉRANT, VICTOR PROSPER (*b. Salins, France, 1808; d. Paris, France, 1893*), social philosopher, Fourierist. Founder of Utopian community of Reunion, near Dallas, Tex., 1855.

CONVERSE, CHARLES CROZAT (*b. Warren, Mass., 1832; d. Highwood, N.J., 1918*), composer, lawyer. Studied music at Leipzig; wrote songs, orchestral pieces, cantatas, and popular hymns, including "What a Friend We Have in Jesus."

CONVERSE, EDMUND COGSWELL (*b. Boston, Mass., 1849; d. Pasadena, Calif., 1921*), inventor, capitalist, philanthropist. Patented lock-joint for gas and water pipes, 1882; organized National Tube Co., 1899. President, Liberty National Bank and Bankers' Trust Co., New York.

CONVERSE, FREDERICK SHEPHERD (*b. Newton, Mass., 1871; d. Westwood, Mass., 1940*), composer of the first American opera performed at New York City's Metropolitan Opera House (*The Pipe of Desire*, 1910) and many other works.

CONVERSE, JAMES BOOTH (*b. Philadelphia, Pa., 1844; d. 1914*), Presbyterian clergyman. Missionary and pastor in Kentucky and east Tennessee; author of *The Bible and Land* (1889), inspired by Henry George's *Progress and Poverty*.

CONVERSE, JOHN HEMAN (*b. Burlington, Vt., 1840; d. 1910*), locomotive builder. From 1870 to 1909, associated with Baldwin Locomotive Works; on its incorporation, 1909, was elected president.

CONWAY, ELIAS NELSON (*b. Greene Co., Tenn., 1812; d. 1892*), politician. Brother of James S. Conway. Went to Arkansas, 1833; served as auditor and administrator of public lands. As Democratic governor, 1852–60, stabilized state's financial affairs.

CONWAY, FREDERICK BARTLETT (*b. Clifton, England, 1819; d. Manchester, Mass., 1874*), actor. Made American debut, 1850; co-starring with his wife, he played in stock in Brooklyn, Philadelphia, Boston, and Cincinnati.

CONWAY, JAMES SEVIER (*b. Greene Co., Tenn., 1798; d. Lafayette Co., Ark., 1855*), politician, planter. Brother of Elias N. Conway. Removed to Arkansas, 1820. As first governor of state of Arkansas, 1836–40, he secured the chartering of the ill-fated State Bank and Real Estate Bank.

CONWAY, MARTIN FRANKLIN (*b. Harford Co., Md., 1827; d. Washington, D.C., 1882*), lawyer, printer. Removed to Kansas, 1854. Was an active Free-Soiler; served as president of Leavenworth constitutional convention, 1858, and as congressman, Republican, from Kansas, 1861–63.

CONWAY, MONCURE DANIEL (*b. near Falmouth, Va., 1832; d. Paris, France, 1907*), preacher. Author of *Life of Thomas Paine* (1892) and editor of Paine's works. He also produced a number of other works on slavery and liberal theology, and an autobiography (1904).

CONWAY, THOMAS (*b. Ireland, 1735; d. ca. 1800*), Revolutionary soldier. Raised in France, he reached rank of colonel in the French army, 1772. On recommendation of Silas Deane, he was appointed brigadier general in the Continental army, arriving in America, April 1777. Washington's opposition to his promotion to major general was overridden by Congress, which commissioned him on Dec. 14, 1777, and appointed him inspector general of the army. Entering into correspondence with Horatio Gates and others, he criticized Washington and contributed to a movement in Congress to oust the commander in chief. Although the movement has gone down in history as the "Conway Cabal," Conway was not the prime mover in the conspiracy but merely the one who was caught. Attached to an abortive expedition against Canada, January 1778, Conway began to intrigue for a separate command; instead, he was ordered back to Peekskill to serve under General McDougall. His resignation from the army was accepted, Apr. 28, 1778. Subsequently, after coming close to death in a duel with General Cadwalader over his conduct, he wrote Washington a full apology for the injury he had done him and returned to France.

CONWELL, HENRY (*b. Moneymore, Ireland,* ca. *1745; d. Philadelphia, Pa., 1842*), Roman Catholic clergyman. Consecrated bishop of Philadelphia, 1820; was involved in struggle over lay trusteeism, 1821–26.

CONWELL, RUSSELL HERMAN (*b. South Worthington, Mass., 1843; d. 1925*), Union soldier, Baptist clergyman. Pastor of Philadelphia's Grace Baptist Church *post* 1880; founded Temple University; author of famous "Acres of Diamonds" lecture.

CONYNGHAM, GUSTAVUS (*b. Co. Donegal, Ireland,* ca. *1744; d. Philadelphia, Pa., 1819*), naval officer, privateer. Successful as captain of the cutter *Revenge,* 1777–78; made daring escape from Mill Prison, Plymouth, 1779.

COODE, JOHN (*d. 1709*), adventurer. As captain of militia of a "Protestant Association," Coode seized control of the government of Maryland, 1689.

COOK, ALBERT STANBURROUGH (*b. Montville, N.J., 1853; d. 1927*), scholar. Graduated Rutgers, 1872; studied at Göttingen, Leipzig, London, and Jena (Ph.D., 1882). Organized English department at Johns Hopkins; taught at California and at Yale, 1889–1921; specialist in Old and Middle English.

COOK, CLARENCE CHATHAM (*b. Dorchester, Mass., 1828; d. 1900*), art critic, journalist. His *New York Tribune* art column (1863–69) was feared by American artists. Editor, *The Studio,* 1884–92; author of *The House Beautiful* (1878).

COOK, FLAVIUS JOSEPHUS (*b. Ticonderoga, N.Y., 1838; d. 1901*), lecturer. Gave Boston Monday lectures at Tremont Temple on relation of science to religion, *post* 1874.

COOK, FREDERICK ALBERT (*b. Hortonville, N.Y., 1865; d. New Rochelle, N.Y., 1940*), physician and polar explorer. Surgeon and ethnologist on the 1891–92 Greenland expedition of Robert E. Peary. After several later exploratory expeditions, Cook, accompanied by two young Eskimos, claimed to have reached the North Pole, April 1908. Almost simultaneously with Cook's announcement, Peary claimed to be the first to have reached the pole, and challenged Cook's claim. The controversy raged for years. Cook failed to convince official and scientific opinion that he was telling the truth.

COOK, GEORGE CRAM (*b. Davenport, Iowa., 1873; d. Greece, 1924*), founder and director of Provincetown (Mass.) Players; established Macdougal Street (New York City) playhouse, 1915, for encouragement of American dramatic talent.

COOK, GEORGE HAMMELL (*b. Hanover, N.J. 1818; d. 1889*), geologist, educator. As professor of chemistry at Rutgers, 1853–89, promoted establishment of agricultural college and experiment station; was state geologist, 1864–89. Author of many lucid and practical reports, and of *Geology of New Jersey* (1872).

COOK, ISAAC (*b. Long Branch, N.J., 1810; d. Eureka Springs, Ark., 1886*), politician, wine merchant. Prospered in Chicago, *post* 1834; president, American Wine Co., St. Louis, Mo., 1859–86.

COOK, JAMES MERRILL (*b. Ballston Spa, N.Y., 1807; d. 1868*), capitalist, New York Whig politician. As superintendent of State Banking Department, 1856–61, stabilized state finances.

COOK, JOHN WILLISTON (*b. near Oneida, N.Y., 1844; d. 1922*), educator. Removed to Illinois, 1851. Taught at Illinois State Normal University; edited *Illinois Schoolmaster* and *Illinois School Journal*; president of National Education Association, 1904.

COOK, JOSEPH. *See* COOK, FLAVIUS JOSEPHUS.

COOK, MARTHA ELIZABETH DUNCAN WALKER (*b. Northumberland, Pa., 1806; d. Hoboken, N.J., 1874*), author, editor, translator. Sister of Robert J. Walker.

COOK, PHILIP (*b. Twiggs Co., Georgia, 1817; d. Georgia, 1894*), lawyer, Confederate soldier. Congressman, Democrat, 1873–83; secretary of state of Georgia, 1890–94.

COOK, ROBERT JOHNSON (*b. near Cookstown, Pa., 1849; d. Belle Vernon, Pa., 1922*), publisher, rowing coach at Yale. Originator of Bob Cook stroke.

COOK, RUSSELL S. (*b. New Marlboro, Mass., 1811; d. Pleasant Valley, N.Y., 1864*), Congregational clergyman. Corresponding secretary, American Tract Society, 1839–56; popularized "colportage."

COOK, LADY TENNESSEE CELESTE CLAFLIN. *See* WOODHULL, VICTORIA.

COOK, WALTER (*b. Buffalo, N.Y., 1846; d. New York, N.Y., 1916*), architect. Graduated Harvard, 1869; studied at Paris and Munich. *Post* 1877, headed several firms, ultimately Cook & Welch. Designed DeVinne Press Building, New York Life Insurance Building, Andrew Carnegie's residence, and the Choir School of the Cathedral of St. John the Divine, all in New York City.

COOK, WALTER WHEELER (*b. Columbus, Ohio, 1873; d. Tupper Lake, N.Y., 1943*), law professor. B.A., Columbia, 1894; M.A., 1899; LL.M., 1901. Taught at Nebraska, Missouri, Wisconsin, Chicago, Columbia, Yale, and Northwestern. Member of the faculty of the Institute of Law, Johns Hopkins, 1928–33. A principal formulator of the legal realism school of jurisprudence.

COOK, WILL MARION (*b. Washington, D.C., 1869; d. New York, N.Y., 1944*), musician, composer. A son of the first black man to practice law in Washington, D.C., Cook studied at Oberlin Conservatory of Music, in Berlin under Josef Joachim, and briefly under Anton Dvořák in New York. Realizing that race prejudice limited his chances of success as a classical violinist and composer, he decided to write in the black idiom for popular audiences. His successful music comedy *Clorindy,* with a libretto by Paul L. Dunbar, was produced with an all-black cast in 1898. Over the next ten years, he composed much of the music for a series of black musical shows featuring the great team of Bert Williams and George Walker; these included *In Dahomey* (1903), which was a European as well as an American success, and

Abyssinia (1906). His Broadway career languished as ragtime gave way to other forms.

COOK, ZEBEDEE (*b. Newburyport, Mass., 1786; d. South Framingham, Mass., 1858*), insurance man, horticulturist. A founder of Massachusetts Horticultural Society.

COOKE, EBENEZER (*b. ca. 1670; d. ca. 1732*), poet. His *Sotweed Factor* (1708) and *Sotweed Redivivus* (1730) give a satirical picture of Maryland in the early 18th century.

COOKE, ELISHA (*b. Boston, Mass., 1637; d. 1715*), physician. Took leading part in overthrow and imprisonment of Andros and Dudley, 1689; agent of Massachusetts in London, 1690–92; an opponent of clericalism and royal prerogative.

COOKE, ELISHA (*b. Boston, Mass., 1678; d. Boston, 1737*), physician, statesman. Son of Elisha Cooke (1637–1715), whose ideas of popular government he inherited. Served for 18 years in Massachusetts General Court and on the Council; opposed Governors Shute and Belcher.

COOKE, GEORGE WILLIS (*b. Comstock, Mich., 1848; d. Revere, Mass., 1923*), Unitarian clergyman, lecturer. A liberal in theology and a socialist, he was author of a life of Emerson (1881) and *Unitarianism in America* (1902).

COOKE, HENRY DAVID (*b. Sandusky, Ohio, 1825; d. 1881*), journalist, banker. Brother of Jay Cooke, for whom he lobbied in Washington, D.C.

COOKE, JAY (*b. Sandusky, Ohio, 1821; d. 1905*), banker, financier. In 1839 entered banking firm in Philadelphia; from 1861 to 1873 was head of Jay Cooke & Co., one of the country's best-known banking houses. After success in negotiating a government loan in 1861, Cooke was appointed treasury agent in 1862 and succeeded by extensive advertisement in distributing a $500 million government loan, a feat which he repeated in 1865. After the Civil War he entered general banking with branches in New York and London. The failure of his project to finance a northern railroad route from Duluth to Tacoma and the consequent collapse of his firm precipitated the panic of 1873.

COOKE, JOHN ESTEN (*b. Bermuda, 1783; d. 1853*), physician. Came to Virginia, 1791; M.D., University of Pennsylvania, 1805. Author of *Treatise on Pathology* (1828), said to have been earliest American systematic textbook on medicine; taught at Transylvania University and Louisville, Ky., Medical Institute.

COOKE, JOHN ESTEN (*b. Winchester, Va., 1830; d. 1886*), novelist, Confederate soldier. Son of John R. Cooke. Author of *Leather Stocking and Silk* (1854), *The Virginia Comedians* (1854), *Surry of Eagle's Nest* (1866), *Mohun* (1869), and other works.

COOKE, JOHN ROGERS (*b. Bermuda, 1788; d. 1854*), lawyer. Brother of John E. Cooke (1783–1853) and Philip St. George Cooke. A leading lawyer of western Virginia *post* 1812, he removed to Richmond, 1840. He was particularly distinguished as a delegate of the Virginia constitutional convention, 1829–30.

COOKE, JOSIAH PARSONS (*b. Boston, Mass., 1827; d. Newport, R.I., 1894*), chemist, teacher. Graduated Harvard, 1848; Erving professor there *post* 1850; pioneered in the classification of elements by their atomic weights (1854). Author of *Elements of Chemical Physics* (1860), *The New Chemistry* (1874), and other works.

COOKE, MORRIS LLEWELLYN (*b. Carlisle, Pa., 1872; d. Philadelphia, Pa., 1960*), consultant engineer, government official. Studied at Lehigh University. An expert in electrical power and scientific management techniques, Cooke was an advisor to the Tennessee Valley Authority and headed the Mississippi Valley Committee Commission in the Public Works Administration under President Franklin Roosevelt. From 1935 to 1937, he was the first head of the Rural Electrification Administration. Cooke proposed a total national plan for the use of power, watershed, soil erosion, and public works.

COOKE, PHILIP PENDLETON (*b. Martinsburg, Va., now W.Va., 1816; d. 1850*), poet, lawyer. Son of John R. Cooke. His romantic poems were published in *Froissart Ballads* (1847).

COOKE, PHILIP ST. GEORGE (*b. Leesburg, Va., 1809; d, 1895*), soldier. Brother of John E. (1783–1853) and John R. Cooke. Graduated West Point, 1827. Served in the frontier West and in far-western phase of Mexican War; was Union brigadier general in Civil War; retired, 1873. Author of *Cavalry Tactics* (1861) and *The Conquest of New Mexico and California* (1878).

COOKE, ROBERT ANDERSON (*b. Holmdel, N.J., 1880; d. 1960*), physician. Studied at Rutgers College (D.Sc., 1925) and at Columbia (M.D., 1904). A pioneer in allergy treatment, Cooke founded the first clinic for allergic diseases at New York Hospital in 1919. In 1932, the clinic was associated with Roosevelt Hospital. In 1949, Cooke assumed directorship of the Robert A. Cooke Institute of Allergy in New York. Cooke developed the first treatment for the desensitization for hay fever. He founded the American Academy of Allergy and was its first president.

COOKE, ROSE TERRY (*b. near Hartford, Conn., 1827; d. Pittsfield, Mass., 1892*), story writer, poet.

COOKE, SAMUEL (*b. the Ukraine, Russia, 1898; d. Cheltenham, Pa., 1965*), businessman. Immigrated to the U.S. with his family in 1908. In 1927, with Morris and Isaac Kaplan, he founded the Penn Fruit Company, serving as its president until 1960. He was one of the originators of the self-service supermarket and was a pioneer in techniques of getting fruits and vegetables from the farm to the store quickly. When Cooke retired as president, Penn Fruit operated eighty supermarkets in Pennsylvania, Maryland, Delaware, New Jersey, and New York.

COOLBRITH, INA DONNA (*b. Nauvoo, Ill., 1841; d. Berkeley, Calif., 1928*), poet. Niece of Joseph Smith. Removed to California, 1851; was coeditor of Bret Harte's *Overland Monthly*, 1868, and later a librarian in Oakland and San Francisco.

COOLEY, EDWIN GILBERT (*b. Strawberry Point, Iowa, 1857; d. Chicago, Ill., 1923*), educator. Superintendent of Chicago schools, 1900–09; accomplished many reforms.

COOLEY, LYMAN EDGAR (*b. Canandaigua, N.Y., 1850; d. 1917*), civil engineer. Graduated Rensselaer Polytechnic, 1874. First chief engineer of Chicago Sanitary and Ship Canal, and associated with the work of the Chicago Sanitary District, 1885–1916. With James B. Angell and John E. Russell established feasibility of a Great Lakes–Atlantic ship canal. Was prolific writer on engineering subjects.

COOLEY, MORTIMER ELWYN (*b. near Canandaigua, N.Y., 1855; d. Ann Arbor, Mich., 1944*), engineering educator, public utilities expert. Brother of Lyman E. Cooley. Graduated Annapolis, 1878. Professor of engineering at University of Michigan, 1881–1928. As dean of the School of Engineering *post* 1904, he made it one of the most important schools in the university. Commissioned by the governor of Michigan to make a statewide evaluation of railroad properties, 1900, Cooley developed procedures for the purpose which became the model for later utilities surveys. Also active as a member of many government boards and commissions and headed the American Engineering Council, 1922–24.

COOLEY, THOMAS BENTON (*b. Ann Arbor, Mich., 1871; d. Bangor, Maine, 1945*), pediatrician. Son of Thomas M. Cooley. B.A., University of Michigan, 1891; M.D., 1895. Practiced in Detroit, Mich., where he headed the staff of the Children's Hospital, and was professor of pediatrics at Wayne University College of Medicine *post* 1936. Among his contributions to pediatrics, the most important was his identification (1925) of the familial anemia that bears his name. He was also the first to find and report a case of sickle-cell anemia in a child of white ancestry.

COOLEY, THOMAS MCINTYRE (*b. near Attica, N.Y., 1824; d. Ann Arbor, Mich., 1898*), jurist. Removed to Michigan, 1843; admitted to the bar, 1846; practiced in Michigan and Ohio. Became official reporter of Michigan Supreme Court, 1858; edited *Michigan Reports*, 1858–64. Justice, Michigan Supreme Court, 1864–85; professor of law at University of Michigan, 1859–84; professor of American history and constitutional law, 1885–98. He wrote *A Treatise on . . . Constitutional Limitations* (1868); *The General Principles of Constitutional Law* (1880); an authoritative *Treatise on the Law of Torts* (1879); and other works. As chairman of the Interstate Commerce Commission, 1887–91, he made it into an effective judicial tribunal.

COOLIDGE, ARCHIBALD CARY (*b. Boston, Mass., 1866; d. 1928*), historian. Taught at Harvard; was director of Harvard Library *post* 1910 and the first editor of *Foreign Affairs*.

COOLIDGE, CALVIN (*b. Plymouth Notch, Vt., 1872; d. Northampton, Mass., 1933*), president of the United States. Son of parents who operated a general store and post office, he grew up with the traits of his ancestors and those of the community: frugality, taciturnity, industry, piety, and honesty. Prepared for college in Vermont private schools, he entered Amherst in the class of 1895 and graduated *cum laude*. After studying law for 20 months, he was admitted to the bar and opened his own office in Northampton, Mass., in 1898. In 1905 he was married to Grace Anna Goodhue.

After filling various local offices Coolidge was elected to the Massachusetts House of Representatives, 1906, served two terms as mayor of Northampton, and went to the Massachusetts Senate in 1911. He became lieutenant governor of the state in 1915. By party loyalty, industry, and an ingrained conservatism, Coolidge impressed the leaders of his Republican party. Pushed by Frank Waterman Stearns, he was elected governor of Massachusetts in 1918 and made a national reputation by settling the controversial Boston police strike in 1919. His statement that "there is no right to strike against the public safety by anybody, anywhere, anytime" sounded a popular chord, and he was reelected.

At the 1920 Republican National Convention in Chicago he was nominated for vice president in a revolt against boss dictation and, when elected, profited by being the antithesis of President Harding. His advent to the presidency on Aug. 4, 1923, saved the Republican party the full obloquy of the exposure of corrupt oil leases and other scandals under the late president.

In the campaign of 1924 Coolidge's appearance of thrift, caution, honesty, industry, self-reliance, and homely sagacity won him nomination on the first ballot. Few lamented his total want of leadership or perceived that his democracy was combined with an extraordinary deference to big business.

The following four years were those of a national inertia which Coolidge administered. He opposed subsidizing the farmers, action to punish business excesses, government operation of Muscle Shoals, measures to assist the League of Nations or World Court in international stabilization, and reduction of tariffs. His few recommendations to Congress were generally ignored. As speculation

pushed the stock market higher, his statements encouraged it. In foreign affairs Coolidge left the direction of policy primarily to Secretaries Hughes and Kellogg.

Although his popularity remained high and he probably could have been reelected in 1928, Coolidge knew that the country needed bolder leadership and he decided to retire. His last four years after leaving the White House were spent mainly in writing his *Autobiography* and articles preaching individualism, economy, and laissez faire.

COOLIDGE, CHARLES ALLERTON (*b. Boston, Mass., 1858; d. Locust Valley, N.Y., 1936*), architect. Worked for Henry Hobson Richardson, 1883–86, subsequently forming with various partners his own firm, which became in 1924 Coolidge, Shepley, Bulfinch & Abbott. The firm specialized in designs for college, public, and commercial buildings, among them the Ames Building, Boston; the Chicago Public Library and Art Institute; various buildings for the Rockefeller Institute, New York City, and for the University of Chicago, Stanford, and Harvard universities.

COOLIDGE, ELIZABETH PENN SPRAGUE (*b. Chicago, Ill., 1864; d. Cambridge, Mass., 1953*), patron of the arts. In 1916 Coolidge established the Berkshire Chamber Music Festival; in 1924, the name was changed to the South Mountain Association; its first festival featured Fritz Kreisler. In 1925, she funded and built an auditorium for chamber concerts in the Library of Congress; the Elizabeth Sprague Coolidge Foundation was formed at that time. Coolidge sponsored festivals throughout Europe and the United States. Composers receiving her assistance included Samuel Barber, Béla Bartók, Benjamin Britten, Authur Honneger, Arnold Schoenberg, and Heitor Villa-Lobos. She commissioned many works for ballet, including Stravinsky's *Apollon Musagète*, Copland's *Appalachian Spring*, and Milhaud's *Imagined Wing*. Among the performers who received her support were Myra Hess and Rudolph Serkin, as well as the Pro Arte, the Kolisch, and the Budapest quartets.

COOLIDGE, JULIAN LOWELL (*b. Brookline, Mass., 1873; d. Cambridge, Mass., 1954*), mathematician. Studied at Harvard College and Oxford (B.Sc., 1897), and the University of Bonn (Ph.D., 1904). Taught at Harvard, 1899–1940; chairman of the mathematics department, 1927. He was appointed the first house master of Lowell House in 1930. Coolidge delighted in teaching and inspired many students with a love of mathematics.

COOLIDGE, THOMAS JEFFERSON (*b. Boston, Mass., 1831; d. 1920*), merchant, financier, diplomat. Active in cotton-spinning industry, banking, railroad management; served as minister to France, 1892–96.

COOLIDGE, THOMAS JEFFERSON (*b. Manchester, Mass., 1893; d. Beverly, Mass., 1959*), financier, government official. Studied at Harvard. Chairman of the Old Colony Trust Co. (part of the First National Bank of Boston, 1940). Trustee and president of the board of the Boston Museum of Fine Arts (1921–34). Undersecretary of the Treasury (1934–36). Opposed to the New Deal, Coolidge resigned, though he continued to play a role as advisor to the government on fiscal matters. Overseer of Harvard from 1926 to 1932.

COOMARASWAMY, ANANDA KENTISH (*b. Colombo, Ceylon, 1877; d. Needham, Mass., 1947*), art historian, metaphysician. Raised in England, B.Sc., University of London, 1900; D.Sc., 1906. Trained as a geologist, he was director of the Mineralogical Survey of Ceylon, *ca.* 1904–06. Outraged at weakening of the indigenous culture by English colonial influence and inspired by the example of William Morris, he founded a society for the revival of Sinhalese and Tamil culture and edited its journal, the *Ceylon National Review*. He also undertook research for books

(*Mediaeval Sinhalese Art*, 1908; *Rajput Painting*, 1916) which established his reputation as a pioneer in Indian art-historical scholarship. He came to the United States in 1917 as keeper of Indian and Islamic art at Boston Museum of Fine Arts. *The Dance of Shiva* (1918) served to introduce Indian culture to a general American audience. His main concern until the 1930's was the scholarly interpretation of the art of India. *Post* 1932, his writings and study were concerned with development and expression of a philosophy of consciousness which would serve as the point of unity for all other studies, both empirical and speculative.

COOMBE, THOMAS (*b. Philadelphia, Pa., 1747; d. London, England, 1822*), Anglican clergyman, Loyalist, poet. Left America in 1779. A forceful preacher, his *The Peasant of Auburn* (London, 1783) recounted the unhappy fate of immigrants to the Ohio region.

COONTZ, ROBERT EDWARD (*b. Hannibal, Mo., 1864; d. Bremerton, Wash., 1935*), naval officer. Graduated Annapolis, 1885. Chief of naval operations, 1919–23.

COOPER, EDWARD (*b. New York, N.Y., 1824; d. New York, 1905*), manufacturer, metallurgist. Son of Peter Cooper. Invented regenerative hot-blast stove for blast furnaces; helped break "Tweed Ring"; was mayor of New York, 1879–81.

COOPER, ELIAS SAMUEL (*b. near Somerville, Ohio, 1820; d. San Francisco, Calif., 1862*), surgeon. Brother of Jacob Cooper. Founded first medical college on Pacific Coast, 1858; pioneered with alcoholic wound dressings and use of metallic sutures for fractures.

COOPER, EZEKIEL (*b. Caroline Co., Md., 1763; d. 1847*), Methodist clergyman. Agent of Methodist Book Concern, 1789–1808; vigorously opposed slavery.

COOPER, GARY (*b. Helena, Mont., 1901; d. Los Angeles, Calif., 1961*), actor. Attended Wesleyan College at Bozeman, Mont., and Grinnell College in Grinnell, Iowa (1920–24) before moving to Los Angeles, where he worked as a salesman. In 1925 he joined two friends to work as an extra in motion picture westerns. He decided to become an actor and changed his name from Frank to Gary. His first significant role was in *The Winning of Barbara Worth* (1926), after which he signed a contract with Paramount Pictures. In *Wings* (1927), Cooper managed to steal the show although he appeared for only 127 seconds. One of his first talking pictures was *The Virginian* (1929), which helped stereotype him as the classic cinema man of the West. This was followed by *Morocco* (1930) and *A Farewell to Arms* (1932). Between 1936 and 1943 he enjoyed a succession of box office and critical triumphs. For director Frank Capra he starred in *Mr. Deeds Goes to Town* (1936) and *Meet John Doe* (1941). He won an Academy Award and a New York Film Critics Prize for best actor playing *Sergeant York* (1941). Cooper portrayed Lou Gehrig in *The Pride of the Yankees* (1942) and paired with Ingrid Bergman in *For Whom the Bell Tolls* (1943).

Over the next decade Cooper was wracked by an unhappy personal life and ill health, and he was not well served by such films as *Casanova Brown* (1944), *Good Sam* (1948), and *Dallas* (1950). However, with his portrayal of the tortured marshal in *High Noon* (1952), Cooper captured his second Academy Award for best actor. He drew mixed notices for *Vera Cruz* (1954) and *Man of the West* (1958) and good reviews in *Friendly Persuasion* (1956). In 1961 he narrated a widely hailed television documentary, "The Real West," and starred in *The Naked Edge*. By box office figures, Cooper was the most popular male film star of the 1930's, 1940's, and 1950's.

COOPER, HENRY ERNEST (*b. New Albany, Ind., 1857; d. Long Beach, Calif., 1929*), lawyer. Helped organize Hawaii revolution, 1893; promoted American annexation of Hawaii and was first secretary of the territory.

COOPER, HUGH LINCOLN (*b. Sheldon, Minn., 1865; d. Stamford, Conn., 1937*), hydroelectric engineer. Designer of pioneer low-head hydroelectric plants; consultant on many foreign power projects.

COOPER, JACOB (*b. near Somerville, Ohio, 1830; d. 1904*), Presbyterian clergyman, educator. Studied at Yale, Berlin, Halle, Edinburgh; taught Greek at Centre College, Ky., and Greek and moral philosophy at Rutgers, 1866–1904.

COOPER, JAMES (*b. Frederick Co., Md., 1810; d. Camp Chase, Ohio, 1863*), lawyer, Union soldier, Pennsylvania legislator, U.S. senator, Whig, 1849–55.

COOPER, JAMES FENIMORE (*b. Burlington, N.J., 1789; d. Cooperstown, N.Y., 1851*), novelist. Grew up at Otsego Hall, Cooperstown, N.Y., the residence of his father, William Cooper, who held land in that area for development. Cooper's youth was spent in a manorial house located at the edge of the frontier wilderness; thus, the elements of the pioneer and the gentleman were provided to serve as a theme of struggle throughout Cooper's life. Educated in the Albany household of an Episcopal rector of Federalist, anti–New England sentiments, he attended Yale for three years, then shipped before the mast, 1806. A navy midshipman, 1807, he served on Lake Ontario, Lake Champlain, and the Atlantic. Married to Susan A. De Lancey in 1811, he resigned from the navy; he and his wife settled down to country life at Mamaroneck, N.Y., and subsequently at Cooperstown and Scarsdale, N.Y.

In 1822 he went to New York City to pursue his literary interest. He had published his first novel *Precaution* in 1820, but the book, conventional in manner and content, was not a success. With *The Spy* (1821), Cooper turned to an American setting and the period of the American Revolution, producing a story of romantic adventure and suspenseful excitement. The book also revealed his social attitudes, a curious mixture of democratic profession and aristocratic condescension. The vigor of Cooper's narrative and his characteristic formula of flight and pursuit made *The Spy* a success. In 1823 *The Pioneers* appeared, introducing the great character Natty Bumppo (Leather-Stocking), and also *The Pilot*, which set the mode for later sea stories. *The Spy*, *The Pioneers*, and *The Pilot* drew on the three regions of memory with which Cooper was most familiar: respectively, the New York past, the northern frontier, the high seas.

Having won a reputation as an author, Cooper founded the Bread and Cheese Club in New York City, served on the welcoming committee for Lafayette in 1824, and received an honorary master of arts degree from Columbia College. In 1825 he published *Lionel Lincoln*, a story dealing with the Boston of Bunker Hill days. In *The Last of the Mohicans* (1826), Cooper revived the character of Natty Bumppo and portrayed him as youthful, competent scout during the French and Indian War. In *The Prairie* (1827), the same character appears in a setting beyond the Mississippi as an old trapper of wide benevolence, a type of the wisdom attained through having lived in the boundless wilderness. In these books the forest is the symbol of whatever is spacious and elevated in life, the breeding ground of heroism. Cooper's Indian characters were meant to be figures of romance rather than portraits and were shown as chivalrous, noble, and uncorrupted by civilization.

From 1826 to 1833 Cooper lived in Europe, chiefly in Paris. He traveled to England, Switzerland, Italy, and Germany. During these years he wrote several romances: *The Red Rover* (1828); *The Wept of Wish-ton-Wish* (1829); *The Water-Witch* (1831); *The Bravo* (1831); *The Heidenmauer* (1832); *The Headsman* (1833);

and the satiric *Notions of the Americans* (1828). While his work abroad displayed much bumptious, ardent patriotism, and endorsed republican principles, his European experiences also stiffened some of his early aristocratic prejudices. He experienced a profound shock on his return to America. He missed the simplicity, the decorum, the private and public virtue, the enlightened patriotism which he had romantically declared to be natural to Americans. He now discovered that the ideal wilderness of his fantasy did not exist. In his efforts to preach reform and a return to the old virtues, he grew intemperate and shrill, as in *A Letter to His Countrymen* (1834). In *The Monikins* (1835), *Sketches of Switzerland* (1836), *Gleanings in Europe: France* (1837), *Gleanings in Europe: England* (1837), and *Gleanings in Europe: Italy* (1838), he savagely poured out his judgments on Europe, to which he had preferred his mythical America, and also on that actual America which was so unlike his dream. He sought to state his thesis of democratic decline directly in *The American Democrat* (1838) and to illustrate it in the novels *Homeward Bound* (1838) and *Home as Found* (1838). Often justified in his accusations of American vulgarity, stupidity, dishonesty, and cruelty, he made his protagonists show a patriotism so confused with snobbishness as to be beyond sympathy or respect. The American public punished him by neglecting his works, and newspapers attacked him violently and libelously. Cooper, however, emerged victorious in a series of libel suits against the offending papers, produced a scholarly *History of the Navy of the United States of America* (1839), and brought out *The Pathfinder* (1840) and *The Deerslayer*) (1841). These novels show a marked gain in portraiture and round out the full character of Leather-Stocking, completing the outline of the most truly epical figure in American fiction. The real triumph of Cooper's craft lies in the variety of inventive devices by which he fills the existence of his heroes with enough actions, desires, fears, victories, defeats, sentiments, and thoughts to make the barren frontier seem a splendid stage.

From 1840 to 1846 other books appeared in rapid succession. *Mercedes of Castile* (1840) went back to Columbus' first voyage; *The Two Admirals* (1842) concerned itself with the British navy before the Revolution; *The Wing-and-Wing* (1842) told of a French privateer; *Ned Myers* (1843) was the biography of an actual sailor who had sailed with Cooper long before; *Lives of Distinguished American Naval Officers* (1846) carried on the naval history theme; *Afloat and Ashore* (two parts, 1844) dealt with the evils of impressment and with life in early New York. *Le Mouchoir* (1843) described fashionable contemporary Manhattan. The *Little-Page Manuscripts* trilogy (*Satanstoe*, 1845; *The Chainbearer*, 1845; *The Redskins*, 1846) attempted a cyclic scheme similar to that of the Leather-Stocking books. *Satanstoe* must still be considered one of America's most distinguished historical novels in its vivid recreation of the life of the New York gentry in the mid-18th century.

After 1846 Cooper grew more bigoted in his opinions and in his anti–New England bias. He carried his animosities into the plots of his latest novels—*The Crater* (1848), *The Oak Openings* (1848), *The Sea Lions* (1849), *The Ways of the Hour* (1850)—and lost all touch with the magical, mythical wilderness which he himself had created.

COOPER, JAMES GRAHAM (*b. New York, N.Y., 1830; d. Hayward, Calif., 1902*), physician, naturalist. Made pioneer contributions to the botany, zoology, and geology of California and Washington.

COOPER, JOHN MONTGOMERY (*b. Rockville, Md., 1881; d. Washington, D.C., 1949*), ethnologist, Roman Catholic clergyman. Educated at St. Charles College, Maryland, and North American College, Rome (Ph.D., St. Thomas Academy, 1902; S.T.D., Propaganda, 1905). Ordained in Rome, he served as curate in Washington, D.C., 1905–18. Stressed the need for attention to social problems and the importance of social action as a necessary extension of Christian love, especially as teacher of religious education at Catholic University of America. His first notable contribution to ethnology, *Analytical and Critical Bibliography of the Indians of Tierra del Fuego* (1917), evidenced the qualities which marked all his work—mastery of scholarly techniques, clarity of expression, and critical judgment. Taught anthropology at Catholic University *post* 1923; he also headed the graduate department of religion, 1930–37. Primarily an ethnologist and ethnographer, he did his fieldwork mostly among the Algonquians. Author of numerous papers on their culture. Theoretical interests led him to grapple with questions of distribution and historical reconstruction (see *Temporal Sequence and Marginal Culture*, 1941). Founder of *Anthropological Quarterly*.

COOPER, JOSEPH ALEXANDER (*b. Whitley Co., Ky., 1823; d. Stafford Co., Kans., 1910*), soldier. An East Tennessee Unionist farmer, he served brilliantly during Civil War; was breveted major general.

COOPER, KENT (*b. Columbus, Ind., 1880; d. West Palm Beach, Fla., 1965*), journalist. Attended Indiana University, then began working as a reporter in Indianapolis. Became a traveling agent for the United Press (UP) in 1907. In 1910 he joined the Associated Press (AP) as traveling inspector. He later became chief of the traffic department (1912), general manager (1925), and executive director (1943). In his forty-one-year career, Cooper transformed AP from the most parochial of American news agencies into a dominant international force. He introduced the first teletype machines in the news industry and developed the idea of sending pictures directly over the wires. He wrote *Barriers Down* (1942), *The Right to Know* (1956), and his autobiography, *Kent Cooper and the Associated Press* (1959).

COOPER, (LEON) JERE (*b. Dyer County, Tenn., 1893; d. Dyersburg, Tenn., 1957*), congressman. Received LL.B. from Cumberland University (1914). After serving in France during World War I, Cooper entered private practice and local politics until he ran for Congress as a Democratic candidate in 1928; he served in the House from 1929 to 1957. In 1932, he was appointed to the Ways and Means Committee; chairman from 1955 to 1957. A supporter of the New and Fair Deal measures, Cooper was for a liberal trade policy and for more equitable tax laws. He supported the subversive activities control bill and the tidelands oil bill (1950). In 1955, he became chairman of the Democratic Committee on Committees.

COOPER, MARK ANTHONY (*b. Hancock Co., Ga., 1800; d. Etowah, Ga., 1885*), businessman, politician. Engaged in cotton-milling, banking, railroading, iron-manufacturing, coal-mining; was Whig, later Calhoun-Democratic congressman, 1839–43.

COOPER, MYLES (*b. Cumberland Co., England, 1737; d. England, 1785*), Episcopal clergyman, Loyalist. Able president of King's College (Columbia), New York City, 1763–75. An ardent propagandist for the royal cause, he returned to England in May 1775.

COOPER, OSWALD BRUCE (*b. Mount Gilead, Ohio, 1879; d. Chicago, Ill., 1940*), letterer and typographic designer.

COOPER, PETER (*b. New York, N.Y., 1791; d. 1883*), manufacturer, inventor, philanthropist. Worked with his father as hatter, brewer, storekeeper, and brick-maker; was apprenticed to a New York coachmaker. He then began a cloth-shearing business of his own, and in 1813 opened a retail grocery store. Next he bought a glue factory and soon won a monopoly for his superior

American-made glue and isinglass. In 1828 he and two partners erected the Canton Iron Works at Baltimore, Md.; here in 1829–30 Cooper built "Tom Thumb," the first steam locomotive built in America. In 1836 he sold the Canton Works for stock of the Baltimore & Ohio Railroad. He then acquired a wire manufactory in Trenton, N.J.; blast furnaces in Phillipsburg, Pa.; a rolling mill in New York; foundries at Ringwood, N.J., and Durham, Pa., and iron mines in New Jersey. In 1854 he rolled the first structural iron for fireproof buildings. Cooper served as president of the New York, Newfoundland & London Telegraph Co. (Atlantic cable), and of the North American Telegraph Co. He invented a washing machine, a machine for mortising hubs, and others for propelling ferryboats, for utilizing the tide for power, and for moving canal barges by an endless chain. Cooper served as New York City alderman, advocated paid police and fire departments, sanitary water conditions, and public schools. He was a presidential candidate on the Greenback ticket in 1876. His greatest monument is the Cooper Union (or Cooper Institute) of New York City, a free educational institution uniquely combining general scientific education with practical training, which he founded, 1857–59.

COOPER, SAMUEL (*b. Boston, Mass., 1725; d. 1783*), clergyman, Revolutionary patriot, pastor of Boston's Brattle Square Church, 1743–83.

COOPER, SAMUEL (*b. Hackensack, N.J., 1798; d. Alexandria, Va., 1876*), Confederate soldier. Served many years as staff officer in Washington, D.C. In 1861 went with the South and was appointed adjutant general and inspector general of the Confederate army, in which his long experience in administration was highly valued.

COOPER, SARAH BROWN INGERSOLL (*b. Cazenovia, N.Y., 1836; d. 1896*), philanthropist, founder of kindergartens. Removed to San Francisco, 1869; was president of Woman's Congress and, in 1892, of International Kindergarten Union.

COOPER, SUSAN FENIMORE (*b. Westchester Co., N.Y., 1813; d. 1894*), author, daughter of James Fenimore Cooper. Was her father's amanuensis; wrote *Rural Hours* (1850) and prefaces to Household Edition (1876–84) of Cooper's works.

COOPER, THEODORE (*b. Cooper's Plain, N.Y., 1839; d. 1919*), civil engineer, bridge-builder. Graduated Rensselaer Polytechnic, 1858. Served as navy engineer, 1861–72; introduced wheel-load instead of uniform load analysis for railway bridges.

COOPER, THOMAS (*b. Westminster, England, 1759; d. Columbia, S.C., 1839*), agitator, scientist, educator. Studied at Oxford; took up medicine in London and Manchester. Entered a firm of calico-printers, was a barrister, and dabbled in philosophy and chemistry. Joseph Priestley nominated him for the Royal Society, but Cooper's materialist philosophy, his Unitarian theology, and his revolutionary political thought rendered him unacceptable. He agitated for abolition of the slave trade and repeal of the Corporation and Test Acts, and was attacked by Burke for instituting a correspondence between the Manchester Constitutional Society and the French Jacobins, 1792. Disgusted with the Terror in France and the conservative reaction in England, he went with Priestley to the United States in 1794. He practiced law and medicine in Pennsylvania, and by 1800 emerged as a Jeffersonian pamphleteer, attacking the Sedition Law, under which he himself was imprisoned and fined. As a Pennsylvania county commissioner, 1801–04, and state judge, 1804–11, he became identified with the conservative faction in opposition to the more radical democrats who attacked the judiciary. Removed from office, he turned to science and teaching. He was professor of chemistry at Carlisle (now Dickinson) College, 1811–15, and professor of applied chemistry and mineralogy at the University of

Pennsylvania, 1815–19. He was honored by membership in the American Philosophical Society and by Jefferson's unsuccessful attempts to appoint him at the University of Virginia. In January 1820 he went to South Carolina College; shortly thereafter he was elected its president and taught chemistry, mineralogy, and political economy until 1834. He helped found the state's first medical school and first insane asylum. Embroiled in controversy with the Presbyterian clergy over his biblical criticism and materialist doctrines, he strengthened his position through his defense of the extreme states' rights party, of slavery, and of the southern view on the tariff question. The academic philosopher of states' rights, he favored nullification and, valuing union too little because he loved liberty too well, became one of the first advocates of secession. After his retirement from the college in 1834, he edited the South Carolina statutes, supported the second Bank of the United States against Jackson, and conspired with Nicholas Biddle to bring about the latter's nomination for the presidency in 1840. Cooper's chief influence came through his masterly use of the pen in political controversies. Always a passionate hater of tyranny, he wrote a pioneer American textbook, the *Lectures on the Elements of Political Economy* (1826).

COOPER, THOMAS ABTHORPE (*b. Harrow-on-the-Hill, England, 1776; d. Bristol, Pa., 1849*), actor, theatrical manager. Raised by William Godwin; trained and coached by Thomas Holcroft. Came to America, 1796; by 1800 he was recognized as the unrivaled tragic actor of America and rapidly made a fortune. *Post* 1815, he devoted himself entirely to starring engagements in America and abroad; he last appeared on the New York stage in 1835 after a decade of waning popularity and financial reverses. Thereafter he held several minor government posts. He is best known for his powerful portrayals of Macbeth, Hamlet, and Othello.

COOPER, WILLIAM (*b. Byberry, Pa., 1754; d. Albany, N.Y., 1809*), jurist, landowner. Father of James Fenimore Cooper. Founded and settled Cooperstown, N.Y.

COOPER, WILLIAM JOHN (*b. Sacramento, Calif., 1882; d. Kearney, Nebr., 1935*), educator. U.S. commissioner of education, 1929–33.

COOPER-POUCHER, MATILDA S. (*b. Blauveltville, N.Y., 1839; d. Oswego, N.Y., 1900*), educator. Devoted herself to the successful work of the Oswego State Normal School; served there as critic, teacher, placement director, and preceptor.

COOTE, RICHARD (*b. 1636; d. New York, N.Y., 1701*), Earl of Bellomont, colonial governor. A supporter of William of Orange, he received extensive land grants in Ireland and was member of Parliament, 1688–95. In 1697 he was appointed governor of New York, Massachusetts, and New Hampshire. By restraining the dealing of New York merchants with pirates, he aroused the hostility of merchants; since he seemed to appease the "Leisler democrats," the landed proprietors opposed his efforts to secure a more orderly conduct of colonial affairs.

COPE, ARTHUR CLAY (*b. Dunreith, Ind., 1909; d. Washington, D.C., 1966*), organic chemist. Studied at the University of Indianapolis and the University of Wisconsin; was at Harvard (1932–34) on a National Research Council Fellowship. Taught at Bryn Mawr (1934–41), where he discovered the "Cope rearrangement." Moved to Columbia as associate professor in 1941; during World War II joined the Office of Scientific Research and Development and became technical aide and section chief of Division 9 of the National Defense Research Committee. In 1945 he became chairman of the chemistry department at the Massachusetts Institute of Technology, and in 1965 he was named the first Camille Dreyfus Professor of Chemistry. In 1947 Cope was elected to the National Academy of Sciences. He was on the editorial board of *Organic Syntheses* and was a consultant to the Central Research Department of the Du Pont Company. He served in many capacities with the American Chemical Society.

COPE, CALEB (*b. Greensburg, Pa., 1797; d. Philadelphia, Pa., 1888*), merchant, financier. Active in numerous Philadelphia business and charitable enterprises.

COPE, EDWARD DRINKER (*b. Philadelphia, Pa., 1840; d. Philadelphia, 1897*), zoologist, paleontologist. Student of S. F. Baird and Joseph Leidy; authority on extinct vertebrates of the Far West; owner and editor of *American Naturalist*.

COPE, THOMAS PYM (*b. Lancaster, Pa.,1768; d. 1854*), merchant, philanthropist. Established first regular packet line between Philadelphia and Liverpool, 1821; promoted canal and railroad construction; served in state legislature.

COPE, WALTER (*b. Philadelphia, Pa., 1860; d. 1902*), architect. Designed notable buildings chiefly in adaptation of English Collegiate Gothic for Bryn Mawr, University of Pennsylvania, Princeton, and Washington University at St. Louis.

COPELAND, CHARLES TOWNSEND (*b. Calais, Maine., 1860; d. Waverly, Mass., 1952*), college professor. Graduated Harvard, 1882. Joined the Harvard English department in 1893 after working as a literary reviewer in Boston. One of Harvard's most famous teachers; his students included Maxwell E. Perkins, Conrad Aiken, T. S. Eliot, Walter Lippmann, Robert Benchley, John Dos Passos, Brooks Atkinson, Robert Sherwood, and Helen Keller. Copeland, always known as "Copey" to his students, received little recognition from Harvard; but his reputation as one of the great teachers of our time lives through his students.

COPELAND, CHARLES W. (*b. Coventry, Conn., 1815; d. 1895*), naval engineer. Designed machinery of the *Fulton*, the first steam war vessel built (1836) under navy supervision; also designed record-breaking transatlantic merchant steamers.

COPELAND, ROYAL SAMUEL (*b. near Dexter, Mich., 1868; d. Washington, D.C., 1938*), physician, teacher, and medical writer. M.D., University of Michigan, 1889. Removed to New York, 1908. New York City public health commissioner, 1918–22; U.S. senator from New York, Democrat, 1922–38.

COPLEY, IRA CLIFTON (*b. Copley Township, Knox County, Ill., 1864; d. Aurora, Ill., 1947*), public utility executive, newspaper publisher, congressman. B.A., Yale, 1887; LL.B., Union College of Law, Chicago, 1889. Built failing family gas company into a utilities empire, consolidated in 1921 as the Western United Corporation. Conducted parallel careers in publishing and politics. Served six consecutive terms in the U.S. House of Representatives (1911–23); a liberal Republican, he was author of a child labor bill. Purchased first newspaper, *Aurora Beacon*, in 1905, later acquiring papers in Elgin and Joliet, Ill. In 1926 disposed of his interest in the Western United Corporation. Weary of retirement, in 1928 he bought up 24 Southern California newspapers and operated them as the Copley Press, Inc. Kept financial control but gave his publishers and editors considerable autonomy, discouraged "mass thinking," and insisted on the impartial handling of local news.

COPLEY, JOHN SINGLETON (*b. Boston, Mass., 1738[?]; d. London, England, 1815*), painter. Grew up in the Boston home of his stepfather, Peter Pelham, a teacher, portraitist, and engraver. Copley later lamented the limited opportunities for artistic training in Boston, but benefited greatly from his association with craftsmen at his stepfather's home and workshop. He started as a professional portrait painter before he was of age; he worked in oil,

but also was a pioneer American pastelist. The exhibition in England of Copley's *The Boy with the Squirrel* in 1766 led to his election as a fellow of the Society of Artists of Great Britain. Benjamin West urged Copley to come to England for study, but Copley was kept in Boston by his success; the foremost personages of New England came to his painting-room as sitters. Married in 1769 to Susannah Clarke, he established himself in a house on Beacon Hill. He took little or no part in town and church affairs. In 1771 he went to New York for several months of portrait painting and also visited Philadelphia.

With the rise of the revolutionary spirit in Boston, Copley's family connections being Loyalist and his English friends urging him to come to London, he left Boston in June 1774. He traveled and made studies in France, Italy, Germany, and the Low Countries, returning to London; there he was reunited with his family which had left Boston in May 1775, to escape the Revolution. Copley's technique was so well established, his habits of industry so well confirmed, and the reputation that had preceded him from America so extraordinary that he could hardly fail to make a place for himself among British artists. Yet the pictures of his maturity did not always reach the standard of the best works of his youth. He began now to paint historical pieces, best known among which are *A Youth Rescued from a Shark* and *The Death of Lord Chatham*. These and many others were characterized by Copley's painstaking efforts to obtain good personal likenesses and correct historical accessories. He continued to paint portraits, among them those of several members of the royal family and numerous British and American celebrities. Between 1776 and 1815 he sent 43 paintings to exhibitions of the Royal Academy, of which he was elected an associate member in 1776 and a full member in 1783. Copley's industry injured his health and he became nervous from overwork. Personally liberal and sympathetic to the American cause, he was prevented by his professional labor from ever returning to the United States. During the last years of his life, Copley was beset by financial difficulties and was assisted by his son, who is celebrated in English history as Lord Lyndhurst.

COPLEY, LIONEL (*b. 1693*). Colonial governor of Maryland, commissioned 1691. Died in office.

COPLEY, THOMAS (*b. Madrid, Spain, 1595; d. ca. 1652*), Jesuit missionary. Active in settlement of Maryland, 1637–45, where he was for a time superior of the mission. Arrested and carried to England, he returned to Maryland after two years' imprisonment and died there.

COPPÉE, HENRY (*b. Savannah, Ga., 1821; d. Bethlehem, Pa., 1895*), soldier, educator. Graduated West Point, 1845; taught literature and history at West Point and University of Pennsylvania. President of Lehigh University, 1866–75, 1893–95.

COPPENS, CHARLES (*b. Turnhout, Belgium, 1835; d. Chicago, Ill., 1920*), Roman Catholic priest, educator. Entered Society of Jesus at St. Louis, Mo., 1853; ordained, 1865. Taught at Jesuit colleges in Midwest and was author of widely used textbooks and devotional works.

COPPET, EDWARD J. DE. *See* DE COPPET, EDWARD J.

COPWAY, GEORGE (*b. Ontario, Canada, 1818; d. near Pontiac, Mich.[?], ca. 1863*), Chippewa chief, Methodist missionary. Author of *Life, History and Travels of Kah-Ge-Ga-Gah-Bowh* (1847, an autobiography) and other works.

COQUILLETT, DANIEL WILLIAM (*b. Pleasant Valley, Ill., 1856; d. 1911*), entomologist. Helped acclimatize Australian ladybird beetle, which saved California citrus culture; experimented with use of hydrocyanic acid gas against scale insects.

Coram

CORAM, THOMAS (*b. Lyme Regis, England, 1668; d. 1751*), merchant, shipbuilder, colony promoter. Strengthened Anglican church in Massachusetts, where he lived at Taunton, 1697–1703; promoted settlement schemes between Kennebec and St. Lawrence and in Nova Scotia.

CORBETT, HARVEY WILEY (*b. San Francisco, Calif., 1873; d. 1954*), architect. Studied at the University of California and at the École des Beaux Arts in Paris (1900). He was a consultant for the design of Rockefeller Center and Chairman of the Architectural Commission for the Century of Progress Exposition in Chicago. He designed the Metropolitan Life Insurance Company (1932) on Madison Square and the Criminal Courts Building (1934), both in New York. Taught architecture at Columbia (1907–11; 1920–35).

CORBETT, HENRY WINSLOW (*b. Westboro, Mass., 1827; d. 1903*), merchant, banker, railroad promoter, politician. Settled in Oregon, 1851, and became leading businessman of Portland. U.S. senator, Republican, from Oregon, 1867–73.

CORBETT, JAMES JOHN (*b. San Francisco, Calif., 1866; d. Bayside, N.Y., 1933*), pugilist called "Gentleman Jim." Defeated John L. Sullivan for world's heavyweight title, 1892; lost championship to Robert Fitzsimmons, 1897.

CORBIN, AUSTIN (*b. Newport, N.H., 1827; d. near Newport, 1896*), capitalist, railroad executive. Began banking career in Iowa; removed to New York, 1865, where he reorganized Long Island Railroad and the Philadelphia & Reading.

CORBIN, DANIEL CHASE (*b. Newport, N.H., 1832; d. 1918*), financier. Brother and associate of Austin Corbin. Built railroads in Pacific Northwest and developed Spokane, Wash., as transportation and distributing center.

CORBIN, HENRY CLARK (*b. near Batavia, Ohio., 1842; d. New York, N.Y., 1909*), soldier. Adjutant general of the army during Spanish-American War.

CORBIN, MARGARET (*b. Franklin Co., Pa., 1751; d. Westchester Co., N.Y., 1800*), Revolutionary heroine.

CORBY, WILLIAM (*b. Detroit, Mich., 1833; d. 1897*), Roman Catholic clergyman. Chaplain of New York's Irish Brigade, 1861–6; earned title of "second founder" of Notre Dame University as president, 1866–72, 1877–81. Served as U.S. provincial and assistant general of his order, the Congregation of the Holy Cross.

CORCORAN, JAMES ANDREW (*b. Charleston, S.C., 1820; d. Philadelphia, Pa., 1889*), Roman Catholic clergyman, theologian, editor. Secretary of Baltimore councils of 1855, 1858, 1866, and theologian for preparatory commission for Vatican Council; drew up "Spalding formula" on papal infallibility.

CORCORAN, WILLIAM WILSON (*b. Georgetown, D.C., 1798; d. 1888*), banker, philanthropist. Began his career as drygoods merchant, entered banking, and in 1840 opened the successful banking firm of Corcoran & Riggs. The Corcoran Gallery of Art, begun in 1859, was inaugurated in Washington, D.C., 1872; Corcoran's personal collection was its nucleus, and he endowed it. His other philanthropic activities include the founding of the Louise Home for needy "gentlewomen," and donations to universities, churches, and religious institutions.

CORDON, GUY (*b. Cuero, Tex., 1890; d. Washington, D.C., 1969*), U.S. senator. During his youth, moved to Roseburg, Oreg., where he taught himself law and was admitted to the Oregon bar in 1920. A Republican, he was elected county assessor (1916) and district attorney (1923–35). He was appointed to fill the Senate seat of Charles L. McNary in 1944, and he was elected to the seat in 1944 and 1948. He was a member of the Appropriations Committee and the Committee for Interior and Insular Affairs. Cordon was a fiscal and social conservative, and he was President Eisenhower's senior adviser on resource issues during the Eighty-third Congress. Defeated in his bid for reelection in 1954, Cordon practiced law in Washington, D.C., until 1967.

COREY, LEWIS (*b. Galdo, Italy, 1892; d. New York, N.Y., 1953*), economist. Immigrated to New York City in 1895. A self-educated man, Corey wrote under the name Louis C. Fraina until 1926. A Marxist, Corey was the editor and secretary for the Communist Party of America (1919). In 1920, he was a delegate to the Second Congress of the Communist International in Moscow. In 1922, he was forced to leave Russia. Returning to the United States in 1923, he became an economist, eschewing politics. His book *The Decline of American Capitalism* (1934) became a best seller. He worked for six months as an economist for the Works Progress Administration in Washington. 1942–51, he taught economics at Antioch College.

COREY, WILLIAM ELLIS (*b. Braddock, Pa., 1866; d. 1934*), steel manufacturer. Developed a process for toughening armor plate to resist projectiles; president, U.S. Steel, 1903–11.

CORI, GERTY TERESA RADNITZ (*b. Prague, Czechoslovakia, 1896; d. St. Louis, Mo., 1957*), biochemist. Studied at the German University of Prague (M.D., 1920). Immigrated to the U.S. with her husband, Carl F. Cori, in the 1920's. From 1931 Gerty Cori worked in research with her husband at Washington University School of Medicine; she became a full professor in 1947, remaining in this position until her death. In 1938 the couple demonstrated the enzymatic conversion of glucose 1-phosphate to glucose 6-phosphate. The enzyme (phosphorylase) that forms the 1-ester from glycogen was discovered and crystallized in 1942. For these studies, the Coris were awarded half the Nobel Prize in 1947. The disorder of glycogenesis due to a lack of debranching enzyme is frequently called Cori's disease.

CORIAT, ISADOR HENRY (*b. Philadelphia, Pa., 1875; d. Boston, Mass., 1943*), neurologist, psychoanalyst. M.D., Tufts Medical College, 1900. Influenced by Adolf Meyer and, during practice *post* 1905 in Boston, Mass., by Morton Prince and James J. Putnam. By 1913 was convinced of the validity of psychoanalytic theory and helped establish it on a professional basis in Boston. Strong advocate of the healing values of religion. His most original and influential book was *Stammering: A Psychoanalytic Interpretation* (1928).

CORLISS, GEORGE HENRY (*b. Easton, N.Y., 1817; d. 1888*), inventor, manufacturer. His invention of separate rotary valves for steam and exhaust ports and a governor which by a system of levers controlled the valves and the admission of steam to the engine cylinder was made 1846–51. It revolutionized the construction and operation of steam engines. He became president of Corliss Engine Co. in Providence, R.I., 1856. Patents for a gear-cutting machine, an improved boiler, and a pumping engine were also granted him. He is ranked equally with Watt in the development of the steam engine.

CORNBURY, EDWARD HYDE (*b. England, 1661; d. 1723*), viscount, colonial governor of New York and New Jersey, 1702–08. His administration suffered from his arrogance, vanity, and financial dishonesty.

CORNELL, ALONZO B. (*b. Ithaca, N.Y., 1832; d. Ithaca, 1904*), politician. Son of Ezra Cornell. Official of Western Union Co.; as Republican governor of New York, 1879–83, modernized state government.

CORNELL, EZEKIEL (*b. Scituate, R.I., 1733; d. Milford, Mass., 1800*), Revolutionary soldier. Commanded Rhode Island State Brigade; distinguished himself at battle of Rhode Island, Aug. 29, 1778.

CORNELL, EZRA (*b. Westchester Co., N.Y., 1807; d. Ithaca, N.Y., 1874*), capitalist. Began life as a carpenter and millwright. After devising a satisfactory means for insulating telegraph wires on poles, he aided S. F. B. Morse in erecting the Baltimore-Washington line. Thereafter he financed and built other lines and soon became the chief figure in the new industry. In 1855 he joined in the founding of the Western Union Telegraph Co., of which he became a director and was for years the largest stockholder. In association with Andrew D. White he brought about the establishment of Cornell University.

CORNING, ERASTUS (*b. Norwich, Conn., 1794; d. 1872*), businessman, capitalist. Removed to Albany, N.Y., 1814, and began career as iron manufacturer; associated *post* 1837 with John F. Winslow, he built the business into one of the most extensive in the country. As president of the Utica & Schenectady Railroad, 1833–53, Corning was a prime mover in the consolidation of New York lines and was elected first president of the New York Central, a post he held until 1864. He served also as mayor of Albany, state senator, Democratic congressman, and as a regent and vice-chancellor of the University of New York.

CORNOYER, PAUL (*b. St. Louis, Mo., 1864; d. East Gloucester, Mass., 1923*), painter, teacher of art.

CORNSTALK (*b. ca. 1720; d. 1777*), Shawnee Indian chief. Fought English settlers on Ohio-Virginia frontier during French and Indian War, Pontiac's War, Lord Dunmore's War; was loyal to the Americans after the Treaty of Camp Charlotte. His murder at the fort at the mouth of the Kanawha brought down the enmity of the Shawnee on the whites for nearly a score of years.

CORNWALLIS, KINAHAN (*b. London, England, 1839; d. New York, N.Y., 1917*), lawyer, editor, writer.

CORONADO, FRANCISCO VÁZQUEZ (*b. Salamanca, Spain, 1510; d. Mexico, 1554*), explorer. Came to Mexico, 1535. As governor of Nueva Galicia, 1538, he aided Fray Marcos de Nizza, and was named commander of an expedition to check on the friar's alleged explorations. Departing in February 1540, in July he reached and conquered the Zuni pueblos. Members of the expedition explored much unknown territory: the mouth of the Gila River, part of the California peninsula, the Moqui pueblos, the Grand Canyon. After wintering near Isleta, in April 1541 Coronado set out for the fabled Gran Quivira in eastern Kansas. He traversed the Llanos del Cíbola, the Texas Panhandle, and Oklahoma. At Quivira he found only an Indian settlement and, disappointed, returned to Mexico. His journey ranks as one of history's epochal explorations. Removed as governor of Nueva Galicia in 1544, Coronado served until death as a *regidor* in Mexico City.

CORRIGAN, MICHAEL AUGUSTINE (*b. Newark, N.J., 1839; d. New York, N.Y., 1902*), Roman Catholic clergyman. Bishop of Newark, 1873–80; coadjutor bishop of New York 1880–85. Succeeded Cardinal McCloskey as archbishop, 1885. A conservative, a strict canonist, and an able administrator.

CORROTHERS, JAMES DAVID (*b. Calvin, Mich., 1869; d. West Chester, Pa., 1917*), clergyman, poet. Author of verse and prose sketches of black life.

CORSE, JOHN MURRAY (*b. Pittsburgh, Pa., 1835; d. Winchester, Mass., 1893*), Union soldier. Raised in Iowa. Won fame through his gallant defense of Allatoona Pass, October, 1864; was postmaster of Boston's "model post office."

CORSON, HIRAM (*b. Philadelphia, Pa., 1828; d. Ithaca, N.Y., 1911*), educator. Taught literature at Cornell, 1870–1903. Author of *Aims of Literary Study (1895) and other works.*

CORSON, JULIET (*b. Roxbury, Mass., 1842; d. New York, N.Y., 1897*), pioneer teacher of cooking.

CORSON, ROBERT RODGERS (*b. New Hope, Pa., 1831; d. Philadelphia, Pa., 1904*), coal merchant, humanitarian. Active in Civil War relief work and in many reform causes.

CORT, EDWIN CHARLES (*b. Rochelle, Ill., 1879; d. Alexandria, Va., 1950*), medical missionary. B.A., Washington and Jefferson College, 1901; M.A., 1904. M.D., Johns Hopkins, 1907. Appointed to Thailand mission of the Board of Foreign Missions of the Presbyterian church, 1908; in charge of McCormick Hospital, Chiengmai, 1914–49. During most of the years of the Japanese occupation in World War II he worked in India. The outstanding foreign medical expert in Thailand, Dr. Cort concerned himself with medical education and nurse training and made many contributions to tropical medicine.

CORTAMBERT, LOUIS RICHARD (*b. Paris, France, 1808; d. New York, N.Y., 1881*), author, journalist, disciple of Thoreau.

CORTELYOU, GEORGE BRUCE (*b. New York, N.Y., 1862; d. Huntington, N.Y., 1940*), public utility executive, cabinet member. Became stenographer to President Cleveland in 1895, then secretary to Presidents McKinley and Theodore Roosevelt. In 1903 Roosevelt appointed him secretary of the newly created Department of Commerce and Labor. Impressing the president with his administrative ability and political sagacity, Cortelyou managed Roosevelt's 1904 campaign and subsequently was appointed postmaster general, effecting a major reorganization of his department. In 1907 he became secretary of the treasury, acting effectively to meet the financial panic of that year and framing legislation for a central banking system. From 1909 to 1935 Cortelyou was president of what became the Consolidated Edison Co., New York City, greatly expanding the company's business.

CORTHELL, ELMER LAWRENCE (*b. South Abington, Mass., 1840; d. 1916*), civil engineer. Specialist in railroad, bridge, and harbor work.

CORTISSOZ, ROYAL (*b. Brooklyn, N.Y., 1869; d. New York, N.Y., 1948*), art critic. After working in office of McKim, Mead, and White, he became art critic on the *New York Tribune*, 1891, a post which he held until 1944. Devoting most of his long career to educating the public in the virtues of the Renaissance masters and their tradition, he opposed all modernist tendencies. He was author, among other works, of *Augustus Saint-Gaudens (1907), John La Farge (1911), Art and Common Sense (1913), American Artists (1923), and Arthur B. Davies (1932).*

CORWIN, EDWARD SAMUEL (*b. near Plymouth, Mich., 1878; d. Princeton, N.J., 1963*), historian and political scientist. Studied at University of Michigan (Ph.B., 1900) and University of Pennsylvania (Ph.D., 1905). Appointed a preceptor at Princeton by Woodrow Wilson (1905), he was promoted to professor (1911), McCormick Professor of Jurisprudence (1918), and chairman of the new Department of Politics (1924). He was a prominent authority on constitutional law. His books include *National Supremacy: Treaty Power vs. State Power (1913), The Doctrine of Judicial review (1914), French Policy and the American Alliance (1916), The President's Control of Foreign Relations (1917), John Marshall and the Constitution (1919), The Constitution and*

What It Means Today (1920), *The President: Office and Powers,* and *Twilight of the Supreme Court* (1934). He was an adviser to the Public Works Administration (1935) and special assistant and consultant to the attorney general on constitutional issues (1936–37).

CORWIN, EDWARD TANJORE (*b.* New York, N.Y., 1834; *d. 1914*), clergyman, historian. Published many works on Dutch Reformed church in America; edited *Ecclesiastical Records of the State of New York* (1901–16).

CORWIN, THOMAS (*b.* Bourbon Co., Ky., 1794; *d.* Washington, D.C., 1865), lawyer. Raised in Ohio, which state he represented as congressman, Whig, 1831–40, and U.S. senator, 1845–50; he was also secretary of the treasury under Fillmore, and minister to Mexico, 1861–64. He reached the high point of his career as U.S. senator when he denounced the Mexican War as unjust and predicted that a civil war would be one of its effects.

CORY, CHARLES BARNEY (*b.* Boston, Mass., 1857; *d.* 1921), ornithologist. Curator, Chicago's Field Museum; published *Birds of the Americas* (1918–19), a synopsis and synonymy.

COSBY, WILLIAM (*b.* ca. 1690; *d.* 1735/6). Unenlightened royal governor of New York and New Jersey, 1731–1735/6.

COSTAIN, THOMAS BERTRAM (*b.* Brantford, Ontario, Canada, 1885; *d.* New York, N.Y., 1965), editor and novelist. Worked as a journalist and editor in Canada, then went to the United States as an editor of the *Saturday Evening Post* (1920–34). He is best known for his historical novels, which were based on extensive research: *For My Great Folly* (1942), *The Black Rose* (1945), *The Conquerors* (1949), and *The Silver Chalice* (1952).

COSTANSÓ, MIGUEL (*fl.* 1769–1811), Spanish explorer, army engineer. His accounts of an expedition to settle Alta California, 1769, are major contributions to California history.

COSTELLO, LOU (*b.* Paterson, N.J., 1906; *d.* Los Angeles, Calif., 1959), comedian. A vaudeville comedian and movie stunt man, Costello formed the team of Abbott and Costello, with Bud Abbott, in the early 1930's; the two remained together until 1957, appearing in vaudeville, on radio (their own show opened in 1940), television (1952–53), and in thirty-six films. The film *Buck Private* (1941) grossed over $10 million.

COSTER, F. DONALD. *See* MUSICA, PHILIP MARIANO FAUSTO.

COSTIGAN, EDWARD PRENTISS (*b.* near Beulahville, Va., 1874; *d.* Denver, Colo., 1939), lawyer. Brother of George P. Costigan. A Republican turned Progressive, he was a tariff commissioner, 1916–28; then served in U.S. Senate from Colorado as a Democrat, 1930–36.

COSTIGAN, GEORGE PURCELL (*b.* Chicago, Ill., 1870; *d. 1934*), professor of law. Taught at Northwestern University, 1909–22; University of California, 1922–34. Insisted in his teaching on the recognition of human values and social responsibilities by lawyers; was author of a number of casebooks and critical articles on legal problems.

COTTON, JOHN (*b.* Derby, England, 1584; *d.* Boston, Mass., 1652), Puritan clergyman, author. Studied at Trinity College, Cambridge; won fellowship to Emmanuel College, where he became head lecturer and dean; was ordained, 1610, and chosen, 1612, vicar of St. Botolph's Church at Boston, Lincolnshire. By about 1615 he began abandoning practices of the Church of England for the Puritan form of worship. His nonconformism was tolerated by his bishop, although Cotton did not entirely escape

opposition. In 1632, however, summoned to appear before the Court of High Commission, he fled to London; in May 1633, resigned his charge. Having been a friend of John Winthrop, he went to America and landed at Boston in September 1633. He became teacher of the Boston church and quickly rose to a dominant position in the religious and political affairs of the colony. In the antinomian controversy he at first took the side of Anne Hutchinson, but finding himself alone among the colony's leaders, he went over to the side of the persecutors. However honest his opinions may have been, from 1638 on he became narrower and more bitter in his views. In two controversies with Roger Williams he rejected Williams' view that a definite renunciation of the Church of England should be the prerequisite for membership in the church in New England, and insisted in opposition to Williams that the authority of magistrates should extend over religious as well as secular affairs. A tireless worker, he spent up to six hours a day praying and preaching and wrote voluminously. His catechism *Spiritual Milk for Babes* (1646) was a standard textbook for New England children. He wrote many controversial pamphlets, works on prayer, church music, and the theory and methods of Congregationalism as practiced in New England. To the latter belong *The Keyes of the Kingdom of Heaven* (1644), *The Way of the Churches of Christ in New England* (1645), and *The Way of the Congregational Churches Cleared* (1648). Undoubtedly one of the ablest and most influential men of his day in Massachusetts, through a perhaps unconscious desire to retain his prestige and influence he gradually became more and more reactionary. A nonconformist himself in England, he came in later life, like most of the Massachusetts leaders, to uphold staunchly the power of the civil magistrate over the conscience of citizens and was willing to grant the civil authorities power of life and death to bring about conformity. Like Winthrop, he had no faith in the common man and advocated a strong government by the few.

COTTON, JOSEPH POTTER (*b.* Newport, R.I., 1875; *d.* Baltimore, Md., 1931), lawyer. Assistant secretary of state, 1929–31.

COTTRELL, CALVERT BYRON (*b.* Westerly, R.I., 1821; *d.* Westerly, 1893), inventor, manufacturer. Greatly improved the printing press; invented a rotary color press, and a shifting tympan for a web perfecting press.

COTTRELL, FREDERICK GARDNER (*b.* Oakland, Calif., 1877; *d.* Berkeley, Calif., 1948), physical chemist, inventor, philanthropist. B.S., University of California, 1896; Ph.D., Leipzig, 1902. Instructor to assistant professor of physical chemistry at University of California, 1902–11. Organized and administered San Francisco office of the U.S. Bureau of Mines; chief metallurgist of the bureau in Washington, D.C., 1916–20. Chairman of the chemistry division of the National Research Council (1921–22); director U.S. Department of Agriculture's fixed-nitrogen research laboratory (1922–30). Patented in 1907 his electrical precipitation method for disposition and retrieval of noxious but valuable particles in dust and industrial smoke, later adapting the process to dehydrate petroleum. Set up the nonprofit Research Corporation in 1912, turning over to it all his patents and stipulating that the profits from their commercial application be used to support further research that would benefit the human race—thus aiding the development of the cyclotron, the electrostatic generator, the production of cortisone, and the synthesis of Vitamin B_1.

COUCH, DARIUS NASH (*b.* Southeast, N.Y., 1822; *d.* Norwalk, Conn., 1897), Union general. Graduated West Point, 1846. An able division commander, 1861–65, although handicapped by disease contracted during the Mexican War.

COUCH, HARVEY CROWLEY (*b. Calhoun, Ark., 1877; d. near Hot Springs, Ark., 1941*), public utilities promoter. Built up a network of local telephone exchanges in Louisiana and Arkansas which he sold to the Bell System in 1911. By acquiring franchises through political influence and raising capital through local banks and private subscriptions, he expanded his Arkansas Light & Power Company *post* 1913 into an extensive integrated electric system, serving Arkansas, northern Louisiana, and western Mississippi. He was generally regarded as a principal factor in the economic growth of Arkansas and the progress of rural electrification. Unlike many other financiers, he was an enthusiastic supporter of the New Deal.

COUDERT, FREDERIC RENÉ (*b. New York, N.Y., 1832; d. 1903*), lawyer. Graduated Columbia, 1850; made his greatest mark in international law; was long interested in politics as an independent Democrat and served on many international commissions.

COUDERT, FREDERIC RENEÉ (*b. New York, N.Y., 1871; d. New York, 1955*), international lawyer, foreign policy adviser. Studied at Columbia. Deeply involved in advancing world organizations and arbitration as a means of settling international affairs. Worked as a special assistant to the U.S. attorney general before the outbreak of World War I to help ease Anglo-American relations. During the war, worked with Robert Lansing and Frank Polk of the State Department as a legal adviser on problems arising from the British naval blockade and from ship seizure and contraband. A strong interventionist, he supported U.S. entry into the war and, later, into the League of Nations.

COUES, ELLIOTT (*b. Portsmouth, N.H., 1842; d. 1899*), physician, ornithologist. Made outstanding contributions to the knowledge of American birds; author of *Key to North American Birds* (1872), *Birds of the Northwest* (1874), and *Birds of the Colorado Valley* (1878). Edited early source materials for the history of the West.

COULDOCK, CHARLES WALTER (*b. London, England, 1815; d. New York, N.Y., 1898*), actor. Came to America in 1849; remained a public favorite until his death.

COULTER, ERNEST KENT (*b. Columbus, Ohio, 1871; d. Santa Barbara, Calif., 1952*), civic reformer, youth worker. Studied at Ohio State University and at the New York Law School (LL.B., 1904). 1894–1902, he worked in journalism. 1902–12, he was clerk for the New York Children's Court. Coulter helped found the Boy Scouts of America and served on its national committee. In 1946, he founded the Big Brothers of America, later the Big Brothers and Big Sisters Federation serving as president until his death.

COULTER, JOHN MERLE (*b. Ningpo, China, 1851; d. 1928*), botanist. Pupil of Asa Gray. Taught at University of Chicago, 1896–1925; founded and edited *Botanical Gazette*. A morphologist, he trained many of America's leading botanists.

COUNCILMAN, WILLIAM THOMAS (*b. Pikesville, Md., 1854; d. York Village, Maine, 1933*), pathologist. Associate, and resident pathologist, Johns Hopkins University, 1887–92; professor of pathology, Harvard, 1892–1921.

COUPER, JAMES HAMILTON (*b. 1794; d. Georgia, 1866*), planter. Studied methods of water control in Holland; based the operations of his Georgia coastal plantations on scientific diking and drainage. He substituted sugar cane for long-staple cotton, erected a sugar mill, but in 1838 gave up sugar growing for rice. He introduced olive trees and Bermuda grass, and pioneered in the crushing of cottonseed for oil. By 1834 he operated two cottonseed oil mills. His fame as a scientific farmer, experimenter, geologist, and conchologist attracted many noted visitors from Europe. The Civil War brought ruin to his plantations and broke his health and fortune.

COURTNEY, CHARLES EDWARD (*b. Union Springs, N.Y., 1849; d. 1920*), single sculler, rowing coach at Cornell, 1883–1916.

COUTARD, HENRI (*b. Marolles-les-Braults, Sarthe, France, 1876; d. Le Mans, France, 1950*), radiologist. Graduated in medicine, University of Paris, 1902; began research with radium, 1912; headed X-ray department at Radium Institute, University of Paris, 1919–37. A 1921 report, of which he was coauthor, on cases of advanced carcinoma of the larynx which had been controlled by X radiation marked the beginning of acceptance of roentgen therapy as a primary method of treatment. He was a pioneer in application of the time-dose relationship in radiotherapy, known as fractionation or Coutard's method. Worked and taught in the United States, at Chicago Tumor Institute, 1938–41, and Penrose Cancer Hospital, Colorado Springs, 1941–49. Work took a bizarre turn *post* 1941 and eventually he was asked to resign. Returned to France and subsequent work raised doubts about his sanity.

COUZENS, JAMES (*b. Chatham, Canada, 1872; d. Detroit, Mich., 1936*), automobile manufacturer. Removed to Detroit, 1890. In 1903 put up $2,500 of the original capital in the Ford Motor Co.; in 1919 sold out for more than $29 million. Meanwhile, he had served as Ford's business manager and virtual partner. Leaving Ford in 1915, "nauseated" just with "making money," Couzens became police commissioner and then mayor, 1918–22, of Detroit, effecting an unprecedented public improvements program. Appointed to the U.S. Senate from Michigan in 1922 and reelected in 1924 and 1930, Couzens, a Republican, was an unorthodox and controversial political figure. He opposed the Harding and Coolidge tax programs, criticized Hoover's ineffectual depression policies, and became a warm supporter of President Roosevelt's New Deal.

COVICI, PASCAL ("PAT") (*b. Botosani, Rumania, 1885; d. New York, N.Y., 1964*), book publisher and editor. Immigrated to Chicago in 1898. Studied literature at the universities of Michigan and Chicago. Through several firms (Covici-McGee; Pascal Covici, Inc.; and Covici-Friede), he published the likes of Ben Hecht, Wyndham Lewis, Clifford Odets, Gene Fowler, Nathanael West, and John Steinbeck. He became a senior editor at Viking Press in 1938, where he was editor for Steinbeck, Saul Bellow, and Arthur Miller.

COVODE, JOHN (*b. Westmoreland Co., Pa., 1808; d. Harrisburg, Pa., 1871*), manufacturer. Called "Honest John"; served in the Pennsylvania legislature and as congressman, Whig (later Republican), 1854–63, 1867–71. Was chairman of Covode Investigation Committee, 1860; introduced House impeachment resolution against President Johnson.

COWAN, EDGAR (*b. Greensburg, Pa., 1815; d. 1885*), lawyer. U.S. senator, Republican, from Pennsylvania, 1861–67; opposed many Civil War measures; supported Johnson during impeachment proceedings.

COWELL, SIDNEY FRANCES. *See* BATEMAN, SIDNEY FRANCES COWELL.

COWEN, JOHN KISSIG (*b. Holmes Co., Ohio, 1844; d. 1904*), corporation lawyer. *Post* 1876, was general counsel for Baltimore & Ohio Railroad and later its receiver and president.

COWEN, JOSHUA LIONEL (*b. New York, N.Y., 1880; d. Palm Beach, Fla., 1965*), inventor and manufacturer. Studied at the City College of New York and Columbia. His early projects included fuses and batteries. In 1901 he built his first electrified toy train. "Lionel Lines" trains quickly became as much a symbol of Christmas as Santa Claus. The Lionel Corp. claimed in 1960 to have laid more miles of track than any single real railroad.

COWL, JANE (*b. Boston, Mass., 1883; d. Santa Monica, Calif., 1950*), actress, playwright, director. Born Grace Bailey, she was raised in Brooklyn, N.Y.; attended Erasmus Hall High School; married Adolph E. Klauber, 1906. A theater personality in the great romantic tradition, she made her Broadway debut doing a walk-on in *Sweet Kitty Bellairs*, 1903. Continuing to play bit parts in David Belasco's productions, she played her first major role in *Is Matrimony a Failure?*, 1909. Leaving Belasco's management, 1910, she reached stardom in *Within the Law* (1912–13) and *Common Clay* (1915). In collaboration with Jane Murfin, she wrote *Lilac Time* (1917), in which she starred with great success in New York and on tour, and perhaps her greatest success, *Smilin' Through* (1919). Subsequent triumphs were *Romeo and Juliet* (1922); *Easy Virtue* (1925–26); *The Road to Rome* (1927); *First Lady* (1935); and *Old Acquaintance* (1940–41).

COWLES, EDWIN (*b. Austinburg, Ohio, 1825; d. 1890*), journalist. Owner and editor of the *Cleveland Leader* and a founder of the Republican party; later aided sons in development of new methods of electric smelting.

COWLES, GARDNER (*b. Oskaloosa, Iowa, 1861; d. Des Moines, Iowa, 1946*), newspaper publisher. B.A., Iowa Wesleyan College, 1882; M.A., 1885. At first a superintendent of schools in Algona, Iowa, he engaged successfully in a variety of local business activities, in particular banking, before taking up journalism, 1903. In that year, he bought a majority interest in the *Des Moines Register and Leader* which he turned into a profitable paper, subsequently absorbing the *Des Moines Tribune* (1908), the *Daily News* (1924), and the *Capital* (1927). By 1930, the Cowles publications had enveloped the Iowa daily newspaper market and were unusual in that they counted more on revenue from circulation than from advertising. Cowles allowed his staffs much initiative, insisting only on honesty, accuracy, and fair play; he also believed in providing ample space for readers' opinions. The Cowles company pioneered in opinion polling (1925) and in extending maximum benefits to employees; it later entered radio broadcasting, started a syndicate, acquired newspapers in Minneapolis, and published *Look* magazine.

COWLES, HENRY CHANDLER (*b. Kensington, Conn., 1869; d. Chicago, Ill., 1939*), botanist, geographer, pioneer ecologist. Graduated Oberlin College, 1893; Ph.D., University of Chicago, 1898. Taught at Chicago until 1934; was one of a group of geologists and botanists investigating the new field of ecology. Two classic papers by Cowles, one on the Lake Michigan sand dunes (1899), the other on the physiographic ecology of the Chicago area (1901), did much to advance the change in emphasis from the purely descriptive, static study of vegetation to the study of the processes involved in its development and stabilization. Coauthor of the important *Textbook of Botany for Colleges and Universities* (1910–11).

COWLEY, CHARLES (*b. Eastington, England, 1832; d. Lowell, Mass., 1908*), lawyer. Came to America as a child. Championed labor legislation in Massachusetts. Author of many books on local history.

COX, EDWARD EUGENE (*b. Mitchell County, Ga., 1880; d. Bethesda, Md., 1952*), lawyer, judge, congressman. Law degree, Mercer University, 1902; judge of the Georgia Supreme Court (1912–16). Congressman (1924–52). A conservative Democrat, Cox was opposed to the New Deal and Fair Deal legislation of Roosevelt and Truman. He successfully killed most progressive legislation as a member of the powerful Rules Committee. Anticivil rights and anti–Communist, he supported Dixiecrat candidate J. Strom Thurmond for the presidency in 1948.

COX, GEORGE BARNSDALE (*b. Cincinnati, Ohio, 1853; d. 1916*), Ohio politician. Helped build Republican machine in Ohio and dominated it from 1888 to 1910; thereafter devoted himself to business.

COX, HANNAH PEIRCE (*b. Chester Co., Pa., 1797; d. Chester Co., 1876*), Quaker antislavery worker.

COX, HENRY HAMILTON (*b. Ireland, ca. 1769; d. Ireland, 1821*), farmer, poet, religionist. In Pennsylvania from 1799 to 1817; became a Quaker; author of *Metrical Sketches* (1817).

COX, JACOB DOLSON (*b. Montreal, Canada, 1828; d. Maine, 1900*), lawyer, Union general. Graduated Oberlin, 1851. Began his career as high school principal; known for his antislavery sentiments, he helped organize Ohio Republican party and served in state senate. Rose to major general during Civil War. As Republican governor of Ohio, 1866–68, Cox advocated forcible segregation of blacks and lost favor with his party. As secretary of interior, 1869–70, Cox was staunch defender of civil service reform and resigned in protest over Grant's policies. Cox now was identified with the Liberal Republicans, served briefly in Congress, and was dean of Cincinnati Law School, 1881–97. His books on military history are highly regarded.

COX, JAMES MIDDLETON (*b. Jacksonburg, Ohio, 1870; d. Dayton, Ohio, 1957*), publisher, politician. Owner of a newspaper empire that was centered in Ohio, his Canton, Ohio, *News* won the Pulitzer Prize in 1927. Democratic member of Congress (1908–1912); governor of Ohio (1912–14 and 1916–20). Democratic presidential candidate, with Franklin D. Roosevelt as his running mate, in 1920; defeated by Warren Harding. Member of the American delegation to the London World Monetary and Economic Conference in 1933. By the time of his death, Cox owned a chain of flourishing newspapers and numerous radio and television stations in Ohio, Georgia, and Florida.

COX, KENYON (*b. Warren, Ohio, 1856; d. 1919*), painter, art critic. Son of Jacob D. Cox. Studied at Pennsylvania Academy of Fine Arts and at Duran's and Gérôme's ateliers in Paris. Returning to America, he found no buyer for his classic nudes, but fared better with portraits and was instrumental in ushering in a new era of mural decoration. His murals graced the 1893 Chicago Exposition and others can be seen at the New York Appellate Court, the Library of Congress, the Iowa and Minnesota state capitols, and the Wilkes-Barre, Pa., courthouse. An able teacher, lecturer, and writer, he stood for the authority of tradition in an age of license.

COX, LEMUEL (*b. Boston, Mass., 1736; d. Charlestown, Mass., 1806*), mechanic, bridge-builder. Supervised construction of Boston-Charlestown bridge across Charles River, 1785–86, and other massive works in Massachusetts, Maine, and Ireland.

COX, PALMER (*b. Granby, Canada, 1840; d. Granby, 1924*), author, illustrator. Created the "Brownie" stories for *St. Nicholas Magazine*; over a million copies of his books for children were sold, from *The Brownies, Their Book* (1887) to *The Brownies' Many More Nights* (1913).

COX, ROWLAND (*b. Philadelphia, Pa., 1842; d. Plainfield, N.J., 1900*), patent lawyer. Acquired national reputation as expert in trademark and copyright law; wrote *Manual of Trade Mark Cases* (1881).

COX, SAMUEL HANSON (*b. Rahway, N.J., 1793; d. Bronxville, N.Y., 1880*), Presbyterian clergyman, educator. A New School Presbyterian leader, a founder of New York University, and a director of Union Theological Seminary.

COX, SAMUEL SULLIVAN (*b. Zanesville, Ohio, 1824; d. 1889*), lawyer, politician. Called "Sunset" Cox. Graduated Brown, 1846. After brief practice of law and journalism in Cincinnati and Columbus, entered Congress as a Democrat from Ohio, 1857; thereafter, except for 1864–68, he was a member of the lower house, representing a New York district *post* 1868. A liberal, independent thinker, Cox worked for adjustment of sectional differences and the speedy restoration of peace and union *post* 1861; he aided in settling the *Trent* case and was consistently opposed to centralizing tendencies in government and infringement of personal rights. He favored complete amnesty for Confederates, tariff reform, reform of the civil service and of census procedures; he was also active in securing legislation for development of the West.

COX, WILLIAM RUFFIN (*b. Scotland Neck, N.C., 1832; d. 1919*), Confederate soldier, politician. In legal practice at Raleigh, N.C., after distinguished Civil War service; congressman, Democrat, from North Carolina, 1880–86.

COXE, ARTHUR CLEVELAND (*b. Mendham, N.J., 1818; d. 1896*), Episcopal bishop. Son of Samuel Hanson Cox. Consecrated bishop of western New York, 1865; wrote *Christian Ballads* (1840). Rejected contemporary scientific tendencies in his *Holy Writ and Modern Thought* (1892).

COXE, DANIEL (*b. London, England, 1673; d. Trenton, N.J., 1739*), landowner, politician. Came to America, 1702; was commander of forces in West Jersey and in 1706 was appointed to Governor's Council and made associate judge of West Jersey supreme court. Removed from council 1713, he was elected to assembly in 1714, and 1716 was chosen Speaker. Upon urging of Governor Hunter, Coxe was expelled and fled first to Pennsylvania and then to London, where he published *A Description of the English Province of Carolana* (1722), which sets forth what is believed to be the first printed plan for a confederation of North American colonies. Returning to New Jersey, he was candidate for the assembly in 1725 and supreme court judge, 1734–39.

COXE, ECKLEY BRINTON (*b. Philadelphia, Pa., 1839; d. 1895*), mining engineer. Grandson of Tench Coxe. Developed Wilkes-Barre, Pa., anthracite deposits; greatly improved mining techniques.

COXE, JOHN REDMAN (*b. Trenton, N.J., 1773; d. 1864*), physician. Grandson of John Redman. Studied in London, Edinburgh, Paris, and, under Benjamin Rush, Philadelphia. He practiced in Philadelphia, was physician to the Pennsylvania Hospital, and taught chemistry, materia medica, and pharmacy at the University of Pennsylvania. He was an early advocate of vaccination and an expert pharmacist, and is said to have introduced the Jalap plant into the United States. He edited the *Medical Museum* (1805–11) and the *American Dispensatory* (1808); he published a *Medical Dictionary* (1808) and several books on the history of medicine. His library contained the "best collection of the Fathers of Medicine and of Theology" in America.

COXE, RICHARD SMITH (*b. Burlington, N.J., 1792; d. Washington, D.C., 1865*), lawyer. Son of William Coxe. A specialist in real property law, he was prominent as counsel before the Supreme Court.

COXE, TENCH (*b. Philadelphia, Pa., 1755; d. Philadelphia, 1824*), merchant, political economist. Brother of William Coxe. A neutralist during the Revolution, he was a member of the Annapolis Convention and the Continental Congress of 1788. A Federalist from 1788 to 1797, he served as assistant secretary of the treasury and commissioner of the revenue. Dismissed by Adams, he turned Republican and served as purveyor of public supplies, 1803–12. A nationalist in his economic views, he advocated development of native manufactures, a revenue tariff, unrestricted interstate commerce, confinement of import and coastal trade to American vessels. His promotion of cotton culture in the South earned him the title of father of America's cotton industry.

COXE, WILLIAM (*b. Philadelphia, Pa., 1762; d. near Burlington, N.J., 1831*), pomologist. Grandson of Daniel Coxe; brother of Tench Coxe. Outstanding authority on fruit trees; helped introduce Seckel pear into England; served in New Jersey legislature and as Federalist congressman.

COXETTER, LOUIS MITCHELL (*b. Nova Scotia, Canada, 1818; d. Charleston, S.C., 1873*), mariner. The Confederacy's most celebrated privateersman and most successful blockade-runner.

COXEY, JACOB SECHLER (*b. Selinsgrove, Pa., 1854; d. Massillon, Ohio, 1951*), businessman, monetary reformer. A member of the Greenback party, which advocated a non-metal currency, Coxey, during the depressed 1890's, formed and led a group of unemployed workers to Washington to protest the government's neglect of the jobless. These men, who walked from Ohio to the Capitol in Washington, D.C., became known as "Coxey's army" and were unsuccessful in their reform attempt, but managed to rally support for labor that was to surface in later years.

COYLE, GRACE LONGWELL (*b. North Adams, Mass., 1892; d. Cleveland, Ohio, 1962*), social worker and social work theorist. Inspired by the writings of Jane Addams, she studied at Wellesley (B.A., 1914), New York School of Social Work (1915), and Columbia (M.A., 1928; Ph.D., 1931). She taught at Western Reserve University for all but two years from 1934 until her death. She was a leading social group work educator and evolved an original theoretical approach to group work and social engineering. Her dissertation, *Social Process in Organized Groups*, was published in 1930.

COZZENS, FREDERICK SWARTWOUT (*b. Brooklyn, N.Y., 1818; d. 1869*), humorist, wine merchant. Author of *Prismatics* (1853, under pseudonym "Richard Haywarde"); *The Sparrowgrass Papers* (1856); *Acadia; or a Month with the Bluenoses* (1859); *The Sayings of Dr. Bushwacker* (1867).

CRABTREE, LOTTA (*b. New York, N.Y., 1847; d. 1924*), actress. Began her career in California mining camps, 1855; her free, infectious humor made her outstanding in American burlesque and extravaganza until her retirement, 1891.

CRADDOCK, CHARLES EGBERT. See MURFREE, MARY NOAILLES.

CRAFTS, JAMES MASON (*b. Boston, Mass., 1839; d. 1917*), chemist, teacher, administrator. Graduated from Lawrence Scientific School, 1858; studied also at Freiberg, Heidelberg, and Paris. Bunsen and Wurtz were among his teachers. In 1868 he became professor of chemistry at Cornell; in 1871 at Massachusetts Institute of Technology. From 1874 until 1891 he did research at the École des Mines in Paris, and there with Charles Friedel discovered the "Friedel-Crafts reaction." Returning to Cambridge, he taught at, and served as president of, the Massachusetts Institute of Technology and devoted himself to a study of catalysis and accurate thermometry. He was a chevalier of the Legion of Honor and a recipient of the Rumford Medal.

CRAFTS, WILLIAM (*b. Charleston, S.C., 1787; d. Lebanon Springs, N.Y., 1826*), lawyer, South Carolina legislator. Author of local satires and descriptive poems.

CRAIG, AUSTIN (*b. Peapack, N.J., 1824; d. 1881*), clergyman, educator. A staunch foe of denominationalism, he was one of America's best New Testament Greek scholars, an adviser to Horace Mann at Antioch College, and president of the Christian Biblical Institute (Stanfordville, N.Y.), 1869–81.

CRAIG, DANIEL H. (*b. Rumney, N.H., ca. 1814; d. Asbury Park, N.J., 1895*), journalist. Used carrier pigeons to report advance shipping news for the *Boston Daily Mail* and *New York Herald*; was president of Associated Press, 1861–66.

CRAIG, MALIN (*b. St. Joseph, Mo., 1875; d. Washington, D.C., 1945*), army officer. Raised on military posts in Kansas, Arizona, and New Mexico; graduated West Point, 1898. Served with 6th Cavalry in Spanish-American War, Boxer Rebellion, and Philippine Insurrection. After holding a variety of posts, graduating from line and staff schools, and attendance at the Army War College, he was promoted lieutenant colonel and served with great distinction in World War I as chief of staff to Gen. Hunter Liggett (I Corps), and after the armistice as chief of staff of the Third Army. Returned to the United States, 1919; major general and chief of cavalry, 1924. Named commandant of the Army War College, February 1935; in October, succeeded Gen. Douglas MacArthur as Chief of Staff, U.S. Army. His ambitious program of modernization and innovation provided the army with a capacity for efficient expansion by the time he retired in August 1939.

CRAIG, THOMAS (*b. Pittston, Pa., 1855; d. 1900*), mathematician. Taught at Johns Hopkins University; edited *American Journal of Mathematics* (1894–99); eminent geometer.

CRAIG, WINCHELL McKENDREE (*b. Washington Court House, Ohio, 1892; d. Rochester, Minn., 1960*), neurosurgeon. Studied at Ohio Wesleyan University and at Johns Hopkins (M.D., 1919). Member of the staff of the Mayo Clinic in Rochester, Minn., from 1926; headed neurosurgery from 1946 to 1955. Recalled to active duty in the Navy Reserve during World War II, Craig became chief of surgery at the National Naval Medical Center in Bethesda, Md. (1942–45). He retired from the Reserve with the rank of rear admiral. One of the nation's leading neurosurgeons, Craig advanced the field to that of a respected specialty. President of the Society of Neurological Surgeons, 1946.

CRAIGHEAD, EDWIN BOONE (*b. Ham's Prairie, Mo., 1861; d. 1920*), educator. Was college president in South Carolina, Missouri, Louisiana (Tulane), and Montana; in Montana fought business influence on education.

CRAIGIE, ANDREW (*b. Boston, Mass., 1743; d. Cambridge, Mass., 1819*), apothecary, financier, speculator. Apothecary general, Continental army, 1777–83.

CRAIK, JAMES (*b. Arbigland, Scotland, 1730; d. near Alexandria, Va., 1814*), chief physician and surgeon of the Continental army. Immigrated, 1750; served with Braddock's expedition, 1755; was George Washington's friend and personal physician.

CRAM, RALPH ADAMS (*b. Hampton Falls, N.H., 1863; d. Boston, Mass., 1942*), architect, author. Studied in Boston office of architects Arthur Rotch and George T. Tilden, 1881–86. On return from first trip to Europe, abandoned architecture for journalism; served briefly as art critic for *Boston Evening Tran-*

script. He returned to Europe in 1888 as tutor to a friend's stepson. A Christmas Eve midnight mass at San Luigi dei Francesi in Rome gave him a new vision of the world, which was reinforced by stays in Palermo, Monreale, and Venice. He decided to get back into architecture.

Returning to Boston, Cram won second prize for a deplorable entry in a competition for an addition to the Massachusetts State House. In 1890 he formed a partnership with Charles Francis Wentworth and soon began to specialize in the design of churches. He was baptized and confirmed in the Episcopal church and set his sights on an ideal (and largely imaginary) vision of pre-Reformation England, as a guide not only to architecture but to religious and social life.

Cram stoutly believed that the Gothic had been the perfect expression of Northern and Western Christianity for five centuries. It had not suffered a natural death but had been cut off by the classical Renaissance and the Protestant Reformation. An ally appeared, Bertram Grosvenor Goodhue. Cram took him on as a draftsman in 1890; in 1895 the firm became Cram, Wentworth & Goodhue. Goodhue was an invaluable ally in the designing of All Saints', Ashmont (Boston), in 1892 and in a series of Episcopal parish churches. He died in 1924.

The energies of Cram and Goodhue extended beyond architecture into a vision of a hopeful twentieth century, inspired by a compound of Pre-Raphaelitism, William Morris socialism, Wagner, and a passion for the improvement of arts and crafts. He collaborated in the short-lived (1892) periodical *Knight Errant*. In 1893 Cram completed *Excalibur, An Arthurian Drama* (published 1909) and wrote a very fin de siècle fantasy, *The Decadent: Being the Gospel of Inaction* (1893), with decorations by Goodhue. *Black Spirits & White*, a series of antiquarian ghost stories, appeared in 1895. Cram expounded with eloquence and conviction his Gothic vision, as in the essay "Meeting-houses or Churches" (reprinted in *The Gothic Quest*, 1907). Numerous articles written for the *Churchman* were subsequently collected in his *Church Building* (1901). He published in 1898 *English Country Churches: One Hundred Views*, and in 1905 *The Ruined Abbeys of Great Britain*.

Cram and Goodhue produced a design for new parliament houses in Tokyo, and Cram went to Japan. The project was never realized, but Cram produced *Impressions of Japanese Architecture and the Allied Arts* (1905).

The firm won the competition for the rebuilding of the U.S. Military Academy at West Point in 1903. The building gave great impetus to the spread of collegiate Gothic in the United States. St. Thomas' Church on Fifth Avenue, New York, was the last important project on which they worked together. Their partnership was dissolved in 1913.

Cram was appointed supervising architect of Princeton University in 1909, and in 1910 he was entrusted with the design of the new Rice Institute at Houston, Tex., where he forsook Gothic in favor of a style involving Italian and Byzantine elements. He was consulting architect for Bryn Mawr and Wellesley colleges and designed Georgian buildings for Wheaton, Williams, and Sweet Briar colleges and Phillips Exeter Academy.

The extent and variety of Cram's churches can be seen in *The Work of Cram and Ferguson, Architects* (1929) and *American Church Building of Today* (1929). A singularly congenial task was the chapel of St. George's School, Newport, R.I., (1928). The most challenging and extended work in Cram's career was the Cathedral of St. John the Divine, New York, entrusted to him in 1912.

In 1914 Cram, although continuing his active architectural practice, accepted appointments as professor of architecture at the Massachusetts Institute of Technology and chairman of the Boston City Planning Board, posts that he held until 1921. In a number of volumes of essays he offered Christian and Gothic suggestions about the solution to the world's problems: *The Ministry of Art* (1914); *Heart of Europe* (1915); *The Substance of Gothic and the Nemesis of Mediocrity* (1917); *The Great Thousand Years* (1918); *The Sins of the Fathers: Walled Towns,* and *Gold, Frankincense and Myrrh* (1919); and *Towards the Great Peace* (1922).

He was a founder of the Mediaeval Academy of America (1925), which in 1932 published his *Cathedral of Palma de Mallorca: An Architectural Study.* He also published *Convictions and Controversies* (1935), the autobiographical *My Life in Architecture* (1936), and *The End of Democracy* (1937).

CRAMER, MICHAEL JOHN (*b. near Schaffhausen, Switzerland, 1835; d. Carlisle, Pa., 1898*), Methodist clergyman, educator. Came to America as a child. Brother-in-law of Ulysses S. Grant, who named him U.S. minister to Denmark and Switzerland.

CRAMP, CHARLES HENRY (*b. Philadelphia, Pa., 1828; d. 1913*), shipbuilder. Son of William Cramp. President of William Cramp and Sons Shipbuilding Co., 1879–1903; one of the leading naval architects of his day. He built the record-breaking liners *St. Louis* and *St. Paul,* and the battleships *Maine, New York,* Indiana, and *Massachusetts*; installed the first American triple-expansion engine in the yacht *Peerless* and the first American three-screw propulsion system in the cruiser *Columbia.*

CRAMP, WILLIAM (*b. Philadelphia, Pa., 1807; d. Atlantic City, N.J., 1879*), shipbuilder. Founded William Cramp Shipbuilding Co. at Philadelphia, 1830. Successfully adapted his yard to the change in materials from wood to iron to steel.

CRANCH, CHRISTOPHER PEARSE (*b. Alexandria, D.C. [now Va.], 1813; d. 1892*), painter, critic, poet, Unitarian minister. Son of William Cranch; friend of R. W. Emerson and George W. Curtis.

CRANCH, WILLIAM (*b. Weymouth, Mass., 1769; d. Washington, D.C., 1855*), jurist. Nephew of President John Adams. Chief justice of U.S. circuit court of District of Columbia, 1805–55; reporter of U.S. Supreme Court, 1802–17.

CRANDALL, CHARLES HENRY (*b. Greenwich, N.Y., 1858; d. Stamford, Conn., 1923*), poet. Wrote patriotic verse for magazines.

CRANDALL, PRUDENCE (*b. Hopkinton, R.I., 1803; d. Elk Falls, Kans., 1890*), educator, reformer. Fought a losing battle to establish schools for blacks in Connecticut, 1833–34.

CRANE, ANNE MONCURE (*b. Baltimore, Md., 1838; d. Stuttgart, Germany, 1872*), author. Her novels include *Emily Chester* (1864), *Opportunity* (1867), and *Reginald Archer* (1871) and were condemned as immoral in their day.

CRANE, CHARLES RICHARD (*b. Chicago, Ill., 1858; d. Palm Springs, Calif., 1939*), businessman, philanthropist. Left his family's plumbing supply business in 1914 to devote himself to world travel, the cultivation of international friendships, and public service. A supporter of Woodrow Wilson, Crane was a member of a special diplomatic mission to Russia in 1917, served on the Inter-Allied Commission on Mandates in Turkey, 1919, and was minister to China, 1920–21, where he was active in famine relief. His philanthropies were many and included support for the American colleges in Istanbul and the establishment in 1925 of the Institute of Current World Affairs.

CRANE, FRANK (*b. Urbana, Ill., 1861; d. Nice, France, 1928*), Methodist and Congregational clergyman. Author of syndicated inspirational newspaper essays, 1909–28.

CRANE, FREDERICK EVAN (*b. Brooklyn, N.Y., 1869; d. Garden City, N.Y., 1947*), lawyer, judge. LL.B., Columbia Law School, 1889. Practiced in Brooklyn. Elected a judge of the Kings County court on the Republican ticket, 1901, he became a trial judge of the state supreme court, 1906. Appointed a justice of the state court of appeals, 1917, he was elected to a full term in 1920 with bipartisan endorsement and continued to serve until retirement in 1939. In 1934, he was elected chief judge. He was a moderate in the controversy over revising law to suit emergent social needs. In 1935, he presided over a judicial council for improvement of administration of the courts of New York State and effected some reforms.

CRANE, HAROLD HART (*b. Garretsville, Ohio, 1899; d. 1932*), poet. Incompatible parents subjected him to tensions which marked his whole life. He began principal work, *The Bridge* (1930), in 1923; this poem was to be a mystical synthesis of America, a refutation of the disillusion of Eliot's *Waste Land.* Its structure is characterized by free association of images and symphonic organization of rhythms. Despairing of his work and himself, he drowned himself off the Florida coast.

CRANE, JOHN (*b. Braintree, Mass., 1744; d. 1805*), Revolutionary soldier. Associated with Boston's Sons of Liberty; took part in the Boston Tea Party; brevetted brigadier general, 1783, for outstanding service as an artillery officer.

CRANE, JONATHAN TOWNLEY (*b. Connecticut Farms, N.J., 1819; d. Port Jervis, N.Y., 1880*), Methodist clergyman. Father of Stephen Crane.

CRANE, STEPHEN (*b. Newark, N.J., 1871; d. Badenweiler, Germany, 1900*), writer, novelist. Son of Jonathan Townley Crane. Worked as journalist on New Jersey and New York papers; first successful with *Red Badge of Courage* (1895). Became a newspaper syndicate writer, traveling in the Far West and Mexico, and covering Cuban filibustering and the Greco-Turkish War; moved to England, 1898, where he was friend to Joseph Conrad, H. G. Wells, and other writers. War correspondent in Spanish-American War. Died of tuberculosis. Crane's work set fresh standards for American writing in its intensity and its use of startling yet inevitable descriptive phrasing. His books include *Maggie, a Girl of the Streets* (1892); *The Red Badge of Courage* (1895); *The Black Riders and Other Lines* (1895); *The Little Regiment* (1896); *George's Mother* (1896); *The Third Violet* (1897); *The Open Boat* (1898); *Active Service* (1899); *War Is Kind* (1899); *The Monster* (1899); *Wounds in the Rain* (1900); and *Whilomville Stories* (1900).

CRANE, THOMAS FREDERICK (*b. New York, N.Y., 1844; d. 1927*), lawyer, teacher, scholar. Taught modern languages at Cornell University, 1868–1909, and served twice as acting president; pioneer in study of medieval literature and of folklore.

CRANE, WILLIAM HENRY (*b. Leicester, Mass., 1845; d. Hollywood, Calif., 1928*), actor, comedian. Played in partnership with Stuart Robson; his greatest hit was *David Harum,* 1900–03.

CRANE, WILLIAM MONTGOMERY (*b. Elizabeth, N.J., 1784; d. 1846*), naval officer. Served at Tripoli and during War of 1812; commanded Mediterranean Squadron, 1827–29; chief of Bureau of Ordnance and Hydrography, 1842–46.

CRANE, WINTHROP MURRAY (*b. Dalton, Mass., 1853; d. Dalton, 1920*), paper manufacturer. Devised (*ca.* 1879) production process for silk-threaded paper used for U.S. notes. Served on

Republican National Committee; was elected lieutenant governor of Massachusetts in 1896; governor, 1900–02. His personal arbitration of Boston teamsters' strike, 1902, served as model for Roosevelt's action in anthracite strike. As U.S. senator, 1904–12, he was judged the Senate's most influential member. Lost his fight to persuade 1920 Republican National Convention to support U.S. membership in the League of Nations.

CRANSTON, EARL (b. *Athens, Ohio, 1840; d. New Richmond, Ohio, 1932*), Methodist clergyman and bishop. Influential in bringing about reunion of that church's northern and southern branches.

CRANSTON, JOHN (b. *London, England, 1625; d. Rhode Island, 1680*), physician. Immigrated to Rhode Island, *ca.* 1637. Served as major during King Philip's War; was commissioner from Newport in Rhode Island General Assembly, and governor of the colony, 1678–80.

CRANSTON, SAMUEL (b. *Newport, R.I., 1659; d. 1727*). Son of John Cranston. Colonial governor of Rhode Island, 1698–1727. Preserved Rhode Island charter rights, settled boundary disputes with Massachusetts and Connecticut.

CRAPSEY, ADELAIDE (b. *New York, N.Y., 1878; d. Saranac Lake, N.Y., 1914*), poet. Daughter of Algernon S. Crapsey. Graduated Vassar, 1901. Her book *Verse* (1915) employed an original verse form, the cinquain.

CRAPSEY, ALGERNON SIDNEY (b. *Fairmount, Ohio, 1847; d. 1927*), Episcopal clergyman, author. Widely known as preacher, pastor, and missioner, he was deposed after trial for heresy, 1906.

CRARY, ISAAC EDWIN (b. *Preston, Conn., 1804; d. Marshall, Mich., 1854*), lawyer, educator. First congressman from Michigan, 1837–41.

CRATTY, MABEL (b. *Bellaire, Ohio, 1868; d. New York, N.Y., 1928*), social worker. General secretary of YWCA National Board, 1906–28.

CRAVATH, ERASTUS MILO (b. *Homer, N.Y., 1833. d. 1900*), Congregational clergyman, first president of Fisk University. Served as chaplain during Civil War; helped establish Atlanta and Fisk universities.

CRAVATH, PAUL DRENNAN (b. *Berlin Heights, Ohio, 1861; d. Locust Valley, N.Y., 1940*), corporation lawyer. Son of Erastus M. Cravath.

CRAVEN, BRAXTON (b. *Randolph Co., N.C., 1822; d. 1882*), first president of Trinity College (now Duke University).

CRAVEN, FRANK (b. *Boston, Mass., 1875[?]; d. Beverly Hills, Calif., 1945*), actor, playwright, director. As a child, trouped with parents, who were actors; tried business for a while, but returned to stage. After long apprenticeship in minor parts, made Broadway hit in comic role in *Bought and Paid For* (1911). Although more interested in writing plays and sketches for vaudeville, he found that producers would stage his plays only if he acted in them. Works included *Too Many Cooks* (1914), *This Way Out* (1917), and *The First Year* (1920). *Post* 1929, he devoted most of his efforts to motion pictures, functioning as actor, writer, and director. Embodying in his stage persona the homely virtues of small-town American life, he was particularly effective in the role of the Stage Manager in Thornton Wilder's *Our Town* (1938).

CRAVEN, JOHN JOSEPH (b. *Newark, N.J., 1822; d. Patchogue, N.Y., 1893*), inventor, physician. Invented cable insulation for underwater use; as military surgeon attended Jefferson Davis during imprisonment at Fortress Monroe.

CRAVEN, THOMAS TINGEY (b. *District of Columbia, 1808; d. Boston, Mass., 1887*), naval officer. Initiated Annapolis practice cruise; served with Farragut in Mississippi River campaign; retired, 1869, as rear admiral.

CRAVEN, TUNIS AUGUSTUS MACDONOUGH (b. *Portsmouth, N.H., 1813; d. off Mobile, Ala., 1864*), naval officer. Brother of Thomas T. Craven. A leading surveyor and hydrographer of the navy; commanded ironclad *Tecumseh*, 1863–64, and went down with her in Mobile Bay.

CRAWFORD, FRANCIS MARION (b. *Bagni di Lucca, Italy, 1854; d. Sorrento, Italy, 1909*), novelist, historian. Son of Thomas Crawford. Among his more than forty novels, the *Saracinesca* trilogy on 19th-century Rome is outstanding.

CRAWFORD, GEORGE WALKER (b. *near Augusta, Ga., 1798; d. 1872*). As Whig governor of Georgia from 1843 to 1847, excelled as administrator; was secretary of war, 1849–50.

CRAWFORD, JAMES PYLE WICKERSHAM (b. *Lancaster, Pa., 1882; d. Philadelphia, Pa., 1939*), professor of Romance languages, University of Pennsylvania, 1914–39. Author of *Spanish Drama Before Lope de Vega* (1922); first editor, *Hispanic Review* (1933–39).

CRAWFORD, JOHN (b. *North Ireland, 1746; d. Baltimore, Md., 1813*), physician. Worked in Barbados and Demerara; in Baltimore after 1796, he developed a theory of infection through parasitic organisms.

CRAWFORD, JOHN MARTIN (b. *Herrick, Pa., 1845; d. Cincinnati, Ohio, 1916*), physician. Translated Finnish epic *Kalevala* and Estonian epic *Kalevipoeg*; served as consul general in Russia and translated *Industries of Russia* (1893).

CRAWFORD, JOHN WALLACE ("CAPTAIN JACK") (b. *Co. Donegal, Ireland, 1847; d. Brooklyn, N.Y., 1917*), "the poet scout." Came to America as a boy. After service in Union army, 1862–65, went west; succeeded Buffalo Bill Cody as chief of scouts, Sioux campaign, 1876, and served in later Apache wars. Author of sincere but banal verse.

CRAWFORD, MARTIN JENKINS (b. *Jasper Co., Ga., 1820; d. Columbus, Ga., 1883*), lawyer. Congressman, Democrat, from Georgia, 1855–61; later a judge of Georgia district and supreme courts.

CRAWFORD, SAMUEL EARL (b. *Wahoo, Nebr., 1880; d. Hollywood, Calif., 1968*), baseball player. Known as "Wahoo Sam," he played baseball in Nebraska, Canada, Ohio, and Michigan before signing with Cincinnati in the National League in 1899. He played with the Detroit Tigers (1903–17), where his achievements were often overshadowed by his teammate Ty Cobb. Crawford played with the Los Angeles Angels (1917–21) of the Pacific Coast League. In 2,505 major-league games, Crawford batted .309. He was the only player to lead both major leagues in home runs; he still holds the record for most triples in a career (312). Crawford was baseball coach at the University of Southern California (1924–30), an umpire in the Pacific Coast League (1935–38), and treasurer of the Association of Professional Baseball Players (1939–42). In 1957 he was inducted into the Baseball Hall of Fame.

CRAWFORD, SAMUEL JOHNSON (b. *near Bedford, Ind., 1835; d. 1913*), lawyer, Union soldier. Republican governor of Kansas, 1864–68.

CRAWFORD, THOMAS (b. *New York, N.Y., ca. 1813; d. London, England, 1857*), sculptor. Worked as woodcarver and marble cutter in New York; in Rome studied under Thorwaldsen. Charles

Sumner raised subscription in Boston to buy Crawford's *Orpheus* for the Athenaeum. This, like his other works, was idealistically conceived and allegorically or mythologically portrayed. In 1849 Crawford won the Richmond, Va., competition for an equestrian monument to Washington. He was entrusted with the designing of the marble pediment and bronze doors of the Capitol's Senate wing and with the *Armed Liberty* capping the dome. His art was based largely on the imitation of classic forms.

CRAWFORD, WILLIAM (b. Frederick Co., Va., 1732; d. near modern Crawfordsville, Ohio, 1782), Revolutionary soldier. Served on Indian frontier in Braddock's campaign, Forbes's expedition, Pontiac War, Dunmore's War, and Revolutionary War.

CRAWFORD, WILLIAM HARRIS (b. Nelson Co., Va., 1772; d. Georgia, 1834), statesman. A Columbia Co., Ga., plantation owner and circuit court judge, he entered the state legislature in 1803 and allied with the Jackson-Troup faction. As U.S. senator, Democratic-Republican, 1807–13, he advocated conservative financial policies. In 1813 he served as minister to France, in 1815 as secretary of war, and in 1816–25 as secretary of the treasury. In 1816, urged to run against Monroe as the Democratic-Republican nominee for the presidency, he demurred; from 1820 to 1824 Crawford's friends sought again to prepare the ground for Crawford's nomination, this time with his active cooperation. Stricken with paralysis in 1823, friends sought unsuccessfully to nominate him by congressional caucus and failed. An able administrator and financier, Crawford has suffered in reputation by his use as a foil for biographers of Clay, Calhoun, and other of his political rivals.

CRAZY HORSE (b. ca. 1849; d. near Camp Robinson, Nebr., 1877), chief of Oglala Sioux. Fought under Red Cloud in Wyoming, 1865–68; married to a Cheyenne woman, he led Southern Sioux and Northern Cheyenne in their forays off the reservations. Forced General Crook to withdraw from the upper Rosebud, 1876; fought Custer at the Little Bighorn; was driven by Crook to withdraw to the Wolf Mountains, where he was attacked by Colonel Miles and forced to retire. Desertions of his supporters and lack of supplies led him to surrender at the Red Cloud Agency, May 6, 1877. He was fatally wounded when he sought to resist confinement.

CREAMER, DAVID (b. Baltimore, Md., 1812; d. Baltimore, 1887), hymnologist. Wrote *Methodist Hymnology* (1848), a comprehensive study of John and Charles Wesley's poetical works.

CREATH, JACOB (b. near Cumberland, Nova Scotia, 1777; d. 1854), clergyman. Raised in North Carolina; migrated to Kentucky, 1803. As Kentucky evangelist, became leading Campbellite and was excluded from Baptist church; organized Kentucky churches of the Disciples of Christ.

CREATH, JACOB (b. Mecklenburg County, Va., 1799; d. 1886), clergyman. Nephew of Jacob Creath (1777–1854). An intense polemicist, established Campbellite churches in Kentucky and Missouri; wrote *A Blow at the Root of Episcopalianism* (1848).

CREEL, GEORGE (b. Lafayette County, Mo., 1876; d. San Francisco, Calif., 1953), journalist and government official. Self-educated, Creel worked in journalism in Kansas City and Denver, championing liberal causes. A supporter of Woodrow Wilson, he was appointed chairman of the Committee on Public Information, which controlled most information about the U.S. going out of the country during World War I. The committee also oversaw the propaganda efforts for the mobilization.

CREELMAN, JAMES (b. Montreal, Canada, 1859; d. Berlin, Germany, 1915), journalist, war correspondent.

CREESY, JOSIAH PERKINS (b. Marblehead, Mass., 1814; d. Salem, Mass., 1871), sea captain, master of the *Flying Cloud*. Set speed records on New York–San Francisco run, 1851 and 1854.

CREIGHTON, EDWARD (b. Belmont or Licking Co., Ohio, 1820; d. 1874), pioneer telegraph builder, banker, philanthropist. Helped build transcontinental telegraph to Salt Lake City; provided initial capital to found Creighton University, Omaha, Nebr.

CREIGHTON, JAMES EDWIN (b. Pictou, Nova Scotia, 1861; d. 1924), philosopher. Protégé of Jacob G. Schurman. Taught at Cornell, 1889–1924; edited *Philosophical Review*, 1902–24.

CREIGHTON, JOHN ANDREW (b. Licking Co., Ohio, 1831; d. 1907), philanthropist. Brother and associate of Edward Creighton.

CREIGHTON, WILLIAM (b. Berkeley Co., Va., 1778; d. 1851), lawyer. Moved to Chillicothe, Ohio, 1799. Was Ohio's first secretary of state, 1803–08; served as U.S. district attorney and as congressman, Democratic-Republican, 1813–17 and 1827–33. He was later identified with the Whig party.

CRERAR, JOHN (b. New York, N.Y., 1827; d. Chicago, Ill., 1889), financier, philanthropist. An incorporator and director of Pullman Co., left his estate for philanthropic purposes, including the John Crerar Library, Chicago.

CRESAP, MICHAEL (b. Allegany Co., Md., 1742; d. New York, N.Y., 1775), border leader, trader, Revolutionary soldier. Son of Thomas Cresap. Accused of brutality to Indians and death of Logan, 1774.

CRESAP, THOMAS (b. Skipton, England, ca. 1702; d. ca. 1790), trader, pioneer. Came to America, ca. 1717. In his stockaded house on the Appalachian border of Maryland, Cresap acted as intermediary between the colony government, the Iroquois, and the Cherokee.

CRESPI, JUAN (b. Mallorca, Spain, 1721; d. Carmel, Calif., 1782), Franciscan missionary, explorer. His diaries record major Pacific Coast expeditions, 1769–74, the discovery of San Francisco Bay, and the sea route to Alaska.

CRESSON, ELLIOTT (b. Philadelphia, Pa., 1796; d. 1854), Quaker merchant, philanthropist.

CRESSON, EZRA TOWNSEND (b. Byberry, Pa., 1838; d. 1926), entomologist. Helped found first American entomological society, 1859; specialized in the order Hymenoptera.

CRESWELL, JOHN ANGEL JAMES (b. Port Deposit, Md., 1828; d. Elkton, Md., 1891), lawyer, politician. Made sweeping and constructive reforms in Post Office Department as postmaster general, 1869–74.

CRET, PAUL PHILIPPE (b. Lyons, France, 1876; d. Philadelphia, Pa., 1945), architect. Studied at the École des Beaux Arts, Paris. Appointed assistant professor of architectural design, University of Pennsylvania, 1903, and professor, 1907. Associated with the university until his retirement in 1937. His own architectural work was extensive and varied. Impatient with both the conservatism of traditionalists and the pretensions of self-styled moderns, he hoped to see American architecture evolve into a kind of 20th-century classicism. His own search for such a modern American style was exemplified in his Detroit Institute of Arts, the Barnes Foundation Gallery at Merion, Pa., the Integrity Trust Company of Philadelphia, and the Folger Library, Washington, D.C.

CRÉTIN, JOSEPH (*b. Montluel, France, 1799; d. St. Paul, Minn., 1857*), first Roman Catholic bishop of St. Paul, Minn. A missionary at Dubuque, Iowa, and Prairie du Chien, 1839–50; consecrated bishop, 1851.

CRÈVECOEUR, J. HECTOR ST. JOHN. *See* CRÈVECOEUR, MICHEL-GUILLAUME JEAN DE.

CRÈVECOEUR, MICHEL-GUILLAUME JEAN DE (*b. near Caen, France, 1735; d. Sarcelles, France, 1813*), essayist. Served in Canada under Montcalm; went to New York, 1759; traveled in Pennsylvania, New York, and the Carolinas. Lived on a farm in Orange Co., N.Y., from 1769 to 1780. During these years he composed *Letters from an American Farmer* (1782) and most of the *Sketches of Eighteenth Century America* (1925). Crèvecoeur went to France in 1780; returning to America in 1783, he served as French consul in New York until 1790. As a writer, Crèvecoeur is brilliant, excelling in his description of American frontier life as well as in his understanding of new economic and social forces. He was author also of *Voyages dans la Haute Pensylvanie* (Paris, 1801).

CRILE, GEORGE WASHINGTON (*b. near Chili, Ohio, 1864; d. Cleveland, Ohio, 1943*), surgeon. B.A., present Ohio Northern University, 1884; M.D., University of Wooster Medical Department, 1887; studied also in Europe. Taught at Wooster (1889–1900), and was professor of surgery, Western Reserve University School of Medicine, 1900–24. A pioneer in investigation of the role of physiology and emotional factors in surgery, Crile made major contributions to the problem of shock and related conditions.

CRIMMINS, JOHN DANIEL (*b. New York, N.Y., 1844; d. 1917*), contractor, capitalist. Built large part of New York's elevated railroad and subway system.

CRISP, CHARLES FREDERICK (*b. Sheffield, England, 1845; d. 1896*), lawyer, Confederate soldier. Raised in Georgia. Congressman, Democrat, 1883–96; Speaker of the House *post* 1891. A leading advocate of Interstate Commerce Act and of free silver. Ranked among the ablest Georgians of his time.

CRISSINGER, DANIEL RICHARD (*b. Tully Township, Marion County, Ohio, 1860; d. Marion, Ohio, 1942*), lawyer. Through friendship with Warren G. Harding, was appointed comptroller of the currency, 1921. Named governor of the Federal Reserve Board by Harding in 1923, he was incompetent and resigned under fire in 1927.

CRITTENDEN, GEORGE BIBB (*b. Russellville, Ky., 1812; d. Danville, Ky., 1880*), soldier. Son of John J. Crittenden. Graduated West Point, 1832. Served in Black Hawk War, with Texans in 1843, and in Mexican War; joined Confederate army in 1861, and after censure for conduct as brigadier general served without rank.

CRITTENDEN, JOHN JORDAN (*b. near Versailles, Ky., 1787; d. Frankfort, Ky., 1863*), lawyer, statesman. Practiced law with success and held various Kentucky state offices, 1809–35; filled out a term in U.S. Senate, 1817–19; became a friend and supporter of Henry Clay. Elected to the U.S. Senate as a Whig, 1835, he remained a national figure until his death. He served as U.S. senator, 1835–41, 1842–48, and 1854–61; as U.S. attorney general, 1841 and 1849–53; and as congressman, 1861–63. He was for a brief time governor of Kentucky. An advocate of conservative policies, he urged a congressional policy of nonintervention in the territories over slavery. The greatest effort of his life was made during his last three years when he sought to save the Union by the Crittenden propositions and other measures for peace. During the Civil War, he consistently opposed radical policies of both the North and the South.

CRITTENDEN, THOMAS LEONDIDAS (*b. Russellville, Ky., 1819; d. Annandale, N.Y., 1893*), lawyer, soldier. Son of John J. Crittenden. Served with Union army, 1861–64, rising to major general. Reentered army, 1867, and served until retirement, 1881.

CRITTENDEN, THOMAS THEODORE (*b. near Shelbyville, Ky., 1832; d. Kansas City, Mo., 1909*), lawyer. Nephew of John J. Crittenden. Moved to Missouri, 1857, and as Democratic governor, 1881–85, broke up Jesse James gang.

CRITTENTON, CHARLES NELSON (*b. Henderson, N.Y., 1833; d. San Francisco, Calif., 1909*), philanthropist. A successful New York businessman, he founded the Florence Crittenton Missions to save unfortunate women.

CROCKER, ALVAH (*b. Leominster, Mass., 1801; d. 1874*), manufacturer, politician, railroad builder. Built up one of New England's largest paper-manufacturing concerns. Helped establish Fitchburg Mutual Fire Insurance Co.; organized the Turners Falls Co., which developed waterpower of that Massachusetts community. Promoted construction of the Fitchburg Railroad (Boston-Fitchburg, 1843–45), of the Vermont & Massachusetts (Fitchburg-Brattleboro, Vt., 1845–49) and of the Troy & Greenfield Railroad, which included the Hoosac Tunnel. He served also in Massachusetts General Court and as Republican congressman, 1872–74.

CROCKER, CHARLES (*b. Troy, N.Y., 1822; d. Monterey, Calif., 1888*), merchant, railroad builder, capitalist. Established forge in Marshall Co., Ind., near a bed of iron he discovered in 1845; took up gold mining in California in 1850; opened a store in Sacramento, 1852, and by 1854 was one of the town's wealthiest men. Served in city council and state legislature. With Leland Stanford, C. P. Huntington, and Mark Hopkins, built Central Pacific Railroad across the Sierra Nevada, 1863–69. Crocker supervised the actual construction of the line and was president of the Contract and Finance Co. In 1871 he was elected president of the Southern Pacific Railroad of California; in 1884 he consolidated the Central and Southern Pacific. He was interested financially in banking, real estate, irrigation, and industrial projects in California.

CROCKER, FRANCIS BACON (*b. New York, N.Y., 1861; d. 1921*), electrical engineer. Graduated Columbia School of Mines, 1882. In partnership with Charles G. Curtis and, after 1886, with Schuyler S. Wheeler, designed the commercial electric motor of standard specification. As "father of American electrical standards," Crocker helped formulate the National Electric Code, introduced "henry" as name for the international unit of inductance, and at the 1906 International Electrotechnical Commission in London insured international standardization of electrical manufacturing. In 1917 he and Peter Cooper Hewitt developed the first American helicopter capable of flight.

CROCKER, HANNAH MATHER (*b. Boston, Mass., 1752; d. Boston, 1829*), writer. Granddaughter of Cotton Mather. An early advocate of woman's rights, she also championed Freemasonry and warned sailors against intemperance and vice.

CROCKER, URIEL (*b. Marblehead, Mass., 1796; d. 1887*), printer, Boston publisher.

CROCKER, WILLIAM (*b. Montville, Ohio, 1874; d. Athens, Ohio, 1950*), plant physiologist. Graduated Illinois Normal University, 1898. Taught in country schools. B.A., University of Illinois, 1902; M.A., 1903; Ph.D. in botany, University of Chicago, 1906. At Chicago, was influenced by John M. Coulter, in whose department he taught, 1906–21. Director of the Boyce Thompson Institute (Yonkers, N.Y.) for plant study *post* 1921. In addition to planning, building, and administering the institute, he carried on a program of research principally in the physiology of seed plants. In association with others, he made valuable studies on the toxic effects on plant life of illuminating gas, carbon monoxide, and other gases. Equally important were his studies on the dormancy and germination of seeds.

CROCKETT, DAVID (*b. near Rogersville, Tenn., 1786; d. Texas, 1836*), frontiersman. After a wandering youth, married Polly Findlay, *ca.* 1804, and settled down on a rented tract in his home county. Though he was a mighty hunter, he was a poor farmer and did not prosper; he soon moved with his family to Lincoln Co. near the Alabama line. He served with distinction as a scout under Andrew Jackson in the Creek War of 1813–14. After his wife's death in 1815 he married again; settling in Giles Co., he was appointed justice of the peace, elected colonel of the militia and, in 1821, to the Tennessee legislature. Moving further west near the junction of the Obion with the Mississippi, he devoted himself to bear-hunting. He was again elected to the legislature in 1823. Taking seriously a jocular proposal, he ran for Congress and was elected on an anti-Jackson ticket; he served 1827–31 and 1833–35. In April 1834 he commenced his celebrated "tour of the North," visiting Baltimore, Philadelphia, New York, and Boston. His opposition to Jackson brought political defeat in 1835, and Crockett joined the movement for Texas independence. He met his death during the defense of the Alamo. Happily innocent of learning and with little understanding of public questions, Crockett was a man of sterling independence, good nature, and exceptional self-confidence. He excelled as a brave soldier, an able scout, and an expert rifleman. His authorship of the autobiographical writings issued in his name is doubtful.

CROGHAN, GEORGE (*b. Ireland; d. Passyunk, Pa., 1782*), Indian trader and agent, land speculator. Immigrated to Pennsylvania, 1741. His home near Carlisle, Pa., was base for trading operations throughout the upper Ohio country. As representative of Pennsylvania, Croghan was the leading English agent at Indian treaty councils; by arousing the fears of the French for their claims on the Ohio, he drew upon himself and the English settlers the French attack on Pickawillany in 1752. Croghan assisted Washington, Braddock, Forbes, and Bouquet in their Indian campaigns and negotiated with the Northwest tribes. Sent to open the Illinois country, he was taken prisoner, was freed, and made a treaty with Pontiac. In 1772 he turned to land speculation and was a charter member of the Grand Ohio Co. The Revolution reduced him to poverty.

CROGHAN, GEORGE (*b. near Louisville, Ky., 1791; d. New Orleans, La., 1849*), soldier. Nephew of George R. Clark and William Clark. Distinguished himself at Tippecanoe, Fort Defiance, Fort Meigs, and in particular Fort Stephenson (Ohio), August 1813.

CROIX, TEODORO DE (*b. 1730; d. Madrid, Spain, 1792*), Spanish soldier. As commandant general of Provincias Internas of Mexico, 1776–83, he was a highly efficient administrator of Texas, New Mexico, and California.

CROKER, RICHARD (*b. Cloghnakilty, Ireland, 1841; d. 1922*), New York City politician, "Boss Croker." Reared in New York City, he worked as a machinist, was a leader of the "Fourth Avenue Tunnel Gang" and a prize-fighter. In 1868, as a member of Tammany's "Young Democracy," he participated in the struggle to oust Boss Tweed. He became Tammany leader in 1886 and dominated city politics until 1894. He regained his hold from

1897 to 1901. He then moved to England and, later, Ireland, where he devoted himself to his racing stables.

CROLY, DAVID GOODMAN (*b. Cloghnakilty, Ireland, 1829; d. 1889*), journalist. Came to America as a child and was raised in New York City. His books *Miscegenation* (1864) is the first use of the title word, which he coined; he was an ardent positivist.

CROLY, HERBERT DAVID (*b. New York, N.Y., 1869; d. Santa Barbara, Calif., 1930*), editor, author. Son of David G. and Jane C. Croly. Wrote *The Promise of American Life* (1909), a manifesto of liberalism; edited *The New Republic*, 1913–30.

CROLY, JANE CUNNINGHAM (*b. Market Harborough, England, 1829; d. New York, N.Y., 1901*), journalist. Wife of David G. Croly. Founded Sorosis and the Women's Press Club; wrote *History of the Woman's Club Movement in America* (1898).

CROMPTON, GEORGE (*b. Holcombe, England, 1829; d. 1886*), inventor, manufacturer. Came to America, 1839. Son of William Crompton. Trained in Colt's pistol factory at Hartford and in his father's plant at Taunton, Mass., he began loom manufacture at Worcester, Mass. He improved practically every part of the loom, added 60 percent to its producing capacity, and invented many new textile fabrics. Crompton served on Worcester's board of aldermen and on the common council. He was a founder of the Hartford Steam Boiler Inspection & Insurance Co. and a founder and director of the Crompton Carpet Co.

CROMPTON, WILLIAM (*b. Preston, England, 1806; d. Windsor, Conn., 1891*), textile machinery inventor, manufacturer. Came to America, 1836. Employed by Crocker & Richmond at Taunton, Mass., he invented a loom for easily exchangeable fancy patterns. In England from 1837 to 1839, he returned to Taunton and introduced his loom at the Middlesex Mills, Lowell, Mass., 1840. This was probably the first instance of fancy woolens being woven by power.

CROMWELL, DEAN BARLETT (*b. Turner, Oreg., 1879; d. Los Angeles, Calif., 1962*), track and field coach. Graduate of Occidental College (1902), where he was an outstanding athlete (football, baseball, track). Coached football (1909–14) and track (1909–48) at the University of Southern California. During his tenure, USC dominated intercollegiate track and field, winning twelve NCAA championships. Between 1912 and 1948, eight of his athletes won a total of twelve Olympic gold medals. Cromwell was head track and field coach for the 1948 U.S. Olympic team. He was elected to the National Track and Field Hall of Fame in 1974.

CROMWELL, GLADYS LOUISE HUSTED (*b. Brooklyn, N.Y., 1885; d. France, 1919*), poet. Author of *Gates of Utterance* (1915) and *Poems* (1920); in 1918 did Red Cross work at Châlons-sur-Marne.

CROMWELL, WILLIAM NELSON (*b. Brooklyn, N.Y., 1854; d. New York, N.Y., 1948*), lawyer. Worked as an accountant; graduated Columbia Law School, 1876. Entered partnership with A. S. Sullivan, 1879, becoming senior partner on Sullivan's death, 1887. Specialized in supplying advice to increasingly complex business organizations which were trying to reach rapidly expanding markets. More interested in efficient results than in legal doctrine, he was ingenious in salvaging business enterprises in distress, devising for the purpose a form of reorganization, the so-called Cromwell plan, which won him reputation as "the physician of Wall Street." Much criticized for using his Republican party connections to achieve a shift of the proposed isthmian canal from Nicaragua to Panama—thus benefiting a French client. Left most of his nearly $19 million estate to philanthropic causes.

CROOK, GEORGE (*b. near Dayton, Ohio, 1829; d. Chicago, Ill., 1890*), soldier. After graduation from West Point in 1852, served on northwestern frontier. During Civil War rose from rank of major to major general; was distinguished for service with cavalry at South Mountain, Antietam, Chickamauga, Winchester, Fisher's Hill, Cedar Creek, and Appomattox. Pacified the Indians of the Boise district, and the Apache of northern Arizona. Took a prominent part in the Sioux War of 1876. Returned to Arizona, 1882, and until 1885 sought to pacify the Chiricahua Apache. After 1888 he served as commander of the Division of the Missouri. A splendid frontier soldier, he understood the Indians well and advocated for them the granting of full citizenship privileges.

CROOKS, GEORGE RICHARD (*b. Philadelphia, Pa., 1822; d. 1897*), Methodist Episcopal clergyman, educator. Taught historical theology at Drew Seminary; edited *The Methodist*, 1860–75; wrote school texts and theological works.

CROOKS, RAMSAY (*b. Greenock, Scotland, 1787; d. New York, N.Y., 1859*), fur trader. Immigrated to Canada, 1803, and entered fur trade. In 1807 established trading post near Calhoun, Nebr.; in 1810 became partner in Astor's Pacific Fur Co. Discouraged by hardships and poor prospects of the venture at Astoria, he returned to St. Louis in 1813. Appointed general manager of Astor's American Fur Co., 1817, he promoted the establishment of the company's Western Department and in 1834 became president of the Northern Department. A superb manager, he left much interesting historical information in his letters. He also served as president of the Mohawk & Hudson Railroad Co. and as trustee of New York's Astor Library.

CROPSEY, JASPAR FRANCIS (*b. Rossville, N.Y., 1823; d. 1900*), painter. Architect for the Sixth Avenue elevated railroad stations, New York; famous for autumn landscapes.

CROSBY, ERNEST HOWARD (*b. New York, N.Y., 1856; d. 1907*), author, social reformer. Son of Howard Crosby. Championed the single tax, antimilitarism, industrial arbitration, vegetarianism, settlement work.

CROSBY, FANNY (*b. Southeast, N.Y., 1820; d. Bridgeport, Conn., 1915*), hymnist. Taught at New York Institution for the Blind; wrote about 6,000 hymns.

CROSBY, HOWARD (*b. New York, N.Y., 1826; d. New York, 1891*), Presbyterian clergyman, reformer. A Greek scholar, he was pastor, 1863–91, at New York's Fourth Avenue Presbyterian Church; founded Society for the Prevention of Crime.

CROSBY, JOHN SCHUYLER (*b. Albany, N.Y., 1839; d. Newport, R.I., 1914*), Union soldier, public official. Brevetted lieutenant colonel, 1865; resigned from army, 1870. Served as U.S. consul in Florence, Italy, 1876–82, and as territorial governor of Montana, 1882–84.

CROSBY, PEIRCE (*b. Delaware Co., Pa., 1824; d. Washington, D.C., 1899*), naval officer. Distinguished himself under Farragut at New Orleans, 1862, in command of USS *Pinola.*

CROSBY, PERCY LEE (*b. Brooklyn, N.Y., 1891; d. New York, N.Y., 1964*), cartoonist and artist. Attended Pratt Institute and Art Students League in New York. Drew the comic strip "The Clancy Kids" (1915–17) and published two books of war cartoons. Introduced the "Skippy" series in the humor magazine *Life* in 1923. In 1925 "Skippy" became a daily comic strip, and Skippy's popular escapades were featured in the 1931 motion picture *Skippy,* starring Jackie Cooper. Crosby also achieved an international reputation with his drawings, lithographs, etchings, water colors, and oils. He wrote over sixteen books and pamphlets.

CROSBY, WILLIAM OTIS (*b. Decatur, Ohio, 1850; d. 1925*), geologist. Consulting engineer for construction of dams in Idaho, Texas, Mexico, and Keokuk, Iowa.

CROSLEY, POWELL, JR. (*b. Cincinnati, Ohio, 1886; d. Cincinnati, 1961*), manufacturer and baseball club owner. Studied at the University of Cincinnati (1906–07). Made several unsuccessful efforts to manufacture automobiles. Established a profitable mail-order business in 1916. Crosley designed a cheap radio receiver, and by 1922 the Crosley Radio Corp. was the world's largest radio manufacturer. He later added refrigerators (Shelvador) and air conditioners to his line. Briefly produced the Crosley, one of the nation's first compact cars. In 1934 he became president of the Cincinnati Reds baseball team, and in 1936 he bought the controlling interest.

CROSS, ARTHUR LYON (*b. Portland, Maine, 1873; d. Ann Arbor, Mich., 1940*), historian. Instructor and professor at University of Michigan, 1899–1940; specialist in Anglo-American legal history.

CROSS, CHARLES WHITMAN (*b. Amherst, Mass., 1854; d. Rockville, Md., 1949*), geologist, petrologist. Raised in Iowa. B.S., Amherst College, 1875; Ph.D., Leipzig, 1880. Associated with the U.S. Geological Survey, 1880–1925; worked for many years on the volcanic rocks of the San Juan region of southwestern Colorado; collaborated in devising a new and still standard system (the CIPW system) described in *Quantitative Classification of Igneous Rocks* (1903). His meticulously prepared collection of rock specimens became the nucleus of the Smithsonian Institution's petrographic collection.

CROSS, EDWARD (*b. Virginia, 1798; d. Little Rock, Ark., 1887*), Arkansas jurist and Democratic congressman.

CROSS, SAMUEL HAZZARD (*b. Westerly, R.I., 1891; d. Cambridge, Mass., 1946*), government official, educator. B.A., Harvard, 1912; Ph.D. in comparative literature, 1916. An infantry officer in World War I, he served as U.S. trade commissioner in Brussels, Belgium, 1920–25, and as chief of the European division of the Bureau of Foreign and Domestic Commerce in Washington, D.C., 1925–26, and was for a short time in the securities business in Boston. Returning to academic life in 1928 as lecturer in history at Harvard, he was appointed professor of Slavic languages and literatures in 1930 and held that post until his death. Since his field was relatively new in America, his work was primarily one of cultural mediation and preparing the ground for the later vast expansion of Slavic studies. His published scholarly work dealt mainly with medieval Russia. *Post* 1929, assistant managing editor, managing editor, and editor (1936–46) of *Speculum.*

CROSS, WILBUR LUCIUS (*b. Gurleyvill, Conn., 1862; d. New Haven, Conn., 1948*), scholar, educator, governor of Connecticut. B.A., Yale, 1885; Ph.D., 1889. Taught English at Shady Side Academy, Pittsburgh, Pa., 1889–94. Appointed instructor in English at Sheffield Scientific School, Yale, 1894, he became professor of English in 1902 and succeeded Thomas R. Lounsbury as head of the English department in 1907. He retained his Sheffield professorship until 1922, when he was named first Sterling professor of English. On his appointment in 1916 as dean of the graduate school, he began teaching there also. He retired from his Yale posts in 1930. He was author of three major scholarly works: *The Development of the English Novel* (1889); *The Life and Times of Laurence Sterne* (1909, preceded by his edition of Sterne's principal works, 1904); and *The History of Henry Fielding* (1918). Editor of *Yale Review*, 1911–40, which he made an important intellectual force. Elected Democratic governor of Connecticut, 1930, after a grass-roots campaign. Served four terms against machine politics opposition. A strong and humane leader in the worst years of the Great Depression.

CROSSER, ROBERT (*b. Holytown, Scotland, 1874; d. Bethesda, Md., 1957*), U.S. congressman. Immigrated to the U.S. in 1881. Studied at Kenyon College and at the Cincinnati Law School (LL.B., 1901). Democratic member of Congress (1912–18 and 1922–54). An advocate of the rights of labor and later a supporter of the New Deal, Crosser was instrumental in the passage of much labor legislation, including the Railroad Labor Act of 1934. Chairman of the House Committee on Interstate and Foreign Commerce (1949–52).

CROSSWAITH, FRANK RUDOLPH (*b. Frederiksted, St. Croix, Virgin Islands, 1892; d. New York, N.Y., 1965*), labor organizer. Came to the U.S. in 1910. Graduated from Rand School of Social Science (1918), where he taught part-time for many years. Inspired by Eugene Debs, he became a socialist and was active among a group of radical blacks in Harlem. He lectured for the Socialist party and the League for Industrial Democracy, and was a Socialist candidate for several offices. He was the first professional organizer for A. Philip Randolph's Brotherhood of Sleeping Car Porters (1926–28), then became an organizer for the International Ladies' Garment Workers' Union. Crosswaith joined with Randolph in the March on Washington Committee in 1941. He was a founding member of the anti-Communist Union for Democratic Action and served on the New York City Housing Authority for many years.

CROSWELL, EDWIN (*b. Catskill, N.Y., 1797; d. Princeton, N.J., 1871*), journalist, politician. As editor of the Albany *Argus,* was mouthpiece of the Democratic "Albany Regency."

CROSWELL, HARRY (*b. West Hartford, Conn., 1778; d. New Haven, Conn., 1858*), Controversial Federalist editor of the Hudson, N.Y., *Balance* and *The Wasp. Post* 1814, an Episcopal clergyman.

CROTHERS, RACHEL (*b. Bloomington, Ill., 1878; d. Danbury, Conn., 1958*), playwright. Studied at the Stanhope-Wheatcroft School of Acting in New York. Crothers championed the modern woman; her plays were satires and criticisms of the double standard, Freudianism, trial marriage, and divorce. They included *The Three of Us* (1906), *Nice People* (1912), *Mary the Third* (1923), *Let Us Be Gay* (1929), *As Husbands Go* (1931), *When Ladies Meet* (1932), and *Susan and God* (1937). All of these plays were successes on Broadway.

CROTHERS, SAMUEL MCCHORD (*b. Oswego, Ill., 1857; d. Cambridge, Mass., 1927*), Presbyterian and Unitarian clergyman, essayist.

CROUNSE, LORENZO (*b. Sharon, N.Y., 1834; d. Omaha, Nebr., 1909*), jurist. Removed to Nebraska, 1864; served in many state and national offices and in Congress; an independent Republican, his opposition to railroad interests won him the governorship, 1892–94.

CROUSE, RUSSEL MCKINLEY (*b. Findlay, Ohio, 1893; d. New York, N.Y., 1966*), reporter, columnist, author, playwright, and producer. Worked as a reporter and columnist for the *Kansas City Star,* the *Cincinnati Post,* the *New York Globe* (1919–23), and the *New York Evening Post* (1924–31). During this period he also contributed to the *New Yorker.* He collaborated with Morrie Ryskind and Oscar Hammerstein on the musical *The Gang's All*

Here, which opened in 1931. He wrote *Mr. Currier and Mr. Ives* (1930) and *It Seems Like Yesterday* (1931), which he and Corey Ford turned into the successful musical *Hold Your Horses* (1933). In 1932 he compiled *The American Keepsake* and wrote *Murder Won't Out.* He is best known for his collaborations with Howard Lindsay (1934–66), beginning with the musical *Anything Goes* (1934). Their screenplays, often done with other writers, included *Artists and Models Abroad* (1938), *The Big Broadcast of 1938* (1938), and *The Great Victor Herbert* (1939). They wrote the film adaptations of *Anything Goes* (1936), *Life with Father* (1947), *State of the Union* (1948), *Call Me Madam* (1953), and the remake of *Anything Goes* (1956). Their play *Life with Father* (1939) ran for 3,224 performances. They produced *Arsenic and Old Lace* (1940), *The Hasty Heart* (1945), *Detective Story* (1949), and *One Bright Day* (1952). Other plays include *Strip for Action* (1942), *State of the Union* (1945), *Life with Mother* (1948), *Remains to Be Seen* (1951), *The Prescott Proposals* (1953), *The Great Sebastians* (1956), *Happy Hunting* (1956), *The Sound of Music* (1959), *Tall Story* (1959), and *Mr. President* (1962).

CROUTER, ALBERT LOUIS EDGERTON (*b. near Belleville, Canada, 1846; d. 1925*), educator. Superintendent of celebrated Pennsylvania Institution for the Deaf, 1884–1925.

CROWDER, ENOCH HERBERT (*b. Edinburgh, Mo., 1859; d. Washington, D.C., 1932*), army officer, diplomat, lawyer. Graduated West Point, 1881; assigned to frontier duty in Texas. Detailed to teach military science at the University of Missouri, where he received LL.B. degree, 1886. Served as judge advocate in the Philippines during Spanish-American War and as military observer in Russo-Japanese War. Supervised Cuban elections in 1908, heading advisory law commission which drafted most of the organic laws of the island. Appointed judge advocate general of the army in 1911. Chief credit for the draft law of 1917 belongs to Crowder, who was promoted to major general in that year. His term as ambassador to Cuba, 1923–27, and previous service as special representative in Cuba, won him acclaim in both Havana and Washington.

CROWE, FRANCIS TRENHOLM (*b. Trenholmville, Quebec, Canada, 1882; d. Redding, Calif., 1946*), civil engineer. B.S., University of Maine, 1905. Worked for U.S. Reclamation Service, 1905–25 (except for 1908–08, 1920), as construction chief for a number of western dams. When the service discontinued its construction force, Crowe entered private industry. He was in charge of work on 19 dams during his professional career, including Hoover and Shasta.

CROWELL, LUTHER CHILDS (*b. West Dennis, Mass., 1840; d. West Dennis, 1903*), inventor. In 1862 he obtained a patent for an aerial machine; in 1867 for a machine to make paper bags. He devised the square-bottomed bag and the side-seam bag and the machines for manufacturing them, and in 1873 a sheet-delivery and folding mechanism for printing presses. With R. Hoe and Co., 1879–1903, he perfected the double supplement press, double and quadruple presses, and combined pamphlet-printing and wire-binding machines. He obtained over 280 U.S. patents for printing machinery alone. At the time of his death he was working on a wrapping and mailing machine.

CROWNE, JOHN (*b. Shropshire[?], England, 1640; d. London, England, 1712*), Restoration dramatist. Son of William Crowne. First Harvard College playwright; attended Harvard for three years *post* 1657 but did not graduate. Author of *Sir Courtly Nice, The Destruction of Jerusalem,* and other plays. Returned to England, 1661.

CROWNE, WILLIAM (*b. England, ca. 1617; d. Boston, Mass., 1683*), adventurer, land speculator. Lost his property on

Penobscot River through cession of Nova Scotia to France, 1667; resided in America, 1657–61, and 1667–83.

CROWNINSHIELD, BENJAMIN WILLIAMS (*b. Salem, Mass., 1772; d. Boston, Mass., 1851*), merchant, politician. President of Merchants Bank of Salem; served in state and national legislatures; secretary of the navy, 1814–18.

CROWNINSHIELD, FRANCIS WELCH (*b. Paris, France, 1872; d. New York, N.Y., 1947*), magazine editor. Raised in Boston, Mass., and in New York City. Became a bookstore clerk, 1890. Held a number of editorial positions on periodicals, 1895–1913. Appointed editor of *Dress and Vanity Fair*, 1914, he shortened the name to *Vanity Fair* and transformed it into a chic and slick reflection of his own interests in modern art and literature and "the things people talk about at parties." He was a founder and first secretary of New York's Museum of Modern Art. Active in Manhattan social life, he was one of the creators of what came to be known as café society. The onset of the Great Depression caused *Vanity Fair* to operate at a serious loss, and on its merger in 1936 with *Vogue*, Crowninshield, who has already been shorn by the publisher of his editorial autonomy, was named art editor of *Vogue* and "literary adviser" to Condé Nast Publications.

CROWNINSHIELD, FREDERIC (*b. Boston, Mass., 1845; d. Capri, Italy, 1918*), painter, writer. Director of American Academy in Rome, 1900–11.

CROWNINSHIELD, GEORGE (*b. Salem, Mass., 1766; d. Salem, 1817*), sea captain, merchant, pioneer yachtsman. Built first American yacht, the *Jefferson*, and the first seagoing yacht of its class, *Cleopatra's Barge*.

CROWNINSHIELD, JACOB (*b. Salem, Mass., 1770; d. Washington, D.C., 1808*), sea captain, merchant, congressman. Ablest member of this celebrated Salem family; secretary of the navy, 1805–09.

CROY, HOMER (*b. near Maryville, Mo., 1883; d. New York, N.Y., 1965*), journalist and novelist. Studied at the University of Missouri. Moved to New York City and worked for Butterick Publications as editor of *Baseball Magazine* and travel writer. Later he became a writer for the *Saturday Evening Post*. A prolific writer, his better-known novels include *They Had to See Paris* (1926), *Sixteen Hands* (1938), *Family Honeymoon* (1941), and *The Lady from Colorado* (1957). His nonfiction included *Jesse James Was My Neighbor* (1949), *He Hanged Them High* (1952), *Our Will Rogers* (1953), *Wheels West* (1955), *Trigger Marshal* (1957), and *Star Maker: The Story of D. W. Griffith* (1959). His autobiography, *Country Cured*, was published in 1943.

CROZER, JOHN PRICE (*b. West Dale, Pa., 1793; d. 1866*), manufacturer, philanthropist. Crozer Theological Seminary at Chester, Pa., is named for him.

CROZET, CLAUDE (*b. Villefranche, France, 1790; d. 1864*), soldier, engineer. An artillery officer in the French army, 1807–15, the second restoration of the Bourbons prompted him to immigrate to America, where he taught engineering at West Point, 1816–23. Here, as later at the Virginia Military Institute, Crozet introduced the study of descriptive geometry. From 1823 to 1832 he served as Virginia state engineer and planned an inland communication system which gave Virginia one of the best road systems of that time. He also located and built a railroad through the Blue Ridge. As president of the Board of Visitors to the Virginia Military Institute, 1839–45, Crozet modeled its curriculum after that of West Point.

CROZIER, WILLIAM (*b. Carrollton, Ohio, 1855; d. Washington, D.C., 1942*), army officer, inventor. Raised in Leavenworth,

Kans. Graduated West Point, 1876; commissioned in artillery. Developed interest in large-caliber guns, coastal defense, and systematization of military procurement. Chief of ordnance, 1901–18. Conceived of his department as an agent of scientific advance, its manufacturing arsenals as pilot plants which set efficiency standards by which private bids could be appraised. His reorganization and testing and development work contributed substantially to preparedness for World War I. Promoted major general, October 1917. Served on the Supreme War Council, cooperating in the standardization and pooling of all ordnance used by the Allied armies. Codeveloper of the Buffington-Crozier disappearing gun carriage (1896), adopted as standard for U.S. coast defenses.

CRUGER, HENRY (*b. New York, N.Y., 1739; d. New York, 1827*), merchant. Resided in England, 1757–90. As Edmund Burke's fellow member in Parliament for Bristol, Cruger served 1774–80 and 1784–90; in the Commons he was an outspoken friend to America. On his return to New York he was elected to the state senate.

CRUGER, JOHN (*b. New York, N.Y., 1710; d. New York, 1791*), mayor of New York, 1756–65. Speaker of the last New York colonial assembly; first president of New York Chamber of Commerce, 1768. Prominent in resistance to British policies before 1776.

CRUMBINE, SAMUEL JAY (*b. Emlenton, Pa., 1862; d. Queens, N.Y., 1954*), physician, public health officer. Studied at the Cincinnati College of Medicine and Surgery (1889). Kansas Board of Health (1899–1911), head from 1904. He gained national recognition for his efforts against adulterated foods, fraudulent medicines, and unsanitary health habits; he banned public drinking cups and the roller towels. 1911–19, dean of Kansas Medical School. Medical consultant to the American Child Health Association (1923–36); director, 1925. Crumbine advocated national pasteurization of milk.

CRUMP, EDWARD HULL (*b. Holly Springs, Miss., 1874; d. Memphis, Tenn., 1954*), politician. Mayor of Memphis for four terms beginning 1909; elected U.S. congressman (Democrat) in 1930 and 1932. Until his death, he was the acknowledged "boss" of Memphis and of Shelby County, Tenn.

CRUMP, WILLIAM WOOD (*b. Henrico Co., Va., 1819; d. Richmond, Va., 1897*), jurist. A strong secessionist, he served as assistant secretary of the treasury of the Confederacy; excelled as advocate before a jury.

CRUNDEN, FREDERICK MORGAN (*b. Gravesend, England, 1847; d. St. Louis, Mo., 1911*), educator, librarian. Came to America as a child. Chief promoter of the St. Louis Public Library.

CUBBERLEY, ELLWOOD PATTERSON (*b. Antioch, later Andrews, Ind., 1868; d. Palo Alto, Calif., 1941*), educator. Influenced by David Starr Jordan, Cubberley decided on a career in education. Graduated Indiana University, 1891. Taught physical science at Vincennes University; president, 1893–96. Experience as superintendent of schools in San Diego, Calif., 1896–98, convinced him that school boards should be nonpolitical and that administrators need autonomy. Appointed assistant professor of education, Stanford University, 1898. Formed Department of Education. In 1917, the department was made a professional school of the university and he was made dean, serving until 1933. Meanwhile, he had attended Teachers College, Columbia University; Ph.D., 1905. His experience there intensified his evangelical fervor for public education. Viewed education as "social engineering" and schools as instruments of evolutionary progress.

Numerous publications included *Public Education in the United States* (1919) and *The History of Education* (1920).

CUBERO, PEDRO RODRÍGUEZ (*b. Calatayud, Spain, 1645; d. Mexico, 1704*), Spanish governor of New Mexico, 1697–1703.

CUDAHY, EDWARD ALOYSIUS, JR. (*b. Chicago, Ill., 1885; d. Phoenix, Ariz., 1966*), meat packer. At fifteen, kidnapped and held in chains for $25,000 ransom. Studied at Creighton University and entered the family meat-packing business, Cudahy Packing, in 1905. He became vice president in 1916 and president in 1926, by which time the company operated nine plants, had distribution facilities in nearly 100 cities, and owned a fleet of refrigerator and tank cars. During the 1930's the company was hurt by declining meat prices and labor turmoil. Along with other packers, Cudahy was indicted in 1941 for fixing hog prices in Iowa and Nebraska, but the indictments were dropped in 1949. He became board chairman in 1944 and resigned in 1962. Due to the lack of research, long-range planning, or diversification during Cudahy's tenure, the company disintegrated after his retirement.

CUDAHY, MICHAEL (*b. Callan, Ireland, 1841; d. 1910*), meat-packer. Came to America, 1849. Revolutionized industry through introduction of summer curing of meat under refrigeration.

CUFFE, PAUL (*b. Cuttyhunk, Elizabeth Islands, Mass., 1759; d. 1817*), seaman. Prospered as shipowner; founded the Friendly Society, to facilitate emigration of American blacks to Sierra Leone.

CULBERSON, CHARLES ALLEN (*b. Dadeville, Ala., 1855; d. Washington, D.C., 1925*), lawyer, statesman. Son of David B. Culberson. A Democrat, he was Texas attorney general, 1890–94; governor, 1894–98; and U.S. senator 1899–1923.

CULBERSON, DAVID BROWNING (*b. Troup Co., Ga., 1830; d. Jefferson, Tex., 1900*), lawyer, Confederate soldier, statesman. Removed to Dadeville, Ala., 1851, to Upshur Co., Tex., 1856, and to Jefferson, Tex., 1860. A Democrat, he served in Congress, 1875–97. The ablest constitutional lawyer in the House, he was a conservative, interested in judicial reforms and the limitation of tariffs.

CULBERTSON, ELY (*b. Ploesti, Romania, 1891; d. Brattleboro, Vt., 1955*), contract bridge authority, world peace worker. Studied at Yale. An expert on the rules and playing of contract bridge; founded the magazine *Bridge World* in 1919; in 1930, his book *Blue Book* became a best seller. Culbertson worked for the cause of world peace before the outbreak of World War II and championed the formation of the United Nations.

CULBERTSON, JOSEPHINE MURPHY (*b. Bayside, N.Y., 1899; d. New York, N.Y., 1956*), contract bridge expert. The wife of bridge player Ely Culbertson, Josephine helped found and run the magazine *Bridge World* (1929). She wrote a syndicated newspaper column on bridge from 1931 and edited all of her husband's works, including *Contract Bridge Blue Book* (1930).

CULLEN, COUNTÉE PORTER (*b. New York, N.Y., or possibly Louisville, Ky., 1903; d. New York, 1946*), poet, novelist, teacher. Graduated New York University, 1925; M.A., Harvard, 1926. Author of lyric poems which won wide recognition during his school and college years, Cullen worked as assistant editor of *Opportunity: A Journal of Negro Life*, received first Harmon Award of NAACP (1927) and a Guggenheim fellowship (1928). Resident principally in France, 1928–34. Returned to New York City, 1934, and taught French, English, and creative writing at Frederick Douglass Junior High School until his death. A princi-

pal figure in the Harlem Renaissance, he was author, among other works, of *Color* (1925); *Copper Sun* (1927); *Caroling Dusk* (1927, an anthology of Afro-American poetry); *The Black Christ and Other Poems* (1929); *One Way to Heaven* (1932), a novel about life in Harlem; several books for children; and a collection of his work, *On These I Stand* (1947).

CULLEN, HUGH ROY (*b. Denton County, Tex., 1881; d. Houston, Tex., 1957*), oilman, philanthropist. Self-educated, Cullen, through real estate dealings in the Houston area and by acquiring vast tracts of oil lands in west Texas, became one of the state's most successful and wealthy oilmen. His philanthropies include support of the University of Houston and of many hospitals. In 1947 he organized his major philanthropies under the Cullen Foundation, which became the third largest of its type in the nation. A staunch Republican, he supported Hoover and later Eisenhower for the presidency.

CULLEN, THOMAS STEPHEN (*b. Bridgewater, Ont., 1868; d. Baltimore, Md., 1953*), gynecologist. Studied at the University of Toronto (1890). Affiliated with Johns Hopkins University from 1892 to 1939. Member of the board of trustees of the American Medical Association.

CULLINAN, JOSEPH STEPHEN (*b. Sharon, Pa., 1860; d. Palo Alto, Calif., 1937*), corporation executive. Creator and head of three major oil companies: Texas, Magnolia, and American Republics.

CULLIS, CHARLES (*b. Boston, Mass., 1833; d. 1892*), homeopathic physician, leader in faith-cure movement.

CULLOM, SHELBY MOORE (*b. Kentucky, 1829; d. 1914*), lawyer, statesman. Grew up in Illinois; admitted to the bar in Springfield, 1855. Republican after 1858, he served in state legislature, in Congress, as governor of Illinois, 1876–83, and as U.S. senator, 1883–1913. A champion of state regulation of railroads in Illinois, he was instrumental as senator in the establishment of the Interstate Commerce Commission and became chairman of the Senate Interstate Commerce Committee. After 1901 he was chairman of the Committee on Foreign Relations and in 1906 helped secure passage of the Hepburn Act. Independent in his thinking but colorless, his seniority rights gave him a prominent place within the Republican party.

CULLUM, GEORGE WASHINGTON (*b. New York, N.Y., 1809; d. 1892*), author, soldier. Graduated West Point, 1833. Author of *Biographical Register of Officers and Graduates* of West Point (1850, 1868, 1891).

CULPEPER, THOMAS (*b. England, 1635; d. London, England, 1689*). Lord Culpeper, royal governor of Virginia. Commissioned 1675 but served by deputy until 1680. At first conciliatory and popular, he turned dictatorial and was removed from office in 1683 for having left the colony without royal permission.

CUMING, ALEXANDER (*b. ca. 1690; d. London, England, 1775*). Eccentric Scottish baronet who persuaded Cherokee Indians to accept British sovereignty, 1730. Died a debtor and a poor brother of Charterhouse.

CUMING, FORTESCUE (*b. Strabane, Ireland, 1762; d. Vermilionville, La., 1828*), traveler. Author of *Sketches of a Tour to the Western Country* (1810).

CUMMING, ALFRED (*b. Augusta, Ga., 1802; d. near Augusta, 1873*), territorial governor of Utah. Appointed by Buchanan in 1857 to replace Brigham Young; resigned upon Lincoln's inauguration.

CUMMINGS, AMOS JAY (*b. Conkling, N.Y., 1841; d. 1902*), journalist. On staffs of New York *Tribune* and *Sun*; founded and edited evening *Sun*. In Congress as Tammany regular, 1886–88, 1890–94, 1896–1902.

CUMMINGS, CHARLES AMOS (*b. Boston, Mass., 1833; d. 1905*), architect. Author of *History of Architecture in Italy* (1901).

CUMMINGS, E E (*b. Cambridge, Mass., 1894; d. North Conway, N.H., 1962*), poet and painter. Studied at Harvard (B.A., 1915; M.A., 1916), where he contributed poems to the *Harvard Monthly*. As a college student he aligned himself with modernist writers and artists. His first book was a prose work, *The Enormous Room* (1922), modeled on *The Pilgrim's Progress*. The book described his experiences in a French concentration camp in 1917. Cummings developed rapidly as a poet during the 1920's. He began publishing in the *Dial*, and his first collection of poems was *Tulips and Chimneys* 1923), which was followed by *XLI Poems* (1925), *&* (1925), and *Is 5* (1926). From the beginning Cummings established his unique use of typography and language, and over the next forty years he did not appreciably change his style or themes. Through his poems of hate and love he expressed a mystical reverence for the wholeness and immediacy of life. He lived in Europe (1921–23), mostly in Paris, painting and writing. His 1927 play, *Him*, was performed at the Provincetown Playhouse in 1928. In 1931 Cummings exhibited his paintings for the first time in New York and published *CIOPW*, a book of pictures. *Eimi* (1933) was a journal compiled during a 1931 visit to the Soviet Union. In 1938 he published *Collected Poems*. In 1952 he taught at Harvard and delivered lectures about himself, published as *I: Six Nonlectures* (1953). His complete poems were published as *Poems 1923–1954* (1954), followed by *95 Poems* (1958).

CUMMINGS, EDWARD (*b. 1861; d. 1926*), Unitarian minister, student and worker in social ethics. Minister and pastor of Boston's South Congregational Society; promoter of the World Peace Foundation.

CUMMINGS, HOMER STILLÉ (*b. Chicago, Ill., 1870; d. Washington, D.C., 1956*), lawyer, politician. Studied at the Sheffield School at Yale (Ph.B., 1891), and at the Yale Law School (LL.B., 1893). Active in Democratic politics, Cummings served in local Connecticut politics and as vice-chairman (1913–1919) and chairman (1919–20) of the Democratic National Committee. Appointed attorney general of the U.S. by Roosevelt (1933–39), Cummings led the Justice Department through many difficult New Deal cases, including the plan to "pack" the court in 1937.

CUMMINGS, JOHN (*b. Woburn, Mass., 1785; d. 1867*), tanner. Pioneer in the modernization of the leather industry.

CUMMINGS, JOSEPH (*b. Falmouth, Maine, 1817; d. 1890*), Methodist clergyman. President of Genesee College, 1854–57; Wesleyan University, 1857–75; Northwestern University, 1881–90.

CUMMINGS, THOMAS SEIR (*b. Bath, England, 1804; d. Hackensack, N.J., 1894*), painter. An expert miniaturist; helped found National Academy of Design, 1825; taught at University of the City of New York.

CUMMINGS, WALTER JOSEPH (*b. Springfield, Ill., 1879; d. Chicago, Ill., 1967*), banker and industrialist. During World War I bought a company, which became Cummings Car and Coach Company, that manufactured streetcars and buses. Was active in transit-related businesses in the 1920's. During the Depression he was bankruptcy trustee of the Chicago, Milwaukee, and St. Paul Railroad and the Chicago Railways Company. He acquired several Chicago-area transit companies in the early 1930's. In 1933 Cummings entered government service as an executive assistant to Secretary of the Treasury William H. Woodin. Later that year he became the first chairman of the Federal Deposit Insurance Corporation. In 1934 he became treasurer of the Democratic National Committee. Cummings was elected a class-A director of the Chicago Federal Reserve Bank in 1936 and 1939. Also in 1936 he became chairman of the Continental Illinois Bank, from which he retired in 1959.

CUMMINS, ALBERT BAIRD (*b. Carmichaels, Pa., 1850; d. 1926*), lawyer, statesman. Gained reputation in Iowa for his legal victory over the barbed-wire trust; as Republican governor of Iowa, 1901–08, brought progressivism to the state, broke political domination of the railroads, and witnessed adoption of a new primary law. As U.S. senator, 1909–26, Cummins became chairman of the Committee on Interstate Commerce and played an important role in passage of the Transportation Act of 1920. He urged, however, compulsory consolidation and arbitration, provisions which were not adopted.

CUMMINS, GEORGE DAVID (*b. near Smyrna, Del., 1822; d. Lutherville, Md., 1876*), clergyman, founder of the Reformed Episcopal church, 1873.

CUMMINS, MARIA SUSANNA (*b. Salem, Mass., 1827; d. Dorchester, Mass., 1866*). Author of moralistic stories and novels; *The Lamplighter* (1854) had an extraordinary success.

CUNLIFFE-OWEN, PHILIP FREDERICK (*b. London, England, 1855; d. New York, N.Y., 1926*), editor, publicist. An outstanding international interpreter of foreign affairs on the *New York Tribune*, and later in syndicated articles signed "Marquise de Fontenoy."

CUNNINGHAM, ANN PAMELA (*b. Laurens Co., S.C., 1816; d. Laurens Co., 1875*), founder and first regent of Mount Vernon Ladies' Association, which preserved Washington's home for posterity.

CUNNINGHAM, KATE RICHARDS O'HARE. *See* O'HARE, KATE RICHARDS CUNNINGHAM.

CUPPIA, JEROME CHESTER (*b. Pelham Manor, N.Y., 1890; d. Montclair, N.J., 1966*), securities and commodities trader. In 1916 he was a partner in Robertson and Company and became a member of the New York Cotton Exchange. In 1920 he formed the firm of Cuppia and Robertson and in 1923 a new firm, J. C. Cuppia and Company, which in 1926 was merged with E. A. Pierce and Company, which in turn merged in 1940 with other firms to form Merrill Lynch, E.A. Pierce and Cassatt. In 1925 Cuppia purchased a seat on the New York Curb Exchange (which became the American Stock Exchange in 1953) and started speculating in stocks and commodities. He became active in Democratic party politics in the early 1930's. In 1940 Cuppia was served with a warrant of attachment and he resigned from his firm. A 1941 Securities and Exchange Commission investigation uncovered widespread wrongdoing by members of the Curb. Though the scandal was soon forgotten, Cuppia died a broken man.

CUPPLES, SAMUEL (*b. Harrisburg, Pa., 1831; d. St. Louis, Mo., 1912*), merchant, manufacturer, philanthropist.

CUPPY, WILLIAM JACOB (*b. Auburn, Ind., 1884; d. New York, N.Y., 1949*), journalist, humorist, literary critic. Known as Will Cuppy. Ph.B., University of Chicago, 1907; M.A., 1914. A specialist reviewer of detective fiction and true crime narratives, Cuppy was author of a number of humorous essays and sketches, attacking the pretensions of modern gadget-oriented culture and the gullibility and self-destructiveness of modern man. His works include *How to Be a Hermit* (1929); *How to Tell Your Friends from the Apes* (1931); *How to Become Extinct* (1941); and *How to Attract the Wombat* (1949). He also edited several excellent collections of crime fiction.

CURLEY, JAMES MICHAEL (*b. Boston, Mass. 1874; d. Boston, 1958*), politician. Self-educated, Curley was one of the century's most controversial and colorful politicians. Entering politics as a member of the Boston common council in 1899, he went on to serve four terms as Boston's mayor (1914–17, 1922–26, 1930–34, and 1945–49). He served in the U.S. Congress from 1910 to 1914 and from 1943 to 1945. Governor of Massachusetts from 1934 to 1938. Accused of being a big-city political boss, Curley saw Boston through many hard times by pushing through many public works projects that were precursors to the New Deal legislative programs of the 1930's. Often accused of corruption, he was convicted only twice: in 1937 he was convicted of taking a bribe, which he was forced to repay; and in 1947, while serving his last term as mayor, he served five months in prison, having been convicted of receiving a payoff some years earlier. He was pardoned by President Truman and served out his term as mayor. The novel by Edwin O'Connor *The Last Hurrah* (1956), which was also the basis for a film, is an excellent fictionalized account of his life.

CURME, GEORGE OLIVER (*b. Richmond, Ind., 1860; d. White Plains, N.Y., 1948*), scholar, grammarian. B.A., University of Michigan, 1882; M.A., De Pauw University, 1885; studied at University of Berlin, 1890. Taught modern languages at University of Washington, 1884–86, and at Cornell College in Iowa, 1886–96; professor of Germanic philology at Northwestern University, 1896–1934. Won an international reputation for his *Grammar of the German Language* (1905, 1922), and his two-part *Grammar of the English Language* (*Syntax*, 1931; *Parts of Speech and Accidence*, 1935).

CURRAN, JOHN JOSEPH (*b. Hawley, Pa., 1859; d. Wilkes-Barre, Pa., 1936*), Roman Catholic clergyman. Son of a coal miner, he began work as a child in the Pennsylvania coal fields. Graduated, 1882, from St. Vincent College, Latrobe, Pa.; ordained 1887. Serving parishes in Wilkes-Barre from 1895 until his death, Curran actively supported the mine workers and their union. He acted as intermediary in a number of labor disputes, notably the anthracite strikes of 1900 and 1902. A supporter of both Presidents Roosevelt, Curran was characterized by his friend T.R. as "the kind of priest needed in a democracy."

CURRAN, THOMAS JEROME (*b. New York, N.Y., 1898; d. New York, 1958*), lawyer, politician. Studied at Fordham University (LL.B., 1923). An Irish Catholic Republican, Curran was an anomaly in New York City politics. He won terms as an alderman in 1933–34, and served as president and executive chairman of the powerful New York County Republican Committee from 1940 to 1958. From 1942 to 1945, he was secretary of state of New York under Governor Thomas E. Dewey.

CURRIER, CHARLES WARREN (*b. St. Thomas, Virgin Islands, 1857; d. Maryland, 1918*), Roman Catholic clergyman. Active in pastoral work, and for a brief time bishop of Matanzas, Cuba, he was an outstanding Hispanist and enthusiastic promoter of Pan-Americanism.

CURRIER, MOODY (*b. Boscawen, N.H., 1806; d, 1898*), financier, politician. A Manchester, N.H., banker, he served as state senator, and as governor of New Hampshire, 1885–87.

CURRIER, NATHANIEL (*b. Roxbury, Mass., 1813; d. New York, N.Y., 1888*), lithographic printer, publisher. Apprentice in shops of W. S. and John Pendleton, in 1835 he issued his first popular lithograph, drawn by J. H. Bufford, *The Ruins of the Merchants' Exchange*. This was the beginning of the series best-known as Currier & Ives prints, which for nearly seventy years gave a lively picture of manners and history of the American people. J. Merritt Ives became Currier's partner in 1850. Great fires, disasters, the California gold rush, the development of railroads and commerce from the clipper ship to the steamship, political changes, sports, and the making of the West were the subjects portrayed in color by the staff artists of this notable firm.

CURRY, GEORGE LAW (*b. Philadelphia, Pa., 1820; d. 1878*), territorial governor of Oregon, 1854–59. Edited *Oregon Spectator*; founded *Oregon Free Press*, 1848. Remembered for his vigorous defense of the settlers against the Indians, 1855.

CURRY, JABEZ LAMAR MONROE (*b. Lincoln Co., Ga., 1825; d. 1903*), statesman, author, educator. Inspired by Horace Mann's zeal for universal education and John C. Calhoun's theory of politics. After a widely diversified career in law, politics, war, and diplomacy, Curry made an outstanding contribution to educational progress in the South as agent of the Peabody Fund after 1881, as agent of the Slater Fund after 1890, and as supervising director of the Southern Education Board.

CURRY, JOHN STEUART (*b. near Dunavant, Kans., 1897; d. Madison, Wis., 1946*), painter, illustrator. Studied briefly at Kansas City Art Institute and for two years at Chicago Art Institute. Served in army during World War I. Attended Geneva College in Pennsylvania, 1918–20. Began as illustrator of stories for Wild West magazines. After a year's serious study in Paris, he returned to the United States, 1927, and continued study at Art Students League, New York City. Between 1928 and 1936, he produced a volume of easel and mural paintings of the American rural scene and of historical subjects which established him as a leading exponent of the popular regionalism movement. He was artist-in-residence at University of Wisconsin *post* 1936.

CURTIN, ANDREW GREGG (*b. Bellefonte, Pa., 1815[?]; d. 1894*), lawyer, politician. Admitted to the bar, 1839. Campaigned for Harrison in 1840, for Clay in 1844, for Taylor in 1848, and for Scott in 1852. Appointed secretary of Pennsylvania and ex officio superintendent of common schools, 1854. As Republican governor, 1861–67, Curtin secured Pennsylvania's support for the Union, established the Pennsylvania Reserve Corps, and devoted himself to the welfare of the state's soldiers. In 1869 Grant appointed him minister to Russia. Supporting Greeley in 1872, Curtin lost the favor of the Republican party and joined the Democrats. From 1881 to 1887 he served as a Democratic congressman.

CURTIN, JEREMIAH (*b. Detroit, Mich., 1835; d. 1906*), linguist, student of comparative mythology. Contributed primarily to Celtic, Slavonic, Mongolian, and American Indian ethnology; translated Sienkiewicz, Tolstoy, Zagoskin, and others.

CURTIS, ALFRED ALLEN (*b. Pocomoke, Md., 1831; d. Baltimore, Md., 1908*), Roman Catholic clergyman. Bishop of Wilmington, Del., 1886–96.

CURTIS, BENJAMIN ROBBINS (*b. Watertown, Mass., 1809; d. Newport, R.I., 1874*), jurist. Graduated Harvard, 1829; attended Harvard Law School. Practiced in Northfield, Mass., and Boston. Appointed to the U.S. Supreme Court, 1851, Curtis dissented in the Dred Scott decision (1857), holding that residence in a free state enabled an ex-slave to vindicate his freedom in slave-state courts. Curtis also objected to the Court's ruling on the merits of the case after having denied that a slave is a citizen, and resigned from the Court. Thereafter, as a recognized leader of the bar,

Curtis argued many cases before the U.S. and Massachusetts supreme courts, and was President Andrew Johnson's chief counsel during the impeachment proceedings.

CURTIS, CHARLES (*b. North Topeka, Kans., 1860; d. Washington, D.C., 1936*), lawyer. Congressman, Republican, from Kansas, 1892–1907; U.S. senator, 1907–1929; vice president of the United States, 1929–33.

CURTIS, CHARLES PELHAM (*b. Boston, Mass., 1891; d. Boston, 1959*), lawyer, author. Studied at Harvard Law School. Became senior partner of Choate, Hall and Stewart, a prestigious Boston law firm. His books include *Lions Under the Throne* (1947), a study of the U.S. Supreme Court, and *The Oppenheimer Case: The Trial of a Security System* (1955), an indictment of the federal security system. From 1924 to 1935, he was the youngest member of the Harvard Corporation.

CURTIS, CYRUS HERMANN KOTZSCHMAR (*b. Portland, Maine, 1850; d. Wyncote, Pa., 1933*), publisher. Founder and business head of the Curtis Publishing Co.; publisher of the *Ladies' Home Journal* and *Saturday Evening Post*.

CURTIS, EDWARD LEWIS (*b. Ann Arbor, Mich., 1853; d. 1911*), Presbyterian clergyman, educator. Graduated Yale, 1874, and Union Theological Seminary. Taught Hebrew at McCormick Theological Seminary and at Yale; published *Critical and Exegetical Commentary on the Books of Chronicles* (1910).

CURTIS, EDWARD SHERIFF (*b. Whitewater, Wis., 1868; d. Los Angeles, Calif., 1952*), photographer. Self-educated, Curtis became a specialist in photographing the American Indian. In 1909, with the backing of Theodore Roosevelt and J. P. Morgan, he published the first of a twenty-volume work, *The American Indian*.

CURTIS, EDWIN UPTON (*b. Roxbury, Mass., 1861; d. 1922*), lawyer. Carried out major reforms of Boston city government as mayor, 1894–95. As police commissioner, 1918–22, reorganized department after 1919 strike.

CURTIS, GEORGE (*b. Worcester, Mass., 1796; d. Jacksonville, Fla., 1856*), banker. Served in Rhode Island legislature; as president of Continental Bank, New York, drew up "Constitution" of New York Clearing House, 1854.

CURTIS, GEORGE TICKNOR (*b. Watertown, Mass., 1812; d. New York, N.Y., 1894*), lawyer. Brother of Benjamin R. Curtis. A celebrated patent attorney and counsel for plaintiff in Dred Scott case, his reputation rests chiefly on his *Constitutional History of the United States* (1889, 1896).

CURTIS, GEORGE WILLIAM (*b. Providence, R.I., 1824; d. Staten Island, N.Y., 1892*), author, orator. Son of George Curtis. As a young man, spent two years at Brook Farm; traveled for four years in Europe and Near East. Returning to New York, was associated with the *Tribune* and *Putnam's Magazine*, and served as editor of *Harper's Weekly*, 1863–92. Idealist and Puritan, Curtis employed his talents as speaker and writer in numerous movements for reform, beginning with the antislavery campaigns *post* 1855, and including municipal reform, woman's rights and suffrage, and civil service. He was author, among other books, of *Potiphar Papers* (1853), *Prue and I* (1857), and numerous published orations.

CURTIS, HEBER DOUST (*b. Muskegon, Mich., 1872; d. Ann Arbor, Mich., 1942*), astronomer. B.A., University of Michigan, 1892; M.A., 1893; Ph.D., University of Virginia, 1902. Staff of Lick Observatory, 1902–20 (at station in Santiago, Chile,

1906–10); director, Allegheny Observatory, University of Pittsburgh, 1920–30; director, observatory of the University of Michigan *post* 1930. Author of important monographs on the nebulae.

CURTIS, JOHN GREEN (*b. New York, N.Y., 1844; d. 1913*), physiologist. Son of George Curtis; half-brother of George W. Curtis. As professor at College of Physicians and Surgeons, New York, 1883–1909, he made his laboratory there a research center of note; he also contributed to the scholarly study of the history of his specialty.

CURTIS, MOSES ASHLEY (*b. Stockbridge, Mass., 1808; d. Hillsboro, N.C., 1872*), botanist, Episcopal minister. Graduated Williams, 1827. Made valuable contributions to knowledge of fungi; collected unusually complete mycological herbaria.

CURTIS, NEWTON MARTIN (*b. De Peyster, N.Y., 1835; d. Ogdensburg, N.Y., 1910*), Union soldier, New York legislator and congressman.

CURTIS, OLIN ALFRED (*b. Frankfort, Maine, 1850; d. 1918*), Methodist clergyman. Taught at Boston University and Drew Theological Seminary, 1889–1914; the most influential Methodist theologian of his time.

CURTIS, SAMUEL RYAN (*b. near Champlain, N.Y., 1805; d. Council Bluffs, Iowa, 1866*), soldier, lawyer, engineer. Graduated West Point, 1831. Active in railroad construction and river improvement projects; as Union brigadier, defeated Confederates at Pea Ridge, Ark., 1862.

CURTIS, WILLIAM ELEROY (*b. Akron, Ohio, 1850; d. Philadelphia, Pa., 1911*), journalist, traveler, publicist. First director of Pan-American Union, 1889–93.

CURTISS, GLENN HAMMOND (*b. Hammondsport, N.Y., 1878; d. Buffalo, N.Y., 1930*), aviator, inventor. Interest in bicycle and motorcycle racing led to venture in motorcycle manufacture. With Thomas Scott Baldwin, Curtiss built the first army dirigible in 1905. Became director of Alexander Graham Bell's Aerial Experiment Association; developed the *June Bug*, an airplane which won the *Scientific American* trophy in 1908; invented the hydroplane and flying boat, 1911–12. In World War I, the Curtiss Aeroplane and Motor Co. manufactured 5,000 "Jennies," a mass-produced plane. A navy Curtiss flying boat made the first Atlantic crossing by air in 1919. In the development of aviation Curtiss' place is alongside the Wright brothers and Langley.

CURTISS, SAMUEL IVES (*b. Union, Conn., 1844; d. 1904*), theologian. Professor at Chicago Theological Seminary; disciple of Franz Delitzsch; author of *Primitive Semitic Religion Today* (1902).

CURTIZ, MICHAEL (*b. Budapest, Hungary, 1888; d. Los Angeles, Calif., 1962*), film director. Studied acting, languages, and stage production at the Royal Academy of Theater and Art in Budapest (1910–12) and may have directed the first Hungarian feature film. Directed films in Austria (1919–26), then moved to Hollywood in 1926 to work for Warner Brothers. In the 1930's he directed films in a wide variety of genres: *Mammy* (1930), *Dr. X* (1932), *20,000 Years in Sing-Sing* (1933), *The Kennel Murder Case* (1933), *Black Fury* (1935), *Front Page Woman* (1935), *Angels with Dirty Faces* (1938), and *Dodge City* (1939). His most popular films in the decade were his series starring Errol Flynn, including *Captain Blood* (1935) and *The Adventures of Robin Hood* (1938). During the 1940's he directed *Yankee Doodle Dandy* (1942), *Casablanca* (1942), for which he won his only Oscar for best director, *Mission to Moscow* (1943), *Mildred Pierce* (1945), and *Life with Father* (1947). After leaving Warner Brothers he made *White Christmas* (1954), and his final film was *The Comancheros* (1961).

CURWEN, SAMUEL (b. *Salem, Mass., 1715; d. Salem, 1802*), Loyalist. In England, 1775–84; described fellow exiles in his journal and letters.

CURWOOD, JAMES OLIVER (b. *Owosso, Mich., 1878; d. Owosso, 1927*), author of popular adventure novels.

CUSHING, CALEB (b. *Salisbury Township, Mass., 1800; d. Newburyport, Mass., 1879*), statesman. Grew up in Newburyport. Graduated Harvard, 1817. Studied at the Harvard Law School, tutored mathematics at Harvard, and in 1821 began law practice in Newburyport. He also contributed to the *North American Review*, edited the Newburyport newspaper, and delivered many public addresses. As a supporter of John Quincy Adams, he entered the Massachusetts General Court in 1824, and in 1826 became a state senator, but lost election to Congress, 1826. After several bitter contests he was elected to the House of Representatives on the Whig ticket and served, 1835–43.

Conservative by temperament yet morally opposed to slavery, Cushing agreed with Everett, Webster, and other Massachusetts Whigs that the North had no constitutional right to interfere in Southern affairs. He believed the preservation of the Union to be more important than the abolition of slavery, but upheld the rights of his constituents to petition Congress against slavery. Supported Tyler against Clay Whigs, and until the Civil War voted consistently for Democratic principles and candidates.

Accepting the post of commissioner to China, he concluded the commercial Treaty of Wang Hiya in 1844, which opened five Chinese ports to American merchants, settled disputed tariff and trade regulations, and established the principle of extraterritoriality for U.S. citizens in China. After a trip through Wisconsin and Minnesota, he was elected again to the Massachusetts General Court and there advocated military expansion, favored the annexation of Oregon and Texas, and supported President Polk's policy on the Mexican War issue. In 1847 he raised a regiment, and as brigadier general entered Mexico City. Defeated in the gubernatorial elections of 1847 and 1848, in 1851 he became mayor of Newburyport, and in 1852 served as associate justice of the Massachusetts Supreme Judicial Court. Having been instrumental in Franklin Pierce's election in 1852, Cushing was appointed U.S. attorney general. An influential cabinet member, he spoke out against abolitionism and in foreign affairs became the spokesman of "Young America" and the apostle of "manifest destiny." In 1857 he returned to the Massachusetts legislature. Remained a foe of slavery, while condemning Garrison's abolitionists and John Brown's raid.

As permanent chairman of the Democratic National Convention in Charleston and Baltimore (April-June 1860), Cushing vainly labored for compromise. He then chaired the seceding rival convention, which nominated Breckinridge. Unable to prevent passage of the secession ordinance in Charleston (December 1860), he returned to Washington and offered his services to Lincoln. He became a Republican and was legal consultant to both Seward and Lincoln. After the war he conducted a law practice in Washington, was chairman of a commission which revised and codified the U.S. statutes and was one of the chief American negotiators of the *Alabama* claims. He was a major architect of the 1871 Treaty of Washington, which provided for an international tribunal of arbitration. When President Grant nominated Cushing in 1873 to be chief justice of the Supreme Court, Cushing's enemies revived old slanders, and he failed to be confirmed for purely partisan reasons.

From 1873 to 1877 Cushing served as minister to Spain, where he proved to be one of America's most popular and able diplomats. Cushing was an extraordinarily erudite scholar in the most diverse fields, contributing to the *Encyclopedia Americana*, the *American Annual Register*, and the *North American Review*. He wrote *History of Newburyport* (1826), *Review Historical and Political of the Late Revolution in France*, and *Reminiscences of Spain* (1833).

CUSHING, FRANK HAMILTON (b. *North East, Pa., 1857; d. 1900*), ethnologist. Associated for many years with Smithsonian Institution, Bureau of American Ethnology; author of *Zuni Creation Myths* (1896).

CUSHING, HARVEY WILLIAMS (b. *Cleveland, Ohio, 1869; d. New Haven, Conn., 1939*), neurological surgeon. His father, grandfather, and great-grandfather were physicians. After graduating from Yale, 1891, Cushing received M.A. and M.D. degrees cum laude from Harvard Medical School, 1895. His ability to draw anatomical structures with remarkable fidelity early focused attention on his capabilities. Attracted to surgery by an instinctive ability to handle delicate tissues, he interned at the Massachusetts General Hospital, then became a resident at the Johns Hopkins Hospital. Here he learned his slow, meticulous technique under William Stewart Halted and became increasingly interested in cerebral surgery. At Hopkins began Cushing's long association with Dr. William Osler.

Cushing spent the year 1900–01 abroad, meeting many important scientists and doing work on problems of intracranial pressure and cerebral circulation in European laboratories. Upon his return to Baltimore, Cushing began a general surgical practice and continued teaching at the Johns Hopkins Hospital. The earliest of his brain tumor operations were disappointing, but his original and increasingly skillful operative procedures resulted in dramatic reductions in mortality, a record which he continued to better throughout his career and which was equaled by no other neurosurgeon of his time. A successful operation for brain tumor on Gen. Leonard Wood in 1910 enhanced Cushing's reputation, as did his monograph (1912) on the pituitary gland, a field in which he had become increasingly interested.

In 1912 Cushing became surgeon in chief of the Peter Bent Brigham Hospital in Boston and professor of surgery at Harvard Medical School, positions he held until his retirement in 1932. During World War I he served abroad with medical units he had organized. As a result of his many operations he contributed (1918) a classic paper on wartime injuries of the brain. Though the war undermined his health, Cushing returned to a period of intense activity, training young men from all over the world, writing the Pulitzer Prize–winning biography *The Life of Sir William Osler* (1925), and publishing some of his most important monographs. Among them was his description of pituitary basophilism (Cushing's disease), one of his most original contributions to clinical medicine.

In 1933 Cushing became professor of neurology at Yale and, later, director of studies in the history of medicine. Long interested in medical history and in book collecting, his extensive collection became the nucleus of the historical medical library at Yale.

CUSHING, JOHN PERKINS (b. *Boston, Mass., 1787; d. Watertown, Mass., 1862*), merchant, philanthropist. Nephew of Thomas H. Perkins. Made his fortune in China, 1803–30, where he was the most highly respected foreign merchant.

CUSHING, JOSIAH NELSON (b. *North Attleboro, Mass., 1840; d. 1905*), Baptist missionary in Burma. Developed Judson College in Rangoon, translated the Shan Bible, and prepared a Shan Bible Dictionary.

CUSHING, LUTHER STEARNS (b. *Lunenberg, Mass., 1803; d. Boston, Mass., 1856*), jurist. Served in Massachusetts General

Court; was reporter of state supreme court; author of a celebrated *Manual of Parliamentary Procedure* (1844).

CUSHING, RICHARD JAMES (*b. South Boston, Mass., 1895; d. Boston, 1970*), Roman Catholic clergyman. Studied at Boston College and St. John's Seminary in Brighton, Mass.; ordained a priest in 1921. He was assigned to the Boston office of the Society for the Propagation of the Faith; in 1928 he was named director of the office with the title monsignor. He became auxiliary bishop of Boston in 1939 and archbishop in 1944. He added more than eighty churches and brought into the archdiocese more than sixty religious orders. He helped build many secondary schools and chartered three colleges. In 1958 he founded the Missionary Society of St. James the Apostle, which sent priests to Peru, Bolivia, and Ecuador. Cushing built six new hospitals and established in 1947 St. Coletta's School for mentally retarded children, where he is buried. A supporter of Pope John XXIII, Cushing was made a cardinal in 1958. As priest and archbishop, Cushing often turned to Joseph P. Kennedy for gifts to charities, and very early he developed a special fondness for John F. Kennedy. He resigned his post in 1970.

CUSHING, THOMAS (*b. Boston, Mass., 1725; d. Boston, 1788*), merchant, politician. Speaker of Massachusetts General Court, 1766–74; member of First and Second Continental Congresses; served as Massachusetts lieutenant governor, 1780–88.

CUSHING, WILLIAM (*b. Scituate, Mass., 1732; d. Scituate, 1810*), jurist. Graduated Harvard, 1751. Served as register of deeds and probate judge in Lincoln Co., 1760–71; a judge of Massachusetts superior court after 1772, he refused in conformity with instructions from the General Court to accept a royal salary. Cushing was senior associate judge of the new court as reorganized by the revolutionary council, and chief justice, 1777–89. He was vice president of the state convention which ratified the Constitution, and first associate justice appointed to the U.S. Supreme Court. During Jay's absence Cushing administered the oath at Washington's second inauguration. In 1796 he declined appointment as chief justice. He devoted himself chiefly to his duties in the federal circuit courts.

CUSHING, WILLIAM BARKER (*b. Delafield, Wis., 1842; d. Washington, D.C., 1874*), naval officer. During Civil War he carried out brilliant and daring missions, among them the torpedoing of the Confederate ram *Albemarle.*

CUSHMAN, CHARLOTTE SAUNDERS (*b. Boston, Mass., 1816; d. Boston, 1876*), actress. Debut as a singer, Boston, 1835. In New York and Philadelphia, 1837–44, she displayed as actress a "rude, strong, uncultivated talent." Engagements in London disciplined and polished her acting without robbing it of its passionate power to move audiences. She toured the United States, 1849–52, acclaimed as the leading actress of the stage. Resident in London and on the Continent until 1870, she returned at intervals to play American engagements. Tall, deep-voiced, almost masculine in many respects, inheritor of the great acting tradition of Garrick and Kean, she won fame and fortune by the intelligence of her interpretations.

CUSHMAN, GEORGE HEWITT (*b. Windham, Conn., 1814; d. Jersey City Heights, N.J., 1876*), painter of miniatures, engraver. Pupil of Washington Allston and Seth and John Cheney. Second only to Malbone among American miniaturists.

CUSHMAN, JOSEPH AUGUSTINE (*b. Bridgewater, Mass., 1881; d. Sharon, Mass., 1949*), micropaleontologist. Graduated Bridgewater Normal School, 1901; Lawrence Scientific School, Harvard, 1903. Worked as curator, Boston Society of Natural History, 1903–23, and was long associated with U.S. Geological

Survey. Began lifelong study of Foraminifera, 1904, which was of great economic importance to the petroleum industry; author of many papers and of the basic text *Foraminifera, Their Classification and Economic Use* (1928 and subsequent editions). In 1923, he built his own laboratory in Sharon, Mass., where he continued his research, offering use of its facilities to students at Harvard, Radcliffe, and Massachusetts Institute of Technology. For a number of years, he served as a lecturer at Harvard, refusing any stipend.

CUSHMAN, JOSHUA (*b. Halifax, Mass., 1761; d. Augusta, Maine, 1834*), Congregational clergyman. Congressman, Democrat, from Massachusetts and Maine, 1819–25.

CUSHMAN, PAULINE (*b. New Orleans, La., 1833; d. San Francisco, Calif., 1893*), Union spy, actress.

CUSHMAN, ROBERT (*b. Canterbury, England, ca. 1579; d. England, 1625*), an organizer of the Pilgrim migration to America. With John Carver, made financial arrangements with English merchants which the Pilgrims accepted at Leiden, 1620.

CUSHMAN, SUSAN WEBB (*b. Boston, Mass., 1822; d. Liverpool, England, 1859*), actress. Younger sister of Charlotte Cushman, with whose companies she acted until 1848.

CUSHMAN, VERA CHARLOTTE SCOTT (*b. Ottawa, Ill., 1876; d. Savannah, Ga., 1946*), organizer and leader in the YWCA. Graduated Smith College, 1898. Beginning her association with the YWCA while a student at Smith, she had a leading role in the establishment of its national body, and thereafter served as officer and benefactor, both of the national organization and of the YWCA of New York City. Chairman of the YWCA service activities council during World War I; vice president of the World Council, 1924–38.

CUSHNY, ARTHUR ROBERTSON (*b. Fochabers, Scotland, 1866; d. near Edinburgh, 1926*), physician. Educated in Scotland and on the Continent, he taught pharmacology at the University of Michigan from 1893 until 1905 when he accepted the chair of pharmacology at University College, London. In 1918 he succeeded Sir Thomas Fraser at Edinburgh. Cushny's contributions to pharmacology were outstanding. His *Text-Book of Pharmacology and Therapeutics* (1899) has held the field in English almost without a rival; he was author, among other works, of *The Action and Uses in Medicine of Digitalis and Its Allies* (1925) and *The Biological Relation of Optically Isometric Substances* (1926).

CUSTER, GEORGE ARMSTRONG (*b. New Rumley, Ohio, 1839; d. Little Bighorn, 1876*), soldier. Graduated West Point, 1861; rose by merit to major general of volunteers in Civil War. Appointed lieutenant colonel, Seventh Cavalry (regular army), 1866, Custer saw hard service against hostile Plains Indians, 1867–70 and 1873–75. His frank testimony about frauds in the Indian Bureau brought him disfavor of President Grant and removal from independent command in the 1876 expedition to round up hostile Sioux and Cheyenne; he was restored to command of his regiment and permitted to serve in the expedition under General Terry. Encountering a great body of Indians encamped on the Little Bighorn River in present-day southern Montana, Custer attacked them and was defeated, dying with his entire immediate command in a battle which is still the subject of violent controversy. He was author of memoirs of his Civil War service and of *My Life on the Plains* (1874).

CUSTIS, GEORGE WASHINGTON PARKE (*b. 1781; d. Arlington, Va., 1857*), playwright. Son of John P. Custis, George Washington's stepson; father-in-law of Robert E. Lee. Wrote and produced several plays; the most successful, *Pocahontas, or The Settlers of Virginia*, was produced at Philadelphia, 1830.

CUTBUSH, JAMES (*b. Philadelphia, Pa., 1788; d. West Point, N.Y., 1823*), chemist. Author of *Philosophy of Experimental Chemistry* (1813), one of the first chemical textbooks published by an American; professor of chemistry, West Point, 1820–23.

CUTLER, CARROLL (*b. Windham, N.H., 1829; d. 1894*), Congregational clergyman, educator. Graduated Yale, 1854. President, Western Reserve College (later University), 1871–88.

CUTLER, ELLIOTT CARR (*b. Bangor, Maine, 1888; d. Brookline, Mass., 1947*), surgeon, educator. Raised in Brookline, Mass. B.A., Harvard, 1909; M.D., Harvard Medical School, 1913. Interned under Harvey Cushing at Peter Bent Brigham Hospital; served briefly in Paris, 1915, with American Ambulance Hospital; resident at Massachusetts General Hospital; studied immunology at Rockefeller Institute. Returned to France after American entry into World War I. Later was resident surgeon under Cushing at Brigham; associate in surgery, 1921; chairman of the Department of Surgery at Harvard. Professor of surgery at Western Reserve University, 1924–32; active role in the development of the medical school. Succeeded Cushing as Moseley professor of surgery at Harvard, 1932, and as surgeon in chief of Brigham. His Massachusetts system for securing adequate medical help for civilians in the event of disasters during World War II became the model system for the nation. Recalled to military duty, 1942, he served eventually as chief of the professional services division of the European theater of operations. His notable interests in surgical practice were thoracotomy, cardiac surgery, and the treatment of lung abscess.

CUTLER, JAMES GOOLD (*b. Albany, N.Y., 1848; d. Rochester, N.Y., 1927*), architect, inventor, banker. Devised, patented (1883), and manufactured the mail chute used in modern office buildings.

CUTLER, LIZZIE PETIT (*b. Milton, Va., 1831; d. Richmond, Va., 1902*). Author of *Light and Darkness, a Story of Fashionable Life* (1855) and other fiction.

CUTLER, MANASSEH (*b. Killingly, Conn., 1742; d. Hamilton, Mass., 1823*), Congregational clergyman, botanist, Ohio colonizer. Graduated Yale, 1765; studied law and divinity; was ordained, 1771, as pastor of church in Ipswich Hamlet, later Hamilton, Mass.; served as chaplain in Revolution. A versatile man, Cutler practiced medicine and undertook various scientific investigations; he prepared the first systematic account of New England flora. He is best known for his part in founding the Ohio Co., securing for it from Congress in 1787 the right to take up a million and a half acres of land around the junction of the Ohio and Muskingum rivers at cost of about eight cents an acre. He visited the Ohio settlements in 1788–89.

CUTLER, TIMOTHY (*b. Charlestown, Mass., 1684; d. Boston, Mass., 1765*), Congregational and Episcopal clergyman. Graduated Harvard, 1701. Rector of Yale College, 1719–22. After taking Episcopal orders in England, 1723, he served as rector of Christ Church, Boston, Mass., until his death.

CUTTER, CHARLES AMMI (*b. Boston, Mass., 1837; d. Walpole, N.H., 1903*), librarian. Graduated Harvard, 1855. Assisted in Harvard library, 1860–68; librarian of the Boston Athenaeum, 1868–93. Compiled the *Catalogue* of the Athenaeum library (1874–82) and published *Rules for a Printed Dictionary Catalogue* (1875).

CUTTER, EPHRAIM (*b. Woburn, Mass., 1832; d. West Falmouth, Mass., 1917*), physician, inventor of medical and surgical appliances.

CUTTER, GEORGE WASHINGTON (*b. Quebec, Canada, 1801; d. Washington, D.C., 1865*), lawyer, poet.

CUTTING, BRONSON MURRAY (*b. Oakdale, N.Y., 1888; d. Atlanta, Mo., 1935*), U.S. senator from New Mexico, 1927–35. Liberal Republican; vigorous critic of President Hoover's administration; supported the New Deal.

CUTTING, JAMES AMBROSE (*b. Hanover, N.H., 1814; d. Worcester, Mass., 1867*), inventor. Patented the "ambro-type" (1854), an improvement of the collodion process of photography designed to insure greater permanency of picture.

CUTTING, ROBERT FULTON (*b. New York, N.Y., 1852; d. 1934*), financier, New York civic leader, philanthropist.

CUYLER, THEODORE (*b. Poughkeepsie, N.Y., 1819; d. Philadelphia, Pa., 1876*), lawyer. Won fame for his brilliant advocacy in Christiana treason case, 1851. He later became general counsel for the Pennsylvania Railroad.

CUYLER, THEODORE LEDYARD (*b. Aurora, N.Y., 1822; d. 1909*), Presbyterian clergyman, writer. Principal pastorate at Lafayette Avenue Church, Brooklyn, N.Y., *post* 1860. Conservative and a noted preacher.

D

DABLON, CLAUDE (*b. Dieppe, France, 1618 or 1619; d. Quebec, Canada, 1697*), Jesuit missionary. Served among Iroquois, 1655–58; associate of Allouez and Marquette on Ottawa mission and in Wisconsin; superior of Canadian missions, 1671–80 and 1686–93.

DABNEY, CHARLES WILLIAM (*b. Hampden-Sydney, Va., 1855; d. Asheville, N.C., 1945*), chemist, agriculturist, educator. Son of Robert L. Dabney. B.A., Hampden-Sydney College, 1873; studied sciences at graduate school, University of Virginia; Ph.D., Göttingen, 1880. North Carolina state chemist, and director of state agricultural experiment station, 1880–87. President, University of Tennessee, 1887–94 and 1897–1904; assistant secretary, U.S. Department of Agriculture, 1894–97. President, University of Cincinnati, 1904–20. A strong proponent of scientific and professional studies and of the improvement and democratization of education in the South.

DABNEY, RICHARD (*b. Louisa Co., Va., 1787; d. Louisa Co., 1825*), poet. His *Poems* (1812, 1815) include miscellaneous lyrics and translations and reveal more intellectual vigor than metrical talent.

DABNEY, ROBERT LEWIS (*b. Louisa Co., Va., 1820; d. Victoria, Tex., 1898*), Presbyterian theologian, teacher, author. A powerful defender of religious orthodoxy and the Confederate cause; taught at Union Theological Seminary, Virginia, 1853–84, and at University of Texas.

DABNEY, THOMAS SMITH GREGORY (*b. King and Queen Co., Va., 1798; d. 1885*), planter. Removed to Hinds Co., Miss., 1835. Embodiment of southern patrician character in reverses of post–Civil War years.

DABNEY, VIRGINIUS (*b. Gloucester Co., Va., 1835; d. New York, N.Y., 1894*), teacher, author. Son of Thomas S. G. Dabney. A whimsical, shrewd, and wise critic of post–Civil War America, he wrote *The Story of Don Miff* (1886).

DABOLL, NATHAN (*b. Groton, Conn., 1750; d. 1818*), teacher of navigation, mathematician. Edited the *New England Almanack*; *post* 1773 was author of several textbooks.

DABROWSKI, JOSEPH (*b. Zoltance, Poland, 1842; d. Detroit, Mich., 1903*), Roman Catholic priest. Came to America, 1869. Pastor in Wisconsin, 1870–83; founded Sts. Cyril and Methodius Seminary in Detroit, 1884, for training Polish priests in America.

DA COSTA, JACOB MENDEZ (*b. St. Thomas, Virgin Islands, 1833; d. Villanova, Pa., 1900*), physician. A skillful and honored teacher and clinician, Da Costa taught at Jefferson Medical College. Philadelphia, 1872–91. His *Medical Diagnosis* (1864) influenced teaching and clinical methods.

DA COSTA, JOHN CHALMERS (*b. Washington, D.C., 1863; d. Philadelphia, Pa., 1933*), surgeon. Graduated University of Pennsylvania, 1882; M.D., Jefferson Medical College, 1885. Interned at Philadelphia General Hospital and served as assistant physician in Pennsylvania Hospital for the Insane. Starting as assistant demonstrator of anatomy at Jefferson Medical College, he advanced in 1907 to Gross professor of surgery, a position he filled until his death. Known as a great teacher, he made a unique contribution to the literature of surgery with his textbook *A Manual of Modern Surgery, General and Operative* (1894). Encyclopedic in scope and detail, it was the most used text in surgery for 40 years.

DAEGER, ALBERT THOMAS (*b. North Vernon, Ind., 1872; d. Santa Fe, N.Mex., 1932*), Franciscan missionary to the Indians and Mexicans of New Mexico; archbishop of Santa Fe, 1919–32.

DAFT, LEO (*b. Birmingham, England, 1843; d. 1922*), electrical engineer, inventor. Came to America, 1866. His firm supplied apparatus for the first New York Power Co. distributing stations and, for the Massachusetts Electric Power Co., built the first (1884) complete central station for the generation and distribution of electricity for power purposes on a commercial scale. Daft began electric-railroad experiments in 1883; in 1885 he built in Baltimore the first commercially operated electric railroad in the United States. He also invented a process now generally used for vulcanizing rubber onto metal.

DAGG, JOHN LEADLEY (*b. near Middleburg, Va., 1794; d. Hayneville, Ala., 1884*), Baptist clergyman, educator. President, Mercer University, 1844–56.

DAGGETT, DAVID (*b. Attleboro, Mass., 1764; d. New Haven, Conn., 1851*), lawyer, politician, jurist. Best known for his opinion in the case of Prudence Crandall (1833) that free blacks were not citizens of the United States.

DAGGETT, ELLSWORTH (*b. Canandaigua, N.Y., 1845; d. 1923*), mining engineer. Graduated Sheffield Scientific School at Yale, 1864. The first U.S. surveyor general of Utah, Daggett was among the earliest American hydrometallurgists and an advocate of state irrigation projects.

DAGGETT, NAPHTALI (*b. Attleboro, Mass., 1727; d. New Haven, Conn., 1780*), Congregational clergyman. First incumbent of first professorship in Yale College, and its acting president, 1766–77.

DAHL, THEODOR HALVORSON (*b. Baastad, Norway, 1845; d. Minneapolis, Minn., 1923*), Lutheran clergyman. A successful home missionary among Norwegians in America; active in forming the United Norwegian Lutheran Church of America.

DAHLGREN, JOHN ADOLPHUS BERNARD (*b. Philadelphia, Pa., 1809; d. Washington, D.C., 1870*), naval officer, inventor. After service at sea and with the Coast Survey, Dahlgren was assigned to ordnance duty in Washington, 1847, and became chief, Bureau of Ordnance, 1862. His innovations revolutionized naval armament. Two guns of his design, cast-iron and smoothbore, distinguished by great thickness at the breach rapidly diminishing from trunnions to muzzle, were called "Dahlgrens." He commanded at the Washington Navy Yard, 1861–63. Promoted rear admiral, 1863, he succeeded Du Pont in command of the South Atlantic Blockading Squadron, 1863–65.

DAHLGREN, SARAH MADELEINE VINTON (*b. Gallipolis, Ohio, 1825; d. Washington, D.C., 1898*), author. Married John A. B. Dahlgren, 1865.

DAKIN, HENRY DRYSDALE (*b. London, England, 1880; d. Scarborough-on-Hudson, N.Y., 1952*), biochemist. Studied at Victoria University at Leeds and at Heidelburg University. Immigrated to the U.S. in 1905. Working in a private laboratory on the Hudson River, Dakin made significant contributions to enzyme chemistry, intermediate metabolism of fatty acids, protein chemistry, and hormone chemistry, doing some of the first work in synthesizing adrenaline. He never held academic positions nor did he collaborate with colleagues for long periods of time.

DAKIN, JAMES HARRISON (*b. Hudson, N.Y., 1806; d. Baton Rouge, La., 1852*), architect. Pupil of Alexander Jackson Davis. Practiced in Louisiana, *post* 1835, where he designed, among other buildings, St. Patrick's Church, New Orleans, and the Louisiana Capitol.

DALCHO, FREDERICK (*b. London, England, 1770; d. Charleston, S.C., 1836*), physician, Episcopal clergyman, author of *Ahiman Rezon* (1807), a handbook for Freemasons.

DALE, CHESTER (*b. New York, N.Y., 1883; d. New York, 1962*), investment banker and art collector. As a member of the New York Stock Exchange (1918), he became wealthy consolidating power companies and selling their stocks and bonds to the public. With his first wife, Maud Dale, he began to collect American paintings. The Dale Collection, the bulk of which was left to the National Gallery of Art in Washington, D.C., came to include works by Braque, Corot, Cézanne, Dali, Degas, Matisse, Modigliani, Monet, Picasso, Renoir, Toulouse-Lautrec, and van Gogh.

DALE, MAUD MURRAY THOMPSON (*b. Rochester, N.Y., 1875; d. Southampton, N.Y., 1953*), collector. Studied at the Art Students League of New York. Together with her second husband, Chester Dale, Maud Dale collected one of the finest groupings of late-nineteenth- and early-twentieth-century French art in America. In 1931, under the auspices of the French Institute in New York, she opened a gallery, The Museum of French Art, French Institute in the U.S. It included exhibitions of Picasso, Braque, Léger, Degas, Renoir, and Fantin-Latour. The collection was donated to the National Gallery in Washington.

DALE, RICHARD (*b. Norfolk Co., Va., 1756; d. Philadelphia, Pa., 1826*), naval officer. Served with distinction in the American Revolution; was first lieutenant of *Bon Homme Richard* in fight with *Serapis*, 1779. A merchant captain, 1783–94, he returned to the navy but retired in 1802 after a number of disputes over rank.

DALE, SAMUEL (*b. Rockbridge Co., Va., 1772; d. Lauderdale Co., Miss., 1841*), pioneer, soldier. Removed as a boy to frontier Georgia. A scout and trader, he became a guide for immigrants to Mississippi *ca.* 1810 and an Indian fighter; he was later a legislator in both Alabama and Mississippi.

DALE, THOMAS (*d. India, 1619*), baronet, soldier, colonizer, naval commander. Marshal of Virginia, 1611–16. Although the colonists disliked his stern measures, he left Virginia tranquil and prosperous.

DALL, CAROLINE WELLS HEALEY (*b. Boston, Mass., 1822; d. Washington, D.C., 1912*), reformer, woman's rights publicist.

DALL, WILLIAM HEALEY (*b. Boston, Mass., 1845; d. 1927*), naturalist. A specialist in mollusks, he served with the Geological Survey, 1884–1923, and was author of, among other books, *Alaska and Its Resources* (1870).

DALLAS, ALEXANDER JAMES (*b. Jamaica, West Indies, 1759; d. Philadelphia, Pa., 1817*), lawyer, statesman. Immigrated to the United States, 1783; became a lawyer in Philadelphia. Appointed secretary of Pennsylvania, 1791; commissioned U.S. attorney for eastern district of Pennsylvania, 1801. A moderate Democratic-Republican with a record of ability and skill. Dallas became secretary of the treasury, 1814. His measures restored public confidence and provided revenue for the bankrupt treasury. His recommendations in regard to a protective tariff were the basis of American policy for the next 30 years. Dallas resigned the secretaryship in 1816 and returned to practice of law.

DALLAS, GEORGE MIFFLIN (*b. Philadelphia, Pa., 1792; d. Philadelphia, 1864*), lawyer, statesman, diplomat. Son of Alexander J. Dallas. Graduated Princeton, 1810. Secretary to Albert Gallatin on mission to Russia, 1813. After holding several local offices in Pennsylvania, he served as U.S. senator, Democrat, 1831–33, and as minister to Russia, 1837–39. He was vice president of the United States, 1845–49. As minister to Great Britain, 1856–61, Dallas secured a convention clarifying Central American problems under the Clayton-Bulwer Treaty and obtained a final disavowal of the long-disputed right of search.

DALLIN, CYRUS EDWIN (*b. Springvillle, Utah, 1861; d. Arlington Heights, Mass., 1944*), sculptor. Apprentice in Boston, Mass., studio of Truman H. Bartlett; studied in Paris with H. M. Chapu, 1888–90. Practiced and taught thereafter, principally in Boston. Among the first sculptors to choose the American Indian as his subject, Dallin was one of the most successful in portraying them realistically and with dignity.

D'ALOES, CLAUDE JEAN. *See* ALLOUEZ, CLAUDE JEAN.

DALTON, JOHN CALL (*b. Chelmsford, Mass., 1825; d. 1889*), physiologist. Graduated Harvard, 1844; Harvard Medical, 1847. First American physician to devote life to experimental physiology.

DALTON, ROBERT (*b. Cass Co., Mo.[?], 1867; d. Coffeyville, Kans., 1892*), desperado. With his brothers Grattan and Emmett, began as a horse thief in Kansas *ante* 1890; later robbed trains in California and Oklahoma.

DALY, ARNOLD. *See* DALY, PETER CHRISTOPHER ARNOLD.

DALY, AUGUSTIN. *See* DALY, JOHN AUGUSTIN.

DALY, CHARLES PATRICK (*b. New York, N.Y., 1816; d. Sag Harbor, N.Y., 1899*), jurist. Outstanding judge of common pleas, New York City, 1844–85; chief justice, 1858–85. A Democrat, he was legal adviser to Lincoln and W. H. Seward on many occasions.

DALY, JOHN AUGUSTIN (*b. Plymouth, N.C., 1838; d. Paris, France, 1899*), playwright, producer. Author of *Under the Gaslight* (1867), and author and adapter of many other dramas; proprietor of Daly's Theater, New York, whose company and productions were celebrated for taste, 1869–99.

DALY, MARCUS (*b. Ireland, 1841; d. 1900*), miner, capitalist. Came to America, 1856. Organized Anaconda Copper Mining Co. His feud with William A. Clark dominated Montana society and politics from 1888 to 1900.

DALY, PETER CHRISTOPHER ARNOLD (*b. Brooklyn, N.Y., 1875; d. New York, N.Y., 1927*), actor. His productions of G. B. Shaw's plays in New York, 1903–05, marked an important step forward in the American theater.

DALY, REGINALD ALDWORTH (*b. Napanee, Ontario, 1871; d. Cambridge, Mass., 1957*), geologist, petrologist. Studied at the University of Toronto and Harvard University (Ph.D., 1896). Professor of geology at M.I.T. from 1907 to 1912 and at Harvard from 1912 to 1942. An expert in igneous rocks and petrology, Daly's works include *Igneous Rocks and Their Origin* (1914), *The Changing World of the Ice Age* (1934), and *The Floor of the Ocean* (1942). President of the Geological Society of America (1932); member of the National Academy of Sciences from 1925.

DALZELL, JOHN (*b. New York, N.Y., 1845; d. Altadena, Calif., 1927*), lawyer, parliamentarian. Congressman, Republican, from Pennsylvania, 1886–1912; dominant in Rules Committee of the House.

DALZELL, ROBERT M. (*b. near Belfast, Ireland, 1793; d. Rochester, N.Y., 1873*), millwright, inventor. Introduced and perfected the elevator system for storing grain and meal which is now used in all large pots.

DAMON, RALPH SHEPARD (*b. Franklin, N.H., 1897; d. Mineola, N.Y., 1956*), airline executive. Studied at Harvard University. Joined Curtis Aeroplane and Motor Company in 1922; president (1935–36). Vice president of American Airlines from 1936 to 1941; president from 1945 to 1949. During World War II headed Republic Aviation's production of war planes. President of TWA from 1949 to 1956. Introduced air coach travel in 1949, which opened up flying to the mass market.

DAMROSCH, FRANK HEINO (*b. Breslau, Prussia [now Wrocław, Poland], 1859; d. New York, N.Y., 1937*), music educator. Son of Leopold Damrosch. Founder (with James Loeb) of Institute of Musical Art, 1905, later the undergraduate section of the Juilliard School.

DAMROSCH, LEOPOLD (*b. Posen, Poland, 1832; d. New York, N.Y., 1885*), conductor, composer, violinist. Came to America, 1871, as conductor of New York Arion Society. Active in many fields, he raised the standard of musical taste and appreciation in America.

DAMROSCH, WALTER JOHANNES (*b. Breslau, Prussia [now Wrocław, Poland], 1862; d. New York, N.Y., 1950*), musical conductor, composer. Son of Leopold Damrosch. Immigrated to America with his family in 1871. Attended public school in New York City and continued his musical studies principally with his father.

In 1887 he spent three months studying with Hans von Bülow. From the age of 14 he assisted Leopold. He also served as organist at Plymouth Church in Brooklyn (where Henry Ward Beecher was pastor), toured southern cities (1878) as accompanist for the violinist August Wilhelmj, and was named permanent conductor of the 300-voice Newark Harmonic Society. In 1882 he met Liszt at Weimar and attended the first performance of Wagner's *Parsifal* at Bayreuth.

Damrosch conducted German opera for the Metropolitan Opera Association after his father died. He was also asked by the Symphony Society and Oratorio Society to carry on his father's work as their conductor. He traveled to Europe to engage principals for a second season of German opera at the Metropolitan, including the conductor Anton Seidl and such singers as Lilli Lehmann, Max Alvary, and Emil Fischer. The Metropolitan in 1891 reverted to Italian and French opera, and Damrosch left.

In the winter of 1893–94 he successfully staged his own productions of Wagner's *Götterdämmerung* and *Die Walküre* at Carnegie Hall. He then formed his own Wagnerian company, the Damrosch Opera Company, which made its debut in the spring of 1895 at the Metropolitan Opera House. Except for a return to the Metropolitan to conduct the German repertoire for two seasons (1900–02) he put opera-conducting behind him after the turn of the century.

Damrosch produced his opera *The Scarlet Letter* in 1896 and began a second opera, *Cyrano*, but did not complete it until 1913, when it was produced by the Metropolitan. The song "Danny Deever" (to Kipling's poem) remains the best known of all his compositions.

Damrosch determined to establish an orchestra on a permanent basis in New York. Aided by a group of benefactors—led by Harry Harkness Flagler—he reorganized the New York Symphony Society and thus gained his permanent orchestra. He took the New York Symphony to every part of the United States.

During World War I, Damrosch went to France to conduct concerts for American troops and organized a school at Chaumont for training army bandmasters. The fruitful relationship established there between French and American musicians led Damrosch to urge his French friends to find a way to continue after the war. The French responded by establishing the summer music school at Fontainebleau, which was to contribute to the training of a number of America's most distinguished composers. The French government invited Damrosch to brin the New York Symphony to perform in France in 1920. Damrosch took his orchestra—the first American symphony orchestra to be heard in Europe—around the Continent in triumph. Damrosch took pride in introducing musical works to the American public—by both European and American composers. In 1891 he arranged for Tchaikovsky to come to New York to conduct his own music during a festival that inaugurated Carnegie Hall. Damrosch's musical convictions were nevertheless conservative. He was a pioneer in giving concerts for children.

In 1926, the New York Symphony merged with the Philharmonic-Symphony of New York. Damrosch retired but soon emerged to pioneer in a new field: radio broadcasting. He had conducted the New York Symphony in the first broadcast of an orchestral concert. The National Broadcasting Company (NBC) immediately asked him to broadcast a series of Saturday evening concerts in the winter of 1926–1927. NBC estimated a weekly audience of 4 million.

He then suggested a series for young people. On Oct. 26, 1928, Damrosch launched the NBC Music Appreciation Hour broadcasts, which he narrated and conducted until they were discontinued in 1942. The audience grew to over 7 million in the 1930's. Damrosch's grandfatherly "Good morning, my dear children" was familiar in every part of the United States.

In 1937 his opera *The Man Without a Country* was performed. A revised version of *Cyrano* was presented in a concert of the New York Philharmonic in 1941, and in 1942 Damrosch produced a new work, *The Opera Cloak*. His ballad *Dunkirk* was performed in 1943.

His autobiography, *My Musical Life*, was first published in 1923.

DANA, CHARLES ANDERSON (*b. Hinsdale, N.H., 1819; d. Dosoris Island, Glen Cove, N.Y., 1897*), newspaper editor. Matriculated Harvard, 1839; left in junior year because of failing eyesight. Spent five years at Brook Farm and became "the best all-round man" there. Joined staff of *New York Tribune* and stood second to Greeley when he resigned, 1862, to serve in the War Department. As reporter and observer, he gave valuable aid to Grant and Sherman. After an unsuccessful newspaper venture in Chicago, Dana became owner-editor of *New York Sun*, 1868. A perverse, cynical, and often reactionary leader of public opinion, he achieved high distinction as a news editor, especially emphasizing the human-interest story and cleverness of style and reporting technique.

DANA, CHARLES LOOMIS (*b. Woodstock. Vt., 1852; d. Harmon, N.Y., 1935*), neurologist. Brother of John C. Dana. M.D., Columbia University, 1876; College of Physicians and Surgeons, 1877. His clinical descriptions of combined scleroses of the spinal chord and observations of alcoholism are of outstanding importance.

DANA, EDWARD SALISBURY (*b. New Haven, Conn., 1849; d. 1935*), mineralogist. Son of James D. Dana. Graduated Yale, 1870; Ph.D., 1876. His revision (1892) of his father's *System of Mineralogy* (1837) has been, with its appendices, the standard reference in the field.

DANA, FRANCIS (*b. Charlestown, Mass., 1743; d. Cambridge, Mass., 1811*), diplomat, jurist. Son of Richard Dana; nephew of Edmund Trowbridge. Graduated Harvard, 1762; admitted to the bar, 1767. At first in favor of reconciliation with Great Britain, *post* 1776 he took a leading part in the Revolution and was secretary of legislation with John Adams in Paris, 1780. He spent 1781–83 in Russia vainly attempting to obtain recognition of the United States and a treaty. He was associate justice of Massachusetts supreme court, 1785–1806; from 1791 to 1806 he was chief justice of that body. A true Federalist, he supported the Alien and Sedition Acts and regarded Jeffersonians as a national menace.

DANA, JAMES (*b. Cambridge, Mass., 1735; d. New Haven, Conn., 1812*), Congregational clergyman. Leading character in the "Wallingford Controversy," 1758; pastor, First Church, New Haven, 1789–1805.

DANA, JAMES DWIGHT (*b. Utica, N.Y., 1813; d. 1895*), geologist, zoologist. Attended Yale, 1830–33; left to become instructor in the navy. Served as geologist and mineralogist with the U.S. South Seas Expedition under Captain Wilkes, 1838–42. Editor of the *American Journal of Science*. Professor of natural history at Yale, *post* 1849; professor of geology, 1864–90. Despite poor health, Dana was a tireless writer; in addition to his reports from the Wilkes expedition, he wrote standard texts, including *Manual of Geology* (1862) and *Textbook of Geology* (1864). Influential as teacher and scholar, Dana was America's foremost geologist throughout his active life.

DANA, JAMES FREEMAN (*b. Amherst, N.H., 1793; d. 1827*), chemist. Graduated Harvard, 1813. Brother of Samuel L. Dana. Taught chemistry at Harvard, Dartmouth, and the College of Physicians and Surgeons, New York.

DANA, JOHN COTTON (*b. Woodstock, Vt., 1856; d. New York, N.Y., 1929*), librarian, museum director, author, printer. Graduated Dartmouth, 1878. For reasons of health abandoned practice of law; after trials at engineering and newspaper work, became librarian in 1889 of the Denver (Colo.) Public Library, which flourished under his administration. In 1889 he became librarian of the City Library, Springfield, Mass., and in 1902 of the Newark (N.J.) Public Library. He greatly increased the circulation of the Newark library, making it the most effective institution of its kind in the United States. As director of the Newark Museum he made it as popular in its sphere as the library. Author of a standard textbook, *Library Primer* (1896), his pungent style is best represented in *Libraries: Addresses and Essays* (1916).

DANA, NAPOLEON JACKSON TECUMSEH (*b. Eastport, Maine, 1822; d. Portsmouth, N.H., 1905*), soldier, business executive.

Graduated West Point, 1842. Served in Mexican War and was Union major general of volunteers.

DANA, RICHARD (*b. Cambridge, Mass., 1700; d. Boston, Mass., 1772*), lawyer. Graduated Harvard, 1718. A leader at the bar, Dana was an original member of the Sons of Liberty and one of committee which investigated Boston Massacre, 1770.

DANA, RICHARD HENRY (*b. Cambridge, Mass., 1787; d. Boston, Mass., 1879*), poet, essayist. Son of Francis Dana. Educated at Harvard; received degree, 1808; admitted to bar, 1811, but soon abandoned law for literature. Many years associated with *North American Review*. Author of periodical *The Idle Man* (1821); *The Buccaneer and Other Poems* (1827); *Poems and Prose Writings* (1833, 1850).

DANA, RICHARD HENRY (*b. Cambridge, Mass., 1815; d. Rome, Italy, 1882*), author, lawyer. Son of Richard H. Dana (1787–1879). Graduated Harvard, 1837, having interrupted his course to sail around Cape Horn to California as a common sailor. His *Two Years Before the Mast* (1840), written from notes made during this voyage, is a lively, unconventional account of life at sea from the viewpoint of the forecastle which has attained classic stature. His manual, *The Seaman's Friend* (1841), became a standard work on maritime law. A founder of the Free-Soil party, Dana was deeply involved in the antislavery movement. In 1867–68, with William M. Evarts, he was counsel for the United States in the trial of Jefferson Davis. He died before completing projected study of international law.

DANA, SAMUEL LUTHER (*b. Amherst, N.H., 1795; d. Lowell, Mass., 1868*), chemist. Brother of James F. Dana. Introduced improvements in bleaching and calico-printing. Author of *A Muck Manual for Farmers* (1842), an early work on soil chemistry.

DANA, SAMUEL WHITTELSEY (*b. Wallingford, Conn., 1760; d. 1830*), lawyer, statesman. Son of James Dana. Congressman, Federalist, from Connecticut, 1797–1810; U.S. senator, 1810–21.

DANCEL, CHRISTIAN (*b. Cassel, Germany, 1847; d. Brooklyn, N.Y., 1898*), inventor of machines for sewing shoes. His work made the widely used Goodyear welt system a success.

DANDRIDGE, DOROTHY JEAN (*b. Cleveland, Ohio, 1922; d. West Hollywood, Calif., 1965*), singer and actress. Appeared as an extra in her first film, *A Day at the Races* (1937), with the Marx Brothers. With her sister Vivian and Etta Jones performed on Broadway and in nightclubs as the Dandridge Sisters. Dandridge's most important film was Otto Preminger's *Carmen Jones* (1954) for which she received an Academy Award nomination for best actress—the first black actress to be so cited for a leading role. Other films included *Island in the Sun* (1957) and *Porgy and Bess* (1959). For the most part Dandridge found herself limited to roles defined by racial stereotypes. Her autobiography is *Everything and Nothing* (1970).

DANDY, WALTER EDWARD (*b. Sedalia, Mo., 1886; d. Baltimore, Md., 1946*), neurological surgeon. B.A., University of Missouri, 1907; M.D., Johns Hopkins, 1910; M.A., Johns Hopkins, 1911. While assistant to Harvey Cushing in the Hunterian Laboratory of Experimental Medicine and later as Cushing's clinical assistant in neurosurgery at Johns Hopkins Hospital (1910–11), a lifelong personal conflict between them developed; Cushing would appear to have been the antagonist in their quarrel. Appointed to W. S. Halsted's service, Dandy became resident surgeon at the hospital (1916–18). *Post* 1918, although engaged in private practice, he held a succession of professorial posts in neurological surgery at Hopkins and served as visiting surgeon at the hospital. Established an international reputation in 1913, when he and Kenneth D. Blackfan published the first of their papers on the mechanism and pathology of hydrocephalus and its treatment by surgery. He introduced ventriculography, a diagnostic method that many regard as the greatest single contribution ever made to neurological surgery, and pneumoencephalography.

In 1922 Dandy announced a new surgical method that involved total extirpation of acoustic nerve tumors, and successful surgical treatment of trigeminal neuralgia was one of his most brilliant and original contributions. Two years later he introduced a curative operative procedure for glossopharyngeal neuralgia (tic douloureux).

Other accomplishments included development of an operation that would often permanently cure Ménière's disease, his surgical cures for intracranial aneurysms, and his demonstration that a ruptured vertebral disk can cause pain in the lower back and leg.

DANE, NATHAN (*b. Ipswich, Mass., 1752; d. Beverly, Mass., 1835*), lawyer, statesman. Graduated Harvard, 1778; admitted to the bar, 1782. Served in the General Court of Massachusetts, 1782–85. Elected to the Continental Congress, he helped draft the Northwest Ordinance and introduced the article prohibiting slavery in the Northwest Territory. An opponent of the federal Constitution, he retired from Congress, 1788, serving thereafter in the Massachusetts senate, 1790 and 1793–98. His *General Abridgment and Digest of American Law* (1823) was the first comprehensive compendium of law prepared and printed in North America.

DANENHOWER, JOHN WILSON (*b. Chicago, Ill., 1849; d. Annapolis, Md., 1887*), Arctic explorer. Graduated Annapolis, 1870. Author of *Lieutenant Danenhower's Narrative of the Jeannette* (1882).

DANFORTH, CHARLES (*b. Norton, Mass., 1797; d. Patterson, N.J., 1876*), inventor, manufacturer. Invented and developed the cap spinner, an improvement in spinning frames; headed the Danforth locomotive building works, 1852–71.

DANFORTH, MOSELEY ISAAC (*b. Hartford, Conn., 1800; d. 1862*), engraver, painter.

DANFORTH, THOMAS (*b. Framlingham, England, 1623; d. 1699*), deputy governor of Massachusetts, 1679–86. An early supporter and treasurer of Harvard College and a leader of the antiprerogative party.

DANFORTH, THOMAS (*b. Taunton, Mass., 1703; d. ca. 1786*), pewterer. Ancestor of the two largest pewtering families in America, the Danforths and the Boardmans.

DANIEL, JOHN MONCURE (*b. Stafford Co., Va., 1825; d. Richmond, Va., 1865*), journalist, diplomat. Editor of the *Richmond Examiner*, 1847–53 and 1861–65. An ardent secessionist.

DANIEL, JOHN WARWICK (*b. Lynchburg, Va., 1842; d. 1910*), lawyer, Confederate soldier. U.S. senator, Democrat, from Virginia, 1885–1910.

DANIEL, PETER VIVIAN (*b. Stafford Co., Va., 1784; d. Richmond, Va., 1860*), jurist. Associate justice, U.S. Supreme Court, 1841–60.

DANIELS, FRANK ALBERT (*b. Dayton, Ohio, 1856; d. West Palm Beach, Fla., 1935*), musical comedy star. Made his reputation in Hoyt's *The Rag Baby* (1884) and Victor Herbert's first hit, *The Wizard of the Nile* (1895).

DANIELS, FRED HARRIS (*b. Hanover Center, N.H., 1853; d. 1913*), engineer, metallurgist. Inventor of devices for manufacturing steel rods and wire which made possible faster, less costly production.

DANIELS, JOSEPHUS (*b. Washington, N.C., 1862; d. Raleigh, N.C., 1948*), newspaper editor, cabinet officer, diplomat. Raised in Wilson, N.C., where his widowed mother was a seamstress and the village postmistress. Attended a one-room school and the Wilson Collegiate Institute. Published an amateur newspaper, the *Cornucopia*. In 1880 Daniels left school to become editor of the *Wilson Advance*. By 1885 he was a partner in two other rural weeklies and was elected president of the State Press Association.

Daniels spent the summer of 1885 studying law at the University of North Carolina, his only experience with higher education. He thereafter was one of the university's most devoted backers, and was a university trustee for 47 years. Daniels passed the bar examination in October 1885 but never practiced. Backed by Julian S. Carr, a wealthy Durham banker and tobacco manufacturer, he instead took over the *Raleigh State Chronicle*. Daniel's reform crusades and lively editorials soon revived the paper and attracted attention to him. He also took an increasing interest in Democratic politics, and in 1887 he was awarded the contract of state printer. In Raleigh he formed lifelong friendships with other young idealists.

Married in 1889, he started the *North Carolinian*. He used his political connections to secure governmental posts in Washington in the Cleveland administration, first as chief of the appointments division and then as chief clerk in the Department of the Interior. He returned to North Carolina to buy the bankrupt *Raleigh News and Observer* in 1894, with the backing of Carr and other friends.

Daniels was henceforth associated with what North Carolinians soon nicknamed the "Nuisance and Disturber." The leading voice of reform in North Carolina and the upper South and a fervent partisan of the progressive wing of the Democratic party, the *News and Observer* also played a leading role in the disfranchisement of North Carolina blacks in 1900.

Beginning in 1896 Daniels served on the Democratic National Committee. A close friend of William Jennings Bryan, he campaigned hard for him in his bids for the presidency. His party loyalty also led him to take charge of publicity for the 1904 campaign. Daniels early became a supporter of Woodrow Wilson and was instrumental in getting North Carolina Democrats to endorse him. He was floor manager at the Baltimore convention and national director of publicity in the campaign.

Daniels was appointed secretary of the navy and was one of only three cabinet members to serve throughout both of Wilson's terms. Daniels was a highly innovative secretary and instituted a number of significant reforms. He is regarded as one of the few great navy secretaries. He was also probably the most controversial member of Wilson's cabinet and, for a time, the most unpopular. It was charged that Daniels, a near pacifist, inadequately prepared the navy for possible action in World War I. He was investigated by a Senate subcommittee in 1920, but the findings of the highly partisan hearing were inconclusive. Daniels' enemies sometimes received quiet encouragement from his ambitious young assistant secretary, Franklin D. Roosevelt. Daniels overlooked his subordinate's occasional disloyalty, and Roosevelt increasingly respected the older man's sound political judgment, if not always his naval policies.

Returning to his Raleigh newspaper in 1921, Daniels continued to play a prominent role in state and national Democratic politics. He fought the Ku Klux Klan and championed child labor laws, the League of Nations, and the World Court. He reluctantly supported Alfred E. Smith for president despite Smith's opposition to Prohibition. Daniels gave much more enthusiastic backing to Franklin D. Roosevelt. After declining to head a proposed new transportation agency, Daniels settled for the ambassadorship to Mexico, in which post he was a great success. When Mexico expropriated American oil holdings in 1938, he almost single-handedly prevented a diplomatic rupture.

Daniels returned to Raleigh in 1941. He continued to take an active interest in the *News and Observer* and in state and national affairs until his death.

DANIELS, WINTHROP MORE (*b. Dayton, Ohio, 1867; d. Saybrook, Conn., 1944*), economist. B.A., Princeton, 1888; M.A., 1890. Taught political economy at Princeton *post* 1892, and was one of the "young faculty" group led by Woodrow Wilson; served on editorial boards of the *Nation* and the *New York Evening Post*. Appointed to New Jersey Board of Public Utility Commissioners, 1911; served on Interstate Commerce Commission, 1914–23, in which post his aversion to theories and insistence on commonsense realism caused him to be branded a reactionary by reformers. Cuyler professor of transportation, Yale, 1923–35.

DANNREUTHER, GUSTAV (*b. Cincinnati, Ohio, 1853; d. 1923*), violinist, conductor, teacher. Founded Beethoven (later Dannreuther) String Quartet, 1884.

DANON, IDA MAUD (*b. Milwaukee, Wis., 1877; d. Watertown, Mass., 1960*), social worker, medical reformer. Studied briefly at the University of Minnesota and at the Boston (Simmons) School of Social Work. From 1908 to 1945, head of social services for the Massachusetts General Hospital. Wrote *Social Work in Hospitals* in 1913; helped found the American Association of Hospital Social Workers in 1918, president 1920–21; delegate to the White House Conference on Child Health and Protection (1930–31); vice president of the National Conference of Social Work (1938–39). Canon was instrumental in shaping the field of medical social work through her teaching, writings, and forming new programs for many American cities.

DA PONTE, LORENZO (*b. Ceneda, Italy, 1749; d. New York, N.Y., 1838*), poet, librettist, expositor of Italian culture in America. After an adventurous youth, Da Ponte was appointed "Poet to the Italian Theater" in Vienna. As librettist for Mozart he wrote *Le Nozze di Figaro* (1786), *Don Giovanni* (1787), and *Cosí Fan Tutte* (1790). Da Ponte left Vienna for London and in 1805 immigrated to America, where he succeeded as a teacher of Italian after numerous business reverses. Appointed professor of Italian literature at Columbia College in 1825, he imported Italian books, encouraged the study of Dante, and furthered Italian opera in America.

DARBY, JOHN (*b. North Adams, Mass., 1804; d. New York, N.Y., 1877*), educator. Graduated Williams, 1831. Author of *A Botany of the Southern States* (1841), an authoritative manual for the flora of that area, and other textbooks.

DARBY, WILLIAM (*b. Lancaster County, Pa., 1775; d. 1854*), geographer. Darby's surveys and researches were basis for John Melish's map of the United States (1818). Author of *A Tour from . . . New York to Detroit* (1819), and author or editor of many other geographical and statistical studies, 1816–41.

DARE, VIRGINIA (*b. Roanoke, Va., 1587*), the first English child born in America.

DARGAN, EDMUND STROTHER (*b. Montgomery Co., N.C., 1805; d. Mobile, Ala., 1879*), jurist, congressman. Judge, Alabama Supreme Court, 1847–52; chief justice, 1849–52.

DARGAN, EDWIN PRESTON (*b. Barboursville, Va., 1879; d. Chicago, Ill., 1940*), educator. Professor of French literature, University of Chicago, 1911–40; Balzac scholar.

DARKE, WILLIAM (*b. Pennsylvania, 1736; d. 1801*), soldier. Raised near present Shepherdstown, W.Va. Served ably in Revolution; commanded left wing in St. Clair's defeat near Fort Wayne, 1791.

DARLEY, FELIX OCTAVIUS CARR (*b. Philadelphia, Pa., 1822; d. 1888*), illustrator. Early work appeared in periodicals. Facility in caricature shown in work for Carey & Hart's "Library of American Humorous Works" (1840's); displayed more serious ability in *Scenes in Indian Life* (1843) and in illustrations for Judd's *Margaret* and for works by Irving and Cooper. Prolific, versatile, and always a careful craftsman. Darley had an essentially American genius and was at his best in depicting American scenes and characters.

DARLING, FLORA ADAMS (*b. Lancaster, N.H., 1840; d. New York, N.Y., 1910*). Cofounder of Daughters of the American Revolution, 1890; founder of two similar patriotic organizations.

DARLING, HENRY (*b. Reading, Pa., 1823; d. Clinton, N.Y., 1891*), Presbyterian clergyman. Pastor at Albany, N.Y.; Hudson, N.Y.; and Philadelphia, Pa. President, Hamilton College, 1881–91.

DARLING, JAY NORWOOD ("DING") (*b. Norwood, Mich., 1876; d. Des Moines, Iowa, 1962*), cartoonist and conservationist. Graduate of Beloit College (1900). Reported and produced sketches for the *Journal* in Sioux City, Iowa (1900–06), then became cartoonist for the Des Moines *Register and Leader*. He worked for the *New York Globe* syndicate, 1911–13, then returned to the *Register* until 1949. His cartoons appeared in some 130 newspapers nationally, and he twice won Pulitzer Prizes (1923, 1943). He published *Ding Goes to Russia* (1932) and *The Cruise of the Bouncing Betsy* (1937). An activist for the preservation of land and wildlife, Darling served on the Iowa Fish and Game Commission, was chief of the U.S. Bureau of Biological Survey (1934–36), and became the first president of the National Wildlife Federation in 1936.

DARLING, SAMUEL TAYLOR (*b. Harrison, N.J., 1872; d. near Beirut, Syria, 1925*), pathologist, authority on tropical medicine. Graduated M.D., Baltimore College of Physicians, 1903. Joined Isthmian Canal Commission, 1906, and served as chief of laboratories at the Panama Canal Zone until 1915. Appointed, 1915, to the staff of the International Health Board, he studied the cause of anemia common in Southeast Asia. After a period of teaching he became director of the field laboratory for malaria research under the International Health Board. Darling's study of sanitation helped make possible the construction of the Panama Canal. He also contributed significantly to the knowledge and control of hookworm disease.

DARLINGTON, WILLIAM (*b. Dilworthtown, Pa., 1782; d. 1863*), physician, botanist. Wrote *Florula Cestrica* (1826) and memoirs of William Baldwin, John Bartram, and Humphrey Marshall.

DARROW, CLARENCE SEWARD (*b. near Kinsman, Ohio, 1857; d. Chicago, Ill., 1938*), lawyer, social reformer. Attended Allegheny College and law school of University of Michigan; was admitted to bar in Ohio, 1878. Reared in traditions of 19th-century rationalism and self-educated in liberal social doctrines of his time, Darrow embodied a variety of intellectual influences; these included skepticism in religion and philosophy, determinism in psychology, a firm faith in evolutionary doctrine, and an attitude in politics which drew on elements of progressive Democracy, socialism, and anarchism. After nine years' practice in small Ohio towns, he removed to Chicago, Ill., 1887, where his professional rise was rapid. Among his better-known partners were

John P. Altgeld (1897–1902) and Edgar Lee Masters (1903–1911). Successful in civil practice, he lost his first major criminal case (the appeal of the murderer of Carter H. Harrison, 1894) but soon won wide repute in handling labor cases. Among his principal defense efforts in this field were the cases of Eugene V. Debs (argued 1895), William D. Haywood (1906–1907), and the McNamara brothers (1911). Gradually entering the third phase of his career, criminal law, Darrow was counsel in a number of lesser cases but achieved national publicity in the Loeb-Leopold murder case (1924), the Scopes trial in Tennessee (1925), and the Massie trial (Honolulu, Hawaii, 1932). Basing his jury appeals on his view that men are the victims of social and physiological forces which they cannot control, he was successful in making atrocious crimes appear comprehensible; he was also adept at jury selection and was painstaking in pretrial investigations, and in the hope of securing public understanding and sympathy for his clients he deliberately tried his cases in the newspaper headlines. Cherishing as he did the independent rural society into which he had been born, he never could adapt himself to monopolistic and bureaucratic industrial capitalism; out of this basic dilemma arose the many contradictions in thought which appeared in his writings and speeches.

DART, HENRY PALAUCHÉ (*b. Fort St. Philip, La., 1858; d. New Orleans, La., 1934*), lawyer. An outstanding trial advocate; promoted study of Louisiana colonial history.

DARTON, NELSON HORATIO (*b. Brooklyn, N.Y., 1865; d. Chevy Chase, Md., 1948*), chemist, geologist. Educated privately; opened his own consulting laboratory at age 15. Associated with U.S. Geological Survey, 1886–1936 (with U.S. Bureau of Mines, 1910–13). Author of a bibliography of North American geology (USGS) *Bulletin* no. 172, 1896, which initiated the annual *Index to North American Geology*. Made extensive field studies within and outside of the United States. A master of structural geology, he mapped about one-fifth of the nation topographically and about one-quarter geologically.

DARWELL, JANE (*b. Palmyra, Mo., 1880; d. Woodland Hills, Calif., 1967*), actress. Principally a stage actress until embarking on a film career, beginning with *Tom Sawyer* (1930). She appeared with Shirley Temple in *Bright Eyes* (1934), *Curly Top* (1935), *Captain January* (1936), and *Poor Little Rich Girl* (1936). She also appeared in *One More Spring* (1935), *Navy Wife* (1935), *Life Begins at Forty* (1935), *Paddy O'Day* (1935), *The Country Doctor* (1936), *White Fang* (1936), *Ramona* (1936), *Nancy Steele is Missing* (1937), *Slave Ship* (1937), *Dangerously Yours* (1937), *Three Blind Mice* (1938), *Time Out for Murder* (1938), *Gone with the Wind* (1939), and *Jesse James* (1939). She won the academy Award for best supporting actress for her portrayal of Ma Joad in *The Grapes of Wrath* (1940). Other films include *Brigham Young, Frontiersman* (1940), *The Loves of Edgar Allan Poe* (1942), *Captain Tugboat Annie* (1945), *My Darling Clementine* (1946), *Three Godfathers* (1948), *Wagonmaster* (1950), *The Sun Shines Bright* (1953), *The Last Hurrah* (1958), and *Mary Poppins* (1964).

DAUGHERTY, HARRY MICAJAH (*b. Washington Court House, Fayette County, Ohio, 1860; d. Columbus, Ohio, 1941*), lawyer, politician. LL.B., University of Michigan, 1881. Began practice in his hometown and engaged in local Republican politics. Member of Ohio legislature, 1890–94; denied nomination to higher office because of unsavory reputation as lobbyist and disloyalty to party leadership. Maintained a certain importance in politics by his work as a campaigner and the impression that he was able to control one faction of Ohio Republicans. Although his self-proclaimed indispensable agency in securing the presidential nomination of Warren G. Harding in 1920 was a myth, he was named U.S. attorney general in Harding's cabinet and served until April 1924. His tenure was marked by inept and inefficient management of the Department of Justice. Twice brought to court on charges of bribery and defrauding the government, he escaped indictment because he had destroyed important records of the transactions concerned.

DAVEIS, CHARLES STEWART (*b. Portland, Maine, 1788; d. Portland, 1865*), lawyer. Graduated Bowdoin, 1807. Active in settlement of dispute with Great Britain over Maine's northeastern boundary, 1827–42.

DAVEISS, JOSEPH HAMILTON (*b. Bedford Co., Va., 1774; d. Tippecanoe, 1811*), lawyer. As federal district attorney for Kentucky, charged Aaron Burr, 1806, with leading a conspiracy in the western states but failed to get indictment. Killed in battle with Indians. Brother-in-law of John Marshall.

DAVENPORT, CHARLES BENEDICT (*b. near Stamford, Conn., 1866; d. Huntington, N.Y., 1944*), biologist. Raised in Brooklyn, N.Y. B.S., Brooklyn Polytechnic Institute, 1886; B.A., Harvard, 1889; Ph.D., Harvard, 1892, in zoology. Taught at Harvard, 1892–99, and University of Chicago, 1899–1904. A leader in the field of biostatistics, he became one of America's "scientific influentials" as director of the Brooklyn Institute's biological laboratory, the Station for Experimental Evolution, and the Eugenics Record Office, all in Cold Spring Harbor, N.Y. Devoting most of his own efforts *post* 1907 to human genetics, he was an early supporter and propagandist for the eugenics movement. He made few fundamental contributions to the field of genetics, but had importance as an administrator, organizer, and popularizer of science.

DAVENPORT, EDWARD LOOMIS (*b. Boston, Mass., 1815; d. Canton, Pa., 1877*), actor. Made his debut at Providence, R.I., with Junius Brutus Booth in *A New Way to Pay Old Debts, ca.* 1837; first decade in theater was spent in stock companies playing every variety of character. Went to England, 1847, as leading man for Anna Cora Mowatt. Davenport developed as a Shakespearean actor during six years in England and in 1849 married Fanny Vining, a popular English actress. Returning to America, 1854, Davenport took place among America's leading actors, acclaimed for the intelligence of his impersonations.

DAVENPORT, EUGENE (*b. near Woodland, Mich., 1856; d. Woodland, 1941*), educator. Graduated Michigan Agricultural College, 1878; M.S., 1884. A practical farmer, Davenport taught agriculture at his alma mater, and in 1895 became dean of the College of Agriculture, University of Illinois. As dean and, *post* 1896, as director of the university's agricultural experiment station, he made them leaders among the institutions of their kind. He was particularly successful in mobilizing the farmers and farm organizations of the state in support of the work of the college.

DAVENPORT, FANNY LILY GYPSY (*b. London, England, 1850; d. South Duxbury, Mass., 1898*), actress. Daughter of Edward L. Davenport. Played with parents, in stock, and as leading lady in Augustin Daly's company; later headed her own company. Famous in Sardou's *Fédora* and *Tosca*.

DAVENPORT, GEORGE (*b. Lincolnshire, England, 1783; d. 1845*), soldier, fur trader. Came to America, 1804. One of the founders of Davenport, Iowa, which is named for him.

DAVENPORT, HERBERT JOSEPH (*b. Wilmington, Vt., 1861; d. New York, N.Y., 1931*), economist. Distinguished teacher at University of Missouri and Cornell; author of *Value and Distribution* (1908) and *The Economics of Enterprise* (1913).

DAVENPORT, HOMER CALVIN (*b. Silverton, Oreg., 1867; d. 1912*), cartoonist. An advocate of municipal reform, his depictions of Mark Hanna's dollar-marked clothes and the "Trust" figure were permanent contributions to cartoon symbolism.

DAVENPORT, IRA ERASTUS (*b. 1839; d. Mayville, N.Y., 1911*), medium. With his brother William H. H. Davenport (*1841–77*), he performed a spiritualist act which was successful in America and Europe, *ca. 1860–77*.

DAVENPORT, JAMES (*b. Stamford, Conn., 1716; d. 1757*), clergyman. Graduated Yale, 1732. Influenced by George Whitefield, he had a stormy career as itinerant preacher and revivalist.

DAVENPORT, JOHN (*b. Coventry, England, 1597; d. Boston, Mass., 1669/70*), clergyman. Attended Oxford. Active in ministry in London *post* 1619, he interested himself in procuring the Massachusetts Co. charter, 1629; by 1632 he was definitely a nonconformist. In Holland *post* 1633, he returned briefly to England in 1637 and sailed in June of that year in company with Theophilus Eaton for America. After about nine months in Boston, he, Eaton, and their company of emigrants settled an independent colony at present New Haven, Conn.; Eaton was governor and Davenport pastor. In 1661, Davenport sheltered the regicides Whalley and Goffe; he stoutly opposed the "Half-Way Covenant," and in 1662 opposed the absorption of New Haven Colony by Connecticut. Against the will of his congregation, he accepted a call to Boston's First Church in 1667.

DAVENPORT, RUSSELL WHEELER (*b. South Bethlehem, Pa., 1899; d. New York, N.Y., 1954*), writer, editor. Editor *Fortune* (*1930–40*); managing editor (*1937*). Writer for *Life* (*1942–44*). Published poems and novels celebrating democracy and patriotism.

DAVENPORT, THOMAS (*b. Williamstown, Vt., 1802; d. Salisbury, Vt., 1851*), blacksmith, inventor of the electric motor. After experiments with electromagnets *post* 1831, in 1834 he built a little machine composed of four opposed electromagnets connected through a commutator to an electric battery. This device unquestionably embodied the principles of the modern electric motor. After many difficulties, Davenport's motor was patented in 1837. He tried to establish a market for his machine, but never succeeded, although he enlarged and improved it.

DAVENPORT, WILLIAM H. *See* DAVENPORT, IRA ERASTUS.

DAVEY, JOHN (*b. Somersetshire, England, 1846; d. 1923*), "the father of tree surgery in America." Came to America, *ca.* 1872; settled eventually in Kent, Ohio.

D'AVEZAC, AUGUSTE GENEVIÈVE VALENTIN (*b. Santo Domingo, 1780; d. New York, N.Y., 1851*), lawyer. Raised in New Orleans, La. Brother-in-law of Edward Livingston. Held diplomatic posts in the Netherlands and Naples.

DAVID, JOHN BAPTIST MARY (*b. Couêron, France, 1761; d. 1841*), Roman Catholic clergyman, Sulpician, missionary, theologian. Came to America, 1792. Assistant to Bishop Flaget in Bardstown, Ky., 1811–32, David succeeded him, resigning the bishopric, 1833. He founded the Sisters of Charity of Nazareth.

DAVIDGE, JOHN BEALE (*b. Annapolis, Md., 1768; d. Baltimore, Md., 1829*), anatomist, surgeon. Known for his work on yellow fever, Davidge developed several operative techniques; his method of amputation became known as the American method.

DAVIDGE, WILLIAM PLEATER (*b. London, England, 1814; d. Wyoming, 1888*), actor. Came to America, 1850. Played Dick Deadeye in the first American production of *H.M.S. Pinafore*; member of Daly's company (*1869–77*) and others.

DAVIDSON, GEORGE (*b. Nottingham, England, 1825; d. 1911*), geodesist, geographer. Came to America as a child. Headed 1850 survey of the Pacific Coast for purposes of navigation. A noted astronomer, he operated first (*1879*) observatory in California; he also advised on building Lick Observatory.

DAVIDSON, ISRAEL (*b. Yanova, Russia, 1870; d. Great Neck, N.Y., 1939*), Hebrew scholar. Came to America, 1888. Graduated College of City of New York, 1895; Ph.D., Columbia, 1902. Author of *Thesaurus of Mediaeval Hebrew Poetry* (*1924–33*).

DAVIDSON, JAMES WOOD (*b. Newberry Co., S.C., 1829; d. 1905*), author, journalist, Confederate soldier. Edited *Living Writers of the South* (*1869*).

DAVIDSON, JO (*b. New York, N.Y., 1883; d. Bercheron, France, 1952*), sculptor. Considered the finest portrait-sculptor of his time; sculpted Gertrude Stein, Georges Clemenceau, Woodrow Wilson, Benito Mussolini, Mahatma Gandhi, Albert Einstein, and a host of other personages.

DAVIDSON, JOHN WYNN (*b. Fairfax Co., Va., 1823; d. St. Paul, Minn., 1881*), soldier. Graduated West Point, 1845. Served against Indians in the Southwest and as Union major general; distinguished in Arkansas and Missouri campaigns, 1863–65.

DAVIDSON, LUCRETIA MARIA (*b. 1808; d. 1825* and **MARGARET MILLER** (*b. 1823; d. 1838*), poets. Born in Plattsburg, N.Y., both sisters wrote precociously and died of tuberculosis. The sentimental tragedy of their lives held vast appeal to their contemporaries.

DAVIDSON, ROBERT (*b. Elkton, Md., 1750; d. 1812*), Presbyterian clergyman. Professor at Dickinson College and pastor in Carlisle, Pa., *post* 1784.

DAVIDSON, THOMAS (*b. Aberdeenshire, Scotland, 1840; d. 1900*), philosopher, teacher, wandering scholar. Came to the United States, *ca.* 1867. A follower first of W. T. Harris, later of Rosmini.

DAVIDSON, WILLIAM LEE (*b. Lancaster Co., Pa., 1746; d. 1781*), Revolutionary soldier. Served with the North Carolina line and militia; was killed at Cowan's Ford on the Catawba. Davidson College is named for him.

DAVIE, WILLIAM RICHARDSON (*b. Egremont, England, 1756; d. Lancaster Co., S.C., 1820*), lawyer, Revolutionary soldier. Came to America as a child. Federalist governor of North Carolina; called "father" of the University of North Carolina.

DAVIES, ARTHUR BOWEN (*b. Utica, N.Y., 1862; d. Florence, Italy, 1928*), painter. Studied with a local painter in Ithaca, N.Y., at Chicago Art Institute and at Art Students League, New York; encouraged by the dealer William Macbeth and by Benjamin Altman. Early works are small idylls, recalling the quality of Watteau; around 1900, he changed style, producing larger canvases of cooler color and with abstract figures symbolical of poetic ideas. In his third manner, the figure compositions in his mythologies and abstractions are dense and elaborate and tend to assume form of a frieze. He also experimented in cubism and did many admirable lithographs and etchings.

DAVIES, HENRY EUGENE (*b. New York, N.Y., 1836; d. Middleboro, Mass., 1894*), lawyer, Union soldier. Served 1861–65; called "a cavalryman by instinct," he rose to major general of volunteers.

DAVIES, JOHN VIPOND (*b. Swansea, Wales, 1862; d. Flushing, N.Y., 1939*), civil engineering. Came to America, 1889.

With his partner, Charles M. Jacobs, he pioneered in subaqueous and pneumatic foundation work.

DAVIES, JOSEPH EDWARD (*b. Watertown, Wis., 1876; d. Washington, D.C., 1958*), lawyer, diplomat, and author. Studied at the University of Wisconsin (LL.B., 1901). A backer of Woodrow Wilson, Davies was appointed commissioner of corporations in 1913; he was the first chairman of the Federal Trade Commission, from 1915 to 1916. During the 1920's, he practiced law in the capital, specializing in antitrust and international law. In 1936, President Roosevelt appointed him ambassador to the Soviet Union; he was a strong advocate of cooperation with the Soviets against the Axis powers and recognized the strength of the Soviet army in the coming war. He was ambassador to Belgium and minister to Luxembourg from 1938 until the fall of the Low Countries in 1940. After serving as chairman of the President's War Relief Control Board, he met with Stalin in 1943 to lay the groundwork for the Teheran Conference and was later an advisor at the Potsdam Conference.

DAVIES, MARION CECILIA (*b. Brooklyn, N.Y., 1897; d. Hollywood, Calif., 1961*), stage and film actress. A chorus girl in the revue *Stop! Look! Listen!* (1915) when she met publishing magnate William Randolph Hearst, who had her trained by experts and starred her in films. Her first picture was *Cecilia of the Pink Roses* (1918); her biggest successes were *When Knighthood Was in Flower* (1922), *Little Old New York* (1923), and *Janice Meredith* (1924). Her later pictures were *Lights of Old Broadway* (1925), *Zander the Great* (1925), *Beverly of Graustark* (1926), *The Red Mill* (1927), and *Quality Street* (1927). Davies' life with Hearst was parodied in Orson Welles's *Citizen Kane* (1941).

DAVIES, SAMUEL (*b. New Castle Co., Del., 1723; d. Princeton, N.J., 1761*), Presbyterian clergyman. President, College of New Jersey (Princeton), 1759–61.

DAVIESS, JOSEPH HAMILTON. *See* DAVEISS, JOSEPH HAMILTON.

DAVIESS, MARIA THOMPSON (*b. Harrodsburg, Ky., 1872; d. New York, N.Y., 1924*), painter. Author of sentimental romances, of which the best-known was *The Melting of Molly* (1912).

DAVIS, ALEXANDER JACKSON (*b. New York, N.Y., 1803; d. West Orange, N.J., 1892*), architect. Began as draftsman, producing excellent architectural views in lithography and line; was probably apprenticed to J. C. Brady. Employed as draftsman by Ithiel Town, he was associated with him (save for a brief hiatus), 1829–43; thereafter he practiced by himself for more than twenty years. Davis collaborated in design of the North Carolina State Capitol and designed the original buildings of Virginia Military Institute; he produced also a great variety of superior work throughout the United States. His designs were distinguished by versatility and romantic imagination.

DAVIS, ANDREW JACKSON (*b. Blooming Grove, N.Y., 1826; d. 1910*), spiritualist.

DAVIS, ANDREW MCFARLAND (*b. Worcester, Mass., 1833; d. 1920*), lawyer, antiquarian. Brother of John C. B. Davis. Author of many important papers and monographs on the history of currency and banking in the colony of Massachusetts.

DAVIS, ARTHUR POWELL (*b. near Decatur, Ill., 1861; d. 1933*), hydraulic and irrigation engineer. Nephew of John W. and William B. Powell. Topographer in U.S. Geological Survey, 1882–96. Appointed hydrographer, 1896, he supervised all stream measurements in the United States and made rainfall and stream studies for the proposed Nicaraguan and Panamanian Canal routes. On organization of the Reclamation Service, Davis was appointed supervising engineer, 1903, and from 1914 to 1923 was director. The Reclamation Service under his direction built more than 100 dams, including Shoshone and Arrowrock dams and the Gunnison Tunnel.

DAVIS, ARTHUR VINING (*b. Sharon, Mass., 1867; d. Miami, Fla., 1962*), industrialist and philanthropist. With the Pittsburgh Reduction Company, he worked with Charles Martin Hall to produce the first commercial aluminum in 1888. He became general manager, then a director of the firm in 1892. He continued as general manager when the firm became the Aluminum Company of America (Alcoa) in 1907; he became president in 1910 and chairman of the board in 1928. Davis built Alcoa into an industrial giant, and as the company's largest stockholder he amassed great wealth. He was frequently in conflict with the government over antitrust issues. After retiring from Alcoa in 1957 he invested heavily in the Bahamas and Florida.

DAVIS, BENJAMIN OLIVER, SR. (*b. Washington, D.C., 1877; d. Lake County, Ill., 1970*), army officer. Joined the infantry (1898), then enlisted as a private in one of four black units in the regular army. He became second lieutenant of cavalry in 1901. He trained black National Guardsman and taught military science at black colleges. He was military attaché to Liberia (1909–12), reached the rank of major by the time the U.S. entered World War I, and was promoted to colonel in 1930. Davis was appointed to command the 369th (N.Y.) National Guard in 1938, and he was promoted to brigadier general in 1940, becoming the first black to achieve the rank of general. He commanded the Fourth Cavalry Brigade and worked in the Inspector General's Office. During World War II he was a member of the Advisory Committee on Negro Troop Policies (the McCloy Committee). Though he served in a segregated army, he is credited with helping desegregate the U.S. armed forces. In 1948 he was retired with the permanent rank of brigadier general.

DAVIS, CHARLES HAROLD (*b. Amesbury, Mass., 1856; d. Mystic, Conn., 1933*), artist. Created an individual style; was temperamentally akin to Ryder and Blakelock.

DAVIS, CHARLES HENRY (*b. Boston, Mass., 1807; d. Washington, D.C., 1877*), naval officer. Active in scientific work connected with the navy, 1842–56, he also distinguished himself in active administration, planning duties, and command at sea, 1861–65.

DAVIS, CHARLES HENRY (*b. Cambridge, Mass., 1845; d. 1921*), naval officer. Son of Charles H. Davis (1807–77).

DAVIS, CHARLES HENRY STANLEY (*b. Goshen, Conn., 1840; d. Meriden, Conn., 1917*), physician, philologist, orientalist.

DAVIS, CUSHMAN KELLOGG (*b. Henderson, N.Y., 1838; d. 1900*), lawyer. Republican governor of Minnesota, 1873–75; U.S. senator, 1887–1900.

DAVIS, DAVID (*b. Cecil Co., Md., 1815; d. Bloomington, Ill., 1886*), jurist. A graduate of Yale Law School, 1835, Davis set up practice in Bloomington, Ill. From 1848 to 1862 he was judge of eighth judicial circuit, Illinois. During this time he formed a friendship with Abraham Lincoln, and at the Chicago convention in 1860 led the Lincoln forces. Appointed, 1862, to the U.S. Supreme Court, he delivered opinion in the *Milligan* case, 1866, antagonizing the Radical Republicans. Nominated, 1872, for the presidency by the Labor Reform Convention, he withdrew when the liberal Republicans did not endorse him. Elected U.S. senator from Illinois, 1877, he resigned from the Supreme Court and upset the expected composition of the electoral commission created to decide between Hayes and Tilden. He owed his place to the Democrats but generally supported the Republicans before retiring in 1883.

DAVIS, DWIGHT FILLEY (*b. St. Louis, Mo., 1879; d. Washington, D.C., 1945*), sportsman, public official. Graduated Harvard, 1900. National doubles tennis champion, 1899–1901; donor of the Davis Cup, 1900. Devoted all his time to St. Louis civic affairs until World War I, in which he served with great distinction. Appointed assistant U.S. secretary of war, 1923, he succeeded to secretary in 1925 and served until 1929. As governor general of the Philippines, 1929–32, he worked to improve economic conditions there, developing the school system and initiating new banking laws. A trustee of the Brookings Institution, he served *post* 1937 as chairman.

DAVIS, EDMUND JACKSON (*b. St. Augustine, Fla., 1827; d. Austin, Tex., 1883*), lawyer. Raised in Texas. A Unionist and a bitter Radical reconstructionist. Republican governor of Texas, 1860–73.

DAVIS, EDWIN HAMILTON (*b. Hillsboro, Ohio, 1811; d. 1888*), physician, archaeologist. Collaborated with E. G. Squier in a survey of a hundred Indian mounds, *Ancient Monuments of the Mississippi Valley* (1847), the first work issued by the Smithsonian Institution. The book is still valuable in itself and as a record of mounds since sacrificed to farming and building.

DAVIS, ELMER HOLMES (*b. Aurora, Ind., 1890; d. New York, N.Y., 1958*), news commentator, writer. Studied at Franklin (Ind.) College and was a Rhodes scholar, receiving a B.A. from Oxford in 1912. Reporter and columnist for the *New York Times* from 1914 to 1923; afterwards, a free-lance writer and novelist. By 1935, he had published nine novels. It was as a radio commentator that Davis made a national reputation. He was a news analyst for CBS from 1939 to 1942. During World War II, he was head of the Office of War Information in Washington. From 1945 to 1955, he was news commentator for ABC, receiving the Peabody Radio Award in 1951 for his outspoken opposition to the excesses of the McCarthy era. His nonfiction includes *But We Were Born Free* (1954) and *Two Minutes Till Midnight* (1955). He retired from radio in 1955.

DAVIS, ERNEST R. ("ERNIE") (*b. New Salem, Pa., 1939; d. Cleveland, Ohio, 1963*), football player. A graduate of Syracuse (1962) and a star on the Syracuse football team. He established many school records, including some held previously by Jim Brown. He was the first black to be awarded the Heisman Trophy (1961). He signed a contract with the Cleveland Browns, but his death from leukemia prevented him from playing professional football.

DAVIS, FRANCIS BREESE, JR. (*b. Fort Edward, N.Y., 1883; d. Savannah, Ga., 1962*), business executive. Graduate of Sheffield Scientific School at Yale (Ph.B., 1906). Joined the construction engineering department of E. I. du Pont de Nemours and Company in 1909; after World War I became a vice president of the Du Pont Chemical Company. Davis held executive positions with several divisions of Du Pont and companies controlled by Du Pont, including General Motors, the Pyralin division, the Viscoloid (later Du Pont Viscoloid) Company, and the Celastic Corporation. In 1928 he became chairman of the board of directors of the new Pittsburgh Safety Glass Corporation. With the U.S. Rubber Company, controlled by Du Pont since 1927, he served as president (1929–42), chairman of the board (1929–49), and chief executive officer.

DAVIS, GARRET (*b. Mount Sterling, Ky., 1801; d. 1872*), lawyer. Congressman, Whig, from Kentucky, 1839–47. In turn a Know-Nothing and a Radical Unionist, he was U.S. senator, 1861–72. Abandoning his Radical views, 1864, he was thereafter a strong critic of Lincoln and the Republicans and ran as a Democrat, 1867.

DAVIS, GEORGE (*b. Porter's Neck, N.C., 1820; d. Wilmington, N.C., 1896*), lawyer. Attorney general of the Confederacy, 1864–65. Later became counsel to the Atlantic Coast Line in its formative period.

DAVIS, GEORGE BRECKENRIDGE (*b. Ware, Mass., 1847; d. Washington, D.C., 1914*), soldier. Graduated West Point, 1871. Author of several works on military law; supervised publication of *War of the Rebellion: Official Records.*

DAVIS, GEORGE WHITEFIELD (*b. Thompson, Conn., 1839; d. 1918*), soldier, engineer, governor of Canal Zone, 1904–05, and a member of the Isthmian Canal Commission.

DAVIS, HARVEY NATHANIEL (*b. Providence, R.I., 1881; d. New York, N.Y., 1952*), physicist, college president. Harvard (Ph.D., 1906). President of Stevens Institute of Technology, Hoboken, N.J., (1928–1952).

DAVIS, HENRY (*b. East Hampton, N.Y., 1771; d. Clinton, N.Y., 1852*), clergyman. President, Middlebury College, 1809–17; Hamilton College, 1817–32.

DAVIS, HENRY GASSAWAY (*b. Woodstock, Md., 1823; d. Washington, D.C., 1916*), merchant, lumberman, railroad builder. U.S. senator, Democrat, from West Virginia, 1871–83.

DAVIS, HENRY GASSETT (*b. Trenton, Maine, 1807; d. Everett, Mass., 1896*), pioneer orthopedic surgeon. Graduated Yale, M.D., 1839; practiced in Worcester and Millbury, Mass., and later in New York, N.Y., where he founded "traction" school of orthopedic surgery, *ca.* 1856, his work providing the basis for the modern approach to problems of deformity. He influenced, among others, Lewis A. Sayre, Charles Fayette Taylor, and Edward Hickling Bradford. His most important book, *Conservative Surgery* (1867), was first notable textbook in American orthopedics.

DAVIS, HENRY WINTER (*b. Annapolis, Md., 1817; d. Baltimore, Md., 1865*), lawyer, politician, statesman. Congressman, Know-Nothing, from Maryland, 1855–61; Republican, 1863–64. His vote for the Republican candidate for Speaker of the House in 1860 broke a deadlock and made him a national figure; that same year he supported the successful Bell and Everett party in Maryland. Though an ardent Unionist, Davis strenuously opposed Lincoln and his program, especially protesting violations of habeas corpus and the plan for a moderate Reconstruction. Defeated in the congressional elections of 1864, Davis led the attack on Andrew Johnson in the lame duck session. He was author of the Wade-Davis Manifesto (1864).

DAVIS, HORACE (*b. Worcester, Mass., 1831; d. San Francisco, Calif., 1916*), flour manufacturer. Son of John Davis (1787–1854). Removed to California, *ca.* 1849. President, University of California, 1888–90.

DAVIS, JAMES JOHN (*b. Tredegar, South Wales, 1873; d. Takoma Park, Md., 1947*), fraternal order leader, cabinet officer, U.S. senator. Came to the United States with parents, 1881; raised in Sharon, Pa.; worked as puddler in iron mills; attended night schools. Worked, and held both trade union and public offices in Elwood, Ind., 1893–1907. *Post* 1907, he was director general and principal organizer of lodges for the Loyal Order of Moose. A conservative Republican, he was opposed by organized labor when appointed U.S. secretary of labor, 1921, but he served with credit until 1930 and acted to temper Republican antilabor attitudes. As U.S. senator from Pennsylvania, 1930–44, he sponsored the Davis-Bacon Act, and voted for the Social Security, Wagner, and Fair Labor Standards acts, although frequently criticizing the implementation of New Deal programs.

Davis, Jeff (*b. Little River Co., Ark., 1862; d. 1913*), lawyer. Democratic governor of Arkansas, 1901–07; U.S. senator, 1907–13. Excelled in ability to appeal to popular passions and prejudices.

Davis, Jefferson (*b. Christian, now Todd, Co., Ky., 1808; d. New Orleans, La., 1889*), president of the Confederate States of America. Tenth child of Samuel and Jane (Cook) Davis, originally of Georgia, who removed again to Wilkinson Co., Miss., while Jefferson was still very young. His eldest brother, Joseph Emory Davis, prospered in Mississippi and was Jefferson's patron. Sensitive and imaginative, Jefferson Davis studied at St. Thomas' College in Kentucky, at local schools, and at Transylvania University. Nominated to West Point, he graduated in 1828 and performed his early service at Wisconsin and Illinois frontier posts. Stationed at Fort Crawford, Wis., 1833, under Col. Zachary Taylor, Davis fell in love with Taylor's daughter Sarah and married her against her father's wishes, resigning from the army, 1835. Three months after his marriage, his wife died.

From 1835 to 1845, Davis was a planter at "Brierfield" in Mississippi, hardworking and intensely interested in his plantation. Guided by his brother Joseph, who was his neighbor, he became an extensive reader, especially in politics and history. He became devoted to his environment and its social system, and by his marriage to Varina Howell in 1845 associated himself conclusively with the local slaveholding aristocracy. Gentle and patriarchal in his relations with his slaves, he resented the abolitionist attack which emerged at this time, and opposed it with states' rights arguments. A temperamental influence in this decade was his deep-seated love of the army and military life, for which he never lost his zeal. Indeed, in the darkest hours of the Confederacy, Davis believed himself the equal of the greatest generals. Yet his military self-esteem rested on one brief year of service in 1846 and one gallant action in 1847. Elected to Congress as a Democrat in 1845, Davis resigned to command a volunteer regiment in the Mexican War. At the battle of Buena Vista his regiment made a gallant stand which probably turned defeat into victory.

In 1847 Davis withdrew from the army and was chosen U.S. senator from Mississippi. He supported Polk and the policy of seizing Mexican territory, fought proposals to organize the Oregon Territory without slavery, and was one of the ten senators who opposed to the last the admission of California. The debate over California aroused secession sentiment in the South. Extreme states' righters like R. B. Rhett and W. L. Yancey wished their states to secede whether or not other states followed suit. Another faction, the cooperationists, or party of "Southern nationalism," having concluded that it was impossible to effect immediate group secession, wanted to arrest the movement until the whole South could act together. A third party, headed by Sen. Henry S. Foote, who had opposed Davis' stand on California, regarded the Compromise of 1850 as the opening of a satisfactory new chapter in the history of the Union. By September 1851 it was evident that Foote, nominated for governor of Mississippi on a Union antisecession ticket, would carry the election in the contest against the secessionist John A. Quitman. Mississippi Democrats, apparently wishing to retreat from an extreme secession position, persuaded Davis to resign from the Senate and replace Quitman as candidate and party leader of the state. Defeated by Foote, Davis returned to his life as a planter.

Becoming secretary of war in the cabinet of Franklin Pierce, 1853, he entered the happiest phase of his career. His policies were governed by a desire to enlarge the territory, and develop the economy, of the South. He frequently opposed the secretary of state, William L. Marcy, who favored the northern wing of his party. Davis urged a transcontinental railway routed close to the Mexican border and terminating in Southern California. The monumental railroad surveys of the West were made under his supervision. To make a southern route possible, he induced Pierce and Marcy to acquire the Gadsden Purchase.

Davis returned to the Senate in 1857. In the internal wrangles of the Democratic party from the Dred Scott decision in 1857 to the Charleston convention in 1860, Davis and Stephen Douglas championed opposing forces. Ostensibly Douglas defended "popular sovereignty" while Davis held that neither Congress nor local law could interfere with slavery in a territory. His reluctance to support immediate secession in 1860, however, suggests that he may have wished to win "dominion status" for the South. Following Lincoln's election Davis was passive until the president declared there should be no more slave states. This decision, denying the possibility of Southern expansion, determined Davis' choice. When Mississippi seceded, he withdrew from the Senate.

Davis expected war and hoped to become chief commander of the Southern armies. To his disappointment he was chosen provisional president of the Confederacy, inaugurated at Montgomery, Ala., Feb. 18, 1861. A tired man in very delicate health, Davis was unable to control events. He kept a close hand on the management of the army, yet uncompromising in both animosities and friendships, he was not wise in choosing men to trust. His efforts to win support in Europe were failures.

When it became apparent that Davis' loyalty was to the South as a whole, an anti-Davis party formed around the idea of state sovereignty. Davis angered this opposition in a number of ways, notably by proposing and enacting a general conscription law. As economic conditions became increasingly difficult with the fall in value of Confederate money and the tightening of the federal blockade, the opposition grew stronger, and the complaints against the president's so-called egotism and vanity, louder. General elections in 1863 returned to the Confederate Congress a majority hostile to Davis. It had been agreed that the government should not own slaves, but should rent them from their owners and use them as laborers only. One white man from every plantation of 15 or more slaves was exempted to serve as overseer. This law produced envy in men of small property, who also resented the system of hiring substitutes for army service. Davis' annual message in 1864, urging outright government purchase of 40,000 slaves to be freed when the government was through with them, was looked on as one more step toward despotism. His proposal was probably designed to see if the South would endorse arming slaves to reinforce the sadly diminished army. Eventually a bill was passed permitting a levy of 300,000 men "irrespective of color," but omitting any mention of emancipation.

Through the winter of 1864–65, Davis seems to have had no doubt of eventual victory. He reinforced the army by a general order revoking all exemptions, stripping the plantations of overseers, and recalling all furloughed or hospitalized soldiers "except those unable to travel." His efforts to rally the people of the South behind the army only aroused further suspicions that he was planning a coup d'état. He never understood the seriousness of Sherman's march to the sea.

Various attempts at reconciliation were made. In January 1865, Francis P. Blair proposed to Davis a reunion of the states, the abandonment of slavery, and an expedition against Maximilian of Mexico in which Davis should play a leading party. Consequent to this, Davis appointed commissioners to confer with Northern authorities on terms of peace, and the South might have won reconciliation on good terms at the Hampton Roads Conference (Feb. 3, 1865), had not Davis refused to accept any terms short of Confederate independence.

On Apr. 3, 1865, Davis left falling Richmond for Danville, Va., where he issued a final proclamation asking for resistance to the last and promising the recovery of Richmond. Following Lee's surrender, he turned southward and at Charlotte, N.C., on April 24 held his last council with his cabinet. On May 10 he was captured by Union cavalry at Irwinville, Ga., and imprisoned two years in Fortress Monroe. Though put in irons at first, he was later accorded better treatment. He was never brought to trial. His last years were valiant though sad. *The Rise and Fall of the Confederate Government* (1881) is his own account of the great events in which he played a part.

DAVIS, JEFFERSON COLUMBUS (*b. Clark Co., Ind., 1828; d. Chicago, Ill., 1879*), Union soldier. A distinguished and able military man, he failed of further promotion after killing his commanding officer in a Louisville hotel, 1862.

DAVIS, JEROME DEAN (*b. Groton, N.Y., 1838; d. 1910*), Congregational clergyman. Missionary to Japan, 1871–1910; helped found Kobe College and later the Doshisha University, Kyoto.

DAVIS, JOHN (*b. Plymouth, Mass., 1761; d. Boston, Mass., 1847*), jurist. Graduated Harvard, 1781. Judge district court of Massachusetts, 1801–41; president, Massachusetts Historical Society, 1818–35.

DAVIS, JOHN (*b. ca. 1780; d. ca. 1838*), operatic and theatrical manager. Came to New Orleans from San Domingo. Built the Théâtre d'Orléans, 1813, 1819; as manager, made New Orleans the first American city to have an annual opera season.

DAVIS, JOHN (*b. Northboro, Mass., 1787; d. Worcester, Mass., 1854*), lawyer, statesman. Graduated Yale, 1812. Congressman, National Republican, from Massachusetts, 1824–32; governor of Massachusetts, 1833–34 and (as a Whig) 1840–41; U.S. senator, Whig, 1835–40 and 1845–53. Nicknamed "Honest John"; conservative protectionist.

DAVIS, JOHN CHANDLER BANCROFT (*b. Worcester, Mass., 1822; d. Washington, D.C., 1907*), lawyer, diplomatist. Son of John Davis (1787–1854); nephew of George Bancroft. As assistant secretary of state, Davis prepared (1871–72) the American case against Great Britain arising from Confederate cruiser action in Civil War.

DAVIS, JOHN LEE (*b. Carlisle, Ind., 1825; d. Washington, D.C., 1889*), naval officer. Son of John W. Davis, he was among the younger ship commanders of note in the Civil War. Retired as rear admiral, 1887.

DAVIS, JOHN STAIGE (*b. Norfolk, Va., 1872; d. Baltimore, Md., 1946*), surgeon, teacher. Ph.B., Sheffield Scientific School, Yale, 1895; M.D., Johns Hopkins, 1899. One of the first to devote full time to the principles and techniques of plastic and reconstructive surgery, he practiced in Baltimore *post* 1903, and he taught at Johns Hopkins from 1909 until his death. He was particularly concerned with the relief by surgery of the psychological effects of physical deformities. His book *Plastic Surgery: Its Principles and Practice* (1919) was the first definitive textbook on the subject and remains a classic.

DAVIS, JOHN WESLEY (*b. New Holland, Pa., 1799; d. Carlisle, Ind., 1859*), physician, politician. Removed to Carlisle, Ind., 1823. Congressman, Democrat from Indiana; Speaker of the House, 1845–47. Governor of Oregon Territory, 1853–54.

DAVIS, JOHN WILLIAM (*b. Clarksburg, W.Va., 1873; d. Charleston, S.C., 1955*), lawyer, diplomat, U.S. solicitor general, Democratic presidential candidate. Studied at Washington and Lee University. Served as an American commissioner to the German-American Conference on Prisoners of War, 1918; attended the Versailles Peace Conference and played an important role in the formulation of the Rhineland Convention. Appointed ambassador to Great Britain, he was most effective in easing Anglo-American tensions concerning the Irish question and oil in the Middle East. Defeated by Coolidge for the presidency, 1924. Returned to private law practice, often arguing such important cases as *Brown* v. *Board of Education* (1954) before the Supreme Court and as counsel to the physicist Robert J. Oppenheimer, 1954.

DAVIS, JOSEPH ROBERT (*b. Woodville, Miss., 1825; d. 1896*), lawyer, Confederate soldier. Nephew of Jefferson Davis.

DAVIS, KATHARINE BEMENT (*b. Buffalo, N.Y., 1860; d. Pacific Grove, Calif., 1935*), prison reformer. First chairman of New York City Prison Parole Commission, 1915–18.

DAVIS, MARY EVELYN MOORE (*b. Talladega, Ala., 1852; d. New Orleans, La., 1909*), author.

DAVIS, MATTHEW LIVINGSTON (*b. probably New York, N.Y., 1773; d. Manhattanville, N.Y., 1850*), politician, journalist. Friend and biographer of Aaron Burr.

DAVIS, NATHAN SMITH (*b. Greene, N.Y., 1817; d. 1904*), physician, "father of the American Medical Association." Practiced and taught in Chicago, Ill., 1849–1904.

DAVIS, NOAH (*b. Haverhill, N.H., 1818; d. New York, N.Y., 1902*), jurist. New York Supreme Court justice, 1857–68, 1872–86; tried and sentenced William M. Tweed, 1873.

DAVIS, NOAH KNOWLES (*b. Philadelphia, Pa., 1830; d. Charlottesville, Va., 1910*), teacher, author. An effective teacher, he was associated with various Baptist colleges, 1852–72, and professor of moral philosophy at University of Virginia, 1873–1906.

DAVIS, NORMAN HEZEKIAH (*b. Normandy, Tenn., 1878; d. Hot Springs, Va., 1944*), banker, diplomat. Made a fortune in banking and other enterprises in Cuba, 1902–17. Volunteering services to the federal government, he was employed in the treasury department, acting as assistant to Herbert Hoover in negotiations on postwar relief (1918) and as financial adviser to U.S. commission at Paris Peace Conference (1919); served on the Reparations Commission. In 1919, he was made assistant U.S. secretary of the treasury in charge of the Foreign Loan Bureau; in June 1920, appointed undersecretary of state. A strong supporter of the League of Nations, Pan-Americanism, and good Anglo-American relations. Leaving government service after the defeat of the Democrats in 1920, he helped organize the Council on Foreign Relations. He was a delegate to the Geneva Economic Conference, 1927, and to the Geneva Disarmament Conference, 1932, serving as chairman after the election of President Franklin D. Roosevelt; he led the U.S. delegation to the London Naval Conference, 1935–36, and to the Nine-Power Treaty Conference at Brussels, 1937. He headed the American Red Cross and the International Red Cross *post* 1938. He was distinguished in diplomacy for directness, persuasiveness, and patience.

DAVIS, OSCAR KING (*b. Baldwinsville, N.Y., 1866; d. Bronxville, N.Y., 1932*), journalist, Washington and foreign correspondent.

DAVIS, OWEN GOULD (*b. Portland, Me., 1874; d. New York, N.Y., 1956*), playwright. Studied briefly at Harvard. Credited with approximately 200 plays, most published under a pseudonym. From 1899 until the 1920's, he wrote popular melodramas. In 1921, he wrote a serious play, *The Detour*, which was influenced by Eugene O'Neill; in 1923, his play *Icebound* won the Pulitzer Prize and Davis was elected to the National Academy of Arts and Letters. His comedy, *The Nervous Wreck* (1923), was later a Broadway musical, *Whoopee* (1928), and a film, *Up In Arms* (1944).

DAVIS, PAULINA KELLOGG WRIGHT (*b. Bloomfield, N.Y., 1813; d. Providence, R.I., 1876*), editor, suffragist. Established *Una*, 1853, the first distinctively woman's rights paper published in the United States.

DAVIS, PAULINE MORTON SABIN (*b. Chicago, Ill., 1887; d. Washington, D.C., 1955*), political official. Heiress to the Morton Salt fortune; first woman to serve on the Republican National Committee (1923–29). She resigned and formed a powerful women's group opposed to Prohibition. Director of volunteer services of the American Red Cross in World War II.

DAVIS, PHINEAS (*b. Grafton Co., N.H., 1800; d. Maryland, 1835*), inventor. Built prize-winning locomotive "York" for the Baltimore & Ohio Railroad, 1831. Produced in 1832 with Israel Gardner the first of the "Grasshopper" type engines used on the road.

DAVIS, RAYMOND CAZALLIS (*b. Cushing, Maine, 1836; d. Ann Arbor, Mich., 1919*), mariner, librarian. Librarian, University of Michigan, 1877–1905.

DAVIS, REBECCA BLAINE HARDING (*b. Washington, Pa., 1831; d. Mount Kisco, N.Y., 1910*), novelist. Mother of Richard Harding Davis. Her early stories (e.g., *Margaret Howth*, 1862) were pioneer works in American realism.

DAVIS, REUBEN (*b. near Winchester, Tenn., 1813; d. Huntsville, Ala., 1890*), lawyer. Congressman, Democrat, from Mississippi, 1857–61; member of Confederate Congress, 1861–64. A strong critic of Confederate war policy.

DAVIS, RICHARD HARDING (*b. Philadelphia, Pa., 1864; d. Mount Kisco, N.Y., 1916*), journalist, author. Son of Rebecca Harding Davis. Began career as newspaperman, 1886; won fame as reporter, feature writer, traveling correspondent. Covered revolt in Greco-Turkish, Spanish-American, Boer, and Russo-Japanese wars, and opening phases of World War I. His infallible news sense and eye for picturesque detail were joined with a taste for sensation and melodrama. "Popular" appeal in the bad sense marked his skillfully told fiction and dramas. Among his books were *Gallegher, and Other Stories* (1891); *Van Bibber and Others* (1892); *Soldiers of Fortune* (1897); *Cuba in War Time* (1897).

DAVIS, STUART (*b. Philadelphia, Pa., 1894; d. New York, N.Y., 1964*), artist. Inspired by European postimpressionist and cubist painters, he is known for his abstract urban landscapes and jazz-inspired syncopations of color. He was exhibited at the 1913 Armory Show, and his one-man shows were held at the Downtown Gallery in New York City from 1927–62. Davis produced covers for the leftist magazine the *Masses* (1912–16), helped organize the Artists' Union (1934) and the American Artists' Congress (1936), and edited *ART FRONT*. His autobiography is *Stuart Davis* (1945).

DAVIS, VARINA ANNE JEFFERSON (*b. Richmond, Va., 1864; d. Narragansett Pier, R.I., 1898*), daughter of Jefferson Davis and Varina Howell Davis, author.

DAVIS, VARINA HOWELL (*b. near Natchez, Miss., 1826; d. New York, N.Y., 1906*), author, wife of Jefferson Davis.

DAVIS, WATSON (*b. Washington, D.C., 1896; d. Washington, D.C., 1967*), science writer, editor, and popularizer. Received civil engineering degrees from George Washington University (1918, 1920), then worked for the National Bureau of Standards and the *Washington Herald*. In 1921 he joined Science Service, a syndicated news agency, and became editor of its *Science News Letter* (later *Science News*). He became managing editor and secretary (1923), acting president (1929), and president (1933). In 1930 Davis established the "Adventures in Science" radio interview program on the Columbia Broadcasting System. In 1934 he helped create the National Association of Science Writers. In 1941 he turned his attention to the Science Talent Search, science fairs, and Science Clubs of America. He helped create the American Documentation Institute in 1935 and served as its president (1937–47). Science Service lost it preeminence in popular science after World War II, and Davis was forced into retirement in 1966.

DAVIS, WILLIAM AUGUSTINE (*b. Barren Co., Ky., 1809; d. St. Joseph, Mo., 1875*), postmaster. Invented railway post office and railway mail-car, 1862.

DAVIS, WILLIAM HAMMATT (*b. Bangor, Maine, 1879; d. Southwest Harbor, Maine, 1964*), patent attorney and labor mediator. Graduated from George Washington Law School (1901), worked with the law firms of Betts, Betts, Sheffield, and Betts (1903–06) and Pennie and Goldsborough (later Pennie, Davis, Marvin, and Edmonds) (1906–45). He founded the New York City law firm of Davis, Hoxie, Faithfull, and Hapgood in 1945. Davis worked with the U.S. War Department (1917–19) and the National Recovery Administration (1933–34). He chaired the New York State Mediation Board (1937–40). During World War II, Davis was a key figure in the government's effort to maintain peaceful labor relations, working with the National Defense Mediation Board, the National War Labor Board, and the Office of Economic Stabilization. He was a commissioner of the New York City Board of Transportation (1946–47), a member of the patent advisory panel of the Atomic Energy Commission (1947–57), and chairman of the President's Commission on Labor Relations in Atomic Installations (1948–49) and of the Atomic Energy Labor Relations Panel (1949–53). Davis was chairman of the board of trustees of the New School for Social Research (1950–57).

DAVIS, WILLIAM MORRIS (*b. Philadelphia, Pa., 1850; d. Pasadena, Calif., 1934*), geographer, geologist. Graduated, 1870. Lawrence Scientific School, Harvard, as mining engineer. After various expeditions at home and abroad, became in 1876 assistant in geology at Harvard, rising to the Sturgis-Hooper professorship of geology in 1898. Evolved the concept of "the cycle of erosion." *Post* 1898, he traveled widely, studying landforms, and developed his major contribution, the science of geomorphology. Author of the classic *Die erklärende Beschreibung der Landformen* (1912) and *The Coral Reef Problem* (1928); also prepared studies in meteorology and oceanography. Considered himself a geographer and is largely responsible for having made geography a science in America.

DAVIS, WILLIAM THOMAS (*b. Plymouth, Mass., 1822; d. Plymouth, 1907*), lawyer, author. Authority on history of his native town; edited Plymouth records.

DAVIS, WINNIE. *See* DAVIS, VARINA ANNE JEFFERSON.

DAVISON, GEORGE WILLETS (*b. Rockville Centre, N.Y., 1872; d. New York, N.Y., 1953*), lawyer, banker. New York

University (LL.B., 1894). President, Hanover Bank and Trust Co. (1929–33); chairman of the board (1933–39). Director, Federal Reserve Board of New York (1933–38). Helped formulate the Emergency Banking Relief Act (1933).

DAVISON, GREGORY CALDWELL (*b. Jefferson City, Mo., 1871; d. Lyme, Conn., 1935*), naval officer. Graduated Annapolis, 1892. Inventor of the balanced turbine torpedo, the first nonrecoil gun for airplanes, and the Y-gun depth-charge projector.

DAVISON, HENRY POMEROY (*b. Troy, Pa., 1867; d. 1922*), banker. Devised plan of Bankers' Trust Co.; partner in J. P. Morgan and Co.; distinguished as head of Red Cross War Council, 1917–19.

DAVISSON, CLINTON JOSPEH (*b. Bloomington, Ill., 1881; d. Charlottesville, Va., 1958*), physicist. Studied at the University of Chicago and at Princeton (Ph.D., 1908). Taught at the Carnegie Institute of Technology from 1911 until World War I, when he joined the staff of the Western Electric Laboratories in New York City. Davisson, along with George P. Thompson, discovered the wave theory of the electron in the late 1920's. He and Thompson shared the Nobel Prize in 1937. Davisson left Western Electric in 1946 and became professor of physics at the University of Virginia. He retired in 1954.

DAWES, CHARLES GATES (*b. Marietta, Ohio, 1865; d. Evanston, Ill., 1951*), banker. U.S. vice president, ambassador to England. Studied at Marietta College and Cincinnati Law School. Appointed director of the Bureau of the Budget, 1921. Served as chairman of the Committee of Experts of the Allied Reparations Commission, 1923, and formulated the "Dawes Plan" for restructuring the German economy. Awarded the Nobel Prize for Peace in 1925, sharing the honor with Sir Austin Chamberlain. Elected vice president under Coolidge, 1924, and was instrumental in obtaining congressional support for the Kellogg-Briand Peace Pact. Ambassador to England, 1929–32; played important roles in the London naval armaments limitations conference, 1930, and in attempts to settle the Sino-Japanese crisis, 1931. Served under Hoover as director of the Reconstruction Finance Corporation, 1932.

DAWES, HENRY LAURENS (*b. Cummington, Mass., 1816; d. Pittsfield, Mass., 1903*), lawyer, legislator. Massachusetts congressman, Republican, 1857–75, and U.S. senator, 1875–92. Had great influence in House, becoming chairman of Appropriations Committee, 1869, and of Ways and Means Committee, 1871; was a consistent protectionist. At suggestion of Cleveland Abbe, he initiated weather bulletin plan which became U.S. Weather Bureau. As chairman of Senate Indian Affairs Committee, he improved condition of Indians and was author of liberating Dawes Act, 1887.

DAWES, RUFUS CUTLER (*b. Marietta, Ohio, 1867; d. Evanston, Ill., 1940*), businessman, public utilities operator. Assistant to brother Charles G. Dawes on Dawes Plan; president, Chicago World's Fair, 1933–34.

DAWES, WILLIAM (*b. Boston, Mass., 1745; d. Boston, 1799*). With Paul Revere, a warner on night of Apr. 18, 1775.

DAWKINS, HENRY (*fl. New York and Philadelphia, 1753–80*), one of the earliest copper-plate engravers in America. Arrested on suspicion of counterfeiting, 1776.

DAWLEY, ALMENA (*b. Silver Springs, N.Y., 1890; d. Flourtown, Pa., 1956*), sociologist, educator. Studied at Oberlin College and at the University of Chicago. A pioneer in social investigation and child guidance, Dawley supervised the department of social investigation for the Pennsylvania School of Social Services in 1920. With Frederick H. Allen, she founded and was associate director of the Child Guidance Clinic in Philadelphia in 1925; taught at Bryn Mawr from 1928 to 1936.

DAWSON, FRANCIS WARRINGTON (*b. London, England, 1840; d. Charleston, S.C., 1889*), journalist. Came to America, 1861, as volunteer in Confederate navy. Purchased *Charleston News*, 1867, later merged with the *Courier*, and served as editor. A moderate liberal, he urged economic measures for rebuilding the postwar South.

DAWSON, HENRY BARTON (*b. Lincolnshire, England, 1821; d. Tarrytown, N.Y., 1889*), editor. Came to America, 1834. Author of numerous historical works and editor of the *Historical Magazine*, 1866–76. His "revisionist" tendencies and trenchant style provoked controversy.

DAWSON, JOHN (*b. Virginia, 1762; d. 1814*), statesman. Graduated Harvard, 1782. Member of Virginia House of Delegates. An ardent Jeffersonian, he served in Congress, 1797–1814.

DAWSON, THOMAS CLELAND (*b. Hudson, Wis., 1865; d. 1912*), lawyer, diplomat. The "foremost Latin-American diplomat of the government," he served with distinction in many Latin American countries, 1897–1911.

DAWSON, WILLIAM CROSBY (*b. Greene Co., Ga., 1798; d. Greensboro, Ga., 1856*), lawyer. As U.S. senator, Whig, from Georgia, 1849–55, he led in adoption of "Georgia Platform" and in support of Compromise of 1850.

DAWSON, WILLIAM LEVI (*b. Albany, Ga., 1886; d. Chicago, Ill., 1970*), U.S. congressman. Received a B.A. from Fisk (1909) and a law degree from Northwestern (1920). As a Republican he served on the Chicago city council for six years. He became a Democrat and represented Chicago's South Side in the U.S. Congress from 1943 until his death. In 1944 he became the first black to be elected vice-chairman of the Democratic National Committee. He was elected chairman of the House Committee on Government Operations in 1949. Dawson's black political machine was a dominant element in Chicago Democratic affairs, and he was instrumental in engineering the election of Richard Daley as mayor in 1955. A moderate, Dawson remained aloof from the racial crusades of the 1960's.

DAY, ARTHUR LOUIS (*b. Brookfield, Mass., 1869; d. Bethesda, Md., 1960*), geophysicist. Studied at Yale University (Ph.D., 1894). First director of the Physical Laboratory of the Carnegie Institute in Washington, D.C. (1907–36). At the laboratory, Day extended the standard thermometer scale from 1200 to 1600 degrees centigrade. The nitrogen gas thermometer scale remains the thermodynamic standard and is still in use at the laboratory. Day also measured the thermal stability of the major feldspar solid-solution series. Day initiated a major plan to investigate the physiochemical behavior of phases in systems of important oxides in the earth's crust; this study yielded major information needed in the steel, cement, and glass industries. In addition to studies of volcanoes and geysers, Day became vice president of the Corning Glass Works, where he conducted research for the foundation of an American optics industry necessitated by the cut off of German goods during World War I. President of the Geological Society of America, 1938, and elected to the National Academy of Sciences in 1911.

DAY, BENJAMIN HENRY (*b. West Springfield, Mass., 1810; d. New York, N.Y., 1889*), printer. Came to New York City, 1830, and in 1833 began publication of the New York *Sun*, a penny daily. Its success was immediate; by 1835 it boasted the highest circulation in the world. Day sold the *Sun* to Moses Yale Beach in 1838. Not a great journalist, he proved that newspapers at a popular price could be successful.

DAY, CLARENCE SHEPARD (*b. New York, N.Y., 1874; d. 1935*), author. Grandson of Benjamin H. Day. Graduated Yale, 1896. Wrote *This Simian World* (1920); *God and My Father* (1932); *Life with Father* (1935).

DAY, DAVID ALEXANDER (*b. Adams Co., Pa., 1851; d. at sea, 1897*). Lutheran missionary in Liberia, 1874–97.

DAY, DAVID TALBOT (*b. East Rockport, Ohio, 1859; d. Washington, D.C., 1925*), chemist, geologist. Chief, Mineral Resources Division, U.S. Geological Survey, 1886–1907; inaugurated study of oil shales.

DAY, EDMUND EZRA (*b. Manchester, N.H., 1883; d. Ithaca, N.Y., 1951*), economist, educator. Harvard (Ph.D., 1909). Taught Harvard (1910–23); University of Michigan (1923–27), where he organized the graduate school of business administration. Delegate, the World Monetary and Economic Conference, London (1933). President of Cornell University (1937–49). Director of the N.Y. Federal Reserve Board (1937–42). Director of the National Bureau of Economic Research (1939–44).

DAY, FRANK MILES (*b. Philadelphia, Pa., 1861; d. Philadelphia, 1918*), architect. Studied at University of Pennsylvania, and in London. His outstanding work was in collegiate buildings, notably at Princeton, Wellesley, and University of Colorado.

DAY, GEORGE PARMLY (*b. New York, N.Y., 1876; d. New Haven, Conn., 1959*), financier, publisher, university executive. Studied at Yale University. Founded the Yale University Press in 1908; headed the press until 1944. Treasurer of Yale University from 1910 to 1942. Day was responsible for expanding the role of the press from that of an academic elitist service to a high-level educational extension service.

DAY, HENRY NOBLE (*b. New Preston, Conn., 1808; d. New Haven, Conn., 1890*), Congregational clergyman, educator.

DAY, HOLMAN FRANCIS (*b. Vassalboro, Maine, 1865; d. Mill Valley, Calif., 1935*), journalist, novelist.

DAY, HORACE H. (*b. Great Barrington, Mass., 1813; d. Manchester, N.H., 1878*), manufacturer. In 1839, opened a small factory to manufacture rubber fabrics. His interests soon conflicted with those of Charles Goodyear, who had patented (1844) the process of vulcanization. After a series of complicated law suits in which Daniel Webster and Rufus Choate were of counsel, Day was enjoined permanently from further rubber manufacture in 1852.

DAY, JAMES GAMBLE (*b. Jefferson Co., Ohio, 1832; d. Des Moines, Iowa, 1898*), jurist. Judge, Iowa Supreme Court, 1870–84. Overruled a popular prohibition amendment to Iowa constitution as unconstitutional, 1882, and was refused reelection.

DAY, JAMES ROSCOE (*b. Whitneyville, Maine, 1845; d. Atlantic City, N.J., 1923*), Methodist clergyman, educator. A colorful and popular preacher, Day was chancellor of Syracuse University, 1904–22.

DAY, JEREMIAH (*b. New Preston, Conn., 1773; d. 1867*), Congregational clergyman, educator. Graduated Yale, 1795. Tutor and professor at Yale; president, 1817–47. Conservative and unselfish, he exerted great influence by force of character.

DAY, LUTHER (*b. Granville, N.Y., 1813; d. Ravenna, Ohio, 1885*), Ohio jurist.

DAY, STEPHEN (*b. England, ca. 1594; d. Cambridge, Mass., 1668*), first printer in British America. Locksmith by trade, Day immigrated to New England, 1638, under contract to work two years for Rev. Jesse Glover. Glover, who brought with him a printing press, a font of type, and paper, died on the voyage to Boston. His widow settled in Cambridge, where the press was set up. At least 22 imprints, including the *Bay Psalm Book* (1640), were made by the Cambridge Press before 1649, when Samuel Green became the printer. Day's relationship to the press is in doubt. It is presumed that he set it up and managed it for Mrs. Glover.

DAY, WILLIAM RUFUS (*b. Ravenna, Ohio, 1849; d. Mackinac Island, Mich., 1923*), secretary of state, lawyer, jurist. Son of Luther Day. Graduated University of Michigan, 1870; admitted to the bar, 1872. Practicing in Ohio, he became acquainted with William McKinley, who as president appointed Day secretary of state, 1898. Day served with the U.S. commission to make peace with Spain, and in 1903 was appointed associate justice of the U.S. Supreme Court, where he served until 1922. A learned and liberal judge, he was celebrated for the clarity and concision of his opinions.

DAYTON, ELIAS (*b. Elizabeth-Town, N.J., 1737; d. Elizabeth, N.J., 1807*), storekeeper, Revolutionary brigadier general.

DAYTON, JONATHAN (*b. Elizabeth-Town, N.J., 1760; d. Elizabeth, N.J., 1824*), Revolutionary soldier, lawyer, politician, Son of Elias Dayton. Congressman, Federalist, from New Jersey, 1791–99; U.S. senator, 1799–1805. Indicted, 1807, for complicity in Aaron Burr's schemes, but released on nolle prosequi. Dayton, Ohio, is named for him.

DAYTON, WILLIAM LEWIS (*b. Baskingridge, N.J., 1807; d. 1864*), lawyer, politician, diplomat. Great-grandson of Elias Dayton. Graduated Princeton, 1825. U.S. senator, Whig, from New Jersey, 1842–51; Republican nominee for vice president, 1856. As U.S. minister to France, 1861–64, he successfully opposed Confederate attempts to secure French aid and recognition.

DEADY, MATTHEW PAUL (*b. near Easton, Md., 1824; d. Portland, Oreg., 1893*), jurist. Immigrated to Oregon, 1849; practiced law; presided over constitutional convention of Oregon (1857). U.S. district judge for Oregon, 1859–93.

DEALEY, GEORGE BANNERMAN (*b. Manchester, England, 1859; d. Dallas, Tex., 1946*), newspaper publisher. Immigrated to Galveston, Tex., with family, 1870. Employed as office boy by the *Galveston News*, 1874, he rose rapidly in the organization. On his recommendation, the *Dallas Morning News* was founded, 1885; he spent the rest of his career with it, serving as business manager, as general manager, and as president of the corporation that published both the Galveston and Dallas papers. In 1940, he retired as president and became chairman of the board. He made the *News* a model of decent, civic-minded journalism, refusing advertising believed misleading or harmful, supporting all intelligent plans for improvement of Dallas, and speaking out consistently for tolerance (as in his uncompromising resistance to Ku Klux Klan in the 1920's).

DEAN, AMOS (*b. Barnard, Vt., 1803; d. Albany, N.Y., 1868*), lawyer, educator.

DEAN, BASHFORD (*b. New York, 1867; d. Battle Creek, Mich., 1928*), zoologist, ichthyologist, armor expert. Curator of arms and armor, Metropolitan Museum of Art, 1906–27.

DEAN, GORDON EVANS (*b. Seattle, Wash., 1905; d. Nantucket, Mass., 1958*), lawyer, business executive. Studied at the University of Redlands and the University of Southern California (J.D., 1930). Dean worked as special consultant and assistant to the attorney general in the 1930's. In 1945, he was chosen by Supreme Court Justice Robert Jackson to assist him in prosecuting Nazi criminals at Nuremberg. From 1949 to 1953, he was a member and later chairman of the Atomic Energy Commission. In 1953, he organized and became chairman of the board of the Nuclear Science and Engineering Corporation, later a part of General Dynamics. He died in a plane crash in 1958.

DEAN, JAMES BYRON (*b. Marion, Ind., 1931; d. near Cholame, Calif., 1955*), actor. Played Arab boy in Gide's *The Immoralist* on Broadway, 1954. Films include *East of Eden* (1955), *Rebel Without a Cause* (1955), and *Giant* (1957). Received posthumous nominations for the Academy Award for last two films. Died in an automobile accident in California.

DEAN, JULIA (*b. Pleasant Valley, N.Y., 1830; d. 1868*), one of America's most beloved actresses at her peak, 1846–55.

DEAN, "MAN MOUNTAIN." *See* LEAVITT, FRANK SIMMONS.

DEAN, SIDNEY (*b. Glastonbury, Conn., 1818; d. Brookline, Mass., 1901*), Methodist clergyman, congressman, journalist.

DEAN, WILLIAM HENRY, JR. (*b. Lynchburg, Va., 1910; d. New York City, 1952*), economist, U.N. staff member. Studied at Bowdoin College and Harvard University. One of the first blacks to receive a Ph.D. in economics, Dean was denied professional status at Harvard because of his race. Taught at Atlanta University, 1933–42; served on the National Resources Planning Board, 1940–42; joined the Office of Price Administration, 1942, as chief economist in Haiti and the Virgin Islands. Joined the staff of the U.N., 1946, and served as head of the African Unit of the Division of Economic Stability and Development. Focusing on Italian Somaliland, Dean attempted in 1952 to help that country's technical development. Dean was profoundly moved by the plight of the people in that region, but his efforts to help them were stymied by resistance from entrenched whites in authority. His idealism and programs have subsequently served as models for American development efforts.

DEANE, CHARLES (*b. Biddeford, Maine, 1813; d. 1889*), Boston merchant, historian. After retiring from business in 1864, Deane devoted himself to tireless, very able research in American colonial history. Among his works, his discovery and editing of Bradford's *History of Plymouth Plantation* (1856) is considered most important.

DEANE, SAMUEL (*b. Dedham, Mass., 1733; d. Portland, Maine, 1814*), Congregational clergyman, agricultural writer. Author of *The New England Farmer or Georgical Dictionary* (1790), an encyclopedic work, the first of its kind in the United States.

DEANE, SILAS (*b. Groton, Conn., 1737; d. at sea near Deal, England, 1789*), member of the Continental Congress, diplomat. Graduated Yale, 1758. Admitted to the bar, 1761, he began successful practice in Wethersfield, Conn. He married twice; both alliances improved his economic and social situation. Deane was an early leader of the Revolutionary movement in Connecticut. He became a member of the General Assembly, 1772, and in May 1773 was secretary of the newly appointed legislative Committee of Correspondence. He was a delegate to the First and Second Continental Congresses, but, for some reason, the Connecticut Assembly did not reappoint him for 1776.

Unwilling to lose his services, Congress in March 1776 sent him to France as a representative of two separate committees. One, the commercial committee, authorized five merchants (of whom Deane was one) to buy colonial produce with money furnished by Congress, to ship commodities so purchased abroad, and to sell them there and invest the proceeds in supplies needed by the colonies. The other, the Committee of Secret Correspondence, instructed Deane to buy clothing, arms, munitions, and artillery. He was also to discover if an American ambassador would be received in France, and if the French government would form treaties of alliance and commerce with the colonies.

Deane's mission was successful. With the aid of Beaumarchais, he secured eight shiploads of military supplies, which were of material help in the Saratoga campaign of 1777. He also commissioned and sent to America many European military officers, some of whom, especially Lafayette, De Kalb, Steuben, and Pulaski, were valuable to the American cause. Unfortunately, he also sent many soldiers of fortune, who proved an embarrassment to Congress and a liability to the country.

In September 1776, Congress appointed a commission of three—Deane, Benjamin Franklin, and Arthur Lee—to strengthen its connection with France. In February 1778, the commissioners signed two treaties with the French government, one of commerce, the other providing for an offensive and defensive alliance. Soon thereafter, Congress ordered Deane home. The reason for his recall lay in Arthur Lee's insinuations that Deane was charging Congress for supplies which had been intended as free gifts to the Americans by the French government. Because he did not have proper vouchers to cover his financial transactions, Deane was unable to effect a settlement with Congress. After two years, he returned to Europe, hoping to speed up the auditing of his accounts. Embittered and ill, Deane lost confidence in the American cause. In 1781 he wrote friends in America advising them to abandon the war and seek reconciliation with England. These letters, intercepted and printed by a New York Loyalist press, further blackened Deane's reputation in his homeland. After the war Deane lived as a bankrupt exile in Ghent and later in England.

Deane's services to America were substantial and his personal losses heavy. In 1842 Congress made partial restitution to his heirs, voting them the sum of $37,000.

DE ANGELIS, THOMAS JEFFERSON (*b. San Francisco, Calif., 1859; d. 1933*), actor, light-opera comedian. The song "Tammany" from *Fantana* was his greatest personal hit and was always associated with him.

DEARBORN, HENRY (*b. Hampton, N.H., 1751; d. Roxbury, Mass., 1829*), physician, soldier. Served with distinction in the Revolution, eventually joining Washington's staff. Represented the District of Maine in Congress, 1793–97, and served as secretary of war, 1801–09. Given command of the northeast area from the Niagara River to the New England coast in 1812, it was soon apparent that the military ability he had once possessed had disappeared with age and disuse. His failure to implement his own plans for invasion of Canada directly contributed to Hull's defeat at Detroit. After another American defeat at Queenston, mismanagement of a proposed attack at Kingston, and the near capture of Sackett's Harbor, Dearborn was removed in July 1813.

DEARBORN, HENRY ALEXANDER SCAMWELL (*b. Exeter, N.H., 1783; d. Portland, Maine, 1851*), lawyer, politician, author. Son of Henry Dearborn. Collector of the port of Boston, 1812–29.

DEARING, JOHN LINCOLN (*b. Webster, Maine, 1858; d. 1916*), Baptist clergyman. Missionary to Japan, 1889–1916.

DEARTH, HENRY GOLDEN (*b. Bristol, R.I., 1864; d. 1918*), landscape and genre painter, distinguished for unusual skill with color.

DEAS, ZACHARIAH CANTEY (*b. Charleston[?], S.C., 1819; d. 1882*), cotton broker, Confederate soldier. Nephew of James Chesnut, Jr.

DEAVER, JOHN BLAIR (*b. Lancaster Co., Pa., 1855; d. Wyncote, Pa., 1931*), surgeon. M.D., University of Pennsylvania, 1878. A tireless and brilliant operator; one of the first to adopt and develop appendectomy and to insist on prompt surgical interference.

DE BARDELEBEN, HENRY FAIRCHILD (*b. Alabama, 1840; d. 1910*), industrialist. Ward of Daniel Pratt, whose daughter, Ellen, he later married, De Bardeleben managed Pratt's Red Mountain Iron & Coal Co. and the development of the Helena mines. When Pratt died, 1873, De Bardeleben inherited his fortune. He helped organize the Eureka Coal Co. and other coal and iron companies, founded the town of Bessemer, and had extensive holdings of mineral lands. In 1891 he sold his properties to the Tennessee Coal, Iron and Railroad Co. Three years later he lost most of his fortune in an attempt to gain control of that company. De Bardeleben's enterprises were the basis for modern Birmingham, Ala., and its industrial district.

DE BARENNE, JOANNES GREGORIUS DUSSER. *See* DUSSER DE BARENNE, JOANNES GREGORIUS.

DE BERDT, DENNYS (*b. London, England, ca. 1694; d. 1770*), merchant, colonial agent in London for Massachusetts and Delaware. Both colonies acknowledged his services in securing repeal of the Stamp Act.

DE BOW, JAMES DUNWOODY BROWNSON (*b. Charleston, S.C., 1820; d. Elizabeth, N.J., 1867*), editor, statistician. Graduated College of Charleston, 1843. Was admitted to the bar but practiced journalism, becoming editor of the *Southern Quarterly Review*. In 1846 he founded at New Orleans the *Commercial Review of the South and Southwest*, which in three years gained the largest circulation of any magazine published in the South. It occupied a place in its area like that of *Hunt's Merchants' Magazine* in the country at large. De Bow advocated instruction in economics at the University of Louisiana and occupied its chair of political economy. He was also superintendent of the seventh U.S. census. De Bow retained some measure of nationalism in his thinking but drifted with the secessionist tide and became increasingly a violent Southern partisan. During the Civil War, he was chief Confederate agent for the purchase and sale of cotton.

DE BRAHM, WILLIAM GERARD (*b. probably Holland, 1717; d. Philadelphia, Pa., ca. 1799*), surveyor general of the southern district of North America, 1764–83. Founded Bethany settlement, Georgia, 1751; drew first map of Georgia and South Carolina; with Bernard Romans charted the Florida coast and made inland surveys.

DEBS, EUGENE VICTOR (*b. Terre Haute, Ind., 1855; d. Elmhurst, Ill., 1926*), Socialist advocate. Helped organize a lodge of the Brotherhood of Locomotive Firemen, 1875; by 1880 was a national officer of the brotherhood and editor of its magazine. An advocate of "industrial" organization, in 1893 he promoted, and was president of, the American Railway Union, later prominent in strikes against the Great Northern Railroad and the Pullman Co. Debs became a Socialist, 1895; in 1900, 1904, 1908, 1912, and 1920 he was Socialist nominee for president of the United States. He was imprisoned, 1919–21, for publicly denouncing the prosecution of persons charged with sedition. Never an intellectual leader of his party, Debs's character and moral earnestness made him an effective standard-bearer.

DEBYE, PETER JOSEPH WILLIAM (*b. Maastricht, the Netherlands, 1884; d. Ithaca, N.Y., 1966*), physicist and physical chemist. Graduated from the Technical University in Aachen, Germany (1905), where he was strongly influenced by Arnold Sommerfeld. Succeeding Einstein as professor of theoretical physics at the University of Zurich (1911–12), Debye joined the small international elite of physicists pioneering in the study of electricity, radiation, and molecular structure. He held professorships at Utrecht (1912–13), Göttingen (1913–20), the Federal Technical University in Zurich (1920–27), Leipzig (1927–34), and Berlin (1934–39). His major research during this period progressed in three areas: molecular electric dipole moments, X-ray diffraction, and electrolytes. In 1936 he was awarded the Nobel Prize in chemistry. In 1940 Debye moved to the U.S., and he became a citizen in 1946. He headed the Cornell chemistry department (1940–50) and became professor emeritus in 1952. In the U.S. he was particularly involved in the development and utilization of the light-scattering process.

DE CAMP, JOSEPH RODEFER (*b., Cincinnati, Ohio, 1858; d. Bocagrande, Fla., 1923*), painter. Student of Frank Duveneck; a sound, capable portrait painter and an efficient teacher.

DECATUR, STEPHEN (*b. Newport, R.I., 1752; d. near Frankford, Pa., 1808*), privateer, naval officer.

DECATUR, STEPHEN (*b. Sinepuxent, Md., 1779; d. Bladensburg, Md., 1820*), naval officer. Son of Stephen Decatur (1752–1808). Became midshipman, 1798; advanced rapidly and in 1803 assumed his first command. Active throughout the Tripolitan War, Decatur became famous for heroic actions. His capture and burning of frigate *Philadelphia*, 1804, was called "the most bold and daring act of the age." Returning to America, 1805, he was in 1808 given command of naval forces on the southeastern coast. In that same year he was a member of the court-martial that suspended Capt. James Barron after the *Chesapeake-Leopard* incident. During the War of 1812, commanding the *United States* on an independent cruise, he defeated HMS *Macedonian* off Madeira, Oct. 25, 1812, in a celebrated action, but was blockaded with his prize in New London, Conn., soon after his return. Attempting to run the British blockade of New York with the *President* early in 1815, he surrendered after a heavy action with HMS *Endymion* and *Pomone* off Long Island. During the summer of 1815, as commodore commanding a squadron of nine ships, he dictated a treaty with Algiers, ending tribute and requiring full payment for injuries suffered by Americans; he then exacted payment for similar wartime depredations on American commerce from Tunis and Tripoli. Replying to a toast after his return, he spoke the oft-quoted words "Our country . . . may she always be in the right; but our country, right or wrong." Serving thereafter as a navy commissioner, Decatur was killed in a duel by Capt. James Barron.

DE COPPET, EDWARD J. (*b. 1855; d. 1916*), New York banker, stockbroker, patron of music. Founded the Flonzaley Quartet, 1904.

DE COSTA, BENJAMIN FRANKLIN (*b. Charlestown, Mass., 1831; d. 1904*), clergyman, historian. Wrote chiefly on early American discovery and exploration.

DE CUEVAS, MARQUIS (*b. Santiago, Chile, 1885; d. Cannes, France, 1961*), ballet impresario and patron of the arts. Graduated from the Catholic University of Santiago, then established himself as a fashionable dress designer in Paris. Married a granddaughter of John D. Rockefeller and became a U.S. citizen in 1940. Launched Ballet International (1944–45), a critical and financial failure. In 1947 he assumed management of the Nouveau Ballet de Monte Carlo which he renamed the Grand Ballet de Monte Carlo. He relocated the company to Paris in 1950 and renamed it the Grand Ballet du Marquis de Cuevas. In 1958 he again changed the name, to the International Ballet of the Marquis de Cuevas. De Cuevas is remembered more for extravagant productions than for memorable choreography.

DEEMER, HORACE EMERSON (*b. Bourbon, Ind., 1858; d. 1917*), jurist. Judge, Iowa Supreme Court, 1894–1917, the longest continuous tenure in that court.

DEEMS, CHARLES FORCE (*b. Baltimore, Md. 1820; d. New York, N.Y., 1893*), clergyman, teacher. Headed Church of the Strangers, New York City; founded American Institute of Christian Philosophy, 1881.

DEERE, JOHN (*b. Rutland, Vt., 1804; d. 1886*), manufacturer. Left Vermont in 1837 and settled eventually at Grand Detour, Ill., where he opened a blacksmith shop. Contact with farmers revealed that plows brought from the East were unsatisfactory for working prairie soil. Deere, after considerable experiment, began to develop improved plows which became popular. About 1846 Deere established a new company in Moline, Ill. Convinced that better plows could be produced with a higher grade of steel plate, he imported steel from England to test his theory. After a successful trial he began negotiations in Pittsburgh for steel of equal quality and so brought about the first rolling of plow steel in the United States *ca.* 1847.

DEERFOOT (*b. Cattaraugus Reservation, Erie Co., N.Y., 1828; d. Erie Co., 1897*), professional name of Lewis Bennett, a Seneca Indian. A remarkable distance runner, trained under the old Indian system; ran in England, 1861–63.

DEERING, NATHANIEL (*b. Portland, Maine, 1791; d. near Portland, 1881*), author, editor, dramatist.

DEERING, WILLIAM (*b. South Paris, Maine, 1826; d. Cocoanut Grove, Fla., 1913*), manufacturer. After experience as dry-goods merchant, he entered partnership with Elijah H. Gammon, who had purchased rights to manufacture the hand-binding harvester developed by the Marsh brothers. The firm also undertook production of the Gordon wire binder and in 1879, when Deering had become sole owner, began making a twine binder after John F. Appleby's design. Under Deering's tireless management, the business grew steadily. In 1902 it merged with the International Harvester Co.

DE FONTAINE, FELIX GREGORY (*b. Boston, Mass., 1834; d. Columbia, S.C., 1896*), journalist, author. Confederate war correspondent, 1861–65; later worked on New York *Telegram* and *Herald*.

DE FOREST, ALFRED VICTOR (*b. New York, N.Y., 1888; d. Marlborough, N.H., 1945*), metallographer. Nephew of Robert W. De Forest. Graduated Massachusetts Institute of Technology, 1912. Expert in the field of metal testing and inspection, for which he invented a number of electromagnetic devices. Professor of engineering, MIT, *post* 1934.

DE FOREST, DAVID CURTIS (*b. Huntington, Conn., 1774; d. 1825*), merchant. Established the first permanent American commercial house in Buenos Aires. Acted as Argentine consul general to the United States, 1818–22.

DE FOREST, ERASTUS LYMAN (*b. Watertown, Conn., 1834; d. 1888*), mathematician. Graduated Yale, 1854; Sheffield Scientific School, 1856. Known for his studies in the theory of probability and errors, unrecognized by contemporaries but now considered outstanding.

DE FOREST, JOHN KINNE HYDE (*b. Westbrook, Conn., 1844; d. Tokyo, Japan, 1911*), Congregational clergyman, missionary to Japan, 1874–1911.

DE FOREST, JOHN WILLIAM (*b. Humphreysville, Conn., 1826; d. New Haven, Conn., 1906*), author. Published in 1851 a solid *History of the Indians of Connecticut,* and in the decade thereafter several minor novels and reminiscences of travel. Service in the Civil War, 1861–65, won him rank of major; he continued to serve until 1868 as captain in command of a Freedman's Bureau district at Greenville, S.C. His war experiences gave him material for his best work, which is outstanding for its vigorous realism and satiric reading of character. Among his novels are *Miss Ravenel's Conversion from Secession to Loyalty* (1867); *Kate Beaumont* (1872); *Honest John Vane* (1875); *The Bloody Chasm* (1881).

DE FOREST, LEE (*b. Council Bluffs, Iowa, 1873; d. Hollywood, Calif., 1961*), inventor. Studied at Yale (Ph.B., 1896; Ph.D., 1899). A pioneer in wireless telegraphy, telephony, and sound motion pictures, he was awarded more than 300 patents. His first major invention was the responder, which facilitated the transmission of radio waves. He then formed the American De Forest Wireless Telegraphy Company, but he was dismissed in 1905 by the company's directors due to allegations of patent infringement. In 1906 he began applying for patents on the triode Audion, one of the most important and fundamental inventions of the twentieth century. Though de Forest neither fully understood nor appreciated his invention, the triode began the age of electronics. In 1912, working for the Federal Telegraph Company in Palo Alto, Calif., he and his coworkers found that by feeding a triode's output back into its input, they could use it as a powerful generator or transmitter of high-frequency radio signals. This made international telephony possible. De Forest sold long-distance telephony rights to the American Telephone and Telegraph Company in 1913; in 1914 American Telephone acquired the radio signaling rights to the Audion. Turning his attention to motion pictures, de Forest presented the first commercial talking picture in New York City, 1923. Having made fortunes through invention and lost them through development, de Forest changed his strategy in his fifties and began to devote himself primarily to invention, selling the rights to his discoveries to others. His autobiography is *Father of Radio* (1950).

DE FOREST, ROBERT WEEKS (*b. New York, N.Y., 1848; d. 1931*), lawyer, businessman, philanthropist. Patron of art; champion of conservation; leader in the movement for the founding of a national association to fight tuberculosis.

DE GRAFFENRIED, CHRISTOPHER. *See* GRAFFENRIED, CHRISTOPHER BARON DE.

DE HAAS, JACOB. *See* HAAS, JACOB JUDAH AARON DE.

DE HAAS, JOHN PHILIP (*b. Holland, ca. 1735; d. Philadelphia, Pa., 1786*), Revolutionary soldier. Brought to Lancaster Co., Pa., as a child. Served in French and Indian War frontier campaigns. After rising to brigadier general in Continental service, he resigned in 1777.

DE HAVEN, EDWIN JESSE (*b. Philadelphia, Pa., 1816; d. Philadelphia, 1865*), naval officer. In 1850–51 De Haven commanded an Arctic expedition to search for Sir John Franklin and acquire scientific information. Discovered and named Grinnell Land.

DEINDÖRFER, JOHANNES (*b. near Nürnberg, Bavaria, 1828; d. Waverly, Iowa, 1907*), Lutheran clergyman. Came to America, 1851. After differing with the Missouri Synod, he removed from Michigan to Iowa and helped found the German Lutheran Synod at St. Sebald, 1854.

DEITZLER, GEORGE WASHINGTON (*b. Pine Grove, Pa., 1826; d. Arizona, 1884*), antislavery leader in Kansas. Solicited arms for the Free-Soil cause in Boston; fought in Wakarusa War, 1855; served in Free-Soil Kansas territorial legislature, 1857–58, and with distinction in Civil War.

DE KAY, GEORGE COLMAN (*b. in or near New York, N.Y., 1802; d. Washington, D.C., 1849*), mariner. Won engagements at sea while serving the Argentine Republic in its war with Brazil, 1826–27. Brother of James E. De Kay.

DE KAY, JAMES ELLSWORTH (*b. Lisbon, Portugal, 1792; d. Oyster Bay, N.Y., 1851*), naturalist, physician. An intimate of the Knickerbocker writers in New York. Author of the *Zoology of New York* (1842–44). Brother of George C. De Kay.

DE KOVEN, HENRY LOUIS REGINALD (*b. Middletown, Conn., 1859; d. 1920*), composer. His romantic comic opera *Robin Hood* was first heard in Chicago, Ill., 1890. In the years that followed, De Koven wrote many light-opera scores and served as music critic for newspapers in Chicago and New York. His best-known song, "O Promise Me," was interpolated in the *Robin Hood* score.

DE KOVEN, JAMES (*b. Middletown, Conn., 1831; d. Racine, Wis., 1879*), Episcopal clergyman. A representative of High Church views and a defender of ritualism, he was active as clergyman and teacher in Wisconsin *post* 1855.

DE LACY, WALTER WASHINGTON (*b. Petersburg, Va., 1819; d. 1892*), soldier, engineer. Employed in constructing the Mullan Road, 1858, and various western railroads. De Lacy made the first map of Montana (1864–65), which was for many years the best.

DELAFIELD, EDWARD (*b. New York, N.Y., 1794; d. 1875*), opthalmologist, surgeon. Son of John Delafield. A founder of New York Eye Infirmary, 1820, and American Opthalmological Society, 1864; president, College of Physicians and Surgeons, New York, 1858–75.

DELAFIELD, FRANCIS (*b. 1841; d. Noroton, Conn., 1915*), pathologist, physician. Son of Edward Delafield. A graduate of Yale, he received the M.D. degree in 1863 from College of Physicians and Surgeons, New York. He continued medical studies in Europe, where he was influenced by Rudolf Virchow. *Post* 1876, he taught at his alma mater and in 1886 helped found and served as president of the Association of American Physicians. His textbook, *A Handbook of Post Mortem Examinations and of Morbid Anatomy* (1872), was unusually successful. Delafield made contributions of the first importance to pathology, especially of nephritis and of the diseases of the colon.

DELAFIELD, JOHN (*b. England, 1748; d. Long Island, N.Y., 1824*), merchant. Immigrated to New York City, 1783, and prospered in trade, later engaging in insurance.

DELAFIELD, JOHN (*b. New York, N.Y., 1786; d. Geneva, N.Y., 1853*), banker, farmer. Son of John Delafield (1748–1824). Entered banking in London after experience in merchant shipping, 1803–08. Returning to America, 1820, he throve as a banker and a civic leader. Losses in 1838 led to his retirement to Seneca Co., N.Y., where he established a model farm.

DELAFIELD, RICHARD (*b. New York, N.Y., 1798; d. 1873*), military engineer. Son of John Delafield (1748–1824). Graduated West Point, 1818, and served twice as its superintendent. Commanded the Corps of Engineers, 1864–66, until his retirement as major general.

DE LAMAR, JOSEPH RAPHAEL (*b. Amsterdam, Holland, 1843; d. New York, N.Y., 1918*), capitalist.

DELAMATER, CORNELIUS HENRY (*b. Rhinebeck, N.Y., 1821; d. 1889*), mechanical engineer. As a young man, Delamater and his cousin Peter Hogg acquired the Phoenix Foundry in New York City. In 1839 Delamater met John Ericsson, after whose designs the foundry built the first iron boats and the first steam fire engines used in America. During the Civil War, Delamater's foundry built, according to Ericsson's plans, the famous ironclad *Monitor*. During its battle with the *Merrimack*, the *Monitor*'s engines were operated by Delamater's workmen. The firm was noted also for its gunboats, propellers, and air compressors and for building (1881) the first successful submarine torpedo boat designed by John P. Holland.

DE LANCEY, JAMES (*b. New York, N.Y., 1703; d. 1760*), New York colonial political leader. After study in England, he returned to America in 1725 and was admitted to the bar. Appointed to New York Supreme Court, 1731, he became chief justice in 1733 by favor of Gov. William Cosby. During the prosecution of John Peter Zenger, De Lancey's decision to disbar James Alexander and William Smith, leaders of the legal profession, made him unpopular. Granted in 1744 a commission as chief justice for good behavior, De Lancey used his new immunity to control both council and assembly and to block the governor's leadership in the colony. In 1753 he became lieutenant governor of New York and managed to retain both his high offices until his death. The classic division of New York politics into the Episcopalian "De Lancey party" and the Presbyterian "Livingston party" survived him.

DE LANCEY, JAMES (*b. New York, N.Y., 1732; d. Bath, England, 1800*), politician. Son of James De Lancey (1703–60), he was educated in England and acquired sporting tastes. The "father of the New York turf," De Lancey was probably the first to import Thoroughbreds to New York. Becoming head of the powerful De Lancey family upon his father's death, he displayed gifts for dexterous management equaling his father's, and won several political contests. As a member of New York's last provincial assembly, he voted against approval of the proceedings of the First Continental Congress. Shortly thereafter he retired to England.

DE LANCEY, JAMES (*b. New York, 1746; d. Nova Scotia, Canada, 1804*), Loyalist. Cousin of James De Lancey (1732–1800). Leader of a troop, known as De Lancey's Horse, in the irregular partisan warfare about New York, 1777–82.

DE LANCEY, OLIVER (*b. 1718; d. Beverley, England, 1785*), merchant, colonial politician, Loyalist soldier. Brother of James De Lancey (1703–60).

DE LANCEY, WILLIAM HEATHCOTE (*b. Mamaroneck, N.Y., 1797; d. Geneva, N.Y., 1865*), Episcopal clergyman. Grandson of James De Lancey (1703–60). Graduated Yale, 1817; ordained, 1822. Provost of University of Pennsylvania, 1828–33. First bishop of the diocese of western New York, consecrated 1839.

DELAND, MARGARET (*b. near Allegheny, Pa., 1857; d. Boston, Mass., 1945*), author. Maiden name, Margaret Campbell. Studied art at Cooper Union; taught drawing and design at present Hunter College, New York City, 1876–80. Married Lorin F.

Deland, 1880. Settling in Boston, the Delands undertook to assist unwed mothers by taking them and their infants into the Deland home. After the success of her first book, a collection of poems, *The Old Garden* (1886), she turned to fiction and wrote an attack on extreme Calvinism in *John Ward, Preacher* (1888), which excited considerable controversy. Other of her novels were *The Awakening of Helena Richie* (1906) and *The Iron Woman* (1911). She was author also of a number of pleasant short stories reminiscent of her Pennsylvania childhood, which were collected in *Old Chester Tales* (1898), *Dr. Lavendar's People* (1903), and other volumes.

DE LANGLADE, CHARLES MICHEL (*b. Mackinac, Canada, 1729; d. Green Bay, Wis., ca. 1801*), soldier. Son of Augustin Mouet de Langlade and an Ottawa Indian woman, he was educated by Jesuits, wrote a good hand, and was received as a gentleman. As a cadet in the French colonial troops, he drove the English from Pickawillany, 1752; during the French and Indian War, he led the Indian auxiliaries and was credited with defeating Braddock. He also served on the Great Lakes in 1757 and in the Quebec campaign, 1759. After surrendering the Mackinac post to the English, he became a British subject and served the crown faithfully during the Revolution.

DELANO, AMASSA (*b. Duxbury, Mass., 1763; d. Boston, Mass., 1823*), ship captain. Author of *Narrative of Voyages and Travels in the Northern and Southern Hemispheres* (1817).

DELANO, COLUMBUS (*b. Shoreham, Vt., 1809; d. 1896*), lawyer, politician. Raised in Ohio. Congressman from Ohio, Whig, 1845–47; Republican, 1865–69. As secretary of the interior, 1870–75, Delano was criticized for frauds in the Bureau of Indian Affairs.

DELANO, JANE ARMINDA (*b. Townsend, N.Y., 1862; d. France, 1919*), teacher, nurse. As chairman of the National Committee of Red Cross Nurses, directed the recruitment of nurses during World War I.

DELANO, WILLIAM ADAMS (*b. New York, N.Y., 1874; d. New York, 1960*), architect. Studied at Yale and Columbia and at the École des Beaux Arts in Paris. Taught design at Columbia School of Architecture fro 1903 to 1910. Founded, with Chester Aldrich, an architectural firm in 1903; he remained head of the firm until 1950 and consultant until his death. The firm became the foremost twentieth-century exponent of the academic trend in architecture in America. Characterized by the severe Georgian style, Delano's designs included many wealthy estates, hotels (New York's Knickerbocker, 1914), the Japanese Embassy in Washington (1931), the American Embassy in Paris (1933), and La Guardia Field in New York (1937–43). Member of the National Capital Park and Planning Commission (1929–46), and of the National Institute of Arts and Letters.

DELANY, MARTIN ROBINSON (*b. Charlestown, W.Va., 1812; d. Xenia, Ohio, 1885*), physician, journalist, black leader.

DELANY, PATRICK BERNARD (*b. Killavilla, Ireland, 1845; d. South Orange, N.J., 1924*), electrical engineer. Came to America as a child; raised in Hartford, Conn. His inventions for telegraphic systems include the anti-Page relay, anti-induction cables, a synchronous multiplex telegraph; he also invented devices for submarine detection.

DELAVAN, EDWARD CORNELIUS (*b. Westchester Co., N.Y., 1793; d. Schenectady, N.Y., 1871*), reformer, publisher. Helped organize New York State Temperance Society, 1829.

DE LA WARR, THOMAS WEST, BARON (*b. Hampshire[?], England, 1577; d. 1618*), first governor and captain general of the Virginia colony. Author of *The Relation of . . . the Lord De-la-Warre . . . of the Colonie, Planted in Virginea* (1611).

DELEE, JOSEPH BOLIVAR (*b. Cold Spring, N.Y., 1869; d. Chicago, Ill., 1942*), obstetrician. M.D., Chicago Medical College, 1891; made special studies in Berlin, Vienna, and Paris, to further his aim of reforming U.S obstetrical practice. Opened the Chicago Lying-in Dispensary, 1895, a maternity clinic which offered free prenatal care and obstetric service in the patient's homes; he continued to conduct the clinic (later hospital) independently until its affiliation with the University of Chicago Medical School, 1929. Chairman of the Department of Obstetrics and Gynecology at Northwestern University Medical School, 1896–1929, and at University of Chicago, 1929–34. He was a superb, if demanding, teacher. A perfectionist and a selfless humanitarian, he carried on a crusade—by example, formal teaching, and writing—to prevent death in childbirth. He was author of, among other books, *The Principles and Practices of Obstetrics* (1913, and later editions), and edited the *Yearbook of Obstetrics* (1904–41).

DE LEEUW, ADOLPH LODEWYK (*b. Zwolle, Netherlands, 1861; d. Plainfield, N.J., 1942*), engineer. Educated at the Delft Polytechnic and University of Leiden; immigrated to United States, 1890. In a long series of systematic experiments with the milling machine, he established bases for redesign of the cutters employed, thus greatly improving efficiency of the machine and leading to other innovations and improvements. He was chief engineer of several large manufacturing companies and served as an independent consultant for problems of production and management.

DE LEON, DANIEL (*b. Curaçao, 1852; d. New York, N.Y., 1914*), Socialist advocate. Settled in New York City, *ca.* 1874; taught school and studied law, receiving LL.B. from Columbia, 1878. In 1890 joined Socialist Labor party; in 1891 became its national lecturer and in 1892 editor of its weekly, *The People*. He was Socialist candidate for governor of New York in 1891 and 1902. Dominant in the party and a complete doctrinaire, De Leon criticized the leadership and organization of existing trade unions and caused a major split in the Socialist movement. In 1905, he helped to found the Industrial Workers of the World. De Leon's propagandist writings were admired by Lenin.

DE LEON, THOMAS COOPER (*b. Columbia, S.C., 1839; d. Mobile, Ala., 1914*), author, Confederate soldier. Managing editor and, later, editor of the *Mobile Register*; author of Civil War reminiscences, parodies and local-color novels.

DELÉRY, FRANÇOIS CHARLES (*b. St. Charles Parish, La., 1815; d. Bay St. Louis, La., 1880*), physician, writer. Best known for his works on yellow fever; also wrote on educational, philosophical, and political subjects.

DELL, FLOYD JAMES (*b. Barry, Ill., 1887; d. Bethesda, Md., 1969*), novelist, editor, playwright, and social critic. Joined the Socialist party at age sixteen, then dropped out of high school, and within a year became a reporter. Worked as a book reviewer and editor of the *Friday Literary Review*, a supplement of the *Chicago Evening Post* (1909–13). Moving to New York City's Greenwich Village in 1913, he became a managing editor of the radical magazine the *Masses*. With other members of the *Masses* staff he was indicted and twice tried under the Espionage Act of 1917 but was never convicted. He became an associate editor of the *Liberator* in 1918. He held government jobs from 1935–47. Dell's novels include *Moon-Calf* (1920), *Janet March* (1923), *This Mad Ideal* (1925), *Runaway* (1925), *An Old Man's Folly* (1926), *An Unmarried Father* (1927), *Souvenir* (1929), *Love Without Money* (1931), and *Diana Stair* (1932). His nonfiction includes *Women* *as World-Builders* (1913), *Were You Ever a Child?* (1919), *The Briary-Bush* (1921), *Looking at Life* (1924), *Love in Greenwich Village* (1926), *Intellectual Vagabondage* (1926), *The Outline of Marriage* (1926), *Upton Sinclair* (1927), *Love in the Machine Age* (1930), and *Homecoming* (1933).

DELLENBAUGH, FREDERICK SAMUEL (*b. McConnelsville, Ohio, 1853; d. New York, N.Y., 1935*), artist, author, explorer. His *Canyon Voyage* (1908) is the story of Maj. John Wesley Powell's 1871 Colorado River expedition.

DEL MAR, ALEXANDER (*b. New York, N.Y., 1836; d. Little Falls, N.J., 1926*), mining engineer, economist. Author of *A History of the Precious Metals from the Earliest Times to the Present* (1880) and other works on money and coinage.

DELMAS, DELPHIN MICHAEL (*b. France, 1844; d. Santa Monica, Calif., 1928*), lawyer. Moved to San José, Calif., as a child. An accomplished advocate, he achieved notoriety while defending Harry K. Thaw at his 1907 trial for murder of Stanford White.

DELMONICO, LORENZO (*b. Marengo, Switzerland, 1813; d. 1881*), restaurateur. Arrived New York City, 1832; established with two uncles a restaurant which provided food cooked and served in the best European manner of the day. Within twenty years, he set new standards for American dining and made New York famous the world over as a center of good living. Through his example and success, he was largely responsible for the growth of the restaurant as an institution in American cities.

DE LONG, GEORGE WASHINGTON (*b. New York, N.Y., 1844; d. Lena Delta, Siberia, 1881*), Arctic explorer. Graduated U.S. Naval Academy, 1865. Led *Jeannette* expedition, 1879–81. His journal, *The Voyage of the Jeannette*, was published, 1883.

DEL RUTH, ROY (*b. Philadelphia, Pa., 1895; d. Sherman Oaks, Calif., 1967*), motion picture director. Moved to Hollywood to work for the Keystone Film Company (1915–17), writing slapstick comedy scripts and directing shorts. Joined the Fox Film Corporation in 1918, where he wrote and directed 150 two-reel comedies. He directed thirty-seven feature films at Warner Brothers (1925–34), including *Blonde Crazy* (1931), *Taxi* (1932), and *Lady Killer* (1933). He then made two or three films a year for Metro-Goldwyn-Mayer, Twentieth Century-Fox, and Paramount. They included *Broadway Melody of 1936* (1935), *Born to Dance* (1936), *Broadway Melody of 1938* (1937), *Happy Landing* (1938), *My Lucky Star* (1938), *Du Barry Was a Lady* (1943), *Always Leave Them Laughing* (1949), *On Moonlight Bay* (1951), *Starlift* (1951), *About Face* (1952), and *Three Sailors and a Girl* (1953). In his last years he moved into television, directing episodes of "Warner Brothers Hour," "Four Star Theatre," and "Adventures in Paradise."

DE LUCA, GIUSEPPE (*b. Rome, Italy, 1876; d. New York, N.Y., 1950*), operatic baritone. Admitted as a child to the Schola Cantorum, Rome; later studied at the Academy of St. Cecilia. Made professional debut in Gounod's *Faust* at Piacenza, Nov. 6, 1897. An immediate success in Europe and South America, he made his New York debut at the Metropolitan Opera on Nov. 25, 1915, as Figaro in Rossini's *Barber of Seville*. He remained a member of the Metropolitan company until the summer of 1935, giving more than 800 performances. Subsequent to his "retirement," he continued to sing in concert and over the radio, returning to the Metropolitan on Feb. 7, 1940, as Germont in Verdi's *La Traviata* for a memorable performance. *Post* 1947, he taught privately and at the Juilliard School. Considered the greatest exponent in his time of the art of bel canto, he had a fine voice under perfect control, elegance of diction and phrasing, and the art of communicating emotion by acting ability as well as by his music.

DE MÉZIÈRES Y CLUGNY, ATHANASE (*b. Paris, France, ca. 1715; d. San Antonio, Tex., 1779*), soldier, explorer. Arrived Louisiana, *ca.* 1733; was a soldier at Natchitoches, 1743, and also engaged in planting and trading. On surrender of Louisiana to Spain, he entered Spanish service and for ten years ruled the Red River valley, supervising Indian trade and winning to Spanish allegiance the tribes of Louisiana, Texas, Arkansas, and Oklahoma. His diaries and reports in *Athanase de Mézières and the Louisiana-Texas Frontier: 1768–80* (ed. H. E. Bolton, 1914) gave the first definite information about a large part of northern Texas.

DEMILLE, CECIL BLOUNT (*b. Ashfield, Mass., 1881; d. Hollywood, Calif., 1959*), motion picture producer and director. Studied at the American Academy of Dramatic Arts. After acting and collaborating on plays, DeMille joined Samuel Goldwyn and Jesse Lasky in 1914 to film *The Squaw Man*, the first feature-length film shot in Hollywood. In 1915, the Famous Players-Lasky Corporation was formed with DeMille as director general. Early films included *Carmen* (1915), with singer Geraldine Farrar. The Cecil B. DeMille Productions, Inc. was founded in 1922; DeMille was president until 1951. His first epic film, *The Ten Commandments* was filmed in 1923. DeMille was to develop this form with such films as *The King of Kings* (1927); *Cleopatra* (1934); *The Plainsman* (1937); *The Buccaneer* (1938); *Reap the Wild Wind* (1942); *Samson and Delilah* (1949); *The Greatest Show on Earth* (1952); and a remake of *The Ten Commandments* in 1956. He won the Academy Award for *The Greatest Show on Earth* in 1952.

DE MILLE, HENRY CHURCHILL (*b. Washington, N.C., 1853; d. Pompton, N.J., 1893*), playwright. Father of William C. and Cecil B DeMille. Wrote society drama vehicles for skilled actors, often in association with David Belasco.

DEMING, HENRY CHAMPION (*b. Colchester, Conn., 1815; d. Hartford, Conn., 1872*), lawyer, Union soldier, politician. Gifted as an orator.

DEMING, PHILANDER (*b. Carlisle, N.Y., 1829; d. Albany, N.Y., 1915*), lawyer. A pioneer law stenographer and verbatim court reporter, Deming was author of *Adirondack Stories* (1880) and other books.

DEMING, WILLIAM. *See* DENNING, WILLIAM.

DEMME, CHARLES RUDOLPH (*b. Mühlhausen, Germany, 1795; d. 1863*), Lutheran clergyman. Immigrated to Philadelphia, 1818; served at St. Michael's and Zion's Church there, 1822–59, and *emeritus* to 1863. A famous preacher in German and a notable scholar.

DEMPSTER, JOHN (*b. Florida, N.Y., 1794; d. 1863*), Methodist clergyman. Encouraged establishment (1845) of Wesley Theological Institute (which became the Theological School of Boston University); was a founder of Garrett Biblical Institute, 1854–55.

DEMUTH, CHARLES (*b. Lancaster, Pa., 1883; d. Lancaster, 1935*), artist. Studies at Pennsylvania Academy with Anschutz and W. M. Chase and in Paris. Illustrator of Henry James's *Turn of the Screw* and Zola's *Nana*; painter of still lifes semiabstract in character.

DENBY, CHARLES (*b. Mount Joy, Va., 1830; d. Jamestown, N.Y., 1904*), lawyer, Union soldier, diplomat. Graduated Virginia Military Institute, 1850. Removed to Indiana, 1853. Honored by China for services as U.S. minister there, 1885–98.

DENBY, EDWIN (*b. Evansville, Ind., 1870; d. Detroit, Mich., 1929*), lawyer. Son of Charles Denby. As secretary of the navy, 1921–24, was implicated in Teapot Dome scandal. Though not impeached, widespread criticism led to his resignation from office.

DENNETT, TYLER (WILBUR) (*b. Spencer, Wis., 1883; d. Geneva, N.Y., 1949*), historian, government official, educator. Raised in Pascoag, R.I. Graduated Williams College, 1904; B.D., Union Theological Seminary, 1908; Ph.D., Johns Hopkins, 1924. In Congregational ministry, 1908–14. Methodist Episcopal Board of Foreign Missions and Inter-Church World Movement, 1914–20, traveling in Asia. Thereafter wrote a series of articles published as *The Democratic Movement in Asia* (1918). *Americans in Eastern Asia* (1922) established his reputation as expert in U.S.–Far East diplomatic history. He continued his studies with *Roosevelt and the Russo-Japanese War* (1925). His biography *John Hay: From Poetry to Politics* won the 1934 Pulitzer Prize. Editor and chief of publications for the State Department, 1924–29. After teaching international relations at Princeton, 1931–34, he became president of Williams College. Began an energetic reform of Williams, but after three years of conflict with unsympathetic elements on the board of trustees and in the student body, he resigned.

DENNIE, JOSEPH (*b. Boston, Mass., 1768; d. Philadelphia, Pa., 1812*), essayist, editor. Graduated Harvard, 1790. Admitted to the bar, 1794, he soon abandoned practice. After failure of a weekly paper he started in Boston, Dennie settled in Walpole, N.H., where he became center of a group of wits and contributed to the *Farmer's Weekly Museum* a series of essays entitled generally "The Lay Preacher"; in 1796 he became editor of the *Museum*. The strong Federalist bias with which he wrote won him appointment as secretary to Secretary of State Pickering and a staff post on Fenno's Federalist *Gazette of the United States*. He made the necessary move to Philadelphia, 1799, but his bright prospects soon evaporated. As editor of *The Port Folio*, 1801–11, he was constantly in financial difficulties, but he made that magazine a distinguished literary journal and should rank with Freneau and Charles Brockden Brown as a pioneer American man of letters.

DENNING, WILLIAM (*b. 1736; d. Cumberland Co., Pa., 1830*), cannon maker for the Revolutionary army. Said to have made first successful attempt to employ wrought iron in cannon-founding.

DENNIS, ALFRED LEWIS PINNEO (*b. Beirut, Syria, 1874; d. Worcester, Mass., 1930*), historian. Son of James S. Dennis. Specialist in international relations; author of *Adventures in American Diplomacy, 1896–1906* (1928).

DENNIS, EUGENE (*b. Seattle, Wash., 1905; d. New York, N.Y., 1961*), labor organizer and Communist functionary. Joined the Communist party in 1926 and headed the party's Trade Union Unity League in Los Angeles (1929–30). In the Soviet Union (1931–35) he attended the Lenin School in Moscow and was assigned to the Comintern's Far Eastern Section. In 1935 he became state secretary of the Wisconsin Communist party and he served as the U.S. party's representative to the Comintern in 1937 and 1941. In 1938 Dennis was appointed national secretary for political and legislative affairs. He became the party's general secretary in 1946. He was sentenced to one year in prison in 1947 for contempt of Congress, the result of his defiance of the House Committee on Un-American Activities. With eleven other party leaders, Dennis was indicted in 1948 for violation of the Smith Act; he served a five-year prison term. At the time of his death he was national chairman of the Communist party.

DENNIS, FREDERIC SHEPARD (*b. Newark, N.J., 1850; d. New York, N.Y., 1934*), surgeon. Brother of James S. Dennis. M.D., Bellevue Hospital Medical School, 1874; studied at Edinburgh. Introduced Listerian technique of surgery in the United States.

DENNIS, GRAHAM BARCLAY (*b. London, England, 1855; d. 1923*), capitalist. Came to America as a boy. Settled in Spokane, Wash., 1885, and was a leader in mining and other development in the Northwest.

DENNIS, JAMES SHEPARD (*b. Newark, N.J., 1842; d. Montclair, N.J. 1914*), Presbyterian clergyman, missionary to Syria. Author of *Christian Missions and Social Progress* (1897, 1899, 1906), an exhaustive study of the social effect of Protestant missions on non-Christian peoples.

DENNISON, AARON LUFKIN (*b. Freeport, Maine, 1812; d. England, 1895*), pioneer watch manufacturer. Designed and made the first machine-made, factory-produced watches utilizing a system of interchangeable parts, *ca.* 1850 at Roxbury, Mass. His Boston Watch Co., bankrupt in 1857, was continued by others as the American Waltham Watch Co.

DENNISON, HENRY STURGIS (*b. Boston, Mass., 1877; d. Framingham, Mass., 1952*), manufacturer, industrial welfare planner. Advocate of modern management techniques in industry. Co-authored with John Kenneth Galbraith *Modern Competition and Business Policy* (1938). Chairman of the Industrial Advisory Board of the National Recovery Administration. Deputy chairman, Federal Reserve Bank of Boston (1937–45).

DENNISON, WALTER (*b. Saline, Mich., 1869; d. 1917*), educator, scholar. Graduated University of Michigan, 1893; Ph.D., 1897. A distinguished classicist; taught at Oberlin, University of Michigan, Swarthmore.

DENNISON, WILLIAM (*b. Cincinnati, Ohio, 1815; d. Columbus, Ohio, 1882*), businessman. Republican governor of Ohio, 1859–61; took prompt, effective action for the Union at start of Civil War.

DENNY, GEORGE VERNON, JR. (*b. Washington, N.C., 1899; d. Sharon, Conn., 1959*), educator, broadcaster. Studied at the University of North Carolina. Became associate director of the League for Political Education in 1931; the league later became Town Hall, Inc., in 1938, and Denny served as president until 1951. Innovator of the NBC radio program "America's Town Meeting of the Air," Denny led the program with debates on current issues by leading public figures. The program ran from 1935 to 1956.

DENSMORE, FRANCES (*b. Red Wing, Minn., 1867; d. Red Wing, Minn., 1957*), ethnomusicologist. Studied at the Oberlin Conservatory of Music and at Harvard. Originally a pianist and musician, Densmore later devoted her life to recording and writing about American Indian music. Her volumes include *Teton Sioux Music* (1918) and *The American Indians and Their Music* (1926). Her recordings are housed at the Library of Congress.

DENT, FREDERICK TRACY (*b. St. Louis Co., Mo., 1821; d. 1892*), soldier. Graduated West Point, 1843. Brother-in-law of Ulysses S. Grant, whom he served as aide in Civil War and as military secretary during presidency. He retired as colonel, First Artillery, 1883.

DENVER, JAMES WILLIAM (*b. Winchester, Va., 1817; d. Washington, D.C., 1892*), lawyer, soldier. Raised in Ohio; removed to California, 1850. Congressman, Democrat, from California, 1855–57; prominent as chairman of Special Committee on Pacific Railroads. In 1857 he became commissioner of Indian affairs and in 1858 governor of the Kansas Territory. The city of Denver, Colo., was named for him. A brigadier general of volunteers, 1861–63, he served in Kansas and with the Army of the Tennessee. He stayed politically active in the postwar years. Remarkably energetic and farsighted, his fearlessness in discharging public office was fully appreciated in the West.

DE PALMA, RALPH (*b. Troia, Italy, 1883; d. South Pasadena, Calif., 1956*), racing car driver. From 1907 until his retirement in 1934, De Palma participated in 2,889 races and won 2,557, including the Vanderbilt Cup in 1912, 1914, and 1915, and the Indianapolis 500 in 1915. Elected to the Racing Hall of Fame in 1954.

DE PAOLIS, ALESSIO (*b. Rome, Italy, 1893; d. New York, N.Y., 1964*), opera singer. Made his professional operatic debut in 1919. During the 1920's he sang leading lyric tenor roles with the major opera companies in Italy and performed throughout Europe. In the 1930's he devoted himself exclusively to key supporting (comprimario) roles. In 1938 he began a twenty-six-season association with the Metropolitan Opera Company. He sang forty-eight roles in 1,192 performances of forty operas at the Met. He also sang with the Cincinnati Summer Opera (1948), 1952–55), the San Francisco Opera (1940, 1942–56), and in Los Angeles.

DE PAUW, WASHINGTON CHARLES (*b. Salem, Ind., 1822; d. 1887*), manufacturer, banker, philanthropist. Principal benefactor of De Pauw University, named for him in 1884.

DEPEW, CHAUNCEY MITCHELL (*b. Peekskill, N.Y., 1834; d. New York, N.Y., 1928*), lawyer, railway president, wit. Graduated Yale, 1856; admitted to the bar, 1858; began practice in Peekskill. Republican member of New York legislature, 1862–63; New York secretary of state, 1863–65. Appointed first U.S. minister to Japan, 1866, Depew resigned to become attorney and legislative contact man for Commodore Cornelius Vanderbilt's railroads. Rising steadily in the Vanderbilt system, he was president of the New York Central, 1885–98. Elected U.S. senator, Republican, from New York in 1899, he served until 1911. A charming man and an accomplished raconteur, he was widely influential in his day.

DE PEYSTER, ABRAHAM (*b. New Amsterdam, 1657; d. New York, 1728*), colonial merchant. Held almost every office in the city and province of New York between 1685 and 1722.

DE PEYSTER, JOHN WATTS (*b. New York, N.Y., 1821; d. 1907*), author, soldier.

DE PRIEST, OSCAR STANTON (*b. Florence, Ala., 1871; d. Chicago, Ill., 1951*), U.S. congressman. First black member of the Chicago City Council, 1915. Republican congressman (1928–34). Active in Illinois Republican politics until his death.

DE QUILLE, DAN. *See* WRIGHT, WILLIAM.

DERBIGNY, PIERRE AUGUSTE CHARLES BOURGUIGNON (*b. Laon, France, 1767; d. Gretna, La., 1829*), jurist. Emigrated from France to the West Indies, 1793, thence ultimately to Louisiana. Judge of Louisiana's first supreme court, 1813–20; helped revise state civil code; as governor, 1828–29, worked to resolve differences between French and English factions.

DERBY, ELIAS HASKET (*b. Salem, Mass., 1739; d. Salem, 1799*), merchant. Son of Richard Derby. Profits of Revolutionary War privateers and many successful trading voyages made him one of New England's wealthiest merchants. Embarking on extensive pioneering foreign ventures, he sent ships to Russia and the Orient, 1784–86; he later profited by demand for neutral vessels during Napoleonic wars. Astute in seeking out new commercial fields, he was wise also in his choice of superior masters and supercargos. Although his business was destroyed by the Embargo of 1807, the trade he had begun with the Baltic, China, and the East Indies was the foundation of American commerce in those parts of the world.

DERBY, ELIAS HASKET (*b. Salem, Mass., 1766; d. Londonderry, N.H., 1826*), merchant. Son of Elias Hasket Derby (1739–99). Established Derby firm as dominant American commercial house on Île de France (Mauritius).

DERBY, ELIAS HASKET (*b. Salem, Mass., 1803; d. Boston, Mass., 1880*), lawyer. Son of Elias H. Derby (1766–1826). Won distinction in railroad cases; served as president, Old Colony Railroad.

DERBY, GEORGE HORATIO (*b. Dedham, Mass., 1823; d. New York, N.Y. 1861*), army officer, humorist. Graduated West Point, 1846; served with Topographical Engineers, and with distinction in the Mexican War. Sent to California, 1849, he remained on the Pacific Coast until 1856 and there won general fame as a practical joker and wit. Originally published in local newspapers and magazines, his satires and burlesques were gathered into two collections: *Phoenixiana* (1856) and *The Squibob Papers* (1865). The first of these was immensely popular; the latter contains work which he did after his return to the East. His writings are important as representing one of the earliest developments of western humor and had marked influence on later writers of whom Mark Twain is most noteworthy.

DERBY, RICHARD (*b. Salem, Mass., 1712; d. 1783*), merchant, shipowner, Revolutionary patriot. Father of Elias Hasket Derby (1739–1799). Traded successfully to Spain and the West Indies.

DERCUM, FRANCIS XAVIER (*b. Philadelphia, Pa., 1856; d. Philadelphia, 1931*), physician, teacher, writer. M.D., University of Pennsylvania, 1877. Specialist in neurology; produced (1892) the first original contribution on adiposis dolorosa, or Dercum's disease.

DERN, GEORGE HENRY (*b. near Scribner, Nebr., 1872; d. Washington, D.C., 1936*), mine operator in Utah. Democratic governor of Utah, 1924–32, notable for tax revision program. U.S. secretary of war, 1933–36.

DE ROSE, PETER (*b. New York, N.Y., 1900; d. New York, 1953*), composer. Composer of "Deep Purple," "The Lamp Is Low," and "All I Need Is You." Performed on radio series "The Sweethearts of the Air" (1923–39).

DE ROSSET, MOSES JOHN (*b. Wilmington, N.C., 1838; d. New York, N.Y., 1881*), physician, Confederate army surgeon. Specialist in diseases of the eye and ear.

DE SAUSSURE, HENRY WILLIAM (*b. Pocotaligo, S.C., 1763; d. Charleston, S.C., 1839*), lawyer. Studied law in Philadelphia with Jared Ingersoll. Returning to South Carolina, he served in the General Assembly at various times between 1790 and 1808, favoring a program of gradual concessions to the poorly represented up-country settlers. During his term as director of the U.S. Mint (1795), he brought about the first U.S. coinage of gold. He performed notable service in organizing the South Carolina system of equity as chancellor *post* 1808.

DE SCHWEINITZ, EDMUND ALEXANDER. *See* SCHWEINITZ, EDMUND ALEXANDER DE.

DE SCHWEINITZ, GEORGE EDMUND. *See* SCHWEINITZ, GEORGE EDMUND DE.

DESHA, JOSEPH (*b. Monroe Co., Pa., 1768; d. Georgetown, Ky., 1842*), soldier, politician. Raised in frontier Kentucky and Tennessee; settled in Mason Co., Ky., 1792; served in Indian campaigns under Wayne, 1794–95. Congressman, Democratic-Republican from Kentucky, 1807–19; an extreme war hawk. Governor of Kentucky, 1824–28.

DE SMET, PIERRE-JEAN (*b. Termonde, Belgium, 1801; d. St. Louis, Mo., 1873*), Jesuit missionary. Came to America, 1821, entering Jesuit novitiate at Whitemarsh, near Baltimore, Md.; made further studies and was ordained in 1827 at Florissant, Mo. Began work as missionary to the Potawatomie near present Council Bluffs, Iowa. Between 1840 and 1846, he worked in Oregon country, the Rockies, and other areas of the Pacific Northwest, setting up mission stations and affecting almost every tribe in the Columbia Valley and its neighborhood; during the same period he traveled to the East and to Europe on behalf of the missions. By 1850, he was known and respected by the Plains tribes as well and served many times thereafter as a peacemaker in their conflicts with one another and with the whites. His most famous exploit in diplomacy came in 1868 when he was successful in effecting a truce with Sitting Bull's hostile band in the Bighorn Valley.

DE SOTO, HERNANDO (*b. Barcarrota, Spain, ca. 1500; d. 1542*), explorer, soldier, discoverer of the Mississippi River. Accompanied Pedrarias Dávila to Central America, 1519. Participated in conquest of Peru; after sack of Cuzco, returned to Spain with a fortune. In 1537, Charles V commissioned him to conquer Florida; he was also made governor of Cuba. After landing in Florida, May 1539, he marched north, entering successively Georgia, the Carolinas, Tennessee, Alabama, Mississippi, Arkansas, Oklahoma, and Texas; detachments of his party may have entered Missouri and Louisiana. With brief interludes, the march was made in constant warfare with the native peoples. He made the first conscious discovery of the Mississippi River in April 1541. A year later, endeavoring to cross the Mississippi on his way homeward, De Soto died after naming Luis de Moscoso his successor. His body was consigned to the river.

DE SYLVA, GEORGE GARD ("BUDDY") (*b. New York, N.Y., 1896; d. Hollywood, Calif., 1950*), lyricist, librettist, producer, director. Raised in California. Moving to New York City, 1919, he wrote the lyrics for a number of standard hits by Al Jolson, Jerome Kern, George Gershwin, and Victor Herbert. Between 1925 and 1930, he was associated with Lew Brown and Ray Henderson in one of the most successful songwriting collaborations in popular-music history. Among the musical shows for which they wrote the songs were *George White Scandals* (1925, 1926, 1928), *Good News* (1927), *Hold Everything* (1928), *Follow Through* (1929), and *Flying High* (1930). In 1929, they also provided the songs for the screen musicals *The Singing Fool* and *Sunny Side Up.* In 1930, De Sylva went to Hollywood to work as a producer and director, returning to Broadway at intervals as producer and colibrettist for shows such as *Panama Hattie* and *Louisiana Purchase* (both 1940).

DETMOLD, CHRISTIAN EDWARD (*b. Hannover, Germany, 1810; d. New York, N.Y., 1887*), civil engineer. Came to America, 1826. Active in railway surveys; supervising engineer and architect, New York Crystal Palace, 1852–53.

DE TROBRIAND, RÉGIS DENIS DE KEREDERN (*b. near Tours, France, 1816; d. Bayport, N.Y., 1897*), soldier. Came to America, 1841. A volunteer in Union army, 1861–65, he rose to major general and continued in regular army, 1866–79. Author of *Four Years with the Army of the Potomac* (published in French, 1867–68).

DETT, ROBERT NATHANIEL (*b. Drummondsville, Ontario, Canada, 1882; d. Battle Creek, Mich., 1943*), composer, choral conductor. Born of Afro-American parents. Majored in composition at Oberlin, graduating Mus.B., 1908; made later studies at Columbia and Harvard, with Nadia Boulanger in France, and at Eastman School of Music (Mus.M., 1932). Director of music at Hampton Institute, 1913–32, he wrote choral compositions and arrangements for the Hampton choirs which were a major contribution to American music. His "Listen to the Lambs" (1914) is the most popular and perhaps most characteristic example of his use of the black spiritual as the basis for a larger musical form; he was composer of some 22 other comparable works published between 1914 and 1941, and edited a number of collections of spirituals. Except for his "Juba Dance" (from his *In the Bottoms Suite*, 1913), his original piano compositions are in the romantic mode of the late 19th century; his largest choral work, however, the oratorio *The Ordering of Moses*, 1937, draws its melodic idea from a spiritual.

DEUTSCH, GOTTHARD (*b. Kanitz, Austria, 1859; d. 1921*), educator, Jewish scholar. Pupil of Graetz, Weiss, and Jellinek; Ph.D., Vienna, 1881. Professor of history and philosophy of religion, Hebrew Union College, Cincinnati, Ohio, 1891–1921.

DEVANEY, JOHN PATRICK (*b. Lake Mills, Iowa, 1883; d. Milwaukee, Wis., 1941*), lawyer, jurist, politician. B.A., University of Minnesota, 1905; LL.B., 1907; LL.M., 1908. Practiced in Minneapolis; specialized in common-carrier law. Active in politics as a Democrat. Chief justice, Minnesota Supreme Court, 1933–37, he tended to champion the individual against the larger economic interests and became known as a liberal and a legal realist; he was, however, a strong supporter of prompt and unsentimental justice in criminal cases. He was a founder and first president of the National Lawyers Guild, and exerted powerful, local influence in behalf of the policies of Franklin D. Roosevelt.

DE VARGAS ZAPATA Y LUJAN PONCE DE LEON, DIEGO (*b. Madrid, Spain, ca. 1650; d. New Mexico, 1704*), soldier, administrator, Spanish governor of New Mexico, 1688–97 and 1703–04; reconquered the province for Spain, 1692–93.

DEVENS, CHARLES (*b. Charlestown, Mass., 1820; d. Boston, Mass., 1891*), Union soldier, jurist. Graduated Harvard, 1838; admitted to bar, 1840; served in Massachusetts legislature and as U.S. marshal. Won brevet as major general in Civil War. Justice, state superior court, 1867–73; state supreme court, 1873–77. After service as U.S. attorney general, 1877–81, he resumed his place on the state supreme court bench and served until his death.

DE VERE, MAXIMILIAN SCHELE. *See* SCHELE, MAXIMILIAN DE VERE.

DEVEREUX, JOHN HENRY (*b. Marblehead, Mass., 1832; d. Cleveland, Ohio, 1886*), civil engineer. Manager and president of several midwestern railroads, including Lake Shore and Michigan Southern and the "Big Four."

DEVIN, THOMAS CASIMER (*b. New York, N.Y., 1822; d. New York, 1878*), Union soldier. Brigade and division commander of cavalry, Civil War; on frontier service, Eighth and Third Cavalry, 1866–78.

DEVINE, EDWARD THOMAS (*b. near Union, Hardin Co., Iowa, 1867; d. Oak Park, Ill., 1948*), social worker. B.A., Cornell College (Iowa), 1887; Ph.D., University of Pennsylvania, 1893, in economics under Simon N. Patten. As secretary of the New York Charity Organization Society, 1896–1917, he was a leader in the development of social work as a profession and in exerting effective pressure for enactment of social reform legislaexerting effective pressure for enactment of social reform legislation. He founded and edited *Charities*, 1897, which, after absorbing other journals, became the leading national social work journal as the *Survey*. After 1917, he remained active for two more decades as a writer and administrator. An exceptionally versatile social worker, he was an expert on disaster relief.

DE VINNE, THEODORE LOW (*b. Stamford, Conn., 1828; d. 1914*), printer, historian of printing. Author of *The Invention of Printing* (1876), *Historic Printing Types* (1886), and other works.

DEVOTO, BERNARD AUGUSTINE (*b. Ogden, Utah, 1897; d. New York, N.Y., 1955*), historian, critic, and journalist. Writer of the "Easy Chair" column for *Harper's Magazine* (1935–55). Wrote *Across the Wide Missouri* (Pulitzer Prize, 1947) and *The Course of Empire* (National Book Award, 1952). Curator of the Mark Twain papers (1938–46). Editor of *Saturday Review of Literature* (1936–38).

DEVOY, JOHN (*b. Kill, Ireland, 1842; d. Atlantic City, N.J., 1928*), journalist, Fenian leader. After involvement in Irish revolutionary movement, 1861–66, and five years' imprisonment, Devoy came to America in 1871 and worked for the *New York Herald* and other papers. Founder and editor of the *Irish Nation*, 1881–85, and of the *Gaelic American*, 1903–28. Exponent of physical force in Irish revolt. Author of *Recollections of an Irish Rebel* (1929).

DE VRIES, DAVID PIETERSEN (*b. La Rochelle, France, ca. 1592; place and date of death uncertain*), merchant skipper, colonizer of New Netherland. About 1630, entered into partnership with directors of the West India Co. to plant a colony on the Delaware. Thereafter De Vries made three voyages to America (1632–33, 1634–36, 1638–44). He established a small settlement on Staten Island and a colony near Tappan which he called Vriessendael. Both were destroyed in the Indian war of 1643. His account of his voyages, *Korte Historiael . . .* (1655), is a valuable source for the history of New Netherland.

DEW, THOMAS RODERICK (*b. King and Queen Co., Va., 1802; d. Paris, France, 1846*), economist. Graduated William and Mary, 1820; traveled in Europe. Appointed professor of political law at William and Mary, 1827. His *Lectures on the Restrictive System* (1829) upheld the free-trade argument and foretold that disunion would follow if protection were pressed by the industrial North. His "Review of the Debate . . ." (1832), better known after its incorporation in the volume of essays entitled *The Pro-Slavery Argument* (1852), was widely influential; De Bow said that this proslavery essay won for Dew "the lasting gratitude of the whole South." Dew became president of William and Mary in 1836 and substantially increased its enrollment and prosperity.

DEWEES, WILLIAM POTTS (*b. near Pottstown, Pa., 1768; d. Philadelphia, Pa., 1841*), obstetrician. Author of *A Compendious System of Midwifery* (1852), America's first authoritative work on the subject.

DEWEY, CHESTER (*b. Sheffield, Mass., 1784; d. Rochester, N.Y., 1867*), Congregational clergyman, scientist. Graduated Williams, 1806. A born teacher and versatile scientific investigator; first professor of chemistry and natural sciences at the University of Rochester, 1850–61.

DEWEY, GEORGE (*b. Montpelier, Vt., 1837; d. Washington, D.C., 1917*), naval officer. Graduated Annapolis, 1858; served under Farragut during the Civil War. Promoted captain, 1884, he became chief of the Bureau of Equipment, 1889, and president of the Board of Inspection and Survey, 1895. In these posts he became acquainted with the modern battleships, cruisers, and torpedo boats of the "New Navy." Taking command of the Asiatic Squadron early in 1898, he made most careful preparations for any event, and upon receiving news of war with Spain, executed the capture of Manila. His victory made the United States a principal power in the Far East and demonstrated the quality of the new types of ships. Given rank of Admiral of the Navy, he returned home to great ovations in New York and elsewhere; he served as president of the Navy General Board *post* 1900.

DEWEY, JOHN (*b. Burlington, Vt., 1859; d. New York, N.Y., 1952*), philosopher and educator. Dewey's philosophy is often called "experimentalist," placing individual experience at the center of human existence and then applying this concept to all human activities: art religion, politics, logic, and education. Taught at University of Michigan (1884–94), and at the University of Chicago (1894–1904). During this period, he published works on psychology and education: *The School and Society* (1899) and *Studies in Logical Theory* (1903). While at Chicago, he and his wife founded and ran the famous Laboratory School.

From 1905 until his death, he was affiliated with Columbia, writing *Ethics* (1908), *How We Think* (1910), and *Democracy and Education* (1916), which Dewey called the fullest expression of his philosophy, actually stating that philosophy was "the general theory of education." Other works include *Art As Experience* (1934) and *A Common Faith* (1934).

After World War I, Dewey and his wife traveled extensively, lecturing in Japan, China, Turkey, Mexico, and the Soviet Union. In social affairs, Dewey was a charter member of the American Civil Liberties Union and a founder of New York's New School for Social Research.

When Dewey received an honorary doctorate from the University of Paris in 1930, the citation described him as "the most profound and complete expression of American genius."

DEWEY, MELVIL (*b. Adams Center, N.Y., 1851; d. Florida, 1931*), librarian. Graduated Amherst, 1874. After experience as assistant in Amherst library, published *A Classification and Subject Index for Cataloguing and Arranging . . . a Library* (1876). This decimal system of classification, although not original in its essential features, came into wide use because of its workability and because of the missionary zeal of its author's pupils. Secretary of the American Library Association, 1876–90, editor of the *Library Journal*, 1876–80, and organizer of the Library Bureau, Dewey started the first library school in the United States in 1887 while librarian of Columbia College, New York City, 1883–88. Removing the school to Albany, N.Y., 1889, he served as director, New York State Library, 1888–1905. Abounding in energy and self-confidence, he was tactless and indiscreet.

DEWEY, ORVILLE (*b. Sheffield, Mass., 1794; d. Sheffield, 1882*), clergyman, author. Graduated Williams, 1814. Fourth president of the American Unitarian Association, 1845–47. Interested in social questions, he opposed both slavery and abolitionism.

DEWEY, RICHARD SMITH (*b. Forestville, N.Y., 1845; d. La Canada, Calif., 1933*), psychiatrist. M.D., University of Michigan, 1869. Served as surgeon in German army during Franco-Prussian War. Assistant physician, Elgin (Ill.) State Hospital, 1872–79; superintendent at Kankakee, 1879–93, where he introduced the "cottage plan," an innovation which replaced the traditional massive mental hospital building with comparatively small detached cottages. From 1895 to 1920 he directed the Milwaukee Sanitarium, a private institution at Wauwatosa, Wis.

DEWING, FRANCIS (*fl. Boston, Mass., 1716–22*), the first important engraver on copper in America. Engraved Capt. John Bonner's *The Town of Boston*, 1722.

DEWING, MARIA RICHARDS OAKEY (*b. New York, N.Y., 1845; d. New York, 1927*), painter. Best known for flower painting, in which she was rivaled only by La Farge in America and Fantin-Latour in France. Married Thomas W. Dewing, 1881.

DEWING, THOMAS WILMER (*b. Boston, Mass., 1851; d. New York, N.Y., 1938*), figure and portrait painter. Trained as a lithographer; studied in Paris under Lefebvre. His lyrical idealistic work is best represented in the Freer and Gellatly collections, Washington, D.C.

DE WITT, SIMEON (*b. Wawarsing, N.Y., 1756; d. Ithaca, N.Y., 1834*), surveyor general of New York, 1784–1834; surveyor and military mapmaker in Revolutionary War.

DE WOLF, JAMES (*b. Bristol Co., R.I., 1764; d. New York, N.Y., 1837*), slave trader, manufacturer. U.S. senator from Rhode Island, 1821–25. An advocate of high tariffs.

DE WOLFE, ELSIE (*b. New York, N.Y., 1865; d. Versailles, France, 1950*), actress, decorator, hostess. Attended school in Edinburgh, Scotland. Active in amateur theatricals for charity after her return to the United States in 1884, she became a professional in 1890. She left the stage in 1905, and at the suggestion of Elizabeth Marbury, her closest friend, she turned her lifelong interest in design into a profession and became America's first female decorator. She based her work on 18th-century principles of unity, simplicity, and serenity, and a sense of vibrant color and airiness. Her conscious revolt against the dark hangings and crowded fussiness of Victorian decoration was a success, and with publication of *The House in Good Taste* (1913) she became an arbiter of decorative design in the United States. As her decorating business prospered, she spent more and more time in France and became widely known as a hostess for international celebrities at innovative parties at her house in Versailles. She married Sir Charles Mendl, 1926.

DEXTER, FRANKLIN (*b. Charlestown, Mass., 1793; d. Beverly, Mass., 1857*), lawyer. Son of Samuel Dexter (1761–1816).

DEXTER, FRANKLIN BOWDITCH (*b. Fairhaven, Mass., 1842; d. New Haven, Conn., 1920*), antiquarian, historian. Graduated Yale, 1861. His many publications dealt with the history of Yale, its graduates, and the colony and city of New Haven.

DEXTER, HENRY (*b. Nelson, N.Y., 1806; d. Boston, Mass., 1876*), sculptor. A blacksmith by trade, self-taught as a sculptor, Dexter made busts of Longfellow, Agassiz, Charles Dickens, and many other contemporaries. They were distinguished chiefly for verisimilitude.

DEXTER, HENRY (*b. West Cambridge, Mass., 1813; d. New York, N.Y., 1910*), businessman. Consolidated newspaper dealers into the American News Co., of which he was president for many years.

DEXTER, HENRY MARTYN (*b. Plympton, Mass., 1821; d. New Bedford, Mass., 1890*), Congregational clergyman. Editor, *The Congregationalist*, 1851–90.

DEXTER, SAMUEL (*b. Dedham, Mass., 1726; d. Mendon, Mass., 1810*), merchant. Revolutionary patriot.

DEXTER, SAMUEL (*b. Boston, Mass., 1761; d. Athens, N.Y., 1816*), lawyer. Son of Samuel Dexter (1726–1810). Graduated Harvard, 1781. A Federalist congressman from Massachusetts, 1793–95, and U.S. senator, 1799–1800, he served as secretary of war in 1800 and secretary of the treasury from January 1801 to

January 1802. He later attained high eminence at the Massachusetts bar.

DEXTER, TIMOTHY (*b. Malden, Mass., 1747; d. Newburyport, Mass., 1806*), merchant, speculator, eccentric. Author of *A Pickle for the Knowing Ones* (1802).

DEXTER, WIRT (*b. Dexter, Mich., 1832; d. Chicago, Ill., 1890*), lawyer. Grandson of Samuel Dexter (1761–1816). A recognized leader of the Chicago bar.

DE YOUNG, MICHEL HARRY (*b. St. Louis, Mo., 1849; d. 1925*), editor, publisher. Removed to California as a child. With his brother Charles, founded and edited the *Daily Dramatic Chronicle*, 1865, later titled the *San Francisco Chronicle*.

D'HARNONCOURT, RENÉ (*b. Vienna, Austria, 1901; d. New Suffolk, New York, 1968*), museum director. Studied at the University of Graz and the Technische Hochschule in Vienna. Working for an art dealer and collector in Mexico City, he helped stimulate the Mexican folk-art revival of the 1920's; he wrote and illustrated *Mexicana* (1931) and *Hole in the Wall* (1931) and assembled a major exhibition of Mexican folk art that visited various U.S. cities. Moving to New York, he became a close friend and a consultant to Nelson Rockefeller. He taught art history at Sarah Lawrence College and the New School for Social Research, and served as assistant manager and then general manager of the Indian Arts and Crafts Board of the Department of the Interior. D'Harnoncourt helped assemble a major exhibit of Indian art that was installed at the Museum of Modern Art in 1941. He joined the museum as vice president in 1944 and was appointed director in 1949. He retired in 1968.

DIAT, LOUIS FELIX (*b. Montmarault, France, 1885; d. New York, N.Y., 1957*), chef and author. Trained in France and England, Diat immigrated to the U.S. in 1910, where he became the chef at the Ritz-Carlton Hotel in New York, a position he held until the hotel closed in 1951. Supervising a staff of over 100, Diat became the best-known chef in America, contributing the crème à la vichyssoise soup to American menus. His works include *Cooking à la Ritz* (1941) and *French Cooking for America* (1946).

DIAZ, ABBY MORTON (*b. Plymouth, Mass., 1821; d. 1904*), author of *The William Henry Letters* (1870) and other stories for children.

DIBBLE, ROY FLOYD (*b. Portland, N.Y., 1887; d. New York, N.Y., 1929*), teacher. Author of *Strenuous Americans* (1923) and other works.

DIBRELL, GEORGE GIBBS (*b. Sparta, Tenn., 1822; d. Sparta, 1888*), merchant, planter, industrialist. Organized and led Eighth Tennessee Cavalry (Confederate); saw much service under Gen. N. B. Forrest, and succeeded to command of his "Old Brigade" in 1863.

DICK, ELISHA CULLEN (*b. near Marcus Hook, Pa., 1762; d. Alexandria, Va., 1825*), physician. Studied with Benjamin Rush and William Shippen, and at University of Pennsylvania. Called in consultation by Dr. James Craik at George Washington's last illness.

DICK, ROBERT PAINE (*b. Greensboro, N.C., 1823; d. 1898*), jurist. Helped organize Republican party in North Carolina, *post* 1866. Justice, North Carolina Supreme Court, 1868–72; thereafter federal district judge.

DICKERSON, EDWARD NICOLL (*b. Paterson, N.J., 1824; d. near Far Rockaway, N.Y., 1889*), lawyer. Son of Philemon Dickerson. Studied at Princeton, where he met Joseph Henry and was influenced by Henry to study science and mechanics. Admitted to the bar, 1845, his scientific knowledge was basis for his rise to recognition as leading patent lawyer in the United States. Among the important cases in which he acted were *Colt* vs. *Massachusetts Arms Co.* (establishing validity of Samuel Colt's firearms patent) and *Goodyear* vs. *Day* (involving validity of Charles Goodyear's patent for rubber vulcanization). He was later concerned with suits involving electrical patents of Thomas A. Edison, and the rights of the Western Union Co. and of the American Bell Telephone Co.

DICKERSON, MAHLON (*b. Hanover Neck, N.J., 1770; d. Succasunna, N.J., 1853*), lawyer, manufacturer, statesman. Graduated College of New Jersey (Princeton), 1789; licensed as attorney, 1793. Left legal profession to manage family iron works at Succasunna, 1810. An ultraprotectionist for the remainder of his career, he held numerous public offices: governor of New Jersey, 1815–17; U.S. senator, Democrat, from New Jersey, 1817–33; secretary of the navy, 1834–38.

DICKERSON, PHILEMON (*b. Succasunna, N.J., 1788; d. Paterson, N.J., 1862*), jurist. Brother of Mahlon Dickerson. Graduated University of Pennsylvania, 1808; licensed as attorney, 1813. Congressman, Democrat, from New Jersey, 1833–36 and 1839–41; governor of New Jersey, 1836–37; U.S. district judge, 1842–62.

DICKEY, THEOPHILUS LYLE (*b. Paris, Ky., 1811; d. Atlantic City, N.J., 1885*), Illinois jurist, Union soldier.

DICKIE, GEORGE WILLIAM (*b. Arbroath, Scotland, 1844; d. 1918*), engineer, shipbuilder. Came to San Francisco, Calif., 1869; as manager of Union Iron Works, 1883–1905, he was responsible for constructing 11 vessels of the "new" steel navy, including the *Oregon* and *Olympia*.

DICKINS, JOHN (*b. London, England, 1747; d. Philadelphia, Pa., 1798*), Methodist clergyman. Intimate friend and counselor of Francis Asbury. Ordained deacon, 1784; made elder, 1786. His most important contribution to Methodism was in education. He helped in founding of Cokesbury College and, from 1789 to his death, managed the Methodist Book Concern, establishing it as a permanent institution.

DICKINSON, ANNA ELIZABETH (*b. Philadelphia, Pa., 1842; d. Goshen, N.Y., 1932*), orator, actress, playwright. An eccentric egoist, acclaimed as a heroine by the abolitionists, she made wildly emotional platform pleas for harsh treatment of the South.

DICKINSON, ANSON (*b. Milton, Conn., 1779; d. Milton, 1852*), portrait painter in miniature and oils. Influenced by Edward Malbone. Chiefly distinguished as a colorist.

DICKINSON, CHARLES MONROE (*b. near Lowville, N.Y., 1842; d. Binghamton, N.Y., 1924*), lawyer, newspaperman, diplomat. In consular service, 1897–1908, in Bulgaria, Turkey, and the Middle East.

DICKINSON, DANIEL STEVENS (*b. Goshen, Conn., 1800; d. New York, N.Y., 1866*), lawyer, politician. A leading conservative Democrat, he was U.S. senator from New York, 1844–51.

DICKINSON, DONALD MCDONALD (*b. Port Ontario, N.Y., 1846; d. Trenton, Mich., 1917*), lawyer. Raised in Michigan. Graduated University of Michigan Law School and admitted to the bar, 1867. Became a leading lawyer in the Middle West; presented the Homestead Cases before the U.S. Supreme Court. A liberal and active Democrat, he led his party in Michigan *post* 1884.

DICKINSON, EDWIN DE WITT (*b. Bradford, Iowa, 1887; d. St. Helena, Calif., 1961*), professor of international law. Graduate of Carleton College (1909), Dartmouth (M.A., 1911), Harvard (Ph.D., 1918), and the University of Michigan Law School (1919). Taught at Michigan Law School until 1933. At the University of California at Berkeley he taught (1933–36) and was dean of the law school (1936–38). In 1938 President Roosevelt named him U.S. Commissioner on the Permanent Commission of Investigation under the Montevideo Protocol. In Washington, D.C. (1941–44), he served as a special assistant attorney general and as general counsel to the Mexican-American Claims Commission. Dickinson became assistant diplomatic adviser to the United Nations' Relief and Rehabilitation Association in 1944, then was chairman of the United States Alien Enemy Repatriation Hearing Board for Japanese aliens. He returned to teaching at the University of California, then went to the University of Pennsylvania Law School in 1948. He became president of the Association of American Law Schools in 1949. In 1951 he was named to the Permanent Court of Arbitration, and the following year he was elected president of the American Society of International Law. In 1956 Dickinson returned to California, where he taught for a time at Hastings College of Law. His books include *The Equality of States in International Law* (1920), *What is Wrong with International Law?* (1947), and *Law and Peace* (1951).

DICKINSON, EMILY ELIZABETH (*b. Amherst, Mass., 1830; d. Amherst, 1886*), poet. Her father, Edward Dickinson, was dominant and austere; neither Emily nor her sister, Lavinia, married. Educated at Amherst Academy and Mount Holyoke Female Seminary, Emily was early noted for her wit and love of drollery; until her middle twenties she participated freely in village amusements. Thereafter she became increasingly impatient of formal social occasions.

Details of an abortive love affair *ca.* 1854 are unclear. For the rest of her life she lived quietly in Amherst, drifting into a habit of seclusion and finding her satisfactions in nature and "the little toil of love" of household routine. Her preoccupation with poetry, by her own statement, began in 1861–62 and contributed to the desire for "polar privacy," which was deepened by her father's death and mother's invalidism (1874).

Though her outer life seems uneventful, Emily Dickinson's poems reveal an intense inner life and a lively mind capable of deep understanding, metaphysical speculation, and imaginative sympathy. Only two of her poems were printed during her lifetime. One was sent to the *Springfield Republican* (Feb. 14, 1866) by her sister-in-law. Emily's friend Helen Hunt Jackson was responsible for the inclusion of the other, without signature, in G. P. Lathrop's *A Masque of Poets* (1878). By a fortunate decision of her sister, Lavinia, Emily Dickinson's poems were preserved and published after her death in three series: *Poems* (1890), *Poems* (1891), *Poems* (1896). *The Single Hound* (1914) contains messages in swift, spontaneous verse that Emily Dickinson was in the habit of sending across the lawn to her sister-in-law; *Further Poems* (1929) includes a series of love poems reflecting her frustrated attachment. Since that time, several additional collections have been published in which "corrections" by the original editors of her work have been noted critically and a truer text established.

DICKINSON, JACOB MCGAVOCK (*b. Columbus, Miss., 1851; d. 1928*), lawyer. Practiced in Nashville, Tenn., 1874–99; thereafter in Chicago, Ill. Counsel to several railroads; secretary of war, 1909–11.

DICKINSON, JOHN (*b. Talbot Co., Md., 1732; d. Wilmington, Del., 1808*), statesman. Educated at home and in London at the Middle Temple. Returned to Philadelphia, 1757, and entered practice. Elected to the Assembly of the Lower Counties (Delaware), 1760, and became Speaker. Chosen representative from Pennsylvania legislature, 1762, Dickinson led conservative opposition to Franklin and, in the debate of 1764, opposed a change in the proprietary system.

In 1765 he published *The Late Regulations Respecting the British Colonies*, a pamphlet designed to show the injury that would be done to British mercantile interests by enforcement of the Sugar and Stamp acts. Appointed a Pennsylvania delegate to the Stamp Act Congress in 1765, he opposed all violent resistance to the obnoxious law.

In 1767 he began publishing anonymously in the *Pennsylvania Chronicle* the series of essays later known in pamphlet form as *Letters from a Farmer in Pennsylvania to the Inhabitants of the British Colonies* (1768), in which he suggested force as an ultimate remedy, but held that conciliation was possible. In April 1768, at a meeting in Philadelphia, Dickinson urged adoption of the nonimportation and nonexportation agreement. Reelected a member of the legislature, he drafted its 1771 "Petition to the King," which was unanimously adopted. He still opposed resort to force, however, and in 1774 sanctioned only expressions of sympathy to Boston because it had destroyed hope of conciliation. Nonetheless, Dickinson became chairman of the Philadelphia Committee of Correspondence and at the conference of July 1774 wrote three papers representative of conservative sentiment before the Declaration of Independence which were unanimously adopted. They included a series of resolutions stating the principles upon which the colonies based their claim to redress; instructions to congressional delegates to be chosen by the assembly; and a treatise on Great Britain's constitutional power to tax the colonies.

A member of the Continental Congress in 1774, Dickinson drafted the congressional "Petition to the King" and the "Address to the People of Canada." He was chairman of a Committee of Safety and Defense, 1775–76. At the Second Continental Congress, 1775, Dickinson, still seeking a peaceful settlement, wrote the second "Petition to the King," which angered New England members. He also drafted much, if not all, of the "Declaration of the Causes of Taking Up Arms." In the assembly, 1775, he drafted resolutions instructing delegates to the Congress of 1776 to seek means of redressing grievances to avoid measures anticipating separation.

Many Americans felt that separation was the only solution in early 1776, but Dickinson clung to conciliation and voted against the Declaration of Independence as a matter of principle. He was, however, one of the two congressmen who actually volunteered for armed service. In 1781, he was chosen president of the Supreme Executive Council of Delaware and thereafter elected to the same office in Pennsylvania. He was a delegate from Delaware to the Constitutional Convention, 1787, and took an active part in its proceedings.

DICKINSON, JOHN (*b. Greensboro, Md., 1894; d. Baltimore, Md., 1952*), jurist, educator, and public official. Ph.D., Princeton, 1919; LL.B., Harvard, 1921. Apologist for the New Deal, Dickinson was Assistant Secretary of Commerce (1933–35); helped formulate the initial outlines for the National Industrial Recovery Act of 1933. Assistant attorney general (1935–41). General counsel and vice president of the Pennsylvania Railroad (1941–52). Wrote *Hold Fast the Middle Way*, an explanation of the New Deal (1935).

DICKINSON, JOHN WOODBRIDGE (*b. Chester, Mass., 1825; d. 1901*), educator. Secretary of the Board of Education of Massachusetts, 1877–93.

DICKINSON, JONATHAN (*b. Hatfield, Mass., 1688; d. 1747*), Presbyterian clergyman, first president of the College of New Jersey (Princeton), 1747. Graduated Yale, 1706. Ordained pastor at Elizabeth Town, N.J., 1709, and served there until death.

DICKINSON, PHILEMON (*b. Talbot Co., Md.[?], 1739; d. 1809*), lawyer, Revolutionary soldier. Brother of John Dickinson. Major general and commander in chief of New Jersey militia. U.S. senator from New Jersey, 1790–93.

DICKINSON, PRESTON (*b. New York, N.Y., 1889; d. Irún, Spain, 1930*), painter. Influenced by Cézanne and the art of China.

DICKINSON, ROBERT LATOU (*b. Jersey City, N.J., 1861; d. Amherst, Mass., 1950*), gynecologist. M.D., Long Island College Hospital, 1882. Practiced in Brooklyn, N.Y.; held teaching and clinical positions at Long Island College Hospital; was on staffs of several other Brooklyn hospitals. He strongly supported a number of feminist causes and was an early proponent of birth control and scientific programs of sex education.

DICKMAN, JOSEPH THEODORE (*b. Dayton, Ohio, 1857; d. Washington, D.C., 1927*), soldier. Graduated West Point, 1881. An original member of Army General Staff, 1903–06. Among the ablest American generals in France in the World War I.

DICKSON, DAVID (*b. Hancock Co., Ga., 1809; d. Hancock Co., 1885*), farmer, agricultural writer. An extraordinarily successful farmer, Dickson introduced original agricultural methods in the South, including (1846) the use of Peruvian guano as fertilizer.

DICKSON, EARLE ENSIGN (*b. Grandview, Tenn., 1892; d. New Brunswick, N.J., 1961*), inventor of the adhesive bandage. Graduate of Yale (1913) and Lowell Textile Institute (1914). Became a cotton buyer for Johnson and Johnson in 1916. He convinced the company to begin manufacturing adhesive bandages, which he had developed at home. The "Band-Aid" became one of the most widely used products of the twentieth century. Dickson became manager of the hospital sales division (1925) and was named to the board of directors (1929). He retired as a vice president in 1957.

DICKSON, LEONARD EUGENE (*b. Independence, Iowa, 1874; d. Tex., 1954*), mathematician, educator. Ph.D., University of Chicago (1896), where he taught (1899–1939). Chiefly interested in number theory, he published the *History of the Theory of Numbers* (1919–23) and *Modern Elementary Theory of Numbers* (1939).

DICKSON, ROBERT (*b. Dumfries, Scotland, ca. 1765; d. Drummond Island, Mich., 1823*), fur trader. Aided British in capture of Michilimackinac and Detroit during War of 1812.

DICKSON, SAMUEL HENRY (*b. Charleston, S.C., 1798; d. Philadelphia, Pa., 1872*), physician. Founded Medical College of South Carolina, 1833; professor at New York University, 1847–50, and at Jefferson Medical College, 1858–72.

DICKSON, THOMAS (*b. Leeds, England, 1824; d. 1884*), foundryman, machinist, capitalist. Taken to America as a child. President of Delaware and Hudson Canal Co., *post* 1869; developer of coal and other industries at Scranton, Pa.

DIDIER, EUGENE LEMOINE (*b. Baltimore, Md., 1838; d. Baltimore, 1913*). Author of *The Life and Poems of Edgar Allan Poe* (1877), *Poe Cult* (1909), and other works.

DIELMAN, FREDERICK (*b. Hannover, Germany, 1847; d. Ridgefield, Conn., 1935*), painter, illustrator, etcher. Among his best-known works are two overmantels in mosaic, *Law* and *History* in the Library of Congress.

DIETRICHSON, JOHANNES WILHELM CHRISTIAN (*b. Fredrikstad, Norway, 1815; d. Norway, 1883*), Lutheran clergyman. Came to America, 1844. Organized Norwegian Lutheran congregations in Wisconsin, giving them constitutions which became the basis of future development. Author of a volume of travels in the United States (1846). Returned to Norway, 1850.

DIETZ, PETER ERNEST (*b. New York, N.Y., 1878; d. Milwaukee, Wis., 1947*), Roman Catholic clergyman, social reformer. Early interest in social problems encouraged by Walter H. R. Elliott and William J. Kerby; ordained to priesthood, 1904. Believing that the church must engage actively in the fight against social injustice, he worked to create a national Catholic reform organization, to establish close ties between the church and the trade union movement, and to found a Catholic school of social service. A militant partisan of labor, he directed at Cincinnati, Ohio, the American Academy of Christian Democracy for the training of professional social workers. An adjunct of this school was the National Labor College for trade unionists (founded 1922); opposition by local business interests forced the closing of the academy and the college in 1923.

DIGGES, DUDLEY (*b. Dublin, Ireland, 1880; d. New York, N.Y., 1947*), actor, director. A charter member of the Irish National Theater, Digges settled in the United States, 1904. An actor of great skill and intelligence, he was associated with the companies of Ben Greet and George Arliss and, from 1919 until shortly before his death, with the Theater Guild. His acting roles were many and diverse; as director, his handling of several Shaw revivals won the admiration of the playwright himself; he appeared in more than fifty films. In 1946, he gave a masterly performance as the bar owner in O'Neill's *The Iceman Cometh.*

DIKE, SAMUEL WARREN (*b. Thompson, Conn., 1839; d. Auburndale, Mass., 1913*), Congregational clergyman, sociologist. Early a student of American family conditions, Dike founded and conducted the National Divorce Reform League, 1881–1913.

DILL, JAMES BROOKS (*b. Spencerport, N.Y., 1854; d. 1910*), corporation lawyer, jurist. Graduated Yale, 1876; New York University Law School, 1878. Drafted the 1889 New Jersey statute which legalized the holding company and allowed incorporation for almost any purpose. The consequent rush of business to New Jersey inspired Dill to organize the Corporation Trust Co. there— a corporation to organize other corporations. His publications on corporation law were invaluable guides for the business world, since Dill had largely created the law he expounded.

DILLARD, JAMES HARDY (*b. Nansemond Co., Va., 1856; d. Charlottesville, Va., 1940*), educator. First president and director, 1907–31, Negro Rural School Fund (Jeanes Fund); worked to improve race relations.

DILLE, JOHN FLINT (*b. Dixon, Ill., 1884; d. Chicago, Ill., 1957*), newspaper syndicator. Studied at the University of Chicago (Ph.B., 1909). Founded the National Newspaper Syndicate in 1917 of which he was president. Remembered for his formation of the comic strip "Buck Rogers" in 1929. Taken from a novel by Philip Nowlan, *Armageddon 2419 A.D.* (1928) and drawn by artist Richard Calkins, the strip was translated into eighteen languages, published in forty countries, and served as a radio program script.

DILLER, BURGOYNE (*b. New York, N.Y., 1906; d. New York, 1965*), painter and sculptor. Studied at Michigan State College (1925–27) and the Art Students League in New York City (1928–ca. 1932). Influenced by cubism, he became one of the first American-born artists to adopt a purely abstract style. By the mid-1930's he had embraced "neoplasticism," and his painting now consisted of studies in rectangular shape and line in a color range limited to red, yellow, and blue. Diller worked for the Works Progress Administration 1935–42. After serving in the navy during World War II, he joined the art department at Brooklyn College, where he taught until his death. In 1954 he was invited by the Yale School of Art and Architecture to serve as visiting critic.

DILLER, JOSEPH SILAS (*b. near Plainfield, Pa., 1850; d. 1928*), geologist. With U.S. Geological Survey, 1883–1923. Specialist in vulcanology.

DILLINGER, JOHN (*b. Indianapolis, Ind., 1902; d. Chicago, Ill., 1934*), bandit. "Public Enemy Number One"; killed by federal officers.

DILLINGHAM, CHARLES BANCROFT (*b. Hartford, Conn., 1868; d. 1934*), theatrical producer of 200 plays; famous for his lavish, tuneful, and tasteful musical comedies and revues.

DILLINGHAM, WALTER FRANCIS (*b. Honolulu, Hawaii, 1875; d. Honolulu, 1963*), business executive. Studied at Harvard (1898–1900), then joined his father's Oahu Railway and Land Company. He became president of Oahu Railways and associated companies in 1904. In 1902, with several associates, he formed Hawaiian Dredging Company (later Hawaiian Dredging and Construction Company), which became one of the most powerful and influential enterprises in Hawaii. The company's dredging operations made possible the development of Pearl Harbor and Waikiki Beach. In 1961 Hawaiian Dredging merged with the Oahu Railway and Land Company to form the Dillingham Corporation.

DILLINGHAM, WILLIAM PAUL (*b. Waterbury, Vt., 1843; d. Montpelier, Vt., 1923*), lawyer, politician. Republican governor of Vermont, 1888–90; U.S. senator, 1900–23. Advocated quota principle of immigration restriction and incorporated his views in the Dillingham bill, which became the Immigration Act of 1921.

DILLON, JOHN FORREST (*b. Montgomery Co., N.Y., 1831; d. 1914*), jurist. Removed to Iowa as a child. Studied medicine and law; admitted to bar, 1852. Iowa Supreme Court justice, 1862–68; federal circuit judge, 1869–79. Professor of law, Columbia, 1879–82; he engaged thereafter in corporate practice. His reputation rests upon contributions to legal scholarship, especially his monumental *Municipal Corporations* (1872), which created that subject as a separate field of law.

DILLON, SIDNEY (*b. Northampton, N.Y., 1812; d. New York, N.Y., 1892*), railroad-builder, financier. Having worked as foreman on several railroad projects, Dillon contracted to build a section of what is now the Boston & Albany Railroad, completing it in 1840. Thereafter, he built thousands of miles of railroad in America and was principal contractor for the Union Pacific Railroad, 1865–69. He served as director of that road, and as its president, 1874–84, 1890–92.

DIMAN, JEREMIAH LEWIS (*b. Bristol, R.I., 1831; d. 1881*), Congregational clergyman. Graduated Brown, 1851; Andover Theological Seminary, 1856. Gave up brilliant career in ministry to become professor of history and political economy at Brown University, 1864–81.

DIMITRY, ALEXANDER (*b. New Orleans, La., 1805; d. New Orleans, 1883*), educator, public official. First state superintendent of education in Louisiana, 1847–50.

DIMITRY, CHARLES PATTON (*b. Washington, D.C., 1837; d. New Orleans, La., 1910*), journalist, author. Son of Alexander Dimitry.

DINGLEY, NELSON (*b. Durham, Maine, 1832; d. 1899*), publisher. Graduated Dartmouth, 1855. Editor-publisher, *Lewiston Evening Journal.* Republican governor of Maine, 1874−76; congressman, 1881−99. Prepared the protectionist tariff adopted in 1897, commonly known as the Dingley Act.

DINGMAN, MARY AGNES (*b. Newark, N.J., 1864; d. Berea, Ky., 1961*), disarmament and peace activist. Studied at Teachers College, Columbia University (B.S., 1910). Taught elementary school, then joined the Young Women's Christian Association (YWCA) as a traveling secretary. Following World War I she was responsible for all YWCA work in France and Belgium. She was social and industrial secretary of the World Committee at the world YWCA headquarters, 1921−35. At its formation in 1931, Dingman became president of the Peace and Disarmament Committee, Women's International Organizations. In 1940, after returning to the U.S., she became honorary president. She then became involved in efforts to secure favorable congressional action on the United Nations. She served as the representative to the United Nations of the International Union for Child Welfare, 1948−54.

DINSMOOR, ROBERT (*b. Windham, N.H., 1757; d. 1836*), poet. The "Rustic Bard," and friend of John G. Whittier. His verses were published in 1828 and again in 1898.

DINWIDDIE, ALBERT BLEDSOE (*b. Lexington, Ky., 1871; d. 1935*), educator and administrator. Nephew of Albert T. Bledsoe. Graduated University of Virginia, 1889; Ph.D., 1892. President of Tulane University, 1918−35.

DINWIDDIE, COURTENAY (*b. Alexandria, Va., 1882; d. New York, N.Y., 1943*), social worker. Grandson of Albert T. Bledsoe; brother of Albert B. Dinwiddie. B.A., Southwestern Presbyterian University, 1901; graduate study at University of Virginia. In a long and varied career in social work, he displayed particular interest in public health organization and child welfare. Adept at enlisting cooperation between public and private agencies, he exemplified the emerging role of the professional community organizer in initiating social change. Typical of this was his work as secretary of the Cincinnati Social Unit, 1917−20, in which he devised techniques of neighborhood organization involving ordinary citizens in public affairs.

DINWIDDIE, EDWIN COURTLAND (*b. Springfield, Ohio, 1867; d. Washington, D.C., 1935*), Evangelical Lutheran clergyman, lecturer, reformer. Played a significant part in securing the adoption of the 18th Amendment and the Volstead Act.

DINWIDDIE, ROBERT (*b. near Glasgow, Scotland, 1693; d. Bristol, England, 1770*), colonial administrator. Appointed collector of customs for Bermuda, 1727; surveyor general for the southern part of America, 1738. An active and honest public servant, he was named lieutenant governor of Virginia, 1751. By provoking a quarrel with the House of Burgesses over land-patent fees, he lost its cooperation at a critical time. In 1754 Dinwiddie sent troops to prevent French settlement in the Ohio region, but after a defeat near present Pittsburgh in which George Washington played a part, the assembly would not support his measures, nor did neighboring governors help him. Braddock's attempt in 1755 also failed, and until 1757 Dinwiddie had to hold the frontier with companies of rangers, one regiment, and erratic aid from friendly Indians. As an early advocate of intercolonial cooperation and the man who precipitated the struggle leading to the downfall of New France, Dinwiddie is a major figure in American history.

DIRKSEN, EVERETT McKINLEY (*b. Pekin, Ill., 1896; d. Washington, D.C., 1969*), U.S. congressman and senator. Entered politics in 1926 by winning election to the Pekin City Commission. He was elected to the U.S. House of Representatives in 1932 and was appointed to the Appropriations Committee in 1937. He was chairman of the Republican National Congressional Committee (1938−46). Retiring in 1948, he then was elected to the U.S. Senate in 1950 and became a leading McCarthyite. Facing reelection in 1956, he moderated his views and was easily reelected. Dirksen was chosen Republican whip in 1957 and Republican leader in 1959. As Senate minority leader, he was a popular and visible figure during the Kennedy and Johnson administrations.

DISBROW, WILLIAM STEPHEN (*b. Newark, N.J., 1861; d. 1922*), physician, collector. Especially interested in natural sciences, medical history, and numismatics, his collections of books and specimens were distributed among many museums, including the Smithsonian Institution and the Newark Museum.

DISNEY, WALTER ELIAS ("WALT") (*b. Chicago, Ill., 1901; d. Los Angeles, Calif., 1966*), film producer, animator, and amusement park creator. Following service with the Red Cross in World War I, during which he contributed drawings to the army paper *Stars and Stripes*, he took a job with the Kansas City Film Ad Service, which made short cartoon advertisements. With the Dutch draftsman Ub Iwerks, Disney then went into business making short films. In 1923 he moved his studio to a garage in Hollywood, Calif., and with his brother, Roy, he developed the Alice in Cartoonland and Oswald the Rabbit series. With his business in jeopardy, Disney conceived a series of films built around the escapades of an animal; Mickey Mouse made his first appearance in 1928, followed in the 1930's by such characters as Minnie Mouse, Donald Duck, Pluto, Goofy, the Three Little Pigs, and the Big Bad Wolf. Disney's feature-length cartoons began with *Snow White and the Seven Dwarfs* (1937), *Pinocchio* (1940), *Fantasia* (1940), *Dumbo* (1941), and *Bambi* (1942). After World War II the Disney studios produced *Cinderella* (1950), *Alice in Wonderland* (1951), *Peter Pan* (1953), and *Sleeping Beauty* (1959). Live-action films included *Treasure Island* (1950), *20,000 Leagues Under the Sea* (1954), *Old Yeller* (1957), *Pollyanna* (1960), and *Mary Poppins* (1964). Disney received over 30 Oscars. In the early fifties he turned his attention to the creation of Disneyland, which opened in 1955 in Anaheim, Calif., and then Walt Disney World in Orlando, Fla.

DISSTON, HENRY (*b. Tewkesbury, England, 1819; d. 1878*), saw and tool manufacturer. By technological innovations at his factories in and near Philadelphia, Pa., Disston won world markets for his products.

DISTURNELL, JOHN (*b. Lansingburg, N.Y., 1801; d. New York, N.Y., 1877*), publisher and compiler of maps, guidebooks, gazetteers, and resort directories.

DITMARS, RAYMOND LEE (*b. Newark, N.J., 1876; d. New York, N.Y., 1942*), herpetologist. Assistant in entomological department, American Museum of National History, 1893−97; after 1899, rose from assistant curator of reptiles, New York Zoological Society, to curator of reptiles and mammals. Best known as a lecturer and author of popular articles and books which aroused wider interest in herpetology.

DITRICHSTEIN, LEO (*b. Temesvár, Hungary, 1865; d. Auersperg, Yugoslavia, 1928*), actor, dramatist. Made American debut, New York, 1890; thereafter, having gained facility in English, was successful as actor and as adapter of foreign plays.

DITSON, GEORGE LEIGHTON (*b. Westford, Mass., 1812; d. New York, N.Y., 1895*), author, theosophist.

DITSON, OLIVER (*b. Boston, Mass., 1811; d. Boston, 1888*), music publisher.

DITTEMORE, JOHN VALENTINE (*b. Indianapolis, Ind., 1876; d. New York, N.Y., 1937*), business executive, Christian Science leader. Expelled, 1919, from the church's board of directors, he led for a time a rival movement.

DIVEN, ALEXANDER SAMUEL (*b. Catherine, now Watkins, N.Y., 1809; d. 1896*), lawyer, Union soldier, railroad promoter. Financed and oversaw construction of the New York & Erie, 1844–50; was active in promoting and constructing several other railroads including Missouri Pacific. Leading citizen of Elmira, N.Y.

DIVINE, FATHER (*b. rural Georgia, ca. 1878/1880; d. Lower Merion Township, Pa., 1965*), black religious leader. Born George Baker. Though not ordained, using the name Reverend Major J. Devine he organized a religious group that came to be known as the Peace Mission Movement. In 1930 he formally adopted the name Father Divine. With headquarters in Harlem (1933) and then Philadelphia (1942), the Peace Mission attracted thousands of followers, black and white. His teachings rejected matrimony, urged celibacy, and emphasized racial equality.

DIX, DOROTHEA LYNDE (*b. Hampden, Maine, 1802; d. Trenton, N.J., 1887*), humanitarian. At 10 she left an unhappy home to live with grandmother in Boston and at 14 was teaching school in Worcester, Mass. Soon thereafter she established in Boston a school for young girls which she conducted until 1835. Her school stressed the natural sciences and moral character; among her pupils were the children of Rev. William Ellery Channing, to whose congregation she belonged. During this period she also wrote a number of now-forgotten books. When ill-health forced her to abandon the school, she resided for a while in England, returning to Boston in 1838 still an invalid.

In 1841 she undertook a Sunday-school class in the East Cambridge (Mass.) House of Correction. Visiting the jail, she found insane persons in an unheated room, treatment which was not unusual at a time when the insane were regarded as fallen to a brute condition. Having obtained relief for these persons, Dix spent two years investigating the shocking condition of the insane in jails, poorhouses, and similar institutions throughout Massachusetts. Influential men, chosen by her and supplied with the facts she had unearthed, presented a memorial of protest to the state legislature and, over objections and disbelief, a bill was carried for the enlargement of the Worcester insane asylum.

Well aware that the principal reform would come through state asylums staffed by intelligent, trained personnel, she made her work national in scope. She followed the same procedure in each state: thorough, independent research; wise choice of spokesmen; influence of the press. As a result, from 1841 to 1845, three hospitals for the insane were enlarged or reorganized at Worcester, Mass., Providence, R.I., and Utica, N.Y.; three new hospitals were founded at Trenton, N.J., Harrisburg, Pa., and Toronto, Canada. Between 1845 and 1852, 11 state legislatures were induced to vote for erection of state hospitals. Her great effort for a federal land grant whose taxes would be set aside for the care of the insane was defeated by presidential veto in 1854.

Between 1854 and 1857, she traveled in England and on the Continent, investigating care of the insane and effecting reforms. She was active not only in her own field but in many other humanitarian projects. Throughout the Civil War, she served as "superintendent of women nurses," selecting and assigning nurses for hospitals.

DIX, DOROTHY. *See* GILMER, ELIZABETH MERIWETHER.

DIX, JOHN ADAMS (*b. Boscowen, N.H., 1798; d. New York, N.Y., 1879*), soldier, lawyer, statesman. Dix's father, a man of marked individuality and versatile talents, gave his boy a good elementary education and then sent him to the College of Montreal for tuition in French and contact with a different civilization. Recalled at the outbreak of the War of 1812, Dix obtained an army commission and participated in the battle of Lundy's Lane. Having to contribute to the support of his family after his father was killed in the campaign of 1813, he remained in the army, rising to the rank of major. Seeking a larger field for his talents, he studied law and was admitted to the bar in 1824.

In 1826 he married the adopted daughter of John J. Morgan, a New York landowner who offered Dix the position of managing agent at Cooperstown. There Dix settled in 1828, practiced law, became county Democratic leader, and was appointed adjutant general of the state in 1830. From then on his political career prospered. He made an especial mark as New York secretary of state, 1833–39, working to improve the training of teachers in the public schools and taking the first step toward organizing a geological survey of the state.

Dix was elected to the Senate in 1845 for the five unexpired years of Silas Wright's term. Here he displayed a special interest in international affairs and also the Free-Soil sentiments that ultimately put him at odds with the Democratic party. He might have become a leader of the Democrats in the fifties, had not the proslavery wing of the party interfered, preventing his appointment as U.S. secretary of state and as minister to France.

After a decade's concentration on private affairs, he was appointed by Buchanan to straighten out affairs in the New York City post office. In January 1861, he became secretary of the treasury on demand of the alarmed business and money interests of the East. His chief service to the Union was this brief term at the treasury department. His dispatch of Jan. 29, 1861, to a treasury official in New Orleans which ended, "If anyone attempts to haul down the American flag, shoot him on the spot!" was a clarion call to the North. When he turned over his reorganized department in excellent condition to Salmon P. Chase in March, he was made a major general and did excellent, if unspectacular, service, notably as commander of the departments of Maryland and of the East.

After the war he served as minister to France, 1866–69. In 1872, though still a Democrat, he was nominated for governor of New York by the Republicans. Elected, he discharged the routine duties of his office capably until 1874.

DIX, JOHN HOMER (*b. Boston, Mass., 1811; d. Boston, 1884*), ophthalmologist. Performed one of the first operations in America for congenital strabismus, 1840. A leader in his speciality, he is also credited with introducing, 1856–57, the apartment house into the United States.

DIX, MORGAN (*b. New York, N.Y., 1827; d. New York, 1908*), Episcopal clergyman. Son of John A. Dix. Graduated Columbia, 1848; General Theological Seminary, 1852. Assigned to Trinity Parish, New York City, in 1855, he was its rector, 1862–1908.

DIXON, JAMES (*b. Enfield, Conn., 1814; d. Hartford, Conn., 1873*), lawyer, politician. Congressman, Whig, from Connecticut, 1845–49; U.S. senator, Republican, 1856–69. An ardent supporter of Andrew Johnson, he ran for the Senate as a Democrat, 1868, and failed of reelection.

DIXON, JOSEPH (*b. Marblehead, Mass., 1799; d. 1869*), inventor, manufacturer. After long years of experiment, developed and patented graphite crucibles for use in pottery and steel industries (1850, 1858).

DIXON, LUTHER SWIFT (*b. Underhill, Vt., 1825; d. Milwaukee, Wis., 1891*), jurist. Removed to Wisconsin, 1850; commenced practice of law; held minor offices. Chief justice, state supreme court, 1859–74. He appeared thereafter in important railroad cases.

DIXON, ROLAND BURRAGE (*b. Worcester, Mass., 1875; d. 1934*), anthropologist, teacher. Graduated Harvard, 1897, Ph.D., 1900. Author of more than 80 works; especially noted for work on ethnography of California.

DIXON, THOMAS (*b. near Shelby, N.C., 1864; d. Raleigh, N.C., 1946*), clergyman, author, lecturer, theatrical and motion picture producer. M.A., Wake Forest College, 1883. After studying history and political science at Johns Hopkins, acting with a Shakespearean road company, serving a term in the North Carolina legislature, and receiving an LL.B. from Greensboro (N.C.) Law School, 1886, he was ordained in the Baptist ministry. After holding pastorates in North Carolina, Boston, and New York City, he founded his own sect for the "unaffiliated masses," preaching with great success on political topics and urging reforms. Abruptly leaving the ministry, 1899, he wrote a number of polemical historical novels designed, in his view, to correct social evils. His most famous work was the trilogy *The Leopard's Spots* (1902), *The Clansman* (1905), and *The Traitor* (1907), which constituted a defense of southern retaliation against blacks during the Reconstruction period. Other novels attacked socialism, feminism, and pacifism. He produced a stage adaptation of *The Clansman*, 1905–06, which was the basis for D. W. Griffith's classic film *The Birth of a Nation* (1915).

DIXON, WILLIAM (*b. Ohio Co., W.Va., 1850 d. Oklahoma, 1913*), frontiersman, called "Billy" Dixon. Left home as a boy to become a muleskinner and buffalo hunter; fought at second battle of Adobe Walls, 1874; as army scout, won Congressional Medal for bravery.

DIXWELL, JOHN (*b. near Rugby, England, ca. 1607; d. New Haven, Conn., 1688/9*), regicide. A signer of Charles I's death warrant, Dixwell fled, *post* 1660, to Germany; he is first mentioned in America in 1664/5. Soon after, he settled at New Haven under the name of James Davids.

DOAK, SAMUEL (*b. Augusta Co., Va., 1749; d. Bethel, Tenn., 1830*), Presbyterian clergyman, educator. Graduated Princeton, 1775. Began ministry on Tennessee frontier, founding Salem Church near Jonesboro and what was later Washington College; in 1818, he opened Tusculum Academy.

DOANE, GEORGE WASHINGTON (*b. Trenton, N.J., 1799; d. 1859*), Episcopal clergyman. Graduated Union College, 1818; one of the first students at General Theological Seminary, New York, he was ordained, 1823. Consecrated bishop of New Jersey, 1832, he served also as rector of St. Mary's Church, Burlington, N.J. Leader of the High Church party in his time, he was author of a number of well-known hymns.

DOANE, THOMAS (*b. Orleans, Mass., 1821; d. West Townsend, Vt., 1897*), mechanical engineer. Did his principal work for Boston & Maine and other New England railroads; chief engineer, Hoosac Tunnel construction *post* 1863.

DOANE, WILLIAM CROSWELL (*b. Boston, Mass., 1832; d. 1913*), Episcopal clergyman. Son of George W. Doane. Consecrated bishop of Albany, N.Y., 1869.

DOBBIN, JAMES COCHRAN (*b. Fayetteville, N.C., 1814; d. Fayetteville, 1857*), lawyer. As secretary of the navy, 1853–57, he remade that service and greatly increased its technical efficiency. He recommended a radical increase in number of steam vessels, forced an act for reform of personnel procedures through Congress, and generally restored morale.

DOBBS, ARTHUR (*b. Co. Antrim, Ireland, 1689; d. 1765*), colonial governor of North Carolina, 1754–65. An opponent of popular government, his administration was in constant difficulties over questions of crown and governmental prerogative.

DOBIE, GILMOUR (*b. Hastings, Minn., 1878; d. Hartford, Conn., 1948*), football coach. LL.B., University of Minnesota, 1904. An outstanding end and quarterback at Minnesota, he began his career in 1902 as assistant coach there. In 1906 became director of athletics and coach of all sports at North Dakota Agricultural College, beginning of one of the most unusual coaching achievements in collegiate athletics. For two years, Dobie's football team was undefeated; he maintained the same record as football coach at the University of Washington, 1908–16. At the Naval Academy, 1917–19, his teams won 17 games out of 20. At Cornell, 1920–36, he at first continued his success, but his refusal to engage in aggressive recruiting and other factors brought about losing seasons. After a moderate success as coach at Boston College, 1937–39, he retired. Dobie stressed power, timing, and a strong defense, and favored the off-tackle play and used deception and a passing attack only enough to keep the opposition guessing. His teams won 179 games, lost 45, and tied 15.

DOBIE, J(AMES) FRANK (*b. Live Oak County, Tex., 1888; d. Austin, Tex., 1964*), writer and folklorist. Studied at Southwestern University and Columbia (M.A., 1913). Taught English at the University of Texas (1925–47) and was secretary-editor for the Texas Folklore Society (1922–43). After military service (1917–19) he began writing seriously, averaging a volume every year and a half over the next forty years. His books include *A Vaquero of the Brush Country* (1929), *Coronado's Children* (1930), *Apache Gold and Yaqui Silver* (1939), *The Longhorns* (1941), *Guide to the Life and Literature of the Southwest* (1943, 1952), *A Texan in England* (1944), *The Voice of the Coyote* (1949), *The Mustangs* (1952), and *Cow People* (1964).

DOCK, CHRISTOPHER (*no reliable information available as to birth; d. Montgomery Co., Pa., 1771*), Mennonite schoolmaster. Arrived Pennsylvania between 1710 and 1714; taught at Skippack and Salford, Pa. Author of the earliest treatise on school-keeping in America yet discovered, *Schulordnung* (written 1750; published, 1770).

DOCK, LAVINIA LLOYD (*b. Harrisburg, Pa., 1858; d. Chambersburg, Pa., 1956*), nurse, social reformer. Studied at the Bellevue Training School for Nurses in New York City. An ardent suffragist and pacifist, Dock was instrumental in obtaining state registration for nursing; she was assistant director of the nursing school at Johns Hopkins (1890–93); her books include *Materia Medica for Nurses* (1890), *History of Nursing*, with Adelaide Nutting (1907–1912), and *The History of American Red Cross Nursing*, with Clara Barton (1922). She retired in 1922 because of ill health.

DOCKSTADER, LEW (*b. Hartford, Conn., 1856; d. New York, N.Y., 1924*), minstrel. Original name, George Alfred Clapp; one of the most popular comedians of his time.

DOD, ALBERT BALDWIN (*b. Mendham, N.J., 1805; d. Princeton, N.J., 1845*), Presbyterian clergyman. Son of Daniel Dod. Professor of mathematics, Princeton University, 1830–45.

DOD, DANIEL (*b. Virginia, 1778; d. 1823*), inventor, engine-builder. Raised in Mendham, N.J. Nephew of Thaddeus Dod. Trained as a watch and instrument maker, he received (1811 and

1812) U.S. patents for steam engines to be used in steamboats as well as mills. In partnership with Aaron Ogden, Dod built a ferryboat which went in service in 1813. He continued to build machinery for boats, including the engines for the SS *Savannah*, the first steam vessel to cross the Atlantic, despite his bankruptcy, 1819. His death resulted from a boiler explosion on the East River, N.Y.

DOD, THADDEUS (*b. Newark, N.J., 1740; d. Ten Mile Creek, Pa., 1793*), Presbyterian clergyman, educator. Graduated Princeton, 1773; ordained, 1777, for work on western frontier. As pastor at Ten Mile Creek, Dod opened first classical school west of the Alleghenies, 1782; he was later a trustee of Washington Academy and its first principal, 1789–90.

DODD, BELLA VISONO (*b. Picerno, Italy, 1904; d. New York, N.Y., 1969*), union representative, lawyer, and renouncing Communist. Studied at Hunter College (B.A., 1925), Columbia (M.A., 1927), and New York University (LL.B., 1930). Began teaching at Hunter College in 1932, where she worked closely with the Communist party and became legislative representative of the teachers' union. She worked full-time for the union (1938–44). In 1944 she formally joined the Communist party, left the union, and opened a law office. She was elected to the party's National Committee, then was expelled from the party in 1949. In 1952 she returned to the Roman Catholic church, and over the next five years she testified several times before the Senate Internal Security Subcommittee. She taught at St. John's University Law School (1953–61) and published *School of Darkness* (1954). As a Conservative she made several unsuccessful runs for public office.

DODD, FRANK HOWARD (*b. Bloomfield, N.J., 1844; d. 1916*), publisher. *Post* 1870, senior partner of Dodd, Mead & Co.

DODD, LEE WILSON (*b. Franklin, Pa., 1879; d. 1933*), author. Son of Samuel C. T. Dodd. His satiric wit best displayed in *The Great Enlightenment* (1928).

DODD, MONROE ELMON (*b. Brazil, Tenn., 1878; d. Glendale, Calif., 1952*), Southern Baptist preacher. Pastor of the First Baptist Church of Shreveport, La. (1913–50). Founder of Dodd College and president (1926–1935); president of the Southern Baptist Convention (1933–35).

DODD, SAMUEL CALVIN TATE (*b. Franklin, Pa., 1836; d. 1907*), lawyer. Originally an "antirebate" lawyer in Pennsylvania oil regions, he became an attorney for Standard Oil, 1881, and organized the Standard Oil Trust, 1882.

DODD, WILLIAM EDWARD (*b. near Clayton, N.C., 1869; d. Round Hill, Va., 1940*), historian. Graduated Virginia Polytechnic Institute, 1895; Ph.D., Leipzig, 1900. Professor at University of Chicago, 1908–33, specializing in history of the South; ambassador to Germany, 1933–37.

DODDRIDGE, JOSEPH (*b. near Bedford, Pa., 1769; d. 1826*), Methodist and Episcopal clergyman, physician, author. Brother of Philip Doddridge. Author of *Notes on the Settlement and Indian Wars of the Western Parts of Virginia and Pennsylvania* (1824).

DODDRIDGE, PHILIP (*b. near Bedford, Pa., 1773; d. Washington, D.C., 1832*), lawyer, politician. Removed to what is now Wellsburg, W.Va., *ca.* 1790. As a member of the Virginia House of Delegates, an aggressive protagonist of the western, against the tidewater, interests, he was congressman from his section, 1829–32.

DODGE, AUGUSTUS CAESAR (*b. Ste. Genevieve, Mo., 1812; d. Burlington, Iowa, 1883*), politician, diplomat. Son of

Henry Dodge. Removed to Wisconsin, 1827, and to Iowa, 1838. Territorial delegate from Iowa, 1840–46; U.S. senator, Democrat, 1848–54; minister to Spain, 1855–59.

DODGE, DAVID LOW (*b. Brooklyn, Conn., 1774; d. 1852*), dry-goods merchant. Founded New York Peace Society, 1815, said to have been the first organization of its kind.

DODGE, EBENEZER (*b. Salem, Mass., 1819; d. 1890*), Baptist clergyman. President of Madison (now Colgate) University, *post* 1868.

DODGE, GRACE HOADLEY (*b. New York, N.Y., 1856; d. New York, 1914*), philanthropist, social worker. Granddaughter of William Earl Dodge. Among her many interests, her work in support of Teachers College (New York) and the Young Women's Christian Association was outstanding.

DODGE, GRENVILLE MELLEN (*b. Danvers, Mass., 1831; d. 1916*), civil engineer. Employed as a railroad surveyor, Illinois and Iowa; settled as a contractor and merchant in Council Bluffs, *ca.* 1854. Rose to major general of volunteers in Civil War, performing outstanding service as builder of bridges and railroads. Chief engineer, Union Pacific Railroad, 1866–70. Thereafter active as projector, builder, financier, and director of many railroads in the Southwest and West, he was called "ablest railroad lobbyist of his time."

DODGE, HENRY (*b. Vincennes, Ind., 1782; d. 1867*), soldier, pioneer. Raised in Ste. Genevieve district of present Missouri, where his father farmed and mined lead; served as sheriff of district and in War of 1812. Removed to region of present Dodgeville, Wis., *ca.* 1827; commanded mounted volunteers in Winnebago War, 1827, and Black Hawk War, 1832; appointed colonel, U.S. First Dragoons, 1833. Territorial governor of Wisconsin, 1836–41, 1845–48; territorial delegate, Democrat, 1841–45; U.S. senator, state of Wisconsin, 1848–57.

DODGE, HENRY CHEE (*b. New Mexico, 1860; d. Crystal[?], N.Mex., 1947*), Indian leader. Son of a captured Mexican adopted by the Navajo and a mother who was half-Navajo and half-Jemez, he was raised near Fort Defiance, where he was employed as a clerk's assistant. About 1880, he was appointed official interpreter for the Navajo. Intelligent and frugal, he used his savings to enter business for himself in 1890 as a partner in operating the successful Round Rock trading post. He extended his activities to ranching. He was chairman of the Navajo Tribal Council, 1923–28, and again in 1942. He protected and asserted the rights of the tribe against infringement by private corporations, and persuaded the U.S. government of the need for improvement of economic, health, and educational conditions.

DODGE, JACOB RICHARDS (*b. New Boston, N.H., 1823; d. Nashua, N.H., 1902*), agricultural journalist. Editor and statistician, U.S. Department of Agriculture, 1862–93.

DODGE, JOSEPH MORRELL (*b. Detroit, Mich., 1890; d. Detroit, 1964*), banking executive and government official. Worked as an examiner for the Michigan State Banking Department and the Securities Commission (1911–16), then became president of an automotive concern (1917–32). He became president of the Detroit Bank in 1933. Dodge began his government career as a price adjuster for various boards (1942–45), then served as a financial adviser to the Office of Military Government in Berlin and a finance director for American forces in Germany (1945–46). In 1947 President Truman appointed Dodge to head the American delegation to a Big Four advisory commission on reparations, and he served as Secretary of State Marshall's deputy for Austrian affairs. Dodge was a member of the advisory committee on fiscal and monetary problems of the Economic Cooperation Administration, which directed the original Marshall Plan (1948–51). In 1949 he became chief financial and economic adviser to General MacArthur in Japan, where he became the principal American architect of the postwar industrial rehabilitation of Japan. In 1952 President Eisenhower named him director of the Bureau of the Budget and in 1954 chairman of the Council on Foreign Economic Policy. In 1956 he became chairman of the New Detroit Bank and Trust Company.

DODGE, MARY ABIGAIL (*b. Hamilton, Mass., 1833; d. 1896*), journalist. Writer of caustic, clever miscellanies under pseudonym "Gail Hamilton."

DODGE, MARY ELIZABETH MAPES (*b. New York, N.Y., 1831; d. Onteora, N.Y., 1905*), editor, author. Especially remembered for her children's classic *Hans Brinker; or, The Silver Skates* (1865), and for her very able editorship of *St. Nicholas Magazine,* 1873–1905.

DODGE, RAYMOND (*b. Woburn, Mass., 1871; d. Tryon, N.C., 1942*), psychologist. B.A., Williams, 1893; studied with Benno Erdmann at University of Halle (Ph.D., 1896). Professor of psychology at Wesleyan University, 1898–1924, and Yale, 1924–36. Celebrated for his invention and development of instrumental techniques for experimental investigation of eye movements and other processes in human behavior, of which the Erdmann-Dodge tachistoscope was the first.

DODGE, THEODORE AYRAULT (*b. Pittsfield, Mass., 1842; d. near Nanteuil-le-Haudouin, France, 1909*), Union soldier, businessman, military historian. Author of careful studies of Alexander, Gustavus Adolphus, Napoleon, and others.

DODGE, WILLIAM DE LEFTWICH (*b. Liberty, Va., 1867; d. 1935*), artist. Studied at Munich and with Gérôme in Paris. The 24 large murals in the Flag Room of the New York State Capitol are representative of his work.

DODGE, WILLIAM EARL (*b. Hartford, Conn., 1805; d. 1883*), merchant. Son of David L. Dodge. Left wholesale dry-goods business, 1833, to join in Phelps, Dodge & Co., developers of copper and iron properties; maintained lifelong interest in philanthropies and in various reform movements, notably temperance.

DODS, JOHN BOVEE (*b. New York, N.Y., 1795; d. Brooklyn, N.Y., 1872*), spiritualist.

DOE, CHARLES (*b. Derry, N.H., 1830; d. Rollinsford, N.H., 1896*), jurist. Graduated Dartmouth, 1849. Justice, New Hampshire supreme judicial court, 1859–74; chief justice, state supreme court, 1876–96. Made radical and effective reforms in state legal procedure.

DOHENY, EDWARD LAURENCE (*b. near Fond du Lac, Wis., 1856; d. Beverly Hills, Calif., 1935*), oil producer. Developed fields in California and Mexico; with Albert B. Fall, secretary of the interior under President Harding, was tried for conspiracy and bribery in the Teapot Dome scandal.

DOHERTY, HENRY LATHAM (*b. Columbus, Ohio, 1870; d. Philadelphia, Pa., 1939*), public utility engineer, executive. Began work at 12 in Columbus Gas Co. A remarkable example of self-education, he rose to chief engineer, then became general manager of gas and electric properties in some 30 cities. By 1905 he headed his own firm, providing engineering and financial services to utilities. In 1910 he formed Cities Service, a holding company which acquired, reorganized, and refinanced dozens of operating companies, and extended into gas and petroleum pro-

duction. A brilliant and unorthodox engineer, he translated complex new technologies into goods and services by high-pressure financial methods which were sharply curbed by New Deal legislation.

DOLAN, THOMAS (*b. Montgomery Co., Pa., 1834; d. 1914*), capitalist. Successful with Keystone Knitting Mills, he became a major figure in development of public utilities in Philadelphia and elsewhere; he was center of a 1905 Philadelphia gas company scandal.

DOLD, JACOB (*b. Tuttlingen, Germany, 1825; d. Buffalo, N.Y., 1909*), meatpacker. Went to Buffalo, 1844; began own business, 1848, expanding it greatly after Civil War.

DOLE, CHARLES FLETCHER (*b. Brewer, Maine, 1845; d. 1927*), Congregational clergyman. Pastor, First Church, Jamaica Plain, Mass., 1876–1916.

DOLE, JAMES DRUMMOND (*b. Jamaica Plain, Mass., 1877; d. Honolulu, Hawaii, 1958*), businessman. Studied at Harvard. Founded the Hawaiian Pineapple Co. in 1901. Dole was responsible for perfecting the processing of pineapples and popularizing their use around the world. By the time of his death, Hawaii (including his company) was producing 72 per cent of the world's supply of pineapples.

DOLE, NATHAN HASKELL (*b. Chelsea, Mass., 1852; d. Yonkers, N.Y., 1935*), author, editor. Brother of Charles F. Dole. Among the earliest translators who introduced American readers to Russian literature.

DOLE, SANFORD BALLARD (*b. Honolulu, Hawaii, 1844; d. Honolulu, 1926*), lawyer, jurist. Son of an American missionary, Dole was educated in the United States, returning to Hawaii to practice law and engage in public affairs. Elected to the legislature as a reform candidate, 1884 and 1886, he was a leader in the revolution of 1887 whereby King Kalakaua was forced to grant a new constitution under which the monarch was reduced in status. Also in 1887, Dole was appointed a justice of the Hawaii Supreme Court and held that office until 1893 when he became head of the revolutionary provisional government which had overthrown the monarchy. Balked of immediate annexation to the United States by President Cleveland's opposition, Dole accepted presidency of the Republic of Hawaii, 1894, and served until 1900 when he became first governor of the Territory of Hawaii. Resigning in 1903, he was made judge of the U.S. district court for Hawaii.

D'OLIER, FRANKLIN (*b. Burlington, N.J., 1877; d. New Jersey, 1953*), insurance executive. Founder, with Theodore Roosevelt, of the American Legion (1919), and first national commander. Vice president of the Prudential Life Insurance Company of Newark (1926–38); president (1938–46); chairman of the board (1946–53). During World War II, a member of the U.S. Strategic Bombing Survey; awarded the Medal of Merit (1946).

DOLLAR, ROBERT (*b. Falkirk, Scotland, 1844; d. San Rafael, Calif., 1932*), ship owner. Immigrated to Canada, 1858; removed to Michigan, 1882, and to California, 1888. Founded steamship companies bearing his name; began first round-the-world passenger service.

DOLLIVER, JONATHAN PRENTISS (*b. near Kingwood, Va., 1858; d. 1910*), statesman. Removed to Iowa, *ca.* 1878; won local fame as orator in Republican campaign, 1884. As congressman, 1889–1900, Dolliver was a useful member of the conservative Republican group; however, as U.S. senator, 1901–10, he grew increasingly "insurgent" and aligned himself with La Follette and the liberals.

DOLPH, JOSEPH NORTON (*b. Dolphsburg, N.Y., 1835; d. 1897*), lawyer. Settling in Portland, Oreg., after the Civil War, he represented Northwest railroad interests and served as U.S. senator, Republican, from Oregon, 1882–94.

DOMBROWSKI, JOSEPH. *See* DABROWSKI, JOSEPH.

DOMINGUEZ, FRANCISCO ATANASIO *See* ESCALANTE, SILVESTRE VELEZ DE.

DONAHOE, PATRICK (*b. Munnery, Ireland, 1811; d. Boston, Mass., 1901*), editor, publisher. Immigrated to Boston as a child; learned printer's trade; began publication of the Boston *Pilot* with H. L. Devereaux, 1836. Notable for his philanthropies.

DONAHUE, PETER (*b. Glasgow, Scotland, 1822; d. San Francisco, Calif., 1885*), capitalist. Immigrated to America as a child; settled in California, 1849. Founded Union Iron Works, San Francisco, *ca.* 1850; was pioneer also in California public utility development.

DONALDSON, HENRY HERBERT (*b. Yonkers, N.Y., 1857; d. West Philadelphia, Pa., 1938*), neurologist. Graduated Yale, 1879; Ph.D., Johns Hopkins, 1885. Joining the faculty of Clark University in 1889, Donaldson published (1891) a classic anatomical study of the brain of Laura Bridgman, whose hearing had been lost and sight impaired through infection in infancy; this led to his remarkable monograph *The Growth of the Brain* (1895). Donaldson was professor of neurology, University of Chicago, 1892–1906; he then joined the Wistar Institute in Philadelphia. Here he developed the important "Wistar strain" of the albino rat on which he carried out his studies of the growth and development of the nervous system.

DONALDSON, JESSE MONROE (*b. Hanson, Ill., 1885; d. Kansas City, Mo., 1970*), U.S. postmaster general. Worked as a letter carrier in Shelbyville, Ill., and post-office clerk and supervisor in Muskogee, Okla. He was a post-office inspector in Kansas City, Mo. (1915–32), when he became acquainted with Harry Truman (then a judge). He became an inspector in Chattanooga, Tenn., in 1932, then was transferred to Washington, D.C., as deputy second assistant postmaster general (1933–36), deputy first assistant postmaster general (1936–43), chief post-office inspector (1943–45), and first assistant postmaster general (1946–47). In 1947, Truman named Donaldson postmaster general.

DONCK, ADRIAEN VAN DER. *See* VAN DER DONCK, ADRIAEN.

DONELSON, ANDREW JACKSON (*b. near Nashville, Tenn., 1799; d. Memphis, Tenn., 1871*), soldier, lawyer, diplomat. Raised in the home of Andrew Jackson; graduated West Point, served as aide to Jackson in Seminole War. Resigning from army, he studied law and was admitted to the bar, 1823. Served as Jackson's confidential secretary, 1824–28, and as his private secretary in Washington, 1828–36. Handled U.S. relations with Republic of Texas; served as minister to Prussia, 1846–49.

DONGAN, THOMAS (*b. Castletown, Ireland, 1634; d. London, England, 1715*), soldier, colonial administrator. Governor of New York (commissioned, 1682), 1683–88. One of the best of all the colonial governors, Dongan did his utmost to check the growing power of France in North America; during his term, a representative assembly was called and the so-called Dongan Charter of liberties was formulated.

DONIPHAN, ALEXANDER WILLIAM (*b. near Maysville, Ky., 1808; d. Richmond, Mo., 1887*), lawyer, soldier, statesman. Removed to Missouri, 1830, and was successful in practice of law. As colonel, First Missouri Mounted Volunteers, he led a remarkable western campaign during the Mexican War which is still considered one of the most brilliant long marches ever made. He favored Missouri neutrality in the Civil War and opposed secession.

DONLEVY, HARRIET FARLEY. *See* FARLEY, HARRIET.

DONN-BYRNE, BRIAN OSWALD (*b. New York, N.Y., 1889; d. Co. Cork, Ireland, 1928*), author. Among his colorful stories, distinguished for their word-music, are *Stranger's Banquet* (1919); *Messer Marco Polo* (1921); and *Blind Raftery* (1924).

DONNELL, JAMES C. (*b. Ireland, 1854; d. Findlay, Ohio, 1927*), oil producer. Taken to America as a child. Active *post* 1872 in Pennsylvania and Ohio oil fields; later associated with Standard Oil.

DONNELL, ROBERT (*b. Guilford Co., N.C., 1784; d. Athens, Ala., 1855*), Cumberland Presbyterian clergyman; a notable camp-meeting preacher.

DONNELLY, CHARLES FRANCIS (*b. Athlone, Ireland, 1836; d. Boston, Mass., 1909*), lawyer. Immigrated to Canada as an infant; to Providence, R.I., 1848. Graduated Harvard Law School, 1859. In practice in Boston, he served for many years as counsel for the Catholic church in New England, particularly in constitutional matters. He was active also in child welfare and public charities.

DONNELLY, ELEANOR CECILIA (*b. Philadelphia, Pa., 1838; d. West Chester, Pa., 1917*), author. Sister of Ignatius Donnelly.

DONNELLY, IGNATIUS (*b. Philadelphia, Pa., 1831; d. 1901*), politician, reformer. Projected a town (Nininger, Minn.), on whose site he turned farmer after panic of 1857 killed the scheme. As congressman, Republican, 1863–69, he was active in promoting railroad land grants; after his defeat for reelection, he left the Republican party and was successively Liberal Republican, Granger, and Greenbacker in his opinions. He was later active in formation of the Populist party. Among his books, each written to advance some unusual theory, are *Atlantis* (1882); *The Great Cryptogram* (1888); and *Caesar's Column* (1891).

DONOGHUE, JOHN (*b. Chicago, Ill., 1853; d. near New Haven, Conn., 1903*), sculptor. Studied in Chicago and in Paris under Jouffroy. Showed promise but never reached first rank and is remembered chiefly for his *Young Sophokles*.

DONOVAN, JAMES BRITT (*b. Bronx, N.Y., 1916; d. Brooklyn, N.Y., 1970*), lawyer and educator. Studied at Fordham (B.A., 1937) and Harvard (LL.B., 1940). He was general counsel for the U.S. Office of Scientific Research and Development (1942–43), then served in the navy (1943–45). He was an associate prosecutor at the war-crimes trials in Nuremburg, Germany (1945–46) and general counsel for the National Bureau of Casualty Underwriters. In 1951 he formed the law firm of Watters, Cowen, and Donovan in New York City. In 1957 he was appointed to defend Soviet intelligence agent Colonel Rudolf Abel, and in 1962 he successfully negotiated an exchange of Abel for Francis Gary Powers, the American U-2 pilot whose plane was shot down in the Soviet Union in 1960. In 1962–63 he negotiated with Fidel Castro the release of Cuban and American prisoners captured during the abortive Bay of Pigs invasion in 1961. He was elected president of the New York City Board of Education in 1963, and in 1968 he became president of Pratt Institute.

DONOVAN, JOHN JOSEPH (*b. Rumney, N.H., 1858; d. Bellingham, Wash., 1937*), pioneer railroad builder, lumberman, and community leader in the Pacific Northwest.

DONOVAN, WILLIAM JOSEPH (*b. Buffalo, N.Y., 1883; d. Washington, D.C., 1959*), lawyer, soldier, intelligence officer. Studied at Columbia (LL.B., 1907). A military hero of World War I, Donovan practiced law and became active in Republican politics in New York State. In 1924, he became chief of the Criminal Division for the Justice Department and assistant to the attorney general for the antitrust division during the Coolidge and Hoover administrations. During the 1930's, he conducted several secret missions to Europe to assess military situations. In 1941, President Roosevelt asked him to head an intelligence agency that became the Office of Strategic Services in 1942. As head of OSS, Donovan was controversial but effective in his efforts to combat Axis forces. He recommended the formation of a peacetime agency and hoped to head it, but the selection went to Allen Dulles. From 1953 to 1954, Donovan served as ambassador to Thailand.

D'OOGE, MARTIN LUTHER (*b. Zonnemaire, Netherlands, 1839; d. Ann Arbor, Mich., 1915*), Greek scholar. Came to America as a child. Graduated University of Michigan, 1862; Ph.D., Leipzig, 1872. Taught Greek at Michigan, 1867–1912; author of *The Acropolis of Athens* (1908) and other works.

DOOLEY, THOMAS ANTHONY, III (*b. St. Louis, Mo., 1927; d. New York, N.Y., 1961*), physician and writer. Studied at Notre Dame and St. Louis University Medical School (M.D., 1953). Served in the U.S. Navy as a medical corpsman (1944–46) and medical intern (1953–56). Assigned to the ship *Montague*, he assisted refugees leaving North Vietnam for South Vietnam, and he established a refugee camp near Haiphong. His best-selling account of this work is *Deliver Us From Evil* (1956). He resigned from the navy in 1956 and went to Laos to establish two medical clinics. He wrote of his Laotian experiences in *The Edge of Tomorrow* (1958). He then cofounded MEDICO (Medical International Corporation Organization). Dooley wrote about his third clinic in Laos in *The Night They Burned the Mountain* (1960).

DOOLITTLE, AMOS (*b. Cheshire, Conn., 1754; d. New Haven, Conn., 1832*), engraver. Produced prints of battles at Lexington and Concord after Ralph Earle, 1775, and a great variety of maps, book illustrations, and portraits.

DOOLITTLE, CHARLES LEANDER (*b. Ontario, Ind., 1843; d. 1919*), astronomer. Graduated University of Michigan, 1874; taught at Lehigh and at University of Pennsylvania; director, Flower Observatory, 1896–1912.

DOOLITTLE, ERIC (*b. Ontario, Ind., 1869; d. 1920*), astronomer. Son of Charles L. Doolittle.

DOOLITTLE, JAMES ROOD (*b. Washington Co., N.Y., 1815; d. 1897*), lawyer, statesman. After rising to prominence as a leader of the "Barnburner" faction of Democrats in New York, Doolittle removed to Racine, Wis., 1851. Served as U.S. senator, Republican, 1857–69. A friend and adviser of Abraham Lincoln, he sacrificed his political career in support of Andrew Johnson's policies.

DORAN, GEORGE HENRY (*b. Toronto, Ontario, 1869; d. Toronto, 1956*), publisher. Immigrated to the U.S. in 1892. Founded the George H. Doran Company in 1908 in Toronto, moving the headquarters to New York in 1909. Originally trained in the publication of religious works, Doran expanded his lists to include such authors as Stephen Vincent Benét, Du Bose Heyward, W. Somerset Maugham, and Aldous Huxley. In 1925, Doran merged with Doubleday, forming Doubleday, Doran and Company. He resigned in 1930.

DORCHESTER, DANIEL (*b. Duxbury, Mass., 1827; d. 1907*), Methodist clergyman, legislator. An able pastor and preacher, interested in temperance and other reforms, he supervised U.S. Indian Schools, 1889–93. Author of *History of Christianity in the United States* (1888) and other works.

DOREMUS, ROBERT OGDEN (*b. New York, N.Y., 1824; d. 1906*), chemist, inventor, educator. M.D., New York University, 1851. A versatile, inspiring teacher of science at several New York institutions, in particular at College of the City of New York, 1852–1903.

DOREMUS, SARAH PLATT HAINES (*b. New York, N.Y., 1802; d. 1877*), social worker. Active with J. Marion Sims in establishing the Woman's Hospital, 1855; long identified with charitable enterprises in New York.

DORGAN, THOMAS ALOYSIUS (*b. San Francisco, Calif., 1877; d. Great Neck, N.Y., 1929*), cartoonist. Famous as "TAD" for his political satire, his "Indoor Sports" and other series, and his gift for coinage of original slang.

DORION, MARIE (*b. Iowa Nation, ca. 1791; d. near present Salem, Oreg., 1850*), wife and trail companion of Pierre Dorion, interpreter of the Astoria land expedition 1811–12.

DORN, HAROLD FRED (*b. near Ithaca, N.Y., 1906; d. Washington, D.C., 1963*), medical statistician and government administrator. Studied at Cornell (B.S., 1929; M.S., 1930) and the University of Wisconsin (Ph.D., 1933). In 1934 became a research analyst in the Federal Emergency Relief Administration of the Works Progress Administration. In 1936 he became a staff member on the Committee on Population Problems of the National Resources Committee. He then began a lifelong career as a statistician with the U.S. Public Health Service. He was a lieutenant colonel and director of the Medical Statistics Division of the Office of the Surgeon General of the U.S. Army (1943–46) and then returned to the National Institutes of Health, where he played an important role in the growth and staffing of a program in medical statistics. Dorn is probably best known for his development of statistical methodology for large-scale epidemiological studies of cardiorespiratory diseases. With Sidney J. Cutler he published *Morbidity from Cancer in the United States, Parts I and II* (1955, 1959). His discovery of a significant link between lung cancer and smoking provided important evidence leading to announcements by the U.S. surgeon general on the dangers of smoking. In 1959 Dorn became the Cutter Lecturer in Preventive Medicine at Harvard. He became the general secretary of the International Union against Cancer in 1953, and he was a member of the scientific advisory council of the American Cancer Society and of the Joint U.S.-U.K. Board on Cardio-Respiratory Diseases.

DORNIN, THOMAS ALOYSIUS (*b. Ireland, 1800; d. Savannah, Ga., 1874*), naval officer. Retired as commodore, 1862.

DORR, JULIA CAROLINE RIPLEY (*b. Charleston, S.C., 1825; d. Rutland, Vt., 1913*), poet, novelist.

DORR, THOMAS WILSON (*b. Providence, R.I., 1805; d. 1854*), politician, reformer. Graduated Harvard, 1823; studied law under James Kent. As member of state legislature led fight for reform of Rhode Island's archaic suffrage laws, 1834–40; took leading part in agitation in 1840–42 of "People's party" for a constitution. Tried for treason, he was committed to prison, 1844–45. Restored his civil rights, 1851.

DORRELL, WILLIAM (*b. Yorkshire, England, 1752; d. Leyden, Mass., 1846*), founder of the Dorrellites, a fanatical sect which flourished in Franklin Co., Mass., *post* 1794.

DORSCH, EDUARD (*b. Würzburg, Bavaria, 1822; d. Monroe, Mich., 1877*), physician, poet.

DORSET, MARION (*b. Columbia, Tenn., 1872; d. Washington, D.C., 1935*), chemist. Graduated University of Tennessee, 1893; M.D., Columbian University, 1896. Known for his work with the Bureau of Animal Husbandry; he was a pioneer investigator of the chemistry of the tubercle bacillus and developed an effective method of controlling and preventing hog cholera.

DORSEY, ANNA HANSON MCKENNEY (*b. Georgetown, D.C., 1815; d. Washington, D.C., 1896*), author.

DORSEY, GEORGE AMOS (*b. Hebron, Ohio, 1868; d. New York, N.Y., 1931*), anthropologist, teacher. Author of *Why We Behave Like Human Beings* (1925).

DORSEY, JAMES OWEN (*b. Baltimore, Md., 1848; d. 1895*), ethnologist. Expert in linguistics and sociology of Indian tribes of the plains; author of many valuable specialized studies.

DORSEY, JOHN SYNG (*b. Philadelphia, Pa., 1783; d. Philadelphia, 1818*), surgeon. Nephew of Philip Syng Physick, whose student he was; M.D., University of Pennsylvania, 1802. Author of *The Elements of Surgery* (1813), he was associated with the Pennsylvania Hospital as surgeon and taught at University of Pennsylvania.

DORSEY, SARAH ANNE ELLIS (*b. near Natchez, Miss., 1829; d. New Orleans, La., 1879*), author.

DORSEY, STEPHEN WALLACE (*b. Benson, Vt., 1842; d. Los Angeles, Calif., 1916*), businessman, promoter. While active in fraudulent railroad promotions in Arkansas, he served as U.S. senator, Republican, from that state, 1873–76; he was indicted with T. W. Brady in Star Route scandal, 1881.

DORSEY, THOMAS FRANCIS ("TOMMY") (*b. Shenandoah, Pa., 1905; d. Greenwich, Conn., 1956*), trombonist and band leader. Leader of one of the most successful and long-lived big bands from the 1930's through the 1950's, Tommy Dorsey learned to play in his father's band. With his brother, Jimmy, with whom he was affiliated until 1935, he developed a musical style that is a blend of jazz, swing, and ballad. Featured singers included Frank Sinatra, Jo Stafford, and Connie Haines.

DORSHEIMER, WILLIAM EDWARD (*b. Lyons, N.Y., 1832; d. Savannah, Ga., 1888*), lawyer, politician, journalist. Prominent in New York Democratic politics, 1874–88; author of Grover Cleveland's campaign biography, 1884.

DOS PASSOS, JOHN RANDOLPH (*b. Philadelphia, Pa., 1844; d. New York, N.Y., 1917*), lawyer. Left thriving criminal practice to specialize in problems of finance and exchange. Author of a standard *Treatise on the Law of Stockbrokers and Stock Exchanges* (1882) and other works.

DOS PASSOS, JOHN RODERIGO (*b. Chicago, Ill., 1896; d. Baltimore, Md., 1970*), novelist and historian. Studied at Harvard (B.A., 1916) and the Sorbonne in Paris. Service with an ambulance corps during World War I led to his first novels, *One Man's Initiation: 1917* (1920) and *Three Soldiers* (1921). During the 1920's he was part of the literary scenes in both Paris and Greenwich Village, and he wrote *Rosinante to the Road* (1922), *A Pushcart at the Curb* (1922), *Manhattan Transfer* (1925), *The Garbage Man* (1926), and *Airways, Inc.* (1928). In 1926 he joined the editorial board of the radical *New Masses* magazine. During the early 1930's he was involved in Communist party activities, but a 1937 trip to Spain left him embittered toward the Communists. His trilogy *U.S.A.* (1938) was followed by the anti-Communist novel *Adventures of a Young Man* (1939). Beginning with *The*

Living Thoughts of Tom Paine (1940), he wrote frequently about the nation's founding fathers, and his politics became increasingly conservative. *Chosen Country* (1951) is an autobiographical novel and *The Best Times* (1966), a book of memoirs.

DOTY, ELIHU (*b. Berne, N.Y., 1809; d. Amoy, China, 1864*), Dutch Reformed clergyman. Missionary to Borneo and China; author of works on the Amoy dialect.

DOTY, JAMES DUANE (*b. Salem, N.Y., 1799; d. Salt Lake City, Utah, 1865*), politician, lawyer, speculator. Removed to Detroit, 1819, and became a judge in northern Michigan, 1823. Was later the stormy petrel of early Wisconsin politics, serving as delegate to Congress and as governor, and continuously involved in both capacities with promoting his own private interests.

DOUBLEDAY, ABNER (*b. Ballston Spa, N.Y., 1819; d. Mendham, N.J., 1893*), soldier, by tradition inventor of baseball. Graduated West Point, 1842. Served in Mexican War and as division commander in Civil War. Distinguished himself particularly at Gettysburg by holding Confederates in check on first day of battle.

DOUBLEDAY, FRANK NELSON (*b. Brooklyn, N.Y., 1862; d. Coconut Grove, Fla., 1934*), publisher. Founded Doubleday & McClure, 1897, and Doubleday, Page & Co., 1900.

DOUBLEDAY, NELSON (*b. Brooklyn, N.Y., 1889; d. Oyster Bay, N.Y., 1949*), book publisher. Son of F. N. Doubleday. Attended New York University, 1908–10, dropping out to start his own magazine-marketing and book-publishing business. In 1918, after service in World War I, he joined his father's firm, Doubleday, Page & Co.; president, 1928, chairman of the board, 1934. By mass production and sale of popular books, offered through high-volume outlets and a variety of direct-mail book clubs and reprint divisions, he made the firm, which became known as Doubleday and Company, the largest publishing house in the United States.

DOUBLEDAY, NELTJE DE GRAFF (*b. Chicago, Ill., 1865; d. China, 1918*), naturalist. Wife of Frank N. Doubleday.

DOUGHERTY, DENNIS JOSEPH (*b. Ashland, Pa., 1865; d. Philadelphia, Pa., 1951*), Roman Catholic cardinal and archbishop of Philadelphia. Ordained and personally awarded the doctorate of theology by Pope Leo XIII in 1890. From 1903 to 1915, cardinal of the Philippines. From 1915 to 1918, archbishop of Buffalo; from 1918 to 1951, archbishop of Philadelphia; established a system of free high schools for all Catholic children in his archdiocese.

DOUGHERTY, RAYMOND PHILIP (*b. Lebanon, Pa., 1877; d. 1933*), United Brethren clergyman, missionary educator, Assyriologist. Author of *The Sealand of Ancient Arabia* (1932).

DOUGHTON, ROBERT LEE (*b. Laurel Springs, N.C., 1863; d. 1954*), U.S. congressman. Democratic congressman from North Carolina (1910–53). Chairman of the House Ways and Means Committee (1932–53). Treaded a middle ground between conservatives and New Dealers.

DOUGHTY, THOMAS (*b. Philadelphia, Pa., 1793; d. New York, N.Y., 1856*), painter. Rated for a time the foremost landscape painter of the Hudson River school, Doughty was among the first American landscapists to attain general recognition.

DOUGHTY, WILLIAM HENRY (*b. Augusta, Ga., 1836; d. Augusta, 1905*), physician, Confederate army surgeon. An efficient general practitioner, he was also a student of climatology and its relation to medicine.

DOUGLAS, AMANDA MINNIE (*b. New York, N.Y., 1831; d. Newark, N.J., 1916*). Author of the Kathie series, the Little Girl series, and other books for children which reflect her love of domestic life.

DOUGLAS, BENJAMIN (*b. Northford, Conn., 1816; d. Middletown, Conn., 1894*), pump manufacturer. Coinventor of revolving cistern stand pump.

DOUGLAS, HENRY KYD (*b. Shepherdstown, W.Va., 1838; d. 1903*), lawyer, Confederate soldier. Douglas' brigade of Lee's army was the last unit to surrender at Appomattox.

DOUGLAS, JAMES (*b. Quebec, Canada, 1837; d. 1918*), metallurgist, mining engineer, industrialist. Headed the Cooper Queen Consolidated Mining Co. (Arizona).

DOUGLAS, LLOYD CASSEL (*b. Columbia City, Ind., 1877; d. Los Angeles, Calif., 1951*), minister, essayist, novelist. Lutheran minister (1903–32). Wrote popular novels, including *Magnificent Obsession* (1929), *The Robe* (1942), and *The Big Fisherman* (1948). All best sellers, they were made into successful motion pictures.

DOUGLAS, STEPHEN ARNOLD (*b. Brandon, Vt., 1813; d. Chicago, Ill., 1861*), Democratic leader, statesman. Lost father in infancy. Apprenticed to cabinetmaker's trade, he later began study of law. Hopeful of early admission to bar, he journeyed west, 1833, and after many wanderings, settled as schoolmaster in Winchester, Ill. Licensed to practice law at Jacksonville, Ill., 1834, within a year he was elected state's attorney for the first judicial district.

As a politician Douglas owed much to the Democratic political machine in Illinois, which he helped to fashion. Having noted the methods of New York's Albany Regency, he urged party organization and discipline. He was elected to the legislature and soon thereafter became registrar of the land office at Springfield. Nominated for Congress in 1837, Douglas lost the election by only 35 votes. On reorganizing the state supreme court, he received one of the five new judgeships. Elected to Congress in 1843, during his first term he made so favorable an impression as a party orator that he was asked to take an active part in the 1844 presidential campaign for Polk in the West.

Appointed to the U.S. Senate in 1847, Douglas immediately became chairman of the Committee on Territories. In this post, he encountered the active demand of northern political groups that Congress prevent the extension of slavery, while southerners were equally insistent that citizens should not be prevented from taking slaves into the territories. Douglas was acutely conscious of these opposing forces. His wife, Martha Denny Martin, had upon her father's death inherited some 150 slaves; some interpreted his subsequent career by this economic interest. In 1850, Douglas and Congressman McClernand drafted the bills providing territorial governments for Utah and New Mexico, which promised that when they came to be admitted as states, they should be admitted with or without slavery as their constitutions should prescribe. Though Douglas was absent when the vote on the Fugitive-Slave Act was taken, he approved of the act and defended it in a speech at Chicago.

Young men of his generation seemed drawn to Douglas. As the presidential candidate of "Young America" in 1852, he gave Cass and Buchanan supporters some concern, although he was unsuccessful. Reelected senator in 1852; he lost his wife at that time, growing bitter, morose, and careless in personal habits.

Territorial problems now returned to the fore. The speedy organization of the vast territory of Nebraska concerned Missouri politicians, settlers in the region, and promoters of a Pacific railway. Under pressure of many conflicting interests, the Committee on Territories produced a bill (January 1854) with a report stating that the Compromise of 1850 had established the principle that questions of slavery in the territories should be left to the people residing therein. A southern attempt explicitly to repeal the Missouri Compromise by amendment to the new bill led to the Kansas-Nebraska Act which provided for two new territories instead of one and declared the Act of 1820 "superseded." Subsequently the phrase was altered to "inoperative and void." In ensuing debates Douglas coined the phrase "popular sovereignty," to describe the new principle of decision. Independent Democrats in Congress claimed that Douglas' position was motivated by presidential ambition; yet Douglas had nothing to gain by subserviency to the South. Though an opportunist, Douglas had taken his stand on what he believed was a fundamental principle—self-determination. He failed to gauge the attachment of northern Democrats to "a compact binding in moral force" for over 30 years. Though the bill was contested in the House, the mastermind behind its passage was Douglas.

At the convention of 1856 Douglas was a leading contender for the presidency. When Buchanan received a majority, Douglas withdrew his name and in the campaign unreservedly supported the candidate.

Douglas was opposed by Abraham Lincoln in his 1858 campaign for reelection to the Senate. The famous series of debates in which the candidates engaged widened Douglas' breach with the dominant faction of his party by forcing him to deny the full force of the Dred Scott decision as interpreted by the national administration. Douglas won the election, but he was deposed by fellow Democrats from chairmanship of the Committee on Territories. Though he supported party policies where he could, he was eventually forced to declare opposition to any congressional intervention to protect slavery in the territories.

When the Democratic convention of 1860 met at Charleston, S.C., in April, Douglas led the balloting for the presidency but did not command two-thirds of the votes. When the convention reconvened at Baltimore two months later, southern delegations withdrew and Douglas was nominated by acclamation. The bolters nominated John C. Breckinridge. Douglas had hoped to win the South and enough free states to ensure election, but by midsummer a Democratic victory seemed impossible. His efforts were bent upon reorganizing the Democratic party and quashing disunion. The popular vote in 1860 was a personal triumph for Douglas, for he alone among the candidates drew votes from every section of the country and his total vote fell only 489,495 short of Lincoln's.

In the last weeks of Buchanan's administration, Douglas worked for compromise. He urged Lincoln to call a national convention for amendment of the Constitution so as to forbid the federal government from interfering with the domestic institution of slavery in the states. It is to his credit that Douglas gave total support to Lincoln in the early days of his administration. After the outbreak of the Civil War, Douglas, on Lincoln's advice, left Washington to rouse the people of the Northwest to the seriousness of the crisis. Soon after delivering a moving speech at Springfield, Ill. (Apr. 25, 1861), Douglas was stricken with typhoid fever and died.

DOUGLAS, WILLIAM (*b. Plainfield, Conn., 1742/3; d. Northford, Conn., 1777*), merchant, Revolutionary sailor and soldier. Served with credit in Montgomery's Canadian expedition, 1775, and in the defense of New York, 1776.

DOUGLAS, WILLIAM LEWIS (*b. Plymouth, Mass., 1845; d. 1924*), shoe manufacturer. From small beginnings at Brockton, Mass., 1876, Douglas built a business controlling 117 retail shoe stores throughout the country. He was Democratic governor of Massachusetts, 1905–06.

DOUGLASS, ANDREW ELLICOTT (*b. Windsor, Vt., 1867; d. Tucson, Ariz., 1962*), astronomer and dendrochronologist. Studied at Trinity College (Hartford, Conn.) (B.A., 1889). Became principal assistant, then acting director, of the new Lowell Observatory, near Flagstaff, Ariz., where he directed an intensive study of Mars. He joined the University of Arizona faculty in 1906, serving as professor and chairman of physics and astronomy (1906–37), acting president (1910–11), and dean (1915–18). He was instrumental in raising funds for the Steward Observatory, which he directed from 1922–37. He then became director of the newly established Laboratory of Tree-Ring Research at the university, a post he held until his retirement in 1958.

DOUGLASS, DAVID BATES (*b. Pompton, N.J., 1790; d. Geneva, N.Y., 1849*), engineer, soldier, teacher. Planned (1834–36) the Croton water supply system which served New York City for 75 years; planned and laid out Greenwood Cemetery, Brooklyn, N.Y.; taught science and engineering at West Point, New York University, and Hobart College.

DOUGLASS, FREDERICK (*b. Tuckahoe, Md., 1817[?]; d. 1895*), abolitionist, orator, journalist. Son of an unknown white father and a slave who had some Indian blood, he was named Frederick Augustus Washington Bailey but assumed the name of Douglass after escaping from slavery in 1838. In 1841 he successfully addressed a Massachusetts Anti-Slavery Society convention and was employed as its agent. To answer those who doubted that a man of his abilities could ever have been a slave, he wrote his *Narrative of the Life of Frederick Douglass* (1845). He then spent two years lecturing in British Isles. Later, he founded a newspaper, the *North Star*, labored continuously for justice to his race, and assisted other social reforms, including woman suffrage.

DOUGLASS, WILLIAM (*b. Gifford, Scotland, ca. 1691; d. 1752*), physician. Settled in Boston, Mass., 1718. His account of a scarlet fever epidemic (1736) was the first adequate clinical description of the disease; he was author also of a history of colonial settlement and a treatise on colonial currency.

DOULL, JAMES ANGUS (*b. New Glasgow, Nova Scotia, 1889; d. Baltimore, Md., 1963*), epidemiologist. Studied at Dalhousie University (B.A., 1911; M.D., C.M., 1914), Cambridge (D.P.H., *ca.* 1918), and Johns Hopkins (D.P.H., 1921). At Johns Hopkins School of Hygiene, he was associate in epidemiology, associate professor, and director of the John J. Abel Fund for Research on the Common Cold. He was professor of hygiene and public health at Western Reserve University in Cleveland (1930–46). In 1936 he helped to found the Cleveland Health Museum. He became first chief of the Office of International Health Relations of the U.S. Public Health Service in 1946, and in 1948 he became medical director of the Leonard Wood Memorial (American Leprosy Foundation). He is most recognized for his work on leprosy.

DOVE, ARTHUR GARFIELD (*b. Canadaigua, N.Y., 1880; d. Huntington, N.Y., 1946*), painter. Graduated Cornell University, 1903. Began as a magazine illustrator, but continued to study and develop an early talent for painting, in 1908 going to Paris, where he encountered and was influenced by fauvism and the trend to abstract art. He returned to the United States in 1909 and had his first one-man show in February 1912 at Alfred Stieglitz's 291 Gallery in New York City. His series of pastel abstractions was an important early contribution to the new concept. Living a life of relative poverty and comparative isolation, he continued to practice his own special art, using abstract principles to create his uniquely American form, more poetic in quality and intention than the intellectual designs of European abstractionists. Dove's best work was done in the 1940's; and he was beginning to enjoy considerable success when he died.

DOVE, DAVID JAMES (*b. Portsmouth, England, ca. 1696; d. Philadelphia, Pa., 1769*), Philadelphia schoolmaster, pamphleteer. The first person in Pennsylvania (perhaps in the colonies) to offer higher education for women, Dove went to Philadelphia in 1750 and taught there and in Germantown until his death.

DOW, ALEX (*b. Glasgow, Scotland, 1862; d. Ann Arbor, Mich., 1942*), public utility executive. Immigrated to Baltimore, Md., 1882. As engineer for Brush Electric Light Co., designed and installed arc-lighting system for South Park, Chicago, 1893; designed and built city-owned Detroit streetlighting electric plant, 1893–95. Built Detroit Edison Co. into an efficient, successful, and ethically conducted utility system, 1896–1940 (president, *post* 1912), through skills in management and administration.

DOW, HENRY (*b. Ormsby, England, 1634; d. Hampton, N.H., 1707*), soldier, lawyer. Taken to America as a child. Residing in Hampton, N.H., *post* 1644, he held a great number of town and provincial offices.

DOW, HERBERT HENRY (*b. Belleville, Canada, 1866; d. Rochester, Minn., 1930*), chemist. Taken to the United States as an infant. Graduated Case School of Applied Science, 1888; here began his interest in brine analysis. He patented a method for obtaining bromine from brine and in 1892 operated the first commercially successful American electrochemical plant at Midland, Mich. The Dow Chemical Co. was chartered in 1897 for the production of chlorine and bleaching powder. Dow products later developed from brines included insecticides, salicylates, magnesium, the first synthetic indigo in the western hemisphere, and the first iodine produced in the United States.

DOW, LORENZO (*b. Coventry, Conn., 1777; d. Georgetown, Md., 1834*), evangelist. An itinerant eccentric tentatively connected with the Methodists, Dow preached throughout the colonies and in England and Ireland, 1794–1834.

DOW, LORENZO (*b. Sumner, Maine, 1825; d. New York, N.Y., 1899*), inventor, businessman. Obtained the first patent for a waterproof cartridge, 1861. He later developed and marketed type-distributing and type-setting machines invented by his son Alexander.

DOW, NEAL (*b. Portland, Maine, 1804; d. Portland, 1897*), temperance reformer, Union soldier, mayor of Portland. Father of the "Maine Law" (1851, 1858), a prohibition measure.

DOWELL, GREENSVILLE (*b. Albemarle Co., Va., 1822; d. Galveston, Tex., 1881*), surgeon. Remembered for his monograph *Yellow Fever and Malarial Diseases* (1876), which suggested that the disease was transmitted by mosquitoes. Practicing principally in Texas *post* 1853, he developed a radical cure for hernia and designed a number of surgical instruments.

DOWIE, JOHN ALEXANDER (*b. Edinburgh, Scotland, 1847; d. 1907*), founder of the Christian Catholic Apostolic Church in Zion. Immigrated to America, 1888. His sect, centered in Zion City (near Chicago), claimed 50,000 members scattered throughout the world before his self-exposure and downfall, 1903–05.

DOWLING, AUSTIN (*b. New York, N.Y., 1868; d. St. Paul, Minn., 1930*), Roman Catholic clergyman. Bishop of Des Moines, Iowa, 1912–19; archbishop of St. Paul, Minn., 1919–30.

DOWLING, NOEL THOMAS (*b. Ozark, Ala., 1885; d. New York, N.Y., 1969*), constitutional scholar and law professor.

Studied at Vanderbilt (B.A., 1909) and Columbia (M.A., 1911; LL.B., 1912). Taught law at the University of Minnesota (1919–22), then at Columbia, becoming professor of law in 1924, Nash Professor of Law in 1930, and the first occupant of the Harlan Fiske Stone chair in constitutional law in 1946. He retired from teaching in 1958, but continued working with the Columbia University Legislative Drafting Research Fund. He is most remembered as a constitutional scholar; his *Cases on Constitutional Law* (1931) remains one of the most widely used law-school texts.

DOWNER, ELIPHALET (*b. Norwich, now Franklin, Conn., 1744; d. Brookline, Mass., 1806*), physician. Revolutionary army and navy surgeon.

DOWNER, SAMUEL (*b. Dorchester, Mass., 1807; d. 1881*), manufacturer. With Joshua Merrill and the Atwood brothers, introduced hydrocarbon lubricating and illuminating oils on a wide scale in America.

DOWNES, (EDWIN) OLIN (*b. Evanston, Ill., 1886; d. New York, N.Y., 1955*), music critic. Studied at the National Conservatory of Music in New York. Music critic for the *Boston Post* (1906–23); for the *New York Times* (1924–1955). Downes was known for his conservative taste in music, eschewing such modernists as Schoenberg and Stravinsky and favoring the folk classicists such as Moussorgsky and Sibelius, whose American reputation he helped establish. Believing in music for the masses, Downes lectured widely. Radio commentator for broadcasts of the New York Philharmonic and the Boston Symphony Orchestra.

DOWNES, JOHN (*b. Canton, Mass., 1784; d. Charlestown, Mass., 1854*), naval officer. First lieutenant of the *Essex* during her memorable cruise, 1812–13. Led first American engagement in Orient, the attack on Quallah Battoo, Sumatra, 1832.

DOWNEY, JOHN (*b. Germantown, Pa., ca. 1765; d. Harrisburg, Pa., 1826*), educator. His 1797 plan for a state educational system was ahead of its time, but was later commended by Henry Barnard.

DOWNEY, JUNE ETTA (*b. Laramie, Wyo., 1875; d. 1932*), psychologist. Pioneer in the field of personality measurement.

DOWNEY, SHERIDAN (*b. Laramie, Wyoming Territory, 1884; d. San Francisco, Calif., 1961*), U.S. senator. Studied at the University of Wyoming and the University of Michigan Law School (LL.B., 1907). As a Republican, elected district attorney of Albany County, Wyoming (1908). In California, he ran unsuccessfully as a Democrat for lieutenant governor (1934) and as a supporter of the Townsend Plan for Congress (1936). He was elected to the Senate (1938) with the support of pro-pension groups, liberals, and organized labor. He served on the Military Affairs Committee and was chairman of the Civil Service Committee. Downey wrote *Onward America* (1933), *Why I Believe in the Townsend Plan* (1936), *Pensions or Penury?* (1939), *Highways to Prosperity* (1940), and *They Would Rule the Valley* (1948). He retired from Congress in 1950 because of ill health.

DOWNING, ANDREW JACKSON (*b. Newburgh, N.Y., 1815; d. 1852*), landscape gardener, architect, horticulturist. Author of the classic *A Treatise on the Theory and Practice of Landscape Gardening* (1841), which established him as America's authority on "rural art." His *Cottage Residences* (1842) adapted his theories to the needs of humbler folk; *The Fruits and Fruit Trees of America* (1845) was the most complete treatise of its kind at that time. In 1846 Downing became editor of the *Horticulturist*, a new periodical. Increasingly interested in architecture, Downing, with Calvert Vaux, designed and constructed many estates. The first

great American landscape gardener, Downing "made over the face of rural America."

DOWNING, CHARLES (*b. Newburgh, N.Y., 1802; d. 1885*), pomologist, horticulturist, author. Brother of Andrew J. Downing.

DOWNING, GEORGE (*b. Dublin, Ireland, 1623; d. 1684*), baronet, diplomat, member of Parliament. Nephew of John Winthrop. A graduate of the first class (1842) at Harvard, he left New England, 1645. Downing Street, London, is named for him.

DOWSE, THOMAS (*b. Charlestown, Mass., 1772; d. 1856*), bibliophile. Collected a remarkable library which he donated to the Massachusetts Historical Society.

DOYLE, ALEXANDER (*b. Steubenville, Ohio, 1857; d. Boston, Mass., 1922*), sculptor. Designer of a vast number of public monuments.

DOYLE, ALEXANDER PATRICK (*b. San Francisco, Calif., 1857; d. San Francisco, 1912*), Roman Catholic clergyman, Paulist. Editor, *Catholic World*, 1893–1904; cofounder and rector of Apostolic Mission House at Catholic University, Washington, D.C.

DOYLE, JOHN THOMAS (*b. New York, N.Y., 1819; d. San Mateo, Calif., 1906*), lawyer. Graduated Georgetown (D.C.), 1838. Secured restitution from Mexico of proceeds from Spanish colonial Pious Fund.

DOYLE, SARAH ELIZABETH (*b. Providence, R.I., 1830; d. Providence, 1922*), educator. Promoted the establishment of the Women's College in Brown University.

DRAKE, ALEXANDER WILSON (*b. Westfield, N.J., 1843; d. New York, M.Y., 1916*), wood-engraver. Art director of the *Century Magazine*, and a leading figure in the development of American illustration.

DRAKE, BENJAMIN (*b. Mays Lick, Ky., 1795; d. 1841*), lawyer, editor, biographer. Brother of Daniel Drake. Author of *Cincinnati in 1826*, an account which encouraged immigration to Ohio and is still a valuable source; also of *Tales and Sketches from the Queen City* (1838) and lives of Black Hawk, W. H. Harrison, and Tecumseh.

DRAKE, CHARLES DANIEL (*b. Cincinnati, Ohio, 1811; d. 1892*), lawyer, jurist. Son of Daniel Drake. Leader of the radical faction which controlled Missouri from 1865 to 1871. U.S. senator, Republican, 1867–70; thereafter chief justice, U.S. Court of Claims, until 1885.

DRAKE, DANIEL (*b. near Plainfield, N.J., 1785; d. Cincinnati, Ohio, 1852*), physician. Raised in Kentucky; studied medicine at Cincinnati, 1800–04, and practiced there with distinction for the greater part of his life. A teacher of medicine at several institutions, Drake expressed ideals of medical education far ahead of his time. He served at various times as president of the Ohio Medical College, which he founded. He was author of *Notices Concerning Cincinnati* (1810), *Picture of Cincinnati in 1815* (1815), and his principal work, *A Systematic Treatise . . . on the Principal Diseases of the Interior Valley of North America* (1850, 1854).

DRAKE, EDWIN LAURENTINE (*b. Greenville, N.Y., 1819; d. Bethlehem, Pa., 1880*), railroad conductor, pioneer petroleum industrialist. In 1857 he visited properties, near Titusville, Pa., of the Pennsylvania Rock Oil Co., in which he owned stock. He studied salt-well drilling operations, leased land, and formed the Seneca Oil Co. for exploitation of the properties. In 1859 he struck oil at a depth of 69 feet. This was the first time petroleum was tapped at its source and the first proof of oil reservoirs within the earth's surface. Drake developed the use of pipe driven to bedrock to keep clay and quicksand from the drill hole.

DRAKE, FRANCES ANN DENNY (*b. Schenectady, N.Y., 1797; d. near Louisville, Ky., 1875*), actress. Sometimes called the "Star of the West"; the "tragedy queen" of the American stage, 1824–36.

DRAKE, FRANCIS MARION (*b. Rushville, Ill., 1830; d. Centerville, Iowa, 1903*), railroad builder. Union soldier, philanthropist. Removed to Iowa as a child. Promoter and official of several Iowa railroads. Republican governor of Iowa, 1896–97. His donation facilitated incorporation of Drake University, 1881.

DRAKE, FRANCIS SAMUEL (*b. Northwood, N.H., 1828; d. Washington, D.C., 1885*), historian. Son of Samuel G. Drake. Author of, among other works, an excellent *Dictionary of American Bibliography* (1872) and *Tea Leaves* (1884).

DRAKE, JOHN BURROUGHS (*b. Lebanon, Ohio, 1826; d. 1895*), hotel man. Prospered as Chicago, Ill., hotel keeper, 1855–95. Won national fame at Grand Pacific Hotel.

DRAKE, JOSEPH RODMAN (*b. New York, N.Y., 1795; d. New York, 1820*), poet. Friend of Fitz-Greene Halleck, with whom he collaborated on *The Croaker Poems* (1819); a selection of his work appeared in *The Culprit Fay and Other Poems* (1835).

DRAKE, SAMUEL (*b. England, 1768; d. Oldham Co., Ky., 1854*), pioneer actor-manager of the West. Immigrated to America, 1810. Drake brought the first really talented company beyond Pittsburgh and established the drama in Louisville, Lexington, and Frankfort, Ky.

DRAKE, SAMUEL ADAMS (*b. Boston, Mass., 1833; d. Kennebunkport, Maine, 1905*), historian. Son of Samuel G. Drake.

DRAKE, SAMUEL GARDNER (*b. Pittsfield, N.H., 1798; d. 1875*), antiquarian, historian. Author of, among other works, *Indian Biography* (1832), enlarged as *Book of the Indians* (1841). Editor of several classic source works on New England.

DRAPER, ANDREW SLOAN (*b. Westford, N.Y., 1848; d. 1913*), lawyer, politician, educator. Elected first commissioner of education of New York State, 1904, Draper laid the basis of the state's present Department of Education.

DRAPER, DOROTHY (*b. Tuxedo Park, N.Y., 1889; d. Cleveland, Ohio, 1969*), real estate stylist and interior decorator. Became the foremost woman decorator and real estate stylist of her day, even though she had no formal training in art or interior decoration. Her career began when she was commissioned to decorate the Hotel Carlyle in New York City. Dorothy Draper and Company, established in the 1930's, influenced the design of the interiors of hotels, hsopitals, offices, restaurants, and apartment-house lobbies. She is best-known for her work on the thirty-six-story Hampshire House apartment hotel in New York City. She wrote several books as well as articles for *Vogue* and *House and Garden*, and she had a syndicated newspaper column. She was director of the Studio of Architecture, Building, and Furnishing of *Good Housekeeping* magazine (1941–46).

DRAPER, EBEN SUMNER (*b. Milford, now Hopedale, Mass., 1858; d. Greenville, S.C., 1914*), cotton-machinery manufacturer. Republican governor of Massachusetts, 1909–10.

DRAPER, HENRY (*b. Prince Edward Co., Va., 1837; d. 1882*), astronomer, pioneer in astronomical photography. Son of John W. Draper. Graduated New York University, M.D., 1858. Se-

cured his first spectrum photograph of a star, 1872; he also photographed the spectra of the moon, Jupiter, and Venus. In 1874 Draper organized the photographic work of the government expedition to observe the transit of Venus.

DRAPER, IRA (*b. Dedham, Mass., 1764; d. Saugus, Mass., 1848*), textile-machinery inventor, manufacturer. Known as the inventor of the first rotary loom temple, a device which allowed one weaver to attend two looms.

DRAPER, JOHN (*b. Boston, Mass., 1702; d. Boston, 1762*), printer, journalist. Father of Richard Draper. Publisher of the *Boston News-Letter*, 1733–62.

DRAPER, JOHN WILLIAM (*b. St. Helen's, England, 1811; d. 1882*), chemist, author. Studied chemistry, London University; immigrated to America, *ante* 1834. Graduated M.D., University of Pennsylvania, 1836. Taught at Hampden-Sidney College and at New York University. Distinguished in chemical and physical research, he was also a pioneer in American photography and in promotion of long-distance telegraphy. Among his many books were the influential but now outdated *History of the Intellectual Development of Europe* (1863) and *History of the Conflict Between Religion and Science* (1874).

DRAPER, LYMAN COPELAND (*b. New York State, 1815; d. Madison, Wis., 1891*), historian, collector, librarian. Resolving at the age of 23 to devote his life to writing biographies of western heroes and to seek from their living contemporaries data to make his narratives complete, Draper journeyed extensively to find pioneer survivors, whose reminiscences, with other documentary material, filled a long series of manuscript volumes. In addition, he collected account books, letters, diaries, etc., which supplemented his frontier researches. All of his materials, known as the Draper Collection, were bequeathed to the Wisconsin State Historical Society, whose secretary he was, 1854–86, and were the foundation of its great historical library. He was also founder and first editor of *Wisconsin Historical Collections*.

DRAPER, MARGARET GREEN (*fl. 1759–1807*), wife of Richard Draper. Published *The Massachusetts Gazette and Weekly News-Letter*, *post* 1774. Strongly Loyalist, she left Boston in 1776.

DRAPER, RICHARD (*b. Boston, Mass., 1726/7; d. Boston, 1774*), printer. Son of John Draper. Succeeded father as publisher of *Boston News-Letter*, 1762, and continued it under subsequent titles, *The Boston Weekly News-Letter and New England Chronicle* and *The Massachusetts Gazette and Boston News-Letter* and others.

DRAPER, RUTH (*b. New York, N.Y., 1884; d. New York, N.Y., 1956*), monologuist. A member of New York society, Draper did not perform professionally until 1920 in London, at the age of thirty-five. She was a friend of King George V of England, Henry James, and Sarah Bernhardt. Draper always performed her own pieces and alone; her monologues were models of impersonation. She became a Commander of the Order of the British Empire in 1951.

DRAPER, WILLIAM FRANKLIN (*b. Lowell, Mass., 1842; d. Washington, D.C., 1910*), Union soldier, manufacturer, diplomat. Grandson of Ira Draper. Partner and principal executive in the family firm manufacturing textile machinery. Congressman, Republican, from Massachusetts, 1892–97; U.S. ambassador to Italy, 1897–1900.

DRAYTON, JOHN (*b. near Charleston, S.C., 1766; d. Charleston, 1822*), South Carolina jurist, legislator, author. Son of William H. Drayton. Governor of South Carolina, 1800–02 and 1808–10. Responsible for establishment of South Carolina College, 1801, opened 1805. Author of *A View of South Carolina* (1802) and *Memoirs of the American Revolution* (1821).

DRAYTON, PERCIVAL (*b. South Carolina, 1812; d. Washington, D.C., 1865*), naval officer. Son of William Drayton (1776–1846). Unionist in Civil War, in which he served under Du Pont and Farragut, rising to chief of Bureau of Navigation, 1865.

DRAYTON, THOMAS FENWICK (*b. South Carolina, 1808; d. Florence, S.C., 1891*), planter, Confederate brigadier. Son of William Drayton (1776–1846). Graduated West Point, 1848. Friend of Jefferson Davis; president of Charleston and Savannah Railroad, 1853–61.

DRAYTON, WILLIAM (*b. Magnolia Plantation, S.C., 1732; d. 1790*), jurist. Chief justice of East Florida, 1763–77; first U.S. judge, district of South Carolina, 1789–90.

DRAYTON, WILLIAM (*b. St. Augustine, East Florida, 1776; d. Philadelphia, Pa., 1846*), lawyer, soldier. Son of William Drayton (1732–90). Congressman, Democrat, from South Carolina, 1825–33; a foe of nullification.

DRAYTON, WILLIAM HENRY (*b. near Charleston, S.C., 1742; d. Philadelphia, Pa., 1779*), Revolutionary leader. Cousin of William Drayton (1732–90). Educated in England, Drayton returned to South Carolina, 1764, and became a planter. He entered the assembly in 1765. In 1769 he published articles denouncing the nonimportation movement and defending the right of the individual to ignore rules established without legal authority. He then went to England, where he was received as a champion of British rights. Returning to Carolina, he became a member of the council of the province, 1772–75. In 1775 he assumed leadership of the revolutionary movement in Carolina. Elected chief justice of South Carolina in 1776, he represented the state in the Continental Congress after 1778.

DREIER, KATHERINE SOPHIE (*b. Brooklyn, N.Y., 1877; d. Milford, Conn., 1952*), artist, art promoter. Studied at the New York Art Students' League and privately in London and Paris. Exhibited at the Salon des Beaux-Arts in Paris (1911) and at the Dore Gallery in London. First important exhibition in the U.S. was the Armory Show of 1913 in New York. Her early work was strongly influenced by art nouveau. Later she developed an abstract geometric style similar to Kandinsky. Along with Marcel Duchamp and Man Ray, she founded the influential Société Anonyme in 1920, an organization devoted to the promotion of modernist works. The society held over eighty exhibitions in the U.S. and presented a series of lectures and discussions in order to publicize new art. The collection included works by Brancusi, Kandinsky, Malevitch, Mondrian, and Schwitters. In 1941, Dreier and Duchamp gave the entire collection to Yale University.

DREIER, MARGARET. *See* ROBINS, MARGARET DREIER.

DREIER, MARY ELISABETH (*b. Brooklyn, N.Y., 1875; d. Bar Harbor, Maine, 1963*), reformer and philanthropist. From a financially secure family, she focused her personal and philanthropic activities on working women, woman suffrage, and social and civic improvement. She was president of the New York branch of the National Women's Trade Union League (1906–15, 1935) and served on the national board until 1950. In 1915 she committed herself fully to the final drive to achieve the vote for women. In 1917 she became chairman of the New York State Committee on Women in Industry of the Advisory Commission of the Council of National Defense, and she was a member of the executive committee of the New York Council for Limitation of

Armaments (1921–27). Dreier also was involved in the Young Women's Christian Association, the New York Commission for Law Enforcement, the Ellis Island Committee, the Regional Labor Board in New York, the Federal Advisory Council of the U.S. Employment Service, the Women's Joint Legislative Conference, the New York Conference for Unemployment Insurance, the Committee to Defend America by Aiding the Allies, and Promoting Enduring Peace. After Pearl Harbor she chaired the War Labor Standards Committee and served on the Women's Commission. She wrote a biography of her sister, *Margaret Dreier Robins: Her Life, Letters, and Work* (1950).

DREISER, THEODORE (*b. Terre Haute, Ind., 1871; d. Hollywood, Calif., 1945*), novelist. Received early education in German-language parochial schools; attended public schools in Warsaw, Ind. A rebel against his father's gloomy authoritarianism and his own early experiences of religion, he took from his childhood also a lifelong dread of poverty. His mother took in washing and kept house for roomers, which exposed him to harsh lessons in class distinction. At the age of 16, Dreiser left home and went to Chicago. He had a knack for finding people who wanted to educate him. At Indiana University, he began to know his intellectual and personal powers as well as some of the limiting exclusions—from fraternities and social pleasures—that affected his life. After a year he returned to petty white-collar jobs in Chicago, which gave him wide acquaintance with people. As he thought vaguely of becoming a writer, he identified himself with the enormous newly built metropolis, traditionless and daring to make new traditions. Beginning as a reporter for the *Chicago Globe*, Dreiser went from one newspaper to another in Chicago, St. Louis, and elsewhere.

In 1894, he met Arthur Henry of the *Toledo Blade*, who in 1899 turned Dreiser to fiction. But Dreiser first had to complete his education as a journalist. A Pittsburgh phase in 1894 was crucial. There, Dreiser "ate, slept, dreamed, lived" Balzac. A little later came his shattering encounter with Huxley, Tyndall, and Herbert. Yet by the end of that year, with $240 in savings, he set off for New York. Dreiser went to his brother Paul (who, as Paul Dresser, was a successful song-and-dance man and songwriter) with a proposition that his music firm publish a house magazine. He edited *Ev'ry Month* for two years and even provided Paul with a first stanza and chorus for the hit song "On the Banks of the Wabash."

Dreiser continued writing for *Munsey's, Cosmopolitan, Success,* and others, and making a name with his interviews of tycoons and his sketches of the urban poor. In 1898 Dreiser married Sara Osborne White (whom he had met in 1893), despite the fact that the emotion behind his commitment had long since begun to fade. He was a shrewd entrepreneur of his own writing. His first novel, *Sister Carrie,* appeared in 1900. However, the publisher's disapproval almost stopped publication, and only 456 copies were sold. The blow was not only to the inner self; it also spelled economic disaster. His personal and creative life declined until he entered a sanatorium and began to recover.

After six months' physical labor on a railroad, Dreiser became a subeditor at the *New York Daily News.* In 1905 he became editor of *Smith's Magazine*; not long after Paul's death in 1906, he moved to *Broadway Magazine.* Dreiser used his new affluence to back a second edition of *Sister Carrie* (1907), this time finding favorable reviewers and a ready public.

In 1907 Dreiser went to the Butterick Publishing Co. to run three women's magazines. In 1909 he began secretly to edit the *Bohemian*; he invited H. L. Mencken to contribute, but warned him that he wanted no "tainted fiction or cheap sex-struck articles." His official prudery contrasted with his earlier fearlessness and confirmed "varietist" taste in love. His Don Juan compulsion led to his dismissal from Butterick, and he subsequently separated from his wife.

Freed from business and marriage, Dreiser now experienced a surge of creativity. He produced *Jennie Gerhardt* (1911), *The Financier* (1912), *The Titan* (1914), and *The "Genius"* (1915). The novelist's cause, he believed, was truth-telling even more than it was sexual liberation, and educated readers reacted accordingly. The New York Society for the Suppression of Vice had *The "Genius"* withdrawn. One effect of this censorship was that he did not produce another novel for ten years, but he did write plays, poems, stories, memoirs, travel books, and philosophical reflections. Moreover, Dreiser no longer struggled alone: Mencken generaled a campaign with the support of Amy Lowell, Edwin Arlington Robinson, Sinclair Lewis, Sherwood Anderson, Max Eastman, and many others. Dreiser now consciously played his part in "breaking the bonds of Puritanism."

His finest work of the period was *Twelve Men* (1919). He was pursuing his study of science more systematically and coming to focus on psychology; friendships with A. A. Brill and Jacques Loeb date from this period. In 1919 he met 25-year-old Helen Patges Richardson, a second cousin, and entered into the most stable relationship of his life.

He now started work on *An American Tragedy*. Having studied some 15 actual cases, he settled on that of Chester Gillette, who in 1906 had killed his pregnant girlfriend, Grace Brown, when the illicit liaison threatened him socially and economically in his small town. Dreiser's title emphasized his painstaking demonstration that the false values of American society were more responsible for the crime than individual will. The novel, which except perhaps for *Huckleberry Finn* made the most trenchant criticism of American society, ironically was his first popular success.

Increasingly involved in social causes, in his sixtieth year Dreiser became chairman of the National Committee for the Defense of Political Prisoners, and for more than a decade he made himself available as a public supporter of Communist-sponsored causes. He joined the Communist party in 1945, the last year of his life, but he considered his act an affirmation of internationalism, equality, and a reordered social system, not the undertaking of a discipline of power.

In his sixties, Dreiser continued his persistent study of science with a view to making a comprehensive naturalist philosophy of being. In science he got round his analytic deficiencies and reached fundamental affirmations more easily than in politics. This spirit renewed his own creative powers, and in 1942 he resumed work on novels long set aside. He expressed his religious acceptance convincingly in the Quaker piety which informs *The Bulwark*, much less so in the concern with Yoga in *The Stoic*. The same mood affected his awareness of how much he depended on Helen, whom he married at last in 1944. Dreiser had all but finished both of the late novels before he died of a heart attack in 1945.

DRESEL, OTTO (*b. Geisenheim, Germany, ca. 1826; d. 1890*), concert pianist, composer. Came to America, 1848. Resided in Boston, *post* 1852; was for many years a force in that city's musical life.

DRESSEN, CHARLES WALTER (*b. Decatur, Ill., 1898; d. Detroit, Mich., 1966*), baseball player, coach, and manager. Began playing professional baseball and football in 1919. Played major-league baseball (1925–33), principally with the Cincinnati Reds, and batted .272. His first major-league managing position was with Cincinnati in 1934. As manager of the Brooklyn Dodgers (1951–53) Dressen won 298 games, lost only 166, and won the National League championship (1952). He also managed the Oakland Acorns, the Milwaukee Braves, the Toronto Blue Jays, the Detroit Tigers, and the Washington Senators. As a major-league manager, Dressen won 1,037 games and lost 993.

DRESSER, LOUISE KERLIN (*b. Evansville, Ind., 1882; d. Woodland Hills, Calif., 1965*), actress. Achieved great success on Broadway as a musical comedy favorite, beginning in *About Town* (1906). She appeared in *The Girls of Gottenburg* (1909), *Potash and Perlmutter* (1913), and *Hello, Broadway!* (1914). She also toured in vaudeville. Her films included *Prodigal Daughters* (1923), *The City That Never Sleeps* (1924), *The Eagle* (1925), *The Goose Woman* (1925), *Blind Goddess* (1926), *The Third Degree* (1927), *White Flannels* (1927), *Mr. Wu* (1927), *The Air Circus* (1928), *Mother Knows Best* (1928), *A Ship Comes In* (1928), for which she won a "Citation of Merit" at the first Academy Awards, *Not Quite Decent* (1929), *Mammy* (1930), *Lightnin'* (1930), *State Fair* (1933), *Cradle Song* (1933), *The Scarlet Empress* (1934), *David Harum* (1934), *A Girl of the Limberlost* (1934), *The County Chairman* (1935), and *Maid of Salem* (1937).

DRESSLER, MARIE (*b. Cobourg, Canada, 1871; d. 1934*), stage and screen comedian. Her greatest success was on the screen in *Anna Christie* (1930) and as "Tugboat Annie" (1933).

DREW, CHARLES RICHARD (*b. Washington, D.C., 1904; d. near Burlington, N.C., 1950*), surgeon. B.A., Amherst College, 1926; M.D. and C.M., McGill University, 1933. As a student, as an intern at Montreal General Hospital, and later as resident there and at Columbia-Presbyterian Medical Center, New York City, Drew engaged in special study and research on blood typing, problems of transfusion, and the preservation and storage of blood. He also investigated the use of plasma, and in 1939 established Columbia-Presbyterian's first blood bank; for his pioneering work and his thesis on blood preservation, he received the Sc.D. degree from Columbia. Before U.S. entry into World War II, he supervised the procurement and processing of blood, and shipping of plasma, for use in England. Appointed medical director of the American Red Cross blood bank program early in 1941, he resigned when the Red Cross received an official directive to keep non-Caucasian blood separate from other blood donations. A member of the faculty of Howard University Medical College since 1935, he returned there and devoted himself to surgery and teaching; in 1942, he became professor of surgery and chief surgeon at Freedmen's Hospital and subsequently chief of staff and medical director. He died in an auto accident.

DREW, DANIEL (*b. Carmel, N.Y., 1797; d. 1879*), capitalist, speculator. Enlisted in War of 1812 to earn the $100 paid for substitutes. Became a cattle drover and horse trader. With capital supplied by Henry Astor, Drew extended his operations westward, being the first to drive cattle from Ohio, Kentucky, and Illinois across the Alleghenies. In 1834 he entered the steamboat business in competition with Cornelius Vanderbilt. In 1844 he entered Wall St., where he became known as a crafty independent operator and amasser of money. Becoming director of the Erie Railroad in 1857, he shamelessly manipulated stock. His greatest business battle was the "Erie War" with Vanderbilt, 1866–68, which he waged in alliance with Jay Gould and James Fisk. *Post* 1870 his luck failed him and he went bankrupt.

DREW, GEORGIANA EMMA. *See* BARRYMORE, GEORGIANA EMMA DREW.

DREW, JOHN (*b. Dublin, Ireland, 1827; d. Philadelphia, Pa., 1862*), actor. Father of one of the most noted stage families of the United States; made American debut, New York, 1842.

DREW, JOHN (*b. Philadelphia, Pa., 1853; d. San Francisco, Calif., 1927*), actor. Son of John Drew (1827–62) and Louisa L. Drew. Made his debut in Philadelphia, 1873; joined Augustin Daly's New York company, 1875; later accompanied his brother-in-law, Maurice Barrymore, in barnstorming. Drew acted exclusively with Daly's company, 1879–93; his Petruchio, opposite Ada Rehan's Kate, in *The Taming of the Shrew* was a high point of Daly's productions. Starred for the first time in Clyde Fitch's *Masked Ball*, 1892; for two decades thereafter he was managed by Charles Frohman. Best known for ease, grace, and skill in high comedy, Drew played an important part in the growth of the modern American theater.

DREW, LOUISA LANE (b. *London, England, 1820; d. Larchmont, N.Y., 1897*), actress, theatrical manager. Wife of John Drew (1827–62); mother of John Drew (1853–1927) and Georgiana Drew Barrymore. Herself a versatile actress she managed the Arch Street Theatre, Philadelphia, 1861–92.

DREXEL, ANTHONY JOSEPH (b. *Philadelphia, Pa., 1826; d. Carlsbad, Germany, 1893*), philanthropist, banker. Son of Francis M. Drexel. Partner in his father's brokerage house at 21, he guided the successful development of the Drexel Co. in the post–Civil War period. Founded the Drexel Institute, Philadelphia.

DREXEL, FRANCIS MARTIN (b. *Dornbirn, Australia, 1792; d. 1863*), artist, banker. Came to America, 1817. Established brokerage office at Louisville, Ky., 1837, which became famous Philadelphia banking house of Drexel & Co.

DREXEL, JOSEPH WILLIAM (b. *Philadelphia, Pa., 1833; d. 1888*), banker, philanthropist. Son of Francis M. Drexel. Partner in Drexel, Harjes and Co., Paris; also Drexel, Morgan & Co., New York.

DREXEL, KATHARINE MARY (b. *Philadelphia, Pa., 1858; d. Cornwells Heights, Pa., 1955*), philanthropist, nun. Heiress to an immense fortune, Drexel entered the order of the Sisters of Mercy in 1889. In 1891, she founded the order of the Sisters of the Blessed Sacrament. Especially concerned with aiding American Indians and blacks, Sister Drexel founded a boarding school for Pueblo Indians in Santa Fe, N.M., and Xavier University for blacks in New Orleans, La. By 1955, the order had grown to some 500 members living in fifty-one convents, conducting forty-nine elementary schools, twelve high schools, Xavier University, and three houses of social services.

DREYFUS, MAX (b. *Kuppenheim, Germany, 1874; d. near Brewster, N.Y., 1964*), music publisher. Began with a part interest (1901), then assumed control of T. B. Harms, Inc., a music-publishing house. He sold his interest in Harms in 1929, then acquired the British music-publishing concern Chappell and Company with his brother Louis in 1935. Together, they dominated the music-publishing industry in the West. Dreyfus-controlled companies published the works of virtually every major musical theater composer and lyricist except Irving Berlin. Dreyfus helped found the American Society of Composers, Authors, and Publishers (ASCAP) in 1914, on whose board he served until his death.

DRINKER, CATHARINE ANN. *See* JANVIER, CATHARINE ANN.

DRINKER, CECIL KENT (b. *Philadelphia, Pa., 1887; D. Falmouth, Mass., 1956*), experimental physiologist and educator. Studied at Haverford College and University of Pennsylvania (M.D., 1913). Taught at Harvard School of Public Health from 1917 to 1948; dean from 1935 to 1942. An expert in asphyxia and resuscitation, he helped develop the oxygen masks used by the military flyers during World War II; consultant physiologist to the Naval Medical Research Institute (1948–54). Wrote *The Clinical Physiology of the Lungs*, 1954.

DRINKWATER, JENNIE MARIA (b. *Yarmouth, Maine, 1841; d. 1900*), writer of juvenile fiction. Originator of the Shut-in-Society, *ca.* 1874, for promoting correspondence to invalids.

DRIPPS, ISAAC L. (b. *Belfast, Ireland, 1810; d. 1892*), inventor, engineer. Mechanical superintendent, Camden & Amboy Railroad; later of Pennsylvania Railroad. Built the first freight-car truck of the diamond-framed pattern.

DRISLER, HENRY (b. *Staten Island, N.Y., 1818; d. 1897*), educator. Graduated Columbia, 1839, and was associated thereafter with Columbia as professor, dean, and acting president. Jay professor of Greek, 1867–94, he was coeditor of a number of lexicons and textbooks with Charles Anthon and others.

DROMGOOLE, WILLIAM ALLEN (b. *Murfreesboro, Tenn., 1860; d. 1934*), author and journalist. Writer of fiction about the blacks and mountaineers of Tennessee and also stories for children, Miss Dromgoole was a feature writer for the *Nashville Banner* from 1904.

DROPSIE, MOSES AARON (b. *Philadelphia, Pa., 1821; d. 1905*), lawyer. Public spirited and philanthropic, Dropsie left his entire estate for the founding of the Philadelphia college for Hebrew studies which today bears his name.

DROWN, THOMAS MESSINGER (b. *Philadelphia, Pa., 1842; d. Bethlehem, Pa., 1904*), chemist. Graduated M.D., University of Pennsylvania, 1862. Made advanced studies at Yale and Harvard and in Germany. Taught at Lafayette College and Massachusetts Institute of Technology; president, Lehigh University, 1895–1904.

DRUILLETTES, GABRIEL (b. *France, 1610; d. Quebec, Canada, 1681*), Jesuit missionary. Came to Canada, 1643; ministered to the Abenaki and later to western tribes. Author of an account of his diplomatic visits to New England, 1648 and 1651.

DRUM, HUGH ALOYSIUS (b. *Fort Brady, Mich., 1879; d. New York, N.Y., 1951*), army officer, business executive. Studied at Boston College (B.A., 1921). Commissioned in the army in 1898, Drum saw action in the Philippines. Following four years of line duty, he attended the Army School of the Line and Staff College in Ft. Leavenworth (1910–1912). In 1917, Pershing appointed him staff member of the American Expeditionary Force to France, and later, chief of staff of the American First Army. Drum was responsible for all phases of the victorious St. Mihiel and Meuse-Argonne offensives. Appointed deputy chief of staff of the army in 1933, he commanded various areas, including the Second Corps Area and the First Army Headquarters (1938). In 1939, he was considered for the position of chief of staff, but for political reasons the position went to George Marshall. Confined to the home front during World War II, he retired a lieutenant general in 1943 and became president of the Empire State Corporation in New York. He was military advisor to Thomas Dewey in his campaigns of 1944 and 1948.

DRUMGOOLE, JOHN CHRISTOPHER (b. *Granard, Ireland, 1816; d. New York, N.Y., 1888*), Roman Catholic clergyman. Came to America, 1824. Devoted himself to reclaiming incorrigible children; founded Mission of the Immaculate Virgin, New York City and Staten Island.

DRURY, JOHN BENJAMIN (b. *Rhinebeck, N.Y., 1838; d. New Brunswick, N.J., 1909*), Dutch Reformed clergyman, editor.

DRYDEN, JOHN FAIRFIELD (b. *Temple Mills, Maine, 1839; d. 1911*), pioneer of industrial insurance in America. Founded Prudential Insurance Co., 1875. U.S. senator, Republican, from New Jersey, 1902–07.

DRYFOOS, ORVIL E. (b. *New York, N.Y., 1912; d. New York, 1963*), newspaper executive. Studied at Dartmouth (B.A., 1934), then worked for a Wall Street brokerage firm. Following his marriage to a daughter of Arthur Hays Sulzberger and Iphigene Ochs, who held a controlling interest in the *New York Times*, Dryfoos joined the *Times* as a cub reporter. He advanced to assistant to the publisher (1943), vice president (1955), and president (1958). In 1961 he succeeded Sulzberger as publisher of the *Times*.

DUANE, ALEXANDER (*b. Malone, N.Y., 1858; d. 1926*), ophthalmologist. Son of James C. Duane. Graduated Union, 1878; M.D., College of Physicians and Surgeons, New York, 1881.

DUANE, JAMES (*b. New York, N.Y., 1733; d. Schenectady, N.Y., 1797*), jurist. Admitted to the bar, 1754. A conservative throughout the pre-Revolutionary period in New York, he was elected to the Continental Congress, 1774, and served on the committee which wrote the statement of rights of the colonists, being largely responsible for its mild tone; served in Congress almost continuously until 1783. As mayor of New York, 1784–89, he was chiefly concerned with rehabilitating the city. Became first federal judge of the district of New York, 1789.

DUANE, JAMES CHATHAM (*b. Schenectady, N.Y., 1824; d. 1897*), military and civil engineer. Grandson of James Duane. Graduated West Point, 1848. Largely responsible for design of bridges and siege works as chief engineer, Army of the Potomac. Retired as brigadier general and chief of engineers, U.S. Army, 1888.

DUANE, WILLIAM (*b. near Lake Champlain, N.Y., 1760; d. Philadelphia, Pa., 1835*), journalist, politician. After a stormy youth in Ireland, India, and England, he returned to America, 1796, and joined Benjamin Franklin Bache in publishing the *Aurora*. Under Duane, *post* 1798, this newspaper became the most powerful Jeffersonian organ. Energetic, radical, and fearless, Duane materially assisted Jefferson's election in 1800. Disappointed of his hopes for advancement, he continued to edit his paper until 1822.

DUANE, WILLIAM (*b. Philadelphia, Pa., 1872; d. Devon, Pa., 1935*), physicist. Graduate of University of Pennsylvania, 1893; M.A., Harvard, 1895; Ph.D., Berlin, 1897. Studied radioactivity in Marie Curie's laboratory, 1907–13. On his return to the United States, worked at Harvard and with the Cancer Commission until 1934. Devised standards of measurement for dosage in the biological application of radioactivity; his proposals were internationally accepted in 1928. His most important single discovery was the "Duane-Hunt law," which states that there is a sharp upper limit to the frequency of X rays emitted from a target under electron bombardment.

DUANE, WILLIAM JOHN (*b. Clonmel, Ireland, 1780; d. Philadelphia, Pa., 1865*), lawyer. Son of William Duane. Associated with father on the *Aurora* newspaper; author of numerous pamphlets on local affairs. Secretary of the treasury, 1833–35; dismissed from office for refusal to aid Jackson's bank policy.

DUBBS, JOSEPH HENRY (*b. Lehigh Co., Pa., 1838; d. 1910*), clergyman of Reformed church (German), church historian. Professor of history, Franklin and Marshall, 1875–1910.

DUBOIS, AUGUSTUS JAY (*b. Newton Falls, Ohio, 1849; d. 1915*), civil engineer. Professor of engineering, Sheffield Scientific School, 1884–1915. His *Elements of Graphical Statics* (1875) was the first comprehensive work on this subject to appear in the United States.

DUBOIS, JOHN (*b. Paris, France, 1764; d. New York, N.Y., 1842*), Roman Catholic clergyman. Came to America, 1791. After successful missionary career in frontier Maryland, established Mt. St. Mary's at Emmitsburg, Md., 1807. Consecrated bishop of New York, 1826, he experienced great difficulties in coping with the lay trustee system.

DU BOIS, WILLIAM EDWARD BURGHARDT (*b. Great Barrington, Mass., 1868; d. Accra, Ghana, 1963*), historian, sociologist, editor, and political activist. Studied at Fisk University (1885–88), Harvard (Ph.D., 1895), and the University of Berlin (1892–94). He began teaching, as a professor of Latin and Greek, at Wilberforce University in Ohio (1894–96). His dissertation, *The Suppression of the African Slave-Trade to the United States*, was published in 1896. He then accepted a one-year assignment at the University of Pennsylvania to produce a study of blacks in Philadelphia. The result was his *The Philadelphia Negro* (1899), a work that set new standards for the study of African-Americans. Du Bois began teaching economics, history, and sociology at Atlanta University in 1897, and he took charge of the annual Atlanta University Conference for the Study of the Negro Problems.

Du Bois grew to resent the leadership of the most influential black in America, Booker T. Washington. He became Washington's most ideological rival with the publication of *The Souls of Black Folks* (1903). In 1905 he organized the Niagara Movement, which promoted agitation against segregation and other injustice. He also founded two magazines, *Moon* (1905–06) and *Horizon* (1907–10). Stimulated by a commencement address by Franz Boas, Du Bois turned to a deeper concern for African culture. His book *John Brown* was published in 1909. The next year he resigned from Atlanta and joined the newly founded National Association for the Advancement of Colored People (NAACP) as director of publications and research. He also founded *Crisis*, the monthly organ of the NAACP, and remained its editor for twenty-four years.

In 1911 Du Bois briefly joined the American Socialist party. His book *The Negro* (1915) became a kind of Bible of Pan-Africanism. Following World War I, Du Bois was involved in the Pan-African Congress. During this period he openly clashed with the leader of the back-to-Africa movement, Marcus Garvey. His next books were *Darkwater: Voices from Within the Veil* (1920) and *Dark Princess* (1928). A 1926 visit to the Soviet Union led Du Bois to declare "I am a Bolshevik" in *Crisis*. His promotion of voluntary segregation for blacks brought him into conflict with the NAACP, from which he resigned in 1934. Returning to Atlanta University, he wrote his monumental *Black Reconstruction in America* (1935), which was followed by *Black Folk: Then and Now* (1939) and *Dusk of Dawn: An Autobiography of a Concept of Race* (1940). He retired from his Atlanta position in 1944 and returned to the NAACP as director of special research (1944–48). He published *Color and Democracy: Colonies and Peace* (1945) and *The World and Africa* (1947).

Following his dismissal from the NAACP he moved steadily toward Communism. In 1950 he became chairman of the Peace Information Center. Shortly thereafter the State Department revoked his passport, preventing him from traveling abroad until 1958. Turning to fiction, he wrote the first draft of a trilogy, *The Black Flame* (*The Ordeal of Mansart*, 1957; *Mansart Builds a School*, 1959; *Worlds of Color*, 1961). In 1960 Kwame Nkrumah, president of Ghana, invited Du Bois to move to Ghana and begin work on the *Encyclopedia Africana*. He accepted, and his final act before leaving the U.S. was to apply for membership in the Communist Party of the U.S. In 1963 Du Bois renounced his American citizenship and took that of Ghana. Additional books include *The Battle for Peace* (1952) and *The Autobiography of W. E. B. Du Bois* (1968).

DU BOIS, WILLIAM EWING (*b. Doylestown, Pa., 1910; d. Philadelphia, Pa., 1881*), numismatist.

Du Bose, William Porcher (*b. near Winnsboro, S.C., 1836; d. Sewanee, Tenn., 1918*), Episcopal clergyman, theologian. A professor and chaplain, University of the South, 1871–1918; also held administrative posts. In the field of philosophy of the Christian religion, Du Bose was the foremost thinker in the Episcopal church in America.

Du Bourg, Louis Guillaume Valentin (*b. Cap Français, Santo Domingo, 1766; d. Besançon, France, 1833*), Roman Catholic clergyman. Arriving in Baltimore, Md., 1794, he joined Sulpicians. President, Georgetown College, 1796–98; head of St. Mary's College, Baltimore, *ca*. 1800–12, he encouraged Elizabeth Ann Seton in foundation of Sisters of Charity. Appointed administrator apostolic of New Orleans, *ca*. 1812, he was consecrated bishop, 1815, but because of difficulties with local clergy governed from St. Louis, Mo., 1817–20. During his stay in St. Louis and later at New Orleans, he was responsible for extensive building of churches and seminaries and the introduction of teaching orders of nuns and priests. He resigned his see February 1825 and returned to Europe the following year.

Dubuque, Julien (*b. St. Pierre les Brecquets, Canada, 1762; d. Iowa, 1810*), first white settler of Iowa. As early as 1785 was at Prairie du Chien, Wis.; won permission in 1788 from a band of Fox Indians to work lead mines in the Iowa country.

Du Chaillu, Paul Belloni (*b. France, 1835; d. St. Petersburg, Russia, 1903*), African explorer. Came to America, 1852. Traveled through tropical Africa, 1856–59, 1863–65. Author of *Explorations and Adventures in Equatorial Africa* (1861), *Stories of the Gorilla Country* (1868), and other books.

Duché, Jacob (*b. Philadelphia, Pa., 1737/8; d. Philadelphia, 1798*), Anglican clergyman, Loyalist. Chaplain of Continental Congress. Author of *Caspipina's Letters* (1774; published in periodical form, 1772), sermons, and other works. Renounced revolutionary sympathies, 1777.

Duchesne, Rose Philippine (*b. Grenoble, France, 1769; d. St. Charles, Mo., 1852*), teacher, pioneer. Coming to America in 1818 as a religious of the Society of the Sacred Heart, she founded schools of that society in Missouri and Louisiana; also served as a missionary to Indians in Kansas.

Duchin, Edward Frank ("Eddy") (*b. Cambridge, Mass., 1909; d. New York, N.Y., 1951*), pianist and orchestra leader. Studied at the Massachusetts College of Pharmacy. Duchin organized his orchestra in 1931; by 1933, he had a radio series on NBC. A player of refined and sophisticated music, he was popular with society circles and appeared at leading hotels. In 1937, he played at the White House. The orchestra was also featured in films and made recordings for RCA Victor, Brunswick, and Columbia recording studios. During World War II, Duchin saw action on D-Day and in the Pacific. He returned to music as a soloist. A popular movie based on his life, *The Eddy Duchin Story*, was released in 1956.

Dudley, Benjamin Winslow (*b. Spotsylvania Co., Va., 1785; d. near Lexington, Ky., 1870*), surgeon. Graduated M.D., University of Pennsylvania, 1806; studied also in London. Practiced in Kentucky until 1853. Known for his operation for bladder stone, in which he was more successful than any surgeon until that time.

Dudley, Charles Benjamin (*b. Oxford, N.Y., 1842; d. 1909*). Chemist to the Pennsylvania Railroad Co. after 1875, he was the first person to apply chemistry to railroad economy, efficiency, and safety problems.

Dudley, Charles Edward (*b. Stafford, England, 1780; d. Albany, N.Y., 1841*), politician. Often mayor of Albany and a loyal member of the Albany Regency, he served as U.S. senator, Democrat, from New York, 1829–33.

Dudley, Edward Bishop (*b. Onslow Co., N.C., 1789; d. Wilmington, N.C., 1855*), businessman, politician. Congressman, Democrat, from North Carolina, 1829–31; Whig governor, 1837–40. Founder and president of the Wilmington & Weldon Railroad.

Dudley, Joseph (*b. Roxbury, Mass., 1647; d. Roxbury, 1720*), politician. Son of Thomas Dudley. Graduated Harvard, 1665. Served in the General Court, 1673–76, and, after King Philip's War, in the upper house of the legislature until 1684. When the Massachusetts charter was revoked, Dudley became president of the council and governor of Massachusetts, New Hampshire, and the King's Province. Replaced by Andros in 1686, he helped enforce unpopular laws passed under the new governor, thus winning New England's hatred. After a brief period as chief of the Council of New York (1691–92) and some years abroad, Dudley became governor of Massachusetts in 1702. He immediately entered upon a struggle with the General Court over salary and prerogatives which continued until his retirement in 1715.

Dudley, Paul (*b. Roxbury, Mass., 1675; d. Roxbury, 1751*), jurist. Son of Joseph Dudley. Massachusetts attorney general, 1702–18; judge of superior court, 1718–45; chief justice, 1745–51. Founder of Dudleian lectures at Harvard.

Dudley, Thomas (*b. Northampton, England, 1576; d. Roxbury, Mass., 1653*), governor of the colony of Massachusetts Bay. Steward of the earl of Lincoln, parishioner of John Cotton, Dudley immigrated to Massachusetts, 1630, on the *Arbella*. Deputy governor under Governor Winthrop, he resented Winthrop's move of the colony from Newtown to Boston and fixed his own residence at Roxbury. Throughout his life he was almost constantly in public office. He was elected governor in 1634, 1640, 1645, and 1650. Dogmatic and austere, Dudley dominated the community by sheer strength of will.

Dudley, William Russel (*b. Guilford, Conn., 1849; d. 1911*), botanist. Taught at Cornell, Indiana, and Stanford. Active in conservation; founder of the Dudley Herbarium.

Duer, John (*b. Albany, N.Y., 1782; d. Staten Island, N.Y., 1858*), jurist. Son of William Duer. Served on commission to revise New York statutes, 1825–27; judge, superior court, New York City, 1849–58.

Duer, William (*b. Devonshire, England, 1747; d. New York, N.Y., 1799*), merchant, financier. Settled in America, *post* 1773. A patriot, he served in the New York constitutional convention, 1776, and on the Committee of Public Safety. Member of the Continental Congress, 1777–79. Grown rich, he entered on extensive speculations and was instrumental in establishing the Bank of New York, 1784. Secretary to the Board of the Treasury *post* 1786, and briefly assistant secretary of the U.S. treasury, 1789–90, he continued personal dealings and was prime mover in the Scioto land speculation and others. His insolvency and arrest for debt in 1792 precipitated New York's first financial panic.

Duer, William Alexander (*b. Rhinebeck, N.Y., 1780; d. Morristown, N.J., 1858*), jurist, educator. Son of William Duer; grandson of Gen. William Alexander. Judge, New York Supreme Court, 1822–29; president, Columbia College, 1829–42.

Duff, James Henderson (*b. Mansfield, now Carnegie, Pa., 1883; d. Washington, D.C., 1969*), lawyer, governor of Pennsylvania, U.S. senator. Attended Princeton (B.A., 1904), the University of Pennsylvania Law School, and the University of Pittsburgh (LL.B., 1907). Practiced law in Pittsburgh and was long active in Pennsylvania politics. He was appointed attorney general in 1943, was elected governor in 1946, and was elected to the U.S. Senate in 1950. A moderate Republican, he served on the Armed Services and Commerce committees and he spoke out against Senator Joseph R. McCarthy. He was defeated in his reelection bid in 1956.

DUFF, MARY ANN DYKE (*b. London, England, 1794; d. New York, N.Y., 1857*), actress. Made American debut, 1810, at Boston; at her best in tragedy, appeared mainly in the South *post* 1835.

DUFFIELD, GEORGE (*b. Lancaster Co., Pa., 1732; d. Philadelphia, Pa., 1790*), Presbyterian clergyman. A "New Side" Presbyterian, he was chaplain of the Pennsylvania militia and also of the Continental Congress; later pastor, Third Church, Philadelphia.

DUFFIELD, GEORGE (*b. Strasburg, Pa., 1794; d. Detroit, Mich., 1868*), Presbyterian clergyman. Grandson of George Duffield (1732–90). Pastor at Carlisle, Pa., dismissed for views expressed in *Spiritual Life; or, Regeneration* (1832), he had a successful ministry thereafter in Detroit, Mich.

DUFFIELD, SAMUEL AUGUSTUS WILLOUGHBY (*b. Brooklyn, N.Y., 1843; d. 1887*), Presbyterian clergyman, hymnologist. Grandson of George Duffield (1794–1868).

DUFFY, EDMUND (*b. Jersey City, N.J., 1899; d. New York, N.Y., 1962*), cartoonist. Graduate from New York's Art Student's League (1919), then contributed sketches to several newspapers and magazines. He was editorial cartoonist for the *Baltimore Sun* (1924–48), where he won three Pulitzer Prizes (1931, 1934, 1940). Duffy was editorial cartoonist with the *Saturday Evening Post* (1949–57).

DUFFY, FRANCIS PATRICK (*b. Cobourg, Canada, 1871; d. New York, N.Y., 1932*), Roman Catholic clergyman, chaplain of the "Fighting 69th" New York regiment in World War I.

DUFFY, HUGH (*b. River Point, R.I., 1866; d. Allston, Mass., 1954*), baseball player. One of baseball's greatest hitters, Duffy played for several minor league teams before being purchased by the Chicago Blackstockings in 1888. In 1892, he was playing for the Boston franchise of the National League. In 1894, his .440 batting average became the highest one-season average in baseball history. Duffy managed and played for many teams across the country before joining the Boston Red Sox as a scout, coach, and director of the club's rookie instructional school (1924–54). He was elected to the Baseball Hall of Fame in 1945.

DUFOUR, JOHN JAMES (*b. Chatelard, Switzerland, ca. 1763; d. Vevay, Ind., 1827*), pioneer viticulturist. Came to America, 1796, and in Kentucky set up vineyards which failed; later his vineyard colony merged with another at Vevay, Ind. He wrote *The American Vine Dresser's Guide* (1826).

DUGANNE, AUGUSTINE JOSEPH HICKEY (*b. Boston, Mass., 1823; d. New York, N.Y., 1884*), journalist. Author of adventure stories, popular manuals, plays, dime novels, and other writings, of which *Parnassus in Pillory* (1851) and *Camp and Prisons* (1865) have some value.

DUGDALE, RICHARD LOUIS (*b. Paris, France, 1841; d. 1883*), social economist. Come to America, 1851. Attended night classes at Cooper Union, and, interested in sociological subjects, worked for the Prison Association of New York, *post* 1868. Struck with the consanguinity of many criminals, he used private funds to study one large family connection and published "The Jukes: A Study in Crime, Pauperism, Disease and Heredity" (1875) in a Prison Association report. Dugdale believed inheritance was more important than environment in determining character.

DUGGAR, BENJAMIN MINGE (*b. Gallion, Ala., 1872; d. New Haven, Conn., 1956*), botanist and plant pathologist. Studied at Mississippi Agricultural and Mechanical College, Alabama Polytechnical Institute, Harvard, and Cornell (Ph.D., 1908). Taught at Cornell, the University of Missouri, and at the University of Wisconsin. Wrote the first American textbook on plant pathology, *Fungous Diseases of Plants* (1909) and *Plant Physiology* (1911). An expert on the effects of radiation on plant viruses and bacteria. From 1944 to 1948, his search for antibiotic-producing fungi resulted in the isolation and commercial production of the antibiotic Aureomycin.

DUGUÉ, CHARLES OSCAR (*b. New Orleans, La., 1821; d. Paris, France, 1872*), Creole poet and dramatist, educator.

DUHRING, LOUIS ADOLPHUS (*b. Philadelphia, Pa., 1845; d. Philadelphia, 1913*), dermatologist. Published several pioneer works in dermatology, among them a *Practical Treatise on Diseases of the Skin* (1877), the first American textbook in the field.

DUKE, BASIL WILSON (*b. Scott Co., Ky., 1838; d. 1916*), lawyer, Confederate soldier. Served with John Hunt Morgan's Lexington Rifles; published *History of Morgan's Cavalry* (1867).

DUKE, BENJAMIN NEWTON (*b. near Durham, N.C., 1855; d. New York, N.Y., 1929*), industrialist. Brother of James B. Duke, with whom he was associated in business; active *post* 1906 in southern railroad, power, and manufacturing enterprises. Benefactor of Duke University.

DUKE, JAMES BUCHANAN (*b. near Durham, N.C., 1856; d. 1925*), industrialist. Just after the Civil War, Washington Duke and his sons, Benjamin and James, began to retail tobacco off their own farm; by 1889 the firm was producing more than half the cigarettes sold in the United States. Backed by eastern financiers, James B. Duke monopolized the American retail tobacco trade, merging competitors into a series of combines which bore at last the title of the American Tobacco Co. In 1911, the Supreme Court ordered Duke's company dissolved as in restraint of trade; its constituents then continued business as normal competitors. Duke created the Southern Power Co. to develop the waterpower of the southern Piedmont; in 1924 he assigned these holdings in trust for Duke University and for other charitable purposes.

DUKE, VERNON (*b. Parfianovka, near Pskov, Russia, 1903; d. Santa Monica, Calif., 1969*), composer. Immigrated to New York City in 1921, where he played the piano in restaurants and conducted and composed for vaudeville and burlesque. Encouraged by Artur Rubenstein, he moved to Paris in 1924. He composed a ballet for Serge Diaghilev, was one of four pianists at the London premiere of Stravinsky's *Les noces*, composed symphonies, and wrote songs for the London popular stage. He used his Russian name, Vladimir Alexandrovich Dukelsky, on his serious works. He returned to New York in 1929 and wrote film music and songs for the musical theater. His first complete score was for *Walk a Little Faster* (1932). He wrote music for the *Ziegfeld Follies*. His most important musical was *Cabin in the Sky* (1940). His most successful ballet was *Le bal des blanchisseuses* (1946). His autobiography is *Passport to Paris* (1955).

DULANY, DANIEL (*b. Queen's Co., Ireland, 1685; d. Annapolis, Md., 1753*), lawyer. Immigrated to Maryland, 1703. As attorney general and a member of the Maryland Legislative

Assembly, he led the fight against the proprietary government for introduction of English statutes into colony law, *ca. 1722–32.* Thereafter, he held a number of high provincial offices.

DULANY, DANIEL (*b. Annapolis, Md., 1722; d. Baltimore, Md., 1797*), lawyer. Son of Daniel Dulany (1685–1753). Educated at Eton, Cambridge, and the Middle Temple. Opposed popular measures as a member of Maryland Assembly. In Stamp Act crisis, issued *Considerations on the Propriety of Imposing Taxes in the British Colonies* (1765) in support of colonial representation, yet later opposed American revolutionary action and was deprived of his property as a Loyalist.

DULLES, ALLEN WELSH (*b. Watertown, N.Y., 1893; d. Washington, D.C., 1969*), lawyer, foreign-service officer, and intelligence official. A graduate of Princeton (1914), he worked in the foreign service (1916–26). After studying law at George Washington University, he joined his brother, John Foster Dulles, in the Wall Street law firm of Sullivan and Cromwell, becoming a partner in 1930. He served with the Office of Strategic Services in Bern during World War II. In 1947 he helped draft the National Security Act, which created the Central Intelligence Agency, of which he became deputy director for plans in 1951. In 1953 Dulles was appointed the first civilian director of the CIA, masterminding covert actions that overthrew the governments of Iran (1953) and Guatemala (1954), and the U-2 overflights of the Soviet Union beginning in 1956. The Bay of Pigs fiasco in 1961 ended his active career.

DULLES, JOHN FOSTER (*b. Washington, D.C., 1888; d. Washington, D.C., 1959*), lawyer, U.S. senator, secretary of state. Studied at Princeton, the Sorbonne, and George Washington University; specialized in international law with the New York firm of Sullivan and Cromwell, from 1911. Assigned by President Wilson, 1917, to assure the alignment of Central America against any German threat to Panama Canal. Served in World War I as major in the army and on the War Trade Board. Was counsel to the reparations section of the American Commission to Versailles and counsel to the financiers of the Dawes Plan of 1924.

Embraced isolationist policies until Pearl Harbor but subsequently became an active proponent of postwar planning, serving as chairman of the Commission for a Just and Durable Peace established by the Federal Council of Churches. Appointed by New York governor Thomas E. Dewey to serve as U.S. senator, 1949. Drafted and negotiated the peace treaty with Japan for President Harry S. Truman, 1950. Appointed secretary of state by President Eisenhower, 1953, he carried his fervent anticommunism into the international field.

Dulles was convinced of the importance of a strong moral and ideological center to American foreign policy to combat the spread of communism; he believed that military intervention in such crises as the Hungarian Revolt, the East German bread riots, and Suez would lead to war. He preferred a policy of unbending refusal to recognize a permanent communist sphere of influence in Eastern Europe and Southeast Asia. Differing sharply with the policies and economic appeasement of the Soviet Union and China, he hoped to ally American interests with emerging anticolonial forces and to present a united front to communism, a hope largely destroyed by the invasion of Egypt by England, France, and Israel in 1956, and the subsequent identification, by the Third World, of America with the old colonial powers. Responsible for the Southeast Asia Treaty Organization, he died believing he had successfully confronted the spread of communism in that area.

Dulles wrote *War, Peace and Change* (1939) and *War or Peace* (1950).

DULUTH, DANIEL GREYSOLON, SIEUR (*b. St. Germain-en-Laye, France, 1636; d. Montreal, Canada, 1710*), explorer. Cousin of Henry de Tonty. Visited Montreal about 1674 and returned to France. He soon came back to Montreal and in 1678 set out to explore Lake Superior and routes westward. He succeeded in reconciling the Chippewa and Sioux who barred the way, meeting their chiefs near the site of present Duluth, Minn., 1679; he also made alliance with the Sioux and took possession of their territory for Louis XIV. From 1680 to 1690 Duluth made several futile efforts to explore westward from Lake Superior; however, no one did more to establish French control over the region. He retired about 1695 and spent his last years in Montreal. One of the great French explorers, Duluth sought not gain but knowledge in his travels.

DUMAINE, FREDERIC CHRISTOPHER (*b. Hadley, Mass., 1866; d. 1951*), industrialist. Dumaine rose from office boy to chief executive in the Amoskeag Manufacturing Co., Manchester, N.H. The company, one of the world's leading producers of cotton textiles, flourished until Dumaine began to drain off the profits into an investment and trust, ignoring modernization. The company almost went bankrupt. As president of Waltham Watch Company, a New England concern, Dumaine repeated his actions of cutting costs and insuring short-terms profits. Ignoring modernization, he sold his stock at great profit to himself and destruction to his company. In 1948 Dumaine gained control of the New Haven Railroad, but died before he could realize his plans for the line.

DUMMER, JEREMIAH (*b. Newbury, Mass., 1645; d. 1718*), silversmith, engraver, portrait painter, magistrate. A leading citizen of Boston, he produced some of the finest ecclesiastical and convivial silver pieces of his period.

DUMMER, JEREMIAH (*b. Boston, Mass., ca. 1679; d. Plaistow, England, 1739*), colonial agent, author. Son of Jeremiah Dummer (1645–1718). Graduated Harvard, 1699; studied in Utrecht until 1703. Returning to Massachusetts, he found no occupation there and went to England, where he remained and prospered at the law. Became the Massachusetts colonial agent, 1710; also agent for Connecticut, 1712. He persuaded Elihu Yale to bestow money on the college which bears his name. In 1715, when Parliament attacked colonial charters, Drummer wrote his *Defence of the New England Charters* (printed in 1721). His refusal to endorse complaints made by the colony against Governor Shute led to dismissal as Massachusetts agent, 1721. He remained agent for Connecticut until 1730.

DUMONT, ALLEN BALCOM (*b. Brooklyn, N.Y., 1901; d. New York, N.Y., 1965*), electrical engineer and manufacturer. He was an engineer with the Westinghouse Lamp Company (1924–28) and chief engineer with the De Forest Radio Company (1928–31). Working out of a small laboratory in his home, he developed a cathode-ray tube that could be used as a visual tuning aid in radio receivers. The Allen B. Dumont Laboratories, incorporated in 1934, then began manufacturing cathode-ray oscilloscopes, which became widely used in engineering schools. He was instrumental in formulating television standards, and he initiated experimental telecasts in New York City in 1941. He was the first president of the Television Broadcasters Association (1943). Following World War II the Dumont television network was established, which was incorporated as Metropolitan Broadcasting Company in 1955 (later Metromedia). Dumont established assembly plants for television receivers (1947, 1949), which were sold to the Emerson Radio and Phonograph Company in 1958.

DUMONT, MARGARET (*b. Brooklyn, N.Y., 1889; d. Los Angeles, Calif., 1965*), actress. Appeared on Broadway in *The Girl Behind the Counter* (1907), *The Summer Widowers* (1910), *Mary* (1920), *Rise of Rosie O'Reilly* (1923), and *The Four-Flusher* (1925). She then appeared with the Marx Brothers on Broadway in *The Cocoanuts* (1925) and *Animal Crackers* (1928). She played the same roles in the filmed versions of these plays (1929, 1930) and went on to play the stuffy, dignified, society woman in five other Marx Brothers films: *Duck Soup* (1933), *A Night at the Opera* (1935), *A Day at the Races* (1937), *At the Circus* (1939), and *The Big Store* (1941). She also appeared in *Never Give a Sucker an Even Break* (1941), *The Dancing Masters* (1943), and *The Horn Blows at Midnight* (1945).

DUN, ROBERT GRAHAM (*b. Chillicothe, Ohio, 1826; d. 1900*). Began as employee of Tappan's Mercantile Agency, New York, 1850; became sole owner of the credit rating agency, 1859, which he conducted as R. G. Dun and Co.

DUNBAR, CHARLES FRANKLIN (*b. Abington, Mass., 1830; d. 1900*), editor, economist. First professor of political economy at Harvard, *ca.* 1869–1900, he edited the *Quarterly Journal of Economics*, the first American periodical exclusively devoted to economic science. He was active also in the general administration of the university.

DUNBAR, (HELEN) FLANDERS (*b. Chicago. Ill., 1902; d. South Kent, Conn., 1959*), psychoanalyst, Dantean Scholar, and religious educator. Studied at Bryn Mawr, Columbia (Ph.D., 1936), Union Theological Seminary, and at Yale University School of Medicine. She received her M.D. in 1930. Involved in the study of psychosomatics, Dunbar worked with the Council for the Clinical Training of Theological Students. Published *Emotions and Bodily Changes: A Survey of Literature on Psychosomatic Interrelationships: 1910–1933* (1935), *Psychosomatic Diagnosis* (1943), *Symbolism in Medieval Thought and Its Consummation in the Divine Comedy* (1929), and *Psychiatry in the Medical Specialities* (1959).

DUNBAR, MOSES (*b. Wallingford, Conn., 1746; d. near Hartford, Conn., 1777*), only person ever executed in Connecticut for treason. A Loyalist, he was convicted of recruiting for the British service.

DUNBAR, PAUL LAURENCE (*b. Dayton, Ohio, 1872; d. Dayton, 1906*), poet. Both his parents had been slaves in Kentucky. Printed at his own expense his first book of poems, *Oak and Ivy* (1893). His second book, *Majors and Minors* (1895), was reviewed enthusiastically by W. D. Howells. *Lyrics of Lowly Life* (1896) was introduced by Howells, who described Dunbar as the first man of African descent and American training to feel negro life aesthetically and express it lyrically.

DUNBAR, ROBERT (*b. Carnbee, Scotland, 1812; d. Buffalo, N.Y., 1890*), engineer, inventor. Raised in Canada. Expert in the design and construction of grain elevators, he contributed to Buffalo's development as a major grain market after moving to that city in 1834.

DUNBAR, WILLIAM (*b. near Elgin, Scotland, 1749; d. near Natchez, Miss., 1810*), planter, scientist. Immigrating to America in 1771, Dunbar established a plantation in the then British province of West Florida, 1773; after the destruction of this plantation by a series of raids and other misfortunes, he built another near Natchez in 1792. Prospering through scientific improvements in farming methods, he was soon able to devote much time to scientific investigation. First surveyor general of his area and its first meteorological observer, he was a friend and correspondent of Jefferson and a member of the American Philo-

sophical Society. At Jefferson's request, Dunbar, with George Hunter, explored the Oachita River country (1804) and was the first to give a scientific account of the hot springs; in 1805, he was appointed to explore the region bordering on the Red River.

DUNCAN, ISADORA (*b. San Francisco, Calif., 1878; d. Nice, France, 1927*), pioneer of modern dance. At 17 she and her mother journeyed to New York City, where Isadora obtained an engagement in Augustin Daly's company. Two years later she resigned and traveled to London, where applauded private performances were succeeded by similar performances in Paris. Isadora then joined the company of Loie Fuller for a trip through Germany. In 1904 she opened a school of dance for children at Grünewald, Germany. After her two illegitimate children were killed in an accident in Paris, she resolved at last to forget herself in her work, but her plans were interrupted by the outbreak of World War I. In 1922 she married the half-mad Sergei Esenin, who three years later took his own life. Isadora was the author of the autobiography *My Life* (1927) and *The Art of the Dance* (1928). She was killed when her scarf was caught in the wheel of the auto in which she was riding.

DUNCAN, JAMES (*b. Kincardine Co., Scotland, 1857; d. 1928*), labor leader. Immigrated to America, *ca.* 1880. A longtime associate of Samuel Gompers, Duncan played a prominent part in the American Federation of Labor during its formative period and was its first vice president, 1900–28.

DUNCAN, JOSEPH (*b. Paris, Ky., 1794; d. Jacksonville, Ill., 1844*), farmer, politician. Removed to Illinois, 1818. Congressman, Democrat, 1827–34; governor, 1834–38. Subsequently an unsuccessful Whig candidate for the governorship, he was a consistent advocate of public education.

DUNCAN, ROBERT KENNEDY (*b. Brantford, Canada, 1868; d. 1914*), chemist. A well-known popular interpreter of science, he advocated a system of industrial fellowships and inspired the foundation of the Mellon Institute of Industrial Research at University of Pittsburgh.

DUNDEE, JOHNNY (*b. Sciacca, Sicily, 1893; d. East Orange, N.J., 1965*), boxer. Born Giuseppe Carrora, he became a professional boxer in New York City at seventeen. He was the junior lightweight champion (1921–24) and featherweight champion (1923–25). His last fight was in 1932. Of his 321 matches, he won 113, drew 18, lost 31, and had 159 no-decision fights.

DUNGLISON, ROBLEY (*b. Keswick, England, 1798; d. Philadelphia, Pa., 1869*), medical writer, teacher. Made studies in Edinburgh, Paris, London, and Erlangen. Came to America, 1825. Taught at universities of Virginia and Maryland, and was professor of Jefferson Medical College, 1836–68. A voluminous writer and attractive lecturer, he was a pioneer in systematic teaching of physiology.

DUNHAM, HENRY MORTON (*b. North Bridgewater, Mass., 1853; d. 1929*), composer, organist, educator. Teacher at New England Conservatory of Music, 1875–1929. Published two books on organ technique. His organ sonatas are widely known.

DUNIWAY, ABIGAIL JANE SCOTT (*b. near Groveland, Ill., 1834; d. 1915*), leader of the woman suffrage movement in the Pacific Northwest. Removed to Oregon, 1852. Engaged in business in Portland, she edited a newspaper, *The New Northwest*, 1871–87, in support of equal rights for women, thereafter continuing her efforts through political action.

DUNLAP, JOHN (*b. Strabane, Ireland, 1747; d. Philadelphia, Pa., 1812*), printer. Came to America *ca.* 1757. From 1771, publisher of *The Pennsylvania Packet*, which became the first daily newspaper in the United States, 1784. Also printed broadside Declaration of Independence and the Constitution of the United States.

DUNLAP, ROBERT PINCKNEY (*b. Brunswick, Maine, 1794; d. Brunswick, 1859*), lawyer. Democratic governor of Maine, 1834–38; instrumental in obtaining prison reforms, an insane asylum, and the first geological survey of Maine.

DUNLAP, WILLIAM (*b. Perth Amboy, N.J., 1766; d. New York, N.Y., 1839*), playwright, theatrical manager, painter, historian. Showing early artistic promise, Dunlap studied briefly under Benjamin West in London, returning to America *ca.* 1787 fired with a new interest, the stage. For numerous plays written and adapted between then and about 1805, he has an important place in the history of American drama. Between 1796 and 1805, he was proprietor and manager of New York's John Street and Park theaters but met with indifferent financial reward and eventual bankruptcy. Turning again to painting, he served also as assistant to the new manager of the Park Theatre, 1806–11, was employed by the government and had some success as a portrait painter. After 1821, he exhibited a series of subject paintings, and in 1826 helped found the National Academy of Design. He was also author of various valuable biographies and histories. These include *Memoirs of George Fred. Cooke* (1813); *Life of Charles Brockden Brown* (1915); *History of the American Theatre* (1832); and *History of the Rise and Progress of the Arts of Design in the United States* (1834).

DUNLOP, JAMES (*b. Chambersburg, Pa., 1795; d. Baltimore, Md., 1856*), lawyer. Author of *The General Laws of Pennsylvania, 1700–1846* (1847).

DUNMORE, JOHN MURRAY, EARL OF (*b. Scotland, 1732; d. Ramsgate, England, 1809*), colonial administrator. Appointed governor of New York, 1770; next year was appointed governor of Virginia. At first popular, Dunmore offended patriots, 1773, by dissolving House of Burgesses for proposing a committee of correspondence on colonial grievances; in 1774, he again dissolved the House after a dispute over Boston Port Act. Despite these local difficulties, he called out militia to engage hostile Shawnee on frontier of the province and led with Andrew Lewis a successful campaign (1774) against Cornstalk known as Lord Dunmore's War. As revolutionary activity increased in Virginia, he opposed it by force rather than finesse, undertaking several abortive raids against patriot forces in the fall and winter of 1775. In July 1776 he returned to England.

DUNN, CHARLES (*b. Bullitt's Old Lick, Ky., 1799; d. Mineral Point, Wis., 1872*), lawyer, jurist. Removed to Illinois, 1819. Chief justice of territory of Wisconsin, 1836–48; a Democrat, he also served in the Wisconsin legislature, 1853–56.

DUNN, WILLIAM McKEE (*b. Hanover, Ind., 1814; d. Fairfax Co., Va., 1887*), lawyer, Union soldier. Judge advocate general, U.S. Army, 1875–81.

DUNN, WILLIAMSON (*b. near Crow's Station, Ky., 1781; d. 1854*), Indiana pioneer, soldier. Removed to present Hanover, Ind., 1809. Served in important public offices and the state legislature; gave land to establish Hanover College and Wabash College.

DUNNE, FINLEY PETER (*b. Chicago, Ill., 1867; d. New York, N.Y., 1936*), author, humorist. While working on the Chicago *Post* in 1892, he wrote some Irish dialect pieces, his protagonist being "Colonel McNeery," modeled after an actual Chicago saloonkeeper. Increasingly Dunne used the character as a vehicle for his social and political observations; on Oct. 7, 1893, his spokesman became "Mr. Martin Dooley." The genial bartender, with his homely democratic philosophy, his tolerance, his dislike of sham, became increasingly popular. Dooley's first appearance in book form, *Mr. Dooley in Peace and War* (1898), was an instant success at home and abroad. Half a dozen collections of Dooley pieces followed. In 1900 Dunne moved to New York, where he became a contributor to *Collier's*, the *American Magazine*, and other publications.

DUNNING, ALBERT ELIJAH (*b. Brookfield, Conn., 1844; Brookline, Mass., 1923*), Congregational clergyman. Secretary of the Congregational Sunday School and Publishing Society, 1881–89; editor, *The Congregationalist*, 1889–1911.

DUNNING, WILLIAM ARCHIBALD (*b. Plainfield, N.J., 1857, d. 1922*), historian. Graduated Columbia, 1881; Ph.D., 1885. Taught history at Columbia. A founder of the American Historical Association, Dunning was among the first to make a scholarly investigation of the Civil War and Reconstruction.

DUNSTER, HENRY (*b. Bury, England, 1609; d. Scituate, Mass., 1658/9[?]*), first president of Harvard College, 1640–54. Established rules of admission and of granting degrees; shaped college according to form of English universities. Forced to resign because of his adoption of some Baptist principles, he served as minister in Scituate.

DUNWOODY, WILLIAM HOOD (*b. Westtown, Pa., 1841; d. Minneapolis, Minn., 1914*), merchant, miller, financier. During 1877, established permanent trade in flour and wheat between Europe and America; present U.S. export flour business is result of his work. Endowed the Dunwoody Industrial Institute, Minneapolis.

DU PONCEAU, PIERRE ÉTIENNE (*b. St.-Martin, France, 1760; d. Philadelphia, Pa., 1844*), lawyer, author. Came to America, 1777, as secretary to Baron von Steuben; served in Revolution as aide to von Steuben and Greene. Admitted to the bar, 1785, became America's leading expert on international law and practice. Author of various legal treatises and valuable early works on history and philology, particularly of the Indians.

DU PONT, ALFRED IRÉNÉE (*b. near Wilmington, Del., 1864; d. Jacksonville, Fla., 1935*), manufacturer. Grandson of Eleuthère I. du Pont. With cousins Thomas C. and Pierre S. du Pont, incorporated the family gunpowder company in 1902.

DU PONT, ELEUTHÈRE IRÉNÉE (*b. Paris, France, 1771; d. Philadelphia, Pa., 1834*), manufacturer. Worked under Lavoisier at French royal gunpowder works. Came to America, 1799, with father, Pierre Samuel du Pont de Nemours, a publisher and a member of the physiocratic school of economists. After making a study of American gunpowder manufacture and noting the poor quality of the powder produced, Irénée decided that a small efficient plant would yield substantial profit. Securing machinery from France, he established a powder works near Wilmington, Del., 1802. The War of 1812 assured success of the enterprise.

DU PONT, FRANCIS IRÉNÉE (*b. Hagley House, near Wilmington, Del., 1873; d. New York, N.Y., 1942*), chemist, inventor, stockbroker. Great-grandson of E. I. du Pont. Graduated Sheffield Scientific School, Yale, 1895; entered family gunpowder business. As director of Du Pont Co. Experimental Station, 1903–16, he emphasized research and development; he moved the firm to diversify its product and make dyes, paints, plastics, and synthetics. Between 1895 and 1915, he took out almost 50 patents, principally in explosives chemistry and engineering. His invention of a fixation process for conversion of inert nitrogen into chemically active oxides was a major advance in industrial chemistry. Withdrawing from the family firm, 1916, he engaged in explosives manufacture for a time, and then in his Delaware Chemical Engineering Co., a wide-ranging research and development organization which made a number of improvements and inventions in petrochemicals and synthetic rubber. In 1931, he bought a seat on the New York Stock Exchange and did business as Francis I. du Pont and Co., meanwhile continuing his other activities. He advocated political reform and the single tax.

Du Pont, Henry (*b. Wilmington, Del., 1812; d. 1889*), manufacturer. Son of Eleuthère Irénée du Pont. Graduated West Point, 1833. Presided over the family firm, 1850–89, expanding its activities through the Civil War and after.

Du Pont, Henry Algernon (*b. near Wilmington, Del., 1838; d. 1926*), Union soldier, industrialist. Son of Henry du Pont. Graduated West Point, 1861. Congressional Medal winner in Civil War. Entered family business, 1878, and in 1899 brought to fruition his plan to incorporate it so as to retain family control. U.S. senator from Delaware, 1906–17.

Du Pont, Irénée (*b. Nemours, near Wilmington, Del., 1876; d. Granouge, Del., 1963*), industrialist. Studied at Massachusetts Institute of Technology (B.S., 1897; M.A., 1898). Joining the new E. I. du Pont de Nemours Powder Company in 1903, he served as chairman of the new operative committee, head of the development department, and assistant general manager. When his brother Pierre took command of the company in 1914, Irénée became chairman of the executive committee. He was president of the company (1919–26) and vice-chairman, then honorary chairman, of the board of directors. He served on the Du Pont Finance Committee and the Finance Committee of General Motors.

Du Pont, Lammot (*b. Nemours, Del., 1880; d. Fishers Island, N.Y., 1954*), industrialist. Studied at M.I.T. Vice president of the du Pont Company during World War I, a period during which the company became the world's leading producer of explosives. Lammot du Pont successfully invested the company's enormous war earnings in programs of research, diversification, and expansion. He was president of the company in 1926, succeeding his brother; chairman of the board from 1940 to 1948. During his tenure, the company's research laboratories invented nylon, Orlon, and Dacron, revolutionizing the world's textile industry, and developed the first general-purpose synthetic rubber. During World War II, du Pont engineers played a major part in atomic research by constructing the Hanover atomic works in Washington State. Du Pont also served as chairman of the board of General Motors from 1931 to 1937.

Du Pont, Pierre Samuel (*b. Nemours, Del., 1870; d. Wilmington, Del., 1954*), industrialist. Studied at M.I.T. By introducing modern management and financial brilliance to the ailing du Pont family company, Pierre du Pont was successful in making E. I. du Pont de Nemours Powder Co., the nation's largest producer of explosives by the end of World War I. Pierre served as acting president (1909); president (1915–19). From 1920 to 1929, he was president of General Motors, where he used the same techniques of industrial reorganization that had been so successful at du Pont in Delaware: modern management, statistical controls, and a technique in marketing called bracketing, whereby each major division of the company would sell cars in each major price class. In 1923, he became chairman of the board, turning the presidency over to Alfred P. Sloan. The company was soon selling more cars than Ford and had the best profit record in the industry.

In 1933 du Pont served on the Advisory Board of the National Recovery Administration and on the NRA National Labor Board.

Du Pont, Samuel Francis (*b. Bergen Point, N.J., 1803; d. Philadelphia, Pa., 1865*), naval officer. Son of Victor du Pont. Appointed midshipman, 1815. During the Mexican War, commanded Commodore Stockton's flagship and later sloop *Cyane* in California operations. For two decades thereafter he was concerned with improvements in naval education, national defense, lighthouse maintenance, and service personnel efficiency. He was promoted captain, 1855. Assigned to command South Atlantic blockading squadron, 1861, he occupied Port Royal, South Carolina, November 1861, in a notable fleet action against shore defenses; also occupied Beaufort and Tybee Island. Promoted rear admiral, July 1862. After failure to take Charleston, 1863, he was relieved by Adm. John A. Dahlgren and began a long controversy with Secretary of the Navy Welles over responsibility for the failure.

Du Pont, Thomas Coleman (*b. Louisville, Ky., 1863; d. 1930*), capitalist. Merged all military powder plants in superholding company, E. I. du Pont de Nemours Co.; interested financially in many industries. Cousin of Alfred I. du Pont.

Du Pont, Victor Marie (*b. Paris, France, 1767; d. Philadelphia, Pa., 1827*), diplomat, manufacturer. Brother of Eleuthère I. du Pont. Attaché to the first French legation in the United States, 1787; second secretary of the legation, 1791. French consul general in the United States, 1798. Settled in America, 1800; for a time, tried to establish a commission business. After a land development project in New York failed, he became the active director of woolen mills erected by his brother.

Dupratz, Antoine Simon le Page (*fl. 1718–58*), pioneer, historian. Author of *Histoire de la Louisiane* (1758).

Dupuy, Eliza Ann (*b. Petersburg, Va., 1814; d. New Orleans, La., 1881*), novelist.

Durand, Asher Brown (*b. Jefferson Village, N.J., 1796; d. Jefferson Village, 1886*), engraver, painter. Apprenticed to Peter Maverick, 1812; met Samuel Waldo, who instructed him in portrait work. In partnership with Maverick, engraved Trumbull's *Signing of the Declaration of Independence* (1820–23), which established his reputation. His engraving of Vanderlyn's *Ariadne* created a stir in American artistic circles. Durand also produced many superior engraved portraits of eminent men and also banknote designs which established a tradition still apparent in U.S. currency. *Post* 1836, he became a professional painter, producing illustrations for books and landscapes greatly esteemed in their time. Durand was identified with every contemporary movement to foster American arts.

Durand, Cyrus (*b. Jefferson Village, N.J., 1787; d. Irvington, N.J., 1868*), engraver, inventor. To execute his brother Asher B. Durand's designs for banknotes, he invented several machines for ruling geometrical patterns.

Durand, Élie Magloire (*b. Mayenne, France, 1794; d. 1873*), pharmacist, botanist. Came to America, 1816. Conducted a celebrated drugstore in Philadelphia, 1825–52. Made extensive botanical collections which he presented to the Paris Jardin des Plantes, the Philadelphia Academy of Natural Sciences, and other public institutions.

Durand, William Frederick (*b. Bethany, Conn., 1859; d. New York, N.Y., 1958*), mechanical and aeronautical engineer. Studied at the U.S. Naval Academy (1880) and at Lafayette College. Taught mechanical engineering at Michigan State College (1887–91); naval architecture at Cornell (1891–1904), and engineering at Stanford (1904–24). Contributed significant advances to the design of ship propellers, to hydraulic machinery, and to the development of airplane propellers and design. Member of the National Advisory Committee for

Aeronautics from 1915 to 1933 and 1941 to 1945; chairman from 1916 through World War I. Trustee of the Daniel Guggenheim Fund for the Promotion of Aeronautics. Durand was instrumental in advancing the design and public acceptance of aeronautics in the nation, figuring in the resolution of the Billy Mitchell case, which introduced aviation into American defenses. He was a consultant on the construction of Hoover, Grand Coulee, Shasta, and Friant dams. Organized and edited the six-volume *Aerodynamic Theory* (1929–36). Elected to the National Academy of Sciences and the American Philosophical Society in 1917.

Durant, Charles Ferson (b. New York, N.Y., 1805; d. 1873), aeronaut, scientist. The first professional American aeronaut; made balloon flights in New York, 1830–33; also at Albany, Baltimore, and Boston.

Durant, Henry (b. Acton, Mass., 1802; d. Oakland, Calif., 1875), Congregational clergyman. Graduated Yale, 1827. Held pastorate in Byfield, Mass., and was principal of Dummer Academy until 1853 when he removed to California to conduct a school in Oakland. First president, 1870–72, University of California, which he helped to found. Twice mayor of Oakland.

Durant, Henry Fowle (b. Hanover, N.H., 1822; d. 1881), lawyer, evangelist. Successful at the Boston bar, he became a revivalist preacher *ca.* 1864 and gave his fortune to found Wellesley College, whose early development he guided.

Durant, Thomas Clark (b. Lee, Mass., 1820; d. North Creek, N.Y., 1885), a financier and builder of the Union Pacific Railroad. With Henry Farnam, built several midwestern railroads; alone sponsored 1863 surveys of routes for the railroad to the Pacific. Became vice president of the Union Pacific, 1863, and was chief manager of the railroad until 1869. When New York capitalists failed to subscribe funds for the road, Durant organized and was president of the Crédit Mobilier, a funding organization, 1864. A struggle between Boston and New York capitalists for control of the Crédit Mobilier and the road now ensued. Durant, although ousted from the Crédit Mobilier, continued to supervise construction. Two weeks after he joined Leland Stanford in driving the "last spike," May 10, 1869, he was dropped from the directorate of the road.

Durant, Thomas Jefferson (b. Philadelphia, Pa., 1817; d. Washington, D.C., 1882), lawyer, politician. Practiced in New Orleans. A Unionist throughout the Civil War, he was distinguished for his successful argument in the Slaughterhouse Cases, 1873.

Durant, William Crapo (b. Boston, Mass., 1861; d. New York, N.Y., 1947), automobile manufacturer, financier. Raised in Flint, Mich. After success in carriage and wagon manufacturing, he entered the automobile business in 1904 by buying out the manufacturer of the Buick car. His skills in production administration and sales promotion made the Buick Motor Car Co. the largest in the United States. Convinced that the formula for success in the new industry was a large organization making a variety of models and controlling its own sources of parts, he chartered the General Motors Co. in New Jersey in September 1908, merging into it a number of firms: Buick, Cadillac, Oakland, and Oldsmobile, as well as makers of axles, spark plugs, and other parts. Financially overextended because of his attempt to cover all the possible elements, he was forced out of active management by the bankers in 1910. He organized the Chevrolet Motor Car Co. in 1911 and was so successful that he was able to recover control of General Motors and resume its presidency in 1916. A new expansion program included the manufacture of refrigerators and farm machinery. He dispersed his energies and neglected the main business of the firm. He was caught by the depression of 1920, both with respect to the decline of sales and a financial crisis brought about by his efforts to support the price of General Motors stock by huge purchases on margin. In December 1920, he resigned under pressure of his principal stockholders. In 1921 he formed Durant Motors, which was never successful and was liquidated in 1933. He himself filed a bankruptcy petition in 1935.

Duranty, Walter (b. Liverpool, England, 1884; d. Orlando, Fla., 1957), journalist. Studied at Harrow and Cambridge University. Joined the Paris bureau of the *New York Times* in 1913; after covering the French army during World War I, Duranty became interested in the Soviet Union. He was Moscow correspondent for the *Times* in 1922 and remained until 1941. An apologist for Stalinism, Duranty's coverage became increasingly pro-Stalin; though not a leftist, he accepted Stalin's tactics and influenced U.S. governmental opinion. He won the Pulitzer Prize in 1932 for articles on the Soviet Five-Year Plan.

Durbin, John Price (b. Bourbon Co., Ky., 1800; d. New York, N.Y., 1876), Methodist clergyman. Secretary of the Missionary Society, 1850–72.

Durell, Edward Henry (b. Portsmouth, N.H., 1810; d. Schoharie, N.Y., 1887), jurist. Removed to New Orleans, La., 1837, where he practiced and held local office. A Unionist and U.S. judge, 1863–74, he issued the famous 1972 "midnight order" declaring the Louisiana Democratic electoral board illegal and so enabling the Republicans to win control of the state government.

Durfee, Job (b. Tiverton, R.I., 1790; d. Tiverton, 1847), jurist, author. Graduated Brown, 1813. Justice, Rhode Island Supreme Court, 1833–35; chief justice, 1835–47.

Durfee, Thomas (b. Tiverton, R.I., 1826; d. Providence, R.I., 1901), jurist. Son of Job Durfee. Graduated Brown, 1846. Justice, Rhode Island Supreme Court, 1865–75; chief justice, 1875–91. His *Treatisè on the Law of Highways* (1857) was a standard work.

Durfee, William Franklin (b. New Bedford, Mass., 1833; d. 1899), engineer, inventor. Supervised at Wyandotte, Mich., 1864, the manufacture of the first Bessemer steel produced in America; expert also in copper refining, wrought-iron casting, and machinery design. Cousin of Zoheth S. Durfee.

Durfee, Zoheth Sherman (b. New Bedford, Mass., 1831; d. Providence, R.I., 1880), inventor, manufacturer. Led to believe that William Kelly was the real inventor of the Bessemer process, Durfee (with Capt. E. B. Ward) gained control of Kelly's patents, 1861. With Ward and a cousin, William F. Durfee, he formed the Kelly Pneumatic Process Co. In 1864 he gained American control of Robert Mushet's invention for using spiegeleisen as a recarburizing agent. In 1865, persons holding license under Bessemer's patents joined with Durfee in the Pneumatic Steel Association; Durfee was its secretary and treasurer until his death. He originated the use of the cupola instead of a reverberatory furnace for melting pig iron for the converter charge. Interested throughout his life in manufacturing steel, Durfee protected Kelly's interests.

Durham, Caleb Wheeler (b. Tunkhannock, Pa., 1848; d. Peekskill, N.Y., 1910), engineer, inventor. Invented, 1880, the Durham system for house drainage, using screw-jointed pipe to provide a tight, rigid installation.

Durivage, Francis Alexander (b. Boston, Mass., 1814; d. 1881), author, journalist, playwright.

DURKEE, JOHN (*b. Windham, Conn., 1728; d. Norwich, Conn., 1782*), Revolutionary soldier. Led Connecticut emigrants to Wyoming Valley, Pa., and settled Wilkes-Barre, 1769.

DURKIN, MARTIN PATRICK (*b. Chicago, Ill., 1894; d. Washington, D.C., 1955*), labor leader. Durkin was a union official in Chicago, rising to vice president of the Chicago Building Trades Council in 1927. In 1933, he became Illinois director of labor, introducing unemployment compensation and minimum wage laws. He was elected president of the International Association of Government Labor Officials and served until 1955. During World War II, he served on the National Labor Board. In 1953, President Eisenhower appointed him Secretary of Labor. A controversial member of an antilabor cabinet, he resigned after eight months and returned to his post of union president.

DURRETT, REUBEN THOMAS (*b. Henry Co., Ky., 1824; d. Louisville, Ky., 1913*), lawyer, historian. Practiced in Louisville, 1850–80; thereafter built up a magnificent library on western history and founded the Filson Club, 1884.

DURRIE, DANIEL STEELE (*b. Albany, N.Y., 1819; d. Madison, Wis., 1892*). Librarian of the State Historical Society of Wisconsin *post* 1856; with Lyman Draper built up an outstanding collection of historical sources there.

DURSTINE, ROY SARLES (*b. Jamestown, N.Dak., 1886; d. New York, N.Y., 1962*), advertising executive. Studied at Princeton (B.A., 1908), worked as a reporter and copywriter, then directed press relations for Theodore Roosevelt's "Bull Moose" presidential campaign in 1912. Turning to an advertising career, he was a founder of Barton, Durstine, and Osborn (1918), which became Batten, Barton, Durstine, and Osborn in 1928. He served as vice president and general manager, then became president of the agency in 1936. Following his resignation in 1939, he established Roy S. Durstine, Inc. Durstine was one of the first to recognize the potential of radio as an advertising medium in the 1920's. He wrote *Making Advertisements and Making Them Pay* (1920), *This Advertising Business* (1928), and *Red Thunder* (1934).

DURYEA, CHARLES EDGAR (*b. near Canton, Ill., 1861; d. Philadelphia, Pa., 1938*), inventor, automobile manufacturer. Began his career in the bicycle trade, inventing several devices, and launching his own business in Peoria, Ill., moving later to Springfield, Mass. By 1891 he had designed a motor-driven carriage and a gas engine, and with his brother J. Frank built the first successful American car; it was demonstrated in Springfield in September 1893. An improved car, largely of Frank's design, won several races at home and abroad, 1895–96. The Duryea Motor Wagon Co. made the first sale of an American-built automobile in 1896. The brothers parted company in 1898. Charles Duryea later organized the Duryea Power Co., manufacturing until 1914 a three-cylinder car. His brother developed the Stevens-Duryea (1903–14).

DURYEA, HERMANES BARKULO (*b. Brooklyn, N.Y., 1863; d. Saranac Lake, N.Y., 1916*), yachtsman, breeder of racehorses.

DURYEA, JAMES FRANK (*b. Washburn, Ill., 1869; d. Madison, Conn., 1967*), automobile inventor. With his brother, Charles, built the first operational American gasoline-powered highway vehicle (1893), which was replaced by a second car in 1895. The Duryea Motor Wagon Company was formed in 1894, but dissolved the next year due to conflict between the brothers. In 1900 Duryea formed his own company, the Hampden Automobile and Launch Company. The next year he began designing and building automobiles for what became, in 1904, the Stevens-Duryea Motor Car Company, which built four- and six-cylinder luxury cars. He sold the company to Westinghouse in 1915.

DURYÉE, ABRAM (*b. New York, N.Y., 1815; d. New York, 1890*), Union soldier. Colonel, Fifth New York Regiment (Duryée Zouaves) in Civil War.

DU SIMITIÈRE, PIERRE EUGÈNE (*b. Geneva, Switzerland, ca. 1736; d. Philadelphia, Pa., 1784*), artist, antiquary.

DUSSER DE BARENNE, JOANNES GREGORIUS (*b. Brielle, Netherlands, 1885; d. Boston, Mass., 1940*), physiologist. M.D., University of Amsterdam, 1909. Immigrated to America, 1930. Professor at Yale, 1930–40. Pioneering investigator of the functional divisions and interrelations of the cerebral cortex.

DUSTIN, HANNAH (*b. Haverhill, Mass., 1657*), pioneer. Survivor of Indian raid on Haverhill, 1697; escaped after she killed and scalped ten Indians. Said to have survived until after 1729.

DUTTON, CLARENCE EDWARD (*b. Wallingford, Conn., 1841; d. Englewood, N.J., 1912*), Union soldier, geologist. On detail to U.S. Geological Survey, 1875–90, Dutton studied plateau region of Utah and Arizona; was leading advocate of doctrine of isostasy.

DUTTON, HENRY (*b. Watertown, Conn., 1796; d. New Haven, Conn., 1869*), jurist. Kent professor of law at Yale, *post* 1847.

DUTTON, SAMUEL TRAIN (*b. Hillsboro, N.H., 1849; d. 1919*), educator. Graduated Yale, 1873. A national figure in education, he was superintendent of schools, New Haven, Conn., and Brookline, Mass.; professor of administration, Teachers College, Columbia, 1900–15.

DUVAL, WILLIAM POPE (*b. near Richmond, Va., 1784; d. Washington, D.C., 1854*), lawyer, politician. First judge, superior court of East Florida, 1821; civil governor, 1822–34. Outstanding achievement was the peaceable removal of Seminole Indians to South Florida.

DUVALL, GABRIEL (*b. Prince George's Co., Md., 1752; d. Prince George's Co., 1844*), Revolutionary soldier, jurist. Admitted to the bar, 1778. Elected to Maryland House of Delegates, 1787; congressman, Democratic-Republican, from Maryland, 1794–96. Became first comptroller of the treasury, 1802. Appointed to the U.S. Supreme Court by President Madison, 1811, he remained in office until 1835. Although supporting Marshall's constitutional views generally, he dissented from the chief justice in *Trustees of Dartmouth College* v. *Woodward*.

DUVENECK, FRANK (*b. Covington, Ky., 1848; d. Cincinnati, Ohio, 1919*), painter, etcher, sculptor, teacher. Trained as ecclesiastical decorator in Cincinnati; studied at Royal Academy, Munich, 1870–72 and 1875–77. Early celebrated for technical skill and emotional quality of his work. As a teacher successively in Munich, Florence, and Venice, his influence on a generation of American painters was great and good. Returning to America, 1888, he continued his fruitful career as teacher in Cincinnati. Several sculptures, among them a monument to his wife, indicate Duveneck's talent in this field. It was said of him that he had the greatest talent of the brush in his generation.

DUYCKINCK, EVERT AUGUSTUS (*b. New York, N.Y., 1816; d. New York, 1878*), editor, critic. Graduated Columbia, 1835. Edited two outstanding literary magazines, *Arcturus*, 1840–42, and the *Literary World*, 1847 and 1848–53. With brother George, edited *Cyclopaedia of American Literature*, 1855.

DUYCKINCK, GEORGE LONG (*b. New York, N.Y., 1823; d. New York, 1863*). Brother and literary associate of Evert A. Duyckinck; active in Episcopal Sunday-school work.

DWENGER, JOSEPH (*b. in/near Stallotown, Ohio, 1837; d. Fort Wayne, Ind., 1893*), Roman Catholic clergyman. Ordained, 1859; member of Congregation of the Most Precious Blood. Bishop of Fort Wayne, 1872–93, he built up a highly efficient parochial school system there.

DWIGGINS, WILLIAM ADDISON (*b. Martinsville, Ohio, 1880; d. Hingham, Mass., 1956*), calligrapher, book and type designer, author. Studied at the Frank Holme School of Illustration in Chicago. A consulting designer for the publisher Alfred A. Knopf from 1926, Dwiggins' designs for wrappings and bindings made Knopf books among the most attractive of the time. From 1929 until 1946, he worked with the Mergenthaler Linotype Co., designing eleven typefaces, five experimental faces, and three Greek fonts. His work was shown at the Houghton Library at Harvard in 1937 and at the Boston Public Library in 1938. His books include *Layout in Advertising* (1928), which remains a classic in the field.

DWIGHT, ARTHUR SMITH (*b. Taunton, Mass., 1864; d. Hobe Sound, Fla., 1946*), mining and metallurgical engineer. Nephew of Rossiter W. Raymond. M.E., School of Mines, Columbia University, 1885. Worked as superintendent of mining and smelting operations in Colorado, Kansas, Texas, and Mexico. Coinventor of the Dwight-Lloyd sintering process for salvage of metal from fine ore or dust. A consulting engineer in New York City *post* 1906, he helped organize a reserve officers corps for the U.S. Army Engineers and served with distinction in France during World War I.

DWIGHT, BENJAMIN WOODBRIDGE (*b. New Haven, Conn., 1816; d. 1889*), educator, Presbyterian clergyman. Brother of Theodore W. Dwight.

DWIGHT, EDMUND (*b. Springfield, Mass., 1780; d. 1849*), merchant, manufacturer, philanthropist. Established three manufacturing centers in the Connecticut Valley at Chicopee Falls, Chicopee, and Holyoke; erected cotton mills. Promoted Western Railroad from Worcester to Albany. Helped devise Massachusetts School Law of 1837; patron of Horace Mann.

DWIGHT, FRANCIS (*b. Springfield, Mass., 1808; d. 1845*), lawyer, educator. Published *District School Journal of the State of New York* from 1840, the organ of the state common-school system.

DWIGHT, HARRISON GRAY OTIS (*b. Conway, Mass., 1803; d. near Bennington, Vt., 1862*). Resided chiefly in Constantinople as "missionary to Armenians," 1834–62; one of the first American students of Armenian.

DWIGHT, HENRY OTIS (*b. Constantinople, Turkey, 1843; d. Roselle, N.J., 1917*), Congregational missionary, editor. Son of Harrison G. Ohio Dwight. Author of books on Turkey; editor, *Turkish and English Lexicon* (1890) of Sir James Redhouse, and of reference works on missions.

DWIGHT, JOHN SULLIVAN (*b. Boston, Mass., 1813; d. Boston, 1893*), music critic, editor. Graduated Harvard, 1832; Harvard Divinity School, 1836; studied and translated German poetry; spent short time in the ministry. Joined Brook Farm, 1841, and while there, contributed musical and other articles to the *Harbinger*. Founded, 1852, *Dwight's Journal of Music*, which for nearly 30 years exerted an unparalleled influence on the formation of musical taste in America. Long associated with Harvard Musical Association, he was instrumental in the establishment of a professorship of music at Harvard.

DWIGHT, NATHANIEL (*b. Northampton, Mass., 1770; d. Oswego, N.Y., 1831*), physician, educator. Brother of Timothy Dwight (1752–1817).

DWIGHT, SERENO EDWARDS (*b. Fairfield, Conn., 1786; d. Philadelphia, Pa., 1850*), educator, Congregational clergyman. Son of Timothy Dwight (1752–1817). Minister at Park Street Church, Boston, 1817–26; edited writings of Jonathan Edwards, his great-grandfather (1830).

DWIGHT, THEODORE (*b. Northampton, Mass., 1764; d. New York, N.Y., 1846*), lawyer, author, editor. Brother of Timothy Dwight (1752–1817). Practiced law principally in Hartford, Conn.; was one of "Connecticut Wits." Served as secretary to the Hartford Convention, 1814, and in 1833 published its journal.

DWIGHT, THEODORE (*b. Hartford, Conn., 1796; d. 1866*), author, educator. Son of Theodore Dwight (1764–1846). Graduated Yale, 1814. A prolific writer and espouser of numerous causes.

DWIGHT, THEODORE WILLIAM (*b. Catskill, N.Y., 1822; d. Clinton, N.Y., 1892*), lawyer, educator. Grandson of Timothy Dwight (1752–1817). Professor of law, Hamilton College, 1846–58; first professor at Columbia Law School, 1858, and its warden, 1878–91. Emphasized fundamental principles in teaching of law.

DWIGHT, THOMAS (*b. Boston, Mass., 1843; d. 1911*), anatomist. M.D., Harvard, 1867. Taught at Harvard and Bowdoin; succeeded Ohio W. Holmes as Parkman professor of anatomy, Harvard; served 1883–1911. Dwight's chief contributions related to meticulous studies of anatomical variations of the skeleton and joints.

DWIGHT, TIMOTHY (*b. Northampton, Mass., 1752; d. New Haven, Conn., 1817*), Congregational clergyman, author, president of Yale College, 1795–1817. His mother, Mary Edwards Dwight, daughter of Jonathan Edwards, was a woman of remarkable character and mental ability, to whom Dwight said he owed all that he was. Prepared by her for college, he entered Yale at 13 and graduated, 1769. He returned to Yale, 1771, to remain six years as an able and popular tutor.

Dwight's *Dissertation on the History, Eloquence, and Poetry of the Bible* was read upon receiving his master's degree in 1772; he was later to be a prolific member of the literary group known as the Connecticut (or Hartford) Wits. In service, 1777–79, as chaplain of Gen. S. H. Parson's Connecticut Continental Brigade.

In 1783 he became pastor of the Congregational church at Greenfield Hill, Conn.; during his 12 years there his fame as educator, preacher, author, and man of affairs spread. Again he established a school for both sexes, which drew students from middle and southern states as well as New England. A rigid Calvinist and staunch Federalist, Dwight energetically opposed the prevalent rise of democracy and infidelity. His satiric *Triumph of Infidelity, a Poem* (1788) uncorked vials of abuse on Voltaire, Hume, and others. Dwight's views were also set forth in many sermons and addresses.

In 1795, upon the death of Ezra Stiles, Dwight was elected president of Yale. For more than 21 years he administered the college with great ability and exerted an extraordinary influence over the students. Theologically indebted to Jonathan Edwards, Dwight outlined his own system in *Theology, Explained and Defended* (1818–19). His *Travels in New England and New York* (1821–22), written to refute foreign misrepresentations of America, is an astonishingly varied collection of descriptions of natural, agricultural, political, religious, and social conditions, including statistical information.

DWIGHT, TIMOTHY (*b. Norwich, Conn., 1828; d. 1916*), Congregational clergyman, educator. Grandson of Timothy Dwight (1752–1817). Graduated Yale, 1849. Professor of sacred literature, Yale Divinity, 1858–86; president, Yale University, 1886–98, in which time a successful expansion and reorganization of the various schools of the university took place.

DWIGHT, WILLIAM (*b. Springfield, Mass., 1831; d. Boston, Mass., 1888*), manufacturer, Union soldier. Rose to division command under P. H. Sheridan in Virginia, 1864, after gallant service in the peninsula (1861–62) and in the western campaigns (1863) under N. P. Banks.

DWORSHAK, HENRY CLARENCE (*b. Duluth, Minn., 1894; d. Washington, D.C., 1962*), publisher and U.S. congressman and senator. Owned and published the *Burley* (Idaho) *Bulletin* (1924–44). He served as a Republican in the U.S. House of Representatives (1939–47) and Senate (1946–48, 1949–62). A leader of the conservative bloc in the Senate, Dworshak was frequently linked with Senator Joseph R. McCarthy in the early 1950's.

DYAR, HARRISON GRAY (*b. New York, N.Y., 1866; d. Washington, D.C., 1929*), entomologist. Graduated Massachusetts Institute of Technology, 1889; Ph.D., Columbia, 1895. Chief interest, lepidoptera; his main work, *The Mosquitoes of North and Central America and the West Indies* (1912–17).

DYE, WILLIAM McENTYRE (*b. Pennsylvania, 1831; d. Muskegon, Mich., 1899*), soldier. Graduated West Point, 1853. Served with distinction in Union army. Staff officer of the Egyptian army, 1873–78; military adviser to Korea, 1888–99.

DYER, ALEXANDER BRYDIE (*b. Richmond, Va., 1815; d. 1874*), soldier. Graduated West Point, 1837. In ordnance service, *post* 1838. Commanded U.S. arsenal, Springfield, Mass., 1861–64; chief of ordnance, U.S. Army, 1864–74.

DYER, ELIPHALET (*b. Windham, Conn., 1721; d. Windham 1807*), jurist. Prominent in affairs of the Susquehanna Co., 1753–83; member of the Continental Congress; chief justice of Connecticut, 1789–93.

DYER, ISADORE (*b. Galveston, Tex., 1865; d. New Orleans, La., 1920*), physician. Graduated Tulane, M.D., 1889; taught there, 1905–20, and was dean, 1908–20. A successful dermatologist and one of the foremost leprologists of his time.

DYER, LOUIS (*b. Chicago, Ill., 1851; d. 1908*), classical scholar, writer, lecturer. Graduated Harvard, 1874. Associated with Oxford University, *post* 1893.

DYER, MARY (*d. Boston, Mass., 1660*), Quaker preacher and martyr.

DYER, NEHEMIAH MAYO (*b. Provincetown, Mass., 1839; d. 1910*), naval officer. Volunteered in U.S. Navy, 1862. Remaining in service, he was promoted captain, 1897, and commanded the *Baltimore* at Manila Bay. Retired as rear admiral, 1901.

DYKSTRA, CLARENCE ADDISON (*b. Cleveland, Ohio, 1883; d. Laguna Beach, Calif., 1950*), public administrator, educator. B.A., Iowa State University, 1903; did graduate work at University of Chicago in history and political science. Head of the Department of Political Science, University of Kansas, 1909–18; won recognition as a theoretician in state and municipal administration. Between 1918 and 1930, he served as secretary to civic reform groups in Cleveland, Chicago, and Los Angeles. He was highly efficient as city manager of Cincinnati, Ohio, 1930–37, despite the problems of the Great Depression. President of the University of Wisconsin, 1937–45, he devoted most of his time to wartime duties as first director of the Selective Service System and, later, as chairman of the National Defense Mediation Board. *Post* 1945, provost of the University of California at Los Angeles.

DYLANDER, JOHN (*b. Sweden, ca. 1709; d. Southwark, Philadelphia, Pa., 1741*), Lutheran clergyman. Pastor, Gloria Dei Church, Philadelphia, 1737–41.

DYMOND, JOHN (*b. Canada, 1836; d. New Orleans, La., 1922*), Louisiana sugar planter, inventor, editor.

DYOTT, THOMAS W. (*b. England, 1771; d. Philadelphia, Pa., 1861*), patent medicine king, welfare worker, temperance advocate. Came to Pennsylvania *ca.* 1795. The largest dealer in patent medicines in America, Dyott operated the Kensington Glass Works, *post* 1833. He also engaged in eccentric reform activities, including operation of a personal bank maintained entirely on his own credit. Imprisoned briefly after his financial failure in 1836, he returned to his drugstore and again acquired considerable wealth.

E

EADS, JAMES BUCHANAN (*b. Lawrenceburg, Ind., 1820; d. Nassau, Bahama Islands, 1887*), engineer, inventor. Became a purser on a Mississippi River steamboat, 1838; invented a diving bell, which he patented, and in 1842 formed a partnership to engage in steamboat salvage. A student of the laws which governed the Mississippi's flow and determined its deposits, Eads proposed in 1856 to Congress to remove all snags and wrecks from the Mississippi, Missouri, Arkansas, and Ohio rivers and to keep their channels open for some years; the bill, however, died in the Senate.

Summoned to Washington by Lincoln in 1861 to advise upon the best methods of utilizing western rivers for attack and defense, Eads proposed a fleet of armor-plated steam-propelled gunboats. He contracted to construct 7 such vessels ready for armament in 65 days; despite chaotic conditions, the boats were built. In the course of the war he built 14 armored gunboats and armed and built other vessels.

In 1865 a bill was introduced into Congress authorizing construction of a bridge across the Mississippi at St. Louis, Mo. The project was declared impracticable, but Eads's plan for the bridge was approved and construction was successfully completed in 1874. That year, Eads proposed to Congress to open a mouth of the Mississippi and maintain the channel at the sole risk of himself and his associates. The proposition was accepted. In 1879 the project was completed, Eads having devised a system of jetties which caused the river to deposit its sediment where he wanted it. His reports and articles during this work are probably unsurpassed in value as engineering expositions on controlling the flow of water and correct river improvement.

EAGELS, JEANNE (*b. Kansas City, Mo., 1894; d. New York, N.Y., 1929*), actress. Best known for her performance as Sadie Thompson in *Rain*, 1922–26.

EAKINS, THOMAS (*b. Philadelphia, Pa., 1844; d. Philadelphia, 1916*), painter, sculptor, teacher. Attended Pennsylvania Academy of Fine Arts; studied in Paris at the École des Beaux Arts under J. L. Gérôme, Léon Bonnat, and the sculptor A. A. Dumont. While in Spain in 1869 Eakins was impressed by the work of the great Spanish realists, especially Velásquez, Ribera, Goya, and Herrera. Returned to Philadelphia, 1870; studied anatomy at Jefferson Medical College. Knowledge of anatomy brought him the opportunity to teach at the Pennsylvania Academy, where he became dean and was for many years its principal instructor. He also taught at the Art Students League. Eakins worked unsparingly, painting many portraits and eventually more elaborate compositions. Among these the *Clinic of Dr. Gross*, completed in 1875, is generally regarded as his masterpiece. In his painting is displayed the masterly drawing of the human figure in repose or action, which is his chief title to fame. Among many other pictures may be mentioned the *Clinic of Dr. Agnew, Between Rounds, Chess Players, The Pair-Oared Shell, The Biglen Brothers Turning the Stakeboat*, and a long series of fishing subjects.

The virility of his nature appears in his selection of subjects and his strength of characterization. He was able to reveal in each portrait not only an individual personality but a racial type. *The Thinker*, for example, unique in its plainness, is a penetrating study of a native type. Eakins' sense of the dignity and worth of common things and people suggests analogies with the work of Walt Whitman, Winslow Homer, and Ralph Waldo Emerson.

EAMES, CHARLES (*b. New Braintree, Mass., 1812; d. 1867*), lawyer, diplomat. Successful in concluding a treaty with the Hawaiian government in 1849, Eames later practiced international law in Washington, D.C.

EAMES, WILBERFORCE (*b. Newark, N.J., 1855; d. New York, N.Y., 1937*), librarian, bibliographer. Specialist in Americana, New York Public Library, 1895–1937.

EARHART, AMELIA MARY (*b. Atchison, Kans., 1897; d. 1937*), aviator. Made first solo flights *ca.* 1921; was the first woman passenger on a transatlantic flight, June 1928. In May 1932 she made the trip alone, establishing a record of 14 hours, 56 minutes. She followed three record-breaking transcontinental flights (1932–33) by making the first solo flight from Hawaii to the U.S. mainland, January 1935, and the first nonstop flight from Mexico City to Newark, N.J., May 1935. In July 1937 she and her navigator, Frederick Noonan, were lost after leaving New Guinea on the last lap of a globe-circling flight.

EARLE, ALICE MORSE (*b. Worcester, Mass., 1853; d. Hempstead, N.Y., 1911*). Author of a number of valuable studies in colonial costume and customs.

EARLE, EDWARD MEAD (*b. New York, N.Y., 1894; d. New York, 1954*), educator and public official. Columbia (Ph.D., 1923). Taught at Columbia from 1920 to 1934. An authority on international affairs, he served on numerous League of Nations commissions and was vice-chairman of the Foreign Policy Association. In 1934, he joined the faculty of the School of Historical Studies at the Institute for Advanced Study at Princeton. An expert on military affairs, he was a military analyst for the Office of Strategic Services (1941–1942). From 1942 to 1945, he was a special consultant to the commander of the army air forces; he was a consultant to the National War College (1946–49); consultant to the supreme commander of the Allied powers in Europe (1951). His major book is *Makers of Modern Strategy: Military Thought From Machiavelli to Hitler* (1943).

EARLE, JAMES (*b. Paxton, Mass., 1761; d. Charleston, S.C., 1796*), portrait painter. Brother of Ralph Earle. Ranked by contemporaries with Copley and Trumbull, Earle spent his professional life in London, England, and Charleston, S.C.

EARLE, MORTIMER LAMSON (*b. New York, N.Y., 1864; d. 1905*), classical scholar, educator. Taught at Barnard, Bryn Mawr, and Columbia; known for archaeological discoveries as well as paleographical knowledge.

EARLE, PLINY (*b. Leicester, Mass., 1762; d. 1832*), cotton-machinery manufacturer. Invented and patented, 1803, a machine for making wool and cotton cards.

EARLE, PLINY (*b. Leicester, Mass., 1809; d. 1892*), physician, psychiatrist. Son of Pliny Earle (1762–1832). A cofounder of the American Medical Association, Earle led his contemporaries in study of psychiatric institutions and in treatment of the insane.

EARLE, RALPH (*b. Shrewsbury, Mass., 1751; d. 1801*), painter. Brother of James Earle. Designer of crude views of battles at Lexington and Concord engraved by Amos Doolittle; led a rambling life in England and America. Celebrated for portraits of uneven quality.

EARLE, RALPH (*b. Worcester, Mass., 1874; d. Worcester, 1939*), naval officer, educator. Graduated Annapolis, 1896. Chief, Bureau of Ordnance (as rear admiral), 1916–19. Responsible for arming navy in World War I, he developed and procured mines for North Sea blockage and suggested use of naval guns on railroad cars on western front, 1918.

EARLE, THOMAS (*b. Leicester, Mass., 1796; d. 1849*), lawyer. Son of Pliny Earle (1762–1832). Led agitation for reform of the constitution of Pennsylvania, *ante* 1837.

EARLY, JOHN (*b. Bedford Co., Va., 1786; d. Lynchburg, Va., 1873*), Methodist clergyman. Helped found Randolph-Macon College. Active in formation of Methodist Episcopal Church, South, he served as bishop, 1854–66.

EARLY, JUBAL ANDERSON (*b. Franklin Co., Va., 1816; d. Lynchburg, Va., 1894*), lawyer, Confederate soldier. Graduated West Point, 1837. Admitted Virginia bar, 1840. Though against secession in 1861, he joined the Confederate army and for the next three years served with the Army of Northern Virginia, rising to lieutenant general; after June 1864 he was in independent command in the Shenandoah Valley. From this position, his forces threatened Washington and obstructed communications between the capital and the west. He was defeated by Sheridan at Cedar Creek, occasion of the famous "ride." After the war, Early remained a loyal, "unreconstructed" Confederate.

EARLY, PETER (*b. Madison Co., Va., 1773; d. Greensboro, Ga., 1817*), politician, judge. Removed to Georgia, 1795. As governor of Georgia, 1813–15, he supported the War of 1812 and vetoed an unwise stay law for relief of debtors.

EARLY, STEPHEN TYREE (*b. Corzet, Va., 1889; d. Washington, D.C., 1951*), newspaperman, government official. A reporter for the United and Associated press organizations in Washington, Early was Franklin Roosevelt's advance man for the unsuccessful bid for the vice presidency in 1920. In 1933, Roosevelt appointed him assistant secretary in charge of press relations at the White House, where he serve until 1945. Early was successful in informing the public of New Deal programs in spite of a press that was owned by hostile forces. He did this through brilliant use of newsreels, building a strong rapport between the president and the public, and, eventually, the press. After Roosevelt's death, Early became vice president of the Pullman Co.; he returned to government as a chief deputy to Louis Johnson, Secretary of Defense (1949–50), but left when the secretary resigned.

EASLEY, RALPH MONTGOMERY (*b. Schuyler Co., Ill., 1856; d. Rye, N.Y., 1939*), reformer. Founded National Civic Federation, 1900, to improve relations between capital and labor.

EAST, EDWARD MURRAY (*b. Du Quoin, Ill., 1879; d. Boston, Mass., 1938*), plant geneticist. Graduated University of Illinois, B.S., 1901; M.S., 1904; Ph.D., 1907. Trained as a chemist, he became interested in genetics through researches, 1900–04, to improve Indian corn for animal nutrition. As agronomist at Connecticut Agricultural Experiment Station, 1904–08, East continued his corn experiments. Together with independent investigations by George Harrison Shull, they led to the development of hybrid corn, a new method of seed production revolutionizing corn growing throughout the world. East also did important theoretical studies of Mendelian heredity in corn, of self- and cross-incompatibility, species hybridization, cytoplasmic heredity, and heretosis. In 1909 he joined the Bussey Institution of Harvard University.

EASTMAN, ARTHUR MACARTHUR (*b. Gilmanton, N.H., 1810; d. 1877*), firearms manufacturer. During the Civil War, Eastman made a fortune turning old arms into cavalry carbines. He promoted a direct ocean cable between Europe and the United States, which was successfully completed in 1875.

EASTMAN, CHARLES GAMAGE (*b. Fryeburg, Maine, 1816; d. Montpelier, Vt., 1860*), journalist, politician, poet. *Post* 1846, editor of *Montpelier* (Vt.) *Patriot.*

EASTMAN, ENOCH WORTHEN (*b. Deerfield, N.H., 1810; d. 1885*), Iowa lawyer and public official.

EASTMAN, GEORGE (*b. Waterville, N.Y., 1854; d. Rochester, N.Y., 1932*), inventor, manufacturer, philanthropist. Convinced before 1879 of the commercial prospects for photographic dry plates, he invented a machine for coating plates and began their manufacture. After experimenting, 1884, with transparent and flexible film, he marketed the first Kodak, using paper-backed film, 1888. With aid of Henry Reichenbach, he prepared transparent film, 1889, and introduced a daylight-loading film, 1891. The Eastman Co., reorganized as the Eastman Kodak Co., 1893, was remarkably successful, owing largely to Eastman's aggressive fight to control the market in photographic goods. Among the objects of Eastman's philanthropies, on which were spent well over $75 million, were the University of Rochester and its various schools, Massachusetts Institute of Technology, and Hampton and Tuskegee institutes.

EASTMAN, HARVEY GRIDLEY (*b. near Waterville, N.Y., 1832; d. Denver, Colo., 1878*), businessman, politician, promoter. Founded Eastman's National Business College, Poughkeepsie, N.Y., 1859, which aided in development of that town.

EASTMAN, JOHN ROBIE (*b. Andover, N.H, 1836; d. 1913*). One of several astronomers (among them Newcomb and Hall) who established the reputation of the Naval Observatory; served there, 1862–98.

EASTMAN, JOSEPH BARTLETT (*b. Katonah, N.Y., 1882; d. Washington, D.C., 1944*), reformer, public administrator. B.A., Amherst, 1904. After working with Robert A. Woods at South End House, Boston, Mass., he served as secretary of the Public Franchise League, 1905–15, keeping a watchful eye on Massachusetts utilities, exposing stock frauds, blocking unwarranted rate changes, and preparing bills for presentation to the legislature. A member of the Massachusetts Public Service Commission, 1915–18, Eastman joined the Interstate Commerce Commission in 1919. He continued with it until his death, twice serving as chairman. A man of high competence and stern objectivity, he continued to be reappointed by successive presidents, irrespective of politics.

EASTMAN, MAX FORRESTER (*b. Canandaigua, N.Y., 1883; d. Barbados, 1969*), writer and political ativist. Studied at

Williams College and Columbia. As editor of the *Masses* from 1912, transformed a foundering socialist monthly into a lively left-wing periodical that provided a forum for opposition to American entry into World War I. Founded (1918) and was editor of the *Liberator*. Regarded as the chief anti-Stalinist on the American left, 1924–39. In the 1940's Eastman moved steadily to the right, becoming a roving editor of the *Reader's Digest* in 1941. The author of 26 books, including *Marxism: Is It Science?* (1940) and *Stalin's Russia and the Crisis of Socialism* (1940).

EASTMAN, TIMOTHY CORSER (*b.* *Croydon, N.H., 1821; d. Tarrytown, N.Y., 1893*), cattle merchant, meatpacker. A pioneer in shipping livestock and dressed meat in commercial quantities to England and Scotland. His first shipment of dressed meat abroad was made in October 1875.

EASTMAN, WILLIAM REED (*b. New York, N.Y., 1835; d. 1925*), engineer, Presbyterian clergyman. Entering upon a career in library work at 55 years of age, he became a leading authority on library buildings and equipment.

EASTON, JOHN (*b.* ca. *1625; d. Newport, R.I., 1705*), governor of Rhode Island, 1690–95. Son of Nicholas Easton. Author of a *Narrative of the Causes Which Led to Philip's Indian War* (published 1858).

EASTON, NICHOLAS (*b. Wales, 1593; d. Newport, R.I., 1675*), governor of Rhode Island, 1672–74. Came to America, 1634. Built the first house in Newport, 1639, removing there eventually from Massachusetts after involvement in antinomian controversy.

EATON, AMOS (*b. Chatham, N.Y., 1776; d. Troy, N.Y., 1842*), scientist, educator. Graduated Williams, 1799. Author of *Manual of Botany for the Northern States* (1817). Lecturer on scientific subjects; professor at Rensselaer Institute, 1824–42.

EATON, BENJAMIN HARRISON (*b. near Zanesville, Ohio, 1833; d. 1904*), agriculturist, pioneer in irrigation. Settled near present Windsor, Colo., 1864; developed and irrigated extensive holdings in Colorado.

EATON, CHARLES AUBREY (*b. Pugwash, Nova Scotia, 1868; d. Watchung, N.H., 1953*), clergyman, journalist, industrial consultant, statesman. Studied at Acadia University, Newton Theological Institution, and Baylor University (D.D., 1899). While he was pastor of several churches, including the Euclid Baptist Church in Cleveland (1901–1909) and the Madison Avenue Baptist Church in New York, he was also a journalist, writing articles for the *London Times* and the *New York Tribune*. An ardent internationalist, Eaton resigned from the ministry in 1910 and became a full-time journalist. From 1924 to 1953, he was elected Congress as a Republican representative from New Jersey. As a member of the powerful Foreign Affairs Committee (chairman, 1947–53), Eaton became the foremost Republican internationalist. He supported Roosevelt's preparations for World War II and was a delegate to the U.N. Charter Conference in San Francisco in 1945. After the war, he effectively supported the Marshall Plan and Truman Doctrine, and helped legislation for foreign aid—all in the face of hostile Republican and Democratic isolationism.

EATON, DANIEL CADY (*b. Fort Gratiot, Mich., 1834; d. New Haven, Conn., 1895*), botanist. Author of *The Ferns of North America* (1877–80) and numerous shorter works; professor of botany, Yale, 1864–95.

EATON, DORMAN BRIDGMAN (*b. Hardwick, Vt., 1823; d. 1899*), lawyer, civil service reformer. Entitled to share with G. W.

Curtis and Carl Schurz honor of securing national recognition for merit system.

EATON, HOMER (*b. Enosburg, Vt., 1834; d. Madison, N.J., 1913*), Methodist clergyman. Agent, Methodist Book Concern, 1889–1913.

EATON, JOHN (*b. Sutton, N.H., 1829; d. 1906*), educator. Graduated Dartmouth, 1854. Organized Freedmen camps, 1862–65. U.S. commissioner of education, 1870–86.

EATON, JOHN HENRY (*b. North Carolina, 1790; d. Washington, D.C., 1856*), lawyer, politician. Settled in Tennessee, *ca.* 1808. U.S. senator, Democrat, from Tennessee, 1818–29; strong supporter of Andrew Jackson. Appointed secretary of war, 1829, he resigned in 1831 after Washington society's refusal to accept his second wife, Peggy O'Neale, disrupted Jackson's cabinet. Eaton was governor of Florida, 1834–35, and minister to Spain, 1836–40.

EATON, JOSEPH ORIEL (*b. Newark, Ohio, 1829; d. Yonkers, N.Y., 1875*), painter.

EATON, MARGARET L. O'NEILL. *See* O'NEALE, MARGARET L.

EATON, NATHANIEL (*b. Coventry, England, ca. 1609; d. Southwark, London, England, 1674*), first head of Harvard College. Brother of Samuel and Theophilus Eaton. Immigrated to Massachusetts, 1637, where he was welcomed for his learning and made head (though not president) of Harvard College. He was soon in trouble, charged with withholding food from the students and with beating his usher. Removed from office, fined, and excommunicated by the church, he fled Boston for Virginia and later returned to England.

EATON, SAMUEL (*b. Cheshire, England, 1596[?]; d. England, 1664/5*), clergyman. Brother of Theophilus and Nathaniel Eaton. Became colleague of John Davenport at New Haven, Conn., 1637. Returned to England, *ca.* 1640.

EATON, THEOPHILUS (*b. Stony Stratford, England, 1590; d. New Haven, Conn., 1658*), merchant, colonizer. Brother of Samuel and Nathaniel Eaton. A successful merchant in London and an original patentee of the Massachusetts Co., he immigrated in 1637 with his old schoolmate John Davenport and others, including his brothers, to Boston. Eaton's group, the wealthiest and commercially the ablest which had up to that time gone to America, established their own independent colony at what is now New Haven (located, 1637–38, organized 1639). Eaton and Davenport ruled the colony. Eaton was elected civic governor and was annually reelected until his death. His attempt to establish a fur-trading post on the Delaware occasioned conflict with the Dutch of New Amsterdam. His administration of the colony, however, was marked by wisdom, justice, firmness, and prudence.

EATON, WILLIAM (*b. Woodstock, Conn., 1764; d. Brimfield, Mass., 1811*), army officer, diplomat. Graduated Dartmouth, 1790; commissioned captain, U.S. army, 1792. Appointed U.S. consul to Tunis, 1798, he renegotiated an unsatisfactory treaty with aid of James L. Cathcart; at Cathcart's suggestion also, he urged on Congress in 1804 a scheme to win peace with Tripoli by reinstating an exiled pasha. His venture suddenly countermanded after he had led a spectacular march with a motley army from Alexandria, Egypt, to Derna, Eaton returned to America, where he made many political enemies by his complaints about his treatment.

EATON, WYATT (*b. Philipsburg, Canada, 1849; d. Newport, R.I., 1896*), painter. A friend of the French painter Millet, who influenced him, Eaton is known for his portraits of distinguished American and Canadian contemporaries.

EBERLE, EDWARD WALTER (*b. Denton, Tex., 1864; d. Washington, D.C., 1929*), naval officer. Graduated Annapolis, 1885. Wrote the first modern manual of naval gun and torpedo drills and the first instructions for wireless on naval vessels. Superintendent at Annapolis, 1915–19, he was promoted rear admiral, 1919, and was chief of naval operations, 1923–27.

EBERLE, JOHN (*b. Hagerstown[?], Md., 1787; d. Lexington, Ky., 1838*), physician. Author of *Treatise on the Materia Medica and Therapeutics* (1823) and *Notes of Lectures on Theory and Practice of Medicine* (1834). Founded, 1824, Jefferson Medical College, where he taught, 1825–30; taught also at Transylvania and Medical College of Ohio.

ECHOLS, JOHN (*b. Lynchburg, Va., 1823; d. Staunton, Va., 1896*), lawyer, Confederate major general. For many years an official and director of the Chesapeake & Ohio Railway.

ECKART, WILLIAM ROBERTS (*b. Chillicothe, Ohio, 1841; d. Palo Alto, Calif., 1914*), engineer. Associated with B. F. Isherwood during Civil War and after in marine propeller design and other marine engineering projects; specialized in mining machinery design; pioneered in high-head long-distance transmission power plants.

ECKELS, JAMES HERRON (*b. Princeton, Ill., 1858; d. Chicago, Ill., 1907*), lawyer, financier. Efficient comptroller of the currency, 1893–97; headed Commercial National Bank of Chicago, 1897–1907.

ECKERT, THOMAS THOMPSON (*b. St. Clairsville, Ohio, 1825; d. Long Branch, N.J., 1910*), telegrapher. Organized and supervised U.S. military telegraph during Civil War; later administrator of telegraph companies controlled by Jay Gould and others, he was president of Western Union, 1893–1900.

ECKFORD, HENRY (*b. Irvine, Scotland, 1775; d. in Turkey, 1832*), shipbuilder. Settled in New York City, 1796. Ships of his design were famous for strength and speed. Built the *Robert Fulton*, which made first successful steam voyage from New York to New Orleans and Havana, 1822.

ECKSTEIN, JOHN (*b. Mecklenburg[?], Germany, ca. 1750; d. Philadelphia[?], Pa., ca. 1817*), painter, sculptor, engraver.

ECKSTORM, FANNIE HARDY (*b. Brewer, Maine, 1865; d. Brewer, 1946*), ornithologist, authority on the history, folk songs, and Indians of Maine. Graduated Smith College, 1889. Author of *The Penobscot Man* (1904), *The Handicrafts of the Modern Indians of Maine* (1932), and other works.

EDDIS, WILLIAM (*fl. 1769–77*), Maryland Loyalist. Secretary to Gov. Robert Eden. Author of *Letters from America, Historical and Descriptive* (1792).

EDDY, CLARENCE (*b. Greenfield, Mass., 1851; d. Chicago, Ill., 1937*), organist.

EDDY, DANIEL CLARKE (*b. Salem, Mass., 1823; d. Martha's Vineyard, Mass., 1896*), Baptist clergyman. Know-Nothing Speaker of Massachusetts lower house, 1854.

EDDY, HARRISON PRESCOTT (*b. Millbury, Mass., 1870; d. Montreal, Canada, 1937*), sanitary engineer. A leader in the development of water supply and purification and of sewage treatment. Author, with Leonard Metcalf, of *American Sewerage Practice* (1914–15).

EDDY, HENRY TURNER (*b. Stoughton, Mass., 1844; d. 1921*), mathematician, physicist. Applied his learning to engineering problems; taught at Tennessee, Cornell, Princeton, Cincinnati, Minnesota. President, Rose Polytechnic Institute, 1891–94.

EDDY, MANTON SPRAGUE (*b. Chicago, Ill., 1892; d. Fort Benning, Ga., 1962*), army officer. Graduated from the Shattuck Military School in Faribault, Minn., in 1913. One of the most battle-tested army commanders in the European theater during World War II, Eddy led the Ninth Infantry from 1942 through the North Africa, Sicily, and Normandy campaigns. As commander of the XII Corps, he was instrumental to the rapid advance of Lieutenant General Patton's Third Army across France and into Germany in 1944–45. An outstanding military educator, he was named director of the Army Educational System in 1948. Appointed commander in chief of the U.S. Armed Forces in Europe in 1952. Eddy retired a lieutenant general in 1952.

EDDY, MARY MORSE BAKER (*b. New Hampshire, July 16, 1821; d. Chestnut Hill, Mass., Dec. 3, 1910*), founder of the Christian Science church. She was born on a hillside farm, the youngest of six children of Mark Baker and Abigail Barnard Ambrose. As a child she suffered from a nervous ailment, and her education was desultory. She read much, however, and, according to her own statement, studied Hebrew, Greek, and Latin under the tutelage of her brother Albert. She was received into membership in the Tilton Congregational Church at 17, after some doubts had been expressed about her soundness on doctrinal points. In New England at this time the transcendental movement was in full swing; within a few miles of her home were numerous colonies of Shakers and believers in spiritualism. The family physician dabbled in mesmerism and even tried the effect of mental suggestion upon Baker for the relief of hysteria.

In 1843 Baker married George Washington Glover, but after a few months together he died. She returned home, where she gave birth to her son. She soon became a chronic invalid.

In 1853 she married Dr. Daniel Patterson, an itinerant dentist and homeopathist. He was frequently absent and in 1862 was captured by Confederate troops. Mary returned to her sister's home, a helpless invalid. Two or three months in a sanitorium did little for her, and in October 1862 she consulted Dr. Phineas Parkhurst Quimby of Portland, Maine. In a letter published in the *Portland Courier*, Nov. 7, 1862, she declared that by virtue of the great principle discovered by Dr. Quimby, who "speaks as man never spoke and heals as never man healed since Christ," she was on the highway to complete health. She was now an ardent disciple of Quimby. In 1873 she secured a divorce on the ground of desertion. From time to time she sought a livelihood by teaching and practicing what she called a new system of healing. She was still loyal to Quimby and professed no higher purpose than to disseminate his teachings, but as early as 1866 she endeavored to find a publisher for a manuscript which may have been a first draft of *Science and Health*.

On her return to Lynn in 1870, she became partners with Richard Kennedy, who practiced as a doctor, and devoted herself to teaching and writing. It was a profitable alliance and she accumulated enough capital to buy a house at 8 Broad Street. The manuscripts which she put into the hands of her students no longer bore Quimby's name but contained matter of her own composition. She was now trying to give coherent expression to the "metaphysical" system which she believed would mark an epoch in religious thought and practice. Few manuscripts have had a more remarkable influence upon American religious history than that which finally found its way into print in 1875, under the title *Science and Health*. According to the doctrine, disease is caused by mind alone. Science is the wisdom of the Eternal Mind revealed through Jesus Christ, who taught the power of Mind to overcome the illusions of sin, sickness, and death—hence the appropriateness of calling metaphysical science "Christian Science." In subsequent editions, this doctrine was given more pointed application. "We must understand that the cause and cure of all disease rest with the mind." That she owed much to Quimby cannot be doubted, and it is highly probable that she owed much also to the writings of Warren Felt Evans. But she gave a propulsive force to her thought which both Quimby and Evans lacked.

On New Year's Day 1877, she married Asa Gilbert Eddy, a simple man of humble origin. At this time she gave public utterance to a belief in mental malpractice, a strange contrast to her fundamental tenets. She had come firmly to believe in so-called malicious animal magnetism, a mental influence which evil-minded persons could exert to produce disease or misfortune in others. When Asa Eddy's health began to fail, his wife was certain that he was a victim of malicious animal magnetism. A consulting physician reported that he suffered from organic heart disease. On June 3, 1882, Asa Eddy died, and in an interview Mrs. Eddy declared that her husband had died of "mesmeric poisoning."

Though Eddy did not at first desire an organization to support the new faith, the informal group of students who called themselves Christian Scientists formed the Christian Scientists' Association in 1876; and with her active support they sought and secured in 1879 a charter as the Church of Christ, Scientist. In 1881 she secured a charter for the Massachusetts Metaphysical College, which was to be the training school for practitioners, and in 1882 she and the college moved to Boston.

In 1883 appeared the first number of the *Journal of Christian Science*, which carried her influence beyond the confines of New England. The "Healing Department" of the *Journal*, with its reports of cures, undoubtedly won many recruits. Institutes and academies sprang up which became feeders for the Metaphysical College; and every graduate with a diploma became in turn a practitioner and a missionary. In January 1886 the National Christian Science Association was formed and in February a general convention was held in New York.

Never content with her handiwork, Eddy published edition after edition of *Science and Health*. The sixteenth edition was prepared by Rev. James Henry Wiggin, a former Unitarian minister employed as literary adviser and editor by her publisher. Eddy's yearly royalties amounted to nearly $50,000 by 1900. Letters printed in the *Journal* and unsigned editorials were suggesting that Eddy was "God-sent to the world as much as any character of Sacred Writ" and that perhaps it was left to her to supplement the New Testament and explain the miracles of Jesus. "We are witnessing," said one enthusiastic follower, "the transfer of the Gospel from male to female trust."

In 1889 Eddy move to Concord, N.H. "Our dear Mother in God," announced the *Journal*, "withdraws herself from our midst and goes up into the Mount for higher communings." In these years of so-called retirement, she built the church organization, which, next to *Science and Health*, is her most enduring monument.

EDDY, NELSON (*b. Providence, R.I., 1901; d. Miami Beach, Fla., 1967*), singer and actor. An operatic baritone, Eddy made his debut with the Philadelphia Civic Opera Company in 1924. Studied with William Vilonat in Dresden in 1927. On his return to the U.S., signed a contract with Columbia Concerts, and by 1933 had visited almost every major city in the country. Signed a seven-year contract with Metro-Goldwyn-Mayer in 1933. At MGM he was teamed with the soprano Jeanette MacDonald; the duo was hailed as "America's singing sweethearts." They made eight films, including *Rose Marie* (1936), *Sweethearts* (1938), and *I Married an Angel* (1942). Toured with Canadian singer and comedienne Gale Sherwood, 1952–66. Throughout his career, Eddy recorded 25 albums and 284 songs for RCA Victor, Columbia Records, and Everest Records.

EDDY, THOMAS (*b. Philadelphia, Pa., 1758; d. 1827*), insurance broker. Promoted reforms of prisons, hospitals, schools, and penal code of New York; supported DeWitt Clinton's Erie Canal project.

EDEBOHLS, GEORGE MICHAEL (*b. New York, N.Y., 1853; d. 1908*), surgeon. Graduated Fordham, 1871; M.D., College of Physicians and Surgeons, 1875. Specialized in gynecology; originated Edebohls' operation for Bright's disease.

EDEN, CHARLES (*b. England, 1673; d. Bertie Co., N.C., 1722*), colonial governor of North Carolina, 1714–22; last person to receive title Landgrave under John Locke's constitution for Carolina.

EDEN, ROBERT (*b. Durham, England, 1741; d. Annapolis, Md., 1784*), colonial governor of Maryland, 1768–76. His skillful diplomacy and moderation won him friends among the colonial gentry; created a baronet, 1776, he resided in England during the Revolution.

EDES, BENJAMIN (*b. Charlestown, Mass., 1732; d. Boston, Mass., 1803*), journalist. With John Gill, founded *Boston Gazette and Country Journal*, 1755, organ of Massachusetts patriots. His fortunes declined after the Revolution.

EDES, ROBERT THAXTER (*b. Eastport, Maine, 1838; d. Springfield, Mass., 1923*), physician. Graduated Harvard, 1858; M.D., Harvard Medical, 1861. Specialized in diseases of nervous system; foreshadowed modern treatment of psychoneuroses.

EDESON, ROBERT (*b. New Orleans, La., 1868; d. 1931*), actor. Played with Frohman's Empire Theatre company; leading man to Maude Adams and other stars; one of the first stage stars to go into motion pictures.

EDGAR, CHARLES (*b. Metuchen, N.J., 1862; d. Miami, Fla., 1922*), lumberman. Helped develop lumber areas of upper Midwest and of southern pine districts. Invented band saw with teeth on both edges.

EDGE, WALTER EVANS (*b. Philadelphia, Pa., 1873; d. New York, N.Y., 1956*), politician and diplomat. Self-educated, Edge became governor of New Jersey (1917–20 and 1944–47) after a successful career in advertising. He was elected to the U.S. Senate (1920–29). A Republican, Edge was known for progressive policies, transforming the New Jersey state government into a corporate structure. He was appointed ambassador to France in 1929, serving until 1932.

EDGERTON, ALFRED PECK (*b. Plattsburg, N.Y., 1813; d. Hicksville, Ohio, 1897*), businessman, politician. Long active as a "Bourbon" Democrat in Ohio and Indiana politics.

EDGERTON, SIDNEY (*b. New York, N.Y., 1818; d. 1900*), lawyer. Congressman, Republican, from Ohio, 1858–62; chief justice of Idaho, 1863; active in establishment of Montana Territory and its first territorial governor, 1864.

EDGREN, AUGUST HJALMAR (*b. Värmland, Sweden, 1840; d. Stockholm, Sweden, 1903*), soldier, linguist. Volunteered Union army in Civil War; after the war, taught abroad, returning 1870 to graduate Cornell, B.A., 1871; Ph.D., Yale, 1874. Taught subsequently in Sweden and at University of Nebraska. Specialist in Sanskrit and Germanic and Romance languages.

EDISON, CHARLES (*b. Llewellyn Park, N.J., 1890; d. New York, N.Y., 1969*), businessman, U.S. Navy secretary, and governor. Enjoyed a privileged upbringing as the son of Thomas Alva Edison, the inventor, and Mina Miller. Studied at the Massachusetts Institute of Technology, leaving before graduation to join his father in business. Became chairman of the board of the Edison Illuminating Co. in 1915; replaced his father as president of Edison Industries in 1926. From 1917, he assisted his father on the wartime Navy Consulting Board, formed to develop new weapons. As a member of the Democratic party from 1932, was appointed assistant secretary of the Navy under President Roosevelt in 1936; became Navy secretary in 1939. Roosevelt removed Edison from office in 1940, and influenced his nomination for the governorship of New Jersey. As governor, Edison fought corruption in state politics, but his power was limited by an antiquated state constitution and the animosity of Democratic boss Frank Hague. Later he was vindicated in his policies by the adoption of a new constitution and the overthrow of Hague as mayor. Resumed the presidency of Thomas A. Edison Inc. in 1944.

EDISON, THOMAS ALVA (*b. Milan, Ohio, 1847; d. West Orange, N.J., 1931*), inventor. Raised in Michigan, contrary to popular legend, in a "prosperous, changing and beautiful environment." Slow in school, inept in mathematics, but an avid reader, by age ten he had developed a strong taste for chemistry. As a youth, established a profitable business selling newspapers, candy, etc., on railroad trains; became a telegraph operator, 1863; went to work for Western Union in Boston, Mass., 1868. During all this time he had continued to read and experiment in chemistry and in applications of electricity to telegraphy; in 1869, he patented his first invention, an electrographic vote recorder, and also took out patents for an improved stock ticker. In the same year, he took an excellent position in New York as general manager of the Laws Gold Indicator Co.; he also entered partnership with two others in an "electrical engineer" consultation business. His share of the profits of his partnership when it was bought out in 1870 permitted him to set up his own shop and devote himself, with a staff of assistants (who later became famous on their own account), to improvements in telegraphy. In 1874, he made quadruplex telegraphy practicable; in 1875, invented a resonator for analyzing sound waves; in 1876, devised the carbon telephone transmitter. Also in 1876, he moved his laboratory to Menlo Park, N.J.; in 1877, he invented the phonograph, his greatest single achievement from the viewpoint of inventive imagination.

In 1879 he made commercially practicable the incandescent lamp, although he did not invent it. He introduced improvements vital to its common use and cheap production and was responsible for the system by which widely distributed lamps were empowered from central stations, an immense engineering achievement. Edison made his first and only scientific discovery, the "Edison effect," in 1883, whereby he demonstrated that the incandescent lamp could be used as a valve admitting negative but not positive electricity. Seeing no practical use for such a valve, Edison abandoned it, but it was to become later the basis for the vacuum tube, so essential to modern radio. In 1891, he patented a "kinetoscope," an apparatus for exhibiting photographs of moving objects. It had no projector or screen. In 1895 Thomas Armat invented a machine which would project a picture from film to screen, and in the following year Edison acquired the patent, a fact which erroneously caused contemporaries to give him credit for it. Edison did do much for the organization and standardization of the motion picture industry.

In 1887 Edison had moved his laboratory to West Orange. He had put in motion the many commercial companies for manufacturing and selling his many inventions, companies which later were consolidated into the Edison General Electric Co., later the General Electric Co. Having organized the companies, he lost interest in them and turned to investigation of the fluoroscope, ore-mill machinery, magnetic separation of iron, the storage battery, and railway signaling. He devised a dictating machine and mimeograph, and during World War I conducted research on torpedo mechanisms, flamethrowers, and submarine periscopes.

Edison was the idol of the press of his day, and it may be some time before the Edison myth can be divorced from the Edison fact. A trial-and-error inventor who scorned scientific theory and mathematical study which might have saved him time, he had an infinite capacity for hard work but the sensitivity of genius was lacking in him. Seeking devices adapted to commercial use, his approach to invention was economic. His triumphs seem less brilliant now than in the era when his pioneer work was done, but he must be judged with a consciousness of that era and of the society which acclaimed his gifts.

EDMAN, IRWIN (*b. New York, N.Y., 1896; d. New York, 1954*), teacher and writer. Columbia University (Ph.D., 1920). Edman spent his entire career at Columbia as a professor of philosophy. Influenced by his teacher and colleague, John Dewey, and by George Santayana, he considered himself a naturalist and empiricist. His book *Philosopher's Holiday* (1938) was a widely read account of his philosophy reflected through his travels and thoughts on people.

EDMANDS, JOHN (*b. Framingham, Mass., 1820; d. Philadelphia, Pa., 1915*), librarian, bibliographer. Graduated Yale, 1847. Librarian, Philadelphia Mercantile Library, 1856–1915. Author of a classification system, 1883.

EDMONDS, FRANCIS WILLIAM (*b. Hudson, N.Y., 1806; d. Westchester Co., N.Y., 1863*), businessman, genre painter.

EDMONDS, JOHN WORTH (*b. Hudson, N.Y., 1799; d. New York, N.Y., 1874*), jurist. Brother of Francis W. Edmonds. Justice of state supreme court, 1847–52. Published annotated New York *Statutes at Large* (1863), a standard reference.

EDMONDSON, WILLIAM (*b. Nashville, Tenn., 1882?; d. Nashville, 1951*), sculptor. Entirely without training, Edmondson, after working in train yards and as a hospital janitor, turned to carving tombstones out of limestone in 1931. A religious black man, his inspiration was almost all biblical. In 1937, a photographer from *Harper's Bazaar* took photographs and examples back to her magazine in New York. William Randolph Hearst, the magazine's owner, would not allow pictures of blacks to be printed in his publications. The photographer then approached Alfred Barr, curator for the Museum of Modern Art. Edmondson was given his first exhibition in 1937. He was commissioned as a WPA artist (1939–40). Edmondson never left Nashville; he continued to carve in that city until poor health forced him to retire in 1949.

EDMUNDS, CHARLES WALLIS (*b. Bridport, Dorset, England, 1873; d. Ann Arbor, Mich., 1941*), pharmacologist. Came to the United States with parents as a child; raised in Richmond, Ind. M.D., University of Michigan, 1901; B.A., 1904. A member of the Department of Materia Medica and Therapeutics at University of Michigan medical school *post* 1902, he was successively assistant, instructor, and professor; he served also as secretary of the medical school (1911–21) and as assistant dean (1918–21). He made many contributions to the development of pharmacology as a science, his major concern being establishment of drug standards and methods of bioassay of drugs for which chemical assay methods were not available. He was a member of the committee for revision of the U.S. Pharmacopeia, 1910–40. Among the subjects of his research were the action of botulinus and diphtheria toxins and caffeine, the role of chemical structure in the addictive properties of morphine and its derivatives.

EDMUNDS, GEORGE FRANKLIN (*b. near Richmond, Vt., 1828; d. Pasadena, Calif., 1919*), lawyer. Practiced in Vermont, *post* 1849; argued successfully against constitutionality of income tax in *Pollock* v. *Farmers' Loan and Trust Co.*, 1895. As U.S. senator, Republican, from Vermont, 1866–91, made important contributions in domestic legislation. Supported Radical Reconstructionists; arranged procedural rules for President Andrew Johnson's impeachment; secured adoption of Electoral Count Act of 1887; championed Thurman Act of 1878; was principal author of Sherman Antitrust Act, 1890; advocated civil service reform. A Republican reform candidate for presidential nomination in 1884, he drew support of independents away from Blaine. After Fessenden's death, Edmunds was generally considered ablest constitutional lawyer in Congress.

EDSALL, DAVID LINN (*b. Hamburg, N.J., 1869; d. Cambridge, Mass., 1945*), physician, medical educator. B.A., Princeton, 1890; M.D., University of Pennsylvania, 1893. Associated with William Pepper in clinical research at Pennsylvania. Made fundamental studies of nutritional diseases, metabolic abnormalities of children, and the effects of industrial conditions on health. One of the few men of his day who sought to understand the physiological and biochemical processes of disease in order to find basic principles of treatment. Deeply involved in the reforms in medical education set in motion by the famous Flexner report, he resigned the top chair of medicine at Pennsylvania, to which he had been raised in 1910, and in 1911 went to Washington University School of Medicine as professor of preventive medicine. Dissatisfied there, he went in 1912 to Boston as Jackson professor of clinical medicine at Harvard Medical School; he became dean in 1918, and in 1922 also assumed duties as dean of the Harvard School of Public Health. Retired in 1935, after presiding over a notable period of growth and scientific advance at Harvard.

EDWARDS, BELA BATES (*b. Southampton, Mass., 1802; d. Athens, Ga., 1852*), Congregational clergyman, editor. Cofounder of *Bibliotheca Sacra*, 1842, and editor, 1844–52. Taught at Andover Theological Seminary.

EDWARDS, CHARLES (*b. Norwich, England, 1797; d. 1868*), lawyer, author. Settled in New York City after graduation, Cambridge University; studied law. Standing counsel to British consulate general, New York. Author of, among other works, *Edwards' Chancery Reports* (1833–51).

EDWARDS, CLARENCE RANSOM (*b. Cleveland, Ohio, 1860; d. Boston, Mass., 1931*), army officer. Nephew of Oliver Edwards. Graduated West Point, 1883. Successful administrator of Bureau of Insular Affairs; commanded 26th Division in World War I. Retired as major general, 1922.

EDWARDS, EVERETT EUGENE (*b. Waltham Township, Minn., 1900; d. Washington, D.C., 1952*), agricultural historian. Attended Carleton College and Harvard (M.A., 1924). Editor of the quarterly *Agricultural History*, the organ of the Agricultural History Society in Washington (1931–52). Edward edited, wrote numerous monographs, and lectured in his field both at the society and at American University. He is remembered for his monographs, *Washington, Jefferson, Lincoln, and Agriculture* (1937), and *Jefferson and Agriculture* (1943).

EDWARDS, HENRY WAGGAMAN (*b. New Haven, Conn., 1779; d. 1847*), lawyer. Grandson of Jonathan Edwards (1703–58). Congressman, Democratic-Republican, from Connecticut, 1819–23; U.S. senator, 1823–27; governor, 1833, 1835–38.

EDWARDS, JOHN (*b. London, England, ca. 1671; d. Boston, Mass., 1746*), early American silversmith. Immigrated to Boston *ante* 1689.

EDWARDS, JOHN (*b. Stafford Co., Va., 1748; d. Bourbon Co., Ky., 1837*), planter. Removed to Lincoln Co., Ky., 1780; to Bourbon Co., 1785. Led in Kentucky's struggle for independence and statehood; opposed Spanish conspiracy, 1787–88. U.S. senator, 1792–95.

EDWARDS, JONATHAN (*b. East Windsor, Conn., 1703; d. Princeton, N.J., 1758*), Congregational clergyman, theologian, philosopher. Son of Timothy and Esther Stoddard Edwards. Entered Yale College, 1716, where his mind was formed by the idealism of John Locke and the new science of Newton. For Edwards, however, Newton's world of natural law was not a lifeless mechanism, but made up of bodies the substance of which was "the infinitely exact, and precise, and perfectly stable Idea, in God's mind." Reason could interpret the orderly related facts of Newton's science, but excellency—consisting in greatness and beauty, the consent or love of being to being—had to be apprehended independent of intellectual reason. The apprehension of divine beauty was God's redemptive disclosure of himself to the privileged elect.

After graduation, 1720, two years of theological study and a short pastorate in New York, Edwards took over parish duties in Northampton, Mass., in 1726 as a colleague of his grandfather, Rev. Solomon Stoddard. Edwards' emphasis on divine majesty, on personal conversion, and on salvation through supernatural illumination rather than through intellectual effort or "moral sincerity" estranged him from his relatives and congregation. He feared that their tendency to Arminian theology would diminish the doctrinal differences between the Congregational church and the Church of England. He expressed his views in *God Glorified in the Work of Redemption* (1731) and in *A Divine and Supernatural Light, Immediately Imparted to the Soul by the Spirit of God* (1734). One result of his fiery sermons was the Northampton revival of 1734–35. His *Faithful Narrative of the Surprising Work of God in the Conversion of Many Hundred Souls in Northampton* (1737) prepared the ground for Whitefield's "Great Awakening" of 1740–42, the excesses of which and its resulting social and religious divisions prompted Edwards to set down his mature analysis of piety and his psychology of religion. In his *Treatise Concerning Religious Affections* (1746) he described the mind as having two activities: understanding and will. Both must receive light, the former through intellectual study, the latter through a delight in holiness. The resulting birth of a love of God changes the soul's nature. It comes to share in the divine light, in the character of Christ. His theology led Edwards to demand a more rigorous criterion for church membership than many of his colleagues and parishioners were willing to accept. From December 1748 to June 1750 he was involved in a dispute with the Standing Committee of his church. The dispute resulted in Edwards' resignation. After a year of occasional service in Northampton, he went as missionary to the Indians at Stockbridge.

This new activity did not lessen the hardships to which he was exposed. To reduce his financial obligations, his wife and children sold their needlework in Boston. Old animosities of his Northampton days reasserted themselves in Stockbridge when Ephraim Williams, a relative of the Stoddard family, sought to oust Edwards from his church in order to escape the preacher's censure of his greed and intrigues. Edwards, however, prevailed in this struggle and enjoyed the confidence and support of settlers, Indians, commissioners, and the legislature. With his *Freedom of the Will* (1754) Edwards renewed his campaign against Arminianism and revealed himself as the first great philosophic intelligence in American history. The essay maintained the doctrine of unconditional predestination together with the freedom of the mind to act out its choice. Moral responsibility lies in the choice, not in the course of the choice. Liberty means only that man can do what he wills, but, as appears from the fact of divine foreknowledge, volitions are determined. In *The Great Christian Doctrine of Original Sin Defended* (1758), a reply to the English dissenter John Taylor's rejection of Adam's sin, Edwards demonstrated that man's identity is constituted by God with Adam's; that man is born depraved; that sin is infinite, for it is sin against infinite being. In "The Nature of True Virtue" (1765), Edwards reiterated that although all men possess a "natural conscience" which makes them approve justice and benevolence and perceive their beauty, only those whose conscience is enlightened by saving grace may love and taste this beauty. Natural virtues are spurious and rest on self-love. Disinterested love belongs to God and the redeemed. Edwards' aesthetic appreciation, his delight as a lover of beauty, finally found expression in his mystical pantheistic essay "Concerning the Ends for Which God Created the World" (1755). Here he described the universe as an exfoliation of God, an emanation, not a creation out of nothing. The end, therefore, is the manifestation of Himself, the creation of the supreme artist.

Edwards' service in Stockbridge came to an end with his call to the presidency of the College of New Jersey at Princeton. Beginning in January 1758 he conducted a seminar course in theology for seniors until Mar. 22, when he died of the aftereffects of a smallpox inoculation. Thus came to a close the life of America's first philosopher, a theologian admired by many for the saintliness of his disciplined character and hated by others for his pitiless logical consistency. Edwards had created the first great religious revival of modern times; had intensified the power of Calvinism to stem the tide of the world's new thought; had fused the iron logic of that system with a rapture of mystic communion; and had initiated a New England theology as a new chapter in the history of doctrine.

EDWARDS, JONATHAN (*b. Northampton, Mass., 1745; d. Schenectady, N.Y., 1801*), Congregational clergyman, theologian. Son of Jonathan Edwards (1703–58). Graduated Princeton, 1765. After long pastorate in New Haven, Conn., served as president, Union College, 1799–1801. His writings carried his father's doctrine a step further toward "progressive orthodoxy."

EDWARDS, JULIAN (*b. Manchester, England, 1855; d. 1910*), composer. Came to America, 1888. Best known for light operas and for the song "My Own United States."

EDWARDS, JUSTIN (*b. Westhampton, Mass., 1787; d. Bath Alum Springs, Va., 1853*), Congregational clergyman. Writer of pamphlets and tracts on temperance; president, Andover Theological Seminary, 1836–42.

EDWARDS, MORGAN (*b. Trevethin Parish, Monmouthshire, England, 1722; d. Pencader, Del., 1795*), pastor of Philadelphia Baptist Church, 1761–71. Collected and published manuscripts relating to American Baptist history.

EDWARDS, NINIAN (*b. Montgomery Co., Md., 1775; d. Belleville, Ill., 1833*), lawyer. Removed to Kentucky, 1795. Governor of Illinois Territory, 1809–18; U.S. senator from state of Illinois, 1818–24; governor of Illinois, 1826–30. Lacking in judgment, he lost early prestige as spokesman for interests of settlers.

EDWARDS, NINIAN WIRT (*b. Frankfort, Ky., 1809; d. 1889*), lawyer, merchant. Son of Ninian Edwards. Brother-in-law of Mary Todd Lincoln. First Illinois superintendent of public in-

struction, 1854–57, he also served in both houses of the legislature.

EDWARDS, OLIVER (*b. Springfield, Mass., 1835; d. 1904*), Union brigadier general, businessman, inventor. Removed to Warsaw, Ill., 1856. Conspicuous for bravery at Spotsylvania and Winchester.

EDWARDS, PIERPONT (*b. Northampton, Mass., 1750; d. 1826*), lawyer, politician. Son of Jonathan Edwards (1703–58). Directed drafting of liberal 1818 Connecticut Constitution; federal district judge in Connecticut, 1806–26.

EDWARDS, RICHARD STANISLAUS (*b. Philadelphia, Pa., 1885; d. Oakland, Calif., 1956*), naval officer. Graduated from the U.S. Naval Academy (1907). One of the outstanding flag officers of the navy during World War II. Edwards held routine assignments, including commander of Submarine Squadron Six in San Diego (1935–37), and, in 1940 with the rank of rear admiral, commander of the Submarine Patrol Force in New London. Brought to Washington by Admiral Ernest J. King in 1941 as deputy chief of staff, Edwards was promoted to vice admiral and chief of King's staff in 1942. In 1944, he became deputy commander in chief. In 1945 he was promoted to admiral. Edwards made invaluable contributions to the war effort. He retired in 1947.

EDWARDS, TALMADGE (*b. England, 1747; d. Johnstown, N.Y., 1821*), tanner. Originated American glove and mitten industry and the "oil-tan" method for preparing buckskin.

EDWARDS, WELDON NATHANIEL (*b. Northampton Co., N.C., 1788; d. 1873*), planter. Congressman, Democrat, from North Carolina, 1815–27. Thereafter prominent in the state legislature as a conservative, he presided over the first secession meeting at Goldsboro, March 1861.

EDWARDS, WILLIAM (*b. Elizabethtown, N.J., 1770; d. Brooklyn, N.Y., 1851*), tanner, inventor. Grandson of Jonathan Edwards (1703–58). Founder of the hide and leather industry in the United States. Persevering in the face of repeated business failures, he greatly improved the tanning process through inventions, such as rollers for preparing leather, a hide mill for softening dry leather, and an improved sole-leather tanning process.

EDWARDS, WILLIAM HENRY (*b. Hunter, N.Y., 1822; d. 1909*), entomologist, lawyer, businessman. Grandson of William Edwards. Author of *Voyage up the Amazon* (1847) and a classic study, *The Butterflies of North America* (1868–97).

EDWIN, DAVID (*b. Bath, England, 1776; d. Philadelphia, Pa., 1841*), stipple engraver. Came to America, 1797. Worked with Edward Savage and Gilbert Stuart, and for Philadelphia magazines; reputed to be America's "first good engraver of the human countenance."

EELLS, DAN PARMELEE (*b. Westmoreland, N.Y., 1825; d. Cleveland, Ohio, 1903*), banker, capitalist. President, Commercial National Bank of Cleveland, 1868–97.

EGAN, MAURICE FRANCIS (*b. Philadelphia, Pa., 1852; d. Brooklyn, N.Y., 1924*), journalist, diplomat. Graduated La Salle College, Philadelphia, 1873. Professor at Notre Dame and Catholic universities; was "unofficial adviser" to Presidents McKinley and T. Roosevelt. Served as minister to Denmark, 1907–18.

EGAN, MICHAEL (*b. Ireland[?], 1761; d. Philadelphia, Pa., 1814*), Roman Catholic clergyman. A learned Franciscan, his brief term as first bishop of Philadelphia (1810–14) was marred by internal strife and a contest for authority with the trustees of the parishes.

EGAN, PATRICK (*b. Ballymahon, Ireland, 1841; d. New York, N.Y., 1919*), politician, diplomat. A political refugee to America in 1883, he settled in Lincoln, Nebr., and engaged in the grain and milling business. A Republican and friend of James G. Blaine, he served ably as U.S. minister to Chile.

EGGLESTON, EDWARD (*b. Vevay, Ind., 1837; d. Joshua's Rock, Lake George, N.Y., 1902*), clergyman, novelist, historian. Methodist pastor and Bible agent in Indiana and Minnesota, 1856–66; removed to Evanston, Ill., and became a journalist. Resident in Brooklyn, N.Y., 1870–79, where he was pastor of nonsectarian Church of Christian Endeavor, 1874–79, he won fame for a series of popular novels which had an important influence in turning American fiction toward realism. These included *The Hoosier Schoolmaster* (1871); *The Circuit Rider* (1874); *Roxy* (1878); and *The Graysons* (1888). Shifting his interest to history, he planned to write a history of life in the United States but completed only two volumes: *The Beginners of a Nation* (1896) and *The Transit of Civilization* (1901). The emphasis in these books on cultural development helped advance this then-neglected view of the historian's function.

EGGLESTON, GEORGE CARY (*b. Vevay, Ind., 1839; d. New York, N.Y., 1911*), lawyer, Confederate soldier, journalist. Brother of Edward Eggleston. *Post* 1870, worked on various New York newspapers as editor, including the *Evening Post*, the *Commercial Advertiser*, and the *World*. Author of stories for boys, novels of antebellum Virginia life, *The History of the Confederate War* (1910), and several volumes of recollections.

EGLE, WILLIAM HENRY (*b. Lancaster Co., Pa., 1830; d. 1901*), Pennsylvania historian, physician. Edited second and third series of *Pennsylvania Archives*; developed state library as a research center.

EGLESTON, THOMAS (*b. New York, N.Y., 1832; d. 1900*), mineralogist. Founded School of Mines, Columbia University, 1864; preserved New York's Washington Square for recreational purposes; author of *The Metallurgy of Silver, Gold and Mercury in the U.S.* (1887–90).

EHNINGER, JOHN WHETTEN (*b. New York, N.Y., 1827; d. Saratoga Springs, N.Y., 1889*), genre painter, illustrator. Studied in Düsseldorf and Paris under Leutze and Couture.

EHRLICH, ARNOLD BOGUMIL (*b. Wlodawa, Polish Russia, 1848; d. 1919*), Bible exegete, Hebrew scholar. Came to America, 1878. His works, published in Germany, are the most comprehensive and valuable contributions to Old Testament scholarship made in America.

EICHBERG, JULIUS (*b. Düsseldorf, Germany, 1824; d. 1893*), violinist, teacher, composer. Came to America, 1857. Founded Boston Conservatory of Music; wrote *The Doctor of Alcantara* (1862) and other light operas.

EICHELBERGER, ROBERT LAWRENCE (*b. Urbana, Ohio, 1886; d. Asheville, N.C., 1961*), army officer. Graduated from the U.S. Military Academy in 1909. Served with the Eighth Division in Siberia in 1918, to protect American interests during the Russian Civil War. Named superintendent of West Point in 1940. During World War II, commanded the I Corps in New Guinea, 1942–43. Commanded the Eighth Army in New Guinea, participating in several amphibious operations in the Philippines. His retirement in 1948 was followed by a belated promotion to the rank of general in 1954.

EICHOLTZ, JACOB (*b. Lancaster, Pa., 1776; d. 1842*), painter. Produced portraits in the style of Sully and Stuart, also landscapes and historical groups.

EICKEMEYER, RUDOLF (*b. Altenbamberg, Germany, 1831; d. 1895*), inventor, manufacturer. Came to America, 1850. Invented and patented hat-making machinery which gradually revolutionized the hat-making industry throughout the world. Later he carried out experiments in electricity and produced improved armatures and generators and the first direct-connected railway motor. In 1892 his business was consolidated with the General Electric Co. He was the discoverer and first employer of Charles P. Steinmetz.

EIDLITZ, CYRUS LAZELLE WARNER (*b. New York, N.Y., 1853; d. 1921*), architect. Son of Leopold Eidlitz. Designed many important buildings, among them Dearborn Station, Chicago, the Buffalo, N.Y., Library, and the *New York Times* Building, Times Square.

EIDLITZ, LEOPOLD (*b. Prague, Bohemia, 1823; d. 1908*), architect. Came to America, 1843. Designed many churches and other buildings in the Gothic style, his most successful being Christ Church, St. Louis, Mo.; redesigned state capitol at Albany, N.Y.

EIELSEN, ELLING (*b. Vossestranden, Norway, 1804; d. Chicago, Ill., 1883*), Norwegian lay preacher. Came to America, 1839. Preached on the Midwestern frontier; founded Norwegian Evangelical Lutheran Church of North America, 1846.

EIGENMANN, CARL H. (*b. Flehingen, Germany, 1863; d. California, 1927*), ichthyologist, educator. Came to America, 1877. Graduated Indiana University, 1886; Ph.D., 1889. Taught at Indiana University; founded its graduate school and served as dean. Specialized in fishes of South America. Author of *Cave Vertebrates of America* (1909).

EILERS, FREDERIC ANTON (*b. Laufenselden, Germany, 1839; d. 1917*), metallurgist, leader in American lead-silver smelting. Came to America, 1859. Made theoretical as well as mechanical advances in western smelting operations and furnace design.

EILSHEMIUS, LOUIS MICHEL (*b. North Arlington, N.J., 1864; d. New York, N.Y., 1941*), painter. Educated in private schools in New York City and Geneva, Switzerland, and at the Handelschule in Dresden; studied agriculture for two years at Cornell University. Attended Art Students League, New York City, 1884–86, and was influenced by Robert C. Minor; attended Académie Julian, Paris, 1886–88, under Bouguereau, but was strongly attracted to Corot's work. When early showings of his work and publication of his verse and fiction met with public apathy, he became increasingly frustrated and eccentric; in 1921, he gave up painting. About 1932, after he was permanently paralyzed by an auto accident, his work was suddenly "discovered" as foreshadowing some of the later avant-garde movements in American art. His melodramatically fierce canvases, poetic landscapes, and lyrical nudes were shown in more than 25 one-man exhibitions between 1932 and 1941, receiving wide publicity and very gratifying sales.

EIMBECK, WILLIAM (*b. Brunswick, Germany, 1841; d. Washington, D.C., 1909*), geodetic engineer. Came to America, 1857. Originated duplex base apparatus for triangulation; carried out triangulation of the thirty-ninth parallel, 1878–96; engineer, U.S. Coast Survey, 1871–1906.

EINHORN, DAVID (*b. Dispeck, Germany, 1809; d. New York, N.Y., 1879*), rabbi. Came to America, 1855; served congregations in Baltimore, Philadelphia, and New York. The leading theologian of the Reform Judaism of his generation in America.

EINSTEIN, ALBERT (*b. Ulm, Germany, 1879; d. Princeton, N.J., 1955*), theoretical physicist. Studied at the Zurich Eidgenössische Technische Hochschule; Ph.D., University of Zurich (1909). Unable to obtain a post at a university after he finished his studies, Einstein worked at the Swiss Patent Office in Bern (1902). In 1905, he published a series of papers in *Annalen der Physik*, and their combined influence on physics surpassed anything since the time of Newton.

The first, "On a Heuristic Viewpoint Concerning the Production and Transformation of Light," in which Einstein applied the ideas of statistical thermodynamics to light radiation in a cavity, concluded that light energy must be concentrated in the form of particles he called light quanta. The concept of light quanta was revolutionary, and Einstein was awarded the Nobel Prize in Physics for 1921.

In the second paper, "On the Movement of Small Particles Suspended in a Stationary Liquid Demanded by the Molecular-Kinetic Theory of Heat," Einstein applied statistical thermodynamics to the motion of a small object, suspended in a fluid, that is constantly being struck by the moving molecules in the fluid. He showed that the object should undergo a kind of random motion through the fluid, the magnitude of which depends on the number of molecules in the fluid. He thus obtained direct evidence for the existence of molecules in atoms.

Einstein's major work of 1905, "On the Electrodynamics of Moving Bodies," contained what has become known as the special theory of relativity. This theory describes the relationship between the measurements of physical quantities made by two observers moving at constant speed with respect to each other. Einstein believed that all the laws of physics were equally valid for any two such observers, the principle of relativity. The other basis for his theory is that the speed of light will have the same value for all observers in uniform relative motion.

Einstein showed that the principle of relativity required certain changes in the prevailing laws of physics. One such change stated that as its velocity increases, the mass of a body would increase in such a way that it would be impossible to accelerate any object from rest up to the speed of light. This special relativity theory has become a cornerstone of twentieth-century physics, which all subsequent work in physics has had to incorporate or build upon.

Another paper in 1905, "Does the Inertia of a Body Depend Upon its Energy Content?," drew an additional conclusion from the principle of relativity: When the energy content of a body changes, its mass must also change. This conclusion is a special case of the result denoted by the now famous equation $E = mc^2$, which Einstein stated in 1907.

Einstein was given professorships at the University of Zurich (1909), the German University in Prague (1911), and from 1914 to 1933, he was director of scientific research at the Kaiser Wilhelm Institute for physics in Berlin. While there, he completed work on the general theory of relativity, which described the relation between measurements by two observers with any relative motion whatsoever, rather than the uniform relative motion of a special theory. At the same time, it provides a new description of gravitation, in terms of the geometrical properties of space and time. His prediction that a light beam passing near the sun would be deflected from a straight line by a definite amount was tested and verified during a solar eclipse in 1919. The ensuing publicity made Einstein the paragon of the theoretical physicist. This role was uncomfortable for him, since it diverted him from scientific work; but it did aid him in two causes—pacifism and Zionism.

A Jew, Einstein remained in the U.S., where he was visiting when Hitler came to power. He became a member of the Institute for Advanced Study at Princeton where he worked until his death.

At Princeton he worked unsuccessfully on his unified field theory, which he hoped would link electromagnetism and gravity. He ultimately rejected the final version of the quantum theory, because it replaced strictly deterministic predictions of the future with probabilistic ones. In the years following World War II he became active in promoting world peace and in warning of the dangers of nuclear war.

EISENHART, LUTHER PFAHLER (*b. York, Pa., 1876; d. Princeton, N.J., 1965*), mathematician. Studied at Gettysburg College and Johns Hopkins (Ph.D., 1900). Taught at Princeton, 1900–45; named chairman of the department of mathematics in 1929. An expositor and developer of modern differential geometry, Eisenhart wrote a series of important textbooks on the subject.

EISENHOWER, DWIGHT DAVID (*b. Denison, Tex., 1890; d. Washington, D.C., 1969*), army officer and president of the United States. Graduated from West Point in 1915; attended the Command and General Staff School at Fort Leavenworth, Kans. (1925–26), and the Army War College (1927–28). Married Mamie Doud in 1916. Served in the Panama Canal Zone (1922–24) and in Washington, D.C. (1930–35) in the office of the assistant secretary of war and then of Chief of Staff Douglas MacArthur. Served as chief of staff under General MacArthur in the Philippines, 1936–40. Became a full colonel in 1941. Named chief of staff of the Third Army; promoted to brigadier general after figuring prominently in peacetime maneuvers. Called to Washington after the Japanese attack on Pearl Harbor and named to the War Plans Division. Worked with Chief of Staff General George C. Marshall to elaborate the details of the "Europe first" strategy. Named commander of American and Allied forces in Europe in 1942, with the rank of lieutenant general. Promoted to full general upon the successful invasion of North Africa in November 1942, and the Allied attack on Sicily and invasion of Italy. Named supreme commander of the Allied Expeditionary Force in Europe in 1943. Named general of the army in 1945. Succeeded General George C. Marshall as chief of staff of the U.S. Army (1945–48). President of Columbia University (1948–52). Named supreme commander of the armed forces of the North Atlantic Treaty Organization (NATO) in 1950. President of the United States, 1953–61.

An extraordinary technician in the two areas in which he chose to excel, Eisenhower's military life strongly influenced his political career: even in the White House he was known as "the General." His leadership in Europe during World War II secured for him the presidency in 1953.

Eisenhower's greatest military achievement, and one of the most notable in the history of American arms, was his command of Operation Overlord, the Allied invasion across the English Channel in 1944. Following the invasion, the military tactics that would lead to an Allied victory in Europe came up against steady criticism, among them Eisenhower's decision to move into Germany on a broad front rather than make a single thrust toward Berlin. On 16 December 1944, a heavy concentration of German troops broke through the Western front in the Battle of the Bulge. Eisenhower brought the German breakthrough under control in ten days, though many critics described the battle as a near catastrophe, for which he was directly responsible. He also came under fire for failing to take Berlin during the war's last days. He insisted that Berlin was not a military target, and refused to risk American lives for a city that lay in the future Soviet zone.

As president, Eisenhower embraced a domestic policy of "dynamic conservatism," seeking to replace conservative leaders in the House and Senate with moderates. He waged a subtle campaign to marshall support against Senator Joseph R. McCarthy. In fiscal matters he was staunchly conservative. He feared that government deficits would cause inflation, and drastically reduced the military budget after the Korean War. He is also noted for bringing in federal troops to enforce school integration in Little Rock, Ark., in 1957.

His foreign policy often proved contentious. Initiatives included a cease-fire in Korea in 1953, and a summit conference in Geneva in 1955 with the new post-Stalin leadership. The promise of world peace that had come to be known as "the spirit of Geneva" gave way to crisis after crisis in Soviet-American relations: the Suez affair of 1956, the Lebanon crisis of 1958, Khrushchev's showdown over Berlin in 1958, and the U-2 incident in 1960. In 1957 the Soviets launched *Sputnik* and directly challenged American scientific prowess. Critics maintained that Eisenhower's policy turned all large international disputes into nuclear threats. Unknown to his critics at the time, he took a firm position within his administration against the actual use of nuclear weapons, and came to fear a powerful lobby that he saw as aiding and abetting the arms race with the Soviet Union. In his farewell address in 1966 he warned against "the acquisition of unwarranted influence, whether sought or unsought, by the military-industrial complex."

In 1955 Eisenhower suffered a massive heart attack; successive ailments in 1956 and 1957 did not prevent his reelection for a second term. Though his accomplishments as president are not easy to assess, early appraisals that portrayed him as a lazy man (perhaps buttressed by his much-photographed interest in golf) and as a political naif, have given way to the opinion that sees him as a man who worked hard and efficiently at anything he did, transforming the Republican party from a collection of "outs" into a party that was close to the center of American opinion. Eisenhower wrote of his World War II experiences in *Crusade in Europe* (1948), and of the presidency in *Mandate for Change* (1963) and *Waging Peace* (1965).

EISLER, GERHART (*b. Leipzig, Germany, 1897; d. Yerevan, Armenia, 1968*), Soviet espionage agent and East German Communist party official. Active in Communist politics in Weimar Germany during the 1920's, in China in the early 1930's, and in the U.S. during the 1930's and 1940's. Entered the U.S. in 1933 using a fraudulent passport. As the reputed top liaison between the Comintern and the U.S. Communist party, his main missions were to infiltrate labor unions and liberal organizations and to form front organizations for the party. He served as "political commissar" (1936–41) to antifascist Germans fighting in the Spanish Civil War, and led underground antifascist movements in Spain, Czechoslovakia, Austria, and Switzerland. Returned to the U.S. in 1941, and in 1947 was denounced by his sister, the ex-Communist activist Ruth Fischer, as "a most dangerous terrorist." Convicted for contempt of Congress and passport fraud, Eisler jumped bail and escaped to East Germany in 1949, where he became a professor at the University of Leipzig, a leading Communist propagandist, and a member of East Germany's Central Committee.

EKLUND, CARL ROBERT (*b. Tomahawk, Wis., 1909; d. Philadelphia, Pa., 1962*), ornithologist and Antarctic explorer. Studied at Carleton College and the University of Maryland (Ph.D., 1959). As a scientist of the U.S. Antarctic Service under Admiral Byrd, Eklund participated in one of the most important land treks in Antarctic history. Made important contributions to the study of wildlife in regions of bitter cold.

ELBERT, SAMUEL (*b. Prince William Parish, S.C., 1740; d. Savannah, Ga., 1788*), Revolutionary soldier, merchant. Removed to Georgia in early youth. Governor of Georgia, 1785.

ELDER, SAMUEL JAMES (*b. Hope, R.I., 1850; d. 1918*), lawyer, authority on copyright.

ELDER, SUSAN BLANCHARD (*b. Fort Jessup, La., 1835; d. Cincinnati, Ohio, 1923*), author. In many biographies, stories, poems, and dramas expressed her devotion to the South and the Catholic church.

ELDER, WILLIAM (*b. Somerset, Pa., 1806; d. Washington, D.C., 1885*), physician, writer. Contributed to Free-Soil papers; in *Questions of the Day: Economic and Social* (1871), popularized the economic theories of Henry C. Carey.

ELDER, WILLIAM HENRY (*b. Baltimore, Md., 1819; d. Cincinnati, Ohio, 1904*), Roman Catholic clergyman. Ordained Rome, 1846. Served as professor of theology, Mount St. Mary's, Emmitsburg, Md., 1846–57. Consecrated bishop of Natchez, 1857; archbishop of Cincinnati, 1883.

ELDRIDGE, SHALOR WINCHELL (*b. West Springfield, Mass., 1816; d. Lawrence, Kans., 1899*), Kansas leader, Union soldier, businessman.

ELIOT, CHARLES (*b. Cambridge, Mass., 1859; d. 1897*), landscape architect, author. Son of Charles W. Eliot. Active in establishing Boston Metropolitan Park Commission, 1892; associated with Frederick Law Olmsted, under whom he had studied.

ELIOT, CHARLES WILLIAM (*b. Boston, Mass., 1834; d. Northeast Harbor, Maine, 1926*), educational leader. Son of Samuel A. Eliot. Graduated Harvard, 1853; taught there as tutor in mathematics and as assistant professor of mathematics and chemistry, 1854–63. Introduced first written examinations; emphasized laboratory work and elective as well as compulsory instruction. After a trip to Europe during which he made a firsthand study of European methods of education, he returned in 1865 as professor of chemistry at Massachusetts Institute of Technology. His concept of education as embodied in two articles in the *Atlantic Monthly*, 1869, won him the favorable notice of the Harvard Corporation and he was chosen president of Harvard, 1869.

His 40-year tenure transformed the college into a modern university. Primarily an administrator rather than a scholar or teacher, Eliot concentrated all undergraduate studies in the college, and around it grouped the professional schools and research centers. His policy was to give the university coherence by drawing its parts into organic relationship so that they might then be given a larger autonomy under their own deans and faculties. The bachelor's degree was made prerequisite for all graduate and professional studies. He encouraged the teaching of private classes for women by Harvard faculty members, a venture which in 1894 resulted in the founding of Radcliffe College. Eliot greatly improved the quality of the faculty, recruiting good men from all over the United States and from abroad; he also introduced the system of sabbatical leaves and French and German exchange professorships, raised salaries, and inaugurated retirement allowances for professors.

Eliot's most radical reform in the college was the development of the "elective system." Eliot made it almost fully effective by the year 1894. One of Eliot's projects, the three-year college course, encountered difficulties and was not formally adopted. His interest in the elective system led Eliot to pay considerable attention to admission requirements and to the need for improving the work done in secondary and primary schools. He participated in the work of the New England Association of Colleges and Preparatory Schools and in the National Education Association, of which he became president in 1903. He also prepared the report of the "Committee of Ten" of the NEA (1892), which formulated standard programs for secondary instruction and charged the secondary schools with the task of preparing all their students for college.

Eliot's influence was exerted strongly on the graduate schools of the university. In 1872 the degrees of master of arts, doctor of science, and doctor of philosophy were established; in 1890 followed the Graduate School of Arts and Sciences, organized under the same faculty as that of the college and the scientific school. Eliot transformed the divinity school from a denominational training school for ministers into a nonsectarian institution of higher learning. But his most notable contributions were made with the reforms of the law school and the school of medicine. Under Dean C. C. Langdell, a two-year course (1872) and later (1877–78) a three-year course, with admission and graduation examinations, were required of all law students. Adoption of the "case system" was the principal reform in law-school methods of instruction. In like manner, the low standards of the medical school were raised. In 1871, a three-year course, laboratory work, and written examinations were inaugurated, and clinical instruction and internships were gradually made available at the Boston hospitals. By 1892, a four-year course was obligatory.

After retirement from the presidency in 1909, Eliot continued his active public career in the cause of American education as an overseer of Harvard College (1910–16), as a member of the General Education Board, and as a trustee of the Rockefeller Foundation and of the Carnegie Foundation for the Advancement of Teaching. In politics Eliot was independent with a leaning toward the Democratic party; in religion he was Unitarian. He held an optimistic philosophy which put a premium on individual liberty and considered the essence of democratic freedom to consist in the maintenance of social mobility so as to ensure equal opportunities for all. In his annual *Reports of the President of Harvard College* Eliot left a 40-year documentary record of the history of American education. His views on education may be found also in *Educational Reform* (1898); on politics and social issues in *American Contributions to Civilization* (1897); on religion in *The Religion of the Future* (1909), and in *The Durable Satisfactions of Life* (1910). He was also editor of the widely sold Harvard Classics, a series illustrative of his statement that anyone could acquire a liberal education by reading 15 minutes a day from great books which would fit on a "five-foot shelf."

ELIOT, JARED (*b.* Guilford, Conn., 1865; *d.* Killingworth, Conn., 1763), Congregational clergyman, physician. Grandson of John Eliot. Graduated Yale, 1706. Pastor of Killingworth (now Clinton), Conn., 1708–63; became the leading physician in New England. Discovered local black beach sand to be a valuable iron ore; also developed ore beds in northwestern Connecticut. Together with Ezra Stiles, Eliot introduced silk culture into Connecticut. Author of *Essay on the Invention . . . of Making . . . Iron from Black Sea Sand* (1762) and the widely read and esteemed *Essay on Field Husbandry in New England* (1748–59). Yale College owes him its earliest bequest for the permanent endowment of the library.

ELIOT, JOHN (*b.* Widford, England, 1604; *d.* Roxbury, Mass., 1690), missionary to the Indians. A graduate of Cambridge University and influenced by Thomas Hooker, Eliot came to Massachusetts in 1631 and served as pastor and teacher in Roxbury. He preached first to the Indians in 1646. Recognizing the desire of the Indians to live by themselves, he founded the first town of native Christians at Natick, 1651; by 1674, there were 14 such self-governing communities, with a population of about 1,100. King Philip's War reduced the number of these towns to 4, and the "praying Indians" gradually dwindled away. Eliot's celebrated translation of the Bible into the Indian language, the first Bible printed in North America, was published in 1661 (New Testament) and 1663 (Old Testament). His book *The Christian Commonwealth* (1659) was suppressed by the Massachusetts government for its republican sentiments.

ELIOT, SAMUEL (*b.* Boston, Mass., 1821; *d.* Beverly Farms, Mass., 1898), historian, educator, philanthropist. President, Trinity College, Hartford, Conn., 1860–64. Devoted rest of life to educational, religious, and eleemosynary institutions in Boston.

ELIOT, SAMUEL ATKINS (*b.* Boston, Mass., 1798; *d.* Cambridge, Mass., 1862), statesman, man of letters. Father of Charles W. Eliot. Mayor of Boston, 1837–39; served in legislature and briefly in Congress, where he supported Compromise of 1850. Promoted Boston musical life.

ELIOT, T(HOMAS) S(TEARNS) (*b.* St. Louis, Mo., 1888; *d.* London, England, 1965), poet. Studied at Smith Academy, the preparatory department of Washington University (which had been founded by his grandfather), and Harvard. A resident of London from 1914, Eliot became a British citizen in 1927.

Eliot established his early literary reputation in London while holding down a full-time job at Lloyds Bank (1917–25). His collaborative association with Ezra Pound began in 1914. Eliot's essays in the *Egoist*, of which he became assistant editor in 1917, along with the publication of his first volume of poetry, *Prufrock and Other Observations* (1917), brought him to the attention of the Bloomsbury Group. *Poems* (1919) and *Ara Vos Prec* (1920) developed Eliot's early themes of erotic failure and spiritual longing. In 1922 he published a poem that revolutionized English literature: In its technical innovation and expression of postwar disillusionment, "The Waste Land" has become a central document of literary modernism.

With the publication of *The Sacred Wood* (1920) Eliot also became influential as a critic. His essays advanced an "impersonal" theory of poetry; he insisted that contemporary verse should reflect a "historic sense" of the entire Western literary tradition. Terms like "objective correlative" and "dissociation of sensibility" became central to the development of the New Criticism.

Eliot's editorship of the *Criterion* (1922–39) and his long association with the publishing house of Faber and Faber (from 1925) as a director distinguished him as influential in the publication of much of the most important literature of the period.

With his conversion to Anglo-Catholicism in 1927, his critical and creative focus underwent a steady evolution toward religious and social affairs. Poems collected in *Ash Wednesday* (1930) portray the struggle of the new Christian to accept the consequences of religious belief and discipline. A series of verse plays, *The Rock* (1934), *Murder in the Cathedral* (1935), and *The Family Reunion* (1939), demonstrates his efforts to share his Christian vision with a wide, largely secular audience. In lectures published as *The Idea of a Christian Society* (1939) he attacked secular liberalism and outlined a society based on religious principles.

Eliot returned to nondramatic poetry in 1943 with the publication of *Four Quartets*. Considered by many to be his greatest achievement, the poems, which can be read independently or taken as a group, incorporate philosophical, religious, autobiographical, and critical (in their discussion of poetry itself) themes.

Eliot's later criticism is marked by a mellowing of tone. In *On Poetry and Poets* (1957), a collection of essays from the late 1940's and early 1950's, he abandoned the strident moralizing characteristic of the earlier work. Later verse plays include *The Cocktail Party* (1949) and *The Elder Statesman* (1958). Eliot was awarded the Nobel Prize for literature in 1948.

ELIOT, WILLIAM GREENLEAF (*b.* New Bedford, Mass., 1811; *d.* Pass Christian, Miss., 1887), Congregational clergyman. Founded Washington University, St. Louis, Mo.

ELKIN, WILLIAM LEWIS (*b.* New Orleans, La., 1855; *d.* New Haven, Conn., 1933), astronomer. Studied at Stuttgart, Germany; Ph.D., University of Strassburg, 1880. Director of Yale

Observatory, 1896–1910; increased substantially the fund of information regarding stellar distances.

ELKINS, STEPHEN BENTON (*b. Perry Co., Ohio, 1841; d. 1911*), lawyer. Union soldier, industrialist. Raised in Westport, Mo.; graduated University of Missouri, 1860. Began law practice in New Mexico, 1864; was elected to territorial legislature and appointed successively territorial district attorney, attorney general, and U.S. district attorney. Elected Republican delegate to Congress, 1872 and 1874–77. Was founder and president of the Sante Fe First National Bank, and held considerable Colorado land and coal properties. *Post* 1890, he was a resident of West Virginia, where he had many industrial interests. Elkins entered national politics as a supporter of James G. Blaine. He served as U.S. secretary of war, 1891–95, and as Republican senator from West Virginia, 1895–1911. As head of the Interstate Commerce Committee he was author of the Antirebate Act of 1903 and coauthor of the Mann-Elkins Act of 1910.

ELKINS, WILLIAM LUKENS (*b. near Wheeling, W.Va., 1832; d. Philadelphia, Pa., 1903*), oil promoter, capitalist. Refined first gasoline; organized gas and street railway companies in Philadelphia and other cities.

ELLERY, FRANK (*b. Newport, R.I., 1794; d. Castleton, Vt., 1871*), naval officer. Grandson of William Ellery.

ELLERY, WILLIAM (*b. Newport, R.I., 1727; d. Newport, 1820*), lawyer, politician, signer of the Declaration of Independence from Rhode Island. Grandfather of Frank Ellery, W. E. Channing (1780–1842), and R. H. Dana. An expert committeeman on commercial and naval affairs as a member of Congress, 1776–86 (failed of election 1780 and 1782). Collector of customs at Newport, 1790–1820.

ELLET, CHARLES (*b. Penn's Manor, Pa., 1810; d. Cairo, Ill., 1862*), civil engineer. Designed and built innovative suspension bridges over the Schuylkill at Fairmount (1842) and over the Ohio at Wheeling (1849). Urged in *The Mississippi and Ohio Rivers* (1853) flood and navigation control of western rivers through dams and reservoirs. In 1854 built the Virginia Central track across the Blue Ridge. In *Coast and Harbour Defences* (1855), proposed construction of "ram-boats"; in 1862 led a fleet of nine ram-boats down the Mississippi and received surrender of Memphis. During this action he was mortally wounded.

ELLET, ELIZABETH FRIES LUMMIS (*b. Sodus Point, N.Y., 1818; d. New York, N.Y., 1877*). Author of, among other works, *Domestic History of the American Revolution* (1850) and *Queens of American Society* (1867). Translator and critic of French, German, and Italian literature.

ELLICOTT, ANDREW (*b. Bucks County, Pa., 1754; d. West Point, N.Y., 1820*), Revolutionary soldier, surveyor, mathematician. In 1784, aided in completing Pennsylvania-Maryland boundary begun by Mason and Dixon; also served on survey of western and northern Pennsylvania boundary and of islands in the Ohio and Allegheny. Determined southwestern boundary of New York, 1789; from 1791 to 1793 surveyed what was to become the District of Columbia. His revised plan of the "Federal City" (1792) was a redrawn version of L'Enfant's original design. After surveying in Pennsylvania and Georgia and on the United States–Florida frontier, Ellicott served as professor of mathematics at West Point, 1813–20.

ELLICOTT, JOSEPH (*b. Bucks Co., Pa., 1760; d. 1826*), engineer, land agent. Brother and associate of Andrew Ellicott. Served as the Holland Land Co. agent in western New York, 1800–21. Founded Buffalo, N.Y.

ELLIOT, DANIEL GIRAUD (*b. New York, N.Y., 1835; d. 1915*), zoologist. Founded American Ornithologists' Union; author of *Review of the Primates* (1912).

ELLIOT, JAMES (*b. Gloucester, Mass., 1775; d. 1839*), politician, lawyer, soldier. Federalist congressman from Vermont, 1803–09. Author of *Poetical and Miscellaneous Works* (1798).

ELLIOT, JONATHAN (*b. near Carlisle, England, 1784; d. 1846*), editor, publicist. Moved to America, 1802. Produced the *Gazette*, first daily evening paper in Washington, D.C., 1814. Best known as publisher of *Debates . . . on the Adoption of the Federal Constitution* (1827–30, 1845) and *Diplomatic Code of the United States* (1827, 1834).

ELLIOTT, AARON MARSHALL (*b. Wilmington, N.C., 1844; d. 1910*), philologist. A pioneer in scientific study of modern languages and literatures as professor of Romance languages at Johns Hopkins University. Established the Modern Language Association, 1883.

ELLIOTT, BENJAMIN (*b. Charleston, S.C., 1787; d. Charleston, 1836*), lawyer. Nephew of Charles Pinckney; law partner of Robert Y. Hayne. Collaborated in a pioneer defense of slavery, *A Refutation of the Calumnies, etc.* (1822), with E. C. Holland.

ELLIOTT, CHARLES (*b. Co. Donegal, Ireland, 1792; d. Mt. Pleasant, Iowa, 1869*), Methodist clergyman, historian.

ELLIOTT, CHARLES BURKE (*b. Morgan Co., Ohio, 1861; d. 1935*), lawyer, jurist, writer. Associate justice, supreme court of the Philippines, 1909; member of Philippine Commission, 1910–12.

ELLIOTT, CHARLES LORING (*b. Scipio, N.Y., 1812; d. Albany, N.Y., 1868*), painter. His portraits of many famous 19th-century Americans are marked by firm drawing, clean color, and a natural likeness.

ELLIOTT, JESSE DUNCAN (*b. Hagerstown, Md., 1782; d. Philadelphia, Pa., 1845*), naval officer. As commander of *Niagara* during the battle of Lake Erie, 1813, he was accused of failure to come to the aid of Commodore Perry's flagship, and a 30-year controversy ensued. James Fenimore Cooper ably defended Elliott, but Admiral Mahan reached conclusions favorable to Perry. Elliott subsequently held many commands and died as commandant of the Philadelphia navy yard.

ELLIOTT, JOHN (*b. Lincolnshire, England, 1858; d. Charleston, S.C., 1925*), painter. Best known for murals in Boston Public Library and Washington, D.C., National Museum, and for his distinguished portraits.

ELLIOTT, JOHN LOVEJOY (*b. Princeton, Ill., 1868; d. New York, N.Y., 1942*), social worker. Ethical Culture leader. Influenced in youth by Robert Ingersoll and, at Cornell University (from which he graduated, 1892), by Felix Adler. Ph.D., philosophy, University of Halle, 1894. Became Adler's assistant in New York City as teacher, lecturer, and organizer for the Ethical Culture Society. In 1895, he founded one of the early settlement houses, the Hudson Guild, on New York City's West Side "to develop the latent social power" of its members; he continued its successful management while pursuing his duties at the Ethical Culture Society, of which he became senior leader in 1933. A consistent sponsor of reform movements, he was a founder of the American Civil Liberties Union.

ELLIOTT, MAXINE (*b. Rockland, Maine, 1871; d. near Cannes, France, 1940*), actress. Changed name from Jessie Carolyn Dermot. A famous beauty and an astute businesswoman, she starred in drawing-room comedies.

ELLIOTT, SARAH BARNWELL (*b. Georgia, 1848; d. Sewanee, Tenn., 1928*), author, suffragist leader. Shares with Charles Egbert Craddock credit for introducing realistic southern mountaineer characters into literature.

ELLIOTT, STEPHEN (*b. Beaufort, S.C., 1771; d. 1830*), botanist, banker, U.S. senator. Cofounder of the *Southern Review,* 1828; author of *Sketch of the Botany of South Carolina and Georgia* (1821–24).

ELLIOTT, WALTER HACKETT ROBERT (*b. Detroit, Mich., 1842; d. Washington, D.C., 1928*), lawyer, Union soldier, Roman Catholic priest of the Paulist Congregation. Cofounder, Apostolic Mission House at Catholic University, Washington, D.C.; was a celebrated missionary. Author of *Life of Father Hecker* (1891) and other works.

ELLIOTT, WASHINGTON LAFAYETTE (*b. Carlisle, Pa., 1825; d. San Francisco, Calif., 1888*), soldier. Son of Jesse D. Elliott. Served in Mexico, on western frontier, and rose to Union major general of cavalry during Civil War.

ELLIOTT, WILLIAM (*b. Beaufort, S.C., 1788; d. Charleston, S.C., 1863*), planter. Author of *Carolina Sports by Land and Water* (1846) and *Letters of Agricola* (1852).

ELLIS, CALVIN (*b. Boston, Mass. 1826; d. 1883*), physician. Graduated Harvard, 1846; M.D., Harvard Medical, 1849. As dean of Harvard Medical School, *post* 1869, he carried out the reform program of Charles W. Eliot, and made important contributions to scientific medical diagnosis.

ELLIS, CARLETON (*b. Keene, N.H., 1876; d. Miami Beach, Fla., 1941*), chemist, inventor. B.S., Massachusetts Institute of Technology, 1900. After achieving financial success in the invention and manufacture of paint and varnish removers, he organized a company (Ellis-Foster) in 1907 for research in industrial chemistry. With a large staff of chemists and engineers, he produced an average of more than 24 marketable inventions and processes a year. Granted 753 U.S. patents. He wrote a number of basic books on industrial chemistry.

ELLIS, EDWARD SYLVESTER (*b. Geneva, Ohio, 1840; d. Cliff Island, Maine, 1916*). Author of *Seth Jones, or the Captive of the Frontier* (1860) and other dime novels, biographies and histories under many pen names.

ELLIS, GEORGE EDWARD (*b. Boston, Mass., 1814; d. Boston, 1894*), Unitarian clergyman, historian, editor. Professor of theology at Harvard; president of Massachusetts Historical Society, 1885–94.

ELLIS, GEORGE WASHINGTON (*b. Weston, Mo., 1875; d. 1919*), lawyer, sociologist. While secretary of American legation in Liberia, 1902–10, made scientific study of West African tribes; author of *Negro Culture in West Africa* (1914) and other works marked by originality and insight.

ELLIS, HENRY (*b. Ireland, 1721; d. Naples, Italy, 1806*), hydrographer. Searched unsuccessfully for Northwest Passage; active and able royal governor of Georgia, 1757–60.

ELLIS, JOB BICKNELL (*b. near Potsdam, N.Y., 1829; d. Newfield, N.J., 1905*), botanist, mycologist. Graduated Union College, 1851. His *North American Pyrenomycetes* (1892) spread his fame among botanists throughout the world.

ELLIS, JOHN WASHINGTON (*b. Williamsburg, Ohio, 1817; d. New York, N.Y., 1910*), merchant, banker. Headed First National of Cincinnati, 1863–69, and Winslow, Lanier and Co., 1870–83.

ELLIS, JOHN WILLIS (*b. Rowan Co., N.C., 1820; d. Raleigh, N.C., 1861*), lawyer. Served in legislature and as judge of superior court. As Democratic governor of North Carolina, 1858–61, he favored secession; called for volunteers to resist Northern invasion.

ELLIS, POWHATAN (*b. Amherst Co., Va., 1790; d. Richmond, Va., 1863*), jurist, diplomat. Removed to Mississippi, 1816; served on supreme court there, 1818–25, and as U.S. senator, Democrat, 1825–32. U.S. minister to Mexico, 1839–42.

ELLIS, SETH HOCKETT (*b. Martinsville, Ohio, 1830; d. Waynesville, Ohio, 1904*), farmer, politician. Organized first Ohio Grange, 1872, and was active in the movement thereafter. Union Reform party candidate for U.S. presidency, 1900.

ELLMAKER, (EMMETT) LEE (*b. Lancaster, Pa., 1896; d. Philadelphia, 1951*), editor, publisher. Founder, in 1925, of the *Philadelphia Daily News,* and with it an empire that was to include the *Detroit Daily News,* the *New York Evening Graphic,* and the magazines *Woman's World,* *Amazing Stories,* and *Complete Detective.*

ELLSWORTH, ELMER EPHRAIM (*b. Malta, N.Y., 1837; d. Alexandria, Va., 1861*), soldier. Commanded a volunteer Zouave unit in Chicago, Ill.; entered Abraham Lincoln's office as a law clerk, 1860, and was active in the presidential campaign. In 1861, he recruited a Zouave regiment from New York volunteer firemen and was first man of note killed in Civil War.

ELLSWORTH, HENRY LEAVITT (*b. Windsor, Conn., 1791; d. Fair Haven, Conn., 1858*), lawyer, agriculturist. Son of Oliver Ellsworth. Appointed, 1832, as commissioner to superintend resettlement of Indian tribes south and west of Arkansas. As first U.S. commissioner of patents, 1835–45, Ellsworth obtained a congressional appropriation for Morse's telegraph, and made his office assume many functions of an agricultural bureau. Removing to Lafayette, Ind., he became one of the largest landowners in the West and a pioneer advocate of the use of agricultural machinery.

ELLSWORTH, HENRY WILLIAM (*b. Windsor, Conn., 1814; d. New Haven, Conn., 1864*), lawyer, diplomat. Son of Henry L. Ellsworth. Served as chargé d'affaires to Sweden and Norway, 1845–49.

ELLSWORTH, LINCOLN (*b. Chicago, Ill., 1880; d. New York, N.Y., 1951*), polar explorer, civil engineer. Ellsworth was the first man to cross both the North and South poles. In 1926, he flew over the North Pole in a dirigible and proved that there was no substantial landmass north of Alaska. In 1935, he succeeded in reaching Little America by plane; on this and subsequent voyages, he laid the foundation for later U.S. claims to over 430,000 square miles of the continent.

ELLSWORTH, OLIVER (*b. Windsor, Conn., 1745; d. 1807*), statesman, jurist. Graduated Princeton (College of New Jersey), 1766. Admitted to the bar, 1771; opened an office in Hartford, Conn., 1775. By 1780 he had become a member of the Governor's Council, and subsequently served on the state supreme court of errors, on the superior court, and as state's attorney. During the Revolution he acted as a member of Connecticut's Committee of the Pay Table, as delegate to the Continental Congress from 1777 to 1783, and as a member of the Connecticut Council of Safety. As a delegate to the Constitutional Convention, Ellsworth took a prominent part in working out the "Connecticut compromise," and ably defended the plan against the large-state delegates. He favored state rather than national payment of representatives and a three-fifths ratio in counting slaves as a basis of both taxation and representation. He opposed the abolition of the foreign slave trade.

Printed in the *Connecticut Courant* (1787–88) and widely circulated, his "Letters of a Landholder" urged ratification of the new Constitution.

Intimately familiar with organizational and administrative affairs, he enjoyed a predominant position among his colleagues as U.S. senator from Connecticut, 1789–96. He reported the first set of Senate rules, considered a plan for printing a journal, reported back from conference the first 12 amendments, framed the measure which admitted North Carolina, and devised the nonintercourse act that forced Rhode Island into the Union. He reported a bill for government of the territory south of the Ohio, drew up the first bill regulating the consular service, and vigorously defended Hamilton's plans for funding the national debt and for incorporating a bank of the United States. His most important single contribution was his draft of the bill organizing the federal judiciary. In the words of John Adams, Ellsworth was "the firmest pillar of his [Washington's] administration."

Ellsworth resigned from the Senate in 1796 to become chief justice of the United States. In 1799 he was named one of a commission to France to improve American relations with that country. He and his colleagues, W. R. Davie and William Vans Murray, were obliged to accept terms from Napoleon which conformed neither to their hopes nor to their instructions; Ellsworth felt, however, that a possible war with France had been thereby avoided. Broken in health, he resigned from his office as chief justice and, on returning to the United States in the spring of 1801, retired to his home in Windsor.

ELLSWORTH, WILLIAM WOLCOTT (*b. Windsor, Conn., 1791; d. Hartford, Conn., 1868*), lawyer. Son of Oliver Ellsworth. Congressman, Whig, from Connecticut, 1829–34; governor, 1838–42; judge of state supreme court, 1847–61.

ELMAN, HARRY ("ZIGGY") (*b. Philadelphia, Pa., 1914; d. Los Angeles, Calif., 1968*), trumpeter, composer, and bandleader. Born Harry Aaron Finkelman, Elman achieved a strong musical identity by incorporating elements of the Jewish *fralich* (wedding dance) into his work in the age of swing. Played with Benny Goodman and Tommy Dorsey, leading the Goodman band when Goodman became ill. Made a series of recordings in the late 1930's under the name of "Ziggy Elman and His Orchestra." Among the tunes associated with Elman are "Bublitchki" and "Fralich in Swing" (which became "And the Angels Sing," a hit for the Goodman band in 1939).

ELMAN, MISCHA (*b. Talnoye, Ukraine, 1891; d. New York, N.Y., 1967*), violinist. Studied at the Imperial Academy of Music in Odessa, and the St. Petersburg Conservatory of Music. Made his American debut in 1908; became a U.S. citizen in 1923. Achieved world renown for his virtuosic technique and innate musical sensitivity.

ELMAN, ROBERT (*b. Boston, Mass., 1897; d. St. Louis, Mo., 1956*), surgeon, educator. Studied at Harvard and Johns Hopkins, M.D., 1922. Surgeon and teacher at Washington University, 1926–51; chief of staff and director of surgical service at the Homer G. Phillips Hospital in St. Louis, 1951–56. A specialist in pancreatic function and disease, Elman conducted important clinical and experimental studies of intravenous feeding with the amino acids of hydrolized protein.

ELMER, EBENEZER (*b. Cedarville, N.J., 1752; d. Bridgeton, N.J., 1843*), physician, Revolutionary surgeon, New Jersey legislator.

ELMER, JONATHAN (*b. Cedarville, N.J., 1745; d. 1817*), physician, Revolutionary patriot, jurist. Brother of Ebenezer Elmer. Gave up promising medical career for politics; served in Congress, 1776–78, 1781–84, 1787–88. Elected U.S. senator, Federalist,

from New Jersey in 1789, he served until 1791. He was surrogate of Cumberland County for many years.

ELMER, LUCIUS QUINTIUS CINCINNATUS (*b. Bridgeton, N.J., 1793; d. 1883*), jurist, legislator. Son of Ebenezer Elmer. Prominent in New Jersey Assembly as independent Democrat; U.S. attorney for New Jersey, 1824–29. Later congressman and New Jersey attorney general, he was a justice of state supreme court, 1852–59, 1861, 1862–69.

ELMORE, FRANKLIN HARPER (*b. Laurens District, S.C., 1799; d. Washington, D.C., 1850*), banker. Disciple of J. C. Calhoun; served briefly as representative and as U.S. senator from South Carolina.

ELMSLIE, GEORGE GRANT (*b. Huntly, Scotland, 1871; d. Minneapolis, Minn., 1952*), architect. Immigrated to the U.S. in 1885. Unschooled in architecture, Elmslie apprenticed at J. L. Silsbee's firm (1897), where he met Frank Lloyd Wright. Joined the firm of Dankmar Adler and Louis Sullivan in 1890, became Sullivan's assistant in 1893, and served as his principal associate until 1909. Sullivan turned over his domestic commissions to Elmslie, and for a time, their work was indistinguishable. Moved to Minneapolis in 1909 and founded a firm with William G. Purcell and George Feick, Jr., returning the firm to Chicago in 1919. From 1905 to 1915, Elmslie and Purcell dominated the architecture of the Midwest. Best-known works include the Bradley bungalow at Woods Hole, Mass. (1911); the Edison Shop in Chicago (1912); and the Woodbury County Courthouse, Sioux City, Iowa (1915–17). Ignored until after World War II, Elmslie is now considered one of America's foremost architects.

ELSBERG, CHARLES ALBERT (*b. New York, N.Y., 1871; d. 1948*), neurological surgeon. B.A., College of the City of New York, 1890; M.D., College of Physicians and Surgeons, Columbia, 1893. On surgical staff of Mount Sinai Hospital, New York City, 1897–1929; attending surgeon and chief of the Department of Neurosurgery, Neurological Institute of New York, 1909–37. Professor of neurological surgery at Fordham University, New York University, and College of Physicians and Surgeons. Author of several books on his field of specialization, the diseases of the spinal cord.

ELSBERG, LOUIS (*b. Iserlohn, Prussia, 1836; d. 1885*), laryngologist. Came to America, 1849. Graduated Jefferson Medical College, 1857. Studied his specialty at Vienna and pioneered in it thereafter in New York. Author of *Laryngoscopal Surgery* (1865).

ELSON, LOUIS CHARLES (*b. Boston, Mass., 1848; d. Boston, 1920*), music critic, lecturer. Taught theory at New England Conservatory of Music; author of *History of American Music* (1904).

ELVEHJEM, CONRAD ARNOLD (*b. McFarland, Wis., 1901; d. Madison, Wis., 1962*), biochemist and educator. Received B.S. (1923) and Ph.D. (1927) from the University of Wisconsin at Madison, where he went on to teach, becoming chairman of the department of agricultural chemistry (now biochemistry) in 1944, and president of the university in 1958. Studied the role of vitamins and minerals in the treatment of nutritional deficiencies of farm animals and human beings. Contributed heavily to the understanding of folic acid in nutrition, and of the function of metabolic enzymes.

ELWELL, FRANK EDWIN (*b. Concord, Mass., 1858; d. Darien, Conn., 1922*), sculptor. Patronized by Louisa M. Alcott and Daniel C. French; studied in Paris and Ghent. Versatile author of many public monuments and portrait statues.

ELWELL, JOHN JOHNSON (*b. near Warren, Ohio, 1820; d. Cleveland, Ohio, 1900*), physician, lawyer, Union soldier, editor. Specialized in, and taught, medical jurisprudence; wrote standard text, *Medico-Legal Treatise on Malpractice and Medical Evidence* (1860).

ELWYN, ALFRED LANGDON (*b. Portsmouth, N.H., 1804; d. Philadelphia, Pa., 1884*), physician. Student of history, philology, botany; philanthropist. Author of *Glossary of Supposed Americanisms* (1859).

ELY, HANSON EDWARD (*b. Independence, Iowa, 1867; d. Atlantic Beach, Fla., 1958*), army officer. Graduated from West Point, 1891. Served in the Philippine Insurrection (1899–1902) and as major in the Philippine Scouts (1908–12). Chief of staff and combat commander with the American Expeditionary Force under General Pershing, Ely led the American forces in the St. Mihiel salient and the Meuse-Argonne offensive (1918). Commandant of the Army War College in Washington, 1923–27. He retired in 1931 as a major general.

ELY, RICHARD THEODORE (*b. Ripley, N.Y., 1854; d. Old Lyme, Conn., 1943*), economist, reformer. B.A., Columbia, 1876. Studied philosophy at the University of Halle. There Simon N. Patten introduced him to Johannes Conrad, an expert on agrarian economics and a member of the German historical school of economics, which viewed economic behavior as a matter of cultural patterns and governmental policy. Ely moved to the University of Heidelberg, Ph.D., 1879, where he studied under Karl Knies, a leading historical economist. After an additional year at Geneva and Berlin, he returned to the United States. In 1881 Ely joined the faculty of Johns Hopkins University as lecturer on political economy; by 1887 he rose to the rank of associate professor.

Ely became a leader in the development of the "new economics." He cooperated in organizing the American Economic Association in 1885; secretary, 1885–92, president, 1900–01. Economic principles, he thought, must be grounded in the real needs of society and must change as society changes. He viewed society as an organic whole in which all the parts are interdependent and argued that unfettered individualism is a threat to social cohesion. The state should play a positive role in the economy. He envisioned the advent of a cooperative commonwealth and advocated factory regulation, recognition of the rights of labor unions, slum clearance, immigration restriction, and working-class savings banks. Yet he described himself as an "aristocrat rather than a democrat," and believed that the working classes must accept the leadership of an elite of intellect and achievement.

Ely moved in 1892 to the University of Wisconsin, and later served as an informal adviser to Robert M. La Follette in the development of the policies that were known as the "Wisconsin idea." But he became an ardent supporter of preparedness and of American participation in World War I and broke with La Follette. He even helped wage a bitter campaign in 1918 to defeat La Follette's bid for reelection to the Senate. Moreover, by this time Ely had again shifted his attention to a new set of ideas that led to a break with old friends and with the university. In 1925, under attack from La Follette and single-tax forces, Ely moved to Northwestern University.

ELZEY, ARNOLD (*b. Somerset Co., Md., 1816; d. Baltimore, Md., 1871*), soldier. Graduated West Point, 1837. Fought in Seminole and Mexican wars; as a Confederate officer, he led final and successful charge of Kirby Smith's brigade at first battle of Manassas. Promoted major general, 1864, after severe wounding at Cold Harbor; he commanded in Richmond and was later chief of artillery, Army of Tennessee.

EMBREE, EDWIN ROGERS (*b. Osceola, Nebr., 1883; d. New York, N.Y., 1950*), foundation executive. Raised in Berea, Ky. Great-grandson of John G. Fee. B.A., Yale, 1906. Worked on *Yale Alumni Weekly*; held various positions at Yale concerned with alumni affairs, 1911–17. On staff of Rockefeller Foundation, 1917–27. President of the Julius Rosenwald Fund, 1928–48. Author of *Brown America: The Story of a New Race* (1931) and *Brown Americans: The Story of a Tenth of a Nation* (1943); coauthor of *The Collapse of Cotton Tenancy* (1935).

EMBREE, ELIHU (*b. Washington Co., Tenn., 1782; d. 1820*), iron manufacturer, abolitionist. Became leader of Tennessee Manumission Society, editor of *Manumission Intelligencer* (1819) and of the *Emancipator* (1820).

EMBURY, EMMA CATHERINE (*b. New York, N.Y., ca. 1806; d. 1863*), author, leader of literary salon. Her verse suffered from vagueness of imagery and conventionality of theme.

EMBURY, PHILIP (*b. Ballingrane[?], Ireland, ca. 1728; d. near East Salem, N.Y., 1773*), Methodist preacher, carpenter. Came to America, 1760. Reputed to have been the first Methodist preacher in America (1766, New York City).

EMERSON, BENJAMIN KENDALL (*b. Nashua, N.H., 1843; d. Amherst, Mass., 1932*), educator, geologist. Taught at Amherst and Smith colleges.

EMERSON, EDWARD WALDO (*b. Concord, Mass., 1844; d. Concord, 1930*), physician, author. Edited works and journals of his father, Ralph Waldo Emerson; author of *Emerson in Concord* (1889) and other books.

EMERSON, ELLEN RUSSELL (*b. New Sharon, Maine, 1837; d. 1907*), ethnologist. Author of *Indian Myths* (1884) and *Masks, Heads, and Faces* (1891).

EMERSON, GEORGE BARRELL (*b. Wells, Maine, 1797; d. Newton, Mass., 1881*), educator. Graduated Harvard, 1817. Headed a Boston private school, 1823–55; helped organize American Institute of Instruction. Published survey of Massachusetts trees and shrubs.

EMERSON, GOUVERNEUR (*b. near Dover, Del., 1795; d. Philadelphia, Pa., 1874*), physician, agriculturist.

EMERSON, HAVEN (*b. New York, N.Y., 1874; d. Southold, N.Y., 1957*), public health educator, statesman. Studied at Harvard and at Columbia, M.A. and M.D., 1889. Health commissioner of New York City, 1915–18. Wrote *Control of Communicable Diseases in Man* (1917). Director of the Delmar Institute of Public Health (later the Columbia University School of Public Health), 1922–40. Member of the New York City Board of Health, 1937–57.

EMERSON, JAMES EZEKIEL (*b. Norridgewock, Maine, 1823; d. Columbus, Ohio, 1900*), machinist, inventor. Patented the inserted-tooth circular saw, a steel-making process, saw-making machinery, and a steel scabbard for bayonets.

EMERSON, JOSEPH (*b. Hollis, N.H., 1777; d. Wethersfield, Conn., 1833*), Congregational clergyman, educator. Conducted a noteworthy seminary for young women, 1816–33; Zilpah Grant and Mary Lyon were among its graduates.

EMERSON, MARY MOODY (*b. Concord, Mass., 1774; d. Brooklyn, N.Y., 1863*), aunt of Ralph Waldo Emerson, whose education she supervised and on whom she had a strong influence.

EMERSON, OLIVER FARRAR (*b. near Wolf Creek, Iowa, 1860; d. Ocala, Fla., 1927*), philologist. Taught at Cornell and

Western Reserve; wrote extensively on English language and literature.

EMERSON, RALPH (b. Andover, Mass., 1831; d. 1914), inventor, manufacturer. Produced agricultural machines in association with John H. Manny; developed knitting concerns in Rockford, Ill. Founded Emerson Institute for education of black children at Mobile, Ala.

EMERSON, RALPH WALDO (b. Boston, Mass., 1803; d. Concord, Mass., 1882), essayist, poet. Son of William Emerson and Ruth Haskins Emerson; descendant of Peter Bulkeley. Orphaned of his father, 1811, he grew up under strong influence of his aunt, Mary Moody Emerson. Attended Boston Latin School; enrolled at Harvard College, 1817. Helped support himself there as messenger, waiter, and tutor. Among professors who influenced him were George Ticknor, Edward Everett, and Edward Tyrrel Channing. Emerson became a member of the Pythologian Club, a literary society, and graduated as class poet in 1821. From his junior year at the college dates the earliest extant volume of his journals, in which he noted his ideas and sensations and which served through life as the quarry from which he drew his lectures and books. During the next four years he taught school; in 1825 he entered the Harvard Divinity School. He soon found that his strength lay in his oratorical ability and in the exercise of "moral imagination," rather than in reasoning and the defense of church dogma. He was beset by doubts concerning the latter and suffered from ill health. Nevertheless, he was "approbated to preach" in 1826 and gave occasional sermons in churches in Boston and other New England towns. In 1829 he became minister of the Second Church of Boston and held this position until the summer of 1832 when he refused to administer Communion in the accepted fashion. During this period he enjoyed a few happy months of married life, which ended with the death of the first Mrs. Emerson (Ellen Tucker) in February 1831.

Emerson's break with the ministry and recurring poor health prompted him to set off on a journey to Italy, England, and Scotland, where he met, among others, Coleridge, Wordsworth, and Carlyle. From his visit with Carlyle dates their correspondence of nearly 40 years. His European sojourn brought Emerson into direct contact with men and ideas which stimulated his reason and imagination. If liberal American Unitarianism, 18th-century republicanism, and British philosophical skepticism had cleansed his mind of traditional dogmas, then German idealism and Goethean, as well as English, transcendentalism provided the materials and incentives for his future work. These currents of thought, together with insights derived from Montaigne, Plato, and Swedenborg, turned Emerson's attention to a deliberate observation of nature. He strove to establish an original relationship with the visible universe, spending a portion of each day in the woods and along the rivers, seeking to effect a marriage between his thoughts and sensations. He presented the results of his endeavors in his first book, *Nature* (1836). Nature, Emerson declared, was man's greatest teacher. Being the dress God wears, it taught lessons of usefulness and beauty; it had its own language and, being always moral, carried its own discipline.

Emerson enjoyed the company of like-minded friends, the so-called transcendentalists, among whom were Orestes Brownson, Theodore Parker, Bronson Alcott, Margaret Fuller, and James Freeman Clarke. While he was working on *Nature*, Emerson continued preaching every Sunday in different churches and began his career as a lecturer. His journals continued to provide the materials for his lectures on natural history, biography, English literature, and other topics; the lectures themselves were later published in slightly altered form in his *Essays* (1841 and 1844). He now made his home in Concord, and in 1835 married his second wife, Lydia Jackson. He settled down to a daily routine of writing, walking, and enjoying the company of his friends, among whom he also counted Henry David Thoreau, Jones Very, and Nathaniel Hawthorne. In 1837 he delivered his famous Phi Beta Kappa address at Harvard, *The American Scholar*, called by Oliver Wendell Holmes "our intellectual Declaration of Independence." It urged an original relation of the American scholar to philosophy and the arts, and it repudiated American reliance on the culture of Europe and the ancient world. In 1838 Emerson's divinity school address at Cambridge declared the church dead and the ministry outmoded; he called for an end to the scholar's dependence on the church as an institution and for a new revelation for the present age. Emerson's indictment roused the antagonism of many churchmen and made Emerson persona non grata at Harvard for almost 30 years. In 1840 Emerson became a regular contributor to the transcendentalist magazine, *The Dial*; in 1842 he became its editor. Unsympathetic to "practical" reform aspects of the magazine's program, he emphasized poetry and metaphysics. Believing that reforms must spring from the hearts and minds of individuals, he remained cool to the communal reform efforts of his friends and to such projects as Brook Farm and Fruitlands. He did, however, speak on behalf of the abolitionist cause.

Going to England on a lecture tour in 1847, he found himself famous there; he renewed his friendship with Carlyle and made the acquaintance of all the literary notables of the time. His reactions to England and its people were expressed in lectures later (1856) published as *English Traits*. The need to make money for his support by lecturing was not altogether to his taste; he continued, however, to travel the circuit, extending his trips into the West. Meanwhile, he had published *Poems* (1847), which, with *May-Day and Other Pieces* (1867), ranks him in the poetic company of Poe, Whitman, and Emily Dickinson. His output was uneven, but at his best he produced an intellectual poetry burning with what he himself called "aromatic fire."

In 1850, he published *Representative Men*, based on lectures delivered five years previously; in 1855, he was among the first to recognize Walt Whitman's genius. Emerson's chief mental occupation during the 1850's, however, was politics, and his journals are filled with comment on the great issues dividing the nation. He became bolder in his criticism of slavery and its defenders.

Immediately preceding the Civil War, he formed about him a group of men for monthly discussions which was known as the Saturday Club; it numbered Longfellow, Hawthorne, Motley, Dana, Agassiz, O. W. Holmes, and others. He also took pleasure in the outdoor excursions of the Adirondack Club.

After 1866, Emerson did nothing new, although he continued to lecture and, in some measure, write. His poem "Terminus" expresses his mood at this time, and five years thereafter (1871) began the slow erosion of physical and mental powers which marked his declining years. During this period appeared *Parnassus* (1874), an anthology of English poetry which had pleased him, and *Letters and Social Aims* (1876).

Emerson's fame at home and abroad rests on the fact that he had something of importance to say and that he said it with a beautiful, aphoristic freshness. His doctrine that men are exalted creatures, that instinct is to be obeyed, that the soul is a sensible reality, and that man is capable of all things if he but stand erect and go alone is an ideal doctrine, but he clothed it in a durable style and enforced it with a rare power of observation and a subtle sense of humor. His stylistic excellencies will be found most marked in the concluding paragraph of the chapter "Illusions" in *The Conduct of Life* (1860). Few American intellectuals have been more picturesque; none holds a solider position in the history of American life, for the impact of his shining, energizing personality is still strong.

EMERSON, ROLLINS ADAMS (b. Pillar Point, N.Y., 1873; d. Ithaca, N.Y., 1947), agricultural scientist, geneticist. B.Sc., University of Nebraska, 1897; D.Sc., Harvard, 1913. At University of Nebraska as horticulturalist in the Agricultural Experiment Station and head of the Department of Horticulture, 1899–1914 (professor *post* 1905). Professor and head of the Department of Plant Breeding, Cornell University, 1914–42. Dean, Cornell Graduate School, 1925–31. His chief research was done in the genetics of maize. Although he achieved no single major breakthrough, the sum of his work was of capital importance, and he influenced many future geneticists.

EMERSON, WILLIAM (*b. Concord, Mass., 1769; d. 1811*), Unitarian clergyman, father of Ralph Waldo Emerson. Graduated Harvard, 1789. Pastor, First Church, Boston, 1799 until his death. Served as chaplain of the state senate, as editor of the *Monthly Anthology*, and was a founder of the Anthology Club, from whose library grew the Boston Athenaeum.

EMERTON, EPHRAIM (*b. Salem, Mass., 1851; d. 1935*), educator, historian. Professor at Harvard; specialist in Renaissance and Reformation history; emphasized cultural aspects of history in original and influential textbooks and in scholarly monographs.

EMERTON, JAMES HENRY (*b. Salem, Mass., 1847; d. 1930*), naturalist, arachnologist, artist. Authority on the taxonomy and habits of spiders.

EMERY, ALBERT HAMILTON (*b. Mexico, N.Y., 1834; d. Glenbrook, Conn., 1926*), engineer, inventor. Consultant and designer of testing machinery; made principal contribution in ordnance and hydraulic-pressure measuring devices.

EMERY, CHARLES EDWARD (*b. Aurora, N.Y., 1838; d. 1898*), engineer. Consultant to U.S. Navy on steam engines, Coast Survey, and Coast Guard; chief engineer and manager, New York Steam Co., *post* 1879.

EMERY, HENRY CROSBY (*b. Ellsworth, Maine, 1872; d. at sea, 1924*), economist, businessman. Son of Lucilius A. Emery. Graduated Bowdoin, 1892; Ph.D., Columbia, 1896. Taught at Yale; was chairman of Tariff Board, 1909–13; *post* 1915 worked as financier in Russia and China.

EMERY, LUCILIUS ALONZO (*b. Carmel, Maine, 1840; d. 1920*), jurist. Introduced coordinated system of equity pleading and chancery rules in Maine; justice of state supreme court, 1883–1911 (chief justice *post* 1906).

EMERY, STEPHEN ALBERT (*b. Paris, Maine, 1841; d. Boston, Mass., 1891*), teacher, composer. Taught harmony, piano, composition, and theory at New England Conservatory and Boston University; author of *Elements of Harmony* (1879).

EMMET, THOMAS ADDIS (*b. Cork, Ireland, 1764; d. New York, N.Y., 1827*), lawyer. Brother of Robert Emmet, the Irish patriot. Graduated Trinity College, Dublin, 1782; M.D., Edinburgh, 1784. After study at the Temple, was admitted to Irish bar, 1790. Became an Irish national idol for activities on behalf of Society of United Irishmen. After arrest, 1798–1802, he was exiled to the Continent; immigrated, 1804, to the United States. Over opposition of Federalist lawyers Emmet was admitted to the New York bar, where he was very successful. In 1812 he served as state attorney general.

EMMET, THOMAS ADDIS (*b. near Charlottesville, Va., 1828; d. 1919*), physician. Grandson of Thomas A. Emmet (1764–1827). Graduated Jefferson Medical College, 1850. Practiced at Emigrants' Refuge Hospital, New York, and later with J. Marion Sims at the Woman's Hospital. Devised Emmet's operation for the repair of tears in the womb; wrote *Principles and Practice of Gynaecology* (1879). Recognized as outstanding surgeon in America and Europe. Made an important collection of American prints and autographs. An ardent advocate of Irish home rule, Emmet wrote a vitriolic indictment of England, *Ireland Under English Rule* (1903), and was president of the Irish National Federation of America.

EMMET, WILLIAM LE ROY (*b. Travers Island, Pelham, N.Y., 1859; d. Erie, Pa., 1941*), engineer. Great-grandson of Thomas A. Emmet (1764–1827); uncle of Robert E. Sherwood. Graduated U.S. Naval Academy, 1881. After early experience with Frank J. Sprague on electric street railway systems, he was associated *post* 1892 with the General Electric Co. Author of a pioneer textbook *Alternating Current Wiring and Distribution* (1894), he held 122 patents for electrical equipment, steam turbine development, and use of mercury vapor in turbines. He was responsible for General Electric's part in the Niagara Falls power project and for the design of turboelectric propulsion plants for warships.

EMMETT, BURTON (*b. Lee, Ill., 1871; d. Melfa, Va., 1935*), advertising executive, book and print collector.

EMMETT, DANIEL DECATUR (*b. Mount Vernon, Ohio, 1815; d. Mount Vernon, 1904*), one of the originators of the "Negro Minstrel" troupe, 1842–43. Author of "Old Dan Tucker" (*ca.* 1831); "Dixie" (1859); and other minstrel songs.

EMMONS, EBENEZER (*b. Middlefield, Mass., 1799; d. Brunswick Co., N.C., 1863*), geologist, physician, teacher. State geologist of North Carolina, *post* 1851.

EMMONS, GEORGE FOSTER (*b. Clarendon, Vt., 1811; d. Princeton, N.J., 1884*), naval officer. Active in Wilkes's exploring expedition and on Pacific Coast, 1838–50. Author of *The Navy of the United States . . . 1775–1853* (1853). Served with ability on Gulf blockade in Civil War. Retired as rear admiral, 1873.

EMMONS, NATHANAEL (*b. East Haddam, Conn., 1745; d. Franklin, Mass., 1840*), Congregational clergyman, conservative theologian.

EMMONS, SAMUEL FRANKLIN (*b. Boston, Mass., 1841; d. 1911*), geologist, mining engineer. Participated in geological exploration of fortieth parallel and later western surveys; author of *Geology and Mining Industry of Leadville, Colo.* (1886).

EMORY, JOHN (*b. Spaniard's Neck, Md., 1789; d. near Reisterstown, Md., 1835*), Methodist clergyman. Held pastorates in Philadelphia and Baltimore conferences; was agent of Methodist Book Concern; elected bishop, 1832.

EMORY, WILLIAM HEMSLEY (*b. Queen Annes Co., Md., 1811; d. 1887*), soldier. Graduated West Point, 1831. As topographical engineer, participated in northeastern boundary survey; served with Army of the West in Mexican War. Chief astronomer in survey of California–Mexico boundary, 1848–53; commissioner and astronomer under Gadsden Treaty, 1854–57. During Civil War, held brigade, division, and corps commands with high distinction. Author of, among others, *Notes of a Military Reconnaissance from Fort Leavenworth to San Diego* (1848) and *Report on the U.S. and Mexican Boundary Survey* (1857–59). Retired as brigadier general, regular army, 1876.

EMOTT, JAMES (*b. Poughkeepsie, N.Y., 1771; d. 1850*), New York jurist, legislator. Federalist congressman.

EMOTT, JAMES (*b. Poughkeepsie, N.Y., 1823; d. Poughkeepsie, 1884*), jurist, banker. Son of James Emott (1771–1850). First mayor of Poughkeepsie, Whig, 1854; judge, New York Supreme Court, 1856–64. Active in exposure of "Tweed Ring."

ENDECOTT, JOHN (*b. Chagford, England, ca. 1589; d. Boston, Mass., 1665*), governor of Massachusetts. An incorporator of the Massachusetts Bay Colony, he was in charge of the first settlement from colonists' arrival at Naumkeag (Salem), September 1628, until the main body of company arrived in the summer of 1630 and John Winthrop took over as governor. Endecott ruled with sternness and efficiency; he helped organize an independent church after the model of the Pilgrims at Plymouth, and deported two members of his colony who declined to accept Separatism. After Winthrop's succession, Endecott served as his assistant and in military capacities; he was again governor in 1644, 1649, 1651–53, 1655–64. A punitive expedition against the Indians which he led in 1636 proved a complete failure and did much to bring on the Pequot War. Intolerant of religious opinions other than his own, in his persecution of the Quakers he showed himself bloodthirsty and brutal. He was interested in education, urged the establishment of a free school at Salem, and became an overseer of Harvard College. As a public servant Endecott was capable and honest, although unable to conceive of any public good other than as he saw it. In his religious and social views he was a thoroughgoing Puritan, stern and irascible, a man of iron will and little human sympathy.

ENDICOTT, CHARLES MOSES (*b. Danvers, Mass., 1793; d. 1863*), sea captain, antiquarian. Author of the useful and important *Sailing Directions for the Pepper Ports on the West Coast of Sumatra* (1833).

ENDICOTT, JOHN. *See* ENDECOTT, JOHN.

ENDICOTT, MORDECAI THOMAS (*b. Mays Landing, N.J., 1844; d. Washington, D.C., 1926*), naval engineer. Chief of Bureau of Yards and Docks, 1898–1907; completed floating dry dock *Dewey*, largest of its time.

ENDICOTT, WILLIAM CROWNINSHIELD (*b. Salem, Mass., 1826; d. Boston, Mass., 1900*), jurist. Judge, Supreme Judicial Court of Massachusetts, 1873–82; as secretary of war, 1885–89, distinguished himself through his work with the Endicott Board of Fortifications on Atlantic Coast defense work.

ENELOW, HYMAN GERSON (*b. Kovno, Russia, 1877; d. at sea, 1934*), rabbi. Moved to America, 1893. Graduated Hebrew Union College, 1898. Held pastorates in Kentucky and at Temple Emanu-el, New York City. Author of scholarly works and patron of scholars.

ENGEL, CARL (*b. Paris, France, 1883; d. New York, N.Y., 1944*), musicologist, composer. Immigrated to the United States, 1905. Editor, Boston Music Company, 1909–21; chief of music division, Library of Congress, 1922–34; president of G. Schirmer, Inc., music publishers, New York City, 1929–32 and *post* 1934; editor of the *Musical Quarterly post* 1929.

ENGELHARDT, ZEPHYRIN (*b. Bilshausen, Germany, 1851; d. Santa Barbara, Calif., 1934*), Roman Catholic clergyman, Franciscan. Taken to America as an infant. Missionary to the Indians. Author of *The Franciscans in California* (1897), *Missions and Missionaries of California* (1908–16), and many other works.

ENGELMANN, GEORGE (*b. Frankfurt-am-Main, Germany, 1809; d. St. Louis, Mo., 1884*), physician, botanist, pioneer meteorologist. Graduated Würzburg, M.D., 1831. Immigrated to America, 1832; practiced in St. Louis, Mo., *post* 1835. Made important contributions to grape culture. His botanical monographs were published in collected form, 1887.

ENGELMANN, GEORGE JULIUS (*b. St. Louis, Mo., 1847; d. Boston, Mass., 1903*), gynecologist, obstetrician. Son of George Engelmann. Studied medicine in Germany, Austria, France, and England; practiced and taught in St. Louis and Boston. Made extensive researches of Indian mounds in Missouri.

ENGLAND, JOHN (*b. Cork, Ireland, 1786; d. Charleston, S.C., 1842*), Roman Catholic clergyman. Active in Irish nationalist movements and a highly articulate democrat, he was consecrated first bishop of Charleston, S.C., 1820. An indefatigable preacher and vehement controversialist, he roused the spirit of his diocese, instituted a democratic constitution for its guidance by lay and clerical delegates, opened the Philosophical and Classical Seminary of Charleston (an innovating school), brought in Irish Ursulines for the education of girls, and unsuccessfully sought to open a school for free blacks. For practical reasons he accepted slavery as an institution. He was a prolific writer and lecturer, the first priest to address the House of Representatives and a prime mover in calling the Provincial Councils of Baltimore. In 1833–37 he served as apostolic delegate to Haiti. His greatest achievement was the founding of the *United States Catholic Miscellany* (1822–61), the first distinctly Catholic paper in America.

ENGLE, CLAIR WILLIAM WALTER (*b. Bakersfield, Calif., 1911; d. Washington, D.C., 1964*), U.S. congressman and senator. Studied at Hastings College of Law of the University of California (LL.B., 1933). Elected Democratic congressman from California's second district in 1943. From his positions on the Public Lands Committee and the Interior and Insular Affairs Committee (which he chaired, 1955–59), Engle devoted himself to water, land, and reclamation issues. A liberal, Engle advocated federal power development rather than Eisenhower's "partnership" approach, which involved private power utilities. U.S. senator from 1958–64.

ENGLIS, JOHN (*b. New York, N.Y., 1808; d. 1888*), shipbuilder. His Hudson River, Long Island Sound and Great Lakes steamboats were known for speed and grace of line.

ENGLISH, ELBERT HARTWELL (*b. Madison Co., Ala., 1816; d. 1884*), Arkansas lawyer and jurist.

ENGLISH, GEORGE BETHUNE (*b. Cambridge, Mass., 1787; d. Washington, D.C., 1828*), writer, soldier, linguist. Graduated Harvard, 1807. Served as officer of U.S. Marines; converted to Islam and served in Egyptian army; secret U.S. agent in Levant, 1823–27. Versatile but erratic.

ENGLISH, JAMES EDWARD (*b. New Haven, Conn., 1812; d. New Haven, 1890*), clock and brass manufacturer. Congressman, Democrat, 1861–65; U.S. senator, 1875–76; governor of Connecticut, 1867, 1868 and 1870.

ENGLISH, THOMAS DUNN (*b. in or near Philadelphia, Pa., 1819; d. Newark, N.J., 1902*), editor, politician, playwright. Remembered for his poem "Ben Bolt" (1843).

ENGLISH, WILLIAM HAYDEN (*b. Lexington, Ind., 1822; d. Indianapolis, Ind., 1896*), lawyer, banker. Congressman, Democrat, from Indiana, 1852–60; author of "English Bill" (1858). Democratic candidate for vice presidency, 1880. Author of *Life of Gen. George Rogers Clark* (1896).

ENNEKING, JOHN JOSEPH (*b. Minster, Ohio, 1841; d. Boston, Mass., 1916*), landscape and figure painter. A romanticist and impressionist, Enneking has been called the interpreter of New England in painting as Edward MacDowell was in music.

ENO, WILLIAM PHELPS (*b. New York, N.Y., 1858; d. Norwalk, Conn., 1945*), pioneer in traffic regulation. Uncle of Amos Pinchot and Gifford Pinchot. B.A., Yale, 1882. Anticipating the problems to be caused by unregulated traffic as automobiles became common, he proposed a uniform *Rules for Driving* (1903), comprising rules for passing, turning, crossing, stopping, and signaling by hand. Among his other contributions were a system of one-way rotary traffic for multiple intersections and a traffic code for military convoys and ambulances used in both world wars. He founded a nonprofit center for research in traffic engineering, 1921, which was later affiliated with Yale, and wrote a number of books on traffic control and its relation to city planning and the reduction of pollution.

ENSLEY, ENOCH (*b. near Nashville, Tenn., 1836; d. 1891*), planter, manufacturer, economist. A pioneer in industrial development of the South. Author of *What Should Be Taxed* (1873), a novel and important work, very far in advance of its time.

ENTWISTLE, JAMES (*b. Paterson, N.J., 1837; d. Paterson, 1910*), naval engineer. Fleet engineer under Commodore George Dewey at Manila Bay, 1898.

EPPES, JOHN WAYLES (*b. near Petersburg, Va., 1773; d. Buckingham Co., Va., 1823*), lawyer. Nephew of Thomas Jefferson. Congressman, Democratic-Republican, from Virginia, 1803–11 and 1813–15. U.S. senator, 1817–19. Upheld Jefferson's policies against John Randolph of Roanoke's factional group.

EPSTEIN, ABRAHAM (*b. Luban, near Pinsk, Russia, 1892; d. New York, N.Y., 1942*), economist, pioneer in the American social insurance movement. Attended local Hebrew schools. Came to New York City, 1910; worked at odd jobs; secured a position teaching Hebrew in Pittsburgh, Pa. Assisted by a local schoolmaster, he was admitted to the University of Pittsburgh and graduated, B.S., 1917. After graduate study in economics at Pittsburgh, he was executive secretary and research director of the Pennsylvania Commission on Old Age Pensions, 1918–27. His pioneering books *Facing Old Age* (1922) and *The Challenge of the Aged* (1926) and magazine articles and frequent talks to labor union and social welfare groups won him a reputation as an expert on social insurance. In 1927, he founded the American Association for Old Age Security (later the American Association for Social Security), which advocated social and health insurance programs financed and controlled by the government. Critical of the Social Security Act of 1935, many of his suggested changes were made by Congress in 1939.

EPSTEIN, JACOB (*b. New York, N.Y., 1880; d. London, England, 1959*), sculptor. Studied at the New York Art Students League, the École des Beaux Arts and the Académie Julian in Paris. Immigrated to England and became a British citizen in 1907. Remembered for his controversial academic sculptures, Epstein turned to abstract works during the decades 1900–20; his work *Rock Drill* (1913) remains an important work of the period. His fame rests in the portraits of the famous. He was knighted in 1954.

EPSTEIN, PHILIP G. (*b. New York, N.Y., 1909; d. Hollywood, Calif., 1952*), playwright, screenwriter. Studied at Pennsylvania State College. With his twin brother, Julius, Epstein wrote the filmscripts of *Daughters Courageous* (1938), *Saturday's Children* (1940), *Strawberry Blonde* (1941), *The Man Who Came to Dinner* (1942), *Arsenic and Old Lace* (1944), and *Yankee Doodle Dandy* (1942). They received an Academy Award for *Casablanca* (1943).

ERDMAN, CHARLES ROSENBURY (*b. Fayetteville, N.Y., 1866; d. Princeton, N.J., 1960*), educator, theologian. Studied at Princeton University and at Princeton Theological Seminary; ordained, 1891. Accepted the newly created chair of practical theology at Princeton Theological Seminary in 1906; pastor of the First Presbyterian Church of Princeton, 1925–34. A fundamentalist who was not opposed to liberal voices in the seminary, Erdman sought to preserve unity in the organization of the school.

ERICSSON, JOHN (*b. Värmland, Sweden, 1803; d. New York, N.Y., 1889*), engineer, inventor. Received early training as cadet in Swedish corps of mechanical engineers; worked in London, England, 1826–38, where he perfected many mechanical inventions and improvements, among others a steam fire engine, a steam locomotive, and the screw propeller for steam vessels. Came to America, 1839, intending a short visit; remaining, he became a citizen. Prolific, versatile, but incapable of working closely with others, he designed power plants for all purposes, including fire engines, hot-air stationary engines, and the first screw-propelled man-of-war, USS *Princeton*. The Civil War brought him fame as designer of the ironclad, turreted, propeller-driven warship *Monitor*. After the war he developed the forerunner of the modern torpedo boat or destroyer.

ERLANGER, ABRAHAM LINCOLN (*b. Buffalo, N.Y., 1860; d. 1930*), theatrical booking agent, manager, producer. Developed modern centralized booking system; with Klaw, Charles Frohman, and others organized Theatrical Syndicate, 1896, which was denounced as a monopoly.

ERLANGER, JOSEPH (*b. San Francisco, Calif., 1874; d. St. Louis, Mo., 1965*), physiologist. Studied at the University of California and Johns Hopkins (M.D., 1899). As a professor at Washington University School of Medicine from 1910, Erlanger built one of the world's premiere departments of physiology, of which he became chairman. His development of the cathode-ray oscilloscope to study nerve impulse transmission made possible the modern field of neurophysiology. Erlanger shared the Nobel Prize in Medicine or Physiology with his collaborator, Herbert Gasser, in 1944.

ERNST, HAROLD CLARENCE (*b. Cincinnati, Ohio, 1856; d. 1922*), bacteriologist. Graduated Harvard, 1876; Harvard Medical, 1880; studied bacteriology under Koch. Gave first (1885) lectures on bacteriology at Harvard Medical School; was professor of his specialty there, 1895–1922.

ERNST, OSWALD HERBERT (*b. near Cincinnati, Ohio, 1842; d. Washington, D.C., 1926*), soldier, engineer. Graduated West Point, 1864. Specialist in river and harbor improvement; supervised digging of deep-sea channel to Galveston, Tex.; was member of original Isthmian Canal Commission.

ERRETT, ISAAC (*b. New York, N.Y., 1820; d. 1888*), Disciples of Christ clergyman, author. Editor of *The Christian Standard*, 1866–88.

ERROL, LEON (*b. Sydney, Australia, 1881; d. Hollywood, Calif., 1951*), comedian. Studied at Sydney University; immigrated to the U.S. around 1900. Remembered for his vaudeville routines in which he played a drunk, Errol was featured in the *Ziegfeld Follies of 1911*, partnering with black comic Bert Williams. After appearing in many plays on Broadway, including *Fioretta* (1929), he turned to films; made over 100 short comic films, including *Never Give a Sucker an Even Break* (1941) and the *Mexican Spitfire* series (1940–43).

ERSKINE, JOHN (*b. Strabane, Ireland, 1813; d. Atlanta, Ga., 1895*), jurist. Came to America as a child; settled in Georgia, 1855. A foe of secession, he was federal judge in Georgia, 1866–83, where his integrity and fairness won him public confidence and respect.

ERSKINE, JOHN (*b. New York, N.Y., 1879; d. New York, N.Y., 1951*), teacher, author, musician. Graduated from Columbia University, Ph.D., 1903. Taught literature at

Columbia, 1909–51 (emeritus, 1937). Coeditor of the *Cambridge History of American Literature*. Headed Army Education Commission in France during World War I. Introduced the "great books" concept for teaching literature. Published the best-selling novel, *The Private Life of Helen of Troy* (1925). President of the Juilliard School of Music, 1928–37.

ERSKINE, ROBERT (*b. Dunfermline, Scotland, 1735; d. 1780*), geographer, hydraulic engineer. Came to America, 1771, as representative of British interests in the American Iron Co. By 1775 his sympathies for the colonials led to a commission as captain in the New Jersey militia; in 1777 he was named geographer and surveyor general to the Continental army. Erskine's maps of the seat of war were important contributory factors in Washington's ultimate victory.

ERVING, GEORGE WILLIAM (*b. Boston, Mass., 1769; d. New York, N.Y., 1850*), diplomat. Served with ability in U.S. legations at London, Madrid, and Copenhagen; initiated negotiations which culminated in treaty of 1819 with Spain.

ESBJÖRN, LARS PAUL (*b. Delsbo, Sweden, 1808; d. Sweden, 1870*), Lutheran clergyman. Came to America, 1849, with emigrant party; was pastor of settlement at Andover, Ill. First president of Augustana Seminary, Chicago, 1860–63, he is regarded as the founder of the Swedish Lutheran Church in the United States.

ESCALANTE, SILVESTRE VELEZ DE (*fl. 1768–79*), Franciscan missionary, explorer. Born in Spain, Escalante sailed for New Spain in 1768 and served as missionary in Sonora and at the Laguna and Zuñi pueblos, New Mexico. He is celebrated for two exploring expeditions and the reports which he made on them. The first (1775) took him from Zuñi to the Moqui (Hopi) pueblos; the second, which had as object the opening of direct communication between Sante Fe and Monterey, Calif., was performed in 1776. Leaving Sante Fe in July, Escalante and Fray Francisco Dominguez traveled northwest to Utah Lake and thence southwest to Black Rock Springs, where snowfall discouraged their passage over the Sierra Nevada. They returned to Sante Fe on Jan. 2, 1777, by way of the Colorado River, the Moqui towns, and Zuñi.

ESCH, JOHN JACOB (*b. near Norwalk, Wis., 1861; d. La Crosse, Wis., 1941*), lawyer, politician. Graduated University of Wisconsin, 1882; LL.B., 1887. Practiced law in La Crosse and was active in the state guard and in Republican politics. As congressman from the Seventh Wisconsin District, 1899–1921, he had progressive leanings; he made his major contribution as sponsor of the Esch-Townsend bill (1905) to give the Interstate Commerce Commission power to fix maximum railroad rates. The bill failed to pass the Senate. He was author of the Esch-Cummins Act (Transportation Act of 1920), which returned the nation's railroads to private control, leading to his defeat in the 1920 Republican primary in Wisconsin. He was a member of the Interstate Commerce Commission, 1921–27, serving as chairman in 1927.

ESHER, JOHN JACOB (*b. Baldenheim, Alsace, 1823; d. 1901*), bishop of the Evangelical church, 1863–1901.

ESPEJO, ANTONIO DE (*fl. 1581–83*), Spanish merchant in Mexico. After prospecting for ores in the Pueblo Indian region, he stimulated an interest in the territory by his reports which culminated in the conquest of New Mexico under Juan de Oñate.

ESPY, JAMES POLLARD (*b. Pennsylvania, 1785; d. Cincinnati, Ohio, 1860*), educator, meteorologist. Developed convectional theory of precipitation; first used telegraphic bulletins as basis for weather forecasting. Author of *Philosophy of Storms* (1841).

ESTABROOK, JOSEPH (*b. Lebanon, N.H., 1793; d. Anderson Co., Tenn., 1855*), educator. Graduated Dartmouth, 1815. President, East Tennessee College (later University of Tennessee), 1834–50.

ESTAUGH, ELIZABETH HADDON (*b. Southwark, England, ca. 1680; d. Haddonfield, N.J., 1762*), Quaker founder of "a home in the wilderness for travelling ministers" at Haddonfield, 1701.

ESTERBROOK, RICHARD (*b. Liskeard, England, 1813; d. Camden, N.J., 1895*), manufacturer. Organized Esterbrook steel pen company, 1858; was its president, 1858–95.

ESTERLY, GEORGE (*b. Plattekill, N.Y., 1809; d. Hot Springs, S.D., 1893*), inventor, manufacturer. Patented first successful American harvesting machine, 1844, a horse-pushed "header," which won gold medal at 1848 fair of Chicago Mechanics Institute. Subsequently patented a mowing machine, plow, hand-rake reaper, the first sulky cultivator, a seeder, and a self-rake reaper. Erected his own manufacturing plant at Whitewater, Wis., 1858; produced twine binders and mowers; built up a large export trade. In 1892 moved his plant to Minneapolis, Minn., where it failed in the panic of 1893.

ESTES, DANA (*b. Gorham, Maine, 1840; d. Boston, Mass., 1909*), bookseller, publisher. Partner in Boston firms of Estes and Lauriat, and Dana Estes and Co.

ESTEY, JACOB (*b. Hinsdale, N.H., 1814; d. 1890*), pioneer American organ manufacturer. *Post* 1850, developed small melodeon-manufacturing shop into one of the world's largest organ companies.

ETTWEIN, JOHN (*b. Freudenstadt, Germany, 1721; d. Bethlehem, Pa., 1802*), Moravian bishop. Came to America, 1754, as spiritual adviser to children of Moravians; undertook missionary work among Indians in middle and southern colonies; in 1766 was appointed assistant to Bishop Nathanael Seidel at Bethlehem, Pa. In 1772, he led party of Christian Indians to David Zeisberger's settlement in Tuscarawas Valley, Ohio. Known as a Loyalist, he was temporarily imprisoned during Revolution. Successfully negotiated with Continental Congress and Pennsylvania Assembly over refusal of Moravians to bear arms and to subscribe to the Test Oath; served devotedly as chaplain, Continental army hospital at Bethlehem, 1776–77. In 1785, he prevailed upon Congress and the Pennsylvania Assembly to establish reservations for converted Indians. Chosen bishop in 1784, he presided over the Moravian Church of North America until his death and ranks as one of its greatest leaders.

EUSTIS, DOROTHY LEIB HARRISON WOOD (*b. Philadelphia, Pa., 1886; d. New York, N.Y., 1946*), philanthropist. After experience as a breeder of dairy cattle and German shepherd dogs, she was inspired by observation of the use of such dogs in Germany as guides for blinded war veterans to establish the Seeing Eye, 1929. Devoting much of her own fortune to the work, Eustis served as president of the Seeing Eye until 1940 and thereafter as honorary president.

EUSTIS, GEORGE (*b. Boston, Mass., 1796; d. New Orleans, La., 1858*), jurist. Nephew of William Eustis. Louisiana chief justice, 1846–52; held other state offices. Encouraged development of Louisiana educational system.

EUSTIS, GEORGE (*b. New Orleans, La., 1828; d. Cannes, France, 1872*), statesman, diplomat. Son of George Eustis

(1796–1858). Secretary to Confederate legation at Paris, France, during Civil War.

EUSTIS, HENRY LAWRENCE (*b. Boston, Mass., 1819; d. Cambridge, Mass., 1885*), engineer, soldier. Graduated Harvard, 1838; West Point, 1842. Resigned army, 1849, to become professor of engineering, Harvard, where he taught until his death. Commanded Tenth Massachusetts Regiment, 1862–64.

EUSTIS, JAMES BIDDLE (*b. New Orleans, La., 1834; d. Newport, R.I., 1899*), lawyer, statesman, Confederate soldier, diplomat. Son of George Eustis (1796–1858), U.S. senator from Louisiana, Democrat, 1877–79 and 1885–91. Ambassador to France.

EUSTIS, WILLIAM (*b. Cambridge, Mass., 1753; d. Boston, Mass., 1825*), Revolutionary army surgeon, statesman. Graduated Harvard, 1772. Congressman, Democratic-Republican, from Massachusetts, 1801–05 and 1820–23; secretary of war, 1809–12; minister to Holland, 1814–18; governor of Massachusetts, 1823–25.

EVANS, ANTHONY WALTON WHYTE (*b. New Brunswick, N.J., 1817; d. 1886*), civil engineer. Graduated Rensselaer Polytechnic, 1836. Won fame as builder of railroads in Chile and Peru.

EVANS, AUGUSTA JANE (*b. Columbus, Ga., 1835; d. Mobile, Ala., 1909*). Author of turgid and sentimental novels including the best seller *St. Elmo* (1866).

EVANS, CHARLES (*b. Boston, Mass., 1850; d. 1935*), librarian, bibliographer. Author of *American Bibliography* (1903–34).

EVANS, CLEMENT ANSELM (*b. Stewart Co., Ga., 1833; d. Atlanta, Ga., 1911*), lawyer, Confederate soldier, Methodist clergyman, historian. Commander in chief of United Confederate Veterans; edited *Confederate Military History* (1899).

EVANS, EDWARD PAYSON (*b. Remsen, N.Y., 1831; d. New York, N.Y., 1917*), man of letters. An expatriate to Germany, he wrote scholarly works on many abstruse subjects.

EVANS, EVAN (*b. Carnoe, Wales, 1671; d. Harford Co., Md., 1721*), Anglican clergyman. Second rector of Christ Church, Philadelphia, 1700–18; strengthened influence of Church of England in America.

EVANS, FREDERICK WILLIAM (*b. Leominster, England, 1808; d. Mount Lebanon, N.Y., 1893*), reformer, Shaker elder. Brother of George H. Evans. Edited radical reform publications with his brother before becoming prominent Shaker leader.

EVANS, GEORGE (*b. Hallowell, Maine, 1797; d. 1867*), lawyer. Congressman, Whig, from Maine, 1829–41; U.S. senator, 1841–47. Expert in public finance.

EVANS, GEORGE ALFRED (*b. Brooklyn, N.Y., 1850; d. 1925*), physician. Graduated Bellevue Medical College, 1873. Pioneered in sanatorium and climatic treatment of pulmonary tuberculosis; wrote *Handbook of Historical and Geographical Phthisiology* (1888).

EVANS, GEORGE HENRY (*b. Bromyard, England, 1805; d. Granville, N.J., 1856*), reformer. Brother of Frederick W. Evans. Came to America, 1820. Influenced by Thomas Paine's writings, Evans edited a series of papers which were the first labor papers in America. These were *The Man* (Ithaca, N.Y., *ca.* 1822); *Working Man's Advocate* (New York, 1929–45); *Daily Sentinel* and *Young America* (between 1837 and 1853). Championed workingmen's parties and advocated agrarian principles similar to those of Henry George. Opposed doctrines of Fourier and Owen with principles developed from Paine's and Jefferson's individualism and natural rights doctrines. Advocated right of every man to an inalienable homestead, abolition of laws for collection of debts and imprisonment for debt, abolition of chattel and wage slavery, and equal rights for women.

EVANS, HENRY CLAY (*b. Juniata Co., Pa., 1843; d. Chattanooga, Tenn., 1921*), industrialist. Raised in Wisconsin. Settled in Chattanooga, 1870, and prospered in car-building industry. Served as mayor of Chattanooga and as organizer of its school system; was prominent in national Republican politics.

EVANS, HUGH DAVEY (*b. Baltimore, Md., 1792; d. Baltimore, 1868*), lawyer, Protestant Episcopal lay theologian, editor, author.

EVANS, JOHN (*fl. 1703–31*), deputy governor of Pennsylvania, 1703–07. His riotous living, aggressive Anglicanism, and policy of military preparedness antagonized the Quaker Assembly and led to his removal.

EVANS, JOHN (*b. Waynesville, Ohio, 1814; d. 1897*), physician, railroad builder. Prominent in his profession in Indiana and as professor of obstetrics at Rush Medical College, Chicago, he was also an investor in real estate and railroads. Evanston, Ill., was named for him. He took a leading part in founding of Northwestern University, where he endowed two chairs. Removing to Denver, he was territorial governor of Colorado, 1862–65; he supported churches and founded Colorado Seminary (later University of Denver). The Denver Pacific, South Park, and Denver & New Orleans railroads, which saved the city from isolation, were promoted by him.

EVANS, LAWRENCE BOYD (*b. Radnor, Ohio, 1870; d. Washington, D.C., 1928*), lawyer. Taught history and public law at Tufts College; published legal casebooks; codified navigation laws for U.S. Shipping Board.

EVANS, LEWIS (*b. Llangwnadl Parish, Wales, ca. 1700; d. New York, N.Y., 1756*), geographer. In 1749 published "A Map of Pennsylvania, New-Jersey, New-York, and the Three Delaware Counties," which traced the major emigration roads through Lancaster, York, and Carlisle. His best-known map, "A General Map of the Middle British Colonies in America" (1755), was published with an "Analysis" stressing the importance of the Ohio region, was used by Braddock in his campaign, and was generally accepted as standard authority in settling boundary disputes.

EVANS, NATHAN GEORGE (*b. Marion, S.C., 1824; d. Midway, Ala., 1868*), Confederate general. Graduated West Point, 1848. On frontier service with cavalry, 1848–60. Displayed courage and leadership at first Bull Run and Ball's Bluff, but later showed little fitness for command.

EVANS, NATHANIEL (*b. Philadelphia, Pa., 1742; d. Haddonfield, N.J., 1767*), Anglican clergyman, poet. Belonged to Philadelphia group of Francis Hopkinson and Thomas Godfrey; works collected in *Poems on Several Occasions* (1772), edited by William Smith (1727–1803).

EVANS, OLIVER (*b. near Newport, Del., 1755; d. New York, N.Y., 1819*), inventor, America's first steam-engine builder. Apprenticed to a wagon-maker; studied mechanics and mechanics; early determined to develop and extend the use of the steam engine. First worked at perfecting a machine for making card teeth for carding wool, then at improving flour-mill machinery. His improvements (*ca.* 1785) made hand operations unnecessary, but were universally scorned by millers at the time. By 1802 Evans produced his first stationary high-pressure steam engine; in the following year he set up in business as engine builder. He established the Mars Iron Works, 1807; in 1817 he designed and constructed the engine and boilers for Fairmount Waterworks in Philadelphia. By the time of his death 50 of his engines were in operation on the Atlantic Coast. He never received sufficient pecuniary assistance to build his proposed "steam carriage," on which he worked for many years, or to develop his ideas on steam propulsion for boats.

EVANS, ROBLEY DUNGLISON (b. Floyd Court House, Va., 1846; d. 1912), naval officer, "Fighting Bob." Commanded USS *Iowa* at Santiago, 1898; commissioned rear admiral, 1901; commanded U.S. fleet on round-the-world cruise, 1907.

EVANS, THOMAS (b. Philadelphia, Pa., 1798; d. Philadelphia, 1868), Quaker minister and editor. Wrote and edited extensively in defense of orthodox doctrine and reconciliation of Hicksites.

EVANS, THOMAS WILTBERGER (b. Philadelphia, Pa., 1823; d. Paris, France, 1897), dentist, philanthropist. Pupil of Dr. John De Haven White. Practiced in Baltimore, Md., and Lancaster, Pa., removing to Paris, *ca.* 1848, and opening his own office there, 1850. Beginning as dentist to Napoleon III, he came to know and serve the principal royal families of Europe; built up a private fortune; became an amateur diplomat. Aided Empress Eugénie in her escape from Paris, 1870. Provided ambulance and medical services at his own expense during Crimean and Franco-Prussian wars; established first American paper in Paris. His technical contributions to dentistry were considerable, and he left his fortune to establish an institute and museum which are today the Dental School of the University of Pennsylvania.

EVANS, WALTER (b. Barren Co., Ky., 1842; d. 1923), jurist, Union soldier. Congressman, Republican, from Kentucky, 1895–99; helped formulate Dingley Tariff. U.S. judge for district of Kentucky, *post* 1899.

EVANS, WARREN FELT (b. Rockingham, Vt., 1817; d. 1889), clergyman, disciple of Phineas P. Quimby as a mental healer.

EVANS, WILLIAM THOMAS (b. Clough-Jordan, Ireland, 1843; d. 1918), New York City dry-goods merchant, patron of American art.

EVARTS, JEREMIAH (b. Sunderland, Vt., 1781; d. Charleston, S.C., 1831), lawyer, philanthropist. Edited the *Panoplist* (Boston, 1810–21); opposed policy of transferring Indians to western reservations; a founder of American Board of Commissioners for Foreign Missions.

EVARTS, WILLIAM MAXWELL (b. Boston, Mass., 1818; d. New York, N.Y., 1901), lawyer, statesman. Son of Jeremiah Evarts; grandson of Roger Sherman. Graduated Yale, 1837; admitted to New York bar, 1841. Formed partnership, 1842, with Charles E. Butler in a firm which later included Charles F. Southmayd, Joseph H. Choate, and Charles C. Beaman. Early successful in private practice, Evarts entered public life as assistant U.S. attorney for the southern district of New York, 1849–53.

His public career included service as chairman of the New York delegation to the 1860 Republican National Convention and as secretary to the Union Defense Committee. He went to England in 1863 and in 1864 to halt, if possible, the building and equipping of Confederate navy vessels. In 1867 he was a member of the judiciary committee of the New York state constitutional convention; from July 1868 to March 1869, he was attorney general in President Andrew Johnson's cabinet; for ten years after 1870 he

was president of the New York City Bar Association. In this capacity he fought for reform and against the corruption of the "Tweed Ring." He served as President Hayes's secretary of state, 1877–81; as delegate to the Paris Monetary Conference; and as U.S. senator from New York, 1885–89, until his health and eyesight failed.

Evarts' legal career ran parallel to, and was interspersed between, events of his career as a statesman. Among the many outstanding causes in which he was engaged were *People* v. *Draper*, in which he successfully sustained the right of the legislature to create a new metropolitan police district; the case of the Savannah privateers; the prosecution of Jefferson Davis for treason (1867); the Bank Tax, Legal Tender, and Cotton Tax cases before the Supreme Court; and his appearance in the Springbok Case before the mixed commission on British and American claims (1873). Evarts' fame, however, rests on his success in three cases of national and international importance. His eloquence prevented the required two-thirds vote for conviction in the impeachment of President Johnson (1868); his courteous and conciliatory attitude won the respect of the British participants during the Geneva arbitration negotiations (1871–72); and his argument reaffirming the constitutional power of the states to regulate casting and counting of votes prevailed in the Hayes-Tilden presidential dispute (1876–77).

EVE, JOSEPH (b. Philadelphia, Pa., 1760; d. Augusta, Ga., 1835), inventor, scientist, poet.

EVE, PAUL FITZSIMONS (b. near Augusta, Ga., 1806; d. Nashville, Tenn., 1877), surgeon. Graduated University of Pennsylvania, M.D., 1828; studied also in London and Paris. Taught surgery at Medical College of Georgia and at Nashville; served as Confederate army surgeon; credited with being first American to perform hysterectomy.

EVERENDON, WALTER (d. 1725), colonial gunpowder manufacturer. First man to make powder in America; overseer of Neponset, Mass., mill which supplied powder for prosecution of King Philip's War (1675–76).

EVERETT, ALEXANDER HILL (b. Boston, Mass., 1790; d. Canton, China, 1847), editor, diplomat. Brother of Edward Everett. Served in diplomatic posts in Russia, Holland, Spain, Cuba, and China. Edited *North American Review*, 1830–35.

EVERETT, CHARLES CARROLL (b. Brunswick, Maine, 1829; d. 1900), theologian. Graduated Bowdoin, 1850. Author of *Science for Thought* (1869); dean of Harvard Divinity School, 1878–1900.

EVERETT, DAVID (b. Princeton, Mass., 1770; d. Marietta, Ohio, 1813), lawyer, journalist. Author of *Common Sense in Dishabille* (1799); a play, *Daranzel* (performed 1798, 1800; published, 1800); and other works.

EVERETT, EDWARD (b. Dorchester, Mass., 1794; d. Boston, Mass., 1865), Unitarian clergyman, educator, statesman, orator. Graduated Harvard, 1811; was first American to receive Ph.D. degree at Göttingen (1817); taught Greek literature at Harvard; edited *North American Review*. Congressman, Independent, from Massachusetts, 1825–35; Whig governor, 1836–39. American minister to Court of St. James's, 1841–45; president of Harvard College, 1846–49; U.S. secretary of state, 1852–53; senator from Massachusetts, 1853–54. An ardent Unionist, he compromised himself by not voting on the Kansas-Nebraska bill, and resigned his seat. Ran for vice president on Constitutional Union ticket, 1860. Spent last four years of his life speaking in support of the Union; shared platform with Lincoln at Gettysburg, Nov. 19, 1863. A brilliant and magnetic public speaker, he was given to making compromises either because of personal ambition or because of a strain of timidity in his character.

EVERETT, ROBERT (*b. Gronant, Wales, 1791; d. 1875*), Congregational clergyman, publisher. Immigrated to Oneida Co., N.Y., 1823. Advocating abolition and prohibition, he won most of the Welsh Congregationalists in America for the Republican party.

EVERLEIGH, MINNA (*b. 1878; d. New York, N.Y., 1948*), and EVERLEIGH, ADA (*b. 1876; d. Virginia, 1960*), madams. Conducted the Everleigh Club in Chicago, Ill., 1899–1911, the most luxurious and expensive house of prostitution in the United States. Of uncertain origin, but generally believed to have been from Kentucky and originally named Lester, they held themselves out as aristocratic belles from the South. After their establishment was shut down, they lived a quiet life in New York City, devoted to poetry-reading and theatergoing.

EVERMANN, BARTON WARREN (*b. Albia, Iowa, 1853; d. Berkeley, Calif., 1932*), ichthyologist. Graduated University of Indiana, 1886; Ph.D., 1891. Associated with U.S. Bureau of Fisheries, 1891–1914. His principles of conservation prevented extinction of Alaska fur seal. Author of *Fishes of North and Middle America* (1896–1900) and other works.

EVERS, MEDGAR WILEY (*b. Decatur, Miss., 1925; d. Jackson, Miss., 1963*), civil rights leader. Joined the National Association for the Advancement of Colored People (NAACP) in 1954; made field secretary in Mississippi, 1954. A quiet, reasonable, and effective organizer who believed that blacks should rid themselves of their sense of inferiority and seek equality through voting and economic boycotts. The target of white hostility, Evers was assassinated in 1963. The crime energized black political activism in Mississippi and sped the passage of civil rights legislation in Congress.

EWBANK, THOMAS (*b. Durham, England, 1792; d. New York, N.Y., 1870*), inventor, manufacturer, author. Came to America, 1819. As U.S. commissioner of patents, 1849–52, he filled his annual reports with useful essays on historical aspects and industrial applications of inventions.

EWELL, BENJAMIN STODDERT (*b. Georgetown, D.C., 1810; d. 1894*), Confederate soldier, educator. Son of Thomas Ewell. Graduated West Point, 1832. Professor of mathematics at several colleges; chief of staff to Gen. J. E. Johnston. President of William and Mary College, 1854–61, 1865–88; president emeritus thereafter. Preserved the college from extinction during his postwar service.

EWELL, JAMES (*b. near Dumfries, Va., 1773; d. Covington, La., 1832*), physician. Introduced vaccination in Savannah, Ga.; author of *Planter's and Mariner's Medical Companion* (1807); practiced in Washington, D.C., and New Orleans, La.

EWELL, RICHARD STODDERT (*b. Georgetown, D.C., 1817; d. near Spring Hill, Tenn., 1872*), Confederate soldier. Son of Thomas Ewell. Graduated West Point, 1840. Served in Mexican War, and with distinction as brigade, division, and corps commander in Civil War under Jackson and Lee. Promoted lieutenant general, 1863, he commanded II Corps in the Gettysburg and wilderness campaigns; he subsequently commanded the defenses of Richmond.

EWELL, THOMAS (*b. near Dumfries, Va., 1785; d. Centerville, Va., 1826*), physician, businessman. Brother of James Ewell. Edited first American edition of Hume's *Essays* (1817); author of *The American Family Physician* (1824).

EWER, FERDINAND CARTWRIGHT (*b. Nantucket, Mass., 1826; d. 1883*), Episcopal clergyman. After an early career as a California journalist (editor, *The Pioneer*, 1854, and others), he was ordained, 1858, and became a leading exponent of Anglo-Catholicism. He served as rector of parishes in New York City *post* 1862.

EWING, CHARLES (*b. Bridgeton, N.J., 1780; d. 1832*), jurist. Graduated Princeton, 1798. Practiced law in Trenton, N.J.; was chief justice of New Jersey Supreme Court, 1824–32.

EWING, FINIS (*b. Bedford Co., Va., 1773; d. 1841*), farmer, chief founder of Cumberland Presbyterian church, 1810. Pastor in Kentucky, Tennessee, and Missouri; helped shape doctrines of his sect.

EWING, HUGH BOYLE (*b. Lancaster, Ohio, 1826; d. near Lancaster, 1905*), lawyer, Union soldier. Son of Thomas Ewing (1789–1871); foster brother of W. T. Sherman. Attended West Point; practiced law in St. Louis, Mo., Leavenworth, Kans., and Washington, D.C. Division commander in Civil War. U.S. minister to Holland, 1866–70.

EWING, JAMES (*b. Lancaster Co., Pa., 1736; d. Hellam, Pa., 1806*), Revolutionary soldier, Pennsylvania legislator and official.

EWING, JAMES (*b. Pittsburgh, Pa., 1866; d. New York, N.Y., 1943*), pathologist. B.A., Amherst, 1888; M.D., College of Physicians and Surgeons, Columbia, 1891. Influenced by T. M. Prudden. Taught histology and clinical pathology at Columbia; professor of pathology, Cornell University Medical College, 1899–1932. Celebrated for his research on malignancies, he was able with the help of James Douglas to reorganize Memorial Hospital, New York City, an affiliate of Cornell, into a specialized institution for cancer treatment and research. Under Ewing's influence, Memorial Hospital became the world leader in the clinical classification and diagnostic histology of tumors. Among his many publications, his leading work was *Neoplastic Diseases* (1919). He was founder of the American Cancer Society.

EWING, JAMES CARUTHERS RHEA (*b. Rural Valley, Pa., 1854; d. Princeton, N.J., 1925*), Presbyterian missionary in India, 1879–1922. Principal, Forman College, Lahore, 1888–1918; officer of Punjab University.

EWING, JOHN (*b. East Nottingham, Md., 1732; d. Norristown, Pa., 1802*), Presbyterian clergyman. Pastor, First Church, Philadelphia. Provost of University of Pennsylvania and professor of natural philosophy there *post* 1779, he enjoyed high contemporary repute as a scholar and scientist.

EWING, THOMAS (*b. near West Liberty, Va., 1789; d. Lancaster, Ohio, 1871*), lawyer. Raised in Athens Co., Ohio; graduated Ohio University, 1815. Became one of the ablest and most successful lawyers in the West. U.S. senator, Whig, from Ohio, 1831–36, 1850–51; U.S. secretary of treasury, 1841, resigning in contest with President Tyler over recharter of a national bank; secretary of interior, 1849–50. Supported Lincoln; opposed Reconstruction policies.

EWING, THOMAS (*b. Lancaster, Ohio, 1829; d. 1896*), Union soldier, lawyer. Son of Thomas Ewing (1789–1871). Distinguished in fighting in Missouri and Kansas, 1863–64. Leader of Greenback wing of Democratic party, 1870–81.

EYTINGE, ROSE (*b. Philadelphia, Pa., 1835; d. Amityville, N.Y., 1911*), actress, author, teacher. Acted with companies of E. Booth, J. W. Wallack, Augustin Daly; principal success in *Antony and Cleopatra*, produced by her own company, New York, 1877.

EZEKIEL, MOSES JACOB (*b. Richmond, Va., 1844; d. Rome, Italy, 1917*), sculptor, Confederate soldier. Graduated Virginia Military Institute, 1866. Studied at Royal Academy, Berlin. Among his many works are the Jefferson monument at Louisville, Ky., and the Confederate monument at Arlington National Cemetery. Skillful and prolific, he was knighted by both Germany and Italy.

F

FABER, JOHN EBERHARD (*b. Stein, Bavaria, 1822; d. 1879*), pencil manufacturer. Extended family business to America, *ca.* 1848, opening factory in 1861. First to attach rubber erasers to pencils.

FACCIOLI, GIUSEPPE (*b. Milan, Italy, 1877; d. Pittsfield, Mass., 1934*), mechanical and electrical engineer. Came to America *ca.* 1900; was associated thereafter principally with William Stanley and General Electric Co. in design and development of alternating current machinery and high-tension transmission apparatus.

FACKLER, DAVID PARKS (*b. Kempsville, Va., 1841; d. Richmond, Va., 1924*), actuary. Graduated College of the City of New York, 1859. Made notable improvements in life-insurance practice; served as consulting actuary to private companies and governmental investigating committees.

FAESCH, JOHN JACOB (*b. Canton of Basle, Switzerland, 1729; d. 1799*), ironmaster, government contractor. Came to America, 1764. Had charge of Mt. Hope furnaces in New Jersey. Cast shot for Continental army.

FAGAN, JAMES FLEMING (*b. Clark Co., Ky., 1828; d. 1893*), planter, Confederate soldier. Raised in Arkansas. Served in Mexican War and in western campaigns of Civil War; was major general at surrender.

FAGAN, MARK MATTHEW (*b. Jersey City, N.J., 1869; d. Jersey City, 1955*), politician. Colorful mayor of Jersey City, 1901–07, and honorary mayor under a commission government, 1913–17. A Republican, he was known for his "single tax" concept and for machine reforms.

FAGES, PEDRO (*fl. 1767–96*), first *commandante* and later governor of Alta California. Accompanied Portolá to Monterey, 1770; explored San Francisco Bay; as governor, 1782–91, encouraged fur trade, erection of missions and presidios, and education of Indians.

FAGET, JEAN CHARLES (*b. New Orleans, La., 1818; d. New Orleans, 1884*), physician. Graduated in medicine at Paris, 1844; practiced in New Orleans. Discovered a conclusive sign of diagnosis for yellow fever, 1859; chevalier of Legion of Honor.

FAHNESTOCK, HARRIS CHARLES (*b. Harrisburg, Pa., 1835; d. 1914*), banker. Directed New York branch of Jay Cooke & Co., 1866–73; on its failure, he became a vice president and organizer of the First National Bank of New York.

FAIR, JAMES GRAHAM (*b. near Belfast, Ireland, 1831; d. San Francisco, Calif., 1894*), forty-niner, financier. Came to America as a boy of 12. Derived fortune from Consolidated Virginia mine of the Comstock Lode.

FAIRBANK, CALVIN (*b. Allegany, now Wyoming, Co., N.Y., 1816; d. Angelica, N.Y., 1898*), Methodist clergyman, abolitionist, Underground Railroad agent.

FAIRBANKS, CHARLES WARREN (*b. near Unionville Center, Ohio, 1852; d. 1918*), lawyer. Graduated Ohio Wesleyan, 1872. Practiced as railway attorney in Indianapolis, Ind.; was temporary chairman and keynote speaker of convention which nominated McKinley. As U.S. senator, Republican, from Indiana, 1897–1904, he served on Foreign Relations Committee, advocated comprehensive plans for internal improvements, was American chairman of Joint High Commission, 1898. Was U.S. vice president, 1905–09; chairman of Republican platform committee, 1912; and "favorite son" candidate for presidential nomination in 1908 and 1916.

FAIRBANKS, DOUGLAS (*b. Denver, Colo., 1883; d. Santa Monica, Calif., 1939*), motion-picture actor and producer. Changed name from Douglas Ulman. Best known for his costume adventure films, *The Three Musketeers, Robin Hood,* etc.

FAIRBANKS, ERASTUS (*b. Brimfield, Mass., 1792; d. 1864*), manufacturer. Brother of Thaddeus Fairbanks. Headed E. & T. Fairbanks & Co., a firm which he founded with his two brothers and which enjoyed worldwide reputation for the quality of its platform scales. Whig governor of Vermont, 1852–53, his stand on temperance lost him reelection. Running on the Republican ticket, 1860, he returned as governor and ably mobilized the state to support the Union war effort.

FAIRBANKS, HENRY (*b. St. Johnsbury, Vt., 1830; d. 1918*), Congregational clergyman, inventor, manufacturer. Son of Thaddeus Fairbanks. Graduated Dartmouth, 1853. Taught natural philosophy at Dartmouth, 1860–69; patented scales and pulp-manufacturing machines; also invented an alternating current electric generator.

FAIRBANKS, THADDEUS (*b. Brimfield, Mass., 1796; d. St. Johnsbury, Vt., 1886*), inventor. Cofounder with Erastus and Joseph Fairbanks, his brothers, of the E. & T. Fairbanks iron foundry, 1823, later famous as scale manufacturers. Inventor of improved plows, stoves, and a machine for dressing flax and hemp, he was granted a patent for the first platform scale, 1831. He later invented draft mechanism for furnaces, a hot-water heater, and a feedwater heater. With his brothers, he founded and endowed St. Johnsbury Academy.

FAIRBURN, WILLIAM ARMSTRONG (*b. Huddersfield, England, 1876; d. Kezar Lake, Maine, 1947*), naval architect, marine engineer, corporation executive. Came to the United States as a boy with his parents. Served apprenticeship at Bath Iron Works, Bath, Maine. After studying naval architecture and marine engineering at the University of Glasgow, Scotland, he became general superintendent and architect for Bath Iron Works, 1898. In 1900, he became an independent consultant, designing and supervising construction of cargo vessels for James J. Hill and E.

H. Harriman; pioneered in use of the diesel engine for railroading. Retained by the Diamond Match Co. to develop a safety match, 1909, he used patents already owned by the company, and in association with company chemists perfected the match by 1911; he also provided safer packaging for the product. As president of the company *post* 1915, he diversified its activities, contained foreign competition, and put it at the head of the industry.

FAIRCHILD, BLAIR (*b. Belmont, Mass., 1877; d. 1933*), composer. Influenced by Widor and César Franck.

FAIRCHILD, CHARLES STEBBINS (*b. Cazenovia, N.Y., 1842; d. Cazenovia, 1924*), lawyer, financier. New York State attorney general under Governor S. J. Tilden; prosecuted "Canal Ring" frauds. U.S. secretary of the treasury, 1887–89.

FAIRCHILD, DAVID GRANDISON (*b. Lansing, Mich., 1869; d. Coconut Grove, Fla., 1954*), botanist, author, agricultural explorer. Studied at Kansas State College for Agriculture, Iowa State College for Agriculture, and Rutgers. Working for the Department of Agriculture and for the Smithsonian Institution, Fairchild explored for exotic plants and introduced more than 20,000 species into the U.S., including the soybean, hairy Peruvian alfalfa, a variety of dates, the nectarine, flowering cherries, the avocado, and mangoes. Founded the Fairchild Tropical Gardens near Miami (1938), one of the world's finest botanical collections.

FAIRCHILD, FRED ROGERS (*b. Crete, Nebr., 1877; d. Bridgeport, Conn., 1966*), economist and educator. Studied at Doane College in Crete, Nebr., and Yale (Ph.D., 1904). Professor of economics and political economy at Yale from 1904. Chairman of the Department of Social and Political Science (1920–24); the Department of Economics, Sociology, and Government (1924–25); the Department of Economics (1937–39). Seymour H. Knox Professor of Economics (1936–45). Academic works include coauthorsip of *Elementary Economics* (1926). An expert in public finance and a spokesman for business on tax matters, Fairchild was president of the National Tax Association in 1929. Consultant to the Dominican Republic (1917–18) and Colombia (1923) on economic restructuring.

FAIRCHILD, GEORGE THOMPSON (*b. Brownhelm, Ohio, 1838; d. Columbus, Ohio, 1901*), educator. Graduated Oberlin in arts, 1862, and in theology, 1865. President, Kansas Agricultural College, 1879–97.

FAIRCHILD, JAMES HARRIS (*b. Stockbridge, Mass., 1817; d. 1902*), educator. Graduated Oberlin, in arts, 1838, and in theology, 1841. A professor at Oberlin, 1841–98, and president of the college, 1866–89.

FAIRCHILD, LUCIUS (*b. Portage Co., Ohio, 1831; d. Madison, Wis., 1896*), Union soldier, diplomat. Republican governor of Wisconsin, 1866–72. Consul at Liverpool, consul general at Paris; U.S. minister to Spain, 1880–82. National Commander, GAR, 1886.

FAIRCHILD, MARY SALOME CUTLER (*b. Dalton, Mass., 1855; d. 1921*), librarian. Pioneer in professional library training at New York State Library School, Albany, 1889–1905.

FAIRCHILD, MUIR STEPHEN (*b. Bellingham, Wash., 1894; d. Fort Myer, Va., 1950*), army and air force officer. Attended University of Washington, 1913–16. Served on Mexican border; was cadet in aviation section of U.S. Army Signal Corps; commissioned in U.S. Air Service, January 1918. After flying bombing missions in France, where he was wounded, he returned briefly to civilian life. Resuming active duty, 1920, he served as a test pilot and in varied Air Corps engineer assignments; he also completed

courses at the Army Industrial College, the Army War College, and the Air Corps Tactical School, on whose faculty he served, 1937–40. Assigned to staff duty in Washington, July 1940, he was promoted to major general, 1942, and was one of three advisers on global and theater strategy to the Joint Chiefs of Staff during World War II. In January 1946, he was assigned as the first commanding general of the Air University at Maxwell Air Force Base, Alabama. Appointed vice-chief of staff of the Air Force, May 1948, he held this post, with promotion to general, until his death.

FAIRFAX, BEATRICE. *See* MANNING, MARIE.

FAIRFAX, DONALD McNEILL (*b. Virginia, 1821; d. Hagerstown, Md., 1894*), naval officer. Supervised capture of Confederate agents Mason and Slidell from the *Trent*, 1861. Retired as rear admiral, 1881.

FAIRFAX, THOMAS (*b. Leeds Castle, Kent, England, 1693; d. "Greenway Court," Shenandoah Valley, Va., 1781*), sixth Lord Fairfax of Cameron, proprietor of the Northern Neck of Virginia. Came first to Virginia, 1735–37, to protect his property from efforts of the Virginia Assembly to narrow its boundaries; returning in 1747, he settled in the Shenandoah Valley, 1752. Served as justice of the peace and county lieutenant and was an early friend to George Washington. The only resident peer in America, he was accorded all the privileges of Virginia citizenship and was never molested during the Revolution.

FAIRFIELD, EDMUND BURKE (*b. Parkersburg, Va., 1821; d. Oberlin, Ohio, 1904*), Baptist and Congregational clergyman, educator. Second chancellor of University of Nebraska, 1876–82, he resigned over a fundamentalist-modernist controversy among the faculty, in which he stood for the older modes of thought.

FAIRFIELD, JOHN (*b. Saco, Maine, 1797; d. 1847*), lawyer, politician. Congressman, Democrat, from Maine, 1835–38; U.S. senator, 1843–47. As Maine governor, 1838–39 and 1841–42, he clashed with Great Britain over northeastern boundary dispute.

FAIRFIELD, SUMNER LINCOLN (*b. Warwick, Mass., 1803; d. New Orleans, La., 1844*), teacher, poet. Author of *The Last Night of Pompeii* (1832) and others; editor, the *North American Magazine*, 1832–38.

FAIRLAMB, JAMES REMINGTON (*b. Philadelphia, Pa., 1838; d. Ingleside, N.Y., 1908*), composer, organist.

FAIRLESS, BENJAMIN F. (*b. Pigeon Run, Ohio, 1890; d. Ligonier, Pa., 1962*), industrialist. Worked his way through college, graduating from Ohio Northern University in 1909. Fairless rose through the ranks of the Central Steel Company in Ohio, 1914–35, which merged with several firms over the years to become the Republic Steel Corporation in 1930. Fairless left his position as executive vice president of that company to become president of the Carnegie-Illinois Steel Corporation, a subsidiary of United States Steel. He was chairman of the board and chief executive officer, 1952–55. An effective defender of bigness in the steel industry, Fairless battled the unions and the government to resolve several major steel strikes throughout the 40's and early 50's. During his tenure, United States Steel enjoyed swelling profits, plant expansion, and modernization.

FAIRLIE, JOHN ARCHIBALD (*b. Glasgow, Scotland, 1872; d. Atlanta, Ga., 1947*), political scientist. Came to America as a child; raised in Jacksonville, Fla. Graduated Harvard, 1895; Ph.D., Columbia, 1898. Taught administrative law at University of Michigan, 1900–09; associate professor of political science, University of Illinois, 1909–11, and full professor, 1911–41. An authority on state and local government, Fairlie took an active part in movements for reform of municipal and state administration. He was a founder of the American Political Science Association and managing editor of its *Review*, 1916–25. Among his books was the influential *Municipal Administration* (1901).

FALCKNER, DANIEL (*b. Langen-Reinsdorf, Saxony, 1666; d. New Jersey*[?], *ca. 1741*), Lutheran clergyman. Brother of Justus Falckner. Came to America, 1694. Agent for Frankfort Land Co., proprietors of Germantown, Pa.; organized first German Lutheran congregation in Pennsylvania.

FALCKNER, JUSTUS (*b. Langen-Reinsdorf, Saxony, 1672; d. 1723*), Lutheran clergyman. Brother of Daniel Falckner. Came to America, 1700, and was ordained at Philadelphia, 1703. Ministered thereafter to Dutch and German Lutheran congregations in New York, East Jersey, and western Long Island.

FALK, MAURICE (*b. Old Allegheny, Pa., 1866; d. Miami Beach, Fla., 1946*), industrialist, philanthropist. Organized and operated successful companies in the Pittsburgh area for refining nonferrous metals and production of related chemicals; made profitable investments in steel manufacturing and other companies. A generous supporter of Jewish and other philanthropies, he established an outpatient clinic at University of Pittsburgh (1928) and endowed the Maurice and Laura Falk Foundation (1929) to fund research into economics and social problems, medicine, political education, and cultural affairs.

FALK, OTTO HERBERT (*b. Wauwatosa, Wis., 1865; d. Milwaukee, Wis., 1940*), soldier, industrialist. President, Allis-Chalmers Manufacturing Co., 1913–32.

FALKNER, ROLAND POST (*b. Bridgeport, Conn., 1866; d. New York, N.Y., 1940*), economist, statistician. Graduated Wharton School of Finance, University of Pennsylvania, 1885; Ph.D., University of Halle, 1888. Joining the Wharton School faculty, 1888–1900, he became probably first American professor to teach statistics full time. Statistician, subcommittee of U.S. Senate Finance Committee investigating prices and wages, 1891, he made its findings an important milestone in economic statistics. A keen analyst with a gift for expression, Falkner divided his later career between government and private service.

FALL, ALBERT BACON (*b. Frankfort, Ky., 1861; d. El Paso, Tex., 1944*), lawyer, politician, cabinet officer. Moved west, 1881; worked as cattle drover, insurance and real estate agent, grocer; prospected in Mexico and New Mexico. Began practice as attorney in Las Cruces, N.Mex., 1889. Served as a territorial legislator (Democrat), judge, and attorney general, meanwhile engaging in Mexican mining promotions and representing industrial clients. His admiration for Theodore Roosevelt was a principal reason for his shift to the Republican party, 1908. In 1912, he became one of New Mexico's first U.S. senators, demanding forceful protection of U.S. property rights in revolution-torn Mexico and bitterly opposing President Wilson's Mexican policy. One of Warren G. Harding's poker-playing cronies, he was named U.S. secretary of the interior when Harding took office in 1921. In 1922, he turned over rights to drill in the U.S. Navy oil reserve lands at Teapot Dome, Wyo., and Elk Hills, Calif., to oil magnates Harry F. Sinclair and Edward L. Doheny, receiving from them at least $404,000 and other considerations. After he had resigned from the cabinet in 1923, an investigation by Senator Thomas J. Walsh disclosed what became known as the Teapot Dome scandal. Fall maintained that the money was a legitimate business loan, but he was convicted of taking a bribe (1929) and sentenced to a year in prison.

FALL, BERNARD B. (*b. Vienna, Austria, 1926; d. north of Hue, Vietnam, 1967*), historian and war correspondent. Grew up in southern France. Joined the resistance as a teenager in World War II; fought with the regular army in the liberation of France and drive into Germany. Studied at the University of Paris, the University of Munich, Johns Hopkins, and Syracuse University (Ph.D., 1955). Professor of international relations at Howard University (1956–67). Visiting professor at the Royal Institute of Administration, Cambodia (1961–62). Reputation as one of the foremost authorities on Vietnam in the 1960's grew out of his study of the area for his doctoral dissertation (published as *The Viet-Minh Regime* in 1954). Also wrote *Street Without Joy* (1961), *The Two Vietnams: A Political and Military Analysis* (1963), and *Hell in a Very Small Place* (1966). Articles and essays examining the war and the experiences of those who fought it were collected in *Viet-Nam Witness* (1966). Though he remained a French citizen, Fall had great affection for both the United States and Vietnam. His work is noted for its sharp criticism of American policy in Vietnam. He was killed by a Vietminh land mine while accompanying U.S. marines.

FALLOWS, SAMUEL (*b. Pendleton, England, 1835; d. Chicago, Ill., 1922*), Union soldier, Methodist clergyman, bishop of Reformed Episcopal church, 1876–1922.

FANEUIL, PETER (*b. New Rochelle, N.Y., 1700; d. Boston, Mass., 1743*), merchant. Donor of Faneuil Hall, Boston.

FANNIN, JAMES WALKER (*b. Georgia, ca. 1804; d. Goliad, Tex., 1836*), colonel in Texas army. Removed to Texas, 1834. Active in the revolutionary movement, he successfully carried out missions at Gonzales, Concepcion, and west of Trinity River, 1835. Overtaken near Goliad by General Urrea's force, he was defeated, Mar. 19, 1836, and captured. On order of Santa Anna, 330 men of Fannin's force, including Fannin himself, were shot.

FANNING, ALEXANDER CAMPBELL WILDER (*b. Boston, Mass., 1788; d. Cincinnati, Ohio, 1846*), soldier. Graduated West Point, 1812. Served in War of 1812 and Seminole campaigns of 1818 and 1835–39. Brevetted colonel for gallantry on the Withlacoochee, December 1835; defended Camp Monroe, February 1837.

FANNING, DAVID (*b. Beech Swamp, Va., ca. 1755; d. Canada, 1825*), North Carolina Loyalist and partisan leader. Author of *Narrative of Col. David Fanning* (written 1790; first published 1861).

FANNING, EDMUND (*b. Suffolk Co., N.Y., 1739; d. London, England, 1818*), lawyer, North Carolina Loyalist. Graduated Yale, 1757. A favorite of Governor Tryon, he won a North Carolina reputation for avarice and immorality; commanded King's American Regiment of Foot during the Revolution.

FANNING, EDMUND (*b. Stonington, Conn., 1769; d. New York, N.Y., 1841*), sea captain, explorer, promoter. Brother of Nathaniel Fanning. Discovered Fanning Island in the Pacific; promoted South Sea trade.

FANNING, JOHN THOMAS (*b. Norwich, Conn., 1837; d. 1911*), hydraulic engineer. Author of *A Practical Treatise on Water Supply Engineering* (1877). Designed water supply and purification systems for Minneapolis, Des Moines, Omaha, Birmingham, Ala., and many other American cities.

FANNING, NATHANIEL (*b. Stonington, Conn., 1755; d. Charleston, S.C., 1805*), privateersman, naval officer. Won fame as captain of the maintop during the *Bonhomme Richard*'s fight with the *Serapis*, 1779. Author of *Narrative of the Adventures of an American Naval Officer* (1806), later published as *Memoirs of the Life of Captain Nathaniel Fanning* (1808).

FANNING, TOLBERT (*b. Cannon Co., Tenn., 1810; d. 1874*), Disciples of Christ minister, educator, editor.

FARABEE, WILLIAM CURTIS (*b. Washington Co., Pa., 1865; d. 1925*), anthropologist, ethnologist. Graduated Waynesburg, 1894; Ph.D., Harvard, 1903. Taught at Harvard and University of Pennsylvania; carried out important field studies in South America.

FARAN, JAMES JOHN (*b. Cincinnati, Ohio, 1808; d. 1892*), lawyer, politician, editor. Held state offices and was congressman, Democrat, from Ohio, 1845–49. A proprietor and editor of the *Cincinnati Enquirer*, 1844–81.

FARGO, WILLIAM GEORGE (*b. Pompey, N.Y., 1818; d. Buffalo, N.Y., 1881*), expressman. Was messenger and agent for Pomeroy & Co., express firm between Albany and Buffalo; became messenger and co-owner of Wells & Co., first express concern west of Buffalo, 1844, and secretary of first American Express Co., 1850. Helped organize Wells, Fargo & Co. for express service to California, 1852. By 1855 the company controlled western express business, carrying gold dust, mail, packages, and passengers and conducting banking services. After a series of mergers, Wells, Fargo and associated express companies were united as the American Express Co., 1873, with Fargo as president. He also served as Democratic mayor of Buffalo, 1862–66.

FARIBAULT, JEAN BAPTISTE (*b. Berthier, Canada, 1775; d. St. Paul, Minn., 1860*), pioneer fur and lead trader. Influential with the Sioux, he preserved peace on the Minnesota frontier.

FARISH, WILLIAM STAMPS (*b. Mayersvile, Miss., 1881; d. Millbrook, N.Y., 1942*), oil company executive. Entered oil industry at Beaumont, Tex., 1901; by 1916 was one of the leading independent producers in Texas. After failing in an effort to persuade all small producers to pool their oil so as to sell direct to refineries in the East, thus bypassing the restrictive sales contracts imposed by the major companies in Texas, he joined with several other producing firms to form the Humble Oil and Refining Co., 1917. The new firm was successful but outran its capital resources; Farish obtained necessary funds for expansion and a stable market for his product by affiliating with Standard Oil Co. (New Jersey), 1919. A leader in application of scientific research and advanced engineering techniques in the industry and in reform of wasteful practices and the laws governing oil and gas production, he was president of Humble Oil, 1922–33, and chairman of the board of Standard Oil (New Jersey), 1933–37. In 1937, he was elected president of Standard.

FARLEY, HARRIET (*b. Claremont, N.H., 1817; d. New York, N.Y., 1907*), editor, author. Edited the *Lowell Offering*, 1842–45 and 1848–50, publishing contributions from female workers in Lowell, Mass., mills.

FARLEY, JOHN MURPHY (*b. Newtown-Hamilton, Ireland, 1842; d. New York, N.Y., 1918*), Roman Catholic clergyman. Came to America, 1864. Ordained Rome, 1870; served as secretary to Archbishop McCloskey; succeeded him as archbishop of New York, 1902. Created cardinal, 1911.

FARLOW, WILLIAM GILSON (*b. Boston, Mass., 1844; d. 1919*), botanist. Graduated Harvard, 1866. Studied under Asa Gray and De Bary; laid foundation of American phytopathology; built up Harvard's cryptogamic herbarium and library.

FARMAN, ELBERT ELI (*b. New Haven, N.Y., 1831; d. 1911*), jurist, diplomat. Graduated Amherst, 1855. Served as consul general and judge of the international mixed tribunals in Egypt, 1876–84.

FARMER, FANNIE MERRITT (*b. Boston, Mass., 1857; d. 1915*), educator. Director, Boston Cooking School, 1891–1902, and of her own school. Editor, *Boston Cooking School Cook Book* (1896).

FARMER, FERDINAND (*b. Swabia, Germany, 1720; d. Philadelphia, Pa., 1786*), Jesuit priest. Came to America, 1752; changed his name from Steinmeyer. Served in Lancaster, Pa., 1752–58; thereafter worked as missionary out of St. Joseph's parish, Philadelphia. He is believed to have organized first Catholic congregation in New York City in 1775.

FARMER, HANNAH TOBEY SHAPLEIGH (*b. Berwick, Maine, 1823; d. Eliot, Maine, 1891*), philanthropist. Wife of Moses G. Farmer.

FARMER, JOHN (*b. Chelmsford, Mass., 1789; d. Concord, N.H., 1838*), apothecary, antiquarian, genealogist. A *Genealogical Register of the First Settlers of New England* (1829) is his most important work.

FARMER, JOHN (*b. Halfmoon, N.Y., 1798; d. 1859*), surveyor, cartographer. Mapped states of Michigan and Wisconsin, also city of Detroit.

FARMER, MOSES GERRISH (*b. Boscawen, N.H., 1820; d. Chicago, Ill., 1893*), teacher, inventor, pioneer American electrician. Devised machine for printing paper window shades; in 1845 started experiments with electricity, and in 1847 exhibited a practical miniature electric train. Accepted position with new electric telegraph line in Massachusetts between Boston and Worcester, 1848; shortly thereafter took charge of Boston and Newburyport telegraph. Was superintendent of first American electric fire-alarm system in Boston, 1851–53, a system which he had developed in association with Dr. William F. Channing. Devised the duplex and quadruplex telegraph, 1855; in 1856 succeeded in depositing aluminum electrolytically. Invented an incandescent electric lamp, 1858–59, and patented in 1866 the "self-exciting" dynamo, lighting thereby a Cambridge, Mass., residence with 40 of his incandescent lamps arranged in multiple series. As electrician at the U.S. Torpedo Station, Newport, R.I., 1872–81, he greatly advanced the art of torpedo warfare for the U.S. Navy. Thereafter, he acted as consulting electrician for the U.S. Electric Light Co. of New York, giving his attention chiefly to electric power generation and distribution. Interested always in discovering the principles that made his inventions work, he did not profit greatly from any of them.

FARNAM, HENRY (*b. Scipio, N.Y., 1803; d. 1883*), engineer, philanthropist. Built Michigan Southern and other railroads to Chicago, also the Rock Island bridge across the Mississippi; president of Chicago & Rock Island, 1854–63.

FARNAM, HENRY WALCOTT (*b. New Haven, Conn., 1853; d. New Haven, 1933*), economist, philanthropist, reformer. Son of Henry Farnam. Taught at Yale; active in civil service reform.

FARNHAM, ELIZA WOODSON BURHANS (*b. Rensselaerville, N.Y., 1815; d. Milton-on-the-Hudson, N.Y., 1864*), philanthropist. Author of *Woman and Her Era* (1864).

FARNHAM, RUSSEL (*b. Massachusetts, 1784; d. St. Louis, Mo., 1832*), fur trader. One of the "Astorians" of the 1810 expedition. Traveled across Siberia on foot, 1814–16; managed Astor's American Fur Co. on upper Mississippi, 1817–19; thereafter farmed in Missouri.

FARNHAM, THOMAS JEFFERSON (*b. Vermont[?], 1804; d. San Francisco, Calif., 1848*), lawyer, traveler. Author of *Travels in the Great Western Prairies* (1841), describing his 1839 journey across the continent to Oregon.

FARNSWORTH, ELON JOHN (*b. Green Oak, Mich., 1837; d. near Gettysburg, Pa., 1863*), Union soldier. Rose from lieutenant to brigadier general in two years. Killed leading a gallant cavalry charge near Little Round Top.

FARNSWORTH, JOHN FRANKLIN (*b. Eaton, Canada, 1820; d. Washington, D.C., 1897*), lawyer, politician, Union soldier. Raised in Michigan; removed to Illinois, 1842. Congressman, Republican, from Illinois, 1857–61 and 1863–73. An active Radical during the Reconstruction era.

FARNUM, DUSTIN LANCY (*b. Hampton Beach, N.H., 1874; d. 1929*), actor. Famous for his portrayal of *The Virginian*, 1904, and other romantic roles; later became screen actor.

FARNUM, FRANKLYN (*b. Boston, Mass., 1878[?]; d. Los Angeles, Calif., 1961*), silent film actor. Early work on Broadway led to leading roles in 150 silent films, including *Love Never Dies* (1914), *The Fighting Grin* (1918), and *Battling Brewster* (1924). His popularity was as a hero in such westerns as *The Struggle* (1920), *So This Is Arizona* (1922), and *The Gambling Fool* (1925). With the introduction of sound, Farnum worked as an extra in hundreds of talkies. President of the Screen Extras Guild, 1956–59.

FARQUHAR, PERCIVAL (*b. York, Pa., 1864; d. New York, N.Y., 1953*), entrepreneur. Pioneer in transportation, utilities, rubber, cattle, steel, and iron ore exportation. Built and financed railroads, power systems, tramways, and port facilities throughout South America in the early part of the century. Built the Madeira-Mamoré Railway (completed in 1912) through the Amazon jungle in Brazil at a cost of $30 million.

FARRAGUT, DAVID GLASGOW (*b. Campbell's Station, Tenn., 1801; d. Portsmouth, N.H., 1870*), naval officer. Son of George Farragut. Appointed midshipman, 1810; one year later he saw his first sea duty on the *Essex* under Commodore David Porter, his foster father. During the War of 1812 the young midshipman was made master of one of the *Essex*'s prizes; after creditable service during the *Essex*'s losing fight with the *Phoebe* and *Cherub* in the harbor of Valparaiso, 1814, he was taken prisoner. Serviced in the Mediterranean, 1815–20; accompanying his naval schoolmaster, Charles Folsom, to the latter's post as consul to Tunis, he learned to speak French, Italian, Spanish, and Arabic. Serving, 1822–24, in the West Indies against pirates, he obtained his first command of a naval vessel, the *Ferret*. A lieutenant from 1825 to 1841, he conveyed Lafayette to France on the frigate *Brandywine*; served on the sloop *Vandalia* off the coast of Brazil and on the sloop *Natchez* on her visit to Charleston, S.C., during the nullification controversy. In 1838, he commanded the *Erie* on a mission to protect American citizens and property in Mexico during the Franco-Mexican war. On duty on the Brazil station, 1841, he was made commander; he took over the sloop *Decatur*, 1842. During the Mexican War, in disfavor with his commodore, he commanded the *Saratoga* on routine blockade duties. Commissioned captain, 1855, while establishing Mare Island navy yard in California, he returned east in 1859 and took command of the *Brooklyn*.

At home in Norfolk, Va., on waiting orders, 1860–61, Farragut left the state the day after the Virginia Convention had passed its secession ordinance, and was assigned at first to an unimportant post at the New York navy yard. Appointed in January 1862 to command of the West Gulf Blockading Squadron, Farragut was responsible for the area between St. Andrew's Bay, Fla., and the Rio Grande; he had confidential orders to reduce the defenses guarding New Orleans and to take the city. Arriving at Ship Island late in February, on Apr. 18 he began operations with his fleet of 17 vessels and a mortar flotilla by bombarding Fort Jackson. The bombardment appearing ineffective, Farragut, against orders, decided to run by Fort Jackson and Fort St. Philip before they were reduced. He was successful, all but 3 of his ships passing the forts. He destroyed 11 of the enemy's vessels and took New Orleans without further bloodshed.

This victory made him the navy's leading officer and earned him a congressional resolution of thanks and a commission as the first American rear admiral. He continued up the Mississippi and passed the defenses of Vicksburg, but on finding that place impregnable to naval attack he returned to blockade duty in the Gulf. By the end of 1862, he held the whole of the Gulf Coast within the limits of his command, except for Mobile.

After varying success and a furlough in 1863, he hoisted his flag again on the *Hartford* and returned to the Gulf. On Aug. 5, 1864, he led his fleet against the defenses at the entrance to Mobile Bay, forcing his way over the mines with which the passage was sown and inspiring his men with his famous cry "Damn the torpedoes!" Fort Gaines and Fort Morgan surrendered soon after the dispersal of the supporting Confederate flotilla. Mobile Bay was the crowning event of Farragut's career. He had reached a position as preeminent in the American navy as that of Nelson had been in the British. On Dec. 23, 1864, he was made vice admiral; on July 26, 1866, he was commissioned admiral, a grade especially created for him.

The closing months of the Civil War saw Farragut on leave of absence to recover his health and on a mission to guard the James River. After the war, he commanded the European Squadron on a goodwill tour, 1867–68, and in 1869 visited the Mare Island navy yard. He died on a visit to the commandant of the Portsmouth, N.H., navy yard. Farragut was a master of every detail of his profession. His superiority lay in his mental and moral qualities, his courage, initiative, judgment, and willingness to accept responsibility.

FARRAGUT, GEORGE (*b. Ciudadela, Minorca, 1755; d. Point Plaquet, Miss., 1817*), mariner. Naval and army officer in the American Revolution and War of 1812. Father of David G. Farragut.

FARRAND, BEATRIX CADWALADER JONES (*b. New York, N.Y., 1872; d. Bar Harbor, Maine, 1959*), landscape architect. Privately educated, Jones was influenced by her aunt, Edith Wharton, Charles Sprague Sargent, and Gertrude Jekyll. Opened a private practice in Manhattan in 1897. From 1910 to 1930, she designed gardens for the wealthy and for college campuses, including Princeton, Yale, Vassar, and the University of Chicago. She began work on the gardens of umbarton Oaks in 1922.

FARRAND, LIVINGSTON (*b. Newark, N.J., 1867; d. New York, N.Y., 1939*), psychologist, anthropologist, public health administrator. Graduated Princeton, 1888; M.D., College of Physicians and Surgeons, 1891. After graduate work in physiological psychology at Cambridge, England, and Berlin, he taught psychology and, later, anthropology at Columbia, 1893–1913, meanwhile serving (1905–14) as executive secretary of the National Tuberculosis Association. He was president, University of Colorado, 1914–19, and after heading the American Red Cross for two years, he became president of Cornell, 1921–37. A pioneer in the field of public health education, he was especially active in developing the medical schools of the universities he so ably served.

FARRAND, MAX (*b. Newark, N.J., 1869; d. Bar Harbor, Maine, 1945*), historian, library director. Brother of Livingston Farrand. Graduated Princeton, 1892; Ph.D., 1896. After teaching at Wesleyan, Stanford, and Cornell, he was professor of history at Yale, 1908–25. He served as general director of the Commonwealth Fund, 1919–21, and director of its division of education, 1925–27. He was author of, among other works, *Records of the Federal Convention of 1787* (1911, 1937). Director of research, Henry E. Huntington Library, 1927–41, which he made into a leading center for study of Anglo-American civilization.

FARRAR, EDGAR HOWARD (*b. Concordia, La., 1849; d. Biloxi, Miss., 1922*), lawyer. Authority on municipal and corporation law; reformed New Orleans city government.

FARRAR, GERALDINE (*b. Melrose, Mass., 1882; d. Ridgefield, Conn., 1967*), opera singer. Coached by Lilli Lehmann. First appeared in 1901 with the Berlin Royal Opera; became an operatic idol during her five years with that company. Following further European successes, Farrar made her American debut with the Metropolitan Opera in New York City in 1906; reigned as prima donna assoluta at the Met until her retirement in 1922. A lyric soprano with an expansive range, she was not known for her acting ability, but her physically attractive stage presence brought glamour to her performances; she was the first opera singer to star in motion pictures. Among her many films are *Maria Rosa* (1915), *Carmen* (1915), and *Flame of Desert* (1919). Published her autobiography, *Such Sweet Compulsion,* in 1938.

FARRAR, JOHN (*b. Lincoln, Mass., 1779; d. Cambridge, Mass., 1853*), mathematician, physicist, astronomer. Graduated Harvard, 1803, and taught there, 1805–36; translated French scientific literature for textbook use.

FARRAR, TIMOTHY (*b. New Ipswich, N.H., 1788; d. Boston, Mass., 1874*), jurist. Daniel Webster's law partner; author of a report on the Dartmouth College Case (1819); excelled as legislative draftsman.

FARRELL, JAMES AUGUSTINE (*b. New Haven, Conn., 1862; d. New York, N.Y., 1943*), industrialist. Left school at 16 to work in a steel wire mill; removed to Pittsburgh, Pa., 1888. Rose from laborer to general manager of Pittsburgh Wire Company, 1888–93; pioneered in development of foreign sales. On absorption of his then employer by the U.S. Steel Corporation, 1901, he became head of foreign sales for U.S. Steel. Successful and innovative in this post, he was chosen president of the U.S. Steel, 1911, serving until 1932 and remaining a member of the board of directors until his death. Served as chairman, National Foreign Trade Council.

FARRER, HENRY (*b. London, England, 1843; d. Brooklyn, N.Y., 1903*), etcher, landscape painter. Came to America, 1863.

FARRINGTON, JOSEPH RIDER (*b. Washington, D.C., 1897; d. Washington, D.C., 1954*), newspaper publisher and congressional delegate from Hawaii. Publisher and president of the Honolulu *Star Bulletin,* 1933. As territorial delegate from Hawaii, 1942–54, campaigned for statehood until his death.

FARRINGTON, WALLACE RIDER (*b. Orono, Maine, 1871; d. 1933*), newspaperman, governor of Hawaii, 1921–29.

FARSON, NEGLEY (*b. Plainfield, N.J., 1890; d. Georgeham, England, 1960*), journalist. As foreign correspondent for the *Chicago Daily News,* 1924–35, covered many political and natural disasters. Later contributed to the *London Daily Mail.* Author of *The Way of a Transgressor* (1936) and *Mirror for Narcissus* (1956).

FARWELL, ARTHUR (*b. St. Paul, Minn., 1872; d. New York, N.Y., 1952*), composer, musical educator. Composed music based upon American Indian and jazz themes; tone poem based on Walt Whitman's "Once I Passed Through A Populous City"

was performed by the Philadelphia Orchestra in 1928. Wrote over 116 works.

FARWELL, CHARLES BENJAMIN (*b. Mead Creek, N.Y., 1823; d. Lake Forest, Ill., 1903*), businessman, politician. Brother of John V. Farwell and his partner in business. Served without distinction as Republican congressman and U.S. senator from Illinois.

FARWELL, JOHN VILLIERS (*b. Steuben Co., N.Y., 1825; d. Chicago, Ill., 1908*), merchant. Raised in Illinois. Entered dry-goods business in Chicago, 1844; organized John V. Farwell and Co., 1865, Chicago's leading wholesale firm before rise of Marshall Field.

FASSETT, CORNELIA ADÈLE STRONG (*b. Owasco, N.Y., 1831; d. Washington, D.C., 1898*), portrait and figure painter. Pursued successful career in Chicago, Ill., and Washington.

FASSETT, JACOB SLOAT (*b. Elmira, N.Y., 1853; d. Vancouver, Canada, 1924*), lawyer, financier. Antimachine Republican. As New York state legislator, 1883–91, headed exposé of city corruption; was congressman, 1905–11. Edited *Elmira Advertiser,* 1879–96.

FATHER DIVINE. *See* DIVINE, FATHER.

FAULK, ANDREW JACKSON (*b. Milford, Pa., 1814; d. Yankton, S.D., 1898*), lawyer, journalist, post trader. Governor of Dakota Territory, 1866–68.

FAULKNER, CHARLES JAMES (*b. Martinsburg, Va., now W.Va., 1806; d. Martinsburg, 1884*), lawyer. Congressman, Democrat, from Virginia, 1851–59; from West Virginia, 1875–77. U.S. minister to France, 1859–61. Served in Confederate forces as staff officer to Gen. T. J. Jackson.

FAULKNER, CHARLES JAMES (*b. Martinsburg, Va., now W.Va., 1847; d. Martinsburg, 1929*), lawyer. Son of Charles J. Faulkner (1806–84). U.S. senator, Democrat, from West Virginia, 1887–99. Framed first general law (1888–89) against food and drug adulteration.

FAULKNER (FALKNER), WILLIAM CUTHBERT (*b. New Albany, Miss., 1897; d. Byhalia, Miss., 1962*), writer. Faulkner spent most of his life in Oxford, Miss., which provided the regional and family lore that later enriched his fiction. He would come to transmute his "little postage stamp of native soil" into the "aprocryphal" Yoknapatawpha County.

After dropping out of high school in 1915, Faulkner changed the spelling of his name in order to pass as British, and enlisted in the Canadian Royal Air Force (1918). He was discharged shortly after, and enrolled as a special student at the University of Mississippi (1921–24). He worked for a time in a bookstore in New York City (1921), and as postmaster at the University of Mississippi (1921–24). During this time he was writing mostly poetry, and published *The Marble Faun* in 1924. He traveled to Europe in 1925.

Encouraged by the writer Sherwood Anderson, Faulkner began writing short stories and a novel (published as *Soldier's Pay* in 1926), and realized that his true métier was fiction. Encouraged by Anderson to mine his native Mississippi material, Faulkner wrote *Sartoris* (1929), which traced the Sartoris family, whose towering figure, Colonel John Sartoris, was based on Faulkner's great-grandfather, Colonel William Clark Falkner. He went on to write *The Sound and the Fury* (1929), which employed stream of consciousness technique, mythic and biblical references, and a dense texture of symbolism. This novel was followed by *As I Lay Dying* (1930), another brilliantly imaginative tale, in which spoken words were recorded with fidelity to dialect while inner thoughts were rendered with poetic virtuosity. *Light In August* (1932) was a powerful novel of social tensions in Yoknapatawpha County. An enormous body of criticism grew up around *Absalom, Absalom!* (1936), which was seen as an allegory of the South and is considered by some critics to be his crowning masterwork. *The Town* (1957) and *The Mansion* (1959) completed the Snopes trilogy Faulkner had begun with a fragment he had written early in his career entitled "Father Abraham." By the early 1930's Faulkner had gained a national audience, but his books did not sell well. With their exuberant rhetoric and mythic consciousness, they were considered difficult; their subject matter, perverse. He began to sell short stories to national magazines to supplement his income, and in 1932 signed with Metro-Goldwyn-Mayer as a screenwriter. He worked intermittently for MGM, Twentieth Century-Fox, and Warner Brothers throughout his career. He also determined to write a commercially successful novel, and published *Sanctuary* (1931), which he conceived of as a mystery-detective-gangster story. He continued to eke out a precarious existence with film work and short stories, but did not achieve financial security until the age of 51, when he sold the screen rights to *Intruder in the Dust* (1948), a commentary on racial prejudice that showed Faulkner's increasing awareness of and concern about contemporary tensions in the South. In the mid 1950's he became intensely concerned with the civil rights crisis, writing and speaking in an attempt to avert violence and establish a position for moderates.

Faulkner was elected to the National Institute of Arts and Letters in 1939; to the American Academy of Arts and Letters in 1948. He received the 1949 Nobel Prize for literature. He was writer-in-residence at the University of Virginia in 1957 and 1958.

Other books include *Mosquitoes* (1927), *A Green Bough* (1933), *Doctor Martino and Other Stories* (1934), *Pylon* (1935), *The Unvanquished* (1938), *The Wild Palms* (1939), *Go Down, Moses* (1942), *Requiem for a Nun* (1951), *A Fable* (Pulitzer Prize and National Book Award, 1954), and *The Reivers* (1962).

FAUNCE, WILLIAM HERBERT PERRY (*b. Worcester, Mass., 1859; d. Providence, R.I., 1930*), Baptist clergyman. Taught at Chicago, Harvard, Yale; liberal and able president of Brown University, 1899–1929.

FAUQUIER, FRANCIS (*b. England, 1704[?]; d. Williamsburg, Va., 1768*), lieutenant governor of Virginia. Director of the South Sea Co.; fellow of the Royal Society, 1753; writer on economics. Was appointed lieutenant governor of Virginia, 1758, a position which made him governor in fact. His administration was marked by tact and skill in dealing with the colonists and a realistic independence of orders given him by the British Board of Trade.

FAUSET, JESSIE REDMON (*b. Camden County, N.J., 1882[?]; d. Philadelphia, Pa., 1961*), writer, teacher, and editor. First black woman admitted to Cornell (graduated, 1905). Also studied at the University of Pennsylvania (M.A., 1919), the Sorbonne, the Alliance Française, and Columbia. Taught Latin and French at DeWitt Clinton High School in New York City (1927–44). Also taught at Hampton Institute (1949) and Tuskegee Institute. An integral figure in the Harlem Renaissance, Fauset was literary editor of the *Crisis* and *The Brownie's Book*, 1919–26. Best known for her novels *There Is Confusion* (1924), *Plum Bun* (1928), *The Chinaberry Tree* (1931), and *Comedy: American Style* (1933). One of the main black novelists to depict middle-class black society during the 1920's and 1930's, Fauset is nevertheless considered a minor writer whose work was compromised by her assimilation into white society and orientation to white opinion.

FAUST, FREDERICK SHILLER (*b. Seattle, Wash., 1892; d. Santa Maria Infante, Italy, 1944*), author. A prolific writer of popular fiction under the pseudonym "Max Brand" and at least 18 other pen names, he also worked on the scripts of a number of motion pictures, including adaptation of seven of his own "Dr. Kildare" stories. Professing indifference to his fame as "King of the Pulp Writers," he was author of several collections of serious poetry, among them *The Village Street and Other Poems* (1922) and *Dionysus in Hades* (1931). He was killed in action while serving as a war correspondent.

FAVERSHAM, WILLIAM ALFRED (*b. London, England, 1868; d. Bay Shore, N.Y., 1940*), actor. Came to America, 1886. Replaced Henry Miller as leading man of Frohman's Empire Theatre company, 1892, and was successful as romantic lead; achieved greatest success in *The Squaw Man*, 1905–08.

FAVILL, HENRY BAIRD (*b. Madison, Wis., 1860; d. 1916*), physician. Graduated Rush Medical College, 1883, where he later taught. Specialized in internal medicine; had large Chicago practice and enjoyed nationwide reputation.

FAWCETT, EDGAR (*b. New York, N.Y., 1847; d. London, England, 1904*), author. Satirized New York society in some 35 tepid novels and plays. *The Buntling Ball* (1884), a Gilbertian essay in verse, is metrically clever.

FAY, EDWARD ALLEN (*b. Morristown, N.J., 1843; d. 1923*), educator of the deaf. Graduated University of Michigan, 1862. Associated with Gallaudet College, 1866–1920. Author of *Concordance of the Divina Commedia* (1888) and a study of *Marriages of the Deaf in America* (1898).

FAY, EDWIN WHITFIELD (*b. Minden, La., 1865; d. Texas, 1920*), classical scholar. Professor of Latin at Washington and Lee, 1893–99, and thereafter at University of Texas.

FAY, FRANCIS ANTHONY ("FRANK") (*b. San Francisco, Calif., 1897; d. Santa Monica, Calif., 1961*), vaudevillian actor. Began as a single performer in 1917. Known for witty, sophisticated, satirical humor. Numerous Broadway credits include memorable portrayal of the eccentric alcoholic Elwood P. Dowd in *Harvey* (1944). Film credits include *Under a Texas Moon* (1930), a box office success, and starring roles in films of the early 1930's that were not well received. Married to Barbara Stanwyck, (1928–35). Appeared in films through 1951. Wrote and produced several stage productions that were critical and financial failures, including *Frank Fay's Fables* (1922), *The Smart Alec* (1926), and *Tattle Tales* (1933). Nightclub appearances throughout his career. Fay's radio show in 1936 ran for four months. Published *How to Be Poor* in 1945. Censured by the National Council of Actor's Equity in 1945 after a political controversy in which he accused fellow actors of being pro-communist.

FAY, JONAS (*b. Westborough, Mass., 1737 n.s.; d. Bennington, Vt., 1818*), physician, politician. Removed to Vermont, 1766, and was active in independence and statehood movements of Vermont settlers, 1772–85.

FAY, SIDNEY BRADSHAW (*b. Washington, D.C., 1876; d. Lexington, Mass., 1967*), historian and educator. Studied at Harvard (Ph.D., 1900). Professor of history at Dartmouth (1902–14) and Smith (1914–29). Held a joint Harvard–Radcliffe professorship (1929–45). Visiting professor at Yale and president of the American Historical Association for the 1946–47 term. A prolific commentator about and reviewer of works on European history, Fay's essays appeared in *American Historical Review*, the *Nation*, and *Current History*, among others. Best known for his book *The Origins of the World War* (1928), which challenged "the aggression of Germany and her allies" as the sole cause of World War I. Also wrote *The Rise of Brandenburg-Prussia to 1786* (1937) and participated in the editing of the *Guide to Historical Literature* (1931).

FAY, THEODORE SEDGWICK (*b. New York, N.Y., 1807; d. Berlin, Germany, 1898*), author, diplomat. Miscellaneous writer for the *New York Mirror* from 1828. Left America, 1833; served as secretary of legation at London and Berlin, 1837–53, and as minister of Switzerland, 1853–61. Author of *Norman Leslie* (1835) and other books.

FAYERWEATHER, DANIEL BURTON (*b. Stepney, Conn., 1822; d. 1890*), leather merchant. Bequeathed entire estate unconditionally to a score of American colleges.

FAYSSOUX, PETER (*b. Charleston, S.C.[?], 1745; d. 1795*), physician, surgeon. Graduated M.D., Edinburgh, 1769. Served as senior physician with South Carolina forces in Revolution; first president of South Carolina Medical Society, 1790–92.

FAZENDA, LOUISE MARIE (*b. West Lafayette, Ind., 1896; d. Hollywood, Calif., 1962*), film comedienne. Grew up in Los Angeles. Best known for her films with Mack Sennett's Keystone Company, including *Are Waitresses Safe?* (1917), *The Kitchen Lady* (1918), and *Down on the Farm* (1920). Her character often appeared in pigtails, gingham dress, and long pantalettes. Other film credits include *The Gold Diggers* (1923), *Tillie's Punctured Romance* (1928), *The Winning Ticket* (1935), and *Swing Your Lady* (1938).

FEARING, KENNETH FLEXNER (*b. Oak Park, Ill., 1902; d. New York, N.Y., 1961*), poet and novelist. Studied at the University of Illinois and the University of Wisconsin (B.A., 1924). Throughout the late 1920's and 1930's, his work appeared primarily in journals allied with the American Communist party. His poetry was aimed at deepening social consciousness and has been called proletarian. A contributing editor of *New Masses* (1930–33); on the editorial board of *Partisan Review* (1935–36). Poetry appeared regularly in the *New Yorker* in the 1940's. Books of poetry include *Angel Arms* (1929), *Poems* (1935), *Dead Reckoning* (1938), *Afternoon of a Pawnbroker* (1943), and *Stranger at Coney Island* (1948). Novels include *The Hospital* (1939), *The Dagger of the Mind* (1941), and *The Big Clock* (1946).

FEARN, JOHN WALKER (*b. Huntsville, Ala., 1832; d. Hot Springs, Va., 1899*), lawyer, diplomat. Nephew of Leroy P. Walker.

FEATHERSTON, WINFIELD SCOTT (*b. near Murfreesboro, Tenn., 1819; d. Holly Springs, Miss., 1891*), lawyer, Confederate soldier. Congressman, Democrat, from Mississippi, 1847–51; rose to brigadier general in Civil War. Was a leader, 1874–78, in overthrow of Ames regime in Mississippi.

FEBIGER, CHRISTIAN (*b. Fünen, Denmark, 1746; d. Philadelphia, Pa., 1796*), Revolutionary soldier. Came to America, 1772. Served with ability in all theaters of the war, retiring, 1783, as brigadier general. Treasurer of Pennsylvania, 1789–96.

FECHTER, CHARLES ALBERT (*b. London, England, 1824; d. near Quakertown, Pa., 1879*), actor. Successful as innovating actor-manager on French, English, and American stages, 1848–70. His later career was unhappy.

FEE, JOHN GREGG (*b. Bracken Co., Ky., 1816; d. Berea, Ky., 1901*), abolitionist, founder of Berea College (1855).

FEEHAN, PATRICK AUGUSTINE (*b. Killenaule, Ireland, 1829; d. Chicago, Ill., 1902*), Roman Catholic clergyman. Came to America, 1852; was ordained that year in St. Louis, Mo. Consecrated bishop of Nashville, 1865; archbishop of Chicago, 1880. A man of great ability and charity.

FEININGER, LYONEL (CHARLES LÉONELL ADRIAN) *b. New York, 1871; d. New York, N.Y., 1956*), painter. Studied at the Hamburg School of Applied Arts and the Royal Academy of Art in Berlin; spent most of his life in Germany. His earliest work was in cartoons and comic strips. Influenced by cubists, Delaunay's study of prismatic light, and later by the Italian futurists. Teacher and artist-in-residence at the Bauhaus in Weimar and Dessau, 1919–37. Returned to the U.S. in 1937; taught at Mills College and at Black Mountain College.

FEJOS, PAUL (*b. Budapest, Hungary, 1897; d. New York, N.Y., 1963*), film director and anthropologist. Studied at the Royal Hungarian Medical University (M.D., 1921). Directed films for Mobil Studios in Budapest. Immigrated to New York City in 1923; moved to Hollywood in 1926. Directed several films for Universal Studios that were noted for their technical virtuosity, including *Lonesome* (1928), *The Last Performance* (1929), and *Broadway* (1929). Returned to Europe in 1931. Directed ethnographic documentary films in Indonesia and eastern Asia for the Swedish Film Industry (1937–39). Wrote and produced *A Handful of Rice* (1940), during the filming of which he became a self-taught anthropologist and ethnographer. Led Peruvian expeditions sponsored by Axel Wenner-Gren in the early forties. Stressed the importance of photography as an anthropological tool. Director of research for the Viking Fund, 1941–55 (became the Wenner–Gren Foundation for Anthropological Research); and president, 1955–63. Taught anthropology at Stanford University (1943–63), Yale (1949–51), Columbia, and Fordham.

FEKE, ROBERT (*b. Oyster Bay, N.Y., ca. 1705; d. Bermuda, ca. 1750*), portrait painter. A clever draftsman and catcher of likenesses, Feke resided in Newport, R.I., but is known to have worked also in Boston and Philadelphia.

FELCH, ALPHEUS (*b. Limerick, Maine, 1804; d. Ann Arbor, Mich., 1896*), lawyer. Removed to Michigan, 1833. Held state offices, and was Democratic governor, 1846–47; U.S. senator, 1847–53.

FELL, JOHN (*b. New York, N.Y., 1721; d. Coldenham, N.Y., 1798*), merchant, Revolutionary patriot. Member of Continental Congress from New Jersey, 1778–80; judge, court of common pleas, 1766–74 and 1776–86.

FELS, JOSEPH (*b. Halifax Co., Va., 1854; d. 1914*), soap manufacturer. Devoted time and fortune to worldwide spread of Henry George's single tax doctrine.

FELS, SAMUEL SIMEON (*b. Yanceyville, N.C., 1860; d. Philadelphia, Pa., 1950*), soap manufacturer, philanthropist. Raised in Baltimore and Philadelphia. Brother of Joseph Fels, with whom he was associated in the manufacture of Fels-Naptha laundry soap. A benefactor of many charities, he is principally remembered as the founder of the Samuel S. Fels Fund, created to aid research projects in medicine and government. He is reputed to have given more than $40 million to various causes during his lifetime.

FELSENTHAL, BERNHARD (*b. Münchweiler, Bavaria, 1822; d. 1908*), rabbi. Came to America, 1854. Associated with Zion Congregation, Chicago. A leading figure of Reform Judaism in the Middle West, he became a fervent advocate of Zionism.

FELT, JOSEPH BARLOW (*b. Salem, Mass., 1789; d. 1869*), antiquarian, New England historian.

FELTON, CORNELIUS CONWAY (*b. Newbury, Mass., 1807; d. Chester, Pa., 1862*), classical scholar. Graduated Harvard, 1827. Professor of Greek, Harvard, 1832–60; regent of that university, 1849–57, and president, 1860–61. Author of school texts and *Greece: Ancient and Modern* (1867).

FELTON, REBECCA LATIMER (*b. near Decatur, Ga., 1835; d. Atlanta, Ga., 1930*), writer. Wife of William H. Felton. First woman U.S. senator; held two-day ad interim appointment in 1922.

FELTON, SAMUEL MORSE (*b. Newbury, Mass., 1809; d. 1889*), civil engineer. Brother of Cornelius C. Felton. Graduated Harvard, 1834. Built and managed the Fitchburg Railroad; became president of the Philadelphia, Wilmington & Baltimore, 1851, and made it one of the country's best-equipped and most profitable roads. Rendered inestimable service in Civil War transportation of Union troops. Was a developer and director of the Pennsylvania Railroad and later of the Northern Pacific.

FELTON, WILLIAM HARRELL (*b. Oglethorpe Co., Ga., 1823; d. Cartersville, Ga., 1909*), Methodist preacher, physician, farmer, reform politician. As independent legislator and congressman, fought Democratic "ring rule" in Georgia *post* 1874.

FENDALL, JOSIAS (*b. ca. 1620; d. ca. 1687*), colonial governor of Maryland, 1656–60. Attempted overthrow of proprietary government, 1659–60; was later influential among supporters of Nathaniel Bacon and was associate of John Coode.

FENGER, CHRISTIAN (*b. Breininggaard, Denmark, 1840; d. Chicago, Ill., 1902*), surgeon, pathologist. After practice in Europe and Egypt, came to America, 1877, and won fame as a teacher at Chicago's medical schools and at Cook County Hospital. His students numbered some of the greatest names in modern surgery and pathology.

FENICHEL, OTTO (*b. Vienna, Austria, 1897; d. Los Angeles, Calif., 1946*), psychoanalyst. M.D., University of Vienna, 1921. Removed to Los Angeles, 1938. Author of *The Outline of Clinical Psychoanalysis* (1934) and *The Psychoanalytic Theory of Neurosis* (1945).

FENN, WILLIAM WALLACE (*b. Boston, Mass., 1862; d. 1932*), Unitarian clergyman, theologian. Professor, Harvard Divinity School, and dean, 1906–22.

FENNELL, JAMES (*b. London, England, 1766; d. 1816*), actor. Came to America, 1793. His invariable success as an actor in Philadelphia and New York alternated with his failures as a promoter of saltworks, schools, and other enterprises.

FENNEMAN, NEVIN MELANCTHON (*b. Lima, Ohio, 1865; d. Cincinnati, Ohio, 1945*), geographer, geologist. B.A., Heidelberg College, 1883; M.A., University of Chicago, 1900; Ph.D., Chicago, 1901. After teaching in high schools and at the universities of Colorado and Wisconsin, he established the Department of Geology and Geography at the University of Cincinnati, 1907, remaining there for the rest of his life. He was author of two major books and of a number of articles and survey monographs based on his work with the U.S. Geological Survey and several state surveys. Pioneered in application of physiographic generalizations to the analysis of specific regions. Exemplified his concept in *The Physiography of Western United States* (1931) and in a similar work on the eastern United States (1938).

FENNER, ARTHUR (*b. Providence, R.I., 1745; d. Providence, 1805*). Antifederalist governor of Rhode Island, 1790–1805.

FENNER, BURT LESLIE (*b. Rochester, N.Y., 1869; d. Croton-on-Hudson, N.Y., 1926*), architect. Partner in McKim, Mead and White, 1906–26.

FENNER, CHARLES ERASMUS (*b. Jackson, Tenn., 1834; d. New Orleans, La., 1911*), Confederate soldier, jurist. Associate justice, Louisiana Supreme Court, 1880–94. Active trustee of Tulane University and of Peabody Educational Fund.

FENNER, JAMES (*b. Providence, R.I., 1771; d. 1846*), politician. Son of Arthur Fenner. U.S. senator from Rhode Island, 1804–07; governor, 1807–11, 1824–31, and 1843–45.

FENNO, JOHN (*b. Boston, Mass., 1751 o.s.; d. Philadelphia, Pa., 1798*), editor. Published and edited the Federalist *Gazette of the United States* (New York, 1789; Philadelphia, 1790–98) with the aid of Alexander Hamilton as contributor and patron.

FENOLLOSA, ERNEST FRANCISCO (*b. Salem, Mass., 1853; d. London, England, 1908*), poet, student of oriental art. Author of *Epochs of Chinese and Japanese Art* (1912) and translations of verse and dramas published posthumously by his literary executor, Ezra Pound.

FENTON, REUBEN EATON (*b. Carroll, N.Y., 1819; d. Jamestown, N.Y., 1885*), lumberman, politician, banker. As Democratic congressman from New York, 1853–55, seceded from his party over the slavery issue; in 1855 presided over first Republican state convention. Served as Republican congressman, 1857–64, and as governor of New York, 1864–68; built up a powerful political machine. While U.S. senator, 1869–75, he broke with Roscoe Conkling over control of state patronage and was forced out of power.

FENWICK, BENEDICT JOSEPH (*b. near Leonardtown, Md., 1782; d. Boston, Mass., 1846*), Roman Catholic clergyman, Jesuit. Ordained, 1808; served at St. Peter's, New York City, 1809–17, and as president of Georgetown College, 1817–18. After a few years in Charleston, S.C., he served again as president of Georgetown, 1822–25. Consecrated bishop of Boston, 1825, he founded *The Jesuit* (now *The Boston Pilot*), 1829, and administered his diocese with great energy and success.

FENWICK, EDWARD DOMINIC (*b. St. Mary's Co., Md., 1768; d. Wooster, Ohio, 1832*), Roman Catholic clergyman, Dominican. Consecrated first bishop of Cincinnati, 1822. Founded American mother house of Dominican order in Springfield, Ky.

FENWICK, GEORGE (*b. England, 1603; d. England, 1656/7*), colonist. Patentee of part of Connecticut. Resident at Saybrook, 1639–45.

FENWICK, JOHN (*b. Bynfield, England, 1618; d. 1683*), colonist. A Cromwellian trooper turned Quaker, he advocated a Quaker colony in America and was assigned West Jersey in trust for the purpose; he planted first Quaker settlement on the Delaware at Salem, 1675.

FENWICKE, JOHN. *See* FENWICK, JOHN.

FERBER, EDNA JESSICA (*b. Kalamazoo, Mich., 1885; d. New York, N.Y., 1968*), novelist and playwright. Among her novels are *Dawn O'Hara* (1911), *Fanny Herself* (1917), *The Girls* (1921), *So Big* (Pulitzer Prize, 1924), *Show Boat* (1926), *Cimarron* (1930), *Saratoga Trunk* (1941), and *Giant* (1952). Created a memorable character in the short stories of Emma McChesney. Collaborated on nine plays, six of them with George S. Kaufman, including *The Royal Family* (1927), *Dinner at Eight* (1932), and *Stage Door* (1936). Rich in characterization, local color, and historical authenticity, Ferber's creative achievement is notable for its illumination of crucial stages in American history during the twentieth century.

FERGUSON, ALEXANDER HUGH (*b. Manilla, Canada, 1853; d. Chicago, Ill., 1911*), surgeon. Taught in Canada and in Chicago *post* 1894; devised method of treating hernia and improved cleft palate operations.

FERGUSON, ELIZABETH GRAEME (*b. Philadelphia, Pa., 1737; d. Montgomery Co., Pa., 1801*), poet, translator. Acted as go-between in British intrigues during Revolution.

FERGUSON, JAMES EDWARD (*b. near Salado, Tex., 1871; d. Austin, Tex., 1944*), lawyer, politician. Left home at age 16; worked as itinerant laborer, construction gangs member, and farmer. Admitted to the bar, 1897, he established a practice in Belton, Bell Co., Tex. Removing to Temple, Tex. *ca.* 1900, he engaged in local Democratic politics. Elected governor in 1914. His campaign style was at once witty, sarcastic, and slanderous, which made "Farmer Jim" popular with rural audiences. As governor, he was successful in his fight against prohibition, woman suffrage, and laws regulating corporate wealth, but his most constructive efforts were made in improvement of rural education. Reelected in 1916, he was accused of mishandling state funds, receiving loans from brewing interests, and interfering in management of the University of Texas. The legislature impeached and removed him in 1917 and declared him ineligible to hold any state office in future. Unsuccessful in several efforts to return to power, he supported his wife's candidacy for governor in 1924; "Ma" Ferguson, as she was called, was elected and followed out her husband's conservative policies, which now included opposition to the revived Ku Klux Klan, although the Fergusons were white-supremacists. Defeated in 1926 and 1930, she was once again elected governor in 1932. Ferguson himself occupied an office next to his wife's.

FERGUSON, JOHN CALVIN (*b. near Belleville, Ontario, Canada, 1866; d. Clifton Springs, N.Y., 1945*), Methodist clergyman, public official in China, connoisseur of Chinese art. B.A., Boston University, 1886. After service as an associate pastor in Boston, Mass., he left for China to start a college in Nanking for the Methodist mission, serving as first president of Nanking University, 1888–97. His ability and his comprehension of Chinese culture and manners won him the favor of high Chinese officials. Leaving the mission field in 1897, he established, and was first president of, Nanyang College (later Chiaotung University); with the help of his principal Chinese patron, he acquired the Chinese-language newspaper *Sin Wan Pao*, which grew to be the largest daily in Shanghai. Between 1902 and 1911, he held a number of important offices under the imperial government, continuing to serve the new governments as an adviser after the imperial overthrow. He was repatriated to the United States in 1943. He was author of many articles and several books on the arts of China, and made a notable collection of paintings and bronzes which he left to Nanking University.

FERGUSON, MIRIAM AMANDA WALLACE (*b. Bell County, Tex., 1875; d. Austin, Tex., 1961*), governor of Texas. Studied at Salado College and Baylor Female College. Married James Edward Ferguson in 1899; he was elected governor of Texas in 1914, and was reelected in 1916. A controversy over his handling of finances resulted in his impeachment in 1917. Miriam Ferguson went on to become governor (1925–27; 1933–35). Believed by many to be merely a stand-in for her disbarred husband, she nevertheless made an impact on Texas politics. Nicknamed "Ma," the key to her success was thought to be her accessibility to, and identification with, the common people.

FERGUSON, SAMUEL (*b. Exeter, N.H., 1874; d. Lake Wales, Fla., 1950*), utility executive. B.S., Trinity College, 1896; E.E. and M.A., Columbia University, 1899. As an officer of the Hartford Electric Light Co., 1912–50 (president, 1924–35, 1939–46), he aimed to provide the public with reliable low-cost power, at the same time preserving the company from outside control either by the federal government or absentee financial interests.

FERGUSON, THOMAS BARKER (*b. near Charleston, S.C., 1841; d. Boston, Mass., 1922*), Confederate soldier, scientist, diplomat. Carried out valuable researches in fish propagation.

FERGUSON, WILLIAM JASON (*b. Baltimore, Md., 1844; d. Baltimore, 1930*), actor. Sole eyewitness of Lincoln's assassination, 1865.

FERGUSON, WILLIAM PORTER FRISBEE (*b. Delhi, N.Y., 1861; d. 1929*), clergyman, journalist, militant Prohibitionist.

FERMI, ENRICO (*b. Rome, Italy, 1901; d. Chicago, Ill., 1954*), physicist. Studied at the Scuola Normale Superiore of the University of Pisa, and at the universities of Göttingen and Leiden. Developed the Fermi-Dirac statistics, stating that no two particles such as electrons, could occupy precisely the same quantum state. Professor of theoretical physics at the University of Rome, 1927–38; developed a statistical model of the atom (Thomas-Fermi model) and his theory of nuclear beta decay. Searching for ways to induce radioactivity through neutron bombardment, he discovered in 1934 that slow neutrons produced nuclear reactions much more effectively than fast ones; awarded Nobel Prize for this work in 1938. Joined the faculty of Columbia University, 1939. Began investigative work on nuclear fission in 1939 (Manhattan Project) transferring to the University of Chicago in 1942. On Dec. 2, 1942, the first self-sustaining chain reaction created and controlled by man was achieved, and with it, the birth of the atomic age.

Joined J. R. Oppenheimer at Los Alamos, N.Mex., in 1944 in research that led to construction and testing of the first atomic bomb on July 16, 1945, at Alamagordo, N.M. With Oppenheimer, A. H. Compton, and E. O. Lawrence advised President Truman to use the bomb against Japan. In 1945 Fermi returned to the University of Chicago, where he taught until his death.

FERNALD, CHARLES HENRY (*b. Fernald's Point, Maine, 1838; d. 1921*), entomologist. Professor at Massachusetts Agricultural College, 1886–1910. One of first Americans who taught entomology systematically; led fight against gypsy moth in New England.

FERNALD, JAMES CHAMPLIN (*b. Portland, Maine, 1838; d. Upper Montclair, N.J., 1918*), Baptist clergyman, author. Edited *English Synonyms and Antonyms* (1896, 1914).

FERNALD, MERRITT LYNDON (*b. Orono, Maine, 1873; d. Cambridge, Mass., 1950*), botanist. B.S., Harvard, 1897. From 1891 until 1947, Fernald's connection with Harvard was continuous; he was successively instructor, assistant professor, and Fisher professor of natural history, and from junior assistant in the Gray Herbarium rose to curator and director (1935–47). His area of botanical concentration included most of North America east of the Missouri and Mississippi rivers and north of the Carolinas. His crowning achievement was his eighth edition of *Gray's Manual of Botany* (1950), a wholly new work, quite unlike any previous editions.

FERNOW, BERNHARD EDUARD (*b. Inowrazlaw, Germany, 1851; d. Toronto, Canada, 1923*), forester, author, teacher. Trained in Prussian forest service; immigrated to America, 1876; was U.S. pioneer of scientific forestry. Managed Cooper-Hewitt timber lands in Pennsylvania; in 1882 helped organize American

Forestry Congress; in 1886 became chief, Division of Forestry, U.S. Department of Agriculture. Advocated special studies of trees, federal and state protection laws, and the present system of national forests. Shaped federal forest reserve law of 1897. Organized first American collegiate school of forestry at Cornell University, 1898; inaugurated forestry work at Pennsylvania State College, 1906; became head of forestry department, University of Toronto, 1907. Author of *Economics of Forestry* (1902), *A Brief History of Forestry* (1907), *The Care of Trees* (1910), and many government circulars.

FERNOW, BERTHOLD (*b. Inowrazlaw, Germany, 1837; d. Togus, Maine, 1908*), historian, archivist, Union soldier. Specialist in documentary sources for New York and the middle colonies.

FERREE, CLARENCE ERROL (*b. Sidney, Ohio, 1877; d. Baltimore, Md., 1942*), psychologist. B.S., Ohio Wesleyan, 1900; M.S., 1901. Ph.D., Cornell University, 1909. Taught at Bryn Mawr, 1907–28; director of research in physiological optics at Wilmer Ophthalmological Institute, Johns Hopkins Medical School, 1928–36 (professor *post* 1932). Made important contributions as a pioneer in the standardized quantitative study of visual functions, for which he devised a variety of apparatus. In most of his work, his wife, Gertrude Rand, was a collaborator.

FERREL, WILLIAM (*b. Fulton Co., Pa., 1817; d. 1891*), meteorologist. Internationally known for "Essay on the Winds and the Currents of the Ocean" (1856); worked for U.S. Coast and Geodetic Survey.

FERRERO, EDWARD (*b. Granada, Spain, 1831; d. New York, N.Y., 1899*), dancing master, Union soldier.

FERRIS, GEORGE WASHINGTON GALE (*b. Galesburg, Ill., 1859; d. 1896*), civil engineer. Graduated Rensselaer Polytechnic, 1881. Specialist in steel testing and inspection; invented the Ferris wheel.

FERRIS, ISAAC (*b. New York, N.Y., 1798; d. 1873*), Reformed Dutch clergyman. Active on foreign mission board of his church; chancellor of University of the City of New York, 1852–70.

FERRIS, JEAN LÉON GÉRÔME (*b. Philadelphia, Pa., 1863; d. Philadelphia, 1930*), historical painter. Nephew of Edward, Peter and Thomas Moran; studied under Christian Schussele, and in France, Spain, and England. His studies from American history excel in fidelity and accuracy of detail.

FERRIS, WOODBRIDGE NATHAN (*b. near Spencer, N.Y., 1853; d. Washington, D.C., 1928*), educator. Founded Ferris Institute, Big Rapids, Mich.; Democratic governor of Michigan, 1913–17; U.S. senator, 1923–28.

FERRY, ELISHA PEYRE (*b. Monroe, Mich., 1825; d. 1895*), lawyer, Union soldier. Governor of Washington Territory, 1872–80; first governor of state of Washington, 1890–93.

FERRY, ORRIS SANFORD (*b. Bethel, Conn., 1823; d. 1875*), lawyer, Union soldier. Congressman, Republican, from Connecticut, 1859–61, and U.S. senator, 1866–75, shifting from Radical views to a moderate position on Reconstruction.

FERRY, THOMAS WHITE (*b. Mackinac Island, Mich., 1827; d. Grand Haven, Mich., 1896*), businessman. U.S. senator, Republican, from Michigan, 1871–83; financial expert; president pro tempore of the Senate during Hayes-Tilden electoral count, 1877.

FERSEN, HANS AXEL, COUNT VON (*b. Stockholm, Sweden, 1755; d. Sweden, 1810*), soldier, statesman. Aide-de-camp to Rochambeau in America, 1780–83; attempted to rescue French royal family, 1791, by flight to Varennes.

FESS, SIMEON DAVIDSON (*b. Allen Co., Ohio, 1861; d. Washington, D.C., 1936*), educator. Graduated Ohio Northern, 1889; LL.B., 1894. President, Antioch College, 1907–17. Congressman, Republican, from Ohio, 1913–23; U.S. senator, 1923–35. A conservative leader of the "Old Guard" and an ardent prohibitionist, he opposed President Wilson's policies and later attacked progressive spirits in his own party, vehemently supporting the Presidents Harding, Coolidge, and Hoover. Solemn, superior and long-winded, he won respect for his sincerity.

FESSENDEN, FRANCIS (*b. Portland, Maine, 1838; d. 1906*), lawyer, Union major general, biographer of his father, William Pitt Fessenden.

FESSENDEN, JAMES DEERING (*b. Portland, Maine, 1833; d. 1882*), lawyer, Union brigadier general, Maine official and legislator. Son of William Pitt Fessenden.

FESSENDEN, REGINALD AUBREY (*b. East Bolton, Canada, 1866; d. Bermuda, 1932*), inventor, pioneer in radio communication. Educated in Canada, gave up a career in education because of his interest in science. Removed to New York *ca.* 1886. Worked for Thomas A. Edison, Westinghouse Electric Co., and taught at the University of Pittsburgh, where he concentrated on wireless communication. Formed the National Electric Signalling Co., 1902. Believed wireless telephony to be practicable if a continuous flow of high-frequency vibrations were developed; achieved success with an alternator on a frequency of 50,000 cycles, and in 1906 sent out, the first known broadcast of speech and music ever made. Established two-way transatlantic telegraphic communication, 1906. He is credited also with invention of heterodyne reception, the fathometer, and the radio compass.

FESSENDEN, SAMUEL (*b. Fryeburg, Maine, 1784; d. 1869*), lawyer, abolitionist. Father of William Pitt Fessenden.

FESSENDEN, THOMAS GREEN (*b. Walpole, N.H., 1771; d. Boston, Mass., 1837*), poet, journalist, inventor. Graduated Dartmouth, 1796. Contributed under pen name "Simon Spunkey" to Dennie's *Farmer's Weekly Museum*; practiced law. In England, 1801–04, as agent and promoter of inventions; there published the satire *Terrible Tractoration* (1803) and a volume of *Original Poems* (1804; reprinted at Philadelphia, 1806). Returning to Boston, he wrote *Democracy Unveiled* (1805), a virulent Hudibrastic attack on Jefferson; edited a partisan Federalist magazine. During law practice in Brattleboro, Vt., 1809–22, he also edited local newspapers and compiled legal and other works. Established *New England Farmer*, 1822, and other agricultural periodicals; invented a portable hot-water stove. Served as Whig in Massachusetts General Court. Was most important American verse satirist between John Trumbull and James Russell Lowell.

FESSENDEN, WILLIAM PITT (*b. Boscawen, N.H., 1806; d. Portland, Maine, 1869*), lawyer, politician, financier. Son of Samuel Fessenden. Graduated Bowdoin, 1823; admitted to Maine bar, 1827; became one of the state's outstanding lawyers. Entered public life with election to the state legislature on anti-Jackson ticket, 1831; active as a Whig, he accompanied Daniel Webster on western tour in 1837, but later (1852) opposed Webster's presidential nomination. Elected again to Maine legislature, 1839, he was Whig Congressman, 1841–43; he returned to the legislature in 1845–46 and 1853–54. His rise to national fame began when the antislavery faction of the Maine legislature elected him to the U.S. Senate in 1854. There he quickly became known through his eloquent opposition to the Kansas-Nebraska Act, and in 1857 began his notable ten-year service on the Senate

Finance Committee. In poor health, given to displays of irritability, and with a reputation for harshness and austerity, Fessenden was one of the Senate's greatest debaters and intellectual forces. As chairman of the Finance Committee after 1861, he earned a permanent place among America's public financiers. He consistently tried to administer the finances of the Civil War economically and efficiently. He opposed many popular personal and sectional projects and protested against the issue of legal-tender notes, although he later admitted that they presented the only resource available at the time. He foresaw the need for increased taxation and at the beginning of the war proposed the levy of an income tax. Appointed secretary of the treasury, 1864, during his one year of service Fessenden stood firm against further inflation, raised the interest rate on government bonds, and marketed yet another great loan through Jay Cooke and Co.

Reelected to the Senate, 1865, he became chairman of the Joint Committee on Reconstruction. A Radical Reconstructionist, he believed in the power of Congress to change the South's form of government, to punish, to exact security, and to take entire charge of the defeated section. He was not, however, an extremist, and opposed part of the Confiscation Act and the attempt to expel Senator Garrett Davis for treasonable acts. In the impeachment of President Andrew Johnson, he held that impeachment was a judicial process to be motivated by manifestly impeachable offenses and not a device for the summary removal of an unpopular, ill-advised executive. Although he disapproved of President Johnson's policies and conduct, he thought him free of impeachable offenses and so voted, refusing to bow to the opinions and wishes of his constituents in the matter. He courageously faced a storm of popular disapproval in the confident hope that events would justify his course. His death occurred before his term ended.

FETTER, FRANK ALBERT (*b. Peru, Ind., 1863; d. Princeton N.J., 1949*), economist. B.A., Indiana University, 1891; Ph.M., Cornell University, 1892; studied in Paris at the Sorbonne and at the École de Droit; Ph.D., University of Halle, 1894. Taught at Cornell, Indiana, and Stanford; professor of political economy, Princeton, 1911–31. Author of *Principles of Economics* (1904, rewritten as *Economic Principles*, 1915); *The Masquerade of Monopoly* (1931); and other works in which he proposed a new theory of the basis of value and was creatively critical of conventional economic doctrines. He was particularly concerned with the monopoly problem in the United States and was one of the first professional economists to recognize the basing-point system of pricing as an unlawful price-fixing arrangement.

FETTERMAN, WILLIAM JUDD (*b. ca. 1833; d. near Lodge Trail Ridge, Wyo., 1866*), soldier. Ambushed and killed with his command of 80 men by Indian chief Red Cloud while leading a foolhardy attack out of Fort Phil Kearny.

FEUCHTWANGER, LION (*b. Munich, Germany, 1884; d. Pacific Palisades, Calif., 1958*), author. Studied at the universities of Munich and Berlin. Author of *Thomas Wendt*, later retitled *1918* (1918–19), and *Jew Suess* (1920–1921); *Erfolg* (1930) established his reputation as anti-Nazi. Collaborated with Bertolt Brecht on *The Life of Edward the Second of England* in the late 1920's. Immigrated to France and settled in California, where he wrote *Proud Destiny* (1947), *The Devil in Boston* (1948), *This Is the Hour* (1951), and *Jeptha and His Daughter* (1957).

FEW, IGNATIUS ALPHONSO (*b. near Augusta, Ga., 1789; d. Athens, Ga., 1845*), Methodist clergyman. Founder and first president, Emory College.

FEW, WILLIAM (*b. near Baltimore, Md., 1748; d. Fishkill-on-the-Hudson, N.Y., 1828*), statesman, Revolutionary soldier, banker. Raised in North Carolina; removed to Georgia, 1776.

Georgia delegate to Continental Congress and member of Constitutional Convention; U.S. senator from Georgia, 1789–93. Removed to New York, 1799, and engaged in banking.

FEW, WILLIAM PRESTON (*b. Sandy Flat, S.C., 1867; d. Durham, N.C., 1940*), educator. Graduated Harvard 1893; Ph.D., 1896. President, Trinity College, Durham, N.C., 1910–24, and first president of its successor, Duke University.

FEWKES, JESSIE WALTER (*b. Newton, Mass., 1850; d. Forest Glen, Md., 1930*), zoologist, ethnologist. Graduated Harvard, 1875; Ph.D., 1877. Founded the *Journal of American Ethnology and Archaeology*. Became associated with Bureau of American Ethnology, 1895. Introducing zoological methods to archaeology, Fewkes intensively studied Hopi cults as well as pioneering in exploration and conservation of Southwest cliff dwellings and pueblos. Became chief of bureau, 1918; received international recognition. Among his many contributions to anthropology was his demonstration of value of study of living tribes in solving problems of their past.

FFOULKE, CHARLES MATHER (*b. Quakertown, Pa., 1841; d. New York, N.Y., 1909*), wool merchant. Collector of, and authority on, tapestries.

FFRENCH, CHARLES DOMINIC (*b. Galway, Ireland, 1775; d. 1851*), Roman Catholic clergyman, Dominican. *Post* 1812, attended missions in New Brunswick (Canada), New York, New Jersey, and New England; pastor at Lawrence, Mass., *post* 1846.

FIELD, BENJAMIN HAZARD (*b. Yorktown, N.Y., 1814; d. New York, N.Y., 1893*), merchant, philanthropist. Benefactor and officer of New York Home for Incurables, 1866–93; helped found New York Free Circulating Library.

FIELD, CHARLES WILLIAM (*b. Woodford Co., Ky., 1828; d. Washington, D.C., 1892*), Confederate soldier, engineer. Graduated West Point, 1849. Served with cavalry on southwestern frontier. As major general, commanded Hood's old Texas division, 1864–65. Inspector general of Egyptian army, 1875–77.

FIELD, CYRUS WEST (*b. Stockbridge, Mass., 1819; d. 1892*), merchant, capitalist, promoter of first Atlantic cable. Son of David D. Field (1781–1867). Retired from business as paper merchant, 1852, and turned to promotion of an Atlantic cable *post* 1854. In association with Peter Cooper and others, and with advice of M. F. Maury and S. F. B. Morse, Field formed a company to build cable between Newfoundland and Ireland. After many reverses and a partial success in 1858, a fully serviceable cable was in operation by 1866. Field also promoted New York elevated railroads, and with Jay Gould developed the Wabash Railroad. A man of courage and vision, he was easily deceived and his last years were saddened by financial reverses.

FIELD, DAVID DUDLEY (*b. East Guilford, Conn., 1781; d. Stockbridge, Mass., 1867*), Congregational clergyman, historian. Minister at Haddam, Conn., and Stockbridge, Mass. Father of four celebrated Americans: David Dudley, Cyrus West, Stephen Johnson, and Henry Martyn Field.

FIELD, DAVID DUDLEY (*b. Haddam, Conn., 1805; d. 1894*), lawyer. Son of David D. Field (1781–1867). Attended Williams College; admitted to New York bar, 1828; became partner of Robert Sedgwick. Long active in politics as antislavery Democrat, briefly as a Republican, and *post* 1865 as a Democrat again. Field's career was primarily that of a lawyer and law reformer. He was outstanding in the years following the Civil War as counsel in great constitutional cases, defending L. P. Milligan before the Supreme Court in 1867 and contending successfully that military courts were without jurisdiction as long as civilian courts were open. Likewise, he won arguments on usurpations of constitutional rights in the Cummings, McCardle, and Cruikshank cases. During the Erie Railroad litigation of 1869, Field was counsel for Jay Gould and James Fisk, and was accused of unprofessional conduct; the Committee on Grievances of the New York City bar delivered a damaging report on Field, but its recommendations were not adopted. Field's connection with "Boss" Tweed, a codirector of Erie with Gould and Fisk, also laid him open to adverse criticism.

Field served with distinction as counsel for Samuel J. Tilden in the 1876 election dispute; also in the case of *New York* v. *Louisiana* before the Supreme Court, 1882. His permanent fame, however, derives from his fight for codification of municipal and international law. He inspired and personally shaped reformed political, penal, and civil procedural codes for New York; in 1881 the penal code was adopted. The civil code involved Field in a bitter fight in which he almost single-handedly engaged the New York bar. His work has been recognized by wide adoption of his codes both in the United States and abroad. In 1872 he published a *Draft Outline of an International Code*, whose second edition (1876) carried an added part on relations in time of war. In 1873 Field helped found the Association for the Reform and Codification of the Law of Nations and was active in furthering the movement until the end of his life.

FIELD, EUGENE (*b. St. Louis, Mo., 1850; d. Chicago, Ill., 1895*), author. Attended Williams, Knox College, and University of Missouri. Worked as newspaperman in Missouri and on Denver, Colo., *Tribune*, 1873–83. Joined staff of Chicago *Morning News* (renamed *Record*, 1890) with which he remained until his death. His practical jokes, his practice of attributing poems to embarrassed notables, and his uproarious reporting of imaginary events distinguished his column "Sharps and Flats," in which much of his verse originally appeared. As whimsical in his life as in his writings, he was a student of Horace and a bibliophile, and the character of his column set a higher standard for American journalism. His poems are at their best ("Little Boy Blue," "Wynken, Blynken, and Nod") sentimental and pathetic; at their worst, jejune and repetitive. Among his books are *The Tribune Primer* (1882); *Culture's Garland* (1887); *A Little Book of Western Verse* (1889); *Second Book of Verse* (1892); *The Holy Cross and Other Tales* (1893); and a selection from *Sharps and Flats* (1900).

FIELD, FRED TARBELL (*b. Springfield, Vt., 1876; d. Newton Mass., 1950*), lawyer, jurist. B.A., Brown University, 1900; LL.B., Harvard Law School, 1903. After service in the Massachusetts attorney general's office, 1905–12, he entered practice in Boston. Appointed an associate justice of the Massachusetts Supreme Judicial Court, 1929, he was chief justice of that court, 1938–47.

FIELD, HENRY MARTYN (*b. Stockbridge, Mass., 1822; d. 1907*), Presbyterian clergyman. Son of David D. Field (1781–1867). Author of popular travel books and biographies of his brothers David Dudley and Cyrus West Field; owned and edited the *Evangelist*.

FIELD, HERBERT HAVILAND (*b. Brooklyn, N.Y., 1868; d. 1921*), zoologist, bibliographer. Studied at Harvard, Freiburg, Leipzig, Paris; established Concilium Bibliographicum, Zurich, 1895, international center for indexing zoological literature.

FIELD, JOSEPH M. (*b. Dublin, Ireland*[?], *1810; d. Mobile, Ala., 1856*), actor, playwright, journalist. Brought to America in infancy. Played in West and South.

FIELD, KATE. *See* FIELD, MARY KATHERINE KEEMLE.

FIELD, MARSHALL (*b. near Conway, Mass., 1834; d. 1906*), merchant. Removed to Chicago, 1856; was clerk and salesman for dry-goods firm of Cooley, Wadsworth & Co.; became general manager, 1861, and a partner, 1862. Associated with Levi Z. Leiter and Potter Palmer in retail and wholesale firm of Field, Palmer and Leiter until 1867; with Leiter and his own brothers in Field, Leiter and Co. until 1881, when Leiter withdrew and it became Marshall Field and Co. Under his able management, his shop won a reputation for quality merchandise and honest dealing. Like A. T. Stewart and John Wanamaker, Field promoted new trends in merchandising. Prices were marked plainly; sales were for cash or on short credit; goods could be bought on approval and exchanged; large stocks were acquired in anticipation of demand and a demand was then created. Field bought his goods on a worldwide scale and manufactured many of them in his own factories. He was a master of detail, a diplomat in employee relations, and shrewd in his choice of able assistants.

FIELD, MARSHALL, III (*b. Chicago, Ill., 1893; d. New York, N.Y., 1956*), newspaper publisher, philanthropist. Studied at Eton and Cambridge Universities. Inheritor of one of the world's largest fortunes, Field worked first in banking and financial enterprises before becoming a serious liberal and New Dealer. Founded the liberal newspaper *PM* in New York (1940) and the *Chicago Sun* (1941), later the Chicago *Sun-Times*. In 1944, he consolidated his communications and publishing enterprises as Field Enterprises. President, 1935, Child Welfare League of America. Awarded the Silver Star for gallantry under fire in World War I.

FIELD, MARSHALL, IV (*b. New York, N.Y., 1916; d. Chicago, Ill., 1965*), publisher. Son of Marshall Field III, founder and publisher of the *Chicago Sun*, later the *Chicago Sun-Times*; a great-grandson of the founder of Chicago's Marshall Field and Company department store. Studied at Harvard (1934–38), and the University of Virginia (LL.B., 1941). Commissioned an ensign in the Navy in 1942; discharged with the rank of lieutenant commander in 1945. Assistant publisher and associate editor of the *Chicago Sun-Times* in 1949; editor and publisher from 1950. President of Field Enterprises from 1956. Editor and publisher of the *Chicago Daily News* from 1959. The *Sun-Times* and *Daily News* reflected their publisher's centrist Republican attitudes and respect for journalistic decorum.

FIELD, MARY KATHERINE KEEMLE (*b. St. Louis, Mo., 1838; d. Honolulu, Hawaii, 1896*), journalist, author, lecturer, actress. Daughter of Joseph M. Field. Friend of the Brownings, George Eliot, Anthony Trollope, and other distinguished Victorians.

FIELD, MAUNSELL BRADHURST (*b. Peekskill, N.Y.*[?], *1822; d. New York, N.Y., 1875*), lawyer. Served in U.S. Paris legation and as president of U.S. commission to Paris Exhibition, 1855. Did valuable service as assistant in U.S. treasury department, 1861–65. Author of *Memories* (1874).

FIELD, RICHARD STOCKTON (*b. White Hill, N.J., 1803; d. Princeton, N.J., 1870*), lawyer, jurist. Grandson of Richard Stockton. Developed New Jersey's educational system; defended Lincoln's suspension of habeas corpus as U.S. senator, 1862; federal judge, New Jersey district, 1863–70.

FIELD, ROBERT (*b. England, ca. 1769; d. Jamaica, British West Indies, 1819*), painter of portraits in oil, miniaturist, engraver. Led successful professional and social life in Philadelphia, Washington, Baltimore, Boston, 1794–1803; in Halifax, Nova Scotia, 1808–16.

FIELD, ROSWELL MARTIN (*b. St. Louis, Mo., 1851; d. Morristown, N.J., 1919*), journalist. Brother of Eugene Field; collaborator with him in *Echoes from the Sabine Farm* (1891, 1892).

FIELD, STEPHEN DUDLEY (*b. Stockbridge, Mass., 1846; d. Stockbridge, 1913*), electrical engineer, inventor. Nephew of Cyrus W. Field. Active in telegraphy in California, 1863–79, during which time he developed many improvements. Thereafter, designed and built electric railroads; designed a superior stock ticker; invented and installed submarine quadruplex telegraph.

FIELD, STEPHEN JOHNSON (*b. Haddam, Conn., 1816; d. 1899*), jurist. Son of David D. Field (1781–1867). Graduated Williams, 1837; studied law with brother David D. Field and with John Van Buren; admitted to bar, 1841. Removed to California, 1849; became alcalde of Marysville; served in state legislature, where he drafted state civil and criminal practice acts. Elected to state supreme court, 1857, he became known and respected for his pragmatism and disregard for common-law notions, his defense of the power of the legislature to legislate for the general welfare and to adopt measures for the protection of labor. A Union Democrat, he was appointed U.S. circuit judge at San Francisco and U.S. Supreme Court justice in 1863.

In contrast to his previous pragmatism, Field's constitutional position became increasingly doctrinaire. He held the dualistic thesis of "a national government for national purposes, local governments for local purposes," each sovereign in its sphere, neither dependent upon nor subordinate to the other in any degree. The Court could define the spheres of local and national government only acting judicially and as mere mouthpiece of the Constitution. His second major tenet was his natural-rights doctrine derived from the contemporary discussion of freedmen's rights, from the individualism of the classical school of economics, and from his own western experience. The two articles of his creed were not always compatible. Among the noteworthy cases in which Field spoke for the Court were the Test Oath Cases, *Paul* v. *Virginia*, *The Daniel Ball*, Tarble's Case, *Pennoyer* v. *Neff*, *Escanaba Bridge & Transportation Company* v. *Chicago*, *Barbier* v. *Connelly*, *Gloucester Ferry Company* v. *Pennsylvania*, and *Chae Chan Ping* v. *United States*. Among his most important contributions were his dissents in the Slaughterhouse Cases and in *Munn* v. *Illinois*. Field's work as California circuit judge contributed the most dramatic chapters to his career. His defiance of local anti-Chinese feeling and other considerations thwarted his hopes of a Democratic presidential nomination. He retired from the bench in 1897.

FIELD, THOMAS WARREN (*b. Onondaga Hill, N.Y., 1821; d. Brooklyn, N.Y., 1881*), author. Edited several valuable historical works, in particular *An Essay Towards an Indian Bibliography* (1873).

FIELD, WALBRIDGE ABNER (*b. Springfield, Vt., 1833; d. 1899*), jurist. Graduated Dartmouth, 1855. Served as assistant to the U.S. attorney general; as congressman, Republican, from Massachusetts, 1877–78 and 1878–80; and as justice of Massachusetts Supreme Judicial Court, 1881–99, (chief justice *post* 1890).

FIELDS, ANNIE ADAMS (*b. Boston, Mass., 1834; d. 1915*), Boston hostess, author. Wife of James T. Fields. Wrote memoirs of the literary people whom she entertained, a life of her husband, and other works.

FIELDS, JAMES THOMAS (*b. Portsmouth, N.H., 1817; d. Boston, Mass., 1881*), publisher. Head of Ticknor & Fields; editor of *Atlantic Monthly*, 1861–70; author of poems, essays, and *Yesterdays with Authors* (1872).

FIELDS, LEWIS MAURICE. *See* WEBER, JOSEPH MORRIS.

FIELDS, WILLIAM CLAUDE (*b. Philadelphia, Pa., 1880; d. Pasadena, Calif., 1946*), actor. Born William Claude Dukenfield. Ran away from home at 11, began career as a carnival juggler, 1894. Perfecting his skills and adding comedy routines, he was a featured vaudeville performer, with the stage name W. C. Fields, before he was 20; between 1901 and 1914, he made several successful world tours. He appeared in the Ziegfeld *Follies*, 1915–21, and in George White's *Scandals*, 1922. Starred in the Broadway musical comedy *Poppy*, 1923, as "Eustace McGargle," a top-hatted combination of juggler, medicine man, card sharp, and confidence trickster; he made the character his own, both on the stage and in private life. Thereafter, he was known for his muttered asides, reflecting not only on pretension and sentiment but on most of society, and was professedly hostile to children and dogs. He made his first important movie appearance in the silent *Sally of the Sawdust* (1925); from then on, except for appearances in Earl Carroll's *Vanities* (1928) and on a weekly radio program with ventriloquist Edger Bergen in the late 1930's, he devoted his career to motion pictures, for many of which he provided the basic ideas. Among these, *It's a Gift* (1934), *The Man on the Flying Trapeze* (1935), and *The Bank Dick* (1940) were outstanding. He also gave a brilliant performance as Mr. Micawber in *David Copperfield* (1935).

FIFER, JOSEPH WILSON (*b. near Staunton, Va., 1840; d. Bloomington, Ill., 1938*), politician, Union soldier. Republican governor of Illinois, 1889–93.

FILENE, EDWARD ALBERT (*b. Salem, Mass., 1860; d. Paris, France, 1937*), merchant, reformer. Transformed a small family business into a large Boston department store which earned him a fortune, although he lost control of its management in 1928 and was unable to realize his ambition to make it a cooperative enterprise. Idealistic in public affairs, he organized with Lincoln Steffens and others the Boston 1915, a civic reform group, and was a pioneer in the chamber of commence movement. His most lasting contributions were his development of credit unions and his sponsorship of the Twentieth Century Fund, 1919, a fact-gathering organization specializing in the economic field, to which he left the bulk of his fortune.

FILLEBROWN, THOMAS (*b. Winthrop, Maine, 1836; d. 1908*), dentist. Practiced in Boston, Mass. Professor of operative dentistry and oral surgery at Harvard, 1883–1904; author of *A Textbook of Operative Dentistry* (1889).

FILLMORE, CHARLES (*b. near St. Cloud, Minn., 1854; d. Lee's Summit, Mo., 1948*), real estate developer, cofounder with his wife of the Unity School of Christianity.

FILLMORE, JOHN COMFORT (*b. near Franklin, Conn., 1843; d. Taftville, Conn., 1898*), musician, theorist, educator. Authority on music of American Indians.

FILLMORE, MILLARD (*b. Locke, N.Y., 1800; d. Buffalo, N.Y., 1874*), president of the United States. Grew up on the New York frontier, a farmer's son; was admitted to bar, 1823; moved to Buffalo, 1830. Elected Anti-Masonic representative to the legislature, 1828; in 1934, following lead of his mentor Thurlow Weed, he became a Whig. Served in Congress, 1833–35 and 1837–43; as chairman of the House Ways and Means Committee, he took a leading part in framing tariff of 1842. The support of Henry Clay's followers helped him win nomination for vice president in 1848. Shortly after his inauguration Fillmore broke with Weed and was reconciled with Daniel Webster, with whom he had a difference. Fillmore presided over the great slavery debate of 1850 in the Senate with firmness and fairness. Slow in announcing his support for Clay and Webster on the Compromise of 1850, he appointed Webster as secretary of state on his succession to the presidency after Zachary Taylor's death that year, and otherwise demonstrated his alliance with the moderate Whigs who favored compromise. When he signed the Fugitive Slave Law in the fall of 1850, he exposed himself to violent abuse by the abolitionists. Fillmore lost the 1852 Whig presidential nomination to Gen. Winfield Scott. In 1856, nominated by the Know-Nothings, he ran a poor third to Buchanan and Frémont. Always for conciliation as against coercion, he opposed Lincoln's conduct of the Civil War; he supported McClellan in the 1864 presidential campaign and was sympathetic to President Andrew Johnson's policies.

FILSON, JOHN (*b. East Fallowfield Township, Pa.*, ca. *1747; d. on Little Miami River, Ohio, 1788*), explorer, historian. Author of *Discovery, Settlement, and Present State of Kentucke* (1784), which contained the first appearance of Daniel Boone's so-called autobiography and the first map of Kentucky. The map was also issued separately.

FINCH, FRANCIS MILES (*b. Ithaca, N.Y., 1827; d. 1907*), jurist. Associate judge, New York Court of Appeals; wrote popular poems "Nathan Hale" (1853) and "The Blue and the Gray" (1867).

FINCK, HENRY THEOPHILUS (*b. Bethel, Mo., 1854; d. 1926*), author. Music critic for the *Nation*, 1881–1924.

FINDLAY, JAMES (*b. Franklin Co., Pa., 1770; d. Cincinnati, Ohio, 1835*), soldier. Removed to Cincinnati, Ohio, *ante* 1798. Was first U.S. marshal of Ohio and mayor of Cincinnati, 1805–06 and 1810–11. Commended for service in War of 1812, he was later major general of state militia. Congressman, Democrat, 1825–33.

FINDLEY, WILLIAM (*b. North Ireland, 1741; d. Westmoreland Co., Pa., 1821*), Revolutionary soldier, politician. Came to America, 1763; settled near Waynesboro, Pa., and worked as weaver, teacher, and farmer. At close of Revolution, removed to a farm near present Latrobe, Pa. Active as Antifederalist in local and state politics; opposed ratification of the Constitution and Hamilton's financial policies; served in U.S. Congress, 1791–99 and 1803–17; in the Pennsylvania senate, 1799–1803. Upon his recommendation the first standing congressional committee, Ways and Means, was appointed. As spokesman of the frontier he encouraged, and later helped settle, the Whiskey Rebellion of 1794.

FINE, HENRY BURCHARD (*b. Chambersburg, Pa., 1858; d. 1928*), mathematician. Graduated Princeton, 1880; Ph.D., Leipzig, 1885; specialized in logic of mathematics. Professor of mathematics, Princeton, 1891–1928; dean of faculty, 1903–12; dean of scientific departments, 1909–28.

FINK, ALBERT (*b. Lauterbach, Germany, 1827; d. New York, 1897*), railroad engineer, pioneer in U.S. railway economics and statistics. Came to America, 1849. Invented Fink bridge truss, *ca.* 1852. As construction engineer, Louisville & Nashville Railroad, *post* 1857, built Green River bridge near Louisville, then second-largest iron bridge in North America. Carried out successful reconstruction of the road after the Civil War; became general superintendent, 1865, and vice president, 1869. Built mile-long Ohio River bridge at Louisville, the world's longest truss bridge. His 1874 report on costs of transportation is considered the foundation stone of U.S. rail economics. Resigning from the Louisville & Nashville, 1875, he served as commissioner of Southern Railway & Steamship Association and of New York City Trunk Line Association.

FINLAY, CARLOS JUAN (*b. Camagüey, Cuba, 1833; d. 1915*), physician. Educated in France; graduated M.D., Jefferson Medical College, 1855, and University of Havana, 1857. Spent most of his professional career in Havana. Declared the mosquito to be the probable transmitting agent of yellow fever in a paper read in 1881; his theory was received with indifference. His view was triumphantly confirmed by the findings of the Reed Board, 1900.

FINLAY, HUGH (*b. Scotland, ca. 1731; d. 1801*), colonial postmaster. Developed postal service in Quebec, New England, and Maritime Provinces; postmaster general of British North America, 1787–99.

FINLEY, JAMES BRADLEY (*b. North Carolina, 1781; d. Ohio, 1856*), Methodist preacher. Raised in frontier Ohio. Was one of the West's most distinguished evangelical pioneers *post* 1810; cofounder of Wyandot Indian Mission.

FINLEY, JOHN HUSTON (*b. near Grand Ridge, Ill., 1863; d. New York, N.Y., 1940*), educator, editor, author. Graduated, 1887, Knox College, Galesburg, Ill.; returned as president, 1892. He subsequently filled with distinction the following posts: editor of *Harper's Weekly*, 1899–1900; a chair of politics at Princeton, 1900–03; president of City College of New York, 1903–13; New York State commissioner of education, 1913–21; associate editor, 1921–37, and editor in chief, 1937–38, of the *New York Times*. A man of disciplined mind, cultured taste, and active conscience, he was the author of eight books and many articles in the fields of education, politics, and the humanities.

FINLEY, MARTHA FARQUHARSON (*b. Chillicothe, Ohio, 1828; d. Elkton, Md., 1909*), author of popular juvenile series. Wrote the immortal *Elsie Dinsmore* (1868).

FINLEY, ROBERT (*b. Princeton, N.J., 1772; d. 1817*), Presbyterian clergyman, educator. Organizer of the American Colonization Society, 1816; president of University of Georgia, 1817.

FINLEY, SAMUEL (*b. Co. Armagh, Ireland, 1715; d. Philadelphia, Pa., 1766*), Presbyterian clergyman. Came to America, 1734. Friend and fellow worker of Gilbert Tennent, and a notable evangelistic preacher in the "Great Awakening," 1740–43. Pastor at Nottingham, Pa., 1744–61; president of College of New Jersey (Princeton), 1761–66.

FINN, FRANCIS JAMES (*b. St. Louis, Mo., 1859; d. Cincinnati, Ohio, 1928*), Roman Catholic clergyman, Jesuit, educator. Author of *Percy Wynn* (1889), *Tom Playfair* (1892), and other long-popular stories of Catholic schoolboys.

FINN, HENRY JAMES WILLIAM (*b. Sydney, Canada, 1787; d. Long Island Sound, 1840*), actor, playwright, journalist. Raised in New York City. Made stage debut in England; first American appearance, 1817, at Philadelphia. Excelled as eccentric comedian. Author of various melodramas and satires of the *American Comic Annual* (1831).

FINNEY, CHARLES GRANDISON (*b. Warren, Conn., 1792; d. Oberlin, Ohio, 1875*), revivalist, educator. Raised in frontier New York. Abandoned practice of law after a highly emotional conversion; studied theology; was ordained as Presbyterian minister, 1824. Conducted extraordinary revivals in middle and eastern states; became pastor in New York City, 1832. Withdrew from the Presbytery, and was associated, *post* 1837, with Oberlin College, serving as its president, 1851–66, and as pastor of Oberlin's First Congregational Church, 1835–72. A New School Calvinist whose "Oberlin theology" was frequently attacked as tending toward Arminianism and perfectionism, he objected to popular amusements as hindrances to maintenance of "revival pitch" in churches and opposed the use of tobacco, tea, and coffee.

FINNEY, JOHN MILLER TURPIN (*b. near Natchez, Miss.,
1863; d. Baltimore, Md., 1942*), surgeon. Raised in Illinois and
Maryland. Graduated Princeton, 1884; M.D., Harvard Medical
School, 1889. Associated with Johns Hopkins Hospital and Medical School *post* 1889 (professor of clinical surgery, 1912–33), he
practiced in Baltimore. Skilled in all types of operations, he
achieved special renown in gastric surgery; his procedure for relief
of duodenal ulcer remains standard. During World War I service
in France, he was made chief consultant in surgery of the Allied
Expeditionary Force. First president the American College of
Surgeons, 1913–16.

FINOTTI, JOSEPH MARIA (*b. Ferrara, Italy, 1817; d. Colorado, 1879*), Roman Catholic clergyman, bibliographer. Was
literary editor of Boston *Pilot*; compiled *Bibliographia Catholica
Americana, Pt. I, 1784–1820* (1872).

FIRESTONE, HARVEY SAMUEL (*b. Columbiana, Ohio,
1868; d. Miami Beach, Fla., 1938*), rubber manufacturer. Organized Firestone Tire and Rubber Co., 1900, catering to the
growing automobile market; by 1913 the company's annual sales
were $15 million. Firestone weathered the post 1919 depression by
cutting prices and wages; he expanded production and introduced
the balloon tire, 1923. To circumvent the rise in British crude
rubber prices *post* 1924, he acquired extensive rubber plantations
in Liberia, assuming an important role in the country's affairs.

FISCHER, EMIL FRIEDRICH AUGUST (*b. Brunswick, Germany,
1838; d. Hamburg, Germany, 1914*), singer. Principal bass at
New York Metropolitan Opera, 1885–98; at his best in
Wagnerian roles.

FISCHER, LOUIS (*b. Philadelphia, Pa., 1896; d. Hackensack,
N.J., 1970*), journalist and writer. Reporting from the Soviet
Union for the *Nation* during 1924–35, Fisher was sympathetic to
the changes brought about by the Bolshevik Revolution. An
admirer of the Soviet system, his reports deliberately covered up
the severity of Russian social and economic conditions; for him the
attraction of socialism transcended its material shortcomings.
Harboring increasing misgivings about Stalin from 1933, however, he renounced the Soviet Union in 1936. He was the first
American to join the International Brigades, and fought the
Loyalists against Franco during the Spanish Civil War. Fischer
believed that writers and journalists should be involved with
political causes. Among his books are biographies of Gandhi and
Lenin.

FISCHER, RUTH (*b. Leipzig, Germany, 1895; d. Paris,
France, 1961*), writer and ex-Communist activist. Sister of modernist composer Hanns Eisler and Communist activist Gerhart
Eisler. Chairman of the Berlin branch of the German Communist
party in 1921; a Communist delegate to the German Reichstag in
1924; member of the Comintern Presidium (1924–26). Expelled
from the German Communist party in 1926 after leading the "Left
Opposition," in which she dissented from the conservative and
Russian orientation of the German party, the Comintern, and the
Soviet party led by Stalin. Formed the Independent German
Communist party in 1926. Fled to France upon Nazi seizure of
power. Immigrated to the United States in 1941. An emotional
anti-Stalinist, she started and edited a newsletter, *The Network*
(1944–45), renamed *The Russian State Party* (1946–47, in
which she identified individuals, including her brother Gerhart
Eisler, as Soviet agents in the United States. Testified against her
brother before the House Committee on Un-American Activities
in 1947. Published a monography, *Stalin and German Communism* (1948), and in 1958 a study in German of post-Stalin reform
efforts.

FISH, CARL RUSSELL (*b. Central Falls, R.I., 1876; d. Madison, Wis., 1932*), historian. Graduated Brown, 1897; Ph.D.,
Harvard, 1900. Taught at University of Wisconsin, *post* 1900.
Author of *The Development of American Nationality*, a textbook
(1913); *The Rise of the Common Man* (1927); and other works
marked by originality and an emphasis on human and social
aspects.

FISH, HAMILTON (*b. New York, N.Y., 1808; d. 1893*), statesman. Son of Nicholas Fish. Graduated Columbia, 1827; admitted
to the bar, 1830. Congressman, Whig, from New York, 1843–45;
governor of New York, 1849–51. As governor, established statewide free schools; extended canal system; expressed hostility
toward extension of slavery. While U.S. senator, 1851–57, won
no special distinction. Joined Republican party with no enthusiasm. Served on New York Union Defense Committee during
Civil War and as federal commissioner for relief of prisoners.

Appointed U.S. secretary of state, 1869, he acted until 1877
with efficiency, caution, and patience. His most notable achievement was the settlement of the so-called *Alabama* claims against
Great Britain for damages suffered by Northern commerce during
the Civil War through the action of Confederate cruisers fitted out
or supplied in British ports. By the Treaty of Washington, 1871,
these claims were arbitrated by a tribunal at Geneva, which in
1872 levied damages to the amount of $15.5 million against Great
Britain.

Fish faced difficulties over Cuba throughout his term. An
insurrection in Cuba had obliged Fish to press claims on Spain for
redress of injuries to Americans and to contend with Americans
who wanted the United States to recognize the Cuban rebels as
belligerents and intervene in their favor. Fish persuaded President
Grant in 1869 to declare unjustified any recognition of belligerency, and in 1871 reached an agreement for a joint commission to
decide on American claims. In 1873 a new crisis arose when
Spanish authorities in Cuba executed the captain, crew members,
and passengers of the *Virginius*, a steamer under American registry
but belonging to the Cuban revolutionary committee in New
York. Fish succeeded in adjusting the affair peacefully, and in
1874 secured the *Virginius* indemnity claims; in 1875 he
instructed the U.S. minister to Spain to warn that nation of
possible international intervention if the Cuban insurrection continued. Spain complied at last with all American demands, and on
the quelling of the revolt in 1876 the discussion over Cuba ended.

Other achievements during Fish's tenure as secretary of state
concerned the protection of interests of North German citizens in
France during the Franco-Prussian War; the recognition by
Bismarck of the right to pass sealed dispatches through the German
lines around Paris; the agreement of both belligerents to refrain
from extending hostilities to the Far East; the protection of
American rights in China; and the signing of a treaty of commercial reciprocity with Hawaii in 1875. His efforts to secure agreements with Colombia and Nicaragua for an interoceanic canal
failed.

FISH, NICHOLAS (*b. New York, N.Y., 1758; d. 1833*), Revolutionary officer, lawyer. Lifelong friend of Alexander Hamilton;
distinguished in Saratoga and Yorktown campaigns; an active
Federalist politician.

FISH, PRESERVED (*b. Portsmouth, R.I., 1766; d. New York,
N.Y., 1846*), merchant, shipowner. A founder, 1815, of Fish &
Grinnell, foremost New York shipping firm; president,
Tradesman's Bank, 1836–46.

FISH, STUYVESANT (*b. New York, N.Y., 1851; d. 1923*),
railroad executive, banker. Son of Hamilton Fish. Successfully
managed Illinois Central Railroad as president, *post* 1887, until
ousted by E. H. Harriman interests, 1906.

FISHBACK, WILLIAM MEADE (*b. Jeffersonton, Va., 1831; d. Fort Smith, Ark., 1903*), lawyer. Removed to Arkansas, 1858. Unionist in Civil War, but turned against carpetbaggers. Governor of Arkansas, Democrat, 1893–95.

FISHER, ALFRED J. (*b. Norwalk, Ohio, 1892; d. Detroit, Mich., 1963*), and CHARLES T. (*b. Sandusky, Ohio, 1880; d. Detroit, Mich., 1963*), carriage and automobile body builders. Founded the Fisher Body Company in 1908 to manufacture automobile bodies. Reorganized as the Fisher Closed Body Company in 1910; pioneered in the development of closed bodies for power-driven vehicles, and interchangeable body parts, with a level of craftsmanship that made "Body by Fisher" a hallmark of quality. Fisher became the world's largest manufacturer of automobile bodies. Bought by General Motors in 1926.

FISHER, ALVAN (*b. Needham, Mass., 1792; d. Dedham, Mass., 1863*), painter. Brother of John D. Fisher, Specialized in rural landscapes and portraits.

FISHER, CLARA (*b. London, England, 1811; d. Metuchen, N.J., 1898*), actress, singer. Began career as child star in London; in America, *post* 1827, became one of the country's most finished stage artists, retiring in 1889. Author of an autobiography (1897).

FISHER, CLARENCE STANLEY (*b. Philadelphia, Pa., 1876; d. Jerusalem, Palestine, 1941*), archaeologist. B.S., University of Pennsylvania, 1897. Trained as an architect, he served as archaeological architect for the University of Pennsylvania's excavations at Nippur. A leading member of the Harvard University Expedition to Samaria, 1909, he remained in the Near East for the rest of his life, and developed the pioneering research techniques of George A. Reisner while serving as director or adviser to a number of American expeditions. His insistence on the most careful kind of surveying and mapping of ancient sites, the drafting of exact architectural plans of every building and wall, and the recording of the location of every object encountered in an excavated level profoundly affected the development of Palestinian archaeology. *Post* 1925, he was professor of archaeology at the American School of Oriental Research in Jerusalem.

FISHER, CLARK (*b. Levant, Maine, 1837; d. 1903*), naval engineer. Graduated Rensselaer Polytechnic, 1858. Served in U.S. Navy, 1859–71, resigning as chief engineer, after experiments proving value of oil as fuel. A prolific inventor, 1874–91, as head of Eagle Anvil Works.

FISHER, DANIEL WEBSTER (*b. Arch Spring, Pa., 1838; d. Washington, D.C., 1913*), Presbyterian clergyman. President of Hanover College, 1879–1907.

FISHER, DOROTHEA FRANCES CANFIELD (*b. Lawrence, Kans., 1879; d. Arlington, Vt., 1958*), author, moralist. Studied at Ohio State University, Ph.B., 1899, and at Columbia University, Ph.D., 1904, the first woman awarded the degree by Columbia in Romance languages. Served on the American Youth Commission, 1935–41. Advocated adult education and published many works on the subject. Her novels include *The Brimming Cup* (1921) and *The Deepening Stream* (1930). Member of the selection committee of the Book-of-the-Month Club, 1926–50.

FISHER, EBENEZER (*b. Charlotte, Maine, 1815; d. Canton, N.Y., 1879*), Universalist clergyman, educator. Principal of the theological school, St. Lawrence University, 1858–79.

FISHER, FREDERIC JOHN (*b. Sandusky, Ohio, 1878; d. Detroit, Mich., 1941*), industrialist. An expert carriage builder by trade, he and his five brothers were associated in a variety of industrial and financial enterprises. The Fisher Body Co. organized 1908, and its associated companies were the principal providers of bodies for automobiles; the firm pioneered in numerous improvements, including the development of steel body presses, steel-faced dies, and the use of lacquer on auto bodies instead of paint. Fisher Body Corporation became a division of General Motors in 1926, in exchange for $140 million in GM common stock. The brothers were active in large-scale trading on the stock market until 1929. He was a generous contributor to Detroit educational and cultural organizations.

FISHER, FREDERICK BOHN (*b. Greencastle, Pa., 1882; d. Detroit, Mich., 1938*), Methodist clergyman. Active in missions *post* 1910, he was bishop of Calcutta, India, 1920–30.

FISHER, GEORGE JACKSON (*b. North Castle, N.Y., 1825; d. 1893*), physician, book collector. Practiced at Ossining, N.Y.

FISHER, GEORGE PARK (*b. Wrentham, Mass., 1827; d. 1909*), Congregational clergyman, historian. Graduated Brown, 1847; Andover Theological Seminary, 1851. Studied in Germany. Professor of divinity, Yale, 1854–61; of history, Yale Divinity School, 1861–1901, and dean, 1895–1901. Author of numerous works on history and theology.

FISHER, GEORGE PURNELL (*b. Milford, Del., 1817; d. Washington, D.C., 1899*), lawyer. Judge of supreme court of District of Columbia, 1863–70; presided over first trial of John Surratt.

FISHER, HAMMOND EDWARD (*b. Wilkes-Barre, Pa., 1901?; d. 1955*), cartoonist. Creator of the cartoon strip "Joe Palooka." Widely used as a propaganda vehicle during World War II, the strip was carried by 1,000 newspapers by 1955.

FISHER, HARRISON (*b. Brooklyn, N.Y., 1875; d. New York, N.Y., 1934*), illustrator and magazine-cover artist. Creator of the Harrison Fisher Girl, "supernally beautiful and starry-eyed." Collections of his drawings were published in book form, 1907–14.

FISHER, HENRY CONROY (*b. Chicago, Ill., 1884; d. New York, N.Y., 1954*), cartoonist. Creator of the widely syndicated strip "Mutt and Jeff." First published in the Hearst papers in 1907, in the 1980's it was the oldest daily strip still in existence.

FISHER, IRVING (*b. Saugerties, N.Y., 1867; d. New York, N.Y., 1947*), economist. Raised in Peace Dale, R.I., and St. Louis, Mo. Graduated Yale, 1888, and began higher studies there. He was much influenced by Josiah Willard Gibbs and William Graham Sumner. Academically, Fisher found himself drawn to both mathematics and the practical significance of economics and social science. In 1891 he received the Ph.D. with a dissertation entitled "Mathematical Investigations in the Theory of Value and Prices." Fisher developed his ideas without knowledge of earlier work, and his dissertation was recognized as a significant step in the development of the theory of utility and consumer choice. He studied in Berlin and Paris, where he met Walras, Edgeworth, and Pareto.

Returning to Yale, Fisher continued in mathematics until 1895, when he transferred to the Department of Political Economy. He began his investigations of monetary problems, capital and interest, and economic statistics, and demonstrated his two interests: to develop the basic theory of his subject and to serve as a critic and adviser on economic policy. Ill health forced him in 1898 to take three years' leave; he then resumed his work in economics with renewed vigor. A series of major publications followed.

After 1920 his energies were increasingly devoted to the problem of monetary stability. The theory of income, capital, and interest occupied Fisher from an early period. He had considerable influence in reasserting the primacy of income as the central concept of economics and in pointing out that capital is simply the discounted value of future income streams. Analysis of the rate of discount led Fisher inevitably to the theory of interest. "The rate of interest is the mouthpiece at once of impatience to spend income without delay and of opportunity to increase income by delay." Fisher argued that society's investment opportunities are subject to the increase or decrease in resources, the discovery of new resources or means of developing old ones, and change in political conditions.

The contributions of Fisher's studies of money lie in his effort at statistical verification and his advocacy of proposals for monetary stabilization. At a time when the quantity theory of money was under widespread attack, Fisher espoused the theory. Fisher's concern with the purchasing power of money led him to extensive studies of the best index number for measuring price changes. He also undertook extensive studies of the velocity of money. The practical significance of Fisher's work on the purchasing power of money lay in his proposals for stabilizing the value of the dollar. He recognized the hold of the gold standard on people's imagination and the dangers of a paper currency. To avoid monetary instability he advocated a system of 100 percent money.

Fisher's interests led him to extensive work in statistics. Besides his work on index numbers and velocity, his contributions include a critical appraisal of U.S. vital statistics, development of the concept of the distributed lag, and work on the problem of effective graduation of statistical series.

Fisher had a great gift for exposition of even the most technical matters. His work provided the components of a model of the economic system which might have replaced the neoclassical model. Although no Fisherian school of economics developed, Fisher was, in the opinion of many, the leading economic theorist in the United States during the first half of the twentieth century.

FISHER, JOHN DIX (*b. Needham, Mass., 1797; d. Boston, Mass., 1850*), physician. Brother of Alvan Fisher. Graduated Harvard Medical School, 1825; studied in Paris. One of the first in America to use auscultation. Inspired New England Asylum, 1829, later the Perkins Institute for the Blind.

FISHER, JOSHUA FRANCIS (*b. Philadelphia, Pa., 1807; d. 1873*), humanitarian. A founder and lifelong trustee of Pennsylvania Institution for the Blind. Advocated sympathetic understanding of Southern problems and reform of the representative system.

FISHER, PHILIP. *See* COPLEY, THOMAS.

FISHER, SIDNEY GEORGE (*b. Philadelphia, Pa., 1809; d. Philadelphia, 1871*), lawyer, author.

FISHER, SYDNEY GEORGE (*b. Philadelphia, Pa., 1856; d. Essington, Pa., 1927*), lawyer, historian. Son of Sidney G. Fisher. Graduated Trinity (Hartford, Conn.), 1879. Author of many historical studies, notably *The Evolution of the Constitution* (1897); *The True Benjamin Franklin* (1899); and *The Struggle for American Independence* (1908).

FISHER, THEODORE WILLIS (*b. Westboro, Mass., 1837; d. 1914*), psychiatrist.

FISHER, WALTER LOWRIE (*b. Wheeling, W.Va., 1862; d. Winnetka, Ill., 1935*), lawyer, reformer. Son of Daniel W. Fisher. Practiced in Chicago, *post* 1889. Leader in movement to conserve U.S. natural resources; secretary of the interior, 1911–13.

FISHER, WILLIAM ARMS (*b. San Francisco, Calif., 1861; d. Brookline, Mass., 1948*), composer, music editor. Director of publications and editor for the Oliver Ditson Company of Boston,

Mass., 1897–1931. Author of *Notes on Music in Old Boston* (1918) and other works on the history of music in America.

FISK, CLINTON BOWEN (*b. western New York, 1828; d. New York, N.Y., 1890*), banker, Union soldier. Opened school for black freedmen, 1866, which later became Fisk University; presidential candidate on Prohibition party ticket, 1888.

FISK, JAMES (*b. Greenwich, Mass., 1763; d. Swanton, Vt., 1844*), lawyer, politician. Congressman, Democratic-Republican, from Vermont, 1805–09 and 1811–15; served as Vermont federal collector of revenue, 1818–26.

FISK, JAMES (*b. Bennington, Vt., 1834; d. New York, N.Y., 1872*), capitalist, speculator. Began his career as a boastful, flashy peddler and jobber; in 1866 founded brokerage house of Fisk & Belden with support of Daniel Drew. Drawn into the "Erie War" of 1868 between Drew and Cornelius Vanderbilt, Fisk broke Vanderbilt's attempt to corner Erie stock and, with Jay Gould, came to control the Erie Railroad. With Drew and Gould, he launched a campaign in 1868 to tighten credit and raise price of gold; their raids on U.S. Express Co. and Albany & Susquehanna rail stock culminated in an attempted gold corner on Black Friday, September 1869, which affected disastrously the nation's business.

FISK, WILBUR (*b. Brattleboro, Vt., 1792; d. Middletown, Conn., 1839*), Methodist clergyman, educator. Dispelled indifference of eastern Methodists toward education; first president, Wesleyan University, Middletown, Conn., 1830–39.

FISKE, AMOS KIDDER (*b. Whitefield, N.H., 1842; d. 1921*), editor, author. Staff member of *New York Times*, 1869–71 and 1878–97, and of *Journal of Commerce*, 1902–19.

FISKE, BRADLEY ALLEN (*b. Lyons, N.Y., 1854; d. New York, N.Y., 1942*), naval officer. Graduated U.S. Naval Academy, 1874. A competent and reliable officer, almost continuously occupied in sea duty, Fiske won distinction for his technical contributions, based on long study of the sciences. He developed a number of important inventions, including an electric ammunition hoist, electrically controlled gun turrets, an improved ship communication system, and sighting and range-finding devices which made naval gunnery an exact science. Opposition to his innovations by hidebound officials caused him to turn his attention to reform in the system of education for naval officers. Promoted rear admiral, 1911, he served from 1913 to 1915 as aide for operations to the secretary of the navy. He retired from active duty in 1916. He was one of a remarkable group of officers who took the U.S. Navy from archaic complacency into modern times.

FISKE, DANIEL WILLARD (*b. Ellisburg, N.Y., 1831; d. 1904*), scholar, librarian, book collector. Student of Icelandic civilization, newspaperman, book dealer, diplomat, Fiske lived in Italy *post* 1883. He was a principal benefactor of Cornell University library.

FISKE, FIDELIA (*b. Shelburne, Mass., 1816; d. Shelburne, 1864*), missionary to the Nestorians. Graduated Mt. Holyoke Seminary, 1842. Improved condition of women in Persia on tour of duty, 1843–58; wrote *Recollections of Mary Lyon* (1866).

FISKE, GEORGE CONVERSE (*b. Roxbury Highlands, Mass., 1872; d. 1927*), classicist, educator. Graduated Harvard, 1894; Ph.D., 1900. Taught at University of Wisconsin, 1901–27; authority on Roman satire; author of *Lucilius and Horace* (1920) and other works.

FISKE, HALEY (*b. New Brunswick, N.J., 1852; d. 1929*), insurance official, lawyer. Brother of Stephen Fiske. Graduated

Rutgers, 1871. Became vice president of Metropolitan Life Insurance Co., 1891; was instrumental in placing control of company in hands of policyholders, in making payments of bonuses to the insured, in initiating a highly successful national health campaign and in directing the company's capital into housing developmets. By 1919, when he became president, the company was recognized as the world's largest financial institution.

FISKE, HARRISON GREY (*b. Harrison, N.Y., 1861; d. New York, N.Y., 1942*), theatrical journalist, producer, director. Married Minnie Maddern Fiske, 1890. Editor-owner of the weekly New York *Dramatic Mirror*, 1879–1911, in which he consistently championed the creative people of the theater against exploitation by managers and particularly the theatrical trust known as the Syndicate. Also instrumental in founding the Actors' Fund. He and his wife raised the general standards of the American stage by the encouragement they gave new playwrights and by the care and taste with which their productions were designed, cast, staged, and directed.

FISKE, JOHN (*b. Salem, Mass., 1744; d. 1797*), naval commander, merchant. Captain in the Massachusetts navy during the Revolution; commanded the brigantines *Tyrrannicide* and *Massachusetts* on successful cruises, 1776–77.

FISKE, JOHN (*b. Hartford, Conn., 1842; d. Gloucester, Mass., 1901*), philosopher, historian. Born Edmund Fisk Green. Precocious as a linguist. Graduated Harvard, 1863; as a student, became disciple of Herbert Spencer and published articles on evolution in *North American Review*. Lectured on philosophy and history at Harvard and in Boston; in 1872 became assistant librarian at Harvard and published his first book, *Myths and Myth-Makers*. In 1874 followed *The Outlines of Cosmic Philosophy*. After resignation from Harvard, 1879, he became a popular lecturer on history both in the United States and abroad. Profound as neither a thinker nor a scholar, he was America's chief exponent of evolution and remarkable in the field of history chiefly for the lucid freedom of style in his many books.

FISKE, MINNIE MADDERN (*b. New Orleans, La., 1865; d. 1932*), actress. Christened Marie Augusta Davey. Made her stage appearance at age three as "Little Minnie Maddern"; New York debut, 1870; continued to act on and off Broadway until 1890 when she married Harrison Grey Fiske and retired. In 1893 she returned in *Hester Crewe*. Continued with *A Doll's House*, *Tess of the D'Urbervilles*, *Becky Sharp*, and *Salvation Nell* and acted in and directed many others. During the 1920's she toured the country as Mrs. Malaprop in *The Rivals*. One of the most potent forces in the American theater for realism on the stage, she won fame for her grasp of character, intellectual acuteness, emotional sensitivity, and ability as a director.

FISKE, STEPHEN RYDER (*b. New Brunswick, N.J., 1840; d. 1916*), journalist, theatrical manager. Brother of Haley Fiske.

FITCH, ASA (*b. Salem, N.Y., 1809; d. 1879*), physician, entomologist. State entomologist of New York, 1854–70; issued important annual reports on crop pests. Fitch's appointment gave official recognition to applied entomology and represented the first great practical step taken in the United States to investigate the problem of insect damage.

FITCH, CLYDE. *See* FITCH, WILLIAM CLYDE.

FITCH, JOHN (*b. Windsor Township, Conn., 1743; d. Bardstown, Ky., 1798*), metal craftsman, inventor. After an unhappy boyhood and various employments, set up brass shop in East Windsor, 1764; lost money in unsound investments; after further financial setbacks abandoned his family and shop, 1769.

Built up profitable brass and silversmith business in Trenton, N.J., which was wiped out by the Revolution. Entered military service; took charge of Trenton gun factory; profited by selling provisions to the Continental army and invested in Virginia land warrants. While surveying along the Ohio, 1780, acquired 1,600 acres in Kentucky. Captured by Indians, 1782, he was turned over to the British and held prisoner in Canada. After his exchange, settled in Bucks Co., Pa., but organized a land company and surveyed in the Northwest Territory, 1783 and 1785. His projects failed with the adoption of the federal government's township system.

After 1785, Fitch devoted all his attention to inventing a steamboat. Obtained exclusive privileges for use of his proposed boat from Pennsylvania, New York, Delaware, and Virginia; was given financial support by prominent Philadelphia citizens. Launched his first boat successfully on the Delaware near Philadelphia, 1787, and his second, a 60-foot paddle wheeler, 1788. With this vessel, he carried 30 passengers on numerous round trips between Philadelphia and Burlington, N.J. Despite public indifference, Fitch built a third boat in 1790 providing regular service on the Delaware. Received American (1791) and French patents, but lost financial support when his fourth boat was wrecked before completion. After a futile effort to get backing in France, he returned to America, destitute and ill. Built a 4-passenger, screw-propelled steamboat in New York, 1796, but failing once again to win financial support, he moved to Kentucky, where he died.

FITCH, SAMUEL (*b. Lebanon, Conn., 1724; d. London, England, 1799*), lawyer, Boston Loyalist.

FITCH, THOMAS (*b. Norwalk, Conn., ca. 1700; d. 1774*), lawyer. Graduated Yale, 1721. Colonial governor of Connecticut, 1754–66; defeated for reelection, 1766, because of his support of the Stamp Act by taking the oath required in it, he published a pamphlet justifying his conduct.

FITCH, WILLIAM CLYDE (*b. Elmira, N.Y., 1865; d. Châlons-sur-Marne, France, 1909*), playwright. Graduated Amherst, 1886. Wrote *Beau Brummell* for Richard Mansfield (produced, 1890). Many other original plays and adaptations from foreign sources were written by Fitch in rapid succession, all marked by his strong sense of theater and his skill in suiting the taste of the period. *The Moth and the Flame* and *Nathan Hale* opened to great acclaim at the same time in Philadelphia and Chicago, 1898. Other successes followed, notably *Barbara Frietchie* (1898); *The Climbers* (1901); *Captain Jinks* (1901); *The Truth* (1907); and *The City* (1909).

FITE, WARNER (*b. Philadelphia, Pa., 1867; d. Philadelphia, 1955*), educator, philosopher. Studied at Haverford and the University of Pennsylvania (Ph.D., 1894). Professor of philosophy at Princeton, 1915–35. A naturalist, Fite believed that the individual as a conscious agent is the source and measure of all value, and that the interests of conscious individuals are essentially harmonious. Books include *Moral Philosophy—the Critical View of Life* (1925) and *Jesus, the Man* (1943).

FITLER, EDWIN HENRY (*b. Philadelphia, Pa., 1825; d. near Philadelphia, 1896*), cordage manufacturer. Mayor of Philadelphia, 1887–91.

FITTON, JAMES (*b. Boston, Mass., 1805; d. Boston, 1881*), Roman Catholic clergyman. Missionary in New England, 1827–43, he later held pastorates in Providence and Newport, R.I., and in East Boston, Mass. In 1842 he gave Bishop Fenwick the site of Holy Cross College, Worcester, Mass.

FITZ, HENRY (*b. Newburyport, Mass., 1808; d. New York, N.Y., 1863*), telescope maker.

FITZ, REGINALD HEBER (*b. Chelsea, Mass., 1843; d. 1913*), pathologist, clinician. Graduated Harvard, B.A., 1864; M.D., 1868. Studied at Vienna and under Virchow at Berlin. Taught at Harvard Medical School, *post* 1870, and was visiting physician to Massachusetts General Hospital. His paper "Perforating Inflammation of the Vermiform Appendix" (1886) named appendicitis, provided its diagnosis, proved its origin, and advocated radical surgery for its cure. It ranks as a classic of modern medicine. In a second major contribution Fitz described acute pancreatitis. Earliest of Virchow's students to return to America, Fitz was first to introduce the microscope study of diseased tissue, greatly influenced scientific pathology, and advanced rational therapeusis.

FITZGERALD, ALICE LOUISE FLORENCE (*b. Florence, Italy, 1875; d. Bronx, N.Y., 1962*), nurse and international health care administrator. Born to American parents residing in Europe. Studied at the Johns Hopkins Nurses Training School (graduated, 1906). Staff nurse at Johns Hopkins from 1906; became head nurse, 1910. Head nurse at New York's Bellevue Hospital, 1911–12. Superintendent of nurses at Wilkes Barre City Hospital in Pennsylvania, 1912–15; and at Robert W. Long Hospital in Indianapolis, 1915–16. Director of student health at Dana Hall in Wellesley, Mass, 1916. Edith Cavell Memorial Nurse with the British army during World War I. Transferred to the American Red Cross, 1917. Chief Nurse of the American Red Cross for Europe, 1919. Director of nursing of the League of Red Cross Societies in Geneva, 1919–21. She worked for the International Health Board of the Rockefeller Foundation, 1922–29, surveying nursing in the Philippines, Hawaii, China, Japan, Singapore, and Thailand, in an effort to publicize modern nursing, upgrade nursing standards, and establish training facilities. Director of nursing at Polyclinic Hospital in New York, 1931–37. Director of the Nurses' residence at Sheppard-Pratt in Baltimore, 1937–48. Fitzgerald retired in 1948.

FITZGERALD, DESMOND (*b. Nassau, Bahamas, 1846; d. 1926*), hydraulic engineer. Raised in Providence, R.I. Supervised Boston water reservoirs, 1873–1903; did important research work on evaporation and coloration of water.

FITZGERALD, EDWARD (*b. Limerick, Ireland, 1833; d. Hot Springs, Ark., 1907*), Roman Catholic clergyman. Came to America, 1849; ordained, 1857. Served as pastor at Columbus, Ohio, Consecrated bishop of Little Rock, 1867, and served until 1906. Voted *non placet* on doctrine of infallibility at Vatican Council, 1870.

FITZGERALD, EDWIN. *See* FOY, EDDIE.

FITZGERALD, FRANCIS SCOTT KEY (*b. St. Paul, Minn., 1896; d. Hollywood, Calif., 1940*), novelist. Reflected in his work his admiration for wealth as a means of realizing "the promises of life" and his distrust of the insensitivity of the rich.

Entering Princeton in 1913, he achieved some social and literary success but fell behind scholastically, dropped out for a year, and finally left in 1917 to enlist in the army. Training in Alabama, he became engaged to Zelda Sayre. They were married in 1920, on the success of his first novel, *This Side of Paradise* (1920). This first book about "the Jazz Age" made Fitzgerald famous and momentarily rich. Following *The Beautiful and Damned* (1922) and an unsuccessful play, *The Vegetable* (1923), he wrote *The Great Gatsby* (1925), his most brilliant work, though a financial failure.

The Fitzgeralds lived in Europe from 1924 to 1930, when Zelda's mental breakdown brought them back to America. Fitzgerald then began his long, losing struggle against his wife's insanity, his own drinking, and their increasing debts. *Tender Is the Night* (1934), deeply moving but unsuited to the taste of the 1930's, was a financial and critical failure. His fear that his talent was dead, revealed in *The Crack-Up* (1945), led Fitzgerald to Hollywood as a movie writer in 1937. At his death he left the unfinished manuscript *The Last Tycoon* (1941). Of his 160 short stories, four volumes were collected: *Flappers and Philosophers* (1921), *Tales of the Jazz Age* (1922), *All the Sad Young Men* (1926), and *Taps at Reveille* (1935).

FITZGERALD, JOHN FRANCIS (*b. Boston, Mass., 1863; d. 1950*), politician. Nicknamed "Honey Fitz" for his charm of manner and fine singing voice. Began political career as a Boston city councilman, 1892; served as congressman, Democrat, 1895–1901. On leaving Congress, he bought a weekly newspaper, *The Republic*, which provided him with an income and a public forum, and as the "Napoleon of Ward Six" he was a dominant force in city Democratic politics. Elected mayor of Boston, 1905, he backed labor and expanded city services to the poor, but tolerated vice, circumvented civil service regulations, and tried to build his own citywide political machine by patronage and awarding of contracts. Elected to a second term in 1910 despite fierce opposition and continuing charges of corruption, he did not offer his candidacy in 1914 but joined with his old enemies, the Good Government Association, to oppose James M. Curley. He was defeated in senatorial bids in 1916 and his election to the House in 1918 was overturned by a congressional committee. He was unsuccessful Democratic candidate for governor, 1922. In 1930, he again sought the gubernatorial nomination, but lost in the primary to J. B. Ely. At the age of 86 campaigned for his grandson and namesake John Fitzgerald Kennedy in his first congressional campaign.

FITZGERALD, OSCAR PENN (*b. Caswell Co., N.C., 1829; d. Monteagle, Tenn., 1911*), Methodist bishop, author.

FITZGERALD, THOMAS (*b. New York, N.Y., 1819; d. London, England, 1891*), editor, playwright. Published Philadelphia *Evening City Item*; campaigned for local progressive reforms.

FITZGIBBON, CATHERINE. *See* IRENE, SISTER.

FITZHUGH, GEORGE (*b. Prince William Co., Va., 1806; d. Huntsville, Tex., 1881*), lawyer, sociologist. Author of regular articles in *DeBow's Review*, 1857–67, and of *Sociology for the South* (1854). Defended slavery as better suited than socialism to overcome evils of laissez-faire.

FITZHUGH, WILLIAM (*b. Bedford, England, 1651; d. Stafford Co., Va., 1701*), lawyer. Came to Virginia, *ca.* 1670; was successful as lawyer and merchant. His extant letters give valuable insights into business procedures of a Virginia capitalist between 1679 and 1699.

FITZPATRICK, BENJAMIN (*b. Greene Co., Ga., 1802; d. 1869*), lawyer, planter. Removed to Mississippi Territory, 1816; settled near Montgomery, Ala. As Democratic governor of Alabama, 1841–45, reformed state banking system. U.S. senator from Alabama, 1848 and 1853–61; declined nomination for vice president on Douglas ticket, 1860.

FITZPATRICK, DANIEL ROBERT (*b. Superior, Wis., 1891; d. St. Louis, Mo., 1969*), editorial cartoonist. Studied at the Chicago Art Institute and Washington University. Worked for the *Chicago Daily News* (1911–13) and the *St. Louis Post-Dispatch* (1911–56). Widely syndicated, his stark cartoons in the "dripping mud" style dealt with global issues. Concurrent with the rise of realism, urbanism, the ashcan school of art, and post–World War I disillusionment, they expressed Fitzpatrick's indignation at social wrongs and oppression; typical of his dark style were drawings of giant swastikas rolling relentlessly across Europe. Fitzpatrick won two Pulitzers, in 1926 and 1955.

FITZPATRICK, JOHN (*b. Athlone, Ireland, 1870; d. Chicago, Ill., 1946*), labor leader. Came to Chicago, an orphan, in 1882; worked in a meatpacking plant. Deciding to learn the farrier's trade, he served his apprenticeship and became a full member of Local No. 4, International Union of Journeymen Horseshoers; as vice president, treasurer, president, and for five years business agent of his local, he displayed rugged honesty and a complete dedication to the cause of the workingman. Active in the 1896 reform movement which resulted in the formation of the Chicago Federation of Labor, he served as the federation's president, 1899–1901 and 1905–46. Under his leadership, it won a wide reputation for progressivism. Free of all ethnic and craft-oriented bias, Fitzpatrick figured largely in the pre–New Deal efforts to organize mass-production workers; under his acting chairmanship, the Stock Yards Labor Council in 1917 forced the Chicago meatpackers to accept a system of arbitration (later repudiated). A similar effort in 1918 to organize the steel industry on a national scale was a failure. Encouraged by the example of the Labour party in England and thoroughly disillusioned with the labor policies of Woodrow Wilson's administration, Fitzpatrick tried on the state and national levels to establish a political party in labor's interest; this led in 1920 to the formation of the Farmer-Labor party. After the takeover of the party's convention by the Communists in 1923, Fitzpatrick gave up the idea of an independent American labor party and retired to the conventional role of a labor functionary.

FITZPATRICK, JOHN BERNARD (*b. Boston, Mass., 1812; d. Boston, 1866*), Roman Catholic clergyman. Studied at Collège de Montreal and at Saint-Sulpice, Paris; ordained, 1840. Consecrated coadjutor of Boston, 1844, he succeeded to the see, 1846. An intellectual and able administrator, he raised standards of clerical training and prepared Boston to handle the great wave of Irish immigration.

FITZPATRICK, JOHN CLEMENT (*b. Washington, D.C., 1876; d. Washington, 1940*), curator of manuscripts, Library of Congress, 1897–1928. Editor, collected writings of George Washington (39 vols., 1831–44).

FITZPATRICK, MORGAN CASSIUS (*b. Tuscaloosa, Ala., 1868; d. Gallatin, Tenn., 1908*), lawyer, educator. Tennessee Democratic leader and legislator; effect state superintendent of public instruction, 1899–1903.

FITZPATRICK, THOMAS (*b. Co. Cavan, Ireland, ca. 1799; d. Washington D.C., 1854*), trapper, guide, Indian agent. Came to America, *ante* 1816. Served as second in command under Jedediah S. Smith in effective discovery of South Pass, 1824; became partner in Rocky Mountain Fur Co., 1830, with James Bridger, Milton Sublette, and others. After decline of fur trade, served as guide, accompanying the Bidwell-Bartleson pioneer emigrant train (1841), the White-Hastings Oregon party (1842), Frémont's second expedition (1843–44), Kearny's expedition to South Pass and J. W. Albert's expedition (1845), and Kearny's Army of the West (1846). As agent of the Upper Platte and Arkansas Indian agency, *post* 1846, Fitzpatrick was in charge of Cheyenne, Arapaho, and some Sioux. He negotiated the Indian treaties, signed at the Fort Laramie Council (1851) which he helped to arrange, and also peace treaties with the Comanche, Kiowa, and Kiowa Apache at Fort Atkinson (1853). The Indians called him "Broken Hand"; they trusted and respected him. His contemporaries considered him the greatest of the "mountain men."

FITZSIMMONS, JAMES EDWARD ("SUNNY JIM") (*b. Brooklyn, N.Y., 1874; d. Miami, Fla., 1966*), horse trainer. In his 78-year career, Fitzsimmons trained notable horses that won more money than any other trainer's of the time, including Gallant Fox, named Horse of the Year in 1930, Dark Secret, Johnstown, and Bold Ruler, named Horse of the Year in 1957. Horses trained by Fitzsimmons won the Kentucky Derby three times, the Preakness four times, the Belmont Stakes six times, and the Wood Memorial eight times; over 2,000 races, and over $13,000,000 in purses.

FITZSIMMONS, ROBERT PROMETHEUS (*b. Helston, England, 1862; d. Chicago, Ill., 1917*), pugilist. Raised in New Zealand. Came to California, 1890, and won middleweight title, 1891. Defeated Jim Corbett for heavyweight title, 1897; lost it to J. J. Jeffries, 1899.

FITZSIMMONS, OR FITZSIMONS, THOMAS (*b. Ireland, 1741; d. Philadelphia, Pa., 1811*), merchant, Revolutionary soldier and patriot. Immigrated to Philadelphia in youth. Served in Confederation Congress, in Pennsylvania legislature, and in Constitutional Convention of 1787. Congressman, Federalist, from Pennsylvania, 1789–95. Active in establishment of Bank of North America, 1781, he was a founder of Insurance Co. of North America.

FLAD, HENRY (*b. near Heidelberg, Germany, 1824; d. Pittsburgh, Pa., 1898*), engineer, inventor, Union soldier. Came to America, 1849; worked on railway construction. Associated after Civil War with St. Louis, Mo., public improvements. A prolific inventor.

FLAGET, BENEDICT JOSEPH (*b. Contournat, France, 1763; d. 1850*), Roman Catholic clergyman, Sulpician. Came to America after French Revolution; worked at Vincennes, at Georgetown College, and at St. Mary's College, Baltimore. Consecrated bishop of Bardstown (later Louisville), Ky., 1810; save for a year's interlude, served until his death as bishop and active missionary.

FLAGG, AZARIAH CUTTING (*b. Orwell, Vt., 1790; d. 1873*), editor, politician. Democratic assemblyman, secretary of state, state comptroller in New York; comptroller of New York City, 1852–59; a man of "unassailable integrity."

FLAGG, EDMUND (*b. Wiscasset, Maine, 1815; d. 1890*), author, lawyer, journalist, diplomat. His roving life was spent in the Middle West, Berlin, Vienna, Venice, and Virginia.

FLAGG, ERNEST (*b. Brooklyn, N.Y., 1857; d. New York, N.Y., 1947*), architect. Grandnephew of Washington Allston. Left school at 15 to work as office boy in Wall Street. In 1880, he joined the architect Philip G. Hubert in a real estate venture. While designing floor plans for two of their buildings, he used a then novel scheme of two-story "duplex" apartments.

After attending the École des Beaux Arts in Paris, where he studied in the atélier of Paul Blondel, he was commissioned, 1891, to design St. Luke's Hospital, facing the Cathedral of St. John the Divine, New York City. In the same year, he was chosen as architect of a new museum for the Corcoran Gallery of Art, Washington, D.C. In 1897 Flagg designed a building, at the northwest corner of Broadway and Liberty Street, for the Singer Sewing Machine Co. and soon thereafter the Bourne Building to the west. These earlier structures were integrated into Flagg's Singer Tower, for a time the tallest office building in the world. More conservative, but clearly Beaux Arts in style, was the office building and bookstore for Charles Scribner's Sons, at 597 Fifth Avenue, 1913.

Flagg's greatest opportunity came with the commission that he received in 1896 to design a completely new campus for the U.S. Naval Academy at Annapolis. This great, formal complex, centering on a domed chapel, gave many Americans their first taste of design in the grand manner.

From his Beaux Arts training, Flagg also acquired an interest in rational plans for city living. He sought zoning restrictions to prevent skyscrapers from robbing their neighbors of light and turning streets into caverns; and he stressed the need for low-cost housing, fireproofing, and modular design.

Save for one brief interval, Flagg headed his own firm without a partner. He was one of the few American Beaux Arts architects to place his own interpretative stamp on every design he created.

FLAGG, GEORGE WHITING (*b. New Haven, Conn., 1816; d. 1897*), genre painter. Nephew of Washington Allston. Studied in London, Paris, and Italy. Retired after many years' New York residence to Nantucket, Mass., 1879.

FLAGG, JAMES MONTGOMERY (*b. Pelham Manor, N.Y., 1877; d. New York, N.Y., 1960*), illustrator and writer. Studied at the Art Students League of New York. Illustrated leading publications and books; artist of the famous Uncle Sam poster captioned "I Want YOU/for U.S. Army" during World War I.

FLAGG, JARED BRADLEY (*b. New Haven, Conn., 1820; d. New York, N.Y., 1899*), portrait painter, Episcopal clergyman. Brother of George W. Flagg. Author of *Life and Letters of Washington Allston* (1892), whose nephew he was.

FLAGG, JOSIAH (*b. Woburn, Mass., 1737; d. ca. 1795*), musician. Established liaison between New England psalmody and classical musical forms; introduced the anthem to the English colonies. Author of *A Collection of the Best Psalm Tunes* (1764) and *Sixteen Anthems* (1766).

FLAGG, JOSIAH FOSTER (*b. Boston, Mass., 1788; d. 1853*), dentist, anatomical artist, early experimenter in use of dental porcelain. Graduated Boston Medical College, 1815; practiced in Boston. Designed traction apparatus, extracting forceps, and, in 1833, first "mineral teeth."

FLAGG, THOMAS WILSON (*b. Beverly, Mass., 1805; d. Cambridge, Mass., 1884*), naturalist, author.

FLAGLER, HENRY MORRISON (*b. Hopewell, N.Y., 1830; d. West Palm Beach, Fla., 1913*), capitalist, promoter. A grain merchant in Bellevue and Cleveland, Ohio, he became an associate of John D. Rockefeller and his partner in Standard Oil Co. Active *post* 1883 in Florida development. Organized Florida East Coast Railway, which reached Miami, 1896; built a string of resort hotels along the line and transformed beaches and swamps into playgrounds. Completed railroad line to Key West, 1912; dredged Miami harbor; established steamship services to Key West and Nassau, where he also opened hotels.

FLAGLER, JOHN HALDANE (*b. Cold Spring, N.Y., 1836; d. Greenwich, Conn., 1922*), pipe and tube manufacturer, capitalist.

FLAHERTY, ROBERT JOSEPH (*b. Iron Mountain, Mich., 1884; d. Brattleboro, Vt., 1951*), documentary filmmaker. Directed and filmed *Nanook of the North* (1922); other films include *Moana* (1926), *Man of Aran* (1934), and *The Land* (1942). Many critics prefer to call his work film-poems rather than factual documentaries.

FLANAGAN, EDWARD JOSEPH (*b. Leabeg, Co. Roscommon, Ireland, 1886; d. Berlin, Germany, 1948*), Roman Catholic clergyman, founder of Boys Town. Came to the United States, 1904. B.A., Mount St. Mary's College, 1906; M.A., 1908. Studied for the priesthood at University of Innsbruck, Austria, and was ordained there, 1912. Working in Omaha, Nebr., Father

Flanagan turned from efforts to rehabilitate vagrants to provision of preventive care for homeless youths; in December 1917, he opened a home for boys. His humane policies, the welcome given boys of all races, and the absence of denominational proselytizing won his home the support of all tolerant Omahans. In 1921, he moved the home to a farm outside the city, where he gradually developed facilities for elementary, secondary, and vocational education. In 1935, he incorporated the home's property as a municipality, Boys Town, giving unusual legal status to the juvenile government which he had encouraged the boys to institute. He died while inspecting child welfare work in Germany.

FLANAGAN, HALLIE (*b. Redfield, S. Dak., 1890; d. Old Tappan, N.J., 1969*), palywright and national director of the Federal Theatre Project (FTP). Studied at Grinnell College and Radcliffe (M.A., 1924). Professor of drama and founder of experimental theater at Grinnell, 1925. Directed Vassar College's experimental theater, 1925–42. Dean of Smith College from 1942; professor of drama, 1946–55. National director of FTP, part of Franklin Roosevelt's Works Progress Administration, for the life of that program, 1935–39. The relief-program objectives of the FTP were largely achieved under Flanagan. Viewing theater as a vital social force, she pressed for the dramatization of the nation's social conscience. Her theater of ideas was noted for its use of avant-garde techniques, including "Living Newspaper," to pillory intolerance, poverty, and disease. At its best, the project inspired a federation of many theaters catering to different regions, something Flanagan had advocated when helping to found the National Theatre Conference in 1932. Among her plays are *The Curtain* and *E = mc²*.

FLANAGAN, WEBSTER (*b. Claverport, Ky., 1832; d. Texas, 1924*), merchant, cattle-breeder, Confederate soldier. Republican officeholder, and, *post* 1890, leader of Republican party in Texas.

FLANAGIN, HARRIS (*b. Roadstown, N.J., 1817; d. 1874*), lawyer. Settled in Arkansas, 1837; practiced at Greenville and Arkadelphia. Confederate governor of Arkansas, 1862–65.

FLANDERS, HENRY (*b. Plainfield, N.H., 1824; d. 1911*), lawyer. Practiced in Philadelphia, Pa., *post* 1853, specializing in admiralty work. Author of works on maritime law, fire insurance, and legal biography.

FLANDERS, RALPH EDWARD (*b. Barnet, Vt., 1880; d. Springfield, Vt., 1970*), mechanical engineer and United States senator. Learned his trade during an apprenticeship at a machine-tool factory in Rhode Island (1897–99), during which time he studied at night school and took correspondence classes. Contributed articles to machine-shop journals, leading to a position as associate editor of *Machinery* (1905–10) in New York City. Returned to Vermont and married the daughter of the president of the Jones and Lamson Machine Company in 1911; became manager of the firm and later president. Appointed to the Business Advisory and Planning Council in 1933. Served on the War Production Board during World War II. President of the Federal Reserve Bank of Boston, 1944–46. Elected to the Senate in 1946. Sat on Banking and Currency, Finance, Joint Economy, and Armed Services committees, as well as the Armed Services Appropriations Subcommittee. Reelected in 1952 by an overwhelming majority. Best remembered for his introduction of a resolution to censure Republican Senator Joseph McCarthy in 1954. Chose not to run for a third term. His autobiography is *Senator from Vermont* (1961).

FLANDRAU, CHARLES EUGENE (*b. New York, N.Y., 1828; d. St. Paul, Minn., 1903*), jurist, soldier, author. Removed to St. Paul, 1853; settled at Traverse des Sioux, 1854. Was member of

Minnesota constitutional convention and justice of the state supreme court; defended frontier during Sioux outbreak, 1862.

FLANDRAU, CHARLES MACOMB (*b. St. Paul, Minn., 1871; d. St. Paul, 1938*), essayist and traveler. Son of Charles E. Flandrau. Best known for his unorthodox, penetrating account of Mexican life and character: *Viva Mexico* (1908).

FLANNAGAN, JOHN BERNARD (*b. Fargo, N.Dak., 1895; d. New York, N.Y. 1942*), sculptor. Relying on the motivational force of the subconscious and conceiving of himself as the liberator of an image recognized in the material with which he was working, Flannagan sought to express quite abstract ideas by a relatively abstract approach. He was encouraged and assisted by many of the leading American artists of his time. His constant battle with illness and alcoholism ended with his suicide.

FLANNERY, JOHN (*b. Nenagh, Ireland, 1835; d. Savannah, Ga., 1910*), Confederate soldier, banker, cotton factor. Came to America, 1851; settled in Savannah, 1854. Head of John Flannery and Co.; president of Southern Bank and of Cotton Exchange.

FLATHER, JOHN JOSEPH (*b. Philadelphia, Pa., 1862; d. 1926*), mechanical engineer. Graduated Sheffield Scientific School, 1885. Taught at Lehigh, at Purdue, and at University of Minnesota; national authority on transmission and measurement of power.

FLEEMING, JOHN. *See* FLEMING, JOHN.

FLEET, THOMAS (*b. Shropshire, England, 1685; d. Boston, Mass., 1758*), printer. Came to Boston *ca.* 1712. Publisher of *Boston Evening Post,* 1735–58.

FLEGENHEIMER, ARTHUR (*b. New York, N.Y., 1902; d. Newark, N.J., 1935*), gangster, better known as Dutch Schultz. Rose to power as a bootlegger; killed in a gang war.

FLEISCHMANN, CHARLES LOUIS (*b. near Budapest, Hungary, 1834; d. 1897*), yeast manufacturer, capitalist, philanthropist.

FLEISHER, BENJAMIN WILFRID (*b. Philadelphia, Pa., 1870; d. Rochester, Minn., 1946*), newspaper publisher and editor. Associated with the *Japan Advertiser* (Tokyo), 1908–40, which he built into one of the leading English-language papers in Asia. Police surveillance and pressure forced him to sell out, and he returned to the United States in 1940.

FLEMING, ARETAS BROOKS *b. near Middleton, Va., now W.Va., 1839; d. 1923*), jurist, coal operator. Democratic governor of West Virginia, 1890–93.

FLEMING, ARTHUR HENRY (*b. Halton Co., Ontario, Canada, 1856; d. Pasadena, Calif., 1940*), lumber magnate. Removed to the United States, 1879. Founder and chief benefactor (with his wife, Clara Huntington Fowler) of California Institute of Technology.

FLEMING, JOHN (*fl. 1764–1800*), printer, Loyalist. Born in Scotland; arrived in Boston, Mass., 1764. In partnership with John Mein, published *Boston Chronicle,* chief Tory organ, December 1767–June 1770; was officially proscribed and banished, 1778.

FLEMING, JOHN (*b. Mifflin Co., Pa., 1807; d. Ayr, Nebr., 1894*), Presbyterian clergyman. Missionary to Creek, Wea, Chippewa, and Ottawa Indians; first to reduce Creek language to writing, *ca.* 1834.

FLEMING, JOHN ADAM (*b. Cincinnati, Ohio, 1877; d. San Mateo, Calif., 1956*), geophysicist, science administrator. Graduated from the University of Cincinnati (B.S., 1899). Member of the Department of Terrestrial Magnetism of the Carnegie Institution of Washington, D.C., from 1904; acting director, 1929–34; director, 1935–46. One of the world's experts on terrestrial magnetism; designed instruments for measuring magnetism and set up observatories around the world. Led expeditions to observe and record the earth's magnetic fields. Honorary president for life of the American Geophysical Union from 1947.

FLEMING, WALTER LYNWOOD (*b. Brundidge, Ala., 1874; d. 1932*), educator, historian. Graduated Alabama Polytechnic Institute, 1896; Ph.D., Columbia, 1904. Specialist in Civil War and Reconstruction history. Taught at West Virginia, Louisiana State, and Vanderbilt universities.

FLEMING, WILLIAM (*b. Jedburgh, Scotland, 1729; d. Montgomery Co., Va., 1795*), physician, soldier, statesman. Came to America, 1755. Served in the Forbes and Abercromby campaigns and others; practiced medicine at Staunton, Va., 1763–68. Wounded at battle of Point Pleasant. Was member of Virginia Senate and Council and acting governor, 1781.

FLEMING, WILLIAM MAYBURY (*b. Danbury, Conn., 1817; d. New York, N.Y., 1866*), actor, manager, Union soldier.

FLEMING, WILLIAMINA PATON STEVENS (*b. Dundee, Scotland, 1857; d. 1911*), astronomer. Came to America, 1878. At Harvard College Observatory pioneered in analysis of photographs of stellar spectra, discovered 10 novae and over 200 variable stars.

FLETCHER, ALICE CUNNINGHAM (*b. Cuba, 1838; d. Washington, D.C.[?], 1923*), ethnologist, pioneer student of Indian music. Authoritative interpreter of religious and social observances of North American Indians; author of *The Omaha Tribe* (1911) and many other studies.

FLETCHER, BENJAMIN (*b. London, England, 1640; d. near Boyle, Ireland, 1703*), soldier. Colonial governor of New York, 1692–98, and briefly of Pennsylvania; allied himself with conservative elements; accused of excessive land grants and protection of pirates; replaced by Earl of Bellomont.

FLETCHER, CALVIN (*b. Ludlow, Vt., 1798; d. Indianapolis, Ind., 1866*), lawyer, banker. First lawyer to practice in Indianapolis, where he settled in 1821.

FLETCHER, DUNCAN UPSHAW (*b. Sumter Co., Ga., 1859; d. Washington D.C., 1936*), lawyer, politician. Removed to Jacksonville, Fla., 1881. U.S. senator, Democrat, from Florida, 1909–36; sponsored the Fletcher-Rayburn Act, 1934, creating the Securities and Exchange Commission.

FLETCHER, HENRY PRATHER (*b. Greencastle, Pa., 1873; d. Newport, R.I., 1959*), diplomat. Served with Roosevelt's Rough Riders in Cuba. Second secretary to the legation in Havana (1902–03), China (1903–05 and 1908–09), and in Portugal (1905–07). Appointed minister to Chile he became the first U.S. ambassador in Santiago in 1914. Ambassador to Mexico, 1916–20; to Belgium (1922–24) and Italy (1924–29). An advocate of dollar diplomacy, Fletcher capitalized on his contacts with financial circles to promote American business abroad. Headed the Republican National Committee, 1934–36, and attended the Dumbarton Oaks Conference, 1944.

FLETCHER, HORACE (*b. Lawrence, Mass., 1849; d. Copenhagen, Denmark, 1919*), writer and lecturer on nutrition. A successful, world-traveling salesman, he preached a gospel of health through thorough chewing of food.

FLETCHER, JAMES COOLEY (*b. Indianapolis, Ind., 1823; d. Los Angeles, Calif., 1901*), Presbyterian clergyman, missionary, diplomat. Son of Calvin Fletcher. Served in South America, Portugal, Italy; coauthor of *Brazil and the Brazilians* (1857).

FLETCHER, JOHN GOULD (*b. Little Rock, Ark., 1886; d. Little Rock, 1950*), poet. Attended Harvard, 1903–06; took up poetry as a substitute for religion, at first influenced by Arthur Symons and the French symbolists. He settled in London in 1908, became a Fabian, and began to write in the vein of Walt Whitman. In 1913, after publishing five small volumes at his own expense, he met Ezra Pound, who intoduced him to the imagist group. He contributed to the three imagist anthologies sponsored by Amy Lowell (1915, 1916, 1917), and with her developed so-called polyphonic prose. Through her aid, he found an American publisher for his *Irradiations: Sand and Spray* (1915). After publishing several more volumes of poems reflective of his enthusiasm for oriental thought and symbolism, he turned to art criticism; he then undertook mystical religious poetry (as in *Parables*, 1925). In 1926, after a long visit to America, he realized that his future lay in his native land. Committing himself to regionalism and southern agrarianism, he lived *post* 1933 in Little Rock. His *Selected Poems* were awarded the Pulitzer Prize in 1939.

FLETCHER, RICHARD (*b. Cavendish, Vt., 1788; d. 1869*), jurist. Graduated Dartmouth, 1806. A noted trial lawyer, he became a leading Massachusetts practitioner; successfully contested Harvard's claim to an exclusive franchise over Charles River bridge.

FLETCHER, ROBERT (*b. Bristol, England, 1823; d. Washington D.C., 1912*), medical scholar, bibliographer. Member of Royal College of Surgeons, 1844. Came to America, 1947; practiced at Cincinnati, Ohio; was field and hospital surgeon in Civil War. Assistant to John S. Billings in preparing great *Catalogue of Surgeon-General's Library*, 1876–95, he succeeded Billings as editor. Was coeditor of *Index Medicus*, 1879–95, and sole editor thereafter; author also of pioneer papers on medical history.

FLETCHER, ROBERT (*b. New York, N.Y., 1847; d. Hanover, N.H., 1936*), engineering educator. Graduated West Point, 1868. First director, 1871–1918, of Thayer School of Engineering of Dartmouth.

FLETCHER, THOMAS CLEMENT (*b. Herculaneum, Mo., 1827; d. Washington D.C., 1899*), lawyer, Union soldier, Republican governor of Missouri, 1865–69.

FLETCHER, WILLIAM ASA (*b. Plymouth, N.H., 1788; d. 1852*), jurist. Attorney general of Michigan Territory and circuit judge; served as first chief justice of state supreme court, 1836–42.

FLETCHER, WILLIAM BALDWIN (*b. Indianapolis, Ind., 1837; d. Orlando, Fla., 1907*), physician. Son of Calvin Fletcher. Taught at Indiana medical institutions; as superintendent of Indiana Central Hospital for the Insane, introduced many reforms.

FLEXNER, ABRAHAM (*b. Louisville, Ky., 1866; d. Falls Church, Va., 1959*), educational reformer. Studied at Johns Hopkins and Harvard (M.A., 1906) and at the University of Berlin. An expert in medical education, Flexner wrote *Medical Education in the United States and Canada* (1910), which led to widespread reforms of existing medical colleges. Affiliated with the Rockefeller General Educational Board, 1913–28, heading the Division of Studies and Medical Education. Founder and first director (1930–39) of the Institute for Advanced Study at Princeton.

FLEXNER, BERNARD (*b. Louisville, Ky., 1865; d. New York, N.Y., 1945*), lawyer, philanthropist, Zionist leader, Brother of Abraham Flexner and Simon Flexner. LL.B., University of Louisville, 1898. An early supporter of the juvenile court movement. *Post* 1917 lived in New York, where he devoted himself to various Zionist movements and organizations to aid Palestine and world Jewry.

FLEXNER, JENNIE MAAS (*b. Louisville, Ky., 1882; d. New York, N.Y., 1944*), librarian. Niece of Abraham Flexner, Bernard Flexner, and Simon Flexner. On staff of Louisville Public Library, 1905–28; New York Public Library, 1928–44. Inaugurated and headed Readers' Adviser's Office at New York Public Library, to advance adult education through programs of systematic reading.

FLEXNER, SIMON (*b. Louisville, Ky., 1863; d. New York, N.Y., 1946*), pathologist, director of the Rockefeller Institute for Medical Research. Brother of Abraham Flexner and Bernard Flexner. Graduated Louisville College of Pharmacy, 1882; M.D., University of Louisville, 1889.

In 1890 he went to Baltimore to study pathology at the Johns Hopkins Hospital with William H. Welch. By 1892 he was Welch's first assistant and became associate in pathology at the newly opened Johns Hopkins Medical School. In 1893 Flexner briefly studied pathology at Strasbourg and Prague. Returning to Baltimore as resident pathologist at Johns Hopkins Hospital, he continued research in bacteriology and pathology. The Johns Hopkins University promoted him in 1895 to associate professor and in 1898 to professor of pathological anatomy. While at Manila the following year, he discovered a widespread strain of the dysentery bacillus, since known as the Flexner type.

He was professor of pathology at the University of Pennsylvania from 1899 to 1903, and in 1901 headed a governmental commission investigating bubonic plague in San Francisco.

In 1906 the Rockefeller Institute for Medical Research (later Rockefeller University) in New York City opened a permanent new laboratory building and in 1910 a modern research hospital. In this development Flexner, appointed ostensibly to direct the laboratories only, established himself as head of the whole organization. In 1905 New York City was struck with a severe epidemic of cerebrospinal meningitis. Flexner was able to implant the infection in monkeys, and thereby produce a serum against the infection. In 1909 Flexner did work that laid the foundation for the development, 40 years later, of protective poliomyelitis vaccines. In 1905 he was among the first to confirm the discovery of the microscopic parasite of syphilis, the spirochete now called *Treponema pallidum*.

For 19 years, beginning in 1904, he was the chief or sole editor of the *Journal of Experimental Medicine*. During World War I, Flexner was commissioned a lieutenant colonel in the Army Medical Corps and went to Europe to inspect the medical laboratories of the expeditionary forces. After the war his responsibilities at the institute included general direction not only of the laboratories and hospital but also of a large department of animal pathology at Princeton, N.J.

His many honors included membership in the Royal Society of London, the National Academy of Sciences, the American Philosophical Society, and the American Academy of Arts and Sciences. After his retirement from the Rockefeller Institute in 1935, Flexner was appointed Eastman professor at Oxford University for 1937–38. He wrote *The Evolution and Organization of the University Clinic* (1939) and, with the collaboration of his son James T. Flexner, a distinguished biography of his late teacher and friend, *William Henry Welch and the Heroic Age of American Medicine* (1941).

FLICK, LAWRENCE FRANCIS (*b. Cambria Co., Pa., 1856; d. Philadelphia, Pa., 1938*), physician, pioneer tuberculosis specialist. M.D., Jefferson Medical College, Philadelphia, 1879. President, 1901–35, White Haven Sanatorium, Luzerne Co., Pa.; president 1903–10, Henry Phipps Institute, Philadelphia.

FLICKINGER, DANIEL KUMLER (*b. Sevenmile, Ohio, 1824; d. Columbus, Ohio, 1911*), clergyman of United Brethren in Christ. Directed church missions in Africa and Germany.

FLINT, ALBERT STOWELL (*b. Salem, Mass., 1853; d. 1923*), astronomer. Graduated Harvard, 1875, and studied at Princeton with C. A. Young. Did valuable work at Washburn Observatory, University of Wisconsin, 1889–1920.

FLINT, AUSTIN (*b. Petersham, Mass., 1812; d. 1886*), physician, one of the most eminent American practitioners and teachers of his century. Graduated Harvard, M.D., 1833. Practiced in Boston briefly and in Buffalo, N.Y. Taught at Rush Medical College, Chicago; founded Buffalo Medical College, 1847; lectured at University of Louisville and at New Orleans Medical College. Helped found Bellevue Hospital Medical College at New York, 1861, where he taught; also taught at Long Island College Hospital. Was active as hospital physician, teacher, textbook author, and consultant; in 1883–84 served as president of American Medical Association. Published first text on diagnosis of respiratory diseases in 1856, of which eighth edition appeared in 1920 as *A Manual of Physical Diagnosis*. His classic work, *A Treatise on the Principles and Practice of Medicine*, appeared first in 1866 and was many times reissued and revised.

FLINT, AUSTIN (*b. Northampton, Mass., 1836; d. 1915*), physician, physiologist, alienist. Son of Austin Flint (1812–86). Associated with father in teaching in Buffalo, New Orleans, New York; author of *The Physiology of Man* (1867–73).

FLINT, CHARLES LOUIS (*b. Middleton, Mass., 1824; d. Hillman, Ga., 1889*), lawyer, agriculturist. Secretary of Massachusetts Board of Agriculture, 1853–80; helped found Massachusetts Institute of Technology and Massachusetts Agricultural College.

FLINT, CHARLES RANLET (*b. Thomaston, Maine, 1850; d. Washington, D.C., 1934*), industrial capitalist with international connections who provided guns and munitions to foreign governments. Known as "the father of trusts," he arranged many business mergers in the United States, 1892–1928.

FLINT, TIMOTHY (*b. near North Reading, Mass., 1780; d. Salem, Mass., 1840*), missionary, writer. Graduated Harvard, 1800. Pastor at Lunenburg, Mass., 1802–14; served as missionary in New Hampshire, Ohio, Missouri, Arkansas, 1815–25. Published the *Western Monthly Review* (Cincinnati, Ohio, 1827–30); for brief period, edited the *Knickerbocker; or New-York Monthly Magazine*. Wrote romanticized, melodramatic stories of the western border; *Francis Berrian* (1826); *Life and Adventures of Arthur Clenning* (1828); *Shoshonee Valley* (1830); and *George Mason, the Young Backwoodsman* (1829). He was author also of *Recollections of the Last Ten Years . . . in the Valley of the Mississippi* (1826); *The History and Geography of the Mississippi Valley* (1832); *Indian Wars of the West* (1833); and *The Biographical Memoir of Daniel Boone* (1833). He edited *The Personal Narrative of James O. Pattie* (1831).

FLINT, WESTON (*b. Wyoming Co., N.Y., 1835; d. 1906*), librarian, government official. Graduated Union College, 1860. Held various government positions; prepared catalogue of U.S. Patent Office library; helped organize U.S. Civil Service Commission.

FLORENCE, THOMAS BIRCH (*b. Philadelphia, Pa., 1812; d. Washington, D.C., 1875*), politician, editor. Congressman, Democrat, from Pennsylvania, 1851–61. Championed temperance; was popular among workmen as "the widow's friend."

FLORENCE, WILLIAM JERMYN (*b. Albany, N.Y., 1831; d. Philadelphia, Pa., 1891*), actor. Born Bernard Conlin. Comedian, excelling in dialect parts and impersonation; considered among the six leading comedians of his time for skill in vivid drawing of character.

FLOWER, BENJAMIN ORANGE (*b. Albion, Ill., 1858; d. Boston, Mass., 1918*), editor, social reformer. Grandson of George Flower. Edited many reform periodicals, among them *The Arena* (Boston); wrote numerous books; became virulently anti-Catholic and edited *The Menace*.

FLOWER, GEORGE (*b. Hertford, England, 1788; d. Grayville, Ill., 1862*), pioneer. Son of Richard Flower. With Morris Birkbeck, promoted settlement of English and Scandinavian immigrants in Edwards Co., Ill.; resisted introduction of slavery into Illinois.

FLOWER, LUCY LOUISA COUES (*b. Boston, Mass., 1837; d. Coronado, Calif., 1921*), educator. Engaged in philanthropic work in Chicago; member of city school board and trustee of University of Illinois.

FLOWER, RICHARD (*b. England, 1761; d. Albion, Ill., 1829*), reformer. Illinois pioneer. Father of George Flower. Came in 1819 to settlement made in Edwards Co., Ill., by his son and Morris Birkbeck. Founded probably first library in Illinois; negotiated sale of village and lands of Harmony, Ind., to Robert Owen.

FLOWER, ROSWELL PETTIBONE (*b. Theresa, N.Y., 1835; d. Long Island, N.Y., 1899*), banker, stockbroker, politician. began as jeweler and postmaster at Watertown, N.Y.; admitted to New York Stock Exchange, 1873. A Democrat of wealth, he served as congressman from New York, 1881–83; in 1884 and 1885, respectively, Tammany Hall unsuccessfully suggested him as presidential candidate and for governor to offset influence of Grover Cleveland. Returned to Congress, 1889–92; served as governor of New York, 1892–95. In 1896 he headed the New York delegation of gold Democrats at the Indianapolis convention and vigorously protested his party's "surrender to Populism and Anarchy." Always a person of importance in his party, he was denounced by opponents as a "flamboyant millionaire."

FLOY, JAMES (*b. New York, N.Y., 1806; d. New York, 1863*), Methodist Episcopal clergyman, editor, hymnologist.

FLOYD, JOHN (*b. Floyd Station, Ky., 1783; d. 1837*), surgeon. Graduated in medicine. University of Pennsylvania, 1806. Congressman, Democrat, from Virginia, 1817–29, he was first to propose occupation and territorial organization of Oregon, 1821. As governor of Virginia, 1830–34, he came to defend state sovereignty and the proslavery cause.

FLOYD, JOHN BUCHANAN (*b. Smithfield, Va., 1806; d. near Abingdon, Va., 1863*), lawyer. Son of John Floyd. Graduated South Carolina College, 1829. Entered Virginia Assembly, 1847; served as states' rights but antisecession Democratic governor, 1849–52; reentered Assembly, 1855. Secretary of War in Buchanan's cabinet, 1857–Dec. 29, 1860, he resigned over Buchanan's refusal to order evacuation of Fort Sumter, but was subsequently accused of transferring an excessive number of arms from Northern to Southern arsenals and of having tolerated abstraction of Indian trust funds. After Virginia's secession he raised and commanded a volunteer brigade for the Confederate army. Dismissed by President Davis for abandoning his post at Fort Donelson, 1862, he was commissioned major general by the Virginia Assembly.

FLOYD, WILLIAM (*b. Brookhaven, N.Y., 1734; d. Westernville, N.Y., 1821*), landowner, signer of the Declaration of Independence from New York. Member of Continental Congress, 1774–77 and 1778–83; of U.S. Congress, 1789–91. Active also in New York legislature. Lacking brilliance and unusual distinction, he was valued for his reliability and common sense.

FLÜGEL, EWALD (*b. Leipzig, Germany, 1863; d. 1914*), philologist. Ph.D., Leipzig, 1885. Professor at Stanford *post* 1892, he planned and partly executed a historical dictionary of the Chaucerian vocabulary.

FLY, JAMES LAWRENCE (*b. Seagoville, Tex., 1898; d. Daytona Beach, Fla., 1966*), lawyer and government administrator. Graduated from the U.S. Naval Academy in 1920. Served with the Pacific Fleet until his resignation from the Navy in 1923. Studied at Harvard (LL.B., 1926). Associated with the law firm of White and Case of New York City from 1926–29. Appointed a special assistant to the U.S. attorney general in 1929. Appointed general solicitor and head of the Tennessee Valley Authority legal department in 1934; general counsel in 1937. Conducted legal work in two major constitutional challenges to TVA's power program; by 1939 the constitutionality of the power program was firmly established. Appointed chairman of the Federal Communications Commission in 1939; credited with greatly improving FCC regulatory efficiency. Named chairman of the Defense Communications Board (renamed the Board of War Communications) in 1940. Resigned from both the FCC and the board in 1944 to resume private law practice and pursue business interests.

FLYNN, EDWARD JOSEPH (*b. New York, N.Y., 1891; d. Dublin, Ireland, 1953*), political leader. Graduated from Fordham University, LL.B., 1912. Democratic state assemblyman from New York, 1917–21; New York secretary of state, 1929–39; national chairman of the Democratic Party, 1940–43.

FLYNN, ELIZABETH GURLEY (*b. Concord, N.H., 1890; d. Moscow, Russia, 1964*), labor organizer, civil libertarian, suffragette, and political leader. A leading orator and organizer of the Industrial Workers of the World (IWW) from 1906. Fought for women's suffrage, peace, the rights of labor, civil liberties, and socialism. A founder of the American Civil Liberties Union (ACLU) in 1920; member of the board of directors until 1940. A member of the Communist Party of the United States from 1937, Flynn was expelled from the ACLU in 1940. Prosecuted (1951) and convicted (1952) under the Smith Act of 1940 for conspiring to teach, and to advocate, the overthrow of the U.S. government. Sentenced to Alderson Prison, W.Va. (1955–57). Her expulsion from the ACLU was rescinded posthumously in 1978.

FLYNN, ERROL LESLIE (*b. Hobart, Tasmania, Australia, 1909; d. Vancouver, B.C., 1959*), actor. Remembered for his swashbuckling roles; his films include *Captain Blood* (1935), *The Charge of the Light Brigade* (1936), *The Adventures of Robin Hood* (1938), *Dodge City* (1939), *That Forsyte Woman* (1949), and *The Sun Also Rises* (1957).

FLYNN, JOHN THOMAS (*b. Bladensburg, Md., 1882; d. Amityville, N.H., 1964*), journalist and political commentator. Studied at Georgetown University (LL.B., 1902). Reporter, *New Haven Register*, during World War I; city editor and managing editor, the *New York Globe*, in the early 1920's. Free-lance work from 1923. Wrote column "Other People's Money" for the *New Republic* to 1940. Adviser to the Senate Committee on Banking and Currency (1933–34); economic consultant to the Special Senate Committee Investigating the Munitions Industry (1934–35). Chairman of the New York chapter of the America First Committee (from 1940). A polemicist whose historical research and observations of bureaucrats and capitalists led him to

conclude that America was on "the march toward the Fascist society." The author of fourteen books on contemporary affairs, including *As We Go Marching* (1944), Flynn foresaw the growth in power of the Federal Bureau of Investigation and blacklisting. His critique of anti-Communist foreign policy anticipated voices on the left in the 1960's.

FLYNT, JOSIAH.   *See* WILLARD, JOSIAH FLINT.

FOGG, GEORGE GILMAN (*b. Meredith Center, N.H., 1813; d. Concord, N.H., 1881*), lawyer, editor, diplomat. Founded and edited *Independent Democrat* (Concord). Served as U.S. minister to Switzerland, 1861–65.

FOKINE, MICHEL (*b. St. Petersburg, Russia, 1880; d. New York, N.Y., 1942*), dancer, choreographer. Graduated Imperial Ballet School, 1898. While remaining true to the classical traditions of ballet, Fokine was instrumental in rousing ballet from a state of decadence and stagnation and making it a popular and vital theater art. He insisted that each production be artistically coherent and that dance movement, music, stage setting, and costuming all be relevant to the theme, rather than dictated by formalities which were often absurd. He developed his reforming ideas in early work at St. Petersburg but particularly as ballet master with Sergei Diaghilev's company, 1909–14. *Post* 1919, he made his home in the United States, becoming a citizen, 1932. By teaching and by joint appearances with his wife, he had great influence in awakening American interest in ballet. Among the works which he created were *The Dying Swan* (1907); *Les Sylphides* (1908); *Cleopatra* (1909); *Carnaval, Scheherazade,* and *The Firebird* (all 1910); *Le Spectre de la Rose* and *Petrouchka* (1911); *Daphnis and Chloë* (1912); *Le Coq d'Or* (1914); *Don Juan* (1936); *Paganini* (1939); and *Bluebeard* (1941).

FOLGER, CHARLES JAMES (*b. Nantucket, Mass., 1818; d. 1884*), jurist. Moved to Geneva, N.Y., as a boy. Served as New York state senator, and was judge of court of appeals; as secretary of treasury in President Arthur's cabinet, reduced public debt and put department offices under civil service rules.

FOLGER, HENRY CLAY (*b. New York, N.Y., 1857; d. Brooklyn, N.Y., 1930*), lawyer, capitalist. Graduated Amherst, 1879. Long associated with Standard Oil Co., he was president, Standard Oil Co. of New York, 1911–23. Founded and endowed Folger Shakespeare Library, Washington, D.C.

FOLGER, PETER (*b. Norwich, England, 1617; d. 1690*), grandfather of Benjamin Franklin. Came to Massachusetts, *ca.* 1635; settled on Nantucket, 1663, and as teacher and Indian interpreter was island's "indispensable citizen." Author of *A Looking Glass for the Times* (1676).

FOLGER, WALTER (*b. Nantucket, Mass., 1765; d. Nantucket, 1849*), lawyer, jurist, scientist. Built "Folger's astronomic clock," 1788–90, a mechanical marvel; discovered process of annealing wire; served in Massachusetts General Court and as congressman, Democrat, 1817–21.

FOLIN, OTTO KNUT OLOF (*b. Asheda, Sweden, 1867; d. 1934*), biological chemist. Came to America, 1882. Worked on a farm to put himself through school. Graduated University of Minnesota, 1892; studied also in Germany and Sweden; Ph.D., University of Chicago, 1898. For seven years worked at McLean Hospital, Waverly, Mass.; *post* 1907, headed the Department of Biological Chemistry at Harvard School of Medicine. His investigations illuminated the laws governing the composition of normal urine and the fields of the intermediate stages in protein metabolism. He studied part played in health and disease by creatine, creatinine, and uric acid; created methods for the accurate quantitation of the constituents of urine and blood. These methods soon were in general use throughout the world in determining the diagnosis and progress of disease and the effects of treatment.

FOLK, JOSEPH WINGATE (*b. Brownsville, Tenn., 1869; d. New York, N.Y., 1923*), lawyer. Graduated Vanderbilt University Law School, 1890. Practiced corporation law in St. Louis, Mo. Elected that city's chief law-enforcement officer, 1900, he conducted a series of exposures of alliance there between corrupt business and corrupt politics, 1901–02. Supported by rural counties and opposed by city politicians, he was elected Democratic governor of Missouri, 1905, and continued his reforming policies in that office until 1909. Served as chief counsel for Interstate Commerce Commission in first Wilson administration; returned to private law practice after defeat for U.S. senate seat, 1918.

FOLKS, HOMER (*b. Hanover, Mich., 1867; d. Riverdale, N.Y., 1963*), child welfare worker, welfare administrator, and public health crusader. Studied at Albion College and Harvard (graduated, 1890). General superintendant of the Children's Aid Society of Pennsylvania, 1890–93. Headed the New York State Charities Aid Association (SCAA) to 1947. Commissioner of public charities of New York City, 1902–03. Director of the Department of Civil Affairs of the American Red Cross in France, 1917–18. A founder of the National Child Labor Committee; chairman, 1935–44. President of the National Conference of Social Work (terms from 1911 and 1923). Folks revolutionized the care of needy children in the United States, utilizing a preventive approach that stressed the importance of maintaining the family in its entirety. His anti-tuberculosis campaign led to the enactment of laws governing the reporting and treatment of all cases and the building of public institutions. Instrumental in the establishment of juvenile courts in New York State, and in the creation of the nation's first state probation commission. As vice-chairman of the New York Public Health Council, 1913–55, Folks reorganized the state's Health Department, making it the most progressive such body in the nation. His career is unmatched in American social welfare history.

FOLLEN, CHARLES (*b. Giessen, Germany, 1796; d. Long Island Sound, 1840*), first professor of German literature at Harvard, abolitionist, Unitarian clergyman. Came to America, 1824. Taught at Harvard, 1825–35; lectured on law, gave lessons in gymnastics, wrote linguistic textbooks, literary readers, theological and philosophical essays. His vigorous defense of the abolitionists and his "Address to the People of the United States," drafted at the New England Anti-Slavery Society's first convention, caused his severance from Harvard.

FOLLEN, ELIZA LEE CABOT (*b. Boston, Mass., 1787; d. 1860*), author. Prominent in Sunday-school movement and as a Massachusetts abolitionist. Wife of Charles Follen.

FOLLEN, KARL THEODOR CHRISTIAN. *See* FOLLEN, CHARLES.

FOLLET, MARY PARKER (*b. Quincy, Mass., 1868; d. Boston, Mass., 1933*), vocational guidance counselor. Author of *The New State* (1918) and *Creative Experience* (1924).

FOLSOM, CHARLES (*b. Exeter, N.H., 1794; d. Cambridge, Mass., 1872*), librarian, teacher, editor. Served as U.S. Navy chaplain and instructor, later as tutor and librarian at Harvard and as librarian of Boston Athenaeum, 1846–56.

FOLSOM, GEORGE (*b. Kennebunk, Maine, 1802; d. Rome, Italy, 1869*), lawyer, antiquarian. Editor and librarian, American Antiquarian Society and New-York Historical Society; translated *Dispatches of Hernando Cortez* (1843).

FOLSOM, NATHANIEL (*b. Exeter, N.H., 1726; d. 1790*), Revolutionary soldier, New Hampshire politician.

FOLWELL, SAMUEL (*b. ca. 1768; d. Philadelphia, Pa., 1813*), painter of miniatures, engraver.

FOLWELL, WILLIAM WATTS (*b. Romulus, N.Y., 1833; d. 1929*), educator, Union soldier. First president of University of Minnesota, 1869–84; thereafter librarian and professor of political science. Author of *History of Minnesota* (1921–30).

FONDA, JOHN H. (*b. Watervliet, N.Y., ca. 1797; d. Prairie du Chien, Wis., ca. 1868*), frontiersman, soldier. Led a wandering life along frontier from Texas to Green Bay, 1819–31; his reminiscences of early Wisconsin published, 1868.

FONT, PEDRO (*d. Pitique, Sonora, Mexico, 1781*), Franciscan missionary, cartographer. Accompanied de Anza's expedition to San Francisco, Calif., 1775–76; left graphic account of the journey.

FOOT, SAMUEL AUGUSTUS (*b. Cheshire, Conn., 1780; d. Cheshire, 1846*), merchant, farmer, politician. Graduated Yale, 1797. A Democratic legislator and congressman; U.S. senator, 1827–33. In 1829, he offered a resolution on public lands which led to Webster-Hayne debate. Served as governor of Connecticut, 1834–35.

FOOT, SOLOMON (*b. Cornwall, Vt., 1802; d. Washington, D.C., 1866*), lawyer, politician. Served in Vermont legislature. As Whig (later Republican) senator from Vermont, 1850–66, excelled as presiding officer through tact and knowledge of parliamentary law.

FOOTE, ANDREW HULL (*b. New Haven, Conn., 1806; d. New York, N.Y., 1863*), naval officer. Son of Samuel A. Foot. Appointed midshipman, 1822. When first lieutenant on USS *Cumberland*, enforced temperance on shipboard; was largely responsible for abolishment of grog ration in navy, 1862. After duty along African coast, wrote *Africa and the American Flag* (1854); supported agitation against slave traffic. As commander of USS *Portsmouth* in China, 1856–58, led retaliatory raid on four barrier forts below Canton. Commanding naval operations on upper Mississippi, 1861–62, he was at reduction of Fort Henry and Fort Donelson; was wounded in the latter engagement. After fall of Island No. 10 in spring of 1862, he was relieved of duty afloat for reasons of health and promoted rear admiral.

FOOTE, ARTHUR WILLIAM (*b. Salem, Mass., 1853; d. Boston, Mass., 1937*), composer. A typical member of the New England group, his simple lyric forms, romantic in feeling, were rooted in classical tradition.

FOOTE, HENRY STUART (*b. Fauquier Co., Va., 1804; d. Nashville, Tenn., 1880*), lawyer, Mississippi Democratic politician. A personal and political enemy of Jefferson Davis, Foote opposed secession sentiment in his state as U.S. senator, 1847–52, and as governor of Mississippi, 1852–54. After the triumph of the states' rights faction, he removed first to California, then to Tennessee. After failure of his attempts to make peace, 1861, he resided for a time in Europe. Called the "Vallandigham of the South," he was author of *The War of the Rebellion* (1866), *Casket of Reminiscences* (1874), and other books.

FOOTE, JOHN AMBROSE (*b. Archbald, Pa., 1874; d. Washington, D.C., 1931*), physician, pediatrician. M.D., Georgetown, 1906; thereafter taught at Georgetown Medical School; dean, 1929–31.

FOOTE, LUCIUS HARWOOD (*b. Winfield, N.Y., 1826; d. San Francisco, Calif., 1913*), lawyer, diplomat. Active in Republican politics in California; U.S. minister to Korea, 1883–85.

FOOTE, SAMUEL AUGUSTUS. *See* FOOT, SAMUEL AUGUSTUS.

FOOTE, WILLIAM HENRY (*b. Colchester, Conn., 1794; d. Romney, W.Va., 1869*), Presbyterian clergyman. Author of *Sketches of North Carolina, Historical and Biographical* (1846) and *Sketches of Virginia, Historical and Biographical* (1850, 1855).

FORAKER, JOSEPH BENSON (*b. near Rainsboro, Ohio, 1846; d. 1917*), lawyer, Union soldier, politician. Began law practice, Cincinnati, Ohio, 1869; was judge of superior court. Republican governor of Ohio, 1886–90. As U.S. senator, 1896–1908, he was recognized as an outstanding constitutional lawyer and party leader; a supporter of McKinley's policies, he consistently opposed the policies of Theodore Roosevelt. Disclosure of questionable financial ties with Standard Oil led to his resignation in 1908.

FORBES, EDWIN (*b. New York, N.Y., 1839; d. Flatbush, N.Y., 1895*), painter, etcher, writer. Studied with Arthur F. Tait. As Civil War staff artist for *Leslie's*, sketched camp life and battlefields; published *Life Studies of the Great Army* (1876).

FORBES, ESTHER (*b. Westborough, Mass., 1891; d. Worcester, Mass., 1967*), novelist and historian. Studied writing at the University of Wisconsin, 1916–18. Worked on the editorial staff of Houghton Mifflin in Boston, 1919–26. Noted for her meticulous treatment of historical detail in works such as *Paul Revere and the World He Lived In* (1942), a biography that won a Pulitzer Prize for history, and historical novels such as *A Mirror for Witches* (1928) and *Johnny Tremain: A Novel for Young and Old* (1943), which won the Newbery Medal in 1944 and has become a classic of children's literature. Forbes became the first woman member of the American Antiquarian Society in 1960.

FORBES, JOHN (*b. Pittencrieff, Scotland, 1710; d. Philadelphia, Pa., 1759*), British officer. Came to America, 1757, as colonel of the 17th Foot; was promoted brigadier general in America only. Commanded expedition against Fort Duquesne, 1758. Contending with unenthusiastic supporters, continual rainfalls, and his own mortal illness, he penetrated the western Pennsylvania wilderness; cut a road by way of Bedford and Ligonier and over Laurel Hill which later became major emigration highway; safeguarded line of communication by building regularly spaced blockhouses. Upon his arrival the French evacuated Fort Duquesne, and Forbes raised the British flag over the site on Nov. 25, 1758.

FORBES, JOHN (*b. Scotland, 1740[?]; d. England, 1783*), Church of England clergyman. First, and for many years only, English clergyman licensed in East Florida, where he served, 1764–83, also holding high judicial offices in the province.

FORBES, JOHN (*b. Scotland, 1769; d. Cuba, 1823*), merchant. Agent for, and *post* 1792 a partner in, Panton, Leslie and Co., trading with the Creek, Choctaw, and Cherokee on the Spanish-Indian frontier; secured "Forbes Purchase," land grant on Appalachicola River from Spain and the Indians, 1804 and 1811.

FORBES, JOHN MURRAY (*b. St. Augustine, Fla., 1771; d. Buenos Aires, Argentina, 1831*), lawyer, diplomat. Son of John Forbes (1740–83). Was John Quincy Adams' most trusted agent in southern South America; served as agent for commerce, secretary of legation, and chargé d'affaires at Buenos Aires, 1820–31.

FORBES, JOHN MURRAY (*b. Bordeaux, France, 1813; d. 1898*), merchant, capitalist. Grandson of John Forbes (1740–83). Began business career in China; *post* 1846, turned to railroad building and management. With others bought and completed Michigan Central Railroad; financed roads which later became the Chicago, Burlington & Quincy; built the Hannibal & St. Joseph. During Civil War helped organize black regiments in Massachusetts; advised navy department; built a cruiser; organized Loyal Publication Society. After the war, was member of Republican national executive committee. Forbes brought into railroad business sound methods of finance and a broad view of its relation to the public interest.

FORBES, ROBERT BENNET (*b. Jamaica Plain, Mass., 1804; d. 1889*), sea captain, China merchant, shipowner, writer. Brother of John M. Forbes (1813–98). Began career in employ of his uncles (James and Thomas H. Perkins) in the China trade; as head of Russell & Co., at Canton, 1839, during opium war refused to join British boycott of the port. Part-owned or constructed 68 vessels; invented "Forbes rig"; early acquired screw-driven iron steamers. Commanded ship carrying food from Boston to Ireland in famine of 1847; supported coastal lifesaving work; built Union warships during Civil War. Author of numerous pamphlets on China and on nautical subjects and a volume of *Personal Reminiscences* (1876).

FORBES, STEPHEN ALFRED (*b. Silver Creek, Ill., 1844; d. 1930*), entomologist, naturalist. After service in Union army, studied at Rush Medical; *post* 1872, worked at Museum of State Natural History, Normal. Ill; became director of State Laboratory of Natural History. Professor of zoology and entomology, University of Illinois, 1884–1921; state entomologist, 1882–1917. His more than 500 publications cover diverse branches of biology. He was the first writer and teacher in America to stress the study of ecology, the earliest and leading American hydrobiologist, and a pioneer student of the foods of birds and fishes.

FORBES, WILLIAM CAMERON (*b. Milton, Mass., 1870; d. Boston, Mass., 1959*), businessman, government official, diplomat. Graduated from Harvard, 1892. Secretary of commerce and police in the Philippines, 1904; governor general, 1909–13. After completing a study of conditions in the Philippines and Haiti during the 1920's, Forbes was ambassador to Japan, 1930–32. Chairman of the board of trustees of the Carnegie Institution of Washington during the 1930's.

FORBUSH, EDWARD HOWE (*b. Quincy, Mass., 1858; d. 1929*), ornithologist. Author of *The Gypsy Moth* (1896), *Birds of Massachusetts and Other New England States* (1925, 1927), and other works.

FORCE, JULIANA RIESER (*b. Doylestown, Pa., 1876; d. New York, N.Y., 1948*), museum director. Associated *post* 1914 with Gertrude Vanderbilt Whitney in her work to encourage and support the "new movement" in American art through the Friends of the Young Artists, the Whitney Studio Club, the Whitney Studio Galleries, and the Whitney Museum of American Art.

FORCE, MANNING FERGUSON (*b. Washington, D.C., 1824; d. 1899*), Union soldier, jurist. Son of Peter Force. Brevetted major general in recognition of "especial gallantry before Atlanta"; was judge of superior court of Cincinnati, Ohio, 1877–87.

FORCE, PETER (*b. near Passaic Falls, N.J., 1790; d. 1869*), printer, publisher, archivist, historian. Whig major of Washington, D.C., 1836–40. Principally famous for collecting and publishing a series of reprints of rare pamphlets on colonial history, *Tracts and Other Papers*, etc. (1836–46), and for the monumental volumes known as *American Archives*, a most important collection of original materials on American history, originally planned to cover from the 17th century through 1789. Only nine volumes, covering the years 1774–76, appeared (1837–53).

FORD, DANIEL SHARP (*b.* Cambridge, Mass., 1822; *d.* 1899), printer. Edited and published *Youth's Companion* from 1857, building it into the country's most successful family journal. Bequeathed funds for construction of Boston's Ford Hall.

FORD, EDSEL BRYANT (*b.* Detroit, Mich., 1893; *d.* Lake St. Clair, Mich., 1943), industrialist. Son of Henry Ford. Began work at Ford Motor Co., 1912; served as president of the company, 1919–43. Ford Foundation established through his initiative.

FORD, GEORGE BURDETT (*b.* Clinton, Mass., 1879; *d.* New York, N.Y., 1930), architect, city planner. Worked in office of George S. Post. Sponsored a program of urban development in which aesthetic considerations played a large role.

FORD, GORDON LESTER (*b.* Lebanon, Conn., 1823; *d.* Brooklyn, N.Y., 1891), lawyer, businessman, collector of Americana.

FORD, GUY STANTON (*b.* Liberty Corners, Wis., 1873; *d.* Washington, D.C., 1962), editor and educator. Studied at the University of Wisconsin at Madison (1892–95); the University of Berlin (1899–1900), and Columbia (Ph.D., 1903). Instructor of history at Yale (1901–06); and at the University of Illinois (1906–13). Chairman of the history department and dean of the graduate school at the University of Minnesota from 1913; acting president from 1931–32 and 1937–38; president, 1938–41. Gained a reputation for raising the level of intellectual life not only in the university and the state, but also in the nation. Director of civic and educational publications, the Committee on Public Information, Washington, D.C., 1917–19. Member of the Social Science Research Council of the Association of American Universities, 1923–40. Edited *Essays in American History: Dedicated to Frederick Jackson Turner* (1910); editor-in-chief of *Compton's Pictured Encyclopedia* and editor of Harper's *Historical Series* (1922) and of a volume of essays, *Dictatorship in the Modern World* (1935). Went to Germany in 1924 to study postwar university needs in the social sciences, under the sponsorship of the Laura Spelman Rockefeller Foundation. President of the American Historical Association, 1938; executive secretary, editor of the association, and managing editor of the *American Historical Review*, 1941–53.

FORD, HANNIBAL CHOATE (*b.* Dryden, N.Y., 1877; *d.* Kingsport, N.Y., 1955), inventor and engineer. Graduated from Cornell University, B.S., 1903. Coinventor of the gyroscope and of many related navigational instruments; virtually all modern naval vessels employ instruments directly related to his inventions; during World War I, as head of the Ford Instrument Company, he invented many devices to help control the range and accuracy of naval gunfire.

FORD, HENRY (*b.* Greenfield Township, now in Dearborn, Wayne Co., Mich., 1863; *d.* Fair Lane, Dearborn, Mich., 1947), industrialist, automotive pioneer. A farmer's son. Ford attended rural schools, 1871–79. In 1879 he became an apprentice in a Detroit machine shop. He then joined the Detroit Drydock Co., 1880, where he acquired knowledge of power plants. In 1882 he became a road agent for the Westinghouse Engine Co. and spent about a year servicing steam-traction engines for farmers in Michigan. Over the years 1884–86 Ford operated and repaired steam engines, helped his father on the family farm, and occasionally worked in Detroit factories. He abandoned farming and moved with his wife, Clara Bryant Ford, to Detroit, where in September

1891 he became a night engineer with the Edison Illuminating Co. On Nov. 6, 1893, a son and only child, Edsel Bryant Ford, was born to the couple.

His spare time was devoted to efforts to produce an engine suitable for an automobile; he produced an operable car by mid–1899. With the backing of a group of investors, the Detroit Automobile Co. was formed in 1899. After turning out approximately 20 machines, the company went out of business in 1900.

Ford then turned to auto racing. In 1902, at 39 he had a local standing as an authority on motor vehicles and demonstrated ability to attract both investors and coworkers. Ford then designed a car to compete with such popular-priced cars as the Oldsmobile. The Ford Motor Co. was incorporated in 1903, and the first Ford automobile, the Model A, was brought out. Higher-priced models, the B, C, and F, were offered in 1904–05.

The Model T, introduced on Oct. 1, 1908, combined in a standardized utility vehicle the features of lightness, durability, and low cost. From its introduction until 1927, the Model T was the sole model built by the company. Ford designed the car for rural America, and it quickly became the favorite in farm areas and small towns. This versatile car was principally responsible for taking the automobile out of the luxury class and making it an inexpensive necessity for the common man.

In announcing that he would "build a motorcar for the great multitude," Ford became the first automobile manufacturer to concentrate on a single model with a standardized chassis made of interchangeable parts. This revolutionary departure imposed a new set of technological requirements. Between 1910 and 1914 Ford and his production engineers laid down the foundations of automotive mass production and its culminating achievement— the continuously moving assembly. By empirical means, Ford arrived at some of the same principles of work and motion management formulated by Frederick Winslow Taylor and Frank B. Gilbreth. By 1916, when the millionth Model T rolled off the line, Ford production was averaging 2,000 cars a day.

In 1913 Ford recognized that the vast market for the Model T could not be satisfied unless Ford workers had an incentive to submit to the new industrial discipline of the moving assembly line. Primarily from this motive, the Ford Motor Co. announced on Jan. 5, 1914, a basic (and, at the time, very good) wage of $5 a day for all eligible workers in the Ford plants, as well as a reduction in shift time from nine to eight hours. The "five-dollar day" signaled Ford's meteoric rise to fame, and for the first time linked the Ford name on the Model T to a recognizable image and a concrete personality.

In early 1914, Ford was 50 and at the height of his powers. Although completely self-assured with problems of mechanical construction and automotive manufacture, he had little use for conventional formulas and expert authority and preferred to rely upon his "hunches," as he called them. In fields for which he was ill equipped Ford exhibited a narrow materialism, utilitarianism, and anti-intellectualism. His sudden rise to fame, by enhancing his self-importance, made him more inclined to interpret his success and its universal acclaim as proof of his unerring judgment.

In 1915–19 Ford became involved in some of the most controversial episodes of his career. The outbreak of World War I in Europe reawakened his deep aversion to militarism and war, and in the summer of 1915 he issued militant pacifist denunciations. Ford also attacked war "profiteers," but he pledged that in the event of war he would place his factory at the disposal of the government and "operate without one cent of profit."

Nominally a Republican, Ford enthusiastically supported President Wilson for reelection. In June 1918, at Wilson's urging, Ford agreed to enter the Michigan senatorial race. Ford lost the election, but financed an undercover investigation of his opponent that led to his resignation from the Senate. Privately, Ford attributed the European war to "international bankers" and his defeat in the Senate contest to Wall Street "interests" and to "the Jews." His latent bigotry was reinforced in 1919 as a result of his libel suit against the *Chicago Tribune*, which he sued for an editorial it had published on June 23, 1916, calling him an "anarchist" and "an ignorant idealist" because of his anti-preparedness utterances. In August 1919 the *Tribune* was found guilty of libel, but the trial was a humiliating personal ordeal for Ford.

Ford's unfortunate excursions into pacifism, politics, and bigotry did not seriously impair his popularity among his many admirers. "Fordismus" became an international term connoting factory efficiency, high wages, and mass consumption. In the 1920's Ford reached a wide public as the nominal author of books and articles written by amanuenses, chief among them Samuel Crowther, who "collaborated" with Ford on *My Life and Work* (1922). Upon taking full control of the company in 1919, Ford converted it into an organization completely responsive to his autocratic imperatives. By April 1921, Ford had liquid assets of $87.3 million for paying debts amounting to $58 million.

The introduction of the Model A on Dec. 1, 1927, was a tumultuous public event, and within two weeks 400,000 orders had been taken. But Ford ended the year with a net loss, and barely four years later, in August 1931, Ford discontinued the Model A. He was no longer the single most decisive influence in the industry. In March 1932 he introduced a new eight-cylinder engine car, the Ford V-8. Ford sales remained low, and for 1931-33, company losses amounted to $125 million. The V-8 was Ford's last automotive innovation. Ford sales improved in 1934 and 1935, but in 1936 the company settled back into third place in the industry. After 1932, Ford spent less time on company affairs, although he still controlled basic policy decisions. The outside project which absorbed most of his time was his historical museum and village at Dearborn.

At the outbreak of World War II in 1939, Ford urged American aloofness from the conflict, but later supported the isolationist position of the America First Committee. The billion-dollar corporation he created had been brought to a precarious state by years of autocratic rule, and it would remain for others to rebuild it. Ford slipped quietly into retirement, dividing his time between his Fair Lane estate and his Georgia plantation.

Most of Ford's fortune, consisting mainly of company stock, went to the Ford Foundation. Despite shortcomings mostly attributable to a narrow provincialism, Ford will probably be remembered as the greatest revolutionary of the machine age.

FORD, HENRY JONES (*b. Baltimore, Md., 1851; d. Blue Ridge Summit, Pa., 1925*), newspaper editor, publicist, historian. Author of *The Rise and Growth of American Politics* (1898) and other works; professor of politics at Princeton; confidential agent of President Woodrow Wilson and member of Interstate Commerce Commission.

FORD, JACOB (*b. Morristown N.J., 1738; d. Morristown, 1777*), Revolutionary soldier, powder maker, ironmaster. With father, cast shot and shell for Washington's army; operated powder mill by Whippanong River.

FORD, JOHN BAPTISTE (*b. Danville, Ky., 1811; d. 1903*), inventor, manufacturer. Learned saddler's trade in Greenville, Ind.; operated general store, woodworking plant, foundry, and rolling mill. During Civil War built and operated river steamboats; turned to plate-glass manufacture at New Albany, Ind., 1863; lost his fortune in depression of 1873. Established Ford Plate Glass Co. at Creighton, near Pittsburgh, Pa., 1884, and made second large fortune; with his sons, controlled Pittsburgh Plate Glass Co.

Established Michigan Alkali Co. at Wyandotte, Mich.; helped develop gas deposits near Pittsburgh.

FORD, JOHN THOMSON (*b. Baltimore, Md., 1829; d. 1894*), theater manager. Built Baltimore Grand Opera house; managed theaters in Baltimore, Washington, Alexandria and Richmond.

FORD, PATRICK (*b. Galway, Ireland, 1835; d. Brooklyn, N.Y., 1913*), journalist. Came to America as a child. Editor of *Irish World* (New York), *post* 1870; a vehement advocate of complete Irish independence.

FORD, PAUL LEICESTER (*b. Brooklyn, N.Y., 1865; d. New York, N.Y., 1902*), historian, novelist. Son of Gordon L. Ford. Precociously expert, he began bibliographical researches in his father's library of Americana, reprinted many volumes of rare historical materials; produced bibliographical studies on, among others, Noah Webster, Charles Chauncy, Alexander Hamilton, and Benjamin Franklin. He also edited the writings of John Dickinson and Thomas Jefferson and wrote popular works such as *The True George Washington* (1896) and *The Many-Sided Franklin* (1899). Among his successful works of fiction were *The Honorable Peter Stirling* (1894), *Janice Meredith* (1899), and *The Great K. and A. Train Robbery* (1897). Inherited wealth, restless energy, and a gift of painstaking concentration made possible Ford's impressive labors.

FORD, THOMAS (*b. Fayette Co., Pa., 1800; d. Peoria, Ill., 1850*), lawyer, jurist. As governor of Illinois, Democrat, 1842–46, he saved the state's credit by avoiding debt repudiation; he also secured removal of the Mormons in the interest of peace. Author of *History of Illinois* (1854).

FORD, WORTHINGTON CHAUNCEY (*b. Brooklyn, N.Y., 1858; d. at sea, between Lisbon and New York, 1941*), historical editor, bibliographer. Son of Gordon L. Ford; brother of Paul L. Ford. Headed statistical bureaus of U.S. Department of State, 1885–89, and of U.S. Treasury Department, 1893–98; headed Department of Statistics and Manuscripts, Boston Public Library, 1898–1902; chief of the manuscripts division, Library of Congress, 1902–08. Directed a major publication program as editor at Massachusetts Historical Society, 1908–29, thereafter until 1933 serving as European representative of Library of Congress. Outstanding for his work as collector and organizer of historical manuscripts at Library of Congress and for pioneer modern scholarly editions of the writings of George Washington, William Bradford, John Quincy Adams, and others.

FORDNEY, JOSEPH WARREN (*b. near Hartford City, Ind., 1853; d. 1932*), lumberman. Congressman, Republican, from Michigan, 1899–1923. An ardent protectionist, he gave name to the Fordney-McCumber Tariff of 1922, the climax of his legislative career.

FORDYCE, JOHN ADDISON (*b. Guernsey Co., Ohio, 1858; d. New York, N.Y., 1925*), dermatologist, syphilologist. Graduated Adrian College, 1878; M.D., Northwestern, 1881; M.D., Berlin, 1888; studied also in Vienna and Paris. Practiced and taught in New York; organized first adequate American training center for dermatologists.

FOREPAUGH, ADAM (*b. Philadelphia, Pa., 1831; d. 1890*), showman. Began his circus career in 1864; by 1880 was most formidable rival of Barnum's Greatest Show on Earth.

FORESTER, CECIL SCOTT (*b. Cairo, Egypt, 1899; d. Fullerton, Calif., 1966*), biographer and historical novelist. The son of a British official stationed in Egypt, Forester studied at Dulwich College (1915–18) and medicine at Guy's Hospital in London (1918–21). Moved to Southern California after contracting to write screenplays based on his original stories; worked on films such as *Born for Glory* (1935), *Eagle Squadron* (1942), and *Captain Horatio Hornblower* (1951). Historical novels include *Payment Deferred* (1926), *The Gun* (1933), *The African Queen* (1935), *The General* (1936), *The Ship* (1943), and the twelve-book series of seafaring novels that make up the Hornblower Saga, for which he is best remembered. These include *Beat to Quarters* (1937), *A Ship of the Line* (1938), *Flying Colours* (1938), *The Commodore* (1945), and *Lord Hornblower* (1946). Also wrote histories of naval engagements such as *The Age of Fighting Sail* (1956) and *Hunting the Bismarck* (1959). Forester never became an American citizen.

FORESTER, FRANK. *See* HERBERT, HENRY WILLIAM.

FORESTI, ELEUTARIO FELICE (*b. Conselice, Papal States, 1793; d. Genoa, Italy, 1858*), educator. Exiled from Italy as member of the Carbonari, came to America, 1836. Professor of Italian at Columbia and New York universities, 1839–56; appointed U.S. consul to Genoa, 1858.

FORGAN, JAMES BERWICK (*b. St. Andrews, Scotland, 1852; d. 1924*), banker. Vice-president, 1892–1900, and president, *post* 1900, First National Bank, Chicago, Ill.

FORMAN, DAVID (*b. Monmouth Co., N.J., 1745; d. on shipboard, 1797*), Revolutionary soldier. Commanded Jersey militia at battle of Germantown; while suppressing armed Loyalists in Jersey, earned reputation for brutality.

FORMAN, JOSHUA (*b. Pleasant Valley, N.Y., 1777; d. Rutherfordton, N.C., 1848*), lawyer, businessman. Graduated Union College, 1798. Practiced law at present Syracuse, N.Y., of which he is recognized as founder. Was early advocate of Erie Canal and author of New York's Safety Fund plan, 1828–29, insuring redemption of bank notes.

FORMAN, JUSTUS MILES (*b. LeRoy, N.Y., 1875; d. aboard Lusitania, 1915*), author.

FORNEY, JOHN WIEN (*b. Lancaster, Pa., 1817; d. 1881*), Philadelphia journalist, politician. Author of *Anecdotes of Public Men* (1873, 1881).

FORNEY, MATTHIAS NACE (*b. Hanover, Pa., 1835; d. New York, N.Y., 1908*), engineer, editor, inventor. Designed tank locomotive, 1866, used on urban elevated railroads; edited railroad journals. Author of *Catechism of the Locomotive* (1875) and other works.

FORNEY, WILLIAM HENRY (*b. Lincolnton, N.C., 1823; d. 1894*), lawyer. Confederate brigadier general. Practiced law in Jacksonville, Ala. Congressman, Democrat, from Alabama, 1875–93.

FORREST, EDWIN (*b. Philadelphia, Pa., 1806; d. Philadelphia, 1872*), earliest American-born actor of the first rank. Made his debut at Walnut St. Theatre, Philadelphia, Nov. 1820; spent his apprenticeship in frontier theaters and at New Orleans. Supported Edmund Kean at Albany, N.Y., 1825, and received encouragement and advice from him. Forrest's appearance as Othello at New York's Park Theatre, 1826, launched him as a successful, popular star. His aggressive nationalism, animal vigor, and sonorous voice gained him the love of the less critical public, and enabled him to amass a small fortune and to give over $20,000 in prizes for native dramas and plays. Visiting England, 1845, he played Macbeth in London, where he had been previously well received, and was hissed. Believing the English actor Macready to be responsible, Forrest hissed Macready in Edinburgh shortly thereafter and stirred up a hornet's nest of passions. When Mac-

ready played in America in 1848–49, American audiences took sides in the actors' rivalry and interpreted it as a struggle of democracy versus Anglomania. Macready was howled down at his farewell appearance at New York's Astor Place Opera House on May 8, 1849, by a riotous mob of Forrest's adherents. When the Englishman was persuaded to try again on May 10, mob violence broke out and was quelled by the militia only after much bloodshed. This shadow on Forrest's reputation was followed by scandalous divorce proceedings which dragged on from 1851 to 1869. Although he continued to enjoy financial success, he now alternated between periods of acting and of brooding withdrawal in his Philadelphia home. After 1865, he became increasingly crippled by sciatica and the public turned to younger actors. Forrest's strength was his vigorous rendering of strong-willed, elemental characters; his weakness lay in his egocentric passions, vanity, and arrogance.

FORREST, FRENCH (*b. St. Mary's Co., Md., 1796; d. Georgetown, D.C., 1866*), naval officer. Distinguished in the Mexican War at Alvarado and at Vera Cruz landing; as a Confederate officer, commanded Norfolk Navy Yard, 1861–62, and the James River squadron, 1863–64.

FORREST, NATHAN BEDFORD (*b. Bedford Co., Tenn., 1821; d. Memphis, Tenn., 1877*), Confederate general. A self-made wealthy plantation owner, Forrest enlisted as private in Confederate army, 1861; having raised and equipped a mounted battalion, he was appointed lieutenant colonel. Avoided capture at Fort Donelson, 1862, by leading his troops through a gap in the Union encirclement. Brigadier general after July 1862, he carried out daring and tactically brilliant raids behind Union lines, in 1864 penetrating as far north as Paducah, Ky. Defeated superior force at Brice's Cross Roads, Miss., June 1864; commanded Confederate cavalry in Nashville campaign. Promoted lieutenant general, February 1865, he met final defeat at Selma, Ala., in April and surrendered in May. His reputation as courageous soldier and superior cavalry leader is darkened by his failure to prevent the massacre of black soldiers at Fort Pillow, 1864.

FORRESTAL, JAMES VINCENT (*b. Matteawan, now part of Beacon, N.Y., 1892; d. Bethesda, Md., 1949*), investment banker, public servant. Attended Dartmouth and Princeton, 1911–15. Associated with Dillon, Read and Co., 1916–40, as bond salesman, partner, vice president, and president, 1938–40. Called to Washington, 1940, to serve as special administrative assistant to President Franklin D. Roosevelt, he was soon made undersecretary of the navy and became secretary in 1944. As undersecretary he was responsible for the World War II procurement program. He asserted civilian domination over the Navy Department, generating considerable opposition to his actions. Opposed to the unification of the armed forces under a single Department of Defense, he finally accepted the idea in principle but continued to insist on a large measure of service autonomy. Successful in securing such guarantees in the National Security Act of 1947, he became the first U.S. secretary of defense in July of that year. Embroiled in interservice squabbles and at odds with President Harry Truman, he was asked to resign on Mar. 1, 1949. His health shattered, he committed suicide while under treatment for depression.

FORSYTH, JOHN (*b. Fredericksburg, Va., 1780; d. Washington, D.C., 1841*), lawyer, statesman. Graduated Princeton, 1799. Attorney general of Georgia, 1808; congressman, Democrat, from Georgia, 1813–18 and 1823–27; U.S. senator, 1818 and 1829–34; U.S. secretary of state, 1834–41. Served also as minister to Spain, 1819–22; secured ratification of treaty of 1819. Was governor of Georgia, 1827–29. Repudiating early states' rights leanings, he became staunch supporter of President Jackson. Voted against the tariff of 1832, but challenged authority of Georgia's nullification convention and helped to defeat its purposes. Voted for Force Act of 1833; justified Jackson's stand on bank issue. As secretary of state, secured French indemnity payments owing under treaty of 1831; stalled on issue of Texas recognition and annexation. A diplomat and courtier, Forsyth was a gifted orator and powerful debater.

FORSYTH, JOHN (*b. Newburgh, N.Y., 1810; d. Newburgh, 1886*), Reformed clergyman, professor. Pastor in Philadelphia and Newburgh; taught languages, history, theology at Newburgh Seminary, Princeton, Rutgers, and West Point.

FORSYTH, THOMAS (*b. Detroit, 1771; d. St. Louis, Mo., 1833*), Indian agent, explorer. Fur trader in Michigan and Illinois; as agent to Potawatomi, Sauk, and Fox Indians, helped maintain peace along the frontier, 1812–30. He was half brother of John Kinzie.

FORTEN, JAMES (*b. Philadelphia, Pa., 1766; d. Philadelphia, 1842*), sail maker. One of the foremost American blacks of his time. Served in Continental navy; became prominent Philadelphia businessman and an active philanthropist.

FORTESCUE, CHARLES LEGEYT (*b. York Factory, Canada, 1876; d. Pittsburgh, Pa., 1936*), electrical engineer, inventor. His contributions to power transmission include the method of symmetrical components for checking polyphase alternating current systems and a method of protecting lines against lightning.

FORTIER, ALCÉE *b. St. James Parish, La., 1856; d. 1914*), educator, author, historian. Professor of Romance languages at Tulane University. Author of a classic *History of Louisiana* (1904); also textbooks and works on Creole history and customs.

FORWARD, WALTER (*b. Old Granby, Conn., 1786; d. Pittsburgh, Pa., 1852*), lawyer. Congressman, Democrat, from Pennsylvania, 1822–25; advocated high tariff. Played important part in forming Whig party, 1834. U.S. secretary of treasury, 1841–43, he was in constant disagreement with President John Tyler.

FORWOOD, WILLIAM HENRY (*b. Brandywine Hundred, Del., 1838; d. Washington, D.C., 1915*), army medical officer. Saw extensive field service during Civil War and on western reconnaissances, 1879–83; taught surgery at Army Medical School, 1893–98; headed hospitals at Montauk Point, N.Y., Savannah, Ga., and San Francisco, Calif., 1898–1901. Retired in 1902 after brief tenure as surgeon general.

FOSDICK, CHARLES AUSTIN (*b. Randolph, N.Y., 1842; d. Hamburg, N.Y., 1915*), author. Writing under the pen name of "Harry Castlemon," he produced many popular series of boys' books, beginning with *Frank, the Young Naturalist* (1864). Appealed through his brisk, realistic descriptions and Northern patriotism.

FOSDICK, HARRY EMERSON (*b. Buffalo, N.Y., 1878; d. Bronxville, N.Y., 1969*), author, preacher, and churchman. Studied at Colgate University (B.A., 1900), Hamilton Theological Seminary, and Union Theological Seminary (B.D., 1904). Pastor, First Baptist church, Montclair, N.J., 1904–15. Professor, Union Theological Seminary, 1915–46. Preaching minister, First Presbyterian Church in New York City; resigned in 1925 after a controversy during which Fosdick refused to submit to Presbyterian orthodoxy. Pastor of Riverside Church, 1925–46. Began a radio ministry in 1922 that culminated in "National Vespers." Achieved fame as a religious liberal and controversialist, especially in the 1920's, when his sermons routinely challenged the conservative fundamentalist movement. Books include *The Second Mile*

(1908), *The Manhood of the Master* (1913), *Adventurous Religion* (1926), and *On Being a Real Person* (1943).

FOSDICK, WILLIAM WHITEMAN (*b. Cincinnati, Ohio, 1825; d. Cincinnati, 1862*), lawyer, author.

FOSHAG, WILLIAM FREDERICK (*b. Sag Harbor, N.Y., 1894; d. Westmoreland Hills, Md., 1956*), geologist. Graduated from the University of California, Ph.D., 1923. Affiliated with the National Museum (geology department) of the Smithsonian Institution from 1919; assistant curator, 1919–29; curator, 1929–48; head curator, 1948–56. Responsible for bringing the Roebling and Canfield collections of minerals to the museum in 1926. Stimulated and supervised research in mineralogy and crystallography. The major observer and documentator of Paricutín volcano in Mexico, 1943–52, Foshag wrote *Birth and Development of Paricutín Volcano* (1956) with Jenaro González.

FOSS, CYRUS DAVID (*b. Kingston, N.Y., 1834; d. Philadelphia, Pa., 1910*), Methodist Episcopal clergyman. President of Wesleyan University, Middletown, Conn., 1875–80; as bishop, *post* 1880, traveled widely on missionary tours around the world.

FOSS, SAM WALTER (*b. Candia, N.H., 1858; d. 1911*), poet, journalist. Graduated Brown, 1882. Worked as editor and humorous columnist on Massachusetts newspapers; *post* 1898 was librarian in Somerville, Mass. Best known for poem "The House by the Side of the Road" in *Dreams in Homespun* (1898).

FOSTER, ABIEL (*b. Andover, Mass., 1735; d. 1806*), Congregational clergyman. Actively supported Revolution; served in New Hampshire legislature. As congressman from New Hampshire, 1789–91 and 1795–1803, was staunch Federalist.

FOSTER, ABIGAIL KELLEY (*b. Pelham, Mass., 1810; d. 1887*), abolitionist lecturer, woman's rights advocate. Wife of Stephen S. Foster.

FOSTER, BENJAMIN (*b. North Anson, Maine, 1852; d. New York, N.Y., 1926*), landscape painter, art critic. Studied with Abbott Thayer and in Paris. An individual depicter of the quiet, meditative moods of nature.

FOSTER, CHARLES (*b. Fostoria, Ohio, 1828; d. Fostoria, 1904*), merchant. Republican congressman from Ohio, 1871–79; governor of Ohio, 1880–84;; U.S. secretary of the treasury, 1891–93. Efficient in office but unspectacular.

FOSTER, CHARLES JAMES (*b. Bicester, England, 1820; d. Astoria, N.Y., 1883*), sports editor. Came to America, 1848. Authority on history of the turf; wrote for *Porter's* (later *Wilkes's*) *Spirit of the Times.*

FOSTER, DAVID SKAATS (*b. Utica, N.Y., 1852; d. 1920*), merchant. Author of facile, sentimental novels crowded with action and superficial humor.

FOSTER, EPHRAIM HUBBARD (*b. near Bardstown, Ky., 1794; d. 1854*), prominent Nashville, Tenn., lawyer and Whig leader. U.S. senator, 1838–39 and 1843–45; voted against admission of Texas.

FOSTER, FRANK HUGH (*b. Springfield, Mass., 1851; d. 1935*), Congregational clergyman, theologian. Graduated Harvard, 1873; Ph.D., Leipzig, 1882. Author of many books, including *A Genetic History of the New England Theology* 1907.

FOSTER, FRANK PIERCE (*b. Concord, N.H., 1841; d. 1911*), physician, immunologist, editor. Graduated College of Physicians and Surgeons, New York, 1862. Pioneered in use of animal lymph as vaccine; edited *New York Medical Journal*, 1880–1911;

compiled *Illustrated Encyclopedic Medical Dictionary* (1888–94).

FOSTER, GEORGE BURMAN (*b. Alderson, W.Va., 1858; d. 1918*), Baptist clergyman, educator. Professor at McMaster University and University of Chicago; an articulate liberal in theology, he regarded religion as something experimental and almost wholly pragmatically sanctioned.

FOSTER, HANNAH WEBSTER (*b. Boston, Mass., 1759; d. Montreal, Canada, 1840*). Author of *The Coquette: or, The History of Eliza Wharton* (1797), a widely read roman à clef, and *The Boarding School* (1798).

FOSTER, JOHN (*b. Dorchester, Mass., 1648; d. Dorchester, 1681*), printer, earliest wood engraver in English America. Chief among some ten woodcuts attributed to him are a portrait of Richard Mather, a 1677 map of New England, and a view of Boston and Charlestown.

FOSTER, JOHN GRAY (*b. Whitefield, N.H., 1823; d. 1874*), army officer, engineer. Graduated West Point, 1846. Author of an important journal and reports of the attack on Fort Sumter, where he was serving as captain, 1861. He held important field commands in the Union army and was promoted major general, 1862.

FOSTER, JOHN PIERREPONT CODRINGTON (*b. New Haven, Conn., 1847; d. 1910*), tuberculosis specialist. Graduated Yale, 1869; M.D., Yale, 1875. Practiced and taught at Yale; was first in America to experiment with Koch's tuberculin; advocated rest and fresh-air cures.

FOSTER, JOHN WATSON (*b. Pike Co., Ind., 1836; d. 1917*), lawyer, Union soldier, diplomat. Graduated Indiana University, 1855. Practiced at Evansville, Ind., and after Civil War edited *Evansville Daily Journal*. U.S. minister to Mexico, 1873–80; to Russia, 1880–81; to Spain, 1883–84. Acted as U.S. agent in Bering Sea arbitration, and was secretary of state, 1892–93. Author of *A Century of American Diplomacy: 1776–1876* (1900), *Diplomatic Memoirs* (1909), and other works.

FOSTER, JUDITH ELLEN HORTON (*b. Lowell, Mass., 1840; d. 1910*), lawyer, temperance reformer. Practiced in Clinton, Iowa.

FOSTER, LAFAYETTE SABINE (*b. Franklin, Conn., 1806; d. 1880*), lawyer. Graduated Brown, 1828. Practiced at Norwich, Conn.; edited *Norwich Republican*, U.S. senator, Whig, from Connecticut, 1855–67. Justice, state superior court, 1870–76.

FOSTER, MURPHY JAMES (*b. near Franklin, La., 1849; d. New Orleans, La., 1921*), lawyer. Served in state senate, 1880–92, and led fight against renewal of Louisiana lottery charter. Was Democratic governor of Louisiana, 1892–1900; U.S. senator, 1900–13.

FOSTER, RANDOLPH SINKS (*b. Williamsburg, Ohio, 1820; d. 1903*), Methodist Episcopal clergyman. Held pastorates in western Virginia and Ohio, and in and about New York City; was author of popular books on Methodist beliefs. President of Northwestern University, 1857–60, and of Drew Theological Seminary, 1870–72; elected bishop, 1872.

FOSTER, ROBERT SANFORD (*b. Vernon, Ind., 1834; d. Indianapolis, Ind., 1903*), Union soldier. Held brigade and divisional commands in eastern theater of the Civil War, rising to rank of brigadier general in able but unspectacular service.

FOSTER, ROGER SHERMAN BALDWIN (*b. Worcester, Mass., 1857; d. 1924*), lawyer. Graduated Yale, 1878; Columbia Law School, 1880. Practiced in New York City, specializing in tax law, corporation law, and constitutional cases. Drafted New York Tenement House Act, 1895; expressed decisive opinion in Homestead trials, 1892. Author of, among other books, *Commentaries on the Constitution* (1895) which established his reputation as an authority on constitutional law.

FOSTER, STEPHEN COLLINS (*b. Pittsburgh, Pa., 1826; d. New York, N.Y., 1864*), composer. He began as a bookkeeper in his brother's office at Cincinnati, Ohio. After publication of "Louisiana Belle," "O Susanna," "Uncle Ned," and "Away Down South" in *Songs of the Sable Harmonists* (1848), he turned to music for a livelihood. In writing songs for the then popular black minstrel troupes, Foster found his best medium. In 1851, he sold to E. P. Christy the privilege of singing his songs from manuscript before their formal appearance, reserving to himself all publication rights. Among his greatest songs were "The Old Folks at Home" (1851), "Massa's in the Cold Ground" (1852), "My Old Kentucky Home" and "Old Dog Tray" (both 1853), and "Old Black Joe" (1860). Foster probably visited the South only once. Living in New York after 1860, he wrote ceaselessly, but his music grew reiterative and commonplace and he spent his last years in poverty. His best songs gave permanent expression to the nostalgic melancholy of the American black and remain a valuable contribution to the folk literature of American music.

FOSTER, STEPHEN SYMONDS (*b. Canterbury, N.H., 1809; d. 1881*), farmer, reformer. Graduated Dartmouth, 1838. Was associated with extremist wing of abolitionists and second only to W. L. Garrison in activity in early years of agitation. Author of *The Brotherhood of Thieves* (1843), a vitriolic attack on organized religion.

FOSTER, THEODORE (*b. Brookfield, Mass., 1752; d. Providence, R.I., 1828*), lawyer, antiquarian. Rhode Island legislator and jurist. U.S. senator, Federalist, 1790–1803.

FOSTER, THOMAS JEFFERSON (*b. Pottsville, Pa., 1843; d. Scranton, Pa., 1936*), journalist. Founder, 1901, of the International Correspondence Schools.

FOSTER, WILLIAM TRUFANT (*b. Boston, Mass., 1879; d. Jaffrey, N.H., 1950*), educator, writer on economics. B.A., Harvard, 1901; M.A., 1904. Ph.D., Teachers College, Columbia, 1911. First president of Reed College, Portland, Oreg., until 1919; thereafter director of the Pollak Foundation of Economic Research. Coauthor of, among other works, *The Road to Plenty* (1928).

FOSTER, WILLIAM Z. (*b. Taunton, Mass., 1881; d. Moscow, Russia, 1961*), Communist leader and labor organizer. Joined the Socialist party in 1901. Member of the Industrial Workers of the World, 1909–12. Founded the Syndicalist League of North America in 1912, to mobilize radical unionists within the American Federation of Labor. Founded the Independent Trade Union Educational League in 1915. Organized the steel industry for the great strike of 1919. Secretary general of the American Communist party from 1921. The party's presidential candidate in 1924, 1928, and 1932. Party chairman, 1945–46; chairman emeritus, 1957–61.

FOULK, GEORGE CLAYTON (*b. Marietta, Pa., 1856; d. Kyoto, Japan, 1893*), naval officer, diplomat. Graduated Annapolis, 1876. Served under great stress and with ability as naval attaché and head of American mission in Korea, 1885–87; later taught mathematics at Kyoto.

FOULKE, WILLIAM DUDLEY (*b. New York, N.Y., 1848; d. 1935*), lawyer, leader in civic reform. LL.B., Columbia, 1871. Practiced in New York City and *post ca.* 1876 in Richmond, Ind.;

gave special attention to civil service reform and woman suffrage; was associate of Lucius B. Swift and his biographer.

FOULOIS, BENJAMIN DELAHAUF (*b. Washington, Conn., 1879; d. Andrews Air Force Base, Md., 1967*), army officer and aviator. Piloted the army's first dirigible balloon in 1908; given command of *Military Aeroplane No. 1* in 1910. Organized the army's first tactical air unit; commanded the First Aero Squadron in operations in Mexico in 1916. Responsible for drawing up and implementing plans for the rapid expansion of the air arm in 1917; these plans laid the foundation for the postwar Air Service. Commanded Mitchel Field, N.Y., 1925–27. Assistant chief of the Air Corp in 1927; chief of the Air Corp in 1931. Believing that strategic bombing could achieve decisive results in a war, he consolidated all tactical units into an offensive striking force, pushed for development of long-range bombers, and had introduced into service the B-17 in 1935. Retired a major general in 1935.

FOWKE, GERARD (*b. near Maysville, Ky., 1855; d. 1933*), archaeologist. Author of *Archaeological History of Ohio: The Mound Builders and the Later Indians* (1902) and *The Evolution of the Ohio River* (1933).

FOWLE, DANIEL (*b. Charlestown, Mass., 1715; d. 1787*), printer. In partnership with Gamaliel Rogers, 1740–50, published at Boston a number of books and *The American Magazine and Historical Chronicle* (1743–46); also published *The Independent Advertiser*, a weekly newspaper, 1748–50. Fowle removed to Portsmouth, N.H., 1756, and was the first printer in New Hampshire.

FOWLE, WILLIAM BENTLEY (*b. Boston, Mass., 1795; d. Medfield, Mass., 1865*), bookseller, educator. Nephew of William Bentley. Organized a monitorial school in Boston, 1821, in which he introduced blackboards, map drawing, and written spelling lessons, and abolished corporal punishment. In 1823 took charge of Female Monitorial School , which was probably first American school to have adequate scientific apparatus and where he introduced study of vocal and instrumental music, calisthenics, needlework. Wrote more than 50 textbooks and gave scientific lectures. Was publisher, and from 1848 to 1852 editor, of Horace Mann's *Common School Journal*; served as one of Mann's ablest assistants in the Teachers' Institute.

FOWLER, CHARLES HENRY (*b. Burford, Canada, 1837; d. 1908*), Methodist Epicopal clergyman. Gifted administrator and preacher, he was president of Northwestern University, 1873–77, and editor of *Christian Advocate*, 1876–80. Active in missionary work, he was elected bishop, 1884.

FOWLER, FRANK (*b. Brooklyn, N.Y., 1852; d. 1910*), painter, critic. Studied under Edwin White and Carolus Duran; excelled in portraits.

FOWLER, GENE (*b. Denver, Colo., 1890; d. Los Angeles, Calif., 1960*), author, journalist. Studied briefly at the University of Colorado. Reporter for the *Denver Post* (1914–18) before joining the staff of the *New York American* , becoming managing editor in 1925. Left journalism in 1931 and wrote several screenplays, including *Call of the Wild* (1935), *A Message to Garcia* (1936), and *Billy the Kid* (1941). His books include *Shoe the Wild Mare* (1931) and *Goodnight, Sweet Prince* , a best-selling biography of John Barrymore.

FOWLER, GEORGE RYERSON (*b. New York, N.Y., 1848; d. 1906*), surgeon. Graduated Bellevue Hospital Medical College, 1871. Specialized in abdominal surgery; author of classic *Treatise on Appendicitis* (1894) and *Treatise on Surgery* (1906). Introduced class instruction in first aid.

FOWLER, JOSEPH SMITH (*b. Steubenville, Ohio, 1820; d. Washington, D.C., 1902*), educator, lawyer, Unionist. U.S. senator from Tennessee, 1866–71. Supported Reconstruction acts but voted against President Andrew Johnson's impeachment, on grounds that the action was a plot of "mere politicians"; supported Greeley in 1872.

FOWLER, ORIN (*b. Lebanon, Conn., 1791; d. Washington, D.C., 1852*), Congregational clergyman, politician. Pastor in Plainfield, Conn., and Fall River, Mass. As congressman, Free-Soil Whig, from Massachusetts, 1849–52, advocated temperance laws and cheap postage.

FOWLER, ORSON SQUIRE (*b. Cohocton, N.Y., 1809; d. near Sharon Station, Conn., 1887*), phrenologist. An immensely popular lecturer and writer of inordinate self-conceit, he happily interwove scientific facts with popular superstitions and personal fancy.

FOWLER, RUSSELL STORY (*b. Brooklyn, N.Y., 1874; d. Brooklyn, N.Y., 1959*), surgeon. Graduated from the College of Physicians and Surgeons of Columbia University, M.D., 1895. Associated with the German Hospital (later Wyckoff Heights Hospital) in New York from the mid-1890's until his death; specialist in abdominal surgery. A founder and governor of the American College of Surgeons, 1913. Author of *The Operating Room and the Patient* (1906).

FOX, CHARLES KEMBLE (*b. Boston, Mass., 1833; d. New York, N.Y., 1875*), actor. Brother of George W. L. Fox, with whose career he was closely associated.

FOX, DIXON RYAN (*b. Potsdam, N.Y., 1887; d. Schenectady, N.Y., 1945*), historian, educator. Graduated Potsdam Normal School, 1907; Columbia College, 1911. Ph.D., Columbia, 1917. Taught history at Columbia, 1913–34; professor *post* 1927. President of Union College, 1934–45. Author of, among other works, *The Decline of Aristocracy in the Politics of New York* (1919); *Caleb Heathcote: Gentleman Colonist* (1926); and *Yankees and Yorkers* (1940). Coeditor of the History of American Life series (1927–48), which represented his lifelong interest in social and economic forces as shapers of local and national politics. President, New York State Historical Association, 1929–45.

FOX, FONTAINE TALBOT, JR. (*b. Louisville, Ky., 1884; d. Greenwich, Conn., 1964*), cartoonist. Worked for the *Louisville Herald* (1906), the *Louisville Times* (1907–11), and the *Chicago Post* (1911–15). From 1915, he sold his comic strip "Toonerville Folks" to feature syndicates until his retirement in 1955. It appeared in more than 200 daily newspapers with circulations in the millions. A lively and inventive commentary on the people and places along the tracks of a mythical trolley line, the strip's themes reflected a nation suffering the growing pains caused by the shift from an agrarian to an urban society.

FOX, GEORGE WASHINGTON LAFAYETTE (*b. Boston, Mass., 1825; d. Cambridge, Mass., 1877*), actor, manager. An excellent comedian and the greatest pantomimist of his time, he had his principal success in a series of fantasies about "Humpty Dumpty," *post* 1868.

FOX, GILBERT (*b. England, 1776; d. 1807[?]*), engraver, actor, singer. Came to Philadelphia as assistant to Edward Trenchard, 1795; taught drawing; as singer, induced Joseph Hopkinson to write "Hail, Columbia," 1798.

FOX, GUSTAVUS VASA (*b. Saugus, Mass., 1821; d. New York, N.Y., 1883*), naval officer, assistant secretary of the navy, 1861–66. Appointed midshipman, 1841. Resigned from navy, 1856, to enter business as mill agent. Suggested plan for relief of Fort Sumter, February 1861; evacuated Major Anderson and garrison in April. As assistant secretary, *post* August 1861, suggested D. G. Farragut as commander of New Orleans expedition; was early advocate of *Monitor*; gave indispensable support to Gideon Welles.

FOX, HARRY (*b. Westfield, Mass., 1826; d. Salt Lake City, Utah, 1883*), contractor, railroad constructor. Removed to Chicago, Ill., 1856, where he was a leader in the topographical improvement of the city.

FOX, JOHN WILLIAM (*b. Stony Point, Ky., 1863; d. Big Stone Gap. Va., 1919*), novelist. Described life of Kentucky mountaineers in *A Cumberland Vendetta* (1895); *The Little Shepherd of Kingdom Come* (1903); *Trail of the Lonesome Pine* (1908); and other very popular works.

FOX, MARGARET (*b. Canada, 1833; d. Brooklyn, N.Y., 1893*), medium. Raised in upper New York State. Produced "spirit" rappings with her toes; admitted her trickery, 1888, but retracted her confession and continued to practice until her death.

FOX, RICHARD KYLE (*b. Belfast, Ireland, 1846; d. Red Bank, N.J., 1922*), journalist. Came to America, 1874. Made *National Police Gazette* America's most lurid journal, but then gradually transformed it into an intelligent sports and theatrical paper.

FOX, WILLIAM (*b. Tulchva, Hungary, 1879; d. New York, N.Y., 1952*), film producer. Founder of the Fox Film Co. (1915), which became Twentieth Century-Fox in 1935. Producer of *Carmen* (1915), with Geraldine Farrar. Other films include *Seventh Heaven* (1927), *What Price Glory?* (1927), *Evangeline* (1929), *Cleopatra* (1934), *Les Miserables* (1935), and *A Tale of Two Cities* (1935). Pioneered in talking pictures and created Fox Movietone News. Beset by lawsuits related to bankruptcy proceedings, Fox served one year in jail for obstruction of justice, 1941–42.

FOX, WILLIAMS CARLTON (*b. St. Louis, Mo., 1855; d. New York, N.Y., 1924*), diplomat. Served in Germany, Persia, Greece, Ecuador; published *Diplomatic and Consular Review*; was director of Pan American Union.

FOXALL, HENRY (*b. Monmouthshire, England, 1758; d. Handsworth, England, 1823*), iron founder. Came to America, 1797. Operated Columbian Foundry at Georgetown, D.C., 1800–15; produced heavy guns and shot for the government and rendered valuable service in War of 1812.

FOXX, JAMES EMORY (*b. near Sudlersville, Md., 1907; d. Miami, Fla., 1967*), baseball player. Reached stardom in 1929 with the Philadelphia Athletics, who in that year won the first of three straight American League pennants and two straight World Series. His best all-around season was 1932, when Foxx hit .364, drove home 169 runs, and came within two of tying Babe Ruth's all-time season home run record of 60. A highly capable fielder as well, Foxx was voted the American League's Most Valuable Player by the Baseball Writers Association in 1932 and 1933. Traded to the Boston Red Sox in 1935; played with the Chicago Cubs (1944) and Philadelphia's National League team (1945) before retiring in 1945. Foxx's lifetime batting average was .325; he hit 534 career home runs. Named to the Baseball Hall of Fame in 1951.

FOY, EDDIE (*b. New York, N.Y., 1856; d. Kansas City, Mo., 1928*), comedian. Born Edwin Fitzgerald. Raised in Chicago, Ill. His career led him from western towns and mining camps to stardom as eccentric farceur; played vaudeville with his children, billed as the Seven Little Foys, 1913–23.

FRALEY, FREDERICK (*b. Philadelphia, Pa., 1804; d. Philadelphia, 1901*), merchant, banker. Cofounder of Franklin Institute; president of American Philosophical Society, 1880–1901.

FRAME, ALICE SEYMOUR BROWNE (*b. Harput, Turkey, 1878; d. Newton, Mass., 1941*), Congregational missionary, educator. Born of missionary parents; graduated Mount Holyoke, 1900. B.D., Hartford Theological Seminary, 1903. At work in China for the greater part of her life *post* 1905, she headed the North China College for Women, 1922–31. A capable administrator and a strong feminist, she set high standards for her students and fought to maintain the financial and academic autonomy of the college as against Yenching University, with which it was affiliated. In 1913, she married Murray S. Frame, a fellow missionary, who died in 1918.

FRANCHÈRE, GABRIEL (*b. Montreal, Canada, 1786; d. St. Paul, Minn., 1863*), fur trader. As employee of John Jacob Astor, sailed on the *Tonquin* from New York to the Columbia River, 1810–11; helped found Astoria. Returned overland to Montreal, 1814; acted as Astor's agent there and at Sault Ste. Marie. Later established his own fur-trading company in New York. Franchère's published reminiscences of Astoria (*Relation d'un Voyage à la Côte du Nord Ouest de l'Amérique Septentrionale*, 1820) were utilized by Senator Benton during the Oregon controversy, 1846. Washington Irving relied on them as source for his *Astoria*.

FRANCIS, CHARLES SPENCER (*b. Troy, N.Y., 1853; d. 1911*), editor, diplomat. Son of John M. Francis, whom he succeeded as owner and editor of the Troy *Times*. An important figure in state and national Republican politics, he served as U.S. minister to Greece, Romania, and Serbia, and as ambassador to Austria-Hungary.

FRANCIS, CHARLES STEPHEN (*b. Boston, Mass., 1805; d. Tarrytown, N.Y., 1887*), New York City bookseller, publisher, 1826–70.

FRANCIS, CONVERS (*b. Menotomy, Mass., 1795; d. 1863*), Unitarian clergyman, educator. Graduated Harvard, 1815. Succeeded Henry Ware as professor at Harvard Divinity School, 1842–63; an outstanding theologian, he early utilized German scholarship.

FRANCIS, DAVID ROWLAND (*b. Richmond, Ky., 1850; d. 1927*), grain merchant. Democratic mayor of St. Louis, Mo., 1885–89; governor of Missouri, 1889–93; secretary of the interior, 1896. Defended creation of forest reserves. Served under great stress as U.S. ambassador to Russia, 1916–18.

FRANCIS, JAMES BICHENO (*b. Southleigh, England, 1815; d. Lowell, Mass., 1892*), hydraulic engineer. Came to America, 1833. Helped construct Stonington Railroad. Built locomotives for the "Proprietors of the Locks and Canals on the Merrimack River"; as company's chief engineer and general manager *post* 1837, developed waterpower facilities at Lowell, Mass., and contributed heavily to Lowell's rise as industrial center. Designed mixed-flow turbine; published *The Lowell Hydraulic Experiments* (1855). Also devised a pioneer fire-protection water system for Lowell and hydraulic lifts for gates on Pawtucket Canal.

FRANCIS, JOHN BROWN (*b. Philadelphia, Pa., 1791; d. Warwick, R.I., 1864*), merchant. Grandson of John Brown (1736–1803). Anti-Masonic and Democratic governor of Rhode Island, 1833–38; U.S. senator, 1844–45. Strongly influenced education in Rhode Island.

FRANCIS, JOHN MORGAN (*b. Plattsburg, N.Y., 1823; d. 1897*), editor, publicist, diplomat. Father of Charles Spencer Francis. As proprietor-editor of the *Times* of Troy, N.Y., *post* 1851, supported Republican party from its beginnings; served as U.S. minister to Greece, Portugal, and Austria-Hungary.

FRANCIS, JOHN WAKEFIELD (*b. New York, N.Y., 1789; d. New York, 1861*), physician. Graduated Columbia, 1809; studied medicine with David Hosack and was first graduate of College of Physicians and Surgeons, New York, 1811. Was the city's leading obstetrician and active in all phases of the city's social and literary life.

FRANCIS, JOSEPH (*b. Boston, Mass., 1801; d. Cooperstown, N.Y., 1893*), inventor, manufacturer. Early interested in unsinkable boats, he patented an unsinkable lifeboat, 1838, which had great commercial success. In 1845 he received a patent for use of corrugated metal in all types of boat construction; later he adapted this technique for manufacture of watertight army wagons. Extending his business to Europe, he built a fleet of light-draft corrugated iron steamers for use on Aral Sea. Author of a *History of Life-Saving Appliances* (1885).

FRANCIS, KAY (*b. Oklahoma City, Okla., 1905; d. New York, N.Y., 1968*), actress. Started her acting career on Broadway in 1927, made her movie debut in 1929; contracted with Warner Brothers in 1931, where she remained for most of her acting career. Often teamed with William Powell or George Brent, Kay's films were society dramas of the soap opera variety, which stereotyped her as ultrasophisticated and chic. In the 1930's she was one of Hollywood's most popular and highest-paid actresses. Her films include *Jewel Robbery* (1932), *One-Way Pasage* 1932), *The Keyhole* (1934), *The House on 56th Street* (1933), and *Give Me Your Heart* (1936).

FRANCIS, PAUL JAMES (*b. Millington, Md., 1863; d. Graymoor, N.Y., 1940*), Episcopal clergyman, Roman Catholic priest. Founded the Society of the Atonement under the Franciscan rule, 1898; entered the Roman Catholic church with his friars, 1909.

FRANCIS, SAMUEL WARD (*b. New York, N.Y., 1835; d. Newport, R.I., 1886*), physician, author, inventor. Son of John W. Francis. Patented a number of devices, including a "printing machine" which anticipated the typewriter.

FRANCIS, TENCH (*b. Ireland, date unknown; d. Philadelphia, Pa., 1758*), lawyer. Came to America *ante* 1720 as attorney for Lord Baltimore; removed from Talbot Co., Md., to Philadelphia, 1738, and became leader of Pennsylvania bar. Attorney general of Pennsylvania, 1741–55.

FRANCK, JAMES (*b. Hamburg, Germany, 1882; d. Göttingen, Germany, 1964*), physicist. Studied at the University of Berlin (Ph.D., 1906). Professor of physics and director of the Second Physical Institute at the University of Göttingen, 1920–33. Visiting professorships at Johns Hopkins, and at Bohr's institute in Copenhagen (1933–35). Immigrated to the United States in 1935; naturalized in 1941. Professor of physical chemistry at Johns Hopkins (1935–38); and at the University of Chicago (1938–49). Shared the 1925 Nobel Prize with Gustav Hertz, for the discovery of excitation potentials in collisions between electrons and atoms. Formulated the Franck-Condon principle with Edward Condon, which remains fundamental in describing the physical properties of molecules. In charge of the chemistry division of the Manhattan Projects' Metallurgical Laboratory from 1942. Became a symbol of the social responsibility of concerned scientists with the issuance of the "Franck Report" (1945) which counseled against the use of atomic bombs on Japanese cities and advocated international control of nuclear weapons.

FRANCKE, KUNO (*b. Kiel, Germany, 1855; d. Cambridge, Mass., 1930*), historian, philologist. Came to America, 1884, as instructor in German at Harvard; professor of German culture, Harvard, 1896–1917. Author of *Social Forces in German Literature* (1896); founded Harvard Germanic Museum.

FRANK, GLENN (*b. Queen City, Mo., 1887; d. near Greenleaf, Wis., 1940*), editor, publicist. Graduated Northwestern University, 1912; became executive assistant to its president, then a research assistant to the reform-minded Boston merchant Edward A. Filene. Associate editor and editor in chief, *Century* magazine, 1919–25; an optimistic advocate of social reform. As president of the University of Wisconsin, he initiated the Experimental College, 1927–32, and the Short Course in Agriculture. Increasingly critical of the New Deal, he fell into disfavor with the dominant La Follette faction and with the university's board of regents, and was dismissed in 1937. He was seeking the Republican nomination for U.S. senator when he died in an automobile accident.

FRANK, JEROME (*b. New York, N.Y., 1889; d. New Haven, Conn., 1957*), judge, legal philosopher, author. Graduated from the University of Chicago, Ph.B., 1909, and University of Chicago Law School, 1912. General counsel to the Agricultural Adjustment Administration and the Federal Surplus Relief Corporation, 1933–35; special counsel to the Reconstruction Finance Corporation, 1935–36; chairman of the Securities and Exchange Commission, 1939–41. Judge of the U.S. Circuit Court of Appeals for the Second Circuit, 1941–57. An advocate of legal realism, Frank pioneered in applying psychology and social realities to interpretation of the law.

FRANK, LAWRENCE KELSO (*b. Cincinnati, Ohio, 1890; d. Melmont, Mass., 1968*), social scientist and author. Studied at Columbia (B.A., 1912). An effective foundation director associated with the Laura Spelman Rockefeller Memorial (1923–30), the Laura Spelman Rockefeller Fund (1930–31), the General Education Board (1931–36), the Josiah Macy, Jr., Foundation (1936–42), and the Caroline Zachary Institute of Human Development (1945–50). Wrote prolifically on the subject of human development. His work ranged from chatty and informal columns to erudite and provocative essays. Among his books are *Nature and Human Nature* (1951), *Babies Are Puppies, Puppies Are Babies* (1953), and *Feelings and Emotions* (1954). Best remembered for expanding and enriching the role of the foundation both in research and in the implementation of new ideas in social theory, Frank was also a valued collaborator who had a stimulating, critical, and widely acknowledged effect on many prominent thinkers in the social sciences.

FRANK, PHILIPP G. (*b. Vienna, Austria, 1884; d. [?], 1966*), mathematician, physicist, philosopher of science, and educator. Studied at the University of Vienna (Ph.D., 1906) and the University of Göttingen. A productive theoretical physicist, his major interest became the interrelationship between science and philosophy. Published *Das Kausalgesetz und seine Grenzen* (1932), detailing his thoughts on causality as it applied to quantum mechanics. Frank and his colleagues were referred to as logical positivists or logical empiricists; in the late 1920's their group became widely known as the Vienna Circle. Taught at the University of Vienna (1920–12), the German University of Prague (1912–38), and Harvard (1939–54). Contributed to the revision of a standard text for generations of European physics students, Riemann and Weber's *Die Differential- und Integralgleichungen der Mechanik und Physik* (1925–27). Helped found the Institute for the Unity of Science in 1947; president from 1948–65. Editor of *Synthèse* (1946–63); associate editor of the *Journal of Unified Science* (1939–40), and of *Philosophy of Science* (1941–55). Other books include *Einstein: His Life and Times* (1947), and *Philosophy of Science* (1957).

FRANK, TENNEY (*b. near Clay Center, Kans., 1876; d. Oxford, England, 1939*), classical scholar. Graduated University of Kansas, 1898; Ph.D., Chicago, 1903. Taught Latin at Bryn Mawr, 1904–19, and Johns Hopkins, 1919–39. His fresh and revealing interpretations of Roman civilization combine the disciplines of history, literature, and archaeology. His books include biographies of Vergil (1922), Catullus and Horace (1928), *History of Rome* (1923), and *Economic History of Rome to the End of the Republic* (1920). He planned, edited, and wrote two volumes of the series An Economic Survey of Ancient Rome, one of the first large cooperative enterprises in American classical scholarship.

FRANK, WALDO DAVID (*b. Long Branch, N.J., 1889; d. White Plains, N.Y., 1967*), writer. Studied at Yale (B.A. and M.A., 1911). An experimental writer and radical cultural critic of the American scene, Frank established a lifelong pattern of activism coupled with prolific writing. Cofounder and editor of *The Seven Arts*, 1916–17. A regular contributor to the *New Yorker*, the *New Republic*, and the *New Masses*. His books include *Our America* (1919), *Rahab* (1922), *Virgin Spain* (1926), *The Rediscovery of America* (1929), *Death and Birth of David Markand* (1934), *Birth of a World* (1951), and *Cuba: Prophetic Island* (1961).

FRANKFURTER, ALFRED MORITZ (*b. Chicago, Ill., 1906; d. Jerusalem, Israel, 1965*), art critic and connoisseur. Studied at Princeton and the Institute for Art History in Berlin. Over the period of 1927 to 1934, art critic at *International Studio*, *The Antiquarian*, and *Fine Arts*. Editor, *Art News*, 1936–65. With his deputy (and successor) Thomas B. Hess, made *Art News* an important publication in his time, promoting contemporary movements and recruiting high-quality European and U.S. contributors.

FRANKFURTER, FELIX (*b. Vienna, Austria, 1882; d. Washington, D.C., 1965*), legal scholar and Supreme Court justice. Immigrated to the United States in 1894. Studied at the College of the City of New York and Harvard Law School (graduated, 1906). General assistant to Henry L. Stimson in the office of the United States attorney, 1906–09. Served as legal officer of the Bureau of Insular Affairs under Stimson, 1911–13. One of the first contributing editors of the *New Republic*. Professor of law at Harvard, 1914–39. One of the original members of the American Civil Liberties Union, 1920. Adviser to President Franklin D. Roosevelt from 1935. Elected to the U.S. Supreme Court in 1939. Exponent of the doctrine of judicial self-restraint. Retired in 1962. His books include *The Business of the Supreme Court* (with James M. Landis, 1927), *The Labor Injunction* (with Nathan Greene, 1930), and *The Case of Sacco and Vanzetti* (1927).

FRANKLAND, AGNES SURRIAGE (*b. Marblehead, Mass., 1726; d. Chichester, England, 1783*), Boston social figure. Wife of Sir Charles Henry Frankland; heroine of a 'rags-to-riches' romance which has served as basis for a poem by O. W. Holmes and a novel by E. L. Bynner.

FRANKLIN, BENJAMIN (*b. Boston, Mass., 1706; d. Philadelphia, Pa., 1790*), printer, author, philanthropist, inventor, statesman, diplomat, scientist. Son of Josiah and Abiah (Folger) Franklin. Attended Boston Grammar School and George Brownell's school for writing and arithmetic; at age 10 was employed in his father's business of tallow chandler and soap boiler; at 12 was apprenticed in the printing shop of his brother

James. Repeated quarrels with James led Benjamin to leave Boston for Philadelphia, where he arrived in October 1723.

He had already gone far in that close application to study and self-improvement which was one secret of his success. He had read Bunyan, Plutarch, Defoe, Cotton Mather, Tryon on "vegetable diet," Cocker's arithmetic, Seller on navigation, Locke's *Essays*, Shaftesbury and Collins, and Xenophon's *Memorabilia*. He improved his style by rewriting essays in Addison's *Spectator* from memory and checking them against the originals. He was delighted when his brother printed in the *New England Courant* essays which Benjamin had slipped beneath the door of the shop under the pen name of "Silence Dogood."

At Philadelphia, Benjamin obtained employment as a printer; was urged by Governor Keith to set up a shop of his own. On Keith's promise of money to buy equipment, Benjamin went to London, 1724; Keith's promise unfulfilled, he found work as a printer and wrote *A Dissertation on Liberty and Necessity* (1725), a refutation of Wollaston's *Religion of Nature Delineated*. Back in Philadelphia in 1726, he became by 1730 the sole owner of a printing business and of *The Pennsylvania Gazette*. He married Deborah Read in the same year and devoted himself to business until 1748. His thrift and industry won him prosperity; the chief reasons for his success, however, were his capacity for making influential friends, his uncanny instinct for advertising himself and his paper, and, above all, the sense, novelty, and charm of his writings. His almanac, sold as *Poor Richard's* (1732–57) and credited to a supposititious "Richard Saunders," abounded with homely aphorisms which Franklin pilfered and adapted from everywhere, and made the author's name a household word throughout the colonies.

Franklin's efforts at self-improvement led him to study French, Spanish, Italian, and Latin; in the Junto, a debating club which he had founded in 1727, he perfected himself in the arts of oral persuasion. He regarded religion as a useful sanction for the practice of virtue. He believed in one God who made all things and governs the world through His providence; who is to be worshipped by adoration, prayer, and thanksgiving; who will certainly reward virtue and punish vice; and to whom the most acceptable service consists in doing good to men. Franklin believed in the immortality of the soul and devised a list of 13 useful virtues: Temperance, Silence, Order, Resolution, Frugality, Industry, Sincerity, Justice, Moderation, Cleanliness, Tranquillity, Chastity, and Humility. He assiduously devoted himself to practicing one virtue a week and went through "a course compleat in 13 weeks, and four courses a year." The outward expressions of his passion for improvement were his promotion of a city police force; of improved paving, cleaning, and lighting of streets; of a circulating library; of the American Philosophical Society (founded 1743); of a city hospital (1751); and of an Academy for the Education of Youth. He served as clerk of the Pennsylvania Assembly, 1736–51, as member for Philadelphia, 1751–64; he was deputy postmaster at Philadelphia, 1737–53, and, jointly with William Hunter, deputy postmaster general for the colonies, 1753–74.

His interest in science ("natural philosophy") was awakened probably in England. As early as 1737 he was writing in the *Gazette* on earthquakes; by 1741 he had invented the "Pennsylvania fireplace," a stove with an open firebox which heated rooms better at less expense. Every sort of natural phenomenon interested him and called forth some ingenious idea. Feeling that he had a sufficient income from real estate and a partnership arrangement with David Hall, his printing-house foreman, he turned in 1748 to full-time occupation with "philosophical studies and amusements." His leisure lasted only six years, but during this time he made those electrical experiments on which his fame as a scientist rests. He had become interested in electricity *ca.* 1743; thereafter, his correspondence is filled with the record of his varied experiments. He was not the first to suggest the identity of lightning and electricity, but in a letter of 1750 proposed a method of testing the theory by erecting an iron rod on a high tower or steeple. The famous kite experiment, performed in the summer of 1752 and described by Franklin in a letter in the *Pennsylvania Gazette* (Oct. 19), was a simpler employment of the same method. *Experiments and Observations on Electricity . . . by Mr. Benjamin Franklin* (London, 1751, and reprinted with additions in 1753) embodied the results and method of his experiments, was translated into French, and won him general recognition. Harvard and Yale gave him the degree of master of arts, 1753, as did William and Mary, 1756.

Public affairs claimed him thereafter. He had represented Pennsylvania at the Albany Congress, 1754, where his "Plan of Union" was considered to have "too much prerogative in it" for the taste of the colonial assemblies and was judged too democratic in England. In 1757, he went to England to present to Parliament the grievance of the Pennsylvania Assembly against the proprietors of the province, notably the claim of the Penn heirs to be exempt from taxation. This matter was settled in 1760 but Franklin remained in England, becoming intimate with Collinson, Priestly, Strahan, and others, and corresponding with Lord Kames, and Hume, the philosopher. He received degrees of LL.D. from St. Andrews, 1759, and D.C.L. from Oxford, 1762.

He returned reluctantly to Philadelphia, 1762, but was soon sent again to London to obtain recall of the Pennsylvania charter, an effort submerged in the controversy over the Stamp Act. Perceiving the intransigence of the British government, Franklin advised the colonists to accept the tax and even arranged for a friend to become tax collector in Philadelphia. This and his own purchase of stamped paper exposed him to much ill will, but his prestige was restored when the news of his "examination" in February 1766 before the House of Commons reached Philadelphia. Franklin's answers to his questioners portrayed the tax as contrary to custom and as administratively impracticable both on account of the country's circumstances and the settled opposition of the people.

Reappointed in 1766 as agent in London for Pennsylvania, Franklin became in effect ambassador extraordinary for the colonies; he was also appointed agent for Georgia, 1768; New Jersey, 1769; and Massachusetts, 1770. He saw his task as the reconciliation of the colonies with Great Britain, but after the passing of the coercive acts (1774), he began to despair of any reconciliation. His ideas on American rights became more precise and radical. In 1765 he had not doubted the right of Parliament to levy the Stamp Tax. In 1766 he had defended the distinction between internal and external taxes. By 1768 he was convinced, however, "that no middle doctrine can be well maintained." Either Parliament had the power to make all laws, or it had no power to make any. In 1770 he rejected the term "supreme authority of Parliament" and urged the theory that the colonies and England were united only in having a common sovereign. Although he deprecated violence, he agreed with Samuel Adams that good relations could not be reestablished until the repeal of the duty on tea; he welcomed the establishment of committees on correspondence; he distrusted Governor Thomas Hutchinson and sought to discredit him in England. Turning to satire as a means of checking what he considered anti-American excesses, he published his "Edict by the King of Prussia" and the "Rules by Which a Great Empire May Be Reduced to a Small One." These did more to aggravate than to compose the troubles, as did the affair of the "Hutchinson Letters." By the agency of Franklin, letters in which the governor of Massachusetts had advocated drastic measures on the ground that "there must be an abridgement of what are called English Liberties," were printed in

Boston and circulated in London. The ensuing furor caused Franklin to suffer public denunciation and abuse and to lose his office as deputy postmaster general. Supported by his friends and his own conviction of having carried out "one of the best actions of his life," he remained in England, aiding Pitt in his fruitless efforts at conciliation until he left for America in March 1775. Elected a member of the Second Continental Congress, he sketched a plan of union for the colonies; organized the Post Office; and served on the commissions which vainly sought Canadian cooperation and which advised Washington on defense. He served also on the committee appointed to draft the Declaration of Independence; prepared instructions for Silas Deane, colonial commissioner to France; and in December 1776 arrived in France as one of three commissioners to negotiate a treaty.

He was received by the French people as the personification of all the ideas dear to the Age of the Enlightenment. His simplicity of dress and manners, his wit and wisdom, his natural courtesy, all endeared him to his hosts and made him the object of unmeasured adulation. While he and his colleagues negotiated with foreign minister Vergennes, his mere presence in France intensified popular enthusiasm for the Americans and made it increasingly difficult for France to avoid a rupture with Great Britain.

Treaties of commerce and defensive alliance were signed between France and the United States in February 1778. Throughout the negotiations Franklin had to contend with annoying difficulties contrived by Arthur Lee, his fellow commissioner with Silas Deane. Lee took it upon himself to prove the supposed incompetence and venality of his colleagues and of Beaumarchais, the French agent with whom they dealt. Besides suffering Lee's "magisterial snubbings and rebukes," Franklin carried the chief burden of the negotiations with Vergennes, served as consul, judge of admiralty, and director of naval affairs, and negotiated for the exchange of prisoners in England. His task was made easier when on Sept. 14, 1778, Congress appointed him as sole plenipotentiary. Now Franklin found time again to write scientific articles, to correspond with Madame Helvétius and Madame Brillon, and to publish satires and bagatelles for the amusement of his friends. Throughout the next three years his chief tasks were to obtain loans of money from France, to mollify creditors, and to meet the innumerable bills of exchange which were drawn on him by Congress, shipowners, and others engaged in the Revolutionary War. His offered resignation was declined by Congress, March 1781; in June, he, John Jay, and John Adams were appointed to negotiate a peace with Great Britain. Awaiting the arrival of his colleagues, Franklin began preliminary conversations and proposed as a basis of negotiation (1) independence, (2) cession of the Mississippi Valley, (3) fishing rights "on the banks of Newfoundland, and elsewhere." He rejected British claims for recovery of debts and congressional compensation for American Loyalists, but indicated a willingness to consider the second demand favorably if Britain should cede Canada. He kept Vergennes informed of every step in the negotiations. British naval successes and the arrival of Jay, however, injected new factors into the negotiations and strengthened the hands of the British commissioners. Franklin broke the deadlock which resulted by an American counterclaim for war damages, and on Nov. 30 the preliminaries of a treaty were signed. In the interest of harmony Franklin had yielded to his colleagues on his previous agreement to keep the French government informed of the negotiations, because Adams and Jay were convinced that France and Spain were conspiring to restrict the boundaries of the United States to the Alleghenies. Vergennes penned a formal protest, but Franklin replied that although a point of courtesy had been neglected, the agreement had not been broken, since there would be no peace between England and America until France had concluded its own. The final and definitive peace having been signed on Sept. 3, 1783, Franklin asked Congress for recall in December, but did not receive notice until May 1785.

Home in America, he served as president of the executive council of Pennsylvania, 1785–88, and in May 1787, at the age of 81, took his seat in the Constitutional Convention. None of his cardinal ideas was accepted, but his personality and genial humor proved invaluable in soothing tempers and in suggesting compromises. The Constitution, as it finally emerged, was not all to his liking. Reminding himself and his colleagues of human fallibility, Franklin urged nevertheless that it be unanimously adopted. The last five years of his life he spent in his home near Market Street, Philadelphia. He carried on a large correspondence, enjoyed conversations with his friends and many visitors, and, as his last public act, signed a memorial to Congress for the abolition of slavery. He died on Apr. 17, 1790.

Franklin spoke the language of the Enlightenment philosophers, but with a homely accent, a tang of his native soil. His humor was neither brilliant nor corrosive; rather it was genial and kindly, even if cynical. He accepted without question and expressed without effort all the characteristic ideas and prepossessions of his century—its aversion to "superstition" and "enthusiasm" and mystery; its dislike of dim perspectives; its healthy, clarifying skepticism; its passion for freedom and its humane sympathies; its preoccupation with the world that is evident to the senses; its profound faith in common sense, in the efficacy of reason for the solution of human problems and the advancement of human welfare. His pragmatic habit of thought made him shun the ideal conceptions of the philosophers; insatiably curious, knowing neither inhibitions nor repressions, he accepted serenely the world as it was and brought to its understanding and mastery rare common sense, genuine disinterestedness, and a cool, flexible intelligence fortified by exact knowledge and chastened and humanized by practical experience. Rising from poverty to affluence, from obscurity to fame, he was equally at ease with rich and poor, the cultivated and the untutored; he spoke with equal facility the language of vagabonds and kings, politicians and philosophers, men of letters, kitchen girls, and *femmes savantes*. The whole world was his field of activity. He was the most universal and cosmopolitan spirit of his age, a true citizen of the world, and yet remained throughout his life more pungently American than any of his famous countrymen. The secret of Franklin's amazing capacity for assimilating experience lay perhaps in his final refusal to commit himself completely to any issue or cause. No one enterprise ever absorbed all his energies. In all of Franklin's dealings with men and affairs, genuine, sincere, loyal as he surely was, one feels that he was nevertheless not wholly committed; some thought remained uncommunicated, some penetrating observation was held in reserve. This characteristic is plain in his famous *Autobiography*, which is anything but a frank revelation of self, valuable as it may otherwise be. Science alone commanded his unreserved service, and in that endeavor the essential quality of Franklin appears to best advantage. As a literary artist, he possessed rare merit and was master of a style distinguished for clarity, precision, and pliable adhesion to the form and pressure of the idea to be conveyed.

FRANKLIN, BENJAMIN (*b. Belmont Co., Ohio, 1812; d. Anderson, Ind., 1878*), minister of the Disciples of Christ. A prominent evangelist, he edited the *American Christian Review*, 1856–78, and became spokesman of conservative Disciples.

FRANKLIN, EDWARD CURTIS (*b. Geary City, Kans., 1862; d. Stanford, Calif., 1937*), chemist. Graduated University of Kansas, 1888; M.S., 1890; attended University of Berlin, 1890–91, and received his doctorate from Johns Hopkins, 1894.

An unusually effective teacher, he was professor of chemistry at Kansas, 1899–1903, when he went to Stanford University for the remainder of his career. Here Franklin made pioneering investigations in developing the ammonia system of acids, bases, and salts, from which he synthesized and compiled data on many new compounds, and developed new concepts of the structure and relationship of nitrogenous compounds. His monograph *The Nitrogen System of Compounds* (1935) is one of the classics of American chemistry.

FRANKLIN, FABIAN (*b. Eger, Hungary, 1853; d. New York, N.Y., 1939*), mathematician, journalist, publicist. Came to America as an infant. Graduated, Columbian College, 1869; Ph.D., Johns Hopkins, 1880; taught mathematics there until 1895, when, increasingly interested in public affairs, he became editor of the *Baltimore News*. From 1908 to 1917 he was coeditor of the New York *Evening Post* and of the *Nation*. He found his true profession in publicizing his convictions in editorials, articles, pamphlets, and books. A fervent believer in internationalism, personal liberty, low tariffs, women's rights, and laissez-faire in government, he championed Woodrow Wilson's policies and the Allied cause in World War I, and vehemently opposed prohibition and New Deal bureaucracy.

FRANKLIN, JAMES (*b. Boston, Mass., 1696/7; d. Newport, R.I., 1735*), printer. Brother of Benjamin Franklin (1706–90). Published *New England Courant*, 1721–26, a lively, secular paper which offended official dignity; started *Rhode Island Gazette*, 1732.

FRANKLIN, JESSE (*b. Orange Co., Va., 1760; d. North Carolina, 1823*), Revolutionary soldier, politician. U.S. senator, Democratic-Republican, from North Carolina, 1799–1805 and 1807–13; governor, 1821.

FRANKLIN, PHILIP ALBRIGHT SMALL (*b. Ashland, Md., 1871; d. Locust Valley, N.Y., 1939*), shipping executive. Associated with International Mercantile Marine Co., 1903–36; president, *post* 1921. Chairman, Shipping Control Committee in World War I.

FRANKLIN, WILLIAM (*b. 1731; d. 1813*), last royal governor of New Jersey. Reared in household of his father, Benjamin Franklin (1706–90); became comptroller of General Post Office and clerk of Pennsylvania Provincial Assembly; went to England with his father, 1757, studied at Middle Temple and was admitted to bar. Named governor of New Jersey, 1763, he supported improvement of roads and agriculture and laws mitigating imprisonment for debt. In Stamp Act controversy, he upheld British view and became estranged from his countrymen and his father. Arrested 1776 by the Jersey Provincial Congress, he was exchanged, 1778; soon thereafter, he returned to England, where he died.

FRANKLIN, WILLIAM BUEL (*b. York, Pa., 1823; d. Hartford, Conn., 1903*), soldier, business executive. Graduated West Point, 1843; served in topographical engineers. A division and corps commander, 1861–62, he was blamed for the Union debacle at Fredericksburg and sent to subordinate commands in the Southwest. He was manager of Colt's Firearms Co. from his resignation from the army in 1866 until 1888.

FRANZ, SHEHERD IVORY (*b. Jersey City, N.J., 1874; d. California, 1933*), physiological psychologist. Graduated Columbia, 1894; Ph.D., 1899. Noted for his discoveries in brain localization, brain action, and the rehabilitation of persons suffering from brain injuries.

FRARY, FRANCIS COWLES (*b. Minneapolis, Minn., 1884; d. Oakmont, Pa., 1970*), chemical engineer. Studied at the University of Minnesota (Ph.D., 1912), where he was an instructor and researcher until 1915. Director of research for the Oldbury Electrochemical Company (1915–17), and for the Aluminum Company of America (Alcoa) from 1919, whose research department became an independent organization within Alcoa in 1928, called Aluminum Research Laboratories (ARL). Conducted research mainly on primary processes. Some of his most important work, patented in 1925–26, related to development of an electrolytic process for refining aluminum to a purity of more than 99.9 percent, which made it possible to obtain basic information about the characteristics and properties of aluminum and its alloys. Coauthored *The Aluminum Industry* in 1930. President of the Electrochemical Society (1929–30) and the Institute of Chemical Engineers (1941). His many awards included the Perkin Medal of the Joint British and American Society of Chemical Industries (1946). Retired as director of research of ARL in 1951, but remained active as a consultant until 1967.

FRASCH, HERMAN (b. *Gaildorf, Germany, 1851[?]; d. Paris, France, 1914*), pharmacist, chemical engineer, inventor. Came to America, 1868. Developed the Frasch process for desulfurizing petroleum, 1885–94. Also patented processes for producing white lead directly from galena, for producing sodium carbonate from salt, and, most important of all, for mining sulfur by superheated water. His Union Sulphur Co. wrested control of the world sulfur supply from the Anglo-Sicilian monopoly and made the United States an exporter of sulfur.

FRASER, CHARLES (b. *1782; d. 1860*), painter of miniatures. A Charleston, S.C., lawyer and man of letters, his fame rests on his portraits, noted for their subtle, uncompromising, yet sympathetic characterization.

FRASER, JAMES EARLE (b. *Winona, Minn., 1876; d. Westport, Conn., 1953*), sculptor. Studied at the Chicago Art Institute and École des Beaux Arts in Paris, 1895–99. Designer of the buffalo nickel and creator of the equestrian statue of Theodore Roosevelt on the steps of the American Museum of Natural History in New York City. His most famous work is "End of the Trail," a statue of an Indian, the model for which was completed when he was seventeen.

FRASER, LEON (b. *Boston, Mass., 1889; d. North Granville, N.Y., 1945*), lawyer, banker. B.A., Columbia University, 1910; M.A., 1912; Ph.D., 1915. Admitted to New York bar, 1913. After World War I service with the army, he had a varied experience as acting director of the federal Veterans' Bureau, staff member of an international law firm, general counsel for the Dawes Plan, and legal and economic assistant to Owen D. Young in the drafting of the Young Plan. Made a director of the Bank for International Settlements, he served as its president, 1933–35. He was a vice president of the First National Bank of New York, 1935–36, and president thereafter.

FRAUNCES, SAMUEL (b. *West Indies*, ca. *1722; d. Philadelphia, Pa., 1795*). From 1762, kept New York tavern in former De Lancy house; was steward of Washington's presidential households in New York and Philadelphia, 1789–94.

FRAYNE, HUGH (b. *Scranton, Pa., 1869; d. New York, N.Y., 1934*), labor leader. General organizer of the American Federation of Labor, 1901–34; conservative; created a better public understanding of the objectives of labor movement.

FRAZEE, JOHN (b. *Rahway, N.J., 1790; d. Compton Mills, R.I., 1852*), sculptor. From unlettered bricklayer, became stonecutter and sculptor of busts of famous contemporaries. His portrait of John Wells in St. Paul's Church, New York, was the first marble bust carved in this country by a native.

FRAZER, JOHN FRIES (b. *Philadelphia, Pa., 1812; d. Philadelphia, 1872*), scientist, teacher. Editor, *Journal of the Franklin Institute*, 1850–66. Assistant to Alexander D. Bache, whom he succeeded as professor of natural philosophy, University of Pennsylvania, serving 1844–72.

FRAZER, OLIVER (b. *Jessamine Co., Ky., 1808; d. Lexington, Ky., 1864*), portrait painter. Studied with M. H. Jouett and Thomas Sully and in Europe. His work was marked by simplicity of line and firmness of texture.

FRAZER, PERSIFOR (b. *Chester Co., Pa., 1736; d. Chester Co., 1792*), Revolutionary soldier, ironmaster, merchant.

FRAZER, PERSIDOR. (b. *Philadelphia, Pa., 1844; d. 1909*), geologist, metallurgist. Son of John F. Frazer. Graduated University of Pennsylvania, 1862, and attended Royal School of Mines, Freiberg, Germany. Member of Hayden Survey of Colorado and J. P. Lesley's geological survey of Pennsylvania. A prolific writer on science and a handwriting expert.

FRAZIER, CHARLES HARRISON (b. *Germantown, Pa., 1870; d. North Haven, Maine, 1936*), neurological surgeon. M.D., University of Pennsylvania, 1892; studied in Germany under Virchow, 1895–96. Taught at University of Pennsylvania. Pioneer in surgery of the trigeminal nerve and of the spinal cord for relief of pain.

FRAZIER, EDWARD FRANKLIN (b. *Baltimore, Md., 1894; d. Washington, D.C., 1962*), Sociologist and educator. Studied at Howard University (graduated, 1916), Clark University (M.A., 1920), the University of Chicago, and Fisk University (Ph.D., 1931). Professor of sociology at Fisk, 1929–34; professor and head of the Department of Sociology at Howard University, 1934–62. Director of the Mayor's Commission on Conditions in Harlem, 1935; chief of the Division of Applied Social Sciences of the United Nations Educational, Scientific, and Cultural Organization, 1951–53. An authority on the black family and race relations, Frazier's books include *The Negro Family in the United States* (1939), *Black Bourgeoisie* (1957), and *Race and Culture Contacts in the Modern World* (1957).

FRAZIER, LYNN JOSEPH (b. *Steele County, Minn., 1874; d. Riverdale, Md., 1947*), farmer, teacher, politician. Raised in Pembina County, Dakota Territory. Graduated Normal School in Mayville, N.Dak., 1895; University of North Dakota, 1901. Endorsed for governor of North Dakota by the Nonpartisan League and nominated in the primary on the Republican ticket, he was elected in 1916. Entirely committed to the advancement of farmers' rights, he put through a series of laws designed to curb encroachments of industry and finance on agriculture. Reelected in 1918, he continued his first term policies, adding provisions for state ownership and operation of utilities, grain elevators, warehouses, and mills; a state bank for deposit of all public funds; a state housing program; and a number of other reform measures. Elected again in 1920, he faced rising opposition to his policies and he was recalled in a special election, 1921; but he was elected to the U.S. Senate, 1922. He served until 1940, when his antiwar position lost him the election. In the Senate, he continued to press for agricultural justice and aid and against the financial interests; he is best remembered as coauthor of the Frazier-Lemke amendment to the Farm Bankruptcy Act of 1934.

FREAR, WILLIAM (b. *Reading, Pa., 1860; d. 1922*), agricultural chemist, educator. Graduated Bucknell, 1881. Taught at Pennsylvania State College. His greatest work was done in lifetime service with federal and state committees on food and drug standards.

FREAS, THOMAS BRUCE (*b. near Newark, Ohio, 1868; d. 1928*), chemist. Developed the art of laboratory control at University of Chicago. Invented special thermostats and Freas ovens for maintenance of constant temperatures; experimented with a solar motor.

FREDERIC, HAROLD (*b. Utica, N.Y., 1856; d. Henley-on-Thames, England, 1898*), journalist, novelist. London correspondent for *New York Times* from 1884. Author of ten books of fiction, including *In the Valley* (1890), *The Copperhead* (1893), and a study in spiritual deterioration (his masterpiece), *The Damnation of Theron Ware* (1896).

FREED, ALAN J. (*b. Johnstown, Pa., 1921; d. Palm Springs, Calif., 1965*), disc jockey. Called the "Father of Rock 'n' Roll" for naming the new music and popularizing the term. Freed achieved national attention in 1951 with "The Moon Dog Rock 'n' Roll Party" on WJW in Cleveland, Ohio. Beginning in 1952, he staged his "Big Beat" all-black-talent rock 'n' roll shows, which were banned in many cities following a riot at a show in Boston in 1958. His fame exploded as host of "Alan Freed's Rock 'n' Roll Party", 1954–58, on WINS in New York. Implicated and eventually indicted in the "payola" scandal in 1963.

FREEDMAN, ANDREW (*b. New York, N.Y., 1860; d. 1915*), capitalist. Organizer of insurance companies and a promoter of the first New York subway. Left his estate to found a home for aged couples.

FREEMAN, ALLEN WEIR (*b. Lynchburg, Va., 1881; d. Baltimore, Md., 1954*), sanitarian. Graduated from Johns Hopkins School of Medicine, M.D., 1905. Lecturer in public health at the Johns Hopkins School of Hygiene and Public Health, 1921–46; dean, 1934–37. Traveled to Brazil, Italy, and Quebec, surveying health facilities and setting up health programs.

FREEMAN, BERNARDUS (*b. Netherlands[?], date unknown; d. 1741*), Dutch Reformed clergyman. Ordained 1700 as pastor of Albany, N.Y., but served at Schenectady and Long Island. Often involved in controversies; preached successfully to the Mohawk Indians and translated religious texts for their use.

FREEMAN, DOUGLAS SOUTHALL (*b. Lynchburg, Va., 1886; d. Richmond, Va., 1953*), newspaper editor, historian. Studied at Richmond College and Johns Hopkins (Ph.D., 1908). Received Pulitzer Prize in 1935 for his four-volume biography of Robert E. Lee. Editor of the Richmond *News Letter*, 1915–49. Author of *Lee's Dispatches* (1915), *The South to Posterity* (1939), *Lee's Lieutenants* (1942–44), and a seven-volume biography of George Washington (1948–54), which won a posthumous Pulitzer Prize.

FREEMAN, FREDERICK KEMPER (*b. Culpeper Co., Va., 1841; d. Georgia, 1928*), Confederate soldier, journalist. Nephew of James L. Kemper. Editor with his brother Legh of the *Frontier Index*, a newspaper published 1866–69 at successive railheads of the Union Pacific.

FREEMAN, JAMES (*b. Charlestown, Mass., 1759; d. Newton, Mass., 1835*), first Unitarian minister of King's Chapel, Boston, 1787–1826.

FREEMAN, JAMES EDWARDS (*b. Indian Island, New Brunswick, Canada, 1808; d. Rome, Italy, 1884*), genre painter. Studied with William Dunlap and at National Academy of Design, New York. Lived in Italy, *post* 1836. His work was richly colored but largely sentimental.

FREEMAN, JOHN RIPLEY (*b. West Bridgton, Maine, 1855; d. Providence, R.I., 1932*), hydraulic engineer.

FREEMAN, JOSEPH (*b. Poltava, Ukraine, 1897; d. New York, N.Y., 1965*), poet, radical journalist, publicist, and novelist. Immigrated to the United States in 1904; naturalized in 1920. Studied at Columbia (graduated, 1919). Paris correspondent for the *Tribune* and *New York Daily News*, 1920. Wrote for the *Liberator*, 1920–24. Revived the *Masses* as the *New Masses* with Michael Gold in 1926. Publicity director for the American Civil Liberties Union (1924–25; 1940–42). On the staff of the Soviet news agency Tass off and on from 1924 to 1931. Worked in the Soviet Union in the office of the Comintern as a translator in 1926–27. Cofounder of the *Partisan Review* in 1934. Wrote *Dollar Diplomacy: A Study in American Imperialism* with Scott Nearing (1925), *Voices of October* with Joshua Kunitz (1930), *The Soviet Worker* (1932), *An American Testament: A Narrative of Rebels and Romantics* (1936). His novels are *Never Call Retreat* (1943) and *The Long Pursuit* 1947). Committed to the hopeful expectations of a world socialist revolution, during the early 1930's he was active as a writer in explicating Marxist ideas and formulating the principles governing the creation of proletarian literature. Expelled from the Communist party in 1936.

FREEMAN, MARY ELEANOR WILKINS (*b. Randolph, Mass., 1852; d. Metuchen, N.J., 1930*), writer. Through stories in the Harper publications, *post* 1883, she became known as one of the chief exponents of New England rural life. The flat, inland scenery of eastern Massachusetts formed the background of tales which were collected in *A Humble Romance* (1887), *A New England Nun* (1891), and many other volumes. She tried other kinds of writing but without her success in the short story of country life, where she identified herself completely with her material and wrote with subtle and dispassionate objectivity at a time when sentimentality was popular.

FREEMAN, NATHANIEL (*b. Dennis, Mass., 1741; d. 1827*), physician, lawyer, Revolutionary patriot. Practiced in Barnstable Co., Mass.

FREEMAN, THOMAS (*b. Ireland, date unknown; d. Huntsville, Ala., 1821*), civil engineer, astronomer. Came to America, 1784. Accompanied Andrew Ellicott on survey of boundary between United States and Spanish Florida, 1797. Explored the Arkansas and Red rivers, 1806; mapped Tennessee-Alabama boundary, 1807; fought land speculation as U.S. surveyor of southern public lands, 1811–21.

FREER, CHARLES LANG (*b. Kingston, N.Y., 1856; d. 1919*), capitalist. Active in organization of American Car and Foundry Co. Donated Freer Gallery, Washington, D.C., which holds his own unique collections of J. M. Whistler's work, ancient glazed pottery, and oriental art.

FRELINGHUSEN, FREDERICK THEODORE (*b. Millstone, N.J., 1817; d. Newark, N.J., 1885*), statesman. Grandson of Frederick Frelinghuysen. Graduated Rutgers, 1836. Attorney general of New Jersey, 1861–66; U.S. senator, Republican, from New Jersey, 1866–69 and 1871–77. Achieved commanding influence, especially with the "Stalwarts"; supported President Andrew Johnson's impeachment.

Succeeding Blaine as secretary of state, 1881–85, he pursued a less aggressive foreign policy; favored closer reciprocal commercial relations with Latin America; vigorously supported American commercial interests in Germany and France; negotiated for a naval base at Pearl Harbor; opened up treaty relations with Korea; authorized U.S. participation in the Berlin Conference, 1884. Always considerate of the rights of other nations, he aimed to create a feeling of generous goodwill in diplomatic relations.

FRELINGHUYSEN, FREDERICK (*b. near Somerville, N.J., 1753; d. 1804*), lawyer, Revolutionary soldier. Grandson of

Theodore J. Frelinghuysen. Graduated College of New Jersey (Princeton), 1770. Served in Continental Congress, New Jersey state legislature, and U.S. Senate, 1793–96.

FRELINGHUYSEN, THEODORE (*b. Franklin Township, N.J., 1787; d. New Brunswick, N.J., 1862*), lawyer. Son of Frederick Frelinghuysen. Graduated Princeton, 1804. Attorney general of New Jersey, 1817–29; U.S. senator, Whig, 1829–35. Opposed Indian removals; was respected for integrity. President, Rutgers College, 1850–62, after service as chancellor of present New York University, 1839–50.

FRELINGHUYSEN, THEODORUS JACOBUS (*b. Lingen, Germany, 1691; d. ca. 1748*), Dutch Reformed clergyman. Came to America, 1719, to serve in Raritan Valley, N.J. A master revivalist, triumphant in controversy with New York clergyman, he did much to invoke the Great Awakening in the middle colonies.

FRÉMONT, JESSIE BENTON)*b. near Lexington, Va., 1824; d. Los Angeles, Calif., 1902*), writer. Daughter of Thomas Hart Benton. Married John Charles Frémont, 1841; assisted him in writing his reports and in all crises of his career. Contributed regularly to periodicals, *post* 1871.

FRÉMONT, JOHN CHARLES) *b. Savannah, Ga., 1813; d. New York, N.Y., 1890*), explorer, politician, soldier. A precocious youth born out of wedlock, Frémont was raised in Charleston, S.C. Through influence of Joel Poinsett, he was appointed to an instructorship in the navy, resigning to become a second lieutenant in the U.S. Topographical Corps. After assisting in survey of a projected Charleston-Cincinnati railroad and in a reconnaissance of the Cherokee country in 1837–38, he joined J. H. Nicollet's expedition to the upper Mississippi and Missouri rivers, acquiring expert training in astronomical, topographical, and geographical observation.

Through this work he met Thomas Hart Benton, who gave him a new vision of western exploration and expansion to the Pacific. Alarmed by the mutual attachment of Frémont and his daughter Jessie, Benton had Frémont sent to explore the Des Moines River. Secretly married at Washington, D.C., upon Frémont's return in October 1841 the couple was reconciled to Benton, who became Frémont's patron and with others planned his first important expedition to examine the Oregon Trail and to report on rivers, mountains, fertility, positions for forts, and the nature of the mountains in Wyoming.

With Kit Carson as guide, Frémont left the Kansas River in June 1842, traveled by way of the Platte and South Pass, and explored the Wind River Range. Back in Washington by October, he composed with his wife's expert literary help a report (published 1843) which showed zest for adventure and descriptive sparkle and gave him a wide popular reputation.

The departure of his second expedition, May 1843, with Thomas Fitzpatrick as guide, was hastened by a message from Jessie Frémont, who suppressed a War Department order requiring Frémont to return to Washington. Failing to blaze a new trail through northern Colorado, he followed the Oregon Trail, explored Great Salt Lake, and pushed on to the Columbia River. He then struck off through Oregon to Pyramid Lake and into Nevada, reaching the Carson River in January 1844 and daring to cross the Sierra Nevada into California, where he refitted at Sutter's Fort. He returned to St. Louis, Mo., in August 1844 after forming a clear impression of the weakness of the Mexican hold on California. He and Jessie collaborated on a second vivid report.

Frémont's third expedition set out in 1845 as war with Mexico was imminent. He desired to participate in conquering California and claimed in his *Memoirs* (1887) that Benton and George Bancroft intended his scientific force to turn into a military body in case of war. Guided once again by Kit Carson, he went west by way

of Great Salt Lake and the Hastings Cutoff, blazed a new trail across Nevada, and took his men to Monterey and San Jose, Calif. When ordered by Mexican officials to leave, he hoisted the American flag. Moving north, he was overtaken in May 1846 by news that war was expected in a few days and hastened to the Sacramento Valley, where he inspired discontented American settlers to begin the Bear Flag Revolt and in June gave them armed support. With his "California Battalion," he helped in the capture of Los Angeles in August, and in its final capture in January 1847. Involved in the quarrel of Commodore Stockton and Gen. S. W. Kearny, he sided with Stockton, who appointed him civil governor of California. When Kearny was proved to be in command, he arrested Frémont on charges of mutiny and insubordination. A Washington court-martial found him guilty, and though President Polk remitted the penalty, Frémont resigned from the service.

A midwinter expedition in 1848–49 at the expense of Benton and others seeking a Pacific railroad route proved a disastrous venture. Frémont, after much hardship, reached California, settled in Monterey, and began to develop the Mariposa estate recently acquired for him by U.S. consul Thomas Larkin. In a short time he was wealthy through gold mined on the estate and real estate operations in San Francisco. He made a fifth exploring expedition to the mountains in 1853–54. Meanwhile, he had served as U.S. senator from California, September 1850—March 1851.

Frémont's explorations and court-martial had made him a national figure. Nominated for the presidency by the new Republican party in June 1856, with W. L. Dayton as vice presidential candidate, he lost to James Buchanan. Returning to California, he devoted himself to his mines at Mariposa.

His first Civil War appointment was as major general commanding the department of the West, with headquarters at St. Louis. Blamed for federal defeats at Wilson's Creek and Lexington, and justly accused of extravagance, he lost Lincoln's confidence by refusing to rescind a rash proclamation of Aug. 30, 1861, in which he declared the property of rebel Missourians confiscated and their slaves emancipated. He was investigated and removed, to the dismay of radical antislavery men; in deference to these, Lincoln appointed Frémont in March 1862 to command the mountain department in western Virginia. Here he was outmaneuvered by Stonewall Jackson in May and June. Placed subordinate in command to Gen. John Pope, Frémont resigned.

Frémont's prosperity and popularity declined thereafter. He left public life, failed in business, and was saved from poverty by his wife's activities as an author. His whole later career was a tragic anticlimax; his achievements as an explorer remain justly famous. The reports of his earlier expeditions were of particular value in publicizing the fertility of the plains country and the Northwest and in supplying trustworthy information for emigrants.

FRENCH, AARON (*b. Wadsworth, Ohio, 1823; d. 1902*), inventor, manufacturer. Began life as a blacksmith; manufactured first steel springs for railroad cars at Pittsburgh, Pa., *post* 1862; invented and put into use light-weight coiled and elliptic steel springs.

FRENCH, ALICE (*b. Andover, Mass., 1850; d. Davenport, Iowa, 1934*), author. Under pen name "Octave Thanet," wrote realistic stories of life in the Midwest and South. Among her books were *Stories of a Western Town* (1893) and *A Book of True Lovers* (1897).

FRENCH, DANIEL CHESTER (*b. Exeter, N.H., 1850; d. Stockbridge, Mass., 1931*), sculptor. Mainly self-taught, he was helped by Louisa M. Alcott, William Morris Hunt, John Quincy Adams Ward, and William Rimmer. His first important commission was the "Minute Man" memorial, unveiled at Concord,

Mass., 1875. On return after two years' study in Italy, he worked in Washington, D.C., on sculptural groups for the St. Louis Custom House, the Philadelphia Court House, and the Boston Post Office. He was also commissioned to do busts of Emerson and Bronson Alcott. When Emerson saw French's portrayal of him, he said, "That is the face I shave." In 1884 French designed the seated statute of John Harvard at Cambridge.

Post 1888 his work was prolific, and its rich variety continued until he was 80. For the World's Columbian Exposition, 1893, he designed *The Republic* and submitted also his *Death Staying the Hand of the Young Sculptor.* As the leading American sculptor he was selected to design the monumental figure of for the Lincoln Memorial in Washington, D.C.

French's work was modeled on reality but with a touch of idealism subtly interposed; it has poetic feeling and perfection of execution. Probably no other American sculptor has won such appreciative response from the general public.

FRENCH, EDWIN DAVIS (*b. North Attleboro, Mass., 1851; d. Saranac Lake, N.Y., 1906*), engraver on silver; a master of copperplate engraving of bookplates.

FRENCH, LUCY VIRGINIA SMITH (*b. Accomac Co., Va., 1825; d. McMinnville, Tenn., 1881*), author of romantic novels and poems; literary editor of several southern periodicals.

FRENCH, PAUL COMLY (*b. Philadelphia, Pa., 1903; d. Yardley, Pa., 1960*), charity executive. Self-educated, French worked for the *Philadelphia Record,* 1922–36; and was Pennsylvania director of the Federal Writers' Project of the Works Progress Administration, 1937–41. A Quaker, French organized the National Service Board for Religious Objectors and served as executive secretary, 1940–46. As executive director of CARE, 1947–55, he expanded operations to a worldwide distribution of American goods and knowledge.

FRENCH, WILLIAM HENRY (*b. Baltimore, Md., 1815; d. Washington, D.C., 1881*), soldier. Graduated West Point, 1837. Served in Florida and Mexican wars; in Civil War, rose to command III Corps, Army of the Potomac, until failure at Mine Run in 1863 cost him General Meade's confidence.

FRENCH, WILLIAM MERCHANT RICHARDSON (*b. Exeter, N.H., 1843; d. Chicago, Ill., 1914*), secretary and director, Art Institute of Chicago, 1879–1914. Brother of Daniel C. French.

FRENEAU, PHILIP MORIN (*b. New York, N.Y., 1752; d. near Middletown Point, N.J., 1832*), poet, editor, mariner. Graduated College of New Jersey (Princeton), 1771, a classmate of James Madison and H. H. Brackenridge. Collaborated with the latter on the poem "The Rising Glory of America" (published 1772). With the coming of the Revolution he became fiercely active, publishing within a few months eight pamphlet satires, including *General Gage's Soliloquy* and *General Gage's Confession* (1775). An opening as secretary to a planter took him to the West Indies, and in the next three years there he wrote his most significant poems: "Santa Cruz," "The Jamaica Funeral," "The House of Night." The latter, written before the opening of the romantic period in Europe, has all the elements of the new romanticism and places Freneau as a pioneer in the movement.

Returning to find the Revolution in full career, he went to sea; taken by the British, he suffered the brutal imprisonment described in *The British Prison Ship: A Poem* (1781). Exchanged and working in Philadelphia, Pa., he helped edit the *Freeman's Journal,* satirizing the "insolent foe" and writing much patriotic poetry. He took to the sea again in 1784 as master of a brig, surviving storms and shipwreck and writing sea poems. No other American poet has known the ocean so well or pictured it more graphically.

In 1789 he began editing the New York *Daily Advertiser,* which he made an important newspaper. With Jefferson's support and encouragement, he edited the *National Gazette* in Philadelphia, 1791–93, effectively opposing John Fenno's pro-Hamilton *Gazette of the United States.* A passionate Democrat, Freneau, more than any other early journalist, quickened this spirit in the new republic. After service as editor of the *Jersey Chronicle* and the New York *Time-Piece,* he gave up journalism and spent the rest of his life either at sea or on his New Jersey farm.

Freneau's poems were published in collected form in 1786, 1788, 1795, 1809, and 1815. He was the most significant poetic figure in America before William Cullen Bryant.

FREUND, ERNST (*b. New York, N.Y., 1864; d. Chicago, Ill., 1932*), lawyer, professor of law at Columbia and University of Chicago. Excelled in drafting uniform statutes for acceptance by legislative bodies.

FREY, JOHN PHILIP (*b. Mankato, Minn., 1871; d. Washington, D.C., 1957*), labor leader. Joined the International Molders and Foundry Workers Union in 1893 in Massachusetts; vice president, 1900–50. An aide to Samuel Gompers, Frey held great influence in the labor movement. He was instrumental in causing the split between the AFL and CIO and successfully kept the two wings apart until after his retirement. President of the Ohio State Federation of Labor, 1924–28; president of the AFL Metal Trades Department, 1934–50.

FREY, JOSEPH SAMUEL CHRISTIAN FREDERICK (*b. Mainstockheim, Bavaria, 1771; d. Pontiac, Mich., 1850*), clergyman. Converted from Judaism, 1798, he came to America, 1816. As a preacher and agent for the American Society for Meliorating the Condition of the Jews, he traveled extensively in the United States.

FRICK, HENRY CLAY (*b. West Overton, Pa., 1849; d. 1919*), steel manufacturer, capitalist. A coke millionaire at the age of 30, Frick became chairman of Carnegie Brothers in 1889 and reorganized the steel business by building connecting railroads, improving operating methods, employing capable young men, and exploiting labor. He bought out Duquesne Steel, Carnegie's chief competitor, and by 1890 controlled the world's largest coke and steel operation. The notorious Homestead, Pa., strike, 1892, brought much criticism on Frick. A key man in forming the U.S. Steel Corporation, 1901, and a director of many enterprises, he gratified a youthful taste for art by collecting old masters, now housed in the Frick Museum, New York City.

FRIDAY (*b. Kansas-Colorado plains, ca. 1822; d. Wyoming, 1881*), Arapaho subchief. Sent to school in St. Louis, Mo., by Thomas Fitzpatrick, he returned to Indian life; a famous hunter and leader, he remained friendly to the whites.

FRIEDENWALD, AARON (*b. Baltimore, Md., 1836; d. Baltimore, 1902*), physician, ophthalmologist. Practiced in Baltimore; professor of diseases of eye and ear in College of Physicians and Surgeons; cofounder and first president, Maryland Ophthalmological Society.

FRIEDLAENDER, ISRAEL (*b. Kovel, Russian Poland, 1876; d. Kamenetz-Podolsk, Russia, 1920*), Semitist. Educated at Warsaw, Berlin, Strassburg; called to New York, 1903, to chair of biblical literature and exegesis in Jewish Theological Seminary of America. Interested in historical relations between Islam and Judaism, he published many scholarly works. An ardent worker for Jewish education and for Zionism, he felt it his duty to go to the war-and-revolution-torn Ukraine in 1920 as commissioner of the Joint Distribution Committee of America. He was murdered there by Bolshevik soldiers.

FRIEDLAENDER, WALTER FERDINAND (*b. Berlin, Germany, 1873; d. New York, N.Y., 1966*), art historian and educator. Studied at the University of Berlin (Ph.D., 1898). Staff member of the Prussian Historical Institute, 1907–11. Professor of art history at Freiburg University in Germany, 1914–33. Published major works on the seventeenth-century French artist Nicolas Poussin throughout his career, including *Nicolas Poussin* (1914). Also wrote with erudition on Claude Lorraine, Carracci, Rubens, Caravaggio, David, and Delacroix. Explored Italian mannerism, a sixteenth-century style that had been largely disparaged by art historians, and vindicated that period as "autonomous and most meaningful," distinguishing between what he considered its two periods. Served as acting director of the Freiburg Kunsthistorische Institut. Expelled from Germany in 1933 by the Nazis. Immigrated to the United States and became a naturalized citizen. A lecturer in art history at the University of Pennsylvania and a visiting professor of the Institute of Fine Arts at New York University from 1935. Established the Institute's reputation in baroque art.

FRIEDMAN, WILLIAM FREDERICK (*b. Kishinev, Russia, 1891; d. Washington, D.C., 1969*), cryptologist. Immigrated in 1893; naturalized in 1896. Studied at Cornell (M.S., 1915). Headed the genetics department at the Riverbank Laboratories in Geneva, Ill., 1915–17. Married cryptanalyst Elizebeth Smith in 1917; the couple established a school in cryptology for military personnel at Riverbank and coauthored a series of landmark treatises, *Riverbank Publications on Cryptography and Cryptanalyis* (1917–20). A commissioned officer in the army during World War I, Friedman worked on solving German codes and ciphers while in France in 1918. Returned to Riverbank in 1919. Became a civilian cryptologist at Army Signal Corps headquarters in Washington, D.C. in 1921. Recommissioned and appointed the War Department's chief cryptanalyst in 1921. A pioneer in the development of electromechanical enciphering equipment, among his books that became standard references are *Elements of Cryptanalysis* (1926) and *The History of the Use of Codes and Code Language* (1928). Named chief of the Signal Intelligence Service (SIS) in 1930. Instrumental in the solving of "Purple," the complex Japanese cipher for top-priority diplomatic messages, in 1940. Named director of communications research in the army Security Agency, 1945–51; consultant to the Armed Forces Security Agency. Special assistant to the director of the National Security Agency upon its establishment in 1952. Retired in 1955.

FRIES, FRANCIS (*b. Salem, N.C., 1812; d. 1863*), manufacturer. One of a group which sought to implant industry in the antebellum South, he built and operated woolen and cotton mills at Salem *post* 1836.

FRIES, JOHN (*b. Montgomery Co., Pa., ca. 1750; d. Bucks Co., Pa., 1818*), insurgent. An itinerant auctioneer, militia captain, and general rural favorite, he led the Pennsylvania Germans in opposition to the federal property tax of 1798. Assessors were ordered out of Bucks Co., and Captain Fries with a band of followers ejected collectors and liberated federal prisoners. President John Adams sent a force of cavalry and militia in March 1799 to quell the rioters. Fries was arrested, tried for treason in Philadelphia, and twice sentenced to death. President Adams pardoned him against the advice of his cabinet.

FRIESEKE, FREDERICK CARL (*b. Owosso, Mich., 1874; d. Plagny-Château, France, 1939*), painter. His impressionist, essentially orthodox paintings were well received in America and Europe.

FRIEZE, HENRY SIMMONS (*b. Boston, Mass., 1817; d. Ann Arbor, Mich., 1889*), professor of Latin. Graduated Brown, 1841. Thrice acting president of the University of Michigan, 1869–71, 1880–82, and 1887–88, he taught at Michigan *post* 1854.

FRISBIE, LEVI (*b. Ipswich, Mass., 1783; d. 1822*), educator. Graduated Harvard, 1802. Blind from early manhood, he was a teacher of Latin at Harvard, 1805–17, and thereafter Alford professor of natural religion.

FRISSELL, HOLLIS BURKE (*b. South Amenia, N.Y., 1851; d. 1917*), Presbyterian clergyman. Chaplain of Hampton Institute, 1880–93; principal, 1893–1917.

FRITSCHEL, CONRAD SIGMUND (*b. Nürnberg, Germany, 1833; d. Dubuque, Iowa, 1900*), Lutheran clergyman, theologian. Came to America, 1854; helped constitute Evangelical Synod of Iowa. He and his brother Gottfried were principal professors at Wartburg Seminary.

FRITSCHEL, GOTTFRIED LEONHARD WILHELM (*b. Nürnberg, Germany, 1836; d. Mendota, Ill., 1889*), Lutheran clergyman, editor, theologian. Came to America, 1857. Served as colleague of his brother Conrad at Wartburg Seminary and defended its theological position (that of Wilhelm Löhe) against attacks of Missouri Synod.

FRITZ, JOHN (*b. Chester Co., Pa., 1822; d. 1913*), mechanical engineer, ironmaster. Starting as blacksmith and mechanic, he learned all phases of the iron business. As superintendent of Cambria Iron Works, Johnstown, Pa., he raised the mill from bankruptcy, designing solid new machinery and introducing new techniques. He resigned in 1860 to become superintendent and chief engineer for the Bethlehem Iron Co. Fritz was one of a group which revolutionized the steel industry by applying the Bessemer process to American practice. Other outstanding improvements tried out in the Bethlehem plant were open-hearth furnaces, the Thomas basic process, and the Whitworth forging press. He was first recipient of the John Fritz Medal, established in his honor, 1902.

FRIZELL, JOSEPH PALMER (*b. Barford, Canada, 1832, d. Dorchester, Mass., 1910*), hydraulic engineer. Assistant to James B. Francis and trained by him. Author of *Water Power, an Outline* (1900), the first practical book on the subject published in the United States, he had been in government work and general practice *post* 1868.

FROHMAN, CHARLES (*b. Sandusky, Ohio, 1860; d. aboard Lusitania, 1915*), theatrical manager. Acting first as advance agent to road companies, Frohman became an independent manager, 1883; then opened a booking office which was the basis of what later became the "Theatrical Syndicate." *Shenandoah* (1889) was his first independent success. He engaged John Drew as nucleus of his Empire Stock Co., which developed star figures such as Maude Adams, William Faversham, Ethel Barrymore. "The Napoleon of the drama," he produced plays by Belasco, Clyde Fitch, Augustus Thomas, Somerset Maugham, and many others, introducing Sir James Barrie to the American public with Maude Adams in *The Little Minister* (1897). The Barrie-Adams-Frohman combination scored success after success, notably with *Peter Pan*. Frohman was noted for the tasteful lavishness of his productions and for the complete trust to be put in his pledged word.

FROHMAN, DANIEL (*b. Sandusky, Ohio, 1851; d. New York, N.Y., 1940*), theatrical manager and producer. Brother of Charles Frohman. Organized Lyceum Theatre (New York) stock company, 1887. A pioneer in motion-picture production.

FROMM-REICHMANN, FRIEDA (*b. Karlsruhe, Germany, 1889; d. Rockville, Md., 1957*), psychiatrist, psychoanalyst. Studied at Albertus University. Immigrated to the U.S. in 1935. Fromm-Reichmann was influenced by the teachings of Freud and in 1924, with her husband Erich Fromm, founded a progressive psychoanalytic sanitorium in Heidelberg. In 1929, they founded the South-West German Psychoanalytic Institute at Frankfurt. Fromm-Reichmann was associated with the Chestnut Lodge psychiatric hospital near Washington, D.C., from 1935 until her death. A pioneer in the psychoanalytic treatment of severe mental disorders, she was associated with the teachings of Harry Stack Sullivan.

FROST, ARTHUR BURDETT (*b. Philadelphia, Pa., 1851; d. Pasadena, Calif., 1928*), illustrator, humorist. Trained as a wood engraver and lithographer, his illustrating career began with wood engravings for Max Adeler's (Charles H. Clark) *Out of the Hurly Burly* (1874); by 1900 he was probably the country's most popular illustrator.

Frost's illustrations cover a wide range, but his true talent was for American folk pictures—comic line sketches in story sequence or finished illustrations in pen and ink, oils, or watercolor. Selections of his humorous sketches appeared in *Stuff and Nonsense* (1884); *The Bull Calf* (1892); and *Carlo* (1913). His more formal illustrations appeared in *Scribner's, Harper's,* and *Collier's*; a selection of these was published in *A Book of Drawings* (1904). His best-known drawings were for Joel Chandler Harris's "Uncle Remus" books (1892–1918).

FROST, EDWIN BRANT (*b. Brattleboro, Vt., 1866; d. Chicago, Ill., 1935*), astronomer. Graduated Dartmouth, 1885. Director, Yerkes Observatory, 1905–32. His most important work dealt with the spectra of stars.

FROST, HOLLOWAY HALSTEAD (*b. Brooklyn, N.Y., 1889; d. Kansas City, Mo., 1935*), naval officer. Graduated Annapolis, 1910. Specialist in naval strategy and tactics, he wrote and lectured extensively on these subjects.

FROST, ROBERT LEE (*b. San Francisco, Calif., 1874; d. Boston, Mass., 1963*), poet. Professor at Amherst (1917–20, 1923–25, 1926–38); the University of Michigan (1921–23, 1925–26), Harvard (1939–43); Dartmouth (1943–49); lecturer at Amherst (1949–63). In England from 1912 to 1915, Frost developed relationships with Ezra Pound, W. B. Yeats, and Edward Thomas, among others. Published *A Boy's Will* (1913) and *North of Boston* (1914); these poems introduced his experiments with voice tone and colloquial diction. Won Pulitzer Prize for *New Hampshire* (1923), *Collected Poems* (1930), A *Further Range* (1936), and A *Witness Tree* (1942). His greatest contribution to American poetry was in variations with blank verse in his narrative poems. These poems used "sentence sounds," Frost's term for the merger of free-flowing colloquial speech rhythms and the regularity of unrhymed iambic pentameter. In his last years the most admired American poet of the century, Frost was named consultant in poetry in the Library of Congress in 1958. Among his popular triumphs was his reading of "The Gift Outright" at the inauguration of President John F. Kennedy in 1961. Other books are *Mountain Interval* (1916), *West-Running Brook* (1928), A *Masque of Reason* (1945), A *Masque of Mercy* (1947), *Steeple Bush* (1947), and *In the Clearing* (1962).

FROST, WADE HAMPTON (*b. Marshall, Va., 1880; d. Baltimore, Md., 1938*), epidemiologist, M.D., University of Virginia, 1903. Medical officer, U.S. Public Health Service, 1905–28; professor of epidemiology and public health, Johns Hopkins, 1919–38.

FROTHINGHAM, ARTHUR LINCOLN (*b. Boston, Mass., 1859; d. Princeton, N.J., 1923*), scholar, educator. Professor of archaeology at Princeton, 1886–1905. Founded *American Journal of Archaeology*, 1885; wrote prolifically on archaeological subjects.

FROTHINGHAM, NATHANIEL LANGDON (*b. Boston, Mass., 1793; d. 1870*), Unitarian clergyman. Graduated Harvard, 1811. Pastor of the First Church, Boston, 1815–50; an intellectual, much admired by R. W. Emerson, he was author of hymns, metrical translations from Latin and German literature, sermons, and other works.

FROTHINGHAM, OCTAVIUS BROOKS (*b. Boston, Mass., 1822; d. Boston, 1895*), Unitarian and independent clergyman. Son of Nathaniel L. Frothingham. Pastor, Third Congregational Unitarian Society, New York, 1859–79, and a founder and first president of the Free Religious Association (Boston), he was considered the intellectual heir of Theodore Parker.

FROTHINGHAM, PAUL REVERE (*b. Jamaica Plain, Mass., 1864; d. 1926*), Unitarian clergyman. Nephew of Octavius B. Frothingham.

FROTHINGHAM, RICHARD (*b. Charlestown, Mass., 1812; d. 1880*), historian, businessman, legislator. Managing editor of the *Boston Post*, 1852–65; author of meticulously accurate studies of local history, including *History of the Siege of Boston* (1848) and *The Rise of the Republic* (1872).

FRY, BIRKETT DAVENPORT (*b. Kanawha Co., Va., now W.Va., 1822; d. Richmond, Va., 1891*), lawyer, cotton manufacturer, Confederate brigadier general.

FRY, JAMES BARNET (*b. Carrollton, Ill., 1827; d. Newport, R.I., 1894*), soldier, writer. Graduated West Point, 1847. Organized Bureau of the Provost-Marshal-General, 1863, after outstanding field service at first Bull Run, Shiloh, and Perryville. His conduct of the bureau until 1866 was the occasion of celebrated debate in Congress between J. G. Blaine and Roscoe Conkling. He served thereafter in the adjutant general's department. Published much military history.

FRY, JOSHUA (*b. Crewkerne, England, ca. 1700; d. Wilf's Creek [now Cumberland], Md., 1754*), mathematics professor, surveyor, pioneer. Came to Virginia, *ante* 1720. Member of the House of Burgesses; commander of the militia, 1754. Author, with Peter Jefferson, of the celebrated *Map of the Inhabited Parts of Virginia* (1751).

FRY, RICHARD (*fl. 1731–41*), papermaker, bookseller. In Boston jail for debt, he sent to the legislature in 1739 a scheme for a chain of factories to provide New England with a variety of products.

FRY, WILLIAM HENRY (*b. Philadelphia, Pa., 1815; d. Santa Cruz, West Indies, 1864*), composer, journalist. First successful American opera composer; his *Leonara* was produced in Philadelphia and New York, 1845, and revived, 1858.

FRYE, JOSEPH (*b. Andover, Mass., 1711/12; d. 1794*), soldier. At siege of Louisburg, 1744–45; on Kennebec expedition, 1754; survived massacre at Fort William Henry, 1757; served briefly in Revolution. Grantee of Fryeburg, Maine, which was named in his honor, 1777.

FRYE, WILLIAM JOHN ("JACK") (*b. near Sweetwater, Tex., 1904; d. Tucson, Ariz., 1959*), airline and manufacturing executive. First president of Transcontinental and Western Air (TWA), 1934–47. A pioneer in commercial aviation, Frye introduced the DC–3 and the Constellation. The firm was joined in 1939 by

Howard Hughes, who eventually gained control of the airline. Frye resigned in 1947 over differences with Hughes and became president of the General Aniline and Film Company.

FRYE, WILLIAM PIERCE (*b. Lewiston, Maine, 1831; d. Lewiston, 1911*), lawyer. Great-great-grandson of Joseph Frye. As congressman, Republican, from Maine, 1871–81, established himself both as a debater and an industrious committee worker. Chosen U.S. senator, 1881, he served until death as a Senate wheel horse, was one of the Old Guard under Roosevelt and Taft, long chairman of the Committee on Commerce, and a member of the Foreign Relations Committee. An ardent expansionist, he was also a constant supporter of measures to revive the American merchant marine.

FRYER, DOUGLAS HENRY (*b. Willimantic, Conn., 1891; d. Rye, N.Y., 1960*), industrial psychologist. Graduated from Clark University, Ph.D., 1923. Taught at New York University from 1924. Administrative chairman of the University Heights Department of Psychology, 1925–40. Worked with various government personnel programs during World War II. A founding director of Richardson, Bellows, Henry and Co. (1945), a firm of consulting psychologists.

FUERTES, ESTEVAN ANTONIO (*b. San Juan, Puerto Rico, 1838; d. 1903*), engineer, educator. Dean, civil engineering department of Cornell University, 1873–1902; built it into a great technical school, devising courses, installing laboratories, making his idealism and enthusiasm widely felt.

FUERTES, LOUIS AGASSIZ (*b. Ithaca, N.Y., 1874; d. 1927*), artist-naturalist. Son of Estevan A. Fuertes. Illustrated most of the leading bird books published, 1896–1927, with paintings and sketches of extraordinary accuracy.

FULLAM, FRANK L. (*b. West Brookfield, Mass., 1870; d. Princeton, N.J., 1951*), chemist. Expert in smokeless powder explosives; superintendent and then manager (1905–20) of International Smokeless Powder and Chemical Co., a subsidiary of Du Pont. Smokeless powder played an important role in the nation's munitions production during World War I. Directed operations leading to the discovery of Duco automobile lacquer.

FULLER, ANDREW S. (*b. Utica, N.Y., 1828; d. 1896*), horticulturist, editor. Pioneer in strawberry crossbreeding. Author of *Illustrated Strawberry Culturist* (1862); *The Small Fruit Culturist* (1867); *The Nut Culturist* (1896); and other works. An indefatigable experimenter.

FULLER, GEORGE (*b. Deerfield, Mass., 1822; d. Brookline, Mass., 1884*), painter. Pupil of Henry Kirke Brown; studied also at National Academy of Design. After a number of years of wandering and the artist's life, settled at Deerfield as a farmer, 1860–75. Forced back to his profession by financial pressure, he entered on the finest period of his work, producing his masterpiece *Winifred Dysart* in 1881. An elusive, mystical quality distinguishes all his painting.

FULLER, GEORGE WARREN (*b. New York, N.Y., 1868; d. 1934*), engineer. Graduated Massachusetts Institute of Technology, 1890; studied at University of Berlin. An expert in water supply and purification, sewerage and sewage treatment.

FULLER, HENRY BLAKE (*b. Chicago, Ill., 1857; d. 1929*), novelist. His early work was divided between use of romantic materials from his European travels, as in *The Chevalier of Pensieri-Vani* (1890, under pseudonym "Stanton Page"), and *The Chatelaine of La Trinité* (1892), and realistic studies of the raw Middle West. Of the latter, *The Cliff-Dwellers* (1893) and *With the Procession* (1895) are outstanding. His subsequent work expressed his disgust with developing trends in the national culture, culminating in a revival of creativity shortly before his death. *Gardens of This World* and *Not on the Screen*, written in the last year of his life, were published posthumously.

FULLER, HIRAM (*b. Halifax, Mass., 1814; d. Paris, France, 1880*), journalist. Partner of George P. Morris and Nathaniel P. Willis in conducting the *New York Mirror*, 1843–44; continuing as owner-manager of the *Evening Mirror*, he lost all support by pro-Southern utterances and expatriated himself on outbreak of the Civil War.

FULLER, JOHN WALLACE (*b. Harston, England, 1827; d. Toledo, Ohio, 1891*), businessman, Union soldier. Came to America as a child. Colonel, 27th Ohio; brigadier general, commanding "Fuller's Brigade" in western campaigns and on the Atlanta and Carolina campaigns.

FULLER, JOSEPH VINCENT (*b. Knoxville, Tenn., 1890; d. 1932*), historical editor in research section, U.S. State Department. Graduated Harvard, 1914; Ph.D., 1921. Edited diplomatic correspondence of the United States relating to World War I.

FULLER, LEVI KNIGHT (*b. Westmoreland, N.H., 1841; d. 1896*), inventor, manufacturer. Long associated with Estey Organ Co. Republican governor of Vermont, 1892–94.

FULLER, LOIE (*b. Fullersburg, Ill., 1862; d. 1928*), dancer. Her "serpentine" dance brought success *post* 1891. Experimenting with possibilities latent in harmonies of light, color, and movement, she developed school in Paris; was especially popular in Europe.

FULLER, MARGARET. *See* FULLER, SARAH MARGARET.

FULLER, MELVILLE WESTON (*b. Augusta, Maine, 1833; d. Sorrento, Maine, 1910*), jurist. Graduated Bowdoin, 1853. Removed to Chicago, Ill., 1856, where he practiced law. Dignity, courtesy, moderation, learning and a distinct personality marked him at the bar and on the bench. A strong Democrat, on his appointment as chief justice of U.S. Supreme Court by President Cleveland in 1888, he inclined toward strict construction of all governmental powers and insisted that congressional powers were derivable only from specific grants, reasonably construed. He was consistent in support of traditional rights of person and property against the tendency toward regulation and limitation which marked his time.

FULLER, RICHARD (*b. Beaufort, S.C., 1804; d. Baltimore, Md., 1876*), Baptist clergyman, apologist for slavery.

FULLER, ROBERT MASON (*b. Schenectady, N.Y., 1845; d. 1919*), physician, pharmacist. Graduated Albany Medical School, 1865. Originated and worked out the principle of the tablet triturate; introduced the use of the camera in teaching and in forensic medicine.

FULLER, SARAH MARGARET (*b. Cambridgeport, Mass., 1810; d. at sea, 1850*), journalist, critic, social reformer. Forced in her education by her strenuous father, she began her friendships with intellectual leaders like F. H. Hedge, James Freeman Clarke, and W. H. Channing at an early age and was accepted in the transcendentalist circle on a par with Alcott and Thoreau. After several years of teaching, she started her famous "conversations" in 1839 with a group of ladies from cultivated Boston society who met at Elizabeth Peabody's; from their discussions derived *Woman in the Nineteenth Century* (1845), a work often compared to Mary Wollstonecraft's. It touched on all issues of the woman's movement but was too philosophical for the militant enthusiasts.

With R. W. Emerson and George Ripley, Fuller edited the

transcendentalist *Dial*. Invited by Horace Greeley to join the *New York Tribune*, she won a reputation as one of the best American critics. Going to Europe, 1846, she visited Carlyle, Wordsworth, and others, and met Mazini. Settling in Rome, 1847, she joined in the revolution of 1848. Angelo Ossoli, an Italian marchese whom she married at some time during her Italian sojourn, fought with the republican army. Fuller assisted in the organization of hospitals, writing occasionally to the *Tribune* to describe the siege of Rome, 1849.

When the French suppressed the Roman Republic in July, Fuller fled to Florence with Ossoli and their son, then about a year old; she spent the winter writing a history of the Roman Revolution. In May 1850, the family sailed from Leghorn for America. All drowned when the vessel went down off Fire Island, N.Y. An invalid most of her life and a better talker than a writer, Fuller worked prodigiously. Although her eccentricities offended many, her noble and generous personality impressed itself upon her generation. Her critical writings were published in *Papers on Literature and Art* (1846) and in the edition of her works by Horace Greeley (1869).

FULLER, THOMAS CHARLES (*b. Fayetteville, N.C., 1832; d. Raleigh, N.C., 1901*), lawyer. Confederate soldier. Member of Confederate Congress. Justice of court of private land claims dealing with former Mexican territory, 1891–1901.

FULLERTON, GEORGE STUART (*b. Fatehgarh, India, 1859; d. Poughkeepsie, N.Y., 1925*), "new realist" philosopher. Taught at University of Pennsylvania, and was dean of Graduate School; later a research professor at Columbia. Author of *System of Metaphysics* (1904), *The World We Live In* (1912), and other scholarly works.

FULTON, JOHN FARQUHAR (*b. St. Paul, Minn., 1899; d. Hamden, Conn., 1960*), neurophysiologist. Studied at Harvard, B.S., 1921, and at Oxford University as a Rhodes scholar, D.Phil., 1925. Taught at Yale University School of Medicine from 1930; chairman of the department of physiology, 1931; chairman of the department of the history of medicine from 1951. Established the first primate colony in the U.S. to study the correlations between cerebral physiology in apes and human neurological disorders. His research on the behavioral effects of extirpation of the anterior association areas of the frontal lobes led to the development of prefrontal lobotomy for relief of psychosis. With Allen D. Keller, published *The Sign of Babinski* in 1932. Amassed one of the world's most extensive collections of works on physiology.

FULTON, JUSTIN DEWEY (*b. Earlville, N.Y., 1828; d. Somerville, Mass., 1901*), Baptist clergyman. Fanatical opponent of slavery, drink, woman suffrage, the drama, and Roman Catholicism.

FULTON, ROBERT (*b. Lancaster Co., Pa,., 1765; d. New York, N.Y., 1815*), artist, civil engineer, inventor. As a boy, showed genius for drawing; learned gunsmithing; provided mechanical aid and decorative designs much in demand with gunmakers. Went to Philadelphia, 1782; successfully painted portraits, miniatures, landscapes; also made mechanical drawings. Journeying to London, 1786, for his health, he did not return for 20 years.

Friendship with the Duke of Bridgewater and Lord Stanhope encouraged him to devote full time to engineering projects for internal improvements and the devising of mechanical equipment, especially for canals. He patented machines for sawing marble, spinning flax, twisting hemp rope, and raising and lowering canal boats. He invented a dredge for cutting channels and wrote many pamphlets and *A Treatise on the Improvement of Canal Navigation* (1796), profusely illustrated by himself and containing complete computations of construction and operating costs. He also designed low-cost cast-iron aqueducts and bridges.

From 1797 to 1806 Fulton devoted himself principally to the development of the submarine mine and torpedo. Aided by Joel Barlow, he experimented at Brest; then, to support himself in France, obtained French patents on his canal improvements, and saw his plans for the Paris-Dieppe canal adopted. He also painted probably the first panorama, *L'Incendie de Moscow*. About 1799 the Directory rejected his torpedo plans. Following Napoleon's appointment of a commission to examine his schemes, Fulton built a remarkably successful diving boat, *Nautilus*, which descended 25 feet, steered easily under water, and could stay down 4.5 hours. After trials, Napoleon authorized Fulton to proceed against British ships, but when a summer's reconnoitering of the coast brought no British prizes, the French lost interest and Fulton received no pay or expense money.

The British government now made overtures to Fulton, but although he proved the value of his submarine by blowing up a brig near Deal, he failed against the French fleet and this invention was not adopted. During all these negotiations and experiments Fulton kept the United States officially informed.

Fulton now entered into an agreement with Robert R. Livingston to construct a steamboat to navigate between New York and Albany. After one boat launched on the Seine sank because of the weight of machinery, 1803, Fulton built a successful steamboat which proceeded upstream at 4.5 mph. He then ordered an engine from Boulton & Watt for the *Clermont* to be built in New York by Charles Brown. The craft was 133 feet long, 18 feet broad, 7 feet deep. The Watt engine was placed forward of a 20-foot boiler set in brickwork and housed-over. Two side paddle wheels propelled the boat up the Hudson to Albany and back in five days, Aug. 17–22, 1807, the *Clermont* being actually under way only 62 hours.

After the success of the *Clermont*, Fulton was busy establishing commercial lines and directing the building of 17 other steamboats, a torpedo boat, and a ferryboat. He designed a steam warship for New York harbor defense, authorized for construction in 1814; called *Fulton the First*, it was a large vessel, 156 feet long and carrying thirty 32-pounders. During his last years Fulton experimented with firing guns under water. Commonly called the "inventor" of the steamboat, he was rather the man who devised for it a practical design and demonstrated its commercial value.

FULTON, ROBERT BURWELL (*b. Sumter Co., Ala., 1849; d. New York, N.Y., 1919*), educator. Graduated University of Mississippi, 1869. Taught there, and served as chancellor, 1892–1906. Developed system of affiliated high schools; extended curriculum; added three professional schools.

FUNK, CASIMIR (*b. Warsaw, Poland, 1884; d. Albany, N.Y., 1967*), biochemist. Studied at the University of Geneva in Switzerland and the University of Bern (Ph.D., 1904), and the Pasteur Institute in Paris. Publications on protein chemistry and protein metabolism resulted from his collaboration with Emil Abderhalden at the University of Berlin (1906–1907). Biochemist at the Municipal Hospital in Wiesbaden, Germany, 1907–08. Researcher at the Lister Institute of Preventive Medicine in London, 1910–13; then at the London Cancer Hospital Research Institute, 1913–15. Immigrated to the United States in 1915; naturalized in 1920. Worked for the Harriman Research Laboratory in New York City (1915), Calco Company in Bound Brook, N.J. (1916), and Metz and Company in New York City (1917–23). Biochemist at Columbia University, 1918–23. Returned to Warsaw as chief of the Department of Biochemistry at the State Institute of Hygiene, 1923–27. Founded Casa Biochemica in 1928. Biochemist for the Roussel Company, 1927–36. Research consultant to the U.S. Vitamin Corporation of New

York from 1936. Through the corporation's sponsorship, became head of the Funk Foundation for Medical Research from 1947. Retired in 1963. Best known for his work on vitamins (he coined the term). His declaration of the "vitamine Hypothesis" stimulated worldwide interest in the role of vitamins in health and disease.

FUNK, ISAAC KAUFFMAN (*b. Clifton, Ohio, 1839; d. 1912*), Lutheran clergyman, publisher, editor. Founded Funk & Wagnalls Co., 1877, with A. W. Wagnalls. Projected and edited the *Literary Digest* and A *Standard Dictionary of the English Language.*

FUNK, WILFRED JOHN (*b. Brooklyn, N.Y., 1883; d. Montclair, N.J., 1965*), publisher and lexicographer. The son of Isaac Kauffman Funk, cofounder of the publishing firm Funk and Wagnalls. Studied at Princeton (graduated, 1909). Joined Funk and Wagnalls in 1909; secretary in 1912; vice president in 1914; president from 1925–40. Published six volumes of poetry. Editor of *Literary Digest* 1936–37. Founded Wilfred Funk, Inc. in 1940. Sold his interest in the firm to Funk and Wagnalls in 1954. Best known for his books and articles on vocabulary improvement and etymology, Funk wrote 30 *Days to a More Powerful Vocabulary* with Norman Lewis (1942) and *Word Origins and Their Romantic Stories* (1950). He wrote a monthly feature for *Reader's Digest* called "It Pays to Increase Your Word Power" from 1946–65.

FUNSTON, FREDERICK (*b. New Carlisle, Ohio, 1865; d. 1917*), soldier. Raised in Kansas; trained as botanist. Served in Cuban insurrection, 1896–97; commanded a regiment in the Philippines, 1899–1900; received the Congressional Medal and became brigadier general of volunteers. With a small party, he captured Aguinaldo, the insurrectionist leader, in March 1901 and was transferred to the regular army as brigadier general. Commanded the department of California during San Francisco earthquake, 1906; commanded the force sent to hold Veracruz, 1914, and was military governor there. Promoted major general in November 1914, he commanded thereafter on the Mexican border.

FURLOW, FLOYD CHARLES (*b. Americus, Ga., 1877; d. New York, N.Y., 1923*), engineer. Graduated Georgia School of Technology, 1897. Chief engineer, later president, Otis Elevator Co. Inventor of many devices which brought electric elevators to high efficiency.

FURMAN, JAMES CLEMENT (*b. Charleston, S.C., 1809; d. near Greenville, S.C., 1891*), Baptist clergyman. President, Furman University, 1852–79. Son of Richard Furman.

FURMAN, RICHARD (*b. Esopus, N.Y., 1755; d. 1825*), Baptist clergyman, educator. Raised in South Carolina; ordained 1774, he took an active part in the Revolution. A Federalist in politics, Furman also favored strong central authority in his church and was its outstanding leader in the South. He led the movement to found a collegiate school for the Baptist ministry and Furman University, founded a short time after his death, was named for him.

FURNAS, ROBERT WILKINSON (*b. near Troy, Ohio, 1824; d. Lincoln, Nebr., 1905*), agriculturist, Union soldier. Removed to Nebraska, 1856; edited *Nebraska Advertiser.* Republican governor of Nebraska, 1873–75. Noteworthy for a lifelong devotion to the advancement of agriculture and education.

FURNESS, HORACE HOWARD (*b. Philadelphia, Pa., 1833; d. Wallingford, Pa., 1912*), lawyer, Shakespeare scholar. Son of William H. Furness. Graduated Harvard, 1854. Edited the New Variorum Shakespeare, 1871 to his death.

FURNESS, HORACE HOWARD (*b. Philadelphia, Pa., 1865; d. 1930*), Shakespeare scholar. Son of Horace H. Furness (1833–1912). Coeditor, New Variorum Shakespeare, *post* 1901; later succeeded his father as editor.

FURNESS, WILLIAM HENRY (*b. Boston, Mass., 1802; d. 1896*), Unitarian clergyman. Pastor, Unitarian church in Philadelphia, 1825–75; thereafter emeritus. Active in antislavery movement, and a pioneer American student of German literature.

FURST, CLYDE BOWMAN (*b. Williamsport, Pa., 1873; d. 1931*), educator. Known for his work with Carnegie Foundation for the Advancement of Teaching; secretary, *post* 1911. Put teachers' pension systems on sound basis.

FURUSETH, ANDREW (*b. near Romedal, Norway, 1854; d. Washington, D.C., 1938*), labor leader. Changed name from Anders Andreassen. Came to America, 1880. President, International Seamen's Union, 1908–38; crusader for seamen's rights; his ideas embodied in La Follette Seamen's Act, 1915.

FUSSELL, BARTHOLOMEW (*b. Chester Co., Pa., 1794; d. Chester Springs, Pa., 1871*), physician, abolitionist. Active cooperator in the Underground Railroad.

G

GABB, WILLIAM MORE (b. Philadelphia, Pa., 1839; d. Philadelphia, 1878), paleontologist. Studied with James Hall. Served on geological survey of California (Whitney's), 1861–64; worked also in Mexico, Santo Domingo, and Costa Rica.

GABLE, (WILLIAM) CLARK (b. Cadiz, Ohio, 1901; d. Hollywood, Calif., 1960), actor. One of the most famous screen actors of his time, Gable began acting in stock companies; in the early 1930's he made several films cast as a villain; in 1934 he made It Happened One Night , a comedy, for which he was awarded the Academy Award. Other films include Mutiny on the Bounty (1935), San Francisco (1936), Idiot's Delight (1939), and, his most famous film, Gone with the Wind (1939). Gable served in the U.S. Army Air Forces during World War II, discharged as a major. His other films include Run Silent, Run Deep (1958), Mogambo (1953), and The Misfits (1960).

GABRILOWITSCH, OSSIP (b. St. Petersburg, Russia, 1878; d. Detroit, Mich., 1936), concert pianist, orchestra conductor. Son-in-law of Mark Twain. Settled in America, 1914. Director, Detroit Symphony Orchestra, 1918–35.

GADSDEN, CHRISTOPHER (b. Charleston, S.C., 1724; d. 1805), merchant, revolutionary leader. Member of South Carolina Assembly, 1757–58. In the Stamp Act Congress, 1765, Gadsden urged for colonial union and against recognition of Parliament's authority. As leader of the radicals, his integrity, zeal, and courage made him an invaluable champion; the Charleston mechanics followed him enthusiastically. Delegate to the First and Second Continental Congresses, he left in 1776 to serve in the South Carolina forces. The climax of his career came in 1778 when he and William H. Drayton secured the disestablishment of the church and popular election of senators in the South Carolina constitution adopted that year. He was among the few Carolina legislators who opposed confiscation of Loyalist property.

GADSDEN, JAMES (b. Charleston, S.C., 1788; d. Charleston, 1858), soldier, politician. Grandson of Christopher Gadsden. Settled in Florida, 1822–39. As president of the South Carolina Railroad Co., 1840–50, he hoped to form southern railroads into one system connected by a route to the Pacific along the U.S. southern frontier. This would make the West tributary to the South and inaugurate direct trade with Europe. He promoted this idea through a series of so-called railroad and commercial conventions but realized that purchase of Mexican territory was necessary to secure the most practicable westward route. As minister to Mexico under President Pierce, Gadsden was authorized to buy as much border land as possible for $50 million. The Gadsden Purchase was the result of this offer (1853–54).

GAFFNEY, MARGARET. See HAUGHERY, MARGARET GAFFNEY.

GÁG, WANDA HAZEL (b. New Ulm, Minn., 1893; d. New York, N.Y., 1946), artist. Author and illustrator of a number of innovative children's books in which the pictures were integral parts of the hand-lettered text. These included Millions of Cats (1928), Snippy and Snappy (1931), and volumes of translations from Grimm's Kinder und Hausmärchen. She was also a successful artist in watercolor, wood engraving, and lithography.

GAGE, FRANCES DANA PARKER (b. Marietta, Ohio, 1808; d. Greenwich, Conn., 1884), reformer, author. Popular speaker and writer on slavery, temperance, women's rights.

GAGE, LYMAN JUDSON (b. Deruyter, N.Y., 1836; d. San Diego, Calif., 1927), banker. Removed to Chicago, Ill., 1855; was associated post 1868 with First National Bank there, and served as its president, 1891–97. Prominent in moves to reconcile capital and labor, and as director of Chicago Exposition, 1893, he accepted the post of secretary of the treasury from McKinley after staunchly defending the gold standard in the 1896 campaign. During the Spanish-American War he added greatly to his financial reputation and was influential in securing passage of the Act establishing the gold standard, Mar. 14, 1900. He resigned the secretaryship in 1902.

GAGE, MATILDA JOSLYN (b. Cicero, N.Y., 1826; d. Chicago, Ill., 1898), woman's suffrage leader. Coauthor with Elizabeth Cady Stanton and Susan B. Anthony of History of Woman Suffrage (1881–86).

GAGE, THOMAS (b. Firle, England, 1721; d. 1787), soldier, last royal governor of Massachusetts. Came to America, 1754. Fought with distinction on Braddock's expedition and in later campaigns of French and Indian War; was commander in chief in North America, 1763–73. He succeeded Thomas Hutchinson as governor of Massachusetts, 1774, to find the quarrel with the English government in a high state of aggravation, the Boston Port Act having just been announced. Gage's attempts to seize military stores from the colonists resulted in the outbreak of hostilities at Lexington and Concord, April 1775, and the subsequent siege of Boston. He left Boston for England on Oct. 10, 1775.

GAILLARD, DAVID DU BOSE (b. Fulton, S.C., 1859; d. Baltimore, Md., 1913), engineer, soldier. Graduated West Point, 1884. Served on commission reestablishing Mexican boundary; surveyed Portland Channel; commanded regiment of engineers in Spanish-American War. Published valuable standard work, Wave Action in Relation to Engineering Structures (1904). In 1907, he was put in charge of dredging and excavation on the Panama Canal by General Goethals. He energetically organized his areas, presently taking charge of central division, which included cutting through the continental divide. Gaillard progressed in spite of great earth slides and other discouragements, until in July 1913, within sight of the end of the work, he broke under the strain and never recovered.

GAILLARD, EDWIN SAMUEL (b. near Charleston, S.C., 1827; d. 1885), surgeon, medical journalist. Founder and editor, Richmond Medical Journal and American Medical Weekly.

GAILLARD, JOHN (*b. St. Stephen's Parish, S.C., 1765; d. Washington, D.C., 1826f*), planter. U.S. senator, Democratic-Republican, from South Carolina, 1805–26.

GAILLARDET, THÉODORE FRÉDÉRIC (*b. Auxerre, France, 1808; d. Plessis-Bouchard, France, 1882*), journalist, author. As owner-editor, 1840–48, revivified the *Courrier des États-Unis* and gave it national standing as a newspaper for Franco-Americans.

GAILOR, THOMAS FRANK (*b. Jackson, Miss., 1856; d. Sewanee, Tenn., 1935*), Episcopal clergyman. Long associated with University of the South, Sewanee, Tenn. Consecrated bishop of Tennessee, 1893.

GAINE, HUGH (*b. Belfast, Ireland, 1726/27; d. New York, N.Y., 1807*), printer, bookseller. Came to America 1745. Founded the *New-York Mercury*, 1752, and kept the paper going through denominational and Revolutionary difficulties until 1783; was official New York printer for city and province *post* 1768.

GAINES, EDMUND PENDLETON (*b. Culpeper Co., Va., 1777; d. New Orleans, La., 1849*), soldier. Brother of George S. Gaines. In War of 1812, covered the American retreat at Chrysler's Field; conducted defense of Fort Erie. Fought against Creek and Seminole; in Black Hawk War; and in Florida War, 1835. In command of the western department at outbreak of Mexican War, he was court-martialed for raising troops in defiance of War Department reprimands. Defending himself skillfully and vehemently, he was exonerated and later commanded the eastern department. Fiery and unrestrained, he cherished a lifelong feud with Gen. Winfield Scott and the U.S. War Department.

GAINES, GEORGE STROTHER (*b. Stokes Co., N.C., ca. 1784; d. Mississippi, 1873*), Alabama pioneer, Indian agent, merchant, planter. Brother of Edmund P. Gaines. His fair dealing, kindness, adroitness as agent to the Choctaw, 1805–19, won their trade and friendship. His service to pioneers of Mississippi Territory were inestimable. Gainesville, Ala., was named for him.

GAINES, JOHN POLLARD (*b. Augusta Co., Va., 1795; d. near Salem, Oreg., 1857*), lawyer, soldier. Raised in Kentucky. Served in War of 1812 and Mexican War; was congressman, Whig, from Kentucky, 1847–49. Appointed governor of Oregon Territory, he served 1850–53. His single term was marked by disputes, principally over the choice of Salem or Oregon City as the capital.

GAINES, REUBEN REID (*b. Sumter Co., Ala., 1836; d. 1914*), lawyer, Confederate soldier. Removed to Texas, 1868. Chief justice, Texas Supreme Court, 1894–1911.

GAINES, WESLEY JOHN (*b. Wilkes Co., Ga., 1840; d. Atlanta, Ga., 1912*), bishop of the African Methodist Episcopal church. An able organizer and financial agent, and a promoter of education for blacks.

GAITHER, HORACE ROWAN, JR. (*b. Natchez, Miss., 1909; d. Boston, Mass., 1961*), lawyer and foundation executive. Studied at the University of California at Berkeley and the University of California Law School (graduated, 1933). Worked for the Farm Credit Administration in Washington, D.C. (1933–36), and the law firm of Cooley, Crowley, and Supple in San Francisco, Calif. (1936–41). Instructor at Berkeley, 1936–41. Assistant director of the Massachusetts Institute of Technology Radiation Laboratory, 1942–45. Worked for the Ford Foundation from 1948; associate director (1951–53); president (1953–56); chairman of the board (1956–58). Trustee, secretary, and general counsel of the RAND Corporation from 1946; chairman of the board, 1948–59. Headed a security resources panel established by the Science Advisory Committee in 1957; its classified report, "Deterrence and Survival in the Nuclear Age," was declassified and published in 1976. As a foundation director, he was concerned with scientific development and the applications of technology and the social sciences to national security. Due to his efforts, the Ford Foundation contributed to making organized philanthropy a profession.

GALBERRY, THOMAS (*b. Naas, Ireland, 1833; d. New York, N.Y., 1878*), Roman Catholic clergyman. Came to America as a child. Graduated Villanova, 1851. Ordained as Augustinian, 1856. Was rector of Villanova, 1872–75, and Augustinian provincial. Consecrated bishop of Hartford, 1876.

GALBREATH, CHARLES BURLEIGH (*n. near Leetonia, Ohio, 1858; d. Columbus, Ohio, 1934*), Ohio State librarian. Author of *History of Ohio* (1925) and other works.

GALE, BENJAMIN (*b. Jamaica, N.Y., 1715; d. 1790*), physician, political writer. Studied with Jared Eliot at Killingworth, Conn.; succeeded him in practice there. Wrote a valuable paper on smallpox; associated with David Bushnell in early submarine work.

GALE, ELBRIDGE (*b. Bennington, Vt., 1824; d. 1907*), Baptist clergyman, horticulturist. Professor, Kansas State Agricultural College; removed to Florida, 1884, where he raised fruits and succeeded in propagating the Mulgoba mango.

GALE, GEORGE WASHINGTON (*b. Stanford, N.Y., 1789; d. 1861*), Presbyterian clergyman, educator. Graduated Union, 1814. Founded Oneida Institute, Whitesboro, N.Y., 1827; also Knox College, Galesburg, Ill., 1837. Both schools were at first operated on the principle of instruction for students in return for manual labor.

GALE, HENRY GORDON (*b. Aurora, Ill., 1874; d. Chicago, Ill., 1942*), physicist. B.A., University of Chicago, 1896; Ph.D., 1899. Taught at Chicago *post* 1899; professor of physics *post* 1916. At various times, he held deanships in the university's administration. Most of Gale's research work was done in collaboration with others (*e.g.*, George Ellery Hale and Albert A. Michelson), his responsibility being the exacting technical aspects of the experiments. He was coauthor with Robert A. Millikan of several widely used textbooks and edited the *Astrophysical Journal*, 1912–40.

GALE, ZONA (*b. Portage, Wis., 1874; d. Chicago, Ill., 1938*), journalist, novelist. Her best work was done in studies in regional realism such as *Birth* (1918) and *Miss Lulu Bett* (1920), the dramatization of which won a 1921 Pulitzer Prize.

GALES, JOSEPH (*b. Eckington, England, 1761; d. Raleigh, N.C., 1841*), printer, journalist, reformer. Friend of Joseph Priestly. Fled England, 1794, after advocating principles of Thomas Paine and defending French Revolution. Founded Raleigh, N.C., *Register*, 1799; compiled first two volumes of *Annals of Congress* (1834).

GALES, JOSEPH (*b. Eckington, England, 1786; d. 1860*), journalist. Son of Joseph Gales (1761–1841). Sole reporter of U.S. Senate proceedings, 1807–20. Proprietor with W. W. Seaton of *National Intelligencer*, most valuable source of congressional debates to 1833. Published *Annals of Congress* (1834–56) and *American State Papers* (1832–61).

GALL (*b. on the Moreau River, S.Dak., ca. 1840; d. Oak Creek, S.Dak., 1894*), Hunkpapa Sioux war chief. Military leader at Little Bighorn, 1876; later opposed Sitting Bull, became friend of whites, urged education on Indians.

GALLAGHER, HUGH PATRICK (*b. Killygordon, Ireland, 1815; d. San Francisco, Calif., 1882*), Roman Catholic clergyman. Came to America, 1837. Invited to California, 1852, by Bishop Alemany, he became colorful "Father Hugh" of mining camps, frontier towns; was organizer of parishes, schools, orphanages, hospitals.

GALLAGHER, RALPH W. (*b. Salamanca, N.Y., 1881; d. New York, N.Y., 1952*), oil company executive. President and chairman of the board of Standard Oil Company (New Jersey) (1942–45). Began work for Standard Oil subsidiary as a janitor. After retirement, director of W.T. Grant and Company and J.P. Morgan & Co., Inc.

GALLAGHER, WILLIAM DAVIS (*b. Philadelphia, Pa., 1808; d. Louisville, Ky., 1894*), editor, poet, public official. Raised in Ohio. Associated with many short-lived periodicals and newspapers, 1826–39; with the *Cincinnati Gazette*, 1839–50. His principal claim to remembrance is as a poet, among the first of his section, and influential there in encouraging literary expression. His work was collected in *Erato* (three issues, 1835–37); *Miami Woods* (1881); and in his own anthology, *Selections from the Poetical Literature of the West* (1841).

GALLATIN, ABRAHAM ALFONSE ALBERT (*b. Geneva, Switzerland, 1761; d. Astoria, N.Y., 1849*), statesman, diplomat. Early orphaned son of an aristocrat family, Gallatin developed Rousseauistic and republican sympathies and immigrated to America, 1780. At first trading in Maine, he later tutored in French at Harvard; in 1784 he set up a store at Clare's Farm on the Pennsylvania frontier near where he had sunk his patrimony in an extensive and unprofitable land purchase. He began his political career as a radical member of the 1788 Harrisburg conference called to consider revision of the U.S. Constitution and introduced radical resolutions. At the 1789–90 convention to revise the Pennsylvania Constitution, he contributed notably to discussions of suffrage, representation, taxation, and the judiciary. In the state legislature, 1790–92, he prepared the reports and bills of many committees and became leader in financial legislation. Elected to the U.S. Senate, 1793, he was ousted by the Federalists, who for political reasons challenged him on the inadequate time he had been a citizen. During the brief time he sat in the Senate, he angered Hamilton by calling for a detailed statement of the government's finances down to Jan. 1, 1794. Returning home to Fayette Co., 1794, he found western Pennsylvania seething with the Whiskey Rebellion, provoked by the excise bill of 1791. Gallatin courageously faced an armed mob and succeeded in persuading the revolutionary committee to peaceable submission, thus helping to prevent what amounted to civil war.

As congressman, Democratic-Republican, from Pennsylvania, 1795–1801, Gallatin showed an unrivaled grasp of constitutional and international law and great power of argument; he became leader of the minority, but his signal service was in matters of finance, though hindered by Federalist opposition. His insistence on the strict accountability of the Treasury Department to Congress caused the creation of the Ways and Means Committee. He also urged that no moneys be spent except for the purposes for which they had been appropriated.

Appointed secretary of the treasury on Jefferson's accession in 1801 and holding the post until 1814, Gallatin was not content to be a mere financier. He shaped his policy to further the political and social ends which he envisaged as the destiny of the United States. He felt that the nation, highly favored by geographical position and natural resources, would prosper through industry and commerce; without oppressive taxation, therefore, the government could look forward to a surplus to devote to national projects for education and internal improvements. Despite much British and French vexation of American commerce, an inefficient Navy Department, bitter Senate opposition, indifferent support from Jefferson and scarcely any from Madison, all government expenses, including interest on stock for the Louisiana Purchase, had been met, and the treasury surplus was $1 million at the end of Jefferson's first administration.

Gallatin's policies and his calculations for paying off the public debt were wrecked by the events of 1807–13. He had to enforce the Embargo of 1807 by drastic means and extend internal taxes. His plea for the Bank of the United States did not save its charter, and the issue of paper money by state banks brought about a suspension of specie payments outside New England. Senate opposition became so bitter that he asked the president to send him on a mission to Russia and left for St. Petersburg in May 1813.

For the next ten years Gallatin was abroad in the diplomatic service. As a member of the peace commission at Ghent, 1814, Gallatin not only prepared drafts on the most important points in dispute with Great Britain but with great skill maintained some harmony between John Quincy Adams and Henry Clay, his fellow commissioners, who clashed over sectional interests. Henry Adams has called the treaty signed at Ghent (December 1814) "the special and peculiar triumph of Mr. Gallatin." Before revisiting the United States in the fall-winter of 1815, Gallatin worked to conclude a favorable British-American commercial treaty. Declining to return to the Treasury Department, he became U.S. minister to France, where he worked conscientiously in a diplomatic deadlock, 1816–23, unable to press claims for injury done to American commerce by the Napoleonic decrees. He did assist the American minister in London in negotiating the treaty of 1818 which stabilized U.S. relations with Great Britain for a time.

Repelled by the tone of politics at home, Gallatin retired to his home in Pennsylvania until 1826 when he undertook a successful term as U.S. minister to London. When he returned in November 1827, the commercial treaties of 1815 and 1818 had been renewed, joint occupation of Oregon was to be continued indefinitely, and the northeast Canadian boundary was to be settled by the arbitration of the friendly king of the Netherlands. Urged by John Jacob Astor, Gallatin served as president (1831–39) of the new National Bank in New York, using his great influence in banking circles to hasten return to specie payments after the panic of 1837.

The services of this great financier, diplomat, and statesman have never been adequately recognized by his adopted country. He never paraded his patriotism, which was sincere and abiding. He never sought to ingratiate himself with the multitude. His appeal was always to men's reason and judgment, not to their emotions and prejudices. No prospect of political preferment or threat of personal loss could tempt or frighten him from what he felt to be the path of duty, honor, and truth. He was the author also of several pamphlets on currency and on tariffs and was a pioneer in study of American ethnology.

GALLAUDET, EDWARD MINER (*b. Hartford, Conn., 1837; d. 1917*), educator of the deaf. Son of Thomas H. Gallaudet., First principal of the Washington, D.C., school for the deaf, which became Gallaudet College, named after his father.

GALLAUDET, THOMAS (*b. Hartford, Conn., 1822; d. 1902*), teacher, Episcopal clergyman. Son of Thomas H. Gallaudet. Established church for the deaf in New York, 1852, the center of his tireless and widespread missionary work on their behalf.

GALLAUDET, THOMAS HOPKINS (*b. Philadelphia, Pa., 1787; d. 1851*), educator of the deaf. Graduated Yale, 1805. Studied instructional methods at the Institut Royal des Sourds-Muets, Paris, under Abbé Sicard, 1815; returned with the brilliant teacher Laurent Clerc. Together they raised money for the first free American school for the deaf, established at Hartford, Conn., 1817. As principal, 1817–30, Gallaudet trained men who established similar schools, He worked also for black education, public normal schools, manual training in public schools, and higher education for women.

GALLI-CURCI, AMELITA (*b. Milan, Italy, 1882; d. La Jolla, Calif., 1963*), opera singer. Made her Italian debut in 1906; official debut in Rome in 1908. With the Chicago Opera Association, 1916–24; sensational American debut as Gilda in *Rigoletto* established her as the reigning coloratura singer of her time. With the Metropolitan Opera in New York City, 1921–30. Became a U.S. citizen in 1921.

GALLIER, JAMES (*b. Ravensdale, Ireland, 1798; d. at sea, 1868*), architect. Came to New York, 1832; removed to New Orleans, 1834. With James H. Dakin, responsible for the introduction into New Orleans of buildings strongly influenced by Greek revival.

GALLINGER, JACOB HAROLD (*b. Cornwall, Canada, 1837; d. 1918*), physician. Practiced in Concord, N.H. Became power in Republican party, serving as New Hampshire legislator, as congressman, 1885–89, and as U.S. senator, 1891–1918. The embodiment of "stand-pattism," he was active in legislation to improve the District of Columbia.

GALLITZIN, DEMETRIUS AUGUSTINE (*b. The Hague, Netherlands, 1770; d. Loretto, Pa., 1840*), Roman Catholic clergyman. Son of a distinguished Russian diplomat, he was converted to Catholicism, 1787; coming to America, 1792, he entered St. Mary's Seminary, Baltimore, Md., and was ordained, 1795. Founded Catholic colony at Loretto, Pa., 1799, on frontier at the summit of the Alleghenies, persevering against poverty and local opposition. Receiving only a fraction of his expected patrimony from Europe, accepting no salary, and slow to collect land payments from his settlers, he ran into difficulties, although widely known and respected. A public appeal in 1827 brought aid from many sources, and Gallitzin endured every privation in order to pay back his creditors. His *Defence of Catholic Principles* (1816) went through many editions; in this as in his other works he was a model of tolerant controversy.

GALLOWAY, BEVERLY THOMAS (*b. Millersburg, Mo., 1863; d. Washington, D.C., 1938*), pioneer plant pathologist, agricultural research administrator. With U.S. Department of Agriculture, 1887–1933; chief, Bureau of Plant Industry, 1901–13.

GALLOWAY, CHARLES BETTS (*b. Kosciusko, Miss., 1849; d. Jackson, Miss., 1909*), Methodist Episcopal, South, clergyman. Pastor at Jackson and Vicksburg, Miss.; as bishop, *post* 1886, made extensive missionary tours in the Orient and South America; was a noted orator.

GALLOWAY, JOSEPH (*b. West River, Md., ca. 1731; d. England, 1803*), colonial statesman, Loyalist. Rose early to eminence at Philadelphia bar; member of Pennsylvania Assembly, 1756–64 and 1766–76. An able politician, he served interests of his own merchant class. As Speaker of the assembly in 1766–76, he attempted to restore harmony with England, believing that difficulties were basically constitutional and could be solved by provision of a written imperial constitution. Conscience, legalism, and pride forbade his adherence to the American cause, although he was a delegate to the First Continental Congress. Going over to the British, he was of great service to General Howe. He went to England, 1778, where he became spokesman for the American Loyalists. His many tracts and pamphlets are important sources for the history of the Revolution.

GALLOWAY, SAMUEL (*b. Gettysburg, Pa., 1811; d. Columbus, Ohio, 1872*), educator, lawyer, congressman. Reconstructed the entire Ohio school system, 1844–50, raising teaching standards, organizing teachers' institutes, inspiring educators and public to fresh vigor and interest.

GALLUP, JOSEPH ADAMS (*b. Stonnington, Conn., 1769; d. Woodstock, Vt., 1849*), physician, teacher. Graduated Dartmouth Medical College, 1798. Established, 1827, clinical school of medicine at Woodstock, Vt., with free infirmary to give students bedside instruction, an innovation in medical teaching.

GALLY, MERRITT (*b. near Rochester, N.Y., 1838; d. Brooklyn, N.Y., 1916*), Presbyterian clergyman, inventor. Patented the Universal job-printing press, 1869; also a linotype machine, a system of multiplex telegraphy, a long-distance telephone repeater, and devices for automatic musical instruments.

GALPIN, CHARLES JOSIAH (*b. Hamilton, N.Y., 1864; d. Falls Church, Va., 1947*), rural sociologist. B.A., Colgate University, 1885; M.A., 1888. Harvard, 1895. After experience as high school teacher and principal, farmer, and Baptist religious worker, he joined the faculty of the University of Wisconsin, 1911. Taught pioneering courses in problems of country life. Author of *Rural Life* (1918), *Rural Social Problems* (1924), and the basic *Social Anatomy of an Agricultural Community*, which has had lasting influence on rural sociology and social ecology. From 1919 to 1934, he headed the Division of Farm Studies, U.S. Department of Agriculture.

GÁLVEZ, BERNARDO DE (*b. Macharaviaya, Spain, 1746; d. Mexico, 1786*), captain general of Louisiana and the Floridas. Appointed governor of Louisiana, 1776, he strove to weaken the British by supplying arms to American frontier rebels and seizing British ships. When Spain entered the war, 1778, he reduced every British post in West Florida, enabling Spain to secure both Floridas at the peace settlement of 1783. In taking Pensacola, 1781, he crossed the bar alone under the guns of the British fort in a small ship, the *Galveztown*; for this feat he was named Count de Gálvez and Viscount de Galveztown. He was also promoted to captain general of Cuba, and in 1785 was made viceroy of New Spain.

GAMBLE, HAMILTON ROWAN (*b. Winchester, Va., 1798; d. 1864*), lawyer, jurist. Removed to Missouri, 1818. Presiding judge at first Dred Scott suit, he dissented in Scott's favor. As provisional governor, Unionist, 1861–64, he labored to save Missouri for the Union.

GAMBRELL, JAMES BRUTON (*b. Anderson, S.C., 1841; d. Dallas, Tex., 1921*), Baptist clergyman, editor, educator. President, Mercer University, 1893–96; secretary, Baptist General Convention of Texas, 1896–1918.

GAMMON, ELIJAH HEDDING (*b. present Lexington, Maine, 1819; d. 1891*), Methodist clergyman, farm-machinery manufacturer. Removed to Illinois, 1851. *Post* 1858, became a leader in promotion, manufacture, and distribution of harvesters, acquiring rights to sale of the machine devised by Charles W. and William W. Marsh. He was later a partner of William Deering. Devoting much of his wealth to religious and educational purposes, he founded and endowed Gammon Theological Seminary at Atlanta, Ga.

GAMOW, GEORGE (*b. Odessa, Russia, 1904; d. Boulder, Colo., 1968*), physicist. Studied at the University of Leningrad (Ph.D., 1928). Professor of physics at the University of Leningrad, 1931–33. Immigrated in 1934. Professor of physics at George Washington University, 1934–56; at the University of Colorado at Boulder, 1956–68. Developed theory of radioactive alpha decay (1928) and liquid-drop model of the nucleus; contributed to the theory of thermonuclear reaction rates in stellar interiors (1928–29). With Edward Teller, formulated the Gamow-Teller selection rule for beta decay (1936). Applied his knowledge of nuclear physics to astrophysical processes, studying stellar evolution, the expanding-universe theory, and stellar energy production. Proposed a theory of the origin of the universe that led to the prediction of a residual black-body radiation spectrum, the remnant of the primordial big bang (1948). Studies of DNA (from 1954) led to fundamental insight into the nature of genetic coding. His many books include popular-science works such as *Mr. Tompkins in Wonderland* (1939).

GANNETT, EZRA STILES (*b. Cambridge, Mass., 1801; d. 1871*), Unitarian clergyman, editor. Assisted William E. Channing at Federal St. Church, Boston; succeeded him as pastor. Active in organizing American Unitarian Association, 1825; vigorously opposed the transcendental movement.

GANNETT, FRANK ERNEST (*b. Bristol, N.Y., 1876; d. Rochester, N.Y., 1957*), journalist and publisher. Studied at Cornell. Owner of a newspaper empire that included over twenty-seven newspapers, mostly in upstate New York. Gannett was active in Republican politics; during the 1930's, he opposed Franklin D. Roosevelt's plan to pack the Supreme Court and to reorganize the government. He ran unsuccessfully for the Republican nomination for the presidency in 1940, losing to Wendell Willkie.

GANNETT, HENRY (*b. Bath, Maine, 1846; d. 1914*), chief geographer of U.S. Geological Survey, 1882–1914. Graduated Lawrence Scientific School, Harvard, 1869. Topographer to Hayden Survey of Colorado and Wyoming; geographer to tenth, eleventh, and twelfth U.S. censuses, and assisted in Philippine, Cuban, and Puerto Rican censuses. Helped establish U.S. Geographical Board, 1890, to eliminate confusion in place-names and served as its chairman; aided in forming the National Geographic Society, the Geological Society of America, the Association of American Geographers. His work was characterized by zeal for exactitude; under him the maps of the U.S. Geological Survey achieved their high quality.

GANNETT, WILLIAM CHANNING (*b. Boston, Mass., 1840; d. 1923*), Unitarian clergyman, writer. Son of Ezra S. Gannett. Held pastorates in Illinois, Minnesota, and, *post* 1889, Rochester, N.Y. An extreme liberal.

GANO, JOHN (*b. Hopewell, N.J., 1727; d. 1804*), Baptist clergyman, Continental army chaplain. Pastor at Morristown, N.J., and at New York City, 1762–88. Thereafter, preached in Kentucky and North Carolina.

GANO, STEPHEN (*b. New York, N.Y., 1762; d. 1828*), Baptist clergyman. Son of John Gano. Pastor at Providence, R.I., 1793–1828. An energetic pastor of liberal views, he was also active in community and educational affairs.

GANSEVOORT, LEONARD (*b. Albany, N.Y., 1751; d. 1810*), New York legislator, judge. Brother of Peter Gansevoort. Treasurer, Albany Committee of Correspondence; member of New York Provincial Congresses; prominent to the end of his life in state politics.

GANSEVOORT, PETER (*b. Albany, N.Y., 1749; d. 1812*), Revolutionary soldier. Brother of Leonard Gansevoort. Received thanks of Congress for brave defense of Fort Schuyler against British under St. Leger, 1777.

GANSO, EMIL (*b. Halberstadt, Germany, 1895; d. Iowa City, Iowa, 1941*), painter, printmaker. Came to United States, 1912. A baker by trade, he was self-taught as an artist, painting in pastel, watercolor, and oils, and exhibiting vigorous talent for drawing in his wood engravings, etchings, and lithographs. He was a friend of Jules Pascin, who exercised a considerable influence on him. Fundamentally a stylist, he evoked in his work a world of sensuous beauty, entirely without sentimentality.

GANSS, HENRY GEORGE (*b. Darmstadt, Germany, 1855; d. Lancaster, Pa., 1912*), Roman Catholic clergyman, composer. Came to America as an infant. Graduated St. Vincent's College, Latrobe, Pa., 1876, and was pastor in small Pennsylvania towns. His high character, scholarship, and ecclesiastical music made him influential in the church and the musical world.

GANTT, HENRY LAURENCE (*b. Calvert Co., Md., 1861; d. 1919*), engineer, industrial leader. Graduated Johns Hopkins, 1880; Stevens Institute of Technology, 1884. Associated with Frederick W. Taylor in pioneer scientific management. Among his major contributions was a paper, "Training Workmen in Habits of Industry and Cooperation" (1908), in which he broke with Taylor's ideas; also *Work, Wages and Profits* (1913) and *Industrial Leadership* (1916). Gantt devised the "Gantt chart," a widely used analytical presentation of the mechanism of management.

GARAKONTHIE, DANIEL (*b. ca. 1600; d. Onondaga village [N.Y.], 1676*), Iroquois chief, councillor of the Onondaga and of the Confederacy. Friendly to the French, he rescued many white captives from Indian torture and death.

GARCELON, ALONZO (*b. Lewiston, Maine, 1813; d. Medford, Mass., 1906*), physician, farmer, Union soldier, railroad president, editor. Democratic governor of Maine, 1879–80.

GARCÉS, FRANCISCO TOMÁS HERMENEGILDO (*b. Villa Morata del Conde, Aragon, 1738; d. junction of the Colorado and the Gila, 1781*), Spanish missionary-explorer,. Assigned to San Xavier del Bac, 1768. Made four expeditions to points on Gila and Colorado rivers, 1768–74; on the last, he accompanied de Anza to California, and joined him again on the exploration of 1775. He was killed by Indians while founding pueblo missions.

GARDEN, ALEXANDER (*b. Birse, Scotland, ca. 1730; d. London, England, 1791*), physician, naturalist. Graduated Aberdeen, M.D., 1753. Immigrated soon after to Prince William Parish, S.C. Interested in fauna and flora of the region where he practiced, he exchanged notes and specimens with other naturalists; his voluminous correspondence with Linnaeus and John Ellis, the British naturalist, forms a precious scientific document. Ellis named the flower *Gardenia* after him. Garden was elected to the Royal Societies of Uppsala and London. A Loyalist, he left America for England, 1783.

GARDEN, ALEXANDER *b. Charleston, S.C., 1757; d. 1829*), Revolutionary soldier, planter. Son of Alexander Garden (*ca. 1730–91*). His *Anecdotes of the Revolutionary War* (1822) and *Anecdotes . . . , Second Series* (1828) are valuable and entertainingly written sources.

GARDEN, MARY (*b. Aberdeen, Scotland, 1874; d. Aberdeen Scotland, 1967*), opera singer. Immigrated in 1881. Studied voice in Paris. With the Opéra-Comique (1900–07); debut in the title role of Charpentier's *Louise*; chosen to create the role of Mélisande in Claude Debussy's *Pelléas et Mélisande* (1902), for which she is most remembered. American debut at the Manhattan Opera House in Massenet's *Thaïs* (1907). With Chicago Civic Opera Company, 1910–31; director, 1921–22. Honored by the French government for popularizing modern French opera in the United

States. A soprano, she was gifted with a remarkable stage personality and noted for her acting ability.

GARDENER, HELEN HAMILTON (*b. Winchester, Va., 1853; d. Washington, D.C., 1925*), author, suffragette, first woman member of U.S. Civil Service Commission.

GARDINER, SIR CHRISTOPHER (*fl. 1630's*), baronet, agent and spy of Sir Ferndinando Gorges. Preceded the Puritans in 1630 to Massachusetts Bay; arrested by them and imprisoned, he appeared as witness in Gorges' attempt to break the Massachusetts charter, 1632–33.

GARDINER, HARRY NORMAN (*b. Norwich, England, 1855; d. Northampton, Mass., 1927*), philosopher. Came to America, 1874. Graduated Amherst, 1878. Studied at Göttingen, Heidelberg, and Leipzig. Professor of philosophy at Smith, 1884–1924. Author of *Feeling and Emotion—A History of Theories* (1937).

GARDINER, JAMES TERRY (*b. Troy, N.Y., 1842; d. 1912*), engineer. Chief topographer of U.S. Geological Survey of Fortieth Parallel, 1866–73; pioneered, 1880–86, in public health by establishing proper sewerage systems in New York State; was later a leader in the coal industry.

GARDINER, JOHN (*b. Boston, Mass., 1737; d. at sea, 1793*), lawyer. Son of Silvester Gardiner. Called to English bar, 1761; an ardent Whig, he was counsel for John Wilkes. After practicing for some years at St. Christopher, British West Indies, he returned to Boston, 1783, and settled in Maine. Representative for Pownalboro in the Maine General Court, he was a zealous democrat and law reformer.

GARDINER, JOHN SYLVESTER JOHN (*b. Haverfordwest, England, 1765; d. Harrowgate, England, 1830*), Episcopal clergyman. Son of John Gardiner. Came to America, 1783. Minister at Trinity Church, Boston, Mass., 1792–1830; pastor, *post* 1805. Conducted a classical school; president, Anthology Club; a founder of Boston Athenaeum and author of *Remarks on the Jacobiniad* (1795).

GARDINER, LION (*b. England, 1599; d. Easthampton, N.Y., 1663*), colonist, military engineer. Sent to Connecticut to fortify and protect the new colony, he built Saybrook fort, 1636; was cocommander in Pequot War; became proprietor of Gardiner's Island.

GARDINER, ROBERT HALLOWELL (*b. Bristol, England, 1782; d. 1864*), agriculturist. Grandson and heir of Sylvester Gardiner, whose surname he assumed. Came to America, 1792. Developed model Maine farm; fostered agricultural societies; founded Gardiner (Maine) Lyceum, 1821, forerunner of American agricultural and technical schools.

GARDINER, SILVESTER (*b. South Kingston, R.I., 1708; d. Newport, R.I., 1786*), physician, Loyalist, landowner. Practiced in Boston. *Post* 1753, was chief promoter of Kennebec Co., developed a huge grant of land in Maine. Founder of Pittston and Gardiner, Maine.

GARDNER, CALEB (*b. Newport, R.I., 1739; d. 1806*), merchant, Revolutionary soldier. Celebrated for piloting French fleet into Newport, July 1780.

GARDNER, CHARLES KITCHEL (*b. Morris Co., N.J., 1787; d. 1869*), journalist. Author of a manual of infantry tactics and *A Dictionary of All Officers in the Army of the U.S.* for the years 1789–1853 (1853).

GARDNER, ERLE STANLEY (*b. Malden, Mass., 1889; Temecula, Calif., 1970*), writer. Practiced law in Ventura, Calif., 1911–34. Author of more than 140 books, including the best-selling Perry Mason mystery novels, such as *The Case of the Velvet Claws* (1933), *The Case of the Sulky Girl* (1933), and *The Case of the Lucky Legs* (1934). Also wrote a series of novels surrounding the character Doug Selby, including *The D.A. Calls It Murder* (1937) and *The D.A. Goes to Trial* (1940). Wrote the Bertha Cool series under the pseudonym A. A. Fair. The nine-year run of the "Perry Mason" television series (from 1957) was produced by Gardner's Paisano Productions. His 15 works of nonfiction include travel books such as *The Hidden Heart of Baja* (1962) and *Mexico's Magic Square* (1968). Established the Court of Last Resort (1947), a panel of experts that aided persons unjustly accused; published *The Court of Last Resort* (1952; expanded, 1954).

GARDNER, GILSON (*b. Chicago, Ill., 1869; d. Washington, D.C., 1935*), journalist.

GARDNER, HELEN (*b. Manchester, N.H., 1878; d. Chicago, Ill., 1946*), art historian, educator. B.A., University of Chicago, 1901; M.A., 1917. Taught at Brooks Classical School; developed courses in history of art at Art Institute School (Chicago). Author of *Art Through the Ages* (1926, and subsequent editions).

GARDNER, HENRY JOSEPH (*b. Dorchester, Mass., 1818; d. Milton, Mass., 1892*), dry-goods merchant. Prominent organizer in Know-Nothing party and its successful candidate for governor of Massachusetts, 1855–58.

GARDNER, ISABELLA STEWART (*b. New York, N.Y., 1840; d. Boston, Mass., 1924*), art collector, social leader. Married John Lowell Gardner, 1860. Witty, exuberant, clever, she dazzled and often shocked Boston society. Began buying works of art, 1867; was influenced by Charles E. Norton and Edward S. Morse, and aided by Bernard Berenson. To house and display her superb collections, she built Fenway Court, 1899–1903, an Italianate structure referred to as "Mrs. Jack Gardner's Palace." Here she continued her lifelong entertainment of artists, musicians, and visiting celebrities, and on her death left it "for the education and enjoyment of the public forever."

GARDNER, JOHN LANE (*b. Boston, Mass., 1793; d. Wilmington, Del., 1869*), soldier. Served in War of 1812, Florida War; commanded a regiment in Mexico and was twice brevetted. Superseded as commander at Fort Moultrie, 1861, he retired as colonel.

GARDNER, LEROY UPSON (*b. New Britain, Conn., 1888; d. Saranac Lake, N.Y., 1946*), pathologist, authority on tuberculosis and silicosis. B.A., Yale, 1912; M.D., Yale School of Medicine, 1914. Taught pathology at Harvard Medical School and at Yale School of Medicine before entering U.S. Army Medical Corps, 1917. Discharged from service on discovery that he had pulmonary tuberculosis, he entered Trudeau Sanatorium, Saranac Lake, N.Y., for treatment. He remained with the Edward L. Trudeau Foundation *post* 1918, serving first as research pathologist, then as director of the Saranac Laboratory from 1927, and as director of the Foundation from 1938 until his death. His first report on the role of silica dust in tuberculosis (1920) remains a medical classic; in subsequent experiments, he investigated the pathogenicity of a variety of mineral dusts. His work was an important factor in devising and imposing safety measures in mining and quarrying operations.

GARDNER, OLIVER MAXWELL (*b. Shelby, N.C., 1882; d. New York, N.Y., 1947*), lawyer, politician. Known as O. Max Gardner. Successful in his practice of law and in investments in real estate and the textile industry, he was also active in local politics *post* 1907. A moderately progressive Democrat, allied by blood and marriage with what was called the "Shelby dynasty" in North Carolina politics, he served two terms in the state senate and was elected lieutenant governor in 1916. Defeated in several primary bids for the gubernatorial nomination, he was nominated and elected governor in 1928. His success in coping with the problems of the depression won him a favorable national reputation. In 1933, he opened a law office in Washington, D.C., specializing in tax matters, and became one of the capital's most effective lobbyists, maintaining at the same time his reputation for probity of character. A friend and adviser of President Franklin D. Roosevelt, he served on several federal boards and acted on occasion as liaison between Congress and the White House. He was appointed undersecretary of the treasury in 1946. Appointed U.S. ambassador to Great Britain in December 1946, he died before he could assume his new post.

GAREY, THOMAS ANDREW (*b. Cincinnati, Ohio, 1830; d. 1909*), horticulturist. Outstanding in development of citrus industry in Southern California, *post* 1865; introduced and promoted fruit varieties, including the Eureka lemon.

GARFIELD, HARRY AUGUSTUS (*b. Hiram, Ohio, 1863; d. Williamstown, Mass., 1942*), lawyer, educator, public official. Son of James A. Garfield. B.A., Williams College, 1885. Studied law at Columbia University, at Oxford University, and at the Inns of Court in London. Admitted to Ohio bar, 1888; practiced in Cleveland and engaged in municipal reform. Professor of politics, Princeton, 1904–08; president of Williams College, 1908–34. As independent Republican in politics, he supported the Democratic presidential ticket in 1912, 1916, 1920, and 1936. He served as federal fuel administrator, 1917–19. Devoted to the values of good citizenship, public service, and moral leadership as a duty of the educated, which he (like his friend Woodrow Wilson) regarded as essential to effective democratic government, he broadened the scope of Williams in some ways (*e.g.,* the establishment, 1921, of its Institute of Politics), but held it strictly within the 19th-century tradition and ideals in others. This brought him difficulties during the last years of his presidency.

GARFIELD, JAMES ABRAM (*b. Cuyahoga Co., Ohio, 1831; d. Elberon, N.J., 1881*), teacher, Union soldier, president of the United States. Attended Western Reserve Eclectic Institute, Hiram, Ohio; graduated Williams, 1856. Elected to Ohio Senate, 1859, he became known as an effective speaker and an antislavery man. Helped raise 42nd Ohio Volunteer Infantry, 1861; commanded it so ably that he was given a brigade by General Buell and justified the choice by winning a victory at Middle Creek, Ky., 1862. Served as chief of staff in the Army of the Cumberland, 1863; was much praised for his conduct at Chickamauga and made a major general.

Elected by a heavy Republican majority from the nineteenth Ohio district, he entered the House of Representatives, 1863, and sat in Congress until November 1880. He took an important place on the Military Affairs Committee and later served on the Appropriations and Ways and Means committees, training himself in public finance and opposing "greenback" and excessive tariff legislation. Touched by the Crédit Mobilier and DeGolyer paving contract scandals, he yet managed to win reelection to Congress. When James G. Blaine entered the Senate, 1876, Garfield became House minority leader. He had been an active agent in the election of R. B. Hayes, who asked him to postpone his own senatorial ambitions and continue as Republican leader in the lower chamber. Elected to the U.S. Senate in 1880, he never took his seat. As head of Ohio delegation to the 1880 Republican convention and manager for John Sherman, who sought the

presidential nomination, he blocked the path of the "Stalwarts," who were pressing for a third term for Grant, and also Blaine's supporters. A deadlock ensued. On the thirty-fifth ballot, Wisconsin votes were shifted to Garfield, and his nomination became unanimous in a stampede. Not until September, however, did Grant's partisans decide to recognize the candidate. Blaine bore no malice, nor did Sherman at that time. Garfield and his vice presidential running-mate, Chester A. Arthur, carried the country, 214 electoral votes to 155.

Garfield attempted to build a conciliation cabinet with Blaine as secretary of state; however, his recognition of the Stalwarts was less than they desired, and a bitter wrangle ensued over patronage. Garfield stood firm in his determination to maintain the independence of the president in matters of appointment, and the "Star Route" scandal in the Post Office discredited his opponents.

Before his administration could proceed much further, he was shot on July 2, 1881, by a disappointed office seeker, Charles J. Guiteau.

GARFIELD, JAMES RUDOLPH (*b. Hiram, Ohio, 1865; d. Cleveland, Ohio, 1950*), lawyer, politician. Son of James A. Garfield. Graduated Williams College, 1885. Studied law at Columbia University and in a New York City law office. Admitted to the Ohio bar, 1888, he began practice in Cleveland with his brother Harry A. Garfield. A Republican of reformist tendencies, he was elected to to Ohio Senate in 1895 and 1897, but failed twice in bids for a nomination as congressman. Appointed in 1902 to the U.S. Civil Service Commission by President Theodore Roosevelt, he became one of the president's inner circle of advisers, the "tennis cabinet." As commissioner of the Bureau of Corporations *post* 1903, he stood (like Roosevelt) for federal regulation of the trusts, rather than "trust-busting"; he investigated the beef, oil, and steel industries, among others. Of these, he was criticized for his settlements with the beef and steel trusts, but praised for his searching examination of Standard Oil, which led to an antitrust suit. His greatest public service was as U.S. secretary of the interior, 1907–09; he reorganized the department with the aid of Gifford Pinchot, and implemented a full program of conservation and internal improvement. A progressive in politics, 1910–16, he was a vigorous supporter of Roosevelt's bid for the presidency in 1912. After World War I, he gave most of his time to his law practice, but continued to speak out and act in support of conservation policies.

GARFIELD, JOHN b. *New York, N.Y., 1913; d. New York, N.Y., 1952*), actor. Born Jacob Garfinkle. Associated with the Group Theater, 1934. Appeared in Clifford Odets' *Awake and Sing* (1935) and *Golden Boy* (1937); questioned about his activities in the radical theaters of the 1930's by the House Un-American Activities Committee. Films include *Four Daughters* (1938) which won him an Academy Award nomination; *Gentlemen's Agreement* and *Body and Soul* (1947) which won him another nomination for the Academy Award.

GARIS, HOWARD ROGER (*b. Binghamton, N.Y., 1873; d. Amherst, Mass., 1962*), journalist and creator of the Uncle Wiggily stories. Began a fifty-year career as a reporter and special writer with the *Newark Evening News* in 1898. Wrote for the Stratemeyer syndicate from 1905; prolific career in juvenile writing produced more than 700 children's books (many written under pseudonyms), including many of the "Tom Swift" and "Bobbsey Twins" books. Best known for his Uncle Wiggily stories, which began as a daily children's column in the *News* and were nationally syndicated from 1910. Uncle Wiggily, the gentleman rabbit with the striped rheumatism crutch and the silk top hat, was memorable for his unflagging optimism in the face of the "Skillery-scallery" alligator and other villains.

GARLAND, AUGUSTUS HILL (*b. Tipton Co., Tenn., 1832; d. Washington, D.C., 1899*), lawyer, Confederate congressman and senator. Governor of Arkansas, Democrat, 1874–77; U.S. senator, 1877–85; attorney general under Cleveland, 1885–89. Worked industriously for tariff and civil service reform.

GARLAND, HAMLIN (*b. near West Salem, Wis., 1860; d. Los Angeles, Calif., 1940*), novelist. Raised on small farms, first in Wisconsin, then in Iowa, where he early experienced the dehumanizing drudgery of farm life that he later depicted in his novels. His family moved to Dakota Territory in 1881, but Garland went east, settling in Boston in 1884. Association with W. D. Howells and a trip back to Iowa and Dakota encouraged Garland to write some short stories of midwestern farm life. A collection appeared as *Main-Travelled Roads* (1891). Hailed by Howells as an advance in American realism, the book was not widely read, nor were three novels indicting social injustices, published in 1892. In 1893 Garland moved to Chicago, where he remained until his removal to New York in 1916. The lack of success of *Crumbling Idols* (1894), a collection of critical essays, and *Rose of Dutcher's Coolly* (1895), a farm novel, led Garland to write a series of Indian-country romances, stereotyped in character and arbitrarily motivated. Finally, in 1913, he resumed work on an autobiographical account of his youth. Serialized in *Collier's Weekly* and published as *A Son of the Middle Border* (1917), it was recognized as a major contribution to America's knowledge of its recent history. *A Daughter of the Middle Border* (1921), a Pulitzer Prize–winner, and two other sequels, were equally successful. In *A Son of the Middle Border* and *Main-Travelled Roads*, Garland achieves his place as a realistic recorder of a particular aspect of his time and of its spirit.

GARLAND, JUDY (*b. Grand Rapids, Minn., 1922; d. London, England, 1969*), singer and actress. Born Frances Ethel Gumm. Public image as a sweet young woman was built around films such as *The Wizard of Oz* (1939), for which she won a special Oscar at seventeen, *Babes in Arms* (1939) with Mickey Rooney, *Me and My Gal* (1942) with Gene Kelly, and *Meet Me in St. Louis* (1944). During the late 1940's she established herself as a leading musical star in films such as *The Pirate* (1948) with Gene Kelly, and *Easter Parade* (1948) with Fred Astaire. Gave legendary concert performances at the Palladium in London (1951; 1960), the Palace Theater in New York City (1951), and Carnegie Hall (1960). Acclaimed as an actress in films such as *A Star is Born* (1954) and *Judgment at Nuremberg* (1961), for which she received Academy Award nominations. Plagued by emotional problems and illness throughout her career, her erratic behavior was evidenced in public appearances throughout the 1960's. "The Judy Garland Show" television series (1963–64) was regarded as a failure. Her death was attributed to an accidental overdose of barbiturates.

GARLAND, LANDON CABELL (*b. Nelson Co., Va., 1810; d. Nashville, Tenn., 1895*), educator. President, Randolph-Macon College, 1836–46, and of the University of Alabama, 1855–65. Chancellor, Vanderbilt University, 1875–93, which incorporated his plan for a theological seminary for the Methodist Episcopal Church, South.

GARLICK, THEODATUS (*b. Middlebury, Vt., 1805; d. 1884*), plastic surgeon, sculptor, pioneer in pisciculture. Practiced in Ohio, *post* 1834. Invented orthopedic procedures, fashioned surgical instruments, made anatomical models, medallions, busts. Experimented with artificial breeding of trout.

GARMAN, CHARLES EDWARD (*b. Limington, Maine, 1850; d. 1907*), educator. Graduated Amherst, 1872. Taught philosophy there, 1881–1907.

GARMAN, SAMUEL (*b. Indiana Co., Pa., 1843; d. 1927*), zoologist. Pupil of Agassiz; curator of fishes, Harvard Museum of Comparative Zoology; a foremost authority on sharks, skates, and rays.

GARNER, JAMES WILFORD (*b., Pike Co., Miss., 1871; d. 1938*), political scientist, expert on international law. Ph.D., Columbia, 1902. Taught at University of Illinois, 1904–38.

GARNER, JOHN NANCE (*b. Red River County, Tex., 1868; d. Uvalde, Tex., 1967*), vice president of the United States. Uvalde County judge, 1893–96. Democratic member of the Texas House of Representatives (1898–1902); of the U.S. House of Representatives (1903–33); whip (from 1911); member of the Ways and Means committee (from 1913); leader (from 1929); Speaker (1931–33). Vice president of the United States under Roosevelt, 1933–41. Known as "Cactus Jack," in Congress he was considered a diligent and studious legislator and an effective negotiator. Usually considered a moderate liberal, he was relatively influential as vice president, playing a significant role in the establishment of the Federal Deposit Insurance Corporation, despite the president's opposition. After 1936, Garner and Roosevelt increasingly split on policy matters; Garner was an unsuccessful candidate for the Democratic presidential nomination in 1940.

GARNET, HENRY HIGHLAND (*b. New Market, Md., 1815; d. Liberia, 1882*), Presbyterian clergyman. Born a slave, he was educated at Oneida Institute. Became a noted antislavery speaker and the leading black abolitionist before the rise of Frederick Douglass.

GARNETT, ALEXANDER YELVERTON PEYTON (*b. Essex Co., Va., 1819; d. Rehoboth Beach, Del., 1888*), physician. M.D., University of Pennsylvania, 1841. Prominent Confederate medical officer and personal physician to Jefferson Davis. Later greatly esteemed in Washington, D.C., he worked fearlessly to improve standards of medical ethics.

GARNETT, JAMES MERCER (*b. Essex Co., Va., 1770; d. Essex Co., 1843*), agriculturist, educator. Congressman, Democrat, from Virginia, 1805–09; partisan of John Randolph. Wrote many articles on agricultural reform; advocated seed selection, fertilizers, crop rotation. Conducted girls' and boys' schools, urged a state school system.

GARNETT, JAMES MERCER (*b. Aldie, Va., 1840; d. 1916*), philologist, Confederate soldier. Grandson of James M. Garnett (1770–1843). A painstaking and erudite scholar, he was acclaimed for the first American translation of *Beowulf* (1882) and other translations from Anglo-Saxon.

GARNETT, MUSCOE RUSSELL HUNTER (*b. Essex Co., Va., 1821; d. Essex Co., 1864*), lawyer, statesman. Grandson of James M. Garnett (1770–1843). Strict constructionist and defender of slavery; congressman from Virginia, 1856–61, and member of Confederate Congress.

GARNETT, ROBERT SELDEN (*b. Essex Co., Va., 1819; d. Carrick's Ford, Va., 1861*), soldier. Nephew of James M. Garnett (1770–1843). Graduated West Point, 1841. Fought with distinction through Mexican War; commanded Puget Sound and Yakima expeditions, 1855–58. Commanded Confederate forces in northwestern Virginia, 1861; was killed in action.

GARRARD, JAMES (*b. Stafford Co., Va., 1749; d. Mount Lebanon, Bourbon Co., Ky., 1822*), Baptist clergyman, politician. Removed to Kentucky, 1783; was minister at church at Cooper's Run; helped organize other Baptist congregations. Represented Fayette and Bourbon counties in conventions to achieve Kentucky statehood; served as Democratic-Republican governor, 1796–1804, but did not distinguish himself in office.

GARRARD, KENNER (*b. Kentucky, 1828; d. Cincinnati, Ohio, 1879*), Union soldier. Graduated West Point, 1851. After distinguished service in all theaters of the Civil War, resigned as major general, 1866.

GARREAU, ARMAND (*b. Cognac, France, 1817; d. New Orleans, La., 1865*), French novelist, journalist. Resident in New Orleans, ca. 1839–49 and ca. 1858–65. Contributed extensively to New Orleans and French newspapers, wrote several romantic-historical novels, including *Louisiana* (1849).

GARRETSON, AUSTIN BRUCE (*b. Winterset, Iowa, 1856; d. Cedar Rapids, Iowa, 1931*), labor leader. Officer in railway engineers' union; helped bring about the eight-hour day on railroads.

GARRETSON, JAMES EDMUND (*b. Wilmington, Del., 1828; d. Lansdowne, Pa., 1895*), dentist. M.D., University of Pennsylvania, 1859. Professor and dean, Philadelphia Dental College. Originator of oral surgery as a specialty; author of *A System of Oral Surgery* (1873, and many later editions) and other works.

GARRETT, EDMUND HENRY (*b. Albany, N.Y., 1853; d. Needham, Mass., 1929*), painter, illustrator, etcher.

GARRETT, FINIS JAMES (*b. Ore Springs, Tenn., 1875; d. Washington, D.C., 1956*), politician and federal judge. Studied at Bethel College, Tenn. Democratic member of the House of Representatives (1905–29). A staunch backer of Wilson, Garrett was for American membership in the League of Nations, voted for anti-lynching laws and child labor laws. In 1929, he was appointed associate judge on the Federal Court of Customs and Patent Appeals; he became presiding judge in 1937, serving until his retirement in 1955.

GARRETT, JOHN WORK (*b. Baltimore, Md., 1820; d. 1884*), railroad executive, banker. Son of Robert Garrett. President, Baltimore and Ohio Railroad, 1858–84; freed the road of political control and gave it efficient management. In the Civil War, the railroad was a main objective of Southern attack and only Garrett's extraordinary skill and energy prevented its abandonment. The first rail movement of troops in history, the transfer of 20,000 men from the Potomac to Chattanooga, 1863, was a triumph for Garrett. After the war, he secured direct routes to Pittsburgh and Chicago and a line to New York.

GARRETT, ROBERT (*b. Lisburn, Ireland, 1783; d. 1857*), merchant, financier. Came to America as a child; settled in Baltimore, Md., 1800. Alert to that city's business possibilities and energetic in civic enterprises, Garrett established faster transportation to capture western trade and developed own banking house for foreign commerce.

GARRETT, THOMAS (*b. Upper Darby, Pa., 1789; d. Wilmington, Del., 1871*), merchant, abolitionist. Fearless and resourceful, he helped about 2,700 slaves to escape north.

GARRETT, WILLIAM ROBERTSON (*b. Williamsburg, Va., 1839; d. 1904*), Confederate soldier, educator, historian. Graduated William and Mary, 1858. Held numerous educational posts, including Tennessee superintendency of education; dean, Peabody College for Teachers, 1899–1904. Was especially interested in state teachers' institutes and associations.

GARRETTSON, FREEBORN (*b. Maryland, 1752; d. 1827*), itinerant Methodist minister. Admired by John Wesley and Asbury, he traveled for more than 50 years *post* 1776; his outstanding work was in extension of Methodism in New York State.

GARRIGAN, PHILIP JOSEPH (*b. Cavan, Ireland, 1840; d. 1919*), Roman Catholic clergyman. Came to America as a child. Vice-rector, Catholic University; first bishop of Sioux City, Iowa, 1902–19.

GARRISON, CORNELIUS KINGSLAND (*b. Fort Montgomery, N.Y., 1809; d. New York, N.Y., 1885*), financier. Steamship magnate, banker, he carried on financial operations of great variety and magnitude. Accomplished remarkable reforms as mayor of San Francisco, 1853–57.

GARRISON, FIELDING HUDSON (*b. Washington, D.C., 1870; d. Baltimore, Md., 1935*), medical historian bibliographer. Collaborated on *Index* of surgeon general's library. Author of *An Introduction to the History of Medicine* (1913).

GARRISON, LINDLEY MILLER (*b. Camden, N.J., 1864; d. Seabright, N.J., 1932*), lawyer. Graduated University of Pennsylvania, 1885; admitted to the bar, 1886. Practiced in Camden and Jersey City, N.J., 1904–12. U.S. secretary of war, 1913–16. After outbreak of World War I, Garrison stressed the need for a large regular army. President Wilson, who seemed to agree, refused to condemn the Hay bill, which repudiated Garrison's plan, and Garrison resigned. Garrison's clash with Wilson focused public attention on the unpreparedness of the country and contributed to the National Defense Act of 1916.

GARRISON, WILLIAM LLOYD (*b. Newburyport, Mass., 1805; d. New York, N.Y., 1879*), reformer, dominant figure in fight against slavery. A printer and editor by trade, Garrison met Benjamin Lundy ca. 1828, and was moved by him to devote himself to the abolition movement. Was one of earliest abolitionists to demand "immediate and complete emancipation"; denounced slavery harshly and violently in platform speeches and in the weekly *Genius of Universal Emancipation*. Founded *The Liberator*, 1831, in which for 35 years he employed his one weapon of denunciation against the slave power. Its opening manifesto contained the famous words "I am in earnest—I will not equivocate—I will not excuse—I will not retreat a single inch—and *I will be heard*." A founder of the American Anti-Slavery Society, 1833, pacifist and nonresistant by conviction, he braved persecution and threat of bodily harm without fear. His gift for antagonizing extended even to his friends and supporters; to conservatives and the orthodox clergy he was a thorn in the flesh. On July 4, 1854, he publicly burned a copy of the Constitution, exclaiming, "So perish all compromises with tyranny." When the Civil War concluded the abolitionist crusade, Garrison gave his full attention to other reforms in which he had been interested, notably woman suffrage, prohibition, and the improvement of the American Indian. An extremist in all things, he inspired more than he led and is remembered more for his courage and tenacity than for his ideas.

GARRISON, WILLIAM RE TALLACK (*b. Goderich, Canada, 1834; d. Long Branch, N.J., 1882*), financier. Son of Cornelius K. Garrison. Identified with marine and rail transportation interests, he achieved complete unification of New York City elevated railways in Manhattan Railway Co., 1879.

GARRY, SPOKANE (*b. present Spokane Co., Wash., 1811; d. 1892*), Indian leader, missionary, teacher, peace advocate. Leader among Columbia River basin tribes, he promoted peaceful white settlement; later tried to protect his people against white aggression.

GARTRELL, LUCIUS JEREMIAH (*b. Wilkes Co., Ga., 1821; d. 1891*), lawyer, Confederate brigadier general, politician. As legislator, and as congressman, Democrat, from Georgia, 1857–61, he championed ultra-Southern views and was an advocate of secession. After the war he became noted as a criminal lawyer.

GARVEY, MARCUS MOZIAH (b. St. Ann's Bay, Jamaica, B.W.I., 1887; d. London, England, 1940), black leader. Moved to United States, 1916. Organizer of the Universal Negro Improvement Association, which flourished 1917–22. Founded Black Star ship line, newspaper, and other ultimately unsuccessful enterprises as part of his black nationalist program. Started "Back-to-Africa" movement. Sentence for mail fraud commuted by President Coolidge. Deported to Jamaica.

GARVIN, LUCIUS FAYETTE CLARK (b. Knoxville, Tenn., 1841; d. Lonsdale, R.I., 1922), physician. Graduated Amherst, 1862; M.D., Harvard Medical School, 1867. Advocate of Henry George's single-tax theory, he served for many years in the Rhode Island legislature, and as Democratic governor of that state, 1903–05.

GARY, ELBERT HENRY (b. near Wheaton, Ill., 1846; d. 1927), corporation lawyer, financier. Built up a wide practice in Illinois; removed to New York City, 1898, as president of Federal Steel Co. J. P. Morgan entrusted him with major role in organization of U.S. Steel Corp., and Gary dominated its policies until his death; he was chairman of the board, 1903–27. He followed a conservative but fair policy, keeping within the antitrust laws, paying fair wages, and striving for social amelioration, though he insisted upon the open shop. He was much criticized for his unwillingness to negotiate with organized labor, which led to the strike of 1919, yet it was said in his defense that he had early introduced schemes for pensions and purchase of stock by employees. Gary, Ind., was named for him.

GARY, JAMES ALBERT (b. Uncasville, Conn., 1833; d. Baltimore, Md., 1920), cotton manufacturer, banker, Republican politician. U.S. postmaster general, 1897–98.

GARY, MARTIN WITHERSPOON (b. Cokesbury, S.,C., 1831; d. 1881), lawyer, Confederate brigadier general, planter. Post 1876, a South Carolina legislator; favored the "straight-out policy."

GASKILL, HARVEY FREEMAN (b. Royalton, N.Y., 1845; d. 1889), inventor, engineer. Met need for higher steam economy and larger pumping capacity by inventing first crank and flywheel high-duty pumping engine for waterworks, 1882.

GASS, PATRICK (b. Falling Springs, Pa., 1771; d. 1870), soldier, explorer. Author of Journal of the Voyages and Travels of a Corps of Discovery (1807, and many later editions), the first published account by a member of the Lewis and Clark expedition.

GASSER, HERBERT SPENCER (b. Platteville, Wis., 1888; d. New York, N.Y., 1963), physiologist. Studied at the University of Wisconsin and Johns Hopkins (M.D., 1915). Instructor, the University of Wisconsin, (1915–16). Professor, Washington University, St. Louis, 1916–31; Cornell Medical College, 1931–35. Director, Rockefeller Institute, 1935–53. Conducted research on the electrophysiology of nerves. Published Electrical Signs of Nervous Activity (1937), a classic in the field of neurophysiology, with Joseph Erlanger; their contributions to an understanding of "the highly differentiated functions of single nerve fibers" led to their sharing the 1944 Nobel prize for physiology or medicine.

GASSON, THOMAS IGNATIUS (b. Sevenoaks, England, 1859; d. Montreal, Canada, 1930), Jesuit priest, educator. Came to America, 1872; became a Catholic, 1874; ordained, 1891. As president, 1907–14, moved and rebuilt Boston College.

Reorganized Georgetown University graduate school; helped develop Loyola College, Montreal.

GASTON, HERBERT EARLE (b. Halsey, Oreg., 1881; d. Los Angeles, Calif., 1956), journalist, government official, and banking executive. Studied at the University of Washington and the University of Chicago. Reporter and editor for various newspapers in the Northwest and Midwest, Gaston was night editor of the New York World (1929–31). He was hired by Henry Morgenthau, Jr. as secretary of the N.Y. State Conservation Department in 1931. From 1939 to 1945, he was assistant secretary of the Treasury under Morgenthau; from 1945 he was vice-chairman and director of the Export-Import Bank; president and chairman from 1949–1953.

GASTON, JAMES MCFADDEN (b. near Chester, S.C., 1824; d. Atlanta, Ga., 1903), surgeon. Served in Confederate hospitals; lived and practiced in Brazil, 1865–83. Returning to Atlanta, Ga., he taught very successfully at Southern Medical College.

GASTON, WILLIAM (b. New Bern., N.C., 1778; d. Raleigh, N.C., 1844), jurist. Attended Georgetown; graduated College of New Jersey (Princeton), 1796; studied law with F. X. Martin. Served as Federalist legislator; as congressman, North Carolina, 1813–17, his speeches in support of the Bank of the United States and in opposition to the loan bill won him national reputation. Popular opposition in North Carolina to the state supreme court was overcome in 1833 by electing Gaston chief justice, although as a Catholic he was supposedly barred by the thirty-second article of the state constitution. Later he labored in constitutional convention to have all religious restrictions on office-holding removed. Gaston's opinions displayed profound learning, clarity, vigor, and a broad humanitarian spirit. He sought to mitigate the harshness of the slave code and delivered two masterful opinions on the subject.

GASTON, WILLIAM (b. Killingly, Conn., 1820; d. Boston, Mass., 1894), lawyer. Graduated Brown, 1840. Served in Massachusetts legislature; was Democratic mayor of Boston, 1871–72; governor of Massachusetts, 1875–76.

GATES, CALEB FRANK (b. Chicago, Ill., 1857; d. Denver, Colo., 1946), missionary, educator. Graduated Beloit College, 1877; Chicago Theological School, 1881. Served at American Board of Foreign Missions station, Mardin, Turkey, 1881–94; president of Euphrates College, Harput, 1894–1903; president of Robert College, Constantinople, 1903–32, except for 1922–23 when he was adviser to the U.S. high commissioner at the peace conference in Lausanne.

GATES, FREDERICK TAYLOR (b. Maine, N.Y., 1853; d. Phoenix, Ariz., 1929), Baptist clergyman, business executive. Graduated University of Rochester, 1877; Rochester Theological Seminary, 1880. As secretary of Baptist Education Society, he arranged conference of leading Baptist educators and laymen to formulate plan for reconstituted University of Chicago, which won support of the elder John D. Rockefeller. In 1893 Gates became Rockefeller's business associate and a guiding force in many enterprises, notably in developing iron-ore projects in Minnesota. Gates's greatest achievement lay in education and philanthropy. He was president of the General Education Board, first of the Rockefeller foundations, and he conceived the idea of the Rockefeller Institute for Medical Research. Analyzing appeals for aid flowing into Rockefeller's office, Gates developed the principles and policies which led to establishment of the Rockefeller Foundation.

GATES, GEORGE AUGUSTUS (*b. Topsham, Vt., 1851; d. 1912*), minister, educator. Graduated Dartmouth, 1873; Andover Seminary, 1880. President of Iowa (now Grinnell) College, 1887–1900; of Pomona College, 1901–08; of Fisk University, 1909–12.

GATES, HORATIO (*b. Maldon, England, ca. 1728/29; d. New York, N.Y., 1806*), Revolutionary soldier. Godson of Horace Walpole. Entered the British army at an early age, served in Nova Scotia, 1749–50, and in Virginia, 1755; was wounded in Braddock's defeat before Fort Duquesne. Served under Monckton in the conquest of Martinique, 1761. After retirement in England *post* 1764, was advised by George Washington about land in Virginia, and in 1772 moved to a plantation in Berkeley Co.

Gates was drawn to the patriot cause by his personal revolt against the English caste system. Commissioned brigadier general in the Continental army in July 1775, he was at Cambridge, Mass., as adjutant general, organizing the miscellaneous units besieging Boston, showing himself a capable administrator, a loyal and indefatigable supporter of Washington. Commissioned major general in May 1776, he went to command the troops of the broken invasion of Canada who were retreating to Crown Point and Ticonderoga. Here a conflict arose with Gen. Philip Schuyler over command of the northern department which was not settled until Gates relieved Schuyler, August 1777, in time to oppose Burgoyne's expedition. Gates and Benedict Arnold, the dramatic figure of the fighting at Freeman's Farm and Bemis Heights, quarreled over what Arnold regarded as Gates's lack of initiative and failure to appreciate Arnold's services in victory of Saratoga. Criticism of Gates for not notifying Congress and Washington more promptly of the victory was owing to his dilatory messenger and adjutant, James Wilkinson, who was also responsible for a worsening of relations between Gates and Washington in the affair of Gen. Thomas Conway's letter of Oct. 11, 1777. According to Wilkinson, with whom Gates subsequently fought a duel, Gates publicized in his headquarters a letter from Conway criticizing Washington and complaining of the mismanagement of the war. Gates's undignified insistence that the letter had been stolen, and then that it was a forgery, disgusted Washington; Gates's friends in Congress, who were engaged in a scheme to have him supersede Washington, dropped the matter.

Gates commanded the northern and eastern departments, 1778–79. Called in June 1780 to command the southern department, then in straits because of the surrender of Lincoln at Charleston, he raised troops and opposed Cornwallis at Camden, S.C. In a disastrous defeat on Aug. 16, he tried vainly to rally the fleeing militia, who made up more than half his army. Gates was relieved by Nathanael Greene. Congress voted an inquiry into Gates's conduct, but charges were never pressed. Congress repealed its resolve, 1782, ordering Gates to take such command as Washington should direct.

In 1783 he returned home to Virginia and remained there until 1790 when, old doubts about social inequality again besetting him, he emancipated his slaves and moved to an estate on the then outskirts of New York City. Unpopular with many of the best officers in the army, his character was contradictory. At times vigorous and able, at other times he seems to have been wavering and indecisive.

GATES, JOHN WARNE (*b. near Turner Junction, Ill., 1855; d. Paris, France, 1911*), promoter, speculator. Known as "Bet-You-a-Million" Gates. Starting with the manufacture and promotion of barbed wire, he formed through a series of consolidations the American Steel and Wire Co., 1898; became head of the U.S. wire industry. Restless, imaginative and more interested in floating companies than running them, he was a daring speculator, feared on the stock exchange. A manipulation of the Louisville &

Nashville Railroad, which he secretly acquired and resold at a fancy price to J. P. Morgan, ended in his virtual ostracism from New York finance. Thereafter, he removed to Port Arthur, Tex., organized the Texas Co., and controlled the town's industries.

GATES, SIR THOMAS (*b. Colyford, England; d. Netherlands, 1621*), baronet, soldier, governor of Virginia. An investor in the Virginia Co., Gates sailed in June 1609 with a fleet of settlers for Virginia. His ship, separated from the others in a storm, landed in the Bermudas. He reached Virginia at last in May 1610, to find the colonists in deplorable condition, but was prevented from taking them back to England by the arrival of Lord De La Warr, who took over the government from Gates. Returning to England, Gates worked to gain support and settlers for the colony. With a large company he reached Jamestown again in August 1611, resumed the government in a discouraging time, and laid the foundations for the colony's prosperity before his final departure in the spring of 1614.

GATES, THOMAS SOVEREIGN (*b. Germantown, Pa., 1873; d. Osterville, Mass., 1948*), investment banker, university president. Graduated Wharton School of Finance, University of Pennsylvania, 1893; LL.B., University of Pennsylvania, 1896. After serving as officer of an insurance company and president of the Philadelphia Trust Company, he became a partner in Drexel and Co., 1918. Three years later, he joined J. P. Morgan and Co. as a partner. A trustee of the University of Pennsylvania *post* 1921, he retired from business in 1930 to become the university's president. Serving without salary, he reorganized its finances, instituted economies, and took control of intercollegiate sports out of the hands of the alumni association. He also gave greater emphasis to cultural activities, increasing funds available for research, scholarships, and libraries. Retired 1944.

GATLING, RICHARD JORDAN (*b. Hertford Co., N.C., 1818; d. 1903*), inventor. Devised and manufactured farm tools. The Gatling gun, a repeating weapon which he patented in 1862, made him world-famous.

GATSCHET, ALBERT SAMUEL (*b. St. Beatenberg, Switzerland, 1832; d. 1907*), linguist, ethnologist. European-trained, he went to America, 1868; worked as ethnologist in U.S. Geological Survey and Bureau of Ethnology, *post* 1877, on classification of Indian tribes by linguistic families. Author of, among other books, *The Klamath Indians* (1890).

GATTI-CASAZZA, GIULIO (*b. Udine, Italy, 1869; d. Ferrara, Italy, 1940*), general manager of La Scala opera, Milan, 1898–1908; of the Metropolitan Opera, New York, 1908–35.

GAUL, WILLIAM GILBERT (*b. Jersey City, N.J., 1855; d. New York, N.Y., 1919*), painter, illustrator. Ablest American military painter; notable for vivid, accurate Civil War scenes and for studies of Indians and cowboys.

GAUSS, CHRISTIAN FREDERICK (*b. Ann Arbor, Mich., 1878; d. New York, N.Y., 1951*), educator. M.A., the University of Michigan, 1899. Professor of modern languages, Princeton University (1905–46); dean of the college (1925–46). Officer and trustee of the Princeton University Press; national committee member of the American Civil Liberties Union. Best-known book is *A Primer for Tomorrow* (1934), an examination of the modern spirit and contemporary culture.

GAUSS, CLARENCE EDWARD (*b. Washington, D.C., 1887; d. Los Angeles, Calif., 1960*), diplomat. Gauss began his career in 1907 in China, where he served as consul general until 1940. In 1940–41, he was first minister to Australia before he was appointed ambassador to China (1941–44). Serving during the difficult years of the Japanese invasion, Gauss distinguished himself with his thorough knowledge of Chinese affairs; he was opposed to the U.S. backing of Chiang Kai-shek, in particular of Chiang's demands for financial aid. From 1945 to 1952, he was a member of the board of the Export-Import Bank, an important instrument of the U.S. Cold War diplomacy.

GAUT, JOHN MCREYNOLDS (*b. Cleveland, Tenn., 1841; d. 1918*), lawyer. Practiced in Nashville, Tenn. Was authority on law in its relations to church organizations and property; became general counsel to the Presbyterian Church in the United States, 1906.

GAUVREAU, EMILE HENRY (*b. Centerville, Conn., 1891; d. Suffolk, Va., 1956*), newspaper editor. Editor of various scandal-tabloid newspapers including *The New York Evening Graphic* (1924–29), *The New York Mirror* (1929–35), and *The Philadelphia Inquirer* (1936–38). Books include *What So Proudly We Hailed* (1935), a contrast of the Soviet and American systems.

GAVIN, FRANK STANTON BURNS (*b. Cincinnati, Ohio, 1890; d. New York, N.Y., 1938*), Episcopal clergyman, historian. An Anglo-Catholic, and active in ecumenical movements. Professor at General Theological Seminary, New York, *post* 1923.

GAXTON, WILLIAM (*b. San Francisco, 1893; d. New York, N.Y., 1963*), stage and film actor. Made stage debut in vaudeville in 1915. Long list of stage roles included Martin in *A Connecticut Yankee* 1927); Peter Forbes in *Fifty Million Frenchmen* (1929); Billy Crocker in *Anything Goes* (1934); Buckley Joyce Thomas in *Leave It to Me* (1938); Jim Taylor in *Louisiana Purchase* (1940); and Frank Jordan in *Nellie Bly* (1946). Among his films were *Stepping Along* (1926); *Silent Partners* (1932); *Best Foot Forward* (1943); and *Billy Rose's Diamond Horseshoe* (1945). Shepherd (president) of the Lambs, a New York theatrical club (1936–39; 1952–53; 1957–62). Gaxton was also a trustee of the Actor's Fund and a vice president of Parfums Charbert, a perfume manufacturing company.

GAY, EBENEZER (*b. Dedham, Mass., 1696; d. Hingham, Mass., 1787*), Congregational clergyman. Pastor at Hingham, 1718–87. A precursor of the Unitarian movement in New England.

GAY, EDWIN FRANCIS (*b. Detroit, Mich., 1867; d. Pasadena, Calif., 1946*), economic historian. B.A., University of Michigan, 1890; Ph.D., University of Berlin, 1902. Originally planning to specialize in medieval history, Gay studied at several universities during 12 years in Germany and followed an intensive program of independent reading. His dissertation of the English enclosure movement and a subsequent article on that topic in the *Quarterly Journal of Economics* (August 1903) were major revisionist studies. Beginning as instructor of economics at Harvard, 1902, he became professor and chairman of the department in 1906. Helped plan Harvard Graduate School of Business Administration and was first dean, 1908–17. During World War I, he was a member of the U.S. Shipping Board and the director of the Division of Planning and Statistics of the Shipping and War Trade boards; later, as director of the Central Bureau of Planning and Statistics, he helped prepare the economic data used by U.S. representatives at the Versailles conference. After an unhappy experience as editor and president of the New York *Evening Post*, 1919–24, he was professor of economic history at Harvard, 1924–36. *Post* 1936, he was a member of the research staff at the Huntington Library.

GAY, FREDERICK PARKER (*b. Boston, Mass., 1874; d. New Hartford, Conn., 1939*), bacteriologist. Graduated Harvard, 1897; M.D., Johns Hopkins, 1901. Studied also at University of Pennsylvania and Pasteur Institute, Brussels. Professor of pathology, University of California at Berkeley, 1910–23, where he developed bacteriology and immunology as separate disciplines; *post* 1923, professor of bacteriology at Columbia University. Gay's early investigations dealt with the serological phenomena accompanying infection and immunity. Later studies included the phenomenon of anaphylaxis, typhoid fever, the pathogenesis and chemotherapy of hemolytic streptococcus infections, tissue immunity, and virus infections.

GAY, SYDNEY HOWARD (*b. Hingham, Mass., 1814; d. 1888*), journalist. Great-grandson of Ebenezer Gay. Editor, *American Anti-Slavery Standard*, 1843–57; managing editor, *New York Tribune*, through Civil War, and of *Chicago Tribune*, 1867–71. Author of W. C. Bryant's *History of the United States*.

GAY, WINCKWORTH ALLAN (*b. West Hingham, Mass., 1821; d. West Hingham, 1910*), landscape painter. Brother of Sydney H. Gay. Studied with R. W. Weir and, in Paris with Constant Troyon. Among the first Americans to work in the "naturalist" style of landscape painting as practiced by his master and other contemporaries.

GAYARRÉ, CHARLES ÉTIENNE ARTHUR (*b. New Orleans, La., 1805; d. 1895*), lawyer, legislator, historian. Author of *Histoire de la Louisiane* (1846–47), largely a series of documentary extracts. His accurate and readable history of Louisiana in English appeared in four volumes issued in 1848, 1852, 1854, and 1866.

GAYLE, JOHN (*b. Sumter District, S.C., 1792; d. 1859*), lawyer. Democratic governor of Alabama, 1831–35. Under his leadership, the state rejected nullification and upheld the Union. Turning Whig, Gayle served in Congress, 1847–49, and thereafter was a federal district judge.

GAYLER, CHARLES (*b. New York, N.Y., 1820; d. Brooklyn, N.Y., 1892*), playwright. Wrote some 200 tragedies, comedies, melodramas, operettas, exploiting topical material.

GAYLEY, JAMES (*b. Lock Haven, Pa., 1855; d. New York, N.Y., 1920*), engineer, metallurgist, inventor. Graduated Lafayette, 1876. Manager, Edgar Thomson Steel Works; became managing director of Carnegie Steel, 1897. Called "father of American blast furnace practice," he instituted economies of fuel consumption; invented and introduced new appliances, such as the bronze cooling-plate for furnace walls, a casting apparatus for use with the Bessemer converter and, most important, the dry air blast (perfected 1894–1911).

GAYLORD, WILLIS (*b. Bristol, Conn., 1792; d. Camillus, N.Y., 1844*), agricultural writer. Editor, *Genesee Farmer* and *Cultivator*; did much to advance New York State agriculture. With Luther Tucker, wrote *American Husbandry* (1840).

GAYNOR, WILLIAM JAY (*b. near Oriskany, N.Y., 1849; d. on shipboard, 1913*), jurist, mayor of New York City, 1909–13. Noted for reforms in local politics and severe dealing from the bench.

GAYOSO DE LEMOS, MANUEL (*b. Spain, ca. 1752; d. Louisiana, 1799*). Appointed governor of Natchez District, 1787, he served 1789–97. Endeavored to separate the West from the United States with the aid of James Wilkinson and Kentucky dissidents; acted vigorously in defense of Spanish rights. As governor of Louisiana, 1797–99, excluded Americans, encouraged commerce, prepared for invasion by the United States.

GEAR, JOHN HENRY (*b. Ithaca, N.Y., 1825; d. 1900*), businessman. Removed to Iowa as a boy. After service in legislature, was Republican governor of Iowa, 1878–82; congressman, 1887–91 and 1893–95; U.S. senator, 1895–1900.

GEARY, JOHN WHITE (*b. near Mount Pleasant, Pa., 1819; d. 1873*), engineer, soldier. Active militia officer; led assault on Chapultepec in Mexican War. Chosen to establish postal service in California, Geary arrived in San Francisco, 1849; superseded by a Whig postmaster, he was elected "first alcalde," and in 1850, first mayor. He was active in making California a free state and was chairman of the Democratic Territorial Committee; he returned to Pennsylvania in 1852. Declining the governorship of Utah, he accepted that of Kansas Territory, where he found virtual civil war on his arrival in September 1856. He disbanded the proslavery militia, organized his own, and within three weeks could report, "Peace now reigns in Kansas." The enmity of the proslavery group (an overwhelming majority in the legislature) and the refusal of Gen. Persifor Smith to supply more troops so discouraged him, however, that he resigned in March 1857. On the outbreak of the Civil War, Geary became colonel of the 28th Pennsylvania, fought with distinction in many campaigns, and was brevetted major general. Becoming a Republican, he served as governor of Pennsylvania, 1867–73, battling often with the legislature, striving to reduce the state debt and safeguard the treasury. He advocated a general insurance law, state control of gas companies, and safeguards for public health. He also urged that taxes be shifted from business to land, to encourage business growth.

GEDDES, JAMES (*b. near Carlisle, Pa., 1763; d. 1838*), civil engineer. An early producer of salt in Syracuse, N.Y., region. His 1809 report of a survey to the New York legislature established the route adopted later for Erie Canal, of which he was one of the engineers, 1816–22.

GEDDES, JAMES LORAINE (*b. Edinburgh, Scotland, 1827; d. 1887*), soldier, college administrator. Raised in Canada. Distinguished in British service and as Union brigadier general. Officer at Iowa State College, *post* 1870.

GEDDES, NORMAN BEL (*b. Adrian, Mich., 1893; d. New York, N.Y., 1958*), theatrical and industrial designer. Along with Robert Edmond Jones and Lee Simonson, Geddes revolutionized the American theater by using costumes, scenery, and lighting to intensify the mood rather than decorate the set. His productions included work at the Metropolitan Opera (1918); *The Rivals* (1922); *The Miracle*, in collaboration with Max Reinhardt (1923); and *Dead End* (1935). Geddes was the first to remove footlights and substitute high-intensity lights hung from the balcony. He also designed for industry and architecture.

GEERS, EDWARD FRANKLIN (*b. Wilson Co., Tenn., 1851; d. Wheeling, W.Va., 1924*), turfman. World's leading racing driver of his period.

GEHRIG, HENRY LOUIS (*b. New York, N.Y., 1903; d. New York, 1941*), baseball player, better known as Lou Gehrig. Attended Columbia, 1921–23, after excelling in football and baseball at High School of Commerce; joined New York Yankees, 1923. After two years of seasoning at Hartford, Conn., he became the Yankee first baseman, June 1925, and was moved to fourth place in the batting order, 1926. Between 1925 and early 1939, he was in the lineup for every regular game the Yankees played—2,130 games in a row. He hit 493 home runs and had a lifetime batting average of .340. He was American League most valuable player, 1927, 1931, 1934, and 1936, and was elected to the baseball Hall of Fame in 1939. He played his last big-league game against the Washington Senators, Apr. 30, 1939; shortly thereafter, he learned that he was suffering from a progressive and incurable disease of the spinal cord. Highly respected and admired for his personal character as much as for his athletic ability, he

spent the last two years of his life in work with boys' clubs and helping to combat juvenile delinquency.

GEIGER, ROY STANLEY (*b. Middleburg, Fla., 1885; d. Bethesda, Md., 1947*), Marine Corps officer, naval aviator. Graduated Florida State Normal School, 1904; LL.B., John B. Stetson University, 1907. Commissioned second lieutenant, 1909. Completed flight training at Pensacola and designated a naval aviator, June 1917. During World War I, promoted to major; squadron commander of the 1st Marine Aviation Force in France and Belgium. Late in 1941, after acting as official observer with the British in North Africa and the Mediterranean, he became commanding general of the 1st Marine Air Wing, Fleet Marine Force. He and his group played a vital role in the Guadalcanal campaign. In November 1943, promoted major general, he took command of the 1st Marine Amphibious Corps; the next summer and fall, he led the 3rd Marine Amphibious Corps in the Guam and Palau Islands campaigns; and in 1945, during the Okinawa campaign, as deputy, he succeeded to command of the Tenth Army on the death in combat of Gen. S. B. Buckner. Promoted lieutenant general, in July 1945 he was named commander of the Fleet Marine Force, Pacific. Supervised Marine activity in the occupation of Japan and in China. Promoted posthumously to full general.

GELLATLY, JOHN (*b. New York, N.Y., 1853; d. New York, 1931*), businessman, art collector.

GEMÜNDER, AUGUST MARTIN LUDWIG (*b. Ingelfingen, Germany, 1814; d. New York, N.Y., 1895*), and his brother **GEORGE GEMÜNER** (*b. 1816; d. 1899*), immigrated to America, 1846, and were pioneer makers in the United States of the finest violins; they had no contemporary superiors. *Post* 1852, they worked in New York City.

GENÊT, EDMOND CHARLES (*b. France, 1763; d. 1834*), diplomat. A precocious scholar and fashionably liberal in his ideas. Genêt succeeded his father in 1781 as *premier commis* of the bureau of interpretation, department of foreign affairs at Versailles. By the time he was 25, he had made the rounds of the most important courts in Europe. After he was expelled as chargé d'affaires at St. Petersburg, 1792, the Girondist ministry of France appointed him minister plenipotentiary to the United States, where he hoped to press French rights to fit out privateers under the treaties of 1778, a matter of current concern to Washington and his advisers. Arriving at Charleston, S.C., April 1793, he journeyed to Philadelphia, Pa., where he was first made welcome by Jefferson and other French sympathizers. His efforts soon made him a storm center of politics. He worked in South Carolina with dissatisfied local politicians; sent André Michaux to Kentucky to encourage an expedition down the Mississippi to take Louisiana from Spain; planned to send the French fleet to recapture St. Pierre and Miquelon and so provoke a rebellion in Canada. These energetic enterprises proved abortive. He had, however, stimulated the formation of local Jacobin clubs which soon spread and contributed to the growth of the Democratic-Republican party. Recalled home at request of U.S. government, he remained in the United States, becoming a citizen. He settled on Long Island, N.Y., 1794; *ca.* 1800, he moved to a farm in Rensselaer Co., N.Y.

GENIN, JOHN NICHOLAS (*b. New York, N.Y., 1819; d. 1878*), hatter, merchant. A pioneer in the use of novel advertising methods, he built up a large clothing business, starting with a hat shop adjoining Barnum's museum in New York City.

GENOVESE, VITO (*b. Rigliano, Italy, 1897; d. Springfield, Mo., 1969*), reputed Cosa Nostra boss. Immigrated, 1913; naturalized, 1936. Involved from an early age in the Italian underworld in New York City, quickly establishing himself as a reliable and ruthless mob soldier; with Charles ("Lucky") Luciano, gained control of the organized crime ring Cosa Nostra in 1931. Said to have amassed a fortune worth $30 million; he was one of the first underworld figures to establish and operate legitimate businesses to protect himself. Indicted in a federal narcotics smuggling case in 1959; convicted and sentenced to fifteen years. Continued to exert influence on the mob while incarcerated. In 1963 Joseph Valachi turned state's evidence against his former boss, confirming many allegations concerning Genovese and solving a number of murders and disappearances.

GENTH, FREDERICK AUGUSTUS (*b. Wächtersbach, Germany, 1820; d. 1893*), analytical chemist. Studied at Heidelberg, Giessen, and Marburg. Came to America, 1848. At his Philadelphia laboratory, 1850–70, he devoted himself to research, commercial analysis, and the instruction of special students; was professor of chemistry, University of Pennsylvania, 1872–88. Peerless in accuracy and industry, expert in minerals, Genth discovered 23 new mineral species, and published 102 investigations—over 70 on mineral topics. Another group of studies on fertilizers arose from his work with the Pennsylvania Board of Agriculture. His most important work was a study of ammonia-cobalt bases. It was begun in 1847; a preliminary paper was published, 1851; subsequently it was developed jointly with Wolcott Gibbs and issued as a Smithsonian monograph, 1856.

GENTHE, ARNOLD (*b. Berlin, Germany, 1869; d. New Milford, Conn., 1942*), photographer. Ph.D., University of Jena, 1894. After working as a tutor in San Francisco, Calif., 1895–97 (during which time he took up photography as a means of making a visual record of the Chinese quarter of the city), he settled there and opened a professional photographic studio. Soon successful because of the excellence and novelty of his softly focused, naturally posed portraits, he continued documentary work among the Indians of New Mexico and made a unique record of the devastation in San Francisco following the 1906 earthquake. Moving to New York City, 1911, he made portraits of many notable personalities, taking special interest in actors and dancers. His studies of the work of Isadora Duncan and her troupe, Pavlova, Ruth St. Denis, and others, had great documentary importance. His published works include *Pictures of Old Chinatown* (1908); *The Book of the Dance* (1916); *Impressions of Old New Orleans* (1926); and *Isadora Duncan, Twenty-four Studies* (1929).

GENUNG, JOHN FRANKLIN (*b. Willseyville, N.Y., 1850; d. 1919*), Baptist clergyman. Graduated Union, 1870; Ph.D., Leipzig. Beloved teacher of rhetoric at Amherst College, 1882–1917; published biblical and literary studies, and *Working Principles of Rhetoric* (1901).

GEORGE, GLADYS (*b. Patten, Maine, 1904; d. Hollywood, Calif., 1954*), actress. Daughter of a touring theatrical family, George achieved fame for her portrayal of Carol Arden in *Personal Appearance* on Broadway in 1934; films include *Valiant Is the Word for Carrie* (1936) which won her a nomination for the Academy Award; *Madame X* (1937); *Marie Antoinette* (1938); *The Way of All Flesh* (1940); and *The Lullaby of Broadway* (1951).

GEORGE, GRACE (*b. Brooklyn, N.Y., 1879; d. New York, N.Y., 1961*), actress, theater manager, translator, and adaptor. Made New York debut in *The New Boy* (1894). Went on to star in such productions as *The Turtle* (1898); *Divorçons* (1907); *The School for Scandal* (1909); *Sauce for the Goose* (1911); *Major Barbara* (1915); *Mademoiselle* (1932); and *The Velvet Glove* (1949). Married the producer William Aloysius Brady in 1899. Manager of the Playhouse, New York, 1915–16. Translations include *The Nest* (1922), her adaptation of *Les noces d'argent* by Paul Geraldy, and *She Had to Know* (1925), an adaptation of

Geraldy's *Si je voulais*. Directed and starred in *The First Mrs. Fraser* (1929). Costarred with James Cagney in her only film, *Johnny Come Lately* (1943).

GEORGE, HENRY (*b. Philadelphia, Pa., 1839; d. New York, N.Y., 1897*), journalist, economist, reformer. After brief schooling, George began work at 14, but read widely, particularly in poetry. Shipped out to Australia and India, 1855–56. Learned to set type. Sailed to San Francisco, Calif., 1857–58; worked as compositor, storekeeper, prospector. Penniless and jobless, he married Annie Fox, 1861. The desperate years which followed gave him a burning personal knowledge of poverty, which was reflected in all he afterward did and wrote. Starting as printer on the San Francisco *Times*, 1866, he rose to managing editor, 1868.

In that same year, he visited New York City, where he was struck with the "shocking contrast between monstrous wealth and debasing want. Why did progress have its twin in poverty?" Returning to California, he became editor of the Oakland *Transcript*, 1869. He believed he had found the answer to his question in the monopolization of land and natural resources, and published a pamphlet, *Our Land and Land Policy* (1871), which contained the essentials of the philosophy he afterward expanded. It was several years before George could continue writing, but in 1877 he started *Progress and Poverty*, the definitive statement of his thesis: that as all men have an equal right to apply their labor to natural resources, economic rent is robbery, and, by the necessity of paying economic rent, labor, capital, and enterprise receive less return than is their due. To cure this condition, it is not necessary to distribute land; it is necessary only to take economic rent in taxation, abolishing all other contributions to government. This will ensure the smooth working of natural economic laws, which, thus freed, will make for an equitable sharing of wealth; monopoly, being grounded in appropriation of land values, will disappear, and so economic society will not be subject to the recurrent seizures called industrial depressions.

This theory, known in George's version as the single-tax theory, had been anticipated by the 18th-century Physiocrats, the two Mills, Marx, Spencer, and others, but George had never read their works and gave his own statement a singular force and beauty.

Published first in an author's edition of 500 copies in 1879, *Progress and Poverty* was published in a trade edition a year later and soon attracted wide notice. George now became a propagandist. He moved to New York; published *The Irish Land Question* (1881); spent a year in Ireland and England speaking, writing, and becoming a public figure. In 1883 he made a triumphal lecture tour in Britain and in 1884 another. He published *Social Problems* (1883) and *Protection or Free Trade* (1886).

Backed by labor, he ran for mayor of New York in a spectacular campaign, 1886. Following his defeat, he organized Land and Labor Clubs throughout the country and began publishing the weekly *Standard*. After intervening years of intense activity he ran again for mayor, 1897, but illness and strain brought on his death before election day.

GEORGE, HENRY (*b. Sacramento, Calif., 1862; d. 1916*), journalist. Son of Henry George (1839–97). His father's intimate helper; editor of the *Standard*, 1887–92; author of *Life of Henry George* (1900).

GEORGE, JAMES ZACHARIAH (*b. Monroe Co., Ga., 1826; d. 1897*), soldier, jurist. Raised in Mississippi. U.S. senator, Democrat, from Mississippi, 1881–97. Defended 1890 Mississippi constitution in the Senate and workmen's right to organize.

GEORGE, WALTER FRANKLIN (*b. Preston, Ga., 1878; d. Vienna, Ga., 1957*), judge and politician. George studied at Mercer University, law degree, 1901. From 1917 to 1922, he was an associate justice of the Georgia Supreme Court. He served as a Democrat in the U.S. Senate from 1922 to 1956. In the Senate, George represented the basic Southern conservatism of his state; he was opposed to many of the New Deal programs, especially those dealing with labor and racial issues. After 1939, he was an ardent supporter of Roosevelt's interventionist policies in Europe. From 1941 to 1954, he was chairman of the Finance Committee. During the war, he was a member of the Senate Committee of Eight and became an internationalist in favor of the U.N. and NATO. In 1954, he became chairman of the Foreign Relations Committee and helped shape the postwar world by assuring Senate support of the nation's international policies.

GEORGE, WILLIAM REUBEN (*b. West Dryden, N.Y., 1866; d. near Freeville, N.Y., 1936*), businessman, philanthropist. Founded, 1895, the George Junior Republic, an innovation in institutional self-government for adolescents.

GERARD, JAMES WATSON (*b. New York, N.Y., 1794; d. 1874*), lawyer, philanthropist. Graduated Columbia, 1811; admitted to bar, 1816. Early began work in behalf of juvenile offenders; procured incorporation in 1824 of the Society for the Reformation of Juvenile Delinquents, whose House of Refuge was the first institution of its kind in the United States. Devoted himself to many other social causes. In later years his greatest services were in popular education.

GERARD, JAMES WATSON (*b. Geneseo, N.Y., 1867; d. Southampton, N.Y., 1951*), lawyer, diplomat. Studied at Columbia University. Ambassador to Germany, 1913–17. Received Grand Cross of the Order of the Bath, 1917, for his efforts on behalf of prisoners of war and British citizens caught in Germany at the outbreak of the war. Intervened with the Germans on behalf of Belgian relief, winning the praise of Herbert Hoover. Warned of the possible consequences of American sales of munitions to the Allies, postwar German revenge, and of possible German intervention in Latin America. Returned to the U.S. at the request of the German government, 1916, to urge Wilson to press for an early peace, predicting that if the war continued, Germany would unleash unlimited submarine warfare.

GERBER, (DANIEL) FRANK (*b. Douglas, Mich., 1873; d. 1952*); GERBER, DANIEL (FRANK) (*b. Fremont, Mich., 1889; d. 1974*), baby food manufacturers. Frank Gerber founded the Fremont Canning Company in 1901; in 1928, at the suggestion of his son, the company began to make strained baby food. The firm's name was changed to Gerber Products in 1941; by 1973, the company manufactured 60 percent of the U.S. market and was the world's largest producer of baby foods.

GERHARD, WILLIAM WOOD (*b. Philadelphia, Pa., 1809; d. 1872*), physician. Graduated Dickinson, 1826; M.D., University of Pennsylvania, 1830; studied also in Paris. Famous for first distinguishing typhus from typhoid fever, 1837, Gerhard also published a series of papers on the pathology of smallpox, pneumonia in children, tuberculous meningitis.

GERHART, EMANUEL VOGEL (*b. Freeburg, Pa., 1817; d. Lancaster, Pa., 1904*), German Reformed theologian. President, Franklin and Marshall College, 1854–66; Mercersburg Theological Seminary, 1868–1904. Strongly influenced doctrinal development of his church.

GERICKE, WILHELM (*b. Graz, Austria, 1845; d. 1925*), musician. Conductor and director of Boston Symphony Orchestra, 1884–89 and 1898–1906.

GERNSBACK, HUGO (*b. Luxembourg, 1884; d. New York, N.Y., 1967*), publisher, editor, inventor, and author.

Immigrated, 1904. Started Electro Importing Company in New York City (1905), probably the first American radio supply house; patented about eighty electronic devices throughout his career. Founded *Modern Electrics* magazine (1908), which he sold in 1912 to start *Electrical Experimenter*. Also founded *Radio Amateur News* in 1919 (became *Radio News* in 1920). Founded *Amazing Stories* (1926); his reputation as the publisher of the first science fiction (a phrase he coined) magazine in the United States gained him the title "father of science fiction." Also published the pulps *Wonder Stories, Air Wonder Stories,* and *Science Wonder Stories.* Wrote *The Wireless Telephone* (1908), *Radio for All* (1922), and a posthumous novel, *Ultimate World* (1970). Beginning in 1953, the prestigious achievement award annually presented at the World Science Fiction Convention was called a "Hugo" in his honor.

GERONIMO (*b. southern Arizona, 1829; d. Fort Sill, Okla., 1909*), Chiricahua Apache warrior. Indian name, "Goyathlay." Not a Chiricahua by birth, he assumed virtual leadership of the tribe. Their forced removal to San Carlos on the Gila, 1876, started him raiding; after an interval as a farmer, 1877–79, he led other forays in 1880 and 1882–83. He began his bloodiest, most spectacular campaign in May 1885. For ten months he raided outlying settlements until, followed into Mexico, he surrendered on Mar. 27, 1886, only to escape again two nights later. He was not recaptured until early in September. He and his band were imprisoned in Florida and Alabama; later they became orderly farmers and stock-raisers at Fort Sill.

GERRISH, FREDERIC HENRY (*b. Portland, Maine, 1845; d. 1920*), surgeon. M.D., Bowdoin, 1869; taught anatomy and surgery there *post* 1875.

GERRY, ELBRIDGE (*b. Marblehead, Mass., 1744; d. Washington, D.C., 1814*), statesman. Graduated Harvard, 1762; entered family shipping business. Elected to General Court, 1772. An ardent follower of Samuel Adams, he was member of Massachusetts Committee of Correspondence, of the First and Second Provincial Congresses and of the Committee of Safety. He was active in raising troops and efficient in procuring all manner of supplies for the provincial army. Delegate to the Second Continental Congress, he was an industrious member of the Treasury Board and an early advocate of separation from Great Britain. He signed both the Declaration of Independence and the Articles of Confederation.

As the Revolutionary war continued, his experience and faithful attendance made him increasingly valuable in Congress. In foreign policy he opposed the French alliance but was an implacable enemy of England. He worked hard to provide army supplies. Frowning on profiteering, he tried to enforce on others (and observed himself) the schedule of fair prices fixed by the New Haven convention of 1778. Opposed in Congress on this point in 1780, he absented himself for three years, engaging successfully in trade and privateering at home. After the peace, Gerry returned to Congress, where he attempted to carry the stern republicanism of the 1770's into a period when altered problems required other qualities for solution. He retired from Congress, 1793.

In 1797, Gerry was appointed member of the XYZ mission to France because John Adams wanted a nonparty man joined with Marshall and Pinckney. His conduct throughout was questionable. He allowed Talleyrand to negotiate with him singly and in secret, and remained in Paris when his indignant colleagues departed, believing that the Directory would declare war if he left. On his return to American in October 1798, the Federalists snubbed him, but the Massachusetts Republicans, sharing his belief that he had prevented war with France, put him up unsuccessfully for governor in 1800 and each year thereafter until

1804. In 1810, however, he was elected governor and served until April 1812. His second term was immortalized by the "Gerrymander" bill in which the state was redistricted so as to give to the Republicans a number of state senators in excess of their voting strength. Elected vice president on the ticket with James Madison, 1812, Gerry entered into the social life of Washington with zest, but he was in frail health and died Nov. 22, 1814.

GERRY, ELBRIDGE THOMAS (*b. New York, N.Y., 1837; d. 1927*), lawyer, philanthropist. Grandson of Elbridge Gerry. Graduated Columbia, 1857. Energetic legal adviser to the American Society for the Prevention of Cruelty to Animals; procured enabling and subsequent legislation for the New York Society for the Prevention of Cruelty to Children, incorporated 1875, first of its kind in the world. Gerry studied all the phases of child rescue and gradually devoted all his time to the society, molding policy and directing activities as president, 1879–1901, in the face of bitter opposition.

GERSHWIN, GEORGE (*b. Brooklyn, N.Y., 1898; d. Beverly Hills, Calif., 1937*), composer. His first influential music teacher, Charles Hambitzer, recognizing the youth's latent talents, advised him to study harmony and attend concerts. In 1913 Gershwin left high school to work as staff pianist for the Remick music publishing firm. By 1916 one of the many popular songs he had written was published and another appeared in the *Passing Show of 1916*. In 1918 Max Dreyfus, head of the publishing firm of Harms, engaged Gershwin simply to write songs and show them to him. Gershwin's career advanced rapidly. In 1919 he had his first smash song hit, "Swanee," and wrote the score for the musical comedy *La, La Lucille*. From 1920 to 1924 he wrote the music for the annual *George White's Scandals*.

In 1922 Gershwin wrote *Blue Monday*, a one-act opera in the jazz idiom, which was performed once in the *Scandals* but withdrawn because of its somber mood. However, its conductor, Paul Whiteman, was deeply impressed. At his request Gershwin wrote a new symphonic-jazz work, *Rhapsody in Blue*, which Whitman introduced at a concert on Feb. 12, 1924. It made the young composer famous and wealthy, and opened up new horizons for jazz. Other notable concert compositions by Gershwin followed: *Concerto in F* (1925), commissioned by the New York Symphony Society; *Three Piano Preludes* (1926); *An American in Paris* (1928); *Second Rhapsody* (1932); *Cuban Overture* (1932); *Variations on "I Got Rhythm"* (1934); and, perhaps his most enduring work, *Porgy and Bess* (1935).

Meanwhile, Gershwin was also writing scores (his brother Ira writing most of the lyrics) for Broadway stage productions and Hollywood films. His best musical comedies were *Lady Be Good* (1924), *Tip Toes* (1925), *Oh Kay* (1926), *Funny Face* (1927), *Strike Up the Band* (1929), *Girl Crazy* (1930), and *Of Thee I Sing* (1931, the first musical comedy to win the Pulitzer Prize). Gershwin's music is filled with verve, spontaneity, excitement; it is American music to the core. Its continued growth in popularity and artistic stature mark Gershwin as one of the most significant creative figures that American music has produced.

GERSTER, ARPAD GEYZA CHARLES (*b. Kassa, Hungary, 1848; d. 1923*), surgeon. M.D., Vienna, 1872. Came to America, 1873. An early partisan of the antiseptic technique, he published the first textbook in American on the new surgery, *Rules of Aseptic and Antiseptic Surgery* (1888). This epoch-making book contained some of the earliest halftone pictures made from Gerster's own plates. He was professor of surgery at the New York Polyclinic, 1882–94; he became professor of clinical surgery at Columbia, 1916. A superior diagnostician, he excelled in postoperative care.

GERSTLE, LEWIS (*b. Ichenhausen, Germany, 1824; d. 1902*), California pioneer, capitalist. Moved to America, 1847; settled in California, 1850. Promoter and director of many business enterprises; president of the Alaska Commercial Co.

GESELL, ARNOLD LUCIUS (*b. Alma, Wis., 1880; d. New Haven, Conn., 1961*), pediatric psychologist. Studied at the University of Wisconsin (B.Ph., 1903), Clark University, Worcester, Mass. (Ph.D., 1906), and Yale (M.D., 1915). Professor, Yale, 1911–48; founded the Yale Clinic for Child Development in 1911. School psychologist for the Connecticut State Board of Education, 1915–19. Attending pediatrician at the New Haven Hospital, 1928–48. The Gesell Institute of Child Development at Yale was founded in his honor in 1950. A pioneer in the determination of normal ranges of child development and behavioral patterns, he initiated the use of cinematography in evaluating infant development. Among his works are *The Mental Growth of the Pre-school Child* (1925) and the *Atlas of Infant Behavior* (1934), both of which included action photographs.

GEST, MORRIS (*b. Koshedary, near Vilna, Russia, 1881; d. New York, N.Y., 1942*), theatrical producer. Born of Jewish parents and originally named Moses Gershonovitch, he went to Boston, Mass., at the age of 12 to work for an uncle; he credited his education chiefly to the Boston Public Library. Stagestruck almost at once, he held a variety of minor theater jobs; in 1902, he moved to New York City, where he was employed by Oscar Hammerstein, who sent him to Europe to "scout" foreign acts for the Victoria Theater. In partnership with F. Ray Comstock, 1905–28, Gest specialized at first in lavish spectacles, including *The Wanderer* (1917), *Chu Chin Chow* (1917), and *Mecca* (1920). Thereafter, he imported a number of very distinguished foreign artists and productions, among them Balieff's *Chauve-Souris* revues, the Moscow Art Theater (1923–25), the final American tour of Eleonora Duse (1923–24), and Max Reinhardt's *The Miracle* (1924). As an independent producer *post* 1928, he failed to equal his earlier successes.

GETTY, GEORGE WASHINGTON (*b. Georgetown, D.C., 1819; d. Maryland, 1901*), soldier. Graduated West Point, 1840. Fought in Mexican War; served with distinction in Army of the Potomac, 1861–65, especially at siege of Suffolk, Va., 1863.

GEYER, HENRY SHEFFIE (*b. Frederick, Md., 1790; d. 1859*), lawyer. Removed to St. Louis, Mo., *ca.* 1816. Eminent in landtitle litigation; played prominent part in Missouri struggle for statehood. U.S. senator, Whig, from Missouri, 1851–59. Attorney for defendant slave owner in Dred Scott case.

GHENT, WILLIAM JAMES (*b. Frankfort, Ind., 1866; d. Washington, D.C., 1942*), author. A printer by trade, Ghent began to write on social and political topics during the 1890's; his point of view was socialist, but he remained independent of official American socialist doctrine and political efforts until 1904 when he joined the Socialist party. Aligning himself with men like Morris Hillquit and others who opposed violent methods of reform, he helped found and headed (1906–11) the Rand School of Social Science in New York City. Having contracted tuberculosis, he lived in Arizona and California, 1913–24. He continued to lecture and write, and interested himself in the history of the Old West. Meanwhile, he had left the Socialist party in 1916 and become an aggressive opponent of Marxism and Soviet Russia. His books include *Our Benevolent Feudalism* (1902), *Mass and Class* (1904), *The Road to Oregon* (1929), *The Early Far West* (1931), and, in collaboration with L. R. Hafen, *Broken Hand: The Life Story of Thomas Fitzpatrick* (1931). He was also an editor-writer for the *Dictionary of American Biography*.

GHERARDI, BANCROFT (*b. Jackson, La., 1832; d. Stratford, Conn., 1903*), naval officer. Nephew of George Bancroft. Graduated U.S. Naval Academy, 1852. Commended for conduct at Mobile Bay, 1864. Held series of naval posts; rose to rear admiral and command of North Atlantic Squadron, 1889–92.

GHERARDI, BANCROFT (*b. San Francisco, Calif., 1873; d. French River, Ontario, Canada, 1941*), engineer, corporation executive. Son of Bancroft Gherardi and grandnephew of George Bancroft. B.S., Brooklyn Polytechnic Institute, 1891; M.E., Cornell University, 1893. Associated with the New York Telephone Co. and its predecessor firms, 1895–1907, he served thereafter as engineer and administrative officer with the American Telephone and Telegraph Co. In 1919, he became chief engineer of A.T.&T., and in 1920 vice president; he held both positions until his retirement in 1938.

GHOLSON, SAMUEL JAMESON (*b. Madison Co., Ky., 1808; d. Aberdeen, Miss., 1883*), jurist, legislator, Confederate soldier. Federal district judge in Mississippi, 1839–61.

GHOLSON, THOMAS SAUNDERS (*b. Gholsonville, Va., 1808; d. Savannah, Ga., 1868*), Virginia lawyer and jurist. Confederate congressman.

GHOLSON, WILLIAM YATES (*b. Southampton Co., Va., 1807; d. 1870*), lawyer, jurist. Practiced in Mississippi, 1834–44; removing to Cincinnati, Ohio, he won reputation for legal learning and integrity.

GIANNINI, AMADEO PETER (*b. San Jose, Calif., 1870; d. San Mateo, Calif., 1949*), banker, financier. Child of immigrant parents from Genoa, Italy, Giannini lost his father in 1877 and was raised by a stepfather, in whose San Francisco wholesale produce business he became a partner in 1889. Highly successful, he sold his interest in the business in 1901, proposing to retire. In 1902, however, he was asked by the family to manage the estate of his late father-in-law, which included a directorship and stock in the Columbus Savings and Loan Society, a small community bank in North Beach, an Italian neighborhood. Giannini sought, unsuccessfully, to persuade the other directors to make more small loans. He then resigned and organized the Bank of Italy. From the start the bank offered complete banking services; it accepted both savings and commercial (checking) accounts, pursued an easy lending policy, and encouraged small loans. During the 1906 earthquake and fire Giannini transported the bank's coin and currency to the safety of his own house. During the panic of 1907 most of the city's banks were forced to use clearinghouse certificates, but the Bank of Italy continued to issue currency.

By the end of 1918, with 24 branches scattered throughout California and total resources of more than $93 million, the Bank of Italy had become the first statewide branch-banking system in the United States. In 1919 he organized Bancitaly Corporation, a holding company that purchased the East River National Bank in New York City and later acquired a branch system in Italy. In 1924 Giannini retired as president of the Bank of Italy, but remained a director and chairman of its executive committee, as well as president of Bancitaly. He then acquired a new network of branch banks and by 1928 had unified them under the name of Bank of America of California. Two years later Giannini and the directors of Transamerica Corporation—the holding company that succeeded Bancitaly in 1928—merged with the Bank of Italy and the Bank of America of California into the Bank of America National Trust and Savings Association. Several other banks controlled by the corporation but ineligible for inclusion were united in a new state bank called simply the Bank of America. This in turn was later merged into the parent bank. Giannini retired in 1934 as chairman of the board of Bank of America, but continued as board chairman of Transamerica Corporation. By this time, Bank of America had grown into the world's largest commercial bank.

GIBAULT, PIERRE (*b. Montreal, Canada, 1737; d. New Madrid, Spanish Louisiana, 1804*), Roman Catholic clergyman. Vicar general of Illinois mission country, 1769–90. After George Rogers Clark's capture of Kaskaskia, 1778, encouraged French settlers there and at Vincennes to assist the American cause.

GIBBES, ROBERT WISLON (*b. Charleston, S.C., 1809; d. 1866*), physician, author. Son of William H. Gibbes. Graduated South Carolina College, 1827; M.D., Medical College of South Carolina, 1830. Worked as assistant to Thomas Cooper, and won national reputation; his 1842 treatise *On Typhoid Pneumonia* revolutionized treatment. Proprietor and editor, Columbia, S.C., *South Carolinian*.

GIBBES, WILLIAM HASELL (*b. Charleston, S.C., 1754; d. Charleston, 1834*), lawyer, Revolutionary soldier. Rendered important services as master in equity, 1783–1825.

GIBBON, JOHN (*b. near Holmesburg, Pa., 1827, d. Baltimore, Md., 1896*), soldier. Graduated West Point, 1847. Author of *Artillerist's Manual* (1860). As brigadier general, commanded the Union "Iron Brigade" at second Bull Run, South Mountain, Antietam; raised to divisional command, he was wounded at Fredericksburg and Gettysburg. Commanding the new XXIV Corps, 1865, he was named to the commission which arranged details of Lee's surrender. After the war he served mainly in the West. He commanded the expedition which rescued the Custer survivors, 1876, and in 1877 pursued and defeated the Nez Percé under Chief Joseph.

GIBBONS, ABIGAIL HOPPER (*b. Philadelphia, Pa., 1801; d. 1893*), teacher, philanthropist. Daughter of Isaac T. Hopper; wife of James S. Gibbons. An active abolitionist, she engaged in many other forms of humanitarian work, including relief of crippled and blind children and Civil War nursing. Her most important accomplishment was as president of the Women's Prison Association.

GIBBONS, FLOYD (*b. Washington, D.C., 1887; d. near Stroudsburg, Pa., 1939*), war correspondent, radio commentator.

GIBBONS, HERBERT ADAMS (*b. Annapolis, Md., 1880; d. Grunslee, Austria, 1934*), journalist, foreign correspondent.

GIBBONS, JAMES (*b. Baltimore, Md., 1834; d. Baltimore, 1921*), Roman Catholic prelate. Graduated St. Charles College, 1858; studied at St. Mary's Seminary, Baltimore; ordained, 1861. As a local pastor, he soon showed unusual powers. During the Civil War he was chaplain at Fort McHenry, ministering to Union and Confederate alike. Appointed secretary to Archbishop Spalding of Baltimore, 1865, he attracted general notice at the Second Plenary Council of Baltimore, 1866, and was nominated vicar apostolic of North Carolina. Consecrated bishop of Adramyttum, 1868; bishop of Richmond, 1872.

In attendance at Vatican Council, Rome, 1870, he was impressed by the difficulties of church-state relations in Europe as compared with the ease of relations in the United States under the American system. An able administrator, popular with people of all creeds, he was made archbishop coadjutor of Baltimore with right of succession in 1877 only five months before Archbishop J. R. Bayley's death. He then became head of the oldest U.S. archdiocese, the first native of the city to be appointed to the see. He took an active part in civic and humanitarian movements, acquired a wide Washington acquaintance. His exposition of Catholic doctrine, *The Faith of Our Fathers* (1877), leapt into popularity. Sharing the belief of Pope Leo XIII that the future of the church would be among democratic peoples, Gibbons organized the Third Plenary Council of Baltimore, 1884, and presided as apostolic delegate. The decrees of the council have guided the Catholic church in the United States since, and were strong in support of American civil institutions. The Catholic University at Washington, D.C., was also established as an outcome of this council, and Gibbons was head of its board of trustees until his death.

In 1886, Leo XIII made Gibbons the second American cardinal. At his installation in Rome he declared that the progress of the Catholic church in the United States was due in large part to American liberty. Sympathizing with labor's aspirations, he obtained the Vatican assurance that the Knights of Labor would not be condemned as a secret society; he also succeeded in preventing ecclesiastical condemnation of Henry George's *Progress and Poverty*. Back in Baltimore, he was hailed as a champion of labor and representative of American principles. He threw all his influence against the "Cahensly movement" for the appointment of U.S. Catholic bishops on the basis of representation of national immigrant groups. He was in favor of early blending of immigrants with the native population and especially opposed to transplantation of European differences. Through his efforts also, the controversy over "Americanism" in doctrine was exposed as an error and ended. In 1911 at a celebration of his jubilee as cardinal, Gibbons received honors never before accorded any American churchman. His greatest influence was shown as a farsighted leader and administrator and in promoting the spirit of religious toleration.

GIBBONS, JAMES SLOAN (*b. Wilmington, Del., 1810; d. New York, N.Y., 1892*), abolitionist, banker. Son of William Gibbons (1781–1845). Author of works on banking and taxation, and of the famous Civil War song "We Are Coming, Father Abraham."

GIBBONS, THOMAS (*b. near Savannah, Ga., 1757; d. New York, N.Y., 1826*), lawyer, politician. Mayor of Savannah, 1791–92, 1794–95, and 1799–1801; federal judge in Georgia. He moved north and began running steamboats from Elizabethtown, N.J., to New York City, 1818, competing with Aaron Ogden, who had purchased rights to the route from the holders of the New York monopoly on steam navigation in state waters granted to Robert Livingston and Robert Fulton in 1803. Ogden secured an injunction; Gibbons appealed; the case was carried to the Supreme Court in 1824, and Chief Justice John Marshall handed down his famous decision declaring the New York monopoly, with all others of its kind, null and void.

GIBBONS, WILLIAM (*b. Bear Bluff, S.C., 1726; d. 1800*), lawyer, Revolutionary patriot. Practiced in Savannah, Ga.; led in opposition to the crown there. Member of the Provincial Congress, the Committee of Safety, and the Continental Congress, 1784–86.

GIBBONS, WILLIAM (*b. Philadelphia, Pa., 1781; d. 1845*), physician. Practiced in Wilmington, Del. Interested in black emancipation and education.

GIBBS, ARTHUR HAMILTON (*b. London, England, 1888; d. Boston, Mass., 1964*), author. Studied at St. Johns College, Oxford (1907–09). Traveled to the United States in 1912. Served in Europe in World War I. Returned to the United States in 1918; became a citizen, 1931. His book of World War I memoirs, *Gun Fodder* (1919), won critical acclaim for its realism. Published fourteen novels, including *Soundings* (1925), *Labels* (1926), *Harness* (1928), *Chances* (1930), *Way of Life* (1947), and *Obedience to the Moon* (1956). His novels were popular; some were best-sellers, but none were taken seriously by the critics. Also wrote a book of verse, *One Touch of France*, published in 1953.

GIBBS, GEORGE (*b. Newport, R.I., 1776; d. near Astoria, N.Y., 1833*), friend of science. His mineral collection, the largest and most valuable in the country, was deposited at Yale, 1810. Friend and encourager of the elder Benjamin Silliman, Gibbs inspired founding of *American Journal of Science*.

GIBBS, GEORGE (*b. near Astoria, N.Y., 1815; d. New Haven, Conn., 1873*), ethnologist. Son of George Gibbs (1776–1833); brother of Oliver W. Gibbs. Graduated Harvard, 1838. Studied natural history and geology of the Northwest, and the languages and traditions of its Indians. Author of Indian language studies and of *Memoirs of the Administrations of Washington and John Adams* (1846).

GIBBS, GEORGE (*b. Chicago, Ill., 1861; d. New York, N.Y., 1940*), engineer. Nephew of Oliver W. Gibbs. Graduated Stevens Institute, 1882. Associated with Samuel M. Vauclain of Baldwin Locomotive Works, and George Westinghouse, in the development of electric locomotives, *post* 1897. He represented the Westinghouse companies abroad in the electrification of railways in London and Liverpool. From 1901 he played an important part in the electrification of American railways, in particular of the New York Central, Pennsylvania, and Long Island lines leading into New York City. He was consulting engineer for the first New York City subway, and designed and patented the first all-steel subway passenger car.

GIBBS, JAMES ETHAN ALLEN (*b. Rockbridge Co., Va., 1829; d. Raphine, Va., 1902*), inventor. Patented, 1857, chain-and lock-stitch devices and a twisted loop rotary hook which with his partner, James Willcox, he marketed as the Willcox and Gibbs sewing machine.

GIBBS, JOSIAH WILLARD (*b. Salem, Mass., 1790; d. 1861*), orientalist, philologist. Graduated Yale, 1809. Professor of sacred literature at Yale Divinity School, 1826–61.

GIBBS, JOSIAH WILLARD (*b. New Haven, Conn., 1839; d. New Haven, 1903*), mathematician, physicist. Son of Josiah W. Gibbs (1790–1861). Graduated Yale, 1858; Ph.D., 1863; studied at Paris, Berlin, and Heidelberg, 1866–69. Appointed professor of mathematical physics at Yale, 1871, a post he held for 32 years. Few undergraduates were equipped to profit from Gibbs's advanced lectures, and despite his worldwide reputation, he did not draw many graduate students to New Haven. His influence on science came chiefly from his writings.

In his first two scientific papers (1873) he made an exhaustive study of geometrical methods of representing by diagrams the thermodynamic properties of homogeneous substances and established a point of view for his later work. His great memoir "On the Equilibrium of Heterogeneous Substances" appeared in two parts in 1876 and 1878 in the *Transactions of the Connecticut Academy of Arts and Sciences*. This epochal work, with its later supplementary monographs, provided the basic theory for a new branch of science, physical chemistry. Many years passed before some of Gibbs's theoretical developments were experimentally verified, and even today his suggestions have not been exhausted by experimenters.

Gibbs was occupied between 1880 and 1884 with modifying the work of Hamilton on quaternions and of Grassman on geometric algebra into a system of vector analysis especially suited to the need of mathematical physicists, which he printed privately (1881, 1884) for his students and friends. The whole was not published until 1901. Between 1882 and 1889, besides completing the second part of the vector analysis, Gibbs developed his own electrical theory of optics, which he set forth in articles in the *American Journal of Science* (April and June 1882; February 1883; June 1888; February 1889).

His last great work, *Elementary Principles in Statistical Mechanics*, appeared in 1902 in the Yale Bicentennial series.

Gibbs's English style was perfection—brief, precise, free from dogmatic statements, not given to ornamentation, fascinating in its inexorable logic. Little is known of Gibbs's methods of work. He left few notes and would appear to have composed mainly from ideas carried in his head. At the time of his death he had three pieces of work in mind: reedition and amplification of his work on thermodynamics; some developments of multiple algebra, on which he had an original point of view; a revision of the method used in his theory of orbits published in 1889.

GIBBS, OLIVER WOLCOTT (*b. New York, N.Y., 1822; d. 1908*), chemist. Son of George Gibbs (1776–1833); brother of George Gibbs (1815–73). Graduated Columbia, 1841; M.D., College of Physicians and Surgeons, 1845; studied also in Germany and France. Professor at New York City College (Free Academy), 1849–63; Rumford professor at Harvard, 1863–87. Directed Lawrence Scientific School laboratory, inspiring his students with zeal for research and introducing laboratory methods which he had learned in Europe. His chief work was with inorganic compounds, analytical methods, physiological chemistry. With F. A. Genth he conducted classical researches into the nature of the complex compounds of cobalt; his work on the platinum metals was of equal importance. A later series of researches established the nature of the complex acids formed by vanadium, tungsten, molybdenum, phosphorus, arsenic, and antimony.

GIBBS, (OLIVER) WOLCOTT (*b. New York, N.Y., 1902; d. Fire Island, N.Y., 1958*), author, editor, and critic. Copy editor, writer and drama critic for *The New Yorker* from 1927 until his death, Gibbs personified that magazine's style. Published collections of his essays for the magazine and wrote the Broadway play, *Season in the Sun* (1950). As a critic, Gibbs is remembered as a tough, almost venomous judge.

GIBBS, WOLCOTT. *See* GIBBS, (OLIVER) WOLCOTT.

GIBSON, CHARLES DANA (*b. Roxbury, Mass., 1867; d. New York, N.Y., 1944*), illustrator, cartoonist, creator of the "Gibson Girl." Raised in Flushing, Long Island, N.Y. Had a brief apprenticeship with Augustus Saint-Gaudens; studied at Art Students League, New York, with Kenyon Cox, William M. Chase, and Thomas Eakins. Contributed numerous drawings to *Life,* 1886–88, and other humor magazines; on return from a visit to Europe, 1888, began illustrating stories for *Harper's, Scribner's,* and *Century* magazines. Gibson's drawings of square-jawed, manly heroes and elegant, rather queenly women were perfect expressions of the ideals of the period and its dress, manners, and attitudes toward life. With the Gibson Girl he created a distinctive type which still stands as a symbol of 1890's smartness and was a model for countless American women until World War I. He was equally effective as a gentle satirist of the newly rich. Achieving financial independence, he gave up pen-and-ink illustration in 1905 and went abroad to study painting; the loss of his savings in the financial crash of 1907, however, compelled his return to magazine work. During World War I, he directed a federal project for production of posters and drawings to spur the war effort. He was owner and editor in chief of *Life,* 1920–32.

GIBSON, EDMUND RICHARD ("HOOT") (*b. Tekamah, Nebr., 1892; d. Woodland Hills, Calif., 1962*), cowboy and motion picture actor. Worked as a cowboy throughout the West and participated in Wild West shows and rodeos from about 1906. Drawn into the emerging film industry as a stunt rider; first screen appearance was in *Shotgun Jones* (1911). Starred in a series of five-reel Westerns for Universal Pictures, starting with *Action* (1921). In all he made 200 silent and seventy-five talking pictures, including *Long, Long Trail* (1929), *Lariat Kid* (1929), *Mounted*

Stranger (1930), and *The Horse Soldiers* (1959). His pictures captured a vanishing way of life that Gibson knew well; he was among the most popular stars of Westerns.

GIBSON, GEORGE (*b. Lancaster, Pa., 1747; d. Fort Jefferson, Northwest Territory, 1791*), Revolutionary soldier. Brother of John Gibson. Agent for gunpowder purchase at New Orleans, 1776; killed on St. Clair's expedition.

GIBSON, JOHN (*b. Lancaster, Pa., 1740; d. Braddock's Field, Pa., 1822*), frontier soldier. Brother of George Gibson. Indian trader at Fort Pitt. Reported the famous speech of Chief Logan, publicized by Thomas Jefferson; served on frontier during Revolution. Secretary of Indiana Territory, 1800–16.

GIBSON, JOHN BANNISTER (*b. Westover Mills, Pa., 1780; d. Philadelphia, Pa., 1853*), jurist. Justice of Pennsylvania Supreme Court, 1816–53, and chief justice, *post* 1827, he was the dominant figure of the state judiciary, distinguished for breadth of view, independence, originality, and masterful opinions. In hearing over 6,000 cases and delivering reasons for judgment in more than 1,200, he profoundly influenced the development of Pennsylvania law. His opinions range over the whole legal field, those on constitutional problems commanding the greatest respect.

GIBSON, JOSHUA (*b. Buena Vista, Ga., 1911; d. Pittsburgh, Pa., 1947*), baseball player. Raised in Pittsburgh; as a schoolboy, was an expert swimmer and showed natural talent as a hitter in baseball. At age 16 he joined the Gimbels Athletic Club, a local all-black amateur baseball club; in 1929 and 1930, playing with the semiprofessional Crawford Colored Giants of Pittsburgh, his growing reputation as a slugger drew large crowds. His next move was to the Homestead (Pa.) Grays, one of the best black professional clubs; he joined the club in July 1930, and was soon the regular catcher. During the season of 1931, he was credited with 75 home runs, and from then until his death he continued a mighty man at bat; statistics are incomplete, but he is believed to have hit more than 800 home runs in regular season play during his 17 years as a professional. His highest reported number of home runs for a single season was 89. During his career, he played not only for the Grays, but for the Pittsburgh Crawfords (named for the earlier Crawford Giants), and during the winters played with teams in Latin America. One of the preeminent hitters in baseball history, he died of a brain tumor just before the major leagues admitted the first black player.

GIBSON, PARIS (*b. Brownfield, Maine, 1830; d. 1920*), Montana pioneer, conservationist. Introduced sheep farming in northern Montana, 1879; planned city of Great Falls; was closely connected with waterpower, coal mining, and railroad development. U.S. senator, Democrat, 1901–05.

GIBSON, RANDALL LEE (*b. Woodford Co., Ky., 1832; d. Hot Springs, Ark., 1892*), lawyer, painter, Confederate soldier. Congressman, Democrat, from Louisiana, 1875–83; U.S. senator, 1883–92. Worked in Congress to improve Mississippi navigation; was chief agent in founding Tulane University.

GIBSON, WALTER MURRAY (*b. at sea en route from England, 1823; d. 1888*), adventurer, politician. Raised in New York and New Jersey; early orphaned. After a fantastic career in Central America and Sumatra and in Utah as adviser to Brigham Young, he settled in Hawaii, 1861. Opposing nonnatives there, he became premier of the kingdom, 1882, and was deposed in revolution of 1887.

GIBSON, WILLIAM (*b. Baltimore, Md., 1788; d. Savannah, Ga., 1868*), surgeon. Graduated Edinburgh, M.D., 1809; studied also with Bell and Cooper in London. Organized University of

Maryland's medical department and taught there, 1811–19; professor of surgery, University of Pennsylvania, 1819–55.

GIBSON, WILLIAM HAMILTON (*b. Newtown, Conn., 1850; d. Washington, Conn., 1896*), artist, naturalist, popularizer of nature study.

GIDDINGS, FRANKLIN HENRY (*b. Sherman, Conn., 1855; d. Scarsdale, N.Y., 1931*), sociologist, educator. Attended Union College; became first a teacher, then a journalist. Specialized in statistical investigations of social problems. Taught at Bryn Mawr, 1888–94; went to Columbia, 1894, as professor of sociology and served until 1931. His first volume to attract widespread attention was *The Principles of Sociology* (1896); in 11 subsequent volumes he shaped social research and the concepts and teaching of sociology. A disciple of Herbert Spencer and an influential propagandist for the scientific method, he helped to bring sociology out of the theoretical, and into the scientific, stage.

GIDDINGS, JOSHUA REED (*b. Bradford Co., Pa., 1795; d. Montreal, Canada, 1864*), lawyer, abolitionist. Raised in Ashtabula Co., Ohio. Congressman, Whig, and Free-Soil, from Ohio, 1839–54; Republican, 1854–58. A militant crusader against slavery, he opposed the annexation of Texas, the Mexican War, and the compromise on the Oregon boundary. His program called for freedom in the territories, opposition to disunion, and, if war resulted, use of the president's war powers to emancipate all slaves. Lincoln, who had been a student of his speeches, appointed him consul general to Canada, 1861.

GIDEON, PETER MILLER (*b. near Woodstock, Ohio, 1820; d. 1899*), pioneer pomologist. Settled, 1858, on Gideon's Bay, Lake Minnetonka, Minn., where he worked to develop fruit hardy enough to withstand the rigors of northern winters. After many setbacks, he produced from seed of the Siberian crab the "Wealthy" apple, first noticed in the *Western Farmer*, 1869. In quest of a variety with equal size and flavor but with a tougher skin, he also developed "Peter" and "Gideon."

GIDLEY, JAMES WILLIAMS (*b. Springwater, Iowa, 1866; d. 1931*), vertebrate paleontologist. Graduated Princeton, 1898. Associated with U.S. National Museum, *post* 1905. Authority on the history and development of fossil horses in America.

GIESLER-ANNEKE, MATHILDE FRANZISKA (*b. Lerchenhausen, Germany, 1817; d. 1884*), author, German revolutionary, reformer. Married Fritz Anneke, 1847. Came to America, *ca.* 1850. Conducted a girls' school in Milwaukee, Wis., 1865–84.

GIFFORD, ROBERT SWAIN (*b. Naushon Island, Mass., 1840; d. New York, N.Y., 1905*), landscape painter, etcher. Teacher for many years at Cooper Union. His most congenial subject, the Buzzard's Bay, Mass., area, may be seen in such spacious, melancholy paintings as *Dartmouth Moors*.

GIFFORD, SANFORD ROBINSON (*b. Greenfield, N.Y., 1823; d. New York, N.Y., 1880*), landscape painter. Inspired by work of Thomas Cole and F. E. Church; studied with John Rubens Smith. His paintings show some of the scenic manner of Turner, and his work is differentiated from that of others of the Hudson River school by a more subtle perception of values, a greater interest in air and light. Emotional content and glowing color mark his sunny and cheerful landscapes.

GIFFORD, SANFORD ROBINSON (*b. Omaha, Nebr., 1892; d. Chicago, Ill., 1944*), ophthalmologist, microbiologist. Grandnephew of Sanford Robinson Gifford. B.A., Cornell University, 1913; M.D., University of Nebraska, 1918. After service in France and Germany during and after World War I, he began practice in Omaha and was a member of the teaching staff at University of Nebraska College of Medicine, 1919–29. In 1923–24, he studied ocular diseases produced by certain bacteria and fungi, and did research in the biochemistry of the eye, at a number of European clinics and university laboratories. Professor of ophthalmology and department head at Northwestern University Medical School, 1929 until his death. Author of *A Textbook of Ophthalmology* (1938) and some 150 research papers.

GIFFORD, WALTER SHERMAN (*b. Salem, Mass., 1885; d. New York, N.Y., 1966*), corporation executive and diplomat. Studied at Harvard (graduated, 1905). Accounting clerk with the Western Electric Company in Chicago, 1905–06; assistant secretary and treasurer, 1906–11. Chief statistician at AT&T, 1911–15. Supervising director of the Committee on Industrial Preparedness of the Naval Consulting Board; organized the Council of National Defense, 1916–18. Controller of AT&T, (1918–20); vice president in charge of finance, (1920–22); director (1922–25); president (1925–49); chairman of the board (1949–51). Appointed ambassador to Great Britain in 1951. During his presidency AT&T attained nearly universal residential subscribership and conversion to the dial system of automatic switching. His administrative talents created the modern telephone company; his diplomatic talents and position of prestige with American political leaders helped to continue its functioning as a monopoly.

GIHON, ALBERT LEARY (*b. Philadelphia, Pa., 1833; d. 1901*), naval surgeon.

GILBERT, ALFRED CARLTON (*b. Salem, Oreg., 1884; d. Boston, Mass., 1961*), inventor and manufacturer of toys. Studied at Yale (M.D., 1909). Tied for the pole vault gold medal at the Olympic Games in London in 1908. Established the Mysto Manufacturing Company in 1909 (the A.C. Gilbert Company from 1916). Success grew out of his invention of the Erector Set. Went on to produce a number of other instructional toys, and a series of books to go with them, including *Meteorology* (1920), *Magnetic Fun and Facts* (1920), and *75 Electrical Toys and Tricks* (1932). Acquired the American Flyer Company in 1938; redesigned train models that brought his company further success. Became chairman of the board of A.C. Gilbert in 1956, handing over the presidency to his son. Founding president of the Toy Manufacturers' Association of U.S.A., Incorporated, in 1916.

GILBERT, ANNE HARTLEY (*b. Rochdale, England, 1821; d. 1904*), dancer, character actress. Came to America, 1849. Played in western companies, and was a member of Augustin Daly's company, 1869–99. One of "Big Four," which included James Lewis, John Drew, and Ada Rehan.

GILBERT, CASS (*b. Zanesville, Ohio, 1859; d. Brockenhurst, England, 1934*), architect. Attended Massachusetts Institute of Technology, 1878–79; worked as surveyor; traveled in England, France, and Italy; worked as draftsman in office of McKim, Mead and White. Entered partnership as architect in St. Paul, Minn., December 1882; won first success with Minnesota State Capitol, 1896. Removing to New York City, he was successful competitor for design of U.S. Customs House, New York, and was soon engaged in other large work including the Woolworth Building (completed 1913).

In 1910 he was appointed a member of the National Commission of Fine Arts, and through the prestige of this position secured Washington commissions for the U.S. Treasury Annex, 1918–19; the Chamber of Commerce, 1924; and the Supreme Court Building. Other important commissions included the St. Louis Public Library; the New York Life Insurance Building, New York City; and the George Washington Memorial Bridge.

Gilbert's achievements were diversified, generally successful, and often monumental. His early designs showed a leaning to the Romanesque; in his later work he turned to the American concept of the classic. Although his designs were somewhat heavy and uninspired, with little originality, they were generally safe and commonly approved. It is remarkable that one man working without partners could accomplish so much and do it so well.

GILBERT, CHARLES HENRY (*b. Rockford, Ill., 1859; d. 1928*), zoologist. Professor at Stanford, 1891–1925. Participated in intensive investigations of fishes in the waters of the United States, British Columbia, the North Pacific, Hawaii, and Japan.

GILBERT, ELIPHALET WHEELER (*b. New Lebanon, N.Y., 1793; d. Philadelphia, Pa., 1853*), Presbyterian clergyman. Pastor at Wilmington, Del., and later in Philadelphia. President of Newark College (now University of Delaware), 1834 and 1841–47.

GILBERT, GROVE KARL (*b. Rochester, N.Y., 1843; d. 1918*), geologist. Graduated University of Rochester, 1862. Worked with J. S. Newberry on geological survey of Ohio and with the Wheeler Survey, 1871–74. Joined J. W. Powell in U.S. geological and geographical surveys, and continued with the consolidated surveys until 1918. His magnum opus was a monograph on the extinct Lake Bonneville of Nevada and Utah. He also investigated the life history of the Niagara River and recent earth movements in the Great Lakes region. His study of the Coon Butte crater in Arizona illustrates his deliberate, detailed, judicial method. He was unquestionably one of the best-balanced and most philosophical of American geologists.

GILBERT, HENRY FRANKLIN BELKNAP (*b. Somerville, Mass., 1868; d. 1928*), composer. Studied with Edward MacDowell. The first American composer whose work was wholly indigenous, he developed a mature, original style shown in ballet, opera, and orchestral pieces.

GILBERT, JOHN (*b. Logan, Utah, 1897; d. Beverly Hills, Calif., 1936*), film actor. Star of *The Big Parade* (1925), *Flesh and the Devil* (1927), and others; his popularity waned with talking films.

GILBERT, JOHN GIBBS (*b. Boston, Mass., 1810; d. 1889*), actor. Member of Tremont Theatre, Wallack's, and Joseph Jefferson's companies. Famous for elderly roles, his greatest being Sir Anthony Absolute.

GILBERT, LINDA (*b. Rochester, N.Y., 1847; d. Mount Vernon, N.Y., 1895*), philanthropist. The "Prisoners' Friend," she established the Gilbert Library and Prisoners' Aid Society, to provide prison libraries and help ex-convicts obtain employment.

GILBERT, RUFUS HENRY (*b. Guilford, N.Y., 1832; d. 1885*), physician. Union soldier, inventor. Convinced that overcrowding in cities created ill health, he projected the New York City elevated railway as a means of providing rapid transit and spreading out the city's population.

GILBERT, SEYMOUR PARKER (*b. Bloomfield, N.J., 1892; d. New York, N.Y., 1938*), lawyer, financier. Graduated Rutgers, 1912; Harvard Law School, 1915. Assistant secretary of U.S. treasury, 1920–23. Appointed agent general for reparation payments, 1924, he directed with tact and ability the economic rehabilitation of Germany under the Dawes Plan. From 1931 until his death, he was a partner in J. P. Morgan & Co.

GILBERT, WILLIAM LEWIS (*b. Northfield, Conn., 1806; d. Oshawa, Canada, 1890*), capitalist, clock manufacturer, philanthropist.

GILCHRIST, ROBERT (*b. Jersey City, N.J., 1825; d. 1888*), lawyer, Union soldier. Attorney general of New Jersey, 1869–75. An authority on constitutional law, he defined rights of blacks to vote in state and drew up riparian-rights act.

GILCHRIST, WILLIAM WALLACE (*b. Jersey City, N.J., 1846; d. Easton, Pa., 1916*), organist, composer. Founder and conductor, Philadelphia Symphony Society and Philadelphia Mendelssohn Club.

GILDER, JEANNETTE LEONARD (*b. Flushing, N.Y., 1849; d. New York, N.Y., 1916*), journalist. Sister of Richard W. and William H. Gilder.

GILDER, RICHARD WATSON (*b. Bordentown, N.J., 1844; d. New York, N.Y., 1909*), editor, poet. Managing editor, *Scribner's Monthly*, 1870–81; editor, *Century Magazine*, 1881–1909. Active in many civic and social movements. An ardent worker for international copyright, civil service reform and better city government, he performed a notable public service in 1894 as chairman of New York State's Tenement House Committee. Author of *The New Day* (1876) and other volumes of only adequate verse, he published collections of his poetry in 1894 and 1908.

GILDER, WILLIAM HENRY (*b. Philadelphia, Pa., 1838; d. 1900*), journalist. Brother of Jeannette L. and Richard W. Gilder.

GILDERSLEEVE, BASIL LANNEAU (*b. Charleston, S.C., 1831; d. Baltimore, Md., 1924*), philologist, Confederate solider, author, editor. Graduated Princeton, 1849; Ph.D., Göttingen, 1853. Professor of Greek, University of Virginia, 1856–76; university professor of Greek, Johns Hopkins, 1876–1915. Author of many monographs, a *Latin Grammar* (1867), and masterly editions of *Persius* (1875), *Justin Martyr* (1877), and *Pindar* (1885). Of his great work *Syntax of Classical Greek*, Part I appeared in 1900; Part II (with C. W. E. Miller) appeared in 1911. *The American Journal of Philology*, which he founded in 1880 and edited until 1920, printed many of his articles on Attic syntax.

GILDERSLEEVE, VIRGINIA CROCHERON (*b. New York, N.Y., 1877; d. Centerville, Mass., 1965*), college dean. Studied at Barnard College (B.A., 1899). Ph.D. conferred at Columbia in 1908. Taught at Barnard from 1904; dean, 1911–46. Began public affairs work during World War I, coordinating activities of several women's war work organizations, including the Women's Land Army. Helped organize the International Federation of University Women in 1919. During World War II she joined the Committee to Defend America by Aiding the Allies. Helped establish a women's naval reserve, WAVES. Appointed by President Roosevelt in 1945 as one of six American delegates—the only woman—to the conference to draft the Charter of the United Nations. Published her memoirs, *Many a Good Crusade*, in 1954.

GILES, CHAUNCEY (*b. Charlemont, Mass., 1813; d. 1893*), Swedenborgian clergyman, teacher, editor. Held pastorates in Cincinnati, New York City, and Philadelphia, 1853–93.

GILES, WILLIAM BRANCH (*b. Amelia Co., Va., 1762; d. Amelia Co., 1830*), lawyer, statesman. Graduated Princeton, 1781; studied law under George Wythe at William and Mary. Congressman, Democratic-Republican, from Virginia, 1790–98 and 1801; U.S. senator, 1804–15; governor of Virginia, 1827–30. Spurred inquiry into Hamilton's conduct of the treasury, 1793; opposed the Jay Treaty. Favoring Madison's election, 1808, he then opposed him; he vented his hostility also on Gallatin and Monroe. *Post* 1809 he was a "war hawk," but bitterly criticized the administration during the War of 1812. Personal animosity often marred his judgment and rendered his career not only erratic but destructive.

GILL, JOHN (*b. Charlestown, Mass., 1732; d. 1785*), printer, journalist. With Benjamin Edes, printed and published the radical *Boston Gazette*, 1755–75; the Boston Tea Party set forth from their office. *Post* 1776, Gill published the *Continental Journal.*

GILL, LAURA DRAKE (*b. Chesterville, Maine, 1860; d. Berea, Ky., 1926*), educator, pioneer in vocational placement. Started first vocational bureau for college women Boston, Mass., 1910.

GILL, THEODORE NICHOLAS (*b. New York, N.Y., 1837; d. Washington, D.C., 1914*), zoologist. Long associated with George Washington University and with the Smithsonian Institution. Never a field-worker, but in matters of taxonomy he was easily greatest in the world. Among his important papers are "Arrangement of the Families of Mollusks" (1871), "Arrangement of the Families of Mammals" (1872), "Arrangement of the Families of Fishes" (1872), and "A Comparison of Antipodal Faunas" (1893). His published memoirs on fishes alone number 388 titles, and he contributed many articles to American encyclopedias and lexicons.

GILLAM, BERNHARD (*b. Banbury, England, 1856; d. Canajoharie, N.Y., 1896*), political cartoonist. Came to America as a child. His "tattooed man" cartoons of James G. Blaine were influential in 1884 campaign. As director of *Judge*, 1886–96, his work had strong influence on political opinion.

GILLEM, ALVAN CULLEM (*b. Jackson Co., Tenn., 1830; d. near Nashville, Tenn., 1875*), soldier. Graduated West Point, 1851. Served effectively against Confederates in Kentucky and Tennessee, 1861–65; was prominent in reorganizing Tennessee civil government, 1865. As commander, 4th Military District, he was criticized by Northern radicals for refusal to execute Reconstruction policies harshly.

GILLESPIE, ELIZA MARIA. *See* ANGELA, MOTHER.

GILLESPIE, MABEL (*b. St. Paul, Minn., 1867; d. Boston, Mass., 1923*), labor leader. Executive secretary, Boston Women's Trade Union League; active in minimum-wage legislation and in unionizing women workers *post* 1909.

GILLESPIE, WILLIAM MITCHELL (*b. New York, N.Y., 1816; d. New York, 1868*), first professor of civil engineering at Union College, 1845–68. Graduated Columbia, 1834; studied also in France. An unusually effective teacher, he believed engineers should be familiar with the humanities.

GILLET, RANSOM HOOKER (*b. New Lebanon, N.Y., 1800; d. 1876*), lawyer, Democratic politician. New York congressman and federal official. Partner and protégé of Silas Wright.

GILLETT, EZRA HALL (*b. Colchester, Conn., 1823; d. 1875*), Presbyterian clergyman, educator, author. Pastor in Harlem, N.Y., 1845–70. Professor of political science, New York University, 1870–75. Official historian of his church.

GILLETT, FREDERICK HUNTINGTON (*b. Westfield, Mass., 1851; d. 1935*), lawyer. Graduated Harvard Law School, 1877. U.S. congressman, Republican, from Massachusetts, 1893–1925; a leader in the reform of appropriations procedure resulting in the Budget Act of 1921; impartial and tactful Speaker of the House, 1919–25; U.S. senator, 1925–31.

GILLETT, HORACE WADSWORTH (*b. near Penn Yan, N.Y., 1883; d. near Nicholasville, Ky., 1950*), metallurgist. B.A., Cornell University, 1906; Ph.D., 1910. After brief employment in industry, he was chief alloy chemist in charge of the field station of the U.S. Bureau of Mines, Ithaca, N.Y., 1912–24. During this time, he developed and patented, 1915, the rocking arc electric furnace. Chief of the Division of Metallurgy of the U.S. Bureau of Standards, Washington, D.C., 1924–29. First director of the Battelle Institute, Columbus, Ohio, 1929, which he made a world leader in metallurgical research. Resigned the directorship in 1934, but remained chief technical adviser. Devoted himself to research with alloy steels, heat treatment, foundry problems, and metal fatigue. His pioneering study of the "creep" of metals, their gradual deformation and failure under stress at high temperatures, influenced space technology.

GILLETTE, FRANCIS (*b. Bloomfield, Conn., 1807; d. Hartford, Conn., 1879*), farmer, businessman. Graduated Yale, 1829. U.S. senator, Whig and Free-Soil, from Connecticut, 1854–55. Active in formation of state Republican party; championed abolition, temperance, education.

GILLETTE, KING CAMP (*b. Fond du Lac, Wis., 1855; d. Calif., 1932*), inventor, manufacturer. Invented safety razor, *ca.* 1895; organized Gillette Razor Co., 1901.

GILLETTE, WILLIAM HOOKER (*b. Hartford, Conn., 1853; d. Hartford, 1937*), actor, dramatist. Son of Francis Gillette. Famous principally for creating role of Sherlock Holmes, 1899.

GILLIAM, DAVID TOD (*b. Hebron, Ohio, 1844; d. 1923*), surgeon, gynecologist. Practiced in Columbus, Ohio; taught at several medical schools there. Devised, 1899, the Gilliam operation for relief of backward displacement of the uterus, as well as other new techniques and instruments.

GILLIS, JAMES MARTIN (*b. Boston, Mass., 1876; d. New York, N.Y., 1957*), religious editor and writer. Studied at St. John's Seminary, Mass.; editor of the *Catholic World* from 1922 to 1948. A conservative Catholic, Gillis espoused rigorous Catholicism in his articles. Member of the Paulist Fathers.

GILLISS, JAMES MELVILLE (*b. Georgetown, D.C., 1811; d. 1865*), naval officer, astronomer. Placed in charge of the Depot of Charts and Instruments, 1863, Gilliss made observations for evaluation of findings of the Wilkes Exploring Expedition seldom equaled for accuracy; he also planned and equipped the first U.S. Naval Observatory, 1842–44. His *Astronomical Observations* (1846) was the first such volume to be published in America, as was his first catalogue of stars. He headed a South American expedition to determine anew the solar parallax, 1849–52, and was finally given charge of the Naval Observatory in 1861.

GILLISS, WALTER (*b. Lexington, Ky., 1855; d. 1925*), printer. With his brothers, directed the Gilliss Press, 1871–1908, specializing in designing and making books distinguished by care in production and classic taste.

GILLMAN, HENRY (*b. Kinsale, Ireland, 1833; d. Detroit, Mich., 1915*), archaeologist, scientist. Came to America, 1850. Assisted in U.S. survey of Great Lakes, 1851–69, and held other government posts. U.S. consul at Jerusalem, 1886–91. Did important work on Mound Builder culture study.

GILLMORE, QUINCY ADAMS (*b. Black River, Ohio, 1825; d. Brooklyn, N.Y., 1888*), soldier, military engineer. Graduated West Point, 1849, and later taught there. In Civil War gave brilliant service to the Union, rising to rank of major general of regulars. Among his outstanding feats were the reduction of Fort Pulaski, Ga., by rifled cannon fire, the reduction of Morris Island, and the retaking of Fort Sumter. His most important postwar service was as president, Mississippi River Commission, 1879. He was author of a number of technical treatises.

GILLON, ALEXANDER (*b. Rotterdam, Holland, 1741; d. "Gillon's Retreat," S.C., 1794*), Charleston merchant, Revolutionary financial and naval agent for South Carolina.

GILMAN, ARTHUR (*b. Alton, Ill., 1837; d. 1909*), author, editor, educator. Proposed, 1878, and served as executive secretary of the Harvard Annex for higher education of women. On its incorporation as Radcliffe College, 1893, he became regent.

GILMAN, ARTHUR DELEVAN (*b. Newburyport, Mass., 1821; d. 1882*), architect. Designed Boston City Hall, New York Equitable Building, New York State Capitol; important as one of the first American architectural eclectics.

GILMAN, CAROLINE HOWARD (*b. Boston, Mass., 1794; d. Washington, D.C., 1888*), writer, poet. Wife of Samuel Gilman. Edited early children's paper, *Southern Rosebud*, 1832; author of *Recollections of a Southern Matron* (1836) and many other popular works.

GILMAN, CHARLOTTE PERKINS STETSON (*b. Hartford, Conn., 1860; d. Pasadena, Calif., 1935*), social reformer, lecturer. Daughter of Frederick B. Perkins. Author of *Women and Economics* (1898) and other books.

GILMAN, DANIEL COIT (*b. Norwich, Conn., 1831; d. Norwich, 1908*), educator. Graduated Yale, 1852. Spent years 1853–55 abroad; in 1856 was enlisted by James D. Dana to write plan for what was to be the Sheffield Scientific School at Yale. Here he served as professor of physical and political geography; through his efforts it was the first institution to use funds derived from the Morrill Act. He declined presidency of the University of Wisconsin, 1867, and that of the University of California, 1870, but became president of the latter in 1872. Hampered by politics at Berkeley, he showed so much ability that he was called to be first president of Johns Hopkins University, 1875, recommended for the post by Presidents Eliot of Harvard, White of Cornell, and Angell of Michigan. Johns Hopkins was still largely unformed, but according to the will of the founder, was free to develop without legislative supervision.

For a year Gilman searched in Europe and America for the men who were to do a unique piece of creative work in Baltimore. The new university was to put emphasis on graduate study; its students would be already grounded in culture and informed with scholarly purpose; the chief inspiration was to be the freedom of thinking and teaching on which Gilman insisted from the very start.

The Johns Hopkins Medical School, Gilman's second great contribution to the educational development of America, was deferred by the suspension of common-stock dividends by the Baltimore & Ohio Railroad, whose shares formed the bulk of the endowment. Gilman persevered, however, and in 1893 the school opened with William J. Welch, William Osler, William S. Halstead, and Howard A. Kelly on the faculty. Standards of admission were high. Gilman wisely insisted that all matters pertaining to medical instruction should come under the university, while actual care of the sick, clinical opportunities, and residence within the hospital were the responsibility of the Johns Hopkins Hospital.

Gilman retired from the presidency in 1902, but threw himself into the work of founding the projected Carnegie Institution of Washington, of which Carnegie wished him to be president. Finding, however, that he did not have a free hand in unifying the forces of the institution, he resigned he presidency after three years. He was one of the original trustees of the John F. Slater Fund and its president from 1893 until his death, and was a trustee of the Peabody Educational Fund and of the Russell Sage Foundation.

GILMAN, JOHN TAYLOR *b. Exeter, N.H., 1753; d. 1828*), financier. Brother of Nicholas Gilman. Federalist governor of New Hampshire, 1794–1805 and 1813–16.

GILMAN, LAWRENCE (*b. Flushing, N.Y., 1878; d. Franconia, N.H., 1939*), music critic. Nephew of Daniel C. Gilman. On staff of *New York Tribune* (later *Herald Tribune*, 1923–39.

GILMAN, NICHOLAS (*b. Exeter, N.H., 1755; d. Philadelphia, Pa., 1814*), politician. Brother of John T. Gilman. Congressman, Federalist, from New Hampshire, 1789–97; U.S. senator, Democratic-Republican, 1804–14.

GILMAN, SAMUEL (*b. Gloucester, Mass., 1791; d. Kingston, Mass., 1858*), Unitarian clergyman, author. Graduated Harvard, 1811. Minister of Second Independent Church, Charleston, S.C., *post* 1819; published poems and translations. Wrote "Fair Harvard," 1836.

GILMER, ELIZABETH MERIWETHER (*b. Woodstock, Tenn., 1870; d. New Orleans, La., 1951*), newspaper columnist better known as "Dorothy Dix." Wrote for the New Orleans *Picayune* (1896–1901); reporter and columnist for Hearst's New York *Journal* (1901–17). With Hearst, she covered most of the famous American murder trials involving women, including the Stanford White and the Hall-Mills cases. From 1917 until World War II, she wrote a nationally syndicated column on advice to the lovelorn.

GILMER, FRANCIS WALKER (*b. Albemarle Co., Va., 1790; d. 1826*), lawyer, author. Grandson of Dr. Thomas Walker. Procured professors, books, equipment for new University of Virginia on mission to Great Britain at Thomas Jefferson's request, 1824.

GILMER, GEORGE ROCKINGHAM (*b. Broad River Settlement, Ga., 1790; d. Georgia, 1859*), lawyer, congressman. Democratic governor of Georgia, 1829–31 and 1837–39. Author of *Sketches of Some of the First Settlers of Upper Georgia* (1855).

GILMER, JOHN ADAMS (*b. Guilford Co,. N.C., 1805; d. 1868*), lawyer, legislator. Congressman, Whig, from North Carolina, 1857–61. An outstanding southern Unionist who strongly opposed secession, he declined a place in Lincoln's cabinet and urged withdrawal of federal troops from southern forts. He later sat in Confederate Congress.

GILMER, THOMAS WALKER (*b. Albemarle Co., Va., 1802; d. 1844*), legislator, statesman. Whig governor of Virginia, 1840–41; congressman, 1841–43; secretary of the navy, 1844. Killed in gun explosion on USS *Princeton*.

GILMOR, HARRY (*b. near Baltimore, Md., 1838; d. 1883*), soldier. Daring Confederate cavalry raider.

GILMORE, JAMES ROBERTS (*b. Boston, Mass., 1822; d. Glens Falls, N.Y., 1903*), cotton shipper. Writer under pseudonym "Edmund Kirke" of superficial sketches of the South at war. With James F. Jaquess, undertook unofficial mission from Lincoln to Jefferson Davis, seeking peace terms, July 1864.

GILMORE, JOSEPH ALBREE (*b. Weston, Vt., 1811; d. 1867*), railroad executive, legislator. Republican governor of New Hampshire, 1863–65.

GILMORE, JOSEPH HENRY (*b. Boston, Mass., 1834; d. Rochester, N.Y., 1918*), Baptist clergyman, teacher. Professor of rhetoric, University of Rochester, 1868–1908; author of textbooks and of the hymn "He Leadeth Me."

GILMORE, PATRICK SARSFIELD (*b. near Dublin, Ireland, 1829; d. St. Louis, Mo., 1892*), bandmaster. Came to America, ca. 1849. Originator of monster band concerts.

GILMOUR, RICHARD (*b. Glasgow, Scotland, 1824; d. St. Augustine, Fla., 1891*), Roman Catholic clergyman. Came to America as a child. A convert to Catholicism, 1842; consecrated bishop of Cleveland, Ohio, 1872. An aggressive leader and upholder of episcopal prerogatives, he ruled his rapidly growing diocese with a strong hand.

GILPIN, CHARLES SIDNEY (*b. Richmond, Va., 1878; d. Eldridge Park, N.J., 1930*), actor. Managed first black stock company in New York City, 1916. His great triumph was the title role in Eugene O'Neill's *Emperor Jones*, which he created in November 1920.

GILPIN, EDWARD WOODWARD (*b. Wilmington, Del., 1803; d. Dover, Del., 1876*), jurist. Attorney general of Delaware, 1840–50; upheld black rights in *State v. James Whittaker*. Chief justice of Delaware, 1857–76.

GILPIN, HENRY DILWORTH (*b. Lancaster, England, 1801; d. 1860*), Philadelphia lawyer and author. Brother of William Gilpin. U.S. attorney, eastern district of Pennsylvania, 1831–37; U.S. attorney general, 1840–41.

GILPIN, WILLIAM (*b. Brandywine, Pa., 1813; d. Denver, Colo., 1894*), soldier, lawyer, editor. Accompanied J. C. Frémont on 1843 expedition; served with Doniphan's Missouri volunteers in Mexican War. First territorial governor of Colorado, 1861–62, he helped save Colorado for the Union.

GIMBEL, BERNARD FEUSTMAN (*b. Vincennes, Ind., 1885; d. New York, N.Y., 1966*), retail merchant. Born into a family of merchants whose business started with Adam Gimbel's Palace of Trade in Vincennes, Ind., in 1842; by 1907 the family had opened branch stores in Milwaukee and Philadelphia. Studied at the Wharton School of the University of Pennsylvania (graduated, 1907). Began work at the family store in Philadelphia; vice president in 1909. Played a key role in the opening of the New York City store, 1910, which proved an immediate success. Persuaded family to convert Gimbel Brothers into a public corporation, 1922. Engineered purchase of Saks Fifth Avenue in 1923, and of Kaufmann and Baer of Pittsburgh in 1925. President of Gimbels Brothers, Inc., 1927–53; chief executive officer to 1961; chairman of the board, 1961–66. Except for two years during the depression, the firm grew steadily under Gimbel's leadership; by 1966 twenty-seven Gimbels stores and twenty-seven Saks stores were in operation across the nation.

GINN, EDWARD (*b. Orland, Maine, 1838; d. Winchester, Mass., 1914*), textbook publisher. Founded Ginn & Co., 1867. Endowed World Peace Foundation in 1910.

GINTER, LEWIS (*b. New York, N.Y., 1824; d. Richmond, Va., 1897*), tobacconist, philanthropist.

GIOVANNITTI, ARTURO (*b. Ripabottoni, Italy, 1884; d. New York, N.Y., 1959*), poet and labor organizer. Immigrated to the U.S. in 1901. Studied briefly at McGill University and Columbia. As editor of the Italian labor newspaper *Il Proletario* (1911), Giovannitti covered the textile strike at Lawrence, Mass. in 1912; he was accused of being an accessory to murder by inciting to riot when one of the strikers was killed; he was acquitted. While in prison awaiting trial he wrote some of his best poetry, published as *Arrows in the Gale* (1914). He served as secretary for the Italian Labor Education Board from 1916 to 1940. *The Collected Poems of Arturo Giovannitti* were published in 1962.

GIRARD, CHARLES FRÉDÉRIC (*b. Mülhausen, Alsace, 1822; d. Neuilly-sur-Seine, France, 1895*), zoologist, physician. Came to America as assistant to Louis Agassiz, 1847. At Smithsonian Institution, 1850–60, he was chief author of reports on fishes and reptiles collected by Wilkes and Pacific Railroad exploring expeditions.

GIRARD, STEPHEN (*b. Bordeaux, France, 1750; d. Philadelphia, Pa., 1831*), merchant, financier, philanthropist. Served as master in French merchant marine and for Thos. Randall and Son of New York, 1773–76; settled in Philadelphia after the British left that city and established himself in the West Indian, Asian, and European trade. Commerce to him was a subject of vast speculative possibilities, to which he brought great industry, initiative, a genius for detail, and a knowledge of sea markets and political conditions acquired through personal experience and careful study of the reports of his agents. Branching out into banking, real estate, insurance, he grew rich. A strong supporter of the first Bank of the United States, he served on the committee which petitioned for renewal of the bank's charter in 1810. When Congress refused, Girard bought the bank building and started the Bank of Stephen Girard as a private venture. With David Parish and John Jacob Astor, Girard arranged with treasury secretary Gallatin to take over the unsubscribed portion of the U.S. loan for the War of 1812 and dispose of it to the public. This action restored public confidence and averted financial crisis. After the war, Girard rendered a similar service by taking over $3 million worth of stock in the second Bank of the United States.

In the yellow fever epidemic at Philadelphia, 1793, Girard volunteered to superintend the Bush Hill fever hospital, where he nursed the sick day and night. He served Philadelphia in many ways, leaving in his will over $6 million in trust to the city for educating poor white orphan boys. Girard College is the monument to this generosity. He also left sums to Pennsylvania for internal improvements.

GIRARDEAU, JOHN LAFAYETTE (*b. near Charleston, S.C., 1825; d. Columbia, S.C., 1898*), Presbyterian clergyman, theologian. Ministered to blacks in Charleston, 1853–60; served as Confederate chaplain; was professor of theology, Columbia Seminary, 1875–95.

GIRDLER, TOM MERCER (*b. Silver Creek Township, Clark County, Ind., 1877; d. Easton, Md., 1965*), industrialist. Studied at Lehigh University (graduated, 1901). Worked for the Oliver Iron and Steel Company of Pittsburgh (1902–05) and the Colorado Fuel and Iron Company at Pueblo, Colo. (1905–07). Superintendent, the Atlantic Steel Company of Atlanta (1907–08); general manager (1908–14). At Jones and Laughlin Steel of Pittsburgh from 1914; general superintendent (1920–24); general manager (1924–26); a director and vice president in charge of operations (1926–28); president (1928–29). An organizer of the Republic Steel Corporation in 1929; chairman of the board and chief executive officer (1930–56). Chairman of the board and chief executive officer of Vultee and Consolidated (merged in 1943) from 1941. President of the American Iron and Steel Institute (1937–39). Fought against unionization at Republic Steel Corporation until a 1942 War Labor Board order called for certification elections, which the union won.

GIRSCH, FREDERICK (*b. Büdingen, Germany, 1821; d. Mount Vernon, N.Y., 1895*), bank-note engraver.

GIRTY, SIMON (*b. near Harrisburg, Pa., 1741; d. near Amherstburg, Canada, 1818*), "the Great Renegade." An Indian captive, 1756–59, he was employed as an interpreter at Fort Pitt, 1759–74. Served as scout in Dunmore's War and as interpreter for Continental forces, 1776. With Alexander McKee and others, he deserted the American cause in March 1778 and fled to Detroit, where Lieutenant Governor Hamilton used him as interpreter. Active in many forays against the frontier settlers, he was notoriously savage and cruel, encouraging the torture of captives. He remained among the tribes in the Ohio country, opposing any peace with the Americans, and participated in many battles, including St. Clair's defeat and Fallen Timbers.

GISH, DOROTHY (*b. Dayton, Ohio, 1898; d. Rapallo, Italy, 1968*), actress and younger sister of Lillian Gish. Began stage career in 1902. Appeared with Lillian in *An Unseen Enemy* (1912) for film producer D. W. Griffith; signed contract with Griffith in 1912. First real success was in *Hearts of the World* (1918). Starred in a series of comedies released by Paramount, including *Battling Jane* (1918), *The Hope Chest* (1919), and *Boots* (1919), which won her unqualified praise for her comic pantomime genius. Dramatic roles in the classics *Orphans of the Storm* (1922), *Bright Shawl* (1923), and *Romola* (1924). Primarily on the stage from 1928; plays included *Young Love* (1928), *Brittle Heaven* (1934), *The Magnificent Yankee* (1946), *The Story of Mary Surratt* (1947), and *The Chalk Garden* (1956). Other films include *The Country Flapper* (1922), *Remodeling Her Husband* (1920), *Nell Gwyn* (1926), *Our Hearts Were Young and Gay* (1944), and *The Cardinal* (1963).

GIST, CHRISTOPHER (*b. Maryland, ca. 1706; d. South Carolina or Georgia, 1759*), explorer, soldier. The first white American to explore carefully the Ohio River lands and northeastern Kentucky, 1750–51, preceding Daniel Boone by 18 years, his reports show keen observation of topography and native customs; his plats and surveys have been much praised. On a mission to Fort Le Boeuf, 1753–54, Gist twice saved George Washington's life. He was with Washington in the defeat of Jumonville, 1754; at the surrender of Fort Necessity; and on the Braddock campaign.

GIST, MORDECAI (*b. near Reisterstown, Md., 1742/43; d. South Carolina, 1792*), Revolutionary soldier. Nephew of Christopher Gist. This devoted patriot served throughout the war, rising to brigadier general, 1779. The dying De Kalb praised his conduct in the battle of Camden.

GIST, WILLIAM HENRY (*b. Charleston, S.C., 1807; d. Union District, S.C., 1874*), planter, legislator. As governor of South Carolina, 1858–60, he pressed for secession and directed the legislature's proceedings to accomplish it after Lincoln's election.

GITLOW, BENJAMIN (*b. Elizabethport, N.J., 1891; d. Crompond, N.Y., 1965*), radical politician and author. Joined the Socialist party in 1909. Elected to the New York Assembly in 1917; served one term. Helped to organize the Communist Labor party in 1918. The first Communist tried under New York's Criminal Anarchy Act (*Gitlow v. New York*), he was convicted in 1925, served three years in prison; pardoned in 1925. While incarcerated, he was the Communist party's candidate for mayor of New York City and for Congress; the party's vice presidential candidate in 1924 and 1928. Expelled from the party in 1929. Helped to organize the Communist Party, U.S.A. in 1929. Throughout the 1930's Gitlow grew more and more disillusioned with Communism and radical politics; published *I Confess: The Truth About American Communism* in 1940. Testified before the House Committee on Un-American Activities in 1939; during the late 1940's and early 1950's he was one of the most important ex-Communist witnesses in the nation.

GLACKENS, WILLIAM JAMES (*b. Philadelphia, Pa., 1870; d. Westport, Conn., 1938*), painter, illustrator. Worked as an artist-reporter on various Philadelphia newspapers, meanwhile studying painting at Pennsylvania Academy of the Fine Arts under Robert Henri. Later, did magazine and book illustrating in New York; concentrated on painting, *post* 1905. One of "The Eight"; helped organize, and was president of, Society of Independent Artists; was chairman, Selection Committee of the landmark 1913 Armory Show. Although frequently a spokesman for the vanguard of American artists, Glackens was always a painter of gay, pleasant, and elegant scenes, his glowing, luminous impressionism suggesting some of Renoir's coloristic tendencies.

GLADDEN, WASHINGTON (*b. Pottsgrove, Pa., 1836; d. Columbus, Ohio, 1918*), Congregational clergyman, early proponent of the Social Gospel. Graduated Williams, 1859. Held pastorates in New York, Massachusetts, and in Columbus, 1882–1918. Influenced by F. W. Robertson and Horace Bushnell. Active as a popularizer of the new trends in biblical criticism, he is more famous, however, for application of fundamental religious principles to social relations in such books as *Working People and Their Employers* (1876), *The Christian Way* (1877), *Applied Christianity* (1886), *Social Salvation* (1902), and *The Church and Modern Life* (1908). He held that the church's chief business is to Christianize the social order, not by use of force or endorsing a particular program but by inspiring individuals with love of justice and the spirit of service.

GLADWIN, HENRY (*b. Stubbing Court, near Chesterfield, England, 1729; d. Stubbing Court, 1791*), British soldier. Best known for his brilliant defense of Detroit in Pontiac's War, 1763–64, he had previously fought under Braddock and Gage. He refused to serve in the Revolutionary War.

GLASGOW, ELLEN ANDERSON (*b. Richmond, Va., 1873; d. Richmond, 1945*), novelist. Descended on her paternal side from Scots-Irish Presbyterian stock settled in the Shenandoah Valley and on her maternal side from Tidewater Episcopalians, she was the inheritor of two traditions, whose conflicting attitudes were reflected in much of her fiction. She attended private schools for a few months each year, but she received little formal education. In 1889 her hearing began to deteriorate, although she did not become totally deaf until she was past 35.

At the age of 7 she resolved to become a writer and began to make verses. In 1897 she published anonymously *The Descendant*, which reflected Glasgow's Fabian socialism and was for its time a radical work. Her second novel, *Phases of an Inferior Planet* (1898), is the story of a rebellious scientist-philosopher. Later, in a series of novels, her design was to portray "the retreat of an agrarian culture before the conquest of an industrial revolution, and the slow and steady rise of the lower middle class." By the turn of the century she had embarked on a fictional exploration of most of the historical movements, regions, and classes in Virginia in the period 1850–1939. The first of these novels was *The Voice of the People* (1900), which recounts the rise of a poor white to the governorship of Virginia. The second, *The Battle-Ground* (1902), was her "Civil War novel." *The Deliverance* (1904) was her first really good work. In 1902 she published her only volume of poetry, *The Freeman and Other Poems*. She continued to travel nearly every summer, was briefly engaged to a poet, and helped start the woman suffrage movement in Virginia. Meanwhile, Glasgow's commitment to her craft and her "design" reasserted itself. She wrote *The Romance of a Plain Man* (1909), which records the rise of a man from poverty to wealth and social acceptance in Richmond; *The Miller of Old Church* (1911), which deals with changes in the political and economic life of a "plain" farmer; *Virginia* (1913), a portrait of an "ideal" Virginia lady of the 1880's; and *Life and Gabriella* (1916), which deals with a "new woman," the action taking place partly in New York City.

Glasgow spent the summer of 1914 in England, where she was well received by many literary figures, including Conrad and Hardy. Two of her subsequent novels were failures: *The Builders*

(1919), a domestic melodrama; and *One Man in His Time* (1922), a tragicomedy about a radical Virginia governor. In 1923 she published a collection of eight short stories, *The Shadowy Third, and Other Stories.*

In 1922 Glasgow began *Barren Ground* (1925), one of her two best novels. A rural novel, it recounts events that could happen, she declared, "wherever the spirit of fortitude has triumphed over the sense of futility." It brought her critical acclaim and inaugurated her period of greatest accomplishment.

It was followed by *The Romantic Comedians* (1926), *They Stooped to Folly* (1929), and *The Sheltered Life* (1932), which ranks alongside *Barren Ground.* Two other novels were published in her lifetime: *Vein of Iron* (1935), a grim picture of life in the Virginia mountains; and *In This Our Life* (1941), which was awarded the Pulitzer Prize, perhaps more as a recognition of its author's career than of its own merit. In 1943 she published *A Certain Measure*, which defined her artistic ideals, stated her concept of the novel, and made a by no means modest evaluation of her work. Her autobiography was published in 1954 as *The Woman Within.*

Her reputation rests on her witty, epigrammatic style and on the irony that is a pervasive quality in her best work. Hers was the first southern voice to be raised in loving anger against the falseness and sentimentality of the accepted traditions of the region.

GLASPELL, SUSAN KEATING (*b. Davenport, Iowa, 1876; d. Provincetown, Mass., 1948*), author. Ph.B., Drake University, 1899. Worked as reporter for Des Moines *Daily News*; successful as magazine short-story writer, 1903–22; author also of *The Visioning* (1911), *Brook Evans* (1928), and other novels. She is remembered less for her fiction, marked by strong midwestern regional feeling, than for her plays and for *The Road to the Temple* (1927), a life of George Cram Cook, to whom she was married, 1913–24. Associated with the Provincetown Players, which Cook had founded, she wrote seven short plays between 1915 and 1922, including (in collaboration with Cook) *Suppressed Desires* (1915); of her four long plays of this period, the best were *Inheritors* (1921) and *The Verge* (1922). Her finest one-act play was *Trifles* (1916). *Alison's House* (1930), a drama inspired by the life of Emily Dickinson, was awarded the Pulitzer Prize in 1931.

GLASS, CARTER (*b. Lynchburg, Va., 1858; d. Washington, D.C., 1946*), newspaper publisher, statesman. After leaving school at 14, Glass became a printer's devil on his father's paper. In 1880, after working briefly as an auditor's clerk for a railroad, he became a reporter for the *Lynchburg News*. Appointed editor in 1887, he purchased the paper the following year; and by 1895 he had acquired two other Lynchburg papers. He was an unflagging defender of the special heritage of the South and of its states' rights tradition.

Glass was a lifelong member of the Democratic party, and as his newspapers prospered he took a more active role in politics. He served one term (1899–1903) in the state senate; but it was as a delegate to the Virginia constitutional convention of 1901–02 that he first gained political prominence. Elected to Congress, 1902, where he served for the next 16 years, he was assigned to the House Committee on Banking and Currency and became a leading congressional authority. In 1913 Glass was given responsibility for the Wilson administration's measure to reform the nation's banking and currency system. Glass prepared a draft measure providing for a system of reserve banks under the control of the banking industry. Though favoring a decentralized private system of reserve banks, Glass in later years took pride in the title "father of the Federal Reserve System."

Wilson appointed Glass secretary of the treasury in 1919. In 1920 he was appointed to fill a vacancy in the U.S. Senate, where he served until his death. An ardent champion of the League of Nations, Glass drafted the 1920 Democratic platform, which gave strong endorsement to the league. Although personally fond of Franklin D. Roosevelt, he broke with the administration over Roosevelt's decision to decrease the gold value of the dollar; for the rest of his career he was an implacable foe of the New Deal. In the late 1930's he emerged as a leader of the bipartisan "conservative coalition" in Congress that sought to block further New Deal legislation. In matters of foreign policy, Glass was an ardent internationalist. After Pearl Harbor, Glass supported Roosevelt's war measures, particularly as chairman of the Senate Appropriations Committee. Glass was elected president pro tempore of the Senate in 1941.

GLASS, FRANKLIN POTTS (*b. Centreville, Ala., 1858; d. Birmingham, Ala., 1934*), manager, *Montgomery Advertiser*, 1886–1915; editor, *Birmingham News*, 1910–20; publisher, *Montgomery Advertiser*, 1927–34. A forceful, independent journalist.

GLASS, HUGH (*fl. 1823–33*), trapper. Joined Ashley's Missouri River expedition, 1823. Returning to the mouth of the Yellowstone in August with Andrew Henry's party, he was terribly injured by a grizzly bear. His death seeming imminent, he was left in charge of James Bridger and a certain Fitzgerald. They took his rifle and equipment and rejoined the party, reporting him dead and buried. Regaining some strength, Glass began crawling toward Fort Kiowa, more than 100 miles away. He reached it and recuperated, vowing vengeance. He forgave Bridger because of his youth; later, after recovering his favorite rifle, he abated his wrath against Fitzgerald. Glass was subsequently the hero of many encounters with Indians. He is believed to have been killed by Blackfeet on the upper Yellowstone.

GLASS, MONTAGUE MARSDEN (*b. Manchester, England, 1877; d. 1934*), author. Came to America, 1890. Creator of the characters "Potash and Perlmutter," who were famous for a generation in story, stage, and motion pictures.

GLASSFORD, PELHAM DAVIS (*b. Las Vegas, N.Mex., 1883; d. Laguna Beach, Calif., 1959*), army officer and police official. Graduated West Point, 1904. Served with the American Expeditionary Force in France during World War I, earning the Distinguished Service Medal and the Silver Star. Glassford retired as a major in 1931 and was appointed chief of police in Washington, D.C.; after a controversial handling of a veterans' march on the capital, he was forced to resign in 1932 for his soft tactics in handling the marchers.

GLEASON, FREDERIC GRANT (*b. Middletown, Conn., 1848; d. 1903*), composer, organist. Studied with Dudley Buck and in Germany. *Post* 1877, taught and worked in Chicago, Ill.

GLEASON, KATE (*b. Rochester, N.Y., 1865; d. Rochester, 1933*), businesswoman, philanthropist. An energetic promoter and leader in the development of gear-cutting machinery and home-building projects.

GLEAVES, ALBERT (*b. Nashville, Tenn., 1858; d. Haverford, Pa., 1937*), naval officer. Graduated Annapolis, 1877. Authority on ordnance and hydrography; in charge of Atlantic convoy operations, World War I. During his command of Destroyer Force, a successful method of refueling at sea was devised.

GLENN, HUGH (*b. Berkeley Co., Va., 1788; d. Cincinnati, Ohio, 1833*), trader, army contractor. With Jacob Fowler, conducted first successful trading expedition to Mexican provinces, from Verdigris River to Santa Fe, 1821–22.

GLENN, JOHN MARK (*b. Baltimore, Md., 1858; d. New York, N.Y., 1950*), social work leader, foundation director. B.A.,

Washington and Lee University, 1878; M.A., 1879. LL.B., University of Maryland, 1882. After service as officer and director of a number of charitable organizations, private and public, in Maryland, he helped plan and organize the Russell Sage Foundation and served as its director, 1907–31.

GLENNON, JOHN JOSEPH (*b. near Kinnegad, Co. Meath, Ireland, 1862; d. Dublin, Ireland, 1946*), Roman Catholic clergyman. Studied at St. Mary's College, Mulingar, and at All Hallows College, Dublin. Came to the United States, 1883; ordained for the diocese of Kansas City, Mo., 1884. Consecrated coadjutor bishop of Kansas City, 1896, he was appointed coadjutor to the archbishop of St. Louis, 1903. He succeeded to the archbishopric in the fall of that same year and held that position until his death. He was named a cardinal in 1945. An able administrator, he took special interest in the relief of poverty and in efforts to settle immigrants on farms.

GLIDDEN, CHARLES JASPER (*b. Lowell, Mass., 1857; d. 1927*), telephone pioneer, motorist, aviator. Directed test of long-distance telephony for Alexander Graham Bell, 1876; organized first telephone exchange at Lowell, Mass., 1877, which gave satisfactory service with one of first multiple switchboards. The Lowell Co. and other Massachusetts companies established by Glidden, William A. Ingham, and associates were the nucleus of New England Telephone Co. Successful in this and other telephone operations, Glidden turned his attention to motoring and aviation, organizing the first round-the-world motor tour and establishing the Glidden trophy, 1905. He made 46 balloon ascents and was prominent in early air meets. President of World's Board of Aeronautical Commissioners, he also edited *Aeronautical Digest*, 1921–24.

GLIDDEN, JOSEPH FARWELL (*b. Charleston, N.H., 1813; d. 1906*), farmer, inventor, capitalist. Removed *ca.* 1844 to De Kalb, Ill.; managed large Illinois and Texas farms. Invented and patented, 1874, a basic improvement in barbed-wire fencing which made its manufacture feasible and successful.

GLOVER, JOHN (*b. Salem, Mass., 1732; d. Marblehead, Mass., 1797*), Revolutionary soldier. Commanded troop transports in retreat from Long Island; ferried army across Delaware to Trenton, 1776. Promoted brigadier general, 1777, he retired in 1782 after extensive further service.

GLOVER, SAMUEL TAYLOR (*b. Virginia, 1813; d,. 1884*), lawyer. Raised in Kentucky; removed to Missouri, 1837; practiced in Palmyra and St. Louis. Devoted to emancipation; prominent in retaining Missouri in the Union, 1861–65; leading constitutional lawyer of his time in the West.

GLOVER, TOWNEND (*b. Rio de Janeiro, Brazil, 1813; d. Baltimore, Md., 1883*), artist, earliest government entomologist. Educated in England and Germany; came to America, 1836. Served as insect expert in Bureau of Agriculture, 1854–78.

GLUCK, ALMA (*b. Bucharest, Romania, 1884; d. New York, N.Y., 1938*), operatic and concert soprano. Came to America as a child. Married the violinist Efrem Zimbalist, 1914.

GLYNN, JAMES (*b. Philadelphia, Pa., 1801; d. New Haven, Conn., 1871*), naval officer. His reports after rescue of American sailors held captive in Japan, 1849, helped prepare the way for Commodore M. C. Perry's mission, 1853–54.

GLYNN, MARTIN HENRY (*b. Kinderhook, N.Y., 1871; d. Albany, N.Y., 1924*), journalist, lawyer, politician. Graduated Fordham, 1894. Editor and publisher of Albany *Times-Union*, 1897. Astute state comptroller, 1906–08. As Democratic governor of New York, 1913–14, he instituted workmen's compensation law and statewide primary elections.

GMEINER, JOHN (*b. Bärnau, Bavaria, 1847; d. 1913*), Roman Catholic priest, author. Came to America as a child; raised and educated in Wisconsin. An authority on German emigrants, he opposed "Cahenslyism," expressing a stout Americanism as teacher and pastor in Wisconsin and Minnesota.

GOBRECHT, CHRISTIAN (*b. Hanover, Pa., 1785; d. Philadelphia, Pa., 1844*), die-sinker, engraver to the U.S. Mint in Philadelphia, *post* 1836.

GODBE, WILLIAM SAMUEL (*b. London, England, 1833; d. Brighton, Utah, 1902*), merchant, mine operator, Mormon convert and dissenter. Came to Salt Lake City, 1851. Disfellowshipped by Mormons, 1869, for advocating development of mining industry, he championed liberal attitude in his *Utah Magazine* and *Salt Lake Tribune*.

GODDARD, CALVIN HOOKER (*b. Baltimore, Md., 1891; d. Washington, D.C., 1955*), doctor, criminologist, military historian. M.D., Johns Hopkins, 1915. The inventor of methods of identifying the gun that fired a given bullet, Goddard retired from medicine in 1925 to found the Bureau of Forensic Ballistics in New York. In 1930, he established the nation's first crime detection laboratory, which became part of Northwestern University; professor, 1930–34. In 1927, he offered evidence in the controversial Sacco-Vanzetti case. In 1940, Goddard was named military editor of the *Encyclopaedia Britannica*; in 1941, he became the first American on the board of editors of the *Britannica*. Changing careers again, he became chief historian of the Ordnance Department of the army, 1942; assistant chief of the historical branch of the Far East Command, 1947. 1948–50, head of the Far East Criminal Investigation Laboratory. 1950, chief of the historical unit of the Army Medical Service in charge of editing and publishing a forty-volume history of medicine in World War II. He retired a full colonel.

GODDARD, CALVIN LUTHER (*b. Covington, N.Y., 1822; d. Worcester, Mass., 1895*), inventor. Patented, 1866, and marketed indispensable machine for extracting burrs and dust from wool.

GODDARD, HENRY HERBERT (*b. Vassalboro, Maine, 1866; d. Santa Barbara, Calif., 1957*), psychologist. Studied at Haverford College and Clark University (Ph.D., 1899). Introduced the intelligence tests of French psychologist Alfred Binet to the U.S. An expert in mental defects, Goddard coined the term "moron" from the Greek for "slow" or "sluggish." Director of research at the N.J. School for Feeble-Minded Boys and Girls (1906–18); professor, Ohio State University (1922–38). Published *Feeble-mindedness: Its Causes and Consequences* (1914), which stated that retardation was mainly hereditary in nature.

GODDARD, JOHN (*b. Dartmouth, Mass., 1723/24; d. Newport, R.I., 1785*), leading Newport cabinetmaker. Produced unequaled pieces in Santo Domingo mahogany, especially secretaries and kneehole desks. Probably originated the "block front," which he perfected.

GODDARD, LUTHER MARCELLUS (*b. Palmyra, N.Y., 1940; d. 1917*), lawyer. Practiced in Leavenworth, Kans., 1865–78; thereafter in Leadville and Denver, Colo. As district judge, and judge of Colorado supreme court, his commonsense decisions and masterly opinions largely developed into its present form the state law dealing with prospecting and mining claims.

GODDARD, MORRILL (*b. Auburn, Maine, 1865; d. Naskeag Point, Maine, 1937*), journalist. Grandson of Anson P. Morrill. Innovator of the sensational "Sunday supplement" with pictures and comics. City editor and Sunday editor, New York *World*, 1885–89; first editor of the *American Weekly*.

GODDARD, PAUL BECK (*b. Baltimore, Md., 1811; d. Philadelphia, Pa., 1866*), physician, anatomist, pioneer in photography. Discovered and exhibited in 1839 use of vapor of bromine on silvered plate, perfecting Daguerre's process. Made first instantaneous pictures by heliographic process.

GODDARD, PLINY EARLE (*b. Lewiston, Maine, 1869; d. 1928*), ethnologist. Graduated Earlham College, 1892; served as lay missionary to Hupa tribe in California. Became outstanding authority in Athapascan; wrote intensive, uniformly valuable studies, principally of Indian languages; was associated *post* 1909 with American Museum of Natural History, New York.

GODDARD, ROBERT HUTCHINGS (*b. Worcester, Mass., 1882; d. Baltimore, Md., 1945*), rocket and space pioneer. He began a lifelong interest in rocketry with the reading of H. G. Well's *War of the Worlds*. He graduated from Worcester's South High School in 1904, at the age of 21. Completed a general science course at Worcester Polytechnic Institute, 1908; Ph.D. in physics, Clark University, 1911. After an additional year at Clark, Goddard went to Princeton's Palmer Physical Laboratory on a research fellowship. There he devoted his evenings to the theory of rocket propulsion. Ill with tuberculosis, he returned to Worcester in 1913, but he took advantage of his convalescence to convert his Princeton theories on rocketry into patents. At Clark in 1914 Goddard worked on powder rockets and nozzle-equipped steel rockets. In 1916 he obtained a grant from the Smithsonian Institution. To support his application, Goddard had sent the Smithsonian a manuscript entitled "A Method of Reaching Extreme Altitudes," which set forth the theory of rocket propulsion.

During World War I Goddard directed work that led to a demonstration of a recoilless rocket, a direct ancestor of the bazooka of World War II. His 1916 manuscript "A Method of Reaching Extreme Altitudes" appeared in 1919. Goddard suggested that a sufficient amount of flash powder sent by rocket to the moon could be seen by telescope and prove escape from the earth's attraction. He also foresaw automated spacecraft to photograph celestial bodies and manned landings on the planets. Oxygen-hydrogen and ion propulsion would provide the energy necessary to explore the solar system. Thus, by 1920 Goddard had sketched out the potential of space flight.

Goddard became head of the Department of Physics at Clark in 1923. In 1921 he began to concentrate efforts on demonstrating the feasibility of liquid-fuel rockets. On Mar. 16, 1926, he achieved the world's first flight of a liquid-fuel rocket near Auburn, Mass. On July 17, 1929, a larger, more sophisticated model reached twice the 1926 altitude. With an initial grant from the philanthropist Daniel Guggenheim, Goddard took leave from Clark and shifted his small staff to Roswell, N.Mex. There Goddard's first objective was reliable motor performance and flight stability, but from 1935 he felt increasing pressure to achieve high-altitude flights. While he was experimenting in the desert at Roswell, the Germans moved beyond him. Although reluctant to take others into his confidence, Goddard was prompted to present a paper, "Progress in the Development of Atmospheric Sounding Rockets" (1935), and published *Liquid-Propellant Rocket Development* (1936). In 1941 the navy asked him to produce a preliminary model of a liquid-fuel variable-thrust, jet-assist takeoff unit for aircraft. After an unsuccessful flight test that led the navy to turn to solid-fuel units, Goddard sat on the sidelines. In 1944 he read press reports of the German V-I flying bomb and the V-2 rocket. Goddard believed the Germans had copied him, but the similarity reflected the phenomenon of multiple invention.

Goddard's 214 patents are the measure of his accomplishment; it was virtually impossible to construct a rocket without infringing on one or more of them.

GODDARD, WILLIAM (*b. New London, Conn., 1740; d. Rhode Island, 1817*), printer, Whig journalist. Pioneer printer of Providence, R.I., 1762; published *Pennsylvania Chronicle*, 1767–74; established *Maryland Journal*, 1773, at Baltimore.

GODDU, LOUIS (*b. St. Césaire, Canada, 1837; d. Winchester, Mass., 1919*), inventor of shoe-manufacturing machines.

GODEFROY, MAXIMILIAN (*fl. 1805–24*), painter, architect, military engineer. Came to America, 1805. Designed St. Mary's Seminary chapel, Baltimore, Md., 1807, first Gothic revival church built in America; also the Unitarian Church and fortifications in Baltimore, 1814–17, and Richmond, Va., Court House, 1816.

GODEY, LOUIS ANTOINE (*b. New York, N.Y., 1804; d. Philadelphia, Pa., 1878*), publisher of *Godey's Lady's Book*, from 1830, and other magazines.

GODFREY, BENJAMIN (*b. Chatham, Mass., 1794; d. Godfrey, Ill., 1862*), sea captain, merchant, financier, philanthropist. Made and lost several fortunes in Mexico and New Orleans, La. Settled in Alton, Ill., 1832; ruined state bank by using money in speculative schemes to develop Alton. Founded Monticello Female Academy, 1838.

GODFREY, THOMAS (*b. Philadelphia, Pa., 1704; d. 1749*), glazier, mathematician, true inventor of Hadley's quadrant. His natural, uneducated genius for mathematics, astronomy, and optics was encouraged by James Logan. In 1730 Godfrey invented and made a quadrant improved over Davis', which was then in general use. Godfrey's quadrant was tried in Delaware Bay, and Captain Wright carried it to Jamaica, where "he showed and explained it to several Englishmen, among whom was a nephew of Hadley's." The Royal Society being about to reward James Hadley for inventing a similar quadrant in 1734, Governor Logan wrote and claimed recognition for Godfrey.

GODFREY, THOMAS (*b. Philadelphia, Pa., 1736; d. Wilmington, N.C., 1763*), poet, playwright. Son of Thomas Godfrey (1704–49). Under the tutelage of William Smith he joined a group of young men (including Benjamin West and Francis Hopkinson) who pioneered in painting, music, and drama in the middle colonies. He wrote Cavalier love songs, pastorals, and a long poem, *The Court of Fancy* (published 1762), but is remembered for the *Prince of Parthia*, a romantic tragedy which he wrote *ca.* 1758–59 for David Douglass' American Co. The first drama written by a native American to be produced on the professional stage (Philadelphia, 1767), it had already been published in his *Juvenile Poems* (1765).

GODKIN, EDWIN LAWRENCE (*b. Moyne, Ireland, 1831; d. Brixham, England, 1902*), journalist. Came to America, 1856, after experience as a correspondent in Hungary and the Crimea. Edited the *Nation* from its foundation in 1865. Noted for range of scholarship and breadth of view, the influence of the journal was out of all proportion to its circulation. Godkin was also editor in chief of the New York *Evening Post*, 1883–1900. By his entire independence of party and fearless treatment of public questions, Godkin won a unique place in American journalism of his time.

GODMAN, JOHN DAVIDSON (*b. Annapolis, Md., 1794; d. 1830*), naturalist, anatomist. Edited *Western Quarterly Reporter* (Cincinnati, Ohio, 1822), the first medical journal published west of Alleghenies; author of *American Natural History* (1826–28), first original treatise on this subject, and *Rambler of a Naturalist* (1833).

GODOWSKY, LEOPOLD (*b. Soshly, Lithuania, 1870; d. New York, N.Y., 1938*), concert pianist, composer. Taught in the United States, 1891–1900; settled in United States, 1914.

GODWIN, PARKE (*b. Paterson, N.J., 1816; d. 1904*), editor, author. Associated, 1836–81, with New York *Evening Post*; later editor of *Commercial Advertiser*. Edited reference works and the collected works of his father-in-law, William Cullen Bryant (1883–84).

GOEBEL, WILLIAM (*b. Carbondale, Pa., 1856; d. Kentucky, 1900*), lawyer, legislator. Raised in Covington, Ky. Credited with the passing of much reform legislation as a Democratic state senator, 1887–99, he was sponsor of the bitterly denounced Goebel Election Law of 1898. He secured nomination for governor, 1899, by a series of political maneuvers which greatly increased the number of his enemies. An exciting campaign resulted in a contested election and Goebel's murder on Jan. 30, 1900. The legislature declared him legally elected governor before his death.

GOERZ, DAVID (*b. Neu Bereslow, South Russia, 1849; d. California, 1914*), Mennonite clergyman. Came to America, 1873; settled in Kansas. Excelled as organizer and missioner.

GOESMANN, CHARLES ANTHONY (*b. Naumburg, Germany, 1827; d. 1910*), chemist. Ph.D., Göttingen, 1852. Came to America, 1857, and worked in sugar and salt refining. Professor at Massachusetts Agricultural College, 1868–1907, he helped shape the policies of this new type of college and developed its experiment station.

GOETHALS, GEORGE WASHINGTON (*b. Brooklyn, N.Y., 1858; d. 1928*), engineer, soldier, builder of the Panama Canal. Graduated West Point, 1880. Previously assigned to important canal, river, and harbor works, he was appointed by President Theodore Roosevelt chief engineer of the Panama Canal, 1907, with full authority and responsibility for every phase of the work. Tact and intelligence were needed to combat civilian prejudice against an army man; moreover, 30,000 employees of many nationalities had to be housed, fed, amused, and kept healthy. Goethals and his assistants overcame gigantic engineering and personnel problems. Starting in an atmosphere of opposition, Goethals ended his construction days on the Isthmus with the respect and even veneration of his helpers.

The Panama Canal was opened to world commerce in August 1914. Goethals remained as governor of the Canal Zone until the latter part of 1916, having been made a major general by special act of Congress. He retired in November 1916 at his own request, but was recalled in December 1917 as acting quartermaster general and given additional duty as director of purchase, storage, and traffic, supervising transport of all supplies and movement of all troops throughout World War I. He returned voluntarily to the retired list, 1919, but served as consulting engineer on many important works, including the Inner Harbor Navigation Canal of New Orleans; Columbia Basin Irrigation Project; East Bay Municipal Utility District of Oakland, Calif.; and the New York–New Jersey Port and Harbor Development Commission.

GOETSCHIUS, JOHN HENRY (*b. Berneck, Switzerland, 1718; d. New Jersey, 1774*), Dutch Reformed clergyman. Came to America, 1735. Belligerent minister of Long Island and New Jersey churches, he supported the Coetus party, which wished to be free from control of the Classis of Amsterdam.

GOETSCHIUS, PERCY (*b. Paterson, N.J., 1853; d. Manchester, N.H., 1943*), music theorist. Graduated Royal Conservatory, Stuttgart, Germany, 1876; studied piano with Sigmund Lebert and Dionys Pruckner. Immanuel Faisst, with whom he studied composition and theory, exercised a major influence on his development. Engaged in musical journalism in Stuttgart, where he taught harmony, composition, and music history at the conservatory. In 1885, he was named royal professor by the king of Württemberg. Returning to the United States, 1890, he taught at Syracuse University and the New England Conservatory of Music (Boston). Set up a private studio in Boston, 1896. As head of the Department of Theory and Composition at the Institute of Musical Art (New York City, later amalgamated with the Juilliard School), 1905–25, he exerted a wide influence upon musical composition and music education in the United States. Produced more than 15 influential textbooks and the 43-volume Analytic Symphony Series.

GOETZ, GEORGE. *See* CALVERTON, VICTOR FRANCIS.

GOETZ, GEORGE WASHINGTON (*b. Milwaukee, Wis., 1856; d. 1897*), metallurgist, consultant to large steel and iron companies. Pioneered in gas analysis, mechanical puddling, and the "basic" process, which he was first to use successfully in America.

GOFF, EMMET STULL (*b. Elmira, N.Y., 1852; d. 1902*), horticulturist. Noted for research in economic entomology, plant pathology and physiology, fungicides, and insecticides, he was also an effective professor of horticulture at University of Wisconsin, 1889–1902.

GOFF, JOHN WILLIAM (*b. Co. Wexford, Ireland, 1848; d. 1924*), jurist. Came to America as a child. Counsel for Lexow Committee, 1893, which investigated corruption in New York City police department. Last recorder of New York, 1894–1906; New York Supreme Court justice, 1906–19.

GOFFE, WILLIAM (*d. 1679[?]*), Parliamentary soldier, regicide. Fled with Edward Whalley to New England, 1660. He moved secretly from place to place and probably died in Hartford, Conn.

GOFORTH, WILLIAM (*b. New York, N.Y., 1766; d. Cincinnati, Ohio, 1817*), physician. Removed to Kentucky, 1788; *post* 1800, was leading physician in Cincinnati. Teacher of Daniel Drake, he was probably the first to vaccinate in the Northwest Territory (1801).

GOING, JONATHAN (*b. Reading, Vt., 1786; d. 1844*), Baptist clergyman, educator. Graduated Brown, 1809. With John M. Peck planned American Baptist Home Mission Society, 1832, and served as its secretary. President of college at Granville, Ohio, later Denison University, 1837–44.

GOLD, MICHAEL (*b. New York, N.Y., 1893; d. San Francisco, Calif., 1967*), radical journalist and writer. Born Itzok Isaac Granich. Demonstrated a commitment to proletarian art with the one-act plays *Down the Airshaft* and *Ivan's Homecoming* (both 1917), the full-length plays *Hoboken Blues* (1928) and *Fiesta* (1929), and his most important work, the novel *Jews Without Money* (1930), an impassioned plea for a socialist transformation of American society. Established the New Playwrights Theater with John Dos Passos and John Howard Lawson. A contributing editor of the *Liberator* from 1920. Editor of *New Masses* from 1926. Columnist with the *Daily Worker* from 1933. Also known for critical and polemical essays, especially his theoretical pronouncements on "proletarian literature," the most important of which are "Towards Proletarian Art" (*Liberator*, February 1921) and "Proletarian Realism" (*New Masses*, October 1930). Exerted a strong influence both upon the Communist movement and upon the critical life of his time with essays like "Go Left, Young Man" (*New Masses*, January 1929) and "Prophet of the Genteel Christ" (*New Republic*, Nov. 22, 1930).

GOLDBECK, ROBERT (*b. Potsdam, Prussia, 1839; d. St. Louis, Mo., 1908*), pianist, teacher, prolific composer.

GOLDBERG, REUBEN LUCIUS ("RUBE") (*b. San Francisco, Calif., 1883; d. New York, N.Y., 1970*), cartoonist and sculptor. Studied at the University of California at Berkeley (graduated, 1904). Sports cartoonist with the *San Francisco Chronicle*, 1904–05. Illustrator with the *San Francisco Bulletin*, 1906–07. Sports cartoonist and columnist for the *New York Mail*, 1907–21. Syndicated cartoonist from 1921. Political cartoonist at the *New York Sun* from 1938. Comic-strip creations include *Mike and Ike—They Look Alike, Boob McNutt, The Weekly Meeting of the Tuesday Ladies' Club*, and *Lala Palooza*. His best-known character was the inventor known as Professor Lucifer Gorgonzola Butts. Pulitzer Prize in 1948 for the editorial cartoon *Peace Today*. Turned to sculpture at the age of eighty. His work was exhibited at the Smithsonian Institution in 1970.

GOLDBERGER, JOSEPH (*b. Austria, 1874; d. Washington, D.C., 1929*), medical research worker. Came to America as a child. M.D., Bellevue Hospital Medical College, 1895. Served in U.S. Public Health Service and, *post* 1904, with Hygienic Laboratory, Washington. Directed pellagra research campaign, 1913–25, which practically freed southern public institutions of the disease.

GOLDEN, JOHN (*b. New York, N.Y., 1874; d. Bayside, N.Y., 1955*), producer, songwriter, playwright. Produced a series of family-style plays on Broadway, including *Lightnin'* (1918), *Seventh Heaven* (1922), and *Claudia* (1941). Collaborated with Oscar Hammerstein, Jerome Kern, Victor Herbert, and Irving Berlin, writing many Broadway revues and musical shows; song hits included "Poor Butterfly" and "Goodbye, Girls, I'm Through."

GOLDENWEISER, ALEXANDER ALEXANDROVICH (*b. Kiev, Russia, 1880; d. Portland, Oreg., 1940*), anthropologist.

GOLDENWEISER, EMANUEL ALEXANDER (*b. Kiev, Russia, 1883; d. Princeton, N.J., 1953*), economist. Immigrated to the U.S. in 1902. Ph.D., Cornell University, 1907. A pioneer in developing research and analysis as a factor in government economic planning; 1919–45, statistician for the Federal Reserve Board; director of the Division of Research and Statistics, 1926–45. Introduced the Federal Reserve's index of industrial production and the statistics of money flow for major sectors of the economy. During World War II, helped plan the International Monetary Fund; attended the Breton Woods conference as the Federal Reserve Board delegate. Institute for Advanced Study, Princeton, 1945–53. Books include *The Federal Reserve System* (1939–46) and *American Monetary Policy* (1951).

GOLDER, FRANK ALFRED (*b. near Odessa, Russia, 1877; d. Stanford, Calif., 1929*), historian. Came to America as a child. Graduated Bucknell, 1898; Ph.D., Harvard, 1909. Authority on Alaska and Russian expansion in Pacific. Professor of history, Stanford; director, Hoover War Library.

GOLDFINE, BERNARD (*b. Avanta, Russia, 1889; d. Boston, Mass., 1967*), industrialist and influence peddler. Immigrated, mid-1890's; settled in Boston. With Gordon Wayness, established the Strathmore Woolen Company in 1910; acquired the Georges River Woolen Company in Maine in 1929; the Lebanon and Lebandale mills in New Hampshire in 1931; and, later, the Northfield Mills in Vermont. Formed the industrial and commercial real estate East Boston Company and Boston Post Development Company. Cultivated the friendship of New England political figures and was a generous contributor to candidates of both parties. Gained notoriety in 1958 as the central figure in the Eisenhower administration's biggest political scandal, in which it was alleged that Goldfine had received preferential treatment from the Federal Trade Commission and the Securities and Exchange Commission as a result of his longtime friendship with White House Chief of Staff Sherman Adams; Adams later resigned. Served time in the early 1960's for income tax evasion; in 1962 he consented to sell all of his assets to settle $10.3 million in federal tax claims. There is no record that he ever became a U.S. citizen.

GOLDIN, HORACE (*b. near Vilna, Poland, 1873; d. London, England, 1939*), internationally known magician, innovator of "sawing a woman in half."

GOLDMAN, EDWIN FRANKO (*b. Louisville, Ky., 1878; d. New York, N.Y., 1956*), bandmaster and composer. Studied at the National Conservatory of Music. Founded (1911) the New York Military Band which became the Goldman Band in 1922; Goldman conducted the band until 1955. Famous for the Central Park Concerts which were broadcast nationally on radio, Goldman also composed many works for bands, including the famous march *On the Mall* (1923); in addition, he promoted and performed many works by new composers such as Virgil Thomson, Walter Piston, and Vincent Persichetti.

GOLDMAN, EMMA (*b. Kovno, Lithuania, 1869; d. Toronto, Canada, 1940*), anarchist editor and propagandist, lecturer, literary critic. Resided in the United States from 1885 until her deportation to Russia in 1919.

GOLDMAN, MAYER C. (*b. New Orleans, La., 1874; d. New York, N.Y., 1939*), lawyer. Lifetime advocate of a public defender in criminal cases.

GOLDMARK, HENRY (*b. New York, N.Y., 1857; d. Nyack, N.Y., 1941*), civil engineer. Graduated Harvard, 1878; studied at Royal Polytechnic School, Hannover, Germany. Began practice in construction of railroad bridges; made special studies of metallurgy and deep-water technology. As one of the design engineers of the Isthmian Canal Commission, 1906–14, he was responsible for design and installation of the Panama Canal locks and auxiliary equipment. Helped design New Orleans Inner Navigation Canal, 1914–17.

GOLDMARK, RUBIN (*b. New York, N.Y., 1872; d. New York, 1936*), pianist, composer, music teacher. Studied at Vienna Conservatory, and at New York's National Conservatory under Joseffy and Dvořák. Director, Colorado College Conservatory, 1895–1901; of the Department of Theory of New York College of Music, 1911–24; and of the composition department of Juilliard School, 1924–36. Goldmark influenced a number of students who later became distinguished composers and performers. His own compositions reflect his idealism and thorough craftsmanship. His orchestral works include *Hiawatha* (1900), *Samson* (1914), *Gettysburg Requiem* (1919), *Negro Rhapsody* (1922), and *Call of the Plains* (*ca.* 1932).

GOLDSBOROUGH, CHARLES (*b. near Cambridge, Md., 1765; d. near Cambridge, 1834*), lawyer, legislator. Congressman, Federalist, 1805–17; last Federalist governor of Maryland, 1818–19.

GOLDSBOROUGH, LOUIS MALESHERBES (*b. Washington, D.C., 1805; d. 1877*), naval officer. Commanded Atlantic and North Atlantic Blockading Squadrons, *post* 1861; commanded fleet which, with Burnside's troops, captured Roanoke Island and destroyed Confederate fleet, 1862; was later criticized for ineffectiveness at Drewry's Bluff. Retired in 1873 as rear admiral.

GOLDSBOROUGH, ROBERT (*b. near Cambridge, Md.,
1733; d. near Cambridge, 1788*), lawyer, legislator, member of
Continental Congress, 1774–75.

GOLDSBOROUGH, THOMAS ALAN (*b. Caroline County, Md.,
1877; d. Washington, D.C., 1951*), lawyer, congressman, judge.
Law degree, University of Maryland, 1901. Democrat, Congress
(1920–38). Member of the House Banking and Currency Committee, he introduced legislation that led to the creation of the
Federal Deposit Insurance Corporation in 1933. Judge, U.S.
District Court in Washington, D.C., 1939–51. Presided over two
cases of contempt charges brought against John L. Lewis, president of the United Mine Workers, 1946 and 1948; his guilty
verdict was upheld by the Supreme Court.

GOLDSCHMIDT, JAKOB (*b. Eldagsen, Germany, 1882; d. New
York, N.Y., 1955*), international financier. A major figure in the
financial circles of the Weimar Republic; head of securities of the
Nationalbank für Deutschland, 1918; merged with the
Darmstätter Bank to become the Danatbank in 1922, the fourth
largest in Germany. Organized a steel combine, the giant
Vereinigte Stahlwerker in 1926. Involved in over 100 corporations
in Central Europe, he lost his position when foreign investors
withdrew support from German finances with the rise of Hitler. A
favorite target of the Nazis, Goldschmidt, a Jew, fled to the U.S. in
1936, where he had a short and modest career in business. A
member of the Foreign Policy Association, the Academy of
Political Science, the Museum of Modern Art, and the Metropolitan Museum of Art.

GOLDSMITH, MIDDLETON (*b. Port Tobacco, Md., 1818; d.
Rutland, Vt., 1887*), physician, surgeon. Graduated New York
College of Physicians and Surgeons, 1840. With his father,
introduced practice of lithotrity. Taught surgery at Castleton, Vt.,
and Louisville, Ky. During Civil War, as Union army surgeon,
devised a bromine treatment for gangrene which was generally
adopted.

GOLDSTEIN, MAX AARON (*b. St. Louis, Mo., 1870; d.
Frankfort, Mich., 1941*), physician. M.D., Missouri Medical
College (later Wisconsin University School of Medicine), 1892;
postgraduate study in otolaryngology in Berlin, Vienna, Strassburg, and London; began practice in St. Louis, 1895. Professor of
otology, Beaumont Medical College (later St. Louis University
School of Medicine), 1895–1912. Long interested in the problem
of teaching deaf children to communicate, he developed his ideas
at his own Central Institute for the Deaf, founded in 1914.

GOLDTHWAITE, GEORGE (*b. Boston, Mass., 1809; d. 1879*),
jurist. Removed to Montgomery, Ala., ca. 1826. Read law with
brother, Henry B. Goldthwaite, and achieved success as lawyer
and planter. Unsympathetic to slavery, he opposed, but accepted,
secession. Served as U.S. senator, Democrat, from Alabama,
1871–77.

GOLDTHWAITE, HENRY BARNES (*b. Concord, N.H.,
1802; d. 1847*), lawyer. Brother of George Goldthwaite. Removed to Alabama, ca. 1817; won distinction as lawyer in Mobile
and as Alabama Supreme Court justice *post* 1836.

GOLDWATER, SIGISMUND SCHULZ (*b. New York, N.Y.,
1873; d. New York, 1942*), hospital and public health administrator. Studied sociology and economics at the institute founded by
George Gunton; studied political science at Columbia University
and social problems at University of Leipzig. Seeking career in
public health, he entered Bellevue Hospital Medical College
(New York University) and graduated M.D., 1901. After interning
at Mount Sinai Hospital, New York City, he was appointed its
superintendent, 1903. He established a social service department,

1906, reorganized the medical education services, and encouraged the development of an extensive outpatient service. Director,
Mount Sinai, 1917–28. Commissioner of hospitals of New York
City, 1934–40; carried through a complete reorganization and
upgrading of the city's municipal health facilities. Thereafter, he
was president of the Associated Hospital Service, the citywide Blue
Cross organization.

GOMBERG, MOSES (*b. Elisavetgrad, present Kirovograd, Russia, 1866; d. Ann Arbor, Mich., 1947*), organic chemist. Came to
Chicago, Ill., ca. 1884, as refugee. B.S., University of Michigan,
1890; M.S., 1892; Ph.D., 1894. Appointed instructor in chemistry at Michigan, 1893; full professor, 1904; chairman of the
department, 1927–36. He studied in Germany, 1896–97—in
Munich with Adolf von Baeyer and in Heidelberg with Victor
Meyer. He successfully prepared tetraphenylmethane and, in
1897, hexaphenylethane, the next fully phenylated member of the
hydrocarbon series.

In 1900 Gomberg announced the discovery of a stable free
radical, and much of his research effort during the rest of his life
was aimed toward demonstrating the soundness of his interpretation and in gaining new knowledge of organic free radicals. He also
carried out studies on the reducing action on organic compounds
of magnesium iodide mixture, the synthesis of certain dyes, the
properties of the perchlorate radical, and the synthesis of biaryls
(Gomberg reaction). During World War I he participated in gas
warfare research directed by the U.S. Bureau of Mines. His work
on the synthesis of ethylene chlorohydrin led to a method for
commercial preparation, an intermediate in the manufacture of
mustard gas. Later he became a major in the Ordnance Department, where he served as an adviser on the manufacture of high
explosives and smokeless powder.

GOMPERS, SAMUEL (*b. London, England, 1850; d. 1924*),
labor leader. Apprenticed to a cigarmaker; came to America, 1863;
joined Cigarmakers' Union, 1864. Attended Cooper Union lectures, but got the most important part of his education in the skilled
cigarmakers' shops where books, papers, and magazines were
purchased from a common fund and the workmen took turns
reading aloud. Ferdinand Laurell, a onetime leader of the Scandinavian Marxist Socialist organization, interpreted *The Communist Manifesto* for Gompers, taught him the "Marx of trade
unionism," and warned him against joining the Socialist movement. Gompers went to Socialist meetings, was admitted to the
inner circle of a group of European refugees, *die zehn Philosophen*.
From this group "came the purpose and the initiative that finally
resulted in the present American labor movement."

In 1877, local American cigarmakers' unions carried on a
prolonged and fruitless strike against the tenement-house sweating
system. Gompers and Strasser led a reorganization of the cigarmakers, Strasser becoming the international president or traveling organizer, Gompers president of Local 144. In this reorganization, they made international officers supreme over local unions,
greatly increased membership dues to build up a fund, concentrated control of that fund in the national officers, and adopted, or
prepared to adopt, sickness, accident, and unemployment benefits. The cigarmakers' union became a model for others, and in
1881 the Federation of Organized Trades and Labor Unions of the
United States of America and Canada was formed, reorganized in
1886 as the American Federation of Labor (AFL) and operated on
a unique basis of principles. Elected president of the new federation, Gompers remained official head of the American labor
movement, except for one year, until his death. The power he
exerted may be called "moral," a term which in his interpretation
signified organized consent to collective action. He believed that
drastic methods would not bring education and solidarity, that it
was persuasion, not dictation, that unionized. Gompers' moral

influence with the executives of each national union was founded on their knowledge that no "dual union" would be allowed to displace them. Gompers was well aware of the limits beyond which labor organization could not go. Labor could not lift itself as a body into another status. For this reason Gompers was always against theorizers and intellectuals in the organization of labor. Amid all the differences in America of religion, race, language, politics, there was only one direction toward which labor should unite—more wages, more leisure, more liberty. Labor must struggle by collective action toward better living, better citizenship.

Although Gompers held that labor is always right, his conviction that labor could never displace the capitalist in management enabled him to negotiate with capitalists. He felt, too, that labor could not compete with politicians, that its role in politics was to bargain for immunity from interference by legislatures, courts, and executives so that it could use its own power in collective bargaining. With the expansion of the AFL, Gompers became an important public figure. President Wilson appointed him to the Council of National Defense and to the Commission on International Labor Legislation at the Paris Peace Conference. During World War I he was an implacable foe of pacifism and organized the War Committee on Labor. His autobiography, *Seventy Years of Life and Labor* (1925), is an authoritative and important account of the rise and growth of American trade unionism.

GONZALES, AMBROSE ELLIOTT (*b. Colleton Co., S.C., 1857; d. 1926*), newspaper publisher, writer of black dialect stories. His liberal paper, the Columbia, S.C., *State*, opposed the Tillman regime *post* 1891, fought for reforms, and achieved a national reputation.

GOOCH, WILLIAM (*b. Yarmouth, England, 1681; d. Bath, England, 1751*), baronet, colonial governor of Virginia, 1727–49. Favorably regarded by colonists, he staunchly defended them and tried to improve tobacco export conditions.

GOOD, ADOLPHUS CLEMENS (*b. West Mahoning, Pa., 1856; d. Efulen, Cameroons, 1894*), Presbyterian missionary to Africa, naturalist. Unusually effective in his work, he journeyed far into interior; prepared a Bulu primer and translated Gospels into Bulu.

GOOD, JAMES ISAAC (*b. York, Pa., 1850; d. Philadelphia, Pa., 1924*), German Reformed clergyman. Graduated Lafayette, 1872; Union Theological, 1875. Pastor and seminary professor; his greatest work was as historian of the Reformed church. He discovered documents, collected a notable library, published over 20 books.

GOOD, JEREMIAH HAAK (*b. Rehrersburg, Pa., 1822; d. Tiffin, Ohio, 1888*), German Reformed clergyman. Uncle of James I. Good. Studied at Marshall College and Mercersburg. Pastor in Ohio; taught at Heidelberg College. Professor of theology and president, Heidelberg Theological Seminary, 1869–87.

GOOD, JOHN (*b. Co. Roscommon, Ireland, 1841; d. 1908*), inventor, manufacturer of rope. Came to America as a child; raised in Brooklyn, N.Y. Granted more than 100 patents for rope-making machinery, 1869–1908, he revolutionized this hitherto hand industry.

GOODALE, GEORGE LINCOLN (*b. Saco, Maine, 1839; d. 1923*), physician, botanist. Son of Stephen L. Goodale. Graduated Amherst, 1860; M.D., Harvard and Bowdoin, 1863. Taught at Harvard and was Fisher professor of natural history, 1888–1909. Stimulated interest in plant physiology, economic botany, and Harvard Botanical Garden and Museum, which he developed.

GOODALE, STEPHEN LINCOLN (*b. South Berwick, Maine, 1815; d. Saco, Maine, 1897*), agriculturist. Secretary of Maine Board of Agriculture; stimulated scientific approach to all phases of agricultural practice.

GOODALL, HARVEY L. (*b. Lunenburg, Vt., 1836; d. 1900*), journalist. Founded Chicago *Sun* in 1869, and *Drovers' Journal*, pioneer livestock market paper, in 1873.

GOODALL, THOMAS (*b. Dewsbury, England, 1823; d. 1910*), woolen manufacturer, originator of the horse blanket. Came to America, 1846. His mills at Sanford, Maine, were first in country to make carriage robes, mohair, plushes, kersey blankets.

GOODE, GEORGE BROWN (*b. New Albany, Ind., 1851; d. 1896*), ichthyologist, museum administrator, assistant secretary of Smithsonian Institution. Graduated Wesleyan (Conn.), 1870. Author of monographs and books on his specialty and of histories of the Smithsonian (1895 and 1897).

GOODE, JOHN (*b. Bedford Co., Va., 1829; d. 1909*), lawyer, Confederate soldier and congressman, statesman. Congressman, Democrat, from Virginia, 1875–81; president, Virginia Constitutional Convention, 1901–02.

GOODE, JOHN PAUL (*b. near Stewartville, Minn., 1862; d. Little Point Sable, Mich., 1932*), geographer. Graduated University of Minnesota, 1889; Ph.D., University of Pennsylvania, 1901. Taught at University of Chicago, 1903–28. Made his principal reputation as a cartographer in a series of maps for school use which set new standards in design and craftsmanship, and a school atlas. His projections embodied three new devices: the principle of "interruption" in a map grid applied to a sinusoidal projection (1916); a homolosine projection, using the sinusoidal from the equator to nearly 40° north and south, and homolographic thence to the poles (1923); and a polar equal-area projection in which continental lobes were deployed radially from the North Pole (1928).

GOODELL, HENRY HILL (*b. Constantinople, Turkey, 1839; d. on shipboard, 1905*), educator. Son of William Goodell (1792–1867). Graduated Amherst, 1862. Taught at Massachusetts Agricultural College, 1867–86; president, 1886–1905.

GOODELL, WILLIAM (*b. Templeton, Mass., 1792; d. Philadelphia, Pa., 1867*), Congregational clergyman; missionary to Near East, 1823–65. Laid foundation for American Board's work in Turkey with mission at Constantinople; translated Bible into Armeno-Turkish.

GOODELL, WILLIAM (*b. Coventry, N.Y., 1792; d. Janesville, Wis., 1878*), reformer, abolitionist. Edited a great number of temperance and antislavery publications; founded Liberty League, 1847, which opposed slavery, monopoly, tariffs, liquor, war, and secret societies.

GOODENOW, JOHN MILTON (*b. Westmoreland, N.H., 1782; d. New Orleans, La., 1838*), jurist. Removed to Ohio, 1811; admitted to bar, 1813. Successfully opposed Judge Benjamin Tappan's view that, in absence of specific state legislation, crimes under English common law should be held as crimes by Ohio courts.

GOODHUE, BENJAMIN (*b. Salem, Mass., 1748; d. 1814*), merchant, legislator. Congressman, Federalist, from Massachusetts, 1789–96; U.S. senator, 1796–1800. Cousin of Timothy Pickering.

GOODHUE, BERTRAM GROSVENOR (*b. Pomfret, Conn., 1869; d. 1924*), architect. Studied in office of James Renwick, New York City; as a draftsman, soon gained reputation for remarkable facility. Joined new firm of Ralph Adams Cram and Francis Wentworth in Boston, 1889; later he became a partner. Working in the style of the English Gothic revival and influenced by Morris and the arts-and-crafts movement, Goodhue did book design and type design at this period as well as ecclesiastical buildings. This first period of his career culminated in the group of buildings at West Point, commissioned 1903. The superb rugged chapel was Goodhue's particular work, and the group gave a powerful impetus to the adoption of Gothic forms in college architecture.

Goodhue removed to New York *ca.* 1903; the Cram partnership was dissolved in 1913. The detail of St. Thomas' Church, Fifth Avenue, New York, was largely Goodhue's work. His characteristic romantic spirit and design formulas appear in the Chapel of the Intercession, and St. Vincent Ferrer, New York, designed by himself. In St. Bartholomew's, New York, and the University of Chicago Chapel he added Byzantine elements.

As Goodhue grew older he grew dissatisfied with medievalism. The invention of reinforced concrete turned him toward modernism. "I dream," he wrote, "of something very much bigger and finer and more modern and more suited to present-day civilization than any Gothic church could possibly be." In practice he turned toward a kind of classicism shown in the Nebraska Capitol. Essentially a belated romanticist and eclectic, Goodhue was influenced by many styles. He died before achieving a vitally creative modernity.

GOODHUE, JAMES MADISON (*b. Hebron, N.H., 1810; d. 1852*), lawyer, editor. Graduated Amherst, 1833. Removed to Wisconsin and to St. Paul, Minn., 1849, where he published the *Minnesota Pioneer*, first newspaper in the territory. An outstanding frontier figure, he promoted immigration, urged settlement of Indian lands, sharply criticized conditions in rapidly growing St. Paul.

GOODLOE, DANIEL REAVES (*b. Louisburg, N.C., 1814; d. Warrenton, N.C., 1902*), journalist, abolitionist, politician. Edited the *National Era* in succession to Gamaliel Bailey; author of, among many other writings, *Inquiry into the Causes Which Have Retarded the Accumulation of Wealth . . . in the Southern States* (1846).

GOODLOE, WILLIAM CASSIUS (*b. Madison Co., Ky., 1841; d. Lexington, Ky., 1889*), politician. Grandnephew, and for a time secretary, of Cassius M. Clay. Helped organize Kentucky Republican party; killed in a sensational fight with political rival, Armistead M. Swope.

GOODMAN, CHARLES (*b. Philadelphia, Pa., 1796; d. Philadelphia, Pa., 1835*), stipple-engraver, lawyer. Taught by David Edwin. Gave up engraving and dissolved partnership with Robert Piggot, 1819.

GOODMAN, KENNETH SAWYER (*b. Chicago, Ill., 1883; d. 1918*), playwright. Graduated Princeton, 1906. Specialist in one-act play form. His first book, *Quick Curtains* (1915), included "The Game of Chess" and others popular with "little theaters." Plays in which he collaborated with Ben Hecht were published in *The Wonder Hat* (1925).

GOODMAN, LOUIS EARL (*b. Lemoore, Calif., 1892; d. Palo Alto, Calif., 1961*), federal judge. Studied at the University of California at Berkeley and Hastings College of Law (graduated, 1915). Practiced law in San Francisco before being named a judge of the District Court for the Northern District of California in 1942; became chief judge in 1958. Many of his decisions regarded maritime and immigration issues. In *United States* v. *Two Ob-*

scene Books (1951) Goodman ruled that Henry Miller's *Tropic of Cancer* and *Tropic of Capricorn* could not be legally imported. Brought to national prominence with the Caryl Chessman case, in which a man convicted in state court in 1948 challenged the legitimacy of the court's transcription of his case. Goodman repeatedly upheld the accuracy of the transcript, keeping Chessman on Death Row for thirteen years before his execution.

GOODNIGHT, CHARLES (*b. Macoupin Co., Ill., 1836; d. 1929*), cattleman. Removed to Texas, 1846; was cattle-handler, guide, scout, and a member of the Frontier Regiment, Texas Rangers, during Civil War. After the war, he established ranches in New Mexico and Colorado. With Oliver Loving, he laid out the Goodnight Cattle Trail from Belknap, Tex., to Fort Sumner, N. Mex., 1866; he also blazed the Goodnight-Loving Trail into Wyoming, and the New Goodnight Trail from Alamogordo Creek, N. Mex., to Granada, Colo., 1875. With John George Adair, he developed the JA Ranch in the Texas Panhandle, which soon after the formation of their partnership in 1877 embraced nearly 1 million acres and 100,000 head of cattle. Also in 1877, he ran a cattle trail from the JA Ranch to Dodge City, Kans. In extensive breeding experiments he developed one of America's finest beef herds and a large buffalo herd. Goodnight originated in 1880 the first Panhandle stockmen's association, which policed trails, introduced purebred cattle, systematized range work, and kept order.

GOODNOUGH, XANTHUS HENRY (*b. Brookline, Mass., 1860; d. Waterford, Maine, 1935*), sanitary engineer.

GOODNOW, FRANK JOHNSON (*b. Brooklyn, N.Y., 1859; d. Baltimore, Md., 1939*), political scientist. Graduated Amherst, 1879; Columbia Law School, 1882. Taught at Columbia, 1883–1914; president, Johns Hopkins, 1914–29. A pioneer in the study of public administration.

GOODNOW, ISAAC TICHENOR (*b. Whitingham, Vt., 1814; d. near Manhattan, Kans., 1894*), teacher, Kansas pioneer. Led a company of Free-Soil colonists who founded Manhattan, 1855. Helped establish college there which became Kansas State Agricultural College, 1863.

GOODRICH, ALFRED JOHN (*b. Chilo, Ohio, 1847; d. Paris, France, 1920*), musical theorist, composer, teacher, writer.

GOODRICH, ANNIE WARBURTON (*b. New Brunswick, N.J., 1866; d. Cobalt, Conn., 1954*), nurse and educator. Studied at New York Hospital School of Nursing (1892). Taught at Post-Graduate Hospital in New York (1892–1901); 1904–13, lectured at Columbia Teachers College; inspector of nurse training schools for New York State, 1910; during World War I, chief inspector of army hospitals in the U.S., becoming dean of the Army School of Nursing. From 1923 to 1934, she was dean of the Yale University School of Nursing.

GOODRICH, BENJAMIN FRANKLIN (*b. Ripley, N.Y., 1841; d. Manitou Springs, Colo., 1888*), physician, rubber manufacturer. In partnership with J. P. Morris, bought Hudson River Rubber Co., 1867; despite lack of success here and at another small rubber factory at Melrose, N.Y., Goodrich persevered, moving the business to Akron, Ohio, 1870–71. Continued lack of working capital and of local confidence in his enterprise hindered progress until 1880 when adequate backing was secured from G. W. Crouse.

GOODRICH, CHARLES AUGUSTUS (*b. Ridgefield, Conn., 1790; d. Hartford, Conn., 1862*), Congregational clergyman, author. Brother of Samuel G. Goodrich. Wrote many informational and children's books; his *History of the United States* (1822) went through more than 150 editions.

GOODRICH, CHAUNCEY (*b. Durham, Conn., 1759; d. 1815*), lawyer. Son of Elizur Goodrich (1734–97). Graduated Yale, 1776. Congressman, Federalist, from Connecticut, 1795–1801; U.S. senator, 1807–13; lieutenant governor, Connecticut, 1813–15. Prominent at Hartford Convention, 1814.

GOODRICH, CHAUNCEY (*b. Hinsdale, Mass., 1798; d. Burlington, Vt., 1858*), bookseller, publisher, horticulturist. Greatly encouraged and improved fruit-growing in Vermont and northern New York.

GOODRICH, CHAUNCEY (*b. Hinsdale, Mass., 1836; d. 1925*), Congregational clergyman. Nephew of Chauncey Goodrich (1798–1858). Missionary to China, 1865–1925. Leader of committee which translated Bible into Mandarin (published 1919), he also published valuable Chinese language studies.

GOODRICH, CHAUNCEY ALLEN (*b. New Haven, Conn., 1790; d. New Haven, 1860*), Congregational clergyman, educator, lexicographer. Son of Elizur Goodrich (1761–1849). Graduated Yale, 1810; was professor of rhetoric there *post* 1817. Author of several textbooks, he helped in the 1847 revision of the *Dictionary* by Noah Webster, whose daughter he had married, 1816.

GOODRICH, ELIZUR (*b. Wethersfield, Conn., 1734; d. Durham, Conn., 1797*), Congregational clergyman. Graduated Yale, 1752. Pastor at Durham, Conn., 1756–97. Biblical scholar, ardent Whig, keen astronomer, he was greatly interested in Yale and a member of its corporation, *post* 1776.

GOODRICH, ELIZUR (*b. Durham, Conn., 1761; d. New Haven, Conn., 1849*), lawyer, Federalist politician. Son of Elizur Goodrich (1734–97); brother of Chauncey Goodrich (1759–1815). Mayor of New Haven, 1803–22. Secretary of Yale, 1818–46.

GOODRICH, FRANK BOOTT (*b. Boston, Mass., 1826; d. Morristown, N.J., 1894*), journalist, playwright. Son of Samuel G. Goodrich. Author of superficial popular books; as dramatist, collaborated with John Brougham, Dion Boucicault, and others.

GOODRICH, SAMUEL GRISWOLD (*b. Ridgefield, Conn., 1793; d. New York, N.Y., 1860*), author, publisher, known by pen name "Peter Parley." Grandson of Elizur Goodrich (1734–97); brother of Charles A. Goodrich. Mainly self-educated. After several unsuccessful ventures, removed to Boston, 1826, where he published and, save for two years, edited *The Token*, best of the American "annuals." The first of the Peter Parley books, *The Tales of Peter Parley About America* (1827), was followed by more than a hundred others. In these books, which sold by the millions, a kindly, omniscient old gentleman converses with a group of priggishly inquiring children, and instruction is given a thin sugarcoating of fiction. Goodrich's claim to have written all the books which bear his name as author is doubtful.

GOODRICH, SARAH. *See* GOODRIDGE, SARAH.

GOODRICH, WILLIAM MARCELLUS (*b. Templeton, Mass., 1777; d. Boston, Mass., 1833*), organ builder.

GOODRIDGE, SARAH (*b. Templeton, Mass., 1788; d. Boston, Mass., 1853*), painter of miniatures. Sister of William M. Goodrich. Originally self-taught, she improved her technique with help from Gilbert Stuart, 1820–24. Her best work was done before 1840.

GOODRIDGE, WILLIAM MARCELLUS. *See* GOODRICH, WILLIAM MARCELLUS.

GOODSELL, DANIEL AYRES (*b. Newburgh, N.Y., 1840; d. New York, N.Y., 1909*), Methodist clergyman. A force for tolerance in his church, he was made a bishop in 1888.

GOODSPEED, THOMAS WAKEFIELD (*b. near Glens Falls, N.Y., 1842; d. 1927*), Baptist clergyman, educational leader. Graduated University of Rochester, 1863; Rochester Theological Seminary, 1866. With Frederick T. Gates, helped in founding University of Chicago; was secretary of its board of trustees, 1890–1912, and author of its history.

GOODWIN, DANIEL RAYNES (*b. North Berwick, Maine, 1811; d. Philadelphia, Pa., 1890*), Episcopal clergyman. Graduated Bowdoin, 1832; attended Andover Theological Seminary. A professor at Bowdoin, 1835–53, he was ordained to the Episcopal priesthood, 1848. He served as president of Trinity College, Hartford, Conn., 1853–60, and as provost of University of Pennsylvania, 1860–68.

GOODWIN, ELIJAH (*b. Champaign Co., Ohio, 1807; d. near Cleveland, Ohio, 1879*), minister of the Disciples of Christ. As pioneer preacher, traveled and preached widely and energetically in Indiana and Illinois. Edited *Christian Record*, 1847–48 and 1859–66.

GOODWIN, HANNIBAL WILLISTON (*b. Taughannock, N.Y., 1822; d. 1900*), Episcopal clergyman, inventor. Graduated Union College, 1848; General Theological Seminary, 1851. Served parishes in New Jersey and California. Received patent in 1898 for invention of celluloid photographic film.

GOODWIN, ICHABOD (*b. North Berwick, Maine, 1794; d. Portsmouth, N.H., 1882*), merchant, financier, railroad executive. Brother of Daniel R. Goodwin. Whig New Hampshire legislator, and Republican governor, 1859–61.

GOODWIN, JOHN NOBLE (*b. South Berwick, Maine, 1824; d. Paraiso Springs, Calif., 1887*), lawyer, politician. Graduated Dartmouth, 1844. As territorial governor of Arizona, 1863–65, Goodwin showed great tact and ability in conciliating factions, guiding the first legislature, and maintaining a stable government.

GOODWIN, NATHANIEL CARLL (*b. Boston, Mass., 1857; d. 1919*), actor. An impulsive, wayward, much-married personality. "Nat" Goodwin failed in Shakespearean roles but succeeded in contemporary plays, especially those he produced with his second wife, Maxine Elliott, as costar.

GOODWIN, WILLIAM WATSON (*b. Concord, Mass., 1831; d. 1912*), Hellenist. Graduated Harvard, 1851; Ph.D., Göttingen, 1855. Eliot professor of Greek literature at Harvard, 1860–1901. Always zealous for high scholarly standards, as Harvard expanded from college to university Goodwin fought the battle for Greek with wit, clarity, and good nature. His book on Greek syntax (1860) gave new life to American methods of studying Greek. He published a widely used elementary Greek grammar, an excellent *Greek Reader* (1871), translations of *Plutarch's Morals*, the *Birds* and *Clouds* of Aristophanes, and other important studies and textbooks. The Greek constitutional and artistic achievements interested him profoundly, and he gave a course on Greek law. He was a founder of the Archaeological Institute of America and first director of the American School of Classical Studies in Athens.

GOODYEAR, ANSON CONGER (*b. Buffalo, N.Y., 1883; d. Old Westbury, N.Y., 1964*), industrialist and art collector. Studied at Yale (B.S., 1899). After college he entered the lumber manufacturing company of his father and uncle. Became vice president, 1907, of the Goodyear Lumber Company, and president of both the Norwich and Goodyear Lumber Companies upon the death of his father, 1911. He assumed the presidency of one of the country's largest lumber enterprises, the Great Southern Lumber Company, 1920. Goodyear served as vice president of the Buffalo and Susquehanna Railroad, 1907–1910. He was president of the New Orleans Great Northern Railroad Company, 1920–1930. He served as a colonel in the army in World War I, and brigadier general in the National Guard during World War II. Succeeded his father as director of the Buffalo Academy of Fine Arts, 1912. He moved to New York City and became President of the Museum of Modern Art, 1929–39. He remained a trustee of the museum until his death. Goodyear's art collection, a brilliant assemblage of late-nineteenth- and early-twentieth-century art, included paintings by Cézanne, Salvador Dali, Degas, and van Gogh.

GOODYEAR, CHARLES (*b. New Haven, Conn., 1800; d. New York, N.Y., 1860*), inventor. Became interested in rubber, 1834, while designing an improved inflating valve for a rubber life preserver. The rubber industry, after a mushroom growth, *post* 1830, had collapsed because no process was known to prevent India rubber from melting, sticking, and decomposing in heat. Goodyear began experiments enthusiastically, kneading into raw rubber every conceivable material. Despite a succession of failures and the most extreme poverty, he continued undaunted. In June 1837 he obtained Patent No. 240, in which he claimed to eliminate adhesive properties of rubber by superficial application of metals, especially nitric acid with copper or bismuth. In 1838 he began new experiments, combining Nathaniel M. Hayward's method of spreading sulfur on rubber to eliminate stickiness with his own process. Vulcanization was discovered when a mass of sulfur and rubber mixture, dropped accidentally on a hot stove by Goodyear, did not melt. Further experiments with mixes and baking temperatures were made with great difficulty. After three years, however, he produced a uniform product, and in 1844 received his celebrated Patent No. 3,633. Goodyear was so deeply in debt that he had to sell licenses and establish royalties for use of vulcanization at absurdly low figures.

In 1851 Goodyear went to Europe to extend his patent and designed a magnificent exhibit in London with everything made of rubber—furniture, floorcovering, jewelry, books. Napoleon III conferred on him the Grand Medal of Honor and the Cross of the Legion of Honor for a similar exhibit in Paris, 1855. Foreign patents were granted to him in all countries except England, yet despite all his efforts he died in debt.

GOODYEAR, CHARLES (*b. Germantown, Pa., 1833; d. 1896*), industrialist. Son of Charles Goodyear (1800–1860). President of the American Shoe-tip Co. *ca.* 1860, he was convinced of the feasibility of producing a completely machine-made shoe. To this end he purchased patents for stitching machines, encouraged the invention of new ones, and manufactured them himself. Though his experts made progress in inventing machines, the demand for them was small. With the help of Jonathan Munyon, a consolidation with Goodyear's competitor Gordon McKay was effected. *Post* 1880, McKay took care of the turned-shoe business, Goodyear of the welt-shoe business, and Munyon successfully marketed both products.

GOODYEAR, WILLIAM HENRY (*b. New Haven, Conn., 1846; d. 1923*), archaeologist, museum curator, author. Son of Charles Goodyear (1800–60). Proved that deviation, rather than mathematical regularity, was the traditional practice in architecture before modern times.

GOOKIN, DANIEL (*b. England or Ireland, 1612; d. 1686/87*), colonist, soldier, magistrate. Removed from Virginia to Massa-

chusetts, 1644; was for many years assistant to the General Court. His efforts on the Indians' behalf were second only to John Eliot's.

GOOLD, WILLIAM A. (*b. near Glasgow, Scotland, 1830; d. 1912*), coal miner, prospector, operator. Came to America, 1852. Identified *post* 1854 with development of the coal industry in Alabama.

GORCEY, LEO (*b. New York, N.Y., 1917; d. Oakland, Calif., 1969*), actor. Began his career in Sidney Kingsley's play *Dead End* in 1935; acted in the film version, which featured Humphrey Bogart, in 1937. This film introduced a set of characters called the Dead End Kids, of which Gorcey was a member. The Kids appeared in *Angels with Dirty Faces* (1938) with James Cagney, *Hell's Kitchen* (1939), and *Angels Wash Their Faces* (1939) with Ronald Reagan. Formed the Bowery Boys with Huntz Hall in the mid-1940's. Made close to fifty low-budget features that became increasingly slap stick, including *Bowery Bombshell* (1946), *Spook Busters* (1946), *Lucky Losers* (1950), *The Bowery Boys Meet the Monsters* (1954), and *Bowery to Bagdad* (1955). Retired from films in the mid-1950's.

GORDIN, JACOB (*b. Mirgorod, Russia, 1853; d. Brooklyn, N.Y., 1909*), playwright. Came to America, 1891. Characteristically Russian in his approach to the theater, he wrote many successful plays for the Yiddish theaters in New York.

GORDON, ANDREW (*b. Putnam, N.Y., 1828; d. Philadelphia, Pa., 1887*), Presbyterian clergyman. Instituted successful Presbyterian mission in the Punjab, India, 1855.

GORDON, GEORGE ANGIER (*b. Oyne, Scotland, 1853; d. 1929*), Congregational clergyman, author. Came to America, 1871. Graduated Harvard, 1881. Minister of Old South Church, Boston, Mass., 1884–1929; an outstanding champion of religious freedom and theological progress in American Congregationalism.

GORDON, GEORGE BYRON (*b. New Perth, Prince Edward Island, Canada, 1870; d. 1927*), archaeologist. Director of University Museum, Philadelphia; specialist in American anthropology.

GORDON, GEORGE HENRY (*b. Charlestown, Mass., 1823; d. 1886*), soldier, lawyer. Graduated West Point, 1846. Served with credit in Mexican War and at western frontier posts; resigned from army, 1854. Returning 1861 to Union army, he rose to major general, 1865. Author of a three-volume history of Civil War campaigns he had experienced.

GORDON, GEORGE PHINEAS (*b. Salem, N.H., 1810; d. Norfolk, Va., 1878*), printer, inventor. Began experimenting *ca.* 1835 on improvement of presses for card printing; took out the first of more than 50 patents, 1851. He invented and manufactured the "Yankee" and "Firefly" presses, and in 1858 the highly successful "Franklin," later called the "Gordon," job press.

GORDON, GEORGE WASHINGTON (*b. Giles Co., Tenn., 1836; d. 1911*), Confederate brigadier general, lawyer. Distinguished in Civil War service, in particular at battle of Franklin, he practiced law, served as Indian agent, and was congressman, Democrat, from Tennessee, 1907–11.

GORDON, JAMES (*b. Monroe Co., Miss., 1833; d. Okolona, Miss., 1912*), planter, legislator, Confederate soldier. Captured on return from mission to England, 1864, he escaped to Canada and was accused groundlessly of complicity in the murder of Abraham Lincoln.

GORDON, JOHN BROWN (*b. Upson Co., Ga., 1832; d. Miami, Fla., 1904*), lawyer, Confederate lieutenant general, statesman. The idol of Georgia for 40 years and the state's most important military figure, Gordon began service, 1860, as elected captain of a company of mountaineers; he had no previous military experience. His personality and genius for war won him the title "Chevalier Bayard of the Confederate Army." After the war, Gordon was in the thick of the fight to restore home rule to Georgia. He was U.S. senator, Democrat, from Georgia, 1873–80 and 1891–97; governor of Georgia, 1886–90. He represented the rising commercial and industrial, rather than the agrarian, spirit in the state. His *Reminiscences of the Civil War* (1903) is an important source.

GORDON, LAURA DE FORCE (*b. North East, Pa., 1838; d. San Joaquin Co., Calif., 1907*), lawyer, suffragist. Settled in California, *ca.* 1868; founded and edited newspapers in Stockton. Active in securing legislation permitting women to practice law in the state, she was one of first women admitted to California bar, 1879, and to practice before the U.S. Supreme Court.

GORDON, WAXEY. *See* WEXLER, IRVING.

GORDON, WILLIAM (*b. Hitchin, England, 1728; d. Ipswich, England, 1807*), Congregational clergyman, author. Came to America, 1770. As pastor at Roxbury, Mass., was a strong Whig and served as chaplain to Provincial Congress. Collected materials for a history of the Revolution; professing to doubt American reception of an "impartial" work, he published it in England, 1788. Modern research has discovered it to be a plagiarism from the *Annual Register*.

GORDON, WILLIAM FITZHUGH (*b. Germanna, Va., 1787; d. Albemarle Co., Va., 1858*), lawyer, Virginia legislator. As congressman, Democrat, from Virginia, 1830–35, introduced the bill, 1834, which later led to establishment of an independent U.S. treasury.

GORDON, WILLIAM WASHINGTON (*b. Screven Co., Ga., 1796; d. 1842*), lawyer. Graduated West Point, 1815. As president, Central Railroad of Georgia, supervised its planning and construction under great difficulties, 1836–42.

GORDY, JOHN PANCOAST (*b. near Salisbury, Md., 1851; d. New York, N.Y., 1908*), educator. Professor of history of education and American history at New York University, 1901–08.

GORE, THOMAS PRYOR (*b. near Embry, Miss., 1870; d. Washington, D.C., 1949*), lawyer, politician. Partially blinded at age 8, he was totally blinded at 20. He earned a law degree at Cumberland University, 1892. An active Populist in politics, he became known as the "Blind Orator." Removing to Corsicana, Tex., 1895, he practiced law; in 1899, in view of the declining fortunes of the Populists, he joined the Democratic party. Settling in Oklahoma Territory, 1901, he was elected to the territorial council and was soon the leading politician in Oklahoma. In 1907, on the granting of statehood, he became U.S. senator from Oklahoma. A progressive and an antimonopolist, he helped elect Woodrow Wilson president in 1912, but bitterly opposed Wilson's foreign policy, wartime legislation, and the League of Nations. Defeated for renomination in the Democratic primary of 1920, he returned for a final term in 1930, during which he opposed most of the policies of the New Deal. Defeated in his 1936 bid for reelection, he resumed the practice of law in Washington. A strong supporter of aid for farmers and soil conservation, he was also the author of an amendment to the 1918 Revenue Act which instituted the discovery-depletion allowance for the oil industry.

GORGAS, JOSIAH (*b. Dauphin Co., Pa., 1818; d. Tuscaloosa, Ala., 1883*), soldier, educator. Father of William C. Gorgas. Graduated West Point, 1841. An ordnance specialist, he married Amelia, daughter of John Gayle, while in command of the U.S. arsenal near Mobile, Ala., 1853. His Southern marriage and his dislike of abolitionists led him to resign his federal commission, and in April 1861 he was appointed Confederate chief of ordnance. There was no manufacturing arsenal in the Confederate States, only one foundry capable of casting cannon and but two small powder mills. Available cannon were outmoded as were most of the small arms. Cavalry and infantry equipment was practically nonexistent. Because of the blockade, the import of munitions was uncertain; the armies relied chiefly on local manufactures and captured items. Gorgas, with the aid of a remarkable staff of subordinates, established armories at Richmond, Va., and Fayetteville, N.C.; arsenals at Charleston, Augusta, Macon, Atlanta, Columbus, Selma, Baton Rouge, Little Rock, and other places; a cannon foundry and a central laboratory at Macon; and a powder mill at Augusta. Lead, iron, and copper were mined and saltpeter made. By 1863, Gorgas' bureau was operating with high efficiency; despite enormous difficulties, he supplied arms and ammunition to the very end of the war. After the collapse of the Confederacy, he managed an Alabama iron works. In 1869, he joined the staff of the University of the South at Sewanee, Tenn., becoming professor of engineering and vice-chancellor. Elected president of the University of Alabama, 1878, he resigned because of ill health.

GORGAS, WILLIAM CRAWFORD (*b. near Mobile, Ala., 1854; d. England 1920*), sanitarian. Son of Josiah Gorgas. Unable to obtain appointment to West Point, Gorgas joined the Army Medical Corps in 1880 after graduation from the University of the South, 1875, and Bellevue Hospital Medical College, 1879. Early in his career, he survived an attack of yellow fever at Fort Brown, Tex.; thereafter, he was in demand for posts where yellow fever was rife. Placed in charge of a yellow fever camp at Siboney, Cuba, 1898, and soon made chief sanitary officer of Havana, he applied the conventional methods of control: segregation of the sick, quarantine of infected localities, and general cleanliness. In spite of his efforts, the incidence of the disease grew worse. Following proof by the board headed by Walter Reed that the *Stegomyia* mosquito, later named *Aedes aegypti*, was the yellow fever carrier, Gorgas set about to destroy the breeding places of the insect. Within a few months Havana was rid of mosquitoes and fever.

Promoted colonel in recognition of his Cuban achievement, Gorgas studied the sanitary problems of the Panama Canal area. He arrived there with his staff in 1904 when actual work commenced on the Isthmus. Although aware that French failure with the canal project had been caused by disease, the American Canal Commissions were disinclined to support adequate preventive measures. A visitation of yellow fever in late 1904 brought Gorgas some support, but the first two commissions made determined efforts to discredit and supplant him. President Theodore Roosevelt, however, directed active support of his mosquito-control work and after visiting Panama in 1906 made Gorgas a member of the commission. Temporarily he had a free hand, but when George W. Goethals became chief engineer in 1908, he attacked Gorgas' sanitary work on the grounds of its cost. In spite of these difficulties, Gorgas rid the Canal Zone of yellow fever, made the cities of Colón and Panama models of sanitation, and came to be regarded as the foremost sanitary expert in the world. He was appointed U.S. Army surgeon general in 1914. After service during World War I, he retired as a major general. Commissioned by the International Health Board to investigate yellow fever on the west coast of Africa, he was stricken en route and died in Queen Alexandra Hospital, Millbank, England.

GORHAM, JABEZ (*b. Providence, R.I., 1792; d. 1869*), silversmith, merchant. Founder of Gorham Manufacturing Co.; first American silversmith to use machinery in that industry.

GORHAM, JOHN (*b. Boston, Mass., 1783; d. Boston, 1829*), physician. Erving professor of chemistry at Harvard, 1816–27. Taught with conspicuous success, and was author of *The Elements of Chemical Science* (1819–20), a standard textbook for many years.

GORHAM, NATHANIEL (*b. Charlestown, Mass., 1738; d. 1796*), merchant, Massachusetts patriot and legislator. President of Continental Congress, 1786; active in Constitutional Convention, 1787. With Oliver Phelps, purchased the so-called Genesee Country in New York, 1788, for development and settlement.

GORKY, ARSHILE (*b. Khorkom Vari Haiyotz Dzor, Turkish Armenia, 1904/5; d. Sherman, Conn., 1948*), painter. Born Vosdanig Adoian; changed his name to Gorky, 1925. Came to the United States, 1920; attended, among other schools, Rhode Island School of Design. Removed to New York City, 1925; studied and taught at Grand Central School of Art, 1925–31. Received increasing recognition during the years 1934–45. His painting is described as "exploring psychological space" and as providing much of the groundwork for abstract expressionism.

GORMAN, ARTHUR PUE (*b. Woodstock, Md., 1839; d. Washington, D.C., 1906*), politician. Protégé of Stephen A. Douglas. Maryland legislator, 1869–79; president, Chesapeake and Ohio Canal Co.; U.S. senator, Democrat, 1881–99, 1903–06. Conducted Cleveland's campaigns in 1884 and 1892, but opposed his policies.

GORMAN, WILLIS ARNOLD (*b. near Flemingsburg, Ky., 1816; d. St. Paul, Minn., 1876*), lawyer. Removed to Indiana, 1835; practiced in Bloomington. After service in Mexican War, was congressman, Democrat, from Indiana, 1849–53; governor of Minnesota Territory, 1853–57. Interrupted successful practice of law at St. Paul to serve as Union brigadier general, 1861–64.

GORRELL, EDGAR STALEY (*b. Baltimore, Md., 1891; d. Washington, D.C., 1945*), military aviator. Graduated West Point, 1912. Qualified as a military aviator, 1915, and served with the 1st Aero Squadron during the Mexican punitive expedition, 1916. M.S., aeronautical engineering, Massachusetts Institute of Technology, 1917. On U.S. entry into World War I was assigned to the Bolling technical mission sent to Europe to study means of planning U.S. aviation production; he later was in charge of Air Service procurement at Allied Expeditionary Force headquarters, Paris, held other staff posts, and rose to assistant chief of staff, Air Service, and was promoted colonel. Following the armistice, he headed a project at Tours, France, which produced a lengthy history and evaluation of the Air Service's development and combat record. *Post* 1920, he devoted his life to private business. He is noteworthy for a report he wrote in November, 1917, in which he showed himself an early advocate of strategic air power, a view which he later reversed.

GORRIE, JOHN (*b. Charleston, S.C., 1803; d. Apalachicola, Fla., 1855*), physician, pioneer in mechanical refrigeration. Conceived the idea of artificially cooling the air of sickrooms and hospitals to cure and prevent fever, *ca.* 1839; by 1845 was giving his whole time to the problem. From artificially cooling air he turned to artificial ice-making and accomplished it by 1850 with machinery of his own design. Patent No. 8080, granted him in May 1851, was presumably the first U.S. patent on mechanical refrigeration. Gorrie had no capital, and his failure to raise funds for the manufacture of his machinery induced a nervous collapse from which he never recovered.

GORRINGE, HENRY HONEYCHURCH (*b. Barbados, British West Indies, 1841; d. New York, N.Y., 1885*), naval officer. Engineered and directed transportation of Cleopatra's Needle obelisk from Egypt to New York City, 1879–80.

GORTNER, ROSS AIKEN (*b. near O'Neill, Nebr., 1885; d. St. Paul, Minn., 1942*), biochemist. B.S., Nebraska Wesleyan University, 1907; M.S., University of Toronto, 1908; Ph.D., Columbia University, 1909. After five years, 1909–14, spent at the Carnegie Institution's Station for Experimental Evolution, he served from 1917 until his death as professor of agricultural biochemistry at University of Minnesota and head of the division of agricultural biochemistry at the Minnesota Agricultural Experiment Station. A pioneer in application of colloid chemistry to biology, he did extensive research in the nature of proteins; he also studied the chemistry of wood and the pulping process. His work was characterized not by any major theoretical contribution but by a steady series of factual advances. He was author of more than 300 papers and books, among them a major treatise, *Outlines of Biochemistry* (1929).

GORTON, SAMUEL (*b. Gorton, near Manchester, England, ca. 1592; d. Warwick, R.I., 1677*), colonist, founder of Gortonites. His unorthodox religious beliefs brought him into conflict with authorities in Massachusetts Bay, Plymouth, and Newport, 1637–44. He denied the doctrine of the Trinity, denied the fitness of any paid person to be a minister, and also denied the actual existence of heaven and hell. After being several times imprisoned and banished, Gorton sought redress in England. Returning to America, 1648, he bore a letter from the Earl of Warwick ordering Massachusetts to leave him unmolested at Shawomet, R.I., which he renamed Warwick and in which he lived peaceably the rest of his life.

GOSNOLD, BARTHOLOMEW (*fl. 1572–1607*), navigator, colonizer. Made a landfall in the *Concord* on the southern Maine coast, 1602; standing southward, he landed on a foreland which he named Cape Cod, traversed Nantucket Sound, erected a small fort on Cuttyhunk, and searched for a western passage. On returning to England with a cargo of furs, cedar, and sassafras, Gosnold tried to interest others in American settlement. Late in 1606 he sailed as vice admiral of the fleet in command of the *God Speed*, which carried 52 of the Virginia Co. pioneers; they landed at Cape Henry in April 1607. As a member of the council for the colony, he opposed the selection of the island site in the James River for a settlement, but was overruled, and there Jamestown was founded. He died there in August that same year.

GOSS, ALBERT SIMON (*b. Rochester, N.Y., 1882; d. New York, N.Y., 1950*), businessman, agricultural leader. Raised in Spokane, Wash., and Portland, Oreg. Engaged in flour-milling and other businesses until 1914, when he took up dairy farming and became active in the Grange. He was master of the Washington State Grange, 1922–33. As director of the Federal Land Bank in Spokane, 1927–33, he drafted a program of cooperative farm credit that subsequently became a model for the Farm Credit Administration (FCA). He served as land bank commissioner of the FCA, 1933–40. Elected master of the National Grange, 1941, he was a critic of the World War II price-control program; during the postwar years, he opposed farm programs that restricted production in order to maintain prices in the midst of acute world food shortages. Believed that farmers had right to produce abundantly and still get fair prices.

GOSS, JAMES WALKER (*b. Albemarle Co., Va., 1812; d. Piedmont, Va., 1870*), minister of the Disciples of Christ, educator.

GOSSETT, BENJAMIN BROWN (*b. Williamstown, S.C., 1884; d. Charlotte, N.C., 1951*), cotton textile executive. Studied at Clemson College and the U.S. Naval Academy. Commissioned in the marines, 1905. President of several cotton mills, including the family-owned Gossett Mills and Dan River Mills. In the mid-1920's, helped from the Cotton Textile Institute, which helped to stabilize the industry throughout the country; vice president, 1931–33.

GOSTELOWE, JONATHAN (*b. Passyunk, Pa., 1744; d. Philadelphia, Pa., 1795*), cabinetmaker, Revolutionary soldier. Worked in mahogany and walnut, displaying considerable originality at a time when English models were paramount.

GOTSHALL, WILLIAM CHARLES (*b. St. Louis, Mo., 1870; d. 1935*), engineer, specialist in electric railroad work.

GOTTHEIL, GUSTAV (*b. Pinne, Prussia, 1827; d. 1903*), rabbi. Ministered at Temple Emanu-el, New York, 1873–99. Outstanding in the transition of Reform Jewry from German to American standards.

GOTTHEIL, RICHARD JAMES HORATIO (*b. Manchester, England, 1862; d. New York, N.Y., 1936*), Semitics scholar, Zionist leader. Son of Gustav Gottheil. Came to America, 1873. Graduated Columbia, 1881; Ph.D., Leipzig, 1886. Taught at Columbia, 1886–1936; chief, Oriental Division, New York Public Library, 1896–1936.

GOTTSCHALK, LOUIS MOREAU (*b. New Orleans, La., 1829; d. Tijuca, Brazil, 1869*), pianist, composer. Trained in Paris; a pupil and friend of Berlioz, with whom he later gave a series of concerts. Chopin commented favorably on his debut in 1845. Successful European tours included a triumph in Madrid, 1851, where the queen of Spain decorated him. In 1853 he returned to America. Brilliant New York seasons followed and equal success in tours throughout the United States, Canada, Panama, and South America. A prolific composer, largely in bravura style, he was notable, too, as a brilliant performer, decidedly the best American pianist of his period.

GOUCHER, JOHN FRANKLIN (*b. Waynesburg, Pa., 1845; d. 1922*), Methodist clergyman, philanthropist. Pastor in Baltimore, Md. A principal benefactor of Woman's College of Baltimore (later Goucher College) and its second president, 1890–1908. Supported many Far Eastern missions.

GOUDY, FREDERIC WILLIAM (*b. Bloomington, Ill., 1865; d. Marlboro, N.Y., 1947*), lettering artist, type designer, printer. Taught himself bookkeeping, lettering, and the arrangement of type for advertising, while holding a variety of jobs, 1884–99; was coproprietor of an unsuccessful Chicago venture, the Camelot Press, 1895–96. Increasingly successful as a commercial letterer and designer of advertising, in 1903 he established the Village Press. He designed the Kennerley typeface, which brought him international recognition. In 1911 he formed the Village Letter Foundry to sell the 116 typefaces that he designed. From 1920 to 1940, he was art director of Lanston Monotype Machine Co. Author of several books and articles on his craft, he taught lettering at the Art Students League, New York, 1916–24, and graphic arts at New York University, 1927–29.

GOUDY, WILLIAM CHARLES (*b. Indiana, 1824; d. 1893*), lawyer. Raised in Jacksonville, Ill.; admitted to bar, 1847; removed to Chicago, 1859. Authority on real property law and commercial and constitutional law, he was retained in much heavy railroad litigation.

GOUGE, WILLIAM M. (*b. Philadelphia, Pa., 1796; d. Trenton, N.H., 1863*), U.S. treasury official, writer. Author of, among other works, *Short History of Money and Banking in the United States* (1833), in which he opposed banks, paper money, and corporations.

GOUGH, JOHN BARTHOLOMEW (*b. Sandgate, England, 1817; d. Frankford, Pa., 1886*), temperance lecturer.

GOULD, AUGUSTUS ADDISON (*b. New Ispwich, N.J., 1805; d. 1866*), physician, conchologist. Son of Nathaniel D. Gould. Graduated Harvard, 1825; M.D., Harvard Medical School, 1830. Author with Louis Agassiz of *Principles of Zoology* (1848), he was a constant contributor to scientific journals, writing chiefly on mollusks. His *Report on the Invertebrata of Massachusetts* (1841) was chief among his contributions to American science; for it, he penned beautiful illustrations. He also studied and reported on the mollusks obtained by the Wilkes Exploring Expedition and edited the first two volumes of Amos Binney's *Terrestrial Air-Breathing Mollusks*. No one except Thomas Say was more influential in developing the study of American conchology.

GOULD, BENJAMIN APTHORP (*b. Lancaster, Mass., 1787; d. Boston, Mass., 1859*), educator. Graduated Harvard, 1814. As principal of Boston Latin School, 1814–28, he made the school famous. Resigning for reasons of health, he became a successful merchant.

GOULD, BENJAMIN APTHORP (*b. Boston, Mass. 1824; d. Cambridge, Mass., 1896*), astronomer. Son of Benjamin A. Gould (1787–1859). Graduated Harvard, 1844; studied also at Berlin and Göttingen. Founded *Astronomical Journal*, 1849; was in charge of longitude department, U.S. Coast Survey, 1852–67. His observations of the stars in the southern heavens comprise his greatest work. This private project led to the establishment of a national observatory at Córdoba, Argentina, 1870. There, with unfaltering devotion and energy, aided by a corps of enthusiastic assistants, in the short space of 15 years he prepared zone catalogues of 73,160 stars and a general catalogue of 32,448 stars. He brought back photographs of the southern clusters in 1885, and their measurement and reduction occupied much of the last 10 years of his life.

GOULD, EDWARD SHERMAN (*b. Litchfield, Conn., 1805; d. New York, N.Y., 1885*), author. Son of James Gould. Wrote novels, sketches, comedies; also *Good English; or Popular Errors in Language* (1867).

GOULD, ELGIN RALSTON LOVELL (*b. Oshawa, Canada, 1860; d. near North Bay, Canada, 1915*), economist, reformer. Made important studies of production costs, wages, and family budgets for U.S. Department of Labor, 1887–92.

GOULD, GEORGE JAYU (*b. 1864; d. Menton, France, 1923*), financier, railroad executive. Son, and unsuccessful successor, of Jay Gould.

GOULD, GEORGE MILBRY (*b. Auburn, Maine, 1848; d. Atlantic City, N.J., 1922*), ophthalmologist, medical journalist. Friend and patron of Lafcadio Hearn.

GOULD, HANNAH FLAGG (*b. Lancaster, Mass., 1789; d. Newburyport, Mass., 1865*), poet. Sister of Benjamin A. Gould (1787–1859).

GOULD, JAMES (*b. Branford, Conn., 1770; d. 1838*), jurist, law teacher. Graduated Yale, 1791. In 1798, on completing course at Tapping Reeve's Litchfield, Conn., law school, he became Reeve's associate and had sole charge of the school, 1820–33.

GOULD, JAY (*b. Roxbury, N.Y., 1836; d. 1892*), financier. As a youth, learned rudiments of surveying and showed precocious skill in moneymaking. Keen-witted and unscrupulous, he traded first as a tanner and leather merchant and began speculating in railroads *post* 1860. His operations became spectacular when in 1867 with James Fisk he became a director of the Erie Railroad, of which Daniel Drew was treasurer and controlling agent. In the ensuing struggle for control with Cornelius Vanderbilt, Gould supplied the strategic imagination. Defying a court injunction, Gould, Fisk, and Drew broke Vanderbilt's attempted corner by flinging 50,000 Erie shares on the market in March 1868. Gould, by lavish bribes, then effected passage of a bill by the New York legislature legalizing the recent issue of Erie stock and forbidding union of the Erie and the New York Central. To the Gould-Fisk partnership were added Peter B. Sweeney and William M. Tweed as directors, Drew having withdrawn. They looted the Erie by huge stock-watering measures, carried out a daring raid on the credit, produce, and export markets, and in the fall of 1869 attempted to corner the gold market, bringing on the disastrous panic of Black Friday (Sept. 24). This excited general indignation, and litigation commenced over the sale of fraudulent Erie stock. After Fisk's death and the overthrow of the Tweed Ring, Gould was ejected from control of the Erie in March 1872. Between 1874 and 1879 he juggled control of the Union Pacific, Kansas Pacific, Denver Pacific, Central Pacific, and Missouri Pacific railroads. By threatening to extend the Kansas Pacific so as to form a new transcontinental railroad, he compelled the Union Pacific to consolidate with Kansas Pacific at par, then sold his Kansas Pacific stock, clearing an estimated $10 million. By 1890 he owned half of the railroad mileage in the Southwest. He also owned the New York *World*, 1879–83, was practically full owner of the New York City elevated railways by 1886, and controlled the Western Union Telegraph Co. Working almost to the end, he died of tuberculosis. As a young man, he had written *History of Delaware County, and Border Wars of New York* (1856). His hobby was gardening.

GOULD, NATHANIEL DUREN (*b. Bedford, Mass., 1781; d. Boston, Mass., 1864*), conductor, music teacher. Author of *Church Music in America* (1853).

GOULD, ROBERT SIMONTON (*b. Iredell Co., N.C. 1826; d. Austin, Tex., 1904*), jurist, Confederate soldier. Raised in Alabama; removed to Texas, 1850. Associate justice, state supreme court, 1874–82, and briefly chief justice. Professor of law, University of Texas, 1883–1904.

GOULD, THOMAS RIDGEWAY (*b. Boston, Mass., 1818; d. Florence, Italy, 1881*), sculptor.

GOULDING, FRANCIS ROBERT (*b. Midway, Ga., 1810; d. Roswell, Ga., 1881*), Presbyterian clergyman. Author of many books for boys, of which *Robert and Harold* (1852), later titled *The Young Marooners on the Florida Coast*, was extremely popular here and abroad.

GOUPIL, RENÉ (*b. Anjou, France*, ca. 1607; *d. Ossernenon, near present Auriesville, N.Y., 1642*), Jesuit lay brother, martyr. Companion of Father Isaac Jogues; slain by Iroquois after capture while journeying to the Huron missions. Beatified, 1925; canonized, 1930.

GOVAN, DANIEL CHEVILETTE (*b. Northampton Co., N.C., 1829; d. 1911*), planter, Confederate bridgadier general. Raised in Mississippi; settled in Arkansas, *post* 1853. Described by his division commander, P. R. Cleburne, as one of the best officers of the Confederate service.

GOVE, AARON ESTELLUS (*b. Hampton Falls, N.H., 1839; d. 1919*), educator, Union soldier. Graduated Illinois State Normal School, 1861. As Denver superintendent of schools, 1874–1904, he was educational leader and shaper of school policies in Colorado.

GOWANS, WILLIAM (*b. Lanarkshire, Scotland, 1803, d. New York, N.Y., 1870*), bibliophile, bookseller, publisher. Came to America, 1821. Starting with a bookstall on Chatham Street, New York, he was from 1863 to his death the "Antiquarian of Nassau Street," celebrated among collectors for the range of his stock and his interest in Americana.

GOWEN, FRANKLIN BENJAMIN (*b. Mount Airy* [*Philadelphia*], *Pa., 1836; d. Washington D.C., 1889*), lawyer, president of the Philadelphia & Reading Railroad. Procured investigation and trials of the "Molly Maguires," secret Pennsylvania terrorists, 1875–77.

GRABAU, AMADEUS WILLIAM (*b. Cedarburgh, Wis., 1870; d. Peking, China, 1946*), geologist, paleontologist. B.S., Massachusetts Institute of Technology, 1896; M.S., Harvard, 1898; D.Sc., Harvard, 1900. Taught geology at Tufts and Rensselaer Polytechnic Institute. Professor of paleontology, Columbia University, 1905–19, he was forced to leave because of his pro-German sentiments during World War I. *Post* 1920, he was professor of paleontology at the National University, Peking, and simultaneously chief paleontologist of the National Geological Survey of China. Interned by the Japanese during World War II. While at Columbia, he published many valuable studies on the stratigraphy of the Silurian and Devonian of the northeastern United States; he was also one of the first to write extensively on deltaic and continental sedimentation. His subsequent work in China, however, was of greater importance. Among his books were *Principles of Stratigraphy* (1913, 1924), *Stratigraphy of China* (1923, a basic work), and his summary of his pulsation hypothesis entitled *The Rhythm of the Ages* (1940).

GRABAU, JOHANNES ANDREAS AUGUST (*b. Olvenstedt, Prussia, 1804; d. 1879*), Lutheran clergyman. Persecuted in Germany, he was called to be pastor of an emigrant group which settled in Buffalo, N.Y., 1839. Organized Buffalo Synod and founded Martin Luther Seminary.

GRÄBNER, AUGUST LAWRENCE (*b. Frankentrost, Mich., 1849; d. St. Louis, Mo., 1904*), Lutheran theologian, historian. Professor in Wisconsin and Concordia seminaries.

GRACE, EUGENE GIFFORD (*b. Goshen, N.J., 1876; d. Bethlehem, Pa., 1960*), industrialist. Studied at Lehigh University. Executive for Bethlehem Steel from 1908; president, 1913–46; chairman of the board, 1946–57. A brilliant administrator, Grace led Bethlehem Steel through the transition from a small manufacturing concern to the nation's second-largest steelmaker and its largest shipbuilder.

GRACE, WILLIAM RUSSELL (*b. Queenstown, Ireland, 1832; d. 1904*), international merchant, capitalist. With his brother Michael, developed a prosperous trading firm in Callao, Peru. Organized W. R. Grace & Co., New York City, 1865, originally formed to serve as correspondent for the Peru company. As confidential adviser to the Peruvian government, between 1875 and 1879 Grace handled equipment of the army and navy and furnished munitions during war with Chile, 1879. After the unsuccessful outcome of the war he took over the Peruvian national debt, receiving huge concessions in return for funding it. The Grace firm opened offices in practically every Latin American country, establishing worldwide contacts in banking, importing, and exporting, and steamship operation. William R. Grace served as reform mayor of New York City, 1880–88.

GRACIE, ARCHIBALD (*b. New York, N.Y., 1832; d. Petersburg, Va., 1864*), Confederate soldier. Graduated West Point, 1854. Resigned commission, 1856, to enter business at Mobile,

Ala. Served with first Alabama troops to enter Confederate service; promoted brigadier general, 1862.

GRADLE, HENRY (*b. Friedberg, Germany, 1855; d. Santa Barbara, Calif., 1911*), ophthalmologist. Came to America, 1868. M.D., Northwestern University, 1874; studied also in Europe. Professor at Northwestern, 1879–1906. Author of *Bacteria and the Germ of Theory of Disease* (1883), the first book in English to deal with this subject.

GRADY, HENRY FRANCIS (*b. San Francisco, Calif. 1882; d. at sea, 1957*), diplomat, educator, businessman. Studied at St. Mary's University and at Columbia, Ph.D., 1927. Taught at the University of California from 1921 to 1937, becoming dean of the College of Commerce from 1928. After serving in several government positions, Grady was named vice-chairman of the U.S. Tariff Commission in 1937; in 1939, he became assistant secretary of state for general economic matters and trade agreements. He served until 1941. From 1941 to 1947, he was president of the American President Line; he was chairman of the Federal Reserve Bank of San Francisco from 1942 to 1947. In 1945, President Truman appointed him head of the American Section of the Allied Mission for Observing the Greek Elections of 1946. He next went to London as U.S. representative for the Committee on Palestine and Related Problems. From 1947 to 1948, he was the first American ambassador to India; from 1948 to 1950, ambassador to Greece; and from 1950 to 1951, ambassador to Iran. He was successful in overseeing the disbursement of U.S. aid to Greece during that country's difficulties with the Communists, but was denied similar support for his mission to Iran. He retired in 1951.

GRADY, HENRY WOODFIN (*b. Athens, Ga., 1850; d. Atlanta, Ga., 1889*), journalist, orator. Graduated University of Georgia, 1868. After newspaper experience in Georgia and New York, he was lent money by Cyrus W. Field to buy a fourth interest in the Atlanta *Constitution*, 1879. With his unerring sense for news, zeal for ordered progress, and faculty for writing in accord with popular taste, he did much to shatter postwar despair in the South. He encouraged development of local resources, diversification of crops; he also convinced his readers of the need for manufacturing and for a logical adjustment of the racial conflict. His address "The New South," delivered first in New York City, December 1886, expressed the gist of his creed and helped allay intersectional animosities.

GRAEBNER, AUGUST LAWRENCE. *See* GRÄBNER, AUGUST LAWRENCE.

GRAESSL, LAWRENCE (*b. Ruemannsfelden, Bavaria, 1753; d. Philadelphia, Pa., 1793*), Roman Catholic clergyman. Came to America, 1787, on urging of Rev. Ferdinand Farmer; served as assistant at St. Mary's, Philadelphia, and as missionary in Pennsylvania, Delaware, New Jersey. Chosen coadjutor to Bishop John Carroll, Father Graessl died of yellow fever before the formal appointment arrived.

GRAFF, EVERETT DWIGHT (*b. Clarinda, Iowa, 1885; d. Rome, Italy, 1964*), steel company executive, book collector, and philanthropist. Studied at Lake Forest College in Illinois (graduated, 1906). Joined Joseph T. Ryerson and Son steel company, 1906; named president in 1937. Ryerson became a subsidiary of Inland Steel Company in 1935; Graff was a director of both Ryerson and Inland until 1952. Trustee and president of the Art Institute of Chicago (1954–58) and the Newberry Library (1952–64). Bequeathed his extensive collection of Americana books to the Newberry library; the catalog of the Everett D. Graff Collection of Western Americana was published in 1968.

GRAFF, FREDERIC (*b. Philadelphia, Pa., 1817; d. Philadelphia, 1890*), engineer. Son of Frederick Graff, whom he succeeded as chief engineer of the Philadelphia water department.

GRAFF, FREDERICK (*b. Philadelphia, Pa., 1774; d. Philadelphia, 1847*), civil engineer. Associated with Philadelphia water system, 1797–1847; superintendent, *post* 1805. Responsible for the hydraulic system employed, virtually a pioneer effort.

GRAFFENRIED, CHRISTOPHER, BARON DE (*b. Bern, Switzerland, 1661; d. Bern, 1743*), adventurer, colonizer. Combined with Franz Ludwig Michel and Georg Ritter to bring Swiss emigrants and exiled German Palatines as colonists to North Carolina, 1710. A town, New Bern, was laid out, but the colony suffered a series of misfortunes. Graffenried secured a patent from Governor Spotswood of Virginia for lands on the upper Potomac in hope of finding silver and transplanting the New Bern settlers, but as Michel would not support the project and his own resources were exhausted, Graffenried returned to Bern, 1713.

GRAFLY, CHARLES (*b. Philadelphia, Pa., 1862; d. Philadelphia, Pa., 1929*), sculptor. Trained at Pennsylvania Academy of Fine Arts and in Paris, he won reputation as a sculptor of imaginative groups, portraitist and teacher. Among his finest works are the *Pioneer Mother Monument* designed 1915 for a location in San Francisco, Calif., and the heroic General Meade Memorial in Washington, D.C. Probably the foremost American sculptor of male portrait busts. Occupied the chair of sculpture at Pennsylvania Academy and Boston Museum of Fine Arts.

GRAFTON, CHARLES CHAPMAN (*b. Boston, Mass., 1830; d. Fond du Lac, Wis., 1912*), Episcopal clergyman. High Churchman; ordained, 1858. Associated in establishing Society of St. John the Evangelist (Cowley Fathers); founded Sisterhood of the Holy Nativity. Rector, Church of the Advent, Boston, Mass., 1872–88. Bishop of Fond du Lac, 1889–1912.

GRAHAM, CHARLES KINNAIRD (*b. New York, N.Y., 1824; d. Lakewood, N.J., 1889*), Union brigadier general, civil engineer.

GRAHAM, DAVID (*b. London, England, 1808; d. Nice, France, 1852*), lawyer. Brought to America as an infant. Author of *Treatise on the Practice of the Supreme Court of New York* (1832), a masterly text; one of the ablest New York advocates of his time.

GRAHAM, EDWARD KIDDER (*b. Charlotte, N.C., 1876; d. 1918*), educator. Graduated University of North Carolina, 1898. Taught in English department there, 1899–1913. As dean, acting president, and president, 1914–18, gave the university its characteristic social-mindedness, training students and public to consider state and community problems. The advances in education, health, public welfare, and industry which North Carolina made, 1910–30, were owing in large measure to the ideas which Graham urged.

GRAHAM, ERNEST ROBERT (*b. Lowell, Mich., 1866; d. 1936*), architect. Construction supervisor for the Chicago firm of Burnham and Root, *post* 1888; partner, 1894–1912. In 1917, with three former Burnham associates, established partnership of Graham, Anderson, Probst and White. The firm became the leading architects of commercial America, executing such notable commissions in Chicago as the Wrigley Building, Union Station, Post Office, Civic Opera, and Merchandise Mart, as well as civic and commercial buildings in other cities. Their work was predominantly classical in character, reflecting Daniel Burnham's influence. Graham's function was chiefly to organize and administer.

GRAHAM, EVARTS AMBROSE (*b. Chicago, Ill., 1883; d. St. Louis, Mo., 1957*), surgeon. Studied at Princeton, the University of Chicago, and the Rush Medical College, M.D., 1907. Professor and chairman of the department of surgery at Washington University in St. Louis (1919–51). The first surgeon to successfully remove a lung in the treatment of carcinoma (1933). Founded the American Board of Surgery in 1937; member of the National Academy of Sciences, 1941. His studies on the Empyema Commission and his development of the technique of cholecystography were major sources of his recognition.

GRAHAM, GEORGE REX (*b. Philadelphia, Pa., 1813; d. Orange, N.J., 1894*), editor, publisher. Issued first number of *Graham's Magazine* in January 1841, replacing the insipid contents then usual with a variety of original fiction, light essays, verse, biography, travel, art criticism, book notices, editorial chat, and tasteful engravings. He paid writers with unprecedented liberality and had a distinguished staff which included Edgar Allan Poe, R. W. Griswold, and Bayard Taylor. Success was immediate. Graham lived lavishly for a time, but his prosperity was short. By 1848 he had lost control of *Graham's*, though he remained editor. He bought back the magazine in 1850, but he lacked energy and it no longer flourished. He sold out for good in 1853.

GRAHAM, ISABELLA MARSHALL (*b. Lanarkshire, Scotland, 1742; d. 1814*), teacher, philanthropist. Settled in New York City, 1789, where she conducted a school. Active in charity, she promoted societies for relief of widows and orphans, which were among earliest formed in America.

GRAHAM, JAMES (*d. Morrisania, N.Y., 1700/01*), provincial official. Came to New York, 1678. Served as an alderman of the city and its first recorder, as attorney general and a judge of the province, and as Speaker of the first General Assembly of the province.

GRAHAM, JAMES DUNCAN (*b. Prince William Co., Va., 1799; d. Massachusetts, 1865*), army engineer. Graduated West Point, 1817. First assistant on S. H. Long's expedition to the Rockies, 1819–21. Distinguished himself in national border surveys, especially joint demarcation of United States and British provinces. Discovered lunar tide on Great Lakes.

GRAHAM, JOHN (*b. Scotland, ca. 1718; d. Naples, Italy, 1795*), merchant, planter, Loyalist. Came to Georgia, 1753. Served on council of province; was chosen lieutenant governor, 1776; in England 1776–79; resided in Georgia during British occupancy, 1779–82. After a short stay in East Florida, resided in London.

GRAHAM, JOHN (*b. Dumfries, Va., 1774; d. Washington, D.C., 1820*), diplomat. Secretary of Orleans Territory; Thomas Jefferson's confidential agent in thwarting of Aaron Burr's western designs. Chief clerk, U.S. Department of State, 1807–17; minister to Portugal, 1819.

GRAHAM, JOHN ANDREW (*b. Southbury, Conn., 1764; d. 1841*), lawyer. Practiced in New York City *post* 1805, mainly in criminal courts. Forced amendment of code, outlawing use of evidence obtained by private examination of accused persons without aid of counsel.

GRAHAM, JOSEPH (*b. Chester Co., Pa, 1759; d. 1836*), Revolutionary soldier, legislator. Removed to North Carolina as a child. After the Revolution, engaged in iron mining in Lincoln Co., N.C.

GRAHAM, PHILIP LESLIE (*b. Terry, S. Dak., 1915; d. Marshall, Va., 1963*), journalist and publisher. Studied at the University of Florida and Harvard Law School (graduated, 1939). A law clerk of the Supreme Court, 1939–40. Served in World War II; discharged a major in 1945. Married Katharine Meyer, daughter of Eugene and Agnes Ernst Meyer, owners of the *Washington Post*, in 1940. Became associate publisher and then publisher of the *Post* in 1946. With his father-in-law, purchased the *Washington Times-Herald* in 1954; the merger, probably the most successful in modern American journalism, brought the *Post* rapid increases in circulation and advertising, and journalistic influence in national affairs. Graham's personal journalistic influence was at its height when his close friends John F. Kennedy and Lyndon B. Johnson gained the White House in 1960. Acquired *Newsweek* magazine in 1961. Suffered from bouts of depression from 1957; his death was by suicide.

GRAHAM, SYLVESTER (*b. West Suffield, Conn., 1794; d. Northampton, Mass. 1851*), reformer. Began as a temperance lecturer *ca.* 1830, but was soon preaching on biblical subjects, health, personal hygiene, and comparative anatomy. He advocated coarsely ground whole wheat (Graham) flour for bread, hard mattresses, open bedroom windows, cold showers, looser and lighter clothing, daily exercise, vegetables, fresh fruits, rough cereals, pure drinking water, and cheerfulness at meals. He had many adherents, among them Horace Greeley, but his frankness shocked many others. Emerson referred to him as the "poet of bran bread and pumpkins" and he was widely lampooned. His influence waned *post* 1840.

GRAHAM, WILLIAM ALEXANDER (*b. Lincoln Co., N.C., 1804; d. Saratoga Springs, N.Y., 1875*), lawyer, statesman. Son of Joseph Graham. Graduated University of North Carolina, 1824. State legislator, 1833–40; U.S. senator, Whig, from North Carolina, 1840–43; governor, 1845–49. He was an excellent administrator. As secretary of the navy, 1850–52, he reorganized the coastal survey and the personnel of the navy, encouraged the exploration of the Amazon, and supported Perry's expedition to Japan.

After running for vice president on Gen. Winfield Scott's ticket, 1852, Graham returned home and was leader of the moderates in the state until his death. He condemned secession, and his position was so strong nationally that in 1860 New York and Pennsylvania electors were urged to vote for him in the electoral college so as to avert dissolution of the Union. When war came, he ceased to be a Union man, although as a Confederate senator, 1864, he worked toward peace. He remained always a trusted adviser in his state.

GRAHAM, WILLIAM MONTROSE (*b. District of Columbia, 1834; d. Annapolis, Md., 1916*), soldier. Son of James D. Graham. Artilleryman, with extensive record of able service in Army of the Potomac, on frontier duty, and in Spanish-American War.

GRAINGER, GEORGE PERCY (*b. Melbourne, Australia, 1882; d. White Plains, N.Y., 1961*), composer and pianist. Changed name to Percy Aldridge Grainger. Began concert career in London in 1901. Between 1905 and 1907, collected and notated a large body of folk tunes from England, Scotland, Denmark, the Faeroe islands, and Polynesia. By 1915 his compositions for orchestra were the most frequently performed in London of all British composers. Immigrated to the United States in 1914; naturalized in 1918. Associate professor and chairman of New York University's Department of Music, 1932–33. Reputation as an eccentric was underscored by his experiments with "free music," music lacking emphatic beats, with gliding intervals, greater dissonance, and independence of lines. Some of his more unusual pieces are "Random Round" (1913), "The Warriors" (1916), and "Tribute to Foster" (1916). Compositions in a more congenial vein include "Irish Tune from County Derry" (1918), "Children's March" (1919), "Shepherd's Hey" (1918), and "Lincolnshire Posy" (1937).

GRANDGENT, CHARLES HALL (*b. Dorchester, Mass., 1862; d. Cambridge, Mass., 1939*), Romance philologist. Graduated Harvard, 1883; studied also at Leipzig, at Paris, and in Spain. Professor of Romance languages, Harvard, 1886–89 and 1896–1932. Author of an excellent edition of the *Divina Commedia* (1933).

GRANDMA MOSES.   *See* MOSES, ANN MARY ROBERTSON.

GRANGER, ALFRED HOYT (*b. Zanesville, Ohio, 1867; d. Roxbury, Conn., 1939*), architect. Grandnephew of William T. and John Sherman. Graduated Kenyon, 1887; studied at Boston Technical Institute and in Paris. Employed in office of successors to Henry H. Richardson; practiced *post* 1893 in Cleveland, Chicago, and Philadelphia. Designer of Euclid Heights (Cleveland) and of the La Salle Street Station, Chicago; also of many other railroad stations in the West. An eclectic in design.

GRANGER, FRANCIS (*b. Suffield, Conn., 1792; d. Canandaigua, N.Y., 1868*), lawyer, legislator. Son of Gideon Granger. Prominent in New York Anti-Masonic movement; congressman, Whig, from New York, 1835–41 and 1842–43. U.S. postmaster general, 1841.

GRANGER, GIDEON (*b. Suffield, Conn., 1767; d. Canandaigua, N.Y., 1822*), lawyer, politician. As Connecticut legislator, took prominent part in passage of Common School Law, 1795; *post* 1798, led Democratic-Republican minority in the state. Became postmaster general, 1801, and successfully directed an expanding service until 1814.

GRANGER, GORDON (*b. Joy, N.Y., 1822; d. Santa Fe, N.Mex., 1876*), soldier. Graduated West Point, 1845. Served in Mexican War and at western frontier posts. As major general of volunteers, he rose to greatness in September 1863, when his surprise attack at Chickamauga drove back the Confederate forces encircling General Thomas' corps and saved the Union army from annihilation.

GRANGER, WALTER (*b. Middletown Springs, Vt., 1872; d. Lusk, Wyo., 1941*), paleontologist. A self-made scientist, Granger was associated with the American Museum of Natural History from 1890 until his death; *post* 1927, he held the rank of curator. In association with William D. Matthew and Albert Thomson, he revolutionized knowledge of the Age of Mammals in North America. He was best known for his work as second in command and chief paleontologist of the American Museum's Central Asiatic Expeditions, which explored the Gobi Desert.

GRANT, ALBERT WESTON (*b. East Benton, Maine, 1856; d. Philadelphia, Pa., 1930*), naval officer. Graduated Annapolis, 1877. In command of Atlantic Fleet submarine flotilla, 1915–17, he built up its efficiency, provided training schools, and established submarine bases at New London, Conn., and Coco Solo, Panama.

GRANT, ASAHEL (*b. Marshall, N.Y., 1807; d. Mosul, Turkey, 1844*), physician. Presbyterian missionary to the Nestorians of western Persia, 1835–44.

GRANT, CLAUDIUS BUCHANAN (*b. Lebanon, Maine, 1835; d. St. Petersburg, Fla., 1921*), Michigan jurist. Graduated University of Michigan, 1859. State circuit judge, 1881–89, celebrated for stern prosecution of criminals; judge of state supreme court, 1889–1910, and chief justice, 1898–99, 1908.

GRANT, FREDERICK DENT (*b. St. Louis, Mo., 1850, d. New York, N.Y., 1912*), soldier. Son of Ulysses S. Grant. Graduated West Point, 1871. Resigned from army, 1881, to enter business; served as U.S. minister to Austria-Hungary, 1889–93, and as commissioner of police, New York City, 1895–97. Distinguished in Philippine insurrection, 1899–1902, he thereafter held territorial commands as regular major general.

GRANT, GEORGE BARNARD (*b. Gardiner, Maine, 1849; d. Pasadena, Calif., 1917*), mechanical engineer. Graduated Lawrence Scientific School of Harvard, 1873. Invented "Grant's difference engine," a successful calculating machine (exhibited at Philadelphia, 1876); was a founder of the American gear-cutting industry.

GRANT, HARRY JOHNSTON (*b. Chillicothe, Mo., 1881; d. Milwaukee, Wis., 1963*), newspaper executive. Worked for N. W. Ayer and Son advertising agency, 1906–09. Sent to London as British representative of the Rubberset Brush Company, 1909–10. Manager of the American Viscose Company in Marcus Hook, Pa., 1910–12. Vice president of O'Mara and Ormsbee advertising agency, in charge of Chicago office, 1913–16. Advertising manager of the *Milwaukee Journal* in 1916; by 1919, vice president and treasurer of the Journal Company, a stockholder, one of three directors, and publisher. President and editor of the *Journal*, 1935–38; chairman of the board, 1938–63. Director of the Associated Press, 1940–41.

GRANT, JAMES BENTON (*b. Russell Co., Ala., 1848; d. Excelsior Springs, Mo., 1911*), metallurgist, banker. Prominent in Denver's civic and business life, he served as Colorado's first Democratic governor, 1883–85.

GRANT, JOHN THOMAS (*b. Greene Co., Ga., 1813; d. Atlanta, Ga., 1887*), capitalist. *Post* 1844, he developed one of greatest plantations in Georgia; also executed railway-building contracts throughout the South. After the Civil War, he took a prominent part in the growth of Atlanta as a business center.

GRANT, LEWIS ADDISON (*b. Winhall, Vt., 1829; d. 1918*), lawyer, Union soldier. Awarded Congressional Medal for action as brigade commander, Salem Heights, Va., 1863. Practiced law, *post* 1867, in Iowa and at Minneapolis, Minn. Assistant secretary of war, 1890–93.

GRANT, MADISON (*b. New York, N.Y., 1865; d. New York, 1937*), lawyer, naturalist, advocate of immigration restriction. Author of *The Passing of the Great Race* (1916).

GRANT, PERCY STICKNEY (*b. Boston, Mass., 1860; d. Mount Kisco, N.Y., 1927*), Episcopal clergyman. Graduated Harvard, 1883; Episcopal Seminary, Cambridge, 1886. Ordained, 1887. Controversial rector of the Church of the Ascension, New York, 1893–1924.

GRANT, ROBERT (*b. Boston, Mass., 1852; d. Boston, 1940*), jurist, novelist. Graduated Harvard, 1873; Ph.D., 1876; Harvard Law School, 1879. Author of *Unleavened Bread* (1900), *The Chippendales* (1909), and other works of a reforming tendency.

GRANT, ULYSSES SIMPSON (*b. Point Pleasant, Ohio, 1822; d. Mount McGregor, N.Y., 1885*), general of the armies, president of the United States. Son of Jesse Root Grant, a tanner, and Hannah Simpson. Baptized Hiram Ulysses Grant, he accepted the name by which he is known on entry at West Point, 1839, although it was an error of the congressman who appointed him. Upon graduation, 1843, rated as the best rider at the academy, he was assigned for duty with the 4th Infantry. He joined Gen. Zachary Taylor's army in Texas, 1845. Disliking military life and out of sympathy with aims of the Mexican War, he yet distinguished himself at Monterrey. Transferred to Gen. Winfield Scott's army, he marched to Mexico City and was mentioned for bravery. He married Julia Dent, 1848. In 1852 he left for the West Coast with his regiment and, by his energy and resource, prevented even greater loss of life than did occur in a terrible crossing of the Isthmus of Panama. Stationed first at Fort Vancouver, he was promoted to captain, 1853, and transferred to the dreary frontier post at Humboldt Bay, Calif. Lonely for his wife and children, whom he saw no prospect of supporting on his pay, he began to drink; warned by his commanding officer, he resigned from the army.

Unsuccessful in various occupations, the outbreak of the Civil War found him a clerk in his brothers' leather shop at Galena, Ill. His application to Washington for duty got no reply. Appointed colonel of the 21st Illinois Volunteers in June 1861, to his own surprise he was raised to brigadier general in August and given command of a district with headquarters at Cairo, Ill. Nearby Columbus, Ky., was the western end of a line held by Gen. A. S. Johnston to protect the Confederate supply depot at Nashville, Tenn. The line was strong in the flanks, but Fort Henry and Fort Donelson in the center were weak, and Grant proposed their capture to Gen. H. W. Halleck.

Grant took Fort Henry early in February 1862. On Feb. 13, he invested Donelson. A Confederate sortie drove back the Union right and center, but Grant attacked with his left and at the end of a day's fighting possessed the outer line of Confederate trenches. To a request for an armistice, he made his famous reply, "No terms except an unconditional and immediate surrender." The North greeted this victory joyfully, and Lincoln named Grant a major general of volunteers. The advance of Buell's force as well as Grant's caused the Confederates to concentrate at Corinth, Miss. Grant ordered a concentration of all his forces save one division at Pittsburg Landing. Although both Grant and his lieutenant, W. T. Sherman, knew that a superior Confederate force was only 22 miles away, they established no line of defense, set up no reconnaissance system and prepared no plan of action. The night before the battle of Shiloh, Grant telegraphed Halleck, "I have scarcely the faintest idea of an attack . . . being made upon us. . . ." Early in the morning of Apr. 6, 1862, the Confederates attacked and in desperate fighting drove the Union lines steadily back. Grant encouraged his men, but failed to direct the battle. The next day, Union reinforcements having arrived, the Confederates were forced to retreat toward Corinth. No major battle of the Civil War displayed less generalship or more courage on the part of the enlisted men than Shiloh. A storm of denunciation followed, but Lincoln refused to relieve Grant, saying, "I can't spare this man—he fights."

Grant redeemed himself in the Vicksburg campaign, where he was at his best. By capturing Vicksburg, the Union army would control the Mississippi and the Confederacy's only remaining railroad leading east from the river. After the failure of his first try in November 1862, Grant planned and executed in April 1863 one of the boldest movements in modern warfare. Abandoning his communications, he interposed his inferior force between the armies of J. E. Johnston and Pemberton, defeated both, and laid siege to Vicksburg, which surrendered on July 4. Ten days later, Port Hudson surrendered and the Confederacy was cut in two. Promoted to major general in the regular army, Grant proceeded in October to the relief of Rosecrans' army, shut up in Chattanooga. He opened up a supply line and set about at once to drive General Bragg from the approaches to the city. On Nov. 24, Hooker took the Confederate position on Lookout Mountain; that day and the next, Sherman and Thomas seized Missionary Ridge. Bragg was driven back to Dalton, Ga., where he entrenched. Grant received the thanks of Congress, a gold medal, the rank of lieutenant general, and command of all the Union armies.

As general in chief, Grant devised a sound strategy, provided a unity of plan and a concentration of effort. His aim was to cut the Confederacy into fragments, to engage all its armies at the same time, to destroy those armies by following them wherever they might go. He began simultaneous, coordinated movements: Meade's Army of the Potomac against Lee's army in Virginia; Butler's Army of the James against Lee's communications and Richmond; Sherman's Army of the Tennessee against J. E. Johnston's army and Atlanta.

Meade's army, hoping to pass Lee in the dense thickets of the Wilderness, was caught in a terrible battle there on May 5–7, 1864. Undeterred by appalling losses, Grant determined to march by Lee's right flank and interpose his army between him and Richmond. After Spotsylvania, North Anna, and more terrific losses at Cold Harbor, Grant realized he could not dislodge Lee from his position. By June 12, the Wilderness campaign had ended. Though Lee was undefeated and Grant outmaneuvered, the policy of attrition had worn down the enemy and robbed him of any initiative.

Grant withdrew from Lee's front and crossed the James River in a brilliant maneuver. Lee, deceived for four days, at last realized what was happening and brought his army south of Richmond. The long siege of Petersburg, Va., which followed left the Confederates drained of strength and in desperate need of food and transport. Meanwhile, Sherman was on the march through the rich lands of Georgia. Lee abandoned Petersburg on Apr. 2, 1865, and marched west, hoping to join J. E. Johnston, but Grant paralleled the march and blocked the retreat with cavalry. At Appomattox Court House on Apr. 9, Lee surrendered the Army of Northern Virginia on Grant's magnanimous terms. Johnston surrendered to Sherman on Apr. 26 and the Civil War was over.

Congress revived the rank of general, unused since 1799, and it was conferred on Grant, who served directly under Secretary of War Stanton and the president. Grant assumed the secretary's duties when Stanton was suspended by President Johnson in 1867; when the Senate restored Stanton, Grant surrendered the secretaryship, thereby winning Johnson's bitter enmity.

The inevitable Republican presidential nominee in 1868, Grant had no real party affiliation, disliked politics as he disliked war, and was reluctant to give up the lifetime salary of general. He accepted, however, and was elected. He ran his office like an army headquarters, for this was the only method he knew. His choice of cabinet officers was poor, and he passed around other posts with no reference to the Republican party or to popular feeling. On the positive side, however, he took steps to restore the public credit, fought inflation, and frustrated the efforts of gold gamblers and currency raiders. With the exception of his scheme to annex the Dominican Republic in 1869, he supported Secretary of State Hamilton Fish in a firm and wise foreign policy.

In the North and West, a Liberal Republican movement based on disapproval of Reconstruction policies and on a demand for reform in the national administration was growing in influence. Its first objective was the defeat of Grant in 1872, but Grant was easily reelected. Much galling criticism attended his second term. He dismissed capable advisers and continued to show a naive bad taste in his choice of personal associates. His defense of friends caught red-handed in graft and other corrupt practices further hurt his own reputation. Failing to understand why people did not wish him to undertake a third term, he retired without complaint and traveled with his family in Europe, 1877–79. Put forward for the nomination in 1880 by the Republican "Old Guard," he lost to James A. Garfield.

Grant's last years were overshadowed by poverty, misfortune, calumny, and illness. His income failed; he was exploited in business and humiliated by bankruptcy. Shortly before his death, his friends succeeded in reviving his office of general for his benefit. His *Personal Memoirs* (1885–86), one of the most successful of American books and a primary historical source, was written by him in the sickroom during the last year of his life.

GRANT, ZILPAH POLY. *See* BANISTER, ZILPAH POLLY GRANT.

GRASS, JOHN (*b. on the Grand River, S.Dak., 1837; d. near Fort Yates, S.Dak., 1918*), a chief of the Blackfoot (Sihasapa) Sioux. Warrior name, Charging Bear. Early distinguished as an orator, and in battle with the Crow and Mandan, he urged his people to take up settled occupations and strongly opposed war with the whites. After the conflicts of 1876–77 his influence became dominant. He defended Indian rights in many treaty councils and served for years as chief justice of the Court of Indian Offenses at Fort Yates.

GRASSELLI, CAESAR AUGUSTIN (*b. Cincinnati, Ohio, 1850; d. 1927*), manufacturing chemist, banker, philanthropist. Expanded activities of the family business, the Grasselli Chemical Co.; was one of the captains of industry who made Cleveland, Ohio, a manufacturing center.

GRASTY, CHARLES HENRY (*b. Fincastle, Va., 1863; d. London, England, 1924*), editor, publisher, newspaper owner. Warred against municipal corruption in Baltimore (Md.) *News* and *Sun*, 1892–1914. Toured war fronts, 1917, as special correspondent of *New York Times*.

GRATIOT, CHARLES (*b. Lausanne, Switzerland, 1752; d. 1817*), pioneer trader. Came to Canada, 1769. Settled at Cahokia in the Illinois country, 1777; with Father Pierre Gibault, helped George Rogers Clark secure allegiance of the Illinois settlers. Removed to St. Louis, Mo., 1781, and married half sister of Col. Auguste Chouteau. Associated *post* 1795 to his death with the first John Jacob Astor, he was the most widely known of the St. Louis traders.

GRATZ, BARNARD (*b. Langensdorf, Upper Silesia, 1738; d. Baltimore, Md., 1801*), merchant. Brother of Michael Gratz and his partner in business. Came to Philadelphia, Pa., 1754. As a "merchant venturer" did pioneer service in opening the West to trade. Laid cornerstone of first Philadelphia synagogue, 1782.

GRATZ, MICHAEL (*b. Langensdorf, Upper Silesia, 1740; d. Philadelphia, Pa., 1811*), merchant. Came to Philadelphia, Pa., 1759. Like his brother and partner, Barnard Gratz, he was active in coast and western trade and a supporter of the American cause in the Revolution.

GRATZ, REBECCA (*b. Philadelphia, Pa., 1781; d. 1869*), philanthropist. Daughter of Michael Gratz. Traditionally the original of Rebecca in Scott's *Ivanhoe*. Devoted her life to good causes. Helped found Philadelphia Orphan Society, 1815, and was its secretary for 40 years; founded Hebrew Sunday School Society, 1838, first of its kind in the United States, and served as president until 1864; inspired founding of the Jewish Foster Home.

GRAU, MAURICE (*b. Brünn, Austria, 1849; d. 1907*), theatrical and operatic impresario, best known for his brilliant management of the Metropolitan Opera, New York, 1898–1903.

GRAUPNER, JOHANN CHRISTIAN GOTTLIEB (*b. Verden, Hanover, Prussia, 1767; d. Boston, Mass., 1836*), musician. First oboist in Haydn's London orchestra, 1791–92, he immigrated to Canada, 1793. Settling finally in Boston, Mass., 1796, he opened a music store where he sold instruments, gave lessons, and published music. Gathering together amateur and professional instrumentalists, he organized the Philharmonic Society in 1810 or 1811 and directed its Saturday evening sessions. In response to demand for a permanent choral society, Graupner, Thomas Smith Webb, and Asa Peabody organized the Handel and Haydn Society, which gave its first concert in King's Chapel on Christmas, 1815.

GRAVENOR, JOHN. *See* ALTHAM, JOHN.

GRAVES, ALVIN CUSHMAN (*b. Washington, D.C., 1909; d. Del Norte, Colo., 1965*), nuclear physicist. Studied at the University of Virginia; Massachusetts Institute of Technology; and the University of Chicago (Ph.D., 1939). Taught at the University of Texas, 1939–42. Participated in the development of the first nuclear reactor, at the University of Chicago in 1942. In Los Alamos, N.Mex. from 1943, worked on the design and construction of nuclear weapons; present at the first nuclear weapon test in 1945. Deputy scientific director for the first weapons test series conducted by the Atomic Energy Commission (AEC) in 1948. From this time, head of the nuclear weapons testing division of the Los Alamos Scientific Laboratory, and chief scientist on nearly every nuclear weapons test conducted by the United States. Also supervised the testing of reactors for nuclear rocket propulsion and detection of foreign weapons tests. Served on advisory panels to government agencies, including the Committee of Senior Reviewers of the AEC and the Army Science Advisory Panel. Among his many honors was the Department of Defense Medal for Distinguished Service, 1965.

GRAVES, DAVID BIBB (*b. Hope Hull, Montgomery Co., Ala., 1873; d. Sarasota, Fla., 1942*), lawyer, politician. C.E., University of Alabama, 1893; LL.B., Yale, 1896. Owed political advancement to prominence in National Guard; served on Mexican border, 1916; commanded 117th U.S. Field Artillery in France during World War I. An adroit practical politician, he was elected governor of Alabama in 1926 and again in 1934; despite his membership in the Ku Klux Klan, he pursued a moderately progressive course in his first term, 1927–31, and an avowedly New Deal and liberal program in his second, 1935–39, winning a reputation as a notably progressive southern governor.

GRAVES, FREDERICK ROGERS (*b. Auburn, N.Y., 1858; d. Shanghai, China, 1940*), Episcopal clergyman. Missionary in China, *post* 1881. Consecrated bishop of Shanghai, 1893; resigned, 1937.

GRAVES, JAMES ROBINSON (*b. Chester, Vt., 1820; d. Memphis, Tenn., 1893*), Baptist clergyman. Brother of Zuinglius C. Graves. Edited *Tennessee Baptist*; established Southern Baptist Sunday-School Union and Southern Baptist Publication Society. Author of *The Great Iron Wheel* (1855), a very popular tirade against Methodism.

GRAVES, JOHN TEMPLE (*b. Abbeville Co., S.C., 1856; d. Washington, D.C., 1925*), journalist, popular lecturer.

GRAVES, ROSEWELL HOBART (*b. Baltimore, Md., 1833; d. China, 1912*), Southern Baptist missionary in South China, 1856–1912.

GRAVES, WILLIAM PHILLIPS (*b. Andover, Mass., 1870; d. 1933*), gynecologist. Graduated Harvard Medical School, 1899. Chief surgeon, Hospital for Women, Brookline, Mass., 1908–33; professor, Harvard Medical, 1911–32. Author of *Gynecology* (1916).

GRAVES, WILLIAM SIDNEY (*b. Mount Calm, Tex., 1865; d. Shrewsbury, N.J., 1940*), army officer. Graduated West Point, 1889; appointed, 1909, to the General Staff; promoted to major general, 1918. In 1918–20, commanded American Expeditionary Force in Siberia. His troops achieved the limited objective of deterring Japan from dismembering Russia's Far Eastern possessions. Graves wrote of his controversial mission in *America's Siberian Adventure* (1931).

GRAVES, ZUINGLIUS CALVIN (*b. Chester, Vt., 1816; d. 1902*), educator. Brother of James R. Graves. First president of Mary Sharp College, Winchester, Tenn., 1850–96, where he maintained a degree of scholastic integrity nearly unique among U.S. women's schools of that period.

GRAVIER, JACQUES (*b. Moulins, France, 1651; d. Mobile, colony of Louisiana, 1708*), Jesuit priest. Went to Canada, 1685. Assistant to Father Allouez on mission to the Illinois, 1688–89; on Allouez's death in the latter year, became vicar general of the mission, ministering to Kaskaskia, Peoria, and Miami tribes. Superior of western missions, *ca.* 1696–1699, and in Louisiana colony, 1700–02, he returned to the Illinois, where he labored until 1705.

GRAY, ASA (*b. Sauquoit, N.Y., 1810; d. Cambridge Mass., 1888*), botanist. Graduated Fairfield (N.Y.) Medical School, 1831; influenced in choice of botany as a lifework by James Hadley, Lewis C. Beck, John Torrey. Between 1831 and 1835, Gray made a series of botanical journeys, taught, served as Torrey's assistant. His first independent publication, the *North American Gramineae and Cyperaceae* (1834–35), was followed by *Elements of Botany* (1836). He became curator of the New York Lyceum of Natural History and collaborated with Torrey on their *Flora of North America* (published, 1838–40, 1841–43). Having accepted the professorship of botany at the University of Michigan, then being organized, he went to Europe, 1838, to purchase books for the university and to study plants for the *Flora*. He never assumed his duties at the University of Michigan. In 1842 his *Botanical Text-Book* (later called *Structural Botany*) was published, the first of many editions. Its lucid text and telling illustrations from pen drawings by Isaac Sprague became the model for many imitations. He became Fisher professor of natural history at Harvard in the summer of 1842 and held the chair until his death. He created the Department of Botany and trained many eminent botanists of the next generation. To the *American Journal of Science* he contributed reviews, bibliographical notes, news items, and short biographies which constitute an authoritative, readable, detailed history of botany extending over 50 years. His important textbooks—*First Lessons in Botany and Vegetable Physiology* (1857); *How Plants Grow* (1858); *Field, Forest and Garden Botany* (1868); *How Plants Behave* (1872); and another *Elements of Botany* (1887)—did immense service in popularizing botany.

Gray was a pioneer and master in the field of plant geography. His monograph on the botany of Japan and its relations to that of the North Temperate Zone (1859) probably did more than any other one production to give Gray his worldwide reputation. His greatest achievement, however, was his elaboration of the descriptive botany of North America. Most of his more than 350 books, monographs, and shorter papers deal with portions of this vast subject. Most notable were the *Manual of the Botany of the Northern United States* (1848), the most widely used of all his books; *Genera Florae Americae Boreali-Orientalis Illustrata*; and *Synoptical Flora of North America*. He also elaborated the collections of the Wilkes Exploring Expedition (Vol. 15, 1854–75; Vol. 17, 1874). In such work Gray was at the height of his genius.

Charles Darwin wrote Gray the famous letter (Sept. 5, 1857) in which he first outlined his theory of the evolution of species by means of natural selection. Gray became Darwin's chief American advocate but, wiser than others in his time, refused to accept Darwinism as a sort of scientific religion and reached conclusions about variations which looked forward to the discoveries of Mendel and De Vries.

Gray received honorary degrees from Oxford, Cambridge, and Aberdeen. He was a founder of the National Academy of Sciences; president, 1863–73, of the American Academy of Arts and Sciences; president, 1872, of the American Association for the Advancement of Science; regent, 1874–88, of the Smithsonian Institution. He belonged to many learned and scientific societies, ranging from the Royal Society of London to the Polk County Agricultural Society of Iowa. Everywhere he was beloved for his simplicity, good humor, and friendliness, as well as revered for qualities that made him one of the great botanists of the world.

GRAY, CARL RAYMOND (*b. Princeton, Ark., 1867; d. Washington, D.C., 1939*), railway executive. President, Great Northern, 1912–14; Western Maryland, 1914–19; Union Pacific, 1920–37. Director, U.S. Railroad Administration, World War I.

GRAY, ELISHA (*b. Barnesville, Ohio, 1835; d. near Boston, Mass., 1901*), inventor. Partner with E. M. Barton in Gray & Barton, 1872–74; retired to devote whole time to electrical research. He had already invented an automatic self-adjusting telegraphic relay, a telegraph switch and annunciator, a private telegraph line printer, and a telegraphic repeater. From his system of electroharmonic telegraphy for transmitting musical tones (patented 1875) grew the idea of transmitting vocal sounds. On Feb. 14, 1876, Gray filed a caveat with the Patent Office a few hours after Alexander Graham Bell filed a patent application for a speaking telephone. A bitter infringement battle followed; Bell's patent was sustained. Gray continued to invent electrical devices and obtained some 70 patents of which the most important was the telautograph (1888, 1891).

GRAY, FRANCIS CALLEY (*b. Salem, Mass., 1790; d. 1856*), Harvard benefactor, lawyer, Massachusetts legislator. Son of William Gray.

GRAY, GEORGE (*b. New Castle, Del., 1840; d. 1925*), jurist. Graduated Princeton, 1859. Attorney general of Delaware, 1879–85; U.S. senator, Democrat, 1885–99; U.S. circuit court judge, 1899–1914. His reputation rests on his skill and tact as an arbitrator both in domestic and international disputes. Perhaps the outstanding accomplishment of his later career was the successful settlement of the Pennsylvania coal strike of 1902.

GRAY, GEORGE ALEXANDER (*b. Mecklenburg Co., N.C., 1851; d. 1912*), cotton manufacturer. Developed Gastonia, N.C., *post* 1888, into an important cotton town.

GRAY, GILDA (*b. Cracow, Poland, 1899; d. Hollywood, Calif., 1959*), dancer and entertainer. Immigrated to the U.S. in 1907. Known as the "Queen of Shimmy," Gray performed in leading revues in New York City and in vaudeville; her movies include *Piccadilly* (1919) and *Aloma of the South Seas* (1926). Though spectacularly successful in the 1920's, Gray died penniless in Hollywood.

GRAY, GLEN ("SPIKE") (*b. Metamora, Ill., 1900; d. Plymouth, Mass., 1963*), saxophonist and orchestra leader. Studied at the American Conservatory of Music in Chicago and also studied music at Illinois Wesleyan University. An original member of the Casa Loma Orchestra, which more than any other single orchestra set the stage for the big band era. President of the Casa Loma Orchestra Corporation, 1929–42. Leader of the Casa Lomans from 1937 to his retirement in 1950. The orchestra's best known records include "No Name Jive," "Casa Loma Stomp," and the band's theme song, "Smoke Rings." Through Gray's business ability, the band gained a wide following, playing extensive national tours, the "Burns and Allen Radio Show" (1938), and in the motion pictures *Time Out for Rhythm* (1941) and *Gals, Inc.*, (1943). The band also enjoyed success with a large and steady sale of phonograph records, featuring among others trumpeter Louis Armstrong, vocalists Mildred Bailey, Connie Boswell, and Lee Wiley, pianist Frankie Carle, and pianist-composer Hoagy Carmichael.

GRAY, HAROLD LINCOLN (*b. Kankakee, Ill., 1894; d. La Jolla, Calif., 1968*), cartoonist. Created comic strip *Little Orphan*

Annie, which was widely syndicated from 1924. Also produced about a dozen *Annie* books from 1926 through the late 1940's. Gray was tagged an "ultraconservative"; his views made evident through a leading character, Daddy Warbucks. "Communists" and "Democrats" were often indistinguishable epithets in Annie's vocabulary. At the time of Gray's death, Little Orphan Annie, with her frizzy hair and magnetic eyes, had become and American institution.

GRAY, HENRY PETERS (*b. New York N.Y., 1819; d. 1877*), portrait and genre painter. Pupil of Daniel Huntington. Worked according to strict academic canons.

GRAY, HORACE (*b. Boston, Mass., 1828; d. 1902*), jurist. Grandson of William Gray. Graduated Harvard, 1845; admitted to the bar, 1851. An original Free-Soiler, interested in pre–Civil War political conflicts, Gray was appointed associate justice of the Massachusetts Supreme Judicial Court, 1864. In 1873 he became chief justice and during 18 years on the bench wrote far more than his share of the court's published opinions. Appointed to the U.S. Supreme Court, 1881, he was preeminent in his knowledge of former decisions and of the history and development of legal doctrine. His judicial opinions were characterized by a critical and chronological examination of all important decisions bearing on the question at issue.

GRAY, ISAAC PUSEY (*b. Chester Co., Pa., 1828; d. Mexico, 1895*), lawyer, Union soldier. Raised in Ohio; removed to Indiana, 1855. Republican state legislator, 1868–72; Democratic governor of Indiana, 1880–81, 1885–89; U.S. minister to Mexico, 1893–95.

GRAY, JOHN CHIPMAN (*b. Brighton, Mass., 1839; d. 1915*), lawyer, Union soldier, author, teacher. Grandson of William Gray. Graduated Harvard, 1859; Harvard Law School, 1861. Entered partnership in Boston with John C. Ropes, *ca.* 1866. Lecturer, Harvard Law School, 1869–75. Appointed the Story professor of law, 1875, he was transferred to Royall professor, 1883, and held that chair until 1913 when he retired. Gray became the most brilliant exponent of the new case system of legal instruction. He was also the foremost U.S. authority on the law of real property. Among his few but outstanding books were *The Rule Against Perpetuities* (1886); *Select Cases . . . on the Law of Property* (1888–92); and *The Nature and Sources of the Law* (1909).

GRAY, JOHN PURDUE (*b. Center Co., Pa., 1825; d. 1886*), physician, alienist. M.D., University of Pennsylvania, 1849. As superintendent, New York State Lunatic Asylum, Utica, 1854–86, Gray became known as the leading alienist of his day in America. More than any other one man he improved conditions for the insane, insisting on fresh air and exercise, abandoning as far as possible mechanical restraint and solitary feeding, and revolutionizing asylum construction. His asylum became a sort of postgraduate school for training alienists.

GRAY, JOSEPH W. (*b. Bridport, Vt., 1813; d. 1862*), journalist. Owner and editor of the Cleveland *Plain Dealer*, 1842–62. A witty, trenchant writer and a pioneer in use of cartoons.

GRAY, ROBERT (*b. Tiverton, R.I., 1755; d. at sea, 1806*), navigator, fur trader. Sailing from Boston, September 1787, in the sloop *Lady Washington*, with the *Columbia* under Capt. John Kendrick, Gray made the northwest coast, succeeded to command of the *Columbia*, gathered a cargo of sea-otter skins. and returned home by way of China, arriving at Boston harbor in August 1790. He had sailed almost 42,000 miles and had carried the American flag around the world for the first time. After a refit, the *Columbia* sailed again in September 1790, arriving at Vancouver Island in June 1791. In the spring of 1792, Gray sailed his ship through the

difficult passage at the mouth of the Columbia River and made an effectual discovery of that river; this later served as foundation of the U.S. claim to Oregon. He returned home again by way of China, arriving at Boston, July 1793.

GRAY, WILLIAM (*b. Lynn, Mass., 1750 o.s.; d. Boston, Mass., 1825*), merchant, shipowner. Prospered in privateering during Revolution; was among first Salem merchants to trade with Russia, China, India. Broke with Federalists on the Embargo of 1807; was Democratic-Republican lieutenant governor of Massachusetts, 1810–12.

GRAY, WILLIAM SCOTT, JR. (*b. Coatsburg, Ill., 1885; d. Wolf, Wyo., 1960*), educator. Studied at Illinois State Normal University, the University of Chicago, Ph.D., 1916, and at Columbia University. Taught at the University of Chicago from 1917 to 1931; dean of the College of Education from 1917. An early exponent of the "sight method" of reading instruction, Gray was the author of the "Dick and Jane" reading texts which became the basic elementary reading texts in the U.S. and Canada for over half a century.

GRAYDON, ALEXANDER (*b. Bristol, Pa., 1752; d. Philadelphia, Pa., 1818*), Revolutionary soldier. Author of *Memoirs of a Life* (1811), one of the best-known and most valuable historical sources for the Revolutionary period.

GRAYSON, WILLIAM (*b. Prince William Co., Va., 1736[?]; d. Dumfries, Va., 1790*), lawyer, Revolutionary soldier. Aide to George Washington, and on active service, 1776–79; commissioner of Board of War, 1779–81. Served in Virginia legislature; member, Continental Congress, 1785–87. Opposed U.S. Constitution as inimical to southern interests. U.S. senator, Antifederal, from Virginia, 1789–90.

GREATHOUSE, CLARENCE RIDGEBY (*b. Kentucky, ca. 1845; d. Seoul, Korea, 1899*), lawyer, diplomat. Legal adviser to Korean government, 1890–99.

GREATON, JOHN (*b. Roxbury, Mass., 1741; d. Roxbury, 1783*), trader, Revolutionary soldier. Distinguished at siege of Boston, and as colonel, 24th Continental Infantry. Promoted brigadier general, 1783. One of the memorialists to Congress on dissatisfaction of army, 1782.

GREATON, JOSEPH (*b. London, England, 1679; d. Bohemia, Md., 1753*), Jesuit priest. Came to America, *ca.* 1720; first Roman Catholic pastor in Pennsylvania, 1729–49. Built St. Joseph's Church, Philadelphia.

GREELEY, HORACE (*b. Amherst, N.H., 1811; d. 1872*), editor, political leader. Learned printer's trade as apprentice in office of *Northern Spectator*, East Poultney, Vt.; went to New York City as journeyman 1831; formed partnership in printing shop with F. V. Story, 1833, later with Jonas Winchester. Founded with Winchester, 1834, the *New Yorker*, a nonpartisan literary and news weekly which achieved a good circulation but lost money. Married Mary Y. Cheney, 1836. Augmented his income by writing for Whig newspapers and edited the *Jeffersonian* (1838), a Whig campaign weekly which ran a year and exercised real influence. Greeley acquired important political friendships, notably with Thurlow Weed and William H. Seward, and in 1840 published a second Whig weekly, the *Log Cabin*, which gained unprecedented success.

As no Whig penny paper existed in New York, nor any paper offering a choice between the sensationalism of Bennett's *Herald* and the staidness of Bryant's *Evening Post*, Greeley launched his *New York Tribune* on Apr. 10, 1841. After a few anxious days, subscriptions poured in. Greeley labored tirelessly and had the efficient aid of Thomas McElrath as business manager to give the establishment system and to free the editor from routine. The *Tribune* was the best all-round paper in the city by 1846. Its energy in news-gathering, good taste, high morals, and intellectual appeal set a new standard. Editorials were vigorous but temperate, political news exact, book reviews numerous.

Greeley's own radical views were expressed fearlessly in his paper. He was an egalitarian, despising and fearing monopoly of any kind and class dominance; he espoused Fourierism and the agrarian movement; he supported cooperative shops and labor unions, opposed capital punishment, urged restrictions on liquor-selling. A free-trader by conviction, he supported high tariffs as the best means to that end, an apparent paradox. Assisted by a liberal, versatile staff, which included Charles A. Dana, Margaret Fuller, Bayard Taylor, George Ripley, and J. S. Pike, he made the *Tribune* a popular teacher, champion, and moral leader with unrivaled national influence. The greatest element in this success was Greeley's own moral earnestness and interpretive and editorial gifts. Throughout the 1850's, the paper concentrated on the Free-Soil movement. Greeley opposed slavery as immoral and uneconomic; the fight over the Kansas-Nebraska Act aroused his greatest eloquence. Among the first editors to join the Republican party, he insisted on the importance of the Union and strongly attacked Know-Nothingism.

As a public figure Greeley was regarded with a mixture of admiration and affectionate amusement. His mild pink face, fringed by throat whiskers, his broad-brimmed hat, white overcoat, crooked cravat, his shambling gait and absentminded manner were widely caricatured. His naïveté on many subjects and his homely wisdom on others appealed to millions. Some of his phrases, like "Go West, young man," were universally current. By signing many editorials and frequently appearing in public as a lecturer, he gave his work a direct appeal unusual in journalism. His principal defect of character was a thirst for political office which led him to unwise and undignified actions.

At the coming of the Civil War, he supported the Union energetically; his primary demand was that no concessions be made to slavery. Allying himself with the radical antislavery element, he warred against Democrats and moderates. He opposed Lincoln's policy of conciliating the border states and demanded early emancipation. His reputation and influence were injured by his hesitation to support Lincoln in 1864. His peace activities of 1864–65 were even more ill advised and gave people a poor opinion of his judgment. His radical views extended to Reconstruction policies as well; he believed in full black equality and endorsed the 14th and 15th amendments, yet he favored general amnesty, advocated Jefferson Davis' release from custody, and signed his bond.

At first a supporter of U. S. Grant, by 1870 Greeley was critical of the president's public policies and of his support of the Conkling-Cornell machine in New York. Gradually convinced that Grant's administration was demoralized and corrupt, Greeley and the *Tribune* declared against renomination in September 1871; Greeley also encouraged the movement for a new party. As the Liberal Republican movement grew and a coalition with the Democrats seemed possible, he agreed to be a presidential candidate and was nominated by the Liberal Republicans at Cincinnati, Ohio, in May 1872. A disputed Democratic convention endorsed Greeley, but many Democrats bolted. The campaign was exceptionally abusive. Greeley took the merciless attacks on himself much to heart. After a strenuous speaking tour in which he urged full reconciliation of North and South for achievement of reforms, he carried only six states and was profoundly hurt by the feeling that he was "the worst beaten man who ever ran for high office." Shortly after the campaign, Greeley's wife died. The final blow came when on returning to the *Tribune* he found Whitelaw Reid

firmly in charge and realized he had practically, if not nominally, lost the editorship which had been his lifelong pride. His body and mind broke and he died insane.

GREELY, ADOLPHOUS WASHINGTON (*b. Newburyport, Mass., 1844; d. Washington, D.C., 1935*), soldier, explorer, scientist, author. Rose from private to brevet major in important Civil War engagements; remained in army and became major general, 1906. Commanded U.S. expedition for study of Arctic weather and climate, 1881–84; of the ill-fated *Proteus* expedition to Lady Franklin Bay, only six of the participants reached home. Although Greely was at first blamed for the failure, he eventually was honored for his sound judgment under trying conditions. His book *Three Years of Arctic Service* (1885) was a popular account of the adventure.

GREEN, ALEXANDER LITTLE PAGE (*b. Sevier Co., Tenn., 1806; d. 1874*), Methodist clergyman. Influential in locating Southern Methodist publishing houses in Nashville, Tenn., 1854.

GREEN, ANDREW HASWELL (*b. Worcester, Mass., 1820; d. New York, N.Y., 1903*), lawyer. Partner of Samuel J. Tilden. Commissioner and planner of Central Park, New York City; as New York City comptroller, 1871–76, straightened out city finances. Conceived and carried through consolidation of Greater New York.

GREEN, ANNA KATHARINE. *See* ROHLFS, ANNA KATHARINE GREEN.

GREEN, ASA (*b. Ashby, Mass., 1789; d. ca. 1837*), physician, novelist, bookseller. Author of *The Perils of Pearl Street* (1834) and other satires.

GREEN, ASHBEL (*b. Hanover, N.J., 1762; d. Philadelphia, Pa., 1848*), Presbyterian clergyman. Son of Jacob Green (1722–90). Graduated College of New Jersey (Princeton), 1783. Minister of Second Presbyterian Church, Philadelphia, 1787–1812; held many offices in the work of his denomination, and was author of its 1818 declaration against slavery. Composed the plan of Princeton Theological Seminary; served as president of Princeton, 1812–22.

GREEN, BARTHOLOMEW (*b. Cambridge, Mass., 1666; d. Boston, Mass., 1732*), printer, journalist. Chief printer in New England, 1692–1732; printed *Boston News-Letter* from 1704.

GREEN, BENJAMIN EDWARDS (*b. Elkton, Ky., 1822; d. near Dalton, Ga., 1907*), lawyer, diplomat, promoter. Son of Duff Green. After diplomatic experience in Mexico and the West Indies, associated himself in his father's enterprises and was active in industrial development of Georgia. Wrote and translated works on currency and economics.

GREEN, BERIAH (*b. Preston, Conn., 1795; d. Whitesboro, N.Y., 1874*), Congregational clergyman, abolitionist. President of Philadelphia convention which formed American Anti-Slavery Society, 1833; president, Oneida Institute, 1833–43.

GREEN, DUFF (*b. Woodford Co., Ky., 1791; d. near Dalton, Ga., 1875*), journalist, politician, industrial promoter. Prospered as land speculator and merchant in St. Louis, Mo., *post* 1816; admitted to bar, he built up a large practice and was among most influential members of Missouri constitutional convention. Removing to Washington, D.C., 1825, he became editor-publisher of the *United States Telegraph*, an outstanding Democratic leader and a member of Jackson's "Kitchen Cabinet." He followed J. C. Calhoun in his split with Jackson; however, although a radical states' rights man, he opposed extreme nullification views. In

1832, he supported Henry Clay and thereafter stood with the Whigs. In England, 1842–44, he served an an unofficial U.S. agent, seeking to secure commercial treaties, lower duties, direct trade with the South. An expansionist, he welcomed the Mexican War; both before and after the Civil War (during which he conducted ironworks for the Confederacy), he was engaged in developing coal and iron lands and railroads. In the postbellum period, he was especially active in raising capital for reconstruction of the South's economy.

GREEN, FRANCES HARRIET WHIPPLE (*b. Smithfield, R.I., 1805; d. Oakland, Calif., 1878*), author, reformer. Active on behalf of temperance, labor, suffrage, abolition, spiritualism.

GREEN, FRANCIS (*b. Boston, Mass., 1742 o.s.; d. Medford, Mass., 1809*), soldier, merchant, Loyalist. First American to write on methods for instructing the deaf and mute (1783, 1801).

GREEN, FRANCIS MATHEWS (*b. Boston, Mass., 1835; d. Albany, N.Y., 1902*), naval officer, hydrographer. Grandson of Francis Green. Led expeditions, 1876–82, to West Indies, South and Central America, China, Japan, and East Indies to determine longitude by exchange of telegraphic time signals.

GREEN, GABRIEL MARCUS (*b. New York, N.Y., 1891; d. 1919*), mathematician. Graduated College of the City of New York, 1911; Ph.D., Columbia, 1913. Author of a work on projective differential geometry and other papers which showed great promise.

GREEN, HENRIETTA HOWLAND ROBINSON (*b. New Bedford, Mass., 1834; d. New York, N.Y., 1916*), financier. In managing a large inherited fortune, she became known as a Wall Street "character." Although she negotiated several "bull" movements, notably in railroad stocks, her Wall Street business was principally lending money. She was shrewd and eccentric, but the newspapers gave her an exaggerated reputation as a miser.

GREEN, HENRY WOODHULL (*b. Lawrenceville, N.J., 1804; d. 1876*), jurist. Brother of John C. Green. Graduated Princeton, 1820; practiced law in Trenton, N.J. Outstanding as chief justice, New Jersey Supreme Court, 1846–60; chancellor, and judge of prerogative court, 1860–66.

GREEN, HORACE (*b. Chittenden, Vt., 1802; d. Sing Sing, now Ossining, N.Y., 1866*), laryngologist. Graduated Castleton Medical College, M.D., 1825. First American throat specialist. Discovered value of applying silver nitrate solutions locally in catarrhal inflammation of the pharynx and larynx. Author of *Treatise on Diseases of the Air Passages* (1846), a pioneer work.

GREEN, JACOB (*b. Malden, Mass., 1722; d. 1790*), Presbyterian clergyman, physician. Father of Ashbel Green. Pastor at Hanover, N.Y., 1746–90. An outspoken patriot in the Revolution. Leader of "Associated Presbytery" movement, 1780.

GREEN, JACOB (*b. Philadelphia, Pa., 1790; d. Philadelphia, 1841*), chemist, naturalist. Son of Ashbel Green. Graduated University of Pennsylvania, 1807. Professor of chemistry, Princeton, 1818–22; at Jefferson Medical College, 1825–41. An excellent teacher and author of useful textbooks.

GREEN, JAMES STEPHENS (*b. near Rectortown, Va., 1817; d. 1870*), lawyer. Settled in Lewis Co., Mo., ca. 1836; practiced in Monticello. Protégé of Thomas H. Benton, he served in Congress, 1847–51; he led the Democratic revolt in 1849 which broke Benton's hold on the party in Missouri. As U.S. senator, 1857–61, he was recognized as one of the ablest spokesmen for the Breckinridge Democracy.

GREEN, JOHN (*b. Worcester, Mass., 1835; d. St. Louis, Mo., 1913*), ophthalmologist.

GREEN, JOHN CLEVE (*b. Lawrenceville, N.J. 1800; d. New York, N.Y., 1875*), China merchant, financier, philanthropist. Head of Russell and Co., most powerful American house in the China trade, 1834–39; a heavy investor in the railroad enterprises of his old Canton partner, J. M. Forbes. Benefactor of Princeton and Lawrenceville School.

GREEN, JONAS (*b. Boston, Mass. 1712; d. Annapolis, Md., 1767*), printer, journalist. Great-grandson of Samuel Green. Removed to Maryland, 1738, where he became printer to the province. Established the *Maryland Gazette*, 1745. His typographical masterpiece was Thomas Bacon's *Laws of Maryland* (1765).

GREEN, JOSEPH (*b. probably Boston, Mass., 1706; d. London, England, 1780*), merchant, Loyalist. Author of witty occasional satires in verse.

GREEN, LEWIS WARNER (*b. near Danville, Ky., 1806; d. 1863*), Presbyterian clergyman, educator. Graduated Centre College, 1824; studied also in Germany, 1834–36. President of Hampden–Sydney College, 1848–56; Transylvania University, 1856–57; Centre College, 1858–63.

GREEN, NATHAN (*b. Salem, Mass., 1787[?]; d. New York, N.Y., 1825*), privateersman. Commanded the *Grand Turk* of Salem, which shares with the *America* (also of Salem) the honor of being the most successful privateer in the War of 1812.

GREEN, NORVIN (*b. New Albany, Ind., 1818; d. 1893*), physician, legislator. Raised in Kentucky. Among first to conceive of a national consolidation of telegraph lines; formed North American Telegraph Co., 1857; Western Union Telegraph Co., 1866; served as president, Western Union, 1878–93.

GREEN, SAMUEL (*b. England, 1615; d. Cambridge, Mass., 1701/2*), printer. Came to Massachusetts, ca. 1633. Succeeded Stephen Day as manager of the Cambridge press and colony printer.

GREEN, SAMUEL ABBOTT (*b. Groton, Mass., 1830; d. 1918*), physician, author. Practiced in Boston. First Massachusetts physician to volunteer, he was distinguished throughout the Civil War in field and hospital service. Prominent in Massachusetts Historical Society, he served as its librarian, 1868–1918.

GREEN, SAMUEL BOWDLEAR (*b. Chelsea, Mass., 1859; d. 1910*), horticulturist. Graduated Massachusetts Agricultural College, 1879. Professor of horticulture and forestry, University of Minnesota, 1892–1910; active in Minnesota experiment station work and author of textbooks.

GREEN, SAMUEL SWETT (*b. Worcester Mass., 1837; d. 1918*), librarian. Brother of John Green. Graduated Harvard, 1858. Pioneered in modern practice at Worcester Free Library, 1871–1909.

GREEN, SETH (*b. Monroe Co., N.Y., 1817; d. 1888*), pioneer fish culturist. Made fish-breeding a recognized and practical art; transported live shad to the Pacific coast, 1871; experimented with hatching salmon, sturgeon, and other fish.

GREEN, THEODORE FRANCIS (*b. Providence, R.I., 1867; d. Providence, 1966*), governor of Rhode Island and U.S. senator. Studied at Brown University (M.A., 1890), Harvard University Law School, and the universities of Bonn and Berlin. Instructor in Roman law at Brown, 1894–97. President of J. P. Coats (1912–23) and of Morris Plan Bankers' Association (1924–27).

Democratic member of the Rhode Island House of Representatives, 1907. Unsuccessful candidate for governor (1912; 1930) and for Congress (1920). Governor of Rhode Island, 1932–36. Democratic senator from Rhode Island, 1936–60. Member of the Senate Foreign Relations Committee, 1938–59; committee chairman from 1951.

GREEN, THOMAS (*b. New London, Conn., 1735; d. New Haven, Conn., 1812*), printer, editor. Great-great-grandson of Samuel Green. Established *Connecticut* (now *Hartford*) *Courant*, 1764; *Connecticut Journal and New Haven Post Boy*, 1767.

GREEN, WILLIAM (*b. Fredericksburg, Va., 1806; d. 1880*), lawyer. Practiced *post* 1827 in Culpeper Co.; *post* 1855 in Richmond, where he stood at head of the Virginia bar for legal learning.

GREEN, WILLIAM (*b. Coshocton, Ohio, 1870; d. Coshocton, 1952*), labor leader. After rising in the ranks of the United Mine Workers in Ohio, Green was elected to the executive council of the American Federation of Labor in 1913; president, 1934–52. Began the processes of unionizing the automobile industry. In a dispute concerning the recruitment of new unions, John L. Lewis rebelled against Green's control and formed the rival labor movement, the Congress of Industrial Organizations, in 1938. In 1949, Green attended a London conference which set up the International Confederation of Free Trade Unions, designed to aid in the formation of non-Communist labor unions in Europe.

GREEN, WILLIAM HENRY (*b. Groveville, N.J., 1825; d. 1900*), Presbyterian clergyman, Hebrew scholar. Nephew of John C. and Henry W. Green. Graduated Lafayette, 1840; Princeton Theological Seminary, 1846. Professor at Princeton Seminary, 1851–1900; also its acting president for 17 years. Scholarly leader in America of the ultraconservative school of biblical criticism.

GREEN, WILLIAM JOSEPH, JR. (*b. Philadelphia, Pa., 1910; d. Philadelphia, 1963*), U.S. congressman. Government positions in the 1930's included insurance examiner for the Commonwealth of Pennsylvania and U.S. chief deputy marshall. A Philadelphia Democrat, he was elected to Congress in 1944. Lost his seat in 1946; reelected in 1948 and served until his death. As chairman of Philadelphia's Democratic Committee, he shaped a coalition that the *New York Times* called "one of the nation's most powerful political machines." Served on the House Armed Services Committee and the Committee on Ways and Means, where he was able to control important committee assignments. Called by AFL-CIO officials "one of labor's staunchest champions."

GREENBAUM, EDWARD SAMUEL (*b. New York, N.Y., 1890; d. Princeton, N.J., 1970*), lawyer. Son of Samuel Greenbaum, a New York State Supreme Court justice. Studied at Williams College and Columbia Law School (graduated, 1913). Helped establish the New York law firm Greenbaum, Wolff and Ernst; with the firm from 1916–70. A noted trial attorney, his clients included the *New York Times* and Harper and Row. A commissioned officer in the Army from 1918; as executive officer to Secretary of War Robert P. Patterson during World War II, he negotiated many major contracts between the government and private defense firms. Left the Army in 1945 a brigadier general. Involved in public service and legal reform from 1928. Chaired a special committee of the Association of the Bar of the City of New York on court reform in 1952. Worked with the New York State Judicial Conference for a constitutional amendment that overhauled the state's court system in 1961. Headed the New York Alcohol Control Commission, 1933. Assistant to the U.S. Attorney General (1934–38) and a member of the U.S. delegation to the United Nations (1956–57).

GREENE, ALBERT GORTON (*b. Providence, R.I., 1802; d. Cleveland, Ohio, 1868*), poet, jurist, book collector. Author of "Old Grimes" (1818) and other poems.

GREENE, BELLE DA COSTA (*b. Alexandria, Va., 1883; d. New York. N.Y., 1950*), library director, bibliographer. Associated with the Pierpont Morgan Library, New York City, *post* 1905, she served as director of the library, 1924–48, after its incorporation as an educational institution for public use. She was instrumental in enriching and enlarging the great collection.

GREENE, CHARLES EZRA (*b. Cambridge, Mass., 1842; d. Ann Arbor, Mich., 1903*), civil engineer, teacher. Graduated Harvard, 1862; Massachusetts Institute of Technology, 1868. Held chair of civil engineering, University of Michigan, *post* 1872; dean, College of Engineering, *post* 1895. First to apply graphical methods of analysis to problems of roofs, bridges, and arches.

GREENE, CHARLES SUMNER (*b. Brighton, Ohio, 1868; d. Carmel, Calif., 1957*); **GREENE, HENRY MATHER** (*b. Brighton, Ohio, 1870; d. Pasadena, Calif., 1954*), architects. Both studied at M.I.T. Founded the architectural firm of Greene and Greene in Pasadena, Calif., around 1893. Known for their innovations in domestic architecture, they created the California bungalow style, Japanese in inspiration, but with an extensive use of wood and shingles. The best example of their style is the David B. Gamble House for the Gamble family of Proctor and Gamble, Pasadena, Calif. Preeminent in domestic California architecture 1902–09, they have had a lasting influence in that state.

GREENE, CHRISTOPHER (*b. Warwick, R.I., 1737; d. Westchester Co., N.Y., 1781*), Revolutionary soldier. Cited for gallant defense of Fort Mercer against Hessian attack, October 1777.

GREENE, DANIEL CROSBY (*b. Roxbury, Mass., 1843; d. 1913*), Congregational clergyman. Graduated Dartmouth, 1864; Andover Theological Seminary, 1869. Missionary to Japan, 1869–1913.

GREENE, EDWARD LEE (*b. Hopkinton, R.I., 1843; d. Washington, D.C., 1915*), botanist. Taught at University of California, 1885–95; at Catholic University, 1895–1904. Associate of the Smithsonian, 1904–11. A controversial, picturesque scholar, unexcelled in field knowledge of North American flora.

GREENE, FRANCES HARRIET WHIPPLE. *See* GREEN, FRANCES HARRIET WHIPPLE.

GREENE, FRANCIS VINTON (*b. Providence, R.I., 1850; d. New York, N.Y., 1921*), soldier, historian, engineer. Son of G. S. Greene (1801–99). Graduated West Point, 1870. Commanded second Philippine expedition, 1898. His *The Russian Army and Its Campaigns in Turkey in 1877–78* (1879) is the standard authority on its subject.

GREENE, GEORGE SEARS (*b. Apponaug, R.I., 1801; d. Morristown, N.J., 1899*), soldier, civil engineer. Graduated West Point, 1823. The high point of his career as brigade commander, 1862–66, was his holding of Culp's Hill at Gettysburg against repeated Confederate attacks. Worked extensively in New York City on water supply, elevated railways, laying out new streets. He was the father of Francis V., Samuel D., and George S. Greene. (1837–1922)

GREENE, GEORGE SEARS (*b. Lexington, Ky., 1837; d. 1922*), civil engineer. Son of George S. Greene (1801–99). Studied with his father; early devised a drifting head for transits and other improvements in surveying instruments. Notable for his work on the seawall around Manhattan Island and his original method in constructing the New York Chelsea piers.

GREENE, GEORGE WASHINGTON (*b. East Greenwich, R.I., 1811; d. East Greenwich, 1883*), author, educator. Grandson of Gen. Nathanael Greene, whose life he wrote; held first chair of American history to be established in the United States (Cornell University, 1817).

GREENE, JEROME DAVIS (*b. Yokohama, Japan, 1874; d. 1959*), university officer and foundation executive. Studied at Harvard University. Secretary to the Harvard Corporation, 1905–09 and 1934–43. Secretary and executive officer of the Rockefeller Foundation, 1913–17; trustee of Rockefeller Institute until 1932. Helped establish the Institute for Government Research (1916), later called the Brookings Institution, served as trustee until 1945.

GREENE, NATHANAEL (*b. Potowomut [Warwick], R.I., 1742; d. near Savannah, Ga., 1786*), Revolutionary general. Brought up as a member of the Society of Friends; employed as a young man in the family business of iron-founding. Denied officer status in a local militia company he had helped organize, he served as a private, 1774–75. Appointed brigadier general by Rhode Island Assembly, May 1775; commissioned Continental brigadier, June 1775. Served through siege of Boston and commanded army of occupation after evacuation by British, March 1776. Assumed charge of defenses of New York City, May 1776. Promoted major general in August, he was ill during the British attack on Long Island that same month. Subsequent to battle of Harlem Heights, he was given command of the troops in New Jersey with headquarters at Fort Lee. His advice to hold Fort Washington (taken by the British in November 1776) has been sharply criticized by historians.

Green ably left column at battle of Trenton, then wintered with the army at Morristown. In March 1777, he held conference about the army with Congress at Washington's request. After the battle of Brandywine, Greene's skillful disposition of troops insured the safe withdrawal of the army and saved the artillery. There is no evidence that he was at fault in the defeat at Germantown, where he led the left column.

Succeeding Thomas Mifflin as quartermaster general, Mar. 2, 1778, Greene reorganized the department, insisting on monthly returns from his deputies and the appointment of trusted friends John Cox and Charles Pettit to assist him. He established an efficient system of depots so as to draw on the fertile middle states for forage and on New England for manufactured goods. At the battle of Monmouth, June 1778, Greene led the right; in July he assisted with preparations to drive the British from Rhode Island; with General Sullivan he won a victory there in late August. Greene's exertions as quartermaster greatly reduced the army's suffering in winter quarters at Middlebrook, N.J., 1778–79.

Attacked by Congress at Mifflin's instigation in the spring of 1780 for permitting dishonesty on the part of his subordinates, Green replied indignantly. When his enemies in Congress adopted a new quartermaster plan of Timothy Pickering's in July, Green resigned as quartermaster and returned to the line. Appointed to command in the South, October 1780, after Gates's defeat at Camden, S.C., Greene set out on his greatest campaign.

Realizing that the Camden disaster had been due to failure of supplies. Greene in nine days provided a medical department, engineers, artillery, clothing, every detail of equipment, and a cavalry force without which Gates had had inadequate intelligence. He went on to secure the cooperation of the local authorities in Virginia and North Carolina and reorganized Gates's army. Unlike Gates, he showed tact and ability in handling such able, if independent, officers as Henry Lee, Daniel Morgan, and William

Washington, as well as the various partisan corps in the area. The tide turned definitely in January 1781, when Morgan gained a striking victory over Tarleton at Cowpens. Greene's general policy was typical of successful American strategy in the Revolution, which was to withdraw as far as the enemy would pursue and, when he had outrun his communications, to follow and worry him on his retreat. The British under Cornwallis gained costly victories at Guilford Court House and Hobkirk's Hill but were maneuvered out of Camden, which the patriot army entered in triumph. Green captured the British posts in the South one by one until by December 1781 only Charleston remained. Under siege for a year, the town was evacuated on Dec. 14, 1782.

Greene pledged his own fortune for the support of his army, 1782–83, and had to endorse the paper of John Banks, a contractor, to keep the men from starving. When Banks later went bankrupt, Greene became involved in debts he could not pay and was obliged to sell his estates. In 1785 he established himself near Savannah, Ga., at Mulberry Grove, the confiscated property of the Loyalist John Graham, where he died.

GREENE, NATHANIEL (*b. Boscawen, N.H., 1797; d. Boston, Mass., 1877*), Boston newspaper editor, Democratic politician and officeholder, linguist.

GREENE, ROGER SHERMAN (*b. Westborough, Mass., 1881; d. West Palm Beach, Fla., 1947*), diplomat, foundation official. Child of missionary parents, he received his early schooling in Japan, attended Harvard (B.A., 1901; M.A., 1902), and, as a U.S. consular service official, held posts in Brazil, Siberia, Manchuria, Japan, and China, 1902–14. A member of the Rockefeller Foundation's China Medical Board, 1914–34, he served first as resident director in China and *post* 1921 as director; vice president, Foundation in the Far East, 1927–29. Deeply involved in projects directed toward the modernization of China, especially public health, he also kept up a steady correspondence with members of the U.S. State Department responsible for Chinese policy. Returning to the United States, 1935, he soon became a leader in organizations formed to work for the support of China and Great Britain against aggression by Japan and Germany and lobbied with federal officials for U.S. aid to China. During World War II, despite ill health, he served as a consultant to the cultural relations division of the State Department.

GREENE, SAMUEL DANA (*b. Cumberland, Md., 1840; d. Portsmouth, N.H., 1884*), naval officer. Son of George S. Greene (1801–99). Graduated Annapolis, 1859. Executive officer of USS *Monitor* from her launching until she sank. Gunnery officer in fight with *Merrimack*.

GREENE, SAMUEL STILLMAN (*b. Belchertown, Mass., 1810; d. 1883*), educator. Founder of Rhode Island College of Education; long on faculty of Brown University. His progressive ideas on teaching were embodied in many successful textbooks on English grammar.

GREENE, WILLIAM (*b. Warwick, R.I., 1695/6; d. Warwick, 1758*), colonial governor of Rhode Island, 1743–45, 1746–47, 1748–55, and 1757–58.

GREENE, WILLIAM (*b. Warwick, R.I., 1731; d. Warwick, 1809*), legislator, jurist. Son of William Greene (1695/6–1758). Governor of Rhode Island, 1778–86.

GREENE, WILLIAM CORNELL (*b. Chappaqua, N.Y., 1851; d. Cananea, Mexico, 1911*), promoter. After a youth as cowboy, Indian fighter and prospector in Arizona, Greene settled as a rancher in the San Pedro Valley. Convinced that La Cananea, a tract of land in Sonora, Mexico, contained mineral deposits, he filed mining claims, obtained possession, and raised capital for several operating companies, the last being Greene Consolidated Copper Co. Shrewdly appealing to the small investor and exercising his genius for writing prospectuses, he prospered exceedingly *post* 1900, and very rich copper ores were discovered on his claims. His own speculations and raids by other financiers severely affected him, however, and his fall was rapid. In 1906, Amalgamated Copper and other interests forced formation of a new company, Greene-Cananea-Consolidated, from which he was soon squeezed out. The panic of 1907 finished his fortunes.

GREENER, RICHARD THEODORE (*b. Philadelphia, Pa., 1844; d. Chicago, Ill., 1922*), educator, lawyer. The first black to receive a degree from Harvard, 1870, he taught at University of South Carolina, 1873–77, and in law department of Howard University, of which he became dean, 1879. He began to practice law in Washington, D.C., 1882. A fluent speaker, he argued against Frederick Douglass, recommending freedmen to go west and take up fertile land. He served as chief examiner of the New York City civil service board, 1885–90, as U.S. consul at Bombay, and as U.S. commercial agent at Vladivostok.

GREENHALGE, FREDERIC THOMAS (*b. Clitheroe, England, 1842; d. Boston, Mass., 1896*), lawyer. Taken to America, 1855. Practices in Lowell, Mass., where he held several offices. Congressman, Republican, from Massachusetts, 1889–91, he served with zeal and independence as governor of Massachusetts *post* 1894.

GREENHOW, ROBERT (*b. Richmond, Va., 1800; d. San Francisco, Calif., 1854*), physician, linguist, historian. Author of *The History of Oregon and California* (1844), a pioneer work based on original sources.

GREENLAW, EDWIN ALMIRON (*b. Flora, Ill., 1874; d. 1931*), educator. Graduated Northwestern, 1897; Ph.D., Harvard, 1904. Taught at Adelphi College; headed English department, University of North Carolina, 1914–25, and was dean of graduate school; Osler professor of English at Johns Hopkins, 1925–31. Authority on Spenser.

GREENLEAF, BENJAMIN (*b. Haverhill, Mass., 1786; d. 1864*), educator. Graduated Dartmouth, 1813. Author of the *National Arithmetic* (1836) and other popular mathematical textbooks.

GREENLEAF, HALBERT STEVENS (*b. Guilford, Vt., 1827; d. Charlotte, N.Y., 1906*), industrialist, Union soldier. Partner in lock factory of Sargent and Greenleaf, Rochester, N.Y., congressman, Democrat, from New York, 1883–85 and 1891–93.

GREENLEAF, MOSES (*b. Newburyport, Mass., 1777; d. 1834*), mapmaker, jurist, author. Brother of Simon Greenleaf. Removed to Maine, 1790; was active in the settlement of the district's interior. His 1815 map of Maine with its accompanying volume of statistics was influential in promoting Maine statehood; his *Survey of the State of Maine* (1829) is one of the most important books relating to Maine history.

GREENLEAF, SIMON (*b. Newburyport, Mass., 1783; d. 1853*), lawyer, author. Brother of Moses Greenleaf. Educated at Newburyport Latin School; read in law in office of Ezekiel Whitman; admitted to bar, 1806; practiced until 1818 at Standish and Gray, Maine. Removing to Portland, he at once took place as one of the town's most learned practitioners and served as reporter of the Maine Supreme Court, 1820–32. Appointed Royall professor of Law at Harvard, 1833, he held the chair until 1846 when he succeeded Joseph Story as Dane professor. His health declining in 1848, he retired as emeritus. Under the dual leadership of Greenleaf and Story, the Harvard Law School rose to national eminence. Greenleaf's learned *Treatise on the Law of Evidence* (1842–53) became in its completed form the foremost American authority. His revision of *Cruise's Digest of the Law of Real Property* (1849–50) superseded the English original in the United States.

GREENLEAF, THOMAS (*b. Abington, Mass., 1755; d. New York, N.Y., 1798*), printer, journalist. Removed to New York City, 1785; published *New-York Journal*; founded the *Argus*, 1795, in support of Aaron Burr's party and against the Federalists.

GREENOUGH, HENRY (*b. Newburyport, Mass., 1807; d. 1883*), architect, painter. Brother of Horatio and Richard S. Greenough.

GREENOUGH, HORATIO (*b. Boston, Mass., 1805; d. Somerville, Mass., 1852*), sculptor. Brother of Henry and Richard S. Greenough. Washington Allston guided his art studies. After graduation from Harvard, 1825, he went to Rome, where he began serious study of sculpture and had aid of Thorwaldsen. Home within a year with malaria, he modeled from life an excellent likeness of John Quincy Adams and other portraits. In 1828 he returned to Italy and settled in Florence. An early commission from James Fenimore Cooper was a small marble group called *Chanting Cherubs*. The nudity of the cherubs raised much American protest, to which Greenough returned a spirited defense. In 1831 he modeled a bust of Lafayette. American travelers gave him small commissions, and he produced several groups, busts, and figures. Commissioned, 1833, to do a statue of Washington to be placed in the U.S. Capitol, for nearly eight years he gave himself to what he believed the crowning work of his career. The colossal half-draped marble figure, poetically treated, proved too heavy for the Capitol floor and was placed outside, where it met the gibes of an unappreciative public. It was the first colossal work in marble by an American. A second colossal group, *The Rescue*, executed 1837–51, was placed on a buttress of the Capitol portico.

Greenough returned home and settled at Newport, R.I., 1851. His importance lies in his influence, rather than in the artistic merit of his work. He dedicated himself to his art with the utmost earnestness and did much to dignify it in the minds of Americans. He was author of *Aesthetics in Washington* (1851).

GREENOUGH, JAMES BRADSTREET (*b. Portland, Maine, 1833; d. 1901*), lawyer, philologist. Taught Latin at Harvard, *post* 1865; was the first to teach Sanskrit and comparative philology there. Author of *Analysis of the Latin Subjunctive* (1870) and (with Joseph H. Allen) of a famous Latin grammar. Edited many texts.

GREENOUGH, RICHARD SALTONSTALL (*b. Jamaica Plain, Mass., 1819; d. Rome, Italy, 1904*), sculptor. Brother of Henry and Horatio Greenough.

GREENSLET, FERRIS (*b. Glens Falls, N.Y., 1875; d. Cambridge, Mass., 1959*), editor, publisher, biographer, and sportsman. Studied at Wesleyan University and at Columbia (Ph.D., 1900). Editor with the *Atlantic Monthly* (1902–07). Editor with Houghton Mifflin (1907–59); vice president from 1936. As editor, Greenslet worked with such authors as Willa Cather and Henry Adams. He wrote *The Life of James Russell Lowell* (1905) and, his most famous book, *Under the Bridge* (1943).

GREENSTREET, SIDNEY HUGHES (*b. Sandwich, England, 1879; d. Hollywood, Calif., 1954*), actor. Came to the U.S. in 1904 as a member of a Shakespearean acting company. Known for his roles at the Theatre Guild with Alfred Lunt and Lynn Fontanne, Greenstreet appeared in O'Neill's *Marco Millions* (1930), *Lysistrata* (1930), *The Seagull* (1938), and *There Shall Be*

No Light (1940), his last stage appearance. His films include *The Maltese Falcon* (1941), the first in which he was teamed with Humphrey Bogart and Peter Lorre, and which won him an Academy Award nomination; *Casablanca* (1942), *The Mask of Dimitrios* (1944), and *Flamingo Road* (1949).

GREENUP, CHRISTOPHER (*b. probably Loudoun Co., Va.*, ca. *1750; d. Blue Lick Springs, Ky., 1818*), lawyer. Removed to Kentucky near end of the Revolution. Congressman from Kentucky, 1792–97; Democratic governor, 1804–08.

GREENWALD, EMANUEL (*b. near Frederick, Md., 1811; d. Lancaster, Pa., 1885*), Lutheran clergyman. Pastor in Ohio, 1831–54; in Easton, Pa., 1854–67; thereafter at Lancaster, Pa. A conservative, he opposed revivals and other innovations.

GREENWAY, JOHN CAMPBELL (*b. Huntsville, Ala., 1872; d. New York, N.Y., 1926*), mining engineer. Specialist in Southwest copper mining.

GREENWOOD, GRACE. *See* LIPPINCOTT, SARAH JANE CLARKE.

GREENWOOD, ISAAC (*b. Boston, Mass., 1702; d. Charleston, S.C., 1745*). Graduated Harvard, 1721. At instance of Thomas Hollis, was appointed professor of mathematics at Harvard, 1727; served in that capacity, 1728–38. His *Arithmetick, Vulgar and Decimal* (1729) was first textbook of its kind in English by a native-born American.

GREENWOOD, JOHN (*b. Boston, Mass., 1760; d. New York, N.Y., 1819*), dentist. Grandson of Isaac Greenwood. Apprenticed to a cabinetmaker, he established himself in New York City as a dentist, 1784–85. He is credited with originating the foot-power drill, spiral springs to hold plates of artificial teeth in position, and the use of porcelain in the manufacture of dentures. Two sets which he made for George Washington are still in existence and are remarkable examples of dental skill.

GREENWOOD, MILES (*b. Jersey City, N.J., 1807; d. Cincinnati, Ohio, 1885*), ironmaster. Established Eagle Iron Works at Cincinnati, 1832; was early advocate of a paid steam fire department. The first steam fire engine in the United States was made in his factory by Shawk and Latta (in use, May 1852).

GREER, DAVID HUMMELL (*b. Wheeling, Va., now W.Va., 1844; d. New York, N.Y., 1919*), Episcopal clergyman. Rector at Covington, Ky., and Providence, R.I.; at St. Bartholomew's, New York City, 1888–1903. Consecrated coadjutor bishop of New York, 1904, he succeeded to the see, 1908. A conservative Broad Churchman.

GREER, JAMES AUGUSTIN (*b. Cincinnati, Ohio, 1833; d. Washington, D.C., 1904*), naval officer. Graduated U.S. Naval Academy, 1854. After a widely varied career, retired as rear admiral, 1895.

GREGG, ALAN (*b. Colorado Springs, Colo., 1890; d. Big Sur, Calif., 1957*), foundation officer. Studied at Harvard (M.D., 1916). Affiliated with the Rockefeller Foundation from 1919; associate director of the Division of Medical Education (1922–24); head of the Paris office of the Foundation (1924–31); director of the medical sciences division in New York City (1931–51); vice president of the Foundation from 1951 to 1954. Remembered for his progressive leadership in disbursing the Foundation's funds, Gregg thought that his task was to identify the best minds and to create optimal environments in which they could work.

GREGG, ANDREW (*b. near Carlisle, Pa., 1755; d. Bellefonte, Pa., 1835*), farmer, politician. Congressman, Democratic-Republican, from Pennsylvania, 1791–1807; U.S. senator, 1807–13. Strong supporter of agrarian interests.

GREGG, DAVID McMURTRIE (*b. Huntingdon, Pa., 1833; d. 1916*), Union soldier. Grandson of Andrew Gregg. Graduated West Point, 1855. Most conspicuous among the exploits which made Gen. U. S. Grant consider him one of the best cavalry generals in the Union army was his defeat of J. E. B. Stuart's charge against Meade's extreme right at Gettysburg, July 3, 1863.

GREGG, JOHN (*b. Lawrence Co., Ala., 1828; d. near Richmond, Va., 1864*), lawyer, Confederate soldier. Removed to Texas, ca. 1852. Commanded Texas brigade, formerly Hood's, in Longstreet's corps, 1864.

GREGG, JOHN ANDREW (*b. Eureka, Kans., 1887; d. Jacksonville, Fla., 1953*), clergyman and educator. B.A., the University of Kansas, 1902. Bishop of the African Methodist Episcopal Church, 1924, serving in the episcopal diocese of South Africa, 1924–28. First black elected to the presidency of Howard University, 1926, an honor which he declined. President of the Bishops' Council, 1948. President of Edward Waters College, 1913–20; president of Wilburforce College, 1920–24.

GREGG, JOHN ROBERT (*b. Shantonagh, Co. Monaghan, Northern Ireland, 1867; d. New York, N.Y., 1948*), inventor of the Gregg system of shorthand. Worked out the principles of his new system while clerk in a Glasgow, Scotland, law office; opened his own shorthand school in Liverpool, England, 1887; published the first edition of his *Light-Line Phonography*, 1888. Came to the United States, 1893, and by the early 1900's had established his system and had begun to open a chain of schools to teach it. President, Gregg Publishing Co., which printed textbooks, drills, and home-study courses.

GREGG, JOSIAH (*b. Overton, C., Tenn., 1806; d. California, 1850*), Santa Fe trader, author. He made frequent journeys from Independence, Mo., to Santa Fe, 1831–41. A close observer, he kept copious notes of everything that interested him. His book *Commerce of the Prairies* (1844) enjoyed immediate success and is a classic of the frontier. Gregg joined Wool's army at San Antonio, 1846, and saw service in Mexico. In 1849 he made his last trip to Santa Fe, journeying thence to California and the Trinity mines. He died of hunger and exposure after crossing the Coast Range with an exploring party.

GREGG, MAXCY (*b. Columbia, S.C., 1814; d. Fredericksburg, Va., 1862*), lawyer, politician, Confederate brigadier general. Grandson of Jonathan Maxcy. South Carolina states' rights leader and ardent secessionist.

GREGG, WILLIAM (*b. Monongalia Co., Va., now W.Va., 1800; d. Edgefield District, S.C., 1867*), father of southern cotton manufacturing. A watchmaker and silversmith, retired from business, he established himself in Charleston, S.C., 1838. With leisure to think, he became convinced that South Carolina and the whole South should abandon devotion to a staple agriculture and develop cotton manufacturing. Industrial communities, as he saw it, would provide new markets for local products and give employment to unpropertied whites who had been rendered superfluous by the slave system. Embodying his ideas in *Essays on Domestic Industry* (1845), he gave them practical effect by founding Graniteville, near Aiken, S.C., 1846. Using native labor and materials, he erected a mill and provided comfortable housing for his work force, thus creating the first typical southern cotton-mill village and setting an example followed elsewhere in the South. The enterprise was highly successful, owing mainly to Gregg's insistence on specializing in a small range of product for sale direct from the mill in a national or world market. Highly solicitous of his employees, he was a pioneer in improving the condition of the poor whites.

GREGG, WILLIS RAY (*b. Phoenix, N.Y., 1880; d. Chicago, Ill., 1938*), meteorologist. Graduated Cornell, 1903. In service of U.S. Weather Bureau, 1904–38; specialist in aeronautical meteorology.

GREGORY, CASPAR RENÉ (*b. Philadelphia, Pa., 1846; d. Neufchatel-sur-Aisne, France, 1917*), New Testament scholar. Graduated University of Pennsylvania, 1864; Princeton Theological Seminary, 1870. Taught at University of Leipzig, 1884–1914; prepared a celebrated edition of the Greek New Testament, *Novum Testamentum Graece* (Leipzig, 1884, 1890, 1894).

GREGORY, CHARLES NOBLE (*b. Unadilla, N.Y., 1851; d. 1932*), lawyer, educator. Brother of Stephen S. Gregory. Admitted to the Wisconsin bar, 1872. Dean of law at University of Iowa, 1901–11; at George Washington University, 1911–14.

GREGORY, CLIFFORD VERNE (*b. near Burchinal, Iowa, 1883; d. Des Moines, Iowa, 1941*), agricultural journalist, farm leader. Graduated Iowa State College in Ames, 1910. Reestablished the reputation of the *Prairie Farmer* as a major farm journal, urging progressive, adaptive agricultural methods as editor, 1911–37. Also active in promoting farm organizations and as a spokesman for the farmer on federal boards and committees.

GREGORY, DANIEL SEELYE (*b. Carmel, N.Y., 1832; d. 1915*), Presbyterian clergyman, educator, editor. Held many pastorates; president of Lake Forest University, 1878–86; managing editor of *Standard Dictionary of the English Language*, 1889–95.

GREGORY, ELIOT (*b. New York, N.Y., 1854[?]; d. 1915*), painter, essayist, dilettante.

GREGORY, JOHN MILTON (*b. Sand Lake, N.Y., 1822; d. Washington, D.C., 1898*), Baptist clergyman, educational leader. Graduated Union, 1846. First regent (president) of University of Illinois, 1867–80, he labored enthusiastically to make it a true university, not a vocational school.

GREGORY, MENAS SARKAS BOULGOURJIAN (*b. Marash, Turkey, 1872; d. Tuckahoe, N.Y., 1941*), psychiatrist. Born of Armenian parents. Gregory is the anglicized form of Krikorian, his father's surname. B.A., Central Turkey College at Aintab, 1894; M.D., Albany (N.Y.) Medical College, 1898. Associated with the psychopathic department of Bellevue Hospital, New York City, 1902–34; as director *post* 1904, he transformed its facilities from a largely custodial role to one of treatment and rehabilitation. He was professor of psychiatry at Bellevue Medical College (New York University), 1918–37; thereafter he was professor emeritus. An able clinician and teacher, he was for many years among the most influential of those who shaped the development of psychiatry as a profession in the United States.

GREGORY, SAMUEL (*b. Guilford, Vt., 1813; d. Boston, Mass., 1872*), pioneer in medical education of women. Founded in 1848 and directed the Boston Female Medical School, later merged in Boston University School of Medicine.

GREGORY, STEPHEN STRONG (*b. Unadilla, N.Y., 1849; d. 1920*), Chicago lawyer. Raised in Madison, Wis. Outstanding trial counsel; represented Eugene Debs and American Railway Union in case arising out of Pullman strike. Brother of Charles N. Gregory.

GREGORY, THOMAS BARGER (*b. Philadelphia, Pa., 1860; d. Pittsburgh, Pa., 1951*), oil and gas developer and public utility executive. An early developer of natural gas in western Pennsylvania, Gregory, along with Harry J. Crawford, founded a developing company (1895) that was to become the Ohio Fuel Corporation in 1902. Acquiring interests in gas and oil companies across the country, their holdings were consolidated into the Columbia Gas and Electric Corporation in 1926; the company controlled fifty-five affiliated companies, serving 257 cities in New York, Pennsylvania, Ohio, Indiana, Kentucky, and West Virginia.

GREGORY, THOMAS WATT (*b. Crawfordsville, Miss., 1861; d. New York, N.Y., 1933*), lawyer. Graduated Law School, University of Texas, 1885. Practiced in Texas. Was prominent in Democratic politics and helped nominate Woodrow Wilson, 1912. As U.S. attorney general, 1914–19, he ably managed the vastly expanded Department of Justice during World War I.

GREIST, JOHN MILTON (*b. Crawfordsville, Ind., 1850; d. 1906*), inventor, manufacturer. Devised and made efficient sewing-machine attachments for tucking, ruffling, and the like.

GRELLET, STEPHEN (*b. Limoges, France, 1773; d. Burlington, N.J., 1855*), minister of the Society of Friends. Came to America, 1795. Undertook missionary journeys over practically all Europe and the United States.

GRESHAM, WALTER QUINTIN (*b. near Lanesville, Ind., 1832; d. Washington, D.C., 1895*), soldier, jurist, statesman. Union major general of volunteers in Civil War; won respect and friendship of U. S. Grant, who appointed him district judge for Indiana. Was frequently mentioned as a presidential possibility, along with his rival for Indiana Republican leadership, Benjamin Harrison. As postmaster general under President Arthur, 1883–84, he worked many reforms. Prominent in Republican conventions of 1884 and 1888, he grew outspoken in opposition to his party's tariff policy; he supported the Democrats, 1892. As U.S. secretary of state, 1893–95, he proved strong and independent, but he lacked a far-reaching knowledge of foreign affairs and left no enduring mark on American foreign policy.

GREW, JOSEPH CLARK (*b. Boston, Mass., 1880; d. Manchester-by-the-Sea, Mass., 1965*), diplomat and author. Studied at Harvard (graduated, 1902). Joined Foreign Service; appointed to Cairo in 1904. Served as third secretary in Mexico City in 1906; in Moscow in 1907. Promoted to second secretary in Berlin in 1908; first secretary in Vienna in 1911–12. Returned to Berlin in 1912. Appointed secretary to the U.S. Commission to the Versailles Peace Conference in 1918. Minister to Denmark, 1920. Negotiated treaty with Turkey at the Lausanne Conference on Near Eastern Affairs, 1922–23. Undersecretary of state (1924–27; 1944–45). Ambassador to Turkey (1927–32); to Japan (1932–41). Writings include *Sport and Travel in the Far East* (1910) and *Ten Years in Japan* (1944).

GREW, THEOPHILUS d. Philadelphia, Pa., 1759), mathematician, astronomer. First professor of mathematics at the College and Academy of Philadelphia, 1750–59.

GREY, ZANE (*b. Zanesville, Ohio, 1872; d. Altadena, Calif., 1939*), prolific and popular author of western romances, sport and outdoor adventure stories, and juveniles. Among these are *Riders of the Purple Sage* (1912); *Wanderer of the Wasteland* (1923); *West of the Pecos* (1937).

GRIDLEY, CHARLES VERNON (*b. Logansport, Ind., 1844; d. Kobe, Japan, 1898*), naval officer. Graduated U.S. Naval Academy, 1863. As captain of USS *Olympia*, began the battle of Manila Bay, 1898, on receiving Commodore Dewey's command, "You may fire when you are ready, Gridley."

GRIDLEY, JEREMIAH (*b. Boston, Mass., 1701/2; d. Brookline, Mass., 1767*), Massachusetts lawyer. His most famous case was the action over the legality of the Writs of Assistance in 1761; as government counsel, he was opposed by James Otis.

GRIDLEY, RICHARD (*b. Boston, Mass., 1710/11; d. Stoughton, now Canton, Mass., 1769*), military engineer, iron smelter. Headed artillery at siege of Louisburg, 1745; commanded provincial artillery on Crown Point expedition, 1755; also built Lake George fortifications. Commanded provincial artillery at Quebec, 1759. Chief engineer, Massachusetts forces, and chief of artillery, 1775; chief engineer, Continental army, 1775–76, and of the eastern department, 1777–80.

GRIER, ROBERT COOPER (*b. Cumberland Co., Pa., 1794; d. Philadelphia, Pa., 1870*), jurist. Graduated Dickinson College, 1812. As associate justice of the U.S. Supreme Court, 1846–70, his opinions were characterized by concision, clarity, freedom from bias, and citation of few but carefully chosen authorities. He made no concessions to popularity.

GRIERSON, BENJAMIN HENRY (*b. Pittsburgh, Pa., 1826; d. Omena, Mich., 1911*), Union soldier. Enlisting as a private, 1861, he became colonel, 6th Illinois Cavalry, and in 1863 commander of a cavalry brigade. In April and May 1863, he executed his famous raid from La Grange, Tenn., to Baton Rouge, La., piercing the heart of the Confederacy and destroying railroads and stores. "Grierson's Raid" was of great service to Grant in the reduction of Vicksburg. Retired as regular brigadier general, 1890.

GRIERSON, FRANCIS (*b. Birkenhead, England, 1848; d. Los Angeles, Calif., 1927*), musician, author. Came to America as infant; was raised in Illinois and St. Louis, Mo. As Jesse Shepard, had unique musical success in Europe, 1869–80. Changing his name, he embarked on a literary career and produced a series of extraordinary books of which the most notable is *The Valley of Shadows* (1909). He has been described as "a philosophical mystic."

GRIEVE, MILLER (*b. Edinburgh, Scotland, 1801; d. Milledgeville, Ga., ca. 1878*), journalist, diplomat. Came to America, 1817. Edited the Milledgeville *Southern Recorder*, 1833–53, unofficial but influential Whig organ.

GRIFFES, CHARLES TOMLINSON (*b. Elmira, N.Y., 1884; d. 1920*), composer, pianist, teacher. Studies in Berlin; was influenced in study of composition by Humperdinck. On his return to America, 1908, he was piano teacher, organist, choirmaster at Hackley School, Tarrytown, N.Y., where he remained until his untimely death. His first works were songs in German romantic style. Gradually developing his own style, influenced at times by Oriental idioms, he attained a wide recognition by the Boston Symphony's 1919 performance of *The Pleasure-Dome of Kubla Khan*, a symphonic poem. His other large works include *Poem* for flute and orchestra, two sketches on Indian themes for string quartet, and a piano sonata.

GRIFFIN, APPLETON PRENTISS CLARK (*b. Wilton, N.H., 1852; d. 1926*), librarian, bibliographer. Advancing from "runner" to librarian in the Boston Public Library, he joined the staff of the Library of Congress, 1897, became chief bibliographer, 1900, and served as chief assistant librarian, 1908–26.

GRIFFIN, CHARLES (*b. Granville, Ohio, 1825; d. Galveston, Tex., 1867*), Union soldier. Graduated West Point, 1847. A vigorous, bellicose, indiscreet artilleryman, Griffin rose to corps command on sheer merit and, *post* 1866, to command of the military district of Texas.

GRIFFIN, CYRUS (*b. Richmond, Co., Va., 1748; d. Yorktown, Va., 1810*), jurist, legislator. Last president of Continental Congress, *post* January 1788. As federal judge for the district of Virginia, 1789–1810, he presided over Aaron Burr's trial for treason.

GRIFFIN, EDWARD DORR (*b. East Haddam, Conn., 1770; d. Newark, N.J., 1837*), Congregational clergyman. Graduated Yale, 1790. As president of Williams College, 1821–36, he revitalized the institution in every way.

GRIFFIN, EUGENE (*b. Ellsworth, Maine, 1855; d. Schenectady, N.Y., 1907*), electrical engineer, soldier, manufacturer. Graduated West Point, 1875. Author of a government report (1888) which hastened use of electricity for streetcars and railways. Officer in General Electric and Thomson-Houston companies.

GRIFFIN, MARTIN IGNATIUS JOSEPH (*b. Philadelphia, Pa., 1842; d. 1911*), journalist, historian. A meticulous gatherer of facts about Catholic elements in U.S. history.

GRIFFIN, ROBERT STANISLAUS (*b. Fredericksburg, Va., 1857; d. Washington, D.C., 1933*), naval officer. Graduated Annapolis, 1878. Chief, Bureau of Steam Engineering, U.S. Navy, 1913–21; responsible for the construction, repair, and outfitting of the enormously expanded World War I navy.

GRIFFIN, SIMON GOODELL (*b. Nelson, N.H., 1824; d. Keene, N.H., 1902*), Union brigadier general, New Hampshire legislator.

GRIFFIN, SOLOMON BULKLEY (*b. Williamstown, Mass., 1852; d. 1925*), journalist. Managing editor, *Springfield* (Mass.) *Daily Republican*, 1878–1919.

GRIFFING, JOSEPHINE SOPHIE WHITE (*b. Hebron, Conn., 1814; d. 1872*), reformer. Ardent, practical worker for abolition and woman's suffrage; active in formation of the Freedman's Bureau.

GRIFFIS, WILLIAM ELLIOT (*b. Philadelphia, Pa., 1843; d. 1928*), Congregational clergyman, educator. Graduated Rutgers, 1869; Union Theological Seminary, 1877. Interpreter of Japan to America. Author of more than 50 books, of which *The Mikado's Empire* (1876) and *Corea: The Hermit Nation* (1882) are outstanding.

GRIFFITH, BENJAMIN (*b. Cardigan, Wales, 1688; d. 1768*), Baptist clergyman. Came to America, 1710; pastor in Montgomery Co., Pa., 1722–68. His manuscript record of the several churches in the Philadelphia Association is one of the most important sources for early American Baptist history.

GRIFFITH, CLARK CALVIN (*b. Clear Creek, Mo., 1869; d. Washington, D.C., 1955*), baseball player. One of baseball's earliest participants, Griffith, after playing for several minor and major league teams of the day, helped found the American League of Baseball Clubs in 1901. He was player-manager for the Chicago White Sox (1901–03); first manager of the New York Highlanders (later the New York Yankees) (1903–08); and for the Cincinnati Reds (1908–12). From 1912 until his death, he was manager and part owner of the Washington Senators, serving as president in 1950. Elected to the Baseball Hall of Fame, 1946.

GRIFFITH, DAVID WARK (*b. near Beard's Station, present Crestwood, Oldham County, Ky., 1875; d. Los Angeles, Calif., 1948*), motion picture director. His father died in 1882, and his mother settled in Louisville, where she ran a boardinghouse. As a young man Griffith planned to be a writer, but in 1895 he joined an amateur theatrical company. By the turn of the century he was playing bit parts throughout the United States, at first under the name "Lawrence Brayington," then as "Lawrence Griffith." He also wrote plays, short stories, and poems, signing them with his family name. His play about California hop pickers, *The Fool and the Girl*, opened in 1907. Returning to New York, he resumed his stage name. He was hired to act in the motion picture *Rescued from an Eagle's Nest* and in 1908 he was offered a trial assignment to direct for the Biograph Co. and he soon became principal director. Griffith demonstrated increasing mastery of the motion picture medium, and directed nearly 500 one- and two-reel films for the company. Among the players he developed into stars were Mary Pickford, Lillian and Dorothy Gish, Henry B. Walthall, Mae Marsh, and Blanche Sweet.

Griffith developed in a systematic and increasingly effective way such techniques as close-up and long shots, the "switchback" or parallel montage for suspense, the fade-out, and restraint in expression. He freed the motion picture from the spatial limitations of the stage, recreating it as a new and unique art form. He also established the primacy of the director.

In 1913 Griffith became director of production for Reliance-Majestic. *The Birth of a Nation* (1915), a film about the Civil War, was Griffith's epic depiction of the struggle between North and South. *Intolerance*, although not as popular as *The Birth of a Nation*, had even greater influence on other filmmakers.

In 1919 he joined with Charles Chaplin, Douglas Fairbanks, Sr., and Mary Pickford to form the United Artists Corporation. By 1925 he could no longer maintain the expense of his own studio and became a studio director at Paramount Pictures. After three films, the relationship broke off in discord. He joined the Art Cinema Corporation and returned to Hollywood in 1927. In 1931 Griffith independently made *The Struggle*, a disastrously unpopular film which ended his career as a filmmaker.

GRIFFITH, GOLDSBOROUGH SAPPINGTON (*b. Harford Co., Md., 1814; d. Baltimore, Md., 1904*), merchant, prison reformer, philanthropist.

GRIFFITH, WILLIAM (*b. Bound Brook, N.J., 1766; d. Burlington, N.J., 1826*), lawyer, legal writer. Expert on New Jersey land titles.

GRIFFITHS, JOHN WILLIS (*b. New York, N.Y., 1809[?]; d. Brooklyn, N.Y., 1882*), naval architect. Established American shipbuilding on a scientific basis through his writings: *A Treatise on Marine and Naval Architecture* (1849); *The Ship-builder's Manual* (1853); *The Progressive Ship-builder* (1874–75). Content to let others build, he specialized in design, showing amazing versatility. The first "extreme clipper ship," *Rainbow* (launched 1845), and the famous *Sea Witch* (1846) were his work. They proved the fastest ships afloat and strongly affected the subsequent development of the American clipper. Griffiths' influence on steamship design was also important. He incorporated new features, including a straight bow, in the *Arctic*, *Baltic*, and *Pacific*, the fastest, finest steamships of the early 1850's.

GRIGGS, EVERETT GALLUP (*b. Chaska, Minn., 1868; d. Tacoma, Wash., 1938*), lumberman. Proponent of industrial cooperation, reforestation, and other advanced policies.

GRIGGS, JOHN WILLIAM (*b. near Newton, N.J., 1849; d. 1927*), lawyer, statesman. Graduated Lafayette, 1868. After able service in the New Jersey legislature, he was Republican governor of that state, 1896–98; U.S. attorney general, 1898–1901; member of the Permanent Court at The Hague, 1901–12.

GRIGSBY, HUGH BLAIR (*b. Norfolk, Va., 1806; d. probably "Edgehill," Charlotte Co., Va., 1881*), newspaper editor, Virginia historian.

GRIM, DAVID (*b. Zweibrücken, Bavaria, 1737; d. New York, N.Y., 1826*), tavern-keeper, merchant, antiquarian. Came to

New York as a child. Noted for pen-and-ink sketches with descriptive notes of early New York City landmarks.

GRIMES, ABSALOM CARLISLE (*b. Jefferson Co., Ky., 1834; d. St. Louis, Mo., 1911*), Mississippi River pilot. Confederate mail runner. Partner in Mark Twain's brief service with the Confederate armed forces, 1861. Author of a volume of reminiscences (1926).

GRIMES, JAMES STANLEY (*b. Boston, Mass., 1807; d. Evanston Ill., 1903*), erratic philosopher, lecturer. An early evolutionist, opposed to spiritualism, but an ardent student of phrenology and mesmerism.

GRIMES, JAMES WILSON (*b. Deering, N.H., 1816; d. Burlington, Iowa, 1872*), lawyer, legislator. Removed to Iowa, 1836. As Whig governor of Iowa, 1854–58, he established many state institutions, including free schools, and virtually remade the state; he also made it staunchly Republican. U.S. senator, 1859–69, his refusal to vote for President Johnson's impeachment in 1868 was crucial in the outcome of the trial and cost Grimes his political popularity.

GRIMKÉ, ANGELINA EMILY. *See* GRIMKÉ, SARAH MOORE.

GRIMKÉ, ARCHIBALD HENRY (*b. near Charleston, S.C, 1849; d. Washington, D.C., 1930*), lawyer, author, publicist. Nephew of Sarah M. Grimké. Graduated Lincoln University, 1870; Harvard Law School, 1874. A black, Grimké was a lifelong crusader against race discrimination; he was president of the American Negro Academy, 1903–16, and was author of numerous pamphlets and books, including biographies of William Lloyd Garrison and Charles Sumner.

GRIMKÉ, JOHN FAUCHERAUD (*b. Charleston, S.C., 1752; d. Long Branch, N.J., 1819*), Revolutionary soldier, South Carolina jurist and legislator. A stern, unpopular judge, he did his best work as a legal compiler in the period of legal reform following the Revolution. He was author of, among other books, *Public Laws of . . . South Carolina* (1790).

GRIMKÉ, SARAH MOORE (*b. Charleston, S.C., 1792; d. Hyde Park, Mass., 1873*), and her sister, **ANGELINA EMILY** (*b. Charleston, S.C., 1805; d. Hyde Park, Mass., 1879*), abolitionists, advocates of woman's rights. Daughters of John F. Grimké; sisters of Thomas S. Grimké. Dissatisfied with slavery, they left their home in Charleston for Philadelphia, turned Quakers, and found themselves increasingly in sympathy with abolition. Angelina's forceful *Appeal to the Christian Women of the South* (1836) was publicly burned in South Carolina. She began to address small groups of women and was joined by Sarah. Their subsequent appearances on the lecture platform aroused great enthusiasm, especially in New England. Opposition to women speaking in public led them to defend woman's rights as well as abolition, both effectively. Angelina married Theodore Dwight Weld, 1838.

GRIMKÉ, THOMAS SMITH (*b. Charleston, S.C., 1786; d. 1834*), lawyer, legislator, educator, reformer. Brother of Sarah M. and Angelina E. Grimké; son of John F. Grimké. Graduated Yale, 1807. An ardent pacifist, he also conceived a radical plan of education which was grounded in religion and utilitarianism. As early as 1832, he advocated manual training in the schools and an extended treatment of science, modern history, and modern literature.

GRINNELL, FREDERICK (*b. New Bedford, Mass., 1836; d. New Bedford, 1905*), industrialist, engineer. Patented, 1881, the automatic fire-extinguisher sprinkler which bears his name; invented also an automatic fire-alarm system.

GRINNELL, GEORGE BIRD (*b. Brooklyn, N.Y., 1849; d. New York, N.Y., 1938*), naturalist, conservationist. Graduated Yale, 1870; Ph.D., 1880. Editor, *Forest and Stream,* 1876–1911; author of, among others, *The Cheyenne Indians* (1923), *Blackfoot Lodge Tales* (1892); founder, Audubon Society, 1886.

GRINNELL, HENRY (*b. New Bedford, Mass., 1799; d. 1874*), New York merchant, philanthropist. Brother of Joseph and Moses H. Grinnell. Financed Arctic expeditions, one of which discovered Grinnell Land; a founder of American Geographical and Statistical Society.

GRINNELL, HENRY WALTON (*b. New York, N.Y., 1843; d. St. Augustine, Fla., 1920*), naval officer. Son of Henry Grinnell. Served in Civil and Spanish-American wars; served in, and helped develop, Japanese navy, 1868–98.

GRINNELL, JOSEPH (*b. New Bedford, Mass., 1788; d. New Bedford, 1885*), merchant, financier. Brother of Henry and Moses H. Grinnell. Established textile industry in New Bedford. Congressman, Whig, from Massachusetts, 1843–51.

GRINNELL, JOSIAH BUSHNELL (*b. New Haven, Vt., 1821; d. 1891*), Congregational clergyman, abolitionist, railroad promoter. Settled in Iowa, 1854; founded town of Grinnell, Iowa, and Grinnell College. Friend of Lincoln and Horace Greeley, who addressed the historic "Go West, young man" advice to him.

GRINNELL, MOSES HICKS (*b. New Bedford, Mass., 1803; d. 1877*), New York merchant, shipowner, philanthropist, public official. Brother of Henry and Joseph Grinnell.

GRISCOM, CLEMENT ACTON (*b. Philadelphia, Pa., 1841; d. near Philadelphia, 1912*), financier, shipowner. Organized International Mercantile Marine Co.; earlier developed such revolutionary steps in shipbuilding as twin screws, transverse bulkheads, watertight compartments.

GRISCOM, JOHN (*b. Hancock's Bridge, N.J., 1774; d. 1852*), teacher, chemist, philanthropist. Publicized value of iodine in goiter treatment and other chemical discoveries. Helped establish House of Refuge, New York, first U.S. reformatory.

GRISCOM, LLOYD CARPENTER (*b. Riverton, N.J., 1872; d. Thomasville, Ga., 1959*), diplomat, lawyer, newspaper publisher. Studied at the University of Pennsylvania and the New York Law School (LL.B., 1896). Minister to Persia (1901–02); to Japan (1902–06); ambassador to Brazil (1906); and to Italy (1907–09). During World War I, he served in France and in London as General Pershing's liaison to the British War Office. Awarded the Distinguished Service Metal and was made knight commander of St. Michael by King George V. Griscom was president of the Huntover Press, a newspaper chain on Long Island. Books include a volume of memoirs, *Diplomatically Speaking.*

GRISCOM, LUDLOW (*b. New York, N.Y., 1890; d. Cambridge, Mass., 1959*), ornithologist. Studied at Columbia and Cornell. Instructor and assistant curator of ornithology at the American Museum of Natural History (1917–27); his *Birds of the New York City Region* became the standard text on the subject. Research curator at the Museum of Comparative Zoology at Harvard from 1927. Wrote the *Distributional Check List of the Birds of Mexico* (1954–57) and many books on the birds of the Northeastern U.S.

GRISSOM, VIRGIL IVAN ("GUS") (*b. Mitchell, Ind., 1926; d. Cape Canaveral, Fla., 1967*), United States Air Force officer and astronaut. Studied at Purdue University (graduated, 1950). Commissioned a second lieutenant in the air force in 1951. Completed the Air Force Test Pilot School course at Edwards Air Force Base in California in 1957. Became one of the seven military test pilots chosen by the National Aeronautics and Space Administration to be the first American astronauts, 1959. Flew the second suborbital test flight of a Mercury spacecraft in 1961. Command pilot for Gemini flight, 1965. Assigned to command the first test flight of the three-man Apollo spacecraft in 1966; a fire at the launch site during a preflight simulation killed the entire crew; Grissom, Edward White, and Roger Chaffee became the first American astronauts to die in an accident directly related to space activity.

GRISWOLD, ALEXANDER VIETS (*b. Simsbury, Conn., 1766; d. Boston, Mass., 1843*), Episcopal clergyman. Consecrated first and only bishop of Eastern Diocese, 1811; extended his church's influence through all New England.

GRISWOLD, ALFRED WHITNEY (*b. Morristown, N.J., 1906; d. New Haven, Conn., 1963*), scholar and university president. Studied at Yale (B.A. in English, 1929; Ph.D. in history, 1933). English instructor at Yale (1929–33); in history (1933–50). Director of the Foreign Area and Language Curriculum of the Army Specialized Training Program and director of the Army Civil Affairs Training School at Yale during World War II. President of Yale, 1950–63. An outstanding lecturer and a successful university president who tripled the university's endowment and doubled faculty salaries. He was a stout defender of academic freedom and a vigorous opponent of loyalty oaths. In addition to his numerous articles for periodicals, Griswold wrote *The Far Eastern Policy of the United States* (1938), *Farming and Democracy* (1948), and *Liberal Education and the Democratic Ideal* (1959).

GRISWOLD, JOHN AUGUSTUS (*b. Nassau, N.Y., 1818; d. Troy, N.Y., 1872*), iron manufacturer, congressman. Made plates and machinery for the *Monitor* and other ships of its class; controlled use of Bessemer patents in America, *post* 1864, in association with John F. Winslow and others.

GRISWOLD, MATTHEW (*b. Lyme, Conn., 1714; d. Lyme, 1799*), jurist, Revolutionary patriot. Deputy governor and chief justice of Connecticut, 1769–84; governor, 1784–86.

GRISWOLD, ROGER (*b. Lyme, Conn., 1762; d. 1812*), lawyer, politician. Son of Matthew Griswold. Congressman, Federalist, from Connecticut, 1795–1805; as governor of Connecticut, 1811–12, denied command of state militia to federal officers.

GRISWOLD, RUFUS WILMOT (*b. Benson, Vt., 1815; d. New York, N.Y., 1857*), journalist, anthologist. Associated with many newspapers and periodicals; compiled, edited, or wrote upward of 40 volumes. His most substantial original work was *The Republican Court* (1855); he grew conspicuous and influential as editor of *The Poets and Poetry of America* (1842) and other popular anthologies. He is best remembered as literary executor and editor of Edgar Allan Poe, in which capacity he incorporated all the current scandal about Poe, together with many errors, into an inexcusable memoir (1850). Griswold's last years were made miserable by disease, scandal, and domestic trouble.

GRISWOLD, STANLEY (*b. Torrington, Conn., 1763; d. Shawneetown, Illinois Territory, 1815*), Congregational clergyman, editor, politician. Partisan of Jefferson. Secretary of Michigan Territory, 1805–08; U.S. senator from Ohio, 1809–10; U.S. circuit judge, Illinois Territory, 1810–15.

GRISWOLD, WILLIAM MCCRILLIS (*b. Bangor, Maine, 1853; d. Seal Harbor, Maine, 1899*), bibliographer. Son of Rufus W. Griswold, whose valuable correspondence he edited, 1898.

GROESBECK, WILLIAM SLOCUM (*b. near Schenectady, N.Y., 1815; d. Cincinnati, Ohio, 1897*), Ohio lawyer, congressman.

Outstanding among defense counsel for President Andrew Johnson in impeachment trial, 1868.

GRONLUND, LAURENCE (*b. Denmark, 1846; d. New York, N.Y., 1899*), lawyer, socialist writer and lecturer. Came to America, 1867. Author of, among other works, *The Cooperative Commonwealth* (1884), first comprehensive work in English on socialism.

GROPIUS, WALTER ADOLF GEORG (*b. Berlin, Germany, 1883; d. Boston, Mass., 1969*), architect. Worked with architect Peter Behrens in Berlin, 1907–10. Opened his own office in 1910. Appointed to reorganize the Weimar Art School in 1914; headed the Staatliches Bauhaus, 1919–28, for more than a decade the center of creative energy in Europe. Under his leadership an effort was made to unite art and industry, and art and daily life, using architecture as the intermediary. In 1925 the school moved into a complex of buildings designed by Gropius at Dessau. Returned to private practice in 1928; worked with Marcel Breuer through 1934. Joined Maxwell Fry in architectural practice in England, 1934–37. Head of the Department of Architecture at Harvard's Graduate School of Design, 1938–52. Became a U.S. citizen in 1944. Formed architectural firm Architects' Collaborative, 1952. Known for integrating into his designs and his philosophy of education the disparate elements of twentieth-century culture, the repetitive forms of mass-production industries, and the iconoclastic images created by modern artists. Other works include the Fagus Works at Alfeld (1911) and a model factory and office building, the Fabrik, in Cologne (1914).

GROS, JOHN DANIEL (*b. Webenheim, Bavaria, 1738; d. Canajoharie, N.Y., 1812*), German Reformed clergyman, philosopher. Came to America, 1764; held numerous pastorates and served as New York militia chaplain in Revolution. Professor of German, geography, and moral philosophy, Columbia College, *post* 1784; served also as a trustee, 1787–92.

GROSE, WILLIAM (*b. near Dayton, Ohio, 1812; d. Newcastle, Ind., 1900*), lawyer, Indiana legislator. Conspicuous among Indiana's Civil War leaders; had excellent combat record as regimental and brigade commander.

GROSEILLIERS, MÉDART CHOUART, SIERUR DE (*fl. 1625–1684*), explorer. Born at Charly-Saint-Cyr, France, he went to Canada in 1637 or 1641 as assistant in Jesuit mission to the Huron. Formed a fur-trading partnership, 1654, with brother-in-law, Pierre Radisson. Heavily fined and their furs confiscated after an unlicensed journey to the Far West, 1658–60, they entered the service of England. Their joint expedition of 1668, in which Groseilliers alone reached Hudson Bay and secured a cargo of furs, resulted in the organization of the Hudson's Bay Co., 1670. Groseilliers eventually returned to French allegiance and settled down in Canada, where, prior to 1698, it is thought, he died.

GROSS, CHARLES (*b. Troy, N.Y., 1857; d. 1909*), educator, historian. Graduated Williams, 1878; Ph.D., Göttingen, 1883. Taught history at Harvard. Author of *The Gild Merchant* (1890) and the monumental *Sources and Literature of English History from the Earliest Times to about 1485* (1900).

GROSS, MILT (*b. New York, N.Y., 1895; d. at sea, 1953*), cartoonist, illustrator, author. Popularizer of the Yiddish dialect, Gross was the creator of the cartoon strips "Nize Baby" and "Hiawatta" in 1926. His cartoons were issued in book form and became best sellers. In 1931 he created two series for King Features comic strips, "Dave's Delicatessen" and "That's My Pop."

GROSS, SAMUEL DAVID (*b. near Easton, Pa., 1805; d. Philadelphia, Pa., 1884*), surgeon, teacher, author. Graduated Jefferson Medical College, 1828; began practice in Philadelphia. Was author of several translations from French and German, including Tavernier's *Elements of Operative Surgery* (1829), first treatise on operative surgery published in America, and an original work, *Treatise on the Anatomy, Physiology, and Diseases and Injuries of the Bones and Joints* (1830). Became professor of pathological anatomy at Cincinnati Medical College, 1835. Gross's *Elements of Pathological Anatomy* (1839) was the first effort in English to present the subject systematically and was long the chief authority on it. Elected professor of surgery, University of Louisville, 1840, he became the most celebrated surgeon of the South. In 1856 he was appointed professor of surgery at Jefferson Medical College. His contributions to medical literature were numerous and important. *A Practical Treatise on the Diseases and Injuries of the Urinary Bladder, the Prostate Gland, and the Urethra* (1851) became the accepted authority and a standard textbook. His third pioneer work, *A Practical Treatise on Foreign Bodies in Air Passages* (1854), was the first attempt to systematize knowledge on that subject. His *System of Surgery, Pathological, Diagnostic, Therapeutic and Operative* (1859) is one of the greatest surgical treatises ever written. Translated into several languages, it had enormous influence on surgical thought.

Outstanding in practice as in precept, particularly noted for operating for bladder stone, he was one of the first to insist on the proper plan of suturing intestinal wounds and restoring damaged intestines by resection and of suturing tendons and nerves. He invented a number of instruments and was a founder of numerous medical societies, including the American Medical Association and the American Surgical Society.

GROSS, SAMUEL WEISSELL (*b. Cincinnati, Ohio, 1837; d. Philadelphia, Pa., 1889*), surgeon, author, teacher. Son of Samuel D. Gross. Graduated Jefferson Medical College, 1857, where he succeeded father as professor of surgery, 1882. With W. S. Halsted and others, developed present-day radical operation for cancer.

GROSSCUP, PETER STENGER (*b. Ashland, Ohio, 1852; d. at sea, 1921*), jurist. Prominent Chicago lawyer; federal district judge, 1892–98 judge, circuit court of appeals, 1899–1911. Issued injunction in Chicago railway strike, 1894; was friendly to trusts.

GROSSET, ALEXANDER (*b. Windsor Mills, Canada. 1870; d. Riverside, Conn., 1934*), publisher. Founder of Grosset and Dunlap, reprint publishers; president of the firm, 1900–34.

GROSSMANN, GEORG MARTIN (*b. Grossbieberau, Germany, 1823; d. Waverly, Iowa, 1897*), Lutheran clergyman. Came to America, 1852. Helped organize German Lutheran Synod of Iowa, 1854, and served as its president until 1893.

GROSSMANN, LOUIS (*b. Vienna, Austria, 1863; d. Detroit, Mich., 1926*), rabbi. Came to America as a child. Graduated University of Cincinnati, 1884, and Hebrew Union College, 1884, where he served as professor, 1898–1921. Pioneer in modernizing Jewish religious education.

GROSVENOR, CHARLES HENRY (*b. Pomfret, Conn., 1833; d. 1917*), lawyer, Union soldier. Raised in Athens Co., Ohio. As congressman, Republican, from Ohio, 1885–1907, he was renowned as a bitter partisan debater.

GROSVENOR, EDWIN PRESCOTT (*b. Constantinople, Turkey, 1875; d. New York, N.Y., 1930*), lawyer. Graduated Amherst, 1897; Columbia Law School, 1904. Prosecutor of antitrust violations as assistant U.S. attorney general, 1908–13, his principal achievements were in proceedings against the Kentucky night riders and against the "bathtub trust." In *United States* v.

Standard Sanitary Manufacturing Co., he won from the Supreme Court a decision which prevents extension of a patent monopoly beyond the invention or process described in the patent, a landmark in the development of antitrust law. A member of the firm of Cadwalader, Wickersham and Taft *post* 1914, he successfully defended the Fur Dealers Association against the government, and thereby clarified the law affecting trade associations.

GROSVENOR, GILBERT HOVEY (*b. Constantinople, Turkey, 1875; d. Baddeck, Nova Scotia, 1966*), editor and naturalist. Born to American parents in Turkey; the family returned to the United States in 1890. Studied at Amherst College (M.A., 1901). President of the National Geographic Society, 1920–54. Editor of *National Geographic Magazine* 1899–1954; as editor, transformed *National Geographic* from a dull, dry, scholarly journal with a circulation of 900 to a colorful and interesting mainstay of home and school libraries with a circulation of 4.5 million. Magazine revenues increased so much that by 1907 the society was able to sponsor far-reaching expeditions that opened up for Americans much of the physical world and its peoples.

GROSVENOR, JOHN. *See* ALTHAM, JOHN.

GROSVENOR, WILLIAM MASON (*b. Ashfield, Mass., 1835; d. 1900*), journalist, publicist. Editor, *St. Louis Democrat*; associate of Joseph Pulitzer and Carl Schurz in Liberal Republican movement. Economics editor, *New York Tribune*, 1875–1900; editor of *Dun's Review* from 1893. His strictly impartial advice on tariff acts and financial policy was sought frequently by federal officials.

GROSZ, GEORGE (*b. Berlin, Germany, 1893; d. Berlin, Germany, 1959*), painter and caricaturist. Studied at the Royal Saxon Academy of the Fine Arts in Dresden. One of the great caricaturists of his time, Grosz's early works were a reaction to the horrors of World War I. He became a leader of the German Dada movement; he was tried and fined twice by the government for his anti-church and state pictures. Grosz escaped the Nazis in 1933, immigrating to the U.S. where he taught at the Art Students League. Early works include *The Face of the Ruling Classes* (1919), *Ecce Homo* (1922), *Mirror of the Bourgeoisie* (1924), and *Love Above All* (1931). Works in America include *The Ambassador of Goodwill* (the Metropolitan Museum of Art) and the Stickmen series represented by the work *Waving the Flag* (Whitney Museum of American Art). He was given a large retrospective by the Whitney Museum of American Art in 1954; in 1959, he was awarded the gold medal of the Academy of Arts and Letters.

GROTE, AUGUSTUS RADCLIFFE (*b. Liverpool, England, 1841; d. Hildesheim, Germany, 1903*), entomologist. Came to America as a child. A born naturalist, he described over 2,000 new species of American Lepidoptera; his published entomological bibliography includes 201 titles.

GROUARD, FRANK (*b. Paumotu Islands, South Pacific, 1850; d. St. Joseph, Mo., 1905*), army scout. Son of a missionary and a native mother; raised in California. Prisoner of the Sioux, 1869–75; scouted in Wyoming, Montana, and the Dakotas, 1876–95.

GROVER, CUVIER (*b. Bethel, Maine, 1828; d. Atlantic City, N.J., 1885*), Union soldier. Brother of La Fayette Grover. Graduated West Point, 1850. Lifelong army career included exploration in Far West, divisional command in Civil War, and frontier duty.

GROVER, LA FAYETTE (*b. Bethel, Maine, 1823; d. Portland, Oreg., 1911*), lawyer, politician, manufacturer. Brother of Cuvier Grover. Removed to Oregon, 1851; was active in territorial politics. As partisan Democratic governor of Oregon, 1871–77, was a key figure in disputed presidential election of 1876. Represented his state in U.S. House and was U.S. senator, 1877–83.

GROVES, LESLIE RICHARD, JR. (*b. Albany, N.Y., 1896; d. Washington, D.C., 1970*), army officer and director of the Manhattan Project during World War II. Studied at the U.S. Military Academy (graduated, 1918). Commissioned a second lieutenant in the Army Corps of Engineers (1918); captain (1934); brigadier general (1942). Supervised military construction in the United States before being assigned command of the atomic bomb project in 1942. Described in the press as the "Atom General," he was an effective leader whose strategy included naming J. Robert Oppenheimer to direct the central laboratory for bomb design and attempting to ensure security by sequestering the bomb-development scientists in Los Alamos, N. Mex. Retired from the army in 1948. His controversial statements about an American atomic monopoly (soon proved false) and foreign relations exacerbated cold-war tensions. Vice president in charge of research for the Remington division of the Sperry Rand Corporation, 1948–61.

GROW, GALUSHA AARON (*b. Ashford, Conn., 1882; d. 1907*), lawyer, politician. Raised in western Pennsylvania. Graduated Amherst, 1844; became law partner of David Wilmot. Congressman, Democrat, from Pennsylvania, 1851–55; Independent and Republican, 1855–63; Republican, 1893–1901. A frontiersman, his immediate and continuing interest was in public lands. He became one of the most outspoken of the new Republicans in the turbulent sessions preceding the Civil War. During his term as Speaker of the House of Representatives, 1861–63, he saw the Homestead Act, for which he had so long labored, passed. Out of office 30 years, he returned to Congress a picturesque veteran still interested in extending homestead legislation and acquiring new territory.

GRUBE, BERNHARD ADAM (*b. near Erfurt, Germany, 1715; d. Bethlehem, Pa., 1808*), Moravian missionary. Came to America, 1748. Worked among Delaware Indians of Pennsylvania; minister at Gnadenhütten and Head's Creek; later pastor at Lititz and elsewhere in Pennsylvania.

GRUENING, EMIL (*b. Hohensalza, East Prussia, 1842; d. New York, N.Y., 1914*), pioneer ophthalmologist and otologist, teacher. Moved to America, 1862. Graduated New York College of Physicians and Surgeons, 1867; postgraduate student, London, Paris, and Berlin. Made pioneer contributions in surgery of the eye, brain abscess, mastoid; practiced and taught in New York City.

GRUND, FRANCIS JOSEPH (*b. Klosterneuburg, Austria, 1798; d. Philadelphia, Pa., 1863*), author, journalist, politician.

GRUNDY, FELIX (*b. Virginia, 1777; d. 1840*), lawyer, jurist. Raised in Kentucky, where he served as legislator and appeals judge. Removed to Tennessee, 1807, and was Democratic congressman, 1811–15; U.S. senator, 1829–38, 1839–40; U.S. attorney general, 1838–39.

GRUNDY, JOSEPH RIDGWAY (*b. Camden, N.J., 1863; d. Nassau, the Bahamas, 1961*), business leader and senator. Founded the Pennsylvania Manufacturers' Association (PMA) in 1909; president from 1909–47. The PMA was the largest political interest group of its kind in the United States; its methods of influencing legislation became the model for other interest groups, especially labor organizations. Grundy's abilities as a fundraiser and lobbyist made him a major figure among the Republican politicians in Pennsylvania. Served as senator from 1929–30.

GUE, BENJAMIN F. (*b. Greene Co., N.Y., 1828; d. Des Moines, Iowa, 1904*), Iowa legislator and lieutenant governor, journalist. Removed to Iowa, 1852. Author of *History of Iowa* (1903).

GUÉRIN, ANNE-THÉRÈSE (*b. Étables, France, 1798; d. 1856*), educator. Religious name Mother Theodore. Founder of Sisters of Providence of St. Mary-of-the-Woods, Ind., 1840; established first women's academy in the state.

GUERNSEY, EGBERT (*b. Litchfield, Conn., 1823; d. 1903*), physician, medical journalist. M.D., University of the City of New York, 1846. Attempted to bring homeopathy into harmony with the old school of medicine.

GUESS, GEORGE. *See* SEQUOYAH.

GUEST, EDGAR ALBERT (*b. Birmingham, England, 1881; d. Detroit, Mich., 1959*), poet and newspaper columnist. Immigrated to the U.S. in the 1880's. Joined the staff of the *Detroit Free Press* in 1895 where he remained until his death. Guest wrote a column which featured his homey and simple verse. Later he became syndicated and his verses were published in collections. Most popular works were *A Heap o' Livin'* (1916) and *Over Here* (1918). Guest's work was ridiculed by the critics but loved by the public and he was successful financially. Guest never called himself a poet; by his own description he was "a newspaper man who wrote verses."

GUFFEY, JOSEPH F. (*b. Westmoreland County, Pa., 1870; d. Washington, D.C., 1959*), businessman and U.S. senator. Studied briefly at Princeton. Guffey was a powerful figure in Pennsylvania Democratic circles and a speculator in oil before he was elected to the Senate in 1934, remaining there until his defeat in 1946. He was an ardent New Dealer and supporter of Roosevelt. A liberal in politics, at a time when liberalism was synonymous with New Deal idealism, Guffey stood out as a liberal who preached and practiced a tough brand of organization and patronage politics.

GUFFEY, JAMES MCCLURG (*b. Sewickley Township. Pa., 1839; d. 1930*), oil producer. One of largest landowners, producers, and operators in United States, individually and in partnership with John H. Galey, 1880–1905.

GUGGENHEIM, DANIEL (*b. Philadelphia, Pa., 1856; d. near Port Washington, N.Y., 1930*), capitalist, philanthropist. Son of Meyer Guggenheim. Headed American Smelting and Refining Co., also the miscellaneous corporations which in the Guggenheim plan of operations clustered about the central enterprise. One of the foremost representatives of American industrial imperialism, he developed Bolivian tin mines; Yukon gold mines; Belgian Congo diamond fields and rubber plantations; copper mines in Alaska, Utah, Chile; and Chilean nitrate fields. He helped plan the "Guggenheim strategy," *viz.* integration of smelting and refining with exploration for, and control of, sources of supply. Among his notable philanthropies, in the tradition of his father, were the Daniel and Florence Guggenheim Foundation and the Daniel Guggenheim Fund for the Promotion of Aeronautics.

GUGGENHEIM, MEYER (*b. Langnau, Switzerland, 1828; d. Palm Beach. Fla., 1905*), financier. Came to America, *ca.* 1847. Built up import firm of M. Guggenheim's Sons, specializing in Swiss embroideries; became interested in mining and smelting, 1887, and by 1891 had thrown his entire fortune into the new venture. Besides his own abilities, his chief resources were seven sons whom he had trained in business tactics, thus enabling him to maintain personal control of large-scale enterprises. His great success came in 1901; after a severe struggle he gained control of the American Smelting and Refining Co., a trust composed of the country's largest metal-processing plants. His policies were carried on by his sons, among them Daniel Guggenheim, who vastly extended the firm's activities.

GUGGENHEIM, SIMON (*b. Philadelphia, Pa., 1867; d. New York, N.Y., 1941*), business executive, philanthropist. Son of Meyer Guggenheim; brother of Daniel and Solomon R. Guggenheim. Became chief ore buyer for his father's firm, settling in Denver, Colo., 1892. When the family won a controlling interest in the American Smelting and Refining Co., 1901, he was appointed its western representative and company treasurer. Politically ambitious, he was, after several years of political activity, elected to the U.S. Senate as a Republican, serving without distinction from 1907 to 1913. He was president of the American Smelting and Refining Co., 1919–41. Taking an increasing interest in philanthropy as he grew older, he made generous gifts to several hospitals and universities; he is remembered particularly for the establishment and endowment by him and his wife of the John Simon Guggenheim Memorial Foundation, which grants fellowships in the arts, sciences, and humanities to young artists and scholars of proven ability.

GUGGENHEIM, SOLOMON ROBERT (*b. Philadelphia, Pa., 1861; d. Sands Point, N.Y., 1949*), mining magnate, art collector, museum founder. Son of Meyer Guggenheim; brother of Daniel and Simon Guggenheim. Retired in 1919 from full-time activity in his family's business enterprises. Beginning in 1926, he shifted his collecting interests from conventional and established work of the past to the enthusiastic acquisition of modern art on a grand scale. He established Solomon R. Guggenheim Foundation in 1937 to administer a museum in which the public might be "enlightened" concerning nonobjective art, and in 1943 commissioned Frank Lloyd Wright to design and build a permanent home for his collections on upper Fifth Avenue, New York City. The Guggenheim Museum, housing more than 3,000 modern paintings and sculptures, opened in 1959.

GUIGNAS, LOUIS IGNAACE. *See* GUIGNAS, MICHEL.

GUIGNAS, MICHEL (*b. Condom, France, 1681; d. Quebec, Canada. 1752*), Jesuit priest. Came to Canada, 1716. Missionary to the Sioux in Minnesota and Wisconsin, 1727–28 and 1731–37.

GUILD, CURTIS (*b. Boston, Mass., 1827; d. 1911*), journalist, author. Editor-manager of Boston *Commercial Bulletin*, 1859–98; financial authority, antiquarian; founded Bostonian Society.

GUILD, CURTIS (*b. Boston, Mass., 1860; d. 1915*), son of Curtis Guild (1827–1911) and associated with him on *Commercial Bulletin*. Republican governor of Massachusetts, 1905–07; ambassador to Russia, 1911–13. As governor, initiated labor and other reforms; enjoyed great respect and popularity.

GUILD, LA FAYETTE (*b. Tuscaloosa, Ala., 1825; d. Marysville, Calif., 1870*), army medical officer. Graduated University of Alabama, 1845; M.D., Jefferson Medical College, 1848. Joined the army medical service, 1849. Confederate surgeon and inspector of hospitals, 1861; medical director of Lee's Army of Northern Virginia, 1862–65. His service was marked by intelligence, industry, and initiative of a high order. Following the war he went to Mobile, Ala., broken in health, thence to San Francisco, 1869, in hopes of improvement.

GUILD, REUBEN ALDRIDGE (*b. West Dedham, Mass., 1822; d. Providence, R.I., 1899*), librarian of Brown University, 1847–93. A founder of American Library Association.

GUILDAY, PETER KEENAN (*b. Chester, Pa., 1884; d. Washington, D.C., 1947*), Roman Catholic clergyman, church historian. Educated at St. Charles Borromeo Seminary, Philadelphia, and at the University of Louvain. He was ordained to the priesthood at Louvain, 1909, and made his graduate studies in history there, receiving the doctorate in 1914. He then joined Catholic University of America as instructor in history; he became professor in 1923. He concentrated on rehabilitating the study of the history of the Catholic church, which had little professional standing in the United States. He served as principal editor of the *Catholic Historical Review*, 1915–41, and as secretary of the American Catholic Historical Society, 1919–41, and gave example in his own writings of what church history should be. Among his books, his *Life and Times of John England* (1927) is perhaps the best.

GUILFORD, NATHAN (*b. Spencer, Mass., 1786; d. Cincinnati, Ohio, 1854*), lawyer. Graduated Yale, 1812. Settled in Cincinnati. Ohio, 1816. Devoted life to fight for free schools in Ohio; published school textbooks. Public school superintendent, Cincinnati, 1850–52.

GUINEY, LOUISE IMOGEN (*b. Boston, Mass., 1861; d. Chipping Campden, England, 1920*), essayist, poet. Author of, among other books, *Songs at the Start* (1884) and *Happy Ending* (her selected poems, 1909, 1927); her sympathetic critical sense and exquisite prose style are best displayed in *A Little English Gallery* (1894) and *Patrins* (1897). Cavalier England was her country of the mind.

GUINZBURG, HAROLD KLEINERT (*b. New York, N.Y., 1899; d. New York, 1961*), publisher. Studied at Harvard and Columbia Law School (graduated, 1926). Worked for Simon and Schuster in 1924. Founded the Viking Press, Inc., with George S. Oppenheimer in 1925; president from 1925–61. Founded the Literary Guild of America in 1926. Joined the Office of War Information in 1942; chief of the Domestic Bureau of Publications in 1943; director of the London Publications Division in 1944; publishing consultant to 1945. President of the American Book Publishers Council, 1956–58. Guinzburg's directives at Viking saw the creation of many successful publishing enterprises, such as Viking's Portable Library and Compass Books. A juvenile department set up in 1933 produced a distinguished juvenile list. Notable American writers published by Viking in the 1930's included John Steinbeck, Erskine Caldwell, Dorothy Parker, Albert Halper, and Alexander Woollcott.

GUITERAS, JUAN (*b. Matanzas, Cuba, 1852; d. Mantanzas, 1925*), physician, medical teacher. Made valuable contributions to knowledge of tropical medicine; associate of W. C. Gorgas, C. J. Finlay, and Walter Reed in yellow fever study.

GULICK, JOHN THOMAS (*b. Waimea, Hawaii, 1832; d. Honolulu, 1923*), Congregational missionary to Japan and China, naturalist. Graduated Williams, 1859. Brother of Luther H. Gulick (1828–91). Formulated hypothesis that evolution is divergent through influence of segregation.

GULICK, LUTHER HALSEY (*b. Honolulu, Hawaii, 1828; d. Springfield, Mass., 1891*), Congregational clergyman. Brother of John T. Gulick. Medical missionary in Caroline Islands, China, Japan, Spain, Italy, Turkey, Bohemia.

GULICK, LUTHER HALSEY (*b. Honolulu, Hawaii, 1865; d. Maine, 1918*), specialist in physical education, author. Son of Luther H. Gulick (1828–91). Graduated M.D., University of the City of New York, 1889. Active in YMCA work; helped devise game of basketball; founded Camp Fire Girls; promoted school hygiene and physical education.

GULICK, SIDNEY LEWIS (*b. Ebon, Marshall Islands, 1860; d. Boise, Idaho, 1945*), Congregational clergyman. Son of Luther H. Gulick (1828–91). A student of Japanese culture and a zealous promoter of better American-Japanese relations while a missionary there *post* 1887, he accepted appointment in 1914 as secretary of a commission of the Federal Council of Churches, charged to study problems of relations with Oriental peoples from the standpoint of Christian statesmanship and ethics. From then until his retirement in 1934, he was tireless in writing, speaking, and lobbying for improvement of U.S. relations with Japan and China. Active also in world peace movements.

GUMMERE, FRANCIS BARTON (*b. Burlington, N.J., 1855; d. 1919*), philologist. Son of Samuel J. Gummere. Graduated Haverford, 1872; Ph.D., Freiburg, 1881. Taught at Haverford, 1887–1919; distinguished prosodist. Best known for theory of communal origin of English and Scottish ballads.

GUMMERE, JOHN (*b. near Willow Grove, Pa., 1784; d. 1845*), mathematician. Author of *Treatise on Surveying* (1814); headed a successful school at Burlington, N.J., 1814–33 and *post* 1843.

GUMMERE, SAMUEL JAMES (*b. Rancocas, N.J., 1811; d. 1874*), educator. Son of John Gummere. President, Haverford College, 1862–74; nationally known as mathematician and astronomer.

GUMMERE, SAMUEL RENÉ (*b. Trenton, N.J., 1849; d. Wimbledon, England, 1920*), lawyer, diplomat. Played important role in "Perdicaris incident," in Morocco, 1904. First U.S. minister to Morocco, 1905–09. Brother of William S. Gummere.

GUMMERE, WILLIAM STRYKER *b. Trenton, N.J., 1850; d. Newark, N.J., 1933*), lawyer, jurist. Brother of Samuel R. Gummere. Judge, New Jersey Supreme Court, 1895–1933; chief justice, *post* 1901.

GUNN, FREDERICK WILLIAM (*b. Washington, Conn., 1816; d. Washington, Conn., 1881*), schoolmaster. Graduated Yale, 1837. Unconventional, strongly individualistic founder of "the Gunnery" school, 1850.

GUNN, JAMES NEWTON (*b. Springfield, Ohio, 1867; d. 1927*), pioneer industrial and production engineer. Perfected tab-type index card and vertical file; assisted in organization of Harvard Business School.

GUNN, ROSS (*b. Cleveland, Ohio, 1897; d. Washington, D.C., 1966*), physicist. Studied at the University of Michigan and Yale (Ph.D., 1926). Instructor in engineering physics at Yale to 1926. Research physicist at the Naval Research Laboratory in Washington, D.C. (1927–38); superintendent of the mechanics and electricity division (1938–43); of the aircraft electrical division (1943–46); of the physics division (1946–47). Technical director of the Army-Navy Precipitation Project, 1944. Director of physical research of the United States Weather Bureau (1944–55); assistant chief for technical services (1955–56). On the physics faculty of American University (1958–66). Aided military security with researches into uranium fission that earned him the title "father of the nuclear submarine."

GUNN, SELSKAR MICHAEL (*b. London, England, 1883; d. Newtown, Conn., 1944*), public health administrator. S.B. in biology, Massachusetts Institute of Technology, 1905; studied under William T. Sedgwick. Began career as a bacteriologist.

Served as health officer of Orange, N.J., 1908–10. Taught sanitary biology at MIT, 1910–17, serving also in 1911 as consultant to Milwaukee Bureau of Economy and Efficiency under John R. Commons; received national recognition for his papers on housing, communicable disease, and public health administration; edited *American Journal of Public Health*, 1912–17. Thereafter, he was associated with the international public health activities of the Rockefeller Foundation, notably in China, 1932–37.

GUNNISON, FOSTER (*b. Brooklyn, N.Y., 1896; d. St. Petersburg, Fla., 1961*), entrepreneur in the prefabricated housing industry. Studied at St. Lawrence University and the U.S. Naval Academy (graduated, 1919). Cofounder of Cox, Nostrand, and Gunnison (1923), which designed and built electric lighting fixtures; the company became a leading firm in the lighting of major Art Deco buildings in New York. Founded Houses, Inc. in 1934 to stimulate research, construction, management, and financing in prefabricated housing. Formed Gunnison Magic Homes (became Gunnison Housing Corporation) in 1935 in New Albany, Ind., The company became a subsidiary of U.S. Steel Corporation in 1944; Gunnison was president until 1950 and a director until 1953. According to *Architectural Forum* Gunnison "perfected prefabrication on a true mass-production, assembly line basis"; he has been called the Father of Prefab and the Henry Ford of Housing.

GUNNISON, JOHN WILLIAMS (*b. Goshen, N.H., 1812; d. near Sevier Lake, Utah, 1853*), army engineer. Graduated West Point, 1837. Engaged in surveys in Georgia and in lake region of Northwest; in 1849 was topographical engineer with Stansbury survey exploring a central route to the Pacific. Author of *The Mormons, of Latter-day Saints, in the Valley of the Great Salt Lake* (1852). Assigned in 1853 to explore a westward route by way of the Grand and Green River valley to the Santa Clara, he and six of his party were killed by Pahvant Indians who raided their camp.

GUNSAULUS, FRANK WAKELEY (*b. Chesterville, Ohio, 1856; d. Chicago, Ill., 1921*), Congregational clergyman, author. Pastor in Chicago *post* 1887; notable preacher; collector of books and art. A founder and president of Armour Institute of Technology.

GUNTER, ARCHIBALD CLAVERING (*b. Liverpool, England, 1847; d. New York, N.Y., 1907*), playwright, novelist, publisher. Came to America as a child; raised in San Francisco, Calif. His novels had a great contemporary popularity, 1887–94. *Mr. Barnes of New York* (1887) sold more than a million copies.

GUNTHER, CHARLES FREDERICK (*b. Wildberg, Germany, 1837; d. 1920*), candy manufacturer, rare-book collector, Chicago civic and political leader. Taken to America as a child. Made numerous popular confectionery inventions, including the caramel.

GUNTHER, JOHN (*b. Chicago, Ill., 1901; d. New York, N.Y., 1970*), journalist and author. Studied at the University of Chicago (graduated, 1922). Worked as foreign correspondent for the *Chicago Daily News*, 1924–36. Achieved unprecedented success with books that introduced the "Inside" usage into the American vernacular, including *Inside Europe* (1936), *Inside Asia* (1939), *Inside Latin America* (1941), *Inside U.S.A.* (1947), and *Inside Russia Today* (1958). Also wrote novels, juvenile, and various nonfiction books, including an account of the death of his son by brain tumor, published as *Death Be Not Proud* (1949).

GUNTON, GEORGE (*b. Chatteris, England, 1845; d. New York, N.Y., 1919*), editor, economist. Immigrated to Fall River, Mass., 1874; edited *Labor Standard*. Author of *Wealth and Progress* (1887); editor, *Social Economist* (later *Gunton's Magazine*, 1891–1904. His views on wages and hours of labor influenced direction of economic thought in America.

GURLEY, RALPH RANDOLPH (*b. Lebanon, Conn., 1797; d. Washington, D.C., 1872*), philanthropist. Devoted life to American Colonization Society; was expert on Liberia and African colonization.

GURNEY, EPHRAIM WHITMAN (*b. Boston, Mass., 1829; d. 1886*), educator. Graduated Harvard, 1852; taught there *post* 1857, and was first dean of faculty, 1870–86. Aided Charles W. Eliot in his transformation of Harvard into a great university.

GUROWSKI, ADAM (*b. Kalisz, Poland, 1805; d. Washington, D.C., 1866*), author, agitator. Exiled from Poland, he was influenced in Paris by Fourier and the St. Simon group; later he was a propagandist for Pan-Slavism. Came to America, 1849; worked for the New York *Tribune*. Served as adviser to W. H. Seward, 1861; was author of a *Diary* (1862) which criticized Lincoln and Seward and praised Stanton.

GUTHE, KARL EUGEN (*b. Hannover, Germany, 1866; d. Ashland, Oreg., 1915*), physicist. Graduated University of Marburg, Ph.D., 1892, the year he came to America. Taught at universities of Iowa and Michigan; dean of graduate school, Michigan.

GUTHERZ, CARL (*b. Schöftland, Switzerland, 1844; d. Washington, D.C., 1907*), artist. Came to America as a child; raised in Cincinnati, Ohio, and Memphis, Tenn. Muralist, influenced by Puvis de Chavannes; executed ceiling of House Reading Room, Library of Congress.

GUTHRIE, ALFRED (*b. Sherburne, N.Y., 1805; d. Chicago, Ill., 1882*), engineer. Son of Samuel Guthrie. Instituted (1852) a federal system of steamboat inspection; served as first head of enforcement bureau.

GUTHRIE, EDWIN RAY, JR. (*b. Lincoln, Nebr., 1886; d. Seattle, Wash., 1959*), psychologist, educator. Studied at the University of Nebraska and at the University of Pennsylvania (Ph.D., 1912). Taught at the University of Washington from 1914 to 1956; dean of the graduate school from 1945 to 1951. An adherent of the behavioristic approach to the problems of psychology, Guthrie collaborated with Stevenson Smith on the elementary text, *Chapters in General Psychology* (1919), a work that established the two authors as important proponents of a unified theory of learning. The main characteristics of his theory were to be understood as association by contiguity in time; that there is only one type of learning, and the same principle applies in all instances. Largely unproven by laboratory experiments, the theory still exerted influence in the field of behaviorist psychology. Guthrie was president of the American Psychological Association in 1945, and in 1958 was awarded the gold medal of the American Psychological Association.

GUTHRIE, GEORGE WILKINS (*b. Pittsburgh, Pa., 1848; d. Tokyo, Japan, 1917*), lawyer, diplomat. Reform mayor of Pittsburgh, 1906–09. As ambassador to Japan, 1913–17, he calmed intense anti-American feeling provoked by California Alien Land Act.

GUTHRIE, JAMES (*b. Bardstown, Ky., 1792; d. Louisville, Ky., 1869*), lawyer, railroad promoter. Served in Kentucky legislature, 1827–41; strong advocate of state internal improvements. Grew rich through real estate investment and promotion of macadam roads and railways; founded University of Louisville. As U.S. secretary of treasury, 1853–57, he was a ruthless reformer and highly effective. A Unionist, he put his Louisville and Nashville Railroad at the disposal of Union troops, 1861–65, a decisive factor in the conquest of the Southwest. Served as U.S. senator, Democrat, from Kentucky, 1865–68.

GUTHRIE, SAMUEL (*b. Brimfield, Mass., 1782; d. Sacketts Harbor, N.Y., 1848*), chemist, physician. Invented "percussion" pill and lock to explode it, replacing flintlock musket. Discovered chloroform, 1831, antedating independent discoveries by Soubeiran and Liebig.

GUTHRIE, WILLIAM DAMERON (*b. San Francisco, Calif., 1859; d. Lattingtown, N.Y., 1935*), lawyer. Authority on constitutional law and Ruggles professor at Columbia, 1913–22. Argued many leading cases before Supreme Court.

GUTHRIE, WOODY (*b. Okemah, Okla., 1912; d. Queens, N.Y., 1967*), songwriter and singer. Said to have written over a thousand songs between 1932 and 1952, including "Hard, Ain't It Hard," "So Long, It's Been Good to Know You" (one of the celebrated "Dust Bowl Ballads"), "This Land Is Your Land," "Pastures of Plenty," "Union Maid," "Tom Joad," and "Hard Traveling." Joined the Almanac Singers in the early 1940's; with Pete Seeger, Lee Hays, and Millard Lampell promoted leftist songs and performed at factories, union meetings, and antifascist conclaves. Many of his songs were popularized by the Weavers, whose personnel overlapped that of the Almanac Singers, in the 1950's. Wrote *Bound for Glory* (1943), *American Folksong* (1947), *Born to Win* (1965), and *Seeds of Man* published posthumously in 1976). A landmark in American folk balladry, Guthrie was the poet of the Oklahoma Dust Bowl, of unionization and antifascism, and, above all, of the American hobo and the West.

GUY, SEYMOUR JOSEPH (*b. London, England, 1824; d. 1910*), portrait and genre painter. Came to America, 1854; worked in New York. Best known for his pictures of childlife, genuine in sentiment.

GUYOT, ARNOLD HENRY (*b. Boudevilliers, Switzerland, 1807; d. 1884*), geographer. Graduated University of Berlin, Ph.D., 1835. Urged by J. R. L. Agassiz, he came to America, 1848; taught at Princeton, 1854–84. Made important contributions to glacial study; began U.S. weather station system; was author of pioneer textbooks and the classic *The Earth and Man* (1849); emphasized topography in teaching geography.

GUZIK, JACK (*b. Russia, 1886/1888; d. Chicago, Ill., 1956*), criminal entrepreneur. One of the most important figures in the Chicago underworld, Guzik became powerful in the bootlegging circle that included Al Capone and John Torrio. He was sentenced to prison in 1930 for income tax evasion, serving from 1932 to 1935. After Prohibition, Guzik's main business was the publication and distribution of sports material for gamblers. He appeared before the Investigating Committee of Estes Kefauver in 1951, but refused to answer questions. Guzik invested in Miami racetracks and was instrumental in transforming Las Vegas, Nev. into a gambling center after World War II.

GWIN, WILLIAM MCKENDREE (*b. Summer Co., Tenn., 1805; d. New York, N.Y., 1885*), lawyer, physician, politician. Graduated Transylvania, M.D., 1828; practiced in Mississippi. Removed to California, 1849. Represented San Francisco district in California constitutional convention; served as U.S. senator, Democrat, 1850–61. On outbreak of the Civil War he was arrested as a Southern sympathizer; released, he engaged in a scheme to establish settlers from the South in Sonora and Chihuahua, Mexico, which was rejected by Emperor Maximilian, 1864. Arrested again, 1865, he was held prisoner at Fort Jackson for eight months. He died in obscurity.

GWINNETT, BUTTON (*b. Down Hatherly, England, ca. 1735; d. near Savannah, Ga., 1777*), signer of the Declaration of Independence, Georgia merchant and planter. Settled in Savannah, Ga., 1765. Member of the Continental Congress, 1776–77, he was president (governor) of Georgia in March–April 1777. He was killed in a duel with Lachlan McIntosh.

H

HAAN, WILLIAM GEORGE (b. near Crown Point, Ind., 1863; d. Washington, D.C., 1924), soldier. Graduated West Point, 1889. Distinguished in Spanish-American War and in World War I as major general commanding 32nd "Red Arrow" Division.

HAARSTICK, HENRY CHRISTIAN (b. Hohenhameln, Germany, 1836; d. St. Louis, Mo., 1919), businessman. Came to America as a child. Pioneer in Mississippi river barge transportation after Civil War.

HAAS, FRANCIS JOSEPH (b. Racine, Wis., 1889; d. 1953), educator, government official, Roman Catholic bishop. Studied at St. Francis Seminary, Milwaukee; ordained in 1913. Director of the National Catholic School of Social Services in Washington, 1931–35. Member of the Labor Advisory Board of the National Recovery Administration, 1933. An expert on labor mediation. Special commissioner of conciliation for the Department of Labor, 1935–43. First dean of the School of Social Sciences at the Catholic University of America (1937). Appointed bishop of Grand Rapids, Mich., 1943.

HAAS, JACOB JUDA AARON DE (b. London, England, 1872; d. New York, N.Y., 1937), journalist, Zionist leader. Came to America, 1902. Associate of Theodor Herzl, and of Louis D. Brandeis whom he brought actively into the movement.

HABBERTON, JOHN (b. Brooklyn, N.Y., 1842; d. Glen Ridge, N.J., 1921), author, editor. Wrote stories of ordinary people and everyday life; remembered exclusively for Helen's Babies (1876).

HABERSHAM, ALEXANDER WYLLY (b. New York, N.Y., 1826; d. Annapolis, Md., 1883), naval officer, tea and coffee merchant. Great-grandson of James Habersham.

HABERSHAM, JAMES (b. Beverley, England, 1712 o.s.; d. New Brunswick, N.J., 1775), merchant planter, colonial official. Immigrated to Georgia, 1738, with friend George Whitefield with whom he established Bethesda Orphanage, one of the first in America. Organized firm of Harris & Habersham, 1744, the first commercial enterprise in the colony. An outspoken advocate of slavery, he developed large rice plantations after introduction of slaves to Georgia, 1749. A leader in the political life of the colony, held many offices and acted as governor, 1771–73. He was a staunch Loyalist in the years leading up to the Revolution.

HABERSHAM, JOSEPH (b. Savannah, Ga., 1751; d. 1815), merchant, Revolutionary patriot. Son of James Habersham. Associated in business with Joseph Clay. Ardently espoused the American cause; served in provincial congress and as colonel in the Continental Army. Was delegate to the Continental Congress, 1785–86, and to the Georgia convention which ratified the Federal Constitution, 1788. Served as postmaster general, 1795–1801. He is said to have raised and exported the first cotton shipped from America.

HACK, GEORGE (b. Cologne, Germany, ca. 1623; d. Va., ca. 1665), merchant, physician, colonist. Partner of Augustine Herrman in one of largest tobacco trading companies at New Amsterdam; ruined by British Navigation Act, 1651, he returned to practice of medicine.

HACKETT, FRANCIS (b. Kilkenny, Ireland, 1883; d. Virum, Denmark, 1962), literary critic, editor, and novelist. After 1901 he lived alternately in Ireland, Denmark, and the United States, becoming a U.S. citizen in 1948. After working as editor for the Chicago Post (1908–11), in 1913 he participated in the creation of the New Republic. Vigorously supported the cultural radicals, the literary realists, and cultural pluralism. In 1922 resigned from the New Republic, moved to Europe, and began a long career as a freelance writer, authoring a serialized book on Ireland for the New York World; a column, "The Rolling Stone," for the World's famous Op-Ed page; travel material and literary essays; and popular histories. His autobiographical novel, Green Lion (1936), was censored by the Irish. He also wrote I Chose Denmark (1940) and What "Mein Kampf" Means to America (1941). While living in the United States between 1939 and the early 1950's, wrote literary reviews and essays for the New Republic, the New York Times, the American Mercury, and many other magazines.

HACKETT, FRANK WARREN (b. Portsmouth, N.H., 1841; d. Portsmouth, 1926), lawyer, writer. One of Henry Adams' Washington intimates.

HACKETT, HORATIO BALCH (b. Salisbury, Mass., 1808; d. 1875), New Testament scholar. Graduated Amherst, 1830; Andover Theological Seminary, 1834. Taught at Newton and Rochester theological seminaries. Active in American Bible Revision Committee; advocate of scientific exegesis.

HACKETT, JAMES HENRY (b. New York, N.Y., 1800; d. Jamaica, N.Y., 1871), character actor. Debut at New York Park Theater, 1826. Famous for his portrayal of Falstaff. Founded first American-born theatrical family; helped develop American types of comedy character.

HACKETT, JAMES KETELTAS (b. Wolfe Island, Canada, 1869; d. Paris, France, 1926), actor. Son of James H. Hackett. Leading man in romantic "cloak and sword" plays, 1896–1908.

HACKLEY, CHARLES HENRY (b. Michigan City, Ind., 1837; d. 1905), lumberman. Post 1856, identified with Muskegon, Mich.; a principal benefactor of that city.

HADAS, MOSES (b. Atlanta, Ga., 1900; d. Aspen, Colo., 1966), classicist, humanist, and translator. B.A. (1922), Emory; M.A. (1925) and Ph.D. (1930), Columbia; rabbinical degree (1926), Jewish Theological Seminary. Serving in Columbia's Department of Greek and Latin, 1930–66, achieved fame as a scholar, teacher, and popularizer of the classics during a time when they were being banished from the center of the liberal arts to near oblivion. His most enduring scholarly contributions are his dissertation, published as *Sextus Pompey* (1930), his editions of *The Epistle of Aristeas* (1950) and *Third and Fourth Maccabees* (1953), and his own *Hellenistic Culture* (1959). Translated important German works and prepared many prose translations of the classics for modern American readers. His greatest single contribution to humanistic studies in America was his establishment of courses on the classics in translation in the Columbia General Education program.

HADDOCK, CHARLES BRICKETT (*b. Salisbury, N.H., 1796; d. West Lebanon, N.H., 1861*), Congregational clergyman, educator. Nephew of Daniel Webster. Professor at Dartmouth, 1819–50; partisan of public school education in New Hampshire.

HADDON, ELIZABETH. *See* ESTAUGH, ELIZABETH HADDON.

HADFIELD, GEORGE (*b. Leghorn, Italy*, ca. 1764; *d. Washington, D.C.*, 1826), architect. Came to America, 1795, as superintendent of construction, U.S. Capitol; dismissed, 1798. Designed "Arlington" (later the home of R. E. Lee) and a number of public buildings in Washington, D.C.

HADLEY, ARTHUR TWINING (*b. New Haven, Conn.*, 1856; *d. Kobe, Japan*, 1930), economist, president of Yale University, 1899–1921. Son of James Hadley. Graduated Yale, 1876. After a year of graduate study at Yale and two years at University of Berlin, he joined the Yale faculty as tutor. In 1883 he began to teach political science which became his specialty; he served as professor of political science in the college, the graduate school, and the Sheffield Scientific School. From 1892 to 1895 he was dean of the graduate school. His first book, *Railroad Transportation, Its History and Its Laws* (1885), was the earliest comprehensive study of the subject in the United States and established him as an authority in the field. He began his public career as expert witness before the Senate committee that drafted the Interstate Commerce Law in the same year and from 1885 to 1887 was commissioner of labor statistics in the state of Connecticut, publishing two reports that extended his reputation as an economist. While a brilliant and stimulating teacher at Yale, he contributed many articles on railroading and economics to various publications. His second book, *Economics—An Account of the Relations between Private Property and Public Welfare* (1896), was widely used as a text.

In May 1899 he became president of Yale. Though his classroom duties were terminated, audiences on both sides of the Atlantic were given an opportunity to hear him through various lectureships. He gave the Lowell Institute lectures, Boston, 1902; in 1907, he was Roosevelt professor of American history at the University of Berlin. In 1914 he lectured at Oxford. During his administration Yale developed into a great national university. New enterprises inaugurated during his term of office included the School of Forestry, the University Press, the *Yale Review*, and increased endowment and an unprecedented number of new buildings.

In 1921, having seen the university through the difficult period of World War I, he retired from the presidency. He had many interests to keep him occupied. He had been chairman of the Railroad Securities Commission, established by Congress in 1910, and of the commission, commonly called by his name, appointed by President Taft in 1911 to investigate the conditions of the railroads out of which came the railway valuation act of 1913. He was an active director of a number of railroads. He died while on a tour around the world.

HADLEY, HENRY KIMBALL (*b. Somerville, Mass.*, 1871; *d. New York, N.Y.*, 1937), composer, conductor. Received musical education from his father and at the New England Conservatory;

also studied in Germany. Conducted successively the Seattle, San Francisco, New York Philharmonic, and Manhattan Symphony orchestras, 1909–32. A prolific composer, his works include five symphonies, four operas, numerous other orchestral works, chamber music, recital songs and some particularly effective choral music. His work derives from the "Boston group" (musicians schooled in the German tradition of classicism and romanticism) with Hadley's own admixture of geniality and vigor. He was a leader in promoting the interests of American composers.

HADLEY, HERBERT SPENCER (*b. Olathe, Kans.*, 1872; *d. 1927*), lawyer. Attorney general, 1905–09, and Republican governor of Missouri, 1909–13. Chancellor of Washington University. Helped start movement for reform of American criminal justice.

HADLEY, JAMES (*b. Fairfield, N.Y.*, 1821; *d. 1872*), philologist. Father of Arthur T. Hadley. Graduated Yale, 1842; was professor of Greek there, 1851–72.

HA-GA-SA-DO-NI. *See* DEERFOOT.

HAGEDORN, HERMANN LUDWIG GEBHARD (*b. Staten Island, N.Y.*, 1882; *d. Santa Barbara, Calif.*, 1964), poet, novelist, and biographer. His first book of poetry was *The Woman of Corinth, A Tale in Verse* (1908). Thereafter he wrote the novel *Faces in the Dawn* (1914) and a drama, *Makers of Magic* (1914). His books *Where Do You Stand?* (1918) and *The Hyphenated Family* (1960) address the situation of German-Americans during World War I. A close friend of Theodore Roosevelt's, he wrote three biographies of him, the most popular being the 1954 best seller *The Roosevelt Family of Sagamore Hill*. Continued to publish poetry and substantial biographies throughout his life.

HAGEN, HERMANN AUGUST (*b. Königsberg, Germany*, 1817; *d. 1893*), entomologist. Author of *Bibliotheca Entomologica* (1862–63). First man to hold a chair confined to entomology in any college in the United States (at Harvard, *post* 1870).

HAGEN, WALTER CHARLES (*b. Rochester, N.Y.*, 1892; *d. Traverse City, Mich.*, 1969), golfer. Won the U.S. Open (1914, 1919); was Professional Golfers' Association (PGA) champion (1921, 1924, 1925, 1926, 1927) and British Open champion (1922, 1924, 1928, 1929); won the French Open (1920), the Belgian (1924), and the Canadian (1931); won some six state opens in the period 1915–31 as well as three Metropolitan Opens (1916, 1919, 1920); two North and South (1918, 1923), five Western (1916, 1921, 1926, 1927, 1932); one Eastern (1926), and the Gasparilla Open (1935); and was captain (1927, 1929, 1931, 1933, 1935) and nonplaying captain (1937) of the American Ryder Cup team. The first golf superstar, in 1940 he was named one of the charter members of the PGA Hall of Fame.

HAGER, JOHN SHARPENSTEIN (*b. near Morristown, N.J.*, 1818; *d. San Francisco, Calif.*, 1890), lawyer, judge, California legislator. Removed to California, 1849. U.S. senator, anti-monopoly Democrat, 1873–75.

HAGGERTY, MELVIN EVERETT (*b. Bunker Hill, Ind.*, 1875; *d. Minneapolis, Minn.*, 1937), educational psychologist, specialist in intelligence and achievement tests. Graduated Indiana, 1902; Ph.D., Harvard, 1910. Dean, College of Education, University of Minnesota, 1920–37.

HAGGIN, JAMES BEN ALI (*b. Harrodsburg, Ky.*, 1827; *d. Newport, R.I.*, 1914), lawyer, rancher, stock-breeder, capitalist. Removed to California, 1850; practiced law with Lloyd Tevis. Controlled over 100 mines, Alaska to Peru; developed extensive California irrigation projects.

HAGNER, PETER (*b. Philadelphia, Pa., 1772; d. 1850*), third auditor of the Treasury, 1817–49. Known as "watchdog of the Treasury," he rendered valuable service in settlement of important claims against the government.

HAGOOD, JOHNSON (*b. Barnwell Co., S.C., 1829; d. Barnwell Co., 1898*), lawyer, planter, Confederate soldier. Graduated Citadel, 1847. Governor of South Carolina, 1880–82. Helped rebuild the state after Civil War; was leader in development of agriculture and education.

HAGUE, ARNOLD (*b. Boston, Mass., 1840; d. 1917*), geologist. Brother of James D. Hague. Assistant, C. King's Survey of Fortieth Parallel; thereafter with U.S. Geological Survey. Supervised survey of Yellowstone National Park, *post* 1883.

HAGUE, FRANK (*b. Jersey City, N.J., 1876; d. New York, N.Y., 1956*), political boss. As Democratic mayor of Jersey City from 1917 to 1947, Hague built a power base in the state's second largest urban center that enabled him to become the principal political figure in New Jersey. His candidates for state and congregational offices were consistently elected with the backing of his highly organized political machine. By 1924, he was a national Democratic vice-chairman, a post he held until 1952.

HAGUE, JAMES DUNCAN (*b. Boston, Mass., 1836; d. Stockbridge, Mass., 1908*), mining engineer. Brother of Arnold Hague. Contributed classic third volume, *Mining Industry* (1870), to report of Geological Survey of Fortieth Parallel.

HAGUE, ROBERT LINCOLN (*b. Lincoln, R.I., 1880; d. New York, N.Y., 1939*), shipbuilder, ship operator. Manager, marine department, Standard Oil Co. of New Jersey, 1920–37; was later a vice president and director. A leader in modern tanker design, especially of ships convertible to naval auxiliaries.

HAHN, GEORG MICHAEL DECKER (*b. Klingenmünster, Bavaria, 1830; d. Washington, D.C., 1886*), lawyer, editor, Louisiana Unionist. Came to America as a child. Practiced law in New Orleans. Congressman, Republican, 1863 and 1885–86; first Republican governor of Louisiana, 1864–65.

HAID, LEO (*b. near Latrobe, Pa., 1849; d. 1924*), Roman Catholic clergyman, Benedictine. Elected abbot of Belmont Abbey, N.C., 1885; consecrated vicar-apostolic of North Carolina, 1888.

HAIGHT, CHARLES COOLIDGE (*b. New York, N.Y., 1841; d. Garrison-on-Hudson, N.Y., 1917*), architect. Graduated Columbia, 1861; studied in office of E. T. Littell. Adapted English collegiate Gothic to school architecture in America; designed, among others, the General Theological Seminary buildings (New York City) and a number of buildings at Yale and Hobart.

HAIGHT, HENRY HUNTLY (*b. Rochester, N.Y., 1825; d. San Francisco, Calif., 1878*), lawyer. Removed to California, 1850, where he was Democratic governor, 1868–72. Among important acts of his term was establishment of University of California (1868).

HAILMANN, WILLIAM NICHOLAS (*b. Glarus, Switzerland, 1836; d. Calif., 1920*), educator. Came to America, 1852. Leader of the kindergarten movement in the United States. Among his numerous publications, his expositions of Froebel's doctrines are outstanding.

HAINES, CHARLES GLIDDEN (*b. Canterbury, N.H., 1792; d. New York, N.Y., 1825*), lawyer, author, politician. Private secretary to De Witt Clinton. Published one of first American law journals, *United States Law Journal and Civilian Magazine* (1822–23).

HAINES, DANIEL (*b. New York, N.Y., 1801; d. 1877*), jurist. As Democratic governor of New Jersey, 1843–44, 1848–51, he built up educational system and improved governmental machinery of the state. He was a justice of the state supreme court, 1852–66.

HAINES, LYNN (*b. Waseca, Minn., 1876; d. 1929*), publicist, journalist. Editor and executive secretary, National Voters' League.

HAISH, JACOB (*b. near Karlsruhe, Germany, 1826; d. De Kalb, Ill., 1926*), contractor, inventor, manufacturer. Came to America as a boy. Invented "S" barbed wire, patented 1875; was long in litigation with assignees of Joseph F. Glidden's patents.

HALDEMAN, SAMUEL STEMAN (*b. Locust Grove, Pa., 1812; d. Chickies, Pa., 1880*), naturalist, geologist, philologist. First professor of comparative philology, University of Pennsylvania, 1868–80; wrote extensively on orthography, etymology, orthoepy.

HALDEMAN-JULIUS, EMANUEL (*b. Philadelphia, Pa., 1889; d. Girard, Kans., 1951*), publisher, author, and editor. Known for his publications during the 1920's and 1930's of the Little Blue Book series, small, low cost paperback editions of the literary classics and self-improvement books. Sold over 500 million copies, especially in rural areas which lacked libraries. He also published the newspaper, *American Freeman*, a descendant of the socialist paper *Appeal to Reason*, from his press in Girard, Kans.

HALDERMAN, JOHN A. (*b. Fayette Co., Ky., 1833; d. Atlantic City, N.J., 1908*), judge, Union soldier, Kansas legislator, diplomat. Consul general and minister resident to Siam, 1880–85, where he introduced postal and telegraph systems.

HALE, BENJAMIN (*b. Newburyport, Mass., 1797; d. Newburyport, 1863*), Congregational and Episcopal clergyman, educator. Third president of Geneva College, N.Y. (later Hobart), 1836–58; an educational liberal in sympathy with movement to substitute modern languages for classics.

HALE, CHARLES (*b. Boston, Mass. 1831; d. 1882*), journalist, Massachusetts legislator. Son of Nathan Hale (1784–1863); brother of Edward E. and Lucretia P. Hale. Consul general to Egypt, 1864–70; assistant U.S. secretary of state, 1872–74.

HALE, CHARLES REUBEN (*b. Lewistown, Pa., 1837; d. Cairo, Ill., 1900*), Episcopal clergyman. Consecrated bishop of Cairo, Ill, coadjutor to the bishop of Springfield, 1892. A Highchurchman, distinguished for scholarship.

HALE, DAVID (*b. Lisbon, Conn., 1791; d. 1849*), journalist. Cousin of Nathan Hale (1784–1863). Co-owner with Gerard Hallock of *New York Journal of Commerce, post* 1831; initiated new methods of news gathering.

HALE, EDWARD EVERETT (*b. Boston, Mass., 1822; d. Boston, 1909*), author, Unitarian clergyman. Son of Nathan Hale (1784–1863); nephew of Edward Everett. Graduated Harvard, 1839. Minister to South Congregational Church, Boston, 1856–99. Published in the *Atlantic Monthly* (December 1863) "The Man Without a Country," one of the best short stories written by an American. In the vast bulk of his writings, *A New England Boyhood* (1893, 1900), *James Russell Lowell and His Friends* (1899) and *Memories of a Hundred Years* (1902) deserve special mention. He was chaplain of the U.S. Senate, 1903–09.

HALE, EDWARD JOSEPH (*b. near Fayetteville, N.C., 1839; d. 1922*), journalist, Confederate soldier. Editor, *Fayetteville Observer, ca. 1866–1913*. Consul at Manchester, England, 1885–89; minister to Costa Rica, 1913–19.

HALE, EDWIN MOSES (*b. Newport, N.H., 1829; d. 1899*), homeopathic physician and teacher of medicine. Practiced in Michigan and Chicago, Ill.

HALE, ENOCH (*b. Westhampton, Mass., 1790; d. 1848*), physician. Brother of Nathan Hale (1784–1863). Graduated Harvard, M.D., 1813. Practiced in Gardiner, Maine, and Boston; author of the important *Observations on the Typhoid Fever of New England* (1839).

HALE, EUGENE (*b. Turner, Maine, 1836; d. Washington, D.C., 1918*), lawyer, politician, Maine legislator. Admitted to bar, 1857. Congressman, Republican, from Maine, 1869–79; authority on naval affairs and public expenditure; friend of James G. Blaine. U.S. senator, 1881–1911, a conservative and supporter of high tariff, he opposed measures for social and political reform. Hale did work of utmost importance in developing the modern Navy, but after the Spanish-American War his naval enthusiasm declined because of his dislike of American imperialism. His contempt for every progressive idea of the time made him unpopular in the country at large after 1901. After retirement from politics he was a member of the National Monetary Commission.

HALE, FREDERICK (*b. Detroit, Mich., 1874; d. Portland, Maine, 1963*), U.S. senator. B.A. (1896), Harvard; attended Columbia University Law School, 1896–97, and was admitted to the Maine bar, 1899. A Republican, in 1916 he was the first U.S. senator from Maine chosen by popular vote, and his career in the Senate continued till his retirement in 1941. Served on the Rules, Appropriations, and Naval Affairs committees, and was chairman of the latter for nine years and briefly chairman of the Appropriations Committee. Was noted for his strong advocacy of a large navy and his consistent opposition to New Deal spending policies during the 1930's.

HALE, GEORGE ELLERY (*b. Chicago, Ill., 1868; d. Pasadena, Calif., 1938*), astronomer. Graduated Massachusetts Institute of Technology, 1890. Taught astrophysics at University of Chicago, *post* 1892, and planned and directed the Yerkes Observatory there. His most important role was as initiator and director, 1904–23, of Mount Wilson Observatory, near Pasadena, Calif., where he performed many pioneering investigations, among them his discovery of magnetic fields in sunspots. He persuaded the Rockefeller Foundation to establish a 200-inch telescope on Palomar Mountain, Calif., 1928. Hale's bibliography of 450 titles covers a wide range of subjects but deals mainly with solar research; his eminence was international.

HALE, HORATIO EMMONS (*b. Newport, N.H., 1817; d. 1896*), lawyer, ethnologist. Son of Sarah J. B. Hale. On Wilkes Exploring Expedition, 1838–42, he collected data comprised in monumental *Ethnography and Philology* (Vol. VI of the Expedition Report, 1846). His subsequent work aided development of anthropology.

HALE, JOHN PARKER (*b. Rochester, N.H., 1806; d. 1873*), lawyer, politician, diplomat. Graduated Bowdoin, 1827. U.S. district attorney, 1834–41; congressman, Democrat, from Maine, 1843–45. Read out of the party for anti-slavery views, he was elected to the U.S. Senate, 1846, as an independent and served until 1853. Made his most notable speech in reply to Webster on Compromise of 1850; secured abolition of flogging and of the grog ration in the navy. Was presidential candidate of the Free-Soil party, 1852. Returned to the U.S. Senate, 1855, was re-elected, 1858, for a six-year term as a Republican and was chairman of the naval affairs committee. Involved in an influence-peddling scandal, he failed of renomination. While minister to Spain, 1865–69, he was charged with moral delinquencies in-volving the Queen and abuse of his importation franchise, and was recalled.

HALE, LOUISE CLOSSER (*b. Chicago, Ill., 1872; d. Los Angeles, Calif., 1933*), actress, author. Excelled as player of character roles and writer of travel books.

HALE, LUCRETIA PEABODY (*b. Boston, Mass., 1820; d. Boston, 1900*), author. Daughter of Nathan Hale (1784–1863); sister of Edward E. and Charles Hale. Remembered for *The Peterkin Papers* (1880) and *The Last of the Peterkins* (1886).

HALE, NATHAN (*b. Coventry, Conn., 1755; d. New York, 1776*), "Martyr Spy" of the Revolutionary War. Graduated Yale, 1773; was noted for physical and literary prowess. Taught school in Connecticut, 1773–75. Commissioned lieutenant, July 1775; served at siege of Boston and was promoted to captain, January 1776. With Knowlton's Rangers in defense of New York, April to September 1776. When Washington needed information on the strength and designs of the British after the defeat on Long Island, Hale volunteered to get it. Assuming the role of a schoolmaster with his college diploma for credentials, he accomplished his mission on Long Island. Returning to the American position on Harlem Heights, he had almost reached his own lines when he was apprehended as a spy. That he was betrayed by his Tory cousin Samuel Hale, British Deputy Commissioner of Prisoners, was the belief of the times and of his family. Military sketches and notes having been found on his person, Hale declared his name, rank, and mission. Without trial, Gen. Howe gave orders for his execution. At the gallows on the morning of Sept. 22, 1776, Hale made a "spirited and sensible speech" concluding with the memorable words, "I only regret that I have but one life to lose for my country."

HALE, NATHAN (*b. Westhampton, Mass., 1784; d. 1863*), journalist. Nephew of Nathan Hale, (1755–1776); father of Charles, Edward E., and Lucretia P. Hale. Edited *Boston Daily Advertiser*, 1814–54; one of first Americans to introduce editorial articles as a regular feature; helped found *North American Review*, 1815; was active in New England railroad promotion.

HALE, PHILIP (*b. Norwich, Vt., 1854; d. Boston, Mass., 1934*), musician, critic. Music critic and columnist on staff of the *Boston Herald*, 1903–33; author of program notes of the Boston Symphony Orchestra.

HALE, PHILIP LESLIE (*b. Boston, Mass., 1865; d. Boston, 1931*), figure painter, critic, teacher. Son of Edward E. Hale. Author of *Jan Vermeer of Delft* (1913).

HALE, ROBERT SAFFORD (*b. Chelsea, Vt., 1822; d. 1881*), lawyer. Practiced in Elizabethtown, N.Y.; was a Republican member of 39th and 43rd Congresses, and U.S. agent and counsel before American-British Mixed Claims Commission, 1871–73.

HALE, SARAH JOSEPHA BUELL (*b. Newport, N.H., 1788; d. Philadelphia, Pa., 1879*), author, editor. After publication of a novel, *Northwood* (1827), she removed at instance of John Lauris Blake to Boston to edit the *Ladies' Magazine*, first significant publication of its kind. When Louis A. Godey bought it out in 1837, she became literary editor of his famous *Lady's Book* and helped make it the best known of American women's periodicals. Throughout her life she fought for better education for American women, guided their taste and constantly set forth their duties and privileges. Of all the work in her 36 published volumes, the poem "Mary's Lamb" (in *Poems for Our Children*, 1830) is best remembered.

HALE, WILLIAM BAYARD (*b. Richmond, Ind., 1869; d. Munich, Germany, 1924*), Episcopal clergyman, journalist. Early admirer of Woodrow Wilson whose campaign biography he wrote in 1912 and whose *The New Freedom* (1914) he edited. Exposed (1918) as undercover German propaganda adviser in United States.

HALE, WILLIAM GARDNER (*b.* *Savannah, Ga., 1849; d. Stamford, Conn., 1928*), classical scholar. Graduated Harvard, 1870; studied at Leipzig and Göttingen. Professor of Latin, Cornell 1880–92; University of Chicago, 1892–1919. First director, American School of Classical Studies, Rome. Discovered lost Catullus manuscript.

HALL, ABRAHAM OAKEY (*b.* *Albany, N.Y., 1826; d. New York N.Y., 1898*), lawyer, politician, journalist. Known as "Elegant Oakey." Graduated New York University, 1844. New York county district attorney, 1855–58, 1862–68. Previously and successively a Whig, a Know-Nothing, and a Republican, he joined Tammany Hall, 1864. As mayor of New York City, 1868–72, he acted as the mountebank of the "Tweed Ring" covering up ugly facts by his wit and debonair manner. Conducting his own defense, he was acquitted of implication with Tweed, 1872. City editor of the New York *World*, 1879–82, he was later London representative of the *New York Herald* and the New York *Morning Journal*. He wrote a number of books and plays, *The Crucible* (1878) being his best claim to dramatic distinction.

HALL, ARETHUSA (*b.* *Norwich, Mass., 1802; d. Northampton, Mass., 1891*), educator, author. Co-founder of the Brooklyn Heights Seminary.

HALL, ARTHUR CRAWSHAY ALLISTON (*b.* *Binfield, England, 1847; d. Burlington, Vt., 1930*), Episcopal clergyman, member of Cowley Fathers. Came to America, 1874. Consecrated bishop of Vermont, 1894. Widely known canonist and writer, active in Christian unity work.

HALL, ASAPH (*b.* *Goshen, Conn., 1829; d. Annapolis, Md., 1907*), astronomer. Largely self-taught. Worked at Harvard Observatory, 1858–62; at U.S. Naval Observatory, 1862–91. His most spectacular observation was his discovery in 1877 of the two satellites of Mars. Among his 500 published papers are masterly investigations of the orbits of various satellites and of double stars, the mass of Mars and of Saturn's rings, the perturbations of the planets, the advance of Mercury's perihelion, the parallax of the sun, and solutions of mathematical problems these investigations brought up. After 1896, he taught celestial mechanics at Harvard.

HALL, BAYNARD RUSH (*b.* *Philadelphia, Pa., 1798; d. Brooklyn, N.Y., 1863*), Presbyterian clergyman, educator. Author of a frontier classic *The New Purchase* (1843, under pseudonym "Robert Carlton"), *Frank Freeman's Barber Shop* (1852) and other books.

HALL, BOLTON (*b.* *Armagh, Ireland, 1854; d. Thomasville, Ga., 1938*), lawyer, reformer. Son of John Hall. Came to America as a boy; graduated Columbia Law School, 1888. Author of many books and pamphlets on tax and other reforms of which the most successful was *Three Acres and Liberty* (1907).

HALL, CHARLES CUTHBERT (*b.* *New York, N.Y., 1852; d. 1908*), Presbyterian clergyman. Graduated Williams, 1872. Pastor, First Presbyterian Church, Brooklyn, N.Y., 1877–97; president, Union Theological Seminary, 1897–1908.

HALL, CHARLES FRANCIS (*b.* *Rochester, N.H., 1821; d. in Arctic, 1871*), explorer. Went alone to Frobisher Bay area and searched for traces of Sir John Franklin's party, 1860–62; described his expedition in *Arctic Researchers, and Life among the Esquimaux* (London, 1864; New York, 1865). Supported by Henry Grinnell, he left in 1864 on a five-year trip to the north end of Hudson Bay. With aid of Congress and a naval vessel, the *Polaris*, he departed in 1871 for a trip to the North Pole, reaching 82° 11′ N., 61° W., the most northerly point then attained by any vessel. Among the important geographic results of this expedition was the disclosure of the way to the North Pole. With similar limited resources no man has surpassed Hall in Arctic explorations.

HALL, CHARLES HENRY (*b.* *Augusta, Ga., 1820; d. Brooklyn, N.Y., 1895*), Episcopal clergyman. Rector, Church of the Epiphany, Washington, D.C., 1856–69, and of Holy Trinity, Brooklyn. Conducted funeral of friend Henry Ward Beecher.

HALL, CHARLES MARTIN (*b.* *Thompson, Ohio, 1863; d. 1914*), chemist, manufacturer. Graduated Oberlin, 1885. Encouraged by college chemistry professor, F. F. Jewett, Hall discovered the only commercially successful process of making aluminum (patent applied for, 1886; granted, 1889). When the Cowles Smelting Co. gave up an option they had taken on his patent, he secured backing from the Mellons; as Pittsburgh Reduction Co., he began producing fifty pounds of aluminum daily at Kensington, Pa., 1888. Cowles later brought suit against him for stealing the process, but the U.S. circuit approved Hall's originality in an 1893 decision. His process brought aluminum into general use.

HALL, DAVID (*b.* *Edinburgh, Scotland, 1714; d. Philadelphia, Pa., 1772*), printer, bookseller. Came to America, 1743, as journeyman in Benjamin Franklin's shop. Was Franklin's partner, 1748–66, and carried on the business as Hall and Sellers after Franklin sold his interest, 1766.

HALL, DOMINICK AUGUSTIN (*b.* *ca. 1765; d. New Orleans, La., 1820*), lawyer. Practiced in Charleston, S.C. As federal judge in Louisiana, 1804–20, he fined Andrew Jackson $1,000 for overriding writ of habeas corpus, 1815.

HALL, EDWIN HERBERT (*b.* *Great Falls, Maine, 1855; d. Cambridge, Mass., 1938*), physicist. Graduated Bowdoin, 1875; Ph.D., Johns Hopkins, 1880. Taught physics at Harvard, 1881–1921. His Ph.D. thesis was upon an effect he had discovered—a particular interaction between an electric current and a magnetic field that had been sought unsuccessfully by others, including the director of his graduate studies, Henry Augustus Rowland. The Hall effect, hailed as "a discovery comparable with the greatest made by Faraday," was Hall's major activity for the rest of his life, as he worked to fit it and other related effects and phenomena into a unified theoretical picture.

HALL, FITZEDWARD (*b.* *Troy, N.Y., 1825; d. 1901*), philologist. Graduated Rensselaer Polytechnic, 1842; Harvard, 1846. In India as teacher and inspector of public instruction, 1846–62; became professor of Sanskrit, Hindustani and Indian jurisprudence at King's College, London, 1862, and served until 1869. Edited H. H. Wilson's translation of *The Vishńu Puráná* (1864–77). Hall was the first American to edit a Sanskrit text (in 1852); his activity in editing and writing was prodigious. As much an authority on English philology as on Sanskrit, he wrote extensively in that field as well and was a valued contributor to the *Oxford English Dictionary* and other cooperative works.

HALL, FLORENCE MARION HOWE (*b.* *Boston, Mass., 1845; d. High Bridge, N.J., 1922*), author, lecturer. Daughter of Samuel G. and Julia Ward Howe.

HALL, GEORGE HENRY (*b.* *Manchester, N.H., 1825; d. 1913*), genre painter.

HALL, GRANVILLE STANLEY (*b.* *Ashfield, Mass., 1844; d. 1924*), psychologist, philosopher, educator. Graduated Williams,

1867; was influenced there by John Bascom. Entered Union Theological Seminary but left in 1866 for study in Germany. Returned to America, 1871; taught at Antioch College, 1872–76; took Ph.D. at Harvard, 1878. Following further study in Germany and development of a course on pedagogy at Harvard, he was made professor of psychology and pedagogics at John Hopkins, where he continued his researches in experimental psychology, 1883–88, and built up a circle of disciples including John Dewey and Joseph Jastrow. In 1887 he founded the *American Journal of Psychology* and in 1891 became first president of the newly formed American Psychological Association.

Hall attracted wide attention by his article "The Moral and Religious Training of Children" (1882), and by his first study, *The Contents of Children's Minds* (1883). By 1888 he was perhaps the foremost educational critic in the country, a reputation which led to his selection as president of newly founded Clark University, Worcester, Mass. Dissension soon arose between the founder, Jonas G. Clark, and the administration, though the trustees stood unanimously by Hall and gave him full support on all occasions until he resigned in 1919. During these difficult years he devoted himself to the new child-study movement which his writings had inaugurated. *The Pedagogical Seminary* which he founded in 1891 became its organ. His own interest culminated in *Adolescence, Its Psychology and Its Relation to Physiology, Anthropology, Sociology, Sex, Crime, Religion and Education* (1904), a digest of all the literature on that subject. In 1893 he returned to the classroom as head of the Clark psychology department, lecturing on a wide range of subjects including the history of philosophy. Publication of *Educational Problems* (1911) marked a return of his interest from education to psychology, a phase which resulted in *Founders of Modern Psychology* (1912), dealing as much with philosophy as psychology. Hall's place in American psychology is much disputed. In education he made a great impression on his own generation. Through his personality and ideas, he influenced the country's schools more profoundly than any other theorists except W. T. Harris and John Dewey. Hall's original point of view is better described in George E. Partridge, *Genetic Philosophy of Education* (1912), than in any work of his own.

HALL, HAZEL (*b. St. Paul, Minn., 1886; d. Portland, Oreg., 1924*), poet.

HALL, HENRY BRYAN (*b. London, England, 1808; d. Morrisania, N.Y., 1884*), engraver, portrait painter. Came to America, *ca.* 1850. Founded H. B. Hall and Sons, engravers of portraits of American historical figures, notably plates of Washington.

HALL, HILAND (*b. Bennington, Vt., 1795; d. Springfield, Mass., 1885*), jurist. Congressman, Whig, from Vermont 1833–43; Republican governor, 1858–60. Author of *The History of Vermont* (1868), an important work.

HALL, ISAAC HOLLISTER (*b. Norwalk, Conn., 1837; d. 1896*), lawyer, Orientalist. Graduated Hamilton, 1859. An outstanding Syriac scholar, he was also one of first to translate an entire Cypriot inscription. Collaborated with L. P. di Cesnola on Metropolitan Museum catalogs of Cypriot art.

HALL, JAMES (*b. Carlisle, Pa., 1744; d. Bethany, N.C., 1826*), Presbyterian clergyman. Removed to North Carolina as a child. Graduated College of New Jersey (Princeton), 1774. Chaplain in American Revolution; pastor at Bethany, N.C., and neighboring towns, 1776–1826. Established first Protestant mission in lower Mississippi Valley at Natchez, 1800.

HALL, JAMES (*b. Philadelphia, Pa., 1793; d. Cincinnati, Ohio, 1868*), author, jurist, banker. Brother of John E. Hall; son of Sarah E. Hall. Commended for bravery in War of 1812, after which he served with Decatur's expedition against Algiers. Removed to Shawneetown, Ill., 1820, to practice law and edit *Illinois Gazette*; contributed as jurist, state treasurer, and promoter of education to the development of the state, 1820–32. Established the *Illinois Monthly Magazine*, 1830, first literary periodical west of Ohio, to which he contributed half the contents. When its successor, the *Western Monthly Magazine*, lost most of its subscribers in 1835 because of Hall's vigorous defense of Catholics against Lyman Beecher's *A Plea for the West*, Hall withdrew to become cashier of the Commercial Bank, Cincinnati, where he had moved in 1833. In 1853 he became the bank's president. He is remembered chiefly as one of the most important recorders and interpreters of pioneer history, life and legend in Illinois and the Ohio Valley. Of his many published works, probably the most valuable are *Legends of the West* (1832) and *Sketches of History, Life and Manners in the West* (1834, 1835); he collaborated with T. L. McKenney in the celebrated *History of the Indian Tribes of North America* (1836–42; 1884).

HALL, JAMES (*b. Hingham, Mass., 1811; d. 1898*), geologist, paleontologist. Graduated Rensselaer Polytechnic, 1832. His report, *Geology of New York: Part IV, Comprising the Survey of the Fourth Geological District* (1843), became a classic in geological literature. In 1843 he began a fifty-year study of the state's paleontology, embodied in *New York State Natural History Survey: Paleontology* (8 vols. in 13, 1847–94). Served as state geologist of Iowa, 1855–58, and of Wisconsin, 1857–60. Became director of New York State Museum, 1866, and state geologist, 1893. His lifework lay in domain of stratigraphic geology and invertebrate paleontology. His contribution was invaluable; his influence, world-wide.

HALL, JAMES NORMAN (*b. Colfax, Iowa, 1887; d. Tahiti, 1951*); **NORDHOFF, CHARLES BERNARD** (*b. London, England, 1887; d. California, 1947*), coauthors. Writers of the best-selling *Bounty* trilogy (1932–34) which included *Mutiny on the Bounty, Men Against the Sea*, and *Pitcairn's Island*. The books established the team as important adventure-story tellers. Other books include *The Hurricane* (1936), *Botany Bay* (1941) and *High Barbary* (1945). After Nordhoff's death in 1947, Hall published *The Far Lands* (1950) and *The Forgotten One* (1951). Hall studied at Grinnel College (Ph.B., 1910) and Nordhoff at Harvard (1909).

HALL, JOHN (*b. Co. Armagh, Ireland, 1829; d. Bangor, Ireland, 1898*), Presbyterian clergyman. Came to America, 1867; served thereafter as influential pastor of Fifth Avenue Presbyterian Church, New York City.

HALL, JOHN ELIHU (*b. Philadelphia, Pa., 1783; d. Philadelphia, 1829*), lawyer, editor. Brother of James Hall (1793–1868). Published *American Law Journal* (Baltimore, Md., 1808–17) and a number of useful legal treatises; edited the *Port Folio*, 1816–27, also Dennie's *Lay Preacher* (1817).

HALL, JUANITA ARMETHEA (*b. Juanita Armethea Long, Keyport, N.J., 1901; d. Bayshore, N.Y., 1968*), actress and singer. After singing with the Hall Johnson Choir and her own Juanita Hall Choir, became famous for the role of Bloody Mary in the musical *South Pacific* (1949); her singing of "Bali Ha'i" and "Happy Talk" made her a celebrity, and she won a Tony and a Donaldson Award for her performance on Broadway and a Box Office award for her performance in the film version (1958). Played Madame Liang in *Flower Drum Song* (1958) for 600 performances in New York, on a long road tour, and in the film version (1961). Also appeared as a blues singer in New York clubs and made radio history in 1954 when she starred in "The Story of Ruby Valentine," the first program broadcast on the National Negro Network.

HALL, LUTHER EGBERT (*b. near Bastrop, La., 1869; d. 1921*), lawyer, jurist. Democratic governor of Louisiana, 1912–16. A reformer, he reduced patronage, freed the public schools from politics, and bonded state debt.

HALL, LYMAN (*b. Wallingford, Conn., 1724; d. Burke Co., Ga., 1790*), physician. Removed to New England settlement at Sunbury, Ga.; was active in Revolutionary cause and served in Continental Congress; was a signer of the Declaration of Independence. Elected Georgia governor, 1783, he initiated chartering of the state university.

HALL, NATHAN KELSEY (*b. Skaneateles, N.Y., 1810; d. 1874*), jurist. Law partner of Millard Fillmore; U.S. postmaster general, 1850–52; federal judge, Northern District of New York, 1852–74.

HALL, SAMUEL (*b. Medford, Mass., 1740; d. Boston, Mass., 1807*), printer. Apprentice to his uncle, Daniel Fowle. Established first printing-house, Salem, Mass., 1768; published intensely Whig *Essex Gazette,* 1768–75; published also *New England Chronicle, Salem Gazette* and *Massachusetts Gazette.*

HALL, SAMUEL (*b. Marshfield, Mass., 1800; d. 1870*), East Boston shipbuilder. Built *Surprise,* 1850, the first Massachusetts clipper; also *John Gilpin, R.B. Forbes* and other celebrated vessels.

HALL, SAMUEL READ (*b. Croydon, N.H., 1795; d. 1877*), Congregational clergyman, educator. Established a teacher-training school at Concord, Vt., 1823; later another at Phillips Academy, Andover. Was a founder of American Institute of Instruction, Boston, 1830.

HALL, SARAH EWING (*b. Philadelphia, Pa., 1761; d. Philadelphia, 1830*), essayist. Daughter of John Ewing; mother of James Hall (1793–1868) and John E. Hall. Contributor to the *Port Folio,* 1801–27; author of *Conversations on the Bible* (1818).

HALL, SHERMAN (*b. Weathersfield, Vt., 1800; d. Sauk Rapids, Minn., 1879*), Congregational clergyman. Missionary to Chippewa Indians in southern Lake Superior region, 1831–54.

HALL, THOMAS (*b. Philadelphia, Pa., 1834; d. 1911*), inventor, patent attorney. Devised a pioneer typewriter, patented 1867; also the single-keyed "Hall Typewriter" (1880), sewing-machine attachments, an improved mill-grinder and other machinist's tools.

HALL, THOMAS SEAVEY (*b. Upper Bartlett, N.H., 1827; d. Meriden, Conn., 1880*), wool manufacturer, inventor. Perfected a system of electric automatic signals for railroads, patented first in 1867. His most important invention, the electric inclosed disc, or "banjo," signal, was patented, 1869; Later he worked out signals for drawbridges and in 1879 devised a method for highway–crossing protection. The first installation of his automatic block-signalling system was made on a line of the Eastern Railroad of Massachusetts, 1871. The principles Hall developed still prevail in railroad-signalling practice.

HALL, WILLARD (*b. Westford, Mass., 1780; d. Wilmington, Del., 1875*), jurist, legislator. Removed to Delaware, 1803; served as federal district judge, 1823–71. Author of Delaware school law of 1829; lifelong advocate of free public education.

HALL, WILLARD PREBLE (*b. Harpers Ferry, Va., 1820; d. 1882*), lawyer, soldier, congressman. Graduated Yale, 1839. Removed to Missouri, 1840; practiced law at Sparta and St. Joseph, Mo. Served with distinction under Col. A. W. Doniphan in Mexican War. A Unionist, he was lieutenant-governor of Missouri, 1861–64, and provisional governor, 1864–65.

HALL, WILLIAM WHITTY (*b. Paris, Ky., 1810; d. New York, N.Y., 1876*), Presbyterian clergyman, physician, pioneer editor of popular health magazines. Author of many rather dubious publications; edited *Hall's Journal of Health,* 1854–76.

HALLAM, LEWIS *b. England, ca. 1740; d. Philadelphia, Pa., 1808*), theatrical manager. Came to America with his father's theatrical company which first appeared in *The Merchant of Venice* at Williamsburg, Va., Sept. 15, 1752, a date which begins the continuous history of the American theatre. After two years' playing in American cities, the company was in Jamaica, B.W.I., 1754–58. When they returned to the American colonies, Lewis Hallam was leading man, undertaking such roles as Hamlet, which he was probably the first to present in this country, and Romeo to his mother's Juliet. Forced back to Jamaica by the Revolution, the so-called "American company" returned after the war with Hallam as manager. In 1785 he began a stormy partnership with John Henry, a rival manager, playing principally in New York and Boston. Henry in 1794 sold his interest to John Hodgkinson, an even greater source of discord. William Dunlap, a third partner, *post* 1796, tried to act as mediator, but Hallam withdrew from the management, 1797, continuing his connection only as a salaried actor. Parsimonious, crafty, quarrelsome, often the source of his own troubles, Hallam was not a good manager; as an actor, however, he was admired for many years, playing every important character in the dramas then current. His forte was high comedy.

HALLECK, FITZ-GREENE (*b. Guilford, Conn., 1790; d. Guilford, 1867*), poet. Employed, 1811–49, as confidential clerk to Jacob Barker and the first John Jacob Astor. Author, with his friend Joseph Rodman Drake, of "Croaker & Co.," satires on local celebrities which appeared anonymously in N.Y. *Evening Post,* 1819. Halleck published *Fanny,* a social satire, in 1819 (enlarged edition, 1821), and collected his poems in *Alnwick Castle,* 1827. Editions of his work with a few additional poems were numerous; in 1865, his *Young America* was published. He was a gifted talker. Though Thomas Campbell was his literary ideal, his poems show more the influence of Byron and Scott. Overrated by his contemporaries, his best work such as "Marco Bozzaris" and his tributes to Drake and Robert Burns gives him a secure niche among minor American poets.

HALLECK, HENRY WAGER (*b. Westernville, N.Y., 1815; d. Louisville, Ky., 1872*), soldier, lawyer, capitalist. Graduated Union College, 1837; West Point, 1839. After a trip to Europe, 1844, he wrote a "Report on the Means of National Defense," which brought him an invitation to give the Lowell lectures in Boston; these were published as *Elements of Military Art and Science* (1846). On his way to service in California, 1846, he translated Jomini's *Vie Politique et Militaire de Napoléon* (published, 1864). Active in both military and civil affairs in California, 1847–53, and already distinguished as an engineer, he studied law, resigning his captaincy, 1854, to head the principal law firm in the state. He published two books on mining law and in 1861 *International Law, or Rules Regulating the Intercourse of States in Peace and War,* widely used as a textbook.

Eminently successful in law and business, he was commissioned major general, 1861, and in November went to St. Louis to succeed Frémont in command of the Department of Missouri. His prestige enhanced by the success of his subordinates, U. S. Grant, Foote and Pope, his area of command was enlarged in March 1862 into the Department of the Mississippi. The next month he took the field before Corinth, Miss., for his only active campaign, a partial failure through his overcaution. He became military adviser to Lincoln with the title general in chief, July 1862. Cold, impersonal and impartial, nicknamed "Old Brains," he antagonized both politicians and his own subordinates. Devoting his time to details, he lost sight of the need to follow out a grand strategy. Halleck's deficiencies as supreme commander could be painted very black, but it is impossible now to reconstruct the difficulties of what he termed his "political Hell." Dependent on dispatches for knowledge of the battlefields, he was an office general without opportunity to obliterate his mistakes by victories in the field. In March 1864, he was made chief of staff, a demotion he took in good part, fulfilling his duties with unflagging energy. After Appomattox he commanded the Military Division of the James, the Military Division of the Pacific, and in 1869, his last post, the Division of the South. Halleck gave up much when he reentered the army in 1861. Thrust against his will into a treacherous position, he was victim of his limitations.

HALLET, ÉTIENNE SULPICE (*b. Paris, France, 1755; d. New Rochelle, N.Y., 1825*), architect. Came to America, *ca.* 1786–88. Submitted a variety of designs in competition for a federal Capitol building, 1791–92; was commissioned to revise plans of the winner, William Thornton, and supervise erection of the building. His name appears as "Stephen Hallette" on the cornerstone laid at Washington, Sept. 18, 1793, though he was shortly dismissed from his post. In one of Hallet's rejected designs, he created the type of capitol which was to prevail in America: a building with a tall central dome and wings for the two legislative houses; in another, he was first to adopt the classic hemicycle for a modern legislative hall.

HALLET, STEPHEN. *See* HALLET, ÉTIENNE SULPICE.

HALLETT, BENJAMIN (*b. Barnstable, Mass., 1760; d. 1849*), owner of packet lines. Founder *ca.* 1815 of the "Bethel Movement" for religious and social work among seamen in port cities.

HALLETT, BENJAMIN FRANKLIN (*b. Osterville, Mass., 1797; d. 1862*), editor, politician. Son of Benjamin Hallett. Militant, liberal editor of *Providence Journal*, 1821–28, and *Boston Advocate*, 1831–38, he later as editor of *Boston Post* became conservative and docile Democratic party man.

HALLETT, MOSES (*b. Galena, Ill., 1834 d. 1913*), jurist. Chief justice, Colorado Territory supreme court, 1866–77; federal judge, Colorado district, 1877–1906; first dean, University of Colorado Law School.

HALLIDIE, ANDREW SMITH (*b. London, England, 1836; d. San Francisco, Calif., 1900*), engineer, inventor. Immigrated to California, 1853. Designed and built wire suspension bridges and flumes; produced in 1858 the first wire rope made on the Pacific Coast. Invented a rigid suspension bridge and perfected the "Hallidie ropeway" to carry freight over canyons, 1867. Devised, 1871, and installed, 1873, the endless moving cable and mechanical gripping device employed to pull streetcars up San Francisco's hillsides. He was active also in municipal affairs, reform movements and education.

HALLOCK, CHARLES (*b. New York, N.Y., 1834; d. Washington, D.C., 1917*), journalist, author, scientist. Son of Gerard Hallock. Founded *Forest and Stream* magazine, 1873; wrote extensively on outdoor life.

HALLOCK, GERARD (*b. Plainfield, Mass., 1800; d. New Haven, Conn., 1866*), journalist. Brother of William A. Hallock. Graduated Williams, 1819. After editing papers in Boston and New York, became editor of *New York Journal of Commerce*, 1828, of which he and David Hale became proprietors, 1831. A pioneer in the cooperative newsgathering movement, he resigned his editorship, 1861.

HALLOCK, WILLIAM ALLEN (*b. Plainfield, Mass., 1794; d. 1880*), first secretary of the American Tract Society, 1825–70, and director of all its activities.

HALLOWELL, BENJAMIN (*b. Montgomery County, Pa., 1799; d. Sandy Spring, Md., 1877*), educator, minister of the Society of Friends. Conducted his own preparatory school, Alexandria, Va., 1824–58; first president of Maryland Agricultural College, 1859.

HALLOWELL, RICHARD PRICE (*b. Philadelphia, Pa., 1835; d. 1904*), wool merchant. A leader in antislavery agitation in Philadelphia and Boston.

HALPERT, EDITH GREGOR (*b. Edith Gregor Fivoosiovitch, Odessa, Russia, 1900; d. New York, N.Y., 1970*), art dealer. Immigrated to the United States, 1906; became citizen, 1921. In 1926 she and her husband, Samuel Halpert, opened the Downtown Art Gallery, which dealt exclusively in modern American art; virtually all the twentieth-century pioneers of modern art in America appeared at the Downtown Gallery, and in the late 1930's and early 1940's the gallery also gained a reputation for backing socially and artistically progressive work. In 1929 she opened the first gallery devoted to American folk art in an upstairs room at the Downtown Gallery, and in 1951 she sectioned off a portion of the premises to form the Ground Floor Gallery, where she exhibited young, unknown artists. Enjoyed one of the longest and most distinguished careers of any art dealer in New York City.

HALPINE, CHARLES GRAHAM (*b. Oldcastle, Ireland, 1829; d. 1868*), journalist, poet, Union soldier, politician. Came to America, 1851. Member of literary group that included Fitz-Hugh Ludlow and Fitz-James O'Brien. His popular Civil War satires were gathered in *Miles O'Reilly His Book* (1864).

HALSEY, FREDERICK ARTHUR (*b. Unadilla, N.Y., 1856; d. New York, N.Y., 1935*), mechanical engineer. Graduated Cornell, 1878. Devised industrial profit-sharing plan known as the Halsey premium payment plan; influential editor of the *American Machinist*, 1894–1911.

HALSEY, JOHN (*b. Boston, Mass., 1670; d. Madagascar, 1716*), South Sea pirate.

HALSEY, THOMAS LLOYD (*b. Providence R.I., ca. 1776; d. Providence, 1855*), merchant. U.S. consul in Buenos Aires, 1814–18; supplied arms to South American rebels; dismissed from post for privateer activity.

HALSEY, WILLIAM FREDERICK, JR. (*b. Elizabeth, N.J., 1882; d. Fishers Island, N.Y., 1959*), naval leader. Graduated from the U.S. Naval Academy in 1904. Halsey's early career was routine: he served abroad several ships and participated in the global cruise of the "Great White Fleet" from 1907–09. In 1909, he was given command of the torpedo boat *Dupont* and began a twenty-three year career in torpedo warfare and escort duties. During World War I, Halsey commanded antisubmarine ships out of Ireland; he was promoted to commander in 1921 and served as naval attaché in Germany (1921–24) and Norway, Denmark, and Sweden (1923–24). Promoted to captain in 1927, Halsey was assigned to the Naval Academy; he attended the Naval War College (1932–33) and the Army War College (1933–34) and, in 1935, became a naval aviator at age fifty-two. In 1938, he was promoted to rear admiral.

At the outbreak of World War II, Halsey was promoted to vice admiral in command of Aircraft Battle Force and of Carrier Division Two. On board the *Enterprise* in 1941, he placed his command on a war footing. When Pearl Harbor was attacked, his forces were at sea and escaped damage. In 1942 his two-carrier task force raided the Japanese-held Marshall, Gilbert, Wake, and Marcus islands, giving a valuable boost to public morale and earning Halsey a worldwide reputation. In April of 1942, Halsey commanded the carriers *Hornet and Enterprise* as a secret base for James Doolittle's raids on the Japanese mainland. In August of that year, he commanded the South Pacific Force, winning the key naval battles of Santa Cruz and Guadalcanal. Promoted to full admiral in November 1942.

As commander in the South Pacific theater, Halsey successfully secured that area through the campaigns for the Solomon Islands. He became commander of the Third Fleet in 1944. His units provided strategic support for MacArthur's landing in the Philippines. During the Battle of Leyte Gulf (Oct., 1944) Halsey was successfully tricked by a Japanese decoy, which diverted Halsey's forces away from the main battle. Halsey's actions became more controversial when he led the Third Fleet into a disastrous typhoon in December of 1944 and again in June of 1945. The Japanese surrendered on board his flagship *Missouri* in 1945. Retired in 1947 with rank of fleet admiral.

HALSTEAD, MURAT (*b. Butler Co., Ohio, 1829; d. 1908*), journalist, war correspondent. Editor of *Cincinnati Commercial, post* 1853 to 1884; wrote graphic accounts of political conventions, 1860; covered Civil and Franco-Prussian wars. Later edited Brooklyn, N.Y., *Standard-Union*.

HALSTED, GEORGE BRUCE (*b. Newark, N.J., 1853; d. New York, N.Y., 1922*), mathematician, educator. Graduated Princeton, 1875; Ph.D., Johns Hopkins, 1879. Did much to make non-Euclidean geometry theories known in the United States. Taught at Princeton, University of Texas, and a number of other schools.

HALSTED, WILLIAM STEWART (*b. New York, N.Y., 1852; d. 1922*), surgeon. Graduated Yale, 1874; N.Y. College of Physicians and Surgeons, 1877. Probably his greatest contribution was his early development of an operative technique concerned with preserving the power of the patient's tissues to resist weakening and infection. His second great service was his discovery, 1884, that a whole region of the body could be anaesthetized by injecting cocaine into the nerve. As professor of surgery at Johns Hopkins Hospital, 1890–1922, he trained many distinguished surgeons. The range and quality of his later work may be studied in *Surgical Papers by William Stewart Halsted* (1924).

HAMBIDGE, JAY (*b. Simcoe, Canada, 1867; d. 1924*), artist. Advanced theory in "The Natural Basis of Form in Greek Art" (1902) that the "principle of proportion" found in nature's symmetrical forms was used consciously in Greek art and involved a "dynamic" symmetry as opposed to "static" symmetry based on pattern properties of two-dimensional figures. His published works include *Dynamic Symmetry* (1917), an explanation of the mathematical background of his theory, and *The Parthenon and Other Greek Temples: Their Dynamic Symmetry* (1924).

HAMBLETON, THOMAS EDWARD (*b. Maryland, 1829; d. Baltimore, Md., 1906*), Confederate blockade runner, Baltimore financier and traction magnate.

HAMBLIN, JOSEPH ELDRIDGE (*b. Massachusetts, 1828; d. New York, N.Y., 1870*), insurance broker, Union brevet major general.

HAMBLIN, THOMAS SOWERBY (*b. London, England, 1800; d. New York, N.Y., 1853*), actor. Came to America, 1825. Managed Bowery Theatre, New York, 1850–53, except for interruptions when fire twice destroyed it.

HAMER, THOMAS LYON (*b. Northumberland Co., Pa., 1800; d. Mexico, 1846*), lawyer, Ohio legislator, soldier. Con-

gressman, Democrat, from Ohio, 1833–39. Died as division commander in Mexico under Zachary Taylor. Appointed U.S. Grant to West Point.

HAMILTON, ALEXANDER (*b. in or near Edinburgh, Scotland, 1712; d. Annapolis, Md., 1756*), physician, social historian. Came to America, 1738. Author of an *Itinerarium* (written 1744, published 1907), descriptive of a tour through the Northern colonies and sharply observant of the manners of the period.

HAMILTON, ALEXANDER (*b. Nevis, Leeward Islands, 1755 or 1757; d. New York, N.Y., 1804*), statesman. Came to New York, 1772; entered King's College (now Columbia University), 1773. His college career interrupted by the stirrings of the Revolution, he entered into the pamphlet wars of the day with *A Full Vindication of the Measures of Congress, etc* (December 1774) and continued the debate in a reply to Samuel Seabury entiled *The Farmer Refuted* (1775), both brilliant expressions of a moderate point of view. Commissioned to command an artillery company early in 1776, he fought in the fall campaign on Long Island, at Harlem Heights and White Plains, was in the New Jersey retreat, and at Trenton and Princeton. He became secretary and aide-de-camp to Washington on March 1, 1777, with rank of lieutenant colonel. In this position of great responsibility he became the general's trusted adviser and did much to systematize the handling of business at headquarters. He also drafted a series of important reports on the defects of the military system. Between 1777 and 1781, his correspondence with various colonial leaders reveals the growth of his political ideas and the incisiveness of his thought. Though a staunch believer in representative government (then widely distrusted), he insisted from the first that it must act through a highly centralized authority. In a letter of 1780 to James Duane, he made the first proposal for a constitutional convention; also in 1780 he married Elizabeth, daughter of Gen. Philip Schuyler. After a quarrel with Washington (February 1781), in which Hamilton's conduct does him discredit, he resigned from the staff but through Washington's magnanimity was appointed to head an infantry regiment. At Yorktown he conducted a brilliant attack on one of the principal British redoubts.

The fighting over, he went to Albany, N.Y., read law, and was admitted to the bar. In 1783, after one term in the Continental Congress, he retired to private life and opened a law office in New York City, continuing active in the movement for a strong federal government. As a New York delegate to the Annapolis commercial convention, 1786, he secured adoption of a resolution recommending a convention of representatives from all the states to meet in Philadelphia the following May to devise provisions "necessary to render the Constitution of the Federal Government adequate to the exigencies of the Union." It was one of the most adroit of all his strokes. A member of the New York legislature of 1787, he made one of his greatest speeches to secure the state's adherence to an impost measure asked by Congress. Named a delegate from New York to the Philadelphia Convention, his federalist zeal was offset by the states' rights obscurantism of his colleagues Robert Yates and John Lansing. His role at Philadelphia was not of great importance, but his work at home in New York was. He opened the fierce newspaper war over adoption of the Constitution in July 1787 and then planned the "Federalist" series, a magnificent sequence of expository and argumentative articles, the greater part of which he wrote either alone or in collaboration with James Madison. At the New York convention for ratification of the Constitution (Poughkeepsie, 1788), with irresistible speeches he led the successful fight for adoption, one of the few instances in American history of the decision of a deliberative body being changed by sheer power of sustained argument. He sat again in the Continental Congress in 1788 and was much in the foreground until the new government was organized, April 1789.

Appointed secretary of the treasury in September, he devised a plan for establishing the nation's credit on a sound basis which was presented to the House on Jan. 14, 1790. This famous document is one of his greatest state papers. He argued that the government should pay not only the foreign debt, but also fund the domestic debt at par value though many holders of public securities had bought them cheaply for speculation. He also argued that the federal government should assume debts contracted during the Revolution by the states. Several schemes for funding the debt on a basis that would postpone full interest charges were offered by Hamilton. To provide annual operating revenue, he proposed to levy import duties and an excise. His plans met fierce opposition. He carried the bill for assumption of state debts to success at last by his famous bargain with Jefferson and Madison for location of the national capital. The funding and assumption measures became law on Aug. 4, 1791. Meanwhile, Dec. 13, 1790, he had presented his plan for an excise on spirits; the next day, his plan for a national bank; and on Jan. 28, 1791, his report on the establishment of a mint. All three proposals were accepted. As a capstone to his financial and economic structure he presented his report on manufactures at the winter session of 1791–92; its cardinal feature was the proposal of protection for infant industries either by import duties or bounties. Whatever critics may say of Hamilton's system, he must be credited with creating public credit out of a void, putting the government on a firm financial foundation, and giving the country adequate banking and currency facilities and important new industries. If only because he went further than any member of the government in exercising the powers of the Constitution, he must rank as one of the boldest and most farsighted of the nation's founders.

Hamilton's aggressiveness and his belief that he was in effect prime minister of Washington's cabinet led to improper interference with other departments and accentuated party divisions which arose from differences in principles. Hamilton and Thomas Jefferson were natural antagonists; each truly believed that the policies of the other would destroy the government. The struggle between them reached a point of great bitterness. Hamilton encouraged John Fenno to establish the *Gazette of the United States* in 1789; in October 1791, Philip Freneau's *National Gazette* appeared under Jefferson's aegis; both were propaganda organs. The attacks on Hamilton's policies culminated in the House in the presentation by William B. Giles of nine resolutions of censure whose defeat early in 1793 vindicated Hamilton. The wars of the French Revolution and the arrival of Genêt as envoy in April 1793 added fuel to the party flames. Despite the old alliance with France, Hamilton won Washington over to a policy of strict neutrality between France and Great Britain, maintained close relations with the British envoy and had John Jay sent to London to negotiate a trade treaty with England. He carefully controlled Jay's work in the interests of his domestic financial policy. The breach between Jefferson and Hamilton widened. Jefferson resigned as secretary of state in December 1793 and tried to discredit Hamilton's party by connecting it with speculation at home and British interests abroad; in home affairs, however, Hamilton's place was secure. When the Whiskey Rebellion occurred in 1794, he played the chief role in in its suppression, taking the field with the punitive force, since he regarded the rebellion as an opportunity for the federal government to show its strength. Forced to resign from the cabinet in January 1795 because of personal financial pressures, he still did much to advise Washington and helped draft the final form of his Farewell Address.

Hamilton remained out of civil office thereafter, but continued to be a major figure in the country's life and was eminently successful as a lawyer. On bad terms with John Adams throughout his administration, he attempted to meddle in administration affairs by influencing members of Adams' cabinet. When war threatened with France in 1798, through Washington's influence Hamilton was appointed inspector general of the provisional army. His plans for mobilization and the conquest of Louisiana and Florida were dissipated when Adams ended the tension by sending a new minister to France. Later, hearing that Adams accused him of being under British influence, Hamilton harshly arraigned Adams as unfit for the presidency in a letter which was published by the Democrat-Republicans and went through a number of printings in 1800. It was a serious blunder and a surrender to personal irritation without excuse. Yet after this pettiness he magnificently rose above it on two important occasions. In the presidential election of 1800, when the Jefferson-Aaron Burr tie went into the House, Hamilton, in opposition to other Federalists, exerted his influence for Jefferson. When Burr sought the governorship of New York in 1804 and it was suspected, if he were victorious, that he would join with New England malcontents in forming a Northern Confederacy, Hamilton took the offensive and succeeded in getting Burr defeated. Thirsting for revenge, and on the pretext that Hamilton had expressed a "despicable opinion of him," Burr challenged Hamilton to a duel at Weehawken, N.J., July 11, 1804. Mortally wounded, Hamilton died the next day.

Certain of Hamilton's acts which arose from passion and errors in judgment may be counted against him, but apart from these, his character was of the highest and his patriotism unquestioned. His power as an orator was great but he chose to exert it on select bodies of influential men, not on the multitude, whose political capacities he distrusted. His intellect was incisive, logical, and amazingly quick but wanting in subtlety and the higher imagination. His political principles probably laid a clearer impress on the Republic than those of any other single man. As a cabinet member he worked to go beyond the Constitution in invigorating the government and hence proclaimed his doctrine of implied powers which, as developed under John Marshall and since, has tremendously strengthened the national sovereignty. Believing in a powerful federal authority, he thought much of governmental strength, but little of liberty. He believed in governmental measures for helping whole classes grow prosperous, but paid no attention to the aspirations of the individual for greater happiness and opportunity. A hard, efficient realist, his work was invaluable to the nation at the time, but his narrow aristocratic ideas needed correction from the doctrines of Jefferson and Lincoln.

HAMILTON, ALICE (*b. New York, N.Y., 1869; d. Hadlyme, Conn., 1970*), physician, social reformer, and professor of industrial medicine. M.D. (1893), University of Michigan. Was resident of Hull House around the turn of the century, and then began documenting the high mortality and morbidity rates of workers exposed to industrial poisons. Her classic textbook *Industrial Poisons in the United States* (1925) established her as one of the world's leading authorities on the subject. Also became a crusader for public health and an advocate of woman suffrage, birth control, a federal child labor law, state health insurance, and workmen's compensation. As assistant professor of industrial medicine at the Harvard Medical School, 1919–35, she was Harvard's first female professor. Her autobiography, *Exploring the Dangerous Trades*, was published in 1943.

HAMILTON, ALLAN McLANE (*b. Williamsburg, N.Y., 1848; d. Great Barrington, Mass., 1919*), physician, alienist. Grandson of Alexander Hamilton (1757–1804); also of Louis McLane. Graduated N.Y. College of Physicians and Surgeons, 1870. Pioneer in neurology; expert witness in homicide cases.

HAMILTON, ANDREW (*b. Scotland; d. Perth Amboy, N.J., 1703*). Settled in America, 1686. Governor of East and West Jersey, 1692–97, 1699–1702. Deputy-governor Pennsylvania, 1701–03; as deputy postmaster-general of America, *post* 1692, helped organize first postal system.

HAMILTON, ANDREW (*d. "Bush Hill," Philadelphia, Pa., 1741*), lawyer, legislator. Came to America toward end of 17th century. Practiced first in Maryland; appointed attorney general of Pennsylvania, 1717; held numerous other offices. His title to fame is his successful defense in 1735 of John Peter Zenger, publisher of the New York *Weekly Journal*, against a charge of seditious libel brought by the New York authorities. In a masterful speech, Hamilton persuaded the jury, at peril to themselves, to render a "general verdict" on both law and facts at a time when "good law" reduced their role to determining the fact of publication, the libelous character of the words being left as a question of law to the judges. The issue at stake was the freedom of the press as the only orderly means of resistance to an arbitrary, unscrupulous executive.

HAMILTON, ANDREW JACKSON (*b. Madison Co., Ala., 1815; d. 1875*), lawyer, legislator. Removed to Texas, 1847. Unionist leader in Texas and congressman; provisional governor, 1865–66; member of Texas supreme court.

HAMILTON, CHARLES SMITH (*b. Western, N.Y., 1822; d. Milwaukee, Wis., 1891*), soldier. Graduated West Point, 1843. Distinguished in Mexican War; resigned commission, 1853, to enter business; in Civil War served as colonel, 3rd Wisconsin, and rose to corps command and rank of major general in Western campaigns.

HAMILTON, CLAYTON (*b. Brooklyn, N.Y., 1881; d. New York, N.Y., 1946*), teacher, playwright, critic. B.A., Brooklyn Polytechnic Institute, 1900; M.A., Columbia University, 1901. Taught and lectured at a number of schools and colleges; began in 1903 a pioneering course in contemporary drama at Columbia Extension School which he conducted for twenty years. As drama critic at various times for *Forum*, *The Bookman*, *Everybody's Magazine*, *Vogue*, and *Vanity Fair*, he focused on the structures and themes of plays, rather than on their acting or production. He was author of eleven books on the theater, on the technique of fiction, and on playwriting, and author or co-author of a number of produced plays.

HAMILTON, EDITH (*b. Dresden, Germany, 1867; d. Washington, D.C., 1963*), teacher, classicist, and author. A.B. and A.M. (both 1894), Bryn Mawr College. As headmistress and teacher (1896–1922) at the Bryn Mawr School in Baltimore, Md., the nation's first women's college-preparatory school, she built the institution into a leading academic center. At the age of 59 began writing books on the classics that were based almost entirely upon her knowledge of the original-language sources, with little attention to later interpretations. Her works include *The Greek Way* (1930; revised, expanded, and reissued as *The Great Age of Greek Literature*, 1942), *The Roman Way* (1932), *The Prophets of Israel* (1936), *Mythology* (1942), *Witness to the Truth* (1948), and *Spokesmen for God* (1949).

HAMILTON, EDWARD JOHN (*b. Belfast, Ireland, 1834; d. 1918*), Presbyterian clergyman, philosopher. Came to America as a boy. Taught at Hanover (Ind.), Princeton and Hamilton colleges; worked and published in fields of epistemology, logic, metaphysics, ethics. His most ambitious book was *The Human Mind* (1883).

HAMILTON, FRANK HASTINGS (*b. Wilmington, Vt., 1813; d. 1886*), surgeon. Graduated Union, 1830; M.D., University of Pennsylvania, 1835. Practiced and taught at Buffalo, N.Y., and New York City. Civil War medical officer, Union Army. Instituted healing of old ulcers by skin grafting.

HAMILTON, GAIL. *See* DODGE, MARY ABIGAIL.

HAMILTON, JAMES (*b. probably Accomac Co., Va., ca. 1710; d. 1783*), Lieutenant governor of Pennsylvania, 1748–54, 1759–63. Son of Andrew Hamilton (d. 1741). Supported proprietors in colonial difficulties, particularly in their political clashes with back country; neither opposed nor supported American Revolution.

HAMILTON, JAMES (*b. Charleston, S.C., 1786; d. Gulf of Mexico, 1857*), lawyer, statesman. Partner of James L. Petigru. Congressman, Democrat, from South Carolina, 1822–29; leader in Jacksonian opposition to John Q. Adams' administration, in anti-tariff movement, and in states' rights movement; nullificationist. As governor of South Carolina, 1830–32, he called a popular convention on the passage of the 1832 Tariff Act. Calhoun was the intellectual theorist of nullification, but Hamilton interpreted it to the people of the state and won them to it. When the ordinance was passed, he retired from the governorship to command the state's troops. After organizing an armed force of 27,000 men, he changed his mind on nullification and favored the compromise that secured tariff reduction. No more a force in politics, he turned to business and later played an important part in the struggle of Texas for independence.

HAMILTON, JAMES ALEXANDER (*b. New York, N.Y., 1788; d. New York, 1878*), lawyer, politician. Son of Alexander Hamilton (1757–1804). At first a Tammany partisan and a follower of Jackson and Van Buren, *post* 1840, he was identified with the Whig and Republican parties.

HAMILTON, JOHN WILLIAM (*b. Weston, Va., 1845; d. Boston, Mass., 1934*), Methodist clergyman. Bishop in California and New England, 1900–16; chancellor of the American University, Washington, D.C., 1916–22.

HAMILTON, MAXWELL McGAUGHEY (*b. Tahlequah, Iowa, 1896; d. Palo Alto, Calif., 1957*), diplomat. Studied at Princeton University (B.Litt., 1918). Entered the State Department as a Chinese language officer in 1920; retired in 1952. After training in cities in China, Hamilton returned to Washington in 1927 and worked with the Division of Far Eastern Affairs, assistant chief (1931–37), and chief (1937–40). Hamilton was one of the principal policymakers for the Far East during this period; he advocated a course of moderation towards Japan and hoped for American recognition of and cooperation with the Chinese Communists, realizing they would have to be reckoned with after the war. From 1943 to 1944, minister-counselor at the embassy in Moscow; 1945–48, minister to Finland. With the rank of ambassador, he was chairman of the Far Eastern Commission (1949–52).

HAMILTON, PAUL (*b. South Carolina, 1762; d. 1816*), Revolutionary soldier, planter, legislator. Democrat-Republican governor of South Carolina, 1804–06. As secretary of the navy, 1809–12, he was powerless in face of the refusal of Congress to vote funds for his department.

HAMILTON, PETER (*b. Harrisburg, Pa., 1817; d. Mobile, Ala., 1888*), lawyer, legislator. Graduated Princeton, 1835; admitted to Alabama bar, 1838. A leader of conservative Democrats during Reconstruction, he played a great part in restoring Alabama's transportation and credit.

HAMILTON, SCHUYLER (*b. New York, N.Y., 1822; d. New York, 1903*), soldier, engineer. Grandson of Alexander Hamilton

(1757–1804). Graduated West Point, 1841. Distinguished for Mexican War service and as staff and field officer in Civil War.

HAMILTON, WALTON HALE (b. Hiwassee College, Tenn., 1881; d. Washington, D.C., 1958), economist and jurist. Attended Vanderbilt, Texas, and Michigan (Ph.D., 1913). Taught at Michigan (1910–13), Chicago (1914–15), Amherst (1915–23), the Brookings Graduate School of Economics and Government (1923–28), and at the Yale Law School (1928–48). Member of the NRA Advisory Board (1934–35) and special assistant to the U.S. attorney general (1938–45).

HAMILTON, WILLIAM THOMAS (b. Hagerstown, Md., 1820; d. Hagerstown, 1888), lawyer, legislator. Congressman, Democrat, from Maryland, 1849–55. Sympathetic to the South but anti-secession. As U.S. senator, 1869–75, opposed radical Reconstruction; as Democrat governor of Maryland, 1880–84, fought without success for economic and political reform.

HAMILTON, WILLIAM THOMAS (b. England, 1822; d. Columbus, Mont., 1908), trapper, Indian trader, scout. Came to America as a child; raised in St. Louis, Mo. Author of My Sixty Years on the Plains (ed. E. T. Sieber, 1905).

HAMLIN, ALFRED DWIGHT FOSTER (b. near Constantinople, Turkey, 1855; d. 1926), architect. Son of Cyrus Hamlin. Taught at Columbia University, post 1887; influenced teaching of history of architecture and ornament in American schools; author of standard textbooks.

HAMLIN, CHARLES (b. Hampden, Maine, 1837; d. Bangor, Maine, 1911), Union brigadier general, lawyer, businessman. Son of Hannibal Hamlin. Pioneer in organizing building and loan associations.

HAMLIN, CHARLES SUMNER (b. Boston, Mass., 1861; d. Washington, D.C., 1938), lawyer. Graduated Harvard, 1883; LL.B., 1886. Member of the Federal Reserve Board, 1914–36, and its first governor, 1914–16.

HAMLIN, CYRUS (b. near Waterford, Maine, 1811; d 1900), missionary, educator. Graduated Bowdoin, 1834; Bangor Theological Seminary, 1837. Worked in Turkey, 1838–60, 1861–77. Founded Robert College at Bebek, Turkey, 1863, and was its president until 1877; president, Middlebury College (Vt.), 1880–85.

HAMLIN, EMMONS (b. Rome, N.Y., 1821; d. Boston, Mass., 1885), inventor, manufacturer of organs and pianos. Revolutionized "voicing" of organ reeds, increasing variety of stops. Partner, post 1854, with Henry Mason in Mason & Hamlin Organ Co.

HAMLIN, HANNIBAL (b. Paris Hill, Maine, 1809; d. 1891), lawyer, politician. As a Jacksonian Democrat, he represented Hampden in the Maine legislature, serving three terms as speaker, and was a member of Congress, 1843–47. In his first terms as U.S. senator, 1848–57, he wrote important legislation on steamboat inspection and ship-owners' liability. Becoming a Republican, he resigned from the Senate in January 1857 to become governor of Maine for a few weeks; resigning the governorship, he returned to the Senate. Widely prominent in the anti-slavery contest, he was a logical running-mate for Abraham Lincoln in 1860 and served as vice president during Lincoln's first term. Failing of renomination, 1864, he returned to politics on reelection to the U.S. Senate where he served, 1869–81. He supported the Radical group in reconstruction matters and Republican principles in economic issues. He was minister to Spain, 1881–82.

HAMLIN, TALBOT FAULKNER (b. New York, N.Y., 1889; d. Beaufort, S.C., 1956), architect, teacher, and librarian. Studied at Amherst College (B.A., 1910) and the Columbia School of Architecture (B. Arch., 1914). Taught at Columbia, 1916–54; Avery architectural librarian, 1934–45; professor of architecture from 1947. Wrote many books including Architecture Through the Ages (1940) and Benjamin Henry Latrobe (1955), a biography which won him the Pulitzer prize. His Greek Revival Architecture in America (1944) remains the basic book on the subject.

HAMLIN, WILLIAM (b. Providence R.I., 1772; d. Providence, 1869), engraver. His interest to collectors of American prints is chiefly historical.

HAMLINE, LEONIDAS LENT (b. Burlington, Conn., 1797; d. 1865), Methodist clergyman and bishop in Ohio and Iowa; helped found Hamline University.

HAMMER, WILLIAM JOSEPH (b. Cressona, Pa., 1858; d. New York, N.Y., 1934), electrical engineer. Associate of Thomas A. Edison; as chief engineer of the English Edison Co., built the world's first central station for incandescent electric lighting, Holborn, London, 1882.

HAMMERSTEIN, OSCAR (b. Germany, ca. 1847; d. New York, N.Y., 1919), inventor, composer, theatrical manager, opera impresario. Came to America, ante 1865.

HAMMERSTEIN, OSCAR, II (b. New York, N.Y., 1895; d. Doylestown, Pa., 1960), librettist and lyricist. Attended Columbia Law School. One of America's best-known musical comedy writers, Hammerstein entered the theater as a stage manager in 1917; he began to compose lyrics in the 1920's and achieved success with Sigmund Romberg's The Desert Song (1926). In 1927, he collaborated with Jerome Kern to produce Show Boat, a work that revolutionized the musical theater. Hammerstein's partnership with composer Richard Rodgers began with Oklahoma! (1943); other works include Carousel (1945), South Pacific (1949), The King and I (1951), Me and Juliet (1953), Pipe Dream (1955), Flower Drum Song (1958), and The Sound of Music (1959). In Hollywood, Hammerstein received the Academy Award for his lyrics to Rodgers' "The Last Time I Saw Paris" (1941) and "It Might As Well Be Spring" (1945).

HAMMETT, HENRY PINCKNEY (b. Greenville Co., S.C., 1822; d. 1891), cotton manufacturer. Founded Piedmont Manufacturing Co., 1873; its success inspired confidence in practicability of manufacturing cotton in the South.

HAMMETT, SAMUEL ADAMS (b. Jewett City, Conn., 1816; d. Brooklyn, N.Y., 1865), merchant, author. His first book, A Stray Yankee in Texas (1853, published under pseudonym, "Philip Paxton"), was a noteworthy contribution to literature of the Southwestern frontier.

HAMMETT, SAMUEL DASHIELL (b. St. Mary's County, Md., 1894; d. New York, N.Y., 1961), writer. Credited with initiating the hard-boiled school of detective fiction, he is most noted for such tough-skinned but romantic detective figures as the Continental Op (in Red Harvest and The Dain Curse, both 1929), Sam Spade (in The Maltese Falcon, 1930), Ned Beaumont (in The Glass Key, 1931), and Nick and Nora Charles (in The Thin Man, 1934). His reputation was enhanced by the film versions of a number of his stories, most notably The Thin Man (1934), its several sequels, and The Maltese Falcon (1941). While working on film scripts in Hollywood during the 1930's, wrote the screenplay for Watch on the Rhine (1943), based on the play by his lover Lillian Hellman. Then he turned his attention to politics, and by 1937 had joined the Communist party. Appeared before Senator

Joseph McCarthy's Subcommittee on Investigations in 1953, and eventually became blacklisted in Hollywood.

HAMMON, JUPITER (*b.* ca. *1720; d.* ca. *1800*), poet. An African slave, resident in Long Island, N.Y., and Hartford, Conn., his first poem was written late in 1760 and antedates by several years that of Phillis Wheatley, commonly regarded as the first black voice in American literature.

HAMMOND, BRAY (*b. Springfield, Mo., 1886; d. Middlebury, Vt., 1968*), economic historian and banking official. While working for the Board of Governors of the Federal Reserve System in Washington, D.C., 1930–50, wrote speeches and reports, including the first edition of *The Federal Reserve System: Its Functions and Purposes* (1939) and the historical introduction to *Banking Studies* (1941). Thereafter devoted himself to study and writing. Won the Pulitzer Prize in history for his *Banks and Politics in America from the Revolution to the Civil War* (1957), which depicted the destruction of the Second Bank of the United States. Also wrote *Sovereignty and an Empty Purse* (published posthumously, 1970), which described the financing of the Civil War.

HAMMOND, CHARLES (*b. near Baltimore, Md., 1779; d. 1840*), lawyer, journalist. Removed to Ohio, 1810; became leader of Ohio bar. Edited *Cincinnati Gazette*, 1825–40, making it one of most influential papers in the West. He was also an Ohio legislator and was reporter of the state supreme court, *post* 1823.

HAMMOND, EDWARD PAYSON (*b. Ellington, Conn., 1831; d. Hartford, Conn., 1910*), evangelist. Influenced William Booth, founder of Salvation Army.

HAMMOND, EDWIN (*b. Middlebury, Vt., 1801; d. 1870*), breeder of Merino sheep.

HAMMOND, GEORGE HENRY (*b. Fitchburg, Mass., 1838; d. Detroit, Mich., 1886*), meat packer, pioneer (*ca.* 1868) in the use of refrigerator cars.

HAMMOND, JABEZ DELANO (*b. New Bedford, Mass., 1778; d. Cherry Valley, N.Y., 1855*), lawyer, politician. Author of *The History of Political Parties in the State of New York* (Auburn, N.Y., 1842 and Syracuse, N.Y., 1848).

HAMMOND, JABEZ DELANO (*b. New Bedford, Mass., 1839; d. St. Augustine, Fla., 1913*), inventor, manufacturer. Invented the Hammond typewriter, patented 1880.

HAMMOND, JAMES HENRY (*b. Newberry District, S.C., 1807; d. 1864*), lawyer, planter. Graduated South Carolina College, 1825. Early advocate of nullification; Southern nationalist; constant proponent of secession. Considered his attack on the state bank his greatest achievement as Democratic governor of South Carolina, 1842–44. The chief event of his career as U.S. senator, 1857–60, during which he began to doubt the wisdom of secession, was his reply to W. H. Seward, 1858, in which he advanced his theory that Southern slaves and Northern workers were "mudsills of society," and declared, "You dare not make war on cotton . . . Cotton is king."

HAMMOND, JOHN HAYS (*b. San Francisco, Calif., 1855; d. Gloucester, Mass., 1936*), mining engineer. Graduated Sheffield Scientific School, 1876; Royal School of Mines, Freiberg, Saxony, 1879; soon earned a reputation as a mine valuation expert. In South Africa on an assignment, 1893, he became chief consulting engineer for Cecil Rhodes and took part in the abortive "Jameson Raid" against the Kruger government, 1896. On his return to America, 1899, he acquired many important clients, including the Guggenheims. After 1907 his chief interest was in politics and public affairs, especially in the cause of peace.

HAMMOND, NATHANIEL JOB (*b. Elbert Co., Ga., 1833; d. 1899*), lawyer. Leader of Georgia bar; Congressman, Democrat, 1879–87; strong supporter of Georgia educational institutions.

HAMMOND, PERCY HUNTER (*b. Cadiz, Ohio, 1873; d. New York, N.Y., 1936*), drama critic. Wrote with distinction for the *Chicago Tribune*, 1908–21; *New York Tribune* and *Herald Tribune*, 1921–36. "Dramatic criticism," he once wrote, "is the venom of contented rattlesnakes."

HAMMOND, SAMUEL (*b. Farnham's Parish, Va., 1757; d. 1842*), Revolutionary soldier, merchant, Missouri territorial official. Organized first bank in St. Louis. Removed to South Carolina, 1824.

HAMMOND, WILLIAM ALEXANDER (*b. Annapolis, Md., 1828; d. Washington, D.C., 1900*), neurologist. Graduated M.D., University of City of New York, 1848; U.S. army surgeon, 1849–59. Appointed surgeon general, 1862, he accomplished many reforms but clashed with Secretary of War Stanton and was dismissed, 1864. Became a leader in practice of neurology, then in its infancy, and taught at a number of schools until 1888. A prolific writer, his *Treatise on Diseases of the Nervous System* (1871) was described as the "first text-book on nervous diseases in English." He founded and edited a number of medical journals and was a pioneer in modern treatment of mental and nervous diseases in the United States.

HAMMOND, WILLIAM GARDINER (*b. Newport, R.I., 1829; d. St. Louis, Mo., 1894*), lawyer, legal educator. Graduated Amherst, 1849; studied at Heidelberg. Settled in Des Moines, Iowa, *post* 1860. As chancellor, law school of University of Iowa, and dean, law school of Washington University, his teaching methods approached the case system of study later introduced at Harvard. He was leading contemporary America authority on the history of the common law.

HAMPDEN, WALTER (*b. Brooklyn, N.Y., 1879; d. Los Angeles, Calif., 1955*), actor, director, and producer. Studied at Brooklyn Polytechnic Institute. Producer and director of a New York acting company noted for its production of *Cyrano de Bergerac* in 1923, in which Hampden played the lead. Other plays include Ibsen's *An Enemy of the People* and Bulwer Lytton's *Richelieu*. Films include *The Hunchback of Notre Dame* (1940), *All About Eve* (1950), and *Sabrina* (1954).

HAMPTON, WADE (*b. Halifax Co., Va., 1751 or 1752; d. Columbia, S.C., 1835*), planter, Revolutionary soldier. As major general in War of 1812, commanded on Lake Champlain but resigned 1813 after dispute with Gen. James Wilkinson. Reputed wealthiest planter in America.

HAMPTON, WADE (*b. Charleston, S.C., 1818; d. Columbia, S.C., 1902*), planter, statesman, Confederate soldier. Grandson of Wade Hampton (1751/52–1835). Graduated South Carolina College, 1836. As a member of state legislature, he was conservative on questions of Southern policy. Though he had not favored secession, he gave himself and his resources to the Confederacy from the outset, offering his cotton to be exchanged in Europe for arms and raising troops at his own expense. Serving first as an infantry officer, he was wounded at Bull Run and Seven Pines. He became a cavalry officer, July 1862. After September, as second in command, he served in all major movements of Gen. J. E. B. Stuart and became major general, 1863. After Stuart's death (May 1864), Hampton commanded the Confederate cavalry corps. Promoted lieutenant general early in 1865, he covered J. E.

Johnston's retreat and on Johnston's surrender proposed unsuccessfully to join Jefferson Davis and continue resistance from Texas. When a drastic Reconstruction policy was instituted, Hampton came out of retirement and joined in the protests against Republican rule, *post* 1868. In 1876, as a "straight-out" Democrat, he was elected governor. His greatest contribution toward restoration of white supremacy in his state was his influence in avoiding general armed conflict, particularly between the election and the withdrawal of U.S. troops (Apr. 10, 1877) when the Democrats were permitted to take over the government. In 1878 he was reelected governor. Shortly afterward he was made U.S. senator and served until 1891. From 1876 to 1890 the name Wade Hampton was the symbol of the South Carolina political regime, conservative in tradition and practices and of the old rather that the new South. Opposition arose, led by Benjamin R. Tillman, which represented the farmer and artisan strata of society, and Hampton was defeated for reelection to the Senate.

HAMTRAMCK, JOHN FRANICS (*b. Fort Wayne, Ind., 1798; d. Shepherdstown, W.Va., 1858*), soldier, planter, jurist. Graduated West Point, 1819. Indian agent for Osage Indians, 1826–31. Fought in War of 1812 and Mexican War.

HANAFORD, PHOEBE ANN COFFIN (*b. Nantucket Island, 1829; d. Rochester, N.Y., 1921*), Universalist minister, author. First woman to be regularly ordained in New England.

HANBY, BENJAMIN RUSSEL (*b. Rushville, Ohio, 1833; d. 1867*), song writer. Composer of "Darling Nelly Gray" and "Ole Shady, the Song of the Contraband" (1861), a favorite of the Northern armies.

HANCHETT, HENRY GRANGER (*b. Syracuse, N.Y., 1853; d. Siasconset, Mass., 1918*), pianist, music teacher, author. Inventor of the "sostenuto" or third tone-sustaining pedal now used on all grand pianos.

HANCOCK, JOHN (*b. Braintree Mass., 1736/37; d. Quincy, Mass., 1793*), merchant, politician. Nephew of Thomas Hancock. Graduated Harvard, 1754. Entered his uncle's mercantile firm; became a partner in 1763, and headed it, *post* 1764. In 1768, a riot ensued when his sloop *Liberty* was seized for smuggling wine; the episode and an unsuccessful Crown prosecution were important in the prelude to the Revolution and added to Hancock's local popularity. He was elected to the General Court, 1769, and headed the Boston committee of patriots, 1770. Samuel Adams soon became a determining influence in his life, and he became an idol of the populace. President of the Massachusetts Provisional Congress, 1774–75, he was the richest if not the most intelligent New Englander on the patriot side; he was elected president of the Second Continental Congress and signed the Declaration of Independence. Not realizing his limitations, he desired to be made commander in chief of the army. Congress thwarted him by appointing Washington, a slight Hancock never forgave. He resigned the presidency of the Congress in 1777; though still a member, he spent much time in Boston, more interested in local than national politics. In command of a Massachusetts contingent in a Rhode Island action, 1778, his performance was neither able nor creditable. As treasurer of Harvard College, 1773–77, he gave that institution infinite trouble. In 1780 he was elected first governor of Massachusetts state. He served until 1785 when, in the face of troubles culminating in Shays' Rebellion, he had an attack of gout and resigned. After the rebellion, he was again elected governor. In 1788, presiding at the state convention to ratify the Federal Constitution, he maneuvered matters so as to appear popular peacemaker at the divided meeting. He was serving his ninth term as governor when he died.

HANCOCK, JOHN (*b. Jackson Co., Ala., 1824; d. Austin, Tex., 1893*), Texas Unionist, lawyer. Partner of Andrew J. Hamilton; expert in land laws. Congressman, Democrat, from Texas, 1871–77, 1883–85.

HANCOCK, THOMAS (*b. present Lexington, Mass., 1703; d. Boston, Mass., 1764*), merchant, army supplier. Uncle of John Hancock.

HANCOCK, WINFIELD SCOTT (*b. Montgomery Square, Pa., 1824; d. Governors Island, N.Y., 1886*), soldier. Graduated West Point, 1844. Served in Mexican War, Seminole War, and at various Western posts until 1861. Commissioned brigadier general in that year and major general, 1862, he distinguished himself at Fredericksburg and Chancellorsville; at Gettysburg, he won fame as one of the Civil War's great soldiers, selecting the field and diverting Lee from immediate attack. On the second day of Gettysburg he thwarted Lee's nearly successful attack on the Union flank; on July 3 he repulsed the Confederate thrust at the federal center. His volunteer rank was confirmed in the regular army, 1866; thereafter, he commanded various army departments. Democratic presidential candidate in 1880, he was defeated by Garfield.

HAND, AUGUSTUS NOBLE (*b. Elizabethtown, N.J., 1869; d. Middlebury, Vt., 1954*), judge. Law degree from Harvard, 1894. Appointed by Woodrow Wilson as U.S. district judge for the Southern District of New York, Manhattan (1914–27). From 1927 to 1954, he was a judge on the Court of Appeals. Notable decisions include *U.S. v. Kauten* (1943), which held that Congress could constitutionally limit exemption from military service because of religious convictions, and his ruling that James Joyce's novel *Ulysses* was not obscene, although privately he held that it was.

HAND, DANIEL (*b. East Guilford, Conn., 1801; d. 1891*), merchant in Augusta, Ga., and Charleston, S.C. Established Daniel Hand Educational Fund for Colored People, 1888.

HAND, EDWARD (*b. King's Co., Ireland, 1744; d. near Lancaster, Pa., 1802*), physician, Revolutionary soldier. Came to America, 1767, as army surgeon; settled in Lancaster, *post* 1774. Brevet major general, 1783, after outstanding service.

HAND, LEARNED (*b. Albany, N.Y., 1872; d. New York, N.Y., 1961*), jurist. B.A. (1893), Harvard; graduated Harvard Law School (1896). In 1909 was named a district judge in New York by President William Howard Taft. Was an enthusiastic supporter of the 1912 Bull Moose campaign of the Roosevelt Progressives. In 1924 was named to the Court of Appeals for the Second Circuit, which covered New York, Connecticut, and Vermont and which was the leading intermediate appellate court in the nation, especially on commercial and maritime problems.

As chief judge of the court, 1939–51, he became widely regarded as one of the foremost American judges of the twentieth century. His major influence stems from his published opinions, of which he wrote about 3,000, in every area of law. Most of his contributions to the clarification and evolution of of legal doctrine pertain to problems of private law and statutory interpretation, though he was also an important voice in constitutional theory. Probably his greatest constitutional contribution was his controversial decision *Masses Publishing Co. v. Patten* (1917); his ruling, which reflected his deep commitment to free expression, protected the mailing of antiwar materials in the midst of a national atmosphere hostile to dissent. In 1969 his approach, combined with the best elements of Oliver Wendell Holmes's ruling in *Schenk v. United States* (1919), became the modern standard for First Amendment protection: *Brandenburg v. Ohio* (1969).

At Harvard Law School he had been deeply influenced by James

Bradley Thayer's advocacy of judicial self-restraint, and as a result he practiced the modest model of judging, which involved openmindedness, impartiality, skepticism, and restless probing. His decisions were not noted for dramatic overturning of majoritarian sentiments, but rather for his craftsmanlike performance of the more modest task of operating creatively within the confines set by the political branches.

HANDERSON, HENRY EBENEZER (b. *Orange, Ohio, 1837; d. Cleveland, Ohio, 1918*), physician, medical historian.

HANDY, ALEXANDER HAMILTON (b. *Princess Anne, Md., 1809; d. Canton, Miss., 1883*), Mississippi jurist.

HANDY, WILLIAM CHRISTOPHER (b. *Florence, Ala., 1873; d. New York, N.Y., 1958*), songwriter, cornetist, band leader, and musical publisher. Graduated from the Agricultural and Mechanical College in Huntsville, Ala. Handy was responsible for introducing the blues into American music. He composed "Memphis Blues" in 1912, "St. Louis Blues" in 1914; "Beale Street Blues" in 1917. Handy also led many bands, including Handy's Band (Memphis, 1905) and founded a publishing company in Memphis which became the W.C. Handy Music Co. In 1926, he published *Blues: An Anthology*, a definitive work that figured prominently in the Harlem Renaissance of the 1920's.

HANNA, EDWARD JOSEPH (b. *Rochester, N.Y., 1860; d. Rome, Italy, 1944*), Roman Catholic clergyman. Attended North American College, Rome; ordained, 1885; D.D., 1886. While a curate in Rochester, N.Y., his experience with Italian immigrants employed in clothing industry inspired a lifelong concern with social problems. A progressive theologian, Hanna taught at St. Bernard's Seminary, Rochester, 1893–1912; accused, wrongly, of Modernism, he was refused promotion to coadjutor archbishop of San Francisco when nominated in 1907. Appointed auxiliary bishop of San Francisco, 1912, he succeeded as archbishop in 1915 and held the see until his resignation for reasons of health in 1935. He was one of the founders of the National Catholic Welfare Council (later Conference), 1919, and served as chairman of its administrative committee until 1935. Active in California civic affairs, he distinguished himself as a labor mediator and in promoting better understanding between religious groups.

HANNA, MARCUS ALONZO (b. *New Lisbon, Ohio, 1837; d. 1904*), capitalist, politician. A partner in father's grocery and commission firm in Cleveland, Ohio, 1862. Married Charlotte Rhodes, daughter of a Cleveland coal and iron merchant, 1864, and in 1867 transferred all his interests to expansion of new firm of Rhodes & Co. Reorganized the firm as M. A. Hanna & Co., 1885; meantime, he had helped organize the Union National Bank, and had become owner of the *Cleveland Herald* and of the Cleveland Opera House. Quick to see interrelation of business and politics as necessary under new industrialism, he entered politics; by organizing Cleveland businessmen in support of Garfield, 1880, he became an important figure in Ohio Republican politics. Hanna successfully promoted his friend William McKinley for governor in 1891 and got him reelected in 1893. He then launched the McKinley boom for president and in 1894–95 withdrew from business to devote his energies to the pre-convention maneuvers which brought about McKinley's nomination on the first ballot at the St. Louis convention, 1896. Hanna became chairman of the Republican national committee, giving that body new importance; he raised the unprecedented amount of $3,500,000 in a highly organized campaign which included regular assessments on business institutions and assured McKinley's election. Hanna succeeded John Sherman as U.S. senator from Ohio, 1897. He played an active part in the Republican congressional campaign of 1898 and was an important presidential adviser, particularly in

employment of federal patronage to strengthen the party. In 1900, again national chairman, he played a great part in McKinley's reelection. Thereafter, he took a more active role in the Senate, revealing qualities of statesmanship. When Theodore Roosevelt became president on McKinley's death, September 1901, Hanna continued as a presidential adviser and, as chairman of the conciliation committee, National Civic Federation, helped settle disputes in the anthracite coal industry. Hanna believed in the right of labor to organize as a corollary to his advocacy of big business and organized capital, and because it was easier and more efficient to deal with labor's responsible spokesmen than with a mass of employees. Reelected to the Senate, 1903, he died the following year. Hanna played politics according to the rules without any of the instincts of the reformer. In 1902 he declared himself champion of "Standpattism," which carried all the connotations of reactionary politics.

HANNAGAN, STEPHEN JEROME (b. *Lafayette, Ind., 1899; d. Nairobi, Kenya, 1953*), press agent. Popularized the use of cheesecake photographs to publicize events and personalities. His clients included Captain Eddie Rickenbacker, boxer Gene Tunney, and utilities magnate, Samuel Insull. In 1940, he was press agent for Wendell Willkie; in 1944, for Thomas Dewey. Instrumental in the success of the Indianapolis 500, Miami Beach, and Sun Valley.

HANNEGAN, EDWARD ALLEN (b. *Hamilton Co., Ohio, 1807; d. St. Louis, Mo., 1859*), lawyer. Congressman, independent Democrat, from Indiana, 1833–37; U.S. senator, 1843–49. An aggressive expansionist.

HANNEGAN, ROBERT EMMET (b. *St. Louis, Mo., 1903; d. St. Louis, 1949*), lawyer, politician. An effective leader in St. Louis and Missouri Democratic politics, Hannegan was an early supporter of Harry S. Truman. He served as collector of internal revenue in St. Louis, as commissioner of internal revenue, and as chairman of the Democratic national committee secured Truman's nomination for the U.S. vice presidency in 1944. Postmaster general in 1945–47, he retired from his post and from politics for reasons of health.

HANSBERRY, LORRAINE VIVIAN (b. *Chicago, Ill., 1930; d. New York, N.Y., 1965*), playwright. Most noted for her play *A Raisin in the Sun*, which opened on Broadway in 1959 and ran for 530 performances. Was the first black woman to have her work produced on Broadway, and when the play won the Drama Critics' Circle Award, she was the youngest American and the first black to receive that prestigious prize. Also wrote *The Drinking Gourd* (1962), *Les blancs* (1966), and the controversial *The Sign in Sidney Brustein's Window* (1964). After her death her husband, Robert Nemiroff (m. 1953), assembled many of her notes, letters, and scenes into an informal autobiography, *To Be Young, Gifted and Black*, which was adapted for an off-Broadway production in 1969. Was active in the civil rights movement throughout her life.

HANSEN, GEORGE (b. *Hildesheim, Germany, 1863; d. Berkeley, Calif., 1908*), horticulturist, landscape architect. Came to America, 1887. Active in reclamation of exploited central Sierra region of California, 1889–96.

HANSEN, MARCUS LEE (b. *Neenah, Wis., 1892; d. Redlands, Calif., 1938*), historian. Taught at University of Illinois. Pioneer student of American immigration; author of *The Atlantic Migration* (ed. A. M. Schlesinger, 1940).

HANSEN, NIELS EBBESEN (b. *near Ribe, Denmark, 1866; d. Brookings, S.Dak., 1950*), horticulturist, plant explorer. Immigrated to United States with parents, 1873; raised in Des Moines, Iowa. B.S., Iowa State College at Ames, 1887; M.S.,

1895. Professor of horticulture at South Dakota State College, Brookings, and staff member of the Agricultural Experiment Station there, 1895–1937. Introduced and developed new varieties of grains, forage crops, and fruits suitable for growth in the northern American prairies and plains.

HANSEN, WILLIAM WEBSTER (*b. Fresno, Calif., 1909; d. Stanford, Calif., 1949*), physicist. After attending Fresno Technical High School, he entered Stanford University in 1925. A.B., 1929; Ph.D., 1933. He spent eighteen months studying at the Massachusetts Institute of Technology and at the University of Michigan, and returned to Stanford in 1934 as assistant professor of physics. He was made associate professor in 1937 and professor in 1942.

At M.I.T., Hansen became interested in mathematical methods of analyzing emission and absorption of atomic radiation. In addition, he worked on accelerating electrons by electromagnetic resonance, work which led to development of the klystron and, subsequently, radar. After moving east in 1941 to the Sperry Gyroscope Company plant on Long Island, Hansen was invited to M.I.T.'s Radiation Laboratory, which had been formed the previous fall to exploit the possibilities of microwave radar. In the summer of 1943 he also spent some weeks at the University of California as consultant on aspects of atomic energy problems for the Manhattan Project.

After World War II ended, Hansen returned to Stanford as director of the microwave laboratory being established there. Hansen devised the instrumentation used in discovering the existence of nuclear magnetic resonance and made many valuable suggestions that contributed to the successful demonstration of the method of nuclear induction in 1946.

HANSON, ALEXANDER CONTEE (*b. Annapolis, Md., 1749; d. Annapolis, 1806*), jurist. Son of John Hanson. Chancellor of Maryland, 1789–1806. Author of *Remarks on the Proposed Plan of a Federal Government* (1787) and various legal works.

HANSON, ALEXANDER CONTEE (*b. Annapolis, Md., 1786; d. near Elkridge, Md., 1819*), lawyer, editor. Son of Alexander C. Hanson (1749–1806). Graduated St. John's College, 1802. An extreme Federalist; founded *Federal Republican*, Baltimore, 1808. On June 22, 1812, because of an editorial hostile to Madison and the war, a mob destroyed the newspaper building; Hanson secured a new building and made it into an arsenal; on July 28 a member of the mob was killed in an attack on it. That night the offending Federalists within were brutally beaten in the jail where they had consented to go for protection. Among them were Hanson, Gen. J. L. Lingan and Gen. Henry Lee. In reaction to this Republican terrorism, Hanson was elected to Congress (1812), and served as U.S. senator, 1817–19.

HANSON, JAMES CHRISTIAN MEINICH (*b. district of Nord-Aurdal, Norway, 1864; d. Green Bay, Wis., 1943*), librarian. Came to United States, 1873; raised in Decorah, Iowa; B.A., Luther College (Decorah), 1882. Studied also at Concordia Seminary (St. Louis, Mo.) and at Cornell University; received basic library training as member of staff, Newberry, Library, Chicago, 1890–93. Head cataloguer, University of Wisconsin Library, 1893–97. He then became chief of the catalogue division, Library of Congress. He devised the classification system and catalogue format and reorganized the Library bibliographically; worked out a uniform code for library cataloging and was largely responsible for reconciling British and American cataloging codes in a joint system (published as *Catalog Rules, Author and Title Entries*, 1908). In 1910, he became associate director of the libraries at University of Chicago, where he was a professor in the

Graduate Library School, 1928–34. He headed the team of U.S. experts who assisted in the reorganization of the Vatican Library, 1928.

HANSON, JOHN (*b. Charles Co., Md., 1721; d. Prince Georges Co., Md., 1783*), Revolutionary leader. Member of Maryland Assembly, 1757–79; a strong proponent of every revolutionary measure preceding the war. Served in Continental Congress, 1780–82, and as president of Congress under the Articles of Confederation, Nov. 5, 1781–1782. With Daniel Carroll, succeeded in securing relinquishment of claims of Virginia and other states to unsettled territory extending westward to the Mississippi.

HANSON, OLE (*b. near Union Grove, Wis., 1874; d. Los Angeles, Calif., 1940*), politician, real-estate dealer. Removed to Seattle, Wash., 1902, where as mayor, 1919, he broke a general strike which had paralyzed the city.

HANSON, ROGER WEIGHTMAN (*b. Winchester, Ky., 1827; d. 1863*), Confederate brigadier general. Known as "Old Flintlock"; mortally wounded at Murfreesboro, Tenn.

HANUS, PAUL HENRY (*b. Hermsdorf unter dem Kynast, Upper Silesia, Prussia, 1855; d. Cambridge, Mass., 1941*), educator. Came to the United States as a child, raised in Wisconsin and Colorado. B.S., University of Michigan, 1878. Taught in Denver high schools and at University of Colorado; appointed professor of pedagogy, Colorado State Normal School, Greeley, 1890. In 1891, he went to Harvard to teach the history and art of teaching as part of Charles W. Eliot's plan to reform American secondary education. Concerned with the social and vocational relevance of education as opposed to the cultural, and its efficiency as measurable in a scientific manner, he met with strong faculty opposition before his department received recognition. Promoted to professor, 1901, he continued to press for creation of a separate professional faculty of education. He retired in 1921, embittered by Harvard's failure to make him honorary dean of the Graduate School of Education when it was established in 1920.

HAPGOOD, HUTCHINS (*b. Chicago, Ill., 1869; d. Provincetown, Mass., 1944*), journalist. Brother of Norman Hapgood.

HAPGOOD, ISABEL FLORENCE (*b. Boston, Mass., 1850; d. New York, N.Y., 1928*), translator, journalist. Introduced works of Tolstoy, Gogol, Turgenev, and other European authors to English-speaking world.

HAPGOOD, NORMAN (*b. Chicago, Ill., 1868; d. New York, N.Y., 1937*), publicist, reformer. Graduated Harvard, A.B., 1890; LL.B., 1893. Associate of Lincoln Steffens on N.Y. *Commercial Advertiser*, 1897–1902; editor, *Collier's Weekly*, during progressive reform era, 1902–12.

HAPPER, ANDREW PATTON (*b. Washington Co., Pa., 1818; d. Wooster, Ohio, 1894*), Presbyterian missionary. Worked mainly in Canton, China, 1844–84, and again in 1888–91 when he founded Canton Christian College.

HARADEN, JONATHAN (*b. Gloucester, Mass., 1744; d. Salem, Mass., 1803*), Revolutionary naval officer and privateersman. Commanded *Tyrannicide*, 1777–78; *General Pickering*, 1778–81; *Julius Caesar*, 1782.

HARAHAN, JAMES THEODORE (*b. Lowell, Mass., 1841; d. 1912*), railroad official. Pioneer in public relations aspect of railroad management. After Civil War service, held responsible posts with many roads; was president of Illinois Central, 1906–11.

HARAHAN, WILLIAM JOHNSON (*b. Nashville, Tenn., 1867; d. Clifton Forge, Va., 1937*), railroad executive. Son of James T. Harahan. President, Chesapeake and Ohio, 1920–29 and 1935–37; also of Nickel Plate and Pere Marquette railways, 1935–37.

HARASZTHY DE MOKCSA, AGOSTON *b. Futtak, Hungary*, ca. *1812; d. near Corinto, Nicaragua, 1869*), pioneer. Came to America, 1840; founded Sauk City, Wis. Removed to California, 1849, and imported first European grapevines, 1852. Planted first large California vineyard in Sonoma Valley, 1858.

HARBAUGH, HENRY (*b. Washington Township, Pa., 1817; d. Mercersburg, Pa., 1867*), German Reformed clergyman. Author of folk poetry in Pennsylvania-German dialect; popularized "Mercersburg theology."

HARBEN, WILLIAM NATHANIEL (*b. Dalton, Ga., 1858; d. New York, N.Y., 1919*), novelist.

HARBORD, JAMES GUTHRIE (*b. near Bloomington, Ill., 1866; d. Rye, N.Y., 1947*), army officer, corporation executive. Raised in Missouri and Kansas. B.S., Kansas State Agricultural College, 1886. After unsuccessfully trying for an appointment to West Point, he taught school and then enlisted in the army. He moved rapidly through the ranks to quartermaster sergeant, graduating from the Infantry and Cavalry School in 1895 and earning the M.S. degree at his alma mater the same year. During the Spanish-American War, Harbord served as a major in the 2nd Volunteer Cavalry. He was promoted in the regular army to first lieutenant (1898) and formed a friendship with John J. Pershing. In 1917 Harbord was named chief of staff to Pershing, commander of the American Expeditionary Forces. In May 1918 Harbord, now a brigadier general, took over command of the Marine brigade in the 2nd Division and led it during the victorious battle of Belleau Wood. In July, newly promoted to major general, he was given command of the entire 2nd Division, which played a crucial role in the counteroffensive at Soissons.

After serving under Pershing as commander of the Services of Supply, Harbord left the S.O.S. in 1919 and, after a brief second tour as Pershing's chief of staff, became chief of the American Military Mission to Armenia. When Pershing became the army's chief of staff (1921), he named Harbord his executive assistant. After retirement Harbord was president (until 1930) and then chairman of the board (until his retirement in 1947) of the Radio Corporation of America.

HARBY, ISAAC (*b. Charleston, S.C., 1788; d. New York, N.Y., 1828*), journalist, playwright. A founder of Reformed Society of Israelites in Charleston, earliest American movement of its kind.

HARCOURT, ALFRED (*b. Ulster County, N.Y., 1881; d. New York, N.Y., 1954*), publisher. Studied at Columbia (B.A., 1904). Editor for Henry Holt and Co., 1904–19; founder and president of Harcourt, Brace and Co., 1919–42. Harcourt published many of the century's finest thinkers and writers, including Bertrand Russell, Lytton Strachey, Sinclair Lewis, members of the Bloomsbury Group in London (Virginia Woolf, E. M. Forster) T. S. Eliot, and John Maynard Keynes.

HARD, WILLIAM (*b. Painted Post, N.Y., 1878; d. New Canaan, Conn., 1962*), journalist. Began his career in Chicago in 1902, writing articles on reformers, reform issues, workingmen, and women's issues. After 1914, worked out of Washington, D.C., directing his attention to national and international political and economic issues. Participated in the fight against the League of Nations and the debate over Bolshevik Russia. During the 1920's, wrote the "Weekly Washington Letter" for the *Nation* (1923–25) and articles for *Asia, Collier's, Century,* and *Review of Reviews,* among others, and supplied newspapers with Washington correspondence through his own Hard News Service and

David Lawrence's Consolidated News Service. With the coming of radio, became a regular correspondent and commentator for NBC. An outspoken critic of the New Deal, he held Republican party posts in the late 1930's. Thereafter wrote regularly for *Reader's Digest.* Wrote two biographies, *Raymond Robins' Own Story* (1920) and *Who's Hoover?* (1928).

HARDEE, WILLIAM JOSPEH (*b. Camden Co., Ga., 1815; d. Wytheville, Va., 1873*), Confederate soldier. Graduated West Point, 1838. Served ably in Mexican War and as commandant of cadets, West Point, 1856–61. Author of a textbook on infantry tactics. Identified through Civil War with Army of Tennessee, he rose by merit to lieutenant general, 1862. Noted for personal bravery.

HARDENBERGH, HENRY JANEWAY (*b. New Brunswick, N.J., 1857; d. 1918*), architect. Trained in office of Detlef Lienau; designed old Waldorf and Astoria hotels, also the Plaza Hotel, New York. The Fine Arts Building, New York (1896), is characteristic of his best work.

HARDENBERGH, JACOB RUTSEN (*b. Rosendale, N.Y., 1736; d. 1790*), Dutch Reformed clergyman, Revolutionary patriot, first president of Rutgers College, 1786–90. A leader of the Coetus faction, advocating independence from the church of Holland, he brought about chartering of Queens (now Rutgers) College, 1766.

HARDEY, MOTHER MARY ALOYSIA (*b. Piscataway, Md., 1809; d. Paris, France, 1886*), religious of the Society of the Sacred Heart. Cofounder of the first Eastern convent of her congregation at New York, 1841; established many other foundations and served as a provincial and assistant general of the Society.

HARDIE, JAMES ALLEN (*b. New York, N.Y., 1823; d. Washington, D.C., 1876*), Union major general. Graduated West Point, 1843. Served in Mexican War and in California, Oregon and at Eastern posts. A very able staff officer with the Army of the Potomac in the Civil War, he was later chief of the inspector general's office.

HARDIN, BEN (*b. Westmoreland Co., Pa., 1784; d. 1852*), lawyer. Nephew of John Hardin. Raised near Springfield, Ky. Practiced law, *post* 1808, in Bardstown, Ky. An active Kentucky legislator and a congressman. Whig, for five terms between 1815 and 1837.

HARDIN, CHARLES HENRY (*b. Trimble Co., Ky., 1820; d. 1892*), lawyer, Missouri legislator, philanthropist. Democratic reform governor of Missouri, 1875–77.

HARDIN, JOHN (*b. Fauquier Co., Va., 1753; d. at site of Hardin, Ohio, 1792*), Revolutionary soldier, Indian fighter. Settled in present Washington Co., Ky., 1786. Served thereafter, until his murder by the Miamis, on every punitive expedition into Indian territory with the exception of St. Clair's.

HARDIN, JOHN J. (*b. Frankfort, Ky., 1810; d. in battle of Buena Vista, Mexico, 1847*), lawyer, soldier. Son of Martin D. Hardin. Settled in Jacksonville, Ill., 1831. Rival of Abraham Lincoln for Whig leadership in Illinois legislature and for election to Congress, 1845–46.

HARDIN, MARTIN D. (*b. Pennsylvania, 1780; d. 1823*), lawyer. Son of John Hardin. Raised in Kentucky and practiced in Frankfort; served in state legislature and briefly as U.S. senator, National Democrat, 1816–17.

HARDING, ABNER CLARK (*b. East Hampton, Conn., 1807; d. Monmouth, Ill., 1874*), lawyer, financier, railroad builder, Union soldier. Removed to Illinois, 1838. Congressman, Republican, from Illinois, 1865–69.

HARDING, CHESTER (b. Conway, Mass., 1792; d. Boston, Mass, 1866), portrait painter. After a varied career as chair maker, drum manufacturer, tavern keeper, and itinerant house and sign painter, Harding settled as a self-schooled portrait painter in Paris, Ky. His success there and later in St. Louis, Mo., Washington, D.C., and Northampton, Mass., encouraged him to attempt Boston. There, after six busy months of "Harding fever" (a term coined by Gilbert Stuart, whose popularity was momentarily eclipsed), he earned enough to go to England, 1823, where he had a great social success. Finding that his family were not received in the circles where he moved, he returned to Boston, 1826, and settled permanently at Springfield, Mass. His portraits of American celebrities, ranging in time from Daniel Boone to W. T. Sherman, are now in most important collections.

HARDING, GEORGE (b. Philadelphia, Pa., 1827; d. 1902), patent lawyer. Son of Jesper Harding. Prominent in litigation over Morse telegraph, McCormick reaper, and a series of cases involving manufacture of fat acids and glycerin.

HARDING, JESPER (b. Philadelphia, Pa., 1799; d. Philadelphia, 1865), printer, publisher. Editor-proprietor of *Pennsylvania* (later *Philadelphia*) *Inquirer*, post 1829; was largest printer of Bibles in the United States.

HARDING, ROBERT (b. Nottinghamshire, England, 1701; d. 1772), Jesuit priest. Entered Society of Jesus, 1722; worked as missionary in Maryland, 1732–49; pastor, St. Joseph's, Philadelphia, 1749–72. Prominent in civic and intellectual life of Pennsylvania.

HARDING, SETH (b. Eastham, Mass., 1734; d. Schoharie, N.Y., 1814), naval officer. In June 1776, commanding brig *Defence*, he took 3 British transports in Massachusetts Bay, providing Washington with badly needed military stores; later commanded *Oliver Cromwell, Confederacy.*

HARDING, WARREN GAMALIEL (b. Caledonia, now Blooming Grove, Ohio, 1865; d. San Francisco, Calif., 1923), newspaper publisher, politician, president of the United States. Purchased the weekly Marion, Ohio, *Star*, 1884; as the town grew and prospered, so did the paper. Florence Kling De Wolfe, a widow whom he married, 1891, helped him transform it into a daily. Harding grew in importance too, becoming director of local corporations. Genial, "community-minded," he fitted the small-town environment in every respect. A state senator, Republican, 1898–1902, through the efforts of Harry M. Daugherty he was elected lieutenant governor of Ohio, 1903. At the close of his undistinguished term he retired from politics until 1910 when he was defeated for governor. Always friendly to the machine elements of his party, and celebrated for the kind of empty oratory that pleased the unthinking, he was elected U.S. senator, 1914, under Daugherty's guidance. During six years in the senate he was a safe conservative member, a defender of big business and attached to standard Republican policies.

National reaction from tensions of World War I made Harding with his conservative, cautious nationalism, limited ideas, and amiable temperament a potential presidential candidate. Daugherty, at the head of the Ohio Republican machine, began a campaign in his behalf. Nominated at Chicago, June 1920, through agreement of a little two-o'clock-in-the-morning group of Republican senators, he was elected 29th president over the Democrat James M. Cox after a confused and equivocal campaign. His cabinet was a strange mixture of distinguished men, mediocrities, and politicians largely unfit for their offices, such as Daugherty (attorney general) and Albert M. Fall (secretary of the

interior). His policies were less his own than those of the Republican Senate leaders and the three strongest cabinet members, Charles E. Hughes, Andrew Mellon, and Herbert Hoover. Soft mentally, he bowed to authority; moreover, his close associates were an inferior, predatory and disreputable set. His tariff policy, his reduction of taxes policy and his handling of labor and farm problems were all misguided, but his worst single error was his failure to guard the public domain from marauders who acted with the connivance of Secretary of the Interior Fall. In the preliminary steps to calling the Washington Conference, November 1921 (the one memorable achievement of his administration), Harding responded to rather than led Congress.

By spring 1923, difficulties were thickening fast around the president. The administration's legislative program was crippled by a precarious Republican congressional majority; the farm block of radical Republicans held a balance of power with resultant political confusion. Rumors of corruption, extortion, and wholesale looting in high places, and the existence of an illegitimate child added to Harding's anxieties. In June 1923, the president, his wife and a large party set off on a transcontinental tour. Returning from Alaska in July after receipt of a long message in code which deeply disturbed him, he was taken ill in San Francisco and died there on August 2. After a few months, a series of public investigations, of which the chief was an inquiry by the committee under Sen. Thomas J. Walsh into leases to private parties of naval oil reserves by Secretary Fall, revealed how Harding had been victimized by treachery and corruption in his administration. Fall was sent to prison; Attorney General Daugherty escaped prison by a hair; others resigned under fire. These exposures, continuing for several years, disclosed a looseness and dishonesty in government which paralleled the post–Civil War era. A heavy responsibility for Harding's record, however, falls upon the party and the nation which elected a man of moderate abilities, weak judgment, and lack of vigilance to so exacting an office. It was his cruel misfortune to be lifted to a post beyond his powers.

HARDING, WILLIAM PROCTER GOULD (b. Greene Co., Ala., 1864; d. 1930), banker. Grandson of Chester Harding. Federal Reserve Board governor, 1916–22, during difficult period of war and postwar instability. Author of *The Formative Period of the Federal Reserve System* (1925).

HARDING, WILLIAM WHITE (b. Philadelphia, Pa., 1830; d. Philadelphia, 1889), publisher. Son of Jesper Harding. Succeeded him as publisher of *Philadelphia Inquirer*, 1859, and built it into a model journal. He was also identified with first attempts to make paper from wood.

HARDWICK, THOMAS WILLIAM (b. Thomasville, Ga., 1872; d. Sandersville, Ga., 1944), lawyer, politician. An ally of Thomas E. Watson, Hardwick was congressman (Democrat) from Georgia, 1903–14. Elected U.S. senator in 1914, to complete the term of Augustus O. Bacon, he grew increasingly hostile to the policies of President Woodrow Wilson; his defeat when he sought reelection in 1918 was owing in part to an open letter of criticism which the president directed to the Georgia voters. Once again in alliance with Watson, whose nativist views he shared, he was elected governor of Georgia in 1920. His attacks on the terrorist actions of the resurgent Ku Klux Klan brought about his defeat for reelection in 1922.

HARDWICKE, CEDRIC WEBSTER (b. Lye, Stourbridge, Worcestershire, England, 1893; d. New York, N.Y., 1964), stage and film actor. Began his career on the British stage in 1912, playing Shakespearean roles and appearing in first productions of the plays of George Bernard Shaw, with whom he was a close friend. Between 1926 and 1937 he also appeared in sixteen motion pictures. On 1 January 1934 was knighted for his achievements. After 1935 turned his attention to America, making his American film debut in *Becky Sharp* (1935) and his New York stage debut in the comedy *Promise* (1936). Thereafter divided his time between the New York stage and Hollywood and British films. His film career became increasingly undistinguished, but he had some great successes on Broadway, including his performances in *Caesar and Cleopatra* (1949), in Shaw's *Don Juan in Hell* (1951), and in *A Majority of One* (1959). Wrote a two-volume autobiography: *Let's Pretend* (1932) and *A Victorian in Orbit* (1961).

HARDY, ARTHUR SHERBURNE (*b. Andover, Mass., 1847; d. Woodstock, Conn., 1930*), mathematician, novelist, diplomat.

HARDY, OLIVER NORVELL (*b. Harlem, Ga., 1892; d. North Hollywood, Calif., 1957*), film comedian. Attended the Atlanta Conservatory of Music and the University of Georgia. Remembered as the heavyweight member of the Laurel and Hardy comedy team, Hardy first worked with Stan Laurel in the film *Lucky Dog* (1917). They were first billed together in 1927 under the producer Hal Roach; together they made 105 films which included *The Battle of the Century* (1927), *Big Business* (1929), and *Swiss Miss* (1938).

HARDY, SAMUEL (*b. Isle of Wight Co., Va., ca. 1758; d. New York, N.Y., 1785*), lawyer, statesman. Member of Virginia House of Delegates and of Privy Council; briefly lieutenant governor of Virginia, 1782. Virginia delegate to Continental Congress, 1782–85.

HARDY, WILLIAM HARRIS (*b. Collirene, Ala., 1837; d. Gulfport, Miss., 1917*), lawyer, jurist, journalist. Promoted New Orleans and Northeastern, and Gulf and Ship Island railroads to develop the Mississippi pine belt and Gulf Coast regions. Founded Hattiesburg and Gulfport.

HARE, GEORGE EMLEN (*b. Philadelphia, Pa., 1808; d. Philadelphia, 1892*), Episcopal clergyman, educator. Graduated Union, 1826; ordained, 1830; pastor in Princeton, N.J., and Philadelphia. Headmaster, Academy of Protestant Episcopal Church, Philadelphia, 1846–57; headed, *post* 1857, institution which became Divinity School of Protestant Episcopal Church, Philadelphia.

HARE, JAMES H. (*b. London, England, 1856; d. Teaneck, N.J., 1946*), news photographer, war correspondent. Came to New York City, 1889; became a photographer for the *Illustrated American* and a free-lance contributor to newspapers. Sent to Cuba for *Collier's Weekly*, 1898, he won fame as one of the most daring and resourceful of battlefield news photographers; after the Spanish-American War, he covered for *Collier's* the revolutions in Haiti, Venezuela, Panama, and Mexico; the Russo-Japanese War (1904–05); and the Balkan wars of 1912–13. During World War I, he photographed combat in France, Italy, Greece, and Russia for *Leslie's Weekly*. Pioneer in aerial photography.

HARE, JOHN INNES CLARK (*b. 1816; d. Philadelphia, Pa., 1905*), Philadelphia jurist. Son of Robert Hare. Made important contribution to establishment of equity as general system in Pennsylvania.

HARE, ROBERT (*b. Philadelphia, Pa., 1781; d. 1858*), chemist, teacher. Studied with James Woodhouse; friend and associate of Benjamin Silliman. His important inventions included the oxyhydrogen blow-pipe (1801), the calorimotor, the use of the mercury cathode in electrolysis, and an electric furnace. He also did pioneer work on the constitution of salts.

HARE, WILLIAM HOBART (*b. Princeton, N.J., 1838; d. Atlantic City, N.J., 1909*), Episcopal clergyman. Son of George E. Hare; nephew of John H. Hobart. *Post* 1872, missionary bishop in the Sioux country north of Niobrara River; his diocese was later limited to South Dakota.

HARGROVE, ROBERT KENNON (*b. Pickens Co., Ala., 1829; d. Nashville, Tenn., 1905*), bishop of Methodist Episcopal Church, South; president, board of trust, Vanderbilt University, 1889–1905.

HARING, CLARENCE (*b. Philadelphia, Pa., 1885; d. Cambridge, Mass., 1960*), historian. Studied at Harvard (Ph.D., 1916), and as a Rhodes scholar at Oxford. An expert in Spanish colonial policies and history, Haring taught at Bryn Mawr (1912–15), Yale University (1916–23), and Harvard (1923–53). His books include *Trade and Navigation Between Spain and the Indies in the Time of the Hapsburgs* (1918) and *The Spanish Empire in America* (1947).

HARKINS, WILLIAM DRAPER (*b. Titusville, Pa., 1873; d. Chicago, Ill., 1951*), nuclear physicist and physical chemist. Ph.D., Stanford University, 1907. From 1921 to 1951, professor of physics at Chicago. For fifteen years (1913–28) Harkins and his students were the only Americans involved in studies of nuclear reactions and nuclear research. In 1915, he and E. D. Wilson published papers on nuclear synthesis reactions, showing how the stability and abundance of the elements in stars could be predicted from the relative loss of mass in the fusion reactions of atombuilding. Harkins' experimental studies of nuclear reactions included pioneer studies with Wilson cloud chambers in the early 1920's and the construction and operation of a cyclotron in the mid-1930's. During World War II, the cyclotron was turned over to the Manhattan Project. Major field of research was the physical chemistry of liquid and solid surfaces, a study started with Fritz Haber in 1909.

HARKNESS, ALBERT (*b. Mendon, Mass., 1822; d. 1907*), classical scholar. Graduated Brown, 1842; Ph. D. University of Bonn, 1854. Professor of Greek at Brown, 1855–92. Author of Latin textbooks, notably *Latin Grammar* (1865; revised, 1898). A founder of American School of Classical Studies, Athens.

HARKNESS, EDWARD STEPHEN (*b. Cleveland, Ohio, 1874; d. New York, N.Y., 1940*), philanthropist. Son of S. V. Harkness, an associate and partner of John D. Rockefeller, Sr. As president of the family-established Commonwealth Fund, Edward Harkness directed many grants in the fields of health and education. He was largely responsible for the establishment of the Columbia-Presbyterian Medical Center, New York, financing the affiliation of the two institutions, giving the land for the site, and endowing the hospital. His interest in the decentralization of large educational institutions led to vast gifts for that purpose to Harvard, Yale, and Phillips Exeter Academy. His British benefactions included establishing the Pilgrim Trust.

HARKNESS, WILLIAM (*b. Ecclefechan, Scotland, 1837; d. Jersey City, N.J., 1903*), astronomer. Came to America as a child. Associated with U.S. Naval Observatory, 1862–99; was director, *post* 1894.

HARLAN, JAMES (*b. Harlan Station, Ky., 1800; d. 1863*), lawyer, legislator. Congressman, Whig, from Kentucky, 1835–39; held many state offices, including secretary of state and attorney general; opposed secession.

HARLAN, JAMES (*b. Clark Co., Ill., 1820; d. 1899*), lawyer, teacher, college president. Raised on Indiana frontier; settled in Iowa, 1845. U.S. senator, Free-Soil, 1855–61; Republican, 1861–65, 1867–73. During inept term as U.S. secretary of the interior, 1865–66, dismissed Walt Whitman from Indian Office in economy move.

HARLAN, JOHN MARSHALL (*b. Boyle Co., Ky., 1833; d. 1911*), jurist. Son of James Harlan (1800–1863). Graduated Centre College, 1850. Elected county court judge, 1858, his only judicial position prior to Supreme Court appointment. Southern by tradition, a Whig and a slave-holder, he raised and commanded the 10th Kentucky Volunteer Infantry and served on the Union side from 1861 until his father's death in 1863; thereafter until 1867 he served as Kentucky attorney general. Firm for the Union, he was a bitter critic of Lincoln's administration; after 1866, however, he cast his lot with the radical Republicans. In 1871 and 1875 he was defeated for governor. Heading the Kentucky delegation to the Republican National Convention in 1876, he threw its support to R. B. Hayes. As a reward, President Hayes named him to the U.S. Supreme Court where he assumed his seat Dec. 11, 1877. His tenure until 1911 made him a participant in the constitutional controversies of a third of a century. During this time he wrote the opinion of the Court in 703 cases. His legal philosophy was built on an almost religious reverence for the Constitution; he believed that the Constitution—and all legislation—should be construed in accordance with the framers' intention and the dictates of common sense. He tried to hold an even course between strong nationalism and states' rights, a balance of conflicting pressures evident in his opinions on specific constitutional problems. His famous dissent (1895) in the income-tax cases (*Pollock* v. *Farmer's Loan and Trust Co.*, 158 U.S., 601) was a protest against what he regarded as impairment of the vital power of national taxation. But he also believed that firm protection should be given the police power of the states. Therefore, he dissented in a series of cases, including the famous "original package case," in which the states' power to keep intoxicating liquor from being shipped in through channels of interstate commerce was cut down or denied. He supported this principle also in his dissent from the Court's judgment in *Lochner* v. *New York*.

A stern defender of civil liberty, Harlan believed that the constitutional guarantees in its behalf should be strictly construed. This is apparent in his numerous opinions interpreting the clause forbidding impairment of contracts by states or municipalities. He had profound reverence for the jury system and its attributes. For him the Constitution "followed the flags" and he could not conceive of any American territory being deprived of protection of fundamental law. He rendered valiant service in helping discredit the "natural rights" philosophy which Justice Field had struggled to engraft upon American constitutional law and resented with all his vigor what seemed to him judicial legislation.

His first dissent like his last ones, written a few months before his death in the Standard Oil and American Tobacco Co. cases, were all strong denunciations of judicial legislation. It is as the "great dissenter," vigorous, uncompromising, often bitter, that he will be remembered; altogether he dissented in 316 cases. Justice Harlan served as an American representative in the Bering Sea arbitration with Great Britain, 1892, and lectured on constitutional law at Columbian (George Washington) University, 1889–1910.

HARLAN, JOSIAH (*b. Chester County, Pa., 1799; d. San Francisco, Calif., 1871*), physician, soldier, adventurer. Brother of Richard Harlan. Recounted his exploits as secret agent and Afghan general in A *Memoir of India and Afghanistan* (1842).

HARLAN, RICHARD (*b. Philadelphia, Pa., 1796; d. New Orleans, La., 1843*), naturalist, physician. Brother of Josiah Harlan. His major interests were zoology and vertebrate paleontology. A prolific writer, his most notable work was *Fauna Americana* (1825), first systematic treatise on American mammals.

HARLAND, HENRY (*b. St. Petersburg, Russia, 1861; d. San Remo, Italy, 1905*), novelist. Raised in New York City. Editor, *The Yellow Book* (London), 1894–97; author, among other works, of *As It Was Written* (under pseudonym, "Sidney Luska," 1885), *The Cardinal's Snuff Box* (1900) and *My Friend Prospero* (1904).

HARLAND, MARION. *See* TERHUNE, MARY VIRGINIA.

HARLAND, THOMAS (*b. England, 1735; d. 1807*), watch and clock maker, silversmith. Established in Norwich, Conn., *post* 1773. Eli Terry was one of his apprentices.

HARLOW, JEAN (*b. Kansas City, Mo., 1911; d. Los Angeles, Calif., 1937*), "platinum blonde" motion-picture actress; star of *Hell's Angels* (1930), *Bombshell* (1933).

HARLOW, RALPH VOLNEY (*b. Claremont, N.H., 1884; d. Westbrook, Conn., 1956*), historian and educator. Studied at Yale (Ph.D., 1913). Taught at Simmons College (1913–20); Boston University (1920–26); Yale (1926–29); and Syracuse (1929–48). Wrote a controversial biography, *Samuel Adams, Promoter of the American Revolution* (1923) and a widely used text, *The United States From Wilderness to World Power* (1949).

HARMAR, JOSIAH (*b. Philadelphia, Pa., 1753; d. 1813*), soldier. An able Revolutionary officer, he served as commander of the U.S. Army, 1784–91. His 1790 campaign against the Indians in the Maumee valley was a failure.

HARMON, DANIEL WILLIAMS (*b. Bennington, Vt., 1778; d. Montreal, Canada, 1845*), fur trader, explorer. Recorded his experiences as employee and partner of the North-West Co. in *Journal of Voyages and Travels in the Interiour of North America* (1820).

HARMON, JUDSON (*b. Newtown, Ohio, 1846; d. Cincinnati, Ohio, 1927*), jurist. Graduated Denison, 1866; Cincinnati Law School, 1869. Practiced in Cincinnati. U.S. attorney general, 1895–97; Democratic governor of Ohio, 1909–13. An able, conservative reformer.

HARNDEN, WILLIAM FREDERICK (*b. Reading, Mass., 1812; d. 1845*), pioneer expressman. Began parcel service between New York and Boston, 1839; prospered and opened European offices for shipping and exchange. Facilitated movement of 100,000 immigrants to United States.

HARNETT, CORNELIUS (*b. probably Chowan Co., N.C., 1723[?]; d. Wilmington, N.C., 1781*), Revolutionary statesman, "the Samuel Adams of North Carolina." Member of the Assembly, 1754–75; president of N.C. Provincial Congress, 1776; put state on war basis. Served three terms in Continental Congress.

HARNEY, BENJAMIN ROBERTSON (*b. near Middleboro, Ky., 1871; d. Philadelphia, Pa., 1938*), early composer of "ragtime music," which he played and sang in vaudeville. His "You've Been a Good Old Wagon" (1895) was probably the first piece of ragtime to be printed.

HARNEY, WILLIAM SELBY (*b. Haysboro, Tenn., 1800; d. Orlando, Fla., 1889*), soldier. Commissioned lieutenant in 1st Infantry, 1818. Served on numerous expeditions against Florida Indians. Promoted colonel, 1846, he was ranking cavalry officer under Gen. Scott who tried, unsuccessfully, to remove Harney from his command. Harney displayed brilliant, heroic leadership in the war with Mexico. Stationed later in the Platte country, he defeated the Sioux at Sand Hill. Given command of the Department of Oregon and promoted brigadier, 1858, he was soon recalled because of anti-British proclivities and commanded the Department of the West at St. Louis until 1861. Suspected of

Southern sympathies, he was superseded and given no active duty during the Civil War. He was retired in 1863.

HARPER, FLETCHER (*b. Newtown, New York, 1806; d. 1877*), printer, publisher. With James, John, and Joseph Wesley Harper, was partner in Harper & Brothers. Created *Harper's Weekly* (1857), which exerted strong political influence; also *Harper's Bazar* (1867).

HARPER, IDA HUSTED (*b. Fairfield, Ind., 1851; d. Washington, D.C., 1931*), journalist, author. Historian of woman's suffrage movement in which she was prominent.

HARPER, JAMES (*b. Newtown, New York, 1795; d. 1869*), printer, publisher. Started printing business in 1817 which, with his brothers Fletcher, John and Joseph Wesley Harper as partners, was first known as J. and J. Harper and as Harper & Brothers, *post* 1833. Originated *Harper's New Monthly Magazine* (1850). Elected reform mayor. New York City, 1844.

HARPER, JOHN. *See* HARPER, JAMES.

HARPER, JOHN LYELL (*b. Harpersfield N.Y., 1873; d. Niagara Falls, N.Y., 1924*), mechanical and electrical engineer, specialist in hydroelectric work. Graduated Cornell, 1897. Chief engineer, Niagara Falls Hydraulic Power & Manufacturing Co., *post* 1904; chief engineer, Niagara Falls Power Co., *post* 1918. His most important achievement was designing and constructing the company's hydroelectric power plant in the gorge below the Falls, largest in the world at that time. He served as chief engineer of other companies and patented several electric furnaces, one being the Harper Electric Furnace for commercial firing of ceramic materials.

HARPER, JOSEPH WESLEY. *See* HARPER, JAMES.

HARPER, ROBERT FRANCIS (*b. New Concord, Ohio, 1864; d. London, England, 1914*), Assyriologist. Brother of William R. Harper. Graduated University of Chicago, 1883; Ph.D., Leipzig, 1886. Taught at Yale and University of Chicago. Edited monumental *Assyrian and Babylonian Letters Belonging to the Kouyunjik Collections of the British Museum* (14 vols., 1892–1914).

HARPER, ROBERT GOODLOE (*b. near Fredericksburg, Va., 1765; d. Baltimore, Md., 1825*), lawyer, Federalist politician. Graduated Princeton, 1785. Practiced law and entered politics in South Carolina; served in legislature and as congressman, 1795–1801. Elected as a (Democrat) Republican, he almost immediately shifted allegiance and became leader of the Federalists, publishing in 1797 his *Observations on the Dispute Between the U.S. and France*. He married Catherine, daughter of Charles Carroll, 1801, and moved to Baltimore where he was a successful lawyer, prominent in civic affairs. An original member of the American Colonization Society, he was influential in selecting Africa as the place for the Society's colony and suggested Liberia and Monrovia as names for the colony and its capital.

HARPER, WILLIAM (*b. Antigua, 1790; d. 1847*), South Carolina legislator and nullification leader, judge. Graduated South Carolina College, 1808. Chancellor of Missouri Territory and state, 1819–23; chancellor of South Carolina, 1828–30, 1835–47. Author of nullification ordinance at 1832 convention. His *Memoir on Slavery* (1837) is regarded as one of the most important pro-slavery arguments.

HARPER, WILLIAM RAINEY (*b. New Concord, Ohio, 1856; d. 1906*), Hebraist, educator. Brother of Robert F. Harper. Graduated Muskingum College, 1870; Ph.D., Yale, 1874. After work at Masonic College, Macon, Tenn., and Denison University, he

taught Semitic languages at Baptist Union Theological Seminary, Chicago, 1879–86. Prominent in work at Chatauqua, *post* 1885, he gave a summer course there and was president of the college of liberal arts for several years. As a teacher at Yale, 1886–90, he multiplied his activities and won a national reputation as teacher, lecturer, organizer and editor. When, with John D. Rockefeller's encouragement, the new University of Chicago was established, Harper was named president. Before accepting the position he made plain his conception of the new university and his own position in the conflict between orthodoxy and modernism, stipulating that there should be entire academic freedom. His plans included university extension, a university press, university affiliations, division of the year into four quarters, distinction of the two upper years of undergraduate school as the senior college, faculty control of athletics, concentration on a few studies at a time, emphasis on graduate study and research. He expounded his ideas in numerous addresses, the most significant being collected in *The Trend in Higher Education* (1905). A volume of talks to students, *Religion and the Higher Life* (1904), reveals much of his inner self and beliefs. His works on *The Priestly Element in the Old Testament* (1902) and *The Prophetic Element in the Old Testament* (1905) illustrate his enormous industry. His colleagues recognized him as a sound, if not greatly creative Semitic scholar, and a very great teacher who contributed much to the revival of Hebrew scholarship. His *Critical and Exegetical Commentary on Amos and Hosea* (1905) was favorably reviewed by experts.

From 1892 to his death, Harper's life was inseparable from that of the University of Chicago. Within two or three years he assembled a brilliant faculty, established a working library and had an adequate university functioning. He also did what few university presidents have ever done—taught full time as chairman of his department. The demands on his vitality were terrific. His days were filled with administrative problems, "campaigns" for endowment, mediation between a faculty to which he had promised full freedom and alarmed sectarians, and the swift continuous growth of the University. Though Harper was a sturdy man, no constitution could endure a regimen of incessant work, no vacations, little sleep, irregular diet and a perpetual round of dinners and speeches. An appendicitis operation revealed a cancerous infection, and in January 1906 he died.

Like all strong executives, Harper wished to have his own way because it seemed to him the efficient way; but he was always ready to listen to the other side, and was flexible in adapting himself to modifications of his plans. His was a dominating but not a domineering personality. Though a devout Christian, he remained despite calumny a champion of the rights of higher criticism.

HARPSTER, JOHN HENRY (*b. Centerhall, Pa., 1844; d. Philadelphia, Pa., 1911*), Lutheran clergyman. Missionary to India, 1872–76, 1893–1901, 1902–09.

HARPUR, ROBERT (*b. Ballybay, Ireland, 1731?; d. 1825*), educator, Revolutionary patriot, New York legislator. Professor of mathematics, librarian, tutor, King's College, New York, 1761–75; secretary, Regents of University of State of New York, 1784–87; clerk of board of trustees, Columbia College, 1787–95. Member, N.Y. Assembly, 1777–84. Founded Harpursville, N.Y.

HARRAH, CHARLES JEFFERSON (*b. Philadelphia, Pa., 1817; d. Philadelphia, 1890*), promoter, capitalist. Prominent in business in Philadelphia, and in Brazil (1843–73) where he built shipyards, railroads and established first telegraph company, first street railroad and first public school.

HARRELL, JOHN (b. Perquimans Co., N.C., 1806; d. 1876), Methodist clergyman, educator. Labored, post 1831, in western Arkansas and Indian Territory.

HARRIGAN, EDWARD (b. New York, N.Y., 1845; d. New York, 1911), playwright, actor, producer. Began career in California, ca. 1867. Made New York debut, 1870; joined Anthony Cannon ("Tony Hart") in the famous firm of Harrigan and Hart, 1872. The most famous of Harrigan's productions began with *The Mulligan Guards* (1873). The Mulligan cycle of burlesque on Irish and German immigrant types and life had its best expression in *Cordelia's Aspirations* (1883) and *Dan's Tribulations* (1884). Besides variety sketches he wrote 39 plays, in all of which he acted the leading part. The many charming songs interspersed through his plays were set to music by his father-in-law, Dave Braham.

HARRIMAN, EDWARD HENRY (b. Hempstead, N.Y., 1848; d. 1909), railroad executive, capitalist. Son of an Episcopal clergyman. A Wall St. office boy at 14, he bought a seat on the N.Y. stock exchange seven years later. In 1879 he married Mary Averell, whose father was an Ogdensburg, N.Y., banker and president of a railroad. This relationship aroused Harriman's interest in transportation; he began his career as rebuilder of bankrupt railroads with the Lake Ontario Southern, successfully reorganizing it, 1881–82. In 1883 he entered the Illinois Central directorate and was vice president by 1887, a dominant influence in its financial policy. In 1895 he joined in the syndicate which reorganized the Union Pacific, and by 1898 was chairman of the executive committee; from then on his word was law on the Union Pacific system. He was responsible for restoring the physical efficiency of the road, spending $25,000,000 on rails and rolling stock. In 1903 he became president of the Union Pacific, after restoring it physically and financially. In 1901 he had begun buying into the Southern Pacific until the Union Pacific controlled 46 percent of the stock; this carried control of that corporation and ownership of its subsidiary, the Central Pacific, which would make possible an efficient system to the Pacific Coast. He strengthened the financial and operating conditions of both roads and evolved a brilliant administrative organization for the combined system. To secure an entrance into Chicago, he began his fight with James J. Hill of the Northern Pacific for control of the Chicago, Burlington & Quincy. Outgeneraled by Hill, Harriman began buying stock of the Northern Pacific which now held a half interest in the Burlington. The Hill-Harriman struggle for the Northern Pacific resulted in the stock market panic of May 9, 1901. The issue was settled by organization of the Northern Securities Co. to take over the stocks of the Great Northern and the Northern Pacific with the Harriman interests represented on the board of the holding company.

When the Northern Securities Co. was condemned by the Supreme Court in 1904 for effecting a combination in restraint of trade, Harriman sold his interests in the Northwestern roads and emerged with a profit of over $50 million. His purchase of stocks of other railways led to an investigation of the Harriman lines by the Interstate Commerce Commission, 1906–07. The reor of the Chicago & Alton in 1899 was cited as an example of how a road may be drained of its resources for the benefit of insiders. The Commission's report also revealed the range of Harriman's holdings and the extent to which the Union Pacific served as a holding company for securities of other transportation companies. From the standpoint of public welfare, his offense was his use of the resources of the Union Pacific speculatively to purchase other securities instead of devoting them to the road as an agency of transportation.

Harriman's influence extended beyond railroads into banks and insurance companies. He owned a steamship line to the Orient. He was a director of the Equitable Life Assurance Society and was one of those responsible for the change in its ownership and control in 1905. The investigation which followed this change, together with the Interstate Commerce Commission report, made him in popular opinion a personification of all the evils of the existing monopolistic business situation and subjected him to a storm of abuse. Characterized as the last great individualist and the last figure of an epoch, his genius as an administrator made him one of the great railway builders of all time. Self-confident, dominant, cold and ruthless, he spared neither friend nor foe if they blocked his plans.

HARRIMAN, FLORENCE JAFFRAY HURST (b. New York, N.Y., 1870; d. Georgetown, Wash., D.C., 1967), socialite, reformer, diplomat, and political activist. Her social-welfare endeavors included a study of industrial working conditions, particularly for women. Among other political activities in women's organizations of the Democratic party, established and chaired the Women's National Wilson and Marshall Association, which became the Women's Division of the Democratic National Committee. During World War I she campaigned for American preparedness and worked for Allied relief. In the 1920's she began a tradition of Sunday-night dinners at her Washington home, which became the capital city's leading salon. Roosevelt appointed her minister to Norway in 1937, and in 1942 she received the highest honor of Norway, the Great Cross of St. Olav. Was an avid supporter of postwar international organization, and after 1945, of world disarmament. In 1963 President John F. Kennedy awarded her the first Citation for Distinguished Service.

HARRIMAN, WALTER (b. Warner, N.H., 1817; d. Concord, N.H., 1884), Universalist clergyman, businessman, Union soldier. Republican governor of New Hampshire, 1867–69.

HARRINGTON, CHARLES (b. Salem, Mass., 1856; d. Lynton, England, 1908), Boston sanitarian, educator. Graduated Harvard, 1878; Harvard Medical School, 1881, where he taught hygiene, post 1885. Through his writings, he did much to arouse interest in preventive medicine.

HARRINGTON, JOHN LYLE (b. Lawrence, Kans., 1868; d. Kansas City, Mo., 1942), civil and mechanical engineer. Graduated University of Kansas, 1895. A specialist in design and construction of bridges, he made his most important contribution in the development of the vertical lift bridge from the basic invention of John A. L. Waddell, with whom he was in partnership, 1907–14.

HARRINGTON, MARK WALROD (b. Sycamore, Ill., 1848; d. 1926), astronomer, meteorologist, educator. First civilian chief of U.S. Weather Bureau, 1891–95. Established *American Meteorological Journal*, 1884; author of *About the Weather* (1899).

HARRINGTON, SAMUEL MAXWELL (b. Dover, Del., 1803; d. Philadelphia, Pa., 1865), Delaware jurist and railroad promoter.

HARRINGTON, THOMAS FRANCIS (b. Lowell, Mass., 1866; d. 1919), physician, hygienist. Graduated Harvard Medical School, 1888; practiced in Lowell and Boston. Author of a standard history, *The Harvard Medical School* (1905). Pioneer of hygienic physical culture in public schools.

HARRIS, BENJAMIN (fl. 1673–1716), bookseller, publisher, author, first American journalist. After a career in London where he was associated with Shaftesbury and the Whigs as an anti-Catholic and anti-court propagandist, he came to New England, 1686. Successful as bookseller and publisher in Boston, he brought out on Sept. 25, 1690, the first newspaper printed in America, *Publick Occurrences Both Forreign and Domestick*, remarkable because the news was chiefly American. The first issue was suppressed by the governor and the council "because not licensed." Sometime before 1690, Harris had published *The New England Primer*, one of the most popular and influential books ever printed in America. Established as the leading publisher and bookseller of 17th-century America, he returned to London, 1695, and was active as journalist and publisher.

HARRIS, CALEB FISKE (*b. Warwick, R.I., 1818; d. Moosehead Lake, Maine, 1881*), merchant, bibliophile. The American poetry collection formed by him was presented to Brown University Library, 1884.

HARRIS, CHAPIN AARON (*b. Pompey, N.Y., 1806; d. Baltimore, Md., 1860*), dentist, editor. One of the founders of dentistry as an organized profession; practiced in Baltimore from 1839 until his death. Author of *The Dental Art, a Practical Treatise on Dental Surgery* (1839), perhaps the most popular dental textbook ever written. With several New York dentists, established in 1839 the world's first dental periodical, the *American Journal of Dental Science*. With Horace H. Hayden, organized the world's first dental college, the Baltimore College of Dental Surgery, chartered 1840. Harris helped organize the first national dental association, the American Society of Dental Surgeons, also in 1840. His many valuable articles and books include *A Dictionary of Dental Science, Biography, Bibliography and Medical Terminology* (1849).

HARRIS, CHARLES KASSELL (*b. Poughkeepsie, N.Y., 1865; d. New York, N.Y., 1930*), song writer, music publisher. Composed many sentimental popular ballads, of which the most famous were "After the Ball" (1892) and "Break the News to Mother" (1897).

HARRIS, DANIEL LESTER (*b. Providence R.I., 1818, d. Springfield, Mass., 1879*), engineer, Massachusetts legislator. Notable in railroad and bridge construction; president, Connecticut River Railroad, *ca.* 1855–79.

HARRIS, ELISHA (*b. Westminster, Vt., 1824; d. 1884*), pioneer sanitarian. Graduated College of Physicians and Surgeons, New York, 1849. Practiced in New York; was superintendent of New York quarantine hospital; helped organize U.S. Sanitary Commission, 1861. Designed a hospital car to relieve Civil War wounded and also originated an effective national system of records of death and burial of soldiers. Served as registrar of records of New York's board of health and sanitary superintendent of the city. In 1869 he organized the first free public vaccination service. He was an organizer of the American Public Health Association, 1872, becoming president in 1877. In 1880 he was appointed secretary of the new New York State Board of Health and state superintendent of vital statistics.

HARRIS, GEORGE (*b. East Machias, Maine, 1844; d. 1922*), Congregational minister, educator. Nephew of Samuel Harris. Professor of theology, Andover Theological Seminary, 1883–99; president, Amherst College, 1899–1912.

HARRIS, GEORGE WASHINGTON (*b. Allegheny City, Pa., 1814; d. 1869*), humorist. Raised in Knoxville, Tenn. A metal craftsman and engineer by profession, he contributed humorous sketches *post* 1843 in Porter's *Spirit of the Times*. His *Sut Lovingood Yarns* (1867) and many uncollected humorous sketches delineate the localisms, dialect, thoughts and superstitions of the East Tennessee mountain people.

HARRIS, IRA (*b. Charleston, N.Y., 1802; d. Albany, N.Y., 1875*), jurist, New York legislator, legal educator. Justice, state supreme court, 1847–59; U.S. senator, Republican, from New York, 1861–67.

HARRIS, ISHAM GREEN (*b. near Tullahoma, Tenn., 1818; d. 1897*), lawyer, Confederate soldier, politician. Congressman, Democrat, from Tennessee, 1849–53. As governor of that state, 1857–63 (and nominally until 1865), he urged secession and committed Tennessee to the Confederacy by a series of legislative maneuvers, 1861. *Post* 1867, he practiced law in Memphis. Elected to the U.S. Senate, 1877, he served until his death.

HARRIS, JAMES ARTHUR (*b. Plantsville, Ohio, 1880; d. St. Paul, Minn., 1930*), botanist, biometrician. Raised in Kansas. Graduated University of Kansas, 1901; Ph.D., Washington University, St. Louis, 1903. Botanical investigator, Station for Experimental Evolution, Carnegie Institution of Washington, 1907–24; head of botany department, University of Minnesota, 1924–30. Adapted exact techniques of physics and chemistry to study of plant geography. Collaborated with Bureau of Plant Industry, U.S. Department of Agriculture, 1918–30, on problems of cotton and cereal growing in arid and semi-arid regions. Interested early in the application of mathematics to biology, he became America's leading exponent of and contributor to biometric theory and practice. His papers, numbering over 300 titles, include topics pertaining to almost every field of the biological sciences.

HARRIS, JOEL CHANDLER (*b. near Eatonton, Ga., 1848; d. Atlanta, Ga., 1908*), journalist, author. Learned to set type on the weekly *Countryman*, published near his home by the planter Joseph A. Turner. Turner lent him books, schooled him in writing, and gave him the run of the plantation, whence came his sympathetic knowledge of the black dialect and folkways. After varied newspaper experience, 1864–76, Harris was on the staff of the *Atlanta Constitution*, 1876–1900. He published *Uncle Remus: His Songs and His Sayings* in 1880. This volume and its continuation *Nights with Uncle Remus* (1883) are among the unforgettable books of American literature. A whole cycle of Uncle Remus books followed. He also produced several volumes of children's stories, a few poems, magazine articles, and many short stories which were republished in book form, the best of which appear in the collections *Mingo and Other Sketches in Black and White* (1884) and *Free Joe and Other Georgian Sketches* (1887).

HARRIS, JOHN (*b. Harris Ferry, Pa., 1726; d. Harrisburg, Pa., 1791*), Revolutionary soldier, Indian trader. Founder of Harrisburg, Pa.

HARRIS, JOHN WOODS (*b. Nelson Co., Va., 1810; d. Galveston, Tex., 1887*), lawyer. Graduated University of Virginia, 1837. Removed to Texas, 1837. Served in Congress of the Texas Republic, where he had profound influence in framing the laws; was later first attorney general of the State of Texas.

HARRIS, JOSEPH (*b. Shrewsbury, England, 1828; d. near Rochester, N.Y., 1892*), scientific agriculturist, editor. Came to America, 1849. Edited *Genesee Farmer*; partner of Orange Judd in *American Agriculturist*. Among his books are *Harris on the Pig* (1870) and *Talks on Manures* (1878).

HARRIS, JULIAN LA ROSE (*b. Savannah, Ga., 1874; d. Atlanta, Ga., 1963*), journalist and publisher. After working for Atlanta newspapers, launched *Uncle Remus's the Home Magazine* (1907–13) with his father, Joel Chandler Harris. During World War I worked as European correspondent for the *New York Herald*. In 1920 bought into the Columbus, Ga., *Enquirer-Sun*, and within two years was sole owner and editor of this progressive publication, notable for its fearless attacks on the Ku Klux Klan. In 1926 the *Enquirer-Sun* was awarded the Pulitzer Prize for Meritorious Public Service, but the paper was financially unstable, and he sold it in 1929. Worked for the *Atlanta Constitution*, 1930–35, the *Chattanooga Times*, 1935–42, and was southern correspondent for the *New York Times*, 1942–45.

HARRIS, MAURICE HENRY (*b. London, England, 1859; d. 1930*), rabbi. Came to America, *ca.* 1878. Graduated Columbia, 1887; Ph.D., 1889. Minister of Hand in Hand Synagogue (later Temple Israel), New York; a founder of Jewish Institute of Religion; active in social work.

HARRIS, MERRIMAN COLBERT (*b. Beallsville, Ohio, 1846; d. Aoyama, Japan, 1921*), missionary bishop of Methodist Episcopal Church. In Japan, 1873–86; established Pacific Coast and Hawaiian missions, 1886–1904; bishop of Japan and Korea, 1904–16.

HARRIS, MIRIAM COLES (*b. Dosoris N.Y., 1834; d. Pau, France, 1925*), author. Her many novels, popular in the late 19th century, are all of the same melodramatic type. Her reputation rests on *Rutledge* (1860).

HARRIS, NATHANIEL HARRISON (*b. Natchez, Miss., 1934; d. Malvern, England, 1900*), lawyer, Confederate brigadier general.

HARRIS, PAUL PERCY (*b. Racine, Wis., 1868; d. Chicago, Ill., 1947*), lawyer, founder of Rotary International. Raised in Vermont; practiced law in Chicago *post* 1896. Founded Rotary in Chicago, February 1905; served as first president of the national association of Rotary Clubs, 1910–12, and as president emeritus thereafter.

HARRIS, ROLLIN ARTHUR (*b. Randolph, N.Y., 1863; d. 1918*), oceanographer, mathematician. Graduated Cornell, 1885; Ph.D., 1888. Entered U.S. Coast and Geodetic Survey as computer, 1890. Author of the valuable "Manual of Tides" which appeared serially in the Survey Reports, 1894–1907.

HARRIS, SAM HENRY (*b. New York, N.Y., 1872; d. New York, 1941*), theatrical producer. Starting in show business at seventeen as a stagehand at the Bowery Theater, he was also active as a manager of prizefighters; between 1900 and 1904, he was a member of a partnership which produced a number of successful melodramas and burlesques. In a notable partnership with George M. Cohan, 1904–20, he was co-producer of more than fifty plays; in addition, the firm owned theaters in several cities, managed road companies, and ran a music publishing business. After the firm was dissolved, Harris began the most successful part of his career; the list of plays which he produced from 1920 until his death reads like a roster of contemporary hits, and four of them won major awards. As a man, Harris was quiet, generous, and honest; as a producer, he displayed shrewd showmanship and unfailing good taste.

HARRIS, SAMUEL (*b. East Machias, Maine, 1814; d. Litchfield, Conn., 1899*), Congregational clergyman, theologian, educator. Graduated Bowdoin, 1833; studied at Andover Theological Seminary, 1835–38. Professor, Bangor (Maine) Seminary, 1855–67. President of Bowdoin, 1867–71. Resigned to become Dwight professor of systematic theology, Yale Divinity School, 1871–95. Author of *The Philosophical Basis of Theism* (1883), which made a deep impression, and *The Self-Revelation of God* (1887), which carried his philosophical argument into the domain of doctrinal theology; also of *God: The Creator and Lord of All* (1896). He occupied a transitional position between the old dialectical New England theology and the more modern school.

HARRIS, THADDEUS MASON (*b. Charlestown, Mass., 1768; d. 1842*), Unitarian clergyman, author, editor. Graduated Harvard, 1787. Pastor of First Church in Dorchester, Mass., 1793–1836. Librarian, Harvard College, 1791–93, and of Massachusetts Historical Society, 1837–42.

HARRIS, THADDEUS WILLIAM (*b. Dorchester, Mass., 1795; d. 1856*), entomologist, librarian. Son of Thaddeus M. Harris. Graduated Harvard, 1815; M.D., 1820. Interest in ento-

mology inspired by W. D. Peck. Librarian, Harvard College, 1831–56. Became a member of the scientific commission to make a geological and botanical survey of Massachusetts, 1837; from this experience came his classic *Report on the Insects of Massachusetts Injurious to Vegetation* (1841 and later revisions). Probably no 19th-century American work on natural history was better done and the trend of American entomology toward the practical stems from it. Harris' bibliography covers 120 titles on entomological subjects and eight other titles. He is generally considered the father of economic entomology in the United States.

HARRIS, THOMAS LAKE (*b. Fenny Stratford, England, 1823; d. New York, N.Y., 1906*), Universalist clergyman, spiritualist. Founded "Brotherhood of the New Life" and its colony "The Use," located first in New York and *post* 1875 at Santa Rosa, Calif.

HARRIS, TOWNSEND (*b. Sandy Hill, N.Y., 1804; d. New York, N.Y., 1878*), merchant, politician, diplomat. As president, New York City Board of Education, 1846–48, he managed the legislation for College of City of New York. Appointed consul general to Japan, 1855, and minister-resident, 1859, he negotiated earliest U.S. treaties with Japan, 1857–58. Honest and moderate as he showed himself, no foreigner in the East ever so quickly attained such influence over the government of an Oriental people. He resigned his post in 1860.

HARRIS, WILEY POPE (*b. Pike Co., Miss., 1818; d. Jackson, Miss., 1891*), lawyer, judge, congressman.

HARRIS, WILLIAM (*b. Springfield, Mass., 1765; d. 1829*), Episcopal clergyman. Graduated Harvard, 1786. Rector, St. Mark's-in-the-Bowery, New York City, 1802–16. President, Columbia College, 1811–29.

HARRIS, WILLIAM ALEXANDER (*b. Loudoun Co., Va., 1841; d. Chicago, Ill., 1909*), Confederate soldier, engineer, stockman. Imported Scotch Shorthorns and bred a famous herd near Lawrence, Kans,; Congressman, Populist and Democrat, from Kansas, 1893–95; U.S. senator, 1897–1903.

HARRIS, WILLIAM LITTLETON (*b. Elbert Co., Ga., 1807; d. Memphis, Tenn., 1868*), Mississippi jurist.

HARRIS, WILLIAM LOGAN (*b. near Mansfield, Ohio, 1817; d. Brooklyn, N.Y., 1887*), Methodist clergyman. Secretary of General Conferences, 1856–72; elected bishop, 1872; served as secretary to the board of bishops.

HARRIS, WILLIAM TORREY (*b. near North Killingly, Conn., 1835; d. Providence, R.I., 1909*), educator, philosopher. Attended Yale; began to teach in public schools, St. Louis, Mo., 1857, and was appointed superintendent, 1868. After dabbling in mesmerism, spiritualism, and phrenology, he took up study of Hegel under influence of Henry C. Brokmeyer; found life work in exposition of Hegel's thought and application of his principles especially to education. Founded *Journal of Speculative Philosophy*, 1867, in which German thought was critically presented and in which Royce, Peirce, James, and Dewey made debuts as writers. Harris helped establish the Concord (Mass.) School of Philosophy, 1880. After its failure, as U.S. commissioner of education, 1889–1906, he labored to put education on a psychological basis and to relate schools to other departments of institutional life. His *Introduction to the Study of Philosophy* (1889) is the best approach to his views.

HARRISON, ALEXANDER. *See* HARRISON, THOMAS ALEXANDER.

HARRISON, BENJAMIN (*b. Charles City Co., Va., 1726[?]; d. 1791*), planter, Revolutionary statesman. Grandson of Robert Carter of Corotoman. Member, Virginia House of Burgesses, 1749–74; of Continental Congress, 1749–77; of Virginia House of Delegates, 1777–81. A signer of the Declaration of Independence. Governor of Virginia, 1781–84. Reelected to the House of Delegates, he served until his death.

HARRISON, BENJAMIN (*b. North Bend, near Cincinnati, Ohio, 1833; d. Indianapolis, Ind., 1901*), lawyer, statesman, president of the United States. Grandson of William H. Harrison. Graduated Miami University, 1852. Settled in Indianapolis, Ind., 1854; practiced law; entered politics as a Republican. Elected city attorney, 1857; elected, 1860 and 1864, reporter of Indiana supreme court. Colonel of the 70th Indiana Infantry, 1862, he rose to brigade rank on merit; after the Civil War he returned to his profession and built up a lucrative practice, maintaining interest in public affairs and local philanthropy, but regarded as austere and cold in personal relationships. An ardent radical Republican during Johnson's presidency, he fought for sound money and helped keep Indiana Republicans from supporting "Greenback" doctrines. Defeated for governor in 1876, he drew national attention; as chairman of the Indiana delegation to the Republican National Convention, 1880, he played a leading role in James A. Garfield's nomination. A member of the U.S. Senate, 1881–87, he was chairman of the committee on territories and generally aligned himself with the moderate, progressive group of his party. He supported railroad regulation, labor legislation, protective tariff and increased pensions.

Harrison's friends began in 1887 a campaign which secured him the Republican presidential nomination at Chicago in 1888. He set a precedent by conducting a "front porch" campaign, making many short speeches to visiting delegations. He received in the electoral college 233 votes to 169 for Grover Cleveland (although the latter's popular plurality was 100,000), and became the 23rd president of the United States. James G. Blaine was named secretary of state, but most of the other cabinet appointees were little known in national politics, and some were obnoxious to the reform element in the Republican party. Appreciative of the forces sweeping the nation into imperialism, Harrison took pride in the navy of steel ships being built under Secretary Benjamin Tracy and in his own policy of building a merchant marine. The Pan-American Congress was brilliantly conducted by Blaine, who also pushed American claims in Samoa and received credit for the result although his hand was guided by the president. Civil-service reform proved troublesome to Harrison. Though elected on a reform platform, the hunger of his party for office was great. His attempt at a middle course aroused the antipathy of reformers and politicians alike, for which he suffered in the 1892 campaign. His repugnance to wield the "big stick" caused him to avoid policies distinct from those his party advocated in Congress, and he was not skillful in arousing public opinion in support of legislation he desired. His reserved manner limited his influence with congressmen of his party which from 1888 to 1891 were in the hands of leaders he could not control. Important laws passed during his administration included the McKinley Tariff Act (in which he insisted on a reciprocity provision), the Sherman Silver Act and the Sherman Anti-Trust Act. As a result of Republican legislation and general economic conditions, the federal treasury surplus disappeared and the panic of 1893 was foreshadowed.

Moved to seek renomination in 1892 in resentment of the virulent hostility of the Republican bosses, Harrison was soundly defeated by Cleveland. The enmity of labor, the apathy of the Republican bosses, resentment of the McKinley Tariff, and many other factors contributed to his defeat. No other ex-president, however, resumed the practice of law so successfully as Harrison. He was senior counsel for Venezuela before the arbitration tribunal in Paris (1899) in the boundary dispute with England, presenting a masterly closing argument. During his last years he gave his influence to the liberal side of national and international problems, condemned extremes of imperialism, and emphasized the obligations of wealth.

HARRISON, BIRGE. *See* HARRISON, LOVELL BIRGE.

HARRISON, BYRON PATTON (*b. Crystal Springs, Miss., 1881; d. Washington, D.C., 1941*), lawyer, politician. Known familiarly as "Pat" Harrison. Attended Mississippi State College and Louisiana State University; taught school; was admitted to the bar, 1902. Elected to Congress as a Democrat, 1910, he served four terms. In 1918, backed by John S. Williams, he was elected to the U.S. Senate (1919–41). Unlike most Southern politicians he campaigned for Alfred E. Smith and he was an early supporter of Franklin D. Roosevelt. *Post* 1933, as chairman of the Senate Finance Committee, he maneuvered much of the New Deal legislation through to passage. Passed over for the post of Senate majority leader in 1937, he was chosen president pro tempore of the Senate in 1941.

HARRISON, CARTER HENRY (*b. near Lexington, Ky., 1825; d. 1893*), lawyer, businessman, politician. Graduated Yale, 1845. Grew wealthy in Chicago, Ill., real estate ventures. Elected Cook Co. commissioner, 1871; congressman, Democrat, 1874 and 1876. Elected five times mayor of Chicago, 1879, 1881, 1883, 1885, and 1893 when he was shot and killed by a disappointed office seeker. A successful businessman, witty and a liberal, he won support from both propertied and working classes.

HARRISON, CARTER HENRY, JR. (*b. Chicago, Ill., 1860; d. 1953*), politician. Studied in Altenburg, Germany, and at Yale University, law degree, 1883. During the years 1897–1915, he was elected five times as mayor of Chicago. He was instrumental in implementing the Burnham Plan for the revitalization of Chicago's lakefront. A Democrat, he was appointed by Franklin D. Roosevelt as Collector of Internal Revenue for the First Illinois District, 1933–45.

HARRISON, CHARLES CUSTIS (*b. Philadelphia, Pa., 1844; d. Philadelphia, 1829*), financier, educator. Amassed a fortune in sugar refining. As provost, University of Pennsylvania, 1894–1910, he contributed greatly to its expansion and improvement. He served in later years as president of the University Museum and made possible its archeological expeditions.

HARRISON, CONSTANCE CARY (*b. Fairfax Co., Va., 1843; d. Washington, D.C., 1920*), novelist. As Mrs. Burton Harrison, wrote *Flower de Hundred* (1890) and many other popular tales; also an autobiographical volume, *Recollections Grave and Gay* (1911).

HARRISON, ELIZABETH (*b. Athens, Ky., 1849; d. San Antonio, Tex., 1927*), kindergartner. President, National Kindergarten and Elementary College, Chicago. Author of *A Study of Child Nature* (1890).

HARRISON, FAIRFAX (*b. New York, N.Y., 1869; d. Baltimore, Md., 1938*), lawyer. Son of Burton and Constance C. Harrison. President, Southern Railway, 1913–37.

HARRISON, FRANCIS BURTON (*b. New York, N.Y., 1873; d. Flemington, N.J., 1957*), congressman and colonial administrator. Attended Yale and the New York Law School. Democratic member of Congress from New York City, 1902–04 and 1906–14. As a congressman, Harrison was known as an anti-imperialist. He was author of the Harrison Narcotics Act of 1914. Appointed governor general of the Philippines by Woodrow Wilson in 1913. An advocate of Philippine independence, Harrison founded institutions that would lead the islands to that goal, transferring leadership to Philippine nationals whenever possible. He left the islands in 1921, returning in the 1930's as a presidential adviser to Manuel Quezon, a position he resumed after World War II when the Philippines achieved their independence. He was given a state funeral in Manila.

HARRISON, GABRIEL (*b. Philadelphia, Pa., 1818; d. Brooklyn, N.Y., 1902*), theatrical manager, actor, author, painter. Friend of Edgar A. Poe. A force in dramatic, musical, and art life of Brooklyn, N.Y., 1848–88.

HARRISON, GEORGE PAUL (*b. near Savannah, Ga., 1841; d. 1922*), lawyer, Confederate brigadier general, Alabama legislator and congressman.

HARRISON, GESSNER (*b. Harrisonburg, Va., 1807; d. 1862*), teacher, classicist. Graduated University of Virginia, 1828, and served there as professor of ancient languages, 1828–59. The first American college teacher to recognize science of comparative grammar.

HARRISON, HENRY BALDWIN (*b. New Haven, Conn., 1821; d. New Haven, 1901*), lawyer, Connecticut legislator. Graduated Yale, 1846. Republican governor of Connecticut, 1885–87.

HARRISON, HENRY SYDNOR (*b. Sewanee, Tenn., 1880; d. Atlantic City, N.J., 1930*), newspaperman, novelist. Graduated Columbia, 1900. Editorial writer, *Richmond Times-Dispatch*. Author of best-selling *Queed* (1911), *V.V.'s Eyes* (1913), and other works.

HARRISON, JAMES (*b. Bourbon Co., Ky., 1803; d. 1870*), merchant, trader, developer of Missouri mineral resources. Organized the American Iron Mountain Co., 1843, which became one of world's largest iron producers.

HARRISON, JAMES ALBERT (*b. Pass Christian, Miss., 1848; d. Charlottesville, Va., 1911*), philologist. Professor of languages at Randolph-Macon, Washington and Lee, and University of Virginia; an American pioneer in Old-English scholarship; editor in chief of Virginia Edition of E. A. Poe (1902).

HARRISON, JOHN (*b. Philadelphia, Pa., 1773; d. Philadelphia, 1833*), first (1801) manufacturing chemist in the United States.

HARRISON, JOSEPH (*b. Philadelphia, Pa., 1810; d. Philadelphia, 1874*), mechanical engineer. Served as apprentice to a steam-engine builder; after varied working experience became a partner in Eastwick & Harrison, locomotive manufacturers, first to design a practical 8-wheel engine. In 1839 Harrison patented a method for equalizing weight on the driving wheels and made the forward truck flexible so as to meet irregular undulations on rails. The *Gowan and Marx* engine, built by the firm in 1841, pulled 101 loaded coal-cars, an unprecedented feat at that time. Eastwick and Harrison removed their plant to St. Petersburg, Russia, where, in association with Thomas Winans, they completed a huge railroad contract for the Russian government, 1844–51. Harrison returned home in 1852; the sectional Harrison Steam Boiler, which he patented 1859, marked an era in reduction of danger from explosion.

HARRISON, LOVELL BIRGE (*b. Philadelphia, Pa., 1854; d. 1929*), landscape painter. Brother of Thomas A. Harrison. Studied at Pennsylvania Academy of Fine Arts, and in Paris with Carolus-Duran and Cabanel. Specialized in urban subjects and winter scenes; founded the Woodstock, N.Y., art colony.

HARRISON, PAT. *See* HARRISON, BYRON PATTON.

HARRISON, PETER (*b. York, England, 1716; d. New Haven, Conn., 1775*), merchant, architect. Came to Newport, R.I., 1740; engaged in agriculture and trade with his brother, Joseph. In 1761 they moved to New Haven where Peter became collector of customs, 1768. A cultivated amateur of the arts, he made maps of Cape Breton and Newport, 1745, and assisted in the fortification of Newport, 1746. The Redwood Library (1748–50), the Brick Market (1761), and the Synagogue (1762–63), all in Newport; King's Chapel, Boston (1749–54); and Christ Church, Cambridge (1761), were built from his designs and justify his claim to being the most notable architect of colonial America. His buildings were exceptional in America of that time for their purity of detail and monumental qualities.

HARRISON, RICHARD BERRY (*b. London, Canada, 1864; d. 1935*), lecturer, teacher, actor. Created the memorable part of "de Lawd" in Marc Connelly's *The Green Pastures*, 1930.

HARRISON, ROSS GRANVILLE (*b. Germantown, Pa., 1870; d. New Haven, Conn., 1959*), biologist. Studied at Johns Hopkins University (Ph.D., 1894), and at the University of Bonn, Germany (M.D., 1899). The leading experimental embryologist of his generation and a pioneer investigator of still unsolved problems in molecular biology. Taught at Johns Hopkins (1896–1907). At Yale, professor of comparative anatomy and chairman of the department (1907–38). Adapting Gustav Born's technique of uniting parts of amphibian embryos, Harrison studied many different developmental problems, such as the growth and differentiation of the tail, muscle-nerve relationships, and the lateral line system of sense organs. Managing editor of the *Journal of Experimental Zoology* (1904–46); chairman of the National Research Council from 1938.

HARRISON, THOMAS ALEXANDER (*b. Philadelphia, Pa., 1853; d. Paris, France, 1930*), marine and figure painter. Brother of Lovell B. Harrison. Studied at Pennsylvania Academy of Fine Arts, and in Paris with J.L. Gérôme and Bastien-Lepage.

HARRISON, WILLIAM HENRY (*b. Charles City Co., Va., 1773; d. Washington, D.C., 1841*), soldier, statesman, president of the United States. Son of Benjamin Harrison (1726?–1791). Attended Hampden-Sidney College; studied medicine briefly under Benjamin Rush. In August 1791, following his father's death he entered the army and was commissioned ensign in the 1st Infantry. Serving in the Northwest Territory against the Indians, he became a lieutenant and aide-de-camp to Anthony Wayne. After the Treaty of Greenville, 1795, he remained on garrison duty at North Bend and Ft. Washington (Cincinnati). In 1795 he married Anna Symmes, daughter of John Cleves Symmes. On resigning from the army, 1798, he was appointed secretary of the Northwest Territory and was elected first delegate to Congress, 1799. There, as chairman of the committee on public lands, he obtained passage of the act dividing the Northwest Territory into the territories of Ohio and Indiana. He was appointed governor of Indiana in May 1800. Instructed to win the confidence of the Indians and secure justice for them from the settlers, he was also urged to obtain cession of as much land as possible for the government. Harrison did his best, but the two aims of the government were irreconcilable. During his term, he obtained Indian grants of millions of acres in the present states of Indiana and Illinois, but the Indians' resentment of the invading settlers increased. An Indian confederacy under the Shawnee warrior Tecumseh and his brother, the Prophet, began to develop in 1805. Tecumseh's aim was to bind all tribes into an agreement to sell no more land. When Harrison, by the Treaty of Fort Wayne, 1809, secured some 2½ million acres on the Wabash River, Tecumseh warned him that he would oppose occupation, and the Indians encamped in force near the point where Tippecanoe Creek empties into the Wabash. On Nov. 6, 1811, with a force of about 1,000 men, Harrison encamped near the Indian village at Tippecanoe and was attacked next morning by the Shawnees. Though Harrison was able to take possession of their settlement, his losses were heavy and by spring the Indians became bold again. Convinced of the necessity of a general war against the Indians, Harrison urged his plans upon President Madison, but the War of 1812 ended such an idea. He received no regular command at the start of the war, but participated as a brevet major general of Kentucky militia in an action which relieved Fort Wayne, August 1812. Finally, in September he received notice of his appointment as regular brigadier general and supreme commander of the Army of the Northwest.

The task before him was great. The British held Mackinac, Chicago, and Detroit. Harrison had to train and equip an army and transport it across Ohio before winter. His initial mistake was his undertaking a difficult campaign with raw troops. He tried to move his forces in three divisions north through Ohio so as to concentrate at Miami Rapids, but impassable roads and faulty communications proved fatal to such a plan. Gen. James Winchester, on the left wing, reached the rendezvous first and attempted an unsupported advance; at Frenchtown on Jan. 22, 1813, his force was overcome by the British. For six months thereafter, based at Fort Meigs, Harrison pursued a defensive policy, trying to build a force for another offensive. Perry's victory over the British fleet on Lake Erie (Sept. 10, 1813) was a factor of great strategic importance. Harrison felt able to take the offensive. On September 27 he occupied Malden and two days later reoccupied Detroit. Pursuing the retreating British under Procter, Harrison overtook and defeated them at the Thames River in early October. Procter fled and Tecumseh was killed; the British did not again attempt offensive operations in that quarter. Tecumseh's death and the surrender of the Indian allies brought about pacification of most of the Indians of the Northwest. Harrison had been promoted major general in March 1813, and in the same month had been replaced as governor of Indiana by Thomas Posey. On his resignation from the army in May 1814, he returned to his farm in North Bend, Ohio, and engaged in several unfortunate commercial enterprises. Congressman from Ohio, 1816–19, he was in no sense an outstanding figure in the House. As U.S. senator, 1825–28, he was chiefly distinguished by his work as chairman of the military affairs committee. In May 1828, he was appointed minister to Colombia through the influence of Henry Clay, whose political follower he was. Arriving in Bogotá, February 1829, he meddled in the local revolutionary situation and was recalled that summer, not because of his behavior, but because President Jackson desired the place for one of his own supporters.

For some years after his return from Colombia, Harrison encountered a series of financial reverses and family misfortunes. He kept up his interest in politics, however, and in 1836 was an unsuccessful anti–Van Buren candidate for president. In 1840 he was selected over Henry Clay by the Whigs as their presidential candidate. The election of 1840 is famous because of its emphasis on emotional and demagogic appeal. The Whigs drew up no political platform, but emphasized Harrison's military record and alleged frontier character. "Tippecanoe and Tyler too" was the campaign slogan, and the general was pictured seated before a log cabin with a barrel of cider beside him. Elected by a landslide electoral vote, Harrison was inaugurated 9th president of the United States amid tremendous enthusiasm. One month later he died of pneumonia.

HARRISON, WILLIAM POPE (*b. Savannah, Ga., 1830; d. Columbus, Ga., 1895*), Methodist clergyman, editor.

HARRISSE, HENRY (*b. Paris, France, 1829; d. Paris, 1910*), lawyer, bibliographer, historian of the discovery of America.

Author, among other works, of *Bibliotheca Americana Vetustissima* (1866), a monumental study of printed books relating to America before 1550.

HARROD, BENJAMIN MORGAN (*b. New Orleans, La., 1837; d. New Orleans, 1912*), engineer, Confederate soldier. A leading hydraulic engineer and expert on levee construction; member, Mississippi River Commission and Panama Canal Commission; city engineer, New Orleans.

HARROD, JAMES (*b. Big Cove, Pa., 1742; d. 1793*), pioneer, soldier. Founded the first settlement in Kentucky at Harrodsburg, 1774. Took an active part in the war in the West, serving in Bowman's expedition against Chillicothe, 1779, and in George Rogers Clark's invasion of the Shawnee country, 1782.

HARSHBERGER, JOHN WILLIAM (*b. Philadelphia, Pa., 1869; d. Philadelphia, 1929*), botanist, naturalist. Graduated University of Pennsylvania, 1892; Ph.D., 1893. Taught biology and botany at Pennsylvania, 1893–1929. Author, among many other works, of the *Phytogeographic Survey of North America* (1911).

HARSHE, ROBERT BARTHOLOW (*b. Salisbury, Mo., 1879; d. Chicago, Ill., 1938*), artist, teacher. Director, Chicago Art Institute, 1921–38.

HART, ABRAHAM (*b. Philadelphia, Pa., 1810; d. Long Branch, N.J., 1885*), publisher. Partner in Carey and Hart, 1829–49; continued until 1854 under his own name.

HART, ALBERT BUSHNELL (*b. Clarksville, now Clark, Mercer County, Pa., 1854; d. Belmont, Mass., 1943*), historian. Brother of Hastings H. Hart. Removed to Cleveland, Ohio, 1864. Graduated West High School, Cleveland, 1871; went to work as bookkeeper for a Cleveland firm. At Harvard, 1876–80, he befriended Theodore Roosevelt. After a post-graduate year at Harvard, he studied at the University of Freiburg; Ph.D., 1883. His dissertation, *The Coercive Powers of the Government of the United States of America* (1885), he later enlarged and published as *Introduction to the Study of Federal Government* (1891). He returned to Cambridge as instructor in American history. His pupils included many future senators, governors, and a future president, Franklin D. Roosevelt.

With his colleague Edward Channing, Hart published the *Guide to the Study of American History* (1896). Hart also wrote the biography *Salmon Portland Chase* (1899), *Essentials in American History* (1905), and *American History Told by Contemporaries* (5 vols., 1897–1929). He edited the *American Historical Review* and was president of the American Historical Association, 1909. Hart was often called "The Grand Old Man" of American history and his students easily found university posts.

As an editor of historical works, Hart was most significant. For the *Epochs of American History* series, he wrote *Formation of the Union* and persuaded Woodrow Wilson at Princeton to write *Division and Reunion*. His greatest editorial accomplishment was the *American Nation* series (1904–07). Hart had planned an American biographical dictionary, but amiably stood aside when the American Council of Learned Societies undertook to sponsor the *Dictionary of American Biography*.

In 1910 Hart became Eaton Professor of Government, which post he held until his retirement in 1926. His eminence in this field led to his election as president of the American Political Science Association in 1912, and he helped edit the *Cyclopaedia of American Government*.

Hart took an active role in politics and was a delegate to the Republican national convention, where he ardently supported the candidacy of Theodore Roosevelt. Hart was interested in the advancement of black Americans (W. E. B. DuBois was a pupil) and was a trustee of Howard University.

Hart's greatest achievement was in making American history a respected academic subject and providing the materials so that it could be properly taught. He was an educational counterpart to his friend Theodore Roosevelt.

HART, CHARLES HENRY (*b. Philadelphia, Pa., 1847; d. New York, N.Y., 1918*), lawyer, art expert. Authority on historical portraiture; made a special study of work of Gilbert Stuart.

HART, EDMUND HALL (*b. Manchester Bridge, N.Y., 1839; d. 1898*), pioneer Florida horticulturist. Settled at Federal Point, Fla., 1867, as citrus fruit grower; introduced the Valencia orange there. The Choice banana was also an important product of his breeding.

HART, EDWARD (*b. Doylestown, Pa., 1854; d. 1931*), chemist, educator, editor. Ph.D., Johns Hopkins, 1879. Taught at Lafayette College, 1880–1924. Designed a widely used nitric acid condenser; founded and managed the Chemical Publishing Co.

HART, EDWIN BRET (*b. Sandusky, Ohio, 1874; d. Madison, Wis., 1953*), biochemist and nutritionist. Studied at the University of Michigan (B.S., 1897) and at Marburg and Heidelberg with Albrecht Kossel. Professor and chairman of the department of agricultural chemistry at Wisconsin (1906–44). Concentrating on the chemistry of dairy production, his research dealt with the role of minerals in the general nutrition of animals and the role of vitamins and other organic nutrients in animal metabolism. Identified the roles of vitamins A and B in animal physiology.

HART, GEORGE OVERBURY (*b. Cairo, Ill., 1868; d. New York, N.Y., 1933*), painter, etcher. Known as "Pop" Hart. An accomplished draftsman and colorist, he traveled widely recording his sensitive impressions of scenes and people.

HART, HASTINGS HORNELL (*b. Brookfield, Ohio, 1851; d. 1932*), social worker, penologist. A commanding figure in his field; drafted the juvenile court law for Cook County, Ill., the first law of its kind in the world.

HART, JAMES MACDOUGAL (*b. Kilmarnock, Scotland, 1828; d. Brooklyn, N.Y., 1901*), landscape painter. Brother of William Hart. Came to America as a child. Studied at Düsseldorf and made great success in New York *post* Civil War, supplying the new-rich with paintings they could understand.

HART, JAMES MORGAN (*b. Princeton, N.J., 1839; d. Washington, D.C., 1916*), lawyer, philologist. Son of John S. Hart. Graduated Princeton, 1860; J.U.D., Göttingen, 1864. Professor of English, University of Cincinnati, 1876–90; Cornell, 1890–1907. Author of *German Universities: A Narrative of Personal Experience* (1874) and other works.

HART, JOEL TANNER (*b. near Winchester, Ky., 1810; d. Florence, Italy, 1877*), sculptor. Self-taught, Hart was at his best in portrait busts.

HART, JOHN (*b. Stonington, Conn., 1711[?]; d. 1779*), farmer, New Jersey signer of the Declaration of Independence. Member of New Jersey Assembly, 1761–71; of Jersey Provincial Congress, 1774–76; of Continental Congress, 1776. Speaker of the first Assembly of the state of New Jersey.

HART, JOHN SEELY (*b. Stockbridge, Mass., 1810; d. 1877*), educator, editor. Raised in Pennsylvania. Graduated Princeton, 1830; Princeton Theological Seminary, 1834. Principal, Philadelphia Central High School, and State Normal School, Trenton, N.J. Taught also at Princeton. Founder and first editor (1859–71) of the *Sunday School Times*.

HART, LORENZ MILTON (*b. New York, N.Y., 1895; d. New York, 1943*), musical comedy lyricist. In collaboration with Richard Rodgers *post* 1918, Hart contributed to the maturing of the American musical comedy from inane "girlie" shows to witty and intelligent dramas with music. His sharp, often caustic lyrics were finely coordinated with rhythm and melody, and with the plot, mood, and action of the play. He was essentially the bard of the sophisticated, urban generation of the 1920's and 1930's, disillusioned, tart, and at times tragic. His style is exemplified by the musical adaptation of *Pal Joey*.

HART, MOSS (*b. Bronx, N.Y., 1904; d. Palm Springs, Calif., 1961*), playwright. After numerous years of writing plays that were rejected and directing little theater groups, began collaborating with George S. Kaufman. Their first play, *Once in a Lifetime* (1930), was an instant Broadway hit, and they went on to produce a number of moderately successful plays and two big hits: *You Can't Take It with You* (1936) and *The Man Who Came to Dinner* (1939). Severed the tie with Kaufman around 1940 and went on to produce more plays as well as numerous screenplays, including *A Star Is Born* (1954) and the Oscar-winning *Gentleman's Agreement* (1947). He also resumed his role of director, directing *My Fair Lady* (1956) and *Camelot* (1960).

HART, SAMUEL (*b. Saybrook, Conn., 1845; d. 1917*), Episcopal clergyman, theologian. Graduated Trinity College, Hartford, Conn., 1866; Berkeley Divinity School, 1869. Taught at both institutions; was dean of Berkeley *post* 1908. Author of *History of the American Book of Common Prayer* (1910).

HART, VIRGIL CHITTENDEN (*b. Lorraine, N.Y., 1840; d. Burlington, Canada, 1940*), Methodist clergyman. Missionary to China, 1866–87; 1891–1900.

HART, WILLIAM (*b. Paisley, Scotland, 1823; d. 1894*), painter. Brother of James MacDougal Hart. Came to America as a child. Though thin and crude, his work has some of the freshness of the primitive. He was a portraitist, and a landscapist of the "Hudson River" school.

HART, WILLIAM SURREY (*b. Newburgh, N.Y., 1862?; d. Los Angeles, Calif., 1946*), actor, motion picture director. Raised in a succession of small towns from Illinois to the Dakotas, he lived alongside the Sioux in Minnesota and the Dakotas, learning their language, and in the frontier towns of Kansas during the days of the cattle drives. In the mid 1870's his family moved to New York City.

On a trip to England, Hart began to study acting, and he continued his training upon his return to New York. In 1888 he found a place in a touring company. He appeared in 1897 in *The Man in the Iron Mask*, and two years later he played in the New York production of *Ben-Hur*. Engaged to play in the Western melodrama *The Squaw Man*, he thereafter united his passion for the West with his career. He became the quintessential cowboy of the American stage, touring in such Westerns as *The Virginian*, *The Barrier* (1910), and *The Trail of the Lonesome Pine* (1912). Determined to leave the stage and enter motion picture work, he played villains in two short films and then starred in *The Bargain* (1914), which was an immediate hit. Typically he played a "good badman." He then became a famous cowboy star and his screen career, which lasted a dozen years, made him wealthy.

HARTE, BRET. *See* HARTE, FRANCIS BRETT.

HARTE, FRANCIS BRETT (*b. Albany, N.Y., 1836; d. London, England, 1902*), author. Removed to California, 1854; his early experiences there as clerk, teacher, newspaperman were the basis of his literary work. Variously employed in San Francisco, 1860–68, he contributed verse and prose to the *Golden Era* and the *Californian* and published three books: *Outcroppings* (1865, but dated 1866), an anthology of California verse; *The Lost Galleon* (1867), a collection of his own poems; and a volume of parodies, *Condensed Novels* (1867). The work for which he is remembered, the short stories of California life which pointed out the way to a whole school of "local color" writers, appeared between 1868, when he became editor of the *Overland Monthly*, and 1871 when he deserted the West for the East and Europe. The best of these are found in *The Luck of Roaring Camp and Other Sketches* (1870); in the same year appeared his most celebrated poem, "The Heathen Chinee." After his removal eastward, his life as lecturer, journalist, consul, and finally hack storywriter in London, was a study in debt and declining fortunes. His one great achievement was the application of simple, well-tested story formulas to novel material.

HARTFORD, GEORGE HUNTINGTON (*b. Augusta, Maine, 1833; d. Spring Lake, N.J., 1917*), **HARTFORD, GEORGE LUDLAM** (*b. Brooklyn, N.Y., 1864; d. Montclair, N.J., 1957*); **HARTFORD, JOHN AUGUSTINE** (*b. Orange, N.J., 1872; d. New York, N.Y., 1951*), chain food-store magnates. From a small store in New York City which sold tea, Hartford was to found, in 1859, the Great Atlantic and Pacific Tea Company, eventually known as A&P. By 1900, the family owned 200 stores; by 1951, 4,700. For a time, A&P had the largest sales volume of any commercial concern in the nation.

HARTLEY, FRANK (*b. Washington, D.C., 1856; d. 1913*), surgeon. Graduated Princeton, 1877; M.D., Columbia, 1880, where he was teacher and professor, *post* 1886. Devised intracranial method for curing trigeminal neuralgia by bisecting ganglion of the trigeminal nerve.

HARTLEY, FRED ALLEN, JR. (*b. Harrison, N.J., 1903; d. Linwood, N.J., 1969*), congressman and coauthor of the Taft-Hartley Act. Elected to Congress in 1928, he served his New Jersey district as a Republican party loyalist until 1946, when he became chairman of the reorganized Education and Labor Committee and helped draft and pass the Labor Management Relations Act of 1947, better known as the Taft-Hartley Act. When passed, the act outlawed the closed shop, required an anti-Communist oath from labor officials, imposed criminal penalties for corruption, prohibited secondary boycotts, and allowed states to pass right-to-work laws. He succeeded in producing a stricter bill than many, including Taft, had favored or thought possible. Insisting on one omnibus bill to include all important points, he promoted passage by a large bipartisan vote that held together for a record-breaking override of President Truman's veto in 1947, though he exaggerated his role in his book *Our New Labor Policy* (1948).

HARTLEY, JONATHAN SCOTT (*b. Albany, N.Y., 1845; d. 1912*), sculptor. Studied at Royal Academy, London; also at Rome and Paris. Famous for portraits of men.

HARTLEY, MARSDEN (*b. Lewiston, Maine, 1877; d. Ellsworth, Maine, 1943*), painter, poet. Left school at fourteen to work in a shoe factory; removed to Cleveland, Ohio, 1892, where he studied at the Cleveland Art School. Coming to New York City, 1898, he studied at the schools of William M. Chase and of the National Academy of Design; also at the Art Students' League. Vain and insecure and subject to periods of melancholy, he attempted a variety of styles, responding to almost every artistic fashion of his time. Resident in Maine *post* 1936, he developed a distinctive style of his own; broad simplification in seascapes and landscapes, rendered in flat masses enclosed within heavy contours and in rich, glowing colors, conveying symbolic overtones.

HARTLEY, THOMAS (*b. Colebrookdale, Berks Co., Pa., 1748; d. 1800*), lawyer, Revolutionary soldier. Commanded 1st Pennsylvania Brigade; led 1778 expedition to avenge Wyoming Massacre. Congressman, Federalist, 1789–1800.

HARTMANN, CARL SADAKICHI (*b. Nagasaki, Japan, 1867[?]; d. St. Petersburg, Fla., 1944*), author, art critic. Of Japanese and German parentage, he was raised in Hamburg, Germany, and came to the United States in 1882. After acting as a factotum to Walt Whitman, 1884–85, he became a wanderer among art centers here and in Europe until 1923 when he settled somewhat permanently in southern California. Supported by lecturing, and by shameless panhandling, he was almost a parody of a bohemian and an extension of the literary mood of the 1890's. His critical writing, however, was in a different key, and had merit. Among his books were *Japanese Art* (1904) and *The Whistler Book* (1910).

HARTNESS, JAMES (*b. Schenectady, N.Y., 1861; d. 1934*), tool builder, inventor. Associated *post* 1889 with Jones & Lamson Co.; devised many lathe improvements and was active in standardization of screw threads. Republican governor of Vermont, 1921–23.

HARTRANFT, CHESTER DAVID (*b. Frederick, Pa., 1839; d. Wolfenbüttel, Germany, 1914*), Dutch Reformed Church clergyman, educator. President, Hartford Theological Seminary, 1888–1903.

HARTRANFT, JOHN FREDERICK (*b. near Fagleysville, Pa., 1830; d. 1889*), lawyer, Union soldier, politician. Republican governor of Pennsylvania, 1873–79; noted for his attempt to solve industrial labor problems by armed force.

HARTSHORNE, HENRY (*b. Philadelphia, Pa., 1823; d. Tokyo, Japan, 1897*), physician. Graduated Haverford, 1839; M.D., University of Pennsylvania, 1845. Versatile but unstable, he held an extraordinary number of medical and teaching positions.

HARTSUFF, GEORGE LUCAS (*b. Tyre, N.Y., 1830; d. New York, N.Y., 1874*), soldier. Graduated West Point, 1852. Served as Union brigade and corps commander; retired as major general, 1871.

HARTWIG, JOHANN CHRISTOPH (*b. Thüringen, Germany, 1714; d. Clermont, N.Y., 1796*), Lutheran clergyman. Came to America, 1746; served congregations in Hudson Valley until 1748 when he became a nomad, ranging from Maine to Virginia. A friend of Henry M. Mühlenberg, he established Hartwick Seminary.

HARTZELL, JOSEPH CRANE (*b. Moline, Ill., 1842; d. Blue Ash, Ohio, 1928*), Methodist clergyman. Pastor, New Orleans, La., 1870–81; active in Freedmen's Aid Society, 1883–96; missionary bishop for Africa, 1896–1916.

HARVARD, JOHN (*b. London, England, 1607; d. Charlestown, Mass., 1638*), benefactor of Harvard University. Graduated Emmanuel College, Cambridge, B.A., 1631/32; M.A., 1635. Sailed to New England not earlier than May 29, 1637; admitted an inhabitant at Charlestown, Mass., August 1, 1637; became teaching elder of the church at Charlestown. John Harvard left half his estate, a sum estimated at between £400 and £800, and his library of about 400 volumes to the college founded by the colony in the fall of 1636. The General Court named the college after him on March 13, 1638/39.

HARVEY, "COIN." *See* HARVEY, WILLIAM HOPE.

HARVEY, GEORGE BRINTON MCCLELLAN (*b. Peacham, Vt., 1864; d. Dublin, N.H., 1928*), political journalist. Grew wealthy through connections with William C. Whitney and other Wall St. figures. Edited *North American Review* and *Harper's Weekly*; was president of Harper and Brothers, 1900–15. Promoted both Woodrow Wilson and Warren G. Harding for presidency. Ambassador to Great Britain, 1921–23.

HARVEY, HAYWARD AUGUSTUS (*b. Jamestown, N.Y., 1824; d. Orange, N.J., 1893*), inventor, manufacturer. Secured 125 patents on a wide variety of mechanical inventions. The Harvey Process for treating armor plate brought him worldwide reputation.

HARVEY, SIR JOHN (*d. 1646*), baronet, sea captain. Governor and captain general of Virginia, serving 1630–35 and 1637–39. Returned to England, 1641.

HARVEY, LOUIS POWELL (*b. East Haddam, Conn., 1820; d. Savannah, Tenn., 1862*), businessman, legislator. Raised in Ohio; removed to Wisconsin, 1841. Union-Republican governor of Wisconsin, 1861–62.

HARVEY, WILLIAM HOPE (*b. Buffalo, W. Va., 1851; d. Monte Ne, Ark., 1936*), promoter, publicist. Proponent, through "Coin's Financial Series," of free coinage of silver at a ratio of 16 to 1. Number 3 of this pamphlet series, *Coin's Financial School* (1894), had wide circulation and influence.

HARVIE, JOHN (*b. Albemarle Co., Va., 1742; d. near Richmond, Va., 1807*), Revolutionary patriot, Virginia statesman, financier.

HASBROUCK, ABRAHAM BRUYN (*b. Kingston, N.Y., 1791; d. Kingston, 1879*), lawyer. Graduated Yale, 1810. As president of Rutgers, 1840–50, his administration was marked by increasing independence of the college from ecclesiastical (Dutch Reformed) control.

HASBROUCK, LYDIA SAYER (*b. Warwick, N.Y., 1827; d. Middletown, N.Y., 1910*), writer, lecturer. Advocated temperance, woman's suffrage, dress reform; edited the *Sibyl*, a fortnightly reform paper, 1856–64.

HASCALL, MILO SMITH (*b. Le Roy, N.Y., 1829; d. Chicago, Ill., 1904*), soldier, lawyer, banker. Graduated West Point, 1852. Brigade and division commander in Union Army, 1862–64.

HASELTINE, JAMES HENRY (*b. Philadelphia, Pa., 1833; d. Rome, Italy, 1907*), sculptor. Spent most of his life abroad; produced allegorical works, pseudo-classic in type, and busts of well-known contemporaries including Longfellow.

HASELTON, SENECA (*b. Westford, Vt., 1848; d. 1921*), jurist. Graduated University of Vermont, 1871; LL.B., University of Michigan, 1875. Practiced in Burlington, Vt. U.S. minister to Venezuela, 1894–95. Served on Vermont supreme court, 1902–06, 1908–19.

HASENCLEVER, PETER (*b. Remscheid, Prussia, 1716; d. 1793*), iron manufacturer. Resided in America, 1764–68. Established extensive works in New Jersey, New York, and elsewhere for mining and smelting, also for producing potash; engaged in raising flax and hemp. After initial success, the mismanagement of his partners in England and America left him stripped of his properties and loaded with debts.

HASKELL, CHARLES NATHANIEL (*b. Leipsic, Ohio, 1860; d. Oklahoma City, Okla., 1933*), lawyer, railway and telephone promoter. Removed to Oklahoma, 1901. First governor of state of Oklahoma, Democrat, 1907–11.

HASKELL, DUDLEY CHASE (*b. Springfield, Vt., 1842; d. Washington, D.C., 1883*), legislator, politician. Removed to Kansas, 1855. Congressman, Republican, from Kansas, 1877–83; an ardent protectionist.

HASKELL, ELLA LOUISE KNOWLES (*b. Northwood Ridge, N.H., 1860; d. Montana, 1911*), lawyer, Populist politician, crusader for equal rights for women. Graduated Bates College, 1884. Admitted to Montana bar, 1889, by special legislative act

HASKELL, ERNEST (*b. Woodstock, Conn., 1876; d. near Bath, Maine, 1925*), painter, etcher, lithographer. An unusually versatile artist, mainly self-taught, he is best known as an etcher.

HASKELL, HENRY JOSEPH (*b. Huntington, Ohio, 1874; d. Kansas City, Mo., 1952*), journalist and civic leader. Studied at Oberlin College (B.A., 1896). Employed by the *Kansas City Star*, (1898–1952); editor, 1928–52. The paper won the Pulitzer Prize in 1933 for a series on international affairs; Haskell won the Pulitzer Prize for distinguished editorial writing in 1944. Author of a weekly column, "Random Thoughts."

HASKET, ELIAS (*b. Salem, Mass., 1670; d. 1739[?]*), sea captain. Governor of New Providence, Bahamas, 1701. The people revolted, imprisoned and returned him to New York after a four-month tenure of office.

HASKINS, CHARLES HOMER (*b. Meadville, Pa., 1870; d. Cambridge, Mass., 1937*), historian. Graduated Johns Hopkins, A.B., 1887; Ph.D., 1890. Taught at Johns Hopkins, 1889–92; Wisconsin, 1892–1902; and Harvard, 1902–31. Dean of Harvard graduate school, 1908–24. A leading medievalist of his generation, and an outstanding teacher, especially of graduate students, Haskins' work centered on Norman institutions and on the transmittal of Greek and Arabic learning to Western Europe. *Norman Institutions* (1918), *Studies in the History of Mediaeval Science* (1924) and *Studies in Mediaeval Culture* (1929) sum up his work in these fields. He was a prominent member of the group of presidential advisers known as "The Inquiry," 1917. As delegate to the Paris Peace Conference, 1918–19, Haskins advanced the solution eventually adopted for the Saar.

HASSAM, FREDERICK CHILDE (*b. Dorchester, Mass., 1859; d. East Hampton, N.Y., 1935*), artist. A brilliant exponent of the Impressionist school.

HASSARD, JOHN ROSE GREENE (*b. New York, N.Y., 1836; d. 1888*), journalist. Graduated Fordham, 1855. Served literary apprenticeship with George Ripley. Essayist, music critic with *New York Tribune*, 1866–88. His numerous writings include an authoritative biography of Archbishop John Hughes of New York (1866).

HASSAUREK, FRIEDRICH (*b. Vienna, Austria, 1831; d. Paris, France, 1885*), journalist, lawyer, diplomat, politician. Immigrated to America, 1849; published German newspaper at Cincinnati, Ohio; active in Republican politics. Served with distinction as American minister to Ecuador, 1861–64, 1865–66.

HASSELQUIST, TUVE NILSSON (*b. Hasslaröd, Sweden, 1816; d. 1891*), Lutheran clergyman, editor, educator. Came to America, 1852, as pastor at Galesburg, Ill. Ablest leader, most versatile personality of Swedish Lutheran Church in America. President, Augustana College and Seminary, 1863–91.

HASSLER, FERDINAND RUDOLPH (*b. Aarau, Switzerland, 1770; d. Philadelphia, Pa., 1843*), geodesist, mathematician. Came to America, 1805. Nominated to superintend a survey of the United States coast, 1807, he did not receive formal appointment until 1816 when he began work. In 1818 civilians were restricted from the survey, and it came to a virtual halt until 1832 when Hassler again became superintendent and served until his death. The work of the Coast Survey to the present day follows his plan; his field work was of such high precision that it still forms part of the basic network.

HASTINGS, CHARLES SHELDON (*b. Clinton, N.Y., 1848; d. 1932*), physicist. Graduated Sheffield Scientific School, 1870; Ph.D., Yale, 1873. Professor of physics, Sheffield, 1884–1915. A specialist in optics and spectroscopy, he was celebrated for his theory of achromatic lenses, and for contributions to the microscope, including the Aplanat magnifier.

HASTINGS, DANIEL OREN (*b. near Princess Anne, Md., 1874; d. Wilmington, Del., 1966*), U.S. senator. Served in the U.S. Senate, 1928–36, initially aligning himself with the "Young Turks," whose Republican politics rested between the old guard conservatives and progressives. Was assigned to the Judiciary Committee because of his legal expertise and to the Interstate Commerce Committee because of his widespread grasp of railroad problems. Was a consistent supporter of President Herbert Hoover's domestic and foreign policies and thereafter a harsh critic of President Franklin D. Roosevelt and his New Deal programs. After 1936, resumed his law practice in Wilmington, reaching the top of his profession as a lawyer and legal counsel and remaining influential in local, state, and national Republican party activities. Filled more public offices than did any other Delaware politician and wrote *Delaware Politics, 1904–1954* (1964).

HASTINGS, SAMUEL DEXTER (*b. Leicester, Mass., 1816; d. Evanston, Ill., 1903*), businessman, Wisconsin legislator and pubic official, reformer.

HASTINGS, SERRANUS CLINTON (*b. Jefferson Co., N.Y., 1814; d. 1893*), jurist. Removed to Iowa, 1837; to California, 1849. Was first chief justice of California supreme court. Gave endowment to establish Hastings' College of Law at San Francisco, 1878.

HASTINGS, THOMAS (*b. Washington, Conn., 1784; d. New York, N.Y., 1872*), hymnwriter, hymn-book editor, composer. Devoted his life to church music; composed about 1,000 tunes, the best of that time in America except for Lowell Mason's.

HASTINGS, THOMAS (*b. New York, N.Y., 1860; d. Mineola, N.Y., 1929*), architect. Grandson of Thomas Hastings (1784–1872). Graduated École des Beaux-Arts, Paris, 1884, where he met John Carrère with whom he formed a celebrated partnership, 1886. Interested in city planning, he designed the industrial town for the United States Steel Co. at Duluth, Minn. His interest in city beautification is exemplified by his treatment of the Plaza in New York City. The Memorial Amphitheatre in the national cemetery, Arlington, Va., is one of many monuments he designed. Hastings believed in a scholarly, respectful attitude toward the past and in the importance to modern American architecture of the classic tradition.

HASTINGS, WILLIAM WIRT (*b. Delaware District, Cherokee Nation, later Oklahoma, 1866; d. Muskogee, Okla., 1938*), lawyer. Congressman, Democrat, from Oklahoma, 1915–21, 1923–35. A leader in legislation to protect Indian rights.

HASWELL, ANTHONY (*b. Portsmouth, England, 1756; d. Bennington, Vt., 1816*), printer, editor, ballad writer. Came to Boston, Mass., as a boy; was apprentice to Isaiah Thomas. Published newspapers at Worcester and Springfield, Mass.; published the *Vermont Gazette* at Bennington *post* 1783.

HASWELL, CHARLES HAYNES (*b. New York, N.Y., 1809; d. 1907*). First engineer to be appointed in U.S. Navy, 1836; chief engineer, 1844–52. Worked thereafter as a consultant. Author of *Mechanic's and Engineer's Pocket Book* (1842; 74th ed., 1913) and other works.

HATCH, CARL A. (*b. Kirwin, Kans., 1889; d. Albuquerque, N.Mex., 1963*), senator and federal district judge. A Democrat, served as U.S. senator from New Mexico, 1933–49. A strong ally of presidents Franklin D. Roosevelt and Harry Truman, he was especially influential in supporting the latter during the debates on the Truman Doctrine and the Marshall Plan. On the domestic front, was most interested in farm and labor legislation, and is best remembered as the author of the Hatch Acts of 1939 and 1940, which were designed to curb the political influence of governmental, corporate, and labor special interests. Held federal district judgeship in Albuquerque, 1949–63.

HATCH, EDWARD (*b. Bangor, Maine, 1832; d. Fort Robinson, Nebr., 1889*), Union soldier. Colonel, 2nd Iowa Cavalry, 1862–64; participated in Grierson's raid, 1863; rose to major general of volunteers. Commissioned colonel, 9th U.S. Cavalry, 1866; served in Arizona and New Mexico.

HATCH, JOHN PORTER (*b. Oswego, N.Y., 1822; d. New York, N.Y., 1901*), Union soldier. Graduated West Point, 1845. Served in Mexican War, in Oregon, Texas and New Mexico; as brigade commander in Civil War, received Medal of Honor for conduct at South Mountain. Retired, 1886, as colonel of 2nd U.S. Cavalry.

HATCH, RUFUS (*b. Wells, Maine, 1832; d. 1893*), financier, promoter. Removed to Rockford, Ill., 1851; was in business there and in Chicago. *Post* 1864, a New York stockbroker and speculator, he is said to have coined the phrase, "lambs of Wall Street."

HATCH, WILLIAM HENRY (*b. near Georgetown, Ky., 1833; d. 1896*), lawyer, politician, Confederate soldier. Removed to Hannibal, Mo., 1854, where he practiced law. As congressman, Democrat, from Missouri, 1879–95, his chief interest was agricultural legislation; he served during several sessions as chairman of Committee on Agriculture and successfully sponsored the Bureau of Animal Industry Act (1884), the first oleomargarine act (1886), and a meat inspection act (1890). His greatest service was in establishment of federal aid for agricultural experiment stations by the Hatch Act, 1887. He was a leader in agitation to raise the Department of Agriculture to cabinet status.

HATCHER, ORIE LATHAM (*b. Petersburg, Va., 1868; d. Washington, D.C., 1946*), educator, pioneer in vocational guidance. Educated at Vassar College and the University of Chicago. Taught at Bryn Mawr, 1904–15. Promoted standardizing Virginia women's education so that outstanding graduates could attend northeastern women's colleges. Movement eventually extended to both sexes in the Alliance for Guidance of Rural Youth.

HATCHER, ROBERT ANTHONY (*b. New Madrid, Mo., 1868; d. Flushing, N.Y., 1944*), pharmacologist. Raised in New Orleans, La.; Ph.D., Philadelphia College of Pharmacy, 1889. After several years as a druggist in New Orleans, he graduated M.D., Tulane University, 1898. Taught at Cleveland (Ohio) School of Pharmacy and at Western Reserve Medical School; taught at Cornell University Medical College in New York City, 1904–35, professor of pharmacology, *post* 1908. Hatcher's approach to investigating the diverse action of drugs in man developed into the present discipline of clinical pharmacology. Also carried out studies of strychnine, morphine, the cinchona alkaloids, and local anesthetics. He is perhaps best known for his investigations of the action of digitalis.

HATCHER, WILLIAM ELDRIDGE (*b. Bedford Co., Va., 1834; d. Fork Union, Va., 1912*), Baptist clergyman, author. Pastor for many years at Grace Street Baptist Church, Richmond, Va.

HATFIELD, EDWIN FRANCIS (*b. Elizabeth, N.J., 1807; d. Summit, N.J., 1883*), Presbyterian clergyman, hymnologist. New York City pastor; stated clerk of New School Church, 1846–70, and of united church thereafter. Moderator, General Assembly, 1883.

HATHORNE, WILLIAM (*b. Binfield, England, ca. 1607; d. Salem, Mass., 1681*), merchant, colonial official. Immigrated with John Winthrop, 1630; settled in Salem, 1636. Speaker, Massachusetts General Court, 1644–50; commissioner, New England Confederacy, 1650–53; held many other offices, civil and military. Ancestor of Nathaniel Hawthorne.

HATLO, JIMMY (*b. James Cecil Hatlow, Providence, R.I., 1898; d. Pebble Beach, Calif., 1963*), cartoonist. In 1928 created the two-panel cartoon "They'll Do It Every Time," which became nationally syndicated by 1935, eventually running in some 800 papers. Got most of his ideas from readers and always acknowledged his source in a small box in the corner of the cartoon. His sketches were refined by Tommy Thompson and forwarded to cartoonist Bob Dunn in New York for further work; after his death his cartoons were continued by Dunn and two collaborators. Also created "Hatlo's Inferno."

HATTON, FRANK (*b. Cambridge, Ohio, 1846; d. 1894*), journalist. Removed to Iowa, 1866; *post* 1874, published the influential *Burlington Daily Hawk-Eye*; was editor and publisher, *Washington Post*, 1889–94. As assistant postmaster general, 1881-84, created special-delivery system; was postmaster general for a brief period, 1884–85.

HAUGEN, GILBERT NELSON (*b. Plymouth Township, Wis., 1859; d. Norwood, Iowa, 1933*), farmer, businessman. Raised in Iowa. Congressman, Republican, from Iowa, 1899–1933. Chairman of the committee on agriculture for many years. Co-author of McNary-Haugen bill for relief of farm surpluses.

HAUGEN, NILS PEDERSON (*b. Modum, Norway, 1849; d. Madison, Wis., 1831*), lawyer. Came to Wisconsin as a child. Congressman, Republican, from Wisconsin, 1887–95. As a tax commissioner, 1900–21, aided Gov. Robert M. La Follette in reform.

HAUGHERY, MARGARET GAFFNEY (*b. Cavan, Ireland, ca. 1814; d. New Orleans, La., 1882*), philanthropist. Came to America, *ca.* 1822; settled in New Orleans, *ca.* 1836; operated a dairy and a bakery. Established and sustained three orphanages for 600 children and did numerous other charities.

HAUGHTON, PERCY DUNCAN (*b. Staten Island, N.Y., 1876; d. New York, N.Y., 1924*), football coach, broker. Graduated Harvard, 1899, where he played varsity tackle and kicking fullback, earning a reputation as one of the outstanding kickers of all time. Successfully coached Cornell, 1899–1900. As coach at Harvard, 1908–16, he produced winning teams and wrought rules and strategy changes which revolutionized the game. He was coach at Columbia, 1923–24.

HAUK, MINNIE (*b. New York, N.Y., 1852?; d. Lake Lucerne, Switzerland, 1929*), dramatic soprano. Debut at Brooklyn, N.Y., 1866, in *Sonnambula*; was internationally famous, 1868–95. America's first *Carmen*, she also sang in American premières of *Roméo et Juliette* and *Manon*.

HAUPT, ALMA CECELIA (*b. St. Paul, Minn., 1893; d. San Francisco, Calif., 1956*), nurse. Studied at the University of Minnesota (B.A., 1915), the Minnesota School of Nursing, and Johns Hopkins Hospital. A leader in the public health field, Haupt worked in Europe for the Commonwealth Fund and then for the Metropolitan Life Insurance Co., 1935–52, becoming a pioneer in the field of home nursing care.

HAUPT, HERMAN (*b. Philadelphia, Pa., 1817; d. Jersey City, N.J., 1905*), civil engineer, author, inventor. Graduated West Point, 1835. Engaged in railroad construction; wrote *General Theory of Bridge Construction* (1851). After work for Pennsylvania Railroad, he began construction of the Hoosac tunnel, 1856, and developed in 1858 a pneumatic drill superior to any in use to that time. Served as chief of construction and transportation on U.S. military railroad, 1862–63. After the Civil War he held important positions with a number of railroads and other firms. Throughout his career he was a voluminous writer on technical subjects.

HAUPT, PAUL (*b. Görlitz, Germany, 1858; d. 1926*), philologist, Assyriologist. Ph.D., Leipzig, 1878. Taught at Göttingen; was Spence Professor of Semitic Languages and director of the Oriental Seminary, Johns Hopkins, 1883–1926. A prolific author, his bibliography includes 522 titles. Few men have had wider accurate knowledge of Semitic languages and dialects. His contribution to Biblical criticism was, however, inferior to his work in Assyriology and Semitic philology. He was in his time the chief interpreter of the Gilgamesh Epic.

HAUSER, SAMUEL THOMAS (*b. Falmouth, Ky., 1833; d. 1914*), miner, capitalist. After early training as railroad surveyor, he prospected in Idaho and Montana, 1862–63; thereafter, he bought silver mines and built first silver-ore reduction furnace in Montana. He operated coal mines, built toll roads, telegraph lines, railroads and organized banks in the Territory; he also planned the first large irrigation project in Montana, and was one of the first to engage in large-scale stock raising there. He served as territorial governor, 1885–86.

HAVELL, ROBERT (*b. Reading, England, 1793; d. Tarrytown, N.Y., 1878*), engraver, painter. Resided in America, 1839–78. Engraved in aquatint and colored all but ten of the plates in the folio *Birds of America* by J. J. Audubon, completed in 1838. The success of the work owed much to Havell's genius.

HAVEMEYER, HENRY OSBORNE (*b. New York, N.Y., 1847; d. 1907*), sugar refiner, capitalist. Cousin of William F. Havemeyer. President of the "sugar trust," the American Sugar Refining Co. and its predecessor company, 1887–1907.

HAVEMEYER, WILLIAM FREDERICK (*b. New York, N.Y., 1804; d. New York, 1874*), sugar refiner, capitalist. Graduated Columbia, 1823. Formed a partnership in a refinery, 1828; retired, wealthy, 1842. Democratic mayor of New York City, 1845 and 1848. Turning his attention to business, he had coal and railroad interests and was president of the Bank of North America and the New York Savings Bank until 1861. Elected reform mayor, 1872, after outstanding services as an unmasker of the "Tweed Ring," his term was a tragedy. His appointment of police commissioners, previously guilty of public offenses, atounded the city. He wrangled constantly with the Board of Aldermen. A petition sent to Gov. John A. Dix for Havemeyer's removal was ineffectual, however, because there was no evidence of the mayor's personal corruption or dishonesty.

HAVEN, ALICE B.   *See* HAVEN, EMILY BRADLEY NEAL.

HAVEN, EMILY BRADLEY NEAL (*b. Hudson, N.Y., 1827; d. Mamaroneck, N.Y., 1863*), author, editor. Wife of Joseph C.

Neal. Editor, *Neal's Saturday Gazette and Lady's Literary Museum*, 1847–53; contributor to *Sartain's* and *Graham's* magazines and to *Godey's Lady's Book*. After second marriage to Samuel L. Haven, continued work as Alice B. Haven.

HAVEN, ERASTUS OTIS (*b. Boston, Mass., 1820; d. Salem, Oreg., 1881*), educator, Methodist clergyman and bishop. Graduated Wesleyan University, 1842. Editor, *Zion's Herald*, 1856–63. President, University of Michigan, 1863–69, and of Northwestern University, 1869–72; chancellor of Syracuse University, 1874–80.

HAVEN, GILBERT (*b. Malden, Mass., 1821; d. Malden, 1880*), abolitionist, Methodist clergyman. Cousin of Erastus O. Haven. Editor, *Zion's Herald*, 1867–72. As bishop of Atlanta, Ga., 1872–80, he energetically and courageously pressed freedmen's claims to racial equality.

HAVEN, HENRY PHILEMON (*b. Norwich, Conn., 1815; d. 1876*), whaling merchant, capitalist. An outstanding Sunday school superintendent at Second Congregational Church, New London, Conn., 1858–76.

HAVEN, JOSEPH (*b. Dennis, Mass., 1816; d. 1874*), Congregational clergyman, teacher, scholar. Graduated Amherst, 1835, and taught philosophy there, 1851–58. Professor of theology, Chicago Theological Seminary, 1858–70; of philosophy, University of Chicago, 1873–74. A gifted teacher.

HAVENS, JAMES SMITH (*b. Weedsport, N.Y., 1859, d. Rochester, N.Y., 1927*), lawyer, Democratic congressman.

HAVERLY, CHRISTOPHER (*b. near Bellefonte, Pa., 1837; d. Salt Lake City, Utah, 1901*), "Col. Jack H. Haverly," theatrical manager. He began his career by purchasing a variety theatre in Toledo, Ohio, 1864; his first minstrel show opened in Adrian, Mich., in the same year. Thereafter he organized minstrel troupes and acquired theatres all over America. His most famous show was Haverly's Mastodon Minstrels, organized 1878, with which he toured England and Germany, 1880–81. In 1884 his most brilliant company failed in London and his fortunes declined. A daring speculator in stocks and the greatest minstrel manager in America, he died in obscurity.

HAVERLY, JACK H. *See* HAVERLY, CHRISTOPHER.

HAVILAND, CLARENCE FLOYD (*b. Spencertown, N.Y., 1875; d. Cairo, Egypt, 1930*), physician, psychiatrist.

HAVILAND, JOHN (*b. Gundenham Manor, Somersetshire, England, 1792; d. Philadelphia, Pa., 1852*), architect. Came to America, 1816. Designed many buildings in Philadelphia. His most notable work was his creation of the modern prison on the "radiating plan" as exemplified in Eastern State Penitentiary at Cherry Hill, Philadelphia.

HAWES, CHARLES BOARDMAN (*b. Clifton Springs, N.Y., 1889; d. 1923*). Author of *The Dark Frigate* (1923) and other tales of adventure.

HAWES, HARRIET ANN BOYD (*b. Boston, Mass., 1871; d. Washington, D.C., 1945*), archaeologist. Graduated Smith College, 1892; L.H.D., Smith, 1910. The first woman to have been responsible for the direction of an archaeological excavation and the publication of its findings, Mrs. Hawes worked in Crete (principally in 1901, 1903, 1904); the important results were published in *Gournia, Vasiliki, and Other Prehistoric Sites on the Isthmus of Hierapetra* (1908). She taught at various times at Smith, University of Wisconsin, Dartmouth, and at Wellesley (*ca.* 1919–36); she was assistant and later associate director of the Museum of Fine Arts, Boston, 1919–34. Active in movements for political and social justice and served as a volunteer in hospital and relief service during the Greco-Turkish and Spanish-American wars, and in World War I.

HAWKINS, BENJAMIN (*b. Warren Co., N.C., 1754; d. Crawford Co., Ga., 1816*), planter, Indian agent. French interpreter on Washington's staff, 1776–79. Member of Confederation Congress, 1781–84, 1786–87; U.S. senator, Federalist, from North Carolina, 1789–95. As Indian commissioner, he negotiated treaties with Cherokees (1785), Choctaws and Chickasaws (1786), and (with the Creeks) the important treaty of Coleraine (1796). Washington then appointed him agent to the Creeks and general superintendent of all Indians south of the Ohio. His headquarters were first at Fort Hawkins near Macon, Ga., later at the "Old Agency" on Flint River. Known as "Beloved Man of the Four Nations," he semicivilized the Creeks by teaching them agriculture and won their liking and respect. The War of 1812 ruined the work to which he had sacrificed a great part of his life.

HAWKINS, DEXTER ARNOLD (*b. Canton, Maine, 1825; d. Groton, Conn., 1886*), lawyer, educator, political reformer. Champion of public schools, instrumental in establishing national Department of Education, 1867.

HAWKINS, RUSH CHRISTOPHER (*b. Pomfret, Vt., 1831; d. 1920*), lawyer, Union soldier. Practiced law in New York City; commanded 9th New York Volunteers (Hawkins Zouaves), 1861–63. Presented superb collection of incunabula to the Annmary Brown Memorial, Providence, R.I.

HAWKS, FRANCIS LISTER (*b. New Bern, N.C., 1798; d. 1866*), lawyer, Episcopal clergyman, historian. Grandson of John Hawks. Held a number of pastorates in the North and the South; was first president, University of Louisiana, 1844–49; published a number of valuable works on the history of the church in the United States.

HAWKS, JOHN (*b. Dragby, England, 1731; d. New Bern, N.C., 1790*), architect. Came to America, 1764, as designer and builder of the governor's palace at New Bern; completed in 1770, it was one of the finest structures in colonial America. After holding various local offices, Hawks served as first auditor of North Carolina, 1784–90.

HAWLEY, GIDEON (*b. Stratfield [Bridgeport], Conn., 1727; d. Mashpee, Mass., 1807*), Congregational clergyman. Graduated Yale, 1749. Missionary under Jonathan Edwards at Stockbridge, 1752–54; among Six Nations on New York frontier, 1754–56; and as permanent preacher to Mashpees, 1758–1807.

HAWLEY, GIDEON (*b. Huntington, Conn., 1785; d. 1870*), lawyer. Graduated Union College, 1809. Became successful Albany, N.Y., lawyer and a pioneer in New York railroad development, but his most notable service was in education. From 1812 to 1821, as first superintendent of public instruction for New York State, he laid foundations for the public elementary school system. From 1814 to 1841 he was secretary of the Board of Regents, who guided the development of private academies; he served as a member of the Board of Regents of the University of the State of New York, 1842–70. He was largely responsible for establishing the first normal school in the state at Albany.

HAWLEY, JAMES HENRY (*b. Dubuque, Iowa, 1847; d. 1929*), lawyer, Idaho legislator. Governor of Idaho, 1911–13. Nationally prominent as prosecutor of W. D. Haywood and other labor officials for murder of Gov. Steunenberg.

HAWLEY, JOSEPH (*b. Northampton, Mass., 1723; d. Northampton, 1788*), lawyer. Grandson of Solomon Stoddard. Graduated Yale, 1742. Influential in dismissal of his cousin Jonathan Edwards from his church, 1749–50. Guiding spirit of the Revolution in the Connecticut Valley.

HAWLEY, JOSEPH ROSWELL (*b. Stewartville, N.C., 1826; d. Washington, D.C., 1905*), editor, Union soldier. Graduated Hamilton College, 1847. Helped organize Republican party in Connecticut, 1856. Editor, Hartford *Evening Press*, 1857–61; rose to major general in Civil War; editor, *Hartford Courant*, 1867. Elected governor of Connecticut, 1866, he was in politics to the end of his life, serving three times as congressman *post* 1868, and as U.S. senator, 1881–1905. A consistent, able conservative.

HAWLEY, PAUL RAMSEY (*b. West College Corner, Ind., 1891; d. Washington, D.C., 1965*), physician and army officer. M.D. (1914), University of Cincinnati; Ph.D. in public health (1923), Johns Hopkins. In the Army Medical Corps, 1916–46, rose to the rank of major general by 1944 and became chief surgeon of the European Theatre after D-Day. Upon retirement, was named chief medical director of the Veterans Administration, which he completely revitalized. In 1948 became chief executive officer of the Blue Cross and Blue Shield Commission. As director of the American College of Surgeons, 1950–61, he used his position to expose abuses in the medical profession.

HAWLEY, WILLIS CHATMAN (*b. near Monroe, Oreg., 1864; d. Salem, Oreg., 1941*), educator, politician. B.S., Willamette University, 1884; A.B., LL.B., 1888; A.M., 1891. Taught at several schools and at Willamette; president of Willamette, 1893–1902. As a Republican congressman, 1907–33, he achieved considerable influence in his party's councils and was regarded as an expert in taxation and tariff matters; he wrote the agricultural schedule for the Fordney-McCumber Tariff, 1922. An advocate of the protective tariff, he became chairman of the House Ways and Means Committee, 1928, and maneuvered the Smoot-Hawley Tariff bill through the House in 1929.

HAWORTH, JOSEPH (*b. Providence, R.I., 1855?; d. 1903*), actor. Debut with Ellsler's stock company, Cleveland, *ca.* 1873. Supported Barrett, Edwin Booth, McCullough, Modjeska; superior performer of serious roles.

HAWTHORNE, CHARLES WEBSTER (*b. Lodi, Ill., 1882; d. Baltimore, Md., 1930*), painter. Studied at Art Students League, New York, and with William M. Chase. Established Cape Cod School of Art, Provincetown, Mass.

HAWTHORNE, JULIAN (*b. Boston, Mass., 1846; d. 1934*), author. Son of Nathaniel Hawthorne; brother of Rose H. Lathrop.

HAWTHORNE, NATHANIEL (*b. Salem, Mass., 1804; d. Plymouth, N.H., 1864*), novelist. Descended from a New England line that began with William Hathorne who came to Massachusetts in 1630, and included a judge of the Salem witchcraft trials and several sea captains. His father's death, 1808, and his mother's consequent withdrawal from society caused him to grow up in habits of solitude. By the age of 14, he was widely read in novels and romances of all kinds and in the works of the classic authors, French and English. On graduation from Bowdoin, 1825, he settled down in Salem, devoting a dozen years to making himself a man of letters. Yearly he struck out on a kind of wary summer vagabondage, traveling through other districts of New England, across New York to Niagara, and perhaps even so far as Detroit. His *American Note-Books* show him to have used his eyes and ears on his travels, as do many of his tales and sketches. Everywhere he was attentive to manners and customs. He continued to read extensively, particularly in the early history of New England, aiming to enliven and warm the cold record by reconstructing typical "moments of drama . . . clashes between the parties and

ideas which divided the old New England." Though a descendant of the Puritans, he seemed to sympathize with humane and expansive rebels against the order of austerity and orthodoxy. That this was less an historical than a moral position is indicated by the theme of egotism stressed in his short stories. Solitary by habit, he deeply feared that solitude which ends in egotism and is in turn encouraged and deepened by it. Egotism leads to pride; pride by different roads leads always away from nature. Aside from the stories he wrote between 1825 and 1837, there are no events to mark his life in that period. In 1828 he issued, at his own expense and anonymously, the undistinguished novel *Fanshawe*. Though unsuccessful, it got him a publisher, Samuel G. Goodrich of Boston, just then founding an annual, the *Token*, which with the *New England Magazine* was to be Hawthorne's chief publishing outlet. *Twice-Told Tales* (1837), a collection of short masterpieces, marked the end of his years of solitary experiment. Thereafter he wrote with increasing reputation and in 1842 published a second series of *Twice-Told Tales*.

The need of money did as much as anything else to end Hawthorne's career of solitude. He served for seven months during 1836 as editor of Goodrich's *American Magazine of Useful and Entertaining Knowledge* and wrote or compiled the whole of every issue. He compiled *Peter Parley's Universal History* (1837), a piece of hackwork which sold over a million copies. For children he wrote *Grandfather's Chair* (1841), *Famous Old People* (1841), *Liberty Tree* (1841), *Biographical Stories for Children* (1842) and, later, two of the lasting triumphs of their mode, *A Wonder-Book for Girls and Boys* (1852) and *Tanglewood Tales for Girls and Boys* (1853). With the help of Franklin Pierce, he was employed as weigher and gauger in the Boston Custom House, 1839–41. He then went to live at West Roxbury with the Transcendentalists who had founded Brook Farm; after an intermittent year of residence he left, satisfied that the association was not for him. After his marriage to Sophia Peabody of Salem in July 1842, he moved to the Old Manse at Concord. Profoundly happy with his wife, he was not distracted by the presence nearby of the most distinguished group who have ever come together in a single American village. Alcott bored him; he heard Emerson with interest but without the customary reverence; only with Thoreau did he arrive at anything like intimacy. His story collection *Mosses from an Old Manse* (1846) contained an introductory paper describing this pastoral interlude. Pressed for money, he moved to Salem, 1845, and was appointed surveyor of the port; in 1849, when the Democrats went out of power, he was dismissed. Forced into private life, he produced within the next three years the novels which brought his art to its peak.

The novels marked no break with the tales. In style, tempo, themes, Hawthorne proceeded much as he had always done. Only the dimensions were different. *The Scarlet Letter* (1850) is a succession of moments of drama from the lives of the principal characters, bound together by a continuity of mood and firmness of central idea which lift the story to a region more spacious than 17th-century Salem. The novel portrays a clash between elements opposed in old New England, and also, at the same time, the universal clash between egotism and nature with which Hawthorne had dealt in his shorter stories. *The House of the Seven Gables* (1851) is an extended description of such households as he dealt with in many of his sketches. The house, like the household of his own youth, was withdrawn, solitary, declining, haunted by an ancestral curse. Into the story he distilled all the representative qualities of decadent New England without, however, bringing in that New England complacency which made a virtue out of decay and refused to admit the existence of evil in adversity. In *The Blithedale Romance* (1852) he turned to the contemporary world. The setting was more or less what he remembered of Brook Farm. His thesis was that philanthropy, of his character Hollingsworth's sort, is only another egotism which may bring the philanthropist into tragic conflict with nature. *The Scarlet Letter* was written at Salem; he wrote *The House of the Seven Gables* at Lenox in the Berkshires, where he made the acquaintance of Herman Melville, then writing *Moby Dick* at Pittsfield. Here, also, he collected *The Snow Image and Other Twice-Told Tales* (1851) and wrote *A Wonder-Book*. In 1851 he moved to West Newton, Mass., where the third novel was completed; as the novels put money at his command, he bought a house in Concord. After writing with much labor and out of obligation for many favors a campaign *Life of Franklin Pierce* (1852), Hawthorne was appointed U.S. consul at Liverpool, where he served conscientiously, 1853–57. During 1858 and early 1859 he lived in Italy. Here he began *The Marble Faun* (1860), which he completed in England before returning to Concord, 1860.

The four years after his return to America, except for his shrewd, slyly satirical commentary on England, *Our Old Home* (1863), saw nothing further by him. He experimented with four ideas (published posthumously and unfinished as *The Ancestral Footstep, Septimius Felton, Dr. Grimshaws's Secret,* and *The Dolliver Romance*, but he could not fuse or complete them. His imagination was dissolving; his vitality was breaking up. The Civil War weighed upon him, as did the illness of his daughter Una, and Thoreau's death in 1862. He could not survive his era of New England or endure the tumult of its passing. In May 1864, enfeebled and discouraged, he set out from Concord for a carriage trip with his friend Pierce. At Plymouth, N.H., he died in his sleep. Mourned as a classic figure, he has ever since been so regarded.

HAWTHORNE, ROSE. *See* ALPHONSA, MOTHER.

HAY, CHARLES AUGUSTUS (*b. York, Pa., 1821; d. Gettysburg, Pa., 1893*), Lutheran clergyman. Nephew of John Gottlieb Morris. Professor of theology, German, and Hebrew at Gettysburg Seminary, 1844–48, 1865–93.

HAY, GEORGE (*b. Williamsburg, Va., 1765; d. 1830*), jurist, Virginia legislator. Son-in-law of James Monroe. As U.S. attorney for district of Virginia, conducted prosecution of Aaron Burr for treason. Later a federal judge in eastern Virginia and able political writer on the Jeffersonian side.

HAY, JOHN MILTON (*b. Salem, Ind., 1838; d. New Hampshire, 1905*), poet, journalist, historian, statesman. Graduated Brown, 1858. Entered his uncle's law office, Springfield, Ill., 1859. John G. Nicolay, a young friend, persuaded Abraham Lincoln to hire Hay as assistant private secretary. Daily relations with Lincoln during more than four years of national peril gave Hay a wide experience of men and issues and an abiding sense of Lincoln's greatness. In 1864 Hay became assistant adjutant general in the army on detail to the White House. Appointed secretary to the American legation in Paris, March 1865, Hay was influenced by John Bigelow to revive his early ambition to be a writer. In 1867–68 he was chargé d'affaires at Vienna; in June 1869 he became secretary of legation at Madrid, where he collected impressions which he later published as *Castilian Days* (1871). Returning to New York in 1870, he accepted a position as editorial writer and night editor on the *New York Tribune*; in January 1874, he married the wealthy Clara Stone, daughter of Amasa Stone of Cleveland. Within a year he quit journalism and removed to Cleveland to assist his father-in-law in financial matters and to continue his own literary efforts. His best-known verses, "Little Breeches" and "Jim Bludso," after appearing in the *Tribune*, were included in *Pike County Ballads and Other Pieces* (1871) and sounded an original and virile note in American poetry. He published anonymously *The Bread-Winners* (1884), a satirical novel which attacked labor unions and defended economic indi-

vidualism. With John Nicolay he was author of *Abraham Lincoln: A History* (10 vols., 1890), a cooperative work which required ten years of labor. It is a monument to Lincoln and an invaluable narrative of the history of his presidency based on original sources.

Removing to Washington, D.C. 1878, as assistant secretary of state, Hay formed his most important friendship, that with Henry Adams. He had no opportunity to hold office again *post* 1880 until his help to William McKinley's campaign won him appointment as ambassador to Great Britain, 1897. With the outbreak of the Spanish-American War, April 1898, all of Hay's resources were used successfully to secure Great Britain's goodwill. Accepting the post of U.S. secretary of state, he took office in September 1898. An imperialist in his dealings with Spain, he supported President McKinley in his determination that the Philippines should become American. In 1899 he made his proposal to the European powers that a declaration should be made in favor of the "Open Door," or equal trade opportunity for all in China. This policy (actually formulated by W. W. Rockhill) was largely an illusion, but his China policy in 1900 during the Boxer Rebellion was masterful and helped China escape dissolution. It is also to his credit that the United States did not shamefully abrogate the Clayton-Bulwer treaty in 1900, and the successful 1903 settlement of the Alaskan boundary dispute with Canada was his work. He suffered some disappointment in his efforts to clear the way for the Panama Canal by treaties and was in ill-health for several years before his death in office.

HAY, MARY GARRETT (*b. Charlestown, Ind., 1857; d. New Rochelle, N.Y., 1928*), civic worker. Active in woman's suffrage and prohibition movements.

HAY, OLIVER PERRY (*b. near Hanover, Ind., 1846; d. 1930*), paleontologist. Indiana University, Ph.D., 1884. Associated with Field Museum, American Museum of Natural History, Carnegie Institution. Author of notable *Bibliography and Catalogue of the Fossil Vertebrata of North America* (1902), supplemented by *Second Bibliography and Catalogue . . .* (1929–30).

HAYDEN, AMOS SUTTON (*b. Youngstown, Ohio, 1813; d. Collamer, Ohio, 1880*), minister of Disciples of Christ, educator. Brother of William Hayden. A founder and first principal of Hiram College.

HAYDEN, CHARLES (*b. Boston, Mass., 1870; d. New York, N.Y., 1937*), financier, philanthropist. Founded brokerage firm of Hayden, Stone & Co., 1892. Established Hayden Foundation to aid youth work; principal donor of Hayden Planetarium, New York City.

HAYDEN, CHARLES HENRY (*b. Plymouth, Mass., 1856; d. Belmont, Mass., 1901*), landscape painter.

HAYDEN, EDWARD EVERETT (*b. Boston, Mass., 1858; d. Baltimore, Md., 1932*), naval officer, meterologist. Graduated Annapolis, 1879. Established the system of correcting the observatory time-signal transmission on the basis of barometric pressure and temperature.

HAYDEN, FERDINAND VANDIVEER (*b. Westfield, Mass., 1829; d. 1887*), geologist. Graduated Oberlin, 1850; M.D., Albany Medical College, 1853. Influenced by James Hall, went on exploration of Dakota badlands with F. B. Meek, 1853; continued surveys unofficially and as member of Warren expedition (1856–57) and Raynolds survey (1859). Served as surgeon with Union Army, 1861–65; was professor of geology, University of Pennsylvania, 1865–72. Surveyed Nebraska Territory, 1867; in so doing, laid the foundation for U.S. Geological Survey as it exists today. *Post* 1872, Hayden devoted full time to geological and natural-history surveys in the West and Southwest which were outstanding pioneer studies; the act of Congress which set aside the public reservation known as Yellowstone National Park was a result of his efforts. Subsequent to consolidation of government survey work under Clarence King (1879), he took rank as geologist and worked chiefly in Montana.

HAYDEN, HIRAM WASHINGTON (*b. Haydenville, Mass., 1820; d. Waterbury, Conn., 1904*), brass manufacturer. Son of Joseph S. Hayden. Invented pioneer kettle-making machinery by die process, 1851; took out many patents on brass lamp burners.

HAYDEN, HORACE H. (*b. Winsor, Conn., 1769; d. Baltimore, Md., 1844*), dentist, geologist. Started as an architect; removed to New York City, 1792, where he studied dentistry with the help of John Greenwood; began practice of dentistry in Baltimore *ca.* 1800. With Chapin A. Harris and others, established first dental college in the world, the Baltimore College of Dental Surgery (chartered 1840), and was its first president. He also helped organize the American Society of Dental Surgeons, 1840.

HAYDEN, JOSEPH SHEPARD (*b. Foxborough, Mass., 1802; d. Waterbury, Conn., 1877*), inventor and manufacturer of button-making machinery.

HAYDEN, WILLIAM (*b. Westmoreland Co., Pa., 1799; d. Chagrin Falls, Ohio, 1863*), pioneer evangelist of the Disciples of Christ. Brother of Amos S. Hayden.

HAYES, AUGUSTUS ALLEN (*b. Windsor, Vt., 1806; d. 1882*), chemist. Studied chemistry at Dartmouth under James F. Dana. Removed to Boston, 1828, and was director of a chemical plant, consulting chemist to dyeing, bleaching, gas making and smelting firms, and state assayer of Massachusetts. Quicker methods for smelting iron and refining copper were devised by him. His 1837 study of fuel economy in generating steam led to improvements in furnace and boiler construction; his investigations for the Navy Department on the use of copper sheathing in building vessels led to extensive study of the composition of sea water. Among other practical effects of his constant research was a process for manufacturing saltpeter used by the U.S. Navy in the Civil War.

HAYES, CARLTON JOSEPH HUNTLEY (*b. Jericho Farm in Afton, N.Y., 1882; d. Jericho Farm, 1964*), historian and ambassador. B.A. (1904), M.A. (1905), and Ph.D. (1909), Columbia University. Taught at Columbia from 1910 to 1950, becoming Seth Low Professor of History in 1935. His central interest was nationalism, and along with Hans Kohn and Boyd C. Shafer, he was a pioneer in its study. His advanced seminar on modern nationalism won international fame, and his works are regarded as classics, notably *Essays on Nationalism* (1926), *France, A Nation of Patriots* (1930), *The Historical Evolution of Modern Nationalism* (1931), and *Nationalism: A Religion* (1960). Also wrote *British Social Politics* (1913) and *A Generation of Materialism, 1871–1900* (1941), as well as the highly successful textbook *Political and Social History of Modern Europe* (1916), one of the textbooks that virtually monopolized the college history textbook market for years. Received into the Catholic church in 1924, he became a leading Catholic layman. Was ambassador to Spain, 1942–45, an experience he recorded in *Wartime Mission in Spain* (1945).

HAYES, CHARLES WILLARD (*b. Granville, Ohio, 1858; d. Washington, D.C., 1916*), geologist. Associated with U.S. Geological Survey, 1887–1911; thereafter engaged in oil prospecting in Mexico. An able administrator, he took particular interest in physiography.

HAYES, EDWARD CAREY (*b. Lewiston, Maine, 1868; d. 1928*), sociologist. Ph.D., University of Chicago, 1902. Established department of sociology, University of Illinois, 1907. His theoretical outlook will be found in "Sociological Construction Lines," *American Journal of Sociology*, March 1905–July 1906.

HAYES, GABBY (*b. George Francis Hayes, Willing, N.Y., 1885; d. Burbank, Calif., 1969*), actor and comedian. In the 1930's became famous in the role of irascible but amiable geezer in westerns. Made twenty-two pictures as Windy Halliday, William Boyd's garrulous companion in the "Hopalong Cassidy" series, 1935–39; became Gabby and made twenty-six pictures with Roy Rogers, 1939–42, and twenty-four pictures with Wild Bill Elliott. In 1943 was named one of the ten most popular western stars, and in 1945 theater owners voted him second only to Rogers. He had substantial parts, notably in *Don't Fence Me In* (1945), and displayed talent for light drama as well as comedy. Retired from films in 1950, having appeared in 177 features; thereafter appeared on radio and television until 1955.

HAYES, ISAAC ISRAEL (*b. Chester Co., Pa., 1832; d. 1881*), physician, Arctic explorer. Graduated M.D., University of Pennsylvania, 1853; surgeon with the second Arctic expedition of Elisha K. Kane, 1853–55. Hayes described his own early explorations and experiences in *An Arctic Boat Journey* (1860) and *The Open Polar Sea* (1867). During the Civil War he was an army surgeon at Satterlee Hospital, Philadelphia. A third voyage to the Arctic, 1869, provided materials for *The Land of Desolation* (1871); he also wrote an account of his adventures for children, *Cast Away in the Cold* (1868).

HAYES, JOHN LORD (*b. South Berwick, Maine, 1812; d. Cambridge, Mass., 1887*), lawyer, scientist, tariff lobbyist for wool industry.

HAYES, JOHN WILLIAM (*b. Philadelphia, Pa., 1854; d. North Beach, Md., 1942*), labor leader. At various times a railroad brakeman, telegrapher, and grocery storekeeper, Hayes became the chief ally and confidant of Terence Powderly in the Knights of Labor; he was made general secretary-treasurer of the Knights in 1888 and held the post until 1902. Meanwhile, he had joined with the socialist and agrarian elements which ousted Powderly as head of the Knights in 1893. Hayes held the title of general master workman of the Knights during its decline to extinction, 1902–16.

HAYES, MAX SEBASTIAN (*b. near Havana, Ohio, 1866; d. Shaker Heights, Cleveland, Ohio, 1945*), printer, labor editor, socialist leader. Parents' name originally Hoize. A printer's apprentice at thirteen, he went to work at the *Cleveland Press* and joined the International Typographical Union, 1884. He represented his local in the Cleveland Central Labor Union, 1890–1939, and edited the weekly newspaper (the *Cleveland Citizen*, 1892–1939. He believed that socialists should work within the established labor movement for the adoption of socialist principles. He left the Socialist party, 1919, but remained convinced that labor should engage in independent political action. Helped organize the National Labor party, 1919, which in 1920 became a part of the Farmer-Labor party. Farmer-Labor candidate for vice president, 1920.

HAYES, PATRICK JOSEPH (*b. New York, N.Y., 1867; d. Monticello, N.Y., 1938*), Roman Catholic clergyman. Graduated Manhattan College, 1888; ordained priest, 1892. As archbishop of New York 1919–38, he unified Catholic charitable efforts in the city. He was made cardinal, 1924.

HAYES, RUTHERFORD BIRCHARD (*b. Delaware, Ohio, 1822; d. Fremont, Ohio, 1893*), lawyer, statesman, president of the United States. Graduated Kenyon College, 1842; read law for a few months in an an office at Columbus, Ohio, and studied for a year and a half at Harvard Law School. Began practice in Lower Sandusky (later Fremont), Ohio, 1845; opened an office in Cincinnati, 1850, where he prospered. He married Lucy Webb, 1852. At first a Whig, he became a moderate Republican; he believed that war could and should be averted, even by compromising on slavery. When the Civil War began, he helped recruit men, became a major in the 23rd Ohio and later commanded the regiment. His military service was varied and capable but not distinguished; he was commissioned brigadier in 1864 and brevetted major general of volunteers, 1865. Elected to Congress, 1864, though he did not leave his military duties to campaign, he took his seat late in 1865. His best work was as chairman of the library commission. Reelected in 1866, his career was brief; in June 1867, he resigned from Congress to accept Republican nomination for governor of Ohio. Elected after an arduous campaign, he carried through important prison reforms and a measure for better supervision of charities and was reelected, 1869. His reputation as a courageous, liberal and wise administrator grew, and some of his addresses were widely reported and read. An astute politician, though he sympathized with many aims of the Liberal Republicans, he refused to leave his party in 1872 and campaigned for Grant. Elected governor again in 1875 in a campaign which made him a national figure and "available" for the next presidential nomination, he was awarded it at the Republican National Convention, Cincinnati, 1876. His nomination satisfied the different factions of the party and did much to hold it together. The first returns on November 7 seemed to show that the Democrat, Samuel J. Tilden, had won the election. Hayes's hopes revived next day when Zachariah Chandler sent out his telegram "Hayes has 185 votes and is elected." When it became clear that the result hinged on contested returns from South Carolina, Florida, Louisiana and Oregon, Hayes was opposed to any attempt at compromise, as he believed himself "justly and legally" elected. As a result of Carl Schurz's arguments, he consented to the creation of an Electoral Commission to examine the vote and determine the result. There is evidence that as the work of the Commission approached its close, especially after Louisiana's votes were counted for Hayes, Republican party agents made commitments to the Southern Democrats who cared less about the presidency than the restoration of white rule in the contested states of the South. On Mar. 2, 1877, Hayes was awarded the presidency, with 185 electors to Tilden's 184.

Hayes's administration was notable for his policy of Southern pacification, his attention to reform, and his insistence on conservative treatment of financial questions. His first important measure was to carry out "the bargain" which had ended the contested election by withdrawing Federal troops from the South. Though he was fiercely attacked by many Republican leaders, the wisdom of his course was shown by the immediate end of violence and establishment of relative prosperity and contentment in the South. The restoration of full autonomy to the one-time Confederate states was his greatest achievement. He continued to excite hostility among the "Stalwarts" of his own party by his measures of civil-service reform. With his encouragement, Secretary Carl Schurz at once reformed the Interior Department and other department heads took similar action. After an investigation of the New York Custom House, Hayes issued orders forbidding partisan control of the revenue service and all political assessments upon revenue officers. When Chester A. Arthur, collector at New York, and A. B. Cornell, naval officer, defied these orders, Hayes, after a long fight, had them removed. Facing an unsatisfactory monetary situation, Hayes insisted on resumption of specie payments; his determined stand helped prevent the Senate from passing the bill to postpone resumption, but did not defeat the Bland-Allison bill. He did not fully understand the social and economic problems of

the time and did nothing to strike at the root of business distress and labor troubles, but showed firmness in vetoing a popular Chinese exclusion bill as a violation of the Burlingame treaty, and in combating congressional usurpation of the Executive's powers. Gradually his conscientiousness and responsiveness to moral forces impressed the nation and he became genuinely esteemed. Believing that a president could most effectively discharge his duties by refusing to think of a second term, he had expressed at his nomination his determination to serve but one term. He returned to his "Spiegel Grove" estate near Fremont, Ohio, in March 1881, to spend his remaining years devoting much time to his library, filling many speaking engagements, and enlisting in a variety of humanitarian causes.

HAYES, WILLIAM HENRY (*b.* Cleveland, Ohio[?], 1829; *d. at sea,* 1877), trader, swindler, adventurer, commonly known as Bully Hayes. Famous for his rascality through the Pacific and South Sea Islands.

HAYFORD, JOHN FILLMORE (*b.* Rouse's Point, N.Y., 1868; *d.* 1925), geodesist. Graduated C.E., Cornell, 1889. Worked in U.S. Coast and Geodetic Survey and headed engineering school, Northwestern University. Established existence and applications for isostasy.

HAYGOOD, ATTICUS GREEN (*b.* Watkinsville, Ga., 1839; *d.* 1896), bishop of Methodist Episcopal Church, South, educator. President, Emory College, 1875–84. Resigned to act as agent of Slater Fund to aid black education.

HAYGOOD, LAURA ASKEW (*b.* Watkinsville, Ga., 1845; *d.* Shanghai, China, 1900), Methodist missionary to China, *post* 1884. Sister of Atticus G. Haygood.

HAYNE, ISAAC (*b.* Colleton District, S.C., 1745; *d.* Charleston, S.C., 1781), Revolutionary soldier. Condemned and hanged by the British as a spy without benefit of trial, an event which produced a long controversy.

HAYNE, PAUL HAMILTON (*b.* Charleston, S.C., 1830; *d.* 1886), poet. Nephew of Robert Y. Hayne. Edited *Russell's Magazine*, 1857–60. Threnodist of the Southern antebellum regime whose ideals he illustrated in his poetry; his best single volume, *Legends and Lyrics* (1872).

HAYNE, ROBERT YOUNG (*b.* Colleton District, S.C. 1791; *d.* Asheville, N.C., 1839), lawyer, legislator, railroad president. Studied in Charleston office of Langdon Cheves and acquired a large practice. Elected to the South Carolina legislature, 1814, he became speaker in 1818 for one year. After two years as state attorney general, he was elected U.S. senator, Democratic-Republican, in 1822 and again in 1828. His chief endeavor was to check the heightening of protective tariff rates. In 1830, after Daniel Webster shifted with New England from low to high tariff and from strict to broad construction of the Constitution, Hayne was his natural opponent. Foot's resolution to restrain public land sales gave occasion for a trial of eloquence. Thos. H. Benton, for the West, opposed the resolution. Hayne, alert to the southern need of an alliance with the West, supported Benton. Webster replied to Hayne. The forensic duel began in mid-January 1830 and covered a broad range of topics. Hayne indorsed the doctrine of nullification, arguing that the U.S. Constitution was a compact between the several states and the federal government. Webster showed that the federal government was not a party to such a compact. In 1832 when the crisis came, Hayne resigned his seat and became governor of South Carolina, to give Calhoun a place on the Senate floor. He played a leading role in the convention which adopted the nullification ordinance, and as governor defended the state's policy with vigor, yet with temperance. To

Jackson's proclamation he replied in similar form defiantly, and summoned the state to furnish 10,000 troops to repel invasion. But when Clay proposed his compromise, Hayne readily concurred and rescinded the ordinance. After one term as governor, and a year as Charleston's mayor, Hayne's main interest became the project of a railroad to tap the Ohio Valley traffic at Cincinnati, make Charleston rival of New York, and bind the South and the West together. In 1836 the Louisville, Cincinnati, & Charleston Railroad Co. was formed with Hayne as president. Subscriptions to stock did not meet expectations and the panic of 1837 completed the work of ruin. Only a loan by the South Carolina legislature enabled the corporation to survive long enough to build a few miles of track.

HAYNES, GEORGE EDMUND (*b. Pine Bluff, Ark., 1880; d. New York, N.Y., 1960*), sociologist and race relations expert. Studied at Fisk (B.A., 1903) and Yale (M.A., 1904). The first black to graduate from the New York School of Social Work (1910) and the first black to receive a Ph.D. from Columbia (1912). In 1911, he founded the National League on Urban Conditions Among Negroes, which became the National Urban League, serving as its executive secretary until 1917. From 1918 to 1921, with the U.S. Department of Labor; executive secretary of the Commission on the Church and Race Relations of the National Council of Churches (1922–46). Member of the board of trustees of the New York State University system (1948–54); taught at the City College of New York (1950–59).

HAYNES, JOHN (*b. Essex, England, 1594[?]; d. Hartford, Conn., 1653/54*). Came to Massachusetts, 1633; settled at Newtown (Cambridge). As governor of Massachusetts, 1635, banished Roger Williams. Removing to Connecticut, 1637, he was chosen the colony's first governor under the Fundamental Orders, 1639, and elected every alternate year thereafter until his death.

HAYNES, JOHN HENRY (*b. Rowe, Mass., 1849; d. North Adams, Mass., 1910*), archeologist. Graduated Williams, 1876. Did important work in excavations at Nippur; acted as first American consul at Baghdad, 1888.

HAYNES, WILLIAMS (*b. Nathan Gallup Williams Haynes, Detroit, Mich., 1886; d. Stonington, Conn., 1970*), publisher, historian, and economist. In his father's firm, D. O. Haynes and Company, worked as publisher of several chemicals-industry trade journals, 1916–39. During this period he also founded *Chemical Who's Who* (1928) and edited it through five editions; wrote less technical books on the chemical industry; and during World War II wrote several popular books dealing with chemistry and the war effort. In 1939 sold his trade magazines to devote his time to historical projects, in particular *The American Chemical Industry: A History* (6 vols.; 1945–54).

HAYS, ALEXANDER (*b. Franklin, Pa., 1819; d. 1864*), soldier. Graduated West Point, 1844. Served in occupation of Texas and Mexican War. Returning to the army, 1861, after retirement, 1848, he served gallantly in the Civil War and was killed in action at the battle of the Wilderness.

HAYS, ARTHUR GARFIELD (*b. Rochester, N.Y., 1881; d. New York, N.Y., 1954*), lawyer and author. LL.B., Columbia (1905). One of the leading lawyers of his time, Hays was involved in the defense of the Scottsboro boys in Atlanta; assisted Clarence Darrow in the last days of the Scopes trial; and assisted in the defense of Sacco and Vanzetti. He represented William Randolph Hearst when his private telegrams were subpoenaed; Henry Ford in a freedom-of-speech dispute; and defended H. L. Mencken and the *American Mercury* against the Boston Watch and Ward Society, which objected to a story about a prostitute. He repre-

sented the facist German-American Bund while also defending Communist John Strachey's First Amendment freedoms.

HAYS, HARRY THOMPSON (*b. Wilson Co., Tenn., 1820; d. New Orleans, La., 1876*), lawyer, Confederate major general. Brother of John C. Hays.

HAYS, ISAAC (*b. Philadelphia, Pa., 1796; d. Philadelphia, 1879*), physician, opthalmologist. Graduated M.D., University of Pennsylvania, 1820. Editor, *post* 1827, of the valuable *American Journal of the Medical Sciences*. One of first to detect astigmatism and to study color blindness.

HAYS, JOHN COFFEE (*b. Little Cedar Lick, Tenn., 1817; d. near Piedmont, Calif., 1883*), soldier, surveyor. Went to Texas as a volunteer to help in the revolution, 1836. Served four years on the frontier against hostile Mexicans and Indians and was made captain of a Ranger company, 1840, rising to major for gallantry and efficiency. A colonel of Texas volunteer cavalry in the Mexican War, he won special distinction at Monterey. In 1849 he went to California, and after serving as sheriff of San Francisco, 1850–53, and a single term as state surveyor general, he entered the real-estate business. He also had large banking, public service, and industrial interests in Oakland.

HAYS, WILL H. (*b. Sullivan, Ind., 1879; d. Sullivan, Ind., 1954*), attorney, political official, and cinema industry official. Graduated Wabash College, 1900. Republican party state chairman from Indiana, 1910; chairman of the National Committee, 1918. From 1921 to 1922, he was U.S. postmaster general. From 1922 to 1945, he was chairman of the Motion Picture Producers and Distributors of America, Inc., whose job it was to respond to the public's demand for censorship of film content and advertising. Hays and the so-called Hays office policed the industry successfully and thus curtailed the growth of state censorship laws (only seven states passed such laws) or federal action.

HAYS, WILLIAM JACOB (*b. New York, N.Y., 1830; d. New York, 1875*), painter of animals. Studied drawing with John Rubens Smith. Visited the West, 1860, and produced a number of works of historic as well as artistic value. His "The Wounded Buffalo" is one of the best animal paintings ever executed by an American.

HAYS, WILLIAM SHAKESPEARE (*b. Louisville, Ky., 1837; d. Louisville, 1907*), ballad writer, composer.

HAYWARD, GEORGE (*b. Boston, Mass., 1791; d. 1863*), surgeon. First to employ ether anesthesia during a major operation, 1846. Graduated Harvard, 1809; M.D., University of Pennsylvania, 1812. Practice in Boston, and was professor of surgery, Harvard Medical School, 1835–49. His medical writings are of considerable importance.

HAYWARD, NATHANIEL MANLEY (*b. Easton, Mass., 1808; d. Colchester, Conn., 1865*), inventor, manufacturer. Subjected rubber-coated cloth to sulphur fumes to bleach it and found that it did not soften, thus achieving its partial vulcanization. Patenting his process, 1839, he sold it to Charles Goodyear for $1,000. Hayward owned various businesses thereafter, and in 1843 engaged in manufacturing rubber shoes for which he had devised a method of giving luster. He helped organize the Hayward Rubber Co., 1847, was its manager until 1854, and president, 1855–65.

HAYWOOD, ALLAN SHAW (*b. Monk Breton, England, 1888; d. Wilkes-Barre, Pa., 1953*), labor leader. Immigrated to the U.S. in 1906. After working in the mines, he became a professional organizer for the United Mine Workers; he rose to district representative of the national executive board and was a trusted subordinate of John L. Lewis, joining Lewis when he formed the CIO. CIO regional director of New York City, 1937; director of organization for the CIO, 1939–53; vice president in 1942 and executive vice president in 1951. Defeated for the presidency in 1952 by Walter Reuther.

HAYWOOD, JOHN (*b. Halifax Co., N.C., 1762; d. near Nashville, Tenn., 1826*), jurist, historian. Self-taught, and successful as lawyer and judge in North Carolina, he removed to Tennessee, *ca.* 1807, where he prospered and served as state supreme court judge, 1816–26. With Robert Cobbs he compiled *The Statute Laws of the State of Tennessee* (1831). A pioneer in the field of history in the Southwest, his books *The Natural and Aboriginal History of Tennessee* (1823) and *The Civil and Political History of Tennessee* (1823) are of high authority.

HAYWOOD, WILLIAM DUDLEY (*b. Salt Lake City, Utah, 1869; d. Russia, 1928*), labor agitator. Officer in Western Federation of Miners; advocated industrial unionism and violence in labor disputes; presided over founding convention of I.W.W., 1905, and held office in that organization. Acquitted after trial for complicity in murder of Idaho governor, F. R. Steunenberg (1906–07). Jumped bail after conviction for sedition, 1918, and resided *post* 1921 in Soviet Russia.

HAZARD, AUGUSTUS GEORGE (*b. South Kingstown, R.I., 1802; d. Enfield, Conn., 1868*), merchant. Principal owner and president, 1843–68, of the Hazard Powder Co. with departments in practically every state in the Union.

HAZARD, EBENEZER (*b. Philadelphia, Pa., 1744; d. 1817*), editor, businessman, scholar. Graduated College of New Jersey (Princeton), 1762. As surveyor general of the U.S. Post Office, 1776–82, he traveled extensively and collected source materials of early American history. His term as postmaster general, 1782–89, was one of the few in which the post office paid its way. His pioneer *Historical Collections* (1792–94) contain documents relating to the discovery and colonization period of America and records of the New England Confederation edited with conscientious skill.

HAZARD, JONATHAN J. (*b. Narragansett, R.I., ca. 1744; d. Verona, N.Y., post 1824*), Rhode Island political leader.

HAZARD, ROWLAND GIBSON (*b. South Kingstown, R.I., 1801; d. 1888*), woolen manufacturer, author. Brother of Thomas R. Hazard.

HAZARD, SAMUEL (*b. Philadelphia, Pa., 1784; d. Germantown, Pa., 1870*), editor, antiquarian. Son of Ebenezer Hazard.

HAZARD, THOMAS (*b. Rhode Island, 1720; d. South Kingstown, R.I., 1798*), abolitionist. Nicknamed "College Tom." One of first of Society of Friends to work actively against slavery.

HAZARD, THOMAS ROBINSON (*b. South Kingstown, R.I., 1797; d. near Newport, R.I., 1886*), agriculturist, manufacturer, social reformer. Grandson of Thomas Hazard. Nicknamed "Shepherd Tom." Author of *Recollections of Olden Times*, and *The Jonny-Cake Letters* (1882, 1915).

HAZELIUS, ERNEST LEWIS (*b. Neusalz, Prussia, 1777; d. Lexington, S.C., 1853*), Lutheran clergyman. Came to America, 1800. Taught theology, *post* 1807, in several Moravian and Lutheran seminaries.

HAZELTINE, MAYO WILLIAMSON (*b. Boston, Mass., 1841; d. Atlantic City, N.J., 1909*), lawyer, journalist. Literary editor, New York *Sun*, 1878–1909.

HAZELTON, GEORGE COCHRANE (*b. Boscobel, Wis., 1868; d. 1921*), actor, lawyer, playwright, novelist. Coauthor, with J. Harry Benrimo, of *The Yellow Jacket* (1912).

HAZELWOOD, JOHN (*b. England, ca. 1726; d. 1800*), Revolutionary naval officer. Active in planning defense of the Hudson and Delaware rivers; especially distinguished before Philadelphia, Oct. 1777.

HAZEN, ALLEN (*b. Hartford, Vt., 1869; d. Miles City, Mont., 1930*), hydraulic and sanitary engineer. With Gardner S. Williams, developed Williams and Hazen pipeflow formula.

HAZEN, HENRY ALLEN (*b. Sirur, India, 1849; d. Washington, D.C., 1900*), meteorologist. Came to America, 1859. Graduated Dartmouth, 1871. Associated with U.S. Weather Bureau and its predecessor agencies *post* 1881.

HAZEN, MOSES (*b. Haverhill, Mass., 1733; d. Troy, N.Y., 1803*), Revolutionary soldier. A veteran of the French and Indian War and a resident of Canada at outbreak of the Revolution, Hazen took part in Montgomery's attack on Quebec but quarreled with Benedict Arnold. Later as colonel of a Canadian regiment in Continental service, he served with it under Washington's command at various times, 1776–81. He was promoted brigadier general, 1781.

HAZEN, WILLIAM BABCOCK (*b. Vermont, 1830; d. 1887*), soldier. Graduated West Point, 1855. Served in Oregon and Texas, and rose to colonel in regular army and major general of volunteers during the Civil War. As an officer on the frontier, *post* 1865, Hazen denounced exaggerated claims of western land promoters and revealed corruption in the post-trader system which led to Secretary of War Belknap's resignation, 1876. In 1880 Hazen became brigadier general and chief signal officer in the War Department, a post which included managing the Weather Bureau and involved him in a humiliating controversy. For censuring Secretary of War Lincoln for failure to send a third relief partly to find A. W. Greely's expedition stranded in the Arctic since 1881, Hazen was court-martialed and reprimanded, 1885.

HEADLEY, JOEL TYLER (*b. Walton, N.Y., 1813; d. Newburgh, N.Y., 1897*), author. Brother of Phineas C. Headley. Graduated Union, 1839. Prolific, superficial, and popular, he produced over thirty biographies, histories, and travel books. *Napoleon and his Marshals* (1846) reached a 50th edition, 1861. *Washington and His Generals* was another resounding success.

HEADLEY, PHINEAS CAMP (*b. Walton, N.Y., 1819; d. Lexington, Mass., 1903*), Presbyterian clergyman. Brother of Joel T. Headley and like him a facile writer of inspirational biographies.

HEALY, GEORGE PETER ALEXANDER (*b. Boston, Mass., 1813; d. Chicago, Ill., 1894*), portrait painter. Encouraged by Thomas Sully; studied in Paris under Gros where he made his first success. Painted hundreds of portraits as well as historical and genre subjects. "Webster's Reply to Hayne" is his best-known historical composition.

HEAP, SAMUEL DAVIES (*b. Carlisle, Pa., 1781; d. Tunis, 1853*), naval surgeon. Consul at Tunis, 1823–53, except for brief intervals. Negotiated a treaty, 1824, which replaced the treaty of 1797 with Tunis and which stood without amendment for eighty years.

HEARD, AUGUSTINE (*b. Ipswich, Mass., 1785; d. Ipswich, 1868*), sea captain, merchant. Partner in Samuel Russell & Co. and in its successor firm Augustine Heard & Co., Canton, China.

Through maintenance of high ethical standards, the firm was highly regarded by Chinese and prospered, 1840–65.

HEARD, DWIGHT BANCROFT (b. Boston, Mass., 1869; d. Arizona, 1929), investment banker, farmer. Nephew of Franklin F. Heard. Removed to the Southwest, 1894, and exerted a dominating influence on Arizona affairs after settling in Phoenix. A leader in movement resulting in U.S. Reclamation Act, 1902, and in all phases of the development of Arizona as territory and state.

HEARD, FRANKLIN FISKE (b. Wayland, Mass., 1825; d. Boston, Mass., 1889), legal author. Graduated Harvard, 1848. Author of over twenty legal treatises now largely superseded but valuable to the profession in their time. Among these were *A Treatise on Libel and Slander* (1860) the first American work on this subject, and *Equity Pleading* (1882).

HEARN, LAFCADIO (b. Santa Maura Island, Greece, 1850; d. Japan, 1904), author. Son of C. B. Hearn, surgeon major in the British Army, and Rosa Tessima, a Greek. After an unhappy childhood in Ireland, Hearn arrived in New York, 1869, friendless, half-blind, and morbidly shy. Beset by poverty and hardship there and in Cincinnati, he began work for the *Cincinnati Enquirer*, 1873, and became a successful reporter. Commissioned by the *Cincinnati Commercial* to report politics in New Orleans, 1877, he was dismissed and almost died of dengue fever and starvation before he got work on the New Orleans *Item*. The *Times-Democrat* assigned him, 1881, to write a Sunday feature of translations from the French and Spanish, and his initial book, *One of Cleopatra's Nights* (1882), a very able rendering of six stories by Théophile Gautier, was a result of this work. His articles on strange and exotic subjects were collected in *Stray Leaves from Strange Literatures* (1884). *Gombo Zhèbes* (1885), a collection of proverbs in French black patois, followed. *Some Chinese Ghosts*, an exquisitely written group of Oriental legends, appeared in 1887. Hearn lived precariously in Martinique, 1887–89, and produced *Two Years in the French West Indies* (1890), still the most perfect picture of the islands that has been painted; he also wrote *Youma* (1890), a novel of the slave rebellion there. Early in 1890 he went to Japan, married a Japanese girl and became a Japanese citizen under the name of Koizumi Yakumo. He taught at various schools and in 1894 was given the chair of English literature, Imperial University of Tokyo, which he occupied until 1903. Among the twelve books which he wrote during this period are *Glimpses of Unfamiliar Japan* (1894) and the posthumous *Japan: An Attempt at Interpretation* (1904), the summation of all his sympathetic and acute observation of his adopted country.

HEARST, GEORGE (b. near Sullivan, Mo., 1820; d. Washington, D.C., 1891), mining prospector, mine owner, publisher. Father of William Randolph Hearst. Crossed the plains on foot to California, 1850. Engaged in quartz mining and later in placer mining. By 1859, speculating in Nevada strikes, he laid the foundation of a great fortune. His interests spread to other states and to Mexico; his famous holdings, among them the Ophir, Homestake, and Anaconda mines, made him a multimillionaire. In 1880 he acquired the San Francisco *Daily Examiner*. Appointed as a Democrat to the U.S. Senate in March 1886 to fill an unexpired term, in 1888 he was elected for the full term as senator from California.

HEARST, PHOEBE APPERSON (b. Missouri, 1842; d. 1919), philanthropist. Wife of George Hearst.

HEARST, WILLIAM RANDOLPH (b. San Francisco, Calif., 1863; d. Los Angeles, Calif., 1951), publisher. Studied at Harvard. Assumed management of the San Francisco *Examiner*, owned by his father, 1887; expanded operations and in 1895 bought the New York *Evening Journal*. Hearst's publishing style

has been named "yellow journalism," a crude and theatrical appeal to mass audiences, many of them immigrants who had not previously read English and who identified with Hearst's stands against politics and corporations. Often, this style would distort, inflate, and even fake news events.

Hearst's style of journalism had great impact on American foreign policy by exploiting the Cuban Revolution against Spain. To rally public opinion in favor of American intervention, Hearst inundated the press with stories strongly slanted toward the Cubans. When the battleship *Maine* blew up in Havana Harbor, 1898, the *Journal* immediately concluded that the Spanish were responsible and demanded war, which President McKinley declared two months later. There is little doubt that Hearst and yellow journalism were very influential in causing the conflict. During the war, Hearst observed the fighting as a correspondent in Cuba.

Before the U.S. entry into World War I, Hearst's papers took a mildly pro-German stand; the British and French barred his organization from using their cables and mails, 1916; and Canada outlawed distribution of his newspapers. After the war, Hearst strongly opposed U.S. entry into the League of Nations and was instrumental in blocking U.S. participation in the World Court.

HEATH, JAMES EWELL (b. probably Northumberland Co., Va., 1792; d. 1862), author, state auditor of Virginia, 1819–49. Published *Edgehill, or The Family of the Fitzroyals* (1828); gave important assistance to *Southern Literary Messenger* during its first year, 1834.

HEATH, PERRY SANFORD (b. Muncie, Ind., 1857; d. 1927), newspaperman, politician. For directing publicity in McKinley's 1896 campaign, he was appointed first assistant postmaster general and installed the rural free-delivery system. He resigned in 1900 and was later censured for the character of some of his appointees.

HEATH, THOMAS KURTON.   *See* MCINTYRE, JAMES.

HEATH, WILLIAM (b. Roxbury, Mass., 1737; d. Roxbury, 1814), Revolutionary soldier. Active in pre-Revolutionary committees and the Massachusetts Provincial Congress. Served with credit before Boston but, although promoted major general, 1777, proved inept in the field. Commanded Eastern district, 1777–79, and lower Hudson, 1779–83. Author of *Memoirs* (1798), an important source work.

HEATHCOTE, CALEB (b. Derbyshire, England, 1665/66; d. 1720/21), merchant, statesman, churchman. Came to New York, 1692; appointed to the governor's council, he served on it, except 1698–1702, until his death. Prospering as a contractor and farmer of Westchester Co. taxes, he was colonel of militia, 1692–1720, and a county judge. He took up residence in Westchester borough town, 1696, and was its mayor for life. Heathcote patented many large tracts of land including the "Great Nine Partners" tract and the Manor of Scarsdale (1701), the last manor granted in the British Empire. He was mayor of New York, 1711–13. A devoted churchman, he aided the partial establishment of Anglicanism in New York and led in founding Trinity Parish. He set up Episcopal worship in Westchester, Rye, New Rochelle, Eastchester, and Yonkers and was chiefly responsible for planting episcopacy in Connecticut.

HEATON, JOHN LANGDON (b. Canton, N.Y., 1860; d. Brooklyn, N.Y., 1935), newspaper editor, writer. Brilliant editorial writer for New York *World*, 1900–31.

HÉBERT, LOUIS (b. Iberville Parish, La., 1820; d. St. Martin Parish, La., 1901), engineer, Confederate brigadier general. Graduated West Point, 1845. Cousin of Paul O. Hébert.

HÉBERT, PAUL OCTAVE (*b. Iberville Parish, La., 1818; d. New Orleans, La., 1880*), engineer, Confederate brigadier general. Graduated West Point, 1840. Participated in all important battles of Mexican War. Democratic governor of Louisiana, 1853–56.

HECHT, BEN (*b. New York, N.Y., 1894; d. New York, 1964*), journalist, writer, playwright, and screenwriter. As a reporter for the *Chicago Journal* and the *Chicago Daily News*, he gained a reputation as the best writer on this city and became part of the Chicago Renaissance. During this period wrote a variety of works, including the novels *Erik Dorn* (1921) and *Fantazius Mallare* (1922); the latter was banned as obscene. After moving to New York City in 1924, wrote *The Front Page* (1928) with Charles MacArthur; the play remains the best-known work of both men. An adept screenwriter, he wrote or collaborated on some seventy films, including *The Front Page* (1931), *Scarface* (1932), *Wuthering Heights* (1939), *Spellbound* (1945), *Notorious* (1946), and *A Farewell to Arms* (1958). Also wrote several hundred short stories and columns, two autobiographies—*A Child of the Century* (1954) and *Gaily Gaily* (1963)—and a biography of Charles MacArthur, *Charlie* (1957).

HECHT, SELIG (*b. Głogów, then Austrian Poland, 1892; d. New York, N.Y., 1947*), physiologist, biophysicist. Came to New York City with parents, 1898. B.S., College of the City of New York, 1913; Ph.D., Harvard, 1917. Taught physiology at medical school of Creighton University, 1917–21; worked during summers at Marine Biological Laboratory, Woods Hole, Mass. Fellowships in biology, 1921–26, enabled him to carry out research in Liverpool, at Harvard, at the zoological station in Naples, and at Cambridge University. He was associate professor of biophysics at Columbia University, 1926, professor, 1928–47. He and his students investigated visual functions, particularly in man, including dark adaptation, pattern vision, brightness discrimination, and color vision. He brought to the field of photoreception the concept that visual responses take place through physical and chemical processes amenable to quantitative study.

HECK, BARBARA (*b. Ballingrane, Ireland, 1734; d. Augusta, Canada, 1804*), "Mother of Methodism in America." Came to New York, 1760. Inspired Philip Embury to preach, 1766, thus beginning the Wesleyan movement in America.

HECKER, FRIEDRICH KARL FRANZ (*b. Eichtersheim, Germany, 1811; d. Summerfield, Ill., 1881*), German revolutionist, Union soldier, farmer.

HECKER, ISAAC THOMAS (*b. New York, N.Y., 1819; d. New York, 1888*), Roman Catholic priest, founder of the Paulists. Under influence of Orestes Brownson, studied philosophy, engaged in early labor and reform activities; was at Brook Farm, 1843; lived with Thoreau family. Became a Roman Catholic, 1844; was ordained a Redemptorist priest in London, 1849. Missionary to German immigrants in America, 1851–57, he was dismissed from the order for urging need of an English-speaking Redemptorist house. In 1858, with papal approval he founded the Paulist order in New York and served as its superior until his death. Father Hecker conceived of the Catholic Church as essentially democratic, hence uniquely suited to democratic America. He founded the *Catholic World*, 1865, and wrote *Questions of the Soul* (1852) and *Aspirations of Nature* (1857).

HECKEWELDER, JOHN GOTTLIEB ERNESTUS (*b. Bedford, England, 1743; d. Bethlehem, Pa., 1823*), missionary of the Moravian Church to the Indians of Ohio. Came to America, 1754. Served as a messenger to frontier Indian settlements, 1763–71. In his regular mission work as assistant to David Zeisberger, 1771–86, he lived with the Moravian Christian Indians, protecting them as they were forced westward. He served the U.S. government on commissions to arrange peace treaties with the frontier Indians, 1792–93, and recorded his views of Indian life in a number of important publications through which the story of colonial Indian affairs in the Ohio country received a proper perspective in history.

HECKSCHER, AUGUST (*b. Hamburg, Germany, 1848; d. near Lake Wales, Fla., 1941*), mine executive, real estate operator, philanthropist. Came to the United States, 1867, after apprenticeship in a Hamburg exporting firm; became manager of Pennsylvania coal properties owned by his cousins; made highly successful investments in zinc ore lands. Retiring from the mining industry, 1904, he had extraordinary success as an operator of real estate in midtown New York City. Among his philanthropies were the establishment of the Heckscher Foundation for Children (1921), and generous gifts for day nurseries, dental clinics, parks, and playgrounds.

HECTOR, FRANCISCO LUIS. See CARONDELET, FRANCISCO LUIS HECTOR, BARON DE.

HEDDING, ELIJAH (*b. Pine Plains, N.Y., 1780; d. Poughkeepsie, N.Y., 1852*). Methodist Episcopal bishop, 1824–52. One of foremost agents in extending Methodism in New England. Instrumental in founding *Zion's Herald*, Boston, 1823, earliest Methodist periodical.

HEDGE, FREDERIC HENRY (*b. Cambridge, Mass., 1805; d. Cambridge, 1890*), Unitarian clergyman, professor at Harvard. Son of Levi Hedge. Had early education in Germany; graduated Harvard, 1825. With R. W. Emerson and George Ripley, organized Transcendentalist group and imbued it with his own enthusiasm for German philosophy. Of his numerous publications, the most important is *Prose Writers of Germany* (1848), which helped to introduce German literature to America.

HEDGE, LEVI (*b. Warwick, Mass., 1766; d. 1844*), philosopher. Graduated Harvard, 1792; taught there, *post* 1795. His *Elements of Logick* (1816) was a remarkably clear, practical textbook which was far in advance of its time.

HEENAN, JOHN CARMEL (*b. West Troy, N.Y., 1835; d. Green River Station, Wyo., 1873*), pugilist, the "Benicia Boy."

HEFFELFINGER, WILLIAM WALTER ("PUDGE") (*b. Minneapolis, Minn., 1867; d. Blessing, Tex., 1954*), football player. Heffelfinger's legendary feats on the Yale football team (1889–91) earned him election to Walter Camp's All American team for three straight years. A lifetime football enthusiast, he published *This Was Football* in 1954.

HEFLIN, JAMES THOMAS (*b. Louina, Ala., 1869; d. Lafayette, Ala., 1951*), U.S. representative and senator. Alabama secretary of state, 1902–04; Democratic congressman, 1904–20; senator, 1920–30. A liberal in economic matters, but a religious and racial bigot. Heflin was opposed to women's voting rights; he introduced the House resolution creating Mother's Day in 1913. His political career was essentially ended when he refused to support the presidential candidacy of Al Smith in 1928 because of Smith's Catholicism.

HEGEMAN, JOHN ROGERS (*b. Brooklyn, N.Y., 1844; d. Mamaroneck, N.Y., 1919*), president, Metropolitan Life Insurance Co., 1891–1919.

HEILMANN, HARRY (*b. San Francisco, Calif., 1894; d. Detroit, Mich., 1951*), baseball player. First played for the Detroit Tigers in 1914 but played for San Francisco in 1915 because of a contract dispute. Again in Detroit, 1916–29. Cincinnati Reds,

1929–31. From 1934 to 1951, he was the radio broadcaster for the Detroit Tigers. One of baseball's great hitters, Heilman compiled a .342 batting average. Elected to the Baseball Hall of Fame in 1952.

HEILPRIN, ANGELO (*b. Sátoralja-Ujhely, Hungary, 1853; d. New York, N.Y., 1907*), geologist, paleontologist. Son of Michael Heilprin. Came to America as a child. Famous as a traveler, his explorations included Mexico, Alaska, British Guiana, North Africa, the West Indies, and the Arctic with Peary, 1891–92.

HEILPRIN, MICHAEL (*b. Piotrków, Poland, 1823; d. 1888*), scholar, writer, encyclopaedia expert. Came to America, 1856. Began lifelong encyclopaedia work on *New American Cyclopaedia*, 1858; was a valued contributor to the *Nation*.

HEINEMAN, DANIEL WEBSTER ("DANNIE") (*b. Charlotte, N.C., 1872; d. New York, N.Y., 1962*), engineer and industrialist. After graduating from Technical College of Hannover, in Germany (1895), joined the Union-Elektrizitäts-Gesellschaft, a Berlin company affiliated with General Electric. From 1905 to 1955 was chief executive of the Belgian firm Société Financière de Transports et d'Enterprises Industrielle (SOFINA). By the beginning of World War II SOFINA was recognized as one of the corporate giants of electrical equipment, and he as one of the human giants in that field.

HEINEMANN, ERNST (*b. Brunswick, Germany, 1848; d. Fort Wadsworth, N.Y., 1912*), wood engraver.

HEINRICH, ANTONY PHILIP (*b. Schönbüchel, Bohemia, 1781; d. New York, N.Y., 1861*), composer. Came to America, 1805. Led a wandering, erratic life, here and abroad. Published *The Dawning of Music in Kentucky* (1820), a collection of his compositions. He was presumably the first composer to essay "Americanism" in music, and to build a great part of his amazing output on American subjects.

HEINRICH, MAX (*b. Chemnitz, Germany, 1853; d. 1916*), concert baritone. Came to America, 1873. A pioneer in cultivating taste for German lieder.

HEINTZELMAN, SAMUEL PETER (*b. Manheim, Pa., 1805; d. Washington, D.C., 1880*), soldier. Graduated West Point, 1826. Distinguished for gallantry in Mexican War and on Far West frontier duty. As division and corps commander under McClellan, 1862, he lacked initiative and magnified difficulties; his subsequent Civil War service was administrative. Retired as major general, 1869.

HEINTZELMAN, STUART (*b. New York, N.Y., 1876; d. Hot Springs, Ark., 1935*), army officer. Grandson of Samuel P. Heintzelman. Graduated West Point, 1899. Served in Philippine insurrection and Boxer uprising; chief of staff, II Army, World War I. Skilled in training of officers. Promoted major general, 1931.

HEINZ, HENRY JOHN (*b. Pittsburgh, Pa., 1844; d. Pittsburgh, 1919*), manufacturer of prepared food. Founded F. and J. Heinz, 1876 (H. J. Heinz Co., 1888); was a pioneer in the pure-food movement in America; invented advertising slogan "57 Varieties."

HEINZE, FREDERICK AUGUSTUS (*b. Brooklyn., N.Y., 1869; d. Saratoga Springs, N.Y., 1914*), copper miner, speculator. Graduated Columbia School of Mines, 1889. Engaged in successful operations at Butte, Mont., 1892–1906. Lost epic struggle for control of the industry to the Amalgamated Copper Co.

HEINZEN, KARL PETER (*b. Grevenbroich, Rhenish Prussia, 1809; d. 1880*), German revolutionist, journalist, satirist. Resided in America *post* 1850; settled in Boston, 1859. Most intellectual of the German revolutionist exiles, his work became known only to a few. Editor of a radical weekly, the *Pionier*, 1854–79.

HEISS, MICHAEL (*b. Pfahldorf, Bavaria, 1818; d. Milwaukee, Wis., 1890*), Roman Catholic clergyman. Studied under Görres, Döllinger, and Moehler at Munich. Came to America, 1842, and served as pastor and missionary to Germans in Wisconsin. First bishop of La Crosse, 1868–80; archbishop of Milwaukee, 1880–90. Helped establish Catholic University, Washington, D.C.

HELBRON, PETER (*b. Hilbringen, Germany, 1739; d. Carlisle, Pa., 1816*), Roman Catholic clergyman, Capuchin. Came to Pennsylvania, 1787. Pastor in Philadelphia, 1791–96. His later missionary journeys covered all western Pennsylvania and as far as Buffalo; he organized the first congregation at Pittsburgh.

HELBURN, THERESA (*b. New York, N.Y., 1887; d. Norwalk, Conn., 1959*), theatrical producer and director. Studied at Bryn Mawr College and at Radcliffe College. After a few years of writing poetry and plays, Helburn joined the Theatre Guild in 1919; she became executive secretary in 1920 and served as executive director until 1958. Under her leadership, the Guild premiered many of Shaw's works in the U.S., as well as plays by Maxwell Anderson, Eugene O'Neill, and the Rodgers and Hammerstein musical *Oklahoma!* (1943).

HELD, JOHN, JR. (*b. Salt Lake City, Utah, 1889; d. Belmar, N.J., 1958*), cartoonist, illustrator, writer, and artist. Self-educated, Held is remembered for his stylized illustrations of the Flapper during the 1920's. He illustrated F. Scott Fitzgerald's *Tales of the Jazz Age*. His stylish illustrations appeared in most leading periodicals of the time: The *New Yorker*, *Life*, *Liberty*, and *Harper's Bazaar*. His books include *The Saga of Frankie and Johnnie* (1930) and *The Works of John Held, Jr.* (1932).

HELFFENSTEIN, JOHN ALBERT CONRAD *b. Mosbach, Germany, 1748; d. Germantown, Pa., 1790*), German Reformed clergyman. Came to America, 1772; won fame for the eloquence and pungency of his sermons. Served congregations at Lancaster and Germantown, Pa., 1772–90.

HELLER, MAXIMILIAN (*b. Prague, Bohemia, 1860; d. 1929*), rabbi. Came to America, 1879. Graduated University of Cincinnati, 1882; Hebrew Union College, 1884. Pastor of Temple Sinai, New Orleans, 1887–1927. A leader in reform movements and an early Zionist, he was also professor of Hebrew language and literature at Tulane University, 1912–28.

HELLER, ROBERT. *See* PALMER, WILLIAM HENRY.

HELM, CHARLES JOHN (*b. Hornellsvile, N.Y., 1817; d. Toronto, Canada, 1868*), U.S. consul general, 1858–61, and later Confederate agent at Havana, Cuba.

HELM, JOHN LARUE (*b. near Elizabethtown, Ky., 1802; d. 1867*), lawyer, Kentucky legislator. Whig governor of Kentucky, 1850–51; Democratic governor-elect, 1867. President, Louisville and Nashville Railroad, 1854–60.

HELMER, BESSIE BRADWELL (*b. Chicago, Ill., 1858; d. Battle Creek, Mich., 1927*), lawyer, editor, publisher. An important figure in the growth of the American Association of University Women.

HELMPRAECHT, JOSEPH (*b. Niederwinkling, Bavaria, 1820; d. New York, N.Y., 1884*), Roman Catholic clergyman, Redemptorist. Came to America, 1843; served German congregations in Baltimore, Md., Buffalo, N.Y., and elsewhere. American provincial of his order, 1865–77.

HELMUTH, JUSTUS HENRY CHRISTIAN (*b. Helmstedt, Germany, 1745; d. 1825*), Lutheran clergyman. Came to America, 1769. Pastor at Lancaster, Pa., 1769–79; co-pastor of St. Michael's and Zion's, Philadelphia, 1779–1820. Founded *Evangelisches Magazin*, 1812, first Lutheran Church paper in the United States.

HELMUTH, WILLIAM TOD (*b. Philadelphia, Pa., 1833; d. 1902*), surgeon. Great-grandson of Justus H. C. Helmuth. An important figure in teaching and practice of homeopathy in St. Louis, Philadelphia, and New York; edited several homeopathic journals; contributed extensively to literature of medicine and surgery.

HELPER, HINTON ROWAN (*b. Rowan, now Davie, Co., N.C., 1829; d. Washington, D.C., 1909*), author, businessman. Published *The Impending Crisis* (1857), a brief in behalf of non-slaveholding Southern whites in which he attributed the South's economic backwardness to impoverishment of free labor by slavery. Furiously attacked in the South, the book caused a greater sensation than *Uncle Tom's Cabin* and was a powerful contributing cause of the Civil War. Helper was consul at Buenos Aires, 1861–66. Interested in commercial relations with South America, he tried to promote a railroad from Hudson Bay to the Strait of Magellan and almost monomaniacally sacrificed everything to this dream. He died, despondent, by suicide.

HEMENWAY, MARY PORTER TILESTON (*b. New York, N.Y., 1820; d. 1894*), philanthropist. Aided freedmen; instituted sewing, cooking, gymnastics in Boston schools; contributed lavishly to save Old South Meeting House, Boston, and to promote study of U.S. history and ethnology.

HEMINGWAY, ERNEST MILLER (*b. Oak Park, Ill, 1899; d. Ketchum, Idaho, 1961*), novelist and short-story writer. After graduation from high school, worked briefly as cub reporter for the *Kansas City Star* in Missouri. Prevented from enlisting in the armed forces by a congenital eyesight deficiency, volunteered to drive ambulances for the American Red Cross in Italy and was severely wounded on 8 July 1918. After the war returned to the Middle West, beginning to write serious fiction while doing journalistic work. Married Elizabeth Hadley Richardson in 1921 and sailed to France with letters of introduction from Sherwood Anderson to such famous American expatriates as Ezra Pound and Gertrude Stein. Worked in France as foreign correspondent for the *Toronto Star* while writing poems and short stories.

In 1923 three stories and ten poems were published in Paris by Robert McAlmon, and in 1924 eighteen miniature short stories were published as *In Our time* by William Bird's Three Mountains Press. Edmund Wilson's laudatory review of the two Paris chapbooks opened the way for publication in America, and Horace Liveright of the New York house of Boni and Liveright agreed to publish *In Our Time*, containing fourteen short stories interfoliated with the miniatures from *In Our Time*. When Liveright accepted *The Sun Also Rises* but rejected *The Torrents of Spring*, a satirical attack on Sherwood Anderson, Hemingway entered into a contract with Scribner's who published both works. *The Sun Also Rises* (1926) was met with considerable acclaim.

In 1927 divorced Hadley and married Pauline Pfeiffer. Moved to Key West, Fla., where he eventually bought a home at 907 Whitehead Street, and wrote *A Farewell to Arms*. His next novel, *Death in the Afternoon* received mixed reviews. An African safari provided him with the material for *Green Hills of Africa* (1935), a nonfiction narrative that received adverse reviews. He turned to fishing on his boat, the *Pilar*, and wrote "The Snows of

Kilimanjaro," "The Short Happy Life of Francis Macomber," and *To Have and Have Not* (1937).

Upon the outbreak of the Spanish Civil War, returned to Spain, where he wrote feature stories for the North American Newspaper Alliance; worked on a propaganda film, *The Spanish Earth*; and wrote *The Fifth Column*, a melodrama of counterespionage in besieged Madrid. In 1940 bought a house in Cuba, which became a fairly permanent home for the rest of his life; divorced Pauline and married Martha Gellhorn; and published *For Whom the Bell Tolls*, the most successful of his books through 1940. During World War II assisted the war effort in Cuba and the Caribbean, went to England to report for *Collier's* on the activities of the Royal Air Force, and participated in the drive to liberate Paris. Divorced Martha in 1945 and married Mary Welsh in 1946.

His next work, *Across the River and into the Trees* (1950), was not well received, but in 1953 he won the Pulitzer Prize for *The Old Man and the Sea* (1952); the novella was part of a much longer novel, *Islands in the Stream* (1970). After trips to Spain and Africa in 1953–54, began to suffer ill health and was too ill to attend the Stockholm ceremony at which he was awarded the Nobel Prize in 1954. The ensuing years were dogged by recurrent illness, at first physical and at last mental, with severe paranoid symptoms beginning around June 1960. Managed to write *A Moveable Feast* (1964), a series of sketches on his life in Paris in 1921–26, but after being hospitalized and given electric shock therapy twice in 1960–61, on 2 July 1961 took his life with a double-barreled shotgun in the foyer of the house he had bought at Ketchum, Idaho.

As one of America's greatest writers, his influence on other writers has been vast and pervasive, and his works continue to be read by millions of readers.

HEMMETER, JOHN CONRAD (*b. Baltimore, Md., 1863; d. Baltimore, 1931*), physiologist, musical composer. Made early, possibly first, use of Roentgen rays to study the stomach; invented method of intubating the duodenum. M.D., University of Maryland, 1884; Ph.D., Johns Hopkins, 1890.

HEMPEL, CHARLES JULIUS (*b. Solingen, Germany, 1811; d. 1879*), homeopathic physician, author, translator. Came to America, 1835. Graduated M.D., University of the City of New York, 1845. Author of *A New and Comprehensive System of Materia Medica and Therapeutics* (1850).

HEMPHILL, JOHN (*b. near Blackstock, S.C., 1803; d. 1862*), Texas jurist. Removed to Texas, 1838. Chief justice of Texas Supreme Court, 1840–58, he was called "the John Marshall of Texas" for his wisdom in reconciliation of the civil and common law systems there. He served as U.S. senator, 1858–61.

HEMPHILL, JOSEPH (*b. Thornbury Township, Pa., 1770; d. 1842*), lawyer, Philadelphia jurist. Congressman, Federalist, from Pennsylvania, 1801–03; Democrat, 1819–27, 1829–31. Opponent of slavery.

HEMPL, GEORGE (*b. Whitewater, Wis., 1859; d. 1921*), philologist. Graduated University of Michigan, 1879; Ph.D., Jena, 1889. Taught at Michigan, 1889–1906; at Leland Stanford, 1907–21. Published extensively on etymology and usage; studied American dialects.

HENCH, PHILIP SHOWALTER (*b. Pittsburgh, Pa., 1896; d. St. Ann's Bay, Jamaica, 1965*), physician and rheumatologist. Teacher, researcher, and consultant for the Mayo Clinic, 1921–57. A pioneer in the treatment of chronic rheumatism and arthritis, he established that these were among the most severe medical problems in the world. He took part in organizing Ligue International Contre le Rheumatisme, and was a founder and president, 1940–41, of the American Rheumatism Association.

Helped compile and edit the annual *Rheumatism Review* of the American Rheumatism Association, the first issue of which appeared in 1935. With Edward C. Kendall and Tadeus Reichstein, was awarded the 1950 Nobel Prize in physiology or medicine for their discoveries of the effects of 17-hydroxy-11-dehydrocorticosterone (cortisone) in the treatment of rheumatism.

HENCHMAN, DANIEL (*b. Boston, Mass., 1689; d. 1761*), merchant, colonial bookseller, importer, and manufacturer whose records shed a valuable light on colonial commerce. Maternal grandfather of John Hancock.

HENCK, JOHN BENJAMIN (*b. Philadelphia, Pa., 1815; d. Montecito, Calif., 1903*), engineer, educator. Supervised at first with W. S. Whitwell, the filling-in, planning, and paving of Boston's Back Bay, 1855–81. Head of civil engineering department, Massachusetts Institute of Technology, 1865–81.

HENDEL, JOHN WILLIAM (*b. Dürkheim, Germany, 1740; d. Philadelphia, Pa., 1798*), German Reformed clergyman. Came to America, 1765. Held pastorates at Lancaster, Tulpehocken, and Philadelphia, Pa.

HENDERSON, ARCHIBALD (*b. Granville Co., N.C., 1768; d. Salisbury, N.C., 1822*), lawyer. Son of Richard Henderson. Congressman, Federalist, from North Carolina, 1799–1803; was one of the ablest lawyers of his time.

HENDERSON, CHARLES RICHMOND (*b. Covington, Ind., 1848; d. Charleston, S.C., 1915*), Baptist clergyman, sociologist. After pastorates in Terre Haute, Ind., and Detroit, he served as university chaplain and sociology professor at the University of Chicago, 1892–1915. Many of his books and articles were of pioneer importance in penology, industrial insurance and industrial legislation. They include *Introduction to the Study of the Dependent, Defective and Delinquent Classes* (1893); *Modern Methods of Charity* (1904); *Industrial Insurance in the United States* (1907).

HENDERSON, DANIEL McINTYRE (*b. Glasgow, Scotland, 1851; d. Baltimore, Md., 1906*), bookseller, poet. Came to America, 1873. Proprietor, University Book Store, Baltimore. Author of *Poems, Scottish and American* (1888); *A Bit Bookie of Verse* (1905).

HENDERSON, DAVID BREMNER (*b. Old Deer, Scotland, 1840; d. Dubuque, Iowa, 1906*), Iowa pioneer, Union soldier, lawyer. Came to America as a child; raised in Illinois and Fayette Co., Iowa. Congressman, Republican, from Iowa, 1883–1903; speaker of House, 1899–1903. An ardent "stand–patter."

HENDERSON, FLETCHER HAMILTON (*b. Cuthbert, Ga., 1897; d. New York, N.Y., 1952*), band leader and arranger. Leading his own band from 1921 to 1939, Henderson was the first black to achieve national success with a big jazz band. His band featured such artists as Ethel Waters, Louis Armstrong, and Coleman Hawkins and played regularly at the Roseland Ballroom in New York for twenty-four years. From 1939 to 1941 and 1947 to 1950, he was an arranger for Benny Goodman, helping to make Goodman's band the most successful in the "swing era."

HENDERSON, JAMES PINCKNEY (*b. Lincoln Co., N.C., 1808; d. Washington, D.C., 1858*), lawyer, first governor of Texas. Fought in Texas War for independence and Mexican War. Attorney general of Texas Republic and secretary of state; performed important service as Texas agent to England and France, 1837–39. Governor, 1846–47; U.S. senator, 1857–58.

HENDERSON, JOHN (*b. Bridgeton, N.J., 1795; d. Pass Christian, Miss., 1857*), lawyer. Removed as a young man to Missis-

sippi. U.S. senator, Whig, from Mississippi, 1839–45. Stood trial, 1851, for his support of Lopez in filibustering expeditions against Spanish authorities in Cuba.

HENDERSON, JOHN BROOKS (*b. Danville, Va., 1826; d. Washington, D.C., 1913*), lawyer. Removed to Missouri as a child. Served as democrat in state legislature; was in 1861 one of most influential anti-secession forces in Missouri. Appointed U.S. senator, 1862, he was elected for a full term as a Republican, 1863. He quickly became prominent, served on important committees and was responsible for much of the Civil War financial legislation. His great test of courage came in the impeachment trial of President Johnson. A severe critic of Johnson, he voted "not guilty," and was denounced by the Missouri radicals. He returned to practice law in St. Louis and in 1889 retired to Washington, D.C.

HENDERSON, LAWRENCE JOSEPH (*b. Lynn, Mass., 1878; d. Boston, Mass., 1942*), biochemist, physiologist. He attended public schools in Salem and Harvard; A.B., 1898. An interest in biochemistry led him to the Harvard Medical School; M.D., 1902. After two years in Strassburg, he returned to Harvard Medical School as lecturer in biological chemistry. He also began research on heats of combustion of organic molecules in relation to their structure. He returned to Harvard College in 1910 where he remained for the rest of his life. From 1907 to 1910 Henderson was concerned with the balance between acids and bases in the animal organism—the buffer action—and was the first to recognize its importance for all aspects of life. His work on blood, however, was his greatest contribution to biochemistry, and in 1928 he published his comprehensive book *Blood: A Study in General Physiology*. Henderson taught Harvard's first course in the history of science and brought George Sarton to Cambridge.

HENDERSON, LEONARD (*b. Granville Co., N.C., 1772; d. 1833*), jurist. Son of Richard Henderson. Judge of North Carolina Superior Court, 1808–16; supreme court, 1818–33; chief justice, 1829–33. Had great influence as a teacher, conducting a law school in connection with his law office.

HENDERSON, PAUL (*b. Lyndon, Kans., 1884; d. Washington, D.C., 1951*), airmail pioneer and airline executive. After a successful business career in Chicago, Henderson was appointed second assistant postmaster general for the fledgling airmail service, 1922–25. Responsible for the introduction of lighted airfields, he introduced night airmail in 1924 and made the service profitable. In 1925 he joined National Air Transport which was absorbed by United Airlines in 1928. In 1934, he and many other airline officials were forced to resign because of alleged irregularities in the awarding of airmail contracts.

HENDERSON, PETER (*b. Pathhead, Scotland, 1822; d. 1890*), horticulturist, seed merchant. Came to America, 1843. Established New York seed and garden supply house, Peter Henderson & Co. Among his numerous books were *Gardening for Profit* (1866); *Gardening for Pleasure* (1875, 1888); *Henderson's Hand Book of Plants* (1881). He also exerted great influence in his field through a very large personal correspondence.

HENDERSON, RAY (*b. Raymond Brost, Buffalo, N.Y., 1896; d. Greenwich, Conn., 1970*), composer. After adopting the professional name Ray Henderson in 1920, collaborated with a number of different lyricists to create a series of eminently singable and danceable songs that captured the spirit of the post–World War I years, including "That Old Gang of Mine," with lyrics by Billy Rose and Mort Dixon (1923), and "Five Foot Two, Eyes of Blue," with Sam M. Lewis and Joe Young (1925). Is best known for his collaborations with Buddy De Sylva and Lew Brown; the trio's career is depicted in the 1956 film *The Best Things in Life Are*

Free. Writing for numerous Broadway shows and Hollywood films of the late 1920's and early 1930's, the trio produced such well-known songs as "The Birth of the Blues" (1926), "The Varsity Drag" (1927), "The Best Things in Life are Free" (1927), "To Know You Is to Love You" (1928), "Sonny Boy" (1928), and "Button Up Your Overcoat" (1929). The trio broke up in the early 1930's, and thereafter Henderson joined forces with a succession of lyricists, including Ted Koehler and Irving Caesar, with whom he created the Shirley Temple favorite "Animal Crackers in My Soup" for the film *Curly Top* (1935).

HENDERSON, RICHARD (*b. Hanover Co., Va., 1735; d. Nutbush Creek, Granville Co., N.C., 1785*), lawyer, North Carolina jurist. As early as 1764, organized Richard Henderson & Co., a land company, with Daniel Boone as agent, and by 1769 was projecting a colony in Kentucky. In 1773, Henderson retired from his judgeship of the superior court to give full time to western colonization projects, organizing the Louisa (renamed the Transylvania) Company, 1774. In 1775, he signed a treaty at Sycamore Shoals with the Cherokees giving him title to a tract between the Kentucky and Cumberland rivers. Preceded by the trail-blazing Boone, Henderson went through Cumberland Gap and established the first settlement of his projected colony at Boonesborough. North Carolina and Virginia objected to the colony within their chartered limits, and the Revolution ended any chance of English support for the legality of the enterprise. Later, in 1779–80, Henderson promoted colonization in western Tennessee, establishing a settlement at French Lick, later Nashville.

HENDERSON, THOMAS (*b. Freehold, N.J., 1743; d. Freehold, 1824*), physician, Revolutionary soldier. Held many political offices in New Jersey, including acting-governor; was a Federalist congressman, 1795–97.

HENDERSON, WILLIAM JAMES (*b. Newark, N.J., 1855; d. New York, N.Y., 1937*), outstanding music critic of the *New York Times*, 1887–1902, and of the New York *Sun*, 1902–37.

HENDERSON, YANDELL (*b. Louisville, Ky., 1873; d. San Diego, Calif., 1944*), physiologist, toxicologist. Graduated Yale, 1895; Ph.D. in physiological chemistry, 1898; studied also at universities of Marburg and Munich. Taught physiology at Yale Medical School, 1900–21. His early research on the physiology of circulation led him to question current theories of the action of the heart and, in turn, to investigate the physiological role of carbon dioxide in respiration. His studies led to his famous "acapnia theory of shock." He pointed out the role of severe pain in stimulating overventilation and described experiments that led the way to the clinical use of a mixture of carbon dioxide and oxygen after anesthesia. The theory was eventually discarded, but not before he had used it as the basis for his pioneer studies of ventilation, noxious gases, and resuscitation.

HENDRICK (*b. ca. 1680; d. at battle of Lake George, 1755*), Mohawk sachem. His Indian name, Tiyonoga. As spokesman for the Mohawk, his friendship was cultivated by William Johnson and the English colonial governors. Active in his efforts to hold the Six Nations to the English interest against the French menace, he represented his tribe at the numerous councils between the English and the Six Nations which culminated in the Albany Congress of 1754. There he delivered the greatest speech of his career, taking the English to task for neglecting their border defenses and leaving the Mohawk exposed to French reprisals. In the summer of 1755, he lost his life while leading a force of Mohawks in William Johnson's expedition against Crown Point.

HENDRICK, BURTON JESSE (*b. New Haven, Conn., 1870; d. New York, N.Y., 1949*), journalist, author. B.A., Yale, 1895;

M.A., 1897. Reporter on New York *Evening Post*, 1899–1905; on staff of *McClure's Magazine*, 1905–13; chief editorial writer for *World's Work*, 1913–27. Author of a number of factually accurate, detailed, but uncritical biographies, edited memoirs, and popular studies in American history, which had wide popularity, 1920–40.

HENDRICK, ELLWOOD (*b. Albany, N.Y., 1861; d. New York, N.Y., 1930*), chemist, broker, author.

HENDRICKS, THOMAS ANDREWS (*b. near Zanesville, Ohio, 1819; d. Indianapolis, Ind., 1885*), lawyer, Indiana legislator. Nephew of William Hendricks. Raised in Shelby Co., Ind. Congressman, Democrat, from Indiana, 1851–55; commissioner, general land office, 1855–59. As U.S. senator from Indiana, 1863–69, won prominence as a leader of the Democratic opposition, a constant critic of every administration policy. He supported Johnson's plan of reconstruction but opposed the 14th and 15th Amendments. Governor of Indiana, 1873–77, one of the first Democratic governors of a Northern state after the Civil War. Vice president of the United States, 1885.

HENDRICKS, WILLIAM (*b. Ligonier, Pa., 1782; d. Madison, Ind., 1850*), lawyer, Indiana legislator. Removed to Indiana, 1813; was congressman, Democrat, 1816–22, and governor of Indiana, 1822–25. As U.S. senator, 1825–37, he was interested especially in development of roads and canals, and in the cession of public lands to the individual states.

HENDRIX, EUGENE RUSSELL (*b. Fayette, Mo., 1847; d. Kansas City, Mo., 1927*), clergyman of Methodist Episcopal Church, South. Was engaged mainly in administrative work; bishop, 1886–1927. Brother of Joseph C. Hendrix. First president, Federal Council of Churches of Christ in America, 1908–12.

HENDRIX, JIMI (*b. James Marshall Hendrix, Seattle, Wash., 1942; d. London, England, 1970*), guitarist, singer, and songwriter. Played with a number of popular bands in the 1960's before forming his own band, the Jimi Hendrix Experience. In 1968 was named artist of the year by both *Billboard* and *Rolling Stone*, with *Playboy* adding its voice the following year. In 1969 formed the all-black Band of Gypsies, which made its debut at the Fillmore East in New York City and produced one album. An innovator of the improvisatory style known as heavy metal, his major singles include Bob Dylan's "All Along the Watchtower" and "Like A Rolling Stone," and his most popular albums were *Are You Experienced?*, *Electric Ladyland*, and *Axis: Bold as Love*. Died of drug-related causes.

HENDRIX, JOSEPH CLIFFORD (*b. Fayette, Mo., 1853; d. Brooklyn, N.Y., 1904*), banker. Brother of Eugene R. Hendrix. Congressman, Democrat, from New York, 1893–95. President, National Bank of Commerce, New York, 1900–03.

HENEY, FRANCIS JOSEPH (*b. Lima, N.Y., 1859; d. Santa Monica, Calif., 1937*), lawyer. Raised in San Francisco. Practiced first in Arizona Territory; *post* 1895 in California. Prosecuted Oregon land frauds, 1903, and Abe Ruef, 1906–08. Progressive politician, pro-labor, he was long at feud with Hiram Johnson.

HENIE, SONJA (*b. Oslo, Norway, 1912; d. on a plane to Oslo, Norway, 1969*), ice skater and film actress. After 1927, won ten world championships, seven European championships, and Olympic gold medals at St. Moritz (1928), Lake Placid (1932), and Garmisch-Partenkirchen (1936). By incorporating music and dance into the free-skating portion of her routine, she revolutionized figure skating. In 1936 began appearing in motion pictures designed to showcase her skating talent and Nordic beauty.

By 1939 only Clark Gable and Shirley Temple outranked her as a box-office attraction, and in 1937 King Haakon of Norway made her the fifth woman and the youngest person ever to be named a Knight First Class of the Order of St. Olav. Her later films continued to draw sellout crowds, and she earned huge profits with her touring *Hollywood Ice Review* (1937–51) and her *Sonja Henie with Her 1952 Ice Revue*, after which her performances were largely limited to occasional appearances on television. Became a U.S. citizen in 1941. Wrote an autobiography, *Wings on My Feet* (1940).

HENING, WILLIAM WALLER (*b. probably Spotsylvania Co., Va., 1767/68; d. Richmond, Va., 1828*), legal writer. Edited *The Statutes at Large; Being a Collection of All the Laws of Virginia* (13 vols., 1809–23), at instance of Thomas Jefferson.

HENKEL, PAUL (*b. Rowan Co., N.C., 1754; d. New Market, Va., 1825*), Lutheran clergyman. The greatest Lutheran home missionary of his generation; traveled each year through Virginia, North Carolina, Tennessee, Kentucky, Ohio, and Indiana.

HENLEY, ROBERT (*b. Williamsburg, Va., 1783; d. Sullivan's Island, S.C., 1828*), naval officer. Second in command to Commodore Macdonough at battle of Lake Champlain, September 1814, he aggressively commanded the brig *Eagle*.

HENNEPIN, LOUIS (*b. Ath, Flemish province of Hainaut, 1640; d. post 1701*), Recollect friar. Missionary in Canada, 1675–82. Accompanied La Salle, 1679, on his expedition through the Great Lakes into the Illinois country; explored the upper Mississippi, 1680. Captured by Sioux, he was rescued by Duluth after traveling over much of Minnesota. On his return to France, he published *Description de la Louisiane* (Paris, 1683), called "the most minute of all narratives of early American exploration." Two later books, *Nouveau Voyage* (Antwerp, 1696) and *Nouvelle Découverte* (Utrecht, 1697), the latter of which appeared in English as *A New Discovery* (1698), also deal with his North American travels but are filled with false claims. His works have charm and graphic quality but are marred by his garrulity, vanity, mendacity, and appropriating without credit what others had written. He was in Rome in 1701; after that no trace of him has been found.

HENNESSY, JOHN (*b. Bulgaden, Ireland, 1825; d. Dubuque, Iowa, 1900*), Roman Catholic clergyman. Came to America, 1847. Ordained, St. Louis, Mo., 1850. Bishop of Dubuque, 1866–93; archbishop, 1893–1900. Staunch advocate of parochial schools.

HENNESSY, WILLIAM JOHN (*b. Thomastown, Ireland, 1839; d. 1917*), painter, illustrator. Came to America as a child. Successful landscape and genre painter, he made his mark particularly as an illustrator of the works of Tennyson, Longfellow, Whittier, and other 19th-century classic authors.

HENNI, JOHN MARTIN (*b. Misanenga, Switzerland, 1805; d. Milwaukee, Wis., 1881*), Roman Catholic clergyman. Came to America, 1828. Ordained 1829; was pastor in Cincinnati, Ohio. Founded *Wahrheitsfreund*, Cincinnati, 1837, first American German Catholic newspaper. Consecrated bishop of Milwaukee, 1844; archbishop, 1875.

HENNINGSEN, CHARLES FREDERICK (*b. probably Belgium, 1815; d. Washington, D.C., 1877*), soldier, author. Fought in Spain, Caucasus, Hungary; came to America with Kossuth, 1851. Joined William Walker in filibuster to Nicaragua, 1856. Colonel, 59th Virginia Infantry, 1861–62. Wrote extensively on historical and cultural subjects.

HENNY, DAVID CHRISTIAAN (*b. Arnhem, Netherlands, 1860; d. 1935*), hydraulic engineer. Came to America, 1884. Authority on the construction of dams and inventor of the "Henny shear joint" used at Boulder and Grand Coulee dams.

HENRI, ROBERT (*b. Cincinnati, Ohio, 1865; d. New York, N.Y., 1929*), painter, teacher. Studied at Pennsylvania Academy of Fine Arts under T.P. Anschutz and in Paris under Bougereau and Fleury. Taught successfully at Women's School of Design, Philadelphia, Pa., the Art Students League, and other schools, laying emphasis on visual honesty, avoiding imitation and being true to one's self. Associated with John Sloan, A. B. Davies, George Luks, Maurice Prendergast, Shinn, Glackens, and Lawson in the group of realists known as "The Eight." *The Art Spirit* (1923) was compiled from Henri's essays and classroom notes; like his painting, the writing is sketchy but vital. The chief merit of his art is its naturalness and spontaneity.

HENRICI, ARTHUR TRAUTWEIN (*b. Economy, later Ambridge, Pa., 1889; d. Minneapolis, Minn., 1943*), bacteriologist, microbiologist. Graduated University of Pittsburgh Medical School, 1911. Taught at University of Minnesota, 1913–43; professor, *post* 1925. His primary scientific interests lay in the morphology and taxonomy of microorganisms and of certain higher forms such as yeasts and molds. His *Morphologic Variation and the Rate of Growth of Bacteria* (1928) brought order into that then chaotic area of bacteriology and offered fresh points of view; he was author also of *Molds, Yeasts, and Actinomycetes* (1930), and *The Biology of Bacteria* (1934) which was widely used as a college text. He made additional contributions to knowledge of the ecology and taxonomy of freshwater and saltwater microorganisms.

HENROTIN, CHARLES (*b. Belgium, 1843; d. Chicago, Ill., 1914*), banker. Brother of Fernand Henrotin. Came to America as a child. A leader in organizing the Chicago Stock Exchange, he was its first president, 1882–84.

HENROTIN, FERNAND (*b. Brussels, Belgium, 1847; d. 1906*), surgeon. Brother of Charles Henrotin. Came to America as an infant. Graduated Rush Medical School, 1868. A founder of the Chicago Polyclinic. Achieved international reputation in the field of operative gynecology and contributed to its literature.

HENRY, ALEXANDER (*b. New Brunswick, N.J., 1739; d. Montreal, Canada, 1824*), fur trader, explorer in the Great Lakes and Northwest area, 1760–76. Author of *Travels and Adventures* (1809).

HENRY, ALICE (*b. Richmond, Victoria, Australia, 1857; d. Melbourne, Australia, 1943*), journalist, labor leader. A feminist and ardent supporter of labor, she was resident in the United States, 1906–33 (except for a stay in England and Australia, 1924–25) and was associated with the National Women's Trade Union League in various capacities. She was editor of the League's monthly publication *Life and Labor*, 1911–15, and was author of *The Trade Union Woman* (1915) and *Women and the Labor Movement* (1923).

HENRY, ANDREW (*b. York Co., Pa., ca. 1775; d. Harmony Township, Mo., 1833*), fur trapper, lead miner. Removed to Missouri, 1800, and engaged in lead mining. Joined with Manuel Lisa, Pierre Chouteau, and others in St. Louis Missouri Fur Co., 1809. Left that year for the upper Missouri country and in 1810 was with Pierre Ménard in first organized invasion of the Three Forks region. That winter, after crossing the continental divide, he and his party descended Henry's Fork of the Snake River, the first American trappers to operate west of the Rockies. The venture was a failure and Henry returned to his lead mines, 1811. In 1822 he joined W. H. Ashley's first trapping expedition and spent the ensuing two years adventurously in the Western mountains. Discouraged by his lack of success, in 1824 he returned once again to St. Louis and his lead mines. He figures largely in the early annals of the frontier. Few trappers had wider renown as a hero.

HENRY, CALEB SPRAGUE (*b. Rutland, Mass., 1804; d. 1884*), Congregational and Episcopal clergyman, educator, author.

HENRY, EDWARD LAMSON (*b. Charleston, S.C., 1841; d. Ellenville, N.Y., 1919*), historical painter. Studied at Pennsylvania Academy of Fine Arts and in Paris under Gleyre and Courbet. Primarily an illustrator in oils, his pictures were accurate in the most minute detail. His major interest was in the life and customs of the United States, 1800–50.

HENRY, JOHN (*b. Dublin, Ireland, 1746; d. 1794*), actor, theatrical manager. A member of the so-called "Old American" company, partner of Lewis Hallam, 1785–94.

HENRY, JOHN (*b. Dorchester Co., Md., 1750; d. Dorchester Co., 1798*), lawyer. Maryland delegate to the Continental Congress, 1778–81, 1784–87; state senator, 1781–84; U.S. senator from Maryland, 1789–97; governor of Maryland, 1798.

HENRY, JOHN (*fl. 1807–1820*), adventurer. His secret reports on U.S. public opinion to the governor general of Canada, written in 1809, were sold to President Madison for $50,000 in 1811. Their publication influenced the declaration of war in 1812.

HENRY, JOSEPH (*b. Albany, N.Y., 1797; d. Washington, D.C., 1878*), investigator in physics, first secretary and director of the Smithsonian Institution. A graduate of Albany Academy, Henry worked as schoolteacher, private tutor, and surveyor before appointment as professor of mathematics at Albany Academy, 1826. He then took up research in the new field of the relation of electric currents to magnetism. His first notable success was the improvement of William Sturgeon's electromagnet. Henry's method of making magnets was at once adopted everywhere, and the electromagnets of the present day are precisely like those he designed. Discovering a difference in effect when coils were joined in parallel to the battery or successively in a series, he called these two types "quantity" and "intensity" magnets and pointed out as early as January 1831 in the *American Journal of Science* that the intensity magnet was the type to be used in the electromagnetic telegraph. By experiment in 1830 he had discovered the principle of self-induction but, failing to publish his findings, was anticipated by Faraday's announcement of the discovery made independently in 1831. The modern unit of inductance is called the henry in honor of his research. While at Albany, Henry invented an eletromagnetic motor, a little machine he called a "philosophical toy." In 1832 he became professor of natural philosophy at Princeton. His researches, 1838–42, on the induction of a current by another current anticipated modern developments in the science of electricity, notably the action of transformers. In his experiments with inductive effect from a Leyden-jar discharge, he came very near the fundamentals of wireless telegraphy. He is usually credited with discovering the oscillatory nature of a discharge through a spiral. He collaborated with Stephen Alexander in investigating solar radiation and the heat of sun spots and was also greatly interested in capillarity and the cohesion of liquids.

In 1846 he left Princeton to become the first secretary and director of the Smithsonian Institution. The development of the Institution followed the course marked out for it in his first report to the Board of Regents. In that report and afterward, he urged upon the Regents and upon Congress the importance of relieving the Institution of the burden of supporting the museum, art gallery, and library, so freeing the Smithson fund to promote and publish original research. As time went on, his wisdom in regard to these matters was recognized. His duties left him little time for further research in pure science. As director he initiated various enterprises, among them the system of receiving weather reports by telegraph and basing predictions on them. He helped organize the American Association for the Advancement of Science; he was an original member of the National Academy of Sciences and its president, 1868–78. He received many honorary degrees and honorary elections to scientific and literary societies. The Smithsonian Institution published *The Scientific Writings of Joseph Henry* (1886).

HENRY, MORRIS HENRY (*b. London, England, 1835; d. 1895*), physician, surgeon. Came to America, 1852. Graduated University of Vermont, M.D., 1860. Served as a naval surgeon in Civil War. Founded *American Journal of Syphilography and Dermatology*, 1870, a pioneer effort to bring awareness of importance of knowledge of skin and venereal diseases.

HENRY, O. *See* PORTER, WILLIAM SYDNEY.

HENRY, PATRICK (*b. Hanover Co., Va., 1736; d. Red Hill Plantation, Charlotte Co., Va., 1799*), lawyer, Revolutionary statesman, orator. Brought up among frontier farmers; educated at home. After failure as storekeeper and planter, he was licensed to practice law, 1760; opened an office at Hanover Courthouse and won immediate success. The case which brought him fame throughout the colony was one in the Parson's Cause series, 1763. Defending the constitutionality of the vestrymen's right to fix the price of tobacco with which the clergy of the established church were paid, Henry discoursed less upon the law in question than upon the clergy's declining to observe the law of their "country," and above all upon the encroachment of the Crown on the rights of Virginia freemen. On May 20, 1765, he became a member of the House of Burgesses and at once was engaged in a controversy over illegal use by the treasurer of the colony of paper money issued to support the recent war. He caused a strong alignment of the western and northern counties against the tidewater region. In arguing against the Stamp Act, May, 1765, Henry offered seven radical resolutions in a speech which closed with his famous comparison, "Caesar had his Brutus—Charles the first, his Cromwell—and George the third—may profit by their example." The resolutions were publicized in the other colonies and became the basis for violent agitation from Boston to Charleston. Leader of a new party, between 1765 and 1770 Henry was as complete a master of public life in Virginia as Samuel Adams was in Massachusetts. The Townshend Acts and the efforts at resistance which followed them enabled Henry to consolidate the opposition to Great Britain. In May 1774, Governor Dunmore dissolved the Assembly for declaring a day of prayer in sympathy with the closing of the port of Boston. The members assembled at Raleigh Tavern under Henry's leadership to ask all the colonies to meet in a continental congress and to call a Virginia convention, Aug. 1, 1774. At this convention, Henry and six others were chosen delegates to the First Continental Congress at Philadelphia. There he took an active part, always leaning toward radical measures and showing strong nationalist tendencies. On Mar. 23, 1775, at an assembly meeting in Richmond, he offered three resolutions, one of which provided for military defense of the colony. On this occasion he uttered his famous saying: "Give me liberty, or give me death." The colony was armed. In May 1775, after forcing Governor Dunmore to restore to the colony the gunpowder he had seized at Williamsburg, Henry went to the Second Continental Congress at Philadelphia but returned to Virginia in August to help put an army in the field. Appointed colonel of the first regiment, he was superseded in command by political opponents in the Assembly. Resigning his commission, February 1776, he went home to Hanover County. In May, at the Third Revolutionary Convention, he helped draft a new constitution for Virginia and on its completion in June was elected governor. He was twice reelected. As governor he sent George Rogers Clark in 1778 on a military mission to the Illinois country which resulted in expulsion of the British from the Northwest. In 1778–79, when there was intrigue to remove Washington from his command, Henry sent him evidence which defeated the movement. In 1779 Henry retired to Henry County and was succeeded in the governorship by his friend Thomas Jefferson.

In 1781 Henry joined in the criticism of Jefferson's conduct and began the feud which lasted the rest of their lives. To the surprise of his followers, he urged restoration of property to the Loyalists, 1783, proposed an onerous tariff, and opposed Madison's proposal to disestablish the church. As governor again, 1784–86, he opposed a treaty with Spain, seeing in it an alignment of the trading states against the South. He declined election to the Federal Convention. At the Virginia ratifying convention in October 1788, he vigorously led those opposed to adopting the new constitution. As his life drew on to an end, he became increasingly conservative. In October 1795 he refused Washington's offer of the office of secretary of state; three months later, when he also declined the position of chief justice, he made a speech declaring his admiration for Washington which created a sensation and led to fierce party warfare in Virginia. In January 1799, at Washington's request, Henry consented to become a Federalist candidate for the Virginia House of Delegates. He was elected, but death in June prevented his ever taking his seat.

HENRY, ROBERT (*b. Charleston, S.C., 1792; d. 1856*), Presbyterian and Episcopal clergyman, educator. From 1818 to 1856, except for a brief interval, he served South Carolina College, now University of South Carolina, as professor of various subjects and several times as president.

HENRY, WILLIAM (*b. West Caln, Chester Co., Pa., 1729; d. 1786*), gunsmith, Revolutionary patriot. Established a firearms factory at Lancaster, Pa., 1750, which brought him a fortune. An enthusiastic student of science, he made experiments with steam, and by 1763 completed a stern-wheel steamboat. Although its trial on Conestoga Creek was unsuccessful, he was the first person in America to make such an experiment and later encouraged Robert Fulton. Among others whom he aided was Benjamin West. He devised labor-saving machines for his gun factory, invented a screw auger and perfected a steam-heating system. He held important civil and military offices in Pennsylvania. Elected to the Continental Congress in 1784, he died in office.

HENRY, WILLIAM ARNON (*b. near Norwalk, Ohio, 1850; d. San Diego, Calif., 1932*), agriculturist. As professor of agriculture, University of Wisconsin, and dean of its College of Agriculture, he stressed value of silage and promoted efficient methods of raising livestock. Author of *Feeds and Feeding* (1898).

HENRY, WILLIAM WIRT (*b. Charlotte Co., Va., 1831; d. 1900*), lawyer, historian. Author of *Patrick Henry: Life, Correspondence and Speeches* (1891), a still valuable biography of his grandfather.

HENSHALL, JAMES ALEXANDER (*b. Baltimore, Md., 1836; d. Cincinnati, Ohio, 1925*), physician, naturalist. Associated with U.S. Bureau of Fisheries, 1896–1917. Published many books and articles on fish and fishing.

HENSHAW, DAVID (*b. Leicester, Mass., 1791; d 1852*), businessman, politician. Leader of Massachusetts Democrats, 1821–37, 1843–50. Secretary of the navy, July 1843 to February 1844.

HENSHAW, HENRY WETHERBEE (*b. Cambridge, Mass., 1850; d. Washington, D.C., 1930*), ornithologist, ethnologist. Naturalist, Wheeler Survey, 1872–79; associated with Bureau of Ethnology, 1879–93; chief, Bureau of Biological Survey, 1910–16. Contributed important papers on ornithology and ethnology to scientific journals.

HENSON, JOSIAH (*b. Charles Co., Md., 1789; d. Dresden, Canada, 1883*), slave, active in the service of his race, reputed original of Uncle Tom in H. B. Stowe's *Uncle Tom's Cabin*. With his wife and children escaped to Ontario, Canada, 1830. Tried to develop a black community there which failed because of an agent's incompetence. Published *The Life of Josiah Henson . . . Narrated by Himself* (1849); it appeared in subsequent editions with introductory material by H. B. Stowe.

HENSON, MATTHEW ALEXANDER (*b. Charles County, Md., 1886; d. New York, N.Y., 1955*), arctic explorer. A black, Henson became Admiral Robert E. Peary's valet and righthand man in 1887; in 1909, he accompanied Peary and four Eskimos to the North Pole. He received no official recognition until 1944 when he was awarded a medal by Congress. Henson was then granted membership in the Explorers Club, given two honorary degrees, and citations from Presidents Truman and Eisenhower.

HENTZ, CAROLINE LEE WHITING (*b. Lancaster, Mass., 1800; d. Marianna, Fla., 1856*). Author of a number of plays and novels including *Aunt Patty's Scrap Bag* (1846) and *The Planter's Northern Bride* (1854).

HEPBURN, ALONZO BARTON (*b. Colton, N.Y., 1846; d. 1922*), lawyer, banker, philanthropist. As a member of the New York legislature, he wrote the "Hepburn Report," 1879, a landmark in railroad history which influenced the Federal Interstate Commerce Act, 1887. He engaged in lumber and land operations, 1883–89, the foundation of his later fortune, was U.S. bank examiner in New York City, 1889–92, and comptroller of the currency, 1892–93. After holding several important posts in New York banks, he became vice president of the Chase National Bank, 1899. He was its president, 1904–11, and was chairman of board, 1911–22. He became an important international figure, playing a significant role in international diplomacy and finance. Of his many important writings, *A History of Currency in the United States: with a Brief Description of the Currency Systems of All Commercial Nations* (1915) is a classic. His philanthropies were widespread.

HEPBURN, JAMES CURTIS (*b. Milton, Pa., 1815; d. East Orange, N.J., 1911*), Presbyterian medical missionary. Graduated Princeton, 1832; University of Pennsylvania, M.D., 1836. In Malaya and China, 1843–45; in Japan, 1859–92.

HEPBURN, KATHARINE HOUGHTON (*b. Corning, N.Y., 1878; d. Hartford, Conn., 1951*), suffragist and birth control reformer. Studied at Bryn Mawr College (B.A., 1899; M.A. 1900). Mother of six children, one of them the famous actress Katharine Hepburn, she was an ardent fighter for woman suffrage, the end of white slavery, and birth control. Member of the Connecticut Women's Suffrage Association, 1913–18, resigning as president to join the militant Woman's Party; founded the Connecticut Birth Control Movement. In 1934, she served briefly as chairman of the National Committee on Federal Legislation for Birth Control, appearing before a House judiciary committee investigating penal laws for the disbursement of birth control methods. A strong advocate of an Equal Rights Amendment.

HEPBURN, WILLIAM PETERS (*b. Wellsville, Ohio, 1833; d. Clarinda, Iowa, 1916*), lawyer, Union soldier, politician. Raised in Iowa. As congressman, Republican, from Iowa, 1881–87, an opponent of "pork barrel" legislation and advocate of military pensions. He was solicitor of the treasury, 1889–93. In 1892 he was again a congressional candidate and was elected for eight consecutive terms. For 14 years chairman of the interstate and foreign commerce committee and 10 years on the Pacific railroads committee, his work culminated in the Hepburn Rate Law, 1906, his principal achievement. He was also joint author and leading advocate of the Pure Food and Drug Act of 1906.

HEPWORTH, GEORGE HUGHES (*b. Boston, Mass., 1833; d. 1902*). Unitarian and Congregational clergyman, journalist.

HERBERMANN, CHARLES GEORGE (*b. Saerbeck, Germany, 1840; d. New York, N.Y., 1916*), editor, educator, scholar. Came to America as a boy. Graduated St. John's College (Fordham), 1858. Professor of Latin, College of the City of New York, 1869–1914. Editor in chief, *The Catholic Encyclopedia*, 1905–13.

HERBERT, FREDERICK HUGH (*b. Vienna, Austria, 1897; d. Los Angeles, Calif., 1958*), writer. Immigrated to the U.S. in 1920. Author of the play *Kiss and Tell* (1943) which was the basis for the radio program "Meet Corliss Archer," produced by CBS (1943–55). Other works include *The Moon is Blue* (1951), which became a highly controversial film in 1953. Film scripts included *Scudda Hoo! Scudda Hay!* (1948) and *Our Very Own* (1949).

HERBERT, HENRY WILLIAM (*b. London, England, 1807; d. New York, N.Y., 1858*), writer. Graduated Caius College, Cambridge, 1830. Came to America, 1831. A classical scholar, he taught in New York City private schools. His literary output was prodigious and varied. He edited periodicals, made many translations from the French, wrote historical romances and histories. Under the pseudonym "Frank Forester," he began in 1839 in the *American Turf Register* the series of writings on field sports which constitute his chief claim to fame. Among his sporting books are *The Warwick Woodlands* (1845), *My Shooting Box* (1846), *Frank Forester's Field Sports* (London, 1848; New York, 1849), *Frank Forester's Horse and Horsemanship, etc.* (1857).

HERBERT, HILARY ABNER (*b. Laurensville, S.C., 1834; d. Tampa, Fla., 1919*), lawyer. Confederate soldier. Congressman, Democrat, from Alabama, 1877–93; secretary of the navy, 1893–97. Responsible for overcoming congressional opposition to a large navy.

HERBERT, VICTOR (*b. Dublin, Ireland, 1859; d. 1924*), musician. Came to America, 1886, with European reputation as a cellist. Played at Metropolitan Opera and with New York Philharmonic orchestra, and was later conductor of Pittsburgh Symphony. In 1894, with *Prince Ananias* he began his career as a composer of light opera. There followed a long list of immediately successful works which included *The Fortune Teller* (1898), *Babes in Toyland* (1903), *Mlle. Modiste* (1905), *The Red Mill* (1906) and *Naughty Marietta* (1910). He also wrote the musical scores for the Ziegfeld Follies of 1919, 1921 and 1924. His *Natoma* (1911) remains musically one of the best American grand operas. His non-dramatic compositions include a wide variety of musical forms. He attained a popularity which no other American composer had won despite the inadequate librettos with which he worked. He was a founder of the American Society of Composers, Authors and Publishers.

HERBST, JOSEPHINE FREY (*b. Sioux City, Iowa, 1892; d. New York, N.Y., 1969*), radical journalist and novelist. A member of New York City's radical community, in 1920 she began working for H. L. Mencken and George Jean Nathan as a reader for their magazines, which included the *Smart Set*, to which she sold two stories. Her first two novels, *Nothing Is Sacred* (1928) and *Money*

for Love (1929), were highly autobiographical; the first two volumes of her trilogy—*Pity Is Not Enough* (1933), *The Executioner Waits* (1934), and *Rope of Gold* (1939)—were well-received by the critics; and her other works include *Hunter of the Doves*, a novella centering on Nathanael West, and *New Green World* (1954), a biography of John and William Bartram. During the Depression, her politics moved leftward, and she began writing political articles for several radical magazines, including *New Masses*. In the 1930's she gained public attention for her coverage of the underground movement in Cuba, resistance to Hitler in Germany, and the Spanish Civil War.

HERDIC, PETER (*b. Fort Plains, N.Y., 1824; d. New York, N.Y., 1888*), lumberman. Patented, 1880, an improved vehicle, the "Herdic," for city and interurban transportation.

HERFORD, OLIVER BROOKE (*b. Sheffield, England, 1863; d. New York, N.Y., 1935*), author, illustrator, wit. Came to America as a boy. Contributed to *Century Magazine*, *Life*, *Harper's Weekly*, and others. Author of *An Alphabet of Celebrities* (1899), *The Rubáiyát of a Persian Kitten* (1904), *Cupid's Cyclopedia* (1910) and numerous other books.

HERGESHEIMER, JOSEPH (*b. Philadelphia, Pa., 1880; d. Sea Isle City, N.J., 1954*), novelist, short story writer. Studied at Pennsylvania Academy of Fine Arts. From 1914 to 1934, he published some two dozen books including *The Lay Anthony* (1914), *The Three Black Pennies* (1917), *Java Head* (1919), and *The Foolscap Rose* (1934). Using a luxuriant, highly mannered style, his prose was reminiscent of the fin de siècle manner.

HERING, CARL (*b. Philadelphia, Pa., 1860; d. Philadelphia, 1926*), electrical engineer. Son of Constantine Hering.

HERING, CONSTANTINE (*b. Oschatz, Saxony, 1800; d. Philadelphia, Pa., 1880*), physician, a founder of homeopathy in the United States. Educated at Dresden and Leipzig; M.D. Würzburg, 1826. Came to America, 1833. Founder of Hahnemann Medical College, Philadelphia, 1867. Author of *Guiding Symptoms* (10 vols., 1878–91).

HERING, RUDOLPH (*b. Philadelphia, Pa., 1847; d. New York, N.Y., 1923*), pioneer sanitary engineer. Son of Constantine Hering. Graduated Royal Polytechnical School, Dresden, Germany, 1867. After working as civil engineer, he was assistant city engineer at Philadelphia, 1876–80. Because of yellow fever in American cities, the National Board of Health sent him to Europe to study sewage disposal. His *Report on European Sewerage Systems* (1881) was the first comprehensive American writing in the field and for years the chief work on sanitary engineering. On his return he began his practice as consulting sanitary engineer and made reports for over 250 cities and towns in North and South America on water supply and sewage disposal. He wrote extensively on hydraulics for technical journals.

HERKIMER, NICHOLAS (*b. near Herkimer, N.Y., 1728; d. near Oriskany, N.Y., 1777*), Revolutionary officer. Appointed chairman, Committee of Safety of Tryon County, and a brigadier general of militia; charged with defense of the Mohawk Valley; led a force against Sir John Johnson, 1776. In August 1777, marching with 800 men to relieve Fort Schuyler, under attack by General St. Leger's force of Tories and Indians, he was ambushed near Oriskany in a heavily wooded ravine. The battle, long and desperate, was one of the bloodiest of the Revolution, and Herkimer was severely wounded. The Americans retreated, taking him to his home where he died within a fortnight. The battle has been variously described as victory or defeat for either side.

HERMAN, LEBRECHT FREDERICK (*b. Güsten, Germany, 1761; d. Pottstown, Pa., 1848*), German Reformed clergyman. Came to America, 1786; held various Pennsylvania pastorates. Wielded far-reaching influence over his denomination by founding the famous "Swamp College" in his home at Pottstown.

HERNDON, WILLIAM HENRY (*b. Greensburg, Ky., 1818; d. 1891*), lawyer. Became Abraham Lincoln's junior partner, 1844, and worked thereafter to further Lincoln's political ambitions. His claim to fame is as Lincoln's biographer. After Lincoln's death, Herndon traveled in Kentucky and Indiana gathering personal reminiscences of Lincoln's boyhood. He gave these stories freely to other biographers who gave scanty acknowledgment of their debt. As an old man he published (with Jesse W. Weik) *Herndon's Lincoln: The True Story of a Great Life* (1889; revised, 1892). The work met savage criticism, but recent opinion acquits Herndon of serious blunders and endorses his attempt to keep Lincoln human and save him from apotheosis.

HERNDON, WILLIAM LEWIS (*b. Fredericksburg, Va., 1813; d. at sea, 1857*), naval officer. Saw active service in Mexican War and was for a time attached to the Naval Observatory. Detached, 1851, to explore Amazon River system, he reported his findings in *Exploration of the Valley of the Amazon* (1853–54). Lost with his ship, *Central America*, in storm off Cape Hatteras.

HERNE, CHRYSTAL KATHARINE (*b. Dorchester, Mass., 1882; d. Boston, Mass., 1950*), actress. Daughter of James A. Herne, in whose plays *Griffith Davenport* and *Sag Harbor* she made her first stage appearances, 1899; her first engagement as a lead was in Clyde Fitch's *Major André*, 1903. After a brilliant success as leading lady in the series of G. B. Shaw's plays produced by Arnold Daly in 1905–06, she continued to act up to 1936; her fine talent was to a great degree wasted in ephemeral or inferior plays.

HERNE, JAMES A. (*b. Cohoes, N.Y., 1839; d. New York, N.Y., 1901*), actor, playwright. Changed name from James Ahern when he became professional actor, 1859. Played in support of J. B. Booth, Edwin Booth, Forrest, and others; toured country as leading man for Lucille Western. His real talents first showed themselves in San Francisco where with David Belasco he wrote *Hearts of Oak*, produced 1879, a play unusual in its day for its simple, genuine sentiment. *Drifting Apart*, produced New York, 1888, was a second pioneering effort in realism. *Margaret Fleming*, produced by the author, 1890, was written in the spirit of the new Continental naturalist playwrights. A story of marital infidelity, its reality shocked audiences. *Shore Acres*, realistic in method but full of homely sentiment, was first produced in Chicago, 1892 Herne played it successfully for five years. *Griffith Davenport*, produced 1899, a tragic domestic drama of the Civil War, was unsuccessful on the stage; it was succeeded by *Sag Harbor*, a return to the mood of *Shore Acres*, first acted in Boston 1899, with great success. Subsequent developments in the modern American theatre owe much to his pioneering efforts in realism.

HEROLD, DAVID E. *See* BOOTH, JOHN WILKES.

HERON, MATILDA AGNES (*b. Co. Londonderry, Ireland, 1830; d. 1877*), actress. Came to Philadelphia, Pa. as a child. American debut at Walnut Street Theater, 1851. Famed for her interpretation of the title role of *Camille, post* 1857.

HERON, WILLIAM (*b. Cork, Ireland, 1742 d. 1819*), teacher, surveyor, Revolutionary spy. Member of the Connecticut Assembly, 1778–82, he supplied military intelligence to Oliver De Lancey, British secret service head. His duplicity was not discovered until long after his death.

HERR, HERBERT THACKER (*b. Denver, Colo., 1876; d. Philadelphia, Pa., 1933*), mechanical engineer, inventor. Designed safety-braking devices for railroads, improvements in engines and turbines, and a remote-control device whereby ship engines might be operated from the bridge.

HERR, JOHN (*b. West Lampeter, Pa., 1781; d. Humberstone, Canada, 1850*), founded Reformed Mennonites, 1812.

HERRESHOFF, JAMES BROWN (*b. near Bristol, R.I., 1834; d. New York, N.Y., 1930*), chemist, inventor. Brother of John B. and Nathanael Herreshoff. Patented many inventions, as various as a sliding seat for rowboats, 1860, and an apparatus for measuring specific heat of gases, 1872; perfected the fin keel for racing yachts.

HERRESHOFF, JOHN BROWN (*b. near Bristol, R.I., 1841; d. 1915*), shipbuilder, yacht designer. Brother of James B. and Nathanael Herreshoff, with whom, in 1874, he devised an improved tubular marine boiler. The brothers formed the Herreshoff Manufacturing Co., 1878, John handling finance and construction, Nathanael the drafting, engineering, and experimentation. Original in their designs and building methods, they were among the first to build yachts over molds, keel upward, with double skins and iron floors and knees. Among their triumphs in sailing craft design were the *Gloriana* (1891), and the *America's* Cup defenders, *Vigilant, Defender, Columbia, Reliance*. The *Resolute's* victory in 1920 gave the Herreshoffs a record of 18 winners in 20 starts against the fastest English yachts.

HERRESHOFF, NATHANAEL GREENE (*b. Bristol, R.I., 1848; d. Bristol, 1938*), naval architect, marine engineer, shipbuilder. Brother of James B. and John B. Herreshoff; the latter's partner in Herreshoff Manufacturing Co. From the 1890's to 1924, the leading U.S. yacht designer.

HERRICK, EDWARD CLAUDIUS (*b. New Haven, Conn., 1811; d. New Haven, 1862*), librarian, scientist. Yale librarian, 1843–58; treasurer, 1852–62.

HERRICK, MYRON TIMOTHY (*b. Huntington, Ohio, 1854; d. Paris, France, 1929*), lawyer, banker, diplomat. Admitted to the bar, 1878, practiced in Cleveland. Engaged in successful business ventures; became director of several railroads and trust companies; was elected president of American Bankers Association, 1901. Meanwhile he had entered politics, become a friend of William McKinley, and been influential in his election, 1896. Republican governor of Ohio, 1904–06. From 1907 to 1912, while still interested in politics, Herrick was chiefly engaged in large financial transactions and reorganized several railroads. Though he had refused McKinley's offers to make him secretary of the treasury or ambassador to Italy, in 1912 he accepted appointment by President Taft as ambassador to France. Staying on until December 1914 at President Wilson's request, he became a symbol of American good will in a time of French national peril, and was decorated with the Legion of Honor by the French government. During a second term as ambassador to France, 1921–29, the problems of financial settlement resulting from the war, 1914–18, presented many difficulties with which he was particularly fitted to deal. Criticism of the United States caused him much unhappiness, but he served to remind the French of past American kindness, and personally did much to ease the situation. He died in the embassy building which he had purchased and presented to the U.S. government.

HERRICK, ROBERT WELCH (*b. Cambridge, Mass., 1868; d. St. Thomas, Virgin Islands, 1938*), novelist, educator. Graduated Harvard, 1890. Taught at Massachusetts Institute of Technology and University of Chicago. Author of controversial novels of urban middle-class life which include *The Web of Life* (1900), *The Common Lot* (1904), and *Together* (1908).

HERRICK, SOPHIA MCILVAINE BLEDSOE (*b. Gambier, Ohio, 1837; d. 1919*), editor, author. Daughter of Albert T. Bledsoe. Contributor to *Southern Review*, 1868–78; assistant editor, *Scribner's* and *Century* magazines, 1879–1906.

HERRIMAN, GEORGE JOSEPH (*b. New Orleans, La., 1880; d. Los Angeles, Calif., 1944*), cartoonist. Raised in Los Angeles. Employed by the *Los Angeles Herald*, 1897, he began publishing full-color Sunday cartoons as early as 1901; his first comic strip "Lariat Pete" ran in the *San Francisco Chronicle*, 1903. Removed to New York City, he did political and sports cartoons for the *World*. First successful creation was "The Dingbat Family" (1910), out of which emerged "Krazy Kat and Ignatz," 1911. "Krazy Kat's" fans ran the gamut from ordinary readers to President Woodrow Wilson and avant-garde intellectuals.

HERRING, AUGUSTUS MOORE (*b. Covington, Ga., 1867; d. Brooklyn, N.Y., 1926*), pioneer in aviation. Made early experiments with gliders; associated with Samuel P. Langley, 1895; with Octave Chanute, 1896. Applied for a patent on an engine-powered flying machine, 1896. Though the Patent Office found twenty new claims in his design, he had no working model, and the application was rejected. The Herring-Curtiss Co. was formed to build airplanes, *ca*. 1909, Herring contributing his patent applications and attempting to revive the 1896 claim. After a second denial of Herring's petition, the Herring-Curtiss Co. was the unsuccessful defendant in a famous 1910 infringement suit by the Wright brothers.

HERRING, JAMES (*b. London, England, 1794; d. Paris, France, 1867*), portrait painter. Published, in collaboration with J. B. Longacre, *The National Portrait Gallery* (1834–39) which includes some of his own portrait work.

HERRING, SILAS CLARK (*b. Salisbury, Vt., 1803; d. 1881*), safe-manufacturer.

HERRMAN, AUGUSTINE (*b. Prague, Bohemia, ca. 1605; d. Maryland, 1686*), colonial cartographer, merchant, landholder. Served in North and South America for Dutch West India Co.; was agent for Peter Gabry & Sons, 1644–51, at New Amsterdam. In partnership with George Hack, became largest tobacco exporter in America. Ruined by Peter Stuyvesant, Herrman went to Maryland, 1659, and became a citizen of that colony, 1666. His outstanding achievement is the map *Virginia and Maryland as it is Planted and Inhabited This Present Year 1670 . . . [by] Augustin Herrman Bohemiensis*, for which he spent ten years making the surveys. Lord Baltimore rewarded Herrman by granting him over 13,000 acres in northeastern Maryland.

HERRMANN, ALEXANDER (*b. Paris, France, 1844; d. 1896*), magician. Became an American citizen, 1876. Enjoyed world-wide fame.

HERRON, FRANCIS JAY (*b. Pittsburgh, Pa., 1837; d. New York, N.Y., 1902*), youngest major general in Civil War, commissioned 1862 after brilliant service with the 1st and 9th Iowa regiments in Missouri and Arkansas.

HERRON, GEORGE DAVIS (*b. Montezuma, Ind., 1862; d. Munich, Germany, 1925*), Congregational clergyman, Socialist. Influential in founding Rand School, New York City, 1906. American representative to Prinkipo Conference.

HERSCHEL, CLEMENS (*b. Boston, Mass., 1842; d. Glen Ridge, N.J., 1930*), hydraulic engineer. Graduated Lawrence Scientific School, Harvard, 1860; studied at Karlsruhe Technical School. Became chief engineer of the Holyoke Co., *ca*. 1879; constructed the Holyoke testing flume which marked the beginning of scientific study of water turbines, and invented the Venturi meter, a device without moving parts to measure the flow of water in pipes.

HERSEY, EVELYN WEEKS (*b. New Bedford, Mass., 1897; d. Milton, Vt., 1963*), social worker. Executive secretary of the YWCA International Institute of Philadelphia, 1928–39, service director of the American Committee for Christian Refugees in New York City, 1939–43, and special assistant to the U.S. commissioner of immigration and naturalization in Philadelphia, 1943–47. Is most noted for her social work in India, 1948–58, first in the capacity of foreign service reserve officer, with the title social welfare attaché, at the American embassy at New Delhi, India, then as social welfare adviser with the International Cooperation Administration.

HERSHEY, MILTON SNAVELY (*b. Derry Township, Dauphin County, Pa., 1857; d. Hershey, Pa., 1945*), chocolate manufacturer, philanthropist. Apprenticed to a confectioner. After several business failures, he became a successful manufacturer of fresh-milk caramel candies and other confectionery products, *ca*. 1886. He decided in 1903 to concentrate on chocolate based on a formula he had perfected, and built a factory in his native Derry Township for the mass-production of milk chocolate and almond milk-chocolate bars to be sold for five cents. His sales rose rapidly. Around the factory, he constructed a self-sufficient community (Hershey, Pa.), whose commercial community enterprises he operated with enlightened self-interest and paternalism. Hershey left the bulk of his fortune in trust for the Hershey Industrial School (later the Milton Hershey School). The trust later built the Hershey Medical Center.

HERTER, CHRISTIAN (*b. Stuttgart, Germany, 1840; d. 1883*), designer. Came to America, 1860. Head of Herter Brothers, interior decorators, *post* 1870. An influential figure in American art after the Civil War when millionaires' "palaces" were rising in the principal cities of the United States.

HERTER, CHRISTIAN ARCHIBALD (*b. Glenville, Conn., 1865; d. 1910*), physician, biochemist. Son of Christian Herter. Graduated College of Physicians and Surgeons, New York, M.D., 1885. His chief contribution, beyond his *On Infantilism* (1908) and other writings, was the foundation of lectureships for European scientists at Johns Hopkins and Bellevue.

HERTER, CHRISTIAN ARCHIBALD (*b. Paris, France, 1895; d. Washington, D.C., 1966*), congressman, governor of Massachusetts, and U.S. secretary of state. Joined the diplomatic service in 1916. After World War I was secretary to Henry White, one of the five American commissioners at the 1919 Paris Peace Conference, and was promoted to secretary to the entire American Commission to Negotiate Peace; subsequently became a State Department expert on the Treaty of Versailles and the League of Nations. After the U.S. Senate's 1920 defeat of the treaty and the League, left the State Department to become secretary to relief administrator Herbert Hoover. When Hoover was named secretary of commerce in 1921, he became Hoover's special assistant. In 1924 he left government for publishing and other activities, but in 1930 ran for and won a seat in the Massachusetts House of Representatives, where he was one of several eastern Republicans seeking pragmatic accommodation with the policies of President Franklin Roosevelt's New Deal. After Pearl Harbor, was recruited back to Washington as a deputy director of the Office of Facts and Figures, and in 1942 returned to Massachusetts to run for Congress. As a congressman during World War II, he criticized the Office of Price Administration and other wartime agencies for bureaucratic excesses, strongly backed the idea of a postwar United Nations organization, and laid the groundwork for the congressional passage of the Marshall Plan. In domestic affairs, he lined up with other self-styled progressive Republicans in support of civil rights, public works, vigorous antitrust law enforcement, and selected social welfare programs. Was elected governor of Massachusetts in 1952; his governorship was characterized by careful moderation. Became undersecretary and then, upon John Foster Dulles' resignation in 1959, secretary of state, in which position his low-key anti-Communism has been viewed as a historical bridge between the stridency of Dulles and the more flexible cold-war diplomacy of President John F. Kennedy. Kennedy appointed him as the president's special representative for trade negotiations in 1962; retained by President Lyndon Johnson, he participated in the "Kennedy Round" tarriff-reduction negotiations in Geneva, 1964–66.

HERTY, CHARLES HOLMES (*b. Milledgeville, Ga., 1867; d. Savannah, Ga., 1938*), chemist. Graduated University of Georgia, 1886; Ph.D., Johns Hopkins, 1890. Taught at universities of Georgia and North Carolina. His later researches (especially on pine products) and his publicizing of the chemical industry contributed substantially to the South's industrial development.

HERTZ, ALFRED (*b. Frankfurt am Main, Germany, 1872; d. San Francisco, Calif., 1942*), orchestra conductor. Graduated Raff Conservatory, Frankfurt, 1891. After serving as assistant conductor at the Halle and Altenburg operas, he became full conductor at Elberfeld; he was director of the Stadttheater in Breslau, 1899–1902. Conductor of German opera at the Metropolitan Opera House, New York City *post* 1902, he removed to San Francisco, 1915, where he conducted the symphony orchestra until his retirement in 1930. He remained active as a guest conductor. Best known as an interpreter of German music, particularly Richard Wagner, he was hospitable to new works.

HERTZ, JOHN DANIEL (*b. Ruttka, now Czechoslovakia, 1879; d. Los Angeles, Calif., 1961*), transportation executive and financier. Immigrated to the United States in 1884. After purchasing an automobile agency partnership, began using traded-in cars for a chauffeured livery business, and in 1915 organized the Yellow Cab Company of Chicago, the nation's first dependable taxicab service. Began building cabs, and in the 1920's his Yellow Cab Manufacturing Company became the Yellow Truck and Coach Manufacturing Company, a division of General Motors. In 1922 organized the Chicago Motor Coach Company, to operate motor buses; it soon merged with the Fifth Avenue Coach Company of New York to form Omnibus Corporation of America. In 1924 organized the Hertz Drive-Ur-Self Corporation, which he later sold to General Motors.

HESS, ALFRED FABIAN (*b. New York, N.Y., 1875; d. 1933*), pediatrician, pathologist. Graduated Harvard, 1897; M.D., College of Physicians and Surgeons, New York, 1901. After studying abroad, began practice in New York City. Made classic studies of scurvy in infants, devising tests and therapy. Popularized the use of pasteurized milk formulas for infants supplemented with antiscorbutic substances, as well as a supplement of fresh orange juice. Discovered that irradiation of certain foodstuffs caused the formation of antirachitic vitamin D (1924). With Adolf Windaus, identified provitamin D (1927). An outstanding investigator and leader in improving pediatric practice.

HESS, VICTOR FRANZ (*b. Schloss Waldstein, Styria, Austria, 1883; d. Mount Vernon, N.Y., 1964*), physicist. Ph.D. (1906), University of Graz. At the Institute for Radium Research at the University of Vienna and at the University of Graz, conducted research that led him to deduce that radiation has a cosmic and not

a solar or terrestrial origin. Confirmed his research in *The Electrical Conductivity of the Atmosphere and Its Causes* (1928), *Ionization Balance of the Atmosphere* (1933), and a number of important papers. Also verified that sunspot activity has no effect on cosmic radiation and claimed proof for variation in radiation based on differing latitudes. In 1936 shared the Nobel Prize in physics with Carl D. Anderson, whose discovery of the positive electron, or positron, was enabled by Hess's groundwork. Became professor at Fordham University in 1938 and a U.S. citizen in 1944. With Paul Luger, conducted the first tests for radioactive fallout in the United States in 1946.

HESSELIUS, GUSTAVUS (*b. Folkarna, Sweden, 1682; d. Philadelphia, Pa., 1755*), portrait painter, organ builder. Came to Philadelphia, 1711; resided in Maryland, *ca.* 1718–33. His altarpiece "The Last Supper" for St. Barnabas' Church, Prince Georges Co., Md. (1721), was first public art commissioned in colonies.

HESSELIUS, JOHN (*b. probably Prince Georges Co., Md., 1728; d. near Annapolis, Md., 1778*), portrait painter. Son of Gustavus Hesselius. Influenced by John Wollaston. Probably the most prolific painter of the pre-Revolutionary period, his known portraits number nearly a hundred.

HESSOUN, JOSEPH (*b. Vršovice, Bohemia, 1830; d. St. Louis, Mo., 1906*), Roman Catholic clergyman. Came to St. Louis, Mo., 1865. A national, as well as clerical, leader of emigrant Czechs in the Midwest; pastor, journalist, founder of abbeys.

HETH, HENRY (*b. Chesterfield Co., Va., 1825; d. Washington, D.C., 1899*), soldier. Cousin of Gen. George Pickett. Graduated West Point, 1847. Served in the Mexican War and in the West. Resigned his commission, 1861; entered Confederate service and served in West Virginia, Kentucky, and Tennessee. Promoted major general, 1863, his most conspicuous action was at Gettysburg where accidental contact of his division with a superior Union force precipitated that battle.

HEWAT, ALEXANDER (*b. Scotland, ca. 1745; d. London[?], England, ca. 1829*), Presbyterian clergyman, historian. Came to America, 1763; served as pastor in South Carolina until 1775. Author of *An Historical Account of . . . South Carolina and Georgia* (1779), first history of South Carolina.

HEWES, JOSEPH (*b. Kingston, N.J., 1730; d. Philadelphia, Pa., 1779*), businessman, North Carolina legislator and signer of Declaration of Independence. Removed to Edenton, N.C., in the late 1750's. As member of Continental Congress, 1774–77, 1779, he was outstanding as executive head of Continental Navy.

HEWES, ROBERT (*b. Boston, Mass., 1751; d. Boston, 1830*), glassmaker, fencing instructor, bone-setter. Helped organize Essex Glass Works, Boston, 1787, for years the leading cylinder or window-glass firm in America.

HEWETT, WATERMAN THOMAS (*b. Miami, Mo., 1846; d. London, England, 1921*), educator, editor. Graduated Amherst, 1869; studied in Germany and Holland; Ph.D., Cornell, 1879. Professor of German, Cornell, 1879–1910. A pioneer of modern language study, at his best as textbook editor.

HEWIT, AUGUSTINE FRANCIS (*b. Fairfield, Conn., 1820; d. New York, N.Y., 1897*), Roman Catholic clergyman, Paulist. Graduated Amherst, 1839. Influenced by the Oxford Movement, he was converted to Catholicism, 1846, and was ordained, 1847. With Isaac Hecker and others, formed the Paulist congregation; edited *Catholic World*, 1869–74; succeeded Father Hecker as Paulist superior, 1888. A prolific writer, for years one of the foremost Catholic apologists in America.

HEWIT, NATHANIEL AUGUSTUS. *See* HEWIT, AUGUSTINE FRANCIS.

HEWITT, ABRAM STEVENS (*b. Haverstraw, N.Y., 1822; d. Ringwood, N.J., 1903*), iron manufacturer, statesman, philanthropist. Graduated Columbia, 1842. There he formed a friendship with Edward Cooper, son of Peter Cooper who turned over to their partnership of Cooper & Hewitt his own iron works at Trenton. Pioneers in making iron beams and girders, they were successful from the start. In 1862 Hewitt erected at Weston, N.J., the first American open-hearth furnace. Here he produced for the U.S. government all the gun-barrel material it needed at bare production cost, and in 1870 produced the first steel of commercial value in the United States. As the iron and steel industry grew, Cooper, Hewitt & Co. expanded with it, and Hewitt became a force in financial and industrial affairs acting as executive of many corporations. In 1855 he married Peter Cooper's daughter Sarah. When Peter Cooper established Cooper Union, Hewitt took a leading part in the undertaking and for over forty years directed all its financial and educational details. In 1871, with Samuel J. Tilden and Edward Cooper, he joined in a campaign against the "Tweed Ring," and helped reorganize Tammany Hall; he served as congressman, Democrat, from New York, 1875–87, except for one term, winning a position of authority on questions of labor, finance, and national resources. Chairman of the Democratic National Committee, 1876. In 1886 he defeated Henry George and Theodore Roosevelt for the mayoralty of New York City. His vigorous administration was notable for reforms and improvements, which included the plan for the municipal construction of the rapid transit railroad. His reforms and intolerance of partisanship led to a break with Tammany Hall and he retired from politics. The last ten years of his life were devoted to the public interest, especially in education and charity.

HEWITT, JAMES (*b. Dartmoor, England, 1770; d. Boston, Mass., 1827*), violinist, composer. Came to America, 1792. His many compositions included the quasi-opera *Tammany or the Indian Chief* (1794), which became a symbol of Republican protest against the Federalists.

HEWITT, JOHN HILL (*b. New York, N.Y., 1801; d. Baltimore, Md., 1890*), journalist, musician, poet. Son of James Hewitt.

HEWITT, PETER COOPER (*b. New York, N.Y., 1861; d. Paris, France, 1921*), scientist, inventor. Son of Abram S. Hewitt; grandson of Peter Cooper. Educated at Columbia College and Stevens Institute. He is best known for his invention in 1903 of the mercury vapor lamp, bearing his name, which has been widely adopted for industrial illumination. His other inventions include a static converter or rectifier, an electrical interrupter, and a wireless receiver. He was a pioneer in developing hydroplanes and high-speed motor boats. Early interested in the problem of helicopters, he built a successful one in 1918. Appointed to the Naval Consulting Board in 1915, he designed an aerial torpedo. He had large business interests and was director in a number of corporations.

HEYDT, HANS JÖST. *See* HITE, JOST.

HEYE, GEORGE GUSTAV (*b. New York, N.Y., 1874; d. New York, 1957*), museum founder and director. Founder, in 1915, of the Museum of the American Indian in New York City. Heye donated his great collection of American Indian artifacts to the museum in 1916 and served as the museum's director until 1956. The museum is considered the best collection of American Indian materials in the world.

HEYER, JOHN CHRISTIAN FREDERICK (*b. Helmstedt, Germany, 1793; d. Philadelphia, Pa., 1873*), Lutheran clergyman.

Came to America *ca.* 1807. Held pastorates in Pennsylvania, Maryland, and Minnesota; was for many years a missionary to India, founding the first foreign mission of his church, 1842.

HEYWARD, DUBOSE (*b. Charleston, S.C., 1885; d. Tryon, N.C., 1940*), poet, novelist, dramatist. His novel *Porgy* (1924) was the basis of a successful play (1927) and a folk opera as *Porgy and Bess* (1935).

HEYWARD, THOMAS (*b. St. Helena's Parish, S.C., 1746; d. 1809*), Revolutionary soldier, planter, jurist, signer of Declaration of Independence from South Carolina.

HEYWOOD, EZRA HERVEY (*b. Princeton, Mass., 1829; d. Boston, Mass., 1893*), radical pamphleteer. Graduated Brown, 1856. Active Abolitionist, Civil War pacifist. With his wife, wrote and printed an astonishing amount of propaganda on marriage reform, women's rights, labor reform, and others. Edited a monthly journal of reform, *The Word*, 1872–93.

HEYWOOD, LEVI (*b. Gardner, Mass., 1800; d. 1882*), chair manufacturer. Invented many new manufacturing methods for use in his factory, in particular, a machine for bending wood and another for the manipulating of rattan in furniture.

HIACOOMES (*b. ca. 1610; d. 1690*), Pokanauket Indian preacher of Edgartown, Martha's Vineyard, Mass. First convert of the younger Thomas Mayhew, 1643, he aided conversion of other Indians and was ordained in 1670.

HIBBARD, FREEBORN GARRETTSON (*b. New Rochelle, N.Y., 1811; d. 1895*), Methodist clergyman.

HIBBEN, JOHN GRIER (*b. Peoria, Ill., 1861; d. near Rahway, N.J., 1933*), Presbyterian clergyman, philosopher, educator. Graduated Princeton, 1882; Ph.D., 1893. Taught logic at Princeton, 1891–1912; succeeded Woodrow Wilson as president of the university, 1912–32. After the controversies of Wilson's administration, Hibben gave the university peace and academic freedom, greatly expanding it. He combined a rare talent for conciliation with a robust tenacity to principle. His educational philosophy is revealed in *A Defense of Prejudice* (1911). In philosophy his most enduring contribution is *The Philosophy of the Enlightenment* (1910).

HIBBEN, PAXTON PATTISON (*b. Indianapolis, Ind., 1880; d. 1928*), diplomat, journalist. Graduated Princeton, 1903. Embassy secretary in Russia, Colombia, Mexico, Chile, Netherlands. Actively sympathetic with Russian Revolution.

HIBBINS, ANN (*b. Boston, Mass., 1656*). Executed as a witch, because she had "more wit than her neighbors," according to later opinion.

HICHBORN, PHILIP (*b. Charlestown, Mass., 1839; d. Washington, D.C., 1910*), naval officer. Rose from apprentice shipwright to be chief of Navy's Bureau of Construction, 1893–1901. Invented Franklin lifebuoy and Hichborn balanced turrets for battleships. Retired as rear admiral, 1901.

HICKENLOOPER, ANDREW (*b. Hudson, Ohio, 1837; d. 1904*), engineer, Union soldier. Supervised engineering at siege of Vicksburg; brevet brigadier general, 1865. Later a power in business and political life of Cincinnati, Ohio.

HICKOK, JAMES BUTLER (*b. Troy Grove, Ill., 1837; d. Deadwood, Dakota Territory, 1876*), stage driver, soldier, scout, and U.S. marshal, commonly known as "Wild Bill." Removed to Kansas, 1855. Achieved fame as gunfighter while driving over Santa Fe and Oregon Trails; rendered invaluable service as Union scout and spy in Missouri and in campaigns against Western

Indians after the Civil War. As deputy and marshal in turbulent Kansas frontier communities, notably Hays City and Abilene, he controlled the lawless elements by courage and skill. After touring the East with Buffalo Bill Cody, 1872–73, he settled in Deadwood where he was murdered by Jack McCall. Quiet in manner and greatly admired, Hickok never killed a man except in self-defense or in line of duty.

HICKOK, LAURENS PERSEUS (b. Bethel, Conn., 1798; d. Amherst, Mass., 1888), clergyman, philosopher. Graduated Union, 1820. Taught in Western Reserve and Auburn seminaries and at Union College where he was president, 1866–68. As philosopher, the ablest American dialectician of his day; *Rational Psychology* (1849) was his most important work.

HICKOK, "WILD BILL." *See* HICKOK, JAMES BUTLER.

HICKS, ELIAS (b. Hempstead Township, N.Y., 1748; d. Jericho, N.Y., 1830), Quaker preacher, leader of the 1827–28 separation in the Society of Friends. Inclined to extreme Quietism, the inward light became for him the all-important and central feature of religion. By 1815, he was clearly the principal exponent of liberal views within the Society of Friends and opposed doctrinal definition. Both then and later, the term "Hicksite" has been used to designate his following.

HICKS, JOHN (b. Newtown, Pa., 1823; d. Trenton Falls, N.Y., 1890), painter. Studied at Pennsylvania Academy and in Paris under Couture. Of present interest mainly because of the distinguished persons he portrayed.

HICKS, JOHN (b. Auburn, N.Y., 1847; d. San Antonio, Texas, 1917), Oshkosh, Wis., editor, diplomat.

HICKS, THOMAS HOLLIDAY (b. Dorchester Co., Md., 1798; d. Washington, D.C., 1865), politician. Know-Nothing governor of Maryland, 1857–61. Hindered seccessionist movement in Maryland until arrival of Union troops. U.S. senator, 1862–65.

HIESTER, DANIEL (b. Upper Salford Township, Pa., 1747; d. 1804), farmer, Revolutionary patriot, businessman. Congressman, Anti-Federalist, from Pennsylvania, 1789–96; from Maryland, 1801–04.

HIESTER, JOSEPH (b. Bern Township, Pa., 1752; d. Reading, Pa., 1832), merchant. Revolutionary soldier. Cousin of Daniel Hiester. Served in Pennsylvania legislature, and as congressman, 1797–1805, 1815–20. An Independent Republican, he was described by Jefferson as "disinterested, moderate and conscientious." He was governor of Pennsylvania, 1820–23.

HIGGINS, ANDREW JACKSON (b. Columbus, Nebr., 1886; d. New Orleans, La., 1952), industrialist and shipbuilder. Founded the Higgins Lumber and Export Co. in New Orleans in 1910; in order to transport his lumber through shallow river and bayou waters, he designed in 1926 a special shallow draft vessel known as the Eureka boat, which later led to the development of the landing craft (LCVP and LCM) used in World War II.

HIGGINS, DANIEL PAUL (b. Elizabeth N.J., 1886; d. New York, N.Y., 1953), architect. A bookkeeper, Higgins worked for the architectural firm of John Russell Pope from 1905 to 1922, while studying architecture at night at New York University. In 1922 he became a partner of the firm. Commissions included the Roosevelt Memorial at the Museum of Natural History in New York and Constitution Hall, the National Archives, the National Gallery of Art and the Jefferson Memorial in Washington. When Pope died, in 1937, Higgins and Otto R. Eggers founded their own firm, which carried on in the same tradition.

HIGGINS, FRANK WAYLAND (b. Rushford, N.Y., 1856; d. 1907), businessman, New York legislator. Republican governor of New York, 1905–07; promoted insurance legislation, election and taxation reforms.

HIGGINS, MARGUERITE (b. Hong Kong, 1920; d. Washington, D.C., 1966), journalist, war correspondent, and author. As a correspondent for the *New York Herald Tribune*, traveled with the Seventh Army in Europe and gained worldwide attention for her firsthand accounts of such events as the capture of Munich. Was chief of her paper's Berlin bureau after 1947, and in 1950, as the *Herald Tribune*'s Far Eastern correspondent, covered the frontline engagements of the U.S. Army in Korea. Won a 1951 Pulitzer Prize for international reporting and wrote *War in Korea: The Report of a Woman Combat Correspondent* (1951). After serving as Washington correspondent for the *Herald Tribune*, 1958–63, moved to the Long Island daily *Newsday* to write a syndicated thrice-weekly column. Also wrote *Our Vietnam Nightmare* (1965) and the autobiographical *News Is a Singular Thing* (1954).

HIGGINSON, FRANCIS (b. Claybrooke, England, 1586; d. Salem, Mass., 1630), clergyman. Graduated Jesus College, Cambridge, 1610; M.A., 1613. Ordained 1614, he became a nonconformist through association with Thomas Hooker and other Puritans and immigrated to New England, 1629. As religious teacher of Salem (Naumkeag) settlement, he drew up its confession of faith and the covenant of the church. He was author also of *New-Englands Plantation* (1630), a valuable source.

HIGGINSON, HENRY LEE (b. New York, N.Y., 1834; d. 1919), banker, Union soldier. Partner in Lee, Higginson & Co., Boston. Founded the Boston Symphony Orchestra, 1881, and was its sole underwriter until 1918. Benefactor also of numerous colleges and schools.

HIGGINSON, JOHN (b. Claybrooke, England, 1616; d. 1708), clergyman. Son of Francis Higginson, with whom he came to Salem, Mass., as a boy. Religious teacher and pastor at Guilford, Conn.; pastor, Salem, Mass., *post* 1660. Held a high place among Massachusetts clergy.

HIGGINSON, NATHANIEL (b. Guilford, Conn., 1652; d. London, England, 1708), merchant. Son of John Higginson. Graduated Harvard, 1670. Entered service of East India Co., 1683. First mayor of Madras, 1688; governor of Fort Saint George, 1692–98. Returned to England, 1700.

HIGGINSON, STEPHEN (b. Salem, Mass., 1743; d. 1828), Boston merchant, Revolutionary privateer. Descendant of Francis Higginson.

HIGGINSON, THOMAS WENTWORTH (b. Cambridge, Mass., 1823; d. Cambridge, 1911), reformer, author, Unitarian minister, Union soldier. Grandson of Stephen Higginson. Graduated Harvard, 1841; was early advocate of woman suffrage and a violent opponent of slavery; supported disunion movement and participated in riots connected with return of fugitive slave Anthony Burns, 1854. As colonel of the first black regiment in the Union Army, he served in South Carolina, 1862–64. A prominent "magazinist" thereafter, he wrote most frequently for *Atlantic Monthly*. He aided in the discovery of Emily Dickinson and her poetry and was author of a number of books, among them *Life in a Black Regiment* (1870) and *Atlantic Essays* (1871).

HIGH, STANLEY HOFLUND (b. Chicago, Ill., 1895; d. New York, N.Y., 1961), writer and editor. A.B. (1917), Nebraska Wesleyan University; S.T.B. (1923), Boston University School of Theology. In the 1920's wrote from a Christian perspective on international affairs for such magazines as *Travel*, *Christian*

Science Monitor, Outlook, Christian Century, Methodist Review, Nation, and *Asia.* Also wrote *China's Place in the Sun* (1922), *The Revolt of Youth* (1923), and *Europe Turns the Corner* (1925). A supporter of the New Deal, was an unofficial adviser and a top speechwriter, 1935–37, for President Franklin D. Roosevelt and thereafter published a series of friendly but critical articles on the Roosevelt presidency in *Harper's,* later expanded into the book *Roosevelt—and Then?* (1937). Was appointed roving editor for *Reader's Digest* in 1941 and senior editor in 1952. His biography of Billy Graham was published in 1956.

HIGINBOTHAM, HARLOW NILES (*b. near Joliet, Ill., 1838; d. 1919*), merchant, philanthropist. Partner and associate of Marshall Field; president of World's Columbian Exposition, 1893; director of museums; benefactor to Chicago charities.

HILDRETH, RICHARD (*b. Deerfield, Mass., 1807; d. Florence, Italy, 1865*), lawyer, historian. Graduated Harvard, 1826. Editor and writer, *Boston Daily Atlas,* 1832–38. An active Whig in 1840, an advocate of temperance and abolition, he was author of numerous tracts; also *Banks, Banking, and Paper Currencies* (1840) and a novel *The Slave: or Memoirs of Archy Moore* (1836). Engaged in writing his *History of the United States, post* 1844, he published its six volumes, 1849–52. Competent and accurate in detail, his major work is heavy in style and influenced by an unconscious tendency toward socialism.

HILDRETH, SAMUEL CLAY (*b. Independence, Mo., 1866; d. New York, N.Y., 1929*), turfman. Trainer of Zev, Purchase, Grey Lag and other great champions.

HILDRETH, SAMUEL PRESCOTT (*b. Methuen, Mass., 1783; d. Marietta, Ohio, 1863*), physician, naturalist, historian. Began practice in Ohio, 1806. Collected and preserved the oral traditions and papers of Ohio pioneers.

HILGARD, EUGENE WOLDEMAR (*b. Zweibrücken, Bavaria, 1833; d. 1916*), geologist, authority on soils. Son of Theodor E. Hilgard. Came to America as a boy. Studied in Philadelphia, Zürich, Freiberg; Ph.D., Heidelberg, 1853. As director of Mississippi geological survey, published *Geology and Agriculture of the State of Mississippi* (1860, issued 1866). After Civil War, taught at University of Mississippi and again directed the state survey; was one of the first to reorganize relation of soil analysis to agriculture. Professor of agriculture and director of Agricultural Experiment Station at University of California, Berkeley, *post* 1875, he exerted great influence on application of scientific knowledge to agriculture. His *Geology of the Mississippi Delta* (1870) has become a classic; almost as famous as his *Soils, Their Formation, Properties, Composition, and Relations to Climate and Plant Growth in Humid and Arid Regions* (1906).

HILGARD, JULIUS ERASMUS (*b. Zweibrücken, Bavaria, 1825; d. Washington, D.C., 1891*), geodesist. Son of Theodor E. Hilgard. Came to America as a boy. Associated, *post* 1844, with U.S. Coast Survey; superintendent, 1881–85. Active in scientific organizations and in the introduction here of the metric system.

HILGARD, THEODOR ERASMUS (*b. Marnheim, Bavaria, 1790; d. Heidelberg, Germany, 1873*). Father of Eugene W. and Julius E. Hilgard. A prominent lawyer and justice in Germany, he immigrated to Belleville, Ill., 1836, where he became a successful farmer and land speculator.

HILL, AMBROSE POWELL (*b. Culpeper, Va., 1825; d. near Petersburg, Va., 1865*), soldier. Graduated West Point, 1847. Served briefly in Mexican War, and Seminole campaigns. Resigned from U.S. army, 1861, to join Virginia's forces. Promoted major general, May 1862, he participated in all Lee's major battles, opening the Seven Days battle and meeting his death in combat at close of the siege of Petersburg. He served with Jackson at Cedar Mountain, Second Bull Run, and Harpers Ferry; by rapid marching from Harpers Ferry to Sharpsburg (Antietam), he reinforced and saved Lee's yielding right wing. Hill shared in Jackson's famous flanking movement at Chancellorsville. As lieutenant general (promoted, May 1863), he commanded all the Confederate forces during the first day's fighting at Gettysburg. Genial and affectionate in private life, he was a restless and impetuous soldier.

HILL, BENJAMIN HARVEY (*b. Jasper Co., Ga., 1823; d. Atlanta, Ga., 1882*), lawyer, legislator. Opposed secession, but became Davis spokesman in Confederate Senate, 1861–65; was a moderate Southern spokesman as Georgia congressman, Democrat, 1875–77, and U.S. senator, 1877–81.

HILL, DANIEL HARVEY (*b. York District, S.C., 1821; d. Charlotte, N.C., 1889*), soldier, educator. Graduated West Point, 1842. After service in Mexican War, resigned to become professor of mathematics at Washington College, and later at Davidson College. Rose to lieutenant general in Confederate service, 1861–65; published southern regional journals; served as president, University of Arkansas, 1877–84.

HILL, DAVID BENNETT (*b. Montour Falls, N.Y., 1843; d. near Albany, N.Y., 1910*), lawyer, New York legislator. A machine politician and strict party man, he possessed a genius for organization and became recognized leader of the Democratic party in his state. As governor, 1885–91, he showed great administrative efficiency; as U.S. senator from New York, 1892–97, he won a fight with President Grover Cleveland over the control of the New York patronage but was otherwise undistinguished. Aspirant for the presidency in 1892, his high-handed actions to block Cleveland in the Democratic Convention helped, rather than hindered, his rival secure the nomination. He opposed free silver in the Convention of 1896. After W. J. Bryan's nomination, he wrote: "I am a Democrat still—very still."

HILL, DAVID JAYNE (*b. Plainfield, N.J., 1850; d. Washington, D.C., 1932*), educator, diplomat, publicist. Graduated Bucknell, 1874. Taught at Bucknell, and was president, 1879–88; president, University of Rochester, 1888–95. Assistant U.S. secretary of state, 1898–1903. Served, 1903–11, as U.S. minister successively in Switzerland, Netherlands, and Germany. Author of *A History of Diplomacy* (1905, 1906, 1914) and other works.

HILL, EDWIN CONGER (*b. Aurora, Ind., 1884; d. St. Petersburg, Fla., 1957*), journalist and news commentator. After working on various Indiana newspapers, Hill came to New York as a reporter for the *New York Sun* in 1904. He remained there until 1923, when he became director of the Fox Film Corp. newsreels. Returning to the *Sun* in 1927 he expanded his activities to radio news broadcasting, becoming one of the first national broadcasters. He was an influential friend of many presidents and wrote a national syndicated column.

HILL, ERNEST ROWLAND (*b. Pompton, N.J., 1872; d. Orange, N.J., 1948*), electrical engineer. M.E. and E.E., Cornell University, 1893. A pioneer in railroad electrification, at first with the Westinghouse Company, and as partner in Gibbs & Hill, *post* 1911. Electrified the Pennsylvania Railroad main line between New York, Washington, and Harrisburg.

HILL, FRANK ALPINE (*b. Biddeford, Maine, 1841; d. 1903*), educator. Graduated Bowdoin, 1862. As secretary of board of education of Massachusetts, *post* 1894, he worked for more expert supervision of schools and higher qualifications for teachers.

HILL, FREDERIC STANHOPE (*b. Boston, Mass., 1805; d. 1851*), actor, playwright. Two of his adaptations of French melodramas (*The Six Degrees of Crime* and *The Shoemaker of Toulouse*, 1834) became stock pieces for the American theater of his day.

HILL, FREDERICK TREVOR (*b. Brooklyn, N.Y., 1866; d. 1930*), New York lawyer, novelist. Author of *Lincoln, the Lawyer* (1906).

HILL, GEORGE HANDEL (*b. 1809; d. Saratoga Springs, N.Y., 1849*), actor, commonly known as "Yankee" Hill. Popular comedian in America and England, *post* 1832. Unsurpassed in Yankee character parts.

HILL, GEORGE WASHINGTON (*b. Philadelphia, Pa., 1884; d. near Matapedia, Quebec, Canada, 1946*), tobacco executive. His father, Percival Hill, was a partner in the Blackwell Durham Tobacco Company, which he sold to James B. Duke's American Tobacco Company in about 1908. He became one of Duke's executives and moved his family to New York City. George attended Williams College for two years and then took a job with the American Tobacco Company in North Carolina.

In 1927, father and son purchased Butler and Butler, the principal product of which was Pall Mall cigarettes. Advertising cigarettes became George Hill's consuming concern. When Duke reorganized the American Tobacco trust he named the elder Hill president and George became vice president and sales manager of the cigarette division. In 1917 the Hills introduced Lucky Strike to compete against Camel. Aggressive advertising techniques reminiscent of patent medicine promotion assured the success of the new product which briefly in 1939 was the nation's leading seller.

Hill succeeded his father as president of American Tobacco in 1925, and the company was consistently profitable even during the depression of the 1930's.

HILL, GEORGE WILLIAM (*b. New York, N.Y., 1838; d. West Nyack, N.Y., 1914*), mathematician. Graduated Rutgers, 1859. His important contributions to mathematical astronomy were published by the Carnegie Institution, 1905–07.

HILL, GRACE LIVINGSTON (*b. Wellsville, N.Y., 1865; d. Swarthmore, Pa., 1947*), author of eighty novels, employing a mixture of romance, adventure, conflict, and religion to exemplify principles of strict morality and the rewards of virtuous living. During her lifetime, her books sold nearly four million copies; the two most popular were *The Witness* (1917) and *The Enchanted Barn* (1918).

HILL, HENRY BARKER (*b. Waltham, Mass., 1849; d. 1903*), chemist. Son of Thomas Hill (1818–1891). Graduated Harvard, 1869. Professor at Harvard, *post* 1874, he specialized in organic chemistry and qualitative analysis; made distinguished researches in uric acid and in furaldehyde derivatives.

HILL, ISAAC (*b. Cambridge, Mass., 1789; d. Washington, D.C., 1851*), New Hampshire political leader. Editor, *New Hampshire Patriot*, 1809–29; U.S. senator, Democrat, from New Hampshire, 1831–36; governor of New Hampshire, 1836–39. A member of Andrew Jackson's "kitchen cabinet."

HILL, JAMES (*b. Kittery, Maine, 1734; d. 1811*), soldier in colonial and Revolutionary wars, shipbuilder, New Hampshire landowner and legislator.

HILL, JAMES JEROME (*b. near Rockwood, Canada, 1838; d. St. Paul, Minn., 1916*), railroad executive, financier. Settled in St. Paul, 1856. Worked as clerk for a line of Mississippi River steamboats, as a freight agent and as agent for the St. Paul and Pacific Railroad. Operated Northwestern Fuel Co., 1875–78. Began his rise with Norman W. Kittson in the Red River Transpor-

tation Co., freighting to Fort Garry (Winnipeg). Purchased, 1878, the bankrupt St. Paul and Pacific Railroad in association with Kittson, Donald A. Smith (later Lord Strathcona) and George Stephen (later Lord Mount Stephen); through Hill's able management and a wise policy of extension and reconstruction, the opulent Great Northern system was created out of it. Hill served as general manager, 1879–81; vice president, 1881–82; president, 1882–1907; chairman, 1907–12. Hill's belief that the competition of the less successful Northern Pacific was uneconomical, as well as dangerous to his own line, led to his acquisition of stock in that property after formal unification had been enjoined by the courts, 1896. To assure entry for the lines into Chicago and St. Louis, Hill and J. P. Morgan, acting for Great Northern and Northern Pacific respectively, bought 97 percent of the share capital of the Chicago, Burlington and Quincy. E. W. Harriman, denied participation in the Burlington, sought to win control of the vulnerable Northern Pacific by purchase of its shares on the open market, thus precipitating the stock market panic of May 9, 1901. Harriman established a minority interest on the Northern Pacific board in a resulting compromise. The Northern Securities Co., a holding company designed to act virtually as trustee for Hill's far-flung railroad interests, was declared illegal by Supreme Court decision, 1904.

Under Hill's management, his railroad system was the only transcontinental carrier which weathered all financial storms and maintained an uninterrupted dividend record. His success was owing to unceasing watchfulness and attention to detail. He built his lines where he knew that traffic would flow; he selected routes with favorable grades; he held operation costs to a minimum; he was a pioneer in recognizing the value of adequate terminal facilities. The Great Northern made its way without land grants or government aid, and was among the first to run agricultural demonstration trains with expert lecturers. The great part which Hill played in the settling and development of the Northwest brought him the sobriquet of "empire builder."

HILL, JOHN (*b. London, England, 1770; d. near West Nyack, N.Y., 1850*), engraver, aquatinter. Came to America, 1816. Celebrated for the craftsmanship of his *Landscape Album* (1820, after Joshua Shaw) and the *Hudson River Portfolio* (1828, after W. G. Wall).

HILL, JOHN HENRY (*b. New York, N.Y., 1791; d. Athens, Greece, 1882*), Episcopal clergyman, missionary to Greece, *post* 1832. With his wife, founded in Athens the leading girls' school in the Greek-speaking world.

HILL, JOSEPH ADNA (*b. Stewartstown, N.H., 1860; d. 1938*), statistician. Graduated Harvard, 1885; Ph.D., University of Halle, 1892. Associated with U.S Bureau of the Census, *post* 1898; chief of statistical research, 1933–38.

HILL, JOSHUA (*b. Abbeville District, S.C., 1812; d. 1891*), lawyer. Practiced in Madison, Ga. Congressman, Know-Nothing, 1857–61; opposed secession, declined to participate in Civil War. Worked for radical reconstruction policies, and was U.S. senator, Republican, from Georgia, 1868–73.

HILL, LOUIS CLARENCE (*b. Ann Arbor, Mich., 1865; d. Los Angeles, Calif., 1938*), civil and hydraulic engineer. Specialist in design and construction of dams and irrigation projects. As chief engineer, U.S. Reclamation Service, supervised Roosevelt Dam (Arizona), Laguna Dam and Colorado Basin project, 1906–14; later served as consultant.

HILL, NATHANIEL PETER (*b. Montgomery, N.Y., 1832; d. 1900*), metallurgist. Replaced amalgamation process for reducing Colorado ores with smelting process, 1868, thus inaugurating great era of Rocky Mountain mining. Settled in Colorado, 1871, and was U.S. senator, 1879–85.

HILL, PATTY SMITH (*b. Anchorage, Ky., 1868; d. New York, N.Y., 1946*), kindergarten and nursery school educator. Graduated Louisville Collegiate Institute, 1887; departed from a formalized, strictly Froebelian approach as teacher and head (1893–1905) of the Louisville Training School for Kindergarten and Primary Teachers. On the Staff of Teachers College, Columbia University, 1905–35. Warned prospective teachers against tightly structured classroom work and efforts to be too empirical. She devised a "habit inventory" of specific, desirable traits in children and the activities and subjects which would best develop them. With her sister wrote "Happy Birthday to You."

HILL, RICHARD (*b. Maryland*, ca. 1673; *d. Philadelphia, Pa., 1729*), merchant. Settled in Philadelphia, *ca*, 1700. Was four times mayor of that city, an intimate of William Penn, and associate justice of the provincial supreme court.

HILL, ROBERT ANDREWS (*b. Iredell Co., N.C., 1811; d. Oxford, Miss., 1900*), judge, anti-secessionist, moderate reconstructionist. Raised in Tennessee; removed to Mississippi, 1855. Neutral in Civil War, he was U.S district judge, 1866–91.

HILL, THOMAS (*b. New Brunswick, N.J., 1818; d. Waltham, Mass., 1891*), Unitarian clergyman, scientist. Graduated Harvard, 1843. President of Antioch College, 1859–62; of Harvard, 1862–68, where he introduced elective system and encouraged advanced scientific investigation.

HILL, THOMAS (*b. Birmingham, England, 1829; d. Raymond, Calif., 1908*), landscape painter. Came to America as a child. Studied at Pennsylvania Academy. Settled in California, *ca*. 1870. Emphasized romantic elements of Western scenery.

HILL, URELI CORELLI (*b. probably Connecticut* ca. 1802; *d. Paterson, N.J., 1875*), violinist, music teacher. First president, and a founder of Philharmonic Society of New York, 1842.

HILL, WALTER BARNARD (*b. Talbot Co., Ga., 1851; d. 1905*), lawyer, educator. Chancellor, University of Georgia, 1899–1905, in which period he expanded the university's plant and instituted a state college of agriculture.

HILL, WILLIAM (*b. Ireland, 1741; d. York, S.C., 1816*), ironmaster, Revolutionary soldier, politician. Came to America, *ca*. 1761; settled in York Co., S.C., 1762. Operated important mines and ironworks both during and after Revolution; served with distinction as soldier under General Sumter.

HILLARD, GEORGE STILLMAN (*b. Machias, Maine, 1808; d. near Boston, Mass., 1879*), lawyer, orator. A man of talent, friend of Charles Sumner and Nathaniel Hawthorne, he never achieved eminence because of divided aims. Author of *Six Months in Italy* (1853).

HILLEBRAND, WILLIAM FRANCIS (*b. Honolulu, Hawaii, 1853; d. 1925*), chemist. After extensive study in the United States, at Heidelberg (Ph.D., 1875) and elsewhere in Germany, he joined the U.S. Geological Survey as chemist, 1880, soon establishing a reputation for accuracy in analysis. He was first to publish a consistent outline for complete analysis of silicate rock. His work with uraninite led to significant discoveries of his own and of other scientists. Hillebrand's term of service as chief chemist of the Bureau of Standards, 1908–1925, was particularly noteworthy.

HILLEGAS, MICHAEL (*b. Philadelphia, Pa., 1729; d. Philadelphia, 1804*), merchant, Revolutionary patriot. His considerable fortune was acquired from a business inherited from his father and

his own ventures into sugar refining, iron manufacturing and, finally, banking. He performed his patriotic service as treasurer, in turn, of the Philadelphia Committee of Safety, the Province of Pennsylvania, and as U.S. treasurer, 1777–89. During the Revolution he contributed a large part of his fortune to the support of the army.

HILLHOUSE, JAMES (*b. Montville, Conn., 1754; d. New Haven, Conn., 1832*), lawyer, politician, Revolutionary soldier. Congressman, Federalist, from Connecticut, 1791–96; U.S. senator, 1796–1810. Member of Hartford Convention. Administered Connecticut schools fund with great ability. Treasurer, Yale College, 1782–1832.

HILLHOUSE, JAMES ABRAHAM (*b. New Haven, Conn., 1789; d. New Haven, 1841*), poet. Son of James Hillhouse. Graduated Yale, 1808. Author of *Hadad* (1825), a blank verse drama, and other works issued in collected form (1839).

HILLIARD, FRANCIS (*b. Cambridge, Mass., 1806; d. Worcester, Mass., 1878*), legal writer. Abandoned active practice of law to write and publish treatises on numerous and widely separated legal subjects embodying American decisions and showing the extent to which they followed English Common Law. His treatise *The Law of Torts* (1859) was the first work in English on the subject. All of his works were compilations. First in the field, however, they made litigation less difficult and costly.

HILLIARD, HENRY WASHINGTON (*b. Fayetteville, N.C., 1808; d. Atlanta, Ga., 1892*), lawyer, Confederate soldier. Congressman, Whig, from Alabama, 1845–51. Opposed William L. Yancey in political debates, 1840–51. Opposed secession, but supported Confederacy on ground that coercion of a state was wrong. Minister to Brazil, 1877–81.

HILLIS, DAVID (*b. Washington Co., Pa., 1788; d. 1845*), Indiana pioneer, judge, Indian fighter, legislator. Removed to Madison, Ind., *ca*. 1808.

HILLIS, NEWELL DWIGHT (*b. Magnolia, Iowa, 1858; d. 1929*), pastor of Plymouth Church, Brooklyn, N.Y., 1899–1924.

HILLMAN, SIDNEY (*b. Zagare, Lithuania, 1887; d. Point Lookout, N.Y., 1946*), labor leader. He left the famous Hebrew seminary in Kovno at the age of sixteen and began organizing typesetters for the Bund, the outlawed Jewish trade union movement. Imprisoned in 1904 and again during the revolution of 1905, he left Russia. After a brief stay in England he sailed for the United States.

In Chicago, as an apprentice cutter at a men's clothing factory, he was instrumental in persuading the workers to accept a compromise calling for arbitration of a strike. He was promptly elected business agent for the newly formed Local 39, United Garment Workers of America. In 1914 Hillman was called to New York City by the International Ladies Garment Workers Union, and was chosen president of the newly formed Amalgamated Clothing Workers of America. Hillman shrewdly mixed militancy and reasonable negotiation in a sustained organizing campaign, and by 1920 the Amalgamated boasted a membership of 177,000, contracts covering 85 percent of the industry, and a significant rise in labor standards. The Amalgamated Clothing Workers joined the American Federation of Labor (AFL) in 1933, but when internal conflicts became irreconcilable, Hillman helped establish the rival Congress of Industrial Organizations.

In 1936 Hillman helped establish Labor's Non-Partisan League to support the reelection of President Franklin D. Roosevelt. Hillman became the key labor figure in Washington, and in 1940 was appointed labor member of the National Defense Advisory Commission and associate director general of the Office of Production Management. Wartime reorganizations eased Hillman out of administrative power in May 1942. He left Washington and resumed his role as union president and head of the powerful Political Action Committee. Hillman was instrumental in the formation of the World Federation of Trade Unions in 1945.

HILLMAN, THOMAS TENNESSEE (*b. Montgomery Co., Tenn., 1844; d. Atlantic City, N.J., 1905*), Alabama industrialist. In association with H. F. De Bardeleben, built first iron furnace in Birmingham, Ala., 1880; was promoter of consolidations in Alabama steel and coal industries.

HILLQUIT, MORRIS (*b. Riga, Russia, 1869; d. 1933*), Socialist leader, lawyer, author. Came to New York City, 1886; joined the Socialist Labor party; led anti–De Leon faction. Graduated New York University Law School, 1893. Took an active part in trade-union organizations, especially of Jewish garment workers. Opposed American participation in World War I on Socialist grounds; polled high Socialist vote in mayoralty campaign, 1917. Active as attorney in espionage cases and labor cases. Acted as legal adviser to the Soviet Government Bureau in the United States until 1919. Frequently an unsuccessful candidate for public office; long subject to tuberculosis. Author of *History of Socialism in the United States* (1903) and other works.

HILLS, ELIJAH CLARENCE (*b. Arlington, Ill., 1867; d. 1932*), Romance philologist, educator.

HILLYER, JUNIUS (*b. Wilkes Co., Ga., 1807; d. Decatur, Ga., 1886*), lawyer, Georgia Congressman, Democrat, 1851–55; solicitor of U.S. treasury, 1857–61. In letters to Howell Cobb, Jan.–Feb. 1861, he warned that border states would not secede.

HILLYER, ROBERT SILLIMAN (*b. East Orange, N.J., 1895; d. Wilmington, Del., 1961*), poet and critic. His poems were published in *Sonnets and Other Lyrics* (1917), *The Five Books of Youth* (1920), *Alchemy* (1920), *Collected Verse* (1933), for which he won the Pulitzer Prize, *The Death of Captain Nemo* (1949), *The Suburb by the Sea* (1952), *The Relic and Other Poems* (1957), and *Collected Poems* (1961). Also wrote three autobiographical novels and a collection of critical essays, and his *First Principles of Verse* (1938) became a popular textbook. Taught at Harvard, 1928–45, Kenyon College, 1948–51, and the University of Delaware, 1952–61. A minor but true poet who wrote on the eternal verities of love, death, and honor in the great tradition of English sixteenth-century verse, he came under attack by left-wing critics in the 1930's. In the 1950's he attacked Ezra Pound, T. S. Eliot, and the "new criticism," thus triggering a vociferous poetic debate and contributing to the decline of the new criticism.

HILPRECHT, HERMAN VOLRATH (*b. Hohenerxleben, Germany, 1859; d. 1925*), Assyriologist. Came to America, 1886. Professor and curator at University of Pennsylvania, 1887–1911; resigned his post after a controversy which involved John H. Haynes. Author of *Old Babylonian Inscriptions, Chiefly from Nippur* (1893, 1896).

HIMES, CHARLES FRANCIS (*b. Lancaster Co., Pa., 1838; d. Baltimore, Md., 1918*), educator. Graduated Dickinson College, 1855; taught the sciences there, 1865–96. Authority on photography. His elective laboratory courses were among first (1865) offered by American colleges.

HIMES, JOSHUA VAUGHAN (*b. North Kingstown, R.I., 1805; d. Elk Point, S.D., 1895*), Adventist and Episcopal clergyman.

HINDMAN, THOMAS CARMICHAEL (*b. Knoxville, Tenn., 1828; d. Arkansas, 1868*), lawyer, Confederate major general. Raised in Mississippi; removed to Helena, Ark., 1856. Severely wounded in Atlanta campaign; murdered by an assassin after vigorously opposing Reconstruction government.

HINDMAN, WILLIAM (*b. Dorchester Co., Md., 1743; d. Baltimore, Md., 1822*), lawyer, Revolutionary patriot. Congressman, Federalist, from Maryland, 1793–99; U.S. senator, 1800–01.

HINDS, ASHER CROSBY (*b. Benton, Maine, 1863; d. Washington, D.C., 1919*), journalist, politician. Parliamentarian of Congress, 1895–1911. Author of monumental *Hinds' Precedents of the House of Representatives* (1907–08).

HINDUS, MAURICE GERSCHON (*b. Bolshoye Bikovo, Russia, 1891; d. New York, N.Y., 1969*), writer. Immigrated to the United States, 1905; became citizen *ca.* 1910. His books and magazine articles, primarily on Russia, helped to increase American understanding of, and sympathy for, the people of the Soviet Union. His nonfiction works include *The Russian Peasant and the Revolution* (1920), *Humanity Uprooted* (1929), *Red Bread* (1931), *Mother Russia* (1943), *Crisis in the Kremlin* (1953), *House Without a Roof* (1961), and his autobiography, *Green Worlds: An Informal Chronicle* (1938). His four novels are *Moscow Skies* (1936), *Sons and Fathers* (1940), *To Sing with the Angels* (1941), and *Magda* (1951).

HINE, CHARLES DE LANO (*b. Vienna, Va., 1867; d. New York, N.Y., 1927*), railroad official, organizational expert for American railroads. Author of *Modern Organization: An Exposition of the Unit System* (1912).

HINE, LEWIS WICKES (*b. Oshkosh, Wis., 1874; d. Hastings-on-Hudson, N.Y., 1940*), photographer. Specialized in creating social documents; his photographs (1907–14) for Child Labor Committee helped bring legislative reforms. Pioneer in industrial photography.

HINES, DUNCAN (*b. Bowling Green, Ky., 1880; d. Bowling Green, 1959*), restaurant critic. Attended briefly Bowling Green Business College. Hines worked in the printing industry in Chicago until his fifties; in 1936, he published *Adventures in Good Eating*, which earned him his reputation as a critic of restaurants. By 1943, Hines was able to establish the Duncan Hines Foundation to provide scholarships in the study of hotel and restaurant management at Cornell and Michigan State universities. In 1949, he formed the Hines-Park Foods Inc., with Roy H. Park, which licensed manufacturers to use the name Hines on their food products.

HINES, FRANK THOMAS (*b. Salt Lake City, Utah, 1879; d. Washington, D.C., 1960*), army officer and government official. Studied at the Agricultural College of Utah. Hines enlisted in the army in 1898 and rose to the rank of brigadier general, holding the position of chief of the Embarkation Service for the army during World War I, and in 1919, chief of the Army Transportation Service. He retired in 1920. In 1923, President Warren G. Harding appointed him director of the Veterans Bureau, later the Veterans Administration, a position he held until 1945. Appointed ambassador to Panama by President Harry S. Truman, he retired from government service in 1948.

HINES, JAMES J. (*b. New York, N.Y., 1876; d. Long Beach, N.Y., 1957*), politician. The most powerful single leader of New York City's Tammany Hall from 1907 through 1939, Hines began his career by running his father's blacksmith shop which was contracted to shoe the horses of the New York police force. A friend of many underground figures, Hines was convicted in 1939 of conspiracy to protect racketeer Dutch Schultz. He served almost four years in prison before being paroled. Remembered as corrupt by later political reform leaders, Hines was fondly remembered by his constituents as a generous man who, on annual June walks through Central Park, would distribute ice cream to thousands of the city's youth.

HINES, JOHN LEONARD ("BIRDIE") (*b. White Sulphur Springs, W.Va., 1868; d. Washington, D.C., 1968*), army officer. Graduated U.S. Military Academy (1891). Won a Silver Star for gallantry under fire at Santiago, Cuba, during the Spanish-American War. In 1917, was included in the initial group of officers that General Pershing took with him to France to form the American Expeditionary Force (AEF). In France, was repeatedly promoted due to his skillful command of the Sixteenth Infantry Regiment in the First Division, the First Brigade in the First Division, the Fourth Division, and the Third Army Corps. Received the Distinguished Service Cross for extraordinary heroism near Soissons. Was Pershing's deputy chief of staff, 1922–24, and, upon Pershing's retirement, chief of staff, 1924–26. Retired as major general in 1932.

HINES, WALKER DOWNER (*b. Russellville, Ky., 1870; d. Merano, Italy, 1934*), lawyer. Assistant director and director, U.S. Railroad Administration, 1917–20; adviser on railroads to foreign governments.

HINKLE, BEATRICE MOSES (*b. San Francisco, Calif., 1874; d. New York, N.Y., 1953*), psychiatrist, psychoanalyst. Studied at Cooper Medical School. Appointed city physician for San Francisco (1899), she became the first woman public health doctor in the nation. With Charles R. Dana, helped found the first American psychotherapeutic clinic at the Cornell Medical College (1908). After working with Carl Jung in Europe, she became affiliated in 1916 with the Cornell Medical School and the New York Post-Graduate Medical School. Author of *The Recreating of the Individual* (1923), a collection of essays on types that emphasized her interest in women and artists. Practiced privately in New York City and ran a private sanitorium in Connecticut.

HINMAN, ELISHA (*b. Stonington, Conn., 1734; d. Stonington, 1805*), naval officer, privateer in American Revolution.

HINMAN, GEORGE WHEELER (*b. Mount Morris, N.Y., 1864; d. Winnetka, Ill., 1927*), editor, educator. Graduated Hamilton College, 1884; Ph.D., Heidelberg, 1888. On staff New York *Sun*, 1888–98; editor, Chicago *Inter Ocean*, 1898–1912.

HINMAN, JOEL (*b. Southbury, Conn., 1802; d. 1870*), Connecticut legislator and jurist.

HINSDALE, BURKE AARON (*b. near Wadsworth, Ohio, 1837; d. Atlanta, Ga., 1900*), educator. President, Hiram College, 1870–82; superintendent, Cleveland public schools, 1882–86; professor of education, University of Michigan, *post* 1888.

HINSHAW, DAVID SCHULL (*b. near Emporia, Kans., 1882; d. West Chester, Pa., 1953*), public relations counsel, political aide, author. Graduated from Haverford College, B.S., 1911. Corporate public relations counsel in the 1930's for such clients as the Pennsylvania Railroad and the Standard Oil Co., for whom he was director of Latin American public relations. Supported Theodore Roosevelt in 1912 and was a fund raiser and publicist for Calvin Coolidge, Herbert Hoover, Alf Landon, and Thomas Dewey. Author of *The Home Front* (1943), a criticism of Roosevelt's mobilization policies; and *Herbert Hoover: American Quaker* (1950).

HIRES, CHARLES ELMER (*b. near Roadstown, N.J., 1851; d. Haverford, Pa., 1937*), soft-drink manufacturer, popularizer of root beer.

HIRSCH, EMIL GUSTAV (*b. Luxembourg, 1851; d. 1923*), rabbi. Came to America as a boy. Graduated University of Pennsylvania, 1872; studied also at Berlin, Leipzig. Ministered in Philadelphia, Baltimore, Louisville; in Chicago, *post* 1880. Professor of University of Chicago, *post* 1892. An editor of the *Jewish Encyclopedia* and active civic leader, he was the Jewish apostle to the non-Jewish world.

HIRSCH, ISAAC SETH (*b. New York, N.Y., 1880; d. New York, 1942*), radiologist. M.D., College of Physicians and Surgeons, Columbia University, 1902. As radiologist, Bellevue Hospital, New York City, 1910–26, he made its X-ray department one of the finest in the nation; he was director of the X-ray department at New York's Beth Israel Hospital from 1928 until shortly before his death. Author of several textbooks on his specialty, he taught at N.Y. Post-Graduate Medical School and at the College of Medicine, New York University.

HIRSCH, MAXIMILIAN JUSTICE (*b. Fredericksburg, Tex., 1880; d. New Hyde Park, N.Y., 1969*), horse trainer. After a short but successful career as a jockey, became a trainer, and by 1915 his horses were winning important races. The first champion he trained was Sarazen, who won eight stakes races in 1924. He won the Belmont with Vito, 1928, and the Arlington Classic with Attention, 1941, and then trained Assault, often considered his best horse: Assault won the 1946 Kentucky Derby and completed the Triple Crown with victories in the Preakness and Belmont and also won the Pimlico Special and the Westchester Handicap. Trained for many owners, including Robert Kleberg, Jr., of the King Ranch of Texas, for whom he saddled fifty-four stakes winners. In the last sixty years of his career, won over 1,900 races and over $12 million. At the time of his death, horsemen considered him the best.

HIRSCHBEIN, PERETZ (*b. near Klestchel, Grodno Province, Russia, 1880; d. Los Angeles, Calif., 1948*), Yiddish dramatist, novelist, travel writer, lecturer. Resident in the United States, 1911–13, during World War I, and *post* 1930; contributor to newspaper *Der Tag*. Author, among many other works, of *Travels in America* (1918); *Bovel*, a massive novel dealing with the fortunes of a Jewish family after immigration to the United States in 1883 (1942); and two volumes of personal memoirs. Among his plays, the trilogy *Green Fields* (1916), *Two Towns* (1919), and *Levi Isaak* (1923) is considered his best work.

HIRSCHENSOHN, CHAIM (*b. Safed, Palestine, 1857; d. New York, N.Y., 1935*), rabbi. Came to America, 1903. Pastor in Hoboken, N.J. Active in movements for popularizing Hebrew, he was a dedicated Zionist.

HIRST, BARTON COOKE (*b. Philadelphia, Pa., 1861; d. Philadelphia, 1935*), obstetrician, author. Graduated M.D., University of Pennsylvania, 1883; studied also in Germany and Austria. Professor of obstetrics, University of Pennsylvania, 1889–1927, and in graduate school, 1927–35.

HIRST, HENRY BECK (*b. Philadelphia, Pa., 1817; d. Philadelphia, 1874*), poet, lawyer. Eccentric author of *The Coming of the Mammoth* (1845), *Endymion* (1848) and other works.

HIRTH, WILLIAM ANDREW (*b. Tarrytown, N.Y., 1875; d. Columbia, Mo., 1940*), journalist. Removed to Missouri as a child. Publisher, the *Missouri Farmer*; organized Missouri Farmers' Assn., 1917; advocate of the McNary-Haugen farm-surplus plan.

HISCOCK, FRANK HARRIS (*b. Tully, N.Y., 1856; d. Syracuse, N.Y., 1946*), lawyer. B.A., Cornell University, 1875; admitted to bar after study with lawyer uncle, 1878. Appointed judge of state supreme court, 1896, and elected to full fourteen-year term that same year; raised to appellate division, 1901. Appointed auxiliary member of N.Y. court of appeals, 1906, he was elected as associate judge for a full term, 1913. In 1916, he was elected to a ten-year term as chief judge of the court of appeals; during his tenure, he won a reputation for administrative efficiency and a cautious progressivism.

HISE, ELIJAH   (*b. Allegheny Co., Pa., 1801; d. Russellville, Ky., 1867*), lawyer, jurist, diplomat. Raised in Kentucky. Negotiated controversial canal treaty with Nicaragua, 1849, while on mission to Guatemala.

HITCHCOCK, CHARLES HENRY   (*b. Amherst, Mass., 1836; d. Honolulu, Hawaii, 1919*), geologist. Son of Edward Hitchcock (1793–1864). Professor at Dartmouth, 1868–1908, and administrator of New Hampshire geological survey, 1868–78.

HITCHCOCK, EDWARD   (*b. Deerfield, Mass., 1793; d. 1864*), geologist, educator, Congregational clergyman. Professor of science, Amherst, *post* 1825; president, 1845–55. Along with his academic duties, he conducted two geological surveys of Massachusetts; after long investigation, ascribed the sandstone "bird tracks," found in the Connecticut Valley, to dinosauric origin; served as Vermont state geologist, 1856–61. Outstanding among his books were *Elementary Geology* (1840), *Report on Geology of Vermont* (1861) and *Illustrations of Surface Geology* (1857).

HITCHCOCK, EDWARD   (*b. Amherst, Mass., 1828; d. 1911*), educator. Son of Edward Hitchcock (1793–1864). M.D., Harvard, 1853. First professor of physical education in an American college (Amherst, 1861–1911).

HITCHCOCK, ENOS   (*b. Springfield, Mass., 1744; d. Providence, R.I., 1803*), Congregational clergyman, Revolutionary Army chaplain. Author of numerous works including two early didactic novels, *Memoirs of the Bloomsgrove Family* (1790) and *The Farmer's Friend* (1793).

HITCHCOCK, ETHAN ALLEN   (*b. Vergennes, Vt., 1798; d. Sparta, Ga., 1870*), soldier, author. Graduated West Point, 1817. Served on the frontiers, in the Florida war, and with distinction on Winfield Scott's staff in Mexico. His integrity and intelligence brought him often into conflict with his superiors. Retired, 1855, he was commissioned major general of volunteers, 1861, and rendered valuable service in Union Army during Civil War. He wrote extensively on scientific subjects, philosophy, and alchemy.

HITCHCOCK, ETHAN ALLEN   (*b. Mobile, Ala., 1835; d. Washington, D.C., 1909*), businessman. Brother of Henry Hitchcock. An important figure in American steel and glass manufacturing, when he first entered political life, 1897. His friendship with President McKinley led to his appointment as minister to Russia and, in 1898, as secretary of the interior, which office he retained under Theodore Roosevelt. As secretary, he was a vigorous and persistent conservationist. He instituted legal proceedings against officials in the Land Office and secured 126 convictions. He withdrew mineral lands from sale, helped institute reclamation projects, and protected the Five Tribes in their possession of oil lands. It was claimed and denied that Roosevelt welcomed his resignation, 1907.

HITCHCOCK, FRANK.   *See* MURDOCH, FRANK HITCHCOCK.

HITCHCOCK, FRANK HARRIS   (*b. Amherst, Ohio, 1867; d. Tucson, Ariz., 1935*), lawyer, politician. Managed presidential campaign of William H. Taft, 1908. Postmaster general, 1909–12. His businesslike and forward-looking policies included establishment of the first air-mail route and the parcel-post system.

HITCHCOCK, GILBERT MONELL   (*b. Omaha, Nebr., 1859; d. Washington, D.C., 1934*), politician. Son of Phineas W. Hitchcock. Publisher, Omaha *World Herald*. Congressman, Democrat, from Nebraska, 1903–05, 1907–11; U.S. Senator, 1911–23. Spoke and wrote in support of Treaty of Versailles; opposed Senator Lodge's amendments.

HITCHCOCK, HENRY   (*b. Alabama, 1829; d. St. Louis, Mo., 1902*), lawyer, Union soldier. Brother of Ethan Allen Hitchcock (1835–1909). Organized law school of Washington University (St. Louis, Mo.) and served as its first dean.

HITCHCOCK, JAMES RIPLEY WELLMAN   (*b. Fitchburg, Mass., 1857; d. New York, N.Y., 1918*), journalist, publishers' editor, author. Art critic for *New York Tribune*, 1882–90. Editorial adviser to D. Appleton and Co., and Harper and Brothers.

HITCHCOCK, PETER   (*b. Cheshire, Conn., 1781; d. Painesville, Ohio, 1853*), Ohio jurist and legislator. Graduated Yale, 1801. Removed to Ohio, 1806.

HITCHCOCK, PHINEAS WARRENER   (*b. New Lebanon, N.Y., 1831; d. 1881*), lawyer. Removed to Nebraska, 1857; practiced in Omaha. Was territorial delegate, Republican, 1865–67; U.S. senator, 1871–77.

HITCHCOCK, RAYMOND   (*b. Auburn, N.Y., 1865; d. Beverly Hills, Calif., 1929*), actor, comedian.

HITCHCOCK, RIPLEY.   *See* HITCHCOCK, JAMES RIPLEY WELLMAN.

HITCHCOCK, ROSWELL DWIGHT   (*b. East Machias, Maine, 1817; d. Somerset, Mass., 1887*), Congregational clergyman, educator. Graduated Amherst, 1836. Professor of religion, Bowdoin, 1852–55; professor of church history, Union Theological Seminary, New York, 1855–87.

HITCHCOCK, THOMAS   (*b. Aiken, S.C., 1900; d. near Salisbury, England, 1944*), sportsman, military aviator. Grandson of George Eustis (1828–1872). Rejected as too young for U.S. military service, 1917, he joined the Lafayette Escadrille; shot down in March 1918, he made his way back to France and joined the U.S. Air Service. Graduated from Harvard, 1922. Played on the U.S. Polo Association's championship teams, 1919, 1920, 1921, achieving ten-goal rank. Captain, Olympic polo team, 1924; led the U.S. team to victory over the English in 1927 and the Argentines in 1928. *Post* 1932, he was associated with Lehman Brothers, bankers, becoming a partner in 1937. Served in Army Air Corps, World War II. Killed while testing a P-51 plane.

HITE, JOST   (*b. Strasbourg, Alsace; d. Virginia, 1760*), colonizer. Came to America, 1710; promoted settlement in New York and Pennsylvania; colonized area near Winchester, Va., *post* 1732. Litigation with Lord Fairfax over titles to Virginia grants continued for more than fifteen years.

HITT, ROBERT ROBERTS   (*b. Urbana, Ohio, 1834; d. Newport, R.I., 1906*), reporter, diplomat. Congressman, Republican, from Illinois, 1883–1906; chairman, House foreign affairs committee, 1889–91, 1895–1905.

HITTELL, JOHN SHERTZER   (*b. Jonestown, Pa., 1825; d. 1901*), journalist, author, statistician. Brother of Theodore H. Hittell. Removed to California, 1849. On staff of the *Alta California*, 1853–80. Author of *The Resources of California* (1863), *A History of the City of San Francisco, and Incidentally of the State of California* (1878), and other works.

HITTELL, THEODORE HENRY   (*b. Marietta, Pa., 1830; d. 1917*), California lawyer, land-title expert. Brother of John S.

Hittell. Removed to California, 1856. Author of important legal works; also *The Adventures of James Capen Adams* (1860) and the *History of California* (1885–1897).

HOADLEY, DAVID (*b. Waterbury, Conn., 1774; d. Waterbury, 1839*), architect. The North Church in New Haven, the Samuel Russell mansion in Middletown, and many other houses through Connecticut displayed the intuitive genius of this self-taught craftsman and master of styles.

HOADLEY, JOHN CHIPMAN (*b. Martinsburg, N.Y., 1818; d. 1886*), engineer, designer and manufacturer of steam-engines and mill machinery. Author of *The Portable Steam Engine* (1863) and *Steam-Engine Practice in the United States* (1884).

HOADLY, GEORGE (*b. New Haven, Conn., 1826; d. Watkins, N.Y., 1902*), lawyer, Ohio jurist. Nephew of Theodore D. Woolsey. Raised in Ohio; studied law in office of Salmon P. Chase. Democratic governor of Ohio, 1884–86.

HOAG, JOSEPH (*b. Oblong, N.Y., 1762; d. Charlotte, Vt., 1846*), Quaker preacher. Opposed teaching of Elias Hicks; allied himself with "Wilburites" in New York.

HOAGLAND, CHARLES LEE (*b. Benkelman, Nebr., 1907; d. New York, N.Y., 1946*), physician, biochemist. B.S., Washington University (St. Louis, Mo.), 1931; M.D., 1935. Rockefeller Institute, New York City, 1937–46; did brilliant, pioneering work in a study of the chemical structure of the cowpox virus. His search for the cause of progressive muscular dystrophy was interrupted by World War II. Rejected by the navy for medical reasons, he studied and treated navy personnel suffering from infectious hepatitis. Worked out biochemical tests for measuring the extent of liver damage and the rate of repair of the liver during convalescence, thereby effecting a marked improvement in the method of treatment. Giving himself no rest, he died of malignant hypertension.

HOAGLAND, DENNIS ROBERT (*b. Golden, Colo., 1884; d. Berkeley, Calif., 1949*), plant physiologist, soil chemist. B.A., Stanford University, 1907; M.A., University of Wisconsin, 1913. Assistant professor of agricultural chemistry, University of California at Berkeley, 1913–26; professor of plant nutrition thereafter. Made notable advances in the field of plant and soil interrelations; to ensure control in research, perfected the water-culture technique for growing plants without soil; gave particular attention to the process of absorption and accumulation of ions by plants.

HOAN, DANIEL WEBSTER (*b. Waukesha, Wis., 1881; d. Milwaukee, Wis., 1961*), public official and Socialist and Democratic party leader. His experiences as city attorney for Milwaukee, 1910–16, are recorded in *The Failure of Regulation* (1914). As mayor of Milwaukee, 1916–40, launched an aggressive attack on the rising cost of living and on the housing shortage; fostered professional administration, planning, zoning, and city beautification; expanded public services, centralized purchasing, and pay-as-you-go municipal financing; strengthened the water utility with sewage treatment and water filtration systems; built municipal port facilities; and forged a close alliance with organized labor. His experiences are described in *City Government: The Record of the Milwaukee Experiment* (1936). Became an effective local leader of the Socialist party in the late 1920's, but joined the Democratic party in 1944 and succeeded in reviving and liberalizing the Wisconsin Democrats.

HOAR, EBENEZER ROCKWOOD (*b. Concord, Mass., 1816; d. 1895*), lawyer, jurist. Brother of George F. Hoar; son of Samuel Hoar. Graduated Harvard, 1835; Harvard Law School, 1839;. Coined the slogan "Conscience Whig" (1845) but joined the Free

Soil party, 1848, and finally became a Republican. When he was called by President Grant to become attorney general, 1869, he had served on the Massachusetts supreme judicial court for a decade. His demand that federal judgeships not be treated as patronage cost him a seat on the Supreme Court, the Senate refusing confirmation. He retired from the cabinet, 1870.

HOAR, GEORGE FRISBIE (*b. Concord, Mass., 1826; d. 1904*), lawyer, statesman. Son of Samuel Hoar. Graduated Harvard, 1846; Harvard Law School, 1849. Closely associated with founding of Republican party in Massachusetts; was congressman, 1869–77, and U.S. senator, 1877–1904. He was on the congressional electoral commission which settled the Hayes-Tilden controversy and voted for the Republican candidates. In Congress he was considered an able committeeman, and was a respected authority on the judiciary, Civil War claims and privileges and elections. A formidable, successful debater, both at the bar and in Congress, he upheld in speech and conduct the highest traditions of his profession. The bent of his mind was liberal; apparently he did not appreciate the social and economic developments which had changed the party of Abraham Lincoln to that of Mark Hanna and William McKinley.

HOAR, LEONARD (*b. Gloucester, England, ca. 1630; d. Boston, Mass., 1675*), clergyman, scholar. Came to New England as a boy. Graduated Harvard, 1647, and returned to England where he became M.A., Cambridge, 1654, and M.C., 1671. Called to presidency of Harvard, 1672–75, he incurred violent opposition of fellows and undergraduates. Among other reforms, he tried to introduce experimental sciences into Harvard curriculum.

HOAR, SAMUEL (*b. Lincoln, Mass., 1778; d. 1856*), lawyer. Massachusetts congressman, opponent of slavery. Father of Ebenezer R. and George F. Hoar.

HOARD, WILLIAM DEMPSTER (*b. Munnsville, N.Y., 1836; d. Fort Atkinson, Wis., 1918*), editor, educational leader. Removed to Wisconsin, 1857. Founded *Hoard's Dairyman*, 1885, a paper which circulated in every American state and most foreign countries. Introduced alfalfa in Wisconsin; pioneered in use of tuberculin test for cattle; urged use of silos; founded Wisconsin Dairyman's Association, 1872. Governor of Wisconsin, 1888–91.

HOBAN, JAMES (*b. Callan, Ireland, ca. 1762; d. Washington, D.C., 1831*), architect, contractor. Immigrated to Philadelphia, *ante* 1785. Designed old state capitol in Columbia, S.C. 1790–91. Moved to the new Federal City, 1792, and took part in competition for the proposed public buildings there. Designed the White House, supervised its construction, and rebuilt it after its destruction by the British in 1814. Among his later works were the State and War offices, begun 1818.

HOBART, ALICE NOURSE TISDALE (*b. Lockport, N.Y., 1882; d. Oakland, Calif., 1967*), writer and novelist. Wrote a number of books and novels about her experiences living in China during 1908–27. The most popular of these, *Oil for the Lamps of China* (1933) was made into a motion picture (1935, and, as *Law of the Tropics*, 1941). Another popular novel, *The Cup and the Sword* (1942), was made into the movie *This Earth Is Mine* (1959). After moving to California in 1935, wrote historical novels set in California and Mexico. Ten of her novels became best-sellers, and her books sold more than 4 million copies and were translated into a dozen languages. Also wrote numerous articles and stories for magazines.

HOBART, GARRET AUGUSTUS (*b. Long Branch, N.J., 1844; d. Paterson, N.J., 1899*), lawyer. New Jersey legislator, corporation director. Vice president of the United States, 1897–99.

HOBART, JOHN HENRY (*b. Philadelphia, Pa., 1775; d. Auburn, N.Y., 1830*), Episcopal clergyman. Graduated College of New Jersey (Princeton), 1793; A.M., 1796. Installed assistant minister, Trinity Parish, New York, 1801; elected assistant bishop of New York, 1811. His ability, energy in controversy, and devotion to his creed made him a prominent religious figure. In 1816 he was chosen both rector of Trinity and diocesan of New York. He established a society for training ministers, 1806, which later developed into General Theological Seminary, where he taught theology. He succeeded in awakening the loyalty of both clergy and laity in a church which had suffered loss of prestige during the Revolution and the early years of the nation.

HOBART, JOHN SLOSS (*b. Fairfield, Conn., 1738; d. New York, N.Y., 1805*), Revolutionary patriot. Landowner in Suffolk Co., Long Island; member, N.Y. York Provincial Congress, Justice of New York Supreme Court, 1777–98; U.S. senator from New York, 1798; U.S. district judge, 1798–1805.

HOBBS, ALFRED CHARLES (*b. Boston, Mass., 1812; d. Bridgeport, Conn., 1891*), lock expert, manufacturer, mechanical engineer, designer of machine tools.

HOBBY, WILLIAM PETTUS (*b. Moscow, Tex., 1878; d. Houston, Tex., 1964*), governor of Texas, editor, and publisher. After working for the *Houston Post*, in 1907 he became publisher and half-owner of the *Beaumont Enterprise*. Was lieutenant governor, 1914–17, and governor, 1917–20, of Texas. As governor he made 90 percent of Texas "dry" and appointed the first effective administrators of the newly created highway department. Later bought *The Beaumont Journal*, and in 1924 returned to the *Houston Post* as president, in 1939 acquiring ownership as well as control.

HOBSON, EDWARD HENRY (*b. Greensburg, Ky., 1825; d. Cleveland, Ohio, 1901*), businessman, Union brigadier general. Leader of 1863 expedition which pursued Confederate General John H. Morgan for 900 miles through Kentucky and Ohio; captured a major portion of the raider's command.

HOBSON, RICHMOND PEARSON (*b. Greensboro, Ala., 1870; d. New York, N.Y., 1937*), naval officer. Graduated Annapolis, 1889. Won fame for sinking collier *Merrimac* in Santiago, Cuba, channel, 1898; resigned, 1903. Congressman, Democrat, from Alabama, 1907–15.

HOCH, AUGUST (*b. Basel, Switzerland, 1868; d. San Francisco, Calif., 1919*), psychiatrist. M.D., University of Maryland, 1890; studied extensively abroad. Taught at Cornell Medical School, 1905–17.

HOCKING, WILLIAM ERNEST (*b. Cleveland, Ohio, 1873; d. Madison, N.H., 1966*), philosopher and educator. B.A. (1901), M.A. (1902), Ph.D. (1904), Harvard. Taught primarily at Harvard, 1914–43, where he was Alford Professor of Natural Religion, Moral Philosophy, and Civil Polity after 1920. His first major book, which remains his magnum opus, was *The Meaning of God in Human Experience: A Philosophic Study of Religion* (1912). In this book and others, he espoused his own version of Josiah Royce's philosophical idealism, but despite his efforts, that tradition was eclipsed by a less speculative, religiously skeptical, and frequently antimetaphysical empiricism. Thus his twenty books are no longer studied extensively, though many college students read his *Types of Philosophy* (1929; revised 1939 and 1959), and his influence as a pioneer of religious ecumenicity, world harmony, and a global perspective in philosophy remains.

HODES, HENRY IRVING (*b. Washington, D.C., 1899; d. San Antonio, Tex., 1962*), soldier. Graduated U.S. Military Academy (1918). Led the 112th Infantry Regiment in France in 1944 and the 7th Infantry Division during the Korean War, after which he was chief army representative at the armistice negotiations. After 1954 held posts of increasing responsibility in Germany for five years, commanding the VII Corps and then the Seventh Army. Was commander in chief of the U.S. Army in Europe, with the rank of general, 1956–59. His major decorations include three awards of the Distinguished Service Medal, the Legion of Merit twice, the Silver Star for both Normandy and Korea, the British Distinguished Service Order, and the Korean Order of Military Merit.

HODGE, ARCHIBALD ALEXANDER (*b. Princeton, N.J., 1823; d. 1886*), Presbyterian clergyman. Son of Charles Hodge. Graduated Princeton, 1841; Princeton Theological Seminary, 1845, where he taught theology, 1877–86. A severely orthodox writer whose class lectures and theological discussions were audacious, brilliant, and humorous.

HODGE, CHARLES (*b. Philadelphia, Pa., 1797; d. 1878*), Presbyterian clergyman, theologian. Graduated Princeton, 1815; Princeton Theological Seminary, 1819, where he was instructor and professor, 1820–78. Advocated the Calvinistic theology as stated by the Westminster divines and supported it by Scriptural interpretation. He maintained his position with skill at the time when Calvinism was disintegrating and evolutionary ideas were becoming increasingly powerful. His learned, able, controversial writings and success in awakening minds explain his fame as teacher and leader; he was a powerful conservative force on Presbyterianism and on other churches. *Systematic Theology* (1872–73) and *Discussions in Church Polity* (published posthumously) were of outstanding importance among his many books. He contended against the Presbyterian "New School" views and opposed slavery while deprecating Abolitionist policy.

HODGE, HUGH LENOX (*b. Philadelphia, Pa., 1796; d. 1873*), obstetrician. Brother of Charles Hodge. Professor of obstetrics, University of Pennsylvania, 1835–63; designer of obstetrical instruments; author of *The Principles and Practice of Obstetrics* (1864).

HODGE, JOHN REED (*b. Golconda, Ill., 1893; d. Washington, D.C., 1963*), army officer dubbed by reporters "the Patton of the Pacific." As assistant commander of the 25th Division, distinguished himself in the actions of early 1943 that consolidated the American hold on Guadalcanal. In 1943 successfully commanded the 43rd Division, then heavily engaged on New Georgia. In 1944 was given command of the newly formed XXIV Corps, which he led in the invasions of the Philippines and Okinawa. During the war was awarded the Legion of Merit, the Distinguished Service Medal with two oak leaf clusters, and the Air Medal. Following Japan's collapse, was designated by General Douglas MacArthur to receive the surrender of Japanese forces in southern Korea and to occupy and administer the country south of the thirty-eighth parallel, a position he held until a U.N.–supervised election ended military occupation. Retired in 1953 with the rank of full general.

HODGE, WILLIAM THOMAS (*b. Albion, N.Y., 1874; d. near Greenwich, Conn., 1932*), actor, playwright. Famous for characterization of slow-speaking, good-humored, astute American rustic.

HODGEN, JOHN THOMPSON (*b. Hodgenville, Ky., 1826; d. St. Louis, Mo., 1882*), surgeon. Professor and dean, St. Louis Medical College, 1864–82. Developed a splint for fracture of the femur and other surgical aids.

HODGES, COURTNEY HICKS (*b. Perry, Ga., 1887; d. San Antonio, Tex., 1966*), soldier and military commander. Enlisted in the army in 1906. In France during World War I, rose rapidly up the chain of command and led troops in several offensives, earning the Distinguished Service Cross, the Silver Star, and the Bronze Star with three battle stars for his gallantry and leadership. Between the two world wars learned and taught about the use of infantry, artillery, and air support, graduating from the Field Artillery School (1920), the Command and General Staff College (1925), and the Army War College (1933) and becoming assistant commandant (1938) and commandant (1940) of the Infantry School at Fort Benning, Ga. During World War II became commanding general of the First Army, which compiled a record second to none in the European Theater of Operations; though other commanders received more recognition, President Dwight D. Eisenhower eventually hailed him as the "star" of the drive across the Rhine into the heart of Germany, and in the final weeks of the campaign he was promoted to full general. After the war, remained in command of the First Army until his retirement (1949).

HODGES, GEORGE (*b. Rome, N.Y., 1856; d. 1919*), Episcopal clergyman. Influenced by Kingsley and Maurice, he became advocate of the "social gospel" while active minister and as dean of Episcopal Theological Seminary, Cambridge, Mass., *post* 1894.

HODGES, HARRY FOOTE (*b. Boston, Mass., 1860; d. Lake Forest, Ill., 1929*), military engineer. Graduated West Point, 1881. Supervised important work on Ohio, Missouri, and Mississippi rivers; served in Puerto Rico, 1898–99, and was chief engineer in Cuba under Gen. Leonard Wood. Assigned to Panama, 1907, he performed notable service as engineer in charge of design of locks, dams, and regulating works on the Canal. He trained and commanded the 76th Division in World War I, retiring as major general, 1921.

HODGKINSON, FRANCIS (*b. London, England, 1867; d. Toledo, Ohio, 1949*), mechanical engineer. Associated in England with the manufacturers of the Parsons turbine, he came to Pittsburgh, Pa., where he worked for Westinghouse from 1896 to 1936. Holder of more than a hundred patents in steam turbine design, he was author of a number of important papers on his specialty.

HODGKINSON, JOHN (*b. England, ca. 1767; d. near Bladensburg, Md., 1805*), actor, theatrical manager. Trained in English provincial theaters; came to America, 1792. Maneuvered John Henry and Lewis Hallam out of management of their New York company; uneasy partner of William Dunlap, 1797; later played in Dunlap's company and at Charleston, S.C. As an actor, his peculiar province was low comedy, but he was equally capable in high comedy, tragedy, and operatic roles.

HODGSON, WILLIAM BROWN (*b. Georgetown, D.C., 1801; d. New York, N.Y., 1871*), U.S. consular officer, Orientalist. World-pioneer in studies of the Berber languages.

HODSON, WILLIAM (*b. Minneapolis, Minn., 1891; d. Paramaribo, Dutch Guiana, 1943*), welfare administrator. Graduated University of Minnesota, 1913; LL.B., Harvard Law School, 1916. Achieved recognition as chief architect of a new children's code for Minnesota, enacted 1917, and as director of the Minnesota child welfare program, 1918–22. Removing to New York City, he directed the child welfare division and the social legislation department of the Russell Sage Foundation, 1922–25. Director, Welfare Council of New York City, 1925–33; appointed commissioner of welfare of New York City. He was killed in an air crash while on a wartime relief mission. He was a proponent of work relief and public works projects, old-age pensions, unemployment insurance, compulsory federal health insurance, elimination of the means test, and the opening up of new opportunities for disadvantaged groups.

HODUR, FRANCIS (*b. Zarki, Poland, 1866; d. Scranton, Pa., 1953*), founder and Prime Bishop of the Polish National Catholic Church in America. Immigrated to the U.S. in 1892. Studied at St. Vincent Seminary; ordained in 1893. First pastor of St. Stanislaus Bishop and Martyr parish, Scranton, Pa., the first Polish National Church in America, 1897. Excommunicated in 1898. Designated bishop-elect of the First General Synod, 1904. Consecrated as bishop of the Old Catholics in Europe, 1907, thus culminating the first and only major schism in the American Catholic church. Founded a seminary in 1927; established organs of communication; and joined the American and, later, the World Council of Churches. Negotiated the intercommunion with the Church of England and the American Protestant Episcopal Church, 1946.

HOE, RICHARD MARCH (*b. New York, N.Y., 1812; d. Florence, Italy, 1886*), inventor, manufacturer. Son of Robert Hoe (1784–1833). In 1830, he assumed responsibility, together with his cousin, Matthew Smith, for the Hoe printing-press-building establishment. His interest in experimentation led to vast improvements and great prosperity for an already famous company. Hoe was the dominant force in management and active director of policy for more than fifty years. Among his inventions or adaptations were the large cylinder press and the type-revolving press (1847) which caused an immediate revolution in newspaper printing. *Post* 1871, he helped to develop the web press.

HOE, ROBERT (*b. Hoes, England, 1784; d. New York, N.Y., 1833*), founder of R. Hoe & Co., makers of printing presses. Father of Richard M. Hoe. Came to America, 1803. His improved cylinder press succeeded in displacing presses imported from England.

HOE, ROBERT (*b. New York, N.Y., 1839; d. London, England, 1909*), manufacturer, bibliophile. Grandson of Robert Hoe (1784–1833); nephew of Richard M. Hoe. Succeeded his uncle as head of R. Hoe & Co., 1886. Undeterred by unsuccessful experiments, the firm went on to produce a double supplement press, the quadruple newspaper press, then the sextuple machine. A 96–page press for newspapers was perfected, 1901, along with rotary art presses and color presses. Collector of a celebrated library, Hoe was founder and first president of Grolier Club and a founder of Metropolitan Museum of Art.

HOECKEN, CHRISTIAN (*b. Tilburg, Belgium, 1808; d. Missouri River, near mouth of the Platte, 1851*), Jesuit missionary to Kickapoo and Potawatomi Indians in Kansas and Iowa; associate of P. J. De Smet. Came to America, 1833. Composed a grammar and dictionary of the Kickapoo language, prayerbooks and catechisms in Potawatomi language.

HOEN, AUGUST (*b. Höhn, Germany, 1817; d. Baltimore, Md., 1886*), lithographer, map printer. Came to America, 1835; joined cousin in establishment of a firm in Baltimore which developed into A. Hoen & Co. Soon established a reputation in his specialty, lithographing maps and illustrating publications of government bureaus and of Congress. The maps and illustrations in J. C. Frémont's reports (1845 and 1846) and the color charts in U.S. Geological Survey reports were considered outstanding achievements. Hoen produced first colored show cards in this country, 1839. Hoen's research laboratory made important contributions in the field of map symbolism and developed many new processes, and most notable being "Lithokaustic" (1860), which found favor with illustrators and producers of trade labels.

HOENECKE, GUSTAV ADOLF FELIX THEODOR (*b. Brandenburg, Germany, 1835; d. 1908*), Lutheran clergyman. Came to America, 1863. Conservative president and professor at Evangelical Lutheran Seminary, Milwaukee, Wis.

HOERR, NORMAND LOUIS (*b. Peoria, Ill., 1902; d. Cleveland, Ohio, 1958*), histologist, neuroanatomist, educator. Studied at Johns Hopkins University and the University of Chicago, Ph.D., 1929; M.D., 1931. Taught anatomy at the University of Chicago, 1925–39. Influential in research and dissemination of modern organelle chemistry; with R. R. Bensley, Hoerr separated mitochondria from liver cells (1934). Introduced the term cytochemistry, 1943. Taught at Western Reserve University from 1939, where he encouraged the multidisciplinary approach to the study of anatomy. Coeditor of the *New Gould Medical Dictionary*, 1949–56.

HOEY, CLYDE ROARK (*b. Shelby, N.C., 1877; d. Washington, D.C., 1954*), politician. Attended the University of North Carolina; studied law privately. Member of the North Carolina House of Commons, 1897–1902, and Senate, 1902–19; Democratic congressman 1919–21. Governor of North Carolina, 1936–41. U.S. senator, 1944–54. Supported the Marshall Plan and the Taft-Hartley Act of 1947, but opposed Truman's civil rights program.

HOFF, JOHN VAN RENSSELAER (*b. Mount Morris, N.Y., 1848; d. 1920*), army medical officer. Graduated Union, 1871; M.D., Columbia, 1874. A pioneer in establishing proper military rank and status for army doctors.

HOFFMAN, CHARLES FENNO (*b. New York, N.Y., 1806; d. Harrisburg, Pa., 1884*), editor, poet. Author of a number of books including *A Winter in the West* (1835) and *Greyslaer* (1839).

HOFFMAN, CLARE EUGENE (*b. Vicksburg, Pa., 1875; d. Allegan, Mich., 1967*), congressman. Republican congressman from Michigan's Fourth District, 1934–62. A conservative and an isolationist, he vehemently opposed President Franklin D. Roosevelt's domestic and foreign policy. Became noted for his opposition to labor unions during the "Little Steel" strike of 1937. During the Eightieth Congress, became chairman of the House Committee on Expenditures in the Executive Department. In 1947 a bill providing for the reorganization of the army, navy, and air force was introduced and referred to his committee, and he considered his protection of the Marine Corps one of his two chief legislative accomplishments, the other being his work on the Taft-Hartley Act. In 1953 resumed chairmanship of his old committee, which had been renamed the Government Operations Committee. A foe of President Dwight D. Eisenhower's New Republicanism, he opposed Eisenhower on both domestic and foreign policy.

HOFFMAN, DAVID (*b. Baltimore, Md., 1784; d. New York, N.Y., 1854*), lawyer. As professor of law, University of Maryland, at various times between 1823 and 1843, he outlined a course of legal study (1817 and 1836) that was, according to Justice Joseph Story, the most perfect yet offered. Hoffman's basic requirements were systematic reading of legal and social literature, the study of statutes and forms, and an insistence on pleadings in genuine practice courts. His teachings were in advance of the practice of his time and were poorly patronized.

HOFFMAN, DAVID MURRAY (*b. New York, N.Y., 1791; d. Flushing, N.Y., 1878*), jurist. Nephew of Josiah O. Hoffman. Graduated Columbia, 1809. Distinguished commentator on chancery practice and procedure in New York; pioneer commentator on the revision of the New York Code.

HOFFMAN, EUGENE AUGUSTUS (*b. New York, N.Y., 1829; d. 1902*), Episcopal clergyman. Graduated Rutgers, 1847; General Theological Seminary, New York, 1851. Dean of that seminary, 1879–1902, where his efficient administration brought prosperity and success.

HOFFMAN, FREDERICK LUDWIG (*b. Varel, near Bremen, Germany, 1865; d. San Diego, Calif., 1946*), statistician, writer on public health. Immigrated to the United States, 1884. Largely self-educated. His statistical studies of black mortality and susceptibility to disease—published as *Race Traits and Tendencies of the American Negro* (1896)—were used to justify higher premiums for blacks and their disenfranchisement in the South. From 1894 until his retirement in 1934, he held executive positions with the Prudential Insurance Company. Associated also with the Babson Institute and the Franklin Institute (1934–38). He was a prolific writer on actuarial, public health, and demographic subjects, and an implacable opponent of public health insurance and medical care. His statistical studies of many ills, ranging from malaria to industrial health hazards, suicide, and murder, were of value in campaigns for their cure and control. Directly responsible for the founding of the American Cancer Society.

HOFFMAN, JOHN THOMPSON (*b. Sing Sing, N.Y., 1828; d. Wiesbaden, Germany, 1888*), lawyer, Tammany politician. Mayor of New York City, 1865–68; governor of New York, 1869–73. His popularity served as a screen for the Tweed Ring, which he later repudiated.

HOFFMAN, JOSIAH OGDEN (*b. Newark, N.J., 1766; d. 1837*), lawyer. Leader of Federalist party in N.Y. Assembly, 1791–1797. Associate judge, N.Y. superior court, 1828–37.

HOFFMAN, OGDEN (*b. New York, N.Y., 1793; d. New York, 1856*), lawyer. Son of Josiah O. Hoffman. Graduated Columbia, 1812. Served under Commodore Decatur, 1812–16. Practiced in New York City, *post* 1826. District attorney, N.Y. County, 1829–35; congressman, Whig, from New York, 1837–41. Opposed Jackson's stand on U.S. Bank; became in Congress an outstanding enemy of the Sub-Treasury bill. U.S. attorney, N.Y., southern district, 1841–45; N.Y. State attorney general, 1853–55. Hoffman's brilliance was clearly evidenced as trial attorney; he was considered his generation's outstanding criminal lawyer.

HOFFMAN, RICHARD (*b. Manchester, England, 1831; d. Mt. Kisco, N.Y., 1909*), concert pianist, composer, teacher. Came to America, 1847. Accompanied Jenny Lind in her first American concerts.

HOFFMAN, WICKHAM (*b. New York, N.Y., 1821; d. Atlantic City, N.J., 1900*), Union soldier, diplomat, lawyer. Son of David M. Hoffman. Able staff officer throughout Civil War; secretary in important legations, 1866–83; U.S. minister to Denmark, 1883–85.

HOFFMANN, FRANCIS ARNOLD (*b. Herford, Germany, 1822; d. near Jefferson, Wis., 1903*), Lutheran clergyman, banker. Came to America ca. 1840. Agricultural writer under name of Hans Buschbauer. Settled thousands of immigrants on land of Illinois Central. Lieutenant governor, Republican, of Illinois, 1861–65.

HOFMAN, HEINRICH OSCAR (*b. Heidelberg, Germany, 1852; d. 1924*), metallurgist. Came to America, 1882. Professor, Massachusetts Institute of Technology, *post* 1889. His *Metallurgy of Lead and the Desilverization of Base Bullion* (1892, 1918) became a standard work.

HOFMANN, HANS (*b. Weissenberg, Bavaria, Germany, 1880; d. New York, N.Y., 1966*), painter. Created the Hans Hofmann School of Fine Arts in Munich (1915–32). Became one of the leaders of the German abstract movement and was influenced by German expressionist art, evidenced by his portrait drawings of 1926–27. After moving to America (became U.S. citizen, 1944), opened his own art school in 1932 in New York City, and in 1935 founded the highly successful Hans Hofmann Summer School in Provincetown, Mass. Has been cataloged as the father figure and leading theoretician of abstract expressionism. His influence as a teacher was enormous, such handy Hofmann tenets as "forming with color," "push and pull," and the musical "interval" becoming part of the argot of young artists. A collection of his work, numbering forty-five paintings, was opened in 1970 as the Hans Hofmann Wing at the Museum of the University of California at Berkeley.

HOFMANN, JOSEF CASIMIR (*b. Podgorze, Poland, 1876; d. Los Angeles, Calif., 1957*), pianist. Immigrated to the U.S. around 1900. A prodigy, Hofmann concertized in Europe from 1884 to 1887; his first U.S. tour was in 1887. A pupil of Anton Rubinstein, he soon was considered one of the greatest pianists of his day, with an almost universal repertoire. Hofmann also composed several works for piano, at first under the pseudonym, Michel Dvorsky. From 1924 to 1938, associated with the Curtis Institute in Philadelphia; general director and dean from 1926. His last public concert was in New York City in 1946.

HOFSTADTER, RICHARD (*b. Buffalo, N.Y., 1916; d. New York, N.Y., 1970*), historian and author. B.A. (1937), University of Buffalo; M.A. (1938) and Ph.D. (1942), Columbia. In conjunction with honorary positions at other academic institutions, remained associated with Columbia throughout his life, joining the faculty in 1946 and becoming DeWitt Clinton Professor of American History in 1959. His major publications were *Social Darwinism in American Thought, 1860–1915* (1944), his doctoral dissertation, which received the Beveridge Award from the American Historical Association in 1942; *The American Political Tradition and the Men Who Made It* (1948); *The Development of Academic Freedom in the United States* (1955), coauthored with Walter P. Metzger; *The Age of Reform: From Bryan to F.D.R.* (1955), which was awarded the Pulitzer Prize; *Anti-Intellectualism in American Life* (1963), which won a Pulitzer Prize and other awards; *The Paranoid Style in American Politics and Other Essays* (1965); *The Progressive Historians: Turner, Beard, Parrington* (1968); *The Idea of a Party System: Legitimate Opposition in the United States, 1780–1840* (1969); and *America at 1750: A Social Portrait* (1971), published posthumously. The subjects that he addressed were affected above all by the repressive effects of McCarthyism in the 1950's, which motivated him to search for the sources of enmity to independent thought in America's history. In *Anti-Intellectualism* he identified the twin nemeses of intellectual inquiry as sectarianism and provincialism, historically identified with the new democracy of the nineteenth century. In *The Age of Reform*, he saw new hope for independent thought late in the nineteenth century but identified Populism and Progressivism as obstacles to intellectual tolerance. Generally, however, he gave his history a progressive thrust, seeing the New Deal era as a time of positive change in American culture, celebrating the metropolis as the environment that best nourished free inquiry, and identifying the modern university as the bastion of intellectual freedom. Drawing from such disciplines as anthropology, sociology, psychology, and literary analysis, he was a pioneer in the interdisciplinary approach to history, and he improved the art of applying history to public commentary.

HOGAN, JOHN (*b. Mallow, Ireland, 1805; d. 1892*), Methodist preacher, businessman, Missouri politician.

HOGAN, JOHN VINCENT LAWLESS (*b. Philadelphia, Pa., 1890; d. Forest Hills, N.Y., 1960*), electrical engineer and inventor. Studied at Yale University. Remembered as the inventor of single-dial tuning of radio receivers (1912), Hogan was instrumental in researching many aspects of radio transmission and technology. Founded the Institute of Radio Engineers in 1912; president, 1920. Founded New York's experimental high fidelity station, WQXR, in 1936. During World War II Hogan did research on radar and proximity fuses with the Office of Scientific Research and Development led by Vannevar Bush.

HOGE, MOSES (*b. Cedargrove, Va., 1752; d. 1820*), Presbyterian clergyman, educator. President, Hampden-Sydney College, 1807–20. His teaching resulted in founding of Union Theological Seminary in Virginia. A moderate Evangelical.

HOGE, MOSES DRURY (*b. Hampden-Sydney, Va., 1819; d. Richmond, Va., 1899*), Presbyterian clergyman. Grandson of Moses Hoge. Pastor, Second Presbyterian Church, Richmond, Va., 1845–99. Ran blockade during Civil War to bring Bibles for Confederate soldiers.

HOGG, GEORGE (*b. Cramlington, England, 1784; d. Allegheny City, Pa., 1849*), merchant, glass manufacturer, operator of lake and river shipping. Came to America as a young man. A pioneer of chain stores, wholesale and retail.

HOGG, JAMES STEPHEN (*b. near Rusk, Tex., 1851; d. 1906*), lawyer. Texas attorney general, 1887–91; Democratic governor of Texas, 1891–95. Curbed abuses of corrupt corporations, railroads, and land companies.

HOGUE, WILSON THOMAS (*b. Lyndon, N.Y., 1852; d. 1920*), clergyman and bishop of the Free Methodist Church. President, Greenville College, Illinois, 1892–1904.

HOGUN, JAMES (*b. Ireland; d. Haddrell's Point, S.C., 1781*), Revolutionary soldier. Settled in Halifax Co., N.C., ca. 1751. As brigadier general, commanded North Carolina brigade under Washington and Lincoln; taken prisoner at Charleston, S.C., 1780.

HOHFELD, WESLEY NEWCOMB (*b. Oakland, Calif., 1879; d. Alameda, Calif., 1918*), legal scholar. Graduated University of California, 1901; Harvard Law School, 1904. Served as professor of law at Stanford, 1905–14; at Yale, 1914–18. His greatest work was a series of monographs published posthumously, *Fundamental Legal Conceptions as Applied in Judicial Reasoning* (1919, 1923), setting forth the ideas of legal analysis which later became known as the Hohfeld System. Although subjected to much discussion, his terminology was adopted in substance by the American Law Institute.

HOISINGTON, HENRY RICHARD (*b. Vergennes, Vt., 1801; d. Centerbrook, Conn., 1858*), Congregational clergyman. Missionary to Ceylon, 1833–49. Principal, Batticotta Seminary, Ceylon. Translated Tamil religious texts and treatise on Hindu astronomy.

HOKE, ROBERT FREDERICK (*b. Lincolnton, N.C., 1837; d. Raleigh, N.C., 1912*), businessman, Confederate soldier. Rose from second lieutenant, 1861, to major general, 1864; served mainly with Lee's army and was highly regarded by that general.

HOKINSON, HELEN ELNA (*b. Mendota, Ill., 1893; d. Washington, D.C., 1949*), artist. Studied at Chicago Academy of Fine Arts; began as fashion illustrator; removed to New York City, 1920, where she studied with Howard Giles who taught Jay Hambidge's theory of dynamic symmetry. From 1925 until her death in an air crash, she contributed to the *New Yorker* magazine a number of drawings of a gently satirical nature, the best known being of middle-aged suburban clubwomen. She was a truthful observer and not a caricaturist. *Post* 1931, she worked in collaboration with James R. Parker, a *New Yorker* writer who devised the situations and wrote the captions for most of her drawings. Her work was published also in book form.

HOLABIRD, WILLIAM (*b. Amenia Union, N.Y., 1854; d. Evanston, Ill., 1923*), architect. Resigning from West Point, 1875, he moved to Chicago and was employed as a draftsman by William Le Baron Jenney. In association, *post* 1883, with Martin Roche, he took the lead among Chicago architects. Confronted with the demand for a building with profitable floor space, to be constructed on a narrow building lot, the firm designed the first office building in the world to utilize throughout its facades the principles of skeleton construction. This building at La Salle and Madison Streets, completed 1888, established the use of skeleton construction in high buildings. This achievement and the introduction of multiple deep basements were outstanding contributions of Holabird & Roche to structural engineering.

HOLBROOK, ALFRED (*b. Derby, Conn., 1816; d. Lebanon, Ohio, 1909*), pioneer in professional teacher training in Middle West. Son of Josiah Holbrook. Established Lebanon (Ohio) University, 1855, to democratize college education and reduce cost to students.

HOLBROOK, FREDERICK (*b. near East Windsor, Conn., 1813; d. Brattleboro, Vt., 1909*), scientific farmer. Republican governor of Vermont, 1861–63.

HOLBROOK, JOHN EDWARDS (*b. Beaufort, S.C., 1794; d. Norfolk, Mass., 1871*), physician, zoologist, Confederate medical officer. Graduated Brown, 1815; M.D., University of Pennsylvania, 1818. Practiced at Charleston, S.C., and taught at South Carolina Medical College. Author of *North American Herpetology* (1836, 1838), rearranged systematically in five volumes (1842). He also published *Ichthyology of South Carolina* (1855, 1860), an abbreviation of his proposed series on the fishes of the Southern states.

HOLBROOK, JOSIAH (*b. Derby, Conn., 1788; d. near Lynchburg, Va., 1854*), educational reformer, originator of movement known as the American Lyceum. Graduated Yale, 1810. An itinerant lecturer on science, he began the organization, *post* 1826, of community enterprises for mutual improvement and the establishment of museums and libraries. These town lyceums were established throughout the country and became a typical feature of American community life for half a century. The training of teachers was an important phase of his program.

HOLBROOK, STEWART HALL (*b. Newport, Vt., 1893; d. Portland, Oreg., 1964*), journalist and historian. Beginning in 1938 he published more than thirty books and innumerable articles for such publications as *Century* magazine, the *New Yorker*, the *New York Times*, the *New York Herald Tribune*, the *Saturday Evening Post*, *American Mercury*, *American Heritage*, and *American Forests*. Wrote in a nonscholarly but pleasurable and interesting manner for both adults and young readers, his favorite subjects being forests and rivers; heroes of the West, industry, and wars; and popular customs. His books include *Holy Old Mackinaw: A Natural History of the American Lumberjack* (1938), *Lost Men of American History* (1946), *The Story of American Railroads* (1947), *The Yankee Exodus: An Account of Migration from New England* (1950), *The Age of the Moguls* (1953), *Dreamers of the American Dream* (1957), *James J. Hill* (1955), *The Columbia* (1956), and *Mr. Otis* (1958), a book of paintings.

HOLCOMB, AMASA (*b. Southwick, Mass., 1787; d. Southwick, 1875*), instrument maker. Produced telescopes, *ca.* 1835, with focal length of 14 feet; experimented with photographic cameras.

HOLCOMB, SILAS ALEXANDER (*b. Gibson Co., Ind., 1858; d. Bellingham, Wash., 1920*), lawyer, Populist politician. Settled in Nebraska, 1879. Governor of that state, 1895–99; state supreme court judge, 1899–1905. Conservative leader of a radical party and a popular and successful administrator.

HOLCOMBE, CHESTER (*b. Winfield, N.Y., 1844; d. Rochester, N.Y., 1912*), Presbyterian clergyman, missionary to China, 1869–76. Became interpreter, secretary and acting chargé at Peking; helped draft treaty with China, 1880, and first American treaty with Korea, 1882.

HOLCOMBE, HENRY (*b. Prince Edward Co., Va., 1762; d. Philadelphia, Pa., 1824*), Baptist clergyman in South Carolina, Georgia, and Philadelphia, Pa.

HOLCOMBE, JAMES PHILEMON (*b. Powhatan Co., Va., 1820; d. Capon Springs, W.Va., 1873*), lawyer, writer on legal subjects. Professor of law, University of Virginia, 1851–61. Confederate congressman, 1862–64; secret agent in Canada, 1864, with C. C. Clay and Jacob Thompson.

HOLCOMBE, WILLIAM HENRY (*b. Lynchburg, Va., 1825; d. New Orleans, La., 1893*), homeopathic physician, authority on yellow fever. Brother of James P. Holcombe.

HOLDEN, EDWARD SINGLETON (*b. St. Louis, Mo., 1846; d. 1914*), astronomer. Graduated West Point, 1870. Assistant at Naval Observatory, 1873–81, associate of Simon Newcomb; director, Lick Observatory, 1888–97; librarian, West Point, 1901–14.

HOLDEN, HALE (*b. Kansas City, Mo., 1869; d. New York, N.Y., 1940*), lawyer. President, Chicago, Burlington & Quincy Railroad, 1914–18, 1920–29; chairman, Southern Pacific, 1932–39; a notable railway statesman.

HOLDEN, LIBERTY EMERY (*b. Raymond, Maine, 1833; d. 1913*), financier, mine owner, proprietor of *Cleveland Plain Dealer*, *post* 1884.

HOLDEN, OLIVER (*b. Shirley, Mass., 1765; d. Charlestown, Mass., 1844*), carpenter, land owner, preacher, writer and composer of hymns. His *Union Harmony* (1793) contains forty of his compositions including his "Coronation."

HOLDEN, WILLIAM WOODS (*b. Orange Co., N.C., 1818; d. 1892*), journalist. Editor, *North Carolina Standard*, *post* 1843. Governor of North Carolina, 1868–70, when he was impeached for arbitrary action and protection of corrupt elements. A political chameleon, he began as a Whig and was in succession Democrat, Unionist, Republican.

HOLDER, CHARLES FREDERICK (*b. Lynn, Mass., 1851; d. Pasadena, Calif., 1915*), naturalist, sportsman. Son of Joseph B. Holder. Author of popular works on zoology. Founded "Tournament of Roses," Pasadena; developed tuna fishing as a sport.

HOLDER, JOSEPH BASSETT (*b. Lynn, Mass., 1824; d. 1888*), marine zoologist, physician, author. As U.S. army surgeon at Ft. Jefferson, Fla., he made important studies of coral formation.

HOLDREGE, GEORGE WARD (*b. New York, N.Y., 1847; d. Omaha, Nebr., 1926*), Western railroad builder, agricultural promoter.

HOLIDAY, BILLIE (*b. Baltimore, Md., 1915; d. New York, N.Y., 1959*), singer. Blessed with a uniquely flexible and unforgettable voice, Billie Holiday rose from the poverty and obscurity of black America to become perhaps the greatest jazz singer of all time. Her ability to improvise, along with her superb rhythmic authority, were apparent from her first singing engagements in the early 1930's in Harlem. Overnight she was singing with such artists as Benny Carter and Benny Goodman, and in 1933, she was engaged in a recording series for Brunswick with pianist Teddy Wilson. In 1937, she sang with Count Basie and his orchestra. Ill-suited temperamentally for the rigors and discipline of a commercial singer's life, she succumbed to drug addiction, and in 1947 served nine months in prison. On her release, she gave a triumphant concert at Carnegie Hall and had a brilliant tour of Europe in 1956. Continuing deterioration of her health caused her early death in 1959. Her autobiography, *Lady Sings the Blues*, appeared in 1956; a film of her life with the same title was released in 1972.

HOLLADAY, BEN (*b. Carlisle Co., Ky., 1819; d. Portland, Oreg., 1887*), stagecoach master, financier. Starting as Indian trader in Kansas, he expanded operations by supplying Kearny's Army of the West during the Mexican War; later traded with Mormon settlements in Utah and drove cattle to California market. On bankruptcy of Russell, Majors and Waddell, he bought their freight lines and organized the Holladay stagecoach empire which served an area stretching from the Missouri River to the Golden Gate until 1866. After losses by Indian raiding and aware of coming railroad dominance, he sold out to Wells, Fargo and Co. and turned first to ocean transport and then to promoting and constructing the Oregon Central Railroad. The failure of this railroad, after the panic of 1873, broke his financial power.

HOLLAND, CLIFFORD MILBURN (*b. Somerset, Mass., 1883; d. Battle Creek, Mich., 1924*), civil engineer, leader in field of subaqueous construction. Graduated Harvard, 1905; B.S. in civil engineering, 1906. Recommended and constructed the New Jersey–New York vehicular tunnel which bears his name.

HOLLAND, EDMUND MILTON (*b. 1848; d. Chicago, Ill., 1913*), actor, comedian. Son of George Holland.

HOLLAND, EDWIN CLIFFORD (*b. Charleston, S.C., ca. 1794; d. Charleston, 1824*), author. His *Odes, Naval Songs and Other Poems* (Charleston, 1813) marked the beginning of romantic poetry in South Carolina.

HOLLAND, GEORGE (*b. London, England, 1791; d. New York, N.Y., 1870*), comedian. Made American debut, Bowery Theatre, New York, 1827; especially popular in the South. Was with Wallack's company in New York, 1855–67. Refusal of a fashionable church to conduct his funeral was the occasion for the naming of "The Little Church Around the Corner."

HOLLAND, JOHN PHILIP (*b. Liscanor, Ireland, 1840; d. Newark, N.J., 1914*), inventor. While in Ireland, he conceived the idea of a submarine, hoping that it might be used as a means of gaining Irish independence, an idea he retained after emigration to the United States, 1873. The American Fenian Society financed the building of a submarine, the *Fenian Ram* (1881), which embodied the chief principles of the modern submarine in balance, control, and compensation of weight lost in torpedo discharge. Holland's designs for submarines to be built by the Navy Department were uniformly unsuccessful. In 1898, he launched the *Holland*, built by him according to his design and without official meddling, which was successful and clearly demonstrated the practical value of submarines. It was purchased by the Navy Department, 1900.

HOLLAND, JOSEPH JEFFERSON (*b. New York, N.Y., 1860; d. Falmouth, Mass., 1926*), actor. Son of George Holland.

HOLLAND, JOSIAH GILBERT (*b. Belchertown, Mass., 1819; d. 1881*), editor. Abandoned practice of medicine, 1848; associated with Samuel Bowles in editorship of *Springfield Republican*, 1850–ca. 1868. Editor, *Scribner's Monthly, post* 1870, and of the *Century Magazine*, 1881. Author of popular but now forgotten books.

HOLLAND, WILLIAM JACOB (*b. Jamaica, B.W.I., 1848; d. Pittsburgh, Pa., 1932*), naturalist, educator, Presbyterian clergyman. Director, Carnegie Museum of Pittsburgh, 1898–1922. Sponsored fossil explorations in West. Wrote *The Butterfly Book* (1898) and *The Moth Book* (1903).

HOLLANDER, JACOB HARRY (*b. Baltimore, Md., 1871; d. 1940*), economist. Graduated Johns Hopkins, 1891; Ph.D., 1894. Taught at Johns Hopkins, 1894–1940. Served as government adviser in revising Puerto Rico finances, 1900–01, and as financial adviser to Dominican Republic, 1905–10. Built up labor seminar at Johns Hopkins.

HOLLERITH, HERMAN (*b. Buffalo, N.Y., 1860; d. Washington, D.C., 1929*), inventor of tabulating machines. Graduated School of Mines, Columbia, 1879. Became an assistant in the Census of 1880; this work brought him in contact with John Shaw Billings from whom came the suggestion for a machine to do the mechanical work of tabulating population statistics. Invented machines to record statistical items by means of electrical current through a system of punched holes in non-conducting material. These were first used in the Census of 1890 and subsequently improved. Organized the Tabulating Machine Co., 1896, which after consolidations became known as the International Business Machines Corp.

HOLLEY, ALEXANDER LYMAN (*b. Lakeville, Conn., 1832; d. Brooklyn, N.Y., 1882*), mechanical engineer, metallurgist. Graduated Brown, 1853. While in college, drew plans of locomotives and invented a steam cut-off; after practical experience in locomotive plants, became publisher of *Holley's Railroad Advocate*, 1855–57. Thereafter, until the end of his life, he continued to write technical articles, but was progressively more involved in original engineering work. In 1863 he bought American rights to the Bessemer process and was able to reconcile the conflicting claims under the Bessemer and Kelly processes and construct an improved steel mill at Troy, N.Y., 1865. He planned other steel mills and was recognized as the foremost steel-plant engineer in the United States and the "father of modern American steel manufacture."

HOLLEY, HORACE (*b. Salisbury, Conn., 1781; d. at sea, 1827*), Unitarian minister, educator. Brother of Myron Holley. Graduated Yale, 1803. Minister, Hollis Street Church, Boston, 1809–18; outstanding president, Transylvania University, 1818–27.

HOLLEY, MARIETTA (*b. Jefferson Co., N.Y., 1836; d. 1926*), humorist, woman's rights advocate. Author of *My Opinions and Betsy Bobbet's* (1873) and many other books and magazine articles in which as Samantha, "Josiah Allen's wife," her droll, homely humor delighted countless readers.

HOLLEY, MYRON (*b. Salisbury, Conn., 1779; d. 1841*), editor, abolitionist. Brother of Horace Holley. Treasurer, Erie Canal Commission; a leader in the anti-Masonic movement. Largely responsible for formation of Liberty party, 1840; edited *Rochester Freeman* (N.Y.), 1839–41.

HOLLICK, CHARLES ARTHUR (*b. Staten Island, N.Y., 1857; d. 1933*), engineer, paleobotanist. Associated for many years with N.Y. Botanical Garden.

HOLLIDAY, CYRUS KURTZ (*b. near Carlisle, Pa., 1826; d. 1900*), businessman. Removed to Kansas, 1854; builder and promoter of Topeka. He secured charter and federal land grands for the Atchison, Topeka & Santa Fe Railroad; served for a time as president and was director until death.

HOLLIDAY, JUDY (*b. Judith G. Tuvim, New York, N.Y., 1921; d. New York, 1965*), actress. Appeared in numerous films and stage plays, in which she typically played dumb but good-natured characters. Her stage credits include *Kiss Them for Me* (1945), *Born Yesterday* (1946), and *Bells Are Ringing* (1956). Her film credits include *Winged Victory* (1944), *Something for the Boys* (1944), *The Marrying Kind* (1952), *It Should Happen to You* (1954), *Phffft* (1954), *The Sold Gold Cadillac* (1956), *Full of Life* (1957), and *Bells Are Ringing* (1960). She won an Academy Award for best actress for her performance of the movie version of *Born Yesterday* (1950). Her promising career was cut short by throat cancer.

HOLLINGWORTH, LETA STETTER (*b. near Chadron, Nebr., 1886; d. New York, N.Y., 1939*), psychologist. Taught at Teachers College, Columbia, 1919–39; studied individual and group differences, particularly of subnormal and gifted children, and adolescents.

HOLLINS, GEORGE NICHOLS (*b. Baltimore, Md., 1799; d. Baltimore, 1878*), naval officer. Resigned from U.S. Navy, 1861, to enter Confederate service. Commanded Confederate flotilla at New Orleans, 1861, and all naval forces on upper Mississippi, 1862. His advice was ignored in Confederate defense of New Orleans.

HOLLIS, IRA NELSON (*b. Mooresville, Ind., 1856; d. Cambridge, Mass., 1930*), naval engineer, educator. Graduated Annapolis, 1878. Resigned from U.S. Navy, 1893. Harvard professor of mechanical engineering, 1893–1913; president, Worcester Polytechnic Institute, 1913–25.

HOLLISTER, GIDEON HIRAM (*b. Washington, Conn., 1817; d. 1881*), lawyer. Author of *Mount Hope* (1851) and *Kinley Hollow* (1882).

HOLLOWAY, JOHN (*b. England, ca. 1666; d. Virginia, 1734*), colonial official, lawyer, jurist. Despite doubts of his character, he succeeded in practice in Virginia, *post ca.* 1700, and was long a member of the House of Burgesses (speaker for 14 years), and treasurer of the colony, 1723–34.

HOLLOWAY, JOSEPH FLAVIUS (*b. Uniontown, Ohio, 1825; d. Buffalo, N.Y., 1896*), mechanical engineer. Designed and built machinery for steam craft on Great Lakes and the Mississippi, and for oceangoing vessels of all types.

HOLLS, FREDERICK WILLIAM. *See* HOLLS, GEORGE FREDERICK WILLIAM.

HOLLS, GEORGE FREDERICK WILLIAM (*b. Zelienople, Pa., 1857; d. New York, N.Y., 1903*), lawyer, publicist. Aroused President McKinley's interest in Hague International Peace Conference and converted German opposition into support of International Court.

HOLLY, CHARLES HARDIN ("BUDDY") (*b. Lubbock, Tex., 1936; d. near Mason City, Iowa, 1959*), musician. One of rock and roll's first stars and seminal artists, Buddy Holly's first recordings were made in Clovis, N.M. His hits included "That'll Be the Day" (1957), "Peggy Sue" and "Rave On" (1958), and "Oh Boy."

Many of his songs were recorded with the rock group known as the Crickets. Holly was killed at age twenty-two in a plane crash. His influence on later rock singers of the 1960's has been widely acknowledged.

HOLLY, JAMES THEODORE (*b. Washington, D.C., 1829; d. Port-au-Prince, Haiti, 1911*), Episcopal clergyman. A leader in Negro Emigration Conventions, 1854 and 1856. Led emigration of free blacks to Haiti, 1861; consecrated Protestant Episcopal bishop of Haiti, 1874.

HOLLYER, SAMUEL (*b. London, England, 1826; d. 1919*), engraver, etcher. Settled permanently in America, 1866. Published series of antiquarian etchings in *Prints of Old New York* (1904).

HOLMAN, JESSE LYNCH (*b. near Danville, Ky., 1784; d. 1842*), Baptist clergyman, Indiana pioneer and legislator. Federal judge in Indiana, 1834–42.

HOLMAN, WILLIAM STEELE (*b. near Aurora, Ind., 1822; d. 1897*), lawyer, jurist. Congressman, Democrat from Indiana, 1859–65, 1867–77, 1881–95, 1897. Powerful in debate and skilled as a parliamentarian, he expressed the philosophy of Jeffersonian agrarianism in an age dominated by railroad operators, industrial magnates, and leaders of high finance. Denounced by some for "hay-seed statesmanship," hailed by others as "The Watch-dog of the Treasury" and "The Great Objector" to excess appropriations.

HOLME, THOMAS (*b. probably Yorkshire, England, 1624; d. Philadelphia Co., Pa., 1695*). Came to America, 1682, as surveyor general of Pennsylvania. Laid out site of Philadelphia; drafted A *Map of the Province of Pennsylvania* (published London *ca.* 1687) and also on earlier map or plot of Philadelphia, first printed in A *Letter from William Penn . . . to the Committee of the Free Society of Traders* (1683).

HOLMES, ABIEL (*b. Woodstock, Conn., 1763; d. Cambridge, Mass., 1837*), Congregational clergyman, historian. Graduated Yale, 1783. Pastor, First Church, Cambridge, Mass., 1792–1829. He is best known as father of Oliver Wendell Holmes (1809–1894) and as author of *American Annals* (1805), the first serious attempt at an orderly history of America.

HOLMES, BAYARD TAYLOR (*b. North Hero, Vt., 1852; d. Fairhope, Ala., 1924*), surgeon. Raised in Minnesota. Graduated, M.D., Chicago Homeopathic College, 1884; Chicago Medical College, 1888. Professor of pathology and surgery, University of Illinois, 1892–1908. Socialist candidate for mayor of Chicago, 1895.

HOLMES, DANIEL HENRY (*b. New York, N.Y., 1851; d. Hot Springs, Va., 1908*), poet, musician, lawyer.

HOLMES, DAVID (*b. York Co., Pa., 1770; d. near Winchester, Va., 1832*), lawyer. Congressman, (Democrat) Republican, from Virginia, 1797–1809; governor of Mississippi Territory, 1809–17; of State of Mississippi, 1817–20 and 1826; U.S. senator from Mississippi, 1820–25. Instrumental in occupation of Baton Rouge district and in annexation, 1812, of Mobile district by Americans.

HOLMES, ELIAS BURTON (*b. Chicago, Ill., 1870; d. Hollywood, Calif., 1958*), travel lecturer known professionally as Burton Holmes. Founded Burton Holmes Lectures, Inc. (1897–98); later changed to Burton Holmes Travelogues, a term which he coined. Eventually introducing motion pictures into his lectures, Holmes became world famous for his reporting on the world at large. He avoided any social or political comment in his lectures and films. He retired in 1951 after delivering over 8,000 lectures.

HOLMES, EZEKIEL (*b. Kingston, Mass., 1801; d. 1865*), editor, physician, agriculturist. Graduated Brown, 1821; M.D., Bowdoin, 1824. While an undergraduate, he showed an early interest in botany and mineralogy; shortly afterward he discovered the important tourmaline deposit on Mount Mica in Maine. He served as instructor in agriculture and as principal of Gardiner Lyceum, also lectured on scientific subjects at Waterville College, Maine. Settled permanently in Winthrop, Maine, 1832. Started the first farm journal in Maine, 1833, thus embarking on his real mission, the promotion of scientific agriculture in that state. He was instrumental in the establishment of the University of Maine and stimulated American settlement in the disputed Aroostook area.

HOLMES, GEORGE FREDERICK (*b. Straebrock, British Guiana, 1820; d. Virginia, 1897*), educator, scholar. Educated in England; settled in America, 1837. Contributor to *Southern Literary Messenger*. First president, University of Mississippi, 1848; professor of history and political economy, University of Virginia, 1857–97.

HOLMES, ISAAC EDWARD (*b. Charleston, S.C., 1796; d. Charleston, 1867*), lawyer, politician. Vehement opponent of abolition; nullificationist. Congressman, Democrat, from South Carolina, 1839–51. In California, 1851–61; returned to Charleston and was a zealous Confederate.

HOLMES, ISRAEL (*b. Waterbury, Conn., 1800; d. 1874*), Connecticut brass manufacturer. Associated with firms of Holmes and Hotchkiss, Waterbury Brass Co., Holmes, Booth and Atwood, and others. Active in construction of Naugatuck Railroad.

HOLMES, JOHN (*b. Kingston, Mass., 1773; d. Portland, Maine, 1843*), lawyer. Graduated Brown, 1796. Removed to Maine, 1799, and was successful in land-title practice. Opposed Daniel Webster and Hopkinson in Dartmouth College case. Represented Maine in Congress and was active in separation of Maine from Massachusetts, 1816–20. U.S. senator, Democrat, later Whig, from Maine, 1821–27, 1828–33. U.S. attorney, Maine district, 1841–43.

HOLMES, JOHN HAYNES (*b. Philadelphia, Pa., 1879; d. New York, N.Y., 1964*), minister and social reformer. Bachelor of Sacred Theology (1904), Harvard; ordained to the ministry of the American Unitarian Association (1904). In 1907 began a radical social ministry at the prestigious Church of the Messiah in New York City. With Rabbi Stephen S. Wise, helped organize the National Association for the Advancement of Colored People in 1909 and was national vice president for more than fifty years. An ardent pacifist during both world wars, in 1919 he severed his ties with the Unitarians due to their support of the war effort and formed the Community Church of New York. Helped organize the American Civil Liberties Union. Understanding socialism a "political Christianity," he supported Progressive and Socialist party candidates. Wrote more than twenty books, including his autobiography, *I Speak for Myself* (1959), which won the Ainsfield-Wolf Award in race relations (1960).

HOLMES, JOSEPH AUSTIN (*b. Laurens, S.C., 1859; d. Denver, Colo., 1915*), mining engineer. Graduated Cornell, 1881. Professor of geology, University of North Carolina, 1882–92; state geologist, 1891–1904. His testing of fuels in public demonstration at St. Louis World's Fair, 1904, led to an appointment to head testing laboratories of the U.S. Geological Survey; his advocacy of conservation of mineral resources and mine safety

gained him promotion to first director of Bureau of Mines, 1910. His "safety first" campaign was responsible for installation of equipment and devices that reduced U.S. industrial accident rate.

HOLMES, JULIUS CECIL (*b. Pleasanton, Kans., 1899; d. Washington, D.C., 1968*), soldier and diplomat. As a member of General Dwight D. Eisenhower's staff during World War II, was criticized for his association with the infamous "Darlan deal," in which he and Robert Murphy drew up the agreement with Admiral François Darlan that ended Franco-Allied hostilities. After the war Eisenhower made him responsible for developing plans to administer occupied areas, and he is generally identified as the father of the Allied Military Government of the Occupied Territories. In 1948 returned to the State Department and was ambassador to Iran, 1961–62.

HOLMES, MARY JANE HAWES (*b. Brookfield, Mass., 1825; d. Brockport, N.Y., 1907*), popular novelist. Among her books were *Tempest and Sunshine* (1854), *Lena Rivers* (1856), *Ethelyn's Mistake* (1869) and other sentimental tales of small town life.

HOLMES, NATHANIEL (*b. Peterborough, N.H., 1815; d. Cambridge, Mass., 1901*), Missouri jurist. Royall Professor of Law, Harvard, 1868–72. Enthusiast for the Baconian authorship of Shakespeare's plays.

HOLMES, OLIVER WENDELL (*b. Cambridge, Mass., 1809; d. Boston, Mass., 1894*), essayist, poet, teacher of anatomy. Son of Abiel Holmes. Graduated Harvard, 1829; achieved early popularity as a poet. His "Old Ironsides," published in the *Boston Daily Advertiser*, 1830, was copied widely by other newspapers and reprinted and distributed on handbills to help save USS *Constitution* from destruction. His collected early *Poems* appeared in 1836. Deciding upon a medical career, Holmes had studied at Harvard and in Paris under Louis and Larrey; graduated M.D. from Harvard, 1836, he became a teacher and lecturer rather than a practitioner. He wrote, among other medical pieces, a noteworthy and controversial article on "The Contagiousness of Puerperal Fever" (1843) and became deservedly famous for his lectures on anatomy and other medical subjects at Harvard (as Parkman Professor, 1847–82) and as a lyceum lecturer. Meanwhile, he continued to produce verse and literary prose. His twelve Lowell Institute lectures on the English poets (1853) were concluded, each time, with an original poem, a practice later adopted in his *Autocrat* articles. His total production as poet occupied 300 double-column pages in the *Collected Works* of 1895. It contains verse that may be classified as the poetic, the merely fanciful, the deftly humorous, and the *vers d'occasion*; in this last group, the various Class of 1829 poems reveal his gifts as a weaver of felicitous after-dinner verses at their best.

Holmes was brilliant and indefatigable conversationalist with a boundless intellectual curiosity which caused his fellow member of the Saturday Club, James Russell Lowell, to assess correctly his possibilities as an essayist. The first installment of *The Autocrat of the Breakfast Table* appeared in the first issue of *The Atlantic Monthly* under Lowell's editorship (November 1857) and marked the entrance of Holmes into the field of witty "dramatized *causerie*" which he proceeded to make his own. The *Autocrat* essays were published as a book in 1858; *The Professor at the Breakfast Table* (1860) and *The Poet at the Breakfast Table* (1872) were not equal to their prototype. Holmes's best serious poem, "The Chambered Nautilus," appeared in the *Autocrat*; his masterpiece in light verse, "The Deacon's Masterpiece; or The Wonderful One-Hoss-Shay" appeared in another installment of the original series and has been called "a parable of the breakdown of Calvinism."

In the field of fiction Holmes was not so successful, although his first novel *Elsie Venner* (1861) foreshadowed later psychological fiction. Many successively enlarged editions of his poems appeared between 1836 and 1895, and among the mass of his published travel notes, memorial addresses, and other works may be singled out his biographies of *John L. Motley* (1879) and *R. W. Emerson* (1885). His ability to give universal interest to local Boston scenes and topics is the secret of his appeal. A rationalist and a wit, he was in lifelong revolt against the Calvinist view of life which had shadowed his boyhood. He was the father of Justice Oliver Wendell Holmes of the U.S. Supreme Court.

HOLMES, OLIVER WENDELL (*b. Boston, Mass., 1841; d. 1935*), jurist. Son of Oliver Wendell Holmes (1809–1894) and Amelia Lee Jackson. Descended from a long line of New Englanders among whom were Dorothy Quincy and Anne Bradstreet, he was deeply rooted in the Puritan tradition.

Volunteering for the infantry in April 1861, before his graduation from Harvard that year, he was commissioned second lieutenant in July. He served until July 1864 with the 20th Massachusetts. Wounded three times, he was mustered out with the rank of captain. Returning to Boston as a military hero, he shocked patriotic sentimentalists by speaking of war as an "organized bore," but useful so "that we may realize that our comfortable routine is no eternal necessity of things . . . in this time of individualist negations." After his graduation from Harvard Law School, 1866, he visited in England, making friendships with Leslie Stephen, James Bryce, Frederick Pollock, and others. Admitted to the bar, 1867, he practiced in Boston, working with feverish intensity to become a master in his calling. He was editor of the *American Law Review*, 1870–73, worked to bring Kent's *Commentaries* up to date and lectured on law at Harvard. In 1872 he married Fanny Bowditch Dixwell whose influence on his life and career must figure in any account of him.

In his early writings he canvassed issues which are vital to a society devoted to justice according to law. What are the sources of law and what are its sanctions? What are the ingredients, conscious or unconscious, of adjudication? What are the wise demands of precedent and when should the judicial process feel unbound by its past? These were some of the inquiries which guided Holmes's investigations at a time when law was generally treated as a body of settled doctrine from which answers to the new problems of industrialized society were to be derived by logical deduction. While judges boasted a want of philosophy, Holmes realized that decisions are functions of some juristic philosophy, and that awareness of the considerations moving beneath the surface of logical form is the prime requisite of a civilized system of law. He was cognizant of the role of the unconscious more than a generation before Freud began to influence modern psychology, and a half a century before Ogden and Richards wrote *The Meaning of Meaning*. He systematized these pioneer contributions in *The Common Law* (1881), which is a classic in the sense that its stock of ideas has been absorbed and become part of common juristic thought. "The life of the law," he wrote, "has not been logic: it has been experience."

Called to Harvard Law School, 1882, as Weld Professor of Law, he became a justice of the supreme judicial court of Massachusetts in 1883. His Massachusetts opinions (nearly 1,300) if brought together would constitute the most comprehensive and philosophic body of American law for any period of its history. He became chief justice of Massachusetts in 1899, and although his opinions in labor cases (e.g., *Vegelahn* v. *Guntner*) disturbed the conservatism of Boston, they were in part the influences which led President Theodore Roosevelt to appoint Holmes to the U.S. Supreme Court, 1902. He served until Jan. 12, 1932.

He came to the Court at a time when legislative activity reflected changing social conceptions stimulated by technological development. Probably no man on the Court was ever freer of emotional commitments which might compel him to translate his own economic or social views into constitutional commands. His disbelief in ultimate answers to social questions permitted him to exhibit judicial function at its purest. Social development could be an effective process of trial and error only when there was the fullest possible opportunity for the free play of the mind. To Holmes, the Constitution was not a literary document or an occasion for juggling with words but a framework of great governmental powers to be exercised for great public ends. Expressing his opinions with stinging brevity, he was unimpressed by what are called great cases. "My keenest interest is excited . . . by little decisions . . . which have in them . . . the germ of some wider theory . . . some profound interstitial change in the very tissue of law." In deciding cases his aim was "to strike the jugular," to omit in his expression of opinion all but essentials.

Some of his weightiest utterances are dissents that have shaped history, written with "cold Puritan passion": *Adair* v. *United States; Hammer* v. *Dagenhart; U.S.* v. *Schwimmer; Tyson & Bro.* v. *Banton; Baldwin* v. *Missouri*. Some of his most powerful opinions were written in his ninth decade. After his retirement, he continued his life in Washington and Beverly Farms until March 6, 1935, and was buried on his birthday in Arlington Cemetery. Without explanation he left the bulk of his estate to the nation, the largest unrestricted gift ever made to it.

Because Holmes disciplined himself against any kind of parochialism in his thinking, he is a significant figure in the history of civilization, not merely a commanding American legal figure. He is unsurpassed in the depth of his penetration into the nature of the judicial process and in the originality of its exposition. He early rejected legal principles as absolutes. Looking beneath their formulations, he saw them as expressions of conflicting or overlapping social policies; the vital judicial issue, therefore, was apt to be their accommodation and decisions became essentially a matter of drawing lines.

HOLMES, THEOPHILUS HUNTER (*b. Sampson Co., N.C., 1804; d. Cumberland Co., N.C., 1880*), Confederate soldier. West Point classmate of Jefferson Davis, 1829. Cited for bravery in Mexican War; ineffective lieutenant general in Confederate Army, 1862–64.

HOLMES, WILLIAM HENRY (*b. near Cadiz, Ohio, 1846; d. 1933*), archeologist, artist. Served with the Hayden Survey, 1872–77; U.S. Geological Survey, 1880–84; American Bureau of Ethnology, 1889–94. Curator of anthropology, Field Museum, Chicago, 1894–97; Smithsonian Institution, 1897–1920. In 1902, he succeeded J. W. Powell as chief of Bureau of American Ethnology. Director, National Gallery of Art, 1920–32. Author of *Handbook of Aboriginal American Antiquities* (1919) which became the standard treatise on the subject.

HOLSEY, LUCIUS HENRY (*b. near Columbus, Ga., ca. 1842; d. 1920*), an organizer (1870) and bishop (1873) of the Colored Methodist Episcopal Church. Born a slave and self-educated, he founded a number of schools and colleges for his people.

HOLST, HERMANN EDUARD VON (*b. Fellin, Russia [Estonia], 1841; d. Freiburg, Germany, 1904*), historian. Graduated Heidelberg, Ph.D., 1865. Came to America, 1867. Returned to Europe as professor at Strassburg, 1872–74, and at Freiburg, 1874–92. Head of history department, University of Chicago, 1892–99. His voluminous *Constitutional and Political History of the United States* (1873–92) emphasized the moral influence of slavery on American history.

HOLT, ARTHUR ERASTUS (*b. near Longmont, Colo., 1876; d. Chicago, Ill., 1942*), Congregational clergyman, specialist in social ethics. Graduated Colorado College, 1898; Ph.D., University of Chicago, 1904 (under Gerald B. Smith); B.D., McCormick Theological Seminary, 1904. Held pastorates in Colorado, Kansas, and Texas, 1904–19; was secretary of the Social Service Department of the Congregational Education Society in Boston, Mass., 1919–24. Professor of social ethics in both the Chicago Theological seminary and the University of Chicago Divinity School thereafter, he had a predominant concern with rural life and the securing of social justice for agrarian groups; in this he was almost unique among the leaders of the Social Gospel movement.

HOLT, EDWIN BISSELL (b. *Winchester, Mass., 1873; d. Rockland, Maine, 1946*), psychologist. B.A., Harvard, 1896; M.A., Columbia University, 1900; Ph.D., Harvard, 1901. As instructor (1901–05) and assistant professor (1905–18) of psychology at Harvard, he was closely associated with William James and with the work of the psychological laboratory directed by Hugo Münsterberg. Visiting professor at Princeton University, 1926–36. Holt's position is best called philosophic behaviorism; he believed that the phenomena of consciousness could be accounted for wholly in terms of physical and physiological processes. He was author of *The Freudian Wish and Its Place in Ethics* (1915) and *Animal Drive and the Learning Process* (1931).

HOLT, EDWIN MICHAEL (b. *Orange Co., N.C., 1807; d. Alamance Co., N.C., 1884*), cotton manufacturer. First Southern manufacturer to dye yarn; introduced the "Alamance Plaids."

HOLT, HAMILTON BOWEN (b. *Brooklyn, N.Y., 1872, d. Woodstock, Conn., 1951*), editor, internationalist, college president. Studied at Columbia Grammar School and Yale University. Managing editor of New York weekly *Independent*, 1897–1912; editor, 1913–21. A leading internationalist, Holt was never committed to one specific program but supported any idea that might advance his goal. After lecturing and writing extensively on the subject, attended the Second Hague Peace Conference, 1907; founded the World Federation League, 1910, which gained passage of a congressional resolution endorsing a study for combining "the navies of the world" into "an international force for the preservation of universal peace." Involved in other international peace societies as director of the World Peace Federation, 1911–14, and trustee of the Church Peace Union, 1914–51. Instrumental in founding the League to Enforce Peace, 1915; and as vice-chairman did much to enlighten the American public to the need for an international organization after World War I. Attended the Paris Peace Conference, 1919, and sought to influence the drafting of the Covenant of the League of Nations. Promoted U.S. entry into the League, 1919–24, making extensive public appearances on its behalf. President of Rollins College, 1925–49.

HOLT, HENRY (b. *Baltimore, Md., 1840; d. 1926*), publisher. Graduated Yale, 1862. Established firm of Leypoldt and Holt, 1866, later Henry Holt and Co.

HOLT, JOHN (b. *Williamsburg, Va., 1721; d. 1784*), printer, journalist, Revolutionary patriot. Learned the printing art at Williamsburg; moved north, 1754, to become part owner with James Parker and editor of papers in New Haven and New York. He acquired full ownership of the *New-York Gazette and Weekly Post-Boy*, 1762 (later, *The New-York Journal*, Parker resuming the *Gazette* title, 1766). Active as a Whig printer, Holt left New York on the eve of the British occupation, 1776, a procedure which he repeated in New Haven and Danbury, Conn., and Kingston, N.Y.; on each removal his property was destroyed by the enemy. He returned to New York City, 1783, and edited *The Independent New-York Gazette* and its successors. He was interested also in improving the delivery service for newspapers, in postal reforms, and in bookselling.

HOLT, JOSEPH (b. *Breckenridge Co., Ky., 1807; d. Washington, D.C., 1894*), lawyer, politician. Postmaster general, 1859–61; secretary of war, 1861. Sympathetic at first to Southern sentiments, after South Carolina's secession he became a leading Kentucky Unionist. As judge-advocate general, 1862–75, Holt used military commissions effectively in prosecuting citizens accused of disloyalty, the Vallandigham and Milligan cases being notable examples. His prosecution of the alleged assassins of President Lincoln brought him great popularity, but disclosures of perjury on the part of government witnesses and the charge that he had suppressed important evidence favorable to Mrs. Surratt brought him into disfavor.

HOLT, LUTHER EMMETT (b. *Webster, N.Y., 1855; d. Peking, China, 1924*), pediatrician. Graduated M.D., College of Physicians and Surgeons, New York, 1880. First practiced his specialty at the New York Infant Asylum and similar institutions. The Babies Hospital of New York (founded 1887) was, medically speaking, his creation. A teacher by nature, he served as professor at the Polyclinic Hospital and the College of Physicians and Surgeons. As author of popular medical books, he reached a vast audience; his *The Care and Feeding of Children* (1894) and *The Diseases of Infancy and Childhood* (1896) made "Dr. Holt" a household word. Osler alone in the United States exercised a comparable educational influence.

HOLT, WILLIAM FRANKLIN (b. *Mercer County, Mo., 1880; d. Los Angeles, Calif., 1951*), businessman. Entrepreneurial developer of the Imperial Valley region of Southern California, circa 1900. By exploiting the possibilities of irrigation from the Colorado River, Holt successfully built the area into a prosperous farming region. The town of Holtville remains a memorial to the man's influence in the area. He was a tireless entrepreneur involved in a wide variety of businesses, and he was a community leader who helped shape the area's economic institutions.

HOLT, WINIFRED (b. *New York, N.Y., 1870; d. Pittsfield, Mass., 1945*), worker for the blind. Daughter of Henry Holt. Worked as a young girl in a New York City settlement house; resided in Florence, Italy, for a time because of ill health, and while there discovered a special concern for the blind. Returning to New York, 1903, she and her sister began to work with the blind and were soon convinced that their most important need was employment by which they might become self-reliant and financially independent. Organized New York Association for the Blind, 1905. In 1913, the association opened "The Lighthouse," a social settlement for the blind. She established similar centers in France and Italy and toured the world initiating programs for the blind.

HOLTEN, SAMUEL (b. *Salem Village [Danvers], Mass., 1738; d. Danvers, 1816*), physician. Massachusetts legislator and Revolutionary leader; member of Continental Congress, 1778–87. Strongly opposed ratification of Federal Constitution.

HOLYOKE, EDWARD AUGUSTUS (b. *Marblehead, Mass., 1728; d. Salem, Mass., 1829*), physician. Graduated Harvard, 1746. A promoter of medical education in Massachusetts, among his students were N. W. Appleton and James Jackson. Experience, in his view, was the key to medical knowledge.

HOLYOKE, SAMUEL (b. *Boxford, Mass., 1762; d. Concord, N.H., 1820*), teacher, composer of "Arnheim" and other music. Compiled *Harmonia Americana* (1791), the *Columbian Repository of Sacred Harmony* (1802) and other collections of hymns.

HOMER, LOUISE DILWORTH BEATTY (*b. Shadyside, Pa., 1871; d. Winter Park, Fla., 1947*), contralto. After early voice training in Philadelphia, she went to Boston, where she studied voice with W. L. Whitney and musical theory with Sidney Homer, whom she married in 1895. A student in Paris, 1896–97, she made her operatic debut in *La Favorita* at Vichy in June 1898. Other European engagements followed. She made her American debut with the Metropolitan Opera in November 1900. Her career with Metropolitan continued until 1929, but her last regular season was 1918–19. Homer also sang in oratorio and on concert tours and enjoyed great success as a recording artist.

HOMER, WINSLOW (*b. Boston, Mass., 1836; d. Prout's Neck, Maine, 1910*), painter. Apprenticed to Bufford, the Boston lithographer, 1855; set up his own studio in Boston, 1857, and New York, 1858, selling drawings to *Ballou's Pictorial* and to *Harper's Weekly*. Harper's sent him to Washington, 1861, to make drawings of Lincoln's inauguration; thereafter, he sketched camp scenes and early engagements during the Peninsular campaign, and on his return to New York began to paint pictures of war subjects which were exhibited at the National Academy of Design, 1863. He was made an Academician, 1865. *Post* 1867, he produced mainly rural *genre* and landscapes until a stay in England, 1881–82, brought a change in his art. He became increasingly concerned with the drama of the sea. Turning his back on the city, he settled at Prout's Neck, Scarboro, Maine, 1884, and except for seasonal expeditions to Florida, Nassau, Cuba, or Bermuda, lived there until death. From the Maine coast came outstanding works such as *The Life Line* (actually started in England), *The Fog Warning, Banks Fishermen*, the stirring deep-sea classic *Eight Bells*, and *A Summer Night*. The haunting *Gulf Stream* and *Searchlight, Harbor Entrance, Santiago de Cuba* were products of his stays in southern climes. Both in water colors and in oils, Homer's method and style were those of a man who had something to say and who employed no surplus rhetoric; he drove straight to the mark. He echoed no other painter and his work is wholly personal and American. Preeminent as a realistic marine painter, he is never prosaic; his work throbs with the essential elements of poetry, with deep feeling and a sense of the dignity and heroism of man.

HOMES, HENRY AUGUSTUS (*b. Boston, Mass., 1812; d. 1887*). Graduated Amherst, 1830. Missionary to Turkey, 1836–54. Librarian, New York State Library, 1854–87. Author of papers on library administration and historical subjects.

HONE, PHILIP (*b. New York, N.Y., 1780; d. New York, 1851*), auctioneer, diarist. Whig leader; mayor of New York City, 1825; promoter of cultural and commercial enterprises. Principally remembered for his diary (covering 1828–51; first published, in part, 1889) which furnishes a useful view of New York life in its period.

HONTAN, LOUIS-ARMAND DE LOM D'ARCE, BARON DE LA. *See* LAHONTAN, LOUIS ARMAND DE LOM D'ARCE.

HOOD, JAMES WALKER (*b. Kennett Township, Pa., 1831; d. 1918*), bishop, African Methodist Episcopal Zion Church (ordained, 1872). First black to preside over the Ecumenical Conference; assistant superintendent of public instruction, North Carolina, 1868–70.

HOOD, JOHN BELL (*b. Owingsville, Ky., 1831; d. New Orleans, La., 1879*), Confederate soldier. Graduated West Point, 1853; served in California and Texas. As Confederate brigadier general, March 1862, he commanded the "Texas Brigade" which won high reputation on the Peninsula and at Antietam. As major general, October 1862, he was division commander under Longstreet at Gettysburg and directed Longstreet's Corps at

Chickamauga. Lee wrote President Davis that Hood was "a bold fighter" but voiced doubt of his qualifications for high command; yet Hood (promoted lieutenant general, February 1864) was named to replace Gen. J. E. Johnston as leader of the Confederate Army defending Atlanta. Uniformly unsuccessful in this command, he experienced a disastrous defeat at Nashville, December 1864, and was relieved. His subsequent career in Texas and New Orleans was marked by misfortune.

HOOD, RAYMOND MATHEWSON (*b. Pawtucket, R.I., 1881; d. Stamford, Conn., 1934*), architect. Graduated Massachusetts Institute of Technology, 1903; École des Beaux-Arts, 1911. After working for Cram, Goodhue and Ferguson, and other architects, opened office in New York, 1914. Joined J. M. Howells in 1922 competition for Chicago Tribune building and won; its strong composition and late Gothic detail won immediate acclaim. In 1929, has misgivings about traditional styles and joined the "modernists." His conversion was expressed in the American Radiator building, New York, the Beaux-Arts Apartments and, in association with Kenneth Murchison, the New York Daily News building. His last great work was in connection with Rockefeller Center in New York, whose final form owed much to his influence.

HOOD, WASHINGTON (*b. Philadelphia, Pa., 1808; d. Bedford Springs, Pa., 1840*), army officer, topographical engineer. Graduated West Point, 1827. His map of Oregon Territory (compiled 1838) was used as justification for occupation of that territory by the United States.

HOOKER, DONALD RUSSELL (*b. New Haven, Conn., 1876; d. Baltimore, Md., 1946*), physiologist, editor. B.A., Yale, 1899; M.S., 1901. M.D., Johns Hopkins, 1905. After a year at the University of Berlin, he taught at the Johns Hopkins Medical School from 1910 to 1920. In 1926, he returned to Hopkins as lecturer in social hygiene (*post* 1935 in physiology) in the School of Hygiene and Public Health. Hooker devoted his research almost exclusively to the physiology of the circulatory system. For his study of venous pressure, he is recognized as a pioneer. From 1914 to 1946, he served as managing editor of the *American Journal of Physiology*. Also edited *Physiological Reviews* (*post* 1921).

HOOKER, ELON HUNTINGTON (*b. Rochester, N.Y., 1869; d. Pasadena, Calif., 1938*), civil engineer, industrialist. Founded Hooker Electrochemical Co., 1909, producers of chlor-alkali chemicals and plastics.

HOOKER, ISABELLA BEECHER (*b. Litchfield, Conn., 1822; d. Hartford, Conn., 1907*), leading advocate of rights for women. Daughter of Lyman Beecher. Promoter of Connecticut law granting married women equal property rights (1877).

HOOKER, JOSEPH (*b. Hadley, Mass., 1814; d. Garden City, N.Y., 1879*), soldier. Graduated West Point, 1837. Served in Florida War, on Canadian border, and as adjutant at West Point. Distinguished for gallantry and efficiency in Mexican War through part of Taylor's campaign and most of Scott's, he was brevetted lieutenant colonel at Chapultepec. His testimony in the Pillow-Scott controversy gained for Hooker the hostility of Gen. Scott, and he resigned, 1853, to engage in various occupations at Sonoma, Calif., and in Oregon. He returned to service in 1861, as brigadier general of volunteers. During the Peninsular campaign, 1862, he gained the sobriquet of "Fighting Joe" and promotion to major general of volunteers. He was effective as a corps commander at South Mountain and at Antietam, where he was wounded. Returning to active duty, he participated in the assault on Fredericksburg and in the open criticism of Gen. Burnside. Appointed commander of the Army of the Potomac in Burnside's place, January 1863, he was defeated by Lee at Chancellorsville,

May 2–4, 1863, despite a 2 to 1 superiority. The indecision which caused his defeat may be explained in part by the injury he sustained during the course of the battle. He declined to admit defeat and managed to protect Washington and Baltimore from Lee's invading army as it swept into Pennsylvania. Gen. Halleck's refusal to send reinforcements from Harpers Ferry was, he concluded, a breach of faith in him, and Hooker asked to be relieved of his command although the decisive battle at Gettysburg was in immediate prospect. Transferred to the Department of the Cumberland, he served under Thomas and Sherman in all the decisive battles from Chattanooga to the fall of Atlanta. After McPherson's death, Sherman's refusal to award his command to Hooker brought another request for relief from duty, 1864. Thereafter he commanded several northern departments of the army, retiring as regular major general, 1868.

HOOKER, PHILIP (*b. Rutland, Mass., 1766; d. Albany, N.Y., 1836*), architect. Removed to Albany, N.Y., as a child and was associated with that city until his death, transforming it architecturally, *post* 1796, from a Dutch frontier town to the semblance of a New England city. His work derived from Mangin, McComb, and Bulfinch; little of it remains unaltered.

HOOKER, SAMUEL COX (*b. Brenchley, England, 1864; d. Brooklyn, N.Y., 1935*), chemist. Trained abroad; came to America, 1885. Specialist in the chemistry of sugar.

HOOKER, THOMAS (*b. probably Marfield, England, 1586[?]; d. Hartford, Conn., 1647*), Congregational clergyman. Graduated Emmanuel College, Cambridge, 1608; was a fellow there, 1609–18. Developed Puritan leanings there and as rector of Esher, Surrey, *post* 1620. As lecturer at St. Mary's, Chelmsford, 1626–30, his preaching was popular and attracted the enmity of Archbishop Laud. Hooker then opened a school at Little Baddow with John Eliot as assistant. Summoned, nevertheless, to appear before the High Commission, 1630, Hooker forfeited bond and escaped to Holland, whence he returned to England briefly in 1633 before sailing for New England in company with John Cotton and Samuel Stone. Arriving at Boston, September 1633, Hooker quickly established himself as a popular pastor at Newtown; as dissension deepened between his flock and the rest of the Bay Colony, he led the 1636 migration of most of his congregation to Hartford in the Connecticut valley. At the Synod called in 1637 for the purpose of condemning the Hutchinsonian and other heresies, Hooker proposed to John Winthrop a New England Confederation, but his long-cherished plan was not to assume tangible form until 1643. A born democrat, he had much to do with framing the "Fundamental Orders" or constitution of Connecticut, 1639. He was a prolific author of sermons; his introduction to his posthumously published *A Survey of the Summe of Church Discipline* (1648) is considered as clear an exposition of Congregationalism as has ever been given.

HOOKER, WILLIAM (*fl. 1804–1846*), engraver, mapmaker in Newburyport, Mass., and New York, N.Y. Associated with Edmund M. Blunt as engraver of charts for *American Coast Pilot* and maps of the New York area.

HOOKER, WORTHINGTON (*b. Springfield, Mass., 1806; d. 1867*), physician. Graduated Yale, 1825; M.D., Harvard, 1829. Practiced in Norwich, Conn., until 1852; thereafter at New Haven. Professor in Yale Medical School; author, *Rational Therapeutics* (1857).

HOOPER, CLAUDE ERNEST (*b. Kingsville, Ohio, 1898; d. Salt Lake City, Utah, 1954*), broadcast audience analyst. Studied at Amherst College and Harvard School of Business Administration (M.B.A., 1923). Advertising manager, *Scribner's* magazine (1926–29); market research firm of Daniel Starch (1931–34). In

1934, Hooper formed the research firm of Clark-Hooper which became C. E. Hooper in 1938. Hooper developed a technique for measuring the effectiveness of advertising and broadcast audience characteristics by telephoning at random in more than thirty metropolitan areas and inquiring what program was being listened to. By 1946, a good "Hooperating" was considered essential for a radio program's continuance. In 1950, challenged by the new techniques of A.C. Nielsen, Hooper sold his rating service to Nielsen for a reported $600,000.

HOOPER, JESSIE ANNETTE JACK (*b. Winneshiek Co., Iowa, 1865; d. Oshkosh, Wis., 1935*), suffragist. Active in League of Women Voters and world peace societies.

HOOPER, JOHNSON JONES (*b. Wilmington, N.C., 1815; d. Richmond, Va., 1862*), humorist, Alabama journalist, early portrayer of Southern frontier types. Created a celebrated character whose exploits appeared in newspapers and in collected form as *Some Adventures of Captain Simon Suggs, Late of the Tallapoosa Volunteers* (Philadelphia, 1846).

HOOPER, LUCY HAMILTON (*b. Philadelphia, Pa., 1835; d. Paris, France, 1893*), editor, journalist.

HOOPER, SAMUEL (*b. Marblehead, Mass., 1808; d. Washington, D.C., 1875*), merchant, Massachusetts legislator. Congressman, Republican, from Massachusetts, 1861–75. Advocated issue of legal tender notes and establishment of a national banking system; *post* 1865, he urged contraction of greenbacks and was prominent in framing the 1873 currency act.

HOOPER, WILLIAM (*b. Boston, Mass., 1742; d. Hillsboro, N.C., 1790*), lawyer. Practiced in North Carolina, *post* 1764. Member of Continental Congress, 1775–77. Signer of Declaration of Independence. Opposed democratic tendencies as North Carolina legislator.

HOOTON, EARNEST ALBERT (*b. Clemansville, Wis., 1887; d. 1954*), anthropologist. Studied at Lawrence College, the University of Wisconsin (Ph.D. 1911), and at Oxford University as a Rhodes Scholar. Taught at Harvard from 1913 until the end of his career. As a pioneer in physical anthropology, Hooton applied his findings to the social and biological problems facing modern society. Major works include *The Ancient Inhabitants of the Canary Islands* (1915) and *The Indians of Pecos Pueblo* (1930); both were attempts to discover the racial origins of these peoples. He studied the body traits of the American criminal population, of Irish physical types, and of the Harvard undergraduate, the last study becoming the book *Young Man, You Are Normal* (1945). During World War II, he made studies of the normal ranges of the body dimensions for the design of airplanes and military clothing. Other works include *Up From the Ape* (1931) and *Twilight of Man* (1939).

HOOVER, CHARLES FRANKLIN (*b. Miamisburg, Ohio, 1865; d. Cleveland, Ohio, 1927*), physician, diagnostician. Professor of medicine in Western Reserve University, *post* 1907. Prominent as consultant in cardio-respiratory, neurological, and hepatic diseases.

HOOVER, HERBERT CLARK (*b. West Branch, Iowa, 1874; d. New York, N.Y., 1964*), mining engineer, public administrator, and thirty-first president of the United States (the first president born west of the Mississippi). Son of Jesse Hoover and Hulda Minthorn.

After the death of his father (1880) and mother (1884), in 1885 Hoover went to Oregon to live with his uncle and aunt, John and Laura Minthorn, an educated couple who ran a preparatory school in Newberg. He attended their school for about three years.

His uncle soon had Hoover working for his Oregon Land Company in nearby Salem and attending business school at night. Using a small inheritance left by his mother, he was able to enter the first class at Stanford University in 1891. Ill-prepared for college, he attended summer classes in Palo Alto.

At Stanford, Hoover majored in geology. During the summers he worked for the U.S. Geological Survey. He met another geology major, Lou Henry, daughter of a Monterey banker. Married in 1899, they had two sons.

After graduating from Stanford in 1895, Hoover worked as a day laborer in California mines. He was soon given more responsible jobs and went to London to work for the firm of Bewick, Moreing, which sent him to western Australia as a mine "scout." Hoover found gold, particularly in one mine, the Sons of Gwalia, which became one of Australia's richest. He also excelled in developing new technologies for the economical mining of gold.

In 1899, after his success in Australia, Hoover was sent to China as chief engineer for the Chinese Engineering and Mining Company. He discovered rich coal deposits in Chihli Province. He also found himself in the midst of the Boxer Rebellion of 1900. At the same time that he helped to organize relief activities in the foreign settlement of Tientsin, he managed to extract a trustee deed to the coal properties. After the rebellion had run its course, Hoover and his wife took the deed to London, where he was rewarded with a partnership in the firm.

During the next fourteen years Hoover developed mining interests all over the world and spent a sizable portion of his time visiting likely sites. His biggest finds were silver, lead, and zinc in Burma, zinc in Australia, and, just before the outbreak of World War I, copper and petroleum in Russia.

From 1908, Hoover worked on his own. He was known as a "doctor of sick mines," and specialized in bringing their finances into good order. He accumulated some $4 million by 1913. Hoover was also drawn to public service, and labored on such projects as the Panama Pacific Exposition at San Francisco (1915).

In the early years of the twentieth century, Hoover lived principally in London. Important in terms of his social thought was the publication in 1909 of *Principles of Mining*. This textbook, used for decades in mining schools, revealed Hoover's thinking on capital and labor. He endorsed collective bargaining, the eight-hour day, and the importance of safety in mines; he denounced "reactionary capitalists" and "academic economists" who, he claimed, stood in the way of reform. Trying to improve professional standards among mining engineers, financed the publication of new mining journals and eventually assumed high offices in professional mining organizations, including president of the American Institute of Mining and Metallurgical Engineers.

By 1914 his professional standing and his work on the American Citizens Relief Committee made him a logical choice to head the Commission for Relief in Belgium (CRB) after the outbreak of World War I. The CRB had the delicate job of feeding the Belgians, whose country had been overrun by the German army. For more than two years Hoover arbitrated between the warring parties and managed, largely through voluntary contributions and a shrewd manipulation of public opinion, to organize the feeding of some 9 million people. The operation was extended to 2 million more in northern France during the spring of 1915. He so impressed President Woodrow Wilson that after the United States entered the war, he was appointed food administrator in Washington, D.C. (1917).

In this post Hoover emphasized voluntary conservation of food and fuel so that America could feed its soldiers and the Allies. Although he condemned price fixing, with the cooperation of the Lever Food Control Act (August 1917) he in effect set the long-term price of wheat. Working closely with experts from the businesses the government had to deal with, his purpose was to standardize business practices and prices. This foreshadowed the trade association movement of the 1920's, which he supported. Nevertheless, when his approach failed to curb excessive profits, Hoover began to advocate a wartime excess-profits tax.

Hoover was faced with enormous problems. He had to stimulate production, prevent prices from soaring, and at the same time be prepared to dispose of tremendous surpluses should the war come to a sudden end. What saved him was postwar "relief." Hoover seized upon war-ravaged Europe's needs to solve America's problem of overstock, and persuaded Congress to make $100 million in credits available to the Allies. Hoover was appointed chairman of the Inter-Allied Food Council in Paris after the war, and soon took on a multitude of new duties. He served as director general of the American Relief Administration—both the public agency and the private one that succeeded it in July 1919. He was also economic director of the Supreme Economic Council, personal adviser to President Wilson at the Versailles Peace Conference, and chairman of the European Coal Council. The economic reorganization of Europe proceeded in considerable part under Hoover's direction while the peace negotiations dragged on.

Hoover applied all his tactical skills to the problems at hand. He rushed shiploads of food to European ports. He worked to clear the rivers and railroads so as to get food to where it was needed. He supervised the rebuilding of communications and brought in medicines to prevent or eradicate disease. Hoover went ahead with many feeding operations, without any guarantee that governments would take formal responsibility for American loans. Where necessary he engaged in barter to supply food.

Hoover was at his best in advocating food for Germany, which many of the Allies opposed immediately after the war. During the Russian famine in 1921–23, Hoover, now secretary of commerce, helped to save the lives of millions when he supervised the shipment of food to the Soviet Union without any political strings attached.

When Hoover returned to the United States in September 1919, he wrote extensively for magazines, taking a progressive, individualistic line in a time of reaction. His ideas—service to the community and equality of opportunity—reached fruition in *American Individualism* (1922). Hoover opposed sharp class differences and counseled a Jeffersonian meritocracy. He had an optimistic belief in moral and scientific progress, and he opposed the suppression of civil liberties or the use of laissez-faire dogma to restrict equal opportunity for all individuals to develop fully. He refused to accept the popular belief of 1919 that "Reds" were responsible for America's problems.

When Wilson appointed him vice-chairman of the Second Industrial Conference (1919), he urged a federal employment service, a home loan bank, and a fairer distribution of profits between capital and labor. The conference, in a report written chiefly by Hoover, endorsed a minimum wage law, equal pay for men and women, the prevention of child labor, a forty-eight-hour week, better housing, and insurance plans.

During the 1920 presidential campaign, Hoover spoke vigorously for the League of Nations and, when Warren Harding was nominated, pushed him hard in a pro-League direction.

As secretary of commerce in the Harding administration, he tried to apply what he saw as the lessons of the war era: self-regulation, coordination and provision of information, and the use of experts and volunteers to promote "cooperative capitalism."

Hoover's principal device for accomplishing his goals, both as commerce secretary and later as president, was to organize national conferences. His first important conference, held in the middle of the depression of 1920–22, concerned unemployment. Only a few of the recommendations, such as road building, were enacted by Congress, but the educational effects were important.

Much of Hoover's efforts during the 1920's concerned farming and labor problems. He pushed cooperative marketing schemes to aid the agricultural economy, but his ideas did not get a trial until the Agricultural Marketing Act was passed in 1929.

In labor matters Hoover's main success was to embarrass the steel industry into abandoning the twelve-hour day in 1923. Less successful was his attempt to bring stability to the soft-coal industry. The Jacksonville Agreement of 1924 extended wage agreements until 1927, when the influence of nonunion mines brought chaos to the industry.

Among Hoover's major domestic accomplishments as commerce secretary was the Colorado River Commission. He persuaded the various states concerned to build a major dam, and deserves as much credit as Congressman Phil Swing of California for the Boulder Canyon Project Act of 1928. He also spearheaded efforts for a St. Lawrence seaway, which Congress blocked.

Hoover expanded the activities of his department in every direction. He encouraged the trade association movement, his Bureau of Foreign and Domestic Commerce sought new markets abroad, and he fought foreign "monopolies" of raw materials, such as rubber, as detrimental to American consumers. He also worked on commissions to settle foreign debts, and was noteworthy for his generous treatment of Germany.

Hoover began his campaign for the Republican presidential nomination indirectly, by supervising relief efforts in the Mississippi flood of 1927. His trips to the devastated areas received wide coverage in the national press. When President Calvin Coolidge announced that he would not run, Hoover allowed his name to be entered in the primaries. He won the nomination at the Republican National Convention at Kansas City in June, and chose Senator Charles Curtis of Kansas as his running mate.

During the campaign against Democratic nominee Governor Alfred E. Smith of New York, Hoover's major theme was the abolition of poverty through greater productivity. He advanced plans for the aid of depressed agriculture, for regional waterpower projects, and for building highways. On the tariff and war debt issues he took a conservative position, responding to the dominant constituencies in his party and to what he perceived as the weight of public opinion. Hoover's victory resulted from the appeal of prosperity and his own effective campaign uniting disparate Republicans, while Smith failed to build a broad progressive alignment.

The first eight months of the Hoover presidency exhibited a distinct reformist character. How much of a progressive record Hoover would have made had good times continued is impossible to say. But the record is strong in civil rights, conservation, Indian welfare, and prison reform. The first major White House conference dealt with child welfare. A 1931 conference on housing brought 3,700 registrants. Similar conferences met and made recommendations in the areas of education, conservation, and waterpower.

One of Hoover's most important achievements was the passage of the Agricultural Marketing Act of June 1929, which set up a $500 million revolving fund to encourage farm cooperatives. The new Federal Farm Board had the power to enter the commodities market indirectly and to make loans to farm organizations in order to sustain prices. The board, the first government agency to react to the Great Depression, bolstered the prices of wheat, cotton, and several other crops for months after the stock market had crashed. The business community became angry over its activities on the Chicago Board of Trade, and although it continued to function, lack of congressional appropriations hindered its effectiveness after 1931.

Hoover had repeatedly complained of stock market speculation during the 1920's, warning that Federal Reserve policies were encouraging it. He was ignored. Yet, after the market crashed in October 1929, Hoover was quick to take actions to reassure the country. He recommended avoiding strikes and no wage cuts until the cost of living fell, a sharing of work where practicable, and employers providing relief where needed. Hoover asked Congress for more money for public works, and he urged state governors to expedite projects already under way. But he spent most of his energies on trying to revive business rather than on unemployment and relief.

Judging from Hoover's willingness slowly to encourage a more active government role against the Great Depression, we may conclude that he was capable—as he later claimed—of most of the "uncoercive" reforms of the New Deal. The Reconstruction Finance Corporation (RFC) of January 1932, his major legislation against the Great Depression, concentrated on helping bankers and industrialists, pouring vast sums into failing concerns.

There is considerable debate among historians about Hoover's responsibility for the government's slow response to problems of relief. Voluntary relief, he believed, worked more efficiently than bureaucratic government programs. He feared that the subsidy seekers would drain the government treasury; he also wanted to preserve the work ethic. He believed that individual initiative could have as its object not merely personal greed but also acts of sharing.

Hoover's worst problem was the American banking system, whose needs he sought to address through the RFC. Thousands of banks had failed by 1932. By then, weighty international problems had complicated and intensified the banking crisis. Hoover had not helped the international situation by signing the Smoot-Hawley Tariff Act of 1930. It raised many tariff schedules beyond the point where foreign countries could trade with the United States in order to repay war debts. The inevitable crisis came late in 1931, when Hoover was forced to call an eighteen-month moratorium on the repayment of these debts. The European economy had collapsed in 1931, driving Britain off the gold standard. Hoover then persuaded Senator Carter Glass to sponsor an omnibus banking bill to free up credit.

In foreign affairs Hoover sought to improve relations with Latin America and to encourage international disarmament. Unfortunately, despite the successful London Naval Disarmament Conference of 1930, the World Disarmament Conference at Geneva (1932) ended inconclusively; no nation appeared to know how to disarm or what weapons to do away with. The Japanese invasion of Manchuria in 1931 led to the Stimson, or Hoover-Stimson, Doctrine, which declared a more firm refusal to recognize any government established contrary to the Kellogg-Briand Peace Pact. But Hoover would not consider military intervention in Asia.

As the Great Depression worsened, Hoover came to believe that many of the nation's problems had originated abroad. The debt moratorium of June 1931 was a step in the right direction, but Hoover's meeting with France's Premier Pierre Laval—patterned on an earlier, more successful one with Britain's Prime Minister Ramsey MacDonald—failed to secure cooperation.

Then came a dramatic event that insured Hoover's exit from the White House. In the spring of 1932, unemployed veterans and their families flocked to Washington to lobby for early payment of a bonus due in 1945. They lived in abandoned buildings and shantytowns that were then springing up within many cities. When General Douglas MacArthur went beyond Hoover's orders and ejected the demonstrators from their main camp, Hoover remained silent. The veterans became refugees, and the federal government seemed heartless and cruel. Hoover, the great humanitarian, received the blame. The incident helped assure victory for the Democratic candidate, Franklin D. Roosevelt, in the 1932 presidential campaign.

The "interregnum" between Hoover's defeat in early November and Roosevelt's assumption of office the following March was so nearly disastrous that it contributed to passage of the Twentieth Amendment, setting the inauguration of a president in January. The economy continued to sink, while Hoover bickered with a president-elect who seemed unwilling to place the national interest above personal politics. A banking crisis developed just before Roosevelt's inauguration, and thanks only to the similar economic policies of their subordinates was complete collapse averted. Hoover left the White House a lonely and bitter figure, shunned by many former friends.

Moving first to Palo Alto and, in 1934, to the Waldorf Astoria Hotel in New York City, Hoover remained silent during the first year of the new administration. In 1934 he published *The Challenge to Liberty*, a book warning of the threat of fascism within the New Deal. The theme was continued in *Addresses Upon the American Road*, (8 vols., 1936–61).

In his postpresidential years, Hoover tended toward isolationism, or at least nonintervention militarily. Nonetheless, at the request of Truman, Hoover served in an advisory role in post-World War II relief, undertaking the coordination of world food supplies for thirty-eight countries in 1946 and a study of the economic situation of Germany and Austria in 1947.

Under presidents Truman and Dwight D. Eisenhower, Hoover also headed the Hoover Commissions to reorganize and streamline the federal government. The first of the two commissions to reorganize the federal bureaucracy (1947–49) was generally effective; the second (1953–55) was largely ignored owing to its markedly conservative recommendations. Both of these commissions and Hoover's advisory role on post-World War II relief enhanced his reputation as an elder statesman.

Hoover's last years were spent productively. He wrote a work on the life of Woodrow Wilson (1958) and chronicled American relief activities in the four-volume *An American Epic* (1959–64). His best-known memorial—aside from the Herbert Hoover Presidential Library at West Branch, Iowa—is the scholarly Hoover Institute on War, Revolution, and Peace at Stanford, Calif.

HOOVER, HERBERT CLARK, JR. (*b. London, England, 1903; d. Pasadena, Calif., 1969*), engineer, businessman, and undersecretary of state. Son of Herbert Clark Hoover, thirty-first president of the United States. B.A. in petroleum geology (1925), Stanford; M.B.A. (1928), Harvard. An authority on ground-to-air communication, he patented an air radio direction finder in 1931. Also patented devices for the discovery of oil. Was founder and head of the United Geophysical Company and was president (1936–46) of the Consolidated Engineering Corporation. Became special adviser for Secretary of State John Foster Dulles after the Anglo-Iranian oil dispute of the early 1950's. As undersecretary and acting secretary of state, 1954–56, played a particularly significant role in the Egyptian crisis of 1955–56: helped to scuttle Dulles' plans to assist Nasser's development of the Aswan Dam; and after Egypt seized the Suez Canal, attempted to forestall invasion of Egypt.

HOOVER, HERBERT WILLIAM (*b. New Berlin [now North Canton], Ohio, 1877; d. Canton, Ohio, 1954*), manufacturer. Attended Hiram College. Manufacturer of the Hoover vacuum cleaner. Invented by a janitor in the family leather products firm, the vacuum cleaner was introduced as a side item for the company in 1908. By the mid-twentieth century, the Hoover International Corp. operated in sixty-seven nations. Hoover was president (1922–48); chairman of the board (1948–54).

HOOVER, JAMES MATTHEWS (*b. Greenvillage, Pa., 1872; d. Kuching, Borneo, 1935*), Methodist missionary to Malaya.

HOPE, CLIFFORD RAGSDALE (*b. Birmingham, Iowa, 1893; d. Garden City, Kans., 1970*), congressman. Republican representative of the Seventh District of western Kansas in the

U.S. Congress, 1927–56; served on the Committee on Agriculture throughout his tenure. During the Depression, when prices for farm products plunged due to overproduction and decreased demand, sought to restore balance between production and consumption by endorsing a program of economic planning and control through the voluntary cooperation of farmers under government supervision: in 1932 was a sponsor of the Voluntary Domestic Allotment Plot, which became the basis for the Agricultural Act of 1933, and was among those responsible for its successor, the Soil Conservation and Domestic Allotment Act of 1935, which continued farm subsidies. He also coauthored in 1946, the Research and Marketing Act and, in 1948, the compromise Hope-Aiken price-support law; initiated the Farm Credit Act of 1953; coauthored the Hope-Aiken Watershed Act of 1953; and in 1954 was instrumental in securing the passage of the Agricultural Trade Development and Assistance Act.

HOPE, JAMES BARRON (*b. Norfolk, Va., 1829; d. 1887*), poet, newspaperman, Confederate soldier.

HOPE, JOHN (*b. Augusta, Ga., 1868; d. Atlanta, Ga., 1936*), educator. Of mixed white and black blood, Hope might have lived in the white world but chose to devote himself primarily to the education of black youth. Graduated Brown University, 1894. Professor of classics, Atlanta Baptist College (later Morehouse College), in 1906 he became its president. A great schoolmaster and able administrator, Hope became president of Atlanta University, 1929, when Atlanta became the first black graduate school, after affiliation with Morehouse and Spelman colleges. His advocacy through many national black organizations of complete equality for the black was made on an intellectual rather than an emotional basis.

HOPKINS, ARTHUR FRANCIS (*b. Pittsylvania Co., Va., 1794; d. Mobile, Ala., 1865*), lawyer, planter, jurist. Prominent in Alabama Whig party; president, Mobile and Ohio Railway; state agent for Alabama hospitals during Civil War.

HOPKINS, CYRIL GEORGE (*b. near Chatfield, Minn., 1866; d. Gibraltar, 1919*), agricultural chemist, inventor. Graduated South Dakota Agricultural College, 1890; Ph.D., Cornell, 1898. Professor of agronomy, University of Illinois, 1900–19. Devised the "Illinois System" of permanent soil fertility.

HOPKINS, EDWARD (*b. Shrewsbury, England, 1600; d. London, England, 1657*), merchant. Immigrated to New England, 1637, with Theophilus Eaton and John Davenport; settled in Hartford, Conn. Elected many times governor or deputy governor of Connecticut between 1639 and 1654. Returned to England *ca.* 1653. Benefactor to educational institutions in New England.

HOPKINS, EDWARD AUGUSTUS (*b. Pittsburgh, Pa., 1822; d. Washington, D.C., 1891*), naval officer, journalist. Promoter of trade between United States and Latin America. Established steam navigation on Paraná River; built a railroad between Buenos Aires and San Fernando. Son of Bishop John H. Hopkins.

HOPKINS, EDWARD WASHBURN (*b. Northampton, Mass., 1857; d. Madison, Conn., 1932*), orientalist, philologist. Author of *The Religions of India* (1895), *Epic Mythology* (1915), etc.

HOPKINS, ESEK (*b. Scituate, R.I., 1718; d. Providence, R.I., 1802*), sea captain, commander in chief of the Continental Navy, 1775–77. Brother of Stephen Hopkins. An able, energetic seaman, he was impatient and critical as a commander. Regarding his orders from Congress to attack the British ships off Virginia and Carolina as discretionary, he led his command of eight small vessels on an expedition to New Providence, Bahamas, early in 1776; it was on the whole a successful enterprise. Uncertainty of pay by Congress discouraged recruiting, so that Hopkins was unable to man his vessels on his return. He was plagued also by subordination and criticism of his inactivity. The British blockaded his ships in Narragansett Bay, December 1776, and Congress suspended him in March 1777 for acting unwisely and speaking slightingly of authorities in Philadelphia. A loyal patriot, he continued to serve the American cause in his native Rhode Island.

HOPKINS, HARRY LLOYD (*b. Sioux City, Iowa, 1890; d. New York, N.Y., 1946*), social worker, federal administrator, diplomat. After Harry was born, the family settled in Grinnell, Iowa. Attended Grinnell High School and Grinnell College, A.B., 1912.

In 1912 he took a summer camp job for a New York settlement house and became fascinated by social work. He stayed on with the Association for Improving the Condition of the Poor (AICP). In 1914 he became executive secretary of the Board of Child Welfare. During World War I, he was a director of the American Red Cross, and in 1922 director of an AICP study of health conditions. In 1924, Hopkins became executive director of the New York Tuberculosis Association. He amalgamated his group with the New York Heart Committee and changed its name to New York Tuberculosis and Public Health Association.

In the wake of the 1929 stock market crash, Hopkins operated a Red Cross-financed work-relief program that became the model for the New York State Temporary Emergency Relief Administration. In 1933 President Roosevelt appointed Hopkins director of the New Deal Federal Emergency Relief Administration (FERA). Hopkins put much energy into spending the money quickly and stressing some new lines of policy; he tried to provide work not dole. In 1933, Hopkins persuaded the president to permit the development of the Civil Works Authority (CWA). By January 1934, twenty million people were being helped by the combination of federal relief programs.

Hopkins wore many hats and was constantly in controversy. Many projects were indeed inefficient, programs were often hastily planned and loosely managed, and Hopkins insisted on using the federal relief programs to set new standards for the states. The Works Progress (Projects) Administration (WPA) and related Hopkins-dominated agencies, such as the Federal Surplus Relief Corporation, the Rural Rehabilitation Division, and the National Youth Administration, had a direct impact upon more individuals than did any other antidepression programs.

Eventually Hopkins supervised the expenditure of more than $9 billion in federal relief. He played a significant role, as a member of the Committee of Economic Security system. He had hopes for the White House as early as the winter of 1935–36 and came to believe that he was Roosevelt's personal choice for 1940. However, his health was bad and his national image was a problem. When Roosevelt appointed him secretary of commerce in December 1938, the confirmation hearings were difficult and lengthy.

He very quickly became Roosevelt's special projects man. In 1938, he did a secret survey of the aircraft production capacity of the nation. In 1940, he helped develop the Selective Service system and the National Defense Advisory Committee. Resigning as secretary of commerce in 1940 he went to live in New York, but was soon involved with the president's speechwriting team. Roosevelt sent him to England to catalogue British military needs, and in 1941, he was given responsibility for the whole Lend-Lease program. During 1941 he worked as the president's special representative in all the complicated negotiations with the British, and in everything involving the production, transportation, and allocation of military goods.

Throughout the war, Hopkins was the president's alter ego, advising on all matters, discussing everything, and carrying Roosevelt's authority in direct negotiations with Churchill, De Gaulle, Stalin, and Molotov. He had the president's absolute confidence.

Hopkins was one of the principal architects and managers of the New Deal and a major American policy maker in World War II. Because of his much-valued bluntness and clarity, Churchill called him "Lord Root of the Matter."

HOPKINS, ISAAC STILES (*b. Augusta, Ga., 1841; d. 1914*), Methodist clergyman, educator. Initiated technological instruction at Emory College as president, 1884–88; first president, Georgia School of Technology, 1888–96.

HOPKINS, JAMES CAMPBELL (*b. Rutland Co., Vt., 1819; d. 1877*), lawyer. Removed to Wisconsin, 1856. He helped arrange the Wisconsin code of legal procedure, and was federal judge, western Wisconsin district, 1870–77.

HOPKINS, JOHN BURROUGHS (*b. Providence, R.I., 1742; d. 1796*), naval officer. Son of Esek Hopkins. Captain and squadron leader, Continental Navy, 1775–79. Cruised as successful privateer, 1780 and 1781.

HOPKINS, JOHN HENRY (*b. Dublin, Ireland, 1792; d. 1868*), Episcopal clergyman. Came to America as a boy. Successful as ironmaster and lawyer, he abandoned his practice of law when elected rector by Trinity Episcopal Church, Pittsburgh, Pa., 1823. After a year as assistant at Trinity Church, Boston (1831), he became rector of St. Paul's Church, Burlington, Vt., and first bishop of Vermont, 1832. As presiding bishop *post* 1865, he played a leading role in effecting the reunion of the northern and southern members of the Episcopal communion. A High Churchman and a student of patristic literature, he was author of many books.

HOPKINS, JOHNS (*b. Anne Arundel Co., Md., 1795; d. Baltimore, Md., 1873*), merchant, philanthropist. Accumulated a vast fortune as commission merchant, note broker, and warehouseman; was director and largest individual stockholder in Baltimore and Ohio Railroad; became president of the Baltimore Merchants' Bank and director of several others. His interests extended also to life and fire insurance companies and steamship lines. Under his will (1870) he left the bulk of his fortune—some seven million dollars—for the establishment of the university and hospital which bear his name today.

HOPKINS, JULIET ANN OPIE (*b. Jefferson Co., Va., 1818; d. Washington, D.C., 1890*). Wife of Arthur F. Hopkins. Director of Confederate hospitals in Virginia and Alabama.

HOPKINS, LEMUEL (*b. Naugatuck, Conn., 1750; d. Hartford, Conn., 1801*), physician, satirist, one of "Hartford Wits." Removed to Hartford, 1784, where he practiced until his death, specializing in treatment of tuberculosis by a method far in advance of his day. Author of pro-Federalist satires in collaboration with John Trumbull, Richard Alsop, Theodore Dwight, and Joel Barlow.

HOPKINS, MARK (*b. Stockbridge, Mass., 1802; d. 1887*), philosopher, theologian, educator. Graduated Williams, 1824. Except for a brief experience as medical student and doctor, he spent the major portion of his adult life at Williams College, as tutor, 1825–27, as professor of moral philosophy, 1830–87, and as president also, 1836–72. He was not a great scholar or an original thinker although he did evolve an ingenious, rather labored philosophy, over which he had reflected deeply. His fame rests on his skill as a teacher who encouraged his students to make good use of their minds.

HOPKINS, SAMUEL (*b. Waterbury, Conn., 1721; d. Newport, R.I., 1803*), Congregational clergyman, theologian. Graduated Yale, 1741. Pastor at Great Barrington, Mass., 1743–69; at First Church, Newport, R.I., 1770–1803. One of first Congregational ministers to denounce slavery. Chiefly remembered for the profound influence which his philosophy (called Hopkinsianism) had on New England thought. His teachings were presented finally in complete and logical form in his *System of Doctrines Contained in Divine Revelation, Explained and Defended* (1793). His principle that disinterested benevolence should be the motive of the individual possessed great ethical value; his conception of a universe steadily set toward the greatest happiness for all had real spiritual grandeur. An associate of Jonathan Edwards in earlier years, he influenced, in his turn, the youthful William Ellery Channing.

HOPKINS, SAMUEL (*b. Albemarle Co., Va., 1753; d. near Henderson, Ky., 1819*), Revolutionary soldier, lawyer, Kentucky legislator.

HOPKINS, STEPHEN (*b. Providence, R.I., 1707; d. Providence, 1785*), farmer, surveyor, merchant. Brother of Esek Hopkins. Served Rhode Island as assemblyman, chief justice, governor (1755–68, excepting three years); was a staunch advocate of colonial rights. While chief justice he not only refused to apprehend those accused in the *Gaspée* affair, 1772, but suffered no executive officer in the colony to do it. His newspaper, the *Providence Gazette*, founded to express colonial sentiment, published his own early argument for American home rule: *The Rights of the Colonies Examined* (1764; in pamphlet form, 1765). As member of Continental Congress, 1774–76, he signed the Declaration of Independence and served on the committee selected to draw up the Articles of Confederation. As a public-spirited citizen, he fostered literary and scientific enterprises and became first chancellor of Rhode Island College.

HOPKINSON, FRANCIS (*b. Philadelphia, Pa., 1737; d. Philadelphia, 1791*), statesman, judge, author, musician. Received the first diploma from the College of Philadelphia, 1757. Achieved early success as musician and composer; contributed poetry to the *American Magazine* and others, 1757–72. After ill success in business, he rose rapidly in the legal profession, *post* 1773, was appointed a member of the Governor's Council, 1774, and in 1776 was elected to the Continental Congress. A signer of the Declaration of Independence, he served as chairman of the Navy Board, 1776–78, and as treasurer of loans, 1778–81. He was effective also as a witty, satiric essayist and poet. *A Pretty Story* (1774) presented American grievances in allegory; *A Letter to Lord Howe* (1777) protested brutality to noncombatants. Among his satires were also *The Battle of the Kegs* (1778), *Date Obolum Bellesario* (1778) and *Advertisement* (1781). As a graphic artist, he used his talents to design official seals and, in 1777, the American flag. A judge of admiralty, 1779–89, and a federal judge for Pennsylvania thereafter, Hopkinson continued to write and to follow up his musical interests. His most notable essays of this later period were the allegory "The New Roof" (1787) in support of the Federal Constitution, and "Modern Learning" (1784); the *Columbian Magazine* and the *American Museum* published his new works, *post* 1786, and republished many of his earlier works. His book *Seven Songs* (1788) is probably the first book of music published by an American composer. A collected edition of his literary work was published as *The Miscellaneous Essays and Occasional Writings* (1792).

HOPKINSON, JOSEPH (*b. Philadelphia, Pa., 1770; d. Philadelphia, 1842*), lawyer, jurist. Son of Francis Hopkinson. Graduated University of Pennsylvania, 1786. Congressman, Federalist, from Pennsylvania, 1815–19; federal judge, 1828–42. Author of "Hail Columbia," first sung in Philadelphia, 1798.

HOPPE, WILLIAM FREDERICK ("WILLIE") (*b. Cornwall on the Hudson, N.Y., 1887; d. Miami, Fla., 1959*), billiard player.

Hoppe played billiards from early childhood until 1952 and held fifty-one world billiards titles. He won his first world balkline title at age eighteen in 1906. He wrote *Billiards as It Should Be Played* in 1941.

HOPPER, DEWOLF (*b. New York, N.Y., 1858; d. Kansas City, Mo., 1935*), actor, light-opera singer. Known for his rich bass voice, his 10,000 recitations of "Casey at the Bat," and his many marriages.

HOPPER, EDNA WALLACE (*b. San Francisco, Calif., 1864?; d. New York, N.Y., 1959*), entertainer. Hopper began her theatrical career in 1891 in New York; in 1893, she appeared in David Belasco's *The Girl I Left Behind Me*, beginning a series of successes as a leading star of purely popular and escapist theater. During the 1930's, she toured in vaudeville promoting a cosmetics line bearing her name. From 1938 until her death, she was a successful investment broker on Wall Street.

HOPPER, EDWARD (*b. Nyack, N.Y., 1882; d. New York, N.Y., 1967*), painter. Studied illustration, painting, and drawing at the New York School of Art, where he was especially influenced by Robert Henri. Began exhibiting in 1908, and at the 1913 International Exhibition of Modern Art (the Armory Show), sold his first painting. Could not sell another for the next ten years, during which time he took up etching and was more successful with both sales and juried exhibitions. In 1923 began painting watercolors that were well-received in a group show at the Brooklyn Museum (1924) and at his second one-man show at the Frank K. M. Rehn Gallery (Rehn remained his dealer for the rest of his career). Thereupon he turned to painting in oil with renewed ambition. In 1925 the Pennsylvania Academy of Fine Arts purchased his oil *Apartment House*, and that same year he painted *House by the Railroad*. This canvas of a solitary nineteenth-century house standing starkly alone against railroad tracks has become one of the most famous images in American art. When the Whitney Museum of American Art opened in 1931, his *Early Sunday Morning* (1930) was placed on view; this deserted urban street scene is now one of his best-known works. In the early 1930's he began painting oils and watercolors of the Cape Cod area, including *Rooms by the Sea* (1931). During the 1930's critics categorized his art as "American scene" painting, and by the 1940's critics began to emphasize that his painting embodied loneliness, as in his masterpiece, *Nighthawks* (1942), a dramatic canvas depicting people in an all-night diner. With the emergence of the American abstract expressionists, his representational style began to be seen again as "illustrative," and many came to regard his work as representing an obsolete style. The conservative art establishment continued to respect his work, however, and when his third retrospective opened at the Whitney in 1964, revisionist critics in a generation of pop artists and photorealists saw him as the forefather of the new avant-garde. Throughout his career, however, he had pursued his own objective: to create realist paintings that expressed personal meaning.

HOPPER, HEDDA (*b. Elda Furry, Hollidaysburg, Pa., 1885; d. Hollywood, Calif., 1966*), newspaper columnist and actress. Was initially a favorite supporting actress of Broadway and in Hollywood movies, of which she made 110 by 1935, but turned to journalism when she failed to receive top billing. The Esquire Features syndicate signed her to do a column that first appeared in 1938, and her popularity grew by leaps and bounds due to her ruthless reporting on celebrities. She also succeeded in radio with programs for national networks that featured both gossip and drama, 1939–51, and her fame brought her roles in first-rate films such as *The Women* (1939) and *Sunset Boulevard* (1950). Supported the work of the House Un-American Activities Committee and similar organizations. With outrageous hats as her trademark, she became a star, gracing Republican conventions, entertaining with Bob Hope, and making frequent guest appearances on television. Wrote two best-sellers: her autobiography, *From Under My hat* (1952), and *The Whole Truth and Nothing But* (1963; written with James Brough).

HOPPER, ISAAC TATEM (*b. Deptford, N.J., 1771; d. New York, N.Y., 1852*), Quaker Abolitionist, prison reformer. A foremost promoter of the "Underground" method of aiding runaway slaves; operated in Philadelphia and New York, 1800–52.

HOPPIN, AUGUSTUS (*b. Providence, R.I., 1828; d. Flushing, N.Y., 1896*). Popular as magazine and book illustrator, 1852–85. His works include drawings for Curtis's *Potiphar Papers* (1853), Shillaber's *Mrs. Partington* (1854) and Holmes's *Autocrat of the Breakfast Table* (1858).

HOPPIN, JAMES MASON (*b. Providence, R.I., 1820; d. New Haven, Conn., 1906*), Congregational clergyman. Brother of William W. Hoppin. Professor, Yale Divinity School, 1861–79; taught history of art at Yale School of Fine Arts, 1879–99.

HOPPIN, JOSEPH CLARK (*b. Providence, R.I., 1870; d. 1925*), archaeologist, collector. Graduated Harvard, 1893; Ph.D., Munich, 1896. Author of *A Handbook of Attic Red-Figured Vases* (1919) and *Greek Black-Figured Vases* (1924) which are standard reference books.

HOPPIN, WILLIAM WARNER (*b. Providence, R.I., 1807; d. 1890*), lawyer. Brother of James M. Hoppin. Know-Nothing governor of Rhode Island, 1854–56.

HOPSON, HOWARD COLWELL (*b. Fort Atkinson, Wis., 1882; d. Greenwich, Conn., 1949*), utilities executive, financier, lawyer. A student and protégé of John R. Commons, Hopson joined the newly formed Public Service Commission of New York, 1908, and became head of its division of capitalization, 1913. He left the Public Service Commission in 1915 and began a private practice as consultant to the utilities industry. He acquired a small utilities holding company, the Associated Gas and Electric Company, in 1921, and then bought controlling interests in hundreds of operating companies—raising money for the purpose by selling additional Associated securities. The 1929 stock market crash ruined him and the Public Utilities Holding Company Act in 1935 all but shattered what was left of his empire. He was found guilty of fraud the next year, and sentenced to prison.

HOPWOOD, AVERY (*b. Cleveland, Ohio, 1882; d. Jaun-les-Pins, France, 1928*), playwright. Graduated University of Michigan, 1905. Wrote, entirely or in collaboration, 18 successful Broadway plays which include *The Bat* (1920) and *Getting Gertie's Garter* (1921).

HORLICK, WILLIAM (*b. Ruardean, England, 1846; d. Racine, Wis. 1936*), food manufacturer, philanthropist. Innovator (1887) of malted milk.

HORMEL, GEORGE ALBERT (*b. Buffalo N.Y., 1860; d. Los Angeles, Calif., 1946*), meatpacker. Raised in Toledo, Ohio. Settled in Austin, Minn., 1887, as partner in a packing house; organized his own business as George A. Hormel and Company, 1891; turned over active control of the firm to his son, Jay C. Hormel, 1927. Believing it good business to treat labor fairly, he was an industry leader in the movement for shorter hours and higher wages. In 1931, Hormel and Company initiated a "straight-time" plan, offering fifty-two equal paychecks a year regardless of the number of hours worked in a given week, in order to stabilize employment in an industry with seasonal fluctuations.

HORMEL, JAY CATHERWOOD (*b. Austin, Minn., 1892; d. Austin, Minn., 1954*), meatpacker. Studied at Princeton. After inheriting Hormel and Company, Jay Hormel became vice president in 1916; president, 1929; chairman of the board, 1945. He introduced modern management techniques, profit sharing, and modern advertising schemes to the company.

HORN, EDWARD TRAILL (*b. Easton, Pa., 1850; d. Philadelphia, Pa., 1915*), Lutheran clergyman. Pastor in Philadelphia and Reading, Pa., and in Charleston, S.C. Active member of committee which prepared the Lutheran Common Service (1888) and the *Common Service Book* (1917).

HORN, GEORGE HENRY (*b. Philadelphia, Pa., 1840; d. Beesley's Point, N.J., 1897*), entomologist, physician. Graduated M.D., University of Pennsylvania, 1861. Associated with J. L. Le Conte in the *Classification of the Coleoptera of North America* (1883); became world authority on the coleoptera.

HORN, TOM (*b. near Memphis, Mo., 1860; d. Cheyenne, Wyo., 1903*), government scout, interpreter, Wyoming stock detective. Helped negotiate surrender of Geronimo, 1886; controversial figure in Wyoming cattleman-rustler warfare.

HORNADAY, WILLIAM TEMPLE (*b. near Plainfield, Ind., 1854; d. Stamford, Conn., 1937*), naturalist, conservationist. First director, New York Zoological Park, 1896–1926.

HORNBLOWER, JOSEPH COERTEN (*b. Belleville, N.J., 1777; d. Newark, N.J., 1864*), lawyer. Son of Josiah Hornblower. Chief justice, New Jersey Supreme Court, 1832–46. Wrote important decisions on law of remainders and disqualifications of jurors; in *State* v. *Sheriff of Burlington* (1836), held that Congress had no right to pass a fugitive slave law.

HORNBLOWER, JOSIAH (*b. Staffordshire, England, 1729 n.s.; d. 1809*), engineer, mine operator, New Jersey legislator. Came to America, 1753. Assembled first steam engine in America at copper mine near Belleville, N.J., 1753–55.

HORNBLOWER, WILLIAM BUTLER (*b. Paterson, N.J., 1851; d. Litchfield, Conn., 1914*), jurist. Grandson of Joseph C. Hornblower; nephew of Joseph P. Bradley. Graduated Princeton, 1871; LL.B., Columbia, 1875. Practiced successfully in New York. Appointed to U.S. Supreme Court by President Cleveland, 1893, but his nomination was blocked by David B. Hill on partisan political grounds.

HORNER, HENRY (*b. Chicago, Ill., 1878; d. Winnetka, Ill., 1940*), jurist. Judge, probate court, Cook Co., 1914–32; Democratic governor of Illinois, 1932–40. Able and effective depression governor; foe of machine politics.

HORNER, WILLIAM EDMONDS (*b. Warrenton, Va., 1793; d. Philadelphia, Pa., 1853*), physician, anatomist. Graduated M.D., University of Pennsylvania, 1814. Teacher and professor of anatomy, University of Pennsylvania, 1816–53; dean, medical department, 1822–52. Author of *A Treatise on Pathological Anatomy* (1829), first work on this subject to appear in America.

HORNEY, KAREN DANIELSSEN (*b. Hamburg, Germany, 1885; d. New York, N.Y., 1952*), psychoanalyst. Immigrated to the U.S. in 1932. Studied at the universities of Freiburg, Göttingen, and Berlin (M.D., 1911). Affiliated, Berlin Psychoanalytic Institute (1920–32). A critic of what she saw as Freud's masculine bias concerning female psychology, she issued a series of papers in the 1920's attacking Freud's concepts of penis envy and frigidity in women. In "The Dread of Women," 1932, Horney presented considerable evidence, derived from historical and anthropological data, of the basic fear that men have of women, especially evident in taboos concerning menstruation and the "dread of the vagina." Disturbed by these views, Freud unconvincingly attributed them to Horney's own unacknowledged penis envy.

In 1934, Horney settled in New York City as an instructor at the New School for Social Research; in 1941, she was disqualified as a training analyst and instructor by the N.Y. Psychoanalytic Institute because of her rejection of Freud's principles. She immediately founded the Association for the Advancement of Psychoanalysis and its training center, the American Institute for Psychoanalysis. Her books include *The Neurotic Personality of Our Time* (1937), which is a major exposition of her theories of analysis; *New Ways in Psychoanalysis* (1939); *Self-Analysis* (1942); *Our Inner Conflicts* (1945); and, posthumously, *Feminine Psychology* (1967). The Karen Horney Clinic opened in New York City in 1955.

As Americans became increasingly interested n existentialism, Horney's concepts of basic anxiety in the newborn and of self-realization and her phenomenological approach to clinical matters were emphasized. In the late 1960's, with the freer expression of sexual behavior and the liberation of women from many male prejudices, Horney's early concepts of feminine psychology acquired new relevance.

HORNSBY, ROGERS (*b. Winters, Tex., 1896; d. Chicago, Ill., 1963*), professional baseball player. Joined the Cardinals in 1915 and soon became the greatest right-handed hitter baseball had ever known. In his twenty-three years in the big leagues Hornsby led the National League in batting seven times—six years in a row. Three times he hit over .400, reaching .424 in 1924, thus attaining the modern major-league record. In the five seasons from 1921 to 1925 his average was .402. His lifetime average was .358, exceeded only by Ty Cobb's .367. In his career batted in 1,579 runs, a total surpassed at the time he retired by only five other players. Led the National League in home runs in 1922 with 42 and in 1925 with 39, and was the Most Valuable Player in 1925 and 1929. Salary disputes, his irascible personality, and his betting on horse races led to his being frequently released or traded: was manager of the Cardinals (1925–26); was with the New York Giants (1926–28), the Boston Braves (1928), and the Chicago Cubs (1928–32); signed with the Cardinals again (1932–33); became manager of the St. Louis Browns (1933–37); thereafter bounded from job to job as coach and playing manager in the minor leagues; returned to the Browns as manager (1951–52); was briefly manager of the Cincinnati Reds; was a coach with the Cubs (1958–59); and in 1962 became batting coach with the New York Mets. In 1942 was elected to baseball's Hall of Fame.

HORR, GEORGE EDWIN (*b. Boston, Mass., 1856; d. 1927*), Baptist clergyman. Editor, New England Baptist weekly, the *Watchman, post* 1901; president, Newton Theological Institution, 1908–25.

HORROCKS, JAMES (*b. Wakefield, England, ca. 1734, d. Oporto, Portugal, 1772*), Episcopal clergyman, educator. Graduated Trinity College, Cambridge, 1755. Came to America *ca.* 1761. President, College of William and Mary, *post* 1764, a controversial choice. Commissary of bishop of London; member of the Council of Virginia. Advocated an American episcopate, 1771.

HORSFIELD, THOMAS (*b. near Bethlehem, Pa., 1773; d. 1859*), explorer, naturalist. Graduated M.D., University of Pennsylvania, 1798. Spent many years in Java as army surgeon. Curator, East India Company Museum, London, 1820–59. His most important monograph was the beautifully illustrated *Plantae Javanicae Rariores* (1838–1852).

HORSFORD, EBEN NORTON (*b. Moscow, N.Y., 1818; d. Cambridge, Mass., 1893*), chemist. Graduated Rensselaer Polytechnic, 1838. Taught chemistry at Lawrence Scientific School, whose laboratory was among first to teach analytical chemistry systematically to individual students, 1847–63; engaged thereafter in chemical research for industry.

HORSMANDEN, DANIEL (*b. Purleigh, England, 1694; d. Flatbush, N.Y., 1778*), last chief justice of New York Province. Studied law at Middle and Inner Temple, London. Settled in New York, 1731. Held numerous civil and judicial offices, 1733–46. An active member of the DeLancey faction, Horsmanden was stripped of his offices by Governor Clinton, 1747. He managed a financial and political recovery, becoming councilman, member of the New York Supreme Court, 1753, and chief justice, 1763. He achieved popularity when he ruled (1765) against any appeals from supreme court to the governor and council except on error in law. He was author of *A Journal of the Proceedings in the Detection of the Conspiracy, etc.* (1744), an account of the so-called Negro Plot of 1741.

HORST, LOUIS (*b. Kansas City, Mo., 1884; d. New York, N.Y., 1942*), musician and dance educator. As head of the music department at the Denishawn School, 1915–25, began to analyze the relationship of music to dance and formed a "synchoric orchestra" of dancers patterned after a symphonic orchestra, which influenced a trend toward more abstract dance forms. Joined Martha Graham in 1925, and as her accompanist, musical director, composer, and adviser, encouraged her to explore more dramatic materials. As a composer, his most successful pieces were *Primitive Mysteries* (1931), *Celebration* (1934), *Frontier* (1935), and *El Penitente* (1940), done in collaboration with Graham. Taught at numerous schools and founded *Dance Observer* in 1934, serving as managing editor and a major contributor until his death. Wrote *Pre-Classic Dance Forms* (1937), the first text to draw upon musical knowledge for formal principles of choreography, and *Modern Dance Forms in Relation to Other Modern Arts* (1961), with Carroll Russell. Received a Capezio Award in 1955.

HORTON, EDWARD EVERETT, JR. (*b. Brooklyn, N.Y., 1886; d. San Fernando Valley, Calif., 1970*), actor. In the late 1920's he and his brother Winter Davis Horton established a repertory company that presented George Bernard Shaw and Noel Coward comedies, French farces, and Broadway hits to a loyal California following. As a producer and actor, he remained a mainstay of West Coast and regional theaters. Is most famous for his role as Henry Dewlip, the aging, prissy bachelor roué, in Benn W. Levy's comedy *Springtime for Henry* (1931), which he performed in summer stock and touring companies. Also appeared as a comic mainstay in more than 100 films over a twenty-year period, becoming well known for his portrayals of jittery, addlebrained fussbudgets.

HORTON, SAMUEL DANA (*b. Pomeroy, Ohio, 1844; d. Washington, D.C., 1895*), lawyer, economist. Son of Valentine B. Horton. Graduated Harvard, 1864; LL.B., 1868. Lifelong crusader for theory that silver could be restored to importance through formation of international monetary union.

HORTON, VALENTINE BAXTER (*b. Windsor, Vt., 1802; d. 1888*), lawyer. Pioneer bituminous coal operator in Ohio; deviser of "Condor" towboats. Congressman, Whig and Republican, from Ohio, 1855–59, 1861–63. Organized a salt combine which was regarded as an early example of a trust.

HOSACK, ALEXANDER EDDY (*b. New York, N.Y., 1805; d. 1871*), pioneer urological surgeon. Son of David Hosack. Author of classic paper on removal of sensitive tumors from female urethra (*New York Journal of Medicine,* 1839).

HOSACK, DAVID (*b. New York, N.Y., 1769; d. 1835*), physician, teacher. Graduated Princeton, 1789; studied medicine under Samuel Bard, Benjamin Rush, and others. Professor of botany and materia medica, Columbia, 1795–1811; taught practice and theory of medicine at College of Physicians and Surgeons, 1811–26. In practice in New York, he was one of the first American surgeons to use the stethoscope and to advocate vaccination; he was also instrumental in founding Bellevue Hospital. With his pupil and partner John W. Francis, he established the *American Medical Register*, 1810; the Elgin Botanical Garden was founded at his home in Hyde Park, N.Y. He was also prominent in the cultural and social life of New York City.

HOSHOUR, SAMUEL KLINEFELTER (*b. Heidelburg, York Co., Pa., 1803; d. Indianapolis, Ind., 1883*), clergyman, Lutheran and Disciples. Removed to Indiana, 1835, where he was a pioneer educator.

HOSMER, FREDERICK LUCIAN (*b. Framingham, Mass., 1840; d. 1929*), Unitarian clergyman, hymn writer.

HOSMER, HARRIET GOODHUE (*b. Watertown, Mass., 1830; d. 1908*), sculptor. Studied in Boston, at St Louis University, and under John Gibson at Rome, Italy, 1852–59. Her best-known work, a statue of Zenobia, was shown in London, 1862; her pseudo-classic statue of Thomas H. Benton was placed in St. Louis, Mo., 1868. Famous in her day, she had a genius for friendship and a great zest for living.

HOSMER, HEZEKIAH LORD (*b. Hudson, N.Y., 1814; d. San Francisco, Calif., 1893*), jurist. Removed to Ohio, 1830, where he practiced law and journalism, *post* 1835. Controversial chief justice of Montana Territory, 1864–68. Held minor offices in California, *post* 1872.

HOSMER, JAMES KENDALL (*b. Northfield, Mass., 1834; d. Minneapolis, Minn., 1927*), Unitarian clergyman, educator, popular historian.

HOSMER, TITUS (*b. Middletown, Conn., 1737; d. 1780*), lawyer, Connecticut state legislator, Revolutionary statesman, patron of literature.

HOSMER, WILLIAM HOWE CUYLER (*b. Avon, N.Y., 1814; d. Avon, 1877*), lawyer, poet Union soldier. Versified Seneca Indian legends.

HOTCHKISS, BENJAMIN BERKELEY (*b. Watertown, Conn., 1826; d. Paris, France, 1885*), inventor, ordnance manufacturer. Supplied Union Army cannon projectiles, 1861–65; patented machine gun, 1872; perfected magazine rifle, 1875. Considered the leading artillery engineer of his time.

HOTCHKISS, HORACE LESLIE (*b. Auburn, N.Y., 1842; d. San Antonio, Tex., 1929*), financier, New York stock broker. Promoted stock quotation ticker through Gold and Stock Telegraph Co., 1867–71; organized American District Telegraph Co., 1871.

HOTZ, FERDINAND CARL (*b. Wertheim, Germany, 1843; d. Chicago, Ill., 1909*), ophthalmologist. Graduated M.D., Heidelberg, 1865. Establishing a practice in Chicago, 1869, he performed the first plastic operation for the entropion and the first recorded mastoid operation in Chicago. Internationally renowned for plastic surgery of the eye, he taught at Rush Medical College and at Presbyterian Hospital, *post* 1898.

HOUDINI, HARRY (*b. Appleton, Wis., 1874; d. Detroit, Mich., 1926*), magician, author. Actual name, Ehrich Weiss; celebrated for sensational feats as escape artist.

HOUDRY, EUGENE JULES (*b. Domont, France, 1892; d. Upper Darby, Pa., 1962*), inventor and industrialist. In 1927 discovered a method of catalytically "cracking" low-grade crude oil into high-test gasoline, and in 1930 moved to the United States to implement his invention as president and director of research of the Houdry Process Corporation. His process revolutionized the art of making gasoline, enabling refining companies to produce twice as much high-quality gasoline per barrel of crude oil as simple distillation and allowing the utilization of even the poorest grades of crude oil; within a decade catalytic cracking became the standard process for petroleum-refining companies worldwide. During World War II applied his process to the production of high-octane aviation gasoline. Formed the Oxy-Catalyst company to pursue cancer research. With more than 100 patents in his name, he was one of the most prolific inventors of his time.

HOUGH, CHARLES MERRILL (*b. Philadelphia, Pa., 1858; d. New York, N.Y., 1927*), jurist. U.S. district and circuit court judge in New York, 1906–27. Authority on maritime law.

HOUGH, EMERSON (*b. Newton, Iowa, 1857; d. 1923*), journalist. Author of the *Singing Mouse Stories* (1895), the *Mississippi Bubble* (1902) and many other popular novels. His *The Covered Wagon* (1922) became a famous motion picture. He was a lifelong propagandist for conservation and for the national park idea.

HOUGH, FRANKLIN BENJAMIN (*b. Martinsburg, N.Y., 1822; d. 1885*), forester. Graduated Union, 1843; Western Reserve, M.D., 1848. Practiced medicine at Somerville, N.Y., was army surgeon during Civil War. Served as superintendent of 1870 U.S. Census. The Census revealing a need for publicizing rapid depletion of the country's forest reserves, Hough submitted a series of reports on this subject to the federal government even before his appointment as forestry agent in the Department of Agriculture, 1876. Traveling widely through the United States and Europe, he investigated forestry systems and embodied his findings in official reports, books, and pamphlets. His activities paved the way for the successful conservation movement of later years.

HOUGH, GEORGE WASHINGTON (*b. Tribes Hill, N.Y., 1836; d. 1909*), astronomer, inventor of astronomical and meteorological instruments. Made systematic study of surface details of Jupiter as director of Dearborn Observatory, 1879–1909; he also discovered and measured difficult double stars.

HOUGH, THEODORE (*b. Front Royal, Va., 1865; d. Charlottesville, Va., 1924*), physiologist. Graduated Johns Hopkins, 1886; Ph.D., 1893. Taught at Massachusetts Institute of Technology, Simmons College, and University of Virginia; dean of medicine, University of Virginia, 1916–24; an authority on the medical school curriculum.

HOUGH, WALTER (*b. Morgantown, W.Va., 1859; d. 1935*), anthropologist. Graduated West Virginia University, 1883; Ph.D., 1894. Served for many years with the U.S. National Museum; was head curator at his death. Made extensive researches in the Southwest, and was author of a wide range of technical articles.

HOUGH, WARWICK (*b. Loudoun Co., Va., 1836; d. St. Louis, Mo., 1915*), lawyer, Confederate soldier. Justice, supreme court of Missouri, 1874–84; circuit court judge, 1900–06.

HOUGHTON, ALANSON BIGELOW (*b. Cambridge, Mass., 1863; d. South Dartmouth, Mass., 1941*), glass manufacturer, congressman, diplomat. Raised in Corning, N.Y. Graduated Harvard, A.B., 1886; studied political economy at universities of Göttingen, Berlin, and Paris. Joined family business (Corning

Glass Works), 1889; president, 1910; chairman of the board, 1918. He was congressman, Republican, from New York, 1919–22, resigning his seat to accept appointment as U.S. ambassador to Germany (1922–25). Successor to Frank B. Kellogg as U.S. ambassador to Great Britain, he served from 1925 to 1929. In a speech at Harvard, June 1927, he called for new peace machinery, including hundred-year nonaggression pacts which would be submitted to popular referenda, thus putting the issues of war and peace directly into the hands of the people.

HOUGHTON, DOUGLAS (b. Troy, N.Y., 1809; d. 1845), geologist, physician. Graduated Rensselaer Polytechnic, 1829. Removed to Michigan, 1830; was surgeon-botanist on H. R. Schoolcraft's 1831 expedition to the sources of the Mississippi. Professor of geology, University of Michigan, 1838–45; mayor of Detroit, 1842–43.

HOUGHTON, GEORGE HENDRIC (b. Deerfield, Mass., 1820; d. New York, N.Y., 1897), Episcopal clergyman. Founded the New York City parish of the Transfiguration, 1849, known as "The Little Church Around the Corner." Active in charity.

HOUGHTON, HENRY OSCAR (b. Sutton, Vt., 1823; d. North Andover, Mass., 1895), publisher. Established H. O. Houghton & Co., 1852, printers; merged publishing branch of Hurd and Houghton with J. R. Osgood & Co., 1878, becoming Houghton Mifflin and Company, 1880.

HOUK, LEONIDAS CAMPBELL (b. near Boyds Creek, Tenn., 1836; d. 1891), lawyer, Tennessee Unionist and soldier, jurist. Congressman, Republican, from Tennessee, 1879–91. Early advocate of equal rights for former Confederates.

HOURWICH, ISAAC AARONOVICH (b. Vilna, Russia, 1860; d. New York, N.Y., 1924), statistician, lawyer. Came to America, 1890. Author of controversial Immigration and Labor (1912).

HOUSE, EDWARD HOWARD (b. Boston, Mass., 1836; d. Tokyo, Japan, 1901), journalist, musician. Japan's first foreign publicist. Editor, Tokyo Times, 1877.

HOUSE, EDWARD MANDELL (b. Houston, Tex., 1858; d. New York, N.Y., 1938), presidential adviser, known as "Colonel House." Active, 1892–1902, in Texas politics as campaign manager and adviser to Gov. James S. Hogg and his successors. Vigorously supporting Woodrow Wilson's candidacy, 1912, House became the president's most intimate adviser and chief deputy. Primarily interested in foreign affairs, House attempted conciliatory negotiations before and during World War I and he set up an advisory group, "The Inquiry," to formulate peace strategy and policies. Thrown in the shadow by Wilson's presence at the Paris peace talks and more realistic and conciliatory than the president, House broke off relations with Wilson over the conduct of negotiations, June 1919. No other American of his time was on such close terms with so many men of international fame.

HOUSE, HENRY ALONZO (b. Brooklyn, N.Y., 1840; d. Bridgeport, Conn., 1930), inventor, manufacturer. Nephew of Royal E. House. Patented a machine to work buttonholes, 1862, and other sewing-machine inventions. Designed a steam motorcar, 1866; aided building of Maxim steam flying machine, 1896.

HOUSE, ROYAL EARL (b. Rockland, Vt., 1814; d. Bridgeport, Conn., 1895), inventor. Exhibited a printing telegraph, 1844 (patented, 1846), which had extensive standard use; constructed profitable range of telegraph lines; was first to employ stranded wire and also designed a glass screw-socket insulator.

HOUSE, SAMUEL REYNOLDS (b. Waterford, N.Y., 1817; d. Waterford, 1899), physician, Presbyterian clergyman. Medical missionary in Siam, 1846–52; superintendent of a boys' school in Bangkok, which popularized Western education, 1852–1876.

HOUSTON, CHARLES HAMILTON (b. Washington, D.C., 1895; d. Washington, 1950), lawyer, civil rights leader. B.A., Amherst College, 1915; LL.B., Harvard Law School, 1922; S.J.D., Harvard, 1923; D.C.L., University of Madrid, 1924. After training at a black officers' training camp, he served in France during World War I. At Harvard Law School, he was on the editorial board of the Law Review. Practiced with his father in Washington, D.C., 1924–29. As resident vice-dean (1929–32) and dean (1932–35) of Howard University Law School, he raised its standards and gave it rank among the leading schools in the nation. Important civil rights cases in which he participated up to 1935 included Nixon v. Condon and Norris v. Alabama, the second Scottsboro case. As special counsel for the National Association for the Advancement of Colored People, 1935–40, he initiated and organized N.A.A.C.P. legal work in support of civil rights and argued cases before the U.S. Supreme Court. One of the most important of these was Missouri ex rel. Gaines v. Canada. Returning to private practice, 1940, he remained until his death a member of the national legal committee of the N.A.A.C.P.; he was its chairman, 1948–50.

HOUSTON, DAVID FRANKLIN (b. Monroe, N.C., 1866; d. New York, N.Y., 1940), educator, businessman. President, Texas A.&M., 1902–05; University of Texas, 1905–08. U.S. secretary of agriculture, 1913–20, and secretary of treasury, 1920–21. Brought into politics by Edward M. House, he enlarged and reorganized the Department of Agriculture; his conservative policies at the Treasury were blamed for declining farm prices, 1920.

HOUSTON, EDWIN JAMES (b. Alexandria, Va., 1847; d. Philadelphia, Pa., 1914), educator, electrical engineer. Pioneer in laboratory method of instruction in sciences at Central High School, Philadelphia. Inventor, with Elihu Thomson, of an improved system of arc lighting, patented 1881. Author, with A. E. Kennelly, of probably the first elementary electrical textbooks (1895–1906).

HOUSTON, GEORGE SMITH (b. Williamson Co., Tenn., 1811; d. 1879), lawyer, politician. Raised in Alabama. Congressman, Democrat and Unionist, 1841–49, 1851–61. Opposed secession; refused to serve in Confederate Army. Reform Democratic governor of Alabama, 1874–78; U.S. senator, 1878–79.

HOUSTON, HENRY HOWARD (b. Wrightsville, Pa., 1820; d. Philadelphia, Pa., 1895), railroad executive. Innovated through freight-car service over Pennsylvania and Lake Shore systems; promoted the Union Line and the Empire Line.

HOUSTON, SAMUEL (b. Rockbridge Co., Va., 1793; d. Huntsville, Tex., 1863), lawyer, soldier, statesman. Grew up in vicinity of Maryville, Tenn., only a few miles from the Cherokee country; acquired a liking and sympathetic appreciation for Indian life which he retained throughout his career. Served under Andrew Jackson against the Creeks, 1813–14; was wounded at battle of Horseshoe Bend, 1814. Tall and handsome, he had a natural gift for stump speaking. Resigning from the army, 1818, he studied law and was chosen district attorney for the Nashville district. In 1827, he was elected governor of Tennessee on an internal improvements platform after serving, 1823–27, as a Democratic congressman. His wife leaving him for reasons undivulged, he resigned the office and became an Indian trader and adopted son of the Cherokee, 1829. He traded on the Verdigris near Fort Gibson, 1829–34. A confidante of the Indians, he represented them on several missions to Washington. After 1835, Texas commanded both his interest and his services; during that year he assumed command of the Texan army of 400 men, which he managed to expand and improve. Houston's withdrawal before the Mexican invaders under Santa Anna was unpopular, but his surprise attack at Buffalo Bayou on the San Jacinto, Apr. 21, 1836, overthrew the Mexicans and established the fame of the Texas commander. Elevated to the presidency of the republic, 1836, he secured recognition of the new nation. Houston was sent to the Texas Congress, after the expiration of this first presidential term, where he opposed the expensive, expansionist policy of President Mirabeau B. Lamar. Elected president again, 1841, he restored Texas finances. When it was clear that annexation was popular and possible, Houston accepted it, despite earlier doubts of its wisdom. As U.S. senator from the State of Texas, 1846−59, he became a strong Unionist and an increasingly lonely figure among his Southern colleagues. Defeated for reelection to the Senate, 1858, he was elected governor of Texas, 1859. He opposed secession and refused to recognize the authority of the Secession Convention, but resigned his office when the Convention's action was sustained by the voters, 1861. The hero of San Jacinto refused to take an oath of allegiance to the Confederacy since, in his opinion, Texas had resumed the status of an independent nation.

HOUSTON, WILLIAM CHURCHILL (*b. ca. 1746; d. Frankford, Pa., 1788*), lawyer, teacher, Revolutionary leader in New Jersey. Taught at Princeton, 1768−83; practiced law in Trenton, N.J., thereafter.

HOUSTOUN, JOHN (*b. near Waynesboro, Ga., 1744; d. near Savannah, Ga., 1796*), Revolutionary leader, jurist. Governor of Georgia, 1778 and 1784.

HOVE, ELLING (*b. Northwood, Iowa, 1863; d. 1927*), Lutheran clergyman. Professor of theology, Luther Seminary, St. Paul, Minn., 1901−26. His *Christian Doctrine* (1930) puts him in front rank of Lutheran theologians in America.

HOVENDEN, THOMAS (*b. Dunmanway, Ireland, 1840; d. near Norristown, Pa., 1895*), historical and genre painter. Came to America, 1863. Studied in New York, and in Paris under Cabanel. Taught in Pennsylvania Academy; among his pupils was Robert Henri. *The Last Moments of John Brown* is his best-known work.

HOVEY, ALVAH (*b. Greene, N.Y., 1820; d. 1903*), Baptist clergyman. Graduated Dartmouth, 1844; Newton Theological Institution, 1848. Taught at Newton, 1849−1903; served as president, 1868−98.

HOVEY, ALVIN PETERSON (*b. near Mount Vernon, Ind., 1821; d. 1891*), jurist, Union major general. Credited by Grant with key victory at Champion's Hill during Vicksburg campaign. Minister to Peru, 1865−70; Republican governor of Indiana, 1889−91.

HOVEY, CHARLES EDWARD (*b. Thetford, Vt., 1827; d. Washington, D.C., 1897*), educator, Union major general, lawyer. Graduated Dartmouth, 1852. An outstanding Illinois school official, 1854−61; founder of normal school near Bloomington. Practiced law in Washington D.C., *post* 1865.

HOVEY, CHARLES MASON (*b. Cambridge, Mass., 1810; d. 1887*), horticulturist. With his brother Phineas, established a nursery at Cambridge, Mass., 1832. Here, by a definite plan of plant breeding, he originated the Hovey strawberry (1834) and also became well known as an authority on a variety of fruits and ornamentals. He achieved national fame as editor of *The Magazine of Horticulture, Botany, and All Useful Discoveries, etc.,* 1835−68. He was author of *Fruits of America,* which he published in parts, 1847−1856.

HOVEY, OTIS ELLIS (*b. East Hardwick, Vt., 1864; d. New York, N.Y., 1941*), engineer, specialist in design and construction of bridges. B.S., Dartmouth, 1885; C.E., 1889. After varied experience, in particular with the firm of George S. Morison, he joined the Union Bridge Company in 1896. On Union's merger into the American Bridge Company, he became a sign engineer with the new firm (1900), assistant chief engineer (1907), and consulting engineer in 1931. Skilled in every aspect of bridge building, he specialized in large, movable steel structures, and also in dams; he designed and patented three major types of pivots for turntables of "swing" bridges. He was author of *Movable Bridges* (2 vols., 1926, 1927) and *Steel Dams* (1935).

HOVEY, RICHARD (*b. Normal, Ill., 1864 d. New York, N.Y., 1900*), poet. Son of Charles E. Hovey. Graduated Dartmouth, 1885. Author of Dartmouth verse; also of a series of poetic dramas on Arthurian themes. Translated Maeterlinck's dramas. In collaboration with Bliss Carman, published *Songs from Vagabondia* (1894), of which a second series appeared in 1896, and a final volume, *Last Songs,* in 1901.

HOVGAARD, WILLIAM (*b. Aarhus, Denmark, 1857; d. Morristown, N.J., 1950*), naval architect, educator, specialist in design of warships. Graduated Danish Naval Academy, 1879; studied naval architecture and ship construction at Royal Naval College, Greenwich, England, 1883−86; assigned to Royal Dockyard, Copenhagen, 1886−1901 (except for 1895−97, when he managed the Burmeister and Wain shipyard in Copenhagen). Professor of naval design and construction, Massachusetts Institute of Technology, 1902−33. Consultant to U.S. Navy Department thereafter. His course at M.I.T. comprised three elements: historical developments, theory of design, and structural and internal arrangements; his lectures were supplemented by design practice and shipyard visits. He was author, among other works, of *Structural Design of Warships* (1915), *General Design of Warships* (1920), and *Modern History of Warships* (1920).

HOWARD, ADA LYDIA (*b. Temple, N.H., 1829; d. Brooklyn, N.Y., 1907*), educator. Graduated Mount Holyoke Seminary, 1853. First president of Wellesley College, 1875−81.

HOWARD, BENJAMIN (*b. Virginia, 1760; d. St. Louis, Mo., 1814*), soldier, Kentucky legislator and congressman. Governor of District of Louisiana, 1810−12; of Territory of Missouri, 1812−13.

HOWARD, BENJAMIN CHEW (*b. near Baltimore, Md., 1791; d. Baltimore, 1872*), lawyer. Son of John E. Howard. Graduated Princeton, 1809. Congressman, Democrat, from Maryland, 1829−33, 1835−39. Reporter of U.S. Supreme Court Reports covering period 1843−62. These volumes were models of clarity, diction, and thoroughness.

HOWARD, BLANCHE WILLIS (*b. Bangor, Maine, 1847; d. Munich, Germany, 1898*), popular novelist.

HOWARD, BRONSON CROCKER (*b. Detroit, Mich., 1842; d. 1908*), journalist, playwright. First president, American Dramatist's Club. Author of many successful plays, too closely keyed to the taste of his generation to have survived as literature. Among them were *Saratoga* (1870), *The Henrietta* (1887), and *Shenandoah* (1888).

HOWARD, CHARLES PERRY (*b. Harvel, Ill., 1879; d. Colorado Springs, Colo., 1938*), labor leader. President, International Typographical Union, 1923−24, 1926−38; first secretary, Committee (later Congress) for Industrial Organization, 1935.

HOWARD, EDGAR (*b. Osceola, Iowa, 1858; d. Columbus, Nebr., 1951*), politician and editor. Attended Iowa College of Law. Editor and part owner of the *Columbus* (Nebr.) *Telegram* from 1900 until his death. Entered politics as a supporter and personal secretary of William Jennings Bryan. Elected as lieutenant governor of Nebraska in 1916; U.S. congressman (Democrat) from 1922 to 1934. Author of the Wheeler-Howard Act (1934), which reversed the policy of the Dawes Severalty Act of 1887 and reestablished tribal structure as the cornerstone of Indian policy. Howard promoted legislation to benefit his agricultural constituents, to aid Indians, and to provide for the insuring of bank deposits. In foreign policy he remained a staunch isolationist.

HOWARD, GEORGE ELLIOTT (*b. Saratoga, N.Y., 1849; d. 1928*), teacher, scholar. Graduated University of Nebraska, 1876. Professor of history at University of Nebraska, 1879–91; at Stanford University, 1891–1901. Returning to Nebraska, 1904, he was head of political science and sociology departments and taught until 1924. Author of *History of Matrimonial Institutions* (1904).

HOWARD, HENRY (*b. Jamaica Plain, Mass., 1868; d. Cambridge, Mass., 1951*), chemical engineer. Studied at M.I.T. Developer of the "Howard dust chamber" for the efficient and clean burning of pyrites necessary in the production of sulfuric acid; the process was widely used throughout the U.S., Germany, and Belgium. Held eighty-nine patents covering a broad spectrum of chemical processes. Member of the M.I.T. corporation, 1911; president of the Manufacturing Chemists Association and of the American Institute of Chemical Engineers. In World War I, he served on the chemical committees of the Council of National Defense and the War Industries Board.

HOWARD, JACOB MERRITT (*b. Shaftsbury, Vt., 1805; d. Detroit, Mich., 1871*), lawyer, politician. Removed to Detroit, 1832, where he practiced law. An organizer of Republican party, he served as U.S. senator from Michigan, 1862–71; an outspoken Radical, he favored extreme punishment for the South.

HOWARD, JOHN EAGER (*b. Baltimore Co., Md., 1752; d. 1827*), Revolutionary soldier. Federalist governor of Maryland, 1788–91; U.S. senator, 1796–1803; vice presidential candidate, 1816.

HOWARD, JOSEPH KINSEY (*b. Oskaloosa, Iowa, 1906; d. Choteau, Mont., 1951*), newspaper editor, regional historian, social and political critic. Editor of the Great Falls *Leader* (1923–44). Author of *Montana: High, Wide and Handsome* (1943) and *Montana Margins: A State Anthology* (1946). From 1944 to 1946, he was research associate for the Montana Study, a project sponsored by the Rockefeller Foundation and the University of Montana, designed to determine how the quality of small-town and rural life could be improved. *Strange Empire: A Narrative of the Northwest* was published posthumously in 1952. In his work Howard championed the underdog and clearly revealed the dehumanization arising from discrimination against minorities and the dispossessed.

HOWARD, LELAND OSSIAN (*b. Rockford, Ill., 1857; d. Bronxville, N.Y., 1950*), entomologist. Raised in Ithaca, N.Y. Graduated Cornell University, B.S., 1877; M.S., 1883. Assistant entomologist, U.S. Department of Agriculture, 1878–94; chief of the bureau of entomology, 1894–1927; consultant to the Department of Agriculture, 1927–31. He covered a wide range of topics in his lectures and publications, but was particularly interested in biological control and in insects as disease carriers. Among his more than 1,000 publications were books on the mosquito and on the housefly, also the popular *Insect Book* (1901) and *Insect Menace* (1931).

HOWARD, LESLIE (*b. London, England, 1893; d. Bay of Biscay, 1943*), actor, stage and screen director. Stage name of Leslie Howard Steiner (or Stainer). Attended Dulwich College; became a bank clerk. Served as officer in World War I; invalided home, 1917. He made his first appearances in 1917 with a provincial company of *Peg o' My Heart*, and his London debut in 1918 in Pinero's *The Freaks*. In the fall of 1920, he made his New York debut in *Just Suppose*, and continued to appear in New York for several years as juvenile lead in light comedies. In 1925, he played opposite Katharine Cornell in *The Green Hat*. He first starred in *Her Cardboard Lover* (1927, New York, with Jeanne Eagels; 1928, London, with Tallulah Bankhead) and enhanced his reputation with a brilliant performance in Galsworthy's *Escape*. He gave memorable stage performances in *Berkeley Square* (1929), *The Animal Kingdom* (which he directed and co-produced, 1932), *The Petrified Forest* (1935), and his own production of Shakespeare's *Hamlet* (1936). He made his first U.S. film appearance in *Outward Bound* (1930). His outstanding films were *Of Human Bondage* (1934), *The Scarlet Pimpernel* (1935), *Pygmalion* (1938), and *Gone with the Wind* (1939). He returned to his native England in 1939 to aid in the British war effort. Returning from Lisbon, his plane was shot down by German aircraft.

HOWARD, OLIVER OTIS (*b. Leeds, Maine, 1830; d. Burlington, Vt., 1909*), Union soldier. Graduated West Point, 1854, where he served as instructor in mathematics. Promoted brigadier general of volunteers, 1861; in the regular army, 1864. Retired as major general, regular army, 1894. Medal of Honor winner for valor at Fair Oaks, a general officer during major Civil War campaigns, Howard's military reputation has been the subject of controversy. Military critics assign him blame for Union failures at Chancellorsville and during the first day of Gettysburg, although his personal courage has never been questioned. As commissioner of the Freedmen's Bureau, 1865–72, he was charged with inefficiency and over enthusiasm. Instrumental in founding Howard University, he served as its president, 1869–74. He commanded the 1877 expedition against the Nez Percé and in 1878 went against the Bannock and Paiute.

HOWARD, ROY WILSON (*b. Gano, Ohio, 1883; d. New York, N.Y., 1964*), newspaper executive. In 1906 became a Scripps-McRae news service correspondent in New York City, where he was also manager of the Publishers' Press Association. In 1907 those two services and the Pacific Coast Scripps news organization were joined under Scripp's control to form the United Press Association (UP), with Howard as general manager and vice president. In 1921 was advanced to chairman of the board, and in 1922 the Scripps-McRae organization was renamed Scripps-Howard. He then changed his main interest from the UP to management of the newspaper group. Purchased the *New York Telegram* (1927) and the *New York World* (1931) and merged the evening edition of the *World* with the *Telegram*; in 1933 the *World-Telegram* received the Pulitzer Prize for meritorious public service. Acquired the *New York Sun* (1950) and renamed it the *World-Telegram and Sun*. His half-century career contributed significantly to journalism's development, growth, and change.

HOWARD, SIDNEY COE (*b. Oakland, Calif., 1891; d. near Tyringham, Mass., 1939*), dramatist. Graduated University of California, 1915; student in Harvard's famous "47 Workshop." His most successful independent plays, the Pulitzer Prize–winning *They Knew What They Wanted* (1924), *The Silver Cord* (1926), and *Alien Corn* (1933), demonstrate his skill in dealing realistically with the problems and characters of middle-class society. *Yellow Jack* (1934, written with Paul de Kruif) was a strikingly original documentary; *The Late Christopher Bean* (1932, from René Fauchois) and *Dodsworth* (1934) were successful stage adaptations by Howard. He also wrote several notable screen plays, including *Arrowsmith* (1932), *Dodsworth* (1936) and *Gone with the Wind* (1939).

HOWARD, TIMOTHY EDWARD (*b. near Ann Arbor, Mich., 1837; d. 1916*), jurist, Indiana legislator. Graduated Notre Dame, 1862. Justice and chief justice, Indiana Supreme Court; professor of law, University of Notre Dame, 1906–1916.

HOWARD, VOLNEY ERSKINE (*b. Oxford Co., Maine, 1809; d. Santa Monica, Calif., 1889*), lawyer. Removed to Mississippi, 1832. Editor of *Howard's Reports* of decisions of Mississippi appeals court, 1834–43. Served as Texas legislator and congressman; removed to California, 1853, where he unsuccessfully opposed the Vigilantes. He served later as district attorney and judge in Los Angeles.

HOWARD, WILLIAM ALANSON (*b. Hinesburg, Vt., 1813; d. Washington, D.C., 1880*), lawyer, politician. Removed to Detroit, Mich., 1840. Congressman, Republican, from Michigan, 1855–61; was later a land commissioner for railroads. He was governor of Dakota Territory, 1878–80.

HOWARD, WILLIAM TRAVIS (*b. Cumberland Co., Va., 1821; d. Narragansett Pier, R.I., 1907*), gynecologist. Graduated Jefferson Medical College, 1844. Taught at University of Maryland for many years. First to use Tarnier's forceps successfully in the United States; devised the bivalve, or Howard, speculum.

HOWARD, WILLIE (*b. Neustadt, Germany, 1886; d. New York, N.Y., 1949*), comedian, impersonator. Stage name of William Levkowitz, born of Russian Jewish parents while on their emigrant journey to New York City. Expelled from public school at the age of eleven, he worked as a boy soprano. When his voice began to change, he turned to low comedy, doing burlesque imitations of well-known entertainers. His famous partnership with his older brother, Eugene Howard, began in 1903. They appeared also in several of the *Passing Shows*, starting in 1912, and in several of George White's *Scandals*. On his own, Willie acted in *Ballyhoo of 1932*, in the Ziegfeld Follies, and in occasional films (e.g., *Rose of the Rancho* 1936).

HOWE, ALBION PARRIS (*b. Standish, Maine, 1818; d. Cambridge, Mass., 1897*), soldier. Graduated West Point, 1841. Artillery officer in Scott's Mexican campaign and in Army of Potomac campaigns. Retired, 1882, as colonel of 4th Artillery.

HOWE, ANDREW JACKSON (*b. Paxton, Mass., 1825; d. 1892*), surgeon. Graduated Harvard, 1853; M.D., Worcester Medical Institute, 1855. Practiced in Cincinnati, Ohio, *post* 1856. Author of *Art and Science of Surgery* (1876) and many other works.

HOWE, EDGAR WATSON (*b. Wabash Co., Ind., 1853; d. near Atchison, Kans., 1937*), journalist. Editor, Atchison *Daily Globe*, 1877–1911; *E. W. Howe's Monthly*, 1911–33. Author of *The Story of a Country Town* (1883).

HOWE, ELIAS (*b. Spencer, Mass., 1819; d. Brooklyn, N.Y., 1867*), inventor. Apprenticed in cotton-machinery and hemp-carding machine factories, 1835–37. Later, while apprentice and machinist with Ari Davis, Boston maker of watches and scientific apparatus, inspired by a random suggestion, he set to work to invent a sewing machine. By 1845 he had devised and constructed a successful machine whose eye-pointed needle worked in conjunction with a lower thread-loaded shuttle; this shuttle was thrown, accurately and at proper intervals, through loops of thread made by the upper needle—thus making the desired lockstitch. Securing a patent, 1846, he found no interest in his machine from U.S. manufacturers. After one was sold in England to William

Thomas, together with all British rights, Howe was induced to enter Thomas' employ, only to break with him after eight months. Returning to America, Howe found that unauthorized manufacturers were infringing on his patent; with partner, George W. Bliss, he waged a long but successful lawsuit against the pirates, his patent being declared basic, 1854.

HOWE, FREDERIC CLEMSON (*b. Meadville, Pa., 1867; d. Oak Bluffs, Mass., 1940*), lawyer, reformer. Associated with Tom L. Johnson in Cleveland, Ohio, reforms. Removed to New York, 1910. Author, among other books, of *The City: The Hope of Democracy* (1905).

HOWE, FREDERICK WEBSTER (*b. Danvers, Mass., 1822; d. Providence, R.I., 1891*), mechanical engineer, inventor. Designed first commercially exploited universal milling-machine, 1850; also many machine tools of basic design used today.

HOWE, GEORGE (*b. Dedham, Mass., 1802; d. 1883*), Presbyterian clergyman. Professor of Biblical literature, Columbia, (S.C.), Theological Seminary, 1831–83; author of *History of the Presbyterian Church in South Carolina* (1870–1883).

HOWE, GEORGE AUGUSTUS (*b. England, ca. 1724; d. foot of Lake George, N.Y., 1758*), third Viscount Howe, British soldier. Commissioned ensign, 1st Foot Guards, 1745; rose rapidly because of his high connections and his own natural aptitude for the military profession. Appointed colonel, 3rd Battalion of the Royal Americans (60th), he made the campaign of 1757 in upper New York; in September 1757, he became colonel of the 55th Regiment and led an abortive winter expedition against the French at Ticonderoga, February 1758. Accepting the peculiarities of war in the wilderness, he increased the efficiency of his British soldiers by cropping their hair and cutting down their hats and coats. Highly regarded by Pitt, as brigadier general he served as Abercromby's second in command in the summer strike against Ticonderoga, 1758. When he was shot by French skirmishers on July 6, it was said that "the soul of the army seemed to expire." Massachusetts erected a tablet to his memory in Westminster Abbey.

HOWE, HENRY (*b. New Haven, Conn., 1816; d. 1893*), historian. Editor and publisher of a series of *Historical Collections* of New York (1841), New Jersey (1844), Virginia (1845), Ohio (1847), and other sections of the country which still have value for their first-hand narratives and anecdotes and original drawings of subjects treated.

HOWE, HENRY MARION (*b. Boston, Mass., 1848; d. Bedford Hills, N.Y., 1922*), metallurgist, designer of manufacturing plants, teacher. Son of Samuel G. Howe and Julia Ward Howe. His books on the metallurgy of steel (1890) and cast-iron (1916) have been called epoch-making.

HOWE, HERBERT ALONZO (*b. Brockport, N.Y., 1858; d. 1926*), astronomer. Dean, University of Denver, *post* 1891. He discovered double stars, remeasured positions of faint nebulae and engaged in research on Kepler's problem.

HOWE, JOHN IRELAND (*b. Ridgefield, Conn., 1793; d. Birmingham, Conn., 1876*), physician. Inventor of a rotary pin-making machine (patented 1841).

HOWE, JULIA WARD (*b. New York, N.Y., 1819; d. Middletown, R.I., 1910*), poet, reformer, hostess to Boston reform leaders of the Civil War period, leader in woman's suffrage and peace movements. Granddaughter of Samuel Ward (1756–1832); daughter of Samuel Ward (1786–1839); wife of Samuel G. Howe,. She produced her celebrated "Battle Hymn of the Republic" after a visit to a camp near Washington, D.C., in autumn 1861. It was first printed in the *Atlantic Monthly*, February 1862.

HOWE, LOUIS MCHENRY (*b. Indianapolis, Ind., 1871; d. Washington, D.C., 1936*), journalist. Political mentor and secretary to Franklin D. Roosevelt, 1913–30.

HOWE, LUCIEN (*b. Standish, Maine, 1848; d. 1928*), ophthalmologist. Nephew of Albion P. Howe. Graduated Bowdoin, 1870; studied medicine at Harvard, Bellevue, and in Scotland and Germany. Founded Buffalo Eye and Ear Infirmary, 1876. Donor, Howe laboratory for ophthalmic research at Harvard; author, New York Howe Law, obliging application of prophylactic to eyes of newborn children.

HOWE, MARK ANTHONY DE WOLFE (*b. Bristol, R.I., 1808; d. 1895*), Episcopal clergyman. Graduated Brown, 1828. Ordained 1833, he served as pastor in and about Boston, and was rector of St. Luke's, Philadelphia, 1846–71; bishop of Central Pennsylvania, 1871–95.

HOWE, MARK ANTONY DEWOLFE (*b. Bristol, R.I., 1864; d. Cambridge, Mass., 1960*), editor and biographer. Studied at Lehigh University and at Harvard (M.A., 1888). Associate editor of the *Atlantic Monthly*, (1893–95); vice president (1911–29). Biographer of many notable Americans including Oliver Wendell Holmes (1936), James Ford Rhodes (1929), and Annie Adams Fields (1923); also edited many volumes of letters including five volumes of *Memoirs of the Harvard Dead in the War against Germany* (1920–24). Overseer of Harvard (1925–31) and (1933–39); Trustee of the Boston Athenaeum from 1906 and of the Boston Symphony from 1918.

HOWE, MARK DE WOLFE (*b. Boston, Mass., 1906; d. Cambridge, Mass., 1967*), legal historian and civil rights activist. B.A. (1928) and LL.B. (1933), Harvard. Taught at the University of Buffalo Law School, 1937–43, and after 1945 was a professor of law at Harvard. In addition to other writings, edited numerous volumes of the correspondence, diaries, and legal writings of Oliver Wendell Holmes, Jr., and completed two volumes of a projected multivolume biography of Holmes. In the 1950's became a passionate proponent of civil rights; among other more direct forms of participation, helped teach scores of southern trial lawyers how to conduct civil rights litigation.

HOWE, PERCY ROGERS (*b. North Providence, R.I., 1864; d. Belmont, Mass., 1950*), dentist, pioneer in dental research. Raised in Lewiston, Maine. B.A., Bates College, 1887. D.D.S., Philadelphia Dental College, 1890. In 1903 he settled in Boston. Early became convinced that diet and nutrition were important factors in dental health. Howe's work attracted considerable attention, and in 1915 he was appointed chief of research at the newly opened Forsyth Dental Infirmary for Children, in Boston.

Howe investigated the role of oral microorganisms in producing caries, particularly the etiology of pyorrhea. One of his most important contributions was chemotherapeutic treatment of dental caries.

HOWE, ROBERT (*b. Brunswick Co., N.C., 1732; d. 1786*), Revolutionary major general, planter. Unpopular commander of Southern Department, 1776–78, he retained the confidence of Gen. Washington who employed him in various capacities until 1783.

HOWE, SAMUEL (*b. Belchertown, Mass., 1785; d. 1828*), lawyer, Massachusetts jurist.

HOWE, SAMUEL GRIDLEY (*b. Boston, Mass., 1801; d. 1876*), reformer. Husband of Julia Ward Howe. Graduated Brown, 1821; M.D., Harvard, 1824. Participated in Greek revolution of 1827–29. Pioneer in education of the blind; his program at Perkins Institute in Massachusetts became a model for others.

Active in public-school promotion, in prison reform, and in aiding the learning-disabled. An abolitionist, he supported the Free Soldiers in Kansas and aided and abetted the plots of John Brown.

HOWE, TIMOTHY OTIS (*b. Livermore, Maine, 1816; d. Kenosha, Wis., 1883*), lawyer, politician. Removed to Green Bay, Wis., 1845. Judge, state supreme court, 1850–53. U.S. senator, Republican, from Wisconsin, 1861–79; U.S. postmaster general, 1881–83. An early advocate of emancipation.

HOWE, WILLIAM (*b. Spencer, Mass., 1803; d. Springfield, Mass., 1852*), inventor. Uncle of Elias Howe. Designed and patented (1840) a bridge truss with wooden diagonals and vertical iron ties in single or double systems which was used widely until the development of the iron bridge.

HOWE, WILLIAM F. (*b. Boston, Mass., 1828; d. New York, N.Y., 1902*), lawyer. Educated in England; admitted to the bar in New York City, 1859. *Post* 1869, in partnership with Abraham H. Hummel, became notorious, as well as famous, in criminal court practice.

HOWE, WILLIAM HENRY (*b. Ravenna, Ohio, 1846; d. Bronxville, N.Y., 1929*), landscape and cattle painter, follower of Troyon.

HOWE, WILLIAM WIRT (*b. Canandaigua, N.Y., 1833; d. New Orleans, La., 1909*), Union soldier, lawyer. Became leading New Orleans attorney *post* 1865 and a nationally recognized authority on the civil code.

HOWELL, ALBERT SUMMERS (*b. West Branch, Mich., 1879; d. Chicago, Ill., 1951*), inventor and designer of cinematographic equipment. With Don J. Bell, founded the Bell and Howell Company in 1907. Invented a 35-millimeter movie projector around 1907, a 35-millimeter camera in 1909, and an automatic continuous printer for reproducing films in 1911. Howell's work provided both the technical precision and the standardization of equipment that made possible the mass distribution of motion pictures. In 1922, he introduced the first automatic camera for amateur cinematographers (the 16-millimeter camera), and in 1928, the 8-millimeter camera. An honorary life member of the American Society of Cinematograpers, sharing that honor with Thomas Edison and George Eastman. At his retirement in 1938, he held 147 patents.

HOWELL, CLARK (*b. Barnwell Co., S.C., 1863; d. Atlanta, Ga., 1936*), newspaper editor, political leader. Associated *post* 1884 with the *Atlanta Constitution*, at that time controlled by his father, Evan Park Howell, and edited by Henry W. Grady. As managing editor, *post* 1889, and editor in chief, *post* 1897, Clark Howell championed southern industrialization, diversification of agriculture, improvement of education, free silver, and a just resolution of racial problems. Active in state Democratic politics, Howell served in the state assembly, 1886–91, and senate, 1900–06. He was appointed to national commissions by Presidents Harding, Hoover, and Franklin D. Roosevelt.

HOWELL, DAVID (*b. Morristown, N.J., 1747; d. 1824*), lawyer. Taught at Rhode Island College (Brown), *post* 1766; was president, 1791–92. Served also as state attorney general, state judge, and federal judge (1812–1824).

HOWELL, EVAN PARK (*b. Warsaw, Ga., 1839; d. Atlanta, Ga., 1905*), Confederate soldier, lawyer, editor. Associated with the *Atlanta Constitution*, 1876–97, which he and his associates made the most important southern newspaper.

HOWELL, JAMES BRUEN (*b. near Morristown, N.J., 1816; d. 1880*), lawyer, political journalist, called "Horace Greeley of Iowa." Raised in Ohio; settled in Iowa *ca.* 1842. Editor of newspapers in Des Moines and Keokuk, 1845–70. A pronounced Radical Republican.

HOWELL, JOHN ADAMS (*b. Bath, N.Y., 1840; d. Warrenton, Va., 1918*), naval officer. Graduated Annapolis, 1858. Promoted rear admiral, 1898. Invented the Howell torpedo *ca.* 1885, first to use a gyroscopic device; also invented torpedo-launching apparatus, a disappearing gun carriage, and high-explosive shells.

HOWELL, RICHARD (*b. Delaware, 1754; d. 1802*), Revolutionary patriot, soldier, and intelligence agent. Federalist governor of New Jersey, 1793–1801.

HOWELL, ROBERT BOYTÉ CRAWFORD (*b. Wayne Co., N.C., 1801; d. 1868*), leading clergyman in Virginia and Nashville, Tenn.

HOWELL, THOMAS JEFFERSON (*b. near Pisgah, Mo., 1842; d. Portland, Oreg., 1912*), Oregon pioneer, botanist. Discoverer of the weeping spruce; author of *Flora of Northwest America* (1897–1903), the text of which he set in type himself.

HOWELL, WILLIAM HENRY (*b. Baltimore, Md., 1860; d. Baltimore, 1945*), physiologist. A.B., Johns Hopkins University, 1881; Ph.D., 1884. His doctoral dissertation dealt with coagulation of the blood. Appointed assistant professor of biology, John Hopkins, and in 1888 was promoted to associate professor. In 1889 Howell went to the University of Michigan as lecturer in physiology and histology in its medical school; a year later he became professor. He resumed research on the particles in red blood cells now known as Howell-Jolly bodies, the importance of inorganic salts in maintaining the beat of the heart, and the defeneration of peripheral nerve fibers after severance of a nerve.

Howell's short stay of three years at Ann Arbor was followed by another, still more brief, at Harvard Medical School as associate professor of physiology. In 1892 Howell accepted the chair of physiology in the new Johns Hopkins Medical School.

Most of Howell's publications after 1892 dealt with the physiology and pathology of the blood. Howell also secured a purified substance having powerful anticoagulant action, "heparin," and did pioneering work on glands.

Howell was chosen to edit it and brought out in 1896 the first edition of *An American Text-book of Physiology* and in 1900 a second edition. Shortly thereafter he began to write his own textbook, *Physiology for Medical Students and Physicians.* In 1899 Howell became dean of the Johns Hopkins Medical School.

HOWELLS, WILLIAM DEAN (*b. Martin's Ferry, Ohio, 1837; d. New York, N.Y., 1920*), author. Learned printer's trade in his father's country newspaper offices, read diligently, went to common school when he could. Master of no language or no literature in the strict scholar's sense, he was an outstanding example of self-education; his early years are reflected in his *A Boy's Town* (1890) and *My Literary Passions* (1895). Was reporter and editorial writer on *Ohio State Journal*, Columbus, Ohio, 1856–61; published (with John J. Piatt) *Poems by Two Friends* (1860). A successful "campaign biography" of Lincoln, 1860, led to his appointment as consul in Venice, Italy, 1861–65. Returning to America, Howells published *Venetian Life* (1866), served briefly on staff of the *Nation*, and became subeditor of the *Atlantic Monthly* (1866–71) and editor in chief, 1871–81. James Russell Lowell, his friend, felt that he had assimilated completely all that was good in the refined social life of Cambridge; certainly he found a natural affinity there, but the hard working, firm-fibered Westerner in him survived also. His novels published while he lived in Cambridge (among others, *A Chance Acquaintance*, 1873; *The*

Lady of the Aroostook, 1879) are in the main comedies of the incongruities of manners, urbane, subtle in psychology, and humorous. *Post* 1881, he put off the Bostonian quiet and applied himself in fiction to a wider range of more aggressive themes. A *Modern Instance* (1882) and *A Woman's Reason* (1883) are departures, as is his masterpiece *The Rise of Silas Lapham* (1885) in which the old cultured Boston consorts with untutored wealth; thereafter, influenced by his reading of Continental novelists, Howells' work is progressively realistic. His theory of art may be studied in *Criticism and Fiction* (1891); his realism may be summarized in the dictum that everything real in human nature is valuable and that nothing unreal has value except by way of sportive interlude. His ideal novelist-realist is a moralist too, tasteful and cultivated, who uses the helps of a realistic approach to enrich the process and not to pervert the result.

Howells lived in New York, *post* 1891. The range of his subjects during his middle life expanded in two directions: to the use of art itself as theme, and to examination of the economic or class problems of the time. A *Hazard of New Fortunes* (1890), *The Quality of Mercy* (1892), *The Story of a Play* (1898) illustrate these interests; *A Traveler from Altruria* (1894) and other works illustrate an unpartisan, undogmatic socialist trend in his thinking. His abilities did not age with the man. *The Landlord at Lion's Head* (1897) and *The Son of Royal Langbirth* (1904) are among the most vital of his books.

Howells also published five volumes of short tales, thirty-one remarkable closet-dramas, eleven books of travel, two more books of verse, numerous volumes of literary criticism and miscellanies, and several books of reminiscence of which *Literary Friends and Acquaintance* (1900) and *My Mark Twain* (1910) are outstanding. Honored by many colleges and universities, he was first president of the American Academy of Arts and Letters.

HOWEY, WALTER CRAWFORD (*b. Fort Dodge, Iowa, 1882; d. Boston, Mass., 1954*), journalist and inventor. Immortalized as Walter Burns in Hecht and MacArthur's play *The Front Page* (1928), Howey was the editor of numerous newspapers, including the Chicago *Evening American*, the *Tribune* (ten years as city editor), and Hearst's *Herald Examiner* (1917–22) and the *Chicago Herald-American* (1942–44). He was a special editorial assistant to William R. Hearst from 1944 to 1951. In 1931, he patented an automatic photoelectric engraving process, and beginning in 1935, he successfully developed the soundphoto system of transmitting photographs by wire.

HOWISON, GEORGE HOLMES (*b. Montgomery Co., Md., 1834; d. 1916*), philosopher. Graduated Marietta College, 1852; Lane Seminary, 1855. While teaching political economy in St. Louis, Mo., became philosopher under influence of H. C. Brokmeyer and W. T. Harris. Taught at Massachusetts Institute of Technology, Harvard, University of Michigan; organized philosophy department, University of California, and taught there, 1884–1909.

HOWLAND, ALFRED CORNELIUS (*b. Walpole, N.H., 1838; d. Pasadena, Calif., 1909*), artist.

HOWLAND, EMILY (*b. Sherwood, N.Y., 1827; d. 1929*), promoter of education for blacks; founder of school for blacks in Northumberland Co., Va. Educational leader in New York State; advocated woman's suffrage, temperance, world peace.

HOWLAND, GARDINER GREENE (*b. Norwich, Conn., 1787; d. New York, N.Y., 1851*), merchant. Partner with his brother in New York firm of G. C. & S. Howland, 1816–34; promoter, New York & Harlem and Hudson River railroads.

HOWLAND, JOHN (*b. New York, N.Y., 1873; d. 1926*), pediatrician. Graduated Yale, 1894; M.D., New York University,

1897. Associated as an intern with Luther E. Holt, whose assistant he became, 1901; studied also in Vienna and under Czerny in Strassburg where he laid foundations for subsequent research concerning nutritional disorders of infancy. After teaching at Washington University, St. Louis, Mo., he became professor of pediatrics at John Hopkins Medical School, 1912, and held that post until his death. He devoted himself to the study of the chemical aspects of disease and developed a clinic at Johns Hopkins which became the first pediatric clinic in this country. His noteworthy research included studies of chloroform poisoning, chemical and energy metabolism of sleeping children, infantile tetany, acidosis, and rickets. He proved, with Edward A. Park, the effectiveness of cod-liver oil in rickets.

HOWLEY, RICHARD (*b. probably Liberty Co., Ga., 1740; d. Savannah, Ga., 1784*), Revolutionary patriot. Georgia's governor during occupation by British army; member of Continental Congress, 1780–82; chief justice of Georgia, 1782–83.

HOWRY, CHARLES BOWEN (*b. Oxford, Miss., 1844; d. Washington, D.C., 1928*), jurist, Confederate soldier. Justice, Court of Claims, 1897–1915; a man of wide learning whose decisions were often monographs on points of special knowledge.

HOWZE, ROBERT LEE (*b. Overton, Tex., 1864; d. Columbus, Ohio, 1926*), soldier. Graduated West Point, 1888. Cited or decorated for service in Indian Wars, 1890–91, in Cuban and Philippine campaigns, Mexican border expedition, and Meuse-Argonne Offensive where he commanded 38th Division. Promoted major general, 1922.

HOXIE, ROBERT FRANKLIN (*b. Edmeston, N.Y., 1868; d. 1916*), economist, teacher.

HOXIE, VINNIE REAM (*b. Madison, Wis., 1847; d. Washington, D.C., 1914*), sculptor, Washington hostess. Of moderate talent, she made statues of Lincoln, Sequoyah and Farragut (sited in Washington, D.C.); her sitters for portraits included many famous persons of the Civil War era.

HOXIE, WILLIAM DIXIE (*b. Brooklyn, N.Y., 1866; d. at sea, 1925*), marine engineer. Associated with Babcock and Wilcox Co., *post* 1889. Improved water-tube and express-type boilers for use on war and commercial ships; built them by mass production methods.

HOYME, GJERMUND (*b. Vestre Slidre, Norway, 1847; d. Eau Claire, Wis., 1902*), Lutheran clergyman. Came to America as a child. Pastor at Eau Claire, 1876–1902. First president, United Norwegian Lutheran Church of America, 1890–1902; labored to unite all the Norwegian Lutheran Synods.

HOYT, ALBERT HARRISON (*b. Sandwich, N.H., 1826; d. 1915*), antiquarian. An efficient editor and learned contributor to the quarterly *Register* of the New England Historic Genealogical Society.

HOYT, CHARLES HALE (*b. Concord, N.H., 1860; d. Charlestown, N.H., 1900*), playwright. A writer of farces and satires, 1882–98, of which *A Trip to Chinatown* (1891) and *The Texas Steer* (1890) are typical.

HOYT, HENRY MARTYN (*b. Kingston, Pa., 1830; d. 1892*), lawyer, politician, Union soldier. As Republican governor of Pennsylvania, 1879–83, he reduced state debt, prosecuted railroads for rate discrimination, promoted state institutions for youthful offenders.

HOYT, JOHN SHERMAN (*b. New York, N.Y., 1869; d. White Plains, N.Y., 1954*), businessman and philanthropist. Graduated Columbia School of Mines, 1890; graduate work at the University of Berlin. Founder of the American Car and Foundry Co., 1899; director, 1917–51. Served with the YMCA, 1890–1919; responsible for supervising and organizing overseas operations, 1906–19. Helped found the Boy Scouts of America in 1910; member of the national council, serving as vice president, 1926–50. Helped found Columbia Presbyterian Medical Center, 1928.

HOYT, JOHN WESLEY (*b. near Worthington, Ohio, 1831; d. 1912*), educator. Removed to Wisconsin, 1857. Governor of Wyoming Territory, 1878–82; first president, state university of Wyoming, 1887–90; advocate of a national university.

HRDLIČKA, ALEŠ (*b. Humpolec, Bohemia, later part of Czechoslovakia, 1869; d. Washington, D.C., 1943*), physical anthropologist. Immigrated with father to New York City, 1882; worked in a cigar factory and attended night school. Graduated N.Y. Eclectic Medical College, 1892; New York Homeopathic Medical College, 1894. Studied also in Paris, France. Shifting to anthropology, he did fieldwork in Mexico and the U.S. Southwest for the American Museum of Natural History. Became head of the division of physical anthropology in the U.S. National Museum (Smithsonian), 1903; curator, 1910–42. He devoted himself to assembling and studying one of the world's largest collections of human skeletal remains. Produced catalogs of crania and monographs on the antiquity of man in America and on the most ancient skeletal traces in the Old World. Also wrote on physical variation in the American population, with a special interest in Alaskan Eskimos and Indians. Editor-founder of *American Journal of Physical Anthropology* (1918–42). He was distrustful of new methods in anthropology, preferring anthropometry.

HUBBARD, BERNARD ROSECRANS (*b. San Francisco, Calif., 1888; d. Santa Clara, Calif., 1962*), Jesuit priest, explorer, photographer, and lecturer. Became a member of the Jesuit order (1908), received his A.B. (1919) at Los Gatos, Calif., and his M.A. (1921) at Gonzaga University in Spokane, Wash. From 1927 until the mid-1950's made numerous expeditions to Alaska, accumulating a valuable photographic record of its terrain and presenting his photographs primarily in lectures but also in educational films, travel shorts, and magazine articles. Also wrote *Mush, You Malemutes!* (1932) and *Cradle of the Storms* (1935). By his tireless efforts, he put little-known Alaska on the map for the general public.

HUBBARD, DAVID (*b. Old Liberty, Va., ca. 1792; d. Pointe Coupée Parish, La., 1874*), politician, lawyer. Raised in Tennessee; removed to Alabama *ca.* 1819, where he was prominent as a states' rights Democratic legislator and congressman, and champion of the poor whites.

HUBBARD, ELBERT (*b. Bloomington, Ill., 1856; d. at sea, 1915*), author, founder of the Roycroft Shops, editor of *The Philistine*, lecturer. An American disciple of William Morris, whose theories he turned to rather crass practical account, Hubbard is best remembered for his *Message to Garcia* (1899).

HUBBARD, FRANK McKINNEY (*b. Bellefontaine, Ohio, 1868; d. 1930*), humorist, caricaturist. Known as "Kin" Hubbard. Created the character "Abe Martin," whose rustic humor had a vast audience in American newspapers, *post* 1904.

HUBBARD, GARDINER GREENE (*b. Boston, Mass., 1822; d. Washington, D.C., 1897*), lawyer. Graduated Dartmouth, 1841. Became interested in educating the deaf because of his daughter's affliction; this led to association with Alexander G. Bell, *post* 1871, to interest in Bell's invention, and to development of the telephone industry. Hubbard acted as business head of the early telephone companies and instituted policy of renting rather than selling telephones. Resident in Washington, *post* 1879, he devoted his energies to educational and scientific enterprises. He was founder and first president (1888–97), National Geographic Society.

HUBBARD, GURDON SALTONSTALL (*b. Windsor, Vt., 1802; d. 1886*), fur trader, merchant, pioneer meat packer. An apprentice in the fur trade, 1818–23, he became superintendent of American Fur Company's posts in the Illinois country and eventual owner of all the company's interests in Illinois. Hubbard was the last "bartering fur trader" in Illinois and its first purchaser of surplus hogs and other livestock for packing in Chicago. He played a leading role not only in expanding Lake shipping but also in promoting the Canal Bill (1836) which made Chicago the pivotal point for commerce of the Mississippi Valley. His interests grew along with his city, even to banking and insurance; he was ruined, however, by the Chicago fire of 1871.

HUBBARD, HENRY GRISWOLD (*b. Middletown, Conn., 1814; d. 1891*). First (*ca.* 1841–42) manufacturer in the United States to reduce India rubber to thread and weave it into webbing by machinery.

HUBBARD, HENRY GUERNSEY (*b. Detroit, Mich., 1850; d. 1899*), entomologist. Graduated Harvard, 1873; influenced in study of entomology by H. A. Hagen, C. R. Osten Sacken, E. A. Schwarz. Acquired an estate in Florida, *ca.* 1879, and there began successful investigations of insects injurious to cotton and oranges; published *Insects Affecting the Orange* (1855), the most careful study made at the time and the standard since. His fame rests on this work and the "Riley-Hubbard emulsion" he developed as pest preventive.

HUBBARD, JOHN (*b. probably Readfield, Maine, 1794; d. Hallowell, Maine, 1869*), physician. Graduated Dartmouth, 1816; M.D., University of Pennsylvania, 1822. As Democratic governor of Maine, 1849–53, he signed the celebrated Maine Law (1851), outlawing liquor traffic; advocated free lands in Maine, agricultural schools, reform schools, education for women.

HUBBARD, JOSEPH STILLMAN (*b. New Haven, Conn., 1823; d. New Haven, 1863*), astronomer. Associated, *post* 1845, with Naval Observatory. Contributed important works to *Astronomical Journal*, including masterly calculations on orbit of 1843 comet.

HUBBARD, KIN. *See* HUBBARD, FRANK MCKINNEY.

HUBBARD, LUCIUS FREDERICK (*b. Troy, N.Y., 1836; d. Minneapolis, Minn., 1913*), editor, businessman, Union soldier. Removed to Red Wing, Minn., where he founded the *Republican* newspaper, 1857. Republican governor of Minnesota, 1882–87; acted to prevent discriminatory freight rates and unfair grading of wheat.

HUBBARD, RICHARD BENNETT (*b. Walton Co., Ga., 1832; d. 1901*), lawyer, Confederate soldier. Graduated Mercer College, 1851. Settled in Tyler, Texas, *ca.* 1854. Democratic governor of Texas, 1876–79; U.S. minister to Japan, 1885–89.

HUBBARD, RICHARD WILLIAM (*b. Middletown, Conn., 1816; d. 1888*), landscape painter. Studied under Samuel F. B. Morse and Daniel Huntington.

HUBBARD, THOMAS HAMLIN (*b. Hallowell, Maine, 1838; d. 1915*), Union soldier, lawyer. Son of John Hubbard. Graduated Bowdoin, 1857; admitted to New York bar, 1861. Beginning as manager of Mark Hopkins interests in Southern Pacific, 1888, he

was associated thereafter with other railroads here and abroad and was president, International Banking Corp., *post* 1904.

HUBBARD, WILLIAM (*b. England, ca. 1621; d. Ipswich, Mass., 1704*), Congregational clergyman, historian. Came to America as a child. Graduated Harvard, 1642. Ordained minister at Ipswich, 1658, he served as pastor until 1703. Author of *Narrative of the Troubles with the Indians* (1677) and A *General History of New England*, used in manuscript by Cotton Mather, Thomas Prince, and others for information concerning early New England, but not itself published until 1815.

HUBBARD, WYNANT DAVIS (*b. Kansas City, Mo., 1900; d. Miami, Fla., 1961*), naturalist, author, and expert on Africa. Conducted numerous ventures on the African continent: was a professional hunter who specialized in obtaining live specimens for zoos; led an expedition in Africa that led to the release of two films, *Adventures in Africa* and *Untamed Africa*; created a short-lived research station at Ibamba; covered the Italian campaign in Ethiopia as a war correspondent; was president of the Africa Company, an exporting firm (1938–39); was involved in the import and export of minerals; and served the U.S. government on overseas agricultural development. His books on Africa include *Wild Animals: A White Man's Conquest of Jungle Beasts* (1925) and *Wild Animal Hunter* (1958).

HUBBELL, JOHN LORENZO (*b. Pajarito, N.Mex., 1853; d. 1930*). Navajo Reservation post trader, and a trusted friend to Navajos and Hopis for whose work he built up a world market.

HUBBLE, EDWIN (*b. Marshfield, Mo., 1899; d. San Marino, Calif., 1953*), astronomer. Studied at the University of Chicago and at Queens College, Oxford, as a Rhodes scholar (B.A. jurisprudence, 1912). Returning to the University of Chicago, he received a Ph.D. in astronomy in 1917. Staff astronomer, Mount Wilson Observatory in Pasadena, Calif. (1919–53). Hubble was concerned mainly with the mystery of nebulae, which had been found to differ both structurally and in the quality of their light. One of the reasons for this was that nobody could determine exactly how far away they were.

During the early 1920's, Hubble studied the relatively near galactic nebulae, showing that the quality of their light depended on whether the temperature of the star illuminating them was high or low. He then turned to the extragalactic nebulae and determined the distances of three by observing that they contain Cepheids, a kind of star that varies slightly but regularly in light output; the longer the period of light variation, the more luminous the Cepheid is known to be. This period-luminosity relation, based on earlier work by H. S. Leavitt and Harlow Shapley, is a powerful distance indicator because the intrinsically very luminous Cepheids can be detected at great distances. Hubble's preliminary results were announced in 1924 and immediately recognized as conclusive evidence that extragalactic nebulae were indeed island universes.

Hubble's next project was to relate some observed property of galaxies to the curious "red shifts" that Vesto M. Slipher had been finding in the spectra of galaxies. These were the Doppler shifts, changes to longer wavelengths in all their spectral lines, commonly interpreted as indicating motion away from the observer. In 1924, Hubble combined twenty-four distances he had estimated with the corresponding red shifts, and discovered a linear relation between the distances of galaxies and their apparent speeds of recession. This relation is called Hubble's Law, and is widely considered to be the most significant astronomical discovery of the twentieth century. It confirms what cosmologists had predicted on the basis of Einstein's theory of general relativity, namely, that the universe is expanding. If so, the reciprocal of the constant ratio of speed to distance—the ratio known as Hubble's constant—determines the time when the expansion started; revised upward since Hubble's day, that time now appears to be 12 billion years ago.

HUBBS, REBECCA (*b. Burlington Co., N.J., 1772; d. 1852*), traveling Quaker preacher. Resided in Woodstown, N.J.; accredited a minister, 1807; visited meetings in her own state, Pennsylvania, and the Middle West.

HUBER, GOTTHELF CARL (*b. Hubli, India, 1865; d. 1934*), anatomist, educator. Son of a Swiss missionary family; brought to America, 1871. Graduated University of Michigan medical school, 1887; studied also in Berlin and Prague. Taught anatomy, histology, and embryology at Michigan; *post* 1927, was dean of the graduate school. An authority on the sympathetic nervous system, and probably the first American to employ Ehrlich's methylene blue technique. Using the Born method, he made first waxplate reconstruction of a complete uriniferous tubule; demonstrated that practically all the blood to the parenchyma of the kidney passes through a second capillary plexus.

HUBERT, CONRAD (*b. Minsk, Russia, 1855; d. Cannes, France, 1928*), inventor. Changed name from Akiba Horowitz. Successful in Russia as distiller. Came to New York, 1890. Patented various electrical devices, and in 1902 secured basic patents for electric flashlight; organized successful American Ever-Ready Co.; left his estate to charity.

HUBNER, CHARLES WILLIAM (*b. Baltimore, Md., 1835; d. Atlanta, Ga., 1929*), poet, Confederate soldier. His critical volume *Representative Southern Poets* (1906) is his best work.

HUDDE, ANDRIES (*b. Kampen, Netherlands, 1608; d. Apoquenamingh, 1663*), surveyor. Immigrated to New Netherland, 1629; was for a time Dutch commander on the Delaware.

HUDSON, CHARLES (*b. Marlboro, Mass., 1795; d. Lexington, Mass., 1881*), clergyman. Editor, *Boston Daily Atlas*; congressman, Whig, from Massachusetts, 1841–49; held many Massachusetts offices, both elective and appointive. Active as contributor to reports of Massachusetts Historical Society

HUDSON, CLAUDE SILBERT (*b. Atlanta, Ga., 1881; d. Washington, D.C., 1952*), chemist. Studied at Princeton (Ph.D. 1907). After studying in Germany, he joined the Bureau of Chemistry in Washington (1907), and from 1912 to 1918, he headed a carbohydrate laboratory. From 1923 to 1929, he was employed by the Bureau of Standards; 1929–51, analyst for the Hygienic Laboratory of the U.S. Public Health Service. His primary work was the study of those structural characteristics of sugar molecules that are responsible for their observed properties, particularly, optical rotation. By the preparation and study of numerous rare sugars and sugar derivatives Hudson sought to elucidate not only optical rotation but also such structural characteristics as ring size and chemical reactivity. A side effect of the work on rules of rotation was the synthesis of rare new sugars and the clarification of their physical and chemical properties.

HUDSON, DANIEL ELDRED (*b. Nahant, Mass., 1849; d. Notre Dame, Ind., 1934*), Roman Catholic clergyman. Joined congregation of the Holy Cross, 1871. Editor of *Ave Maria* magazine, 1875–1929.

HUDSON, EDWARD (*b. County Wexford, Ireland, 1772; d. Philadelphia, Pa., 1833*), Irish patriot, dentist. Trained in his profession in Ireland where he was a friend and adviser of Thomas Moore. Came to America, 1803; practiced in Philadelphia, 1810–33, setting high professional standards.

HUDSON, FREDERIC (*b. Quincy, Mass., 1819; d. Concord, Mass., 1875*), journalist. Organizer of N.Y. *Herald's* news coverage of the Civil War; author of *Journalism in the United States* (1873). Associated with the *Herald*, 1837–66, Hudson was considered an outstanding gatherer of news and the father of modern American journalism.

HUDSON, HENRY (*d. post June 23, 1611*), English navigator. Hudson sailed May 1, 1607 o.s. on his so-called "First Voyage," made for the English Muscovy Co. in the *Hopewell*, which took him to the coast of Greenland and to Spitzbergen. The Muscovy Co. sent him again in 1608 to seek a northeast passage to the Orient between Spitzbergen and Novaya Zemlya; becalmed for a time, he found it impossible to get through the ice pack. His famous "Third Voyage" was financed by the Dutch East India Co., once again for the purpose of finding a northeast passage. Hudson sailed from Amsterdam early in the spring of 1609 on the *Halve Maen* (*Half Moon*) with a mixed Dutch-English crew of 18. After rounding the North Cape, he was so discouraged by icebergs and snow storms that he despaired of reaching Novaya Zemlya. He decided to disregard his instructions and, after consulting with his crew, sailed westward for America, of whose coast he had been informed by Capt. John Smith. Beset by Atlantic gales the *Half Moon* arrived off Newfoundland without a foremast; Hudson repaired her on the Maine coast and sailed to the southward of Chesapeake Bay, then back up the coast for exploration. He entered Delaware Bay and River but soon concluded that it would not lead to China; then, coasting the Jersey shore, he anchored early in September 1609 in the Lower Bay of New York. Ten days later he stopped at Manhattan, and on Sept. 13–19 sailed slowly up the river which bears his name to anchor near the site of Albany. After a month of exploring in the pleasant valley, he sailed the *Half Moon* back across the Atlantic. Hudson was detained at Dartmouth, England, and forbidden to sail again in other than English employ; his reports and papers, however, were dispatched to Amsterdam during the winter, and an account of the voyage was published. English adventurers staked Hudson's last voyage. Sailing in the *Discovery* in April 1610, Hudson sighted the coast of Greenland in June; he passed the strait which bears his name by August 2, observing next day "a Sea to the Westward" (Hudson Bay) which he explored until the *Discovery* was hauled ashore for the winter on November 1. New explorations were started or in prospect when the ice broke the next spring, but the half-starved crew seized their captain at the instigation of the deposed mate Robert Juet, and set Hudson, his son, and seven others adrift in a shallop "without food, drink, fire, clothing, or other necessaries" on June 23, 1611.

HUDSON, HENRY NORMAN (*b. Cornwall, Vt., 1814; d. 1886*), Shakespearian scholar, Episcopal clergyman, Union Army chaplain. Edited "Harvard Edition" of Shakespeare (1880–81).

HUDSON, MANLEY OTTMER (*b. St. Peters, Mo., 1886; d. Cambridge, Mass., 1960*), judge and professor of international law. Studied at William Jewell College and at Harvard Law School, 1910. In 1918, Hudson attended the Versailles Peace Conference as a member of the American Commission to Negotiate Peace. Taught at Harvard Law School from 1919 until his appointment as a judge from 1936 until 1946. Author of an annual report of the Permanent Court in the *American Journal of International Law* from 1923 to 1959. Engaged in the compilation of the 9-volume work *International Legislation* from 1931 to 1950. Director of the Harvard Research in International Law from 1927 to 1939. Member and first chairman of the U.N. International Law Commission (1948–53).

HUDSON, MARY CLEMMER AMES. *See* CLEMMER, MARY.

HUDSON, THOMSON JAY (*b. Windham, Ohio, 1834; d. Detroit, Mich., 1903*), journalist, lecturer. Author of the *Law of Psychic Phenomena* (1893).

HUDSON, WILLIAM SMITH (*b. near Derby, England, 1810; d. 1881*), mechanical engineer, inventor. Came to America, 1835. Superintendent of Rogers Locomotive Works, Paterson, N.J.; invented many improvements on locomotives including the radius bar and the double-end locomotive.

HUEBNER, SOLOMON STEPHEN (*b. Manitowoc, Wis., 1882; d. Merion Station, Pa., 1964*), insurance teacher and writer. Ph.D. in economics (1905), University of Pennsylvania. Introduced courses in insurance at Wharton School of Finance and Commerce of the University of Pennsylvania, where he taught until 1953. Among other activities that earned him the title "Father of Life Insurance Education," he wrote twelve widely used textbooks on insurance and was editor or coeditor of fifteen works on insurance and related fields. His "Human Life Value Concept" was employed by generations of insurance agents and field underwriters, both in the United States and abroad.

HUEBSCH, BENJAMIN W. (*b. New York, N.Y., 1876; London, England, 1964*), publisher. While working with the family printing firm of D. A. Huebsch and Company, began printing and distributing books by Edward Howard Griggs, starting with *The New Humanism* (1900). Eventually took over and renamed the firm B. W. Huebsch; by World War I it became known for translations of European works, books on socialism, psycholanalysis, and little theater, and literature by the new and experimental writers. Over the next decade the firm published such authors as Van Wyck Brooks, James Joyce, D. H. Lawrence, and Sherwood Anderson. He also published the *Freeman*, a weekly journal of "radical" political and literary opinion. In 1925 Huebsch merged with Viking Press, and became vice president and head of the editorial department, strongly influencing the quality of the Viking lists over the next four decades. His numerous activities on behalf of the book world included his 1919 advancement of the plan that led to the formation of the National Association of Book Publishers.

HUGER, BENJAMIN (*b. Charleston, S.C., 1805; d. Charleston, 1877*), soldier. Son of Francis K. Huger. Graduated West Point, 1825. Chief of ordnance under Gen. Scott in Mexican War. A Confederate major general, he was criticized for dilatory tactics in the Peninsular campaign and for Confederate disaster at Roanoke Island, 1862.

HUGER, DANIEL ELLIOTT (*b. South Carolina, 1779; d. 1854*), jurist, South Carolina Unionist. Nephew of Isaac and John Huger. U.S. senator from South Carolina, 1843–45.

HUGER, FRANCIS KINLOCH (*b. Charleston, S.C., 1773; d. Charleston, 1855*), physician, artillery officer during War of 1812. Nephew of Isaac and John Huger. In association with J. E. Bollman, attempted to liberate Lafayette from Olmütz prison; was captured and imprisoned.

HUGER, ISAAC (*b. Limerick plantation, S.C., 1742/43; d. 1797*), Revolutionary brigadier general. Led important commands at Guildford Court House and Hobkirk's Hill.

HUGER, JOHN (*b. Limerick plantation, S.C., 1744; d. 1804*), Revolutionary leader. Brother of Isaac Huger. Member, South Carolina Council of Safety, *post* 1775; first secretary of state of South Carolina.

HUGGINS, MILLER JAMES (*b. Cincinnati, Ohio, 1879; d. 1929*), lawyer, baseball player. Second baseman for Cincinnati Reds and St. Louis Cardinals. As manager, New York Yankees, 1918–29, rose to national prominence as builder of championship teams.

HUGHES, CHARLES EVANS (*b. Glens Falls, N.Y., 1862; d. Washington, D.C., 1948*), lawyer, governor, U.S. secretary of state, chief justice of the U.S. Supreme Court. His father, David Charles Hughes, was an itinerant evangelical minister. In 1876 he entered Madison (now Colgate) University. In 1878 he transferred to Brown University. Hughes taught school for a year at Delaware Academy in Delhi, N.Y., and read law on the side. In 1882 he entered Columbia Law School, graduating in 1884.

His practice, commercial law, brought him swift prominence in the New York legal community, but the strain of singleminded perfectionism began to show on his health. In 1891 he left the city for two years to teach at the Cornell Law School. Restored, he took up practice again at his usual pace.

In 1905 Hughes led an inquiry as committee counsel into the malpractices of the New York City utilities industry. As counsel for the Armstrong Committee of the state legislature, he next applied his powers of lucid analysis to the scandal-stained complexities of the New York life insurance business.

In 1906 to blunt the drive of William Randolph Hearst to become Democratic governor of New York, Hughes ran for the office and defeated him. Theodore Roosevelt shunned him as a presidential successor in 1908 but insisted on his renomination for governor; Hughes was reelected. When President William Howard Taft offered him a seat on the Supreme Court, in 1910, Hughes accepted with alacrity. Of the 151 opinions he wrote over the next six years, he dissented in only thirty-cases, and in only nine cases was there dissent from his decisions. His most far-reaching decisions untangled complex issues raised by expanding federal regulation of rail transportation. In both the *Minnesota Rate* cases (1913) and the *Shreveport* case (1914) he asserted in his majority opinion the supreme and plenary power of Congress over interstate commerce. Hughes also defined more generously than any colleague the regulatory power of states and cities to curb the scope of privileged contracts.

Hughes rejected feelers about a presidential nomination in 1912, but in 1916 he ran against Woodrow Wilson. After his defeat he returned to private practice. A moderate critic of Wilson's plans for collective security through the League of Nations, he nevertheless favored joining the League. After Warren Harding made him secretary of state in 1921, Hughes dropped his advocacy of League membership, and negotiated a separate peace with Germany. In 1923 Hughes's suggestion that the League's Reparations Commission invite American experts to help untangle Germany's postwar fiscal ills led to adoption of the Dawes Plan.

Hughes's most visible feats as secretary of state occurred at the Washington Conference (1921–22), called mainly at his initiative to deal with naval arms competition and to stabilize relations among Pacific powers. In Latin America, Hughes's actions anticipated the Good Neighbor Policy. In 1925 Hughes left the government to rebuild his fortune in Wall Street law practice.

In 1930 Herbert Hoover chose him to succeed Taft as chief justice. Somewhat more conservative than in his earlier service on the Court, he responded to the legislative tumult of the New Deal years with doctrinal calm and a practiced eye for the Court's reputation. Concerned to maintain an appearance of legal continuity, he often yielded logic in search for fine distinctions to avoid abandoning precedents outright. When Franklin D. Roosevelt proposed his famous court-packing plan in 1937, he discovered in Hughes a skilled rival. As chief justice, Hughes presided with grace over the changing makeup and orientation of the Court. Throughout the decade, he held positions on issues of civil liberties and civil rights that anticipated the Court's later thrust in that realm. He retired in 1941.

HUGHES, CHARLES FREDERICK (*b. Bath, Maine, 1866; d. Chevy Chase, Md., 1934*), naval officer. Graduated Annapolis, 1888. Commanded USS *New York*, Adm. Rodman's flagship, 1916–18; active in North Sea. Fleet commander, 1926–27; chief of naval operations, 1927–30.

HUGHES, CHRISTOPHER (*b. Baltimore, Md., 1786; d. Baltimore, 1849*), wit, diplomat. Secretary, American Peace Commission, Ghent, 1814; secretary and chargé in Sweden, Norway, and the Netherlands, 1816–45.

HUGHES, DAVID EDWARD (*b. London, England, 1831; d. London, 1900*), inventor. Came to America as a child; educated in Virginia and Kentucky. While teaching music, experiments with tuning forks and synchronism led him into telegraphic experimentation, in particular, telegraphic printing. His printing telegraph device, patented 1856, was eventually combined with that of Royal E. House. Hughes became European representative of the company which owned the merged patents and secured adoption of his improved device by the principal European countries, devoting his time to further experimentation in London *post* 1877. Abroad, Hughes is credited with invention of the microphone (1878), and the induction balance (1879).

HUGHES, DUDLEY MAYS (*b. Twiggs Co., Ga., 1848; d. 1927*), farmer. Congressman, Democrat, from Georgia, 1909–17; coauthor of Smith-Hughes bill (Vocational Education Act), 1917; active in other measures for agricultural improvement.

HUGHES, EDWIN HOLT (*b. Moundsville, W.Va., 1866; d. Washington, D.C., 1950*), Methodist Episcopal clergyman. Graduated Ohio Wesleyan, 1889; Boston University School of Theology, 1892. Minister in Newton Center, Mass., and Malden, Mass., 1892–1903. President of De-Pauw University, 1903–08. Elected a bishop, he exercised his considerable administrative talents in San Francisco (1908–16), Boston (1916–24), Chicago (1924–32), and Washington, D.C. (1932–40); he also preached and lectured at many colleges, and helped provide educational opportunities for thousands of Methodist ministers who lacked seminary training. *Post* 1922, he served almost continuously on commissions which sought to unify the several branches of Methodism in the United States. As senior bishop (*post* 1936) of his denomination, he saw the happy effect of his efforts in the reunion of the Methodist Protestant Church, the Methodist Episcopal Church, and the Methodist Episcopal Church, South, in a single communion in 1939.

HUGHES, GEORGE WURTZ (*b. Elmira, N.Y., 1806; d. near Annapolis, Md., 1870*), topographical engineer, soldier, railroad official, congressman. Served on staff of General J. E. Wool in Mexican War and as governor, Jalapa Province; surveyed route for railroad across Isthmus of Panama, 1849.

HUGHES, HECTOR JAMES (*b. Centralia, Pa., 1871; d. 1930*), civil engineer. Graduated Harvard, 1894; Lawrence Scientific School, 1899. Taught hydraulics at Harvard, *post* 1902; was professor of engineering *post* 1914, and dean, Harvard Engineering School, 1920–30.

HUGHES, HENRY (*d. Port Gibson, Miss., 1862*), lawyer, Confederate soldier. Defender of slavery as "warranteeism"; author of *Treatise on Sociology* (1854) and other writings.

HUGHES, HOWARD ROBARD (*b. Lancaster, Mo., 1869; d. Houston, Texas, 1924*), inventor and manufacturer of oil industry equipment. Devised cone-type rock drill and improvements for which he obtained basic patents, 1909.

HUGHES, JAMES (*b. Hamstead, Md., 1823; d. Bladensburg, Md., 1873*), lawyer, Indiana legislator. Practiced in Indiana *post* 1842. A Democrat, he followed proslavery leadership of Jesse Bright until 1860 when he became a vehement Republican. Judge, U.S. Court of Claims, 1859–64.

HUGHES, JAMES LANGSTON (*b. Joplin, Mo., 1902; d. New York, N.Y., 1967*), poet, playwright, and novelist. In 1921–22 began publishing free-verse poems inspired mainly by Afro-American culture and music. The volumes of verse *The Weary Blues* (1926) and *Fine Clothes to the Jew* (1927) made his reputation as the most innovative of the younger black poets. His landmark essay "The Negro Artist and the Racial Mountain" (1926) appeared in the *Nation* and became virtually the manifesto of the movement known as the Harlem Renaissance. His first novel was *Not Without Laughter* (1930). During the 1930's, his Marxist sympathies were apparent in *Scottsboro Limited: Four Poems and a Play* (1932) and *The Ways of White Folks* (1934). In the mid-1930's he began to establish himself as a major Afro-American playwright: wrote the Broadway play *Mulatto* (1935) and founded the Harlem Suitcase Theatre (1938), which staged his *Don't You Want to Be Free?*

Around 1940 his reputation suffered setbacks, including the damaging political controversy over his poem "Goodbye Christ." Thereafter he avoided Marxism in such works as the play *The Sun Do Move* (1942) and the volume of verse *Shakespeare in Harlem* (1942). In 1942 began a weekly column in the black *Chicago Defender* that focused on the black Everyman character "Simple." His work having earlier been overshadowed by that of Richard Wright, over the remainder of his career the accumulation and quality of his work made him again the central figure in Afro-American literature: he was lyricist for the Broadway opera *Street Scene* (1947); his Haitian play was adapted as the opera *Troubled Island* (1949); he published volumes of verse—*Fields of Wonder* (1947), *One-Way Ticket* (1949), and *Montage of a Dream Deferred* (1951); and he edited a number of anthologies, brought out five collections of his Simple columns, wrote about a dozen books for children, translated books of verse, and collaborated on several cantatas and operas.

In his later career he continued to publish poetry but devoted most of his energy to drama and to pioneer fusions of black gospel music, as in *Black Nativity* (1961), *Tambourines to Glory* (1963), and *Jericho—Jim Crow* (1964). Also wrote the books of short stories *Laughing to Keep from Crying* (1952) and *Something in Common* (1963); *A History of the NAACP* (1962), pictorial volumes, and anthologies of new writing by black Africans. Was elected to the National Institute of Arts and Letters, 1961. Wrote a two-volume autobiography—*The Big Sea* (1940) and *I Wonder As I Wander* (1956).

HUGHES, JOHN JOSEPH (*b. Annaloghan, Ireland, 1779; d. New York, N.Y., 1864*), Roman Catholic clergyman. Apprenticed to a gardener; came to America, 1817; worked as a gardener in Maryland. Admitted to seminary at Mt. St. Mary's College, Emmitsburg, Md., 1820. Showing marked ability in study of theology under Simon W. G. Bruté, Hughes was ordained priest, 1826. As pastor of old St. Mary's Church, Philadelphia, he entered into controversies with leading Protestant clergyman over prevalent nativism, notably against Rev. John Breckinridge (1833); he was also successful in settling difficulties over trusteeism, founded the *Catholic Herald*, and was favored for elevation to the sees of Philadelphia and Cincinnati. However, on nomination of the Council at Baltimore, he was consecrated as coadjutor-bishop of New York, 1838. Although he did not succeed to formal command of the diocese until 1842, he immediately took control and won the respect and support of the burgeoning Irish and German immigrant population.

While Hughes managed to temporal concerns of the diocese with skill, his principal value in his time was as a fighter for

Catholic rights; he ended trusteeism in New York by securing state legislation permitting a vesting of church property in the bishop or his appointees, and through his efforts, political as well as polemic, the public schools were secularized after a bitter fight. His assurance that he would protect Catholic institutions by force, if necessary (1844), compelled an inactive mayor to keep New York nativist rioters under control. He committed his people to the development of a parochial school system, brought several order of religious into the diocese to staff schools and hospitals, and founded St. John's College (now Fordham), 1841. Active in Irish famine relief, he urged the American Irish to avoid Irish politics and give their first allegiance to the United States; in opposing the movement of immigrants westward and advising them to stay on the seaboard, he made his greatest error.

When New York was raised to an archdiocese, 1850, Hughes was named archbishop, receiving the pallium on April 3, 1851. In his correspondence with Southern prelates he denounced attempts to justify secession, and on outbreak of the Civil War served President Lincoln as an unofficial agent in Paris, Dublin, and Rome, promoting the Union cause. His personal plea to the rioters during the Draft Riots, 1863, did much to end the disorder. A man of unbending will, a firm clerical disciplinarian, Hughes fought openly for what he believed was right. When he was wrong, he erred in a large way. Yet he succeeded in turning a bewildered, apologetic mass of immigrant people, groping toward active citizenship, into a militant, instructed group aware of their right to social and economic advancement.

HUGHES, PRICE (*d. near mouth of Alabama River, 1715*), frontier adventurer. Came to America *ca.* 1712, concerned with a scheme of Welsh colonization in South Carolina; as a volunteer Indian agent, traveled widely among Cherokees; developed project for British province of Annarea on the Mississippi to supplant French influence. Led a trade offensive, 1713–15, seeking to detach Choctaw and others from French, and intrigued with Indians from Illinois to the Gulf of Mexico. Seized by the French, Hughes was imprisoned for a time at Mobile; released he was slain by a band of Tohome Indians.

HUGHES, ROBERT BALL (*b. London, England, 1806; d. Boston, Mass., 1868*), sculptor. Came to America, 1828 or 1829. His statue of Alexander Hamilton for New York's Merchants' Exchange, 1835, is believed the first marble portrait carved in the United States; his bronze of Nathaniel Bowditch, 1847, was the first bronze statue to be cast here.

HUGHES, ROBERT WILLIAM (*b. Powhatan Co., Va., 1821; d. near Abingdon, Va., 1901*), editor, jurist. States' rights advocate in *Richmond Examiner* and *Washington Union*; was hostile to Jefferson Davis. Later edited Republican papers and served as federal judge, eastern district of Virginia, 1874–98.

HUGHES, RUPERT (*b. Lancaster, Mo., 1872; d. Los Angeles, Calif., 1956*), writer. Studied at Adelbert College (now Case Western Reserve University) and at Yale University (M.A., 1899). Hughes began his career in New York by contributing short stories, articles, verse, and criticism to *Scribner's, Cosmopolitan*, and other periodicals. He wrote a dozen plays including *Excuse Me* (1911) and several screenplays, including *The Patent Leather Kid* which was nominated for an Academy Award in 1927. His most famous work was a three-volume biography of the life of George Washington (1926–30); the work was iconoclastic in its realistic approach to Washington. At first criticized for his realistic portrait of a folk hero, Hughes later won praise for his historical accuracy.

HUIDEKOPER, FREDERIC (*b. Meadville, Pa., 1817; d. Meadville, 1892*), Unitarian clergyman. Son of Harm J.

Huidekoper. Professor of New Testament and church history, Meadville Theological School, 1844–77. Early interested in higher criticism, but basically conservative.

HUIDEKOPER, HARM JAN (*b. Hoogeveen, Holland, 1776; d. 1854*), businessman, theologian. Came to America, 1796; employed by Holland Land Co. and its agent in Meadville, Pa., he became an extensive landholder in that area. Founded Meadville Theological School, 1844.

HULBERT, ARCHER BUTLER (*b. Bennington, Vt., 1873; d. Colorado Springs, Colo., 1933*), historian. Projected and edited *Historic Highways* series, 1902–05. Edited the records of the Ohio Company, 1917. Author of the *Forty-niners* (1931) and many other books.

HULBERT, EDWIN JAMES (*b. Sault Ste. Marie, Mich., 1829; d. Rome, Italy, 1910*), surveyor, mining engineer. Nephew of Henry R. Schoolcraft. Discovered (1858–59) the Calumet conglomerate, copper-bearing deposits in northern Michigan, developed as Calumet and Hecla mine.

HULL, CLARK LEONARD (*b. Akron, Ohio, 1884; d. 1952*), psychologist. Ph.D., University of Michigan, 1918. Taught at the University of Wisconsin, 1914–29, where he specialized in the development of aptitude tests; first major book was *Aptitude Testing* (1928). From 1929 to 1952, he was professor at the Institute of Psychology at Yale, where he developed a theory on the conditioned reflex which showed that the conditioned reflex could provide for adaptive behavior. Ultimately, Hull found it possible to derive a large number of the characteristics of human rote learning from the concatenation of his various principles. He published the full scale descriptions of his theory as *Principles of Behavior* (1943).

HULL, CORDELL (*b. Overton [later Pickett] Co., Tenn., 1871; d. Bethesda, Md., 1955*), lawyer, congressman, senator, secretary of state. Studied at the National Normal University, Lebanon, Ohio, and Cumberland Law School. Served as Democratic congressman, 1907–21 and 1923–31, and senator, 1931–33. Hull was a domestic conservative but was liberal in international affairs. Wrote the income tax section of the Underwood Tariff Act of 1913 and was a strong supporter of Woodrow Wilson, advocating U.S. entry into the League of Nations. Influential in securing the nomination of Franklin D. Roosevelt in 1932. Hull served as secretary of state, 1933–44.

Although under Hull the department grew from 800 employees to 3,700, he was neither an organizer nor a good administrator; the department's lines of control were never clearly drawn under his tutelage. Throughout his secretaryship, he was dominated by Roosevelt who frequently passed him by, and he almost resigned in 1933 after the president undercut him at the London Economic Conference. Hull's special area was Latin America, in which he enjoyed full support from Roosevelt. At the Montevideo Conference of 1933, he introduced the guidelines of the Good Neighbor Policy, based on the concept that the American nations would not interfere in the internal or external affairs of their neighbors. Hull turned this atmosphere of goodwill into hemispheric security arrangements during World War II. Hull's other major diplomatic efforts in the 1930's included the reciprocal trade agreements program, inaugurated in 1934; he believed that although difficult to apply during the decade, the agreements might help avoid the coming war.

Hull warned Congress of war in 1939 and fought for repeal of the neutrality acts. As war neared, he played a smaller part in American foreign relations, although from 1939–41, his was a crucial role in dealing with the Japanese. In the fall of 1941, he was convinced that attack in the Pacific was imminent. Although military advisers urged accommodation with the Japanese until the situation could be improved in America's favor, Hull, who was then negotiating with a delegation from Tokyo, recommended a hard line, yielding to the pressure of China and other nations. The result was the attack on Pearl Harbor before America was prepared for war.

During the war, Hull played a small part in the formulation of foreign policy; he attended very few of the Allied conferences and was often kept ignorant of major policy decisions by Roosevelt. He and the president did agree on their dislike of Charles de Gaulle, on their mutual hatred of colonialism, and on the need to maintain a "hands off" policy towards Indochina. They also agreed on the need to treat China as a future great power. Hull opposed the Morgenthau Plan for the postwar "pastoralization" of Germany and blocked the Potsdam Declaration, which was to have allowed Japan to retain the emperor. This move prompted the Japanese to reject the proposed declaration and led to the prolongation of the war that culminated in the atomic bombings of Hiroshima and Nagasaki and in the Soviet Union's invasion of Manchuria and Korea.

Hull's most enduring achievement was in the formulation, 1943, of the proposal for the United Nations submitted by America at Dumbarton Oaks. Unlike Wilson, who had bypassed the Senate with his concept for the League of Nations and failed to obtain America's entrance into the organization, Hull carefully arranged the Committee of Eight, a subcommittee to the Senate Committee on Foreign Relations, and assured passage of the U.N. measures. This action won him the title of "the father of the United Nations" from Roosevelt. He received the Nobel Prize for Peace in 1945.

HULL, ISAAC (b. Huntington, now Shelton, Conn., 1773; d. Philadelphia, Pa., 1843), naval officer. Nephew and adopted son of William Hull. Appointed lieutenant, U.S. Navy, 1798; served in naval war with France and in attacks on Tripoli (1804) and Derne (1805); promoted captain, 1806. Commanded USS *Constitution*, 1810–12, and was outstanding in action with HMS *Guerrière*, Aug, 19, 1812. After long sea service and command of several shore stations, hauled down his flag as commodore, July 1841.

HULL, JOHN (b. England, 1624; d. Boston, Mass., 1683), merchant, goldsmith. Came to New England, 1635; prospered in his own trade and as a merchant. As mint-master, coined first Massachusetts shillings; served as treasurer of the colony and in other civic capacities.

HULL, JOSEPHINE (b. Newtonville, Mass., 1886?; d. 1957), actress. Studied at Radcliffe College. Hull made her professional debut in 1902 but it was not until the 1930's that she achieved success as one of Broadway's best character actresses, appearing in Hart-Kaufman's *You Can't Take It With You* (1936); Kesselring's play *Arsenic and Old Lace* (1941) and also in the 1944 movie. She acted in Chase's *Harvey* (1944) and in the movie version of 1950 which won her an Academy Award. Her last play was *The Solid Gold Cadillac* (1953) by George Kaufman and Howard Teichmann.

HULL, WILLIAM (b. Derby, Conn., 1753; d. Newton, Mass., 1825), soldier. Participated actively and almost continuously in all the major campaigns of the Revolutionary army in the North, winning the commendations of Washington and Congress. A leading Massachusetts Jeffersonian, he was appointed governor of Michigan Territory, 1805, and was so energetic in securing land cessions as to incur the enmity of the Indians. In the War of 1812, he was persuaded against his wishes to become brigadier general of the newly raised army charged with defense of Michigan and invasion of Canada. Because of faulty strategy, for which he was

partly responsible, and his excessive concern for noncombatants he abandoned the Canadian offensive, withdrew to Detroit, and surrendered the post and army without a blow on Aug. 16, 1812.

HULLIHEN, SIMON P. (b. Northumberland Co., Pa., 1810; d. 1857), plastic surgeon, dentist. Practiced in Canton, Ohio, post 1832; removed to Wheeling, Va., (now W.Va.), 1834. Improved operative techniques for cleft-plate, harelip, deformities of lower jaw, nose, lips; stressed scientific training for dental practitioners.

HUMBERT, JEAN JOSEPH AMABLE (b. Rouvray, France, 1755; d. New Orleans, La., 1823), distinguished French general exiled by Napoleon. Established residence in New Orleans, 1814; served bravely under Jackson in the Battle of New Orleans.

HUME, EDGAR ERSKINE (b. Frankfort, Ky., 1889; d. Washington, D.C., 1952), army medical officer. Studied at Central College, Danville, Ky., at Johns Hopkins University, M.D., 1913, and Ph.D. in public health in 1924; later he received an M.A. in public health and tropical medicine at M.I.T. and Harvard (1920–22). In 1916, Hume joined the Medical Reserve Corps of the army and attended the Army Medical School. In World War I, he commanded an army hospital near Asolo, Italy and served with the British Expeditionary Force in the Meuse-Argonne offensive. After the war, he was chief medical officer and director of the Red Cross mission to Serbia.

During World War II Hume served on Eisenhower's staff as advisor on military sanitation. He assisted in planning the invasions of Sicily and Italy. 1943–45, he was chief of the Allied government of the region occupied by the Fifth Army. A major general by 1949, he became chief surgeon of the Far East Command; 1950, chief surgeon of the U.N. forces in Korea. He retired in 1951. His books include *The Medical Work of the Knights Hospitallers* (1930) and he contributed twelve articles to the *Dictionary of American Biography*. Hume was awarded medals from forty-three foreign countries and twenty-three U.S. Army decorations.

HUME, ROBERT ALLEN (b. Byculla, India, 1847; d. Brookline, Mass., 1929), Congregational clergyman. Missionary at Ahmednagar, India, 1874–1926; founded United Divinity College there.

HUME, WILLIAM (b. Waterville, Maine, 1830; d. 1902), pioneer in salmon industry. With his brothers and Andrew Hapgood, Hume started the salmon canning industry along Sacramento and Columbia rivers, 1864–65.

HUMES, THOMAS WILLIAM (b. Knoxville, Tenn, 1815; d. Knoxville, 1892), Episcopal clergyman. Reopened East Tennessee University as president 1866; remained president after it became University of Tennessee, 1869–83.

HUMISTON, WILLIAM HENRY (b. Marietta, Ohio, 1869; d. 1923), musician, critic. Assistant conductor, New York Philharmonic Society; best known as authority on life and works of Bach and Wagner

HUMMEL, ABRAHAM HENRY (b. Boston, Mass., 1850; d. London, England, 1926), New York lawyer. Devious partner of William F. Howe in their notorious criminal law practice. Convicted of conspiracy, 1905, and imprisoned for one year. Hummel left for England, 1908, where he lived thereafter.

HUMPHREY, DORIS (b. Oak Park, Ill., 1895; d. New York, N.Y., 1958), dancer and choreographer. Studied at the Denishawn School in Los Angeles, led by Ted Shawn and Ruth St. Denis. Founded a dance studio and ensemble in 1928 with Charles Weidman and Pauline Lawrence. Member of the faculty of Bennington College School of the Dance in 1934; artistic adviser to the José Limón dance company from 1946 until 1958; taught at the American Dance Festival at Connecticut College for Women from 1948 to 1951; teacher at the Juilliard School of Music from 1951 until 1955. Wrote *The Art of Making Dances* which was published posthumously in 1959. Along with Martha Graham, Humphrey is considered the leading pioneer in modern American dance. Her analytic approach to dance, known as the technique of "fall and recovery," have given her a prominent place in American dance. Major choreographic works include *The Pleasures of Counterpoint* (1932) and the trilogy collectively titled *New Dance* (1936).

HUMPHREY, GEORGE MAGOFFIN (*b. Cheboygan, Mich., 1890; d. Cleveland, Ohio, 1970*), lawyer, industrialist, and secretary of the treasury. LL.B. (1912), Michigan Law School. Became a partner in his father's law firm, but in 1917 joined the M. A. Hanna Company in Cleveland, becoming president by 1929. He then joined forces with Ernest T. Weir to create the National Steel Corporation; with its sound financial basis and expert management, the corporation continued to expand during the Great Depression, becoming the nation's sixth-largest steel producer. After World War II he created the Pittsburgh Consolidation Coal Company. Dwight D. Eisenhower named him secretary of the treasury in 1952; during his four-year term, military expenditures were reduced, taxes were reduced by some $7.4 billion, inflation was checked, the value of the dollar abroad rose, and for two years the budget was balanced. When at the beginning of his second term Eisenhower, under pressure from the Defense Department, submitted the largest peacetime budget in history, he resigned. Resigned as chairman of National Steel in 1962.

HUMPHREY, HEMAN (*b. Canton, Conn., 1779; d. 1861*), Congregational clergyman. Graduated Yale, 1805. Pastor at Fairfield, Conn., and Pittsfield, Mass. Advocate of temperance. President, Amherst College, 1823–45.

HUMPHREYS, ALEXANDER CROMBIE (*b. Edinburgh, Scotland, 1851; d. 1927*), mechanical engineer, educator. Came to America as a child. Designer and constructor of gas plants in all parts of the world; president, Stevens Institute of Technology, 1902–27.

HUMPHREYS, ANDREW ATKINSON (*b. Philadelphia, Pa., 1810; d. 1883*), soldier, scientist. Grandson of Joshua Humphreys. Graduated West Point, 1831; served in Seminole War; appointed lieutenant, Corps of Topographical Engineers, 1838. Served in Coast Survey and for a time worked on survey of Mississippi delta; during 1854–55, supervised explorations and surveys for transcontinental railroad routes. Renewed his Mississippi River work, 1857, in association with Henry L. Abbot; their joint *Report upon the Physics and Hydraulics of the Mississippi River* (1861) has been basis for later flood control and improvements. Humphreys served with great distinction under McClellan in the Peninsular campaign, and was a divisional commander at Antietam and Fredericksburg; at Gettysburg, his division resisted Longstreet's attack on the afternoon of July 2 (1863). Thereafter as major general he served as chief of staff, Army of the Potomac, until November 1864, when Grant chose him to command the II Corps. From 1866 until his retirement, 1879, he was chief of the Corps of Engineers, U.S. Army.

HUMPHREYS, BENJAMIN GRUBB (*b. Claiborne Co., Miss., 1808; d. 1882*), planter, Mississippi legislator, Confederate brigadier general. First elected post-bellum governor of Mississippi, serving 1865–68, he was ejected from office by federal military authority.

HUMPHREYS, DAVID (*b. Derby, Conn., 1752; d. 1818*), soldier, diplomat, merchant, poet. Graduated Yale, 1771. Served with energy and ability in the Revolutionary War, acting as aide-de-camp to Washington whose close friend he became, and rising to rank of lieutenant colonel. Was secretary to the American commercial treaty commission in France and England, 1784–86; served as a secret U.S. intelligence agent at London, Lisbon, and Madrid, 1790; as commissioner for Algerian affairs, *post* 1793; and as minister to Spain, 1796–1801. Settling in Boston on his return from abroad, he interested himself in the breeding of merino sheep and in mills for cloth manufacture at Humphreysville, Conn. Nature endowed him with the habit of success in everything but poetry; his verses are conscientious, aspiring, and leaden; they may be read, along with his *Life of Israel Putnam* and other writings, in his *Miscellaneous Works* (1804). He is associated with his college contemporaries John Trumbull and Joel Barlow and others with America's first literary coterie, the "Hartford Wits."

HUMPHREYS, JAMES (*b. Philadelphia, Pa., 1748; d. Philadelphia, 1810*), Loyalist printer and publisher. Published first American *Works of Laurence Sterne* (1774), also the Tory *Pennsylvania Ledger*, 1775–76 and December 1777–May 1778. Removing to New York first and later to Nova Scotia, he returned to Philadelphia, 1797, and was employed until his death in book printing.

HUMPHREYS, JOSHUA (*b. Haverford Township, Pa., 1751; d. 1838*), ship builder, naval architect. A leader in his profession by 1776, Humphreys fitted out at his Philadelphia shipyard the Continental fleet which sailed that year under Esek Hopkins. After passage of the act of 1794 providing for a naval force of six frigates, Humphreys suggested improved radical designs which were adopted in building the *United States, Constitution, Chesapeake, Constellation, President,* and *Congress;* the *United States* was built under his personal supervision. Longer, broader, lower in the water, carrying more canvas than any vessels of their class afloat and superior in fire power, these ships became famous for their speed and individual accomplishments. He served as first U.S. naval constructor, 1794–1801.

HUMPHREYS, MILTON WYLIE (*b. Greenbrier Co., W.Va., 1844; d. Charlottesville, Va., 1928*), Confederate soldier, scholar. Professor of Latin and Greek at universities of Washington and Lee, Vanderbilt, Texas; and at University of Virginia, 1887–1912.

HUMPHREYS, WEST HUGHES (*b. Montgomery Co., Tenn., 1806; d. near Nashville, Tenn, 1882*), jurist. Tennessee attorney general and state supreme court reporter, 1839–51; edited *Humphreys' Reports* (1841–1851). Federal judge, Tennessee, 1853–62, he was impeached for accepting a Confederate commission as district judge.

HUMPHREYS, WILLIAM JACKSON (*b. Gap Mills, present W.Va., 1862; d. Washington, D.C., 1949*), physicist, meteorologist, B.A., Washington and Lee University, 1886; C.E., 1888. Ph.D., Johns Hopkins, 1897. Taught physics at University of Virginia, 1897–1905. U.S. Weather Bureau, 1905–35. Besides supervising the Bureau's seismological program (1914–24) and editing the *Monthly Weather Review* (1931–35), he pursued research on problems of atmospheric physics. His most notable contribution was his explanation (1909) of the existence of the isothermal stratosphere as a necessary consequence of radiational equilibrium. He was author of some 250 scholarly articles and such books as *Physics of the Air* (1920). Professor of meteorological physics, George Washington University, 1911–33.

HUMPHRIES, GEORGE ROLFE (*b. Philadelphia, Pa., 1894; d. Redwood City, Calif., 1969*), poet, translator, and scholar. Translated classical literature and the writings of Federico García Lorca.

His minor but well-received volumes of poetry are *Europa, and Other Poems and Sonnets* (1929), *Out of the Jewel* (1942), *The Summer Landscape* (1944), *Forbid Thy Ravens* (1947), *The Wind of Time* (1950), *Poems, Collected and New* (1954), *Green Armour on Green Ground* (1956), *Collected Poems of Rolfe Humphries* (1956), and *Coat on a Stick: Late Poems* (1969).

HUNEKER, JAMES GIBBONS (*b. Philadelphia, Pa., 1860; d. 1921*), musician, critic of art and literature. Author of *Chopin: The Man and His Music* (1900) and many other volumes of critical essays marked by wit, insight, and enthusiasm for new developments in the arts.

HUNNEWELL, HORATIO HOLLIS (*b. Watertown, Mass., 1810; d. 1902*), Boston banker, railroad financier, and specialist in foreign exchange, horticulturist.

HUNNEWELL, JAMES (*b. Charlestown, Mass., 1794; d. 1869*), sea captain, merchant. Sailed a 49-ft. schooner, the *Missionary Packet*, laden with merchandise and missionaries around Cape Horn to Honolulu, 1825–26. Established a Hawaiian commercial house (later C. Brewer and Co.).

HUNT, ALFRED EPHRAIM (*b. East Douglas, Mass., 1855; d. Philadelphia, Pa., 1899*), metallurgist, engineer. Son of Mary H. H. Hunt. Organized pioneer testing laboratory for metals in Pittsburgh; instrumental in developing Hall process for reduction of aluminum.

HUNT, BENJAMIN WEEKS (*b. Chappaqua, N.Y., 1847; d. 1934*), horticulturist. Removed to Eatonton, Ga., *ca.* 1876. Developed livestock farm and was active in eradicating tick menace; his farm and garden became in effect an experimental station where he worked with varieties of fruit.

HUNT, CARLETON (*b. New Orleans, La., 1836; d. New Orleans, 1921*), lawyer, Confederate soldier. Professor and dean, law department, University of Louisiana; a founder of American Bar Association, 1878.

HUNT, CHARLES WALLACE (*b. Candor, N.Y., 1841; d. Staten Island, N.Y., 1911*), mechanical engineer, manufacturer. Developed and manufactured automatic coal-handling system, patented 1872; a pioneer in bucket conveying and industrial railway systems; constructed coal terminals for industry and government.

HUNT, FREEMAN (*b. Quincy, Mass., 1804; d. 1858*), publisher. Edited *Merchants' Magazine and Commercial Review post* 1839; it was known, *post* 1850, as *Hunt's Merchants' Magazine.* Author of *American Anecdotes* (1830), *Lives of American Merchants* (1858), and other books.

HUNT, GAILLARD (*b. New Orleans, La., 1862; d. 1924*), able official of State Department and Library of Congress, 1887–1924. Editor of *Writings of James Madison* (1900–10), *Journal of the Continental Congress* (1910–22); author of biographies of Madison and Calhoun; also of *The Department of State* (1914) and *Life in America One Hundred Years Ago* (1914). Son of William H. Hunt.

HUNT, GEORGE WYLIE PAUL (*b. Huntsville, Mo., 1859; d. Phoenix, Ariz., 1934*), businessman, politician, Arizona legislator. Democratic governor of Arizona, 1912–19, 1923–29, 1931–33. A friend of labor, a masterly politician and almost a legend in the Southwest.

HUNT, HARRIOT KEZIA (*b. Boston, Mass., 1805; d. 1875*), pioneer woman physician, reformer. Began practicing medicine, *ca.* 1934, without formal training; was twice denied admission to Harvard Medical School; advocated woman's suffrage, temperance, abolition.

HUNT, HENRY JACKSON (*b. Detroit, Mich., 1819; d. Washington, D.C., 1889*), soldier. Graduated West Point, 1839. Commended for gallantry, Mexican War. With W. F. Barry and W. H. French, wrote revised light artillery tactics, adopted 1860. A distinguished artillery officer in all major campaigns, Army of the Potomac; at Gettysburg, instrumental in securing the Peach Orchard for the Federals and in breaking Pickett's charge.

HUNT, ISAAC (*b. Bridgetown, Barbados, ca. 1742; d. England, 1809*), author, Church of England clergyman. Father of Leigh Hunt. Graduated Philadelphia Academy, 1763. Effective lampooner of Pennsylvania authorities, 1764–65. As Loyalist writer and lawyer, threatened with tar and feathers, 1775, but escaped to England and took orders.

HUNT, LESTER CALLAWAY (*b. Isabel, Ill., 1892; d. Washington, D.C., 1954*), politician. Studied Illinois Wesleyan University and school of dentistry at St. Louis University. Practiced dentistry in Lander, Wyoming. Democratic secretary of state (1935–43); governor, (1943–49); U.S. senator (1949–54). A member of the Kefauver Crime Investigation Commission, Hunt also championed women's rights and worked for a bipartisan foreign policy, balanced budgets, and federal subsidies for health services. Because of complex personal problems, he committed suicide in Washington in 1954.

HUNT, MARY HANNAH HANCHETT (*b. Canaan, Conn., 1830; d. 1906*), temperance reformer, educator, author of temperance textbooks. Successful in securing state laws requiring teaching of hygiene and temperance in all public schools.

HUNT, NATHAN (*b. Guilford Co., N.C., 1758; d. 1853*), Quaker preacher and mystic. Opposed slavery; founded New Garden School, 1837, now Guilford College.

HUNT, REID (*b. Martinsville, Ohio, 1870; d. Belmont, Mass., 1948*), pharmacologist. B.A., Johns Hopkins University, 1891; Ph.D. in physiology, 1896. M.D., College of Physicians and Surgeons, Baltimore, 1896. Taught physiology at Columbia University College of Physicians and Surgeons. New York City; taught pharmacology at Johns Hopkins, 1898–1904; associate professor, 1901. At various times between 1902 and 1904, he worked in Germany, under Paul Ehrlich.

In 1904 Hunt organized a division of pharmacology of the Hygienic Laboratory of the U.S. Public Health and Marine Hospital Service, Washington D.C. He was made chief of this division and in 1910 was given the title of professor of pharmacology. In 1913 he accepted the chair of pharmacology at the Harvard Medical School, where he served until 1936. His first research dealt with the relation between the inhibitory and the accelerator nerves of the vertebrate heart. He also investigated the reflex decrease in blood pressure resulting from stimulation of afferent nerves, the subject of his Ph.D. thesis and of his later (1918) fundamental studies on vasodilator reactions. The scientific work that brought him international fame was the discovery of the powerful biological activity of acetylcholine and the elucidation of the relation between chemical structure and pharmacological action of choline derivatives upon the autonomic system.

Hunt discovered that mice fed thyroid tolerated an amount of acetonitrile several times the lethal dose, and for two decades he employed this "acetonitril reaction" to study the physiology and pharmacology of thyroid function. His work led to the recognition that thyroid preparations could be made therapeutically reliable. In a study of poisonous plants made for the Department of Agriculture in 1902, Hunt found that the death of livestock ascribed to liliaceous plants of the genus *Zygadenus* (poison camas) was caused by alkaloids similar to those of the genus *Veratrum*.

Hunt made important contributions to the revision of *The Pharmacopeia of the United States of America*. He served as president of the United States Pharmacopeial Convention (1920–30) and was a member of the permanent standards commission of the League of Nations Health Committee.

Hunt, Richard Morris (*b. Brattleboro, Vt., 1827; d. 1895*), architect. Brother of William M. Hunt. His artistic interests stimulated by association with his own talented family, he started architectural study in Geneva, Switzerland, at 16. Admitted to the Beaux-Arts, 1846, during his nine-year residence in Paris he worked with Couture and the sculptor Antoine Barye. He returned to America, 1855, and took his first job as draftsman, under T.U. Walter, during construction of additions to the Capitol, Washington, D.C. He opened his first studio in New York, but did not feel ready to enter upon a career as architect in that city until 1858 after further study in Paris.

A lawsuit against a cheating client brought his name to the attention of wealthy New Yorkers. Newport, R.I., houses designed for Ogden Goelet, Cornelius Vanderbilt, Oliver H. P. Belmont, and Mrs. William Vanderbilt were successful efforts; the most ambitious of all his country houses was "Biltmore," at Asheville, N.C. (1890), which he designed in the French Renaissance style. The Fifth Avenue, New York, town houses of Elbridge T. Gerry, John Jacob Astor, and William K. Vanderbilt came from the office of Hunt; the Vanderbilt residence, at Fifth Ave. and Fifty-second St., was called his masterpiece. Many important public buildings were constructed from his designs: among them, the main portion of the New York Metropolitan Museum of Art, the old Lenox Library Building, the Naval Observatory in Washington, the Administration Building at Chicago World's Fair (1893) and the base of the Statue of Liberty. Hunt was an outspoken advocate of better training methods for architects and for the need among them of general artistic education as well as technical training. Establishing a studio in his own office, he actually taught some of the men who later carried on his tradition.

Hunt, Robert (*b. ca. 1568; d. Jamestown, Va., 1608*), Church of England clergyman. Chaplain of the Jamestown expedition; sailed with the expedition Dec. 19, 1606. A zealous minister, he was overcome by the physical hardships of the new settlement.

Hunt, Robert Woolston (*b. Fallsington, Pa., 1838; d. Chicago, Ill., 1923*), metallurgist, Union soldier. Established at Cambria Iron Co., the first analytical laboratory to form an integral part of an iron works, 1860; pioneer in manufacture of Bessemer steel in America; producer of first commercial order for steel rails, 1867; developed automatic rail mills.

Hunt, Theodore Whitefield (*b. Metuchen N.J., 1844; d. 1930*), educator. Graduated Princeton, 1865. Taught English at Princeton *post* 1868, becoming professor emeritus in 1918. A pioneer in reintroduction of Old English studies into American college curricula.

Hunt, Thomas Sterry (*b. Norwich, Conn., 1826; d. 1892*), chemist, geologist. With geological survey of Canada, 1847–72; professor of geology, Massachusetts Institute of Technology, 1872–78. Published papers on many phases of theoretical chemistry, especially on diatomic molecules of gaseous elements and on structure of compounds of the water type.

Hunt, Ward (*b. Utica, N.Y., 1810; d. 1886*), lawyer, New York jurist. Appointed a justice of the U.S. Supreme Court, 1872, he served actively until the end of 1878. Thereafter a paralytic, he was on inactive status until pensioned by Congress, 1882

Hunt, Washington (*b. Windham, N.Y., 1811; d. New York, N.Y., 1867*), lawyer, politician. Whig governor of New York, 1851–53.

Hunt, William Gibbes (*b. Boston, Mass., 1791; d. 1833*), journalist. Graduated Harvard, 1810. Settled at Lexington, Ky., 1815. As editor, *Western Review and Miscellaneous Magazine*, Lexington, Ky., 1819–21, he was literary spokesman of the Ohio Valley region. He later was editor and publisher of *Nashville Banner* (Tenn.) and successors.

Hunt, William Henry (*b. Charleston, S.C., 1823; d. Russia, 1884*), jurist. Practiced law in New Orleans, La., 1844–78. Successively a Whig and a Know-Nothing, he was a Southern Unionist, 1860–65. A Republican during Reconstruction, he served as judge of U.S. Court of Claims, 1878–81, as secretary of the navy, 1881, and as minister to Russia, 1882–84.

Hunt, William Morris (*b. Brattleboro, Vt., 1824; d. Isles of Shoals, N.H., 1879*), painter. Brother of Richard M. Hunt. The eldest child in an artistic family, he learned to draw at an early age. After living in southern France and Rome, he entered the Düsseldorf Academy of Art, 1845. In France, 1846–56, he studied with Thomas Couture, mastering that artist's famous method. Jean François Millet's friendship and association became a major factor in the career of the young American. Hunt's style of painting eventually became a composite of Couture's method plus Millet's ponderous virility, on which was superimposed his own serious and ardent nature. On returning to America, Hunt set up his studio finally in Boston. Ahead of his time in taste, Hunt was dissatisfied with his own progress although he made Boston conscious of Millet, Corot, Rousseau, and the other Barbizon painters, and provided a market for them in America before they were accepted in France. His solid worth as a painter is demonstrated in his portraits of Chief Justice Shaw, Francis Gardner, and Mrs. Charles Francis Adams. His large murals at the Capitol in Albany, N.Y., were the most important and perhaps the best that had been done in the U.S. up to that time.

Hunt, Wilson Price (*b. Hopewell, N.J., 1782[?]; d. 1842*), fur trader, merchant. Removed to St. Louis, Mo., 1804; ran a general store there until 1809. As partner, Pacific Fur Co., he went westward in 1810, establishing winter camp near present St. Joseph, Mo., in September. On Apr. 21, 1811, he and his party started up the Missouri River as far as the Arikara villages. Thereafter they traveled to the Snake River overland. Hunt's attempt to navigate that turbulent steam forced the expedition to divide. The various groups reached Astoria, after extreme privation, early in 1812. After two years of unsatisfactory activity on the Pacific Coast and in the Sandwich Islands, during which the post at Astoria was lost to the British, he returned to St. Louis and became prosperous in general business.

Hunter, Andrew (*b. York Co., Pa., 1751; d. Washington, D.C., 1823*), Presbyterian chaplain in both army and navy. Commended by Washington for conduct at battle of Monmouth; first chaplain-schoolmaster in U.S. Navy, 1811–23; taught also in College of New Jersey (Princeton).

Hunter, Croil (*b. Casselton, N. Dak., 1893; d. St. Paul, Minn., 1970*), airline executive. Was appointed traffic manager of Northwest Airways in 1932 and promoted to vice president and general manager in 1933, when the enterprise was reorganized as Northwest Airlines. Thereafter was president and general manager, 1937–53, and chairman of the board, 1953–65. Pursued an aggressive policy of new route acquisition, fleet expansion, and technological innovation. His most significant achievement was his success in connecting the American Midwest with a number of Asian destinations by following the "Great Circle Route" via

Alaska. In 1939 he applied for such a route to the Civil Aeronautics Board, and during World War II Northwest solidified its claims to preferment by transporting military personnel and cargo to Alaska. Even before the end of the war, Northwest was granted a route from Milwaukee to New York, making it the fourth transcontinental air carrier, and by 1947 the Great Circle Route to Asia had materialized, thus making the airline familiarly known as Northwest Orient.

HUNTER, DAVID (*b. Washington, D.C., 1802; d. Washington, 1886*), Union soldier, Son of Andrew Hunter, nephew of Richard Stockton. Graduated West Point, 1822. Served at Midwestern posts and in Mexican War. During the Civil War, in which he rose to major general, his principal success was in the taking of Fort Pulaski, Ga., 1862, and at Piedmont, Shenandoah Valley, 1864. He was president of military commission which tried Lincoln's assassins.

HUNTER, ROBERT (*b. Hunterston, Scotland; d. Jamaica, British West Indies, 1734*), colonial governor. Distinguished himself as soldier under Marlborough. Appointed lieutenant governor of Virginia, 1707, he was captured en route and imprisoned in France. Released, he was appointed governor of New York and New Jersey, 1709. Arriving New York City, 1710, he served until 1719. He was a successful administrator and one of the few popular royal governors in American colonial history. In furtherance of his defense of the frontiers against the French, Hunter endeavored to influence neighboring colonies to lend assistance and instituted an express between Boston and Albany, possibly the first organized postal service in the English colonies. A man of wit, he was author, with Lewis Morris, of *Androborus* (1714), a satiric farce and the first play known to have been written and printed in British America. He served as governor of Jamaica, 1727–34.

HUNTER, ROBERT (*b. Terre Haute, Ind., 1874; d. Montecito, Calif., 1942*), social worker, socialist. B.A., Indiana University, 1896. Served as organizing secretary of Chicago Board of Charities, 1896–1902; head worker at University Settlement, Rivington Street, New York City, 1902–03. As chairman of the Child Labor Committee set up by New York social workers, he directed its successful campaign for a statewide child labor law, enacted in 1903. His *Poverty* (1904) was the first general statistical survey of America's poor and an important analytical study of the problem. He was active in the American Socialist party, 1905–14.

HUNTER, ROBERT MERCER TALIAFERRO (*b. Essex Co., Va., 1809; d. near Lloyds, Va., 1887*), lawyer, statesman. Nephew of James M. Garnett. Studied law with Henry St. George Tucker; admitted to the bar, 1830. After service in the Virginia legislature, and in Congress as a States-Rights Whig (he was speaker of the House for a single term), Hunter's particularism became pronounced as did his devotion to John C. Calhoun's principles. When he returned to Congress, 1845, it was as a Democrat; from 1847–61 he was U.S. senator from Virginia. He wavered, 1850–61, between his natural conservatism and a spirited defense of Southern interests when threatened. He served the Confederacy briefly as a senator. With A. H. Stephens and J. A. Campbell, he attended the Hampton Roads conference, 1865. After the war, he aided the local conservatives and was treasurer of Virginia, 1874–80.

HUNTER, THOMAS (*b. Ardglass, Ireland, 1831; d. New York, N.Y., 1915*), educator. Came to America, 1850. Famous teacher and principal, P.S. No. 35 in New York City; organized first evening high school, 1866; founded Normal College of New York City, 1869, now called Hunter College in his honor.

HUNTER, WALTER DAVID (*b. Lincoln, Nebr., 1875; d. El Paso, Tex., 1925*), entomologist. Graduated University of Nebraska, 1895. Served with great ability as director of U.S. Department of Agriculture investigation of the boll weevil and other cotton pests, 1901–25.

HUNTER, WHITESIDE GODFREY (*b. near Belfast, Ireland, 1841; d. Louisville, Ky., 1917*), physician, Union soldier, Kentucky legislator and Republican congressman from Kentucky. Minister to Guatemala and Honduras, 1897–1903.

HUNTER, WILLIAM (*b. Newport, R.I., 1774; d. 1849*), lawyer, Rhode Island legislator. U.S. senator, Federalist, from Rhode Island, 1812–21; chargé d'affaires and minister to Brazil, 1834–45.

HUNTER, WILLIAM C. (*b. Kentucky, 1812; d. Nice, France, 1891*), merchant. Worked in Canton, China, 1825–44, latterly as a partner in Russell and Co. Author of several excellent accounts of life in the Canton "Factories."

HUNTINGTON, COLLIS POTTER (*b. Harwinton, Conn., 1821; d. 1900*), railroad magnate, capitalist. Began life as a peddler; kept a store at Oneonta, N.Y., 1842–49. Removing to California, he set up a retail and jobbing business at Sacramento; under the name of Huntington & Hopkins, it soon became a prosperous enterprise. Exploiting, *post* 1860, the opportunity presented by Theodore D. Judah's proposal for a railroad to cross the Sierra Nevada as part of a transcontinental route, he joined Leland Stanford, Charles Crocker, and Mark Hopkins in financing a survey of the route and in securing government support. This so-called Huntington group won exclusive control, 1863, when Judah died. Eastern capital was secured by the activities of Huntington in New York; Stanford acted as president of the company; Crocker took charge of construction. The railroad known as the Central Pacific was completed to a junction with the Union Pacific, 1869. Thereafter, Huntington's group became involved in even greater enterprises, for which he secured capital from both private investors and the government. Railway lines were expanded in California, then to El Paso and New Orleans. The Central Pacific was actually overshadowed by this new enterprise known as the Southern Pacific Co. (organized as such, 1884). Huntington was active in discouraging government aid to competing lines to the Pacific Coast. An active, profane, and cynical advocate of his company's interest before Congress, he was a firm believer in the power of money to influence legislation. In 1890 he displaced Leland Stanford as president of the Southern Pacific; meanwhile he had extended his control over transportation companies in eastern America and on the high seas. He was greatly interested in developing the Chesapeake & Ohio and, as his wealth increased, became more an more outstanding in the business world. Vindictive, sometimes untruthful, he was a persistent opponent of the idea that his railroads were to any degree burdened with obligations to the public.

HUNTINGTON, DANIEL (*b. New York, N.Y., 1816; d. 1906*), painter. Brother of Jedediah V. Huntington; grandson of Jedediah Huntington. Encouraged in art by Charles L. Elliott; studied with Samuel F. B. Morse and Henry Inman. His subjects, when not portraits, were historic in nature and moral in character.

HUNTINGTON, EDWARD VERMILYE (*b. Clinton, N.Y., 1874; d. Cambridge, Mass., 1952*), mathematician. Studied at Howard and the University of Strasbourg (Ph.D., 1901). Member of Harvard faculty (1910–41); professor of mechanics (1919). Huntington was interested in the mathematical study of mechanics. His work *The Continuum, and Other Types of Serial Order, With an Introduction to Cantor's Transfinite Numbers* (1917), introduced several generations of students to the theory of sets of points and transfinite numbers. President of the Mathematical Association of America, and vice president of the American Mathematical Society (1924). Huntington's most influential contribution outside of pure mathematics was a theory of the apportionment of representatives in Congress.

HUNTINGTON, ELISHA (*b. Topsfield, Mass., 1796; d. 1865*), physician, long-time mayor of Lowell, Mass., where he practiced *post ca.* 1825.

HUNTINGTON, ELLSWORTH (*b. Galesburg, Ill., 1876; d. New Haven, Conn., 1947*), geographer. Graduated Beloit College, 1897; M.A., Harvard, 1902; Ph.D., Yale, 1909. Assistant to the president, Euphrates College, Harpoot, Turkey, 1897–1901. He mapped the area around Harpoot and journeyed down the Euphrates in 1901 on a raft made of inflated sheepskins. Between 1903 and 1906, he was a member of expeditions to Transcaspia, and through the Himalayas into the Tarim Basin. Wrote *The Pulse of Asia* (1907). Yale University, 1907–15, 1919–47. He is remembered for twenty-eight books and other writings detailing his research into the origin, distribution, longevity, and accomplishments of civilization. He believed he had found a triadic causation for progress; climate, the quality of people, and culture; his concern for the second of these led him into the eugenics movement. His *Mainsprings of Civilization* (1945) was the first of a projected two-volume synthesis of his life's work; the second, *The Pace of History*, was incomplete at his death.

HUNTINGTON, FREDERIC DAN (*b. Hadley, Mass., 1819; d. Hadley, 1904*), Unitarian and Episcopal clergyman. Resigned his Harvard professorship and post as college preacher, 1860, and was ordained to the Episcopal priesthood, 1861. Organized Emmanuel Church, Boston; consecrated bishop of Central New York, 1869; founded St. John's School, Manlius, N.Y.

HUNTINGTON, HENRY EDWARDS (*b. Oneonta, N.Y., 1850; d. Philadelphia, Pa., 1927*), railroad executive, financier, founder of Huntington Library and Art Gallery, philanthropist. Nephew of Collis P. Huntington, with whom he was associated in business. Developed San Francisco and Los Angeles street railways. After his uncle's death, 1900, he sold his Southern Pacific control to E. H. Harriman. Disposing of later Southern California interurban developments, 1910, he turned his energies to electric power and real estate. An enthusiastic collector of books and art, he acquired many famous collections both in America and Europe, now housed at San Marino, Calif., for public use.

HUNTINGTON, JABEZ (*b. Norwich, Conn., 1719; d. 1786*), merchant, Connecticut legislator. Revolutionary major general and commander of Connecticut militia, 1777–79.

HUNTINGTON, JEDEDIAH (*b. Norwich, Conn., 1743; d. 1818*), merchant, Revolutionary brigadier general. Son of Jabez Huntington. Collector, port of New London, 1780–1818.

HUNTINGTON, JEDEDIAH VINCENT (*b. New York, N.Y., 1815; d. Pau, France, 1862*), novelist, editor. Grandson of Jedediah Huntington; brother of Daniel Huntington. A convert to Catholicism, 1849. Author of *Lady Alice* (1849), *Rosemary* (1860), and other novels.

HUNTINGTON, MARGARET JANE EVANS (*b. Utica, N.Y., 1842; d. 1926*), educator. Raised in Minnesota. Professor of English and dean, Carleton College, 1874–1908. Organizer, Minnesota Federation of Women's Clubs, 1895; vice president, General Federation, 1898. Leader in library and missionary organizations.

HUNTINGTON, SAMUEL (*b. Windham, Conn., 1731; d. Norwich, Conn., 1796*), lawyer, Connecticut legislator and jurist,

signer of Declaration of Independence. Member, Continental Congress, 1775–84; president of Congress, 1779–81; governor of Connecticut, 1786–96.

HUNTINGTON, SAMUEL (*b. Coventry, Conn., 1765; d. Painesville, Ohio, 1817*), jurist, Ohio legislator. Nephew and adopted son of Samuel Huntington (1731–1796). Graduated Yale, 1785. Removed to Ohio *ca.* 1801. Democratic-Republican governor of Ohio, 1808–10, he represented the conservative element of his party.

HUNTINGTON, WILLIAM EDWARDS (*b. Hillsboro, Ill., 1844; d. 1930*), Methodist clergyman. Nephew of Frederic D. Huntington. Graduated University of Wisconsin, 1870; B.D., Boston University, 1873, and Ph.D., 1882. Dean, Boston University, 1882–1904; president, 1904–11; dean, graduate school, 1911–17.

HUNTINGTON, WILLIAM REED (*b. Lowell, Mass., 1838; d. 1909*), Episcopal clergyman. Son of Elisha Huntington. Graduated Harvard, 1859; studied theology under Frederic D. Huntington. Rector, All Saints, Worcester, Mass., 1862–83; Grace Church, New York City, 1883–1909. A leader in revision of Prayer Book (1892). The unity of Christendom was the dominant interest of his life and thought.

HUNTON, EPPA (*b. Fauquier Co., Va., 1822; d. Richmond, Va., 1908*), lawyer, Confederate brigadier general. U.S. congressman, Democrat, from Virginia, 1873–81; U.S. senator, 1892–95.

HUNTON, GEORGE KENNETH (*b. Claremont, N.H., 1888; d. Brooklyn, N.Y., 1967*), lawyer, editor, and civil rights activist. LL.B. (1910), Fordham. From 1934 to 1962 was first executive secretary of the Catholic Interracial Council (CIC) and editor of its official journal, the *Interracial Review*. His primary aims were to educate Catholics about the oppression of blacks and to inform his coreligionists about the glaring discrepancy between Catholic theory and Catholic practice toward blacks; deserves substantial credit for the fact that the Catholic church became a vital force in the civil rights movement. The *Interracial Review* served as his principal weapon; within a decade it became a kind of national clearinghouse of information for the Roman Catholic church. His activities also went beyond strictly Catholic concerns, and in 1955 the National Association for the Advancement of Colored People selected him as a member of its national board of directors.

HUNTON, WILLIAM LEE (*b. Morrisburg, Canada, 1864; d. 1930*), Lutheran clergyman, editor, author.

HUPP, LOUIS GORHAM (*b. Kalamazoo, Mich., 1872; d. Detroit, Mich., 1961*), automobile pioneer. With his brother Robert Craig Hupp, formed the Hupp Motor Car Corporation, which brought out the Hupmobile in 1909. The Hupmobile was extremely popular due to its durability, simple construction, and innovative design (it was easily identified by the uncommonly tall filler necks on the radiator and by the unusual fan-shaped tail lamps). By 1925 the Hupp company was among the top ten American automobile producers, but sales slumped throughout the Great Depression, and the last Hupmobile was built in 1941.

HURD, JOHN CODMAN (*b. Boston, Mass., 1816; d. Boston, 1892*), publicist. Graduated Yale, 1836. His legal treatise *Law of Freedom and Bondage in the United States* (1858, 1862) is unexcelled as a study of chattel slavery in its constitutional and statutory aspects.

HURD, NATHANIEL (*b. Boston, Mass., 1730; d. 1777*), silversmith, engraver chiefly of bookplates.

HURLBERT, WILLIAM HENRY (*b. Charleston, S.C., 1827; d. Cadenabbia, Italy, 1895*), journalist, Graduated Harvard, 1847. Staff writer for *Putnam's Magazine* and *New York Times, ante* 1861; war and foreign correspondent; editor, *New York World,* 1876–93. Brilliant but erratic.

HURLBUT, JESSE LYMAN (*b. New York, N.Y., 1843; d. Bloomfield, N.J., 1930*), Methodist clergyman, editor, author. Associated, *post* 1875, with the Chautauqua movement.

HURLBUT, STEPHEN AUGUSTUS (*b. Charleston, S.C., 1815; d. Lima, Peru, 1882*), lawyer, Union major general, Illinois legislator. Accused of corruption while commanding in Louisiana, 1864. Inept minister to Colombia and Peru. First commander Grand Army of the Republic, 1866–68,

HURLEY, EDWARD NASH (*b. Galesburg Ill., 1864; d. Chicago, Ill., 1933*), industrialist. Organized Standard Pneumatic Tool Co., 1896, manufacturing the first piston air drills; successful also in other businesses. Served on Federal Trade Commission, 1915–17, and was chairman of U.S. Shipping Board and president of Emergency Fleet Corporation, 1917–19. Hurley's achievement made possible the transportation of the U.S. Army and supplies to Europe in World War I.

HURLEY, JOSEPH PATRICK (*b. Cleveland, Ohio, 1894; d. Orlando, Fla., 1967*), Roman Catholic clergyman. Ordained a priest in 1919, he served as assistant pastor at three Ohio churches (1919–27); secretary to Edward A. Mooney, apostolic delegate to India (1928–31) and Japan (1931–33); chargé d'affaires of the apostolic delegation in Japan (1933–34); and attaché to the Papal Secretariat of State in Vatican City (1934–40). As sixth bishop of the Diocese of St. Augustine, Fla. (1940–67), he reorganized the diocese with few resources, conducted papal diplomacy in Yugoslavia, effectively responded to the 1950's Florida Catholic population boom and to the diocesan split caused by the 1958 creation of the Diocese of Miami, and attended the Second Vatican Council.

HURLEY, PATRICK JAY (*b. near Lehigh, Okla., 1883; d. Santa Fe, N. Mex., 1963*), lawyer and diplomat. B.A. (1905), Indian University; LL.B. (1908), National University. Was national attorney for the Choctaws, 1911–17. Became active in the Republican party and in 1928 helped carry Oklahoma for Herbert Hoover, who rewarded him with appointment as assistant secretary of war. After the 1932 defeat of Hoover, became acquainted with President Franklin D. Roosevelt, who in the early 1940's sent him on diplomatic and fact-finding missions to New Zealand, the Soviet Union, the Middle East, and China, and appointed him ambassador to China (1944–45). His most significant mark on American history came in 1940 when, as private secretary for the Sinclair Oil Company, he negotiated a settlement of its claims with the government of Mexico. This agreement broke an impasse between American oil companies and Mexico that had followed the 1938 Mexican expropriation of American oil properties.

HURST, FANNIE (*b. Hamilton, Ohio, 1889; d. New York, N.Y., 1968*), novelist. Beginning her writing career in 1920, she wrote eighteen novels, an autobiography, and over 400 short stories, plays, movie scripts, and articles. Also had her own radio and television programs. In the 1920's she and F. Scott Fitzgerald were the two most highly paid short-story writers in America, and into the 1940's her work sold well. A formulaic and sentimental writer preoccupied with the theme of women suffering for love, she will be remembered for her portrayal of women and their conflicts in the first half of the century. Her novel *Back Street* (1931) was filmed three times, and her novel *Imitation of Life* (1933), twice. In her later years, she took on the role of social critic and reformer, involving herself in issues of war and peace, racial discrimination, poverty in America, and women's rights.

HURST, JOHN FLETCHER (*b. near Salem, Md., 1834; d. 1903*), Methodist clergyman. Graduated Dickinson College, 1854. Professor, Drew Seminary, and president, 1873–80. Elected bishop, 1880. Founded American University, Washington, D.C., and was chancellor, 1891–1901. Author of *History of the Christian Church* (1897–1900).

HURSTON, ZORA NEALE (*b. Eatonville, Fla., 1901?; d. Fort Pierce, Fla., 1960*), novelist and folklorist. Studied at Harvard University and at Barnard College. A figure in the Harlem Renaissance of the 1920's and 1930's, Hurston combined her interests in fiction and black American folklore. She published several novels, the best of which, *Their Eyes Were Watching God* (1937), dealt with black life in Florida. Her works in folklore include *Mules and Men* (1935) and *Tell My Horse* (1938). Her autobiography, *Dust Tracks on a Road* appeared in 1942. She became increasingly alienated from the new awareness in black America, resenting the emphasis on "color." From this perspective she criticized school integration, wrote articles suggesting that black votes in the South were sold or misused, and campaigned for right-wing Republican candidates. Her writing underscored the sensitivity and complexity of the Afro-American social systems.

HUSBANDS, HERMON (*b. probably Cecil Co., Md., 1724; d. 1795*), farmer, leader of the North Carolina Regulators, 1768–71.

HUSE, CALEB (*b. Newburyport, Mass., 1831; d. Highland Falls, N.Y., 1905*), soldier. Graduated West Point, 1851. Because of Southern associations, entered Confederate Army, 1861; acted as arms-purchasing agent in Europe. Returning to the United States, 1868, he conducted a successful preparatory school for West Point *post* 1876.

HUSING, EDWARD BRITT ("TED") (*b. Bronx, N.Y., 1901; d. Pasadena, Calif., 1962*), radio announcer. In 1924 began as announcer for stations WJY-WJZ in New York City, and when WJY-WJZ became part of NBC in 1926, was one of the pioneers of broadcasting, specializing in sports announcing but also covering special events and introducing dance bands, among other duties. Resigned in 1927 and soon thereafter joined CBS, where he became the network's "name" sports broadcaster, covered important events, and participated in prime-time entertainment programming. After quitting CBS in 1946, worked as a disc jockey for station WHN in New York; his "Ted Husing's Bandstand" continued into the 1950's. During the late 1940's and early 1950's he continued to broadcast sports events.

HUSK, CHARLES ELLSWORTH (*b. Shabbona, Ill., 1872; d. Laredo, Tex., 1916*), physician. Graduated Chicago College of Physicians and Surgeons, 1898. Worked mainly in Mexico. As municipal health officer of Santa Barbara. State of Chihuahua, he instituted campaigns against smallpox and worked until death with the anti-typhus commission sent by Mt. Sinai Hospital, New York, to study the disease.

HUSMANN, GEORGE (*b. Meyenburg, Prussia, 1827; d. Napa, Calif., 1902*), viticulturist. Came to America as a boy. Operated vineyards in Missouri; taught pomology and forestry at the State University, Columbia, Mo. Removed to California, 1881. His reputation as viticulturist was second only to that of Nicholas Longworth.

HUSSEY, CURTIS GRUBB (*b. near York, Pa., 1802; d. 1893*), physician, merchant. Raised in Ohio; practiced in Indiana. Settled in Pittsburgh, 1840. Opened first Lake Superior copper mine ca. 1843. Engaged in copper rolling and perfected, *post* 1859, the "direct process" for manufacturing crucible steel.

HUSSEY, OBED (*b. Maine, 1792; d. 1860*), inventor. Acting on a suggestion made to him *ca.* 1830, he worked on a device to cut grain, perfecting its design in Baltimore, Md., and starting construction of a full-sized reaper at Cincinnati, Ohio, 1832–33. Successfully employed in the harvest of 1833, the Hussey reaper was patented in December of that year, six months before the issue of the McCormick reaper patent. Bitter competition developed between Hussey and McCormick. Improvements were made to both machines, but Hussey's refusal to purchase improvement inventions of others led to decline and sale of his business in 1858.

HUSSEY, WILLIAM JOSEPH (*b. Mendon Ohio, 1862; d. 1926*), astronomer. Director of observatories, University of Michigan and La Plata, Argentina; discovered nearly 1400 double stars.

HUSTING, PAUL OSCAR (*b. Fond du Lac, Wis., 1866; d. 1917*), lawyer. Democratic legislator who supported La Follette's Progressive program in Wisconsin; U.S. senator, 1915–17; conservationist.

HUSTON, CHARLES (*b. Philadelphia, Pa., 1822; d. Coatesville, Pa., 1897*), physician. Partner in Lukens Iron and Steel Mills; one of the first steel manufacturers to make scientific studies of the properties of his product; recommended standard tests for boiler-plate (1877).

HUSTON, WALTER (*b. Toronto, Canada, 1884; d. Beverly Hills, Calif., 1950*), actor. After success, *post* 1909, in a big-time vaudeville song-and-dance act, he rose to stage stardom as Ephraim Cabot in Eugene O'Neill's *Desire Under the Elms*, 1924. Gifted in the portrayal of lonely, ruggedly masculine, intensely American individuals, he found his next important role in the film *Abraham Lincoln*, which D. W. Griffith directed in 1930; between 1929 and 1934, he was continually employed on the screen. He returned to the stage in 1934 as the lead in *Dodsworth*, an adaptation of the Sinclair Lewis novel; this was one of his finest performances, which he repeated in a motion picture version, 1936. After another triumph as Peter Stuyvesant in the musical *Knickerbocker Holiday*, 1938, he made few appearances. Huston did continue to grace the films directed by his son, John Huston; these included *The Treasure of Sierra Madre*, 1948, in which his portrayal of the grizzled prospector won him an Academy Award.

HUTCHESON, WILLIAM LEVI (*b. Saginaw, Mich., 1874; d. Indianapolis, Ind., 1953*), labor leader. President of the United Brotherhood of Carpenters and Joiners, the nation's second largest union (1915–52). Opposed the formation of the CIO by John L. Lewis in 1938. Hutcheson was indicted under the Sherman Antitrust Act in 1940 for boycotting the Anheuser-Busch Co.; the charges were dismissed by the Supreme Court. An opponent of the New Deal, he resigned in 1936 as tenth vice president of the AFL; rejoined the AFL in 1939 as first vice president but remained in conflict with the other leaders over jurisdictional issues and reconciliation with the CIO.

HUTCHINS, HARRY BURNS (*b. Lisbon, N.H., 1847; d. 1930*), lawyer, educator. Graduated University of Michigan, 1871; taught history there, 1872–76, and law, 1884–87. First dean, Cornell Law School, 1887–95; dean, University of Michigan Law School, 1895–1910. Outstanding president, University of Michigan, 1910–20.

HUTCHINS, THOMAS (*b. Monmouth Co., N.J., 1730; d. Pittsburgh, Pa., 1789*), military engineer. Officer in Pennsylvania colonial forces, 1757–59; in regular British service until 1780. Produced important maps and travel journals, among them *A*

Topographical Description of Virginia, Pennsylvania, Maryland, and North Carolina (London, 1778) and *An Historical . . . Description of Louisiana and West-Florida* (Phila., 1784). During the American Revolution, he declined a British majority, was imprisoned in England, and escaped to France whence he came to Charleston, S.C., 1781, and served under Gen. Greene. Appointed "Geographer to the United States," July 1781, he surveyed Pennsylvania-Virginia and New York–Massachusetts boundaries. In charge of surveys under the Ordinance of 1785, he ran the famous "east-west line" and drew the plats of the first ranges, 1786–87.

HUTCHINSON, ANNE (*b. Alford, England, 1591; d. Pelham Bay, N.Y., 1643*), pioneer, religious liberal. Born Anne Marbury; married William Hutchinson, 1612. Immigrated to Massachusetts Bay colony, 1634. Advocated preaching of a "covenant of grace," i.e., religion based on the individual's direct intuition of God's grace and love; her criticism of the Massachusetts clergy and assertions of her own doctrine caused her to be labeled an antinomian. Supported at first by John Cotton, John Wheelwright, and Henry Vane, a synod of the churches denounced her views; thereafter the General Court sentenced her to banishment after a travesty of a trial. Early in the spring of 1638, she removed with her family to Aquidneck (Rhode Island); after her husband's death in 1642, she removed first to Long Island and then to the New York mainland on the shore of what is now Pelham Bay. There, in August or September 1643, she and all but one of her household were murdered by Indians.

HUTCHINSON, BENJAMIN PETERS (*b. Middleton, Mass., 1829; d. 1899*), meat packer, commodity speculator. Settled in Chicago, Ill., 1858; prospered in Civil War demand for pork products. *Post* 1876, took lead in organizing "call market" for dealing in futures; attempted numerous "corners" and was successful with September wheat, 1888; he declined in fortunes, *post* 1890.

HUTCHINSON, CHARLES LAWRENCE (*b. Lynn, Mass., 1854; d. 1924*), Chicago banker, merchant. Son of Benjamin P. Hutchinson, in whose office he was trained. President of Chicago Board of Trade, 1888; of Corn Exchange Bank, 1886–98. Sponsor and president, Chicago Art Institute; chairman, Fine Arts Committee, World's Columbian Exposition; active in planning and carrying out Chicago lake front improvement, 1907–22; treasurer, University of Chicago, 1893–1924.

HUTCHINSON, JAMES (*b. Wakefield, Bucks Co., Pa., 1752; d. Philadelphia, Pa., 1793*), physician, Revolutionary patriot. Surgeon general of Pennsylvania, 1778–84; died while fighting yellow-fever epidemic.

HUTCHINSON, PAUL (*b. Madison, N.J., 1890; d. Beaumont, Tex., 1956*), editor and writer. Studied at Lafayette College and at the Garrett Bible Institute in Evanston, Ill. An editor for religious publications, Hutchinson spent 1916–21 in Shanghai editing the *China Christian Advocate*. Managing editor of the *Christian Century* from 1924 to 1947; editor from 1947 to 1956. Author of numerous books on religion, especially the state of Christianity in the Far East, Hutchinson was a leader in the ecumenical movement.

HUTCHINSON, THOMAS (*b. Boston, Mass., 1711; d. England, 1780*), merchant, colonial official. Great-great-grandson of Anne Hutchinson. Graduated Harvard, 1727, and by systematic reading obtained a wide and exact knowledge of history and literature. Served in Massachusetts legislature, 1737–49; was speaker, 1746–48. Represented the province in England, 1740–41, pressing claims against New Hampshire; strongly opposed a "soft" currency and the Land Bank scheme (1740–41) whose collapse ruined the elder Samuel Adams and turned Adams's son into Hutchinson's bitter enemy. In 1749, owing to Hutchinson's persistence, a stable Massachusetts currency was established. Now a leader among the conservative class, he was chosen for the Council and thereafter sat continuously until 1766. Appointed judge of probate and justice of common pleas, he represented the province at the Albany Congress, 1754, and was named lieutenant governor, 1758; in 1760, he became chief justice. Although he merited these multiple offices, he could be, and was, rightly charged with having appropriated too many salaried posts; his appointment as chief justice angered and alienated James Otis. Although he opposed the Sugar Act and the Stamp Act as harmful to empire trade, he was too much of a "prerogative man" to deny the right of Parliament to govern and tax the colonies as it saw fit; the popular leaders, therefore, concluded that he was subservient to ministerial pressure, and the feeling against him led to the sack of his house by a Boston mob (Aug. 26, 1765) during which he barely escaped with his life. The experience left him embittered and convinced him that more strenuous measures were needed to reduce the "common sort" to obedience.

Dropped from the Council, 1766, he served as acting-governor, 1769–71, received his commission as governor, 1771, and served in that office until 1774. Following his instructions without question, he became more and more unpopular, yet he tended to ascribe his troubles and the disturbed state of the province to the machinations of James Otis and Samuel Adams rather than to an aroused public feeling. After a cessation of controversy, 1770–72, his wrangling with the legislature over trivialities revived the revolutionary spirit as much as any overt acts of its proponents; his position became untenable after publication of his letters to friends in England (published with Benjamin Franklin's agency, 1773) which revealed that he was secretly urging the use of sterner measures by the British government.

Succeeded *pro tem* by Gen. Gage as governor, Hutchinson went to England in 1774, expecting to return. Homesick for New England, he never saw it again. Honorable and kindly, he was also unusually attached to property although scrupulously honest in his dealings with it. Among his writings, his *History of the Colony of Massachusetts Bay* (Boston, 1764 and 1828; London, 1765) is outstanding.

HUTCHINSON, WOODS (*b. Selby, England, 1862; d. Brookline, Mass., 1930*), physician. Immigrated with family to Iowa as a boy. Graduated Penn College, 1880; M.D., University of Michigan, 1884. Practiced and taught in Des Moines, Iowa, and New York City; author of books and syndicated articles on medicine for the layman, with emphasis on preventive medicine.

HUTSON, RICHARD (*b. Beaufort District, S.C., 1748; d. Charleston, S.C., 1795*), jurist, Revolutionary patriot. Justice of state chancery court, 1784–93; senior chancellor, 1791–93.

HUTTON, EDWARD FRANCIS (*b. New York, N.Y., 1875; d. Westbury, N.Y., 1962*), stockbroker and business executive. In 1904 organized his own brokerage house, E. F. Hutton and Company; was senior partner until 1921 and then a special partner until his death. During the 1920's helped revitalize the Postum company and brought about the merger of fifteen food and grocery manufacturing companies that resulted in the General Foods Corporation (1929). At various times was chairman and director of Zonite Products and director of Chrysler, Manufacturers Trust, and Coca-Cola.

HUTTON, FREDERICK REMSEN (*b. New York, N.Y., 1853; d. New York, 1918*), engineer. Graduated Columbia, 1873; Columbia School of Mines, E.M., 1876; Ph.D., Columbia, 1881. Taught engineering at Columbia, 1877–1907; head of mechani-

cal engineering department, 1892–1907. Author of widely used textbooks in his field.

HUTTON, LAURENCE (*b. New York, N.Y., 1843; d. 1904*), editor, bibliophile, dramatic critic. Author of dramatic biographies and ephemeral essays on literature.

HUTTON, LEVI WILLIAM (*b. Batavia, Iowa, 1860; d. 1928*), mine operator, philanthropist. Early orphaned, Hutton went West *ca.* 1878 and made a fortune, *post* 1901, in Idaho mines and Spokane, Wash., real estate. Founded the Hutton Settlement for underprivileged children, 1917.

HUXLEY, ALDOUS LEONARD (*b. Laleham, Sussex, England, 1894; d. Los Angeles, Calif., 1963*), writer. Early novels such as *Crome Yellow* (1921) established him as the novelist who best expressed the disillusioned mood of the 1920's in England. Attempted to put forward a more optimistic and humanistic standpoint in the novel *Point Counter Point* (1928), but pessimism recurs in his best-known work, the futuristic novel *Brave New World* (1932). The publication of *Eyeless in Gaza* (1936) marked the beginning of his interest in religious mysticism. After moving to the United States in 1937, he preached the virtues of mysticism, pacifism, and the correct use of consciousness-enhancing drugs in such works as *After Many a Summer Dies the Swan* (1939), *Time Must Have a Stop* (1944), *The Doors of Perception* (1954), *Brave New World Revisited* (1958), and *Island* (1962).

HYATT, ALPHEUS (*b. Washington, D.C., 1838; d. 1902*), zoologist, palaeontologist, Union soldier. Influenced in his career by Louis Agassiz, S. H. Scudder, A. E. Verrill; graduated Harvard, B.S., 1862. In charge, *post* 1865, of fossil cephalopods at Museum of Comparative Zoology, Cambridge, Mass.; a great part of his research work was done in this collection. Assisted in founding Peabody Academy of Sciences and *American Naturalist*, of which he was an editor, 1867–71; associated in several capacities with Boston Society of Natural History, 1870–1902. Taught zoology and palaeontology at Massachusetts Institute of Technology and at Boston University; helped found marine biological laboratory at Woods Hole, Mass. Hyatt's main interest in all his work was based on his desire to discover the laws which governed the development of the individual and the evolution of groups. Among his many technical monographs were "Genesis of the Arietidae" (1889), dealing with cephalopods, and "Phylogeny of an Acquired Characteristic" (1894), which discussed stages in development and their controlling laws.

HYATT, JOHN WESLEY (*b. Starkey, N.Y., 1837; d. Short Hills, N.J., 1920*), inventor. After experimentation with nitrocellulose as a foundation for plastics, he discovered celluloid-molding process and designed special machinery for its manufacture (first patent, July 12, 1870). Also patented a process for filtration and purification of water, and in 1891–92 devised a widely used type of roller bearing. Among his other inventions were a sugar-cane mill, a multiple-stitch sewing machine, and a machine for cold rolling and straightening steel shafting.

HYDE, ARTHUR MASTICK (*b. Princeton, Mo., 1877; d. New York, N.Y., 1947*), lawyer, businessman, politician. B.A., University of Michigan, 1899; LL.B., State University of Iowa, 1900. Entered practice with his father in Princeton, Mo., and became a leader among rural Republicans and a strong supporter of prohibition. Elected governor of Missouri in 1920, he improved rural schools, increased distribution of technical information to farmers, and constructed more than 7,500 miles of highways. Removing to Kansas City, 1925, he continued to practice law and became head of the Sentinel Life Insurance Company in 1927. As U.S. secretary of agriculture, 1929–33, he was hampered by his conservative principles in dealing with depression problems. He vigorously opposed New Deal agricultural programs.

HYDE, CHARLES CHENEY (*b. Chicago, Ill., 1873; d. New York, N.Y., 1952*), international lawyer and teacher. Studied at Yale (M.A., 1898) and at Harvard (LL.B., 1898). Private practice as international lawyer in Chicago (1898–1920); unsalaried professor of law at Northwestern University (1899–1925). Admitted to the bar of the U.S. Supreme Court (1916). Solicitor to the Department of State (1923–25). From 1925 to 1945, professor at Columbia. In 1922, he completed his major work, *International Law, Chiefly as Interpreted and Applied by the United States.* Portions printed in 1918 were circulated as confidential documents at the Paris Peace Conference. The work was revised in 1945.

HYDE, EDWARD (*b. England, ca. 1650; d. North Carolina, 1712*), colonial official. Designated deputy governor of North Carolina, 1709; on arrival in Virginia, 1710, learned that Governor Tynte had died and assumed governorship. His action was approved by the Lords Proprietors, 1710, and by the Privy Council, 1711. He resolved political divisions in the colony and died while preparing to subdue an outbreak of the Tuscarora Indians.

HYDE, EDWARD. *See* CORNBURY, EDWARD HYDE, VISCOUNT.

HYDE, HELEN (*b. Lima, N.Y., 1868; d. Pasadena, Calif., 1919*), artist. Spent early life in California and lived many years in Japan. Worked as color etcher and was an American pioneer in making woodblock prints after Japanese manner.

HYDE, HENRY BALDWIN (*b. Catskill, N.Y., 1834; d. 1899*), founded, and was dominant personality in, the Equitable Life Assurance Society, 1859–99; served as president, *post* 1874.

HYDE, JAMES NEVINS (*b. Norwich, Conn., 1840; d. Prouts Neck, Maine, 1910*), physician, U.S. Navy surgeon. Graduated Yale, 1861; M.D., University of Pennsylvania, 1869. Pioneer specialist in dermatology; practiced in Chicago, Ill., and taught his speciality at Rush Medical College *post* 1873. Author of *Practical Treatise on Diseases of the Skin* (1883).

HYDE, WILLIAM DeWITT (*b. Winchendon, Mass., 1858; d. 1917*), Congregational clergyman, educator. Graduated Harvard 1879; Andover Theological Seminary, 1882. Professor of philosophy, Bowdoin; president of the college, 1885–1917.

HYER, ROBERT STEWART (*b. Oxford, Ga., 1860; d. 1929*), scientist. Graduated Emory College, 1881. Professor of science, Southwestern University (Georgetown, Texas), 1882–1911; president, 1898–1911. As first president, Southern Methodist University, 1911–20, Hyer planned the campus, supervised erection of buildings, and procured an endowment.

HYLAN, JOHN FRANCIS (*b. near Hunter, N.Y., 1868; d. Forest Hills, N.Y., 1936*), lawyer, politician. Democratic mayor of New York City, 1917–24; supported by William Randolph Hearst.

HYRNE, EDMUND MASSINGBERD (*b. South Carolina, 1748; d. St. Bartholomew's Parish, S.C., 1783*), Revolutionary soldier, distinguished in campaigns under Sumter and Greene.

HYSLOP, JAMES HERVEY (*b. Xenia, Ohio, 1854; d. Upper Montclair, N.J., 1920*), philosopher, psychologist, investigator of psychics phenomena.

HYVERNAT, HENRI (*b. St. Julien-en-Jarret, Loire, France, 1858; d. Washington, D.C., 1941*), Roman Catholic clergyman, orientalist. Studied for the priesthood at Sulpician seminaries in Issy and Paris, 1877–82, D.D., Pontifical University, Rome, 1882. Professor of Assyriology and Egyptology at the Roman Seminary, 1885–87. He joined the faculty of the new Catholic University of America as professor of Semitics, 1889; head of the department of Semitic and Egyptian languages and literatures, 1895–1941. A specialist in Coptic studies, he helped establish the *Corpus Scriptorum Christianorum Orientalium*, 1903.

I

IBERVILLE, PIERRE LE MOYNE, SIEUR D' (*b. Montreal, Canada, 1661; d. Havana, Cuba, 1706*), explorer, soldier. Brother of Jean, Sieur de Bienville. After a decade of service at sea with the French royal navy, Iberville returned to his native Canada and in 1686 joined in an expedition against the British trading posts in James Bay. He made further military expeditions to the north in 1689, 1691, 1694, and 1697; meanwhile he had gone as a volunteer on the French raid against Schenectady, N.Y., 1690, and led the successful attacks on Pemaquid and on Fort St. John's, Newfoundland, 1696. His broad vision of New France led him on to succeed where LaSalle had failed. In 1698 he founded a new colony, Louisiana, at the mouth of the Mississippi which Bienville supervised after his death from fever during a campaign against the West Indies. Iberville has been called "the first great Canadian."

ICKES, HAROLD LE CLAIR (*b. Frankstown Township, Pa., 1874; d. Washington, D.C., 1952*), journalist, attorney, cabinet officer, author. Graduated from University of Chicago, B.A., 1897; LL.D., 1907. Practiced law in Chicago, 1907–33. A Republican, he supported Franklin D. Roosevelt and was Secretary of the Interior, 1933–46. Headed Public Works Administration; described as a "builder to rival Cheops," he oversaw the expenditure of over $6 billion for such works as New York's Triborough Bridge and Lincoln Tunnel, Grand Coulee Dam, the overseas Key West highway, hundreds of schools, public buildings, sewer systems, and hospitals. Member of the NAACP. Resigned from the cabinet after a dispute with President Truman; he wrote a political column for the *New Republic* until his death.

IDDINGS, JOSEPH PAXON (*b. Baltimore, Md., 1857; d. Montgomery Co., Md., 1920*), geologist, petrologist. Graduated Sheffield Scientific School, Yale, 1877; served with U.S. Geological Survey in association with Arnold Hague, 1880–95. Made reputation in survey of Yellowstone National Park. A leader in American petrology, he taught that subject at University of Chicago, 1895–1908.

IDE, HENRY CLAY (*b. Barnet, Vt., 1844; d. St. Johnsbury, Vt., 1921*), lawyer, Vermont legislator, diplomat. Successful U.S. commissioner and chief justice in Samoa; member of Philippine Commission, 1900–06, in charge of finance and justice; governor general of Philippines, April to September, 1906. U.S. minister to Spain, 1909–13.

IDE, JOHN JAY (*b. Narragansett Pier, R.I., 1892; d. New York, N.Y., 1962*), aeronautical consultant and author. Studied at Columbia (Certificate of Architecture, 1913) and the École des Beaux Arts in Paris. After service in the navy, 1917–20, he became technical representative in Europe for the National Advisory Committee for Aeronautics (NACA), attached to the American embassy in Paris, and served as a bridge between the American and European aeronautical communities for nearly twenty years. Recalled to active duty with the navy (1940–46), he then returned to NACA as a technical representative and consultant. Published a number of articles on the history of architecture.

IGLESIAS, SANTIAGO (*b. La Coruña, Spain, 1872; d. Washington, D.C., 1939*), Puerto Rican labor leader and resident commissioner in Congress, 1933–39. Immigrated to Puerto Rico from Cuba, 1896. A Socialist, he worked closely with Samuel Gompers and the American Federation of Labor.

IK MARVEL. *See* MITCHELL, DONALD GRANT.

ILLINGTON, MARGARET (*b. Bloomington, Ill., 1879; d. Miami Beach, Fla., 1934*), actress. Wife of Daniel Frohman; after divorce, 1909, married Edward J. Bowes.

ILPENDAM, JAN JANSEN VAN. *See* VAN ILPENDAM, JAN JANSEN.

IMBER, NAPHTALI HERZ (*b. Zloczow, Polish Galicia, 1856; d. 1909*), Hebrew poet. Lived in the United States, 1892–1909, mainly on New York's East Side. Author, among other works, of the national anthem "Hatikvah."

IMBERT, ANTOINE (*b. Calais, France; d. New York, N.Y.[?], ca. 1835*), marine artist, lithographer. Came to America ca. 1824; established first New York lithographic establishment. Printer and publisher of A. J. Davis's "Views of Public Buildings, etc.," 1826–28, and of maps, caricatures and other works.

IMBODEN, JOHN DANIEL (*b. near Staunton, Va., 1823; d. Damascus, Va., 1895*), Confederate brigadier general. Played important part in first battle of Bull Run, 1861; conducted "Imboden Raid," 1863, securing cattle and horses for Gettysburg campaign; covered Confederate retreat from Gettysburg. After the war, encouraged development of Virginia resources by foreign and domestic capital.

IMLAY, GILBERT (*b. Monmouth Co., N.J., ca. 1754; d. probably on island of Jersey, Channel Islands, 1828*), adventurer, author. Speculated in Kentucky land, 1784–85; fled court jurisdiction to Europe. Published A *Topographical Description of the Western Territory of North America* in London, England, 1792; also a novel *The Emigrants* (1793). Plotted with Brissot's party in Paris to seize Spanish Louisiana. Was father, by Mary Wollstonecraft, of Fanny Imlay (born, 1794).

INGALLS, JOHN JAMES (*b. Middleton, Mass., 1833; d. Las Vegas, N.Mex., 1900*), lawyer, Kansas legislator. Graduated Williams, 1855. Removed to Kansas, 1858; became celebrated for denunciatory oratory. Not so much the controlling leader of the Republican party in Kansas as its figurehead, he served as U.S. senator, 1873–91.

INGALLS, MARILLA BAKER (*b. Greenfield Centre, N.Y., 1828; d. 1902*), Baptist missionary to Burma, 1851–56 and *post* 1858.

INGALLS, MELVILLE EZRA (*b. Harrison, Maine, 1842; d. Hot Springs, Va., 1914*), lawyer. As railroad executive, was associated with Vanderbilt interests; headed "Big Four" line, 1889–1905, and Chesapeake & Ohio, 1888–1900.

INGALS, EPHRAIM FLETCHER (*b. Lee Center, Ill., 1848; d. 1918*), physician, pioneer in bronchoscopy. Graduated Rush Medical College, 1871, and taught there for the remainder of his life; as comptroller *post* 1898, was largely responsible for affiliation of the college with the University of Chicago.

INGERSOLL, CHARLES JARED (*b. Philadelphia, Pa., 1782; d. 1862*), lawyer, Pennsylvania legislator and congressman, author. Son of Jared Ingersoll (1749–1822). In political life, he was a Democrat and champion of causes which were unpopular in his own environment; he strongly opposed extremists on both sides of the slavery controversy. His writings include a tragedy *Edwy and Elgiva* (produced at Philadelphia, 1801); an anti-British *View of the Rights and Wrongs, Power and Policy of the United States* (1808); *Inchiquin, the Jesuit's Letters* (1810), a declaration of our literary, social, and moral independence which was widely discussed; another play, *Julian: A Tragedy* (1831); and a history of the War of 1812.

INGERSOLL, EDWARD (*b. Philadelphia, Pa., 1817; d. Germantown, Pa., 1893*), lawyer, legal writer. Son of Charles J. Ingersoll.

INGERSOLL, JARED (*b. Milford, Conn., 1722; d. New Haven, Conn., 1781*), lawyer, public official, Loyalist. London agent for Connecticut, 1758–61 and 1764–65; opposed Stamp Act, but accepted post as stamp master for Connecticut from which he was compelled by force to resign; judge of vice-admiralty *post* 1768, he officiated at Philadelphia, 1771–75. Paroled at New Haven, 1777–81.

INGERSOLL, JARED (*b. New Haven, Conn., 1749; d. Philadelphia, Pa., 1822*), jurist. Son of Jared Ingersoll (1722–1781). Distinguished as a lawyer, he was of counsel in many of the the early leading cases before the U.S. Supreme Court; he was also a member of the Continental Congress and a delegate to the Federal Convention, 1787. The attorney general of Pennsylvania, 1790–99 and 1811–17, he held a number of other offices both in the state and in Philadelphia municipal government.

INGERSOLL, ROBERT GREEN (*b. Dresden, N.Y., 1833; d. Dobbs Ferry, N.Y., 1899*), lawyer, Union soldier, professional agnostic, and lecturer. Characterized James G. Blaine as the "plumed knight" in presidential nominating speech, 1876.

INGERSOLL, ROBERT HAWLEY (*b. Delta, Mich., 1859; d. Denver, Colo., 1928*), merchant, manufacturer. Introduced and promoted sale of the famous "dollar Ingersoll" watch.

INGERSOLL, ROYAL RODNEY (*b. Niles, Mich., 1847; d. La Porte, Ind., 1931*), naval officer. Graduated Annapolis, 1868. As ordnance specialist, took prominent part in reform of naval gunnery *post* 1900; was chief of staff to Admiral R. D. Evans in world cruise, 1907–08; retired as rear admiral, 1909.

INGERSOLL, SIMON (*b. Stanwich, Conn., 1818; d. 1894*), inventor. Patented the Ingersoll rock drill, 1871, and various improvements to it, 1873–93; sold his rights for a nominal sum.

INGHAM, CHARLES CROMWELL (*b. Dublin, Ireland 1796; d. New York, N.Y., 1863*), portrait painter, miniaturist. Worked in New York City, 1816–63; his work was rich in coloring, weak in line.

INGHAM, SAMUEL DELUCENNA (*b. near New Hope, Pa., 1779; d. Trenton, N.J., 1860*), paper manufacturer, politician. Democratic congressman from Pennsylvania, 1813–18 and 1823–29; U.S. secretary of the treasury, 1829–31. Resigned in the controversy over Mrs. John H. (Peggy O'Neale) Eaton. Later, helped develop Pennsylvania anthracite fields.

INGLE, RICHARD (*b. England, 1609; d. post 1653*), rebel, pirate. Came first to the colonies as a tobacco merchant *ca.* 1631; appeared in Maryland as master of ship *Eleanor*, March 1641/42. He was arrested and his ship *Reformation* seized on warrant of high treason, January 1643/44, but Maryland juries refused to convict. Under Parliamentary letters-of-marque, Ingle raided Maryland early in 1644/45, compelling Governor Calvert to flee into Virginia; professing to act as protector of Protestant rights, he pillaged the province before returning to England.

INGLIS, ALEXANDER JAMES (*b. Middletown, Conn., 1879; d. 1924*), educator. Graduated Wesleyan University, 1902; Ph.D., Teachers College, Columbia, 1911. Professor of education at Rutgers and Harvard; made important surveys of the educational systems of South Dakota, Washington, Indiana, and Virginia.

INGLIS, CHARLES (*b. Donegal, Ireland, 1734; d. Halifax, Canada, 1816*), Anglican clergyman, Loyalist. Came to America *ca.* 1755, as a teacher; was ordained in London, England, 1758, and returned to serve as missionary in Dover, Del., 1759–65. As assistant to the rector of Trinity Church, New York City, 1765–77, Inglis worked with Rev. Thomas B. Chandler for establishment of an American episcopate. After the outbreak of Revolution, he answered Paine's *Common Sense* with *The True Interest of America Impartially Stated* (1776). Succeeding Rev. Samuel Auchmuty as rector of Trinity, 1777, he continued to write against the American cause over the pen-name "Papinian." He departed for England, 1783, and was consecrated first bishop of Nova Scotia, 1787.

INGRAHAM, DUNCAN NATHANIEL (*b. Charleston, S.C., 1802; d. Charleston, 1891*), naval officer. Nephew of Joseph Ingraham. Compelled release of Koszta at Smyrna, 1853; served in Confederate Navy, 1861–65.

INGRAHAM, EDWARD DUFFIELD (*b. Philadelphia, Pa., 1793; d. Philadelphia, 1854*), lawyer, legal writer and editor.

INGRAHAM, JOSEPH (*b. Boston, Mass., 1762; d. at sea, 1800*), navigator, Northwest Coast trader. Mate under Capt. John Kendrick and Capt. Robert Gray on the *Columbia*, 1787–90; as captain of the *Hope*, 1791–93, discovered the Washington Islands in the Marquesas; lost on the USS *Pickering*.

INGRAHAM, JOSEPH HOLT (*b. Portland, Maine, 1809; d. Holly Springs, Miss., 1860*), Episcopal clergyman, author. A writer of many blood-and-thunder novels, among which *Lafitte* (1836) may be singled out, Ingraham also produced an interesting regional study, *The South-West, by a Yankee* (1835), and three religious romances which enjoyed great popularity. These were *The Prince of the House of David* (1855); *The Pillar of Fire* (1859); *The Throne of David* (1860).

INGRAHAM, PRENTISS (*b. Adams Co., Miss., 1843; d. 1904*), Confederate soldier of fortune. Son of Joseph H. Ingraham. After an adventurous life, became one of the most prolific writers for Beadle's dime-novel factory; principally remembered as the friend and literary celebrant of Buffalo Bill (William F. Cody).

INGRAM, JONAS HOWARD (*b. Jeffersonville, Ind., 1886; d. San Diego, Calif., 1952*), naval officer. Graduated from the U.S. Naval Academy, 1907. Commander of the South Atlantic Force, U.S. Atlantic Fleet during World War II; instrumental in winning Brazil over to the side of the U.S. during the war. Appointed commander in chief of the Atlantic Fleet, 1944. Retired as full admiral in 1947. Commissioner of the All-American Football

Conference, 1947–49; vice president of the Reynolds Metals Company.

INMAN, GEORGE (*b. Boston, Mass., 1755; d. St. George, Grenada, British West Indies, 1789*), Loyalist, British soldier.

INMAN, HENRY (*b. Utica, N.Y., 1801; d. 1846*), portrait, landscape and genre painter. Brother of John Inman. Apprentice and assistant to John Wesley Jarvis. Except for Gilbert Stuart, few American portraitists have had a more distinguished list of sitters than Inman. He died as he was at work on the first of a series of historical paintings for the Capitol, Washington, D.C. Facile in exact drawing, Inman's work was likened to that of Sir Thomas Lawrence, but it is often commonplace and at times meretricious.

INMAN, HENRY (*b. New York, N.Y., 1837; d. Topeka, Kans., 1899*), Union soldier, journalist. Son of Henry Inman (1801–1846). Author of *The Old Santa Fe Trail* (1897) and other books of frontier adventure.

INMAN, JOHN (*b. Utica, N.Y., 1805; d. 1850*), journalist. Brother of Henry Inman (1801–1846). An editor of Morris's *New York Mirror*, of the New York *Commercial Advertiser* and other newspapers and periodicals; associate of the Knickerbocker group of writers.

INMAN, JOHN HAMILTON (*b. Dandridge, Tenn., 1844; d. New Canaan, Conn., 1896*), cotton merchant, financier. Brother of Samuel M. Inman. Promoted Southern industrial development, notably railroads, through provision of Northern capital.

INMAN, SAMUEL MARTIN (*b. Jefferson Co., Tenn., 1843; d. Atlanta, Ga., 1915*), cotton merchant, financier, philanthropist. Brother of John H. Inman. An organizer and director of the Southern Railway system. Benefactor of Georgia School of Technology and many other educational institutions.

INNES, HARRY (*b. Caroline Co., Va., 1752 o.s.; d. 1816*), lawyer. Brother of James Innes. Removed to Kentucky, 1785; served as U.S. district judge, Kentucky, 1789–1816. Threatened with impeachment for possible implication in schemes of Aaron Burr, James Wilkinson, and Benjamin Sebastian, 1806.

INNES, JAMES (*b. Caroline Co., Va., 1754; d. Philadelphia, Pa., 1798*), lawyer, orator, Revolutionary solder, Virginia legislator. Considered equal of Patrick Henry in addressing popular groups, he served as Virginia attorney general *post* 1786 and was also a Jay Treaty commissioner.

INNESS, GEORGE (*b. Newburgh, N.Y., 1825; d. Bridge of Allan, Scotland, 1894*), landscape painter. Pupil of Régis Gignoux in New York City; set up his own studio, 1845; spent a year in Italy, 1847–48, and made numerous trips abroad thereafter. Strongly influenced by Rousseau, Corot, and Daubigny. Beginning as a follower of the scenic and literal "Hudson River" school, his style underwent a steady development in direction of lyricism and individuality through Barbizon influence and his own recognition of the value of suggestion in portraying nature. In his later work the poetic intensity of his temperament dominated; by common consent he came to occupy first place among American landscapists. His best work has a power and charm which defy analysis.

INNOKENTĬĬ *b. near Irkutsk, Siberia, 1797; d. 1879*), Alaska pioneer and missionary, Russian Orthodox monk and bishop. In secular life, Ioann Evsieevich Popov-Veniamïnov, he took his name in religion when he became a monk, 1839. Previously he had served as pastor at Unalaska and Sitka, 1823–38, making valuable scientific and linguistic studies as well. Returning to Alaska, 1841, as bishop of Kamchatka and the Kurile and Aleutian islands, he was raised to archbishop, 1850; *post* 1853, his work

centered more on the mainland in the Amur River region, and in 1868 he was called to Moscow to receive appointment as metropolitan.

INSHTATHEAMBA.   *See* BRIGHT EYES.

INSKIP, JOHN SWANNEL (*b. Huntington, England, 1816; d. Ocean Grove, N.J., 1884*), Methodist clergyman. Came to America as a child. Served in Philadelphia, Ohio and New York conferences. A leader in the "holiness movement" and promoter of camp-meetings *post* 1864.

INSULL, SAMUEL (*b. London, England, 1859; d. Paris, France, 1938*), public utility magnate. Became Thomas A. Edison's private secretary on coming to America, 1881; advanced to presidency of Chicago Edison Co., 1892. Initiated many new techniques and concepts which became basic economic principles of the electric power industry. By 1907 Chicago's electricity was entirely Insull-operated; soon thereafter he pioneered in unified rural electrification. In the 1920's Insull turned to large-scale public financing of his utilities holdings, which included gas and traction interests. He became overextended financially and the Insull empire collapsed in 1932. His receivership became a political issue and he fled to Europe. On return to America, he was tried on mail fraud, bankruptcy, and embezzlement charges, and acquitted.

ĬOASAF, JAN (*b. Strazhkovo, Russia, 1761; d. at sea between Unalaska and Kodiak, 1799*), Alaska pioneer and missionary, Russian Orthodox monk and bishop. In secular life, Ivan Ilyich Bolotov. First Russian missionary to Aleutians and Alaska, serving at Kodiak, 1794–*ca.* 1797; consecrated bishop of Kodiak at Irkutsk, Siberia, 1799, he died returning to his diocese.

IOOR, WILLIAM (*b. St. George's Parish, S.C.; fl. 1780–1830*), playwright. Author of *Independence* (first performed Charleston, S.C., 1805, published 1805); *The Battle of Eutaw Springs* (published 1807, first recorded production at Philadelphia, Pa., 1813). These were early examples of the American comedy of manners and of patriotic drama.

IREDELL, JAMES (*b. Lewes, England, 1751; d. Edenton, N.C., 1799*), jurist, statesman. Comptroller of customs at Edenton, 1768–74; collector of the port, 1774–76. Active in the Revolutionary cause. Served also as a state attorney general, 1779–81, and collected and revised all state acts in force (revisal issued, 1791). A strong partisan of the new federal constitution, he issued over signature "Marcus" in 1788 his *Answers to Mr. Mason's Objections to the New Constitution*, and was floor leader of the Federalists in the North Carolina ratifying convention. Associate justice of the U.S. Supreme Court, 1790–99, he had no superior on that bench as a constitutional lawyer. His most notable opinions were given in *Calder* v. *Bull* (that a legislative act unauthorized by, or in violation of, the Constitution was void) and in *Chisholm* v. *Georgia* (an enunciation of all the leading principles of state-rights doctrine).

IRELAND, JOHN (*b. near Millerstown, Ky., 1827; d. Seguin, Tex., 1896*), lawyer, Confederate soldier, Texas legislator. Removed to Texas, 1853. Democratic governor of Texas, 1883–87.

IRELAND, JOHN (*b. Burnchurch, Ireland, 1838; d. St. Paul, Minn., 1918*), Roman Catholic clergyman. Came to America, 1849, settling with his family in St. Paul, Minn., 1853. Graduated Séminaire de Meximieux, France, and the Scholasticat à Montbel; ordained T. Paul, 1861. Chaplain, 5th Minnesota Volunteers, 1862–63. Made pastor, St. Paul Cathedral, 1867; consecrated coadjutor-bishop of St. Paul, 1875; succeeded to the see, 1884, and was named archbishop, 1888. Waged war against

political corruption and the liquor interests; organized total abstinence societies; participated actively in civic affairs. Was an
advocate of Western settlement by immigrants and encouraged
them to move out of the slums of Eastern cities through his
Catholic Colonization Bureau. Strongly supported Catholic University, Washington, D.C.; opposed retention of native languages
by immigrants, notably the Germans, and any appointment of
bishops on racial grounds as attempts to foster foreignism in the
United States for European political reasons. With Cardinal
Gibbons and others, defended right of labor to organize, yet
insisted on labor's recognition of its obligations as well. Projected
Faribault plan of parochial school support, 1891. Maintained a
strong liberal attitude in task of reconciling the spirit of the age with
religion. A Republican in politics, he was an adviser and friend of
Presidents McKinley and Theodore Roosevelt.

IRELAND, JOSEPH NORTON (*b. New York, N.Y., 1817; d.
Bridgeport, Conn., 1898*), businessman. Author of *Records of the
New York Stage: 1750–1860* (1866–67), a valuable work of
research.

IRENE, SISTER (*b. London, England, 1823; d. 1896*), Sister of
Charity, philanthropist. In secular life, Catherine Fitzgibbon.
Came to America as a child; entered Roman Catholic community
of Sisters of Charity, 1850. First directress, New York Foundling
Hospital, 1869–96, and an innovator in methods of foundling
care.

IRONSIDE, HENRY ALLAN (*b. Toronto, Canada, 1876; d.
Rotu Rua, New Zealand, 1951* evangelist. Worked for the
Salvation Army in Southern California, before joining the Open
Brethren, a fundamentalist group. Visiting lecturer at the Dallas
Theological Seminary, 1925–43; pastor of the Moody Memorial
Church in Chicago, 1930–48. Often called the "archbishop of
fundamentalism," Ironside traveled extensively, preaching and
spreading his fundamentalist creed.

IRVINE, JAMES (*b. Philadelphia, Pa., 1735; d. Philadelphia,
1819*), Revolutionary soldier, Pennsylvania legislator.

IRVINE, WILLIAM (*b. near Enniskillen, Ireland, 1741; d. Philadelphia, Pa., 1804*), surgeon, Revolutionary brigadier general.
Practiced medicine *post* 1764 at Carlisle, Pa.; served in Continental Army, 1776–83. Advised purchase by Pennsylvania of the
"triangle" tract which gave the state an outlet to Lake Erie; served
in both Continental and federal congresses; active as an arbitrator
and as commander of state troops in quelling Whiskey Rebellion,
1794.

IRVINE, WILLIAM MANN (*b. Bedford, Pa., 1865; d. 1928*),
educator. Graduated Princeton, A.B., 1888; Ph.D. 1891.
Headmaster, Mercersburg Academy, 1893–1928.

IRVING, JOHN BEAUFAIN (*b. Charleston, S.C., 1825; d.
1877*), portrait, genre and historical painter. Pupil of Leutze at
Düsseldorf; strongly influenced by work of Meissonier; worked in
New York City after the Civil War.

IRVING, JOHN DUER (*b. Madison, Wis., 1874; d. 1918*),
mining geologist. Son of Roland D. Irving. Graduated Columbia,
A.B., 1896; Ph.D., 1899. Worked with U.S. Geological Survey,
1899–1907, mainly in South Dakota and Colorado; taught at
Wyoming, Lehigh, and Yale universities; died in service during
World War I.

IRVING, JOHN TREAT (*b. New York, N.Y., 1812; d. 1906*),
lawyer, author. Nephew of Washington Irving.

IRVING, PETER (*b. New York, N.Y., 1772; d. 1838*), physician, journalist. Brother of Washington Irving and William

Irving; an important formative influence on Washington Irving.
Owner-editor, New York *Morning Chronicle*, 1802; also *The
Corrector*, 1804. Lived abroad, 1809–36, and served his famous
younger brother as companion and adviser during European
sojourns.

IRVING, PIERRE MUNRO (*b. New York, N.Y., 1803; d.
1876*), lawyer. Son of William Irving; nephew and biographer of
Washington Irving. Assisted his uncle in collecting materials for
Astoria (1836) and managed his financial and literary affairs *post*
1846.

IRVING, ROLAND DUER (*b. New York, N.Y., 1847; d. 1888*),
geologist, mining engineer. Grandson of John Duer; related on
father's side to Washington Irving. Graduated Columbia, School
of Mines, 1869. Taught geology at University of Wisconsin *post*
1870, made important surveys of iron- and copper-bearing rocks,
Lake Superior region; was an American pioneer in genetic petro-
graphy.

IRVING, WASHINGTON (*b. New York, N.Y., 1783; d. Tarrytown, N.Y., 1859*), author. Brother of Peter and William
Irving. Superficially educated in various New York City schools,
but quick to observe and learn and precocious in sensibility. Irving
studied drawing with Archibald Robertson. As a youth he stole
away from the Scottish Covenanting atmosphere of his home to
attend secretly the little theater in John Street. In 1798 he entered
the law office of Henry Masterson, but he soon wearied of the law.
After leaving the law office he wrote for his brother Peter's
newspapers (contributing *The Letters of Jonathan Oldstyle to the
Morning Chronicle*, went in society, and traveled. His health
beginning to fail, he toured France and Italy (May 1804–March
1806), returning home with restored health and a series of notes of
backgrounds, observations, and anecdotes. In 1807–08, he was a
moving spirit in the publication of *Salmagundi*, a whimsical
periodical miscellany of essays, fables, and verse which commented on life in New York and in which he was associated with
his brother William and James Kirke Paulding. While engaged on
the first of his books to bring him fame, the comic *A History of New
York* (1809), allegedly by Diedrich Knickerbocker, Irving suffered
the loss of his betrothed, Matilda Hoffman. Thereafter, for six
years he was restless, engaging in hackwork, dabbling in politics,
and serving briefly as aide-de-camp to Governor Daniel Tompkins
of New York.

From 1815 to 1832, Irving was in Europe. At first in Liverpool,
England, and until 1818 assisting in the English branch of his
brothers' business, he realized the romantic dreams of his boyhood
in the English landscape, English houses, and the English way of
life; a visit to Sir Walter Scott at Abbotsford, 1817, stimulated his
desire to write, fixed in him a predilection for legendary themes,
and introduced him to German literature. Compelled to earn his
own living by the failure of his brothers' firm, 1818, he composed
the essays and tales of *The Sketch Book*, publishing them in New
York in part-issues (1819, 1820) and in London collectively
(1820). Success was immediate in both countries. Irving, under
his pen name "Geoffrey Crayon," found himself a distinguished
and sought-after man of letters, admired for his style and for the
apparent originality of such stories as "Rip Van Winkle" and "The
Legend of Sleepy Hollow." *Bracebridge Hall* (1822) increased his
reputation, even if its sketches pictured an English way of life that
had no existence save in the author's romantic imagination. He
spent the period between July 1822 and August 1823 in a pleasant
but unfruitful tour of Germany; the succeeding nine months he
spent in Paris. After the failure of his *Tales of a Traveller* (1824), he
made a further sojourn in France while he sought vainly for a
means of retrieving his literary reputation and his financial
stability. Early in 1826, he went to Madrid, Spain, as attaché in

the U.S. embassy with the purpose of translating the collection of scholarly documents on the life of Christopher Columbus gathered and published by Don Martín Fernández de Navarrete. Skillfully adapting these materials, he produced his charming and popular *History of the Life and Voyages of Christopher Columbus* (1828); meanwhile, fascinated by the country and its history, he made notes for his *Chronicle of the Conquest of Granada* (1829) and *The Alhambra* (1832). Between 1829 and 1832, he served as secretary of the U.S. legation in London.

On his return to his native land, he was greeted as the supreme figure in American letters, went much in society, established himself in his "Sunnyside" home near Tarrytown, N.Y., but found himself restless. Profiting by current literary fashion, he produced a series *The Crayon Miscellany* (*A Tour on the Prairies*; *Abbotsford ad Newstead Abbey*; *Legends of the Conquest of Spain*; all 1835). *Astoria* (1836) and *The Adventures of Captain Bonneville* (1837) were written from materials furnished by John J. Astor and from Bonneville's papers; they were frankly hackwork. His readjustment to American life was imperfect and he welcomed his appointment, 1842, as U.S. minister to Spain. After four years of competent service in the troubled Spain of the Regency, he returned to quiet "Sunnyside," there to end his career with the issue of the pleasant but tame *Oliver Goldsmith* (1849), *Mahomet and His Successors* (1849–50), *Wolfert's Roost* (1855), and a five-volume life of George Washington which he had conceived of in 1825 and whose last volume appeared in the year of his death. His life and career were notable for a marked, if limited, literary talent and the coincidence of that talent with the formative years of American letters.

IRVING, WILLIAM (*b. New York, N.Y., 1766; d. 1821*), poet, merchant, politician. Patron of his brother Washington Irving. Contributed verse to *Salmagundi*, 1807–08. Congressman, Democrat, from New York, 1814–19.

IRWIN, ELISABETH ANTOINETTE (*b. Brooklyn, N.Y., 1880; d. New York, N.Y., 1942*), educator. A.B., Smith College, 1903; M.A., Columbia University, 1923. After several years in settlement house work, she joined the staff of the Public Education Association of New York City, which was working to establish progressive education as an agency of social reform. Between 1910 and 1922, she was engaged in projects for testing, classifying, and instructing public school children on the basis of I.Q. tests. In 1922, she began an experiment in revising the public school curriculum and teaching methods on the assumption that the social and emotional adjustment of children was the overriding concern and that intellectual development and the learning of basic skills could be taken for granted. Her school, nicknamed the "Little Red School House," was a widely heralded example of progressive education. When the city withdrew its support, in 1932 she continued it as a private school, adding a high school department in 1941.

IRWIN, GEORGE LE ROY (*b. Fort Wayne, Mich., 1868; d. off Port of Spain, Trinidad, 1931*), soldier. Graduated West Point, 1889. Served in Philippines, Cuba, and Mexico; identified with use and development of modern field artillery. Particularly distinguished in France, 1918, commanding the 57th F.A. Brigade; promoted to major general, 1928.

IRWIN, MAY (*b. Whitby, Canada, 1862; d. New York, N.Y., 1938*), actress and music-hall entertainer, popularizer of many ragtime songs. Real name, Ada Campbell. Appeared in one of earliest motion pictures, a close-up filmed for Edison's Vitascope, 1895.

IRWIN, ROBERT BENJAMIN (*b. Rockford, Iowa, 1883; d. Port Orchard, Wash., 1951*), educator. Studied at the University of Washington and at Harvard, M.A., 1907. Totally blind from the age of five, Irwin was the nation's leading educator of the visually handicapped. In 1909, he became superintendent of public school classes for the blind in Cleveland, Ohio; president of the American Association of Workers for the Blind 1923–27; executive director, American Foundation for the Blind from 1929 until his retirement. Founded the Howe Publishing Co. which produced books in Braille, and was responsible for many federal laws aiding the blind. Executive director of the American Foundation for Overseas Blind, 1946. Awarded the Legion of Honor, 1947, for his work with the blind in Europe.

IRWIN, WILLIAM HENRY (*b. Oneida, N.Y., 1873; d. New York, N.Y., 1948*), journalist, author. Known as Will Irwin. Raised in Colorado; Stanford University, 1899. On staff of *The Wave*, a literary weekly in San Francisco, 1899–1900; staff of the *San Francisco Chronicle*, 1901–04. Removing to New York City, 1904, he joined the *New York Sun*, for which he performed his most remarkable journalistic feat, writing column after column on the San Francisco earthquake by filling out the few facts as they became available with data drawn from his own intimate knowledge of that city. He received national attention for his *The City That Was*. Managing editor of *McClure's* magazine, 1906–07, he left to write for *Collier's*, where he produced the muckraking series "The Power of the Press." He was an outstanding battlefront correspondent during World War I. He also wrote fiction, popular biographies, and political and social commentary, and was coauthor of two plays, *The 13th Chair* and *The Lute Song*.

ISAACS, ABRAM SAMUEL (*b. New York, N.Y., 1851; d. Paterson, N.J., 1920*), educator, editor. Son of Samuel M. Isaacs. Graduated New York University, 1871; Ph.D., 1878, after studies at Breslau. Editor, N.Y., *Jewish Messenger*, 1878–1903. Professor of Hebrew and German, New York University.

ISAACS, SAMUEL MYER (*b. Leeuwarden, Netherlands, 1804; d. 1878*), rabbi. Educated in England; came to New York City, 1839, where he held a pastorate until his death and was renowned as an orthodox teacher. Founder and editor, *Jewish Messenger* 1857–78.

ISBRANDSTEN, HANS JEPPESEN (*b. Drago, Denmark, 1891; d. Wake Island, 1953*), shipping executive. Immigrated to the U.S. in 1914. With Danish shipowner Arnold Maersk, founded the Isbrandtsen-Moller Co. in 1929. An independent shipowner, Isbrandtsen was often in conflict with the Federal Maritime Commission and the shipping authorities of various nations. After World War II, founded Isbrandtsen Lines, which grew to fifteen owned ships and thirty to fifty chartered vessels. The line was taken over by Isbrandtsen's son Jacob in 1953 and subsequently failed.

ISHAM, RALPH HEYWARD (*b. New York, N.Y., 1890; d. New York, N.Y., 1955*), manuscript collector. Studied at Cornell and Yale. Collector of the papers of Boswell, Isham published an eighteen-volume edition of the manuscripts, 1928–34. His entire collection was bought by Yale University in 1949.

ISHAM, SAMUEL (*b. New York, N.Y., 1855; d. Easthampton, N.Y., 1914*), landscape, figure, and genre painter. Author of authoritative *History of American Painting* (1905).

ISHERWOOD, BENJAMIN FRANKLIN (*b. New York, N.Y., 1822; d. New York, 1915*), mechanical engineer, naval architect. Entered Engineer Corps, U.S. Navy, 1844; promoted chief engineer, 1848. Published *Engineering Precedents* (1859), the first systematic attempt to ascertain distribution of energy and losses in steam engines and boilers by actual measurements under operating conditions; author also of *Experimental Researches in Steam*

Engineering (1863, 1865) which became a standard text and a new basis for further experimental research. Isherwood was first chief, Navy Bureau of Steam Engineering, 1862–70, and responsible for design and construction of propulsion machinery for the expanded Civil War Navy. He retired as chief engineer (commodore), 1884.

ISOM, MARY FRANCES (*b. Nashville, Tenn., 1865; d. 1920*), librarian. Made Portland, Oreg., Public Library an important community institution; established libraries in camps and war hospitals, 1917–18.

IVERSON, ALFRED (*b. probably Liberty Co., Ga., 1798; d. Macon, Ga., 1873*), lawyer, Georgia legislator, and jurist. As U.S. senator, Democrat, 1855–61, represented a radical position on Southern rights and was an early advocate of secession.

IVES, CHARLES EDWARD (*b. Danbury, Conn., 1874; d. New York, N.Y., 1954*), composer. Studied composition at Yale with Horatio Parker. Founded Ives and Myrick, an insurance firm, in 1909 and headed it until 1930. He composed prolifically until 1918, when he suffered a heart attack and contracted diabetes.

Won the Pulitzer Prize for his Third Symphony, 1947. Ives' music absorbed the patriotic songs, church hymns, popular ballads, and folk songs of his immediate surroundings; and his style embraced polytonality and atonality years before they became fashionable.

Major compositions include *The Unanswered Question* (1908), *Tone Roads, Three Places in New England* (1903–14), the piano sonata *Concord* (1900–15), and many songs.

IVES, CHAUNCEY BRADLEY (*b. Hamden, Conn., 1810; d. Rome, Italy, 1894*), sculptor.

IVES, ELI (*b. New Haven, Conn., 1778; d. 1861*), physician. Graduated Yale, 1799. Influential in establishing the medical school at Yale, he taught materia medica and botany there, 1813–29, 1852–61. He was professor of medical practice, 1829–52.

IVES, FREDERIC EUGENE (*b. near Lichfield, Conn., 1856; d. Philadelphia, Pa., 1937*), inventor. Devised (1885) the crossline-screen halftone process for photoengraving, which, with later technical improvements, came into general use. Ives also invented the modern short-tube binocular microscope, the parallax stereogram, and many processes relating to three-color printing and color photography.

IVES, HALSEY COOLEY (*b. Montour Falls, N.Y., 1847; d. London, England, 1911*), artist, teacher, art museum administrator. Began in 1874, at St. Louis, Mo., a free drawing class which developed into the St. Louis Museum and School of Fine Arts; headed art department at Chicago (1893) and St. Louis (1904) world's fairs.

IVES, IRVING MCNEIL (*b. Bainbridge, N.Y., 1896; d. Norwich, N.Y., 1962*), U.S. senator. Studied at Hamilton College (B.A., 1920), and then served eight terms as a Republican in the New York Assembly, 1930–45. Was dean of the New York State School of Industrial and Labor Relations at Cornell, and in 1946 was elected to the first of two terms in the U.S. Senate. Helped establish the Senate Select Committee on Improper Activities in the Labor or Management Field, and served as its vice-chairman.

IVES, JAMES MERRITT (*b. New York, N.Y., 1824; d. 1895*), partner of Nathaniel Currier in Currier & Ives, lithographers of popular prints; directed the firm's art staff.

IVES, JOSEPH CHRISTMAS (*b. New York, N.Y., 1828; d. New York, 1868*), explorer, soldier. Graduated West Point, 1852. Assistant to A. W. Whipple in Pacific Railroad survey, 1853–54; commanded exploration of Colorado River, 1857–58, of which his report is a classic of description. He served the Confederate Army as engineer and presidential aide-de-camp.

IVES, LEVI SILLIMAN (*b. Meriden, Conn., 1797; d. 1867*), Episcopal bishop of North Carolina, 1831–52. Influenced by Oxford Movement, he resigned his see and became a Catholic, serving thereafter as teacher at Fordham and other Catholic institutions.

IVINS, ANTHONY WOODWARD (*b. Toms River, N.J., 1852; d. Utah, 1934*), Mormon leader.

IVINS, WILLIAM MILLS (*b. Freehold, N.J., 1851; d. 1915*), lawyer, political reformer. In practice in New York City *post* 1873, he fought for election law and municipal government reform, also for effective control of public utilities.

IZARD, GEORGE (*b. near London, England, 1776; d. Arkansas, 1828*), soldier. Son of Ralph Izard. Educated in military schools in England, Germany, and France; entered U.S. Army *ca.* 1797. Senior American general, Canadian border, 1814; resigned over interference from War Department. Territorial governor of Arkansas, 1825–28.

IZARD, RALPH (*b. near Charleston, S.C., 1741/42; d. near Charleston, 1804*), rice and indigo planter, Revolutionary patriot, diplomat. Grandson of Robert Johnson. Resided in London, 1771–76; after outbreak of Revolution, moved to Paris and was appointed U.S. commissioner to Tuscany. Insisting on his equal status with other American representatives in France, he was repeatedly checked by Franklin, but was friendly with Arthur Lee. Recalled, 1779, he persuaded Washington to put General Greene in command of Southern Army. A strong Federalist, he supported the new Constitution; he was U.S. senator, from South Carolina, 1789–95.

J

JACK, CAPTAIN. *See* CAPTAIN JACK.

JACKLING, DANIEL COWAN (*b. near Appleton, Mo., 1869; d. Woodside, Calif., 1956*), mining engineer, industrialist. Studied at the Missouri School of Mines. The inventor of a process for the mass-production recovery of low-grade porphyry copper, Jackling helped to found the Utah Copper Co. in 1903; he built this concern into a mining empire that included branches in Montana, Nevada, Arizona, and New Mexico. He also built several supporting railroads for his mines. After becoming president of Kennecott Copper, he expanded his operations to include banking and oil. Jackling was also a director of Chase National Bank of New York and of Sinclair Consolidated Oil.

JACKMAN, WILBUR SAMUEL (*b. Mechanicstown, Ohio, 1855; d. 1907*), educator. Graduated Harvard, 1884. Pioneer teacher of nature studies in elementary schools; advocate of reform in teaching methods; dean, College of Education, University of Chicago, 1901–04.

JACKSON, ABRAHAM REEVES (*b. Philadelphia, Pa., 1827; d. 1892*), physician, pioneer gynecologist, Union surgeon. Practiced in Chicago, Ill., *post* 1870. Founder and surgeon in chief, Woman's Hospital of Illinois. Immortalized by Mark Twain as witty doctor in *Innocents Abroad*.

JACKSON, ABRAHAM VALENTINE WILLIAMS (*b. New York, N.Y., 1862; d. New York, 1937*), orientalist, philologist. Graduated Columbia, 1883; Ph.D., 1886; studied also in Germany. Taught at Columbia, 1886–1937. Specialist in Indo-Iranian languages and literature.

JACKSON, ANDREW (*b. Waxhaw Settlement, S.C., 1767; d. "The Hermitage," Nashville, Tenn., 1845*), soldier, seventh president of the United States. His father, an emigrant from the north of Ireland in 1765, died shortly before Andrew's birth. His brother Hugh was killed in 1779; he and his brother Robert took part in the battle of Hanging Rock, were taken by the British, and suffered smallpox in prison from which Robert died. The death of his mother, 1781, left him alone in the world. He began to study law at Salisbury, N.C., but devoted more time to horse racing and carousing with his friend John McNairy than to Blackstone. In 1788 he and McNairy removed to Jonesboro, Tenn.; they settled in Nashville, then a stockaded log village, late in the fall. Jackson's landlady, the widow of Col. John Donelson, had a daughter Rachel who had made an unfortunate marriage. After her divorce, Jackson married her; a technical flaw in their marriage led to a long-lived scandal.

Jackson soon became prosecutor for the district (then still part of North Carolina); on erection of the territorial government, his appointment was renewed in 1791. Among other land speculations in which he engaged at the time, he bought the Hermitage tract which was thereafter his home. In 1796 he was delegate to the convention which framed Tennessee's first constitution and was elected representative in Congress; he owed his rise to the favor of Sen. William Blount. On Blount's expulsion, 1797, Jackson secured a place in the U.S. Senate, but resigned it in April 1798 and was elected a superior judge of Tennessee. He became major general of Tennessee militia, 1802, thus provoking the enmity of John Sevier. Jackson resigned from the bench, 1804, and lived the life of a planter until the War of 1812, when, given command of the Tennessee militia expedition against the Creek Indians, he defeated them at Horseshoe Bend, 1814. Commissioned major general, U.S. Army, he defended New Orleans against the British, defeating the invaders Jan. 8, 1815, and becoming a national figure. Tall, slender, narrowfaced, kind to friends and implacable to enemies, he was able, when he chose, to restrain his high temper or play it up for the sake of effect. Although he denied he sought office, it was clear that he was a presidential possibility. His chances were somewhat dashed by his rash invasion of Spanish Florida, 1818, and his hanging of two British subjects for inciting Indian hostility on the border. After the excitement died down and Florida had been acquired by the United States, Jackson served as its first territorial governor for six months in 1821.

The Panic of 1819 had left hordes of debtors in the West and state banks whose paper money issues were to assist the needy had been established. Jackson opposed the bank in Tennessee, aligning himself with the conservatives even though the great popular movement which bears his name was already getting under way. Thanks to a committee including William B. Lewis, John H. Eaton, and John Overton, Jackson's nomination for the presidency was moved by the Tennessee legislature in 1822. A wave of revulsion against the older school of politicians was rising all through the country; in consequence, at the 1824 election, Jackson received the highest popular vote against Henry Clay, John Q. Adams, and W. H. Crawford. However, a majority electoral vote was lacking; the election being thrown into the House of Representatives, Clay's admirers supported Adams, who became president. Sending up a cry of "corrupt bargain," Jackson's friends campaigned in a crusading spirit, issuing no program, asserting no principles, their sole aim the vindication of "Old Hickory." In 1828, supported by Martin Van Buren of New York and by the followers of Crawford in Virginia and Georgia, Jackson swept to victory; John C. Calhoun was elected vice president. For the first time the great mass of Americans had been aroused to active interest in politics; they demanded a share of the spoils, and the new administration satisfied them by removing government employees wholesale and replacing them with its friends. Early in its course the administration ran into trouble over the refusal of the Cabinet ladies to receive the wife of John H. Eaton, secretary of war. A more basic trouble was the tariff measure of 1828 which aroused South Carolina's resistance to a protection policy and led to the nullification struggle which climaxed 1830–32 and revealed Jackson as no friend to states' rights. Jackson had also, in his first message to Congress, opposed renewal of the charter of the Bank of the United States, but appeared to favor establishment of a government-owned bank with limited operations. The efforts of Clay and Nicholas Biddle to hasten recharter of the Bank turned the question into the leading issue of the 1832 campaign. The president's anti-Bank stand appeared democratic and was popular. Jackson was reelected over Clay, defeating his opposition even in New England. Van Buren succeeded Calhoun in the vice presidency, as he had earlier succeeded him in Jackson's confidence.

Immediately after election, the tariff of 1832 brought the nullification question to a head. South Carolina forbade collection of the tariff duties; Jackson swore to uphold the law by force, if necessary. Clay's compromise tariff of 1833 averted the danger. In order to prevent exercise of power by the Bank (which had until 1836 to live), Jackson withdrew from it all federal deposits and distributed them to state banks. Although he thus humbled the "money power," this and his specie circular, July 1836, in part precipitated panic in 1837. The administration's diplomatic history was highly successful; Indian removals west of the Mississippi were accomplished; the British West Indies were opened to trade; and U.S. claims against France were finally paid. Jackson's dictation of the choice of Martin Van Buren to succeed him alienated many of his friends who joined with the Clay-Adams forces to form the Whig party.

Under Jackson, the nation and the office of president grew stronger. No theorist, he met issues as they arose and was unconscious of his inconsistencies. He had little understanding of the democratic movement named for him and he supported it primarily because it supported him. He was not interested in the will of the people unless it coincided with his own, yet the common man believed in him implicitly and remained his faithful follower. Veering for expediency's sake between strict and liberal constructionism, he left the Democratic party with a heritage of strict-constructionism. The partisan alignment established in his day persisted for many years; even to the present time, the Democratic party retains some of the principles which he adopted. After seeing Van Buren elected and inaugurated, he retired to "The Hermitage" where his strength gradually failed; there he died and was buried.

JACKSON, CHARLES (*b. Newburyport, Mass., 1775; d. 1855*), lawyer. Brother of James Jackson (1777–1867) and Patrick T. Jackson. Graduated Harvard, 1793; read law with Theophilus Parsons. Judge, Massachusetts supreme court, 1813–23; chairman, commission to revise Massachusetts statutes, 1833–35.

JACKSON, CHARLES DOUGLAS (*b. New York, N.Y., 1902; d. New York, 1964*), journalist and diplomat. Studied at Princeton (B.A., 1924) and joined the Luce publishing organization in 1931. Became general manager of *Life* (1937), vice president of Time, Inc., (1940), managing director of Time-Life International (1945), publisher of *Fortune* (1949), and vice president in charge of general management (1954). In 1959 was promoted to administrative vice president, and from 1960 until his death held the post of publisher of *Life*. Jackson took frequent leaves of absence from the Luce empire to devote himself to public service. During World War II he was deputy chief of the Psychological Warfare Branch of the Office of War Information, and helped organize the Psychological Warfare Division of Supreme Headquarters Allied Expeditionary Force. He was a special assistant to President Eisenhower, 1953–54, and a member of the American delegation to the United Nations in 1954.

JACKSON, CHARLES REGINALD (*b. Summit, N.J., 1903; d. New York, N.Y., 1968*), novelist and short-story writer. He was a staff writer for the Columbia Broadcasting System, 1936–39. His novels are *The Lost Weekend* (1944), *The Fall of Valor* (1946), *The Outer Edges* (1948), and *A Second-Hand Life* (1967). Collections of short stories are *The Sunnier Side* (1950) and *Earthly Creatures* (1953). Despite receiving little attention from literary critics, he is

remembered for his sympathetic portrayal of tormented characters.

JACKSON, CHARLES SAMUEL (*b. Middlesex Co., Va., 1860; d. 1924*). Immigrating to Oregon, 1880, he became proprietor of a newspaper at Pendleton; settling in Portland, 1902, he built up the successful *Oregon Daily Journal* as the recognized Democratic organ in the area.

JACKSON, CHARLES THOMAS (*b. Plymouth, Mass., 1805; d. 1880*), chemist, geologist. Graduated Harvard Medical School, 1829, after study with James Jackson and Walter Channing. Studied also in Paris at the Sorbonne and the École des Mines. Established an experimental laboratory at Boston, 1836. Conducted important geological surveys of Maine, Massachusetts, Rhode Island, and New Hampshire. Claimed prior discovery of electric telegraph in controversy with S. F. B. Morse. Suggested possible use of ether to W. T. G. Morton, 1846, later claiming to be true discoverer of surgical anaesthesia.

JACKSON, CHEVALIER (*b. Pittsburgh, Pa., 1865; d. Philadelphia, Pa., 1958*), physician. Studied at the University of Western Pennsylvania and at Jefferson Medical College. A laryngologist, Jackson developed the bronchoscope in 1899. He simultaneously held positions at Jefferson Medical College, the University of Pennsylvania, Temple University and the Women's College of Pennsylvania, of which he became president, 1935–41.

JACKSON, CLAIBORNE FOX (*b. Fleming Co., Ky., 1806; d. near Little Rock, Ark., 1862*), businessman, Missouri legislator. Pro-slavery opponent of Thomas H. Benton *post* 1846; Democratic governor of Missouri, 1860–61.

JACKSON, CLARENCE MARTIN (*b. What Cheer, Iowa, 1875; d. Minneapolis, Minn., 1947*), anatomist. B.S., University of Missouri, 1898; M.S., 1899; M.D., 1900; graduate study at universities of Chicago, Leipzig, and Berlin. Taught anatomy at University of Missouri; dean of medical school, 1909–13. As head of department of anatomy, University of Minnesota Medical School, 1913–41, he was responsible for a revolutionary reorganization of the school, encouraging graduate work and interest in research. His own research, reported in more than a hundred publications, dealt chiefly with the effects of chronic malnutrition. His *Effects of Inanition and Malnutrition upon Growth and Structure* (1925) was for many years the definitive treatise on the subject.

JACKSON, DAVID (*b. Oxford, Pa., 1747[?]; d. Philadelphia, Pa., 1801*), physician, apothecary, Revolutionary patriot. First graduate in medicine, College of Philadelphia (later University of Pennsylvania), 1768; associated, 1793, with David Rittenhouse and others in organizing first U.S. Democratic society.

JACKSON, DUGALD CALEB (*b. Kennett Square, Pa., 1865; d. Cambridge, Mass., 1951*), electrical engineer, educator. Studied at Pennsylvania State College and Cornell University. A pioneer in electrical engineering in academic circles, Jackson headed the departments of electrical engineering at the University of Wisconsin (1891–1907) and at M.I.T. (1907–35), when he retired. President, American Institute of Electrical Engineers, 1911. Awarded the Edison Medal, 1938.

JACKSON, DUNHAM (*b. Bridgewater, Mass., 1888; d. Minneapolis, Minn., 1946*), mathematician. B.A., Harvard, 1908; M.A., 1909. Ph.D., University of Göttingen, 1911. Taught mathematics at Harvard, 1911–18; captain, ordnance department, U.S. Army, 1918–19; professor of mathematics, University of Minnesota, 1919–46. Active in editorial and organizational activities of professional societies; a dedicated and able teacher on both graduate and undergraduate levels. He wrote extensively on orthogonal polynomials, trigonometric sums, and their relation to the theory of approximations; however, he showed substantial diversity in his explorations of the connections of these topics with boundary value problems, the solutions of linear differential equations, functions of several complex variables, and even mathematical statistics.

JACKSON, EDWARD (*b. West Goshen, Pa., 1856; d. Denver, Colo., 1942*), ophthalmologist, surgeon. C.E., Union College, 1874; M.D., University of Pennsylvania, 1878. Began general practice in West Chester, Pa.; removed to Philadelphia, Pa., 1884, to practice ophthalmology. Author of *Skiascopy and Its Practical Application to the Study of Refraction* (1895) and other works in the field of refraction. Appointed professor of ophthalmology, Philadelphia Polyclinic and School of Graduates, 1888, and surgeon to Wills Eye Hospital, 1890, he was influential in raising the standards of professional training for ophthalmology and in establishing it as a separate specialty in medicine. Removing permanently to Denver, Colo., 1898, he continued his professional activities there as professor of ophthalmology, University of Colorado Medical School, 1905–21.

JACKSON, EDWARD PAYSON (*b. Erzerum, Turkey, 1840; d. 1905*), educator. Son of missionary parents; served as instructor in science, Boston Latin School, 1877–1904, showing much originality in methods.

JACKSON, GEORGE K. (*b. Oxford, England, 1758; d. 1822*), organist, music teacher, composer. Came to America, 1796; settled in Boston, Mass., *ca.* 1815, after serving at St. George's, New York City, and was organist at King's Chapel, Trinity, and St. Paul's.

JACKSON, GEORGE THOMAS (*b. New York, N.Y., 1852; d. New York, 1916*), physician. Brother of Samuel M. Jackson. An outstanding specialist in dermatology, which he taught at Woman's Medical College and at the College of Physicians and Surgeons, New York.

JACKSON, HALL (*b. Hampton, N.H., 1739; d. 1797*), physician, surgeon. Practiced in Portsmouth, N.H., after study in London, England; specialized in smallpox. Chief surgeon, New Hampshire troops in Continental Army, 1775–83. Was among first to raise foxglove (digitalis) in America.

JACKSON, HELEN MARIA FISKE HUNT (*b. Amherst, Mass., 1830; d. 1885*), author, better known as Helen Hunt Jackson, or as "H. H." A neighbor and schoolmate of Emily Dickinson, Helen Fiske married Edward B. Hunt, 1852. After the death of her husband and children, she was encouraged to write by T. W. Higginson, publishing her first book *Verses* in 1870 and becoming a valued contributor of stories and essays to the magazines. After her marriage to William S. Jackson, 1875, she resided in Colorado Springs, Colo. Her novel *Mercy Philbrick's Choice* (1876) is said to deal with the life of Emily Dickinson; her *A Century of Dishonor* (1881) and the very popular *Ramona* (1884) reflect her passionate espousal of the cause of the Indians against mistreatment by the U.S. government.

JACKSON, HENRY ROOTES (*b. Athens, Ga., 1820; d. 1898*), jurist, diplomat, Confederate brigadier general. Nephew of James Jackson (1757–1806). U.S. minister to Austria, 1853–58; to Mexico, 1885–86. Supporter of Joseph E. Brown in Georgia politics.

JACKSON, HOWELL EDMUNDS (*b. Paris, Tenn., 1832; d. near Nashville, Tenn., 1895*), jurist. Brother of William H. Jackson. U.S. senator, Democrat from Tennessee, 1881–86; federal judge, 6th circuit, 1886–91; first presiding judge, circuit court of appeals at Cincinnati, 1891–93. Justice, U.S. Supreme Court, 1893–95.

JACKSON, JAMES (*b. Moreton Hampstead, England, 1757; d. Washington, D.C., 1806*), lawyer, Revolutionary soldier, Georgia legislator. Immigrated to Georgia *ca.* 1772; studied law with George Walton after outstanding service with Georgia state troops. Bitter opponent of Yazoo land frauds. U.S. senator, independent Democrat-Republican, 1793–95, 1801–06; governor of Georgia, 1798–1801.

JACKSON, JAMES (*b. Newburyport, Mass., 1777; d. 1867*), physician. Brother of Charles and Patrick T. Jackson. Graduated Harvard, 1796; attended Harvard Medical School (M.B., 1802; M.D., 1809); was apprentice to Edward A. Holyoke and studied in London, England, with Cline and Astley Cooper. Began practice in Boston, Mass., 1800; was one of first in America to investigate vaccination in a scientific spirit. Hersey Professor at the reorganized Harvard Medical School, 1812–33, he was largely responsible for founding Massachusetts General Hospital. His *Letters to a Young Physician* (1855) is a medical classic.

JACKSON, JAMES (*b. Jefferson Co., Ga., 1819; d. Atlanta, Ga., 1887*), jurist, Georgia legislator. Grandson of James Jackson (1757–1806).

JACKSON, JAMES CALEB (*b. Manlius, N.Y., 1811; d. Dansville, N.Y., 1895*), Abolitionist editor, reformer, hydropathic physician.

JACKSON, JOHN ADAMS (*b. Bath, Maine, 1825; d. Pracchia, Italy, 1879*), sculptor of portrait busts and ideal figures in the pseudoclassic manner.

JACKSON, JOHN BRINCKERHOFF (*b. Newark, N.J., 1862; d. Switzerland, 1920*), diplomat, lawyer. Graduated Annapolis, 1883. Secretary of legation and embassy, Berlin, 1890–1902; U.S. minister to Greece, 1902–07. Served thereafter as minister to Cuba, Persia, Roumania, Servia, and Bulgaria, resigning in 1913; was special aide to U.S. embassy in Berlin 1915–17.

JACKSON, JOHN DAVIES (*b. Danville, Ky., 1834; d. Danville, 1875*), physician, Confederate surgeon. Reviewed and vindicated (1873) the claim of Ephraim McDowell to recognition as pioneer in ovariotomy and abdominal surgery.

JACKSON, JOHN GEORGE (*b. near Buckhannon, [W.Va.], 1777; d. 1825*), surveyor, jurist, Virginia legislator. Congressman, (Democrat) Republican, from Virginia, 1803–10, 1813–17; first U.S. judge for Western District of Virginia, 1819–25; active in developing Virginia's natural resources. Brother-in-law of James Madison.

JACKSON, JOSPEH HENRY (*b. Madison, N.J., 1894; d. San Francisco, Calif., 1955*), editor, literary critic, writer. Studied at Lafayette College. Literary editor for the *San Francisco Chronicle*, 1930–55. Judge for the O. Henry Memorial Award, 1935, 1942, and 1951; member of the Pulitzer Prize fiction jury, 1949–51. Held nationally broadcast program, "Bookman's Guide," 1924–43. Author of several books on California history and travel books.

JACKSON, MERCY RUGGLES BISBE (*b. Hardwick, Mass., 1802; d. 1877*), homeopathic physician. Adjunct professor of diseases of children. Boston University Medical School, 1873–77.

JACKSON, MORTIMER MELVILLE (*b. Rensselaerville, N.Y., 1809; d. 1889*), jurist. Removed to Wisconsin, 1838; served as territorial attorney general, 1841–45, and as a state circuit and supreme court judge, 1848–53. As U.S. consul at Halifax, Canada, 1861–82, Jackson did outstanding service during the Civil War and in later adjustment of the disputes over fisheries.

JACKSON, PATRICK TRACY (*b. Newburyport, Mass., 1780; d. Beverly, Mass., 1847*), merchant, financier. Brother of Charles Jackson and James Jackson (1777–1867). With Nathan Appleton, Francis Cabot Lowell, and others, organized Boston Manufacturing Co., 1813, whose Waltham mill on the Charles River was probably the first in which all operations for turning raw cotton into finished cloth were done in one factory. Jackson was prime mover in founding Lowell, Mass., 1820. He also built the Boston & Lowell Railroad, and was active in Boston realty speculation.

JACKSON, ROBERT HOUGHWOUT (*b. Spring Creek, Pa., 1892; d. Washington D.C., 1954*), lawyer, jurist. Studied at Albany Law School (1911) before practicing in Jamestown, N.Y. Appointed general counsel to the Bureau of Internal Revenue, 1934; served successively (1935–38) as special counsel to the Department of the Treasury and to the Securities and Exchange Commission, and as assistant attorney general in charge of the Tax and Anti-Trust Divisions. Solicitor general, 1938–40; attorney general, 1940–41. Appointed to the Supreme Court in 1941, Jackson emerged as both a strong nationalist and a conservative apostle of judicial self-restraint. He supported the Court's decision declaring unconstitutional a California law that made it a misdemeanor to transport into the state any person without visible means of support. Strongly in favor of the federal government in commercial cases, he was rather conservative in labor issues. He supported the separation of church and state, internment of Japanese Americans during World War II, and the rights of accused persons. Chief of counsel for the U.S. at the Nuremberg trials, 1945–46, before returning to the Supreme Court.

JACKSON, ROBERT R. (*b. Malta, Ill., 1870; d. Chicago, Ill., 1942*), Black political and civic leader. Raised in Chicago. Entering the U.S. Post Office, 1888, he advanced in nine years to the post of assistant superintendent of a Chicago postal station; he was also active in the Illinois national guard, in local politics, and in a number of business ventures through which he prospered. He left the postal service in 1909. He is best known as a protégé of Edward Wright in the Republican machine which dominated black political activity in Chicago from about the turn of the century until the advent of the New Deal. As a member of the state legislature and of the city council, he worked to represent and advance the interests of his black constituents while at the same time giving vital political support to the machine bosses. He believed that blacks should work within the existing system and spurned radical reform movements as utopian and impractical.

JACKSON, SAMUEL (*b. Philadelphia, Pa., 1787; d. Philadelphia, 1872*), physician. Son of David Jackson. Graduated University of Pennsylvania, 1808; taught physiology there, 1827–63.

JACKSON, SAMUEL MACAULEY (*b. New York, N.Y., 1851; d. 1912*), Presbyterian clergyman, church historian. Brother of George T. Jackson. Disciple of Philip Schaff, and his associate in the *Dictionary of the Bible* (1880) and the several editions of the Schaff-Herzog *Encyclopedia*. Author also of numerous works including *Huldreich Zwingli* (1901).

JACKSON, SHELDON (*b. Minaville, N.Y., 1834; d. Asheville, N.C., 1909*), Presbyterian clergyman. Pastor in Minnesota; missionary in Rocky Mountain states. Missionary in Alaska, and first U.S. superintendent of public instruction there, 1885–1909. Introduced domesticated reindeer into Alaska, 1892.

JACKSON, SHIRLEY HARDIE (*b. San Francisco, Calif., 1919; d. North Bennington, Vt., 1965*), writer. Studied at the University of Rochester and Syracuse (B.A., 1940). Her first novel was *The Road Through the Wall* (1948), but it was her short story "The Lottery" (1948) that made her reputation. She was a master of the understated psychological horror tale, and her fiction contained a powerful feminist tendency. Other books include *Hangsaman* (1951), *Life Among the Savages* (1953), *The Bird's Nest* (1954), *Raising Demons* (1957), *The Sundial* (1958), *The Haunting of Hill House* (1959), and *We Have Always Lived in the Castle* (1962).

JACKSON, THOMAS JONATHAN (*b. Clarksburg, Va., now W. Va., 1824; d. Guiney's Station, Va., 1863*), "Stonewall" Jackson, Confederate soldier. Graduated West Point, 1846. Became major by brevet within 18 months after distinguished Mexican War service at Vera Cruz, Cerro Gordo, Chapultepec; resigned from army, February 1852; became professor of artillery tactics and natural philosophy at Virginia Military Institute, Lexington, Va. A devout Presbyterian, grave and slightly stiff in his public manner, Jackson took no part in public affairs prior to the Civil War beyond that of commanding the cadet corps at the hanging of John Brown, 1859. He deplored the prospect of war which he described as the "sum of all evils."

Ordered to Richmond, April 21, 1861, with part of the cadet corps, he was soon sent to Harpers Ferry as colonel of infantry; on June 17, 1861, he was made brigadier general. Bringing his command to high efficiency, he sustained a Union assault at a critical moment during the first battle of Bull Run, thus winning his famous sobriquet from Brigadier General B. E. Bee. Promoted major general, Oct. 7, 1861, Jackson assumed command in the Shenandoah Valley. General J. E. Johnston's retreat to the line of the Rappahannock early in March 1862 forced Jackson to abandon Winchester, Va., and enter upon his celebrated "Valley Campaign" which many critics regard as the most remarkable display of strategic science and tactics in all American military history. Marching up the Valley, Jackson turned on his pursuer, the federal force under Major General James Shields, and was defeated with heavy loss at Kernstown on March 23. Criticism of Jackson as irresponsibly reckless failed to take into account the effect of his action in alarming the federal command and causing the retention of force in northern and western Virginia which would otherwise have supported McClellan's attack on Richmond. In further development of this strategy, Jackson continued on the offensive, attacking the federal force under Brigadier General N. P. Banks at Front Royal on May 23, driving it back through Winchester to the Potomac and threatening the safety of Washington. Menaced in the rear from both east and west by superior forces, Jackson withdrew rapidly up the Valley and engaged each opponent separately; the force under Frémont was checked at Cross Keys on June 8, and Shield's advanced guard was defeated at Port Republic on June 9.

Meanwhile, General R. E. Lee had succeeded to command of the forces defending Richmond. An admirer of Jackson, Lee summoned him to join in the Seven Days' Campaign late in June, but Jackson's failures at Beaver Dam Creek and White Oak Swamp were disappointing. After an inconclusive action at Cedar Run, Aug. 9, Jackson was detached and executed the most famous of all his marches, destroying the federal base at Manassas Junction, Aug. 27, holding off the enemy at Groveton, and on Aug. 30–31 sharing in the offensive against General Pope at the second battle of Bull Run which permitted Lee to carry the war into the enemy's country. By this time, Jackson was a legend. Eccentric in behavior and appearance, he was known as "Old Jack" to his adoring soldiers, but his trusted lieutenant, Ewell, was convinced that he was insane.

Leading Lee's advance into Maryland, Jackson took Harpers Ferry, Sept. 15, 1862, and distinguished himself at Antietam (Sept. 17) and at Fredericksburg. Promoted lieutenant general,

Oct. 10, he now commanded one of the two corps into which the Army of Northern Virginia had been divided. On renewal of the federal offensive in the spring of 1863, Jackson in concert with Lee planned to attack the rear of General Hooker's advanced guard as it lay near Chancellorsville. Before dawn on May 2, he began the last of his great marches and near sunset surprised the rear of the Union right, so threatening Hooker's line that a retreat was inevitable. Returning from the front in the dusk, Jackson was severely wounded by the fire of his own men and died of pneumonia eight days later. Although his career in high field command was limited to less than 25 months, he is listed by all critics among the greatest American soldiers.

JACKSON, WILLIAM (b. *Cumberland, England, 1759; d. Philadelphia, Pa., 1828*), Revolutionary soldier, public official. Came to America as a youth; raised in South Carolina. Served as aide to General Benjamin Lincoln, and as secretary to John Laurens on European mission, 1781. Was secretary to Federal Convention, 1787, and personal secretary to President Washington, 1789–91. Thereafter was employed in business, in the customs, and in journalism.

JACKSON, WILLIAM (b. *Newton, Mass., 1783; d. 1855*), tallow chandler, promoter of Massachusetts railroads, Massachusetts legislator and congressman.

JACKSON, WILLIAM ALEXANDER (b. *Bellows Falls, Vt., 1905; d. Cambridge, Mass., 1964*), bibliographer and librarian. Attended Williams College, where he prepared the bibliographical catalog of the Chapin Library collection. Also worked at the Huntington Library and prepared a bibliographical catalog of Carl H. Pforzheimer, Sr.'s library of English literature. In 1937 Jackson became assistant college librarian and associate professor of bibliography at the Harvard University Library. In 1957 he published his edition of *Records of the Court of the Stationers' Company, 1602–1640.* Throughout his life he worked on a revision of *A Short Title Catalogue of Books Printed in England . . . 1475–1640,* but he did not live to see its completion.

JACKSON, WILLIAM HENRY (b. *Keeseville, N.Y., 1843; d. New York, N.Y., 1942*), photographer. Jackson received his early schooling in Peru, N.Y., where he first began to draw and paint. He then worked for photographers in Troy, N.Y., and Rutland, Vt. After limited service in the Civil War he made his way West on wagon trains as a bullwhacker. He arrived in Los Angeles in 1867 but soon began the return journey East. In Omaha he took a job with a photographer, and in 1868 he bought a photographic studio and hired a portrait artist. He began to make a photographic record of the development of the West. Fitting up a horsedrawn wagon as laboratory and darkroom, he traveled widely, photographing Indians, frontiersmen, and the construction of the transcontinental railroad. His photographs, long appreciated for their value as ethnological, geological, and geographical documents, were first exhibited as works of art by the Museum of Modern Art, New York City, 1942.

JACKSON, WILLIAM HICKS (b. *Paris, Tenn., 1835; d. Belle Meade, Tenn., 1903*), Confederate general, planter, stockbreeder. Brother of Howell E. Jackson. Graduated West Point, 1856. After outstanding service in Mississippi, Tennessee, and the defense of Atlanta, in which he rose to divisional command, Jackson returned to manage family plantations. *Post* 1868, he was associated in development of the famous Belle Meade thoroughbred horse farm.

JACOB, RICHARD TAYLOR (b. *Oldham Co., Ky., 1825; d. 1903*), Kentucky soldier, Unionist.

JACOBI, ABRAHAM (b. *Hartum-in-Minden, Germany, 1830; d. 1919*), pediatrician. Graduated Bonn, M.D., 1851. After two years' imprisonment for revolutionary activity, escaped and made his way to England; settled in New York, N.Y., ca. 1855. Identifying himself from the first with treatment of infants' and children's diseases, he won international fame in his speciality. He became the first professor of diseases of children in this country at New York Medical College, 1860, and established there the first free clinic for such diseases; from 1870 until 1902 he was professor of pediatrics, College of Physicians and Surgeons, New York. He was a prolific contributor to medical journals, and the author of several books.

JACOBI, MARY CORINNA PUTNAM (b. *London, England, 1842; d. 1906*), physician. Daughter of George P. Putnam; wife of Abraham Jacobi. Graduated Female Medical College of Pennsylvania, 1864; École de Médecine, Paris, France, 1871, the second woman to receive its degree. Served as professor, Woman's Medical College, New York, 1871–88. The leading woman physician of her generation.

JACOBS, HENRY EYSTER (b. *Gettysburg, Pa., 1844; d. Philadelphia, Pa., 1932*), Lutheran clergyman, theologian. Professor at Gettysburg College, 1870–83; professor, dean, and president, Lutheran Theological Seminary, Philadelphia, *post* 1883. Had strong influence in the liturgical development of Lutheran bodies in the United States.

JACOBS, HIRSCH (b. *New York, N.Y., 1904; d. Miami, Fla., 1970*), horse trainer, breeder, and stable owner. Formed a partnership in 1928 with Isidor ("Beebee") Bieber, which lasted thirty years. Jacobs owned and bred his own horses, and became the winningest trainer in American history (3,569 winners). By the time of his retirement in 1966, horses he had trained had won over $15 million.

JACOBS, JOSEPH (b. *Sydney, New South Wales, 1854; d. 1916*), historian, folklorist. Graduated St. John's College, Cambridge, 1876; studied in Berlin; won early fame for Jewish anthropological and historical studies. Was editor of numerous and valuable collections of fairy tales. *Post* 1900, Jacobs lived in the United States where he served as revising editor of the *Jewish Encyclopedia* and was editor of the *American Hebrew*, 1913–16.

JACOBS, JOSEPH (b. *Jefferson, Ga., 1859; d. 1929*), pharmacist, drugstore chain proprietor, collector of works by and about Robert Burns.

JACOBS, MICHAEL (b. *near Waynesboro, Pa., 1808; d. Gettysburg, Pa., 1871*), Lutheran clergyman. Professor of mathematics and science, Gettysburg College, 1832–66.

JACOBS, MICHAEL STRAUSS (b. *New York, N.Y., 1880; d. Miami Beach, Fla., 1953*), sports promoter. Promoter of heavyweight boxer Joe Louis from 1935 to 1949. Jacobs controlled leases for virtually all commercial boxing events in the New York area during the 1930's and 1940's. His backing of Joe Louis helped open the world of sports to blacks.

JACOBS, WILLIAM PLUMER (b. *York Co., S.C., 1842; d. 1917*), Presbyterian clergyman. Pastor in Clinton, S.C., *post* 1864; founded Thornwell Orphanage, 1875, and Clinton College (later Presbyterian College of South Carolina), 1880.

JACOBSON, JOHN CHRISTIAN (b. *Burkhall, Denmark, 1795; d. 1870*), Moravian bishop, educator. Came to America, 1816; taught at Nazareth and Bethlehem, Pa., and at Salem, N.C.; brought European standards to Moravian education.

JACOBY, LUDWIG SIGMUND (*b. Altstrelitz, Germany, 1813; d. St. Louis, Mo., 1874*), Methodist clergyman. Came to America, 1838; was converted to Methodism in Cincinnati, Ohio, 1839; worked among Germans in upper Mississippi valley, 1841–48. Evangelized in Germany, 1849–71.

JADWIN, EDGAR (*b. Honesdale, Pa., 1865; d. Canal Zone, 1931*), soldier, engineer. Graduated West Point, 1890. Assistant to G. W. Goethals in Panama Canal construction; built channel through Gatun Lake, Gatun Dam, and breakwater at Atlantic terminus. As brigadier general, 1917–18, Jadwin supervised vast wartime construction projects in France; he served as chief of engineers, 1926–29, retiring as lieutenant general.

JAEGER, WERNER WILHELM (*b. Lobberich, Niederrhein, Prussia, 1888; d. Boston, Mass., 1961*), classicist. Studied at Marburg (1907) and the University of Berlin (1907–11). Taught at the University of Basel, Christian-Albrechts University, and the University of Berlin, 1921–36, where he sought to restore classical humanism to the center of German intellectual life (the Third Humanism). He founded the journals *Die Antike* and *Gnomon*. Leaving Germany, he taught at the University of California at Berkeley, 1934–36, the University of Chicago, 1936–39, and Harvard, 1939–60. His writings in English include *Aristotle: Fundamentals of the History of His Development* (1934), *Demosthenes: The Origin and Growth of His Policy* (1938), *Paideia* (3 vols., 1939–44), *The Theology of the Early Greek Philosophers* (1947), the Oxford edition of Aristotle's *Metaphysics* (1957), *Scripta Minora* (1960), and *Early Christianity and Greek Paideia* (1961). He also spent much of his life on the critical edition of Gregory of Nyssa.

JAGGAR, THOMAS AUGUSTUS, JR. (*b. Philadelphia, Pa., 1871; d. Honolulu, Hawaii, 1953*), geologist, volcanologist. Studied at Harvard (Ph.D., 1897) and at the universities of Munich and Heidelberg. Taught geology at Harvard, 1895–1906; head of the geology department, M.I.T., 1906–12. Director of the Hawaiian Volcano Observatory, 1912–40. Jaggar's discoveries and techniques have become standard; his theory that volcanic eruptions result from steam blasts caused by heated groundwater is still generally accepted. He published *Steam Blast Volcanic Eruptions* in 1949.

JAMES, ARTHUR CURTISS (*b. New York, N.Y., 1867; d. New York, 1941*), financier, yachtsman, philanthropist. Son of Daniel Willis James. Joined Phelps, Dodge & Company after graduation from Amherst College, 1889; served as an officer and director and was the largest single stockholder. Principally interested in the financing of railroad systems in the West, by 1931 he had fiscal control of over 40,000 miles of rails. During his lifetime he gave more than twenty million dollars to various institutions; at the liquidation in 1965 of the James Foundation, which he had set up in his will, the foundation had disbursed more than $144 million to those institutions, which included Union Theological Seminary, Amherst College, Hampton Institute, and the Children's Aid Society of New York.

JAMES, CHARLES (*b. near Northampton, England, 1880; d. 1928*), chemist. Came to America *ca.* 1906. Professor at University of New Hampshire, 1906–28. Won international recognition for his work in study of rare earths.

JAMES, CHARLES TILLINGHAST (*b. West Greenwich, R.I., 1805; d. Sag Harbor, N.Y., 1862*), engineer. Expert in textile machinery construction; advocate of steam power for cotton mills. U.S. senator, Democrat, from Rhode Island, 1851–57.

JAMES, DANIEL WILLIS (*b. Liverpool, England, 1832; d. 1907*), merchant, philanthropist. Born of U.S. parents resident in England; educated in England and Scotland. Came to America, 1849; became partner in Phelps, Dodge & Co., 1854. A lifelong, anonymous donor to charities, in particular to the Children's Aid Society and Union Theological Seminary, New York.

JAMES, EDMUND JANES (*b. Jacksonville, Ill., 1855; d. Covina, Calif., 1925*), economist, educator. Graduated University of Halle, Ph.D., 1877. Taught at Wharton School, University of Pennsylvania, and University of Chicago; founded American Academy of Political and Social Science, 1889–90. Served as president, Northwestern University, 1902–04; University of Illinois, 1904–19.

JAMES, EDWARD CHRISTOPHER (*b. Ogdensburg, N.Y., 1841; d. 1901*), lawyer, Union soldier. Practiced in New York City *post* 1882; a notable cross-examiner in all types of cases.

JAMES, EDWIN (*b. Weybridge, Vt., 1797; d. Rock Spring, Iowa, 1861*), physician, explorer, naturalist. Graduated Middlebury, 1816; studied botany and geology with John Torrey and Amos Eaton at Albany, N.Y. Surgeon-naturalist on Stephen H. Long's expedition to explore region between Mississippi and Rocky Mountains, 1820. Author of *Account of an Expedition from Pittsburgh to the Rocky Mountains* (1822–23), the official record of the survey. Later, as army surgeon at Prairie du Chien and Mackinac, James studied and wrote on the Indian languages; he settled near Burlington, Iowa, *ca.* 1838.

JAMES, EDWIN LELAND (*b. Irvington, Va., 1890; d. New York, N.Y., 1951*), journalist. Graduated from Randolph Macon College, 1909. Reporter for the *New York Times*, 1915–32; managing editor, 1932–51. During World War I, James was the *Times* war correspondent in France; he remained chief European correspondent until 1930, covering such events as Lindbergh's flight.

JAMES, GEORGE WHARTON (*b. Gainsborough, England, 1858; d. 1923*), author, lecturer. Came to America, 1881; was a Methodist minister in California and Nevada until 1889. Thereafter he became widely known as an enthusiast for the history and spirit of the Southwest and as a friend of the Indians.

JAMES, HENRY (*b. Albany, N.Y., 1811; d. Cambridge, Mass., 1882*), author, lecturer, philosopher. Father of Henry James (1843–1916) and William James. Graduated Union, 1830. Employed Swedenborg's interpretation of Christianity as a framework for his own speculations; was intimate with Horace Greeley, Albert Brisbane, and the New York Fourierist circle, also with R. W. Emerson, Thomas Carlyle, and other leaders in the thought of his time.

JAMES, HENRY (*b. New York, N.Y., 1843; d. London, England, 1916*), novelist. Son of Henry James (1811–1882); brother of William James. Educated in accordance with his father's theory that children destined to cosmopolitanism should not be allowed to take root in any religion, political system, ethical code, or set of personal habits. From boyhood he interested himself in the sensitive observation of subtle human relationships; constantly on the move, he was able to form impressions in a variety of American cities and abroad in Geneva, London, Paris, Boulogne, and Bonn. Mathematics and drawing interested him at the outset, but while residing at Cambridge, Mass., he was influenced by Charles E. Norton and William D. Howells to a gradual awareness of his vocation in literature. Kept from service in the Civil War by physical infirmity, he felt himself cast in the role of a spectator on life. Between 1865 and 1869 he wrote criticism for the *Nation* and stories for the *Atlantic Monthly* and the *Galaxy* magazines; his early fiction derived from Hawthorne and Balzac and inclined to melodrama. The earliest story to reveal

James's essential traits and his predominant theme of a raw traveler making contact with older cultures was "A Passionate Pilgrim" (*Atlantic Monthly*, 1871). In 1875 he left America for Paris but felt himself too much a foreigner there; in 1876 he settled for good in England. An overconsciousness of national qualities and a too great concern with superficial elements of international differences appear in the works produced during the first period of his European residence; only *The Portrait of a Lady* (1881) rises clearly above these prepossessions. *Roderick Hudson* (1876), *The American* (1877), *Daisy Miller* (1879), *An International Episode* (1879), all suffer despite their merits from the author's concern with matters which are not of first importance for a novelist.

Moving as he did in a world withdrawn from the rougher phases of life, he grew more and more absorbed in his special society. He had conceived of himself as writing in a cosmopolitan capital but having elsewhere a vast native province to draw upon, much as Turgenev drew on Russia; gradually, however, he lost this sense of America as a spiritual reservoir. *The Princess Casamassima* (1886) indicated how far James had gone in his saturation with English life and is the high point of his idealization of it. *The Tragic Muse* (1890) is more critical of the world of leisure and fashion, and here James sets forth his concept of the aristocracy of art and artists as more important and more desirable then anything in those "dense categories of dark arcana" which he had gone to Europe to penetrate. Except for *Daisy Miller*, none of his books had had popular acclaim either in England or America; a personal resentment dictated his siding with fellow-artists against the public, and the years 1886–96 saw this resentment grow and finally surrender to a kind of philosophic stoicism. During these years he confined himself largely to unsuccessful plays, distinguished critical essays, and short narratives of unique delicacy, skill and beauty. *The Author of Beltraffo* (1885), *The Aspern Papers* (1888), *The Lesson of the Master* (1892), and *Embarrassments* (1896) contain what he himself described as "multitude of pictures of my time."

After this decade, reconciled to the fact that his art was for the few, he settled down to practice it as he pleased, to write without conflict in his own way for his own audience. *The Two Magics* (1898) contained "The Turn of the Screw." It was preceded by *The Spoils of Poynton* (1897) and *What Maisie Knew* (1897), and followed by the three novels in which he brought his art to its peak: *The Wings of the Dove* (1902), *The Ambassadors* (1903), and *The Golden Bowl* (1904). Again and again in his later books he dealt with the adventures of exquisite souls in a rough world and their defeat by vulgarity and vice.

James traveled in America, 1904–05; the fruit of his observations was *The American Scene* (1907). The New York edition of his works, 1907–1909, presented a selection of what he judged his best with the addition of prefaces which throw valuable light on the art of fiction. His three autobiographical works, *A Small Boy and Others* (1913), *Notes of a Son and Brother* (1914), and *The Middle Years* (1917), are of great importance for an understanding of James. The First World War ended his career; as a gesture of sympathy with his long-loved England, he became a British citizen, 1915.

In his meticulous examinations of motives, atmospheres, and backgrounds, James did not seek deliberately to be obscure. Obscurity and esoteric reputation were his destiny, not his design. He had set out to identify and represent certain subtle relationships which he had perceived binding men and women together in the human picture before his eyes, and he would not call it his fault if his perceptions proved to be more delicate than those of the reading public at large.

He must be thought of as something more than a merely Anglo-Saxon phenomenon. Balzac and Turgenev furnished examples in which he found what his own art needed to employ or avoid. His originality lay, first, in his choice of his terrain, that international triangle which has London, Paris, and New York at its points and which embraces a homogeneous civilization which before James had never had a great novelist concerned with it as entity and whole. He was original too in his attitude toward the English-American novel as an art form; he found it an unconscious and left it a fully conscious form of art. By example, and in his critical writings, he called attention to the finer details of craftsmanship, generalized the practices of individuals into principles, and brought the whole art of the novel into the region of esthetics. His influence upon numerous followers, in Europe and in America, has been weighty and persistent.

JAMES, JESSE WOODSON (*b. near Kearney, Mo., 1847; d. St. Joseph, Mo., 1882*), desperado, trainrobber. With his brother Alexander Franklin (Frank) James, was a member of Confederate guerrillas under W. C. Quantrill; became leader of a gang of robbers which included Coleman Younger, 1866. They operated successfully until 1876, when all but Jesse and Frank were killed in an attempted holdup of bank at Northfield, Minn. Led a new gang of outlaws, 1879–81; was shot from behind by Robert Ford, a member of his band.

JAMES, LOUIS (*b. Tremont, Ill., 1842; d. Helena, Mont., 1910*), actor. Made debut, Louisville, Ky., 1864. Accomplished his best work under management of Augustin Daly, 1871–75; played in support of Edwin Booth, Lawrence Barrett, and many others.

JAMES, MARQUIS (*b. Springfield, Mo., 1891; d. Rye, N.Y., 1955*), author. Remembered for his biography of Sam Houston, *The Raven*, which received the Pulitzer Prize in 1930; and his two-volume biography of Andrew Jackson (*The Border Captain*, 1933, and *Portrait of a President*, 1937); the latter volume won the Pulitzer Prize in 1938. Wrote biographies of John Nance Gardner (1939) and Alfred I. du Pont (1941).

JAMES, OLLIE MURRAY (*b. Crittenden Co., Ky., 1871; d. 1918*), lawyer, politician. Congressman from Kentucky, Democrat, 1903–12; U.S. senator, 1912–18. One of the most popular campaign orators of his day.

JAMES, THOMAS (*b. Maryland, 1782; d. Monroe City, Ill., 1847*), trapper, Santa Fe trader. Author of *Three Years Among the Indians and Mexicans* (1846), an important source for early frontier history.

JAMES, THOMAS CHALKLEY (*b. Philadelphia, Pa., 1766; d. Philadelphia, 1835*), physician. Grandson of Thomas Chalkley. Graduated University of Pennsylvania, B.M., 1787; awarded doctor's degree, 1811. Served as ship's surgeon; studied in England under Dr. John Hunter and the famous obstetricians Osborne and John Clark, and also in Edinburgh. Gave first regular course on obstetrics at Philadelphia, 1802; served as obstetrician, Pennsylvania Hospital, 1810–32; by teaching and example, laid firm foundation for practice of scientific obstetrics in America.

JAMES, THOMAS LEMUEL (*b. Utica, N.Y., 1831; d. 1916*), businessman, newspaper publisher. Highly efficient postmaster, New York City, 1873–81; as postmaster general, 1881, helped put end to Star Route frauds.

JAMES, THOMAS POTTS (*b. Radnor, Pa., 1803; d. Cambridge, Mass., 1882*), wholesale pharmacist, botanist. Specialized in study of mosses; with C. L. Lesquereux, prepared classic *Manual of North American Mosses* (1884).

JAMES, WILL RODERICK (*b. St. Nazaire de Acton, Quebec, Canada, 1892; d. Hollywood, Calif., 1942*), author, artist. Born Joseph Ernest Nephtali Dufault, he was raised in Montreal, where his father kept a small hotel. According to his own self-propagated myth, however, his father was a Texas cattle drover, and after his death he had been raised by an itinerant trapper in the Mackenzie and Peace River country of Canada. James lived in Montreal until 1907. His early life was spent as a drifter in western Canada and the United States. He seems to have been arrested in connection with the fatal wounding of a drunken sheepherder, and he spent nearly a year in prison for cattle rustling. After a brief interim as a stunt man in Western movies he resumed his drifting life until 1918, when he was inducted into the army.

Seeking to become an artist in the style of Frederic Remington and Charles Russell, James attended the California School of Fine Arts in San Francisco in 1919. His first published sketch appeared in *Sunset Magazine* (January 1920), and he continued to sell occasional sketches while working on ranches. In 1921 he received a scholarship to the Yale Art School, but soon dropped out and, after a brief stay in New York, returned to Reno, Nev., in 1922.

His real success began when he tried writing and illustrating his own material. *Scribner's Magazine* published his first article, "Bucking Horses and Bucking-Horse Riders" (March 1923). Stories and articles for *Scribner's*, the *Saturday Evening Post*, *Sunset*, and *Redbook* followed. Under the guidance of Maxwell Perkins, James began to publish books for Charles Scribner's Sons in 1924. *Cowboys, North and South* was followed by *The Drifting Cowboy* (1925), a series of short stories, and his first and best novel, *Smoky* (1926). James's apocryphal autobiography, *Lone Cowboy* (1930), fooled even his wife and went unexposed until 1967. He died of alcoholic complications.

JAMES, WILLIAM (*b*. *New York, N.Y.*, *1842*; *d*. *Chocorua, N.H.*, *1910*), philosopher, psychologist. Eldest son of Henry James (1811–82); brother of Henry James (1843–1916). Influenced by father's preoccupation with problems of life and religion, he was exposed to an irregular, intermittent education but frequented art galleries and theatres, and observed life in many European cities. Entered studio of William M. Hunt, Newport, R.I., 1860, and worked with John LaFarge; although talented as painter, he decided to pursue a scientific career and entered Lawrence Scientific School, 1861, thus beginning his lifelong association with Harvard. After studying chemistry under Charles W. Eliot and comparative anatomy under Jeffries Wyman, he entered Harvard Medical School, 1864, but interrupted studies to participate in a zoological expedition to the Amazon basin, directed by Louis Agassiz. He acquired from Wyman and Agassiz his respect for facts and firsthand observation, which became a fixed element in his intellectual composition. Failure of health interrupted his medical study; he occupied himself in studying experimental physiology in Germany, 1867–68. This was a period of indecision and discouragement for the young student; he became convinced that his poor health eliminated any prospect of sustained laboratory work. Reentering Harvard Medical School, he received his degree, 1868, but felt unable to engage in medical practice. Another, more prolonged period of ill health and nervous depression followed, but his readings in the fields of the sciences, literature, and philosophy would have taxed the capacity of any well person. In 1870, Charles Renouvier's *Traité de Psychologie Rationelle* delivered him from his melancholia and philosophic doubt.

Accepting an instructorship in physiology in Harvard College, 1872, for the next ten years he taught comparative anatomy, comparative physiology, and hygiene. At that time the theory of evolution was the central topic in the field of biology, and psychology had received a new impulse from increased knowledge of the physiology of the senses and nervous system. James offered a course entitled "Relations between Physiology and Psychology," 1875, established the first psychology laboratory in America, and in 1880 became assistant professor of philosophy. He began work

on his *Principles of Psychology*, 1878, published 12 years later. Sections of this work were first published in learned journals and given in lectures; the immense popularity of the *Principles* was due mainly to the author's learning and skillful use of citation and his success in giving an adequate summary of the state of the science of psychology at the end of the 19th century. An abridged section was for many years the most popular textbook on the subject in America. James's *Talks to Teachers on Psychology* (1899) spread the vogue of his ideas and gave powerful impulse to the new subject of educational psychology. In 1884, two articles of great importance had been contributed by James to *Mind*. The first presented for the first time his insistence on the continuity of the stream of consciousness. The second expressed the so-called "James-Lange Theory" of emotion.

After 1890 there was a gradual shift in emphasis in James's teaching and writing from psychology to philosophy. As a philosopher, he was solicited on the one side by religion and on the other by science. Firmly stationed on the side of empiricism by temperament, he was aware of the need for a new empiricism freed from associationism. He had accepted the Shadworth Hodgson dictum that "realities are only what they are known as"; repelled by Hodgson's determinism, he concluded that conscious experience must be supplemented by freedom of the will. Experience may be considered knowledge, but James held that it must be supplemented by faith to satisfy man's moral and emotional nature. His first step toward a philosophy was to reject the pretensions and negations of science. The affirmation of man's freedom was, to James, a first step in the cogitative as well as moral life. Renouvier's belief that natural processes really begin and end discontinuously had suggested, to the troubled younger James, that a nature so consistent with novelty and creativity implied also free will. His philosophy now developed into a more radical union of empiricism and voluntarism. His ideas, originally published in articles, appeared in book form as *The Will to Believe and Other Essays* (1897). This volume presented reasons for a firm belief in freedom, in the triumph of righteousness and in the God which guarantees this belief. In *Varieties of Religious Experience* (1902), he presented a masterly exposition of the data of conversion, saintliness, and other characteristics of man's religious life. The most important effect of this book was to shift the emphasis from religious dogmas and external forms to the unique states of mind associated with it. In 1904–05 he published the articles later issued as *Essays in Radical Empiricism* (1912); in 1907 he published his famous *Pragmatism*, a doctrine adumbrated in the concluding chapter of his *Principles of Psychology*. The meaning of an idea, says James, consists of the particular consequences to which it leads. Truth should properly be applied as a term, not to reality, but to our beliefs about it. A particular truth must be about something in particular; secondly, it must "work," that is, satisfy the purpose for which it was adopted. He defended this position and its corollaries in *The Meaning of Truth* (1909). James's effort to give a systematic statement of his metaphysics was published as *A Pluralistic Universe* (1909).

Although this volume is popular in style, it affords the best and the final synopsis of his *Weltanschauung* and of his general philosophical orientation. He pays his respects to Hegel and to the absolutists generally, setting forth the failure of their arguments, and the "thinness" of their results. To reject the absolute does not imply the rejection of every hypothesis of a "superhuman consciousness." But instead of the dialectical method used by the Hegelians to establish such a consciousness, James commended the method of empirical analogy and free speculation used by Fechner in his doctrine of an "earth-soul"; and, instead of a superhuman consciousness that is in some unintelligible sense "all-embracing," James proposed that it should be finite like human consciousness. In that case it may without contradiction have those relations to an environment other than itself, and that freedom from evil, which have in fact always been attributed to it by the religious worshipper. It was far from James's intention to increase the distance between man and God. Man is a part, or is capable under certain conditions of becoming a part, of an enveloping spiritual life; and that life is like his own—different in degree, but similar in kind. The probability of such a hypothesis is supported by the mystical state, and by allied abnormal and supernormal experiences to which modern psychology has called attention, as well as by the moral and emotional demands which it satisfies. James ends upon the note of pluralism, in which the "each" is preferred to the "all," and the world is a "multiverse"; which corresponds to the actual appearances of things and satisfies the creed of individualism and freedom, but without that complete disintegration that has usually been supposed to be the only alternative to monism. This was James's solution of that problem which he had set himself at the beginning of his philosophical career, the union, namely, of the empirical temper and method of science with the essential ideals and beliefs of religion.

James is commonly grouped with Jonathan Edwards and R. W. Emerson as a leader in American thought, a distinction owing in great part to his cosmopolitanism and to his literary style. His style is that of a brilliant talker, concrete, witty, and giving the effect of spontaneity. As a person, he was humorous and totally lacking in either self-consciousness or self-righteousness. He responded warmly to humanity in all its forms. He has been fortunate in that the direction of his thought coincided with that of his posterity. The application of an empirical study of human nature to human affairs; a shift of emphasis in philosophy from pure intellect to perception; a recognition of the significance of religious experience; an acknowledgment of the play of will and feeling in formation of belief; these are a few of the major items in the record of James's permanent achievement. He continued to teach at Harvard until January 1907.

JAMESON, HORATIO GATES (*b. York, Pa., 1778; d. New York, N.Y., 1855*), Baltimore, Md., physician, surgeon, teacher. Founded Washington Medical College (Baltimore, 1827–51).

JAMESON, JOHN ALEXANDER (*b. Irasburgh, Vt., 1824; d. Hyde Park, Ill., 1890*), jurist. Practiced law in Illinois *post* 1853; judge, chancery division, superior court of Chicago (later Cook Co.), 1865–83. Author of *The Constitutional Convention* (1867), an exhaustive historical study.

JAMESON, JOHN FRANKLIN (*b. Somerville, Mass., 1859; d. Washington, D.C., 1937*), historian. Graduated Amherst, 1879; Ph.D., Johns Hopkins, 1882. After teaching at Johns Hopkins, Brown, and Chicago universities, he was director, 1905–28, of the department of historical research of the Carnegie Institution. Here he led the campaign for a National Archives building, and directed the publication of guides to foreign archives and of many significant American historical documents. A leader in American historical scholarship, Jameson was chief of the Manuscripts Division of the Library of Congress, 1928–37; managing editor, 1895–1901, 1905–28 of the *American Historical Review*; and, as chairman of the Committee of Management, a guiding spirit in the planning and execution of the *Dictionary of American Biography*.

JAMISON, CECILIA VIETS DAKIN HAMILTON (*b. Yarmouth, Canada, 1837; d. Roxbury, Mass., 1909*), portrait painter, author.

JAMISON, DAVID (*b. Scotland, 1660; d. New York, N.Y.[?], 1739*), lawyer. Came to America as a bondsman, 1685. Defended Francis Makemie for preaching without license, 1707; was chief justice of New Jersey, 1711–23, also recorder of New York City and acting attorney general *post* 1712. Active in establishing Church of England in New York.

JAMISON, DAVID FLAVEL (*b. Orangeburg District, S.C., 1810; d. 1864*), planter, South Carolina legislator, author. Friend of William Gilmore Simms. President, South Carolina secession convention.

JANAUSCHEK, FRANZISKA MAGDALENA ROMANCE (*b. Prague, Bohemia, 1830; d. Amityville, N.Y., 1904*), actress, better known as Fanny Janauschek. A leading German tragedienne, she came to America, 1867, playing in German; in 1870 she began her career in English under Augustin Daly's management, acting in *Mary Stuart* at the New York Academy of Music. *Post* 1880, she made the United States her home. Unable to adapt her heroic style of acting to changing tastes, she gradually lost favor with American audiences.

JANES, LEWIS GEORGE (*b. Providence, R.I., 1844; d. Eliot, Maine, 1901*), lecturer, teacher. Associated with the Ethical Association and other free religious groups. Author of *Health and a Day* (1901).

JANEWAY, EDWARD GAMALIEL (*b. New Brunswick, N.J., 1841; d. Summit, N.J., 1911*), physician. Graduated Rutgers, 1860; M.D., College of Physicians and Surgeons, New York, 1864. Professor of pathological anatomy, Bellevue; later held chair of principles and practice there, and was dean, 1898–1905, after consolidation with New York University. A notable diagnostician and consultant.

JANEWAY, THEODORE CALDWELL (*b. New York, N.Y., 1872; d. 1917*), physician. Son of Edward G. Janeway. Distinguished professor and innovator in methods at New York University, College of Physicians and Surgeons (New York), and Johns Hopkins. Made special studies of tuberculosis.

JANIN, LOUIS (*b. New Orleans, La., 1837; d. Santa Barbara, Calif., 1914*), mining engineer. Trainer and mentor, among others, of Herbert Hoover and John Hays Hammond.

JANIS, ELSIE (*b. Columbus, Ohio, 1889; d. Hollywood, Calif., 1956*), actress. Privately educated, Janis began performing in vaudeville and on Broadway in 1900; she was successfully playing in London in *The Passing Show of 1914*. During World War I she performed in many shows on the Western Front. Toured Europe and was writer and production supervisor on early talkies. Made last professional appearance in the film *Women in War* (1940).

JANNEY, ELI HAMILTON (*b. Loudoun Co., Va., 1831; d. Alexandria, Va., 1912*). Inventor of the modern railroad car-coupler. Basic patents were granted him, 1868 and 1873; his device became standard by agreement of the railroads, 1888.

JANNEY, OLIVER EDWARD (*b. Washington, D.C., 1856; d. Baltimore, Md., 1930*), physician, Quaker reformer, and philanthropist.

JANNEY, RUSSELL DIXON (*b. Wilmington, Ohio, 1885; d. New York, N.Y., 1963*), author and theatrical producer. A graduate of Yale (1906), his first big success as a producer came with *The Vagabond King* (1925). He backed *Ballyhoo* (1927), *White Eagle* (1927), and *The O'Flynn* (1934). He wrote *Miracle of the Bells* (1946) and *So Long as Love Remembers* (1953), both novels, and *The Vision of Red O'Shea* (1949), a verse drama.

JANNEY, SAMUEL MCPHERSON (*b. Loudoun Co., Va., 1801; d. 1880*), educator, Hicksite Quaker minister. Author of lives of William Penn (1852) and George Fox (1853), and a history of the Society of Friends.

JANSEN, REINIER (*b. Alkmaar, Holland; d. Philadelphia, Pa., 1706 n.s.*), merchant. Came to Pennsylvania, 1698. Operated a printing press for the Society of Friends in Philadelphia, his first imprints bearing the date 1699.

JANSKY, KARL GUTHE (*b. Norman, Okla., 1905; d. Red Bank, N.J., 1950*), electrical engineer and founder of radio astronomy. B.S., University of Wisconsin, 1927; M.S., 1936. Associated with Bell Telephone Laboratories *post* 1928. Assigned to trace the source of atmospherics (natural static) that interfered with radiotelephone communication, he observed in 1931 a steady hiss-type static that was not caused by the action of thunderstorms. After a series of experiments, he published three papers in 1933 in which he suggested the strong probability that the "starnoise" as he called it originated in the constellation Sagittarius. He extended his theory in 1935 with the suggestion that the radiation arose in interstellar space from the thermal motion of charged particles. His work led to the exploration of space to distances of billions of light-years.

JANSON, KRISTOFER NAGEL (*b. Bergen, Norway, 1841; d. 1917*), poet, novelist, Unitarian clergyman. Served as Unitarian missionary in Minnesota, 1879–80 and 1881–93, returning to Norway in the latter year.

JANSSENS, FRANCIS (*b. Tilburg, North Brabant, 1843; d. at sea, 1897*), Roman Catholic clergyman. Graduated Louvain; ordained, 1867. Came to America, 1868, and was pastor in Richmond, Va. Bishop of Natchez, Miss., 1881–88; archbishop of New Orleans, 1888–97.

JANVIER, CATHARINE ANN DRINKER (*b. Philadelphia, Pa., 1841; d. Merion, Pa., 1922*), painter, author. Wife of Thomas A. Janvier. Enthusiast for Provençal culture and literature.

JANVIER, MARGARET THOMSON (*b. New Orleans, La., 1844; d. Moorestown, N.J., 1913*), author. Sister of Thomas A. Janvier. Wrote, under pseudonym of Margaret Vandegrift, a variety of juvenile stories and verses.

JANVIER, THOMAS ALLIBONE (*b. Philadelphia, Pa., 1849; d. New York, N.Y., 1913*), journalist. Author, among other books, of *Color Studies* (1885); *The Aztec Treasure House* (1890); *In Old New York* (1894); *At the Casa Napoleon* (1914). A graceful and sympathetic observer of New York City's 19th-century Bohemia, Janvier was also a student and admirer of the literature of Provence.

JAQUESS, JAMES FRAZIER (*b. near Evansville, Ind., 1819; d. St. Paul, Minn., 1898*), Methodist clergyman, Union soldier. Made two unsuccessful attempts to end Civil War by peace missions to Jefferson Davis, 1863 and 1864.

JARDINE, WILLIAM MARION (*b. Oneida Co., Idaho, 1879; d. San Antonio, Tex., 1955*), educator, secretary of agriculture, diplomat. Studied at the Agricultural College of Utah. Faculty member 1910–18, and president, 1918–25, of Kansas State Agricultural College. Secretary of Agriculture, 1925–29; minister to Egypt, 1930–33. President of the University of Wichita, 1934–49.

JARRATT, DEVEREUX (*b. New Kent Co., Va., 1733; d. Dinwiddie Co., Va., 1801*), Episcopal clergyman. Rector of Bath Parish (Dinwiddie Co.), 1763–1801. An advocate of vital religion and a friend to early American Methodists.

JARRELL, RANDALL (*b. Nashville, Tenn., 1914; d. Chapel Hill, N.C., 1965*), writer and teacher. Studied at Vanderbilt (B.S., 1935; M.A., 1939). He taught at Kenyon College (1937–39), the University of Texas (1939–42), Sarah Lawrence (1946–47), and the Women's College of the University of North Carolina (1947–65). His only novel was *Pictures from an Institution* (1954). Collections of poems and essays include *Blood for a Stranger* (1942), *Little Friend, Little Friend* (1945), *Losses* (1948), *The Seven-League Crutches* (1951), *Poetry and the Age* (1953), *Selected Poems* (1955), *The Woman at the Washington Zoo* (1960), *A Sad Heart at the Supermarket* (1962), *The Lost World* (1965), *The Complete Poems* (1969), and *The Third Book of Criticism* (1969). Jarrel also wrote children's books and published many translations.

JARVES, DEMING (*b. Boston, Mass., 1790; d. Boston, 1869*), inventor, leader in American glass industry. Partner in New England Glass Co., Boston and Sandwich Glass Co., Cape Cod Glass Co.; attempted to claim credit for invention of pressed-glass machine, 1826–27; developed red-lead manufactory; a brilliant experimenter in color compounding and technical innovation.

JARVES, JAMES JACKSON (*b. Boston, Mass., 1818; d. Switzerland, 1888*), journalist, critic, pioneer art collector. Son of Deming Jarves. Traveled widely as young man; edited *Polynesian*, first newspaper published in Hawaii, 1840–48. Settling in Florence, Italy, he began career as art critic and collector early in the 1850's. His important collection of early Italian masters became Yale's property, 1871, and is today regarded as priceless. Jarves's declared purpose was the "diffusion of artistic knowledge and aesthetic taste in America." Among his many books were *Scenes and Scenery in California* (1844); *Art Studies* (1861); *The Art Idea* (1864, 1865).

JARVIS, ABRAHAM (*b. Norwalk, Conn., 1739 o.s.; d. 1813*), Episcopal clergyman. Graduated Yale, 1761. Rector at Middletown, Conn. Bishop of Connecticut, *post* 1797.

JARVIS, CHARLES H. (*b. Philadelphia, Pa., 1837; d. Philadelphia, 1895*), concert pianist, teacher.

JARVIS, EDWARD (*b. Concord, Mass., 1803; d. Dorchester, Mass., 1884*), physician, alienist, statistician. Reformer of procedures in U.S. Census.

JARVIS, JOHN WESLEY (*b. South Shields, England, 1781; d. New York, N.Y., 1839*), portrait painter. Came to America as a child. Encouraged in art by Matthew Pratt and others; apprenticed to print publisher Edward Savage, in whose shop he learned drawing and engraving from David Edwin. Successful as painter of portraits in New York City, Baltimore, Md., Charleston, S.C., and New Orleans, La.; prodigiously facile, his work is uneven in quality. Extravagant and reckless, he died in poverty.

JARVIS, THOMAS JORDAN (*b. Jarvisburg, N.C., 1836; d. 1915*), lawyer, Confederate soldier, North Carolina legislator. Gave strong and progressive leadership as Democratic governor of North Carolina, 1879–85. U.S. minister to Brazil, 1885–89.

JARVIS, WILLIAM (*b. Boston, Mass., 1770; d. 1859*), Boston merchant. U.S. consul at Lisbon, Portugal, 1802–11. Introduced Merino sheep in large numbers to the United States and effected their distribution in this country.

JARVIS, WILLIAM CHAPMAN (*b. Fortress Monroe, Va., 1855; d. Willet's Point, N.Y., 1895*), physician, pioneer laryngologist and rhinologist. Graduated University of Maryland, M.D., 1875; did postgraduate work at Johns Hopkins. Devised a famous "snare" which revolutionized treatment of intranasal tumors, 1881. Professor at New York University *post* 1886. His career was marked by a long series of innovations in diagnosis and treatment of nasal and laryngeal diseases.

JASPER, WILLIAM (*b. near Georgetown, S.C., ca. 1750; d. near Savannah, Ga., 1779*), Revolutionary soldier. Enlisted, and appointed sergeant, in the 2nd South Carolina Infantry under William Moultrie, 1775; distinguished himself during British bombardment of Fort Sullivan (now Fort Moultrie), June 1776, recovering flag after it had been shot down, and remounting it over the fort in face of heavy fire. Declining a commission because of his lack of education, he was made a scout and performed valuable service under Generals Moultrie, Marion, and Lincoln. Accompanying the latter and D'Estaing in the assault on Savannah, 1799, he was killed planting his regiment's colors upon an enemy redoubt.

JASTROW, JOSEPH (*b. Warsaw, Poland, 1863; d. Stockbridge, Mass., 1944*), psychologist. Brother of Morris Jastrow. A.B., University of Pennsylvania, 1882; Ph.D., Johns Hopkins University, 1886. Professor of experimental and comparative psychology, University of Wisconsin, 1888–1927. After his retirement, he moved to New York City, taught at the New School for Social Research (1927–33) and, at Columbia, developed a syndicated newspaper column "Keeping Mentally Fit," and produced a number of useful books on psychology directed to the general public. His earlier books included *Fact and Fable in Psychology* (1900); *The Subconscious* (1906); *The Qualities of Men* (1910); *Character and Temperament* (1915); and *The Psychology of Conviction* (1918).

JASTROW, MARCUS (*b. Rogasan, Posen, Poland, 1829; d. Philadelphia, Pa., 1903*), rabbi, lexicographer. Educated in Poland and Germany; imprisoned and exiled by the Russians for patriotic Polish activities. Came to America, accepting a call from Congregation Rodeph Shalom, Philadelphia, 1866. His militant conservative Judaism soon engaged him in controversy with reform Judaism. He helped organize Maimonides College, where he taught religion and Jewish history, and made his synagogue a center of conservative Judaism. After 1876 he concentrated on his monumental *Dictionary of the Targumim, the Talmud Babli and Yerushalmi and the Midrashic Literature* (1886–1903), illustrative of a millennium of Hebrew and Aramaic literature. His declining years found Jastrow fervently espousing Herzlian Zionism.

JASTROW, MORRIS (*b. Warsaw, Poland, 1861; d. Philadelphia, Pa., 1921*), Semitic scholar. Son of Marcus Jastrow. Graduated University of Pennsylvania, 1881; Ph.D., Leipzig, 1884. Taught at University of Pennsylvania, 1892–1921. One of the most influential Orientalists of his time; author of *Religion Babyloniens und Assyriens* (1905, 1912) and other works in English on related subjects which revealed rare skills in linguistics, criticism, and literary insight.

JAY, ALLEN (*b. Mill Creek, Ohio, 1831; d. Richmond, Ind., 1910*), Quaker preacher, educator. Contributed greatly to Quaker revival, late 19th century; developed endowment of Earlham College and other Quaker schools.

JAY, SIR JAMES (*b. New York, N.Y., 1732; d. Springfield, N.J., 1815*), baronet, physician. Brother of John Jay (1745–1829). Suspected, 1782, of working against American independence.

JAY, JOHN (*b. New York, N.Y., 1745; d. Bedford, N.Y., 1829*), statesman. Brother of James Jay; sixth son of Peter and Mary (Van Cortlandt) Jay and thus a scion of two of colonial New York's wealthiest and most influential families. His father was a leading merchant who carefully guided his upbringing and education under private tutors. Bookish and pious, Jay early developed the aristocratic self-confidence and self-satisfaction that characterized his later career. Graduating from King's College,

1764, he prepared for the bar in a New York law office, where he evidenced the powerful and stubborn mental qualities, along with a lucidity of literary expression, which already marked him as a man of unusual force and intellectual ability.

Jay practiced law from 1768 until the American Revolution, which embarked him on a career of public service. He was one of New York's delegates to the first and second Continental Congresses, where he reflected the interests of conservative colonial merchants who opposed independence through fear that it might precipitate a social upheaval and democratic rule. As member of New York provincial congress, he supported the Declaration of Independence unreservedly and helped ratify it. He then guided the framing of New York's constitution and served as state chief justice until 1779. Resuming his seat in the Continental Congress, December 1778, Jay was elected its president, holding that position until chosen minister plenipotentiary to Spain nine months later. Jay began his diplomatic career with a mission which was hopeless from the start. His two chief points, according to the Spanish foreign minister, Florida-blanca, were: "Spain, recognize our independence; Spain, give us more money." Jay obtained a small loan, but Spain had no intention of recognizing America's independence.

In the spring of 1782 Jay was summoned to Paris to join Franklin on the joint commission to negotiate peace with Great Britain. His participation in this secret negotiation remains controversial. His insistence that the British representative, Richard Oswald, be given powers to treat with representatives of the "United States of America" rather than the "Colonies" may have wrecked Franklin's prospect of gaining the cession of Canada. Distrusting French foreign minister Vergennes, Jay privately communicated with the British prime minister, thereby delaying negotiations until events in Europe had greatly strengthened Britain's bargaining position. Whether the British government would have agreed to Franklin's proposal regarding Canada is questionable; but Jay's victory in a matter of form was of dubious value.

Jay and John Adams then convinced Franklin that they should sign preliminary articles of peace without Vergennes's knowledge. This was a violation of their instructions to negotiate only with the full confidence of the French ministry but not technically a violation of the Franco-American treaty of alliance, for the peace was not to become effective until France had also made terms with Britain. France could not make peace until Spain agreed, and the American preliminaries undoubtedly helped bring Spain into line. France and Spain separately signed preliminaries of peace with Great Britain on Jan. 20, 1783.

Declining new diplomatic appointments in order to return to his law practice, Jay came home in July 1784 to discover that he had been drafted by Congress as secretary of foreign affairs. He retained this position until Jefferson became secretary of state in the new federal government, 1790. During his six-year tenure, Jay labored mostly over relations with Britain and Spain. The former retained the Northwest Posts in violation of the peace treaty; Spain occupied territory claimed by the United States and in addition closed the Mississippi to navigation by Americans. Protracted negotiations between Jay and Gardoquí, the Spanish minister, failed when Congress rejected a proposed treaty which would have denied Americans the navigation of the Mississippi for 25 years—a project which earned Jay the lasting distrust of the West and South.

Seriously handicapped by the weakness of government under the Confederation, Jay became one of the strongest advocates of a new constitution. In 1787 he joined with Hamilton and Madison and contributed five of the "Federalist" papers. Under the new government, he became the first chief justice of the United States, presiding over the Supreme Court during its first five formative years. His most important case was *Chisholm* v. *Georgia*, in which he pointed out that the Constitution specifically gave a citizen of one state the right to sue another state, and that suitability and state sovereignty were incompatible. This vigorous exposition of nationalism so alarmed several of the states that the 11th Amendment was quickly added to the Constitution.

Still chief justice, Jay was sent to dissipate the war crisis with Britain which arose in 1794 mainly over continuing occupation of the Northwest Posts and increasing British depredations on American commerce. Since Hamilton's new credit system depended on tariff revenue, and as nine-tenths of it came from British imports, the Federalists were determined to avert a British war and even to prevent adoption of a Republican-sponsored program of commercial retaliation which might have suspended all intercourse. Jay, undercut by disclosures made by Hamilton to the British minister at Philadelphia, eventually signed a treaty which failed to uphold America's neutral rights under international law and thereby led to a serious crisis with France. Jay's Treaty (1794), which might more appropriately be called Hamilton's Treaty, provided for the evacuation of the Northwest Posts and for the establishment of mixed claims commissions to dispose of other mutual grievances. Jay and his treaty were enormously unpopular, but the Senate ratified it and history has justified it as a necessary evil.

Jay returned home to find himself again drafted for another post, that of governor of New York. Nominated and elected *in absentia* in 1795, he served two terms, for a total of six years. He gave his state an upright, conservative administration and thereafter retired to private life, preferring not to involve himself in the imminent Federalist debacle of 1800. His last public act bore witness to his uncompromising moral rectitude. Knowing that the newly elected Republican legislature would choose Jeffersonian electors, Hamilton asked Jay to summon the expiring Federalist legislature to choose Federalists, but Jay merely noted on his friend's letter: "Proposing a measure for party purposes which I think it would not become me to adopt." An able man, but not a genius, he brought intellectual vigor and moral tone into every office which he held.

JAY, JOHN (*b. New York, N.Y., 1817; d. 1894*), lawyer. Grandson of John Jay (1745–1829). Active in the antislavery movement and civil-service reform; an organizer of the Republican party in New York. U.S. minister to Austria, 1869–74.

JAY, PETER AUGUSTUS (*b. Elizabeth Town, N.J., 1776; d. 1843*), New York lawyer. Son of John Jay (1745–1829); served him as secretary during 1794 mission to England.

JAY, WILLIAM (*b. New York, N.Y., 1789; d. 1858*), jurist. Son of John Jay (1745–1829). Active in antislavery and other reform movements. Author of *The Life of John Jay* (1833) and other books.

JAYNE, HORACE FORT (*b. Philadelphia, Pa., 1859; d. 1913*), biologist. Graduated M.D., University of Pennsylvania, 1882; studied at Leipzig and Jena. Heir to a patent medicine fortune, he was professor of biology, dean, and a benefactor of the University of Pennsylvania; also director, Wistar Institute, 1894–1904.

JEANES, ANNA T. (*b. near Philadelphia, Pa., 1822; d. 1907*), Quaker philanthropist. Among many other benefactions, established Negro Rural School Fund *ca.* 1907.

JEFFERS, JOHN ROBINSON (*b. Pittsburgh, Pa., 1887; d. near Carmel, Calif., 1962*), poet. Studied at the University of Western Pennsylvania, Occidental College (B.A., 1905), University of Southern California, University of Zurich, University of Southern California Medical School, and University of Washington. His poetry collections include *Flagons and Apples* (1912), *Californians* (1916), *Tamar and Other Poems* (1924), *Roan Stallion, Tamar and Other Poems* (1925), *The Women at Point Sur* (1927), *Cawdor and Other Poems* (1928), *Dear Judas and Other Poems* (1929), *Thurso's Landing and Other Poems* (1932), *Give Your Heart to the Hawks and Other Poems* (1933), *Solstice and Other Poems* (1935), *Such Counsels You Gave to Me* (1937), *The Selected Poetry of Robinson Jeffers* (1938), *Be Angry at the Sun* (1941), *The Double Axe and Other Poems* (1948), and *Hungerfield and Other Poems* (1954). Influenced by Nietzche and Spengler, Jeffers professed a philosophy labeled "inhumanism." In the 1930's and 1940's he preached isolationism.

JEFFERS, WILLIAM MARTIN (*b. North Platte, Nebr., 1876; d. Pasadena, Calif., 1953*), railroad executive. Employed by the Union Pacific Railroad from 1890 until his death, Jeffers rose from a callboy to become president of the company, 1937–46, and vice-chairman of the board of directors, 1946–53. Director of the synthetic rubber industry for the War Production Board, 1942–43.

JEFFERS, WILLIAM NICHOLSON (*b. Swedesboro, N.J., 1824; d. Washington, D.C., 1883*), naval officer, ordnance expert. Graduated Naval Academy, 1846. Commanded USS *Monitor* in James River operations *post Merrimac* battle. Chief of Bureau of Ordnance, 1873–81.

JEFFERSON, CHARLES EDWARD (*b. Cambridge, Ohio, 1860; d. Fitzwilliam, N.H., 1937*), Congregational clergyman. Pastor in Chelsea, Mass., and at Broadway Tabernacle Church, New York, 1898–1930. A conspicuous Protestant liberal.

JEFFERSON, JOSEPH (*b. Plymouth, England, 1774; d. Harrisburg, Pa., 1832*), actor. Came to America, 1795; made New York debut, 1796. A pillar of Philadelphia's Chestnut Street Theatre, 1803–30.

JEFFERSON, JOSEPH (*b. Philadelphia, Pa., 1829; d. Palm Beach, Fla., 1905*), actor. Grandson of Joseph Jefferson (1774–1832). Debut at Washington, D.C., 1833, with "Jim Crow" Rice. In 71 years on the stage, Jefferson gained fame and fortune and became one of the best-loved figures in American life. His genius as a comedian was instantly recognized with his first appearance as Rip in Boucicault's version of *Rip Van Winkle* in 1865. From that time until his death, Jefferson in *Rip Van Winkle* provided a practical ideal of dramatic entertainment drawn from native sources, and humor, pathos, even poetry, extracted from the common lot. He succeeded Edwin Booth as president of the Players' Club, 1893, and hence as America's premier actor. Among other parts in which he was celebrated were Asa Trenchard (*Our American Cousin*), Caleb Plummer (*The Cricket on the Hearth*), and Bob Acres (*The Rivals*).

JEFFERSON, MARK SYLVESTER WILLIAM (*b. Melrose, Mass., 1863; d. Ypsilanti, Mich., 1949*), geographer. Interrupted studies at Boston University to work in Argentina, 1883–89; after taking bachelor's degree, taught in several Massachusetts schools, 1890–96. Studied geography and geology at Harvard under William Morris Davis (B.A., 1897; M.A., 1898). As professor of geography at Michigan State Normal School, Ypsilanti, 1901–39, he won for the college the appellation "nursery of American geographers"; some 15,000 students took his courses. He was a vigorous and enthusiastic fieldworker, and the author of about 120 books and articles; his work in urban geography was of particular importance. He was chief cartographer for the U.S. peace commission at Paris, 1918–19.

JEFFERSON, THOMAS (*b. Goochland, now Albemarle, Co., Va., 1743; d. "Monticello," Albemarle Co., Va., 1826*), statesman, diplomat, author, scientist, architect, apostle of freedom and enlightenment.

Jefferson's father, Peter Jefferson, was of good stock but not wealthy; a surveyor, he had moved from Henrico Co. to

Goochland, where he patented 1,000 acres on the Rivanna River and by 1734 was a magistrate. He married Jane Randolph, first cousin of his friend William Randolph of "Tuckahoe," thus connecting himself with perhaps the most distinguished family of the province and assuring the social standing of his children. He helped Joshua Fry continue the boundary line between Virginia and North Carolina and with him made the first accurate map of Virginia. From his father, Jefferson doubtless acquired much of his zest for exploring and drawing.

Jefferson was tutored privately until 1760, when he entered the College of William and Mary, graduating 1762. There, Dr. William Small aroused the scientific interest which remained active all his life and introduced him to the "familiar table" of Governor Francis Fauquier and to George Wythe, Virginia's most noted teacher of law, under whom Jefferson prepared himself for practice. A recognized and companionable member of the close-knit social group of the children of Virginia's great families, his natural seriousness soon asserted itself and he early formulated a stern code of personal conduct and disciplined himself to rigorous study habits. His legal preparation was thorough and, admitted to the bar in 1767, he was quite successful until he ceased practicing on the eve of the Revolution.

In 1772 Jefferson married Martha Wayles Skelton, a widow who, in their ten years of married life, bore him six children, of whom only three survived her and only two (Martha and Mary) reached maturity. Jefferson settled his bride at Monticello, the mountaintop home begun in 1770 and whose construction was to extend over a generation. The 5,000 acres left him by his father were doubled in 1774, when he received from his father-in-law's estate holdings practically equivalent to his own. With these, however, came a huge debt from whose effects he never entirely escaped. All through his long lifetime he was most methodical in recording everything connected with his plantations.

Jefferson served in the House of Burgesses from 1769 until it ceased to function in 1775. Not an effective public speaker, he performed best in committees, employing his marked talents as a literary draftsman. A member of the aggressive anti-British group, he was active in creating the Virginia Committee of Correspondence and in subsequent anti-British moves of the House. His most notable contribution to the Revolutionary cause before 1776 was his *A Summary View of the Rights of British America*, composed for the Virginia convention of 1774 and containing his views regarding the colonies' relationship to England. Denying all parliamentary authority over the colonies, he insisted that the King, to whom the colonies had voluntarily submitted, supplied the only political tie with Great Britain. Emphasizing "rights as derived from the laws of nature," he advocated freedom of trade in articles Britain could not use and the relinquishment of all British claims in regard to taxation.

Sent to Congress by the Virginia convention in 1775, he was elected to the committee to draft a declaration of independence after the introduction of Richard Henry Lee's resolution on June 7, 1776. His reputation of a masterly pen was one reason for his selection as its major draftsman. John Adams and Franklin, and Congress itself, made changes in his draft of the Declaration, but its composition belongs indisputably to Jefferson. The doctrines are essentially those of John Locke, the source of current revolutionary philosophy. No believer in absolute equality, Jefferson believed in government by popular consent which would insure the inalienable rights of man, including the pursuit of happiness rather than of property as an end in itself. Notable for its clarity and felicity of expression, the Declaration is Jefferson's noblest literary monument.

In September 1776 Jefferson left Congress to further the "reformation" of Virginia and served in the House of Delegates from October 1776 until his election as governor in June 1779. He favored the end of the artificial aristocracy of wealth and birth and its replacement by one of talent and virtue, supported by an enlightened electorate. Assuming the leadership of the progressives in the House, he deserves the chief credit for an unparalleled program of reform and an almost unequaled record of legislative achievement. Succeeding in abolishing landholding in fee tail, he moved the revision of the laws. For two years he labored with a committee of five, eventually producing a report comprising 126 bills, of which at least 100 were eventually enacted in substance. Primogeniture was abolished in 1785 and his Bill for Establishing Religious Freedom, passed in 1786, he regarded as one of his greatest contributions to humanity. His educational bills were unsuccessful, but he may properly be termed the architect of Virginia government.

The qualities which accounted for Jefferson's preeminence as a legislative leader and prophet were of little avail as executive. Hesitant and reluctant in the exercise of authority, as war governor he was also handicapped by constitutional limitations and the diminution of the state's resources. Reelected in 1780, he managed well enough until the British invasion of Virginia in the spring of 1781. Early in June, he was succeeded in the governorship by General Thomas Nelson after his virtual abdication. Meeting later at Staunton, the Assembly ordered an investigation of charges that he had been lacking in military precaution and expedition, but he was formally vindicated and a resolution of thanks finally adopted. Retired from public life, Jefferson found leisure to organize the memoranda concerning Virginia which he had made over many years. In 1782–83 he enlarged them; in 1785 the *Notes on the State of Virginia* were printed in France, laying the foundation of his fame as a universal scholar. Along with unbounded optimism regarding his country's future, his picture of 18th-century Virginia included strictures on slavery and on Virginia's government.

Seeking relief from the woe caused by the death of his wife, 1782, Jefferson accepted an appointment as peace commissioner to Europe. The mission became unnecessary, but the next year he was elected to Congress, where he performed notable service (advocated adoption of the dollar unit; anticipated Ordinance of 1787 in report of March 22, 1784) until appointed, 1784, to assist Franklin and Adams in Paris in negotiating treaties of commerce.

In 1785 Congress appointed Jefferson to succeed Franklin as U.S. minister to France. He unsuccessfully contended against French commercial exclusiveness, negotiated the Consular Convention of 1788, and reported home in detail on the course of the French Revolution till his departure in October 1789. Intimate and sympathetic with the moderate reformers, he deplored the violence of the Revolution's later phases but remained convinced that it had done more good than ill. He left Europe convinced of the value of American cultivation of France as a counterpoise to Britain, and believing that Britain and Spain could be made to pay for American neutrality in future European conflicts, from which therefore the United States would greatly benefit. From his observations abroad, he had gained an emotional stimulus and returned to his own country much strengthened in his civic faith.

Before he reached his beloved Monticello in December, Jefferson received Washington's offer of the secretaryship of state which, despite his distaste for political strife, he accepted on patriotic grounds. Although he regarded the government of the Confederation as "without comparison the best existing or that ever did exist," he favored the movement to strengthen it and approved the new Constitution, objecting mainly to the absence of a bill of rights, soon remedied. At first he strove to cooperate with Alexander Hamilton, who had already assumed first place among Washington's counselors, but he soon concluded that Hamilton was aiming at a monarchy. His subsequent statement that he was duped into trading approval of Hamilton's assumption policy for the location of the capital on the Potomac is unconvincing, as his contemporary letters show that he regarded some compromise as essential to peace and unity.

The first serious difference between Jefferson and Hamilton came over the use of commercial discrimination against Britain to force her to surrender the Northwest Posts and grant commercial privileges. Jefferson supported a movement to this end, led in Congress by James Madison; Hamilton's influence against the measure, based on his fear of losing revenue from British imports, defeated it. Soon after, at Washington's request, the two men presented opinions on the constitutionality of a national bank. Jefferson argued that Hamilton's bill assumed powers not enumerated by the Constitution and thus committed himself to a narrow and literal interpretation of that instrument which he later found in practice would have rendered the government feeble and inflexible. By mid-1792 the hostility between the two men, sharpened by Hamilton's constant interference in Jefferson's domain of foreign affairs, had become implacable. Hamilton published a series of ferocious anonymous attacks on his colleague in the newspapers. Jefferson's friends defended him, but he himself refrained from newspaper controversy. He probably had a part, however, in drafting the resolutions of William Branch Giles which were severely critical of Hamilton's conduct of the Treasury.

Jefferson's hostility to Hamilton stemmed from the conviction that the latter's system "flowed from principles adverse to liberty, and was calculated to undermine and demolish the republic, by creating an influence of his department over the members of the legislature." At the earnest insistence of George Washington, who valued and utilized both his subordinates, Jefferson agreed to remain in office only until the end of 1793. The outbreak of general war in Europe (Feb. 1793) brought a series of crises. Jefferson, like Washington and Hamilton, believed neutrality was imperative but was determined that his country should not oppose the principles of the French Revolution. He kept the word "neutrality" out of Washington's proclamation, April 1793, and persuaded the president to receive the new French minister Edmond Genet without qualification, though he agreed with Hamilton in refusing to anticipate payments on the debt to France. He welcomed Genet and rejoiced in the popular enthusiasm for democracy which Genet kindled; he came near conniving in the Frenchman's projected expeditions against Louisiana. Eventually, however, he lost patience with Genet and joined in asking his recall. He failed to solve the problems of British relations and pronounced the subsequent Hamilton-inspired Jay Treaty an ignominious surrender of American rights. Equally unsuccessful in negotiations with Spain, the objectives he sought were attained in the treaty of 1795.

Believing his second retirement (Dec. 31, 1793) final, Jefferson devoted himself to the continual improvement of Monticello and to agriculture. Early in 1795 he told Madison that the "little spice of ambition" he once had was gone, but he remained the symbol of anti-Hamilton and Republican political faith and did not refuse the presidential nomination in 1796. He would serve if elected so as "to put our vessel on her republican tack before she should be thrown too much to leeward of her true principles." He was surprisingly content to run second to Adams in the presidential race, whom perhaps he regarded as the only barrier to Hamilton. The vice president's salary, which he undoubtedly needed, and the relative leisure the position afforded, were welcomed but he played no part in the administration, which Hamilton continued to dominate.

Federalists continued to regard him as the personification of the Republican party and seized every opportunity, notably the "Mazzei letter" incident (1797), to vilify him. He approved Monroe's conduct in France and privately condemned the "XYZ frenzy,"

which the Federalists aggravated to discredit the Republicans. When the Alien and Sedition Acts were passed, menacing his most cherished ideals, he drafted the Kentucky Resolutions of 1798 while Madison supplied similar resolutions in Virginia. Though the constitutional doctrines contained in the famous Resolutions later gave comfort to proponents of nullification, their purpose was to denounce the offensive laws as an unconstitutional attack upon individual freedom. In fact, they constituted a somewhat extravagant party platform, pointing to the coming election.

Federalist dissensions contributed to a Republican victory in 1800, to which Jefferson was anything but indifferent. Due to the electoral machinery, he and Aaron Burr received an identical vote, but the Federalist House eventually yielded to Republican preference and to its own grudging feeling that Jefferson was the safer man and elected him president. His election, variously interpreted since then, was immediately significant by its vindication of political opposition and its repudiation of a reactionary regime. Walking from his boardinghouse to the uncompleted Capitol to take the oath of office from his cousin and inveterate political foe, Chief Justice John Marshall, Jefferson felt that the danger of monarchy was now removed; his benevolent first inaugural address wooed the more moderate Federalists into acceptance of the majority will. In keeping with his views of the negative function of government, he lived in the Executive Mansion in sartorial indifference and dispensed generous but informal hospitality, to the consternation of tradition-bound diplomats.

Madison, the secretary of state, and Albert Gallatin, who as secretary of the treasury carried out his economy program with considerable success, were his chief collaborators. It was to Robert R. Livingston and Monroe that Jefferson gave chief credit for the outstanding accomplishment of his administration, the purchase of Louisiana, 1803. Hearing of the retrocession of Louisiana to France by Spain, Jefferson had written to Livingston that the possessor of New Orleans was the natural enemy of the United States and even felt compelled to consider a rapprochement with Britain in order to preserve the open navigation on the Mississippi which was secured by the purchase. The problem of constitutional powers bothered him, for he was aware that broad construction of the Constitution would void a major safeguard against tyranny, but overwhelming public approval crowned his pragmatic statesmanship. Aware of inconsistency in this matter, he seems to have viewed the achievement with little pride. His handling of the Florida question was inept and diminished his influence on Congress; on the other hand, he acted with force and success against the Barbary powers.

Triumphantly reelected, 1804, the difficulties facing Jefferson in his second administration as a neutral during a ruthless European war were probably unsolvable. After 1805, the United States stood in an intolerable position between British Orders in Council and Napoleonic decrees. Even after the *Chesapeake* incident, 1807, Jefferson remained committed to peaceful diplomacy and economic coercion to maintain American rights. The Embargo (December 1807) and the Non-Importation Act, however, though daring measures, were practical failures. Convinced that the Embargo had not received a fair trial, he nevertheless yielded to a rebellious Congress and signed the Non-Intercourse Act, Mar. 1, 1809, just before he left office.

During the remaining years of his life, spent in continuing financial stringency, Jefferson never ventured far from Monticello, maintaining a voluminous correspondence with friends in America and Europe, where his reputation as a patron of learning continued high, and devoting much time to promoting popular education, which he regarded as a guarantor of freedom. He tirelessly promoted a liberal, modern university for his "country," Virginia, and attended every stage of the formation of the University of Virginia with a paternal care. Upon his death, appropriately on the fiftieth anniversary of the Declaration of Independence, this most enigmatic and probably most versatile of great Americans was buried at Monticello, under a stone describing him as he wished to be remembered—as the author of the Declaration of Independence and the Virginia statute for religious freedom, and the father of the University of Virginia.

The popularity and political success of Jefferson, whose diffidence and lack of spectacular qualities would have constituted in a later day an insuperable handicap, and whose relative freedom from personal ambition makes it impossible to characterize him as a demagogue, was due in part to his identification of himself with causes for which time was fighting, and also to his remarkable sensitiveness to fluctuations in public opinion, combined with an ability to utilize and to develop agencies of popular appeal. As a practical politician he worked through other men, whom he energized and who gave him to an extraordinary degree their devoted cooperation. His unchallenged leadership was due, not to self-assertiveness and imperiousness of will, but to the fact that circumstances had made him a symbolic figure, and that to an acute intelligence and unceasing industry he joined a dauntless and contagious faith.

Over the course of his public life this earnest advocate of a free press was one of its principal victims. Long regarded in ecclesiastical circles, especially in New England, as the embodiment of foreign infidelity, he was also charged by the Federalist press with cowardice, drunkenness, sexual immorality, and plain dishonesty. These largely groundless charges were widely believed, especially by the "better sort of people." In fact, Jefferson was anything but an infidel and had he lived a generation later would have been more at home in New England liberal religious circles than anywhere else in America.

During his lifetime Jefferson received international honors for scholarship. Although much of this was owing to his political prominence, he could properly claim the reputation of scholar. He served as president of the American Philosophical Society from 1797 until 1815. Modern scholars have recognized Jefferson as an American pioneer in numerous branches of science, notably paleontology, ethnology, geography, and botany. Living before the age of specialization, he was for his day a careful investigator, no more credulous than his learned contemporaries, and notable among them for his effort in all fields to attain scientific exactitude. In state papers he is commonly the lawyer, pleading a cause; in the heat of political controversy he doubtless compromised his intellectual ideals and certainly indulged in exaggeration; but his procedure in arriving at his fundamental opinions, the habits of his life, and his temperament were essentially those of a scholar. As secretary of state, he was in effect the first commissioner of patents and the first patent examiner. He himself invented or adapted to personal uses numerous ingenious devices, the best known of which is his polygraph.

He was at home in French, Italian, and Spanish, as well as Greek and Latin. He owned one of the best private collections of paintings and statuary in the country, and has been termed "the first American connoisseur and patron of the arts." Besides the Virginia state capitol, "Monticello," and the original buildings of the University of Virginia, he designed wholly or in part numerous Virginia houses, among them his own "Poplar Forest," "Farmington," "Edgemont," "Barboursville," and perhaps the middle section of "Brandon." Before the advent of professional architects in America, he began to collect books on architecture and discovered Palladio, from whom his careful and extensive observations abroad never weaned him. He did more than any other man to stimulate the classical revival in America. His own work, while always ingenious, is academic, precise, and orderly, but, because of the fortunate necessity of using brick and wood, the new creation was a blend, with a pleasing domesticity.

Few other American statesmen have been such careful and unremitting students of political thought and history as was Jefferson, or have been more concerned with ultimate ends. Yet he has left no treatise on political philosophy, and all general statements about his theoretical position are subject to qualification. It is impossible to grant eternal validity to the "principles" adduced by him to support his position in particular circumstances; he was always more interested in applications than in speculation, and he was forced to modify his own philosophy in practice. A homely aristocrat in manner of life and personal tastes, he distrusted all rulers and feared the rise of an industrial proletariat, but, more than any of his eminent contemporaries, he trusted the common man, if measurably enlightened and kept in rural virtue. Although pained and angered when the press made him the victim of its license, he was a passionate advocate of human liberty and laid supreme stress on the individual. Although he clearly realized the value of union, he emphasized the importance of the states and of local agencies of government. An intellectual internationalist, he gave wholehearted support to the policy of political isolation, and anticipated the development on the North American continent of a dominant nation, unique in civilization. He is notable, not for his harmony with the life of his age, but rather for his being a step or several steps ahead of it; no other American more deserves to be termed a major prophet, a supreme pioneer. A philosophical statesman rather than a political philosopher, he contributed to democracy and liberalism a faith rather than a body of doctrine.

JEFFERY, EDWARD TURNER (*b. Liverpool, England, 1843; d. New York, N.Y., 1927*), railroad executive. Came to America as a child. General manager, Illinois Central; controversial president, Denver & Rio Grande, 1891–1912; involved in Western Pacific fiasco, 1905–13.

JEFFREY, EDWARD CHARLES (*b. St. Catherines, Ontario, 1866; d. Cambridge, Mass., 1952*), botanist, educator. Studied at the University of Toronto and Harvard (Ph.D., 1899). Taught at Harvard, 1902–33, becoming chairman of the plant morphology department in 1907. Jeffrey attained reputation as a comparative plant anatomist and phylogenist during the first decade of the century, but because of his incautious attacks on the mutation theories of H. M. de Vries and T. H. Morgan he was not elected to the National Academy of Sciences.

JEFFREY, JOSEPH ANDREW (*b. Clarksville, Ohio, 1836; d. Columbus, Ohio, 1928*), banker, manufacturer of coal-mining machinery.

JEFFREY, ROSA GRIFFITH VERTNER JOHNSON (*b. Natchez, Miss., 1828; d. Lexington, Ky., 1894*), poet, novelist.

JEFFRIES, BENJAMIN JOY (*b. Boston, Mass., 1833; d. 1915*), ophthalmic surgeon. Grandson of John Jeffries. Writer of a treatise on color blindness (1879) which was long the standard authority.

JEFFRIES, JAMES JACKSON (*b. Carroll, Ohio, 1875; d. Burbank, Calif., 1953*), boxing champion. Defeated Bob Fitzsimmons for the heavyweight title in 1899; held championship until his retirement in 1905. Known as the "great white hope" in his match against black fighter Jack Johnson, Jeffries was defeated and retired for good in 1910.

JEFFRIES, JOHN (*b. Boston, Mass., 1744/45; d. 1819*), physician, scientist. Graduated Harvard, 1763; M.D., Aberdeen, 1770. A Loyalist with service on the British side during the Revolution, he became interested in aerostation while in England ca. 1782–90, and made two balloon ascents with the French aeronaut Blanchard. The first was over London, November 1784; the second carried him across the English Channel, January 1785.

Jeffries made observations of temperature, pressure, and humidity, constituting the first scientific data of the free air, to a height of 9,309 feet. He returned to Boston *ca.* 1790 where he practiced medicine.

JELLIFFE, SMITH ELY (*b. New York, N.Y., 1866; d. Huletts Landing, N.Y., 1945*), neurologist, psychoanalyst, medical editor. Graduated in civil engineering from Brooklyn Polytechnic Institute, 1886; A.B., Brooklyn Polytechnic, 1896. M.D., College of Physicians and Surgeons, New York City, 1889. Ph.D., Columbia University, 1899. He began general practice in Brooklyn, N.Y., *ca.* 1891. In 1894 Jelliffe was appointed instructor of pharmacognosy and materia medica in the New York College of Pharmacy, and from 1897 to 1901 he edited the *Journal of Pharmacology*. Meanwhile he had spent the summer of 1896 at the Binghamton (N.Y.) State Hospital. Although Jelliffe acted as an alienist in the courts, he was primarily a neurologist.

In 1907 Jelliffe gave up teaching pharmacology and until 1913 was clinical professor of mental diseases in the ill-fated Fordham University Medical School. While there he helped bring Carl G. Jung for a lecture series (1912) that precipitated the famous break between Jung and Freud. In 1913 Jelliffe took up the practice of psychoanalysis and advocated the psychoanalytic viewpoint. Always the physician, he ultimately became more "medical" than his psychiatric colleagues and earned the title of "Father of Psychosomatic Medicine."

From 1900 to 1905 he served as editor of the weekly *Medical News*, and for the following four years as co-editor of its successor, the *New York Medical Journal*. In 1899 he had begun editorial work on the *Journal of Nervous and Mental Disease*, and in 1902 he became its owner and managing editor. Acknowledged as unexcelled in America in his grasp of neurological literature, Jelliffe's influence on physicians was exerted chiefly through his editorial work and by the textbook *Diseases of the Nervous System*, which went through six editions between 1915 and 1935.

JEMISON, ALICE MAE LEE (*b. Silver Creek, N.Y., 1901; d. Washington, D.C., 1964*), American Indian journalist and activist. Coming from a conservative Seneca background, she became a leading Indian opponent of the New Deal. As editor of the newsletter *The First American*, 1937–40 and 1953–55, she advocated the abolition of the Bureau of Indian Affairs and preached the sanctity of Indian treaty rights. Jemison became a lobbyist in Washington, D.C., for the tribal council of the Seneca in 1934 and also lobbied for the American Indian Federation, 1935–39. Her militancy presaged much of the Red Power movement of the late 1960's and 1970's.

JEMISON, MARY (*b. at sea, en route to Philadelphia from Belfast, 1743; d. Buffalo Creek Reservation, N.Y., 1833*), "the White Woman of the Genesee." Was captured in Pennsylvania and adopted by Indians, 1758. In 1762 she was taken to the Seneca tribal home on the Genesee River near present Geneseo, N.Y. Twice married to Indians, in 1797 she was granted a large tract of land near Castile, N.Y.; her land-title was confirmed by the New York legislature, 1817, when she was also naturalized. One of the most extensive landholders in the region, she became a tradition in western New York, largely through publication of her story as told to James Everett Seaver. *A Narrative of the Life of Mrs. Mary Jemison* (1824) was one of the most popular Indian "captivities."

JENCKES, JOSEPH. *See* JENKS, JOSEPH.

JENCKES, JOSEPH (*b. probably near Hammersmith, England, 1632; d. 1717*), founder of Pawtucket, pioneer iron manufacturer of Rhode Island. Came to America *ca.* 1650. Set up sawmill and forge near Pawtucket Falls, 1671. Son of Joseph Jenks.

JENCKES, JOSEPH (*b. Pawtucket, R.I., 1656; d. 1740*), surveyor. Son of Joseph Jenckes (1632–1717). Deputy governor of Rhode Island, 1715–27; governor, 1727–31. Opposed excessive issue of paper currency.

JENCKES, THOMAS ALLEN (*b. Cumberland, R.I., 1818; d. 1875*), jurist, Rhode Island legislator. Graduated Brown, 1838; rose rapidly in the field of patent litigation. Congressman, Republican, from Rhode Island, 1863–71. Among the earliest proponents of civil service reform, he successfully campaigned for a national bankruptcy law, and initiated competitive examinations for admission to West Point.

JENIFER, DANIEL OF ST. THOMAS (*b. Charles Co., Md., 1723; d. Annapolis, Md., 1790*), Maryland political leader. Nephew of John Hanson. Held many colonial offices; active in Revolutionary cause; member, Continental Congress, 1778–82. Played minor part in Federal Convention, 1787; advocated three-year term for members of the national House of Representatives.

JENKINS, ALBERT GALLATIN (*b. Cabell Co., Va., now W.Va., 1830; d. near Cloyd's Mountain, Va., 1864*), lawyer, farmer. Congressman, Democrat, from Virginia, 1857–61. As Confederate brigadier general, commanded cavalry raid into Ohio, August–September 1862. Died as result of surgery after a severe wound.

JENKINS, CHARLES JONES (*b. Beaufort District, S.C., 1805; d. 1883*), jurist, Georgia legislator. Governor of Georgia, 1865–68. Removed for refusing compliance with Reconstruction acts of 1867.

JENKINS, EDWARD HOPKINS (*b. Falmouth, Mass., 1850; d. New Haven, Conn., 1931*), agricultural chemist. Graduated Yale, 1872; Ph.D., 1879; studied also in Germany. Introduced shade-grown tobacco into Northern states among other achievements during lifelong association with Connecticut Agricultural Experiment Station.

JENKINS, HOWARD MALCOLM (*b. Gwynedd, Pa., 1842; d. 1902*), newspaper editor, historical writer. As editor in chief of the *Friends' Intelligencer*, became a distinguished Quaker leader. Wrote extensively on Pennsylvania history.

JENKINS, JAMES GRAHAM (*b. Saratoga Springs, N.Y., 1834; d. Milwaukee, Wis., 1921*), lawyer. Grandson of Reuben H. Walworth. Moved to Milwaukee, 1857, soon after his admission to the bar. A Democratic leader in Wisconsin, he served as U.S. district judge, eastern district of Wisconsin, 1888–93, and as U.S. circuit judge, 1893–1905. His name is associated with two important cases: *Pillsbury v. Pillsbury Washburn Company, Ltd.*, in which his decision involving unfair competition remains a landmark of American jurisprudence; and the so-called Northern Pacific receivership (*Farmers Loan and Trust Co.* v. *Northern Pacific*), in which a strike order he granted, later affirmed by the Supreme Court, involved him in a controversy with Congress. He was dean of the law school, Marquette University, 1908–15.

JENKINS, JOHN (*b. probably East Greenwich, Conn., 1728; d. Orange Co., N.Y., 1785*), pioneer, surveyor. Leading spirit in efforts by Susquehanna Co. of Connecticut to settle Wyoming Valley in Pennsylvania, 1762–69. Driven from the valley, 1778.

JENKINS, JOHN (*b. New London, Conn., 1751 o.s.; d. Exeter, Pa., 1827*), Revolutionary soldier, pioneer, surveyor. Son of John Jenkins (1728–85). Leader of the Connecticut settlers of the Wyoming Valley after his father's retirement. Helped plan General Sullivan's campaign against the Indians, 1779.

JENKINS, JOHN STILWELL (*b. Albany, N.Y., 1818; d. Syracuse, N.Y., 1852*), lawyer, newspaper editor. Compiled many historical popularizations and abridgments of longer works.

JENKINS, MICAH (*b. Edisto Island, S.C., 1835; d. 1864*), Confederate soldier. Commanded 5th South Carolina and Palmetto Sharpshooters; promoted brigadier general, 1862; commanded Hood's division at Chickamauga; killed at the Wilderness.

JENKINS, NATHANIEL (*b. Boston, Mass., 1812; d. 1872*), inventor, manufacturer. Developed rubber compound packing for water faucets, steam valves; invented the Jenkins valve (patented 1868).

JENKINS, THORNTON ALEXANDER (*b. Orange Co., Va., 1811; d. 1893*), naval officer, lighthouse expert. Chief, Bureau of Navigation, 1865–69. Commanded USS *Hartford* at Port Hudson, March 1863; retired as rear admiral, 1873.

JENKS, GEORGE CHARLES (*b. London, England, 1850; d. 1929*), journalist. Came to America, 1872. As writer of dime novels *post* 1886, was one of group which produced the endless adventures of Nick Carter and Diamond Dick.

JENKS, JEREMIAH WHIPPLE (*b. St. Clair, Mich., 1856; d. New York, N.Y., 1929*), economist, teacher. Graduated University of Michigan, 1878; Ph.D., Halle, 1885. Taught at Indiana, Cornell, and New York universities. First American academic economist to serve extensively on government boards and commissions, Jenks was influential in shaping legislation on trusts, immigration, and the white-slave trade; he also advised foreign governments on currency and other economic problems.

JENKS, JOSEPH (*b. probably Colnbrook, England, 1602; d. Saugus, Mass., 1683 n.s.*), inventor. Father of Joseph Jencks (1632–1717). A skilled iron-worker, Jenks was induced to come to America, 1642, to assist in establishing the first iron works near Lynn, Mass., but he soon occupied himself with original projects. His reputation caused his selection to cut dies for the first coins minted in Boston and to build the first fire engine. In his own forge, Jenks in 1655 produced a scythe of a new, improved type which has long remained standard.

JENKS, TUDOR STORRS (*b. Brooklyn, N.Y., 1857; d. 1922*), lawyer. Author of a large number of juvenile books; associate editor of *St. Nicholas*, 1887–1902.

JENKS, WILLIAM (*b. Newton, Mass., 1778; d. 1866*), Congregational clergyman, antiquarian. Graduated Harvard, 1797. Pastor in Bath, Maine; later, a Boston pioneer in religious work among seamen. An outstanding Biblical and Oriental scholar, he was author of *Comprehensive Commentary on the Holy Bible* (1835–1838) and other works.

JENNEY, WILLIAM LE BARON (*b. Fairhaven, Mass., 1832; d. Los Angeles, Calif., 1907*), architect, inventor, Union soldier. Studied art and architecture in France. After serving as an engineer throughout the Civil War on staffs of Generals Grant and Sherman, he established himself in Chicago as an architect, 1868. For the Home Insurance Building in Chicago, he devised a method of skeleton construction in which each story was carried independently on columns. This building (1883–84) was the first high building to use such a method as the basic principle of its design; as such it was the first skyscraper. Jenney also introduced the use of Bessemer steel beams in building construction.

JENNINGS, HERBERT SPENCER (*b. Tonica, Ill., 1868; d. Santa Monica, Calif., 1947*), biologist. Jennings taught in district schools in Iowa and Illinois, and attended Illinois State Normal School, 1887–88. In 1889 he taught at Texas Agricultural and Mechanical College; and in 1890 he entered the University of Michigan, where he studied biology and received an assistantship in zoology. In 1891 he headed the U.S. Fish Commission's survey of the Great Lakes.

After receiving his B.S., 1893, Jennings stayed on at Michigan for a year as a graduate assistant. He then entered Harvard; M.A., 1895; Ph.D., 1896. His doctoral thesis was a description of the early development of a rotifer. He spent the year 1896–97 studying physiology, psychology, and doing experiments at Jena and Naples. During this important year he began investigations on behavior and responses to stimuli in unicellular and other lower organisms. The work of this period was summarized in his book *Behavior of Lower Organisms* (1906).

Jennings returned from Europe to become professor of botany at Montana State Agricultural and Mechanical College (1897–98), and then successively instructor in zoology at Dartmouth (1898–99) and instructor (1899–1901) and assistant professor (1901–03) in zoology at the University of Michigan. In 1901 he collaborated on *Anatomy of the Cat*. In 1903 Jennings was called to the University of Pennsylvania as assistant professor of zoology, with the first year on leave in Naples under a grant from the Carnegie Institution of Washington. In 1906 he went to Johns Hopkins as associate professor and a year later became professor of experimental zoology. He remained there until his retirement in 1938, from 1910 as Henry Walters Professor and director of the zoological laboratory. At Johns Hopkins, Jennings did research on genetics and evolution in unicellular organisms, chiefly *Paramecium* and *Difflugia*. He also demonstrated the genetic constancy of the clone. The work and thought of these years were summarized in the book *Life and Death: Heredity and Evolution in Unicellular Organisms* (1920).

During his last two decades at Johns Hopkins, Jennings did work as a biometrician for the Food Administration (1917–18); wrote *Genetics of the Protozoa* (1929); and published laboratory studies on fecundity and aging in a rotifer, genetic consequences of conjugation in *Paramecium*, and an extension of his earlier studies on inheritance in *Difflugia*. In 1938, he became research associate at the University of California, Los Angeles. There he discovered the first system of multiple interbreeding mating types. He also contributed abundant data on mating-type inheritance and made an exhaustive study of the factors determining clonal vigor and length of life. Jennings also wrote *Prometheus, or Biology and the Advancement of Man* (1925); *The Biological Basis of Human Nature* (1930); *The Universe and Life* (1933); and a textbook, *Genetics* (1935).

JENNINGS, JAMES HENNEN (*b. Hawesville, Ky., 1854; d. 1920*), mining engineer. Graduated Lawrence Scientific School, 1877. Instituted the cyanide process for recovering gold which made South Africa's Rand district profitable.

JENNINGS, JOHN (*b. probably Philadelphia, Pa., ca. 1738; d. Philadelphia, 1802*), public official, Revolutionary soldier. A prominent figure in the Pennamite War in Pennsylvania against settlers from Connecticut, 1761 and 1769.

JENNINGS, JONATHAN (*b. either Hunterdon Co., N.J., or Rockbridge Co., Va., 1784; d. near Charlestown, Ind., 1834*), lawyer. Removed to Northwest Territory, 1806. Territorial delegate to Congress from Indiana, 1809–15; first governor of Indiana, 1816–22; congressman, 1823–31.

JENSEN, BENTON FRANKLIN ("BEN") (*b. Marion, Iowa, 1892; d. Washington, D.C., 1970*), U.S. congressman. Served as a conservative Republican congressman from Iowa's Seventh District, 1938–64. Was the ranking Republican on the Appropriations Committee; served as chairman of the Interior and

Government Corporations subcommittees; and was the ranking minority member of the Interior, Deficiencies, Atomic Energy, and Public Works subcommittees.

JENSEN, JENS (*b. Dybbøl, Schleswig [now Denmark], 1860; d. Door County, Wis., 1951*), landscape designer. Immigrated to the U.S. in 1884. Worked for the Chicago West Park Commission, 1886–1900. Established his principles of landscape art in a series of private estates (1900–07); he emphasized the importance of local plants, insisted on purity in the handling of water, space, and rock work, and rejected all formalism. Superintendent and landscape architect, West Park Commission, 1907–20. Designed Henry Ford's estate in Dearborn and the Lincoln Memorial Gardens in Springfield, Ill. Founded The Clearing, a school of landscape design, in Door County, Wis. in 1936.

JENSEN, PETER LAURITS (*b. Falster, Denmark, 1886; d. Western Springs, Ill., 1961*), pioneer in radio and electronics. Worked as an apprentice, then assistant, in the laboratory of Valdemar Poulsen in Copenhagen. Moving to California, Jensen met Edwin Pridham, an electrical engineer. Their research firm developed the first dynamic horn loudspeaker. In 1917 they became chief engineers of the newly formed Magnavox Company. Jensen founded the Jensen Radio Manufacturing Company in 1927 and then founded Jensen Industries, which manufactured phonograph needles. He was chief consultant to the U.S. War Production Board's radio and radar division during World War II.

JEPSON, WILLIS LINN (*b. near Vacaville, Calif., 1867; d. Berkeley, Calif., 1946*), botanist. Ph.B., University of California at Berkeley, 1889; Ph.D., 1899. Taught botany at University of California, 1890–1937; was professor *post* 1918. Jepson dedicated himself to interpreting the flora of California. Among his books were *The Silva of California* (1910); A *Manual of the Flowering Plants of California* (1925); and A *Flora of California* (published in parts through 1943, but never completed). He was a pioneer in the conservation movement and an early proponent of better forest management.

JEROME, CHAUNCEY (*b. Canaan, Conn., 1793; d. 1868*), clock maker, inventor. Devised the "bronze looking-glass clock" *ca.* 1825; invented a one-day brass clock movement *ca.* 1838.

JEROME, WILLIAM TRAVERS (*b. New York, N.Y., 1859; d. New York, 1934*), lawyer. Anti-Tammany foe of corruption; assistant to J. W. Goff, 1894; controversial and unconventional but effective district attorney in New York City, 1901–09.

JERVIS, JOHN BLOOMFIELD (*b. Huntington, N.Y., 1795; d. Rome, N.Y., 1885*), engineer. Began his career on the survey for the Erie Canal, rising rapidly to section engineer and then superintendent. Became associated with the projected Delaware & Hudson canal and railway system, 1825; built the railroad, drawing up the specifications for all equipment including the first locomotive to run in America. This was the "Stourbridge Lion," tested August 1829. For the Mohawk & Hudson Railway, he invented the four-wheel, "bogie" truck used on the locomotive "Experiment," 1832. As chief engineer of the Chenango (N.Y.) Canal, he did original work in determining the amount of rainfall available to supply artificial reservoirs for the upper levels. He was chief engineer of the Croton Aqueduct and consulting engineer for the Boston water supply; he also directed construction of the Hudson River Railroad, the Michigan Southern, the Chicago & Rock Island and others.

JESSE, RICHARD HENRY (*b. Lancaster Co., Va., 1853; d. 1921*), educator. Graduated University of Virginia, 1875. Taught at Tulane. President of University of Missouri, 1891–1907, where he established pioneer schools of education and journalism.

JESSUP, HENRY HARRIS (*b. Montrose, Pa., 1832; d. Beirut, Syria, now Lebanon, 1910*), Presbyterian missionary to Syria, 1855–1910. A founder of the present American University of Beirut, 1866.

JESSUP, WALTER ALBERT (*b. Richmond, Ind., 1877; d. New York, N.Y., 1944*), educator, foundation executive. B.A., Earlham College, 1903; M.A., Hanover College, 1908; Ph.D., Teachers College, Columbia University, 1911. Professor and dean of school of education at Indiana University, 1911; at State University of Iowa, Iowa City, 1912–16. As president of the State University of Iowa, 1916–34, he was successful in winning support for its improvement and enlargement. In 1934 he became president of the Carnegie Foundation for the Advancement of Teaching; in 1941 he took on the additional duty of president of the Carnegie Corporation.

JESUP, MORRIS KETCHUM (*b. Westport, Conn., 1830; d. 1908*), capitalist, philanthropist. Made his fortune in New York City in banking before retiring in 1884 to sponsor philanthropies. An original incorporator of the American Museum of Natural History (1868) in which he was primarily interested, he gave it a total of $2,000,000 and supported many of its scientific investigations. He contributed to Peary's discovery of the North Pole, aided the New York conservation movement which resulted in the Adirondack Preserve, was a supporter of the Audubon Society, and gave assistance to many educational institutions, particularly the American University at Beirut and the Union Theological Seminary in New York.

JESUP, THOMAS SIDNEY (*b. Berkeley Co., Va., now W. Va., 1788; d. Washington, D.C., 1860*), soldier. Entered the U.S. Army, 1808; served with distinction in War of 1812. In December 1814 he was sent to Connecticut to watch the Hartford Convention and was able to dispel President Madison's fears concerning secession. In 1818 he began an unequaled 42 years as quartermaster general of the army and soon organized that department on a sound military and business basis. His service as quartermaster general was interrupted during the Seminole War by field commands, 1836–38; he was wounded in 1838. Resuming his duties in Washington, he served until his death. *Post* 1828, he held rank of major general.

JETER, JEREMIAH BELL (*b. Bedford Co., Va., 1802; d. 1880*), Baptist clergyman, editor. Pastor in Richmond, Va., 1836–49, 1852–70. A leader in organizing the Southern Baptist Convention, 1845.

JEWELL, HARVEY (*b. Winchester, N.H., 1820; d. 1881*), lawyer. Brother of Marshall Jewell. Whig and Republican leader in Massachusetts; appointed by President Grant to Court of Commissioners of Alabama Claims (1875–76); practiced in Boston.

JEWELL, MARSHALL (*b. Winchester, N.H., 1825; d. 1883*), leather belting manufacturer, capitalist. Brother of Harvey Jewell. Republican governor of Connecticut, 1869–70; 1871–73. U.S. minister to Russia, 1873–74; efficient U.S. postmaster general, 1874–76.

JEWETT, CHARLES COFFIN (*b. Lebanon, Maine, 1816; d. Braintree, Mass., 1868*), bibliographer, librarian. Brother of John P. Jewett. Published first extended collection of statistics on American libraries at Smithsonian Institution, 1851; projected a union catalogue, 1852; directed Boston Public Library, 1858–68.

JEWETT, CLARENCE FREDERICK (*b. Claremont, N.H., 1852; d. New York, N.Y., 1909*), projector of historical works.

Best known for fostering Justin Winsor's *Narrative and Critical History of America* (1886–1889).

JEWETT, DAVID (*b. New London, Conn., 1772; d. 1842*), naval officer. Served in U.S. Navy, 1799–1801; entered Argentine service, 1815; *post* 1822 was in naval service of Brazil.

JEWETT, FRANK BALDWIN (*b. Pasadena, Calif., 1879; d. Short Hills, N.J., 1949*), telephone engineer, industrial research administrator. Graduated from present California Institute of Technology, 1898. Ph.D., University of Chicago, 1902; worked as research assistant to Albert A. Michelson. After further study and a teaching appointment at Massachusetts Institute of Technology, he joined the engineering department of the American Telephone and Telegraph Company in Boston, Mass., 1904, rising to head the department in 1906. Jewett played a major role in the 1915 establishment of transcontinental telephone service. An advocate of industrial research by trained scientists, Jewett headed the Bell Telephone Laboratories from their founding in 1925 until his retirement in 1944. He was president of the National Academy of Sciences, 1939–47, and gave distinguished service during World War II as a member of the National Defense Research Committee.

JEWETT, HUGH JUDGE (*b. Harford Co., Md., 1817; d. Augusta, Ga., 1898*), lawyer, Ohio legislator. Held executive posts in various Midwestern railroads; successful reorganizer of the Erie, 1874–84.

JEWETT, JOHN PUNCHARD (*b. Lebanon, Maine, 1814; d. Orange, N.J., 1884*), publisher. Brother of Charles C. Jewett. An Abolitionist, he brought out *Uncle Tom's Cabin* in book form, 1852, but was thereafter relatively unsuccessful.

JEWETT, MILO PARKER (*b. St. Johnsbury, Vt., 1808; d. 1882*), educational pioneer. Graduated Dartmouth, 1828. Largely responsible for the establishment of Vassar College, of which he was first president, 1861–67. Thereafter he served in several Wisconsin educational posts.

JEWETT, SARAH ORNE (*b. South Berwick, Maine, 1849; d. 1909*), author. Taught by her father to observe every detail of her surroundings, she possessed at the outset of her career an almost complete knowledge of her environment. Beginning with her first real success, *Deephaven* (1877), and continuing to the classic *The Country of the Pointed Firs* (1896), she gave permanence through her writings to a disappearing order of New England, the remote provincial life which had lingered a few years after the dissolution of the West Indian trade before being engulfed by the new civilization of smoke and steam. The artistic discipline displayed in her sketches of villages and villagers is possibly the most impressive quality in her achievement.

JEWETT, WILLIAM (*b. East Haddam, Conn., 1792; d. Jersey City, N.J., 1874*), portrait painter. Worked in partnership with his teacher, Samuel L. Waldo.

JEWETT, WILLIAM CORNELL (*b. New York, N.Y., 1823; d. Geneva, Switzerland, 1893*), publicist. Known as "Colorado Jewett." Gained notoriety by his efforts to end the Civil War through European intervention; arranged Niagara Falls meeting between Horace Greeley and Confederate commissioner J. P. Holcombe, July 1864.

JOCELYN, NATHANIEL (*b. New Haven, Conn., 1796; d. 1881*), portrait painter, bank-note engraver. Teacher of, among others, Thomas Rossiter and William O. Stone.

JOGUES, ISAAC (*b. Orléans, France, 1607; d. Ossernenon, now Auriesville, N.Y., 1646*), Jesuit missionary, martyr. Came to Canada, 1636. Began mission among Huron Indians on Georgian Bay. Captured by hostile Iroquois, 1642, together with René Goupil, he was tortured and kept a slave for a year, until rescued by the Dutch at Fort Orange. Repatriated to France, he was honored by the queen regent and the pope, but soon returned to his labors in Canada. After visiting the Iroquois as an ambassador of the governor, he obtained permission to undertake a mission to the Mohawks, who killed him on his arrival at one of their villages. He was beatified, 1925; canonized, 1930.

JOHNS, CLAYTON (*b. New Castle, Del., 1857; d. Boston, Mass., 1932*), composer. Prominent in music circles of Boston.

JOHNS, JOHN (*b. New Castle, Del., 1796; d. 1876*), Episcopal clergyman. Son of Kensey Johns (1759–1848). Graduated Princeton, 1815; ordained, 1819; pastor at Frederick and Baltimore, Md. Assistant bishop of Virginia, 1842–62; bishop, 1862–76. President of College of William and Mary, 1849–54.

JOHNS, KENSEY (*b. West River, Md., 1759; d. 1848*), Delaware jurist. Studied law with Samuel Chase and George Read. Served 1799–1830, as chief justice of the supreme court of Delaware, was chancellor, 1830–32.

JOHNS, KENSEY (*b. New Castle, Del., 1791; d. Sussex, Del., 1857*), Delaware jurist, congressman. Son of Kensey Johns (1759–1848). Graduated Princeton, 1810; studied law with his uncle Nicholas Van Dyke. Chancellor of Delaware, 1832–57.

JOHNSEN, ERIK KRISTIAN (*b. near Stavanger, Norway, 1863; d. St. Paul, Minn., 1923*), Lutheran theologian. Came to America, 1892. Professor at Red Wing Seminary; and at Luther Theological Seminary, St. Paul, Minn., 1900–23.

JOHNSON, ALBERT (*b. Springfield, Ill., 1869; d. American Lake, Wash., 1957*), newspaper editor, politician. Worked as a reporter and editor before becoming editor and publisher of the *Grays Harbor Washingtonian*, 1909–34. U.S. Congressman, 1913–33; chairman of the House Committee on Immigration and Naturalization, 1919–33. A vehement racist and nativist, and especially opposed to immigration of Orientals, Johnson was instrumental in ending the open-door immigration policy. In 1924, the Johnson-Reed Act, restricting immigration to 150,000 per year by 1927 and eventually excluding Orientals, was passed.

JOHNSON, ALEXANDER (*b. Ashton-under-Lyne, Lancashire, England, 1847; d. Aurora, Ill., 1941*), social worker. Brother-in-law of Edward R. Johnstone. Educated at Mechanics' Institute and Owens College, Manchester. Immigrated to Canada, 1869; moved to Chicago, Ill., *ca.* 1872, and to Cincinnati, Ohio, *ca.* 1877. At first employed in manufacture of clothing, he began his career in social work as a volunteer with the Cincinnati Associated Charities, 1882; general secretary, 1884–86. After work with a similar agency in Chicago, and with the Indiana State Board of Charities, he was made superintendent of the Indiana State School for the Feeble-Minded, Fort Wayne, 1893–1903, where he endeavored to institute training courses in useful occupations. Removing to New York City, he was associate director of the New York School of Philanthropy, 1904–06. As secretary of the National Conference of Charities and Correction, 1904–12, he brought the organization to the forefront of progressive social reform. He served as field secretary of the Vineland (N.J.) Training School, 1912–17, spreading word of its techniques for the education of the mentally defective. From 1918 until his retirement in 1922 he worked for the American Red Cross.

JOHNSON, ALEXANDER BRYAN (*b. Gosport, England, 1786; d. 1867*), Utica, N.Y., banker. Came to America, 1801.

Wrote extensively on a variety of subjects ranging from religion to finance.

JOHNSON, ALEXANDER SMITH (*b.* Utica, N.Y., 1817; *d. Nassau, Bahama Islands, 1878*), New York jurist. Son of Alexander B. Johnson. Held several state and federal judicial posts, including U.S. circuit judge, 2nd Judicial Circuit, 1875–78.

JOHNSON, ALLEN (*b.* Lowell, Mass., 1870; *d.* Washington, D.C., 1931), teacher and writer of history, biographer. Graduated Amherst, 1892; Ph.D., Columbia, 1899. Studied also at Leipzig and Paris. Editor of the *Chronicles of America* (1918–1921) and first editor of the *Dictionary of American Biography*. Professor of history at Grinnell College, Bowdoin, and Yale.

JOHNSON, ANDREW (*b.* Raleigh, N.C., 1808; *d. near Carter Station, Tenn., 1875*), seventeenth president of the United States. The younger son of a bank porter and sexton who died leaving his sons in poverty, Johnson removed to Tennessee, 1826; settled finally at Greeneville, Tenn. Self-educated, ambitious, he gradually accumulated a small estate by thrift in his management of a tailor shop he established. Neat in appearance and courteous, he was a powerful speaker, though in his early years often crude in thought and diction.

Championship of the working men of Greeneville against the aristocratic element brought about Johnson's election as alderman and then mayor. Beginning in 1835, he was successively representative to the Tennessee legislature; state senator; Democratic congressman, 1843–53; governor of Tennessee, 1853–57, and U.S. senator, 1857–62. Johnson's ability rather than the support of others advanced him; although a Jacksonian Democrat who nearly always voted with his party, Johnson quarreled with so many Democratic leaders that he lacked friends.

Johnson favored a change to the "white basis" of representation instead of the standard count of five slaves as three whites (East Tennessee had relatively few slaves) and supported the formation of East Tennessee into a new state. Yet he claimed orthodoxy regarding slavery and frequently denounced the Abolitionists. He favored the election of federal judges and of senators by popular vote, and the abolition of the electoral college in presidential elections. He became the special advocate of the "homestead" law for the granting of public lands to actual settlers, skillfully appealing to the interest of the laboring classes of the East as well as the frontier states. Throughout his life, he manifested a strong dislike of superiority claimed by right of wealth or birth and was a consistent friend of labor.

In 1860, the Tennessee delegation presented Johnson's name for the presidential nomination. After the split in the Democratic party, he supported Breckinridge and Lane, while favoring compromise between North and South. While the South Carolina secession convention was meeting in December 1860, Johnson declared for the Union in the Senate; when the other Southern senators withdrew, he alone remained. The North at once welcomed him as a powerful ally in the tradition of Jackson, while Southern extremists denounced him as a traitor. In the special session of July 1861, Johnson introduced a successful resolution declaring the war to be only for the defense and maintenance of the supremacy of the Constitution and the Union. During the following winter, he devoted much time to the joint committee on conduct of the war.

Early in 1862, President Lincoln appointed Johnson military governor of Tennessee, which was in Confederate hands with Unionist East Tennessee overrun by Confederates and under martial law. After Grant's victories in secessionist West Tennessee, Johnson began his efforts at reconstruction. Constantly at odds with Union military authorities, he succeeded in restoring civil government by state action after the defeat of the Confederate

armies. By 1865, a constitutional convention adopted amendments abolishing slavery which were later ratified by popular vote. Meanwhile, in recognition of the services of Southern Unionists and to help relieve the party of its sectional character, the National Union Convention nominated Johnson as Lincoln's vice presidential running mate, 1864. Exhaustion and ill health were responsible for Johnson's being under the influence of liquor when he took the oath of office, giving malice something later to feed upon. The day after Lincoln's assassination, April 15, 1865, Johnson took the oath of office and announced that he would retain Lincoln's cabinet and continue Lincoln's policies.

At first Johnson shared the vindictive Northern rage at the assassination, reportedly stating: "Treason must be made infamous, and traitors must be impoverished." Soon freed of hysteria, however, Johnson began to execute Lincoln's plan for re-establishing government in the states that had seceded. He issued a general proclamation of amnesty, excepting 14 classes of persons requiring special pardons; he also issued a proclamation for the establishment of loyal government in North Carolina and followed it by similar proclamations for other of the seceded states. Supervised by Johnson's provisional governors, elections for state conventions were held, new constitutions adopted, and state governments organized through the legislatures. Ordinances of secession were repealed, slavery abolished, the 13th Amendment ratified by all Southern states except Mississippi, and Confederate state debts repudiated. The extension of suffrage to the black was left a power belonging exclusively to the states.

Johnson addressed Congress in December 1865 in a conciliatory spirit, holding that acts of secession had been null and void and that the Southern states should be invited back into the Union, their ratification of the 13th Amendment serving as a pledge of perpetual loyalty and peace. But some radical Republican congressmen led by Thaddeus Stevens, who believed that the Southern states should rejoin the Union as new states or remain conquered provinces, were determined to block Johnson's plan. Stevens secured the establishment of the joint committee of 15— the "Central Directory" of the radicals—which was to dominate Reconstruction and institute reform by force.

The war-expanded power of the executive, altruistic concern for the freedmen, and the threat to the Republican party's control of the government by the return of larger Democratic representations to Congress from the Southern states, all combined to make inevitable a struggle between Congress and a president who was a Southerner and a states' rights Democrat. The Civil Rights Act, designed to provide federal protection of the civil rights of freedmen, was passed over Johnson's veto, Apr. 9, 1866, and was followed by the 14th Amendment. Strengthened in the elections of 1866, the radicals passed over the president's veto the Reconstruction Act of 1867 and a succession of supplementary acts, including a Tenure of Office Act forbidding the president to remove any Senate-approved office holder without the Senate's concurrence.

During a congressional recess in August 1867, Johnson defied the Tenure of Office Act by attempting to oust War Secretary E. M. Stanton, the radicals' informer and adviser within the president's cabinet. The attempt failed, an effort to secure a judicial test of the Act miscarried and the radicals used the incident to introduce impeachment proceedings against Johnson by the House of Representatives. With Chief Justice Chase presiding, the Senate, sitting as a court of impeachment, began the president's trial, since characterized as a "solemn theatrical fiasco," in March 1868. Attorney General Stanberry had resigned his post to lead Johnson's defense, while the notorious General Ben Butler and Thaddeus Stevens played leading parts for the prosecution. Impeachment failed in May by one vote (35–19), seven Republicans voting with the Democrats.

The National Union Republican convention had already nominated General U. S. Grant as its presidential candidate and Johnson had made no effort to secure the Democratic nomination, though he received 65 votes on the first ballot. Returning to Tennessee after a bitter valedictory on leaving office, March 1869, Johnson was drawn again into state politics and in 1874 became a successful candidate for the U.S. Senate. He returned to the Senate on March 5, 1875, but within five months suffered a fatal paralytic attack while visiting a daughter in Tennessee. His last public utterance was a Senate speech in which he attacked Grant's Reconstruction policies in Louisiana and closed with the plea: "Let peace and prosperity be restored to the land. May God bless this people; may God save the Constitution."

JOHNSON, BENJAMIN PIERCE (*b. Canaan, N.Y., 1793; d. 1869*), lawyer, agriculturist. Long-time officer of New York State Agricultural Society and representative of that state at international exhibitions.

JOHNSON, BRADLEY TYLER (*b. Frederick, Md., 1829; d. Amelia, Va., 1903*), lawyer, Virginia legislator, Confederate brigadier general of cavalry. Practiced law in Richmond, Va., and Baltimore, Md., after the Civil War.

JOHNSON, BUSHROD RUST (*b. Belmont Co., Ohio, 1817; d. Brighton, Ill., 1880*), educator, soldier. Graduated West Point, 1840. As Confederate brigadier general, commanded at Fort Henry; escaped after fall of Fort Donelson. Distinguished at Chickamauga and in defense of Richmond, 1864–65.

JOHNSON, BYRON BANCROFT (*b. Norwalk, Ohio, 1864; d. St. Louis, Mo., 1931*). President of the American League of Professional Base Ball Clubs, 1900–27; established World Series.

JOHNSON, CAVE (*b. near Springfield, Tenn., 1793; d. Clarksville, Tenn., 1866*), lawyer. Congressman, Democrat, from Tennessee, 1829–37, 1839–45. Postmaster general, 1845–49, under President Polk, to whom he was confidential friend and adviser; introduced use of postage stamps. Active in support of James Buchanan for presidency.

JOHNSON, CHAPMAN (*b. Louisa Co., Va., 1779; d. Richmond, Va., 1849*), Virginia lawyer and legislator. Championed democratic western against aristocratic eastern Virginia in constitutional convention, 1829–30.

JOHNSON, CHARLES SPURGEON (*b. Bristol, Va., 1893; d. Louisville, Ky., 1956*), sociologist, educator. Graduated from the University of Chicago, Ph.B., 1918. National research director of the Urban League from 1922; founded and edited the periodical *Opportunity*, a publication that encouraged such black writers as Countee Cullen (an assistant editor), Langston Hughes, James Weldon Johnson, and Claude McKay during the Harlem Renaissance. Became professor of sociology and director of the social sciences department at Fisk University, 1928, and elevated the department into a major force in combating racial discrimination; president of the university, 1946–56. Member of the first American delegation to UNESCO at Paris, 1946.

JOHNSON, DAVID BANCROFT (*b. La Grange, Tenn., 1856; d. Rock Hill, S.C., 1928*), educator. Founder and president, 1886–1928, of Winthrop College at Rock Hill, a woman's state college originally established to train teachers.

JOHNSON, DOUGLAS WILSON (*b. Parkersburg, W. Va., 1878; d. Sebring, Fla., 1944*), geologist, geomorphologist, geographer. Attended Denison University, 1896–98. B.S., University of New Mexico, 1901; Ph.D., Columbia University, 1903. Taught geology at Massachusetts Institute of Technology (1903–07), Harvard (1907–12), and Columbia University *post*

1912, becoming professor in 1919. An associate and firm follower of William Morris Davis, Johnson won fame as a geomorphologist by his application and extension of Davis' approach. During World War I, as major in U.S. Army intelligence, he made evaluations of the strategic importance of land formation on the chief European fronts. He also served as chief of the division of boundary geography in the U.S. delegation to the Paris peace conference, 1918–19. He was author of *Shore Processes and Shoreline Development* (1919); *The New England-Acadian Shoreline* (1925); and *Stream Sculpture on the Atlantic Slope* (1931).

JOHNSON, EASTMAN. *See* JOHNSON, JONATHAN EASTMAN.

JOHNSON, EDWARD (*b. Canterbury, England, 1598; d. Woburn, Mass., 1672*), colonial chronicler. Immigrated to Boston, 1630. Author of *The Wonder-Working Providence of Sion's Saviour in New England*, published in London, 1654, as *A History of New England*. The book was written to encourage the friends of the colonies by stories of marvelous evidences of success.

JOHNSON, EDWARD (*b. Salisbury, Va., 1816; d. Richmond, Va., 1873*), soldier, farmer. Graduated West Point, 1838. Resigned captaincy in U.S. Army, 1861; as Confederate brigadier general (1861) and major general (1863), served until capture at Nashville, 1864. Particularly distinguished at the Wilderness and Spotsylvania.

JOHNSON, EDWARD (*b. Guelph, Ontario, 1878; d. Guelph, 1959*), operatic tenor, general manager of the Metropolitan Opera. Studied law at the University of Western Ontario. Achieved great success in Europe as a singer, using the name of Edoardo di Giovanni. Made his debut at the Chicago Opera in 1919 and at the Metropolitan Opera in 1922. As general manager of the Metropolitan Opera, 1935–50, saw radio broadcasts of the Opera becoming a national institution, initiated the Met Auditions of the Air, aided the founding of the Metropolitan Opera Guild, under Mrs. August Belmont, and raised money to buy the opera house from the stockholders. Encouraged and employed many American singers.

JOHNSON, EDWARD AUSTIN (*b. near Raleigh, N.C., 1860; d. New York, N.Y., 1944*), educator, lawyer, politician. Son of black slave parents, he graduated from Atlanta University, 1883; while serving as teacher and principal of schools in Atlanta and Raleigh, he studied law; after receiving the LL.B. degree from Shaw University (Raleigh), 1891, he joined the Shaw faculty; in 1893, he became dean of the law school. Active also in Republican politics, he was a member of the Raleigh board of aldermen and for seven years an assistant U.S. attorney for the eastern district of North Carolina. Removing to New York City, 1907, he practiced law; he was elected state assemblyman in 1917, the first black to sit in that body. Failing of reelection, he resumed his law practice; in 1925, he became blind. He was author of several books dealing with the black experience, including *A School History of the Negro Race in America: 1619–1890* (1891).

JOHNSON, EDWIN CARL (*b. near Scandia, Kans., 1884; d. Denver, Colo., 1970*), governor of Colorado and U.S. senator. A Democrat, he served in the Colorado House of Representatives (1923–31) and then was lieutenant governor (1931–33). Was governor of Colorado (1933–37, 1955–57), and also served in the U.S. Senate (1937–55). Known as a maverick, he was a member of the Congressional Joint Committee on Atomic Energy.

JOHNSON, EDWIN FERRY (*b. Essex, Vt., 1803; d. New York, N.Y., 1872*), civil engineer. One of foremost railroad engineers of his day. Promoter and chief engineer of Northern Pacific Railroad which he had advocated as early as 1854.

JOHNSON, ELDRIDGE REEVES (*b. Wilmington, Del., 1867; d. Moorestown, N.J., 1945*), inventor, businessman. Trained as an expert machinist in Philadelphia, he became full proprietor of his own shop in Camden, N.J., 1894. Beginning as supplier of a spring-driven motor, which he had developed for use in the Berliner Gramaphone, he made further improvements in the "talking machine" and by 1898 was manufacturing 600 complete gramaphones per week for the Berliner Company. In 1901 he founded and became president of the Victor Talking Machine Company, acquiring title to the Berliner patents. For the next twenty years, under Johnson's direction, Victor was the leader of the American phonograph industry and the Victor trademark— a dog listening to "His Master's Voice"—became famous throughout the world. Johnson retired in 1925. In 1927 Victor was merged with the Radio Corporation of America.

JOHNSON, ELIAS HENRY (*b. Troy, N.Y., 1841; d. Philadelphia, Pa., 1906*), Baptist theologian. Professor at Crozier Seminary and a leader in organizing the Baptist Congress.

JOHNSON, ELIJAH (*b. probably New Jersey, ca. 1780; d. Monrovia, Liberia, 1849*), pioneer settler and one of the founders of Liberia, 1820. Commander of the colony's defense force and associate of Jehudi Ashmun in its early government.

JOHNSON, ELLEN CHENEY (*b. Athol, Mass., 1829; d. London, England, 1899*), educator, prison reformer. Campaigned for separate women's prisons; made Sherborn (Mass.) Reformatory a model institution as superintendent, 1884–99.

JOHNSON, FRANKLIN (*b. Frankfort, Ohio, 1836; d. Brookline, Mass., 1916*), Baptist clergyman, author, educator. Scholarly writer and contributor to theological publications; professor of church history at University of Chicago, 1892–1908.

JOHNSON, GEORGE (*b. Toledo, Ohio, 1889; d. Washington, D.C., 1944*), Roman Catholic clergyman, educator. Graduated St. John's University (Toledo), 1910; studied for priesthood at St. Bernard's Seminary (Rochester, N.Y.) and at North American College, Rome; ordained in 1914. Ph.D., Catholic University of America, 1919. Superintendent of schools, diocese of Toledo, 1919–21; professor of education, Catholic University of America, 1921–44. As director of the department of education, National Catholic Welfare Conference (*post* 1928) and secretary general of the National Catholic Educational Association (*post* 1929), he served as a national spokesman for Catholic views on educational reforms and legislation. He believed that Catholic education should achieve a total integration of Catholic culture and American society.

JOHNSON, GEORGE FRANCIS (*b. Milford, Mass., 1857; d. Endicott, N.Y., 1948*), shoe manufacturer. Left school at age thirteen to work in a boot factory; was appointed production and sales manager of a Binghamton, N.Y., boot and shoe firm, 1890, when it was acquired by Henry B. Endicott. A partner in the firm by 1899, he succeeded Endicott as president in 1920. Under his management the firm of Endicott-Johnson became an outstanding exponent of industrial democracy, and his labor policies became widely known. He consistently paid the highest salaries in the shoe industry, instituted a unique and equitable profit-sharing plan, and provided numerous other benefits for his employees. He was equally unorthodox in his political views, supporting the presidential candidacies of Woodrow Wilson, Alfred E. Smith, and Franklin D. Roosevelt.

JOHNSON, GUY (*b. Ireland, ca. 1740; d. London, England, 1788*), Northern superintendent of Indian affairs, 1774–82, Loyalist. Son-in-law of Sir William Johnson. Organized Iroquois to fight on British side during American Revolution.

JOHNSON, HAROLD OGDEN ("CHIC"). *See* OLSEN, JOHN SIGVARD ("OLE"), AND JOHNSON, HAROLD OGDEN ("CHIC").

JOHNSON, HELEN LOUISE KENDRICK (*b. Hamilton, N.Y., 1844; d. New York, N.Y., 1917*), author, educator, antisuffragist.

JOHNSON, HENRY (*b. Gardiner, Maine, 1855; d. Brunswick, Maine, 1918*), teacher at Bowdoin College, poet. His most important works were translations, particularly Dante's *Divine Comedy* in blank verse (1915).

JOHNSON, HERSCHEL VESPASIAN (*b. Burke Co., Ga., 1812; d. 1880*), jurist. Democratic governor of Georgia, 1853–57; accepted 1860 Democratic vice presidential nomination; opposed secession but served in Confederate senate, 1862–65. Denied seat in U.S. Senate, 1866. A consistent moderate states' rights man of sound judgment and high integrity.

JOHNSON, HIRAM WARREN (*b. Sacramento, Calif., 1866; d. Bethesda, Md., 1945*), lawyer, politician. After attending the public schools of Sacramento and working for two years in his father's law office, Johnson went on in 1884 to the University of California at Berkeley. He dropped out and for two years worked as a shorthand reporter and read law in his father's office. Johnson was admitted to the California bar in 1888, and soon made a reputation as a skillful trial lawyer. He managed his father's successful campaign for Congress in 1894. In 1901 he was appointed Sacramento city attorney.

In 1906 he joined in the effort to rid San Francisco of political corruption and as chief prosecutor secured the conviction of Abraham Ruef, the political boss.

By 1910 he ran for governor, centering his campaign around the slogan "Kick the Southern Pacific out of politics." The Public Utilities Act, passed in his first administration, created one of the most effective systems of railroad control in the country.

Johnson supported the announced candidacy of Robert La Follette for the Republican presidential nomination, but he preferred Theodore Roosevelt. He was part of the inner circle of the ex-President's advisers, and at the turbulent 1912 Republican national convention, Johnson was nominated as the Progressive party's vice presidential candidate.

Reelected governor in 1914, Johnson moved in 1916 to the Senate. As a new senator uneasily supporting President Wilson's call for a declaration of war against Germany, Johnson remained a liberal critic of the administration, especially of Wilson's foreign policy.

In 1920 Johnson won the California Republican contest and picked up enough outside support to win third place on the first four ballots at the Republican national convention. After Harding's nomination, the possibility of Johnson's nomination for the vice presidency was broached, but he refused in disgust. Although his party was in power for twelve years after the 1920 election, Johnson was never sympathetic to its leadership and rarely with its policies.

Johnson became increasingly critical of the Hoover administration and the New York bankers whom he blamed for much of the economic distress of the depression. He refused personally to contest the renomination of Hoover and advocated the election of Franklin D. Roosevelt. He was offered the secretaryship of the Interior, which he refused. Johnson cooperated with the early New Deal, but from 1934 on, events in California propelled him toward the conservative side of the political spectrum. By 1936 his enthusiasm for the New Deal had so waned that he refused to take any part in the presidential contest. In 1940 Johnson vehemently opposed a third Roosevelt term, but he was almost as displeased with the Republican ticket. The subsequent Roosevelt victory, the passage of the Lend-Lease Act, and the signing of the Atlantic

Charter, all of which he denounced, increased his bitterness. Johnson loyally supported the war effort but maintained his dogged opposition to Roosevelt's foreign policy.

Johnson's reputation as an incorruptible independent was a priceless political asset, and the voters of California never failed him.

JOHNSON, HUGH SAMUEL (*b. Fort Scott, Kans., 1882; d. Washington, D.C., 1942*), army officer, federal administrator. Raised in Kansas and Oklahoma. Graduated West Point, 1903; commissioned in cavalry. Served in the West and in the Philippines; was executive officer of Yosemite National Park (1910–12) and superintendent of Sequoia National Park (1911). Attended University of California Law School and graduated with honors, 1916; served as judge advocate on staff of General John J. Pershing in campaign in Mexico; as a newly promoted captain on the army's legal staff in Washington, wrote the key sections of the Selective Service Act, 1917. Promoted major, he was judge advocate in charge of directing the World War I draft; also serving as army representative on the War Industries Board, he began his long association with its head, Bernard Baruch. Playing an important role in the war mobilization as chief of military purchase and supply, he rose swiftly in rank and became the youngest brigadier general since the Civil War. He took command of the 8th Division in the fall of 1918, but the war ended as he was about to embark for France. Resigning from the army in February 1919, he was associated in business with George N. Peek, and *post* 1927 with Bernard Baruch. Becoming a member of Franklin D. Roosevelt's "brain trust" in July 1932, he was appointed in 1933 to administer the National Industrial Recovery Act, which he had helped draft. As head of the National Recovery Administration (NRA), he worked tirelessly to establish and supervise the codes for more than 500 industries and made the "Blue Eagle" symbol of the NRA a household emblem. Truculent, self-assured, and given to excess in denunciation of leaders of business and labor who ventured to thwart him, he became an embarrassment to the Roosevelt administration; his tenure as NRA administrator was ended in October 1934. His subsequent career was anticlimactic. Devoting most of his time to writing a syndicated column for the Scripps-Howard newspapers, and to radio broadcasting, he was a sharp critic of the New Deal and a prominent supporter of Wendell L. Willkie's presidential bid in 1940.

JOHNSON, JACK (*b. Galveston, Tex., 1878; d. Raleigh, N.C., 1946*), boxer, first black heavyweight champion of the world. Ring name of John Arthur Johnson. First became interested in boxing while working as a longshoreman; practiced in local gyms; barnstormed with other black boxers in exhibition matches; became contender for championship, 1902. Despite the bar imposed by his color, Johnson had defeated all other contenders by 1908. In that year he won the heavyweight title by defeating Tommy Burns, the champion, in Sydney, Australia; he later stilled any disputes over his right to it by defeating retired champion James J. Jeffries at Reno, Nevada, on July 4, 1910. Dislike of Johnson because of his open association with white women climaxed in his trial, allegedly for abducting his third wife, in 1913, and his sentence to one year in prison. Considering the conviction unjust, he jumped bail and lived abroad until 1920, when he returned and served out his term. Meanwhile he had lost the heavyweight title to Jess Willard in a controversial bout at Havana, Cuba, Apr. 5, 1915. After 1920, he gave exhibition bouts and eked out a living in a variety of ways. Some boxing experts have rated him the greatest of all heavyweights.

JOHNSON, JAMES (*b. Orange Co., Va., 1774; d. 1826*), soldier. Removed to Kentucky as a boy. Hero of battle of the Thames, 1813, where he served under his brother, Richard M. Johnson.

JOHNSON, JAMES WELDON (*b. Jacksonville, Fla., 1871; d. Wiscasset, Maine, 1938*), lawyer, author, educator. Graduated Atlanta University, 1894. Removed to New York City, 1901; with his brother J. Rosamond Johnson, collaborated on some 200 popular songs for their own song-and-dance act and for other shows. Served as U.S. consul in Venezuela, and Nicaragua, 1906–12. A key figure in National Association for the Advancement of Colored People, 1916–30, Johnson did much to secure black rights by his literary and organizational talents. He had wide influence upon other black writers and in winning respect for the blacks' contribution to American culture. He was author of *The Autobiography of an Ex-Colored Man* (1912), *Fifty Years and Other Poems* (1917), *God's Trombones* (1927), *Along This Way* (1933), and other books of high merit.

JOHNSON, SIR JOHN (*b. Mohawk Valley, N.Y., 1742; d. Montreal, Canada, 1830*), baronet, Loyalist. Son of Sir William Johnson. Was knighted, 1765; inherited his father's baronetcy and estates, 1774, along with post of major general of New York militia. At outbreak of Revolution, he fled to Montreal. Commissioned lieutenant colonel, he raised the "Royal Greens," and served with St. Leger in 1777. During 1778–81, he led raids in upper New York, thoroughly devastating the country. Johnson was commissioned "Superintendent General and Inspector General of the Six Nations Indians and those in the province of Quebec," in 1782. As compensation for confiscated property, the British government granted him land in Canada, where he continued to influence Indian affairs and promoted relief measures for Loyalists.

JOHNSON, JOHN ALBERT (*b. near St. Peter, Minn., 1861; d. 1909*), newspaper editor. Democratic governor of Minnesota, 1904–09. Beloved in his state, he attracted national attention as a public speaker and Chautauqua lecturer.

JOHNSON, JOHN BUTLER (*b. near Marlboro, Ohio, 1850; d. Pier Cove, Mich., 1902*), civil engineering professor, Washington University, St. Louis, 1883–99. Dean of Engineering, University of Wisconsin, 1899–1902. Wrote several widely used engineering reference books and made important studies of strength of timber.

JOHNSON, JOHN GRAVER (*b. Philadelphia, Pa., 1841; d. Philadelphia, 1917*), lawyer, art collector. Argued many important cases before the Supreme Court as attorney for trusts. Built up an extraordinary collection of paintings which he left to the city of Philadelphia.

JOHNSON, JONATHAN EASTMAN (*b. Lovell, Maine, 1824; d. 1906*), portrait and genre painter. Began his career in Boston at the age of 16 in Bufford's lithograph shop. By 1845 he was in Washington, D.C., drawing crayon portraits of statesmen and government officials. Studied with Leutze at Düsseldorf, 1849–51; traveled; declined position as Dutch court painter. Returned to New York, 1858; soon gained a reputation which continued to grow. Traveling in the South to study black life, he painted some of his most successful genre pictures, including his "Old Kentucky Home," exhibited in Paris, 1867, and Philadelphia, 1876. His portraits of many eminent Americans were similarly notable for human interest and sound technical qualities of color, drawing, and composition.

JOHNSON, JOSEPH (*b. Mount Pleasant, S.C., 1776; d. Pineville, S.C., 1862*), physician. Brother of William Johnson (1771–1834). Practiced in Charleston where he was active in civic life and a leader of the Union party. Author of *Traditions . . . of the American Revolution in the South* (1851) and other works.

JOHNSON, JOSEPH FRENCH (*b. Hardwick, Mass., 1853; d. 1925*), educator, writer on finance. As dean of New York University School of Commerce, 1903–25, he brought it to a high degree of success, developing night-school courses and generally instituting a more practical training for business.

JOHNSON, LEVI (*b. Herkimer Co., N.Y., 1786; d. 1871*), shipbuilder and trader. Initiator of regular navigation on Great Lakes at Cleveland, Ohio, *post* 1814.

JOHNSON, LOUIS ARTHUR (*b. Roanoke, Va., 1891; d. Washington, D.C., 1966*), lawyer and U.S. secretary of defense. Studied at the University of Virginia (LL.B., 1912). Elected as a Democratic member of the West Virginia House of Delegates in 1917. Served in the army during World War I and was elected national commander of the American Legion for 1932 and 1933. Was assistant secretary of war, 1937–40, and secretary of defense, 1949–50. Then he returned to his law practice.

JOHNSON, MAGNUS (*b. near Karlstad, Sweden, 1871; d. Litchfield, Minn., 1936*), farmer, agrarian reformer. Came to America, 1891. U.S. senator, Farmer-Labor, from Minnesota, 1923–24; congressman, 1933–35.

JOHNSON, MARMADUKE (*d. Boston, Mass., 1674*), printer. Came to Massachusetts, 1660. With Samuel Green, printed John Eliot's Indian translation of the Bible, 1663.

JOHNSON, SIR NATHANIEL (*b. Kibblesworth, England, ca. 1645; d. Carolina, 1713*), baronet, colonial official. Governor of Carolina, 1702–08; active in defense of colony during Queen Anne's War; encouraged Indian trade and helped establish Church of England in Carolina.

JOHNSON, OLIVER (*b. Peacham, Vt., 1809; d. Brooklyn, N.Y., 1889*), antislavery leader, editor. Close associate of William L. Garrison and a founder of New England Anti-Slavery Society; active also in movements for world peace and women's rights.

JOHNSON, OSA (*b. Chanute, Kans., 1894; d. New York, N.Y., 1953*), explorer, author. Together with her explorer-photographer husband, Martin Johnson, made some of the first films of primitive people in the South Seas and Africa, including *Simba, Congorilla,* and *Baboona.* Books include *Cannibal Lands* (1922), *Lion* (1929), and *Over African Jungles* (1935). The Johnsons discovered Paradise Lake in Africa and spent four years there filming wild life for the Museum of Natural History in New York. After her husband's death in 1937, Osa Johnson continued the work on films and wrote the best-selling *I Married Adventure* (1940).

JOHNSON, OWEN MCMAHON (*b. New York, N.Y., 1878; d. Vineyard Haven, Mass., 1952*), novelist, short story writer. Studied at Yale, B.A., 1900. Known primarily as the author of the Lawrenceville stories, which depicted life at a prep school in New Jersey, and the satirical novel *Stover at Yale* (1911). Although commercially successful, Johnson was never treated seriously by the critics. Wrote *The Spirit of France* (1915) and was awarded the French Legion of Honor in 1919.

JOHNSON, REVERDY (*b. Annapolis, Md., 1796; d. Annapolis, 1876*), constitutional lawyer, diplomat. Graduated St. John's College, Annapolis, 1811; admitted to bar, 1815; practiced in Baltimore, Md. His most famous case was *Dred Scott v. Sanford;* he was allegedly the major influence in the Supreme Court's decision. He served as U.S. senator from Maryland, Whig, 1845–49, and was briefly attorney general under President Taylor. He later became a Union Democrat and worked for reconciliation of North and South. Returning to the Senate, 1863, he generally supported Presidents Lincoln and Johnson, although called "trimmer" because of his inconsistencies. He worked effectively against Johnson's impeachment. As U.S. minister to Great

Britain, 1868–69, he negotiated a series of agreements on financial claims and other points in dispute which were not ratified but served as bases for later treaties.

JOHNSON, RICHARD MENTOR (*b. Beargrass, now Louisville, Ky., 1780; d. 1850*), lawyer, soldier. Admitted to the bar, 1802. Congressman, (Democrat) Republican, from Kentucky, 1807–19; Democrat, 1829–37; U.S. senator from Kentucky, 1819–29. Won military reputation at battle of the Thames, War of 1812, where he is said to have killed Tecumseh. An intimate friend and on occasion personal agent of Andrew Jackson, whom he often supported despite contrary personal views, his nomination as Van Buren's running mate was dictated by Jackson but his vice presidential career, 1837–41, was inconspicuous.

JOHNSON, RICHARD W. (*b. near Smithland, Ky., 1827; d. St. Paul, Minn., 1897*), Union soldier. Graduated West Point, 1849; served mainly in Texas and Indian Territory. Distinguished as brigade and division commander in Tennessee and Georgia campaigns, 1863–64, *Post* 1867, he served as professor of military science at the universities of Missouri and Minnesota.

JOHNSON, ROBERT (*b. England, ca. 1676; d. 1735*), popular colonial governor of Carolina, 1717–19, and first royal governor of South Carolina, 1731–35. He was son of Sir Nathaniel Johnson.

JOHNSON, ROBERT UNDERWOOD (*b. Washington, D.C., 1853; d. New York, N.Y., 1937*), editor, poet. Associate editor, *Century Magazine,* 1881–1909; editor, 1909–13. Co-editor, *Battles and Leaders of the Civil War* (1887). Director, Hall of Fame, *post* 1919; secretary, American Academy of Arts and Letters.

JOHNSON, ROBERT WARD (*b. Scott Co., Ky., 1814; d. 1879*), lawyer. Nephew of James and Richard M. Johnson. Removed to Little Rock, Ark., 1835. Congressman, Democrat, from Arkansas, 1847–53; U.S. senator, 1853–61. Served in Confederate Senate.

JOHNSON, SAMUEL (*b. Guilford, Conn., 1696; d. Stratford, Conn., 1772*), minister of the Church of England in colonial Connecticut, president of King's College, New York, 1754–63. Ranks with Jonathan Edwards as one of the two most important exponents of the idealist philosophy in colonial America. First ordained a Congregationalist pastor, he took orders in the Church of England, 1723, serving a small mission in Stratford, Conn., 1724–54, and leading the Church of England movement in New England. On retirement from King's College, he resumed duties as rector at Stratford. Among his works were *Ethices Elementa* (1746), augmented, 1752, with a new section under title *Elementa Philosophica.*

JOHNSON, SAMUEL (*b. Salem, Mass., 1822; d. 1882*), independent liberal preacher, author. Friend of Samuel Longfellow. Too radical an individualist ever to affiliate with any denomination, his associations were Unitarian and his philosophy thoroughly Transcendentalist.

JOHNSON, SAMUEL WILLIAM (*b. Kingsboro, N.Y., 1830; d. 1909*), agricultural chemist. Studied at Yale where John P. Norton encouraged his interest in chemistry; also at Leipzig and Munich. Professor, analytical chemistry, Yale, *post* 1856. Author of the classic volumes *How Crops Grow* (1868) and *How Crops Feed* (1870). His lectures and his publications greatly influenced the development of scientific agriculture in America. He became the founder of agricultural regulatory work in this country and was the leader in the movement leading to the establishment of agricultural experiment stations, directing Connecticut's new state experiment station at New Haven, 1877–99.

Johnson, Seth Whitmore (*b. Middle Haddam, Conn., 1811; d. 1907*), shipbuilder. Removed to Cleveland, Ohio, 1834. Successor of Levi Johnson (no kin) as a pioneer in the Great Lakes ship-building industry.

Johnson, Thomas (*b. Calvert Co., Md., 1732; d. near Frederick, Md., 1819*), lawyer, Maryland legislator. Elected, 1774, to represent Maryland in the Continental Congress; placed Washington's name in nomination for command of army, 1775. Though not in Philadelphia when the Declaration of Independence was adopted, he voted in Annapolis, July 6, 1776, to separate Maryland from the mother country. He served in the state convention of 1776 which framed Maryland's declaration of rights and constitution. Elected first governor of Maryland, 1777, he served until November 1779. In 1791 Washington, his friend and business associate, appointed him to the Supreme Court and to the board of commissioners of the Federal City. He resigned as associate justice of the Supreme Court, 1793, and in 1795 refused the secretaryship of state.

Johnson, Tom Loftin (*b. Blue Spring, Ky., 1854; d. 1911*), inventor, street-railroad operator, steel producer, congressman. Influenced by Henry George. As mayor of Cleveland, Ohio, 1901–09, he made it the best governed city in America. Proponent of municipal traction ownership, public ownership of railroads, and woman's suffrage, he was perhaps the most outstanding city executive America has produced and was certainly the most spectacular in American life, 1890–1910.

Johnson, Treat Baldwin (*b. Bethany, Conn., 1875; d. Bethany, 1947*), chemist. Ph.B., Sheffield Scientific School, Yale, 1898; Ph.D., Yale University, 1901. Taught at Yale, 1902–43; professor *post* 1914, and Sterling professor of chemistry *post* 1928. His scientific contribution was in the area of synthetic organic chemistry, especially as it related to biologically important materials. He was nationally known for his researches in pyrimidine chemistry and in the chemistry of the tubercle bacillus. His study of germicides and antiseptics resulted in the grant of some fifteen patents dealing with medicinal products; one of these was for a synthesis for substituted resorcinols that led to the commercial production of hexylresorcinol.

Johnson, Virginia Wales (*b. Brooklyn, N.Y., 1849; d. 1916*), novelist, writer of travel books.

Johnson, Walter Perry (*b. Humboldt, Kans., 1887; d. Washington, D.C., 1946*), baseball player. Pitched while at Fullerton (Calif.) Union High School and with semiprofessional teams in California and Idaho. In 1907 his overpowering fast ball accounted for eighty-six consecutive scoreless innings at Weiser, Idaho, and he was signed by the Washington Senators of the American League. He soon established himself as one of baseball's superstars and his honesty, decency of life, and sportsmanship made him a national celebrity and model for youth. He remained with the Senators until his active playing career ended in 1927; his work as a manager thereafter was undistinguished. He was credited overall with 414 wins. He started 802 major-league games, completed 532, relieved in many others, and amassed a total of 5,923 innings pitched. From 1910 to 1919 he won twenty or more games each season; in nine of these years he led the American League in strikeouts.

Johnson, Wendell Andrew Leroy (*b. near Roxbury, Kans., 1906; d. Iowa City, Iowa, 1965*), psychologist and educator. Studied at McPherson College and the University of Iowa (B.A., 1928; M.A., 1929; Ph.D., 1931). Taught at the University of Iowa, 1931–65, where he directed the program in speech pathology and audiology, 1943–55, and became an authority on stuttering. He wrote *People in Quandaries* (1946), *Speech Handicapped Children* (1948), *Stuttering in Children and Adults* (1955), *Your Most Enchanted Listener* (1956), *The Onset of Stuttering* (1959), *Stuttering and What You Can Do About It* (1961), *Diagnostic Methods in Speech Pathology* (1963). In later years was a consultant to a number of government agencies.

Johnson, Sir William (*b. Smithtown, Ireland, 1715; d. near present Johnstown, N.Y., 1774*), baronet, Mohawk valley pioneer, colonial superintendent of Indian affairs. Came to America *ca.* 1738; assumed charge of an estate in the lower Mohawk River valley of New York which was owned by his uncle, Sir Peter Warren. He soon purchased a tract of his own, set up a store to trade with the Indians and other settlers and laid the foundations of a large fortune. He became intimately acquainted with the neighboring tribes of the Six Nations, particularly the Mohawks. During King George's War, 1744–48, he was largely responsible for preventing the Six Nations from supporting the French. Governor Clinton made him colonel of the Six Nations, 1746, transferring to him the conduct of Indian affairs. In 1750 he was appointed a member of the Council of New York and soon after resigned his management of Indian affairs. The Indians in attendance at the Albany Congress (1754) requesting his reappointment as agent, General Braddock gave him in 1755 the "sole Management & direction of the Affairs of the Six Nations of Indians & their Allies" and command of an expedition against Crown Point. At Lake George a French and Indian force under Dieskau attacked him and was defeated. Though he failed to capture Crown Point, he had warded off the French threat to the Northern colonies; the King made him a baronet, and commissioned him once again colonel of the Six Nations and "Sole Agent and Superintendent of the said Indians and their Affairs." In 1759 he commanded the force which captured Niagara and in 1760 accompanied Amherst's expedition against Montreal.

Henceforth, Johnson worked to create a centralized and independent Indian department and to centralize control of the fur trade, ideals which were never realized and could only have been of temporary effect in stabilizing the westward rush of settlement and preventing white encroachment on hunting grounds reserved to the Indians.

An imperialist unquestionably loyal to the Crown, Johnson was a man of energy and versatility. He aided in opening the Mohawk valley to settlement; his services in helping to drive the French from North America were invaluable; and he did much to facilitate the difficult transition from French to English rule north of the Ohio following the conquest of Canada. He had also shown interest in the Indians for their own sake, aiding projects for their education and religious training.

Johnson, William (*b. Middletown, Conn., 1769; d. 1848*), law reporter. Associated with Chancellor Kent in the work of New York's supreme court and court of chancery; his reports distinguished by accuracy and good sense.

Johnson, William (*b. Charleston, S.C., 1771; d. Brooklyn, N.Y., 1834*), jurist. Brother of Joseph Johnson. Studied law with Charles Cotesworth Pinckney; served in South Carolina legislature, 1794–98, and as judge of the state court of common pleas until 1806, when President Jefferson appointed him associate justice of the U.S. Supreme Court. Though personally and politically close to Jefferson, his legal opinions leaned toward Federalism; however, he opposed the strong views of Marshall and Story, as well as the doctrines of secession and nullification. Among his ablest opinions was his dissent in *Fletcher* v. *Peck*.

JOHNSON, WILLIAM BULLEIN (*b. Beaufort Co., S.C., 1782; d. Greenville, S.C., 1862*), Baptist preacher, pioneer educator in South Carolina. President of the Southern Baptist Convention, 1845–52; helped found present Furman University and Johnson Female University.

JOHNSON, WILLIAM RANSOM (*b. Warren Co., N.C., 1782; d. Mobile, Ala., 1849*), known as "The Napoleon of the Turf." Leading horse-breeder and -racer of his generation; Southern manager, North-South matches, 1823–34.

JOHNSON, WILLIAM SAMUEL (*b. Stratford, Conn., 1727; d. 1819*), statesman, jurist. Son of Samuel Johnson (1696–1772). Graduated Yale, 1744. Without formal training, he became a leader at the Connecticut bar. He represented Stratford in the house of representatives, 1761, 1765; in 1766 he became the first Anglican ever elected to the Council.

Though Johnson's conservative background made the problems of the Revolutionary era particularly difficult, he was a member of the Stamp Act Congress and later served as Connecticut's colonial agent in London, 1767–71. In 1771 he was re-elected to the Council and made judge of the superior court. Elected to the Continental Congress, 1774, he declined to serve, believing the Congress would "tend to widen the breach already much too great between the parent state and her colonies." After the radical party gained control in Connecticut, he went into political retirement.

From 1785 to 1787 he served in the Confederation Congress, exercising more influence than any other Connecticut delegate. The crowning event of his career was the Federal Convention, where he was one of the most generally respected members. He contributed greatly to the compromise on representation, was one of two Connecticut signers of the Constitution, and worked effectively for ratification, emphasizing that the federal system formed "one new nation out of the individual States." He became one of the first two senators from Connecticut, but resigned in 1791.

In 1787 Johnson had become the first president of Columbia College, bringing to the post the prestige of his distinguished public career, a reputation for scholarship, and a paternal interest in young men. By the close of his administration in 1800, when he retired on account of ill health, the college was on a sound footing.

JOHNSON, WILLIAM WOOLSEY (*b. Owego, N.Y., 1841; d. 1927*), mathematician. Professor at the U.S. Naval Academy, 1881–1921; one of the best-known expository mathematicians of his time and author of a number of textbooks and monographs.

JOHNSON, WILLIS FLETCHER (*b. New York, N.Y., 1857; d. 1931*), journalist. Graduated New York University, 1879. Associated with the *New York Tribune*, 1880–1931, in many editorial capacities.

JOHNSTON, ALBERT SIDNEY (*b. Washington, Ky., 1803; d. 1862*), soldier. Graduated West Point, 1826. Served in the Black Hawk War but resigned his commission, 1834, because of his wife's illness. Thereafter, went to Texas, became commander of the Texan army, 1837, and was secretary of war of the Republic of Texas, 1838–40. During the Mexican War he was colonel in the U.S. Army; he later commanded the Department of Texas. As brevet brigadier general he served as commander of the punitive expedition against the Mormons, 1858–60. Assigned to command of the Department of the Pacific, he resigned when Texas seceded. Appointed general in the Confederate Army, commanding the Western Department, he suffered a series of apparent reverses before routing the Federals at the first day of Shiloh, where he was fatally wounded. His loss was regarded as a mortal blow to the Confederacy.

JOHNSTON, ALEXANDER (*b. Brooklyn, N.Y., 1849; d. 1889*), historian, professor of jurisprudence and political economy at the College of New Jersey (Princeton), 1883–89. A prolific writer, he was author of the popular *History of American Politics* (1879).

JOHNSTON, ANNIE FELLOWS (*b. Evansville, Ind., 1863; d. 1931*), author of books for children, notably the series which began with *The Little Colonel* (1895).

JOHNSTON, AUGUSTUS (*b. Amboy, N.J., ca. 1730; d. ca. 1790*), lawyer. Attorney general for the colony of Rhode Island, 1757–1766. Served as stamp distributor, 1765, and was later interned as a Loyalist.

JOHNSTON, DAVID CLAYPOOLE (*b. Philadelphia, Pa., 1799; d. Dorchester, Mass., 1865*), engraver, lithographer, actor. Achieved a reputation for his comic sketches, modeled after the English caricaturist George Cruikshank, but pointedly satiric on American themes and excellently drawn.

JOHNSTON, ERIC ALLEN (*b. Washington, D.C., 1896; d. Washington, 1963*), businessman and motion picture executive. Studied at the University of Washington (LL.B., 1917) and served in the Marine Corps, 1917–22. In the 1920's and early 1930's was president of the Columbia Electrical and Manufacturing Company and the Brown-Johnston Company. He became a national director (1934), vice president (1941), and president, (1942–46) of the U.S. Chamber of Commerce. He served in various capacities in the Roosevelt, Truman, and Eisenhower administrations. In 1945 Johnston became president of the Motion Picture Association of America. He wrote *America Unlimited* (1944) and *We're All in It* (1948).

JOHNSTON, FRANCES BENJAMIN (*b. Grafton, W. Va., 1864; d. New Orleans, La., 1952*), photographer. Studied at Notre Dame Convent and the Académie Julien in Paris (1884–85). Primarily a photographer of architecture, she was commissioned to record the early American styles in Old Falmouth, Chatham, Fredericksburg, and throughout the South. Her prints are housed in the Library of Congress and led, in 1929, to a grant from the Carnegie Corporation that established a collection of photographs of early American architecture.

JOHNSTON, GABRIEL (*b. Scotland, 1699; d. 1752*), journalist. Coeditor, *The Craftsman, post* 1726. Royal governor of North Carolina, 1734–52. His tenure was featured by a long controversy over quitrents, causing practical rebellion of the whole colony.

JOHNSTON, GEORGE BEN (*b. Tazewell, Va., 1853; d. Richmond, Va., 1916*), surgeon. M.D., University of the City of New York, 1876; professor, Medical College of Virginia, 1884–1914. Virginia pioneer in antiseptic operations; also contributed much information to surgery of the kidney and spleen.

JOHNSTON, HENRIETTA (*b. 1728/29, buried Charleston, S.C.*), artist. Probably the first woman painter in North America; painted pastel portraits, mostly of colonial South Carolina grandees. Little is known of her lineage and education.

JOHNSTON, HENRY PHELPS (*b. Trebizond, Turkey, 1842; d. 1923*), educator, Union soldier, historian. Born of missionary parents; graduated Yale, 1862. Taught history of the College of the City of New York, 1879–1916. Author of *The Campaign of 1776* (1878), *The Battle of Harlem Heights* (1897); edited letters and public papers of John Jay.

JOHNSTON, JOHN (*b. New Galloway, Scotland, 1791; d. Geneva, N.Y., 1880*), agriculturist. Came to America, 1821; started farming near Geneva. Known as "father of American tile-draining" because of his introduction (1835) of this technique of underdraining land. He was among the first to employ other new methods of cultivation: the use of lime and plaster, the surface application of manure, the purchase of oil meal to feed cattle and sheep, and early cutting of hay.

JOHNSTON, JOHN (*b. Perth, Scotland, 1881; d. Bar Harbor, Maine, 1950*), chemist, metallurgist. B.S., University of St. Andrews, 1903; D.Sc., 1908. On staff of geophysical laboratory, Carnegie Institution, Washington, D.C., 1908–16; headed research department of American Zinc, Lead, and Smelting Company, 1916–17; held numerous posts with National Research Council, 1917–19 (resuming membership at intervals through 1943); Sterling professor of chemistry, Yale University, 1919–27. As organizer and director of the research laboratory of the U.S. Steel Corporation, 1927–46, he was responsible for notable contributions to both process and physical metallurgy.

JOHNSTON, JOHN TAYLOR (*b. New York, N.Y., 1820; d. 1893*), railroad executive, art collector. First president of the Metropolitan Museum of Art, New York; benefactor of New York University.

JOHNSTON, JOSEPH EGGLESTON (*b. Prince Edward Co., Va., 1807; d. Washington, D.C., 1891*), soldier, Confederate general. Son of Peter Johnston. Graduated West Point, 1829. Served in Florida campaign, 1838, and in the Mexican War; appointed quartermaster general and brigadier general, 1860. Resigning from the U.S. Army when Virginia seceded, he was named Confederate brigadier general. His leadership and tactical skill at the first battle of Bull Run, July 1861, won him promotion to general and the command in northern Virginia. Passive in conducting defense of Richmond, spring 1862, his excellent plan of counterattack failed in May because of his faulty supervision of subordinates. Assigned in November 1862 to command Confederate forces in Tennessee and Mississippi, his failure to supersede ineffective subordinate generals contributed to loss of Vicksburg. He then commanded the Confederate withdrawal from Chattanooga to Atlanta, where he was relieved in July 1864 for failing to arrest Sherman's advance. Reassigned to the Army of the Tennessee, February 1865, he surrendered to Sherman on April 26. He served as congressman from Virginia, 1879–81, and in 1885 became a U.S. commissioner of railroads.

JOHNSTON, JOSEPH FORNEY (*b. Lincoln Co., N.C., 1843; Washington, D.C., 1913*), lawyer, Confederate soldier, businessman. Removed to Alabama *ca.* 1861. Studied law with William H. Forney; was identified with development of Birmingham, Ala. Democratic governor of Alabama, 1896–1900; U.S. senator, 1907–13.

JOHNSTON, JOSIAH STODDARD (*b. Salisbury, Conn., 1784; d. on Red River above Alexandria, La., 1833*), Louisiana jurist and legislator. Half-brother of Albert S. Johnston. Graduated Transylvania, 1802; studied law with William T. Barry of Lexington, Ky.; removed to Louisiana, 1805. A supporter of Henry Clay, he served as congressman from Louisiana, 1821–23; U.S. senator, 1823–33.

JOHNSTON, MARY (*b. Buchanan, Va., 1870; d. near Warm Springs, Va., 1936*), novelist. Best known as author of popular historical novels about Virginia and the Civil War, which include *To Have and to Hold* (1900), *The Long Roll* (1911), *Cease Firing* (1912), and *The Great Valley* (1926).

JOHNSTON, OLIN DEWITT TALMADGE (*b. near Honea Path, S.C., 1896; d. Columbia, S.C., 1965*), governor and U.S. senator. Studied at Wofford College (B.A., 1921) and the University of South Carolina (M.A., 1923; LL.B., 1924). Served in the South Carolina House of Representatives, 1923–24 and 1927–30, and

was elected governor in 1934 and in 1942. Johnston was elected to the Senate in 1944, where he served until his death. He maintained a strong labor following, supported the New Deal, and opposed civil rights legislation.

JOHNSTON, PETER (*b. Osborne's Landing on James River, Va., 1763; d. 1831*), Revolutionary soldier, Virginia legislator and circuit judge. Strenuously advocated Virginia Resolutions of 1798 in House of Delegates. Father of Joseph E. Johnston.

JOHNSTON, RICHARD MALCOLM (*b. near Powelton, Ga., 1822; d. 1898*), lawyer, educator. Graduated Mercer University, 1841. Taught at University of Georgia, 1857–61; conducted a successful school for boys near Sparta, Ga., 1862–67. Encouraged by his friend Sidney Lanier, he wrote *Dukesboro Tales* (1871), *Old Times in Middle Georgia* (1897), and other sensitive and perceptive sketches of life in his native state.

JOHNSTON, ROBERT MATTESON (*b. Paris, France, 1867; d. Cambridge, Mass., 1920*), historian, author. Graduated Pembroke College, Cambridge, England, 1889. Came to America, 1902; taught, mainly at Harvard, 1902–20. Specialist in military history and the French Revolution.

JOHNSTON, SAMUEL (*b. Dundee, Scotland, 1733; d. 1816*), lawyer, Revolutionary leader. Nephew of Gabriel Johnston. Came to America as an infant. North Carolina legislator; governor, 1787–89; U.S. senator, 1789–93. A legalist, of vigorous intellect and strong convictions, he was a central figure in North Carolina during the Revolution and led the conservative faction in the period of constitutional reorganization which ensued.

JOHNSTON, SAMUEL (*b. Shelby, N.Y., 1835; d. Buffalo, N.Y., 1911*), inventor. Patented rake and reel improvements for harvesters, 1863 and 1865; practically all reapers in the world were altered to use the Johnston system. In 1868 he established a factory at Syracuse, N.Y., to manufacture his harvester rake but later moved it to Brockport, N.Y. In addition to his work on harvesters, he patented rotary and disc harrows and devised new metalworking processes, cold rolling mills, rolled forging mills, and casting machinery.

JOHNSTON, THOMAS (*b. Boston, Mass., ca. 1708; d. 1767*), organ-builder, topographical engraver.

JOHNSTON, WILLIAM ANDREW (*b. Pittsburth, Pa., 1871; d. Chicago, Ill., 1929*), journalist. Wrote mystery novels, humorous books; was active in New York City civic and welfare work. Associated with *New York World*, 1900–27.

JOHNSTON, WILLIAM HARTSHORNE (*b. Cincinnati, Ohio, 1861; d. Nice, France, 1933*), army officer. Retired as major general, 1925; distinguished in service in Philippines and World War I.

JOHNSTON, WILLIAM HUGH (*b. Westville, Nova Scotia, Canada, 1874; d. Washington, D.C., 1937*), labor leader. Came to America as a boy. President, 1912–26, International Association of Machinists; socialist, proponent of industrial unionism and political action by labor.

JOHNSTON, WILLIAM PRESTON (*b. Louisville, Ky., 1831; d. Lexington, Va., 1899*), lawyer, Confederate soldier, educator. Son of Albert S. Johnston. Aide-de-camp to Jefferson Davis, 1862–65. Taught at Washington and Lee University, 1867–77; served as president of Louisiana State University, 1880–83, and of Tulane University *post* 1884.

JOHNSTON, ZACHARIAH (*b. near Staunton, Va., 1742; d. 1800*), farmer, Virginia legislator, Revolutionary soldier. Active in fight for Virginia's "Act for Establishing Religious Freedom," 1786; also in Virginia ratification of the federal Constitution.

JOHNSTONE, EDWARD RANSOM (*b. Galt, Ontario, Canada, 1870; d. Vineland, N.J., 1946*), pioneer educator of the feebleminded. Raised in Cincinnati, Ohio. Became principal of the education department, Indiana State School for the Feeble-Minded, 1893, on invitation of the superintendent, Alexander Johnson, who was his brother-in-law. Associated with the Vineland, New Jersey, Home for the Education and Care of Feeble-Minded Children, 1898–1944, as successively vice-principal, superintendent, and executive director, he continued his crusade to provide better training for his pupils; instituted summer courses in special methods for public school teachers; established a laboratory for research in the psychology of the mentally retarded (the first in the nation, 1906); organized a workshop in which physicians could learn the problems of retarded children and their families; and publicized the need for better understanding and care of the mentally disadvantaged. He was active also in other aspects of New Jersey welfare work and in penal reform.

JOHNSTONE, JOB (*b. Fairfield District, S.C., 1793; d. Newberry, S.C., 1862*), South Carolina jurist, advocate of nullification.

JOLINE, ADRIAN HOFFMAN (*b. Sing Sing, N.Y., 1850; d. 1912*), N.Y. lawyer, book and autograph collector. Specialized in railroad and trust practice. Author of *The Diversions of a Booklover* (1903) and other works on his hobbies.

JOLLIET, LOUIS (*b. near Beaupré, Canada, 1645; d. 1700*), explorer. Traveled to Lake Superior region, 1669; met Father Jacques Marquette at Sault Ste. Marie; on journey back, was first to pass down Great Lakes by way of Detroit River into Lake Erie. Was chosen, 1672, to find "the great Western river"; collaborated with Father Marquette on plans; traveled by canoe to the upper Fox River, where guides showed them the portage to the Wisconsin River, which carried them to the Mississippi. They floated south to the Arkansas River, returning by way of the Illinois and Des Plaines rivers and portaging at the site of Chicago. In 1697 Jolliet was appointed royal hydrographer for Canada. His fame rests on his services in opening the Great Lakes and the Mississippi Valley to civilization and has been overshadowed by Marquette's because of his loss of his notes and journals, 1674, when returning from his great voyage of discovery.

JOLSON, AL (*b. Srednike, Russia, later part of Lithuania, 1886; d. San Francisco, Calif., 1950*), singer. Stage name of Asa Yoelson. Came to America with his family, 1890, to escape anti-Jewish persecution; raised in Washington, D.C., where his father had secured a position as cantor in a synagogue. Jolson's exceptional voice and musical sense were evidenced early when he sang ballads on the street corners to earn spending money. Hoping to join his brother in show business, he ran away to New York. He first appeared on the stage in 1899 as an extra in a Jewish epic, *Children of the Ghetto*. At fifteen he began touring the vaudeville circuits. In 1906, his apprenticeship behind him, Jolson opened in San Francisco as a "single." His sentimental interpretations of popular songs, combined with his impudent charm, immediately appealed to the public.

Following a tour with Dockstader's Minstrels in the conventional role of end man, Jolson struck out on his own again, this time in New York, making his debut at Hammerstein's Victoria. In 1911 the Shuberts included Jolson in a review, *La Belle Paree*, but soon found a better vehicle for him called *Vera Violetta*. In 1912 he was featured in *The Whirl of Society* at the Winter Garden. In this revue Jolson's blackface character acquired the name of Gus, which would follow him in future shows. In *Honeymoon Express* (1913) Jolson may have first used the fall to one knee, arms extended in pathetic appeal, which was to become his hallmark. Other productions followed: *Dancing Around* (1914), *Robinson Crusoe, Jr.* (1916), *Sinbad* (1918), *Bombo* (1921), and *Big Boy* (1925). In the late 1920's, however, his appeal began to fade. His last two stage shows were *Wonderbar* (1931) and *Hold on to Your Hats* (1940).

Jolson starred in the first of the "talking" motion pictures, a sentimentalized version of his life story, *The Jazz Singer* (1927), and made a number of other films for the Warner Brothers studios. His involvement with radio began in 1932 in a series of programs for the Columbia Broadcasting System. His film popularity slipped during the 1930's, but the release of a film biography, *The Jolson Story* (1946), evoked new interest in him.

JONES, ABNER (*b. Royalston, Mass., 1772; d. Exeter, N.H., 1841*), physician. Led a movement for undenominational Christianity in New England, *post* 1801, which had theological affiliations with the later "Christian Connection."

JONES, ALEXANDER (*b. North Carolina, ca. 1802; d. 1863*), author, news reporter, physician. Filed first news message by telegraph from New York to Washington, 1846; pioneered in organizing cooperative press service and market reporting by wire among American cities.

JONES, ALFRED (*b. Liverpool, England, 1819; d. New York, N.Y., 1900*), line engraver. Came to America as a young man. Invented a process for producing directly from a photograph a plate that could be printed with type.

JONES, ALLEN (*b. Halifax Co., N.C., 1739; d. Northampton Co., N.C., 1807*), Revolutionary soldier, planter, North Carlonia legislator. Brother of Willie Jones, yet a strong Federalist.

JONES, AMANDA THEODOSIA (*b. East Bloomfield, N.Y., 1835; d. Junction City, Kans., 1914*), author, inventor. Patented, 1873, the Jones Preserving Process for fruit and meat; also patented a liquid fuel burner, 1880.

JONES, ANSON (*b. Great Barrington, Mass., 1798; d. Houston, Tex., 1858*), physician, Texas legislator. Settled in Texas, 1833; served at San Jacinto. Texas secretary of state, 1841; last president of Republic of Texas, 1844–46.

JONES, BENJAMIN ALLYN (*b. Parnell, Mo., 1882; d. Lexington, Ky., 1961*), horse breeder and trainer. Began breeding and racing thoroughbred horses, graduating to the Chicago circuit around 1925. Trained horses at Woolford Farm for Herbert M. Woolf during 1932–39, then was hired as head trainer by Warren Wright, owner of Calumet Farm in Lexington, Ky., where he remained until retiring in 1960. Jones is credited with having trained the winners of 1,528 races. During his tenure at Calumet Farm, the stable topped the money-winning owners' list eleven times and was the leading breeder according to amount of money won fourteen times.

JONES, BENJAMIN FRANKLIN (*b. Claysville, Pa., 1824; d. 1903*), leader in the iron and steel industry. Founded Jones & Lauth, 1851, which became Jones & Laughlin, 1857.

JONES, CALVIN (*b. Great Barrington, Mass., 1775; d. near Bolivar, Tenn., 1846*), physician, North Carolina legislator, planter. Removed to North Carolina, 1795; retired to Tennessee, 1832.

JONES, CATESBY A. P. ROGER (*b. Fairfield, Va., 1821; d. Selma, Ala., 1877*), naval officer. Nephew of Thomas ap Catesby Jones. Assisted in perfecting Dahlgren gun. Commanded the

Confederate ironclad *Merrimac* in her duel with the *Monitor*, March 1862; supervised Confederate gun works, Selma, Ala.

JONES, CHARLES COLCOCK (*b. Savannah, Ga., 1831; d. Augusta, Ga., 1893*), lawyer, historian. Brother of Joseph Jones (1833–1896). Author of *History of Georgia* (1883) and other works.

JONES, DAVID (*b. New Castle Co., Del., 1736; d. 1820*), Baptist clergyman, chaplain in Revolution and War of 1812. Pastor in New Jersey and Pennsylvania. Author of, among other works, *A Journal of Two Visits to Some Nations of Indians . . . in the Years 1772 and 1773* (1774).

JONES, DAVID RUMPH (*b. Orangeburg District, S.C., 1825; d. Richmond, Va., 1863*), Confederate major general. Graduated West Point, 1846. Supposedly hauled down the national colors at Ft. Sumter.

JONES, ERNEST LESTER (*b. East Orange, N.J., 1876; d. 1929*). Director, U.S. Coast and Geodetic Survey, 1915–29.

JONES, EVAN WILLIAM (*b. Monmouthshire, Wales, 1852; d. Portland, Oreg., 1908*), mechanical engineer. Came to America as a child. Invented mechanical underfeed stoker for boiler furnaces.

JONES, FRANK (*b. Barrington, N.H., 1832; d. Portsmouth, N.H., 1902*), brewer, capitalist. Chief promoter and first president, Portsmouth & Dover Railroad, subsequently Boston & Maine; served as president of the latter, 1889–92 and 1893.

JONES, GABRIEL (*b. near Williamsburg, Va., 1724; d. Augusta Co., Va., 1806*), lawyer, adviser, and executor for Lord Fairfax. King's attorney on Virginia frontier, 1745–75; sponsored George Washington's entry into public life, 1758.

JONES, GEORGE (*b. near York, Pa., 1800; d. Philadelphia, Pa., 1870*), Episcopal clergyman, naval chaplain, author. First chaplain of U.S. Naval Academy, 1851; accompanied Commodore Perry to Japan.

JONES, GEORGE (*b. Poultney, Vt., 1811; d. 1891*), newspaper publisher. Cofounder of the *New York Times*, 1851. Was responsible for overthrowing the "Tweed Ring" and was the first conspicuous business-type newspaper proprietor.

JONES, GEORGE HEBER (*b. Mohawk, N.Y., 1867; d. Miami, Fla., 1919*), Methodist clergyman. Missionary in Korea, 1887–1909.

JONES, GEORGE WALLACE (*b. Vincennes, Ind., 1804; d. 1896*), pioneer miner, merchant, legislator. Michigan Territory delegate to Congress, 1835; secured organization of Wisconsin Territory, 1836, and of Iowa Territory. U.S. senator, Democrat, from Iowa, 1848–59; U.S. minister to New Granada, 1859–61. A representative of the Southern point of view, he lost influence in Iowa *post* 1854.

JONES, HARRY CLARY (*b. New London, Md., 1865; d. 1916*), physical chemist. Established at Johns Hopkins University, 1895, the first distinctive department of physical chemistry in America; specialized in hydrates in solution.

JONES, HERSCHEL VESPASIAN (*b. Jefferson, N.Y., 1861; d. 1928*), journalist, bibliophile. Associated with *Minneapolis Journal*, 1885–1928, as editor, publisher, and owner. Collected three notable libraries.

JONES, HILARY POLLARD (*b. Hanover Co., Va., 1863; d. Washington, D.C., 1938*), naval officer. Graduated Annapolis, 1884. Commander in chief, U.S. Fleet, 1922–23; adviser at naval conferences at Geneva (1927) and London (1930).

JONES, HUGH (*b. ca. 1670; d. 1760*), Anglican clergyman, mathematician, historian. Came to Virginia, 1716; taught at William and Mary. Author of *The Present State of Virginia* (1724) and *A Short English Grammar* (1724), the first English grammar written in America. Pastor in Virginia and Maryland; rector, 1731–60, of St. Stephen's, Cecil Co., Md.

JONES, HUGH BOLTON (*b. Baltimore, Md., 1848; d. New York, N.Y., 1927*), landscape painter.

JONES, JACOB (*b. near Smyrna, Del., 1768; d. Philadelphia, Pa., 1850*), physician, naval officer. Appointed midshipman, 1799; served in Tripolitan War; commanded the *Wasp* in its victory over the British *Frolic*, 1812.

JONES, JAMES CHAMBERLAYNE (*b. near the Davidson and Wilson county lines, Tenn., 1809; d. near Memphis, Tenn., 1859*), farmer. Whig governor of Tennessee, 1841–45; U.S. senator, 1851–57.

JONES, JAMES KIMBROUGH (*b. Marshall Co., Miss., 1829; d. Washington, D.C., 1908*), lawyer, Arkansas legislator. Congressman, Democrat, from Arkansas, 1879–85; U.S. senator, 1885–1903; advocated tariff reform and free silver.

JONES, JEHU GLANCY (*b. Caernarvon Township, Pa., 1811; d. Reading, Pa., 1878*), Episcopal clergyman, lawyer. Congressman, Democrat, from Pennsylvania, 1851–53, 1854–58; helped his friend Buchanan obtain the Democratic nomination for president, 1856. U.S. minister to Austria, 1858–61.

JONES, JENKIN LLOYD (*b. Wales, 1843; d. 1918*), Unitarian clergyman. Came to America as an infant; raised in Wisconsin. Principal pastorate in Chicago, Ill.; editor, 1880–1918, of *Unity*, religious weekly dedicated to "Freedom, Fellowship and Character in Religion." Accompanied the Ford Peace Ship Mission, 1915–16.

JONES, JESSE HOLMAN (*b. Robertson County, Tenn., 1874; d. Houston, Tex., 1956*), businessman, public official. Self-educated, Jones built his small lumber company into a real estate and banking empire, the Texas Trust Company, by 1909. Gained prominence in the Democratic Party through his backing of Woodrow Wilson. Appointed director of the Reconstruction Finance Corporation, 1932. Member of the National Emergency Council 1933–39; from 1936, chairman of the Export-Import Bank of Washington. From 1939, administrator of the Federal Loan Agency. Secretary of commerce, 1940–45, Jones was forced to resign because of a public dispute with vice president Wallace.

JONES, JOEL (*b. Coventry, Conn., 1795; d. 1860*), lawyer. Practiced in Easton and Philadelphia, Pa.; Pennsylvania district court judge, 1835–47. First president, Girard College, 1848–49.

JONES, JOHN (*b. Jamaica, N.Y., 1729; d. 1791*), surgeon. Received most of his medical education abroad, obtaining his degree, 1751, at the University of Rheims. He became a successful lithotomist in New York, served as surgeon throughout the French and Indian War, and in 1767 became professor of surgery and obstetrics at King's College when its medical department was organized. He petitioned for the charter of New York Hospital, 1770, and became one of its attending physicians. Too frail for active service, he helped organize the medical department of the Continental Army. More important was his authorship (1775) of the first surgical textbook written in the American colonies (*Plain . . . Remarks on the Treatment of Wounds and Fractures*). He practiced in Philadelphia, Pa., *post* 1780. A personal friend of George Washington, he was Benjamin Franklin's personal physician.

JONES, JOHN B. (*b. Fairfield District, S.C., 1834; d. Tex., 1881*), Confederate soldier. Appointed major of Texas Rangers Frontier Battalion, 1874; cleared out Indians and badmen from Red River to Rio Grande; broke up Sam Bass gang, 1878. Adjutant general of Texas, 1879–81.

JONES, JOHN BEAUCHAMP (*b. Baltimore, Md., 1810; d. Burlington, N.J., 1866*), journalist. Author of many novels, including a minor classic of the frontier, *Wild Western Scenes* (1841); was the author of *A Rebel War Clerk's Diary* (1866).

JONES, JOHN PAUL (*b. Kirkbean, Scotland, 1747; d. Paris, France, 1792*), merchant captain, naval officer. Known as John Paul until about 1773. At outbreak of Revolution, went to Philadelphia where, through influence of Joseph Hewes and Robert Morris, he was commissioned lieutenant, 1775. He served on the *Alfred*, first U.S. naval vessel to fly the Continental flag, and was at capture of New Providence, 1776. Given command of the *Providence*, 1776, he was promoted captain and on one cruise captured 16 prizes. In June 1777 Congress gave him command of the *Ranger*, and the marine committee ordered him to France, to report to the American commissioners at Paris. In April 1778 he began raids on English ports and shipping from his base at Brest. In February 1779 the French king placed under his command a wornout East Indiaman of 40 guns, which he renamed the *Bonhomme Richard* in honor of Benjamin Franklin. That summer Jones sailed with a small squadron around Ireland and Scotland, taking 17 prizes. Off Flamborough Head, Yorks., on September 23 he fell in with a large British Baltic convoy escorted by the *Serapis*, 44 guns, and the *Countess of Scarborough*, 20 guns. Jones maneuvered the outclassed *Bonhomme Richard* alongside the *Serapis* and, in one of the most desperate and sanguinary sea-fights in naval history, forced the Britisher to surrender, though his own ship was so badly damaged she sank two days later. Putting in to neutral Holland, where the French government took possession of the prizes, prisoners, and fleet, except for the *Alliance* to which Jones transferred his flag, he returned to L'Orient early in 1780 after a short cruise off Spain. At Paris, Jones was received as a popular hero; overstaying his time, he sailed for Philadelphia, arriving in February 1781 after an absence of more than three years. He was then chosen to command the *America*, the first and only 74-gun ship in the Continental Navy, then building at Portsmouth, N.H. After more than a year supervising the construction, Jones launched the vessel, which was then presented to the French government.

Out of the Navy in 1783, Jones was recommended by Congress to the American minister at Paris as agent to solicit payment for prizes taken by his ships. He last visited America in 1787, when Congress resolved unanimously to present him with a gold medal to commemorate his brilliant services. He was the only Continental naval officer so honored. Returning to France, he was offered a commission in the Russian navy, then fighting the Turks, by the Empress Catherine. As rear admiral, he commanded the sail squadron on the Black Sea May–October 1788. Because of the jealousies and intrigues of rivals, Jones's experience in Russia was unhappy and he returned to Paris, 1790.

No longer a popular hero, Jones lived comfortably in Paris, though in declining health. On June 1, 1792, Jefferson as secretary of state wrote that President Washington had appointed him commissioner to treat with Algiers on peace and ransoming of prisoners. Before the letter reached Paris, however, he was dead. He was buried in Paris, but in 1905 what are thought to be his remains were brought to Annapolis and in 1913 entombed in the crypt of the Naval Academy chapel.

JONES, JOHN PERCIVAL (*b. Herefordshire, England, 1829; d. 1912*), miner, California legislator. Raised in Cleveland, Ohio. Removed to California, 1849; made fortune in Crown Point mine, Nevada. U.S. senator, Republican, from Nevada, 1873–1903; author of an important report on bimetallism, 1877–79.

JONES, JOHN PETER (*b. Wrexham, Wales, 1847; d. Hartford, Conn., 1916*), Congregational clergyman. Missionary in India, 1878–1914.

JONES, JOHN PRICE (*b. Latrobe, Pa., 1877; d. Philadelphia, Pa., 1964*), journalist and fund raiser. Studied at Harvard (B.A., 1902), then worked as a reporter in New York City, 1903–17. In early 1919 he became general manager of the Harvard Endowment Fund. Later that year, Jones and some associates from Harvard moved to New York City and incorporated the John Price Jones Corporation. Jones perfected techniques for raising money for colleges, hospitals, and other causes. He organized relief drives during the Great Depression and played a major part during World War II in both United Service Organizations and Red Cross campaigns. In 1945–47 he made the American Cancer Society into a leading medical appeal.

JONES, JOHN TAYLOR (*b. New Ipswich, N.H., 1802; d. Bangkok, Siam, 1851*), Baptist clergyman. First American missionary to Siam (1833–51); prepared a Siamese grammar and translated the New Testament from the Greek into Siamese.

JONES, JOHN WILLIAM (*b. Louisa Court House, Va., 1836; d. Columbus, Ga., 1909*), Baptist clergyman, Confederate soldier. Author of *Personal Reminiscences . . . of Gen. Robert E. Lee* (1874) and *Life and Letters of Robert Edward Lee* (1906).

JONES, JOHN WINSTON (*b. Amelia Co., Va., 1791; d. 1848*), lawyer. Congressman, Democrat, from Virginia, 1835–45; speaker of the House, 1843–45.

JONES, JOSEPH (*b. King George Co., Va., 1727; d. 1805*), Revolutionary statesman, jurist. Uncle of James Monroe. Particularly remembered for preventing Virginia's revocation of the cession of the Northwest Territory to the United States.

JONES, JOSEPH (*b. Liberty Co., Ga., 1833; d. New Orleans, La., 1896*), physician, sanitarian. Brother of Charles C. Jones. Graduated Princeton, 1853; M.D., University of Pennsylvania, 1856. Taught at University of Louisiana *post* 1872. As president of the state board of health, 1880–84, and thereafter as a private citizen, he engaged in a thankless struggle for the sanitary improvement of New Orleans.

JONES, JOSEPH STEVENS (*b. Boston, Mass., 1809; d. Boston, 1877*), physician, dramatist, actor. Won transitory and largely local fame as the author of about 150 plays.

JONES, KIMBROUGH (*b. Marshall Co., Miss., 1829; d. Washington, D.C., 1908*), lawyer, Arkansas legislator. Congressman, Democrat, from Arkansas, 1879–85; U.S. senator, 1885–1903; advocated tariff reform and free silver.

JONES, LEONARD AUGUSTUS (*b. Templeton, Mass., 1832; d. 1909*), jurist, legal writer. Published an exhaustive exposition of the law of securities; also a manual on conveyancing (1886) widely used and known as "Jones Legal Forms." Judge of the Massachusetts land court *post* 1898.

JONES, LEWIS RALPH (*b. Brandon, Wis., 1864; d. Orlando, Fla., 1945*), plant pathologist. Ph.B., University of Michigan, 1889; Ph.D., 1904. Taught botany at University of Vermont,

1889–1910 (professor *post* 1893); headed department of plant pathology at University of Wisconsin, 1910–35. While at Vermont he conducted a long experimental program which made possible a much greater control of diseases of potatoes, carrots, and other vegetables; at Wisconsin he concentrated on the development of disease-resistant plants, also continuing his study of the role of environmental factors in plant pathology. His investigation of cabbage yellows was one of the earliest to demonstrate the relationship between soil temperature and plant diseases.

JONES, LINDLEY ARMSTRONG ("SPIKE") (*b. Long Beach, Calif., 1911; d. Los Angeles, Calif., 1965*), bandleader, composer, and comedian. Worked in radio-show bands before turning to musical satire and slapstick with his group named Spike Jones and His City Slickers. The band made movies and toured with their *Musical Depreciation Revue.* "The Spike Jones Show" appeared on television in 1951, 1954, 1957, 1958 (as the "Club Oasis" show), 1960, and 1961. Jones then abandoned comedy and turned to Dixieland.

JONES, LYNDS (*b. Jefferson, Ohio, 1865; d. Oberlin, Ohio, 1951*), ornithologist. Studied at Grinnell College (then Iowa College), Oberlin (1892) and the University of Chicago, (Ph.D., 1905). Worked and taught at Oberlin, 1892–1930. Founded the Wilson Ornithological Club in 1888; editor of the *Wilson Bulletin,* 1888–1900; 1902–24. Taught ornithology and ecology at Oberlin. Author of *A Revised Catalogue of the Birds of Ohio,* 1902. Fellow of the American Ornithologists' Union, 1905.

JONES, MARY HARRIS (*b. Cork, Ireland, 1830; d. Silver Spring, Md., 1930*), labor leader known and beloved as "Mother Jones." Came to America as a child; raised in Canada. Active in U.S. labor movement, 1871–1923, as organizer and orator.

JONES, NOBLE WYMBERLEY (*b. near London, England, ca. 1724; d. Savannah, Ga., 1805*), physician, planter, Georgia patriot and legislator. Came to Georgia as a youth; was patronized by General Oglethorpe. Opposed British colonial policy *post* 1765, serving as member of provincial congresses and of the Council of Safety.

JONES, RICHARD FOSTER (*b. Salado, Tex., 1886; d. Menlo Park, Calif., 1965*), educator. Graduated from the University of Texas (1903) and Columbia (M.A., 1910; Ph.D., 1918). Taught at Western Reserve University, 1914–18, and Columbia, 1918–19, then moved to Washington University in 1919, and served as dean of the graduate school, 1941–45. As executive head of the Department of English at Stanford, 1945–51, was instrumental in founding the Stanford Creative Writing Center. His publications include *Lewis Theobald* (1919), *Seventeenth-Century Literature* (1929), *Eighteenth-Century Literature* (1929), *Ancients and Moderns* (1936), *The Seventeenth Century* (1951), and *The Triumph of the English Language* (1953).

JONES, ROBERT EDMOND (*b. Milton, N.H., 1887; d. Milton, N.H., 1954*), theatrical designer and stage director. Graduated from Harvard (1910) and attended Max Reinhardt's Deutsches Theater in Berlin, 1913. Preeminent among modern theatrical designers, Jones pioneered in breaking away from the traditional realism of American design. In association with producer Arthur Hopkins, 1915–34, he designed *Hedda Gabler, The Wild Duck, Anna Christie,* and *The Hairy Ape.* He designed the inaugural production at the Radio City Music Hall in 1932; designed and directed at the Play Festival at the old opera house in Central City, Colo., 1932–42. His plays for the Theatre Guild include *Mourning Becomes Electra, The Seagull, The Philadelphia Story,* and *Othello.*

JONES, ROBERT REYNOLDS ("BOB") (*b. Skipperville, Ala., 1883; d. Greenville, S.C., 1968*), evangelist and college founder. Held his first revival at twelve. He studied at Southern University in Greensboro, Ala., 1901–04, then became a popular evangelist who preached against liquor, gambling, Catholicism, and Protestant liberalism. In 1926 he opened Bob Jones College in St. Andrews, Fla. The school moved to Cleveland, Tenn., in 1933, and in 1947 was relocated to Greenville, S.C., and renamed Bob Jones University.

JONES, RUFUS MATTHEW (*b. South China, Maine, 1863; d. Haverford, Pa., 1948*), philosopher, scholar of mysticism, Quaker historian, social reformer. B.A., Haverford College, 1885; M.A., 1886. Influenced by Pliny E. Chase. After teaching for a year at Oakwood Seminary, Union Springs, N.Y., Jones went to Europe to study. After attending lectures in philosophy in Heidelberg (1887), he returned to teach at the Friend's School in Providence, R.I. In 1889 he was named principal of Oak Grove Seminary, Vassalboro, Maine. That same year his first book, *Eli and Sybil Jones, Their Life and Work,* was published. In 1890 he was recognized as a minister.

In 1893 Jones became the editor of the *Friend's Review* and an instructor in philosophy at Haverford College. He then combined the *Friends' Review* with the *Christian Worker* (Chicago) to form the *American Friend,* with which he continued his editorial work until 1912. In 1897 he planned a scholarly history of the Religious Society of Friends. Carried to its conclusion in 1921, these volumes, with subsequent revisions, have been regarded as the standard history of the Society of Friends.

After a sabbatical at Harvard, Jones received his M.A. in philosophy, 1901, and was named to fill the new T. Wistar Brown chair in philosophy at Haverford. In 1898 he had begun a half century of service on the board of trustees of Bryn Mawr College (chairman, 1916–36). In 1904 his *Social Law in the Spiritual World* was published. Five years later there appeared his *Studies in Mystical Religion* (1909), which gained him immediate recognition as a scholar of mysticism. Subsequently he published *The Quakers in the American Colonies* (1911) and *Spiritual Reformers in the Sixteenth and Seventeenth Centuries* (1914).

When the United States entered World War I in 1917, Jones was chosen as chairman of the American Friends Service Committee (AFSC). He continued to serve as chairman until 1928 and again from 1935 to 1944. In 1947, after World War II, the AFSC was awarded the Nobel Peace Prize jointly with the Friends Service Council in London.

Jones's *The Later Periods of Quakerism* appeared in 1921, followed by *The Church's Debt to Heretics* (1924) and *New Studies in Mystical Religion* (1927). In 1932 he shared in an interdenominational survey of missions in the Far East and contributed to the published report, *Rethinking Missions* (1932).

He retired from Haverford College after taking part in the centennial celebrations, for which he wrote *Haverford College, A History and an Interpretation* (1933). The following year, in Europe, he gave lectures, interspersed with additional study of the continental mystics. *The Flowering of Mysticism* (1939), about a small group of fourteenth-century mystics called the Friends of God, was the result of this research. In 1937 he presided at the second Friends World Conference, held at Swarthmore and Haverford colleges. The following year he traveled to South Africa, and in an attempt to intervene on behalf of the Jews, visited Nazi Germany. His last book, *A Call to What is Vital,* appeared shortly after his death in 1948.

JONES, SAMUEL (*b. Fort Hill, N.Y., 1734; d. 1819*), lawyer, New York legislator. With Richard Varick, published a basic revision of New York statutes; was recorder of New York City, 1789–96, and comptroller, 1797–1800.

JONES, SAMUEL (*b. New York, N.Y., 1770; d. Cold Spring, N.Y., 1853*), New York jurist. Son of Samuel Jones (1734–1819). Chancellor of New York, 1826–28; state supreme court justice, 1847–49.

JONES, SAMUEL MILTON (*b. Carnarvonshire, Wales, 1846; d. 1904*), inventor, manufacturer, reformer. Came to America as an infant. Made a fortune in manufacture of oilwell machinery. In his factory at Toledo, Ohio, instituted reforms such as the eight-hour day, a minimum wage, and vacations with pay; was called "Golden Rule" Jones; advocated trade unionism, a cooperative insurance plan, and sick benefits. He believed that the state should assume ownership of trusts which are logical outgrowths of modern business competition and should operate them for all the people. Elected mayor of Toledo, 1897, he served until his death in 1904. During his administration, he established civil service, an eight-hour day, and a minimum wage for city employees.

JONES, SAMUEL PORTER (*b. Chambers Co., Ala., 1847; d. 1906*), itinerant Methodist evangelist. Operated throughout the country, 1872–1906, and was perhaps the foremost American public speaker of his type in his generation.

JONES, SYBIL (*b. Brunswick, Maine, 1808; d. near Augusta, Maine, 1873*), Quaker preacher. One of the principal factors in the great Quaker revival, 1840–80.

JONES, THOMAS (*b. Fort Neck, South Oyster Bay, N.Y., 1731; d. Hoddesdon, England, 1792*), jurist, Loyalist. Author of *History of New York during the Revolutionary War*, a biased Tory work which was not published until 1879. Son-in-law of Chief Justice James de Lancey, he became a judge of the New York supreme court in 1773. Persecuted during the Revolution, he removed to England in 1781.

JONES, THOMAS AP CATESBY (*b. Westmoreland Co., Va., 1790; d. Sharon, Va., 1858*), naval officer. Appointed midshipman, 1805. Distinguished at New Orleans, La., Dec. 14, 1814, for opposing entrance of British into Lake Borgne; seized Monterey, Calif., October 1842, in advance of war with Mexico; commanded Pacific squadron during war with Mexico. Court-martialed, 1850, but restored, 1853.

JONES, THOMAS GOODE (*b. Macon, Ga., 1844; d. Montgomery, Ala., 1914*), Confederate soldier, Alabama legislator. Democratic governor of Alabama, 1890–94; federal district judge, 1901–14; opponent of B. B. Comer over railroad legislation.

JONES, THOMAS P. (*b. Herefordshire, England, 1774; d. Washington, D.C., 1848*), editor, *Journal of the Franklin Institute*, 1826–48. As editor and U.S. patent office official, he gave valuable encouragement to the development of genuinely useful inventions and exposed unworthy projects.

JONES, WALTER (*b. Northumberland Co., Va., 1776; d. Washington, D.C., 1861*), lawyer. Studied law with Bushrod Washington; served as U.S. attorney, for District of Columbia, 1802–21. Practicing with distinguished success in Washington, D.C., he was of counsel in many famous cases including *McCulloch* v. *Maryland*, the Girard Will case, and the litigation over the will of Daniel Clark. A founder of the American Colonization Society (1816), he later strongly opposed secession.

JONES, WESLEY LIVSEY (*b. near Bethany, Ill., 1863; d. 1932*), lawyer. Removed to State of Washington, 1889. Congressman, Republican, from Washington, 1899–1909; U.S. senator, 1909–32.

JONES, WILLIAM (*b. Newport, R.I., 1753; d. 1822*), merchant, Revolutionary soldier, and Federalist governor of Rhode Island, 1811–17. Defied national government over War of 1812 and other policies.

JONES, WILLIAM (*b. Philadelphia, Pa., 1760; d. Bethlehem, Pa., 1831*), Revolutionary soldier and privateersman, merchant. Hopelessly inefficient as secretary of the navy and of the treasury, 1813–14, and as first president of the second United States Bank, 1816–19.

JONES, WILLIAM (*b. Sac and Fox Indian reservation in present Oklahoma, 1871; d. Philippine Islands, 1909*), Indian ethnologist. Graduated Harvard, 1900; Ph.D., Columbia, 1904. Made major contributions to knowledge of Algonquian language and lore.

JONES, WILLIAM ALFRED (*b. New York, N.Y., 1817; d. Norwich Town, Conn., 1900*), author. A critic admired by Poe and Irving, Jones did not bear out his early promise. Served as librarian at Columbia University, 1851–65. His *Characters and Criticisms* (1857) contains the bulk of his work.

JONES, WILLIAM PALMER (*b. Adair Co., Ky., 1819; d. Nashville, Tenn., 1897*), physician, psychiatrist. President, medical faculty, University of Tennessee, 1876–96.

JONES, WILLIAM PATTERSON (*b. Philadelphia, Pa., 1831; d. Fullerton, Nebr., 1886*), educator and U.S. consul in China, 1862–68. Founded Northwestern Female College (later absorbed by Northwestern University), 1855, at which he introduced teaching methods far in advance of his time. Among his students were Frances E. Willard and May W. Sewall.

JONES, WILLIAM RICHARD (*b. Hazleton, Pa., 1839; d. Pittsburgh, Pa., 1889*), engineer, Union soldier, steelman. Became assistant to superintendent, Cambria Iron Co., Johnstown, Pa., 1872; later went to Pittsburgh as master mechanic, Edgar Thomson Steel Co. Became general superintendent of the company at Braddock, Pa., 1875; *post* 1888 was also consulting engineer to Carnegie, Phipps & Co. Characterized as "probably the greatest mechanical genius that ever entered the Carnegie shops," he patented numerous devices and processes, including the Jones mixer, 1889. His pre-eminence, however, rested primarily on his ability as a manager of men, demonstrated most notably in rescue work during the Johnstown Flood.

JONES, WILLIE (*b. Northampton Co., N.C., ca. 1741; d. Raleigh, N.C., 1801*), Revolutionary leader, planter, merchant. A man of wide influence and an ardent supporter of colonial rights from the beginning of the quarrel with the mother country. An important member of each of the provincial congresses, he served on the committee to draft a North Carolina constitution and has been credited with its authorship. Undisputed leader of the dominant democratic element in North Carolina, he served frequently in the legislature. Declining election to the federal convention, he led the successful opposition to the federal Constitution in the North Carolina convention of 1788, fearing it would check the development of political democracy, to which, though an aristocrat, he was passionately attached. He was a brother of Allen Jones.

JOPLIN, JANIS LYN (*b. Port Arthur, Tex., 1943; d. Hollywood, Calif., 1970*), singer. Began singing blues and folk tunes. In 1966 she first appeared as lead singer for a new band called Big Brother and the Holding Company. Following successes at the Monterey International Pop Festival (1967) and the Newport Folk Festival (1968), they released their first album, *Cheap Thrills* (1968). Later that year Joplin formed her own band, which appeared at the

Woodstock festival and released *I Got Dem Old Kozmic Blues Again Mama* (1969). Her album *Pearl* was released after her death which had been caused by heroin-morphine intoxication.

JORDAN, DAVID STARR (*b. near Gainesville, N.Y., 1851; d. Stanford University, Calif., 1931*), described himself as naturalist and explorer first, teacher second, and minor prophet of Democracy third. He taught botany while still an undergraduate at Cornell University from which he graduated, 1872. After further study, including a brief period under the elder Agassiz and the publication of his *Manual of the Vertebrates of the Northern U.S.* (1876), he went to Indiana University, 1879, as head of the natural science department and became president, 1885. In 1891 he became first president of Leland Stanford University. He had become the greatest living authority on ichthyology, and was always to be a student of the problems of geographic distribution of animal and plant species. He introduced the "major-professor" system and other innovations in higher education at both Indiana and Stanford, chose and trained outstanding faculties, was able in financial administration, and yet found time to serve frequently on government and private special commissions. After 1898 he became an indefatigable crusader for international peace. He retired from the presidency of Stanford, 1913, becoming chancellor.

JORDAN, EBEN DYER (*b. Boston, Mass., 1857; d. West Manchester, Mass., 1916*), merchant. Head of Jordan, Marsh & Co.; as patron of music, aided the New England Conservatory of Music and contributed much to establishing opera in Boston.

JORDAN, EDWIN OAKES (*b. Thomaston, Maine, 1866; d. Lewiston, Maine, 1936*), bacteriologist, sanitarian. Graduated Massachusetts Institute of Technology, 1888; Ph.D., Clark University, 1892. Headed division of hygiene and bacteriology at University of Chicago where he taught, 1892–1933. Jordan made important contributions to public health, investigating water pollution and water-borne disease, food poisoning, and influenza. His efforts helped secure for Chicago high-grade diphtheria antitoxin and a clean and pasteurized milk supply.

JORDAN, JOHN WOOLF (*b. Philadelphia, Pa., 1840; d. 1921*), librarian, editor, antiquary. Librarian, Historical Society of Pennsylvania, 1903–21; edited many important manuscript sources for *Pennsylvania Magazine of History and Biography*, of which he was editor, 1887–1921.

JORDAN, KATE (*b. Dublin, Ireland, 1862; d. Mountain Lakes, N.J., 1926*), novelist, playwright.

JORDAN, THOMAS (*b. Luray, Va., 1819; d. 1895*), soldier, journalist. Graduated West Point, 1840. Served as Gen. Beauregard's chief of staff, 1862–65; later led Cuban insurgents. Conducted *Financial and Mining Record*, New York City, 1870–92.

JORDAN, VIRGIL JUSTIN (*b. Olean, N.Y., 1892; d. Southern Pines, N.C., 1965*), economist. Studied at the College of the City of New York (B.S., 1912), the University of Wisconsin, Columbia, and Cambridge. Was an associate editor of *Everybody's Magazine*, 1914–20, then joined the staff of the National Industrial Conference Board as editor of publications in 1920, serving also as chief economist, 1924–29. Later was economist at *Business Week*, 1929–33, and president of the Conference Board, 1933–48. Jordan's writings include *The Inter-Ally Debt and the United States* (1925), *The Agricultural Problem in the United States* (1926), and *Manifesto for the Atomic Age* (1946); in the latter, he pessimistically foresaw the dissolving of all social values.

JORDAN, WILLIAM GEORGE (*b. New York, N.Y., 1864; d. 1928*), editor, author. Campaigned for educational reform.

JOSEFFY, RAFAEL (*b. Hunfalu, Hungary, 1852; d. New York, N.Y., 1915*), concert pianist, teacher, editor. Studied at Budapest, Leipzig, and in Berlin under Tausig; came to America, 1879. Excelled in playing Bach and Mozart, introduced Brahms's works in America; edited, among others, the *Complete Works of Chopin* (1915).

JOSEPH (*b. probably Wallowa Valley, Oreg., ca. 1840; d. Nespelim, Colville reservation, Wash., 1904*), Nez Percé chief. Generally regarded as the greatest of Indian strategists. As leader of the "non-treaty" Nez Percé, who refused to recognize the 1863 agreement ceding their lands and confining them to a reservation in Idaho, Joseph was drawn into hopeless resistance. Recognizing that his 200 warriors were no match for the military power opposed to him, he planned to escape with women and children to Canada. In 1877, he led a brilliant retreat more than 1,000 miles through Montana, Idaho, and Yellowstone Park, eluding one U.S. Army unit under General O. O. Howard, defeating another under General John Gibbon at Big Hole, Mont.; and finally surrendering after a five-day siege only 30 miles from safety. Noted for his humaneness in warfare, he thereafter gave his efforts to help his people learn peaceful ways.

JOSSELYN, JOHN (*fl. 1638–1675*), traveler and writer. Author of two volumes dealing with New England, based on his observations during two visits there in 1638–39 and 1663–71. *New-Englands Rarities Discovered*, published 1672, was the first systematic account of botanical species of the region. *An Account of Two Voyages to New-England* (1674) was a rather strange compound of scientific lore, suggestions for settlers, bits of local history, and much general observation.

JOUBERT DE LA MURAILLE, JAMES HECTOR MARIE NICHOLAS (*b. Saint Jean d'Angely, France, 1777; d. 1843*), Roman Catholic clergyman, Sulpician. Came to Baltimore, Md., *ca.* 1805; ordained, 1810; taught at St. Mary's College. Founded the Oblate Sisters of Providence, Baltimore, Md., 1828.

JOUETT, JAMES EDWARD (*b. near Lexington, Ky., 1826; d. Sandy Spring, Md., 1902*), naval officer. Son of Matthew H. Jouett. Served in Mexican War and was distinguished as captain of USS *Metacomet* on blockade duty, Gulf of Mexico, 1863–65. Recipient of Farragut's "Damn the torpedoes!" order at Mobile Bay, 1864.

JOUETT, JOHN (*b. Albermarle Co., Va., 1754; d. 1822*), Revolutionary patriot. Outpaced Tarleton's British horse, 1781, to save Governor Jefferson and the Virginia legislature from capture at Charlottesville. Removed to Kentucky, 1782, where he became a stockbreeder and legislator.

JOUETT, MATTHEW HARRIS (*b. near Harrodsburg, Ky., 1787; d. Lexington, Ky., 1827*), portrait painter. Son of John Jouett. Studied with Gilbert Stuart; worked extensively in the South.

JOUTEL, HENRI (*b. Rouen, France, ca. 1645; d. Rouen, post 1723*), soldier. Was La Salle's lieutenant and the journalist of his last expedition to America and of his last days and death. He joined La Salle, 1684, in an expedition to form a settlement at the mouth of the Mississippi. They reached the Gulf of Mexico but missed the river mouth, landed in Matagorda Bay on the Texas coast, and began a colony. La Salle made several efforts to find the Mississippi, but early in 1687 he was murdered by conspirators among his own men. Joutel and La Salle's brother and nephew were allowed to escape, crossed what is now Arkansas, and eventually reached Quebec by way of the Mississippi and Tonty's Fort on the Illinois River. Joutel returned to France, 1688. In 1713 he published an account of his adventures, issued in English, 1714, as *A Journal of the Last Voyage Performed by M. de la Sale.*

JOY, AGNES ELIZA. *See* SALM SALM, AGNES ELIZA JOY, PRINCESS.

JOY, CHARLES TURNER (*b. St. Louis, Mo., 1895; d. San Diego, Calif., 1956*), naval officer. Attended the U.S. Naval Academy, commissioned ensign in 1916. An ordnance specialist, Joy had several sea and shore assignments until the outbreak of World War II; headed the Pacific Plans Division in Washington, 1943–44; and as commander of Cruiser Division 6 in the Pacific, participated in the seizures of Iwo Jima and Okinawa. In 1949, he was appointed commander of the U.S. Naval Force in the Far East; Allied naval commander during the Korean War. Won international recognition as senior U.N. negotiator at the Korean Armistice Conference, 1951. Superintendent of the U.S. Naval Academy, 1952–54.

JOY, HENRY BOURNE (*b. Detroit, Mich., 1864; d. Grosse Pointe Farms, Mich., 1936*), financier and industrialist. Son of James F. Joy. General manager, 1903–09, and president, 1909–16, Packard Motor Car Co.

JOY, JAMES FREDERICK (*b. Durham, N.H., 1810; d. Detroit, Mich., 1896*), lawyer, Western railroad builder. Removed to Detroit, 1836; was active in financing the Michigan Central and organizing Chicago, Burlington and Quincy. Constructed the "Joy System," the first important Western railroad combination.

JOY, THOMAS (*b. probably Hingham, England, ca. 1610; d. 1678*), architect, builder. Came to Boston, Mass., *ca. 1636 o.s.* Designed and built the first "statehouse" in Boston, 1657, and considerably influenced early Boston architecture.

JOYCE, ISAAC WILSON (*b. Hamilton Co., Ohio, 1836; d. Minnesota, 1905*), Methodist clergyman. Rode circuits and held pastorates in Indiana and Ohio, 1858–88; elected bishop, 1888. Noted as a preacher and revivalist.

JOYNES, EDWARD SOUTHEY (*b. Accomac Co., Va., 1834; d. 1917*), Southern educator, Confederate official, textbook writer. Exerted important influence *post* 1880 in upbuilding of schools and colleges, particularly in Virginia, Tennessee, and South Carolina.

JUDAH, SAMUEL (*b. New York, N.Y., 1798; d. 1869*), lawyer, Indiana legislator. Graduated Rutgers, 1816. Removed to Indiana, 1818; settled in Vincennes, where he practiced until his death.

JUDAH, SAMUEL BENJAMIN HELBERT (*b. New York, N.Y., ca. 1799; d. New York, 1876*), lawyer. Author of several plays and dramatic poems and of the libelous satire *Gotham and the Gothamites* (1823).

JUDAH, THEODORE DEHONE (*b. Bridgeport, Conn., 1826; d. New York, N.Y., 1863*), engineer, railroad builder. Initiated and successfully promoted the first realized plan for constructing a railroad across the Sierra Nevada, 1862; associated with C. P. Huntington, Leland Stanford, and others in Central Pacific Railroad Co.

JUDAY, CHANCEY (*b. near Millersburg, Ind., 1871; d. Madison, Wis., 1944*), limnologist. B.A., Indiana University, 1896; M.A., 1897. After a short time as biologist with the Wisconsin Geological and Natural History Survey, he went West to recuperate from tuberculosis; he taught at the universities of Colorado and California, 1902–05. Returning to his Wisconsin

post, he collaborated with Edward A. Birge in lake studies; he also taught at University of Wisconsin, 1908–41 (professor of limnology *post* 1931) and was director of the Trout Lake Limnological Laboratory, 1925–41. His objective was to determine the most significant factors influencing biological productivity in lakes; for this, he collected vast amounts of data on the standing crops of plankton, bottom organisms, and aquatic plants, and endeavored to correlate these with environmental conditions.

JUDD, CHARLES HUBBARD (*b. Bareilly, India, 1873; d. Santa Barbara, Calif., 1946*), educational psychologist. Child of Methodist missionary parents; raised in Binghamton, N.Y. B.A., Wesleyan University, 1894. Ph.D., University of Leipzig, 1896, under Wilhelm Wundt, whose concepts of voluntarism and creative synthesis he adopted, as also his interest in social psychology. Judd was successively instructor in philosophy at Wesleyan (1896–98), professor of psychology in New York University's School of Pedagogy (1898–1901), professor of psychology and pedagogy at the University of Cincinnati (1901–02), and instructor (*post* 1907 professor) of psychology at Yale, 1902–09. Appointed professor of education and director of the University of Chicago's School of Education, 1909, he served in these capacities until his retirement in 1938. Meanwhile he oversaw investigations into reading and number consciousness, and was author of *The Psychology of Social Institutions* (1926) and *The Psychology of Secondary Education* (1927, a revision of a work first published in 1915). He and his colleagues at Chicago played a major part in moving the study of education in America out of the domain of philosophy and into the fields of the social and behavioral sciences. To his mind the school was society's agent for civilizing the young by laying out a program of subject matter and formulating standards of performance for pupils that would enable them to master the problems of life and society; the subject matter of the curriculum should consist of the products of social evolution (such as language, number, and the social studies), which can be altered by the application of trained human intelligence.

JUDD, EDWARD STARR (*b. Rochester, Minn., 1878; d. Chicago, Ill., 1935*), surgeon. M.D., University of Minnesota, 1902. Lifelong associate at Mayo Clinic. Outstanding in field of abdominal surgery.

JUDD, GERRIT PARMELE (*b. Paris, N.Y., 1803; d. 1873*), physician, Hawaiian statesman. Went to Hawaii as medical missionary, 1827; became trusted adviser of the Hawaiian king, serving in the highest offices of state, 1842–53.

JUDD, NORMAN BUEL (*b. Rome, N.Y., 1815; d. 1878*), railroad lawyer, diplomat. Removed to Chicago, Ill., 1836, and was first city attorney; served also in state legislature. Managed Lincoln's campaign for Republican nomination, 1860; was U.S. minister to Prussia, 1861–65.

JUDD, ORANGE (*b. near Niagara Falls, N.Y., 1822; d. Chicago, Ill., 1892*), agricultural editor and publisher. A pioneer in relating chemistry to agriculture, he became joint editor of the *American Agriculturist*, 1853, and was owner and publisher of the *New York Times*. After the Civil War he published *Hearth and Home* and a number of agricultural books. He devised the crop-reporting percentage system later adopted by nearly all nations. A benefactor of Wesleyan University, he made possible the establishment there of the first of the State Agricultural Experiment Stations serving Connecticut. *Post* 1884 he edited the *Prairie Farmer* and the *Orange Judd Farmer*. He also pioneered (1857) in the raising of sorghum.

JUDD, SYLVESTER (*b. Westhampton, Mass., 1813; d. 1853*), Unitarian clergyman. Propagated his idea of the "birthright church" and other religious and social views as pastor in Augusta,

Maine. Author of *Margaret* (1845), *Richard Edney* (1850), novels of New England life. An idealist, he opposed war, abolitionism, and capital punishment.

JUDGE, THOMAS AUGUSTINE (*b. South Boston, Mass., 1868; d. Washington, D.C., 1933*), Roman Catholic clergyman, Vincentian. Active as missionary; founded Missionary Servants of the Most Holy Trinity and a similar community of nuns.

JUDGE, WILLIAM QUAN (*b. Dublin, Ireland, 1851; d. 1896*), lawyer, theosophist. Came to America as a boy. Established branches of the Theosophical Society in every large American city; remained loyal to Mme. Blavatsky after her exposure.

JUDSON, ADONIRAM (*b. Malden, Mass., 1788; d. at sea, 1850*), Baptist missionary. Graduated Brown, 1807; was a leader in movement resulting in forming of American Board of Commissioners for Foreign Missions. Going to Calcutta in 1812 as a Congregationalist missionary to Burma, he became a Baptist. He later reached Rangoon, where he set about learning Burmese and eventually translated the Bible into Burmese (completed 1834) and completed his *Dictionary, English and Burmese* (1849). He had married twice, enjoying marital associations remarkable for their intellectual and spiritual compatibility, before his return to America in 1845, when he married once more. The following year he returned to Maulmain, which had earlier become the center of American Baptist activities in Burma.

JUDSON, ADONIRAM BROWN (*b. Maulmain, Burma, 1837; d. 1916*), surgeon. Son of Adoniram Judson. Graduated Brown, 1859; M.D., Jefferson Medical College, 1865; M.D., College of Physicians and Surgeons, N.Y., 1868. Served in Civil War as naval surgeon. Specialized in orthopedic surgery in New York; was instrumental in forming the American Orthopedic Association, 1887.

JUDSON, ANN HASSELTINE (*b. Bradford, Mass., 1789; d. Amherst, Burma, 1826*), missionary to Burma, first wife of Adoniram Judson. Author of *Account of the American Baptist Mission to the Burman Empire* (1823).

JUDSON, EDWARD (*b. Maulmain, Burma, 1844; d. 1914*), Baptist clergyman. Son of Adoniram Judson. After a teaching career and a pastorate at Orange, N.J., became pastor of Berean Baptist Church, New York City, 1881; as pastor of Judson Memorial Church, New York City, *post* 1890, made it a laboratory for readjusting relations of city churches with their communities.

JUDSON, EDWARD ZANE CARROLL (*b. Stamford, N.Y., 1823; d. Stamford, 1886*), adventurer. Led a roving and discreditable career. *Post* 1846, composed hundreds of dime novels under pseudonym Ned Buntline. He was the friend and exploiter of Buffalo Bill Cody.

JUDSON, EGBERT PUTNAM (*b. Syracuse, N.Y., 1812; d. San Francisco, Calif., 1893*), inventor and manufacturer of explosives. Patented Giant Powder, 1873; also a less shattering explosive for railroad construction, marketed as "Judson's RRP."

JUDSON, EMILY CHUBBUCK (*b. Eaton, N.Y., 1817; d. Hamilton, N.Y., 1854*), writer, Baptist missionary. Author of a number of works under penname "Fanny Forester." Third wife of Adoniram Judson, whom she married in 1846 and accompanied to Burma.

JUDSON, FREDERICK NEWTON (*b. St. Mary's, Ga., 1845; d. St. Louis, Mo., 1919*), corporation lawyer, legal writer. Raised in Connecticut; began legal practice in St. Louis, Mo., 1873. Victoriously defended strikers in Wabash Railroad Case, 1903; served on many state and national commissions.

JUDSON, HARRY PRATT (*b. Jamestown, N.Y., 1849; d. 1927*), educator. Graduated Williams, 1870. Was dean and professor, and later president (1906–23), University of Chicago.

JUDSON, SARAH HALL BOARDMAN (*b. Alstead, N.H., 1803; d. St. Helena Island, 1845*), missionary to Burma. Second wife of Adoniram Judson whom she married in 1834.

JUENGLING, FREDERICK (*b. Leipzig, Saxony, 1846; d. New York, N.Y., 1889*), wood-engraver. Came to America, 1866. Won international recognition as a leading American wood-engraver of the "new school" of his art.

JUILLIARD, AUGUSTUS D. (*b. at sea en route from France to America, 1836; d. 1919*), textile merchant, capitalist, patron of music. An active supporter of Metropolitan Opera, New York; established Juilliard Foundation to promote music education.

JULIA, SISTER (*b. Inver, Ireland, 1827; d. Peabody, Mass., 1901*), educator. Name in religion of Susan McGroarty. Came to America as a child; raised in Cincinnati, Ohio; entered congregation of sisters of Notre Dame de Namur. Founded many convents and schools, including Trinity College for women, Washington, D.C.

JULIAN, GEORGE WASHINGTON (*b. near Centerville, Ind., 1817; d. Irvington, Ind., 1899*), abolitionist leader. Entered Indiana legislature, 1845, as a Whig and began to attack slavery in newspaper articles. Elected to Congress as a Free-Soiler, 1848, he opposed the Compromise of 1850 and lost his seat in that year. He helped organize the Republican party, 1856. Reelected to Congress as a Republican, 1860, he urged Emancipation, contributed to passage of Homestead Act (1862), and served on committee on conduct of the war; he helped draw articles of impeachment against President Johnson, 1867. Failing of renomination, 1870, he joined the Liberal Republican movement, supporting Horace Greeley, 1872, and S. J. Tilden, 1876. He published several books and articles championing reform and was surveyor general of New Mexico under President Cleveland.

JUMEL, STEPHEN (*b. France, ca. 1754; d. New York, N.Y., 1832*), wine merchant. Remembered chiefly as husband of the charming but unscrupulous Mme. Jumel who later married Aaron Burr.

JUNE, JENNIE. *See* CROLY, JANE CUNNINGHAM.

JUNEAU, SOLOMON LAURENT (*b. L'Assomption, near Montreal, Canada, 1793; d. Menominee Indian reservation, 1856*), founder of Milwaukee, Wis., which grew from his trading agency, established there, 1818.

JUNGMAN, JOHN GEORGE (*b. Hockenheim, Germany, 1720; d. Bethlehem, Pa., 1808*), Moravian missionary. Came to America as a boy; joined Bethlehem community, 1743. Taught and preached among Indians on Pennsylvania, Connecticut, and Ohio frontiers, 1746–85.

JUNKIN, GEORGE (*b. Cumberland Co., Pa., 1790; d. Philadelphia, Pa., 1868*), Presbyterian clergyman, educator. First president of Lafayette College, 1832–41 and 1844–48; served also as president of Miami University, Ohio (1841–44) and Washington College, Lexington, Va. (1848–61). An uncompromising "Old School" leader.

JUST, ERNEST EVERETT (*b. Charleston, S.C., 1883; d. Washington, D.C., 1941*), zoologist. Child of black parents. A.B., Dartmouth College, 1907; Ph.D., University of Chicago, 1916. Taught biology at Howard University, 1907–12; thereafter was professor of zoology, serving also as professor of physiology in the medical school, 1912–20. From 1909 to 1929 he was a student at the Marine Biological Laboratory, Woods Hole, Mass. A brilliant experimentalist, he had an extraordinary knowledge of the embryology of marine organisms and developed new techniques for their study. He arrived at the concept that the ectoplasm of an animal egg cell is the prime factor in the initiation of development, and through its interplay with cytoplasm is a causative factor in differentiation and in the building up of nuclear material. Thus, in this view, both differentiation and the action of the gene in heredity result from an interplay of ectoplasm and nucleus with the cytoplasm. He set forth his concept in *Biology of the Cell Surface* (1939). Embittered by American attitudes toward blacks, he gave up teaching in the early 1930's and went to live and work in Europe, returning to the United States in the year of his death.

K

KAEMPFFERT, WALDEMAR BERNHARD (*b. New York, N.Y., 1877; d. New York, N.Y., 1956*), science editor, author. Studied at the College of the City of New York and at New York University, LL.B., 1904. Editor, *Popular Science Monthly*, 1915–20. Science editor, the *New York Times*, 1927–28 and 1931–56. From 1928 to 1931, Kaempffert was the first director of the Museum of Science and Industry in Chicago. President of the National Association of Science Writers, 1937. Books include *Science Today and Tomorrow* (1939) and *Explorations in Science* (1953).

KAFER, JOHN CHRISTIAN (*b. Trenton, N.J., 1842; d. Trenton, 1906*), engineer, educator. Served in U.S. Navy at sea, 1863–68; instructor, steam engineering at Annapolis, 1868–74, 1876–82; assistant to chief, Bureau of Steam Engineering, U.S. Navy.

KAGAN, HENRY ENOCH (*b. Sharpsburg, Pa., 1906; d. Pittsburgh, Pa., 1969*), rabbi, psychologist, and promoter of interfaith understanding. Studied at the University of Cincinnati (B.A., 1928), Hebrew Union College, West Virginia University (M.A., 1934), and Columbia (Ph.D., 1949). In 1937 Kagan became rabbi of the Sinai Temple in Mount Vernon, N.Y. He pioneered in promoting the integration of the rabbinical ministry and psychotherapy. He founded both the Committee on Psychiatry and Religion of the Central Conference of American Rabbis and the Counseling Center of the New York Federation of Reformed Synagogues. He wrote *Changing the Attitude of Christian Toward Jew: A Psychological Approach Through Religion* (1952).

KAH-GE-GA-GAH-BOWH. *See* COPWAY, GEORGE.

KAHN, ALBERT (*b. Rhaunen, Westphalia, Germany, 1869; d. Detroit, Mich., 1942*), architect. immigrated with parents to Detroit, *ca.* 1880; attended art school kept by Julius Melchers, father of Gari Melchers; went to work as office boy in architectural office of Mason and Rice, 1885. Kahn soon became a draftsman. A scholarship in 1890 provided a year's study in Europe, where he traveled and sketched monuments. Upon his return he went back to Mason and Rice, but left in 1896 to form a partnership with two fellow employees. In 1898 Kahn codesigned a private library for the newspaper publisher James E. Scripps. The partnership dissolved, however, and in 1902 Kahn began practice on his own.

Employing a superior system of reinforced concrete, Kahn designed factories for the burgeoning automobile industry, including the Packard factory in Detroit and the Highland Park plant (1909–14) for the Ford Motor Company. Although closely related to his industrial architecture, Kahn's commercial architecture frequently departed from the utilitarian simplicity that distinguished his factory buildings. He believed that commercial buildings, as a prominent feature on the urban landscape, demanded more elaborate treatment. Kahn's admiration of the Italianate work of McKim, Mead and White was clearly reflected in his Detroit Athletic Club (1915), Detroit Trust Company (1915), and William L. Clements Library in Ann Arbor (1923).

As Kahn became older, he relied more upon tradition, rejecting the experimental and bizarre tendencies of contemporary commercial architecture. His Fisher Building (1928), with its peaked Gothic roof, won him the silver medal of the Architectural League of New York in 1929.

By 1937 Kahn's architectural firm was handling 19 percent of all architect-designed industrial buildings in America. With the coming of World War II, Kahn designed bases for the navy, employing techniques that he had already perfected.

KAHN, FLORENCE PRAG (*b. Salt Lake City, Utah, 1866; d. San Francisco, Calif., 1948*), teacher, politician. Child of Polish Jewish parents who had immigrated to California first and returned there in 1869. Graduated University of California at Berkeley, 1887. Married Julius Kahn, Republican congressman from San Francisco's 4th District, 1899. Following his death in 1924, she was elected to Congress in his place (February 1925) and reelected to five successive Congresses. Famous for her wit in debate, she was a respected member of important committees, sensibly liberal in her opinions, and responsible for much legislation which materially benefited the people of her district.

KAHN, GUSTAV GERSON (*b. Coblenz, Germany, 1886; d. Beverly Hills, Calif., 1941*), popular song lyric writer. Came to Chicago with Jewish parents, *ca.* 1891; worked as a clerk; in 1907 published his first song, with music by Grace Le Boy, later his wife. His first substantial hits were written to music by Egbert Van Alstyne ("Memories," 1915, and "Pretty Baby," 1916); thereafter, he wrote lyrics to the music of many Broadway composers, notably Walter Donaldson and Isham Jones. *Post* 1933 he worked chiefly in Hollywood. Kahn was one of the most successful and prolific lyricists of his time; over a twenty-year period, he averaged six hits a year; he published in all more than five hundred songs.

KAHN, JULIUS (*b. Kuppenheim, Germany, 1861; d. 1924*), actor, lawyer. Came to California as a child. Congressman, Republican, from California, for 12 terms between 1898 and 1924. An advocate of military preparedness, he was author of the Selective Draft Act of 1917.

KAHN, OTTON HERMAN (*b. Mannheim, Germany, 1867; d. New York, N.Y., 1934*), banker, art patron. Came to America, 1893. Became partner in Kuhn, Loeb & Co., 1897.

KAISER, ALOIS (*b. Szobotist, Hungary, 1840; d. 1908*), cantor, composer. Pupil of Solomon Sulzer, Vienna; came to Baltimore, Md., 1866, where he was cantor of Oheb Shalom synagogue. He was the leading American exponent of the modification of the Jewish musical tradition by German oratorio and operatic standards.

KAISER, HENRY JOHN (*b. Canajoharie, N.Y., 1882; d. Hawaii, 1967*), industrialist. Began his career as a salesman for a paving contractor in Spokane, Wash. In 1914 he set up his own construction company in Vancouver and soon extended it along the Pacific Coast. Known as the New Deal's favorite businessman,

Kaiser had a genius for building government-funded works projects efficiently. In 1931 he organized the Six Companies combine that would build Hoover Dam. During the 1930's he built piers for the Oakland–San Francisco Bay Bridge and headed the companies that constructed Parker, Bonneville, and Grand Coulee Dams. In 1939 he formed the Seattle-Tacoma Shipbuilding Corporation, with A. L. Todd, which turned out over 1,000 Liberty ships during World War II. He built the first integrated steel plant west of the Rockies. After World War II he formed the Kaiser-Frazer Corporation, with Joseph W. Frazer, to manufacture automobiles (the corporation failed in 1955). He also bought an aluminum plant from the government, and founded the country's largest health-maintenance organization, now known as Kaiser Permanente.

KALANIANAOLE, JONAH KUHIO (*b. Kauai, Hawaii, 1871; d. 1922*), delegate to Congress from Hawaii, 1902–22. A native prince, he exerted a great influence in reconciling the Hawaiians to their loss of independence as a nation.

KALB, JOHANN (*b. Hüttendorf, Germany, 1721; d. Camden, S.C., 1780*), Revolutionary general known as Baron de Kalb. After leaving home at 16, he appears, 1743, as Lieutenant Jean de Kalb of a regiment of French infantry. He served throughout the War of the Austrian Succession and the Seven Years' War, and in 1764 retired as lieutenant colonel to live near Paris. In 1768 he traveled in the British colonies in America for about four months on a secret mission of observation for the Duc de Choiseul. Made a French brigadier general, 1776, he was soon engaged by Silas Deane as major general. With his protégé Lafayette and other companions, he sailed to America, arriving in 1777 to discover that Congress refused to ratify Deane's contracts. Congress, however, received Lafayette as major general and eventually elected Kalb to a new major generalship. He saw some action before Philadelphia and spent the winter at Valley Forge. Constantly with the army until 1780, he was ordered on April 3rd of that year to relieve Charleston, S.C., then under siege. In North Carolina he was joined by the new commander for the South, General Gates, who, despite his advice, determined to march to Camden, S.C., to attack the British. In the sudden encounter with Lord Cornwallis's army, Gates's militia fled. Kalb repeatedly charged the enemy, finally falling, mortally wounded.

KALISCH, ISIDOR (*b. Krotoschin, Posen, Prussia, 1816; d. Newark, N.J., 1886*), reform rabbi. Came to America, 1849. Held many pastorates; by his writing contributed greatly to the shaping of reform Judaism in America, combatting both radical reform and orthodox Judaism.

KALISCH, SAMUEL (*b. Cleveland, Ohio, 1851; d. 1930*), jurist. Son of Isidor Kalisch. Graduated Columbia Law School, 1870; practiced in Newark, N.J. Justice, supreme court of New Jersey, 1911–30; active in Democratic politics and in reform.

KALMUS, HERBERT THOMAS (*b. Chelsea, Mass., 1881; d. Los Angeles, Calif., 1963*) and **KALMUS, NATALIE MABELLE DUNFEE** (*b. Norfolk, Va., 1883; d. Boston, Mass., 1965*), inventors. Herbert studied at the Massachusetts Institute of Technology (B.S., 1904; Ph.D., 1906), and Natalie studied at Stetson University, the Boston School of Art, the Curry School of Expressionism, and the University of Zurich. They were married in 1902. An aggressive entrepreneur and dynamic inventor, Herbert formed a consulting engineering firm with two partners in 1912. In 1915 his firm became a partner in the Technicolor Motion Picture Corporation, whose first laboratory developed the Technicolor process. Natalie was often called the codeveloper of Technicolor because of her efforts on behalf of both production and promotion of color films. The Kalmuses were divorced secretly in 1921, but contin-

ued to work closely to develop good color film. Kalmus moved his operations to Hollywood in 1927. The breakthrough came in 1929 when Jack Warner used the Kalmus two-color process to make *Gold Diggers of Broadway*, followed by *On with the Show*. Walt Disney used the Kalmus three-color technology to make *The Three Little Pigs* (1933) and *The Big Bad Wolf* (1934). In 1935 Kalmus' process was completed and displayed in David O. Selznick's *Becky Sharp*, the first true color film. Kalmus had exclusive control of color motion-picture production after World War II. Natalie retired in 1948 and moved to the East Coast. Herbert retained control of Technicolor and it subsidiaries until his retirement in 1959.

KALTENBORN, HANS VON (*b. Milwaukee, Wis., 1878; d. New York, N.Y., 1965*), radio news commentator. Graduated from Harvard (1909). Worked for the *Merrill* (Wis.) *Advocate*, 1898–1902, as a reporter, editor, and foreign correspondent. He then worked for the *Brooklyn Eagle* (1902–05, 1909–30), where he came to focus increasingly on foreign affairs, and in 1930 joined the Columbia Broadcasting System as a full-time radio commentator. He became popularly known as the "Suave Voice of Doom." He was hired by the National Broadcasting Corporation in 1940, where he broadcast regularly until 1955.

KAMAIAKAN (*b. near present Lewiston, Idaho, ca. 1800; d. ca. 1880*), Yakima chief. Organized Indian resistance to cession of Yakima lands, 1856–58.

KANE, ELISHA KENT (*b. Philadelphia, Pa., 1820; d. Havana, Cuba, 1857*), naval officer, physician. Son of John K. Kane. Graduated University of Pennsylvania, M.D., 1842. Served as U.S. Navy surgeon; *post* 1850 attached to U.S. Coast Survey. Medical officer to first Grinnell Arctic expedition; commanded the second, 1853–55. Pioneer of the American route to North Pole. Author, *Arctic Explorations* (1856).

KANE, HELEN (*b. New York, N.Y., 1904; d. New York, 1966*), singer and film actress. At fifteen she appeared in a review with the Four Marx Brothers. She became a hit on Broadway in 1928, known for her baby voice and lyrics ("boop-boop-a-doop"). Her films include *Nothing But the Truth* (1929), *Sweetie* (1929), *Pointed Heels* (1929), *Paramount on Parade* (1930), *Dangerous Dan McGrew* (1930), and *Heads Up* (1930). On vaudeville she appeared with Clayton, Jackson, and Durante; Bill Robinson; Ruth Etting; and Ken Murray, and her voice was used on the sound tracks of movie cartoons. She retired in 1935.

KANE, JOHN (*b. West Calder, Scotland, 1860; d. 1934*), landscape painter. Came to America, 1879. Worked as laborer and house painter. Received first recognition, 1927, as important figure in modern art.

KANE, JOHN KINTZING (*b. Albany, N.Y., 1795; d. Philadelphia, Pa., 1858*), jurist. Graduated Yale, 1814; studied law with Joseph Hopkinson; admitted to the bar, 1817, and practiced in Philadelphia. Assisted President Andrew Jackson in preparation of state papers, particularly in fight against Bank of the United States. Judge, U.S. district court in Pennsylvania, 1846–58.

KANE, THOMAS LEIPER (*b. Philadelphia, Pa., 1822; d. Philadelphia, 1883*), lawyer, Union major general, abolitionist. Son of John K. Kane.

KAPP, FRIEDRICH (*b. Hamm, Westphalia, Germany, 1824; d. Berlin, Germany, 1884*), publicist, historian. Resided in America, 1850–70. Helped unite German Americans in support of the Union, 1860–65; wrote valuable studies in American history.

KARFIOL, BERNARD (*b. near Budapest, Hungary, 1886; d. Irvington-on-Hudson, N.Y., 1952*), painter. Raised in Brooklyn, Karfiol studied at the Pratt Institute and the National Academy of Design. In 1900 he traveled to Paris, where he was the youngest exhibitor at the Grand Salon in 1904; he returned to the U.S. in 1906 and exhibited at the famous Armory Show in 1913. Representative canvases of his mature years include *Seated Nude* (1929; Museum of Modern Art), *Hilda* (1929; Whitney Museum), *Babette* (1931; Detroit Institute of Arts), and *Christina* (1936; Carnegie Institute). A frequenter of Gertrude Stein's salon in Paris, Karfiol knew Picasso and Matisse.

KARLOFF, BORIS (*b. William Henry Pratt, London, England, 1887; d. Midhurst, Sussex, England, 1969*), actor. Came to Los Angeles in 1917, and appeared in plays and films, often playing a villain of exotic ethnic origins. His most famous role came in *Frankenstein* (1931). Other films, most of them horror films, include *The Criminal Code* (1931), *Five-Star Final* (1931), *The Mad Genius* (1931), *The Yellow Ticket* (1931), *Scarface* (1932), *The Mummy* (1932), *The Mask of Fu Manchu* (1932), *The Old Dark Horse* (1932), *The Ghoul* (1933), *The Black Cat* (1934), *The Lost Patrol* (1934), *The House of Rothschild* (1934), *The Bride of Frankenstein* (1935), *The Raven* (1935), *The Invisible Ray* (1936), *The Walking Dead* (1936), *The Man They Could Not Hang* (1939), *Son of Frankenstein* (1939), *The Tower of London* (1939), *Before I Hang* (1940), *The Devil Commands* (1941), *The House of Frankenstein* (1945), *The Body Snatcher* (1945), *Isle of the Dead* (1945), *Bedlam* (1946), *The Secret Life of Walter Mitty* (1947), *Unconquered* (1947), *The Strange Door* (1951), *The Raven* (1962), *The Terror* (1962), *Black Sabbath* (1963), *Comedy of Terrors* (1964), and *Die, Monster, Die* (1965).

KÁRMÁN, THEODORE (TODOR) VON (*b. Budapest, Hungary, 1881; d. Aachen, Germany, 1963*), physicist, engineer, and applied mathematician. Graduated from the Palatine Joseph Polytechnic (1902) and the University of Göttingen (Ph.D., 1908). While a privatdocent at Göttingen, he produced his theory of vortex streets (1911), probably his best-known theory. He held the chair of aeronautics and mechanics at the Technische Hochschule in Aachen, Germany, 1913–14 and 1919–29. He joined Robert A. Millikan at the California Institute of Technology as director of the Guggenheim Aeronautical Laboratory, 1930–49, and director of research of the Guggenheim Airship Institute. In 1942 he and several colleagues formed Aerojet Engineering Corporation, which later, under new owners, became Aerojet-General Corporation. After World War II, Kármán chaired the Scientific Advisory Group. He was instrumental in establishing the RAND corporation in 1948, and in 1952 helped establish the Advisory Group for Aeronautical Research and Development as a part of NATO. He played a significant role in founding and giving direction to the American space program.

KASSON, JOHN ADAM (*b. Charlotte, Vt., 1822; d. Washington, D.C., 1910*), lawyer, diplomat. Congressman, Republican, from Iowa, 1863–66; 1873–77; 1881–84. Was effective U.S. minister to Austria-Hungary, 1877–81, and represented this country in numerous foreign negotiations thereafter as special envoy. Had important part in framing Republican platform, 1860.

KATCHEN, JULIUS (*b. Long Branch, N.J., 1926; d. Paris, France, 1969*), concert pianist. At eleven he made his public debut with Eugene Ormandy and the Philadelphia Orchestra. He studied at Haverford College (B.A., 1946) and the Paris Conservatoire. Settled in Paris, and toured extensively throughout Europe and recorded for Decca. His early reputation rested on his dynamic interpretations of large-scale virtuosic works, especially those of Russian composers, but is best remembered for his interpretations of Brahms.

KATTE, WALTER (*b. London, England, 1830; d. New York, N.Y., 1917*), civil engineer. Came to America, 1849. One of the world's foremost railroad and bridge construction engineers; supervised Eads bridge, St. Louis, Mo., and New York Central right-of-way construction, Park Avenue, New York City.

KATZER, FREDERIC XAVIER (*b. Ebensee, Upper Austria, 1844; d. Fond du Lac, Wis., 1903*), Roman Catholic clergyman. Came to America, 1864; was seminary professor in Milwaukee, Wis., *post* 1866, and an official in that diocese. Bishop of Green Bay, 1886–90; archbishop of Milwaukee, 1891–1903. Opposed Bennett law.

KAUFFMAN, CALVIN HENRY (*b. Lebanon Co., Pa., 1869; d. 1931*), botanist, mycologist. Taught at University of Michigan, *post* 1904. Author of many major monographs and *The Agaricaceae of Michigan* (1918).

KAUFMAN, GEORGE S. (*b. Pittsburgh, Pa., 1889; d. New York, N.Y., 1961*), playwright, director, screenwriter, and essayist. Worked as a columnist and reporter and studied at the Alveine School of Dramatic Art in New York and Columbia. Worked with producer George C. Tyler, 1917–22, rewriting scripts. Collaborating with Marc Connelly, 1921–24, he wrote several hit plays and musical comedies, including *Dulcy* (1921). He then began a writing relationship with Edna Ferber that produced six plays, including *The Royal Family* (1927) and *Dinner at Eight* (1932). Kaufman's only major noncollaborative work was *The Butter and Egg Man* (1925). With Morrie Ryskind he wrote *The Cocoanuts* (1925), *Animal Crackers* (1928), and *A Night at the Opera* (1935) for the Marx Brothers and the Pulitzer-Prize winning musical *Of Thee I Sing* (1931). Kaufman successfully directed *The Front Page* in 1928, and thereafter staged all but two of his own plays. He wrote *June Moon* (1929) with Ring Lardner, *The Channel Road* (1929) and *The Dark Tower* (1933) with Alexander Woollcott, and the film *Roman Scandals* (1933) with Robert E. Sherwood. With Moss Hart he wrote *Once in a Lifetime* (1930), the Pulitzer-Prize winning *You Can't Take It with You* (1936), and *The Man Who Came to Dinner* (1939). In 1950 he directed *Guys and Dolls*. He worked with Leueen MacGrath on *Silk Stockings* (1955) and Howard Teichmann on *The Solid Gold Cadillac* (1953). In 1957 Kaufman directed Peter Ustinov's *Romanoff and Juliet*.

KAUTZ, AUGUST VALENTINE (*b. Ispringen, Germany, 1828; d. Seattle, Wash., 1895*), soldier. Came to America as an infant; raised in Ohio. Graduated West Point, 1852. Civil War brigade and division commander of cavalry; breveted major general, 1865. Served principally in West and Southwest thereafter until retirement, 1892.

KAVANAUGH, EDWARD (*b. Damariscotta Mills, District of Maine, 1795; d. 1844*), lawyer, Maine legislator, diplomat. Democratic governor of Maine, 1843. As commissioner, helped negotiate Maine boundary with Webster and Ashburton.

KAY, EDGAR BOYD (*b. Warriors Mark, Pa., 1860; d. Washington, D.C., 1931*), educator, sanitary engineer. Taught engineering at Union, Cornell, and University of Alabama. Invented the U.S. Standard Incinerator; was recognized as a leader in sanitation and incineration.

KAYE, FREDERICK BENJAMIN (*b. New York, N.Y., 1892; d. Boston, Mass., 1930*), scholar, author. Graduated Yale, 1914; Ph.D., 1917. Professor of English at Northwestern University; achieved international reputation for scholarship in neoclassical English literature (late-17th, early-18th century).

KEAGY, JOHN MILLER (b. *Strasburg, Pa., 1792; d. 1837*), physician, educator. Influenced movement toward professionalizing education in Pennsylvania and shaping it according to the ideas of Pestalozzi.

KEAN, JEFFERSON RANDOLPH (b. *Lynchburg, Va., 1860; d. Washington, D.C., 1950*), military surgeon. M.D., University of Virginia, 1883; commissioned assistant surgeon, U.S. Army, 1884. Served in the West with 9th Cavalry, in Florida, and in Cuba during the Spanish-American War and afterward during the military and provisional governments there. While on duty in the Surgeon General's Office, 1902–06 and 1909–13, he was responsible for the organization of the Medical Reserve Corps and for setting up a system for stockpiling field supplies for emergency use; in 1916, assigned to the American Red Cross, he organized and equipped thirty-two base hospitals. During World War I he served in France, was promoted to brigadier general, and rose to deputy chief surgeon of the American Expeditionary Force. A descendent of Thomas Jefferson, he was organizer and first president of the Monticello Association and a member of the commission that created the Jefferson Memorial in Washington.

KEANE, JAMES JOHN (b. *Joliet, Ill., 1857; d. 1929*), Roman Catholic clergyman. Pastor in St. Paul and Minneapolis; bishop, Cheyenne, Wyo., 1902–11; archbishop of Dubuque, 1911–29.

KEANE, JOHN JOSEPH (b. *Ballyshannon, Ireland, 1839; d. Dubuque, Iowa, 1918*), Roman Catholic clergyman. Came to Baltimore, Md., as a child. Graduated St. Mary's Seminary; ordained, 1866. Appointed bishop of Richmond, Va., 1878, he did much to promote the project of a Catholic university, and when one was founded at Washington, D.C., 1889, he served as its first rector until the end of 1896. Stationed in Rome, 1897–99, he returned to serve as archbishop of Dubuque, 1900–11.

KEARNEY, DENIS (b. *Oakmount, Ireland, 1847; d. Alameda, Calif., 1907*), labor agitator. Settled in San Francisco *ca.* 1868. Was leader in organizing Workingmen's Party of California, 1877 (often called the Kearney movement), and served as its president.

KEARNS, JACK (b. *Waterloo, Mich., 1882; d. Miami, Fla., 1963*), boxing promoter. Fought sixty-seven professional bouts, then became one of the most important and successful managers in the history of boxing. Kearns managed six world champions: Jack Dempsey, Mickey Walker, Jackie Fields, Benny Leonard, Joey Maxim, and Archie Moore.

KEARNY, FRANCIS (b. *Perth Amboy, N.J., 1785; d. Perth Amboy, 1837*), engraver in line and aquatint. Brother of Lawrence Kearny; nephew of James Lawrence. Worked in Philadelphia, 1810–33.

KEARNY, LAWRENCE (b. *Perth Amboy, N.J., 1789; d. Perth Amboy, 1868*), naval officer. Brother of Francis Kearny; nephew of James Lawrence. Appointed midshipman, 1807; promoted captain, 1832. While commanding the East India Squadron, initiated the Open Door Policy in China by actions at Canton, 1842; facilitated conclusion of first Sino-American treaty, 1844.

KEARNY, PHILIP (b. *New York, N.Y., 1814; d. Chantilly, Va., 1862*), soldier. Nephew of Stephen W. Kearny. Prevented by family opposition from entering West Point; graduated Columbia, 1833. Commissioned second lieutenant, 1st Dragoons, 1837, he served on the frontier; studied at French cavalry school, Saumur, and saw action in Algiers, 1840. Returning to America, he was aide to General Macomb and Winfield Scott. Commanding Scott's bodyguard in Mexican War, he lost his left arm at Churubusco. Resigning from the U.S. Army, 1851, he won the cross of the Legion of Honor for service with Napoleon III's

cavalry, Italian campaign, 1859. Returning home at outbreak of Civil War, he was named brigadier general, 1861, and major general, 1862; he participated in at least twelve engagements in the Virginia campaigns and was killed while reconnoitering a new position. General Scott called him "a perfect soldier." The divisional shoulder patch, now in general use, was introduced by Kearny.

KEARNY, STEPHEN WATTS (b. *Newark, N.J., 1794; d. St. Louis, Mo., 1848*), soldier. Cousin of Lawrence Kearny. Commissioned first lieutenant, 13th Infantry, 1812, distinguished at Queenston Heights; promoted captain, 1813. Except for an occasional detail in the East, he served exclusively on the Western frontier, 1819–46, becoming brigadier general commanding Army of the West, 1846. In the war with Mexico, he set out from Fort Leavenworth and occupied Santa Fe, N. Mex., in August 1846; striking for California, he was blocked by superior forces at San Pasqual but relieved by U.S. troops sent by Com. R. F. Stockton with whom he later quarreled over the chief command. In concert with Stockton, he took Los Angeles early in 1847; thereafter he quarreled also with John C. Frémont, whom he deposed as civil governor of California and ordered court-martialed. Kearny then served briefly as civil governor of Vera Cruz and of Mexico City. He was the uncle of Philip Kearny. Fort Kearny (Kearney), Nebr., was named for him.

KEARSLEY, JOHN (b. *Greatham, England, 1684; d. 1772*), physician, architect, teacher. Came to America, 1711; settled in Philadelphia, Pa., 1717. Maintained a medical office called "the first college" of Pennsylvania and trained many physicians; designed, financed, and built Christ Church, Philadelphia.

KEATING, JOHN MCLEOD (b. *Kings Co., Ireland, 1830; d. Gloucester, Mass., 1906*), journalist. Came to America, 1848. Edited newspapers in Memphis, Tenn., 1859–91, notably the *Memphis Appeal.*

KEATING, JOHN MARIE (b. *Philadelphia, Pa., 1852; d. Colorado Springs, Colo., 1893*), physician. Grandson of René La Roche. Graduated University of Pennsylvania, M.D., 1873. Practiced, taught, and wrote principally on obstetrics and children's diseases.

KEATING, WILLIAM HYPOLITUS (b. *Wilmington, Del., 1799; d. London, England, 1840*), mineralogical chemist, businessman. Geologist of Stephen H. Long's 1823 expedition, of which he wrote *Narrative of an Expedition to the Source of St. Peter's River, . . .* (1824). He helped inaugurate the Franklin Institute of Pennsylvania.

KEATON, JOSEPH FRANCIS ("BUSTER") (b. *Picqua, Kans., 1895; d. Woodland Hills, Calif., 1966*), stage and screen comedian. At four began appearing with his parents in medicine shows and vaudeville. He received no formal education. Began making films for Roscoe ("Fatty") Arbuckle in 1917, then directed and acted in a series of two-reel comedies: *One Week* (1920), *The Boat* (1921), *Cops* (1922), *The Electric House* (1922), *Our Hospitality* (1923), *Sherlock, Jr.* (1924), *The Navigator* (1924), and *The General* (1927), widely considered his masterpiece. A loss of artistic control over his pictures and alcoholism contributed to a decline in his career. Between 1947 and 1954 he earned acclaim for appearances at the Cirque Medrano in Paris, and he then appeared in *Sunset Boulevard* (1950) and *Limelight* (1952). He appeared regularly on television variety shows.

KEDZIE, ROBERT CLARK (b. *Delhi, N.Y., 1823; d. 1902*), physician, chemist, sanitarian. Raised in Michigan. Associated, *post* 1863 with the Michigan State Agricultural College and in public health work.

KEEFE, DANIEL JOSEPH (*b. Willowsprings, Ill., 1852; d. Elmhurst, Ill., 1929*), labor leader, industrial arbitrator. Dominant figure in National (now International) Longshoremen's Association, 1892–1908; U.S. commissioner general of immigration, 1908–13.

KEELER, JAMES EDWARD (*b. La Salle, Ill., 1857; d. 1900*), astronomer. Devised many improvements and made many important spectroscopic studies at Lick Observatory; was director at Lick *post* 1898.

KEELER, RALPH OLMSTEAD (*b. on site of present Custar, Ohio, 1840; d. at sea, 1873*), journalist, foreign correspondent. Author of autobiographical *Vagabond Adventures* (1870) and other works.

KEELEY, LESLIE E. (*b. St. Lawrence Co., N.Y., 1832; d. Los Angeles, Calif., 1900*), physician. Graduated Rush Medical College, 1864; practiced at Dwight, Ill. Exploited commercially the "Keeley Cure" for chronic alcoholism and drug addiction.

KEELY, JOHN ERNST WORRELL (*b. probably Philadelphia, Pa., 1827; d. 1898*), inventor and imposter. Claimed discovery of a new physical force; organized Keely Motor Co., *post* 1874, to exploit it; mulcted thousands of trusting investors.

KEEN, MORRIS LONGSTRETH (*b. Philadelphia, Pa., 1820; d. near Stroudsburg, Pa., 1883*), inventor, wood-pulp manufacturer. Patented several papermaking processes; established American Wood Paper Co., 1863.

KEEN, WILLIAM WILLIAMS (*b. Philadelphia, Pa., 1837; d. 1932*), surgeon. M.D., Jefferson Medical, 1862. Served as Union medical officer. Was professor of surgery at his alma mater, 1889–1907. Said to have performed the first (1887) successful operation for brain tumor in the United States. Coauthor and editor of numerous works.

KEENAN, JAMES FRANCIS (*b. Dubuque, Iowa, 1858; d. 1929*), character actor, better known as Frank Keenan. Particularly popular as a "road star," and active in motion pictures, 1915–29.

KEENE, JAMES ROBERT (*b. Chester, England, 1838; d. 1913*), stock-market speculator, turfman. Came to America as a boy; made fortune on San Francisco Exchange, 1866–76. Later acted as market manipulator in New York for the Havemeyers, J. P. Morgan, James J. Hill.

KEENE, LAURA (*b. England, ca. 1826; d. 1873*), actress. Trained in Mme. Vestris's company; came to America, 1852, as member of James W. Wallack's New York company. Enjoyed brilliant success as comedy star; was a pioneer woman theater manager in New York, 1855; encouraged native authors. Played at Ford's Theatre, Washington, D.C., on night Lincoln was assassinated.

KEENE, THOMAS WALLACE (*b. New York, N.Y., 1840; d. Castleton, Staten Island, N.Y., 1898*), actor. Made countrywide tours in Shakespeare repertory, 1880–98, playing in the old, robust style of an earlier day.

KEENER, WILLIAM ALBERT (*b. Augusta, Ga., 1856; d. New York, N.Y., 1913*), lawyer, educator. Graduated Emory, 1874; Harvard Law School, 1877. Was distinguished professor of law at Harvard and Columbia; helped reorganize law teaching on case system for which he edited a series of standard textbooks. Dean, Columbia Law School, 1891–1901.

KEEP, HENRY (*b. Adams, N.Y., 1818; d. New York, N.Y., 1869*), financier. *Post* 1850, was one of the boldest and most successful Wall Street operators in railroad stocks.

KEEP, ROBERT PORTER (*b. Farmington, Conn., 1844; d. Farmington, 1904*), educator. Graduated Yale, 1865; Ph.D., 1869. Progressive principal, Free Academy of Norwich, Conn., 1885–1902.

KEFAUVER, (CAREY) ESTES (*b. near Madisonville, Tenn., 1903; d. Bethesda, Md., 1963*), lawyer and U.S. senator. Studied at the University of Tennessee (B.A., 1924) and Yale Law School (LL.B., 1927). In 1939 became state commissioner of finance and taxation, then was elected to the U.S. Congress as a New Deal Democrat. He served on the House Judiciary Committee and the Select Committee on Small Business, and was reelected to the U.S. Senate in 1948, 1954, and 1960. Served on the Armed Forces, Judiciary, and Appropriations committees; chaired the Juvenile Delinquency, Constitutional Amendments, and Antitrust and Monopoly subcommittees. The 1951 Kefauver Committee's investigations into organized crime made him a national figure. In 1952 and 1956 he unsuccessfully sought to be the Democratic candidate for president; he was the nominee for vice-president in 1956.

KEFAUVER, GRAYSON NEIKIRK (*b. Middletown, Md., 1900; d. Los Angeles, Calif., 1946*), educator. B.A., University of Arizona, 1921; M.A., Leland Stanford Junior University, 1925; Ph.D., University of Minnesota, 1928. Taught at Minnesota and at Teachers College, Columbia University; professor of education and dean of the School of Education, Stanford University, 1933–46 (resigning the deanship, 1945). Early active in the campaign to define and secure a proper world role for education after the end of World War II, he was a leading member of the U.S. delegation to the conference for the establishment of the United Nations Educational and Cultural Organization (London, November 1945).

KEHEW, MARY MORTON KIMBALL (*b. Boston, Mass., 1859; d. 1918*), leader in constructive social movements, especially for women in industry; was moving spirit of Women's Educational and Industrial Union, 1892–1918.

KEIFER, JOSEPH WARREN (*b. near Springfield, Ohio, 1836; d. 1932*), lawyer, Union soldier. Congressman, Republican, from Ohio, 1877–85, 1905–11. Served as mediocre speaker of the House, 1881–83.

KEIMER, SAMUEL (*b. London, England, 1688; d. Barbados, British West Indies, ca. 1739*), printer. Immigrated to Philadelphia, Pa., 1722; employed Benjamin Franklin in his shop, 1723, and at a later period. Removed to Barbados after bankruptcy, 1729.

KEITH, ARTHUR (*b. St. Louis, Mo., 1864; d. Silver Spring, Md., 1944*), geologist. Raised in Quincy, Mass. A.B., Harvard, 1885; A.M., 1886. Associated with U.S. Geological Survey, 1887–1934. His work on the geological structure of the Appalachian Mountain chain placed him in the front rank of field geologists. He had charge of the survey's mapping program for the whole United States, 1906–12, thereafter until 1921 directing the work on the section east of the 100th meridian. He then returned to full-time research on the Appalachians.

KEITH, BENJAMIN FRANKLIN (*b. Hillsboro Bridge, N.H., 1846; d. Palm Beach, Fla., 1914*), theater owner, vaudeville manager. Presented first "continuous performance" shows in America at Gaiety Theatre, Boston, Mass., *post* 1883; organized

Keith Circuit; partner in Keith and Proctor *post* 1906. Raised standard of taste in vaudeville entertainment.

KEITH, GEORGE (*b. Peterhead, Scotland,* ca. *1638; d. England, 1716*), founder of "Christian Quakers," schoolmaster, Anglican missionary. Became a Quaker, 1664; was associated with Quaker founders, Fox, Penn, and Barclay. Appointed New Jersey surveyor general *ca.* 1685, he settled in Philadelphia, Pa., 1689; was headmaster o the school founded there by William Penn. Critical of Quaker failure to appreciate Christ, he entered into controversy with Quaker leaders, his followers becoming known as "Christian Quakers" or "Keithians." Disowned by the Quakers, he took Anglican orders, 1700, and worked as a missionary in America, 1702–04.

KEITH, JAMES (*b. near Warrenton, Va., 1839; d. 1918*), Confederate soldier, jurist. Virginia circuit judge; president, state supreme court of appeals, 1895–1916; exercised a paramount influence on Virginia jurisprudence.

KEITH, MINOR COOPER (*b. Brooklyn, N.Y., 1848; d. 1929*), capitalist, Central American railroad builder and banana planter. A founder of United Fruit Co.

KEITH, SIR WILLIAM (*b. probably Peterhead, Scotland, 1680; d. London, England, 1749*), royal customs official. Governor of Pennsylvania and Delaware, 1717–26; espoused popular interests against the proprietors. Advised British government on colonial matters after his return to England, 1728.

KEITH, WILLIAM (*b. Old Meldrum, Scotland, 1839; d. 1911*), landscape painter, engraver. Came to America as a boy. Removed, 1859, to California whose scenery was theme of his numerous paintings. Friend of George Inness, John Burroughs, John Muir, he painted with poetic intensity and a wealth of color.

KEITT, LAWRENCE MASSILLON (*b. Orangeburg District, S.C., 1824; d. Cold Harbor, Va., 1864*), lawyer. Congressman. Democrat, from South Carolina, 1853–60; a "tempestuous" radical slavery leader and secessionist. Killed as colonel, 20th South Carolina Volunteers.

KELLAND, CLARENCE BUDINGTON (*b. Portland, Mich., 1881; d. Scottsdale, Ariz., 1964*), writer. Studied at Detroit College of Law (L.B., 1902), then practiced law, and worked as a reporter and editor. His first novel was *Mark Tidd, His Adventures and Strategies* (1913). He wrote the Catty Atkins books in the early 1920's, then created his most popular character, Scattergood Baines. He wrote over sixty novels and two hundred short stories, and several of his works were made into films: *Speak Easily* (1932), *Mr. Deeds Goes to Town* (1936), and *Strike Me Pink* (1936), adapted from *Dreamland* (1935). Kelland became a conservative Republican leader and was involved in many business ventures.

KELLER, ARTHUR IGNATIUS (*b. New York, N.Y., 1867; d. New York, 1924*), painter, book and magazine illustrator.

KELLER, HELEN ADAMS (*b. Tuscumbia, Ala., 1880; d. Easton, Conn., 1968*), author and lecturer. In her nineteenth month she suffered a high fever that left her deaf and blind. In 1887 Anne Sullivan, a recent graduate of the Perkins Institute for the Blind, became her tutor. Because of Keller's astonishing progress, Sullivan earned the sobriquet "the Miracle Worker." The enthusiastic writings of Michael Anagnos, Alexander Graham Bell, and Edward Everett Hale made Keller a celebrity before she was ten. Keller attended the Wright-Humason School in New York City, 1894–95, and the Cambridge School for Young Ladies, 1896–97, then entered Radcliffe in 1900 (B.A. cum laude, 1904). Keller depended on touch to communicate. She read the American one-handed manual alphabet by placing her hand over the speller's, and responded by spelling or speaking. She also communicated by reading raised letters and braille and by typewriting. She learned French, German, Greek, Italian, and Latin, in addition to English. Her relationship with Sullivan lasted until Sullivan's death in 1936. Keller's companion from 1914 to 1960 was Polly Thompson. In 1909 Keller joined the Socialist party, and on the eve of World War I she joined the Industrial Workers of the World. She was also a leading figure in the suffragist movement. Keller wrote and lectured throughout her life. Her books include *The Story of My Life* (1903), *The World I Live In* (1908), *My Religion* (1927), *Midstream: My Later Life* (1929), and *Teacher* (1955). Keller's story was told in the 1953 documentary film *The Unconquered.* William Gibson's television drama "The Miracle Worker" (1957) was adapted for the stage (1959) and became a successful film (1962).

KELLER, KAUFMAN THUMA (*b. Mount Joy, Pa., 1885; d. London, England, 1966*), automotive executive. Trained as a machinist, he joined the central staff of General Motors in 1911. In 1916 he was hired by Walter P. Chrysler as general master mechanic for the Buick division of General Motors. He became a member of the central mechanical engineering staff of GM (1919), vice-president of Chevrolet (1921), and general manager for Canadian operations (1924). In 1926 he became vice-president in charge of manufacturing for the new Chrysler Corporation. He joined the Chrysler board of directors (1927), became president of the Dodge division (1929), general manager (1930), president (1935), and chief executive officer (1940). Keller was responsible for pushing the massive Detroit tank plant into production in 1941 and became an active member of the Army Ordnance Association. He became chairman of the board in 1950 and retired in 1956.

KELLER, MATHIAS (*b. Ulm, Württemberg, 1813; d. Boston, Mass., 1875*), composer, songwriter. Came to America, 1846. Author of a number of Civil War anthems and other patriotic compositions.

KELLERMAN, KARL FREDERIC (*b. Göttingen, Germany, 1879; d. Washington, D.C., 1934*), plant physiologist. Born of American parents; graduated Cornell, 1900. Served in Bureau of Plant Industry, U.S. Department of Agriculture *post* 1901; developed *Journal of Agricultural Research.* Among many programs which he directed was that in which the Oriental citrus canker disease was brought under control in the United States, the first instance of a substantially complete eradication of a widespread destructive bacterial plant disease.

KELLETT, WILLIAM WALLACE (*b. Boston, Mass., 1891; d. Philadelphia, Pa., 1951*), aviation executive, pioneer builder of autogiros and helicopters. Graduated from Princeton, 1913. Joined the Seversky (later Republic) Aircraft Corporation in 1931; president, 1939–43; chairman of the board, 1943–45. Founded the Kellett Aircraft Corp. in 1929. Trained and provided opportunities for the first generation of helicopter engineers. Member of the Institute of Aeronautical Sciences.

KELLEY, ALFRED (*b. Middlefield, Conn., 1789; d. 1859*), lawyer, Ohio legislator, canal and railroad builder. His many enterprises deeply affected the material welfare of Ohio, especially Cleveland where he settled, 1810; he resided in Columbus, Ohio, *post* 1830. He founded Ohio's state canal system, saved its public credit (1841–43), and was author of its system of banking and taxation.

KELLEY, EDGAR STILLMAN (*b. Sparta, Wis., 1857; d. New York, N.Y., 1944*), composer, music critic, and teacher. A composer of refinement and taste, he wrote light opera (*Puritania,* 1892), incidental music for the theater (for dramatization of *Ben Hur,* 1899), suites, tone poems, oratorios, and symphonies. Some of his scores achieved great popularity during his lifetime. Among other teaching appointments, he headed the music theory department at the Cincinnati Conservatory, 1911–34.

KELLEY, EDITH SUMMERS (*b. Toronto, Canada, 1884; d. Los Gatos, Calif., 1956*), novelist. Graduated from the University of Toronto, 1903. Secretary to Upton Sinclair, 1906–07, Kelley published only one work, *Weeds* (1923), during her lifetime. Her other novel, *The Devil's Hand*, was published in 1974. Her works concerned the plight of rural farmers in the South and West during the 1920's and 1930's. Kelley died forgotten and penniless; her works were revived by the Southern Illinois University Press series on Lost American Fiction.

KELLEY, FLORENCE (*b. Philadelphia, Pa., 1859; d. 1932*), social worker. Daughter of William D. Kelley. Member of the Hull-House group in Chicago and the Henry Street Settlement in New York; helped establish U.S. Children's Bureau.

KELLEY, HALL JACKSON (*b. Northwood, N.H., 1790; d. 1874*), teacher, surveyor. Became obsessed *ca.* 1829 with a plan for colonizing Oregon; incorporated American Society for Encouraging the Settlement of the Oregon Territory, 1831, enlisting prospective emigrants, of whom only Nathaniel J. Wyeth actually made the journey. Traveling to Mexico and thence to California, Kelley himself reached Fort Vancouver, October 1834. Cared for during the winter by a Hudson's Bay Co. official, he was transported home by sea, returning to Boston, 1836. Subsequently, he wrote a "Memoir" (published with Caleb Cushing's report on Oregon in *House Report No. 101, 25 Cong., 3 Sess., App.*), and many petitions for reimbursement of his losses. An impressive fanatic with some real ability, he exerted appreciable influence in favor of American occupation of Oregon.

KELLEY, JAMES DOUGLAS JERROLD (*b. New York, N.Y., 1847; d. New York, 1922*), naval officer. Graduated Annapolis, 1868. Writer on yachting and maritime history; pioneer in development of wireless telegraphy.

KELLEY, OLIVER HUDSON (*b. Boston, Mass., 1826; d. Washington, D.C., 1913*), farmer, land speculator, founder of the Grange. Removed to Minnesota, 1849; became an enthusiastic advertiser of its advantages to settlers. As clerk in U.S. Bureau of Agriculture, 1864–66, he traveled in Minnesota and the South, surveying agricultural conditions. Conceiving the idea of organizing farmers into a fraternal organization, in the winter of 1867 he founded and became secretary of the National Grange of the Patrons of Husbandry. The depression of the 1870's and the order's usefulness in the fight against monopolies caused farmers to join in numbers; by 1874 there were over 20,000 Granges. Kelley resigned as secretary, 1878.

KELLEY, WILLIAM DARRAH (*b. Philadelphia, Pa., 1814; d. Washington, D.C., 1890*), Philadelphia jurist, politician. Congressman, Republican, from Pennsylvania, 1861–90; was called "Pig Iron" because of his high protectionist sentiments. He was also an advocate of inflationary financial policies.

KELLOGG, ALBERT (*b. New Hartford, Conn., 1813; d. Alameda, Calif., 1887*), physician, botanist. Settled in California, 1849; practiced in San Francisco. Wrote first botanical account of California's *silvas*.

KELLOGG, CLARA LOUISE (*b. Sumterville, S.C., 1842; d. New Hartford, Conn., 1916*), dramatic soprano. Trained in America. Made New York debut in Verdi's *Rigoletto* as Gilda, 1861; identified with role of Marguerite in *Faust*.

KELLOGG, EDWARD (*b. Norwalk, Conn., 1790; d. Brooklyn, N.Y., 1858*), businessman, financial reformer. Invented the "in-

terconvertible bond plan of financial reform"; was the intellectual father of Greenbackism. Author of *Labor and Other Capital* (1849).

KELLOGG, ELIJAH (*b. Portland, Maine, 1813; d. 1901*), Congregational clergyman. Author, among other works, of "Spartacus to the Gladiators" (published 1846 in E. Sargent's *School Reader*) and a number of excellent adventure stories for boys of which *Lion Ben* (1869) is representative.

KELLOGG, FRANK BILLINGS (*b. Potsdam, N.Y., 1856; d. St. Paul, Minn., 1937*), lawyer. Raised in Minnesota. Law partner of Cushman K. Davis *post* 1887; active in "trust busting," 1905–12, notably in compelling dismemberment of Standard Oil. U.S. senator, Republican, from Minnesota, 1917–23; U.S. ambassador to Great Britain, 1923–25; secretary of state, 1925–29; cosigner of Kellogg-Briand Pact outlawing war, 1928.

KELLOGG, JOHN HARVEY (*b. Tyrone Township, Livingston County, Mich., 1852; d. Battle Creek, Mich., 1943*), surgeon, health propagandist. When he was four years old, his father, a convert to the Seventh-day Adventist Church, moved his family to Battle Creek, which was soon to become Adventist world headquarters. At the age of twelve he began learning the printing trade in the Adventist publishing house, where he progressed from printer's devil to editorial assistant.

At sixteen Kellogg spent a year teaching at a rural school. Subsequently he finished his high school course at Battle Creek and in 1872 enrolled in the teacher training program at Michigan State Normal College in Ypsilanti. That same year church leaders sponsored him in a five-month course at Dr. Russell Trall's Hygeio-Therapeutic College in Florence Heights, N.J. Rejecting the Trall system, Kellogg turned to a career in orthodox medicine. After a year at the University of Michigan Medical School, he transferred to Bellevue Hospital Medical College in New York City, where he took his degree in 1875 with a thesis arguing that disease is a natural defense mechanism of the body.

While still a medical student, Kellogg became editor of the Adventist monthly the *Health Reformer*, whose name he changed in 1879 to *Good Health*. In 1876 he became medical superintendent of the Western Health Reform Institute in Battle Creek, which he renamed the Battle Creek Sanitarium. There Kellogg applied his health teachings, which he called "biologic living" or "the Battle Creek Idea." To a much larger degree than earlier health reformers, Kellogg attempted to construct a scientific foundation under his teachings. His sharp mind and great manual dexterity allowed him to develop into a skilled surgeon. In the 1890's he set a record of 165 successive abdominal operations without a fatality. He was elected to the American College of Surgeons in 1914.

For the first two decades of his health crusade, Kellogg enjoyed wide Adventist support. Church leaders, however, expressed doubts about the wisdom of concentrating Adventist health and education facilities in Battle Creek, and urged Kellogg to curb his desire for ever-expanding programs. Policy differences were exacerbated by his combative and suspicious temperament and by religious issues; and after several open clashes, Kellogg was excommunicated on Nov. 10, 1907, and subsequently waged battles with the church over control of the sanitarium. Kellogg had established an experimental food laboratory at the sanitarium in an effort to develop a wide variety of nutritious food products. There, in the early 1890's, he developed the first flaked cereal, beginning with wheat and then applying the process to corn and rice. His younger brother Will, who had assisted him, went on to make corn flakes the cornerstone of a great prepared breakfast-food industry. Policy differences led to a split of the brothers' food manufacturing interests, and in a series of lawsuits Will secured the right to market his products under the Kellogg name.

KELLOGG, MARTIN (*b. Vernon, Conn., 1828; d. Berkeley, Calif., 1903*), Congregational clergyman. Graduated Yale, 1850. Taught *post* 1861 at present University of California; was also dean, 1869–85, and president, 1893–99.

KELLOGG, PAUL UNDERWOOD (*b. Kalamazoo, Mich., 1879; d. New York, N.Y., 1958*), editor, social reformer. Studied at Columbia University. Editor of *Charities* (later *Charities and the Commons*; renamed *Survey* in 1909); editor in chief, 1912–52. Director of the *Pittsburgh Survey*, 1910–14, a record of the first in-depth survey of an American urban community. Member of the advisory committee that helped shape the Social Security Act of 1935. Played a major part in the organization of the American Civil Liberties Union and served on the national board for many years. President of the National Conference of Social Work, 1939.

KELLOGG, SAMUEL HENRY (*b. Quogue, N.Y., 1839; d. Landour, India, 1899*), Presbyterian clergyman. Missionary to India for various tours of duty, 1864–99; compiled a monumental *Grammar of the Hindi Language* and other works.

KELLOGG, WILLIAM PITT (*b. Orwell, Vt., 1830; d. Washington, D.C., 1918*), lawyer, Union soldier. Conspicuous as a carpetbag politician after the Civil War. Served as U.S. senator from Louisiana, 1868–72, 1877–83; also as controversial Republican governor, 1873–77.

KELLOGG, WILL KEITH (*b. Battle Creek, Mich., 1860; d. Battle Creek, 1951*), cereal manufacturer, philanthropist. With his brother, J. H. Kellogg, founded and directed the Kellogg cereal empire. Beginning with the manufacture of health foods in Michigan and the founding of the Battle Creek Toasted Corn Flakes Co. in 1905, the Kellogg Company had net sales of over $1 billion in 1974. Set up a permanent philanthropic structure, the W. K. Kellogg Foundation (1930), to apply existing knowledge to contemporary problems of people, rather than to support basic research. He gave approximately $47 million to the foundation, including the residue of his estate.

KELLOR, FRANCES (ALICE) (*b. Columbus, Ohio, 1873; d. 1952*), sociologist, reformer. Graduated from Cornell University, LL.B., 1897, and studied at the University of Chicago. A champion of black women workers and newly arrived immigrants, she was appointed to the New York Commission on Immigrants in 1908. This work led to the formation of the Bureau of Industries and Immigration in the Department of Labor, of which Kellor became chief investigator in 1910. Her book *Out of Work* (1905) led to stronger laws governing employment agencies. An expert in arbitration, she also wrote *Code of Arbitration* (1931) and *Arbitration in Action* (1941).

KELLY, ALOYSIUS OLIVER JOSEPH (*b. Philadelphia, Pa., 1870; d. 1911*), physician, pathologist. Graduated La Salle College, 1888; M.D., University of Pennsylvania, 1891; studied also in Vienna. Instructor and professor of medicine, University of Pennsylvania, 1896–1911; occupied a high position in medical literature as editor and writer; taught also at University of Vermont and a Woman's Medical College of Pennsylvania.

KELLY, EDMOND (*b. Blagnac, France, 1851; d. near Nyack, N.Y., 1909*), lawyer, political reformer, sociologist.

KELLY, EDWARD JOSEPH (*b. Chicago, Ill., 1876; d. Chicago, 1950*), politician. Went to work at twelve years of age; attended night classes in mathematics and engineering while employed by the Chicago Sanitary District (the water supply and sewers authority), rising to post of assistant engineer, 1908, and chief engineer,

1920. Early active in Democratic politics, he had a close relationship with Patrick A. Nash in what its critics called the "Kelly-Nash machine," which dominated local politics with great efficiency and the customary accompaniments of graft and nepotism. Appointed mayor of the city in 1933 to fill out the term of the assassinated Anton J. Cermak, he remained mayor until 1947, winning reelection easily in 1935, 1939, and 1943. He restored the city's financial position, pushed through a vast program of physical improvements, and encouraged the building of public housing in which discrimination was not tolerated; on the other hand, the city was "wide open," the police force inefficient, and the school system under constant fire from professional educators.

KELLY, EUGENE (*b. Co. Tyrone, Ireland, 1808; d. 1894*), banker, philanthropist. Came to America as a young man. Prospered in California, 1850–57; conducted private bank in New York City thereafter. A founder and benefactor of Catholic University.

KELLY, HOWARD ATWOOD (*b. Camden, N.J., 1858; d. Baltimore, Md., 1943*), gynecologist, surgeon. Kelly received his A.B. degree in 1877 from the University of Pennsylvania, where he subsequently graduated in medicine in 1882. In 1886–89 he made several visits to Europe to observe gynecological work, especially in Germany. Following methods learned in Germany, he performed the first successful caesarian section in Philadelphia under antiseptic conditions.

In 1888 Kelly was appointed associate professor of obstetrics at the University of Pennsylvania. The following year, however, he was called to the newly opened Johns Hopkins Hospital as gynecologist-in-chief as well as professor of gynecology in the projected medical school of the Johns Hopkins University, which opened in 1893. Kelly devised the "Kelly pad" for obstetrical and surgical tables, the bisection method for excising the densely adherent uterus, and numerous diagnostic procedures in urology.

In 1892 Kelly took over a small private sanatorium near his home on Eutaw Place, Baltimore, which he developed into a large hospital and clinic. There he had the first X-ray apparatus used in Baltimore for diagnostic purposes. About 1903, when the medical uses of radium became apparent, he was one of the first American physicians to employ it in treating cancer. He was president of the American Gynecological Society in 1912. He continued to hold his positions at the medical school and hospital until 1919. Kelly wrote or edited several books, of which the most important is the *Dictionary of American Medical Biography* (with Walter L. Burrage, 1928).

KELLY, JOHN (*b. New York, N.Y., 1822; d. 1886*), New York politician and congressman. Became dictator of Tammany Hall after the "Tweed Ring" had discredited it; ruled it autocratically, 1873–82.

KELLY, JOHN BRENDAN (*b. Philadelphia, Pa., 1889; d. Philadelphia, Pa., 1960*), building contractor, athlete, politician. Self-educated, Kelly founded the John B. Kelly Co. in 1919; the construction firm eventually made him a millionaire. He was an Olympic champion rower at the Antwerp (1920) and Paris (1924) Olympics. From 1934 to 1941, he was Democratic party chairman of Philadelphia. His daughter, Grace, became an actress and princess of Monaco.

KELLY, LUTHER SAGE (*b. Geneva, N.Y., 1849; d. Paradise, Calif., 1928*), army scout, known as "Yellowstone Kelly." His memoirs of service in the old West were published in 1926.

KELLY, MACHINE GUN (*b. Memphis, Tenn., 1895; d. Leavenworth, Kans., 1954*), gangster. Studied at Tennessee A. and M. Kelly's most famous crime was the kidnapping of Oklahoma oil millionaire Charles F. Urschel in 1933. Urschel was freed, and Kelly and his wife were captured two months later in Memphis. He died in prison after a famous trial that was one of the first tests of the Lindbergh kidnapping law.

Kelly, Michael J. (*b. Troy, N.Y., 1857; d. Boston, Mass., 1894*), baseball player, known as "King Kelly" and the "Ten Thousand Dollar Beauty." Popular idol of the Chicago White Stockings; object of the slogan, "Slide, Kelly, slide!"

Kelly, Myra (*b. Dublin, Ireland, 1875; d. Torquay, England, 1910*), teacher. Came to America as a child. Author of *Little Citizens* (1904), *Little Aliens* (1910), and other stories about immigrant children she knew while teaching on New York's East Side.

Kelly, William (*b. Pittsburgh, Pa., 1811; d. Louisville, Ky., 1888*), original inventor of the "airboiling process," later known as the Bessemer process, of steel making. With his brother, purchased Kentucky iron-ore land and a furnace and developed the Suwanee Iron Works & Union Forge, manufacturing sugar kettles. Worrying over high costs of production of wrought iron and a diminishing charcoal supply, he noticed one day that the air blast in his furnace blowing on molten iron with no charcoal covering raised the iron to white heat. Further experiments revealed that the carbon contained in molten cast iron could be employed under air blast as a fuel, and in burning out could make the molten mass much hotter. Failing to convince his relatives and customers of the significance of his discovery, he began building the first of seven experimental converters which he secretly constructed between 1851 and 1856. Though the Englishman Henry Bessemer was granted a U.S. patent on the same process in 1856, Kelly convinced patent officials of his priority and on June 23, 1857, was granted a patent and declared to be the original inventor. He later interested Daniel J. Morrell in his process and was encouraged to work it out at the Cambria Iron Works, Johnstown, Pa. An eighth experimental converter was a failure, but on a second trial succeeded; for the first time soft steel could be made cheaply and in the large quantities necessary for rails and other products of the great "Steel Age" just beginning. Steel under the Kelly patent was first blown commercially at the Wyandotte Iron Works near Detroit, Mich., in the fall of 1864.

Kelpius, Johann (*b. near Schässburg, Transylvania, 1673; d. 1708*), mystic. Saintly leader of a community established near Germantown, Pa., 1694, to await the Millennium.

Kelser, Raymond Alexander (*b. Washington, D.C., 1892; d. Philadelphia, Pa., 1952*), microbiologist, veterinarian. Studied at George Washington University, D.V.M., 1914, and at American University, Ph.D., 1923. Served with the U.S. Army veterinarian corps, 1918–46, retiring as brigadier general (the first general in the corps). Chief of the veterinary laboratory division of the Army Medical School, 1921–25 and 1928–33. In the Philippines he developed a successful vaccine for the control of rinderpest; his work on the transmission of viruses by insects led to significant understanding of viral diseases and to the control of mosquitoes. Wrote *Manual of Veterinary Bacteriology* (1927). Dean of bacteriology of the University of Pennsylvania veterinary school, 1946. Elected to the National Academy of Sciences, 1948.

Kelsey, Francis Willey (*b. Ogden, N.Y., 1858; d. 1927*), classicist, archaeologist. Graduated University of Rochester, 1880. Professor of Latin, University of Michigan, 1889–1927; instituted its *Studies: Humanistic Series* and organized its Near Eastern expeditions.

Kelsey, Rayner Wickersham (*b. Western Springs, Ill., 1879; d. Haverford, Pa., 1934*), Quaker minister, teacher. Professor of history at Haverford College *post* 1911.

Kelton, John Cunningham (*b. Delaware Co., Pa., 1828; d. Washington, D.C., 1893*), soldier. Graduated West Point, 1851. Served on frontier duty and as instructor at West Point; was a staff officer to General H. W. Halleck, 1861–65. Inventor of many improvements for the service rifle and revolver; adjutant general, U.S. Army, 1889–92.

Kemble, Frances Anne (*b. London, England, 1809; d. London, 1893*), actress, author. A member of one of the great English stage families, Fanny Kemble came to America, 1832, on tour with her father, and won high acclaim as Bianca in *Fazio*, as Juliet, and especially as Julia in *The Hunchback*. She married Pierce Butler, a wealthy American, in 1834, and retired from the theater, a profession she acutely disliked despite her success. In 1835 she published *Journal of a Residence in America*, a record of her tour which criticized American customs; during a winter on her husband's Georgia plantation (1838–39), she kept a second journal expressive of her revulsion at slavery. This appeared as a book in 1863 and was issued to influence British public opinion in the Civil War. Meanwhile, she climaxed estrangement from her husband by leaving him, 1846; after a brief return to the stage and a divorce, 1849, she entered on a highly successful career of public readings from Shakespeare which she continued until 1869.

Kemble, Gouverneur (*b. New York, N.Y., 1786, d. Cold Spring, N.Y., 1875*), cannon founder, congressman. Established the West Point Foundry at Cold Spring, N.Y., 1818. Friend of Washington Irving and J. K. Paulding.

Kemeys, Edward (*b. Savannah, Ga., 1843; d. Georgetown, D.C., 1907*), sculptor. First American to specialize in animal sculpture; self-taught, he studied his subjects in natural habitats.

Kemmerer, Edwin Walter (*b. Scranton, Pa., 1875; d. Princeton, N.J., 1945*), economist. Graduated Wesleyan University, 1899. Ph.D., Cornell University, 1903. As financial adviser to the U.S. Philippine Commission, 1903–06, he drafted the act for the reorganization of the Philippine currency and was chief (1904–06) of the division of currency of the islands' government. Assistant professor of political economy at Cornell, 1906–09, and professor, 1909–12, he removed to Princeton University and taught there until his retirement in 1943. He is best known for his missions as adviser on financial matters to underdeveloped countries, which won him international renown as the "money doctor." In 1924 he served as banking and monetary expert of the Dawes Commission on European reparations. Central to his thinking was his view that the great monetary disease was inflation and that the ordinary citizen suffered more from it than did any other group or interest. Among his books, his *Money: The Principles of Money and Their Exemplification in . . . Monetary History* (1935) expresses most of his views in succinct form.

Kemp, James (*b. Keith Hall, Aberdeenshire, Scotland, 1764; d. 1827*), Episcopal clergyman. Graduated Marischal College, Aberdeen, 1786. Came to America as a tutor, 1787; ordained at Philadelphia, 1789; rector at Great Choptank, Md., 1790–1813. Assistant bishop and bishop of Maryland, 1814–27.

Kemp, James Furman (*b. New York, N.Y., 1859; d. Great Neck, N.Y., 1926*), geologist, mining engineer. Professor of geology, Columbia University, 1892–1926; specialist in study of ore deposition and alteration.

Kemp, John (*b. Auchlossan, Scotland, 1763; d. New York, N.Y., 1812*), educator. Came to America, 1783, on graduation from Marischal College, Aberdeen. Professor, Columbia College, New York, 1785–1812; taught mathematics, geography, and the natural sciences. Influenced De Witt Clinton in projecting Erie Canal.

KEMP, ROBERT H. (*b. Wellfleet, Mass., 1820; d. Charlestown, Mass., 1897*), shoe dealer. Director of "Old Folks' Concerts" of sacred music, originally given at Reading, Mass.

KEMPER, JACKSON (*b. Pleasant Valley, N.Y., 1789, d. Delafield, Wis., 1870*), Episcopal clergyman. Graduated Columbia, 1809; ordained, 1814; served first in Philadelphia parish. Developed early interest in West, making missionary journeys into frontier Pennsylvania, Virginia, and Ohio; visited Indian Mission near Green Bay, Wis., 1834. Elected missionary bishop of "the Northwest," 1835, he was until 1859 a familiar and beloved figure throughout Missouri, Indiana, Wisconsin, and Iowa. In 1854 he became diocesan of Wisconsin, devoting himself exclusively to that see *post* 1859. He established seven dioceses, founded three colleges to train clergymen, opened numerous schools and academies and planted the Episcopal Church firmly in the Northwest.

KEMPER, JAMES LAWSON (*b. Madison Co., Va., 1823; d. Orange Co., Va., 1895*), lawyer, Virginia legislator, Confederate major general. Democratic governor of Virginia, 1874–77, he provided an administration marked by independence and integrity.

KEMPER, REUBEN (*b. probably Loudoun or Fauquier Co., Va., date unknown; d. Natchez, Miss., 1827*), controversial figure on the West Florida border, associated 1800–02 with John Smith (*ca. 1735–ca. 1824*). Led filibustering attempts to subvert Spanish rule, 1804 and 1810.

KEMPFF, LOUIS (*b. near Belleville, Ill., 1841; d. Santa Barbara, Calif., 1920*), naval officer. Attended Naval Academy, 1857–61; served on Civil War blockade duty. As senior American naval officer at Taku during Boxer troubles (1900), refused to join attack of international fleet on Chinese forts.

KEMPSTER, WALTER (*b. London, England, 1841; d. Milwaukee, Wis., 1918*), physician, psychiatrist. Came to America as a boy. Graduated Long Island College Hospital, 1864, after Civil War service. Practiced in Milwaukee *post* 1884.

KENDALL, AMOS (*b. Dunstable, Mass., 1789; d. 1869*), journalist. Graduated Dartmouth, 1811. Migrated to Kentucky, 1814; edited *Argus of Western America* at Frankfort, 1816–29; helped carry Kentucky for Andrew Jackson in 1828. For the next twelve years Kendall was closely identified with the Jacksonian regime, as treasury auditor, as postmaster general, but most importantly as a member of the "Kitchen Cabinet." The most capable and successful of Jackson's administrators, he prepared many public papers, including the veto message of July 10, 1832, and other documents relative to Jackson's war on the Bank of the United States. Engaged in journalism and farming, 1840–45, he entered in the latter year on a new phase of his career as business agent of Samuel F. B. Morse, by 1859 becoming a rich man. A vigorous War Democrat, 1860–65, he devoted the closing years of his life to church work and to the school for mutes now called Gallaudet College. His "Letter to Rutherford" (1868) was a keen and searching criticism of Republican policy toward the South.

KENDALL, GEORGE WILKINS (*b. Mount Vernon, N.H., 1809; d. Texas, 1867*), journalist. Learned printing in Vermont and worked in Washington, D.C., and New York City before going south about 1832. He founded the first cheap daily in New Orleans, the *Picayune*, whose first number appeared in January 1837. His instinct for news and ardor for adventure led him to join the ill-fated 1841 raid into Mexico which he chronicled in the widely read *Narrative of the Texan Santa Fé Expedition* (1844). He campaigned through the *Picayune* for war with Mexico; when it came, he attached himself to the army. The *Picayune* became famous for its war news, and "Mr. Kendall's express" often out-

sped government dispatches. His *The War between the United States and Mexico* (1851) is celebrated for its splendid illustrations by Nebel.

KENDRICK, ASAHEL CLARK (*b. Poultney, Vt., 1809; d. 1895*), scholar, classicist. Graduated Hamilton, 1831. Taught Greek language and literature at present Colgate University, 1831–50, and at University of Rochester, 1850–88; developed a new method for its study.

KENDRICK, JOHN (*b. Harwich, Mass., ca. 1740; d. Honolulu Harbor, Hawaii, 1794*), navigator, Revolutionary privateersman, trader. Commanded expedition of *Columbia* and *Lady Washington* from Boston to Nootka, 1787–89, in association with Robert Gray. First to fly the American flag in Japan, 1791; traded between the Northwest Coast and the Orient, 1789–94. Killed by accidental cannon fire.

KENDRICK, JOHN BENJAMIN (*b. Cherokee Co., Tex., 1857; d. near Sheridan, Wyo., 1933*), rancher. Democratic governor of Wyoming, 1915–17; U.S. senator, 1917–33.

KENEDY, PATRICK JOHN (*b. New York, N.Y., 1843; d. 1906*), Catholic bookseller and publisher. Directed present firm of P. J. Kenedy & Sons, New York, 1866–1904.

KENNA, JOHN EDWARD (*b. Kanawha Co., Va., now W.Va., 1848; d. 1893*), lawyer. Congressman, Democrat, from W. Virginia, 1877–83; U.S. senator, 1883–93. Championed federal railroad regulation and aid for slack-water navigation on the Kanawha.

KENNAN, GEORGE (*b. Norwalk, Ohio, 1845; d. 1924*), explorer, journalist. Author of *Tent Life in Siberia* (1870) and *Siberia and the Exile System* (1891), which were important original contributions to the world's knowledge of Russia.

KENNEDY, ARCHIBALD (*b. Scotland, 1685; d. 1763*), British colonial official. Came to New York *ante* 1710. Served as collector of customs and member of the Council; was author of pamphlets dissenting from the methods of British mercantilist policy.

KENNEDY, JOHN DOBY (*b. Camden, S.C., 1840; d. Camden, 1896*), lawyer, Confederate brigadier general, South Carolina legislator. Helped restore white supremacy after the Civil War.

KENNEDY, JOHN FITZGERALD (*b. Brookline, Mass., 1917; d. Dallas, Tex., 1963*), U.S. president. Kennedy grew up in a household where parental insistence on self-improvement, competition, and victory became legendary. His father, Joseph P. Kennedy, was a talented Wall Street promoter and corporate reorganizer who served the Roosevelt administration in a variety of capacities. John Kennedy spent much of his childhood sick in bed, surrounded by books. Scarlet fever, appendicitis, bronchitis, measles, whooping cough, parotitis, hives, jaundice, and later a back injury sustained while playing football at Harvard dogged his early years. Although an omnivorous reader, he was casual and unconcerned as a student. After illness forced him to drop out of the London School of Economics, and later Princeton, Kennedy entered Harvard in 1936; he graduated cum laude in 1940. His senior honors essay, a study of Great Britain's appeasement policy, was published as *Why England Slept* (1940), and was briefly a best-seller.

Entering the navy in 1941, by 1943 Lieutenant (junior grade) Kennedy was in command of his own PT boat in the South Pacific. That year a Japanese destroyer rammed Kennedy's PT-109 in Blackett Strait, west of New Georgia in the Solomon Islands, and the crew was plunged into waters aflame with burning gasoline.

Kennedy's courageous feat of towing one of the crew to safety and his resourcefulness until rescue came were later celebrated by John Hersey in a *New Yorker* article. Malaria and further back problems followed.

Demobilized in 1945, Kennedy was elected to the U.S. Congress the next year from the eleventh Massachusetts district. In his three terms in the House, he took a consistent liberal line on social and economic issues. In foreign affairs he supported the Truman Doctrine and the Marshall Plan. In 1952 he was elected to the U.S. Senate, defeating the incumbent, Henry Cabot Lodge, Jr., The following year he married Jacqueline Lee Bouvier.

As he had in the House, Kennedy held himself apart from his colleagues in the Senate. He pursued his interests in social and economic policy, but remained aloof from growing opposition to Senator Joseph McCarthy's witch-hunting. In 1954 he underwent surgery on his back, and during the convalescence he began work, with research assistance, on a series of sketches of American politicians who had risked their careers in the cause of principle. The result was *Profiles in Courage* (1956) which became a bestseller and received the Pulitzer Prize for biography in 1957.

Kennedy was an incisive critic of the policies of Secretary of State John Foster Dulles. He opposed American military intervention in Indochina in 1954 and advocated independence for Algeria and Vietnam. He unsuccessfully sought the vice-presidential nomination in 1956.

Buoyed by his overwhelming reelection to the Senate in 1958, Kennedy began planning for the presidential nomination in 1960. Conventional politicians held his youth, his Roman Catholic religion, and his independence against him, but Kennedy went on to obtain the Democratic nomination on the first ballot. He selected Lyndon Johnson of Texas as his running mate.

The 1960 campaign was marked by a striking innovation in American politics—four televised "debates" in which Kennedy and Vice-President Richard M. Nixon, the Republican candidate, responded to questions asked by panels of reporters. Kennedy won the popular vote by only 119,057 votes, and in 1961 the youngest man ever elected president took office; he was also the first Roman Catholic president. His inaugural address included the memorable injunction, "And so, my fellow Americans, ask not what your country can do for you; ask what you can do for your country."

In foreign policy, Kennedy was a transitional figure. He had an acute sense of the limitations of American power, and he had no illusions about a pax Americana. Viewing the Third World as the decisive battleground between democracy and communism, he hope to encourage the developing countries of Latin America, Asia, and Africa to turn to democratic methods in their quest for independence. Foreign assistance concentrated on economic rather than on military aid. The Peace Corps channeled the idealism of individual Americans into face-to-face cooperation in the developing countries. An expanded Food for Peace program used the American agricultural surplus to foster development in emergent nations.

The Alliance for Progress was designed to use American economic aid to advance development and democracy in the western hemisphere. The Alliance called for economic planning and structural change within a democratic framework. The problem remained, as Washington saw it, of protecting the fragile democratization process against Communist disruption. In 1961 Kennedy allowed a band of 1,400 Cubans, trained by the Central Intelligence Agency, to invade Cuba in an effort to overthrow Fidel Castro. The affair was a perfect failure and to many an indefensible exercise in intervention. At Kennedy's instruction the CIA then undertook small-scale covert operations intended to encourage resistance and sabotage in Cuba.

In Vietnam, the Saigon government of Ngo Dinh Diem was under assault by Communist Vietcong guerrillas. Kennedy began increasing the number of American military advisers. By 1962 American helicopters and personnel were taking a limited part in the fighting. At the end of 1963 there were 16,732 military advisers in Vietnam, and 73 Americans had been killed in combat.

In Kennedy's view, the point of stopping Cuban subversion in Latin America and Communist guerrilla action in Southeast Asia was to secure the stability of the existing world balance. He also discarded the Eisenhower strategy of relying on nuclear weapons to deter war. He substituted the doctrine of "flexible response"— the diversification of military force so that the level of reaction could be graduated to meet the level of threat.

In 1962 Kennedy learned that the Russians had sent offensive weapons to Cuba, and he decided to insist that they be removed. The Cuban Missile Crisis was resolved when Nikita Khrushchev agreed to remove the missiles if the United States would end its naval quarantine and agree not to invade Cuba. Kennedy then turned his attention to a test-ban treaty, and in 1963 the United States, the Soviet Union, and Great Britain agreed on a treaty outlawing nuclear tests in the atmosphere, in outer space, and underwater.

The competition between the superpowers produced at least one benign by-product. In April 1961 the Russians put the first astronaut into space orbit. In May, Kennedy committed the United States "to achieving the goal, before this decade is out, of landing a man on the moon and returning him safely to earth."

In domestic policy, Kennedy proceeded with circumspection. He had been elected by a thin popular margin and was confronted in the House of Representatives by the coalition of Republicans and southern Democrats that had frustrated social legislation since 1938. In 1963 he concluded that if structural poverty was to be relieved, general tax reduction required a counterpart program for those too poor to pay income taxes. The planning set in motion that year led to the "war on poverty" of later years.

The administration pursued steadily expansionist economic policies, which fostered the longest peacetime growth of the American economy since World War II. Unemployment declined from 8.1 percent of the labor force when he became president to 5.2 percent in 1964.

A particular concern of Kennedy's, shared by his wife, was to give the arts a place of honor. He appointed a special consultant on the arts, whose recommendations led to the establishment of the National Endowments for the Arts and Humanities.

Kennedy's most signal domestic achievement lay in the field of racial justice. As senator he had supported civil rights legislation, although without great personal commitment. As president he began by concentrating on executive rather than legislative action, with Attorney General Robert Kennedy as his chief agent. The Kennedys ended segregation in interstate transportation and sent federal troops to Oxford, Miss., to protect a black student's right to attend the University of Mississippi. Kennedy issued an executive order ending discrimination in housing supported by federal loans and guarantees. But the moral dynamism of the civil rights cause outstripped the actions of the administration. In 1963 Kennedy launched a fight for new and sweeping civil rights legislation.

On Nov. 22, 1963, while riding with his wife in an open car through Dallas, Tex., Kennedy was shot and killed by Lee Harvey Oswald. In the years after his death, Kennedy's place in history became a subject of contention. Revisionist historians portrayed him as a rigid and embattled "cold warrior"; others found this an unpersuasive assessment in the light of the movement toward détente after the missile crisis. Some scholars, noting his limited legislative success, dismissed his leadership in domestic affairs as more style than substance; others, pointing to his narrow margins of support in Congress, argued that the perseverance with which he addressed such issues as civil rights, aid to education, tax reduction, and Medicare laid the groundwork for legislation in the next administration.

KENNEDY, JOHN PENDLETON (*b. Baltimore, Md., 1795; d. Newport, R.I., 1870*), author, statesman. Wrote three outstanding pieces of fiction: *Swallow Barn* (under pseudonym "Mark Littleton," 1832), *Horse-Shoe Robinson* (same pseudonym, 1835) and *Rob of the Bowl* (1838). He was author also of *Memoirs of the Life of William Wirt* (1842) and various minor works. He served as congressman, Whig, from Maryland, 1838 and 1841–45. As secretary of the navy, 1852–53, he organized four important expeditions, including Com. Perry's to Japan. He strove to prevent secession and supported the Union but favored "amnesty and forgiveness" after the Civil War.

KENNEDY, JOHN STEWART (*b. Blantyre, Scotland, 1830; d. 1909*), capitalist, philanthropist. Settled in America, 1857, as banking partner of Morris K. Jesup; important in Western railroad building as head of J. S. Kennedy and Co., 1868–83.

KENNEDY, JOSEPH CAMP GRIFFITH (*b. Meadville, Pa., 1813; d. 1887*), statistician. Superintendent of the censuses of 1850 and 1860. Helped organize the First International Statistical Congress (Brussels, 1853).

KENNEDY, JOSEPH PATRICK (*b. Boston, Mass., 1888; d. Hyannis, Mass., 1969*), entrepreneur and government official. Studied at Harvard (B.A., 1912) and in 1914 became president of a small bank. As assistant general manager of Bethlehem Steel's Quincy, Mass., shipyards in 1917 he met Assistant Secretary of the Navy Franklin D. Roosevelt. He worked as an investment banker and in the motion-picture business, becoming very wealthy. In 1932 he made a significant financial contribution to Roosevelt's presidential campaign. He was a member and first chairman of the Securities and Exchange Commission (1934–35), chairman of the United States Maritime Commission (1937), and U.S. ambassador to Great Britain (1938–40). In the 1950's his political support went largely to right-wingers, including Senator Joseph McCarthy. His second son, John, was elected U.S. president in 1960.

KENNEDY, ROBERT FOSTER (*b. Belfast, Northern Ireland, 1884; d. New York, N.Y., 1952*), neurologist. Studied at Queen's University and the Royal Irish University, M.D., 1911. Immigrated to the U.S. in 1910. Best known by the "Kennedy syndrome," a neurological phenomenon resulting in the loss of vision in one eye, resulting from compression of its optic nerve, which is rendered atrophic by an adjacent tumor. Identification of the syndrome made possible a nearly certain diagnosis of a brain tumor under one frontal lobe (1911). Chief of the neurological division of Bellevue Hospital in New York, 1915–49. President of the American Neurological Association, 1940.

KENNEDY, ROBERT FRANCIS (*b. Brookline, Mass., 1925; d. Los Angeles, Calif., 1968*), U.S. attorney general and U.S. senator. The seventh of nine children, he served in the naval reserve, 1943–46, then studied at Harvard (B.A., 1948) and the University of Virginia Law School, graduating in 1951. After brief service in the Department of Justice's criminal division, he made his political debut in 1952 as manager of his brother John's successful campaign for the Senate from Massachusetts. The next year he went to work for the Senate Subcommittee on Investigations, headed by Joseph McCarthy. Kennedy resigned in 1953 and the next year became counsel for the Senate Democratic minority. In 1957 he became chief counsel of the Senate Select Committee on Improper Activities in the Labor or Management Field (the Rackets Committee). His relentless investigation of the Teamsters led to a feud with Jimmy Hoffa and resulted in the Labor Law Reform Act of 1959.

In 1960 John Kennedy drafted his younger brother to run his 1960 campaign for the presidency. Once elected, John made Robert attorney general. In 1961 Robert Kennedy dispatched federal marshals to the South to protect freedom riders, and he persuaded the Interstate Commerce Commission to issue regulations ending segregation in interstate bus terminals. Under Kennedy's leadership, Department of Justice lawyers encouraged voter-registration drives and filed suit when voting rights were denied. Kennedy publicly defended Martin Luther King, Jr., when King was accused of being controlled by Communists, but privately he ordered the Federal Bureau of Investigation to wiretap King's telephones. In 1961 and 1962, Kennedy spurred on the Central Intelligence Agency to undertake covert actions against Cuba.

Devastated by his brother's assassination in 1963, he resigned from the cabinet in 1964 and successfully ran for a Senate seat from New York. In the Senate he criticized the U.S. intervention in the Dominican Republic in 1965 and concluded that President Lyndon Johnson had abandoned the reform aims of John Kennedy's Alliance for Progress. As American involvement in Vietnam grew, Kennedy called for bombing pauses and for negotiations. He entered the race for the Democratic presidential nomination in 1968, challenging Eugene McCarthy and Hubert Humphrey. Following his victory over McCarthy in the California primary on June 4, he was shot by Sirhan Sirhan. He died the following day.

KENNEDY, ROBERT PATTERSON (*b. Bellefontaine, Ohio, 1840; d. Columbus, Ohio, 1918*), Union brigadier-general lawyer, Republican congressman. Lieutenant governor of Ohio, 1886–87.

KENNEDY, WILLIAM SLOANE (*b. Brecksville, Ohio, 1850; d. West Yarmouth, Mass., 1929*), biographer, anthologist. Intimate friend of Walt Whitman; author of *Reminiscences of Walt Whitman* (1896) and other volumes on the poet and his work.

KENNELLY, ARTHUR EDWIN (*b. Colaba, India, 1861; d. Boston, Mass., 1939*), electrical engineer. Left school at 13 to work in office of Society of Telegraph Engineers, London; studied physics in his spare time. Worked for Eastern Telegraph Co. as operator and in submarine cable work, 1876–86. In 1887 he came to the United States and was chief electrical assistant to Thomas A. Edison until 1894. After some years as consulting engineer in partnership with Edwin J. Houston, Kennelly in 1902 became professor of engineering at Harvard, retiring in 1930. He also taught at Massachusetts Institute of Technology.

Kennelly contributed to electrical engineering as an originator, but especially as an interpreter. His careful choice of nomenclature, clarity of exposition, and meticulous mathematical presentations made possible the general use of abstruse methods of analysis by many in his profession. For example, in the field of circuit theory Kennelly's paper on impedance (1893) crystallized the application of the so-called imaginary and complex variables to alternating currents, and led to the wide use of complex numbers in analyzing alternating-current phenomena. Similarly, his application of complex hyperbolic functions to the solution of line problems advanced the development of electrical engineering by many years. In 1902 Kennelly proposed the theory that the conducting properties of the ionized rarefied upper atmosphere reflected electromagnetic waves. The theory, also advanced by the English physicist and electrician Oliver Heaviside, was later verified experimentally. Kennelly's publications included twenty-eight books and over 350 technical papers.

KENNER, DUNCAN FARRAR (*b. New Orleans, La., 1813; d. New Orleans, 1887*), sugar planter, Louisiana legislator. Originated an unsuccessful project, 1864–65, to obtain recognition of the Confederacy by England and France in return for abolition of slavery.

KENNEY, MARY. *See* O'SULLIVAN, MARY KENNEY.

KENNICOTT, ROBERT (*b. New Orleans, La., 1835; d. Fort Nulato, Alaska, 1866*), naturalist, explorer. A founder (1856) of Chicago Academy of Sciences; collected fauna from British North America and Alaska which became part of its collections.

KENRICK, FRANCIS PATRICK (*b. Dublin, Ireland, 1796; d. 1863*), Roman Catholic clergyman. Brother of Peter R. Kenrick. Came to America after ordination in Rome, 1821; worked in Kentucky. Bishop-coadjutor and bishop of Philadelphia, 1830–51; became archbishop of Baltimore, 1851. Effective in fight against trusteeism (1831) and against nativism, 1844; noted as preacher and scholar.

KENRICK, PETER RICHARD (*b. Dublin, Ireland, 1806; d. 1896*), Roman Catholic clergyman. Brother of Francis P. Kenrick. Came to America, 1833; was pastor in Philadelphia, Pa., and vicar general of the diocese. Bishop-coadjutor of St. Louis, Mo., 1841–43; bishop, 1843–47; archbishop thereafter until *ca.* 1891. A prominent opponent of infallibility at Vatican Council, 1870.

KENRICK, WILLIAM (*b. Newton, Mass., 1789; d. Newton, 1872*), nurseryman. Author of *The New American Orchardist* (1833).

KENSETT, JOHN FREDERICK (*b. Cheshire, Conn., 1816; d. 1872*), landscape painter, engraver. Associate of A. B. Durand, John W. Casilear, T. P. Rossiter, and Benjamin Champney; studied in Paris, England, and Italy, 1840–47. Painted somewhat thin, atmospheric canvases imbued with the sincerest love of nature.

KENT, ARTHUR ATWATER (*b. Burlington, Vt., 1873; d. Los Angeles, Calif., 1949*), inventor, radio manufacturer. Attended Worcester (Mass.) Polytechnic Institute; established Atwater Kent Manufacturing Works in Philadelphia, Pa., 1902, to make electrical devices. By 1920 his firm had become one of the major suppliers of electrical systems to the automobile industry. Between 1922 and 1930 he was phenomenally successful in mass-producing and selling radio receivers of high quality.

KENT, CHARLES FOSTER (*b. Palmyra, N.Y., 1867; d. 1925*), Biblical scholar, educator. Graduated Yale, 1889; Ph.D., 1891. Taught at University of Chicago, Brown, and Yale. Founded National Council on Religion in Higher Education. Made the results of modern Biblical study widely accessible in a number of readable, popular books.

KENT, EDWARD (*b. Concord, N.H., 1802; d. Bangor, Maine, 1877*), lawyer, Maine legislator and jurist. Whig governor of Maine, 1838–39 and 1841–42.

KENT, JAMES (*b. Fredericksburgh, now Southeast, N.Y., 1763; d. New York, N.Y., 1847*), jurist, legal commentator. Graduated Yale, 1781. Earlier, his reading of *Blackstone's Commentaries* had inspired him to become a lawyer. After three years in the Poughkeepsie law office of Attorney General Egbert Benson, Kent was admitted to the New York bar and practiced in Poughkeepsie until 1793, when he removed to New York City. He had already established political affiliations with Federalist leaders and became an admirer of Alexander Hamilton. Though three times elected to the New York Assembly, his political influence was exerted through judicial office. Stoutly conservative, he fought always for the rights of the individual as distinguished from those of the people. Briefly in financial straits, in December 1793

he secured appointment as first professor of law at Columbia College. The failure of his courses to attract students led him to resign early in 1798, shortly after Gov. Jay appointed him a judge of the New York supreme court. He became chief justice of the court, 1804, and chancellor of the New York court of chancery, 1814.

Kent's record as judge is to be found in the three sets of law reports published by William Johnson. His reports span the years 1799–1823, and preserve a line of decisions in law and equity which are basic in American jurisprudence. As chancellor, Kent was practically the creator of equity jurisdiction in the United States. "I took the court," he wrote, "as if it had been a new institution, and never before known in the United States. I had nothing to guide me, and was left at liberty to assume all such English Chancery powers and jurisdiction as I thought applicable under our Constitution. This gave me grand scope, and I was checked only by the revision of the Senate, or Court of Errors." At a time when English law and legal institutions were regarded here with distrust, Kent preserved their best features and justified his work by his own high standard of integrity and judicial conduct.

Forced to retire as chancellor by New York constitutional provision in 1823, he accepted reappointment to the law professorship at Columbia. He delivered three courses of lectures (1824–26) before again abandoning a task which he disliked. Urged by his son, he began the rewriting and expansion of his law lectures into a work on which his reputation rests no less firmly than on his judicial decisions, the *Commentaries on American Law* (1826–28, 1830). Many times revised, the *Commentaries* was of fundamental importance and still remains the foremost American institutional legal treatise.

KENT, JOSEPH (*b. Calvert Co., Md., 1779; d. near Bladensburg, Md., 1837*), physician. Congressman from Maryland, Federalist, 1811–15; (Democrat) Republican, 1819–26. National Republican leader and friend of Henry Clay *post* 1824, he served as governor of Maryland, 1826–28, and as U.S. senator, 1833–37.

KENT, WILLIAM (*b. Philadelphia, Pa., 1851; d. Gananoque, Canada, 1918*), mechanical engineer. Established Pittsburgh Testing Laboratory *ca.* 1882, the pioneer commercial physical testing laboratory. Author of *Mechanical Engineers' Pocket-Book* (1895), first modern handbook.

KENTON, SIMON (*b. probably Fauquier Co., Va., 1755; d. near Zanesfield, Ohio, 1836*), frontiersman, Indian fighter. Hunted along the Ohio until 1774, when he served as a scout in Dunmore's War. Settled in Boonesborough, Ky., 1775; was appointed a scout by Daniel Boone and participated in all local encounters with the Indians. Accompanied George R. Clark to Kaskaskia, 1778, and scouted on the Little Miami; captured, he was taken to Detroit by the British but escaped to scout for Clark again in 1780 and 1782. Established himself at Maysville, Ky., 1785; served with Wayne's expedition, 1794. Removing to Ohio, 1798–99, he was made brigadier general of militia, 1805. In the War of 1812 he fought with General Shelby's Kentuckians at the battle of the Thames. His latter years were spent in poverty.

KENYON, JOSEPHINE HEMENWAY (*b. Auburn, N.Y., 1880; d. Boulder, Colo., 1965*), pediatrician. Studied at Pritchett College (B.A., 1898; M.A., 1899), Bryn Mawr, and Johns Hopkins Medical School (M.D., 1904). She had a private practice in New York City, 1911–45, and taught child care and social hygiene at Columbia University Teachers College, 1913–37. A pioneer in the field of sex education, she worked with the Young Women's Christian Association during World War I. She is best known for her writings on child rearing. She wrote for *Good*

Housekeeping (1923–52) and published *Healthy Babies Are Happy Babies* (1934).

KENYON, WILLIAM SQUIRE (*b. Elyria, Ohio, 1869; d. Maine, 1933*), lawyer, jurist. Raised in Iowa. U.S. senator, progressive Republican, from Iowa, 1911–22. Supported labor; *post* 1918, organized and led "farm bloc" of western and southern senators. As U.S. circuit judge, 1922–33, he cancelled the Teapot Dome leases.

KEOKUK (*b. Sauk village on Rock River, Ill., ca. 1790; d. Sauk Agency, Franklin Co., Kans., probably 1848*), Sauk war leader. Succeeded Black Hawk as chief; consistently aided government Indian policy.

KEPHART, EZEKIEL BORING (*b. Clearfield, Co., Pa., 1834; d. 1906*), United Brethren clergyman, educator. Brother of Isaiah L. Kephart. President, Western College, Western, Iowa, 1868–81; rendered his greatest service as bishop of the United Brethren Church, 1881–1905.

KEPHART, ISAIAH LAFAYETTE (*b. Clearfield Co., Pa., 1832; d. 1908*), United Brethren clergyman. Brother of Ezekiel B. Kephart. Editor, the *Religious Telescope*, 1887–1908.

KEPHART, JOHN WILLIAM (*b. Wilmore, Cambria County, Pa., 1872; d. Philadelphia, Pa., 1944*), jurist. Graduated Dickinson Law School (Carlisle, Pa.), 1894. After service as Cambria County solicitor and judge of the state superior court, he was elected to the Pennsylvania supreme court in 1918. He remained on the bench until retirement in 1940, rising through seniority to chief justice in 1936.

KEPPEL, FREDERICK (*b. Tullow, Ireland, 1845; d. 1912*), print dealer, art critic. Immigrated to Canada, 1862; removed to Utica, N.Y., 1864; thence to New York City where he opened his first print shop, 1868.

KEPPEL, FREDERICK PAUL (*b. Staten Island, N.Y., 1875; d. New York, N.Y., 1943*), educator, foundation executive. Son of Frederick Keppel. A.B., Columbia University, 1898. After two years' employment as editor in a publishing house, he returned to Columbia as assistant secretary (1900–02), secretary (1902–10), and dean of Columbia College, 1910–17. During World War I he served Newton D. Baker as confidential clerk and was promoted to the post of Third Assistant Secretary of War; after the war he became vice-chairman and director of foreign relations for the American Red Cross (1919–20) and U.S. delegate to the International Chamber of Commerce (1921–22). In December 1922 he became president of the Carnegie Corporation of New York. An opponent of bureaucracy and overspecialization in foundation giving, he put great reliance on professional advice from outside his organization and was always sympathetic to the innovative and the unorthodox; among his "hunches" were grants that led to the discovery of insulin and to the writing of Gunnar Myrdal's report on the American black. He was particularly interested in fostering adult education, a more general appreciation of the fine arts, and improvement in the quality and usefulness of American libraries. He retired in 1941. Among his books were *The Foundation: Its Place in American Life* (1930) and *Philanthropy and Learning* (1936).

KEPPLER, JOSEPH (*b. Vienna, Austria, 1838; d. New York, N.Y., 1894*), caricaturist. Came to America, 1867. Founded several German comic papers, achieving success with *Puck*, 1876 (issued also in English *post* 1877), for which he lithographed cartoons in colors and provided an exuberant German flavor and satirical sense in comment on public affairs.

KERBY, WILLIAM JOSEPH (*b. Lawler, Iowa., 1870; d. Washington, D.C., 1936*), Roman Catholic clergyman, sociologist. Graduated Loras College, 1889; ordained 1892. Pupil of Thomas J. Bouquillon at Catholic University of America; Ph.D., Louvain, 1897. Taught sociology at Catholic University, 1897–1936. His interest in social reform led him to organize National Conference of Catholic Charities, 1910, of which he was secretary, 1910–18. For participating in social welfare conferences and advocating legislative reforms Kerby was sometimes criticized, but he in turn criticized "Catholic isolationism." His efforts led to the founding (1921) of the National Catholic School of Social Service. He was a pioneer in arousing the American Catholic social conscience.

KERENS, RICHARD C. (*b. Kilberry, Ireland, 1842; d. Merion, Pa., 1916*), railroad builder, Republican politician. Came to America as an infant. After Civil War service with Union Army, prospered in southern overland mail contract hauling, 1866–76; thereafter in West Virginia and other railroads. *Post* 1876, he was influential and active in Missouri politics.

KERFOOT, JOHN BARRETT (*b. Dublin, Ireland, 1816; d. Meyersdale, Pa., 1881*), Episcopal clergyman. Came to America as a child; was protégé of William A. Muhlenberg. Principal of St. James Hall, Md., 1842–64; briefly president, Trinity College. First bishop of Pittsburgh, 1866–81.

KERLIN, ISAAC NEWTON (*b. Burlington, N.J., 1834; d. 1893*), pioneer psychiatrist. Graduated University of Pennsylvania, M.D., 1856. Made important contributions toward understanding and care of the mentally deficient; superintended the Pennsylvania Training School at Elwyn.

KERN, JEROME DAVID (*b. New York, N.Y., 1885; d. New York, 1945*), composer. Studied piano and harmony at New York College of Music, 1902; took additional academic training in Germany, 1903, and worked in London, England, on musical comedies for Charles Frohman. Returning to the United States, 1904, he worked as a song-plugger and arranger for music publishers and wrote songs for interpolation into shows by other composers. By 1911 he was working on his own shows; his first success was *The Girl from Utah*, 1914, which included "They Didn't Believe Me." Highly polished and romantically melodic, his music was obviously superior to the standard product. At this point he was commissioned to write the scores for a series of musical comedies to be produced at the small Princess Theater in New York; the librettists were Guy Bolton and P. G. Wodehouse. The result of their collaboration was a new form of musical theater, in which the action dealt with modern people in believable situations and the songs and music were an integral part of the action. This technique was employed with great success in, among other shows, *Very Good Eddie* (1915) and *Oh, Boy!* (1917). Kern continued to write scores of outstanding quality, of which *Show Boat* (1927) and *Roberta* (1933), and the motion pictures *Swing Time* (1936) and *Cover Girl* (1944), are typical. Inventive in dance idioms as in the romantic ballad, he never catered to the popular taste but led it to new levels of discrimination.

KERN, JOHN WORTH (*b. Alto, Ind., 1849; d. Asheville, N.C., 1917*), lawyer, Indiana legislator. U.S. senator, Democrat, from Indiana, 1911–17; a leader of the progressives and a fighter for social justice.

KERNAN, FRANCIS (*b. Wayne, now Tyrone, N.Y., 1816; d. 1892*), lawyer, New York legislator. Practiced in Utica, N.Y. Associate of Samuel J. Tilden in breaking the Tweed Ring. Denied governorship by religious prejudice, he served as U.S. senator, Democrat, from New York, 1875–81.

KERNEY, JAMES (b. Trenton, N.J., 1873; d. Baltimore, Md., 1934), editor of Trenton Evening Times, post 1903; adviser and friend of Woodrow Wilson.

KEROUAC, JACK (b. Lowell, Mass., 1922; d. St. Petersburg, Fla., 1969), novelist, poet, and essayist. Studied at Columbia, 1940–42, and befriended the novelist William Burroughs and the poet Allen Ginsberg. In 1946 he met Neal Cassady, who became the subject of several of Kerouac's novels. The Town and the City (1950) contrasted Kerouac's Lowell and early New York City life. On the Road (1957), completed in three weeks, recounts the cross-country hitchhiking, car rides, freight rides, all-night conversations, sexual and comradely escapades, commitments, and failures of Kerouac, Cassady, Ginsberg, Burroughs, and others in their circle. In a 1958 article on writing, Kerouac proposed "sketching," much like a visual artist, only with words. Other novels include Big Sur (1962), The Vanity of Duluoz (1968), and Pic (1971). His fiction is valuable as a chronicle of the Beat Generation.

KERR, JOHN GLASGOW (b. near Duncansville, Ohio, 1824; d. 1901), Presbyterian missionary, physician. Headed Medical Missionary Society's hospital at Canton, China, 1855–98; pioneered there in treatment of the insane.

KERR, ROBERT SAMUEL (b. near the present town of Ada, Okla., 1896; d. Washington, D.C., 1963), oil executive, governor, and U.S. senator. Received a degree from East Central Normal School (1911) and studied law at the University of Oklahoma for one year. He practiced law until 1929, when he cofounded the Anderson-Kerr Drilling Company, which eventually resulted in the establishment of Kerr-McGee Oil Industries. A Democrat, he was governor of Oklahoma, 1943–49, and U.S. senator, 1949–63. He served on the Public Works Committee, the Senate Finance Committee, the Democratic Policy Committee, and became chairman of the Aeronautical and Space Sciences Committee in 1961.

KERR, SOPHIE (b. Denton, Md., 1880; d. New York, N.Y., 1965), writer. Studied at Hood College (B.A., 1898) and the University of Vermont (M.A., 1901). She worked as an editor on the Pittsburgh Chronicle-Telegraph and Pittsburgh Gazette-Times and was managing editor of Woman's Home Companion. Much of her magazine writing was published in Ladies' Home Journal, Collier's, and Saturday Evening Post. Her novels include The Blue Envelope (1917), One Thing Is Certain (1922), Mareea-Maria (1929), Girl into Woman (1932), and As Tall as Pride (1949).

KERR, WALTER CRAIG (b. St. Peter, Minn., 1858; d. 1910), engineer. Graduated Cornell, 1879. Moving spirit in organizing Westinghouse, Church, Kerr and Co., first firm to undertake entire contracts for construction of large engineering properties.

KERR, WASHINGTON CARUTHERS (b. Guilford Co., N.C., 1827; d. Asheville, N.C., 1885), geologist. As North Carolina state geologist ca. 1865–82, produced the state survey map, 1882, and advertised North Carolina resources.

KERSHAW, JOSEPH BREVARD (b. Camden, S.C., 1822; d. Camden 1894), Confederate major general, South Carolina legislator, jurist. Commanded "Kershaw's Brigade" with Army of Northern Virginia and also in Tennessee campaign, 1863–64.

KESTER, PAUL (b. Delaware, Ohio, 1870; d. Lake Mohegan, N.Y., 1933), playwright. Brother of Vaughan Kester; cousin of William D. Howells. Romantic author of such hits as Sweet Nell of Old Drury (1900) and When Knighthood Was in Flower (1901).

KESTER, VAUGHAN (b. New Brunswick, N.J., 1869; d. Fairfax Co., Va., 1911), journalist. Author of The Prodigal Judge (1911) and other fiction significant for depiction of frontier types and accurate rendering of their idiom. Brother of Paul Kester.

KETTELL, SAMUEL (b. Newburyport, Mass., 1800; d. Malden, Mass., 1855), author. Hack writer for Samuel G. Goodrich. Edited Specimens of American Poetry (1829), the first comprehensive anthology of native verse.

KETTERING, CHARLES FRANKLIN (b. near Loudenville, Ohio, 1876; d. Dayton, Ohio, 1958), inventor, engineer. Studied at Ohio State University. Invented the electric starter for automobiles (1911). Founded the Dayton Engineering Laboratories Co. (1909), which was absorbed in 1918 by General Motors and became the General Motors Research Laboratories; Kettering was vice president of GM and head of the laboratories. Other achievements of the lab include the discovery of the knock-suppressing property of tetraethyl lead for gasoline (1921) and the development of the refrigerant Freon and of fast-drying automobile paint. Kettering founded, with Alfred P. Sloan, the Sloan-Kettering Institute for Cancer Research. He retired from GM in 1947.

KEY, DAVID McKENDREE (b. Greene Co., Tenn., 1824; d. Chattanooga, Tenn., 1900), lawyer, Confederate soldier. U.S. senator, Democrat, from Tennessee, 1875–77; U.S. postmaster general, 1877–80; U.S. district judge, east and middle Tennessee, 1880–94.

KEY, FRANCIS SCOTT (b. "Terra Rubra," present Carroll Co., Md., 1779; d. Baltimore, Md., 1843), lawyer. Nephew of Philip B. Key. Wrote "The Star Spangled Banner" during British naval bombardment of Fort McHenry, Baltimore, September 1814.

KEY, PHILIP BARTON (b. near Charlestown, Md., 1757; d. Georgetown, D.C., 1815), lawyer, Maryland legislator, jurist. Loyalist soldier during the Revolution; congressman, Federalist, from Maryland, 1807–13. Uncle of Francis S. Key.

KEY, VALDIMER ORLANDO, JR. (b. Austin, Tex., 1908; d. Brookline, Mass., 1963), educator and political scientist. Studied at the University of Texas (B.A., 1929; M.A., 1930) and the University of Chicago (Ph.D., 1934). He taught at the University of California at Los Angeles (1934–36), Johns Hopkins (1938–49), Yale (1949–51), and Harvard (1951–63). Also served with the Bureau of the Budget, 1942–45, and in 1958 was elected president of the American Political Science Association. His books include The Initiative and the Referendum in California (with W. W. Crouch, 1939), Politics, Parties, and Pressure Groups (1942), Southern Politics in State and Nation (1949), A Primer of Statistics for Political Scientists (1954), American State Politics (1956), Public Opinion and American Democracy (1961), and The Responsible Electorate (1966).

KEYES, EDWARD LAWRENCE (b. Fort Moultrie, Charleston, S.C., 1843; d. 1924), surgeon. Son of Erasmus D. Keyes. Graduated Yale, 1863; M.D., New York University, 1866; associate of William H. Van Buren; professor at Bellevue, New York City. An American pioneer in dermatoloy and in male genitourinary surgery; wrote papers of international importance on syphilis treatment.

KEYES, ELISHA WILLIAMS (b. Northfield, Vt., 1828; d. Madison, Wis., 1910), lawyer, politician. Postmaster of Madison, 1861–82, 1898–1910. Autocratic chairman of Wisconsin Republican central committee, 1867–1877.

KEYES, ERASMUS DARWIN (b. Brimfield, Mass., 1810; d. Nice, France, 1895), soldier, businessman. Graduated West Point, 1832. Performed a wide variety of services in the West and South until 1861. As brigadier general, commanded IV Corps in Peninsular Campaign and was promoted major general, 1862.

Resigning 1864, he entered business in San Francisco, Calif. Author of *Fifty Years' Observation of Men and Events* (1884).

KEYES, FRANCES PARKINSON (*b. Charlottesville, Va., 1885; d. New Orleans, La., 1970*), writer and editor. In 1904 she married Henry Wilder Keyes, who was governor of New Hampshire (1917–19) and U.S. senator (1919–37). In 1920 she began writing "Letters from a Senator's Wife," a monthly column in *Good Housekeeping*. She was an associate editor at *Good Housekeeping*, 1923–35, and in 1937 became editor of the *Daughters of the American Revolution Magazine*, which she renamed *National Historical Magazine* and converted into a forerunner of *American Heritatge*. She resigned in 1939. Her first novel was *The Old Gray Homestead* (1919). Keyes wrote over fifty novels, which sold in excess of 20 million copies. She also wrote religiously oriented books, verse, and four autobiographical works.

KEYS, CLEMENT MELVILLE (*b. Chatsworth, Ont., 1876; d. New York, N.Y., 1952*), journalist, financier, airline executive. Graduated from the University of Toronto, B.A., 1897. Immigrated to the U.S. in 1901. After a career in journalism, Keys entered the fledgling aviation industry in the 1920's, acquiring controlling stock in the Curtiss Aeroplane and Motor Co. (later Curtiss-Wright), North American Aviation, its subsidiary, Transcontinental Air Transport (the principal ancestor of Trans World Airways), and National Air Transport. Keys lost control of all of his aviation holdings during the 1930's.

KEYT, ALONZO THRASHER (*b. Higginsport, Ohio, 1827; d. Cincinnati, Ohio, 1885*), physician, physiologist. Graduated Medical College of Ohio, M.D., 1848. Made many important contributions to knowledge of blood circulation; perfected clinical methods of diagnosis of circulatory diseases.

KHARASCH, MORRIS SELIG (*b. Kremenets, Russia, 1895; d. Copenhagen, Denmark, 1957*), organic chemist. Immigrated to the U.S. in 1907. Graduated from the University of Chicago, Ph.D., 1919. Taught at the University of Maryland, 1922–28, and at the University of Chicago, 1928–57. A pioneer in the study of free-radical chemistry, he contributed significantly to the development of synthetic rubber and to the plastics industry. Elected to the National Academy of Sciences in 1946. A founder of the *Journal of Organic Chemistry*.

KIAM, OMAR (*b. Monterrey, Mexico, 1894; d. New York, N.Y., 1954*), fashion designer. Designer of costumes for *Dinner at Eight* (1932) and *The Man Who Came to Dinner* (1939) on Broadway and for several movies, including *Wuthering Heights* (1939). Active in the New York fashion world under the label Reig-Kiam. His designs were exhibited at the Metropolitan Museum of Art in 1942 and 1945. Winner of an American Fashion Critics Award, 1946.

KICKING BIRD (*d. 1875*), Kiowa chief. Accepted reservation life in Oklahoma; kept most of his tribe at peace in south plains outbreaks, 1873–74.

KIDD, WILLIAM (*b. Greenock, Scotland, ca. 1645; d. London, England, 1701*), "Captain Kidd," the most celebrated pirate in English literature. A ship owner and sea captain in New York by 1690, Kidd rendered England and the colony useful service in the West Indies and elsewhere during King William's war with France. Since the war had precluded sending a man-of-war to protect East India Co. shipping in the Red Sea and the Indian Ocean, William III authorized the outfitting of a private expedition for the purpose, at the same time appointing the Earl of Bellomont governor of New England with special instructions to suppress piracy. Bellomont signed an agreement with Kidd on October 10, 1695, whereby Kidd accepted command of an expe- dition for which Bellomont undertook to raise four-fifths of the necessary investment; the net profits were to be similarly divided. Bellomont's partners were high-placed Whig members of British society; their names were kept from public knowledge. Kidd then obtained the 34-gun *Adventure Galley* and sailed for New York from Plymouth in April 1696; he filled out his crew in New York and began his mission against the pirates in September.

By spring he had reached the Comoro Islands, having avoided the pirate-infested eastern coast of Madagascar and without capturing a prize. Now, threatened by a mutinous crew, he became a pirate and determined to plunder the ships he had been sent to protect. After taking a few small vessels, he captured the rich Armenian merchantman *Quedagh Merchant* early in 1698. Scuttling his own ship, he continued his activities aboard the *Quedagh*; in September 1698, he left Madagascar for the West Indies, where he arrived in April 1699 and learned that he had been already proclaimed a pirate. Protesting his innocence, he went to Boston; after failing to convince Bellomont of his innocence, Kidd was sent to London. Tried and found guilty of murder and five instances of piracy on clear and weighty evidence, he was hanged and his property confiscated by the Crown.

KIDDER, ALFRED VINCENT (*b. Marquette, Mich., 1885; d. Cambridge, Mass., 1963*), archaeologist. Studied at Harvard (A.B., 1908; M.A., 1912; Ph.D., 1914), and in 1914 was curator of North American archaeology at the Peabody Museum. He was director of the Pecos excavation project in New Mexico, 1915–29. In 1926 joined the Carnegie Institution as a research associate and in 1929 became head of the division of historical research. Also served on the faculty of the Peabody Museum at Harvard, 1939–51. He retired from the Carnegie Institution in 1950. He was the foremost archaeologist of his time and published over 200 articles and books.

KIDDER, DANIEL PARISH (*b. South Pembroke, now Darien, N.Y., 1815; d. Evanston, Ill., 1891*), Methodist clergyman, educator. Organized the Sunday School work of his church; taught at Methodist seminaries.

KIDDER, FREDERIC (*b. New Ipswich, N.H., 1804; d. Melrose, Mass., 1885*), businessman, local historian.

KIEFT, WILLEM (*b. Amsterdam, Holland, 1597; d. in shipwreck on the Welsh coast, 1647*), fifth governor of New Netherland, 1637–45. On arriving at New Amsterdam, 1638, he assumed absolute control in order to reform the dilapidated colony, but his administration is principally noted for the cruel massacre of the Indians and their retaliatory destruction of outlying settlements. Between 1639 and 1644 there were only five months of peace. In 1642 he dissolved the Board of Twelve Men and prohibited public meetings. After the murder of eighty Indians in February 1643, the people elected a new Board which complained to the States-General in Holland. Peter Stuyvesant replaced Kieft.

KIENTPOOS. *See* CAPTAIN JACK.

KIER, SAMUEL M. (*b. Indiana Co., Pa., 1813; d. Pittsburgh, Pa., 1874*), industrialist, pioneer oil refiner. Owned and operated canal boats on the Pennsylvania State Canal; *post* 1850, developed refined oil by a distillation process for use as illuminant.

KILBOURNE, JAMES (*b. New Britain, Conn., 1770; d. Worthington, Ohio, 1850*), surveyor, Episcopal clergyman, Ohio pioneer. As congressman, introduced the first Homestead Bill, 1814; was early prominent as a Whig leader.

KILBY, CHRISTOPHER (*b. Boston, Mass., 1705; d. Dorking, England, 1771*), merchant, colonial agent.

KILDAHL, JOHAN NATHAN   (*b. Beitstaden, Norway, 1857; d. St. Paul, Minn., 1920*), Lutheran clergyman. Came to America as a boy. Worked to unite Lutheran bodies; became vice-president of United Norwegian Lutheran Church of America and professor of dogmatics at St. Paul Seminary.

KILGALLEN, DOROTHY MAE   (*b. Chicago, Ill., 1913; d. New York, N.Y., 1965*), newspaperwoman, television and radio personality. Began working for William Randolph Hearst's New York *Evening Journal* in 1931, quickly becoming a popular reporter. In 1938 she took over the syndicated gossip column "The Voice of Broadway." With her husband, Richard Tompkins Kollmar, she broadcast the "Breakfast with Dorothy and Dick" radio program, 1945–53. In 1950 Columbia Broadcasting System picked Kilgallen for the popular television program "What's My Line?"

KILGORE, HARLEY MARTIN   (*b. Brown, W. Va., 1893; d. Bethesda, Md., 1956*), politician, judge. Studied at West Virginia University, LL.B., 1914. Practiced law and was elected judge of the Raleigh County Criminal Court in 1938. Democratic senator from West Virginia, 1941–56. An ardent New Deal supporter, Kilgore was also a member of special investigating committees concerned with war mobilization and was instrumental in persuading Roosevelt to establish the Office of War Mobilization in 1943. Responsible for the establishment of the National Science Foundation in 1950. From 1955, chairman of the Senate Judiciary Committee and a ranking member of the Appropriations Committee.

KILMER, ALFRED JOYCE   (*b. New Brunswick, N.J., 1886; d. near Seringes, France, 1918*), poet, critic, soldier. Graduated Columbia, 1908. Author, among other works, of *Trees and Other Poems* (1914). Convert to Roman Catholicism, 1913. By death in battle, became for Americans a symbol of soldierly courage and poetic idealism.

KILPATRICK, HUGH JUDSON   (*b. near Deckertown, N.J., 1836; d. Santiago, Chile, 1881*), soldier, diplomat. Graduated West Point, 1861. Rose to major general in almost continuous brilliant service as Union cavalry commander in Civil War; initiated raid on Richmond to rescue captives from Libby Prison, 1863. U.S. minister to Chile, 1865–68 and 1881.

KILPATRICK, JOHN REED   (*b. New York, N.Y., 1889; d. New York, 1960*), sports executive. Studied at Yale University, B.A., 1911. A famous football player at Yale, Kilpatrick was named to the All-American Team in 1910 and 1911. During World War I, he served in France as the chief regulating officer of the Allied Expeditionary Force. Became a member of the board of directors of Madison Square Garden in 1927; president, 1933–55; chairman of the board from 1955. Lead the Garden through the troubles of the Great Depression by diversifying the activities of the arena which eventually included entertainment as well as major sports events.

KILPATRICK, WILLIAM HEARD   (*b. White Plains, Ga., 1871; d. New York, N.Y., 1965*), educator and theorist and philosopher of education. Studied at Mercer University (B.A., 1891; M.A., 1892) and Columbia (Ph.D., 1909). He taught in public schools, at Johns Hopkins, and at Mercer, where he served as acting president, 1904–06. At Columbia, 1909–38, he became a pioneer in progressive education, disdaining the fixed curriculum and advocating pupil-centered learning. He was involved in the creation of Bennington College, 1923, and chaired that school's board of trustees, 1931–38. He helped found the journal *Social Frontier* and served as president of the New York Urban League (1941–51), as chairman of the Bureau of Intercultural Education (1940–51) and of the American Youth for World Youth (1946–51), and was on the board of directors of the League for Industrial Democracy.

KILTY, WILLIAM   (*b. London, England, 1757; d. Annapolis, Md., 1821*), Revolutionary army surgeon, jurist. Came to America *ante* 1775. Compiled *The Laws of Maryland* (1799–1800) and supplementary works; was chancellor of Maryland, 1806–21.

KIMBALL, DAN ABLE   (*b. St. Louis, Mo., 1896; d. Washington, D.C., 1970*), business executive and secretary of the navy. Served in the army during World War I, then took a sales job with General Tire and Rubber Company, where he progressed through corporate ranks as Los Angeles area manager and then manager of the western region. During World War II became vice-president of General Tire and Rubber and executive vice-president and general manager of its subsidiary, Aerojet Engineering Corporation. Kimball was assistant secretary of the navy for air, 1949, undersecretary of the navy, 1949–51, and secretary of the navy, 1951–53. In 1953 he became president of Aerojet-General Corporation, becoming chairman before his retirement in 1969.

KIMBALL, DEXTER SIMPSON   (*b. New River, New Brunswick, 1865; d. Ithaca, N.Y., 1952*), mechanical engineer, educator. Graduated from Stanford University, 1896. Taught at Cornell University, 1898–1901, and 1904–36; dean of the college of engineering, 1920–36. Combining expertise in the practical elements of machine design and the newer scientific education and industrial management, Kimball soon became a leader in the new field of mechanical engineering. President of the American Society of Mechanical Engineers, 1921–22; vice president of the Federated American Engineering Societies, 1920–22. In 1942 he was appointed chief of the priority section, Machine Tool Division, of the War Production Board.

KIMBALL, GILMAN   (*b. New Chester, now Hill, N.H., 1804; d. 1892*), surgeon. Graduated Dartmouth, M.D., 1827; studied also in Paris. Practiced in Lowell, Mass., *post* 1830. A pioneer in difficult gynecological and traumatic surgery.

KIMBALL, HEBER CHASE   (*b. Sheldon, Vt., 1801; d. Utah, 1868*), Mormon leader. Joined the church, 1832; was ordained one of its twelve apostles, 1835; served as missionary in England and accompanied first migration to Utah, 1847. Was one of Brigham Young's chief counselors.

KIMBALL, NATHAN   (*b. Fredericksburg, Ind., 1823?; d. Ogden, Utah, 1898*), physician. Served in Mexican War. Colonel, 14th Indiana, in Civil War, he was promoted brigadier general after defeat of Stonewall Jackson at Kernstown, 1862; he won distinction also at Antietam, Fredericksburg, and Vicksburg, and commanded a division in Atlanta campaign. *Post* 1873, he served as surveyor general of Utah and postmaster of Ogden.

KIMBALL, RICHARD BURLEIGH   (*b. Plainfield, N.H., 1816; d. New York., N.Y., 1892*), lawyer, author. Founded Kimball, Texas; headed first Texas railroad, 1854–60.

KIMBALL, (SIDNEY) FISKE   (*b. Newton, Mass., 1888; d. Munich, Germany, 1955*), art historian, architect. Studied at Harvard and at the University of Michigan, Ph.D., 1915. As director of the Philadelphia Museum of Art, 1925–55, made the museum into one of the world's leading art institutions. Professor of art at the University of Virginia, 1919–23, where he established the department of architecture; professor and chairman of the department of fine arts at New York University, 1923–25. An expert on Jefferson, he published *Thomas Jefferson, Architect* (1916). Involved in the restoration of Colonial Williamsburg and Monticello; served on the advisory board for Rockefeller Center. Author of the definitive *The Creation of the Rococo* (1943).

KIMBALL, SUMNER INCREASE (*b. Lebanon, Maine, 1834; d. Washington, D.C., 1923*), lawyer, public official. Organizer of the U.S. lifesaving service; served as its general superintendent, 1878–1915.

KIMBALL, WILLIAM WIRT (*b. Paris, Maine, 1848; d. 1930*), naval officer. Graduated U.S. Naval Academy, 1869. A specialist in ordnance, he was a friend of John P. Holland and an early promoter of submarines; he commanded the first U.S. torpedo boat flotilla, 1897–98, and (as rear admiral) the Nicaragua Expedition, 1909–10.

KIMMEL, HUSBAND EDWARD (*b. Henderson, Ky., 1882; d. Groton, Conn., 1968*), naval officer. A graduate of the U.S. Naval Academy (1904), he attended the Naval War College for postgraduate instruction in ordnance. A distinguished career as a naval officer followed. In 1941 Kimmel was named commander in chief of the Pacific Fleet, stationed in Pearl Harbor. Following the Japanese attack on Pearl Harbor, he was relieved of command and subsequently found guilty of "dereliction of duty." He retired from the navy in 1942 and was hired by a marine consulting engineering firm in New York. He defended himself in a short book, *Admiral Kimmel's Story* (1955).

KING, ALBERT FREEMAN AFRICANUS (*b. Oxfordshire, England, 1841; d. Washington, D.C., 1914*), physician. Came to America as a boy. Graduated from National Medical College, Washington, D.C., 1861; M.D., University of Pennsylvania, 1865. Taught obstetrics at National Medical College, 1870–1914; pioneered in linking mosquito to malaria, 1882.

KING, ALEXANDER (*b. Vienna, Austria, 1900; d. New York, N.Y., 1965*), author, illustrator, editor, and raconteur. Immigrated to the United States in 1913, and at seventeen became a cartoonist on *The Big Stick*, a humorous Jewish weekly. He did sketches for the Socialist newspaper *Call* and sold a few covers to *Smart Set*. He also did book illustrations for publisher Horace Liveright. Later edited an erratically published magazine, *Americana*, 1932–33, was managing editor of *Stage* magazine, assistant editor of *Vanity Fair*, and associate editor of *Life*, 1937–40. Publication of his first book, *Mine Enemy Grows Older* (1958) was followed by an explosive appearance on the Jack Paar television show in 1959, in which he captivated the audience by a flow of witty, sardonic comments on a great range of topics. King later had his own television show in New York City, "Alex in Wonderland." His other books are *Alexander King Presents Peter Altenberg's Evocations of Love* (1960), *May This House Be Safe from Tigers* (1960), *I Should Have Kissed Her More* (1961), *The Great Ker-Plunk* (1962), *Is There Life After Birth?* (1963), and *Rich Man, Poor Man, Freud and Fruit* (1965).

KING, AUSTIN AUGUSTUS (*b. Sullivan Co., Tenn., 1802; d. St. Louis, Mo., 1870*), lawyer, jurist, Missouri legislator and congressman. Grandson of John Sevier. As ardent Jacksonian Democrat and member of Sen. Benton's wing of the party in Missouri, he served as governor, 1848–52.

KING, BASIL. *See* KING, WILLIAM BENJAMIN BASIL.

KING, CAROL WEISS (*b. New York, N.Y., 1895; d. New York, N.Y., 1952*), lawyer. Graduated from Barnard College (1916) and New York University Law School (1920). A staunch defender of immigrants and civil liberties law, King played a key role in numerous Supreme Court decisions, including the "Scottsboro Boys" trial, 1932. Organized the *International Judicial Association Bulletin* (1932), devoted to legal problems in labor, civil liberties, rights of blacks, and immigration.

KING, CHARLES (*b. New York, N.Y., 1879; d. Frascati, Italy, 1867*), merchant. Son of Rufus King (1755–1827); brother of James G. and John A. King. Editor, *New York American*, 1823–45; president of Columbia College, 1849–64. His administration marked the conscious beginning of Columbia University with the broadening of curriculum and addition of professional schools.

KING, CHARLES WILLIAM (*b. probably New York, N.Y., ca. 1809; d. at sea, 1845*), merchant. Grandson of Samuel King. Spent almost whole life *post* 1826 in Canton, China; visualized more clearly than any other contemporary American the significance and complicated relationships of Eastern Asia.

KING, CLARENCE (*b. Newport, R.I., 1842; d. Arizona, 1901*), geologist, mining engineer. Nephew of Charles W. King. Graduated Yale, 1862. Worked in Nevada and California in association with James T. Gardiner and W. H. Brewer, 1863–66. His survey of an area about 100 miles in width over the Cordilleran ranges from eastern Colorado to the California boundary line was undertaken between 1867 and 1877. His 7-volume *Report of the Geological Exploration of the Fortieth Parallel* (1870–80) reached perhaps the highest standard yet attained by government publications. He introduced into mapping the system of denoting topography by contour lines and extensively used the laboratory in the solution of geophysical problems. In 1878 Congress combined all the western surveys in a U.S. Geological Survey under King. After organizing the new survey, he resigned in 1881 and entered private engineering practice. His close friends included Henry Adams, John Hay, John La Farge, and William Dean Howells. His literary gifts were displayed in his book of sketches *Mountaineering in the Sierra Nevada* (1872).

KING, DAN (*b. Mansfield, Conn., 1791; d. 1864*), physician, pamphleteer. Prominent in the Rhode Island suffrage movement *ca.* 1837–41. Author of *The Life and Times of Thomas Wilson Dorr* (1859).

KING, EDWARD LEONARD (*b. Bridgewater, Mass., 1873; d. Fort McPherson, Ga., 1933*), soldier. Graduated West Point, 1896. Distinguished in the Philippines and in World War I; active in army school system, commanding at Cavalry School and at General Staff School.

KING, EDWARD SKINNER (*b. Liverpool, N.Y., 1861; d. 1931*), astronomer. Graduated Hamilton, 1887. Associated with the Harvard Observatory, 1887–1931; author of *Photographic Photometry* (1912) and *Manual of Celestial Photography* (1931).

KING, EDWARD SMITH (*b. Middlefield, Mass., 1848; d. 1896*), journalist, foreign and war correspondent. Author, among other books, of *The Great South* (1875); literary discoverer of George W. Cable.

KING, ERNEST JOSEPH (*b. Lorain, Ohio, 1878; d. Portsmouth, N.H., 1956*), naval officer. Graduated from the U.S. Naval Academy, 1901. Began his study of submarines and submarine warfare, 1922. Commander of the submarine base in New London, 1923–26; chief of the Bureau of Aeronautics, 1933–36. Appointed commander in chief of the Atlantic Fleet with the rank of admiral (1941), commander in chief of the U.S. Fleet (1941), and chief of naval operations (1942). Participated in conferences held in Washington (1942); at Casablanca, Washington, Quebec, Cairo, and Teheran (1943); and at Malta, Yalta, and Potsdam (1945). Retired from active duty in 1945.

KING, FRANKLIN HIRAM (*b. near Whitewater, Wis., 1848; d. 1911*), agricultural scientist, educator. Devised the round silo; was author of various works on soils and ventilation, and of *Farmers of*

Forty Centuries (1911), the best account of soil management in the Orient.

KING, GRACE ELIZABETH (*b. New Orleans, La., 1851; d. 1932*), author of fiction and historical studies on creole and southern themes which include *Monsieur Motte* (1888) and *Balcony Stories* (1893).

KING, HENRY (*b. Salem, Ohio, 1842; d. 1915*), journalist, Union soldier. As editor of the *St. Louis Globe-Democrat*, 1897–1915, made it a great conservative force in American journalism.

KING, HENRY CHURCHILL (*b. Hillsdale, Mich., 1858; d. Oberlin, Ohio, 1934*), theologian. President of Oberlin College, 1903–27.

KING, HENRY MELVILLE (*b. Oxford, Maine, 1838; d. 1919*), Baptist clergyman. Pastor in Roxbury, Mass., Albany, N.Y., and Providence, R.I.; was eminent in his denomination's educational and missionary fields.

KING, HORATIO (*b. Paris, Maine, 1811; d. Washington, D.C., 1897*), editor, lawyer, postal official.

KING, JAMES GORE (*b. New York, N.Y., 1791; d. 1853*), financier, railroad president. Son of Rufus King (1755–1827); brother of Charles and John A. King. Associated with firm of Prime, Ward and King, New York bankers, *post* 1824. Secured British loan of specie for relief of panic of 1837.

KING, JOHN (*b. New York, N.Y., 1813; d. North Bend, Ohio, 1893*), physician. A founder of the eclectic school of medicine; author of *The American Dispensatory* (1852) and other works.

KING, JOHN ALSOP (*b. New York, N.Y., 1788; d. Jamaica, N.Y., 1867*), lawyer, farmer. Son of Rufus King (1755–1827); brother of Charles and James G. King. As a politician, was allied in turn with the Democrats, Anti-Masons, National Republicans, Whigs, and Republicans; served as New York legislator, congressman, and as Republican governor, 1857–59.

KING, JOHN PENDLETON (*b. near Glasgow, Ky., 1799; d. Summerville, Ga., 1888*), lawyer. Removed to Georgia *ca.* 1817; served as U.S. senator, Democrat, 1833–37. As cotton manufacturer and railroad president, was one of the constructive industrial leaders in the antebellum South.

KING, JONAS (*b. near Hawley, Mass., 1792; d. 1869*), Congregational clergyman. Conducted a mission in Greece *post* 1830.

KING, MARTIN LUTHER, JR. (*b. Atlanta, Ga., 1929; d. Memphis, Tenn., 1968*), Baptist minister and civil rights leader. A gifted child, King entered Atlanta's Morehouse College at fifteen, thinking he might become a physician or a lawyer. In 1947, however, he was ordained as a minister and was made assistant pastor of Atlanta's Ebenezer Baptist Church, where his father was pastor. Graduating from Morehouse in 1948, he attended Crozer Theological Seminary (B.A., 1951). At Crozer, King was influenced by the writings of Social Gospeler Walter Rauschenbusch and became an ardent disciple of Gandhi, whose teachings about nonviolent resistance and redemptive love became the foundations of King's own philosophy. He earned a Ph.D. in systematic theology from Boston University in 1955.

While serving as pastor of Dexter Avenue Baptist Church in Montgomery, Ala., in 1955, King became the leader of a boycott by blacks of Montgomery's segregated city buses. During this campaign he sharpened his nonviolent strategy and discovered his extraordinary oratorical powers. The boycotters won a resounding moral victory in 1956 when the U.S. Supreme Court nullified the Alabama laws that enforced segregated buses.

In 1957 King and 115 other black leaders met in Montgomery and formed the Southern Christian Leadership Conference (SCLC), with King as its presiding and guiding spirit. King's *Stride Toward Freedom: The Montgomery Story* (1958) was widely read and acclaimed. Following a pilgrimage to India in 1959, King moved to Atlanta in 1960 so that he could devote most of his time to the SCLC and civil rights. He also served as copastor of his father's Ebenezer Baptist Church. In 1960 he helped a group of southern black students to form the Student Nonviolent Coordinating Committee (SNCC). Through 1961 and 1962 King pressured the Kennedy administration to support a tough civil rights bill. Campaigns in Albany, Ga., and Birmingham, Ala., helped produce the 1964 Civil Rights Act, which desegregated public facilities. In 1965 King launched a drive in Selma, Ala., in support of a federal voting rights law for blacks. The Selma campaign culminated in a mass march to Montgomery, the state capital. Later that year Congress passed the Voting Rights Act, which outlawed impediments to black voting and empowered the attorney general to supervise federal elections in seven southern states where blacks were kept from the polls.

In 1963, the director of the Federal Bureau of Investigation, J. Edgar Hoover, learned of King's sexual indiscretions and claimed that King was a hypocrite and a dangerous subversive under Communist influence. Under Hoover's orders, FBI agents conducted a ruthless secret crusade to discredit King. They tapped his and SCLC's telephones, planted microphones in hotel rooms, and circulated malicious statements to journalists. But in August 1963, standing before the Lincoln Memorial, King electrified an interracial crowd of 250,000 with perhaps his greatest speech, "I Have a Dream." In 1964, he won the Nobel Peace Prize.

As a champion of world peace, King first condemned the Vietnam War in 1965, and by 1967 he was devoting entire speeches to denunciations of the conflict. His teachings came under fire by young militants in SNCC, the Congress of Racial Equality (CORE), and Malcolm X, who advocated "black power," but King responded by reaffirming his commitment to nonviolence. In 1968 he worked out a plan for a Poor People's Campaign, in which SCLC would lead an interracial army of poor people to Washington to dramatize poverty. In the midst of his preparations, King went to Memphis, Tenn., to help striking black sanitation workers. There, at the Lorraine Motel, he was assassinated by James Earl Ray.

KING, PRESTON (*b. Ogdensburg, N.Y., 1806; d. New York, N.Y., 1865*), lawyer, politician, New York legislator. Congressman, Democrat, 1843–47, and Free Soiler, 1849–53; U.S. senator, Republican, 1857–63. An important figure in the Republican party organization *post* 1856.

KING, RICHARD (*b. Orange Co., N.Y., 1825; d. 1885*), steamboat captain. Founded the King Ranch in Nueces Co., Texas, 1852. The original tract of 75,000 acres had grown to more than half a million at the time of his death.

KING, RUFUS (*b. Scarboro, Maine, 1755; d. Jamaica, N.Y., 1827*), lawyer, Federalist statesman. Father of Charles, James G., and John A. King. Graduated Harvard, 1777; studied law under Theophilus Parsons at Newburyport, Mass., where he practiced *post* 1780. As a Massachusetts congressman, 1784–86, he renewed Jefferson's original suggestion prohibiting slavery in the Northwest Territory; his motion was later incorporated in the Ordinance of 1787. Probably the most eloquent orator in the Constitutional Convention, he urged a vigorous central government and contributed powerfully to the Constitution's ratification by Massachusetts.

Having married Mary Alsop, the daughter of a wealthy New York merchant, King moved to that city *ca.* 1786, was elected to the N.Y. Assembly and was chosen by the legislature to serve as U.S. senator, 1789. He became the ablest Federalist in the Senate, upholding Alexander Hamilton in all his financial measures, earnestly defending Jay's 1794 Treaty with England, and winning reelection to the Senate, 1795. Hamilton recommended him in 1796 to succeed Thomas Pinckney as U.S. minister to Great Britain. Said to have been one of the most effective representatives the United States ever had at London, he remained there until relieved at his own request in 1803. Federalist candidate for vice president, 1804, he retired to Jamaica, Long Island, after his defeat, but ran unsuccessfully a second time with C. C. Pinckney in 1808. Opposed like all his party to the War of 1812, he returned to the U.S. Senate in 1813 to become opposition leader; later he supported measures for defense. In 1816 he was the last Federalist candidate for president. Reelected to the U.S. Senate in 1820, he worked to secure a halt to further extension of slavery and proposed a plan for emancipation and resettlement of blacks. Declining reelection at the end of his term, he was prevailed upon by President John Quincy Adams to become minister to Great Britain once again. Shortly after his arrival in Liverpool, 1825, however, he became ill. Returning home, he died within a year.

KING, RUFUS (*b. New York, N.Y., 1814; d. 1876*), soldier, editor, diplomat. Son of Charles King; grandson of Rufus King (1755–1827). Graduated West Point, 1833. Edited *Milwaukee* (Wis.) *Sentinel*, 1845–61; was one of first regents, University of Wisconsin. Organized famous "Iron Brigade," 1861; commanded a Union division, 1862; resigned from army because of illness, 1863. U.S. minister to Papal States 1863–67.

KING, SAMUEL (*b. Newport, R.I., 1748; d. Newport, 1819*), portrait painter, maker of nautical instruments, teacher of art.

KING, SAMUEL ARCHER (*b. Tinicum, Pa., 1828; d. Philadelphia, Pa., 1914*), aeronaut. Made first balloon ascent, Philadelphia, 1851; labored to prove feasibility of Atlantic crossing by balloon.

KING, SAMUEL WARD (*b. Johnston, R.I., 1786; d. 1851*), physician. As Whig governor of Rhode Island, 1840–43, played colorless role in suppression of the so-called Dorr's Rebellion.

KING, STANLEY (*b. Troy, N.Y., 1883; d. Gay Head, Martha's Vineyard, Mass., 1951*), industrialist, college president. Studied at Amherst College and Harvard Law School, M.A., 1906. Affiliated with the International Shoe Co. before becoming president of Amherst College, 1932–46. During his presidency, the college expanded its endowment and physical plant.

KING, THOMAS BUTLER (*b. Palmer, Mass., 1800; d. Waresboro, Ga., 1864*), lawyer, planter, Georgia legislator. Nephew of Zebulon Butler. Settled in Georgia, 1823. Congressman, Whig, 1839–43, 1845–49. U.S. collector at San Francisco, Calif., 1851–52.

KING, THOMAS STARR (*b. New York, N.Y., 1824; d. 1864*), Unitarian clergyman, lyceum lecturer. Pastor in Charlestown and Boston, Mass., 1846–60; in San Francisco, Calif., 1860–64. His eloquence is credited as a prime factor in keeping California loyal to the Union.

KING, WILLIAM (*b. Scarboro, Maine, 1768; d. 1852*), ship owner, Maine legislator. Half brother of Rufus King (1755–1827). *Post* 1800, a resident of Bath, Maine, he amassed a large fortune, was a leader in the movement for separation of Maine from Massachusetts, and served as Maine's first governor, 1820–21.

KING, WILLIAM BENJAMIN BASIL (*b. Charlottetown, P.E.I., Canada, 1859; d. Cambridge, Mass., 1928*), Episcopal clergyman, popular novelist. Rector in Canada and at Christ Church, Cambridge, Mass., 1892–1900; author thereafter of some twenty novels and the widely read *The Conquest of Fear* (1921).

KING, WILLIAM RUFUS DEVANE (*b. Sampson Co., N.C., 1786; d. Dallas Co., Ala., 1853*), planter, statesman. Congressman, (Democrat) Republican, from North Carolina, 1811–16; U.S. senator, Democrat, from Alabama, 1820–44; an ardent follower of Andrew Jackson. After competent service as U.S. minister to France, 1844–46, King returned to the Senate in 1848; he resigned in 1852 after election as vice president of the United States.

KING OF WILLIAM, JAMES (*b. Georgetown, D.C., 1822; d. San Francisco, Calif., 1856*), journalist. Removed to California, 1848; prospered as a San Francisco banker, 1849–53; served as executive member, first Vigilante committee. As editor-publisher of the *Evening Bulletin* after Oct. 8, 1855, King attacked in blistering language and by name the corrupt elements in the city's business and political life. His murder by J. P. Casey on May 14, 1856, brought about the revival of the Vigilantes.

KINGSBURY, ALBERT (*b. near Morris, Ill., 1862; d. Greenwich, Conn., 1943*), mechanical engineer. Attended present University of Akron and Ohio State University in intervals of work as machinist; graduated with M.E. degree from Cornell University, 1889. Taught mechanical engineering at present University of New Hampshire, and was professor of applied mechanics at Worcester (Mass.) Polytechnic Institute; worked with the Westinghouse Company, 1903–14; was an independent consultant, 1914–17; thereafter was president of the Kingsbury Machine Works. He was the inventor and developer of the tilting-pad thrust bearing (patent applied for in 1907; issued after a controversy over priority, 1910), which won general acceptance for hydroelectric turbines and generators *post* 1912, and was adopted by the U.S. Navy for use on propeller shafts, 1917.

KINGSBURY, JOHN (*b. South Coventry, Conn., 1801; d. 1874*), educator. Graduated Brown, 1826. Principal of an innovating girl's high school in Providence, R.I., 1828–59; active also in improvement of Rhode Island public schools. President, Washington Insurance Co., Providence, R.I., *post* 1859.

KINGSFORD, THOMAS (*b. Wickham, Kent, England, 1799; d. Oswego, N.Y., 1869*), inventor, manufacturer. Came to America, 1831; became superintendent of starch factory. Perfected process for producing cornstarch, 1842; produced it for food purposes, 1850.

KINGSLEY, CALVIN (*b. Annsville, N.Y., 1812; d. Beirut, Syria, 1870*), Methodist bishop, educator.

KINGSLEY, DARWIN PEARL (*b. near Alburg, Vt., 1857; d. 1932*), insurance executive. President of New York Life Insurance Co., 1907–30.

KINGSLEY, ELBRIDGE (*b. Carthage, Ohio, 1842; d. Brooklyn, N.Y., 1918*), wood engraver, landscape painter.

KINGSLEY, ELIZABETH SEELMAN (*b. Brooklyn, N.Y., 1871; d. New York, N.Y., 1957*), inventor of the Double-Crostic puzzle. Graduated from Wellesley College and New York University, M.A., 1905. Invented the Double-Crostic in the early 1930's; the puzzles were popularized in the *Saturday Review* from 1934 and later in the *New York Times Magazine*.

KINGSLEY, JAMES LUCE (*b. Scotland, Conn., 1778; d. 1852*), educator. Graduated Yale, 1799. First professor of languages at Yale, appointed 1805 and serving until 1851; *post* 1835, devoted himself exclusively to Latin.

KINGSLEY, NORMAN WILLIAM (*b. Stockholm, N.Y., 1829; d. Warren Point, N.J., 1913*), dentist. Practiced in New York, N.Y., *post* 1852. *Post* 1858, specialized in oral deformities. Perfected gold obturator and soft-rubber artificial velum for cleft palates; author of *A Treatise on Oral Deformities* (1880), for many years the standard textbook on orthodontia.

KINKEAD, EDGAR BENTON (*b. Beverly, Ohio, 1863; d. Atlanta, Ga., 1930*), jurist. Judge, common pleas court of Ohio, 1908–30; a prolific writer on legal subjects, particularly in field of procedure; professor of law, Ohio State University.

KINLOCH, CLELAND (*b. Charleston, S.C., 1760; d. "Acton" in High Hills of Santee, 1823*), rice planter. Among first to adopt Dupont system of flooding rice fields by tidal movement; built and improved one of the first tidal rice-pounding mills.

KINLOCH, ROBERT ALEXANDER (*b. Charleston, S.C., 1826; d. Charleston, 1891*), surgeon, teacher of surgery at Medical College of South Carolina.

KINNE, LA VEGA GEORGE (*b. Syracuse, N.Y., 1846; d. Des Moines, Iowa, 1906*), Iowa jurist, teacher of law, and Democratic political leader.

KINNERSLEY, EBENEZER (*b. Gloucester, England, 1711; d. Philadelphia, Pa., 1778*), Baptist clergyman, educator. Came to America as a child. Raised in Lower Dublin, Pa., he was educated by his father. His experiments in electricity were second in importance only to Franklin's; he published a syllabus of his lectures on the subject in 1764 as *A Course of Experiments in . . . Electricity* and was the inventor of an electrical air thermometer. He taught English and oratory in the College of Philadelphia, 1753–73.

KINNEY, ELIZABETH CLEMENTINE DODGE STEDMAN (*b. New York, N.Y., 1810; d. 1889*), poet, essayist. Daughter of David L. Dodge; mother by her first marriage of Edmund C. Stedman; married William B. Kinney, 1841.

KINNEY, WILLIAM BURNETT (*b. Speedwell, N.J., 1799; d. New York, N.Y., 1880*), journalist, diplomat. Literary adviser, Harper and Bros., 1825–35; editor, Newark, N.J., *Daily Advertiser*; U.S. chargé d'affaires at Turin, Italy, 1850–53. Resided thereafter in Turin and Florence until 1865 when he returned to America. Associate of the Browning circle at Florence.

KINNICUTT, LEONARD PARKER (*b. Worcester, Mass., 1854; d. Worcester, 1911*), chemist, educator. Graduated Massachusetts Institute of Technology, 1875; studied under Bunsen at Heidelberg and specialized in organic chemistry at Bonn. Taught at Worcester Polytechnic *post* 1882; was authority on sewage disposal and sanitation of air, water, and gas.

KINO, EUSEBIO FRANCISCO (*b. Segno, Italy, ca. 1645; d. Magdalena River Mission, Mexico, 1711*), Jesuit missionary, explorer, cartographer. Entered Jesuit order at Freiburg, 1665; assigned to Mexican missions, 1678; arrived in Vera Cruz, 1681. After early experience in Lower California, 1683–85, Kino worked in present northern Sonora and southern Arizona. Between 1687 and 1711, from headquarters at Mission Dolores, he founded missions in the San Miguel, Magdalena, Altar, Sonóita, Santa Cruz, and San Pedro river valleys. On his missionary journeys he discovered and wrote the first description of the Casa Grande; as a result of two expeditions which he made to the lower Colorado River, he determined that California was a peninsula and not an island. His autobiography appears in *Kino's Historical Memoir of Pimería Alta* (edited by H. E. Bolton, 1919).

KINSELLA, THOMAS (*b. Co. Wexford, Ireland, 1832; d. Brooklyn, N.Y., 1884*), journalist. Came to America, 1849. Editor, *Brooklyn Daily Eagle*, 1861–84; helped organize Liberal Republican movement, 1871–72.

KINSEY, ALFRED CHARLES (*b. Hoboken, N.J., 1894; d. Bloomington, Ind., 1956*), entomologist, researcher in human sexual behavior. Graduated from Bowdoin College and Harvard, Sc.D., 1920. Taught Zoology at Indiana University from 1920 until his death. An expert on the gall wasp, Kinsey published *The Gall Wasp Genus Cynips* (1930) before turning to the field of sexual research. Working through the auspices of the university and obtaining grants, Kinsey formed the Institute for Sexual Research in 1947; published *Sexual Behavior in the Human Male* (1948) and *Sexual Behavior in the Human Female* (1953). Both works were controversial but were gradually accepted as landmarks in the field of social research. Kinsey was the first to use the interview method as a source of information on sexuality.

KINSEY, JOHN (*b. Burlington, N.J., 1693; d. Burlington, 1750, o.s.*), lawyer, New Jersey and Pennsylvania legislator. Chief justice, supreme court of Pennsylvania, 1743–50; leader of the Quaker party in Pennsylvania Assembly; prepared first compilation of New Jersey laws, 1732.

KINTPUASH. *See* CAPTAIN JACK.

KINZIE, JOHN (*b. Quebec, Canada, 1763; d. Chicago, Ill., 1828*), fur trader. Changed name from McKenzie. Traded on Maumee and St. Joseph rivers *post* 1781; removed to site of present Chicago, 1804.

KIP, WILLIAM INGRAHAM (*b. New York, N.Y., 1811; d. 1893*), Episcopal clergyman, author. Graduated Yale, 1831; General Theological Seminary, New York, 1835. Consecrated missionary bishop of California, 1853, he accepted the election of the diocese, 1857, and served until his death. As rector of Grace Church, San Francisco, 1862, he established it as his cathedral, the first cathedral of the Episcopal Church in America.

KIPHUTH, ROBERT JOHN HERMAN (*b. Tonawanda, N.Y., 1890; d. New Haven, Conn., 1967*), swimming coach and physical educator. Studied physical education at Silver Bay, N.Y., (1911), Harvard (1912), and Buffalo (1913–16). At Yale, he became a physical education instructor (1914), swimming coach (1917), and varsity swimming coach (1918). He became an assistant professor at Yale (1932), associate professor and director of the Payne Whitney Gymnasium (1940), and athletic director (1946). A regular coach of the U.S. Olympic swimming team, Kiphuth's greatest Olympic achievement came in London in 1948, when the U.S. men's team took first place in all six swimming and both diving events. He is considered the greatest swimming coach in history. In forty-two years at Yale his squads won 528 dual meets while losing only 12. He wrote *The Diagnosis and Treatment of Postural Defects* (with Dr. Winthrop Phelps, 1932), *How to Be Fit* (1942), and *Basic Swimming* (with Harry M. Burke, 1950).

KIPLINGER, WILLARD MONROE (*b. Bellefontaine, Ohio, 1891; d. Bethesda, Md., 1967*), journalist and publisher. A graduate of Ohio State (1912), he worked for the Columbus *Ohio State Journal*, then joined the Associated Press. He was a member of the AP Washington bureau, 1916–19, and then worked for New York's National Bank of Commerce, 1920–23. In 1923 he launched the *Kiplinger Washington Letter* and later added *Tax Letter* (1925), *Agricultural Letter* (1929), *Florida Letter* (1956), and *California Letter* (1965) to his news empire. In 1947 Kiplinger founded the monthly magazine *Changing Times*. His books include *Inflation Ahead!* (1935), *Washington Is Like That* (1942),

Kiplinger Looks to the Future (1958), and *Kiplinger Sees Prosperity Ahead* (1959).

KIRBY, EPHRAIM (*b. Litchfield Co., Conn., 1757; d. Fort Stoddart, Mississippi Territory, 1804*), lawyer, law reporter, Revolutionary soldier, Connecticut legislator. Edited *Reports of Cases Adjudged in the Superior Court and Court of Errors of the State of Connecticut, 1785–1788* (1789), the first fully developed volume of law reports to be published in the United States.

KIRBY, GEORGE HUGHES (*b. Goldsboro, N.C., 1875; d. 1935*), psychiatrist. M.D., Long Island College Medical School, 1899. Director of New York State Psychiatric Institute, 1917–31.

KIRBY, J. HUDSON (*b. off Sandy Hook, aboard ship as his parents were immigrating to America, 1819; d. London, England, 1848*), actor. Made debut at Walnut Street Theatre, Philadelphia, *ca.* 1837. A favorite of the gallery gods at the Bowery and Chatham Theatres, New York City, for his strenuous style; origin of the slogan, "Wake me up when Kirby dies."

KIRBY, ROLLIN (*b. Galva, Ill., 1875; d. New York, N.Y., 1952*), cartoonist, illustrator. Studied in the N.Y. Art Students League and in Paris. Famed political and social cartoonist for the *New York World*, 1913–31. Won three Pulitzer Prizes for his cartoons in 1922, 1924, 1928. Work exhibited at the Museum of the City of New York, 1944.

KIRBY-SMITH, EDMUND (*b. St. Augustine, Fla., 1824; d. Sewanee, Tenn., 1893*), Confederate soldier, educator. Grandson of Ephraim Kirby. Graduated West Point, 1845; fought under Taylor and Scott in Mexican War. After teaching mathematics at West Point and service on the frontier, he resigned on the secession of Florida. Commissioned Confederate colonel of cavalry, 1861, he was promoted brigadier general in June, was wounded at first Bull Run, and as major general commanded a division under Beauregard. After the campaign for Nashville, 1862, where he acted with Bragg's force, cleared Cumberland Gap and occupied Lexington, Ky., he was made lieutenant general. In February 1863, he took command of the Trans-Mississippi Department. Cut off after the fall of Vicksburg, he became virtual civil and military ruler of the area, administering it ably and repelling Union efforts at invasion. Promoted general, 1864, he surrendered the Confederacy's last military force on June 2, 1865. He became president of University of Nashville, 1870; *post* 1875, he taught mathematics at University of the South.

KIRCHHOFF, CHARLES WILLIAM HENRY (*b. San Francisco, Calif., 1853; d. near Asbury Park, N.J., 1916*), mining engineer, metallurgist. Chief editor, *Iron Age*, 1889–1910; made it the recognized authority on the American iron and steel industry.

KIRCHMAYER, JOHN (*b. Bavaria, ca. 1860; d. Cambridge, Mass., 1930*), wood carver. Came to America *ca.* 1895. An outstanding artist and craftsman, patronized by Stanford White, Ralph A. Cram, and other architects.

KIRCHWEY, GEORGE WASHINGTON (*b. Detroit, Mich., 1855; d. New York, N.Y., 1942*), law educator, criminologist, penologist. B.A., Yale, 1879; studied law at Yale and at Albany (N.Y.) Law School. After a period of practice, he taught at and was dean of the Albany Law school; removing to New York City, he was professor of law at Columbia University Law School, 1891–1916, serving also as dean, 1901–10. He was head of the department of criminology at the New York School of Social Work, 1918–32. Devoted to penal reform and an opponent of capital punishment, he helped establish the study of criminology in the United States as a scientific discipline and was a constant advocate of methods of penal treatment based on rehabilitative care rather than deterrence.

KIRK, ALAN GOODRICH (*b. Philadelphia, Pa., 1888; d. New York, N.Y., 1963*), naval officer and diplomat. A graduate of the U.S. Naval Academy (1909), he became a career officer, retiring in 1946 with the rank of full admiral. He commanded the U.S. Naval Task Force during the assault on the Normandy beaches in June 1944. His first diplomatic assignment was in 1939 as naval attaché at the American embassy in London. He was U.S. ambassador to Belgium and minister to Luxembourg (1946–49) and ambassador to the Soviet Union (1949–51) and Nationalist China (1962–63).

KIRK, EDWARD NORRIS (*b. New York, N.Y., 1802; d. Boston, Mass., 1874*), clergyman, revivalist. Pastor of Presbyterian and Congregational churches in New York and Massachusetts; at Mount Vernon Church, Boston, *post* 1842.

KIRK, JOHN FOSTER (*b. Fredericton, N.B., Canada, 1824; d. 1904*), author, editor. Secretary and research assistant to William H. Prescott, 1848–59. Kirk's *History of Charles the Bold* (1864–68) won high praise from contemporaries; he served as editor of *Lippincott's Magazine*, 1870–86, and helped prepare *Lippincott's New Dictionary*.

KIRK, NORMAN THOMAS (*b. Rising Sun, Md., 1888; d. Washington, D.C., 1960*), surgeon. Received M.D. from the University of Maryland in 1910. An army doctor, Kirk specialized in bone and joint surgery, serving in the Philippines and various army hospitals in the U.S. Became head of the surgical service at Walter Reed Hospital, 1941; appointed surgeon general of the Army in 1943. During World War II, Kirk was credited with reducing the fatality rate of wounded soldiers to half that of World War I. Other accomplishments include preventive medicine measures and the development of convalescent programs. Retired a major general in 1947.

KIRKBRIDE, THOMAS STORY (*b. Pennsylvania shore of Delaware River opposite Trenton, N.J., 1809; d. 1883*), physician, psychiatrist. M.D., University of Pennsylvania, 1832. Made major contributions as superintendent, Pennsylvania Hospital for the Insane, 1840–83.

KIRKLAND, CAROLINE MATILDA STANSBURY (*b. New York, N.Y., 1801; d. New York, 1864*), author. Granddaughter of Joseph Stansbury. A resident on the Midwest frontier *ca.* 1831–43, she wrote vivid sketches of the pioneers in *A New Home—Who'll Follow* (1839, under pseudonym of Mrs. Mary Clavers) and *Forest Life* (1842). Her later works were commonplace.

KIRKLAND, JAMES HAMPTON (*b. Spartanburg, S.C., 1859; d. Magnetawan, Canada, 1939*), educator. Ph.D., Leipzig, 1885. Chancellor, Vanderbilt University, 1893–1937.

KIRKLAND, JOHN THORNTON (*b. near Little Falls, N.Y., 1770; d. Boston, Mass., 1840*), Congregationalist and Unitarian clergyman. Son of Samuel Kirkland. Graduated Harvard, 1789. As president of Harvard, 1810–28, he gave the college a university status during an administration known as Harvard's "Augustan Age"; introduced lecture method and the first electives. A man of broad culture, he was one of the founders of the *Monthly Anthology* and the Boston Athenaeum.

KIRKLAND, JOSEPH (*b. Geneva, N.Y., 1830; d. 1894*), Chicago businessman, lawyer, writer. Son of Caroline M. S. Kirkland. A factor in development of realism in American fiction. Author of, among other works, *Zury* (1885); *The McVeys* (1888); *The Captain of Company K* (1891).

KIRKLAND, SAMUEL (*b. Norwich, Conn., 1741; d. 1808*), Congregationalist clergyman. Father of John T. Kirkland. Missionary to the Senecas, 1764–66; to the Oneidas, 1766–1808. Helped prevent Lord Dunmore's War (1774–75) from becoming a general Indian uprising. Through his efforts, the Oneidas and Tuscaroras remained neutral during the Revolution; Kirkland also served as chaplain at Fort Stanwix and to General Sullivan's expedition, 1779. After the Miamis' victory over St. Clair, 1791, Kirkland helped keep the Six Nations friendly to the United States. He obtained a charter for an academy (later Hamilton College) for the coeducation of white and Indian boys in 1793.

KIRKMAN, MARSHALL MONROE (*b. Morgan Co., Ill., 1842; d. Chicago, Ill., 1921*), railroad executive. Comptroller, Chicago and North Western R.R., 1881–1910; standardized railroad accounting; author of many pamphlets and books on all phases of the railroad business.

KIRKPATRICK, ANDREW (*b. Minebrook, N.J., 1756; d. New Brunswick, N.J., 1831*), jurist. Studied law in office of William Paterson. A judicial conservative, he was associate justice, New Jersey supreme court, 1798–1804, and chief justice, 1804–24.

KIRKWOOD, DANIEL (*b. Harford Co., Md., 1814; d. Riverside, Calif., 1895*), astronomer. Taught at Indiana University and Leland Stanford. Established connection between comets and meteors (1861, 1867, 1873) among many other contributions to mathematical astronomy.

KIRKWOOD, JOHN GAMBLE (*b. Gotebo, Okla., 1907; d. New Haven, Conn., 1959*), physical chemist. Studied at California Institute of Technology, the University of Chicago, and the Massachusetts Institute of Technology, Ph.D., 1929. Taught chemistry at Cornell University, 1934–37 and 1938–47; at California Institute of Technology, 1947–51; and at Yale University, 1951–59, where he was head of the chemistry department. An expert in the nature of intermolecular forces as affected by such internal factors as molecular shapes, distribution of electrical charges, and location of reactive centers, and by such external factors as temperature, pressure, and electrical environment.

KIRKWOOD, SAMUEL JORDAN (*b. Harford Co., Md., 1813; d. Iowa City, Iowa, 1894*), lawyer, miller. Settled in Iowa, *ca.* 1855. Republican governor of Iowa, 1859–63, 1875–77; U.S. senator, 1866–67, 1877–81; secretary of the interior, 1881–82. Crushed Iowa "Copperhead" movement, 1862–63.

KIRLIN, JOSEPH LOUIS JEROME (*b. Philadelphia, Pa., 1868; d. 1926*), Roman Catholic clergyman. Pastor in Philadelphia; author of devotional works and *Catholicity in Philadelphia* (1909), a diocesan history.

KIRSTEIN, LOUIS EDWARD (*b. Rochester, N.Y., 1867; d. Boston, Mass., 1942*), merchant, civic leader. After successful experience in the optical supply business and in clothing manufacturing, he joined Filene's, the Boston retail store, in 1912 as a manager (partner) and vice president; eventually, he was in charge of the entire merchandising operation of the firm. He served on numerous city, state, and national boards and commissions, was active in support of hospitals and welfare organizations, and a member of the visiting committee of the Harvard Business School.

KIRTLAND, JARED POTTER (*b. Wallingford, Conn., 1793; d. Rockport, Ohio, 1877*), physician, naturalist, Ohio legislator. A founder of Cleveland Medical College, 1843, and a member of its faculty until 1864. Made important studies of zoology of Ohio.

KISS, MAX (*b. Kisvárda, Hungary, 1882; d. Atlantic Beach, N.Y., 1967*), pharmacist and pharmaceutical manufacturer. Immigrated to New York City in 1897. He worked as a druggist and studied at the Columbia University College of Pharmacy (Ph.G., 1902). Kiss put phenolphthalein, whose laxative properties had only recently been discovered, into a pleasant-tasting chocolate tablet to create Ex-Lax. Incorporated in 1908, Ex-Lax went on to become the largest-selling laxative in the world, and Kiss went on to create a diversified pharmaceutical company.

KITCHIN, CLAUDE (*b. near Scotland Neck, N.C., 1869; d. Wilson, N.C., 1923*), lawyer. Brother of William W. Kitchin. Congressman, Democrat, from North Carolina, 1901–23; was reputed the most powerful debater in the House; chairman, ways and means committee and majority leader, 1915–19.

KITCHIN, WILLIAM WALTON (*b. near Scotland Neck, N.C., 1866; d. Scotland Neck, 1924*), lawyer. Brother of Claude Kitchin. Congressman, Democrat, from North Carolina, 1897–1909; governor of North Carolina, 1909–13. Antitrust and antimachine in politics, he worked to satisfy the economic needs of the common man.

KITTREDGE, GEORGE LYMAN (*b. Boston, Mass., 1860; Barnstable, Mass., 1941*), scholar, educator. Graduated Harvard, 1882. He had concentrated on the classics, especially Greek, but his career as teacher and scholar was determined by his courses with Francis James Child, Harvard's first professor of English. Graduating first in his class, Kittredge began graduate study, but lack of money forced him to give it up after a few months. In 1883 he became a teacher of Latin at Phillips Exeter Academy, where he remained, except for a year of study in Europe, until 1888. He returned to Harvard in 1888 as instructor in English. He became assistant professor in 1890 and professor in 1895; in 1917 he was named the first Gurney Professor of English Literature, a chair he held until his retirement in 1936.

Kittredge's first important book, *Observations on the Language of Chaucer's Troilus* (1894), was followed by *Chaucer and His Poetry* (1915), still one of the best criticisms and interpretations of Chaucer. From his study and teaching of medieval romance came *A Study of Gawain and the Green Knight* (1916). The history of witchcraft early drew his attention, and his investigations culminated in *Witchcraft in Old New England* (1929).

For generations of Harvard students, Kittredge and Shakespeare were synonymous, and it is for his work on Shakespeare that he remains best known. His *Shakespeare: An Address* (1916) stands beside the *Preface* of Dr. Johnson (whom Kittredge greatly admired) in its concise, trenchant, and sensible criticism. When his *Complete Works of Shakespeare* appeared in 1936, it contained the soundest text of the plays hitherto available.

The history and folklore of New England engaged Kittredge's attention in his *Old Farmer and His Almanack* (1904) to the more austere account of *Doctor Robert Child, the Remonstrant* (1919). With the classicist James B. Greenough, Kittredge wrote *Words and Their Ways in English Speech* (1901).

KITTSON, NORMAN WOLFRED (*b. Chambly, Canada, 1814; d. 1888*), fur trader. Associate of James J. Hill in Red River steamboating and in reorganization of St. Paul and Pacific R.R., 1878–79.

KLAUDER, CHARLES ZELLER (*b. Philadelphia, Pa., 1872; d. Philadelphia, 1938*), architect. Specialist in college architecture. Designed Dining Hall-Holder Hall group at Princeton, 1916, and University of Pittsburgh, 1934.

KLAW, MARC (*b. Paducah, Ky., 1858; d. Sussex, England, 1936*), theatrical booking agent, manager, producer. With his partner, Abraham L. Erlanger, and others, organized the Theatrical Syndicate *post* 1896.

KLEIN, AUGUST CLARENCE (*b. Jersey City, N.J., 1887; d. Montego Bay, Jamaica, 1948*), mechanical engineer. M.E., Stevens Institute of Technology, 1908. Associated *post* 1920 with Stone and Webster Engineering Corporation, he worked on the design and construction of major industrial power plants and chemical works. He is particularly remembered for his services as project engineer of the Manhattan Project's Oak Ridge plant, which had to be constructed even as ongoing research necessitated complicated alterations in design.

KLEIN, BRUNO OSCAR (*b. Osnabrück, Germany, 1858; d. 1911*), pianist, composer. Settled in New York, N.Y., 1884, after touring the U.S. in concert, 1878–83. Church organist and teacher of piano, he composed numerous works for piano and instrumental groups; also church music and an opera *Kenilworth*.

KLEIN, CHARLES (*b. London, England, 1867; d. aboard Lusitania, 1915*), dramatist. Came to America as actor, 1883. Author of *The Auctioneer* (1901), *The Music Master* (1904), *The Lion and the Mouse* (1905) and many other ephemeral plays concerned with contemporary life in the United States.

KLEIN, CHARLES HERBERT ("CHUCK") (*b. near Southport, Ind., 1904; d. Indianapolis, Ind., 1956*), baseball player. An outfielder, Klein began professional career in 1928 with the Philadelphia Phillies. He also played for the Chicago Cubs (1934–36) and the Pittsburgh Pirates (1936–44) before retiring with a .320 batting average, 2,076 hits, and 300 home runs in 1,753 games.

KLEIN, JOSEPH FREDERIC (*b. Paris, France, 1849; d. Bethlehem, Pa., 1918*), mechanical engineer. Came to America as a child. Graduated Sheffield Scientific School, Yale, 1871. Created and developed engineering school at Lehigh University *post* 1881.

KLEM, WILLIAM J. (BILL) (*b., Rochester, N.Y., 1874; d. Coral Gables, Fla., 1951*), baseball umpire. The first umpire elected to the National Baseball Hall of Fame in 1953, Klem was umpire for the National League from 1905 to 1940. He officiated in eighteen world series and contributed much to the rules and protocol of the game.

KLINE, FRANZ JOSEF (*b. Wilkes Barre, Pa., 1910; d. New York, N.Y., 1962*), painter. Studied at Boston University, the Boston Art Students League, and Heatherley's Art School in London. His first show was in 1942 at the National Academy's Annual Exhibition in New York City, and his first completely abstract work was *The Dancer* (1946). Along with Jackson Pollock and Willem de Kooning he was a quintessential "action painter" or abstract expressionist. His works include *Nijinsky* (1950), *Chief* (1950, *Mahoning* (1956), and the sixteen-foot-wide *1960 New Year's Eve Night Wall* (1960).

KLINE, GEORGE (*b. Germany, ca. 1757; d. Carlisle, Pa., 1820*), frontier newspaper editor and book publisher. Settled in Carlisle, 1785. In the same year, established *The Carlisle Gazette*, first newspaper in Pennsylvania published west of the Susquehanna River.

KLINGELSMITH, MARGARET CENTER (*b. Portland, Maine, 1859; d. 1931*), lawyer, author. Librarian, Biddle Law Library, University of Pennsylvania, 1899–1931.

KLIPPART, JOHN HANCOCK (*b. near Canton, Ohio, 1823; d. 1878*), agricultural writer. Secretary, Ohio State Board of Agriculture, 1856–78; edited its superior series of reports.

KLIPSTEIN, LOUIS FREDERICK (*b. Winchester, Va., 1813; d. Florida, 1878*), philologist. First American to publish works on Anglo-Saxon, including a *Grammar* (1848) and a number of texts.

KLOPSCH, LOUIS (*b. Lübben, Germany, 1852; d. 1910*), publisher, humanitarian. Came to America as a child. Prospered as manager of a press syndicate. As editor and proprietor of the *Christian Herald post* 1890, made the paper a medium of American bounty to the needy throughout the world.

KNAB, FREDERICK (*b. Würzburg, Bavaria, 1865; d. 1918*), landscape painter, entomologist. Came to America as a boy. Made important discoveries in biology of Northern mosquitoes; a coauthor of *The Mosquitoes of North and Central America and the West Indies* (1912–17).

KNABE, VALENTINE WILHELM LUDWIG (*b. Kreuzburg, Prussia, 1803; d. 1864*), piano manufacturer. Came to America, 1833. Established reputation as one of best pianomakers by 1860; virtually controlled antebellum piano business in the southern states from headquarters in Baltimore, Md.

KNAPP, BRADFORD (*b. Vinton, Iowa, 1870; d. Lubbock, Tex., 1938*), agriculturist, educator, lawyer. President, Oklahoma Agricultural and Mechanical College, 1923–28, Alabama Polytechnic Institute, 1928–32, Texas Technological College, 1932–38.

KNAPP, GEORGE (*b. Montgomery, N.Y., 1814; d. at sea, returning from Europe, 1883*), journalist. Raised in St. Louis, Mo. Worked on the *Missouri Republican, post* 1826, becoming one of its proprietors, 1837.

KNAPP, HERMAN (*b. near Wiesbaden, Germany, 1832; d. Mamaroneck, N.Y., 1911*), ophthalmologist. Graduated University of Giessen, M.D., 1854; was pupil of Helmholtz and later taught at Heidelberg. Resided and practiced in New York, N.Y., *post* 1868; taught at New York University and at College of Physicians and Surgeons, New York. Established Ophthalmic and Aural Institute which was his clinic; founded *Archives of Ophthalmology and Otology*.

KNAPP, JOSEPH PALMER (*b. Brooklyn, N.Y., 1864; d. New York, N.Y., 1951*), publisher, philanthropist. Studied briefly at Columbia University. Built a publishing empire that began with the American Lithographic Co., 1895, and which ultimately included the Crowell-Collier Publishing Company purchased in 1906. His publications included the *Associated Sunday Magazine, This Week* (which at his death had a circulation of over six million through syndication), *Collier's Weekly*, and *Woman's Home Companion*. Through the Knapp Foundation he contributed generously to projects in education and ecology.

KNAPP, MARTIN AUGUSTINE (*b. Spafford, N.Y., 1843; d. 1923*), lawyer. Practiced in Syracuse, N.Y.; specialized in transportation problems. Served on Interstate Commerce Commission, 1897–1916; was federal circuit judge assigned to Commerce Court, 1910–13, and U.S. circuit court of appeals justice thereafter.

KNAPP, PHILIP COOMBS (*b. Lynn, Mass., 1858; d. 1920*), neurologist. Graduated Harvard, 1878; Harvard Medical School, 1883. An American pioneer in his field, he published in 1891 the first U.S. treatise on the pathology, diagnosis, and treatment of brain tumors. He taught at Harvard, 1888–1913.

KNAPP, SAMUEL LORENZO (*b. Newburyport, Mass., 1783; d. Hopkinton, Mass., 1838*), lawyer, politician, writer. Author, among much ephemera, of *Lectures on American Literature* (1829), an early attempt to weigh critically the national literary output.

KNAPP, SEAMAN ASAHEL (*b. Schroon Lake, N.Y., 1833; d. Washington, D.C., 1911*), agriculturist, educator. Removed to

Iowa *ca.* 1867. Drafted first experiment-station bill, 1882 (introduced in Congress by C. C. Carpenter). Developed rice industry in the Southwest *post* 1886; inaugurated the Farmer's Cooperative Demonstration Work in the Department of Agriculture as part of fight against the boll weevil.

KNAPP, WILLIAM IRELAND (*b. Greenport, N.Y., 1835; d. Paris, France, 1908*), teacher, scholar. Graduated Colgate, 1860. Taught modern languages at Colgate, Vassar, Yale; first professor of Romance languages at University of Chicago, 1892–95. Was biographer and editor of George Borrow.

KNAPPEN, THEODORE TEMPLE (*b. Minneapolis, Minn., 1900; d. New York, N.Y., 1951*), civil and hydraulic engineer. Studied at the University of California, West Point (1920) and Rensselaer Polytechnic Institute. As a civilian member of the Corps of Engineers, 1928–37, Knappen was engineer for the federal Mississippi flood control project and the Muskingum flood control project in Ohio. Contributed to knowledge of soil mechanics and the building of levees. Founded the Knappen Engineering Co. (1942), which designed hydroelectric and irrigation projects throughout the world.

KNAUTH, OSWALD WHITMAN (*b. New York, N.Y., 1887; d. Beaufort, S.C., 1962*), economist and businessman. Studied at Harvard (A.B., 1909) and Columbia (Ph.D., 1913). He taught at Princeton, 1913–16, was an editorial writer for the *New York Evening Post*, and wrote for the *Dial* and the *Nation*. He founded the National Bureau of Economic Research, of which he was a staff member, 1919–22, director, and president. With R. H. Macy and Company, 1922–34, he was economist, executive vice-president, treasurer, director, and merchandising counsel. Knauth was president of Associated Dry Goods Corporation, 1936–43, and he also taught at Columbia, 1948–54. His books include *Policy of the United States Toward Industrial Monopoly* (1914), *Distribution of Income by States* (1923), *Managerial Enterprise* (1948), and *Business Practices, Trade Position, and Competition* (1956).

KNEASS, SAMUEL HONEYMAN (*b. Philadelphia, Pa., 1806; d. Philadelphia, 1858*), civil engineer, architect. Son of William Kneass; brother of Strickland Kneass. Trained in office of William Strickland. Primarily a railroad and canal builder, he helped construct the Philadelphia and Wilmington R.R., the Delaware and Schuylkill Canal, and many other major projects.

KNEASS, STRICKLAND (*b. Philadelphia, Pa., 1821; d. 1884*), civil engineer, Pennsylvania Railroad official. Son of William Kneass; brother of Samuel H. Kneass to whom he served for a time as assistant. As chief engineer and surveyor of Philadelphia, 1855–70, he designed a new drainage system for the city, and also bridges over the Schuylkill River.

KNEASS, WILLIAM (*b. Lancaster, Pa., 1780; d. Philadelphia, Pa., 1840*), engraver, diesinker. Did superior work for the *Port-Folio* and *Analectic* magazines; employed *post* 1824 by the U.S. Mint.

KNEELAND, ABNER (*b. Gardner, Mass., 1774; d. near Farmington, Iowa, 1844*), Universalist clergyman, antitheist. Leader of the Boston, Mass., "First Society of Free Enquirers"; lectured and wrote on rationalism; edited *Boston Investigator*, 1831–*ca.* 1834, first American rationalist journal.

KNEELAND, SAMUEL (*b. Boston, Mass., 1697; d. 1769*), printer. Nephew of Bartholomew Green. Publisher, *Boston Gazette, or Weekly Advertiser*, 1741–55, which he had printed at intervals *post* 1720; for many years the official provincial printer.

KNEELAND, SAMUEL (*b. Boston, Mass., 1821; d. Hamburg, Germany, 1888*), Boston physician, zoologist, teacher.

KNEELAND, STILLMAN FOSTER (*b. South Stukely, Canada, 1845; d. 1926*), lawyer. Admitted to bar, Albany, N.Y., 1869; practiced in New York City *post* 1872 as authority on commercial law.

KNEISEL, FRANZ (*b. Bucharest, Rumania, 1865; d. 1926*), violinist, teacher. Studied at Bucharest and Vienna conservatories; came to America, 1855, as principal violinist, Boston Symphony. Formed Kneisel Quartet for chamber music, 1885.

KNICKERBOCKER, HERMAN (*b. probably Albany, N.Y., 1779; d. Brooklyn, N.Y., 1855*), lawyer, jurist, New York legislator. A leading citizen of Troy, N.Y.

KNIGHT, AUSTIN MELVIN (*b. Ware, Mass., 1854; d. Washington, D.C., 1927*), naval officer. Graduated Annapolis, 1873. Author of *Modern Seamanship* (1901). As admiral commanding U.S. Asiatic fleet, 1917, was in charge of early American operations at Vladivostok and in Siberia.

KNIGHT, DANIEL RIDGWAY (*b. Philadelphia, Pa., 1840; d. Rolleboise par Bonniers, France, 1924*), painter. Studied at Pennsylvania Academy; also in Paris with Charles Gleyre and Meissonier. Resided in France *post* 1872. Received international recognition for story telling paintings of French life.

KNIGHT, EDWARD COLLINGS (*b. Collingswood, N.J., 1813; d. Cape May, N.J., 1892*), wholesale grocer, capitalist. Established Southwark Sugar Refinery in Philadelphia; invented "Knight" railroad sleeping-car, 1859.

KNIGHT, EDWARD HENRY (*b. London, England, 1824; d. Bellefontaine, Ohio, 1883*), mechanical expert, Patent Office official, patent attorney. Settled in Cincinnati, Ohio, 1845. Author of *Knight's American Mechanical Dictionary* (1874–76 and 1882–84) and other works on various subjects.

KNIGHT, FREDERICK IRVING (*b. Newburyport, Mass., 1841; d. 1909*), physician, laryngologist. Graduated Yale, 1862; M.D., Harvard, 1866; worked with Austin Flint and Henry I. Bowditch. Taught at Harvard Medical School, 1872–92; was clinical professor of laryngology *post* 1886. A pioneer in early days of the war against tuberculosis.

KNIGHT, GOODWIN JESS ("GOODIE") (*b. Provo, Utah, 1896; d. Englewood, Calif., 1970*), attorney and governor of California. Studied at Stanford (B.A., 1919) and Cornell (1919–20) and formed a partnership in 1925 with a Stanford classmate. He was appointed to the Los Angeles Superior Court in 1934, and then twice elected to the superior court. He hosted popular radio discussion programs in Los Angeles and in San Francisco. He was elected lieutenant governor in 1946, then became governor in 1953 when Governor Earl Warren was appointed to the U.S. Supreme Court. Knight was elected governor in 1954, but he was defeated for reelection in 1958.

KNIGHT, HENRY COGSWELL (*b. probably Newburyport, Mass., 1789; d. Rowley, Mass., 1835*), writer, Episcopal clergyman. His poems in *The Cypriad* (1809) and *The Broken Harp* (1815) have curious parallels with Blake and Coleridge. He was author also of *Letters from the South and West* (1824).

KNIGHT, JONATHAN (*b. Bucks Co., Pa., 1787; d. East Bethlehem, Pa., 1858*), civil engineer. Self-educated. Employed on extension of the National Road to Wheeling, Va. (now W.Va.), and *post* 1825 to Illinois; surveyed route of Baltimore and Ohio R.R. and was its chief engineer, 1829–42.

KNIGHT, JONATHAN (*b. Norwalk, Conn., 1789; d. 1864*), physician. A founder of the American Medical Association and of Yale Medical School. Connecticut's leading surgeon *post* 1838.

KNIGHT, LUCIAN LAMAR (*b. Atlanta, Ga., 1868; d. Clearwater, Fla., 1933*), Georgia historian, archivist.

KNIGHT, RIDGWAY. *See* KNIGHT, DANIEL RIDGWAY.

KNIGHT, SARAH KEMBLE (*b. Boston, Mass., 1666; d. probably New London, Conn., 1727*), teacher, diarist. Author of a classic account of New England colonial manners and idiom (*ca.* 1704) which first appeared as *The Journals of Madam Knight . . . ,* New York, 1825.

KNOPF, BLANCHE WOLF (*b. New York, N.Y., 1893; d. New York, 1966*), editor and publisher. In 1916 she married Alfred A. Knopf, who the previous year had started his own publishing house. Blanche worked in the business from the outset, and is credited with the creation of the noted Borzoi imprint on Knopf books. In 1921 she became a vice-president and director of the corporation. The firm first made its reputation by publishing European authors in attractively designed books, and much of the English and French flavor of Knopf's list was due to Blanche's influence. Among the French writers she published were André Gide, Jean-Paul Sartre, Jules Roy, Simone de Beauvoir, and Albert Camus. In 1960 the firm merged with Random House, with control going to the latter, but Blanche Knopf retained the presidency she had held since 1957. During her career the firm published more than 5,000 titles. Borzoi imprints won eighteen Pulitzer Prizes and six National Book Awards. Eleven of Knopf's authors were Nobel Prize winners.

KNOTT, ALOYSIUS LEO (*b. near Newmarket, Md., 1829; d. 1918*), lawyer, Maryland legislator. Practiced in Baltimore, Md., *post* 1855. Helped form Conservative-Democratic party, 1866, and in ensuing legislative session took lead in freeing Maryland from military rule. Was dean, Baltimore Law School, 1905–*ca.* 1918.

KNOTT, JAMES PROCTOR (*b. near Raywick, Ky., 1830; d. Lebanon, Ky., 1911*), lawyer. Congressman, Democrat, from Kentucky, 1867–71, 1875–83; governor of Kentucky, 1883–87; professor and first dean, Centre College law school, 1894–1901.

KNOWLES, LUCIUS JAMES (*b. Hardwick, Mass., 1819; d. Washington, D.C., 1884*), inventor, steam-pump and loom manufacturer.

KNOWLTON, CHARLES (*b. Templeton, Mass., 1800; d. 1850*), physician. Graduated Dartmouth, M.D., 1824. Author of *Fruits of Philosophy* (1832), an early and influential work in favor of birth control.

KNOWLTON, FRANK HALL (*b. Brandon, Vt., 1860; d. Ballston, Va., 1926*), paleontologist, pioneer paleobotanist, author, Graduated Middlebury, 1884. Associated with U.S. National Museum and U.S. Geological Survey. Advanced an original hypothesis on evolution of geologic climates, 1919.

KNOWLTON, MARCUS PERRIN (*b. Wilbraham, Mass., 1839; d. Springfield, Mass., 1918*), lawyer, jurist. Graduated Yale, 1860. Justice, supreme court of Massachusetts, 1887–1911; effective and distinguished as chief justice, *post* 1902.

KNOWLTON, THOMAS (*b. West Boxford, Mass., 1740; d. Harlem Heights, New York, N.Y., 1776*), Revolutionary soldier. Veteran of Seven Years' War. As captain, Ashford Company, protected line of colonial retreat at Bunker Hill; was commissioned major, 20th Continentals, Jan. 1, 1776, and commanded a celebrated raid into Charlestown, Mass., on Jan. 8, 1776. Orga-nized "Knowlton's Rangers" late in August after promotion to lieutenant colonel; was killed at battle of Harlem Heights, Sept. 16.

KNOX, DUDLEY WRIGHT (*b. Walla Walla, Wash., 1877; d. Bethesda, Md., 1960*), naval officer, historian. Graduated from the U.S. Naval Academy, 1896. Pioneered in the operations of destroyers, transforming them from a scouting force into a powerful offensive weapon. During World War I, served on the staff of Admiral Sims in London. As head of the Office of Naval Records and Library, 1921–46, transformed the archives into a major source of naval history with the highest standards of scholarship. Author of *History of the United States Navy* (1936).

KNOX, FRANK (*b. Boston, Mass. 1874; d. Washington, D.C., 1944*), journalist, politician. Christened William Franklin Knox; raised in Grand Rapids, Mich. Interrupted studies at Alma College to enlist for Spanish-American War; served in Cuba with Theodore Roosevelt's Rough Riders. Upon his return he worked on the *Grand Rapids Herald* as reporter, city editor, and circulation manager. In 1902 he became co-owner of the Sault Ste. Marie (Mich.) *Evening Journal* (renamed the *Evening News*, 1903); he ran it as a progressive Republican paper, engaging in successive reform crusades. He became chairman of the Republican State Central Committee in 1910, and in 1912 was active in Theodore Roosevelt's Bull Moose party. Knox sold the *Evening News* and moved to Manchester, N.H., on the invitation of several of the state's leading Progressives. There he was cofounder of a new Progressive paper, the *Manchester Leader*. Within a year he took control of the major competitive paper. In the amalgamation that followed, the *Manchester Union* became a leading state newspaper, while the evening *Leader* served the city of Manchester.

Knox served in France as major in the 78th Division. Upon his return to New Hampshire in 1919, he became a leader, at the Republican National Convention of 1920, in the unsuccessful campaign of Leonard Wood for the presidential nomination. In 1924 Knox entered the New Hampshire Republican gubernatorial primary against the liberal John G. Winant; after losing, he declared that he was through with politics.

Three years later Knox became publisher of the Hearst papers in Boston, and in less than a year was promoted to the position of general manager of the Hearst system. He resigned in 1930 when he disagreed with William Randolph Hearst's business methods. The following year Knox bought the controlling interest in the *Chicago Daily News*.

Knox soon cast aside his earlier vow to avoid politics. He believed that with Hoover's support he could win the 1936 Republican presidential nomination. He failed, however, to win Hoover's backing, and was instead given the vice-presidential nomination on a ticket headed by Alfred M. Landon. After a strenuous campaign, the Landon-Knox 1936 Republican ticket met overwhelming defeat.

Although Knox disagreed vigorously with Franklin D. Roosevelt's domestic policies, he supported the President's foreign policy and his naval preparedness program. In July 1940 Roosevelt appointed him Secretary of the Navy, a post he held until his death in 1944.

Believing that by visiting the navy wherever it operated he would understand the service better and at the same time boost the morale of the men, Knox flew, during his four years as secretary, over 200,000 miles, from Guadalcanal in the Pacific to the coast of Italy near Salerno.

With Roosevelt's backing, Knox countered successfully most attempts by the admirals to increase military authority at the expense of civilian control. He considered support of the president's wartime policies essential, made many speeches on behalf of these policies, and frequently testified before Congressional committees in support of Roosevelt's proposals.

KNOX, GEORGE WILLIAM (*b. Rome, N.Y., 1853; d. Seoul, Korea, 1912*), Presbyterian clergyman. Missionary to Japan, 1877–93; served as seminary professor in Tokyo. Professor of philosophy and history of religions, Union Theological Seminary, New York, 1899–1911.

KNOX, HENRY (*b. Boston, Mass., 1750; d. near Thomaston, Maine, 1806*), bookseller, soldier. As second-in-command, Boston Grenadier Corps, made special study of military science and engineering, 1772–75; rose rapidly in American army after volunteering, June 1775; was close friend and adviser of George Washington. As colonel of artillery, brought captured guns from Ticonderoga for use in terminal stage of siege of Boston; his services thereafter were given in almost every Northern operation of the Revolution, and his handling of the artillery received general praise. Promoted major general in November 1781; conceived and organized Society of the Cincinnati, May 1783; chosen secretary of war by Congress, 1785. Confirmed in that post under the new Constitution, he served until 1794.

KNOX, JOHN JAY (*b. Augusta, N.Y., 1828; d. New York, N.Y., 1892*), financier, U.S. treasury official. Comptroller of the currency, 1872–84.

KNOX, PHILANDER CHASE (*b. Brownsville, Pa., 1853; d. Washington, D.C., 1921*), lawyer. Graduated Mount Union College, Ohio, 1872. Became one of the country's ablest corporation lawyers and was appointed U.S. attorney general, 1901, by his friend President McKinley. An active and successful prosecutor of antitrust cases, he resigned the office, 1904, to accept appointment as U.S. senator, Republican, from Pennsylvania. In 1909, he was appointed President Taft's secretary of state, retiring in March 1913. He reorganized his department; extended the merit system; conducted foreign relations by "dollar diplomacy," first in the Far East and then in Latin America. He extended the Monroe Doctrine to apply to aggressions of Asian nations and settled the Bering Sea and North Atlantic fisheries controversies. Returning to the Senate, 1917, he helped lead the fight against the Treaty of Versailles.

KNOX, ROSE MARKWARD (*b. Mansfield, Ohio, 1857; d. Johnstown, N.Y., 1950*), manufacturer, business executive. Cofounder with her husband, Charles B. Knox, of the Knox Gelatin Company, 1890. On her husband's death in 1908, she continued in full control of the business as its president until 1947, pioneering in industrial research, expanding the uses of her product, and maintaining a most enlightened labor policy.

KNOX, SAMUEL (*b. Ireland, 1756; d. 1832*), Presbyterian clergyman, educator. Settled in Maryland *ca.* 1795; held pastorates and taught at Bladensburg, Frederick, and elsewhere. Campaigned (1799) for a uniform system of national education with state colleges and a national university.

KNOX, THOMAS WALLACE (*b. Pembroke, N.H., 1835; d. New York, N.Y., 1896*), traveler, journalist, war and foreign correspondent.

KNUDSEN, WILLIAM S. (*b. Copenhagen, Denmark, 1879; d. Detroit, Mich., 1948*), automobile manufacturer, government administrator. Christened Signius Wilhelm Paul Knudsen, he was reared in a household shaped by the values of frugality, self-reliance, and Lutheran piety. Immigrating to the United States early in 1900, Knudsen worked as a bench hand in the John R. Keim Mills in Buffalo, N.Y., a factory specializing in the manufacture of bicycle parts, where he rose within a few years to assistant superintendent. With the decline of the "bicycle craze" after 1904, the Keim plant began to manufacture automobile parts. Knudsen visited the Detroit plant of Ford Motor Company in 1906 and obtained an order for crankcases and rear-axle housings for the future Model T. Ford purchased the Keim Mills in 1911, and thus also acquired the talents of Knudsen. In 1913 Ford called him to Detroit and soon put him in charge of laying out and installing manufacturing operations in Ford assembly plants.

After the United States entered World War I, Knudsen supervised the production of army war matériel at Highland Park and directed the construction of navy-designed submarine patrol vessels known as "Eagle Boats." After the war, as head of manufacturing operations at Highland Park, Knudsen found himself in a thickening atmosphere of intrigue. Early in 1921, when Knudsen was on the verge of resigning, Ford ordered his discharge. A year later (after an interim job as general manager of a Detroit firm making automobile parts) Knudsen joined the General Motors Corporation as a staff adviser. Within three weeks he was named vice president of the Chevrolet division in charge of operations. Knudsen quickly improved the division's sales and profit performance. He strengthened the dealer organization, made a survey of consumer preferences, and introduced new mechanical and styling features, including an improved four-cylinder engine and semielliptic springs. In January 1924 he was made president and general manager of the Chevrolet division and a vice president and director of General Motors.

In 1933 Knudsen became executive vice president of General Motors in charge of all car, truck, and body operations in the United States and Canada, a position second only to that of Alfred P. Sloan, Jr. In 1937 he succeeded Sloan as president of General Motors—by then the world's largest manufacturing corporation.

In 1940 Knudsen was appointed to the National Defense Advisory Commission. Knudsen resigned all of his posts at General Motors and throughout the summer of 1940 concentrated on removing bottlenecks in the production of war matériel.

In January 1941 Knudsen was named director general of the Office of Production Management. Like the NDAC, the OPM institutionalized the diffusion of authority over industrial mobilization. The OPM came to an end after Pearl Harbor with the creation of the War Production Board (1942). Knudsen prepared to return to Detroit, but instead was induced to accept an army commission as a lieutenant general (the only civilian in American history appointed directly to that rank). In 1944 he became director of the Air Technical Service Command, and was given the responsibility of purchasing, distributing, and maintaining all aircraft and other equipment used by the Army Air Forces. After retiring from the army in May 1945, Knudsen was elected to the board of directors of General Motors. A year later he joined the Hupp Corporation, a manufacturing firm based in Detroit and Cleveland, and became its chairman.

KNUTSON, HAROLD (*b. Skien, Norway, 1880; d. Wadena, Minn., 1953*), newspaper publisher, congressman. Published the Wadena *Pioneer Journal* for most of his life. U.S. Congressman from Minnesota, 1916–48. A powerful isolationist and anticommunist, Knutson opposed U.S. entry into both world wars. As chairman of the House Ways and Means Committee, 1946–48, he was opposed to the Marshall Plan and the Truman Doctrine.

KOBBÉ, GUSTAV (*b. New York, N.Y., 1857; d. near Bay Shore, N.Y., 1918*), music critic, music historian. Author of *Wagner's Life and Works* (1890) and a number of other less important books in general and musical literature.

KOBER, GEORGE MARTIN (*b. Alsfeld, Germany, 1850; d. 1931*), physician. Came to America, 1866. Served as U.S. Army hospital aide; graduated Georgetown University, M.D., 1873; was army surgeon until 1886. Gave up practice, 1893, to engage in public welfare work; was dean of medical department, Georgetown, 1901–28.

KOCH, FRED CONRAD (*b. Chicago, Ill., 1876; d. Chicago, 1948*), biochemist. B.S., University of Illinois, 1899; M.S., 1900. Ph.D., University of Chicago, 1912. Taught physiological chemistry at University of Chicago, 1912–41 (professor *post* 1923); headed department of physiological chemistry and pharmacology, 1919–41; thereafter directed biochemical research at Armour and Company. His research covered a wide range, chiefly in the areas of internal secretions, including hormones, vitamins, and quantitative analytical methods. His laboratory is best known for its work *ca.* 1928 on the male hormone testosterone; other research involved work on secretin, thyroid and pituitary hormones, and on the activation of pepsin, rennin, and trypsinogen. He also worked on blood chemistry.

KOCH, FREDERICK HENRY (*b. Covington, Ky., 1877; d. Miami Beach, Fla., 1944*), educator, proponent of American folk plays. Raised in Peoria, Ill. A.B., Ohio Wesleyan University, 1900; graduated Emerson School of Oratory (Boston, Mass.), 1903; A.M., Harvard, 1909. As instructor in English at University of North Dakota, 1905–18, he organized and directed a faculty-student dramatic society that produced plays of a regional character written by the members. Moving to the University of North Carolina at Chapel Hill in 1918, he taught dramatic literature and playwriting, stressing plays that were concerned with "the legends, customs, superstitions, environmental differences, and the vernacular of the common people." His Carolina Playmakers, modeled on his earlier group in North Dakota, wrote and staged such plays at the university and on tour; among his students were Thomas Wolfe, Paul Green, and Betty Smith. He also helped school and civic groups in North Carolina to develop their own local programs, and strongly influenced the creation of outdoor pageant plays based on historical themes, such as Paul Green's *The Lost Colony* and Kermit Hunter's *Unto These Hills*.

KOCH, VIVIENNE (*b. New York, N.Y., 1911; d. New York, 1961*), critic and novelist. Studied at New York University's Washington Square College (B.A., 1932) and Columbia (M.A., 1933), with further graduate work at Columbia and the University of Maryland. She taught at Mount Holyoke College, the University of Maryland, Columbia, 1945–48, and New York University, 1947–57. She founded, and for a time was president of, New York University's Poetry Center. Her critical writing includes *William Carlos Williams* (1950) and *W. B. Yeats: The Tragic Phase* (1951). She also wrote a novel, *Change of Love* (1960).

KOCHERTHAL, JOSUA VON (*b. Bretten, Germany, 1669; d. 1719*), Lutheran clergyman. Leader of the Palatine immigration to the province of New York, 1708 and 1710.

KOEHLER, ROBERT (*b. Hamburg, Germany, 1850; d. Minneapolis, Minn., 1917*), painter. Came to America as a child. As director, Minneapolis School of Fine Arts, 1893–1917, was a pioneer in art instruction and appreciation in the Northwest.

KOEHLER, SYLVESTER ROSA (*b. Leipzig, Germany, 1837; d. Littleton, N.H., 1900*), museum curator, writer, artist. Built up print department of Boston Museum of Fine Arts as curator *post* 1887.

KOEMMENICH, LOUIS (*b. Elberfeld, Germany, 1866; d. 1922*), musician. Came to America, 1890. Served as conductor of New York Oratorio Society and other choral groups; composed songs and choruses.

KOENIG, GEORGE AUGUSTUS (*b. Willstätt, Baden, Germany, 1844; d. 1913*), chemist, mineralogist. Came to America, 1868. Taught at University of Pennsylvania and Michigan College of Mines; discovered thirteen new species of minerals; developed a number of improved processes for treatment of ores.

KOENIGSBERG, MOSES (*b. New Orleans, La., 1878; d. New York, N.Y., 1945*), journalist. Child of Jewish immigrant parents; raised in San Antonio, Texas. Extraordinarily precocious, he had worked on newspapers in eight major cities before settling in St. Louis, Mo., 1895. After service in the Spanish-American War, he continued to wander until 1903 when he became city editor of William Randolph Hearst's *Chicago American*. Successful in that post, he was transferred to Hearst's executive staff in New York City, 1907. In 1913 he founded his own Newspaper Feature Service, which operated semi-independently within the Hearst empire; in 1915 he founded an additional Hearst service, King Features Syndicate, which was highly profitable. In April 1919 he was given further responsibility as manager of the ailing International News Service, which he gradually restored to solvency and reliability. By the mid-1920's he was managing a total of eight Hearst services. Resigning from the Hearst organization in 1928, he roved from job to job after the stock market crash of 1929 aborted a project to build a chain of newspapers.

KOERNER, GUSTAVE PHILIP. *See* KÖRNER, GUSTAV PHILIPP.

KOFFKA, KURT (*b. Berlin, Germany, 1886; d. Northampton, Mass., 1941*), psychologist, one of the founders of Gestalt psychology. Studied at University of Berlin and at University of Edinburgh; Ph.D., Berlin, 1908. On leaving Berlin he worked at Freiburg and Würzburg; in 1910, as assistant to Friedrich Schumann in Frankfurt, he was associated with Wolfgang Köhler and Max Wertheimer. From their collaboration developed the Gestalt approach to psychology, which challenged both the traditional atomistic approach and, later, the oversimplifications of behaviorism. He taught at the University of Giessen, 1911–27; he was professor of psychology at Smith College and resident for the most part in the United States from 1927 until his death. Among his books was the monumental *Principles of Gestalt Psychology* (1935).

KOFOID, CHARLES ATWOOD (*b. near Granville, Ill., 1865; d. Berkeley, Calif., 1947*), zoologist. B.A., Oberlin College, 1890. M.A., Harvard, 1892; Ph.D., 1894. Taught briefly at University of Michigan; headed biological station of University of Illinois at Havana, Ill.; taught zoology at University of Illinois, Urbana, 1897–1900, becoming in 1898 superintendent of the Illinois State Natural History Survey. At invitation of William Emerson Ritter, Kofoid joined the faculty of University of California at Berkeley, 1900, as assistant professor of histology and embryology; in 1910 he became professor of zoology and chairman of the department; he retired in 1936. As a close associate of Ritter's, he shared in the development of the Marine Biological Station at La Jolla (presently the Scripps Institution of Oceanography) and served for several years as assistant director.

Much of his research in Illinois had been quantitative and statistical studies of the distribution and movement of freshwater plankton; in California he shifted to the study of marine plankton. He also engaged in research related to public health and other practical problems. Long interested in the intestinal protozoans of termites and some of the higher animals, he expanded his interest to include human parasitic protozoans, tapeworms, and other intestinal parasites; subsequent to his service as a major in the U.S. Army Sanitary Corps during World War I, he directed a laboratory of parasitology for the California State Board of Health, which trained medical technicians in that field. Other researches in the public interest were studies of marine borers, of the life history of termites, and of methods for detection and control of plankton organisms that could contaminate the San Francisco reservoirs. His passion for detail may have deterred him from truly great research achievements; his work was the accumulation and cataloging of facts, not synthesis. His fields of interest were broad, so that he left a large body of data to be classified later by other workers; he was also open to criticism for his tendency to break groups down into too fine classes, hence to name too many new species.

KOHLBERG, ALFRED (*b. San Francisco, Calif., 1887; d. New York, N.Y., 1960*), importer, publisher, political organizer. Studied briefly at the University of California. Through his travels as a silk importer and his activity in the American Bureau for Medical Aid to China, Kohlberg became an ardent supporter of the Chinese nationalists. Published many papers accusing the Institute of Pacific Relations of communist infiltration. Helped organize the American China Policy Association (1946) and founded the journal *Plain Talk*, which merged with *The Freeman* in 1950. A member of the Joint Committee Against Communism, Kohlberg played a prominent role during the McCarthy era, testifying before two Senate investigations. Known as "the China lobby man."

KOHLER, ELMER PETER (*b. Egypt, Pa., 1865; d. Boston, Mass., 1938*), organic chemist. Graduated Muhlenberg, 1886; Ph.D., Johns Hopkins, 1892. Distinguished teacher at Bryn Mawr, 1892–1912, and Harvard, 1912–14, 1919–38.

KOHLER, KAUFMANN (*b. Fürth, Bavaria, 1843; d. New York, N.Y., 1926*), rabbi. Early mastered Talmudic knowledge. At universities of Munich, Berlin, and Erlangen (Ph.D., 1867), broke with orthodox Judaism. Called to congregation Beth-El in Detroit, he came to America, 1869; in 1879 he became rabbi of Temple Beth-El, New York. Continuing his battle against conservative and orthodox critics, he particularly attacked Alexander Kohut's definition of traditional Judaism. Kohler called the Pittsburgh Conference which adopted the radical Pittsburgh Platform (1885), later accepted as a statement of principles by American reform Judaism. In 1903 he became president of Hebrew Union College, Cincinnati, and served until 1921. A productive, mature scholar, he was author of many monographs and books, of which the principal was *Jewish Theology* (1918).

KOHLER, MAX JAMES (*b. Detroit, Mich., 1871; d. Long Lake, N.Y., 1934*), lawyer, publicist, author. Son of Kaufmann Kohler; grandson of David Einhorn. Authority on immigration law; defender and protector of immigrants and minority rights.

KOHLER, WALTER JODOK (*b. Sheboygan, Wis., 1875; d. Kohler, Wis., 1940*), manufacturer of plumbing fixtures. Republican governor of Wisconsin, 1928–30; opposed by the La Follettes. Built model industrial town of Kohler, Wis.; opposed trade unions.

KÖHLER, WOLFGANG (*b. Reval, Estonia, 1887; d. Enfield, N.H., 1967*), psychologist. Studied at the universities of Tübingen, Bonn, and Berlin (Ph.D., 1909). In 1909 became assistant at the Psychological Institute at Frankfurt am Main, where his collaboration with Max Wertheimer and Kurt Koffka marked the beginning of Gestalt psychology. In 1913 Köhler became director of the Anthropoid Station of the Prussian Academy of Sciences on the island of Tenerife. During this period he wrote *Mentality of Apes* (1917) and *Die physischen Gestalten in Ruhe und im stationären Zustand* (1920). He returned to Germany in 1920 as acting director of the Psychological Institute of the University of Berlin, then taught at Göttingen (1921) before becoming professor of philosophy and director of the Psychological Institute at Berlin. The institute flourished under Köhler, and

the journal *Psychologische Rorschung* was founded. Köhler taught at Clark University, 1925–26, Harvard, 1934–35, and Chicago, 1935. He wrote *Gestalt Psychology* (1929) in English and his Harvard lectures were published as *The Place of Value in a World of Facts* (1938). After an unsuccessful battle to save the institute from the Nazis, Köhler immigrated to the United States in 1935. He taught at Swarthmore College, 1935–58, and continued his work at Dartmouth. His *The Task of Gestalt Psychology* (1969) is perhaps the best summary of Gestalt psychology for the beginner.

KOHLMANN, ANTHONY (*b. Kaiserberg, Alsace, 1771; d. 1836*), Jesuit priest, educator, missionary. Worked in America, 1806–24. Administered diocese of New York, 1808–14; was president of Georgetown College, 1818–20; taught at Gregorian University, Rome, *post* 1824. Defendant in celebrated legal action ensuring secrecy of confession made to a priest.

KOHLSAAT, HERMAN HENRY (*b. Albion, Ill., 1853; d. Washington, D.C., 1924*), restaurateur, editor. An influential Republican, publisher of several Chicago newspapers *post* 1891, including the *Inter-Ocean* and the *Times-Herald*; claimed authorship of Republican gold plank, 1896.

KOHUT, ALEXANDER (*b. Félegyháza, Hungary, 1842; d. New York, N.Y., 1894*), rabbi, lexicographer. Graduated Jewish Theological Seminary, Breslau, 1867; Ph.D., University of Leipzig, 1870. Elected to the Hungarian parliament, 1885, he was called the same year to Ahawath Chesed Congregation, New York. Shocked by the vagaries of radical reform Judaism in America, he established his leadership of conservative Jewry in a series of sermons on "The Ethics of the Fathers." Reform, led by Kaufmann Kohler, replied with the Pittsburgh Program. Kohut then organized the Jewish Theological Seminary of America, 1887, where he was professor of Talmud. He published his encyclopedic modern version of the *Aruch Hashalem*, 1878–92; it was reissued, 1926.

KOHUT, GEORGE ALEXANDER (*b. Stuhlweissenberg, Hungary, 1874; d. 1933*), rabbi, scholar. Son of Alexander Kohut. Came to America as a boy. Promoter of Jewish intellectual activities in many fields.

KOLB, DIELMAN (*b. Palatinate, Germany, 1691; d. 1756*), Mennonite preacher. Came to America, 1717; throve in Pennsylvania as weaver and farmer; assisted Swiss and German immigration to America.

KOLB, REUBEN FRANCIS (*b. Eufaula, Ala., 1839; d. Montgomery, Ala., 1918*), planter, Confederate soldier, farm leader. Fought for a progressive democracy in Alabama against the so-called "Organized Democrats" *post* 1890.

KOLLE, FREDERICK STRANGE (*b. Hanover, Germany, 1872; d. New York, N.Y., 1929*), physician. Came to America as a youth. Graduated Long Island College Hospital, M.D., 1893. Pioneer in radiography and modern plastic surgery; author of *Plastic and Cosmetic Surgery* (1911).

KOLLER, CARL (*b. Schüttenhofen, Bohemia, later Susice, Czechoslovakia, 1857; d. New York, N.Y., 1944*), ophthalmologist. Raised in Vienna, Austria-Hungary. M.D., University of Vienna, 1882. Made aware of the need for a local anesthetic in eye surgery, he conducted a number of experiments with various substances while a student and as an intern at the Allgemeines Krankenhaus. These resulted in his discovery that a few drops of a cocaine solution placed in the eye rendered the area insensitive to pain. He presented his findings in a brief paper that was read before a meeting of the German Ophthalmology Society of Heidelberg on Sept. 15, 1884. Owing in part to the prevalent anti-Semitism in

Vienna, he came to New York City, 1888, where he was appointed to the staff of Mount Sinai Hospital, became noted as a diagnostician and surgeon, and developed a successful clinical practice.

KOLLOCK, SHEPARD (*b. Lewes, Del., 1750; d. Philadelphia, Pa., 1839*), journalist, Revolutionary patriot. Nephew and apprentice of William Goddard. Published *New Jersey Journal* at various places *post* 1779 up to 1818; issued numerous books at New York, N.Y., and Elizabeth, N.J.

KOOPMAN, AUGUSTUS (*b. Charlotte, N.C., 1869; d. Étaples, France, 1914*), painter, etcher.

KOOWESKOWE. *See* ROSS, JOHN.

KOREN, JOHN (*b. Washington Prairie, near Decorah, Iowa, 1861; d. at sea, 1923*), Lutheran clergyman, statistician. Son of Ulrik V. Koren. Expert special agent, Bureau of the Census, 1903–12; worked for better data in criminal statistics.

KOREN, ULRIK VILHELM (*b. Bergen, Norway, 1826; d. 1910*), Norwegian Lutheran clergyman. Came to America, 1853. Was influential in Norwegian Synod (president, 1894–1910); pastor at Washington Prairie, Iowa, 1853–1910.

KÖRNER, GUSTAV PHILIPP (*b. Frankfurt am Main, Germany, 1809; d. 1896*), jurist, statesman, historian. Came to America, 1833; settled in Belleville, Ill., where he practiced law. Was state supreme court judge, 1845–50, and lieutenant governor of Illinois, Democrat, 1852–56. Joining Republican party, 1856, he influenced German-Americans to follow his example. A close friend of Abraham Lincoln. Served as U.S. minister to Spain, 1862–64; later in life, wrote on history of German influence in the United States and composed a valuable autobiography.

KORNGOLD, ERICH WOLFGANG (*b. Brünn, Austria, 1897; d. Hollywood, Calif., 1957*), composer. Widely hailed as a child prodigy, Korngold wrote operas and other musical works from an early age; his most famous work, *Die tote Stadt* was produced in 1920. In 1934, Korngold came to the U.S. to compose the music for Max Reinhardt's film *A Midsummer Night's Dream*; other film scores include *Anthony Adverse* (1936) and *The Adventures of Robin Hood* (1938), both of which won Academy Awards, and *Of Human Bondage* (1946).

KOŚCIUSZKO, TADEUSZ ANDRZEJ BONAWENTURA (*b. Palatinate of Breesc, Grand Duchy of Lithuania, 1746; d. Switzerland, 1817*), Revolutionary soldier, Polish patriot. Graduated Royal School, Warsaw, as captain, 1769; received further training in engineering and artillery at Mézières, France. Stirred by the American Revolution, he came to America, 1776, and soon was commissioned colonel of engineers, Continental Army. He contributed greatly to the victory over Burgoyne at Saratoga, 1777; designed works at West Point, 1778–80; served with Greene in the South, 1780–83. Promoted brigadier general, 1783, he returned to Europe, 1784. In 1792 and 1794 he led the Poles in their resistance to the Russians. Becoming liberal dictator of Poland in the latter year, he was defeated at Maciejowice in October. He revisited America, 1797–98, after imprisonment by the Russians, and spent the rest of his life in exile working for Polish freedom.

KOUSSEVITZKY, SERGE ALEXANDROVITCH (*b. Vyshni Volotchek, Russia, 1874; d. Boston, Mass., 1951*), orchestra conductor. Studied at the Moscow Philharmonic School. Immigrated to the U.S. in 1924. Conductor of the Boston Symphony, 1924–49. Affiliated the symphony with the Berkshire Music Festival (later Tanglewood) in 1936; founded the Berkshire Music Center, 1940. Promoted many unknown composers and was instrumental in making the works of contemporary Americans popular concert items. At the Berkshire Center, taught such composers and conductors as Lukas Foss and Leonard Bernstein.

KOVACS, ERNIE (*b. Trenton, N.J., 1919; d. Los Angeles, Calif., 1962*), television comedian. Attended the New York School of Theater, 1935–37, then joined a theater troupe, worked as a radio announcer, and wrote for the *Trentonian*. He hosted a cooking show on a Philadelphia television station, 1949–51, and did television programs for the National Broadcasting Company, 1951–57. He turned to fiction and films, writing the novel *Zoomar* (1957) and starring in *Our Man in Havana* (1960), before returning to TV with the American Broadcasting Company in 1959. He starred in and produced a series of comedy specials sponsored by Dutch Masters, 1961–62.

KOYL, CHARLES HERSCHEL (*b. Amherstburg, Canada, 1855; d. Evanston, Ill., 1931*), civil engineer. Pioneer in treatment of industrial water supplies, especially in connection with railroad operations.

KRACAUER, SIEFGRIED (*b. Frankfurt am Main, Germany, 1889; d. New York, N.Y., 1966*), social scientist. Received a doctorate form the Berlin-Charlottenburg Technische Hochschule in 1915 and practiced architecture. He then worked for the *Frankfurter Zeitung*, 1920–33. Influenced by various strands of Marxism, his close associates were intellectuals clustered around the Institut für Sozialforschung. He wrote *Sociology as Science* (1922), the novel *Ginster* (1928), and *The Employees* (1930). Moving to New York City in 1941, he wrote *From Caligari to Hitler* (1947), which saw in almost all pre-Nazi German films protofascist tendencies. Kracauer worked for the Evaluation Branch of the Voice of America, 1950–52, and was a senior staff member of Columbia University's Bureau of Applied Social Research, 1953–58. Other books include *Satellite Mentality* (with Paul Berkman, 1956), *Theory of Film* (1960), *History: The Last Things Before the Last* (1969), and the novel *Georg* (1977).

KRAEMER, HENRY (*b. Philadelphia, Pa., 1868; d. 1924*), botanist, pharmacognosist. Graduated Girard College, 1883; Philadelphia College of Pharmacy, 1889. Taught at Northwestern, at Philadelphia College of Pharmacy and University of Michigan; edited and reported for pharmaceutical publications.

KRAFT, JAMES LEWIS (*b. Fort Erie, Ont., 1874; d. Chicago, Ill., 1953*), businessman, inventor. Immigrated to the U.S. in 1904. The inventor of a method of grinding and pasteurizing natural cheese, Kraft became the world's largest cheese merchant. Founded the J.L. Kraft Brothers and Co. in 1909 (now Kraft Foods Co.); retired as chairman of the board in 1951.

KRANTZ, PHILIP. *See* ROMBRO, JACOB.

KRAPP, GEORGE PHILIP (*b. Cincinnati, Ohio, 1872; d. 1934*), educator. Graduated Wittenberg College, 1894; Ph.D., Johns Hopkins, 1899. Professor of English language at Columbia for many years. Author of *The Pronunciation of Standard English in America* (1919), *The English Language in America* (1925), and many scholarly texts.

KRAUS, JOHN (*b. Nassau, Germany, 1815; d. New York, N.Y., 1896*), educator. Came to America, 1851. As an official of U.S. Bureau of Education, 1867–73, promoted Froebel's kindergarten theory; *post* 1873, with wife Maria Kraus-Boelté, conducted a seminar for kindergarten teachers.

KRAUS-BOELTÉ, MARIA (*b. Hagenow, Germany, 1836; d. Atlantic City, N.J., 1918*), educator, Froebel kindergarten disciple. Came to America, 1872. Established, with her husband John Kraus, the Normal Training Kindergarten and its model schools, New York City, ca. 1873.

KRAUSE, ALLEN KRAMER (*b. Lebanon, Pa., 1881; d. Providence, R.I., 1941*), physician. A.B., Brown University, 1901; A.M., 1902. M.D., Johns Hopkins, 1907. After little more than a year as instructor in pathology at Johns Hopkins, he developed pulmonary tuberculosis and moved to Saranac Lake, N.Y., for treatment. Influenced by Edward L. Trudeau, Edward R. Baldwin, and Lawrason Brown, he devoted himself to investigation of his disease; as assistant director of the Saranac Laboratory, 1909–16, he carried out studies of resistance and immunity to tuberculosis that made him a leading authority. Returning to Johns Hopkins in 1916 as associate professor of medicine, director of the tuberculosis laboratory, and physician-in-charge of the Phipps Tuberculosis Dispensary, he and an associate, Henry S. Willis, made joint researches which were classics of the time and shed new light on the pathogenesis of the disease. He left Johns Hopkins in 1929 to become president of the Desert Sanatorium, Tucson, Ariz., with additional responsibilities as clinical professor of medicine at Stanford University and University of Southern California. Overburdened, his health failed. He returned to Johns Hopkins Hospital in 1936, but his health continued to deteriorate. A prolific writer, he was also the editor *post* 1916 of the *American Review of Tuberculosis.*

KRAUSKOPF, JOSEPH (*b. Ostrowo, Prussia, 1858; d. 1923*), rabbi, leader in reform Judaism. Came to America as a boy. Graduated Hebrew Union College, 1883. Engaged in innumerable public activities, especially in Philadelphia, Pa., where he ministered *post* 1887. Founded National Farm School at Doylestown, Pa., 1896.

KRAUTH, CHARLES PHILIP (*b. New Goshenhoppen, Pa., 1797; d. 1867*), Lutheran clergyman. First president of Pennsylvania (now Gettysburg) College, 1834–50; professor in Gettysburg Theological Seminary, 1850–67.

KRAUTH, CHARLES PORTERFIELD (*b. Martinsburg, Va., now W.Va., 1823; d. Philadelphia, Pa., 1883*), Lutheran clergyman, theologian, educator, author. Son of Charles P. Krauth. Graduated Gettysburg Theological Seminary, 1841. Champion of reaction of U.S. Lutheranism from a developing American type of liberalism to an older European form of confessional conservatism. As editor in chief of *Lutheran and Missionary,* as first professor of "systematic divinity" at the new (1864) theological seminary at Mt. Airy (Philadelphia), for almost 20 years, and through his writings, especially *The Conservative Reformation and Its Theology* (1871), he influenced a generation of American Lutheran ministers.

KREHBIEL, CHRISTIAN (*b. Weierhof, Palatinate, Germany, 1832; d. near Halstead, Kans., 1909*), Mennonite preacher. Came to America *ca.* 1850; resided in Iowa and Illinois. Responsible for establishment of Mennonite immigrant settlements in Kansas *post* 1872; active in charitable work.

KREHBIEL, HENRY EDWARD (*b. Ann Arbor, Mich., 1854; d. 1923*), music critic, historian, author, lecturer. Associated with New York *Tribune,* 1880–1923; edited A. W. Thayer's *Life of Beethoven* (1921); wrote numerous original works of criticism.

KREISLER, FRITZ (*b. Vienna, Austria, 1875; d. New York, N.Y., 1962*), violinist and composer. Entered the Vienna Conservatory at seven, then attended Paris Conservatoire, 1885–87. At twelve he had completed his formal musical education. He soon began maintaining an enormous concert schedule, but his career sufffered from anti-German sentiment during and after World War I. He wrote several operettas, and although initially opposed to recording, is believed to have been the first to record an entire violin concerto. His series of one-disc instrumental miniatures was a great popular success. Kreisler moved to the United States in 1939, and performed radio concerts for Bell Telephone, 1944–50. His legacy includes some 200 original works, transcriptions, and arrangements.

KREMERS, EDWARD (*b. Milwaukee, Wis., 1865; d. Madison, Wis., 1941*), chemist, reformer of American pharmaceutical education. Apprenticed to a pharmacist in Milwaukee; Ph.G., University of Wisconsin, 1886; B.S., 1888. Ph.D., University of Göttingen, 1890. Beginning as an instructor in pharmacy at University of Wisconsin, he became professor and director of the pharmacy program, 1892. Resolved to raise pharmacy to equal rank with other academic professions, he limited enrollment to high school graduates, lengthened the ordinary course to two full academic years, and offered a pioneering, elective, four-year program that led to a B.S. degree; for this degree course, botany, physics, and other sciences were required, in addition to chemistry, and a graduation thesis based on original laboratory research. His example was soon followed in other state universities and a number of Kremers' students proceeded to the doctorate in pharmaceutical chemistry and pharmacy. His own research interests lay in the fields of structural organic chemistry, particularly phytochemistry, and in the history of pharmacy.

KRESGE, SEBASTIAN SPERING (*b. Bald Mount, Pa., 1867; d. East Stroudsburg, Pa., 1966*), merchant and philanthropist. Graduated from Eastman Business College in Poughkeepsie, N.Y., and worked as a salesman. He went into business with J. G. McCrory, an early chain-store merchant, then took full charge of the Detroit store. By 1912, S. S. Kresge operated eighty-five stores, and when Kresge stepped down as president in 1925 to become chairman of the board, the company operated over 300 stores. Kresge was involved with his company almost to the end of his life. In 1961 he approved a deal for financing a line of discount stores called K-Marts, and in 1963 the company began Jupiter stores. The S. S. Kresge Company later became the largest chain-store company in the country.

KRESS, SAMUEL HENRY (*b. Cherryville, Pa., 1863; d. New York, N.Y., 1955*), merchant, art collector, philanthropist. Founder (1916) of the S. H. Kress Co., a leading nickel-and-dime retail chain. A famous art collector, Kress was president of the National Gallery of Art, 1945–55, and director of the Metropolitan Museum of Art in New York. Established the Kress Foundation (1929), which conveyed his art collections to the public and funded medical research. Remained chairman of the board of the S. H. Kress Co. until his death.

KREYMBORG, ALFRED FRANCIS (*b. New York, N.Y., 1883; d. Milford, Conn., 1966*), poet, editor, dramatist, and literary historian. Published his first volume of poetry, *Love and Life and Other Studies* (1908), at his own expense. He was editor of the magazine *Glebe,* 1913–14, which published poems by Ezra Pound, James Joyce, and William Carlos Williams. In 1915 he began publishing *Others: A Magazine of New Verse,* which became one of the most influential little magazines in the United States. With his wife and the puppeteer Remo Buffano, Kreymborg created his own puppet theater. He published *Plays for Poem-Mimes* (1918), *Plays for Merry Andrews* (1920), and *Puppet Plays* (1923). He was editor of *Broom: An International Magazine of the Arts* (1921–22). He then published *Less Lonely* (1923), *Troubadour: An Autobiography* (1925), *Scarlet and Mellow* (1926), *The Lost Sail* (1928), and *Our Singing Strength* (1929). In 1935 he joined the Federal Theater Project in New York, working as a director in poetic theater. Other publications include *The Four Apes, and Other Fables of Our Day* (1939), *Selected Poems, 1912–1944* (1945), *Man and Shadow: An Allegory* (1946), and *No More War, and Other Poems* (1950).

KREZ, KONRAD (*b. Landau, Rhenish Bavaria, 1828; d. Milwaukee, Wis., 1897*), lawyer, Union soldier, Wisconsin legislator, poet in the German language. Immigrated to America, 1851.

KRIMMEL, JOHN LEWIS (*b. Ebingen, Germany, 1789; d. near Germantown, Pa., 1821*), painter. Came to America, 1810. Painted portraits and humorous genre pieces of American scenes, types, and occasions.

KROEBER, ALFRED LOUIS (*b. Hoboken, N.J., 1876; d. Paris, France, 1960*), anthropologist. Studied at Columbia University, Ph.D., 1901. The first member of the department of anthropology at the University of California (1901–46), Kroeber directed the museum, dominated the department, and generally led the field of American anthropology for forty years. The successor of Boas, he contributed little to original scholarship, seeking instead to popularize the field of anthropology. His works include *Anthropology* (1923), *The Nature of Culture* (1952), and *Style and Civilizations* (1957).

KROEGER, ADOLPH ERNST (*b. Schwabstedt, Duchy of Schleswig, 1837; d. St. Louis, Mo., 1882*), journalist. Came to America as a child. A minor figure in the St. Louis philosophical movement, he translated some of Fichte's works.

KROEGER, ERNEST RICHARD (*b. St. Louis, Mo., 1862; d. 1934*), musician, composer, conductor, teacher. Son of Adolph E. Kroeger.

KROGER, BERNARD HENRY (*b. Cincinnati, Ohio, 1860; d. Wianno, Mass., 1938*), businessman. Founded in Cincinnati a chain of grocery stores extending through the Middle West and into the South.

KROL, BASTIAEN JANSEN (*b. Harlingen, Friesland, 1595; d. 1674*), Dutch colonial official. Commissary and director at Fort Orange (Albany, N.Y.) at various periods, 1626–ca. 1643.

KRUEGER, WALTER (*b. Flatow, West Prussia [now Złotów, Poland], 1881; d. Valley Forge, Pa., 1967*), army officer. Immigrated to the United States in 1889. He enlisted in the army in 1898, then joined the regular army as a private in 1899. He held a variety of command, staff, training, and academic assignments. In 1943 General Douglas MacArthur selected Krueger to organize and command the Sixth Army, which executed MacArthur's grand design to return to the Philippines. Krueger led the campaigns of Leyte and Luzon. He retired in 1946.

KRUELL, GUSTAV (*b. near Düsseldorf, Germany, 1843; d. San Luis Obispo, Calif., 1907*), wood engraver. Came to America, 1873. Was particularly successful in portraiture.

KRUESI, JOHN (*b. Speicher, Switzerland, 1843; d. Schenectady, N.Y., 1899*), mechanical expert, inventor. Came to America, 1870. Was associated with Thomas A. Edison *post* 1871 and responsible for mechanical execution of many of his ideas. Devised system of underground electric cables; superintended Edison Machine Works, 1886–95.

KRUG, JULIUS ALBERT (*b. Madison, Wis., 1907; d. Knoxville, Tenn., 1970*), government administrator. Studied at the University of Wisconsin (B.A., 1929; M.A., 1930). Worked for the Wisconsin Telephone Company, the Wisconsin Public Utilities Commission, and the Federal Communications Commission, 1935–37. Also worked for Kentucky governor A. B. Chandler and reorganized the Kentucky Public Service Commission. In 1937 Krug joined the Tennessee Valley Authority as chief power engineer; he supervised TVA construction projects and was TVA's chief witness at congressional hearings. During World War II he served in Washington, D.C., as power coordinator, deputy director for priorities control, and director of the Office of War Utilities for the War Production Board. He was chairman of the WPB, 1944–46, and secretary of the interior, 1946–49.

KRÜSI, JOHANN HEINRICH HERMANN (*b. Yverdon, Switzerland, 1817; d. Alameda, Calif., 1903*), educator. Came to America, 1854. Did notable work in Object Teaching at Oswego (N.Y.) State Normal School, 1862–87.

KRUTCH, JOSEPH WOOD (*b. Knoxville, Tenn., 1893; d. Tucson, Ariz., 1970*), writer. Studied at the University of Tennessee (B.A., 1915) and Columbia (M.A., 1916; Ph.D., 1924). He taught at Brooklyn Polytechnic Institute, 1923–24, then became associate editor of the *Nation* (1924–37), where his responsibilities included drama criticism. He also taught at Columbia, 1937–52. His books include *Edgar Allan Poe* (1926), *The Modern Temper* (1929), *Was Europe a Success?* (1934), *Samuel Johnson* (1944), *Henry David Thoreau* (1948), *The Twelve Seasons* (1949), *The Desert Year* (1952), *The Measure of Man* (1954), *Human Nature and the Human Condition* (1959), *If You Don't Mind My Saying So* (1964), and *And Even If You Do* (1967).

KUGELMAN, FREDERICK BENJAMIN. *See* KAYE, FREDERICK BENJAMIN.

KUHN, ADAM (*b. Germantown, Pa., 1741; d. Philadelphia, Pa., 1817*), physician, botanist. Pupil of Linnaeus at Uppsala; M.D., University of Edinburgh, 1767. Practiced and taught in Philadelphia *post* 1768.

KUHN, JOSEPH ERNST (*b. Leavenworth, Kans., 1864; d. San Diego, Calif., 1935*), army officer. Graduated West Point, 1885; entered Engineer Corps. President of Army War College, 1917; commanded 79th Division, World War I. Retired as major general.

KUHN, WALT (*b. Brooklyn, N.Y., 1877; d. White Plains, N.Y., 1949*), painter, Christened Walter Francis Kuhn. Made principal early studies at Royal Academy in Munich, Germany. After working as a cartoonist for humor magazines and for several newspapers, he quit a regular job as *New York World* cartoonist, 1909, to devote himself to painting; at this time his art was a derivative continuation of French impressionism. As executive secretary of the Association of American Painters and Sculptors, which he had helped initiate late in 1911, he traveled in Europe in the fall of 1912 to select (along with Arthur B. Davies, president of the Association, and Walter Pach) examples of the most advanced European painting and sculpture to be shown along with progressive American work at a New York City exhibit. This was the famous Armory Show of 1913, a turning point in the history of American art. Thereafter, Kuhn's style, like that of Davies, changed abruptly in the endeavor to assimilate European modernism; up to about 1925, his art reflects in a most eclectic manner the various cubist experiments, as well as the influence of Matisse, Cézanne, Dufy, Derain, and Signac. After a trip abroad in 1925 for the express purpose of studying the old masters in the Louvre and the Prado museums, he succeeded by 1929 in creating an idiom of his own which he practiced with success until shortly before his death. His portraits of circus performers, and in particular clowns (*The White Clown*, 1929; *The Blue Clown*, purchased by the Whitney Museum, 1932) were his most successful artistic achievements.

KUMLER, HENRY (*b. Lancaster Co., Pa., 1775; d. near Trenton, Ohio, 1854*), bishop of the United Brethren in Christ. Removed to Ohio, 1819; was largely responsible for the planting and nurture of United Brethren churches in southwestern Ohio.

KUNIYOSHI, YASUO (*b. Okayama, Japan, 1893; d. New York, N.Y., 1953*), painter. Immigrated to the U.S. in 1906. Studied at the Los Angeles Art School and at the Art Students' League, 1916–20. Kuniyoshi's work is a blend of Japanese traditions and Western styles, strongly influenced by the expressionism of Chagall and Campendonk. Major pieces include *I'm Tired* (Whitney Museum, 1938), *Upside-Down Table and Mask* (Museum of Modern Art, 1940), and *Exit* (Metropolitan Museum, 1948–50). Taught at the Art Students' League and the New School for Social Research. The first living American accorded a retrospective exhibition at the Whitney Museum of American Art (1948).

KUNZ, GEORGE FREDERICK (*b. New York, N.Y., 1856; d. 1932*), authority on gems and ancient jewelry.

KUNZE, JOHN CHRISTOPHER (*b. Artern on the Unstrut, Saxony, 1744; d. New York, N.Y., 1807*), Lutheran clergyman. Came to America, 1770, as coadjutor to Henry M. Muhlenberg at Philadelphia; was pastor in New York *post* 1784. Advocate of training in English for Lutheran clergymen; prepared first Lutheran hymn book in the English language (1795).

KUNZE, RICHARD ERNEST (*b. Altenburg, Germany, 1838; d. near Phoenix, Ariz., 1919*), eclectic physician, naturalist. Came to America *ca.* 1854. Specialized *post* 1896 in study of Southwest reptiles and flora, especially cactus.

KURTZ, BENJAMIN (*b. Harrisburg, Pa., 1795; d. Baltimore, Md., 1865*), Lutheran clergyman. Editor, *Lutheran Observer*, 1833–58; a leader of evangelical "American Lutheranism."

KUSKOV, IVAN ALEKSANDROVICH (*b. Totma, Vologda Government, Russia, 1765; d. Totma, 1823*), assistant to A. A. Baranov in Alaska, *post* 1791. Founder (1812) and first manager of the Russian settlement called "Fort Ross" in California; returned to Russia, 1822.

KUYKENDALL, RALPH SIMPSON (*b. Linden, Calif., 1885; d. Tucson, Ariz., 1963*), historian. Studied at the College of the Pacific (B.A., 1910), Stanford, and the University of California at Berkeley (M.A., 1918; Ph.D., 1921). As executive secretary of the Hawaiian Historical Commission he produced A *History of Hawaii* (1926) and *Hawaii in the World War* (with Lorin Tarr Gill, 1928). Taught at the University of Hawaii, 1923–50. He wrote *The Hawaiian Kingdom, 1778–1854: Foundation and Transformation* (1938), *The Hawaiian Kingdom, 1854–1874: Twenty Critical Years* (1953), and *The Hawaiian Kingdom, 1874–1893: The Kalakaua Dynasty* (completed by Charles H. Hunter, 1967).

KYLE, DAVID BRADEN (*b. Cadiz, Ohio, 1863; d. 1916*), laryngologist. Professor of laryngology, Jefferson Medical College, 1904–16; wrote a widely used textbook on nose and throat diseases.

KYLE, JAMES HENDERSON (*b. near Xenia, Ohio, 1854; d. Aberdeen, S.Dak., 1901*), Congregational clergyman. U.S. senator, Populist-Republican, from South Dakota, 1891–1901; chairman of National Industrial Commission.

KYNE, PETER BERNARD (*b. San Francisco, Calif., 1880; d. San Francisco, Calif., 1957*), author. After serving in the army during the Spanish-American War, Kyne published the first of more than sixty stories (1910) that appeared in the *Saturday Evening Post*. *Three Godfathers*, his first novel, appeared in 1913. Kyne wrote about businessmen, seamen, and lumbermen; his theme was often racial, and his works were never accepted seriously by the critics.

KYNETT, ALPHA JEFFERSON (*b. Adams Co., Pa., 1829; d. Harrisburg, Pa., 1899*), Methodist clergyman, reformer, prohibitionist.

L

LA BARGE, JOSEPH (b. St. Louis, Missouri Territory, 1815; d. St. Louis, Mo., 1899), Missouri River navigator, fur trader.

LA BORDE, MAXIMILIAN (b. Edgefield, S.C., 1804; d. Columbia, S.C., 1873), physician, writer, educator. Associated for over 50 years with South Carolina College as student, trustee, and professor; wrote History of South Carolina College (1859).

LACEY, JOHN (b. Buckingham, Pa., 1755; d. New Mills, now Pemberton, N.J., 1814), Revolutionary soldier, public official in Pennsylvania and New Jersey.

LACEY, JOHN FLETCHER (b. near New Martinsville, Va., now W.Va., 1841; d. Oskaloosa, Iowa, 1913), Union soldier, lawyer. Congressman, Republican, from Iowa, 1889–91, 1893–1907; a strong conservative, he opposed Gov. A. B. Cummins' progressive "Iowa Idea."

LACHAISE, GASTON (b. Paris, France, 1882; d. 1935), sculptor. Studied at École des Beaux Arts with G. J. Thomas. Came to America, 1906. His work distinguished by its robust, earthy, exaggerated anatomies and candid, opulent voluptuousness.

LACKAYE, WILTON (b. Loudoun Co., Va., 1862; d. 1932), actor. Changed name from William A. Lackey. Made debut in New York, 1883. One of the most illustrious stage villains; remembered for his brilliant Svengali in Trilby.

LACLEDE, PIERRE (b. Bedous, lower Pyrenees, France, ca. 1724; d. Mississippi River near mouth of the Arkansas, 1778), trader. Came to New Orleans, 1755; founded St. Louis, Mo., 1764.

LACOCK, ABNER (b. Cub Run, near Alexandria, Va., 1770; d. near Freedom, Pa., 1837), farmer, Pennsylvania legislator. Congressman, Democrat, 1811–13; U.S. senator, 1813–19. An early advocate of state-built canals to connect the Delaware and Ohio rivers.

LACY, DRURY (b. Chesterfield Co., Va., 1758; d. Philadelphia, Pa., 1815), educator, Presbyterian clergyman. Graduated Hampden-Sydney College, 1788; served as its acting president, 1789–97. Established his own academy nearby, 1797, and taught many students later eminent in the professions.

LACY, ERNEST (b. Warren, Pa., 1863; d. 1916), lawyer, playwright, educator. Pioneered in developing rational public speaking and debating in Philadelphia public schools.

LADD, ALAN WALBRIDGE (b. Hot Springs, Ark., 1913; d. Palm Springs, Calif., 1964), film actor. By 1942 had appeared in several "B" pictures, but his role in This Gun for Hire made him a star. In 1943 led a national poll as most popular male star; best remembered for his role in Shane (1953). In Shane, he had probably his most remembered role: a mysterious stranger who helps a turn-of-the-century farming family ward off a landgrab by a group of villainous cattlemen. His final movie was The Carpetbaggers (1964).

LADD, CARL EDWIN (b. McLean, N.Y., 1888; d. near Freeville, N.Y., 1943), agricultural educator. Graduated Cortland (N.Y.) Normal School, 1907. B.S. in agriculture, Cornell University, 1912; Ph.D., 1915. Influenced by ideas of George F. Warren. Directed regional New York state schools of agriculture, 1915–20; returned to Cornell as extension professor of farm management, 1920. Appointed director of extension work for the colleges of agriculture and home economics at Cornell, 1924, he worked closely with the county units of the Farm Bureau Federation, making the advice of specialists available to the individual farmers; he also helped to formulate specific research projects at the colleges to fit the expressed needs of farmers. Dean of the colleges of agriculture and home economics from 1932 until his death, he kept Cornell in the forefront of agricultural research.

LADD, CATHERINE (b. Richmond, Va., 1808; d. near Winnsboro, S.C., 1899), South Carolina schoolmistress, writer of fugitive verse.

LADD, EDWIN FREMONT (b. Starks, Maine, 1859; d. 1925), chemist. Removed to Fargo, N.D., 1890; active in state and national fight against adulterated food. U.S. senator, Republican and Non-Partisan, from North Dakota, 1921–25.

LADD, GEORGE TRUMBULL (b. Painesville, Ohio, 1842; d. 1921), Congregational clergyman, psychologist, philosopher. Maintained a connection with Yale University, 1881–1921, interpreting and systematizing the work of German post-Kantian idealists and helping introduce study of psychology as an experimental science based on physiology.

LADD, JOSEPH BROWN (b. Newport, R.I., 1764; d. 1786), physician, poet. Author of Poems of Arouet (1786), which show influence of English preromantics. Practiced in Charleston, S.C., post 1783.

LADD, KATE MACY (b. New York, N.Y., 1863; d. Far Hills, N.J., 1945), philanthropist. Sister of Valentine E. Macy; great-granddaughter of Josiah Macy. Gave financial support to projects of Martha Berry and Lillian Wald; established the Josiah Macy, Jr. Foundation, 1930, for the support of fundamental research in the areas of health and medicine; was active in funding many hospitals and visiting-nurse services.

LADD, WILLIAM (b. Exeter, N.H., 1778; d. Portsmouth, N.H., 1841), sea captain, farmer. Founded American Peace Society, 1828; prophesied the development of international organization in his Essay on a Congress of Nations (1840).

LADD, WILLIAM SARGENT (b. Holland, Vt., 1826; d. 1893), merchant, banker. Removed to Portland, Oreg., 1851. Became leading promoter of transportation and industrial enterprises in the Pacific Northwest, particularly in Portland.

LADD-FRANKLIN, CHRISTINE (*b. Windsor, Conn., 1847; d. 1930*), logician, psychologist. Graduated Vassar, 1869; qualified for Ph.D., Johns Hopkins, 1882. Married Fabian Franklin, 1822. Made a major original contribution to logic, the "antilogism," 1883; developed a controversial color theory, 1892. Lectured at Johns Hopkins and Columbia.

LAEMMLE, CARL (*b. Laupheim, Germany, 1867; d. Beverly Hills, Calif., 1939*), pioneer exhibitor, distributor, and producer of motion pictures. Founder and head, 1912–36, of Universal Pictures.

LA FARGE, CHRISTOPHER GRANT (*b. Newport, R.I., 1862; d. Saunderstown, R.I., 1938*), architect. Son of John La Farge. Designer, with George Lewis Heins, of original Romanesque plans for Cathedral of St. John the Divine, New York, and of many other buildings.

LA FARGE, CHRISTOPHER GRANT (*b. New York, N.Y., 1897; d. Providence, R.I., 1956*), novelist. Studied at Harvard and at the School of Architecture of the University of Pennsylvania. From 1924 to 1931, he worked as an architect before beginning his career as a novelist. His first book, a verse novel, *Hoxie Sells His Acres*, was published in 1934. Other works include *Each to the Other* (1939), *The Wilsons* (1941), and *The Sudden Guest* (1946). Most of La Farge's works concern the region of Rhode Island. Other works of poetry and short stories appeared in leading periodicals.

LA FARGE, JOHN (*b. New York, N.Y., 1835; d. Providence, R.I., 1910*), painter, worker in stained glass, writer. Graduated Mount St. Mary's College, Emmitsburg, Md., 1853; trifled with legal studies; went to Paris, 1856, where relatives introduced him into the stimulating French literary world and he studied painting briefly under Thomas Couture. Thereafter he toured northern Europe, studying the paintings of the old masters. Returning to America, 1858, he practiced painting at Newport, R.I., with William M. Hunt. Married Margaret Mason Perry, 1860. Disqualified for Civil War service, he turned his mind to studies of light and color. His "Paradise Valley" (1866–68) reveals the influence of his discoveries; it anticipated the formula of Monet and the French impressionists who had yet to make their impact upon American art. His early work included landscapes, flowers, and a few figure subjects; he also did magazine illustrations marked by imagination and technical skill.

Invited by H. H. Richardson, builder of Trinity Church, Boston, to decorate the interior, 1876, La Farge produced a scheme of murals astonishingly unified and of great warmth and dignity. This was the forerunner of other important commissions, including "The Ascension" in the Church of the Ascension, New York City, the greatest mural painting of a religious subject produced anywhere in his time. He was also much occupied with work in stained glass, and it was owing to his genius and invention that one of the noble crafts of the Middle Ages was revived in America and lifted to a high plane. His Watson Memorial window won him the Legion of Honor at the Paris Exposition, 1889. In his glass work, his ability as designer and colorist came uniquely into its own. La Farge visited Japan with his friend Henry Adams and later went with him to the South Seas, recording what he saw and his own thoughts in *An Artist's Letters from Japan* (1897) and *Reminiscences of the South Seas* (1912). He was author also of a number of works on art and artists. In his many-sided activity, La Farge maintained an intellectuality which gave balance to everything he did and enriched his work with subtle implications and overtones. His sensibility was matched by the delicate French precision with which he defined his thought, either in words or in the language of art. He could work with complete simplicity, or in the grand style, as the theme required. He was the first American master of the fusion of decorative art with architecture, a colorist and designer who developed remarkable powers in collaboration with builders.

LAFARGE, JOHN (*b. Newport, R.I., 1880; d. New York, N.Y., 1963*), clergyman, editor, and author. Attended Harvard (B.A., 1901) and pursued theological studies at University of Innsbruck, Austria; ordained a priest in 1905. Leading American Catholic spokesman on the race question who devoted his life to the betterment of race relations. Editor of *America*, influential Jesuit weekly, 1926–48; author of *Interracial Justice* (1937).

LA FARGE, OLIVER HAZARD PERRY (*b. New York, N.Y., 1901; d. Albuquerque, N.Mex., 1963*), author and anthropologist. Graduated from Harvard (1924). While working at Tulane as a linguist and ethnologist, wrote fiction, including *Laughing Boy* (1929), which won a Pulitzer Prize. Director (1930) of the Eastern Association on Indian Affairs (later the Association on American Indian Affairs) and president (1937–42, 1948–63). Opposed the Truman and Eisenhower administrations' attempts to curtail Indian rights and became champion of the Indian cause nationwide.

LAFAYETTE, MARIE JOSEPH PAUL YVES ROCH GILBERT DU MOTIER, MARQUIS DE (*b. chateau of Chavaniac, Auvergne, France, 1757; d. Paris, France, 1834*), statesman, soldier. Descended from noted ancient French families. His father was killed, 1759, in the Seven Years' War; his mother died in 1770. Shy and awkward, yet eager to follow his family's military tradition, he entered the King's Musketeers, 1771, and was promoted captain shortly after his marriage, 1774, to Marie Adrienne Françoise de Noailles, an heiress of one of the old regime's most powerful families. At a dinner in honor of the Duke of Gloucester in August 1775, his imagination was stirred by the Duke's sympathetic talk of the American insurgents. Sensing the possibility of avenging France's defeat in the Seven Years' War, moved by romantic enthusiasm for regeneration of society, and hopeful of satisfying his own love of *la gloire*, he decided to help the Americans. Withdrawing from active service with the army, June 1776, he undertook through Silas Deane and Arthur Lee to serve in the colonies without pay. He sailed for America on April 20, 1777. Commissioned major general by Congress on July 31, he met General George Washington in Philadelphia who virtually adopted him and attached him to his staff. Slightly wounded at the Brandywine in September, he took command on December 1 of the division of Virginia light troops. During the winter at Valley Forge he won the title of "the soldier's friend." He was a valuable liaison officer between the American army and the French force under D'Estaing during and after the unsuccessful operation against Newport, R.I., in August 1778.

In January 1779, he left for France with an elegant sword voted him by Congress and a letter of appreciation to Louis XVI. Acclaimed and consulted at Paris and Versailles, he acquiesced in Rochambeau's appointment to lead a French expeditionary army and returned to America, April 1780, to prepare for its arrival. Congress restored him to his old command, and he served Washington as intermediary with Rochambeau at Newport during conferences with the French general in September. Going with Washington to West Point, he served on the court-martial after Benedict Arnold's treason and voted for André's death. After leading an unsuccessful campaign to capture Arnold at Hampton Roads, March 1781, he was ordered south to join Greene and reached Richmond just in time to prevent its capture by the British. He retreated slowly northward before Cornwallis's advancing army, but after meeting Wayne's force at Rapidan River he turned on Cornwallis, who retired to the coast. He then held Cornwallis in check until the arrival of Washington's and

Rochambeau's armies and De Grasse's fleet which resulted in the British surrender at Yorktown, Oct. 19, 1781, and the virtual end of Revolutionary military operations.

In December, Lafayette sailed for France, to enter on a long, eventful and rather checkered career which belongs to French rather than American history. He revisited the United States in 1784, and again, on President Monroe's invitation, in 1824, when he made an epochal tour of the country. His grave in Picpus Cemetery in Paris was covered with earth from Bunker Hill.

LAFEVER, MINARD (*b. Morristown, N.J., 1798; d. Williamsburg [Brooklyn], N.Y., 1854*), architect. Established in New York *post* 1828. Did much miscellaneous work, but is famous for Gothic churches built after 1835 in Brooklyn, of which his masterpieces are Holy Trinity (1844–47) and Church of the Saviour (1844). His chief influence on American architecture came more from his books, of which the best known are *The Modern Builder's Guide* (1833), *The Beauties of Modern Architecture* (1835), and *The Architectural Instructor* (1856).

LAFFAN, WILLIAM MACKAY (*b. Dublin, Ireland, 1848; d. 1909*), journalist, art connoisseur. Came to America, 1868; worked on San Francisco, Calif., and Baltimore, Md., papers. *Post* 1877, he became successively dramatic critic, publisher, and proprietor of the New York *Sun*. He was also chief art adviser to J. P. Morgan, Sr., and Henry Walters.

LAFFITE, JEAN (*b. probably Bayonne, France, ca. 1780; d. ca. 1821*), adventurer, outlaw. Established in New Orleans by 1809, he became chief of Barataria Bay pirates *ca.* 1810; operated out of Galveston *post* 1817. A shrewd, successful merchant on the Spanish Main as well as the last of the great freebooters, he was responsible for the service of many of his followers in the defense of New Orleans, Dec. 1814–Jan. 1815.

LAFITTE, JEAN.   *See* LAFFITE, JEAN.

LA FLESCHE, SUSETTE.   *See* BRIGHT EYES.

LA FOLLETTE, PHILIP FOX (*b. Madison, Wis., 1897; d. Madison, 1965*), governor of Wisconsin. Attended University of Wisconsin (LL.B., 1922). Elected governor (1930); secured enactment of first comprehensive unemployment insurance law in the United States. Defeated for reelection (1932); formed the Progressive Party of Wisconsin (1934); reelected governor (1935–39); launched National Progressives of America, which few endorsed; defeated for reelection (1940). Spokesman for American First Committee before Pearl Harbor. Director and president of Hazeltine Corporation, 1955–59.

LA FOLLETTE, ROBERT MARION (*b. Primrose, Wis., 1855; d. Washington, D.C., 1925*), governor of Wisconsin, U.S. senator, Progressive candidate for president, was born to the hard labor of pioneer poverty. He worked his way into, and through, the University of Wisconsin, graduating in 1879. After studying law a few months, he was admitted to the bar. He married a classmate, Belle Case, who earned a law degree from the state university, 1885, and worked with her in law and politics; it became a tradition that her sound judgment was the family's most valuable asset. In 1880 he was elected district attorney of Dane County and on renomination in 1882 was the only Republican elected in the county. In 1884 he was elected to Congress and twice reelected. Still relatively a conservative, he was defeated in the Democratic landslide of 1890.

In 1891 La Follette broke with Senator Philetus Sawyer, state Republican leader, claiming that Sawyer had attempted through him to bribe a judge in a corruption suit against several former state treasurers. Thereafter, he increasingly opposed the party bosses and developed a vision of a new political system. During the years

before his inauguration as governor in 1901 he elaborated a reform program: direct-primary nominations protected by law; the equalization of taxation of corporate property with that of other property; the regulation of railroad charges; and the erection of commissions of experts to regulate railroads. He failed to win the Republican nomination for governor in 1896 and 1898, but in 1900 he was nominated by acclamation and elected. His associates in the state government, however, were "Stalwart Republicans" who had surrendered nothing. He took office committed to direct-primary legislation, tax reform, and railroad control, measures partly reminiscent of Populism and partly anticipatory of Progressivism. Attacking the Republican leaders as greedy and corrupt, he created a lasting party schism; his Stalwart legislature refused to implement his platform. He took his case to the people and was so successful that his chief lieutenant became speaker of the Assembly in 1903. By 1905 the "Wisconsin Idea" of reform was a reality in prospect, and La Follette was elected to the U.S. Senate, to be thrice reelected. His program made his state a model. A surprising number of his reforms were adopted nationally, while the regulatory commissions and technical experts he advocated changed to some extent the whole aspect of American government.

La Follette hoped to succeed Theodore Roosevelt whom he regarded as a lukewarm reformer; he feared that the unrestrained greed of businessmen would drive the nation into Socialism and must be checked. In 1912 he was the logical leader of liberal, insurgent Republicans openly at war with the party leadership. The revolt against Taft no longer appeared hopeless, but many of La Follette's supporters seized on a pretext to switch to Roosevelt at the Progressive Convention in Chicago and La Follette was shunted aside. He never forgave Roosevelt for what he considered a betrayal. Supporting the Democrats on many occasions, he opposed Wilson's 1916–17 diplomatic course and voted against war with Germany. He supported all the other war measures, however, and sought to make the war a charge on the current income of the rich rather than upon posterity. He opposed joining the League of Nations and the World Court. In 1924, at the highest point of his prestige, he decided to run independently for president as a Progressive with the hope of throwing the election into the House of Representatives where the insurgents might determine the choice. He received one-sixth of the votes cast.

LA FOLLETTE, ROBERT MARION, JR. (*b. Madison, Wis., 1895; d. Washington, D.C., 1953*), U.S. senator. Studied for a time at the University of Wisconsin. The son of senator and progressive leader Robert La Follette, "Young Bob" inherited the liberal Republican ideology of his father. He was elected to the Senate in 1930 and served until his defeat in 1946 by Joseph R. McCarthy. Opposed in the pro-business policies of Hoover, La Follette supported Roosevelt and the New Deal vigorously, although he felt that the New Deal was not enough for the country's needs. He was an isolationist until the outbreak of World War II. Heading the La Follette Civil Liberties Committee, he championed the cause of organized labor. In 1934, La Follette led the progressive Republicans into a schism with the Republican party to form the Wisconsin Progressive party; this faction held power in the state until 1940. After his defeat, La Follette served as a business consultant and foreign aid advisor to President Truman. He died of a self-inflicted gunshot wound in his home in Washington.

LAFON, THOMY (*b. New Orleans, La., 1810; d. New Orleans, 1893*), black financier, philanthropist. Bequeathed the bulk of his large estate to charitable and educational institutions in New Orleans.

LA GUARDIA, FIORELLO HENRY (*b. New York, N.Y., 1882; d. New York, 1947*), politician, mayor of New York City.

Child of immigrant parents; his father a former Catholic from Foggia, Italy, his mother of Jewish extraction from Trieste in what was then Austria-Hungary. He was raised on U.S. Army posts in the West, where his father served as an enlisted bandmaster, 1885–98; he was educated through the eighth grade in the public schools of Prescott, Ariz. Upon his father's discharge, the family recrossed the Atlantic to Trieste, and La Guardia grew to manhood in the Austro-Hungarian empire. A member of the American consular service from age seventeen through twenty-three, he was stationed in Budapest, then in Fiume, with short assignments in Trieste and Croatia. In 1906 he returned to New York. In 1910, after putting himself through New York University Law School, he began practicing law on the Lower East Side. There he formed a lasting association with the emerging clothing workers' trade unions. Hostile to Tammany's corruption, he joined his local Republican club. In 1915, three years after his debut as an election district captain in his native Greenwich Village, La Guardia was appointed a deputy state attorney general.

Thereafter his career turned on elective office, and the multilingual, Western-bred, Balkan-plated Episcopalian of Italian-Jewish descent started with the advantage of being a balanced ticket in himself. Unlike previous New York mayors, he rose to prominence in national politics before entering City Hall. In 1916 he became the first Republican since the Civil War to be elected to Congress from the Lower East Side. He also took leave of absence from the House to serve as a pilot-bombardier on the Italian-Austrian front in World War I. Returning home a much decorated major in 1918, he was reelected to Congress, but resigned the following year to run for president of the New York City Board of Aldermen. He won, by appealing to normally Democratic nationality groups. In 1921, however, he lost the Republican primary for mayor. The next year he was returned to Congress, this time from the 20th Congressional District. He served five consecutive terms until 1932.

In the 1920's, as his party led the country in disavowing the Progressive era, East Harlem's representative gave the impression of moving to the left. In 1924 he supported the Progressive party presidential candidacy of Robert M. La Follette, and himself stood for reelection as a Progressive. The following year he showed further contempt for the G.O.P. by endorsing the Socialist Norman Thomas in New York's mayoral race. Although La Guardia returned to the Republican party in 1926, he remained a maverick. A New Dealer before that term was coined, La Guardia came into his own during the Great Depression. In 1932 he led the House in defeating President Hoover's proposed sales tax. More significant still, the Norris–La Guardia Anti-Injunction Act, for which he and the Nebraska senator had agitated throughout the "age of normalcy," was passed in the same year. Yet, at the very peak of his congressional career, La Guardia lost his bid for reelection in 1932. In 1933, when an anti-Tammany Fusion slate was formed, La Guardia was its nominee. This time he was elected. Reelected in 1937 and again in 1941, he was the first reform mayor in New York's history to succeed himself. New York was vital for the New Deal's recovery program, and his high standing with the Roosevelt administration released a flow of federal funds for projects dear to him. He opened New York's first major airport in northern Queens (later named La Guardia Airport), and in 1942 ground was broken for Idlewild (Later John F. Kennedy International) Airport in southern Queens. Besides raising the quality of urban life, La Guardia's public improvements put men and women back to work in a time of mass unemployment.

La Guardia's third term fell below the standards of his first two. As World War II approached, La Guardia no longer cared to be the mayor. He hoped that President Roosevelt would appoint him secretary of war. Appointed director of civil defense instead (1941), he applied for an army general's commission and was deeply disappointed when his application was rejected.

So hostile to injecting party politics into municipal government that he allowed neither himself nor his appointees to hold party office, La Guardia's nonpartisanship turned out to be non-self-sustaining. When he left City Hall in 1945, there was no party leader to succeed him and no reform machine to carry on what he had started. Unwilling to retire, he served unhappily as director general of the United Nations Relief and Rehabilitation Administration in 1946.

LAGUNA, THEODORE DE LEO DE (*b. Oakland, Calif., 1876; d. Hardwick, Vt., 1930*), philosopher. Taught at Bryn Mawr College, 1907–30; characterized his philosophy as "The Way of Opinion." He denied existence of truth in general, holding that there are only truths of particular propositions; he also denied validity of induction.

LAHEY, FRANK HOWARD (*b. Haverhill, Mass., 1880; d. Boston, Mass., 1953*), surgeon. Studied at Harvard Medical School. (M.D., 1904). Taught at Harvard and at Tufts Medical School Founded the Lahey Clinic in Boston, which specialized in team surgery. A specialist in thyroid surgery, Lahey gained a reputation as the best American teacher of surgery. At his death, he was perhaps the most famous surgeon in the world. A consultant on President Roosevelt's health, Lahey was President of the A.M.A., 1941–42. Chairman of the War Manpower Commission's Medical Procurement and Assignment Service. He was opposed to President Truman's compulsory national health insurance plan.

LAHONTAN, LOUIS-ARMAND DE LOM D'ARCE, BARON DE (*b. Lahontan, France, 1666; d. probably Hanover, Germany, ca. 1713*), soldier, explorer. Came to Canada, 1683; served in La Barre's and Denonville's expeditions against Iroquois; was commandant at Fort St. Joseph on St. Clair River and explored farther westward beyond Mackinac. Deserted the French service, 1693, after assignment to Newfoundland. Author of *Nouveaux Voyages, etc.* (The Hague, 1703), a well-written and popular mixture of fact and fiction about New France and the western country which exerted a strong influence on the literature of France and England and contributed to 18th-century primitivism.

LAHR, BERT (*b. Irving Lahreim, New York, N.Y., 1895; d. New York, 1967*), comic actor. By 1917 was called the "boy wonder of burlesque"; an overnight success in Broadway musical debut (1927); his last musical role was in *Foxy* (1964, Tony Award for Best Actor in a Musical). Appeared in a score of motion pictures, beginning in 1931, but is best known for his role as the Cowardly Lion in *The Wizard of Oz* (1939). He also appeared in dramatic roles (*Waiting for Godot*, 1956) and on radio and television, including Ed Sullivan's variety show. Dubbed the King of Clowns, elected to the Theatre Hall of Fame (1972).

LAIMBEER, NATHALIE SCHENCK (*b. New York, N.Y., 1882; d. New York, 1929*), banker, financial writer.

LAIT, JACQUIN LEONARD (JACK) (*b. New York, N.Y., 1883; d. Beverly Hills, Calif., 1954*), newspaper writer, editor. Studied at Lewis Institute (later the Illinois Institute of Technology). After working on newspapers in Chicago and writing plays and novels, he became the editor-in-chief of the *New York Mirror* (1936–52). Best known for his books exposing the seamy side of American urban life: *New York Confidential* (1948), *Chicago Confidential* (1950), *Washington Confidential* (1951), and *U.S.A. Confidential* (1952). The books generated numerous lawsuits and were criticized for their sensationalism and inaccuracies.

LAJOIE, NAPOLEON ("LARRY") (*b. Woonsocket, R.I., 1875; d. Daytona Beach, Fla., 1959*), baseball player. Began major league baseball in 1896 with the Philadelphia Phillies. One of the most famous second basemen in baseball's history, Lajoie played with the Phillies, the Athletics, and the Cleveland Blues before retiring in 1918. Elected as a charter member to the Baseball Hall of Fame in 1937.

LAKE, KIRSOPP (*b. Southampton, England, 1872; d. South Pasadena, Calif., 1946*), New Testament scholar, paleographer, archaeologist. B.A., Lincoln College, Oxford, 1895; M.A., 1897. Ordained priest in Church of England, 1896; served as curate in Lumley, Durham, and in Oxford (1897–1904); was also a cataloguer of Greek manuscripts in the Bodleian Library and edited a number of Greek texts. In 1904, he became professor of early Christian literature and New Testament exegesis at the University of Leyden; in 1913, he was appointed professor of early Christian literature at Harvard Divinity School; between 1919 and 1932, he held the Winn chair of ecclesiastical history at Harvard. Thereafter until 1938, he was a member of the history department at Harvard College. Among his many publications were: *The Text of the New Testament* (1900); *The Earlier Epistles of St. Paul* (1911); two volumes in the Loeb Classical Library (*The Apostolic Fathers* and the first volume of Eusebius' *Ecclesiastical History*); he also served as coeditor of *The Beginnings of Christianity* (five volumes, 1902–33).

LAKE, SIMON (*b. Pleasantville, N.J., 1866; d. Bridgeport, Conn., 1945*), inventor, submarine pioneer. Left school at fourteen to work in father's machine shop; in 1887, took out first of some 200 patents granted him (an improved steering device for bicycles). Submitted his first plans for a submarine in a competition, 1893, but was unsuccessful. Encouraged by the performance of a wooden prototype which he built, he had his *Argonaut I* constructed to his specifications. Launched in August 1897, she traveled more than 2,000 miles and made the passage by open sea from Cape May to Sandy Hook. He organized the Lake Torpedo Boat Company, 1900, and in 1902 at Bridgeport, Conn., launched his *Protector*, first of a new breed of submarines; they were equipped with hydroplanes fore and aft to achieve submergence while maintaining an even keel, and with an early form of the periscope. Owing to the U.S. Navy's commitment to John P. Holland and the Electric Boat Company, he could not sell his vessel here and sold it and a number of others to Russia. Up until about 1911, he concentrated on the European market. In 1911, he sold the *Seal* to the United States; over the next eleven years, the navy bought twenty-eight more Lake submarines. The disarmament policies of the 1920's put an end to his work with undersea craft, and he was increasingly unsuccessful with other ventures.

LALOR, ALICE. *See* TERESA, MOTHER.

LAMAR, GAZAWAY BUGG (*b. Richmond, Co., Ga., 1798; d. New York, N.Y., 1874*), ship owner, banker, cotton merchant. Introduced the first iron steamship in American waters (the *John Randolph*, Savannah, Ga., 1834); was an incorporator of the Iron Steamboat Co. of Augusta, 1835. Removed to New York City, 1845, where he became president of the Bank of the Republic; remained in New York as Confederate intelligence agent until after the Civil War began. Back in Savannah, he engaged in banking and blockade running. When General Sherman occupied Savannah, Lamar immediately took the oath of allegiance to save his property; later imprisoned on bribery charges, he was released by President Johnson.

LAMAR, JOSEPH RUCKER (*b. Elbert Co., Ga., 1857; d. Washington, D.C., 1916*), jurist. Attended University of Georgia; graduated Bethany College, W.Va., 1877. Admitted to Georgia bar, 1878, he practiced in Augusta and rose rapidly in his profession. As one of three commissioners appointed, 1893, to recodify the laws of Georgia, he undertook the major task of preparing the civil code. Appointed associate justice of state supreme court, 1904, after two years he resigned. In 1911 he became an associate justice of the U.S. Supreme Court. His decisions were terse, clear and just; among them, *Gompers* v. *Bucks Stove Co.* and *U.S.* v. *Midwest Oil Co.* were outstanding. He served as a U.S. commissioner to the Niagara Falls mediation conference to adjust U.S.-Mexican difficulties in May–June 1914.

LAMAR, LUCIUS QUINTUS CINCINNATUS (*b. Putnam, Co., Ga., 1825; d. Macon, Ga., 1893*), lawyer, statesman. Nephew of Mirabeau B. Lamar. Graduated Emory College, 1845; admitted to the bar in Georgia, 1847. Settled permanently in Mississippi, 1855; was congressman, Democrat, 1857–60. Although conservative by temperament, he was determined to preserve what he considered the rights of the Southern states and drafted and reported the Mississippi ordinance of secession. Appointed Confederate special commissioner to Russia after military service, 1861–62, he spent several months in London and Paris, 1863, but was recalled before going to St. Petersburg. For a period after the end of the Civil War, he practiced law and taught at University of Mississippi. Elected to Congress, 1872, he labored to achieve sectional reconciliation and good will; as U.S. senator, 1877–85, he continued to impress the country with the desire of the new South to serve the interests of a common nationality and was outstanding as an orator. He was an able secretary of the interior, 1885–87. Appointed to the U.S. Supreme Court late in 1887, he served with great distinction until his death.

LAMAR, MIRABEAU BUONAPARTE (*b. Warren Co., Ga., 1798; d. Richmond, Tex., 1859*), statesman, planter. Uncle of Lucius Q. C. Lamar. Early active in Georgia politics; edited *Columbus* (Ga.) *Enquirer*. Removed to Texas, 1836; commanded cavalry at San Jacinto; served as secretary of war in provisional cabinet of President Burnet. Elected vice president of Texas, 1836; served as president of the republic, December 1838–December 1841. Originally opposed to U.S. annexation, he planned a comprehensive system of education; began successful negotiations for recognition by France, England, and Holland; founded city of Austin, 1840. He was, however, unable to solve the growing financial problems of Texas and failed to gain recognition of the republic's independence by Mexico. His career after his presidency was relatively uneventful.

LAMB, ARTHUR BECKET (*b. Attleboro, Mass., 1880; d. Brookline, Mass., 1952*), chemist. Received Ph.D. degrees from Tufts College and Harvard in 1904; attended the universities of Leipzig and Heidelberg. Taught at New York University, 1906–12, and at Harvard, 1912–48. During World War I, he worked for the Bureau of Mines in Washington developing poison gases and gas masks. Dean of Harvard Graduate School of Arts and Sciences from 1940 to 1943. President of the American Chemical Society in 1933; editor (1917–49) of the *Journal of the American Chemical Society.*

LAMB, ISAAC WIXOM (*b. Hartland, Mich., 1840; d. Perry, Mich., 1906*), Baptist clergyman. Patented, 1863, the first successful flat (as contrasted to circular) knitting machine to be designed in the United States. *Post* 1869, he was engaged in pastoral work in Michigan.

LAMB, JOHN (*b. New York, N.Y., 1735; d. 1800*), Revolutionary patriot, soldier, merchant. An active leader of the Sons of Liberty *post* 1765, Lamb was commissioned captain of artillery in July 1775, and served under General Richard Montgomery in the invasion of Canada that year. Described as "very turbulent and troublesome," he was wounded, captured, and paroled; exchanged in 1777, he was made colonel of 2nd Continental Artillery. Promoted brigadier general, 1783, he became collector of customs at port of New York, 1784. Although an anti-Federalist, his appointment was confirmed under the new Constitution, and he served in the post of collector until his resignation, 1797, by reason of a defalcation by his deputy.

LAMB, MARTHA JOANNA READE NASH (*b. Plainfield, Mass., 1829; d. New York, N.Y., 1893*), author. Her principal work was the popular and still valuable *History of the City of New York* (1877–81); she was distinguished also as editor of the *Magazine of American History*, 1883–93.

LAMB, WILLIAM FREDERICK (*b. Brooklyn, N.Y., 1883; d. New York, N.Y., 1952*), architect. Studied at Williams College, Columbia College of Architecture, and the École des Beaux Arts in Paris, degree, 1911. Known as the principal designer of New York's Empire State Building. Member of the firm of Shreve and Lamb, founded 1924; Arthur Loomis Harmon joined 1929. Appointed member of the Federal Commission of Fine Arts by President Roosevelt, 1937–45.

LAMBDIN, JAMES REID (*b. Pittsburgh, Pa., 1807; d. near Philadelphia, Pa., 1889*), portrait painter, miniaturist. Pupil of Thomas Sully. Long associated with Artists' Fund Society, Philadelphia, and with Pennsylvania Academy of the Fine Arts.

LAMBEAU, EARL LOUIS ("CURLY") (*b. Green Bay, Wis., 1898; d. Sturgeon Bay, Wis., 1965*), football player, coach, and founder of the Green Bay Packers. Received a football scholarship to Notre Dame (1918), but illness forced him to drop out. In 1919 he and several high-school friends organized the Packers, a semi-professional team, on which he served as coach, player, and manager. Packers entered the American Professional Football Association (forerunner of National Football League) in 1921. The team won six league championships (1929–31, 1936, 1939, 1944), largely due to his imaginative and demanding coaching, but it began to decline after World War II due to his absences. He resigned in 1950. Also coach of Chicago Cardinals, 1950–51, and Washington Redskins, 1952–54. Elected to Pro Football Hall of Fame in 1963.

LAMBERT, LOUIS ALOISIUS (*b. Charleroi, Pa., 1835; d. Newfoundland, N.J., 1910*), Roman Catholic clergyman, author. Ordained 1859 for diocese of Alton, Ill.; served as Civil War chaplain, 18th Illinois Infantry; was pastor for many years at Waterloo, N.Y. Wrote effectively against fashionable infidelism of Robert G. Ingersoll and was first American Catholic apologist to reach a wide audience outside his own communion; edited New York *Freeman's Journal*, 1894–1910. Engaged in controversy with Bishop Bernard J. McQuaid.

LAMBERTON, BENJAMIN PEFFER (*b. Cumberland Co., Pa., 1844; d. Washington, D.C., 1912*), naval officer. Graduated U.S. Naval Academy, 1864. Was chief of staff to Com. Dewey at battle of Manila Bay, 1898; retired as rear admiral, 1906.

LAMBING, ANDREW ARNOLD (*b. Manorville, Pa., 1842; d. Wilkinsburg, Pa., 1918*), Roman Catholic clergyman, pastor in western Pennsylvania, historian of the Catholic Church in that area.

LAMBUTH, JAMES WILLIAM (*b. Alabama, 1830; d. Kobe, Japan, 1892*), clergyman, Methodist Episcopal Church, South. Graduated University of Mississippi, 1851. Missionary to China and Japan, *post* 1854.

LAMBUTH, WALTER RUSSELL (*b. Shanghai, China, 1854; d. Yokohama, Japan, 1921*), bishop, Methodist Episcopal Church, South. Son of James W. Lambuth. Graduated Emory and Henry College, 1875; M.D., Vanderbilt, 1877; M.D., Bellevue Hospital Medical College, New York, 1881. Missionary to China; with his father, inaugurated missionary work of his church in Japan, 1885–86. Returning to the United States, 1891, he was general secretary, Board of Missions, 1894–1910. Elected bishop, 1910, he superintended mission work in Brazil and projected a new field in tropical Africa.

LAMME, BENJAMIN GARVER (*b. near Springfield, Ohio, 1864; d. Pittsburgh, Pa., 1924*), engineer, inventor. Graduated Ohio State, M.E., 1888. Joined Westinghouse Electric Co., 1889, and was that organization's chief engineer at the time of his death. A master of analytical work and computing, he became an outstanding designer of electrical machinery. He was leader in development of motors for railways, a pioneer in designing rotary converters and among the first to produce a commercially successful induction motor. He transformed the ideas of Nikola Tesla into commercial form and was the creator of the single-phase railway system.

LAMON, WARD HILL (*b. Frederick Co., Va., 1828; d. near Martinsburg, W.Va., 1893*), lawyer. Settled in Danville, Ill., 1847; associate and friend of Abraham Lincoln. As U.S. marshal of District of Columbia, 1861–65, he was a conspicuous Washington figure. Law partner of Jeremiah S. Black, 1865–79. Lamon's *Life of Abraham Lincoln* (1872) was written by Chauncey F. Black and based chiefly upon material which Lamon bought from W. H. Herndon.

LAMONT, DANIEL SCOTT (*b. Cortland Co., N.Y., 1851; d. Millbrook, N.Y., 1905*), New York state official, politician, financier. Private secretary to President Grover Cleveland, 1885–89; prospered in street-railway ventures as employee of William C. Whitney. Served effectively as secretary of war, 1893–97, and was thereafter vice president of Northern Pacific Railway Co. and a close associate of James J. Hill.

LAMONT, HAMMOND (*b. Monticello, N.Y., 1864; d. New York, N.Y., 1909*), educator, journalist. Graduated Harvard, 1886. Taught English at Harvard and Brown; was managing editor, New York *Evening Post*, 1900–09; editor, the *Nation*, 1906–09. Author of *English Composition* (1906).

LAMONT, THOMAS WILLIAM (*b. Claverack, N.Y., 1870; d. Boca Grande, Fla., 1948*), banker. B.A., Harvard, 1892. Starting as a reporter on the *New York Tribune*, he rose to assistant night city editor. In 1894 he became secretary of Cushman Brothers, New York City, agents for manufacturers of food products. By 1898 the firm was in serious financial trouble, and one of its major creditors asked Lamont to reorganize and manage it. In 1903 he joined the newly organized Bankers Trust Company as secretary and treasurer. He remained with Bankers Trust until 1909, rising in 1905 to a vice presidency and a directorship. In that year he accepted similar posts with the First National Bank, but left in 1911 to become a partner in J. P. Morgan and Company. Shortly after the outbreak of World War I, when Britain and France appointed the House of Morgan as their representative and purchasing agent in the United States, Lamont participated in planning and selling international loans. In 1917 he went to London and Paris to serve as advisor on financial and economic matters to Col. Edward M. House in negotiations to coordinate the American war effort with that of Britain and France. In 1919 Lamont was appointed as a representative to the U.S. Treasury on the American delegation to the Paris Peace Conference. He returned in June 1919 to the United States and to J. P. Morgan and Company. Still the nation's leading private investment banking house, the firm between 1919 and 1933 offered the public some $6 billion in securities, approximately one-third of which were foreign government and corporate issues. No one played a more important role in negotiating these offerings than Lamont. In 1940 when J. P. Morgan and Company became incorporated as a commercial bank and trust company, Lamont became chairman of the executive committee. In 1943 he was elected chairman of the board of the firm.

Lamont helped establish the Bank for International Settlements (1931), and he was a delegate to the World Economic Conference that met in London in June 1933. Although a critic of New Deal fiscal policies, he favored Secretary of State Cordell Hull's liberal trade program of the 1930's, and in 1940 he helped organize the committee to Defend America by Aiding the Allies. In 1918 Lamont bought the *New York Evening Post*, but had to sell out four years later. In 1924 he helped establish and finance the *Saturday Review of Literature*, which he continued to support until 1938. He was an officer or trustee of numerous institutions, among them the Carnegie Foundation for the Advancement of Teaching, the American School of Classical Studies (Athens), the Metropolitan Museum of Art, and the Academy of Political Science.

LA MOUNTAIN, JOHN (*b. Wayne Co., N.Y., 1830; d. 1870*), aeronaut. Became interested early in ballooning; with O. A. Gager and John Wise, constructed balloon *Atlantic* in which they flew from St. Louis, Mo., to Henderson, N.Y., July 1–2, 1859, longest air voyage on record to that date. La Mountain served as a balloon observer with the Army of the Potomac in the Civil War.

LAMOUREUX, ANDREW JACKSON (*b. Iosco, Mich., 1850; d. Ithaca, N.Y., 1928*), journalist. Edited liberal *Rio News*, English newspaper in Rio de Janeiro, Brazil, *post* 1877. Returned to the United States, 1902, and was for many years reference librarian, College of Agriculture, Cornell University.

LAMPSON, SIR CURTIS MIRANDA (*b. New Haven, Vt., 1806; d. London, England, 1885*), merchant. Removed to London, 1830; grew wealthy as an importer. Created a baronet, 1866, for his ten years' work in financing and seeing through to success the Atlantic Cable project.

LAMY, JOHN BAPTIST (*b. Lempdes, France, 1814; d. Santa Fe, N.Mex., 1888*), Roman Catholic clergyman. Ordained at Clermont-Ferrand, 1838; volunteered for mission work in lower Ohio, 1839. Appointed vicar-apostolic of New Mexico, 1850; named bishop of Santa Fe., 1853, and archbishop, 1875. Overcame resentment of turbulent native Catholics against an American bishop and performed long journeys of great difficulty in doing the work of his vast diocese; resigned his see, 1885. Willa Cather's *Death Comes for the Archbishop* (1927) is based on his career.

LANCASTER, HENRY CARRINGTON (*b. Richmond, Va., 1882; d. Baltimore, Md., 1954*), literary historian. Studied at the University of Virginia and at Johns Hopkins University. Ph.D., 1907. Taught at Amherst College, 1907–19; at Johns Hopkins, 1918–47. Chairman of the department of Romance languages. Editor of *Modern Language Notes*, 1919–54. Began publishing nine-volume *History of Dramatic French Literature in the Seventeenth Century* in 1929. President of the Modern Language Association, 1939.

LANDAIS, PIERRE (*b. St. Malo, France, ca. 1731; d. New York, N.Y., 1820*), naval officer. After long service in French Navy, accepted captain's commission in Continental Navy, 1777; commanded frigate *Alliance*, 1778–79. Moody, indecisive and jealous, he was formally accused by John Paul Jones of insubordination and treachery during action with British off Flamborough Head, 1779. Court-martialed and discharged from the service, January 1781, he later served creditably with the French Navy. He

returned to New York City, 1797, where he lived thereafter in poverty, pressing his claims against the government for prize money and restitution of rank.

LANDER, EDWARD (*b. Salem, Mass., 1816; d. Washington, D.C., 1907*), jurist. Brother of Frederick W. Lander. Graduated Harvard, 1835; LL.B. 1839. Removed to Indianapolis, Ind., 1841. Served as justice of supreme court, Washington Territory, 1853–58; engaged in controversy over supremacy of civil law with Gov. I. I. Stevens.

LANDER, FREDERICK WEST (*b. Salem, Mass., 1821; d. in camp on Cacapon River, Va., 1862*), engineer, explorer, Union soldier. Brother of Edward Lander. After work on Eastern railroad surveys, Lander led or participated in five Western survey expeditions, including I. I. Stevens' survey of a Northern route for a Pacific Railroad, 1853; the exploration of a feasible route for a railway from the Mississippi via South Pass to Puget Sound, 1854; he served as superintendent and chief engineer of the overland wagon road, 1855–59. Appointed brigadier general of volunteers, 1861, he was cited for gallantry in operations on the upper Potomac and died while preparing to move his force into the Shenandoah Valley to assist Banks's campaign.

LANDER, JEAN MARGARET DAVENPORT (*b. Wolverhampton, England, 1829; d. Lynn, Mass., 1903*), actress. Wife of Frederick W. Lander. Made American debut in New York City as child prodigy, 1838; was first American "Camille" (1853).

LANDIS, HENRY ROBERT MURRAY (*b. Niles, Ohio, 1872; d. Bryn Mawr, Pa., 1937*), physician. Graduated Amherst, 1894; M.D., Jefferson Medical College, 1897. Pioneer investigator (Phipps Institute, Philadelphia) of tuberculosis among blacks, and of silicosis and anthracosis. Professor of University of Pennsylvania *post* 1910. Coauthor *Diseases of the Chest, etc.* (1917).

LANDIS, JAMES MCCAULEY (*b. Tokyo, Japan, 1899; d. Harrison, N.Y, 1964*), law professor and federal administrator. Son of missionary parents, attended Princeton (1921) and Harvard Law School (S.J.D., 1925). Clerked for Supreme Court Justice Louis D. Brandeis (1925); joined Harvard law faculty (1926). He was the youngest dean in the law school's history (1937–41, 1945–46); shifted the curriculum from an emphasis on common law to the needs of public administration. A leading theorist and staunch defender of federal regulation, he was appointed to the Federal Trade Commission (1933), Securities and Exchange Commission (1934–37), and the Civil Aeronautics Board (1946–47). In the 1950's he was an adviser to Joseph P. Kennedy, and he returned to federal service as special assistant to President John F. Kennedy.

LANDIS, KENESAW MOUNTAIN (*b. Millville, Ohio, 1866; d. Chicago, Ill. 1944*), jurist, first commissioner of organized baseball. Attended the Y.M.C.A. Law School, Cincinnati, Ohio, and Union College of Law, Chicago; admitted to Illinois bar, 1891; served as private secretary to U.S. secretary of state, Walter Q. Gresham, 1893–95; practiced law in Chicago, 1895–1905. Through friendship of Frank O. Lowden, he was appointed federal district judge for northern Illinois and served in a spirit of Rooseveltian liberalism and with considerable courtroom showmanship until 1921. In 1921, following on the "Black Sox" scandal in connection with the 1919 World Series, on invitation of the owners of the major league baseball clubs he became the all-powerful censor and arbiter of the game. He continued until his death to smell out corruption, impose standards of conduct for players both on and off the field, and berate club owners whenever he judged it necessary. As "the man who cleaned up baseball," he remained widely popular with the public, if somewhat less so with owners and players.

LANDIS, WALTER SAVAGE (b. Pottstown, Pa., 1881; d. Old Greenwich, Conn., 1944), chemical engineer. Took degrees of metallurgical engineer (1902) and M.S. (1906) at Lehigh University; studied also at University of Heidelberg (1904–05) and at the Technische Hochschule at Aachen (1909). Taught mineralogy and metallurgy at Lehigh, leaving in 1912 to join Frank S. Washburn in the American Cyanamid Company as chief technologist; he became vice president of the firm in 1923. He is particularly remembered as the developer of the cyanamide process of nitrogen fixation in the United States, and for the key role he played in exploring avenues for utilizing the basic product of his company. He made outstanding contributions to the production of concentrated fertilizers, to metallurgy and gold mining, and to the development of synthetic resins and numerous other organic compounds.

LANDON, MELVILLE DE LANCEY (b. Eaton, N.Y., 1839; d. Yonkers, N.Y., 1910), journalist, humorous lecturer, and writer under pseudonym "Eli Perkins."

LANDOWSKA, WANDA ALEKSANDRA (b. Warsaw, Poland, 1879; d. Lakeville, Conn., 1959), harpsichordist and musician. Studied at the Warsaw Conservatory. Landowska is considered primarily responsible for the revival of the harpsichord and its music in our time. She taught at the Hochschule für Musik in Berlin from 1913 to 1919, and at the École Normale de Musique in Paris. In 1925, she founded the École de Musique Ancienne outside of Paris. Her first concert tour of the U.S. was in 1923. She gave the first integral performance of the complete Goldberg Variations by Bach in 1933 and, at age seventy-five, she recorded Bach's complete Well-Tempered Clavier. Moved to the U.S. in 1941 and gave concerts and lectures throughout the country. Her writings include "Sur l'interprétation des oeuvres de clavecin de J.S. Bach" (1905) and, with her husband, Henri Lew, *La musique ancienne*, (1912).

LANDRETH, DAVID (b. Philadelphia, Pa., 1802; d. Bristol, Pa., 1880), agriculturist. Proprietor *post* 1828 of nursery and seed business established by his father, 1784; was active in agricultural societies.

LANDSTEINER, KARL (b. Vienna, Austria, 1868; d. New York, N.Y., 1943), pathologist, immunologist. M.D., University of Vienna, 1891. In 1891–92 he worked at Zurich with Emil Fischer, and in 1892–93, at Munich, with Eugen von Bamberger and Arthur Hantsch. At Vienna, Landsteiner spent a year (1894–95) in the 1st University Surgical Clinic; in 1896–97 he was an assistant in the Institute of Hygiene under Max von Gruber. He then settled down in the University Institute of Pathology, where he remained until 1907.

Landsteiner published numerous studies on antigenantibody reactions such as agglutination and precipitation of bacteria and red blood cells by immune sera. Out of this work came the discovery that certain basic types of human blood existed, a discovery announced in 1901 and subsequently refined by him. In 1930 he received the Nobel Prize for this discovery of the blood cell groups. Among Landsteiner's other achievements of the fruitful decade 1897–1907 were an explanation of a peculiar blood disturbance, paroxysmal hemoglobinuria; a notable improvement of the Wassermann test for syphilis; and introduction of the dark-field microscope for study of *Treponema pallidum*, the microorganism causing that disease.

In 1908 he was appointed prosector (pathologist) to the Wilhelmina Hospital in Vienna and in the following year was named associate professor at the University of Vienna. At the Wilhelmina Hospital he helped establish the viral nature of poliomyelitis and led others, years later, to the preparation of effective vaccines. He also explained (1918–20) that new "syn-thetic" antigens may be produced when proteins are altered by chemical combination with relatively simple substances. As pathologist to a hospital at The Hague, Netherlands (1919), he managed to continue his researches in basic immunochemistry. In 1922 he became a member of the Rockefeller Institute. While there he found a new series of factors in human blood in addition to those characteristic of the four groups first known, (A, B, AB, and O). In a continuing search for new blood factors, Landsteiner was the cofounder of the Rh factor. In the 1920's Landsteiner succeeded in synthesizing chains of amino acids (the "building stones" of proteins) that were sufficiently large to serve as antigens. He retired from membership in the Rockefeller Institute in 1939, but went on working in his laboratory until his death.

LANE, ARTHUR BLISS (b. Bay Ridge, N.Y., 1894; d. New York, N.Y., 1956), diplomat and author. Studied at Yale University; member of the foreign service diplomatic corps from 1916 to 1945. Major assignments included secretary to the American embassy in Mexico, 1924; minister to Nicaragua (1933–36) during the rise of the Somoza family; minister to Yugoslavia (1937–41); and ambassador to Poland, 1944 until his retirement. The last years of his life were spent actively opposing communism. He wrote *I Saw Poland Betrayed* (1948) and campaigned for Senator Joseph R. McCarthy.

LANE, FRANKLIN KNIGHT (b. near Charlottetown, Canada, 1864; d. Rochester, Minn., 1921), lawyer, statesman. Removed as a child to California; was raised in Napa and Oakland. Attended University of California, 1884–86, and Hastings College of Law; was admitted to bar, 1888. After a brief, unsuccessful period as a newspaper publisher and editor, he practiced law in San Francisco. Served three terms as Democratic city and county attorney; won national notice in vigorous but unsuccessful campaigns for governor of California and mayor of San Francisco, 1902 and 1903. Appointed to Interstate Commerce Commission, 1905, he served with outstanding ability, 1906–13; his decisions largely determined the constitutional powers of the government in the regulation of common carriers. As secretary of the interior in President Wilson's cabinet, 1913–20, Lane favored conservation, worked to develop Alaska and pressed for a more liberal Indian policy. He was notable also for his ability to inspire in his subordinates his own enthusiasm for honest public service.

LANE, GEORGE MARTIN (b. probably Northampton, Mass., 1823; d. 1897), classicist. Graduated Harvard, 1846; Ph.D., Göttingen, 1851. Professor of Latin, Harvard, 1951–94. A notable teacher. Author of *Latin Pronunciation* (1871) and an important *Latin Grammar* (1898). Hero of the "Lay of the Lone Fishball."

LANE, GERTRUDE BATTLES (b. Saco, Maine, 1874; d. New York, N.Y., 1941), magazine editor, publishing executive. Associated with the *Woman's Home Companion* from 1903 until her death, she was editor in chief *post* 1912. She was successful alike in shaping the editorial policy of the magazine to suit the needs of American housewives in her time, and in securing large advertising revenues.

LANE, HENRY SMITH (b. near Sharpsburg, Ky., 1811; d. 1881), lawyer, banker. Removed to Crawfordsville, Ind., 1834. Congressman, Whig, from Indiana, 1840–43. As Republican, presided over national convention, 1856, and was U.S. senator from Indiana, 1861–67.

LANE, HORACE M. (b. Readfield, Maine, 1837; d. São Paulo, Brazil, 1912), physician. Presbyterian missionary educator in Brazil *post* 1886; organized Mackenzie College, São Paulo, 1891.

LANE, JAMES HENRY (b. probably Lawrenceburg, Ind., 1814; d. 1866), soldier, Kansas political leader. Served creditably in Mexican War; was Democratic lieutenant governor of Indiana, 1849–53, and congressman, 1853–55. Immigrating to Kansas Territory, he joined Free-State movement and soon was directing its campaign to unite all antislavery factions and secure a "free" constitution preliminary to statehood. President of Topeka constitutional convention, he emerged from the crisis of the so-called Wakarusa War as a radical. In late summer, 1856, he led "Lane's Army of the North" into Kansas in atrocious attacks on proslavery strongholds; when the Free-State party won control of the Assembly, he was elected major general of the militia. Elected to the U.S. senate, he served from 1861 until his death by suicide. Meanwhile, he was a pioneer in advocating emancipation of slaves and their use as soldiers, and was a strong supporter of Lincoln.

LANE, JAMES HENRY (b. Mathews Court House, Va., 1833; d. 1907), Confederate brigadier general, educator. Graduated Virginia Military Institute, 1854; University of Virginia, 1857. Served with Lee's army throughout Civil War. Taught at several schools, and was professor of civil engineering at Alabama Polytechnic Institute, 1882–1907.

LANE, JOHN (b. Fairfax, Co., Va., 1789; d. Vicksburg, Miss., 1855), Methodist clergyman, merchant, A founder of Vicksburg, Miss., as administrator of estate of Newet Vick, his father-in-law.

LANE, JOSEPH (b. Buncombe Co., N.C., 1801; d. Oregon, 1881), soldier, governor, legislator. Raised in Henderson Co., Ky. Settled in Vanderburg Co., Ind., 1820; prospered as farmer and flatboat merchant; was frequently elected to the legislature. One of the Mexican War's outstanding heroes, he won a brevet of major general. Commissioned governor of Oregon Territory, 1848, he resigned in 1850 to be chosen delegate to Congress. Reelected three times, he became U.S. senator, 1859, on Oregon's admission as a state. In 1860 he ran for vice president on the Breckinridge ticket as an avowed partisan of secession, and his public career was ended. One of the ablest men of his time in the West, he was an independent thinker on public questions. His alleged connection with the "Pacific Republic" scheme to aid the Confederacy is legend rather than fact.

LANE, LEVI COOPER (b. near Somerville, Ohio, 1830; d. 1902), surgeon. Graduated Jefferson Medical College, 1851. Associated with his uncle Elias S. Cooper in San Francisco, Calif., 1859–64; was considered leading surgeon on Pacific Coast. Benefactor of Medical College of Pacific, where he taught.

LANE, SIR RALPH (b. England, ca. 1530; d. Dublin, Ireland, 1603), colonist. Accompanied Sir Richard Grenville to Virginia, 1585; commanded settlement on Roanoke Island until it was abandoned the following year.

LANE, TIDENCE (b. near Baltimore, Md., 1724; d. 1806), pioneer Baptist minister of Tennessee. Organized Buffalo Ridge Church in present Washington Co. ca. 1779; was pastor at Bent Creek, 1785–1806.

LANE, WALTER PAYE (b. Co. Cork, Ireland, 1817; d. Marshall, Tex., 1892), soldier, merchant. Came to America as a child; was raised in Fairview, Ohio. Served in Texan war of independence and as a Confederate brigadier.

LANE, WILLIAM CARR (b. Fayette Co., Pa., 1789; d. St. Louis, Mo., 1863), physician. First mayor of St. Louis, 1823; reelected many times. Governor of New Mexico Territory, 1852.

LANG, BENJAMIN JOHNSON (b. Salem, Mass., 1837; d. Boston, Mass., 1909), musician, organist at Old South and King's Chapel, Boston. Conductor of the Apollo Club, the Cecilia Society and the Handel and Haydn Society; introduced much new music as pianist and orchestra leader.

LANG, HENRY ROSEMAN (b. St. Gall, Switzerland, 1853; d. 1934), philologist. Came to America ca. 1875. Ph.D., University of Strasbourg, 1892. Taught Romance languages, Yale, 1893–1922. His many publications deal mainly with Portuguese and Spanish literature of the earlier periods.

LANG, LUCY FOX ROBINS (b. Kiev, Russia, 1884; d. Los Angeles, Calif., 1962), labor activist. Arrived in the United States in 1893, and at an early age identified with the anarchist movement; moved in radical circles in New York and California, 1905–17. About 1917 she came under the influence of Samuel Gompers, president of the American Federation of Labor, which caused her to shift from radical left-wing politics to a commitment to furthering the cause of the American worker. She also worked to secure amnesty for Socialist leader Eugene V. Debs.

LANGDELL, CHRISTOPHER COLUMBUS (b. New Boston, N.H., 1826; d. Cambridge, Mass., 1906), lawyer, legal author. Attended Harvard College and Law School, 1851–54; practiced law in New York City, 1854–70. Called to Harvard, 1870, to become Dane Professor (afterwards dean) in the Law School, he introduced striking changes, requiring examinations for the law degree and training his students to use original authorities for their derivation and understanding of legal principles. For teaching by his case method, he edited and published A Selection of Cases on the Law of Contracts (1871), A Selection of Cases on Sales of Personal Property (1872) and Cases on Equity Pleading (1875). At first opposed by the bar and other law school teachers, his method gained popularity, particularly through the use of it by William A. Keener and James B. Ames.

LANGDON, COURTNEY (b. Rome, Italy, 1861; d. Providence, R.I., 1924), educator. Son of William C. Langdon. Taught modern and Romance languages at Lehigh and Cornell, and at Brown University post 1890. Published translation of Dante's Divine Comedy (1918–21).

LANGDON, HARRY PHILMORE (b. Council Bluffs, Iowa, 1884; d. Los Angeles, Calif., 1944), motion picture comedian. Left home as a boy to join a traveling medicine show; spent more than twenty-five years in vaudeville. Under contract to Mack Sennett, he made twenty-five, two-reel films between 1924 and 1926 which established him as one of the most popular comedians of the great period of the silent movies. Wide-eyed and innocent, he acted the role of a helpless child-man buffeted by a world he does not understand yet emerging from his difficulties unharmed and through no will of his own. In 1926 he left Sennett, taking with him several of Sennett's most talented staff members, and organized his own company to produce feature-length comedies; of these, the first three were successful, but owing to a dispute with Frank Capra, the director who was best able to bring out his talent, his team of associates broke up and he never regained his standing in the industry.

LANGDON, JOHN (b. Portsmouth, N.H., 1741; d. 1819), merchant, Revolutionary patriot, politician. Brother of Woodbury Langdon. Organized and financed Stark's expedition against Burgoyne, 1777; was speaker of New Hampshire legislature and member of Continental Congress. Governor of New Hampshire, 1785, 1788, 1805–08, 1810–11; U.S. senator, (Democrat) Republican, 1789–1801.

LANGDON, SAMUEL (b. Boston, Mass., 1723; d. Hampton Falls, N.H., 1797), Congregational clergyman. President of Harvard, 1774–80, appointed as a "zealous whig" to counterbalance pro-British college officers.

LANGDON, WILLIAM CHAUNCY (*b. Burlington, Vt., 1831; d. Providence, R.I., 1895*), patent lawyer, Episcopal clergyman. Graduated Transylvania University, 1850; ordained, 1859. Took lead in founding American Confederation of Y.M.C.A., 1854, and was first general secretary. Resided in Europe as rector of Episcopal churches in Rome, Florence and Geneva, 1859–62, 1865–76. A partisan of Christian reunion.

LANGDON, WOODBURY (*b. Portsmouth, N.H., 1738 or 1739; d. 1805*), merchant, New Hampshire legislator and official. Brother of John Langdon.

LANGE, ALEXIS FREDERICK (*b. Lafayette Co., Mo., 1862; d. 1924*), educator. Director and dean, University of California School of Education; originated junior high school movement; helped begin junior college movement.

LANGE, DOROTHEA (*b. Dorothea Margaretta Nutzhorn, Hoboken, N.J., 1895; d. Berkeley, Calif., 1965*), photographer. Began taking documentary photographs of people during the Great Depression, including one of her best-known pictures, "White Angel Bread Line." Worked for several government agencies and took her best-known photo, "Migrant Mother," while working for the Resettlement Administration (1936). First woman photographer to receive a Guggenheim grant (1941) and have a retrospective exhibit at the Museum of Modern Art (1966).

LANGE, LOUIS (*b. Hesse, Germany, 1829; d. St. Louis, Mo., 1893*), printer, periodical editor. Came to America *ca.* 1846; settled in St. Louis, 1859. His German language publications, *Die Abendschule* and *Die Rundschau*, had wide influence.

LANGER, WILLIAM (*b. near Everest, N. Dak., 1886; d. Washington, D.C., 1959*), politician. Studied at the University of North Dakota and at Columbia. Twice elected Republican governor of North Dakota (1933 and 1937), Langer had to overcome accusations of corruption before he could take his seat in the U.S. Senate in 1940. Remembered for his ardent isolationism during World War II, he was an opponent of the Marshall Plan, the Truman Doctrine, and U.S. membership in the U.N. A populist, he was successful in representing his rural constituency. He served as chairman of the Senate Judiciary Committee (1953–54).

LANGFORD, NATHANIEL PITT (*b. Westmoreland, N.Y., 1832; d. St. Paul, Minn., 1911*), businessman, explorer, first superintendent of Yellowstone National Park. Removed to St. Paul, 1854. Joined Fisk's Northern Overland Expedition to Salmon River gold fields, 1862; at Bannack, Mont., was an organizer of vigilantes for law administration and enforcement as described in his *Vigilante Days and Ways* (1890). He was best known for his early (1870) exploration of the Yellowstone Park area and his pioneer description of it in *Diary of the Washburn Expedition to the Yellowstone and Fire Hole Rivers* (1905). His articles and political efforts helped bring about creation of the area as a national park, 1872. He served without pay as its superintendent, 1872–76, and preserved the natural wonders from exploitation and misuse.

LANGFORD, SAMUEL (*b. Weymouth Falls, Nova Scotia, 1883; d. Cambridge, Mass., 1956*), boxer. Immigrated to Boston in 1899. Employed as a janitor in a Boston boxing gymnasium, Langford became one of the first black professional boxers in 1902. In 1906, he lost a fifteen-round decision to future heavyweight champion Jack Johnson. His last fight was in 1928, after touring England, Europe, Australia, and South America. Known to boxing writers as "the greatest fighter who never fought for the championship," Langford died blind and penniless shortly after being elected into the Boxing Hall of Fame Old Timers Division in 1955. His ring nickname was the "Boston Tarbaby."

LANGLADE, CHARLES MICHEL DE. *See* DE LANGLADE, CHARLES MICHEL.

LANGLEY, JOHN WILLIAMS (*b. Boston, Mass., 1841; d. Ann Arbor, Mich., 1918*), chemist, educator. Brother of Samuel P. Langley. Graduated Lawrence Scientific School, Harvard, 1861. Taught at present Pittsburgh University, at Michigan and at Case School; engaged in chemical and metallurgical research in iron and steel.

LANGLEY, SAMUEL PIERPONT (*b. Roxbury, Mass., 1834; d. Aiken, S.C., 1906*), scientist, aviation research pioneer, author, third secretary of the Smithsonian Institution. Brother of John W. Langley. Read omnivorously; attended several private schools and graduated from Boston High School, 1851; had no college training. Engaged in engineering and architectural work, 1851–64. After a tour of Europe visiting scientific institutions with his brother, 1864–65, he took charge of the small observatory at the U.S. Naval Academy during 1866. He then went to Western University of Pennsylvania as professor of physics and astronomy and director of the Allegheny Observatory, where he remained 20 years.

As an astronomer, his great achievement was in the field of spectral measurements of solar and lunar radiation. He invented the bolometer, 1878, with which he began an epochal series of experiments on the distribution of radiation in the solar spectrum, the transparency of the atmosphere to the different solar rays and the enhancement of their intensity at high altitudes and even outside the atmosphere altogether. In an expedition to Mt. Whitney, California, 1881, he was able to amplify his findings on the solar constant. Thereafter, he made studies of the lunar spectrum and did considerable popular lecturing and writing on astronomical subjects; his *The New Astronomy* (1888) became a classic in astronomical literature.

In 1887 Langley went to the Smithsonian Institution, becoming secretary the same year and remaining until his death. He early established the National Zoological Park and the Astrophysical Observatory, where he carried forward his studies of solar radiation and observation of solar eclipses. Before leaving Allegheny Observatory, he had begun the series of investigations into the possibilities of flight in heavier-than-air machines which he continued with conspicuous results at Washington. The greatness of his contribution to aviation depends on his pioneering laboratory investigations and successful long-distance flights of large power-driven models (1896), and also on the fact that one of his reputation should have ventured in a field so much ridiculed at the time. Persuaded to undertake with Charles M. Manly the construction of a man-carrying airplane, Langley abandoned his efforts after the mechanical failure of their machine in trials during October and December 1903.

LANGLIE, ARTHUR BERNARD (*b. Lanesboro, Minn., 1900; d. Seattle, Wash., 1966*), attorney, politician, and publisher. Attended University of Washington (LL.B., 1926); admitted to Washington State bar. Elected to Seattle city council (1935); then was mayor (1938) and governor of Washington (1940–44, 1948–56). An active Republican and supporter of Dwight D. Eisenhower, he was the keynote speaker at the 1956 national convention. President (1957–61) and chairman (1961–65) of McCall Corporation, publisher of *McCall's Magazine*.

LANGMUIR, IRVING (*b. Brooklyn, N.Y., 1881; d. Woodshole, Mass., 1957*), chemist and physicist. Studied at Columbia School of Mines and at the University of Göttingen, Germany, Ph.D., 1906. Taught at Stevens Institute of Technology (1906–09). Researcher of the General Electric Research Laboratory in Schenectady, N.Y. (1909–50); associate director of the lab from

1929. Langmuir was the first to discover hydrogen in its atomic form, the first to explain thermionic emission and space charge; he was among the first to experiment with aggregation of ionized gases he named plasmas; and he introduced the concept of electron temperature and invented a device (the Langmuir probe) for studying it. Langmuir also invented the gas-filled incandescent lamp and a whole family of high-vacuum radio tubes. From 1919 to 1921, he put forth the "octet" theory of atomic structure. He clarified for the first time the true nature of surface adsorbtion and discovered the existence of monolayers, for which he was awarded the Nobel Prize in 1932. After World War II he worked with his assistant, V. J. Schaefer, in seeding clouds, attempting "artificial rainmaking." Langmuir remained active until his death in 1957.

LANGNER, LAWRENCE (*b. Swansea, South Wales, 1890; d. New York, N.Y., 1962*), chartered patent agent, playwright, and theatrical producer. Came to the United States in 1911 and advised the U.S. government on patents, 1917–58. Better known for his career in theater; founded Washington Square Players in New York City (1914), which from 1915 to 1918 presented plays written by him and other young writers, such as Eugene O'Neill. Formed the Theatre Guild (1919), one of the world's major art theaters, and supervised production of more than two hundred plays, including *Mourning Becomes Electra* (1931), *Porgy and Bess* (1935), *Oklahoma!* (1943), *Come Back, Little Sheba* (1950), and *Picnic* (1953). Founded the New York Repertory Company (1931–33); worked on the radio show "Theatre Guild on the Air" (1945–54); produced television plays; and founded the American Shakespeare Festival Theater and Academy (1950).

LANGSTON, JOHN MERCER (*b. Louisa Co., Va., 1829; d. 1897*), lawyer, educator, diplomat. Graduated Oberlin, 1849; Oberlin theological department, 1853. Admitted to the Ohio bar, 1854, he was nominated and elected clerk of Brownhelm Township, 1855, probably the first black chosen to an elective office in the United States. After service as inspector general of the Freedmen's Bureau, 1868, he was professor of law and dean at Howard University, 1869–76. Appointed U.S. minister to Haiti, 1877, he remained in the diplomatic and consular service until 1885. He was thereafter president of Virginia Normal and Collegiate Institute and served a single term as Republican congressman from Virginia, 1889–91.

LANGSTROTH, LORENZO LORRAINE (*b. Philadelphia, Pa., 1810; d. Dayton, Ohio, 1895*), Congregational clergyman, educator, apiarist. Invented the moveable-frame beehive, which revolutionized the method of keeping bees.

LANGWORTHY, EDWARD (*b. in or near Savannah, Ga., ca. 1738; d. Baltimore, Md., 1802*), Revolutionary patriot, educator. Georgia member of Continental Congress, 1777–79; published *Memoirs of the Life of the Late Charles Lee* (London, 1792).

LANGWORTHY, JAMES LYON (*b. Windsor, Vt., 1800; d. Dubuque, Iowa, 1865*), lead miner, Iowa pioneer. Prospected near site of Dubuque, 1830; settled there, 1833, and was prominent in its civic affairs and development.

LANHAM, FREDERICK GARLAND ("FRITZ") (*b. Weatherford, Tex., 1880; d. Austin, Tex., 1965*), lawyer and U.S. congressman. Attended Weatherford College, Vanderbilt, University of Texas (B.A., 1900), and University of Texas Law School; gave up formal law studies in 1907, but was admitted to bar in 1909. Elected to Congress for fourteen terms (1919–47); lobbied for government support of helium production and the dirigible industry; was a member of the House Committee on patents, revising and reforming national policy on trademarks; and was chairman of the Public Buildings and Grounds Committee.

LANIER, JAMES FRANKLIN DOUGHTY (*b. Washington, N.C., 1800; d. New York, N.Y., 1881*), lawyer, financier. Raised in Eaton, Ohio; removed to Madison, Ind., 1817. A successful lawyer, he became largest shareholder in new State Bank of Indiana, 1833, and was president of its Madison branch. As it was one of the few banks in the Mississippi Valley to weather the panic of 1837, Lanier and the other officers won high repute. He later went to Europe and arranged to restore Indiana's shaken financial credit. In 1848 he moved to New York, where he helped found Winslow, Lanier & Co., a pioneer firm in the floating of railway securities. During the Civil War, he advanced large sums to the State of Indiana to equip and support troops.

LANIER, SIDNEY (*b. Macon, Ga., 1842; d. Lynn, N.C., 1881*), poet, musician, critic. Musically precocious, Lanier graduated from Oglethorpe University, 1860. He had intended to fit himself for teaching by study at a German university, but on the outbreak of the Civil War, enlisted in the Confederate Army. Captured in 1864, he spent four dreary months in a federal prison, (described in *Tiger-Lilies*, 1867). Already consumptive, his next eight years were a tragic experience as he moved restlessly from one occupation to another; in 1873 his father agreed to help him devote himself to the "two sublime arts," music and poetry. He played the flute in the Peabody Orchestra, Baltimore, and his poems "Corn" and "The Symphony," published in *Lippincott's Magazine*, 1875, marked the definite beginnings of his poetic career. Thereafter he continued to produce verses written in accordance with his theories of identity between the technical laws of music and poetry until his early death. His works include *The Science of English Verse* (1880) and *The English Novel* (1883), fruit of his 1879 lectureship at Johns Hopkins; his poems were published in a small book in 1877 and were issued in collected form, 1884.

LANIGAN, GEORGE THOMAS (*b. St. Charles, on the Richelieu River, Canada, 1845; d. Philadelphia, Pa., 1886*), journalist, humorist. Author of the celebrated "Threnody for the Ahkoond of Swat."

LANMAN, CHARLES (*b. Monroe, Mich., 1819; d. Georgetown, D.C., 1895*), writer, amateur explorer, artist. Author of *Private Life of Daniel Webster* (1852) and many other books.

LANMAN, CHARLES ROCKWELL (*b. Norwich, Conn. 1850; d. Belmont, Mass., 1941*), orientalist. B.A., Yale, 1871; Ph.D., 1873 (studied Sanskrit under William D. Whitney). Spent three years in study at Berlin, Leipzig, and Tübingen; taught at Johns Hopkins University, 1876–80. Professor of Sanskrit at Harvard, 1880–1926. He is chiefly remembered for his editorship of the Harvard Oriental Series, which he began in 1891, and for which he enlisted the talents of a wide range of scholars here and abroad. No other American has yet done more to provide the West with an accurate knowledge of ancient India.

LANMAN, JOSEPH (*b. Norwich, Conn., 1811; d. Norwich, 1874*), naval officer. Served in Mexican War and Civil War; as commodore, led second division of Porter's squadron in attacks on Fort Fisher, 1864–65. Retired as rear admiral, 1872.

LANSING, GULIAN (*b. Lishaskill, N.Y., 1825; d. Cairo, Egypt, 1892*), Associate Reformed Church and United Presbyterian clergyman. Missionary to Syria and Egypt *post* 1850.

LANSING, JOHN (*b. Albany, N.Y., 1754; disappeared, New York City, 1829*), jurist. Admitted to practice in Albany, 1775. Served six terms in N.Y. Assembly, 1780–88; was a member of Congress, 1784–85, and mayor of Albany, 1786–90. A delegate to the Philadelphia Convention, 1787, with Alexander Hamilton and Robert Yates, he and Yates withdrew on grounds that the convention was exceeding its authority by drafting a new constitution rather than amending the articles of Confederation. As a member of New York ratifying convention in 1788, he opposed the federal constitution. He was justice of the N.Y. supreme court, 1790–1801, and chief justice in 1798; named chancellor of New York, 1801, he retired, 1814. Although he owed his political preferment to the Clinton faction, he remained a man of independent mind.

LANSING, ROBERT (*b. Watertown, N.Y., 1864; d. Washington, D.C., 1928*), lawyer. Graduated Amherst, 1886; was admitted to the bar, 1889. His marriage to the daughter of John W. Foster in 1890 brought him into the international field where he won distinction; from 1892 to 1914 he served frequently as U.S. counsel or agent on international arbitration tribunals. He helped found American Society of International Law (1906) and was an editor of its *Journal*, 1907–28. He became counselor for the State Department, 1914, and succeeded William J. Bryan as secretary, serving 1915–20. President Wilson decided major policy himself and handled delicate negotiations informally through Edward M. House, but he and Lansing worked in outward harmony until the Peace Conference. Lansing's view that the proposed League of Nations was unimportant brought about estrangement, and when Lansing held cabinet meetings during the President's illness, Wilson demanded his resignation.

LANSTON, TOLBERT (*b. Troy, Ohio, 1844; d. Washington, D.C., 1913*), lawyer, inventor. Worked in U.S. Patent Office, 1865–87; was granted patents on variety of devices, 1870–83. In 1887, he patented the monotype machines for composing printing type; he received further patents for improvements, 1896, 1897, 1899, 1900, 1902, 1910. His perfected machines were introduced commercially, 1897.

LAPCHICK, JOSEPH BOHOMIEL (*b. Yonkers, N.Y., 1900; d. Monticello, N.Y., 1970*), basketball player and coach. Entered professional basketball in 1919 and played with the New York Celtics (1923–27, 1930–36). He was coach at St. John's University in New York City (1936–47, 1956–65), and his teams won a record four National Invitational tournament championships. He was also head coach of the professional New York Knickerbockers (1947–56), reaching the championship finals three times.

LAPHAM, INCREASE ALLEN (*b. Palmyra, N.Y., 1811; d. Oconomowoc, Wis., 1875*), canal builder and engineer, pioneer Wisconsin scientist. Removed from Ohio to Milwaukee, Wis., 1836, as assistant to Byron Kilbourn in surveying, platting, and promoting the area. Made some of the first and best maps of Wisconsin and wrote on the state's geology, mineralogy, and Indian remains. The U.S. Weather Bureau was established at his insistence, 1869.

LAPHAM, WILLIAM BERRY (*b. Greenwood, Maine, 1828; d. Togus, Maine 1894*), physician. Expert local historian and genealogist of Maine.

LARAMIE, JACQUES (*b. probably Canada; d. on Laramie River, Wyo., 1821*), pioneer trapper. Entered the unknown country of southeastern Wyoming *ca.* 1819; reputed to be first white man to visit upper course of the Laramie River. In the legendry of the West, he became an important figure, but little factual information about him has been discovered.

LARCOM, LUCY (*b. Beverly, Mass., 1824; d. Boston, Mass., 1893*), author, teacher. Contributed first to the *Operative's Magazine* of Lowell, Mass., *ca.* 1840, and to its successor the *Lowell Offering and Magazine*. Her verses were popular and were published collectively in 1869 and 1884, but her *New England Girlhood* (1889) has greater value as literature and social history.

She was coeditor with her friend John G. Whittier of several successful verse anthologies.

LARD, MOSES E. (*b. Bedford Co., Tenn., 1818; d. Lexington, Ky., 1880*), minister of Disciples of Christ, editor.

LARDNER, JAMES LAWRENCE (*b. Philadelphia, Pa., 1802; d. Philadelphia, 1881*), naval officer. Appointed midshipman, 1820; retired as rear admiral. A type of the navy career man, active in varied service, 1820–72.

LARDNER, JOHN ABBOTT (*b. Chicago, Ill., 1912; d. New York, N.Y., 1960*), journalist. Studied at Harvard and the Sorbonne. The son of writer Ring Lardner, John Lardner became a celebrated sportswriter with his syndicated column written from the mid–1930's until 1948. During World War II he was a war correspondent for *Newsweek*; after the war, he wrote exclusively for magazines: *Newsweek* (from 1938 until his death), *Look*, and the *New Yorker*. He published three collected sets of essays and is remembered for his superb writing style.

LARDNER, RINGGOLD WILMER (*b. Niles, Mich., 1885; d. East Hampton, N.Y., 1933*), journalist, author. Known as Ring Lardner. Began career, 1905, as sports reporter in South Bend, Ind.; thereafter worked on several Chicago papers and wrote a successful sports column for the *Chicago Tribune*, 1913–19. Began contributing "Jack Keefe" letters about baseball to the *Saturday Evening Post ca.* 1914; they were later published in book form as *You Know Me Al* (1916) and others. He was author also of *Treat 'Em Rough* (1918) and *The Real Dope* (1919). His broad humor later grew mordant and ironical in *How to Write Short Stories* (1924), *The Love Nest* (1926), and *Round Up* (1929). Accuracy in using the vernacular, humor, and the exposure of dullness and sham through self-revelation by the characters of his stories are the outstanding virtues of his work.

LARKIN, JOHN (*b. Newcastle-upon-Tyne, England, 1801; d. New York, N.Y., 1858*), Roman Catholic clergyman, Sulpician, and Jesuit. Ordained Baltimore, Md., 1827; entered Society of Jesus in Kentucky, 1840. Taught at Fordham (St. John's College), 1846; founded Xavier School, New York City, 1847; was president of Fordham, 1851–53.

LARKIN, THOMAS OLIVER (*b. Charlestown, Mass., 1802; d. 1858*), merchant, diplomatic agent. Removed to California, 1832; played a part in the machinations preliminary to the U.S. acquisition of California. He served as U.S. consul at Monterey, 1844–48; confidential agent, 1846–48; naval storekeeper, 1847–48; navy agent, 1847–49. He watched British and French diplomatic agents closely, fearful of their designs on California *post* 1844. James Buchanan's secret dispatch of October 1845 appointed him "confidential agent in California," under authority of which he launched a propaganda campaign to separate California from Mexico in furtherance of President Polk's expansionist policy.

LARNED, JOSEPH GAY EATON (*b. Thompson, Conn., 1819; d. New York, N.Y., 1870*), lawyer, industrialist. Inventor, promoter and manufacturer of steam fire engines, 1856–63.

LARNED, JOSEPHUS NELSON (*b. Chatham, Canada, 1836; d. Buffalo, N.Y., 1913*), librarian, journalist. Pioneered at Buffalo, N.Y., library in use of Dewey system and other improvements. Author of *History for Ready Reference* (1894–95) and *The Literature of American History* (1902).

LARNED, WILLIAM AUGUSTUS (*b. Summit, N.J., 1872; d. New York, N.Y., 1926*), lawn tennis champion. Among first ten U.S. players, 1892–1912; a master of ground strokes.

LaRoche, René (*b. Philadelphia, Pa., 1795; d. 1872*), physician, musician. M.D., University of Pennsylvania, 1820. An erudite and prolific writer on medical subjects; his *Yellow Fever* (1855) is a classic treatise.

La Ronde, Louis Denis, Sieur de (*b. Quebec, Canada, 1675; d. Quebec, 1741*), French naval officer. Accompanied Iberville to Hudson's Bay, 1697, and to Louisiana, 1700–01. Discovered copper in Lake Superior region, *ca.* 1734.

Larpenteur, Charles (*b. near Fontainebleau, France, 1807; d. Harrison Co., Iowa, 1872*), fur trader. Came to America as a boy. His autobiography, *Forty Years a Fur Trader on the Upper Missouri* (1898), is a valuable primary historical source.

Larrabee, Charles Hathaway (*b. Rome, N.Y., 1820; d. California, 1883*), lawyer, Union soldier, Wisconsin jurist and Democratic congressman. Helped frame constitutions for Wisconsin (1847) and Washington (1877–78).

Larrabee, William (*b. Ledyard, Conn., 1832; d. 1912*), businessman, Iowa legislator. Removed to Iowa, 1853. Forceful Republican governor of Iowa, 1886–90; early proponent of railroad regulation by law. Author of *The Railroad Question* (1893).

Larrabee, William Clark (*b. Cape Elizabeth, Maine, 1802; d. Indiana, 1859*), Methodist clergyman, educator, editor. First state superintendent, Indiana public school system, 1852–54, 1856–58.

Larrazolo, Octaviano Ambrosio (*b. Allende, Mexico, 1859; d. Albuquerque, N.Mex., 1930*), jurist, educator, political leader. Republican governor of New Mexico, 1918–21; U.S. senator, 1929–30. Long-time champion of native Spanish-Americans.

Larrínaga, Tulio (*b. Trujillo Alto, Puerto Rico, 1847; d. Santurce, Puerto Rico, 1917*), engineer, architect, government official. Second resident commissioner for Puerto Rico in the United States, 1905–11.

Larsen, Peter Laurentius (*b. Christiansand, Norway, 1833; d. Decorah, Iowa, 1915*), Norwegian Lutheran clergyman, educator. Came to America, 1857. *Post* 1863, associated with Luther College as professor and president.

Larson, Laurence Marcellus (*b. Spjutøy, Norway, 1868; d. Urbana, Ill., 1938*), historian. Came to America as a child. Graduated Drake University, 1894; Ph.D., Wisconsin, 1902. Taught at University of Illinois, 1907–37. Specialist in the interaction between the cultures of northern and western Europe.

La Salle, Robert Cavelier, Sieur de (*b. Rouen, France, 1643; d. on Brazos River, Tex., above mouth of the Navasota, 1687*), explorer. Entered the Society of Jesus as a novice; not liking its discipline, he left the Society, 1665. His elder brother, a Sulpician, having gone to Montreal, Robert followed him there in the summer of 1666. He at first lived the life of a pioneer farmer in New France, but in the summer of 1669 sold his seigniory and went exploring to Niagara, the western shores of Lake Ontario, and by his own statement to the Ohio; on this expedition he first met Louis Jolliet. His activities from 1669 to 1673 are not known.

Count de Frontenac, appointed governor of New France, 1672, on arriving at Quebec encouraged La Salle to present his hopes for a western empire to the authorities at Paris. When La Salle returned to Canada, 1675, he brought a grant of Fort Frontenac on Lake Ontario as a seigniory and exclusive permission for trade there. Three years thereafter, he journeyed again to France and obtained a patent permitting him to explore and exploit the regions of the West. Back in Canada in the summer of 1678, he and Frontenac began extensive preparations for that task. In the fall of 1679, La Salle, in concert with his lieutenant Henri de Tonty, explored Lake Michigan to St. Joseph River and proceeded by the Kankakee and Illinois rivers to Lake Peoria, where they built Fort Crèvecoeur, January 1680. Thence La Salle sent three men, including Father Louis Hennepin, to explore the upper Mississippi, himself returning to Fort Frontenac on foot. Going back to Illinois country late autumn, he found the ruins of Fort Crèvecoeur, whence all had fled before an Iroquois invasion. La Salle and Tonty were reunited in June 1681 at Mackinac; they returned to the Illinois country and rebuilt their fort, this time on the upper Illinois River near present Ottawa. From here they set out early in 1682 to explore the Mississippi River to its mouth. On their arrival at the Gulf of Mexico on April 9, they took possession of the entire river valley for the king of France and named in Louisiana in his honor. This was the climax of La Salle's career.

Frontenac was replaced in 1682 by Governor de la Barre, who deprived La Salle of many of his concessions and privileges. Having returned to France, La Salle reestablished his position at the French Court, and on July 24, 1684, sailed at the head of an expedition of fours ships and 200 colonists to plant a settlement at the mouth of the Mississippi. The expedition missed its mark and landed on the Texas coast. While La Salle was seeking an overland route to the Mississippi River, his men mutinied and murdered him. In many respects an heroic figure, he was a dreamer with magnificent ideas and hopes. His vision of a great French empire in the heart of the continent, and his accomplishments as an explorer and publicity agent, all merit praise. His failures, however, reflected his lack of administrative ability and his habit of uncertainty of judgment at critical moments.

Lasater, Edward Cunningham (*b. Goliad Co., Tex., 1860; d. Ardmore, Okla., 1930*), cattleman, land developer. Served briefly under Herbert Hoover on U.S. Food Administration, 1917; differed violently with Hoover's policies. A fighter for reforms in both politics and business practices, Lasater was also an authority on range problems.

Lashley, Karl Spencer (*b. Davis, W. Va., 1890; d. Poitiers, France, 1958*), physiological and theoretical psychologist. Studied at the University of West Virginia, the University of Pittsburgh, and at Johns Hopkins University (Ph.D., 1914). Taught at the University of Minnesota, at the University of Chicago, and at Harvard University; director of the Yerkes Laboratories of Primate Biology. Lashley formed theories of the hierarchical conception of behavior which made him the leading physiological psychologist of his time.

Lasker, Albert Davis (*b. Freiburg, Germany, 1880; d. New York, N.Y., 1952*), advertising executive, philanthropist, art collector, sportsman, and political partisan. Acquired ownership of the Chicago advertising firm of Lord and Thomas in 1905. Handling such clients as Palmolive Soap, the American Tobacco Co., Quaker Oats, and Pepsodent Toothpaste, he built the firm into one of the most successful in the country. A part owner of the Chicago Clubs, collector of modern art, donor to medical research, and an ardent supporter of the State of Israel, Lasker dissolved his firm in 1942.

Lasky, Jesse Louis (*b. San Francisco, Calif., 1880; d. Beverly Hills, Calif., 1958*), motion picture industry executive. Lasky began making films in 1913 with Cecil B. De Mille and Samuel Goldwyn. The first of his 1,000 films for the Lasky Company, later the Lasky Famous Players Company, was *Squaw Man* (1913), the first feature length film shot in Hollywood. The Lasky Company eventually became Paramount Pictures; Lasky was forced to resign during the Depression. As an independent producer he made *Sergeant York* (1941) and *The Great Caruso* (1951). Performers whose careers he guided include Maurice Chevalier, Gary Cooper, Pola Negri, and Gloria Swanson.

LASSER, JACOB KAY (b. *Newark, N.J., 1896; d. New York, N.Y., 1954*), accountant and tax expert. Studied at Pennsylvania State College and at New York University. Founded J. K. Lasser and Co. in 1924, specializing in the tax problems of the publishing industry. Published *Your Income Tax* in 1938, which sold over 13 million copies. Founded the Institute of Federal Taxation for attorneys and accountants at New York University, 1942; adjunct professor, 1942–54. Lasser was instrumental in simplifying the language of tax codes and regulations, and through his writings and lectures he contributed to the education of a generation of tax lawyers and accountants.

LATANÉ, JOHN HOLLADAY (b. *Staunton, Va., 1869; d. New Orleans, La., 1932*), historian, educator. Graduated Johns Hopkins, 1892; Ph.D., 1895. Professor of history, Randolph-Macon, 1898–1902; Washington and Lee University, 1902–1913; Johns Hopkins, *post* 1913. His chief interest was in the problems of international relations; he was a champion of the ideas and policies of Woodrow Wilson. His books and numerous articles reflected his keen interest in the contemporary world. Aside from three widely used textbooks which he wrote, his most influential work was *America as a World Power: 1897–1907* (1907).

LATHAM, MILTON SLOCUM (b. *Columbus, Ohio, 1827; d. 1882*), lawyer, financier. Removed to California, 1850. Democratic congressman, 1853–55; collector of port of San Francisco, 1855–57; governor of California, Jan. 9–14, 1860; U.S. senator, 1860–63. Suggested independence for California in event of dissolution of Union (April 1860).

LATHBURY, MARY ARTEMISIA (b. *Manchester, N.Y., 1841; d. East Orange, N.J., 1913*), teacher, author of juvenile stories and verses, hymn writer.

LATHROP, FRANCIS AUGUSTUS (b. *at sea en route to Honolulu, 1849; d. Woodcliffe Lake, N.J., 1909*), mural painter. Brother of George P. Lathrop. Student of Whistler and Madox Brown; associate of Burne-Jones and William Morris. Noted for his wall panels, mosaics and stained-glass windows.

LATHROP, GEORGE PARSONS (b. *near Honolulu, Hawaii, 1851; d. New York, N.Y., 1898*), author, editor. Brother of Francis A. Lathrop; husband of Mother Alphonsa (Rose Hawthorne). Active in work of American Copyright League and a founder of Catholic Summer School of America.

LATHROP, JOHN (b. *Boston, Mass., 1772; d. Georgetown, D.C., 1820*), lawyer, poet, educator.

LATHROP, JOHN HIRAM (b. *Sherburne, N.Y., 1799; d. Columbia, Mo., 1866*), pioneer in midwestern higher education. Graduated Yale, 1819. Served *post* 1841 as president of universities of Missouri, Wisconsin, and Indiana.

LATHROP, JULIA CLIFFORD (b. *Rockford, Ill., 1858; d. 1932*), social worker. Graduated Vassar, 1880. Entered social work in association with Jane Addams at Hull House, Chicago; was first woman member, Illinois Board of Public Charities, 1893–1909. She took an active part in many movements for social improvement including the mental hygiene movement, the establishment of juvenile courts, and woman suffrage. Appointed chief of federal Children's Bureau, 1912, she served until 1921 and made her department a strong force for regulation of child labor, assistance to working mothers and all manner of welfare legislation.

LATHROP, ROSE HAWTHORNE. *See* ALPHONSA, MOTHER.

LATIL, ALEXANDRE (b. *New Orleans, La., 1816; d. 1851*), Louisiana poet. A victim of leprosy; author of *Les Ephémères* (1841).

LATIMER, MARY ELIZABETH WORMELEY (b. *London, England, 1822; d. Baltimore, Md., 1904*), writer. Settled in the United States *ca.* 1845. Author of numerous popular studies of 19th-century European history.

LATIMER, WENDELL MITCHELL (b. *Garnett, Kans., 1893; d. Oakland, Calif., 1955*), chemist. University of Kansas and the University of California (Ph.D., 1918). Taught at Berkeley (1916–49); dean of the college of chemistry (1941–49). An expert in the temperatures and liquefaction of gasses, he published *The Oxidation States of the Elements and Their Potentials in Aqueous Solutions* (1938–1952). In 1920, he set forth the characteristics of the hydrogen bond as distinguished from the interaction between ordinary dipoles, and eventually supplied the basis for understanding the genetic code. Director of the Manhattan Engineering Division project on plutonium of the University of California (1943–47).

LA TOUR, LE BLOND DE (b. *France, late-17th century; d. New Orleans, La., 1723*), engineer. Came to province of Louisiana, 1720; as engineer in chief, planned Biloxi, Miss., and supervised development of New Orleans.

LATOURETTE, KENNETH SCOTT (b. *Oregon City, Oreg., 1884; d. Oregon City, 1968*), historian and educator. Attended McMinnville (later Linfield) College, Oreg. (B.A. in chemistry, 1904), and Yale (B.A. in history, 1906; Ph.D., 1909); ordained a Baptist minister (1918). On the faculties of Yale-in-China at Changsha (1910–12), and Yale Divinity School (1921–53), retiring as Sterling Professor of Missions and Oriental History. A respected sinologist and church historian, he helped introduce Asian studies into university curricula in the United States. Author of the standard text *The Development of China* (1917) and the seven-volume *A History of the Expansion of Christianity* (1937–45).

LATROBE, BENJAMIN HENRY (b. *Fulneck, England, 1764; d. New Orleans, La., 1820*), architect, engineer. Grandson of Henry Antes. Spent his boyhood in England and his youth in Germany, where he received an excellent education. Returning to England *ca.* 1786, he studied both architecture and engineering under outstanding masters. Immigrated to Norfolk, Va., 1796; was soon employed on important works. In 1797, among other projects, he designed the penitentiary to be built at Richmond, one of the earliest to adopt the principle of solitary confinement. In December 1798 he settled in Philadelphia, where he designed and supervised the construction of a new building for the Bank of Pennsylvania (completed 1801); this building has been termed the first monument of the Greek revival in America. Also in 1798, he wrote and published a pamphlet advocating a city water supply (the first in America); work was begun on it in March 1799 with Latrobe as engineer. This water system functioned successfully, 1801–15; it was superseded by a larger plant designed by one of Latrobe's pupils. In 1801 and 1802 he supervised the improvement of the Susquehanna River, clearing the channel for downstream navigation from Columbia to tidewater; he also designed several large homes in and about Philadelphia.

As early as 1800 Latrobe was at work on designs for the federal government. Some of these plans were not accepted, but President Jefferson came to think highly of his work, and created for Latrobe in 1803 the post of surveyor of U.S. public buildings. His first task was to build the Capitol's south wing. Latrobe and Jefferson found themselves in bitter conflict with William Thornton, who had won the original competition for the design in 1792–93 and balked at necessary changes. Jefferson and Latrobe eventually carried their point and brought the building to a worthy completion. For the east basement vestibule, Latrobe designed in 1809 his "American order" of maize, promptly christened by admiring members of Congress the "corn-cob capitals." Meanwhile he had worked on the President's house, on the Washington City Canal, and *post* 1804 as "engineer of the Navy Department" had done work at the yards in Washington, New York, and elsewhere. He built fireproof vaults for the State Department, 1810, and drew plans for the Marine Hospital in Washington, 1812.

During these years he also executed an increasing flood of private commissions. He designed churches, including the Catholic Cathedral in Baltimore, Md., college buildings, and beautiful homes. It was his custom to draw plans for religious and educational buildings free of charge. On the outbreak of the War of 1812 and the suspension of his government work, Latrobe entered partnership with Robert Fulton, Robert R. Livingston, and Nicholas I. Roosevelt to build a steamboat adapted to navigation of the Ohio River above the falls, but increasing costs and the death of Fulton brought this work to a close. Latrobe lost all of his private means in this venture and was left with many debts. In the spring of 1815 he was invited to return to Washington and take charge of the rebuilding of the Capitol, a task he resigned in 1817. Harassed by his debts, he took advantage of the new insolvency act, 1818, and then removed to Baltimore where he had several commissions awaiting him.

As early as 1809, Latrobe had been consulted about a water supply for New Orleans. In 1810 he sent his son, Henry, to pursue the project. The work was delayed by the war, and the son died of yellow fever in 1817, his task unfinished. The father determined to go to New Orleans and finish it, but he too was attacked by fever and died on Sept. 3, 1820, soon after he reached Louisiana.

Latrobe found architecture in America a polite accomplishment of gentlemen amateurs; he left it a profession, with professional standards and practices, largely in the hands of his own pupils. Few American architects before the great organizations of the past generation have had so wide and varied a practice. Apprenticeship in his office constituted the first important professional training in engineering and architecture in America. He was a good linguist; he drew with facility and accuracy, and his reports on engineering and architectural projects are models of technical exposition.

LATROBE, BENJAMIN HENRY (*b. Philadelphia, Pa., 1806; d. Baltimore, Md., 1878*), lawyer, civil engineer. Son of Benjamin H. Latrobe (1764–1820). Obtained a position in the engineer corps of the Baltimore and Ohio Railroad, 1831; an excellent mathematician, he became assistant to Jonathan Knight, chief engineer of the road. The Thomas Viaduct at Relay, Md., was his design. *Post* 1842, he was chief engineer in succession to Knight and had charge of building many miles of difficult track, including the extensions to the Ohio River and to Pittsburgh. He was the first to employ the present type of railroad ferry (1835), originated the "ton mile" work unit, served as consultant in the planning of the first transcontinental railroads, and was a member of the committee to which Roebling submitted the plan of the Brooklyn Bridge.

LATROBE, CHARLES HAZLEHURST (*b. Baltimore, Md., 1834; d. Baltimore, 1902*), civil engineer, Confederate soldier. Son of Benjamin H. Latrobe (1806–1878). A specialist in bridge construction, noted for the structural beauty of his work.

LATROBE, JOHN HAZLEHURST BONEVAL (*b. Philadelphia, Pa., 1803; d. Baltimore, Md., 1891*), lawyer, inventor, public servant. Son of Benjamin H. Latrobe (1764–1820). Studied law with Robert G. Harper. Helped draft charter of the Baltimore and Ohio Railroad, 1827; served as its legal adviser *post* 1828 and was widely recognized as a railroad and patent attorney. He was also of help to S. F. B. Morse in installation of first telegraph, invented the Latrobe stove, was active in many philanthropic societies, including the American Colonization Society, and practiced the arts of painting and design.

LATTA, ALEXANDER BONNER (*b. near Chillicothe, Ohio, 1821; d. Ludlow, Ky., 1865*), machinist. Made many improvements on locomotives; invented and manufactured steam fire engines, 1852–60, supplying his first engine to Cincinnati, Ohio, 1852.

LATTIMORE, WILLIAM (*b. near Norfolk, Va., 1774; d. Amite Co., Miss., 1843*), physician, Mississippi territorial delegate to Congress. Played a major role in establishing boundary line between Mississippi and Alabama, 1817.

LAUDONNIÈRE, RENÉ GOULAINE DE (*fl. 1562–1582*), a French Huguenot who was sent to establish a colony in Florida, is little known except for the narratives of his expedition. Jean Ribaut's lieutenant in the establishment of Charlesfort (now Port Royal, S.C.), 1562, Laudonnière established Fort Caroline on St. John's River, 1564, and was in command when the Spanish under Menendez attacked it, Sept 20, 1565. Most of the French were massacred, but the wounded Laudonnière eventually made his way back to France. His account of the Florida expeditions is contained in his *L'Histoire notable de la Floride* (Paris, 1586), translated the following year by Hakluyt.

LAUFER, BERTHOLD (*b. Cologne, Germany, 1874; d. Chicago, Ill., 1934*), Sinologist. Studied at Berlin, and at Leipzig where he received the Ph.D. degree, 1897. Came to America, 1898. Associated with American Museum of Natural History, New York, and Columbia University, 1898–1908, he became staff member of the Field Museum, Chicago, Ill., and curator of anthropology there. The outstanding Sinologist in the United States, he was concerned chiefly with the cultural exchanges between the Chinese and other peoples prior to the 19th century. His long list of publications includes work on Far Eastern linguistics, art, religion, magic; his most important monographs were *Sino-Iranica* (1919) and *Jade* (1912).

LAUGHLIN, HARRY HAMILTON (*b. Oskaloosa, Iowa, 1880; d. Kirksville, Mo., 1943*), eugenist. B.S., Kirksville State Normal School, 1900. M.S., Princeton University, 1916; D.Sc., 1917. Associate of Charles B. Davenport, and superintendent of the Eugenics Record Office at Cold Spring Harbor, N.Y., 1910–39. A fanatical propagandist for sterilization of the mentally and physically unfit, and for the limitation of immigration according to racial origin.

LAUGHLIN, JAMES LAURENCE (*b. Deerfield, Ohio, 1850; d. Jaffrey, N.H., 1933*), economist. Graduated Harvard, 1873; won Ph.D., 1876, for work under Henry Adams in Anglo-Saxon law. Taught political economy at Harvard, 1878–88. After a brief interval at Cornell, he became professor and head of department of political economy, University of Chicago, 1892, and served until 1916. Founder of the *Journal of Political Economy*, his classroom work was overshadowed by his seminar for doctoral candidates. Author of a number of books of which *The History of Bimetallism in the United States* (1886) and *The Principles of Money* (1903) were outstanding, Laughlin strongly influenced much federal legislation; he was responsible for preparation of the *Report of the Monetary Commission of the Indianapolis Convention* (1898) and was prominent in the educational campaign leading to the Federal Reserve Act (1913). His monetary theory shows a tendency toward propaganda against silver and paper money; although he saw the growing importance of credit, which he described as "a refined system of barter," he insisted that the price of an article is arrived at by comparing its value with that of the gold standard.

LAUGHTON, CHARLES (*b. Scarborough, Yorkshire, England, 1899; d. Hollywood, Calif., 1962*), actor. A leading stage actor in London by 1930, he came to New York in 1931 and was besieged by Hollywood offers. He had an affinity for characters of misfits, outsiders, or physical or mental cripples, and was quickly typed for such roles. His fifty-two films include *The Private Lives of Henry VIII* (1933, for which he won an Academy Award), *The Barretts of Wimpole Street* (1934), *Les Miserables* (1935), *Mutiny on the Bounty* (1935), *The Hunchback of Notre Dame* (1939), and, his final appearance, *Advise and Consent* (1962). He directed the film *The Night of the Hunter* (1955) and made *The Caine Mutiny Court-Martial* a Broadway and national success.

LAUNITZ, ROBERT EBERHARD SCHMIDT VON DER (*b. Riga, Russia, 1806; d. 1870*), sculptor. Came to America ca. 1828. Served as journeyman to John Frazee; later was his partner in monument and stone-carving firm. Taught Thomas Crawford.

LAURANCE, JOHN (*b. near Falmouth, England, 1750; d. New York, N.Y., 1810*), Revolutionary soldier, lawyer. Came to America, 1767. Son-in-law of Alexander Macdougall. Judge advocate general on Washington's staff, 1777–82. Congressman, Federalist, from New York, 1789–93; U.S. senator, 1796–1800.

LAUREL, STAN (*b. Arthur Stanley Jefferson, Ulverston, Lancashire, England, 1890; d. Santa Monica, Calif., 1965*), vaudeville and screen comedian. He is best remembered as the scrawny, bewildered member of the Laurel and Hardy comedy team. First appeared on stage with British vaudeville troupes; while on tour in America, 1912–13, he decided to stay and toured the U.S. circuit. His first film, *Nuts in May* (1917), launched him into a series of silent-screen comedies. Beginning with *Putting Pants on Philip* (1927), he was teamed with Oliver Hardy; their partnership lasted over twenty-five years through about one hundred comedies, including *The Music Box* (1932, Academy Award for Best Comedy Short Subject), *Babes in Toyland* (1934), and *A Chump at Oxford* (1940). Unlike other comedians, the team successfully made the transition to the sound era. They completed their last film together, *Robinson Crusoe-Land*, in 1951. Hardy died in 1957, and Laurel, unwilling to perform without his partner, retired.

LAURENS, HENRY (*b. Charleston, S.C., 1724; d. South Carolina, 1792*), merchant, planter, Revolutionary statesman. Probably the leading merchant of Charleston, Laurens gradually withdrew from commerce *post* 1764 and concentrated his attention on his plantations and on the political events of the period. Accepted as a leader of the Revolutionary movement in the South, he took a middle ground between radicals like Gadsden and conservatives who favored little if any action. His "constitutional stubbornness" against the policies of the British ministry was heightened by his disgust with the corruption of the British ruling class as observed by him during a stay in London, 1771–74. Returning home late in 1774, within a month he was elected to the first Provincial Congress and thereafter was active in all early phases of the Revolution in his section; he took part in the successful defense of Charleston, June 1776. A year later he took his seat in the Continental Congress and served nearly three years, part of the time as president. On many important committees, he demonstrated great ability and high patriotism; at times however he resorted to partisan maneuvers and was hampered in legislative

and diplomatic activity by his tendency to be self-righteous and oversensitive. On his way abroad to negotiate a treaty with the Dutch, he was captured by the British in September 1780, confined to prison and treated harshly. Exchanged for Lord Cornwallis, 1782, he joined Franklin, John Adams, and Jay in Paris and was responsible for several wise stipulations in the preliminary articles of peace. For the next year and a half he acted as a sort of unofficial minister to England, returning to New York in August 1784. After making his report to Congress, he returned to his home on Cooper River. Broken in health, saddened by the death of his son John, his wealth reduced by the heavy property losses he had suffered, he lived on for seven years, the recipient of honors and public recognition.

LAURENS, JOHN (*b. Charleston, S.C., 1754; d. South Carolina, 1782*), Revolutionary soldier, diplomat. Son of Henry Laurens. Served on a military mission to France, 1780–81; killed in a nameless skirmish against British partisans.

LAURIE, JAMES (*b. near Edinburgh, Scotland, 1811; d. Hartford, Conn., 1875*), civil engineer. Came to America ca. 1833. Active in American railroad building; first president, American Society of Civil Engineers, 1852.

LA VÉRENDRYE, PIERRE GAULTIER DE VARENNES, SIEUR DE (*b. Three Rivers, Canada, 1685; d. Canada, 1749*), soldier, explorer. Served in Canada and Europe, returning to Canada, 1711. Assigned to a frontier post north of Lake Superior, 1726, he heard from the Indians accounts of lands to the far west and the routes thither. Between 1731 and 1734, after securing permission to explore at his own expense, Vérendrye and his sons set up forts in the region west and north of Lake Superior. Persistence in the face of great discouragements enabled him to become between 1738 and 1744 the discoverer of Manitoba, the Dakotas, the western plains of Minnesota, the northwest territories of Canada and probably part of Montana. His labors opened up a vast region to French fur traders and pointed the way to the overland route to the Pacific.

LAW, ANDREW (*b. Milford, Conn., 1748/49; d. Cheshire, Conn., 1821*), composer and teacher of sacred music. Author or compiler of widely published hymnals.

LAW, EVANDER MCIVOR (*b. Darlington, S.C., 1836; d. 1920*), Confederate major general, educator. Founded South Florida Military Institute.

LAW, GEORGE (*b. Jackson, now Shushan, N.Y., 1806; d. New York, N.Y., 1881*), contractor, financier. Founded with Marshall O. Roberts the U.S. Mail Steamship Co., 1847; later active in Panama Railroad and in New York City horse-car lines. A prominent Know-Nothing politician.

LAW, JOHN (*b. New London, Conn., 1796; d. Evansville, Ind., 1873*), lawyer, Indiana jurist and congressman. Grandson of Richard Law. Author of *Colonial History of Vincennes* (1858); prosecuted Francis Vigo's claims.

LAW, JONATHAN (*b. Milford, Conn., 1674; d. 1750*), lawyer, Connecticut jurist. Deputy governor of Connecticut, 1724–41; governor, 1741–50; an able conservative.

LAW, RICHARD (*b. Milford, Conn., 1733; d. New London, Conn., 1806*), Revolutionary patriot, Connecticut legislator and jurist. Son of Jonathan Law. Editor, with Roger Sherman, of *Acts and Laws of the State of Connecticut* (1784).

LAW, SALLIE CHAPMAN GORDON (*b. Wilkes Co., N.C., 1805; d. Memphis, Tenn., 1894*), organizer of Confederate hospital and relief services.

LAWES, LEWIS EDWARD (*b. Elmira, N.Y., 1883; d. Garrison, N.Y., 1947*), prison administrator. Son of a guard at Elmira State Reformatory; educated at local schools. After service in U.S. Army (1901–04), he was appointed to Clinton Prison, Dannemora, N.Y., 1905.

In 1906 Lawes accepted a post as guard at Auburn prison, but, six months later, dismayed by the spirit of negativism and repression that characterized New York's penitentiaries for adult offenders, he successfully sought an assignment among younger delinquents, at Elmira Reformatory. He remained there until 1915, when he was appointed overseer of the New York City Reformatory for male delinquents on Hart's Island. He subsequently gained consent to establish a new reformatory at New Hampton in Orange County.

In 1920 Lawes became warden of the state penitentiary, Sing Sing, at Ossining, N.Y., which he transformed into what was probably the most progressive institution of its type in the United States. The chief basis for Lawes's success was his skillful administration of day-to-day life at Sing Sing, which he tried to make as similar to normal outside conditions as possible. Lawes wrote *Man's Judgement of Death* (1924), a critique of capital punishment, and the partly autobiographical *Twenty Thousand Years in Sing Sing* (1932).

LAWLEY, GEORGE FREDERICK (*b. London, England, 1848; d. South Boston, Mass., 1928*), yacht builder. Came to America as a child. Built *America's* Cup defenders *Puritan* (1885), *Mayflower* (1886), and many other vessels.

LAWRANCE, CHARLES LANIER (*b. Lenox, Mass., 1882; d. East Islip, N.Y., 1950*), aeronautical engineer, business executive, B.A., Yale, 1905; diploma in architecture, École des Beaux Arts, Paris, 1914. After earlier experimental work with automobiles, he turned to aeronautics, forming the Lawrance Aero-Engine Company in 1917 to develop an air-cooled engine of his own design. Fully developed in 1921, the Lawrance J-1 is regarded as the prototype of all modern, radial, air-cooled engines. The Wright Aeronautical Corporation bought Lawrance's company in 1923.

He served thereafter as an officer of Wright, and as president from 1925 until its merger with Curtiss in 1929. After a brief period as vice president of Curtiss-Wright Corporation, he left to form and head the Lawrance Engineering and Research Corporation.

LAWRANCE, JOHN. *See* LAURANCE, JOHN.

LAWRANCE, MARION. *See* LAWRANCE, URIAH MARION.

LAWRANCE, URIAH MARION (*b. Winchester, Ohio, 1850; d. Portland, Oreg., 1924*), businessman. Promoter of organized Sunday School activity.

LAWRENCE, ABBOTT (*b. Groton, Mass., 1792; d. 1855*), merchant, manufacturer, philanthropist. Brother of Amos and William Lawrence. Partner in Boston firm of A. and A. Lawrence, *post* 1814. During its first decade the firm was chiefly interested in the importation of English manufactures; gradually it began to deal in cottons and woolens manufactured in New England and in 1830 commenced the making, as well as the sale, of domestic textiles. Associating themselves with the Lowells, Appletons, Jacksons, and other rising manufacturers, the Lawrences were active in the development of New England industry. Abbott Lawrence took the lead in founding the great textile city that bears the family name, 1845, and in establishing there the mills that made Lawrence the principal rival of Lowell, Mass., founded a quarter century earlier. He was also a leader in New England railroad promotion and in the construction of municipal water works. His ability and public spirit made him a chief spokesman for Boston merchants and manufacturers in political and business discus-

sions. A prominent member of the Whig party, he served in Congress, attended national conventions, and was a leading candidate for the vice-presidential nomination in 1848. Refusing the offer of cabinet post by President Taylor, he served as U.S. minister to Great Britain, 1849–52. Strongly opposed to slavery, he was a man of firm religious principles. Among his principal benefactions were the founding of chairs at Harvard for the teaching of science and the endowment of the Lawrence Scientific School there.

LAWRENCE, AMOS (*b. Groton, Mass., 1786; d. 1852*), merchant. Brother of Abbott and William Lawrence. Original partner in A. and A. Lawrence. Retired in 1831 and devoted himself chiefly to philanthropy.

LAWRENCE, AMOS ADAMS (*b. Boston, Mass., 1814; d. 1886*), merchant, philanthropist. Son of Amos Lawrence. Graduated Harvard, 1835. Principal partner in Mason & Lawrence, selling agents for several of the largest textile mills in the country, Lawrence also engaged independently in textile manufacturing, notably in the field of knit goods. Active in many philanthropic enterprises, he established Lawrence University (Appleton, Wis.), and also a college at Lawrence, Kans., which became the nucleus for the state university. The success of the New England Emigrant Aid Society was largely owing to his efficiency as treasurer, yet despite his early zeal against slavery, he opposed the Republicans in 1856 and 1860, supported the Constitutional Union party and worked for the Crittenden compromise. When the Civil War broke out he loyally supported the administration.

LAWRENCE, DAVID LEO (*b. Pittsburgh, Pa., 1889; d. Pittsburgh, 1966*), politician. An ardent Democrat, his interest in politics began at age fourteen as an office boy for the Democratic chairman of Allegheny County, Pa., a position he later held (1920–32). Chairman of the Democratic State Committee (1933) and national committeeman (1940). Elected mayor of Pittsburgh (1945) and served four terms, during which he implemented the reconstruction of downtown Pittsburgh. He became Pennsylvania's first Catholic governor (1957–62) and was influential in securing the presidential nomination of John F. Kennedy (1960). He returned to his role as party leader in 1962, but his political power had begun to decline.

LAWRENCE, ERNEST ORLANDO (*b. Canton, S. Dak., 1901; d. Palo Alto, Calif., 1958*), physicist. Studied at the University of South Dakota, the University of Minnesota, and at Yale (Ph.D., 1925). Taught at Yale (1927–28), and at Berkeley from 1928 until his death in 1958. One of the world's leading nuclear scientists, Lawrence conceived the cyclotron in 1929; the first working model was completed in 1932. By the end of the 1930's, Lawrence had perfected his techniques of studying the atom through the cyclotron. He was elected to the National Academy of Sciences in 1934 and awarded the Nobel Prize for Physics in 1939. Key discoveries in nuclear physics of the 1930's were confirmed and exploited at Berkeley under Lawrence's leadership: the neutron (1932), the disintegration of lithium by protons (1932), and induced radioactivity by alpha particles and neutrons (1934). During World War II, the Berkeley scientists became the group responsible for the development of nuclear weapons; most of the uranium 235 used in the Hiroshima bomb was produced in the 184-inch cyclotron at Berkeley. The transuranic element of atomic number 103 was named lawrencium in his honor after its discovery at Berkeley.

LAWRENCE, GEORGE NEWBOLD (*b. New York, N.Y., 1806; d. New York, 1895*), ornithologist, wholesale druggist.

LAWRENCE, GERTRUDE (*b. London, England, 1898; d. New York, N.Y., 1952*), actress and singer. Best known for her association with British composer and playwright Noel Coward, she starred in his *Private Lives* (1930) and set the standard for the 1930's comedy of manners. Other roles include Cole Porter's *Nymph Errant* (London, 1933), the Moss Hart-Kurt Weil-Ira Gershwin *Lady in the Dark* (1941), and *The King and I*, (1951).

LAWRENCE, JAMES (*b. Burlington, N.J., 1781; d. at sea off Boston, Mass., 1813*), naval officer. Appointed midshipman, 1798; promoted lieutenant, 1802. Distinguished in war with Tripoli, 1801–05, as second in command of two daring operations: Porter's boat attack on Tripoli and the burning of the *Philadelphia*. In the War of 1812, commanding the *Hornet*, he defeated and sank HMS *Peacock* on Feb 24, 1813; soon after, he was promoted captain and ordered to relieve the commander of the *Chesapeake* at Boston. Disobeying specific orders with respect to *Chesapeake*'s mission, he put to sea on June 1 to engage HMS *Shannon*, then blockading Boston. In an action that lasted less than fifteen minutes, the *Shannon* was victorious and Lawrence was mortally wounded. His words, "Don't give up the ship," said to have been uttered when he was carried below, became a popular slogan.

LAWRENCE, RICHARD SMITH (*b. Chester, Vt., 1817; d. Hartford, Conn., 1892*), gunsmith. Inventor of machine tools for large-scale manufacture of rifles and carbines.

LAWRENCE, WILLIAM (*b. Groton, Mass., 1783; d. 1848*), merchant. Brother of Abbott and Amos Lawrence. A director of the Suffolk Bank System, 1818–48.

LAWRENCE, WILLIAM (*b. Mount Pleasant, Ohio, 1819; d. Kenton, Ohio, 1899*), Ohio jurist and legislator. As congressman, Republican, from Ohio, 1865–71, 1873–77, he was virtual author of the law creating the Department of Justice, drafted the law granting homesteads to Civil War veterans from reserved sections of railroad land grants, and secured indemnification of the government by the railroads for public lands improperly granted them (1876).

LAWRENCE, WILLIAM (*b. Boston, Mass., 1850; d. Milton, Mass., 1941*), Protestant Episcopal clergyman, bishop of Massachusetts. Son of Amos Adams Lawrence. A.B., Harvard, 1871. His decision to enter the ministry reflected both the religious character of his upbringing (his father was a convert from Unitarianism) and the great influence of Phillips Brooks, then rector of Trinity Church, Boston. To broaden his background, Lawrence began his theological studies at a Congregational institution, the Andover (Mass.) Theological Seminary (1872–74); he continued them at the Episcopal Divinity School in Philadelphia (1874–75), with a final three months at the Episcopal Theological School in Cambridge, where he received the B.S. degree in 1875. He was ordained priest in 1876. From 1876 to 1883 he served first as assistant and then as rector of Grace Church in Lawrence, Mass. In 1884 he returned to Cambridge as professor of homiletics and pastoral care in the Episcopal Theological School. Upon becoming dean in 1889, he introduced the elective system and other reforms. In 1893 he was elected bishop of Massachusetts, a post he was to hold for thirty-four years. Lawrence's administrative talents made him a national leader in the Episcopal Church; from 1904 to 1910 he was chairman of its House of Bishops. His greatest effort was the establishment of the Church Pension Fund to replace a variety of local funds and charities for the clergy of the Episcopal Church and their dependents.

One of Lawrence's greatest interests was Harvard University. In 1924 he secured the gift from George F. Baker that built the Harvard Business School. He was the recipient of two Harvard honorary degrees: an S.T.D. in 1893 when he became bishop and an LL.D. in 1931 when he resigned from the Harvard Corporation. Lawrence wrote an autobiography, *Memories of a Happy Life* (1926). He resigned as bishop in 1927, but he continued until 1930 as chairman of the board of trustees of St. Mark's School, and until 1940 as a trustee of Groton School.

LAWRENCE, WILLIAM BEACH (*b. New York, N.Y., 1800; d. 1881*), lawyer, public official, writer on international law.

LAWRIE, ALEXANDER (*b. New York, N.Y., 1828; d. Lafayette, Ind., 1917*), landscape and portrait painter.

LAWS, SAMUEL SPAHR (*b. Ohio Co., Va., 1824; d. Asheville, N.C., 1921*), Presbyterian clergyman, educator. Invented the stock-market "ticker" for reporting sales. Was president, among other institutions, of University of Missouri, 1876–89. A scholar of remarkable versatility.

LAWSON, ALEXANDER (*b. Ravenstruthers, Scotland, 1773; d. Philadelphia, Pa., 1846*), line engraver. Came to America, 1794. Established reputation by engraving plates for Alexander Wilson's *American Ornithology* (1808–14) and for the continuation by C. L. Bonaparte (1825–33).

LAWSON, ANDREW COWPER (*b. Anstruther, Scotland, 1861; d. San Leandro, Calif., 1952*), geologist and educator. Studied at the University of Toronto and Johns Hopkins University (Ph.D., 1888). As a member of the Geological Survey of Canada, Lawson, at the age of twenty-two, achieved fame with his new interpretation of the Precambrian era with his observations of the Lake of the Woods and Rainy Lake in Ontario (presented in 1888). Professor at the University of Calif., 1890; emeritus, 1928. Chairman of the State Earthquake Investigation Commission, 1908, which studied the great San Francisco quake of 1906. President of the Geological Society of America, 1926; elected to the National Academy of Sciences, 1924.

LAWSON, ERNEST (*b. San Francisco, Calif., 1873; d. Miami Beach, Fla., 1939*), painter. Studied with John H. Twachtman and J. A. Weir. One of "The Eight," 1908; a sponsor of the Armory Show, 1913. His style, based on impressionism, was characterized by glowing color and thick impasto.

LAWSON, JAMES (*b. Glasgow, Scotland, 1799; d. Yonkers, N.Y., 1880*), accountant, insurance expert. Came to America, 1815. A lifelong amateur in literature and friend to literary men.

LAWSON, JOHN (*b. England, d. North Carolina, 1711*), pioneer, associate of Christopher de Graffenried in settlement of New Bern, N.C. Author of *A New Voyage to Carolina, etc.* (1709), useful for study of Indian life and customs.

LAWSON, LEONIDAS MERION (*b. Nicholas Co., Ky., 1812; d. Cincinnati, Ohio, 1864*), physician, teacher of medicine. Author of *Phthisis Pulmonalis* (1861), a valuable treatise.

LAWSON, ROBERT RIPLEY (*b. New York, N.Y., 1892; d. Westport, Conn., 1957*), illustrator and author. Studied at the New York School of Fine and Applied Art. During the 1920's, Lawson did commercial work; in the 1930's, he concentrated entirely on book illustration; his works include illustrations for Munro Leaf's *Story of Ferdinand* (1936), a book with political overtones which was attacked as communist propaganda, an argument for pacifism, and a glorification of fascist militarism. In 1939 he wrote and illustrated his own book, *Ben and Me*; other works include *Rabbit Hill* (1944) and *The Tough Winter* (1954).

LAWSON, THOMAS (*b. Virginia, ca. 1781 or 1785; d. Norfolk, Va., 1861*), surgeon. In U.S. Army service *post* 1811; a forceful and efficient surgeon general, 1836–61. Lawson obtained military rank for members of the medical department and was responsible for the publication of valuable statistical reports on army sickness and mortality.

LAWSON, THOMAS WILLIAM (*b. Charlestown, Mass., 1857; d. 1925*), stockbroker, speculator. Associated with Standard Oil interest; author of the exposé *Frenzied Finance* (1904–05).

LAWSON, VICTOR FREEMONT (*b. Chicago, Ill., 1850; d. 1925*), journalist. Proprietor, *Chicago Daily News*, 1876–88; proprietor and editor thereafter. President, Associated Press, 1894–1900. A powerful influence in civic reform.

LAWTON, ALEXANDER ROBERT (*b. Beaufort District, S.C., 1818; d. Clifton Springs, N.Y., 1896*), Confederate brigadier general, lawyer, Georgia legislator. Graduated West Point, 1839; Harvard Law School, 1842. A leading Georgia secessionist, Lawton served ably in the field, 1861–63, and as Confederate quartermaster general, 1863–65. Thereafter he was in the first rank of the national bar and served as U.S. minister to Austria, 1887–89.

LAWTON, HENRY WARE (*b. near Toledo, Ohio, 1843; d. San Mateo, Philippine Islands, 1899*), soldier. Raised in Fort Wayne, Ind. Medal of Honor winner for gallantry at Atlanta in Civil War; served in frontier Indian wars; received surrender of Geronimo, 1886. Commanded 2nd Division, V Corps, at Santiago, Cuba, 1898, as major general of volunteers; was killed in action during Philippine Insurrection.

LAY, BENJAMIN (*b. Colchester, England, 1677; d. near Abington, Pa., 1759*), Quaker reformer. Settled in Pennsylvania, 1731. Made dramatic, eccentric protests against slavery.

LAY, HENRY CHAMPLIN (*b. Richmond, Va., 1823; d. Baltimore, Md., 1885*), Episcopal clergyman. Rector in Huntsville, Ala., he was chosen missionary bishop for Arkansas and Indian Territory, 1859, and served until 1869. Thereafter he was bishop of Easton (Maryland).

LAY, JOHN LOUIS (*b. Buffalo, N.Y., 1832; d. New York, N.Y., 1899*), inventor. While in Union naval service, 1861–65, Lay perfected the torpedo used to destroy Confederate ram *Albemarle*, October 1864; he later received patents for an electrically driven torpedo, the vessel from which it could be launched and other devices. *Post* 1870, he lived mainly in Europe.

LAZARUS, EMMA (*b. New York, N.Y., 1849; d. 1887*), poet. Author of *Poems and Translations* (1866, 1867), *Admetus and Other Poems* (1871), *Songs of a Semite* (1882), translations from Heinrich Heine and other literary work. A sonnet written by her was placed on the pedestal of the Statue of Liberty, 1886. *Post* 1881, she became a prominent defender of Judaism and an organizer of relief efforts for Jewish immigrants.

LAZEAR, JESSE WILLIAM (*b. Baltimore Co., Md., 1866; d. Quemados, Cuba, 1900*), physician. John Hopkins, A.B., 1889; Columbia, M.D., 1892; studied also at Pasteur Institute, Paris. Showed great promise in bacteriological research. Appointed assistant surgeon in the army, 1900, he was a member of the Yellow Fever Commission in Cuba with Walter Reed, James Carroll, and Aristides Agramonte. His death from the fever, after being stung by an infected mosquito, went far to convince the Commission that they were on the right path to proof of the mosquito transmission theory and effective control of the disease.

LEA, HENRY CHARLES (*b. Philadelphia, Pa., 1825; d. Philadelphia, 1909*), publisher, historian. Son of Isaac Lea; grandson of Mathew Carey. Active in family publishing firm and in movements for municipal and civil-service reform. Author of a number of important scholarly studies which include A *History of the Inquisition of the Middle Ages* (1888), *The Moriscos of Spain* (1901) and A *History of the Inquisition of Spain* (1906–07).

LEA, HOMER (*b. Denver, Colo., 1876; d. near Los Angeles, Calif., 1912*), soldier. Removed to China, 1899; rose to general's rank in Chinese army and was a confidential adviser to Sun Yat Sen. Author of *The Valor of Ignorance* (1909), a warning against Japanese aggression.

LEA, ISAAC (*b. Wilmington, Del., 1792; d. 1886*), malacologist, publisher. Son-in-law of Mathew Carey; father of Henry C. and Mathew C. Lea. Partner in M. Carey and Sons and successor firms, 1821–51.

LEA, LUKE (*b. Nashville, Tenn., 1879; d. Nashville, 1945*), lawyer, newspaper publisher, politician. B.A., University of the South, 1899; M.A., 1900. LL.B., Columbia University Law School, 1903. Began practice in Nashville. A leader of the Democratic faction that demanded statewide prohibition and other reforms, he founded the *Nashville Tennessean* in 1907 to advocate overthrow of the "regular" Democrats; in 1910 he was a leader of the insurgents who helped elect a Republican governor pledged to reform. Elected to the U.S. Senate by the legislature, 1911, he supported progressive measures and was an early supporter of Woodrow Wilson. In 1915 he was defeated for reelection. After outstanding service with the army during World War I, he helped organize the American Legion, resumed his activities as publisher of the *Tennessean*, and remained a power in local politics. In association with one Rogers Caldwell, he engaged in a vast scheme to control numerous banks, newspapers, and other properties, which resulted in a failure in 1930 and Lea's conviction for conspiracy to defraud in 1931.

LEA, MATHEW CAREY (*b. Philadelphia, Pa., 1823; d. Philadelphia, 1897*), chemist. Son of Isaac Lea; grandson of Mathew Carey. A pioneer in photochemistry, he also made important studies in the platinum metals and was an active investigator in the domain of pure physics.

LEACH, ABBY (*b. Brockton, Mass., 1855; d. 1918*), classicist. Professor of Greek at Vassar, 1889–1918.

LEACH, DANIEL DYER (*b. Bridgewater, Mass., 1806; d. 1891*), Episcopal clergyman, educator. Superintendent of schools in Providence, R.I., 1855–83; pioneer in modern public-school administration; author of many widely used elementary school textbooks.

LEACH, SHEPHERD (*b. Easton, Mass., 1778; d. Easton, 1832*), iron founder, capitalist.

LEADBELLY. *See* LEDBETTER, HUDDIE.

LEAHY, WILLIAM DANIEL (*b. Hampton, Iowa, 1875; d. 1959*), naval officer. Attended the U.S. Naval Academy, class of 1897. Saw action during the Spanish-American War, the Philippine Insurrection, and the Nicaraguan Revolution. Appointed head of the Bureau of Ordinance, 1927; the Bureau of Navigation, 1933; and chief of naval operations, 1937. Retired in 1939 but appointed governor of Puerto Rico, 1939–41; from 1941 to 1942, he was a controversial ambassador to the Vichy government in France. Appointed chief of staff to the president and chairman of the Joint Chiefs of Staff from 1942 to 1949. A realistic and articulate nationalist, Leahy opposed accommodation to the Russians and decreases in military spending after World War II. His diary, *I Was There*, was published in 1950.

LEAMING, JACOB SPICER (*b. near Madisonville, Ohio, 1815; d. 1885*), farmer, seedsman. Developed the famous "Leaming corn," 1856.

LEAMING, JEREMIAH (*b. near Durham, Conn., 1717; d. New Haven, Conn., 1804*), Episcopal clergyman, Loyalist. First choice of Connecticut clergy for consecration as bishop, 1783.

LEAMING, THOMAS (*b. Cape May Co., N.J., 1748; d. Philadelphia, Pa., 1797*), Revolutionary soldier, lawyer, merchant.

LEAR, BEN (*b. Hamilton, Ontario, Canada, 1879; d. Murfreesboro, Tenn., 1966*), army officer. Moved to the United States in 1881; enlisted in U.S. Army (1898) and was immediately made a first sergeant. He served in the Philippines, Cuba, and the border campaign against Pancho Villa. During World War I he was on the army general staff and became a brigadier general in 1936; by 1940 he was commander of the Second Army. In 1943 replaced Lt. Gen. Leslie McNair as commander of army ground forces in France and was later appointed deputy commander of the European theater. Retired in 1945.

LEAR, TOBIAS (*b. Portsmouth, N.H., 1762; d. Washington, D.C., 1816*), consular officer. Graduated Harvard, 1783. George Washington's confidant and secretary, 1785–93, 1798–99. U.S. consul to Santo Domingo, 1801–02; U.S. consul general at Algiers, 1803–12. His conduct of affairs with Morocco, Algiers, and Tunis was able; his 1805 treaty with Tripoli, however, was harshly criticized. On his return home, Lear was made an accountant in the war department. He committed suicide, 1816.

LEARNED, EBENEZER (*b. Oxford, Mass., 1728; d. Oxford, 1801*), Revolutionary soldier. Colonel, 3rd Continental Infantry; led entry into Boston after siege, 1776; held brigade command in Saratoga campaign. Resigned commission for physical disability, March 1778.

LEARNED, MARION DEXTER (*b. near Dover, Del., 1857; d. 1917*), philologist, historian, editor. Head of German department, University of Pennsylvania, *post* 1895.

LEARY, JOHN (*b. St. John, N.B., Canada, 1837; d. Riverside, Calif., 1905*), lawyer, capitalist. Removed to Seattle, Wash., 1869; became a leader in industrial and commercial development of Puget Sound area.

LEASE, MARY ELIZABETH CLYENS (*b. Ridgway, Pa., 1853; d. Callicoon, N.Y., 1933*), Populist leader in Kansas, 1890–96, professional radical, lecturer.

LEATHERS, WALLER SMITH (*b. near Charlottesville, Va., 1874; d. Nashville, Tenn., 1946*), medical educator, public health physician. M.D., University of Virginia, 1895. As professor and dean of the medical school, University of Mississippi, and later at Vanderbilt University, he was a leader in conforming the medical and public health institutions of Mississippi and Tennessee, and indeed of the South generally, to modern practice and standards.

LEAVENWORTH, FRANCIS PRESERVED (*b. Mt. Vernon, Ind., 1858; d. 1928*), astronomer. A distinguished teacher at Haverford College and University of Minnesota.

LEAVENWORTH, HENRY (*b. New Haven, Conn., 1783; d. on Washita River, near junction with the Red, 1834*), lawyer, solider. Entered U.S. Army at start of War of 1812, rising to rank of colonel; *post* 1819, was almost continuously on frontier service. He built Forts Snelling and Leavenworth and was for a time post commander at Jefferson Barracks; he was put in command of the entire southwestern frontier in 1834. While making an effort to negotiate peace among warring Indian tribes of the region, he was stricken with bilious fever and died. A man of broad and varied culture, he holds a place second only to Henry Atkinson in the military annals of the early frontier.

LEAVITT, DUDLEY (*b. Exeter, N.H., 1772; d. 1851*), almanac maker, mathematician, author, teacher.

LEAVITT, ERASMUS DARWIN (*b. Lowell, Mass., 1836; d. Cambridge, Mass., 1916*), mechanical engineer. Associated with Calumet and Hecla Mining Co., 1874–1904; specialized in pumping and mining machinery design.

LEAVITT, FRANK MCDOWELL (*b. Athens Ohio, 1856; d. Scarsdale, N.Y., 1928*), mechanical engineer, inventor. Graduated Stevens Institute of Technology, 1875; was associated with E. W. Bliss & Co., *post* 1884. Over 300 patents were granted him between 1875 and 1921; he perfected much sheet-metal-working machinery and was the first to build a successful automatic tin-can body-making machine. Most of his attention *post* 1900 was given to the improvement of torpedoes. His last engineering work was the design for an aircraft steam boiler.

LEAVITT, FRANK SIMMONS (*b. New York, N.Y., 1889; d. Norcross, Ga., 1953*), wrestler, football player, and actor. Known as Man Mountain Dean, Leavitt was a gaudy and theatrical wrestler during the 1920's and 1930's. He appeared in bit parts in Hollywood films, most notably, *The Gladiators* (1938), with Joe E. Brown.

LEAVITT, HENRIETTA SWAN (*b. Lancaster, Mass., 1868; d. 1921*), astronomer. Graduated Radcliffe, 1892; joined staff of Harvard Observatory, 1902; became head of department of photographic stellar photometry. Discovered more than 2,400 variable stars and made measurements of sequences of stars.

LEAVITT, HUMPHREY HOWE (*b. Suffield, Conn., 1796; d. Springfield, Ohio, 1873*), Ohio federal jurist, legislator.

LEAVITT, JOSHUA (*b. Heath, Mass., 1794; d. 1873*), Congregational clergyman, abolitionist. Graduated Yale, 1814. An active journalist and supporter of many reform movements; office editor of the *Independent*, 1848–73.

LEAVITT, MARY GREENLEAF CLEMENT (*b. Hopkinton, N.H., 1830; d. Boston, Mass., 1912*), educator, temperance reformer. As a result of her efforts as traveling representative, the W.C.T.U. became a world organization.

LEBRUN, FEDERICO ("RICO") (*b. Naples, Italy, 1900; d. Malibu, Calif., 1964*), painter, muralist, and sculptor. Attended night classes at the Naples Academy of Fine Arts, where impressionism was the prevailing vogue, but he took the baroque traditions of the seventeenth century as a foundation for his art. Came to the United States in 1922 and within a few years was a highly paid magazine illustrator. In the early 1930's he turned to purely "creative art" and established his own studio (1933). Joined the faculty of the Chouinard Art Institute in California (1938). From the powerful realism of his drawings of the early 1940's, his art by 1950 had become a mixture of abstraction and expressionism. In 1947 he began his "Crucifixion cycle," and an exhibition of that work (1950) won him an international reputation. He began impressive sculpting in wax and bronze two years before his death.

LE BRUN, NAPOLÉON EUGÈNE HENRY CHARLES (*b. Philadelphia, Pa., 1821; d. 1901*), architect. Studied under Thomas U. Walter; practiced in Philadelphia *post* 1841, in New York City *post* 1864. In partnership with sons, designed many notable churches and civil buildings; his Metropolitan Life Building, New York City (1889–1909) was an early success in skyscraper design.

LECHFORD, THOMAS (*fl. 1629–1642*), lawyer. Immigrated from England to Boston, Mass., 1638. The first professional lawyer in Massachusetts Bay, he was held in low esteem by the clergy and returned to England, 1641. Author of *Plain Dealing: or, Newes From New-England* (1642).

LE CLEAR, THOMAS (*b. Owego, N.Y., 1818; d. Rutherford Park, N.J., 1882*), portrait and genre painter, particularly effective as a portraitist of men.

LE CONTE, JOHN (*b. Liberty Co., Ga., 1818; d. 1891*), physician, scientist. Brother of Joseph LeConte; cousin of John L. LeConte. Professor of physics at several universities, notably at University of California *post* 1869, where he served also as president, 1875–81. Made important acoustical studies.

LE CONTE, JOHN LAWRENCE (*b. New York, N.Y., 1825; d. 1883*), entomologist, physician. Cousin of John and Joseph LeConte. M.D., N.Y. College of Physicians and Surgeons, 1846. Interested in the geographic distribution of species, he made numerous studies and wrote a variety of monographs relative to the subject; he was the first biologist to map faunal areas of western part of the United States. His patient and original investigations may be said to have culminated in his monographic revision of the *Rhynchophora* (1876) and his *Classification of the N.A. Coleoptera* (1883). In addition to studies in entomology, LeConte published essays dealing with mineralogy, geology, radiates, recent fossil mammals, and ethnology. He was recognized at home and abroad as the greatest entomologist America had produced.

LE CONTE, JOSEPH (*b. Liberty Co., Ga., 1823; d. Yosemite Valley, Calif., 1901*), physician, geologist. Brother of John LeConte; cousin of John L. LeConte. M.D., N.Y. College of Physicians and Surgeons, 1845. Taught at Georgia University and College of South Carolina; professor of geology, University of California, 1869–96. Author of numerous articles on a wide variety of scientific topics.

LEDBETTER, HUDDIE (*b. near Mooringsport, La., 1885; d. New York, N.Y., 1949*), folk singer, guitarist, composer. Born of black parents; maternal grandmother was a Cherokee; nicknamed "Leadbelly" because of his powerful bass voice.

LEDERER, JOHN (*fl. 1686–1671*), traveler, explorer. Came to Virginia from Germany, 1668; made several journeys into western Virginia and North Carolina, 1669–70. Author of *The Discoveries of John Lederer, etc.* (London, 1672).

LE DUC, WILLIAM GATES (*b. Wilkesville, Ohio, 1823; d. Hastings, Minn., 1917*), agriculturist, Union soldier, railroad promoter. Settled in St. Paul, Minn., 1850; was active in development of the region. Secured first charter for a railway in Minnesota territory, 1853; was first miller to manufacture and introduce flour made from Minnesota spring wheat, 1856. U.S. commissioner of agriculture, 1877–81.

LEDYARD, JOHN (*b. Groton, Conn., 1751; d. Cairo, Egypt, 1789*), explorer. Nephew of William Ledyard. Went to sea *ca.* 1773; joined Capt. James Cook in expedition, 1776. At Nootka Sound, 1778, realized vast possibilities of northwest fur trade. On arrival in London late in 1780, he was confined to barracks two years for refusal to fight against Americans. Returning home, December 1782, he tried to obtain means for a sailing venture to Northwest Coast. Journeyed to Spain, June 1784, and to France; received encouragement from Thomas Jefferson and John Paul Jones but all projects failed. Proposed to walk across Siberia, for which he sought passport from Russians who refused it. Went to Hamburg, 1786, then by way of Norway, Sweden, and Lapland to St. Petersburg. Permitted to go on from there in 1787, he was arrested in Siberia by order of Empress Catherine and brought back. Engaged in London to explore sources of Niger River, he reached Cairo where he died. Author of *A Journal of Captain Cook's Last Voyage* (1783).

LEDYARD, WILLIAM (*b. Groton, Conn., 1738; d. Groton, 1781*), Revolutionary soldier. Uncle of John Ledyard. Killed after his heroic defense of Fort Griswold, Connecticut, against a superior British force.

LEE, ALFRED (*b. Cambridge, Mass., 1807; d. Wilmington, Del., 1887*), Episcopal clergyman. Consecrated first bishop of Delaware, 1841. A strong Evangelical, he served as presiding bishop, 1884–87.

LEE, ANN (*b. Manchester, England, 1736; d. Watervliet, N.Y., 1784*), foundress of Shakers in America, 1774–76.

LEE, ARTHUR (*b. Westmoreland Co., Va., 1740; d. Middlesex Co., Va., 1792*), diplomat. Great-grandson of Richard Lee. Brother of Richard H., Francis L., and William Lee. M.D., University of Edinburgh, 1764. Began practice of medicine, Williamsburg, Va., 1766; went to London, 1768, and studied law at Lincoln's Inn and Middle Temple. Admitted to bar, 1775. Chosen agent of Massachusetts in London, 1770, he wrote *An Appeal to the Justice and Interests of the People of Great Britain* (1774), followed in the next year by the *Second Appeal*. Associated, 1776, in Paris with Benjamin Franklin and Silas Deane as a commissioner to seek foreign aid, he went to Spain, 1777, and to Berlin where he was refused recognition. Returning to Paris, he commenced making complaints against his colleagues and out of his fervid imagination convinced himself that Franklin, Deane, and others were plundering the public. In consequence, Deane was recalled, and Congress split into hostile factions, comprised of the supporters of Lee and the supporters of Deane. Lee was superseded, 1779. On return to America, he was elected to the Virginia House of Delegates, 1781, then to the Continental Congress in which he served until 1784.

LEE, CANADA (*b. New York, N.Y., 1907; d. New York, N.Y., 1952*), actor. One of the first successful black actors, Lee was first a racing jockey, then a successful boxer before entering the theater. His most notable roles were in Richard Wright's *Native Son* (1941), *South Pacific* (1943), Alfred Hitchcock's film *Lifeboat* (1944), *Body and Soul* (1947) in which he starred with John Garfield, and the film of *Cry, The Beloved Country*, 1952. Plagued by prejudice and persecution during the McCarthy era because of his liberal politics, Lee was denied further employment on the stage, screen, and television. His politics were judged not by his convictions about racial justice in America but by the company he kept. Among his friends were such well-known and outspoken communists as Benjamin J. Davis, Jr., and Richard Wright, author of *Native Son*. Lee was also associated with the Civil Rights Congress and other left-wing Harlem organizations.

LEE, CHARLES (*b. Dernhall, England, 1731; d. Philadelphia, Pa., 1782*), soldier of fortune, Revolutionary general. Served in America, 1755–61; with British in Portugal, 1762–63; and as soldier of fortune in Poland. Returned to America, 1773; took up land in Berkeley Co., Va., 1775. Vehement in support of patriot cause, he was made major general, Continental Army, 1775. He served during siege of Boston, at New York, and in the South, returning to Washington's army just before battle of White Plains, October 1776. After White Plains, he was posted with his division at Philipsburg, N.Y. Consistent with his view that Americans could not stand in pitched battle against the British, he was slow to rejoin main army, explaining that he could do better by hanging on British flanks and harassing them. Taken prisoner in his New Jersey headquarters by British in December 1776, Lee was kept in

New York for a year. During this time he became intimate with Sir William Howe and presented to him a plan detailing how Americans might best be defeated. Lee's purpose in doing this has long been a subject of controversy. Exchanged, 1778, he went to York, Pa., in May and appeared before Congress. He returned to the army at Valley Forge just before the Monmouth campaign. His withdrawal of his forces during battle of Monmouth caused a rout of the Americans which was stopped only by Washington's prompt action. Court-martialed, July–August 1778, Lee was found guilty of disobeying orders, misbehavior in face of the enemy, and disrespect to the commander in chief. Suspended from the army for twelve months, he intrigued with Congress and otherwise conducted himself with so much enmity to Washington that he was challenged to a duel and wounded by Col. John Laurens. Retiring to his Virginia estate, July 1779, he was dismissed from the army, January 1780, in consequence of an insulting letter to Congress. One of the most contradictory characters in American history, Lee had an exaggerated sense of his own ability and great luck in impressing his own view of himself upon other people. On the credit side of his character, he was extremely generous to his friends and considerate to his soldiers.

LEE, CHARLES (*b. Prince William Co., Va., 1758; d. near Warrenton, Va., 1815*), jurist. Brother of Henry Lee (1756–1818) and Richard B. Lee. Graduated College of New Jersey, 1775. Federalist attorney general of the United States, 1795–1801; one of defense lawyers in trial of Aaron Burr and in impeachment of Judge Chase.

LEE, CHARLES ALFRED (*b. Salisbury, Conn., 1801; d. 1872*), physician, teacher of medicine. Author of *Catalogue of Medicinal Plants . . . in the State of New York* (1848).

LEE, ELIZA BUCKMINSTER (*b. Portsmouth, N.H., ca. 1788; d. 1864*), writer. Sister of Joseph S. Buckminster. Author of family biographies and religious works and of popular translations from German.

LEE, FITZHUGH (*b. Fairfax Co., Va., 1835; d. Washington, D.C., 1905*), soldier. Nephew of Robert E. Lee. Graduated West Point, 1856; commissioned in cavalry. Resigned from U.S. Army, 1861; commissioned lieutenant in Confederate Army, 1861; promoted brigadier general, July 1862. Lee's reconnaissance before Chancellorsville was largely responsible for Jackson's success in that battle; he was promoted major general, 1863, and is generally ranked among the best dozen cavalry officers born in America. Engaged in farming after the Civil War, he was elected governor of Virginia, 1885, served until 1890, and did much to secure continued Democratic control of Virginia government. Consul general to Havana, Cuba, 1896–98, he was commissioned major general of volunteers, May 1898, and fought in the Spanish-American War.

LEE, FRANCIS LIGHTFOOT (*b. Westmoreland Co., Va., 1734; d. Richmond Co., Va., 1797*), Virginia legislator, Revolutionary patriot. Brother of Richard H., Arthur, and William Lee. Member of the Continental Congress, 1775–79, and a signer of the Declaration of Independence.

LEE, FREDERIC SCHILLER (*b. Canton, N.Y., 1859; d. Waverly, S.C., 1939*), physiologist. Graduated St. Lawrence University, 1878; Ph.D., Johns Hopkins, 1885. Spent a year in Karl Ludwig's physiology laboratory, Leipzig. Taught physiology, at College of Physicians and Surgeons, Columbia University, 1891–1938; helped extend physiology courses into other fields besides medicine. Lee was best known for his studies of fatigue, particularly in its application to industrial occupations. As a result of his investigations he became an advocate of the eight-hour working day as conducive to more and better work.

LEE, GEORGE WASHINGTON CUSTIS (*b. Fortress Monroe, Va., 1832; d. Fairfax Co., Va., 1913*), soldier, educator. Son of Robert E. Lee. Graduated West Point, 1854; assigned to engineers. Served in Confederate Army, 1861–65, notably as aide-de-camp on staff of President Jefferson Davis. President of Washington and Lee University, 1871–97.

LEE, GYPSY ROSE (*b. Rose Louise Hovick, Seattle, Wash.[?], 1914; d. Los Angeles, Calif., 1970*), entertainer and writer. Entered show business with her sister (later known as June Havoc) about 1918 under the management of their mother, Rose. Toured the vaudeville circuit with her sister as the lead until 1928, when "Dainty June" eloped; Rose took over the act's lead. Performed her first solo strip act at age fifteen; under the name Gypsy Rose Lee, became the best-known burlesque queen of her era. Appeared at Minksy's Theater (1931), in Ziegfeld's *Follies* (1936); in several "B" films (1937–66); and in Las Vegas and on television in the 1950's and 1960's. During World War II and the Vietnam War, toured for the United Services Organizations (USO). Began her writing career in 1940 with Walter Winchell, which led to two mystery novels; several articles in the 1940's and 1950's in *American Mercury, Harper's*, and the *New Yorker*; and her autobiography, *Gypsy: A Memoir* (1957), on which a motion picture and Broadway musicals were based.

LEE, HANNAH FARNHAM SAWYER (*b. Newburyport Mass., 1780; d. 1865*), author of miscellaneous works, including tracts on thrift and self-improvement.

LEE, HENRY (*b. Prince William Co., Va., 1756; d. Cumberland Island, Ga., 1818*), soldier, statesman. Better known as "Light-Horse Harry" Lee. Brother of Richard B. and Charles Lee (1758–1815); father of Robert E. Lee. Graduated College of New Jersey (Princeton), 1773. Won fame in Revolution as commander of irregular cavalry known as "Lee's Legion"; sent south to aid Nathaniel Greene, 1780, his subsequent story is the entire history of the campaign in the South. He was particularly effective at Guildford Courthouse, March 1781, and at Eutaw Springs, September 1781; he was present at the siege of Yorktown and at the surrender of Cornwallis. Active after the war as a Federalist politician in Virginia, he served as governor, 1792–95, and in 1794 was chosen to command the army assembled to put down whiskey rebellion in Pennsylvania. Resolutions offered by John Marshall on Washington's death, 1799, were drawn up by Lee and contained the description "first in war, first in peace and first in the hearts of his countrymen." Harassed by debt *post* 1800, he was seriously injured in the Baltimore riot, 1812, during his attempt to help Alexander C. Hanson defend the Federalist press in that city against a mob. He was author of *Memoirs of the War in the Southern Department, etc.* (1812).

LEE, HENRY (*b. Beverly, Mass., 1782; d. 1867*), Boston merchant, publicist. Brother-in-law of James (1777–1867), Charles, and Patrick T. Jackson. Author of "Boston Report" (1827) opposing tariff increases; leader in free-trade movement.

LEE, HENRY (*b. Westmoreland Co., Va., 1787; d. Paris, France, 1837*), soldier, Virginia legislator. Son of Henry Lee (1756–1818); half brother of Robert E. Lee. Graduated William and Mary, 1808. Served in War of 1812; was an active writer for newspapers in Andrew Jackson's behalf. Author of *Observations on the Writings of Thomas Jefferson* (1832).

LEE, IVY LEDBETTER (*b. Cedartown, Ga., 1877; d. New York, N.Y., 1934*), publicity expert. Adviser on public relations to leading industrialists, *post* 1904. His clients included the Pennsylvania Railroad, John D. Rockefeller, Bethlehem Steel Co., and the Guggenheim interests.

LEE, JAMES MELVIN (*b. Port Crane, N.Y., 1878; d. 1929*), magazine editor, teacher of journalism. Author of *History of American Journalism* (1917).

LEE, JAMES WIDEMAN (*b. Rockbridge, Ga., 1849; d. 1919*), Methodist clergyman, editor. Held pastorates in St. Louis, Mo., and Atlanta, Ga. Author of *The Religion of Science* (1912).

LEE, JASON (*b. Stanstead, Canada* [then conisered part of Vermont], *1803; d. Stanstead, 1845*), missionary, Oregon pioneer. Chosen to head a mission to the Flathead Indians, 1833, Lee left Independence, Mo., in April 1834 in company with N. J. Wyeth's second expedition. The Missionary group arrived at Fort Vancouver in September, and on abandonment of the Flathead project settled in October some ten miles northwest of the present city of Salem, Oreg. Additional missionary settlers came in June 1837, and missions were established in the Clatsop country and at The Dalles on the Columbia River. Lee journeyed overland to the East in 1838, presented a settlers' petition for territorial organization to the authorities at Washington and addressed many Methodist groups for support of his mission; he returned to Oregon by sea with additional missionary-settlers in May 1840. A decline in missionary effort and a concentration on building up the material side of the settlements ensued, with Lee in a leading role as promoter, developer, advocate of Americanization; he presided over the meeting for territorial organization held at Champoeg, Feb. 7, 1841, and was influential in bringing about completion of a provisional government, July 5, 1843. Returning East, 1844, he learned en route that he had been superseded in his mission post. His character and his influence on early Oregon have been themes of much controversy.

LEE, JESSE (*b. Virginia, 1758; d. near Hillsborough, Md., 1816*), Methodist preacher, apostle of Methodism in New England. Author of *A Short History of the Methodists in the United States of America* (1810).

LEE, JOHN CLIFFORD HODGES (*b. Junction City, Kans., 1887; d. York, Pa., 1958*), army officer. Attended West Point, commissioned in 1909. During World War I served as chief of staff at the Eighty-second Division, responsible for planning the St. Mihiel and Argonne-Meuse offensives. During World War II the controversial head of the Services of Supply of the European Theater of Operations. As such, Lee was responsible for the logistical support of the Allied invasion of Europe. He was criticized as being lax and unconcerned about the needs of the army. Later, under investigation by the Inspector General, he was defended by General Eisenhower and cleared of allegations. After the war, he was appointed commanding general of the Mediterranean Theater of Operations and deputy supreme commander of Allied Forces, Mediterranean. He retired in 1947.

LEE, JOHN DOYLE (*b. Kaskaskia, Ill., 1812; d. Mountain Meadows, Utah, 1877*), Mormon elder. Tried and executed for his part in the Mountain Meadows Massacre, 1857.

LEE, JOSEPH (*b. Brookline, Mass., 1862; d. Cohasset, Mass., 1937*), social worker, "father of American playgrounds." Cousin of Richard C. Cabot. President of Playground Association of America (later National Recreation Association), 1910–37.

LEE, LUTHER (*b. Schoharie, N.Y., 1800; d. Flint, Mich., 1889*), Methodist clergyman, abolitionist. First president of Wesleyan Methodist Connection, elected 1844. Returned to the parent church, 1867.

LEE, PORTER RAYMOND (*b. Buffalo, N.Y., 1879; d. Englewood, N.J., 1939*), social worker. Director, New York School of Social Work, 1916–38.

LEE, RICHARD (*d. 1664*), Virginia planter and legislator; ancestor of the Lees of Virginia. Immigrated *ca.* 1641; settled in York Co.; removed to Northumberland Co. *ca.* 1651.

LEE, RICHARD BLAND (*b. Prince William Co., Va., 1761; d. Washington, D.C., 1827*), planter, Virginia legislator. Brother of Henry (1756–1818) and Charles Lee (1758–1815). Congressman, Federalist, from Virginia, 1789–95. His change of vote, 1789, secured Hamilton necessary votes to put through assumption bill and to create District of Columbia.

LEE, RICHARD HENRY (*b. Westmoreland Co., Va., 1732; d. Chantilly, Va., 1794*), lawyer, Virginia legislator, Revolutionary statesman. Brother of Arthur, Francis L., and William Lee. Educated by private tutors and in English schools, he entered the Virginia House of Burgesses, 1758, where he opposed the spread of slavery and acted with Patrick Henry on many issues. His opposition to the Stamp Act placed him at once in the forefront of the defenders of colonial rights. In February 1766, he drew the citizens of his own county into the "Westmoreland Association," binding themselves to import no British goods until the Stamp Act should be repealed. He opposed the Townshend Acts even more firmly, branding them "arbitrary, unjust, and destructive of that mutual beneficial connection which every good subject would wish to see preserved." As early as 1768 he was advocating committees for intercolonial correspondence. Between 1768 and 1773, with Patrick Henry and Thomas Jefferson, he was active in the radical wing of the House of Burgesses.

Elected to the First Continental Congress, Lee was attracted to John Adams and formed a lifelong friendship with Samuel Adams. He was a member of many of the most important committees and was among the foremost proponents of strong measures against England. Openly advocating independence in the spring of 1776, Lee was chosen to move the independence resolutions in Congress. On June 13, 1776, he left Philadelphia to take part in forming the new state government in Virginia; returning to Congress, he furthered the idea of confederation by urging Virginia's surrender of her claim to Western lands. In foreign affairs he supported his brother Arthur in the latter's controversy with Silas Deane.

He left Congress in 1779 and was active in Virginia's public affairs, strangely enough on the conservative side. Elected to Congress, 1784, he played an important role in passage of the Northwest Ordinance but refused to attend the Constitutional Convention, and led in Virginia's opposition to the new Constitution. His *Letters of the Federal Farmer* (1787, 1788) became an anti-Federal textbook. He served in the U.S. Senate 1789–92, his chief concern being for the ideas embodied in the Bill of Rights.

LEE, ROBERT EDWARD (*b. "Stratford," Westmoreland Co., Va., 1807; d. Lexington, Va., 1870*), soldier. Son of Henry Lee (1756–1818); half brother of Henry Lee (1787–1837). Two strong influences affected him in childhood: the sense of responsibility engendered by need to care for a sickly mother, and mingled admiration and pity for his father—a great soldier who had never been able to cope adequately with civilian life. Quick in his studies at school, he graduated second in his West Point class, without a single demerit, 1829. The years that followed his commission as second lieutenant of engineers were such as might have been spent by any young officer of that service who combined a fine presence with social graces, exemplary conduct, energy, and ability. In 1831 he married Mary Ann Randolph Custis, a descendant of Martha Washington. The marriage was a happy one. Association with the Washington traditions at the Custis home, "Arlington," made his father's old commander Lee's ideal; he seems consciously to have emulated Washington in his bearing and in his conception of duty.

Lee's first important independent assignment (July 1837) was to be superintending engineer over river and harbor work at St. Louis, Mo. On the outbreak of the Mexican War he was ordered to San Antonio, Texas, as assistant engineer to General John E. Wool. He won much praise for his reconnaissance work at Buena Vista. Transferred to General Winfield Scott's Vera Cruz expedition, Lee distinguished himself in nearly every engagement from Vera Cruz to Chapultepec. In 1855, after further duty in fortress construction and a tour as superintendent at West Point, Lee was glad to change from the staff to the line as lieutenant colonel of the 2nd Cavalry. When the secession movement began, Lee had no sympathy with it, yet he was fixed in the belief that he could never bear arms against his native state. When he was offered field command of the U.S. Army, April 18, 1861, he refused acceptance; two days later, on learning to his sorrow that the Virginia convention had voted for secession, he resigned from the army.

Virginia chose Lee as commander of her forces on April 23; he accepted and threw all his energies into organizing her defense. For a time, he served as military consultant to President Jefferson Davis with the rank of general; in operations against a threatened invasion from western Virginia he lost popular reputation; from November 1861 to March 1862 he organized the South Atlantic seaboard defense. Returning to Richmond as military adviser to Davis, he worked out in concert with T. J. Jackson a plan to cripple General McClellan's plans to besiege that city. On June 1, 1862, Lee succeeded General Joseph E. Johnston, wounded the previous day, in command of the field force which Lee promptly named the "Army of Northern Virginia." During the next 34 months, the odds against Lee were to be always 3 to 2 and sometimes 3 to 1, yet seldom was he in a more precarious position than when he took command. McClellan, with 100,000 Union men, was but seven miles from Richmond. Three separate forces were threatening T. J. Jackson in the Valley of Virginia. Jackson won two quick actions and dispelled the threat; Lee took the offensive and in the Seven Days' Battles drove the Federals back on Washington. This campaign was the most important period in Lee's military education. Strategically sound in principle though demanding too much of untrained officers, the campaign was tactically bad. It taught Lee the necessity of simpler methods and organization. Ridding himself of inefficient division commanders, and with his first display of skill in the difficult military art of troop movement, lee outmaneuvered General John Pope and with T. J. Jackson's help routed him at the second battle of Bull Run, August 30, 1862. Lee might have smashed Pope's army, but he yielded to General James Longstreet's stubbornness and disclosed for the first time his one great weakness as field commander—his inability to work with unwilling subordinates. Longstreet insisted on a day's delay in the general assault; a further day was lost in regrouping after the battle; and a rainstorm at Chantilly on the afternoon of September 1 then kept Lee from overtaking the fleeing Pope.

During the invasion of Maryland in September 1862, Lee made his only serious blunder in logistics in miscalculating the time required for troop movements. In spite of this, he was able to retreat to Virginia after the bloody fight at Antietam, Sept 17, 1862. Reorganizing his forces, he awaited the next Federal move. In offensive operations against Lee, General A. E. Burnside was badly whipped at Fredericksburg on Dec. 13, and General Joseph Hooker was beaten at Chancellorsville on May 2–4, 1863, in the most brilliant of Lee's victories. Lee suffered a serious loss in the latter battle, however, when T. J. "Stonewall" Jackson was mortally wounded. Lee had worked in complete understanding with Jackson, whom he regarded as a perfect executive officer, and he was never able to replace him. The next month, June 1863, Lee made his second and final invasion of the North. He was met by General George Meade at Gettysburg, Pa., and suffered his worst defeat in the crucial battle of July 1, 2, and 3. Defective staff work,

Ewell's caution, J. E. B. Stuart's absence, Longstreet's obduracy, all helped to explain the defeat. Lee assumed full responsibility, however, and sought unsuccessfully to resign.

Lee was never again able to take the offensive. On May 4, 1864, General U. S. Grant with a force twice that of Lee's army crossed the Rapidan and headed for Richmond. For the next eleven months Lee was always on the defensive. He fought brilliantly and doggedly, but the Confederate cause grew more hopeless. Short of artillery, low on all supplies including food and munitions, plagued by the impossible task of replacing manpower in numbers and staff officers in quality, Lee fought on. Intuitively sensing Grant's maneuvers, constructing excellent field fortifications, but never able to catch Grant on the move or to attack the Federals in detail, he repulsed Grant's attacks time after time. On Feb. 6, 1865, Lee became general in chief of all the Confederate armies, but it was too late. He evacuated Petersburg and Richmond, Va., on April 2–3, and on April 9, reduced to 7,800 men able to bear arms, he surrendered at Appomattox Court House.

In September 1865, Lee became president of Washington College in Lexington, Va. He rebuilt the college, shunned publicity, and set an example of obedience to civil authority. His supreme interest was in restoring the economic, cultural, and political life of the South, and in him the South still sees the embodiment of all its best ideals.

Lee's place in history is that of a great soldier and a Christian gentleman in the widest sense of that term. Self-control was second nature to him. As soldier, he excelled as a strategist; his reputation is not dependent on able seconding of his plans by Stonewall Jackson. Lee devised; Jackson executed. Lee's one great weakness was his inability to persuade stubborn, contrary minds to accept his view of a situation and achieve his purpose. His strategical power sprang from his ability to put himself in his opponents' place, to analyze military intelligence, and to make accurate judgments of the strength of opposing forces.

LEE, SAMUEL PHILLIPS (*b. Fairfax Co., Va., 1812; d. Silver Spring, Md., 1897*), naval officer. Grandson of Richard Henry Lee. Remained loyal to Union; was distinguished at attack on New Orleans, 1862, and in both passages of Vicksburg by Union fleet. Commanding blockade squadron off Virginia and North Carolina, 1862–64, he is credited with placing second cordon of blockade ships at sea to intercept runners who had escaped first cordon. Promoted rear admiral, 1870, he retired in 1873.

LEE, STEPHEN DILL (*b. Charleston, S.C., 1833; d. Vicksburg, Miss., 1908*), Confederate soldier, educator. Grandson of Thomas Lee. Graduated West Point, 1854. Commissioned captain in Confederate Army, 1861, he rose to lieutenant general (1864) after distinguished service, principally with cavalry and in the western campaigns *post* 1862. After the war, he was active in the Mississippi legislature and served as president, Mississippi A. and M. College, 1880–99.

LEE, THOMAS (*b. Charleston, S.C., 1769; d. Charleston, 1839*), jurist, banker. Grandson of Jeremiah Theus. Became president, Bank of South Carolina, 1817; was appointed federal judge for South Carolina district, 1823; held both offices until his death. Opposed nullification.

LEE, THOMAS SIM (*b. Prince George's Co., Md., 1745; d. 1819*), planter, Revolutionary patriot. Great-grandson of Richard Lee. Governor of Maryland, 1779–83 and 1792–94.

LEE, WILLIAM (*b. Westmoreland Co., Va., 1739; d. 1795*), merchant, diplomat. Brother of Richard H., Francis L., and Arthur Lee. Resident in London *post* 1768, he was made alderman of that city, 1775, the only American who ever held that office. Appointed joint commercial agent at Nantes, France,

1777; became involved in controversy between Silas Deane and his brother Arthur Lee. The unratified treaty of commerce between the United States and Holland which he proposed was the ostensible cause of war between England and Holland. He was later unsuccessful in efforts to secure recognition of the United States by Prussia and Austria. In 1783, he returned to Virginia.

LEE, WILLIAM GRANVILLE (*b. Laprairie, Ill., 1859; d. Cleveland, Ohio, 1929*), labor leader. Official in Brotherhood of Railroad Trainmen *post* 1895; president, 1909–28.

LEE, WILLIAM HENRY FITZHUGH (*b. Arlington, Va., 1837; d. near Alexandria, Va., 1891*), Confederate soldier, politician. Son of Robert E. Lee. Served in Confederate cavalry, 1861–65. Promoted brigadier general, 1862, major general, 1864, he was a cool, scientific fighting man who had the perfect confidence of his men. Congressman, Democrat, from Virginia, 1887–91.

LEE, WILLIAM LITTLE (*b. Sandy Hill, N.Y., 1821; d. Hawaii, 1857*), jurist. Removed to Hawaii, 1846; became chief justice, superior court of law and equity, 1847; drafted Hawaiian penal code, 1850. Lee was one of the little group of statesmen who created the Hawaiian constitutional monarchy.

LEE, WILLIS AUGUSTUS (*b. Natlee, Ky., 1888; d. Casco Bay, Maine, 1945*), naval officer. Graduated U.S. Naval Academy, 1908. Early service included Vera Cruz, 1914; World War I assignment with destroyer forces at Brest, France; sea duty in command of several destroyers, and as navigator and executive officer of battleship *Pennsylvania*. Promoted captain, 1936, he was director of fleet training on eve of World War I. When new battleships became available in 1942, he commanded the first division (USS *Washington* and *South Dakota*) and took the ships to the Southwest Pacific; on Nov 15. 1942, he commanded a task force off Guadalcanal that defeated a Japanese force and prevented the landing of reenforcements on that island. Advanced to vice admiral, March 1944, he commanded a battleship squadron in support of fast carrier task forces, and in island bombardment operations. After a brief leave in May 1945, he was assigned to a special antikamikaze project at Casco Bay, where he died of a heart attack.

LEEDOM, BOYD STEWART (*b. Alvord, Iowa, 1906; d. Arlington, Va., 1969*), lawyer. Attended Black Hills Teachers College and University of South Dakota (LL.B., 1929). Served for two years in South Dakota state senate, later was appointed to the state's Supreme Court (1951–54). As chairman of the National Labor Relations Board, 1955–61, he expanded the right of employers to communicate with employees during labor disputes and tightened the rules on permissible picketing and the secondary boycott.

LEEDS, DANIEL (*b. Leeds, England, 1652; d. Burlington, N.J., 1720*), surveyor, almanac maker. Came to America in third quarter of seventeenth century; settled in Burlington, N.J., 1677; appointed surveyor general, Province of West Jersey, 1682. He was also a member of the assembly and of the governor's council and author of pamphlets attacking the Quakers.

LEEDS, JOHN (*b. Talbot Co., Md., 1705; d. Wade's Pt., Md., 1790*), mathematician, astronomer. Served on joint commission to mark off boundary between Maryland and Pennsylvania, 1762–68. Appointed surveyor general of Maryland *ca.* 1766, he served until his death, excepting the period of the Revolutionary War, when his Loyalist sympathies caused his suspension from office.

LEES, ANN. *See* LEE, ANN.

LEESER, ISAAC (*b. Neuenkirchen, Prussia, 1806; d. 1868*), rabbi, author. Came to America, 1824; served congregation Mikveh Israel, Philadelphia, 1829–50. Headed faculty of Maimonides College. A strong advocate of traditional Jewish doctrine.

LEETE, WILLIAM (*b. Dodington, England, ca. 1613; d. Hartford, Conn., 1683*), colonist. Came to America, 1639. Was a founder of Guilford, Conn.; held numerous colonial offices and was deputy governor, New Haven Colony, 1658–61; governor, 1661–64. After acceptance of Connecticut Charter by New Haven, Leete served as deputy governor, Connecticut Colony, 1669–76, governor, 1676–83.

LEFEVERE, PETER PAUL (*b. Roulers, Belgium, 1804; d. Detroit, Mich., 1869*), Roman Catholic clergyman. Came to America, 1828; ordained, St. Louis, Mo., 1831. Worked among immigrants in northeastern Missouri, southern Iowa, western Illinois. Consecrated bishop of Detroit, Mich., 1841. Associated with Bishop J. L. Spalding in founding American College at Louvain.

LEFFEL, JAMES (*b. Botetourt Co., Va., 1806; d. Springfield, Ohio, 1866*), manufacturer, inventor. Raised in Ohio. Patented an improved water wheel, 1845; perfected double turbine wheel, patented 1862.

LEFFERTS, GEORGE MOREWOOD (*b. Brooklyn, N.Y., 1846; d. 1920*), laryngologist. Son of Marshall Lefferts. M.D., N.Y. College of Physicians and Surgeons, 1870. Studied laryngology in London, Paris, and Vienna; practiced in New York *post* 1873; taught at College of Physicians and Surgeons, 1874–1904.

LEFFERTS, MARSHALL (*b. Brooklyn, N.Y., 1821; d. 1876*), engineer. Associated with many early telegraph companies; became president, Gold and Stock Telegraph Co., 1871.

LEFFINGWELL, RUSSELL CORNELL (*b. New York, N.Y., 1878; d. New York, N.Y., 1960*), lawyer, banker, and government official. Studied at Yale and Columbia University Law School, LL.B., 1902. Assistant secretary of the Treasury (1917–20). Associated with J.P. Morgan and Co. from 1923; chairman of the board from 1948; director of Morgan and Co. and of its successor, the Morgan Guaranty and Trust Co., until his death. Helped found the Council on Foreign Relations and served as its chairman. On Wall Street, Leffingwell was considered a business intellectual who gained his points by persuasion, not by table pounding.

LEFFLER, ISAAC (*b. Washington Co., Pa., 1788; d. Chariton, Iowa, 1866*), lawyer, Virginia and Iowa legislator. Brother of Shepherd Leffler. Presided over meeting at Burlington, Iowa, 1837, at which resolutions were adopted for establishment of Iowa Territory.

LEFFLER, SHEPHERD (*b. Washington Co., Pa., 1811; d. 1879*), lawyer, Iowa legislator. Brother of Isaac Leffler. Congressman, Democrat, from Iowa 1846–51.

LEFFMANN, HENRY (*b. Philadelphia, Pa., 1847; d. 1930*), chemist. Graduated Jefferson Medical College, 1869. Distinguished as a teacher of chemistry in Philadelphia medical schools and colleges, he served also as port physician of Philadelphia and made numerous contributions to chemical literature.

LEFLORE, GREENWOOD (*b. Jackson, Miss., 1800; d. 1865*), Choctaw chief, Mississippi planter and legislator, Unionist.

LEGARÉ, HUGH SWINTON (*b. Charleston, S.C., 1797; d. 1843*), lawyer, South Carolina legislator. Graduated South Carolina College, 1814; studied also in Edinburgh and Paris. Associated with Stephen Elliott as editor, *Southern Review*, 1828–32. Fought J. C. Calhoun over issue of nullification, although himself a believer in states' rights and an opponent of protective tariffs. Served as U.S. chargé d'affaires in Belgium, 1832–36. On his return home, he served briefly in Congress; identified himself with Whig party and was active in campaign of 1840. Appointed U. S. attorney general by President Tyler, 1841, he served with distinction until death.

LeGENDRE, CHARLES WILLIAM (*b. Oullins, France, 1830; d. Seoul, Korea, 1899*), Union soldier, diplomat. U.S. consul at Amoy, China, 1866–72. Served as foreign adviser to Japanese government, 1872–75; as adviser to the King of Korea, 1890–99.

LEGGE, ALEXANDER (*b. Dane Co., 1866; d. Hinsdale, Ill, 1933*), manufacturer. Associated, *post* 1891, with the antecedent firms of International Harvester Co., of which he was elected president, 1922. During World War I, he served as chief assistant to Bernard M. Baruch on the War Industries Board and was manager of the Allied Purchasing Commission.

LEGGETT, MORTIMER DORMER (*b. near Ithaca, N.Y., 1821; d. 1896*), Ohio lawyer, Union soldier. U.S. commissioner of patents, 1871–74. First president of Brush Electric Co., *post* 1884.

LEGGETT, WILLIAM (*b. New York, N.Y., 1801; d. 1839*), journalist. Midshipman in U.S. Navy, 1822–26; part owner and assistant editor under William Cullen Bryant of N.Y. *Evening Post*, 1829–36. Combative, energetic and independent, he became oracle of radical Democrats, writing in support of free trade, direct taxation, the right of working men to organize, and abolition. His collected political writings were published, 1840. After leaving the *Post*, he edited the *Plaindealer* (1837) and a daily paper, the *Examiner*.

LEGLER, HENRY EDUARD (*b. Palermo, Italy, 1861; d. 1917*), journalist, librarian. Came to America as a boy; was raised in La Crosse, Wis. Secretary, Milwaukee school board, 1890–1904; distinguished as secretary, Wisconsin Free Library Commission, 1904–09; directed Chicago Public Library system, 1909–17.

LEHMAN, ADELE LEWISOHN (*b. New York, N.Y., 1882; d. Purchase, N.Y., 1965*), philanthropist and art collector. Honorary vice-president of Federation for Jewish Philanthropies, one of whose founders was her husband, Arthur Lehman (brother of Herbert Henry Lehman); member of board of directors of New York Service for Orthopedically Handicapped; founder of Arthur Lehman Counseling Service for people in need of psychiatric help. An ardent art collector; much of her family's collection was given to the Metropolitan Museum of Art and Fogg Museum.

LEHMAN, ARTHUR (*b. New York, N.Y., 1873; d. New York, 1936*), investment banker. Partner, *post* 1901, in Lehman Brothers; played large part in the firm's rise to major status.

LEHMAN, HERBERT HENRY (*b. New York, N.Y., 1878; d. New York, 1963*), investment banker and politician. Attended Dr. Julius Sach's Collegiate Institute and Williams College (B.A., 1899). Joined the family firm, Lehman Brothers, in 1908. During World War I, founded Joint Distribution Committee, which collected and disbursed funds for Jewish relief, and was a textile procurer for the army and a member of the War Claims Board. Elected lieutenant governor of New York (1928–32) on Franklin D. Roosevelt's ticket, then governor (1932–42), presiding over an impressive "Little New Deal" and turning a fiscal debt of $90

million in 1933 to a surplus of $6 million by 1938, despite implementing a 25 percent reduction in the state income tax. Director of Office of Foreign Relief and Rehabilitation Administration (1942) and of the United Nations Relief and Rehabilitation Administration (1943–46). Elected to U.S. Senate (1946–57), he was one of the first to speak out against McCarthyism. Awarded Presidential Medal of Freedom (1963).

LEHMAN, IRVING (*b. New York, N.Y., 1876; d. Port Chester, N.Y., 1945*), jurist, Jewish community leader. Brother of Arthur Lehman and Herbert Lehman; son-in-law of Nathan Straus. A.B., Columbia University, 1896; A.M., 1897; LL.B., 1898. Elected as a Democrat to the N.Y. State Supreme Court, 1908; reelected with bipartisan endorsement, 1922. Elected, again with bipartisan support, a justice of the N.Y. State Court of Appeals, 1923. Reelected in 1937, he served as chief justice *post* 1940. Although not a seminal thinker in the law, he stood for a reasonable instrumentalist approach which would facilitate necessary social legislation in economic matters; he was also a zealous upholder of civil liberties.

LEHMAN, ROBERT (*b. New York, N.Y., 1891; d. Sands Point, N.Y., 1969*), investment banker. Attended Yale (B.A., 1913). Joined family's firm, Lehman Brothers, in 1919; became principal partner in 1925. Initiated the recruitment of the firm's first nonfamily partners; involved the bank with retail businesses, such as Federated Department Stores and F. W. Woolworth; created the nation's largest vaudeville circuit; began a long involvement with the air transportation industry, and acquired what later became American Airlines; also underwrote the initial offerings of such conglomerates as Litton Industries. His art collection, valued at between $50 million and $100 million was donated to the Metropolitan Museum of Art in 1969.

LEHMANN, FREDERICK WILLIAM (*b. Prussia, 1853; d. St. Louis, Mo., 1931*), lawyer. Came to America as a child. Practiced first in Iowa and *post* 1890 in St. Louis, Mo. U.S. solicitor general, 1910–12. Independent in politics, learned and witty.

LEIB, MICHAEL (*b. Philadelphia, Pa., 1760; d. 1822*), physician, Pennsylvania legislator. Congressman, Democratic-Republican, 1799–1806; U.S. senator, 1809–14. Collaborated with William Duane as political dictator of Philadelphia *post* 1796; his violence and avarice, however, soon wrecked the Jeffersonian party in Pennsylvania. He later opposed Thomas McKean, Gallatin's fiscal policies, and James Madison's administration.

LEIBER, FRITZ (*b. Chicago, Ill., 1882; d. Pacific Palisades, Calif., 1949*), actor, theatrical producer. Trained in stock, and with Ben Greet's Players; supported Julia Marlowe and Robert Mantell. Most effective in classic roles, particularly Shakespearian, he played with a nervous force that was sometimes called flamboyant, and was more successful on the road than in New York. His productions were tasteful and employed modern stage techniques to good effect; his Chicago Civic Shakespeare Society (1929–32) was the first resident Shakespearian repertory company in the United States. *Post* 1935, he acted mainly in motion pictures.

LEIDY, JOSEPH (*b. Philadelphia, Pa., 1823; d. 1891*), naturalist, foremost American anatomist of his time. M.D., University of Pennsylvania, 1844. Professor of anatomy, University of Pennsylvania, 1853–91. Distinguished as an anatomist, he was scarcely less at home in other fields of science, notably vertebrate paleontology and parasitology. A tireless worker, he was nearly devoid of any ambition but for the collection of facts; he was not given to theory and disliked controversy. Among his numerous published works were *Elementary Treatise on Human Anatomy* (1861), his monograph "On the Extinct Mammalia of Dakota and Nebraska" (1869) and his *Fresh Water Rhizopods of North America* (1879).

LEIGH, BENJAMIN WATKINS (*b. Chesterfield Co., Va., 1781; d. 1849*), lawyer, Virginia legal codifier and legislator. As U.S. senator from Virginia, 1834–36, he refused to obey the legislature's order to vote for expunging of censure of Andrew Jackson over removal of government deposits from the Bank of the United States and denounced the measure in outstanding speeches. His integrity cost him his political career.

LEIGH, VIVIAN (*b. Vivian Mary Hartley, Darjeeling, India, 1913; d. London, England, 1967*), actress. Attended Royal Academy of Dramatic Art in London, 1931–33; made her stage debut in 1935; became a star after her appearance in *The Mask of Virtue* (1935). Often appeared with her husband, Laurence Olivier, with whom she made her first film, *Fire Over England* (1937). Won Academy Awards for her roles as Scarlett O'Hara in *Gone With the Wind* (1939) and as Blanche DuBois in *A Streetcar Named Desire* (1951). Won an Antoinette Perry Award for her role in the Broadway musical *Tovarich* (1963).

LEIGH, WILLIAM ROBINSON (*b. Falling Waters, W. Va., 1866; d. New York, N.Y., 1955*), painter, author, illustrator. Studied at the Maryland Institute, Baltimore, and the Royal Academy of Fine Arts, Munich, Germany. Best known for his paintings of the American West, Leigh ranks with Frederick Remington in that genre. Best known works include *The Master Hand* and *The Fate of the Nation Was Riding That Night*, his famous painting of the ride of Paul Revere. Leigh also painted the panoramas for the habitat groups in the African Hall in the Museum of Natural History in New York. His reputation as an illustrator was established with his sketches for articles published in *Scribner's* magazine, 1897–98. Leigh was also a prolific writer and in 1933 *The Western Pony* was selected by the American Institute of Graphic Arts as one of the fifty best books of the year.

LEIGHTON, WILLIAM (*fl. 1825–1868*), glassmaker. Employed by New England Glass Co., Cambridge, Mass., he hit upon an original formula for ruby glass *ca.* 1849. Removing to Wheeling, W. Va., 1863, he worked at a new formula for lime-flint glass which he produced, 1864.

LEIPER, THOMAS (*b. Strathaven, Scotland, 1745; d. Delaware Co., Pa., 1825*), tobacco merchant, Revolutionary soldier.

LEIPZIG, NATE (*b. Stockholm, Sweden, 1873; d. New York, N.Y., 1939*), magician. Came to America as a boy; was raised in Detroit, Mich. Internationally recognized as the most skillful sleight-of-hand performer of his time.

LEIPZIGER, HENRY MARCUS (*b. Manchester, England, 1854; d. 1917*), educator, lecturer. Came to America as a boy. Graduated College of the City of New York, 1873; LL.B., Columbia, 1875. Superintendent, Hebrew Technical Institute, 1884–91; assistant superintendent of schools, New York City, 1891–96. Thereafter, he supervised public evening lectures given in the schools, a work which he had inaugurated.

LEISERSON, WILLIAM MORRIS (*b. Revel, Estonia, 1883; d. Washington, D.C., 1957*), labor economist and mediator. Immigrated to the U.S. in 1890. Studied at the University of Wisconsin and at Columbia, Ph.D. in economics. Taught at Antioch College (1925–33). Helped draft National Recovery Administration (NRA) labor codes and was appointed chairman of the National Mediation Board, 1934–39. Appointed to the National Labor Relations Board (NLRB) from 1939 to 1943. Leiserson was committed to traditional collective bargaining and minimal government interference. Taught at Johns Hopkins University, 1944–47. Published *American Trade Union Democracy* in 1959.

LEISHMAN, JOHN G. A. (*b. Pittsburgh, Pa., 1857; d. Nice, France, 1924*), steel manufacturer, diplomat. Associated with Carnegie interests. U.S. minister to Switzerland, 1897–1900; to Turkey, 1900–09, rising to ambassador, 1906. U.S. ambassador to Italy, 1909–11; to Germany 1911–13.

LEISLER, JACOB *b. Frankfort, Germany, 1640; d. New York, N.Y., 1691*), soldier, merchant. Came to New Amsterdam 1660. Married a wealthy widow, 1663; became thereby associated with leading Dutch families, among them the Bayards and Van Cortlandts. Soon numbered among richest men in the colony, he was at odds with his wife's relatives over his claim for a share of her first husband's estate. The Revolution of 1688 in England becoming known in New York, Leisler at head of the militia seized the fort at New York. On the flight of Lt. Gov. Francis Nicholson, Leisler on his own authority proclaimed William and Mary. Acting as leader of various discontented elements in the colony and named commander-in-chief, Aug. 1689, by a committee of safety representing his faction in New York, he governed the province by military force until the arrival of the officially appointed new governor, Sloughter, in March 1691. Tried for his arbitrary seizure of authority and refusal to give it up at the first demand of the new governor, he was condemned to death for treason and executed with his son-in-law and aid, Jacob Milborne. The bitter feeling aroused by Leisler's career and fate was long a factor in New York politics.

LEITER, JOSEPH (*b. Chicago, Ill., 1868; d. Chicago, 1932*), capitalist. Son of Levi Z. Leiter. Attempted a corner in wheat, 1897–98, which failed disastrously; was notable for the numerous litigations in which he engaged.

LEITER, LEVI ZEIGLER (*b. Leitersburg, Md., 1834; d. 1904*), merchant. Removed to Springfield, Ohio, 1854; to Chicago, Ill., 1855. Serving as a clerk in a firm of wholesale dry-goods merchants, he met Marshall Field, 1856. Both men became partners in the concern, leaving it in 1865 to establish firm of Field, Palmer & Leiter. The new firm prospered remarkably under Field's direction as merchant, Leiter's as credit manager. Retiring from the firm, 1881, a wealthy man, Leiter risked his fortune on the continued growth of Chicago and increased it in Chicago real estate. He was active in the promotion and support of cultural institutions in the city.

LE JAU, FRANCIS (*b. Angers, France, 1665; d. 1717*), Anglican clergyman, educator. Rector of Goose Creek parish, S.C., *post* 1706. Interested himself in education of blacks and Indian slaves and exposed cruel practices against them.

LEJEUNE, JOHN ARCHER (*b. Raccourci, Pointe Coupée Parish, La., 1867; d. Baltimore, Md., 1942*), Marine Corps officer. Graduated U.S. Naval Academy, 1888; appointed second lieutenant, U.S.M.C., 1890. In continuous active service, he had risen to brigadier general by 1916; as assistant to the Commandant, 1915–17, he was responsible for legislation which enlarged the Marine Corps and made it ready for World War I. In 1918 he commanded the 4th Marine Brigade in France, and later (promoted to major general) the 2nd Infantry Division which he led to notable victories at St. Mihiel and Blanc Mont and in the Meuse-Argonne. As Commandant of the Marine Corps, 1920–29, he modernized its officer education and selection procedures, and instituted its development of amphibious warfare doctrine, tactics, and techniques. Retiring in 1929, he was chosen superintendent of Virginia Military Institute and served until 1937.

LELAND, CHARLES GODFREY (*b. Philadelphia, Pa., 1824; d. Florence, Italy, 1903*), writer. Graduated Princeton, 1845; studied also at Heidelberg, and Munich. Active in New York and Philadelphia journalism, 1849–69; resided in Europe, 1869–79, and *post* 1884. His published books cover a wide range of subjects, all written with ability and zest. He is remembered particularly for his translations of Heinrich Heine, for the humorous dialect poems collected in *The Breitmann Ballads* (1871) and his numerous works on gypsy lore and language. A genial giant of a man, he was interested to the end of his life in anything mysterious or occult.

LELAND, GEORGE ADAMS (*b. Boston, Mass., 1850; d. Boston, 1924*), physician, otologist, educator. M.D., Harvard Medical School, 1878; made special studies in laryngology and otology at Vienna, Heidelberg and elsewhere in Europe. Professor of laryngology, Dartmouth Medical School, 1893–1914.

LELAND, JOHN (*b. Grafton, Mass., 1754; d. Cheshire, Mass., 1841*), Baptist clergyman. As minister at Orange, Va., 1777–91, played a prominent part in disestablishing Episcopal Church in Virginia; similarly, as minister in Cheshire, Mass., *post* 1791, he labored for the complete disestablishment of the Congregational Standing Order. He obtained considerable celebrity, 1801, when he traveled to Washington to present Thomas Jefferson with a mammoth cheese made by the women of Cheshire.

LELAND, WALDO GIFFORD (*b. Newton, Mass., 1879; d. Washington, D.C., 1966*), historian and archival theorist. Attended Brown (B.A., 1900) and Harvard (M.A., 1901). Began a twenty-four-year association with the Carnegie Institution of Washington in 1903. *The Guide to the Archives of the Government of the United States in Washington* (1904), written with Claude H. Van Tyne, established him as the nation's leading authority on federal archives. General secretary of the American Historical Association (1909–20); president of Society of American Archivists in the 1940's; president of the International Committee of Historical Sciences (1938–48); and secretary (1927–39) and director (1939–46) of the American Council of Learned Societies. Delegate to the conference (1945) that led to the establishment of the United Nations Educational, Scientific, and Cultural Organization.

LEMKE, PETER HENRY (*b. Rhena, Mecklenburg, 1796; d. Carrolltown, Pa., 1882*), Roman Catholic clergyman. A convert to Catholicism, 1824, he was ordained priest, 1826. Volunteering for the American missions, he came to New York, 1834, and by his own choice was assigned to assist Demetrius A. Gallitzin in his Pennsylvania backwoods mission. Inspiring Boniface Wimmer to make the first settlement of Benedictines in Pennsylvania, 1846, Lemke himself joined the Benedictines, 1851. Departing for Kansas, 1855, he took up land near Atchison, where subsequently was established St. Benedict's Abbey. Returning to Pennsylvania, 1858, he served as missionary and pastor until his retirement *ca.* 1876.

LEMKE, WILLIAM FREDERICK (*b. Albany, Minn., 1878; d. Fargo, N. Dak., 1950*), agrarian leader, lawyer, politician. Raised in Towner County, Dakota Territory. B.A., University of North Dakota, 1902; LL.B., Yale, 1905. Established practice in Fargo. After acquiring land in Mexico for colonization by Americans, Lemke applauded the seizure of power by Victoriano Huerta in 1913 and vainly urged President Wilson to recognize the Huerta regime. Lemke expressed his bitterness toward Wilson in his book *Crimes Against Mexico* (1915).

Lemke became an attorney for the Society of Equity, a manifestation of Midwestern agrarian discontent. He was chairman of the Republican state committee (1916–20) and a member of the Nonpartisan League's national executive committee (1917–21). He was the chief architect of the league's legislative program, enacted in 1919, which created the state-owned Bank of North Dakota, a state grain mill and elevator, the Workmen's Compensation Bureau, a state hail insurance program, an industrial commission to oversee state industries, and machinery for rural credit loans and the building of low-cost houses for farmers. In 1920 he was elected attorney general of North Dakota. In 1922 he unsuccessfully ran for governor; thereafter he engaged in several business ventures, most of them unfruitful. Lemke ran for Senate in 1926 as candidate of the short-lived Farmer-Labor party, but was defeated. In the presidential election of 1928 he backed Alfred E. Smith. An early supporter of Franklin D. Roosevelt, Lemke was elected in 1928 to the House of Representatives as a Republican. Save for 1940, when he ran unsuccessfully for the Senate, he was regularly returned to the House until his death. He lined up sufficient support to secure passage of the Frazier-Lemke Farm Bankruptcy Act (1934) and, when it was declared unconstitutional, its successor, the Farm Mortgage Moratorium Act (1935). In 1936 he accepted the presidential nomination of the vaguely agrarian-inflationary Union party, but his candidacy drew less than 900,000 votes. After World War II, as a member of the House Public Lands Committee, he sponsored a number of conservation measures, including several bills for the betterment of American Indians and to repay them for land taken in the construction of Garrison Dam, which he had worked to finance.

LEMMON, JOHN GILL (*b. Lima, Mich., 1832; d. 1908*), botanist, teacher. After Civil War service, removed to California, 1866. Self-educated, he made botanical explorations of wide areas of California, Nevada, and Arizona, and was encouraged by Asa Gray. Two of his reports as botanist of the California board of forestry, "Pines of the Pacific Slope" (1888) and "Conebearers of California" (1890), attracted worldwide attention. His many booklets and pamphlets helped to prepare public opinion for an established forestry policy which came after his death.

LeMOYNE, FRANCIS JULIUS (*b. Washington, Pa., 1798; d. 1879*), physician, reformer. Early American advocate of cremation.

LE MOYNE, JEAN BAPTISTE. *See* BIENVILLE, JEAN BAPTISTE LE MOYNE, SIEUR DE.

LE MOYNE, PIERRE. *See* IBERVILLE, PIERRE LE MOYNE, SIEUR D'.

LE MOYNE, WILLIAM J. (*b. Boston, Mass., 1831; d. Inwood-on-Hudson, N.Y., 1905*), actor, master of the art of makeup.

LENEY, WILLIAM SATCHWELL (*b. London, England, 1769; d. near Montreal, Canada, 1831*), engraver. Came to America *ca.* 1805. Worked in New York City for publishers and as bank-note engraver up to 1820.

L'ENFANT, PIERRE CHARLES (*b. Paris, France, 1754; d. Prince Georges Co., Md., 1825*), soldier, engineer. Son of one of the "painters in ordinary to the King of his Manufacture of the Gobelins," L'Enfant received some instruction in both engineering and architecture. Coming to America, 1777, as a volunteer engineer in Continental service, he served at his own expense. Wounded while leading an American column in the advance on Savannah, Oct. 9, 1779, he was taken prisoner on fall of Charleston, S.C., May 1780. Exchanged early in 1782, he was promoted major by special act of Congress and retired from the army, January 1784.

One of the early members of the Society of the Cincinnati, L'Enfant designed its insignia and diploma, and was charged by

Washington to have the designs executed abroad. Here, for perhaps the first time, one of his major defects appeared. Blessed with great enthusiasm and imagination, he had little business sense or judgement, and the work proved to be overly expensive. Returning to New York, he found increasing occupation for his artistic talents; among other commissions, he converted the old City Hall into Federal Hall, temporary seat of the new national government *post* 1789.

L'Enfant now received his great opportunity, and proved himself worthy of it in imagination and prophetic foresight if not in discretion. Called on by Washington to survey the site and make the plan for the new Federal City, he submitted his complete design to the President, August 1791. The plan was greatly influenced by the layout of Versailles. L'Enfant set about at once to clear the principal sites and avenues, but difficulties arose over the scope of his activities and his refusal to heed suggestions. On Feb 27, 1792, he was informed that his services were at an end. The city of Washington grew slowly through the 19th century, and often not in accord with L'Enfant's plan. His genius was justified, however, when the Park Commission of 1901 endorsed the merits of his original design and recommended its restoration and extension.

Alexander Hamilton and Robert Morris retained their faith in L'Enfant, and each secured commissions for him. In almost every case, L'Enfant conceived brilliantly but wrought so well and so expensively that the task was never completed. Robert Morris, bankrupt, plaintively wrote of the house L'Enfant began for him, "A much more magnificent house than I ever intended to have built." Subsequently, L'Enfant planned some fortifications for the government and was offered a professorship at West Point (1812) which he declined. He died forgotten and in poverty.

LENKER, JOHN NICHOLAS (*b. Sunbury, Pa., 1858; d. 1929*), Lutheran clergyman, historian. A leader in the pan-Lutheran movement.

LENNON, JOHN BROWN (*b. Lafayette Co., Wis., 1850; d. Bloomington, Ill., 1923*), labor leader, temperance reformer. Settled in Denver, Colo., 1869; was active in organizing tailor's union. Held office in his own local and in the national union; was treasurer, American Federation of Labor, 1890–1917.

LENNOX, CHARLOTTE RAMSAY (*b. New York, possibly in Albany, 1720; d. London, England, 1804*), novelist, dramatist, translator. Removed to England *ca.* 1735. A London 'bluestocking," she was a friend of Samuel Johnson, Samuel Richardson, and Henry Fielding. Author, among other books, of *The Female Quixote* (1752) and *Shakespear Illustrated* (1753), an early study of Shakespeare's sources.

LENOX, JAMES (*b. New York, N.Y., 1800; d. New York, 1880*), merchant, real estate investor, book collector. Graduated Columbia, 1818. Ranks with John Carter Brown and George Brinley as a pioneer in collecting Americana. His splendid Lenox Library is now part of New York Public Library.

LENROOT, IRVINE LUTHER (*b. Superior, Wis., 1869; d. Washington, D.C., 1949*), lawyer, politician, jurist. Born of Swedish immigrant parents; his father had simplified his original name of Linderoth. In 1887 he enrolled at Parsons Business College in nearby Duluth, Minn. Becoming an expert shorthand stenographer, he worked during the 1890's for a Superior law firm and then as reporter for the county court. He was admitted to the bar in 1898. In 1900 Lenroot was elected to the state assembly. He was twice reelected, and from 1903 to 1907 he served as speaker of the assembly.

In 1908 Lenroot won election to the House of Representatives, where he served until 1918. A foe of special interests, he opposed the Republican party's commitment to a high tariff and supported progressive railroad regulatory laws. In 1918 Lenroot ran for the Senate in a special election to fill a vacant seat. He won, and was reelected for a full term in 1920. Lenroot made positive contributions in the areas of conservation and agriculture. He contributed importantly to the Federal Water Power Act (1920) and to the Mineral Leasing Act (1920). He was chiefly responsible for the Agricultural Credits Act of 1923, and as a member of the Senate Committee on Public Lands and Survey, Lenroot participated in the Teapot Dome hearings. In 1926 he was defeated for renomination, and after the expiration of his Senate term he entered law practice in Washington. In 1929 President Hoover appointed him a judge of the federal Court of Customs and Patent Appeals in New York City, a post he held until his retirement in 1944.

LENTHALL, JOHN (*b. District of Columbia, 1807; d. Washington, D.C., 1882*), naval architect. Chief, U.S. Navy bureau of construction, 1853–71. Responsible for design of wooden steam frigates of *Merrimac* class; able, blunt, and incorruptible.

LENZ, SIDNEY SAMUEL (*b. Chicago, Ill., 1873; d. New York, N.Y., 1960*), authority on contract bridge. Retiring from business at age thirty-one, Lenz became famous as the first bridge columnist for the *New York Times* beginning in 1923. He published his most important book, *Lenz on Bridge* in 1926. In 1931, he and his partner were defeated in perhaps the most famous bridge match in history with Ely and Josephine Culbertson, rivals in the bridge world. The match at the Chatham Hotel in New York ran from Dec. 7, 1931, until Jan. 8, 1932; it lasted more than 150 rubbers and attracted wide public attention. Lenz also had an interest in magic, practicing sleight of hand for an hour a day until his last illness.

LEONARD, CHARLES LESTER (*b. Easthampton, Mass., 1861; d. 1913*), physician. M.D., University of Pennsylvania, 1889; also studied abroad for three years. Became interested in X rays, 1896; was perhaps the first to demonstrate the presence of stones in the kidney by means of this agent (1898). His powers of observation and interpretation were almost uncanny; he was a prolific writer on X-ray technique, a generous teacher, and a founder or officer of many medical societies. Excessive exposure to X rays caused serious ulcers on his hands and eventually induced cancer, from which he died.

LEONARD, DANIEL (*b. Norton, Mass., 1740; d. London, England, 1829*), lawyer, Massachusetts colonial legislator, Loyalist. Graduated Harvard, 1760. Practiced law in Taunton, Mass.; served as member of the General Court. Appointed a mandamus councilor, 1774, he was forced to flee his home by his Whig neighbors and go to Boston. A series of articles by him in defense of Crown policies was published in the *Massachusetts Gazette*, 1774–75, over signature "Massachusettensis." Removing to Halifax, N.S., 1776, and later to England, he was appointed chief justice of Bermuda, a post which he held, 1782–1806. Eventually he became dean of English barristers.

LEONARD, GEORGE (*b. Plymouth, Mass., 1742; d. New Brunswick, Canada, 1826*), Loyalist. Directed Loyalist privateering during the Revolution; associated with life and politics of New Brunswick, *post* 1783.

LEONARD, HARRY WARD (*b. Cincinnati, Ohio, 1861; d. New York, N.Y., 1915*), electrical engineer, inventor. Graduated Massachusetts Institute of Technology, 1883. Worked with Thomas A. Edison in introduction of central-station power systems; established Ward Leonard Electric Co., 1894. Among his numerous inventions are the first electric train-lighting system, patented 1889; a system of motor control, patented 1891; an electric elevator-control device, patented 1892; the double-arm circuit breaker, patented 1902.

Leonard, Helen Louise.   *See* Russell, Lillian.

Leonard, Levi Washburn (*b. Bridgewater, Mass., 1790; d. Exeter, N.H., 1864*), Unitarian clergyman, educator. Pastor in Dublin, N.H., *post* 1820; a dominant figure in the life of that town.

Leonard, Robert Josselyn (*b. San José, Calif., 1885; d. 1929*), educator. Graduated State Normal School, San José, 1904; Ph.D., Columbia, 1923. Specialist in vocational and adult education. Taught at University of Indiana, University of California, and at Teachers College, Columbia University, where he directed the school of education and organized the first course in college administration.

Leonard, Sterling Andrus (*b. National City, Calif., 1888; d. Madison, Wis., 1931*), educator. Graduated University of Michigan, 1908; Ph.D., Columbia, 1928. Professor of English, University of Wisconsin, 1920–31. Author of textbooks in composition.

Leonard, William Andrew (*b. Southport, Conn., 1848; d. Gambier, Ohio, 1930*), Episcopal clergyman. Held pastorates in Brooklyn, N.Y., and Washington, D.C. Consecrated bishop of Ohio, 1889.

Leonard, William Ellery (*b. Plainfield, N.J., 1876; d. Madison, Wis., 1944*), poet, translator, educator. B.A., Boston University, 1898. M.A., Harvard, 1899. After study of languages and philology in Germany, 1900–02, he took the Ph.D. at Columbia University, 1904. From 1906 until his death, he was a member of the English department at University of Wisconsin. A conscious imitator of the modes of thought and life-style of the German Romantic poets, he exhibited all the liberal attitudes of his time; he was particularly effective as a teacher in arousing enthusiasm for literature among his students. His creative work was largely autobiographical. Among his books were *Two Lives* (a sonnet sequence, 1925), *The Locomotive-God* (1927), and verse translations of Lucretius, *Beowulf*, and the epic of Gilgamesh.

Leonard, Zenas (*b. near Clearfield, Pa., 1809; d. Sibley, Mo., 1857*), trapper, author. His *Narrative of the Adventures of Zenas Leonard* (1839) is a highly valuable contemporary depiction of trapper life and early Western travel.

Leonty, Metropolitan (*b. Kremenets, Russia, 1876; d. Syosset, N.Y., 1965*), primate of the Russian Orthodox Eastern Church of America. Ordained in 1905 and selected in 1906 to be dean of the first Russian Orthodox theological seminary in the United States, in Minneapolis. Consecrated bishop of Chicago and Minneapolis (1933) and raised to archbishop of New York and ruling bishop of the Council of Bishops (1945). Elected metropolitan of America and Canada in 1950. Adamantly opposed any compromise with the Soviet regime and Communist ideology and insisted on complete autonomy of the American church.

Leopold, (Rand) Aldo (*b. Burlington, Iowa, 1886; d. Wisconsin, 1948*), ecologist, environmental philosopher. B.S., Sheffield Scientific School, Yale, 1908; master of forestry, Yale, 1909. Entered U.S. Forest Service and worked in Arizona and New Mexico, taking a lead in starting the game protection movement in the Southwest. His ideas about wildlife management were premised on the idea of balance and long-term stability. He interrupted his Forest Service career in 1918 to become secretary of the Albuquerque (N. Mex.) Chamber of Commerce, but he rejoined the service in the summer of 1919. He served as associate director and field consultant of the U.S. Forest Products Laboratory in

Madison, Wis., from 1924 to 1928, when he became game consultant for the Sporting Arms and Ammunition Manufacturers' Institute. During the next three years he made game surveys in various states. His *Report on Game Survey of the North Central States* (1931) was one of the first intensive studies of game population ever undertaken in America. During this period, he also developed a national game management policy for the American Game Protective Association.

Following a year of private practice as a consulting forester, Leopold was appointed in 1933 as professor of wildlife management at the University of Wisconsin. He wrote *Game Management* (1933), a textbook that described the art of harvesting game species in such a way as to leave their reproductive capacity unimpaired. Although he published versions of his system of environmental "ethics" in articles during the 1930's, full formulation awaited publication of his *Sand County Almanac* (1949). He served on the council of the Society of American Foresters (1927–31), and in 1946 was elected a fellow. He was a director of the National Audubon Society and a vice president of the American Forestry Association. He helped organize the Wilderness Society in 1935 and was also an organizer of the Wildlife Society in 1937.

Le Page Du Pratz, Antoine Simon.   *See* Dupratz, Antoine Simon Le Page.

Le Roux, Bartholomew (*b. probably Amsterdam, Holland, ca. 1665; d. New York, N.Y., 1713*), goldsmith and silversmith. Settled in New York *ante* 1687; held numerous city offices.

Le Roux, Charles (*b. New York, N.Y., 1689; d. New York, 1745*), engraver, silversmith. Son of Bartholomew Le Roux. Official silversmith, New York City, 1720–43; active in New York City politics and in the Reformed Dutch Church.

Léry, Joseph Gaspard Chausse-Gros de (*b. Canada, 1721; d. Quebec, Canada, 1797*), engineer, employed, 1743–59, in fortification work in Canada; author of nine travel journals descriptive of his journeys to Detroit, the Ohio country, and elsewhere.

Leschi (*b. on Nisqually River in present state of Washington, date unknown; d. 1858*), Nisqualli chief. Commanded rebel Indian forces west of the Cascades, 1855. On failure of the uprising, he received amnesty but was twice tried on a charge of murder, convicted (March 1857) and hanged January 1858.

Lesley, J. Peter.   *See* Lesley, Peter.

Lesley, Peter (*b. Philadelphia, Pa., 1819; d. 1903*), Presbyterian clergyman, geologist. Taught at University of Pennsylvania, *post* 1859; dean of Towne Scientific School, *post* 1875. State geologist of Pennsylvania, 1873–87; superintended issue of 77 volumes of reports, with auxiliary atlas volumes, and also a final report in three volumes, 1892–95. Author also of *A Manual of Coal* (1856), *The Iron Manufacturer's Guide* (1859), and works on philology and philosophy.

Leslie, Charles Robert (*b. London, England, 1794; d. London, 1859*), painter, author. Brother of Eliza Leslie. Brought to America as a child; raised in Philadelphia, Pa. Returning to London, 1811, he studied under Fuseli and Benjamin West; was roommate of Samuel F. B. Morse. Highly successful and able in genre painting, Leslie took his subjects from the works of classic English authors, notably Shakespeare, Sterne, Goldsmith, and Fielding. A Royal Academician, he came to the United States, 1833, as teacher of drawing at West Point; after a few months he returned to England and in 1847 became professor of painting,

Royal Academy. Author of *A Handbook for Young Painters* (1855) and *Memoirs of the Life of John Constable* (1843).

LESLIE, ELIZA (*b. Philadelphia, Pa., 1787; d. Gloucester, N.J., 1858*), author. Sister of Charles R. Leslie. A prolific writer of books on domestic economy and stories for young people.

LESLIE, FRANK (*b. Ipswich, England, 1821; d. 1880*), wood engraver, pioneer publisher of illustrated journals. Christened Henry Carter; came to America, 1848. Employed in Boston on *Gleason's Pictorial* and in New York on the *Illustrated News*, he devised method of rapid woodcut engraving whereby current events could be pictured the day following their occurrence. After two unsuccessful attempts, 1854 and 1855, he brought out first issue of *Frank Leslie's Illustrated Newspaper*, Dec. 15, 1855. The newspaper was particularly effective in its coverage of the Civil War; its artists were found wherever the campaigns were hottest. Leslie published a number of other journals and was successful up to about 1877; however, he died bankrupt.

LESLIE, MIRIAM FLORENCE FOLLINE (*b. New Orleans, La., ca. 1836; d. 1914*), author, publisher. Widow of Frank Leslie, whom she married, 1874. Assuming management of her husband's business, together with his debts, she was highly successful as manager and editor of the Leslie publications. A flamboyant figure in the life of her time, she left the bulk of her fortune to the cause of woman suffrage.

LESQUEREUX, LEO (*b. Fleurier, Switzerland, 1806; d. Columbus, Ohio, 1889*), paleobotanist. Came to America, 1848, a recognized authority on peat bogs and an associate of J. L. R. Agassiz and Arnold H. Guyot. Became recognized authority on coal plants and on entire Appalachian coal field.

LESTER, CHARLES EDWARDS (*b. Griswold, Conn., 1815; d. Detroit, Mich., 1890*), Presbyterian clergyman, journalist, author.

LESUEUR, CHARLES ALEXANDRE (*b. Le Havre, France, 1778; d. Le Havre, 1846*), artist, naturalist. Came to America, 1816, as traveling companion and co-worker of William Maclure. While employed as teacher and engraver in Philadelphia, Pa., 1817–25, Lesueur served also as curator of the Academy of Natural Sciences. Consenting to join the projected community at New Harmony, Ind., Lesueur set out from Pittsburgh with Thomas Say, Gerard Troost, Robert Dale Owen, and others, arriving in January 1826. At the community he taught drawing, engraved the plates for Say's works. He made extensive study trips up and down the Mississippi valley, 1826–37, returning to France, 1837. Lesueur was the first to study the fishes of the Great Lakes of North America and one of the first systematic zoologists to work in this country.

LE SUEUR, PIERRE (*b. Artois, France, ca. 1657; d. at sea, ca. 1705*), explorer, trader. Came to Canada, 1679. Traded among the Sioux on the upper Mississippi River *post* 1681; was responsible for securing peace between Sioux and Chippewa, 1695.

LETCHER, JOHN (*b. Lexington, Va., 1813; d. 1884*), lawyer, newspaper editor, politician. Congressman, Democrat, from Virginia, 1851–59. As member of ways and means committee, he was an opponent of government spending and was known as "Honest John, Watchdog of the Treasury." Elected governor of Virginia, 1859, he opposed secession until Lincoln's call for troops to coerce seceding states. A zealous supporter of the Confederate war effort, he resumed practice of law after 1865 and served in the Virginia legislature, 1875–76 and 1876–77.

LETCHER, ROBERT PERKINS (*b. Goochland Co., Va., 1788; d. 1861*), lawyer, Kentucky legislator. Congressman, from Kentucky, 1823–35; supporter of Henry Clay; Whig governor of Kentucky, 1840–44; U.S. minister to Mexico, 1849–52.

LETCHWORTH, WILLIAM PRYOR (*b. Brownville, N.Y., 1823; d. 1910*), businessman, philanthropist. Labored *post* 1869, by private and public effort, to improve condition of New York State dependent and delinquent children, epileptics, and the insane poor.

LETTERMAN, JONATHAN (*b. Canonsburg, Pa., 1824; d. 1872*), military surgeon. M.D., Jefferson Medical College, 1849; appointed assistant surgeon, U.S. Army, 1849. Served on frontiers until start of Civil War. As medical director, Army of the Potomac, 1862–64, he completely reorganized field medical service, created mobile hospital organization, instituted ambulance service. His basic plan has influenced medical service in every modern army.

LEUPP, FRANCIS ELLINGTON (*b. New York, N.Y., 1849; d. Washington, D.C., 1918*), journalist. Outstanding as a Washington correspondent, 1885–1904; active and able U.S. Indian commissioner, 1905–09.

LEUTZE, EMANUEL (*b. Gmünd, Württemberg, 1816; d. Washington, D.C., 1868*), historical and portrait painter. Came to America as an infant; was raised in Fredericksburg, Va., and in Philadelphia, Pa. Studied and worked in Düsseldorf, Germany, 1841–59. Famous for large historical compositions dealing with American history, such as his "Washington Crossing the Delaware." Though full of anachronisms, few modern historical pictures have been more popular in the United States.

LEVENE, PHOEBUS AARON THEODORE (*b. Sagor, Russia, 1869; d. New York, N.Y., 1940*), biochemist. M.D., Imperial Military Medical Academy, St. Petersburg, 1891. Came to America, 1892. Staff member, Rockefeller Institute for Medical Research, 1905–40, and head of its division of chemistry.

LEVER, ASBURY FRANCIS (*b. near Springhill, S.C., 1875; d. Lexington Co., S.C., 1940*), politician. Congressman, Democrat, from South Carolina, 1901–19. A sponsor of important farm legislation as chairman of the House Committee on Agriculture, 1913–19.

LEVERETT, FRANK (*b. Denmark, Iowa, 1859; d. Ann Arbor, Mich., 1943*), glacial geologist. B.S., Iowa State College at Ames, 1885. After serving as field assistant to Thomas C. Chamberlin, 1886–90, he received a permanent appointment with the U.S. Geological Survey which he held until his retirement in 1929. He was also lecturer in geology at University of Michigan, 1909–29. His great contribution was in the realm of observation rather than theory; his work was thorough, systematic, and scrupulously accurate. From his maps of glacial and associated deposits throughout the upper Mississippi valley and the Great Lakes area, he established a temporal classification which, with slight modification, remains the standard for the Pleistocene period in North America. Among his professional publications were *The Illinois Glacial Lobe* (1899); *Glacial Formations and Drainage Features of the Erie and Ohio Basins* (1902); and, with Frank Taylor, *The Pleistocene of Indiana and Michigan and the History of the Great Lakes* (1915).

LEVERETT, JOHN (*b. Boston, England, 1616; d. Boston, Mass., 1679*), governor of Massachusetts, 1673–79. Immigrated to New England, 1633. In England, 1644–48, as officer in Parliamentary army. Held numerous colony offices, both political and military; opposed activities of Edward Randolph.

LEVERETT, JOHN (*b. 1662; d. 1724*), educator, lawyer. Grandson of John Leverett (1616–1679). Graduated Harvard,

1680; in 1685, was appointed fellow and tutor. After disagreement with the Mathers, Leverett was dropped from the College, 1700, and practiced law. His rise was rapid; he served as provincial councillor, judge of the superior court, judge of probate. In 1707 he became the first lawyer and judge to hold the Harvard presidency. His tenure was marked by liberal policy and progressive action which included a liberalized curriculum, enlarged student body, increased physical plant and endowment. He was long engaged in a clerico-political battle against the Mathers and their allies; his victory did much to assist religious and intellectual freedom at Harvard.

LEVERING, JOSEPH MORTIMER (*b. Hardin Co., Tenn., 1849; d. 1908*), Moravian bishop, historian. Author of *A History of Bethlehem, Pennsylvania, 1741–1892* (1903).

LEVERMORE, CHARLES HERBERT (*b. Mansfield, Conn., 1856; d. Berkeley, Calif., 1927*), educator, peace advocate. Founder and president of Adelphi College, Brooklyn, N.Y., 1896–1912; won Bok Peace Award, 1924.

LEVIN, LEWIS CHARLES (*b. Charleston, S.C., 1808; d. 1860*), lawyer. Settled in Philadelphia, 1838. Know-Nothing editor and congressman.

LEVINS, THOMAS C. (*b. Drogheda, Ireland, 1789; d. 1843*), Roman Catholic clergyman. Came to America as Jesuit *ca.* 1822; left the Society and became diocesan priest in New York, 1825. Active in early Catholic journalism. Suspended, 1834, he worked as an engineer until resumption of clerical office, 1841.

LEVINSON, SALMON OLIVER (*b. Noblesville, Ind., 1865; d. Chicago, Ill., 1941*), lawyer, peace advocate. Graduated Yale, 1888. LL.B., Chicago College of Law, 1891. After achieving great success as a specialist in reorganization of business corporations, he directed his major effort to the promotion of international peace. This he hoped to attain by stripping war of its legitimacy by a general outlawry of war as an instrument of policy. His campaign both here and abroad took effect in the Kellogg-Briand pact, signed in 1928.

LEVITT, ABRAHAM (*b. Brooklyn, N.Y., 1880; d. Great Neck, N.Y., 1962*), lawyer and contractor. Attended New York University Law School (LL.B., 1903); admitted to New York State Bar (1903); practiced real estate law until 1929. Founded the successful construction firm Levitt and Sons in 1929, which won national and international fame from the construction (1947–51) of Levittown, a community of more than seventeen thousand four- and five-bedroom houses. By 1962 the firm had built more than 100,000 houses in the United States and abroad. The Levitt house-community building revolution was based on well-designed, functional, and attractive communities, with houses that had standardized interiors behind a variety of facades. The firm maintained a "white only" policy as long as it was legal to do so.

LEVY, JOSEPH LEONARD (*b. London, England, 1865; d. 1917*), rabbi. Came to America, 1889; served congregations in Sacramento, Calif., and Philadelphia, Pa., rabbi of Temple Rodeph Shalom, Pittsburgh, Pa., 1901–17. A leader of Reform Judaism and in community social welfare.

LEVY, LOUIS EDWARD (*b. Stenowitz, Bohemia, 1846; d. 1919*), photochemist. Came to America as a boy. Inventor, with his brother Max, of the Levy halftone screen, patented 1893.

LEVY, MAX (*b. Detroit, Mich, 1857; d. Allenhurst, N.J., 1926*), photoengraver. Brother of Louis E. Levy, with whom he worked on invention of halftone screen. Patented the hemocytometer, 1917.

LEVY, URIAH PHILLIPS (*b. Philadelphia, Pa., 1792; d. New York, N.Y., 1862*), naval officer. Served on merchant ships, 1802–11; commissioned sailing master, 1812. His long service in the navy was punctuated with quarrels and difficulties, but he rose to rank of Flag Officer, 1860.

LEWELLING, HENDERSON. *See* LUELLING, HENDERSON.

LEWELLING, LORENZO DOW (*b. Salem, Iowa, 1846; d. 1900*), Quaker reformer, teacher, public servant. Nephew of Henderson Luelling. Populist governor of Kansas, 1893–95.

LEWIN, KURT (*b. Mogilno, Prussia, later Poland, 1890; d. Newtonville, Mass., 1947*), psychologist. Ph.D., University of Berlin, 1916; studied with Karl Stumpf, with whom he was associated later in the Psychological Institute. Visiting professor at Stanford in 1932 when Hitler came to power, he remained in the United States, working for two years at Cornell University, serving 1935–44 as professor of child psychology at University of Iowa, and moving with a group of associates to Massachusetts Institute of Technology in 1944 to establish there the Research Center for Group Dynamics. He and his collaborators were pioneers in what has come to be called "action research" and group dynamics, i.e., empirical studies of human behavior in a social context.

LEWIS, ALFRED HENRY (*b. Cleveland, Ohio, ca. 1858; d. New York, N.Y., 1914*), journalist. Author of *Wolfville* (1897), *Wolfville Nights* (1902), and other popular tales of cowboy life.

LEWIS, ANDREW (*b. Ireland, 1720; d. 1781*), soldier, Revolutionary patriot. Came to America as a boy; raised near Staunton, Va. Defeated Indians in battle of Point Pleasant, 1774; served as Continental brigadier general, 1776–77.

LEWIS, ARTHUR (*b. London, England, 1846; d. New York, N.Y., 1930*), actor, theatrical manager.

LEWIS, CHARLES BERTRAND (*b. Liverpool, Ohio, 1842; d. Brooklyn, N.Y., 1924*), humorist, printer, Detroit and New York newspaper editor. Wrote under pen name "M. Quad."

LEWIS, CHARLTON THOMAS (*b. West Chester, Pa., 1834; d. Morristown, N.J., 1904*), Methodist clergyman, classicist, editor, lawyer.

LEWIS, CLARENCE IRVING (*b. Stoneham, Mass., 1883; d. Menlo Park, Calif., 1964*), philosopher and educator. Attended Harvard (Ph.D., 1910). On faculty of University of California at Berkeley (1911–20) and Harvard (1921–53). His central philosophical concern was with the questions bearing on the validity and the justification of claims to knowledge. Made significant contributions to logic, theory of knowledge, and ethics. His books include *Mind and the World-Order* (1929), *Symbolic Logic* (1932), and *An Analysis of Knowledge and Valuation* (1946).

LEWIS, DEAN DE WITT (*b. Kewanee, Ill., 1874; d. Baltimore, Md., 1941*), surgeon. A.B., Lake Forest College, 1895. M.D., Rush Medical College, 1899. Taught at Rush (then affiliated with University of Chicago), 1901–24, with distinguished service, 1918–19, in France as head of several U.S. Army evacuation hospitals. Professor of surgery, Johns Hopkins University medical school, and surgeon in chief of Johns Hopkins Hospital, 1925–39. Editor of *Archives of Surgery* (1920–40), *International Surgical Digest* (1926–41), and *Practice of Surgery* (1932).

LEWIS, DIOCLESIAN (*b. near Auburn, N.Y., 1823; d. 1886*), temperance reformer, pioneer in physical culture. Author of *New Gymnastics*, 1862; founder of Boston Normal Institute for Physical Education.

LEWIS, DIXON HALL (*b. probably Dinwiddie Co., Va., 1802; d. New York, N.Y., 1848*), lawyer, Alabama legislator. Leader of states'-rights faction in Alabama; congressman, Democrat, 1829–44; U.S. senator, 1844–48. Opposed protective tariffs and internal improvements by the federal government.

LEWIS, ED ("STRANGLER") (*b. Wisconsin, 1890[?]; d. Muskogee, Okla., 1966*), wrestler. Entered professional wrestling at age fourteen; held the heavyweight title numerous times from 1919 to 1933. Fought in an estimated 6,200 matches until 1947. Known for his headlock hold, which was banned at one time.

LEWIS, EDMUND DARCH (*b. Philadelphia, Pa., 1835; d. Philadelphia, 1910*), landscape painter, collector of art objects.

LEWIS, ELLIS (*b. Lewisberry, Pa., 1798; d. 1871*), lawyer. Pennsylvania supreme court justice, 1851–57; chief justice *post* 1854.

LEWIS, ENOCH (*b. Radnor, Pa., 1776; d. 1856*), mathematician, educator. Author of textbooks, and of miscellaneous works applying Quaker principles to moral and political issues; founded and edited *Friends' Review*, 1847–56.

LEWIS, ESTELLE ANNA BLANCHE ROBINSON (*b. near Baltimore, Md., 1824; d. London, England, 1880*), poet and magazine writer under pen names, "Stella" and "Sarah A. Lewis." A friend and admirer of Edgar Allan Poe.

LEWIS, EXUM PERCIVAL (*b. Edgecombe Co., N.C., 1863; d. 1926*), physicist, educator. Graduated Columbian University (present George Washington), 1888; Ph.D., Johns Hopkins, 1895, specializing in spectroscopy under H. A. Rowland. Taught physics at University of California *post* 1895, becoming full professor, 1908. He published no books, but was the author of papers on diverse subjects; many of his chief contributions related to the spectra of gases under various conditions of excitation, purity, etc. He was a pioneer in infrared and far ultraviolet spectroscopy and did work also in study of ionization and conductivity of gases.

LEWIS, FIELDING (*b. Gloucester Co., Va., 1725; d. Fredericksburg, Va., ca. 1782*), Revolutionary patriot. Brother-in-law of George Washington.

LEWIS, FRANCIS (*b. Llandaff, Wales, 1713; d. 1802*), New York merchant. Came to New York, 1738; prospered as businessman and government contractor. Active in pre-Revolutionary agitation; New York delegate to Continental Congress, 1775–79; signed Declaration of Independence.

LEWIS, FRANCIS PARK (*b. Hamilton, Ontario, Canada, 1855; d. Port Jefferson, N.Y., 1940*), ophthalmologist. Student of Herman Knapp; practiced in Buffalo, N.Y. Pioneer in development of organized efforts to prevent blindness.

LEWIS, FULTON, JR. (*b. Washington, D.C., 1903; d. Washington, 1966*), radio commentator and newspaperman. Attended University of Virginia and George Washington School of Law. Joined the *Washington Herald* in 1924 as a reporter; became city editor in 1927. Was Washington Bureau chief of Universal News Service, 1929–37. Wrote a syndicated column, "The Washington Sideshow," 1933–36; made regular news commentaries in Washington on "The Top of the News" beginning in 1937, becoming the first Washington-based national news commentator. Persuaded Congress to have radio newsmen admitted to the House and Senate press galleries (1939). During World War II advanced his isolationist views, reflecting conservative Republican outlook. Launched private investigations of official bungling and boondoggling; in the 1950's publicized the anti-Communist activities of Senator Joseph McCarthy; after McCarthy's censure, Lewis' influence and audience diminished.

LEWIS, GEORGE WILLIAM (*b. Ithaca, N.Y., 1882; d. Lake Winola, Pa., 1948*), aeronautical engineer. M.E., Cornell University, 1908; master of mechanical engineering, 1910. Associated with the National Advisory Committee for Aeronautics *post* 1917, he became its executive officer in 1919 and was its director of aeronautical research from 1924 to 1947. As such, he presided over the design, construction, and use of some of the world's outstanding wind tunnels for study of aerodynamics; the practical results of this research were notable, taking form in improved wing design, streamlining, and braking devices for aircraft. He was responsible also for the establishment and plan of the flight propulsion laboratory (Cleveland, Ohio, completed in 1942), which bears his name, and for the plan and design of the Ames Aeronautical Laboratory at Moffett Field in California. By 1944 he was directing a staff of some 6,000 researchers, most of whom he had recruited and trained himself.

LEWIS, GILBERT NEWTON (*b. Weymouth, Mass., 1875; d. Berkeley, Calif., 1946*), physical chemist. Attended preparatory school of the University of Nebraska, and completed sophomore year at that university; B.A., Harvard, 1896. After teaching for a year at Phillips Academy, Andover, Mass., he returned to Harvard for graduate work in chemistry and received the Ph.D. in 1899, staying on for an additional year as instructor. He then went abroad to study at Leipzig and Göttingen. He returned to Harvard as an instructor for three more years and then went to Manila (1904–05) as superintendent of weights and measures and chemist in the Bureau of Science of the Philippine Islands. In 1905 he received an appointment in the Massachusetts Institute of Technology, where he was made assistant professor (1907), associate professor (1908), and professor (1911). In 1912 he accepted an appointment as professor of chemistry and dean of the College of Chemistry in the University of California at Berkeley.

Lewis's two most important contributions were in the fields of chemical thermodynamics and of valence and the electronic structure of molecules. In 1923 he was the coauthor of *Thermodynamics and the Free Energy of Chemical Substances*. Lewis presented his theory of the chemical bond in greater detail in his *Valence and the Structure of Atoms and Molecules* (1923). In 1908 he published several papers on Einstein's theory of relativity. In 1919 he discovered the tetratomic oxygen molecule; and in 1933 he made the first preparations of pure heavy water (deuterium oxide), and collaborated in the first use of the deuteron, accelerated in the cyclotron, as a tool for the study of the properties of atomic nuclei. Lewis also showed that the fluorescence of organic molecules involves an excited triplet state, and measured the paramagnetism of this triplet state.

LEWIS, HARRY SINCLAIR (*b. Sauk Centre, Minn., 1885; d. Rome, Italy, 1951*), novelist. Graduated Yale (1908). The author of many of the most famous novels of the century, Lewis published his first great success, *Main Street*, in 1920 for Harcourt and Brace. *Main Street* was the first of a series of satirical novels about America and protested the meanness and conformity of small town life in the nation. In 1922, he published *Babbitt*, an exposé of the inner life of the American businessman; *Arrowsmith*, in 1925, was an inquiry into the medical profession and won the Pulitzer Prize, which he refused for the earlier denial of the prize to *Main Street* and *Babbitt*. *Elmer Gantry*, 1927, was an attack on evangelism and religious hypocrisy. The 1920's also saw the publication of *The Man Who Knew Coolidge* (1928) and *Dodsworth* (1929). After these books, Lewis' powers declined and he was never again able to recapture the public's imagination nor sense the national mood. He continued to write, publishing *Cass Timberlane* in 1945 and

Kingsblood Royal in 1947, among other novels. In 1930, he was awarded the Nobel Prize for literature, the first American to be so honored.

LEWIS, ISAAC NEWTON (*b. New Salem Pa., 1858; d. Hoboken, N.J., 1931*), soldier, inventor. Graduated West Point, 1884; ordnance expert. Patented Lewis depression position finder, 1891, and the Lewis machine gun, 1911; also fire-control systems and torpedo improvements.

LEWIS, JAMES (*b. Troy, N.Y., 1837; d. West Hampton, N.Y., 1896*), actor. Born James Lewis Deming; a principal comedian with Augustin Daly's company *post* 1869.

LEWIS, JAMES HAMILTON (*b. Danville, Va., 1863; d. Washington, D.C., 1939*), lawyer. Removed to Seattle, Wash., *ca.* 1885; served as congressman, Democrat, from Washington, 1897–98. Resident in Chicago, Ill., *post* 1903, he was U.S. senator, Democrat, from Illinois, 1913–19, 1931–39. Despite a deliberately cultivated eccentricity of dress and manner, Lewis was an excellent parliamentary tactician (twice serving as majority whip) and a supporter of the New Deal.

LEWIS, JOHN FRANCIS (*b. near Port Republic, Va., 1818; d. Rockingham Co., Va., 1895*), planter, lawyer, Virginia Unionist. U.S. senator, Republican-Conservative, 1870–75; helped overthrow rule of William Mahone, 1889.

LEWIS, JOHN LLEWELLYN (*b. Cleveland, Iowa, 1880; d. Washington, D.C., 1969*), labor leader. Began working in coal mines in 1897; elected secretary of a United Mine Workers (UMW) local in 1901; built a union machine in Illinois that elected him to the presidency of one of the largest locals in the the state. President of the UMW (1920–60); led the largest national coal strike in U.S. history (1922), but the union grew weaker as coal production increased in non-union fields. In the 1930's he rebuilt the UMW and won contracts all over the country. Elected a vice-president of the American Federation of Labor (1934), then created the Committee for Industrial Organizations (1935) and resigned his AFL post. CIO affiliates in 1937 won collective-bargaining agreements with anti-union General Motors and U.S. Steel. An evolving rift with President Franklin D. Roosevelt undermined his power in the labor movement; Lewis stepped down as CIO president in 1940. In the 1940's he led coal miners in strikes that President Harry Truman condemned as threats to national security and for which Lewis was twice cited and convicted for contempt. By the mid-1950's he had become an apostle of "cooperative capitalism" and turned the UMW into a friendly collaborator with the mine owners.

LEWIS, JOSEPH HORACE (*b. near Glasgow, Ky., 1824; d. 1904*), lawyer, Confederate brigadier general, Kentucky legislator and congressman. Judge, Kentucky court of appeals, 1881–99.

LEWIS, LAWRENCE (*b. Philadelphia, Pa., 1856; d. near West Chester, Pa., 1890*), lawyer, author of valuable studies in Pennsylvania legal history.

LEWIS, LLOYD DOWNS (*b. Pendleton, Ind., 1891; d. near Libertyville, Ill., 1949*), journalist, biographer. B.A., Swarthmore College, 1913. After working on the Philadelphia *North American* and the *Chicago Record-Herald*, World War I naval service, and some years as publicity man for a Chicago movie theater chain, he joined the staff of the Chicago *Daily News* in 1930. He served the paper as drama critic, amusement editor, sports editor, and finally as managing editor in 1943–45. He was author of *Myths After Lincoln* (1929); *Chicago, The History of Its Reputation* (1929, in collaboration with Henry Justin Smith); *Sherman, Fighting Prophet* (1932); and *Captain Sam Grant*

(1950), the first part of his projected life of Ulysses S. Grant. He was also coauthor of a play with Sinclair Lewis (no relation), *Jayhawker*, produced in 1935.

LEWIS, MERIWETHER (*b. Albemarle Co., Va., 1774; d. central Tennessee, 1809*), explorer, soldier. Raised in upper Georgia, where he became an expert hunter and early showed both scientific and literary tastes; studied under private tutors in Virginia, 1787–92. Served in militia during Whiskey Rebellion; entered regular army as ensign, May 1795. Appointed President Jefferson's private secretary (1801) after duty on the Western frontiers, he arrived in Washington soon after the inauguration and took up residence in the White House.

The discussions and councils to which he was witness were a liberal education for the President's young friend. Exploration for a land route to the Pacific Ocean was often discussed, and Jefferson proposed to Congress a journey of discovery on Jan. 18, 1803. Lewis made the estimate of expenses and Congress quickly appropriated the $2,500 he thought necessary. Jefferson's high opinion of Lewis's qualifications to lead such an expedition determined his choice and was later stated in Jefferson's memoir written for the 1814 history of the enterprise. Lewis chose William Clark as his companion officer and their names and fame are inseparably united.

Mustering in Illinois, the men enlisted for the journey were drilled for their work during the winter of 1803–04. In the spring of 1804, the expedition started up the Missouri River. Successfully evading Sioux efforts to block progress, Lewis and Clark wintered in the Mandan villages in North Dakota where they secured the services of Sacajawea as guide to the upper river. They resumed travel on April 7, 1805. By August they were at the head of navigation but Sacajawea obtained horses to cross the divide from her Shoshone relatives. Arriving at the Columbia River, they built canoes and descended to the ocean. They spent the winter at Fort Clatsop, not far from Astoria, and returned overland to St. Louis on Sept 23, 1806, to the great joy of the entire nation, which had long given them up for lost.

The abilities of Lewis and Clark complemented each other in an unusual manner, yet Lewis was the ultimate authority on every question. On his resignation from the army after making his report in Washington, he was appointed governor of Louisiana. He was successful in his brief administration there. En route to Washington in October 1809, he met a mysterious death which is still the subject of scholarly controversy. His observations and journals display his intellectual ardor and scientific spirit; they form, together with those of William Clark, the basis of the *History of the Expedition* (Phila., 1814; ed. Nicholas Biddle and Paul Allen).

LEWIS, MORGAN (*b. New York, N.Y., 1754; d. New York, 1844*), Revolutionary soldier, jurist, political leader. Son of Francis Lewis. Graduated College of New Jersey (Princeton), 1773. Married Gertrude, daughter of Robert R. Livingston, 1779, an alliance which furthered his career in New York politics; served as state attorney general and as justice and chief justice of state supreme court. Elected governor, 1804, he proved unable to navigate in deep political waters and alienated the powerful Clinton faction. He failed of reelection. After service as major general in the War of 1812, he passed the rest of his long life in relatively private activity.

LEWIS, ORLANDO FAULKLAND (*b. Boston, Mass., 1873; d. 1922*), social worker, penologist, author of professional studies and of short stories.

LEWIS, OSCAR (*b. New York, N.Y., 1914; d. New York, 1970*), educator and anthropologist. Attended City College of New York and Columbia (Ph.D., 1940). Primarily concerned with the problem of personality and its relationship to culture.

Studied the Blackfoot Indians (1939) and Tepoztecans of Mexico (1943). Founded the anthropology department at University of Illinois. Advanced the theory of the culture of poverty, which he applied to the poor in the United States and which sparked considerable debate. His books include the classic *Life in a Mexican Village: Tepoztlán Restudied* (1951), *Five Families* (1959), and *The Children of Sánchez* (1961).

LEWIS, SAMUEL (*b. Falmouth, Mass., 1799; d. 1854*), lawyer, educator. Leader, *post* 1826, in founding free public school system of Ohio; first Ohio superintendent of common schools, 1837–39. Antislavery leader and an organizer of the Liberty party.

LEWIS, SINCLAIR. *See* LEWIS, HARRY SINCLAIR.

LEWIS, TAYLER (*b. Northumberland, N.Y., 1802; d. 1877*), lawyer, educator, Orientalist. Graduated Union, 1820. Professor of Greek, University of the City of New York, 1838–50; professor of Greek, Oriental languages, and Bible at Union, 1850–77.

LEWIS, WILFRED (*b. Philadelphia, Pa., 1854; d. at sea, 1929*), mechanical engineer. Graduated Massachusetts Institute of Technology, 1875. An expert in the mechanics of gears.

LEWIS, WILLIAM (*b. near Edgemont, Pa., 1751, o.s.; d. Philadelphia, Pa., 1819*), lawyer, Pennsylvania Federalist legislator. Counsel for John Fries, 1799.

LEWIS, WILLIAM BERKELEY (*b. Loudoun Co., Va., 1784; d. near Nashville, Tenn., 1866*), planter, politician. Friend and supporter of Andrew Jackson; a member of the "Kitchen Cabinet." A Unionist in the Civil War.

LEWIS, WILLIAM DAVID (*b. Christiana, Del., 1792; d. near Florence, N.J., 1881*), merchant, banker. Resided in Russia, 1814–24; translated poems of Pushkin and other Russian writers (published 1849).

LEWIS, WILLIAM DRAPER (*b. Philadelphia, Pa., 1867; d. Northeast Harbor, Maine, 1949*), lawyer, scholar. B.S., Haverford College, 1888. In 1891, he received both a law degree and a Ph.D. in economics from the University of Pennsylvania. As professor of law (1896–1923) and dean of the law school (1896–1914) at University of Pennsylvania, he improved the school both academically and physically and was, at the same time, author or editor of a number of publications. An unqualified admirer of Theodore Roosevelt, and a lifelong crusader against the evils of American society, he served as chairman of the platform committee at the national Progressive party conventions of 1912 and 1916. In 1923 he left the law school at Pennsylvania to direct the American Law Institute, a new organization that he had helped to found and whose purpose was to produce a massive restatement of the common law, a critical summary and evaluation of the state of legal doctrine under different topical headings. The Institute completed its first restatement (24 volumes, covering 9 broad topics ranging from contracts to property) in 1944. Lewis resigned as director in 1947.

LEWIS, WILLIAM GASTON (*b. Rocky Mount, N.C., 1835; d. Goldsboro, N.C., 1901*), engineer, Confederate brigadier general.

LEWIS, WILLIAM HENRY (*b. Berkeley, Va., 1868; d. Boston, Mass., 1949*), lawyer, public official. Born of black parents; father a Baptist clergyman. B.A., Amherst College, 1892. LL.B., Harvard Law School, 1895. Winner of scholastic honors and captain of football at Amherst, he continued to excel as student and football player at Harvard; he was chosen all-American by Walter Camp in 1892 and 1893. In practice in Boston, Mass., he was active in local politics, serving three terms on the Cambridge common council and a single term in the Massachusetts legislature. He was appointed by President Theodore Roosevelt as assistant U.S. attorney for Massachusetts (1903–06); he served next as assistant U.S. district attorney for the six New England states (1907–11), and as assistant U.S. attorney general, 1911–13. Returning to Boston, he continued the practice of law, winning reputation as a defense attorney through his impressive courtroom presence and oratorical powers.

LEWIS, WINSLOW (*b. Wellfleet, Mass., 1770; d. Boston, Mass., 1850*), sailor, lighthouse designer and builder.

LEWISOHN, ADOLPH (*b. Hamburg, Germany, 1849; d. near Upper Saranac Lake, N.Y., 1938*), capitalist, art collector, philanthropist. Came to America, 1867, joining New York branch of his family's Hamburg importing business. Recognizing the importance of copper in the commercial future of electricity, Adolph and his brother Leonard formed the Montana Copper Co., 1879, and subsequently organized the United Metals Selling Co. and the American Smelting & Refining Co. Conducting his affairs independently *post* 1901, Adolph Lewisohn was president of copper mines in Tennessee, Arizona, and South America, and senior member of Adolph Lewisohn & Sons, a brokerage and investment house. He devoted himself chiefly, *post* 1916, to philanthropy, prison reform, music and the collection of modern French paintings.

LEWISOHN, LUDWIG (*b. Berlin, Germany, 1882; d. Miami, Fla., 1955*), teacher, literary critic, novelist, editor, Zionist. Immigrated to the U.S. in 1890. Studied at the College of Charleston and at Columbia (M.A., 1903). Taught at Ohio State University (1911–19); drama editor for the *Nation* (1919–24). An ardent Zionist, Lewisohn was editor of the *New Palestine* from 1943 to 1948 and of the *American Zionist* from 1947. His novels include *The Island Within* (1928) and *Stephen Escott* (1930); they were widely read and discussed but were never critical or commercial successes. His most important work was *Expression in America* (1932), later revised as *The Story of American Literature* (1937). From 1948 until his death, he was professor of comparative literature at Brandeis University.

LEWISOHN, SAM ADOLPH (*b. New York, N.Y., 1884; d. Santa Barbara, Calif., 1951*), industrialist, financier, penologist, philanthropist, and art patron. Graduated Princeton (1904); LL.B., Columbia Law School (1907). Entering his father's mining concern in 1910, Lewisohn soon became influential in the nation's affairs. He was a member of President Roosevelt's National Advisory Council and helped to frame the Social Security Act; he was also a reformer of prisons and helped secure the passage of the Hawes-Cooper Bill of 1929, banning the use of prisoners for private gains. Lewisohn also had numerous connections with the art world, amassed one of the most distinguished collections of art in the nation, and wrote a book, *Painters and Personality* (1937).

LEXOW, CLARENCE (*b. Brooklyn, N.Y., 1852; d. 1910*), lawyer, New York legislator. As Republican chairman of a state senate special committee, he gave his name to a famous investigation of corruption in New York City, 1894, which was actually managed by John W. Goff.

LEY, WILLY (*b. Berlin, Germany, 1906; d. New York, N.Y., 1969*), writer and rocket scientist. Attended University of Berlin and University of Königsberg. Embarked on a career of investigations into space travel. Fled Germany (1935) and wrote articles for several magazines in New York City. Was science editor of the newspaper *PM*, 1940–44, and author of many popular science books, including *The Lungfish and the Unicorn* (1941), *Rockets: The Future of Travel Beyond the Stratosphere* (1944), *Conquest of Space* (1949), and the Adventures in Space series for children.

Director of engineering at Washington Institute of Technology (1944–47), then joined the office of technical services of the Department of Commerce. In the 1950's he was a lecturer at the Hayden Planetarium and technical adviser for the television program "Tom Corbett, Space Cadet." Credited with devising the basic principles that led to the development of the liquid-fuel rocket and for accurately predicting space travel.

Leyendecker, Joseph Christian (*b. Montabaur, Germany, 1874; d. New Rochelle, N.Y., 1951*), artist and illustrator. Immigrated to the U.S. in 1882. Studied at the Art Institute of Chicago and at the Académie Julien in Paris. Remembered for his covers for the *Saturday Evening Post* (1899–1942), especially the famous New Year's baby who appeared in various guises on the cover every year from 1907 to 1943. Leyendecker was a preeminent illustrator in high-class artwork in advertising during the 1920's and 1930's. Creator of the meticulously well-dressed "Arrow Collar Man."

Leyner, John George (*b. Boulder Co., Colo., 1860; d. Littleton, Colo., 1920*), inventor, manufacturer. Devised and marketed many improvements in mining machinery, notably a compressed air rock-drilling machine (patented 1899), the hollow drill or "jackhammer" (*ante* 1902), and a drill-sharpening machine.

Leypoldt, Frederick (*b. Stuttgart, Germany, 1835; d. 1884*), publisher, book-trade bibliographer. Came to America, 1854. Published translations and textbooks; was in partnership with Henry Holt, 1866–68. Founded *Publishers' Weekly*, 1873; the *Library Journal*, 1876; was also responsible for *Publishers' Trade List Annual*.

L'Halle, Constantin de (*d. Detroit, Mich., 1706*), Roman Catholic missionary. Came to Canada, 1696. A Recollect priest, he served as chaplain at Detroit from about 1703 until his death.

L'Halle, Nicolas Benoit Constantin De. *See* L'Halle, Constantin De.

Lhévinne, Josef (*b. Orel, Russia, 1874; d. Kew Gardens, Queens County, New York, N.Y., 1944*), pianist, teacher. Graduated Moscow Conservatory, 1891, thereafter spending the next several years in study with Anton Rubinstein, in concert tours, and in military service. Married Rosina Bessie, 1898, who was also his partner in two-piano concerts and in teaching. Professor at the Moscow Conservatory, 1902–05, he made his American debut in Carnegie Hall, New York City, Jan. 27, 1906, following it with a highly successful tour. Resident in Germany, 1906–19, he made concert tours in Europe and the United States until World War I, during which he and his family were interned as enemy aliens. Settling in New York City, 1919, the Lhévinnes became U.S. citizens, continued to concertize, and *post* 1924 were members of the faculty of the Juilliard School. Ranked with the greatest virtuosos of his day, Josef was famed for his performances of Chopin and Tchaikovski; his playing was marked by flawless brilliance of technique, clarity of style, beauty of tone, and power of emotional projection.

L'Hommedieu, Ezra (*b. Southold, N.Y., 1734; d. Southold, 1811*), lawyer, New York legislator, agriculturist. Brother-in-law of William Floyd. Continuously in public service from 1775 until his death, he was the principal author of the measure establishing the reconstituted University of the State of New York, 1787.

Libbey, Edward Drummond (*b. Chelsea, Mass., 1854; d. 1925*), glass manufacturer, philanthropist. Founded Libbey Glass Co. at Toledo, Ohio, 1888. Developed business framework for exploitation of glass-making inventions of Michael J. Owens. Principal benefactor of Toledo Museum of Art.

Libby, Orin Grant (*b. Hammond, Wis., 1864; d. 1952*), historian. Studied at the University of Wisconsin (Ph.D., 1894). Taught at the University of Wisconsin (1895–1902); the University of North Dakota (1902–45). His doctoral thesis, *The Geographical Distribution of the Vote of the Thirteen States on the Federal Constitution, 1787–88*, became a landmark in the development of the present view of the origins and character of the Constitution. In 1926 Libby launched the *North Dakota Historical Quarterly*, which he edited until 1944.

Libman, Emanuel (*b. New York, N.Y., 1872; d. New York, 1946*), cardiologist, pathologist, bacteriologist. B.A., College of the City of New York, 1891. M.D., College of Physicians and Surgeons, Columbia University, 1894. Interned at Mount Sinai Hospital, New York City; studied in Berlin, Munich, Vienna, and Graz, 1896–97. Served Mount Sinai Hospital as pathologist, and as adjunct, attending, and consulting physician. Discovered causative organism of infant diarrheas, 1898; published many studies on infections, blood cultures, and heart ailments (bacterial endocarditis and Libman-Sacks disease); most noted as a diagnostician and mentor of postgraduate studies. He also endowed lectureships both here and abroad and maintained a lifelong interest in Judaism.

Lick, James (*b. Fredericksburg, Pa., 1796; d. 1876*), piano maker, California real-estate investor. Came to California *ante* 1848. Left the bulk of his estate for charitable and educational purposes, notably for creation of the Lick Observatory.

Lie, Jonas (*b. Moss, Norway, 1880; d. New York, N.Y., 1940*), painter. Came to America as a boy; studied at National Academy of Design and at Art Students League, New York. Artistically a traditionalist, he aimed "not to symbolize nature, but in portraying nature to impart a sense of what is within and beyond."

Lieb, John William (*b. Newark, N.J., 1860; d. New York, N.Y., 1929*), mechanical engineer. Graduated Stevens Institute of Technology, 1880. Worked with Thomas A. Edison on pioneer electric-lighting power plants, 1881–82; was in Italy, 1882–94, as chief engineer and later as manager and technical director of the Italian Edison Co. Returning to New York, Lieb held many responsible positions in the various Edison companies until his death. Under his direction, some of the earliest experiments were undertaken in parallel operation of large direct-driven alternators and in long-distance transmission of high-tension alternating current by underground cables. In his later career, he directed all research and development work for the New York Edison and affiliated companies.

Lieber, Francis (*b. Berlin, Germany, 1800; d. 1872*), political scientist, reformer, educator. Fought as a schoolboy under Blücher at Waterloo; graduated Jena, Ph.D., 1820. Volunteered to aid Greeks in war of liberation, 1822; was tutor in Rome to son of the historian Niebuhr, 1823. Persecuted as a liberal in Prussia, he came to America, 1827, and won success as editor of the *Encyclopedia Americana* (1829–33). Lieber became professor of history and political economy at South Carolina College, 1835, and wrote the first systematic works on political science as such that had appeared in America up to that time. They won him high contemporary reputation; the best known of them was *On Civil Liberty and Self-Government* (1853). In 1857 he was appointed to a chair in Columbia College; in 1865, he transferred to Columbia Law School where he remained for the rest of his life. His *Code for the Government of Armies* (1863) was long standard as a basis of international understanding on the conduct of war.

LIEBLING, ABBOTT JOSEPH (*b. New York, N.Y., 1904; d. New York, 1963*), journalist and author. Attended Dartmouth (1920–23), Columbia School of Journalism (B.Litt., 1925), and the Sorbonne (1926–27). Worked for the *New York Times* (1925), *Providence Journal* and *Evening Bulletin* in Rhode Island (1927–30), and *New York World Telegram* (1931–35). Hired by the *New Yorker* (1935), where he remained for the rest of his life. His books, mostly anthologies of *New Yorker* articles, include *Back Where I Came From* (1938) and *Telephone Booth Indian* (1942), both about New York City. After World War II wrote "The Wayward Press," a *New Yorker* department, in which he exposed the vagaries and shortcomings of newspapers and newspapermen.

LIEBLING, EMIL (*b. Pless, Germany, 1851; d. 1914*), pianist, teacher, composer. Came to America, 1867. Studied in Europe, 1873–76, under Liszt and others. A brilliant interpreter of Bach, Chopin, and Beethoven.

LIEBLING, ESTELLE (*b. New York, N.Y., 1880; d. New York, 1970*), soprano and voice teacher. Studied voice in Europe and made operatic debut in Dresden. Appeared three times at the Metropolitan Opera (1902–04). Continued on the concert stage, where she was a popular recitalist. Reached largest audiences as soloist with John Philip Sousa's band. Most renowned as a voice teacher; opened a studio for operatic and nonoperatic performers in 1921, and taught until the 1960's. Among her most famous students were Amelita Galli-Curchi, Max Lorenz, and Beverly Sills.

LIEBMAN, JOSHUA LOTH (*b. Hamilton, Ohio, 1907; d. Boston, Mass., 1948*), American reform rabbi, radio preacher, Zionist. B.A., University of Cincinnati, 1926; ordained from Hebrew Union College, Cincinnati, 1930; studied also at Harvard, Columbia, and the Hebrew University in Jerusalem. Taught at University of Cincinnati, at Hebrew Union (from which he received his doctoral degree in 1939) and at University of Chicago; served as rabbi of a Chicago congregation, 1934–39. He was then called to Temple Israel in Boston, Mass., where he served until his death. His national fame rests upon his book *Peace of Mind* (1946); a popular statement of contemporary psychological theory with practical application, together with an affirmation and demonstration of the need for religion in the search for moral and emotional maturity.

LIENAU, DETLEF (*b. Ütersen, Germany, 1818; d. New York, N.Y., 1887*), architect. Came to America, 1848. Fortunate in his American social connections, Lienau developed a very large practice, 1849–85, designing domestic, industrial, and educational buildings. His work was basically eclectic and influenced by the Parisian examples of his student days, but it was restrained and marked always by excellent planning, good composition, and thoroughness.

LIGGETT, HUNTER (*b. Reading, Pa., 1857; d. San Francisco, Calif., 1935*), soldier. Graduated West Point, 1879. After efficient service at Western frontier posts and in the Spanish-American War and Philippine insurrection, he reached rank of lieutenant colonel, 1909. Marked by superiors for his consistent application to professional studies, on graduation from Army War College, 1910, he was detailed to the general staff and selected as a director of the War College. Promoted colonel, 1912, he was made president of the College and less than a year later became a brigadier general. Promoted major general, March 1917, he preceded his men of the 41st Division to France. After a period of observation duty on the Western Front, he took command of the I Army Corps, January 1918. His Corps participated in the Champagne-Marne operation in July and in the counteroffensive known as the Second Battle of the Marne. In the reduction of St. Mihiel salient during mid-September and in the Meuse-Argonne offensive, September–November, his men were highly effective in defeating a stubborn, experienced enemy. On assignment to command of the I Army, October 1918, he was promoted lieutenant general. Under his command, the Army broke the Hindenburg Line and forced the Germans to withdraw across the Meuse. General John J. Pershing cited Liggett as conspicuous for personality, leadership, and efficiency. Thereafter, he commanded the Army of Occupation until it was disbanded, July 1919. He retired in 1921.

LIGGETT, LOUIS KROH (*b. Detroit, Mich., 1875; d. Washington, D.C., 1946*), businessman. As salesman and general manager of a firm of patent medicine distributors, Liggett dealt with retail druggists and saw the potential if they were to combine their buying power. In 1901 he established Drug Merchants of America, a central buying agency, in which one druggist in each town or city held stock and was given an exclusive right to trade with the agency. He soon expanded the idea to include the manufacture of a line of the association's own drug and toilet preparations, which the stockholder-druggists could purchase at factory prices. For this, he organized the United Drug Company in 1903, and through able promotion and advertising made "Rexall" (the trademark on both the products and the shops that sold them) a household word. By 1920 the Rexall system was vastly successful. Recovering after some fiscal problems in 1921, it continued successful until the depression years, which again brought economic problems. Liggett was president of the firm from 1904 until 1928; he resumed the presidency in 1933 and held it until 1941.

LIGGETT, WALTER WILLIAM (*b. Benson, Minn., 1886; d. Minneapolis, Minn., 1935*), journalist, editor. After a varied and restless career on many newspapers in many places, Liggett published (1932–35) the *Mid-West American*, a small personal weekly paper which contained almost unrestrained attacks on Minnesota state, county, and city officials, denouncing their alleged connections with crime. He was shot to death by unknown assassins.

LIGHTBURN, JOSEPH ANDREW JACKSON (*b. near West Newton, Pa., 1824; d. West Virginia, 1901*), farmer, Union brigadier general, Baptist clergyman. Resident in Lewis Co., W. Va., *post* 1840.

LIGON, THOMAS WATKINS (*b. Prince Edward Co., Va., 1810; d. near Ellicott City, Md., 1881*), lawyer, Maryland legislator. Congressman, Democrat, 1845–49; governor of Maryland, 1853–57. Opposed Know-Nothingism at expense of his own political future.

LILE, WILLIAM MINOR (*b. Trinity, Ala., 1859; d. Hallsboro, Va., 1935*), lawyer. Professor of law, University of Virginia, 1893–1932; dean of department of law, *post* 1904.

LILIENTHAL, MAX (*b. Munich, Bavaria, 1815; d. Cincinnati, Ohio, 1882*), rabbi. University of Munich, Ph.D., 1837. Came to America, 1845. Pastor in Cincinnati *post* 1855; strove to promote good will between Jews and Christians; helped to found Hebrew Union College and Union of American Hebrew Congregations.

LILLIE, FRANK RATTRAY (*b. Toronto, Ontario, Canada, 1870; d. Chicago, Ill., 1947*), biologist, research administrator. B.A., University of Toronto, 1891; Ph.D. in zoology, University of Chicago, 1894. Taught at University of Michigan (1894–99) and at Vassar College (1899–1900). Appointed assistant professor of embryology at University of Chicago, 1900, he became professor in 1906. He was chairman of the department of zoology,

1910-31, and dean of the division of biological sciences from 1931 until his retirement in 1935. His research contributions were impressive and influential; they included studies of cell lineage, of fertilization in various marine species, and of the development of the chick. His discovery of embryonic sex hormones gave great impetus to the emerging science of endocrinology. He was associated *post* 1891 with the Marine Biological Laboratory at Woods Hole, Mass., serving as director (1908-25) and in other official capacities, notably as fund-raiser; he was also active in initiating and developing the Oceanographic Institution at Woods Hole. He was president of the National Academy of Sciences, 1935-39, and chairman of the National Research Council, 1935-36.

LILLIE, GORDON WILLIAM (*b. Bloomingdale, Ill., 1860; d. near Pawnee, Okla., 1942*), frontiersman, Wild West showman, known as "Pawnee Bill." Left home, 1875, intending to become a cowboy; lived with the Pawnee tribe in Indian Territory for a year; worked in present Oklahoma and in the Texas panhandle as a buffalo hunter, teacher, and interpreter at the Pawnee Agency, and as a cattle rancher. For several years *post* 1883, he toured with Buffalo Bill Cody's Wild West and other shows as interpreter and guardian of the Pawnee Indians employed by them; in 1888 he launched a Wild West show of his own that failed. Returning to Wichita, Kansas, he took an active role in the "boomer" movement to open unassigned lands in Indian Territory to white settlers, and in 1889 led a group of settlers there in their "run" to stake claims. From 1890 to 1909 he managed a revised version of his Wild West show, which became one of the best-paying properties of its kind; after merger with Buffalo Bill's show in 1909, it continued until 1913 and was then disbanded. Lillie then retired to a ranch he had acquired near Pawnee, Okla., and devoted himself to local civic interests and the breeding of prize stock.

LILLY, JOSIAH KIRBY (*b. Greencastle, Ind., 1861; d. Indianapolis, Ind., 1948*), pharmaceutical manufacturer. Ph.G., Philadelphia College of Pharmacy, 1882. Starting in the laboratory of the family firm, Eli Lilly and Company, manufacturers of prescription drugs, he became president, 1898, and continued in that office until 1932 when he became chairman of the board. Under his direction the company both contributed to and benefited from the chemotherapy revolution in medicine during the early decades of the 20th century. After World War I the company assisted in the development and preparation of insulin on the invitation of its discoverer, F. G. Banting; also of barbiturates, ephedrine preparations, and liver extracts. Lilly was active in civic and philanthropic work; with his sons, he established a foundation for charitable and educational purposes, the Lilly Endowment, Inc., in 1937.

LINCECUM, GIDEON (*b. Hancock Co., Ga., 1793; d. Washington Co., Tex., 1874*), frontier physician, naturalist. Early in life a merchant and Indian trader; practiced in vicinity of Columbus, Miss., 1830-48; settled in Texas, 1848. Made special studies of the mound-building ant.

LINCOLN, ABRAHAM (*b. Hardin, now Larue, Co., Ky., 1809; d. Washington, D.C., 1865*), sixteenth president of the United States. Thomas Lincoln, his father, was a powerful, barely literate, unambitious frontiersman. Nancy Hanks, his mother, was of uncertain paternity; there is little reliable evidence concerning her. She seems to have had some intellectual vigor and has been described as spiritually inclined, affectionate, and amiable.

When Abraham Lincoln was seven, the family moved to the Indiana woods, spending the first winter in a rough lean-to, known as a "half-faced camp," in what is now Spencer County. Here, in October 1818, his mother died of fever. Thomas Lincoln soon married Sarah Bush Johnston, a Kentucky widow who brought her own three children to live in the floorless cabin. This stepmother, a woman of energy and ambition, improved the living conditions

and closely supervised the lives of the children. From reminiscences of friends and neighbors, recorded much later, we may reconstruct a fairly definite picture of Lincoln as an easy-going backwoods youth—tall, strong, and ungainly—who did his stint of hard labor on the homestead, performed odd jobs for neighbors, shunned the vociferous camp meetings of the time, avoided membership in the church, and used his leisure for self-improvement by the reading of a few good books. He attended school whenever possible, but his entire schooling probably did not exceed one year. Somehow he grew up without the usual frontier vices, although he was uncommonly sociable.

In 1830 the Lincolns moved to Illinois, settling on the Sangamon River not far from Decatur. Abraham helped move, build the new cabin, clear the land, and fence it. He remained through the next winter, and then left home to shift for himself. He assisted one Denton Offutt in building a flatboat and navigating it to New Orleans; on his return to Illinois, he settled at the village of New Salem. Here he spent six picturesque and formative years (1831-37), managing a mill, conducting a store which left him burdened with debt, all in all eking out a scanty living. He read law meanwhile, studied grammar, widened his acquaintance, and increased his ability to work with people. His skill in sports, especially wrestling, gave him stature among the rough frontiersmen. In 1834 he was elected to the Illinois legislature and served four terms (1834-41), becoming a power in the minority Whig party. In 1836 he was licensed to practice as an attorney; in 1837 he moved to Springfield. At New Salem occurred Lincoln's over-romanticized engagement to Ann Rutledge, who died in 1835; in Springfield he met the vivacious, popular, and socially prominent Mary Todd. Confused testimony, much of it attributable to W. H. Herndon, surrounds their courtship. They were married on Nov. 4, 1842. In spite of Mary's atrocious temper and Abraham's diffidence, untidiness, and lack of dignity, their marriage seems to have been a happy one, their love for each other deep and sincere. Of their four sons, only Robert Todd Lincoln grew to manhood.

Abraham Lincoln served in Congress, 1847-49, the only Whig elected from Illinois. He did not move among the great in Washington, nor did he rise above the obscurity of the average congressman. Supporting the official Whig line, he joined in the attack on the Mexican War and President Polk's policies and so antagonized the Illinois voters that he did not even try for a second term. He campaigned for Zachary Taylor for president in 1848, but there is evidence that he had little influence, even in his own district in Illinois. His return to Springfield was the ebb point of his life: politically unpopular, in debt, his law practice diminished.

Within three or four years, however, Lincoln rose by merit to the front rank of lawyers in his own state. He was associated with capable partners: John Todd Stuart first; then Stephen T. Logan; finally William H. Herndon. In practice before the state supreme court and in the federal courts, he showed qualities that mark the outstanding attorney: a searching thoroughness of investigation, a familiarity with pertinent judicial doctrines, and a knack of so stating a legal question as to brush away its technicalities and get at the core of the controversy. In his journeys on circuit, he rebuilt his popularity and extended it among all classes of people. His important cases included defenses of the Illinois Central R.R. against county taxes and of the McCormick Reaper Co. against patent infringement.

The Lincoln of the prairies was a man of marked individuality. Standing six feet four, with uncommon length of arms and legs, his figure loomed in any crowd, while the rugged face bespoke a pioneer origin and an early life of toil and poverty. In a head not overlarge, each feature was rough and prominent; his face showed deep hollows and heavy shadows. The craggy brow, tousled hair, drooping eyelids, melancholy gray eyes, large nose and chin, heavy lips, and sunken, wrinkled cheeks produced an effect not easily forgotten. He was fond of droll yarns and skilled in telling them. Indifferent to social niceties, he was thought to lack "dignity." He was conservative in his attitude on the slavery question and disliked abolition doctrines. As a stump speaker, he was outstanding.

In the agitation that swept the country on the repeal of the Missouri Compromise, Lincoln emerged from political inactivity and launched upon a new and larger career. Still calling himself a Whig, he competed unsuccessfully for the U.S. senatorship from Illinois in 1855. The next year he identified himself with the new Republican party, wherein he rose rapidly to leadership and received considerable support for the vice-presidential nomination with Frémont. The senatorial election of 1858 was a major turning point in Lincoln's career. Obtaining the Republican nomination to oppose Stephen A. Douglas, he waged an astute campaign. In a carefully prepared speech of acceptance at Springfield on June 16, he made the oft-quoted statement: "A house divided against itself cannot stand. I believe this government cannot endure permanently, half-slave and half-free." After trailing Douglas in the early weeks, Lincoln challenged him to a series of public debates. Between August 21 and October 15, the seven "joint debates" which were held captured the imagination not only of Illinois but of large segments of the nation. In them, Lincoln was conservative; he disavowed abolition doctrines, but shrewdly pointed up the inconsistencies of his opponent's position on slavery.

The Republicans carried the majority of the voting population, but as a result of previous gerrymandering the Democrats were able to organize the state legislature and elect Douglas. Lincoln, however, emerged as a national figure and was increasingly mentioned for the presidency during the next year. It was as a presidential candidate that he delivered his New York speech at Cooper Union, Feb. 27, 1860, in which he formulated the issues on which the Republicans could do battle. He spoke with the greatest clarity, eloquence, and dignity.

A combination of factors led to Lincoln's success in the 1860 Republican convention at Chicago. He was so free from radicalism, had been so careful to avoid offense, and yet withal so skillful in inspiring enthusiasts, that he proved to be precisely the type of candidate to which a convention turns after others have proved unavailable. On the third ballot, the delegates stampeded to Lincoln, who became the convention's choice amid scenes of wild excitement. In the fury of the ensuing campaign, with the Democratic party split between North and South, and disunion threatened in case of Republican success, Lincoln remained quietly at Springfield. He made little effort to reassure the South. Chosen president, Nov. 6, 1860, by a considerable majority in the electoral college, he received only a minority of the popular vote.

In the critical interval between his election and his inauguration Lincoln continued his policy of silence, making no speeches and avoiding public statements as to his policy, even as disunion was effected by formation of a Southern Confederacy. To measures of compromise proposed in Congress, he gave scant encouragement. On Feb. 11, 1861, Lincoln left Springfield for Washington. His speeches en route did little to reassure the skeptical East and, by making it clear that the government would resist secession, had a distinctly unfavorable effect in the South. His secret night ride into the capital (occasioned by rumors of a plot against his life) humiliated his friends and was a subject of ridicule for his opponents. In a conciliatory inaugural address, although he denounced secession as anarchy, he disclaimed any intention of interfering with slavery in the states.

Inexperienced in management of great affairs, untrained in executive functions requiring vigorous action, the new president was soon borne down by pressure of miscellaneous duties and of a horde of officeseekers, although the Fort Sumter crisis was crying out for solution, and peace or war hung in the balance. Meanwhile, W. H. Seward, secretary of state, was arrogating authority and making promises to the Southern leaders which the administration could not possibly keep, thereby laying Lincoln open to the suspicion of bad faith. After some vacillation and much muddling, deciding that Fort Sumter should not be surrendered, he attempted to send food to the garrison without aggressively strengthening it. The South regarded this an an act of war.

Since Congress did not convene until July 1861, Lincoln met the issue with a series of purely executive measures. Treating the conflict as a massive "insurrection," he summoned the militia, proclaimed a blockade, suspended *habeas corpus*, and undertook a multifold series of military measures. As the war progressed, Lincoln extended his executive powers until many called him a dictator; in general, however, he acted with restraint against disloyal elements and used the suspension of *habeas corpus* more as a preventive precaution than as a punitive weapon. Many difficulties beset the administration. There was continual friction within the cabinet, opposition in Congress, and from the "radicals" of the Republican party, hysterical demands by the abolitionists, bitter attacks in the press, and a constant revelation of profiteering and graft. It is in his reaction to these difficulties and in his constant effort to keep the spirit of vindictiveness out of war policy that we find the measure of Lincoln's qualities as president: his unaffected kindness; his fairness toward opponents; his poise, humor, and largeness of soul; his refusal to get angry; and his ability to maintain that well-tempered morale, which is indispensable in a leader of a desperate cause. Lax as an administrator, he was able to keep the disparate elements of his administration in approximate harmony.

The military phase of his task was a sore problem. Inadequate organization, undue state interference with troops, confusion and experimentation in the central control of the army, jealousy and petty strife in the higher command, a poor system of manpower procurement, and constant interference by Congress were only a few of the factors that contributed to the months of Union defeat in the field. The pressure of military responsibility thrust on Lincoln was more than any president of a republic should bear, and his search for a winning general is a painful story. His undeniable blunders in military matters were attributable to political pressure or unsatisfactory human material; they were partly offset by his attention to the Western phases of the war and his final support of U. S. Grant in face of withering criticism. Moderate politicians were very often disappointed by his "pliancy" in yielding to distasteful measures of the radical Congress, yet the radicals never in any sense controlled him. He was an adept in yielding on relatively minor points in order to make a firm stand on major issues. His policy toward slavery illustrates his reluctance to form hasty conclusions, or to take hasty and overemphatic action. The Emancipation Proclamation (Jan 1, 1863) was the result of much thought and was issued when Lincoln considered it wise and expedient. It did not abolish slavery, nor did it declare slavery an evil, it appeared only a half-measure, yet it did change the moral character of the war at home and had great effect on European opinion of the Union cause. Lincoln gave little direct attention to foreign affairs, delegating this work in the main to Secretary Seward.

His manners as president remained much what they had always been—homely and unconventional. His melancholy deepened as the war ground on, and he sought eagerly for relaxation in rough jokes and the repetition of favorite passages from literature. He made few public addresses but most of these were effective—notably his two inaugurals, the Gettysburg Address (Nov. 19, 1863), and his last speech delivered at Washington, D.C. on April 11, 1865. He was also able to influence public opinion by means of letters, written to individuals or delegations but intended for publication.

His renomination in 1864, though opposed, was finally unanimous in convention. The first strength of a popular campaign to replace him was sapped by the news of the fall of Atlanta. He was reelected by a popular majority of more than 400,000 over the Democrat, General George B. McClellan.

At his second inauguration, March 4, 1865, Lincoln delivered a brief address which ranks among his greatest state papers. Refusing to blame the South for the war, he counseled his countrymen to leniency. More than a year before, he had promoted organization of "loyal" governments in the seceded states, requiring that they abolish slavery but standing ready to welcome them back into the Union even though their "loyal" nucleus constituted no more than 10% of their voters in 1860. Later he had killed by pocket veto the Wade-Davis bill providing for severe punitive measures against the South. In several informal peace negotiations, he had insisted only on reunion and the end of slavery, on collateral issues he had shown great generosity, even to compensation of slaveholders for their property loss. On the last day of his life, the subject of Southern reconstruction was considered in a cabinet meeting and a project was considered which resembled the plan later announced (May 29, 1865) by Pres. Andrew Johnson. The war, meanwhile, had to all intents and purposes ended with the surrender of General R. E. Lee.

With opposition growing in his own party and threatening the ruin of his generous plans for reunion, Lincoln was removed by assassination which silenced all criticism. At Ford's Theater, Washington, D.C., he was shot by John Wilkes Booth and died the next morning, April 15, 1865. (Details will be found under the entry *Booth, John Wilkes*.) The early crystallization of the Lincoln tradition was illustrated by Edwin M. Stanton's comment, "Now he belongs to the ages!"

In even the shortest list of American liberal leaders, Abraham Lincoln takes eminent place. Liberalism with him was no garment; it was of the fiber of his mind. His hold upon the affections of his own people has not been due merely to the fact that he, a backwoods lad, rose to the highest office in the land. It is doubtful whether any other leader of the North could have matched him in dramatizing the Civil War to the popular mind, in shaping language to his purpose, in smoothing personal difficulties by a magnanimous touch or a tactful gesture, in avoiding domestic and international complications, in persisting courageously in the face of almost unendurable discouragements, in maintaining war morale while refusing to harbor personal malice against the South. His political philosophy was close akin to the creed of Thomas Jefferson. Not inappropriately, he has become a symbol both of American democracy and of the Union.

LINCOLN, BENJAMIN (*b. Hingham, Mass., 1733; d. 1810*), farmer, Massachusetts legislator, Revolutionary major general. Served in provincial military forces *post* 1755; appointed brigadier general, February 1776, and major general, May 1776. Commissioned major general in the Continental service, February 1777. His maneuvers on Burgoyne's flank prepared way for victory at Saratoga by cutting enemy line of communication with Canada. Appointed to command of American forces in the Southern department, September 1778, he failed in operations before Savannah, Ga.,; shut up in Charleston, S.C., he was captured with his whole army, May 1779. Exchanged, November 1779, he commanded under Washington in the neighborhood of New York, 1780, and took part in the Yorktown campaign. He served as secretary of war, 1781–83, and *ca.* Jan. 1, 1787, was appointed to lead Massachusetts troops in suppression of Shays's Rebellion. His plea for leniency to the rebels was disregarded by the legislature. Thereafter he served on several federal commissions and as lieu-

tenant governor of Massachusetts, 1788. He was collector of the port of Boston, 1789–1809.

LINCOLN, ENOCH (*b. Worcester, Mass., 1788; d. Augusta, Maine, 1829*), lawyer, Maine politician. Son of Levi Lincoln (1749–1820). Removed to District of Maine, 1812. Congressman, (Democrat) Republican, from that part of Massachusetts, 1818–20; from Maine as a state, 1820–26. Governor of Maine, 1827–29. A popular and efficient executive.

LINCOLN, JOHN LARKIN (*b. Boston, Mass., 1817; d. 1891*), educator, Latinist. Graduated Brown, 1836; studied also at Halle and Berlin. Professor of Latin at Brown *post* 1845; made his teaching of Latin a medium for appreciation of beauty in all literatures.

LINCOLN, JOSEPH CROSBY (*b. Brewster, Mass., 1870; d. Winter Park, Fla., 1944*), novelist. Author of more than forty unpretentious, well-told, humorous tales of Cape Cod as he remembered it from boyhood. His books, which were very popular, included *Cap'n Eri* (1904); *Partners of the Tide* (1905); *Extricating Obadiah* (1917); *Galusha the Magnificent* (1921); and *The Bradshaws of Harniss* (1943).

LINCOLN, LEVI (*b. Hingham, Mass., 1749; d. Worcester, Mass., 1820*), lawyer, Massachusetts legislator. Graduated Harvard, 1772. Early successful as a trial lawyer, he was of counsel, 1781, in three cases which involved the question of the right to hold a black in slavery; a supreme court decision upholding the contentions of Lincoln and Caleb Strong was regarded as a landmark in the struggle against slavery. A leader of the Massachusetts (Democrat) Republicans, Lincoln served as U.S. attorney general, 1801–04; in *Letters to the People, by a Farmer* (1802), he assailed political activity of the clergy. Lieutenant governor of Massachusetts, 1807–08, he was offered a place on the U.S. Supreme Court, 1812, which he refused because of failing eyesight.

LINCOLN, LEVI (*b. Worcester, Mass., 1782; d. Worcester, 1868*), lawyer, politician. Son of Levi Lincoln (1749–1820). Graduated Harvard, 1802. Active in state politics as a (Democrat) Republican, he served several terms in the legislature; having become a National Republican, he was elected governor of Massachusetts, 1825, and reelected annually until 1834. As governor he showed notable executive capacity and a liberal point of view. Entering the national House of Representatives, 1834, he served until 1841 as congressman from Massachusetts.

LINCOLN, MARY JOHNSON BAILEY (*b. South Attleboro, Mass., 1844; d. 1921*), teacher. First principal, Boston Cooking School, 1879–85; author of *Mrs. Lincoln's Boston Cook Book* (1884) and other works on domestic economy.

LINCOLN, MARY TODD (*b. Lexington, Ky., 1818; d. Springfield, Ill., 1882*), wife of Abraham Lincoln. Resident in Springfield *post* 1839, she lived with her sister, who was daughter-in-law of Gov. Ninian Edwards. She was married to Lincoln Nov. 4, 1842, and within limits of her unstable temperament, was a devoted wife. *Post* 1871, her mental instability became more pronounced owing to the successive losses of husband and children; adjudged insane, she was later declared competent and after some years of foreign travel died in the home of Mrs. Edwards.

LINCOLN, ROBERT TODD (*b. Springfield, Ill., 1843; d. 1926*), lawyer, businessman, diplomat. Son of Abraham and Mary Todd Lincoln. Graduated Harvard, 1864. Practiced at the Chicago bar *post* 1867. U.S. secretary of war, 1881–85; U.S. minister to Great Britain, 1889–93. On his return, he continued as counsel for leading business firms and was for a time president of the Pullman Co.

LINCOLN, RUFUS PRATT (*b. Belchertown, Mass., 1840; d. 1900*), physician, laryngologist, Union soldier. Graduated Amherst, 1862; M.D., Harvard Medical School, 1868. Practiced in New York in partnership with Willard Parker; later specialized in intranasal surgery.

LIND, JOHN (*b. Kånna, Sweden, 1854; d. 1930*), lawyer. Immigrated to Minnesota as a boy. Congressman, Republican, from Minnesota, 1887–93; Democrat, from Minnesota, 1903–05. Democratic governor of Minnesota, 1899–1901. Despite party designations, Lind was an independent progressive. He served as Pres. Woodrow Wilson's agent in overturning the Huerta government in Mexico, 1913.

LINDABURY, RICHARD VLIET (*b. near Peapack, N.J., 1850; d. 1925*), New Jersey corporation lawyer.

LINDBERG, CONRAD EMIL (*b. Jönköping, Sweden, 1852; d. 1930*), Lutheran clergyman. Came to America, 1871. A leader in the Augustana Synod of his church, he taught theology at its Rock Island, Ill., seminary *post* 1890. He served from 1901 to 1910 as the seminary's vice-president; as dean, 1920–30.

LINDBERGH, CHARLES AUGUSTUS (*b. Stockholm, Sweden, 1859; d. 1924*), lawyer, politician. Father of Charles A. Lindbergh (1902–74). Came to America as an infant; raised near Melrose, Minn. Graduated University of Michigan Law School, 1883; practiced in Little Falls, Minn. Congressman, Republican, from Minnesota, 1907–17. An active and able progressive reformer, he was temporarily unpopular for denouncing war propaganda, 1916–17.

LINDE, CHRISTIAN (*b. near Copenhagen, Denmark, 1817; d. Oshkosh, Wis., 1887*), pioneer Wisconsin physician. A political refugee, Linde immigrated to the vicinity of Oshkosh, 1842, where he planned to establish a landed estate. Called on to treat neighboring settlers and Indians, he resumed practice. A skillful surgeon as well as a busy practitioner, he is credited with discovering the value of animal tendons for surgical sutures.

LINDEMAN, EDUARD CHRISTIAN (*b. St. Clair, Mich., 1885; d. New York, N.Y., 1953*), social philosopher and educator. Studied at Michigan Agricultural College. After working for the YMCA, Lindeman published *Social Discovery: An Approach to the Study of Functional Groups* (1924), and joined the faculty of the New York School of Social Work. A pioneer in the field of adult education, he published *The Meaning of Adult Education* in 1926. A pragmatist as well as a scholar, Lindeman's teaching and writing demonstrated such diverse influences as liberal Christianity, consumer's cooperation, the Danish folk schools, and the philosophies of Mary Parker Follett and John Dewey.

LINDENKOHL, ADOLPH (*b. Niederkaufungen, Germany, 1833; d. 1904*), cartographer, oceanographer. Came to America, 1852. Associated as draftsman with the U.S. Coast and Geodetic Survey, 1854–1904, he executed many distinguished maps and made the first transverse polyconic map of the United States.

LINDENTHAL, GUSTAV (*b. Brünn, Moravia, Austria, 1850; d. 1935*), civil engineer. Came to America, 1874. Reputed by 1890 to be one of the great bridge builders of his time; among his principal works are the Queensboro Bridge over the East River, New York, and the railway bridge over Hell Gate.

LINDERMAN, HENRY RICHARD (*b. Pike Co., Pa., 1825; d. 1879*), physician. Chief clerk, Philadelphia mint, 1853–65; director, Philadelphia mint, 1867–69. First director, Bureau of the Mint, 1873–79.

LINDGREN, WALDEMAR (*b. Kalmar, Sweden, 1860; d. Brookline, Mass., 1939*), geologist. Came to America, 1883. Chief geologist, U.S. Geological Survey, 1911–25; headed department of geology, Massachusetts Institute of Technology, 1912–33. Advocated hydrothermal theory of ore deposition.

LINDHEIMER, FERDINAND JACOB (*b. Frankfurt-am-Main, Germany, 1801; d. New Braunfels, Texas, 1879*), botanist. Came to America, 1834; fought in Texan war for independence; edited a German newspaper at New Braunfels, 1852–70. Encouraged by George Engelmann, he undertook systematic collection of Texas botanical specimens.

LINDLEY, CURTIS HOLBROOK (*b. Marysville, Calif., 1850; d. 1920*), lawyer, jurist. Authority on mining law; author of *Treatise on the American Law Relating to Mines and Mineral Lands* (1897).

LINDLEY, DANIEL (*b. Washington Co., Pa., 1801; d. 1880*), Presbyterian clergyman. Missionary to South Africa, 1835–59 and 1862–73. Principally active among the Zulus.

LINDLEY, JACOB (*b. Washington Co., Pa., 1774; d. Connellsville, Pa., 1857*), Presbyterian clergyman. Graduated College of New Jersey (Princeton), 1800. Active *post* 1805 in founding Ohio University at Athens; served in its preparatory department as instructor and on college faculty, 1822–28.

LINDSAY, HOWARD (*b. Waterford, N.Y., 1889; d. New York, N.Y., 1968*), playwright, actor, and director. Attended Harvard (1907–08) and the American Academy of Dramatic Arts (1908). Toured as an actor beginning in 1909 and briefly worked in the movies. Began directing his own plays in 1927, but his most important collaboration was with Russel Crouse, which began in 1934 with *Anything Goes*. They created fifteen plays, including *Life with Father* (1939), *Arsenic and Old Lace* (1941), *State of the Union* (1945, Pulitzer Prize winner), *Call Me Madam* (1950), and *The Sound of Music* (1959).

LINDSAY, NICHOLAS VACHEL (*b. Springfield, Ill., 1879; d. Springfield, 1931*), poet. Known as Vachel Lindsay. Studied first for the ministry, then for a career in art. In 1906, unable to obtain work, he tramped through the South distributing poems in exchange for bed and board; this experience was basis for his later *A Handy Guide for Beggars* (1916). His first volume of poems, *General William Booth Enters into Heaven* (1913), attracted little attention. *The Congo and Other Poems* (1914) met with wide popular success by reason of its technical innovations, notably a new ragtime poetic music, a blend of speech and song expressive of the energetic idealism of the period. His later books were notably uneven and seemed almost parodies of his better work.

LINDSAY, VACHEL. *See* LINDSAY, NICHOLAS VACHEL.

LINDSAY, WILLIAM (*b. near Lexington, Va., 1835; d. 1909*), lawyer, Kentucky jurist and legislator, Confederate soldier. U.S. senator, Democrat, from Kentucky, 1893–1901.

LINDSEY, BENJAMIN BARR (*b. Jackson, Tenn., 1869; d. Los Angeles, Calif., 1943*), jurist, social reformer, better known as Ben B. Lindsey. Admitted to the Colorado bar, 1894; practiced in Denver. Active in Democratic politics, he was appointed to a county judgeship, 1901, and retained that post until the mid-1920's. Largely through his efforts, the court over which he presided evolved into the Juvenile and Family Court of Denver, and he became widely known as a leader in the juvenile court movement. Lindsey drafted and mobilized public support behind almost every major item of child care legislation enacted in Colorado; it was his fixed opinion that the major cause of crime was economic injustice. A foe of public utilities companies, he was also peripherally associated with other reform "causes" of the time such as woman suffrage and the abolition of capital punishment; after World War I he became an advocate of compulsory sex education and liberalized divorce laws, attracting much publicity for his books *The Revolt of Modern Youth* (1925) and *The Companionate Marriage* (1927). Removing to California, 1930, he was elected to a county judgeship in Los Angeles, 1934. From 1939 until his death he presided over the Los Angeles division of the Children's Court of Conciliation, for which he had drafted the enabling legislation.

LINDSEY, WILLIAM (*b. Fall River, Mass., 1858; d. Boston, Mass., 1922*), textile manufacturer, author.

LINDSLEY, JOHN BERRIEN (*b. Princeton, N.J., 1822; d. Nashville, Tenn., 1897*), physician, Presbyterian clergyman, educator. Son of Philip Lindsley. Graduated University of Nashville, 1839; M.D., University of Pennsylvania, 1843. Organized medical department, University of Nashville, 1850, first school of its kind south of Ohio River; was chancellor of the University, 1855–70. Active in public health and educational work.

LINDSLEY, PHILIP (*b. near Morristown, N.J., 1786; d. Nashville, Tenn., 1855*), Presbyterian clergyman, educator. Graduated College of New Jersey (Princeton), 1804. Taught languages at Princeton, and served as acting president but in 1823 declined election to presidency. President, University of Nashville, 1825–50.

LINGELBACH, ANNA LANE (*b. Shelbyville, Ill., 1873; d. Philadelphia, Pa., 1954*), historian and civic leader. Studied at the University of Indiana and at Pennsylvania University (Ph.D., 1916). Taught at Temple University (1922–52). First woman member to serve on the Philadelphia Board of Education (1920–50). Active in many local civic organizations, she also wrote historical articles and nineteen biographical sketches for the *Dictionary of American Biography*.

LINING, JOHN (*b. Scotland, 1708; d. 1760*), physician, pioneer physiologist. Came to South Carolina, *ca.* 1730. Practiced in Charleston; made a study of yellow fever and sent abroad earliest account (1748) from America of its symptoms and pathology (published Edinburgh, 1753). Reports made by him on the effect of climatic conditions upon his own metabolism (published by the Royal Society in London, 1743 and 1745) were the first published records of the weather in America. He was also an early experimenter in electricity.

LINK, HENRY CHARLES (*b. Buffalo, N.Y., 1889; d. Port Chester, N.Y., 1952*), industrial psychologist. Ph.D., Yale, 1916. A pioneer in industrial psychology and employee testing, Link wrote *Employment Psychology* (1919), *Education and Industry* (1923), and *The New Psychology of Selling and Advertising* (1932). Link's efforts brought stability and respectability to the field. A moralist, he wrote *The Return to Religion* (1936) which sold over 500,000 copies. He was an executive with the Psychological Corp. in New York, and was in charge of the marketing and social research division. His best-known innovation was the Psychological Barometer, a poll inaugurated in 1932 and later renamed the Link Audit of Public Opinion.

LINN, JOHN BLAIR (*b. Shippensburg, Pa., 1777; d. 1804*), Presbyterian clergyman, poet. Brother-in-law of Charles Brockden Brown. Graduated Columbia, 1795. Among the numerous publications of this minor poet were *The Poetical Wanderer* (1796), *The Powers of Genius* (1801, 1802), *Valerian* (1805).

LINN, LEWIS FIELDS (*b. near Louisville, Ky., 1795; d. Missouri, 1843*), physician, authority on Asiatic cholera. Practiced in southeastern Missouri. U.S. senator, Democrat, from Missouri, 1833–43. A sincere exponent of Manifest Destiny. His bill providing for the occupation and settlement of Oregon passed the Senate on Feb. 28, 1843.

LINN, WILLIAM ALEXANDER (*b. Deckertown, now Sussex, N.J., 1846; d. 1917*), journalist, author. Associated as editor with N.Y. *Evening Post, post* 1871, he became managing editor, 1891, and retired, 1900. Under his editorship, the paper was celebrated for the reliability of its news.

LINTNER, JOSEPH ALBERT (*b. Schoharie, N.Y., 1822; d. Rome, Italy, 1898*), manufacturer, entomologist. Appointed New York State entomologist, 1880, he was famous for thoroughness of his annual reports.

LINTON, RALPH (*b. Philadelphia, Pa., 1893; d. New Haven, Conn., 1953*), anthropologist and popular writer. Studied at Swarthmore College, Columbia, and Harvard (Ph.D., 1925). Taught at the University of Wisconsin (1928–37); Columbia (1938–46); Yale (1946–53). A popularizer of cultural anthropology, he published many works: *Study of Man* (1937), *Cultural Background of Personality* (1945), and *The Tree of Culture* (1955). Linden is remembered more for his story telling than for his accurate and scientific scholarship.

LINTON, WILLIAM JAMES (*b. London, England, 1812; d. New Haven, Conn., 1897*), wood engraver. Came to America, 1866, after a notable career as artist and radical political reformer. Engraved illustrations for a number of books, many after his own designs; opposed the "new school" of American wood engraving. Author of *The History of Wood Engraving in America* (1882).

LIPMAN, JACOB GOODALE (*b. Friedrichstadt, Russia, 1874; d. New Brunswick, N.J., 1939*), soil scientist, agricultural educator. Came to America, 1888. Graduated Rutgers, 1898; Ph.D., Cornell, 1903. Meanwhile he had organized (1901) a department of soil chemistry and bacteriology at the New Jersey Agricultural Experiment Station, and had taught agricultural chemistry at Rutgers. As director, *post* 1911, of the Experiment Station, and first dean (*post* 1915) of the N.J. State College of Agriculture at Rutgers, Lipman attracted international acclaim as a scientist and administrator. He founded (1916) and edited *Soil Science*, which became the outstanding journal of its kind in the world. Of his more than one hundred published studies on soil bacteriology and agronomy, many were of a pioneering nature.

LIPPARD, GEORGE (*b. Chester Co., Pa., 1822; d. Philadelphia, Pa., 1854*), novelist, journalist. Author of a number of fantastic works, which include *The Monks of Monk Hall* (1844), reprinted as *The Quaker City* (1845); *Washington and His Generals* (1847); *Washington and His Men* (1850); *New York: Its Upper-Ten and Lower Million* (1854). An enemy of capitalism, he originated a political philosophy and a religion of his own.

LIPPINCOTT, JAMES STARR (*b. Philadelphia, Pa., 1819; d. Greenwich, N.J., 1885*), horticulturist, meteorologist, agricultural writer.

LIPPINCOTT, JOSHUA BALLINGER (*b. Juliustown, N.J., 1813; d. Philadelphia, Pa., 1886*), publisher. Founder of J. B. Lippincott & Co., 1836; was interested also in banking, insurance, and railroads.

LIPPINCOTT, SARA JANE CLARKE (*b. Pompey, N.Y., 1823; d. New Rochelle, N.Y., 1904*), author. Pseudonym, "Grace Greenwood." Contributed widely to magazines; was one of the first women in the United States to become a regular newspaper correspondent. Among her many books, *Greenwood Leaves* (1850) is representative.

LIPPITT, HENRY (*b. Providence, R.I., 1818; d. 1891*), cotton manufacturer, financier. Governor of Rhode Island, 1875–77.

LIPSCOMB, ABNER SMITH (*b. Abbeville District, S.C., 1789; d. 1856*), lawyer. Alabama legislator and jurist, 1811–38. Removed to Texas *ca.* 1839; served as secretary of state, Republic of Texas, and was influential in framing the Texas state constitution, 1845. Justice, Texas supreme court, 1845–56.

LIPSCOMB, ANDREW ADGATE (*b. Georgetown, D.C., 1816; d. Athens, Ga., 1890*), Methodist clergyman. Chancellor, University of Georgia, 1860–74.

LISA, MANUEL (*b. New Orleans, La., 1772; d. St. Louis, Mo., 1820*), fur trader. Removed to St. Louis, Mo., *ca.* 1790; held a Spanish patent for monopoly of trade with the Osage Indians. Led expedition up Missouri River, 1807–08, during which he placed a trading house at mouth of Big Horn River and built fort later known as Fort Manuel, first structure of its kind on upper Missouri. Joined with Andrew Henry, Pierre Chouteau, and others in Missouri Fur Co., 1808; was appointed, 1814, to post of subagent for Indian tribes on the Missouri above mouth of Kansas River. Between 1807 and his death, he made some 13 trips on the Missouri, amounting to about 26,000 miles of river travel.

LIST, GEORG FRIEDRICH (*b. Reutlingen, Germany, 1789; d. Tyrol, Austria, 1846*), journalist, economist. An influential German liberal and a friend of Lafayette, List immigrated to America, 1825. Settling in Reading, Pa., 1826, he very ably edited the *Readinger Adler*. One of the foremost advocates of the protectionist movement, he achieved national recognition for his *Outlines of American Political Economy* (1827) and other publications. Turning his attention to business, he developed anthracite deposits near Tamaqua, Pa., and organized, 1828, the progenitor of the modern Reading Railroad. Returning to Europe in 1831 as a consular official, he divided his energies between literary work and the promotion of a German railway system. List's theory of productive forces, of the economic importance of nations as against the individualism of Adam Smith, and his application of the historical method, all advanced the study of economics. He ranks next to Alexander Hamilton as the most constructive thinker among the early advocates of protectionism in America.

LISTEMANN, BERNHARD (*b. Schlotheim, Germany, 1841; d. 1917*), violinist, conductor, educator. Studied at Leipzig Conservatory, and at Vienna under Joseph Joachim and Henry Vieuxtemps. Came to America, 1867; founded Boston Philharmonic Club, 1875, from which grew Boston Philharmonic Orchestra; served briefly as concert master, Boston Symphony. Removed to Chicago, 1893, where he had successful career as teacher and performer.

LITCHFIELD, ELECTUS BACKUS (*b. Delphi Falls, N.Y., 1813; d. 1889*), financier, railroad builder. Built up, with aid of his two brothers, a remarkable network of railroads in Michigan, Indiana, Ohio, and Illinois, the most impressive organization of its kind before the Civil War. Overextended when the panic of 1857 occurred, the Litchfields lost control of their system in subsequent reorganization; thereafter they turned to development of street railways and real estate in Brooklyn, N.Y. The St. Paul & Pacific Railroad, built by the Litchfields, *post* 1862, after many vicissitudes was sold by them to James J. Hill; its lines became nucleus of the Great Northern system. Brooklyn's famous Prospect Park was constructed on land purchased from the Litchfields.

LITCHFIELD, PAUL WEEKS (*b. Boston, Mass., 1875; d. Phoenix, Ariz., 1959*), rubber manufacturer. Studied at the Massachusetts Institute of Technology. Associated with Goodyear Rubber from 1900; president, 1926; chairman of the board, 1930–58. Under Litchfield's leadership, Goodyear became one of the world's leading rubber manufacturers: he introduced the pneumatic tire for trucks in 1916; the airplane tire in 1910; the Goodyear blimps; the manufacture of synthetic rubber during World War II; and diversified the company's interests into plastics, electronics, and atomic energy.

LITTAUER, LUCIUS NATHAN (*b. Gloversville, N.Y., 1859; d. near New Rochelle, N.Y., 1944*), glove manufacturer, politician, philanthropist. Congressman, Republican, from New York, 1897–1907. Among his benefactions were the establishment of the Littauer Foundation, of the Nathan Littauer professorship of Jewish literature and philosophy at Harvard, and of the Harvard Graduate School of Public Administration.

LITTELL, ELIAKIM (*b. Burlington, N.J., 1797; d. Brookline, Mass., 1870*), publisher. *Littell's Living Age* (founded 1844) and his earlier *Museum* (1822–43) reprinted materials from European periodicals and brought foreign thought to the attention of Americans during the early period of development of the national culture.

LITTELL, SQUIER (*b. Burlington, N.J., 1803; d. Bay Head, N.J., 1886*), physician, ophthalmic surgeon. Brother of Eliakim Littell.

LITTELL, WILLIAM (*b. New Jersey, 1768; d. 1824*), Kentucky lawyer and compiler of law books. Author also of *Epistles of William* (1806), a series of satirical essays on prominent men of the time, and *Political Transactions In and Concerning Kentucky* (1806).

LITTLE, ARTHUR DEHON (*b. Boston, Mass., 1863; d. Northeast Harbor, Maine, 1935*), chemical engineer. A recognized leader in paper technology, he was an organizer and partner in Arthur D. Little, Inc., the largest unendowed commercial industrial research laboratory in the U.S.

LITTLE, CHARLES COFFIN (*b. Kennebunk, Maine, 1799; d. 1869*), publisher. Associated with James Brown (1800–1855) in firm of Little, Brown & Co.; supervised legal publications of the firm.

LITTLE, CHARLES JOSEPH (*b. Philadelphia, Pa., 1840; d. 1911*), Methodist clergyman, theologian, educator. Graduated University of Pennsylvania, 1861; taught at Dickinson College and Syracuse University. Professor of church history, Garrett Biblical Institute, 1891–95; president of the Institute, 1895–1911.

LITTLE, CHARLES SHERMAN (*b. Webster, N.H., 1869; d. Thiells, N.Y., 1936*), psychiatrist. M.D., Dartmouth, 1896. First superintendent, 1910–36, of Letchworth Village in Rockland Co., N.Y., pioneering school for the mentally retarded.

LITTLE, GEORGE (*b. Marshfield, Mass., 1754; d. Weymouth, Mass., 1809*), naval officer. Served in Massachusetts navy during the Revolution. Appointed, 1799, captain in U.S. Navy, he served with great distinction in command of frigate *Boston* during naval war with France.

LITTLE, WILLIAM LAWSON, JR. (*b. Newport, R.I., 1910; d. Pebble Beach, Calif., 1968*), golfer. Nicknamed "Cannonball," his thirty-one amateur championships included the U.S. Open (1929) and the British and U.S. amateur championships (1934, 1935). Became a professional and won the Canadian Open in

1936 and the U.S. Open in 1940. Inducted into Professional Golfers Association Hall of Fame (1961).

LITTLE CROW V (*b. ca. 1803; d. near Hutchinson, Minn., 1863*), chief of Mdewakanton Sioux. A drunkard and habitual liar but a persuasive orator, he was chiefly responsible for the Minnesota outbreak of the Sioux in August–September 1862.

LITTLE TURTLE (*b. on Eel River, northwest of Ft. Wayne, Ind., ca. 1752; d. Ft. Wayne, 1812*), Miami Indian chief. Tribal name, Michikinikwa. A principal leader at defeat of General Harmar, 1790, and of General St. Clair, 1791. Led attack on Ft. Recovery, 1794. Thereafter counseling peace, he lost his leadership in council, and his prestige among his people declined. He is, however, credited with keeping the Miami from joining the confederacy of Tecumseh.

LITTLEDALE, CLARA SAVAGE (*b. Belfast, Me., 1891; d. New York, N.Y., 1956*), journalist and editor. Studied at Smith College. After working for the *New York Evening Post*, serving as press chairman for the National American Woman Suffrage Association, and serving as a reporter for *Good Housekeeping*, Littledale became managing editor of *Children, the Magazine for Parents* in 1926. The name was changed to *Parents' Magazine* in 1929, and Littledale became chief editor, serving until her death. The magazine was the most widely read in its field and had a circulation of 1,675,000 by the 1950's. The magazine regularly carried articles dealing with such subjects as the prohibition of the exploitation of child labor, increased federal aid to education, and articles supporting UNICEF.

LITTLEFIELD, GEORGE WASHINGTON (*b. Panola Co., Miss., 1842; d. 1920*), cattleman, banker, Confederate soldier. Raised in Gonzales Co., Texas. Engaged in trail-driving cattle *post* 1871; established cattle ranch near Tascosa, 1877. Locating on the Pecos River in New Mexico, 1882, and soon ranging some 40,000 head of cattle, he spread the fame of his LFD brand the length of the West. Removing to Austin, Texas, 1883, he organized the American National Bank, 1890, of which he served as president until his death. He was a generous supporter of historical research and a benefactor of the University of Texas.

LITTLEJOHN, ABRAM NEWKIRK (*b. Florida, N.Y., 1824; d. Williamstown, Mass., 1901*), Episcopal clergyman. Consecrated bishop of Long Island, 1869. Secured interest of Alexander T. Stewart in building Cathedral Church of the Incarnation, Garden City, N.Y., 1885.

LITTLEPAGE, LEWIS (*b. Hanover Co., Va., 1762; d. Fredericksburg, Va., 1802*), adventurer. Educated at College of William and Mary. Served with Spanish army in siege of Gibraltar, 1782; was confidential emissary of Stanislaus II Poniatowski, King of Poland, 1786–95. Returned to Virginia, 1801.

LITTLETON, MARTIN WILEY (*b. Roane Co., Tenn., 1872; d. 1934*), lawyer, Democratic politician. Self-educated, Littleton resided in Brooklyn, N.Y., *post* 1897, where his rise as legal practitioner, particularly in criminal practice, was rapid. He received national notice for his speech nominating Alton B. Parker for the presidency at the Democratic convention, St. Louis, Mo., 1904.

LIVERIGHT, HORACE BRISBIN (*b. Osceola Mills, Pa., 1886; d. 1933*), bond salesman, theatrical producer, publisher. Partner in Boni & Liveright, 1918–30. A vivid figure in the literary world of the 1920's, he was first publisher to take interest in works of Eugene O'Neill and helped advance reputations of Ben Hecht and Theodore Dreiser.

LIVERMORE, ABIEL ABBOT (*b. Wilton, N.H., 1811; d. Wilton, 1892*), Unitarian clergyman. President, Theological School, Meadville, Pa., 1863–90.

LIVERMORE, ARTHUR (*b. Londonderry, N.H., 1766; d. Campton, N.H., 1853*), lawyer, New Hampshire legislator, congressman, and jurist. Son of Samuel Livermore (1732–1803), brother of Edward St. L. Livermore.

LIVERMORE, EDWARD ST. LOE (*b. Portsmouth, N.H., 1762; d. Tewksbury, Mass., 1832*), lawyer, New Hampshire jurist and Federalist congressman. Son of Samuel Livermore (1732–1803), brother of Arthur Livermore.

LIVERMORE, GEORGE (*b. Cambridge, Mass., 1809; d. 1865*), wool merchant, book collector.

LIVERMORE, MARY ASHTON RICE (*b. Boston, Mass., 1820; d. Melrose, Mass., 1905*), teacher, woman's rights advocate, reformer. Active in work of U.S. Sanitary Commission. Author of *My Story of the War* (1888) and *The Story of My Life* (1897).

LIVERMORE, SAMUEL (*b. Waltham, Mass., 1732; d. Holderness, N.H., 1803*), lawyer, New Hampshire legislator and jurist. Father of Edward St. L. and Arthur Livermore. Practiced law in Portsmouth, N.H., *post ca.. 1757*; served as judge advocate in Admiralty and attorney general of province, 1769–74. Elected state attorney general, 1776, he continued to hold state office almost continuously until his death. He served as U.S. congressman from New Hampshire, 1789–93; elected to the U.S. Senate, 1793, he resigned, 1801, because of failing health.

LIVERMORE, SAMUEL (*b. Concord, N.H., 1786; d. Florence, Ala., 1833*), lawyer, legal writer. Son of Edward St. L. Livermore. Graduated Harvard, 1804. Successful as a lawyer in New Orleans *post* 1822, Livermore wrote the first American work on agency and auctions (1811); also the first American work on the conflict of laws (1828).

LIVINGSTON, BURTON EDWARD (*b. Grand Rapids, Mich., 1875; d. Baltimore, Md., 1948*), plant physiologist. B.S., University of Michigan, 1898; Ph.D., University of Chicago, 1901. Taught at Chicago, 1901–05; was briefly with the bureau of soils of the U.S. department of agriculture, and with the Tucson, Ariz., Desert Laboratory of the Carnegie Institution. In 1909 he became professor of plant physiology at Johns Hopkins University, and in 1913 director of the university's laboratory of plant physiology; he retired in 1940. Experiments conducted by Livingston and his students and associates studied the effects of numerous environmental factors on the physiological functions of plants; in addition, he devised a number of new pieces of equipment that were put in use by scientists all over the world. He helped edit several scientific journals and was coauthor of *The Distribution of Vegetation in the United States, as Related to Climatic Conditions* (with Forrest Shreve, 1921).

LIVINGSTON, EDWARD (*b. Columbia Co., N.Y., 1764; d. Dutchess Co., N.Y., 1836*), lawyer, statesman. Son of Robert R. Livingston (1718–1775). Graduated College of New Jersey (Princeton), 1781; studied law at Albany under John Lansing. Practiced law in New York City *post* 1785. Congressman, (Democrat) Republican, from New York, 1795–1801. Acting (1801–03) simultaneously as U.S. attorney for New York and as mayor of New York City, he was held responsible for the defalcation of an agent and gave up all his own property to be sold in order to make restitution of the loss to the Treasury. Removing to New Orleans, La., 1804, he began practice of the law there, struggling meanwhile under a weight of private as well as public debt. Falsely accused of abetting Aaron Burr in his 1806 activities, Livingston no sooner cleared himself of these charges before he was brought into controversy with President Jefferson over the rights to certain alluvial lands at New Orleans which Livingston claimed. Dispossessed of the property, he published pamphlets on the subject and complained of his treatment in the courts and before Congress.

As chairman of the New Orleans committee of public defense, Livingston organized the people of Louisiana in their resistance to British invasion, 1814. At the battle of New Orleans he served Andrew Jackson as aide-de-camp, interpreter, and adviser. Commissioned, 1821, to revise the Louisiana penal law, he completed a code in 1825 which aimed at the prevention rather than the punishment of crime. Although it was not adopted, the publication of the code brought him wide fame. As a Democrat, he represented the New Orleans district in the U.S. House of Representatives, 1823–29, and was chosen by the legislature to be U.S. senator, 1829–31. As U.S. secretary of state, 1831–33, he drafted the celebrated 1832 proclamation to the South Carolina nullifiers; he also secured an admission by the French Government in 1831 of the justice of American claims for spoliation under the Berlin and Milan decrees. His last public service was as U.S. minister to France, 1833–35.

LIVINGSTON, HENRY BROCKHOLST (*b. New York, N.Y., 1757; d. Washington, D.C., 1823*), lawyer, Revolutionary soldier. Son of William Livingston (1723–1790). Graduated College of New Jersey (Princeton), 1774. Justice, New York supreme court, 1802–06; justice, U.S. Supreme Court, 1807–23. Opinions written by Livingston dealt mainly with questions of maritime and commercial law; his decisions on the circuit court were considered more noteworthy than those he made on the Supreme bench.

LIVINGSTON, JAMES (*b. probably Montreal, Canada, 1747; d. Schuylerville, N.Y., 1832*), Revolutionary soldier, New York legislator. Responsible, 1780, for failure of H.M.S. *Vulture* to wait for Major André, thus contributing to his later capture.

LIVINGSTON, JOHN HENRY (*b. near Poughkeepsie, N.Y., 1746; d. New Brunswick, N.J., 1825*), Dutch Reformed clergyman, educator. Graduated Yale, 1762; doctor of theology, University of Utrecht, 1770. Professor of theology to the General Synod, 1784–1825; president of Queens College (now Rutgers University), 1810–25. A principal factor in guiding the Dutch Reformed Church to a complete and independent American organization.

LIVINGSTON, JOHN WILLIAM (*b. New York, N.Y., 1804; d. New York, 1885*), naval officer.

LIVINGSTON, PETER VAN BRUGH (*b. Albany, N.Y., 1710; d. Elizabethtown, N.J., 1792*), merchant, Revolutionary patriot. Brother of Philip Livingston and William Livingston (1723–1790). Graduated Yale, 1731. Made a fortune in privateering and government contracting during French wars. Followed lead in New York politics of his brother William, John M. Scott, and William Smith, Jr.

LIVINGSTON, PHILIP (*b. Albany, N.Y., 1716; d. York, Pa., 1778*), New York legislator, Revolutionary patriot, signer of the Declaration of Independence. Brother of Peter Van B. Livingston and William Livingston (1723–1790). Graduated Yale, 1737. Among the first to advocate founding of King's College (Columbia) to which he was a benefactor; also helped organize N.Y. Society Library, 1754, and N.Y. Chamber of Commerce, 1768. In politics, he supported the Whig Presbyterian faction against the Anglicans as represented by the De Lancey interest but was not so intense a partisan as his brother William. A member of the New York provincial congress, he served also in the Continental Congress, 1774–78, where he was active in committee work. Too dignified and austere to win popularity, he pledged his personal credit to maintain confidence in the Congress and was honored in his own generation for ability and integrity.

LIVINGSTON, ROBERT (*b. Ancrum, Roxburghshire, Scotland, 1654; d. 1728*), landowner, trader, New York legislator. Raised in Rotterdam, Holland, where his father was pastor of a Presbyterian congregation; came to New England, 1673; appeared in Albany, N.Y., 1674. Appointed town clerk and secretary of the board of commissioners for Indian affairs, he came to have influence with the successive governors of the province. By careful purchase of Indian claims to lands along the Hudson, and by his marriage to the widowed sister of Peter Schuyler, he rose in fortune and prominence. He secured a patent raising his landholdings into the manor and lordship of Livingston, 1686. Among other activities in which he engaged were government contracting and tax farming as well as private trade with the Indians and French. As speaker of the New York Assembly, 1718–25, he showed a marked tendency to support the Assembly in its frequent quarrels with the royal governor. Grasping and shrewd, he was also a courtier and diplomat of no mean ability.

LIVINGSTON, ROBERT R. (*b. New York, 1718; d. 1775*), jurist, New York legislator, Revolutionary patriot. Grandson of Robert Livingston. A leader of the Whig interest, he was ready to go as far as necessary to assure the economic welfare of the colonies but was opposed to revolution merely for the sake of abstract principle. During the Stamp Act controversy, he was chairman of the New York committee of correspondence and author of the address to the King presented by the Stamp Act Congress.

LIVINGSTON, ROBERT R. (*b. New York, N.Y., 1746; d. 1813*), lawyer, diplomat, agriculturist. Son of Robert R. Livingston (1718–1775); brother of Edward Livingston. Graduated King's College (Columbia), 1765. Admitted to the bar, 1770; practiced at first in partnership with John Jay. Member of Continental Congress, 1775–76, 1779–81, 1784–85. Serving on the congressional committee appointed to draft a declaration of independence, he considered the course inexpedient and was one of the principal speakers for its postponement. Few members of Congress were more conscientious or more in demand as committee members; of his many reports, the most important was that of Dec. 14, 1779, describing the financial problems of the general government and urging methods of solving them. From August 1781 until May 1783, he served as secretary of the newly created Department of Foreign Affairs. In this office he set up a system for business and arranged for the dissemination of news to all departments, innovations which marked an advance in the development of American executive machinery. Throughout his life he was also deeply involved in New York affairs, helping to govern the state in the period after British withdrawal, to settle boundary disputes with Massachusetts and Vermont, and active on the committee to draft first New York constitution, 1777. He held post of chancellor of New York State, 1777–1801. Excepting Alexander Hamilton, no individual contributed more toward New York's ratification of the Federal Constitution. Irked by what he considered the slights of the administration, he became a (Democrat) Republican sometime *ante* 1791. As U.S. minister to France, 1801–04, he scored the greatest diplomatic success recorded in American history by seizing the opportunity offered the United States for the purchase of Louisiana. After his retirement, he conducted agricultural experiments and was a pioneer in the import of Merino sheep and the use of gypsum as fertilizer. His technical as well as financial aid made possible the experiments of Robert Fulton in France and later the success of the steamboat *Clermont* on the Hudson.

LIVINGSTON, WILLIAM (*b. Albany, N.Y., 1723; d. Elizabethtown, N.J., 1790*), lawyer, New York legislator. Grandson of Robert Livingston; brother of Philip and Peter Van B. Livingston; father-in-law of John Jay. Graduated Yale, 1741; studied law under James Alexander and William Smith (1697–1769). Like his brothers a leader in opposition to New York conservatives and an advocate of Whig principles, he was an intense and impatient partisan. The 1751 proposal to place the new King's College of New York under trustees of Episcopalian sentiment and sympathy appeared to him the first step toward establishment of the Anglican Church; his views were ably presented in the weekly publication *Independent Reflector* (1752), in the "Watch Tower" column in the *New York Mercury*, and in other satirical publications. After the 1769 defeat of the Whigs in the New York Assembly, he removed to an estate near Elizabethtown, N.J., quickly rising to a position of leadership in New Jersey. He was a member of the First Continental Congress and of the Second Continental Congress until June 5, 1776, when for a brief period he commanded the New Jersey militia. Elected first governor of New Jersey, 1776, he served until his death. A delegate to the Federal Convention, 1787, he supported the New Jersey plan and worked for a compromise that would be acceptable. Among his contemporaries, he was honored for a high moral courage, for wit, and for a sense of social responsibility.

LIVINGSTONE, BELLE (*b. Kansas, 1875; d. New York, N.Y., 1957*), adventuress. Raised by foster parents in Chicago, Livingstone (a pseudonym for Isabelle Graham) pursued a theatrical career before leaving for Europe in 1897, where she remained for the next thirty years, the "confidant" of such notables as King Leopold II of Belgium, Lord Kitchener, and the Prince of Wales. After several unsuccessful financial adventures, including three marriages, she returned to the U.S. in 1927 and became the proprietress of several speakeasies and "salons," all of which were closed by federal agents who constantly harassed Livingstone for violation of prohibition laws. She served a month in jail in 1931; undaunted, she opened more night spots in New York City, Reno, Nev., and East Hampton, N.Y. All of them failed. Livingstone died in obscurity in New York, her headline-making abilities having faded with the repeal of Prohibition.

LIVINGSTONE, WILLIAM (*b. Dundas, Ontario, Canada, 1844; d. 1925*), Great Lakes shipowner and operator; Detroit, Mich., newspaper owner and banker.

LLEWELLYN, KARL NICKERSON (*b. West Seattle, Wash., 1893; d. Chicago, Ill., 1962*), legal philosopher and teacher. Attended University of Paris (1914) and Yale (LL.B., 1918; J.D., 1920). Began teaching career at Yale and became assistant professor in the Law School (1922); Betts professor of jurisprudence at Columbia (1930–51); University of Chicago Law School (1951–62). Represented New York State (1926–51) in the Conference of Commissioners on Uniform State Laws and was a life member; most important work in this area was the Uniform Commercial Code. One of his most popular books, *The Bramble Bush* (1930), introduced first-year law students to the challenge of the law. Wrote with E.A. Hoebel *The Cheyenne Way* (1941), an examination of where custom and tradition end and formal law begins.

LLOYD, ALFRED HENRY (*b. Montclair, N.J., 1864; d. 1927*), philosopher. Graduated Harvard, 1886; studied also in Germany. Taught at University of Michigan, 1891–1927; served also as dean of graduate school, *post* 1915. Author of *Dynamic Idealism* (1898), *Philosophy of History* (1899), and *The Will to Doubt* (1907), an answer to William James.

LLOYD, DAVID (*b. Manafon, Wales, ca. 1656; d. Chester, Pa., 1731 o.s.*), lawyer, Pennsylvania legislator. Commissioned by William Penn attorney general of Pennsylvania, 1686, he was soon appointed clerk of county and provincial courts and began in 1694 his long intermittent career as speaker of the Assembly. Removed from his position as attorney general, 1700, he became an enemy of Penn and of James Logan and was recognized leader of the antiproprietary party *post* 1703. He served as chief justice of Pennsylvania, 1717–31. Long regarded as a quarrelsome demagogue, he is today represented as a pioneer in the fight for democratic principles in America, because of his steady resistance to the efforts of the governors and council to control the judiciary and encroach upon the powers of the Assembly.

LLOYD, EDWARD (*b. Talbot Co., Md., 1744; d. 1796*), Maryland legislator, Revolutionary patriot.

LLOYD, EDWARD (*b. Talbot Co., Md., 1779; d. Annapolis, Md., 1834*), landowner, Maryland legislator. Son of Edward Lloyd (1744–1796). Congressman, (Democrat) Republican, from Maryland, 1806–09; governor of Maryland, 1809–11; U.S. senator, 1819–26.

LLOYD, HENRY DEMAREST (*b. New York, N.Y., 1847; d. 1903*), journalist, lawyer, opponent of monopoly. Author of the "Story of a Great Monopoly" (*Atlantic Monthly*, March 1881) and *Wealth against Commonwealth* (1894), he was the first and perhaps the best of the "muckrakers." Resident in Chicago, Ill., and its vicinity *post* 1873, he engaged in constant struggle for the rights of labor and made worldwide studies of social experiments. He formally joined the Socialist party in 1903.

LLOYD, JAMES (*b. Oyster Bay, N.Y., 1728; d. Boston, Mass., 1810*), pioneer obstetrician and surgeon. Apprenticed in medicine at Boston, Mass.; studied in London, England, with leading surgeons. On his return to Boston, 1752, he introduced new methods of surgery there and was the first physician to practice midwifery in America.

LLOYD, JOHN URI (*b. North Bloomfield, N.Y., 1849; d. Van Nuys, Calif., 1936*), pharmacist, plant chemist, drug manufacturer, novelist. Active proponent of Eclectic school of medicine. Author, among other works, of *Stringtown on the Pike* (1900).

LLOYD, MARSHALL BURNS (*b. St. Paul, Minn., 1858; d. Menominee, Mich., 1927*), inventor of machines for weaving wire and wicker.

LLOYD, THOMAS (*b. Dolobran, Wales, 1640 o.s.; d. Philadelphia, Pa., 1694 o.s.*), physician, politician. A Quaker, he immigrated to Philadelphia, 1683, and served as president of the provincial council, 1684–88, 1690–91. Appointed deputy governor of Pennsylvania, 1691, he was superseded, 1693. An opponent of usurpation of power by the executive branch of the government, he was the ablest and most popular political leader of his time in Pennsylvania.

LOCHMAN, JOHN GEORGE (*b. Philadelphia, Pa., 1773; d. Harrisburg, Pa., 1826*), Lutheran clergyman. Took leading part in organization of the General Synod at Frederick, Md., 1821, and was chosen its president.

LOCKE, ALAIN LEROY (*b. Philadelphia, Pa., 1886; d. New York, N.Y., 1954*), philosopher and educator. Studied at Harvard (Ph.D., 1918). The first black Rhodes scholar, he received a B. Litt., 1910, from Oxford. Professor of philosophy at Howard University (1912–53); chairman of the department, 1918. A figure in the Harlem Renaissance of the 1920's, Locke edited many literary collections and wrote *Negro Art: Past and Present* (1936) and *The Negro in Art* (1940). He treated African music, as well as the music of American blacks and world folk music, in *The Negro and His Music* (1936). He was the first black president of the American Association for Adult Education, 1945; in 1950, he was a guest professor of philosophy at the Harvard Academic Festival in Salzburg, Austria.

LOCKE, BESSIE (*b.* West Cambridge, Mass., 1865; *d.* New York, N.Y., 1952), educator and association director. Studied for a time at Columbia. Pioneer in kindergarten education in the U.S., Locke helped open more than 3,260 kindergartens in the country. She was organizer, director, and executive director of the National Kindergarten Association from 1911 until her death. Chief of the division of kindergartens of the U.S. Bureau of Education (1913–19). Director of the National Council of Women (1921–46).

LOCKE, DAVID ROSS (*b.* Vestal, N.Y., 1833; *d.* Toledo, Ohio, 1888), journalist, political satirist. Pseudonym, "Petroleum V. Nasby." His attacks on Copperheads and Democrats, *post* March 1861, were admired by Abraham Lincoln. Numerous collections of his satirical letters appeared in book form, beginning with *The Nasby Papers* (1864). Marked by humor, aggressive malice, and merciless insistence on a few points, "Nasby's" satires have not survived their own day. For many years, Locke was editor of the *Toledo Blade*, in which he owned a controlling interest.

LOCKE, JOHN (*b.* Lempster, N.H., 1792; *d.* Cincinnati, Ohio, 1856), physician, scientist, inventor. M.D., Yale, 1819. Settling in Cincinnati, Ohio, *ca.* 1822, he conducted a girls' school there until 1835 and was professor of chemistry, Medical College of Ohio, 1835–53. During this time Locke was also employed in geological surveying for Ohio and for the federal government. He was inventor of a number of instruments, notably his so-called electromagnetic chronograph (1844–48), a device which completely changed the art of determining longitudes.

LOCKE, MATTHEW (*b.* 1730; *d. near* Salisbury, N.C., 1801), Revolutionary patriot, North Carolina legislator. Congressman, radical Jeffersonian Republican, from North Carolina, 1793–99.

LOCKE, RICHARD ADAMS (*b.* East Brent, England, 1800; *d.* Staten Island, N.Y., 1871), journalist. Immigrated to New York City, 1832. As a writer for the New York *Sun*, he was author of the celebrated "Moon Hoax" (August 1835).

LOCKHART, CHARLES (*b.* Cairn Heads, Scotland, 1818; *d.* 1905), pioneer oil producer. Came to America, 1836. A successful oil producer *post* 1853, he leased land in Oil Creek soon after the discovery at Titusville, Pa., 1859, and built up a large export trade. With an associate, he built the Brilliant Refinery (first important refinery erected) and also the Atlantic Refinery in Philadelphia. He was an early partner in Standard Oil.

LOCKHEED, ALLAN HAINES (*b.* Niles, Calif., 1889; *d.* Tucson, Ariz., 1969), airplane manufacturer. With his brother Malcolm and John K. Northrop, built the Model G seaplane, F-1 flying boat, and S-1 high-wing plane. Founded Lockheed Aircraft with Northrop (1920) and built the Vega; company was sold in 1920. Remained associated with aviation as a consultant through World War II.

LOCKHEED, MALCOLM (*b.* Niles, Calif., 1887[?]; *d.* Mokelumne Hill, Calif., 1958), aircraft manufacturer and inventor. Founded the Loughead Aircraft Mfg. Co. in 1916; experimented with the Model F-1 until 1919. The company was the precursor of the Lockheed company, founded in 1934. Lockheed left the company in 1919 and lived the life of a recluse until his death.

LOCKREY, SARAH HUNT (*b.* Philadelphia, Pa., 1863; *d.* 1929), surgeon, worker for woman suffrage.

LOCKWOOD, BELVA ANN BENNETT (*b.* Royalton, N.Y., 1830; *d.* 1917), teacher, lawyer, suffragist. Admitted to the Washington, D.C., bar, 1873, she was first woman admitted to practice before U.S. Supreme Court, 1879. As nominee of the National Equal Rights party, 1884 and 1888, she was the first woman candidate for the presidency of the United States.

LOCKWOOD, JAMES BOOTH (*b.* Annapolis, Md., 1852; *d.* Cape Sabine, E. Ellesmere Island, Canada, 1884), army officer, Arctic explorer. Commissioned second lieutenant, U.S. Army, 1873; served at various posts in the West. Volunteered, 1881, for duty with Greely Expedition, on which he distinguished himself in the explorations and in particular during the winter of starvation at Cape Sabine.

LOCKWOOD, RALPH INGERSOLL (*b.* Greenwich, Conn., 1798; *d.* New York, N.Y., 1858[?]), lawyer, expert in equity practice. Author of several works on law and of two novels: *Rosine Laval* (1833), and *The Insurgents* (1835) which deals with Shays's Rebellion.

LOCKWOOD, ROBERT WILTON (*b.* Wilton, Conn., 1861; *d.* 1914), portrait and flower painter. Studied with John La Farge and at Art Students League, N.Y.; studied also in Paris and Munich. Worked in Boston, Mass., *post* 1896.

LOCKWOOD, SAMUEL DRAKE (*b.* Poundridge, N.Y., 1789; *d.* Batavia, Ill., 1874), jurist. Removed to Illinois, 1818; held various state offices, 1821–24. Justice, Illinois supreme court, 1825–48. A man of great reputation in his state, Lockwood was a principal contributor to the revision of the Illinois statutes, 1826–29.

LOCKWOOD, WILTON. *See* LOCKWOOD, ROBERT WILTON.

LOCY, WILLIAM ALBERT (*b.* Troy, Mich., 1857; *d.* 1924), zoologist. Taught at Northwestern University *post* 1896. Author of numerous important scientific papers, he wrote three studies in the historical development of biology: *Biology and Its Makers* (1908), *The Main Currents of Zoology* (1918) and *Growth of Biology* (1925).

LODGE, GEORGE CABOT (*b.* Boston, Mass., 1873; *d.* 1909), poet. Son of Henry Cabot Lodge. Published, among other books, *The Song of the Wave* (1898), *Cain, a Drama* (1904), *Herakles* (1908). His collected *Poems and Dramas* were published, 1911, in which year appeared a biography of him by Henry Adams.

LODGE, HENRY CABOT (*b.* Boston, Mass., 1850; *d.* Cambridge, Mass., 1924), lawyer, politician, author. Great-grandson of George Cabot. Graduated Harvard, 1871; Harvard Law School, 1874. At invitation of Henry Adams, worked as assistant editor, *North American Review*, 1873–76. Received first degree of Ph.D. granted by Harvard in political science, 1876. Author of *Life and Letters of George Cabot* (1877), *Alexander Hamilton* (1882), *Daniel Webster* (1882), and *George Washington* (1888). Although he continued to write, his works were marred by increasing partisanship.

After service as a Republican in the Massachusetts legislature and a failure to secure nomination for Congress, 1882, he managed the 1883 Republican gubernatorial campaign in Massachusetts with political adroitness of a high order. Delegate to the Republican National Convention, 1884, he worked with Theodore Roosevelt to prevent choice of James G. Blaine, but put aside his principles to support the national ticket in the campaign. Elected to Congress, 1886, he spoke often and effectively and became notable in the House of Representatives before his first term was finished. Serving in the House until 1893, he outraged practical politicians by championing civil service reform. Chosen U.S. senator, January 1893, by the Massachusetts legislature, his hold on the post was never thereafter seriously in doubt until his death, with the exception of 1911 at the time of the Progressive upheaval. Lodge helped draft the Sherman Anti-Trust Law, 1890, the Pure Food and Drugs Law, and several tariff measures—in particular the tariff of 1909. He was a thoroughgoing protectionist and an opponent of free silver. He viewed all proposals for compulsory international arbitration or disarmament with suspicion, supported the taking of the Philippines, and assisted Roosevelt's successful intrigue in Panama. He voted against the direct election of senators, opposed womans' suffrage, and voted against adoption of the Eighteenth Amendment.

Lodge's judgment on international affairs was highly valued by Theodore Roosevelt. Early finding a place on the Foreign Relations Committee, he did not become chairman until late in his career, when his leadership in the fight against ratification of the Peace Treaty and Covenant, 1919, made him a national figure. He was convinced that his opposition to the coupling of the treaty of peace with a guarantee of United States participation in the proposed League of Nations (which in principle he approved) represented majority American opinion and that President Wilson was opposing the popular will. His part in effecting the rejection of the League gained for him at the time both admiration and bitter resentment. Lodge was one of those who were chiefly responsible for the nomination of Warren G. Harding. An excellent practical politician, he was not always scrupulous in his choice of means provided they served his end; he was rarely receptive to reform proposals of any sort and was ruthlessly vindictive toward those whom he opposed or disliked.

LODGE, JOHN ELLERTON (*b. Nahant, Mass., 1876; d. Washington, D.C., 1942*), art museum director, orientalist. Son of Henry Cabot Lodge; brother of George Cabot Lodge. On staff of Boston Museum of Fine Arts, 1911–31, he was curator of Chinese and Japanese art *post* 1916. He was also director of the Freer Gallery of Art in Washington, D.C., 1921–42, building up its collections of Chinese, Indian, and Near Eastern art objects, and forming it into a valuable research center.

LOEB, JACQUES (*b. Mayen, Germany, 1859; d. Bermuda, 1924*), physiologist. Came to America, 1891. Taught at Bryn Mawr and University of Chicago; accepted a call to University of California, 1902; was a member of Rockefeller Institute for Medical Research, 1910–24. Author of the "tropism" theory of behavior. Made pioneer experiments in artificial fertilization.

LOEB, JAMES (*b. New York, N.Y., 1867; d. Murnau, Bavaria, Germany, 1933*), banker, philanthropist. Graduated Harvard, 1888. After working in family banking firm of Kuhn, Loeb & Co., 1888–1901, he devoted himself to artistic pursuits and numerous philanthropies; *post* 1905, he resided abroad. His outstanding contribution to humanistic studies was the Loeb Classical Library, founded in 1910, which provided competently edited texts and translations of Greek and Latin literature in convenient pocket size.

LOEB, LEO (*b. Mayen, Germany, 1869; d. St. Louis, Mo., 1959*), pathologist and experimental biologist. Studied at the University of Freiburg, the University of Edinburgh, and the University of Zurich (M.D., 1897). Immigrated to the U.S. in the 1890's. Taught at the University of Pennsylvania from 1904 to 1910; director of the pathological laboratory of the Barnard Skin and Cancer Hospital in St. Louis (1915–24); and taught at George Washington University (1924–37). One of the founders of experimental pathology and of cancer research in America. Loeb was one of the earliest experimenters to make successful serial transfers

of tumors from animal to animal. Published *The Biological Basis of Individuality* in 1945, in which he applied his wide knowledge of animal organs and tissues to the problem of individual differences in structure and behavior in man and the higher animals.

LOEB, LOUIS (*b. Cleveland, Ohio, 1866; d. Canterbury, N.H., 1909*), painter. Studied at Art Students League, N.Y., and in Paris under J. L. Gérôme. Illustrated with rare taste and skill works by Mark Twain and F. Marion Crawford.

LOEB, MORRIS (*b. Cincinnati, Ohio, 1863; d. New York, N.Y., 1912*), chemist. Graduated Harvard, 1882; Ph.D., Berlin, 1887; studied the new field of physical chemistry at Heidelberg and Leipzig. An American pioneer in physical chemistry, he taught at Clark University and New York University *post* 1890 and was author of a number of papers, notably on molecular weights. He was a benefactor of Harvard.

LOEB, SOPHIE IRENE SIMON (*b. Rovno, Russia, 1876; d. New York, N.Y., 1929*), social worker, journalist. Came to America as a child; was raised in McKeesport, Pa. As reporter and unselfish lobbyist, she secured more constructive welfare legislation than any other woman in America of her time.

LOEFFLER, CHARLES MARTIN (*b. Mülhausen, Alsace, 1861; d. Medfield, Mass., 1935*), violinist, composer. Came to America, 1881, bearing a letter of introduction from his teacher, Joseph Joachim, to Leopold Damrosch, who employed him in his concerts. Associated with the Boston Symphony Orchestra, 1882, Loeffler devoted his major attention to it until he retired to teach and compose, 1903. Although his musical idiom was so Gallic in spirit that it can hardly be considered American in character, it represented something rare at a time when the best American composers excepting MacDowell were largely academic. Loeffler was an independent thinker, an artistic hermit; his sparkling and colorful scores were polished to a refinement which approached perfection. Among his numerous works are *Pagan Poem* (first composed, 1901, but taking its final form, 1907) and *Hora Mystica* (1916.

LOESSER, FRANK (*b. New York, N.Y., 1910; d. New York, 1969*), composer and lyricist. His reputation as a lyricist for motion pictures grew quickly, beginning in 1936; among dozens of songs, he wrote "Two Sleepy People" and "Heart and Soul" (with Hoagy Carmichael). "Praise the Lord and Pass the Ammunition" was one of the most popular songs of World War II. After the war, began writing words to his own music, including the Academy Award-winning "Baby, It's Cold Outside" (1940). Wrote his first Broadway musical in 1948, and *Guys and Dolls* (1950) is recognized as one of the greatest. Other musicals include *The Most Happy Fella* (1956) and *How to Succeed in Business Without Really Trying* (1961), which won a Pulitzer Prize.

LOEW, MARCUS (*b. New York, N.Y., 1870; d. Glen Cove, N.Y., 1927*), theater owner, motion-picture pioneer.

LOEWENTHAL, ISIDOR (*b. Posen, Prussia, ca. 1827; d. Peshawar, India, 1864*), Presbyterian missionary. Came to America, 1846, as a political refugee. Graduated Lafayette, 1848; Princeton Theological Seminary, 1851. Worked in India *post* 1855.

LOEWI, OTTO (*b. Frankfurt am Main, Germany, 1873; d. New York, N.Y., 1961*), neurobiologist and neuropharmacologist. Attended University of Strassburg (M.D., 1896). Worked at University of Marburg (1898–1905), where his work on amino acids and nutrition established his reputation. Accepted the chair of pharmacology (1909) in Graz, Austria; his work on the study of acetycholine and chemical transmission across synapses led to the Nobel Prize in Physiology or Medicine (1936). Arrested by Nazis (1938), he traded his property and Nobel Prize for permission to leave Germany; arrived in the United States in 1940 and became a professor at New York University School of Medicine.

LOGAN, BENJAMIN (*b. Augusta Co., Va.*, ca. *1743; d. Shelby Co., Ky., 1802*), Kentucky pioneer, Indian fighter. Joined with other frontiersmen in settlement of Transylvania colony, 1775; was a leader in retaliatory expeditions against Ohio Indians, 1778, 1780, 1782. Throughout the Revolution the most influential and trusted of Kentucky leaders, he failed to hold his position after the peace and occupied a minor place in public life.

LOGAN, CORNELIUS AMBROSE (*b. Deerfield, Mass., 1832; d. Los Angeles, Calif., 1899*), physician, Union army surgeon, politician. Son of Cornelius Ambrosius Logan; cousin of John A. Logan. Removed to Kansas, 1857. As first president, Kansas State Medical Society, he worked *post* 1867 to raise standards of the profession and quality of medical instruction in the state. U.S. minister to Chile, 1873–77 and 1882–85, he served also as minister resident to Central American states, 1879–82.

LOGAN, CORNELIUS AMBROSIUS (*b. probably Baltimore, Md., 1806; d. near Marietta, Ohio, 1853*), actor, dramatist, manager.

LOGAN, DEBORAH NORRIS (*b. 1761; d. "Stenton," near Germantown, Pa., 1839*), historian. Granddaughter of Isaac Norris; wife of George Logan. Preserved, deciphered, copied, and annotated Logan family papers at "Stenton"; these were later published by Historical Society of Pennsylvania.

LOGAN, GEORGE (*b. "Stenton," near Germantown, Pa., 1753; d. "Stenton," 1821*), physician, Pennsylvania legislator. Grandson of James Logan (1674–1751). M.D., University of Edinburgh, 1779; studied also in Paris where he enjoyed close friendship with Benjamin Franklin. On return to Philadelphia, 1780, he applied himself to study of improved methods of farming and was a founder of Philadelphia Society for Promotion of Agriculture. He served in Pennsylvania legislature as a friend and follower of Thomas Jefferson. A strict Quaker and a friend to peace, he attempted, at his own expense and on his own authority, to bring about better understanding with France, 1798. This mission was the object of much hostile criticism; in consequence of it, on Jan. 30, 1799, Congress passed the so-called "Logan Act" forbidding private citizens to undertake diplomatic negotiations without official sanction. He served as U.S. senator, (Democrat) Republican, from Pennsylvania, 1801–07.

LOGAN, JAMES (*b. Lurgan, Ireland, 1674; d. near Germantown, Pa., 1751*), colonial statesman, scholar. Became William Penn's secretary, 1699; was his confidential adviser and the counselor of his descendants for more than fifty years. Immigrating to Pennsylvania, 1699, he served as secretary of the Province and clerk of the Provincial Council, 1701–17. Supervisor of the Penn family interests in Pennsylvania, Logan was a voting member of the Council, 1702–47; he became in time its senior member and president. Among numerous executive and judicial posts which he held was that of chief justice of the Supreme Court, 1731–39. He amassed a fortune in land investment and in trade with the Indians. Subsequent to his retirement from the Council, he lived at the estate which he had established at "Stenton," near Germantown. Botany was his special field of interest in science; he was a friend of John Bartram and his botanical investigations were recognized by Linnaeus. He published two works of scholarship: *Cato's Moral Distiches, Englished* (1735) and *M.T. Cicero's Cato Major* (1744), the latter

of which is considered the finest specimen of printing from Franklin's press.

LOGAN, JAMES (*b. probably Shamokin, now Sunbury, Pa., ca. 1725; d. 1780*), Mingo orator. Son of Shikellamy. Early a friendly collaborator of the whites, Logan turned against his former friends after the Yellow Creek massacre, April 1774, in which members of his family were killed. More successful in his retaliatory raids against the settlements than were Cornstalk and his warriors, Logan refused to become reconciled after the battle of Point Pleasant, November 1774. During the Revolution he was active on behalf of the British at Detroit. He became famous through Jefferson's use (in *Notes, on the State of Virginia*, edition of 1800) of an alleged reply which he made to John Gibson and from extensive newspaper quotation of the speech prior to this publication.

LOGAN, JAMES HARVEY (*b. near Rockville, Ind., 1841; d. Oakland, Calif., 1928*), California jurist, horticulturist. Developed the loganberry ca. 1881.

LOGAN, JOHN ALEXANDER (*b. Jackson Co., Ill., 1826; d. Washington, D.C., 1886*), lawyer, Union soldier, politician. Congressman, Democrat, from Illinois, 1859–61. Entering the Civil War as colonel, 31st Illinois, he was made brigadier general after Fort Donelson and major general after Vicksburg, and succeeded to command of the Army of the Tennessee, 1864. Relieved of this command on recommendation of General W. T. Sherman because of what Sherman termed his active political interests and his contempt for logistics, Logan, after discharge from the army, 1865, returned to political life, serving as congressman, Republican, from Illinois, 1867–71, and as U.S. senator, 1871–77 and 1879–86. He ran as Republican candidate for the vice-presidency, 1884. A regulation stalwart Republican, he associated himself with all matters of veteran relief; the idea of Memorial Day was conceived by him and he inaugurated it, May 30, 1868.

LOGAN, OLIVE (*b. Elmira, N.Y., 1839; d. Banstead, England, 1909*), actress, lecturer, journalist. Daughter of Cornelius Ambrosius Logan; sister of Cornelius Ambrose Logan.

LOGAN, STEPHEN TRIGG (*b. Franklin Co., Ky., 1800; d. Springfield, Ill., 1880*), jurist, Illinois legislator. Grand-nephew of Benjamin Logan. Removed to Springfield, Ill., ca. 1833; was law partner of Abraham Lincoln, 1841–44.

LOGAN, THOMAS MULDRUP (*b. Charleston, S.C., 1808; d. Sacramento, Calif., 1876*), sanitarian, climatologist. M.D., Medical College of South Carolina, 1828. Practiced in Charleston and in New Orleans, La., before removing to Sacramento, Calif., 1850. Active in public health work, he made complete studies of the epidemiology of California.

LOGAN, THOMAS MULDRUP (*b. Charleston, S.C., 1840; d. New York, N.Y., 1914*), Confederate brigadier general, lawyer, capitalist. Nephew of Thomas M. Logan (1808–1876). *Post* 1878, organized and managed a railway system in the South which adopted its present name, the Southern Railway, 1894. Worked for many years on development and promotion of the telautograph.

LOGUEN, JERMAIN WESLEY (*b. Davidson Co., Tenn., ca. 1813; d. Saratoga Springs, N.Y., 1872*), black leader. Escaped from slavery, ca. 1835, to Canada where he began his education. Settling in Syracuse, N.Y., ca. 1840, he became one of the local managers of the Underground Railroad; he was an associate of Gerrit Smith and John Brown. Loguen held several pastorates in the African Methodist Episcopal Zion Church and was elected a bishop, 1868.

LOMAX, JOHN AVERY (*b. Goodman, Miss., 1867; d. Greenville, Miss., 1948*), teacher, bond salesman and dealer, collector of American folk songs. Raised near Meridian, Texas. B.A., University of Texas, 1897; M.A., 1906. M.A., Harvard, 1907. Interested since boyhood in the songs and folklore of the people among whom he was raised, he was encouraged by Barrett Wendell and G. L. Kittredge at Harvard to make formal study of them. His travels up and down the country with notebook and recording machine (*post* 1932 with the support of the Library of Congress and the American Council of Learned Societies) resulted in his collection of thousands of songs which established a new dimension in American literature and music. Among his books were *Cowboy Songs and Other Frontier Ballads* (1910); *American Ballads and Folk Songs* (1934); *Negro Folk Songs as Sung by Lead Belly* (1936); and *Our Singing Country* (1941).

LOMAX, JOHN TAYLOE (*b. Caroline Co., Va., 1781; d. Fredericksburg, Va., 1862*), Virginia jurist. First professor of law at University of Virginia, 1826–30; later a judge of the state circuit court.

LOMAX, LOUIS EMANUEL (*b. Valdosta, Ga., 1922; d. Santa Rosa, N.Mex., 1970*), journalist and author. Attended Paine College (B.A., 1942), American University (M.A., 1944), Yale (M.A., 1947). Reporter on the *Afro-American* (1942); feature writer for the *Chicago American* (1947–58). First black television newsman (1958); hosted the television program "Louis Lomax" (1967). Syndicated columnist for North American Newspaper Alliance in the 1960's. His books on black history include *The Reluctant African* (1960) and *To Kill a Black Man* (1968). Used television and other media to arouse northern white interest in Jim Crow laws and in segregationist policies of the South and North.

LOMAX, LUNSFORD LINDSAY (*b. Newport, R.I., 1835; d. Washington, D.C., 1913*), Confederate major general. Graduated West Point, 1856. After hard and effective Civil War service, he was a farmer near Warrenton, Va., 1865–85, and president of Virginia Agricultural and Mechanical College, 1885–99. He worked on the compilation of official records of the Union and Confederate Armies (published as *War of the Rebellion* by the War Department), 1899–1905.

LOMBARD, CAROLE (*b. Fort Wayne, Ind., 1908; d. in plane crash near Las Vegas, Nev., 1942*), film actress. Stage name of Jane Alice Peters. Attended high school and drama school in Los Angeles, Calif., given first lead in *Hearts and Spurs* (a Buck Jones Western), 1925; developed comic skills in Mack Sennett two-reel films, 1927–28. She displayed her full talent in *Twentieth Century* (1934); thereafter, in *My Man Godfrey* (1936), *True Confession* and *Nothing Sacred* (both 1937), she reached the peak of her career as a comedienne. Married to actor William Powell, 1931–33, she married Clark Gable in 1939. Accepting fewer film roles after her second marriage, she remained popular with audiences and proved her versatility by a noncomic appearance in *They Knew What They Wanted* (1940). At the outbreak of World War II she was one of the first Hollywood stars to contribute to the war effort and made several cross-country trips selling war bonds.

LOMBARD, WARREN PLIMPTON (*b. West Newton, Mass., 1855; d. Ann Arbor, Mich., 1939*), physiologist. Graduated Harvard, 1878; M.D., Harvard, 1881. Taught at Columbia and Clark universities, and at University of Michigan, 1892–1923. Made important studies of the knee jerk, of fatigue, blood pressure, and metabolism; devised special apparatus for delicate measurements.

LOMBARDI, VINCENT THOMAS (*b. Brooklyn, N.Y., 1913; d. Washington, D.C., 1970*), professional football coach. Attended Fordham University (B.S., 1937), where he later coached, 1947–49. Coached at U.S. Military Academy, 1949–54; was offensive coach of the New York Giants professional team, 1954–59. Became head coach and manager of the Green Bay Packers (1959), and rebuilt the team by disciplining and motivating players; the team won the NFL championship in 1961 and 1962 and the first two Super Bowls, in 1967 and 1968. Head coach and executive president of Washington Redskins (1969). Elected to NFL Hall of Fame (1971).

LONDON, JACK (*b. San Francisco, Calif., 1876; d. Sonoma Co., Calif., 1916*), writer, novelist. Spent his youth in acute poverty; read voraciously in public library but had major part of his education along the Oakland waterfront. Worked successively, when he did work, as seaman aboard a sealing vessel, as a jute mill hand, and as a janitor; was for a while a hobo, at which time he roamed over eastern part of the United States. Returning to Oakland, he attended high school, became a Socialist, spent a brief time at University of California, Berkeley. During 1897–98, he joined the gold rush to the Klondike. On his return, unable to get a job of any sort, he worked furiously at writing and was successful in selling a story of the Yukon to the *Overland Monthly*, December 1898. During the next year he published eight stories in the magazine. Acceptance by the *Atlantic Monthly* of "An Odyssey of the North" in July 1899 and publication of his volume of collected stories, *The Son of the Wolf* (1900), convinced London that he now had his vocation. Between 1899 and 1903 he wrote extensively and successfully for periodicals. He also published eight volumes, five of which dealt with the Klondike. In Europe briefly, 1902, he was engaged January–June, 1904 as a correspondent in the Russo-Japanese War. Thereafter, except for a long cruise in the South Seas, California was his home and his ranch his chief interest. His vast output of some fifty books contains, besides fiction, volumes of Socialist propaganda and miscellaneous essays. Several of his books are autobiographical: *The Road* (1907), *Martin Eden* (1909), and *John Barleycorn* (1913). The best of his fiction is for the most part taken direct from firsthand experience, either in the Far North or at sea. Almost all his writing, masterful in swift and vivid depiction of action, deals with the primitive and reversion to savagery. His insistence is constant upon the importance of brute force. *The Call of the Wild* (1903), *The Sea Wolf* (1904), *White Fang* (1906), together with the works already cited, are representative of London's work.

LONDON, MEYER (*b. Suwalki Province, Russian Poland, 1871; d. New York, N.Y., 1926*), Socialist, labor leader. Immigrated to New York City, 1891. Admitted to the bar, 1898. Opposing Socialist leadership of Daniel DeLeon, London became one of the founders of the Socialist Party of America. His activity as legal counsel and adviser to unions in the "needle trades" made his influence felt in the entire labor movement. Congressman, Socialist, from New York, 1915–19 and 1921–23, he advocated numerous useful reforms, but was consistent with his principles in voting against the declaration of war, 1917, and the conscription laws. An enemy to communism in theory and practice, he vigorously denounced the allied policy towards Russia immediately after the Russian Revolution on grounds that it had rallied the Russian people to support of the Bolshevists.

LONESOME CHARLEY. *See* REYNOLDS, CHARLES ALEXANDER.

LONG, ARMISTEAD LINDSAY (*b. Campbell Co., Va.., 1825; d. Charlottesville, Va., 1891*), Confederate brigadier general. Graduated West Point, 1850. Served as military secretary to General Robert E. Lee, 1861–63, and as brigadier general, commanding artillery, 1863–65. Author of *Memoirs of Robert E. Lee* (1886), a valuable source book.

LONG, BRECKINRIDGE (b. *St. Louis, Mo., 1881; d. Laurel, Md., 1958*), diplomat. Studied at Princeton University and at Washington University Law School. Active in Missouri and national Democratic politics, Long was appointed third assistant secretary of state (1917–20), supervising the Bureau of Accounts and the Far East. Twice a candidate for the U.S. Senate from Missouri (1920 and 1922), Long never attained elected political office. A strong backer of Franklin Roosevelt, he was appointed ambassador extraordinary and minister plenipotentiary to Italy in 1933, serving until 1936. At first an admirer of Mussolini, he later became an ardent critic of fascism and predicted accurately the coming war in Europe. In 1940, he returned to the State Department as a special assistant to handle emergency war matters, especially the Visa Section dealing with immigrants. He was opposed to open immigration of Jews from Europe. Long retired in 1944.

LONG, CHARLES CHAILLÉ. *See* CHAILLÉ-LONG, CHARLES.

LONG, CRAWFORD WILLIAMSON (b. *Danielsville, Ga., 1815; d. Athens, Ga., 1878*), surgeon, pioneer anaesthetist. Graduated Franklin College (University of Georgia), 1835; M.D., University of Pennsylvania, 1839. Practiced *post* 1841 in rural Georgia, removing in 1850 to Athens, Ga. Performed eight operations with the help of sulphuric ether *ante* September 1846, the earliest in 1842. He did not publish his experience with ether, however, until December 1849, when a controversy had already arisen over the claims of W. T. G. Morton to priority in anaesthesia.

LONG, EARL KEMP (b. *Winnfield, La., 1895; d. Alexandria, La., 1960*), politician. Studied briefly at Loyola University Law School. The brother of politician and Louisiana governor, Huey Long, Earl Long was a salesman from 1912 to 1927. During the early thirties, he assisted his brother in legal and political matters. Elected lieutenant governor in 1936 after his brother's assassination; appointed governor in 1940. Elected in three terms as governor from 1948. A populist, Long initiated many programs to aid the poor of his state. Ultimately political tensions generated by racial struggle broke Long's health, and his behavior became erratic and eccentric. Elected to Congress in 1960, one week before his death.

LONG, HUEY PIERCE (b. *near Winnfield, La., 1893; d. Baton Rouge, La., 1935*), politician. Son of a landowning farmer, Long came from a culturally meager background, which was most strongly marked by Baptist evangelicalism and a Populistic animosity toward the wealthy. In his early career as a traveling salesman, he acquired canvassing experience which was later to be a political advantage. After eight months of study at Tulane University Law School, he passed a special bar examination, May 1915, and began practice at Winnfield. Elected railroad commissioner, 1918, he was reelected, 1924, and served as chairman of the Louisiana commission now known as the Public Service Commission, 1921–26. In this post he performed highly creditable services in control of utilities and attracted widespread attention by furious attacks upon the Standard Oil Co.

Defeated for governorship in 1924, Long renewed his candidacy in 1928, and became governor in May of that year. As governor, he aroused violent opposition. Charges of improper influence upon legislators through patronage and the use of state funds for personal expenditures brought about his impeachment at a special session of the legislature, 1929. He escaped conviction on a technicality, meanwhile claiming that he was being persecuted by Standard Oil. Between 1930 and 1934 Long ruled Louisiana by an alliance with the old regular Democrats. Retaining the governorship after his 1930 election as U.S. senator, in order to prevent succession of a hostile lieutenant governor, he expanded his highway program, began construction of a $5,000,000 capitol and sponsored the growth of Louisiana State University. He entered the U.S. Senate, January 1932. Appearing to many Americans primarily a country clown who carried out his nickname "Kingfish," Long brought with him a serious program for the redistribution of wealth; when the Senate rejected drastic tax proposals, he resigned his committee posts in rebellion against the Democratic leader, Joseph T. Robinson. Pres. F. D. Roosevelt's refusal to support Long's proposed redistribution of wealth or to satisfy his expectations of patronage caused Long loudly to denounce Roosevelt by August 1933, although he had campaigned for him a year earlier.

By January 1934, in disfavor with the federal administration and having lost the support of the old regular Democratic machine in Louisiana, Long brought about a reorganization of the Louisiana legislature whereby he created the most complete absolutism that has ever existed in a state of the United States. Local government was abolished, and Long was given control of the appointment of every employee in the state, of the militia, the judiciary, the election officials, and the tax-assessing bodies. To his decrees there was no redress, either electoral or legal. In January 1934 he organized a Share-Our-Wealth Society, which promised homestead allowances and minimum annual income for every American family. This economically fallacious scheme he used as a goad for the administration in Washington, declaring in 1935 that he would bolt the party if Roosevelt were renominated and announcing his own candidacy in August of that year. On a visit to the Louisiana state capitol in the fall for a special session of his legislature, despite the constant protection of bodyguards, he was shot by Dr. Carl A. Weiss on the night of Sept, 8 and died two days later.

Ruthless, violent, and unprincipled, Long was possibly emotionally sincere in championing the cause of the underdog. Flagrantly corrupt, his campaign for the improvement of Louisiana was administered with relative efficiency. His rise was aided by the ineffectuality of his opponents who might have been more polite but were certainly not more ethical than he. He found his opportunity as spokesman of a long-standing agrarian discontent that flared up in the ill wind of the great depression.

LONG, JAMES (b. *North Carolina*[?], ca. 1793; d. *Mexico, 1822*), military adventurer. Attempted to open Texas to American settlement, 1819. Proclaimed a republic at Nacogdoches with himself as president and commander in chief, June 23. After a period of military alliance with Mexican revolutionary leaders, he was killed while on a visit of negotiation to Mexico City.

LONG, JOHN DAVIS (b. *Buckfield, Maine, 1838; d. Hingham, Mass., 1915*), lawyer, Massachusetts legislator. Republican governor of Massachusetts, 1880–82; congressman, 1883–89. Appointed secretary of the navy, 1897, he served until 1902 with tact and ability; here as in his governorship he showed himself an efficient if unspectacular administrator.

LONG, JOHN HARPER (b. *near Steubenville, Ohio, 1856; d. 1918*), chemist. Graduated University of Kansas, 1877; studied chemistry in Germany, receiving D.Sc., 1879, from Tübingen. Professor of chemistry, Northwestern University, *post* 1881. Did extensive work on treatment of sewage and on the influence on health of alum, sodium benzoate, and other adulterants. This latter work was of great benefit in administration of the later Food and Drugs Act. He was author of many textbooks and research papers.

LONG, JOHN LUTHER (b. *Hanover, Pa., 1861; d. Philadelphia, Pa., 1927*), writer, dramatist. His short story "Madame Butterfly" (*Century Magazine*, January 1898) was basis for David Belasco's dramatization (produced, March 1900) and for the libretto of Puccini's opera.

LONG, JOSEPH RAGLAND (*b. Charlottesville, Va., 1870; d. Boulder, Colo., 1932*), lawyer, legal writer. Professor of law, Washington and Lee University, 1902–23; University of Colorado, 1923–32.

LONG, PERRIN HAMILTON (*b. Bryan, Ohio, 1899; d. Chappaquiddick Island, Mass., 1965*), physician. Attended University of Michigan (M.D., 1924). Began medical career in Boston, 1925–27, then joined the staff of Rockefeller Institute and began work in the field of infectious diseases. Joined the faculty of Johns Hopkins Medical School (1929), where he began pioneering studies with Eleanor Bliss on sulfonamide drugs in managing bacterial infections. Government consultant at Pearl Harbor (1941) to advise on care of casualties; received awards from the U.S., French, and British governments for work during the war. Returned to Johns Hopkins. Chairman of Department of Medicine of Downstate Medical Center, 1951–61.

LONG, STEPHEN HARRIMAN (*b. Hopkinton, N.H., 1784; d. Alton, Ill., 1864*), explorer, engineer. Graduated Dartmouth, 1809. Entered army as second lieutenant of engineers, 1814, and continued with the topographical engineers throughout remainder of his life, becoming chief of the corps and colonel, 1861. Commanding an expedition to the Rocky Mountains, 1820, he discovered the peak which bears his name, journeyed south to neighborhood of Colorado Springs, headed east by way of the Arkansas and its tributaries. *Account of an Expedition from Pittsburgh to the Rocky Mountains* (1822–23) by Edwin James contains a vivid narrative of the journey. In 1823, Long examined the sources of the Minnesota River and the adjacent northern boundary of the United States, as described in *Narrative of an Expedition to the Source of the St. Peter's River, etc.* (1824) by W. H. Keating. Thereafter, Long worked as consulting engineer for various railroad enterprises; in association with Jonathan Knight, he selected the route for the Baltimore & Ohio.

LONGACRE, JAMES BARTON (*b. Delaware Co., Pa., 1794; d. Philadelphia, Pa., 1869*), line and stipple engraver. His chief work is found in the series of volumes entitled *The National Portrait Gallery of Distinguished Americans* (published 1834–39 in association with James Herring). He was chief engraver, U.S. Mint, *post* 1844.

LONGCOPE, WARFIELD THEOBALD (*b. Baltimore, Md., 1877; d. Lee, Mass., 1953*), physician and educator. M.D., Johns Hopkins University, 1901. From 1904 to 1911, director of the Ayer Clinical Lab., Pennsylvania Hospital. 1909–11, professor of clinical medicine at the University of Pennsylvania. From 1911 until his death, professor of medicine at Columbia; director of medical service at Presbyterian Hospital, 1914. Applied the results of research to the practice of medicine. His laboratory activities included studies in pathology, biochemistry, bacteriology, and serology. A pioneer in immunology, he was a founder of the American Academy of Allergy. He made important contributions to the knowledge of unusual types of pneumonia, the contraction of kidneys resulting from pyelonephritis, and Boeck's sarcoid.

LONGFELLOW, ERNEST WADSWORTH (*b. Cambridge, Mass., 1845; d. Boston, Mass., 1921*), painter. Son of Henry Wadsworth Longfellow.

LONGFELLOW, HENRY WADSWORTH (*b. Portland, Maine, 1807; d. Cambridge, Mass., 1882*), poet. Son of Stephen Longfellow; grandson of Peleg Wadsworth. Published verses as early as his 13th year. Graduated Bowdoin, 1825. Offered professorship of modern languages at Bowdoin on condition he study abroad, he spent years 1826–29 in France, Spain, Italy, and Germany. While professor at Bowdoin, 1829–35, he prepared textbooks and contributed essays and sketches to magazines. He married Mary S. Potter, September 1831; she died four years later. Having accepted professorship of modern languages and belles lettres at Harvard, 1835, Longfellow went abroad and made extensive study of German literature before returning home, 1836. Taking up residence in the Craigie House, Cambridge, he worked hard at his teaching but went much into society, an immaculate jaunty figure. Among his friends were Cornelius C. Felton, Charles Sumner, George S. Hillard; *post* 1837, his relations with Nathaniel Hawthorne were increasingly friendly. Published *Hyperion*, a semi-autobiographical romance, 1839; also, *Voices of the Night*, his first book of verse, in the same year.

In July 1843 he married Frances Elizabeth Appleton, daughter of a Boston merchant. For a number of years thereafter his outward life flowed on pleasantly and placidly; he resigned his professorship, 1854, giving his whole time to study and work in poetry. The tragic death of his wife, July 1861, left the care and upbringing of their six children to him. His grief over his loss persisted for many years, during which he continued to work and to achieve an international reputation which few poets have won. The gentleness and sweetness of Longfellow's character have always received due emphasis, although he was afflicted lifelong with an extreme nervous sensibility. He worked steadily so far as moods allowed and with a conscientious craftsmanship; he could never "twang off a lyric" at will or mechanically grind out a long poem. Longfellow's writings belong to the Romantic Movement in its milder phases; they have nothing of the storm-and-stress mood except in *Hyperion*. Except for the abolition of slavery (which inspired his *Poems on Slavery*, 1842), social reforms did not much interest him. His unspeculative nature and his Unitarian faith combined to save him alike from the theological struggles of his contemporaries Tennyson and Arnold, and from the paganism of Swinburne. His technical indebtedness to Goldsmith and Keats is plain, but the example of Wordsworth may have quickened his sympathy with common men and women. The strongest single foreign influence on him was that of Goethe and the German romantic lyrists; his use of hexameters, an innovation in American verse, was doubtless due to their success in German narrative poems. When Longfellow fails as a poet it is usually because he has turned to preaching in verse or because he insists on pinning a moral to an incident or a portrait which requires none. His nature poetry is often purely sensuous; his sea poems have a rare felicity and his ballads are spirited. Of all his contributions to our culture, his interpretation of the Old World to the New is perhaps his greatest. His long poems are too often "literary" and smell of the library, but the pictures of American life in his popular short poems are truthful and vivid. His later poems have much more merit than is commonly recognized; the thought is broader and maturer, the style often has more distinction and strength. Longfellow was particularly effective in the sonnet form. Among the many books which he published during his lifetime, the principal are *Hyperion* (1839), *Voices of the Night* (1839), *Ballads and Other Poems* (1842), *Evangeline* (1847), *The Song of Hiawatha* (1855), *The Courtship of Miles Standish* (1858), *Tales of a Wayside Inn* (1863), *The Divine Comedy of Dante Alighieri* (a translation, issued 1865–67), *Kéramos and Other Poems* (1878), *Ultima Thule* (1880), and *In the Harbor* (1882).

LONGFELLOW, SAMUEL (*b. Portland, Maine, 1819; d. Portland, 1892*), Unitarian clergyman, teacher. Son of Stephen Longfellow; brother of Henry Wadsworth Longfellow, whose biography he wrote (published, 1886–87).

LONGFELLOW, STEPHEN (*b. Gorham, Maine, 1776; d. 1849*), lawyer, Massachusetts legislator. Graduated Harvard, 1798. Father of Henry Wadsworth and Samuel Longfellow.

LONGFELLOW, WILLIAM PITT PREBLE (*b. Portland, Maine, 1836; d. East Gloucester, Mass., 1913*), architect, writer on architecture. Nephew of Henry Wadsworth Longfellow.

LONGLEY, ALCANDER (*b. Oxford, Ohio, 1832; d. Chicago, Ill., 1918*), printer, social reformer. Early adopted Fourieristic ideas. After several attempts to organize utopian colonies along the line of cooperatives, he turned to communism and made five essays at establishing a Communist society in Missouri, 1868–85. He publicized his program in *The Communist*, published irregularly *post* 1868; its name was changed to *The Altruist*, 1885, and he continued its publication until 1917.

LONGSTREET, AUGUSTUS BALDWIN (*b. Augusta, Ga., 1790; d. Oxford, Miss., 1870*), lawyer, Methodist clergyman, educator. Son of William Longstreet; uncle of James Longstreet. Published anonymously a series of sketches called "Georgia Scenes" in Milledgeville and Augusta newspapers *post* 1827. Humorous, often crudely realistic, and dealing with life in Georgia as Longstreet knew it, the sketches were at once widely popular and are among the earliest examples in America of the humor later manifested by Mark Twain, Bret Harte, and Joel C. Harris. They appeared in book form, still anonymously, at Augusta, 1835; in 1840 a New York edition appeared under the author's name. Longstreet served as president, Emory College, 1839–48; of Centenary College, Louisiana, 1849; of University of Mississippi, 1849–56; of University of South Carolina, 1857–65. A vigorous proponent of secession, the actuality of the Civil War dismayed him, although he wrote extensively *post* 1865 to prove that the South had always been right and the North always wrong.

LONGSTREET, JAMES (*b. Edgefield District, S.C., 1821; d. Gainesville, Ga., 1904*), soldier. Nephew of Augustus B. Longstreet. Graduated West Point, 1842; saw action in Mexican War with Zachary Taylor until after battle of Monterrey; served then with Scott in campaign against Mexico City. Commissioned Confederate brigadier general, 1861, his excellent leadership at first battle of Bull Run brought him promotion to major general and command of a division under J. E. Johnston. He enhanced his prestige at Yorktown and Williamsburg, but diminished it by tardiness at Seven Pines. During the Seven Days' Battles, June–July 1862, he won R. E. Lee's entire confidence.

At the second battle of Bull Run, Longstreet maneuvered well but delayed a day in taking the offensive. Examined in detail, his reasons for the delay are defensible and may be valid, but his general attitude showed for the first time the greatest defect of his military character. Though he was vigorous and effective when his judgment approved the plans of his superior, he was slow to yield his own opinions and equally slow to move when he thought his commander's course was wrong. Fighting well at Antietam, he failed to impress in his first semi-independent command southeast of Richmond, and was not present at Chancellorsville. The reasons for Confederate defeat at Gettysburg will be long argued but Longstreet's delays on July 2 and 3, 1863, were certainly among them. After further service in Georgia and Tennessee, he returned to Virginia in April 1864 and executed excellent defensive fighting during the last year of the war.

Longstreet prospered in business for a time after the war. Ostracized socially when he became a Republican, for 35 years he held a series of federal political appointments. His differences with Lee, the Southern idol, and the claims made in *From Manassas to Appomattox* (1896), his military autobiography, brought him much unpopularity in the South. He had military weaknesses, but excelled as a combat officer and was an almost ideal corps commander.

LONGSTREET, WILLIAM (*b. near Allentown, N.J., 1759; d. Augusta, Ga., 1814*), inventor. Experimented with a steam engine *ca.* 1780; adapted it to operate cotton gins, sawmills, and boats in Georgia, *post* 1788.

LONGWORTH, NICHOLAS (*b. Newark, N.J., 1782; d. 1863*), lawyer, landowner, horticulturist. Settled in Cincinnati, Ohio, *ca.* 1803. His practice of accepting land for legal fees brought him great wealth in time. He devoted himself *post* 1828 to grape culture and wine manufacture; he also introduced new varieties of the strawberry and the raspberry.

LONGWORTH, NICHOLAS (*b. Cincinnati, Ohio, 1869; d. 1931*), lawyer, Ohio legislator. Great-grandson of Nicholas Longworth (1782–1863). Graduated Harvard, 1891. Congressman, Republican, from Ohio, 1909–13, 1915–31; Republican floor leader of the House, 1923–25, and speaker, 1925–31. A strong protectionist and a partisan Republican, he served as speaker with complete fairness and tact. He married Alice Roosevelt, daughter of Theodore Roosevelt, February 1906.

LONGYEAR, JOHN MUNROE (*b. Lansing, Mich., 1850; d. 1922*) surveyor, capitalist. Best known for his part in opening and developing the Menominee and Gogebic iron ranges and for his promotion of the "Longyear Process" for using low-grade ores.

LOOMIS, ARPHAXED (*b. Winchester, Conn., 1798; d. 1885*), lawyer, New York legislator. A member, with David Graham and David D. Field, of the N.Y. commission for legal reform which produced Code of Civil Procedure, effective July 1848.

LOOMIS, CHARLES BATTELL (*b. Brooklyn, N.Y., 1861; d. Hartford, Conn., 1911*), journalist, humorous lecturer.

LOOMIS, DWIGHT (*b. Columbia, Conn., 1821; d. near Waterbury, Conn., 1903*), lawyer, Connecticut legislator and congressman. Judge, superior court of Connecticut, 1864–75; supreme court of errors, 1875–91. Served thereafter as state referee.

LOOMIS, ELIAS (*b. Connecticut, 1811; d. New Haven, Conn., 1889*), mathematician, astronomer, benefactor of Yale. Graduated Yale, 1830. Taught at Yale, Western Reserve, Princeton, New York University; exerted his greatest influence through excellent textbooks on natural philosophy, astronomy, the calculus, and other subjects.

LOOMIS, ELMER HOWARD (*b. Vermillion, N.Y., 1861; d. 1931*), physicist. Graduated Madison (now Colgate) University, 1883; Ph.D., University of Strassburg, 1893. Taught physics at Princeton, 1894–1929.

LOOMIS, MAHLON (*b. Oppenheim, N.Y., 1826; d. Terre Alta, W. Va., 1886*), dentist. *Post* 1860, experimented with electricity; carried on two-way communication without wires for distance of 18 miles between two mountains in Virginia, 1868. Unable to find financial backing for exploitation of his device, he died in distress.

LOOP, HENRY AUGUSTUS (*b. Hillsdale, N.Y., 1831; d. Lake George, N.Y., 1895*), portrait and figure painter. Studied in New York City under Henry P. Gray; *post* 1857 studied in Paris under Thomas Couture. Worked in New York City *post* 1860.

LOOS, CHARLES LOUIS (*b. Woerth-sur-Sauer, Lower Alsace, France, 1823; d. 1912*), clergyman of the Disciples of Christ, educator. Came to America as a boy; raised in Ohio. Graduated Bethany College, 1846. Held several pastorates; taught at Bethany, 1858–80; president of Kentucky University, 1880–97.

LOPEZ, AARON (*b. Portugal, 1731; d. near Providence, R.I., 1782*), colonial merchant. Immigrated to Newport, R.I., 1752. Prospering in the coastwise and West Indies trade, by 1775 he had interest in over thirty ships.

LORAS, JEAN MATHIAS PIERRE (b. Lyons, France, 1792; d. 1858), Roman Catholic clergyman. A seminary professor and president in France, he came to America, 1829, and served seven years in the diocese of Mobile, Ala. Consecrated bishop of Dubuque, 1837, he administered the new diocese, which reached then from the northern boundary of Missouri to Canada and from the Mississippi River to the Missouri, with great ability and devotion.

LORD, ASA DEARBORN (b. Madrid, N.Y., 1816; d. Batavia, N.Y., 1875), teacher, educational leader. Superintendent of schools, Columbus, Ohio, 1847–56; organized first public high school in Columbus; published a variety of educational journals. Post 1856, specialized in education of the blind.

LORD, CHESTER SANDERS (b. Romulus, N.Y., 1850; d. Garden City, N.Y., 1933), editor, educator. Associated post 1872 with New York Sun, Lord received editorial training from Charles A. Dana and became managing editor of the newspaper, 1881. Except for a brief period, he continued at this post until his retirement, 1913. Selecting his staff with scrupulous care, he built up a group of brilliant writers who were particularly effective in reporting human interest features of any story and "making literature out of news." Under Lord, the Sun became a pioneer school of journalism whose graduates were accepted anywhere. As a regent of the University of the State of New York, 1897–1904, 1909–21, and as chancellor post 1921, he played an important part in shaping and supervising New York educational policies.

LORD, DANIEL (b. Stonington, Conn., 1795; d. 1868), lawyer. Beginning as an attorney for the first John Jacob Astor, he became the favorite counsel of influential New York businessmen.

LORD, DAVID NEVINS (b. Franklin, Conn., 1792; d. 1880), New York merchant, theologian. Brother of Eleazar Lord.

LORD, ELEAZAR (b. Franklin, Conn., 1788; d. Piermont, N.Y., 1871), businessman, author of books on currency and banking, theological writer. Brother of David N. Lord. President of the Erie Railroad, 1833, 1839–41, 1844–45; lobbyist for the protective tariff.

LORD, HENRY CURWEN (b. Cincinnati, Ohio, 1866; d. 1925), astronomer. Grandson of Nathan Lord. Graduated University of Wisconsin, 1889. Long associated with Ohio State University and with its observatory.

LORD, HERBERT MAYHEW (b. Rockland, Maine, 1859; d. Washington, D.C., 1930), financial administrator. Director and chief of finance for U.S. War Department, 1917–22; director of the budget, 1922–29.

LORD, JEREMY. See REDMAN, BENJAMIN RAY.

LORD, JOHN (b. Portsmouth, N.H., 1810; d. Stamford, Conn., 1894), historical lecturer. Nephew of Nathan Lord. Graduated Dartmouth, 1833. Author of a number of books of which Beacon Lights of History (a series, 1884–96) are the best known.

LORD, NATHAN (b. So. Berwick, Maine, 1792; d. 1870), Congregational clergyman, educator. Graduated Bowdoin, 1809; Andover Theological Seminary, 1815. Pastor at Amherst, N.H., 1816–28; president of Dartmouth, 1828–63. An able executive and disciplinarian, he stood for ideas and attitudes which were rapidly passing. His support of slavery as a divinely ordained institution not to be questioned brought him widespread censure and compelled his resignation from office.

LORD, OTIS PHILLIPS (b. Ipswich, Mass., 1812; d. 1884), lawyer, Massachusetts Whig legislator, jurist.

LORD, PAULINE (b. Hanford, Calif., 1890; d. Alamagordo, N. Mex., 1950), actress. Made her first professional appearance in 1903 with the Belasco Stock Company at the Alcazar Theater, San Francisco; toured with Nat Goodwin's company and acted with stock companies in Milwaukee, Wis., and Springfield, Mass. Her New York debut was in a now-forgotten play The Talker, Jan. 8, 1912. Regarded by critics with almost reverence, she was singularly unfortunate in her casting; with four exceptions, she was far superior to the works in which she appeared. These exceptions were her memorable performance as the lead in Eugene O'Neill's Anna Christie (1921); her portrayal of Amy in Sidney Howard's They Knew What They Wanted (1924); her Nina Leeds in O'Neill's Strange Interlude (in succession to Lynn Fontanne, on tour in 1928 and 1929); and her Zenobia in the dramatization of Edith Wharton's Ethan Frome (1936). She also acted in films, among them Mrs. Wiggs of the Cabbage Patch (1934).

LORD, WILLIAM PAINE (b. Dover, Del., 1839; d. 1911), lawyer, Union soldier, Oregon jurist. Settled in Salem, Oreg., 1868. Served as justice, state supreme court, 1880–94; Republican governor of Oregon, 1895–99. U.S. minister to the Argentine Republic, 1899–1902. Compiled Lord's Oregon Laws (1910).

LORD, WILLIAM WILBERFORCE (b. Madison Co., N.Y., 1819; d. New York, N.Y., 1907), Episcopal clergyman, Confederate chaplain. Held several pastorates in the South, notably rectorate of Christ Church, Vicksburg, Miss., 1854–63.

LOREE, LEONOR FRESNEL (b. Fulton City, Ill., 1858; d. West Orange, N.J., 1940), railroad executive, President, Baltimore & Ohio Railroad, 1901–03; president, Delaware and Hudson Company, 1907–38.

LORILLARD, PIERRE (b. New York, N.Y., 1833; d. New York, 1901), merchant, breeder of race horses, developer of Tuxedo Park, N.Y.

LORIMER, GEORGE CLAUDE (b. Edinburgh, Scotland, 1838; d. Aix-les-Bains, France, 1904), Baptist clergyman. Came to America as an actor ca. 1855. Highly effective as preacher and pastor, notably at Tremont Temple, Boston, Mass., 1873–79 and 1891–1901.

LORIMER, GEORGE HORACE (b. Louisville, Ky., 1867; d. Wyncote, Pa., 1937), editor. Became literary editor, 1898, of the Saturday Evening Post, "an elderly and indisposed magazine" which had just been purchased by Cyrus H. K. Curtis. As editor in chief, 1899–1936, Lorimer made the Post an extraordinarily successful magazine, interpreting the America of his time to Americans, with a particular accent on conservatism and the role of business. By his policy of prompt decision and payment on acceptance, he attracted a great variety of first-rate writers of fiction and discovered many new talents.

LORIMER, WILLIAM (b. Manchester, England, 1861; d. Chicago, Ill., 1934), Illinois political boss. Came to America as a child. Adept at political organization, Lorimer cultivated the immigrant population of Cook County and became a power in the state Republican party; he was elected congressman, 1894, re-elected in 1896 and 1898 and after a defeat in 1900, served from 1903 until 1909. Chosen U.S. senator by the Illinois legislature, 1909, he was accused, 1910, of obtaining his seat by corrupt means and ousted, July 1912, after a series of investigations which substantiated the charge.

LORIMIER, PIERRE LOUIS (b. Lachine, Canada, 1748; d. 1812), Indian trader. Established at a post in the present Shelby Co., Ohio, post 1769, he led Shawnee and Delaware Indians against American frontiers during Revolutionary War. Settled near present St. Mary's, Mo., 1787. Founded town of Cape Girardeau, Mo., 1808.

LORING, CHARLES HARDING (*b. Boston, Mass., 1828; d. Hackettstown, N.J., 1907*), naval officer. Holding rank of chief engineer, 1861, he was made fleet engineer on North Atlantic station; later became inspector of ironclad steamers under construction, which included supervision over "monitors." A report in whose preparation he shared brought about abandonment of wooden naval ships, 1881. Appointed U.S. Navy engineer in chief, with rank of rear admiral, 1884, he resigned in the following year.

LORING, CHARLES MORGRIDGE (*b. Portland, Maine, 1832; d. Minneapolis, Minn., 1922*), businessman. Removing to Minneapolis, Minn., 1860, he became nationally known as a worker for civic betterment through his planning of parks and playgrounds in that city *post* 1864.

LORING, EDWARD GREELY (*b. Boston, Mass., 1837; d. New York, N.Y., 1888*), ophthalmologist. Began study of medicine, 1859, in Italy; M.D., Harvard Medical School, 1864. Practiced mainly in New York. His greatest contribution to medicine was his improvement of the ophthalmoscope; he brought out the first practical instrument of the type, *ca.* 1869, and a further improved form of it, 1874. He was author of *A Text Book on Ophthalmoscopy* (1886, 1891).

LORING, ELLIS GRAY (*b. Boston, Mass., 1803; d. 1858*), Boston lawyer, antislavery advocate, liberal.

LORING, FREDERICK WADSWORTH (*b. Boston, Mass., 1848; d. 1871*), journalist. Graduated Harvard, 1870. As correspondent for *Appletons' Journal*, 1871, Loring was killed by Apaches between Wickenburg and La Paz, Ariz., while returning from his coverage of the Wheeler Expedition.

LORING, GEORGE BAILEY (*b. No. Andover, Mass., 1817; d. 1891*), physician, Massachusetts legislator. Congressman, Republican, from Massachusetts, 1877–81; served with intelligent ability as U.S. commissioner of agriculture, 1881–85. Founded New England Agricultural Society, 1864, and served as its president until 1889. U.S. minister to Portugal, 1889–90.

LORING, JOSHUA (*b. Boston, Mass., 1716; d. Highgate, England, 1781*), Loyalist, captain in British navy. Commanded operations in Lakes George, Champlain, and Ontario, 1759–60; participated in capture of Quebec and subsequent conquest of Canada. Removed to England after evacuation of Boston, 1776.

LORING, JOSHUA (*b. Hingham, Mass., 1744; d. Berkshire, England, 1789*), Loyalist. Son of Joshua Loring (1716–1781). After service in the army, 1761–68, he held various offices under the Crown and was one of the addressers to Gov. Hutchinson and General Gage. Appointed vendue master and auctioneer, October 1775, Loring went with the Royal army to Halifax, March 1776; appointed British commissary of prisoners early in 1777, he made himself detested by the colonial leaders who charged him with excessive cruelty. Banished from Massachusetts, he spent the last years of his life in England.

LORING, WILLIAM WING (*b. Wilmington, N.C., 1818; d. New York, N.Y., 1886*), soldier. Raised in Florida. Served against Seminoles and with distinction as commander of the Mounted Rifles in campaign from Vera Cruz to Mexico City, 1847. He also commanded the 1849 march of the Mounted Rifles to Oregon and headed the Oregon department, 1849–51. After service in Texas and New Mexico and in the Mormon Expedition, 1858–59, he resigned from the army, 1861, and was commissioned brigadier general in the Confederate service. Promoted to major general,

1862, he served as a corps commander in Georgia, Mississippi, and Tennessee; in April 1865, serving under General J. E. Johnston in the Carolinas, he surrendered to W. T. Sherman. Entering the army of the Khedive of Egypt, 1869, as brigadier general, he rose to rank of general of division and Pasha before mustering out, 1879, and returning to the United States.

LORRE, PETER (*b. Laszlo Lowenstein, Rosenberg, Hungary, 1904; d. Hollywood, Calif., 1964*), film actor. In the 1920's appeared in amateur productions in Vienna, and then played the lead in Fritz Lang's *M* (1931) and won worldwide renown. Appeared in character parts in more than seventy films, including *The Man Who Knew Too Much* (1934), the Mr. Moto series (beginning in 1938), *The Maltese Falcon* (1941), and *Casablanca* (1942).

LOSKIEL, GEORGE HENRY (*b. Angermuende, Courland, Russia, 1740; d. Bethlehem, Pa., 1814*), bishop of the Moravian Church. Consecrated bishop, 1802, he came to Bethlehem, Pa., in that year to take charge of the work of the Church in North America. He was first of Moravian bishops to strive for Americanization and a separate polity from the European establishment.

LOSSING, BENSON JOHN (*b. Beekman, N.Y., 1813; d. 1891*), wood engraver, author. A prolific writer and editor of popular books on American history, among them the *Pictorial Field Book of the Revolution* (1850–52) and the *Pictorial Field Book of the War of 1812* (1868).

LOTHROP, ALICE LOUISE HIGGINS (*b. Boston, Mass., 1870; d. Newtonville, Mass., 1920*), social worker, expert in disaster relief.

LOTHROP, AMY. *See* WARNER, ANNA BARTLETT.

LOTHROP, DANIEL (*b. Rochester, N.H., 1831; d. 1892*), publisher. Established D. Lothrop & Co., 1868, at Boston, Mass. Specialized in juvenile books and periodicals; founded *Wide Awake* (1875).

LOTHROP, GEORGE VAN NESS (*b. Easton, Mass., 1817; d. Detroit, Mich., 1897*), lawyer. Removed to Michigan, 1839; practiced in Detroit. U.S. minister to Russia, 1885–88.

LOTHROP, HARRIETT MULFORD STONE (*b. New Haven, Conn., 1844; d. San Francisco, Calif., 1924*), author of books for children under penname "Margaret Sidney." Married Daniel Lothrop, 1881. Of her many works, *Five Little Peppers and How They Grew* (1881) was the most popular.

LOTHROPP, JOHN (*b. Yorkshire, England, 1584; d. Barnstable, Mass., 1653*), Nonconformist clergyman. Came to New England, 1634. Served as pastor at Scituate, 1635–39, and thereafter at Barnstable, Mass.

LOTKA, ALFRED JAMES (*b. Lemberg, Austria-Hungary, later Lvov, Poland, 1880; d. Red Bank, N.J., 1949*), chemist, physicist, biologist, statistician. Born of American parents who had spent most of their lives in Europe as missionaries. B.Sc., Birmingham University (England), 1901; M.A., Cornell University, 1909; D.Sc., Birmingham, 1912. Did independent study and research at University of Leipzig and at Johns Hopkins. A man of wide-ranging interests and talents, Lotka's enduring reputation rests on his contributions to demography; he is regarded as the father of demographic analysis. Central to his demographic studies and subsequent mathematical demography was the analysis of the structure of a stable population, a hypothetical population formed by constant age-specific birth and death rates, and unaffected by migration—a concept approached in previous studies but never fully developed before Lotka. In works like his *Elements of Physical*

Biology (1925), he provided analyses of the interrelationship of the sciences which looked forward to such modern concepts as cybernetics and information theory. *Post* 1924, he worked in the statistical bureau of the Metropolitan Life Insurance Company, of which he was supervisor, 1933–47.

LOTTA *See* CRABTREE, CHARLOTTE.

LOUCKS, HENRY LANGFORD (*b. Hull, Canada, 1846; d. Clearlake, S. Dak., 1928*), agrarian politician. Homesteaded, 1884, in Deuel Co., Dakota Territory. Active in reform movements on behalf of farmers of his section, he organized them into the Independent political party (later identified with the Populist party) which played an important part in South Dakota and national politics *post* 1890. He was a leader in the National Farmers' Alliance and a strong advocate of temperance.

LOUDON, SAMUEL (*b. probably Ireland, ca. 1727; d. near Middletown Point, N.J., 1813*), merchant, printer. Came to America *ante* 1753. Published *The New York Packet* (January 1776–August 1776) at New York City, and (January 1777–1783) at Fishkill, N.Y. As state printer, he printed first New York State constitution (Fishkill, 1777); also several issues of state paper money. When the British removed from New York City, he returned there and continued his printing business along with a bookshop and circulating library.

LOUDOUN, JOHN CAMPBELL, EARL OF (*b. Loudoun Castle, Ayrshire, Scotland, 1705; d. Loudoun Castle, 1782*), British soldier. A veteran field officer and a major general, he accepted the post of commander in chief of all forces in North America, January 1756, together with the sinecure post of governor general of Virginia. He had a dual task; to mold the British forces in North America into an efficient fighting unit and to unite the colonies in support of the war with France and her colonies (French and Indian War) then raging. Successful as a trainer of troops and organizer of military services, his insistence on his authority and his outbursts of temper alienated many colonial representatives. His military campaigns were completely unsuccessful and he was recalled, December 1757. He later commanded with better success in Portugal, 1762–63, and was promoted general in 1770.

LOUGHRIDGE, ROBERT McGILL (*b. Laurensville, S.C., 1809; d. Waco, Texas, 1900*), Presbyterian clergyman, educator. Raised in Alabama. Worked as a missionary among the Creek Indians, 1843–61 and 1881–88.

LOUIS, MORRIS (*b. Baltimore, Md., 1912; d. Washington, D.C., 1962*), artist. Attended Maryland Institute of Fine and Applied Arts, 1929–33, but did little until 1954 that indicated his later greatness as an abstract artist. First successful paintings were called "Veils," in which he placed color in an eerie succession of large washes. He had numerous exhibitions and one-man shows.

LOUNSBURY, THOMAS RAYNESFORD (*b. Ovid, N.Y., 1838; d. 1915*), Union soldier, educator, philologist. Graduated Yale, 1859. Professor of English, Sheffield Scientific School, 1871–1906. A brilliant and unconventional teacher, Lounsbury taught his students to recognize in literature the record of a life as real as their own. As a scholar, he was recognized internationally as a master in several fields of English language and literature; in the latter part of his career he showed an increasing interest in questions of spelling, pronunciation, and usage. His scholarship was marked by common sense, regard for fact, and an unshakable sense of values. Among his books were *History of the English Language* (1879, 1894, 1907); *James Fenimore Cooper* (1882); and *Studies in Chaucer* (1892), one of the most important works in its field to appear in the 19th century.

LOVE, ALFRED HENRY (*b. Philadelphia, Pa., 1830; d. 1913*), merchant, radical pacifist. Founded the Universal Peace Union, 1866, and served as its president until his death.

LOVE, EMANUEL KING (*b. near Marion, Ala., 1850; d. 1900*), Baptist clergyman. Graduated Augusta (Ga.) Institute, 1877. His most distinctive work and greatest influence came while pastor, First African Baptist Church, Savannah, Ga., 1885–1900. He was especially interested in securing liberal education for blacks.

LOVE, ROBERTUS DONNELL (*b. near Irondale, Mo., 1867; d. St. Louis, Mo., 1930*), journalist. Author of *The Rise and Fall of Jesse James* (1926).

LOVEJOY, ARTHUR ONCKEN (*b. Berlin, Germany, 1873; d. Baltimore, Md., 1962*), philosopher and historian of ideas. Attended University of California at Berkeley and Harvard (M.A., 1897). Taught at Stanford (1899–1901); Washington University, St. Louis (1901–07); Columbia (1907–08); University of Missouri at Columbia (1908–10); and Johns Hopkins (1910–38). Major works include *The Revolt Against Dualism* (1939), a defense of epistemological and psychophysical dualism, and *The Great Chain of Being* (1936). Instrumental in formation of American Association of University Professors (1915) and served as its secretary and president (1919). President of the American Philosophical Association (1916). Supported national efforts in the 1950's to keep Communists from teaching on university faculties, believing they endangered academic freedom.

LOVEJOY, ASA LAWRENCE (*b. Groton, Mass., 1808; d. Portland, Oreg., 1882*), lawyer, Oregon legislator. Nephew of Abbott Lawrence. Visited Oregon, 1842; accompanied Marcus Whitman on his famous ride eastward, 1842–43. A founder of the city of Portland, Lovejoy was long active in Oregon public life after his settlement there in fall, 1843.

LOVEJOY, ELIJAH PARISH (*b. Albion, Maine, 1802; d. Alton, Ill., 1837*), abolitionist martyr. Brother of Owen Lovejoy. After studying for the ministry, he served as editor of a Presbyterian weekly, the *St. Louis Observer*, 1833–36, making the paper a vehement voice against slavery, intemperance, and "popery." St. Louis, Mo., river port for the lower South, was not the place for such a newspaper. Rather than moderate his tone, Lovejoy moved to Alton, Ill., 1836, and edited the *Alton Observer* as an active Abolitionist organ. Harassed by destruction of his printing press several times, Lovejoy was shot dead in defense of yet another press which had been sent him by the Ohio Anti-Slavery Society.

LOVEJOY, OWEN (*b. Albion, Maine, 1811; d. 1864*), Congregational clergyman, Abolitionist, Illinois legislator. Brother of Elijah P. Lovejoy. Urged Abraham Lincoln as early as 1854 to assume leadership of the new political movement which became the Republican party; remained Lincoln's loyal supporter and friend until his death. He served as congressman, Republican, from Illinois, 1857–64.

LOVEJOY, OWEN REED (*b. Jamestown, Mich., 1866; d. Biglerville, Pa., 1961*), minister, social worker, and reformer. Attended Albion College (M.A., 1894); entered Methodist ministry (1891). A man with a passionate concern for human rights, he was sent in 1904 to the Pennsylvania coal fields by the National Child Labor Committee; troubled by the conditions he encountered, he gave up his parish in Mount Vernon, N.Y., and became a full-time NCLC assistant secretary, then general secretary, 1907–26. Traveled throughout the nation to present the child labor problem to the American people. Secretary of Children's Aid Society of New York, 1927–35; associate director of the American Youth Commission, 1935–39.

LOVELACE, FRANCIS (*b. England*, ca. *1621*; *d. probably Woodstock, England, 1675*), colonial governor. Brother of the English poet Richard Lovelace. Appointed governor of New York, 1667, he arrived in the colony, March 1668. A conscientious tolerant man, Lovelace interested himself in better transportation by land and by water and in regulation of trade. He instituted the first New York merchants' exchange and promoted shipbuilding; the first continuous post road between New York and Boston under a postmaster was one of his numerous innovations. While he was visiting in Connecticut, New York was retaken by a Dutch naval force, July–August 1673; held responsible for negligence in this matter, he was recalled and suffered persecution and imprisonment.

LOVELAND, WILLIAM AUSTIN HAMILTON (*b. Chatham, Mass., 1826; d. Lakeside, Colo., 1894*), merchant, Colorado legislator. After a wandering youth, he settled in Colorado, 1859, where he prospered as a merchant and real estate investor; he was also owner of the Denver *Rocky Mountain News*, promoter of the Colorado Central Railroad, and a leader in the Democratic party.

LOVELL, JAMES (*b. Boston, Mass., 1737; d. Windham, Maine, 1814*), schoolmaster, politician. Son of John Lovell. Graduated Harvard, 1756. Delivered first Boston Massacre oration, 1771; arrested as an American spy by the British, 1775, he spent a year as prisoner in Halifax. As delegate to the Continental Congress, 1777–82, he was a zealous partisan of General Horatio Gates and a participant in the so-called Conway Cabal. He was also one of the congressional group which was opposed to Benjamin Franklin and Silas Deane. A useful member of Congress in many ways, and diligent in foreign affairs committee work, he was too fond of intrigue for its own sake. *Post* 1789, he served as naval officer for Boston district.

LOVELL, JOHN (*b. Boston, Mass., 1710; d. Halifax, Nova Scotia, 1778*), schoolmaster, Loyalist. Graduated Harvard, 1728. Master of the South Grammar or Latin School, Boston, 1734–75.

LOVELL, JOHN EPY (*b. Colne, England, 1795; d. Milwaukee, Wis., 1892*), educator. Came to America *ante* 1822, in which year he started a successful Lancasterian school in New Haven, Conn. He was author of a number of textbooks, in particular *The United States Speaker* (1833).

LOVELL, JOSEPH (*b. Boston, Mass., 1788; d. 1836*), surgeon. Grandson of James Lovell. Graduated Harvard, 1807; Harvard Medical School, 1811. Entering U.S. Army, 1812, as surgeon, 9th Infantry, he made a reputation in administration of hospitals. Appointed surgeon general, 1818, on establishment of the army medical department, he held that office until his death. A man of vision and scholarship, he will be remembered for his aid to William Beaumont in the latter's study of gastric physiology and for his institution of a system of quarterly reports of weather and of the incidence of disease.

LOVELL, MANSFIELD (*b. Washington, D.C., 1822; d. 1884*), soldier, civil engineer. Son of Joseph Lovell. Graduated West Point, 1842. After service in Mexican War and on the frontiers, he resigned from army, 1854, worked as engineer in iron works, and served as New York City street commissioner. Appointed major general, Confederate Army, 1861, he was put in command of the garrison at New Orleans, La. Held responsible for the evacuation and loss of that city, April 1862, although absolved of blame by a military court, he received no further important commands.

LOVEMAN, AMY (*b. New York, N.Y., 1881; d. New York, N.Y., 1955*), editor and author. B.A., Barnard College, 1901. In 1924, a founder and editor of the *Saturday Review of Literature*, a position she held until her death. In 1926, assumed major responsibilities for the Book-of-the-Month-Club, joining the editorial board in 1951. Published *I'm Looking for a Book* in 1936. One of America's finest book reviewers, she was responsible for the high standards of the *Saturday Review*. Her purpose was to promote the role of books in support of truth and civilized life.

LOVERING, JOSEPH (*b. Charlestown, Mass., 1813; d. 1892*), educator. Graduated Harvard, 1833. Hollis professor of mathematics and natural philosophy, Harvard, 1838–88. Secretary, American Association for Advancement of Science, 1854–73; president, American Academy of Arts and Sciences, 1880–92.

LOVETT, ROBERT MORSS (*b. Boston, Mass., 1870; d. Chicago, Ill., 1956*), educator and editor. Studied at Harvard. Taught at the University of Chicago from 1893 to 1936. A Christian socialist, Lovett associated himself with a wide range of social causes including various peace movements. As a result, he was often accused of being a communist and was harassed by state and government officials. In 1935, an Illinois Senate committee recommended that he be dismissed from the University of Chicago. From 1939 to 1943, he was government secretary of the Virgin Islands and was relieved of his duties, having been labeled a subversive by the Dies Committee. Later, in 1946, the Kerr committee vindicated him and authorized payment of back salary. From 1944 to 1946, he was visiting professor at the University of Puerto Rico. Lovett was the author of several books and enjoyed a long editorial association with the *New Republic* (1921–29).

LOVETT, ROBERT SCOTT (*b. near San Jacinto, Texas, 1860; d. 1932*), lawyer. Protégé and confidant of E. H. Harriman, Lovett served as general counsel and as president of the Southern Pacific and Union Pacific railroads.

LOVETT, ROBERT WILLIAMSON (*b. Beverly, Mass., 1859; d. Liverpool, England, 1924*), orthopedic surgeon, medical writer. Graduated Harvard, 1881; Harvard Medical School, 1885. *Post* 1899, he concentrated on work in Boston Children's Hospital; taught his specialty at Harvard Medical School; was a leader in orthopedic restoration for victims of infantile paralysis. His crowning work, prepared in cooperation with his friend Sir Robert Jones, was *Orthopedic Surgery* (1923).

LOVEWELL, JOHN (*b. Dunstable, Mass., now part of Nashua, N.H., 1691; d. near "Lovewell's Pond" on Saco River, Maine, 1725*), Indian fighter. Killed on the third of his punitive expeditions against the Pequawkets in Maine. Lovewell and the sad fate of his company were subjects for several early ballads.

LOW, ABIEL ABBOT (*b. Salem, Mass., 1811; d. Brooklyn, N.Y., 1893*), merchant. Served as clerk and partner, Russell & Co., Canton, China, 1833–40. A profitable enterprise engaged in with the mandarin Houqua enabled Low to begin business in New York on his own account. The firm of A. A. Low & Brothers soon gained leading position in tea and silk trade with China and Japan; Low also shared in financing the first Atlantic cable and in the building of the Chesapeake and Ohio Railroad through West Virginia.

LOW, FREDERICK FERDINAND (*b. Frankfort, now Winterport, Maine, 1828; d. San Francisco, Calif., 1894*), merchant, banker. Immigrated to California, 1849; was successful as a merchant in San Francisco and Marysville. Congressman, Union Republican, from California, 1862–63; governor of California, 1863–67. As governor, much credit is due him for the later founding of University of California and for preserving the site of Golden Gate Park. He served as U.S. minister to China, 1870–74.

LOW, ISAAC (*b. near New Brunswick, N.J., 1735; d. Isle of Wight, England, 1791*), merchant. A delegate to the Stamp Act Congress, 1765, and representative of moderate opinion against the policy of the English ministry, Low served as a delegate from New York to the First Continental Congress but showed himself hostile to independence and, unlike his brother Nicholas Low, went over to the British, 1776. He was a founder of the N.Y. Chamber of Commerce.

LOW, JOHN GARDNER (*b. Chelsea, Mass., 1835; d. 1907*), painter. Designer and manufacturer of art tiles and other ceramic products.

LOW, JULIETTE GORDON (*b. Savannah, Ga., 1860; d. Savannah, 1927*), founder (1912) of the Girl Scouts of America.

LOW, NICHOLAS (*b. near New Brunswick, N.J., 1739; d. New York, N.Y., 1826*), merchant, land speculator, New York legislator. Brother of Isaac Low.

LOW, SETH (*b. Brooklyn, N.Y., 1850; d. Bedford Hills, N.Y., 1916*), merchant, political reformer. Son of Abiel A. Low. Graduated Columbia,, 1870. A partner in his father's business, 1876–87, Low served as mayor of the then city of Brooklyn, N.Y., 1881–1885. He introduced the merit system in the municipal service, reduced the city debt and completely reformed the public school system. Standing for a separation of local and national politics, Low disclaimed the Republican label as mayor, although he was a Republican, and refused to support the candidacy of James G. Blaine in 1884. As the president of Columbia, 1890–1901, he reorganized graduate and professional instruction and brought into association with the university Teachers College, Barnard and the College of Physicians and Surgeons; he was also responsible for the purchase of the new site on Morningside Heights, 1892. Victorious as independent candidate for New York City mayoralty, 1901, his administration marked a brief era of civic reform, but he failed of reelection, 1903. An active philanthropist, he worked to improve the condition of blacks and labor-capital relations.

LOW, WILL HICOK (*b. Albany, N.Y., 1853; d. Bronxville, N.Y., 1932*), artist. Studied in Paris, 1872–77, with Gérôme and Carolus-Duran; was friend of Robert Louis Stevenson. Outstanding as a decorative painter, Low was author of *A Chronicle of Friendships* (1908) and *A Painter's Progress* (1910).

LOWDEN, FRANK ORREN (*b. near Sunrise City, Minn., 1861; d. Tucson, Ariz., 1943*), lawyer, politician, agricultural leader. Raised in Point Pleasant, Iowa. Graduated University of Iowa, 1885; Union College of Law (Chicago, Ill.,), 1887. Practiced successfully in Chicago. Married Florence Pullman, daughter of George M. Pullman, 1896. Following his father-in-law's death in 1897, Lowden managed a number of the "Car King's" enterprises and organized several large manufacturing corporations. In 1902 he moved to "Sinnissippi," an estate near Oregon, Ill. In 1904 he narrowly missed the Republican gubernatorial nomination in Illinois. Two years later he was chosen to a vacant Congressional seat. His constituency reelected him in 1908, but two years later he declined to run again because of ill health. While in Washington perhaps his most notable achievement was his successful fight to reform and upgrade the State Department's Consular Service. Yielding to pressure from leaders of his party, Lowden sought the governorship in 1916 and defeated the Democratic incumbent.

After an unsuccessful bid for the Republican presidential nomination (1920), Lowden refused to seek a second term as governor. He also declined, over the next few years, an opportunity to run for the Senate, several important diplomatic posts, including the ambassadorship to Great Britain, and the Republican vice-presi-

dential nomination in 1924. Instead he devoted his energies to the improvement of agriculture and the machinery of government. He worked closely with the National Institute of Public Administration and helped establish the Public Administration Clearing House. His entire political career, in both state and national politics, exemplified a basic problem of his party, its uneasy alliance between industrialists and farmers. Lowden served for a decade as one of the court-appointed trustees of the bankrupt Chicago, Rock Island, and Pacific Railway.

LOWE, CHARLES (*b. Portsmouth, N.H., 1828; d. 1874*), Unitarian clergyman. Helped organize National Conference, American Unitarian Association, 1865; served as the Association's first executive secretary, 1865–71.

LOWE, RALPH PHILLIPS (*b. Warren Co., Ohio, 1805; d. Washington, D.C., 1883*), lawyer. Settled in Iowa, 1840. Republican governor of Iowa, 1858–60; justice, supreme court of Iowa, 1860–68, acting in 1860 and 1866–68 as chief justice.

LOWE, THADDEUS SOBIESKI COULINCOURT (*b. Jefferson Mills, N.H., 1832; d. Pasadena, Calif., 1913*), aeronaut, meteorologist. Chief of aeronautic section, Army of the Potomac, 1861–63, he made valuable air observations and was first in the United States to take photographs from a balloon. After the Civil War he became interested in manufacture of artificial ice, constructing a plant for this purpose as early as 1866; he also made several later improvements in the manufacture of gas and coke.

LOWELL, ABBOTT LAWRENCE (*b. Boston, Mass., 1856; d. Boston, 1943*), lawyer, political scientist, educator. Grandson of Abbott Lawrence; brother of Amy and Percival Lowell. Entered Harvard in 1873, after preparatory studies at George W. C. Noble's private classical school. Inspired by the mathematics classes of Benjamin Pierce, Lowell took second-year honors in mathematics and graduated cum laude with highest final honors in that field. He entered the Harvard Law School in 1877 and won an LL.B. cum laude in 1880, ranking second in the class. After apprentice work in a Boston law firm, he became a copartner in his own firm in 1880. Working chiefly in probate and investment management for charitable bodies, he was a self-described failure as a lawyer. He followed his father as a member of the Corporation of the Massachusetts Institute of Technology in 1890 and as sole trustee of the Lowell Institute, a foundation for adult education, in 1900. In 1895 he was elected to the Boston School Committee with the backing of the Democrats; three years later he failed of reelection.

In collaboration with F. C. Lowell he published *The Transfer of Stock in Private Corporations* (1884). More suggestive of his shifting interest was his *Essays on Government* (1889). Lowell turned much of his energy to the writing of *Governments and Parties in Continental Europe* (2 vols., 1896), the first comprehensive study of Continental government published by an American. It established Lowell's reputation as a scholar and brought a momentous invitation to teach at Harvard in 1897. He immediately resigned from his law firm, even though the appointment was a part-time, nonpermanent lectureship. In 1900 he accepted a professorship in government.

Lowell's scholarship flourished alongside his teaching. Two short books, *The Government of Dependencies* (1899) and *Colonial Civil Service* (1900), applied Lowell's knowledge of comparative government to America's new colonial problems. *The Government of England*, Lowell's major work, appeared in 1908. Like his study of 1896, it sought to treat government as a functioning machine, to emphasize actual workings rather than objectives or historical development. The appearance of this scholarly monument conveniently enhanced Lowell's candidacy for the Harvard presidency, vacated in 1909 after a forty-year tenure by Charles W.

Eliot. Lowell had already made his educational views known. Without a serious competitor, Lowell was elected president of Harvard in January 1909 and took up his duties in May. To counter the view that course-taking was equivalent to education, Lowell helped establish general examinations in fields of concentration; this requirement led logically to the tutorial system. In his efforts to renew the sense of community, Lowell instituted the Harvard House Plan. Resembling the colleges at Oxford and Cambridge, each "house" had its own master, resident tutors, dining room, and library. While still a professor, he had been instrumental in founding the Graduate School of Business Administration, and he supported its expansion, insisting that business be considered a profession. In regard to ethnic variety at Harvard, he twice held stubbornly to restrictive positions that aroused strong opposition. Although residence in freshman halls was supposedly compulsory, black freshmen were not allowed to live there. At the same time Lowell recommended an admission quota for Jewish students, which was blocked by the Overseers.

In politics Lowell called himself an independent Republican, and he voted for Cleveland in 1884 and 1892 and for Wilson at least once. The effort to found an international peacekeeping body involved Lowell in his most strenuous political activity. He played a major part in creating and naming the League to Enforce Peace. When the League of Nations Covenant emerged from the Paris Peace Conference, he campaigned in its behalf. In 1927 he served on the advisory committee that investigated the trial of Nicola Sacco and Bartolomeo Vanzetti, radicals convicted of murder. In a formal report Lowell and the committee concluded that the trial was fair, the refusals to grant a new trial justified, and the defendants guilty.

Lowell's retirement as president of Harvard in 1933 was brightened by the creation during his last year of the Society of Fellows, which provided postgraduate fellowships. Lowell published two series of lectures, *Public Opinion and Popular Government* (1913) and *Public Opinion in War and Peace* (1923). *Conflicts of Principle* (1932) reasserted his resistance to absolutes. In retirement he continued writing and public speaking. *At War With Academic Traditions in America* (1934) and *What a University President Has Learned* (1938) helped continue interest in his educational theories.

LOWELL, AMY (*b. Brookline, Mass., 1874; d. Brookline, 1925*), poet, critic. Granddaughter of Abbott Lawrence; sister of Abbott L. and Percival Lowell; descendant of John Lowell (1769–1840). Educated at private schools; traveled extensively. The supreme interest of her life *post* 1902 was the art of poetry. Alive to the new movements at that time, she turned from the more or less conventional tendencies of her earliest attempts at literature to work of a markedly original character both in verse and prose. Having met Ezra Pound in England, 1913, she became associated with the Imagist school whose work she endeavored to publicize in the United States. *Post* 1914, her poems are phrased in free verse or, as she preferred to call it, "unrhymed cadence." The principles on which she worked were defined in the preface to her *Sword Blades and Poppy Seed* (1914); this volume also contained her experiments in what she termed "polyphonic prose." Later in her career her work showed the influence of her studies in Chinese and Japanese poetry. From 1915 until her death, she lectured and gave readings from her work, defending her poetic creed and technique with great vigor and verve. During these years she was the most striking figure in contemporary American letters, her serene independence of conventional opinion and her Elizabethan outspokenness occasioning considerable comment. Her important publications besides those already cited are her first book, *A Dome of Many-Coloured Glass* (1912), *Can Grande's Castle* (1918), *Pictures of the Floating World* (1919),

Legends (1921), and her most important critical work, *John Keats* (1925).

LOWELL, EDWARD JACKSON (*b. Boston, Mass.,, 1845; d. Cotuit, Mass., 1894*), historian. Grandson of Francis C. Lowell. Graduated Harvard, 1867. Author, among other books, of *The Eve of the French Revolution* (1892).

LOWELL, FRANCIS CABOT (*b. Newburyport, Mass., 1775; d. Boston, Mass., 1817*), textile manufacturer. Son of John Lowell (1743–1802). Graduated Harvard, 1793. During a journey to England, 1810, he studied textile machinery in Lancashire; on return to America, 1812, he determined to establish a cotton factory. Forming the Boston Manufacturing Co. with his brother-in-law, Patrick T. Jackson, he purchased land at Waltham, Mass., and designed and built (with the aid of Paul Moody) necessary spinning machinery and a practical power loom. When the factory was in complete operation *ca.* 1814, it was believed to be the first mill in the world which combined all operations of converting raw cotton into finished cloth.

LOWELL, GUY (*b. Boston, Mass., 1870; d. Madeira Islands, 1927*), architect. Son of Edward J. Lowell. Graduated Harvard, 1892; department of architecture, Massachusetts Institute of Technology, 1894. Received diploma, École des Beaux Arts, Paris, 1899; had immediate success on his return to America. Among his notable works are the buildings at Phillips Academy, Andover, Mass., and the New York County Court House, designed 1913. A confirmed classicist, Lowell also engaged in landscape architecture.

LOWELL, JAMES RUSSELL (*b. Cambridge, Mass., 1819; d. Cambridge, 1891*), poet, educator, public servant, foremost American man of letters in his time. Grandson of John Lowell (1743–1802); brother of Robert T. S. Lowell. Graduated Harvard, 1838; Harvard Law School, 1840. Married Maria White, 1844, whose enthusiasm for the antislavery movement and for poetry inspired and encouraged him; her influence is noted in his early publications, *A Year's Life* (1841) and *Poems* (1844). His first book of literary criticism, *Conversations on Some of the Old Poets*, was published, 1845. He had made his debut as an editor in *The Pioneer*, a magazine published briefly in 1843. In the year 1848 Lowell published *Poems: Second Series*; the rollicking critical satire, *A Fable for Critics*; the first volume of *The Biglow Papers*; and *The Vision of Sir Launfal*. All of this work was highly competent and some of it was brilliant, yet there was truth in Margaret Fuller's criticism that "his great facility at versification has enabled him to fill the ear with a copious stream of pleasant sound. But his verse is stereotyped; his thought sounds no depth." In *The Biglow Papers* Lowell reproduced Yankee dialect with extreme exactness, and his satiric criticism of the national government in its conduct of the Mexican War was remarkably telling. Nearly twenty years later the second series of *The Biglow Papers* (written, 1864; first published in book form in the United States, 1867) dealt with equal skill with the Civil War. These satires may be regarded as his most distinctive contribution to the literature of his time.

Dealt a desolating blow by the death of his wife, 1853, Lowell busied himself with writing for the magazines and with much social bustle. He succeeded H. W. Longfellow as Smith professor of French and Spanish and professor of belles lettres at Harvard, 1855, and, in 1857, became editor of the *Atlantic Monthly*. Nominally he held his Harvard chair from 1855 to 1886, when he became emeritus for the remainder of his life; actually there were several intermissions in his teaching. He left the *Atlantic Monthly*, 1861, but renewed editorial work, 1864, in association with Charles E. Norton, in conduct of the *North American Review*. The emphasis in his work shifted from creation to criticism more and more as his career went on, although in his "Ode Recited at the Harvard Commemoration, July 21, 1865" (first published, *Atlantic Monthly*, September 1865) he attained a high point in his own poetic achievement and produced a work which stands in the front rank of its genre. Highly rated as a critic in his own day, his stature has diminished with the passage of the years; the scholar of today finds him highly impressionistic and only analytic under pressure of challenge. *Among My Books* (1870), *My Study Windows* (1871), and *Among My Books*, second series (1876), were all gatherings of literary essays, most of which had appeared in the *Atlantic* and the *North American Review*. The books which he published subsequent to 1876 did not materially affect his place in American letters. Lowell's permanent reputation as poet or prose writer has suffered because of his extraordinary versatility and cleverness—the very qualities which gave him so great an influence in his own time.

His career as a public servant began with his service as U.S. minister to Spain, 1877–80. Adapting himself to his new profession with skill and zest, he moved on to England, serving as U.S. minister to the Court of St. James's, 1880–85. Despite an earlier literary antipathy to England and the English, Lowell performed a notable mission of good will as minister in London, showing himself an excellent public speaker both on formal and informal occasions. Among his many addresses, one of the best is "Democracy," Oct. 6, 1884.

LOWELL, JOHN (*b. Newburyport, Mass., 1743; d. Roxbury, Mass., 1802*), Massachusetts legislator, jurist. U.S. judge, district of Massachusetts, 1789–1801; chief judge, first circuit, 1801–02. Father (by successive marriages) of John (1769–1840) and Francis C. Lowell; grandfather of James R. and Robert T. S. Lowell.

LOWELL, JOHN (*b. Newburyport, Mass., 1769; d. 1840*), lawyer, Federalist political writer. Son of John Lowell (1743–1802); half brother of Francis C. Lowell. Graduated Harvard, 1786. His many vigorous pamphlets and letters to the press won him the title of the "Boston Rebel," but were of influence only in New England.

LOWELL, JOHN (*b. Boston, Mass., 1799; d. Bombay, India, 1836*), businessman. Son of Francis C. Lowell. Founder of the Lowell Institute, to which he left half of his estate in trust.

LOWELL, JOHN (*b. Boston, Mass., 1824; d. 1897*), lawyer. Grandson of John Lowell (1769–1840); grandson also of Francis C. Lowell. Graduated Harvard, 1843; Harvard Law School, 1845. Independent, learned, and courteous as U.S. judge, district of Massachusetts, 1865–78, and as judge for the first circuit, 1878–84. Particularly effective in commercial, marine, and bankruptcy cases.

LOWELL, JOSEPHINE SHAW (*b. West Roxbury, Mass., 1843; d. 1905*), philanthropist, reformer. Sister of Robert G. Shaw; married nephew of James Russell Lowell, 1863. First woman appointed to New York State Board of Charities; founder of Charity Organization Society; one of the organizers of the Consumer's League.

LOWELL, PERCIVAL (*b. Boston, Mass., 1855; d. 1916*), astronomer, businessman. Grandson of Abbott Lawrence; brother of Abbott L. and Amy Lowell. Graduated Harvard, 1876. Successful in business, he spent the years 1883–93 in travel in the Far East both as private citizen and diplomat; his books, *Chöson—The Land of the Morning Calm* (1885) and *Soul of the Far East* (1888), show remarkable insight into the Oriental mind. He devoted himself to astronomy subsequent to the early 1890's and built an observatory near Flagstaff, Ariz., where he and a staff of astronomers carried on a most valuable program of research *post* 1894.

LOWELL, ROBERT TRAILL SPENCE (*b. Boston, Mass., d. 1891*), Episcopal clergyman, author. Brother of James R. Lowell. Graduated Harvard, 1833. Pastor in Newfoundland and at churches in New York and New Jersey. Headmaster, St. Mark's School, 1869–73; professor of Latin, Union College, 1873–79. Author, among other books, of *The New Priest in Conception Bay* (1858) and *Poems* (1864).

LOWER, WILLIAM EDGAR (*b. Canton, Ohio, 1867; d. Cleveland, Ohio, 1948*), surgeon. Cousin and later partner of George W. Crile. M.D., Wooster University, 1891. Skillful and conservative, he specialized in urology and devised a number of improved surgical instruments in his field; with Crile, he pioneered in the use of spinal anaesthesia. He taught at the medical school of Western Reserve University and was associate professor of genito-urinary surgery there, 1910–31. After World War I service in France, he joined with Crile and others in forming the Cleveland Clinic Foundation of which he was administrative officer.

LOWERY, WOODBURY (*b. New York, N.Y., 1853; d. Taormina, Sicily, 1906*), lawyer, legal editor, historian. Grandson of Levi Woodbury. Graduated Harvard, 1875. Author of *The Spanish Settlements Within the Present Limits of the United States, 1513–61* (1901, 1905). Bequeathed his valuable collection of early maps to the Library of Congress.

LOWES, JOHN LIVINGSTON (*b. Decatur, Ind., 1867; d. Boston, Mass., 1945*), literary scholar. A.B., Washington and Jefferson College, 1888; A.M., 1891. Graduated from Western Theological Seminary, 1894. After study at the universities of Leipzig and Berlin, he taught at Hanover College in Indiana, 1895–1902. In 1902 he went to Harvard for graduate work in English, receiving the doctorate in 1905; his dissertation was on the prologue to Chaucer's *Legend of Good Women*. He served as professor of English at Swarthmore College, 1905–09, and at Washington University (St. Louis, Mo.), 1909–18. Appointed to the Harvard faculty in 1918, he remained until retirement in 1939; he was named Francis Lee Higginson Professor in 1930.

In 1918 Lowes gave the Lowell Institute lectures in Boston. These became his first book, *Convention and Revolt in Poetry* (1919), in which he discussed the role of traditional and original forms in English poetry, distilled some of his medieval lore and some of his later interest in Coleridge and other romantic poets, and dealt at length with the new Imagists. His collected papers, *Essays in Appreciation* (1936), further attest to his range of sympathy. Lowes's masterwork, *The Road to Xanadu* (1927), an analysis of Coleridge's notebooks, stands as the finest product of the kind of scholarship in which its author had grown up.

LOWIE, ROBERT HARRY (*b. Vienna, Austria, 1883; d. San Francisco, Calif., 1957*), ethnologist. Studied at the City College of New York and at Columbia (Ph.D., 1908). Associated with the American Museum of Natural History from 1906 to 1921. An expert on American Indians, Lowie went on several expeditions to the far West to observe and record the social structures of the Plains Indian culture. Taught at Berkeley from 1921; chairman of the department of anthropology from 1925. Wrote *Culture and Ethnology* (1917), *Primitive Society* (1920), *Primitive Religion* (1924), and *The Origin of the State* (1927). Remembered for his term "multilinear evolution" and for his methods of data handling and analysis. Lowie also wrote several ethnological examinations of German culture, including *The German People* (1945) and *Toward Understanding Germany* (1954).

LOWNDES, LLOYD (*b. Clarksburg, Va., 1845; d. 1905*), lawyer, financier. Practiced *post* 1867 at Cumberland, Md. Congressman, Republican, from Maryland, 1873–75; Republican governor of Maryland, 1896–1900.

LOWNDES, RAWLINS (*b. St. Kitts, British West Indies, 1721; d. 1800*), lawyer, South Carolina legislator. Raised in Charleston, S.C., where he practiced *post* 1754. A conservative, he hoped that the American colonies would be satisfied with a redress of grievances, yet he served on the local revolutionary committees and was a member of the legislative council, 1776–78 and president of the state of South Carolina, 1778. A member of the legislature after the revolution, he opposed ratification of the Constitution because he considered it "ruinous to the liberty of America."

LOWNDES, WILLIAM (*b. Colleton, Co., S.C., 1782; d. at sea, 1822*), planter, South Carolina legislator. Son of Rawlins Lowndes. Congressman, Democratic-Republican, from South Carolina, 1811–22. With Langdon Cheves, John C. Calhoun, and others, formed nucleus of the "War Hawks." A very able congressional debater, he spoke with particular effectiveness in the debate over Missouri, 1820. Highly respected by his contemporaries, he was nominated by the South Carolina legislature for the presidency in December, 1821.

LOWREY, MARK PERRIN (*b. McNairy Co., Tenn., 1828; d. Middleton, Tenn., 1885*), Baptist clergyman, Confederate brigadier general.

LOWRIE, JAMES WALTER (*b. Shanghai, China, 1856; d. Paotingfu, China, 1930*), Presbyterian clergyman. Grandson of Walter Lowrie. Missionary to China *post* 1883.

LOWRIE, WALTER (*b. Edinburgh, Scotland, 1784; d. New York, N.Y., 1868*), businessman, Pennsylvania legislator. Came to America as a boy. U.S. senator, Democrat, from Pennsylvania, 1819–25; outspoken opponent of slavery and of cash-sale basis for public lands. Secretary of the Senate, 1825–36, he became secretary of the Board of Foreign Missions of the Presbyterian Church in 1836 and served with great efficiency and success until 1868.

LOWRY, HIRAM HARRISON (*b. near Zanesville, Ohio, 1843. d. Peking, China, 1924*), Methodist clergyman. Missionary to China *post* 1867; superintendent of North China mission, 1873–93; head of Peking university, 1893–1918.

LOWRY, ROBERT (*b. Chesterfield District, S.C., 1830; d. Jackson, Miss., 1910*), lawyer, Confederate brigadier general. Raised in Tennessee and Mississippi. Governor of Mississippi, Democrat, 1882–90.

LOWRY, THOMAS (*b. Logan Co., Ill., 1843; d. 1909*), lawyer, capitalist. Settled in Minneapolis, Minn., 1867. Active *post* 1875 in local rapid transit and other transportation interests.

LOY, MATTHIAS (*b. Cumberland Co., Pa., 1828; d. Columbus, Ohio, 1915*), Lutheran clergyman, theologian, leader in the Ohio Synod.

LOYD, SAMUEL (*b. Philadelphia, Pa., 1841; d. 1911*), better known as Sam Loyd, composer of chess problems and inventor of puzzles and games including "Pigs in Clover" and "Parchesi."

LOZIER, CLEMENCE SOPHIA HARNED (*b. Plainfield, N.J., 1813; d. 1888*), homeopathic physician, feminist. Founded New York Medical College and Hospital for Women, 1863; the school was later merged with New York Homeopathic Medical College.

LUBBOCK, FRANCIS RICHARD (*b. Beaufort, S.C., 1815; d. 1905*), rancher, businessman, politician, Confederate soldier. Removed to Texas, 1836; served as clerk of Texas Congress and comptroller of the republic, 1837. Democratic lieutenant governor of Texas, 1857–59; governor, 1861–63. During his term he mobilized the state's manpower and resources in support of the Confederacy; at its close, he served as a staff officer in the Confederate Army and was one of those captured with President Davis, May 1865. Elected state treasurer of Texas, 1878, he held office until his retirement. 1891.

LUBIN, DAVID (*b. Klodowa, Russian Poland, 1849; d. Rome, Italy, 1919*), agriculturist. Came to America as a child; removed to California, 1865; returned East. Went West again to Sacramento, Calif., 1874, where he built up the largest mail-order merchandising business on the Pacific Coast. Leader of a revolt of the fruit-growers against discriminatory railroad rates and other evils including protective tariffs, he later campaigned successfully for creation of an international agricultural organization which was effected, 1910, under a treaty ratified by 46 nations.

LUBITSCH, ERNST (*b. Berlin, Germany, 1892; d. Los Angeles, Calif., 1947*), actor, motion picture director. Interested in the theater from boyhood, he studied acting, and worked as apprentice in the Berlin Bioscope Studios, 1909–11. He was a comedian with Max Reinhardt's Deutsches Theater company, 1911–12; played comic Jewish roles in Union-Film (Berlin) silent movies, 1913; began directing comedies, 1914. His direction of a series of historical dramas starring Pola Negri, 1918–22 (including *Madame DuBarry*, 1919, which was considered the most important European motion picture made up to that time), made them both famous. Coming to the United States in 1922 to direct Mary Pickford in *Rosita*, he was inspired by Charles Chaplin's *A Woman of Paris* (1923) to attempt work of similar sophistication and psychological realism. His films *The Marriage Circle* (1924), *Lady Windermere's Fan* (1925), *So This Is Paris* (1926), and others established him as a director of sophisticated comedy and an innovator in comic styles. With the advent of sound in motion pictures, he was able to employ dialogue and music without compromising the inventive visual techniques he had developed during the silent period. His first sound film, the operetta *The Love Parade* (1929), was followed by four other successful musicals. He also directed during this period a classic comedy which many critics consider his masterpiece, *Trouble in Paradise* (1932). After a period during which his work was not so well received either by audiences or by critics, he recovered what had come to be called "the Lubitsch touch" (brevity, lighthearted wit, the comedy of surprise, and visual effects that are remembered long after the plot of a film is forgotten) in *Ninotchka* (1939), *The Shop Around the Corner* (1940), and *To Be or Not to Be* (1942).

LUCAS, ANTHONY FRANCIS (*b. Spalato, Austria, 1855; d. 1921*), Austrian naval officer, geologist, engineer. Came to America, 1879; became American citizen and engaged first in lumbering, then as consulting engineer. His examination of low mounds, or "domes," in Gulf Coastal Plain areas of Louisiana and Texas led him to believe they were natural reservoirs of petroleum. Prosecuting his investigations, he brought in the famous Spindletop oil strike near Beaumont, Texas, Jan. 10, 1901.

LUCAS, DANIEL BEDINGER (*b. near Charles Town, Va., 1836; d. 1909*), West Virginia legislator, jurist, Confederate soldier. Author of quantity of poetry and some minor dramas.

LUCAS, ELIZA. *See* PINCKNEY, ELIZA LUCAS.

LUCAS, FREDERIC AUGUSTUS (*b. Plymouth, Mass., 1852; d. 1929*), naturalist. Associated with Henry A. Ward at Rochester, N.Y., 1871–82; held curatorial posts at U.S. National Museum, 1882–1904; curator, Brooklyn Museum, 1904–11; director, American Museum of Natural History, New York City, 1911–29. Had lasting influence on conduct of American museums; stressed the teaching function of exhibits.

LUCAS, JAMES H. (*b. Pittsburgh, Pa., 1800; d. 1873*), St. Louis banker, capitalist. Son of John B. C. Lucas.

LUCAS, JOHN BAPTISTE CHARLES (*b. Pont-Audemer, France, 1758; d. St. Louis, Mo., 1842*), Pennsylvania legislator, Missouri jurist. Came to America 1784. Congressman, (Democrat) Republican, from Pennsylvania, 1803–05. Appointed U.S. judge for northern district of Louisiana, 1805, he removed to St. Louis, Mo., and served on the bench until 1820; also a member of the commission for land titles, he acquired as much real estate as he could and died possessed of large property.

LUCAS, JONATHAN (*b. Cumberland, England, 1754; d. 1821*), millwright. Came to Charleston, S.C., *ca.* 1790. As rice planters were then handicapped by slow, expensive methods necessary to remove the husks from the grain, Lucas designed tidemill machinery by which three persons could beat 16 to 20 barrels of rice on a single tide. He and his son later developed many improvements in his mill, including the first steam rice mill (1817). In all essentials, later rice mills adhered to his plans, and the rice industry owed as much to him as the cotton industry to Eli Whitney.

LUCAS, JONATHAN (*b. England, 1775; d. Surrey, England, 1832*), millwright. Son and assistant of Jonathan Lucas (1754–1821); accompanied him to South Carolina *ca.* 1790. Patented a machine for rice cleaning without pounding by pestles, 1808, which was adopted with great success in England.

LUCAS, ROBERT (*b. Shepherdstown, Va., 1781; d. near Iowa City, Iowa, 1853*), surveyor, farmer, Ohio legislator. Democratic governor of Ohio, 1832–36; governor and superintendent of Indian affairs, territory of Iowa, 1838–41. Served as member of the 1844 Iowa constitutional convention.

LUCAS, SCOTT WIKE (*b. Cass County, Ill., 1892; d. Rocky Mount, N.C., 1968*), attorney and U.S. congressman and senator. Attended Illinois Wesleyan (LL.B., 1914). Elected an Illinois state attorney (1920) and U.S. Congressman (1934–38). Elected to U.S. Senate (1938–50), where he was Democratic whip (1946) and majority leader (1949). Strongly represented the interests of farmers and businessmen, supported the Truman administration's domestic proposals, but had difficulty grappling with domestic Communism; encountered the enmity of Senator Joseph McCarthy, who was instrumental in Lucas' defeat for reelection in 1950.

LUCE, HENRY ROBINSON (*b. Tengchow, China, 1898; d. Phoenix, Ariz., 1967*), editor and publisher. Son of missionary parents, he came to the United States in 1913; later attended Yale (B.A., 1920) and Oxford (1920–21). Became a reporter on the *Chicago Daily News*, then worked at the *Baltimore News* with college friend Britton Hadden, with whom he started a new journalistic enterprise—a weekly news magazine to synthesize and evaluate the most important events. *Time* was launched in 1923, the foundation of Time, Inc. Lacking an editorial page, Luce and Hadden usually favored a moderate Republicanism. Launched *Fortune*, a business monthly, in 1930. Produced radio and newsreel services in the 1930's, including *The March of Time* (radio version, 1931–45; newsreel version, 1935–51). *Life*, a photoessay magazine, appeared first in 1936. Luce took an active interest in politics, sometimes criticizing presidential administrations, but he never commanded great influence. He was a great admirer of Chiang Kai-shek, but the Truman's administration ignored his pleas for military aid to Chiang. In 1954, Luce began publishing *Sports Illustrated*. His magazines came under increasing attack in the 1950's because they tended to be "middle-brow," critical of most American intellectuals and avant-garde movements in the arts. After the successful launch of the world's first artificial satellite by the Soviet Union in 1957, *Life* championed a space race with Russia and later gained exclusive rights to the stories of first American astronauts. In 1964 Luce stepped down as editor in chief of *Time*. Perhaps the most innovative publisher in twentieth-century America, Luce helped reshape the news to make a complicated world seem comprehensible.

LUCE, HENRY WINTERS (*b. Scranton, Pa., 1868; d. Haverford, Pa., 1941*), Presbyterian clergyman, missionary educator. B.A., Yale, 1892; B.D., Princeton Theological Seminary, 1896. Taught at mission colleges in China, 1897–1915; vice-president of Shantung Christian University, 1915–17, and of Yenching University, 1919–27. Active in promotion of interdenominational cooperation in missionary education work, and as a fund raiser. Professor in Chinese department, Kennedy School of Missions of Hartford (Conn.) Theological Foundation, 1928–35. Father of Henry Robinson Luce.

LUCE, STEPHEN BLEECKER (*b. Albany, N.Y., 1827; d. Newport, R.I., 1917*), naval officer. Appointed midshipman, 1841; served in varied sea and shore duty until assignment just before the Civil War as head of department of seamanship, U.S. Naval Academy, Newport, R.I. His book *Seamanship* (1863) became standard treatise on the subject. After serving in commands at sea, 1863–65, he was commandant of midshipmen, U.S. Naval Academy, Annapolis, 1866–69, and occupied with various training duties thereafter until 1884. During all this time he worked in the face of marked opposition to secure better training for naval officers and advocated establishment of a school for advanced studies. Promoted commodore, 1881, Luce was appointed first president of the Naval War College on its establishment, 1884, at Newport, R.I. With Capt. A. T. Mahan as lecturer, the College struggled on, providing officers with instruction in history, international law, and higher command, "teaching the navy to think." Commissioned rear admiral, 1886, Luce retired in 1889.

LUCHESE, THOMAS (*b. Palermo, Sicily, 1899[?]; d. Lido Beach, Long Island, N.Y., 1967*), organized crime leader. Immigrated to the United States in 1911. Served in several of the Mafia's New York families, and his power and influence grew steadily. Instrumental in the election of New York Mayor Vincent R. Impellitteri (1950). As head of his own Mafia family, beginning in 1953, he used legitimate businesses as a cover for his involvement in narcotics distribution, gambling, and racketeering.

LUCIANO, CHARLES ("LUCKY") (*b. Lercara Friddi, Sicily, 1897[?]; d. Naples, Italy, 1962*), organized crime leader. Came to the United States *ca.* 1906 and after 1914 became involved in criminal activities; by 1926 had reached the upper echelons of the Mafia. Involved in bootlegging, hijacking, narcotics, and prostitution. Prostitution ring shattered (1926) and sentenced to thirty to fifty years, but still wielded power from his jail cell. Sentence commuted in 1946, provided he be deported to Italy; in 1951 the Kefauver Committee learned that the flow of heroin from Italy to the United States had increased since Luciano's deportation. Maintained his American underworld connections until his death.

LUCKENBACH, J(OHN) LEWIS (*b. Kingston, N.Y., 1883; d. New York, N.Y., 1951*), shipping executive. Graduated Princeton (1906). Inherited the Luckenbach shipping company and was vice president in charge of maintenance (1920–25). Executive vice president, the American Bureau of Shipping (1927–32); president (1932–51). An advocate of a strong American merchant marine; he received the navy's Distinguished Public Service Award (1943). Luckenbach represented the United States at a number of important international meetings, among them the International Conference for the Safety of Life at Sea (1948).

LUDELING, JOHN THEODORE (*b. New Orleans, La., 1827; d. near Monroe, La., 1891*), Louisiana jurist, Unionist. Republican chief justice of Louisiana, 1868–77.

LUDLOW, DANIEL (*b. New York, N.Y., 1750; d. Skaneateles, N.Y., 1814*), merchant. A Loyalist during the Revolution, Ludlow built up a very large importing trade as Daniel Ludlow & Company, 1790–1808. Active in the organization of the Manhattan Company, 1799, he was chosen its first president and served until 1808 when he fell into financial difficulties.

LUDLOW, FITZ HUGH (*b. New York, N.Y., 1836; d. Geneva, Switzerland, 1870*), writer. Author, among other works, of *The Hasheesh Eater* (1857), an autobiographical work strongly influenced by DeQuincey.

LUDLOW, GABRIEL GEORGE (*b. probably New York City, 1736; d. 1808*), Loyalist soldier. Half-brother of Daniel Ludlow; brother of George D. Ludlow. *Post* 1784, a councilor of the province of New Brunswick, Canada.

LUDLOW, GEORGE DUNCAN (*b. probably New York City, 1734; d. near Fredericton, New Brunswick, Canada, 1808*), Loyalist, jurist. Brother of Gabriel G. Ludlow; half-brother of Daniel Ludlow. Justice, supreme court of New York Colony, 1769–78; chief justice, province of New Brunswick, 1784–1808.

LUDLOW, NOAH MILLER (*b. New York, N.Y., 1795; d. St. Louis, Mo., 1886*), actor, theatrical manager. *Post* 1815, played through Kentucky and Tennessee; a company formed by him gave the first performances in English by professionals in New Orleans, La., 1817. He was in partnership with Sol Smith, 1835–53, and assisted in management of theatres in Mobile, St. Louis, Cincinnati, New Orleans. Author of *Dramatic Life as I Found It* (1880).

LUDLOW, ROGER (*fl. 1590–1664*), lawyer. Little is known of Ludlow's early life. He was baptized at Dinton, Wiltshire, England, 1590; entered Balliol College, Oxford, 1610; was admitted to the Inner Temple, 1612. He arrived at Massachusetts Bay, May 30, 1630, aboard the *Mary and John*. One of the founders of Dorchester, he took an active part in early government of the colony and was elected deputy-governor, 1634. Removing, 1635, to the new Connecticut River settlements, he presided at Windsor, April 1636, over the first court held in Connecticut. He is credited with having drafted the Fundamental Orders adopted by the colony, January 1638/39. He was author also of "Ludlow's Code," the first gathering together of Connecticut laws, issued 1650. Having settled at Fairfield, 1639, Ludlow resided there until 1654, when he returned to England and took office as a member of the parliamentary commission for seizing forfeited lands in Ireland. He resided in Dublin, 1654–64; the time and place of his death are unknown.

LUDLOW, THOMAS WILLIAM (*b. New York, N.Y., 1795; d. Yonkers, N.Y., 1878*), lawyer, financier. A founder of New York Life Insurance Co., 1845; first president, Panama Railroad Co., 1849; also a promoter of other railroads including the Illinois Central.

LUDLOW, WILLIAM (*b. Islip N.Y., 1843; d. Convent Station, N.J., 1901*), soldier, engineer. Graduated West Point, 1864. In a single year of Civil War service with the Union Army, he won brevets up to lieutenant colonel for services in the Georgia campaign and in the Carolinas. As chief engineer, Department of Dakota, 1872–76, he made important surveys of Yellowstone National Park and the Black Hills country. After a wide experience in engineering work *post* 1876, Ludlow as brigadier general commanded the first brigade in the attack on El Caney, Cuba, 1898. Commissioned major general of volunteers, September 1898, he was made military governor of Havana and served until May 1900; he also saw extensive service during the Philippine insurrection.

LUDLOWE, ROGER. *See* LUDLOW, ROGER.

LUDWELL, PHILIP (*fl. 1660–1704*), planter, Virginia councillor. Born in Somersetshire, England, he immigrated to Virginia *ca.* 1660 and acquired estates in James City County. Led resistance to Lord Howard of Effingham, 1686–87; went to England, 1689, to present the charges of the Burgesses against Howard; was chosen governor of the northern part of Carolina by the Lords Proprietors, December 1689. In 1691 his commission was altered to make him governor of the entire province of Carolina. Effective in restoring a state of comparative peace in the colony, he was recalled, 1694, and ultimately returned to England where he died.

LUDWICK, CHRISTOPHER (*b. Giessen, Germany, 1720; d. Philadelphia, Pa., 1801*), baker, philanthropist. Settled in Philadelphia, 1754. An active patriot, he caused hundreds of Hessians to desert the British, 1776. Congress appointed him superintendent of bakers, Continental Army, May 1777; in this capacity he served until the end of the war. Prospering thereafter in business, he left his entire fortune for the education of poor children.

LUELLING, HENDERSON (*b. Randolph Co., N.C., 1809; d. San Jose, Calif., 1878*), nurseryman. Transported by ox team a stock of young trees and shrubs from Iowa to near present Portland, Oreg., April–November 1847. After success in operations there, he removed to vicinity of Oakland, Calif., 1854.

LUFBERY, RAOUL GERVAIS VICTOR (*b. Clermont, France, 1885; d. Maron, France, 1918*), aviator, American ace in World War I. Son of an American father; raised in France. After a roving life, enlisted in French air force, December 1914; having qualified as a pilot, he joined the *Escadrille Lafayette*, May 1916, and was officially credited with 17 victories. Commissioned major, U.S. Army air force, January 1918, he was shot down in combat.

LUGOSI, BELA (*b. Lugos, Hungary, 1882; d. Los Angeles, Calif., 1956*), actor. Remembered for his portrayal of the vampire, Count Dracula, Lugosi came to the U.S. in 1921, forced to leave Hungary by the revolution of 1919. Previous to this he had acted with the Hungarian National Theater. He made several silent films before appearing in the lead of the play *Dracula* in 1927. The movie version (1931) established his reputation as a horror film actor. Other films include *Murders in the Rue Morgue* (1932), *The Black Cat* (1934), *The Raven* (1935), and *Son of Frankenstein* (1939).

LUHAN, MABEL DODGE (*b. Buffalo, N.Y., 1879; d. Taos, N.Mex., 1962*), writer and patron of the arts. Held gatherings in her villa in Italy, New York City apartment, and New Mexico home that attracted writers, artists, and other intellectuals, including André Gide, Gertrude Stein, Lincoln Steffens, Walter Lippmann, Margaret Sanger, Georgia O'Keefe, and D. H. Lawrence. Her books include *Intimate Memories*, 4 vols. (1933–37).

LUKEMAN, HENRY AUGUSTUS (*b. Richmond, Va., 1871; d. New York, N.Y., 1935*), sculptor. Worked in studio of Launt Thompson and as assistant to Daniel Chester French. Among his many works, the statue of Manu on the Appellate Court House, New York City, and the relief of General Robert E. Lee on Stone Mountain, Georgia, are notable.

LUKENS, REBECCA WEBB PENNOCK (*b. Coatesville, Pa., 1794; d. Coatesville, 1854*), iron manufacturer. Headed Brandywine Rolling Mill *post* 1825, becoming first woman in United States to engage in iron industry.

LUKS, GEORGE BENJAMIN (*b. Williamsport, Pa., 1867; d. New York, N.Y., 1933*), painter. Studied at Pennsylvania Academy of the Fine Arts and in Düsseldorf, London, and Paris; was an ardent admirer of Rembrandt and Franz Hals. Adventurous, turbulent, he painted anything from circus wagons to comic strips for a living; the serious work of Luks dealt with the common life about him, particularly the colorful life of New York's East Side. Reacting from fashionable Impressionism, he associated himself with the group of painters known derisively as the "ash-can school." Though his output was uneven, all of his pictures show an inescapable vitality.

LULL, EDWARD PHELPS (*b. Windsor, Vt., 1836; d. 1887*), naval officer. Graduated U.S. Naval Academy, 1855. Served with credit in Union Navy during Civil War; thereafter had a varied experience as explorer and surveyor, notably in Nicaragua.

LUMBROZO, JACOB (*fl. 1656–1665*), physician, planter, merchant. Born in Lisbon of Jewish ancestry, he immigrated first to Holland, and from Holland to Maryland, 1656. One of the first Jews to settle in Maryland and the first physician to practice there.

LUMMIS, CHARLES FLETCHER (*b. Lynn, Mass., 1859; d. 1928*), journalist, author. Removed to Los Angeles, Calif., 1885; to New Mexico, 1888; lived among Pueblo Indians, and was associated in ethnological work with Adolph Bandelier. Through his books, *The Land of Poco Tiempo* (1893), *The Spanish Pioners* (1893), and others, he aroused interest in the romantic history of the Southwest. Founded the Southwest Museum, Los Angeles.

LUMPKIN, JOSEPH HENRY (*b. Oglethorpe Co., Ga., 1799; d. 1867*), lawyer. Brother of Wilson Lumpkin. Graduated College of New Jersey (Princeton), 1819. Practiced mainly in Athens, Ga. Chief justice, supreme court of Georgia, 1845–67. During his tenure he and his associates, by the wisdom of their decisions, firmly established their court in the good graces of the people of Georgia who had traditionally opposed any court of review.

LUMPKIN, WILSON (*b. Pittsylvania Co., Va., 1783; d. Athens, Ga., 1870*), lawyer, planter, Georgia legislator. Brother of Joseph H. Lumpkin. Congressman, Democrat, 1815–17, 1827–31; governor of Georgia, 1831–35; U.S. senator, 1837–41. An extreme states' rights advocate.

LUNA Y ARELLANO, TRISTAN DE (*fl. 1530–1561*), Spanish explorer. Came to New Spain *ca.* 1530; served as captain under Francisco Coronado. Appointed governor and captain general of Florida, he led the ill-fated expedition which attempted a settlement around Pensacola Bay, 1559–61.

LUNCEFORD, JAMES MELVIN (*b. Fulton, Mo., 1902; d. Seaside, Oreg., 1947*), musician, bandleader. Studied music while a high school student in Denver, Colo., under W. J. Whiteman, father of Paul Whiteman. By 1926, when he graduated with a B. Mus. degree from Fisk University, he was a capable performer on saxophones, flute, trombone, and guitar. Prominent in all sports at Fisk, he became an athletic instructor as well as a teacher of music at a Memphis, Tenn., high school. Forming a band from among his pupils and recent graduates of Fisk University, he instilled a sense of responsibility in his men, stressing the value of teamwork and insisting on it. He was ably supported by his arrangers, Willie Smith and Ed Wilcox, and especially Sy Oliver who joined the band in 1933. The Lunceford "style" soon won public acclaim and recognition by the critics; the band was also notable for the attention it gave to entertainment values, and was virtually a show in itself. A long series of recordings gave it international reputation as one of the most exciting of U.S. jazz bands. The difficulties occasioned by World War II were responsible for a decline in its fortunes.

LUNDEBERG, HARRY (*b. Oslo, Norway, 1901; d. San Francisco, Calif., 1957*), labor leader. Immigrated to the U.S. in 1923. A sailor, Lundeberg joined the Sailors' Union of the Pacific in 1926, rising to secretary-treasurer by 1935. By 1938, he was president of the newly formed Seafarers' International Union, an affiliate of the AFL. Through a series of major strikes in 1936, 1946, and 1952, Lundeberg was able to win major salary and working condition improvements for the sailors' union. Lundeberg was an anticommunist Republican; he remained the leader of the Pacific union until his death. A critic of "tuxedo unionism," he appeared everywhere in the standard sailor's garb of gray cap, shirt sleeves, and black dungarees.

LUNDEEN, ERNEST (*b. Beresford, S. Dak., 1878; d. near Lovettsville, Va., 1940*), lawyer, Minnesota legislator. Congressman, Republican, from Minnesota, 1917–19; Farmer-Labor, 1933–36. U.S. senator, Farmer-Labor, 1936–40). A progressive isolationist, humorless and independent, Lundeen was in domestic affairs to the left of the New Deal, favoring nationalization of banks, high taxes, and a broad program of unemployment insurance.

LUNDIE, JOHN (*b. Arbroath, Scotland, 1857; d. New York, N.Y., 1931*), engineer. Came to America *ca.* 1880. Laid out first low-level drainage system for Chicago; was connected with water-supply projects elsewhere. Established Lundie formula for train resistance; designed first combined electric hoist and tractor (telpher) *ca.* 1898.

LUNDIN, CARL AXEL ROBERT (*b. Venersborg, Sweden, 1851; d. 1915*), optician. Came to America, 1873. Became chief instrument-maker for Alvan Clark & Sons, Cambridgeport, Mass.; in that post worked on many of the largest telescope lenses made in his time.

LUNDY, BENJAMIN (*b. Sussex Co., N.J., 1789; d. Illinois, 1839*), Abolitionist. A saddler of Quaker stock, Lundy removed to Ohio, 1815. An ardent anti-slavery agitator subsequent to 1815, he traveled widely in search of a place where freed blacks might be colonized, meanwhile publishing *post* 1821 an Abolitionist paper, *The Genius of Universal Emancipation*; it ceased publication, 1835. Between 1836 and 1838, Lundy published *The National Enquirer* in opposition to what he claimed were plots of slaveholders to take Texas from Mexico; in March 1838 this paper became *The Pennsylvania Freeman*. Lundy revived *The Genius of Universal Emancipation* in Illinois in 1839 shortly before his death. He was the most active figure in the antislavery movement during the 1820's, and his enlistment of W. L. Garrison as an associate (1828) brought to the cause its chief protagonist.

LUNN, GEORGE RICHARD (*b. near Lenox, Iowa, 1873; d. Rancho Santa Fe, Calif., 1948*), Presbyterian clergyman, Socialist and Democratic party politician. Left school at age twelve to sell newspapers in Des Moines. In 1892 he entered Bellevue College near Omaha, and during the following five years he completed the B.A. degree while supporting himself by various jobs. In 1897 he entered the Princeton Theological Seminary in New Jersey. His training was interrupted by the Spanish-American War, when he joined the unit of Nebraska volunteers. He resumed his studies at Union Theological Seminary in New York City in 1899 and graduated with the B.D. degree in 1901. He was ordained that year in the Presbyterian ministry and became an associate pastor in Brooklyn. In 1903 he moved to Schenectady, N.Y. where he became a leading spokesman of reform. His new role caused friction with his congregation; he resigned at the beginning of 1910 and founded an independent Peoples' Church. He continued in the ministry until 1915. Meanwhile, in 1910 Lunn began publication of the *Citizen* and joined the Socialists.

The next year, as the party's mayoral candidate, he led a Socialist ticket to victory in the municipal elections. He was defeated for reelection in 1913 by a coalition of Republicans and Democrats. He was renominated and reelected in 1915, but the following year the state Socialist organization expelled him.

Lunn never again professed socialism, but in 1916 he was elected to Congress as a Democrat. During his single term in office he served on the House Military Affairs Committee, supported American entry in World War I, and worked for a selective service act. Running as a Democrat, he was twice returned to the office of mayor of Schenectady, in 1919 and 1921. In 1922 he was elected lieutenant governor, but he was defeated for reelection in 1924.

LUNT, GEORGE (*b. Newburyport, Mass., 1803; d. 1885*), lawyer, journalist, author. Editor, *Boston Daily Courier*, 1857–63.

LUNT, ORRINGTON (*b. Bowdoinham, Maine, 1815; d. Evanston, Ill., 1897*), businessman, philanthropist. Removed to Chicago, Ill., 1842, where he prospered in various mercantile activities. Active in establishment of Northwestern University.

LURTON, HORACE HARMON (*b. Newport, Ky., 1844; d. Atlantic City, N.J., 1914*), lawyer, Confederate soldier, jurist. Practiced at Clarksville, Tenn., 1867–86. Justice, supreme court of Tennessee, 1886–93; chief justice, 1893. U.S. circuit judge, 1893–1909. During service on the federal bench, his abilities impressed the presiding judge of the circuit, William H. Taft. Appointed by Taft a justice of U.S. Supreme Court, 1909, Lurton served ably until his death. A strict constitutionalist, he had little sympathy with those who wished to adjust the machinery of government to changing conditions of life and thought by judicial interpretation.

LUSK, GRAHAM (*b. Bridgeport, Conn., 1866; d. 1932*), physiologist. Son of William T. Lusk. Graduated School of Mines, Columbia, 1887; Ph.D., Munich, 1891. Taught physiology at Yale, New York University, and Cornell. His studies in animal and clinical calorimetry extended over a period of 44 years and dealt with a great variety of topics such as basal metabolism, specific dynamic action of various foodstuffs, and the like. His book *The Elements of the Science of Nutrition* (1906) had a marked influence on medical research in the United States and in promoting an appreciation of the value of laboratory methods in explaining the inner processes in disease.

LUSK, WILLIAM THOMPSON (*b. Norwich, Conn., 1838; d. 1897*), obstetrician, Union soldier. Graduated Bellevue Hospital Medical College, 1864; studied also at Edinburgh and Vienna. Junior partner of Benjamin F. Barker, 1866–73; professor of obstetrics, Bellevue, 1871–97; held numerous hospital appointments. His classic work *The Science and Art of Midwifery* (1882) was considered the most learned textbook of the day in English.

LUTHER, SETH (*fl. 1817–1846*), carpenter, pioneer labor reformer. Born probably in Providence, R.I., Luther traveled widely through the United States, 1817–30. His first pamphlet, *An Address to the Working-men of New England* (1832), was an attack on the abuses of the incipient factory system. In the following year he published *An Address on the Right of Free Suffrage* and in 1834 *An Address on the Origin and Progress of Avarice*. His deadly sincerity and biting sarcasm made his pamphlets valuable weapons in the labor movement.

LUTKIN, PETER CHRISTIAN (*b. Thompsonville, Wis., 1858; d. Evanston, Ill., 1931*), musical composer and conductor, educator. As professor of music and dean of school of music, Northwestern University, *post* 1891 (dean, *post* 1897), he developed the school into one of the important musical institutions of the country. He also established the Chicago North Shore Festival Association, 1908, of which he was the choral conductor until 1930.

LUTZ, FRANK EUGENE (*b. Bloomsburg, Pa., 1879; d. New York, N.Y., 1943*), entomologist. A.B., Haverford College, 1900. A.M., University of Chicago, 1902; Ph.D., 1907. Studied also in London and Berlin. Staff member of Carnegie Institution's Station for Experimental Evolution, Cold Spring Harbor, L.I., N.Y., 1904–09; associated with American Museum of Natural History, New York City, *post* 1909, as assistant and associate curator in department of invertebrate zoology, and as curator of his own department of insects and spiders. He also served for many years as editorial director of the Museum's scientific publications. He was author, among other works, of *Field Book of Insects* (1918).

LYALL, JAMES (*b. Auchterardar, Scotland, 1836; d. New York, N.Y., 1901*), inventor, manufacturer. Came to New York, N.Y., as a small child. Invented a positive-motion loom (patented, 1868, 1871, 1872) which abolished use of picking sticks and permitted great widths of fabric to be woven. Lyall made other improvements in textile machinery and in machines for manufacture of jute twine; he also patented a new type of woven fabric for pneumatic tires and fire hose, 1893–96.

LYBRAND, WILLIAM MITCHELL (*b. Philadelphia, Pa., 1867; d. Stamford, Conn., 1960*), public accountant. Taught by accountant John Heins, Lybrand founded his own firm in 1891 which became the international public accounting firm Coopers and Lybrand. Responsible for changing the status of accountants into an accepted profession, Lybrand helped found the Pennsylvania Association of Public Accountants in 1897, and later, the American Association of Public Accountants. In 1904, the Wharton School at the University of Pennsylvania incorporated the educational program for accountants begun by Lybrand. Along with protection through legislation, this step helped ensure the professional status of the accountant.

LYDENBERG, HARRY MILLER (*b. Dayton, Ohio, 1874; d. Westerville, Ohio, 1960*), librarian. Studied at Harvard. Associated with the New York Public Library from 1896; reference librarian from 1908; director from 1934 to 1941. Under Lydenberg's directorship, the library became one of the world's greatest reference and research institutions. Secretary-treasurer of the American Council of Learned Societies (1937–41); president of the American Library Association (1932–33). After leaving the library in 1941, Lydenberg was librarian for the Biblioteca Benjamin Franklin in Mexico City (1941–43). He then did work with foreign libraries in Europe and Latin America. Books include *The Origins of Printing and Engraving* (1940).

LYDSTON, GEORGE FRANK (*b. Jacksonville, Calif., 1857; d. Los Angeles, Calif., 1923*), physician. Graduated Bellevue Hospital Medical School, 1879; practiced in Chicago, Ill., *post* 1881. A specialist in genito-urinary surgery, he wrote vehemently on many subjects. He was the Peck's Bad Boy of the medical profession of his time and engaged in a number of intra-professional controversies.

LYMAN, ALBERT JOSIAH (*b. Williston, Vt., 1845; d. 1915*), Congregational clergyman. Pastor at Milford, Conn., 1869–73; at South Church, Brooklyn, N.Y., 1874–1915. A man of practical ability rather than a theologian, he was a leader in Congregationalism through many years.

LYMAN, BENJAMIN SMITH (*b. Northampton, Mass., 1835; d. Philadelphia, Pa., 1920*), geologist, mining engineer. As general geologist for the Japanese government, 1873–80, he discovered many coal and other mineral deposits in Japan and assisted in their development.

LYMAN, CHESTER SMITH (*b.* Manchester, Conn., 1814; *d. New Haven, Conn.*, 1890), Congregational clergyman, astronomer, physicist. Graduated Yale, 1837. Traveling widely in search of health, he worked in Hawaii and in California. His letter, published in *American Journal of Science and Arts* (September 1848), is said to be the first credible account of the discovery of gold in California received in the East. As professor of physics and astronomy, Sheffield Scientific School *post* 1859, he invented a number of instruments for demonstrating physical theory and also the first combined transit and zenith instrument for determining latitude by Talcott's method. His journal of his travels was published as *Around the Horn to the Sandwich Islands and California* (1924).

LYMAN, EUGENE WILLIAM (*b. Cummington, Mass.,* 1872; *d. Sweet Briar, Va.,* 1948), educator, philosopher of religion, liberal Protestant spokesman. Graduated Amherst College, 1894. B.D., Yale Divinity School, 1899; made advanced studies in theology at universities of Halle, Berlin, and Marburg. Ordained in the Congregational ministry, 1901, he was professor of philosophy at Carleton College, 1901–04. Thereafter, he taught philosophy and theology at the Congregational Church College of Canada (Montreal), at Bangor Theological Seminary in Maine (1905–13), and at the Oberlin School of Theology (1913–18). He was professor of the philosophy of religion at Union Theological Seminary, New York City, 1918–40. An effective and innovative teacher, he was author of numerous articles, of several short books, and of *The Meaning and Truth of Religion* (1933), which expressed his characteristic modernist eagerness to effect a synthesis of varying theoretical and doctrinal emphases, and also the liberal tendency to make philosophy do most of the work of theology. His struggle to find firmer empirical grounding for theology than either idealism or pragmatism could supply was resolved in a synthesis that was one prominent expression of an attitude called theological realism. In Lyman's case, this realism insisted upon the independent reality of natural objects, of intuitively grasped moral values, and of divine revelation—even though each of these areas of experience was thought to "criticize and supplement" the others. He came to define God as a "cosmic creative spirit" whose nature combined purposiveness and open-ended creativity. A steady advocate of the Social Gospel, he generally lent his support to the activist social radicals among his colleagues.

LYMAN, JOSEPH BARDWELL (*b. Chester, Mass.,* 1829; *d. Richmond Hill, N.Y.* 1872), lawyer, Confederate soldier, agriculturist. After the Civil War, as agricultural editor of several newspapers and periodicals, notably the N.Y. *Weekly Tribune*, he impressed on American farmers the need of sustaining home manufactures and of diversifying crops.

LYMAN, PHINEAS (*b. near Durham, Conn.,* 1715; *d.* 1774), lawyer, Connecticut legislator. Graduated Yale, 1738. Commanding Connecticut provincial troops during the Seven Years' War, he won reputation of being ablest general in Northern colonies and aided in defeat of the French at Lake George, 1755. Accompanied Amherst against Crown Point, 1759; later commanded at Ticonderoga. In 1762, he led all the provincial troops on expedition to Havana. *Post* 1763, he planned a series of colonies for discharged provincial soldiers along the Mississippi, especially at the mouth of the Ohio.

LYMAN, THEODORE (*b. Boston, Mass.,* 1792; *d.* 1849), Massachusetts legislator, author, philanthropist. Graduated Harvard, 1810. A Federalist and opponent of John Q. Adams,

Lyman became a supporter of Andrew Jackson *post* 1828, but soon cooled in his affection for the Democrats. He served as mayor of Boston, 1834–35, an able but undistinguished term of office during which he was bitterly assailed by the Abolitionists.

LYMAN, THEODORE (*b. Waltham, Mass.,* 1833; *d. Nahant, Mass.,* 1897), Union soldier, zoologist. Son of Theodore Lyman (1792–1849). Graduated Harvard, 1855. Worked under Louis Agassiz in Lawrence Scientific School. Recognized as an authority on the Ophiuridae. Served on state fisheries commission and in other civic capacities; was an original trustee and later treasurer of the Museum of Comparative Zoology.

LYMAN, THEODORE (*b. Brookline, Mass.,* 1874; *d. Brookline, Mass.,* 1954), experimental physicist. Ph.D., Harvard, 1900. Professor at Harvard (1907–25); director of the Jefferson Physical Laboratory from 1910 to 1947. Lyman's scientific work was in the area of the extreme ultraviolet. By 1915 he had extended the known spectrum to 600 angstroms and by 1917 to 500 angstroms. He identified the "Lyman" or the fundamental series of hydrogen in the vacuum ultraviolet. *The Spectroscopy of the Extreme Ultraviolet* appeared in 1914.

LYNCH, ANNA CHARLOTTE. *See* BOTTA, ANNA CHARLOTTE LYNCH.

LYNCH, CHARLES (*b. near present Lynchburg, Va.,* 1736; *d. Virginia,* 1796), Virginia legislator, planter, Revolutionary patriot. Presiding over an extra-legal court in Bedford Co., Va., during the Revolution, Lynch gave his name to the use of summary unauthorized process in punishing lawlessness.

LYNCH, JAMES DANIEL (*b. Boydton, Va.,* 1836; *d. Sulphur Springs, Texas,* 1903), Confederate soldier, author of numerous works on the history of Mississippi and Texas.

LYNCH, JAMES MATHEW (*b. Manlius, N.Y.,* 1867; *d. Syracuse, N.Y.,* 1930), labor leader. As president, International Typographical Union, 1900–14, 1924–26, he won for its members the eight-hour day (1906–08), established an old-age pension system, provided better apprentice education and greatly strengthened its financial position. He served on the New York State Industrial Commission, 1915–21.

LYNCH, JOHN ROY (*b. Concordia Parish, La.,* 1847; *d. Chicago, Ill.,* 1939), A black, Lynch served as congressman from Mississippi, 1873–77, 1882–83. He was active in Republican politics through 1900, and was chosen temporary chairman of the national Republican convention, 1884. After service as a U.S. army officer, 1901–11, he practiced law in Chicago.

LYNCH, PATRICK NEESON (*b. Clones, Ireland,* 1817; *d. Charleston, S.C.,* 1882), Roman Catholic clergyman. Came to America as an infant; was raised in Cheraw, S.C. Ordained in Rome, 1840, he served as pastor in Charleston *post* 1845, and was consecrated bishop of Charleston, 1858. A successful administrator and a forceful preacher and writer, he carried a letter from President Davis to Pope Pius IX, 1863, expressing desire of the Confederacy for peace. After the Civil War, he was an effective promoter of better feeling between North and South.

LYNCH, ROBERT CLYDE (*b. Carson City, Nev.,* 1880; *d. near Richmond, Ky,* 1931), physician. M.D., Tulane University, 1903; also made studies of the eye, ear, nose, and throat in France, Germany, and England. Taught rhinology and otolaryngology at Tulane *post* 1911; developed radical frontal sinus operation known as the "Lynch operation" and was first to make successful moving pictures of larynx and vocal cords.

LYNCH, THOMAS (*b. Berkeley Co., S.C., 1727; d. Annapolis, Md., 1776*), planter, South Carolina legislator. With Christopher Gadsden and John Rutledge, represented South Carolina in Stamp Act Congress, 1765, at New York City; also served as member of First and Second Continental Congresses, 1774–76.

LYNCH, THOMAS (*b. Winyaw, S.C., 1749; d. at sea[?], 1779*), planter. Son of Thomas Lynch (1727–1776). Educated at Eton and Cambridge and at the Middle Temple (1764–72). A member of the Second Continental Congress, 1776–77, he was a signer of the Declaration of Independence, but soon became an invalid and retired from public life.

LYNCH, WILLIAM FRANCIS (*b. Norfolk, Va., 1801; d. Baltimore, Md., 1865*), naval officer. Appointed midshipman, 1819. Author of *Official Report of the U.S. Expedition to Explore the Dead Sea and the River Jordan* (1852), which dealt with investigations he had made in 1848 and described in an earlier popular work (1849). He served in the Confederate navy during the Civil War.

LYND, ROBERT STAUGHTON (*b. New Albany, Ind., 1892; d. Warren, Conn., 1970*), sociologist and author. Attended Princeton, Union Theological Seminary (D.D., 1923), and Columbia (Ph.D., 1931). A missionary preacher in Elk Basin, Mont., in 1923, he shifted his interest from religion to sociology. He and his wife began to study urban society; their landmark work was *Middletown* (1929), a factual sociological description of life in Muncie, Ind., the first objective examination of an American city. Taught at Columbia, 1931–60.

LYNDE, BENJAMIN (*b. Salem, Mass., 1700; d. Salem, 1781*), Massachusetts colonial legislator and jurist. Graduated Harvard, 1718. Justice, Massachusetts superior court, 1746–72; presided over trial of British soldiers involved in Boston Massacre.

LYNDE, FRANCIS (*b. Lewiston, N.Y., 1856; d. near Chattanooga, Tenn., 1930*), novelist. Drew on his early life experiences on Western railroads in *David Vallory* (1919), *The Wreckers* (1920), and other works.

LYNDS, ELAM (*b. Litchfield, Conn., 1784; d. South Brooklyn, N.Y., 1855*), prison administrator. Originator of so-called Auburn system of prison keeping.

LYON, CALEB (*b. Lyonsdale, N.Y., 1821; d. Staten Island, N.Y., 1875*), politician, New York legislator and congressman. A polished misfit as second territorial governor of Idaho, 1864–66.

LYON, DAVID GORDON (*b. Benton, Ala., 1852; d. 1935*), educator, Orientalist. Graduated Howard College, 1875; attended Southern Baptist Theological Seminary, Louisville, Ky; Ph.D., Leipzig, 1882. Inaugurated teaching of Assyriology in the United States, 1882, at Harvard, where he taught Semitic languages and history until his retirement, 1922.

LYON, DAVID WILLARD (*b. Ningpo, China, 1870; d. Claremont, Calif., 1949*), founder of the YMCA in China, Presbyterian clergyman. Born of missionary parents. B.A., College of Wooster, 1891; attended McCormick Theological Seminary; served as educational secretary for the Student Volunteer Movement, 1894–95; ordained, 1895. Founded a student YMCA at Tientsin, 1896, and helped organize others throughout the country; shaped the organization so that it was self-governing and staffed and led by Chinese; regarded it as a force in the modernizing and reform of Chinese society. He served as general secretary, and then associate secretary of the national committee of the Chinese YMCA, 1901–30.

LYON, FRANCIS STROTHER (*b. Stokes Co., N.C., 1800; d. Demopolis, Ala., 1882*), lawyer, Alabama politician. Nephew of George S. Gaines. Congressman, Whig, from Alabama, 1835–39; served also in the Confederate Congress, 1861–65. His principal public service was as liquidator of the involved Bank of the State of Alabama, *post* 1844, when by shrewd management he saved the state from bankruptcy and many of the bank's creditors from ruin.

LYON, HARRIS MERTON (*b. Santa Fe, N. Mex., 1883; d. 1916*), journalist. Graduated University of Missouri, 1905. His short fiction as contained in *Sardonics* (1908) and *Graphics* (1913) displayed literary powers of a high order.

LYON, JAMES (*b. Newark, N.J., 1735; d. 1794*), Presbyterian clergyman, psalmodist. Pastor, principally at Machias, Maine. Author of *Urania* (Philadelphia, probably 1761; second edition, 1767).

LYON, JAMES BENJAMIN (*b. Pennsylvania Furnace, Pa., 1821; d. 1909*), Pittsburgh glass manufacturer. First to make pressed glass the chief output of his factory, *post* 1849.

LYON, MARY (*b. Buckland, Mass., 1797; d. 1849*), educator. Studied in academies at Ashfield and Amherst, Mass.; attended Byfield Seminary, 1821. After 13 years of practical teaching, she conceived of a permanent female college which would not be beyond the scope of girls of moderate means, and set about to achieve it. She opened Mount Holyoke Seminary in November 1837, at South Hadley, Mass., with a curriculum based on that followed at Amherst College. Her contribution to the education of women was threefold; the opening to women of the highest educational opportunities; the conviction that these opportunities should be used as preparation for service; the conception of such education as the development of all the powers of an individual.

LYON, MATTHEW (*b. Co. Wicklow, Ireland, 1750; d. Spadra Bluff, Ark., 1822*), Revolutionary soldier, Vermont and Kentucky legislator. Came to America, 1765; was an indentured servant in Connecticut; removed to Vermont, 1774. A leading businessman, he was elected congressman, (Democrat) Republican, from Vermont, 1797. Insulted and badgered by Federalists, his retaliation on Roger Griswold on the floor of the House, Jan. 30, 1798, was probably the first personal encounter of its kind. Prosecuted under the Sedition Act, Lyon served four months in jail, October 1798–January 1799, and was fined; reelected triumphantly to Congress, he continued his vigorous opposition to John Adams's administration and cast the decisive vote of Vermont for election of Thomas Jefferson. Removing to Kentucky, 1801, at the head of a colony, he soon became a political power there and served as congressman, 1803–11. In his many able speeches he denounced antidemocratic tendencies but opposed the War of 1812.

LYON, NATHANIEL (*b. Ashford, Conn., 1818; d. near Wilson's Creek, Mo., 1861*), Union brigadier general. Graduated West Point, 1841. After serving in Mexican War, and in California, he was stationed in Kansas, 1854–61. Assigned, February 1861, to the St. Louis (Mo.) Arsenal, he took command in May of all local Union forces and by constant pressure against the Confederates did much to hold Missouri for the Union. He was killed in action.

LYON, THEODATUS TIMOTHY (*b. Lima, N.Y., 1813; d. 1900*), pomologist, businessman. Removed to Michigan as a youth; engaged in pioneer railroad building there. Although self-taught, he came to be considered the most critical and accurate of American pomologists. Removing to South Haven, Mich., 1874, he assembled a collection of fruit varieties which was an important factor in the rapid development of orcharding in that region.

LYON, WILLIAM PENN (*b. Chatham, N.Y., 1822; d. Edenvale, Calif., 1913*), lawyer, Union soldier, Wisconsin legislator and jurist.

LYONS, PETER (*b. Co. Cork, Ireland*[?], *1734/35; d. Hanover Co., Va., 1809*), Virginia lawyer and jurist. Licensed to practice in Virginia county courts, 1756; served as plaintiff's attorney in the "Parsons' Cause." Appointed judge of general court of Virginia, 1779; he served as president of the court, *post* 1803.

LYSTER, HENRY FRANCIS LE HUNTE (*b. Co. Wexford, Ireland, 1837; d. 1894*), physician, Union Army surgeon. Came to America as an infant. Graduated University of Michigan, A.B., 1858; M.D., 1860. Practiced and taught mainly in Detroit, Mich.

LYTLE, WILLIAM HAINES (*b. Cincinnati, Ohio, 1826; d. Chickamauga, Tenn., 1863*), lawyer, Union brigadier general, Ohio legislator. Author of *Poems* (1894). Killed in action.

LYTTELTON, WILLIAM HENRY (*b. England, 1724; d. Hagley, Worcestershire, England, 1808*), colonial official, author. Appointed governor of South Carolina, 1755, he caused renewed Indian war along the borders of the colony by his high-handed detention of Cherokee chiefs who had come on a peace mission, 1759. In April 1760, he left the colony to assume the governorship of Jamaica.

M

Maas, Anthony J. (b. Bainkhausen, Westphalia, Germany, 1858; d. Poughkeepsie, N.Y., 1927), Roman Catholic clergyman, Jesuit educator. Came to America ca. 1877. Provincial of Jesuit Maryland–New York province, 1912–18, he spent most of his life as a seminary professor.

Mabery, Charles Frederic (b. New Gloucester, Maine, 1850; d. Portland, Maine, 1927), chemist. Graduated Lawrence Scientific School, 1876; Sc.D., 1881. Taught at Case School, Cleveland, Ohio, 1883–1911. Authority on petroleum and on the electric furnace.

Mabie, Hamilton Wright (b. Cold Spring, N.Y., 1845; d. 1916), lawyer, editor, essayist. Associated with the Christian Union after 1893, the Outlook), 1879–1916.

McAdams, Clark (b. near Otterville, Ill., 1874; d. St. Louis, Mo., 1935), journalist, conservationist. Associated in a number of capacities from reporter to editor with the St. Louis Post-Dispatch, 1898–1935.

McAdie, Alexander George (b. New York, N.Y., 1863; d. Elizabeth City, Va., 1943), meteorologist. A.B., College of the City of New York, 1881; A.M., 1884; A.M., Harvard, 1885. Enlisted in U.S. Army Signal Service, 1882, and served as assistant in its Washington, D.C., physical laboratory; taught physics and meteorology at Clark University, 1889–91; meteorological physicist and assistant to the director, U.S. Weather Bureau, 1891–95. Served as director and forecaster in San Francisco office of the U.S. Weather Bureau, 1895–1913, becoming an authority on the climate of California. Professor of meteorology at Harvard, and director of the Blue Hill Observatory, 1913–31. He pioneered in use of kites to explore the air at high altitudes, developed and patented devices to protect fruit from frost, studied smoke as an air pollutant, and advocated standardization of the physical units employed in meteorological notation. His books included The Climatology of California (1903) and The Principles of Aerography (1917).

McAdoo, William Gibbs (b. Marietta, Ga., 1863; d. Washington, D.C., 1941), lawyer, businessman, politician. Raised in Milledgeville, Ga. Attended University of Tennessee, 1879–82, studied law in office of Chattanooga, Tenn., attorney; admitted to the bar, 1885. Invested his profits from a local real estate transaction in a Knoxville streetcar line, but the venture failed, forcing McAdoo into bankruptcy. In 1892 he moved to New York City, where he established a practice as partner in the law firm of McAdoo and McAdoo. By 1901 he had brought together the capital and engineering skills for completion in 1909 of four tunnels under the Hudson River. In 1910 he supported Woodrow Wilson in his race for governor of New Jersey and was Wilson's campaign manager in the presidential race of 1912. Later, as secretary of the treasury, McAdoo proposed a central bank operated out of the treasury, and though his plan made little headway, it dramatized the importance of public control. The

Federal Reserve Act (1913) was a compromise, but its centralized and public features owed as much to McAdoo as to anyone else. In 1914 McAdoo married Eleanor Randolph Wilson, daughter of the president.

During the war years McAdoo was, in addition to secretary of the treasury, chairman of the Federal Reserve Board and director general of the railroads after their takeover by the government in 1917. His most important job was the financing of the war by borrowing extensively from the public in four Liberty Loan drives. He resigned from the cabinet effective January 1919 and resumed the practice of law in New York. Although he was widely mentioned as Wilson's likely political legatee, he lost the presidential nomination three times. He had established a power base in California, and in 1932 he returned there to win a Senate seat that fall. He supported the New Deal loyally for six years. He was defeated in the Democratic primary of 1938. While continuing the law practice he had begun in Los Angeles in 1922, McAdoo also served as chairman of the board of the government-owned American President Lines until his death in 1941.

Despite his association in 1924 with much that was reactionary and outdated, McAdoo was a transitional figure between two liberal reform movements. His analytical powers and organizational ability matched Wilson's, and helped restore the Democratic party's reputation as a party capable of governing; his flexibility, his problem-solving pragmatism, and his hospitality to innovation kept his talents unencumbered by theories.

McAfee, John Armstrong (b. Marion Co., Mo., 1831; d. 1890), Presbyterian clergyman, educator. Cofounder of Park College, of which he was president, 1875–90.

McAffee, Robert Breckinridge (b. present Mercer Co., Ky., 1784; d. Mercer Co., 1849), lawyer, Kentucky legislator. Author of A History of the Late War in the Western Country (1816).

Macalester, Charles (b. Campbeltown, Scotland, 1765; d. 1832), merchant, shipowner. Immigrated to Philadelphia, Pa., ante 1786. Designer of the ship Fanny, ca. 1800, fastest merchant vessel of its day.

Macalester, Charles (b. Philadelphia, Pa., 1798; d. Philadelphia, 1873), banker. Son of Charles Macalester (1765–1832). Philadelphia agent and correspondent for George Peabody. Donated site of Macalester College, Minneapolis, Minn., 1873.

McAlexander, Ulysses Grant (b. Dundas, Minn., 1864; d. Portland, Oreg., 1936), army officer. Graduated West Point, 1887. Awarded Silver Star for gallantry in action in Santiago campaign, 1898. Known as the "Rock of the Marne," following his brilliant conduct as colonel commanding 38th Infantry in the Surmelin Valley, France, July 15–16, 1918. McAlexander retired as major general, 1924.

MacALISTER, JAMES (*b. Glasgow, Scotland, 1840; d. at sea, 1913*), educator. Came to America as a boy. Graduated Brown, 1856. Notably successful as superintendent of public schools in Milwaukee, Wis., and Philadelphia, Pa.; developed programs of industrial training. President, Drexel Institute, 1890–1913.

McALLISTER, CHARLES ALBERT (*b. Dorchester, N.J., 1867; d. New York, N.Y., 1932*), marine engineer. Chief engineer, Revenue-Cutter Service, 1902–16; U.S. Coast Guard, 1916–19. As vice president and president of American Bureau of Shipping *post* 1919, he took a leading part in agitation for government support of American merchant marine.

McALLISTER, HALL (*b. Savannah, Ga., 1826; d. near San Rafael, Calif., 1888*), lawyer. Son of Matthew H. McAllister; brother of Samuel W. McAllister. Practiced with great success in San Francisco, Calif., *post* 1849.

McALLISTER, MATTHEW HALL (*b. Savannah, Ga., 1800; d. San Francisco, Calif., 1865*), lawyer, Georgia legislator. Father of Hall and Samuel W. McAllister. U.S. circuit judge in California, 1855–62.

McALLISTER, SAMUEL WARD (*b. Savannah, Ga., 1827; d. 1895*), lawyer, leader of New York society. Son of Matthew H. McAllister; brother of Hall McAllister. On the strength of a fortune made at San Francisco in partnership with his father and brother, 1850–52, he removed to New York and by the late 1860's had made himself arbiter of the post–Civil War "new money" society of New York. He originated the phrase the "Four Hundred" *ca.* 1892, to describe the numerical limits of the city's social world.

McALPINE, WILLIAM JARVIS (*b. New York, N.Y., 1812; d. New Brighton, N.Y., 1890*), civil engineer. Apprenticed to John B. Jervis, 1827, he succeeded his teacher in 1836 as chief engineer of the eastern division of the Erie Canal. In this post and later as chief engineer of the government dry dock, Brooklyn, N.Y., he established himself as one of the leading engineers of his time. He served as engineer in charge and as consultant for many railroads; planned water supply systems for Chicago, San Francisco, and many smaller cities; was in charge of some of the greatest bridge projects of the time. He superintended construction of the New York State Capitol, Albany, 1873, and later built Riverside Drive, New York City.

McANALLY, DAVID RICE (*b. Grainger Co., Tenn., 1810; d. 1895*), Methodist clergyman, educator. Editor, *St. Louis Christian Advocate*, 1851–95.

McANDREW, WILLIAM (*b. Ypsilanti, Mich., 1863; d. Mamaroneck, N.Y., 1937*), educator. Graduated University of Michigan, 1886. A vigorous, if not always popular, administrator, McAndrew made a notable reputation as principal of Pratt Institute, Brooklyn, N.Y., and as organizer of a girls' technical high school (Washington Irving), New York City. He served as associate superintendent of New York City schools, 1914–24. Called to Chicago, Ill., 1924, as superintendent of schools, he fell afoul of Mayor W. H. ("Big Bill") Thompson; his dismissal, 1927, was subsequently overruled by the courts. A colorful personality, he stood out as one of the most rugged individualists in public education.

MacARTHUR, ARTHUR (*b. Springfield, Mass., 1845; d. Milwaukee, Wis., 1912*), soldier. Father of Douglas MacArthur. Raised in Wisconsin. Served with 24th Wisconsin Infantry throughout Civil War; recipient of many honors for gallantry, including the Medal of Honor, he entered the regular army as second lieutenant, 1866, and served mainly on western frontier duty up to 1898. After outstanding service in Philippine Islands, 1898–99, MacArthur was military governor of the islands, 1900–01. On his return to the United States, he held various departmental commands, retiring, 1909, with the rank of lieutenant general.

MacARTHUR, CHARLES GORDON (*b. Scranton, Pa., 1895; d. New York, N.Y., 1956*), journalist, playwright, motion picture writer and producer. After working on Chicago newspapers from 1914 to 1922, MacArthur went to New York for the *New York American;* he became involved with the literary circle at the Algonquin Hotel and began to collaborate with playwright Ben Hecht. Their major success was the 1928 play, *The Front Page;* in 1932, they wrote *Twentieth Century.* In 1931, he wrote the screenplay for *The Sin of Madelon Claudet* which starred his wife, Helen Hayes, and won her the Academy Award. He won an Academy Award for his script of *The Scoundrel,* starring Noel Coward, in 1934. From 1948 to 1950, he was editor of the magazine *Theatre Arts.*

MacARTHUR, DOUGLAS (*b. Little Rock, Ark., 1880; d. Washington, D.C., 1964*), army officer. Studied at the U.S. Military Academy (graduated, 1903); commissioned a second lieutenant in the U.S. Army Corps of Engineers. Promoted to colonel (transferred from engineers to infantry); commanded 42nd Infantry ("Rainbow") Division in France, 1918–19. Promoted to brigadier general (1918), later superintendent, U.S. Military Academy (1919–22). Promoted to major general (1925). Commander of the Philippine Department (1928–30); general and chief of staff, U.S. Army (1930–35); military adviser to the Philippines (1935–37); field marshal in the Philippine Army from 1936. Retired, U.S. Army (1937). Recalled to active duty (July 1941) as lieutenant general, commander of U.S. Army forces in the Far East. To Australia (1942); commander of the Southwest Pacific Area. Promoted to general of the army (1944); commanded all U.S. Army forces in the Pacific beginning in April 1945. Supreme Commander, Allied Powers (SCAP); presided over the Japanese surrender on Sept. 2, 1945; commanded the ensuing Allied occupation of Japan (to 1951). Commander in chief of the United Nations Command, Korea (1950–51). Relieved of his command by President Truman in April 1951. Chairman of the board of Remington Rand (later Sperry-Rand) from 1952.

MacArthur's career was one of the longest and most controversial of any American military figure. His leadership and bravery under fire won him recognition in World War I, and his stubborn defense of the beleaguered Philippines against the invading Japanese in World War II led to his emergence as the first American hero of that war; his famous proclamation "I shall return" (to the Philippines) upon his arrival in Australia in 1942 set forth at the outset the determined, aggressive spirit that would characterize his strategy for the rest of the conflict—bold and imaginative campaigns, with minimum logistical support, that brought about the liberation of most of the South Pacific islands by early 1944. Six months after his forces invaded Leyte (October 1944), most of the Philippine Islands were free.

His genius as a leader was also demonstrated in his pioneering reforms as superintendent of the U.S. Military Academy. Arriving at West Point at the low point in its history, he inaugurated changes in the tactical, athletic, and disciplinary systems, and elevated academic standards to make it a pacesetter among the world's military schools.

MacArthur's personality so dominated his headquarters during the occupation of Japan that the Japanese people generally came to view the occupation as personified by his image. To them he seemed to provide strong, inspiring leadership at a time when they had despaired of their old leaders. He initiated lasting political and economic reforms, and even attempted to westernize Japanese society and culture—one of his most quixotic plans was to Christianize Japan, but few converts were won.

Possessed of tragic flaws as well as monumental gifts, among his more serious limitations were an almost paranoid reaction to criticism, condescension toward superiors that often approached insubordination, and an inability to adjust to a strategy of limited warfare. As army chief of staff in the early 1930's, his outspoken criticism of pacifism produced a lasting image of him as a militarist. His strong character often caused him to clash with other leaders of the time, most notably, perhaps, President Truman, whose views differed sharply on the strategic direction of the Korean War and on civil-military relations.

McARTHUR, DUNCAN (*b. Dutchess Co., N.Y., 1772; d. near Chillicothe, Ohio, 1839*), surveyor, land speculator, Ohio legislator. Raised in the vicinity of Pittsburgh, Pa.; settled near Chillicothe, Ohio, 1796. As brigadier general in War of 1812, he defended Fort Meigs; he succeeded to command of army in the Northwest, 1814. Anti-Jackson governor of Ohio, 1830–32.

McARTHUR, JOHN (*b. Bladenock, Scotland, 1823; d. Philadelphia, Pa., 1890*), architect. Came to America as a child; apprenticed to a carpenter in Philadelphia, Pa. Self-taught, he was established in his profession by winning a competition for design of House of Refuge, Philadelphia, 1848. His most notable work was the Philadelphia City Hall.

McARTHUR, JOHN (*b. Erskine, Scotland, 1826; d. 1906*), manufacturer, Union major general. Immigrated to Chicago, Ill., 1849, where he became a partner in Excelsior Iron Works; rose to colonel in the militia. Promoted brigadier general, 1862, he distinguished himself at Shiloh and in Vicksburg campaign, his attack against Hood's left wing at Nashville, December 1864, turned the battle into a Confederate rout.

MacARTHUR, ROBERT STUART (*b. Dalesville, Canada, 1841; d. Daytona Beach, Fla., 1923*), Baptist clergyman. Graduated University of Rochester, 1867; Rochester Theological Seminary, 1870. Pastor, Calvary Baptist Church, New York City, 1870–1911. President, Baptist World Alliance, *post* 1911.

McARTHUR, WILLIAM POPE (*b. Ste. Genevieve, Mo., 1814; d. at sea off Panama, 1850*), naval officer, hydrographer. Nephew of Lewis F. Linn. Detailed to U.S. Coast Survey, 1840, he participated in surveys of the Gulf Coast, and commanded the first scientific reconnaissance of the Pacific Coast from Monterey to the Columbia River, 1848–50.

MACAULEY, EDWARD YORKE. *See* McCAULEY, EDWARD YORKE.

McAULEY, JEREMIAH (*b. Ireland, ca. 1839; d. New York, N.Y., 1884*), reformed criminal. Conducted Water St. Mission, New York City, 1872–82; a second mission on West 32nd Street, 1882–84. Author of *Transformed, or the History of a River Thief* (1876).

McAULEY, THOMAS (*b. Ireland, 1778; d. 1862*), Presbyterian clergyman, educator. Came to America *ante* 1799. Graduated Union College, 1804; taught there, 1805–22; thereafter held pastorates in New York City and Philadelphia. A leader of the "new school" party in his church, he was a founder of Union Theological Seminary, New York City, 1835, and its first president, 1836–40.

McBAIN, HOWARD LEE (*b. Toronto, Canada, 1880; d. 1936*), political scientist. Raised in Richmond, Va. Graduated Richmond College, 1900; Ph.D., Columbia, 1907. Taught at George Washington University and University of Wisconsin. At Columbia *post* 1913, he held chairs of municipal science and constitutional law and was dean of graduate faculties, 1929–36. Among his books, *The Law and the Practice of Municipal Home Rule* (1916) and *The Living Constitution* (1927) were outstanding.

McBRIDE, F(RANCIS) SCOTT (*b. Carroll County, Ohio, 1872; d. St. Petersburg, Fla., 1955*), clergyman and social reformer. Studied at Muskingum College and at the Pittsburgh Theological Seminary (1901). Active in the Anti-Saloon League on the state and national levels, McBride was a spokesman for the evangelical members of the League, supporting harrassment of drinkers and advocating strong anti-drink legislation.

McBRIDE, HENRY (*b. West Chester, Pa., 1867; d. New York, N.Y., 1962*), art journalist. Art critic for the New York *Sun* (1913–50). Also wrote for the *Dial* (1920–29) and *Creative Art* (1930–32. Columnist for *Art News* (1950–55). Known for his dry, subhumorous, and subtle art criticism. A brilliant apologist for the School of Paris, he wrote perceptively on modern art and the work of Marcel Duchamp and Jean Arp. Mostly identified with the New York art word and known for championing such rising American painters as Bradley Tomlin, Mark Rothko, and Jackson Pollock.

McBRYDE, JOHN McLAREN (*b. Abbeville, S.C., 1841; d. New Orleans, La., 1923*), agriculturist, educator, Confederate soldier. While professor of agriculture, University of Tennessee, 1879–82, his 1880 report on application of scientific methods to agriculture marked an epoch in the history of southern husbandry. President of South Carolina College, 1882–91, he reorganized the college and expanded it into a modern university. He accepted the presidency of Virginia Agricultural and Mechanical College, 1891, and by 1907, turned a moribund institution into a high-grade polytechnic institute. He became president emeritus, 1907. Few southern college executives contributed more to the cause of education along so many different lines.

McBURNEY, CHARLES (*b. Roxbury, Mass., 1845; d. Brookline, Mass., 1913*), surgeon. Graduated Harvard, 1866; M.D., College of Physicians and Surgeons, New York, 1870; made postgraduate studies in surgery at Vienna, Paris, and London. Taught surgery at College of Physicians, 1880–1907, and was a leader in the diagnosis and treatment of appendicitis. First described his diagnostic pressure point, known as "McBurney's point," in the *New York Medical Journal* (December 1889); developed "McBurney's incision," 1894.

McBURNEY, ROBERT ROSS (*b. Castle Blayney, Ireland, 1837; d. Clifton Springs, N.Y., 1898*), Young Men's Christian Association secretary. Came to America, 1854. *Post* 1865, he was a principal factor in YMCA growth and organization in North America and throughout the world.

McCABE, CHARLES CARDWELL (*b. Athens, Ohio, 1836; d. New York, N.Y., 1906*), Methodist clergyman. Became nationally known as chaplain, 122nd Ohio Volunteers in the Civil War; lectured widely on his experiences in Libby Prison. Gifted as a money-raiser and promoter, he was active in extension work and missions, *post* 1868; elected bishop, 1896.

McCABE, JOHN COLLINS (*b. Richmond, Va., 1810; d. Chambersburg, Pa., 1875*), Episcopal clergyman, Confederate chaplain. A frequent contributor to the *Southern Literary Messenger* and an intimate friend of Edgar A. Poe.

McCABE, WILLIAM GORDON (*b. Richmond, Va., 1841; d. 1920*), schoolmaster, Confederate soldier. Son of John C. McCabe. Conducted the University School, 1865–1901, at Petersburg, and later at Richmond, Va.

McCaffrey, John (*b. Emmitsburg, Md., 1806; d. Emmitsburg, 1881*), Roman Catholic clergyman, educator. Associated all his life with Mount St. Mary's College, Emmitsburg, as professor, rector, and governor. A sound, conservative theologian, he was responsible for the training of no small proportion of the hierarchy; his *Catechism of Christian Doctrine* (1865) was widely used in elementary school classes.

McCaine, Alexander (*b. Ireland, ca. 1768; d. Augusta, Ga., 1856*), clergyman, controversialist. Immigrated to Charleston, S.C., *ca.* 1788; *post* 1797, rode circuits in the Carolinas and Virginia. Withdrew from the ministry, 1806, but later reentered it. A strong opponent of episcopacy, he was a leader in founding the Methodist Protestant church, 1830.

McCaleb, Theodore Howard (*b. Pendleton District, S.C., 1810; d. "Hermitage Plantation," Miss., 1864*), jurist, educator. Studied law under Rufus Choate in Salem, Mass. Removed to New Orleans, 1832, where he practiced. Appointed U.S. judge for the District of Louisiana, 1841, he served until 1861. One of the original members of the law school faculty of the University of Louisiana (present Tulane), he taught admiralty and international law there, 1847–64.

McCall, Edward Rutledge (*b. Beaufort, S.C., 1790; d. Bordentown, N.J., 1853*), naval officer. Appointed midshipman, 1808. Took over command of USS *Enterprise*, September 1813, when its captain was killed in the taking of HMS *Boxer*. Performed mainly shore duties thereafter until he went on waiting orders as captain, 1835.

McCall, John Augustine (*b. Albany, N.Y., 1849; d. 1906*), insurance official. After rapid advancement in New York State Department of Insurance, he became comptroller of Equitable Life Insurance Co., New York, 1885, succeeding to presidency of New York Life Insurance Co., 1891. Although the company made great progress under McCall, revelations of irregularities in its management which were made during the New York State insurance investigation of 1905 compelled his resignation.

McCall, Samuel Walker (*b. East Providence, Pa., 1851; d. 1923*), lawyer, Massachusetts legislator. Graduated Dartmouth, 1874; practiced law in Boston. Congressman, Republican, from Massachusetts, 1893–1913. A strict constitutionalist and enemy of paternalism, he acted with independence in Congress and at the height of Theodore Roosevelt's popularity pointed out dangers of executive encroachment. As Republican governor of Massachusetts, 1916–18, he supported Woodrow Wilson's policies and advocated ratification of Versailles Treaty. He was author of *Thaddeus Stevens* (1898) and *The Life of Thomas Brackett Reed* (1914).

McCalla, Bowman Hendry (*b. Camden, N.J., 1844; d. Santa Barbara, Calif., 1910*), naval officer. Graduated U.S. Naval Academy, 1864. After varied sea service and shore duty, he distinguished himself in the landing at Guantanamo, Cuba, 1898, and was promoted captain. After aiding in suppressing Philippine Insurrection, 1899, he commanded the American force which marched to Peking during the Boxer Rebellion in 1900. Promoted rear admiral, 1903, he retired, 1906.

McCalla, William Latta (*b. Jessamine Co., Ky., 1788; d. near Bayou Bidal Church, La., 1859*), Presbyterian clergyman, controversialist. A militant leader of the "old school" party.

McCallum, Daniel Craig (*b. Renfrewshire, Scotland, 1815; d. 1878*), engineer. Immigrated to Rochester, N.Y., as a boy. Originated and patented an inflexible arched truss bridge, 1851; specialized thereafter in bridge construction. Appointed military director of railroads, 1862, with rank of colonel in the Union army, he superintended operation and repair of more than 2,000 miles of railroad, and bossed a construction corps of some 10,000 men. One of his most important achievements was the supplying of General W. T. Sherman's army during the Atlanta campaign. At the end of the war he received a brevet of major general.

MacCallum, William George (*b. Dunville, Ontario, Canada, 1874; d. Baltimore, Md. 1944*), pathologist. A.B., University of Toronto, 1894. M.D., Johns Hopkins, 1897. Studied in Felix M. Marchand's laboratory at Leipzig. Associate professor of pathology, Johns Hopkins, 1902–09; professor of pathology, College of Physicians and Surgeons, Columbia, and pathologist of Presbyterian Hospital, New York City, 1909–17; professor of pathology and bacteriology, Johns Hopkins (succeeding his mentor, William H. Welch), 1917–43. MacCallum made a number of classic studies, among them studies on the microscopic anatomy of the lymphatic system, on the independent functions of the thyroid and parathyroid glands (with Carl Voegtlin), and of epidemic pneumonia among army personnel during World War I. He was author of an innovating *Textbook of Pathology* (1916), and of a life of William S. Halsted.

MacCameron, Robert (*b. Chicago, Ill., 1860; d. New York, N.Y., 1912*), figure and portrait painter. Raised in rural Wisconsin, he studied at the YMCA in Chicago, Ill., and was successful as an illustrator. *Post* 1889 he resided in France, studied under J. L. Gérôme, and won critical recognition and success, 1904–07. His best work was done in the portrayal of the unfortunate and destitute.

McCann, Alfred Watterson (*b. Pittsburgh, Pa., 1879; d. 1931*), journalist, pure-food reformer.

McCann, William Penn (*b. Paris, Ky., 1830; d. New Rochelle, N.Y., 1906*), naval officer. Distinguished *post* 1848 in general service; promoted commodore, 1887; retired, 1892.

McCardell, Claire (*b. Frederick, Md., 1905; d. New York, N.Y., 1958*), fashion designer. One of the first American designers to win name recognition, McCardell studied at Parsons School of Design and in Paris. Remembered for popularizing the casual American look in fashion, her best designs, the "popover" housedress and the "diaper" wrap-and-tie bathing suit, won her the American Fashion Critics Award in 1944, and the Neiman-Marcus Award in 1948.

McCarran, Patrick Anthony (*b. near Reno, Nev., 1876; d. Hawthorne, Nev., 1954*), lawyer, jurist, U.S. senator. Studied at the University of Nevada. Justice of the Nevada Supreme Court (1913–18); chief justice (1916–18). U.S. senator, Democrat (1932–54). One of the most important right-wing dissenters in the Senate during the New Deal and the Cold War. Chairman of the Judiciary Committee (1943), through which passed 40 percent of all national legislation, and head of the key Appropriations Subcommittee, which authorized funds for the departments of Commerce, State, and Justice.

An ardent anti-Communist, McCarran joined forces with Senators Joseph McCarthy and William Jenner. Author of the Internal Security Act (the McCarran-Wood Act) of 1950, which was an omnibus act against subversion, including detention of persons believed likely to commit sabotage and espionage. Author of the Immigration and Nationality Act (the McCarran-Walter Act) (1952) which retained the national origin system for immigration to the U.S.

McCarren, Patrick Henry (*b. East Cambridge, Mass., 1847; d. 1909*), politician, New York legislator. Succeeded Hugh

McLaughlin as Democratic boss of Brooklyn, N.Y., 1903; thereafter fought successfully to keep Tammany from securing control of Brooklyn.

McCARROLL, JAMES (*b. Lanesboro, Ireland, 1814; d. 1892*), journalist, dramatist. Immigrated to Canada *ca.* 1831. Active toward the end of his life in New York City journalism.

McCARTEE, DIVIE BETHUNE (*b. Philadelphia, Pa., 1820; d. San Francisco, Calif., 1900*), Presbyterian medical missionary. M.D., University of Pennsylvania, 1840. Missionary to China, 1843–72, during which time he served also in U.S. consular offices. Professor of law and science, Imperial University at Tokyo, Japan, 1872–77. Thereafter he enjoyed a varied career as diplomat and missionary executive.

McCARTHY, CHARLES (*b. Brockton, Mass., 1873; d. Prescott, Ariz., 1921*), political scientist, publicist. Graduated Brown, 1896; Ph.D., University of Wisconsin, 1901. Organized at Madison, Wis., for the use of legislators, the first official reference library and bill-drafting bureau in the United States, which he directed until his death. Author of *The Anti-Masonic Party* (1903) and *The Wisconsin Idea* (1912).

McCARTHY, CHARLES LOUIS (CLEM) (*b. East Bloomfield, N.Y., 1882; d. New York, N.Y., 1962*), radio sportscaster. Broadcast the first Kentucky Derby ever heard on radio, for KYW in Chicago, in 1928. Sportscaster for NBC, 1929–47, and CBS, 1947–50. By the early 1930's McCarthy's voice was associated with horse racing and boxing events everywhere there were radios, and his announcement "R-r-r-racing fans" became an American institution.

McCARTHY, DANIEL JOSEPH (*b. Philadelphia, Pa., 1874; d. Ventnor, N.J., 1958*), neurologist, neuropsychiatrist, educator. Studied at the University of Pennsylvania (M.D., 1895), and at the universities of Paris, Vienna, Berlin, and Leipzig. Taught medical jurisprudence at the University of Pennsylvania Medical School from 1904 to 1940. Remembered as an expert on medical jurisprudence, in particular the judicial aspects of insanity, McCarthy gained experience during World War I as consultant neurologist and commanding officer for the American Expeditionary Force Hospital in Vichy, France. Wrote *Medical Treatment of Mental Diseases: The Toxic and Organic Basis of Psychiatry* (1955); in this work his theories that mental disorders are physiological in origin, not psychological, were synthesized.

McCARTHY, JOSEPH RAYMOND (*b. Grand Chute, Wis., 1908; d. Bethesda, Md., 1957*), politician. Studied at Marquette University (LL.B., 1935). McCarthy's first political office was a judgeship on the Tenth Judicial Circuit in Wisconsin (1939–42). During World War II, he served in the Marine Corps in the Pacific. He returned to civilian duty and entered Republican politics, finally capturing a seat in the U.S. Senate in 1946, unseating Senator Robert M. La Follette, Jr. As a senator, McCarthy gained a national reputation for a speech delivered in Wheeling, W.Va., in 1950, in which he accused members of the State Department of being Communists. McCarthy was able to rally considerable support for his accusations; by 1953, he was the chairman of the Senate Committee on Government Operations and the Permanent Subcommittee on Investigations. April to June (1954), he was locked in a struggle with the U.S. military in what has come to be known as the Army-McCarthy Hearings. During the proceedings, McCarthy, his lawyer Roy Cohn, and his aide, G. David Schine were thoroughly discredited, and their accusations against government officials were proven mostly false. McCarthy was censured by the Senate in December of that year. He died of ruined health and alcoholism at the naval hospital. The term "McCarthy Era" has become synonymous with the policy of accusing government officials of being Communists and with the concept of witchhunts in general. His fear tactics reached into every branch of American public life: from government and diplomacy to entertainment, the arts, and the universities. His legacy includes the erosion of civil liberties, the restriction of dissent, and a foreign policy of reflexive anticommunism.

McCARTNEY, WASHINGTON (*b. Westmoreland Co., Pa., 1812; d. Easton, Pa., 1856*), lawyer, mathematician, Pennsylvania educator and jurist.

McCAULEY, CHARLES STEWART (*b. Philadelphia, Pa., 1793; d. Washington D.C., 1869*), naval officer. Nephew of Rear Admiral Charles Stewart. As commandant of Norfolk, Va., navy yard, 1860–61, he scuttled the ships therein and abandoned the post without a defense after secession of the state of Virginia. Censured for this single questionable action in a long, honorable career, he was retired in 1862.

MacCAULEY, CLAY (*b. Chambersburg, Pa., 1843; d. Berkeley, Calif., 1925*), Unitarian clergyman, Union soldier. Graduated Princeton, 1864; Presbyterian Theological Seminary of the Northwest, 1867. Held numerous pastorates; made studies of Seminole Indians of Florida; served as missionary in Japan, 1889–1920.

McCAULEY, EDWARD YORKE (*b. Philadelphia, Pa., 1827; d. Conanicut Island, Narragansett Bay, R.I., 1894*), naval officer, Egyptologist. Nephew of Charles S. McCauley.

McCAULEY, MARY LUDWIG HAYS (*b. near Trenton, N.J., 1754; d. 1832*), Revolutionary heroine, better known as "Molly Pitcher." While carrying water to soldiers at battle of Monmouth, June 28, 1778, she took her husband's place when he fell overcome by the heat and served his gun ably through the rest of the battle.

McCAUSLAND, JOHN (*b. St. Louis, Mo., 1836; d. Mason Co., W.Va., 1927*), Confederate brigadier general. Graduated Virginia Military Institute, 1857. On a raid into Pennsylvania, he burned the town of Chambersburg, July 30, 1864, under specific orders from General Jubal Early.

McCAW, JAMES BROWN (*b. Richmond, Va., 1823; d. Richmond, 1906*), physician, educator. Supervised Confederate Chimborazo Hospital, the largest in use during the Civil War; was associated, *post* 1865, as professor and dean, with Medical College of Virginia.

McCAWLEY, CHARLES GRYMES (*b. Philadelphia, Pa., 1827; d. Rosemont, Pa., 1891*), soldier. Appointed second lieutenant, U.S. Marine Corps, 1847, he served with great ability and gallantry in both Mexican and Civil wars. Made colonel commandant of Marine Corps, 1876, he retired, 1891.

McCAWLEY, CHARLES LAURIE (*b. Boston, Mass., 1865; d. 1935*), soldier, Marine officer. Son of Charles G. McCawley. Served in Cuba during Spanish-American War and in the Philippine Insurrection; military aide to President Theodore Roosevelt. Commissioned colonel, 1913, and brigadier general, 1916, he served as quartermaster, U.S. Marine Corps, 1913–29.

McCAY, CHARLES FRANCIS (*b. Danville, Pa., 1810; d. Baltimore, Md., 1889*), mathematician, actuary. Brother of Henry K. McCay. Graduated Jefferson College, 1829. Taught mathematics and science at Lafayette College, at University of Georgia, and at South Carolina College, where he was president, 1855–57. Thereafter, he was active as a banker and as consulting actuary to life insurance companies. He prepared what is believed to have been the first "select and ultimate" table of life insurance mortality in the United States, 1887.

McCay, Henry Kent (*b. Northumberland Co., Pa., 1820; d. 1886*), lawyer. Confederate soldier. Brother of Charles F. McCay. Removed to Georgia *ca.* 1839. Justice, Georgia Supreme Court, 1868–75; U.S. judge, northern district of Georgia, 1882–86.

McClain, Emlin (*b. Salem, Ohio, 1851; d. 1915*), lawyer, Iowa jurist. Professor of law, State University of Iowa, 1881–1901; justice, Iowa Supreme Court, 1901–13. Author of a number of authoritative texts and annotations on Iowa law.

McClatchy, Charles Kenny (*b. Sacramento, Calif., 1858; d. near Sacramento, 1936*), journalist. Editor of the *Sacramento Bee*; from 1884, also co-owner; an outspoken independent progressive.

McClellan, George (*b. Woodstock, Conn., 1796; d. 1847*), anatomist, surgeon. Graduated Yale, 1816; M.D., University of Pennsylvania, 1819. Founded Jefferson Medical College, Philadelphia, 1825, at which he taught until 1839; helped establish Pennsylvania College medical school at Gettysburg. Made early use of clinical methods in teaching.

McClellan, George (*b. Philadelphia, Pa., 1849; d. 1913*), anatomist, physician. Grandson of George McClellan (1796–1847). Graduated University of Pennsylvania, 1869; Jefferson Medical College, 1870. Founded Pennsylvania School of Anatomy and Surgery, 1881, and taught there with great success until 1898. He taught anatomy also at Pennsylvania Academy of the Fine Arts and Jefferson Medical College. Author of *Regional Anatomy* (1891, 1892).

McClellan, George Brinton (*b. Philadelphia, Pa., 1826; d. Orange, N.J., 1885*), soldier. Son of George McClellan (1796–1847); cousin of Henry B. McClellan. Graduated West Point, 1846; was assigned to the Engineers. Serving in General Winfield Scott's command during the war with Mexico, he was often mentioned in dispatches and won brevet of captain. Assistant instructor in military engineering, West Point, 1848–51, he went in March 1852 with R. B. Marcy's expedition to explore sources of the Red River in Arkansas; thereafter, he undertook varied duties until his appointment as captain of cavalry, 1855. He was detailed in April 1855 as a member of a board sent to study European military systems. While abroad he made a complete study of the siege of Sevastopol and on his return proposed a new type of cavalry saddle, which was then adopted and remained standard. Resigning his commission, January 1857, he became chief engineer of the Illinois Central Railroad and, in 1860, president of the Ohio and Mississippi Railroad.

Appointed major general of Ohio Volunteers, Apr. 23, 1861, he was named (as of date May 3) major general of the regular army in command of the department of the Ohio. His prompt action in his department helped keep Kentucky and western Virginia in the Union; his success in the campaign of Rich Mountain led to his appointment to command the Division of the Potomac. Arriving in Washington on July 26, after the defeat at Bull Run, he found the troops in utter confusion but with great energy began their reorganization and retraining. On retirement of General Winfield Scott in November, McClellan became general in chief in his place. Overestimating the strength of the Confederates, McClellan refused to make any decisive move, despite the impatience of President Lincoln, with whom he disagreed also on the proper strategy to employ. Lincoln believed that the army should move directly against Confederates at and about Manassas; McClellan urged that he should transport the army by water to the lower Rappahannock and advance on Richmond from the east. Lincoln

consented at last to such a move by way of Fortress Monroe but imposed conditions to maintain the security of the city of Washington. Relieved as general in chief, McClellan took the field with his Army of the Potomac early in April 1862 but was hampered by the withdrawal of McDowell's corps for the defense of Washington.

On the advance from Fortress Monroe, McClellan was delayed for a month before Yorktown but then moved up the peninsula toward Richmond. Further delays were caused by heavy rains and impassable roads; on the Chickahominy River there was another long delay. The first Union troops to cross had heavy fighting at Seven Pines on May 31, 1862, and at Fair Oaks on June 1, but a position almost at the gates of Richmond was occupied and entrenched. The arrival of Confederate General T. J. Jackson in support of General R. E. Lee encouraged the Confederate command to attack McClellan's army on the left bank of the river, June 26. After a Union defeat at Gaines' Mill, the Confederate pursuit was finally checked at Malvern Hill on July 1. This ended the campaign known as the Seven Days' Battles, and the Union army established itself at Harrison's Landing, McClellan in dispatches charged failure of support from Washington, insisting that he was outnumbered and demanding for a further offensive a greater reinforcement than the president or General Halleck was willing to provide. On Aug. 3, the Army of the Potomac was ordered withdrawn and its troops were assigned to General Pope's Army of Virginia. After Pope's defeat at the second battle of Bull Run, McClellan was called upon again to reorganize the army and defend Washington. Pope's retreating soldiers received him with enthusiasm and between Sept. 1 and Sept. 13 he restored their morale. Learning that the Confederates were much scattered, he moved to take advantage of this but too slowly. Lee succeeded in concentrating his forces and was able to avoid destruction in the fierce battles of South Mountain and Antietam (Sept. 17, 1862). McClellan, overcautious as ever, permitted Lee to withdraw his army across the Potomac and did not follow until late in October. Superseded by General Burnside at Warrenton, Va., on Nov. 7, he was never again employed in the field.

Nominated as Democratic candidate for the presidency, 1864, he ran on a peace platform but carried only the states of New Jersey, Delaware, and Kentucky against Abraham Lincoln. He held various employments as an engineer thereafter, and from January 1878 to January 1881 served as governor of New Jersey. An excellent linguist and a scholar of his military profession, he was also well informed in archaeological research and exploration. As a soldier, he took the best of care of his men and had the faculty of inspiring confidence and loyalty in them. His concepts of strategy and of tactics were clear and sound, but he was never satisfied with what he had; he could always see the way in which he might make an improvement if he were given time, and he took time at the expense of losing opportunity. He accepted too readily the strength estimates given him by his intelligence service, which consistently placed the number of Confederates too high. It should be remembered that up until the time of the Civil War he had held no actual field commands. It is probable that he came to supreme command too early in his career. Robert E. Lee, who was very well aware of McClellan's deficiencies, set him down as the best commander who faced him during the war.

McClellan, George Brinton (*b. Dresden, Saxony, 1865; d. Washington, D.C., 1940*), politician, educator. Son of George B. McClellan (1826–85). Graduated Princeton, 1886. A sachem and prominent orator of Tammany Hall, McClellan was elected president of the New York City board of aldermen, 1892, and served as a congressman from New York, 1895–1903. Running against Seth Low for mayor of New York, 1903, McClellan won easily and served until 1909; *post* 1905, he showed a pronounced independence of Tammany and accomplished a program of public works with efficiency and imagination. His flouting of Charles F. Murphy, the Tammany boss, cost him any further chances he might have had for political preferment. He served as professor of economic history at Princeton, 1912–31. He was author of, among other books, *The Oligarchy of Venice* (1904) and *Venice and Bonaparte* (1931).

McClellan, Henry Brainerd (*b. Philadelphia, Pa., 1840; d. 1904*), Confederate soldier, educator. Cousin of George B. McClellan (1826–85). Graduated Williams, 1858. Entering the Confederate army as a private, 1861, he rose to rank of major and served as chief of staff to Generals J. E. B. Stuart and Wade Hampton. He was principal of Sayre Female Institute, Lexington, Ky., 1870–1904.

McClellan, Robert (*b. near Mercersburg, Pa., 1770; d. Missouri, 1815*), Indian trader, scout. Won rank of lieutenant for bravery in General Anthony Wayne's campaign of 1794–95; was active in Indian trade on the upper Missouri, 1807–10. Accompanied Pacific Fur Co. expedition to Astoria, 1811–13.

McClelland, Robert (*b. Greencastle, Pa., 1807; d. Detroit, Mich., 1880*), lawyer, Michigan legislator. Removed to Monroe, Mich., 1833; was active in organizing the new state government and the Democratic party there. Served as congressman, Democrat, from Michigan, 1843–49; became chief lieutenant of Lewis Cass. As governor of Michigan, 1851–53, he brought his fellow Michigan Democrats to endorse the compromise measures of 1850. Appointed U.S. secretary of the interior, 1853, he reorganized the department; reduced corruption and waste in the land, Indian, and pension bureaus; and called for special legislation to prevent reoccurrence of difficulties. None of his major recommendations were adopted by Congress. A conservative, he joined W. L. Marcy in urging President Pierce to follow a neutral policy in Kansas. *Post* 1857, he practiced law in Detroit.

McClenahan, Howard (*b. Port Deposit, Md., 1872; d. Winter Park, Fla., 1935*), educator. Taught physics at Princeton, 1897–1925; was made dean of the college, 1912. Served as secretary of Franklin Institute, Philadelphia, 1925–35.

McClernand, John Alexander (*b. near Hardinsburg, Ky., 1812; d. Springfield, Ill., 1900*), lawyer, Illinois legislator, Union soldier. Raised in Illinois; admitted to the bar, 1832. A staunch Jacksonian, he hated abolitionists. As congressman, 1843–51 and 1859–61, he urged conciliation between the sections and popular sovereignty as a remedy for the slavery crisis. Leaving Congress on the outbreak of the Civil War, he accepted a brigadier general's commission and by vigor and personal bravery rose to major general, March 1862. Ambitious, tactless, he disliked West Pointers and was critical of General Grant in letters to President Lincoln and to General Halleck. Unauthorized by Grant, with navy support he reduced Arkansas Post, January 1863, and continued to conduct himself independently. Charged by Grant with tardiness and responsibility for heavy loss in the Vicksburg campaign, he was ordered back to Illinois, June 1863, but early in 1864 regained command of the XIII Corps scattered between New Orleans and the Rio Grande. Sickness prevented his participation in the Red River expedition, April 1864, and he resigned his commission in November.

McClintic, Guthrie (*b. Seattle, Wash., 1893; d. Sneden's Landing, N.Y., 1961*), theatrical producer and director. Studied at the American Academy of Dramatic Arts in New York City (graduated, 1912). Began an association with the producer Winthrop Ames in 1913, as a stage manager and later a talent scout for Ames, who backed his first production, A. A. Milne's *The Dover Road* (1921). Married actress Katharine Cornell in 1921; Cornell starred in 28 of his 100 productions. During the 1930's and 1940's

McClintic ranked as one of the most successful directors and producers in the United States. His productions included George Bernard Shaw's *Candida* (1933, 1937, 1942, 1946), and *Saint Joan* (1936); Maxwell Anderson's *Saturday's Children* (1928); Anton Chekov's *The Three Sisters* (1942); Noel Coward's *Fallen Angels* (1927); and Tennessee Williams' *You Touched Me!* (1945); as well as several of the best stagings of Shakespeare produced in the twentieth century.

McClintock, Emory (*b. Carlisle, Pa., 1840; d. 1916*), mathematician, actuary. Son of John M'Clintock. Associated for many years as actuary with Northwestern Life Insurance Co. of Milwaukee and Mutual Life Insurance Co. of New York, he was at the head of his profession in his time.

McClintock, James Harvey (*b. Sacramento, Calif., 1864; d. Sawtelle, Calif., 1934*), Arizona journalist, soldier. Commanded a troop of Roosevelt's Rough Riders, 1898; was active in Arizona National Guard activities.

M'Clintock, John (*b. Philadelphia, Pa., 1814; d. 1870*), Methodist clergyman, educator. Taught at Dickinson College, 1836–48; editor, *Methodist Quarterly Review*, 1848–56. First president, Drew Theological Seminary, 1867–70. Coeditor, with Dr. James Strong, of celebrated *Cyclopedia of Biblical, Theological and Ecclesiastical Literature* (1853–70).

McClintock, Oliver (*b. Pittsburgh, Pa., 1839; d. 1922*), Pittsburgh merchant, political reformer. Led fight, *ca.* 1885–95, against corrupt political ring headed by Christopher L. Magee.

McCloskey, John (*b. Brooklyn, N.Y., 1810; d. near Yonkers, N.Y., 1885*), Roman Catholic clergyman, first American cardinal. Graduated Mount St. Mary's College, Emmitsburg, Md., 1828; attended Gregorian University, Rome, 1835–37. Consecrated coadjutor to Bishop John Hughes of New York, March 1844, he was a conservative dependable counselor; on erection of Albany, N.Y., into a separate see in 1847, McCloskey was given charge of that diocese. Succeeding as archbishop of New York on the death of Hughes, 1864, he continued on a conservative course. During his incumbency there was great progress in the building of charitable institutions; owing largely to his efforts, St. Patrick's Cathedral was completed and made ready for dedication, May 1879. Created cardinal, March 1875, he continued active in the management of the New York archdiocese until 1884.

McCloskey, William George (*b. Brooklyn, N.Y., 1823; d. 1909*), Roman Catholic clergyman. First rector of the American College in Rome, 1859–68; bishop of Louisville, Ky., 1868–1909.

McClung, Clarence Erwin (*b. Clayton, Calif., 1870; d. Swarthmore, Pa., 1946*), biologist. Ph.G., University of Kansas, 1892; A.B., 1896. M.A., Columbia University, 1898. Ph.D., University of Chicago, 1903. Taught zoology at University of Kansas, 1898–1912; professor *post* 1906. Professor of zoology and director of the zoological laboratories, University of Pennsylvania, 1912–40. First director of the division of biology and agriculture of the National Research Council, 1919–21. Celebrated for his researches in the cytological aspects of chromosome behavior, notably his observation of the accessory chromosome and his hypothesis that it was determinant of sex (announced in 1902). He also made numerous contributions to microscopic improvements and technique.

McClure, Alexander Kelly (*b. Sherman's Valley, Pa., 1828; d. 1909*), newspaper editor, Pennsylvania Republican legislator, lawyer. Helped switch Pennsylvania vote to Abraham Lincoln at Republican convention, Chicago, 1860. As chairman of state committee, perfected organization of Republican machine in Pennsylvania. Chairman, Liberal Republican delegation from Pennsylvania, 1872.

McClure, Alexander Wilson (*b. Boston, Mass., 1808; d. Canonsburg, Pa., 1865*), Congregational and Dutch Reformed clergyman, editor.

McClure, George (*b. near Londonderry, Ireland*, ca. *1770; d. Elgin, Ill., 1851*), merchant, soldier. Came to America ca. 1790; removed to Bath, N.Y., ca. 1793. Serving as brigadier general of New York militia in War of 1812, he was responsible for burning of Newark, Canada, which brought about British reprisals against Buffalo, N.Y.

McClure, Robert Alexis (*b. Matoon, Ill., 1897; d. Huachuca, Ariz., 1957*), military officer. Studied at the Kentucky Military Institute; commissioned in the Army (1915). After serving in the Philippines, McClure returned to the U.S. and furthered his studies at the Army Infantry School, the Army Cavalry School, the Command and General Staff School, and at the Army War College, where he was an instructor from 1935 to 1940. At the beginning of World War II, he was a military attaché in London. By 1942, he was chief of intelligence for the American forces in Europe under Eisenhower. As such, he was responsible for the security of the invasion of North Africa. In 1944, he became the head of psychological warfare for the Supreme Headquarters of the Allied Expeditionary Force with the rank of brigadier general. From 1950 to 1953, he was chief of the Psychological Warfare Division in the Pentagon. From 1953 to 1956, he was head of the military mission in Teheran. He retired in 1956 with the rank of major general.

McClure, Samuel Sidney (*b. Frocess, Co. Antrim, Ireland, 1857; d. New York, N.Y., 1949*), editor, social crusader. Raised near and in Valparaiso, Ind. As a student at Knox College, Galesburg, Ill., he edited the college newspaper, organized and issued an intercollegiate news bulletin, and formed the Western College Associated Press, of which he was chosen president. Moving to Boston, Mass., after graduation, he worked for a bicycle manufacturer and edited *The Wheelman*, a magazine devoted to the cycling craze of the early 1880's. Leaving the bicycle firm, he was employed briefly by the DeVinne press and the Century Co. in New York City; in October 1884 he began his own literary syndicate, proposing to supply fiction and other literary features of high quality to newspapers in serial form at low cost to the individual outlet. The syndicate was well enough established by 1887 for McClure to engage a college classmate, John S. Phillips, as helper; he himself then went abroad to make contracts with noted European writers; in this and many later trips to Europe and in the United States, he succeeded in signing up the best writers of the period. In May 1893 he began to publish *McClure's Magazine*, which grew steadily in circulation through the 1890's, featuring new works by many of the writers who were producing for the syndicate. The issue of January 1903 set *McClure's* on the course that made it famous. The leading article was Lincoln Steffens' "The Shame of Minneapolis"; the issue also contained an installment of Ida Tarbell's exposé of the Standard Oil Co., and Ray Stannard Baker's "The Right to Work." McClure, in an accompanying editorial, pointed out that the three articles highlighted a growing contempt for law, for which Americans would have to pay a high price unless it was checked. So began the intense period of revelatory reform journalism (in which other periodicals soon followed *McClure's* lead), during which the reading public was introduced to scandalous corruption in government on all levels, in finance and industry, in the judicial system, and even in the press. In 1906 Theodore Roosevelt belittled these efforts at reform as "muckraking," a term which is still used to describe the move-

ment. After Steffens, Baker, Phillips, and others left *McClure's* to found the *American Magazine* later in 1906, *McClure's* declined, was suspended in 1914, was revived, and after other vicissitudes finally ceased publication in the mid–1920's. Almost forgotten in his old age, McClure was honored in 1944 by the National Institute of Arts and Letters for his recognition of new talent as editor and his creation of a new type of journalism.

McClurg, Alexander Caldwell (*b. Philadelphia, Pa., 1832; d. St. Augustine, Fla., 1901*), bookseller, publisher, Union soldier. Cousin of Joseph W. McClurg. Graduated Miami University, Ohio, 1853. Removed to Chicago, Ill., 1859. After winning recognition as an able staff officer in western campaigns, 1862–65, he built up in Chicago one of the leading bookselling businesses in the Middle West.

McClurg, James (*b. near Hampton, Va.*, ca. *1746; d. Richmond, Va., 1823*), physician, Revolutionary soldier. As a Virginia delegate to the Constitutional Convention, 1787, McClurg advocated a life tenure for the executive and strove to keep the executive as far removed from legislative control as possible.

McClurg, Joseph Washington (*b. St. Louis Co., Mo., 1818; d. Lebanon, Mo., 1900*), merchant, Republican politician. Cousin of Alexander C. McClurg. As congressman, Republican, from Missouri, 1863–68, he became an ardent disciple of Thaddeus Stevens and a strenuous supporter of carpetbag policies. During his term as governor of Missouri, 1869–71, he was dominated by Charles D. Drake and other Radical Republicans; the memory of the proscriptions which he sponsored was responsible for Democratic success in Missouri over the following 30 years.

McComas, Louis Emory (*b. near Williamsport, Md., 1846; d. 1907*), lawyer. Congressman, Republican, from Maryland, 1883–91; justice, District of Columbia Supreme Court, 1892–99; U.S. senator from Maryland, 1899–1905. Active in congressional committee work, he was especially interested in currency problems, the suppression of alien contract labor, civil service reform, and antitrust legislation.

McComb, John (*b. New York, N.Y., 1763; d. 1853*), architect. Began independent practice, 1790; won competition for design of New York City Hall, 1802, in association with Joseph F. Mangin; superintended execution of the design until completion, 1812. Thereafter, McComb designed many churches and public buildings in New York City which illustrated the persistence of American colonial tradition, with strong British influence, into the 19th century.

McConnel, John Ludlum (*b. present Scott Co., Ill., 1826; d. 1862*), lawyer, novelist. Author of, among other works, *Talbot and Vernon* (1850), *The Glenns* (1851), and *Western Characters; or Types of Border Life* (1853), which are of value as studies of life on the frontier.

McConnell, Francis John (*b. Trinway, Ohio, 1871; d. Lucasville, Ohio, 1953*), church leader. Studied at Ohio Wesleyan University and Boston University (Ph.D., 1899). In 1912, elected bishop in the Northern Methodist Episcopal Church. In the 1930's, was probably the best-known champion of the social gospel in American Protestantism. A champion of the rights of labor and the unemployed. President, 1928, of the Federal Council of the Churches of Christ in America. Sought to temper the teachings of Marx with Christianity. Wrote *Evangelicals, Revolutionists and Idealists* (1942).

McConnell, Ira Welch (*b. Schell City, Mo., 1871; d. 1933*), engineer. C. E., Cornell, 1897. Worked with U.S.

Reclamation Service, 1903–09, and later with private firms as an irrigation and hydraulics expert. Associated, *post* 1918, with Dwight P. Robinson & Co. and United Engineers & Constructors in many large projects in United States and abroad.

McCOOK, ALEXANDER McDOWELL (*b. Columbiana Co., Ohio, 1831; d. Dayton, Ohio, 1903*), soldier. Graduated West Point, 1852. As divisional commander, Army of the Ohio, he performed outstanding service at Corinth, Nashville, and Shiloh; commanding XIV and later XX Corps in Army of the Cumberland, he was relieved in October 1863, for failure at Chickamauga, but was exonerated by a military court. After the Civil War he performed varied military service in the West. Promoted major general, 1894, he retired the following year.

McCOOK, ANSON GEORGE (*b. Steubenville, Ohio, 1835; d. New York, N.Y., 1917*), lawyer, Union soldier. Brother of Edward M., Henry C., and John J. McCook; cousin of Alexander McD. McCook. For service in many engagements in all theaters of the Civil War, he received brevet of brigadier general of volunteers, 1865. In practice in New York *post* 1873, he served creditably as a Republican congressman from that state, 1877–83; was secretary of the U.S. Senate, 1884–93. For many years he was editor of the *Daily Register*, later the *New York Law Journal*.

McCOOK, EDWARD MOODY (*b. Steubenville, Ohio, 1833; d. Chicago, Ill., 1909*), lawyer, Union brigadier general, financier. Brother of Anson G., Henry C., and John J. McCook; cousin of Alexander McD. McCook. An outstanding cavalry commander in Army of the Cumberland, he performed his most brilliant exploit by cutting off Atlanta from reinforcement when under siege. After the war, he held several federal administrative and diplomatic posts, including governorship of Colorado Territory, 1869–73 and 1874–75. Thereafter, he was very successful as a financier.

McCOOK, HENRY CHRISTOPHER (*b. New Lisbon, Ohio, 1837; d. 1911*), Presbyterian clergyman, naturalist. Brother of Anson G., Edward M., and John J. McCook; cousin of Alexander McD. McCook. Held pastorates in Midwest and at Tabernacle Presbyterian Church, Philadelphia, Pa., 1870–1902. Author of many valuable technical papers on spiders and ants, he published a number of popular works as well as on natural-history subjects and *The Latimers* (1897), a story of the Whiskey Rebellion.

McCOOK, JOHN JAMES (*b. New Lisbon, Ohio, 1843; d. 1927*), Episcopal clergyman, Union soldier, educator. Brother of Edward M., Anson G., and Henry C. McCook; cousin of Alexander McD. McCook. Rector at St. John's Church, East Hartford, Conn., 1868–1927; taught at Trinity College, Hartford, 1883–1923.

McCORD, DAVID JAMES (*b. St. Matthew's Parish, S.C., 1797; d. 1855*), lawyer, South Carolina legislator. Under his editorship *post* 1823, the *Columbia Telescope* became the most violent of all nullification newspapers. He edited Volumes 6–10 of the *Statutes at Large of South Carolina* (1839–42).

McCORD, JAMES BENNETT (*b. Toulon, Ill., 1870. d. Oakham, Mass., 1950*), medical missionary (Congregational). Graduated Oberlin College, 1891; studied medicine at Northwestern University; practiced in Lake City, Iowa, 1895–99. Assisted by his wife, he served the Zulus in Natal, South Africa, 1899–1940, establishing a hospital for nonwhites in Durban, securing facilities for medical education of Africans, and engaging in movements for improvement of race relations and general education.

McCORD, LOUISA SUSANNA CHEVES (*b. Charleston, S.C., 1810; d. Charleston, 1879*), writer. Daughter of Langdon Cheves; second wife of David J. McCord. Contributor of conservative proslavery essays to antebellum Southern journals.

McCORMACK, JOHN FRANCIS (*b. Athlone, Ireland, 1884; d. Booterstown, near Dublin, Ireland, 1945*), lyric tenor. Studied briefly in Milan, Italy; operatic debut, Jan. 13, 1906, in Mascagni's *L'Amico Fritz* at Savona; had first notable success at a London concert, Mar. 1, 1907; appeared at Royal Opera House, Covent Garden, in Mascagni's *Cavalleria Rusticana*, Oct. 15, 1907; American operatic debut as Alfredo in Verdi's *La Traviata* with Manhattan Opera Company, New York City, Nov. 10, 1909. Although he continued to appear on the operatic stage through about 1913, he owed his wide recognition and financial success to his recordings and the arduous schedule of concert tours which he maintained until 1937. Largely self-taught, he possessed a naturally fine voice which he developed through intelligent practice and with a degree of musicianship foreign to most singers. His tone was rich and clear, his articulation and diction extraordinarily precise, his breath control remarkable. He never condescended to his material, but would sing the simple ballads for which he was famous with the same degree (but not the same kind) of expertness and sincerity that he gave to art songs or operatic arias.

McCORMACK, JOSEPH NATHANIEL (*b. near Howard's Mill, Ky., 1847; d. Louisville, Ky., 1922*), physician. M.D., Miami University, 1870. As a member of Kentucky State Board of Health and as its secretary, 1883–1913, he won national reputation in public health work, particularly in rural districts. Brought about rehabilitation of the American Medical Association during his chairmanship of the association's committee on organization, 1899–1913.

McCORMICK, ANNE ELIZABETH O'HARE (*b. Wakefield, England, 1882; d. New York, N.Y., 1954*), journalist. Studied at the College of St. Mary of the Springs. First woman member of the editorial board of the *New York Times* (1936) and the first woman journalist to receive the Pulitzer Prize (1937). Covering the events leading to World War II in Europe during the 1920's and 1930's, McCormick interviewed such leaders as Mussolini, Roosevelt, Hitler, Stalin, Eisenhower, and Truman. Named Woman of the Year in 1939.

McCORMICK, CYRUS HALL (*b. Rockbridge Co., Va., 1809; d. Chicago, Ill., 1884*), inventor, manufacturer. Son of Robert McCormick. After his father's abandonment of plan to perfect a reaping machine, Cyrus McCormick constructed a crude machine on different principles, which was successful in use on his home farm in the fall of 1831. After introducing improvements, he exhibited his machine on several farms near Lexington, Va., 1832; on hearing of similar work by Obed Hussey, 1833, he took out a patent for his reaper, June 21, 1834. *Post* 1837, McCormick turned seriously to exploitation of his invention. After unfortunate experiences with licensees, he erected his own factory in Chicago, Ill., 1847, closed out other manufacturing contracts, and by 1850 had succeeded in building up a national business. Although he had to compete against Hussey's reaper and at least 30 other rival manufacturers, by hard work and constant improvement of his machine he managed to hold his premier place among reaping-machine manufacturers. McCormick was a pioneer in modern business methods. He was among the first to introduce use of field trials, guarantees and testimonials in advertising, and deferred payments for merchandise, to promote the invention and use in his factory of laborsaving machinery. He was an active benefactor of the Presbyterian church and took a part in Democratic party councils until his death.

McCORMICK, CYRUS HALL   (*b. Washington D.C., 1859; d. Lake Forest, Ill., 1936*), farm-machinery manufacturer. Son of Cyrus H. McCormick (1809–84). After serving as assistant to his father, he became president of McCormick Harvesting Machine Co., 1884. In 1902, with William Deering and other industry leaders, he brought about organization of the International Harvester Co., of which he became president until 1918, when he assumed chairmanship of board of directors. Under his direction the company defended itself against a succession of rugged antitrust suits, expanded its research departments, and instituted numerous employee benefits.

McCORMICK, JOSEPH MEDILL   (*b. Chicago, Ill., 1877; d. Washington, D.C., 1925*), journalist, politician. Son of Robert S. McCormick; grandson of Joseph Medill. Graduated Yale, 1900. Associated all his life with the family newspaper, *Chicago Tribune*; shared in ownership of several Cleveland, Ohio, newspapers. An ardent follower of Theodore Roosevelt, he returned to the Republican party, 1914, and served as congressman from Illinois, 1917–19, and as U.S. senator, 1919–25. He opposed the League of Nations and the Versailles Treaty; sponsored the bill providing for creation of the Bureau of the Budget, 1921. He also encouraged the proposed "Great Lakes to Gulf waterway" and favored the child-labor amendment.

McCORMICK, LEANDER JAMES   (*b. Rockbridge Co., Va., 1819; d. Chicago, Ill., 1900*), manufacturer, philanthropist. Son of Robert McCormick; brother of Cyrus H. McCormick (1809–84). Aided his father and brother in construction of reapers. *Post* 1849, he supervised the manufacturing department of the McCormick Harvesting Machine Co.

McCORMICK, LYNDE DUPUY   (*b. Annapolis, Md., 1895; d. Newport, R.I., 1956*), naval officer. Studied at the U.S. Naval Academy; commissioned in 1915. During World War II, he was war plans officer for Admiral Chester W. Nimitz in the Pacific; he saw action in the Battles of the Coral Sea and Midway; promoted to rear admiral in 1943. After the war he commanded Naval District 12 in San Francisco; in 1949, appointed by President Truman as deputy chief of naval operations with the rank of admiral. Commander in chief of the Atlantic Fleet, and later for NATO (1951–54). From 1954 until his death, president of the Naval War College in Newport, R.I.

McCORMICK, MEDILL.   *See* McCORMICK, JOSEPH MEDILL.

McCORMICK, RICHARD CUNNINGHAM   (*b. New York, N.Y., 1832; d. Jamaica, N.Y., 1901*), journalist, businessman, politician. Acted as war correspondent for New York newspapers in the Crimea and with Army of the Potomac, 1861–62. An early and enthusiastic Republican, he was appointed secretary of Arizona Territory, 1863, and governor, 1866. He served as territorial delegate to Congress, 1869–75. A progressive and intelligent executive, he urged improvement of communications, development of agriculture along with mining, a conservation policy, and humane treatment of the Indians.

McCORMICK, ROBERT   (*b. Rockbridge, Co., Va., 1780; d. Rockbridge Co., 1846*), inventor. Father of Leander J. and Cyrus H. McCormick (1809–84). After developing and patenting a number of agricultural implements, including hempbrake and a threshing machine, he abandoned a 20-year effort to devise a power implement for reaping grain in 1831. His son, Cyrus H. McCormick, was inspired by his efforts to invent in that same year a workable reaper, which the father manufactured, *post* 1837, on a contract basis.

McCORMICK, ROBERT RUTHERFORD   (*b. Chicago, Ill., 1880; d. Chicago, Ill., 1955*), newspaper publisher. Studied at

Yale University and Northwestern University Law School. Heir to the McCormick reaper fortune, Robert McCormick took over the ownership and management of the *Chicago Tribune* in 1911, shaping that paper into the leading newspaper in the Midwest. After World War I, McCormick launched the *New York Daily News*, which was run by his cousin, Joseph M. Patterson. McCormick introduced such features as comic strips and advice columns to his newspapers; these efforts, along with owning his own source of newsprint, made the *Tribune* a profitable enterprise. McCormick fought in France during World War I and was discharged a colonel. His politics were conservative: he was an isolationist and was opposed to the New Deal, the Truman administration's foreign policy, and Eisenhower's connection with the Eastern establishment. A vigorous defender of the freedom of the press, McCormick defended his reporters and editors and paid salaries that were among the highest in the profession.

McCORMICK, ROBERT SANDERSON   (*b. Rockbridge Co., Va., 1849; d. Chicago, Ill., 1919*), diplomat. Grandson of Robert McCormick; nephew of Leander J. and Cyrus H. McCormick (1809–84). U.S. ambassador to Austria-Hungary, 1902; to Russia, 1902–05; to France, 1905–07.

McCORMICK, RUTH HANNA.   *See* SIMMS, RUTH HANNA McCORMICK.

McCORMICK, SAMUEL BLACK   (*b. Westmoreland Co., Pa., 1858; d. near Pittsburgh, Pa., 1928*), Presbyterian clergyman, educator. Graduated Washington and Jefferson College, 1880. President, Coe College, 1897–1904. Chancellor, Western University of Pennsylvania (University of Pittsburgh), 1904–20, he was responsible for its great expansion and modernization both in scope and physical plant.

McCORMICK, STEPHEN   (*b. Auburn, Va., 1784; d. 1875*), inventor, manufacturer. Invented, *ante* 1816, a cast-iron plow on which he took out his first patent, 1819. His plow, made of detachable parts, consisted of a cast-iron mold board, to the bottom of which was fastened an adjustable wrought-iron point whereby the furrow was deepened and the soil more thoroughly pulverized. Manufactured chiefly between 1826 and 1850, McCormick's plows were widely used in Virginia and other southern states.

McCOSH, ANDREW JAMES   (*b. Belfast, Ireland, 1858; d. 1908*), surgeon. Son of James McCosh. Came to America as a boy. Graduated Princeton, 1877; M.D., New York College of Physicians and Surgeons, 1880. Long associated with New York Presbyterian Hospital, he was a professor of surgery at New York Polyclinic and at College of Physicians and Surgeons. His published papers cover every department of major surgery.

McCOSH, JAMES   (*b. Ayrshire, Scotland, 1811; d. Princeton, N.J., 1894*), Presbyterian clergyman, philosopher. Educated at Glasgow and Edinburgh universities. Licensed to preach by the Church of Scotland, 1834, he was one of those who seceded from it to set up the Free Church of Scotland, thereby sacrificing his living and his prospects. Independent in philosophy as he was in church polity, McCosh reacted against his first teacher, William Hamilton, and adopted the intuitionism of Reid and the Scottish school. His first book, a critique of John Stuart Mill, led to his appointment as professor of logic and metaphysics, Queen's College, Belfast, Ireland, a post which he held 1852–68. Firmly established as a philosopher by his work at Belfast, McCosh accepted the presidency of the College of New Jersey (Princeton), 1868. During his 20 years' administration, the faculty was strengthened; a balanced system of elective studies and graduate work was instituted; schools of science, philosophy, and art were organized; fellowships and other means for stimulating research were provided; and the physical plant of the university was greatly extended. During the early 1870's, McCosh stood almost alone among U.S. ministers in defense of the doctrine of evolution, insisting that the doctrine was not directly or by implication a denial of God. He became president emeritus, 1888.

McCoy, Elijah (*b. Canada, 1843; d. Eloise, Mich., 1929*), inventor. McCoy engaged in mechanical work at an early age and soon showed marked inventive talent. Resident in Ypsilanti, Mich., *ca.* 1870, he began experiments with lubricators for steam engines and obtained six patents for lubricating devices, 1872–76. McCoy is regarded as the pioneer in devising means for steady supply of oil to machinery in intermittent drops from a cup. Active in Detroit, Mich., 1882–1926, he received 44 additional patents, which included a locomotive steam dome, a wheel tire, and an improved airbrake lubricator.

McCoy, Isaac (*b. near Uniontown, Pa., 1784; d. Louisville, Ky., 1846*), Baptist missionary, Indian agent. In his *Remarks on the Practicability of Indian Reform* (1827), he advanced a plant to remove eastern Indians west of the Mississippi River and to form an Indian state for them. Appointed U.S. agent to assist Indians in their westward migration, 1830, he surveyed, or caused to be surveyed, most of the Indian reservations in Kansas and the Cherokee Outlet in Oklahoma, but his plan for a separate state never materialized.

McCoy, Joseph Geating (*b. Sangamon Co., Ill., 1837; d. Kansas City, Mo., 1915*), pioneer cattleman. Founded terminal point for cattle drives at Abilene, Kans., 1867; established cattle drives to Cottonwood Falls and to Wichita; helped open Chisholm Trail. Author of *Historic Sketches of the Cattle Trade* (1874), an important source work.

MacCracken, Henry Mitchell (*b. Oxford, Ohio, 1840; d. Orlando, Fla., 1918*), Presbyterian clergyman, educator. Graduated Miami University, 1857; studied also at Princeton Theological Seminary and universities of Tübingen and Berlin. *Post* 1881, he turned from pastoral to educational work. Becoming professor of philosophy, University of the City of New York (present New York University), 1884, he was appointed vice-chancellor, 1885, and chancellor, 1891. Between 1885 and 1910, MacCracken completely transformed and greatly expanded New York University, removing the college to University Heights, establishing a graduate school and schools of pedagogy and commerce, and bringing the medical school in combination with Bellevue Hospital Medical College under direct control of the university council.

McCracken, Joan (*b. Philadelphia, Pa., 1922; d. New York, N.Y., 1961*), actress, singer, and dancer. With the Littlefield (later the Philadelphia) Ballet, 1932–41; in the corps de ballet of the Radio City Music Hall, 1941–42; with Eugene Loring's Dance Players, 1942. Danced in the Broadway production of *Oklahoma!*; costarred with Mitzi Green in *Billion Dollar Baby* (1945). Won critical acclaim for dramatic roles in the Experimental Theatre's production of *Galileo* by Bertolt Brecht and in Clifford Odet's *The Big Knife*, starring John Garfield. Costarred with June Allyson in the screen adaptation of the musical *Good News* (1947). Her television series, "Claudia," aired in 1952.

McCrady, Edward (*b. Charleston, S.C., 1833; d. 1903*), lawyer, Confederate officer, South Carolina legislator. Author of *The History of South Carolina* (1897, 1899, 1901, 1902). Despite its neglect of manuscript sources and its pedestrian style, this work (which covers 1670–1783) is one of the best narrative histories of the original commonwealths.

McCrae, Thomas (*b. Guelph, Canada, 1870; d. Philadelphia, Pa., 1935*), physician. Graduated University of Toronto, 1891; M.B., 1895; M.D., 1903. Associated with Johns Hopkins Hospital, 1896–1912; professor of medicine, Jefferson Medical College, 1912–35. Joint author with William Osler in revisions of *The Principles and Practice of Medicine*.

McCrary, George Washington (*b. near Evansville, Ind., 1835; d. 1890*), lawyer, Iowa legislator. Congressman, Republican, from Iowa, 1869–77; U.S. secretary of war, 1877–79; U.S. circuit judge, Eighth Judicial Circuit, 1879–84.

McCreary, James Bennett (*b. Madison Co., Ky., 1838; d. Richmond, Ky., 1918*), lawyer, Confederate soldier, Kentucky legislator. Democratic governor of Kentucky, 1875–79 and 1911–15; congressman from Kentucky, 1885–97, and U.S. senator, 1903–09. A sound money Democrat, McCreary favored international bimetallism; as governor he strove for liberal reforms.

McCreery, Charles (*b. near Winchester, Ky., 1785; d. West Point, Ky., 1826*), pioneer Kentucky physician. Practiced in Hartford, Ky., *post* 1810; performed first U.S. operation for complete extirpation of the clavicle, 1813.

McCreery, James Work (*b. Indiana Co., Pa., 1849; d. 1923*), lawyer, Colorado legislator, authority on irrigation law.

McCullagh, Joseph Burbridge (*b. Dublin, Ireland, 1842; d. St. Louis, Mo., 1896*), journalist, Union soldier. Came to America *ca.* 1853. Won repute as a Civil War correspondent and as Washington correspondent for Cincinnati, Ohio, papers; worked later in Chicago and St. Louis. Editor of *St. Louis Globe-Democrat*, 1875–96.

McCullers, Carson (*b. Lula Carson Smith, Columbus, Ga., 1917; d. Nyack, N.Y., 1967*), novelist, short-story writer, and playwright. Author of novels *The Heart Is a Lonely Hunter* (1940), *Reflections in a Golden Eye* (1941), *The Member of the Wedding* (1946), and *Clock Without Hands* (1961). Short stories include "Wunderkind" (1936), "The Jockey" (1941), "A Tree. A Rock. A Cloud." (1942), and the novella *The Ballad of the Sad Café* (1944). Wrote play version of *The Member of the Wedding* (New York Drama Critics' Circle Award, 1950), and *The Square Root of Wonderful* (1957). Suffered from depression as well as a variety of illnesses throughout her life, including a stroke in 1947 that resulted in a partial loss of sight and paralysis. Noted for eccentricities in her life as in her work. Won critical acclaim for distinctly southern fiction that emphasized the negative and bizarre aspects of life; loneliness, violence, and the grotesque.

McCulloch, Ben (*b. Rutherford Co., Tenn., 1811; d. Elkhorn Tavern, Ark., 1862*), surveyor, soldier. Served in Texas army at battle of San Jacinto. Settled at Gonzales, 1838; became one of the most popular figures in Texas as an Indian-fighting ranger; commanded a company of rangers with Zachary Taylor's army in Mexican War. In California, 1849–52; U.S. marshal, coast district of Texas, 1853–59. Commissioned brigadier general, Confederate army, he commanded at battle of Wilson's Creek, August 1861. Died in battle at Elkhorn Tavern.

McCulloch, Hugh (*b. Kennebank, Maine, 1808; d. Prince Georges Co., Md., 1895*), lawyer, banker. Removed to Fort Wayne, Ind., 1833; won high reputation for management of State Bank of Indiana in panics of 1837 and 1857. Visiting Washington, D.C., 1862, to oppose projected national banking legislation, he was asked by Salmon P. Chase in March 1863 to accept office as comptroller of currency and launch the new system himself. Successful in this task because of his influence with existing state banks. McCulloch held office until March 1865 when he became secretary of the treasury, serving until 1869. He at once recommended retirement of wartime U.S. notes and return to the gold standard. Failing to get congressional support for his policy, McCulloch concentrated on reduction of the funded public debt, readjustment of public revenue, and reintroduction of federal taxation in the South. Active in banking *post* 1869, he served again as secretary of the treasury, October 1884–March 1885. During his second term he warned the nation of the peril to its currency inherent in the Silver Coinage Act of 1878.

McCULLOCH, OSCAR CARLETON (*b. Fremont, Ohio, 1843; d. Indianapolis, Ind., 1891*), Congregational clergyman. Pastor of Plymouth Church, Indianapolis, *post* 1877, he founded or organized practically all the philanthropic enterprises created in that city during the time of his pastorate.

McCULLOUGH, ERNEST (*b. Staten Island, N.Y., 1867; d. 1931*), structural engineer, specialist in use of reinforced concrete and structural steel. Edited a number of technical periodicals *post* 1909 and wrote extensively on engineering subjects.

McCULLOUGH, JOHN (*b. near Coleraine, Ireland, 1832; d. Philadelphia, Pa., 1885*), actor. Came to America, 1847; made professional debut, Arch Street Theatre, Philadelphia, August 1857. His rise in his profession was slow but steady, the result of close study and hard work. Chosen by Edwin Forrest to act second parts, 1861, he traveled with Forrest several seasons and was then partner with Lawrence Barrett in management of the California Theatre, San Francisco. He acted as sole manager, 1870–75. Successor to Forrest in "strong" characters, his talent was always effective, though it fell short of genius.

McCULLOUGH, JOHN GRIFFITH (*b. Newark, Del., 1835; d. New York, N.Y., 1915*), lawyer, railroad executive, politician. Removed to California *ca.* 1859; served in California legislature and as state attorney general, 1863–67. Associated with his father-in-law, Trenor W. Park, in the Panama Railroad, McCullough removed to Bennington, Vt., in the 1870's. He was associated, 1895, with the successful reorganization of the Erie Railroad. Prominent in Republican politics, he served in the Vermont legislature and was governor of that state, 1902–04.

McCUMBER, PORTER JAMES (*b. Crete, Ill., 1858; d. 1933*), lawyer, North Dakota legislator. U.S. senator, Republican, from North Dakota, 1899–1923. Active in passage of Pure Food and Drugs Act of 1906; as chairman of Senate Finance Committee, was sponsor of the Fordney-McCumber Tariff.

MacCURDY, GEORGE GRANT (*b. Warrensburg, Mo., 1863; d. Plainfield, N.J., 1947*), anthropologist, archaeologist. Graduated State Normal School, Warrensburg, 1887. B.A., Harvard, 1893; M.A., 1894. With aid of Edward E. Salisbury, studied in Europe, 1894–98, with special attention to paleoanthropology; continued graduate work at Yale, receiving the Ph.D., 1905. He spent most of his professional life at Yale, where he served as instructor in anthropology, 1898–1900; lecturer, 1902–10; assistant professor of prehistoric archaeology, 1910–23; and professor, 1923 until his retirement in 1931. He served also as curator of the anthropological collections at the Peabody Museum of Natural History at Yale. In 1921 he was a cofounder of the American School of Prehistoric Research in Paris, France; he was its director in 1921 and 1924–45. A prolific contributor to the literature of anthropology, he was author of, among other books, *Human Origins: A Manual of Prehistory* (1924).

McCURDY, RICHARD ALDRICH (*b. New York, N.Y., 1835; d. Morristown, N.J., 1916*), lawyer, insurance official. Held various posts in Mutual Life Insurance Co.; was president,

1885–1905. Escaped criminal prosecution for improper use of company funds subsequent to investigation of life insurance companies by New York legislature, 1905–06.

McCUTCHEON, GEORGE BARR (*b. near Lafayette, Ind., 1866; d. New York, N.Y., 1928*), novelist. Author of, among other books, the best-selling romances *Graustark* (1901), *Brewster's Millions* (1902), and *Beverly of Graustark* (1904).

McDANIEL, HATTIE (*b. Wichita, Kans., 1898; d. San Fernando Valley, Calif., 1952*), actress and singer. Remembered for her many film roles as black maids, McDaniel appeared in such films as *Alice Adams* (1935), *Show Boat* (1936), and *Gone With the Wind* (1939). She was the first black woman to receive an Academy Award which she received for her role as Mammy in *Gone With the Wind*. She played many roles on radio and television that were usually centered around her characterization of Beulah, a black maid.

McDANIEL, HENRY DICKERSON (*b. Monroe, Ga., 1836; d. Monroe, 1926*), lawyer, Confederate soldier, Georgia legislator, industrialist. Labored, *post* 1865, for restoration of home rule and for material rehabilitation of Georgia. Democratic governor of Georgia, 1883–86, in which time he reduced the state bonded debt and the tax rate. He was for many years chairman of the board of trustees, University of Georgia.

McDILL, JAMES WILSON (*b. Monroe, Ohio, 1834; d. Creston, Iowa, 1894*), lawyer, Iowa jurist. Removed to Afton, Iowa, 1857. As congressman, Republican, from Iowa, 1873–77, he did useful service on Pacific Railroad and public lands committees. Appointed in 1878 to the railroad commission created to implement Iowa's Granger Laws, he served (except for brief period in which he filled a U.S. Senate vacancy) until 1886. Influential in creation of Interstate Commerce Commission, he served on it, 1892–94.

MacDONALD, BETTY (*b. Boulder, Colo., 1908; d. Seattle, Wash., 1958*), author. Studied briefly at the University of Washington. Author of the popular novel, *The Egg and I* (1945) which described the rigors and infelicities of simple rural life and became a best-seller, later made into a popular motion picture. The film led to the creation of the "Ma and Pa Kettle" movies. Other works include *The Plague and I* (1948) and *Onions in the Stew* (1955).

MACDONALD, CHARLES BLAIR (*b. Niagara Falls, Canada, 1856; d. Southampton, N.Y., 1939*), golfer, golf-course designer, stockbroker.

McDONALD, CHARLES JAMES (*b. Charleston, S.C., 1793; d. Marietta, Ga., 1860*), Georgia jurist and legislator. Democratic governor of Georgia, 1839–43; justice of Georgia Supreme Court, 1855–59. Restored Georgia's credit after panic of 1837. An advocate of secession, he led the Georgia delegation to Nashville Convention, 1850, and with Rhett, Barnwell, and Colquitt attempted to commit the convention to extreme measures.

McDONALD, JAMES GROVER (*b. Coldwater, Ohio, 1886; d. New York, N.Y., 1964*), diplomat, educator, and internationalist. Studied at Indiana University (M.A., 1910) and Harvard. Taught at Indiana University (1910; 1915–18) and Harvard (1911–14). Helped form a study group in 1918 that became the Foreign Policy Association in 1921; executive officer, 1919–33. Gave weekly radio talks on "The World Today" for NBC (1928–32). With the League of Nations (1933–36) as high commissioner for refugees. Member of the editorial board of the *New York Times* (1936–38). President (1938–42) of the Brooklyn Institute of Arts and Sciences. Member of the Board of Education of New York City (1940–42). From 1938 to 1945, served as vice-chairman of the

National Council for the Prevention of War, trustee of the World Peace Foundation, and chairman of the Presidential Advisory Committee on Political Refugees. Gave daily radio news analyses for NBC from 1942 to 1944. Member of the Anglo-American Committee of Inquiry on Palestine (1945–47). Special U.S. representative in Israel (1948–49); ambassador extraordinary and plenipotentiary (1949–51). Adviser to the Development Corporation for Israel (1951–61).

MacDonald, James Wilson Alexander (*b. Steubenville, Ohio, 1824; d. Yonkers, Ill., 1908*), sculptor. Won reputation, 1854, for a marble portrait bust of Thomas H. Benton. Removing from St. Louis, Mo., where he had done his early work, he settled permanently in New York City, 1865. His portrait statues and busts of celebrated contemporaries were valued for their realistic correctness. He often signed his works "Wilson MacDonald."

MacDonald, Jeanette Anna (*b. Philadelphia, Pa., 1907; d. Houston, Tex., 1965*), singer and actress. Song and dance appearances in Broadway musical comedies in the 1920's brought her to the attention of Hollywood director Ernst Lubitsch, who cast her in leading roles in *The Love Parade* (1929), *Monte Carlo* (1930) and *One Hour with You* (1931). Her clear soprano voice, exhibited in films such as *Love Me Tonight* (1932), *The Merry Widow* (1934), and *The Cat and the Fiddle* (1934), commanded favorable notices from both general audiences and critics. Known especially for her films with Metro-Goldwyn-Mayer, in which she was teamed with baritone Nelson Eddy, the pair made a series of light opera films, including *Naughty Marietta* (1935), *Rose Marie* (1936), and *Maytime* (1937). Sang for Columbia Radio Network on a weekly program, "Vick's Open House," in 1937. Left filmmaking in 1942 for a concert tour of the United States and Europe. Made several operatic appearances, including singing Juliet in Gounod's *Romeo and Juliet* with the Chicago Civic Opera in 1944. Returned to films briefly in 1947, but thereafter limited her public appearances to guest spots on television and some nightclub performances.

McDonald, John Bartholomew (*b. Fermoy, Ireland, 1844; d. New York, N.Y., 1911*), contractor. Came to America as a child; rose to front rank among railroad constructors, 1870–90. His most remarkable achievement was the Baltimore belt-line railroad, 1890–94; he was also builder of the first New York City subway, 1900–10.

McDonald, Joseph Ewing (*b. Butler Co., Ohio, 1819; d. Indianapolis, Ind., 1891*), lawyer, politician, Indiana congressman and attorney general. A consistent but fair critic of the Lincoln administration, he helped reorganize the Democratic party in his state after the Civil War and served as U.S. senator from Indiana, 1875–81. An advocate of hard money and a protective tariff, he served on the committee investigating the disputed Hayes-Tilden election, 1876.

MacDonald, Ranald (*b. Ft. George [Astoria], Oreg., 1824; d. near Toroda, Wash., 1894*), adventurer. MacDonald, who was half Indian and half white, ran away to sea, 1841, and in 1848, entered the kingdom of Japan by stratagem. Seized and imprisoned, he taught English to Japanese government interpreters. Rescued, 1849, he lived thereafter a wandering life in Australia, Canada, and the United States.

McDonogh, John (*b. Baltimore, Md., 1779; d. 1850*), merchant, philanthropist. Removed to New Orleans, La., ca. 1800, where he traded successfully and built up a large estate in land. Retiring from business, 1817, he worked out a practical plan whereby his slaves might achieve their own emancipation. He left his property for the foundation of schools in New Orleans and Baltimore.

McDonough, Thomas (*b. The Trap, present Macdonough, Del., 1783; d. at sea, 1825*), naval officer. Entered the navy as midshipman, 1800; distinguished himself in the war with Tripoli, taking part under Stephen Decatur in burning of the *Philadelphia*; promoted lieutenant, 1807. Ordered to command the fleet on Lake Champlain, he arrived at the lake early in October 1812 and worked under great difficulties to fit out ships and maintain superiority over the enemy. By the spring of 1814 he had built or otherwise obtained a superior fleet of 13 small vessels (flagship *Saratoga*, 26 guns), but by September the enemy had regained the advantage, a strong British army cooperating with British ships having advanced to the vicinity of Plattsburg. By superior tactics, Macdonough defeated the invading squadron on Sept. 11 in one of the most decisive engagements ever fought by the American navy. His victory caused the enemy's army to retreat into Canada and upset the British plan to claim sovereignty over the Great Lakes. Promoted captain for his services at Plattsburg, he held various other sea and shore commands. His health, which had been seriously impaired in the War of 1812, declined rapidly in the last year of his life. He died aboard a merchantman while returning home from his command in the Mediterranean.

McDougal, David Stockton (*b. Chillicothe, Ohio, 1809; d. San Francisco, Calif., 1882*), naval officer. While commanding USS *Wyoming* in search of Confederate cruiser *Alabama* in Far Eastern waters, McDougal destroyed Japanese land batteries and armed vessels at Shimonoseki, July 16, 1863, because of local violation of treaty pledges to the United States.

McDougall, Alexander (*b. Islay, Scotland, 1732; d. New York, N.Y., 1786*), merchant, Revolutionary agitator and soldier. Immigrated to New York as a child. Came into prominence, 1769, as author of a broadside attacking the General Assembly which was declared libelous. Called by his supporters the "Wilkes of America," he whipped up New York City public opinion in favor of the colonial cause, 1774–75. Appointed colonel of the 1st New York Regiment, 1775, he was made a Continental brigadier general, 1776, and major general, 1777. His most important military service was in the Highlands of the Hudson, where he commanded during most of the war; he succeeded Benedict Arnold as commander at West Point. Increasingly conservative as he grew older, he was an organizer and first president of the Bank of New York and president of the New York Society of the Cincinnati from its organization until his death.

McDougall, Alexander (*b. Islay, Scotland, 1845; d. Duluth, Minn., 1923*), Great Lakes mariner, shipbuilder, inventor. Came to Canada as a boy; *post* 1871, was a resident of Duluth, Minn. Patented basic design for "whaleback" freight vessels, 1881; *post* 1888, engaged in their construction. McDougall built the first steel-ship yard in the Northwest, 1892, and founded the city of Everett, Wash.; he patented, 1888–1900, 40 forty inventions pertaining to ship construction, ore, and grain-loading apparatus, and dredging machinery. Between 1903 and 1907 he perfected and patented a successful process for washing and cleaning sand iron ores; he later brought suit for infringement of this process against a subsidiary of U.S. Steel.

McDougall, Frances Harriet. *See* Green, Frances Harriet Whipple.

McDougall, William (*b. Chadderton, England, 1871; d. Durham, N.C., 1938*), psychologist. Studied physiology, anatomy, and anthropology for B.A. degree, 1894, at Cambridge University and went on to win medical degrees there, 1897. His interest turning to psychology, after further study at Cambridge and Göttingen he taught psychology at University College, London, and at Oxford *post* 1904, simultaneously conducting his own researches, principally in the psychophysics of vision. He published *An Introduction to Social Psychology* (1908), in which he described human action in terms of basic, inherited instincts. McDougall became professor of psychology at Harvard, 1920. Here he incurred the hostility of the press and of American psychologists by his lectures on national eugenics (published, 1921, as *Is America Safe for Democracy?*), in which, on the basis of army mental tests, he proclaimed the superiority of the Nordic race and made class distinctions in mental endowment. In *Outline of Psychology* (1923) and *Modern Materialism and Emergent Evolution* (1929), he developed a "hormic" psychology based on the concept that purposive action is a "form of causal efficiency distinct in nature from all mechanistic causation."

McDougall taught at Duke University *post* 1927. During his last 17 years he experimented, inconclusively, to prove the inheritance of acquired characteristics. His support of indeterminism and free will in an era of deterministic behaviorism and his unpopular theories of race obscured his contributions during his lifetime, but later acceptance of his theories of instinct, of innate capacities, of purposive action, and of the dynamic nature of mental processes mark him as one of the most original and productive of 20th-century psychologists. Other books by McDougall include *Body and Mind: A History and a Defense of Animism* (1911), *The Group Mind* (1920), *Outline of Abnormal Psychology* (1926), *The Energies of Men* (1932), and *Psycho-Analysis and Social Psychology* (1936).

McDowell, Charles (b. Winchester, Va., ca. 1743; d. 1815), Revolutionary soldier, partisan leader in North Carolina. Brother of Joseph McDowell. His initiative and that of Isaac Shelby brought together the force which made possible an American victory at King's Mountain, October 1780.

MacDowell, Edward Alexander (b. New York, N.Y., 1861; d. New York, 1908), musician, composer. Studied with Teresa Carreño and Paul Desvernine; at Paris Conservatory, 1876–78; at Wiesbaden, 1878–79. Entering Frankfurt Conservatory, he studied composition with Joachim Raff and piano with Carl Heymann. Recommended by Heymann to succeed him, MacDowell was denied the post on grounds of youth and inexperience; he served as head piano teacher at the Darmstadt Conservatory, 1881. Franz Liszt approved his Piano Concerto no. 1, Op. 15, and recommended his First Modern Suite, Op. 10, for a program at Zurich, 1882. Publishing two of his suites, 1883, he turned seriously to composition. He visited America to wed former Frankfurt pupil Marian Nevins, 1884. Residing in and near Wiesbaden, 1885–88, he produced such works as Piano Concerto no. 2., Op. 23, and the symphonic poem *Lancelot and Elaine*; he also stored up inspiration for many later compositions.

MacDowell returned to America, 1888, with his reputation established; he composed, taught, and performed successfully in Boston, Mass., 1888–96. To this period belong his *Indian Suite*, *Sonata Eroica*, and *Woodland Sketches*. As his more serious works were played by orchestras at home and abroad, he gained more acclaim than any previous American musician. Appointed to the newly created chair of music at Columbia University, 1896, he assumed that his function was to train musicians. Trying "to make music function in the academic community," he grew disillusioned over college students' inadequate musical background and the reluctance of his colleagues to recognize the value of the arts. He resigned his chair, 1904, after failure of his plan to establish an independent faculty of fine arts. In addition to his academic work, he conducted the Mendelssohn Glee Club, gave occasional performances, taught private pupils, and continued to compose. To this period belong his *Norse* Sonata and his *Keltic* Sonata, many of his finest songs, and a suite for string orchestra which he left unfinished. In failing health *post* 1905, he found his happiest refuge in his farm at Peterboro, N.H.

MacDowell's music is highly original and extremely colorful. The popularity of some of his small things, such as "To a Wild Rose," has obscured his large qualities, but musicians have always shown respect for the orchestral works, for the Piano Concerto no. 2, for the greater piano pieces (especially the sonatas), and for the best of the songs. In all his work the quality is lyrical. He turned away deliberately from the extreme experimentation of the music of his day.

McDowell, Ephraim (b. Rockbridge Co., Va., 1771; d. Danville, Ky., 1830), physician. Raised in Kentucky. Made first studies of medicine in Staunton, Va.; attended lectures at University of Edinburgh, 1793–94. Returning to America, 1795, without a degree, he settled in Danville and became known as best surgeon west of Philadelphia. McDowell was not a writer and did not even keep case notes; the five cases upon which he performed pioneer ovariotomy were described by him very inadequately in the *Eclectic Repertory* as late as April 1817 and October 1819, although descriptive of operations performed as early as 1809. Justly considered the founder of abdominal surgery, McDowell by 1829 had performed ovariotomy 12 times with but a single death and had repeatedly performed radical operations for nonstrangulated hernia. He also performed at least 32 operations for bladder stone without a death.

McDowell, Irvin (b. Columbus, Ohio, 1818; d. San Francisco, Calif., 1885), soldier. Graduated West Point, 1838. Served on Canadian frontier, at the Military Academy, and as aide-de-camp to General Wool in Mexican War; he was on headquarters staff duty, 1848–61. Highly regarded by General Winfield Scott, he was promoted brigadier general, 1861, and assigned to command of the troops assembled south of the Potomac, later known as the Army of the Potomac. Forced by political pressure to attempt a dislodgement of Confederate forces at Manassas Junction, Va., he undertook the brief campaign which ended in the first Union disaster at Bull Run. Superseded by General George B. McClellan, he remained with the army as a division commander and later a corps commander. Later in 1862 his force was separated from McClellan's command and designated as the Army of the Rappahannock. Commanding the III Corps of General Pope's Army of Virginia, McDowell was severely criticized and relieved of command for his actions at the second battle of Bull Run, August 1862. Exonerated by a court of inquiry, he was never afterward employed in the field. He retired as major general, 1882. Able, energetic, honest, McDowell had never held a command of his own, even of a company, until he took over the Army of the Potomac. His failure at the first battle of Bull Run (which came very near being a success) may have been owing to his tendency to defer too much to the views of subordinates as well as to his inexperience in field command.

McDowell, James (b. Rockbridge Co., Va., 1795; d. near Lexington, Va., 1851), planter, Virginia legislator, orator. An early opponent of slavery as a cause of national dissension, he also opposed nullification. As Democratic governor of Virginia, 1843–46, he devoted himself largely to problems of internal improvements. Elected congressman from Virginia, 1846, to fill out an unexpired term, he served until his death.

McDowell, John (b. Cumberland, present Franklin Co., Pa., 1751; d. Franklin Co., 1820), lawyer, educator. Graduated College of Philadelphia, 1771. First principal, St. John's College, Annapolis, 1789–1806; professor of natural philosophy and provost, University of Pennsylvania, 1806–10.

McDowell, John (b. Bedminster, N.J., 1780; d. 1863), Presbyterian clergyman. Graduated College of New Jersey (Princeton), 1801. Pastor at Elizabethtown, N.J., 1804–33, and at Philadelphia churches thereafter. A loyal supporter of the "old school."

McDowell, Joseph (b. Winchester, Va., 1756; d. 1801), Revolutionary soldier, North Carolina legislator. Brother of Charles McDowell. Commanded his brother's troops at battle of King's Mountain, October 1780. A leader of the Democratic-Republican party in western North Carolina, he served as congressman, 1797–99.

MacDowell, Katherine Sherwood Bonner (b. Holly Springs, Miss., 1849; d. Holly Springs, 1883), short-story writer, novelist under pseudonym "Sherwood Bonner."

McDowell, Mary Eliza (b. Cincinnati, Ohio, 1854; d. Chicago, Ill., 1836), settlement house founder. Head, University of Chicago Settlement, 1894–1929.

McDowell, William Fraser (b. Millersburg, Ohio, 1858; d. Washington, D.C., 1937), Methodist clergyman. Bishop *post* 1904; a noted preacher and leader in Methodist reunion.

McDuffie, George (b. probably Columbia Co., Ga., 1790; d. Sumter District, S.C., 1851), lawyer, South Carolina legislator. Congressman, Democrat, from South Carolina, 1821–34; governor of South Carolina, 1834–36; U.S. senator, 1842–46. Entering Congress as a strong nationalist, McDuffie was soon attacking the tariff and opposing internal improvements. Holding that the tariff affected cotton growers most unfairly because it subtracted from their profits by forcing them to sell their produce in exchange for a reduced purchasing power, he argued that the southern planters, in paying import duties on what they purchased, gave to the government or to northern manufacturers 40 out of every 100 bales of cotton they produced. His speech of May 19, 1831, at Charleston is frequently said to have brought John C. Calhoun to open advocacy of nullification. Delegate to the nullification convention, 1832, he wrote the address to the people of the other states in which, after severely condemning the protective tariff, he warned the states that secession might well follow. He stated that if the federal government employed force South Carolina would rather be "the cemetery of freemen than the habitation of slaves." A ready, eloquent, and sensational debater, his speeches were characterized by their sound and fury and extravagance of phrase. John Q. Adams said of him that he had a "gloomy churlishness" in his character; this may well have been caused by a chronic dyspepsia from which he suffered. In the first session of the 19th Congress he made furious charges of a "corrupt bargain" between John Q. Adams and Henry Clay, and proposed a constitutional amendment which would provide for direct election of a president in order to prevent a recurrence of the situation which had resulted in the election of Adams. He broke off relations with Andrew Jackson on the questions of nullification and the recharter of the Bank of the United States. After the expiration of his term as governor, he began to lose influence in South Carolina while Calhoun gained it.

McElrath, Thomas (b. Williamsport, Pa., 1807; d. 1888), publisher. Partner of Horace Greeley in publication of the *New York Tribune*; was its efficient business manager, 1841–57.

McElroy, John (b. Enniskillen, Ireland, 1782; d. Frederick, Md., 1877), Roman Catholic clergyman, Jesuit. Came to America, 1803; entered Society of Jesus, 1806. Pastor at Frederick, Md., 1822–46; Mexican War chaplain; pastor of St. Mary's Church, Boston, Mass. A forceful preacher and retreat master.

McElroy, John (b. Greenup Co., Ky., 1846; d. 1929), journalist, Union soldier. Author of *Andersonville* (1879), descriptive of his prison experiences; *The Struggle for Missouri* (1909); and other books. Held editorial posts in Chicago, Ill. and Toledo, Ohio; editor-publisher of the *National Tribune*, Washington, D.C..

McElroy, Robert McNutt (b. Perryville, Ky., 1872; d. Lihue, Hawaii, 1959), historian, publicist. Studied at Princeton University (Ph.D., 1900); taught at Princeton (1901–14); (1919–25); and again from 1939 until his retirement. Taught at Oxford University, England (1925–39). Educational director of the National Security League from 1914 to 1919. An advocate of America's preparedness for World War I and later an anticommunist, McElroy was in favor of a strong League of Nations and American membership. Wrote biographies of Grover Cleveland, Levi P. Morton, and Jefferson Davis.

McElwain, William Howe (b. Charlestown, Mass., 1867; d. 1908), shoe manufacturer. Without knowledge of the work of F. W. Taylor, McElwain applied principles of scientific management in his factories *post* 1900, thereby obtaining largest output of product in the shoe industry, 1908.

McEnery, Samuel Douglas (b. Monroe, La., 1837; d. New Orleans, La., 1910), jurist, Confederate soldier, politician. Democratic governor of Louisiana, 1881–88; justice, state supreme court, 1888–96; U.S. senator, 1897–1910.

McEntee, James Joseph (b. Jersey City, N.J., 1884; d. Jersey City, N.J., 1957), labor leader and government official. A member and officer of the International Association of Machinists Union from 1911, McEntee was appointed by President Wilson to the New York Arbitration Board in 1917. In 1933, Roosevelt appointed him assistant director of the Civilian Conservation Corps; he was director from 1940 to 1942, when the Corps was abolished. President Truman appointed him to the National Production Authority from 1952 to 1954.

McEntee, Jervis (b. Rondout, N.Y., 1828; d. Rondout, 1891), landscape painter. Studied with Frederick E. Church. Noted for winter and autumn scenes of a marked poetic character.

Macfadden, Bernarr (b. near Mill Spring, Mo., 1868; d. Jersey City, N.J., 1955), physical culturist and publisher. A popularizer of physical health and exercise, Macfadden founded several health farms and, in 1899, the magazine *Physical Culture*, a magazine which helped revive the natural approach to health. In 1919, he founded *True Story*; in 1924, a tabloid, based on sex and violence, the *New York Evening Graphic*, which ran until 1932. He established the Macfadden Corp. in 1924 which oversaw his publications which had a circulation of 35 to 40 million. Losing control of his enterprise during the Depression, Macfadden founded a new religion, the Cosmotarian Fellowship, "a religion through happiness," and was known to deliver sermons to congregations while standing on his head.

McFadden, Louis Thomas (b. Troy, Pa., 1876; d. New York, N.Y., 1936), banker. Congressman, Republican, from Pennsylvania, 1915–36; coauthor of controversial McFadden-Pepper Act, 1927, liberalizing powers of the national banks.

McFarland, George Bradley (b. Bangkok, Siam, now Thailand, 1866; d. Bangkok, 1942), physician, lexicographer. Born of Presbyterian missionary parents. Attended Washington and Jefferson College. M.D., Western Pennsylvania Medical School, 1890; studied surgery at Baltimore College of Physicians and Surgeons, and dental medicine at Chirurgical College of Dentistry, 1891. Resident thereafter for the most part in Thailand, he made major contributions to the development there of modern hospital administration and medical education. Among his numerous literary works was an unabridged Thai-English dictionary (Bangkok, 1941; repr., 1944) which has become standard.

McFARLAND, JOHN HORACE (*b. McAlisterville, Pa., 1859; d. Harrisburg, Pa., 1948*), printer, political and social reformer, conservationist, horticulturist. Active in national associations for good government and conservation of the aesthetic and the economic resources of the country, he had a major role in the establishment of the National Park Service, 1916. He was an international authority on rose culture.

McFARLAND, JOHN THOMAS (*b. Mount Vernon, Ind., 1851; d. Maplewood, N.J., 1913*), Methodist clergyman, educator. President, Iowa Wesleyan, 1884–91. *Post* 1904, he edited Methodist Sunday-school literature, which he reformed and liberalized.

McFARLAND, SAMUEL GAMBLE (*b. Washington Co., Pa., 1830; d. Canonsburg, Pa., 1897*), Presbyterian clergyman. Missionary to Siam, 1860–78; principal of royal school at Bangkok, 1878–96.

McFARLAND, THOMAS BARD (*b. near Mercersburg, Pa., 1828; d. San Francisco, Calif., 1908*), lawyer. Removed to California, 1850. Held several district judgeships; justice, California Supreme Court, 1886–1908.

MACFARLANE, CHARLES WILLIAM (*b. Philadelphia, Pa., 1850; d. Philadelphia 1931*), engineer, builder, author of a number of works in philosophy and economics. Chief theoretical work was *Value and Distribution* (1899), an exposition of the Austrian school.

MACFARLANE, ROBERT (*b. Rutherglen, Scotland, 1815; d. Brooklyn, N.Y., 1883*), dyer. Came to America, 1835. Editor, *Scientific American*, 1848–65; author of works on dyeing and marine propulsion by steam.

McFAUL, JAMES AUGUSTINE (*b. Larne, Ireland, 1850; d. 1917*), Roman Catholic clergyman. Came to America as an infant. Served *post* 1877 as curate and pastor in numerous New Jersey parishes and was consecrated bishop of Trenton, 1894. He interested himself particularly in work among immigrant Poles, Hungarians, and Italians; was liberal in spirit; and took an active part in municipal and state reforms.

McFEE, WILLIAM (*b. at sea [birth registered in Islington, London], 1881; d. New Milford, Conn., 1966*), writer. In the United States from 1912 (but for service in the British naval reserve during World War I); became a U.S. citizen in 1925. Worked at various jobs, including chief engineer for the United Fruit Company, commuting on cargo and passenger ships between New York City and the Spanish Main (1920–22). Books offer a nostalgic account of seafaring life in the early twentieth century, and include *Letters from an Ocean Tramp* (1908), *Casuals of the Sea* (1916), *Captain Macedoine's Daughter* (1920), *The Harbourmaster* (1931), *The Beachcomber* (1935), *Derelicts* (1938), *Spenlove in Arcady* (1941), and *Family Trouble* (1949).

McFERRIN, JOHN BERRY (*b. Rutherford Co., Tenn., 1807; d. Nashville[?], 1887*), Methodist clergyman. Editor, *Southwestern Christian Advocate*, 1840–58. Active thereafter in missionary work and as agent for the publishing interests of his denomination, which he restored to solvency, 1878–87. Author of *History of Methodism in Tennessee* (1869–73).

MACGAHAN, JANUARIUS ALOYSIUS (*b. Perry Co., Ohio, 1844; d. Constantinople, Turkey, 1878*), war correspondent.

Cousin of General Philip Sheridan. His reporting of Turkish massacres in Bulgaria, 1876, for the London *Daily News*, prepared British sentiment to approve war between Russia and Turkey which resulted in Bulgarian independence.

McGARRAH, GATES WHITE (*b. near Monroe, N.Y., 1863; d. New York, N.Y., 1940*), banker. Chairman, Chase National Bank, 1926–27; first president, Bank for International Settlements, 1930–33.

McGARVEY, JOHN WILLIAM (*b. Hopkinsville, Ky., 1829; d. Lexington, Ky., 1911*), Disciples of Christ clergyman, educator, writer. A strong conservative influence in his denomination.

McGEE, WILLIAM JOHN (*b. near Farley, Iowa, 1853; d. 1912*), geologist, hydrologist, anthropologist. Associated with U.S. Geological Survey, 1883–94, he conducted important studies of the Atlantic coastal plain. He was chief ethnologist, Bureau of American Ethnology, 1893–1903. Thereafter he served on the Inland Waterways Commission and supervised a study of U.S. water resources for the Department of Agriculture.

McGEEHAN, WILLIAM O'CONNELL (*b. San Francisco, Calif., 1879; d. 1933*), journalist, sports columnist. Began career on San Francisco newspapers; removed to New York, 1914, where he wrote for *New York Herald-Tribune* and its predecessor papers. His work was notable for literary quality and turn of satire; he coined memorable phrases such as "the cauliflower industry" and "the manly art of modified murder" as definitions of boxing.

McGHEE, CHARLES McCLUNG (*b. Monroe Co., Tenn., 1828; d. Knoxville, Tenn., 1907*), Confederate soldier, financier, executive of Tennessee railroads.

McGIFFERT, ARTHUR CUSHMAN (*b. Sauquoit, N.Y., 1861; d. Dobbs Ferry, N.Y., 1933*), Presbyterian clergyman, historian. Graduated Western Reserve, 1882; Union Theological Seminary, New York, 1885. Ph.D., University of Marburg, Germany, 1888. Taught church history at Lane Theological Seminary and at Union Theological Seminary; president, Union Theological, 1917–26. Author of ten books covering the development of Christian religious ideas, among them *A History of Christianity in the Apostolic Age* (1897) and *A History of Christian Thought* (1932–33).

McGIFFIN, PHILO NORTON (*b. Washington, Pa., 1860; d. New York, N.Y., 1897*), naval officer. Graduated Annapolis, 1882. Honorably discharged, 1884, he took a commission in the Chinese navy, 1885, serving as naval constructor and professor of gunnery and seamanship. As executive officer, but in fact commander, of the battleship *Chen Yuen*, he fought with rare skill a losing action off the Yalu River, Sept. 17, 1894, compelling the retreat of the Japanese main squadron.

McGILL, JOHN (*b. Philadelphia, Pa., 1809; d. 1872*), Roman Catholic clergyman, lawyer. Raised in Kentucky; served there as curate and pastor until 1850 when he was consecrated bishop of Richmond, Va. Although opposed to slavery, he was a Confederate sympathizer; he did notable work in the reconstruction of his diocese subsequent to the Civil War.

McGILL, RALPH EMERSON (*b. Igou's Ferry, Tenn., 1898; d. Atlanta, Ga., 1969*), journalist. With the *Atlanta Constitution* from 1929; editor in chief from 1942. A Democratic partisan, he was a spokesman for the South against segregation and all forms of discrimination. Won Pulitzer Prize (1959) for an editorial on the bombing of an Atlanta synagogue.

McGILLIVRAY, ALEXANDER (*b. ca. 1759; d. Pensacola, Fla., 1793*), Creek Indian chieftain, Loyalist. From 1784 to his death,

McGillivray's career possessed international significance. His immediate purpose was to form a confederation of southern Indians and, with the aid of Spain or perhaps Great Britain, compel the United States to restore the Indian boundary line as it existed in 1773—in other words, to evacuate a large part of Georgia, Tennessee, and Kentucky. Trusting to Spanish support, he precipitated a war along the American frontier from Georgia to the Cumberland, 1786; his power was at its height when the attacks of his warriors almost succeeded in destroying the stations on the Cumberland River, 1787. McGillivray signed a peace treaty at New York, August 1790, which was satisfactory to the United States but failed of Indian approval. Influenced by British arguments and Spanish money, McGillivray repudiated the Treaty of New York in July 1792. He died during the negotiations for formation of a confederation of southern Indians in alliance with Spain against the United States.

McGILVARY, DANIEL (*b. Moore Co., N.C., 1828; d. Chiengmai, Siam, 1911*), Presbyterian clergyman. Missionary in Siam, 1858–1911, he was known as "the Apostle to the Lao."

McGIVNEY, MICHAEL JOSEPH (*b. Waterbury, Conn., 1852; d. Thomaston, Conn., 1890*), Roman Catholic clergyman. Leader in organizing, January 1882, the Knights of Columbus, which he served as national chaplain until his death.

McGLOTHLIN, WILLIAM JOSEPH (*b. near Gallatin, Tenn., 1867; d. Gastonia, N.C., 1933*), Baptist clergyman, professor of church history. President, Furman University, 1919–33.

McGLYNN, EDWARD (*b. New York, N.Y., 1837; d. Newburgh, N.Y., 1900*), Roman Catholic clergyman, social reformer. Educated in New York City schools and at College of the Propaganda, Rome, Italy; ordained, Rome, 1860. Active in charitable and humanitarian affairs, McGlynn was appointed pastor of St. Stephen's parish, New York City, 1866. Becoming acutely aware of the disruption of morals attributable to unemployment and poverty, he became an adherent of Henry George and accepted the single-tax doctrine as fundamental remedy for social evils. His active part in George's 1886 campaign for mayor of New York City brought him into open conflict with Archbishop M. A. Corrigan. Suspended from exercise of his priestly functions, he was removed from his pastorate, January 1887, and summoned to Rome to explain views which he had propagated upon the land questions. His refusal to go, on advice of counsel, coupled with a misunderstanding over his failure to reply to the summons, resulted in his excommunication in July 1887. For five years following this censure he continued to defend the single-tax doctrine; in December 1892, after a review of his teachings and of the facts, he was reinstated. Thereafter, as pastor of St. Mary's Church at Newburgh, N.Y., he was a frequent speaker at single-tax meetings and made it quite clear that Rome had not required him to retract his views on the ownership of land.

McGOVERN, JOHN (*b. Troy, N.Y., 1850; d. Chicago, Ill., 1917*), journalist, Chicago editor.

McGOWAN, SAMUEL (*b. Laurens District, S.C., 1819; d. Abbeville, S.C., 1897*), lawyer, South Carolina legislator, Confederate brigadier general. Justice, South Carolina Supreme Court, 1879–93.

McGRANERY, JAMES PATRICK (*b. Philadelphia, Pa., 1895; d. Palm Beach, Fla., 1962*), U.S. congressman, federal judge, and U.S. attorney general. A prominent Irish Catholic Democrat. Studied at Temple University Law School (graduated, 1928). Established a successful law practice in Philadelphia in 1928. Served on the Pennsylvania Democratic Central Committee (1928–32). Elected to the U.S. House of Representatives

(1936; returned in 1938, 1940, and 1942). Assistant to the U.S. attorney general, 1943–46, federal judge for the Eastern District of Pennsylvania in 1946; attorney general under Harry S. Truman, 1952–53. Practiced law in Washington, D.C., and Philadelphia after 1953.

McGRATH, JAMES (*b. Co. Tipperary, Ireland, 1835; d. Albany, N.Y., 1898*), Roman Catholic clergyman, Oblate. Came to Canada, 1856. After extensive missionary service in Canada and the United States, he was appointed pastor at St. John's, Lowell, Mass., 1870, and erected there the Church of the Immaculate Conception in 1872, and was elected first provincial of the American province of the Oblate Fathers, 1883. He served for ten years.

McGRATH, JAMES HOWARD (*b. Woonsocket, R.I., 1903; d. Narragansett, R.I., 1966*), governor of Rhode Island and U.S. senator and attorney general. Studied at Providence College and Boston University Law School (LL.B., 1929). Began practicing law in Rhode Island in 1929. City solicitor of Central Falls, R.I. (1930–34); U.S. attorney for the district of Rhode Island (1934–40); governor of Rhode Island (1940–45); solicitor general of the United States (1945–46); U.S. senator (1946–49); U.S. attorney general (1949–52). President Truman asked for, and received, McGrath's resignation as attorney general after McGrath fired Newbold Morris, an independent special assistant hired to investigate corruption charges in the Bureau of Internal Revenue and the Justice Department. A Democratic senator, McGrath was known as a liberal who consistently supported Truman administration policies. As U.S. attorney general, he was a strong advocate of civil rights.

McGRATH, MATTHEW J. (*b. Nenagh, Tipperary, Ireland, 1876; d. New York, N.Y., 1941*), police officer, athlete. Came to the United States, 1897; joined New York Police Department, 1902, rising to rank of inspector, 1936. Expert on urban traffic problems. Represented the United States in the four Olympics between 1908 and 1924, setting a hammer-throw record at Stockholm, 1912, and placing second at Paris, 1924.

McGRAW, JAMES HERBERT (*b. Panama, N.Y., 1860; d. San Francisco, Calif., 1948*), book and magazine publisher. Graduated State Normal School, Fredonia, N.Y., 1884. President of the McGraw Publishing Co. (*post* 1917 the McGraw-Hill Publishing Co.), 1899–1928; chairman of the board, 1928–35.

McGRAW, JOHN HARTE (*b. Penobscot Co., Maine, 1850; d. 1910*), lawyer. Removed to Seattle, Wash., 1876. Republican governor of Washington, 1893–97. His term was a stormy period of strikes and riots, which he handled with skill and courage; he fought hard against legislative extravagance.

McGRAW, JOHN JOSEPH (*b. Truxton, N.Y., 1873; d. New Rochelle, N.Y., 1934*), baseball player, manager. Celebrated for his work at third base for Baltimore, 1891–99, McGraw served as manager of the New York Giants, 1902–32. In that time he won ten National League pennants and three World Series.

McGREADY, JAMES (*b. western Pennsylvania, c. 1758; d. Henderson Co., Ky., 1817*), Presbyterian preacher, revivalist. Raised in Guilford Co., N.C. Pastor in Orange Co., N.C., ca. 1790–96, he removed in the latter year to Kentucky, where he conducted a series of revivals in Logan Co., 1797–99. These were the forerunners of the Great Revival of 1800. After a period of alliance with the Cumberland Presbytery, McGready returned to orthodoxy and founded pioneer churches in southern Indiana, 1811–16, preaching almost up to his death.

McGROARTY, SUSAN. *See* JULIA, SISTER.

McGuffey, William Holmes (*b. Washington Co., Pa., 1800; d. 1873*), educator, compiler of school readers. Raised near Youngstown, Ohio; graduated Washington College, 1826; was licensed to preach in the Presbyterian church, 1829. Professor of languages, Miami University, 1826–36; president, Cincinnati College, 1836–39; president, Ohio University, 1839–43; professor of moral philosophy, University of Virginia, 1845–73. Associated with Samuel Lewis and others in promoting common school education in Ohio, he continued his interest in public schools throughout his life. He is most widely known for his series of *Eclectic Readers* for elementary schools. These books, the first and second of which were published in 1836, the third and fourth in 1837, the fifth in 1844, and the sixth in 1857, went through edition after edition, were revised and enlarged, and reached a sale of more than 120 million copies. Their influence contributed much to the shaping of the American mind in the 19th century.

McGuire, Charles Bonaventure (*b. Dungannon, Ireland, 1768; d. Pittsburgh, Pa., 1833*), Roman Catholic clergyman, Franciscan. After a life of adventure and peril during the French Revolution and after, he volunteered for the American missions and arrived in Pennsylvania, 1817. Cosmopolitan and highly educated, he served as pastor in Pittsburgh, Pa., *post* 1820.

McGuire, Hunter Holmes (*b. Winchester, Va., 1835; d. Richmond, Va., 1900*), surgeon. Commissioned a Confederate medical officer, 1861, he was chief surgeon of "Stonewall" Jackson's commands until the latter's death; he was also Jackson's personal physician. Subsequently he served as surgeon and medical director under Generals Ewell and Early, and was professor of surgery, Virginia Medical College, 1865–78. Active in establishment of the College of Physicians and Surgeons, Richmond, Va., 1893, he was its president and professor of surgery at the time of his death.

McGuire, Joseph Deakins (*b. Washington, D.C., 1842; d. 1916*), lawyer, anthropologist. Expert in aboriginal technology.

McHale, Kathryn (*b. Logansport, Ind., 1889; d. Washington, D.C., 1956*), educator, psychologist, administrator. Ph.D., Columbia University (1926). Taught at Goucher College from 1920 to 1935; professor from 1927. At Goucher, McHale developed the McHale Vocational Interest Test for College Women, a test that became widely used in the U.S. From 1929 to 1950, director of the American Association of University Women. After World War II, she served on the executive committee of the U.S. National Commission for UNESCO. From 1950 to 1956, she served on the Subversive Activities Control Board; as such, she served as the chairman of a committee to determine whether the U.S. Communist Party was under foreign domination.

Machebeuf, Joseph Projectus (*b. Riom, France, 1812; d. 1889*), Roman Catholic clergyman. Accompanied J. B. Lamy to Cincinnati, Ohio, 1839, and worked as a missionary in northern Ohio until 1850 when he went with Lamy to New Mexico to serve him as assistant and vicar general. A prodigy for work, Machebeuf traveled widely through the Southwest on missionary tours in addition to serving as pastor in the cathedral at Santa Fe. *Post* 1860, he worked in Colorado and Utah, building churches in Denver, Central City, and other towns, besides establishing chapels in the new agricultural villages which were springing up in those territories. Consecrated vicar apostolic of Colorado and Utah, 1868, he was made bishop, 1887.

Machen, John Gresham (*b. Baltimore, Md., 1881; d. Bismarck, N. Dak., 1937*), Presbyterian clergyman, theologian. Suspended from the ministry as a schismatic, 1935, he formed, with others, the Orthodox Presbyterian church.

McHenry, James (*b. Ballymena, Ireland, 1753; d. Fayetteville, Md., 1816*), physician, Revolutionary soldier, Maryland legislator. Immigrated to America, 1771; studied medicine in Philadelphia with Benjamin Rush; served as surgeon, 5th Philadelphia, 1776–77. Appointed secretary to General George Washington, 1778, he served on Lafayette's staff in a similar capacity and continued in active service until 1781. Congressman from Maryland, 1783–86, he was a strong campaigner for adoption of the federal Constitution by Maryland. As U.S. secretary of war, 1796–1800, he supported Alexander Hamilton on all major matters of policy.

McHenry, James (*b. Larne, Ireland, 1785; d. Larne, 1845*), physician, poet, novelist. Resident in Baltimore, Md., Pittsburgh and Philadelphia, Pa., 1817–43. Author of several American historical tales. A conservative poet and critic, he was at his best in *The Pleasures of Friendship* (1822).

McHugh, Rose John (*b. Marshall, Mich., 1881; d. Washington, D.C., 1952*), social worker. Received Ph.B. from the University of Chicago in 1905. McHugh specialized in child welfare and showed great skill in bringing about cooperation between local, state, and federal government agencies and private organizations. Director of the Central Division of the American Red Cross; member of the National Catholic Welfare Conference; served as Chief, Special Standards Section in the Social Security Administration of the Federal Security Agency.

McIlvaine, Charles Pettit (*b. Burlington, N.J., 1799; d. Florence, Italy, 1873*). Protestant Episcopal clergyman. Graduated Princeton, 1816; ordained, 1823; served parishes in Washington, D.C., and Brooklyn, N.Y. His theology was strongly evangelical, alienating some High Churchmen. Consecrated bishop of Ohio, 1832, he ably administered Kenyon College and was a strenuous opponent of tractarian doctrine. Sent to England at Lincoln's request during the *Trent* affair crisis, 1861, he was able to win friends for the American cause among the higher clergy. His best-known printed works were *Evidences of Christianity* (1832) and *Oxford Divinity* (a defense of evangelical doctrines, 1841).

McIlwaine, Richard (*b. Petersburg, Va., 1834; d. Richmond, Va., 1913*), Presbyterian clergyman, Confederate chaplain. President, Hampden-Sydney College, 1883–1904.

McIntire, Ross (*b. Salem, Ore, 1889; d. Chicago, Ill., 1959*), physician. M.D., Willamette (now Oregon) University Medical School (1912). Served in the U.S. Navy from 1917. Appointed personal physician to President Franklin Roosevelt (1933–45). Surgeon general of the navy and chief of the Bureau of Medicine and Surgery from 1938 to 1946. He retired a vice admiral, the first medical officer to achieve that rank. From 1947 to 1951, head of the American Red Cross blood program. From 1947 to 1954, President Truman's appointee as chairman of the President's Committee for Employment of the Physically Handicapped, a position of particular importance for the employment of disabled World War II veterans. The last years of McIntire's life were spent as executive director of the International College of Surgeons.

McIntire, Samuel (*b. Salem, Mass., 1757; d. Salem, 1811*), architect, wood-carver. Designed the classical Peirce house (a notable contribution to Salem architecture), 1779, and won the lifelong patronage of merchant prince Elias H. Derby. Noted for boldness and simplicity of design, his Doric and Ionic porticoes and pilasters came to adorn many of Salem's leading homes. McIntire commenced public and semipublic building with a concert hall, 1782, and the Salem Court House, 1785; in 1792 he submitted an able plan (not unlike that later used for the White House) for the U.S. Capitol. Speedily recognizing and adopting the style of Charles Bulfinch, McIntire displayed in all his works a refined and delicate elegance. Many of the ornaments—grape sprays, eagles, cornucopias, and the baskets of fruit which became almost a hallmark—he carved himself. Early dwellings which showed the Bulfinch influence (and that of the Adam brothers) were the Nathan Read house and, in Waltham, the home of Theodore Lyman. When Mrs. E. H. Derby demanded a house in the new fashion, he combined features in drawings by Bulfinch and several New York architects, and drafted final plans for what came to be called the "Mansion." This palatial dwelling (1795–98), its front modeled after the Provost's House in Dublin, was to contemporaries perhaps McIntire's masterpiece, although it was razed for newer buildings a few years after his death. Following their parents' deaths the Derby children had McIntire build or remodel homes for them; "Oak Hill," for Mrs. Nathaniel West, in Peabody, Mass., rivaled even the "Mansion" in ornateness. Other clients came to him; the Cook and Gardner houses (1804–05) are among his finest works, and his remodeled parlor in the Peirce house is considered a superb example of the Adam style. He built or reconstructed several Salem churches, and designed the gateways to Washington Square. His later structures (including the Woodbridge and Tucker houses and numerous business buildings) were all of brick; they seemed to reveal the restraint of growing classicism with their sober, almost austere, treatment, but his homes and furniture continued to display elaborate wood carvings and furniture work.

MACINTOSH, DOUGLAS CLYDE (*b. Breadalbane, Ontario, Canada, 1877; d. Hamden, Conn., 1948*), Baptist clergyman, theologian, philosopher of religion. B.A., McMaster University, Toronto, 1903. Ph.D., University of Chicago, 1909, where he was strongly influenced by George B. Foster. Appointed assistant professor of systematic theology at Yale in 1909, he became successively Dwight Professor of Theology, 1916–32, and professor of theology and the philosophy of religion, 1933–42. One of the important modernist liberal theologians in American Protestantism in his time, he sought a way of preserving the abiding essence of Christian belief by using contemporary scientific and philosophical methods and by restructuring Christian doctrine so as to bring it into harmony with modern knowledge. He was author of, among other works, *Theology as an Empirical Science* (1919) and *The Pilgrimage of Faith in the World of Modern Thought* (1931).

McINTOSH, JOHN BAILLIE (*b. Florida, 1829; d. 1888*), Union soldier. Served in U.S. Navy during Mexican War. As brigadier general of cavalry, distinguished himself at Kelly's Ford, 1863, at Gettysburg, and at Winchesther, 1864.

McINTOSH, LACHLAN (*b. Raits, Scotland, 1725; d. Savannah, Ga., 1806*), Revolutionary soldier. Came to America as a boy; raised in Georgia. As brigadier general, Continental, he commanded at Fort Pitt, 1778–79, and fought in southern theater, 1779–80. Suspended from service by George Walton's influence, he was vindicated by Congress, 1784. Killed Button Gwinnett in duel, 1777.

McINTOSH, WILLIAM (*b. present Carroll Co., Ga., ca. 1775; d. Carroll Co., 1825*), Creek chieftain. Son of a British agent and an Indian woman, McIntosh led friendly Lower Creek against British and Indians in War of 1812. He served as U.S. brigadier general under Jackson against the Seminole, 1817–18, and cooperated with his cousin, Governor George M. Troup, to remove Indians from western Georgia. His faction signed treaty of land cession, 1825. The Upper Creek protested his disinterestedness, and when the treaty was approved, they raided his home and killed him. McIntosh's life epitomized the tragedy of the half-breed friendly to whites and viewed by Indians as a renegade.

McINTYRE, ALFRED ROBERT (*b. Hyde Park, Mass., 1886; d. Boston, Mass., 1948*), book publisher. Graduated Harvard, 1907. President, Little, Brown and Company, 1926–48.

McINTYRE, JAMES (*b. Kenosha, Wis., 1857; d. near Southampton, N.Y., 1937*), and **THOMAS KURTON HEATH** (*b. Philadelphia, Pa., 1853; d. Poquott, N.Y., 1938*), blackface comedians, partners in a variety act for more than fifty years. Their celebrated skit "The Ham Tree" was made into a musical revue, 1906.

McINTYRE, OSCOR ODD (*b. Plattsburg, Mo., 1884; d. New York, N.Y., 1938*), journalist. His syndicated column, "New York Day by Day," appeared in more than 500 newspapers and brought "Broadway to Main Street."

McIVER, CHARLES DUNCAN (*b. Moore Co., N.C., 1860; d. 1906*), southern educator. Graduated University of North Carolina, 1881. A zealous advocate of teacher training, universal public education, and women's higher education, he served as president, North Carolina College for Women, 1892–1906. He was also secretary, Southern Education Board.

MacIVER, ROBERT MORRISON (*b. Stornoway, Isle of Lewis, Scotland, 1882; d. New York, N.Y., 1970*), political philosopher and sociologist. Studied at the University of Oxford and Edinburgh University (Ph.D., 1915). Taught at Kings College, Aberdeen (1907–15). Professor of political science at the University of Toronto, Canada (1915–27). Head of the Department of Economics and Sociology at Barnard College (1927–29); professor of political theory at Columbia University (1929–50). Became a U.S. citizen ca. 1927. President of New School for Social Research (1963–65); chancellor (1965–66). Books include *Community* (1917), *The Modern State* (1926), *The Contribution of Sociology to Social Work* (1931), *Leviathan and the People* (1939), *Towards an Abiding Peace* (1943), *The Web of Government* (1947), and *Democracy and the Economic Challenge* (1952).

MACK, CONNIE (*b. East Brookfield, Mass., 1862; d. Germantown, Pa., 1956*), baseball manager and club owner. Legendary manager and owner of the Philadelphia Athletics, Mack joined the club in 1901, retiring as owner in 1954. Under his leadership and his management, the Athletics won nine league championships and five World Series titles. Mack was elected to the National Baseball Hall of Fame in 1938.

MACK, JULIAN WILLIAM (*b. San Francisco, Calif., 1866; d. New York, N.Y., 1943*), lawyer, jurist, leader in social welfare causes and in Jewish affairs. He graduated from Cincinnati's Hughes High School in 1884 and then attended the Harvard Law School, where he was a founding editor and the first business manager of the *Harvard Law Review*. He received an LL.B. degree in 1887, graduating at the top of his class and receiving the coveted Parker Fellowship. In 1890 he settled in Chicago and joined the law firm of Julius Rosenthal, who was at the time the leading spokesman for Chicago Jews on public matters. He became a professor of law, first at Northwestern University Law School, 1895–1902, and then on the original law school faculty of the University of Chicago, 1902–11. His continuing activities on behalf of Jewish charities brought him into national prominence. He early became associated with Jane Addams and the Hull House circle, and in 1892 he helped establish the Maxwell Street Settlement (later merged with Hull House) to serve the immigrant residents of Chicago's west-side Jewish ghetto. In 1904 he was elected president of the National Conference of Jewish Charities. In 1911 he succeeded Jane Addams as president of the National Conference of Social Workers. That same year he was appointed by President Taft to the newly created Commerce Court. In 1913 he became an ambulatory circuit court judge, assigned for a time to various circuits throughout the country but after 1918 mainly in New York City.

Concurrently with his judicial activities, Mack was closely associated with Zionism. As the first president of the Zionist Organization of America, 1918−21, and of the newly formed American Jewish Congress, 1919, he was a member of the delegation representing American Jewry at the 1919 Paris Peace Conference. He aided Jewish war relief during World War I, served on the federal Board of Inquiry on Conscientious Objectors, and at the same time headed the National Organization of Young Men's and Young Women's Hebrew Associations. During World War II he devoted a great deal of energy to helping German Jewish refugees enter the United States.

MACKAY, CLARENCE HUNGERFORD (*b. San Francisco, Calif., 1874; d. New York, N.Y., 1938*), capitalist, philanthropist, society leader. Son of John W. Mackay.

McKAY, CLAUDE (*b. Sunny Ville, Jamaica, British West Indies, 1889; d. Chicago, Ill., 1948*), poet, novelist. After publication of two volumes of poetry in Jamaican dialect (*Constab Ballads* and *Songs of Jamaica*, both 1912), he came to the United States to study agriculture. He spent a few months at Tuskegee Institute and two years at Kansas State University; he then settled for a time in Harlem, New York City. His poems appeared, sometimes under the pseudonym "Eli Edwards," in *Seven Arts*, *Pearson's Magazine*, and *The Liberator*. During a visit to England in 1919, he took a job writing for a Communist publication, *The Worker's Dreadnought*; he also published a volume of poems, *Spring in New Hampshire* (1920). Returning to the United States, he became assistant editor of *The Liberator*, and in 1922 published *Harlem Shadows*, a book of poems which ranks among his major works. That same year he was made coeditor of *The Liberator*, but resigned in June and traveled in Russia, where he was lionized; in 1923 he went to Germany and then to France, where he lived until 1929. Turning to fiction, he wrote *Home to Harlem* (1928) and *Banjo* (1929), which were successful but criticized by some black critics as exploitative of baser elements in black life. *Gingertown*, a collection of stories, appeared in 1932. In poor health, McKay returned to the United States in the early 1930's, but did not end his wandering until the mid-1940's. In 1944 he joined the Roman Catholic church. His final books were *Banana Bottom* (1933), a novel; *A Long Way from Home* (1937), an autobiography; and *Harlem: Negro Metropolis* (1940), a sociological study. An important figure in the so-called Harlem Renaissance of the 1920's, he is best represented by his poetry, of which a sampling may be found in *Selected Poems of Claude McKay* (1953).

McKAY, DAVID OMAN (*b. Huntsville, Utah, 1873; d. Salt Lake City, Utah, 1970*), missionary and ninth president of the Church of Jesus Christ of Latter-Day Saints (LDS). Studied at the University of Utah (graduated, 1897). Missionary for the LDS Church in Scotland (1897−99). Instructor and later principal instructor at Weber Stake Academy (now Weber State College), 1899−1906. In the LDS Church served as member of the Council of the Twelve Apostles (1906−34); member of the First Presidency (1934−50); senior apostle (1950−1951); and president (1951−70). Under his leadership, membership in the LDS Church rose from 1.1 million to 2.9 million; the number of stakes (dioceses) increased from 184 to 500; the missionary force expanded from 2,000 to 13,000; and more than 3,750 chapels, seminaries, and other buildings were constructed, including temples in Switzerland, England, New Zealand, and California.

McKAY, DONALD (*b. Shelburne Co., Nova Scotia, 1810; d. Hamilton, Mass., 1880*), shipbuilder, master builder of the clipper. Immigrated to New York, N.Y., 1827; became shipwright, working among others for Jacob Bell. Entered partnership at

Newburyport, Mass., 1841, to build packet ships; established shipyard at East Boston, Mass., 1844. In December 1850, he launched the *Stag Hound*, his first clipper, and in April 1851 the *Flying Cloud*, which made San Francisco in less than 90 days' passage from New York. Among other famous clippers from McKay's yard were *Sovereign of the Seas* (1852), *Great Republic* (1853), and *James Baines* and *Lightning* (1854−55). The last two vessels were also world record holders for speed under sail. McKay not only designed his ships but oversaw every detail of construction; he had an innate sense of beauty and proportion. An early advocate of steam screw naval ironclads of the largest class, he was not successful in urging their construction on the government. *Glory of the Seas* (1869) was his last great sailing ship.

McKAY, GORDON (*b. Pittsfield, Mass., 1821; d. Newport, R.I., 1903*), industrialist, inventor. Grandson of Samuel Dexter. Purchased Lyman Blake patent for sewing shoe soles to uppers, 1859, and improved it to stitch around toes and heels. Obtained Civil War shoe contracts; manufactured and leased his machines on royalty to other manufacturers. With royalties from over 60 factories, he soon became a millionaire. Retiring from business in 1895, he engaged in philanthropies which included an institute for educating black youths and a trust fund for Harvard.

MACKAY, JAMES (*b. Kildonan, Scotland, ca. 1759; d. 1822*), explorer, fur trader. Immigrated to Canada, *ca.* 1776. Explored Louisiana Territory for Spain, 1795−97, preparing maps later used by Lewis and Clark.

McKAY, (JAMES) DOUGLAS (*b. Portland, Ore., 1893; d. Salem, Ore., 1959*), politician and government official. Studied at Oregon State College. After a successful career in business and serving in the Oregon state government, McKay was elected governor of Oregon from 1948 to 1952; in 1952, President Eisenhower appointed him secretary of the interior. A fiscal conservative and friend of business, McKay earned much criticism for his anticonservationist stands on such projects as Hell's Canyon and Echo Park Dam. He retired in 1956 and was defeated by Wayne Morse in a race for the U.S. Senate.

McKAY, JAMES IVER (*b. Bladen Co., N.C., 1792; d. Goldsboro, N.C., 1853*), planter, North Carolina legislator. Influential debater as congressman, Democrat, 1831−49; famous, while Ways and Means Committee chairman, for insistence on rigid governmental economy.

MACKAY, JOHN WILLIAM (*b. Dublin, Ireland, 1831; d. London, England, 1902*), miner, capitalist. Came to New York, N.Y., as a boy; removed to California, 1851. Became expert in timbering Nevada mines. Joined with James G. Fair and others, 1868, in scheme to make low-grade ore pay by reworking Comstock Lode with up-to-date equipment. Reinvesting profits in nearby mines, the group struck the "Big Bonanza," 1873. Mackay became overnight the most spectacular success in western mining. He acquired real estate, became a banker and railroad director. Forming the Commercial Cable Co., 1883, and the Postal Telegraph Co., 1886, he made his greatest constructive contribution by breaking the Jay Gould−Western Union communications monopoly.

MacKAYE, JAMES MORRISON STEELE (*b. Buffalo, N.Y., 1842; d. Timpas, Colo., 1894*), playwright, actor, inventor. Wrote *Hazel Kirke* (produced 1880); introduced stage and lighting innovations; preached drama's social values. Established first U.S. dramatic school at old Lyceum Theater, New York City.

MacKAYE, PERCY WALLACE (*b. New York, N.Y., 1875; d. Cornish, N.H., 1956*), poet, playwright, essayist. Studied at Harvard University. Author of twenty-five plays, and over a hundred books of poetry, essays, and biography, MacKaye championed a democratic, poetic drama for America. Plays include *The Scarecrow* (1911), *Yankee Fantasies* (1912), and a series of masques including *Wakefield*, the first play commissioned by the federal government (1932). From 1920, MacKaye taught literature at Miami University in Oxford, Ohio.

MACKAYE, STEELE. *See* MACKAYE, JAMES MORRISON STEELE.

MCKEAN, JAMES WILLIAM (*b. Scotch Grove, Iowa, 1860; d. Long Beach, Calif., 1949*), Presbyterian medical missionary. Graduated Lenox College, Iowa; M.D., Bellevue Hospital Medical School, New York City, 1882. Practiced in Omaha, Nebr., before appointment to the Siam Mission of the Presbyterian church, 1889. Assigned to the remote north of present Thailand, he established McCormick Hospital in Chiengmai, radically reduced the prevalence of smallpox and malaria in the region, and in 1908 began a model leprosarium which achieved worldwide fame. He retired in 1931.

MCKEAN, JOSEPH BORDEN (*b. New Castle, Del., 1764; d. Philadelphia, Pa., 1826*), Pennsylvania jurist. Son of Thomas McKean. Attorney general of Pennsylvania, 1800–08; Philadelphia district judge, 1817–26, presiding for much of this time. Promoted coalition of Federalists and moderate Democratic-Republicans, 1805.

MCKEAN, SAMUEL (*b. Huntingdon Co., Pa., 1787; d. West Burlington, Pa., 1841*), merchant, Pennsylvania legislator. Congressman, Democrat, 1823–29; U.S. senator, 1833–39. High-tariff advocate; opposed the Bank of the United States, but voted to restore deposits; enemy of antislavery agitation.

MCKEAN, THOMAS (*b. Chester Co., Pa., 1734; d. Philadelphia, Pa., 1817*), lawyer, statesman, signer of the Declaration of Independence. Entered political life shortly after admission to the bar, 1754; became clerk of the Delaware Assembly, 1757; served as member of Assembly, 1762–79. Noted for radical opposition to the Stamp Act, he led movement in Delaware for a Continental Congress and represented the state in Congress almost continuously throughout the Revolution. An advocate of independence by early 1776, he sent for Caesar Rodney to break a tie vote so that Delaware's delegation would approve Lee's motion of July 1. He supported the Articles of Confederation in Congress and presided briefly over that body, 1781.

While active in Delaware politics McKean had established a home in Philadelphia, and there his interests turned. Increasingly conservative, he opposed Pennsylvania's radical constitution of 1776, though he served as chief justice under it, 1777–99 (for a time holding Delaware offices simultaneously). Strongly favoring the U.S. Constitution, and noted for decisions stressing judicial integrity, Francophile sentiments led him into the Jeffersonian ranks and he was nominated for governor of Pennsylvania, 1799. Elected after a bitter fight, he removed enemies from office and fastened the spoils system upon Pennsylvania. Despite Democratic-Republican divisions occasioned by editor William Duane's domination of the party and McKean's defense of executive and judicial prerogatives, he was reelected, 1802. When radicals demanded a new state constitution, moderates rallied behind him and he was again elected, 1805. McKean then turned on his Democratic-Republican foes, dismissing them from office and appointing Federalist supporters; this produced charges of nepotism (his son had been attorney general since 1800) and abuse of power. Libel suits against his accusers led to counterdemands for impeachment, but these charges were skillfully postponed by the legislature. He retired from office, 1808. Stormy petrel of Pennsylvania politics, McKean furthered education and internal improvements, but his chief accomplishment was the prevention of excesses of radicalism in his state.

MCKEAN, WILLIAM WISTER (*b. Philadelphia, Pa., 1800; d. near Binghamton, N.Y., 1865*), naval officer. Son of Joseph B. McKean; cousin of Franklin Buchanan. Headed Naval Asylum for instructing midshipmen, Philadelphia, 1843–44; recommended founding of naval school at Annapolis.

MCKECHNIE, WILLIAM BOYD (*b. Wilkinsburg, Pa., 1886; d. Bradenton, Fla., 1965*), baseball manager. Managed the Pittsburgh Pirates (1922–26), St. Louis Cardinals (1928–29); Boston Braves (1930–37), and Cincinnati Reds (1938–46). Won National League pennants with Pittsburgh, St. Louis, and Cincinnati, and achieved World Series victories with the Pirates and Reds. Inducted into the Baseball Hall of Fame in 1962.

MCKEE, JOHN (*b. Rockbridge Co., Va., 1771; d. near Boligee, Ala., 1832*), Indian agent, Alabama congressman. Cousin of Sam Houston. Cherokee and Choctaw agent; pacified tribes during Creek War. Furthered trans-Mississippi removal of Five Civilized Tribes *post* 1815.

MCKEEN, JOSEPH (*b. Londonderry, N.H., 1757; d. Brunswick, Mass. [Maine], 1807*), Congregational clergyman. Graduated Dartmouth, 1774; eminent pastor, Beverly, Mass., 1785–1802. First president, Bowdoin College, 1802–07.

MCKELLAR, KENNETH DOUGLAS (*b. near Richmond, Ala., 1869; d. Memphis, Tenn., 1957*), politician, lawyer. Studied at the University of Alabama (LL.B., 1892). McKellar practiced law in Memphis until his election as a Democrat to the U.S. Congress (1911–17). He served in the Senate from 1917 until his defeat in 1952. As chairman of the Post Office and Post Roads Committee and, from 1937, of the House Appropriations Committee, he achieved considerable power. Remembered for his opposition to David E. Lilienthal as chairman of the Tennessee Valley Authority and later of the Atomic Energy Commission, McKellar accused Lilienthal of being a Communist. McKellar was an ardent backer of the TVA and successful representative of Tennessee's interests.

MACKELLAR, PATRICK (*b. Scotland, 1717; d. Minorca, 1778*), British military engineer. Accompanied Braddock's expedition, 1755; captured at Oswego, 1756. Exchanged, he directed siege operations at Louisbourg and was Wolfe's chief engineer at Quebec, 1759.

MACKELLAR, THOMAS (*b. New York, N.Y., 1812; d. 1899*), printer, type-founder, poet. As partner in MacKellar, Smiths and Jordan, Philadelphia, Pa., *post* 1860, he made that firm the leading American manufactory of type. He edited and printed the *Typographic Advertiser*, 1855–84, and his textbook, *The American Printer* (1866), went through many editions.

MCKELWAY, ST. CLAIR (*b. Columbia, Mo., 1845; d. 1915*), newspaperman. Edited *Albany Argus*, 1878–84; *Brooklyn* (N.Y.) *Daily Eagle*, 1884–1915. He closely identified the latter paper with Brooklyn, yet gave it national standing.

MCKENDREE, WILLIAM (*b. King William Co., Va., 1757; d. Sumner Co., Tenn., 1835*), first American-born Methodist bishop. Served as soldier in the Revolution. Converted to Methodism *ca.* 1776, he was appointed, 1788, a helper circuit preacher; ordained deacon, 1790, and elder, 1791. Under James O'Kelly's influence he joined a movement to limit bishop's powers, but close association with Bishop Francis Asbury changed his views. He served on various circuits for many years and became a leader in the trans-Allegheny revival movement. Elected bishop,

1808, he introduced practice of episcopal addresses at conferences and the consulting of elders in appointments.

McKenna, Charles Hyacinth (*b. Fallalea, Ireland, 1835; d. Jacksonville, Fla., 1917*), Roman Catholic clergyman, Dominican. Came to America, 1851. A powerful missionary preacher and ascetical writer, he was associated with the growth of the Holy Name Society and the Rosary Confraternity.

McKenna, Joseph (*b. Philadelphia, Pa., 1843; d. Washington, D.C., 1926*), California legislator, congressman, jurist. U.S. attorney general, 1897. Justice, U.S. Supreme Court, 1898–1925. Branded as prorailroad, his appointment was widely criticized, but his record on the bench won approval for sound, if slow, judgment and social vision.

McKennan, Thomas McKean Thompson (*b. Dragon Neck, Del., 1794; d. Reading, Pa., 1852*), lawyer. Congressman, Whig, from Pennsylvania, 1831–39 and 1842–43. U.S. secretary of interior, 1850. President, Hempfield Railroad (eventually absorbed by Baltimore and Ohio).

McKenney, Thomas Loraine (*b. Hopewell, Md., 1785; d. New York, N.Y., 1859*), businessman, author. Much-criticized superintendent of Indian trade, 1816–22; headed U.S. Bureau of Indian Affairs, 1824–30; was joint commissioner with Lewis Cass at Treaty of Butte des Morts, 1827. Author of text to *History of the Indian Tribes of North America* (with James Hall, 1836–44), *Memoirs* (1846), and other works.

McKenzie, Alexander (*b. New Bedford, Mass., 1830; d. 1914*), Congregational clergyman. Pastor; First Church, Cambridge, Mass., 1867–1914. Affirmative preaching and civic-mindedness gave him influence comparable to that of colonial ministers.

Mackenzie, Alexander Slidell (*b. New York, N.Y., 1803; d. 1848*), naval officer, author of travel books and naval biographies. Brother of John Slidell. As commander of brig *Somers*, he executed son of Secretary of War John Canfield Spencer for mutiny, December 1842.

Mackenzie, Donald (*b. Scotland, 1783; d. Mayville, N.Y., 1851*), fur trader. Partner with John Jacob Astor in Pacific Fur Co., 1810. With Wilson P. Hunt, led overland adventurers to Fort Astoria, 1812; sold post to North West Co., 1814. Later served as governor of Red River Colony for Hudson's Bay Co.

Mackenzie, George Henry (*b. North Kessock, Scotland, 1837; d. New York, N.Y., 1891*), chessplayer, British and Union army officer. American, 1871–80, and world, 1887, chess champion.

Mackenzie, James Cameron (*b. Aberdeen, Scotland, 1852; d. New York, N.Y., 1931*), Presbyterian clergyman, educator. Graduated Lafayette, 1878. Organizer and headmaster, Lawrenceville School, 1882–99. Established "Upper House" system, giving older boys greater freedom in preparation for college.

Mackenzie, John Noland (*b. Baltimore, Md., 1853; d. Baltimore, 1925*), physician, pioneer laryngologist. M.D., University of Virginia, 1876; studied also at Metropolitan Throat Hospital, New York; Munich; and Vienna. Chief of clinic at London Throat Hospital, he helped Sir Morell Mackenzie prepare *Manual of the Diseases of the Throat and Nose* (1880–84). Founded Baltimore Eye, Ear and Throat Charity Hospital; was surgeon at University of Maryland Hospital, 1887–97, and at Johns Hopkins Hospital, 1889–1912, and professor at their associated medical schools. Mackenzie edited various medical journals and wrote numerous papers on laryngorhinology (particularly on

vasomotor neuroses of the nose, on sinuses, and on laryngeal cancer), opposing excessive surgery for nose and throat conditions.

Mackenzie, Kenneth (*b. Ross and Cromarty, Scotland, 1797; d. St. Louis, Mo., 1861*), fur trader, merchant. Joined North West Co. (Canada), 1816; organized Columbia Fur Co., St. Louis, Mo., 1822. Associated with American Fur Co. *post* 1827, he built Fort Union and administered the Upper Missouri trade until 1834. Thereafter, he engaged in various business concerns in St. Louis.

Mackenzie, Murdo (*b. Ross and Cromarty, Scotland, 1850; d. Denver, Colo., 1939*), cattleman. Came to America, 1885. Manager, Matador Land and Cattle Co., 1891–1911 and 1922–37; managed Brazil Land, Cattle and Packing Co. at São Paulo, 1912–18.

Mackenzie, Ranald Slidell (*b. New York, N.Y., 1840; d. Staten Island, N.Y., 1889*), soldier. Son of Alexander S. Mackenzie. Graduated West Point, 1862. Assigned to engineer corps, he was brevetted seven times for gallantry in eastern Civil War campaigns, attaining divisional command as a cavalry officer; Grant considered him the "most promising young officer in the army." After the Civil War, as colonel of the 4th Cavalry, Mackenzie campaigned in western Texas and opened the Staked Plains area to white settlement. He pacified hostiles in Indian Territory and vanquished Sioux bands at Chadron Creek and also Dull Knife's Cheyenne in the Big Horn Mountains after Custer's death, 1876. He fought with marked success against the Ute, 1879–81, and in New Mexico and Arizona. He retired for disability as brigadier general, 1884. Perhaps the ablest Indian fighter, Mackenzie avoided publicity but was recognized as a master tactician by army colleagues.

Mackenzie, Robert Shelton (*b. Co. Limerick, Ireland, 1809; d. Philadelphia, Pa., 1881*), journalist. Came to America, 1852. A pioneer European correspondent, he served as literary and foreign editor for the Philadelphia *Press*, 1857–78; he was author of a number of popular biographies and an able editor of literary causeries.

McKenzie, Robert Tait (*b. Almonte, Canada, 1867; d. Philadelphia, Pa., 1938*), physician, sculptor. Graduated McGill, 1889; M.D., 1892. Director of physical education, 1904–31, and professor of physical therapy, University of Pennsylvania.

Mackenzie, William (*b. Philadelphia, Pa., 1758; d. Philadelphia, 1828*), merchant, book collector. Bequeathed many rare examples of early printing to Philadelphia institutions.

Mackey, Albert Gallatin (*b. Charleston, S.C., 1807; d. Old Point Comfort, Va., 1881*), physician. Author of Masonic histories, manuals, and the *Encyclopedia of Freemasonry* (1874).

McKim, Charles Follen (*b. Isabella Furnace, Pa., 1847; d. St. James, N.Y., 1909*), architect. Son of James M. McKim. Educated in Philadelphia public schools, at Lawrence Scientific School (Harvard), and in Paris at the École des Beaux Arts, 1867–70. On his return, he worked in Henry H. Richardson's office, New York City. Forming a partnership with William Rutherford Mead, 1878, he was joined by Stanford White, 1879. Convinced that Wren's modified classical style of architecture (as brought over by English colonists and exhibited by Charles Bulfinch in his work) was best suited for American homes and public buildings, McKim and his firm consistently maintained this doctrine, although a tendency toward the Italian Renaissance was also shown in some work. They broke with the Richardson tradition because they felt that his style was brilliant but undisciplined. McKim's own method was first to study a proposed structure's purpose, then to consider its exterior. Members of the firm cooperated on design and details after determination of a basic plan. Their reputation established by a group of Italian Renaissance buildings for Henry Villard on Madison Ave., New York, N.Y., the firm was commissioned to design the Boston Public Library, 1887. This structure, with its classical exterior and its perfect siting, was McKim's first masterpiece; he envisaged its murals and sculpture as essential parts of the building rather than mere adornment and enjoyed the collaboration on details of Augustus Saint-Gaudens and the leading artists of the time. The Columbian Exposition at Chicago, 1893, which helped set American architectural patterns for years and ushered in the city-planning movement, owed much of its effectiveness to McKim's designs. In 1901 he participated in plans for developing Washington, D.C., assuming responsibility for the area between the Capitol and the Potomac. His White House restoration, 1902–03, showed respect for the spirit and good work of capable predecessors. Columbia University's Morningside Heights campus, with subordinate brick buildings surrounding a monumental stone library, demonstrated McKim's ingenious use of terrain. Many critics, however, consider New York's University Club his finest achievement. He designed New York's Morgan Library and Pennsylvania Railway Station (then the world's largest building erected at one time), both in 1903; in each case he persuaded strong-willed clients to accept his own concept of the finished structure. The office of McKim, Mead and White was widely recognized as America's outstanding training school for young architects. Ever modest, aware of his own limited training, McKim's fondest dream was to found an American Academy in Rome where artists of promise might study amid masterpieces of all time; supported by him and by other private contributions, the idea became an eventual reality. The deaths of White, 1906, and Saint-Gaudens, 1907, broke his closest ties; overwork led him to retire, 1908, acclaimed the preeminent American architect of his day.

McKim, Isaac (*b. Philadelphia, Pa., 1775; d. Washington, D.C., 1838*), Baltimore merchant, Maryland legislator and congressman. Helped organize Baltimore & Ohio Railroad; built the *Ann McKim*, 1832, prototype of later Yankee clipper ships.

McKim, James Miller (*b. Carlisle, Pa., 1810; d. Orange, N.J., 1874*), Presbyterian clergyman, abolitionist leader. Helped form American Anti-Slavery Society, 1833; was active thereafter in work for the abolition cause and for freedmen. Father of Charles F. McKim.

McKinley, Albert Edward (*b. Philadelphia, Pa., 1870; d. Germantown, Pa., 1936*), historian. Professor of history, University of Pennsylvania, 1915–36; editor and a founder, 1909, of the magazine which became *Social Studies.*

McKinley, Carlyle (*b. Newman, Ga., 1847; d. 1904*), journalist, essayist, poet. Correspondent, associate editor, Charleston, S.C., *News and Courier*, from 1875. An optimistic southern romantic.

McKinley, John (*b. Culpeper Co., Va., 1780; d. Louisville, Ky., 1852*), lawyer, Alabama legislator. U.S. senator, Democrat, from Alabama, 1826–31; congressman, 1833–35. Hardworking and conscientious justice of the U.S. Supreme Court, 1837–52.

McKinley, William (*b. Niles, Ohio, 1843; d. Buffalo, N.Y., 1901*), president of the United States. Of Scotch-Irish stock, McKinley was educated at Allegheny College; he taught briefly in a rural school before enlisting in the 23rd Ohio Volunteer Infantry, with which he served throughout the Civil War. Mustered out as major by brevet, he studied law in Ohio and at Albany (N.Y.)

Law School, commencing practice in Canton, Ohio, immediately following admission to the bar, 1867.

McKinley's political career began with his election as Stark Co. prosecuting attorney, 1869. In 1871 he married Ida Saxton, to whom he remained devoted, despite her later chronic invalidism. An active supporter of his old regimental commander, Rutherford B. Hayes, in Ohio politics, McKinley was a successful Republican candidate for Congress, 1876, and served (though unseated in 1882 by a Democratic House) for seven terms, 1877–91. A leading supporter of the protective tariff (to him no tool of privilege but a sound national policy), he grew in public stature and was given a place on the Ways and Means Committee, 1880. As chairman of the Committee on Resolutions at the Republican National Convention, 1888, he was steadfast in support of John Sherman for the presidency, protesting votes cast for himself. Although the Sherman movement failed, McKinley gained the friendship of Marcus A. Hanna, a Cleveland businessman with funds to spend for furthering the policy of protection. McKinley, in 1889–90 the chairman of the Ways and Means Committee, was largely responsible for the tariff act bearing his name. Its higher rates proved unpopular and he lost his congressional seat in the 1890 Democratic landslide. With Hanna's aid, however, he was elected governor of Ohio, 1891, and reelected, 1893; the governorship served as his sounding board and point of vantage in attaining the Republican presidential nomination.

Uninjured politically after Hanna and others raised money, 1893, to redeem notes he had endorsed for a friend, McKinley held the commanding position in his party after the death of James G. Blaine. Unfortunately for him, protection was being overshadowed as an issue by free silver, on which his record was ambiguous. Despite this, Hanna obtained McKinley's nomination in 1896 on a prearranged gold platform, and during the campaign against the Democrat William J. Bryan, the Republican orators played on eastern fear of a devalued dollar. McKinley's placid, uncommitted "front-porch campaign" avoided mistakes. Improved agricultural conditions helped secure his election to the presidency with 271 electoral votes against 176 for Bryan. He received more than 7 million popular votes out of about 14 million cast.

Orthodox and at first undistinguished, McKinley's conciliatory "businessman" administration (never appreciably ahead of public opinion) enjoyed good relations with Congress. A special session immediately enacted the Dingley Tariff, 1897, but establishment of the gold standard had to be deferred as the Cuban question demanded increasing attention. Secretary of State John Sherman proved inadequate in handling problems arising from the insurrection there. McKinley soon had either to defy popular clamor and the party jingoists or lead America into a war he personally opposed. He referred the matter to a Congress enthusiastic for war with Spain; the ensuing conflict found him acting as "his own chief of staff" because of an incompetent secretary of war. Luckily Spain was weak, and presidential embarrassments over military mobilization, supply, and management soon gave way to problems of the peace. Reluctant at first to annex any territory, he came to believe that the retention of the Philippines was demanded by the people and by the very dictates of conscience. Encouraged by an improvement in the economy, a strengthened Republican congressional majority adopted the gold standard, 1900, and legislated for the government of the newly acquired insular possessions. The armed forces were reorganized. Negotiations commenced for unilateral construction of an isthmian canal. The Platt Amendment to the Army Act of 1901 (providing for intervention in Cuba) heralded the legal beginnings of a new imperialism. The new Secretary of State John Hay's "Open Door" policy of equal trading privileges in China and intervention during the Boxer Rebellion there demonstrated that the nation was now irrevocably involved in the worldwide rivalry among the great powers.

Imperialism proved a tame issue in 1900. McKinley was easily reelected and the administration was soon strengthened by Supreme Court decisions upholding his territorial policies. Booming business might have had some misgivings after McKinley's Buffalo speech of Sept. 5, 1901, which appeared to suggest lowered tariffs; next day, however, the president was shot by an anarchist and on his death eight days later was succeeded by Vice President Theodore Roosevelt. Kindly and well meaning, McKinley inspired an unusual affection among his associates which persisted long after his death, but he was essentially a "party" man and a follower.

McKINLEY, WILLIAM BROWN (*b. Petersburg, Ill., 1856; d. Martinsville, Ind., 1926*), utility operator, philanthropist, politician. Developed the Illinois Traction System, largest electric interurban system in the world, *ca.* 1900–10. Elected to Congress as a Republican from Illinois, 1904, he served until 1921 with the exception of the years 1913–15, always regular in his support of Republican policies. As U.S. senator, 1921–26, he became a warm advocate of world peace. McKinley was widely esteemed for generosity toward charitable causes and notably as a benefactor of the University of Illinois.

McKINLY, JOHN (*b. north Ireland, 1721; d. Wilmington, Del., 1796*), physician, Revolutionary legislator. Came to Delaware *ante* 1747. Chosen first president (governor) of Delaware, February 1777, he was captured by the British a few months later, imprisoned, and paroled, 1778. Resuming the practice of medicine, he took no further part in politics.

McKINSTRY, ALEXANDER (*b. Augusta, Ga., 1822; d. Mobile, Ala., 1879*), lawyer, Confederate soldier, Alabama legislator and lieutenant governor. Identified himself with the Radical party *post* 1865.

McKINSTRY, ELISHA WILLIAMS (*b. Detroit, Mich., 1825; d. San Jose, Calif., 1901*) jurist. Removed to California, 1849; held district and county judgeships. Justice of the California Supreme Court, 1873–88. Delivered opinion of the court in many important cases, including *Ex Parte Wall.*

McKNIGHT, ROBERT (*b. Augusta Co., Va., ca. 1789; d. 1846*), Santa Fe trader, copper miner. Joined Santa Fe trading expedition from St. Louis, Mo., without passports, 1812; was seized at Santa Fe and imprisoned in Mexico for nine years. Denied aid or redress by the United States, he settled in Mexico after a brief visit home in 1822 and an expedition with Thomas James.

MACKUBIN, FLORENCE (*b. Florence, Italy, 1861; d. Baltimore, Md., 1918*), portrait and miniature painter.

McLAGLEN, VICTOR (*b. Tunbridge Wells, England, 1886; d. Newport Beach, Calif., 1959*), actor. Immigrated to the U.S. in 1924. The first of McLaglen's 115 film roles was in *Call of The Road* in 1920. Other films include *Beau Geste* (1926), *What Price Glory* (1926), *Gunga Din, The Informer* (1935), for which he received the Academy Award, *The Quiet Man* (1952), and *She Wore a Yellow Ribbon* (1949). A large man, McLaglen was known for his portrayals of boxers and tough men.

McLANE, ALLAN (*b. Philadelphia, Pa., 1746; d. Wilmington, Del., 1829*), Revolutionary soldier. Celebrated as a scout and as commander of small raiding parties. U.S. marshal of Delaware, 1789–97; U.S. customs collector at Wilmington, 1797–1829.

McLANE, LOUIS (*b. Smyrna, Del., 1786; d. Baltimore, Md., 1857*), lawyer, statesman, diplomat. Son of Allan McLane.

Attended Newark (Del.) College; studied law under James A. Bayard. As congressman, Democratic-Republican, from Delaware, 1817–27, he as a rule upheld the party program, yet championed the Bank of the United States. As U.S. senator, 1827–29, he supported Andrew Jackson. Appointed U.S. minister to Great Britain, 1829, he negotiated a West Indian trade agreement and returned to become U.S. secretary of the treasury, 1831. Differing with Jackson over the recharter of the bank, McLane was shifted to secretary of state, 1833. He advocated stern measures in French spoliation claims, ably reorganized departmental procedures, but failed to adjust northeast boundary question with Great Britain. Resigning in 1834, he held several canal and railroad presidencies. As U.S. minister to Great Britain, 1845–46, he negotiated the Oregon boundary compromise. An efficient executive, he was frequently precipitate and uncooperative.

McLANE, ROBERT MILLIGAN (*b. Wilmington, Del., 1815; d. Paris, France, 1898*), lawyer, soldier, politician, diplomat. Son of Louis McLane. Congressman, Democrat, from Maryland, 1847–51. U.S. commissioner to China and Japan, 1853–54. As U.S. minister to Mexico, 1859–60, he recognized the Juarez government there, but his treaty was not ratified. Subsequent to the Civil War, he served again in Congress, 1879–83, and was advocate of lower tariffs; he was also governor of Maryland, 1884–85, and U.S. minister to France, 1885–89.

McLAREN, JOHN (*b. near Stirling, Scotland, 1846; d. San Francisco, Calif., 1943*), horticulturist, landscape architect. Came to the United States, *ca.* 1869; Superintendent of parks of San Francisco, 1887–1943, he developed Golden Gate Park and about 45 smaller parks about the city. He won international recognition for his landscaping of the Panama-Pacific Exposition, 1915. His book *Gardening in California: Landscape and Flower* is the best treatise in its field.

McLAREN, WILLIAM EDWARD (*b. Geneva, N.Y., 1831; d. 1905*), Episcopal clergyman. A Presbyterian missionary and pastor, 1860–72, he was ordained to the Episcopal priesthood, October 1872. Consecrated bishop of Illinois (later Chicago), 1875, he was a leader of the High Church party.

McLAUGHLIN, ANDREW CUNNINGHAM (*b. Beardstown, Ill., 1861; d. Chicago, Ill., 1947*), historian. Raised in Muskegon, Mich. In 1878 he entered the University of Michigan at Ann Arbor. Graduating in 1882, he returned to Muskegon as principal of the local high school; the following year he went back to Ann Arbor to take a law degree. In 1887 he began teaching in the history department at Ann Arbor. Although from the beginning he taught constitutional history, his early books explored the history of the Old Northwest. In 1901 he became managing editor of the *American Historical Review*, a post that he held for five years, and in 1903 he moved to Washington to head up the new Bureau of Historical Research of the Carnegie Institution. He then wrote *The Confederation and the Constitution* (1905), which won immediate academic acclaim. In 1929 he retired formally from his professorship. His books include *Courts, Constitution, and Parties* (1912) and *America and Britain* (1919). *Foundations of American Constitutionalism* (1932), the Anson Phelps lectures at New York University, remains the most original and provocative of his books. Three years later came his magisterial *Constitutional History of the United States*, which was awarded a Pulitzer Prize. In 1914 he associated himself with Albert Bushnell Hart in editing *The Cyclopedia of American Government* (1914).

McLAUGHLIN, HUGH (*b. Brooklyn, N.Y., ca. 1826; d. 1904*), political boss. Maintained at least partial, sometimes complete, control of Brooklyn, N.Y., Democratic machine, 1862–1903.

McLaughlin, James (*b. Avonmere, Ontario, Canada, 1842; d. Washington, D.C., 1923*), Indian agent. Removed to Minnesota, 1863; joined U.S. Indian service, 1871. As agent at Devils Lake and Standing Rock, he won the confidence of the Sioux and their acceptance of land cessions and education. *Post* 1895, he served as Indian reservation inspector and negotiator for the Interior Department. His book *My Friend the Indian* (1910) is an important study.

McLaurin, Anselm Joseph (*b. Brandon, Miss., 1848; d. 1909*), lawyer, legislator. U.S. senator, Democrat, from Mississippi, 1894–95 and 1901–09. Governor of Mississippi, 1896–1900.

Maclaurin, Richard Cockburn (*b. Lindean, Scotland, 1870; d. 1920*), physicist. After a distinguished career at Cambridge University (England) and in New Zealand, he served briefly at Columbia University as professor of mathematical physics, 1908–09. Chosen president, Massachusetts Institute of Technology in 1909, he directed that institution through a vast program of expansion until his death. He also played a leading part in organizing the Students Army Training Corps, 1917–18.

McLaws, Lafayette (*b. Augusta, Ga., 1821; d. 1897*), soldier. Graduated West Point, 1842. Served in Mexican War and on the western frontier. Entering the Confederate service, 1861, he became major general, May 1862, commanded a division in all the larger operations of Lee's army, 1862–63, and was outstanding at Antietam and Fredericksburg. Relieved of command and court-martialed for failure in the Confederate attempt to relieve Knoxville, Tenn., he was exonerated; commanding the defense of Savannah, Ga., he failed in his efforts to oppose General W. T. Sherman's operations, 1864.

Maclay, Edgar Stanton (*b. Foochow, China, 1863; d. Washington, D.C., 1919*), journalist. Son of Robert S. Maclay. Author of works on naval history.

Maclay, Robert Samuel (*b. Concord, Pa., 1824; d. San Fernando, Calif., 1907*), Methodist clergyman. Missionary in China, Korea, and Japan, 1847–88, founded colleges in Foochow and Tokyo.

Maclay, Samuel (*b. Franklin Co., Pa., 1741; d. Buffalo Valley, Pa., 1811*), surveyor, landowner, Revolutionary patriot, Pennsylvania legislator. Brother of William Maclay. As congressman, Democratic-Republican, 1795–97, Maclay favored France and opposed the Jay Treaty; in U.S. Senate, 1803–09, he was a consistent supporter of the administration.

Maclay, William (*b. Chester Co., Pa., 1734; d. Harrisburg, Pa., 1804*), lawyer, soldier, legislator. Brother of Samuel Maclay. Served in French and Indian War on Pennsylvania frontier. Laid out town of Sunbury, Pa., 1772; settled in Harrisburg, Pa., 1786. After holding numerous state offices, he was active in the first U.S. Congress, 1789–91, as senator from Pennsylvania. Maclay's private journal (not published until 1880) is of the greatest importance, since it is the only continuous report of Senate deliberations of that period. His diary reveals Maclay to have been a stout antagonist of Alexander Hamilton's program and a strong defender of the agricultural interest. His comments on all the leaders of that time, including Washington, are invaluable sidelights on the contest over interpretation of the new Constitution, the funding of the debt, the tariff, enlivened with a caustic wit.

Maclay, William Brown (*b. New York, N.Y., 1812; d. 1882*), lawyer, editor. As a member of the New York Assembly, 1839–41, he obtained passage of an act which gave New York City full benefit of the state law providing for publicly supported, publicly controlled schools. A consistent Jacksonian Democrat, he served five terms in Congress between 1843 and 1859, advocating reduced postal rates, the distribution of public lands in the form of gratuitous homesteads, and the annexation of Texas. He was a vigorous opponent of the Know-Nothings.

McLean, Angus Wilton (*b. Robeson Co., N.C., 1870; d. Washington, D.C., 1835*), lawyer, businessman. As Democratic governor of North Carolina, 1925–29, he brought all state departments and agencies under centralized executive fiscal control; he also took effective steps against lynching.

McLean, Archibald (*b. near Summerside, Prince Edward Island, Canada, 1849; d. Battle Creek, Mich., 1920*), clergyman and missionary executive of the Disciples of Christ.

McLean, Edward Beale (*b. Washington, D.C., 1886; d. Towson, Md., 1941*), newspaper publisher. Undistinguished publisher of the *Cincinnati Enquirer* and *Washington Post*, which he inherited from his father; friend and supporter of Warren G. Harding.

MacLean, George Edwin (*b. Rockville, Conn., 1850; d. Washington, D.C., 1938*), Congregational clergyman, educator. Professor of English, University of Minnesota, 1833–95; chancellor, University of Nebraska, 1895–99; president, State University of Iowa, 1899–1911.

Maclean, John (*b. Glasgow, Scotland, 1771; d. Princeton, N.J., 1814*), chemist. Studied at Glasgow, Edinburgh, London, and Paris. Immigrated to America, 1795. At suggestion of Benjamin Rush, settled in Princeton, N.J., where he served the then College of New Jersey as professor of chemistry and natural history, 1795–1812. He was the first professor of chemistry in any American college other than a medical institution. Benjamin Silliman regarded him as his earliest master in chemistry.

McLean, John (*b. Morris Co., N.J., 1785; d. 1861*), politician, jurist. Raised in Kentucky and Ohio. McLean was largely self-educated; admitted to Ohio bar, 1807, he began practice in Lebanon. As congressman, Democrat, from Ohio, 1813–16, he vigorously supported the war against England. After service as judge, Ohio Supreme Court, 1816–22, and a brief period as commissioner of the land office, McLean became U.S. postmaster general, 1823, and won a national reputation as an able administrator. Appointed a justice of the U.S. Supreme Court, 1829, he served until his death. Fearless, able, and conscientious, he was not a great judge, but his circuit decisions were seldom reversed. In the famous Dred Scott case, he dissented from the majority of the Court and in an opinion of his own held that slavery had its origins merely in force and was contrary to right. During his long term on the bench, he was frequently mentioned as a presidential possibility.

Maclean, John (*b. Princeton, N.J., 1800; d. Princeton, 1886*), Presbyterian clergyman, educator. Son of John Maclean (1771–1814); nephew of William Bainbridge. Graduated College of New Jersey (Princeton), 1816. Taught at Princeton *post* 1818, handling at various times mathematics, natural philosophy, and languages; founded Alumni Association of Nassau Hall, 1826. Appointed vice president of the college, 1829, Maclean acted in effect as dean and was an effective force in improving the standards of the school. Elected president, 1853, he remained in office until 1868. The profits of his book *History of the College of New Jersey* (1877) were left by him to found scholarships for poor students.

McLean, Walter (*b. Elizabeth, N.J., 1855; d. Annapolis, Md., 1930*), naval officer. Graduated Annapolis, 1876. Admiral Dewey's supply and communications officer at Manila, 1898;

commanded Norfolk navy yard and Hampton Roads base, World War I.

McLean, William Lippard (*b. Mount Pleasant, Pa., 1852; d. Germantown, Pa., 1931*), newspaper publisher, philanthropist. Published the Philadelphia *Evening Bulletin* from 1895; made it noted for honesty, independence. Helped reorganize Associated Press, 1900.

McLellan, Isaac (*b. Portland, Maine, 1806; d. 1899*), sportsman. Author of *Poems of the Rod and Gun* (1886) and *Haunts of Wild Game* (1896).

McLeod, Alexander (*b. Mull, Inner Hebrides, Scotland, 1774; d. 1833*), Reformed Presbyterian clergyman. Came to America, 1792. Graduated Union College, 1798. Pastor in New York City, *post* 1800. An eloquent preacher and opponent of slavery.

McLeod, Hugh (*b. New York, N.Y., 1814; d. Dumfries, Va., 1862*), soldier. Raised in Georgia; graduated West Point, 1835. Resigning from the army, he removed to Texas, 1836, and served in the army of that republic. Commissioned brigadier general, 1841, he headed the ill-fated expedition sent to Santa Fe in that year to open a trade route. A minor officeholder thereafter and a member of the legislature, he was chiefly known for his violent tirades against Sam Houston. He died while in Confederate service as colonel of the 1st Texas Infantry.

McLeod, Martin (*b. near Montreal, Canada, 1813; d. near Fort Snelling, Minn., 1860*), fur trader, Minnesota pioneer and legislator.

McLevy, Jasper (*b. Bridgeport, Conn., 1878; d. Bridgeport, 1962*), Socialist politician. Member of the American Federation of Labor and the Socialist party from 1900; led the conservative wing of the party as first head of the Social Democratic Federation. Mayor of Bridgeport, 1933–57; elected on a Socialist platform that was not radical but stressed the elimination of waste, inefficiency, and corruption in government; the merit system and civil service; municipal ownership of public utilities; open public meetings of governing boards and commissions; and home rule for the city. Credited with running a tight-fisted administration and restoring the city's credit rating during the Great Depression.

McLoughlin, John (*b. Rivière du Loup, Quebec, Canada, 1784; d. 1857*), fur trader, physician. As chief factor of the Hudson's Bay Co., he took charge of the Columbia District, where he remained in control, 1825–46. *Post* 1825, Fort Vancouver (within present city of Vancouver, Wash.) was the capital of his far-flung domain. Obliged to monopolize and exploit the fur trade in his area as completely as possible, McLoughlin was generally successful in keeping peace among the numerous Indian tribes and in preventing American competition from affecting the interests of his company. Merciless as a business competitor, he gave all his rivals personally the most generous treatment; by extending credit to the early American settlers for supplies and provisions, he kept many of them from perishing. This humane attitude and his encouragement of missionaries brought on him the censure of his superiors. Retiring from the Hudson's Bay Co., 1846, he failed to make good a claim for lands which he had improved, and it was not until 1862 that his heirs were able to secure the property. A man of extraordinary dignity and appearance, McLoughlin was known to the Indians as the White Eagle.

McLoughlin, Maurice Evans (*b. Carson City, Nev., 1890; d. Hermosa Beach, Calif., 1957*), tennis player. Studied briefly at the University of California. The first to use the "big serve" in tennis, McLoughlin played his first national competition in 1909 in Newport, R.I. In 1913, he and Harold Hackett won the Davis Cup for the U.S.; in 1912 and 1913, he won the American championships. He retired from professional tennis in 1919 and was elected to the Tennis Hall of Fame in 1957.

McClure, William (*b. Ayr, Scotland, 1763; d. near Mexico City, 1840*), merchant, geologist, patron of science. Settled in America *ca.* 1796; became a U.S. citizen *ante* 1803. After making observations throughout the entire United States east of the Mississippi, Maclure produced a geological map of the country, the first of its scope, which was published with an explanatory text in Volume 1 of the *Transactions* of the American Philosophical Society and appeared in a revised form, 1817 and 1818. He was president of the Academy of Natural Sciences of Philadelphia, 1817–40, and presented to the academy the greater part of his valuable library and collections of specimens; he was also responsible for the introduction of Pestalozzian methods of education in America. Becoming interested in Robert Owen's projected community at New Harmony, Ind., he persuaded a number of other scientists to accompany him there, where he hoped to test out a plan for a great agricultural school. After the failure of Owen's venture, Maclure spent most of the rest of his life in Mexico.

McMahon, Bernard (*b. Ireland, date unknown; d. Philadelphia, Pa., 1816*), horticulturalist. Immigrating to America, 1796, McMahon settled in Philadelphia, where he conducted a seed and general nursery business in a shop which served as a club or meeting place for the prominent botanists of the time. He was author of the first notable American horticultural book, *American Gardener's Calendar* (1806).

McMahon, Brien (*b. Norwalk, Conn., 1903; d. Washington, D.C., 1952*), lawyer, politician. Studied at Fordham University and at Yale (LL.B., 1927). Assistant attorney general in charge of the Criminal Division (1936–39). A liberal Democrat, he was elected to the U.S. Senate in 1944. Supporting almost all of the policies of the Truman administration, McMahon secured the chairmanship of the Special Committee on Atomic Energy in 1945; in 1946, he played a leading role in shaping the Atomic Energy Act which gave control of the atom to the Atomic Energy Commission headed by civilians. McMahon continued to fight for buildup in the nation's atomic weapons systems at the same time calling for arms treaties. He was under serious consideration for the presidential nomination when he died of cancer.

McMahon, John Van Lear (*b. Cumberland, Md., 1800; d. Cumberland, 1871*), lawyer, Maryland legislator. Author of *Historical View of the Government of Maryland* (1831).

McManes, James (*b. Co. Tyrone, Ireland, 1822; d. Philadelphia, Pa., 1899*), Philadelphia Republican politician. Held dominant position, 1866–81, in city politics.

McManus, George (*b. St. Louis, Mo., 1884[?]; d. Santa Monica, Calif., 1954*), comic artist. Creator of the comic strip "Bringing up Father," featuring Maggie and Jiggs, in 1913 for the Hearst paper the *New York American*. The strip was possibly the most successful in history; it was syndicated in many countries around the world and brought McManus great wealth and fame.

McMaster, Guy Humphreys (*b. Clyde, N.Y., 1829; d. 1887*), New York jurist, poet.

McMaster, James Alphonsus (*b. Duanesburg, N.Y., 1820; d. New York, N.Y., 1886*), journalist, lawyer. An associate of Isaac Hecker and Clarence Walworth, McMaster was received into the Catholic church, 1845, and served as editor of the independent Catholic paper, the *Freeman's Journal*, 1847–86. Courageous and able, McMaster made his paper an outstanding organ, even though his utter frankness brought upon him at times the criticism of the clergy, the laity, and Irish activists. A picturesque editor of the old school, MaMaster was bitter and prejudiced, stubborn in support of principle, firm in friendship.

McMASTER, JOHN BACH (*b. Brooklyn, N.Y., 1852; d. Darien, Conn., 1932*), historian. Graduated College of the City of New York, 1872. Practiced engineering and taught it at Princeton, 1877–83; professor of American history, University of Pennsylvania, 1883–1920. McMaster is remembered for his monumental *History of the People of the United States* in eight volumes, published at irregular intervals between 1883 and 1913. The earlier volumes in particular hold a unique place in the field of social and economic history, which up until their publication had been largely neglected for war and politics. Working independently and using many contemporary sources, McMaster made effective use of newspapers, magazines, memoirs, narratives of travel, and letters. His contribution to history included a number of excellent textbooks which, like his larger works, showed originality and breadth of conception.

McMATH, ROBERT EMMET (*b. Varick, N.Y., 1833; d. Webster Groves, Mo., 1918*), civil engineer. A specialist in river hydraulics, he is best known for the formula which he devised to help in determining proper size for storm sewers, 1886.

McMICHAEL, MORTON (*b. Bordentown, N.J., 1807; d. Philadelphia, Pa., 1879*), journalist, Whig and Republican politician. Edited several magazines including *Godey's Lady's Book*; also edited and managed Philadelphia *North American*, 1847–79. Held many local offices in Philadelphia, including the mayoralty, 1866–69.

McMILLAN, JAMES (*b. Hamilton, Canada, 1838; d. 1902*), manufacturer, financier. Removed to Detroit, Mich., 1855; managed successful freight-car building company; was partner of John S. Newberry in varied transport and manufacturing enterprises. As state committee chairman, he reorganized the Michigan Republican party, 1886, and was thereafter its effectual leader. Serving as U.S. senator, 1889–1902, he was a member of an influential informal conservative group of senators who determined Republican policies *post* 1890. McMillan promoted the Great Lakes "20-foot channel" and also secured adequate channel entrances to Atlantic harbors. As member of the Senate Committee on the District of Columbia, he secured creation of a notable commission for the development of Washington, D.C.; the resulting "McMillan Plan" (based on L'Enfant's plan of 1792) was the basis for subsequent improvements in the capital.

McMILLAN, JAMES WINNING (*b. Clark Co., Ky., 1825; d. Washington, D.C., 1903*), Union soldier. Organized 21st Indiana Infantry, 1861; resigned from service, 1865, as brevet major general of volunteers. A brave, tenacious, and able brigade commander.

McMILLIN, ALVIN NUGENT ("BO") (*b. Prairie Hill, Tex., 1895; d. Bloomington, Ind., 1952*), football player and coach. Attended Centre College in Danville, Ky., where he led the team in a famous upset over Harvard University in 1921. McMillin went on to coach for several small colleges and Kansas State College (1928–33); he was head coach for Indiana University from 1934 to 1948. In 1948, he became coach and general manager for the Detroit Lions, and in 1950, head coach for the Philadelphia Eagles.

McMILLIN, BENTON (*b. Monroe Co., Ky., 1845; d. 1933*), lawyer, Tennessee legislator. Congressman, Democrat, from Tennessee, 1879–99; governor of Tennessee, 1899–1903. U.S. minister to Peru, 1913–19; to Guatemala, 1919–22. As con-

gressman, favored free silver and advocated an income tax; as governor, reduced the state debt and instituted factory inspection and minimum working age laws.

McMINN, JOSEPH (*b. Chester Co., Pa., 1758; d. 1824*), Tennessee pioneer and legislator. Governor of Tennessee, 1815–21; a just and benevolent U.S. agent to the Cherokee, 1823–24.

MacMONNIES, FREDERICK WILLIAM (*b. Brooklyn, N.Y., 1863; d. New York, N.Y., 1937*), sculptor. Began as studio boy to Augustus Saint-Gaudens, who instructed him and encouraged him to enter night classes at the National Academy of Design and the Art Students League; at 20 he went to Paris to study under Alexandre Falguière at the École des Beaux Arts. By 1991 MacMonnies' work was known at home and abroad; in that year he became the first American to win a medal at the Paris Salon for his statues *J. S. T. Stranahan* and *Nathan Hale* (the latter for New York's City Hall Park). In 1893 Saint-Gaudens chose MacMonnies to design and execute a large fountain for the Chicago World's Fair. The sculptor created a symbolic ship of state, bearing Columbia, and many other elaborate figures, which was the sensation of the fair. Other notable commissions included two fountains for the New York Public Library, *Sir Henry Vane* for the Boston Public Library, *Shakespeare* for the Library of Congress, and, in Grand Army Plaza, Brooklyn, N.Y., two groups and a quadriga for the Memorial Arch. His lovely but pagan *Bacchante* was rejected by staid Boston, and the later *Civic Virtue* aroused a similar controversy in New York. Most ambitious was his war memorial at Meaux, France, his gift to his second country, 1926. Noted for its vigor, ardor, and boldness, MacMonnies' art, as Lorado Taft observed, "is essentially plastic. He delights in the 'feel' of the clay, and he handles it like a magician."

McMURRICH, JAMES PLAYFAIR (*b. Toronto, Canada, 1859; d. Toronto, 1839*), biologist, anatomist. Professor of anatomy at University of Michigan, 1894–1907; at University of Toronto, 1907–30. First dean of School of Graduate Studies at Toronto (1922–30).

McMURRY, FRANK MORTON (*b. near Crawfordsville, Ind., 1862; d. Quaker Hill, N.Y., 1936*), educator. Graduated Jena, Ph.D., 1889. Exponent of Herbartian pedagogy; professor of elementary education, Teachers College, Columbia University, 1898–1926.

McMURTRIE, DOUGLAS CRAWFORD (*b. Belmar, N.J., 1888; d. Evanston, Ill., 1944*), typographer, bibliographer. Son of William McMurtrie. Attended Massachusetts Institute of Technology. Associated over the years as director or typographer with a number of printing firms, he served as editor of the American Imprints Inventory for the Works Progress Administration; he also directed another WPA project for the indexing of printing periodicals. Among his many publications were *The Golden Book* (1927, reissued and revised in 1938 as *The Book*) and A *History of Printing in the United States* (1936, the second volume only, of a projected four). He was active also in work for the rehabilitation of the crippled.

McMURTRIE, WILLIAM (*b. near Belvidere, N.J., 1851; d. New York, N.Y., 1913*), chemist. Associated with Department of Agriculture, 1871–82; *post* 1888, chemist and official of Royal Baking Powder Co. His 1880 report on the foreign beet-sugar industry was instrumental in starting production in the United States.

McNAIR, ALEXANDER (*b. present Juniata Co., Pa., 1775; d. 1826*), merchant. Settled in St. Louis, Mo., 1804; held many public offices there. Defeated William Clark for governorship of Missouri, 1820, in the first state election; served until 1824.

McNair, Fred Walter (*b. Fennimore, Wis., 1862; d. near Buda, Ill., 1924*), mathematician, educator. Graduated University of Wisconsin, 1891. President, Michigan College of Mines, 1899–1924. Assisted in developing a gun fire director for battleships during World War I.

McNair, Frederick Vallette (*b. Jenkintown, Pa., 1839; d. Washington, D.C., 1900*), naval officer. Appointed midshipman, 1853; received commendation for notable Civil War service; was assigned thereafter to positions of unusual responsibility. Promoted rear admiral, 1898, he held the superintendency to U.S. Naval Academy, 1898–1900.

McNair, Harley Farnsworth (*b. Greenfield, Pa., 1891; d. Chicago, Ill., 1947*), historian. Raised in California. Ph.B., University of Redlands, 1912; M.A., Columbia University, 1916; Ph.D., University of California, Berkeley, 1922. Taught history at St. John's University in Shanghai, China, 1912–27, and at University of Washington, 1927–28. Thereafter, until his death, he was professor of Far Eastern history and institutions at the University of Chicago. Author of a number of books on international relations of the Far East, he was primarily a gifted teacher.

McNair, Lesley James (*b. Verndale, Minn., 1883; d. Normandy, France, 1944*), army officer. Graduated West Point, 1904; commissioned in artillery. For most of the decade after graduation, McNair was with the 4th Field Artillery. In 1916–17 he took part in the expedition of General John J. Pershing into northern Mexico. During World War I McNair's acquaintance with Pershing led to his assignment to the 1st Division, with which he went to France in June 1917. He served with Pershing's general headquarters and became the second-youngest brigadier general in the American Expeditionary Forces. For his work on the coordination of field artillery fire with infantry combat he earned the Distinguished Service Medal. He attended the Army War College, from which he was graduated in 1929. For the next four years, he was assistant commandant of the Field Artillery School at Fort Sill. From August 1940 until March 1942 he served as chief of staff of General Headquarters and thereafter until July 1944 as commanding general of the Army Ground Forces. He was promoted to major general in September 1940, lieutenant general in June 1941, and (posthumously) general in 1945.

In organizing American forces for action, McNair stressed economy and simplicity. Though an artilleryman, he viewed the infantry as the arm of decisive action; and he opposed the proliferation of specialized units that could not be welded into a combined arms team built around the infantry. Five weeks after the Normandy invasion McNair was named commanding general of the 1st Army Group. McNair soon crossed to Normandy to get a frontline view of the action; on his first day at the front, July 25, 1944, he was killed when American bombs fell short of their targets.

McNamee, Graham (*b. Washington, D.C., 1888; d. New York, N.Y., 1942*), radio announcer. Raised in St. Paul, Minn. Trained as a singer, he became an announcer at station WEAF, New York City, in 1923. His enthusiastic, informal style made him by 1937 the best-known announcer in the industry, covering sports, political conventions, and news events such as Lindbergh's flight to Paris. During the 1930's he was a leading master of ceremonies for radio variety and humor programs.

McNary, Charles Linza (*b. near Salem, Oreg., 1874; d. Fort Lauderdale, Fla., 1944*), lawyer, politician. A full orphan by 1883, he attended public school in Salem and spent the year 1896–97 at Stanford University. Having read law in the office of his older brother, McNary was admitted to the bar in 1898, after

which he practiced with his brother in Salem. He was appointed to the state supreme court in 1913 to fill a vacancy and failed by one vote to win the Republican nomination to that post in 1914. Upon the death of Larry Lane in 1917, McNary was appointed to his seat in the U.S. Senate. Save for a few weeks in 1918, he remained in the Senate for the rest of his life.

Although McNary had been president of the Oregon Taft-Sherman Club in 1912, he called himself a progressive in 1917. In the Committee on Agriculture and Forestry (of which he was chairman, 1926–33) he presided over the investigation of forest resources that led to the McNary-Clarke Act for fire protection, reforestation, forest management, and acquisition of forest lands, 1924; the McNary-Woodruff Act for the purchase of lands for national forests, 1928; and the McNary-Sweeney Act for forest research, 1928. Best known in the 1920's as leader of the "farm bloc" in Congress, he was cosponsor of the McNary-Haugen bill, which sought to stabilize farm prices by subsidizing the sale of surplus crops abroad. McNary ran for reelection in 1936 independently of the state Republican organization and gave only limited support to Alfred M. Landon, the Republican presidential candidate. When in 1940 the Republicans nominated Wendell Willkie for president, they picked McNary for vice president.

Macnaughtan, Myra Kelly. *See* Kelly, Myra.

MacNeil, Hermon Atkins (*b. near Chelsea, Mass., 1866; d. College Point, N.Y., 1947*), sculptor. Graduated Massachusetts Normal Art School, Boston, 1886; studied in Paris with Henri Chapu and Jean Falguière, 1888–92. Assisted Philip Martiny in sculptures for the Chicago Exposition, 1893; taught at the Chicago Art Institute, 1893–96. A student at the American Academy in Rome, 1896–1900, he produced there several of the pieces on American Indian subjects for which he was noted, including the *Sun Vow*. Returning to the United States, he enjoyed a successful career and received many honors for work in the Beaux-Arts style, to which he added a vital naturalism and colorful details. He gained fame as well as a portraitist (portraits of Roger Williams, Francis Parkman, James Monroe, and Rufus Choate in the Hall of Fame, New York University, are outstanding) and as a designer and sculptor of memorials. During his career he taught at the National Academy of Design, Pratt Institute, and the Art Students League in New York City.

McNeill, Daniel (*b. Charlestown, Mass., 1748; d. Boston, Mass., 1833*), Revolutionary privateersman, naval officer. As captain of privateer *General Mifflin*, he took 13 prizes, 1778–1779. Commissioned captain, U.S. Navy, 1798, he served until 1802, commanding the *Portsmouth* and the frigate *Boston*.

McNeill, George Edwin (*b. Amesbury, Mass., 1837; d. Somerville, Mass., 1906*), labor leader. Active in eight-hour-day movement, 1863–74, as speaker, writer, and organizer for appropriate legislation. The Knights of Labor adopted his declaration of labor principles, 1874. McNeill drafted a plan for cooperation of the Knights with the American Federation of Labor, 1886; when this failed, he joined the Federation, whose nonpolitical program appealed to him. He arbitrated a number of labor disputes, edited the Boston *Labor Leader* and wrote several books. His book *The Labor Movement* (1887) was the first systematic history of American labor organizations.

McNeill, Hector (*b. Co. Antrim, Ireland, 1728; d. at sea, 1785*), Revolutionary naval officer, privateersman. Came to Boston, Mass., as a child. Commanded frigate *Boston* in John Manley's squadron, 1777; was court-martialed and dismissed from the service for conduct during action with the British ship *Rainbow*, July 7, 1777.

McNeill, John Hanson (*b. Hardy Co., Va., 1815; d. Harrisonburg, Va., 1864*), livestock raiser, Confederate partisan. Removed to Missouri, 1848. Served in Missouri campaigns, 1861–62. Captured and imprisoned, he escaped to western Virginia, where he organized the McNeill Partisan Rangers, an independent command which engaged in successful raiding activities against Union forces.

McNeill, William Gibbs (*b. Wilmington, N.C., 1801; d. Brooklyn, N.Y., 1853*), civil engineer. Graduated West Point, 1817. In association with George W. Whistler, McNeill worked on the projection of most new railways in the eastern United States, 1828–37.

MacNeven, William James (*b. Co. Galway, Ireland, 1763; d. New York, N.Y., 1841*), physician. Educated at universities of Prague and Vienna; practiced in Dublin *post* 1784. After imprisonment for Irish revolutionary activities *post* 1798, he served briefly in the French army and in 1805 went to New York City, where he was successful in practice and as a teacher in the College of Physicians and Surgeons, 1808–26.

McNicholas, John Timothy (*b. near Kiltimagh, Co. Mayo, Ireland, 1877; d. Cincinnati, Ohio, 1950*), Roman Catholic clergyman, archbishop of Cincinnati. Came with his parents to Chester, Pa., as a child; attended school there, followed by high school with the Jesuits in Philadelphia. He entered the Dominican Order at St. Rose's priory, Springfield, Ky. His philosophical and theological studies were made in St. Joseph's house of studies, Somerset, Ohio, where he was ordained on Oct. 10, 1901. Following ordination, he studied at the Minerva University in Rome, where he earned his lectorate in sacred theology in 1904. Upon returning to the United States, he was named master of novices at Somerset. Named national director of the Holy Name Society, he established headquarters in New York City and founded and edited the *Holy Name Journal*. In 1913 he was appointed pastor of St. Catherine's Parish, New York.

In 1918 Pope Benedict XV appointed McNicholas bishop of the diocese of Duluth, Minn. In May 1925 he was nominated to the diocese of Indianapolis, Ind., but on July 8 he was elevated to the archdiocese of Cincinnati and installed there as the see's archbishop on Aug. 12. He furthered the educational tradition, which he inherited with the see of Cincinnati. The archdiocese was a model of Roman Catholic education on the grade school, high school, and college levels. He served as episcopal chairman of the department of education of the National Catholic Welfare Conference (1930–35, 1942–45). He was also a five-term president general of the National Catholic Educational Association (1946–50). He played the major role in founding the National Legion of Decency, had a hand in the revision of the Calloner-Rheims version of the New Testament, and directed the writing and editing of the Baltimore catechism. The annual statements issued in the name of the Catholic hierarchy of America for many years owed much of their form and forcefulness to his gifted mind. In 1935 he established the Institutum Divi Thomae as a postgraduate school of theology and science.

MacNider, Hanford (*b. Mason City, Iowa, 1889; d. Sarasota, Fla., 1968*), businessman and army officer. Studied at Harvard (B.A., 1911). Worked at family-owned First National Bank in Mason City, Iowa (1911–16). Elected second lieutenant in the Iowa National Guard (1916). Enlisted in the regular army in 1917; joined the Ninth Regiment of the Second (Indianhead) Division. Discharged in 1919. Iowa state commander, the American Legion (1920–21); national commander (1921–22). Chairman of the Republican Service League (1924); assistant secretary of war (1925–28); American minister to Canada (1930–32). Recalled to active duty in 1942; brigadier general. Commanded

the Warren Force of the 128th Infantry Regiment and the 158th Regimental Combat Team in the Pacific in World War II. In the U.S. Army Reserves from 1945; commanded the 103rd Infantry (Reserve) Division; retired a major general in 1951. In the 1930's MacNider reorganized his family's major holding, the Northwestern States Portland Cement Company, nurturing its growth into one of America's largest producers.

McNulty, Frank Joseph (*b. Londonderry, Ireland, 1872; d. Newark, N.J., 1926*), labor leader. As president, International Brotherhood of Electrical Workers, 1903–19, McNulty succeeded in raising its membership from the condition of a nonskilled labor group and in furthering the settlement of disputes by negotiation instead of by strikes.

McNulty, John Augustine (*b. Lawrence, Mass., 1895; d. Wakefield, R.I., 1956*), journalist, writer. Studied briefly at Colby College and Columbia. After working as a reporter in the Midwest, McNulty came to New York to work for the *New Yorker*, the *New York Daily Mirror*, and the *New York Daily News*. The first of his stories for *The New Yorker* appeared in 1941. Subsequent collections of his observations of New York City life appeared as *Third Avenue, New York* (1946), *A Man Gets Around* (1951), and *My Son Johnnie* (1955).

McNutt, Alexander (*b. probably Londonderry, Ireland, ca. 1725; d. ca. 1811*), colonial land promoter. Came to America *ante* 1753; settled near Staunton, Va. Promoted settlement of Irish Protestants and others in Nova Scotia; helped foment rebellion there, 1778–81.

McNutt, Paul Vories (*b. Franklin, Ind., 1891; d. New York, N.Y., 1955*), lawyer, diplomat. Studied at Indiana University and Harvard Law School. As Democratic governor of Indiana, 1933–37, achieved national recognition by changing the state's finances from a debt of $3 million to a $17-million surplus. Named high commissioner to the Philippines by President Franklin D. Roosevelt, 1937; suggested that American policy of rapid independence for the islands should be reexamined. Served as head of the Federal Security Agency, 1939–45. Campaigned for the presidency, 1940, but withdrew when Roosevelt decided on a fourth term and declined the vice-presidential nomination in favor of Henry Wallace.

Returned as high commissioner to the Philippines, 1945; oversaw the smooth transition of the islands to an independent nation, while lobbying for trade and war rehabilitation legislation that would give advantages to American business. Ambassador to the Philippines, 1946–47, before returning to private law practice.

Macomb, Alexander (*b. Detroit, 1782; d. Washington, D.C., 1841*), soldier. Commissioned cornet and second lieutenant, U.S. Army, 1799; recommissioned, 1801; commissioned first lieutenant, Corps of Engineers, 1802. One of the first student officers to be trained at West Point, Macomb remained on duty there until 1805 when he was promoted captain and engaged thereafter until 1812 on coast fortifications in the Carolinas and Georgia. Made colonel of artillery, 1812, he served in minor capacities on the Canadian frontier until 1814 when he was promoted brigadier general and stationed with his brigade in the Lake Champlain region. His defense of Plattsburg, N.Y., against a superior British invading force, Sept. 11, 1814, was skillfully conducted, but the retreat of the British was probably due rather to the destruction of their supporting fleet by U.S. naval forces under Thomas Macdonough and resultant danger to their communications than to the effectiveness of the small American army. Engaged in various types of service, 1814–21, in the latter year he became head of the Corps of Engineers. In 1828 he was designated senior major general and commanding general of the U.S. Army, a position which he filled until his death. His ability was primarily of the organizing, systematizing kind, which the army of his day greatly needed.

MACOMBER, MARY LIZZIE (*b. Fall River, Mass., 1861; d. Boston, Mass., 1916*), painter of symbolic decorative panels and portraits.

MACON, NATHANIEL (*b. Edgecomb, now Warren, Co., N.C., 1758; d. Warren Co., 1837*), lawyer, North Carolina legislator, Revolutionary soldier. A follower of Willie Jones, Macon opposed the Convention of 1787 and advocated rejection of the U.S. Constitution. Congressman, Democratic-Republican, from North Carolina, 1791–1815, and U.S. senator, 1815–28, he was for years the outstanding leader of his party in the House and served as Speaker, 1801–07. A supporter in its entirety of the foreign policy of the Jefferson and Madison administrations, Macon, as chairman of the Foreign Relations Committee, 1809, reported the two celebrated bills which bear his name, although he was the author of neither. He opposed recharter of the Bank of the United States in 1811 and 1816, voted against any form of protective tariff, and opposed a policy of internal improvements; he was also an earnest defender of slavery and voted against the Missouri Compromise. Important as he was in Congress for many years, he was not a constructive force but a negative radical, rural and local-minded.

McPHERSON, AIMEE SEMPLE (*b. near Ingersoll, Ontario, Canada, 1890; d. Oakland, Calif., 1944*), evangelist. Christened Aimee Elizabeth Kennedy. Married R. J. Semple, 1908, with whom she conducted revival meetings until his death, 1910, while on a mission to Asia. Returning to America, she continued revival activity in New York, Chicago, and elsewhere until her marriage to H. S. McPherson, 1912. Renewing her revival work, she began in 1916 to travel up and down the eastern seaboard in her "gospel automobile"; in 1918, after an itinerant transcontinental evangelizing tour, she settled in Los Angeles, Calif., which was thereafter her headquarters. From Los Angeles, she and her mother set off on repeated cross-country tours, conducting revivals in most major American cities; she and her husband were divorced in 1921. In 1923 her work, which she now called the Foursquare Gospel movement, achieved a permanent home in Angelus Temple, Los Angeles, with an accompanying radio station and Bible school. Much of her success was owing to her flair for publicity and the flamboyance of the methods with which she offered an updated version of Protestant fundamentalism. Despite numerous personal and financial difficulties, she continued as leader of her movement until her death.

McPHERSON, EDWARD (*b. Gettysburg, Pa., 1830; d. 1895*), Pennsylvania journalist and political statistician. Congressman, Republican, from Pennsylvania, 1859–63; clerk of the House of Representatives, 1863–75, 1881–83, 1889–91. Author of several political histories of the period *post* 1861 and of the *Political Manual* (1866–69) and the *Handbook of Politics* (biennially, 1868 through 1894).

McPHERSON, JAMES BIRDSEYE (*b. Sandusky Co., Ohio, 1828; d. near Atlanta, Ga., 1864*), Union soldier. Graduated West Point, 1853; was assigned to Corps of Engineers. After service at start of Civil War as aide to General H. W. Halleck, McPherson was chief engineer in U. S. Grant's Tennessee campaign, 1862, and from that time on was constantly in the field. Promoted brigadier general and major general, 1862, he served with particular distinction in the campaigns which led up to the taking of Vicksburg. Assuming command of the Army of the Tennessee, March 1864, McPherson led it through the entire

subsequent campaign up to the fortifications of Atlanta, where he met his death in action. Recognized as one of the ablest generals in the Union army, McPherson welcomed responsibility and service.

McPHERSON, LOGAN GRANT (*b. Circleville, Ohio, 1863; d. New York, N.Y., 1925*), railway statistician and economist.

McPHERSON, SMITH (*b. near Mooresville, Ind., 1848; d. Redoak, Iowa, 1915*), lawyer, jurist. Iowa attorney general, 1881–85; federal judge, southern district of Iowa, 1900–15. An able active judge, his decisions were markedly conservative.

McQUAID, BERNARD JOHN (*b. New York, N.Y., 1823; d. Rochester, N.Y., 1909*), Roman Catholic clergyman. Held various pastorates in New Jersey; was consecrated bishop of Rochester, 1868. A zealous prelate, McQuaid ruled his diocese ably but exactingly; he was particularly notable because of his ardor for the establishment of parochial schools and for his conflicts of opinion with more liberal Catholic prelates and clergymen of his time. A rigid canonist and conservative, he opposed secret societies, Irish patriotic groups, and the Knights of Labor.

McQUILLEN, JOHN HUGH (*b. Philadelphia, Pa., 1826; d. Philadelphia, 1879*), dentist. Graduated Jefferson Medical College, M.D., 1852. Helped organize American Dental Association, 1859; founded Philadelphia Dental College, 1863, and served there as dean and professor until death. Edited *Dental Cosmos*, 1865–72.

McRAE, DUNCAN KIRKLAND (*b. Fayetteville, N.C., 1820; d. Brooklyn, N.Y., 1888*), lawyer, Confederate soldier. U.S. consul at Paris, 1853–57. Disabled by wounds, he resigned command of 5th North Carolina Regiment, 1862, to serve abroad in the succeeding year as a successful purchasing and commercial agent for his state. *Post* 1865, he practiced law principally in Memphis, Tenn.

MACRAE, JOHN (*b. Richmond, Va., 1866; d. New York, N.Y., 1944*), book publisher. President, E. P. Dutton and Co., *post* 1923.

McRAE, MILTON ALEXANDER (*b. Detroit, Mich., 1858; d. La Jolla, Calif., 1930*), publisher. Associate of James E. and Edward W. Scripps in development of newspapers and newspaper chains. The Scripps-McRae Press Association, formed in 1897, of which he was president, later developed into the United Press.

McRAE, THOMAS CHIPMAN (*b. Union Co., Ark., 1851; d. 1929*), lawyer, politician. Congressman, Democrat, from Arkansas, 1886–1903, McRae held important committee posts and worked for conservation policies, for the recovery of public lands, and for the imposition of a graduated income tax. As Democratic governor of Arkansas, 1921–25, he was successful in abolishing a number of useless offices and instituting a systematic and economical financial administration.

McREYNOLDS, JAMES CLARK (*b. Elkton, Ky., 1863; d. Washington, D.C., 1946*), lawyer, justice of the U.S. Supreme Court. B.S., Vanderbilt University, 1882; graduated in law from University of Virginia, 1884. Developed an extensive practice in Nashville, Tenn. A low-tariff, sound-money, limited-government Cleveland Democrat, he ran as a "Gold Democrat" nominee for Congress in 1896, but met defeat. From 1900 to 1903 he taught at Vanderbilt Law School. In 1903 he was appointed assistant to the attorney general of the United States. In 1910 he took part in the antitrust prosecution of the American Tobacco Co. He then moved to New York City to open his own law office. In 1913 he was appointed attorney general of the United States. He proved to be a zealous foe of the trusts. In August 1914, President

Woodrow Wilson elevated McReynolds to the Supreme Court, where he aligned himself with the conservative wing. He viewed the Constitution as an immutable body of principles that should be interpreted chiefly as limitations on the exercise of governmental power. To a Cleveland Democrat like McReynolds, the New Deal was anathema. In every crucial New Deal case, he voted against the administration. As the last survivor on the Court of the conservative "Four Horsemen," he protested in vain against the "Constitutional Revolution" which saw the Court sanction an enormous range of governmental authority over the economy at the same time that it safeguarded an ever-widening scope of civil liberties. Two days after Roosevelt was inaugurated for a third term, McReynolds resigned.

McReynolds, Samuel Davis (b. Bledsoe Co., Tenn., 1872; d. Washington, D.C., 1939), lawyer, Tennessee jurist. Congressman, Democrat, from Tennessee, 1923–39. Advocated limiting immigration, 1924; was chairman of Foreign Affairs Committee post 1932. Served most ably as administration spokesman on neutrality legislation, 1935–37.

MacSparran, James (b. probably Co. Derry, Ireland, 1693; d. South Kingston, R.I., 1757), Presbyterian and Anglican clergyman. Served briefly as a minister of the Congregational church, Bristol, R.I., 1718. Refused ordination because of Cotton Mather's enmity, MacSparran returned to England, was ordained in the Church of England, 1720, and came out to America again as a missionary of the Society for the Propagation of the Gospel in Foreign Parts. Arriving at Narragansett, R.I., in April 1721, he proved to be one of the ablest of the missionaries sent to America by the society. He served as rector of St. Paul's parish and ministered to the surrounding country thereafter until his death. He was author of, among other works, *America Dissected* (1753), an account of the colonies in a series of letters to friends.

McTammany, John (b. Kelvin Row, Scotland, 1845; d. Stamford, Conn., 1915), inventor, Union soldier. Came to America, 1862. Conceived the idea of the player piano, 1863, embodying such elements as a flexible sheet on rolls, a wind motor, foot pedals, and other important features. After 13 years of experimentation, he filed a caveat but neglected to obtain a patent and his invention was extensively pirated. After long and costly litigation which reduced him to poverty, he was declared the original inventor, 1880, and received patents, 1881. In 1892 McTammany received a basic patent for a pneumatic registering voting machine employing a perforated roll. The first machine to be used in an election, it was adopted in several states, but its manufacture provided little or no return to the inventor.

McTyeire, Holland Nimmons (b. Barnwell Co., S.C., 1824; d. Nashville, Tenn., 1889), clergyman and bishop of the Methodist Episcopal Church, South. The chief agent in the founding of Vanderbilt University, McTyeire served as president of the university's board of trustees, 1873–89.

Macune, Charles William (b. Kenosha, Wis., 1851; d. Fort Worth, Tex., 1940), farm leader. Drifted about the country post 1865, ranching, cattle driving, house painting, and studying law and medicine. Settling in Milam Co., Tex., ca. 1885, he soon became a leader in the Farmers' Alliance, merging the Texas Alliance with other state farm groups. By 1890 Macune was president of an organization of more than a million members. Moving to Washington, D.C., he edited the Alliance's weekly newspaper, pressing for farm credit legislation. Charged with undermining the Populist cause, Macune dropped out of the Alliance in 1893. From 1900 to 1918 he was a Methodist preacher in Texas.

MacVeagh, Charles (b. West Chester, Pa., 1860; d. near Santa Barbara, Calif., 1931), lawyer, diplomat, philanthropist. Son of Isaac W. MacVeagh. Graduated Harvard, 1881; practiced corporation law in New York, N.Y., post 1886. U.S. ambassador to Japan, 1925–29.

MacVeagh, Franklin (b. near Phoenixville, Pa., 1837; d. 1934), lawyer, businessman. Brother of Isaac W. MacVeagh. Removed to Chicago, 1866, where he engaged in the wholesale grocery business and was active in civic reform movements. Independent in his political thinking, MacVeagh left the Republican party, 1884, but rejoined it in reaction to the policies of William Jennings Bryan; however, he supported Alfred E. Smith, 1928. As U.S. secretary of the treasury, 1909–13, MacVeagh reorganized his department in the direction of efficiency and economy and provided a spark of progressivism in an otherwise conservative cabinet.

MacVeagh, Isaac Wayne (b. near Phoenixville, Pa., 1833; d. 1917), lawyer. Brother of Franklin MacVeagh; son-in-law of Simon Cameron. Graduated Yale, 1853. Appointed U.S. minister resident in Turkey, 1870, he resigned, 1871, in protest against political conditions under the Grant administration and began a lifelong career of "insurgency" by opposing the Cameron Republican machine in Pennsylvania. Active under President R. B. Hayes in bringing an end to Reconstruction in Louisiana, he served briefly as U.S. attorney general, 1881. MacVeagh's growing interest in civil service and other reforms impelled him to leave the Republican party and to support Grover Cleveland in the campaign of 1892. During a two-year term as U.S. ambassador to Italy post December 1893, he preserved good relations, despite Italian excitement over treatment of their immigrant compatriots in the United States at the time. Subsequent to 1897, he practiced law, continued his interest in reforms, and was as persistent a nonconformist in the Democratic party as he had been in the Republican. He served as chief counsel for the United States in the Venezuela arbitration, 1903.

McVey, Frank Lerond (b. Wilmington, Ohio, 1869; d. Lexington, Ky., 1953), economist and university president. Studied at Ohio Wesleyan University and at Yale (Ph.D., 1895). Taught at the University of Minnesota (1896–1907). President of the University of North Dakota (1907–17). President of the University of Kentucky (1917–40). Published *Financial History of Great Britain, 1914–1918*, in 1918. President of the National Association of State Universities.

MacVicar, Malcolm (b. Dunglass, Scotland, 1829; d. 1904), Baptist clergyman, educator. Came to Canada as a child; graduated University Of Rochester, 1859. Notably successful as a teacher in upstate New York, he organized and administered state normal schools in New York and Michigan. Returning to his ministerial profession in 1881, he taught at, and headed, several Baptist colleges and was superintendent of the educational work of the American Baptist Home Mission Society.

McVickar, John (b. New York, N.Y., 1787; d. New York, 1868), Episcopal clergyman, economist. Graduated Columbia, 1804; studied theology with John H. Hobart; was ordained, 1812. A teacher at Columbia, 1817–64, McVickar was one of the earliest professors of political economy in the United States, treating the subject as a branch of moral philosophy. He was author of a life of John H. Hobart and of an important economic essay, *Hints on Banking* (1827), among other works.

McVickar, William Neilson (b. New York, N.Y., 1843; d. Beverly Farms, Mass., 1910), Episcopal clergyman. Graduated Columbia, 1865; General Theological Seminary, New York, 1868. An intimate friend of Phillips Brooks, he was rector of Holy Trinity, Philadelphia, 1875–97. Elected coadjutor bishop of Rhode Island, 1897, he succeeded as bishop, 1903.

McVicker, James Hubert (*b. New York, N.Y., 1822; d. 1896*), actor, theatrical manager. A specialist in Yankee comedy parts, McVicker made his most notable success as a manager in Chicago, Ill., *post* 1857. His stock companies were among the best in the United States.

MacWhorter, Alexander (*b. New Castle Co., Del., 1734 o.s.; d. Newark, N.J., 1807*), Presbyterian clergyman, Revolutionary patriot. Pastor at Newark, N.J., 1759–1807.

Macy, Jesse (*b. near Knightstown, Ind., 1842; d. 1919*), philosopher, political scientist. Professor at Grinnell College, Iowa, 1870–1912. Advocated teaching of government in public schools by observation of the workings of local government and application of scientific method to study of politics.

Macy, John Albert (*b. Detroit, Mich., 1877; d. Stroudsburg, Pa., 1932*), editor, critic, poet. Graduated Harvard, 1899. A Socialist iconoclast, he is remembered for his *The Spirit of American Literature* (1913), a plea for realism and for a profounder examination of American life by American writers.

Macy, Josiah (*b. Nantucket, Mass., 1785; d. Rye, N.Y., 1872*), merchant captain. Founder of New York shipping and commission firm of Josiah Macy & Son, 1828.

Macy, Valentine Everit (*b. New York, N.Y., 1871; d. near Phoenix, Ariz., 1930*), capitalist, philanthropist. Performed notable service as a public official in Westchester Co., N.Y.

Madden, John Edward (*b. Bethlehem, Pa., 1856; d. New York, N.Y., 1929*), Kentucky horse breeder. Leading American breeder of winning Thoroughbred racers, 1916–27; outstanding among his horses were Zev and Princess Doreen.

Madden, Martin Barnaby (*b. Darlington, England, 1855; d. Washington, D.C., 1928*), politician. Came to America as a child; was raised in Cook Co., Ill., where he prospered as a quarryman. Active in Republican politics *post* 1889, he broke with the Cook Co. machine, 1897, and helped destroy it. As congressman, 1905–28, he was in the main a party regular but served with ability as member and chairman of the Appropriations Committee *post* 1919.

Madden, Owen Victor ("Owney") (*b. Liverpool, England, 1892; d. Hot Springs, Ark., 1965*), gang leader and racketeer. Immigrated to New York City in 1903; granted citizenship in 1943. Leader of the Gopher Gang in the Hell's Kitchen area of New York City from 1910; organized beatings, robberies, extortions, killings, and gang raids—by the time he was twenty-three, he was said to have killed five men, earning him the nickname "Owney the Killer." Convicted of murder in 1914 and sentenced to ten to twenty years in Sing Sing Prison. Paroled in 1923; established the Phoenix Brewery with William Vincent ("Big Bill") Dwyer; owned the Cotton Club nightclub in Harlem with Arnold Rothstein. Also owned a large part of the Italian heavyweight boxing champion Primo Carnera, with Bill Duffy and George ("Big French") DeMange. Employed in 1932 by Charles Lindbergh to help find his kidnapped son, but sent back to Sing Sing for parole violation. Released in 1933. In Hot Springs, Ark., from 1934, he operated casinos in a spa that became a refuge for gangsters.

Madigan, Laverne (*b. Clifton, N.J., 1912; d. Orleans, Vt., 1962*), administrator and Indian rights advocate. Studied at New York University (M.A., 1941). Relocation officer with the War Relocation Authority in New Jersey, 1941–45. With the Associa-

tion on American Indian Affairs (AAIA) from 1951; executive director, 1956–62. As director of the AAIA, she emphasized education as the best and most lasting mechanism for improving human relations, establishing a scholarship fund for Indians wanting a college eductation. Her monograph *The American Indian Relocation Program* (1956) presented a balanced and well-researched picture of federal efforts to aid Indians in finding work and housing in white America. Most important contribution is considered to be her work with Alaskan natives; she broadened the AIAA perspective on native rights by supporting their land and treaty claims, thereby bringing American Indians together with Alaskan Eskimo and Aleuts for the first time.

Madison, Dolly Payne (*b. present Guilford Co., N.C., 1768; d. Washington, D.C., 1849*), hostess. Raised in Hanover Co., Va.; married John Todd, Jr., a lawyer, 1790; was widowed, 1793. Married James Madison, 1794. She became a social figure of the first importance when her husband assumed U.S. secretaryship of state in 1801; acting as hostess for President Jefferson, who was a widower, her charm and social gifts served to relieve the excessive plainness of the Jeffersonian social regime. Her friendliness, her remarkable memory of persons and their interests, and her unfailing tact were of great service to her husband also during his terms as president. From Madison's retirement, 1817, until his death, 1836, she remained with him at Montpelier, living the busy, hospitable life of the mistress of the plantation. In 1837 she returned to Washington and became again a noted and honored figure there until her own death.

Madison, James (*b. near Staunton, Va., 1749; d. 1812*), Episcopal clergyman, Revolutionary patriot, educator. Cousin of James Madison (1750/1–1836). Graduated William and Mary, 1771. Ordained in England, 1775, he was elected president of William and Mary, 1777, and held this office until his death. Noted among the scientific men of his day, he made surveys from which was made the *Map of Virginia* (1807), commonly known as "Madison's Map" and standard for many years. Under his leadership, the College of William and Mary was brought to a high degree of efficiency; its reorganization and revival after the chaotic period of the Revolution were owing to him. Consecrated first bishop of Virginia, 1790, he was hampered in his efforts to rebuild the church by the pressure of his duties at the college; this and other factors resulted in a gradual weakening of the Episcopal church in Virginia in the time of his episcopate.

Madison, James (*b. Port Conway, Va., 1750/1; d. "Montpelier," Orange Co., Va., 1836*), president of the United States. Descendant of independent, but not wealthy, ancestors, Madison attended school in Virginia and graduated from the College of New Jersey (Princeton), 1771. A diligent student, especially of history and government, he continued another year at Princeton after graduation, studying Hebrew and ethics. After a period of melancholy depression following on his return to Virginia, he was aroused to activity by the political struggle with the British and by the local controversy over religious toleration. Elected to the Orange Co. Committee of Safety, he was chosen a member of the Virginia Convention, 1776, where he served on the committee which framed the Virginia Constitution and Declaration of Rights. His chief contribution was a resolution which made the free exercise of religion a matter of right rather than of toleration. A member of the first Virginia Assembly under the new constitution, Madison was elected to the Governor's Council, 1778, and in 1780 was chosen a delegate to the Continental Congress. Almost constantly in attendance, March 1780–December 1783, he was a consistent advocate of a federal revenue to be raised by duties on imports; he supported Virginia's claims to western territory against the assaults of the smaller states;

and he was instrumental in working out the compromise of September 1783 by which Congress accepted Virginia's cession of its western lands. When a change of the basis of state contributions from land values to population numbers was urged, he suggested the three-to-five "federal" ratio of free persons to slaves, which was later incorporated in the U.S. Constitution.

On returning to Virginia, December 1783, he took up the study of law. Elected within a few months to the House of Delegates, he led in efforts to develop the state's resources, to improve commerce, to complete disestablishement of the Anglican church, and to block paper-money legal-tender laws; he favored communcations to the West, Kentucky statehood, and the natural right of the West to the use of the Mississippi River outlet. He failed in his efforts to achieve a public school system, to honor debts to British creditors, and to ensure payment of Virginia's obligations to the federal government. As he saw clearly that the effectual regulation of commerce and the securing of commercial concessions from foreign nations depended on the adoption by the states of a united commercial policy, he urged that the Assembly grant Congress the power to regulate commerce and he took a prominent part in bringing about the interstate conferences which led through the Annapolis Convention, 1786, to the Constitutional Convention at Philadelphia, 1787. Once again a congressman, February to May 1787, Madison fought the Jay-Gardoqui agreement that the United States should forgo the right to use the Mississippi River.

Named a member of the Virginia delegation to the Convention of 1787, Madison was fearful that its failure would be disastrous to the United States and he set forth constructive preliminary suggestions in letters to Thomas Jefferson, Edmund Randolph, and George Washington in March and April 1787. His principal proposals were (1) a change in the principle of representation which would give the large states a more equitable influence; (2) the arming of the national government with positive and complete authority in all cases which required uniformity; (3) a negative in all cases whatsoever on the legislative acts of the states, perhaps to be lodged in the less numerous house of the legislature; (4) the extension of the national supremacy to the judiciary departments; (5) a legislature of two houses with differing terms of office; (6) a national executive; (7) an article expressly guaranteeing the tranquillity of the states against internal as well as external dangers; (8) an express declaration of the right of coercion; and (9) ratification obtained from the people and not merely from the authority of state legislatures. These suggestions were in substance embodied in resolutions drawn up by the Virginia delegates and submitted to the convention on May 29, known thereafter as the Virginia Plan. Madison became the acknowledged leader of the group in the convention which favored a strong central government. While many of his ideas failed of adoption, his influence upon the work of the convention was so great that he may aptly be described as the "masterbuilder of the Constitution." His most conspicuous quality was perhaps his practical sense, which sought solutions to problems in the realm of past experience rather than in untried theories. Madison was also the chief recorder of the convention's proceedings; although he was not official secretary of the body, his *Journal of the Federal Convention* (first published, 1840) is by far the most complete record of the proceedings.

Although convinced that the new Constitution would neither sufficiently strengthen the national government nor prevent "local mischiefs," Madison threw himself energetically into the fight for its adoption; among his efforts to overcome opposition was his share in the series of essays published in several New York newspapers over the signature of "Publius," which were later collected and published as *The Federalist* (1788). These celebrated essays, in which he cooperated with Alexander Hamilton and John

Jay, have long been accepted as an authoritative exposition of the U.S. Constitution and Madison's share in them was particularly noteworthy. His combination of faith in popular government with a clear-eyed realization that a popular majority can be quite as tyrannical as any monarch is not the least of his virtues. He also emphasized the dual nature of the new government (federal in the extent of its powers, national in their operation) and stressed the idea that the legislative, executive, and judicial branches must not be entirely distinct but must be interrelated if they were to form effective checks on one another. In the Virginia ratifying convention, Madison upheld the Constitution against Patrick Henry and George Mason and overthrew their oratory and arguments with quiet but cogent reasoning. Although Henry attempted to block his election to the 1st Congress, Madison from the beginning participated in the new government, taking a leading part during the first session in the passage of revenue legislation, in the creation of the executive departments and in the framing of the first ten amendments to the Constitution. In the second session and thereafter, Madison was increasingly critical of Hamilton's financial measures; from being an ardent Federalist, he became leader of the opposition, the Jeffersonian or Democratic-Republican party. Wholly out of sympathy with the pro-British trend of Hamilton's policy, his sympathies in the European conflicts which arose at the time of the French Revolution were with France. He opposed assumption of the state debts by the federal treasury; he opposed creation of the Bank of the United States; he criticized Washington's Neutrality Proclamation, 1793; he advocated harsh retaliation against British violations of American rights; he voted against the measures for putting the Jay Treaty into effect.

Madison's marriage to Dolly Payne Todd, September 1794, was the beginning of an extraordinarily happy domestic life. After two more years in Congress, he voluntarily retired from public service, March 1797, expecting to devote his time to scientific farming and the pleasures of rural life. However, repressive legislation initiated by the Federalists against critics of their administration (the Alien and Sedition Acts) brought him back to politics. The chief answer to the Federalist policy was the resolutions drawn up by Madison and Jefferson in 1798 and adopted by the Virginia and Kentucky legislatures, respectively. The states' rights doctrine of these resolutions was to become a matter of controversy; Madison himself in defending them against hostile criticism, 1799, stated that they were mere expressions of opinion. Later, when the South Carolina nullifiers appealed to the authority of the resolutions as supporting their doctrine, Madison denied this and explained that he and Jefferson had proposed no more than cooperation among the states for securing the repeal of laws or the amendment of the Constitution.

Madison returned to a prominent position in public life when Jefferson was elected president, 1800. Appointed U.S. secretary of state in March 1801, and at once confirmed by the Senate, he was opposed from the outset by a hostile faction headed by William Duane of Pennsylvania and W. B. Giles of Virginia, joined later by John Randolph of Roanoke and by Robert and Samuel Smith of Maryland. The principal foreign policy problems which confronted him arose from the relation of the United States to the war between Great Britain and Napoleonic France and to the disregard by both belligerents of the rights of neutrals on the high seas. Madison believed that peace with both warring nations was possible, resting that faith in part upon the supposed vital need each had for the goods and services of the United States. He played only a formal part in the purchase of Louisiana, 1803. On the renewal of the European war, 1803, after the brief respite of the Peace of Amiens, American commerce and seamen were again subjected to mistreatment by Great Britain and France. Madison's diplomatic notes were able presentations of the legal arguments against the British orders in council and the French imperial decrees, but their ineffectiveness was aptly summed up by John Randolph when he characterized one of Madison's treatises as "a shilling pamphlet hurled against eight hundred ships of war." American exasperation was guided by President Jefferson and Madison into the ineffectual Embargo Act, Dec. 22, 1807, which closed American ports and forbade American ships to go to sea. When this measure was repealed, Mar. 1, 1809, administration proposals for a war against both Great Britain and France were defeated in Congress.

Jefferson had chosen Madison as his successor to the presidency. There was little opposition to the choice, and Madison entered upon his new duties, Mar. 4, 1809. Observers at the inauguration noted that he appeared careworn, aging, spiritless, and exhausted. He was to have in the presidency eight difficult years and considerable tragedy. Necessary changes in the cabinet added strength to the faction that had opposed him from his entrance into the administration. Foreign relations steadily grew worse. After holding out a promise to trade with whichever belligerent would repeal its obnoxious measures, Congress, in May 1810, resolved to trade with both; it authorized the president, if either France or Great Britain should reform its practices, to revive nonintercourse against the other. On the strength of what appeared to be an assurance from Napoleon that the objectionable decrees were revoked insofar as they affected the United States, Madison, on Nov. 2, 1810, naively issued a proclamation of nonintercourse against Great Britain. This error was not the only cause of war in 1812. Indian outbreaks in the Ohio Valley were ascribed to British intrigues; the West raised a cry that the British must be driven from Canada and their Spanish allies from Florida. Pressure for war was at its height, November 1811 to June 1812. In his message of Nov. 5, 1811, Madison had warned Congress of the danger and had counseled preparations; in a special message of June 1, 1812, he advised a declaration of war against Great Britain, assigning as principal causes the impressment of American seamen, interference with American trade, and the incitement of the Indians to border hostilities. Acting upon the president's advice in the June message, Congress declared war on June 18. Congress had neglected to follow Madison's previous counsel to put the United States into a state of preparation, however, and the president, despite his many admirable qualities, was not the man to lead his country through such an ordeal. Six months of failure ensued before the War and Navy departments were cleared of incompetent executives; another year went by before men of talent in the army found their way to the top. Federalists opposed the war; northern Democratic-Republicans and Madison's personal enemies within his own party thwarted the administration's efforts to seize what remained of the Floridas. Southerners, including James Monroe the secretary of state, felt little enthusiasm for the conquest of Canada and the creation of more northern states.

The war along the Canadian border was mismanaged until the summer of 1814, and by the time the army became competent, it was too late for victory. Great Britain had disposed of Napoleon and could give the United States its undivided attention. Moreover, a few weeks after the declaration of war, it was learned that Great Britain had in fact repealed the orders in council; the war might have been halted then, in August 1812, had the war spirit in the West been less powerful. An offer of the British government to negotiate directly with the United States led in time to negotiations at Ghent from August to December 1814, and a treaty of peace was signed, Dec. 24, 1814, on the basis of the surrender of occupied territory only. Thus, not a single declared aim of the war was attained; indeed the city of Washington had been captured and the president and his family forced to flee to the woods. Victories during the closing months of the conflict, however, at Plattsburg, N.Y., and Fort Erie and in particular at

New Orleans, gave an illusion of glory and sent "Mr. Madison's War" down to posterity in school histories as an American triumph. The Hartford Convention held by the New England Federalists in the closing months of the war weighed heavily upon Madison, who regarded it properly as a gesture of sedition. The end of the war marked the end of the Federalists as a party, but many of their principles were adopted by the Democratic-Republicans. Madison shared partially in this conversion. He signed a bill providing for a new Bank of the United States and also the Tariff Act of 1816; he also approved measures strengthening the permanent military and naval establishments. His retirement from the presidency, Mar. 4, 1817, brought his political career to a close except for his share in the Virginia Constitutional Convention, 1829. He supported Thomas Jefferson in the founding of the University of Virginia, of which he became rector after Jefferson's death, 1826. He was interested in the work of the American Colonization Society as a solution to the problem of blacks. During the controversy over nullification, he denied the validity of those doctrines and of the doctrine of peaceful secession, maintaining the general beneficence of the Constitution and the Union which he had done so much to create. As the years went by, he was under the necessity of reducing his scale of living and selling part of his farm because of straitened circumstances. The most important work of his later years was the arrangement and preparation for publication of his notes on the Convention of 1787.

A small man, Madison was never impressive in appearance. A poor public speaker, he was a delightful conversationalist. His work as architect of the U.S. Constitution overshadowed in importance and success his labors as secretary of state and president. A note entitled "Advice to My Country," which was found among his papers after his death concluded as follows; "The advice nearest to my heart and deepest in my convictions is, that the Union of the states be cherished and perpetuated. Let the open enemy of it be regarded as a Pandora with her box opened, and the disguised one as the serpent creeping with his deadly wiles into paradise."

MAEDAR, CLARA FISHER.   *See* FISHER, CLARA.

MAES, CAMILLUS PAUL (*b. Courtrai, Belgium, 1846; d. 1915*), Roman Catholic clergyman. Went to America, 1869; worked as missionary and pastor in Michigan. Consecrated bishop of Covington, Ky., 1885, he was active in promoting the American College at Louvain, and Catholic University at Washington, D.C.

MAFFITT, DAVID (*d. Philadelphia, Pa., 1838*), privateersman in the War of 1812, commanding schooner *Atlas* and brig *Rattlesnake*.

MAFFITT, JOHN NEWLAND (*b. at sea, between Dublin and New York, 1819; d. near Wilmington, N.C., 1886*), naval officer. Appointed midshipman, 1832; served on detached duty with Coast Survey, 1842–58. Resigning from U.S. Navy, 1861, he was commissioned lieutenant in the Confederate navy and performed with brilliance as commander of combat ships and in blockade-running. Among his principal exploits were his 1862 run of the cruiser *Florida* from Nassau to Mobile, and his final trip in the blockade-runner *Owl* , 1865, in which he sought harbor for his cargo all the way from Wilmington to Galveston.

MAGEE, CHRISTOPHER LYMAN (*b. Pittsburgh, Pa., 1848; d. 1901*), politician, political agent for Pennsylvania Railroad and other business interests. Controlled the politics of Pittsburgh and Allegheny Co. with scarcely a break, 1882–99; *post* 1876, he sat as a delegate in every Republican National Convention.

MAGIE, WILLIAM JAY (*b. Elizabeth, N.J., 1832; d. Elizabeth, 1917*), lawyer, New Jersey legislator and jurist. Justice of the state supreme court, 1880–97; chief justice, 1897–1900. New Jersey chancellor, 1900–08.

MAGILL, EDWARD HICKS (*b. Bucks Co., Pa., 1825; d. New York, N.Y., 1907*), educator. Graduated Brown, 1852. President of Swarthmore College, 1871–89. His administration of Swarthmore as a coeducational institution was successful and constitutes his chief service. He founded, 1887, the College Association of Pennsylvania which in time became the Association of Colleges and Preparatory Schools of the Middle States and Maryland.

MAGINNIS, CHARLES DONAGH (*b. Londonderry, Ireland, 1867; d. Boston, Mass., 1955*), architect. Immigrated to the U.S. in 1888. Self-educated, he became a member of the Boston firm of Maginnis and Walsh in 1908 (Maginnis, Walsh, and Kennedy in 1954). Maginnis was a typical late Victorian eclectic architect whose buildings reflected the historical styles of the past. He was awarded medals for his church designs by the American Institute of Architects in 1925 and 1927. He became president of the Institute from 1937 to 1939. Maginnis considered the spread of modern architecture to be the spread of universal monotony and remained outside of the mainstream of twentieth-century architecture.

MAGINNIS, MARTIN (*b. Wayne Co., N.Y., 1841; d. Los Angeles, Calif., 1919*), Union soldier, Montana politician and Democratic congressman.

MAGNES, JUDAH LEON (*b. San Francisco, Calif., 1877; d. New York, N.Y., 1948*), rabbi, communal leader, educator. B.A., University of Cincinnati, 1898; attended Hebrew Union College concurrently, and was ordained a Reform rabbi, 1900. Ph.D. in Semitics and philosophy, University of Heidelberg, 1902; also studied at the Lehrenstalt in Berlin. Committed to the advancement of Jewish culture and to Zionism as a cultural force, he sought to bring together in community the divergent and often antagonistic elements among the Jewish Americans of his time; to this end, he directed the negotiations which led to the establishment of the Kehillah of New York City (a structure for coordinating and improving Jewish philanthropic, religious, and educational services) and was its leader, 1908–22. Meanwhile, he served as minister to congregations in New York City, 1904–*ca.* 1912, leaving the active rabbinate on a point of principle; to him, principle had always to be placed above institutional interest or political gain. He left with his family for Palestine, 1922. Elected chancellor of the Hebrew University in Jerusalem on its opening, 1925, he served until 1935, when he was elected its first president; under his administration, the university developed into a major academic center. He spoke and wrote in support of the establishment of a binational state in Palestine in which the essential interests of both Jews and Arabs would be guaranteed (a far from popular position with either party), later opposing partition and urging a United Nations trusteeship. On establishment of the state of Israel, he drafted a plea calling for a confederation of sovereign Jewish and Arab states in Palestine. He died in the midst of efforts to rally support for this position. Guided in his work by religious and social precepts which drew on Jewish sources and on the American experience, he was honored for his integrity and candor even by those who opposed him.

MAGOFFIN, BERIAH (*b. Harrodsburg, Ky., 1815; d. Harrodsburg, 1885*), lawyer, farmer. Active in Kentucky Democratic politics *post* 1839; elected governor of Kentucky, 1859. Taking office on the eve of secession Magoffin did what he could to prevent Democratic disruption at the Charleston Convention; he then favored the Crittenden Compromise. He refused Lincoln's call for troops, Apr. 15, 1861, and a week later refused Davis' call for troops, though he secretly permitted Confederate recruiting in Kentucky. After the state's proclaimed neutrality was broken many times by both sides, the Confederates invaded Kentucky; Magoffin vetoed a resolution of the legislature calling upon him to order the Confederates out. His subsequent opposition to the predominant Union sentiment of the state resulted in his loss of power and resignation August 1862. His advocacy after the Civil War of Kentucky's ratification of the Thirteenth Amendment and the granting of civil rights to blacks lost him the friendship of many Democrats.

MAGOFFIN, JAMES WILEY (*b. Harrodsburg, Ky., 1799; d. San Antonio, Tex., 1868*), trader, Texas pioneer. Brother of Beriah Magoffin. Traded extensively with Mexico, where he resided, 1825–44; by clever diplomacy, assisted U.S. Army capture of Santa Fe, August 1846; resided in Texas *post* 1847.

MAGONIGLE, HAROLD VAN BUREN (*b. Bergen Heights, N.J., 1867; d. Vergennes, Vt., 1935*), architect, sculptor, critic. Studied in offices of Calvert Vaux, Charles C. Haight, and McKim, Mead & White. Celebrated for design of a series of important memorials beginning with the McKinley Memorial, 1904, and climaxing in the Liberty War Memorial, Kansas City, Mo., 1923. He also designed a great deal of important residential work.

MAGOON, CHARLES EDWARD (*b. Steele Co., Minn., 1861; d. Washington, D.C., 1920*), lawyer. After outstanding service as a law officer of the War Department, 1899–1904, Magoon served on the Isthmian Canal Commission, as governor of the Canal Zone, 1905–06, and as provisional governor of Cuba, 1906–09. In all his assignments he was noted for his tact and ability to handle complicated economic problems.

MAGOUN, GEORGE FREDERIC (*b. Bath, Maine, 1821; d. 1896*), Congregational clergyman, educator. Graduated Bowdoin, 1841. President of Iowa (Grinnell) College, 1862–84.

MAGRATH, ANDREW GORDON (*b. Charleston, S.C., 1813; d. Charleston, 1893*), jurist. Graduated South Carolina College, 1831; studied law in office of James L. Petigru. As judge, U.S. district court, 1856–60, he raised that court from a position of disfavor in the state to one of distinction. He opposed secession as inexpedient when advocated by R. B. Rhett, 1852; but on Lincoln's election he accepted the view that there were sufficient grounds for separation and that the welfare of South Carolina required its secession. During service as South Carolina secretary of state, 1860–61, he directed much of the official correspondence over disposition of Fort Sumter. Some of his decisions as judge of the Confederate district courts in South Carolina, 1861–64, ran counter to the policy of the Richmond government and lost him its favor. Chosen governor of South Carolina by the legislature, 1864, he took an extreme states' rights position within the Confederacy. Arrested in May 1865, he was imprisoned for a short time; on his release, he resumed the practice of law.

MAGRUDER, GEORGE LLOYD (*b. Washington, D.C., 1848; d. Washington, 1914*), physician. Graduated Gonzaga College, 1868; M.D., Georgetown, 1870. Professor, dean, and treasurer of Georgetown Medical School *post* 1871. Magruder was a strong influence in promoting sanitary conditions in Washington, in particular, a pure water supply and effective regulation of the sale of milk.

MAGRUDER, JOHN BANKHEAD (*b. Winchester, Va., 1810; d. Houston, Tex., 1871*), soldier. Graduated West Point, 1830. Served in occupation of Texas and in Seminole War; in Mexican War, commanded light artillery of Pillow's division. Nicknamed

"Prince John" for his devotion to society. Magruder resigned his commission, March 1861, to accept appointment as colonel in the Confederate army. His handling of troops on the Virginia Peninsula up to the spring of 1862 won him promotion to major general; his failures during the Seven Days' Battles around Richmond seriously hampered Lee's operations against McClellan. Transferred to command of the district of Texas, October 1862, he was reasonably successful in small operations. At the close of hostilities, refusing to seek parole, Magruder went to Mexico and became a major general under Maximilian.

MAGRUDER, JULIA (b. Charlottesville, Va., 1854; d. Richmond, Va., 1907), novelist, short-story writer. Niece of John B. Magruder.

MAGUIRE, CHARLES BONAVENTURE. See McGUIRE, CHARLES BONAVENTURE.

MAHAN, ALFRED THAYER (b. West Point, N.Y., 1840; d. Washington, D.C., 1914), naval officer, historian. Son of Dennis H. Mahan. Graduated U.S. Naval Academy, 1859. After Civil War service mainly on blockade duty, Mahan followed a routine of sea and shore duty until 1885 when he was promoted captain. Appointed lecturer on tactics and naval history of the newly established Naval War College, Newport, R.I., he delivered his first lectures in the autumn of 1886. Succeeding Admiral Luce as president, 1886–89, he supported the college against the hostility of the secretary of the navy and the indifference of the service itself. He published his lectures in 1890 as *The Influence of Sea Power upon History, 1660–1783*. The book won immediate recognition, far greater in Europe than in America, and with its successor, *The Influence of Sea Power Upon the French Revolution and Empire, 1793–1812* (1892), made him world famous. Mahan's power of generalization and his ability to subordinate details to the central theme and to indicate the significance of events for later times made him the first "philosopher of sea power." He served a second term as president of the Naval War College, 1892–93, and retired, 1896. He returned to duty, 1898, to serve as a member of the strategy board directing naval operations in the Spanish-American War. Mahan wrote a number of other books, among them his memoirs, *From Sail to Steam* (1907). Few other historians have so widely influenced the policies of their own time as did Mahan; however, there will always be a question as to how much his success was due to the value of his books as propaganda for naval expansion already under way in Great Britain, Germany, and the United States.

MAHAN, ASA (b. Vernon, N.Y., 1799; d. Eastbourne, England, 1889), Congregational clergyman. Graduated Hamilton, 1824; Andover Theological Seminary, 1827. First president of Oberlin College, 1835–50, he required that the college receive students without discrimination as to color or sex. He served also as president of Adrian College, 1860–71.

MAHAN, DENNIS HART (b. New York, N.Y., 1802; d. by drowning in Hudson River, 1871), soldier, educator. Half brother of Milo Mahan; father of Alfred T. Mahan. Graduated West Point, 1824; studied also in French army engineering school, Metz. Associated almost all his life with West Point as professor of civil and military engineering, Mahan was best known as the author of pioneering textbooks on fortification, outpost duty, and general engineering.

MAHAN, MILO (b. Suffolk, Va., 1819; d. Baltimore, Md., 1870), Episcopal clergyman, educator. Half brother of Dennis H. Mahan. Professor of ecclesiastical history, General Theological Seminary, New York, 1851–64; thereafter, rector, St. Paul's Church, Baltimore. Author of church histories.

MAHLER, HERBERT (b. Chatham, Ontario, Canada, 1890; d. New York, N.Y., 1961), labor organizer and radical. Immigrated to the state of Washington in 1915. Joined the Industrial Workers of the World (IWW) in 1915; secretary and organizer for several IWW locals in the Seattle area, 1916–17. Secretary-treasurer of the IWW's Everett Defense Committee, which assisted a large group of "Wobblies" accused of murder in the Everett, Wash., "massacre" in 1916. Participated in IWW lumber and copper strikes that tied up the production of vital war supplies during World War I. Convicted of espionage and sedition and sentenced to twelve years in prison in 1918. President Coolidge commuted his sentence in 1923. Returned to the IWW in 1923, working out of Chicago; named secretary of the General Defense Committee and then general secretary-treasurer (1931–32). Organized the Kentucky Mines Defense Committee (1937) on behalf of four union coal miners serving life sentences for murder.

MAHONE, WILLIAM (b. Southampton Co., Va., 1826; d. Washington, D.C., 1895), railroad executive, Confederate major general, politician. Graduated Virginia Military Institute, 1847. President of the Norfolk-Petersburg Railroad. At the outbreak of the Civil War, Mahone proved himself an able field commander and capable administrator; he was particularly distinguished during July 1864 in the Wilderness and at the Crater. Following the war he organized the lines which later became the Norfolk and Western Railroad and developed a strong following in the state legislature. In 1879, he organized and led the "Readjusters," who advocated a partial repudiation of the state's debt and popular social and economic legislation. Frowned on by the regular party machines and by the wealthy, this movement swept the state, 1879 and 1881. Elected to the U.S. Senate, 1880, Mahone traded his vote for offices and committee assignments, thereby angering the Democrats. By his control of state and federal patronage, he built a political machine which thereafter dominated the Republican party in Virginia, of which he was absolute boss.

MAHONEY, JOHN FRIEND (b. Fond du Lac, Wis., 1889; d. Staten Island, N.Y., 1957), physician, public health official. Studied at Milwaukee University and Marquette Medical College (M.D., 1914). A commissioned officer in the U.S Public Health Service (1917–49); director of the Venereal Disease Research Laboratory in Staten Island, N.Y., from 1929 to 1949. After spending years trying to improve the testing for and treatment of syphilis, Mahoney was one of the first to discover and research the cure for the disease with penicillin in 1943. From 1949 until his death, he was director of the Bureau of Laboratories for the New York City Health Department. From 1949 to 1954, he was New York City Health Commissioner.

MAIER, WALTER ARTHUR (b. Boston, Mass., 1893; d. St. Louis, Mo., 1950), Lutheran clergyman. A member of the Missouri Synod. B.A., Boston University, 1913. Graduated Concordia Theological Seminary (St. Louis), 1916; ordained, 1917. M.A., Harvard, 1920; Ph.D., 1929. Edited the Walther League's *Messenger*, 1920–45; professor of Old Testament interpretation and history, Concordia Theological Seminary, 1922–44; regular preacher on the radio "Lutheran Hour," 1930–31 and *post* 1935. Influential in shifting missionary orientation of the Missouri Synod from German immigrants to native-born Americans.

MAILLY, WILLIAM (b. Pittsburgh, Pa., 1871; d. 1912), journalist, Socialist. National secretary, Socialist party, 1903–05.

MAIN, CHARLES THOMAS (b. Marblehead, Mass., 1856; d. Winchester, Mass., 1943), mechanical engineer. Specialist in design and construction of textile mills and hydroelectric plants.

MAIN, JOHN HANSON THOMAS (b. Toledo, Ohio, 1859; d. 1931), educator. Ph.D., Johns Hopkins, 1892. Taught Greek in

Iowa (Grinnell) College; served as acting president, 1900–02, as dean, 1902–06, and as president of Grinnell, 1906–31.

MAISCH, JOHN MICHAEL (*b. Hanau, Germany, 1831; d. 1893*), pharmacist. Came to America *ca.* 1850. Able manager of U.S. Army Laboratory, 1863–65; professor, Philadelphia College of Pharmacy, 1866–93, eventually becoming dean. Editor, *American Journal of Pharmacy,* 1871–93, and author of *A Manual of Organic Materia Medica* (1882).

MAJOR, CHARLES (*b. Indianapolis, Ind., 1856; d. 1913*), popular novelist, lawyer. Author of, among other books, the best-selling *When Knighthood Was in Flower* (1898) and *Dorothy Vernon of Haddon Hall* (1902).

MAJORS, ALEXANDER (*b. near Franklin, Ky., 1814; d. Chicago, Ill., 1900*), freight–line operator, promoter of the Pony Express. Raised in Missouri, Majors began freighting from Independence, Mo., to Santa Fe., N.Mex., 1848; *ca.* 1855, he entered partnership with William H. Russell; in 1858, the partnership became Russell, Majors & Waddell. The firm took over operation of a daily stagecoach line from Fort Leavenworth to Denver, 1859, afterward including in their schedules Atchison, Kans., Salt Lake City, Fort Kearney, and Fort Laramie. On Apr. 3, 1860, they established the famous Pony Express, which lasted only 18 months and was a financial failure. The firm itself failed in 1861.

MA-KA-TAI-ME-SHE-KIA-KIAK. *See* BLACK HAWK.

MAKEMIE, FRANCIS (*b. near Ramelton, Ireland, ca. 1658; d. 1708*), Presbyterian clergyman, regarded as chief founder of the Presbyterian Church in America. Arriving in Maryland, 1683, Makemie worked as an evangelist there and in North Carolina, Virginia, and Barbados. Settling in Virginia, 1698, he secured a license to preach and thus became the first dissenting minister licensed under the Toleration Act; he labored as well in Maryland. In 1706, Makemie united with two young ministers who had come to Maryland through his agency, along with four others, to form the first American presbytery. He was arrested in January 1707 and imprisoned six weeks for preaching in the colony of New York without a license. His vigorous defense of himself brought about legislation which made another such persecution impossible in New York.

MALBONE, EDWARD GREENE (*b. Newport, R.I., 1777; d. Savannah, Ga., 1807*), painter of miniatures. Self-taught, Malbone began business in Providence, R.I., 1794; his earliest work shows the use of fine stipple for modeling the face and scrupulous regard to detail in finish, costume, and background painting. His success in Providence was followed by continuing success in Boston, 1796–98, and at New York and Philadelphia, 1798–99. In the autumn of 1800 he went to Charleston, S.C. His technique by this time had changed from a stiff, detailed style to a freer method in which delicate interwoven lines of color performed the double function of creating form as well as providing color. He visited London, 1801 where his work won the praise of Benjamin West. A third style becomes recognizable in his painting on his return to Charleston in December 1801; the same delicate lines of color are used in painting the face, but the stroke is even freer and somewhat broader. Malbone spent most of the years 1804 and 1805 in Boston, returning once more to Charleston in December 1805; during the following March, he contracted tuberculosis and was forced to give up painting. His genius as a technician is undisputed; his continual and thoughtful experimentation is one of his chief claims to superiority over other miniature painters.

MALCOLM, DANIEL (*b. Georgetown, Maine, 1725; d. Boston, Mass., 1769*), Revolutionary patriot, merchant, sea captain. A leader in Boston of overt defiance of British trade regulations, 1766–68.

MALCOLM, JAMES PELLER (*b. Philadelphia, Pa., 1767; d. England, 1815*), engraver, author, Loyalist. Removing to England *ca.* 1787, Malcolm became an engraver of illustrative plates for magazines and an industrious compiler of books on antiquarian subjects.

MALCOLM X (*b. Malcolm Little, Omaha, Nebr., 1925; d. New York, N.Y., 1965*), black leader. Known as Malcolm X from 1952; El-Hajj Malik El-Shabazz from 1964. Began a process of self-education while imprisoned for burglary, 1946–52; converted to the Lost-Found Nation of Islam (known as the Black Muslims). An effective recruiter for the Nation of Islam from 1952; assistant minister of Detroit's Temple Number One, 1953–54. Brilliant oratorical skill and organizational ability led to his appointment as minister of Harlem's Temple Number Seven in 1954; the rise in popularity of Malcolm X through the 1950's brought the movement national attention. Differences between integrationist groups such as the National Association for the Advancement of Colored People and the separatist, nationalistic Muslims were quickly manifested in the climate of the emerging civil rights movement. Dissatisfied with the Muslim policy of "general nonengagement" from active involvement in confronting racism, Malcolm X cited "internal differences within the Nation of Islam" and left the movement in 1964, departing to tour the Middle East and Africa. While there, meetings with Islamic practitioners who appeared to be without racial prejudice prompted him to moderate his extremist views. Upon returning to the United States, he formed the Organization of Afro-American Unity (1964), accepted the idea of interracial brotherhood, and envisioned the possibility of cooperation with progressive white organizations. Assassinated at the Audubon Ballroom in Harlem.

MALCOM, DANIEL. *See* MALCOLM, DANIEL.

MALCOM, HOWARD (*b. Philadelphia, Pa., 1799; d. Philadelphia, 1879*), Baptist clergyman, educator. President of Georgetown (Kentucky) College, 1840–49; of Lewisburg (Bucknell) University, 1851–57; of Hahnemann Medical College, 1874–79. Author of a number of books, including the popular *Dictionary of Important Names, Objects and Terms Found in the Holy Scriptures* (1830).

MALCOM, JAMES PELLER. *See* MALCOLM, JAMES PELLER.

MALIN, PATRICK MURPHY (*b. Joplin, Mo., 1903; d. New York, N.Y., 1964*), teacher, administrator, and civil libertarian. Studied at the University of Pennsylvania (graduated, 1924). With the International Young Men's Christian Association (1924–29). Professor of economics, Swarthmore College (1930–40). Member of the National Council on Religion in Higher Education (from 1925); director (1937–43); president (1939–43). Vice-chairman of the American Friends Service Committee (1936–38), and director of the International Migration Service (1940–42). With the Franklin Delano Roosevelt administration from 1942, in various posts including director of the Export-Import Price Control Office in the Office of Price Administration. Member of the American Civil Liberties Union from 1920; executive director, 1950–62. President of American-operated Robert College in Istanbul, Turkey, 1962–64.

MALL, FRANKLIN PAINE (*b. near Belle Plaine, Iowa, 1862; d. Baltimore, Md., 1917*), anatomist, embryologist. M.D., University of Michigan, 1883; made further studies at Heidelberg and Leipzig. Fellow in pathology and later instructor at Johns Hopkins Hospital, Mall taught anatomy at Clark University, 1889–92. After a brief service in the new University of Chicago as professor of anatomy, he returned to Baltimore as head of the Department of Anatomy, Johns Hopkins Medical School. He was appointed, in addition, director of the Department of Embryology of the Carnegie Institution, Washington, 1914. Mall vitalized the study of anatomy in America. In medical education, he stood for freedom of curriculum, concentration of courses, broad electives; his anatomy department at Johns Hopkins was the first to bring into one discipline cytology, histology, embryology, and adult structure. His own researches were numerous and important; he first traced the embryologic origin of the thymus gland, added to knowledge of the structure and function of the intestines, introduced the idea of histological units in organs, and worked out the muscular system of the heart.

MALLARY, ROLLIN CAROLAS (*b. Cheshire, Conn., 1784; d. Baltimore, Md., 1831*), lawyer. Congressman from Vermont, 1820–31. As chairman, House Committee on Manufactures, he reported Tariff of Abominations, 1828, and was largely responsible for its passage.

MALLERY, GARRICK (*b. Wilkes-Barre, Pa., 1831; d. 1894*), lawyer, Union soldier, ethnologist. On staff of Bureau of Ethnology, 1879–94, Mallery wrote notable papers on Indian pictography and sign language.

MALLET, JOHN WILLIAM (*b. near Dublin, Ireland, 1832; d. Virginia, 1912*), chemist. Highly trained in Ireland and Germany, Mallet came to America, 1853. He was professor of chemistry, Alabama University, 1855–60, and made an exhaustive scientific study of cotton culture (published 1862). After serving as general superintendent of Confederate ordnance laboratories, 1862–65, he returned to teaching, retiring as professor emeritus, University of Virginia, 1908.

MALLINCKRODT, EDWARD (*b. near St. Louis, Mo., 1845; d. St. Louis, 1928*), chemical manufacturer, philanthropist.

MALLINCKRODT, EDWARD, JR. (*b. St. Louis, Mo., 1878; d. St. Louis, 1967*), chemist, chemical manufacturer, and philanthropist. Son of Edward Mallinckrodt, owner of Mallinckrodt Chemical Works, founded in 1867. Studied at Harvard University (M.A., 1901). In charge of technical activities at Mallinckrodt Chemical Works from 1901; chairman of the board, 1928–65; honorary chairman, 1965–67. Research in ether as an anesthetic led to his development of the first continuous distillation equipment for the production of ether. Mallinckrodt Chemical processed uranium from 1942, including that used in the first self-sustaining nuclear reaction; produced nuclear fuels for military use and power plants (to 1961). By 1966, the company was producing sales of $59 million and earnings of $3.6 million. Mallinckrodt made generous gifts to education and medicine totaling millions of dollars, including an endowment to establish the Mallinckrodt Institute of Radiology in St. Louis.

MALLORY, ANNA MARGRETHE ("MOLLA") BJURSTEDT (*b. Norway, 1892; d. Stockholm, Sweden, 1959*), tennis player. Immigrated to the U.S. in 1914. Mallory won seven national outdoor singles titles, five national indoor singles titles, one national indoor doubles title, two national outdoor doubles titles, and three national outdoor mixed doubles titles. She was also named to the U.S. Wightman Cup team for five years, was the number-one ranked woman player for seven years, and from 1915 to 1927, was one of the three top-ranked U.S. competitors.

MALLORY, CLIFFORD DAY (*b. Brooklyn, N.Y., 1881; d. Miami Beach, Fla., 1941*), shipping executive, yachtsman. Associated with several family shipping concerns until World War I, when he served as assistant to the director of the U.S. Shipping Board; founded C. D. Mallory and Co., 1919, which became the largest and most successful independent shipping house under the American flag.

MALLORY, FRANK BURR (*b. Cleveland, Ohio, 1862; d. Brookline, Mass., 1941*), pathologist. B.A., Harvard, 1886; M.D., Harvard Medical School, 1890. Appointed assistant in the department of pathology at Harvard Medical School and at Boston City Hospital, 1891, he remained at both institutions until retirement in 1932; he became associate professor at the medical school in 1901, and full professor in 1928. A leader of histologic pathology and pathologic techniques in the United States, 1900–30, he developed many of the differential tissue stains now widely used and laid the foundations for the development of histochemistry as related to pathologic states; he took a special interest in classification of human cancers, in tropical diseases, and in liver disease. Author of *Pathological Technique* (1897, with J. H. Wright) and *The Principles of Pathologic Histology* (1914), he was also for many years editor of the *American Journal of Pathology*.

MALLORY, STEPHEN RUSSELL (*b. Trinidad, ca. 1813; d. Pensacola, Fla., 1873*), lawyer. Raised in Florida, where he practiced law from *ca.* 1840. As U.S. senator, Democrat, from Florida, 1851–60, he was active in congressional naval reform; in February 1861, he was named Confederate secretary of the navy. Vehement and forceful, Mallory employed the talents of John M. Brooke and others so well that the Confederacy, which started without ships or yards, was able to prevent penetration of the Virginia rivers by the Union navy; also, he encouraged development of torpedoes and submarines. He failed, however, in his efforts to build up a sizable ironclad fleet. After the war and a brief imprisonment, he resumed his law practice.

MALONE, DUDLEY FIELD (*b. New York, N.Y., 1882; d. Culver City, Calif., 1950*), lawyer, politician. Beginning his career as an anti–Tammany Hall Democrat, he helped organize Woodrow Wilson's presidential primary campaigns, 1912. After a brief period as an assistant secretary of state, he served as collector of the Port of New York, 1913–17, and tried to use the patronage of his office to oust Tammany from control of the Democratic party in New York. Parting company with Wilson in 1917, allegedly over the administration's disregard for civil liberties, he pursued an increasingly erratic political course and became more of a colorful personality than a force.

MALONE, SYLVESTER (*b. Trim, Ireland, 1821; d. Brooklyn, N.Y., 1899*), Roman Catholic clergyman. Came to America, 1839; ordained, New York, 1844. An outstanding Williamsburg (Brooklyn), N.Y., pastor, he was a Republican and a strong Civil War Unionist. Later a prolabor liberal and civic reformer, he served as a regent of the University of the State of New York, 1894–99.

MALONE, WALTER (*b. DeSoto Co. Miss., 1866; d. Memphis, Tenn., 1915*), Tennessee circuit court judge, poet. Wrote *Songs of North and South* (1900) and epic *Hernando De Soto* (1914).

MALONEY, MARTIN (*b. near Thurles, Ireland, 1847; d. Spring Lake, N.J., 1929*), industrialist, public utilities operator, philanthropist.

MALTER, HENRY (*b. near Sabno, Galicia, Austria, 1864; d. 1925*), scholar, teacher. Graduated Heidelberg, Ph.D., 1894; studied also at Berlin and made special rabbinical studies. Came to America, 1900. Professor of Jewish philosophy and Oriental languages, Hebrew Union College, Cincinnati, Ohio, 1900–07; professor of rabbinical language and literature, Dropsie College, Philadelphia, Pa., 1909–25. Author of, among other works,

Saadia Gaon (1921); projected a method for creation of a critical text of the Talmud.

MANATT, JAMES IRVING (*b. Millersburg, Ohio, 1845; d. Providence, R.I., 1915*), classicist. Professor of Greek literature and history, Brown, 1893–1915. Coauthor of *The Mycenaean Age* (1897).

MANDERSON, CHARLES FREDERICK (*b. Philadelphia, Pa., 1837; d. at sea, returning to America, 1911*), lawyer, Union soldier. Practiced law first in Canton, Ohio, and *post* 1869 in Omaha, Nebr. As U.S. senator, Republican, from Nebraska, 1883–95, advocated nationally built highways; on leaving office, became general solicitor for Burlington Railroad.

MANEY, GEORGE EARL (*b. Franklin, Tenn., 1826; d. Washington, D.C., 1901*), lawyer, Confederate brigadier general, diplomat. U.S. minister resident to Columbia, 1881–82; to Bolivia, 1882–89; to Paraguay, 1889–90. He served thereafter until 1894 in Paraguay with rank of envoy extraordinary and minister plenipotentiary.

MANGIN, JOSEPH FRANÇOIS (*fl. 1794–1818*), engineer, architect. Came to New York from France at an undetermined date, possibly as a refugee from the Revolution; served *post* 1795 as chief engineer of New York fortifications and as one of the city's surveyors, in which capacity he produced the official city map (published 1803). He is best known for his connection with the New York City Hall; his share in the design of this work is still a matter of controversy. His only other known important work was the design for the first St. Patrick's Cathedral, Mott Street (built 1809–15).

MANGUM, WILLIE PERSON (*b. Orange, now Durham, Co., N.C., 1792; d. 1861*), lawyer, jurist. Congressman, Democrat, from North Carolina, 1823–27; U.S. senator, Democrat, 1831–35. Breaking with Andrew Jackson over the force bill and the removal of federal deposits from the Bank of the United States, Mangum subsequently identified himself with the Whig party and served again in the U.S. Senate as a Whig, 1841–53. As president pro tempore of the Senate, May 1842–March 1845, he served as acting vice-president of the United States. An astute politician and effective debater, he was known for his power as a campaign speaker; owing in part to his urging, Daniel Webster made his celebrated Mar. 7 speech.

MANIGAULT, ARTHUR MIDDLETON (*b. Charleston, S.C., 1824; d. Georgetown Co., S.C., 1886*), soldier, merchant, planter. Descendant of Pierre Manigault. Served in Mexican War. In Confederate service, 1861–64, he was mainly with the armies in the West and was promoted brigadier general, April 1863.

MANIGAULT, GABRIEL (*b. Charleston, S.C., 1704; d. Charleston, 1781*), merchant, planter, Revolutionary patriot, South Carolina legislator. Son of Pierre Manigault.

MANIGAULT, PETER (*b. Charleston, S.C., 1731; d. London, England, 1773*), lawyer. Son of Gabriel Manigault. Studied law at the Inner Temple; was called to the English bar, 1754. In practice at Charleston, 1754–73, he served as a member of the South Carolina Assembly, 1755–72. During the last seven years of his membership, he was Speaker.

MANIGAULT, PIERRE (*b. La Rochelle, France, date unknown; d. Charleston, S.C., 1729*), merchant. Removed to Charleston from London, England, *ca.* 1695. Starting as a brandy distiller, he branched out into general trade and died wealthy.

MANKIEWICZ, HERMAN JACOB (*b. New York, N.Y., 1897; d. Los Angeles, Calif., 1953*), newspaperman, playwright, screenwriter. Graduated Columbia (1917). Reporter for the *New York Times* in the 1920's, Mankiewicz wrote several unsuccessful plays and was a member of the Algonquin Round Table. He went to Hollywood in 1925, where he wrote the scripts for the Marx Brothers films *Monkey Business* and *Horse Feathers*, as well as the adaptation of *Dinner at Eight*. His most famous film was *Citizen Kane* (1941), written with Orson Welles, which won Mankiewicz the Academy Award for screenwriting. Other films include *Pride of the Yankees* and *Pride of St. Louis*.

MANLEY, JOHN (*b. probably Boston, Mass., ca. 1734; d. Boston, 1793*), naval officer. Commanding schooner *Lee*, he captured in November 1775 the first valuable prize taken by Americans in the Revolutionary War, the brigantine *Nancy*, laden with a cargo of military stores. Appointed captain, Continental navy, April 1776, Manley was made prisoner aboard frigate *Hancock*; exchanged, March 1778, he commanded successful privateers, was twice captured and exchanged, and in 1783 (again a naval officer, commanding the frigate *Hague*) took the last valuable prize to be taken by a Continental ship.

MANLEY, JOSEPH HOMAN (*b. Bangor, Maine, 1842; d. 1905*), lawyer, journalist, Maine legislator. Editor and half-owner of the *Maine Farmer* from 1878. Chairman, Republican National Committee, 1896–1904. James G. Blaine's closest political friend.

MANLY, BASIL (*b. near Pittsboro, N.C., 1798; d. Greenville, S.C., 1868*), Baptist clergyman, educator. Held pastorates in South Carolina, principally in Charleston; helped found Furman University; president, University of Alabama, 1837–55. As pastor in Montgomery, Ala., he delivered prayer at inauguration of Jefferson Davis, February 1861.

MANLY, BASIL (*b. Edgefield District, S.C., 1825; d. Louisville, Ky., 1892*), Baptist clergyman, educator. Son of Basil Manly (1798–1868). Held numerous pastorates; helped organize Southern Baptist Theological Seminary, Greenville, S.C., 1859, and served it as professor at various times, 1859–92.

MANLY, BASIL MAXWELL (*b. Greenville, S.C., 1886; d. Washington, D.C., 1950*), government official, publicist. Grandson of Basil Manly (1798–1868); brother of Charles M. Manly and John M. Manly. B.A., Washington and Lee University, 1906. Engaged for most of his career in federal government work, and a Wilson–La Follette–New Deal liberal in personal views, he was author of the "Manly Report" of the U.S. Commission on Industrial Relations (1913–15) and of the report (1918) of the Federal Trade Commission's investigation of the meatpacking industry. As a member of the Federal Power Commission, 1933–45 (vice-chairman, 1933–36, 1941–44; chairman, 1944–45), he supervised the first national electric rate survey in 1934, and in general was a successful advocate of stronger federal regulation of the electric power and natural-gas industries.

MANLY, CHARLES MATTHEWS (*b. Staunton, Va., 1876; d. 1927*), mechanical engineer. Grandson of Basil Manly (1798–1868). Graduated Furman University, 1896; M.E., Cornell, 1898. Associated with Samuel P. Langley as pilot in the unfortunate trials of Langley's machine, October and December 1903. His permanent contribution to aviation, however, was his design and construction of a five-cylinder water-cooled radial gasoline engine of 52 horsepower weighing only 125 pounds; this engine has been characterized as the first modern aircraft engine. Manly also invented and patented, 1902, the Manly drive, a hydraulic device for transmitting power at variable speeds from a constant-speed motor.

MANLY, JOHN MATTHEWS (*b. Sumter Co., Ala., 1865; d. Tucson, Ariz., 1940*), philologist. Grandson of Basil Manly (1798–1868). Graduated Furman University, 1883; Ph.D., Harvard, 1890. Taught at Brown, 1890–98; first head, Department of English, University of Chicago, 1898–1933. Notable as Chaucer scholar; with Edith Rickert, edited critical edition of *Canterbury Tales* (1940).

MANN, AMBROSE DUDLEY (*b. Hanover Court House, Va., 1801; d. Paris, France, 1889*), lawyer, diplomat. An active and efficient consular representative and special American agent in central Europe, 1842–53, and an assistant U.S. secretary of state, 1853–56, Mann became increasingly identified thereafter with the fight for Southern rights and the economic independence of the South. As a Confederate commissioner in England and Belgium, 1861–65, he showed himself credulous and lacking in penetration.

MANN, HORACE (*b. Franklin, Mass., 1796; d. Yellow Springs, Ohio, 1859*), lawyer, Massachusetts legislator, educator. After an unhappy childhood marked by poverty and repression and by the ignorance and stultifying methods of district schoolmasters, Mann began to prepare himself for college in 1816. Graduating from Brown University, 1819, he studied law, was admitted to the bar, 1823, and practiced with great success at Dedham and Boston, Mass., until 1837. Meanwhile, he served in the Massachusetts legislature, as a member of the House, 1827–33, and of the Senate, 1833–37. As president of the Senate, 1836–37, he signed the epochal education bill which became a law, Apr. 29, 1837. This bill provided for a state board of education which was empowered to appoint a secretary. Through the influence of Edmund Dwight, Mann was appointed to this post. Between 1837 and 1848, when he resigned the secertaryship, he almost completely transformed the decaying Massachusetts public school system. His first task was to arouse and educate public opinion with reference to the purpose, value, and needs of public education. He organized, therefore, annual educational conventions in every county which were attended by teachers, school officials, and the public and which were addressed by civic leaders and men of intellectual distinction. To improve the teaching profession, he brought about the establishment of teachers' institutes and of the first three state normal schools in the United States. He also started and edited a semimonthly magazine, the *Common School Journal*, and prepared a series of annual reports which widely influenced American opinion on public education.

Progress was amazing. A six months' minimum school year was established, educational appropriations were doubled, 50 new high schools were founded, curricula and methods were revamped, and teachers' salaries were greatly increased. Mann's efforts, especially his advocacy of nonsectarian instruction and his commendation of German and Swiss educational methods, produced bitter opposition, but his proposals triumphed.

Resigning his school post, 1848, he served in Congress as an antislavery Whig, 1848–53; he was defeated as Free-Soil candidate for governor, 1852. He served *post* 1853 as president, also professor of a variety of subjects, at Antioch College. Mismanagement, insufficient funds, and dissension caused sale of the college for debt, 1859; exhausted, Mann died shortly thereafter. Interested in numerous humanitarian reforms, Mann was at his best in achieving a revival of American public school education.

MANN, JAMES (*b. Wrentham, Mass., 1759; d. Governor's Island, N.Y., 1832*), army surgeon. Served with 4th Massachusetts Regiment, 1779–82; headed medical department on northern frontier, War of 1812. Author of *Medical Sketches of the Campaigns of 1812, 13, 14* (1816).

MANN, JAMES ROBERT (*b. near Bloomington, Ill., 1856; d. 1922*), lawyer. Congressman, Republican, from Illinois, 1897–1922; an effective if excessively "stand pat" minority leader, 1912–18. Among the major measures with which he was associated were the Mann-Elkins Act, the Pure Food and Drugs Act of 1906, the Mann Act, and the resolution providing for the woman-suffrage amendment.

MANN, LOUIS (*b. New York, N.Y., 1865; d. 1931*), actor, playwright. Celebrated in dialect roles.

MANN, MARY TYLER PEABODY (*b. Cambridge, Mass., 1806; d. Jamaica Plain, Mass., 1887*), educator. Sister of Elizabeth P. Peabody; married Horace Mann, 1843. Collaborated with, and influenced profoundly, her husband's life and thought. Author of *Life and Works of Horace Mann* (1865–68).

MANN, NEWTON (*b. Cazenovia, N.Y., 1836; d. Chicago, Ill., 1926*), Unitarian clergyman, early advocate of Darwinism. Held principal pastorates in Rochester, N.Y., and Omaha, Nebr.

MANN, WILLIAM JULIUS (*b. Stuttgart, Germany, 1819; d. Boston, Mass., 1892*), Lutheran clergyman. Came to America, 1845, at urging of Philip Schaff; held pastorates in Philadelphia, Pa. Professor, Philadelphia Lutheran Theological Seminary, 1864–84. Author of *Life and Times of Henry Melchior Mühlenberg* (1887).

MANNERS, JOHN HARTLEY (*b. London, England, 1870; d. New York, N.Y., 1928*), actor, dramatist. Author of, among other plays, *Peg O' My Heart*, produced first in 1912.

MANNES, CLARA DAMROSCH (*b. Breslau, Silesia, 1869; d. New York, N.Y., 1948*), pianist, music educator. Daughter of Leopold Damrosch; sister of Frank Damrosch and Walter Damrosch. Married David Mannes, 1898, with whom she directed the David Mannes School of Music, New York City, *post* 1916.

MANNES, DAVID (*b. New York, N.Y., 1866; d. New York, 1959*), educator, conductor, violinist. Studied music privately in New York, Berlin, and Brussels. Played the violin for the New York Symphony Orchestra from 1891 to 1911; concertmaster from 1902. Inaugurated and conducted free concerts at the Metropolitan Museum from 1919 to 1949. Cofounder of the David Mannes Music School in Manhattan (1916); director of the school until his retirement in 1949. Founded the Music Settlement for Colored People in Harlem in 1912. Mannes was one of the country's leading proponents of music and musical education, as well as an accomplished violinist.

MANNES, LEOPOLD DAMROSCH (*b. New York, N.Y., 1899; d. Martha's Vineyard, Mass., 1964*), pianist, composer, inventor, and music educator. The son of David Mannes and Clara Damrosch, internationally known musicians who founded the Mannes School of Music in 1916. Studied at the Institute of Musical Art; the Mannes School; with several prominent musicians including Alfred Cortot (1924–25); and at Harvard (B.A., 1920). Taught piano and composition at the Mannes School, 1920–27, and the Institute of Musical Art, 1927–31. Associate director of the Mannes School (the Mannes College of Music from 1953) from 1940; president from 1948. Conducted research in color photography at the laboratories of Eastman Kodak in Rochester, N.Y. (1930–41). With Leopold Godowsky invented the Kodachrome process of color photography in 1935. Patented a sound track of gold that improved the sound quality of color motion pictures in 1941. Formed the Mannes Trio with Vittorio Brero and Luigi Silva in 1949; became the Mannes-Gimpel-Silva Trio when Bronislav Gimpel replaced Brero in 1950. His known compositions include *Suite for Two Pianos* (1924) and *String Quartet* (1928).

MANNING, DANIEL (*b. Albany, N.Y., 1831; d. 1887*), journalist, politician, banker. Became part owner of the *Albany Argus*, 1865. Virtually succeeded Samuel J. Tilden as leader of the New York Democratic party, 1877. Grover Cleveland was greatly indebted to Manning for his nomination as New York governor and for his first nomination to the presidency. Appointed U.S. secretary of the treasury, 1885, he served with great ability and loyally endorsed Cleveland's views. His resignation in 1887, allegedly owing to ill health, was actually caused by Cleveland's resentment of Tilden's desire to be the power behind the throne; as Manning was Tilden's friend, he was therefore proscribed.

MANNING, JAMES (*b. Piscataway, N.Y., 1738; d. Providence, R.I., 1791*), Baptist clergyman. Graduated College of New Jersey (Princeton), 1762. Elected president of the new Rhode Island College, 1765, he served until his death and showed administrative ability of a high order in his management of the school both at Warren, R.I., and at Providence. Serving also as pastor of the First Baptist Church in Providence, he took a firm stand (along with Isaac Backus and others) against the oppression suffered by Baptists under the "Standing Order" in Connecticut and Massachusetts.

MANNING, MARIE (*b. Washington, D.C., 1873[?]; d. Washington, 1945*), newspaperwoman. Associated with the Hearst organization *post* 1898, she originated, and for many years conducted, the "Beatrice Fairfax" column.

MANNING, RICHARD IRVINE (*b. Camden District, S.C., 1789; d. Philadelphia, Pa., 1836*), planter. Governor of South Carolina, 1824–26, Manning attached himself to the Union party *post* 1826 and was one of the leaders of the opposition to nullification. As a congressman, 1834–36, he supported Henry L. Pinckney's 1836 gag resolution.

MANNING, RICHARD IRVINE (*b. Sumter Co., S.C., 1859; d. Columbia, S.C., 1931*), planter, South Carolina legislator. Grandson of Richard I. Manning (1789–1836). A progressive Democrat and an opponent of the faction led by B. R. Tillman, Manning served as governor of South Carolina, 1915–19, and gave the state its most notable administration since the time of Wade Hampton. Among other constructive acts, he emphasized law enforcement and the suppression of lynching, set up a board of labor conciliation, a tax commission, a board of welfare, and reformed state care of the insane and retarded.

MANNING, ROBERT (*b. Salem, Mass., 1784; d. 1842*), businessman, pomologist. Uncle of Nathaniel Hawthorne. Established a pomological garden at Salem in 1823 with the aim of securing specimens of all varieties of fruit hardy enough to withstand the Massachusetts climate. At the time of his death he possessed the finest collection of fruit trees in America and one of the best in the world. He helped found the Massachusetts Horticultural Society and was author of the *Book of Fruits* (1838). To him, more than to any other man of his time, the fruitgrowers of America were indebted for the introduction of new and choice varieties, for correcting the nomenclature of fruits, and for identifying many varieties.

MANNING, THOMAS COURTLAND (*b. Edenton, N.C., 1825; d. New York, N.Y., 1887*), lawyer, Confederate soldier. Practiced in Louisiana *post* 1855; chief justice, Louisiana Supreme Court, 1877–80. Appointed, 1882, to the newly constituted supreme bench of Louisiana, he served until 1886 when he was appointed U.S. minister to Mexico.

MANNING, VANNOY HARTROG (*b. Horn Lake Depot, Miss., 1861; d. 1932*), topographer. Served *post* 1885 with U.S. Geological Survey. Transferring to the newly created Bureau of Mines, 1910, he succeeded Joseph A. Holmes as director of the bureau in 1915 and served until 1920. Under his direction, the bureau did notable research and other work for the U.S. War Department, 1917–18; resultant from this work were a wide variety of chemical weapons, the production of better airplane motor fuels, and the production of helium gas for use in lighter-than-air craft.

MANNING, WILLIAM THOMAS (*b. Northampton, England, 1866; d. New York, N.Y., 1949*), Episcopal clergyman. Immigrated to the United States with parents, 1882; resided in Nebraska and California. Studied at University of the South under William P. Dubose; ordained priest, 1891; returned to University of the South, 1893, after a short rectorate in Redlands, Calif., to take the B.D. degree and to serve as professor of theology. Feeling that his vocation lay rather in parish work, he left in 1894 to be rector successively of churches in Cincinnati, Ohio, Lansdowne, Pa., and Nashville, Tenn. Called in 1903 to be vicar of St. Agnes' Chapel of Trinity Parish, New York City, he was chosen assistant rector of Trinity, 1904, and rector, 1908. Coping at once with the charge that Trinity Parish was exploiting the poor through ownership of tenement properties, he invited a full investigation by the impartial New York Charity Organization Society, instituted a number of reforms, and sought other sources of income. Outside the parish he became known for his encouragement of Christian unity along the lines of historic faith and order. In 1921 he was consecrated bishop of the Diocese of New York, having previously declined election as bishop of western New York and bishop of Harrisburg.

Manning's insistence on doctrinal purity and strict church order quickly brought him into conflict with the liberals. His most conspicuous public achievement was the building of the nave of the Cathedral Church of St. John the Divine on Morningside Heights, begun in 1892. In 1927 he was a member of the Episcopal delegation to the first World Conference on Faith and Order at Lausanne, but took no further active part in the movement (now part of the World Council of Churches), of which he was one of the founders.

MANSELL, WILLIAM ALBERT (*b. Moradabad, India, 1864; d. Bareilly, India, 1913*), Methodist clergyman. Missionary and educator in India from 1889.

MANSFIELD, EDWARD DEERING (*b. New Haven, Conn., 1801; d. near Morrow, Ohio, 1880*), lawyer. Son of Jared Mansfield. Graduated West Point, 1819; College of New Jersey (Princeton), 1822. Practiced law in Cincinnati, Ohio, *post* 1825, and was associated with Benjamin Drake in newspaper publications there. A promoter of Cincinnati and its area, he was coauthor with Drake of *Cincinnati in 1826* (1827), a valuable study of the locality which greatly affected immigration thereto.

MANSFIELD, JARED (*b. New Haven, Conn., 1759; d. New Haven, 1830*), mathematician, physicist. A schoolteacher in New Haven, 1786–1802, he was brought to prominence by his book *Essays, Mathematical and Physical* (1801), which is considered to be the first book of original mathematical researches by a native-born American. Appointed captain of engineers, U.S. Army, by President Jefferson, 1802, he was professor of mathematics and natural philosophy at West Point, 1802–03 and 1812–28. He was surveyor general of the United States, 1803–12, assigned to service in the survey of Ohio and the Northwest Territory.

MANSFIELD, JAYNE (*b. Vera Jayne Palmer, Bryn Mawr, Pa., 1933; d. near New Orleans, La., 1967*), actress and entertainer. In addition to making twenty-five films, she acted on Broadway, as the dizzy blond heroine of George Axelrod's *Will Success Spoil Rock Hunter?* (1955–56; film version 1957), and appeared nude in *Playboy* magazine (at intervals from 1955 until 1964). Her accomplishment as an actress is negligible compared with her fame as a "sex goddess." Films include *Hell on Frisco Bay* (1955), *The Girl Can't Help It* (1956), *The Wayward Bus* (1957), *Kiss Them for Me* (1957), *The Loves of Hercules* (1960), *It Happened in Athens* (1962), and *Single Room Furnished* (1968; released posthumously). She died in an auto accident, the grotesque details of which were widely exploited in the press.

MANSFIELD, JOSEPH KING FENNO (*b. New Haven, Conn., 1803; d. near Sharpsburg, Md., 1862*), military engineer. Nephew of Jared Mansfield. Graduated West Point, 1822. Served with the highest distinction in Mexican War as chief engineer of the army under General Zachary Taylor; was inspector general of the army, 1853–61. Commissioned brigadier general, regular army, 1861, and major general of volunteers, July 1862, Mansfield commanded the Union XII Corps at the battle of Antietam, where he was mortally wounded.

MANSFIELD, RICHARD (*b. New Haven, Conn., 1723; d. Derby, Conn., 1820*), Episcopal clergyman, Loyalist. Rector, St. James Church, Derby, 1748–1820. First Episcopalian to receive degree of Doctor of Divinity from Yale, 1792.

MANSFIELD, RICHARD (*b. Berlin, Germany, 1854; d. New London, Conn., 1907*), actor. Son of a London wine merchant and a noted opera-singer mother, Mansfield resided in Boston, Mass., 1872–77. Returning to London in the latter year, he sang in touring Gilbert and Sullivan companies and played small parts in London and the provinces. His U.S. professional debut was in New York, September 1882, in the operetta *Les Manteaux Noirs*; his first success was as Baron Chevrial in *A Parisian Romance*, also 1882. Failing in an early attempt as a manager, he reached the rank of star in legitimate drama in 1886. Thereafter, until the end of his life, he was his own manager and producer. He first acted his most spectacular role, that of Dr. Jekyll and Mr. Hyde, in May 1887 at the Boston Museum. In London, March 1889, he made his Shakespearean debut in *Richard III* and brought the production to the United States that autumn. Among his other outstanding roles were Beau Brummell, Shylock, Cyrano de Bergerac, Monsieur Beaucaire. He produced *Arms and the Man* at the Herald Square Theatre, New York, September 1894, the first play by G. B. Shaw ever seen in America. In October 1906 he began his season in Chicago with the first American production of Ibsen's *Peer Gynt*. Although Mansfield represented more brilliantly and persistently than any actor of his day the romantic tradition and the grand style in plays and playing, he also helped usher in a new and different era in the history of drama. His performances in Shaw plays were as mordantly modern as the plays themselves. He had a splendid voice under perfect command yet he indulged in numerous eccentricities of speech. In addition to his natural gifts as a mime, he had a certain electric quality which informed all his characterizations from the wistful young prince of *Old Heidelberg* to his portrayal of Brutus haunted by remorse. High-strung, nervous, always carrying the whole weight of his productions, Mansfield was not popular with his fellow actors, but he was at bottom a generous and kindly man.

MANSHIP, PAUL HOWARD (*b. St. Paul, Minn., 1885; d. New York, N.Y., 1966*), sculptor. Won American Prix de Rome (1909); studied on scholarship at the American Academy of Rome (1909–12). Works include *Dancer and Gazelles* (1916), *Abraham Lincoln, the Hoosier Youth* (in Fort Wayne, Ind., 1932), *Prometheus Fountain* (at Rockefeller Plaza in New York, 1934), the *Paul J. Rainey Memorial Gateway* (at the New York Zoological Park, 1934), the *Woodrow Wilson Memorial Celestial Sphere* (at the League of Nations in Geneva, Switzerland, 1939), and portrait busts of John D. Rockefeller (1918) and John Barrymore (1918).

MANSON, OTIS FREDERICK (*b. Richmond, Va., 1822; d. Richmond, 1888*), physician, Confederate surgeon. Graduated medical department, Hampden-Sydney College, 1840; practiced in rural North Carolina until 1862. Early observing importance of malaria as causative agent and complicating force in other diseases, he presented his findings to the profession in numerous controversial writings. Professor of pathology and physiology, Medical College of Virginia, 1869–82.

MANTELL, ROBERT BRUCE (*b. Irvine, Scotland, 1854; d. Atlantic Highlands, N.J., 1928*), actor. Made American debut at Albany, N.Y., November 1878, in Helena Modjeska's company. Was identified with the American stage *post* 1884, principally as an interpreter of Shakespeare. His interpretations depended more upon force of action and vigor of voice than upon intellectual subtlety.

MANTLE, (ROBERT) BURNS (*b. Watertown, N.Y., 1873; d. Forest Hills, N.Y., 1948*), drama critic, theater annalist. Worked as a compositor for several newspapers in Denver, Colo.; began professional career as drama critic on the *Denver Times*, 1898; was successively on staffs of the *Chicago Inter-Ocean*, the *Chicago Tribune*, the *New York Evening Mail*; was drama critic of the *New York Daily News*, 1922–45. A genial, friendly man, he regarded himself not as a dictator of the drama but as an instructed theatergoer; whenever possible, he reviewed plays affirmatively. He is remembered in particular for his *Best Plays* series, yearly summaries of each theatrical season on Broadway, together with much other information, which he edited from 1919 through 1947 and which has become an invaluable reference work.

MANVILLE, THOMAS FRANKLYN ("TOMMY"), JR. (*b. Milwaukee, Wis., 1894; d. Chappaqua, N.Y., 1967*), wealthy eccentric and playboy. Son of Thomas Franklyn Manville, "the asbestos king," owner of the international Johns-Manville Corporation; at his death in 1925, Manville inherited a fortune of approximately $10 million. Became an object of journalistic interest due to his extravagant lifestyle and thirteen marriages.

MAPES, CHARLES VICTOR (*b. New York, N.Y., 1836; d. 1916*), agricultural chemist, manufacturer. Son of James J. Mapes; brother of Mary Mapes Dodge. A pioneer in developing fertilizers adapted to the peculiar needs of different crops and different soils.

MAPES, JAMES JAY (*b. Maspeth, N.Y., 1806; d. New York, N.Y., 1866*), agriculturalist, chemist. Edited *The Working Farmer*, 1849–63, in which he published results of his experimental farming and stressed the scientific principles underlying his practice. Among other contributions to agriculture, he developed a formula for nitrogenized superphosphate, which was probably the first complete plant food among artificial fertilizers used in the United States.

MAPPA, ADAM GERARD (*b. Delft, Holland, 1754; d. present Trenton, N.Y., 1828*), soldier, typefounder. Came to New York City, 1789, and established the first type foundry in that place. After its failure, he removed to Oneida Co., N.Y., where he farmed and acted as agent of the Holland Land Co., *post* 1794.

MARANVILLE, WALTER JAMES VINCENT ("RABBIT") (*b. Springfield, Mass., 1891; d. New York, N.Y., 1954*), baseball player. Flamboyant shortstop for many major league teams (Boston Braves, 1912–21 and 1929–34). Maranville played for twenty-three seasons. He was elected to the National Baseball Hall of Fame in 1954.

MARBLE, ALBERT PRESCOTT (*b. Vassalboro, Maine, 1836; d. 1906*), educator. Graduated Waterville (now Colby) College, 1861. His success as superintendent of public schools in Worcester, Mass., and in Omaha, Nebr., resulted in his appointment as superintendent of New York City high schools, 1896. He was author of *Sanitary Conditions for School Houses* (1891).

MARBLE, DANFORTH (*b. East Windsor, Conn., 1810; d. Louisville, Ky., 1849*), actor. Skillful in roles requiring Yankee dialect, he scored his greatest success in *Sam Patch*, written especially for him by E. H. Thompson, 1836.

MARBLE, MANTON MALONE (*b. Worcester, Mass., 1835 d. England, 1917*), journalist. Editor and owner, New York *World*, 1862–76, Marble opposed many of the policies of the Lincoln administration and was later active in exposing the Tweed Ring. He was credited with having written the Democratic national platform in 1876 and 1884.

MARBURG, THEODORE (*b. Baltimore, Md., 1862; d. Vancouver, British Columbia, Canada, 1946*), civic leader, philanthropist, advocate of international peace. U.S. minister to Belgium, 1912–13. A founder of the League to Enforce Peace, 1915, and later an active supporter of the work of the League of Nations, Marburg was a leader in the cultural and civic life of Baltimore. He organized the city's Municipal Art Society (a city-planning body), was a trustee and benefactor of Johns Hopkins University, and was instrumental in establishing Baltimore's Museum of Art.

MARBURY, ELISABETH (*b. New York, N.Y., 1856; d. 1933*), author's agent, theatrical producer. Beginning as agent for Frances H. Burnett, Marbury came in time to be representative of the most celebrated dramatists of her day; among her clients were Sardou, Rostand, Oscar Wilde, Bernard Shaw, Somerset Maugham, J. M. Barrie. She pioneered also in production of the "revue."

MARBUT, CURTIS FLETCHER (*b. Verona, Mo., 1863; d. Harbin, Manchuria, 1935*), geologist, soil expert. Associated *post* 1905 with the Bureau of Soils, U.S. Department of Agriculture, Marbut was a leader in mapping the soils of the United States and with others developed an international system of soil study known as pedology. His most extensive publication was *Soils of the United States* (1935).

MARCANTONIO, VITO ANTHONY (*b. New York, N.Y., 1902; d. New York, 1954*), politician. Studied at New York University Law School (1925). A protégé of New York's Mayor La Guardia, Marcantonio was a radical politician, though his first years were spent as a member of the Republican party. He was elected to Congress in 1934, and except for one term, served until 1950. A spokesman for the American Left, Marcantonio was highly critical of the proposals of the New Deal and of the Truman administration, but supported them because they were closest to his leftist ideals. He was ardently opposed to the excesses of the McCarthy era, and lost most of his popularity by failing to support the defense of South Korea. In 1938, he was read out of the Republican party, but continued to win the party primaries and often ran on both the Republican and Democratic slates.

MARCH, ALDEN (*b. Sutton, Mass., 1795; d. Albany, N.Y., 1869*), surgeon, anatomist, teacher of surgery. Practiced at Albany *post* 1820; held principal teaching appointments at Vermont Academy of Medicine and Albany Medical College.

MARCH, FRANCIS ANDREW (*b. Worcester Co., Mass., 1825; d. 1911*), philologist. Graduated Amherst, 1845. After several years in legal study and practice, he became a tutor at Lafayette College and in 1857 was appointed professor of the English language and comparative philology there, a post which he held until his retirement, 1906. March seems to have been the first to apply scientific methods of exegesis to the classroom study of English literary monuments; his chief title to fame, however, rests on his researches in the field of English historical grammar. He was author of *A Comparative Grammar of the Anglo-Saxon Language* (1870), a piece of research of the first rank; he also did much valuable work in English lexicography.

MARCH, FRANCIS ANDREW (*b. Easton, Pa., 1863; d. Easton, 1928*), lexicographer. Son of Francis A. March (1825–1911). Taught English at Lafayette College *post* 1882; served on staffs of *Century* and *Standard* dictionaries; edited *A Thesaurus Dictionary of the English Language* (1902).

MARCH, PEYTON CONWAY (*b. Easton, Pa., 1864; d. Washington, D.C. 1955*), soldier. Graduated from Lafayette College (1884) and the U.S. Military Academy (1888). Served with distinction in the Spanish-American War; joined MacArthur's staff and helped put down the Philippine Insurrection. As a major general, became chief of artillery of the American Expeditionary Force, 1917. Given the temporary rank of full general and appointed chief of staff in Washington, 1918. March's efforts to mobilize and supply the American forces in Europe were quite successful, though his tactics earned him many enemies, especially General Pershing and legislators. He retired in 1921; his memoirs, *The Nation at War* (1932), were highly critical of Pershing.

MARCH, WILLIAM EDWARD. *See* CAMPBELL, WILLIAM MARCH.

MARCHAND, JOHN BONNETT (*b. Greensburg, Pa., 1808; d. Carlisle, Pa., 1875*), naval officer. Appointed midshipman, 1828; retired as commodore, 1870, after varied service mainly at sea. Commanded USS *Lackawanna* on blockade duty in Gulf of Mexico, 1863–64.

MARCHANT, HENRY (*b. Martha's Vineyard, Mass., 1741; d. Newport, R.I., 1796*), lawyer, Revolutionary patriot, member of Continental Congress. U.S. district judge in Rhode Island, 1790–96.

MARCIANO, ROCKY (*b. Rocco Francis Marchegiano, Brockton, Mass., 1923; d. in airplane crash en route from Chicago to Des Moines, Iowa, 1969*), heavyweight boxer. Turned professional in 1947; won heavyweight title from "Jersey Joe" Walcott in 1952; defended his title six times, against boxers such as Roland La Starza, Ezzard Charles, Don Cockell, and Archie Moore. Retired with a record of forty-nine victories (forty-three knockouts) and no defeats. Marciano perfected a crouching style marked by relentless, aggressive pursuit, a good left hook, and an awkward but powerful overhand right punch.

MARCOSSON, ISAAC FREDERICK (*b. Louisville, Ky., 1876; d. New York, N.Y., 1961*), journalist and interviewer. With the *Louisville Times* (1894–1903); staff writer with *World's Work* in New York (1903–07); with the *Saturday Evening Post* (1907–10; 1913–36); an editor at *Munsey's* (1910–13). Earned reputation as a journalistic "lionhunter" for *Post* interviews with prominent world (but especially European) political and industrial leaders, including David Lloyd George, Leon Trotsky, Sun Yat-sen, Benito Mussolini, and Paul von Hindenburg. Published writings on cancer in *Reader's Digest* and *Woman's Home Companion* beginning in 1931; elected to the Board of Managers of New York's Memorial Hospital for the Treatment of Cancer and Allied Diseases; became its first director of public relations. Books include *How to Invest Your Savings* (1907), *The Rebirth of Russia* (1917), *Copper Heritage* (1955), and *Anaconda* (1957).

MARCOU, JULES (*b. Salins, France, 1824; d. Cambridge, Mass., 1898*), geologist. Made collections in America for Paris Jardin des Plantes, 1848–50; *post* 1860, was employed as field geologist in western surveys and at Harvard Museum of Comparative Zoology. Author of many articles and books, including a life of his mentor Louis Agassiz (1895).

MARCUS, BERNARD KENT (*b. New York, N.Y., 1890[?]; d. Hunter, N.Y., 1954*), banker. Graduated from Columbia University, B.A., 1911. Affiliated with the Bank of United States; president, 1927–30. Because of mishandling of funds, the bank was closed by the state of New York in 1930. Convicted in 1931 of misapplying funds and sentenced to six years in prison, Marcus was paroled in 1935 and pardoned in 1941.

MARCY, HENRY ORLANDO (*b. Otis, Mass., 1837; d. 1924*), surgeon, gynecologist, Union medical officer. Graduated Harvard Medical School, 1864; studied also in Berlin, London, and Edinburgh, where he became first American pupil of Joseph Lister. Practicing in Boston and, *post* 1880, Cambridge, Mass., Marcy was notable in introduction of Lister's methods to the United States, as a pioneer in antiseptic treatment of wounds, and as the developer of absorbable animal sutures.

MARCY, RANDOLPH BARNES (*b. Greenwich, Mass., 1812., d. West Orange, N.J., 1887*), soldier. Graduated West Point, 1832. Served on Michigan and Wisconsin frontier; saw Mexican War service in Texas; was on active duty in the Southwest, 1847–57. Opened new trail, Fort Smith to Santa Fe, 1849; led exploration to headwaters of Red and Canadian rivers, 1852. Made a famous winter march through the Rockies, 1857–58, to reprovision A. S. Johnston's army operating against Mormons in Utah. Served as chief of staff to son-in-law, General George B. McClellan, in Civil War Peninsular and Antietam campaigns. Retired as brigadier general, 1881. Author of valuable official reports on his explorations in the Red-Canadian region; also of *The Prairie Traveler* (1859) and two volumes of reminiscences.

MARCY, WILLIAM LEARNED (*b. Sturbridge, present Southbridge, Mass., 1786; d. Ballston, N.Y., 1857*), lawyer, statesman. A graduate of Brown, 1808, he removed to Troy, N.Y., where he read law and was admitted to the bar, 1811. Active in support of Jeffersonian principles, Marcy held local and state offices. He became friendly *ca.* 1818 with Martin Van Buren and helped to organize the dominant Democratic political group known as the "Albany Regency." Skillful in restraining the rise of public debt as New York state comptroller, 1823–29, he served with marked ability as a justice of the state supreme court, 1829–31. As U.S. senator, December 1831–December 1832, he defended Van Buren's appointment as minister to London, stating that he could see nothing wrong in the rule that "to the victor belong the spoils of the enemy," whence the term "spoils system" as used in American politics. Outstanding as governor of New York, 1833–38, Marcy organized the state's first geological survey, settled the boundary dispute with New Jersey, refused to extradite abolitionists for Southern trial but reprobated abolitionism. He was an effective conciliator in disputes over Mexican claims, 1840–42, and as secretary of war, 1845–49, won national prestige, despite a controversy with General Winfield Scott.

Appointed secretary of state by President Pierce, Marcy handled with distinction a series of great issues between 1853 and 1857. He was responsible for negotiation of 24 treaties, the largest number ratified within an administration up to that time; among them, the Gadsden (1853), the Reciprocity (with Great Britain, 1854), and

treaties with the Netherlands (1855) and Denmark (1857) were most significant. During Marcy's term, three delicate cases involving international relations were settled: the Koszta case with Austria; the *Black Warrior* case with Spain; the Patrice Dillion case with France. In the matter of the sensational Ostend Manifesto, (March 1855), Marcy was indirectly at fault for putting trust in Pierre Soulé and John Y. Mason, who were bent on acquiring Cuba by any means for southern interests. Reckoned among the nation's foremost men at the time of his death, he ranks among the ablest of secretaries of state.

MARDEN, CHARLES CARROLL (*b. Baltimore, Md., 1867; d. 1932*), philologist. Graduated Johns Hopkins, 1889, Ph.D., 1894. Taught Hispanic studies at Johns Hopkins, Princeton, University of Chicago; edited medieval texts.

MARDEN, ORISON SWETT (*b. near Thornton, N.H., 1850; d. 1924*), hotel operator, journalist. Publicized "the will to succeed" in various books and in his magazine *Success* (1897–1912, 1918–24).

MARÉCHAL, AMBROSE (*b. near Orléans, France, 1764; d. 1828*), Roman Catholic clergyman, Sulpician. Served as missioner and seminary teacher in Maryland, 1792–1803; after returning to France, was recalled to St. Mary's Seminary, Baltimore, 1812. As archbishop of Baltimore, 1817–28, he administered his archdiocese with zeal and firmness and showed himself wholly American in sympathies; during his term, the Baltimore Cathedral was completed (1821).

MAREST, PIERRE GABRIEL (*b. Laval, France, 1662, d. Kaskaskia Mission, 1714*), Roman Catholic clergyman, Jesuit, pioneer priest in Illinois.

MARETZEK, MAX (*b. Brünn, Austria, present Czechoslovakia, 1821; d. Staten Island, N.Y., 1897*), composer, conductor. First successful impresario of Italian opera in New York, 1848–79.

MARGOLIS, MAX LEOPOLD (*b. Merech, Russia, 1866; d. 1932*), biblical scholar, educator. Studied in Warsaw and Berlin; came to America, 1889; graduated Columbia, Ph.D., 1891. Essentially a philologist, he taught Semitic languages at Hebrew Union, University of California, and Dropsie College, and was author of a number of scholarly works on the Bible.

MARIGNY, BERNARD (*b. New Orleans, La., 1785; d. New Orleans, 1868*), planter, Louisiana legislator. Putative introducer of game of craps to the United States *ca.* 1802.

MARIN, JOHN (CHERI) (*b. Rutherford, N.J., 1870; d. Cape Split, Maine, 1951*), artist. Studied at Stevens Institute, the Pennsylvania Academy of Fine Arts, and in Paris. Marin's early career was marked by a representational style and was greatly influenced by Whistler. Exhibited with Stieglitz at the "291" gallery in 1909, before breaking with representational art around 1913. His mature style included, among others, cubism and postimpressionism. Paintings include *The Brooklyn Bridge* (Metropolitan Museum, N.Y.), *Municipal Building* (Philadelphia Museum of Art), and *Nudes in Sea* (Art Institute in Chicago). Honored by a retrospective exhibition at the Museum of Modern Art in New York, 1936.

MARION, FRANCIS (*b. probably St. John's Parish, Berkeley Co., S.C., ca. 1732; d. St. John's Parish, 1795*), planter, Revolutionary soldier, South Carolina legislator. Nicknamed the "Swamp Fox." Served against the Cherokee, 1759 and 1761; appointed captain, 2nd South Carolina Regiment, 1775. After service in and near Charleston, he commanded the regiment in attack on Savannah, 1779. Detailed by General Gates to command militia between Santee and Pee Dee rivers, after the

American disaster at Camden in 1780, Marion prevented effective organization of South Carolina Tories and disrupted British communications by guerrilla operations. At the battle of Eutaw Springs, 1781, he led the militia and was thereafter General Greene's chief aide for outpost duty until the evacuation of Charleston.

MARKHAM, CHARLES HENRY (*b. Clarksville, Tenn., 1861; d. Altadena, Calif., 1930*), railroad executive. President, Illinois Central, 1911–18 and 1919–26; improved facilities and service; began modernization of Chicago terminal and yards.

MARKHAM, EDWIN (*b. Oregon City, Oreg., 1852; d. Staten Island, N.Y., 1940*), poet. Author of "The Man with the Hoe," one of the most popular poems of all time, first published in *San Francisco Examiner*, and issued separately in a special supplement to that newspaper on Jan. 15, 1899.

MARKHAM, WILLIAM (*b. England, ca. 1635; d. Philadelphia, Pa., 1704*), Pennsylvania official. Cousin of William Penn. As deputy governor, arrived at present Chester, Pa., 1681; presided over first provincial council; helped select site of Philadelphia; reverted to office of councillor at Penn's arrival, 1682. Served thereafter as provincial secretary, 1685–91; as deputy governor of Lower Counties (Delaware), 1691–93; as lieutenant governor or governor of both Pennsylvania and the Lower Counties, 1693–99. Probably the chief author of the "Frame of Government."

MARKOE, ABRAHAM (*b. St. Croix, Virgin Islands, 1727; d. Philadelphia, Pa., 1806*), capitalist, Revolutionary patriot. Removed to Philadelphia, *ca.* 1770; organized Philadelphia Light Horse (First Troop), 1774.

MARKOE, PETER (*b. St. Croix, Virgin Islands, ca. 1752; d. Philadelphia, Pa., 1792*), poet, dramatist. Son of Abraham Markoe. Author of *The Patriot Chief* (published 1784, a tragedy); *Miscellaneous Poems* (1787); *The Times* (1788, a satire); *The Reconciliation* (1790, an early comic opera), and other works.

MARKS, AMASA ABRAHAM (*b. Waterbury, Conn., 1825; d. Sound Beach, Conn., 1905*), inventor and manufacturer of improved artificial limbs.

MARKS, ELIAS (*b. Charleston, S.C., 1790; d. Washington, D.C., 1886*), physician, educator. Founded South Carolina Female Institute, 1828, for higher education of women.

MARLAND, ERNEST WHITWORTH (*b. Pittsburgh, Pa., 1874; d. Ponca City, Okla., 1941*), lawyer, oil operator, politician, LL.B., University of Michigan, 1893. Worked as appraiser of coal lands; educated himself in geology; struck oil in West Virginia Panhandle (Congo field), 1906. After losing his gains from this operation in the panic of 1907, he started afresh in Oklahoma, made his first strike in May 1911, and by 1920 had opened the Blackwell, Newkirk, Petit, and Burbank fields. He had also extended his interests to production in other states and overseas, and his Marland Oil Company grew to be the largest independent company, controlling one-tenth of the world's supply. A generous employer and public benefactor, he found his financial resources strained and was obliged to yield participation in management and stock interest to J. P. Morgan and Co. in return for a large loan, 1923. As oil prices dropped through 1927 and 1928, he was unwilling to retrench and was forced to resign as operating head of the firm. Turning to politics, he ran for Congress as a New Deal Democrat, 1932, and was elected from the Eighth Oklahoma District. At the end of his term, he ran for the governorship of Oklahoma as an enemy of the "money trust" and won easily. He began a wide-scale program of reforms and public works, including an oil conservation project, but expense outran income and he lost favor with the national administration. He left the governorship in January 1939 in sad financial straits, and died in comparative poverty.

MARLATT, ABBY LILLIAN (*b. Manhattan, Kans., 1869; d. Madison, Wis., 1943*), home economist. B.S., Kansas State College, 1888; M.S., 1890. Taught at Utah State College and at Providence (R.I.) Technical High School. As head of the home economics department in the agricultural college of University of Wisconsin, 1909–39, she built it into one of the largest and best in the nation, expanding the curriculum to include courses in the sciences and in languages and promoting research in problems of nutrition.

MARLING, ALFRED ERSKINE (*b. Toronto, Canada, 1858; d. 1935*), real estate operator. President, H. S. Ely & Co., New York, 1904–31.

MARLING, JOHN LEAKE (*b. Nashville, Tenn., 1825; d. Nashville, 1856*), journalist, diplomat. Editor, Nashville *Gazette* and *Daily Union*; opposed secessionist sentiment at Nashville Convention, 1850. U.S. minister resident in Guatemala, 1854–56.

MARLOWE, JULIA (*b. Caldbeck, Cumberlandshire, England, 1866; d. New York, N.Y., 1950*), actress. Born Sarah Frances Frost, she was known as Fanny Brough after her immigration with her parents to Missouri, *ca.* 1871; the family later moved to Cincinnati, Ohio. At age 11 she joined a juvenile company performing Gilbert and Sullivan's *Pinafore* and trouped with it through the Midwest. In 1887, as Julia Marlowe, she made her debut as Parthenia in *Ingomar*. She subsequently played in *Romeo and Juliet* and as Viola in *Twelfth Night*. By joining an all-star cast of *The Rivals* for a four-week tour, she reaped financial benefit. She appeared in plays of more general appeal. *The Countess Valeska*, adapted from a German play, displayed her powers in 1898 to the applause of crowded houses. After touring in this success, she returned to New York to revive *As You Like It* and *Romeo and Juliet*. It was through plays like *Barbara Frietchie* (1899) by Clyde Fitch, and the adaptation of Paul Kester of the best-selling novel *When Knighthood Was in Flower* (1900) that her name became a household word. Her art had its roots in Shakespeare, and in his plays alone she realized her theatrical self. In the fall of 1904 she opened a new phase of her career when she appeared with Edward H. Sothern (whom she married in 1911) in *Romeo and Juliet*. Upholding the classic and romantic traditions of the stage, Julia Marlowe made Shakespeare's heroines credible to a modern age. Poor health forced her to announce her retirement in 1916, although she gave subsequent performances. During World War I she entertained at benefits for wounded troops, and in the seasons of 1919–20 and 1923–24 she and Sothern resumed the theatrical trail in their favorite repertory, but these farewell appearances drained her of her last energy.

MARMADUKE, JOHN SAPPINGTON (*b. near Arrow Rock, Mo., 1833; d. Jefferson City, Mo., 1887*), Confederate major general, businessman. Graduated West Point, 1857; served with infantry in Utah and New Mexico. Entering Confederate service, 1861, he was distinguished at Shiloh and later in small but effective actions in Arkansas and western Missouri. As Democratic governor of Missouri, 1885–87, he secured needed legislation for regulation of railroads.

MARQUAND, ALLAN (*b. New York, N.Y., 1853; d. New York, 1924*), art historian. Son of Henry G. Marquand. Graduated Princeton, 1874; Ph.D., Johns Hopkins, 1880. Taught at Princeton *post* 1881 and was director and patron of the Department of Art and Archaeology there. Author of many scholarly studies; also of

Greek Architecture (1909) and of a monumental series of catalogs of sculptures by the Della Robbia family.

MARQUAND, HENRY GURDON (*b. New York, N.Y., 1819, d. 1902*), capitalist, philanthropist. Benefactor of the Metropolitan Museum of Art (New York) and of Princeton University; president, Metropolitan Museum, 1889–1902.

MARQUAND, JOHN PHILLIPS (*b. Wilmington, Del., 1893; d. Newbury, Mass., 1960*), novelist. Studied at Harvard University. Creator of the Japanese detective, Mr. Moto. Marquand's first novel was *The Unspeakable Gentleman*, published in 1922 by Scribners. Other works include *The Late George Apley* (1937) which won the Pulitzer Prize in 1938, *Point of No Return* (1949), *Melville Goodwyn, USA* (1951), *Thirty Years* (1954), and *Sincerely, Willis Wade* (1955).

MARQUETT, TURNER MASTIN (*b. Clark Co., Ohio, 1829; d. Lincoln, Nebr., 1894*), lawyer, Nebraska territorial legislator and attorney for the Burlington Railroad.

MARQUETTE, JACQUES (*b. Laon, France, 1637; d. at mouth of Pere Marquette River, near present Ludington, Mich., 1675*), Jesuit missionary, explorer. Came to Quebec, 1666; learned Indian languages at Three Rivers; appointed to mission among the Ottawa Indians, 1668. After wintering at Sault Ste. Marie, he went to the mission of La Pointe at Chequamegon Bay on the south shore of Lake Superior, where he first encountered Indians from the Illinois country. In the summer of 1671, he founded the mission of St. Ignace on the north shore of the Straits of Mackinac; there, in December 1672, he encountered for the second time Louis Jolliet, who brought him news that the governor had commissioned them both to go in search of a great river to the west, of which Marquette had already heard from the Illinois Indians. They set forth in May 1673 by way of Green Bay and Fox River, portaged to the Wisconsin, and on June 17, 1673, reached the Mississippi. Turning their canoes southward, they reached the mouth of the Arkansas by mid-July; there, learning that the river entered the Gulf of Mexico and that Spaniards were on the lower river, they turned back. They reached Lake Michigan by the Illinois River and the Chicago portage, coasted the lake shore, and rested at the mission of St. Francis Xavier at DePere. Marquette remained there for more than a year, restoring his health and writing his journal. In October 1674, he set out to found a mission among the Illinois Indians. After suffering many hardships and serious illness, Marquette reached the Illinois village, spent Easter of 1675 there, but died on his way back to the mission of St. Ignace. Marquette is the most renowned of all the Jesuit missionaries in the West, in part because of his early death and saintly nature, in part because he and Jolliet were the first to follow the course of the Mississippi River and to make their journey known by journals, maps, and letters.

MARQUIS, ALBERT NELSON (*b. Brown County, Ohio, 1855: d. Evanston, Ill., 1943*), publisher. Established his own publishing business in Chicago, Ill., 1884, after an earlier venture in Cincinnati, Ohio; specialized in business and city directories. Founded *Who's Who in America*, of which the first volume appeared in 1899, and personally supervised it as editor in chief until 1940.

MARQUIS DE CUEVAS. *See* DE CUEVAS, MARQUIS.

MARQUIS, DONALD ROBERT PERRY (*b. Walnut, Ill., 1878; d. Forest Hills, N.Y., 1937*), journalist, humorist. Worked on Washington, D.C., and Atlanta, Ga., newspapers, 1899–1909; in New York City thereafter. Wrote "Sun Dial" column in New York *Evening Sun*, 1913–22. Author of *archy and mehitabel*

(1927), also volumes of fiction, light verse, and several plays, all of a high order. Called "a belated Elizabethan."

MARQUIS, JOHN ABNER (*b. Dinsmore, Pa., 1861; d. New York, N.Y., 1931*), Presbyterian clergyman, educator. President, Coe College, 1909–20; secretary, Presbyterian Board of Home Missions, 1917–23, and of National Missions *post* 1923.

MARRIOTT, WILLIAMS MCKIM (*b. Baltimore, Md., 1885; d. San Francisco, Calif., 1936*), biochemist, pediatrician. Graduated University of North Carolina, 1940; M.D., Cornell, 1910. Taught biochemistry at Washington University Medical School, 1910–14. Wishing to apply biochemistry to medical problems, he became aide to Dr. John Howland in pediatrics department, Johns Hopkins Medical School. Their joint work on acidosis in infancy won international recognition, as did Marriott's later work at Washington University, where he returned as professor of pediatrics, 1917. Here he discovered the cause of "alimentary intoxication" and revolutionized infant feeding by introducing simplified procedures and inexpensive ingredients such as evaporated milk and corn syrup.

MARSH, CHARLES WESLEY (*b. near Trenton, Ontario, Canada, 1834; d. 1918*), inventor, manufacturer, editor. Settled with his parents in De Kalb Co., Ill., 1849. With his brother William, he patented first practical hand-binding harvester, 1858. After the failure of companies which he set up to manufacture his machine, Marsh became editor of the *Farm Implement News*, 1885, and later president of the company which published it.

MARSH, FRANK BURR (*b. Big Rapids, Mich., 1880; d. Dallas, Tex., 1940*), historian. Graduated University of Michigan, 1902; Ph.D., 1906. Taught at University of Texas, 1910–40; author of *The Founding of the Roman Empire* (1922) and other works.

MARSH, GEORGE PERKINS (*b. Woodstock, Vt., 1801; d. Vallombrosa, Italy, 1882*), lawyer, diplomat. Cousin of James Marsh. Graduated Dartmouth, 1820; admitted to bar, 1825; practiced in Burlington, Vt. As congressman, Whig, from Vermont, 1843–49, he supported high tariffs and opposed slavery and the Mexican War. Serving as U.S. minister to Turkey, 1849–54, he arranged for the departure of Kossuth to America and acted with fairness but discretion in the cases of Jonas King and Martin Koszta. Appointed first U.S. minister to the kingdom of Italy, 1860, he served there with success for the remainder of his life. Marsh was a conscientious and erudite scholar in many fields. Notable among his books was *Man and Nature* (1864), revised as *The Earth as Modified by Human Action* (1874), which has been described as "the fountainhead of the conservation movement."

MARSH, GRANT PRINCE (*b. Chatauqua Co., N.Y., 1834; d. Bismarck, N.Dak., 1916*), Mississippi and Missouri river pilot and steamboat captain, friend of Mark Twain.

MARSH, JAMES (*b. Hartford, Vt., 1794; d. Burlington, Vt., 1842*), philosopher, educator. Cousin of George P. Marsh. Graduated Dartmouth, 1817. During his presidency of the University of Vermont, 1826–33, that institution became a leader in educational reform both in New England and in the Middle West. His edition of Coleridge's *Aids to Reflection* (1829), with its preliminary essay, was read with enthusiasm by Emerson and other young intellectuals of the period and had a strong influence upon the transcendentalist movement.

MARSH, JOHN (*b. Wethersfield, Conn, 1788; d. Brooklyn, N.Y., 1868*), Congregational clergyman, temperance reformer.

MARSH, JOHN (*b. South Danvers, Mass., 1799; d. near Martinez, Calif., 1856*), physician, adventurer, California pioneer.

MARSH, OTHNIEL CHARLES (*b. Lockport, N.Y., 1831; d. New Haven, Conn., 1899*), paleontologist. Nephew of John Marsh (1799–1856). Graduated Yale, 1860; did graduate work in science there and studied at Berlin, Breslau, and Heidelberg, 1863–66. He returned from Germany to become America's first professor of paleontology, holding that chair at Yale, 1866–99. Organizing numerous scientific expeditions (at first financed by his own means, augmented by an inheritance from a maternal uncle, George Peabody), he uncovered almost unlimited fossil material in Nebraska, Wyoming, Colorado, and California. He actually accumulated fossils more rapidly than he could study them, and his published bibliography is less comprehensive than might be expected. Besides many papers in the *American Journal of Science*, he wrote the monographs *Odontornithes* (1880) and *Dinocerata* (1884); his best single paper was the *Introduction and Succession of Vertebrate Life in America* (1877); other works had only just been begun at his death. Marsh was the first to describe remains of fossil serpents and flying reptiles in western North America; American museums owe to his almost compulsive collecting the fact that they now often have fossil skeletons as complete as those of animals now living. In 1882 Marsh was appointed vertebrate paleontologist to the U.S. Geological Survey. President of the National Academy of Sciences, 1883–95, recipient of foreign awards, he put the collection and preparation of vertebrate fossils upon a truly scientific basis.

MARSH, REGINALD (*b. Paris, France, 1898; d. Bennington, Vt., 1954*), painter, graphic artist, teacher. Graduated from Yale, A.B., 1920. Became staff artist for the *New York Daily News*, 1925, and a member of the original *New Yorker* staff, 1925. After studying at the Art Students League in New York, Marsh turned seriously to painting. His realistic style depicted the common man of the city. Paintings include *Why Not Take the L?* and *Twenty Cent Movie* (Whitney Museum of Art, N.Y.), *Coney Island Beach* (Yale University Art Gallery), and *Merry-Go-Round* (National Gallery of Art, Washington, D.C.). Also designed and executed frescoes for the Washington, D.C., Post Office (1935) and the New York Custom House (1937).

MARSH, SYLVESTER (*b. Campton, N.H., 1803; d. Concord, N.H., 1884*), inventor, meatpacker, grain dealer. Invented devices for handling and drying grain and meal; devised and constructed cogwheel railroad up Mount Washington, N.H., 1869.

MARSH, WILLIAM WALLACE (*b. near Trenton, Ontario, Canada, 1836; d. Sycamore, Ill., 1918*), inventor, manufacturer. Removed as a boy to De Kalb Co., Ill. Partner with his brother, Charles W. Marsh, in the invention and manufacture of the first practical hand-binding harvester.

MARSHALL, BENJAMIN (*b. Huddersfield, England, 1782; d. Troy, N.Y., 1858*), merchant, cotton textile manufacturer. Came to America, 1803; settled in New York, N.Y., and engaged in import-export trade. A partner with Jeremiah Thompson and others in the Black Ball Line, 1817–33, Marshall was thereafter principally concerned with the manufacture of high-quality cotton goods at Utica and Troy, N.Y.

MARSHALL, CHARLES HENRY (*b. Nantucket Island, 1792; d. New York, N.Y., 1865*), sea captain, shipping executive. Commanded packet ships of the Black Ball Line, 1822–34; served thereafter as New York City agent of that line and became its principal owner.

MARSHALL, CHRISTOPHER (*b. probably Dublin, Ireland, 1709; d. Philadelphia, Pa., 1797*), pharmacist, Revolutionary patriot. Came to America *ca.* 1727; settled in Philadelphia. Best known for the *Diary* which he kept during the Revolution, one of the most valuable sources for the period. Published in part in 1839 and 1849, the comprehensive edition is that of 1877.

MARSHALL, CLARA (*b. West Chester, Pa., ca. 1848; d. 1931*), physician. Graduated Woman's Medical College of Pennsylvania, 1875; practiced for many years in Philadelphia, Pa. Joining the faculty of her alma mater immediately after graduation, she remained there as professor until 1923 and served also as dean, 1888–1917. The success of the school was owing largely to her energy and enthusiasm.

MARSHALL, DANIEL (*b. Windsor, Conn., 1706; d. 1784*), pioneer "Separate Baptist" preacher. Brother-in-law of Shubael Stearns. Leading a wandering life *post* 1744, Marshall settled in Kiokee Creek, Ga., 1771, where he founded the first Baptist church in that state, 1772.

MARSHALL, FRANK JAMES (*b. New York, N.Y., 1877; d. Jersey City, N.J., 1944*), chess player. Raised in Montreal, Canada, where he attended school and began his career in chess; returned to New York City, 1896, where he soon established himself as a top player in the metropolitan area. Won his first international tournament, 1904; ranked as U.S. champion, 1909–36. Directed the Marshall Chess Club, New York City, *post* 1922. His most famous game was played against S. Lewitsky at Breslau in 1912. His main contributions to chess theory were in the Max Lange opening, the Marshall gambit in the semi-Slav defense, and the Marshall counterattack in the Ruy Lopez opening.

MARSHALL, GEORGE CATLETT, JR. (*b. Uniontown, Pa., 1880; d. Washington, D.C., 1959*), general and army chief of staff, secretary of state, secretary of defense. Studied at the Virginia Military Institute. Commissioned second lieutenant of infantry and served in the Philippines, 1902. Attended and taught at the School of the Line, Fort Leavenworth, Kans., 1906–10. Served as chief planning officer in the Philippines, 1916; as aide to Major General Liggett; and as his chief of operations with the First Army in France. Helped plan the battle of the St. Mihiel salient and was highly successful in organizing the movements of large Allied armies. Served as Pershing's principal aide, 1919–24, outlining defense legislation for congressional committees. As executive officer in Tientsin, China, 1924–27, he became familiar with the problems of the Far East. During the 1930's, Marshall directed Civilian Conservation Corps camps in many areas and headed National Guard units. Summoned to Washington, 1938, as chief of the War Plans Division. Appointed chief of staff, 1939, and became general of the army, 1944.

Throughout World War II, Marshall held firmly to a policy of "Europe first" as far as men and supplies went, while still achieving victory in the Pacific. He played a leading part in the great war conferences and became a chief advocate of the cross-channel attack. He appointed Eisenhower as Allied commander in Europe; and while he wished to command the Normandy invasion himself, he remained in Washington at Roosevelt's request. He is generally regarded as the most important figure in arming the United States and is held chiefly responsible for the Allied victories of 1944 and 1945.

Sent to China, 1946, in an unsuccessful attempt to help bring about a coalition government. As secretary of state, 1947–49, he effectively reorganized the department and developed the highly successful European Recovery Plan, which, although the product of many minds, bears his name. Later served as president of the American Red Cross; but in 1950, with the outbreak of the Korean

War, was appointed secretary of defense. Always enjoying strong support in Congress, Marshall reshaped the army for that conflict and backed Truman's dismissal of MacArthur. Received Nobel Prize for Peace, 1953.

MARSHALL, HENRY RUTGERS (*b. New York, N.Y., 1852; d. 1927*), architect, writer on aesthetics. Executive secretary, New York City Municipal Art Commission, 1914–27.

MARSHALL, HUMPHREY (*b. Fauquier Co., Va., 1760; d. Lexington, Ky., 1841*), lawyer, Kentucky landowner and legislator. Nephew of Thomas Marshall; cousin of John and Louis Marshall. U.S. senator, Federalist, from Kentucky, 1795–1801. Instrumental in exposing motives of Aaron Burr, 1806. Author of *The History of Kentucky* (1812, 1824).

MARSHALL, HUMPHREY (*b. Frankfort, Ky., 1812; d. Louisville, Ky., 1872*), soldier, lawyer, diplomat. Grandson of Humphrey Marshall (1760–1841); nephew of James G. Birney. Graduated West Point, 1832, but resigned his commission a year later. Served with credit in the Mexican War. Congressman, Whig, from Kentucky, 1849–52; U.S. minister to China, 1853–54; congressman, Know-Nothing, 1855–59. Commissioned a Confederate brigadier general, 1861, he resigned his commission, 1863, because he could not secure an independent command. He served in the second Confederate Congress, 1864–65.

MARSHALL, HUMPHRY (*b. Chester Co., Pa., 1722 o.s.; d. Chester Co., 1801*), botanist. Cousin of John Bartram. Proprietor of a notable botanic garden at Marshallton, Pa.; author of *Arbustrum Americanum: The American Grove* (1785), which has been called the first truly indigenous botanical essay to be published in the western hemisphere.

MARSHALL, JAMES FOWLE BALDWIN (*b. Charlestown, Mass., 1818; d. Weston, Mass., 1891*), merchant, educator. In business at Honolulu, Hawaii, 1838–59; as representative of Hawaiian native government, helped foil British annexation attempt, 1843. Returning to Boston, he engaged in Civil War service and after the war joined Samuel C. Armstrong at Hampton Institute, where he served as resident trustee and in other capacities, 1870–84.

MARSHALL, JAMES MARKHAM (*b. Fauquier Co., Va., 1764; d. Fauquier Co., 1848*), landholder, Kentucky legislator. Son of Thomas Marshall; brother of John and Louis Marshall; son-in-law of Robert Morris. Acquired large holdings by purchase of Fairfax estates in the Northern Neck section of Virginia.

MARSHALL, JAMES WILSON (*b. Hunterdon Co., N.J., 1810; d. near Coloma, Calif., 1885*), mechanic, discoverer of gold in California. Starting westward in search of adventure and fortune *ca.* 1831, Marshall settled for a brief period in Indiana and Illinois and for a longer time near Fort Leavenworth. His health failing, he struck out along the Oregon Trail, 1844, wintered at Fort Hall and reached the Willamette Valley in the spring. Early in July 1845, Marshall reached Sutter's Fort, site of the present city of Sacramento, after traveling across the Klamath Mountains under guidance of James Clyman. Entering partnership with John A. Sutter for construction and operation of a sawmill near Sutter's Fort on the south fork of the American River, Marshall began operations only to discover early in 1848 that the tailrace would have to be deepened. During excavation for this purpose, gold was discovered on Jan. 24, 1848. The discovery was kept secret for a short time, but the news soon got out and by the end of the year settlers were pouring in from all the neighboring regions. The discovery of gold by Marshall was an epochal event, but it brought only misfortune to the discoverer.

MARSHALL, JOHN (*b. near Germantown, Va., 1755; d. Philadelphia, Pa., 1835*), lawyer, chief justice of the United States, principal founder of judicial review and of the American system of constitutional law. Son of Thomas Marshall; brother of James M. and Louis Marshall (1773–1866); related on his mother's side to William Randolph. Raised on the sparsely settled Virginia frontier, Marshall attributed much of his own success in life to the example and teaching of his father, who was a man of superior ability and force of character. Tutored by his father and a local clergyman, Marshall learned early to enjoy the Latin classics and the English literature popular in that time, notably the moral essays of Alexander Pope. His father was one of the subscribers to the first (1772) American edition of Blackstone's *Commentaries*, and it is likely that John Marshall began his self-education in the law about that time. The eldest of 15 children, he grew up in an environment of thrift and mutual helpfulness; the careless dress, love of debate, and easy "slouching" manners characteristic of his later life were natural consequences of his upbringing in a frontier society. Helping to raise his brothers and sisters developed in him a skill in putting his own ideas into the minds of others unconscious of his purpose, a skill later the distinctive feature of his leadership of the Supreme Court. His youthful view on politics was that of his father, which was in turn the view of Patrick Henry.

A member of the Culpeper minutemen, John Marshall was mustered into the 3rd Virginia Continental Regiment, July 30, 1776, and rose to captain in service (among other engagements) at the Brandywine, Germantown, and Monmouth; he was also at Valley Forge and participated in the taking of Stony Point. While awaiting a new command in 1780, he studied law briefly at the College of William and Mary under George Wythe; this was his only institutional instruction of any sort.

Mustered out of the service, 1781, he was elected to the state assembly, 1782, married Mary Ambler, January 1783, and soon afterward began practice in Richmond, Va. He was soon recognized as a leading attorney. Since British legal precedents were in disfavor following the Revolution, while there were as yet few if any American precedents, what was chiefly demanded of counsel was not learning but a capacity for absorbing material suited to the immediate occasion and then of spinning it out in a web of argumentation. Marshall developed much skill in making his daily practice in court educate him in the law, and he was able to inform himself from the knowledge displayed by his adversaries. Impressed with the need for a strong central government by his army experiences, and now, as an assemblyman, disgusted with the way state legislatures ignored treaty obligations and encouraged interstate commercial wars, Marshall became an eager advocate of constitutional reform. Through his efforts in the Virginia Assembly, 1787, the U.S. Constitution was submitted to the state ratifying convention without hampering instructions with respect to amendments. In the ratifying convention itself he argued for adoption, significantly stressing the concept of judicial review as a preventive of abuse of power by Congress. Strong in support of Washington's administration and of the financial measures of Alexander Hamilton, Marshall became the recognized Federalist leader in Virginia; in 1797 he served as one of the XYZ commissioners to France. Elected to Congress, 1799, he refused nomination as secretary of war but accepted appointment as secretary of state under John Adams, May 12, 1800.

Nominated to the post of chief justice of the United States, Jan. 20, 1801, Marshall took his seat on Feb. 4 after a reluctant confirmation by the Senate. He continued as secretary of state until the end of the Adams administration, though he did not draw the salary of that office; he served as chief justice until his death. A contemporary described him at this time as "tall, meager, emaciated, inelegant in dress, attitudes, gesture, of swarthy complexion, his countenance pervaded with great good humor and hilarity." He enjoyed, according to the same biographer, the faculty of developing a subject by a single glance of his mind. Another contemporary comments upon his "simplicity of manners and convivial habits" and his indolence. He may well have appeared indolent to the casual view, but the fresh energy of mind with which he met the larger occasions of his career is one of his most striking characteristics. Contrary to the previous procedure of the Supreme Court whereby the justices frequently delivered their opinions one after the other, the new chief justice spoke "for the Court," beginning with the August term, 1801. One of the last acts of the Adams administration had been to enlarge the lower federal judicial establishment; one of the early acts of the Jefferson administration was to abolish these new courts (April 1802). At the same time, in order to prevent any judicial test of the constitutionality of the Repeal Act, Congress postponed the next term of the Supreme Court to February 1803. Marshall, seeing in the action of Congress a dangerous challenge to the prestige of the Supreme Court and to the principle that it was the final authoritative interpreter of Constitution, took the first opportunity to vindicate the Court's authority. This opportunity was the celebrated case of *Marbury* v. *Madison*, which came before the Court in February 1803 and in which Federalist appointees to abolished judicial posts requested an order compelling the secretary of state to deliver their commissions of office. Marshall's opinion in this case was a very cleverly contrived document. While conceding that Marbury was entitled to the remedy he sought, Marshall, speaking for the Court, held that the Court could not award the remedy, since to do so would be to assume original jurisdiction in a case not within the categories enumerated by the Constitution. He avoided a direct clash with President Jefferson over the matter, but at the same time he read him a lecture on his legal duty. By holding the constitutional enumeration of cases in which the Supreme Court has original jurisdiction to be exclusive, he put a spoke in Republican plans to abolish the lower federal judiciary and parcel out its jurisdiction between the Supreme Court and the state courts. Most important of all, by holding Section 13 of the Judiciary Act of September 1789 to be unconstitutional, he brought to the support of the Union the important proposition that the Constitution has one final interpreter, at the same time seizing for the Supreme Court its greatest prerogative—the right of judicial review. After acting with a little less than courage during the impeachment trial of Judge Samuel Chase, 1804, Marshall seized the opportunity of the trial of Aaron Burr, 1807, for a renewed attack against the administration of President Jefferson. Marshall's conduct of the proceedings from start to finish was one prolonged baiting of the president, whose unholy zeal to hang Burr fairly exposed him to such treatment. In the process of saving Burr's neck, however, Marshall permitted the whole common-law view of treason as a conspiracy to be junked, with the monstrous result that it becomes impossible to convict the procurer of a treason who is canny enough to leave the overt acts to his agents and dupes. Meantime, Marshall had been busying himself in his leisure time with writing *The Life of George Washington* (1804–07), a hastily written and badly proportioned work which was celebrated in its own time but which recent scholarship has shown to be meretricious.

Since the sittings of the Supreme Court until 1827 were fairly brief, none of the justices resided in Washington; they took lodgings during term time, sometimes all in the same boardinghouse and living in the closest intimacy. These circumstances allowed Marshall to bring to bear upon his associates all his charm of personality and superiority in debate, thus further establishing his dominant position. In his great decisions subsequent to *Marbury* v. *Madison*, he set forth a body of constitutional doctrine which possesses internal consistency to a notable extent and which may be summarized generally as follows: The Constitu-

tion was the act of the people of the United States, although in bringing about its establishment they naturally made such use of existing governmental machinery as convenience dictated. It springs therefore from the ultimate source of authority in the country and possesses such characteristics as this authority chose to stamp upon it. By its own terms it is law and supreme law, wherefore its provisions control all governments and governmental agencies within the territory of the United States. Furthermore, being law, it is directly enforceable by courts in the decision of cases. Indeed, its clear intention is to designate the Supreme Court as the one final authoritative expositor of its terms; and while the Court has no will of its own apart from that of the law, it is nonetheless under obligation always to remember that "it is a constitution" which it is expounding and that this Constitution was "intended to endure for ages to come" and hence to be "adapted to the various *crises* of human affairs." Especially should a narrow rendition of its terms be avoided when questions of the advancement of national unity and power or of the security of private, especially property rights, are involved. These were the interests which had suffered most acutely at the hand of the states during the period of the Confederation and concern for which had brought about the convention that framed the Constitution. By the same token, state power must be sternly repressed whenever it entrenches upon the field of powers delegated by the Constitution to "the government of all" or when it menaces the principles on which public and private faith depends. The designated organ to effect these ends is the Supreme Court.

The immediate target, indeed, of all Marshall's great opinions following 1809 was furnished by the pretensions of state legislatures, the seat then, as in 1787, of localizing and democratic tendencies. His system of constitutional doctrine has continued the vehicle to the present time both of his ingrained conservatism and of his love of the Union.

Marshall's further basic constitutional opinions are to be read in the following cases: *Fletcher* v. *Peck* (6 *Cranch*, 87), *McCulloch* v. *Maryland* (4 *Wheaton*, 316), *Sturges* v. *Crowninshield* (17 *U.S.*, 122), and *Dartmouth College* v. *Woodward* (17 *U.S.*, 518), the latter three delivered at the single term of 1819; *Cohens* v. *Virginia* (6 *Wheaton* 264), given in the 1821 term; *Gibbons* v. *Ogden* (9 *Wheaton*, 1) and *Osborn* v. *U.S. Bank* (22 *U.S.*, 738), rendered in 1825; *Brown* v. *Maryland* (25 *U.S.*, 419), and *Ogden* v. *Saunders* (25 *U.S.*, 213, Marshall's sole dissenting opinion in the constitutional field), rendered in 1827.

A constantly increasing group of Americans, however, began to find Marshall's reading of the Constitution less and less acceptable. The slogan of the day was "states' rights" or "state sovereignty," and one of the most notable spokesmen against Marshall's views was John Taylor of Caroline, who spoke for the dissidents in Virginia. There was hardly a congressional session *post* 1821 in which some proposal for weakening the Court, or at least Marshall's influence over it, was not made. He made a few concessions to the spirit of the hour, but returned to his strong position in *Craig* v. *Missouri* (4 *Peters* 410) and *Worcester* v. *Georgia* (6 *Peters*, 515). With respect to the latter, the word ran round that President Jackson had declared "John Marshall has made his decision, now let him enforce it." Marshall saw the Union crumbling in such developments as these and in the contemporary nullification movement in South Carolina. His life's work was seemingly being destroyed. However, when in 1833 Joseph Story published his *Commentaries on the Constitution of the United States*, Marshall saw his version of the Constitution systematized therein and given its historical setting.

While official propriety forbade that Marshall should express himself publicly on political issues, it is known from his correspondence that he would have welcomed the Federalist nomination for the presidency in 1812 and that in 1832 he was hoping against hope for the election of Henry Clay so that Andrew Jackson would not have the appointment of his own successor. When Jackson was elected, he determined to stick it out to the end and did so. He took a leading role in the Virginia constitutional convention of 1829, and it was due to his and Madison's efforts that manhood suffrage was defeated and that the oligarchic system of county justices was fastened upon the state more tightly than ever.

MARSHALL, LOUIS (b. *Fauquier Co., Va., 1773; d. Woodford Co., Ky., 1866*), physician, educator. Son of Thomas Marshall; brother of James M. and John Marshall. As president, Washington College (now Washington and Lee University), 1830–34, his effort to develop individualism in the students by a total absence of discipline failed to succeed. Later he taught at Transylvania University and at other schools in Kentucky. A man of great intellectual attainment, he was eccentric in manners and speech.

MARSHALL, LOUIS (b. *Syracuse, N.Y., 1856; d. Zurich, Switzerland, 1929*), lawyer, publicist, Jewish leader. Completed the course of Columbia Law School in a single year, 1876–77; was admitted to the bar, 1878. Practiced in New York City *post* 1894 as a member of the firm of Guggenheimer, Untermyer & Marshall. In his practice before the U.S. Supreme Court no contemporary succeeded so frequently as Marshall in striking down measures which violated the federal or state constitutions; he was particularly interested in cases involving discrimination against minorities, corporate abuses, and the rights of immigrants. Active in the American Jewish Committee, he served as its president from 1912 until his death; he was also one of the reorganizers of the Jewish Theological Seminary and served as chairman of its board of directors. At the Paris Peace Conference, 1919, he cooperated with the committee on new states in drafting antidiscrimination clauses for insertion into the treaties with Poland, Romania, and other East European states. He was also a leader in the Zionist movement.

MARSHALL, THOMAS (b. *Westmoreland Co., Va., 1730; d. 1802*), surveyor, Virginia and Kentucky pioneer and legislator, Revolutionary soldier. Father of James M., John and Louis Marshall (1773–1866). Removed to the Virginia frontier *ca.* 1754; to the Kentucky frontier, 1783. A friend of George Washington and a man of marked intellectual stature, Marshall had a strong formative influence on the mind of his son John, the later chief justice.

MARSHALL, THOMAS ALEXANDER (b. *Kentucky, 1794; d. Louisville, Ky., 1871*), jurist, Kentucky legislator. Son of Humphrey Marshall (1760–1841). Congressman, Whig, from Kentucky, 1831–35; held orthodox Whig opinions. As justice, Kentucky court of appeals, 1835–56, he was twice named chief justice of that court. A Unionist during the Civil War, he again served briefly as chief justice of the state court of appeals, 1866–67.

MARSHALL, THOMAS RILEY (b. *North Manchester, Ind., 1854; d. Washington, D.C., 1925*), lawyer, vice president of the United States. Graduated Wabash College, 1873. Admitted to the bar, 1875, he practiced for many years at Columbia City, Ind. A loyal Democrat ("Democrats, like poets, are born, not made," he once said), he supported his party for many years without any desire to hold office. Elected governor of Indiana, 1908, he opposed "dry" legislation, pushed an extensive program of labor and social enactments through the legislature, and tried to secure adoption of a much-needed new state constitution. Nominated for vice president on the Woodrow Wilson ticket, 1912, Marshall was elected and was reelected, 1916, the first vice president in nearly a century to succeed himself. Presiding over the Senate with grace and tact, he exerted personal influence most effectively on behalf of many administration measures; he was perhaps the most popular vice president that the United States has ever had. Generous, kindly, and tolerant, he possessed a never-failing sense of humor. Among his most quoted remarks were, "What this country needs is a really good 5 cent cigar," and "It's got so it's as easy to amend the Constitution of the United States as it used to be to draw a cork."

MARSHALL, WILLIAM EDGAR (b. *New York, N.Y., 1837; d. New York 1906*), portrait painter, engraver. Best known for his portrait of Abraham Lincoln, painted from photographs and descriptions, which had enormous circulation as an engraving. Marshall helped many struggling painters, notably Albert P. Ryder.

MARSHALL, WILLIAM LOUIS (b. *Washington, Ky., 1846; d. Washington, D.C., 1920*), soldier, engineer. Served in 10th Kentucky Cavalry, 1862–63; graduated West Point, 1868. As assistant to G. M. Wheeler in exploration of the Rocky Mountains, 1872–76, he discovered Marshall Pass and also the gold placers in the Marshall Basin, San Miguel River, Colo. After working on river improvement projects in the South, 1876–84, he was placed in charge of river and harbor improvements in Wisconsin and Illinois. In his construction of the Hennepin Canal, 1890–99, he pioneered in the use of concrete masonry; at New York City, 1899–1908, he completed the Ambrose Channel and the extension of Governor's Island, and improved the coast defenses. Commissioned chief of engineers, July 1908, with the rank of brigadier general, he retired from active service, 1910.

MARSHALL, WILLIAM RAINEY (b. *Boone Co., Mo., 1825; d. Pasadena, Calif., 1896*), Union soldier, Minnesota pioneer. Republican governor of Minnesota, 1866–70.

MARTEL, CHARLES (b. *Zurich, Switzerland, 1860; d. Washington, D.C., 1945*), librarian. Name adopted by Karl David Hanke at some time after his immigration to the United States, 1879. Joined staff of Newberry Library, Chicago, Ill., 1892, where his linguistic skills and bibliographic knowledge brought him recognition. Appointed to staff of Library of Congress, 1897, as chief classifier, he was principally responsible for devising the system of book classification and cataloging presently in use there and for supervising the changeover from the older system. From 1912 to 1930, he held the title of chief of the catalog division; thereafter until shortly before his death, he continued his work under title of consultant.

MARTIN, ALEXANDER (b. *Hunterdon Co., N.J., 1740; d. Rockingham Co., N.C., 1807*), lawyer, planter, Revolutionary soldier, North Carolina legislator. Removed to North Carolina, *ca.* 1757, where he held judicial offices under the crown. Resigning his commission as a Continental colonel, 1777, he was active during the rest of the Revolution as a North Carolina legislator and as acting governor, 1781–82. A moderate Federalist *ante* 1790, he was elected governor in 1782 and reelected, 1783 and 1784; again elected governor, 1789, he served through 1792. A master of the art of conciliation, he drifted with the current of opinion in the General Assembly. He served as U.S. senator, Democratic-Republican, 1793–99.

MARTIN, ANNE HENRIETTA (b. *Empire City, Nev., 1875; d. Carmel, Calif., 1951*), suffragist, author, social critic. Graduated from the University of Nevada and Stanford University, M.A., 1897. After teaching in Nevada and traveling in Europe (where she worked with suffragist Emmeline Pankhurst), Martin became involved in the suffragist movement and women's politics, and was the first national chairwoman of the National Woman's Party. The first woman to run for the U.S. Senate, Martin, as an independent, was unsuccessful in her tries in 1918 and 1920.

Member of the national board of the Women's International League for Peace and Freedom, 1926–36.

MARTIN, ARTEMAS (*b. Steuben Co., N.Y., 1835; d. Washington, D.C., 1918*), mathematician. Publisher and editor of the *Mathematical Visitor*, 1877–94, and of the *Mathematical Magazine*, 1882–1913; associated *post* 1885 with U.S. Coast and Geodetic Survey; authority on early mathematical textbooks.

MARTIN, EDWARD SANDFORD (*b. near Auburn, N.Y., 1856; d. New York, N.Y., 1939*), poet, essayist. A regular contributor to *Life, Scribner's Magazine, Harper's Weekly*. Author of *A Little Brother of the Rich* (1890) and other books.

MARTIN, ELIZABETH PRICE (*b. Philadelphia, Pa., 1864; d. 1932*), civic leader, philanthropist. Grand-daughter of Eli K. Price (1797–1884). Active in Pennsylvania welfare movements and in Republican politics; founded Garden Club of America.

MARTIN, EVERETT DEAN (*b. Jacksonville. Ill., 1880; d. Claremont, Calif., 1941*), adult educator, social psychologist. Ordained a Congregational minister, 1907, he left the ministry in 1914 to write on social questions. From 1916 until 1934 he was associated with the People's Institute, New York City, becoming its director, 1922. He headed the Department of Social Philosophy at Cooper Union, 1934–38, and was professor of social philosophy at the Claremont graduate school *post* 1938. His books included *The Behavior of Crowds* (1920) and *The Meaning of a Liberal Education* (1926).

MARTIN, FRANÇOIS-XAVIER (*b. Marseilles, France, 1762; d. New Orleans, La., 1846*), jurist. Immigrated to America *ca.* 1780; settled in New Bern, N.C., where he built up a printing and publishing business. Admitted to the bar, 1789, he wrote or edited a variety of law texts, was successful in practice, and was employed by the state to make his well-known "Revisal" of the *Laws of the State of North Carolina*. Appointed a federal judge for Mississippi Territory, 1809, he was transferred to the Territory of Orleans, 1810. He was the first attorney general of Louisiana, 1813, and became a judge of the state supreme court, 1815. Named chief justice, 1836, he retired, 1846. Martin played a great part in creating a jurisprudence for Louisiana out of the tangle of French, Spanish, and Anglo-American codes which applied there. He began to publish reports of cases decided by the courts, 1811, and continued them until 1830; he also published poorly written and badly arranged historical studies of Louisiana and North Carolina.

MARTIN, FRANKLIN HENRY (*b. Ixonia, Wis., 1857; d. Phoenix, Ariz., 1935*), surgeon. Graduated Chicago Medical College, 1880. An American pioneer in aseptic surgery and in a number of gynecological operations, Martin founded *Surgery, Gynecology and Obstetrics*, 1905, and served as its editor in chief until his death. He was largely instrumental in forming the American College of Surgeons, 1913.

MARTIN, FREDERICK TOWNSEND (*b. Albany, N.Y., 1849; d. London, England, 1914*), lawyer, philanthropist. Author of, among other works, *The Passing of the Idle Rich* (1911).

MARTIN, GLENN LUTHER ("CY") (*b. Macksburg, Iowa, 1886; d. Baltimore, Md., 1955*), aviator, aircraft manufacturer. The third person to fly in the U.S. (after the Wright Brothers). Martin built his own airplane and was a barnstormer from 1909 to 1915. By 1912, he had an aircraft factory in Los Angeles, which became the Wright-Martin Corp. in 1917, with Martin as vice president. The company was unsuccessful and Martin set up his own company in Cleveland in 1917, moving to Middle River, Md., in 1929. Developed the MB-2 and B-10 bombers; in 1935,

Martin developed the *China Clipper*. During World War II, he built the B-26 Marauder medium bomber.

MARTIN, HENRY AUSTIN (*b. London, England, 1824; d. Boston, Mass. 1884*), physician, surgeon. Came to America as a boy. Graduated Harvard Medical School, 1845, and practiced thereafter in Roxbury, Mass. His principal service to American medicine was his study of vaccination and conditions essential for standardizing its procedure.

MARTIN, HENRY NEWELL (*b. Newry, Ireland, 1848; d. Yorkshire, England, 1896*), physiologist. Educated at University of London and at Cambridge University; served as assistant to T. H. Huxley, 1874. As professor of biology, Johns Hopkins, 1876–93, he laid down broad foundations for instruction and research in the biological sciences there. He held that physiology should be studied without regard to its applications to medicine, as a pure science absolutely independent of so-called practical affiliation. His own researches were mainly in the field of cardiac physiology.

MARTIN, HOMER DODGE (*b. Albany, N.Y., 1836; d. St. Paul, Minn., 1897*), landscape painter. Largely self-schooled, Martin was a practicing landscapist at the age of 16. Following Thomas Cole's predilection for wild scenery and large spaces, for some 20 years he tramped on sketching tours through the Adirondacks, the Catskills, and the Berkshires. Removing to New York City, 1865, he began to change his style of painting, simplifying his compositions by eliminating needless detail and experimenting with recondite colors. His work in the new style, although a vast improvement over the old, was considered eccentric by contemporaries and his patronage fell off. Further refinement in handling and tonality followed a trip to England, 1876, during which he met Whistler and was somewhat influenced by him. Never properly supported by his serious work, Martin eked out his living by magazine illustration. A resident in France, 1882–86, brought about a further change in Martin's style; his scale grew more intimate and less panoramic, his method grew richer and somewhat impressionistic. Misfortune continued to dog him after his return to America, but despite his failing eyesight and the onset of a fatal sickness, he filled the few years left of his life with the creation of masterpieces. Within a few years of his death, his erstwhile unsalable paintings had become the sensation of the art market. A poet in his painting, drawing from the contemplation of nature a soothing and noble melancholy, Martin is the most distinguished American artist in the imaginative tradition of landscape painting, although he lacked the vigorous construction of George Inness at his best and of Winslow Homer.

MARTIN, JAMES GREEN (*b. Elizabeth City, N.C., 1819; d. Asheville, N.C., 1878*), soldier, lawyer. Graduated West Point, 1840. Served with distinction in the Mexican War and on the western frontier. Resigning his commission in June 1861, he performed brilliant service in the preparation, training, and arming of North Carolina militia. Appointed Confederate brigadier general, May 1862, he held commands principally in North Carolina until the end of the war.

MARTIN, JOHN ALEXANDER (*b. Brownsville, Pa., 1839; d. 1889*), journalist, Union soldier. Removed to Kansas, 1857, *post* 1858 edited the Atchison *Champion*. Long prominent in the Republican party, Martin served as governor of Kansas, 1885–89. He made prohibition the settled policy of the Republican party in the state, advocated legal reforms, and opposed excessive state financing of railroads and monopolies.

MARTIN, JOHN HILL (*b. Philadelphia, Pa., 1823; d. 1906*), lawyer, Pennsylvania local historian.

MARTIN, JOHNNY LEONARD ROOSEVELT ("PEPPER") (*b. near Temple, Okla., 1904; d. McAlester, Okla., 1965*), baseball player. With the St. Louis Cardinals, 1928–40; played center field and third base. Career totals mark him as a good ballplayer but no superstar; his fame rests on a ten-day period in 1931 when he dominated the World Series against the Philadelphia Athletics. He sparked his team by stealing five bases and setting a new World Series record of twelve base hits in twenty-four times at bat; he was directly responsible for three of the four Cardinal victories that brought the team the championship, prompting sportswriter "Red" Smith to write in the *St. Louis Star* that he was "the greatest one-man show the baseball world has ever known." Later moved into minor-league managing, and one year as assistant manager of the Chicago Cubs (1956).

MARTIN, JOSEPH WILLIAM, JR. (*b. North Attleboro, Mass., 1884; d. Hollywood, Fla., 1968*), Speaker of the House of Representatives. Editor and publisher of *North Attleboro Evening Chronicle* from 1908. Member of the Massachusetts House of Representatives (1911–13), Senate (1914–16, and U.S. House of Representatives (1925–67). Was speaker in 1947–49 and 1953–55. A Republican who wielded considerable influence, he gained recognition as one of the party's shrewdest and most effective legislators.

MARTIN, JOSIAH (*b. 1737; d. London, England, 1786*), British army officer. Commissioned royal governor of North Carolina, 1771, he was soon in conflict with the North Carolina Assembly over a number of issues on which his commission would not permit him to yield. Fleeing from New Bern, he took refuge aboard a British ship in Cape Fear River, July 1775. After the failure of several of his plans for recapturing the colony, he served as a volunteer under Clinton and Cornwallis in the Carolina campaigns, 1779–81.

MARTIN, LUTHER (*b. near New Brunswick, N.J., ca. 1748; d. New York, N.Y., 1826*), lawyer, Revolutionary patriot. Graduated College of New Jersey (Princeton), 1766. Taught school in Maryland and Virginia; admitted to the bar in Virginia, 1771, he practiced in Maryland until the outbreak of the Revolution. As attorney general of Maryland, 1778–1805, he resided in Baltimore. A delegate to the Convention of 1787 at Philadelphia, he opposed the plan for a strong central government and later made a futile effort to prevent Maryland's ratification of the Constitution. Because of his bitter enmity against Thomas Jefferson, Martin allied himself with the Federalist party and aided Justice Samuel Chase in his impeachment trial, 1804; in 1807, he was one of the lawyers who defended Aaron Burr at his treason trial. Serving again as Maryland attorney general, 1818–22, Martin, in his last important case (*McCulloch v. Maryland*), opposed Daniel Webster, William Pinkney, and William Wirt. Ruined by drink and extravagance, Martin died in the house of Aaron Burr. Eminent as a lawyer, an opponent of slavery, and a generous loyal friend, Martin was his own worst enemy—"the rollicking, witty, audacious attorney general of Maryland . . . drunken, generous, slovenly, grand; bulldog of Federalism . . . the notorious reprobate genius."

MARTIN, THOMAS COMMERFORD (*b. London, England, 1856; d. Pittsfield, Mass., 1924*), scientific writer. Came to America *ca.* 1877; served as assistant in laboratory of Thomas A. Edison, 1877–79. Edited the *Electrical Engineer* and the *Electrical World*, 1883–1909; was author of a number of books and articles on electricity and inventions.

MARTIN, THOMAS STAPLES (*b. Scottsville, Va., 1847; d. 1919*), lawyer, politician. U.S. senator, Democrat, from Virginia, 1895–1919. A conservative of great personal integrity, Martin led the Democratic "machine" in Virginia. Majority floor leader, 1917–19, he also served as chairman of the Committee on Appropriations during World War I.

MARTIN, VICTORIA CLAFLIN WOODHULL. *See* WOODHULL, VICTORIA CLAFLIN.

MARTIN, WARREN HOMER (*b. Goreville, Ill., 1901; d. Los Angeles, Calif., 1968*), clergyman and first elected president of the United Automobile Workers (UAW). Ordained a Baptist minister in 1922. Pastor of the Baptist church in Leeds, Mo., from 1932; he encouraged his congregation, a good part of which was made up of workers from the Kansas City, Mo., Chevrolet plant, to unionize. Removed as pastor in 1934, he went to work at the Chevrolet plant, where he became an active union organizer and was president of the American Federation of Labor local. Discharged in 1934 for union activities. In Detroit, Mich., from 1935; elected first president of the newly organized UAW. Martin was popular among the workers, but colleagues came to regard him as incompetent and unstable, and unable to work with others. He suspended fifteen members of the UAW's executive board in 1939; that group gained the support of the Congress of Industrial Workers and was the nucleus from which the future union sprang. Martin was forced to retire from the labor movement in April 1940.

MARTIN, WILLIAM ALEXANDER PARSONS (*b. Livonia, Ind., 1827; d. Peking, China, 1916*), Presbyterian clergyman. Missionary and educator in China *post* 1850.

MARTIN, WILLIAM THOMPSON (*b. Glasgow, Ky., 1823; d. Natchez, Miss., 1910*), lawyer, Confederate major general of cavalry, Mississippi legislator and railroad builder.

MARTINDALE, JOHN HENRY (*b. Hudson Falls, N.Y., 1815; d. Nice, France, 1881*), lawyer, Union soldier. Graduated West Point, 1835. Practiced law *post* 1838 in Batavia and Rochester, N.Y. During the Civil War, Martindale took an active part in training volunteer regiments, served with credit as governor of the District of Columbia and in the field, and rose to corps command before his resignation for ill health in the fall of 1864.

MARTINELLI, GIOVANNI (*b. Montagnana, Italy, 1885; d. New York, N.Y., 1969*), tenor. Concert debut in Rossini's *Stabat mater* in Milan, and opera debut in *Ernani* at Milan's Teatro dal Verme, both 1910. First appeared in the United States as Cavaradossi in *Tosca*, in Philadelphia with the Chicago-Philadelphia Opera Company (1913). With the Metropolitan Opera, in New York City, for thirty-two seasons (1913–45), most often as Radames (*Aida*), Don José (*Carmen*), Canio (*Pagliacci*), and Manrico (*Il trovatore*). Also sang regularly at the San Francisco Opera, the Chicago Civic Opera, and major European opera houses, as well as in the concert hall.

MARTINY, PHILIP (*b. Strasbourg, Alsace, France, 1858; d. New York, N.Y., 1927*), sculptor. Coming to America as a young man, Martiny worked as a carver under Augustus Saint-Gaudens and won reputation as the foremost decorative sculptor of the day for his work for the Agricultural Building at the Chicago World's Fair, 1893. Thereafter he received numerous commissions from McKim, Mead and White and other architects. Among his noted works are the high-relief marble carvings of the balustrade, entrance hall, Library of Congress; the Soldiers' and Sailors' Monument, Jersey City, N.J.; the south pair of bronze doors, St. Bartholomew's Church, New York City; the World War I memorials in Abingdon Square and Chelsea Park, New York City; the cornice and entrance figures of the New York City Hall of Records.

MARTY, MARTIN (*b. Schwyz, Switzerland, 1834; d. St. Cloud, Minn., 1896*), Roman Catholic clergyman, Benedictine.

Came to the monastery at St. Meinrad, Ind., 1860; was chosen its first mitred abbot, 1870. Led a group of Benedictines to work among the Sioux at Standing Rock agency, 1873. Vicar apostolic of the Dakota Territory, 1880–90; first bishop of Sioux Falls, 1890–95. Bishop of St. Cloud, Minn., *post* 1895.

MARTYN, SARAH TOWNE SMITH (*b. Hopkinton, N.H., 1805; d. New York, N.Y., 1879*), author. Editor of religious and reform publications.

MARVEL, IK. *See* MITCHELL, DONALD GRANT.

MARVIN, CHARLES FREDERICK (*b. Putnam, later part of Zanesville, Ohio, 1858; d. Washington, D.C., 1943*), meteorologist. M.E., Ohio State University, 1833. Appointed junior professor of meteorology, U.S. Army Signal Service, 1884, he became chief of its instrument division, 1888, and retained that post subsequent to the transfer in 1891 of the weather service to civilian control of the Weather Bureau. He served as chief of the Weather Bureau, 1913–34. A tactful, able administrator, he made his chief contributions to meteorological science in the invention, improvement, and standardization of the instruments used.

MARVIN, DUDLEY (*b. Lyme, Conn., 1786; d. Ripley, N.Y., 1852*), lawyer. Congressman, National Republican (Adams Democrat), from New York, 1823–29. Coming under the influence of Henry Clay, he became a Whig and advocated a protective tariff and the limitation of slavery. Again in Congress as a Whig, 1847–49, he defended the right of the federal government to exclude slavery from the territories acquired from Mexico.

MARVIN, ENOCH MATHER (*b. present Warren Co., Mo., 1823; d. 1877*), Methodist clergyman. Pastor of several congregations in Missouri, 1855–62; served as Confederate army chaplain. Stationed at Marshall, Tex., after the Civil War, he was elected bishop, Methodist Episcopal Church, South, 1866.

MARWEDEL, EMMA JACOBINA CHRISTIANA (*b. near Göttingen, Germany, 1818; d. San Francisco, Calif., 1893*), leader in the kindergarten movement. Came to America *ca.* 1869. Established kindergartens and kindergarten normal classes in Washington, D.C., and at various places in California. The recognition which California gained as a leader in the kindergarten movement was largely the result of her work.

MARX, ADOLF ARTHUR ("HARPO") (*b. New York, N.Y., 1893; d. Los Angeles, Calif., 1964*) and **MARX, LEONARD ("CHICO")** (*b. New York, N.Y., 1891; d. Hollywood, Calif., 1961*), vaudeville and motion picture performers. With brothers Groucho and Gummo performed in a vaudeville variety act (from 1914) characterized by an energetic assortment of physical gags, outrageous puns, and ad-libbed mayhem, and incorporating Chico's piano playing. World War I temporarily broke up the act, which resumed with the youngest brother, Zeppo, replacing Gummo. Producer Charles Dillingham signed them to do a Broadway show, *I'll Say She Is* (1924), which was followed by *The Cocoanuts* (1925) and *Animal Crackers* (1928). Took their act to films with *The Cocoanuts* (1929), *Animal Crackers* (1930), *Monkey Business* (1931), *Horse Feathers* (1932), and *Duck Soup* (1933) for Paramount Pictures. Harpo, Chico, and Groucho went on to make *A Night at the Opera* (1935), *A Day at the Races* (1937), *A Day at the Circus* (1939), *Go West* (1941), and *The Big Store* (1941) for Metro-Goldwyn-Mayer, after which the team disbanded. During World War II Chico and Harpo performed for servicemen and at war bond rallies. Chico returned to vaudeville and Harpo acted in several short-run revivals of plays, including *The Man Who Came to Dinner* (1941). The brothers were reunited in *A Night in Casablanca* (1946) and *Love Happy* (1950) for United Artists.

MARZO, EDUARDO (*b. Naples, Italy, 1852; d. New York, N.Y., 1929*), composer, organist, teacher of music. Settled in the United States, 1869. After touring the country for a number of years as director of opera and concert companies and as accompanist of leading solo artists, Marzo devoted himself *post* 1882 to composition, voice teaching, and work as a church organist in New York.

MASCHKE, HEINRICH (*b. Breslau, Germany, 1853; d. Chicago, Ill., 1908*), mathematician. Studied at Heidelberg, Berlin, and Göttingen. Came to America, 1891, as an electrical technician; taught mathematics at University of Chicago *post* 1892. His original work in pure mathematics dealt with the theory of finite groups of linear substitutions and the theory of quadratic differential quantics.

MASLIANSKY, ZVI HIRSCH (*b. Slutzk, province of Minsk, Russia, 1856; d. Brooklyn, N.Y., 1943*), preacher, writer, Zionist. Became a speaker for the nascent Zionist movement after the Russian pogroms of 1881, and a professional propagandist for the movement, 1891. Ordered to leave Russia, 1894, he settled in New York City, 1895, bringing with him a reputation as the finest Yiddish orator of his time. As a lecturer at the Educational Alliance, and later as coeditor of *The Jewish World* (1902–05), he became an interpreter of Americanism to the immigrants from East Europe, but he was equally concerned with their preservation of Jewish tradition and their commitment to Zion. He continued active in Jewish charitable and educational affairs and was a frequent contributor to Yiddish and Hebrew newspapers and periodicals.

MASLOW, ABRAHAM H. (*b. Brooklyn, N.Y., 1908; d. Menlo Park, Calif., 1970*), founder of humanistic psychology. Studied at the University of Wisconsin (Ph.D., 1934). Taught at Brooklyn College, 1937–51, and was head of the psychology department at Brandeis University, 1951–61. Developed a conception of personality that, in contrast to "the analytic-dissecting-atomistic-Newtonian approach" of behaviorism and Freudian psychoanalysis, emphasized the holistic character of human nature. Defined and explained "the need hierarchy," in which D (deficit) needs must be met before B (becoming) needs come into play; "self-actualization"; and "peak experiences." Books include *Principles of Abnormal Psychology* (with Bela Mittelman, 1941), *Motivation and Personality* (1954), *Religions, Values, and Peak-Experiences* (1964), and *The Farther Reaches of Human Nature* (1971).

MASON, ARTHUR JOHN (*b. Melbourne, Australia, 1857; d. 1933*), engineer, inventor, agriculturalist. Came to America, 1881. Invented and designed excavating and ore-handling machinery; *post* 1910, experimented extensively on mechanized systems for agriculture which would guard against soil erosion.

MASON, CHARLES (*b. Pompey, N.Y., 1804; d. 1882*), jurist. Graduated West Point, 1829; was admitted to New York bar, 1832. Removed to present Burlington, Iowa, 1837. On the organization of the Iowa Territory in 1838 he was appointed chief justice of its supreme court and served until early in 1847. A member of the commission which drafted the 1851 Iowa Code, he served for a time as a county judge. After acting as federal commissioner of patents, 1853–57, he engaged in the practice of patent law.

MASON, CLAIBOURNE RICE (*b. Chesterfield Co., Va., 1800; d. Swope's Station, Va., 1885*), contractor, Confederate soldier, bridge and railroad construction engineer. Showed great resourcefulness as a military bridge constructor while serving with General T. J. Jackson's commands.

MASON, DANIEL GREGORY (*b. Brookline, Mass., 1873; d. Greenwich, Conn., 1953*), composer, professor, author. Graduated from Harvard, A.B., 1895. Taught at Columbia University, 1909–42; chairman of the music department from 1929. Composer of many works that were nineteenth-century in style, Mason was adamantly opposed to what he considered decadent twentieth-century music of Stravinsky, Ravel, and Scriabin. His *Third Symphony* (1937) was introduced by Sir John Barbirolli in New York. Books include *Contemporary Composers* (1918), *Dilemma of American Music* (1928), and *Tune In, America* (1931).

MASON, FRANCIS (*b. York, England, 1799; d. Burma, 1874*), Baptist clergyman. Came to America, 1818. Prepared for the ministry at Newton Theological Institution; was missionary to Burma *post* 1831.

MASON, FRANK STUART (*b. Weymouth, Mass., 1883; d. Boston, Mass., 1929*), musician. Taught at New England Conservatory of Music and elsewhere in Massachusetts with notable success.

MASON, GEORGE (*b. England, ca. 1629; d. Virginia, ca. 1686*), Virginia legislator and official. The first mention of Mason in the colonial records is in a patent for land in Westmoreland Co., March 1655. He later secured other large tracts of adjacent lands and was active in the defense of the government of the colony. He is chiefly remembered as an Indian fighter and as the precipitator of events culminating in Bacon's Rebellion.

MASON, GEORGE (*b. Fairfax Co., Va., 1725; d. Fairfax Co., 1792*), planter, statesman, political philosopher. Fourth in descent from George Mason (*ca. 1629–ca. 1686*). Privately tutored, 1736–39, Mason educated himself in the main by avid reading in his uncle's library; although never licensed as an attorney, he was a notably competent counsel of questions of public law throughout his life. Settling at "Gunston Hall," a new house which was completed to his taste in 1758, Mason personally managed his large and practically self-sufficient plantation; he also held county, town, and parish offices. Becoming a member of the Ohio Co., 1752, he served as its treasurer until 1773; in the latter year, when the crown abrogated the company's rights and regranted the area it covered to a Pennsylvania group, Mason produced his first major state paper in protest. He shunned office in the colonial government prior to the Revolution, allegedly because of chronic ill health but most probably because of the low rating he put upon human nature acting in committee. Offstage, however, he played a highly important part in the Revolutionary movement *post* 1765. He drafted the nonimportation association which Virginia adopted at the time of the dispute over the Townshend duties; he wrote the Fairfax Resolves of July 1774, which were accepted ultimately by the Continental Congress as a definition of the constitutional position of the colonies as against the crown; he exerted a constant word-of-mouth influence over all with whom he came in contact, including George Washington, Thomas Jefferson, and others of the Virginia dynasty.

Serving on the Committee of Safety, which took over the executive powers vacated by Governor Dunmore, 1775, Mason achieved his outstanding contribution as a constitutionalist by framing the Declaration of Rights, 1776, and the major part of the constitution of Virginia. The Declaration of Rights was drawn upon by Jefferson in the first part of the Declaration of Independence, became the basis for the first ten amendments to the U.S. Constitution, and had a considerable influence in France at the time of the French Revolution. Between 1776 and 1780 Mason was in the forefront of legislative activity, a close

collaborator of Jefferson, Patrick Henry, and George Wythe. He was responsible in large degree for the securing of the Northwest Territory through the efforts of George Rogers Clark, and it was he who sketched the plan out of which grew the cession to the United States by Virginia of its western lands and also Jefferson's ordinance for their government.

Disgusted at the conduct of public affairs *post* 1781, Mason went into retirement. His return to the Assembly, 1786, was motivated by his wish to prevent Virginia from indulging in further orgies of inflation and his growing conviction, despite his lifelong attachment to states' rights, that the Articles of Confederation were an inadequate basis for the central government. A member of the Convention of 1787, he was one of the five most frequent speakers in the debates at Philadelphia and exerted on the Constitution a marked constructive influence. Until the final days of the convention, he fought for the inclusion of certain clauses and the exclusion of others which he regarded as, respectively, essential and evil. Deciding not to sign the final document, he campaigned against ratification of the Constitution in the Virginia Convention, 1788. Mason's insistence on the necessity of a bill of rights bore fruit in the first ten amendments. The Eleventh Amendment, 1798, testifies to the correctness of his criticism of one part of the judiciary article. His principal reason for refusing to sign the Constitution, however, was that it incorporated a compromise between the New England states and those of the extreme South on the tariff and the slave trade; his opposition to slavery was perhaps the most consistent feature of his public career, and the Civil War served later as a sad justification of his views. More than perhaps any other American statesman of the period, Mason represented the rationalistic spirit, the Enlightenment in its American manifestation.

MASON, HENRY (*b. Brookline, Mass., 1831; d. Boston, Mass., 1890*), piano manufacturer. Son of Lowell Mason; brother of William Mason (1829–1908). Founded the Mason & Hamlin Co. with Emmons Hamlin, 1854.

MASON, JAMES MURRAY (*b. Georgetown, D.C., 1798; d. near Alexandria, Va., 1871*), lawyer, Virginia legislator. Grandson of George Mason (1725–92). Congressman, Democrat, from Virginia, 1837–39; U.S. senator, 1847–61. Long associated with the Southern-rights wing of the Democratic party, Mason was influenced particularly by John C. Calhoun. He drafted the Fugitive Slave Law of 1850 and considered the dispute between the North and the South to be a basically uncompromisable conflict between two social and economic systems, one of which was agrarian and the other industrial. His high social position, his ten years as chairman of the Senate Foreign Relations Committee, and his friendship with Jefferson Davis resulted in his appointment as Confederate diplomatic commissioner to England, 1861. En route to his post on board a British ship, the *Trent*, he and John Slidell, who was bound to France on a similar mission, were seized by a U.S. ship of war. This action very nearly caused a war between Great Britain and the United States. On his release from confinement at Boston, Jan. 1, 1862, Mason proceeded to England, where he cultivated the leading members of Parliament, the great merchants and manufacturers and the newspapermen; he also acted as central agent for the various naval and military purchasing agents of the Confederacy. He was, however, never received officially by the British government. After the Civil War, Mason lived for a time in Canada, returning to Virginia, 1868.

MASON, JEREMIAH (*b. Lebanon, Conn., 1768; d. Boston, Mass., 1848*), lawyer, New Hampshire legislator. Graduated Yale, 1788; studied law with Simeon Baldwin and with Stephen R. Bradley. Practiced in Portsmouth, N.H., *post* 1797. U.S.

senator, Federalist, from New Hampshire, 1813–17. Removed to Boston, Mass., 1832. Associated with Daniel Webster in the so-called Dartmouth College Case, Mason was considered by Webster and by Rufus Choate and Joseph Story as one of the greatest lawyers of his time.

MASON, JOHN (*b. England* ca. 1600; *d. Norwich, Conn.,* 1672), colonial soldier and magistrate. Came to Massachusetts *ante* 1633; was a leader in the migration thence to found Windsor on the Connecticut River, 1635. He is remembered principally for his part in the victory over the Pequot Indians near the Mystic River, 1637. His history of the war was printed in A *Relation of the Troubles That Have Hapned in New England* (1677) by Increase Mather; it was reprinted by Thomas Prince under the title A *Brief History of the Pequot War* (1736).

MASON, JOHN (*b. Orange, N.J.,* 1858; *d. Stamford, Conn.,* 1919), actor. Grandson of Lowell Mason. Gifted with much self-possession and a wonderful sense of timing, Mason played with great success *post* 1879, notably with the Boston Museum company and with the Lyceum Theatre company, New York.

MASON, JOHN MITCHELL (*b. New York, N.Y.,* 1770; *d. New York,* 1829), clergyman, educator. Held Associate Reform and Presbyterian pastorates; established forerunner of Union Theological Seminary, New York City, 1804. Provost, Columbia College, 1811–16; president, Dickinson College, 1821–24.

MASON, JOHN YOUNG (*b. Greensville Co., Va.,* 1799; *d.* 1859), lawyer, Virginia legislator, diplomat. Congressman, Democrat, from Virginia, 1831–37; secretary of the navy, 1844 and 1846–49; U.S. attorney general, 1845–46. As congressman, supported Jacksonian measures with exception of the force bill; introduced bill recognizing independence of Texas. While undistinguished U.S. minister to France, 1853–59, he joined with James Buchanan and Pierre Soulé in signing the Ostend Manifesto, October 1854.

MASON, JONATHAN (*b. Boston, Mass.,* 1756; *d. Boston,* 1831), lawyer, Massachusetts legislator. Graduated College of New Jersey (Princeton), 1774; read law with John Adams and Josiah Quincy. U.S. senator, Federalist, from Massachusetts, 1800–03; congressman, 1817–20. Was member of syndicate which developed Beacon Hill section of Boston *post* 1795; was also active in development of Dorchester.

MASON, LOWELL (*b. Medfield, Mass.,* 1792; *d. Orange, N.J.,* 1872), musical educator, hymnwriter. Resident in Savannah, Ga., 1812–27; thereafter until 1851, identified with musical life of Boston, Mass., where he was president of Handel and Haydn Society, founder of Boston Academy of Music (1833), and promoter of musical education for public school children and for the general public. He was author of *Boston Handel and Haydn Society's Collection of Church Music* (1822); *Manual of Instruction* (1834, for teaching music by Pestalozzian methods); and more than 50 books of tunes, sacred and secular. Not a great composer, Mason is remembered for "From Greenland's Icy Mountains" and "Nearer, My God, to Thee"; his chief importance, however, was in his service to musical education as teacher and method-planner and as an originator of the musical "convention" for training of teachers.

MASON, LUCY RANDOLPH (*b. Clarens, Va.,* 1882; *d. Atlanta, Ga.,* 1959), social worker, publicist. General secretary of the National Consumers League, an organization dedicated to improving women's rights in industry, 1932–37; before becoming the public relations officer for the southeastern branch of the newly formed Congress of Industrial Relations; she served until her retirement in 1951. Mason was an effective spokesman for the CIO in the antilabor South; her southern credentials and persuasive manner helped the labor movement win victories throughout the region.

MASON, LUTHER WHITING (*b. Turner, Maine,* 1828; *d. Buckfield, Maine,* 1896), music teacher. Supervised public school musical instruction in Louisville, Ky., Cincinnati, Ohio, Boston, Mass.; edited "National System" of music charts and books; organized teaching of music in Japanese public schools, 1879–82.

MASON, MAX (*b. Madison, Wis.,* 1877; *d. Claremont, Calif.,* 1961), mathematician and astrophysicist. Studied at the University of Wisconsin and the University of Göttingen (Ph.D., 1903). Taught mathematics at the Massachusetts Institute of Technology (1903–04), Yale (1904–08), and the University of Wisconsin (1908–09). Professor of mathematical physics at the University of Wisconsin (1909–25), president of the University of Chicago (1925–28), director and later president of the Division of Natural Sciences at the Rockefeller Foundation (1928–36), and head of the Observatory Council at the California Institute of Technology (1936–49). Worked on the problem of submarine detection during World War I; credited with inventing the sonar detector. Studied the relation between algebra of matrices and integral equations, differential equations, calculus of variations, existence theorems, oscillation properties, and asymptotic expressions. Principal scholarly work, written with Warren Weaver, was *The Electromagnetic Field* (1929).

MASON, OTIS TUFTON (*b. Eastport, Maine,* 1838; *d. Washington, D.C.,* 1908), ethnologist, educator. Associated *post* 1872 with Smithsonian Institution; as its curator of ethnology *post* 1884, classified and regulated National Museum; author of numerous papers on aboriginal technology.

MASON, RICHARD BARNES (*b. Fairfax Co., Va.,* 1797; *d. Jefferson Barracks, Mo.,* 1850), soldier. Great-grandson of George Mason (1725–92). Commissioned in regular army, 1817; served in Black Hawk War; as colonel, 1st Dragoons, served under General S. W. Kearny in conquest of New Mexico and California, 1846. Somewhat hidebound during his term as civil and military governor of California, 1847–49, Mason was the author of the most authentic story of the discovery of California gold (in his report at Monterey, Aug. 17, 1848).

MASON, SAMUEL (*b. Virginia,* ca. 1750; *d.* 1803), desperado, river pirate. Headed gang at Cave-in-Rock (Ohio River), 1797; thereafter pillaged travelers on Natchez Trace and on lower Mississippi until his murder by an accomplice.

MASON, STEVENS THOMSON (*b. Stafford Co., Va.,* 1760; *d. Philadelphia, Pa.,* 1803), lawyer, Virginia legislator. Son of Thomas Mason; nephew of George Mason (1725–92). As U.S. senator Democratic-Republican, from Virginia, 1794–1803, Mason was a strong partisan and achieved notoriety for publishing an abstract of the terms of Jay's Treaty while it was still under consideration by the Senate.

MASON, STEVENS THOMSON (*b. Loudoun Co., Va.,* 1811; *d. New York, N.Y.,* 1843), lawyer, politician. Grandson of Stevens T. Mason (1760–1803). Raised in Kentucky. Succeeded father as secretary of Michigan Territory, 1831; pressed movement for statehood; by intransigence over boundary with Ohio, secured Upper Peninsula for Michigan. As first governor of Michigan, 1836–40, followed a liberal policy on civic rights and education, but was held accountable for failing to check speculation and for the hardships following the panic of 1837.

MASON, THOMSON (*b. Prince William Co., Va., 1733; d. 1785*), lawyer, Revolutionary patriot, Virginia legislator. Brother of George Mason (1725–92).

MASON, WALT (*b. Columbus, Canada, 1862; d. La Jolla, Calif., 1939*), journalist, newspaper humorist. His widely syndicated "prose poems" first appeared in the *Emporia* (Kans.) *Gazette*, 1907.

MASON, WILLIAM (*b. Mystic, Conn., 1808; d. Taunton, Mass., 1883*), inventor, manufacturer. Designed and built specialized power looms; patented the self-acting mule for spinning cotton, 1840 and 1846. Began manufacture of high-quality locomotives, 1852; also produced tubular-spoke car wheels.

MASON, WILLIAM (*b. Boston, Mass., 1829; d. New York, N.Y., 1908*), musician. Son of Lowell Mason. Studied in Boston and abroad, was pupil of Franz Liszt. Founded (with Theodore Thomas) Mason-Thomas chamber music recital series, 1855–56. An outstanding teacher, he was author of *Touch and Technic* and other piano textbooks.

MASON, WILLIAM ERNEST (*b. Franklinville, N.Y., 1850; d. 1921*), lawyer. Raised in Iowa; practiced law in Chicago, Ill., *post* 1872. Congressman, Republican, from Illinois, 1887–91 and 1917–21; U.S. senator, 1897–1903. Independent, antimachine proponent of intervention in Cuba, 1898; later fought imperialism, and in 1917 opposed U.S. entry into World War I.

MASQUERIER, LEWIS (*b. Paris, Ky., 1802; d. probably New York, N.Y., date unknown*), pioneer in phonetic spelling, anarchic agrarian reformer. An early disciple of George H. Evans. Author of *The Phonotypic Spelling and Reading Manual* (1867), as well as earlier pamphlets on phonetics; author also of *Sociology* (1877).

MASSASOIT (*date of birth unknown; d. 1661*), chief of the Wampanoag Indians. Native name, Ousamequin (Yellow Feather). Resided mainly at Pokanoket (Mount Hope), near Bristol, R.I.; father of Metacomet (King Philip). Accompanied Samoset and Squanto to Plymouth, March 1621, and there negotiated a peace treaty with the settlers which he never broke.

MASSEY, GEORGE BETTON (*b. Kent Co., Md., 1856; d. 1927*), physician, pioneer in electrotherapeutics. Practiced in Philadelphia, Pa., *post* 1879.

MASSEY, JOHN EDWARD (*b. Spotsylvania Co., Va., 1819; d. 1901*), Baptist clergyman, Virginia legislator. A founder of the "Readjuster" movement, Massey rebelled against leadership of William Mahone and aided in restoration of a liberalized Democratic regime.

MASSON, THOMAS LANSING (*b. Essex, Conn., 1866; d. Glen Ridge, N.J., 1934*), humorist. Managing editor, *Life*, 1893–1922.

MAST, PHINEAS PRICE (*b. Lancaster Co., Pa., 1825; d. Springfield, Ohio, 1898*), inventor and manufacturer of farm machinery. Published *Farm and Fireside* (*post* 1879); also *Woman's Home Companion*.

MASTERS, EDGAR LEE (*b. Garnett, Kans., 1869; d. Melrose, Pa., 1950*), poet, novelist, lawyer. Raised in Petersburg and Lewistown, Ill.; admitted to the bar, 1891; removed to Chicago, 1892, hoping for a career in journalism. Practiced law, 1893–*ca.* 1920; associated with Clarence Darrow's law firm, 1903–11. Author of a number of works, both poetry and prose, he is remembered for a series of 244 epitaphs in free verse, published first under the pseudonym "Webster Ford" in *Reedy's Mirror* (St.

Louis, Mo.), 1914, and published in book form as *Spoon River Anthology*, 1915. Critically acclaimed, the work reflected its author's liberal sympathies, his nostalgia for a "lost America" of agrarian and democratic peace and freedom, and his conception of himself as an idealist doomed to continual disappointment in a materialistic society. Among his later books, none of which achieved similar renown, were *Domesday Book* (1920), *The New Spoon River* (1924), and studies of Vachel Lindsay, Walt Whitman, and Mark Twain.

MASTERSON, WILLIAM BARCLAY ("BAT") (*b. Iroquois Co., Ill., 1853; d. New York, N.Y., 1921*), frontier peace officer, gambler, sportswriter. Worked as buffalo hunter and contractor; won fame for bravery at battle of Adobe Walls, June 1874; served as U.S. Army scout. Between 1876 and 1885, Masterson was marshal or sheriff in a number of frontier towns, including Dodge City, Deadwood, and Tombstone. After his removal to New York City, 1902, he worked as sportswriter and editor, New York *Morning Telegraph*.

MASTIN, CLAUDIUS HENRY (*b. Hunstville, Ala., 1826; d. Mobile, Ala., 1898*), surgeon. M.D., University of Pennsylvania, 1849. Served in Confederate army medical branch, 1861–65. Devised instruments for genitourinary surgery; pioneered in use of metallic sutures. Practiced principally in Mobile.

MASURY, JOHN WESLEY (*b. Salem, Mass., 1820; d. New York, N.Y., 1895*), paint manufacturer, inventor. Devised metal paint containers which made feasible the marketing of ready-mixed paints, and invented an improved mill (patented 1870) for fine grinding of colors.

MATAS, RUDOLPH (*b. Bonnet Carre, La., 1860; d. New Orleans, La., 1957*), physician, surgeon. Studied at the University of Louisiana (now Tulane University), M.D., 1881. Taught at Tulane, 1884–1927; chairman of the department of surgery from 1894. Matas was the first surgeon to conduct the operation known as endoaneurysmorrhaphy (1888) and the first American to use spinal analgesia.

MATEER, CALVIN WILSON (*b. Cumberland Co., Pa. 1836; d. Tsingtao, China, 1908*), Presbyterian clergyman, educator. Missionary to China *post* 1863; author of *Mandarin Lessons* (1892) and other textbooks.

MATHER, COTTON (*b. Boston, Mass. 1662/3; d. Boston, 1727/8*), Puritan clergyman, scholar, author. Son of Increase Mather; grandson of Richard Mather and John Cotton. Influenced profoundly as a boy by his family tradition of leadership in the church, sensitive and self-conscious, Mather was more popular at Harvard with his tutors than with his classmates. Graduating, 1678, he took the degree of M.A., 1681, and was ordained, 1685, at the Boston Second Church, where he held office for the rest of his life, serving as his father's colleague until 1723. A tract written by him, *The Declaration of the Gentlemen, Merchants, and Inhabitants of Boston* (1689), served as the manifesto of the insurgents against the rule of Sir Edmund Andros. Elected a fellow of Harvard, 1690, he was recognized, in spite of his youth, as one of the most eminent divines in New England. The accession of a new governor, Sir William Phips, 1692, gave Cotton Mather an opportunity for exerting political influence; he wrote in defense of the new (1691) Massachusetts charter and of Phips's acts as governor. Despite the common opinion of Mather's actions during the Massachusetts witchcraft, prosecution of 1692, he had in fact endeavored to impose on the court a fairer set of evidential rules than were employed and he had also suggested milder punishments. As earlier writings of his, however, had excited the public mind on the subject of witchcraft and as he uttered no public protest against the trials or the sentences and indeed defended some of the verdicts in his book *Wonders of the Invisible World* (1693), he must be assigned a sufficient share of the blame.

Popular dissatisfaction with the new charter, a general weakening of clerical dominance in New England, and Mather's own too frequent arrogance of tone combined to lessen his popularity and political influence. Finding that he could not manage Joseph Dudley, who had become governor, 1702, Mather endeavored to oust him, but was unsuccessful. Passed over several times in the choice of a president for Harvard, he came to look upon Yale as the hope of the Congregational education in which he believed. Despite frustrated ambitions, failure in politics and the loss of personal popularity, he remained a leader in the church; he projected societies for various good causes—the maintenance of peace, the building of churches in poor communities, the relief of needy clergymen, and the like. He set up and supported a school for the education of slaves and gave generously of money and time to the poor.

His tireless activity as a writer gave him reputation abroad as well as at home. When smallpox broke out in Boston, 1721, he interested Dr. Zabdiel Boylston in inoculation and defended ably in print what seemed to him a beneficent medical practice. The greater part of his more than 450 books was published *post* 1692; his works reveal him an able editor, a historian, an amateur in many fields of knowledge, and a prose writer with a definite theory of style. His *Magnalia Christi Americana* (published London, 1702) was the mightiest American literary achievement up to its time; his *Bonifacius* (1710), under its later title, *Essays To Do Good*, had great popularity and was praised by Benjamin Franklin.

Constantly overworking himself, plagued by domestic tragedies, vain, unstable, and pedantic, Cotton Mather was consistently more tolerant in deed than in word, and his tolerance grew as he aged. None of the charges made against his honesty in money matters and even his sexual morality has ever been substantiated. Essentially a conservative, he was always torn between allegiance to inherited ideals and the realization that the newer time demanded new standards. Though bred in Calvinism, he expounded in his *Christian Philosopher* (1721) doctrines which represent a step toward deism. However unlovable he may appear at the present, he commands respect for his studiousness, his industry, and his self-forgetfulness in his work.

MATHER, FRANK JEWETT, JR. (*b. Deep River, Conn., 1868; d. Princeton, N.J., 1953*), author, museum director. Studied at Williams College and Johns Hopkins University, Ph.D., 1892. After working in journalism, Mather joined the faculty of Princeton in the history of art department, 1910–33. First director of the Museum of Historic Art (now the Princeton University Museum of Art), 1922–46. A great collector, Mather became the dean of American art critics. Author of *Estimates in Art* (1916–31), *History of Italian Painting* (1923), and *Modern Painting* (1927).

MATHER, FRED (*b. present Rensselaer, N.Y., 1833; d. near Lake Nebagomain, Wis., 1900*), pisciculturist. Supervised New York State hatchery. Cold Spring Harbor, N.Y., 1833–95, where he developed and improved methods of propagation; was author of a number of technical works and popular books on outdoor life.

MATHER, INCREASE (*b. Dorchester, Mass., 1639; d. Boston, Mass., 1723*), Puritan clergyman, politician, author. Son of Richard Mather; father of Cotton Mather. Graduated Harvard, 1656; M.A., Trinity College, Dublin, 1658. Served as Puritan pastor in Devonshire, as chaplain to the garrison at Guernsey and in several other posts in England. Returning to Boston, Mass., September 1661, he became teacher of the Second Church, 1664. In 1681, he refused to leave his congregation to accept the offered presidency of Harvard. Drawn into politics by the crisis produced

by the quo warranto issued against the Massachusetts charter, 1683, he exhorted the citizens of Boston not to submit to the king. Appointed acting president of Harvard, 1685, and a year afterward rector, he encouraged the study of science and showed willingness to make the college something more than a training school for ministers; at the same time, he resisted successfully all efforts to undermine its Congregationalism.

In 1688, he was chosen to take petitions to the king from the Congregational churches in Massachusetts requesting the return of the charter. In London at the fall of James II and the accession of William III, Mather gave assurances of New England's loyalty to the new king and secured the exception of Massachusetts from Andros' rule. Appointed an official agent from Massachusetts, 1690, he and his fellow agents accepted a new charter framed by William III, which, while it took away the colonists' right to elect their own governors, preserved most of the power of the representative assembly elected by the voters. Mather was given by the king the privilege of nominating the governor and all other officers to be appointed for the first year of the new government. He thus secured unique influence in American politics.

On his return to Boston, May 1692, with Sir William Phips, the royal governor whom he had nominated, Mather found himself the object of a campaign of opposition and discredit conducted by Elisha Cooke and others who regarded the old charter as the foundation of Massachusetts liberties and who resented the political influence of Mather and his family. His enemies centered their attack on an attempt to oust him from the rectorship at Harvard. During the celebrated Salem witchcraft trials, Increase Mather, like his son Cotton, was slow to make a public protest, even though he disapproved of the type of evidence admitted. In October, however, Increase wrote and issued the most outspoken and the earliest public utterance issued in New England against the practices of the witchcraft court—*Cases of Conscience Concerning Evil Spirits*. It was first circulated in manuscript, perhaps even printed, before the end of 1692, although the printed version bears the date 1693.

His political prestige, like Cotton Mather's, declined *post* 1692 and for the same reasons. He was committed to the new charter, which he had helped to obtain, and he was a supporter of Governor Phips, whom he had nominated; he shared in their unpopularity. Surrendering his presidency of Harvard, 1701, he continued to exercise his ministry and to write. He took less of a part in politics, although he shared in his son's unsuccessful campaign against Governor Dudley. Increase Mather was unequaled in reputation and power by any native-born American Puritan of his generation. Hot-tempered, self-confident, favoring an ecclesiastical oligarchy, he was yet charitable and sometimes even conciliatory; in civil affairs, he argued for the preservation of democratic institutions. As an author his style was simple and direct, but without brilliance. Among his many books and pamphlets, the most interesting of them today are his political tracts written in connection with his agency in London and his two histories: *A Brief History of the Warr with the Indians* (1676) and *A Relation of the Troubles That Have Hapned in New England by Reason of the Indians There* (1677).

MATHER, RICHARD (*b. Lowton, Lancashire, England, 1596; d. Dorchester, Mass., 1669*), Puritan clergyman, author. Father of Increase Mather; grandfather of Cotton Mather. Originally a schoolmaster at Toxteth Park, now part of Liverpool, he began to preach in November 1618. Ordained soon afterward, he developed Puritan tendencies, but continued to preach at Toxteth and elsewhere in Lancashire until 1633 when he was suspended from his ministry. Removing to Boston, Mass., 1635, he became teacher of the church in Dorchester, August 1636, and continued to minister there until his death. He was, from the first, a leader of Massachusetts Congregationalism; his *Church-Government and*

Church-Covenant Discussed (1643) was the first elaborate defense and exposition of the New England theory of the church to be put forth in print. He was a collaborator with John Eliot and Thomas Welde in *The Whole Booke of Psalmes* (1640), better known as the *Bay Psalm Book*; he also wrote the original draft of the Cambridge Platform, which amended and adopted by a synod at Cambridge, 1646, was for many years the basic document of New England Congregationalism. Richard Mather's practical approach to ecclesiastical affairs was shown in his advocacy of the Half-Way Covenant, which permitted a limited church membership to those who gave no acceptable proof of spiritual regeneration.

MATHER, SAMUEL (*b. Boston, Mass., 1706; d. Boston, 1785*), Congregational clergyman, author. Son of Cotton Mather. Graduated Harvard, 1723. Chosen pastor at the Second Church, Boston, 1732, he was dismissed, 1741; a number of his congregation withdrawing with him, he established a new church where he ministered until his death. The last of the Mather dynasty, Samuel Mather had neither wide public influence nor preaching skill. He published a number of books and pamphlets that displayed erudition rather than distinction or intellectual strength.

MATHER, SAMUEL (*b. Cleveland, Ohio, 1851; d. 1931*), iron merchant, financier. Son of Samuel L. Mather. Associated *post* 1873 with numerous interests controlled by his family, notably the Cleveland Iron Mining Co. and its successors and subsidiaries. He was a benefactor of Kenyon College, Western Reserve University, and the Cleveland Community Fund.

MATHER, SAMUEL HOLMES (*b. Washington, N.H., 1813; d. 1894*), lawyer, banker. Removed to Cleveland, Ohio, 1835. Helped organize Cleveland Society for Savings, 1849; served it from the first as secretary and chief officer, and was president *post* 1884.

MATHER, SAMUEL LIVINGSTON (*b. Middletown, Conn., 1817; d. Cleveland, Ohio, 1890*), capitalist. Removing to Cleveland as an agent for his family and other interests who owned land in Ohio, he helped organize the Cleveland Iron Mining Co., *ca.* 1850, and by 1853 had become the driving force in the organization. The beginning of the city of Cleveland's industrial prominence may be attributed to Mather's company more than to any other single enterprise; his foresight and business ability in developing the ore lands in the Lake Superior region and improving the means of shipping their product revolutionized the iron industry in the United States. In 1869 Mather became president and treasurer of the company and held these offices until his death.

MATHER, STEPHEN TYNG (*b. San Francisco, Calif., 1867; d. Brookline, Mass., 1930*), organizer of the National Park Service. Graduated University of California, 1887; achieved success as a borax company executive. Named an assistant U.S. secretary of the interior, 1915, he was assigned to coordinate the 14 national parks under a single bureau; at Secretary Franklin K. Lane's insistence, he became director of the newly created National Park Service and served from 1917 to 1929. He secured definition of national parks as areas of the highest scenic value, to be preserved forever in their primitive condition. He opposed attempts to include tracts of lesser scenic importance, educated America in national parks ideals, and established and maintained service standards.

MATHER, WILLIAM WILLIAMS (*b. Brooklyn, Conn., 1804; d. Columbus, Ohio, 1859*), geologist. Graduated West Point, 1828; taught there and at the University of Louisiana and Ohio University. Directed geological surveys of Ohio, Kentucky, and New York, 1836–44.

MATHER, WINIFRED HOLT. *See* HOLT, WINIFRED.

MATHESON, WILLIAM JOHN (*b. Elkhorn, Wis., 1856; d. at sea, 1930*), chemist, financier. Active in American production of synthetic dyes; headed National Aniline & Chemical Co. and helped organize Allied Chemical & Dye Corp. Established, 1927, a fund for an international study of encephalitis.

MATHEWS, ALBERT (*b. New York, N.Y., 1820; d. Lake Mohonk, N.Y., 1903*), lawyer, author. Wrote minor essays, legends, and fiction under pen name "Paul Siogvolk."

MATHEWS, CORNELIUS (*b. Port Chester, N.Y., 1817; d. New York, N.Y., 1889*), author. Graduated University of the City of New York (New York University), 1834. A regular contributor to the *Knickerbocker Magazine* and other periodicals, he founded and edited with his friend E. A. Duyckinck the monthly *Arcturus* (1840–42).

MATHEWS, GEORGE (*b. Augusta Co., Va., 1739; d. Augusta, Ga., 1812*), Revolutionary soldier, politician. Removed to Georgia, 1785; served as governor of Georgia, 1787, as congressman, and as governor again, 1793–96. Falling into disfavor because of his connection with the Yazoo Act and suspected connection with the Blount Conspiracy, Mathews returned to prominence in 1810. Employed in official negotiations for transfer of West Florida, he continued irregular activities in East Florida on the failure of his primary mission. These included the stirring up of an insurrection and its support from nearby Georgia. The "insurgents" declared independence of Spain and between March and June 1812 occupied portions of the province. They had come within sight of St. Augustine before Secretary of State James Monroe disavowed the whole proceeding.

MATHEWS, HENRY MASON (*b. Greenbrier Co., Va., 1834; d. Lewisburg, W.Va., 1884*), lawyer, Confederate soldier. Democratic governor of West Virginia, 1877–81.

MATHEWS, JOHN (*b. Charleston, S.C., 1744; d. 1802*), lawyer, Revolutionary patriot and legislator. Governor of South Carolina, 1782–83; chancellor, 1784–91; judge of the court of equality, 1891–97.

MATHEWS, JOHN ALEXANDER (*b. Washington, Pa., 1872; d. Scarsdale, N.Y., 1935*), metallurgist, expert in steel alloys.

MATHEWS, SAMUEL (*b. England, ca. 1600; d. Virginia, 1660*), colonial planter. Came to Virginia, 1622; became a member of the council, 1623; was leader of the council in a revolt against the governor, Sir John Harvey, 1635. A Puritan and an early convert to the cause of the British Parliament, he became governor of Virginia, March 1658, and served with honesty and ability until his death.

MATHEWS, SHAILER (*b. Portland, Maine, 1863; d. Chicago, Ill., 1941*), theologian. B.A., Colby College, 1884. Graduated from Newton (Mass.) Theological Institute, a Baptist seminary, 1887. Although licensed, he never sought ordination or committed himself to the ministry. Deciding to become a teacher, he secured a position at Colby as associate professor of rhetoric. In 1889 he became professor of history and political economy, and the following spring he was granted a year's leave to study at the University of Berlin; this resulted in the publication of *Select Mediaeval Documents* (1892). His interest in social forces later found reflection also in his book *The French Revolution* (1901). On his return to Colby, Mathews continued to teach history and economics. In 1894 he became associate professor of New Testament history and interpretation at the University of Chicago. He became professor in 1897 and, in 1906, professor of historical and comparative theology. Two years later he was made dean of the

Divinity School, an office he filled with distinction until his retirement in 1933.

Mathews viewed Christianity not as a body of truth but as a religious movement subject to social forces; a study of the evolution of Christian doctrine ought therefore to begin with its social background. He elaborated his thesis in four books: *The Faith of Modernism* (1924), *The Atonement and the Social Process* (1930), *The Growth of the Idea of God* (1931), and his 1933 Barrows Lectures in India, *Christianity and Social Process* (1934). He wrote a series of articles on "Christian Sociology," published in book form as *The Social Teaching of Jesus* (1897).

Under Mathews' direction, the University of Chicago Divinity School engaged in a crusade to educate the public in a critical understanding of religion and the Bible. From 1903 to 1911 he edited the *World To-day*, a Chicago journal concerned with political and social trends, and from 1913 to 1920 he was editor of the *Biblical World*. A strong ecumenist, he was president of the Federal Council of the Churches of Christ in America (1912–16) and an active participant in international church gatherings.

MATHEWS, WILLIAM (*b. Waterville, Maine, 1818; d. Forest Hills, Mass., 1909*), journalist, teacher. Author of a number of works of literary criticism and of *Getting On in the World* (1873).

MATHEWS, WILLIAM SMYTHE BABCOCK (*b. Loudon, N.H., 1837; d Denver, Colo., 1912*), music teacher and author. Identified with music in Chicago, Ill., 1867–1910; raised standards of musical education in the West.

MATHEWSON, CHRISTOPHER (*b. Factoryville, Pa., 1880; d. Saranac, N.Y., 1925*), baseball player. Pitcher, New York Giants, 1900–16; won 511 games in National League career. Celebrated for sportsmanship; improved tone of professional baseball by encouraging employment of college-trained players.

MATHEWSON, EDWARD PAYSON (*b. Montreal, Canada, 1864; d. Tucson, Ariz., 1948*), metallurgist, mining engineer. Graduated McGill University in mining engineering, 1885. After extensive experience in management of lead, copper, and nickel smelting and refining operations for the Guggenheim interests, Anaconda Copper, and other corporations, he served as professor of administration of mineral industries at University of Arizona, 1926–42.

MATIGNON, FRANCIS ANTHONY (*b. Paris, France, 1753; d. Boston, Mass., 1818*), Roman Catholic clergyman, Sulpician. Came to America, 1792. Pastor in Boston, Mass., *post* 1792. His scholarship, kindness, and humility did much to make Catholicism acceptable in New England.

MATLACK, TIMOTHY (*b. Haddonfield, N.J., ca. 1734; d. Philadelphia, Pa., 1829*), merchant, Revolutionary patriot, Pennsylvania official. Assistant secretary of Continental Congress; probably engrossed Declaration of Independent. Active in forming Society of Free Quakers, 1781.

MATTESON, JOEL ALDRICH (*b. Watertown, N.Y., 1808; d. Chicago, Ill., 1873*), businessman, Illinois legislator. Removed to Illinois *ca.* 1833. As Democratic governor of Illinois, 1853–57, Matteson reduced state debt, introduced free schools. Implicated, 1858, in theft and refunding of state canal warrants, he devoted his efforts thereafter to railroad operation and banking.

MATTESON, TOMPKINS HARRISON (*b. Peterboro, N.Y., 1813; d. Sherburne, N.Y., 1884*), genre and portrait painter. Used patriotic or American country-life themes; painted *Spirit of '76*, *The First Sabbath of the Pilgrims*, and other popular works.

MATTHES, FRANÇOIS EMILE (*b. Amsterdam, the Netherlands, 1874; d. El Cerrito, Calif., 1948*), geologist. B.S.,

Massachusetts Institute of Technology, 1895. Associated with the U.S. Geological Survey, 1896–1947, he achieved distinction both as geologist and as topographer; the draftsmanship of his maps of national park areas has probably never been equaled. As geologist, he was author of a classic monograph on the Yosemite Valley (1930), and a treatise on glaciers; he considered his demonstration that the eastern escarpment of the Sierra Nevada had resulted from early Pleistocene faulting to be his foremost contribution.

MATTHES, GERARD HENDRIK (*b. Amsterdam, the Netherlands, 1874; d. New York, N.Y., 1959*), hydraulic engineer. Immigrated to the U.S. in 1888; graduated from the Massachusetts Institute of Technology, 1895. After working with the U.S. Geological Survey, the U.S. Reclamation Service, and private industry, Matthes joined the Army Engineer Office in 1929; head engineer for the Mississippi River Commission (1932) and consultant for flood control for the Tennessee Valley Authority (1936). Matthes was one of the first engineers to map regions from aerial photographs.

MATTHEW, WILLIAM DILLER (*b. St. John, New Brunswick, Canada, 1871; d. San Francisco, Calif., 1930*), vertebrate paleontologist. Graduated University of New Brunswick, 1889; Ph.B., School of Mines, Columbia, 1893, and Ph.D., Columbia, 1895. Associated *post* 1895 with American Museum of Natural History; argued against existence of former land bridges between continents.

MATTHEWS, BRANDER. *See* MATTHEWS, JAMES BRANDER.

MATTHEWS, CLAUDE (*b. Bethel, Ky., 1845; d. 1898*), stockbreeder. Democratic governor of Indiana, 1893–97; used state troops to restore order in coalminers' and Pullman strikes; reformed state tax laws.

MATTHEWS, FRANCIS PATRICK (*b. Albion, Nebr., 1887; d. Omaha, Nebr., 1952*), lawyer, secretary of the navy, diplomat. Studied at Creighton University. Active in many Catholic humanitarian and fraternal activities; designated papal chamberlain, 1944, by Pope Pius XII. Although critical of Roosevelt and Truman's handling of communism, Matthews was allegedly instrumental in swinging the Nebraska delegation to Truman at the 1948 convention. Appointed secretary of the navy, 1949; resigned, 1951, because of heavy criticism over his hard line stand against communism and his advocacy of widening the war in Korea. Ambassador to Ireland, 1951–52.

MATTHEWS, FRANKLIN (*b. St. Joseph, Mich., 1858; d. 1917*), journalist. Reporter, editor, correspondent, New York *Sun*, 1890–1912; thereafter, teacher of journalism, Columbia University.

MATTHEWS, JAMES BRANDER (*b. New Orleans, La., 1852; d. New York, N.Y., 1929*), educator, dramatist, critic. Graduated Columbia, 1871; Columbia Law School, 1873. Active in literary life of United States and England *post* 1880; intimate of major writers of the 1880's and 1890's; associate in authorship with Henry C. Bunner and Laurence Hutton. Taught literature and drama at Columbia, 1892–1924, and was author of many critical works in addition to plays and fiction.

MATTHEWS, JOHN (*b. London, England, 1808; d. 1870*), manufacturer and inventor of soda-water dispensing machinery. Immigrated to New York, N.Y., *ca.* 1832.

MATTHEWS, JOSEPH BROWN (*b. Hopkinsville, Ky., 1894; d. New York, N.Y., 1966*), author and reformer. Ordained a Methodist minister in 1915; missionary in Indonesia, 1915–21. Studied at Union Theological Seminary and Columbia University

(M.A., 1924). Taught at Scarritt College, Nashville, Tenn. (1924–27). Left Methodist church in 1927; joined Socialist party in 1929; claimed membership in numerous united-front organizations from 1933 onward. Vice president and member of the Board of Directors of Consumers' Research (1934–38); blacklisted by left-wing organizations after denouncing an employee strike in 1935. Testified before the House Un-American Activities Committee (HUAC) in 1938. Chief investigator and staff director under Martin Dies, Chairman of HUAC (through 1945). Executive director of the Senate Permanent Subcommittee on Investigations under Senator Joseph R. McCarthy (1953). His ideological journey from evangelical Protestantism to left-wing socialism to militant and obsessive anti-Communism ended in the maintenance of an extensive file of alleged Communist subversives that can be seen as a central document of McCarthyism. A regular contributor to right-wing periodicals *American Mercury*, *American Opinion*, and the *National Review* throughout the 1950's.

MATTHEWS, JOSEPH MERRITT (b. *Philadelphia, Pa., 1874; d. San Diego, Calif., 1931*), chemist, textile expert. Author of, among other works, *The Textile Fibres* (1904).

MATTHEWS, NATHAN (b. *Boston, Mass., 1854; d. Boston, 1927*), lawyer, city official, reformer. As Democratic mayor of Boston, 1891–95, he demonstrated the need for a strong executive in municipal government to secure effective reforms; he advocated department consolidations, civil service, and a remodeled charter.

MATTHEWS, STANLEY (b. *Cincinnati, Ohio, 1824; d. Washington, D.C., 1889*), lawyer, Union soldier, Ohio legislator and jurist. Graduated Kenyon College, 1840. As U.S. attorney in Ohio southern district, 1858–61, he gained unpopularity for Fugitive Slave Law enforcement; during Civil War he resigned colonelcy of 51st Ohio to become judge of Cincinnati's superior court, 1863–65. He won national attention as counsel for the electoral commission of 1877, contending that Congress should not go behind returns of state electors. U.S. senator, Republican, from Ohio, 1877–79, he was responsible for the Matthews Resolution of 1878, making silver legal tender. Appointed U.S. Supreme Court justice in 1881 after being earlier rejected by the Senate, he demonstrated fairness and ability during a period of expanding federal authority through liberal constitutional interpretations of the commerce clause and government borrowing powers.

MATTHEWS, WASHINGTON (b. *Killiney, Ireland, 1843; d. Washington, D.C., 1905*), army surgeon, ethnologist. Came to America as an infant; was raised in Iowa. M.D., University of Iowa, 1864. Serving in western frontier posts, he became an authority on the Indians of the plains and the Southwest. Author of numerous papers, notably *Navaho Legends* (1897); pioneered in physical anthropology.

MATTHEWS, WILLIAM (b. *Aberdeen, Scotland, 1822; d. Brooklyn, N.Y., 1896*), bookbinder, scholar. Came to America, 1843. Celebrated for craftsmanship and learning, he headed the bindery of D. Appleton and Co., 1853–90.

MATTHIESSEN, FRANCIS OTTO (b. *Pasadena, Calif., 1902; d. Boston, Mass., 1950*), scholar, teacher, critic. Graduated Yale, 1923. A Rhodes scholar, he received a B.Litt. in English at New College, Oxford, 1925. After graduate work at Harvard (M.A., 1926; Ph.D., 1927), he taught English at Yale, 1927–29. For the rest of his life he taught at Harvard, attracted there by the possibilities he saw in undergraduate honors field in history and literature, by the tutorial system, and by Harvard's commitment to the study of literature within its cultural contexts. As teacher, he was concerned primarily with communicating the experience of literature, conceived both as art and as the creation of individuals who lived in a specific society at a particular time. Appointed as instructor, 1929, he was made professor of history and literature, 1942. Among his books were *Sarah Orne Jewett* (1929); *The Achievement of T. S. Eliot* (1935, 1947); and *American Renaissance* (1941), his principal work, best described by its subtitle, "Art and Expression in the Age of Emerson and Whitman." A worker for numbers of liberal, pacifist, or radical causes, he became severely depressed *post* 1948 and took his own life.

MATTHIESSEN, FREDERICK WILLIAM (b. *Altona, Germany, 1835; d. La Salle, Ill., 1918*), metallurgist. Came to America, 1857. Pioneered in U.S. commercial production of zinc, 1858; built first zinc rolling mill in America at La Salle, 1866; founded Western Clock Manufacturing Co.

MATTICE, ASA MARTINES (b. *Buffalo, N.Y., 1853; d. New York, N.Y., 1925*), mechanical engineer. Graduated in engineering, U.S. Naval Academy, 1874; taught engineering at Annapolis and with John C. Kafer developed course in mechanical drawing there. After service at sea, worked with George W. Melville on design of machinery for new naval vessels. Resigning from the navy, 1890, he worked as machine designer and engineer for a number of corporations, including Westinghouse, Allis-Chalmers, and Remington Arms.

MATTINGLY, GARRETT (b. *Washington, D.C., 1900; d. Oxford, England, 1962*), historian. Studied at Harvard (Ph.D., 1935). Professor of English and history at Northwestern University, 1926–28, and Long Island University, 1928–42, Professor of European History at Columbia University, 1947–62, and visiting professor at Oxford, 1962. An internationally acknowledged master in the field of European diplomatic history. Author of *Bernard De Voto, a Preliminary Appraisal* (1938), *Further Supplement to the Letters, Dispatches, and State Papers of Henry VIII* (1940), *Catherine of Aragon* (1941), *Renaissance Diplomacy* (1955), and *The Armada* (1959).

MATTISON, HIRAM (b. *Norway, N.Y., 1811; d. Jersey City, N.J., 1868*), Methodist clergyman, controversialist, reformer.

MATTOCKS, JOHN (b. *Hartford, Conn., 1777; d. 1847*), lawyer, Vermont legislator and congressman. Antislavery Whig governor of Vermont, 1843–44. An important figure at the Vermont bar, he tried to establish Thanksgiving Day on Dec. 25.

MATTOON, STEPHEN (b. *Champion, N.Y., 1816; d. Marion, Ohio, 1889*), Presbyterian clergyman. With Samuel R. House, founded Presbyterian mission in Siam, where he served, 1847–65. First U.S. consul at Bangkok, 1856–59.

MATTSON, HANS (b. *Skåne, Sweden, 1832; d. 1893*), Minnesota pioneer, Union soldier, immigration agent. Came to America, 1851; removed from Illinois to Minnesota Territory as leader of a group of Swedish immigrants, 1853. Remained to the end of his life a power among Swedish Americans.

MATZELIGER, JAN ERNST (b. *Dutch Guiana, 1852; d. Lynn, Mass., 1889*), inventor. Born of a white father and a black mother, he immigrated to the United States ca. 1872. Between 1880 and 1883, he invented and developed a lasting machine which made it possible to manufacture shoes completely by machinery.

MAURAN, JOHN LAWRENCE (b. *Providence, R.I., 1866; d. Peterboro, N.H., 1933*), architect. Graduated Massachusetts Institute of Technology, 1889. Organized his own firm in St. Louis, Mo., 1900; conducted a large and varied practice there.

MAURER, JAMES HUDSON (*b. Reading, Pa., 1864; d. Reading, 1944*), labor leader, socialist. A machinist and steamfitter by trade, Maurer was active *post* 1880 in the Knights of Labor and in the Greenback and Populist parties; in 1899 he organized a local of the Socialist Labor party, shifting in 1901 to the newly organized Socialist party. Elected to his party's state committee, 1903, and to the national executive committee, 1904, he was Socialist candidate for governor of Pennsylvania in 1906. Failing of election, he ran for the legislature in 1910 and was successful; defeated for reelection, 1912, he won again in 1914 and 1916. As president of the Pennsylvania State Federation of Labor, 1912–28, he made it an important pressure group for labor legislation. As a legislator, he led in obtaining Pennsylvania's first workmen's compensation act, 1915, and worked for industrial health laws, child labor regulation, and old-age pensions. An outspoken opponent of U.S. participation in World War I, he continued his political activities thereafter and was Socialist candidate for U.S. vice president in 1928 and 1932; in 1934 he ran for the U.S. Senate. He resigned from the Socialist party in 1936 when it advocated a united front with the Communists.

MAURIN, PETER ARISTIDE (*b. Oultet, France, 1877; d. Newburgh, N.Y., 1949*), philosopher, teacher, reformer. A member of the teaching order of Christian Brothers, 1893–1903, he left the order to devote himself to the work of Le Sillon, a youth movement supportive of democracy as inspired by the spiritual values of Catholicism. After an attempt at homesteading in western Canada, 1909, he entered on a phase of wandering and casual labor; he came to the United States in 1911. About 1926, after much reading and thought about the problem of community in a world increasingly depersonalized by technology and social institutions, he arrived at a concept of a cooperative world in which ideas and labor would be shared in a Christian and agrarian utopia. Man, he believed, could be made good only by spiritual change effected in his individual personality, not through "social engineering" of whatever the ideological kind. In 1933 he was cofounder with Dorothy Day of the Catholic Worker movement, which gave practical application to his ideas and has been a major influence on Catholic life and thought in the United States.

MAURY, DABNEY HERNDON (*b. Fredericksburg, Va., 1822; d. Peoria, Ill., 1900*), Confederate soldier. Nephew of Matthew F. Maury. Graduated West Point, 1846. Served with credit in Mexican War; taught at West Point, 1847–52; served thereafter in Texas and New Mexico until 1861 when he entered the Confederate army. Promoted major general, November 1862, he became commander of the district of the Gulf, July 1863, and served in this capacity for the rest of the war. He organized the Southern Historical Society, 1868, was author of *Recollections of a Virginian* (1894), and served as U.S. minister to Columbia, 1885–89.

MAURY, FRANCIS FONTAINE (*b. near Danville, Ky., 1840; d. 1879*), surgeon. Graduated Centre College, 1860; M.D., Jefferson Medical College, 1862. Chief surgeon, Philadelphia Hospital, *post* 1865; performed many complex operations for the first time in America; headed surgical clinic at Jefferson Medical College.

MAURY, MATTHEW FONTAINE (*b. near Fredericksburg, Va., 1806; d. Lexington, Va., 1873*), naval officer, oceanographer. Raised in Tennessee. Appointed midshipman, 1825, he saw extensive service at sea; promoted lieutenant, 1836, in the same year he published his *A New Theoretical and Practical Treatise on Navigation*, which met with immediate favor. Assigned to harbor survey duty, he published a number of articles under the pen name "Harry Bluff," 1838, which scored inefficiency in the navy and suggested specific reforms. Appointed superintendent of the De-

pot of Charts and Instruments, 1842, he began a series of researches on winds and currents; in 1847, he issued his *Wind and Current Chart of the North Atlantic*, which was followed in the next year by explanatory sailing directions in *Abstract Log for the Use of American Navigators*. Demonstration of the practical utility of these charts and sailing directions secured for Maury the cooperation of many seamen in noting the winds and currents they encountered in various regions. By 1853, a uniform system of recording oceanographic data which he advocated had been adopted for naval vessels and merchants ships of the whole world by a congress at Brussels, Belgium. On the basis of data now coming in from all quarters, Maury revised his previous charts and drew up another for the Indian Ocean. Great savings of time and money resulted from the shorter passages made possible by Maury's researches. He published *The Physical Geography of the Sea* (1855), now recognized as the first textbook of modern oceanography, and served as a consultant in the laying of the Atlantic cable.

Deeply interested in the development of Southern commerce, Maury hoped for the opening of the Amazon Valley to free trade, believing that one effect of such a measure would be to draw slaves from the United States to Brazil. As antagonism mounted between North and South, he favored conciliation; however, on the secession of Virginia, he resigned from the U.S. Navy and accepted a commission as commander in the navy of the Confederate States. His worldwide reputation made him an effective spokesman for the Southern cause during his service as agent in England, 1862–65; he was also instrumental in securing warships for the Confederacy and was engaged in a series of experiments with electric mines. At the end of the war, Maury sought service with Mexico but returned to England, 1866. Accepting the professorship of meteorology at the Virginia Military Institute, 1868, he served in that capacity and as a lecturer until his death.

MAUS, MARION PERRY (*b. Burnt Mills, Md., 1850; d. New Windsor, Md., 1930*), soldier, celebrated Indian fighter. Graduated West Point, 1874. Served in campaigns against the Sioux, the Nez Percé, and the Apache; received the Congressional Medal of Honor for his actions in the Geronimo campaign, 1885–86. After a further career of exceptionally varied duties, he retired as brigadier general, 1913.

MAVERICK, (FONTAINE) MAURY (*b. San Antonio, Tex., 1895; d. San Antonio, Tex., 1954*), congressman, mayor. Studied at the University of Texas. As a congressman with liberal-radical views, 1934–38, he opposed Roosevelt's plan to pack the Supreme Court. His own group, known as Mavericks, were instrumental in passing the Public Utility Holding Company Act of 1935. Maverick was the only southern Democrat in the House to vote for the Gavigan antilynching bill in 1937. Reform mayor of San Antonio, 1939–41. Author of the best-selling autobiography *A Maverick American* (1937) and *In Blood and Ink* (1939). While chairman of the Smaller War Plants Corp. (1942–46) of the War Production Board, he introduced the term "gobbledygook" in an attempt to combat the use of bureaucratic language.

MAVERICK, PETER (*b. New York, N.Y., 1780; d. New York, 1831*), engraver, one of the founders of the National Academy of Design.

MAVERICK, SAMUEL (*b. ca. 1602, d. ca. 1676*), colonist. Came from England to America *ca.* 1624, settling on Boston Bay; welcomed John Winthrop and his party, 1630; was described by John Josselyn as "the only hospitable man in all the country." Became a freeman of the colony of Massachusetts, 1632, but joined in protest against limitation of citizenship to church members and other violation of civil and religious rights,

1646–47. Removing from Massachusetts, *ca.* 1650, he returned to England, *ca.* 1660, where he recommended a more rigid supervision of the colonies. He revisited Massachusetts in 1664, as one of four royal commissioners sent out to hear and determine complaints.

MAXCY, JONATHAN (*b. Attleborough, Mass., 1768; d. Columbia, S.C., 1820*), Baptist clergyman. Brother of Virgil Maxcy. Graduated Rhode Island College (Brown University), 1787, and served as president of that institution, 1792–1802. After a brief term as president of Union College, he became first president of the University of South Carolina, 1804. Able and broadly tolerant, Maxcy introduced the study of the sciences and also recommended establishment of chairs of law and political economy.

MAXCY, VIRGIL (*b. Attleborough, Mass., 1785; d. aboard USS Princeton, 1844*), lawyer, Maryland legislator, diplomat. Brother of Jonathan Maxcy. Graduated Brown, 1804; studied law with Robert G. Harper. First solicitor of U.S. Treasury, 1830–37; U.S. chargé d'affaires at Brussels, Belgium, 1837–42. Killed by explosion of a gun aboard the *Princeton* while a guest of President John Tyler.

MAXEY, SAMUEL BELL (*b. Tompkinsville, Ky., 1825; d. Eureka Springs, Ark., 1895*), lawyer, Confederate major general, friend of the Indians. Graduated West Point, 1846; after service in Mexican War, resigned his commission. Removed to Paris, Tex., 1857. On the outbreak of the Civil War, he organized the 9th Texas Infantry and after active engagement in the campaigns of 1862–63 in Tennessee and Mississippi and was appointed commander in Indian Territory, December 1863. Organizing three brigades of Indians, he persuaded them that victory for the South was essential to their own safety and gained their goodwill as no other Texan had done since the days of Sam Houston. As U.S. senator, Democrat, from Texas, 1875–87, he advocated economy but did not fail to obtain appropriations for Texas projects; he was among the first to favor individual farms as the ultimate solution of the Indian question.

MAXIM, HIRAM PERCY (*b. Brooklyn, N.Y., 1869; d. La Junta, Colo., 1936*). Son of Hiram S. Maxim. Inventor of the "silencer" for gunfire and many electrical devices; developed gas- and electric-powered automobiles for the Pope Manufacturing Co., Hartford, Conn., 1895–1907.

MAXIM, HIRAM STEVENS (*b. near Sangerville, Maine, 1840; d. Streatham, England, 1916*), Anglo-American inventor, engineer. Brother of Hudson Maxim. As a youth he learned and practiced several trades. Turning to engineering, he worked with machines for illuminating gas, invented a locomotive headlight, and devised a process for equalizing carbon deposit on incandescent lamp filaments. Residing in England *post* 1881, he made scores of inventions, notably the automatic Maxim gun, 1883. This first efficient weapon of its class loaded, fired, and ejected cartridges by using the recoil of the barrel as each shot was fired. In 1894 he built an airplane that lifted itself from the ground, but its steam engine proved too heavy for practicable use.

MAXIM, HUDSON (*b. Orneville, Maine, 1853; d. 1927*), inventor, explosives expert. Brother of Hiram S. Maxim. Supplemented irregular schooling with training in science and engineering; entered a partnership in the job-printing business, also selling writing style charts and colored ink powders. *Real Pen-Work Self-Instructor* (1881), published by his firm, was highly successful. After studying manufacture of French smokeless gunpowder at his brothers gun factory in England, he returned to the United States in 1888 and became its first American producer; his plant and patents were sold to the Du Pont Co., 1897, for whom he became consultant. He had earlier produced a safer dynamite, and now

perfected the armor-piercing high explosive Maximite. Among his other inventions were a device for driving torpedoes, an automobile, improved cartridges, and a process for manufacturing calcium carbide.

MAXWELL, AUGUSTUS EMMETT (*b. Elberton, Ga., 1820; d. Chipley, Fla., 1903*), lawyer, Florida legislator. Raised in Alabama; removed to Tallahassee, Fla., 1845, where he entered politics. After inconspicuous service as congressman from Florida, 1853–57, he resumed practice of law and served throughout the Civil War as member of the Confederate Senate. A law partner of Stephen R. Mallory, *post* 1866, he became a Florida circuit judge, 1877, and served in various posts until 1891.

MAXWELL, DAVID HERVEY (*b. Garrard Co., Ky., 1786; d. Bloomington, Ind., 1854*), physician, Indiana legislator. Chiefly remembered for his long and unflagging interest in Indiana higher education.

MAXWELL, ELSA (*b. Keokuk, Iowa, 1883; d. New York, N.Y., 1963*), hostess, songwriter, author, and entertainer. Hostess whose knack for bringing together members of "high" and "café" societies brought her fame as the "arbiter of international society" (from *ca.* 1907). Composed music, including the score for the musical *Melinda and Her Sisters* (1916), and the songs "Carry On" and "The Sum of Life." Moved to Hollywood in 1938; appeared in movies such as *Elsa Maxwell's Hotel for Women* (1939) and *Public Deb No. 1* (1940). Also lectured, wrote a syndicated gossip column, and broadcast celebrity news on her radio program, "Elsa Maxwell's Party Line." Books include *R.S.V.P.—Elsa Maxwell's Own Story* (1957), *How to Do It—or the Lively Art of Entertaining* (1957), and *The Celebrity Circus* (1963).

MAXWELL, GEORGE HEBARD (*b. Sonoma, Calif., 1860; d. Phoenix, Ariz., 1946*), lawyer, conservationist. Admitted to the California bar, 1882, he became an expert on water rights; his experience with private irrigation organizations convinced him that a national program was essential, and he gave up his practice in 1899 to direct the National Irrigation Association (later called the National Reclamation Association). He was influential in the framing and passing of the Reclamation Act of 1902; he also organized the Salt River Valley Water Users' Association (Arizona), 1903, whose pattern and articles of incorporation served as a model for later cooperative bodies in dealing with the federal government. Flood control, drainage, and river regulation in general were his other interests.

MAXWELL, GEORGE TROUP (*b. Bryan Co., Ga., 1827; d. Jacksonville, Fla., 1897*), physician, Florida legislator, Confederate soldier.

MAXWELL, HUGH (*b. Paisley, Scotland, 1787; d. New York, N.Y., 1873*), lawyer, New York Whig politician. Came to America as a child. District attorney, New York Co., 1817–18 and 1821–29.

MAXWELL, LUCIEN BONAPARTE (*b. Kaskaskia, Ill., 1818; d. Fort Sumner, N.Mex., 1875*), frontiersman, rancher. Grandson of Pierre Menard. Friend of Kit Carson and hunter for John C. Frémont's first expedition. Maxwell married, 1842, the heiress of the vast Beaubien-Miranda tract in New Mexico. An active and valuable member of Frémont's force in the events culminating in the conquest of California, 1845–46, he then settled down to the management of his father-in-law's estate. In 1864, he became sole owner of what has ever since been known as the Maxwell Grant, later the subject of much litigation. Brave and self-reliant as a hunter and Indian fighter, Maxwell was improvident and unwise in handling his business affairs.

MAXWELL, SAMUEL (*b. Lodi, N.Y., 1825; d. Fremont, Nebr., 1901*), lawyer, Nebraska legislator. Justice of Nebraska Supreme Court, 1873–94, he served much of the time as chief justice. Originally a Republican, he took up Populist doctrines and was elected with Populist help to Congress, where he served, 1897–99.

MAXWELL, WILLIAM (*b. near Newtown Stewart, Ireland, ca. 1733; d. Lansdown, N.J., 1796*), Revolutionary soldier, New Jersey legislator. Came to America as a boy; settled with his parents in present Warren Co., N.J. Served in British and provincial regiments during French and Indian War; at its close, was attached to British commissary at Mackinac with rank of colonel. Returning to New Jersey, 1774, he was a member of the Provincial Congress, 1775, served on the expedition against Canada, 1776, and was commissioned brigadier general by Congress, October 1776. He resigned from the army, July 1780, after performing notable service as a soldier, particularly at the battle of Monmouth and in General Sullivan's campaign against the Six Nations in Pennsylvania and New York, 1779.

MAXWELL, WILLIAM (*b. New York or New Jersey ca. 1755; d. Greene Co., Ohio, 1809*), printer. Removed to Lexington, Ky., 1792, where he published several pamphlets; removing again to Cincinnati, Ohio, he issued the first number of *The Centinel of the North-Western Territory*, Nov. 9, 1793, which he published weekly until 1796. He was publisher also of the *Laws of the Territory of the United States, Northwest of the Ohio* (1796), since known as the Maxwell Code, the first book published in the Northwest Territory.

MAXWELL, WILLIAM (*b. Norfolk, Va., 1784; d. near Williamsburg, Va., 1857*), lawyer, Virginia legislator. Graduated Yale, 1802. President, Hampden-Sydney College, 1838–44.

MAXWELL, WILLIAM HENRY (*b. Stewartstown, Ireland, 1852; d. 1920*), educator, journalist. Graduated Queen's College, Galway, 1872. Came to America, 1874. Associate superintendent of schools, Brooklyn, N.Y., 1882–87; superintendent, 1887–98. Superintendent of schools, New York City, 1898–1917. Promoted vocational education, building of playgrounds; raised requirements for teachers and established them on civil service.

MAY, ANDREW JACKSON (*b. Langley, Ky., 1875; d. Prestonburg, Ky., 1959*), congressman. Graduated from Southern Normal University Law School, 1898. Practiced law and served in local politics and as a judge. Democratic congressman, 1930–46. Member of the House Military Affairs Committee from 1933; chairman, 1938–46. Opposed the TVA and in 1939 sponsored legislation that severely limited its power. Supported Roosevelt's policies of preparedness and Lend-Lease. Convicted in 1947 of bribery in connection with war contracts; served a nine-month prison term, 1949–50; pardoned in 1952 by President Truman. Returned to private law practice in Kentucky, 1952–59.

MAY, EDWARD HARRISON (*b. Croydon, England, 1824; d. Paris, France, 1887*), historical and portrait painter. Came to America as a boy. Studied under Daniel Huntington and under Thomas Couture in Paris. Among examples of his elaborate compositions are the *Last Days of Christopher Columbus* (1861) and *Milton Dictating to his Daughters* (1883).

MAY, MORTON JAY (*b. Denver, Colo., 1881; d. Clayton, Mo., 1968*), merchant. Son of David May, department store owner. The May Company was incorporated in 1910, and Morton May became a member of the board of directors; president, 1917–51; chief executive officer, 1927–57; and chairman of the board, to 1967. While he was president, the chain grew to twenty-five stores; by 1968 the May chain, with eighty stores and sales of $1 billion, was the fourth-largest chain in the United States. May engaged in a variety of philanthropic enterprises, including the bestowal of large benefactions on St. Louis, Washington, Brandeis, and Fisk universities.

MAY, SAMUEL JOSEPH (*b. Boston, Mass., 1797; d. 1871*), Unitarian clergyman, reformer. Advocated temperance, women's rights, improved popular education, international peace; was an ardent abolitionist and active agent of the Underground Railroad. Held pastorates in Connecticut, Massachusetts, and Syracuse, N.Y.

MAY, SOPHIE. *See* CLARKE, REBECCA SOPHIA.

MAYBANK, BURNET RHETT (*b. Charleston, S.C., 1899; d. Flat Rock, S.C., 1954*), governor, U.S. Senator. Graduated from the College of Charleston. Democratic governor of South Carolina, 1938–41. U.S. senator, 1941–54. Regarded as a conservative supporter of the New Deal and Fair Deal. Member of the Armed Services Committee, 1944–54; chairman of the Senate Banking and Currency Committee, 1949–52; member and chairman of the Appropriations Committee, 1951–54. Maybank generally voted with the Democrats, though he opposed the party majority in voting for the Taft-Hartley Act.

MAYBECK, BERNARD RALPH (*b. New York, N.Y., 1862; d. Berkeley, Calif., 1957*), architect. Studied at the École des Beaux Arts in Paris. Opened his own firm in San Francisco around 1889. Taught drawing at the University of California, Berkeley, 1894–1903. Instrumental in an architectural renaissance in the San Francisco area. Maybeck's style was eclectic, utilizing the classic styles but also combining such new materials as laminated wooden construction and reinforced concrete. His most notable work is the Palace of the Fine Arts (1915) in San Francisco.

MAYER, ALFRED GOLDSBOROUGH. *See* MAYOR, ALFRED GOLDSBOROUGH.

MAYER, ALFRED MARSHALL (*b. Baltimore, Md., 1836; d. 1897*), physicist. Nephew of Brantz Mayer; protégé of Joseph Henry. Taught at various colleges and was professor at Stevens Institute of Technology, 1871–97. Leading American authority on acoustics.

MAYER, BRANTZ (*b. Baltimore, Md., 1809; d. Baltimore, 1879*), lawyer, author. A founder of Maryland Historical Society, 1844. Author of *Mexico As It Was and As It Is* (1844), *Captain Canot* (1854), and other volumes on Mexican and Maryland history.

MAYER, CONSTANT (*b. Besançon, France, 1829; d. Paris, France, 1911*), artist. Worked in New York N.Y., 1857–95; was noted for competent but commonplace genre paintings and portraits.

MAYER, EMIL (*b. New York, N.Y., 1854; d. New York, 1931*), laryngologist. M.D., New York University, 1877; associated with New York Eye and Ear Infirmary and Mount Sinai Hospital. Pioneer in submucous resection of the nasal septum; made valuable report on local anaesthesia (1926).

MAYER, LEWIS (*b. Lancaster, Pa., 1783; d. York, Pa., 1849*), German Reformed clergyman. Founded denomination's first theological seminary, Carlisle, Pa., 1829 (later Marshall College, Mercersburg).

MAYER, LOUIS BURT (*b. near Minsk, Russia, 1885[?]; d. Los Angeles, Calif., 1957*), motion picture producer and executive. Immigrated to the U.S. in 1904. Starting as a junk dealer in the Boston area, Mayer began his career as a theater manager in 1907 in Haverhill, Mass. Soon he was handling the output of Jesse Lasky-Samuel Goldfish (later Goldwyn)-Cecil B. DeMille production company. Began producing films in 1916. A founder of Metro-Goldwyn-Mayer, 1924, which became the most successful Hollywood studio. Financial and personal difficulties forced Mayer's resignation in 1951. An ardent anticommunist, Mayer supported Senator McCarthy during the days of the infamous Hollywood "blacklistings."

MAYER, OSCAR GOTTFRIED (*b. Chicago, Ill., 1888; d. Evanston, Ill., 1965*), meat packer. Studied at Harvard (graduated, 1909). With Oscar Mayer and Company, which his father had built from a small meat market and sausage factory established in 1883, as assistant superintendent (1909–12); secretary, director, and general manager (1912–21); vice president in charge of operations (1921–28); president (1928–55); and chairman of the board (to 1965). Under Mayer's leadership the company grew from 900 employees and annual sales of $21.5 million to 8,500 employees and annual sales of $220.2 million. Pioneered methods of processing and packaging prepared meats that were adopted throughout the industry, including the introduction of the vacuum-sealed plastic package.

MAYER, PHILIP FREDERICK (*b. New York, N.Y., 1781; d. 1858*), Lutheran clergyman. Graduated Columbia, 1799; studied theology with John C. Kunze. Pastor, St. John's Church, Philadelphia, Pa., 1806–58.

MAYES, EDWARD (*b. near Jackson, Miss., 1846; d. 1917*), lawyer, professor of law. Chancellor, University of Mississippi, 1889–92. Author of a number of works, including a life of his father-in-law, Lucius Q. C. Lamar (1896).

MAYES, JOEL BRYAN (*b. near present Cartersville, Ga., 1833; d. 1891*), Cherokee chief, Confederate soldier, stockbreeder. Raised in Indian Territory (Oklahoma). Justice, Cherokee Supreme Court; worked for his tribe's educational and material betterment.

MAYHEW, EXPERIENCE (*b. Chilmark, Martha's Vineyard, Mass., 1673 n.s.; d. 1758*). Grandson of Thomas Mayhew (*ca. 1621–57*). Outstanding missionary to Martha's Vineyard Indians, 1694–1758; translated Psalms into native tongue. Author of *Indian Converts* (1727) and *Grace Defended* (revealing modified Calvinist beliefs, 1744).

MAYHEW, JONATHAN (*b. Chilmark, Martha's Vineyard, Mass., 1720; d. Boston, Mass., 1766*), clergyman. Son of Experience Mayhew. Graduated Harvard, 1744. Pastor of West Church, Boston, 1747–66. Vigorous as thinker and writer, he preached a rational and practical religion, rejecting the Trinitarian view and Calvinistic predestinarianism. He detested episcopacy, condemning Anglican mission activities in the colonies; he was also a staunch supporter of civil liberty against arbitrary rule. Influencing such patriot leaders as James Otis, Josiah Quincy, and the Adamses, he recommended, 1766, that the Massachusetts lower house send out circular letters to further intercolonial cooperation in defense of their rights. Able as a pamphleteer in religious and political controversy, he was a harbinger of the American Revolution.

MAYHEW, THOMAS (*b. Wiltshire, England, 1593; d. Martha's Vineyard, Mass., 1682*), colonial governor, missionary. Settled in Medford, Mass., *ante* 1632. Purchased, 1641, present-day Dukes and Nantucket counties in Massachusetts; settling in Martha's Vineyard, 1646, he served there as chief magistrate and governor.

MAYHEW, THOMAS (*b. England, ca. 1621; d. at sea, en route to England, 1657*), Congregational clergyman, first English missionary to the Indians of New England. Son of Thomas Mayhew (*1593–1682*). Came to America with his father *ante* 1632; led first settlers to his father's purchase of Martha's Vineyard, 1642. Serving also as pastor of the settlement, he turned his attention to the Indian inhabitants of the Vineyard and islands adjacent; his first convert was made in 1643, three years before John Eliot began work. Devoting almost his entire time to missionary activities, he neglected his personal concerns and paid the expenses of his mission out of his private purse.

MAYNARD, CHARLES JOHNSON (*b. West Newton, Mass., 1845; d. West Newton, 1929*), taxidermist, naturalist. Author of *Naturalist's Guide* (1870), *The Birds of Florida* (1872–78), *Manual of North American Butterflies* (1891), and many other useful works.

MAYNARD, EDWARD (*b. Madison, N.Y., 1813; d. Washington, D.C., 1891*), dental surgeon. Practiced in Washington, D.C., *post* 1836. A profound research student, as early as 1836 he announced the existence of dental fevers; he was the first to fill teeth with gold foil, 1838, and introduced the practice into Europe, 1845. He was also inventor of many improvements in dental instruments and was professor of theory and practice of dentistry, Baltimore College of Dental Surgery, *post* 1857. Maynard's work in improving firearms was equally notable. He patented the Maynard tape primer, 1845, and an improvement in breechloading rifles, 1851, which, with the subsequent improvements he made, brought about adoption of the Maynard rifle throughout the world.

MAYNARD, GEORGE WILLIAM (*b. Brooklyn, N.Y., 1839; d. Boston, Mass., 1913*), mining engineer.

MAYNARD, GEORGE WILLOUGHBY (*b. Washington, D.C., 1843; d. New York, N.Y., 1923*), portrait, figure, and mural painter. Son of Edward Maynard. An assistant to John LaFarge in the decoration of Trinity Church, Boston, Maynard painted a number of important decorative murals in New York and Boston public buildings. His principal work was the exterior decoration of the Agricultural Building at the Chicago World's Fair, 1893; he also painted the Pompeian panels in the second-floor corridors of the Library of Congress, Washington.

MAYNARD, HORACE (*b. Westboro, Mass., 1814; d. 1882*), lawyer, Tennessee Unionist. Removed to Tennessee, 1838. Congressman, Whig and Know-Nothing, from Tennessee, 1857–63; attorney general of Tennessee, 1863–65. Returning to Congress, July 1866, he aligned himself with the radical Republicans and served until 1875. He was U.S. minister to Turkey, 1875–80, and U.S. postmaster general briefly in the last months of President Hayes's administration.

MAYO, AMORY DWIGHT (*b. Warwick, Mass., 1823; d. Washington, D.C., 1907*), Unitarian clergyman, educator, promoter of public education in the southern states.

MAYO, CHARLES HORACE. *See* MAYO, WILLIAM JAMES.

MAYO, FRANK (*b. Boston, Mass., 1839; d. near Grand Island, Nebr., 1896*), actor. Stage name of Frank McGuire. Made debut at Adelphi Theatre, San Francisco, 1856; New York debut, 1865. One of the most popular actors on the American stage, Mayo was effective in classical roles but at his best in American character parts, particularly in the title roles in *Davy Crockett* and the stage version of *Puddin'head Wilson*.

MAYO, GEORGE ELTON (*b. Adelaide, Australia, 1880; d. Guildford, Surrey, England, 1949*), educator, social scientist.

Resident in the United States, 1922–47, he was a research associate at University of Pennsylvania, 1923–26, and professor of industrial research at Harvard University Graduate School of Business Administration, 1926–47. He made many studies of the psychological and social problems of life and work in industrial societies, of group behavior, and of the attitudes of workmen and supervisors in relation to their output and to one another. His work at the Harvard Fatigue Laboratory paralleled the physiological investigations of Lawrence J. Henderson. Among his books were *The Human Problems of an Industrial Society* (1933); *The Social Problems of an Industrial Society* (1945); and *Some Notes on the Psychology of Pierre Janet* (1948).

MAYO, HENRY THOMAS (*b. Burlington, Vt., 1856; d. Portsmouth, N.H., 1937*), naval officer. Graduated Annapolis, 1876. Rose through the grades to rear admiral, 1913. Central figure in "Tampico Incident" with Mexico, 1914, Mayo's firm stand was backed by the Wilson administration and he became vice admiral, 1915. From 1916 through World War I, Mayo served as commander in chief, Atlantic Fleet. He was regarded in the navy as restrained, judicious, and the most competent flag officer of his time.

MAYO, MARY ANNE BRYANT (*b. near Battle Creek, Mich., 1845; d. 1903*), teacher, pioneer Grange and Farmer's Institute worker.

MAYO, SARAH CARTER EDGARTON (*b. Shirley, Mass., 1819; d. Gloucester, Mass., 1848*), author. Wife of Amory D. Mayo. Editor, *The Rose of Sharon: A Religious Souvenir* (1840–48).

MAYO, WILLIAM (*b. Wiltshire, England, ca. 1684; d. 1744*), surveyor. Immigrated to Barbados *ante* 1712; removed to Virginia *ca.* 1723. Associated with William Byrd (1674–1744) in survey of Virginia–North Carolina boundary, 1728; accompanied Byrd in the founding of Richmond and Petersburg, Va.; made a general map of the Fairfax proprietary.

MAYO, WILLIAM JAMES (*b. Le Sueur, Minn., 1861; d. Rochester, Minn., 1939*), and **CHARLES HORACE** (*b. Rochester, Minn., 1865; d. Chicago, Ill., 1939*), surgeons, founders of the Mayo Clinic. Second and third sons of William W. Mayo. After William's graduation from the University of Michigan medical school in 1883 and Charles's from the Chicago Medical College in 1888, they joined their father and gradually took over his large practice. When Rochester, Minn., acquired a new hospital, 1889, the Drs. Mayo were the entire medical staff, giving them control of the only adequate surgical facilities in an area comprising several states. At this time new methods of antiseptic surgery, based on the principles of Joseph Lister, were making many ailments amenable to cure, and a stream of new operations were being developed in the hospitals and clinics of Europe and America. The Mayo brothers made a point of traveling every year to study the new surgical techniques, bringing them back to Rochester; they were especially adept at synthesizing and refining the surgical methods they had learned from others. Their reports of improved techniques and remarkable results were at first hardly believed, but skeptical eastern doctors were convinced when observing the volume and quality of the Mayo surgery, and Rochester became world famous. As the number of patients grew to exceed their personal capacities, the Mayo brothers engaged new men to help them, choosing the best-qualified doctors they could find and providing them with opportunities for travel and study. Thus, the Mayo Clinic evolved, a group of some 200 trained specialists engaged in the cooperative private practice of medicine. Before their retirement the Mayos changed the clinic from a partnership to an independent, self-governing association.

In 1915 the brothers, wishing to provide a planned course of graduate study leading to an advanced degree in medicine, established the Mayo Foundation for Medical Education and Research. Originally endowed with $1.5 million (eventually with $2.5 million), the foundation became affiliated with the University of Minnesota. The brothers were completely unlike in personality. Dr. Will was reserved, imperturbable, decisive, the chief in fact as well as in name; Dr. Charlie's supreme gift was the common touch. Each appreciated the complementary strengths of the other, and their phenomenal success was won as a team.

MAYO, WILLIAM KENNON (*b. Drummondtown, Va., 1829; d. Washington, D.C., 1900*), naval officer. Nephew of Abel P. Upshur. Appointed midshipman, 1841, Mayo saw active service throughout the Mexican War and performed several tours of duty as instructor in the U.S. Naval Academy. Remaining loyal to the Union in the Civil War, he engaged effectively in blockade duty. He retired as commodore, 1886.

MAYO, WILLIAM STARBUCK (*b. Ogdensburg, N.Y., 1811; d. New York, N.Y., 1895*), physician. Graduated College of Physicians and Surgeons, New York, 1932; practiced mainly in New York City. Mayo is remembered principally for his novels, which had a large contemporary success; they include *Kaloolah* (1849), *The Berber* (1850), and *Never Again* (1873).

MAYO, WILLIAM WORRELL (*b. Manchester, England, 1819; d. Rochester, Minn., 1911*), surgeon. Came to America *ca.* 1845. Father of William J. and Charles H. Mayo. M.D., University of Missouri, 1854. Removing in 1855 to St. Paul, Minn., he took part in the further organization of the territory and became within a decade the leading physician and surgeon in and about Rochester, Minn. A liberal Democrat, he took an active interest in politics, serving as mayor of Rochester several times and as state senator twice.

MAYOR, ALFRED GOLDSBOROUGH (*b. near Frederick, Md., 1868; d. Dry Tortugas, Fla., 1922*), biologist. Son of Alfred M. Mayer. Graduated Stevens Institute of Technology, 1899, as an engineer; accompanied Alexander Agassiz on scientific voyages. After engaging in curatorial work in several museums, he served, 1904–22, as organizer and director of the Carnegie Institution's marine laboratory at Dry Tortugas, Fla. His own researches included studies of butterflies, jellyfishes, and the formation of coral reefs. He was author of, among other works, *Medusae of the World* (1910).

MAYO-SMITH, RICHMOND (*b. Troy, Ohio, 1854; d. New York, N.Y., 1901*), statistician, economist. Graduated Amherst, 1875; was drawn to economics and allied subjects by John W. Burgess. Taught political science at Columbia University, 1877–1901, with marked success in both graduate and undergraduate courses. His course in statistics, said to be the first given in an American university, provided training for many subsequently distinguished statisticians. His *Statistics and Sociology* (1895) contained one of the first systematic applications of statistics to social problems; his *Statistics and Economics* (1899) was designed to show what economic problems could be treated by statistical inquiry. He was author also of many scholarly papers on statistics and economics, including *Emigration and Immigration* (1890).

MAYTAG, FREDERICK LOUIS (*b. Elgin, Ill., 1857; d. Los Angeles, Calif., 1937*), pioneer manufacturer of washing machines. Began business, 1907; organized Maytag Co., 1909.

MAZUREAU, ÉTIENNE (*b. France, 1777; d. New Orleans, La., 1849*), lawyer, Louisiana legislator. Settled in New Orleans, 1804; was law partner of Edward Livingston. Appointed attorney general of Louisiana, 1815, he held that position repeatedly but not successively throughout his life.

MAZZEI, PHILIP (*b. Poggio-a-Caiano, Italy, 1730; d. Pisa, Italy, 1816*), physician, merchant, horticulturist. A wine merchant in London for a number of years, he removed to Virginia, 1773, to introduce there the culture of grapes, olives, and other fruits. Settling on a plantation east of Charlottesville, adjoining Jefferson's "Monticello," he became an ardent supporter of the Revolutionary movement in Virginia. Sent abroad in June 1779 by Patrick Henry to borrow money for the Commonwealth of Virginia, he was unsuccessful in the mission, but busied himself in gathering political and military information, which he sent to Governor Jefferson. Mazzei returned to America late in 1783; disappointed in hopes of a consular office, he sailed for Europe in June 1785, never to return. Thereafter, he was in the service of the king of Poland and, *post* 1802, was a pensioner of the czar of Russia. Among his writings was *Récherches historiques et politiques sur les États-Unis de l'Amérique septentrionale* (1788), which was based in part on materials furnished by Thomas Jefferson. An indiscreet letter to him from Jefferson written on Apr. 24, 1796, became famous in the history of American political controversy.

MAZZUCHELLI, SAMUEL CHARLES (*b. Milan, Italy, 1806; d. 1864*), Roman Catholic clergyman, Dominican. Came to America, 1828; ordained at Cincinnati, Ohio, 1830. Served as a missionary to the Canadians and Indians in the neighborhood of Mackinac and Green Bay; built the first church in the area of Prairie du Chien, 1835; served the settlements of Galena and Dubuque. Acted as vicar general to Bishop Loras. Founded Sinsinawa Mound College, 1845; founded a congregation of teaching sisters, the Dominican Congregation of the Most Holy Rosary. Father Mazzuchelli was also the architect of the county courthouse at Galena, built the bishop's residence in Dubuque, and designed the first Iowa capitol at Iowa City.

MEAD, CHARLES MARSH (*b. Cornwall, Vt., 1836; d. 1911*), Congregational clergyman, biblical scholar and reviser.

MEAD, EDWIN DOAK (*b. Chesterfield, N.H., 1849; d. Boston, Mass., 1937*), reformer, author. Cousin of William R. and Larkin G. Mead. Editor, *New England Magazine* (1890–1901); edited *Old South Leaflets*.

MEAD, ELWOOD (*b. near Patriot, Ind., 1858; d. Washington, D.C., 1936*), irrigation engineer. Graduated Purdue, 1882; C.E., Iowa State College, 1883. In 1890, as a government engineer in Wyoming, he helped secure and administered a state water law which became a model for the West. He headed the U.S. Office of Irrigation Investigation, 1899–1907, and spent the years 1907–15 in Australia inaugurating a program of water conservation and reclamation. As head of California's Land Settlement Board, 1917–23, he initiated cooperative group settlements on newly irrigated tracts. He directed the U.S. Bureau of Reclamation *post* 1924.

MEAD, GEORGE HERBERT (*b. South Hadley, Mass., 1863; d. 1931*), educator, philosopher. Graduated Oberlin, 1883; Harvard, 1888. Studied also at universities of Berlin and Leipzig. Taught philosophy at University of Michigan, 1891–94, and at University of Chicago *post* 1894. Developed concept that human thinking and the characteristically human forms of social activity are aspects of the same fundamental process, the development of communication. Though Mead emphasized the philosophical implications of his social psychology and in particular its congruence with pragmatic speculation, his description and analysis of the relations between individual and social development have been useful to sociologists who disregarded or rejected the accompanying philosophy.

MEAD, JAMES MICHAEL (*b. Mount Morris, N.Y., 1885; d. Lakeland, Fla., 1964*), U.S. senator. Member of the New York State Assembly, 1914–18. Served ten consecutive terms as a member of the U.S. House of Representatives, from 1918. Elected to the U.S. Senate in 1938; reelected to a full term in 1940. A democrat, he was a consistent supporter of Franklin D. Roosevelt and the New Deal. Ran for governor of New York in 1942 and 1946. Chairman of the Senate War Investigating Committee, 1942–45. Appointed to the Federal Trade Commission in 1949; chairman to 1955. Director of the Washington, D.C., office of the New York State Commerce Department, 1955–56.

MEAD, LARKIN GOLDSMITH (*b. Chesterfield, N.H., 1835; d. Florence, Italy, 1910*), sculptor. Nephew of John H. Noyes; brother of William R. Mead. Among his many works in the pseudoclassic style are the statues of *Vermont* and *Ethan Allen* for the capitol at Montpelier, Vt., and also the Lincoln Monument at Springfield, Ill.

MEAD, WILLIAM RUTHERFORD (*b. Brattleboro, Vt. 1846; d. Paris, France, 1928*), architect. Graduated Amherst, 1867; studied architecture in New York and in Florence, Italy, where he lived with his brother, Larkin G. Mead. Returning to America, 1872, he became associated with Charles F. McKim and Stanford White in professional practice. Mead managed the office, often conceived the basic scheme of the plan, and acted as efficient critic of the work of both his creative partners.

MEADE, GEORGE (*b. Philadelphia, Pa., 1741; d. Philadelphia, 1808*), merchant, Revolutionary patriot. Brother-in-law and partner in business of Thomas Fitzsimons. Instrumental in building of St. Mary's Church, Philadelphia, one of the oldest Catholic churches there.

MEADE, GEORGE GORDON (*b. Cadiz, Spain, 1815; d. Philadelphia, Pa., 1872*), soldier. Son of Richard W. Meade, U.S. naval agent in Spain. Graduated West Point, 1835; served in Seminole War; resigned commission, 1836. After working as a civilian engineer, 1836–42, he applied for reinstatement in the army. As lieutenant, Topographical Engineer Corps, he helped survey the northeastern boundary, constructed lighthouses on Delaware Bay, and fought under Taylor and Scott in the Mexican War. Further lighthouse work and Great Lakes surveys occupied him until the Civil War, when he became brigadier general of Pennsylvania volunteers, August 1861. His brigade worked on the Washington defenses and participated in McClellan's Peninsular campaign, in which Meade was seriously wounded at Glendale. He rejoined his command before full recovery, fighting at second Bull Run and displaying ability as temporary division and corps commander in the Antietam campaign. Following the Fredericksburg disaster, December 1862, as major general he commanded V Corps, which acquitted itself well at Chancellorsville, May 1863.

When Lee again invaded the North, Meade was awakened early in the morning of June 28 with orders to take command of the Army of the Potomac. Protesting the order, unfamiliar with General Joseph Hooker's previous plans, he began gathering his forces along the Emmitsburg-Hanover line to defend Washington and Baltimore. Advance elements of the hostile armies collided by accident near Gettysburg, Pa., on July 1, and Meade concentrated his troops in a strong defensive position to repulse the Confederates in what is usually considered the Civil War's decisive battle (July 1–3, 1863). Despite his own recent assumption of command and the exhaustion of his men, he has been criticized for not counterattacking and for permitting Lee's escape; indisputably, however, he avoided mistakes that conceivably could have lost the war. Commander of the Army of the Potomac throughout the remaining hostilities, Meade was subordinated to General U. S.

Grant *post* March 1864, and his functions were thenceforward tactical in nature. Notwithstanding the anomalous situation and his own high-strung temperament, he loyally and competently carried out Grant's orders. Promoted major general in the regular army, August 1864, he commanded the Military Division of the Atlantic, 1865–68, and the 3rd Military District in the South, 1868–69, where his firm justice made almost tolerable the difficult Reconstruction administration. Serving again as commander, Military Division of the Atlantic at Philadelphia (where he beautified Fairmount Park), he died at his post. Never popular, undiplomatic but of absolute honesty, he was a sound, steadfast commander.

MEADE, RICHARD KIDDER (*b. Nansemond Co., Va., 1746; d. Frederick Co., Va., 1805*), Revolutionary soldier, aide-de-camp to General George Washington, 1777–83.

MEADE, RICHARD WORSAM (*b. Chester Co., Pa., 1778; d. Washington, D.C., 1828*), merchant. Son of George Meade; father of George G. and Richard W. Meade (1807–70). U.S. naval agent at the port of Cadiz, Spain, 1806–16.

MEADE, RICHARD WORSAM (*b. Cadiz, Spain, 1807; d. 1870*), naval officer. Son of Richard W. Meade (1778–1828); brother of George G. Meade.

MEADE, RICHARD WORSAM (*b. New York, N.Y., 1837; d. Washington, D.C., 1897*), naval officer. Son of Richard W. Meade (1807–70). Graduated U.S. Naval Academy, 1856. Commanded naval battalion which subdued draft riots in New York City, July 1863. After long and varied service at sea and on shore, he retired as rear admiral, 1895.

MEADE, ROBERT LEAMY (*b. Washington, D.C., 1841; d. Lexington, Mass., 1910*), officer, U.S. Marine Corps. Son of Richard W. Meade (1807–70). Graduated U.S. Naval Academy, 1856. Made prisoner in unsuccessful night attack upon Fort Sumter, Sept. 8, 1863; he was exchanged after 15 months' imprisonment. After service in the Spanish-American War as fleet marine officer, North Atlantic Squadron, he was promoted colonel, 1899, and in 1900, took part in the China Relief Expedition. He retired as brigadier general, 1903.

MEADE, WILLIAM (*b. Frederick, later Clarke, Co., Va., 1789; d. 1862*), Episcopal clergyman, third bishop of the Diocese of Virginia. Son of Richard K. Meade. Graduated College of New Jersey (Princeton), 1808. A principal factor in the revival of the Episcopal church in Virginia *post* 1814, he was elected assistant bishop of Virginia, 1829, and from 1841 until his death was bishop of the diocese, which included the present states of Virginia and West Virginia. Bishop Meade was the leader of the Low Church party in his denomination. Although opposed to secession in principle, he went with his state when Virginia seceded. He became presiding bishop of the Protestant Episcopal Church in the Confederate States. Among his numerous writings the best known is *Old Churches, Ministers, and Families of Virginia* (1857).

MEAGHER, THOMAS FRANCIS (*b. Waterford, Ireland, 1823; d. near Fort Benton, Mont., 1867*), politician, lawyer, Union soldier. A leader in the Young Ireland movement, he was arrested for sedition and banished to Tasmania, 1849. Escaping to New York City, 1852, he was naturalized, studied and practiced law, and became a leader among the Irish-Americans. At the outbreak of the Civil War, he organized a volunteer Zuoave company (later part of the 69th New York); he became commander of the famed Irish Brigade, February 1862. When the brigade was so decimated as to be noneffective (after Chancellorsville), he resigned his commission; recommissioned brigadier

general early in 1864, he took over command of the district of Etowah and was mustered out of the service with the coming of peace. Appointed territorial secretary of Montana, 1865, he arrived there in October and served for a year as temporary governor. He was drowned while making a reconnaissance on the Missouri River.

MEANS, GASTON BULLOCK (*b. Blackwelder's Spring, N.C., 1879; d. Springfield, Mo., 1938*), private detective, swindler. His notorious career culminated in a ransom money swindle in the Lindbergh kidnapping case.

MEANY, EDMOND STEPHEN (*b. East Saginaw, Mich., 1862; d. 1935*), educator, Washington legislator, Seattle journalist.

MEARNS, EDGAR ALEXANDER (*b. Highland Falls, N.Y., 1856; d. Washington, D.C., 1916*), army surgeon, naturalist. His principal contribution was made as a gatherer of materials in the Southwest, the Philippines and Africa for the use of specialists in systematic zoology and botany.

MEARS, DAVID OTIS (*b. Essex, Mass., 1842; d. 1915*), Congregational and Presbyterian clergyman, prohibitionist, Anti-Saloon League organizer.

MEARS, HELEN FARNSWORTH (*b. Oshkosh, Wis., 1872; d. New York, N.Y., 1916*), sculptor. Acted as assistant to Augustus Saint-Gaudens. Created statue of Frances Willard in the U.S. Capitol Washington, and also the Fountain of Life at the St. Louis Exposition, 1904.

MEARS, JOHN WILLIAM (*b. Reading, Pa., 1825; d. Clinton, N.Y., 1881*), Presbyterian clergyman, educator. A "new school" minister in New Jersey, Maryland, and Delaware; served as professor of philosophy, Hamilton College, 1871–81.

MEARS, OTTO (*b. Courland, Russia, 1840; d. Pasadena, Calif., 1931*), Colorado pioneer. Immigrated to California as a boy; established a sawmill and a gristmill at Conejos, Colo., 1865. Beginning with a road over Poncho Pass, he constructed a series of toll roads to the newly opened mining districts in Colorado, operated freighting outfits and pack trains over them, and constructed the Rio Grande Southern and the Silverton Northern railroads in southwestern Colorado.

MEASE, JAMES (*b. Philadelphia, Pa., 1771; d. Philadelphia, 1846*), physician. Graduated University of Pennsylvania, 1787; M.D., 1792. Although he wrote, edited, or compiled several medical works, he is principally remembered for his *Picture of Philadelphia* (1811) and for his pioneering *Geological Account of the United States* (1807).

MEASON, ISAAC (*b. probably Virginia, 1742; d. 1818*), pioneer ironmaster west of the Alleghenies. Settled in western Pennsylvania *ca.* 1771; established Union Furnace on Dunbar Creek *ca.* 1791; financed first mill for puddling and rolling bar iron in Pennsylvania, 1816.

MECHEM, FLOYD RUSSELL (*b. Nunda, N.Y., 1858; d. 1928*), lawyer, educator. Admitted to the Michigan bar, 1879; practiced in Battle Creek and in Detroit until 1893. Taught law at University of Michigan, 1892–1903, and at University of Chicago, 1903–28. Internationally known as an authority on agency, partnership, sales, and corporations, he was author of *Treatise on the Law of Agency* (1889), *Treatise on the Law of Sale of Personal Property* (1901), and a number of other important text and casebooks. In a period when contemporary thought was submerging the individual for the sale of "social good," Mechem held firmly that the important ultimate values were individual and not social.

MECOM, BENJAMIN (*b. Boston, Mass. 1732; place and date of death unknown*), printer. Nephew of Benjamin Franklin. After apprenticeship to James Parker of New York City, Mecom managed his uncle's printing officer in Antigua, 1752–56; he worked in Boston, Mass., 1757–62. Failing thereafter in New York, New Haven, and Philadelphia, he removed to Burlington, N.J., where he was employed by Isaac Collins.

MEDARY, MILTON BENNETT (*b. Philadelphia, Pa., 1874; d. Philadelphia, 1929*), architect. Graduated University of Pennsylvania, 1894; apprentice in office of Frank Miles Day. Noted for his use of Gothic, he designed, among other structures, the Washington Memorial Chapel, Valley Forge, and the carillon tower at Mountain Lake, Fla. He served also as a member of several commissions for the development of Washington, D.C.

MEDARY, SAMUEL (*b. Montgomery Co., Pa., 1801; d. Columbus, Ohio, 1864*), editor, Ohio legislator. Removed to Ohio, 1825; edited the *Ohio Sun* and the *Ohio Statesman*; became Democratic party dictator in Ohio, supporting the annexation of Texas, the reoccupation of Oregon, the Mexican War. Governor of Minnesota Territory, 1857–58, and of Kansas Territory, 1858–60, he favored the Lecompton Constitution for Kansas and vetoed a bill prohibiting slavery there. Returning to Ohio, he edited the *Crisis*, opposed the Civil War, and was an active "Peace Democrat."

MEDILL, JOSEPH (*b. near St. John, New Brunswick, Canada, 1823; d. San Antonio, Tex., 1899*), journalist. Raised in Stark Co., Ohio, Medill studied law and was admitted to the bar, 1846. With his three younger brothers, he bought the *Coshocton Whig*, 1849; within two years he removed to Cleveland and established there the *Daily Forest City*, later the *Cleveland Leader*. Possibly the first man to advocate use of the name Republican for a new antislavery party, he was a founder of that party, and in the winter of 1854–55 bought an interest in the *Chicago Tribune*, making that paper a Republican organ. He played an important part in the campaign of 1856, and in 1860 strongly promoted the nomination of Abraham Lincoln. An active supporter of the Republican Civil War policy, Medill favored emancipation and the confiscation of Southern property and continually urged more-radical courses of action on the administration, both during the war and in the Reconstruction period which followed. Acquiring a majority of the stock of the *Tribune*, 1874, he remained actively in charge of the paper until the day of his death.

MEEHAN, THOMAS (*b. England, 1826; d. 1901*), botanist. Immigrated to Philadelphia, Pa., 1848; establishing nurseries at Upper Germantown, Pa., *ca.* 1853, he was successful in business. Author of the *American Handbook of Ornamental Trees* (1853) and *The Native Flowers and Ferns of the United States* (1878–80); edited gardening magazines.

MEEK, ALEXANDER BEAUFORT (*b. Columbia, S.C., 1814; d. 1865*), lawyer, Alabama legislator, author. A leader *post* 1853 in founding Alabama's public school system.

MEEK, FIELDING BRADFORD (*b. Madison, Ind., 1817; d. Washington, D.C., 1876*), paleontologist. After serving as assistant to David Dale Owen and James Hall, Meek was associated *post* 1858 with Ferdinand V. Hayden and worked with him on his surveys in Nebraska, Wyoming, and the Rocky Mountain regions.

MEEK, JOSEPH L. (*b. Washington Co. Va., 1810 d. Hillsboro, Oreg., 1875*), Oregon pioneer. Removed to St. Louis, Mo., 1828; was employed as a trapper, 1829–40. Journeying to Oregon, 1840, he settled as a farmer on the Willamette. A dominating influence in the Champoeg convention of May 2, 1843, he was sheriff in the territory and elected to the legislature in 1846 and 1847. Appointed special messenger to Washington after the Whitman massacre, he set out on Jan. 4, 1848, and reached the capital in May. Appointed U.S. marshal by President Polk after the passage of the Oregon bill in August, Meek lost his office when the Pierce administration came in. A natural leader of great courage, he failed to obtain high office because of his lack of education and excess of humor.

MEEKER, EZRA (*b. near Huntsville, Ohio, 1830; d. Seattle, Wash., 1928*), Oregon and Washington pioneer. Immigrated from Indiana to Oregon, 1851–52; was a farmer most of his life near Puyallup on Puget Sound. *Post* 1906, he gave his time to commemorative marking of the Oregon Trail.

MEEKER, JOTHAM (*b. Hamilton Co., Ohio, 1804; d. near Ottawa, Kans., 1855*), Baptist missionary, printer. Printed first pamphlet and first book in what is now Kansas, near present Kansas City, Kans., March 1834.

MEEKER, MOSES (*b. New Haven, N.J., 1790; d. Shullsburg, Wis., 1865*), lead-miner, physician. Developed lead deposits in Fevre River region, Ill., 1823; removed to Iowa Co., Wis., *post* 1832, where he erected one of the first smelting furnaces in the territory, 1837.

MEEKER, NATHAN COOK (*b. Euclid, Ohio, 1817; d. White River Reservation, Colo., 1879*), journalist, Indian agent. A disciple of Fourierism and a lecturer on the subject, Meeker led a roving life until *ca.* 1865, when he joined the staff of the *New York Tribune* as agricultural editor. Supported by Horace Greeley and the *Tribune*, he organized and set up a cooperative agricultural colony known as the Union Colony, December 1869, siting it the next year at Greeley, Colo. Accepting appointment as agent at White River Reservation, 1878, he attempted to carry out his ideas of the proper method of managing Indians. The Utes, hostile to his plans, massacred him together with the other white men at the agency.

MEERSCHAERT, THÉOPHILE (*b. Russignies, Belgium, 1847; d. 1924*), Roman Catholic clergyman. Came to America, 1872; worked as a missionary in Mississippi and was vicar general, diocese of Natchez, 1887–91. Made vicar apostolic of Indian Territory, 1891, he became the first bishop of Oklahoma, 1905, and served until his death.

MEES, ARTHUR (*b. Columbus, Ohio, 1850; d. New York, N.Y., 1923*), choral and orchestral conductor, organist, teacher of music.

MEES, CHARLES EDWARD KENNETH (*b. Wellingborough, England, 1882; d. Honolulu, Hawaii, 1960*), photographic scientist, industrial research administrator. Studied at University College, London, D.Sc., 1906. Immigrated to the U.S. in 1912 to head the research laboratories of the Eastman Kodak Company; director until 1947; vice president in charge of research and development, 1934–55. Author of *The Organization of Industrial Research* (1920) and coauthor of *The Theory of the Photographic Process* (1942).

MEGAPOLENSIS, JOHANNES (*b. 1603; d. New York, 1670*), Reformed Dutch clergyman. After serving in parishes in Holland, 1634–42, he came to America as minister to the colony at Rensselaerswyck; he served there until 1649. A charitable man and a friend to the Indians, he rescued the Jesuit Father Jogues from captivity, 1642. At the persuasion of Governor Peter Stuyvesant and the Governor's Council, he removed to New Amsterdam as minister, in which post he continued until his death.

MEGRUE, ROI COOPER (*b. New York, N.Y., 1883; d. 1927*), dramatist. Graduated Columbia, 1903. Author of popular topical dramas, including *Under Cover* (first produced Boston, 1913), *It Pays to Advertise* (1914), and *Under Fire* (1915).

MEIÈRE, MARIE HILDRETH (*b. New York, N.Y., 1892; d. New York, 1961*), muralist. Studied at the Art Students League (1912–13), the California School of Fine Arts (1913–16), the New York School of Applied Design for Women (from 1919), and the Beaux Arts Institute of Design. A designer of mosaics and architectural decoration, her works are in such places as the Nebraska State Capitol; the National Academy of Sciences, Washington, D.C.; Rockefeller Center's Music Hall; Smith College; the Education and Science Building of the New York World's Fair (1939); the Travelers Insurance Building in Hartford, Conn.; St. Patrick's Cathedral in New York City; and the National Cathedral in Washington, D.C. Helped found the Liturgical Arts Society in 1928. Chaired the National Society of Mural Painters exhibition at the Grand Central Art Galleries in New York City (1935). Became the first woman to sit on the New York City Municipal Art Commission in 1946. Received the American Institute of Architects Fine Arts Medal in 1956.

MEIGGS, HENRY (*b. Catskill, N.Y., 1811; d. Peru, 1877*), lumber merchant, railroad builder. Removed to California, 1849, and prospered in San Francisco during the first boom there. Absconded, October 1854, leaving behind him debts of almost a million dollars. Gaining reputation as superintendent of Chilean railroads, he undertook construction of railroads in Peru *post* 1868 and by a combination of ruthlessness and executive genius produced works which remain among the engineering wonders of the world. Before the Peruvian lines were completed, however, both the nation and the builder were bankrupt.

MEIGS, ARTHUR VINCENT (*b. Philadelphia, Pa., 1850; d. Philadelphia, 1912*), physician. Brother of William M. Meigs. M.D., University of Pennsylvania, 1871; studied also in Vienna. By patient analysis of milks, he succeeded in modifying cow's milk so as to make it generally wholesome for infants.

MEIGS, CHARLES DELUCENA (*b. St. George, Bermuda, 1792; d. Hamanassett, Pa., 1869*), physician. Son of Josiah Meigs. Graduated University of Georgia, 1809; studied medicine privately and at University of Pennsylvania. Practiced in Philadelphia; was professor of obstetrics, Jefferson Medical College, 1841–61. Author of *The Philadelphia Practice of Midwifery* (1838) and other works.

MEIGS, JAMES AITKEN (*b. Philadelphia, Pa., 1829; d. 1879*), physician, anthropologist. Graduated Jefferson Medical College, 1851. A general practitioner in Philadelphia, he became especially noted for his work in obstetrics; he also taught physiology in several Philadelphia schools.

MEIGS, JOHN (*b. near Pottstown, Pa., 1852; d. near Pottstown, 1911*), educator. Graduated Lafayette, 1871. Associated *post* 1876, with the Hill School as director and teacher; developed it into one of the most extensive and best-equipped schools in the United States.

MEIGS, JOHN FORSYTH (*b. Philadelphia, Pa., 1818; d. 1882*), physician. Son of Charles D. Meigs; brother of Montgomery C. Meigs. M.D., University of Pennsylvania, 1838. Assisted his father in practice, later specializing in pediatrics. Author of *A Practical Treatise on the Diseases of Children* (1848).

MEIGS, JOSIAH (*b. Middletown, Conn., 1757; d. Washington, D.C., 1822*), lawyer, editor, educator, public official. Father of Charles D. Meigs; brother of Return J. Meigs (1740–1823). Graduated Yale, 1778. Edited *New Haven Gazette*, 1784–88, in which appeared many of the literary productions of the "Hartford Wits." Resident in Bermuda, 1789–94, he returned to be professor of mathematics and science at Yale, but resigned in 1800 because of the excessive Federalist tone of the University. Removing to Georgia, he served as president of the state university, 1801–10. Appointed surveyor general of the United States, 1812, he was made commissioner of the General Land Office, 1814, and from 1819 until his death, was president of the Columbian Institute.

MEIGS, MONTGOMERY CUNNINGHAM (*b. Augusta, Ga., 1816; d. Washington, D.C., 1892*), soldier, engineer. Son of Charles D. Meigs; brother of John F. Meigs. Graduated West Point, 1836. Transferring from the artillery to the engineer corps, he carried through a number of important federal projects, including the Washington Aqueduct and the building of the wings and dome of the Capitol at Washington, D.C. Promoted to brigadier general, May 1861, he served throughout the Civil War as quartermaster general, Union army, with splendid efficiency and complete integrity.

MEIGS, RETURN JONATHAN (*b. Middletown, Conn., 1740; d. Cherokee Agency, Tenn., 1823*), Revolutionary soldier, Ohio pioneer. Brother of Josiah Meigs. U.S. agent to the Cherokee *post* 1801.

MEIGS, RETURN JONATHAN (*b. Middletown, Conn., 1764; d. Marietta, Ohio, 1824*), Ohio pioneer, politician. Son of Return J. Meigs (1740–1823). Removed to Marietta, Ohio, 1788; held several posts under the territorial government and served as chief justice of the state supreme court, 1803–04. After representing Ohio in the U.S. Senate, 1808–10, he was elected governor by a fusion of Federalists and conservative Democratic-Republicans. Reelected, 1812, he resigned in March 1814 to accept the post of U.S. postmaster general in which he served rather inefficiently until 1823.

MEIGS, RETURN JONATHAN (*b. near Winchester, Ky., 1801; d. Washington, D.C., 1891*), lawyer. Nephew of Return J Meigs (1764–1824). Removing to Tennessee *ca.* 1823, he practiced in Nashville, served as attorney general of the state and as U.S. attorney, and was coauthor of the *Code of Tennessee* (1858). A Whig in politics, he was prominent in the encouragement of educational, cultural, and economic movements for improvement of Tennessee. Loyal to the Union, he left the state, 1861. Appointed clerk of the supreme court of the District of Columbia, 1863, he continued in this office until his death.

MEIGS, WILLIAM MONTGOMERY (*b. Philadelphia, Pa., 1852; d. 1929*), lawyer, historian. Son of John F. Meigs; brother of Arthur V. Meigs. Author of numerous articles on the courts and the U.S. Constitution, he also produced scholarly biographies of Josiah Meigs (1887), Thomas Hart Benton (1904), and John C. Calhoun (1917).

MEIKLEJOHN, ALEXANDER (*b. Rochdale, England, 1872; d. Berkeley, Calif., 1964*), educator and polemicist. Immigrated to Rhode Island in 1880. Studied at Brown University (M.A., 1895) and Cornell (Ph.D., 1897). Instructor of philosophy at Brown (1897–1901); dean of students (1901–05); full professor (1905–12). President of Amherst College (1912–23), head of the "experimental college" at the University of Wisconsin (1926–32). Cofounded the San Francisco School of Social Studies in 1932; ran the school through 1935. Taught philosophy at the University of Wisconsin (1935–37).

MEINZER, OSCAR EDWARD (*b. near Davis, Ill., 1876; d. Washington, D.C., 1948*), geologist. B.A., Beloit College, 1901. Ph.D., University of Chicago, 1922. Associated with the U.S. Geological Survey, 1907–46, he was the leader in transforming the study of groundwater into a science. He was author of two publications on the subject which became standard references: *Outline of Ground Water Hydrology, with Definitions* (1923) and *The Occurrence of Ground-Water in the United States, with a Discussion of Principles* (1923).

MELCHER, FREDERIC GERSHOM (*b. Malden, Mass., 1879; d. Montclair, N.J., 1963*), editor, publisher, and bookseller. With Estes and Lauriat Bookstore in Boston, Mass. (1895–1913). Member of the Boston Booksellers' League; president (1912–13). Manager of W. K. Stewart Company in Indianapolis (1913–18). Vice president of the R. R. Bowker Company in New York City (1918–34); president (1934–59); chairman of the board (1959–63). Editor of *Publishers Weekly* (1918–63). Originated, with Franklin K. Mathiews, Children's Book Week, in 1922. Originator and donor of the annual Newbery Medal, beginning in 1922; of the annual Caldecott Medal, beginning in 1937.

MELCHERS, GARI (*b. Detroit, Mich., 1860; d. Falmouth, Va., 1932*), landscape, genre, and portrait painter. Studied at Düsseldorf and Paris. Grounded in habits of fine draftsmanship and sound design, Melchers expressed his own candid character in his work, whose unforced, deeply felt quality won him many honors here and abroad.

MELISH, JOHN (*b. Methven, Scotland, 1771; d. Philadelphia, Pa., 1822*), merchant, traveler, geographer. After several periods of extensive travel in the United States, Melish settled in Philadelphia, 1811. His *Travels in the United States of America* (1812) was praised for its truthfulness and accuracy; he was also author of numerous statistical and descriptive accounts of regions of the United States illustrated with his own maps. His most notable undertaking was *The State Map of Pennsylvania* (1822).

MELL, PATRICK HUES (*b. Walthourville, Ga., 1814; d. Athens, Ga., 1888*), Baptist clergyman, educator, Confederate soldier. Professor of classics at Mercer College, 1841–55; at University of Georgia, 1856–88. Served also as a vice-chancellor and chancellor of the university.

MELL, PATRICK HUES (*b. Penfield, Ga., 1850; d. Fredericksburg, Va., 1918*), scientist, educator. Son of Patrick H. Mell (1814–88). Graduated University of Georgia, 1871; Ph.D., 1880. Taught geology and botany at State College Auburn, Ala.; directed Alabama weather service, originating system of weather signals long in use by U.S. Weather Bureau; was associated with, and for a time directed, Alabama Agricultural Experiment Station. President, Clemson College, 1902–10. Distinguished for his work in hybridizing cotton and on the climatology of Alabama.

MELLEN, CHARLES SANGER (*b. Lowell, Mass., 1851; d. Concord, N.H., 1927*), railroad executive. After training in the business and traffic departments of New England railroads, he became general manager, New York and New England Railroad, 1892. Under the influence of J. Pierpont Morgan, he became president of the Northern Pacific, 1897, improving the physical aspects of that road during his term. Appointed president, New York, New Haven and Hartford Railroad, 1903, he won notoriety for that road by his monopolistic policies and by his neglect of adequate maintenance for which he was censured in a report of the Interstate Commerce Commission.

MELLEN, GRENVILLE (*b. Biddeford, Maine, 1799; d. New York, N.Y., 1841*), author, minor poet.

MELLEN, PRENTISS (*b. Sterling, Mass., 1764; d. Portland, Maine, 1840*), lawyer. A leading attorney in Biddeford and later Portland, Maine, Mellen served in the executive council of Massachusetts and as U.S. senator from Massachusetts, 1818–20. In 1820, when Maine became a state, he was named chief justice of the Maine Supreme Court and held office until 1834.

MELLETTE, ARTHUR CALVIN (*b. Henry Co., Ind., 1842; d. Pittsburg, Kans., 1896*), lawyer, journalist, Indiana legislator. Removing to Dakota Territory, 1879, he was active in movements toward statehood, was named governor of Dakota Territory, 1889, and in the same year was elected first governor of the state of South Dakota. He served until 1893 with ability and economy.

MELLON, ANDREW WILLIAM (*b. Pittsburgh, Pa., 1855; d. Southampton, N.Y., 1937*), industrialist, financier, art collector. Son of Thomas and Sarah Jane (Negley) Mellon. A lawyer who had also served as judge of the common pleas court of Allegheny Co., Thomas Mellon established a private banking house in Pittsburgh, 1869. Andrew Mellon attended public schools and the Western University of Pennsylvania (later the University of Pittsburgh) and in 1874 entered the family bank. Judge Mellon, recognizing his son's financial talents, transferred ownership of T. Mellon & Sons to Andrew, 1882. Quick to grasp opportunities to supply capital in a growing industrial area, Andrew Mellon was especially adept at assessing the worth of new ideas and fostering enterprises that others neglected. His backing of the inventor of the electrolytic process of aluminum manufacture resulted in the formation of the Aluminum Co. of America, with the Mellons as principal stockholders. Similar support brought him stock control of the Carborundum Co. Other enterprises which he helped to establish included the Gulf Oil Corporation, the Union Steel Co., and the American organization of the German inventor Heinrich Koppers. T. Mellon & Sons was incorporated as the Mellon National Bank, with Andrew Mellon as president, 1902. Other Pittsburgh banks soon joined with Mellon, forming one of the great financial powers of the nation.

A generous contributor to the Republican machine in Pennsylvania, Mellon became increasingly interested in national politics through his close friend and legal counsel Philander C. Knox. When Warren G. Harding became president in 1920, he accepted Knox's advice that Mellon be made secretary of the treasury. Though hardly one citizen in a thousand had heard of the retiring Pittsburgh banker, Mellon became the dominant figure in the Harding and Coolidge administrations. His immense wealth and technical expertness in complex financial matters impressed a nation embarking on perhaps the most materialistic period in its history. Mellon emphasized economy and tax reduction, based on his belief that business was the mainspring of national well-being and that it would prosper in proportion to the lightening of its tax load, thus bringing benefits that would filter down to workingmen and farmers. Although his initial tax program, favoring repeal of the excess-profits tax and cuts in taxes on high incomes, aroused violent controversy, many of its objectives were attained. Prosperity and peace helped him in a steady lowering of the national debt, a reduction of federal spending, and further reduction of income tax rates. He was applauded by upper and middle income groups but assailed by Democrats and progressive Republicans, and by veterans and farmers for his opposition to veterans' bonus and farm relief legislation. His program of settlements of World War I debts with foreign nations was less successful. Remittances by the onetime allies to the United States depended on payments to them of German reparations, which in turn depended on loans from the United States. Yet the United States recognized no connection between reparations and debt and refused to lower tariffs to permit European debtors to dispose of goods which would help finance their payments. Eventually the debt settlement problem was engulfed in the Great Depression and World War II, but Mellon in his time showed no great imagination or foresight in this area. Neither did he foresee the depression or take precautionary measures. It could even be asked whether his policies, favoring rapid accumulation and investment, had not stimulated stock-market speculation and inflation. Hoover and Mellon met the depression by emphasizing retrenchment. By 1931, large borrowings became necessary, and Mellon was increasingly criticized. His undersecretary, Ogden L. Mills, replaced him in February 1932, and Mellon accepted the ambassadorship to Great Britain, which post he occupied, gracefully but uneventfully, until March 1933. His later years were marked by an unpleasant tax wrangle over an alleged underpayment of some $2 million on his 1931 income tax. Mellon carried his case to the Board of Tax Appeals, which soon after his death unanimously vindicated his actions, although on other technical grounds it added $485,809 to his 1931 tax.

Over the years Mellon had acquired one of the world's great art collections. In 1937 he announced the gift of his collection to the nation, together with funds to erect a building and establish a $5 million endowment. Construction of the National Gallery of Art, Washington, D.C., began before his death.

MELLON, WILLIAM LARIMER (*b. East Liberty, Pa., 1868; d. Pittsburgh, Pa., 1949*), businessman, oil executive. Nephew of Andrew W. Mellon. Active in the oil industry *post* 1889, he protected the Mellon investment in the J. M. Guffey Petroleum Co. and its associated Gulf Refining Co. by taking over their management, *ca.* 1903. After purchase of the Guffey interest in the firms and their absorption into the new Gulf Oil Corporation, 1907, he was highly successful as president of Gulf, 1909–30, and as chairman of the board, 1930–48.

MELSHEIMER, FRIEDRICH VALENTIN (*b. Negenborn, Duchy of Brunswick, 1749; d. Hanover, Pa., 1814*), Lutheran clergyman, entomologist. Coming to America as chaplain with the Brunswick forces hired by the British to serve in the Revolution, he was taken prisoner at the battle of Bennington, August 1777. He became pastor of several small Lutheran congregations in Dauphin Co., Pa., 1779, and later held pastorates at Manheim, New Holland, and Hanover, Pa. His book *Catalogue of Insects of Pennsylvania* (1806) was the first volume published on the entomology of North America.

MELTON, JAMES (*b. Moultrie, Ga., 1904; d. New York, N.Y., 1961*), tenor. One of radio's most popular singing attractions in the late 1920's and through the 1930's; starred in his own show, "The Seiberling Singers," in 1928. Made operatic debut in Cincinnati, Ohio, as Pinkerton in *Madame Butterfly* in 1938. With the Metropolitan Opera in New York, 1942–48; debuted as Tamino in *The Magic Flute*, which became his most famous role. Starred in the motion pictures *Stars over Broadway* (1935), *Sing Me a Love Song* (1936), *Melody for Two* (1937), and *Ziegfeld Follies* (1946).

MELTZER, SAMUEL JAMES (*b. Ponevyezh, Russia, 1851; d. 1920*), physician, physiologist. M.D., University of Berlin, 1882. Came to New York, N.Y., 1883, where he practiced until 1906. His experimental work in physiology won him wide recognition; *post* 1906, he served as head, Department of Physiology and Pharmacology, Rockefeller Institute of Medical Research.

MELVILLE, DAVID (*b. Newport, R.I., 1773; d. Newport, 1856*), pewterer, inventor. After experimentation with use of gas for illumination, Melville received first U.S. patent for apparatus for making coal gas, March 1813. His efforts to turn his invention to practical account met with no success.

MELVILLE, GEORGE WALLACE (*b. New York, N.Y., 1841; d. Philadelphia, Pa., 1912*), naval officer. Entered Engineer Corps, U.S. Navy, 1861. Served as chief engineer of *Tigress*, 1873, in search for crew of the *Polaris*; again volunteered for Arctic service, 1879, as chief engineer of the *Jeanette*. During the ship's two years icebound in the Arctic Ocean, Melville's energy and skill were largely responsible for keeping the vessel afloat. After it sank, the lifeboat which he commanded was one of the two which reached Siberia, and he was the only boat commander to survive and bring his crew to safety. He later led a fruitless expedition in search of George W. DeLong and finally succeeded in finding and burying his dead shipmates. In 1884, he served as chief engineer of the *Thetis* in the Greely relief expedition. Appointed chief of the Bureau of Steam Engineering, 1887, he served until 1903. Among innovations which he introduced, often in opposition to conservative opinion, were the water-tube boiler and the triple-screw system; he superintended design of the machinery of 120 ships and was influential in merging the Engineer Corps with the line. He retired as rear admiral, 1903.

MELVILLE, HERMAN (*b. New York, N.Y., 1819; d. New York, 1891*), author. Melville's paternal grandfather, Maj. Thomas Melville of Boston, was the model for O. W. Holmes's poem "The Last Leaf"; his maternal grandfather was General Peter Gansevoort, famous for defense of Fort Stanwix in the Revolution. Left in care of his unsympathetic mother when his bankrupt father died, 1831. Melville had scant schooling at the Albany Academy but read much in his father's library. Commencing work, 1834, he was a bank clerk, assistant in his brother's fur store, farmhand, schoolteacher. In 1837 he shipped as cabinboy on a New York–Liverpool voyage, returning with a taste for the sea and experiences which influenced much of his later writing. After more teaching, he shipped out of Fairhaven, Mass., aboard the whaler *Acushnet* (1841), deserting with a shipmate at the Marquesas Islands 18 months later. After struggling through the jungle, he spent an idyllic month among friendly cannibals in beautiful Typee Valley, escaping to Tahiti on an Australian whaler. There he worked for a time as a field laborer and studied the island life; eventually he enlisted in the U.S. Navy on the frigate *United States* and returned to Boston, 1844.

His nearly four years' wandering had made him a romantic figure and furnished material for his great books. He commenced writing immediately and the success of *Typee* (1846), based on his Marquesas experience, convinced him that destiny had intended him for a literary career. This book and *Omoo* (1847), which fictionalized the Tahitian episode, made him famous, but also a target of criticism for his attacks on missionaries. In 1847 Melville married Elizabeth, daughter of Lemuel Shaw, chief justice of Massachusetts; removing to New York, he continued writing. *Mardi* (1849), *Redburn* (1849), and *White-Jacket* (1850)—all created from his South Seas adventures and naval service—appeared in rapid succession. He visited England and France briefly and then purchased "Arrowhead" farm in Pittsfield, Mass., where he became a friend of Nathaniel Hawthorne and completed his classic *Moby Dick* (1851). This marked his peak; the autobiographical *Pierre* (1852) revealed the strain and soul-searching bred of his youthful disappointments and family troubles and also inaugurated a gradual decline of his literary powers. Overworked, seeking religious solace, he visited the Holy Land, 1856–57, tried unavailingly to obtain a consulship and took to lecturing to supplement his income. *Moby Dick* did not sell well and was misunderstood by the critics; the plates and unsold copies of his books were destroyed by fire, 1853. His later volumes were largely ignored, though *Israel Potter* (1855), a Revolutionary novel, was distinguished by excellent writing about the sea and by remarkable characterizations of Benjamin Franklin and John Paul Jones. He turned to writing poetry, much of it obscure, and withdrew almost completely from society and the literary life. Working as a customs inspector in New York, 1866–85, he completed a remarkable short novel, *Billy Budd*, shortly before his death. It was not published until 1924. Virtually forgotten in America (though not in England) for seven decades, his mastery of prose became recognized *ca.* 1920, partially as a result of a sudden vogue for South Seas travel books.

Moby Dick, with its haunting allegory of the great whale's pursuit, is considered Melville's masterpiece, but all his earlier works show vivid portraiture, well-organized observations, enthusiasm, and a good, classical style. He was the first literary artist to write of Polynesia, glorifying the virtues of primitive man and providing unforgettable pictures of island life. *Mardi* departs from the reporting of *Typee* and *Omoo* and employs the background of the earlier books to tell of a quest for happiness. It contains many pages of profound speculation and symbolic beauty and has been likened in structure and intention to the work of Rabelais. *The Piazza Tales* (1856) contains some grimly powerful sketches, notably "Benito Cereno" (the most successful of Melville's shorter works) and "The Encantadas." *The Confidence Man* (1857) is a muddled satire on commercialism. The value of Melville's poetry is in process of reassessment; neglected for a long time, *Battle Pieces* (1866) is now recognized as important, and the subjective *Clarel* (1876) is significant in reflecting the theological strivings of the age. Melville wrote nothing entirely devoid of quality, but his supreme work was *Moby Dick*, whose rhythm and epic qualities bear comparison with the great Scandinavian sagas.

MEMBRÉ, ZENOBIUS (*b. Bapaume, France, 1645; d. 1687[?]*), Roman Catholic missionary, Recollect. Assigned to Canada, 1675. Membré went to Fort Frontenac, 1678; he ministered to La Salle's men on their expedition, 1679–80, to the site of present-day Peoria, Ill. There (at Fort Crèvecoeur) Membré and Henri Tonty escaped from an Iroquois attack, rejoining La Salle at Mackinac, 1681, and accompanying him to the mouth of the Mississippi, 1681–82. Returning to France with La Salle, Membré was made superior of the Recollect missionaries who accompanied La Salle in his attempt to found a settlement at the Mississippi's mouth, 1684. Missing its objective, the expedition built Fort Saint Louis (Lavaca Bay, Tex.); there Membré died presumably, since the colony perished at some time after La Salle's departure in 1687. Membré's detailed journals were incorporated in *Premier Établissement de la Foy dans la Nouvelle France* (1691) by Chrétien Le Clercq; they give details of La Salle's expeditions not to be found elsewhere.

MEMMINGER, CHRISTOPHER GUSTAVUS (*b. Nayhingen, Duchy of Würtemberg, 1803; d. Charleston, S.C., 1888*), lawyer, South Carolina legislator. Came to Charleston, S.C., in infancy; graduated South Carolina college, 1819. Practiced law in Charleston; opposed nullification, 1830–32. As a state legislator, he urged laws requiring specie payments by banks; gained reputation as sound financier; also improved public school system in Charleston and the state. Earlier a foe of secession, he advocated joint Southern defensive measures following John Brown's raid. A member of the committee which drafted the Confederacy's provisional constitution, he was named Confederate secretary of the treasury, 1861. Disliking paper money, he was forced to issue treasury notes when Confederate bonds sold slowly. Comprehensive tax laws were enacted too late; military reserves depreciated the currency, requiring still more notes; funding schemes failed because of the Union blockade and for other reasons. Although Memminger is customarily blamed for the Confederacy's credit

collapse, probably no financier could have averted it. He resigned his post, June 1864.

MENARD, MICHEL BRANAMOUR (*b. Laprairie, Lower Canada, 1805; d. Galveston, Tex., 1856*), Indian trader, Texas pioneer. Nephew of Pierre Menard. Removing to Kaskaskia, Ill., 1823, as employee of his uncle, trading among Delaware and Shawnee; was adopted by Shawnee and elected a chief. Going southward with them to Arkansas, Louisiana, and Texas, he settled at Nacogdoches, where he prospered as trader and land operator; in 1833 he settled as miller and trader on Menard Creek above Liberty on the Trinity River. A signer of the Texas Declaration of Independence, 1836, he helped draft the Texas Constitution and served in the Texas Congress. An able businessman and authority on land titles, he founded the city of Galveston, claiming its site in 1834 and organizing a company for its development, 1838.

MENARD, PIERRE (*b. St. Antoine, Quebec, Canada, 1766; d. Kaskaskia, Ill., 1844*), fur trader, merchant, statesman. Removed to Vincennes, Ind., *ca.* 1787; was employed by Francis Vigo. Opened a store in Kaskaskia, 1791. Active as a militia officer and as a county judge, 1801–71, Menard was a partner in the St. Louis Missouri Fur Co. *post* 1809; with Andrew Henry he led the first organized invasion of trappers to the Three Forks of the Missouri, 1810. He served as first president of the Illinois legislative council, 1812–18, and as first lieutenant governor of the state of Illinois.

MÉNARD, RENÉ (*b. Paris, France, 1605; d. probably present Taylor Co., Wis., 1661*), Roman Catholic missionary, Jesuit. Came to Canada, 1640; ministered first to the Huron; attempted an Iroquois mission, 1656–58. First Jesuit missionary to the Ottawa near Lake Superior, 1660–61.

MENCKEN, HENRY LOUIS (*b. Baltimore, Md., 1880; d. Baltimore, 1956*), journalist, editor, critic, linguist. A leader of the social and cultural revolution that climaxed in the 1920's. Mencken, who received only a high school education, began his career as a reporter for the *Baltimore Morning Herald*, 1899–1906; from 1906 to 1948, he was reporter, critic, and columnist for the *Baltimore Sun*. Book reviewer, 1908–14, and coeditor, 1914–23, of the literary magazine *Smart Set*, which published such authors as James Joyce, Aldous Huxley, Somerset Maugham, Theodore Dreiser, Sherwood Anderson. Willa Cather, F. Scott Fitzgerald, and Eugene O'Neill. Mencken constantly defied the genteel notion that American letters must be primarily Anglo-Saxon, optimistic, and morally uplifting. He ridiculed literary commercialism, dramatized the view that an essential function of art is to challenge accepted axioms, and conducted a boisterous onslaught against the "snouters" who favored literary censorship. Editor of the magazine *American Mercury*, 1924–33, designed chiefly as a forum for extensive commentary on American life. Author of *Philosophy of Friedrich Nietzsche* (1908), *A Book of Burlesques* (1916), *A Book of Prefaces* (1917), *The American Language* (1919), *Prejudices* (1919–27), *Treatise on the Gods* (1930), and *Treatise on Right and Wrong* (1934).

MENDEL, LAFAYETTE BENEDICT (*b. Delhi, N.Y., 1872; d. 1935*), physiological chemist. Graduated Yale, 1891; Ph.D., 1893. Began a teaching career of 42 years at Yale as assistant in the chemistry laboratory of Sheffield Scientific School, 1893; was appointed Sterling professor of physiological chemistry, 1921. Celebrated for his work in nutrition, he was, with Thomas B. Osborne, one of the first in America to recognize the existence of vitamins and their relation to health and disease. Equally far-reaching was their joint work on the nutritive value of the different food proteins and the differences in content of amino acids in proteins and their effect on growth.

MENDELSOHN, ERICH (OR ERIC) (*b. Allenstein, East Prussia, 1887; d. San Francisco, Calif., 1953*), architect. Studied at the Technische Hochschules of Berlin and Munich. Immigrated to the U.S. in 1941. Greatly influenced by German expressionism, Mendelsohn designed many buildings during World War I that were then impossible to construct; his concepts were finally realized by such architects as Pier Luigi Nervi, Eero Saarinen, and Le Corbusier. Designed the Einstein Tower in Potsdam, 1919–1924; the De La Warr Pavilion at Bexhill, England, 1933; and the Hadassah University Medical Center in Jerusalem, 1936. Designed a number of synagogues in the U.S. that changed concepts of Jewish religious architecture. Excluded from the modern movement because of his romanticism, Mendelsohn was not appreciated until long after his death.

MENDELSOHN, SAMUEL (*b. Chicago, Ill., 1895; d. Glen Ridge, N.J., 1966*), inventor and manufacturer. Invented a three-cell, dry-battery-powered flashgun that replaced the manganese-powder devices then used by photographers, and owned and operated the Mendelsohn Speedgun Company (1932–51) in Bloomfield, N.J., which manufactured it. The holder of nearly thirty patents, he also developed microwave components and coaxial connections, and a number of devices for aircraft and target controls as well as for radar systems.

MENDENHALL, CHARLES ELWOOD (*b. Columbus, Ohio, 1872; d. 1935*), physicist. Son of Thomas C. Mendenhall. Graduated Rose Polytechnic, 1894; Ph.D., Johns Hopkins, 1898. After teaching briefly at Williams College, he became assistant professor of physics, University of Wisconsin, 1901, and remained at Wisconsin as professor and chairman of the department until his death. His research interests were so extremely broad that he was called "one of the few remaining natural philosophers." His investigations were concerned with gravity measurements, galvanometer design, melting-point determinations, and radiation. He originated the V-wedge black body, of great value in certain problems in pyrometry.

MENDENHALL, THOMAS CORWIN (*b. near Hanoverton, Ohio, 1841; d. Ravenna, Ohio, 1924*), physicist, educator. Largely self-educated, he taught mathematics and science in Ohio high schools; as physics professor at Ohio State University, 1873–78 and 1881–84, he helped popularize science in the Midwest and organized and directed the state weather bureau. He held the chair of physics at the Imperial University, Tokyo, Japan, 1878–81. Serving as president, Rose Polytechnic Institute, 1886–89, he became superintendent of the U.S. Coast and Geodetic Survey, where he developed improved means for measuring gravity and inaugurated high scholastic standards as prerequisite for entry into the survey's technical force. Resigning, 1894, he served as president of Worcester Polytechnic Institute until 1901. Mendenhall made a number of significant contributions to science, especially in seismology, gravity, and electricity.

MENDES, FREDERIC DE SOLA (*b. Montego Bay, Jamaica, British West Indies, 1850; d. New Rochelle, N.Y., 1927*), rabbi, author. Brother of Henry P. Mendes. Graduated London University, 1869; Ph.D., Jena, 1871. Went to America, 1873, and ministered in New York City; established and edited *American Hebrew* magazine, 1879–85. Conservative theologically, he opposed radical Reform Judaism.

MENDES, HENRY PEREIRA (*b. Birmingham, England, 1852; d. Mount Vernon, N.Y., 1937*), rabbi. Brother of Frederic De Sola Mendes. Minister to Congregation Shearith Israel, New York City 1877–1920; cofounder, Jewish Theological Seminary

of America, 1887; first president, Union of Orthodox Jewish Congregations; an early supporter of Zionism.

MENEELY, ANDREW (*b. West Troy, now Watervliet, N.Y. 1802; d. West Troy, 1851*), bell-founder. Established a foundry, 1826, whose work won international reputation.

MENÉNDEZ DE AVILÉS, PEDRO (*b. Avilés, Spain, 1519; d. Santander, Spain, 1574*), naval officer, Florida colonizer. Appointed captain general of Spain's Indies fleet, 1554, he was commissioned in 1565 to resist French encroachments in Florida. He surprised and scattered Jean Ribaut's fleet off St. John's River in August, commenced a fort at St. Augustine in September, and reduced Fort Caroline. Capturing many survivors from the wrecked French fleet, including Ribaut, he killed them after exacting their unconditional surrender. Between 1565 and 1572 he built two other posts in Florida, explored the coast, and attempted to evangelize the Indians (with whom he dealt honorably), but received little help from Cuba or Spain for his settlements. Successful in establishing Spanish power in Florida, he is remembered chiefly for his massacre of the French captives.

MENETREY, JOSEPH (*b. Freiburg, Switzerland, 1812; d. St. Ignatius Mission, Mont., 1891*), Roman Catholic missionary, Jesuit. Came to Oregon, 1847; ministered to Indians, miners, and settlers in Idaho, Washington, and Montana.

MENEWA (*fl. 1814–35*), half-breed Creek chief. Famed for Tennessee border raids; as second chief of his people, commanded at battle of Horseshoe Bend, 1814; killed William McIntosh, 1825, for ceding tribal lands.

MENGARINI, GREGORY (*b. Rome, Italy, 1811; d. Santa Clara, Calif., 1886*), Roman Catholic missionary, Jesuit, educator. Came to America, 1840; accompanied Pierre de Smet to St. Mary's Mission, Idaho, 1841, where he served until 1850. He compiled several Indian-language dictionaries and a Flathead grammar, and helped found College of Santa Clara in California, first collegiate institution on the Pacific slope.

MENJOU, ADOLPHE JEAN (*b. Pittsburgh, Pa., 1890; d. Beverly Hills, Calif., 1963*), motion picture actor. Appeared in more than two hundred films, beginning his career as an extra at the New York movie studios, from 1914. Moved to Hollywood in 1920; appeared in minor roles in a series of films including *The Faith Healer* (1921) and *Bella Donna* (1923). His first starring role was in Charlie Chaplin's *A Woman of Paris* (1923), a sophisticated comedy that established his image as the suave, well-dressed man with the elegant waxed moustache. Other films include *Mon Gosse de Père* (1930), *The Front Page* (Academy Award nomination, 1931), *A Farewell to Arms* (1932), *Little Miss Marker* (1934), *Sing, Baby, Sing* (1936), and *A Star is Born* (1937). His last film was Walt Disney's *Pollyanna* (1960). At his death he was considered one of the wealthiest men in Hollywood.

MENKEN, ADAH ISAACS (*b. probably Milneburg, La., 1835[?]; d. Paris, France, 1868*), actress, poet. Uninhibited beauty of the mid-nineteenth-century stage; famed in *Mazeppa*. Author of *Infelicia* (collected poems 1868); noted for marriages, divorces, and friendships with major literary figures of the time.

MENNINGER, CHARLES FREDERICK (*b. Tell City, Ind., 1862; d. Topeka, Kans., 1953*), physician. Studied at the Hahnemann Medical School in Chicago and the University of Kansas Medical School, M.D., 1908. Founder of the Menninger Clinic in Topeka, Kans., around 1908. Although he specialized in internal medicine, the clinic, because of the influence of his two sons who had became psychiatrists, became one of the foremost psychiatric research and training centers in the U.S.

MENNINGER, WILLIAM CLAIRE (*b. Topeka, Kans., 1899; d. Topeka, 1966*), psychiatrist. Studied at Columbia (M.A., 1922) and Cornell (M.D., 1924); then was intern in medicine and surgery at Bellevue Hospital in New York City, 1924–26. Returned to Topeka in 1926 and served at the Menninger Clinic, which had been founded by his father and brother in 1919. Did postgraduate work in psychiatry at St. Elizabeths Hospital in Washington, D.C.; at Queens Square Hospital, London; and the Chicago Psychoanalytic Institute (1934–35). Was director of the Menninger Sanitarium (1930–45) and professor at the Menninger School of Psychiatry (1946–66). Studied poliomyelitis, paralysis, Alzheimer's disease, brain tumor, and syphilis, and examined the role of psychological factors in numerous diseases. During World War II was promoted to chief psychiatrist for the army (1944), and after the war became one of the nation's leading figures in the fight against mental illness, applying the lessons of psychiatry to issues in family relations, business and public relations, and other problems in personal development and social interaction. Was elected president of the American Psychiatric Association in 1946, and became president of the Menninger Foundation in 1957. Publications include *Fundamentals of Psychiatry* (1943), *Psychiatry in a Troubled World* (1948), and *Human Understanding in Industry* (1956).

MENOCAL, ANICETO GARCIA (*b. Cuba, 1836; d. New York, N.Y., 1908*), naval officer, civil engineer. Graduated Rensselaer Polytechnic, 1862. An engineer officer in the U.S. Navy, 1874–98, he engaged officially and privately in surveys and negotiations for an interoceanic canal in Panama and Nicaragua. He favored Nicaraguan route.

MENOHER, CHARLES THOMAS (*b. Johnstown, Pa., 1862; d. 1930*), soldier. Graduated West Point, 1886. Commanded 42nd (Rainbow) Division, World War I; as chief of Air Service, 1919–22, was troubled by controversy with Col. William Mitchell. Retired as major general, 1926.

MERCER, CHARLES FENTON (*b. Fredericksburg, Va., 1778; d. Fairfax Co., Va., 1858*), lawyer, businessman, Virginia legislator. Son of James Mercer. Congressman, Federalist and Whig, from Virginia, 1817–39; favored free black colonization, suppression of slave trade, internal improvements.

MERCER, HENRY CHAPMAN (*b. Doylestown, Pa., 1856; d. Doylestown, 1930*), archaeologist, antiquarian, inventor.

MERCER, HUGH (*b. Aberdeenshire, Scotland, ca. 1725; d. near Princeton, N.J., 1777*), physician, Revolutionary soldier. Educated at University of Aberdeen, Mercer joined the Jacobite army in 1745 and was present at the battle of Culloden. Immigrating to America *ca.* 1746, he settled near present Mercersburg, Pa., where he practiced his profession. During the French and Indian War, he served gallantly in the line and, as commandant at Fort Pitt, conducted important negotiations for peace with the Six Nations and other tribes. At the suggestion of George Washington, Mercer removed his practice to Fredericksburg, Va., after the war. Elected colonel, 3rd Virginia Regiment, January 1776, he was named brigadier general by the Continental Congress in June. Commanding the Flying Camp in northern New Jersey, he accompanied Washington's army on its retreat across the state in the fall of 1776 and led a brigade at the battle of Trenton. Attempting to rally his disordered command at the battle of Princeton, Jan. 3, 1777, he was mortally wounded.

MERCER, JAMES (*b. Stafford Co., Va., 1736; d. Richmond, Va., 1793*), Revolutionary patriot, Virginia jurist. Half brother of John F. Mercer.

MERCER, JESSE (*b. Halifax Co., N.C., 1769; d. Butts Co., Ga., 1841*), Baptist clergyman. Raised in Wilkes Co., Ga., he was ordained there, 1789, and held a number of frontier pastorates. A tactful leader in his denomination, he was a benefactor of Mercer University, which was named in his honor.

MERCER, JOHN FRANCIS (*b. Stafford Co., Va., 1759; d. Philadelphia, Pa., 1821*), Revolutionary soldier, Virginia and Maryland legislator. Half brother of James Mercer. After serving as a member of Congress from Virginia, 1782–85, he removed to Anne Arundel Co., Md. As delegate from Maryland to the Constitutional Convention, 1787, he strongly opposed the centralizing character of the U.S. Constitution and spoke and voted against its ratification. Congressman, Democratic-Republican, from Maryland, 1791–94, he was chosen governor of Maryland, 1801, and served until 1803.

MERCER, LEWIS PYLE (*b. Kennett Square, Pa., 1847; d. Cincinnati, Ohio, 1906*), Swedenborgian clergyman. Active in the ministry *post* 1870, notably in Detroit, Mich., Chicago, Ill., and Cincinnati.

MERCER, MARGARET (*b. Annapolis, Md., 1791; d. near Leesburg, Va., 1846*), antislavery worker, educator. Daughter of John F. Mercer.

MERCIER, CHARLES ALFRED (*b. McDonogh, La., 1816; d. New Orleans, La., 1894*), physician, Creole author. Brother-in-law of Pierre Soulé. Founder of the Athénée Louisianais, 1876.

MERCK, GEORGE WILHELM (*b. New York, N.Y., 1894; d. West Orange, N.J., 1957*), chemical industry executive. Graduated from Harvard University, B.A., 1915. The heir to a German-based chemical firm, Merck became vice president of Merck and Company in 1918; president in 1925; and chairman of the board in 1949. Founded (1933) extensive research laboratories in Rahway, N.J., attracting many leading scientists. The laboratories synthesized several vitamins and substances, were the first to produce penicillin in this country, and had an important role in the discovery of cortisone. Appointed director of the War Research Service, 1942, and head of the Biological Warfare Committee, 1944.

MERCUR, ULYSSES (*b. Towanda, Pa., 1818; d. Wallingford, Pa., 1887*), Pennsylvania jurist. As congressman, Republican, from Pennsylvania, 1865–72, he was an active advocate of extreme Reconstruction measures. Justice, Pennsylvania Supreme Court, 1872–83; chief justice, 1883–87.

MEREDITH, EDNA C. ELLIOTT (*b. Des Moines, Iowa, 1879; d. Des Moines, 1961*), hostess and publisher. Married Edwin Thomas Meredith in 1896. The Meredith Publishing Company had its beginnings in a newspaper Edwin Meredith's grandfather had given the couple as a wedding gift. By 1924, the company was publishing the magazines *Better Homes and Gardens* and *Successful Farming*. Edwin Meredith's political aspirations led to his appointment as secretary of agriculture under President Woodrow Wilson, 1920; Edna Meredith acquired fame in Washington, D.C., as an elegant hostess. When her husband sought the Democratic nomination for the presidency in 1928, Edna Meredith received national attention as a potential first lady. Upon her husband's death in 1928, she inherited a major interest in the company, serving as business manager and, later, director of the corporation. A successful book division was inaugurated under her direction in 1930 when the company brought out *The Better Homes and Gardens Cookbook*. The *Better Homes and Gardens Baby Book* followed in 1943.

MEREDITH, EDWIN THOMAS (*b. near Avoca, Iowa, 1876; d. 1928*), journalist, publisher. Founded *Successful Farming*, 1902; *Better Homes and Gardens*, 1922. Forced a reform in the type of advertising handled by farm papers; served as U.S. secretary of agriculture, 1920–21.

MEREDITH, SAMUEL (*b. Philadelphia, Pa., 1741; d. Mount Pleasant Township, Pa., 1817*), Revolutionary soldier, financier. Pennsylvania legislator. Brother-in-law of George Clymer. First treasurer of the United States, 1789–1801.

MEREDITH, WILLIAM MORRIS (*b. Philadelphia, Pa., 1799; d. Philadelphia, 1873*), lawyer, Pennsylvania legislator and official. A leading Whig, Meredith was U.S. secretary of the treasury, March 1849–July 1850; in his annual report for 1849 he set forth an elaborate argument for the protective tariff. He served as attorney general of Pennsylvania, 1861–67.

MERGENTHALER, OTTMAR (*b. Hachtel, Germany, 1854; d. Baltimore, Md., 1899*), maker of watches and scientific instruments, inventor of the linotype. Came to America, 1872. Completed the first direct-casting linotype, July 1884; received first patent for it, August 1884; with associates, organized National Typographic Co. for its manufacture, 1885. The first of 12 machines made by the company for the *New York Tribune* was used to compose a part of the issue of the paper on July 3, 1886. After resigning from the manufacturing company in 1888, Mergenthaler continued to add to the value of his invention by devising more than 50 patented improvements to it.

MERGLER, MARIE JOSEPHA (*b. Mainstockheim, Bavaria, 1851; d. Los Angeles, Calif., 1901*), physician. Came to America as a child. Graduated Woman's Medical College, Chicago, Ill., 1879; practiced medicine *post* 1881 in Chicago. Taught gynecology at Woman's Medical College and at Northwestern University; was notable for her success in abdominal surgery.

MERRIAM, AUGUSTUS CHAPMAN (*b. Leyden. N.Y., 1843; d. Athens, Greece, 1895*), philologist, archaeologist. Graduated Columbia, 1866. *Post* 1868, taught Greek and Latin at Columbia; *post* 1876, taught Greek only; appointed professor of Greek archaeology and epigraphy, Columbia, 1890. A productive scholar, Merriam was author of a number of research monographs which won him international reputation.

MERRIAM, CHARLES (*b. West Brookfield, Mass., 1806; d. 1887*), publisher. Established a printing house and bookshop in Springfield, Mass., 1831, which became G. & C. Merriam, 1832. Acquiring the rights to publish Noah Webster's *American Dictionary of the English Language* in 1843, the Merriams, with the editorial assistance of Chauncey A. Goodrich, republished the work in unabridged revised form with the greatest success.

MERRIAM, CHARLES EDWARD, JR. (*b. Hopkinton, Iowa, 1874; d. Rockville, Md., 1953*), political scientist. Studied at the State University of Iowa and at Columbia University, Ph.D., 1900. Taught at the University of Chicago from 1900 until his death. The university's first designated political scientist, Merriam is acknowledged as the father of the behavioral movement of political science. President of the American Political Science Association, 1924–25. Author of *American Political Ideas: 1865–1917* (1920); *New Aspects of Politics* (1925); and *Political Power: Its Composition and Incidence* (1934). Founder of the Social Science Research Council in 1923; president, 1924–27. The council contributed many studies to government and was financed by the Rockefeller Foundation. Leader of the National Resources Planning Board, 1933–43. Appointed to the President's Committee on Administrative Management, 1936.

MERRIAM, CLINTON HART (*b. New York, N.Y., 1855; d. Berkeley, Calif., 1942*), naturalist. Nephew of Augustus C. Merriam. Accompanied Hayden survey in Utah, Idaho, and Wyoming, 1872; attended Sheffield Scientific School, Yale; M.D., College of Physicians and Surgeons, Columbia, 1879. Headed Biological Survey division (later bureau), U.S. Department of Agriculture, 1885–1910, in its investigations of American plants and animals; instituted and edited series of North American Fauna publications; held endowed post as researcher at Smithsonian Institution, 1910–39. Author of, among many other works, *The Mammals of the Adirondack Region* (1884) and *Life Zones and Crop Zones of the Unites States* (1898).

MERRIAM, HENRY CLAY (*b. Houlton, Maine, 1837; d. Portland, Maine, 1912*), soldier. Serving in the Union army, 1862–65, Merriam received the Congressional Medal for bravery in leading assault at Fort Blakely, April 1865. Commissioned major, 1866, he served on the western frontiers, rising to the rank of brigadier general, June 1897. He organized the Philippines Expeditionary Force, 1898, and suppressed labor riots at Coeur d'Alène mines, 1899, and retired as major general, 1901.

MERRIAM, JOHN CAMPBELL (*b. Hopkinton, Iowa, 1869; d. Oakland, Calif., 1945*), paleontologist, science administrator, conservationist. B.S., Lenox College, 1887; Ph.D., University of Munich, 1893, in vertebrate paleontology. Taught at University of California, 1894–1920; was professor and chairman of the Department of Paleontology *post* 1912; played a key role in developing and publicizing paleontological study on the West Coast. President, Carnegie Institution of Washington, 1920–38; president, Save-the-Redwoods League, 1917–42. Author of, among other works, classic studies on the stratigraphy of the John Day Basin (Oregon) and on the remains found in the La Brea tar pits (Los Angeles, Calif.)

MERRIAM, WILLIAM RUSH (*b. Wadham's Mills, N.Y., 1849; d. Fort Sewall, Fla., 1931*), banker, Minnesota legislator. Raised in St. Paul, Minn. Republican governor of Minnesota, 1889–93; highly efficient director of the twelfth census, 1899–1903.

MERRICK, EDWIN THOMAS (*b. Wilbraham, Mass., 1808; d. New Orleans, La., 1897*), lawyer. Admitted to Ohio bar, 1833; practiced in Clinton, La., *post* 1838. Chief justice of Louisiana, 1855–65.

MERRICK, FREDERICK (*b. Wilbraham, Mass., 1810; d. Delaware, Ohio, 1894*), Methodist clergyman, educator. Identified with Ohio Wesleyan University *post* 1843 as professor of science and moral philosophy; as president, 1860–73; and as lecturer on religion thereafter.

MERRICK, PLINY (*b. Brookfield, Mass., 1794; d. 1867*), lawyer, Massachusetts jurist and legislator. Senior counsel to Prof. John W. Webster at his trial for the murder of Dr. George Parkman, 1850. Judge, Massachusetts Supreme Judicial Court, 1853–64.

MERRICK, SAMUEL VAUGHAN (*b. Hallowell, Maine, 1801; d. Philadelphia, Pa., 1870*), engine manufacturer, railroad executive. An early promoter of the Pennsylvania Railroad Co., Merrick served as its first president, 1847–49.

MERRILL, CHARLES EDWARD (*b. Green Cove Springs, Fla., 1885; d. Southampton, N.Y., 1956*), stockbroker, investment banker. Studied at Amherst College. Founded (1915) the investment firm of Merrill Lynch and Co., later known as Merrill Lynch, Pierce, Fenner, and Smith. One of the nation's largest brokerage firms, Merrill Lynch introduced innovative techniques such as advertising, catering to the small investor, and training sales personnel. Helped found the magazine *Family Circle*, 1932.

MERRILL, DANIEL (b. Rowley, Mass., 1765; d. Sedgwick, Maine, 1833), Congregational and Baptist clergyman, Revolutionary soldier. Took the lead, 1813, in securing charter and land grant for Maine Literary and Theological Association, later Colby College.

MERRILL, ELMER DREW (b. East Auburn, Me., 1876; d. Forest Hills, Mass., 1956), botanist, taxonomist, educator. Studied at the University of Maine, M.S., 1904. Professor of botany at the University of the Philippines, 1902–24; dean of the College of Agriculture at the University of California, 1923–26; professor of botany at Columbia University, 1930–35, and at Harvard University, 1935–48. Director of the Bureau of Science in Manila, 1902–24, and of the New York Botanic Garden, 1930–35. Major works include *Bibliography of Eastern Asiatic Botany* (1938) and *Index Rafinesquianus* (1949).

MERRILL, ELMER TRUESDELL (b. Millville, Mass., 1860; d. Santa Barbara, Calif., 1936), Episcopal clergyman, educator, classicist, church historian. Graduated Wesleyan University, 1881; studied also at Yale and at University of Berlin. His two principal teaching positions were at Wesleyan (professor of Latin), 1888–1905, and at University of Chicago, 1908–25. He was best known for his work on Catullus and the younger Pliny.

MERRILL, FRANK DOW (b. Hopkinton, Mass., 1903; d. Fernandina Beach, Fla., 1955), soldier, highway engineer. Graduated from the U.S. Military Academy at West Point, 1929. Joined Lt. General Joseph Stilwell's forces in Burma in 1941. Took part in Stilwell's retreat from Burma by foot in 1942; became Stilwell's operations officer in 1942. Commander of the 5307th Composite Unit (Provisional) in 1943, which saw intensive action in Burma. Chief of staff of Stilwell's Tenth Army (1945–46) on Okinawa, where he planned the invasion of Japan. Retired from the military, 1948. Appointed New Hampshire commissioner of public works and highways, 1949. President of the American Association of Highway Officials, 1955.

MERRILL, GEORGE EDMANDS (b. Charlestown, Mass., 1846; d. Hamilton, N.Y., 1908), Baptist clergyman. Graduated Harvard 1869. After holding pastorates in several Massachusetts cities and in Colorado, he served as president of Colgate University, 1901–08.

MERRILL, GEORGE PERKINS (b. Auburn, Maine, 1854; d. Auburn, 1929), geologist. Graduated University of Maine, 1879. Joining the staff of the U.S. National Museum, 1881, he remained there the rest of his life, becoming head curator, 1897, and developing the Department of Geology and Paleontology into one of the great collections of the world. Merrill was also a pioneer in research on building stones and the processes of rock weathering, on meteorites, and on the history of American physical geology. He was author of, among other works, *A Treatise on Rock, Rockweathering and Soils* (1897), *Non-metallic Minerals* (1904), and *The First One Hundred Years of American Geology* (1824).

MERRILL, GRETCHEN VAN ZANDT (b. Boston, Mass., 1925; d. Windsor, Conn., 1965), figure skater. Began skating in 1935; trained in Berkeley, Calif., and from 1941 with Maribel Vinson Owen. A popular champion, she was known for her technical mastery; her school figures enabled her to enter the free-skating portions of competitions with comfortable leads. Won six consecutive National Senior Ladies Figure Skating Championships beginning in 1943. Retired in 1949.

MERRILL, JAMES CUSHING (b. Cambridge, Mass., 1853; d. Washington, D.C., 1902), army surgeon, ornithologist. Librarian, U.S. Surgeon General's Office, 1897–1902.

MERRILL, JAMES GRISWOLD (b. Montague, Mass., 1840; d. Mountain Lakes, N.J., 1920), Congregational clergyman, educator. After holding a number of pastorates, Merrill served as editor of the *Christian Mirror*; he became professor of logic and dean at Fisk University, 1898. Named acting president of the university in 1899, he served as president, 1901–08. Among his outstanding achievements in office were the improvement of the endowment, confirmation of the policy of having a biracial faculty, and promotion of the Fisk Jubilee Singers.

MERRILL, JOSHUA (b. Duxbury, Mass., 1820; d. 1904), chemist, pioneer oil refiner. Partner and successor of Samuel Downer. Developed many important technological processes, among them the invention, 1869, of a method of distilling by steam without partial decomposition, thereby producing less odorous paraffin lubricating oils.

MERRILL, SAMUEL (b. Peacham, Vt., 1792; d. Indianapolis, Ind., 1855), lawyer, Indiana official and legislator. Removed to Vevay, Ind., 1816. Successful in business and public life, particularly as president of the State Bank of Indiana, Merrill purchased a bookstore, 1850, which became a constituent of the Bowen-Merrill, later the Bobbs-Merrill, publishing company.

MERRILL, SELAH (b. Canton Center, Conn., 1837; d. near East Oakland, Calif., 1909), Congregational clergyman, archaeologist. U.S. consul at Jerusalem, 1882–1907, except during President Cleveland's two terms; author of *Ancient Jerusalem* (1908).

MERRILL, STEPHEN MASON (b. near Mount Pleasant, Ohio, 1825; d. Keyport, N.J., 1905), Methodist clergyman. A midwestern leader of his denomination, Merrill was elected bishop, 1872, and made his headquarters thereafter in St. Paul, Minn., and Chicago, Ill. He was celebrated for his encyclopedic knowledge of Methodist law.

MERRILL, STUART FITZRANDOLPH (b. Hempstead, N.Y., 1863; d. Versailles, France, 1915), French symbolist poet. Raised in Paris and educated there, he returned to live in New York City, 1884–89, but resided in France thereafter, save for occasional visits. The only book which he wrote in English was *Pastels in Prose* (1890, with a preface by W. D. Howells).

MERRILL, WILLIAM BRADFORD (b. Salisbury, N.H., 1861; d. 1928), newspaper editor and manager. Managing editor, Philadelphia *Press*, 1884–91; *New York Press* (1891–1901; *New York World*, 1901–08. Attracting the attention of William R. Hearst because of his financial abilities, Merrill became manager of the *New York American*, 1908, and in 1917 was made general manager of all the Hearst papers. He retired in 1927.

MERRILL, WILLIAM EMERY (b. Fort Howard, Wis., 1837; d. 1891), soldier, engineer. Graduated West Point, 1859. Served with distinction as a military engineer throughout the Civil War and as chief engineer of the Division of the Missouri; *post* 1870, he devoted himself mainly to river and harbor improvement work. Originated, 1878–79, the idea of canalizing the Ohio River from Pittsburgh to its mouth; inaugurating the project in 1879, he worked on it until his death.

MERRIMON, AUGUSTUS SUMMERFIELD (b. Cherryfields, N.C., 1830; d. 1892), lawyer, North Carolina politician, U.S. senator and jurist.

MERRITT, ANNA LEA (*b. Philadelphia, Pa., 1844; d. London, England, 1930*), painter, etcher.

MERRITT, ISRAEL JOHN (*b. New York, N.Y., 1829; d. New York, 1911*), salvage expert, inventor. Patented, 1865, a pontoon device for raising sunken vessels by displacement, which completely revolutionized the salvage business.

MERRITT, LEONIDAS (*b. Chautauqua Co., N.Y., 1844; d. Duluth, Minn., 1926*), prospector. Raised in Oneota, Minn. After working as lumberman and iron prospector, Merritt with his brothers located deposits of iron ore in the Mesabi Range, 1887. The brothers organized the Mountain Iron Co. to exploit their find, July 1890, and secured the financial participation of John D. Rockefeller. In 1893, Rockefeller obtained full control of the mining and transportation enterprises initiated by the Merritts.

MERRITT, WESLEY (*b. New York, N.Y., 1834; d. Natural Bridge, Va., 1910*), soldier. Raised in Illinois. Graduated West Point, 1860. Served as aide-de-camp to General P. St. G. Cooke, 1861; promoted captain, 1862; commissioned brigadier general of volunteers, 1863. Commanded reserve cavalry at Gettysburg; following continual service in Virginia rose to brevet rank of major general. After frontier service in the west, 1866–79, he was superintendent at West Point, 1882–87. Commissioned brigadier general, regular army, 1887, he commanded successively the departments of Missouri, Dakota, Missouri again, and the East. In command of the first Philippine expedition, 1898, supported by Admiral George Dewey, he took the city of Manila in August in a campaign complicated by the presence of the Philippine insurgent army. After a short tour as military governor of the Philippines, Merritt resumed his old command of the Department of the East and retired as major general, 1900.

MERRY, ANN BRUNTON (*b. London, England, 1769; d. Alexandria, Va., 1808*), actress, theatrical manager. Made debut at Bath, England, 1785; married Robert Merry, a minor poet, 1791. Came to America as member of Philadelphia Co., 1796. Widowed, she married Thomas Wignell, director of the Philadelphia Theatre, 1803; on his death, she married William Warren, 1806. A woman of great charm and integrity, Merry was one of the notable players on the early American stage.

MERRY, WILLIAM LAWRENCE (*b. New York, N.Y., 1842; d. Battle Creek, Mich., 1911*), sea captain, merchant. Principal protagonist for Nicaraguan isthmian canal, 1890–95; served as U.S. minister to Nicaragua, Costa Rica, and El Salvador, 1897–1907, remaining as minister to Costa Rica until 1911.

MERTON, THOMAS (*b. Prades, France, 1915; d. Bangkok, Thailand, 1968*), clergyman and writer. Born to New Zealand father and American mother, he moved to Long Island, N.Y., in 1916. Studied at Columbia University (M.A., 1939). Baptized into the Roman Catholic Church (1938), entered Trappist monastery of Our Lady of Gethsemani in Kentucky and received the religious name Louis (1941), ordained a priest in 1949. Became a U.S. citizen in 1951. Wrote about contemplative experience and social responsibility; during the 1960's was a leader in the struggle for racial justice, world peace, and nonviolence as a way of life. Books include *Thirty Poems* (1944), *The Seven Storey Mountain* (1948), *Seeds of Contemplation* (1949), *The Ascent to Truth* (1951), *The Sign of Jonas* (1953), *No Man Is an Island* (1955), *Seeds of Destruction* (1964), and *Mystics and Zen Masters* (1967). He died by accidental electrocution, while visiting Bangkok where he was invited to speak at a meeting of monks and sisters.

MERVINE, WILLIAM (*b. Philadelphia, Pa., 1791; d. Utica, N.Y. 1868*), naval officer. Headed landing detachment of marines and sailors at Monterey, Calif., July 1846; in October, com-

manded landing party which engaged the Mexicans near Los Angeles. Commanded Gulf Blockading Squadron, May–September 1861. Retired as rear admiral, 1866.

MERZ, KARL (*b. Bensheim, Germany, 1836; d. Wooster, Ohio, 1890*), musician, teacher of music. Came to America, 1854. After teaching at various towns in Pennsylvania and Virginia, Merz directed musical studies at Oxford Female College, Ohio, 1861–82, and at Wooster University, 1882–90. He was author of a number of musical textbooks and of *Music and Culture* (1890).

MESERVE, FREDERICK HILL (*b. Boston, Mass., 1865; d. New York, N.Y., 1962*), businessman and collector of historical photographs and Lincolniana. Worked for Deering, Milliken, and Company in New York, 1893–1962, with one interruption, 1909–19, when he held a seat on the New York Stock Exchange with the brokerage firm Charles W. Turner. Collected photographs from the period 1850–1900, and published them in *Photographs of Abraham Lincoln* (privately printed in 1911), *Historical Photographs* (a twenty-eight-volume work with six extant sets, produced in 1917 and 1944), and *The Photographs of Abraham Lincoln* (1941).

MESERVE, NATHANIEL (*b. Newington, N.H., ca. 1705; d. Louisbourg, Cape Breton Island, Canada, 1758*), shipwright, colonial soldier. Constructed frigate *America* at Portsmouth, N.H., 1749; served as master constructor under Loudoun and Amherst, 1756–58.

MESSER, ASA (*b. Methuen, Mass., 1769; d. Providence, R.I., 1836*), Baptist clergyman, educator. Graduated Rhode Island College, 1790. After teaching there, 1791–1802, Messer was made president and served until 1826. During his term, the institution made sure progress, Nicholas Brown became its patron, and its name was changed to Brown University. Messer resigned because of antagonism aroused by his alleged Arianism.

MESSERSMITH, GEORGE STRAUSSER (*b. Fleetwood, Pa., 1883; d. Houston, Tex., 1960*), diplomat. Studied at Delaware State College. Taught in the Delaware public schools until he entered the foreign service in 1913. Consul general for Belgium, 1925–28; in Buenos Aires, 1928–30; in Berlin, 1930–34; and in Vienna, 1934–37. Ambassador to Cuba, 1940–42; to Mexico, 1942–46; and to Argentina, 1946–47, during the rise of Juan Perón. Resigned because of differences with Secretary of State Marshall over Argentina's role in World War II. Chairman of the board of the Mexican Power and Light Company, 1947–55.

MESSLER, THOMAS DOREMUS (*b. Somerville, N.J., 1833; d. Cresson, Pa., 1893*), railway executive. Evolved the "Messler system" of railroad accounting, 1857, while auditor of the Pittsburgh, Fort Wayne and Chicago Railway.

MESSMER, SEBASTIAN GEBHARD (*b. Goldach, Switzerland, 1847; d. Goldach, 1930*), Roman Catholic clergyman. Educated at University of Innsbrück, Austria. Came to America, 1871; taught theology and canon law at Seton Hall College until 1889 and at Catholic University of America, 1889–91. Consecrated bishop of Green Bay, 1892, he became archbishop of Milwaukee, 1903. A broadminded man, sympathetic with labor and trade unionism, he upheld progressive reforms and was notable for his encouragement of educational institutions.

MEŠTROVIĆ, IVAN (*b. Vrpolje, Croatia, 1883; d. South Bend, Ind., 1962*), sculptor. Studied at the Vienna Academy of Fine Arts (1900–04). Immigrated to the United States in 1947; naturalized in 1954. Taught at Syracuse University, 1947–55, and the University of Notre Dame, 1955–62. Works include *The Maiden of*

Kossovo (1907, marble), *The Archers of Domagoj* (1917, plaster), *Gregory, Bishop of Nin* (1926, bronze), and *Job* (1945, bronze).

METALIOUS, GRACE (*b.* Manchester, N.H., 1924; *d.* Boston, Mass., 1964), writer. Author of *Peyton Place* (1956), *Return to Peyton Place* (1959), *Tight White Collar* (1960), and *No Adam in Eden* (1963), all iconoclastic, sex-ridden treatments of small-town life, which, by the time of her death, had sold some 15 million copies. A successful motion picture and television series were based on *Peyton Place*. By no means an important writer, the most lasting influence of her books is in the marketing techniques used to promote and sell them in the legion of similar writers who have followed her.

METCALF, HENRY HARRISON (*b.* Newport, N.H., 1841; *d.* 1932), New Hampshire editor. Published a number of Democratic newspapers and the *Granite Monthly*, 1877–1919.

METCALF, JOEL HASTINGS (*b.* Meadville, Pa., 1866; *d.* Portland, Maine, 1925), Unitarian clergyman, astronomer.

METCALF, THERON (*b.* Franklin, Mass., 1784; *d.* 1875), Massachusetts jurist. Graduated Brown, 1805. Practiced in Massachusetts *post* 1808, principally at Dedham. Compiled *Reports of Cases Argued . . . Supreme Judicial Court of Massachusetts* (1841–50); served on Massachusetts supreme bench, 1848–65.

METCALF, WILLARD LEROY (*b.* Lowell, Mass., 1858; *d.* 1925), landscape and figure painter.

METCALF, WILLIAM (*b.* Pittsburgh, Pa., 1838; *d.* Pittsburgh, 1909), metallurgist, steel manufacturer. Graduated Rensselaer Polytechnic, 1858. As general superintendent, Fort Pitt Foundry, 1859–65, he supervised production of more than 3,000 heavy guns for the United States, no one of which was ever reported as failing in service. Thereafter, he was associated with the Crescent Steel Works and the Braeburn Steel Co. He was one of the first practical experts to stress the importance of mechanical treatment and heat treatment of steel as compared with chemical composition, and the different effects of different kinds of tests of strength.

METCALFE, SAMUEL LYTLER (*b.* near Winchester, Va., 1798; *d.* Cape May, N.J., 1856), chemist, physician. Author of the *Kentucky Harmonist* (1820), *A Collection of Some of the Most Interesting Narratives of the Indian Warfare in the West* (1821), and *Caloric* (1837, 1843), an elaborate study of the nature of heat.

METCALFE, THOMAS (*b.* Fauquier Co., Va., 1780; *d.* Nicholas Co., Ky., 1855), stonemason, Kentucky politician and legislator. A strong exponent of Western democracy while a Kentucky congressman, 1819–28, he followed Henry Clay in voting for John Q. Adams, 1825. Nominated for governor by the Adams-Clay convention, 1827, he was elected and served, 1828–32. As governor, he endorsed protective tariffs and federal aid for internal improvements; he denounced nullification and Jackson's general policy. As U.S. senator, Whig, from Kentucky, 1848–49, he denounced secession, declaring that Kentucky would uphold the Union.

METTAUER, JOHN PETER (*b.* Prince Edward Co., Va., 1787; *d.* 1875), physician, surgeon. M.D., University of Pennsylvania, 1809. Entering practice in his native county, he continued to work there except for brief intervals until his death. A daring and original surgeon, he was a pioneer in genitourinary surgery, and in lithotomy was regarded as second only to Benjamin W. Dudley. He first performed an operation for vesicovaginal fistula in August 1838, and was called by J. Marion Sims one of two men who "stand out in bold relief amongst those who have devoted some time" to such surgery. In 1837 Mettauer organized Prince Edward Medical Institute, which became the medical department

of Randolph-Macon College, 1847. Eccentric but respected, he wore on all occasions, even while operating, a high stovepipe hat; his daughter said she had never seen him without it, and he left instructions that he be buried in it.

METZ, CHRISTIAN (*b.* Neuwied, Prussia, 1794; *d.* Amana, Iowa, 1867), founder of the Christian communist community of Amana. Leader *post* 1823 of a German pietist sect, Metz immigrated with his followers to America *ca.* 1842, settling at Ebenezer near Buffalo, N.Y. Seeking cheaper land and greater seclusion, he led his brethren westward to Iowa, 1854, where, with extraordinary executive ability and sincere piety, he presided over the most successful experiment in communal living attempted in 19th-century America.

MEYER, ADOLF (*b.* Niederweningen, near Zurich, Switzerland, 1866; *d.* Baltimore, Md., 1950), psychiatrist. M.D., Zurich, 1892, after study in Paris, Edinburgh, and London. Deciding to pursue his career in the United States, he accepted a fellowship at the University of Chicago, 1892–93, and served as pathologist at Illinois Eastern Hospital, Kankakee, 1893–95. From 1895 to 1902 he taught at Clark University, working also at the state hospital in Worcester, Mass., he stressed careful study of patients' symptoms and needs, introduced bedside note-taking, and trained his assistants to record cases accurately, concisely, and by a uniform method. In 1898 he published his classic *Critical Review of the Data and General Methods and Deductions of Modern Neurology*, which contained the essence of his integrative theory and the nucleus of his psychobiological doctrine. Between 1902 and 1910 he directed the Pathological Institute in New York City (renamed the Psychiatric Institute in 1908), and transformed the New York insane asylums into modern mental hospitals; he taught the established descriptive psychiatry, but opened the minds of physicians to the promise of dynamic psychiatry and prepared the United States to accept psychoanalysis. He also fought for guidance for families of patients and for continual hospital contact after discharge. As professor of psychopathology at Cornell Medical College, 1904–09, he organized an outpatient service, the first mental clinic in New York City. *Post* 1910 he was chairman of the Department of Psychiatry at Johns Hopkins Medical School and director of the Henry Phipps Clinic.

MEYER, AGNES ELIZABETH ERNST (*b.* New York, N.Y., 1887; *d.* Mount Kisco, N.Y., 1970), journalist, writer, and philanthropist. Studied at Barnard College (graduated, 1907). Reporter for the *New York Morning Sun* (1907–08). Married (1910) Eugene Meyer, a financier and owner of the *Washington Post* (from 1933). Chairman of the Recreation Commission of Westchester County (1923–41). Contributed articles to a number of publications, and wrote often for the *Post*, and for the Associated Press (1942). With her husband, created the Eugene and Agnes E. Meyer Foundation in 1944. Books include *Out of These Roots* (1953), *Chinese Painting as Reflected in the Thought and Art of Li Lung-mien* (1923), *Journey Through Chaos* (1944), and *Education for a New Morality* (1957).

MEYER, ALBERT GREGORY (*b.* Milwaukee, Wis., 1903; *d.* Chicago, Ill., 1965), cardinal of the Roman Catholic Church. Studied at the North American College in Rome, the Urbanian College of the Sacred Congregation de Propaganda Fide (Ph.D., 1927), and the Pontifical Biblical Institute in Rome (licentiate's degree in Sacred Scripture, 1930). Ordained in 1926; appointed assistant pastor of a Waukesha, Wis., parish. Named to the faculty of St. Francis Seminary in Milwaukee in 1931; rector from 1937. Sixth bishop of Superior, 1946–53; archbishop of Milwaukee, 1953–58; of Chicago, 1958–59; and cardinal from 1959. Effectively advanced the renewal of the Church during the Second Vatican Council. Member of the Central Preparatory Commission and the Secretariat de Concilii Negotiis Extra Ordinem, 1961–62, and, in 1963, appointed one of twelve presidents of the council. Advocated the use of vernacular languages in the liturgy, recognition of the contributions of contemporary biblical exegesis, and admission in theory and in practice of the collegial nature of the episcopal order. His efforts helped to ensure passage of the declaration on religious liberty, and caused him to emerge from the third session (1964, the last he attended) of the council the intellectual leader of the American hierarchy.

MEYER, ANNIE NATHAN (*b. New York, N.Y., 1867; d. New York, 1951*), writer and educator. Founded Columbia University's Barnard College for Women in 1889 and was a member of the board of trustees until her death. Meyer was an antisuffragist who believed that the women's movement was motivated by sex envy and sex hatred. She wrote two novels, twenty plays (three staged on Broadway), and a dozen short stories.

MEYER, EUGENE ISAAC (*b. Los Angeles, Calif., 1875; d. Washington, D.C. 1959*), investment banker, government official, and publisher. Founding his investment firm in New York in 1901, Meyer soon built a financial empire, being the chief organizer of the Allied Chemical Co., among other pursuits. He left business for government service during World War I; President Wilson named him director of the War Finance Corporation in 1918, a position he held until 1927. In 1930, he became head of the Federal Reserve Board, and later, the first head of the Reconstruction Finance Corporation. Leaving government in 1933, Meyer bought *The Washington Post*, eventually building that paper into one of the great papers in the world. He served briefly as head of the World Bank in 1946.

MEYER, GEORGE VON LENGERKE (*b. Boston, Mass., 1858; d. 1918*), banker, Massachusetts legislator, diplomat. Graduated Harvard, 1879. Active in Republican politics, Meyer was appointed U.S. ambassador to Italy, 1900; he served with success in this post and was the means by which President Theodore Roosevelt's peace proposals were presented to the czar of Russia, 1905. As U.S. postmaster general, 1907–09, Meyer served with ability and efficiency, as he did in the post of secretary of the navy, 1909–13.

MEYER, HENRY CODDINGTON (*b. Hamburg, Germany, 1844; d. Montclair, N.J., 1935*), dealer in plumbing fixtures, Union soldier, pioneer in sanitary engineering. Founded *Plumber and Sanitary Engineer*, 1877, which, after various changes of title, became the *Engineering Record*, 1890.

MEYER, MARTIN ABRAHAM (*b. San Francisco, Calif., 1879; d. San Francisco, 1923*), rabbi, Semitic scholar. Ministered at Albany and Brooklyn, N.Y.; served Temple Emanu-el, San Francisco, *post* 1910. Active in philanthropy and as Zionist.

MEYERHOF, OTTO (*b. Hannover, Germany, 1884; d. Philadelphia, Pa., 1951*), biochemist. Immigrated to the U.S. in 1940. M.D., University of Heidelberg (1909). Director of the department of physiology at the Kaiser Wilhelm Institute for Medical Research in Heidelberg (1929–38). Taught at the University of Pennsylvania (1940–51). Won the Nobel Prize for physiology or medicine (shared with Archibald V. Hill) for his work on the chemical processes involved in muscles. In 1925 he extracted from muscle the enzymes that convert glycogen to lactic acid; the pathway proposed for this process became known as the Embden-Meyerhof pathway. Meyerhof's work permitted the first quantitative estimates to be made of the efficiency of the muscle as a chemical machine.

MEZES, SIDNEY EDWARD (*b. Belmont, Calif., 1863; d. Altadena, Calif., 1931*), educator. Graduated University of California, 1884; Ph.D., Harvard, 1893; taught philosophy at University of Texas *post* 1894, serving also as dean and as president, 1908–14. As president of the College of the City of New York, 1914–27, he oversaw it during a period of extraordinary growth and was responsible for the establishment of its schools of technology, business, and education. At the request of his brother-in-law, Edward M. House, and by direction of President Woodrow Wilson, he brought together the body of experts known as the Inquiry, 1917. This group, which collected data that might be needed eventually at the peace conference, was later constituted at Paris under Mezes as a special research section. A good part of the credit for the able service which these men rendered both before and during the negotiations at Paris belongs to Mezes, who selected and trained them.

MIANTONOMO (*d. near Norwich, Conn., 1643*), Narragansett Indian chief. Nephew of Canonicus. Gave aid to the English in the Pequot War, 1637; in March 1638, signed deed to William Coddington and his associates for the island of Rhode Island.

MICH, DANIEL DANFORTH (*b. Minneapolis, Minn., 1905; d. New York, N.Y., 1965*), magazine editor. Worked for the *Wisconsin State Journal* and the *Muscatine* (Iowa) *Journal* before joining the editorial staff of *Look* magazine in 1937. Editorial director of *Look* (1942–50); of *McCall's* (1950–54). Editorial director and vice president of *Look* from 1954; elected to the board of directors in 1955; editor (1964–65). A pioneer in photojournalism. Wrote *Technique of the Picture Story* with Edwin Eberman in 1945.

MICHAEL, ARTHUR (*b. Buffalo, N.Y., 1853; d. Orlando, Fla., 1942*), chemist. Resided in Europe, 1871–80; studied at Heidelberg with R. W. Bunsen, at Berlin with A. W. von Hofmann, and at Paris with C. A. Wurtz. Professor of chemistry at Tufts College, 1881–89 and 1894–1907; at Clark University, 1890–91. Professor of organic chemistry, Harvard, 1912–36. Undertaking most of his research in his own laboratory and at his own expense, Michael made many important contributions to organic chemistry theory and technique, but received more recognition in Europe than at home. His more than 200 articles were published mainly in German scientific journals.

MICHAELIS, LEONOR (*b. Berlin, Germany, 1875; d. New York, N.Y., 1949*), physical chemist, medical scientist. M.D., University of Berlin, 1896. Studied with, and was assistant to, Oskar Hertwig and Paul Ehrlich. While bacteriologist at Berlin City Hospital, 1905–22, he carried out basic research in enzyme action and other subjects that gained him international reputation. He then served as professor of biochemistry at the medical school in Nagoya, Japan, 1922–25. After a lecture tour in the United States, he became resident lecturer at Johns Hopkins, 1926–29; from 1929 to his retirement in 1940, he was a member of the Rockefeller Institute. His work at the institute dealt chiefly with the reactions involved in the oxidation and reduction of organic substances. He was elected to the National Academy of Sciences, 1943.

MICHAËLIUS, JONAS (*b. Grootebroek, Holland, 1584; date and place of death unknown*). Went to New Amsterdam, 1628, as first minister of the Dutch Reformed church to serve there. After conflict with Peter Minuit and the members of the council, Michaëlius returned to Holland, 1632, and denounced them to the West India Co. as oppressors and frauds.

MICHAUX, ANDRÉ (*b. Versailles, France, 1746; d. Madagascar, 1802*), explorer, silviculturist. After extensive travels in Europe and the Near East, Michaux came to New York, 1785, directed by the French government to make a study of forest trees of North America. Between the year of his arrival and 1793 he made collecting journeys in the southern Appalachians, in Spanish Florida, in the Carolina mountains, in the Bahamas, and in Canada, even visiting the vicinity of Hudson Bay. A supporter of the French Revolution, he acted as an emissary from Edmond C. Genêt to George Rogers Clark, 1793; he traveled extensively in the Midwest, 1793–96, before returning to France. His manuscript journals, crude and laconic in form, remained unpublished until 1889.

MICHAUX, FRANÇOIS ANDRÉ (*b. Versailles, France, 1770; d. France, 1855*), silviculturist, traveler, botanist. Son of André Michaux. Accompanied his father to America; resided in New York and vicinity and in Charleston, S.C., 1785–90. Returning to France, he became an ardent partisan of the French Revolution. Coming again to America, 1801, commissioned by the French government to sell the tree nurseries which his father had established in the United States, he traveled extensively through Ohio, Kentucky, Tennessee, and the Carolinas before going back to France, 1803. Michaux made another voyage of travel and study in the United States, 1806–09. He was author of, among other books, *Voyage à l'ouest des monts Alléghanys* (Paris, 1804) and *Histoire des Arbres forestiers de l'Amérique Septentrionale* (1810–13). The second book is better known as *The North American Sylva*; it was later supplemented by Thomas Nuttall.

MICHAUX, LIGHTFOOT SOLOMON (*b. Buckroe Beach, Va., 1885[?]; d. Washington, D.C., 1968*), clergyman, social activist, radio personality, and real estate developer. Began evangelical ministry in Hopewell, Va., in 1917; established headquarters of his Church of God and Gospel Spreading Association in Washington, D.C., in 1929. Made daily radio broadcasts on station WSJV from 1929; "The Happy Am I Preacher and His Famous Choir" program was heard weekly on network radio beginning in 1931, and on British Broadcasting Company radio, 1936–38. Sermons stressed interracial social and political action to battle immorality and poverty. Noted for spectacular baptisms conducted in the Potomac River and, from 1938, in Griffith Stadium, Washington, D.C. Known for his ability to attract prominent white supporters; his influence in Washington, D.C., secured for his organizations large government loans to complete housing developments Mayfair Mansions (1946) and Paradise Manor (1964).

MICHEAUX, OSCAR (*b. near Metropolis, Ill., 1884; d. Charlotte, N.C., 1951*), author and film producer. A black, Micheaux produced the first all-black full-length American film, *The Homesteader* (1919), from his novel of the same name. His first novel was *The Conquest: The Story of a Negro Pioneer, by the Pioneer* (1913). He produced over thirty-three films, including *Body and Soul* (1924) starring Paul Robeson.

MICHEL, VIRGIL GEORGE (*b. St. Paul, Minn., 1890; d. Collegeville, Minn., 1938*), Roman Catholic clergyman, Benedictine, philosopher, educator. Organized liturgical movement in America; founded, 1925 and edited *Orate Fratres*.

MICHEL, WILLIAM MIDDLETON (*b. Charleston, S.C., 1822; d. 1894*), physician, Confederate surgeon. Graduated École de Médecine, Paris, 1845; Medical College of the State of South Carolina, 1846. Opened Summer Medical Institute of Charleston, 1847, in which he lectured on anatomy, physiology, and obstetrics until 1860. Professor of physiology and histology, Medical College of South Carolina, 1868–94.

MICHELSON, ALBERT ABRAHAM (*b. Strelno, Prussia, 1852; d. Pasadena, Calif., 1931*), physicist. Came to America as a child; raised in California and Nevada. Graduated Annapolis, 1873. After serving as instructor in physics and chemistry there, 1875–79, Michelson studied at the universities of Berlin, Heidelberg, and Paris. He was professor of physics at Case School,

1883–89, at Clark University, 1889–92, and was head of the Department of Physics, University of Chicago, 1892–1931. Michelson also served on international scientific committees, received 11 honorary degrees and numerous medals, and was member or officer of the world's leading scientific societies. His major work dealt with light; 68 of his 80 significant papers were on that subject. His experiments in measuring velocity of light demonstrated ingenuity and unusual precision; the general confidence in his integrity and ability was so great that his self-checked results were invariably accepted. His other studies in light concerned optical interference. Like other experts, he first believed that light consists of electromagnetic wave motion carried though ether and that its velocity could serve as a constant for measuring cosmical motions. His experiments refuted this point of view and resulted in new basic theories leading to the relativity concept. Michelson's echelon spectroscope gave direct evidence of the effect of heat upon molecular motion and disclosed the effect of a magnetic field upon a source of radiation. He developed a method for measuring diameters of stars, adopted wavelength of cadmium light as standard measuring unit, determined earth's rigidity and viscosity to be comparable to that of steel, and established a center for producing high-grade diffraction gratings.

MICHELSON, CHARLES (*b. Virginia City, Nev., 1868; d. Washington, D.C., 1948*), journalist, political publicist. Brother of Albert A. Michelson. After a long, colorful, and successful career as reporter, correspondent, and editor with the Hearst newspapers, he became chief Washington correspondent for the *New York World* (1917–29). He is particularly remembered for his work as publicity director for the national committee of the Democratic party, 1929–42, during which his office turned out a steady flow of sharply phrased and aggressive statements and speeches against the Republicans and in favor of the New Deal.

MICHENER, EZRA (*b. Chester Co., Pa., 1794; d; near Toughkenamon, Pa., 1887*), physician, botanist. M.D., University of Pennsylvania, 1818. Invented apparatus for treatment of femur fractures; was one of first physicians to use ergot as a uterine tonic.

MICHIE, PETER SMITH (*b. Brechin, Scotland, 1839; d. West Point, N.Y., 1901*), Union soldier. Came to America as a child; was raised in Cincinnati, Ohio. Graduated West Point, 1863. Received brevet of brigadier general for able Civil War service. Instructor in science at West Point, 1867–1901, he was author of a number of textbooks on mechanics, physics, and astronomy.

MICHIKINIKWA. *See* LITTLE TURTLE.

MICHLER, NATHANIEL (*b. Easton, Pa., 1827; d. Saratoga Springs, N.Y., 1881*), Union officer. Graduated West Point, 1848. Performed notable work as a topographical engineer and as a builder of defensive fortifications throughout the Civil War. He was regarded as one of the leading military topographers of his time.

MIDDLETON, ARTHUR (*b. Charleston, S.C., 1681; d. 1737*), South Carolina official and legislator. Headed movement in South Carolina Assembly to overthrow control of proprietors, 1716–19. President of the council under Governor Francis Nicholson and later under Governor Johnson, he administered the colony as acting governor, 1725–29. In constant difficulties with the legislature over currency disputes, he was effective in subduing Indian troubles on the border and in counteracting French influence. His acquisitiveness and earlier revolutionary activity, however, embarrassed him in his appeals for loyal support from the assembly.

MIDDLETON, ARTHUR (*b. "Middleton Place," near Charleston, S.C., 1742; d. Goose Creek, S.C., 1787*), Revolutionary leader. Son of Henry Middleton (1717–84). Read law at the Middle Temple, London, returning in 1763 to serve as justice of the peace and as a member of the South Carolina Assembly. Active *post* 1772 in all the movements toward revolution, Middleton was elected to the Continental Congress, 1776, and was a signer of the Declaration of Independence. He continued to be elected to Congress, but was irregular in his attendance and left little mark on the records of that body.

MIDDLETON, HENRY (*b. probably "The Oaks," near Charleston, S.C., 1717; d. 1784*), planter, South Carolina legislator. Son of Arthur Middleton (1681–1737). A great landowner, a churchman, and a conservative, he became a leader in opposition to British policy *post* 1770. Chosen to represent South Carolina in the Continental Congress, July 1774, he became second president of the Congress and served, October 1774–May 1775. A moderate, hoping for accommodation with Britain, he resigned from Congress, February 1776. He continued public service as president of the congress of South Carolina, of the legislative council, and *post* January 1779, of the newly created state senate. After the surrender of Charleston, 1780, he "took protection" under the British, but lost no reputation thereby.

MIDDLETON, HENRY (*b. London, England, 1770; d. Charleston, S.C., 1846*), South Carolina legislator, diplomat. Son of Arthur Middleton (1742–87). Served as governor of South Carolina, 1810–12, as congressman, 1815–19, and then as U.S. minister to Russia. As minister, he negotiated the convention of 1824 to regulate Pacific trade and fisheries. Returning to the United States in 1830, he became a leader of the Union party in opposition to Calhoun's nullification policy.

MIDDLETON, JOHN IZARD (*b. near Charleston, S.C., 1785; d. Paris, France, 1849*), painter, archaeologist. Son of Arthur Middleton (1742–87). Author and illustrator of *Grecian Remains in Italy* (1812).

MIDDLETON, NATHANIEL RUSSELL (*b. Charleston, S.C., 1810; d. Charleston, 1890*), planter, educator. Great-grandson of Henry Middleton (1717–84). Graduated College of Charleston, 1828; served as its president, 1857–80.

MIDDLETON, PETER (*b. Scotland; d. New York, N.Y., 1781*), physician. M.D., University of St. Andrews, 1752. Practiced in New York City *post* 1752, in which year (or possibly later) he and Dr. John Bard made in New York one of the first dissections of a human body for the purposes of medical instruction on record in America. A founder of the Medical School of King's College (Columbia), 1767, Middleton taught physiology, pathology, and materia medica there. He was also one of the incorporators of New York Hospital, 1771.

MIDDLETON, THOMAS COOKE (*b. Philadelphia, Pa., 1842; d. Villanova, Pa., 1923*), Roman Catholic clergyman, Augustinian. Identified for most of his life with Villanova College, he was a founder and first president, 1884–90, of the American Catholic Historical Society.

MIDGLEY, THOMAS (*b. Beaver Falls, Pa., 1889; d. Worthington, Ohio, 1944*), inventor, chemist. Grandson of James E. Emerson. M.E., Cornell University, 1911. Joined Dayton Engineering Laboratories Co. (Delco), 1916; formed lifelong scientific and personal association with Charles F. Kettering. Assigned to investigate the cause and cure of "knock" in gasoline and kerosene engines, he began a long course of experiments (interrupted by war work, 1917–18), which resulted in his production of ethyl gasoline, made commercially available in 1923. For the Frigidaire division of General Motors, he developed Freon (dichlorodifluoromethane) in 1930, for use in refrigerators and air conditioners. He also devised a technical process for extraction of bromine from seawater and did significant research on synthetic rubbers.

MIELATZ, CHARLES FREDERICK WILLIAM (*b. Breddin, Germany, 1860; d. New York, N.Y., 1919*), etcher. Came to America as a child; studied at the Chicago School of Design. Celebrated for his renderings of picturesque corners of New York City.

MIELZINER, MOSES (*b. Schubin, Posen, Germany, 1828; d. Cincinnati, Ohio, 1903*), rabbi, educator. Studied with his father and at University of Berlin; Ph.D., University of Giessen, 1859. Came to America, 1865. After ministering for a short time in New York and conducting a private boys' school there, he became professor of the Talmud at Hebrew Union College, 1879, and held that chair until his death. Chairman of the committee of editors of the *Union Prayerbook* (1892–94) and author of a number of works, Mielziner served as president of Hebrew Union, 1900–03.

MIES VAN DER ROHE, LUDWIG (*b. Aachen, Germany, 1886; d. Chicago, Ill., 1969*), architect. In the office of architects Bruno Paul, Berlin (1905–08) and Peter Behrens (1908–12). Opened own office in Berlin, 1913. Designed Barcelona Pavilion for international exposition (1929); and Tugendhat House, Brno, Czechoslovakia (1930). Organized and directed the Weissenhofsiedlung project in Stuttgart (1927), and was director of the Bauhaus school in Dessau and Berlin (1930–33). Immigrated to the United States in 1938; naturalized, 1944. Director of the Armour Institute of Technology (from 1940 the Illinois Institute of Technology) in Chicago (1938–58). Furniture designs include the famous Barcelona chair. Building designs embraced modern materials (steel and glass), problems (tall buildings and vast buildings), and aesthetics (space and light), and focused on two types: tall, repetitive structures, such as the 860–880 Lake Shore Drive apartment houses in Chicago (1951), and the Seagram Building in New York (1958); and low, large-span special-use structures, such as the Farnsworth House in Plano, Ill. (1950), Crown Hall on the IIT campus (1956), and the New National Gallery in West Berlin (1968).

MIFFLIN, LLOYD (*b. Columbia, Pa., 1846; d. Columbia, 1921*), painter, poet. Studied art with Thomas Moran and at Düsseldorf, Germany. Author of a number of volumes of verse in the sonnet form from which he made a selection, *Collected Sonnets* (1905).

MIFFLIN, THOMAS (*b. Philadelphia, Pa., 1744; d. Lancaster, Pa., 1800*), merchant, Pennsylvania legislator, Revolutionary soldier. Graduated College of Philadelphia (University of Pennsylvania), 1760. Conspicuous in opposition to British policy *post* 1765, he was one of the youngest and most radical members of the first Continental Congress and helped to draft the Association of 1774. Entering military service, 1775, he was read out of meeting by his fellow Quakers. Appointed Washington's aide-de-camp, June 1775, he became quartermaster general of the Continental army in August and held that post (except for a brief period) until March 1778. Promoted major general, February 1777, he assisted in the defense of Philadelphia. Involved in the congressional plot to advance Gates over Washington, Mifflin aided the cabal as a member of the board of war but soon disclaimed all part in it. He then met criticism of his record as quartermaster with a demand for a formal inquiry, which was never made. He resigned definitely from military service, August 1778, and turned to state politics. A member of Congress, 1782–84, he served as its president, December 1783–June 1784; a member of the Constitutional Convention, 1787, he was a strong supporter of the new U.S. Constitution. During three terms as Democratic-Republican governor of Pennsylvania, 1790–99, he sympathized with Jeffersonian ideas, openly favored the French, and, after first evading action in the Whiskey Rebellion, called for speedy action against the insurgents. His last three years as governor were marked by increasing negligence and laxity. He died penniless.

MIFFLIN, WARNER (*b. Accomac Co., Va., 1745; d. near Camden, Del., 1798*), farmer, Quaker reformer, antislavery worker.

MIGNOT, LOUIS REMY (*b. Charleston, S.C., 1831; d. Brighton, England, 1870*), landscape painter. Studied in Holland, 1851–55; was associate and follower of Frederick E. Church. Sympathetic to the Confederacy, Mignot resided abroad *post* 1862.

MILBURN, WILLIAM HENRY (*b. Philadelphia, Pa., 1823; d. Santa Barbara, Calif., 1903*), Methodist clergyman. Rode circuit in Illinois, 1843–44; held numerous pastorates in both north and south; was chaplain of Congress four times.

MILES, EDWARD (*b. Yarmouth, England, 1752; d. Philadelphia, Pa., 1828*), painter of miniatures. Court painter in both England and Russia. Miles's work was distinguished for good drawing and exquisite finish. He came to Philadelphia, Pa., 1807, where he worked as a drawing master thereafter.

MILES, GEORGE HENRY (*b. Baltimore, Md., 1824; d. near Emmitsburg, Md., 1871*), poet, playwright, educator.

MILES, HENRY ADOLPHUS (*b. Grafton, Mass., 1809; d. Hingham, Mass., 1895*), Unitarian clergyman. Author of *Lowell As It Was and Is* (1845), a rosy picture of the development of industry at that place.

MILES, JOHN. *See* MYLES, JOHN.

MILES, MANLY (*b. Homer, N.Y., 1826; d. probably Lansing, Mich., 1898*), physician, naturalist, agriculturist. Raised in Michigan. Graduated Rush Medical College, 1850. Held first chair of practical agriculture in the United States (Michigan State, 1865–74); served later as professor of agriculture at University of Illinois and at Massachusetts Agricultural College. A constant collector of natural-history specimens, he was author of several books, chief among which were *Stock Breeding* (1879), *Silos, Ensilage and Silage* (1889), and *Land Drainage* (1892).

MILES, NELSON APPLETON (*b. near Westminster, Mass., 1839; d. Washington, D.C., 1925*), soldier. Volunteering at outbreak of Civil War, he was commissioned captain of infantry and served through the Peninsular campaign on General O. O. Howard's staff. For gallantry at Fair Oaks (May 31–June 1, 1862), he won promotion to lieutenant colonel of the 61st New York Volunteers; he was made colonel in September. Distinguished at Antietam, Fredericksburg, Chancellorsville, the Wilderness, and Petersburg, Miles was promoted brigadier general of volunteers, May 1864; in October 1865, he was made major general, commanding the II Army Corps. Commissioned colonel, regular army, July 1866, he assumed command of the 5th Infantry, 1869. Thereafter, he served against the hostile Indians west of the Mississippi until 1891. Notable among his Indian campaigns were those against the Nez Percé, 1877, and against the Apache under Geronimo, 1886. Promoted major general, 1890, he commanded the troops which quelled the riots accompanying the Pullman strike at Chicago, 1894. Becoming by seniority commander in chief of the army, 1895, Miles directed organization and training of troops for the Spanish-American War and led the force which pacified Puerto Rico. Advanced to lieutenant general, 1901, he retired, 1903.

MILES, RICHARD PIUS (*b. Prince George's Co., Md., 1791; d. Nashville, Tenn., 1860*), Roman Catholic clergyman, Dominican. Raised in Kentucky. After service as a missionary-pastor in Ohio *post* 1828, he became a superior in his order, 1883, and was elected provincial, 1837. Consecrated first bishop of Nashville, 1838, he served ably until his death.

MILES, WILLIAM PORCHER (*b. Walterboro, S.C., 1822; d. Ascension Parish, La., 1899*), educator, sugar planter, politician. Graduated College of Charleston, 1842; taught mathematics there, 1843–55. Conservative Democratic mayor of Charleston, 1855–57, Miles served as congressman from South Carolina, 1857–60. Eloquent in support of slavery and secession, he was chairman of the foreign relations committee of the South Carolina secession convention, signed the ordinance of secession, and was one of the three commissioners who arranged the terms of the surrender of Fort Sumter. He represented the Charleston district in the Confederate Congress during its entire existence. President of the University of South Carolina, 1880–82, he resigned to manage his father-in-law's extensive sugar plantations.

MILHOLLAND, INEZ. *See* BOISSEVAIN, INEZ MILHOLLAND.

MILLAY, EDNA ST. VINCENT (*b. Rockland, Maine, 1892; d. Austerlitz, N.Y., 1950*), poet. Her first published poem, "Forest Trees," written when she was 14, appeared in *St. Nicholas Magazine* (October 1906). Within the next four years *St. Nicholas* published five more of her poems. In early 1913 she prepared at Barnard College for entrance examinations to Vassar College and was admitted in the fall of 1913. In 1917 she received the B.A. from Vassar. Her fist book of poetry, *Renascence and Other Poems*, was published in the same year. She joined the Provincetown Players, directing her own allegorical and experimental play *Aria da Capo* in 1919. Under the pseudonym "Nancy Boyd," she also began a series of prose sketches and stories. With the publication of *A Few Figs from Thistles* (1920), she became the spokesman for a younger generation exuberantly defiant of convention. From January 1921 to February 1923 she traveled in Europe writing for *Vanity Fair*. Her third book of poems, *Second April* (1921), received favorable reviews. The Nancy Boyd articles written during this time were collected in 1924 as *Distressing Dialogues*. While in Europe, she completed *The Lamp and the Bell*. In 1922 she contributed eight sonnets to *American Poetry: A Miscellany*, and *The Ballad of the Harp-Weaver* was also published that year. For these, she received the Pulitzer Prize for 1922.

Throughout the late 1920's and the 1930's, Millay published major works of poetry; *The Buck in the Snow* (1928), *Fatal Interview* (1931), *Wine from These Grapes* (1934), and *Huntsman, What Quarry?* (1939), as well as her earlier drama, *The Princess Marries the Page* (1932), and a closet drama, *Conversation at Midnight* (1937). In the 1940's her poems were intended to arouse national patriotism. *Make Bright the Arrows: 1940 Notebook* (1940) and *The Murder of Lidice* (1942) contain a variety of these verses. She was elected to the American Academy of Arts and Letters (1940) and received the gold medal of the Poetry Society of America (1943). Her *Collected Poems* appeared in 1956.

MILLEDGE, JOHN (*b. Savannah, Ga., 1757; d. near Augusta, Ga., 1818*), lawyer, Georgia legislator, Revolutionary soldier. Congressman, Democratic-Republican, from Georgia, 1792–93, 1795–99, 1801–02; governor of Georgia, 1802–06; U.S. senator, 1806–09. A principal benefactor of the University of Georgia and donor of its site.

MILLEDOLER, PHILIP (*b. Rhinebeck, N.Y., 1775; d. Staten Island, N.Y., 1852*), clergyman, educator. Graduated Columbia, 1793; studied theology under John D. Gros. Held Presbyterian and Dutch Reformed pastorates in New York and Philadelphia;

was professor of theology at Dutch Reformed Seminary, New Brunswick, N.J., 1825–40, and simultaneously president of Rutgers College.

MILLER, CHARLES HENRY (*b. New York, N.Y., 1842; d. New York, 1922*), physician, landscape painter, etcher. Distinguished for his studies of Long Island scenery.

MILLER, CHARLES RANSOM (*b. Hanover Center, N.H., 1849; d. 1922*), journalist. Graduated Dartmouth, 1872. Served on staff of *Springfield Daily Republican*; was associated in a number of capacities with the *New York Times* from 1875, and editor in chief of that paper, 1883–1922. His editorial style was marked by strong conviction, forceful reasoning, and clarity.

MILLER, CINCINNATUS HINER (*b. Liberty, Ind., 1839; d. 1913*), poet, known as Joaquin Miller. Raised in Oregon, he led a drifting life through the mining camps of northern California *ca.* 1856–59; thereafter, he taught school, practiced law, dabbled in journalism, and served as a county judge in Oregon until 1870, when two volumes of verse which he had published, *Specimens* (1868) and *Joaquin et al.* (1869), attracted some attention in literary circles in San Francisco. Journeying to London, England, he was taken up by the critics there as a genuine phenomenon of the American West. His *Songs of the Sierras* (1871) won high praise from the British, despite its cheap rhythms and mock-Byronism. After traveling abroad for some time and publishing a number of other works of verse and prose, he returned to America and settled permanently in Oakland, Calif., 1886. He published his complete poetical works in 1897.

MILLER, DAVID HUNTER (*b. New York, N.Y., 1875; d. Washington, D.C., 1961*), businessman, lawyer, diplomat, editor, and historian. Became a partner in the family firm Walter T. Miller and Company in 1898. Studied at the New York Law School (LL.B., 1910; LL.M., 1911). Established a law firm in New York with Gordon Auchincloss in 1915. Participated in State Department affairs as a special assistant from 1917. Technical adviser to the American delegation at the Paris Peace Conference (1919); involved in composing the Covenant of the League of Nations. One of the most vocal American supporters of the League of Nations and the Treaty of Versailles. Editor of treaties in the State Department, (1929–44); historical adviser to the State Department, (1931–38).

MILLER, DAYTON CLARENCE (*b. Strongsville, Ohio, 1866; d. Cleveland, Ohio, 1941*), physicist. Ph.B., Baldwin College, 1886; M.A., 1889. D.Sc., Princeton University, 1890. Professor of physics, Case School of Applied Science, *post* 1892. Made important contributions to X-ray use and to precise measurement and analysis of sound waves; was an authority on architectural acoustics. He also carried out research in optics in collaboration with Edward W. Morley.

MILLER, EDWARD (*b. near Dover, Del., 1760; d. New York, N.Y., 1812*), physician. Brother of Samuel Miller (1769–1850). M.D., University of Pennsylvania, 1789; removed to New York City, 1796, where he practiced thereafter. He was a cofounder with Samuel L. Mitchill and E. H. Smith of the *Medical Repository*, 1797, and gave aid in establishment of the New York College of Physicians and Surgeons, 1807, which he served as first professor of the practice of medicine.

MILLER, EMILY CLARK HUNTINGTON (*b. Brooklyn, Conn., 1833; d. Northfield, Minn., 1913*), author. Helped secure charter for Evanston College for Ladies, 1871. After the college had been united with Northwestern University, Miller taught English literature there and was dean of women, 1891–98.

MILLER, EZRA (*b. near Pleasant Valley, N.J., 1812; d. Mahwah, N.J., 1885*), civil engineer. Patented, 1863–65, a railroad-car platform coupler and buffer, which was widely used before superseded by the Janney coupler.

MILLER, GEORGE (*b. Pottstown, Pa., 1774; d. Union Co., Pa., 1816*), Evangelical Association preacher and compiler of that sect's Book of Discipline (1809).

MILLER, GEORGE ABRAM (*b. near Lynville, Pa., 1863; d. Urbana, Ill., 1951*), mathematician. Studied at Eureka College, Eureka, Ill., and at Cumberland University (Ph.D., 1892). Taught at Eureka College, Cornell University, Stanford University, and at the University of Illinois (1906–31); professor emeritus (1931–47). A specialist in the determination of substitute numbers and group theory, Miller published over 820 journal articles on the subjects; his books include *Historical Introduction to Mathematical Literature* (1916).

MILLER, GERRIT SMITH, JR. (*b. Petersboro, N.Y., 1869; d. Washington, D.C., 1956*), mammalogist and museum administrator. Studied at Harvard University. From 1894 to 1898, Miller worked with the Biological Survey with the U.S. Department of Agriculture. From 1898 to 1940, he was with the National Museum; curator of mammals from 1909. An expert on insectivorous bats, Miller became one of the nation's leading mammalogists. Major works include *The Families and Genera of Bats* (1907); *Catalogue of the Land Mammals of Western Europe (Exclusive of Russia) in the Collection of the British Museum* (1912); and *List of North American Land Mammals in the United States National Museum* (1912).

MILLER, GILBERT HERON (*b. New York, N.Y., 1884; d. New York, 1969*), theatrical producer and director. Son of Henry Miller, an actor-manager, and Helene Stoepel, an actress. Made debut as a producer in London with *Daddy Long-Legs* (1916). Went on to produce some 200 shows in New York and London, including the Broadway productions *The Constant Wife* (1927), *Journey's End* (1929), *Victoria Regina* (1936), *The Cocktail Party* (1950), *The Caine Mutiny Court-Martial* (1956), and *The Rope Dancers* (1957). Earned a reputation for fine performances that utilized Broadway's leading players and generally met with critical and financial success. Known for selecting plays with literate dialogue; produced such playwrights as Somerset Maugham, Philip Barry, Dylan Thomas, T. S. Eliot, and Sherwood Anderson.

MILLER, GLENN (*b. Clarinda, Iowa, 1904; d. 1944*), dance band conductor of the "big band" era. Attended University of Colorado; left to play trombone with a series of bands, including Ben Pollack's, for which he wrote arrangements; settled in New York City, 1928, where he studied arranging with Joseph Schillinger. After working in radio and recording studios, and as trombonist and arranger for Red Nichols and His Five Pennies, he helped Tommy and Jimmy Dorsey organize their band in 1934 and worked in it as an arranger and one of the trombone section. After an unsatisfactory association with Ray Noble, 1935–36, he organized his own band in March 1937. It was unsuccessful. Encouraged by Tommy Dorsey, he tried again in March 1938. This time, he had worked out a distinctive style (incorporating influences of Tommy Dorsey, James Lunceford, and Count Basie) and got his big break in 1939, playing at the Glen Island Casino in New Rochelle, N.Y. and on the radio from coast to coast. For the next three years, the band had extraordinary success, playing in leading hotels, ballrooms, and theaters, appearing on a radio show and in motion pictures, and making hit recordings. In the fall of 1942 Miller joined the U.S. Army Air Force. He was lost on a duty flight from England to Paris in December 1944, en route to make advance arrangements for a scheduled appearance of the Air Force band that he had formed.

MILLER, HARRIET MANN (*b. Auburn, N.Y., 1831; d. Los Angeles, Calif., 1918*), naturalist, author. Under pen name "Olive Thorne Miller," wrote a number of excellent studies of bird life, of which *In Nesting Time* (1888) is typical.

MILLER, HEINRICH. *See* MILLER, JOHN HENRY.

MILLER, HENRY (*b. Glasgow, Ky., 1800; d. Louisville, Ky., 1874*), physician. A leading obstetrician and gynecologist, Miller taught at Louisville Medical College and at its predecessor institutions; he was author of *Principles and Practice of Obstetrics* (1858).

MILLER, HENRY (*b. London, England, 1860; d. New York, N.Y., 1926*), actor, theatrical manager. Came as a boy to Canada; made stage debut *ca.* 1878; was strongly influenced by Dion Boucicault's example. Miller's career falls into three main divisions: his connection as leading man with the Empire Theatre stock company, New York City, in the early nineties; his period as a Broadway star, 1899–1906; and finally his success as actor-manager *post* 1906. His productions of William V. Moody's *The Great Divide* (1906) and *The Faith Healer* (1910) and with C. R. Kennedy's *The Servant in the House* (1908) exhibited his varied talents at their climax and represented a great artistic advance for the American theatre.

MILLER, JAMES ALEXANDER (*b. Roselle Park, N.J., 1874; d. Black Point, Conn., 1948*), physician. B.A., Princeton University, 1893; M.A., 1894. While working as research chemist for the New York City Board of Health, he studied at the College of Physicians and Surgeons, Columbia University, and graduated M.D., 1899. Influenced by Edward L. Trudeau, and while in private practice in New York City, he organized a separate tuberculosis clinic in the outpatient department of Bellevue Hospital, 1903, which he directed until 1938. In addition to medical attention, the clinic investigated and ameliorated unsanitary home conditions of patient, provided education in hygiene, and gave material relief to the families of the sick. Miller was also active in many professional and philanthropic organizations.

MILLER, JAMES RUSSELL (*b. Harshaveille, Pa., 1840; d. Philadelphia, Pa., 1912*), Presbyterian clergyman. Editorial superintendent, Presbyterian Board of Publication, 1887–1912.

MILLER, JOAQUIN. *See* MILLER, CINCINNATUS HINER.

MILLER, JOHN (*b. Berkeley Co., Va., now W.Va., 1781; d. near Florissant, Mo., 1846*), journalist, soldier. Removed to Ohio, 1803; served in War of 1812 as colonel, 19th U.S. Infantry; resigned from army, 1818, and in 1821 became register of the land office at Franklin, Mo. Democratic governor of Missouri, 1825–32, he advocated a well-organized militia, withdrawal of state paper money from circulation, protection of trade and travel on the Santa Fe Trail, the encouragement of educational activities, and the exclusion by the federal government of all British traders from the fur-trading regions of the Rocky Mountains. As congressman, 1837–43, he worked for improvement of river navigation and opposed the growing tendency toward sectionalism.

MILLER, JOHN (*b. Princeton, N.J., 1819; d. Princeton, 1895*), Presbyterian clergyman, Confederate chaplain. Son of Samuel Miller (1769–1850). Withdrew from Presbyterian church, 1877, on doctrinal grounds; served as pastor of an independent congregation at Princeton, 1880–95.

MILLER, JOHN FRANKLIN (*b. South Bend, Ind., 1831; d. Washington, D.C., 1886*), lawyer, Indiana legislator, Union major general. Collector of the port of San Francisco, 1865–69; able president, Alaska Commercial Co., 1869–81. As U.S. senator, Republican, from California, 1881–86, his name is linked with efforts to modify the Burlingame Treaty with China and with the Exclusion Act of 1882.

MILLER, JOHN HENRY (*b. Rheden, Germany, 1702; d. Bethlehem, Pa., 1782*), printer, editor. After several brief stays in America *post* 1741, Miller set up a printing establishment in Philadelphia, 1760. Publisher of a German-language newspaper, he also published a yearly German almanac and, among other books, Thomas Godfrey's *Juvenile Poems* (1765). His newspaper, by a fortunate accident, was the first to announce the adoption of the Declaration of Independence (*Pennsylvanische Staatsbote*, issue of July 5, 1776).

MILLER, JOHN PETER (*b. probably Zweibrücken, Germany, 1709; d. Ephrata, Pa., 1796*), German Reformed clergyman. Came to Philadelphia, Pa., 1730; was ordained in that year by three Presbyterian ministers; was minister to German congregations on the Pennsylvania frontier *post* 1731. Coming under influence of Johann C. Beissel, Miller renounced the Reformed church, 1735, and, after living a while as a hermit, joined Beissel at the Ephrata Community. Miller succeeded Beissel as head of the community, 1768.

MILLER, JONATHAN PECKHAM (*b. Randolph, Vt., 1796; d. Montpelier, Vt., 1847*), lawyer, Vermont legislator. Volunteer soldier in the Greek revolutionary army, 1824–26; antislavery advocate.

MILLER, KELLY (*b. Winnsboro, S.C., 1863; d. Washington, D.C., 1939*), educator. Son of a free black father and a slave mother, Miller graduated from Howard University, 1886. After further study of mathematics, physics, and astronomy with Simon Newcomb and at Johns Hopkins, he taught at Howard, 1890–1934. He served as dean, 1907–18, and *post* 1918 devoted most of his time to sociology. As a writer and lecturer on behalf of blacks, he directed his arguments to the reason and conscience of his fellow Americans; as a theorist on black education, he took a middle course in the controversy between "higher" and "industrial" education.

MILLER, KEMPSTER BLANCHARD (*b. Boston, Mass., 1870; d. Pasadena, Calif., 1933*), engineer. Graduated Cornell, 1893. An expert in telephone design, construction, and operation, Miller also designed and built several hydroelectric plants and was the designer of the New York City fire-alarm system.

MILLER, KENNETH HAYES (*b. Oneida, N.Y., 1876; d. New York, N.Y., 1952*), painter and teacher. Studied at the Art Students League in New York and at the New York School of Art. Taught at the Art Students League from 1911 to 1951. Miller's paintings combined urban genre subject matter with the principles of the High Renaissance: balanced composition and full sculpturesque treatment of form. His pupils included Edward Hopper, Isabel Bishop, and Reginald Marsh. He was given a retrospective exhibition by the National Academy of Design in 1953.

MILLER, LESLIE WILLIAM (*b. Brattleboro, Vt., 1848; d. Martha's Vineyard, Mass., 1931*), painter, educator. Organized the School of Industrial Art, Philadelphia, Pa.; made it one of the leading institutions in its field as its director, 1880–1920.

MILLER, LEWIS (*b. Greentown, Ohio, 1829; d. New York, N.Y., 1899*), inventor, farm-implement manufacturer. Conceiving the idea of combining recreation with some form of education, in 1874 he invited John H. Vincent to join him in organizing a general assembly, as distinct from a Sunday-school teachers' assembly, to meet on Lake Chautauqua, N.Y. This was the beginning of the Chautauqua movement, a pioneer force in adult education.

MILLER, NATHAN LEWIS (*b. Solon, N.Y., 1868; d. New York, N.Y., 1953*), lawyer, judge, politician. Self-educated, Miller served on the New York Supreme Court, as a judge on the Appellate Division, and on the Court of Appeals. He placed the name of Herbert Hoover in nomination for the presidency in 1920; from 1920 to 1922, Republican governor of the state of New York, defeating Al Smith. In 1925, director and general counsel of the board of the U.S. Steel Co. In 1952, defended the steel companies in the seizure case, *Youngstown Sheet and Tube Co. et al. v. Sawyer*, before the U.S. Supreme Court.

MILLER, OLIVE THORNE. *See* MILLER, HARRIET MANN.

MILLER, OLIVER (*b. Middletown, Conn., 1824; d. Ellicott City, Md., 1892*), jurist. Admitted to the Maryland bar, 1850, he became reporter of the state court of appeals, 1852, and established a reputation as editor of *Maryland Reports*, 1853–62. Elected chief judge of the fifth judicial circuit of Maryland, 1867, he served until 1892. His opinions are among the best known in the judicial annals of Maryland.

MILLER, PERRY GILBERT EDDY (*b. Chicago, Ill., 1905; d. Cambridge, Mass., 1963*), teacher and scholar of American literature and intellectual history. Studied at the University of Chicago (Ph.D., 1931). Professor at Harvard University, 1931–63. Studied the history of Puritanism. Works include *Orthodoxy in Massachusetts* (1933), *The New England Mind: The Seventeenth Century* (1939), and *The New England Mind: From Colony to Province* (1953). Also studied American romanticism.

MILLER, PETER. *See* MILLER, JOHN PETER.

MILLER, SAMUEL (*b. near Dover, Del., 1769; d. 1850*), Presbyterian clergyman, educator, author. Brother of Edward Miller. Educated chiefly at home; attended University of Pennsylvania. Ordained, 1793, he served as collegiate pastor in New York City until 1809 and was sole pastor of the Wall Street congregation until 1813. Thereafter he was professor of church history, Princeton Theological Seminary, of which he had been a founder. His writings covered a broad range; chief among them was the very important *Brief Retrospect of the Eighteenth Century* (1803). Long the official historian of the Presbyterian General Assembly, he became its moderator, 1806.

MILLER, SAMUEL (*b. Lancaster, Pa., 1820; d. Bluffton, Mo., 1901*), horticulturist. His best-known plant contribution is perhaps the Captain Jack strawberry; most of his plant-breeding work was practiced with grapes. He was particularly notable for his generous disinterested efforts in testing types and varieties sent him by their owners.

MILLER, SAMUEL FREEMAN (*b. Richmond, Ky., 1816; d. Washington, D.C., 1890*), physician, lawyer, U.S. Supreme Court justice. M.D., Transylvania, 1838; practiced medicine in neighborhood of Barbourville, Ky. After studying law and admission to the Knox Co. bar, 1847, he found the proslavery atmosphere of that section uncongenial and removed to Keokuk, Iowa, 1850. There he practiced law with success and engaged in the organization of the Republican party. Appointed an associate justice of the U.S. Supreme Court, 1862, he was strong in support of the national authority, upholding the constitutionality of the loyalty oath in *Ex parte Garland* and voting with the majority in the Legal Tender Cases. Yet, within the limits of common sense,

he upheld the rights of the individual and the need to maintain an ample autonomy for state governments. He was strong in his belief that it was not the function of federal courts to sit in judgment on state courts expounding state law. Always more concerned with the practical result of a decision than with its doctrinal basis, he was disposed to let no technicality stand in the way of what seemed just. The dominant personality on the bench in his time, he sometimes showed a blunt impatience with lesser minds and with futile arguments.

MILLER, STEPHEN DECATUR (*b. Lancaster District, S.C., 1787; d. Raymond, Miss., 1838*), lawyer, South Carolina legislator, U.S. representative and senator. As a member of Congress, 1817–19, he became a convert to the nullification doctrine of J. C. Calhoun and did much to inflame the state against Congress while governor, 1829–30. As U.S. senator, anti-Jackson Democrat, 1831–33, he opposed the 1832 tariff and was active in the state nullification convention.

MILLER, WARNER (*b. Hannibal, N.Y., 1838; d. New York, N.Y., 1918*), paper manufacturer, politician. Congressman, "Half-Breed" Republican, from New York, 1878–81; U.S. senator, 1881–87. Favored Chinese exclusion, development of the U.S. merchant marine, and the protective tariff.

MILLER, WEBB (*b. near Pokagon, Mich., 1892; d. London, England, 1940*), journalist, foreign correspondent. Appointed to staff of United Press, 1916, for excellent free-lance work during Pancho Villa incident on Mexican border. Covered World War I; managed UP Paris and London bureaus; was general European news manager of UP *post* 1930. Author of *I Found No Peace* (1936).

MILLER, WILLIAM (*b. Pittsfield, Mass., 1782; d. Hampton, N.Y., 1849*), farmer, leader of the Adventists, or "Millerites." Raised in Washington Co., N.Y. Preached doctrine that Christ's second coming would take place in 1843 or 1844. Publicized by Joshua V. Himes, Miller drew a large following from the orthodox Protestant churches; he headed the Adventist church at its founding, 1845.

MILLER, WILLIAM HENRY HARRISON (*b. Augusta, N.Y., 1840; d. Indianapolis, Ind., 1917*), lawyer. Practiced in Indiana *post* 1865; was partner of Benjamin Harrison. As U.S. attorney general, 1889–93, Miller's advice was largely responsible for the excellence of President Harrison's federal bench appointments. An impartial and vigorous law officer, Miller was held in high respect by his subordinates.

MILLER, WILLIAM SNOW (*b. Sterling, Mass., 1858; d. Madison, Wis., 1939*), anatomist, medical historian. M.D., Yale, 1879; studied also with Francis Delafield and Franklin P. Mall; attended University of Leipzig and Johns Hopkins Medical School. Taught at University of Wisconsin, 1892–1924. Author of an important study, *The Lung* (1937), which summarized his lifelong research on the anatomy of that organ.

MILLER, WILLOUGHBY DAYTON (*b. near Alexandria, Ohio, 1853; d. Newark, Ohio, 1907*), dentist. Graduated University of Michigan, 1875; studied also at universities of Edinburgh and Berlin; D.D.S., University of Pennsylvania, 1879. Practiced in Germany, 1879–1907, where he received high scholarly and professional honors and was recognized as one of the leading dental authorities and bacteriologists of his day. Among results of his research was the demonstration that tooth tissue is destroyed by fermentative acids formed by bacteria in the mouth; also findings on the action of diseased teeth as foci of infection and the etiology of dental erosion. Accepting appointment as dean, Dental College, University of Michigan, he died before he took up his duties.

MILLET, FRANCIS DAVIS (*b. Mattapoisett, Mass., 1846; d. at sea aboard* Titanic, *1912*), painter, illustrator, journalist. Graduated Harvard, 1869; studied art at Royal Academy, Antwerp, and at Rome and Venice. Correspondent, Russo-Turkish War, 1877; associate of E. A. Abbey, John S. Sargent, Henry James in colony at Broadway, England; director of decorations of White City, Chicago World's Fair, 1893; correspondent in Philippines, 1899. Director, American Academy in Rome, 1911–12.

MILLIGAN, ROBERT (*b. Co. Tyrone, Ireland, 1814; d. Lexington, Ky., 1875*), Disciples of Christ clergyman, educator. Came to America as a child; raised in Ohio. Taught at Washington College (Pa.), Indiana University, Bethany College; president, Kentucky University, 1859–65.

MILLIGAN, ROBERT WILEY (*b. Philadelphia, Pa., 1843; d. Annapolis Md., 1909*), naval officer. Chief engineer of USS *Oregon* on famous cruise around South America, 1898, and in battle of Santiago. Retired as rear admiral 1905.

MILLIKAN, CLARK BLANCHARD (*b. Chicago, Ill., 1903; d. Pasadena, Calif., 1966*), physicist and aerodynamicist. Son of physicist Robert Andrews Millikan. Studied at Yale University and the California Institute of Technology, or Caltech (Ph.D., 1928). At Caltech as assistant professor (1928–34), associate professor (1934–40), and professor of aeronautics (1940–66); acting director (from 1944) and director (from 1949) of the Guggenheim Aeronautical Laboratory; cofounder of the Jet Propulsion Laboratory. Director of the Southern California Cooperative Wind Tunnel from 1945. Honored for contributions to the field of rocket and jet propulsion development during World War II. Author of *Aerodynamics of the Airplane* (1941). Member of the Air Force's Scientific Advisory Board and adviser to the National Aeronautics and Space Administration. Contributed to Caltech's rise to world leadership in aeronautical education and research.

MILLIKAN, ROBERT ANDREWS (*b. Morrison, Ill., 1868; d. San Marino, Calif., 1953*), physicist and educator. Studied at Oberlin College and at Columbia University (Ph.D., 1895); further study at the University of Berlin (1896). Taught at the University of Chicago (1896–1921). During World War I, director of research for the National Research Council of the National Academy of Sciences in Washington, directing development of a successful submarine listening device.

One of Millikan's first projects as a researcher was to obtain an accurate measurement of the charge of the electron and to determine whether this charge is, in fact, the basic unit of all electrical charges. He discovered that every measured charge was a whole-number multiple of a basic unit of charge—the charge of a single electron—which he could measure with high precision. The results, published in 1913, became one of the most important constants in atomic physics. From 1912 to 1916, Millikan conducted experiments to confirm Einstein's photoelectric equation; he was awarded the Nobel Prize for physics in 1923, only the second American to be so honored.

In 1921, Millikan became head of Throop College in California, transforming that institution into California Institute of Technology, one of the world's leading technical institutions. His first project at Caltech was the study of the ionization of air at high altitudes, which he and others thought might be caused by radiation reaching the earth from outer space. He soon confirmed his theory, and in 1925 named those radiations "cosmic rays." During World War II, Millikan oversaw Caltech's highly successful research projects in jet propulsion, artillery rockets, and antisubmarine warfare.

MILLIKIN, EUGENE DONALD (*b. Hamilton, Ohio, 1891; d. Denver, Colo., 1958*), lawyer and politician. Studied at the University of Colorado. After serving with the army in France during World War I, Millikin set up private law practice in Denver, becoming active in state Republican politics; in 1941, he was appointed to fill a vacant seat in the U.S. Senate. He won reelection until 1950. In the Senate, he was an isolationist who gave minimal support to America's involvement in world affairs after World War II. Millikin accepted liberalized trade policies but was able to enact legislation with specific protectionist laws. He retired in 1956 because of poor health.

MILLINGTON, JOHN (*b. near London, England, 1779; d. Richmond, Va., 1868*), engineer, educator. Came to America, *ca.* 1833, after distinguished career as scientist and teacher of science. Taught engineering and the sciences at William and Mary, the University of Mississippi, and Memphis (Tenn.) Medical College. Author of, among other works, *Elements of Civil Engineering* (1839).

MILLIS, HARRY ALVIN (*b. Paoli, Ind., 1873; d. Chicago, Ill., 1948*), labor economist, arbitrator. B.A., Indiana University, 1895; M.A., 1896. Ph.D., University of Chicago, 1899. Influenced by study under John R. Commons and Thorstein Veblen. Taught economics at University of Arkansas, 1902–03; Stanford University, 1903–12; University of Kansas, 1912–16; professor of economics, University of Chicago, 1916–38. An investigator, not a theorist, Millis directed research studies in several fields, but his major work was in industrial relations; he collaborated with R. E. Montgomery on the three-volume *Economics of Labor* (1938, 1938, 1945). Thorough in scholarship, he made his greatest contribution to labor relations as an arbitrator; a pioneer in this work, he laid much of the groundwork for present-day grievance and arbitration procedures in settling contract disputes. He was a member of the first National Labor Relations Board, 1934–35, and with his colleagues laid down the principles of collective bargaining that were incorporated in the Wagner Act. He served as chairman of the new board, created under the Wagner Act, from 1940 to 1945.

MILLIS, WALTER (*b. Atlanta, Ga., 1899; d. New York, N.Y., 1968*), writer. Studied at Yale (graduated, 1920). Editorial writer for the *Baltimore News* and the *New York Sun* (to 1924); on staff of the *New York Herald Tribune* (1924–54). Author of the novel *Sand Castle* (1929), and nonfiction books including *The Martial Spirit* (1931); *Road to War: America, 1914–1917* (1935), called "revisionist" for arguing the needlessness and futility of America's entry into World War I; *Why Europe Fights* (1940), which urged Americans to be prepared to intervene on the Allied side in World War II; and *This Is Pearl!* (1947). A Democrat and an outspoken member of the American Civil Liberties Union, he contributed frequently to the *Saturday Review* and other journals of opinion.

MILLS, ANSON (*b. near Thorntown, Ind., 1834; d. Washington, D.C., 1924*), Union army officer, Indian fighter, inventor. As surveyor in Texas, 1857–61, made original plat of El Paso and gave city its name; patented, 1866, and manufactured first cartridge belt adopted by U.S. Army.

MILLS, BENJAMIN (*b. Worcester Co., Md., 1779; d. Frankfort, Ky., 1831*), lawyer, Kentucky legislator. Associate justice, Kentucky Court of Appeals, 1820–28; opposed legislature's dissolution of court during contest over debtor relief in 1820's.

MILLS, BENJAMIN FAY (*b. Rahway, N.J., 1857; d. Grand Rapids, Mich., 1916*), interdenominational evangelist.

MILLS, CHARLES KARSNER (*b. Philadelphia, Pa., 1845; d. Philadelphia, 1931*), neurologist. M.D., University of Pennsylvania, 1869; Ph.D., 1871. Taught at Pennsylvania, 1877–1915; was professor of neurology emeritus thereafter. Created famed Philadelphia school of neurology; was president of the American Neurological Association, 1887 and 1924. Author of *The Nervous System and Its Diseases* (1898).

MILLS, CHARLES WRIGHT (*b. Waco, Tex., 1916; d. West Nyack, N.Y., 1962*), sociologist and social critic. Studied at Texas A and M University, the University of Texas at Austin, and the University of Wisconsin (Ph.D., 1942). Associate professor of sociology at the University of Maryland (1941–45). Director of the Labor Research Division of the Bureau of Applied Social Research at Columbia University (1945–48); assistant professor (1946–50); associate professor (1950–56); professor of sociology (1956–62). Visiting appointments at the University of Chicago (1949), Brandeis University (1953), and the University of Copenhagen (1956–57). An exponent of the sociological imagination, which entails, he felt, a comprehensive effort to "grasp history and biography and the relations between the two within society." Works include *The New Men of Power* (1948), *White Collar* (1951), *The Power Elite* (1956), and *The Sociological Imagination* (1959).

MILLS, CLARK (*b. Onondaga Co., N.Y., 1810; d. Washington, D.C., 1883*), sculptor, pioneer bronze founder. His monument to Andrew Jackson, the first large equestrian statue to be cast in bronze in the United States, stands in Lafayette Square, Washington, D.C. With this statue (dedicated in 1853) virtually began the U.S. bronze-casting industry. Mills thereafter created a replica of the Jackson piece for New Orleans (dedicated in 1856), an equestrian statute of Washington for the capital city in 1860, and a bronze casting of Crawford's colossal *Liberty* for the Capitol dome (dedicated in 1863). Numerous portrait busts by him include those of Calhoun, Webster, and Crittenden.

MILLS, CYRUS TAGGART (*b. Paris, N.Y., 1819; d. Oakland, Calif., 1884*), Presbyterian missionary to Ceylon and Hawaii, educator, businessman. Administered (with wife, Susan Mills) Oahu College near Honolulu; founded Mills Seminary near Oakland, Calif., 1871.

MILLS, DARIUS OGDEN (*b. North Salem, N.Y., 1825; d. 1910*), merchant, banker, philanthropist. From the post of cashier in a Buffalo, N.Y., bank, Mills removed to California in 1849 and founded the bank of D. O. Mills & Co. at Sacramento, 1850. Accumulating a fortune, 1850–60, he served as president of the Bank of California at San Francisco, 1864–73; he resumed the presidency in 1875 to reorganize the bank after difficulties caused by his successor, W. C. Ralston. Residing in New York City *post* 1878, Mills became an investor and director in eastern banking, railway, and industrial concerns. To his many benefactions was added in 1888 financial support of the Mills Hotels, where people of low income could get inexpensive board and lodging.

MILLS, ELIJAH HUNT (*b. Chesterfield, Mass., 1776; d. Northampton, Mass., 1829*), lawyer, Massachusetts legislator. Congressman, Federalist, from Massachusetts, 1815–19; U.S. senator, 1820–27.

MILLS, ENOS ABIJAH (*b. near Kansas City, Kans., 1870; d. Colorado, 1922*), naturalist, author, conservationist. Creator of Rocky Mountain National Park.

MILLS, HIRAM FRANCIS (*b. Bangor, Maine, 1836; d. Hingham, Mass., 1921*), hydraulic and sanitary engineer. Graduated Rensselaer Polytechnic, 1856. As chief engineer at Lowell and Lawrence, Mass., Mills initiated far-reaching experiments on sewage, water purification, and hydraulics. His work, among other effects, reduced the threat of typhoid fever and advanced the development of the turbine.

MILLS, LAWRENCE HEYWORTH (*b. New York, N.Y., 1837; d. 1918*), Episcopal clergyman, Iranian scholar. Resident abroad *post* 1872. Distinguished student of the Avesta; professor of Zend philology, Oxford University, England, 1897–1918.

MILLS, OGDEN LIVINGSTON (*b. Newport, R.I., 1884; d. New York, N.Y., 1937*), lawyer, New York legislator. Grandson of Darius O. Mills; nephew of Whitelaw Reid. Graduated Harvard, 1905; LL.B., 1907. Congressman, Republican, from New York, 1921–27. Exerted substantial influence on fiscal policies of Coolidge and Hoover administrations as assistant secretary of the treasury, 1927–32. Succeeding Andrew Mellon as secretary in February 1932, Mills continued Mellon's general policies until his retirement, 1933.

MILLS, ROBERT (*b. Charleston, S.C., 1781; d. Washington, D.C., 1855*), architect, engineer. Unique among native-born Americans of his era, Mills undertook regular training for the career of a professional architect with James Hoban, with Thomas Jefferson at "Monticello," and with Benjamin H. Latrobe, in whose office he served as draftsman and clerk from 1803 to 1808. From Latrobe, the father of the Greek revival in America, he received not only his knowledge of Greek forms but also his principle of professional practice and scientific engineering skill. During his period of training, Mills shared an architectural prize for a South Carolina College building, 1802, and designed, 1804, the "Circular" Congregational Church in Charleston.

In independent practice in Philadelphia, 1808–17, Mills designed or helped to engineer several churches and public structures in that city and in Richmond, Va. Entering the winning design for the first important public monument to George Washington (Baltimore, Md., 1814), he resided in Baltimore, 1817–20, supervising construction of the colossal Doric column, first of its type. Commissions for Baltimore churches followed, together with the presidency of the city water company.

In 1820 Mills returned to Charleston to become a member of the Board of Public Works of his native state. He is referred to in public documents of that period as "State Engineer and Architect" and as "Civil and Military Engineer of the State." South Carolina had entered on an extensive scheme of internal improvements, with annual appropriations exceeding $100,000, spent chiefly on roads and on river and canal development. To his interest in the latter subject Mills had already testified in his *Treatise on Inland Navigation*, published in 1820 before his departure from Baltimore. Extensive works were built under his direction on the Saluda, Broad, and Catawba rivers with numerous locks, and the rivers and bays were connected by several canals. The Board of Public Works had charge also of the public buildings of the state. Those erected from 1820 to 1830 were after designs made by Mills or revised by him; they included the Fireproof Record Building in Charleston, a wing of the Charleston prison planned for solitary confinement, and the State Hospital for the Insane at Columbia, which embodied many modern and humane ideas. While in Charleston, Mills issued a number of valuable publications relative to his state: *Internal Improvement of South Carolina* (1822); an accurate *Atlas of the State of South Carolina* (1825); and *Statistics of South Carolina* (1826).

With the cessation of state appropriations for public works in 1830 Mills removed to Washington, D.C. A staunch Jacksonian as he had been a loyal Jeffersonian, he had hopes of federal employment, which were not disappointed. In 1836 he was appointed "Architect of Public Buildings," a position he held until 1851. In this office, he designed three of the principal 19th-century buildings in Washington: the Treasury, the Patent Office, and the Post Office. The crowning success of his life was his victory in competition, 1836, for the design of the Washington Monument at the capital.

Mills is outstanding as the first U.S.-born professional architect and as one of the chief exponents of the Greek revival. His works now appear a little stereotyped and arid, but very sober, competent, and dignified—contributing to that austere tradition still powerful in American architectural style.

MILLS, ROBERT (*b. Todd Co., Ky., 1809; d. Galveston, Tex., 1888*), merchant, planter. Removed to Texas, 1830, where in partnership with his brothers he built up a great trading and banking business. Bankrupt, 1873, he died in poverty.

MILLS, ROGER QUARLES (*b. Todd Co., Ky., 1832; d. Corsicana, Tex., 1911*), lawyer, Confederate soldier. Congressman, Democrat, from Texas, 1873–92; U.S. senator, 1892–99. Author of the Mills bill, 1887, providing for tariff reduction; an advocate of governmental economy and lower taxes.

MILLS, SAMUEL JOHN (*b. Torringford, Conn., 1783; d. at sea, 1818*), Congregational clergyman, father of American Protestant foreign missionary work. Chiefly responsible for formation of American Board of Commissioners for Foreign Missions, *ca.* 1810, and of the American Bible Society, 1816.

MILLS, SUSAN LINCOLN TOLMAN (*b. Enosburg, Vt., 1826; d. Oakland, Calif., 1912*), missionary, educator. Wife of Cyrus T. Mills. President, Mills College, 1890–1909.

MILLSPAUGH, CHARLES FREDERICK (*b. Ithaca, N.Y., 1854; d. 1923*), physician, botanist. Nephew of Ezra Cornell. A noted botanical specimen collector and artist-naturalist, he served as curator of botany, Field Museum, Chicago, Ill., 1893–1923.

MILMORE, MARTIN (*b. Co. Sligo, Ireland, 1844; d. Boston Highlands, Mass., 1883*), sculptor. Came to Boston, Mass., as a child; was a protégé of Thomas Ball. A good but unimaginative workman, Milmore did his most significant work on the Soldiers' and Sailors' Monument, erected on Boston Common, 1877.

MILNER, JOHN TURNER (*b. Pike Co., Ga., 1826; d. Newcastle, Ala., 1898*), civil engineer, industrialist. Served as city surveyor, San Jose, Calif., 1849–54. Removing to Alabama, he built the Montgomery and West Point Railroad and, on the basis of an 1858 survey, projected a railroad through the coal and iron region from Decatur, Ga., to Elyton, Ala. Construction was suspended during the Civil War. After the war, despite political opposition, Milner and his associates successfully completed the line according to their original plan and formed the Elyton Land Co., which in 1871 founded Birmingham. Milner was also associated with first production of coke pig iron in Birmingham, 1876.

MILNER, MOSES EMBREE. *See* CALIFORNIA JOE.

MILNER, THOMAS PICTON. *See* PICTON, THOMAS.

MILROY, ROBERT HUSTON (*b. Washington Co., Ind., 1816; d. Olympia, Wash., 1890*), lawyer, Union major general, Indian agent. Held field command throughout Civil War, mainly in western Virginia, where he suppressed guerrilla warfare ruthlessly; supervised Indian affairs in the state of Washington, 1872–85.

MILTON, GEORGE FORT (*b. Chattanooga, Tenn., 1894; d. Washington, D.C., 1955*), journalist and historian. Managing editor, president and part owner of the *Chattanooga News* (1919–39). A supporter of the New Deal in the 1930's, Milton was friendly with President Roosevelt and received many political appointments. His greatest contribution was as a historian: he published *The Age of Hate: Andrew Johnson and the Radicals* (1930), a well-written study of the Reconstruction; *The Eve of Conflict: Stephen A. Douglas and the Needless War* (1934);

Conflict: The American Civil War (1941); and *Abraham Lincoln and the Fifth Column* (1942).

MILTON, JOHN (*b. Jefferson Co., Ga., 1807; d. 1865*), lawyer. Removed to Jackson Co., Fla., 1846, where he resided until his death. As Democratic governor of Florida, 1861–65, he was a vigorous defender of states' rights against the Confederate government, at the same time giving it maximum military and economic support.

MINER, ALONZO AMES (*b. Lempster, N.H., 1814; d. Boston, Mass., 1895*), Universalist clergyman, antislavery and temperance reformer. President of Tufts College, 1862–74.

MINER, CHARLES (*b. Norwich, Conn., 1780; d. near Wilkes-Barre, Pa., 1865*), journalist, Pennsylvania legislator. Editor and proprietor of a number of Pennsylvania newspapers *post* 1802, Miner served as a Federalist congressman from Pennsylvania, 1825–29. He is remembered principally for his humorous sketches published as a book under the title *Essays from the Desk of Poor Robert the Scribe* (1815), in which the phrase "to have an axe to grind" was first used; he was author also of a standard *History of Wyoming* (1845) and in other of his writings did much to popularize use of anthracite coal.

MINER, MYRTILLA (*b. Brookfield, N.Y., 1815; d. Washington, D.C., 1864*), promoter of black education. Founded a normal school for free black girls, 1851, in Washington, D.C.

MING, JOHN JOSEPH (*b. Gyswyl, Switzerland, 1838; d. Parma, Ohio, 1910*), Roman Catholic clergyman, Jesuit, sociologist. Came to America, 1872; taught in various Jesuit schools and at St. Louis University, where he gained recognition as a pioneer Catholic sociologist.

MINNIGERODE, LUCY (*b. near Leesburg, Va., 1871; d. Virginia, 1935*), nurse. Superintendent of the Department of Nurses, U.S. Public Health Service, 1919–35.

MINOR, BENJAMIN BLAKE (*b. Tappahannock, Va., 1818; d. Richmond, Va., 1905*), lawyer, educator. LL.B., William and Mary, 1839; practiced mainly in Richmond. As editor, *Southern Literary Messenger*, 1843–47, he identified that magazine with Southern writers and Southern views. After service as president, University of Missouri, 1860–62, he engaged in teaching, public lecturing, and business in Missouri, returning to Richmond, 1889.

MINOR, JOHN BARBEE (*b. Louisa Co., Va., 1813; d. 1895*), legal educator and author. Brother of Lucian Minor. Established high reputation of law school of University of Virginia as professor there *post* 1845. Author of, among other works, the *Institutes of Common and Statute Law* (1875–95).

MINOR, LUCIAN (*b. Louisa Co., Va., 1802; d. 1858*), temperance advocate, lawyer, teacher of law. Brother of John B. Minor. Author of *Reasons for Abolishing the Liquor Traffic* (1853).

MINOR, RALEIGH COLSTON (*b. Charlottesville, Va., 1869; d. Charlottesville, 1923*), lawyer, author. Son of John B. Minor. Teacher of law at University of Virginia *post* 1893. His principal subjects were real property, constitutional law, conflict of laws, and international law. He stands as one of America's three pioneers in the field of private international law. In 1901 he achieved international recognition through the publication of his *Conflict of Laws*, an American legal classic, which clarified the existing chaotic condition of that difficult branch of jurisprudence. Among his other books were *The Law of Tax Titles in Virginia* (1898), *The Law of Real Property* (1908), and *A Republic* *of Nations* (1918), in which he advocated prevention of war through a supranational union of nations.

MINOR, ROBERT (*b. San Antonio, Tex., 1884; d. Ossining, N.Y., 1952*), cartoonist and radical politician. Self-educated, Minor was a cartoonist for the *St. Louis Post Dispatch* and the *New York World*; he covered events in Europe during World War I. A radical and anarchist, he joined the Communist movement n 1920, becoming the Party's delegate to the Communist International in Moscow (1922–24). Editor of the *Daily Worker* (1928–30). A supporter of civil rights for blacks during the 1930's, Minor published many articles on the subject. In the 1930's, he covered events in Spain for the *Daily Worker*. He was associated with the defense of the party's leaders during the trials of 1948 held under the Smith Act.

MINOR, ROBERT CRANNELL (*b. New York, N.Y., 1839; d. Waterford, Conn., 1904*), landscapist. Studied in Antwerp and Paris. Deeply influenced by Diaz and the Barbizon school, he excelled in painting the New York and Connecticut countryside.

MINOR, VIRGINIA LOUISA (*b. Goochland Co., Va., 1824; d. St. Louis, Mo., 1894*), woman suffragist. Early in 1867, she led the organization of the Woman Suffrage Association of Missouri (the first organization in the world to make its exclusive aim that of enfranchising women), of which she was elected president. Denied suffrage in Missouri, 1872, she sued for damages in the circuit court at St. Louis. Although her feeble legal case met with defeat here as well as later in the U.S. Supreme Court when Chief Justice Waite's elaborate opinion upheld the Missouri decisions, the publicity accompanying it contributed to the ultimate victory of woman suffrage.

MINOT, CHARLES SEDGWICK (*b. Boston, Mass., 1852; d. 1914*), biologist, educator. Graduated Massachusetts Institute of Technology, 1872; Sc.D., Harvard, 1878. Taught embryology in Harvard Medical School, 1880–1914. Author of *Human Embryology* (1892); made prolonged studies of senility.

MINOT, GEORGE RICHARDS (*b. Boston, Mass., 1758; d. Boston, 1802*), Massachusetts jurist, historian. Graduated Harvard, 1778. Served with ability as clerk of first Massachusetts House of Representatives after adoption of new state constitution, 1780; also as secretary of the Massachusetts convention ratifying the U.S. Constitution, 1788. His fame as historian comes from his *History of the Insurrection in Massachusetts* (Shays's Rebellion), published first in 1788, and his *Continuation of* [Thomas Hutchinson's] *History of the Province of Massachusetts Bay, from the year 1748* (1798, 1803).

MINOT, GEORGE RICHARDS (*b. Boston, Mass., 1885; d. Brookline, Mass., 1950*), physician, medical scientist. Great-grandson of James Jackson (1777–1867); cousin of Charles S. Minot. B.A., Harvard, 1908; M.D., 1912. After internship at Massachusetts General Hospital, he did a year's research on problems of blood coagulation at Johns Hopkins, continuing his studies on his return to Massachusetts General in 1915. In 1917 he began working at the Collis P. Huntington Memorial Hospital in Boston, where he became increasingly involved in study of leukemia; he was chief of the medical service at Huntington, 1923–28. *Post* 1928, he was director of the Thorndike Memorial Laboratory at Boston City Hospital, resigning because of ill health in 1948. Along with his research, he engaged in private practice and taught at Harvard Medical School, 1918–48. Around 1922, suffering from diabetes, he began the study that led to his most important achievement, a cure for pernicious anemia. Interested in the problem since his days as an intern and stimulated by the work of George H. Whipple, Minot and an assistant, W. P. Murphy, proved by experiment that the disease yielded to a diet of liver (later

in form of liver extract). For the discovery of liver therapy in anemias (reported in 1926), Whipple, Minot, and Murphy were jointly awarded the Nobel Prize, 1934.

MINTO, WALTER (*b. Cowdenknowes, Scotland, 1753; d. Princeton, N.J., 1796*), mathematician. Came to America, 1786. Professor of mathematics and natural philosophy, College of New Jersey (Princeton), 1787–96.

MINTON, SHERMAN (*b. near Georgetown, Ind., 1890; d. New Albany, Ind., 1965*), U.S. Supreme Court justice and U.S. senator. Studied at Indiana University (LL.B., 1915) and Yale (LL.M., 1916). Practiced law in New Albany, Ind., from 1919. Appointed counselor of the Indiana Public Service Commission, 1933–34. U.S. senator, 1934–40; democratic whip and assistant majority leader. On staff of President Roosevelt in 1941. Judge of the Seventh Circuit of the U.S. Court of Appeals, 1941–49; U.S. Supreme Court justice, 1949–56.

MINTURN, ROBERT BOWNE (*b. New York, N.Y., 1805; d. New York, 1866*), merchant. Beginning work in the countinghouse of Preserved Fish and Joseph Grinnell, 1829. Minturn became a partner upon their retirement in 1832. Renamed Grinnell, Minturn & Co., the firm became one of the greatest of the New York commercial houses, extending its influence into almost all parts of the world and sharing leadership in American shipowning with the Welds of Boston. The greatest of the clippers, Donald McKay's *Flying Cloud*, sailed under the Grinnell, Minturn house flag.

MINTY, ROBERT HORATIO GEORGE (*b. Co. Mayo, Ireland, 1831; d. Jerome, Ariz., 1906*), Union brigadier general, railroad official. Immigrated to Michigan, 1853, after service as British officer. Rose to division command in cavalry; helped capture Jefferson Davis.

MINUIT, PETER (*b. Wesel, Duchy of Cleves, 1580; d. off St. Christopher, West Indies, 1638*), first official director general of the Dutch colony of New Netherland, governor of New Sweden. Through his purchase of Manhattan Island, 1626, from the Indian sachems for trinkets valued at 60 guilders ($24), the accomplished fact of Dutch occupation received a semblance of legality which the West India Co. was eager to acquire. Minuit made New Amsterdam the rallying point for other Dutch settlements and instituted peaceful relations with Plymouth Colony. Embroiled in a quarrel with Jonas Michaëlus and other Dutch Reformed ministers and with the provincial secretary, he was dismissed in 1631. He next was chosen to lead a Swedish company which established New Sweden (1638), building Fort Christina where Wilmington, Del., now stands.

MIRANDA, CARMEN (*b. Marco Canavores, Portugal, 1909; d. Los Angeles, Calif., 1955*), singer. Remembered for her colorful South American costumes (especially hats and shoes), Miranda made many films including *That Night in Rio* (1941), *The Gang's All Here* (1944), and *Copacabana* (1947), and she appeared in nightclub acts throughout the country. At her funeral in Rio de Janeiro in 1955, an estimated one million people paid their respects.

MIRÓ, ESTEBAN RODRÍGUEZ (*b. Catalonia, 1744; d. Spain, 1795*), Spanish governor of Louisiana. His administration, which began with his appointment as acting governor in 1782 and included the intendancy after 1788, encouraged commerce and agriculture; his conduct toward the United States and its frontiersmen was not so aggressive, independent, or venal as sometimes described. Toward the Southern Indians, whom he sought to control through Alexander McGillivray, his policy was purely defensive. His notorious intrigue with James Wilkinson was begun on the initiative of the latter and carried on (as were all important matters in which Miró acted) under minute orders from Madrid. His term ended in 1791.

MITCHEL, JOHN (*b. Camnish, Ireland, 1815; d. 1875*), journalist, Irish nationalist. An advocate of armed resistance to England *post* 1845, he escaped to America, 1853, from Van Diemen's Land, where he had been transported for treason. Constantly engaged in journalistic and other intrigue against the English, he was a Confederate sympathizer during the Civil War and served as editor of the *Richmond Enquirer* and also of the *Richmond Examiner*, 1862–65. After further essays in journalism, revolution, and politics, he returned to Ireland, 1875. A man who cared nothing for liberty in the abstract or humanity at large, Mitchel was motivated throughout his life by a desire for vengeance against England.

MITCHEL, JOHN PURROY (*b. Fordham, N.Y., 1879; d. Lake Charles, La., 1918*), lawyer, politician. Grandson of John Mitchel. Graduated Columbia, 1899; New York Law School, 1901. After making his name as a special investigator into conduct of borough officials in New York City, 1906, Mitchel had a spectacular rise in city politics, culminating in his election as mayor on a fusion ticket, 1913. Embarking on a program of municipal reform and ignoring party ties, he and his administration became increasingly unpopular. Defeated for reelection, 1917, he was killed while training for World War I service in the air corps.

MITCHEL, ORMSBY MACKNIGHT (*b. Morganfield, Ky., 1809; d. Beaufort, S.C., 1862*), astronomer, educator, Union major general. Graduated West Point, 1829. Taught mathematics and astronomy at Cincinnati (Ohio) College; by his lectures and writings, stimulated establishment of observatories in Harvard, Washington, D.C., and Cincinnati. Commanded Department of the Ohio, 1861; was later subordinate to General D. C. Buell. Promoted major general of volunteers, 1862, for brilliant capture of Huntsville, Ala., in April. Died of yellow fever soon after assuming command of X Army Corps and the Department of the South.

MITCHELL, ALBERT GRAEME (*b. Salem, Mass., 1889; d. Cincinnati, Ohio, 1941*), pediatrician, educator. M.D., University of Pennsylvania, 1910. Practiced pediatrics in Philadelphia, Pa.; served in France with U.S. Army Medical Corps, World War I; resumed practice, 1919, and was instructor and associate at the University of Pennsylvania in pediatrics department at the Children's Hospital. Appointed Rachford professor and head of the Department of Pediatrics at University of Cincinnati, 1924, he developed and coordinated health services for children in the Cincinnati area in a way that stands as a model for administration of unified community health facilities, established within a teaching and research framework. His most important contribution to the literature was his part in preparing the second edition (1927) of J. P. C. Griffith's *The Diseases of Infants and Children*, and subsequent editions, including those under the title *Textbook of Pediatrics*.

MITCHELL, ALEXANDER (*b. Ellon, Aberdeenshire, Scotland, 1817; d. New York, N.Y., 1887*), banker, railroad builder, politician. Came to America, 1839, engaging first in the insurance business at Milwaukee, Wis. By 1861, one of the principal bankers in that state, Mitchell served with great success as president of the Chicago, Milwaukee and St. Paul Railroad, 1865–87; he served also as congressman, Democrat, from Wisconsin, 1871–75.

MITCHELL, DAVID BRYDIE (*b. Perthshire, Scotland, 1766; d. Milledgeville, Ga., 1837*), lawyer, Georgia legislator. Immigrated to Georgia, 1783. Active in the state militia, he served as Democratic-Republican governor, 1809–13, and 1815–17; he was a liberal supporter of internal improvement, education, and frontier defense. As agent to the Creek Indians, 1817–21, he concluded the land-cession treaty of 1818.

MITCHELL, DAVID DAWSON (*b. Louisa Co., Va., 1806; d. 1861*), fur trader, soldier. Built Fort Mackenzie, 1832; settled in St. Louis, Mo., 1840. Except for an interval of conspicuous service in the Mexican War, he served as U.S. superintendent of Indian affairs, central division, 1841–53.

MITCHELL, DONALD GRANT (*b. Norwich, Conn., 1822; d. near New Haven, Conn., 1908*), author, agriculturist. Grandson of Stephen M. Mitchell. Graduated Yale, 1841. Under pseudonym "Ik Marvel," he wrote a number of contemporaneously popular works, which included *Reveries of a Bachelor* (1850), *Dream Life* (1851), and *My Farm of Edgewood* (1863). *Post* 1855, he devoted a great deal of time to arousing his countrymen to a sense of beauty in farming, homebuilding, and town-planning.

MITCHELL, EDWARD CUSHING (*b. East Bridgewater, Mass., 1829; d. 1900*), Baptist clergyman, Old Testament scholar. Grandson of Nahum Mitchell. Active in furthering the higher education of blacks, notably at Leland University, where he was president, 1887–1900.

MITCHELL, EDWARD PAGE (*b. Bath, Maine, 1852; d. New London, Conn., 1927*), journalist, editor. Graduated Bowdoin, 1871. After apprenticeship on Boston, Mass., and Maine newspapers, Mitchell joined the staff of the New York *Sun* on invitation of Charles A. Dana in October 1875. He remained with the *Sun* until his death as editorial writer and policymaker, and as editor in chief, 1903–20.

MITCHELL, EDWIN KNOX (*b. Locke, Ohio, 1853; d. Hartford, Conn., 1934*), Presbyterian clergyman. A pupil of Adolf Harnack, Mitchell was professor of ancient and early church history, Hartford Theological Seminary *post* 1892. He translated Harnack's *Outlines of the History of Dogma* (1893) and was author of other scholarly works in his field.

MITCHELL, ELISHA (*b. Washington, Conn., 1793; d. Mitchell's Falls, N.C., 1857*), Presbyterian clergyman, geologist, botanist. Graduated Yale, 1813. Professor of mathematics and the sciences, University of North Carolina, 1818–57. His activity in exploring and surveying much of the state is commemorated in Mount Mitchell, highest peak in the eastern United States, which he was the first to measure.

MITCHELL, GEORGE EDWARD (*b. present Eklton, Md., 1781; d. Washington, D.C., 1832*), physician, Maryland legislator, soldier. Remembered for his brilliant defense of Fort Oswego, N.Y., 1814. Congressman, Democrat, from Maryland, 1823–27 and 1829–32. Author of resolutions honoring Lafayette and inviting him to visit America, 1824.

MITCHELL, HENRY (*b. Nantucket, Mass., 1830; d. New York, N.Y., 1902*), engineer, hydrographer. Son of William Mitchell (1791–1869); brother of Maria Mitchell. Associated with U.S. Coast Survey, 1849–88, he specialized in tide and current investigations in North Atlantic harbors and came to be recognized as the leading American hydrographer. He was author of *Tides and Tidal Phenomena* (1868) and numerous other works.

MITCHELL, HINCKLEY GILBERT THOMAS (*b. Lee, N.Y., 1846; d. 1920*), Methodist clergyman, educator, Hebrew scholar. Graduated Wesleyan University, 1873; Boston University school of theology, 1876; Ph.D., Leipzig, 1879. Taught Hebrew at Boston University and at Tufts College; was attacked as champion of the higher criticism and for Unitarian tendencies.

MITCHELL, ISAAC (*b. near Albany, N.Y., ca. 1759; d. Poughkeepsie, N.Y., 1812*), journalist. Author of "Alonzo and Melissa," an early American piece of fiction, first published in the Poughkeepsie, N.Y., *Political Barometer*, June 1804 through October 30, 1804. The tale was published in book form as *The Asylum, or Alonzo and Melissa* (1811); a pirated edition (also 1811) was issued at Plattsburg, N.Y.

MITCHELL, JAMES PAUL (*b. Elizabeth, N.J., 1900; d. New York, N.Y., 1964*), businessman and secretary of labor. With the Western Electric Company in Kearny, N.J., 1926–32 and 1936–38. Emergency Relief Administration director in Union County, N.J. (1932–36); director of the industrial relations department of the New York City Works Progress Administration (1938–40); and director of the Industrial Personnel Division of the Army Service Forces (1942–45). After the war was director of personnel and industrial relations at R. H. Macy and Company (1945–47), and vice president in charge of labor relations and operations at Bloomingdale Brothers (1947–53). Served as secretary of labor under President Eisenhower (1953–60), then was consultant and director of industrial relations (1961), and vice president for corporate relations (from 1962) for the Crown Zellerbach Corporation. Under Mitchell the Department of Labor maintained excellent relations with both organized labor and management; journalist and editor Harry Hamilton called him the "social conscience of the Republican party."

MITCHELL, JAMES TYNDALE (*b. near Belleville, Ill., 1834; d. Philadelphia, Pa., 1915*), Pennsylvania jurist. Edited *American Law Register*, 1863–88, and *Weekly Notes of Cases*, 1875–99. After holding several Philadelphia judgeships, he served as justice of the Pennsylvania Supreme Court, 1888–1910, sitting as chief justice, 1903–10. Described once as "a brake on the wheels of progress," Mitchell's principal positive influence was in connection with legal procedure, on which he was an authority.

MITCHELL, JOHN (*b. probably in the British Isles, date unknown; d. England, 1768*), physician, botanist, cartographer. Practiced medicine successfully at Urbanna, Va., 1735–46; thereafter he resided chiefly in or near London, England. Mitchell's method of treating yellow fever was practiced later by Benjamin Rush in Philadelphia; he was a correspondent of Cadwallader Colden and Benjamin Franklin. He wrote with versatility on several scientific subjects, but his most important work was his *Map of the British and French Dominions in North America*, which he began to make in 1750 and published at London, 1755. This map was many times reprinted, copied, and plagiarized and because of its subsequent use in scores of diplomatic and other controversies (including the peace negotiations at the end of the American Revolution) is considered the most important map in American history.

MITCHELL, JOHN (*b. Braidwood, Ill., 1870; d. New York, N.Y., 1919*), labor leader. Began work in coal mines at the age of 12; joined Knights of Labor, 1885. Joined United Mine Workers, 1890, and helped lead the union in its first victorious national strike, 1897. President of the United Mine Workers, 1898–1908, he won national celebrity for his tact and ability in the anthracite coal strike, Pennsylvania, 1902.

MITCHELL, JOHN AMES (*b. New York, N.Y., 1845; d. Ridgefield, Conn., 1918*), artist, author. Founded *Life* magazine, 1883, whose success was owing largely to Mitchell's ability as editor to anticipate trends in American popular thought and give expression to them in humorous form.

MITCHELL, JOHN HIPPLE (*b. Washington Co., Pa., 1835; d. 1905*), lawyer, politician. Settled in Oregon, 1860. Served intermittently as U.S. senator, Republican, from Oregon, 1872–1905. An adroit, disreputable, and very popular political leader.

MITCHELL, JOHN KEARSLEY (*b. Shepherdstown, Va., now W.Va., 1793; d. 1858*), physician, chemist, physiologist. M.D., University of Pennsylvania, 1819. Practiced in Philadelphia; was professor of medicine, Jefferson Medical College, 1841–58.

MITCHELL, JONATHAN (*b. Halifax, England, 1624; d. 1668*), Congregational clergyman. Went to America as a boy; graduated Harvard, 1647. Pastor at Cambridge, Mass., *post* 1650, he was a leading advocate of the Half-Way Covenant.

MITCHELL, LANGDON ELWYN (*b. Philadelphia, Pa., 1862; d. Philadelphia, 1935*), playwright. Son of Silas W. Mitchell. Author of a number of once-popular plays, which included *Becky Sharp* (produced, New York, 1899) and *The New York Idea* (produced, New York, 1906).

MITCHELL, LUCY MYERS WRIGHT (*b. Urumiah, Persia, 1845; d. Lausanne, Switzerland, 1888*), missionary, historian. Born of missionary parents; resided mainly abroad. Author of *A History of Ancient Sculpture* (1883).

MITCHELL, LUCY SPRAGUE (*b. Chicago, Ill., 1878; d. Palo Alto, Calif., 1967*), educator. Graduated from Radcliffe College. Dean of Women, the University of California at Berkeley (1904–10). Married economist Wesley Clair Mitchell in 1912. Founded the Bureau of Educational Experiments (incorporated in 1950 as the Bank Street College of Education) in 1916; president to 1950; on board to 1956. Cofounded the Cooperative School for Teachers (1931). Author of *Here and Now Story Book* (1921), *Our Children and Our Schools* (1950), and *Two Lives: The Story of Wesley Clair Mitchell and Myself* (1953).

MITCHELL, MARGARET JULIA (*b. New York, N.Y., 1837; d. New York, 1918*), actress, known generally as Maggie Mitchell. Made debut in New York, June 1851; was long a favorite actress, especially in the South. Famous for performance in title role of *Fanchon the Cricket*.

MITCHELL, MARGARET MUNNERLYN (*b. Atlanta, Ga., 1900; d. Atlanta, 1949*), author. Attended Smith College briefly; on staff of *Atlanta Journal* as feature writer for the Sunday magazine, 1922–26. Author of *Gone with the Wind* (1936), a romantic novel set in the time of the Civil War and the Reconstruction of the South, which was an immediate success and is said to have replaced *Uncle Tom's Cabin* as America's all-time best-selling work of fiction. It was awarded the Pulitzer Prize.

MITCHELL, MARIA (*b. Nantucket, Mass., 1818; d. Lynn, Mass., 1889*), astronomer, educator. Daughter of William Mitchell (1791–1869); sister of Henry Mitchell. First professor of astronomy at Vassar College *post* 1865.

MITCHELL, NAHUM (*b. East Bridgewater, Mass., 1769; d. Plymouth, Mass., 1853*), Massachusetts legislator and jurist, composer. Coeditor of the "Bridgewater Collection" of hymns, first published in 1802; author of *History of the Early Settlement of Bridgewater* (1840).

MITCHELL, NATHANIEL (*b. near Laurel, Del., 1753; d. Laurel, 1814*), Revolutionary soldier, Delaware legislator and public official. Governor of Delaware, 1805–08.

MITCHELL, ROBERT BYINGTON (*b. Mansfield, Ohio, 1823; d. Washington, D.C., 1882*), lawyer, Union brigadier general. Settled at Paris, Kans., 1856; was a conservative Free-State man. His governorship of New Mexico Territory, 1866–69, was marked by quarrels with the legislature over his alleged arbitrary rule.

MITCHELL, SAMUEL AUGUSTUS (*b. Bristol, Conn., 1792; d. Philadelphia, Pa., 1868*), geographer, publisher of geographical works.

MITCHELL, SIDNEY ZOLLICOFFER (*b. Dadeville, Ala., 1862; d. New York, N.Y., 1944*), public utility executive. Graduated U.S. Naval Academy, 1883; resigned from the navy, 1885, to work for Thomas A. Edison as sales agent. To create a market for Edison products, he organized electric power companies in the Pacific Northwest; in 1886 he established the Northwest Electric Supply and Construction Co. Responding to mounting demands for electric service and to such technological innovations as the changeover from direct to alternating current, Mitchell became absorbed in the problem of financing the expansion of the facilities. Favoring the consolidation of existing electric companies in order to eliminate wasteful competition, increase efficiency, and make utilities more attractive to potential investors, he handled the consolidation of the Tacoma Railway & Power Co. He left General Electric in 1902 to head the Tacoma company. He returned to General Electric in 1905 to help set up and manage the Electric Bond & Share Co. Mitchell consolidated operating companies and then organized subholding companies under Bond & Share to manage their financial affairs. His enterprises expanded rapidly, and by 1924 the Bond & Share system controlled more than 10 percent of the nation's electric utility business. In 1923, at the request of the State Department, he established the American & Foreign Power Co., which controlled electric utilities in Latin America, and two years later organized the Electric Power & Light Corporation.

MITCHELL, SILAS WEIR (*b. Philadelphia, Pa., 1829; d. 1914*), physician, neurologist, author. Son of John K. Mitchell. Graduated Jefferson Medical College, 1850; began practice as assistant to his father; served as Union army surgeon. Mitchell's contributions to medical literature covered many different fields; his 119 papers included studies in neurology, pharmacology, physiology, and toxicology. He devoted over 40 years of service to Philadelphia Orthopedic Hospital; under his influence it became a center for the treatment of nervous disorders. He was distinguished also in the field of literature, particularly in fiction. Among his novels the following are outstanding: *Roland Blake* (1886); *Hugh Wynne* (1898); *The Adventures of François* (1899); *Constance Trescott* (1905).

MITCHELL, STEPHEN MIX (*b. Wethersfield, Conn., 1743; d. Wethersfield, 1835*), Connecticut legislator and judge of Hartford County court, 1779–93; of state superior court, 1795–1814 (chief justice *post* 1807).

MITCHELL, THOMAS DUCHÉ (*b. Philadelphia, Pa., 1791; d. 1865*), physician. M.D., University of Pennsylvania, 1812. Taught medicine and chemistry in a number of schools in Pennsylvania, Ohio, and Kentucky.

MITCHELL, THOMAS GREGORY (*b. Elizabeth, N.J., 1892; d. Beverly Hills, Calif., 1962*), actor, playwright, and director. Roles in Broadway productions included Tony in *Under Sentence* (1916), Christopher Mahon in *The Playboy of the Western World* (1921), Willy Loman in *Death of a Salesman* (1949 and 1950), and Rollie Evans in *Cut of the Axe* (1960). Received a "Tony" Award for his performance in the musical *Hazel Flagg* (1953). Probably most famous for his screen portrayal of Scarlett O'Hara's father in *Gone with the Wind* (1939). Other films include *The Hurricane* (Academy Award nomination, 1938), *Stagecoach* (Academy Award, 1939), and *Pocketful of Miracles* (1961). Appeared on television in "The O'Henry Playhouse" and the series "Mayor of the Town" and "Glencannon"; received an "Emmy" as best actor of the year in 1952. Wrote *Glory Hallelujah* with Bert

Bloch in 1925, *Little Accident* with Floyd Dell in 1928, and *Cloudy with Showers* (1932). Directed plays including *Nightstick*, *Fly Away Home*, and *At Home Abroad*.

MITCHELL, WESLEY CLAIR (*b. Rushville, Ill., 1874; d. New York, N.Y., 1948*), economist. Entering the University of Chicago in 1892, Mitchell came under the influence of Thorstein Veblen and J. Laurence Laughlin in economics and John Dewey and his disciple George H. Meade in philosophy. After receiving his B.A. in 1896, Mitchell accepted a fellowship at Chicago for graduate study in economics; but Dewey also wanted him, and so Mitchell minored in philosophy. For his doctoral dissertation he undertook to study the history of the greenbacks. After receiving his Ph.D. summa cum laude in 1899, he accepted a post in the U.S. Census Office. He published *A History of the Greenbacks, with Special Reference to the Economic Consequences of Their Issue: 1862–65* in 1903. While working on this treatise and its sequel, *Gold, Prices, and Wages Under the Greenback Standard* (1908), he developed a significantly new technique in economic analysis. In 1903 he became an assistant professor of economics at the University of California in Berkeley. Rising to the rank of professor by 1909, he remained at California until 1912. In 1905 he began a study of the economic consequences of different monetary standards, but quickly shifted his aim to an analysis of changes in the price level and their consequences. The study occupied Mitchell for about five years, culminating in 1910 with the delivery at Stanford University of the paper "The Money Economy and Civilization." From a discussion of economic psychology and economic theory came the essay "The Rationality of Economic Activity" (1910), a stimulating exposition of how the economic man of classical theory is a one-sided reflection of the impact of pecuniary institutions upon the activities and minds of men. The largest segment of the study was woven into *Business Cycles* (1913), a landmark both in its thesis and in its systematic use of quantitative analysis of the workings of the entire economy.

Mitchell accepted a post in 1913 as lecturer at Columbia University. The next year, he was made a full professor, a post he held for all but three years until his retirement in 1944. In his early period at Columbia he wrote *The Making and Using of Index Numbers* (1915), which has long been a requisite for economic statisticians. In 1919 he helped found the New School for Social Research in New York. He taught there for a time, but in 1922, after urgent requests from his former colleagues, he returned to Columbia. In 1920 he was a principal founder of that landmark institution for quantitative economics, the National Bureau of Economic Research.

During World War I he headed the Price Section of the Division of Planning and Statistics of the War Industries Board. After the war he supervised the preparation of a *History of Prices During the War*. Under his direction the National Bureau of Economic Research prepared the comprehensive surveys *Business Cycles and Unemployment* (1923) and *Recent Economic Changes in the United States* (1929). In 1929 President Hoover appointed him chairman of the President's Research Committee on Social Trends, and the outcome was *Recent Social Trends in the United States* (1933). During World War II he served as chairman of the President's Committee on the Cost of Living, whose report, in general, defended the accuracy of the official index numbers of changes in the cost of living prepared by the U.S. Bureau of Labor Statistics. In 1938 he was elected to the presidency of the American Association for the Advancement of Science, an honor only held once before by a social scientist.

MITCHELL, WILLIAM (*b. Nantucket, Mass., 1791; d. Poughkeepsie, N.Y., 1869*), teacher, businessman, amateur astronomer. Father of Henry and Maria Mitchell.

MITCHELL, WILLIAM (*b. Billquay, England, 1798; d. 1856*), actor, dramatist. Made American debut in New York, 1836. As manager of New York Olympic Theatre, 1839–50, Mitchell devised a type of burlesque entertainment, topical in character, which was highly successful.

MITCHELL, WILLIAM (*b. New York, N.Y., 1801; d. Morristown, N.J., 1886*), lawyer. Elected judge of the New York Supreme Court, 1849, he became presiding justice of that court, 1854, and continued to preside until retirement in 1857.

MITCHELL, WILLIAM (*b. Welland Co., Ontario, Canada, 1832; d. Lake Alexandria, Minn., 1900*), railroad official, jurist. Minnesota district court judge, 1874–81; learned and liberal judge of the Minnesota Supreme Court, 1881–99.

MITCHELL, WILLIAM (*b. Nice, France, 1879; d. New York, N.Y., 1936*), army officer, aviator. Grandson of Alexander Mitchell; raised in Milwaukee, Wis. Left college, 1898, to enlist in war with Spain. Commissioned in regular army, 1901, Mitchell was associated with Signal Corps duty. He learned to fly, 1916, and for a while commanded the tiny aviation section of the Signal Corps. Planner of the Allied Expeditionary Force aviation program, 1917, he made a brilliant record in World War I as pilot and strategist, advancing in rank to brigadier general. Appointed assistant chief of the Air Services, 1919, he sought to secure a greater autonomy for military aviation and was increasingly outspoken in his criticism of the role of the navy in national defense. The significance of bombing tests conducted by him against surface ships in July and September 1921, became a national issue. Branded a troublemaker, he was relieved of his post, 1925. In September 1925, Mitchell, by a public statement attacking the War and Navy departments, precipitated his court-martial; found guilty, he was sentenced to a five-year suspension, but on Feb. 1, 1926, he resigned from the army. He continued to propagate his ideas while a civilian, and the significant results of his long campaign were the Army Air Force of World War II and the Department of Defense, established in 1947.

MITCHELL, WILLIAM DeWITT (*b. Winona, Minn., 1874; d. Syosset, N.Y., 1955*), lawyer and government official. Studied at Yale University and the University of Minnesota Law School (LL.B., 1895). Solicitor general (1925–29); 1929–33, attorney general of the U.S. As attorney general, Mitchell was given the thankless task of enforcing Prohibition, a job that took too much time and sapped the resources of his department. In 1932, he was responsible for the expulsion of the Bonus Army; his subsequent defense of the government's actions was controversial. He returned to private practice in New York, and in 1938 wrote a revision to private practice in New York, and in 1938 wrote a revision of the federal rules of civil procedure which ranks as a major reform in the administration of justice. Headed for a time the congressional investigation of the Japanese attack on Pearl Harbor.

MITCHILL, SAMUEL LATHAM (*b. North Hempstead, N.Y., 1764; d. 1831*), physician, New York legislator. Studied medicine in New York City with Samuel Bard; M.D., Edinburgh, 1786. Active all his life in the progress of medical education and the sciences, Mitchill served as congressman, Democratic-Republican, from New York, 1801–04 and 1810–13; he was U.S. senator, 1804–09. Characterized by contemporaries as "a living encyclopedia" and "a chaos of knowledge," he made no epochal discoveries and his theories were often erroneous; he was, however, sincere and amiable and did his best to popularize scientific inquiry.

MITROPOULOS, DIMITRI (*b. Athens, Greece, 1896; d. Milan, Italy, 1960*), composer and conductor. Studied at the Athens Conservatory of Music and in Berlin with Ferruccio Busoni. His major composition was an opera, *Soeur Béatrice* (1919), which enabled him to study in Paris and Berlin. In 1930, he turned from composing to conducting, and, in 1934, he made his American debut with the Boston Symphony Orchestra. From 1937 to 1949, he was director of the Minneapolis Symphony; from 1949 to 1958, he was director of the New York Philharmonic. An eclectic in musical tastes, Mitropoulos interpreted the works of Debussy, Richard Strauss, Mahler, Bruckner, and the Second Vienna School. He became an American citizen in 1946.

MITSCHER, MARC ANDREW (*b. Hillsborough, Wis., 1887; d. Norfolk, Va., 1947*), naval officer, aviator. Graduated U.S. Naval Academy, 1910. Requesting transfer to aviation duty, he trained at Pensacola, Fla. During World War I he served successfully as head of the aviation department on the cruiser *Huntington* and as commander of naval air stations on Long Island and in Florida. He was promoted to lieutenant commander, 1918. In 1922 he undertook the first of four tours of duty at the Bureau of Aeronautics. Most important for the future was his work in the development of techniques of carrier air operations, as air officer and then executive officer of the experimental carrier *Langley*, 1926, 1929–30, and of the newly commissioned *Saratoga*, 1926–1929, 1934–35. He was promoted to captain in 1938; in 1941, after two years as assistant chief of the Bureau of Aeronautics in charge of aircraft procurement, he became the first commanding officer of the carrier *Hornet*. Early in 1944 he was placed in command of the Fast Carrier Task Force, Pacific Fleet. In the great battle for Leyte Gulf, Oct. 23–26, which followed the American landings, Mitscher's force sank 13 enemy ships, including 4 carriers and a battleship. In June 1945 he assumed the post of deputy chief of naval operations for air. Promoted to admiral in 1946, he gladly left Washington to assume command of the Eighth Fleet and in September became commander in chief, Atlantic Fleet, the second naval aviator to hold a major fleet command.

MITTEN, THOMAS EUGENE (*b. Brighton, England, 1864; d. near Milford, Pa., 1929*), street-railway official. Came to America as a boy; was raised in Indiana. After a successful career in the Midwest, he headed the Philadelphia Rapid Transit Co. *post* 1911. Under investigation at the time of his death, his management was described as "a colossal conspiracy against the tax-payers."

MIX, TOM (*b. Mix Run, Pa., 1880; d. near Florenze, Ariz., 1940*), cowboy, motion-picture star. An outstanding box-office attraction, *ca.* 1916–28.

MIXTER, SAMUEL JASON (*b. Hardwick, Mass., 1855; d. Grand Junction, Tenn., 1926*), surgeon. Graduated Massachusetts Institute of Technology, 1875; M.D., Harvard, 1879. On the staff of Massachusetts General Hospital, 1886–1926, Mixter made important contributions to neurological surgery, to the technique of skin-grafting, and to surgery for intestinal obstruction.

MIZNER, ADDISON (*b. Benicia, Calif., 1872; d. Palm Beach, Fla., 1933*), architect, adventurer. Mainly self-trained, Mizner arrived in New York City, 1904; there, with the aid of wealthy contacts provided by Stanford White and others, he commenced practice but without immediate success. Removing to Palm Beach, Fla., 1918, he succeeded in making his personal vision of Spanish art and architecture the fashionable style for ambitious Florida house-builders in the boom era *post* World War I. After his triumphs at Palm Beach, he and his brother Wilson Mizner developed Boca Raton as a resort. His prosperity ended with the collapse of the Florida land bubble.

Modjeska, Helena (*b. Kraków, Poland, 1840; d. East Newport, Calif., 1909*), Polish-American actress. The reigning actress of Poland, 1868–70, she came to America, learned to speak English in six months, and began in 1877 a long series of successful theatrical tours in a wide range of parts. In Polish she had a repertoire of over a hundred roles; in English she played nine heroines of Shakespeare, from Juliet to Cleopatra, and such well-known parts as Adrienne Lecouvreur, Camille, Mary Stuart, and, for the first time in America, Ibsen's Nora.

Modjeski, Ralph (*b. Kraków, Poland, 1861; d. Los Angeles, Calif., 1940*), bridge engineer. Son of Helena Modjeska.

Moeller, Henry (*b. Cincinnati, Ohio, 1849; d. 1925*), Roman Catholic clergyman. Archbishop of Cincinnati, 1904–25; a skilled administrator and promoter of education.

Moffat, David Halliday (*b. Washingtonville, N.Y., 1839; d. New York, N.Y., 1911*), capitalist. Settled in Denver, Colo., 1860; prospered as banker and as investor in mining properties, farmlands, and Denver real estate. Although he promoted and financed a number of Colorado railroads, his name is associated principally with the Denver, Northwestern & Pacific.

Moffat, James Clement (*b. Glencree, Scotland, 1811; d. Princeton, N.J., 1890*), Presbyterian clergyman, church historian, educator. Came to America, 1833. Graduated Princeton, 1835; taught thereafter at Princeton, at Lafayette, and at Miami University until 1852 when he returned to Princeton as professor of classics. Appointed professor of church history at Princeton, 1861, he continued to teach until the year before his death.

Moffat, Jay Pierrepont (*b. Rye, N.Y., 1896; d. Ottawa, Canada, 1943*), diplomat. Attended Harvard, 1915–17. After wartime experience as secretary to the U.S. minister to the Netherlands, he became a career officer in the foreign service and won reputation as a dependable and skillful diplomat in posts all over the world. As head of the division of European affairs of the State Department from 1937, he was a cautious internationalist who believed in limited U.S. involvement in measures for collective security. He was appointed U.S. minister to Canada in June 1940.

Moffatt, James (*b. Glasgow, Scotland, 1870; d. New York, N.Y., 1944*), biblical scholar, church historian. Distinguished abroad as a teacher and as the scholarly author of *An Introduction to the Literature of the New Testament* (1911) and other works, he was Washburn professor of church history at Union Theological Seminary, New York City, 1927–28. Author of a rather coldly received translation of the Bible (New Testament, 1913; Old Testament, 1924–25), he served as executive secretary of the American Standard Bible Committee, which produced in 1946 the Revised Standard Version of the Bible. His work on this project was extensive, effective, and largely unacknowledged.

Moffett, Cleveland Langston (*b. Boonville, N.Y., 1863; d. Paris, France, 1926*), journalist. Author of mystery stories and of a number of successful plays of an ephemeral nature.

Moffett, William Adger (*b. Charleston, S.C., 1869; d. aboard dirigible Akron off New Jersey coast, 1933*), naval officer. Graduated Annapolis, 1890. Served with great distinction at Manila, 1898; at Veracruz, Mexico, 1914; and as a training officer in World War I. As rear admiral and chief of the Bureau of Aeronautics, 1921–33, he was largely responsible by his vision, enthusiasm, and sound policies for the high efficiency and morale of U.S. naval aviation.

Moholy-Nagy, László (*b. Bacsbarsod, Hungary, 1895; d. Chicago, Ill., 1946*), artist, teacher. Probably the most versatile figure in the 20th-century modernist movement in the arts, he came to Chicago in 1937 after a European career in which he had made his mark as abstract painter, photographer, typographer, moviemaker, advertising designer, designer of theater sets, and faculty member, 1923–28, at the Weimar Bauhaus. After the failure of the Chicago "New Bauhaus" school, which he had been invited to direct, he opened his own School of Design in February 1939, in which he proposed to provide an education wherein art, science, and technology were fully integrated. The school succeeded, was renamed the Institute of Design in 1944, and eventually became a division of the Illinois Institute of Technology. During his American period his artistic productions were principally free-form sculptures, often in plastic materials, and multidimensional abstract paintings; he also wrote many articles and a book, *Vision in Motion* (1947).

Mohr, Charles Theodore (*b. Esslingen, Württemberg, 1824; d. Asheville, N.C., 1901*), botanist, pharmacist. Came to America, 1848; settled in Mobile, Ala., 1857. His extensive and important studies were embodied in several official reports and principally in *Plant Life of Alabama* (1901).

Moïse, Penina (*b. Charleston, S.C., 1797; d. 1880*), poet. Her most characteristic work is found in *Hymns Written for the Use of Hebrew Congregations* (1856).

Moisseiff, Leon Solomon (*b. Riga, Latvia, 1872; d. Belmar, N.J., 1943*), engineer, designer of long-span bridges. Immigrated with Jewish parents to New York City, 1891. C.E., Columbia University, 1895. Chief draftsman and assistant designer, New York Department of Bridges, 1898–1910; design engineer, 1910–15; associated during this period with construction of the Williamsburg, Queensboro, and Manhattan bridges across the East River. In practice as consulting engineer thereafter, he worked on many of the largest and most spectacular bridges built in his time, including the Delaware River bridge at Philadelphia; the George Washington, Bayonne, Triborough, and Bronx-Whitestone bridges, all New York City; the Ambassador bridge, Detroit; the Maumee River bridge, Toledo; and the Golden Gate and San Francisco–Oakland Bay bridges, San Francisco. Of a number of these, he was the principal designer.

Moldehnke, Edward Frederick (*b. Insterburg, East Prussia, 1836; d. Watchung, N.J., 1904*), Lutheran clergyman. Came to America, 1861, as missionary in Wisconsin and Minnesota. Pastor, Zion and St. Peter's Church, New York City, 1871–1904.

Moldenke, Richard George Gottlob (*b. Watertown, Wis., 1864; d. Plainfield, N.J., 1930*), metallurgist. Son of Edward F. Moldehnke (*sic*). Stimulated scientific study of foundry problems, especially in gray-iron industry; wrote *The Principles of Iron Founding* (1917).

Mollenhauer, Emil (*b. Brooklyn, N.Y., 1855; d. Boston, Mass., 1927*), violinist. Conductor of Boston Festival Orchestra; also of the Handel and Haydn Society, 1899–1927. A talented, versatile, conservative musician.

Möllhausen, Heinrich Baldwin (*b. near Bonn, Germany, 1825; d. Berlin, Germany, 1905*), traveler, author, artist. Came to America, 1849; led roving life in region of Kaskaskia River, Ill.; joined expedition of duke of Württemberg to the Rocky Mountains, 1851. After a brief return to Germany, he served as topographer to Lt. A. W. Whipple's division of the Pacific Railroad survey, 1853–54. In the years 1857 and 1858 he went out as assistant on the exploration and survey of the Colorado River headed by Lt. J. C. Ives. The sketches which he drew as illustrations to the reports of these expeditions rank high as documents of the topography of the Old West. After his return to Germany, 1858, he produced a great number of novels and novelettes which deal with Indian and emigrant life in the West; among them are *Der Halbindianer* (1861) and *Das Mormonenmädchen* (1864).

MOLYNEUX, ROBERT (*b. near Formby, England, 1738; d. 1808*), Roman Catholic clergyman, Jesuit. Coming to America, 1771; served at the Maryland missions and succeeded Robert Harding as pastor in Philadelphia, Pa., 1773. He served twice as president of Georgetown College and was named American superior of the Society of Jesus, 1805.

MOMBERT, JACOB ISIDOR (*b. Cassel, Germany, 1829; d. Paterson, N.J., 1913*), Episcopal clergyman. A pastor for many years *post* 1859 in Pennsylvania and New Jersey, Mombert was author of several learned theological works, some popular biographies, and a *History of Lancaster County* (1869).

MONCKTON, ROBERT (*b. probably England, 1726; d. 1782*), British lieutenant general. Came to Nova Scotia, 1752. With a small force of regulars and a large number of New England militia, he took Fort Beauséjour in June 1755 and was active in removal of the French inhabitants of the island southward. He commanded in Nova Scotia during Amherst's siege of Louisburg, 1758, and was appointed second in command of the Quebec expedition of 1759. Governor of New York, 1761–63, he commanded the successful expedition against Martinique which resulted in the surrender of that island, February 1762. Offered the chief command in North America, 1773, he refused it.

MONCURE, RICHARD CASSIUS LEE (*b. Stafford Co., Va., 1805; d. Stafford Co., 1882*), lawyer, Virginia legislator and jurist. Judge, state supreme court of appeals, 1851–65; presiding judge, 1870–82. Outstanding in equity cases.

MONDELL, FRANK WHEELER (*b. St. Louis, Mo., 1860; d. Washington, D.C., 1939*), lawyer, mine operator. Settled in Wyoming *ca.* 1888 and pioneered there in development of oil and coal deposits. Congressman, Republican, from Wyoming, 1895–97 and 1899–1923. As congressman, and as floor leader *post* 1919, Mondell was a model of unenlightened conservatism.

MONETTE, JOHN WESLEY (*b. near Staunton, Va., 1803; d. Louisiana, 1851*), physician, historian. Author of the monumental *History of the Discovery and Settlement of the Valley of the Mississippi* (1846).

MONEY, HERNANDO DE SOTO (*b. Holmes Co., Miss., 1839; d. Mississippi, 1912*), lawyer, newspaper editor. Confederate soldier. Congressman, Democrat, from Mississippi, 1875–85 and 1893–97; U.S. senator, 1897–1911. A singularly independent figure in Congress, Money was a leader in the destruction of the "star route" system of mail handling and held a number of important committee assignments.

MONIS, JUDAH (*b. Algiers or Italy, 1683; d. Northborough, Mass., 1764*), Hebrew scholar, educator. Educated in Jewish schools of Leghorn and Amsterdam; settled in New York, 1715/6, as a merchant; removed to Massachusetts *ante* 1720. Monis was the first Jew to receive a Harvard degree (M.A., 1720); he was the first Harvard teacher to bear the title of instructor (taught Hebrew, 1722–60); and he was author of the first Hebrew grammar published in America (1735).

MONROE, HARRIET (*b. Chicago, Ill., 1860; d. Arequipa, Peru, 1936*), poet. Founder and editor, 1912–36, of *Poetry: A Magazine of Verse*, which became a principal vehicle of 20th-century movements in poetry.

MONROE, JAMES (*b. Westmoreland Co., Va., 1758; d. New York, N.Y., 1831*), statesman, president of the United States. His parents were respectable but not distinguished Virginians. At 16 he entered the College of William and Mary, but his academic career was interrupted by the Revolution, in which he participated during the campaign of 1777 and 1778, rising from lieutenant to major and receiving a wound at the battle of Trenton. From 1780 to 1783 he studied law with Thomas Jefferson and formed the close and fruitful friendship that lasted until Jefferson's death.

The first phase of Monroe's political career, 1782–94, saw him established as a strong member of the Antifederalist faction. Guided by caution, strong localism, and fear of centralization, he served successively in the Virginia legislature, 1782, 1787–90; the Confederation Congress, 1783–86; the Annapolis conference of 1786; the Virginia convention to ratify the federal Constitution, 1788; and the U.S. Senate, 1790–94. His opposition to the Constitution before its ratification seems to have reflected the strong sectional sentiment of his district and his suspicion that a strengthened federal government would give up the American claim to navigation of the Mississippi. As a senator he drew even closer to Jefferson and severely criticized the Washington administration. He opposed the Bank of the United States and the appointments of Gouverneur Morris and John Jay as U.S. ministers, and he took a leading and somewhat equivocal part in the senatorial investigation of Alexander Hamilton's handling of the public funds.

Upon his appointment as minister to France, 1794, Monroe began his career as an important but seldom successful diplomat. Though at the outset of his mission he was relatively successful in securing redress for the grievances of American commerce and the hardships suffered by American citizens, he soon suffered from what the French considered to be the Anglophile policy of the American administration as evidenced in the Jay Treaty and other actions. During his last year in France he satisfied neither the authorities in Paris nor those at home. Recalled in 1796, he published a vindication of his mission, *A View of the Conduct of the Executive in the Foreign Affairs of the United States* (1797). He served as governor of Virginia, 1799–1802. He returned to France early in 1803 to cooperate with Robert R. Livingston in the discussions that led to the Louisiana Purchase. The next year found him in Madrid with Charles Pinckney to negotiate for the cession of East Florida, an almost impossible task that, given his discourteous treatment by the Spanish government, he had to abandon. Another extremely difficult assignment was given him in 1805—the settlement of a number of vexing disputes between the United States and Great Britain. The resulting treaty of 1806 did not outlaw the practice of impressment of seamen by Britain and was so unsatisfactory to Jefferson and Madison that it never reached the Senate. He was associated in this negotiation with William Pinkney.

Monroe's career in politics was renewed with his unsuccessful candidacy against James Madison for the presidency in 1808. The confidence of his Virginia supporters was never shaken by his diplomatic defeats and discomfitures. Refraining from criticizing Madison's administration and avoiding factional disputes within the Democratic-Republican party in his home state (which he again served as governor in January–March 1811), he was brought to a reconciliation with Madison, who offered him in 1811 the post of secretary of state. Disappointed as secretary in his hopes for a reconciliation with Great Britain, Monroe seems to have been convinced by December 1811 that war would come. When it did in June 1812, he was in a measure involved in General George Mathews' unsavory attempt to revolutionize West Florida, which activity he was compelled to disavow. Although he continued to justify the war because of British impressments even after the obnoxious British orders in council were withdrawn, he was willing with Madison to accept Russian mediation in 1813. He had little influence upon the peace negotiations, but he can be partly credited with the selection of the very able American delegation at Ghent. Throughout the war Monroe had strong presidential ambitions. American military victories at Plattsburg and New Orleans enhanced his personal prestige because he was also holding the post of secretary of war, August 1814–March 1815. In the congressional caucus of 1816, with administration support, he won the presidency by only 11 votes over William H. Crawford.

He had now reached the summit of his ambition. As chief executive, he showed a capacity for administration and for accurately interpreting the national mood. Few great domestic political issues confronted him in eight years of office. His policies were marked by a characteristic middle-of-the-road viewpoint, notably with regard to internal improvements, in the advocacy of which he modified his earlier strict constructionism ("Views on the Subject of Internal Improvements," 1822, and "Survey Act," 1824). Although his sympathies were naturally with the South in the struggle over the admission of Missouri, 1819–20, his conception of his presidential duties led him to abstain from all interference with the Missouri bill until he reluctantly signed it, undoubtedly the most momentous act of his administration. Despite the economic depression of 1819, Monroe had been almost unanimously reelected to the presidency in 1820. Political strength came through his abandonment of his earlier sectionalism and his choice of excellent advisers—J. C. Calhoun, William Wirt, W. H. Crawford, and particularly John Quincy Adams, to whom he gave large discretion while maintaining presidential supervision over foreign affairs.

In the field of foreign policy, several important settlements were made during his presidency: the Rush-Bagot agreement for limitation of armaments on the Great Lakes, 1817; liquidation of the Newfoundland and Labrador fisheries dispute, 1818; joint occupation of the Northwest, and (following Andrew Jackson's invasion of Florida, during which Monroe maintained a somewhat equivocal silence) the acquisition of Florida, 1819. Out of his slow recognition of the independence of the revolted Spanish colonies, March 1822, grew the events leading to his famous message of Dec. 2, 1823, enunciating what has come to be known as the Monroe Doctrine. Both the initiative and the responsibility for the famous declaration belong to Monroe, but the principle that the American continents were no longer subject to European colonization owes its origin to John Q. Adams. Upon leaving the presidency Monroe returned to private life in Virginia, became a visitor of the University of Virginia, 1828, and was president of the Virginia constitutional convention, 1829–30, wherein he supported the conservatives on suffrage and slavery.

Lacking high imagination, unpretentious in appearance, far from brilliant in speech, without any genuine graces, Monroe yet attained distinction. "Untiring application and indomitable perseverance" were a part of his character. Although the tribute to the soundness of his judgment which was applied to the rising Virginia politician by his wide circle of admirers seems not wholly deserved, it is difficult not to accept it with regard to his years in the presidency. By the doctrine which bears his name, he is indissolubly connected with one of the major dogmas of American foreign policy. While he promulgated nothing very novel, he consolidated and fortified existing views and gave expression to a growing popular sentiment in striking form. No colorless personality could have left behind him so favorable a judgment on the part of so many persons of such diverse views and temperaments as did Monroe. Less intellectual than either Jefferson or Madison, he surpassed them both as an administrator. If he can never be assigned a place among the great men who have held the presi-

dency, he must be numbered among the more useful and the more successful.

MONROE, MARILYN (*b.* *Norma Jean Mortensen, Los Angeles, Calif.*, 1926; *d.* *Brentwood, Calif.*, 1962), actress. Used surname Baker until 1946. Sex-symbol status originated in a full-length shot of her in the nude, which was sold as a calendar picture in 1950. Studied with Lee and Paula Strasberg of the Actors Studio in New York in the late 1950's. Earned recognition as a comedienne of high quality, but her love-goddess image was never erased. Married to Joe Di Maggio (1954) and Arthur Miller (1956–60). Symptoms of personal deterioration became increasingly evident about 1960; an autopsy determined that the cause of her death was an overdose of barbiturates. Films include *Niagara* (1953), *Gentlemen Prefer Blondes* (1953), *How to Marry a Millionaire* (1953), *The Seven Year Itch* (1955), *Bus Stop* (1956), *The Prince and the Showgirl* (1957), *Some Like it Hot* (1959), *Let's Make Love* (1960), and *The Misfits* (1961).

MONROE, PAUL (*b.* *North Madison, Ind.*, 1869; *d.* *Goshen, N.Y.*, 1947), educator, historian of education. B.S., Franklin College (Indiana), 1890; Ph.D., University of Chicago, 1897. Beginning as instructor in history at Teachers College, Columbia University, 1897, he became adjunct professor, 1902. He was named Barnard professor of education, 1925, and professor emeritus, 1935. Insisting on the highest standards of scholarship in his seminars, he was a principal factor in establishing history of education as a recognized discipline. He was also active in the administration of Teachers College and in international education. He was author of, among other books, *The Founding of the American Public School System* (1940), and editor in chief of the comprehensive and important *Cyclopedia of Education* (1911–13).

MONSKY, HENRY (*b.* *Omaha, Nebr.*, 1890; *d.* *New York, N.Y.*, 1947), lawyer, Jewish leader, philanthropist. LL.B., Creighton University, 1912. Practiced in Omaha. Active in the work of B'nai B'rith *post* 1911, he held various offices in that society, and was its international president, 1938–47. In 1943 he established the American Jewish Conference and served as its chairman until his death. He was active also in local and national nonsectarian charitable organizations, in work for reform, and in interfaith religious conferences.

MONTAGUE, ANDREW JACKSON (*b.* *Campbell Co.*, Va., 1862; *d.* *Urbanna, Va.*, 1937), lawyer, politician. Reforming Democratic governor of Virginia, 1902–06; congressman, 1913–37. Made a strong effort as governor to destroy the machine headed by Thomas S. Martin.

MONTAGUE, GILBERT HOLLAND (*b.* *Springfield, Mass.*, 1880; *d.* *New York, N.Y.*, 1961), lawyer and book collector. Studied at Harvard Law School (graduated, 1904). Practiced law in New York from 1904; established himself as a leading practitioner of antitrust law. His books include *Rise and Progress of the Standard Oil Company* (1903) and *Business Competition and the Law* (1917). From an extensive personal library, he donated many manuscripts and book collections to Harvard, including a fourteenth-century copy of the Magna Charta and more than 900 items of Emily Dickinson.

MONTAGUE, HENRY JAMES (*b.* *Staffordshire*[?], *England*, 1843; *d.* *San Francisco, Calif.*, 1878), actor. Stage name of Henry Mann. Made American debut at Wallack's Theatre, New York, 1874, and was an immediate success as a leading man.

MONTAGUE, WILLIAM PEPPERELL (*b.* *Chelsea, Mass.*, 1873; *d.* 1953), philosopher and educator. Studied at Harvard University, (Ph.D., 1898). Taught at Barnard College and Columbia (1903–47). A member of the school of the "new realism," Montague explored and developed variations of the reality of a world independent of thought; the possibility of knowing the world without endangering its independence; rejection of the thesis that all relations are internal in character; acceptance of scientific method as providing the normative model and foundation for knowledge; and the conviction that the universe is pluralistic. By incorporating Platonism, Montague concluded: "one high certainty that is quite philosophy's own: *Ideals are eternal things,* and the life that incarnates them attains an absolute value that time alone could not create and that death is powerless to destroy."

Montague liked to think of philosophy as a form of vision that should be logically precise, but held that rigorous science and imaginative metaphysics belong together.

MONTEFIORE, JOSHUA (*b. London, England, 1762; d. St. Albans, Vt., 1843*), lawyer, author, British officer. Immigrated to America at end of the War of 1812; practiced law, settling eventually in Vermont.

MONTEUX, PIERRE BENJAMIN (*b. Paris, France, 1875; d. Hancock, Maine, 1964*), orchestra conductor. Studied at the Conservatoire National de Paris (graduated, 1896). Principal conductor for Sergei Diaghilev's Ballet Russe (1911–14; 1916; 1924); conducted world premieres of *Petrouchka* (1911), *Daphnis et Chloé* (1912), *Le Sacre du Printemps* (1913), and *Le Rossignol* (1914). In French army (1914–16). Conductor with the Metropolitan Opera in New York (1917–19); with the Boston Symphony Orchestra (1919–24). Coconductor with Willem Mengelberg and Bruno Walter of the Concertgebouw Orchestra of Amsterdam (1924–34). Founder, conductor, and music director of the Orchestre Symphonique de Paris (1929–38). Founded the École Monteux in Paris in 1932. Principal conductor and musical director of the San Francisco Symphony (1936–52). Became a U.S. citizen in 1942. Principal conductor of the London Symphony (1961–64). Promoted such contemporary masters as Igor Stravinsky, Sergei Prokofiev, Arthur Honegger, Maurice Ravel, and Claude Debussy.

MONTGOMERY, DAVID HENRY (*b. Syracuse, N.Y., 1837; d. Cambridge, Mass., 1928*), writer of history textbooks, benefactor of Harvard.

MONTGOMERY, EDMUND DUNCAN (*b. Edinburgh, Scotland, 1835; d. near Hempstead, Tex., 1911*), physician, philosopher. Came to America, 1870; settled in Texas, 1872. Author of *Philosophical Problems in the Light of Vital Organization* (1907).

MONTGOMERY, GEORGE WASHINGTON (*b. Alicante, Spain, 1804; d. Washington, D.C., 1841*), diplomat, consular official, translator of Washington Irving's works into Spanish.

MONTGOMERY, JAMES (*b. Ashtabula Co., Ohio, 1814; d. Mound City, Kans., 1871*), Campbellite minister, Jayhawker, Union soldier.

MONTGOMERY, JAMES ALAN (*b. Germantown, Pa., 1866; d. Philadelphia, Pa., 1949*), Episcopal clergyman, Old Testament scholar. B.A., University of Pennsylvania, 1887; Ph.D., 1904. Graduated Philadelphia Divinity School, 1890; studied also in Germany; ordained priest, 1893. Taught at Philadelphia Divinity School, 1899–1935; at University of Pennsylvania, Semitics department, 1909–39; was long associated with the American Schools of Oriental Research (president, 1921–34). He also served as editor of the *Journal of Biblical Literature*, 1909–13, and of the *Journal of the American Oriental Society*, 1916–21, 1924. Among his many works, distinguished for linguistic skill, accuracy, and good judgment, his commentaries on the books of

Daniel and Kings in the International Critical Commentary series were contributions to the permanent literature of biblical scholarship.

MONTGOMERY, JOHN BERRIEN (*b. Allentown, N.J., 1794; d. Carlisle, Pa., 1873*), naval officer. Appointed midshipman, 1812; saw long and varied service at sea. Commanding USS *Portsmouth,* he raised American flag at San Francisco, July 9, 1846. Retired as captain, 1861, he served throughout Civil War as commodore on shore duty and was promoted rear admiral, 1866.

MONTGOMERY, RICHARD (*b. Co. Dublin, Ireland, 1738; d. Quebec, Canada, 1775*), soldier. Served in French and Indian War with British regular forces; sold his commission, 1772, and settled in New York; married Janet, daughter of Robert R. Livingston (1718–75). In full sympathy with the colonial cause, Montgomery was elected a member of the New York Provincial Congress, 1775; in June of the same year, he was appointed a Continental brigadier general. Appointed second in command to General Philip Schuyler in the expedition against Canada, he took full command on Schuyler's illness, captured Montreal, and in December joined the force under General Benedict Arnold at Point-aux-Trembles. The combined forces then laid siege to Quebec. Montgomery was killed on the last day of the year during the American assault on that city. He was a capable soldier of high personal character.

MONTGOMERY, THOMAS HARRISON (*b. New York, N.Y., 1873; d. 1912*), zoologist, educator. Taught at universities of Pennsylvania and Texas; noted for brilliant cytological investigations and studies of heredity.

MONTGOMERY, WILLIAM BELL (*b. Fairfield District, S.C., 1829; d. Mississippi, 1904*), agriculturist. Introduced new grasses and cattle breeds to Mississippi. Founded *Live Stock Journal,* 1875.

MONTRÉSOR, JAMES GABRIEL (*b. Fort William, Scotland, 1702; d. Teynham, Kent, England, 1776*), British military engineer. Served in America, 1754–60, as chief engineer to the forces; was skillful in adapting European systems of fortifications to frontier conditions.

MONTRÉSOR, JOHN (*b. Gibraltar, 1736; d. England, 1799*), British military engineer. Son of James G. Montrésor, with whom he came to America, 1754. Saw extensive scouting service in French and Indian War and Pontiac's War. Worked on surveying details and on improvement of fortifications at New York, Boston, and Philadelphia *post* 1766; commissioned chief engineer in America, 1775. During the Revolution, the British made little use of his long and valuable experience and he returned to England, 1778.

MOOD, FRANCIS ASBURY (*b. Charleston, S.C., 1830; d. Waco, Tex., 1884*), Methodist Episcopal, South, clergyman, educator.

MOODY, (ARTHUR EDSON) BLAIR (*b. New Haven, Conn., 1902; d. Ann Arbor, Mich., 1954*), journalist. Studied at Brown University. Reporter for the *Detroit News.* Covering world events during World War II, Moody's main base was Washington, D.C.; his regular columns analyzed the U.S. role in world affairs and the peacetime efforts to build a full-employment economy. Appointed U.S. senator to replace Arthur Vandenberg in 1951, Moody carried on the internationalist views of his predecessor. He ran unsuccessfully for reelection in 1952.

MOODY, DWIGHT LYMAN (*b. Northfield, Mass., 1837; d. Northfield, 1899*), evangelist. Accompanied by the organist and singer Ira D. Sankey, he preached to millions throughout urban America and the British Isles between 1873 and 1899. A layman of great business ability with early experience as a successful shoe salesman, Moody inspired businessmen as well as ministers. Unacademic, he yet commanded the admiring cooperation of university people. He founded Northfield Seminary, 1879, and Mount Hermon School, 1881, and stimulated Young Men's Christian Associations on college campuses as well as in Chicago, where, in 1860, he had resigned from business to become an independent city missionary. He believed in personal evangelism; his preaching was direct, forceful, intimate, with emphasis on God's fatherly love.

Moody, James (*b. New Jersey, 1744; d. Weymouth, Nova Scotia, Canada, 1809*), British spy during American Revolution. Rejecting the compulsory state oath of allegiance, 1777, Moody fled from Sussex Co. to Bergen Co., N.J., where he enlisted in General Cortlandt Skinner's Loyalist brigade and served, 1777–81. He spied on the troops of Washington, Sullivan, and Gates, achieving some small but spectacular successes, and was engaged in various abortive schemes to capture patriot officials and their public papers. After capture, 1780, and imprisonment, he escaped and was promoted to lieutenant, 1781. With impaired health he visited England, where he published a *Narrative* (1782, 1783) of his sufferings and exertions.

Moody, John (*b. Jersey City, N.J., 1868; d. La Jolla, Calif., 1958*), financial editor and publisher. Self-educated, Moody began on Wall Street as a clerk and securities analyst. In 1900 he published his *Manual of Industrial and Miscellaneous Securities*, a guide for investors and brokers. In 1905, Moody added railroads to his work; in 1919, he merged with Poor's, under which name the publication is still known. Moody also wrote *The Railroad Builders* (1919) and *The Masters of Capital* (1921), both of which are included in the Yale Chronicles of America series.

Moody, Paul (*b. Newbury, Mass., 1779; d. Lowell, Mass., 1831*), inventor of a number of valuable improvements in cotton-mill machinery. Associated *post* 1814 with Francis C. Lowell.

Moody, William Henry (*b. Newbury, Mass., 1853; d. Haverhill, Mass., 1917*), lawyer, cabinet officer, U.S. Supreme Court justice. Graduated Harvard, 1876; studied law in office of Richard H. Dana, Jr. Served with ability as district attorney, eastern district of Massachusetts, 1890–95; was congressman, Republican, from Massachusetts, 1895–1902. His service as member of the Appropriations Committee won him notice of President Theodore Roosevelt who became his close friend. Appointed U.S. secretary of the navy, 1902, he succeeded Philander C. Knox in 1904 as U.S. attorney general. Roosevelt's antitrust activities reached their high point while Moody held this post, 1904–06, and the president described his work as comparable to that of any other man who had ever held office. His antitrust activities aroused opposition to his appointment to the U.S. Supreme Court, but he was confirmed by the Senate in December 1906. Before his resignation because of ill health, 1910, Moody wrote a number of opinions of which the principal were his dissent in the Employer's Liability Cases and his majority opinion in *Twining* v. *New Jersey*.

Moody, William Vaughan (*b. Spencer, Ind., 1869; d. Colorado Springs, Colo., 1910*), poet, playwright, educator. Graduated Harvard, 1893; M.A., 1894. Taught English at University of Chicago, 1895–99 and 1901–07. Moody's lyric poetry and his dramas were written out of moral conviction and mental necessity; he was constantly striving to come to grips with the spirit of the age and to express his insights with force and beauty. He succeeded in his prose dramas in expressing philosophic ideas in contemporary terms and in bringing to the American theater new spiritual values. His first published book was a drama in verse, *A Masque of Judgment* (1900); he next published *Poems* (1901) and another essay in poetic drama, *The Fire-Bringer* (1904). His play *The Great Divide* (produced 1906) was at once recognized as an important advance in American drama and he moved to leadership among contemporary American dramatists with *The Faith Healer* (produced, Cambridge, Mass., 1909 and New York, 1910). Moody's early death cut short a career that might have risen to greatness, for he was a thinker as well as a conscientious artist.

Moon, Parker Thomas (*b. New York, N.Y., 1892; d. New York, 1936*), historian. Graduated Columbia, 1913; Ph.D., 1921. A specialist in international relations, Moon taught at Columbia *post* 1915.

Mooney, James (*b. Richmond, Ind., 1861; d. 1921*), ethnologist. Associated with the Bureau of American Ethnology, 1885–1921, Mooney was a sympathetic and able student of American Indian language, folklore, and material culture, in particular that of the Cherokee and the Kiowa. He took an active part in preparation of the *Handbook of American Indians* (edited F. W. Hodge, 1907–10).

Mooney, Thomas Joseph (*b. Chicago, Ill., 1882; d. San Francisco, Calif., 1942*), labor radical. Apprenticed as an ironmolder; became a socialist, 1907; settled in San Francisco, 1911. Identified with left-wing socialist factions, he was arrested with his wife, Warren K. Billings, and others, and charged with complicity in the fatal bombing on Steuart Street during the San Francisco Preparedness Day parade, July 22, 1916. In separate trials, Billings was sentenced to life imprisonment, Mrs. Mooney acquitted, and Mooney sentenced to death. Although it was later established that a key prosecution witness in Mooney's trial had perjured himself and was otherwise of bad character, a retrial was denied. In the long legal battle that ensued, Mooney's original left-wing defenders were joined by many concerned attorneys and others who felt that due process had been violated; his case also became an international left-wing cause. In November 1918 the governor of California commuted the sentence to life imprisonment. During the next 20 years Mooney's supporters continued to clamor for his release from prison, which was finally accomplished when Governor Culbert Olson pardoned him early in January 1939; that October, Billings was freed by commutation of sentence.

Mooney, William (*b. probably New York, N.Y., 1756; d. New York, 1831*), upholsterer, politician. A leader in founding the New York Tammany Society, 1786, he was chosen its first grand sachem, 1789.

Moore, Addison Webster (*b. Plainfield, Ind., 1866; d. London, England, 1930*), philosopher. Graduated DePauw University, 1890; Ph.D., University of Chicago, 1898. A teacher at the University of Chicago thereafter until his retirement as professor emeritus, 1929, Moore allied himself with the Chicago school of instrumental pragmatism, of which John Dewey was the creator. The most complete statement of his point of view is in *Pragmatism and Its Critics* (1910).

Moore, Alfred (*b. New Hanover Co., N.C., 1755; d. Bladen Co., N.C., 1810*), planter, Revolutionary soldier, U.S. Supreme Court justice. Son of Maurice Moore. North Carolina attorney general, 1782–91; shared leadership of the North Carolina bar with William R. Davie. Appointed associate justice of U.S. Supreme Court, 1799, he resigned, 1804.

Moore, Andrew (*b. near Staunton, Va., 1752; d. 1821*), lawyer, Revolutionary soldier, Virginia legislator. A leader in politics in the Valley section of Virginia, Moore was a principal supporter of James Madison; he served as congressman, Democratic-Republican, 1789–99 and 1804; U.S. senator, 1804–09. He was largely instrumental in the permanent establishment of the school which later became Washington and Lee University.

MOORE, ANNE CARROLL (*b. Limerick, Maine, 1871; d. New York, 1961*), librarian. Studied at the Pratt Institute Library School in Brooklyn, N.Y. (1895–96). Children's librarian at the Pratt Institute Free Library, 1897–1906, and superintendent of work with children at the New York Public Library, 1906–41. Known for her promotion of quality children's literature; her innovative programs became common in public libraries throughout the United States.

MOORE, ANNIE AUBERTINE WOODWARD (*b. Montgomery Co., Pa., 1841; d. Madison, Wis., 1929*), musician, student of Scandinavian music.

MOORE, (AUSTIN) MERRILL (*b. Columbia, Tenn., 1903; d. Quincy, Mass., 1957*), psychiatrist and poet. Studied at Vanderbilt University and Vanderbilt Medical School (M.D., 1928). Editor of *The Fugitive* (1922–25). Associated with Allen Tate, John Crowe Ransom, and Donald Davidson, Moore confined his poetry to the sonnet form. He became a practicing psychiatrist in Boston in 1935 and taught neurology and psychiatry at Harvard in the 1930's and 1940's. Combining medicine with poetry, Moore produced thousands of sonnets which appeared in various collections: *The Noise That Time Makes* (1929), *M: One Thousand Autobiographical Sonnets* (1938), and *Illegitimate Sonnets* (1950).

MOORE, BARTHOLOMEW FIGURES (*b. Halifax Co., N.C., 1801; d. 1878*), lawyer, North Carolina legislator and Unionist. A leader in the state convention of 1865–66, he was author of the 1866 constitution which failed of ratification.

MOORE, BENJAMIN (*b. Newtown, N.Y., 1748; d. Greenwich Village, N.Y., 1816*), Episcopal clergyman, Loyalist. Served without distinction as president pro tempore of King's College (Columbia), 1775–84, and as actual president of Columbia, 1801–11. Accepting the rectorship of Trinity Church, New York City, 1800, he was consecrated bishop of New York, 1801. Incapacitated by paralysis, 1811, his duties as bishop were assumed by his assistant, John H. Hobart.

MOORE, CHARLES (*b. Ypsilanti, Mich., 1855; d. Gig Harbor, Wash., 1942*), journalist, biographer, historian, city planner. B.A., Harvard, 1878. M.A., George Washington University, 1899; Ph.D., 1900. Engaged in journalism in Ypsilanti and Detroit, 1879–89; secretary of U.S. Senator James McMillan, 1889–1903; held various executive positions in business and industry, 1903–14. Thereafter, he served as, among other things, a member of the federal Fine Arts Commission, from 1910 and as its chairman, 1915–37. As secretary to Senator McMillan, he played a leading part in the establishment of the Senate Park Commission, 1901, and its work to revive the original L'Enfant plan for the development of Washington, D.C., in particular the creation of the mall from the Capitol to the Potomac River. He was active also in city-planning projects for Chicago and Detroit, and was author of, among other books, biographies of the architects Daniel Burnham and Charles F. McKim.

MOORE, CHARLES HERBERT (*b. New York, N.Y., 1840; d. Winchfield, England, 1930*), artist, educator. Taught principles of art at Harvard, 1874–1909; was first curator of Fogg Art Museum and its director, 1896–1909. Author of, among other works, *Development and Character of Gothic Architecture* (1890).

MOORE, CLARENCE LEMUEL ELISHA (*b. Bainbridge, Ohio, 1876; d. 1931*), mathematician. Graduated Ohio State, 1901; Ph.D., Cornell, 1904. Taught at Massachusetts Institute of Technology *post* 1904. Noted for his work in geometry, he was one of the first American mathematicians to recognize the importance of the methods of Ricci in the geometry of hyperspace.

MOORE, CLEMENT CLARKE (*b. New York, N.Y., 1779; d. Newport, R.I., 1863*), Hebrew scholar, poet. Son of Benjamin Moore. Graduated Columbia, 1798. A principal benefactor of the General Theological Seminary, New York City, Moore taught there, 1823–50. He is chiefly remembered for his ballad "A Visit from St. Nicholas," first published in the *Troy Sentinel*, Dec. 23, 1823, several times reprinted thereafter, and included in a collection of Moore's verse, *Poems* (1844).

MOORE, CLIFFORD HERSCHEL (*b. Sudbury, Mass., 1866; d. 1931*), classicist, professor of Greek and Latin. Graduated Harvard, 1889; Ph.D., University of Munich, 1897. Taught at Harvard, 1898–1931. *Post* 1918, he served with outstanding ability as dean of the Harvard Graduate School and of the Faculty of Arts and Sciences.

MOORE, EDWARD MOTT (*b. Rahway, N.J., 1814; d. Rochester, N.Y., 1902*), surgeon, teacher of medicine. Made original contributions in studies of fracture and dislocation; was first president, New York State Board of Health. M.D., University of Pennsylvania, 1838. Practiced and taught in a number of places, principally in Buffalo and Rochester, N.Y.

MOORE, EDWIN WARD (*b. Alexandria, Va., 1810; d. New York, N.Y., 1865*), naval officer. Served in U.S. Navy, 1825–39, when he accepted command of the navy of the Republic of Texas. After four years of stirring service against Mexico in the Gulf, he was suspended from command, 1843, and spent much of the rest of his life prosecuting claims against the governments of Texas and of the United States.

MOORE, ELIAKIM HASTINGS (*b. Marietta, Ohio, 1862; d. 1932*), mathematician. Graduated Yale, 1883; Ph.D., 1885; studied also at Berlin and Göttingen. Taught mathematics at Yale and Northwestern universities; headed Department of Mathematics at University of Chicago *post* 1892. Under his leadership, the department became one of the leading centers in America for teaching and research. His interest in integral equations led to the formulation of his so-called general analysis, a theory which included as special cases the classical integral equation theory and numerous other chapters of mathematics. Far ahead of his time, he set forth ideas which other writers have rediscovered and developed since his death.

MOORE, ELY (*b. near Belvidere, N.J., 1798; d. Lecompton, Kans., 1860*), printer, labor leader. Elected president of newly formed New York City General Trades' Union, 1833; edited its official organ, the *National Trades' Union*; was chairman of national convention of trade unions, New York, 1834. Running as a unionist with Tammany Hall support, he served as congressman from New York, 1835–39. Removing to Kansas *ca.* 1850, he held various federal offices until his death.

MOORE, FRANK (*b. Concord, N.H., 1828; d. Waverly, Mass., 1904*), author, editor. Son of Jacob B. Moore; brother of George H. Moore. Edited a number of useful compilations, which include *Songs and Ballads of the American Revolution* (1856), *Diary of the American Revolution* (1859–60), and *The Rebellion Record* (1861–68).

MOORE, FREDERICK RANDOLPH (*b. Prince William County, Va., 1857; d. New York, N.Y., 1943*), journalist, politician.

Born in slavery, he was educated in the public schools of the District of Columbia, became a messenger in the U.S. Treasury Department *ca.* 1875, and was a confidential aide to Secretary Daniel Manning, who employed him *post* 1887 in the Western National Bank. Removing to New York City, 1904, he was chosen by Booker T. Washington to serve as a traveling organizer for the National Negro Business League and as editor of the *Colored American Magazine.* In 1907 he became editor and part owner of the New York *Age,* the nation's leading black newspaper. Active in Republican politics, he served as a delegate to national conventions and was twice elected to the New York City Board of Aldermen, 1927 and 1929. Retaining his early faith in the ideal of a thriving black capitalist economy and society, he also supported the progressive interracial social service organizations at work in New York City.

MOORE, GABRIEL (*b. Stokes Co., N.C., 1785[?]; d. probably Caddo, Tex., 1845[?]*), lawyer, Alabama legislator. Removed to Huntsville, then in Mississippi Territory, *ca.* 1810. A leader of the Jacksonian faction, he served as congressman from Alabama, 1821–29, and as governor of the state, 1829–31. He advocated the graduation system for the sale of public lands and opposed nullification; locally, he supported beginning of canal construction around Muscle Shoals and the opening of the state university. While U.S. senator, 1831–37, he broke with the Jackson forces and so ended his political career.

MOORE, GEORGE FLEMING (*b. Elbert Co., Ga., 1822; d. Washington, D.C., 1883*), lawyer, Confederate soldier. Settled in Texas, 1846. Associate justice and chief justice, Texas Supreme Court, 1862–67 and 1874–81. An independent and courageous judge, he excelled in equity cases.

MOORE, GEORGE FOOT (*b. West Chester, Pa., 1851; d. 1931*), theologian, historian of religions. Studied at Yale and Union Theological Seminary; was Presbyterian pastor at Zanesville, Ohio, 1878–83; Old Testament professor at Andover Theological Seminary, 1884–1901; professor of the history of religion at Harvard, 1902–28. Eminent as a critical scholar in the fields of Hebrew and the Old Testament, he was assistant editor of the *Andover Review,* 1884–93, and editor of the *Harvard Theological Review,* 1908–14 and 1921–31. His chief works include *Critical and Exegetical Commentary on Judges* (1895), *History of Religions* (1913–19), and *Judaism in the First Centuries of the Christian Era* (1927–30).

MOORE, GEORGE HENRY (*b. Concord, N.H., 1823; d. 1892*), librarian, historian, bibliographer. Son of Jacob B. Moore; brother of Frank Moore. Active in work of New-York Historical Society, 1841–91; superintendent of Lenox Library, New York, N.Y., *post* 1872.

MOORE, GRACE (*b. Slabtown, Tenn., 1901; d. Copenhagen, Denmark, 1947*), singer. After early engagements in a nightclub and in musical comedies, she studied for a time in Europe and was encouraged by Mary Garden. She made her Metropolitan Opera debut on Feb. 7, 1928, as Mimi in *La Bohème.* After touring abroad and a second season at the Metropolitan, she starred in several minor Hollywood films. She then resumed her operatic career, appearing also in a Broadway operetta *The Dubarry* (1932). In 1934 she won acclaim for her performance in the film *One Night of Love,* which pioneered in its use of operatic excerpts. Critical notices of her work were mixed throughout her professional life, but she was sensationally successful with the public. Among her other notable roles were Manon, Marguerite, Madame Butterfly, and the title role in Charpentier's *Louise.*

MOORE, SIR HENRY (*b. Vere, Jamaica, British West Indies, 1713; d. New York, 1769*), colonial official. Educated at Eton

and University of Leiden. Served successively as member of Jamaica Assembly, as councilman, and as secretary of the island; was acting governor, 1756–62, in which time he quelled a black insurrection. Created baronet, 1764, he was appointed governor of New York, 1765, and served until his death. Patient and conciliatory during the Stamp Act disturbances, he was accused of "caressing the demagogues." Thereafter, he devoted time to settlement of boundary disputes with neighboring provinces and to Indian policy; his controversy with the New York Assembly over its failure to pass the quartering bill led to the prorogation of the assembly, December 1766, and to the restraining act, signed by the king in the summer of 1767.

MOORE, HENRY LUDWELL (*b. Moore's Rest, Md., 1869; d. Cornwall, N.Y., 1958*), economist. Studied at Randolph-Macon College, at Johns Hopkins University (Ph.D., 1896), and at the University of Vienna. Taught at Smith College (1898–1902), and at Columbia University (1902–29). A founder of the new field of econometrics, Moore used the methods of economic theory, mathematics, and statistics in the analysis of economic phenomena and the testing of theoretical hypotheses. Major works include *Laws and Wages: An Essay in Statistical Economics* (1911), *Forecasting the Yield and Price of Cotton* (1917), and *Synthetic Economics* (1929).

MOORE, JACOB BAILEY (*b. Andover, N.H., 1797; d. Bellows Falls, Vt., 1853*), New Hampshire journalist, printer. Brother of John W. Moore; father of George H. and Frank Moore. Removed to New York City, 1839. After holding federal offices in Washington, D.C., and New Hampshire, he was elected librarian of New-York Historical Society, 1848. He resigned in 1849 to set up the U.S. post office in California and served as deputy postmaster, San Francisco, 1850–53.

MOORE, JAMES (*b. probably Ireland, date unknown; d. Charleston, S.C., 1706*), Indian trader, colonial official. Settled at Charleston *ca.* 1675; was soon prominent in movements of protest against the proprietors. Elected governor of South Carolina by the council, 1700, he served until 1703. Ambitious and adventurous, he led the force which besieged St. Augustine during Queen Anne's War.

MOORE, JAMES (*b. New Hanover Co., N.C., 1737; d. Wilmington, N.C., 1777*), Revolutionary soldier, North Carolina provincial legislator. Brother of Maurice Moore. Directed American maneuvers in campaign ending in victory at Moore's Creek Bridge, February 1776.

MOORE, JAMES (*b. probably Virginia, 1764; d. Lexington, Ky., 1814*), Episcopal clergyman, educator. Removed to Kentucky *ante* April 1792; was ordained to Episcopal ministry, 1794. Served *post* 1792 as principal of Transylvania Seminary and of Kentucky Academy; headed both schools when united under name of Transylvania University, 1799–1804. Became first resident Episcopal rector in Kentucky, 1809.

MOORE, JAMES EDWARD (*b. Clarksville, Pa., 1852; d. 1918*), surgeon. M.D., Bellevue Hospital Medical College, 1873. Practiced in Minneapolis, Minn., *post* 1882; taught orthopedics and clinical surgery at University of Minnesota from 1888 until his death. Author of *Orthopedic Surgery* (1898).

MOORE, JOHN (*b. England, ca. 1659; d. Philadelphia, Pa., 1732*), colonial official. Immigrated *ca.* 1680 to South Carolina, where he held provincial offices; removed to Philadelphia *ca.* 1696. Appointed advocate of the court of vice admiralty for Pennsylvania and West Jersey, 1698, he and his friend Robert Quarry, who was the judge of this court, were closely associated in leadership of the Anglican party and in efforts to enforce the acts of trade and navigation. King's attorney general for Pennsylvania, 1700–04, Moore continued to serve in lucrative provincial posts until his death, despite his opposition and disloyalty to the proprietors and unpopularity with the people of Pennsylvania. He belongs in the same class with Edward Randolph, Joseph Dudley, and other early American Tories who combined a lust for office with a sincere devotion to the cause of imperial unity.

MOORE, JOHN (*b. Rosmead, Ireland, 1834; d. 1901*), Roman Catholic clergyman. Immigrated to Charleston, S.C., 1848; ordained in Rome, 1860; served as curate and rector in Charleston, 1860–77. Able and liberal bishop of St. Augustine, Fla., 1877–1901.

MOORE, JOHN BASSETT (*b. Smyrna, Del., 1860; d. New York, N.Y., 1947*), international lawyer, jurist. Attended University of Virginia, 1877–80, leaving for reasons of health without a degree; continued study of law in office of former Delaware state district attorney and was admitted to the bar in 1883. Two years later he successfully took the examination for a clerkship in the Department of State. As clerk in the Diplomatic Bureau, 1885–86, and as third assistant secretary, 1886–91, he was exposed to every major item of American diplomatic and consular business. In addition, he developed his scholarly talents by helping Francis Wharton compile A *Digest of the International Law of the United States* (1886) and edit *The Revolutionary Diplomatic Correspondence of the United States* (1889), which was completed by Moore after Wharton's death.

In 1891 Moore became the first Hamilton Fish professor of law and diplomacy at Columbia University. His *History and Digest of International Arbitrations* (1898) was followed by the *Digest of International Law* (1906). His interest in American foreign policy led to the publication of *American Diplomacy: Its Spirit and Achievements* (1905) and *Four Phases of American Development* (1908). Seeing the emerging world role of the United States, he stressed the need for a concurrent expansion of its diplomatic machinery and urged abandonment of isolationism in favor of participation in a variety of world legal, economic, and cultural associations. In 1898 he accepted appointment as assistant secretary of state. As an official foreign policy adviser during the early 1900's, Moore was forced by events to reconcile his belief in international legality with the realities of international politics, especially in regard to Latin America. He helped draft the first Hay-Pauncefote Treaty, 1900, and in 1903 provided Theodore Roosevelt with legal justification for a planned seizure of the Isthmus of Panama. In 1910 he accepted limited assignments as delegate to the Fourth International Conference of American States. In 1912 President Taft named Moore a member of the Permanent Court of Arbitration, The Hague. He returned to the State Department as counselor in 1913, but resigned after one year. Maintaining his faith in the value of international adjudication, he supported the establishment of the Permanent Court of International Justice (the World Court) at The Hague. Yet he opposed its parent organization, the League of Nations. From 1921 to 1928 he was the first American judge of the World Court. In 1928 Moore retired from the court (he had retired from Columbia University in 1924) in order to devote full time to the preparation of his last major editorial work, *International Adjudications* (1936).

MOORE, JOHN TROTWOOD (*b. Marion, Ala., 1858; d. Nashville, Tenn., 1929*), journalist. Resident of Tennessee *post* 1885. Author of *The Bishop of Cottontown* (1906), *Uncle Wash, His Stories* (1910), *The Gift of the Grass* (1911), and other authentic, regional novels, tales, and verse.

MOORE, JOHN WEEKS (*b. probably Andover, N.H., 1807; d. Manchester, N.H., 1889*), printer, newspaper publisher, editor of musical journals and collections. Brother of Jacob B. Moore.

MOORE, JOSEPH EARLE (*b. Philadelphia, Pa., 1892; d. Baltimore, Md., 1957*), physician, educator. Studied at the University of Kansas and Johns Hopkins Medical School (M.D., 1916). During World War I, Moore served in France with the venereal disease control facilities; after the war, he returned to Johns Hopkins and became associated with the syphilis division of the Medical School and Hospital; director from 1929 until 1957. Major works include *The Modern Treatment of Syphilis* (1933) and *Penicillin in Syphilis*, written after World War II. Instrumental in making the study and treatment of syphilis a more rational affair. Moore was also one of the first to use an outpatient clinic for research.

MOORE, JOSEPH HAINES (*b. Wilmington, Ohio, 1878; d. Oakland, Calif., 1949*), astronomer. B.A., Wilmington College, 1897. Ph.D., Johns Hopkins University, 1903. Appointed assistant in spectroscopy to William W. Campbell at Lick Observatory of University of California, 1897, he remained at Lick until 1945; he became assistant director in 1936 and director in 1942. From 1945 to 1948 he taught courses in astronomy at the University of California, Berkeley. During the period 1909–13 he was astronomer in charge of the observatory's D. O. Mills station in Chile. He collaborated with W. W. Campbell in the Lick catalog of radial velocities of stars brighter than visual magnitude 5.51 and was solely or in part responsible for other catalogs of fundamental value in astronomy.

MOORE, MAURICE (*b. New Hanover Co., N.C., 1735; d. 1777*), North Carolina jurist and provincial legislator, Revolutionary patriot. Brother of James Moore (1737–77); father of Alfred Moore. Initially sympathetic toward the Regulator movement, he served as a judge at the special court in Hillsboro that sentenced 12 Regulators to death after the May 1771 battle of Alamance. Thereafter, however, he opposed Governor Tryon's policy toward the insurgents and actively promoted a policy of leniency toward their leaders. A member of several important committees in the patriot interest *post* 1775, he was too conservative to approve actual separation from Great Britain.

MOORE, NATHANIEL FISH (*b. Newtown, N.Y., 1782; d. 1872*), scholar, librarian, author, educator. Nephew of Benjamin Moore. Graduated Columbia, 1802; taught classical languages there, 1817–35, and served as president, 1842–49.

MOORE, NICHOLAS. *See* MORE, NICHOLAS.

MOORE, PHILIP NORTH (*b. Connersville, Ind., 1849; d. St. Louis, Mo., 1930*), mining engineer. Did important work in stimulating production of strategic minerals through War Minerals Committee, 1917.

MOORE, RICHARD BISHOP (*b. Cincinnati, Ohio, 1871; d. Lafayette, Ind., 1931*), chemist. Son of William T. Moore. Educated mainly abroad; studied under William Ramsay at London, 1886–90, and became interested in rare gases and radium. After teaching chemistry at several institutions, he entered U.S. government service, 1911, and went with the Bureau of Mines as physical chemist, 1912. In government service until 1923, he supervised preparation of the first radium salts produced in the United States, was among the first to advocate the use of helium in balloons and airships, and as chief chemist of the Bureau, *post* 1919, organized the cryogenic laboratory in Washington and directed work of reducing the cost of helium production. *Post* 1926, he served as professor of chemistry and dean of the school of science at Purdue University.

MOORE, RICHARD CHANNING (*b.* *New York, N.Y., 1762; d. Lynchburg, Va., 1841*), Episcopal clergyman, physician. Zealous and strongly evangelical, he was consecrated bishop of Virginia, 1814, and served until his death. Together with John J. Hobart and Alexander V. Griswold, he is credited with reconstructing the Episcopal church in the United States both in spirit and in character.

MOORE, SAMUEL PRESTON (*b.* *Charleston, S.C., 1813; d. Richmond, Va., 1889*), army surgeon. Graduated Medical College of South Carolina, 1834; commissioned, U.S. Army assistant surgeon, 1835. After long service on the western frontiers and in the Mexican War, he resigned his commission early in 1861 and accepted the post of surgeon general of the Confederate army, in which he served until 1865. Strict and exacting, he did the best he could in a most difficult task.

MOORE, THOMAS OVERTON (*b.* *Sampson Co., N.C., 1804; d. near Alexandria, La., 1876*), planter. Removed to Louisiana, 1829, where he became an important sugar grower. As Democratic governor of Louisiana, 1860–64, he led in making his state a member of the Confederacy and in securing its resources for Confederate use even after the Union seizure of New Orleans and its neighborhood.

MOORE, THOMAS PATRICK (*b.* *Charlotte Co., Va., 1796[?]; d. Harrodsburg, Ky., 1853*), lawyer, soldier in War of 1812 and Mexican War, Kentucky politician and legislator. An ardent Jacksonian, he served as U.S. minister to Colombia, 1829–33, where he obtained important commercial concessions for the United States.

MOORE, VERANUS ALVA (*b.* *Hounsfield, N.Y., 1859; d. 1931*), pathologist, leader in veterinary science. Graduated Cornell, 1887; M.D., Columbian (now George Washington University) Medical School, 1890. Professor of comparative pathology, bacteriology, and meat inspection in the veterinary college at Cornell, 1896–1929, he also held the position of dean, 1908–29. Under his administration the college became outstanding and Moore won international reputation in his fields. His researches were of incalculable value to the livestock industry.

MOORE, VICTOR FREDERICK (*b.* *Hammonton, N.J., 1876; d. East Islip, N.Y., 1962*), actor. Began his career in vaudeville, where he perfected the comic timing he later brought to Broadway roles. His special gift was for playing politicians, and he received great acclaim for his portrayal of the ineffectual, but lovable, Alexander Throttlebottom in George Gershwin's *Of Thee I Sing* (1931). Other musical comedy appearances included *Let 'Em Eat Cake* (1933), *Anything Goes* (1934), *Leave It to Me* (1938), and *Louisiana Purchase* (1940). Won the New York Drama Critics Circle Award for his portrayal of Gramps in Paul Osborn's *On Borrowed Time* (1938). Film appearances included *We're Not Married* (1952) and *The Seven Year Itch* (1955).

MOORE, WILLIAM (*b.* *Philadelphia, Pa., 1699; d. near Valley Forge, Pa., 1783*), Pennsylvania provincial legislator and jurist. Son of John Moore (*ca.* 1659–1732). Opposed Quaker-dominated Assembly over frontier defense, 1755–58; was a passive Loyalist during Revolution.

MOORE, WILLIAM (*b.* *Philadelphia, Pa., ca. 1735; d. Philadelphia, 1793*), merchant, Revolutionary patriot. Vice president, 1779–81, and president, 1782, of Pennsylvania supreme executive council. A conservative constitutionalist, he was a jealous guardian of executive privilege and was active in promoting plans to solve Pennsylvania's financial difficulties.

MOORE, WILLIAM HENRY (*b.* *Utica, N.Y., 1848; d. New York, N.Y., 1923*), lawyer, capitalist, promoter. After successful practice of corporation law in partnership with his brother in Chicago, Moore turned *post* 1887 to the development and exploitation of industrial mergers. The first important venture of the Moore brothers, who continued to work together, was the reorganization of the Diamond Match Co., in whose stock they formed a pool; after much manipulation and publicity the price of the stock was forced up with the intention of unloading it at top price on the unwary. Failure of this scheme resulted in the closing of the Chicago Exchange, August 1896. Forced out of Diamond Match, Moore organized a merger of various biscuit and cracker companies into the National Biscuit Co., 1898, which was immensely successful, achieving as it did a monopoly control of 90 percent of the nation's business in that commodity. Turning to the steel industry, he organized in rapid succession, 1898–99, the American Tin Plate Co., the National Steel Co., and the American Steel Hoop Co. Although the stock of all three companies was plentifully watered and represented anticipated profits rather than actual properties, it was oversubscribed. After failure in attempting to buy the Carnegie-Frick properties, the Moores created the American Sheet and Steel Co., 1900, and the American Can Co., 1901. When J. P. Morgan succeeded in buying out Carnegie and launching the new U.S. Steel Corporation, 1901, the Moore companies were included in the merger and their sale brought the brothers enormous wealth. Later activities of the Moores in railroad properties were equally daring and unscrupulous. Their looting of the Rock Island system resulted in their arraignment by the Interstate Commerce Commission, 1916.

MOORE, WILLIAM THOMAS (*b.* *Henry Co., Ky., 1832; d. Orlando, Fla., 1926*), clergyman of the Disciples of Christ, educator, promoter of missionary work.

MOORE, ZEPHANIAH SWIFT (*b.* *Palmer, Mass., 1770; d. 1823*) Congregational clergyman, educator. Graduated Dartmouth, 1793; served as pastor at Leicester, Mass., 1797–1811. Professor of learned languages at Dartmouth, 1811–15, he was then elected president of Williams College, a post which he filled with high efficiency until 1821. Chosen as first president of Amherst College, he saw that institution successfully under way before his death in office.

MOOREHEAD, WILLIAM GALLOGLY (*b.* *near Rix Mills, Ohio, 1836; d. Xenia, Ohio, 1914*), United Presbyterian clergyman, biblical scholar. Taught at Xenia Theological Seminary, and served as its president, 1899–1914.

MOORHEAD, JAMES KENNEDY (*b.* *Halifax, Pa., 1806; d. Pittsburgh, Pa., 1884*), canal builder, pioneer in commercial telegraphy, politician. President *post* 1846 of Monongahela Navigation Co.; president, Atlantic and Ohio Telegraph Co. and subsidiary companies *post* 1853. Congressman, Republican, from Pennsylvania, 1859–69.

MOOSMÜLLER, OSWALD WILLIAM (*b.* *Aidling, Bavaria, 1832; d. Wetaug, Ill., 1901*), Roman Catholic clergyman, Benedictine. Came to America, 1852; was educated at St. Vincent's Abbey, Latrobe, Pa.; ordained, 1856. Led an active, wandering life, during which he held many positions as an official of his order and as missionary and army chaplain. Organized Cluny monastery, Wetaug, Ill., 1892.

MORAIS, SABATO (*b.* *Leghorn, Italy, 1823; d. 1897*), rabbi of Mikveh Israel congregation, Philadelphia, Pa., 1851–97. A founder of the Jewish Theological Seminary, New York City, 1886, he served it as president of the faculty and professor of the Bible until his death.

Moran, Benjamin (*b. Chester Co., Pa., 1820; d. England, 1886*), diplomat. Served as clerk, secretary, and chargé d'affaires at the U.S. legation in London, 1853–74, and as U.S. minister resident to Portugal, 1874–76. On discontinuance of his office, he became chargé d'affaires at Lisbon, resigning in 1882. Moran's journal (covering 1857–74) provides invaluable material on contemporary relations between the United States and Great Britain. A staunch Unionist, Moran played no little part in preventing open rupture with Great Britain during the Civil War.

Moran, Daniel Edward (*b. Orange, N.J., 1864; d. Mendham, N.J., 1937*), civil engineer, specialist in foundation work.

Moran, Edward (*b. Bolton, England, 1829; d. 1901*), marine painter. Brother of Peter and Thomas Moran. Came to America, 1844; worked as a weaver; was encouraged to paint by several landscapists in Philadelphia. Removing to New York City, 1872, he was a conspicuous figure in the art life there until his death. His important group of 13 large paintings illustrating salient episodes in American history is owned by the Pennsylvania Museum of Art and betrays influence of the British painters Turner and Stanfield.

Moran, Eugene Francis (*b. Brooklyn, N.Y., 1872; d. Palm Beach, Fla., 1961*), tugboat and shipping industry executive. Joined the Moran Towing and Transportation Company, which had been founded by his father, in 1889; president, 1906–40; chairman of the board from 1930. Member (and for fifty years chairman) of the Committee on Rivers, Harbors and Piers of the Maritime Association of the Port of New York. Wrote, with Louis Reed, an autobiography entitled *Tugboat* (1956).

Moran, Peter (*b. Bolton, England, 1841; d. Philadelphia, Pa., 1914*), landscape and animal painter, etcher. Brother of Edward and Thomas Moran. Came to America as a child; studied with his elder brothers, who had become established as painters. Won high repute in field of animal painting and as one of the best American workers in etching and drypoint of his time.

Moran, Thomas (*b. Bolton, England, 1837; d. Santa Barbara, Calif., 1926*), landscape painter, etcher. Brother of Edward and Peter Moran. Came to America as a child; was apprenticed to a wood engraver in Philadelphia. Began to paint under tutelage of his brother Edward. In England, 1862, he copied Turner's pictures, whose influence remained with him throughout his life. After a later European tour, he returned to the United States and in 1871 accompanied the U.S. Geological Expedition under F. V. Hayden to the Yellowstone region; in 1873, he made an expedition to the Grand Canyon of the Colorado. Panoramic landscapes of the Yellowstone and Colorado canyons which he painted were purchased by Congress and are of importance as the most adequate pictorial records of the scenery of those then unfamiliar regions. His success with these and similar Far West subjects was owing in large measure to his assimilation of the grand style of Turner, with its daring color, visible atmosphere, and splendor of effect. He did excellent work also as an illustrator, and was an etcher and original lithographer of more than common merit.

Morawetz, Victor (*b. Baltimore, Md., 1859; d. Charleston, S.C., 1938*), lawyer, specialist in railroad and corporation law.

Mordecai, Alfred (*b. Warrenton, N.C., 1804; d. Philadelphia, Pa., 1887*), soldier, engineer. Graduated West Point, 1823. After serving with great ability as an engineer and ordnance expert, he resigned from the army in May 1861 on the conscientious ground that he could fight against neither his country nor his state. Thereafter, he worked as an engineer in railroad construction and as an official of canal and coal companies controlled by the Pennsylvania Railroad.

Mordecai, Moses Cohen (*b. Charleston, S.C., 1804; d. Baltimore, Md., 1888*), merchant, shipowner, Charleston official and South Carolina legislator. Removed to Baltimore, Md., 1865, where he recouped losses suffered in the Civil War.

More, Nicholas (*b. England, date unknown; d. Moreland Township, Philadelphia Co., Pa., 1689*), Pennsylvania jurist. Immigrated to Pennsylvania, 1682. Appointed chief justice of Pennsylvania and the lower counties (Delaware), 1684, he became involved in a dispute with the Pennsylvania Assembly which ended in the first impeachment trial in American history, May 1685. The provincial council refused to sanction the impeachment proceedings; he was retained in office and in 1686 was appointed one of five commissioners who were to act as the executive of the province. His health failed and he was unable to serve.

More, Paul Elmer (*b. St. Louis, Mo., 1864; d. Princeton, N.J., 1937*), literary critic, philosopher. Graduated Washington University, 1887; M.A., 1892. M.A., Harvard, 1893. After teaching for a short time, he retired to Shelburne, N.H., for two years of study and meditation, 1898–1900. He then became successively literary editor of the *Independent* and the New York *Evening Post*, and editor of the *Nation*, 1904–14. From 1914 until his retirement in 1934, he gave lectures and graduate seminars at Princeton University. His penetrating, judicious essays in criticism are embodied in the *Shelburne Essays* (8 vols., 1904–21) and *New Shelburne Essays* (3 vols., 1928–36). Associated in the public mind with his lifelong friend Irving Babbitt as a leader of the crusade for the "New Humanism," More regarded himself as the spokesman of enduring tradition in literature; he sought to evaluate given authors in relation to the stream of historical tendency. His final position in religious philosophy was a sort of working compromise between Platonism and Christianity.

Moreau de Saint-Méry, Médéric-Louis-Élie (*b. Fort Royal, Martinique, 1750; d. Paris, France, 1819*), publisher, historian, French Revolutionary politician. Resident in Philadelphia, Pa., 1794–98, as a refugee from revolutionary excesses in Paris, he set up as a bookseller and stationer; his shop became the rendezvous of French émigrés. He published in excellent style a number of books and pamphlets written by him or by his friends, among them his own two books of the history of Santo Domingo. Threatened with deportation under the Alien Act, he returned to France in August 1798, where he was prominent as a diplomat and official in the early days of Napoleon's rule.

Moreau-Lislet, Louis Casimir Elisabeth (*b. Cap Français, Santo Domingo, 1767; d. New Orleans, La., 1832*), Louisiana jurist and legislator. Coauthor of several valuable works on the criminal and civil law of Louisiana.

Morehead, Charles Slaughter (*b. Nelson Co., Ky., 1802; d. near Greenville, Miss., 1868*), lawyer, Kentucky legislator. Congressman, Whig, from Kentucky; 1847–51; governor, Know-Nothing, 1855–59. Approved Kentucky neutrality, 1861; was imprisoned briefly, 1861, for his public criticism of cutting off trade with the South.

Morehead, James Turner (*b. near Shepherdsville, Ky., 1797; d. Covington, Ky., 1854*), lawyer, Kentucky legislator. National Republican governor of Kentucky, 1834–36; U.S. senator, Whig, 1841–47. A consistent supporter of the policies of Henry Clay.

Morehead, John Motley (*b. Pittsylvania Co., Va., 1796; d. 1866*), lawyer, North Carolina legislator and railroad promoter. Whig governor of North Carolina, 1841–45.

Morehead, John Motley (*b. Spray, N.C., 1870; d. Rye, N.Y., 1965*), chemical engineer, inventor, industrialist, and philanthropist. Studied at the University of North Carolina at Chapel Hill (graduated, 1891). Devised the first large-scale commercial means of producing calcium carbide in 1892. Designed an apparatus for analyzing gases in 1899; published *Analysis of Industrial Gases* in 1900. Engineer with Union Carbide, 1897–1925, in charge of technical research and development of new processes; consultant engineer, 1933–65. Mayor of Rye, N.Y. (1925–30), and minister to Sweden (1930–33). Established the John Motley Morehead Foundation at the University of North Carolina in 1945.

Morehouse, Henry Lyman (*b. Stanfordville, N.Y., 1834; d. Brooklyn, N.Y., 1917*), Baptist clergyman, promoter of Baptist home mission work.

Morehouse, Ward (*b. Savannah, Ga., 1899; d. New York, N.Y., 1966*), theater critic, newspaper columnist, and playwright. Reporter for the *Atlanta Journal* (1916–19); for the *New York Tribune* and the *New York Herald-Tribune* (to 1926). Wrote "Broadway After Dark" column for the *New York Sun* (1926–50), and for the *New York World-Telegram and Sun* (1950–56). Broadway critic and columnist for the S. I. Newhouse newspaper chain (1956–66). Wrote plays *Gentlemen of the Press* (1928, adapted for motion picture, 1929), *Miss Quis* (1937), and *U.S. 90* (1941). Worked as a scenarist for Universal, Warner Brothers, and Paramount Pictures during the late 1920's and early 1930's. Author of books that established him as a theater historian as well as a critic, including *Matinee Tomorrow: Fifty Years of Our Theater* (1949), *George M. Cohan: Prince of the American Theater* (1943), and *Just the Other Day* (1953).

Morell, George Webb (*b. Cooperstown, N.Y., 1815; d. Scarborough, N.Y., 1883*), engineer, lawyer, Union major general. Grandson of Samuel B. Webb.

Morey, Samuel (*b. Hebron, Conn., 1762; d. Fairlee, Vt., 1843*), lumberman, contractor, inventor. Built and operated several vessels driven by steam, 1793–97; claimed that his ideas were stolen by Robert Fulton. Received one of first American patents for an internal combustion engine, 1826.

Morfit, Campbell (*b. Herculaneum, Mo., 1820; d. near London, England, 1897*), pioneer industrial chemist. Taught applied chemistry at University of Maryland, 1854–58; assisted James C. Booth in preparing *The Encyclopedia of Chemistry* (1850) and was sole author of a number of technical treatises on fertilizers, the manufacture of paper and soap, and oil refining. Resided in England *post* 1861.

Morford, Henry (*b. New Monmouth, N.J., 1823; d. 1881*), journalist. Author of a number of successful travel guides—*The Rest of Don Juan* (1846), a continuation of Byron's poem; and three novels which attempted to express the mood of the Civil War: *Shoulder-Straps* (1863), *The Days of Shoddy* (1863), and *The Coward* (1864).

Morgan, Abel (*b. Cardiganshire, South Wales, 1673; d. Pennsylvania, 1722*), Baptist clergyman. Immigrated to Philadelphia, 1712; became a leader among Pennsylvania Baptists and also established churches in Delaware and New Jersey. Author of the first real concordance to the Welsh Bible, published posthumously (1730).

Morgan, Anne (*b. Highland Falls, N.Y., 1873; d. Mount Kisco, N.Y., 1952*), war relief organizer. The third daughter of J. Pierpont Morgan, Anne Morgan was privately educated. She became active in women's organizations, founding, with Mrs. August Belmont, the Working Girls Vacation Association in 1910, later the American Women's Association. She was president, 1928–43. After World War I, Morgan organized extensive relief programs for France. She was awarded the Croix de Guerre in 1917 and was the first American woman to be made a commander of the Legion of Honor in 1932. After World War II, she again organized efforts to aid the French.

Morgan, Charles (*b. Killingworth, now Clinton, Conn., 1795; d. New York, N.Y., 1878*), shipping magnate, railroad owner. Built up successful line of steamers plying to Gulf ports of the United States and to Mexico *post* 1835; with C. K. Garrison, engaged in a commercial war against Cornelius Vanderbilt and George Law to secure control of the Nicaragua Transit, 1853–55. After profiting heavily by the Civil War, Morgan started the Morgan Line from New York to New Orleans and extended his activities to include Texas railroads. By the time of his death, he had established a virtual monopoly of Texas transportation.

Morgan, Charles Hill (*b. Rochester, N.Y., 1831; d. Worcester, Mass., 1911*), engineer. Designed an automatic machine for making paper bags, 1860, whose success placed paper-bag manufacturing on a commercial footing for the first time. With Fred H. Daniels, patented improvements in wire-rolling mills which were combined in the Morgan Mill. Founded Morgan Construction Co. for manufacture of rolling-mill machinery, 1891.

Morgan, Daniel (*b. probably Hunterdon Co., N.J., 1736; d. 1802*), Revolutionary soldier. Removed as a youth to the Shenandoah Valley of Virginia; accompanied Braddock's expedition as an independent wagoner, 1755; served as lieutenant in Pontiac's War. Commissioned captain of Virginia riflemen, June 1775, he was taken prisoner during the ill-fated assault on Quebec in that year. Exchanged in autumn, 1776, he commanded a corps of sharpshooters, distinguishing himself particularly in the Saratoga campaign. Resigning from the army, July 1779, in a dispute over promotion, he returned to active service, 1780. As brigadier general commanding the troops in western North Carolina, he won the decisive victory of Cowpens, January 1781. Later a large landowner in western Pennsylvania and Virginia, he assisted in suppressing the Whiskey Rebellion, 1794.

Morgan, Edwin Barber (*b. Aurora, N.Y., 1806; d. Aurora, 1881*), merchant, philanthropist. Cousin of Edwin D. Morgan. Associated with Henry Wells in the express business, he was first president of Wells, Fargo, 1852; he was active also in the U.S. Express Co. and in the American Express Co. As a stockholder of the *New York Times*, he supported editor George Jones in the fight against Boss Tweed, 1871. He was a principal benefactor of Wells College and of Auburn Theological Seminary.

Morgan, Edwin Denison (*b. Washington, Mass., 1811; d. New York, N.Y., 1883*), merchant, banker, New York legislator. Cousin of Edwin B. Morgan. As Republican governor of New York, 1859–63, he displayed independence and statesmanship, improving New York's credit and giving maximum support to the Lincoln administration in the Civil War. He served with ability as U.S. senator, 1863–69, and was a generous benefactor of Williams College, Union Theological Seminary, and several New York City hospitals.

Morgan, Edwin Vernon (*b. Aurora, N.Y., 1865; d. Brazil, 1934*), diplomat. Grandson of Edwin B. Morgan. After serving as a teacher of history, 1893–98, Morgan formally entered the U.S. diplomatic service, 1900. Among the numerous posts which he held, he was most effective as U.S. minister to Brazil, 1912–33.

MORGAN, GEORGE (*b.* *Philadelphia, Pa., 1743; d. near Washington, Pa., 1810*), land speculator, Indian agent. Brother of John Morgan. Partner *post* 1763 in trading firm of Baynton, Wharton, and Morgan, representing it in the Illinois country; named secretary-agent of the Indiana Co. with headquarters at Fort Pitt, 1776. Served during the Revolution as Indian agent for the United States in the middle department and as deputy commissary general of purchases for the western district, resigning in 1779. Founded colony of New Madrid in present Missouri, 1789. Refused overtures of Aaron Burr to join him in his western schemes.

MORGAN, GEORGE WASHINGTON (*b.* *Washington Co., Pa., 1820; d. Fortress Monroe, Va., 1893*), lawyer, diplomat, soldier. Removed to Mount Vernon, Ohio, 1843. Received brevet of brigadier general for gallantry in Mexican War; served as U.S. consul at Marseilles, 1856–58, and as U.S. minister to Lisbon, 1858–61. Commissioned Union brigadier general, November 1861, he rose to division and corps command in the western campaigns of the Civil War before his resignation, June 1863. As congressman, Democrat, from Ohio, 1867–68 and 1869–73, he opposed harsh Reconstruction measures.

MORGAN, HELEN (*b.* *Danville, Ill., 1900; d. Chicago, Ill., 1941*), popular singer, actress. Began her career in Chicago speakeasies; was in chorus of *Sally* on Broadway, 1920, and after a return to work in Chicago nightclubs won a small singing part in *George White's Scandals*, 1925. That year she also sang in Billy Rose's Backstage Club in a room so crowded that she had to sit on the piano while performing; the perch became her trademark. Her small voice, with its suggestion of forlornness and loss, was ideally suited to the torch song and crooning styles that were coming into vogue. She was much more, however, than a café entertainer whose talent suited a particular time. She gave outstanding performances as Julie in *Show Boat* (1927–28) and its film version, and in *Sweet Adeline* (1929), in which she starred. On the surface the typical "shopworn angel" of the 1920's, she was a warmly emotional and extravagantly generous woman.

MORGAN, JAMES DADA (*b.* *Boston, Mass., 1810; d. Quincy, Ill., 1896*), merchant, banker, Union soldier. Removed to Quincy, Ill., 1834; served with credit in Mexican War. Entering Civil War as colonel of 10th Illinois Infantry, he received brevet of major general, March 1865, for saving the left wing of Sherman's army at Bentonville, N.C.

MORGAN, JAMES MORRIS (*b.* *New Orleans, La., 1845; d. 1928*), Confederate naval officer. Half brother of Philip H. Morgan. Author of *Recollections of a Rebel Reefer* (1917).

MORGAN, JOHN (*b.* *Philadelphia, Pa., 1735; d. Philadelphia, 1789*), physician. Brother of George Morgan. Graduated College of Philadelphia (University of Pennsylvania), 1757; served medical apprenticeship under John Redman and studied under outstanding medical men in England and Italy; M.D., University of Edinburgh, 1763. Proposed establishment of a medical school in connection with College of Philadelphia, 1765; on adoption of the project, was appointed professor of the theory and practice of medicine there. In line with this work, he published his classic *Discourse upon the Institution of Medical Schools in America* (1765), in which he advocated separating the functions of physician, surgeon, and apothecary. Elected by Congress director general of hospitals and chief physician of the American army, October 1775, he made a drastic reorganization of the medical department and by his exacting methods provoked the jealousy and antagonism of his subordinates. After a curtailment of his authority in October 1776, he was removed from his posts, January 1777. Publishing a vindication of his conduct, he withdrew from public life, confining himself to his private practice and his duties as professor and as physician at the Pennsylvania Hospital.

MORGAN, JOHN HARCOURT ALEXANDER (*b.* *Kerrwood, Ontario, Canada, 1867; d. Belfast, Tenn., 1950*), agricultural economist, educator, federal administrator. B.S., Ontario Agricultural College at Guelph, 1889. Taught entomology at Louisiana State University, 1889–1905; became a leading authority in the region on pest control. Professor of entomology and zoology, and director of the agricultural experiment station, University of Tennessee, 1905 and after, he was named dean of the college of agriculture, 1913, and president of the university, 1919. Concentrating on external relations, he made his institution favorably known throughout the state; through his close association with farmers and their problems, he was convinced that man was interfering dangerously with the earth's ecosystems by excessive cultivation of soil-depleting cash crops, overconsumption of finite natural resources, and overcrowding into cities. Appointed a director of the Tennessee Valley Authority (with David E. Lilienthal and Arthur E. Morgan), 1933, he shaped the agricultural portion of the authority's program according to his ideas how best to promote rural progress, deliberately allying the authority with the established agricultural interests of the region rather than with the innovative New Deal farm agencies. Tactful and self-effacing, he was a realist, determined to work with the materials at hand, and with the people as they were. He served as chairman of the TVA, 1938–41, and retired in 1948.

MORGAN, JOHN HUNT (*b.* *Huntsville, Ala., 1825; d. Greenville, Tenn., 1864*), businessman, Confederate raider. Early in 1862, as captain of cavalry he began his famous raids in Tennessee and Kentucky during which he harassed the Union army by penetrating its lines, capturing men and trains, and destroying supplies. His rapidity in action, his dispersal of his command after securing his objectives, and his policy of avoiding fighting wherever possible account for his remarkable success. His most memorable raid took place in July 1863 through part of Ohio. Although it ended in his capture, it saved east Tennessee to the Confederacy for several months. After his escape from Ohio State Penitentiary at Columbus, Morgan was assigned to command the Department of Southwest Virginia in April 1864. He organized an efficient force, raided Kentucky in June, but was killed in action while preparing to attack Union forces near Knoxville.

MORGAN, JOHN PIERPONT (*b.* *Hartford, Conn., 1837; d. Rome, Italy, 1913*), banker, connoisseur of art. Son of Junius S. Morgan; grandson of John Pierpont. Entered father's firm in London, 1856; returned to New York, 1857, to work for American representatives of George Peabody & Co.; acted as New York agent for father's firm, 1860–64. Member of firm of Dabney, Morgan & Co., 1864–71; formed firm of Drexel, Morgan & Co., with Anthony J. Drexel, 1871. Closely associated with correspondent firms in Philadelphia, Paris, and London, the firm (*post* 1895 known as J. P. Morgan & Co.) became one of the most powerful banking houses in the world.

J. P. Morgan, although he engaged in several dubious pieces of business during the Civil War period, was essentially an organizer and stabilizing force in business. His prominence may be said to date from 1873, when, by securing a division of a U.S. treasury loan between a Morgan syndicate and one organized by Jay Cooke, he broke the monopoly of that financier in the refunding operations of the government. After Cooke's failure, the Morgan firm became dominant in government financing and managed a long series of railroad and other corporate reorganizations with a view to the restoration of faith abroad in American securities. Morgan was also able to establish some community of interest among railroads hitherto engaged in ruthless and wasteful competition. His efforts were particularly valuable in the reorganizations required after the panic of 1893, although the methods which he employed resulted in a vast concentration of power in his own hands. In 1895, on extremely harsh terms, he formed a syndicate which effectively halted a drain of gold from the reserves of the U.S. treasury. One of his most daring and imperial undertakings was the formation of the U.S. Steel Corporation, 1901, which, although heavily overcapitalized, proved highly successful to investors. Among his less successful activities were the International Mercantile Marine, 1902, and his struggle for control of the Northern Pacific Railroad with Edward H. Harriman. Morgan's personal influence was a decisive factor in overcoming the money panic of 1907 and after Harriman's death Morgan stood without a rival in the public mind as the symbol of financial power.

Investigated by Congress, 1912, he emerged with unimpaired personal credit and prestige. His statements under examination that "the first requisite of credit is character" and that he "would not lend money to a man he didn't trust" were characteristic of him. Implicit faith was reposed in his word; his very physique was commanding and he dealt in ultimatums. He was capable of violent dislikes as well as likes, but despite his prejudices he was gifted in choosing talented partners. He was a ruthless force making for centralized control of industry and credit, yet he contributed to corporate stability. He was not interested in social reform nor did he care for public opinion; he had an instinctive shrinking from personal publicity. As a collector of books and art, he displayed good personal taste and the same powers of imagination and instant decision which marked his business career. A major benefactor of the Metropolitan Museum of Art, New York, he left his superb personal library to be administered as a public reference library. An enthusiastic yachtsman and traveler, he was also one of the most active lay members of the Episcopal church.

MORGAN, JOHN PIERPONT (b. Irvington, N.Y., 1867; d. Boca Grande, Fla., 1943), investment banker. Son of John Pierpont Morgan (1837–1913); nicknamed "Jack" to distinguish him from his father. B.A., Harvard, 1889. Became partner in father's firm, 1892, soon leaving for London, England, to study banking in the firm of J. S. Morgan & Co. Upon the death of his father in 1913, he became the head of J. P. Morgan & Co. and presided over the banking house during World War I. Through his initiative, it became the sole purchasing agent in America for the British and French. In the postwar period the firm carried on important work in foreign government finance, and Morgan gained a reputation for recapitalizing national debts much like his father's for recapitalizing railroad debts. He served at Paris in 1922 on a committee of bankers that sought to adjust German reparations, an important preliminary to the Dawes committee of 1924. He was an American delegate to the reparations conference in 1929, which created the plan for the Bank of International Settlements. During the 1930's both Morgan and his firm were subjected to close governmental and public scrutiny. Since the Banking Act of 1933 had ordered a separation of investment and deposit banking, the following year J. P. Morgan & Co. withdrew from the investment banking field to become a private commercial bank, with Morgan as its head. He continued to build the holdings of the Morgan Library in New York, begun by his father, and in 1923 transformed it from a personal collection into a permanent, endowed institution. He donated art objects to the Metropolitan Museum of Art and the Wadsworth Atheneum in Hartford, Conn., By the mid-1930's Morgan was devoting much time to his avocations, leaving the direction of the Morgan bank increasingly to other partners; it was incorporated in 1940.

MORGAN, JOHN TYLER (b. Athens, Tenn., 1824; d. 1907), lawyer, Confederate brigadier general. Raised in Calhoun Co., Ala., he studied law with William P. Chilton. In 1855, he removed to Selma, Ala., where he resided until his death. As U.S. senator, Democrat, from Alabama, 1877–1907, he advocated states' rights views with independence and courage, fought to reclaim unearned land grants which the railroads were holding, sponsored legislation in support of education, and was long identified with the fight for an isthmian canal over the Nicaragua route. He was a strong expansionist and an ardent supporter of free silver.

MORGAN, JULIA (b. San Francisco, Calif., 1872; d. 1957), architect. Studied at Berkeley, and at the École des Beaux Arts, Paris, being the first woman admitted to that institution. One of America's first woman architects, Morgan spent her career in California where she designed over 700 projects. Her work included projects for the University of California campus in Berkeley, many buildings for the Young Women's Christian Association, various churches (St. John's Presbyterian, Berkeley, 1907–16), Mills College, and the Hearst family estate at San Simeon, her most famous work.

MORGAN, JUNIUS SPENCER (b. West Springfield, Mass., 1813; d. Monte Carlo, Monaco, 1890), international banker. Father of John Pierpont Morgan. After business experience in Hartford and Boston, Morgan became a partner in the London international banking firm of George Peabody & Co., 1854; on Peabody's retirement, 1864, Morgan headed the firm under the name of J. S. Morgan & Co. until his own death. The remark "Never sell a bear on the United States" is attributed to him.

MORGAN, JUSTIN (b. near West Springfield, Mass., 1747; d. Woodstock, Vt., 1798), schoolteacher. In return for a debt, Morgan accepted, 1795, the colt which was the progenitor of the breed known as the Morgan horse.

MORGAN, LEWIS HENRY (b. near Aurora, N.Y., 1818; d. 1881), lawyer, New York legislator, ethnologist, anthropologist. Graduated Union, 1840. Author of a number of pioneering books based on serious scientific study, which include The League of the . . . Iroquois (1851), Systems of Consanguinity and Affinity of the Human Family (in Smithsonian Contributions to Knowledge, Vol. 17, 1871), Ancient Society (1877, 1878), and Houses and House-Life of the American Aborigines (1881). He was author also of a number of monographs and of The American Beaver (1868). He has been called the "father of American anthropology."

MORGAN, MATTHEW SOMERVILLE (b. London, England, 1839; d. New York, N.Y., 1890), artist, correspondent, cartoonist. Worked in America, 1870–90; famous for Civil War cartoons in London Fun.

MORGAN, MORRIS HICKY (b. Providence, R.I., 1859; d. 1910), classicist. Graduated Harvard, 1881; Ph.D., 1887. Taught classical languages and philology at Harvard, 1887–1910; translator-editor, Vitruvius, the Ten Books on Architecture (1914).

MORGAN, PHILIP HICKY (b. Baton Rouge, La., 1825; d. New York, N.Y., 1900), jurist, diplomat. Half brother of James M. Morgan; nephew of Thomas M. T. McKennan. Opposed secession; as Louisiana Supreme Court judge, 1873–76, upheld Reconstruction policies. A judge of the international court in Egypt, 1877–80, he served as U.S. minister to Mexico, 1880–85.

MORGAN, THOMAS HUNT (b. Lexington, Ky., 1866; d. Pasadena, Calif., 1945), zoologist, geneticist. Nephew of John Hunt Morgan. After receiving the B.S. degree in 1886 from the State

College (later University) of Kentucky, he went to the Johns Hopkins University for graduate work, spending the intervening summer at the marine laboratory at Annisquam, Mass., predecessor of the Marine Biological Laboratory at Woods Hole, Mass. In 1890 he received the Ph.D. degree with a thesis on the embyology of sea spiders. In 1891 he became associate professor of biology at Bryn Mawr College. In 1904 he was appointed professor of experimental zoology at Columbia University, where he was to remain for the next 24 years. For a half a dozen years at Columbia, Morgan continued to work in experimental embryology—regeneration, self-sterility in *Ciona*, gynandromorphism, differentiation and sex determination in aphids and phylloxerans. In 1909–10 he found a white-eyed mutant of *Drosophila* to be a sex-linked recessive. Within the next two years he discovered many additional mutant traits, and worked out their modes of inheritance. In 1915 Morgan was the coauthor of *The Mechanism of Mendelian Heredity*, which marked a high point in the development of genetics. In 1928 he moved to the California Institute of Technology in Pasadena to help create a new division of biology; five years later he received the Nobel Prize in physiology. In his last book, *Embryology and Genetics* (1934), he embodied his views on the two fields in which he made his chief scientific contributions.

MORGAN, THOMAS JEFFERSON (*b. Franklin, Ind., 1839; d. 1902*), Union brigadier general, Baptist clergyman. Active *post* 1872 in educational work, he was U.S. commissioner of Indian affairs, 1889–93; thereafter he was corresponding secretary, American Baptist Home Mission Society, until his death.

MORGAN, WILLIAM (*b. probably Culpeper Co., Va., 1774[?]; d. possibly in vicinity of Batavia, N.Y., 1826[?]*), central figure in the anti-Masonic agitation, 1826–38. Morgan's disappearance and alleged murder just before publication of his book *Illustrations of Masonry*, an exposé of the secrets of Freemasonry, had a profound effect on the politics of the time.

MORGENTHAU, HENRY (*b. Mannheim, Germany, 1856; d. New York, N.Y., 1946*), lawyer, realtor, diplomat. Settled with his parents in New York City, 1866; attended College of the City of New York; graduated Columbia Law School, 1877. Highly successful in real estate transactions, he engaged also in movements for reform of housing and working conditions of labor, and in settlement house work. An adherent of Reform Judaism, he was a founder and first president of the Free Synagogue (for Rabbi Stephen S. Wise). In 1912 he was chairman of the finance committee of the Democratic National Committee and an ardent supporter of Woodrow Wilson for the presidency. As U.S. ambassador to Turkey, 1913–16, he found himself also responsible for the interests of nine other countries after the outbreak of World War I and won high praise for his humane efforts to provide aid and relief for internees; he resigned out of disgust with Turkish massacres of Armenians, which he tried vainly to stop. Thereafter, he was identified with numerous movements; for Near East relief, for U.S. support of the League of Nations, and for establishment of the International Red Cross. In 1923 he supervised a mass resettlement of Greeks driven out of Turkish territory after the Greco-Turkish War and made them self-supporting through international loans. In his later years he was an admirer and supporter of Franklin D. Roosevelt and a vigorous campaigner for the New Deal.

MORGENTHAU, HENRY, JR. (*b. New York, N.Y., 1891; d. Poughkeepsie, N.Y., 1967*), secretary of the treasury. Son of Henry Morgenthau, diplomat who prospered in real estate. Farmed his own property in East Fishkill, N.Y., from 1913. Published the *American Agriculturalist* (1922–33). Was chairman of the New York Agricultural Advisory Commission (1928–30); conservation commissioner (1930–32); and governor of the Farm Credit Administration (1933). As U.S. secretary of the treasury, 1934–45, Morgenthau advocated restraint in federal spending and acquired his reputation as a conservative because of his resistance to Keynesian economic theories.

MORIARTY, PATRICK EUGENE (*b. Dublin, Ireland, 1804; d. Chestnut Hill, Pa., 1875*), Roman Catholic clergyman, Augustinian, temperance reformer. Came to Philadelphia, Pa., 1839; was pastor of St. Augustine's Church there and superior of Augustinian mission work. Founded Villanova College, 1842.

MORINI, AUSTIN JOHN (*b. Florence, Italy, 1826; d. Rome, Italy, 1909*), Roman Catholic clergyman, Servite. Came to the United States in 1870 to establish a foundation for the Servites in the diocese of Green Bay, Wis.; established Servite mother house in Chicago, Ill., 1874.

MORISON, GEORGE SHATTUCK (*b. New Bedford, Mass., 1842; d. 1903*), engineer, lawyer. Regarded at the time of his death as the leading bridge engineer in America and internationally renowned as a railway and waterway expert, Morison received his engineering training as principal assistant to Octave Chanute. Active in consulting practice *post* 1880, he was responsible for the building of more than a score of great railroad bridges over the principal U.S. rivers; his work in bridging the Missouri River at some nine points is considered his outstanding achievement. He was a pioneer in the use of steel for bridge construction.

MORLEY, CHRISTOPHER DARLINGTON (*b. Haverford, Pa., 1890; d. Roslyn Heights, N.Y., 1957*), writer and editor. Studied at Haverford College and at Oxford University as a Rhodes scholar. An editor for Doubleday, Page, and Co., for the *Ladies' Home Journal* (1917), and a columnist for the *Philadelphia Evening Public Ledger*, Morley also wrote eighteen works of fiction, sixteen volumes of poetry, and thirteen volumes of essays. His most famous novel was *Kitty Foyle* (1939) which was made into a movie. Judge, Book-of-the-Month-Club (1926–54); edited eleventh edition of *Bartlett's Familiar Quotations* (1937). Published fictionalized autobiography, *John Mistletoe* in 1931.

MORLEY, EDWARD WILLIAMS (*b. Newark, N.J., 1838; d. West Hartford, Conn., 1923*), chemist, physicist. Professor of natural history and chemistry at Western Reserve University, 1869–1906, Morley displayed great ingenuity in constructing apparatus and in making accurate measurements. His magnum opus was a study of densities of oxygen and hydrogen and the ratio in which they combine to form water (Smithsonian Contributions, No. 980, 1895). He made studies of the variation of the oxygen content of the atmosphere by which he substantiated the Loomis-Morley hypothesis of oxygen deficiency at times of high atmospheric pressure. He collaborated with A. A. Michelson in development of the interferometer and in subsequent experiments to measure lengths in terms of the wavelength of light. Morley also determined the velocity of light in a magnetic field (with Dayton C. Miller), and studied thermal expansion of air, nitrogen, oxygen, and carbon dioxide, devising a new form of manometer for this purpose.

MORLEY, FRANK (*b. Woodbridge, England, 1860; d. Baltimore, Md., 1937*), mathematician. Graduated King's College, Cambridge, 1884; Sc.D., 1898. Came to America, 1887, to join faculty of Haverford College, where he remained until 1900; he then transferred to Johns Hopkins, where he taught until his retirement, 1928. He was a specialist in application of complex numbers to the treatment of problems of plane geometry.

MORLEY, MARGARET WARNER (*b. Montrose, Iowa, 1858; d. Washington, D.C., 1923*), teacher. Wrote pioneering grade-school textbooks on nature study; those on sex and birth, such as *Song of Life* (1891), shocked contemporaries.

MORLEY, SYLVANUS GRISWOLD (*b. Chester, Pa., 1883; d. Santa Fe, N.Mex., 1948*), archaeologist, epigrapher. C.E., Pennsylvania Military College, 1904. B.A., Harvard, 1907; M.A., 1908. As a fellow of the School of American Research of the Archaeological Institute of America, 1909–14, he received field training and began the investigations into Maya civilization which were his lifework. *Post* 1914 his research was supported by the Carnegie Institution of Washington. He made numerous expeditions into the tropical jungles of Central America to examine Maya sites and institute excavations, notably that at Chichén Itzá, which he supervised, 1924–34. His study of Maya hieroglyphic texts resulted in numerous papers and several long monographs, which were distinguished by his extraordinary talent for chronology. His last book, *The Ancient Maya* (1946), was the most ambitious and detailed presentation of Maya civilization produced up to that time. In 1947 he was appointed director of the School of American Research.

MORPHY, PAUL CHARLES (*b. New Orleans, La., 1837; d. New Orleans, 1884*), lawyer, chess player. After a brilliant campaign in Europe, 1858–59, Morphy was recognized as chess champion of the world and an unparalleled genius of the game. Disappointed in a normal career, he virtually ceased play in 1864.

MORRELL, BENJAMIN (*b. Rye, N.Y., 1795; d. Mozambique, 1839*), sealing-ship captain, explorer. Author of *A Narrative of Four Voyages to the South Sea* (1832).

MORRIL, DAVID LAWRENCE (*b. Epping, N.H., 1772; d. Concord, N.H., 1849*), Congregational clergyman, physician, New Hampshire legislator. U.S. senator, Democratic-Republican, from New Hampshire, 1817–23; governor of New Hampshire, 1824–27. A moderate antislavery advocate, he vigorously disapproved the Missouri Compromise. He was an unusual combination of scholar and man of affairs.

MORRILL, ANSON PEASLEE (*b. Belgrade, Maine, 1803; d. Augusta, Maine, 1887*), woolen-mill owner. Brother of Lot M. Morrill. Breaking with the Democratic party on the issues of slavery and temperance, Morrill was elected governor of Maine in 1854 by a fusion of Whigs, Free-Soilers, and temperance Democrats. Reelected, 1855, by a popular plurality, he was set aside by the Democratic state senate. He served as congressman, Republican, from Maine, 1861–63, and later headed the Maine Central Railroad.

MORRILL, EDMUND NEEDHAM (*b. Westbrook, Maine, 1834; d. San Antonio, Tex., 1909*), businessman, Union soldier, Kansas legislator. Removed to Kansas, 1857. As congressman, Republican, from Kansas, 1883–91, he devoted his time almost exclusively to pension legislation; as anti-Populist Republican governor of Kansas, 1895–97, he met problems of the local farmers arising from drought and high rates of mortgage interest with the statement "When the government has protected the individual in his life and property he ought to hustle for himself to get bread."

MORRILL, JUSTIN SMITH (*b. Strafford, Vt., 1810; d. Washington, D.C., 1898*), merchant, farmer, politician. Elected to the U.S. House of Representatives, 1854, as an antislavery Whig, he began an unbroken service of 12 years in the House and almost 32 years in the U.S. Senate, to which he was first elected in 1866. In the House he became an important member of the Ways and Means Committee, of which he served as chairman, 1865–67; in the Senate he served as a member of the Committee on Finance, of which he was chairman, 1877–79, 1881–93, and 1895–98. A

conscientious and fair-minded protectionist and an authority on finance, he was influential throughout his congressional career in tariff legislation, especially in the acts of 1861 and 1883; he consistently opposed inconvertible money and financial inflation. He made his greatest contribution in the Morrill Act, for the creation of land-grant colleges, first introduced in 1857 and vetoed by Buchanan but signed in a similar form by Abraham Lincoln, 1862. He was responsible also for an amplification of federal aid to education by grants of public lands in 1890, when he introduced the so-called Second Morrill Act.

MORRILL, LOT MYRICK (*b. Belgrade, Maine, 1812; d. Portland, Maine, 1883*), lawyer, Maine legislator. Brother of Anson P. Morrill. After achieving power in the Democratic party in Maine, he left the party formally in 1856 in protest against its platform of that year. Republican governor of Maine, 1858–61, he was U.S. senator, 1861–March 1869, and September 1869–July 1876. A strong adherent of congressional Reconstruction, he served briefly as U.S. secretary of the treasury at the end of President Grant's second term and was thereafter collector of customs at Portland, Maine.

MORRIS, ANTHONY (*b. London, England, 1654; d. 1721*), Quaker leader and minister, brewer, Pennsylvania jurist. Mayor of Philadelphia, 1703–04.

MORRIS, ANTHONY (*b. Philadelphia, Pa., 1766; d. near Georgetown, D.C., 1860*), merchant, Pennsylvania legislator. Unofficial U.S. representative to Spain, 1810–14; suggested purchase of East and West Florida, as eventually realized in Treaty of 1819.

MORRIS, CADWALADER (*b. Philadelphia, Pa., 1741 o.s.; d. Philadelphia, 1795*), merchant, Revolutionary patriot. Aided establishment of the Pennsylvania Bank, 1780; a founder and a director of the Bank of North America, 1781–87.

MORRIS, CASPAR (*b. Philadelphia, Pa., 1805; d. 1884*), physician, Philadelphia philanthropist. Aided in planning of Johns Hopkins Hospital, Baltimore.

MORRIS, CHARLES (*b. Woodstock, Conn., 1784; d. 1856*), naval officer. Appointed midshipman, 1799; assisted Stephen Decatur in destruction of frigate *Philadelphia*, 1803; promoted to captain after exemplary service as first lieutenant of USS *Constitution* in War of 1812. After further sea duty, he served at various times *post* 1823 as a member of the Board of Navy Commissioners; *post* 1844 he headed the Bureau of Construction and the Bureau of Ordnance. He was called by Admiral Farragut the "ablest sea officer of his day."

MORRIS, CLARA (*b. Toronto, Canada, 1848; d. New Canaan, Conn., 1925*), actress. Raised in Cleveland, Ohio, made first stage appearance there, 1862. Later famous with Daly's company and on the road as the most prominent emotional actress on the American stage, she was able, despite distinctly limited abilities, to play with great effect on the feelings of her audiences.

MORRIS, EDMUND (*b. Burlington, N.J., 1804; d. Burlington, 1874*), newspaper editor, agricultural writer.

MORRIS, EDWARD DAFYDD (*b. Utica, N.Y., 1825; d. Columbus, Ohio, 1915*), Presbyterian clergyman. Held responsible teaching and other positions at Lane Theological Seminary, Cincinnati, Ohio, *post* 1863; was a vigorous exponent of "new school" theology.

MORRIS, EDWARD JOY (*b. Philadelphia, Pa., 1815; d. Philadelphia, 1881*), lawyer, Pennsylvania legislator, diplomat. Congressman, Whig, from Pennsylvania, 1843–45; congressman,

Republican, 1857–61. U.S. minister to Turkey, 1861–70. Author of, among other books, *Notes of a Tour Through Turkey, Greece, Egypt, . . . (1842)*.

MORRIS, ELIZABETH (*b. probably England*, ca. *1753; d. Philadelphia, Pa., 1826*), actress. Known on the stage as Mrs. Owen Morris. Made her first American stage appearance, Philadelphia, 1772, with the American Co. Joined Wignell's company, 1791; shared in first Boston, Mass., theatrical season, 1792; was associated mainly with Chestnut St. Theatre, Philadelphia, 1794–1810. Mrs. Morris was regarded in her time as the greatest attraction on the American stage and was especially effective in high comedy.

MORRIS, GEORGE POPE (*b. Philadelphia, Pa., 1802; d. 1864*), journalist, poet. Founded *New-York Mirror*, 1823, which he published until 1842; founded the *New Mirror* 1843, edited by himself and Nathaniel P. Willis, but discontinued, 1844; was associated also with Willis in the *Home Journal* (original title, the *National Press*) from 1846. General Morris, as he was known in his day, was a writer of popular song lyrics; his most famous individual poem is "Woodman, Spare that Tree." He was author also of a volume of prose sketches, *The Little Frenchman and His Water Lots* (1839). His verses were published in numerous editions.

MORRIS, GEORGE SYLVESTER (*b. Norwich, Vt., 1840; d. Ann Arbor, Mich., 1889*), educator, philosopher. Taught at University of Michigan *post* 1870; was a champion of Kantian idealism. His point of view may be regarded as akin to that of W. T. Harris and the St. Louis Hegelians and to English philosophers like T. H. Green and F. H. Bradley.

MORRIS, GOUVERNEUR (*b. Morrisania, N.Y., 1752; d. 1816*), statesman, diplomat. Grandson of Lewis Morris (1671–1746); half brother of Lewis (1726–98) and Richard Morris. Brilliance, the influence of his prominent landed New York family, unfailing self-assurance, and remarkable social aptitude all combined to make a political career inevitable for him. But for the constant interruptions of politics and diplomacy, he could have achieved the foremost rank of lawyers in his day, as attested by his successful practice in New York City after graduation from King's College, 1768, and admission to the bar, 1771. Originally a conservative and reluctant to countenance a break with Great Britain, after the clash at Lexington he showed himself a nationalist before the birth of the nation, seeking to resolve tension between radicals and loyalists in the New York provincial congress, May 1775, and appealing for a united front in support of the Continental Congress at Philadelphia. In July 1776, he sat in the New York State constitutional convention and, with John Jay and Robert R. Livingston, drafted, 1777, the frame of government that lasted nearly 50 years. Thereafter he served diligently on the Council of Safety.

During his membership in the Continental Congress, 1778–79, Morris turned his talents and soundness of judgment to financial, military, and diplomatic matters, chairing several leading committees and drafting many important foreign-policy documents. His army inspection trip to Valley Forge, 1778, brought him close to Washington, to whom he remained devoted for life. Defeated for reelection to the Continental Congress, 1779, he transferred his citizenship to Pennsylvania, resumed the practice of law, and cultivated polite society in Philadelphia. His articles on Continental finances in the *Pennsylvania Packet* (February–April, 1780) led Robert Morris (not a relative), the new superintendent of finance, to request his service as assistant. In this position, 1781–85, the younger Morris initially planned the U.S. decimal coinage system. As Pennsylvania delegate to the Constitutional Convention, 1787, he participated frequently in debate,

favoring strong, centralized government in the hands of the rich and well-born, with suffrage limited to freeholders. Although Morris loyally accepted the compromises embodied in the U.S. Constitution (which he wrote out in its final form), his cynical contempt for democracy barred him from high office under it. Consequently, he forsook public life to attend to various commercial ventures, purchased the family mansion at Morrisania, N.Y., and returned there to live, 1788. Soon, as business agent for Robert Morris, he left for Europe, where, in pursuit of business, diplomatic duties, and recreational travel, he remained for nearly a decade.

Arriving in Paris, February 1789, he saw the French Revolution begin. His fame as a founder of the American Republic had preceded him and his affability, family connections, command of French, and intellectual versatility opened all doors to him. After Jefferson's return to America in late 1789, Morris was the most influential American in Paris and he worked to improve Franco-American business and financial relations. Freedom from diplomatic responsibility allowed him to criticize and counsel without offense. His voluminous diary of the early revolutionary period (first published, 1888) is highly informative.

Named U.S. minister to France by President Washington, 1792, Morris was almost rejected by the Senate, owing to his sympathy with the French monarchy and his unsuccessful commercial negotiations at London, 1790–91. No one at Paris, however, could have represented the United States better than Morris did in the stormy years 1792–94. He weathered the Terror with dignity and courage. Recalled, 1794, in return for Washington's dismissal of "Citizen" Edmond Genêt, he remained abroad until 1798. After serving as Federalist senator from New York, 1800–02, he retired to his Morrisania estate to cultivate his friends and nurse his hatred of Republicans and their measures.

MORRIS, JOHN GOTTLIEB (*b. York, Pa., 1803; d. Lutherville, Md., 1895*), Lutheran clergyman. Held several pastorates in Baltimore, Md., 1827–73; founded *Lutheran Observer*, 1831, and the Lutheran Historical Society. A notable student, Morris was librarian of the Peabody Institute, 1860–65.

MORRIS, LEWIS (*b. near New York, N.Y., 1671; d. near Trenton, N.J., 1746*), colonial landowner and official, first lord of the manor of Morrisania, N.Y. (erected 1697). Holder of numerous offices in colonial New York and New Jersey, Morris' principal services were given as chief justice of the supreme court of New York Province, 1715–33 and as governor of New Jersey, 1738–46. Long involved in provincial political disputes, Morris strongly opposed unscrupulous crown officials such as the governors Lord Cornbury and William Cosby, and in general served with great contentiousness and ability as a champion of the popular cause against the "court party." His administration was marked by bitter, wordy quarrels with the assembly over taxation, support of the militia, bills of credit, and validity of land titles.

MORRIS, LEWIS (*b. Morrisania, N.Y., 1726; d. Morrisania, 1798*), landowner, statesman, third and last lord of the manor of Morrisania. Grandson of Lewis Morris (1671–1746); half brother of Gouverneur Morris. Graduated Yale, 1746. Active in provincial politics *post* 1762, he grew increasingly critical of British policy, secured appointment of deputies from Westchester Co. to the New York provincial convention in April 1775, and served as a New York delegate to the Continental Congress, 1775–76. Absent from Philadelphia when the Declaration of Independence was finally adopted, he signed it for New York late in 1776. As congressman, he was particularly effective in handling of Indian affairs. Brigadier general of the militia of Westchester Co., N.Y., he served also as a county judge, 1777–78, and was intermittently a member of the New York State Senate from 1777 until 1790.

MORRIS, LEWIS RICHARD (*b. Scarsdale, N.Y., 1760; d. Springfield, Vt., 1825*), landowner, Vermont legislator. Son of Richard Morris. Congressman, Federalist, from Vermont, 1797–1803. His abstention from voting allowed Thomas Jefferson's election as president by the House of Representatives, February 1801.

MORRIS, LUZON BURRITT (*b. Newtown, Conn., 1827; d. 1895*), lawyer, Connecticut legislator. Democratic governor of Connecticut, 1893–95.

MORRIS, MARY PHILIPSE. *See* MORRIS, ROGER.

MORRIS, MRS. OWEN. *See* MORRIS, ELIZABETH.

MORRIS, NELSON (*b. Hechingen, Germany, 1838; d. Chicago, Ill., 1907*), stockbreeder, meatpacker. Came to America as a boy. Settling in Chicago, he worked in the Union Stock Yards and soon rose to a leading position in the live-cattle trade. A pioneer in transporting dressed beef from Chicago to the Atlantic seaboard, he opened one of the first packinghouses in the Chicago Stock Yards, owned a number of large cattle ranches, and established packing plants also in Missouri and Kansas.

MORRIS, RICHARD (*b. probably Morrisania, N.Y., 1730; d. Scarsdale, N.Y., 1810*), jurist. Brother of Lewis Morris (1726–98); half brother of Gouverneur Morris. Graduated Yale, 1748. Judge of the vice admiralty court having jurisdiction over New York, Connecticut, and New Jersey, 1762–75; succeeded John Jay as chief justice, New York Supreme Court, 1779; retired from public life, 1790.

MORRIS, RICHARD VALENTINE (*b. Morrisania, N.Y., 1768; d. Morrisania, 1815*), naval officer, diplomat. Son of Lewis Morris (1726–98). Unsuccessful negotiator with Barbary powers as commodore commanding Mediterranean squadron, 1802–03. Author of *A Defense of the Conduct of Commodore Morris* (1804).

MORRIS, ROBERT (*b. in or near Liverpool, England, 1734; d. Philadelphia, Pa., 1806*), financier of the American Revolution. Joined his father, a tobacco exporter, in Maryland, ca. 1747. After brief schooling in Philadelphia he went into service of the Willings, shipping merchants, and rose to partnership in their firm, 1754. To Willing, Morris & Co., and its successors under other names, he gave his interest for 39 years and, for a large part of that period, his active direction. His prudence and resolution brought him wealth, and the firm, a leading position in the trade of Philadelphia and America. The house concentrated upon importing British manufactures, exporting American goods, shipowning, and a general exchange and banking business.

Morris' public career began when he signed the nonimportation agreement of 1765, opposing the Stamp Act. Uncommitted to the "Patriot" cause as late as 1774, he became a leader in it with the battle of Lexington, April 1775. A member of the Council of Safety, appointed by the Pennsylvania Assembly, June 30, 1775, his commercial experience was of immediate use in the committee charged with procuring munitions and he frequently acted as its banker. In Benjamin Franklin's absence he presided over the council. In November 1775, the Assembly sent Morris as delegate to the Continental Congress. He signed the Declaration of Independence in August 1776, after initial disapproval. Throughout his term in Congress he provided strong financial leadership, especially after Congress fled from Philadelphia in December 1776, when he remained to carry on committee work, buying supplies and borrowing money despite appalling difficulties, and providing Washington and his lieutenants the moral support and material assistance without which the army must have been dispersed. Morris profited greatly as a middleman from the deals which he directed through his committee for the procurement of munitions and naval armaments. He did this, however, at great personal financial risk and without lessening his colleagues' confidence in him. John Adams wrote, "He . . . no doubt pursues mercantile ends, which are always gain; but he is an excellent Member of our Body." Morris signed the Articles of Confederation on behalf of Pennsylvania, March 1778. Ineligible for reelection to Congress, he was elected to the Pennsylvania Assembly, November 1778. Attacks upon him in 1779 by Thomas Paine for improper commercial enterprises in public office, and upon his firm by Henry Laurens for fraud, diminished his political popularity, although he and the firm were acquitted by a congressional investigating committee.

With the treasury empty, credit gone, and the Union a "rope of sand," Congress recognized that a financial dictator was needed and chose Morris to be superintendent of finance, February 1781. Accepting the unique office with stipulations that he might retain his private commercial connections and could control the personnel of his department, Morris initiated a program which included the laying of federal taxes in specie to be used in paying interest on the debt; requisitions from the states to be used to carry on the war; a possible loan from France; and vigilant economy. To save expense to the government he himself accepted the agency of marine. He assumed the task of buying all supplies for the armies; he used notes which circulated only upon his own credit; he pressed the states for their cash contributions; he put vigor, as well as order, into civil administration. Continuously he was driven to greater risks and to daring financial sleight of hand. Disgusted with the impotence of Congress and with the states' failure to meet obligations, Morris resigned in September 1784, but not before he had financed the victorious Yorktown campaign, formed the Bank of North America (January 1782) with a French loan, and undergone severe press abuse for his announced wish to resign.

His remaining years in public office saw him a member of the Pennsylvania General Assembly, 1785–86; a delegate to the Annapolis Convention, 1786; a member of the Constitutional Convention with Federalist convictions, 1787; and U.S. senator from Pennsylvania, 1789–95. *Post* 1785, he held a monopoly of the American tobacco trade with France. His financial downfall came when extensive land speculations in which he was engaged collapsed, and his prestige was demolished when a small creditor caused him to be confined (February 1798–August 1801) in the Philadelphia debtors' prison. Broken in body and spirit, he died a nearly forgotten and much-pitied man.

MORRIS, ROBERT (*b. New Brunswick, N.J., ca. 1745; d. New Brunswick, 1815*), jurist. Natural son of Robert H. Morris. Chief justice, New Jersey Supreme Court, 1777–79; federal judge, New Jersey district, 1789–1815.

MORRIS, ROBERT (*b. near Boston, Mass., 1818; d. La Grange, Ky., 1888*), Masonic writer and lecturer.

MORRIS, ROBERT HUNTER (*b. Morrisania, N.Y., ca. 1700; d. Shrewsbury, N.J., 1764*), jurist, politician. Son of Lewis Morris (1671–1746). Chief justice of New Jersey, 1738–64, Morris was a belligerent defender of the royal prerogative and of property rights. Despite his absence as governor of Pennsylvania, 1754–56, and during a long visit to England, 1757–58, he was never considered to have surrendered his commission as chief justice.

MORRIS, ROGER (*b. England, 1727; d. Yorkshire, England, 1794*), British soldier, Loyalist. Came to America, 1755; served with credit in the French and Indian War; married Mary Philipse, heiress of Frederic Philipse, 1758. His American property, which came to him by his marriage, was confiscated by an act of attainder of the New York state legislature soon after the outbreak of the Revolution. He left America permanently in 1783.

MORRIS, THOMAS (*b. Berks Co., Pa., 1776; d. 1844*), lawyer, Ohio legislator. Raised near Clarksburg, now in West Virginia; removed to Ohio, 1795. A partisan of Andrew Jackson, Morris served as U.S. senator from Ohio, 1833–39; he was an opponent of lotteries, monopolies, imprisonment for debt, and the extension of slavery. His speech defending the abolitionists against the charges of Henry Clay, made on Feb. 9, 1839, ended his political career, but he was active in the campaign of 1844 as vice-presidential nominee of the Liberty party.

MORRIS, THOMAS ARMSTRONG (*b. Nicholas Co., Ky., 1811; d. San Diego, Calif., 1904*), engineer, Union brigadier general, Indiana canal and railroad builder.

MORRIS, WILLIAM HOPKINS (*b. New York, N.Y., 1827; d. Long Branch, N.J., 1900*), Union major general. Son of George P. Morris. Graduated West Point, 1851. Author of several works on infantry tactics.

MORRISON, DELESSEPS STORY (*b. New Roads, La., 1912; d. Ciudad Victoria, Mexico, 1964*), public official and diplomat. Studied at Louisiana State University Law School (graduated, 1934). Formed a law partnership in New Orleans with Hale Boggs in 1935. Member of the Louisiana House of Representatives, 1940–46, mayor of New Orleans, 1947–61, and ambassador to the Organization of American States, 1961–63. Leader of the reform faction in New Orleans that opposed the state administration dominated by Huey Long and his family.

MORRISON, FRANK (*b. Franktown, Ontario, Canada, 1859; d. Washington, D.C., 1949*), printer, labor leader. Settled in Chicago, Ill., 1881; while working as a compositor, attended Lake Forest University law school and graduated LL.B., 1894. Meanwhile, he had joined Typographical Union no. 16 in 1886, and his honesty and dedication to union work helped him become prominent in Chicago labor circles. In 1896 he was elected secretary of the American Federation of Labor; he was reelected to the post without interruption until 1939, and also held the position of treasurer, 1935–39. As secretary, he provided the AFL with an efficient administrative structure during its period of growth and development, keeping all books and records, receiving all funds and preparing financial statements, convening the annual conventions, and performing countless other tasks. A liberal in politics, he lobbied in Congress for laws favorable to labor and favored active political participation by the AFL.

MORRISON, JOHN IRWIN (*b. near Chambersburg, Pa., 1806; d. Knightstown, Ind., 1882*), educator, promoter of public school legislation in Indiana.

MORRISON, NATHAN JACKSON (*b. Sanbornton, now Franklin, N.H., 1828; d. Wichita, Kans., 1907*), Congregational clergyman, educator. President, Olivet (Michigan) College, 1864–72; Drury College, Springfield, Mo., 1873–88; Fairmont Institute, Wichita, Kans., 1895–1907.

MORRISON, WILLIAM (*b. Doylestown, Pa., 1763; d. Kaskaskia, Ill., 1837*), merchant. Removed to Kaskaskia *ante* August 1790 and there built up a flourishing trading business; was first U.S. citizen to attempt opening trade with Sante Fe, N.Mex., 1804; joined Pierre Menard in backing Manuel Lisa for upper Missouri venture, 1807. Led political faction opposed to William H. Harrison in Old Northwest.

MORRISON, WILLIAM MCCUTCHAN (*b. near Lexington, Va., 1867; d. Luebo, Congo Free State, 1918*), Southern Presbyterian clergyman, missionary to the Congo. Denounced treatment of natives by Congo government and its concessionary companies;

supplied part of data to Mark Twain for *King Leopold's Soliloquy* (1905).

MORRISON, WILLIAM RALLS (*b. near Waterloo, Ill., 1824[?]; d. Waterloo, 1909*), lawyer, Union soldier. Congressman, Democrat, from Illinois, 1863–65 and 1873–87. Popularized idea of tariff reform by introducing generally unsuccessful bills in Congress which called for abandonment of protection principle. As member of the Interstate Commerce Commission, 1887–89 (chairman *post* 1892), he conducted a vigorous but temporarily unsuccessful campaign against railroad privilege and attacked discriminations and rebates.

MORRISSEY, JOHN (*b. Templemore, Ireland, 1831; d. 1878*), gambler, prizefighter, politician. Came to Canada as a child; was raised in Troy, N.Y. Claimed heavyweight championship of the world after beating Yankee Sullivan in 37 rounds at Boston Four Corners, N.Y., October, 1853; defeated John C. Heenan in Canada, October 1858. Profiting by financial advice given him by Cornelius Vanderbilt, he made successful speculations and grew wealthy. He served two terms in Congress, 1867–71, and served also in the New York legislature. *Post* 1870, he occupied himself principally with gambling and racetrack interests in Saratoga, N.Y.

MORROW, DWIGHT WHITNEY (*b. Huntington, W.Va., 1873; d. Englewood, N.J., 1931*), lawyer, banker, diplomat. Graduated Amherst, 1895; Columbia Law School, 1899. Successful in corporation law practice through his ability to find common ground on which claims of divergent interests could be resolved, Morrow, among other public services, drafted New Jersey's workmen's compensation law of 1911 and effected reforms in administration of penal institutions. Associated with J. P. Morgan & Co., 1914–27, he served during World War I as adviser to the allied Transport Council and was awarded the Distinguished Service Medal for rationalizing the Allied tonnage situation. He effected the restoration of the Cuban economy *post* 1920; was chairman of the Aircraft Board, whose 1926 report led to separate control for military and commercial aviation; and as U.S. ambassador to Mexico, 1927–30, restored harmonious U.S. relations with that republic and resolved difficulties between the Mexican government and the Roman Catholic church. He was U.S. senator, Republican, from New Jersey, 1930–31.

MORROW, EDWIN PORCH (*b. Somerset, Ky., 1877; d. Frankfort, Ky., 1935*), lawyer. Nephew of William O. Bradley. Republican governor of Kentucky, 1919–23.

MORROW, JEREMIAH (*b. near Gettysburg, Pa., 1771; d. near Lebanon, Ohio, 1852*), surveyor, farmer, Ohio legislator. Removed to Ohio, 1794; was leader in movement for statehood. Congressman, Democratic-Republican, from Ohio, 1803–13; U.S. senator, 1813–19; governor of Ohio, 1822–26. Expert in matters pertaining to the public lands, he advocated the sale of land in smaller units, cash payments, and lower prices; as governor, he inaugurated the state canal-building program and was influential in establishing the public school system. A supporter of John Q. Adams, 1828, he later became a Whig and, as such, served again in Congress, 1840–43.

MORROW, PRINCE ALBERT (*b. Mount Vernon, Ky., 1846; d. 1913*), physician, dermatologist, sociologist. Nephew of Thomas V. Morrow. M.D., New York University, 1874; began practice in New York City, 1875. A specialist in diseases of the skin, he taught this subject at New York University, 1882–90. Early recognizing the social, moral, and economic problems brought about by venereal diseases, he labored to overcome prejudice against open discussion of them and to arouse greater public interest in their prevention.

MORROW, THOMAS VAUGHAN (*b. Fairview, Ky., 1804; d. Cincinnati, Ohio, 1850*), physician, pioneer in eclectic medicine. Studied under Wooster Beach; practiced at Hopkinsville, Ky.; helped to found and taught at eclectic medical schools in Ohio. First president, National Eclectic Medical Association, 1848.

MORROW, WILLIAM W. (*b. near Milton, Ind., 1843; d. San Francisco, Calif., 1929*), California jurist, congressman. Removed to California, 1859. Federal district judge in California, 1891–97; circuit judge, 1897–1923.

MORSE, ANSON DANIEL (*b. Cambridge, Vt., 1846; d. Amherst, Mass., 1916*), educator. Brother of Harmon N. Morse. Graduated Amherst, 1871; taught political science and history there, 1876–1907. Author of *Parties and Party Leaders* (1923) and a number of articles on the theory of political action by parties.

MORSE, CHARLES WYMAN (*b. Bath, Maine, 1856; d. Bath, 1933*), financial promoter, speculator. His American Ice Co., formed 1899, was one of the earliest and most flagrant instances of corrupt promotion in the American trust movement. After this primary success, turning to banking and shipping, he made a number of rapid consolidations of individual firms, either through peaceful or forceful penetration. Pyramiding assets and forming syndicates to float the overcapitalized stock of his consolidated companies, he managed to obtain before 1907 close to a monopoly of Atlantic coastal shipping and also won control of a number of New York banks. After the Morse banks had become the storm center of the panic of 1907, Morse was indicted for criminal misapplication of funds and sentenced to a 15-year term in Atlanta Penitentiary, November 1908. Released from jail two years later through fraud and collusion, Morse reentered Wall Street. He found a golden opportunity on U.S. entrance into World War I, when he accepted contracts for construction of merchant vessels and borrowed the money to build them from the government. In the shadow of an indictment for conspiracy to defraud the government in these matters, Morse went to Europe, 1922. Arrested on his attempt to return to the United States, he became subject to two indictments but was acquitted of criminal charges. The government won heavy judgments against him, however, in civil suits.

MORSE, EDWARD SYLVESTER (*b. Portland, Maine, 1838; d. 1925*), zoologist, authority on Japanese art. Director, Peabody Museum, Salem, Mass., *post* 1880; curator Japanese pottery collection, Boston Museum of Fine Arts *post* 1892.

MORSE, FREEMAN HARLOW (*b. Bath, Maine, 1807; d. Surbiton, England, 1891*), carver of figureheads for ships, politician. Congressman, Whig, from Maine, 1843–45; congressman, Republican, 1857–61. U.S. consul at London, England, 1861–70.

MORSE, HARMON NORTHROP (*b. Cambridge, Vt., 1848; d. Chebeague, Maine, 1920*), organic chemist. Brother of Anson D. Morse. Graduated Amherst, 1873; Ph.D., Göttingen, 1875. Taught chemistry at Johns Hopkins, 1876–1916. Devised new methods of quantitative analysis; made extended research on permanganic acid and its salts *post* 1896. Developed electrolytic method for depositing semipermeable membranes, which he used for accumulating accurate experimental data on osmotic pressure of aqueous solutions.

MORSE, HENRY DUTTON (*b. Boston, Mass., 1826; d. Jamaica Plain, Mass., 1888*), diamond cutter. The first American to learn the technique of diamond-cutting. Morse invented machinery for sawing and polishing stones and cut the first modern full-fashioned brilliants with 56 facets.

MORSE, JEDIDIAH (*b. Woodstock, Conn., 1761; d. New Haven, Conn., 1826*), Congregational clergyman. Graduated Yale, 1783; served briefly as tutor at Yale; was pastor, First Church, Charleston, Mass., 1789–1819. Opposed Unitarian and other heresies in the Congregational churches; edited the *Panoplist*, 1805–10; was a founder of Andover Theological Seminary. The pamphlet *American Unitarianism* (1815), issued by him but extracted from another work, resulted in driving many Unitarian churches from the Congregational fold. As conservative in politics as in religion, Morse was a strong Federalist and contributed to the popular hysteria aroused in the United States during the 1790's by the events of the French Revolution. He is best remembered, however, as the "father of American geography." His *Geography Made Easy* (1784) was the first geography to be published in the United States and went through many editions, as did its larger successor *The American Geography* (1789). During Morse's lifetime, his geographies virtually monopolized their field in the United States. He was father of Samuel F. B. and Sidney E. Morse.

MORSE, JOHN LOVETT (*b. Taunton, Mass., 1865; d. Newton, Mass., 1940*), pediatrician. Graduated Harvard, 1887; Harvard Medical School, 1891. As a teacher at Harvard Medical School and in his work at Boston Children's Hospital, Morse was one of the pioneers in the development of pediatrics as a specialty.

MORSE, JOHN TORREY (*b. Boston, Mass., 1840; d. Needham, Mass., 1937*), biographer, editor, lawyer. Graduated Harvard, 1860. Projected and edited the American Statesmen series (34 vols., 1882–1916).

MORSE, SAMUEL FINLEY BREESE (*b. Charlestown, Mass., 1791; d. New York, N.Y., 1872*), artist, inventor. Son of Jedidiah Morse. Graduated Yale, 1810. Studied painting under Washington Allston and at the Royal Academy of London, 1811–15. Returning to America, he found that portraits were the only works of art which Americans would buy; he achieved initial successes as a portraitist in Charleston, S.C., where he spent the winters, 1818–21, and in New York City, where he made his headquarters *post* 1823. The general excellence of his portraits is high, displaying insight into character and a free and delicate technique; his landscapes and subject pictures are fewer in number and for the most part cold and unimaginative. Leading spirit among the founders of the National Academy of Design, Morse served as its first president, 1826–42. Despite his success in the intellectual and art circles of New York, his income was small and irregular. After spending the years 1829–32 in European travel and study, he returned to New York to accept a nominal post as professor of painting and design at New York University and to engage in some extremely ill-judged nativist and anti-Catholic agitation. He abandoned painting as a profession *ca.* 1837.

Morse's preoccupation with the telegraph dates from October 1832, when a conversation with Charles T. Jackson aboard ship suggested to Morse's mind the concept of an electromagnetic recording telegraph for the rapid transmission of intelligence. What he knew of electricity at this time was solely what he had learned in attending a course of lectures on the subject given by James F. Dana, 1827; he was ignorant of Joseph Henry's discoveries in electromagnetism and of the several European experiments which were being conducted with electromagnetic needle telegraphs. The essential features of Morse's invention as set down in his 1832 notebook were (1) a sending apparatus to transmit signals by the closing and opening of an electric circuit; (2) a receiving apparatus operated by an electromagnet to record the signals as dots and spaces on a strip of paper moved by clockwork; (3) a code translating the dots and spaces into numbers and letters. From this original concept, Morse brought his invention through elaboration to eventual simplicity. Early in the process, he noticed that signals could also be read by ear and worked out an efficient sounder. The code, too, went through a series of changes before it became the "Morse code." Initially the inventor did not dream of the telegraph as a convenience; it was to be government-controlled and used only for communications of great importance. In consequence, he wasted a great deal of time devising a semisecret code that required the use of a huge dictionary for translation. With the assistance of Leonard Dunnell Gale and Joseph Henry, Morse finally reduced his invention to practical working form and he filed a caveat for it in the patent office, 1837. In the same year, he took Alfred Vail into partnership with him. Several years of discouragement followed, in which Morse was denied European patent protection for his work, before Congress voted an appropriation for an experimental line from Washington to Baltimore in 1843. The line was built by Ezra Cornell and on May 24, 1844, Morse sent over it the famous greeting "What hath God wrought!" The further development of the telegraph was neglected by the government, however, and left to private enterprise. With the help of Amos Kendall as business manager, Morse ultimately became rich as a result of the practical exploitation of his invention, despite much litigation in which his rights were challenged and during which he lost the friendship of Joseph Henry.

MORSE, SIDNEY EDWARDS (*b. Charlestown, Mass., 1794; d. 1871*), inventor, author. Son of Jedidiah Morse; brother of Samuel F. B. Morse.

MORTIMER, MARY (*b. Trowbridge, England, 1816; d. Milwaukee, Wis., 1877*), educator, pioneer in higher education of women. In collaboration with Catharine E. Beecher, Mortimer instituted the Milwaukee Female College, 1850–51.

MORTON, CHARLES (*b. Cornwall, England, 1626/7; d. 1698*), Puritan clergyman, schoolmaster. Came to Boston, Mass., 1686, after serving *post* 1666 as master of the famous Dissenting academy at Newington Green. Named minister at Charlestown, Mass., he was elected a fellow of Harvard, 1692, and vice-president of the college, 1697.

MORTON, CHARLES GOULD (*b. Cumberland, Maine, 1861; d. San Francisco, Calif., 1933*), soldier. Graduated West Point, 1883. After serving in a number of posts abroad and at home, Morton rose to rank of major general, May 1917. Appointed to command the 29th Division in July, he trained the unit and actively commanded it in France, 1918–19. His successful operations east of Verdun prevented an increase of German strength between the Argonne and the Meuse and aided the American offensive there, September–November 1918.

MORTON, CHARLES WALTER (*b. Omaha, Nebr., 1899; d. London, England, 1967*), author and editor. Reporter for the *Boston Herald* and the *Boston Evening Transcript* (from 1928). Headed the information service of the U.S. Social Security Board in Boston, 1936–41. On staff of *Atlantic Monthly*, 1941–66; on board of directors from 1948; wrote feature "Accent on Living" from 1943. Collaborated with *Boston Herald* cartoonist Francis Dahl on *Dahl's Boston* (1946) and *Dahl's Brave New World* (1947). *Atlantic*, *New Yorker*, and *Punch* essays are collected in *How to Protect Yourself Against Women and Other Vicissitudes* (1951) and *A Slight Sense of Outrage* (1955). Also wrote the autobiography *It Has Its Charms ...* (1966).

MORTON, FERDINAND JOSEPH ("JELLY ROLL") (*b. New Orleans, La., 1885[?]; d. Los Angeles, Calif., 1941*), jazz musician, composer. Christened Ferdinand Joseph La Menthe. Born of parents whose families were long settled in Louisiana; attended grammar school in New Orleans; became a skillful guitarist and studied piano. When he was about 17 he began working as a piano player in Storyville, the red-light district of New Orleans. He cultivated a "barrelhouse" style, which he considered different from ragtime, and by 1902 or 1903 he had begun composing. Some of his most popular works of the period were "New Orleans Blues," "King Porter Stomp," "Wolverine Blues," and "Jelly Roll Blues." By 1904 he had begun to travel in other parts of the South. For a decade before 1917 he wandered through the Midwest and Southwest, working in minstrel shows and in vaudeville. He also began making written arrangements of his compositions; his "Jelly Roll Blues," published in 1915, was probably the first jazz orchestration ever printed.

In 1917 Morton played in Los Angeles nightclubs and established one of his own. He then returned to Chicago, which had become the new center of jazz, and entered the most successful phase of his career. Between 1926 and 1930 he formed the small band known as the Red Hot Peppers; they recorded some of his most original compositions, including "Black Bottom Stomp" and "Grandpa's Spells." Morton took his Red Hot Peppers on successful tours, but his popularity declined in the 1930's. He spent much of that decade in New York City, which had displaced Chicago as the jazz capital. Morton was the first jazz composer, one who wrote not merely tunes but carefully structured orchestrations. Many of his compositions—including "Milneburg Joys," "The Pearls," "Shoe Shiners Drag," "Wild Man Blues," and "Kansas City Stomps"—became standards in the jazz repertory.

MORTON, FERDINAND QUINTIN (*b. Macon, Miss., 1881; d. Washington, D.C., 1949*), lawyer, politician. Raised in Washington, D.C. Graduated Phillips Exeter Academy, 1902; attended Harvard College, 1902–05. Moved to New York City, 1908, where he worked as a law clerk; admitted to the bar, 1910. Through activity as a campaign speaker and in the United Colored Democracy (an organization of black Democrats, which he headed, 1915–33), he became the leading black Democratic politician in New York City. He served as an assistant district attorney for New York County, 1916–21, resigning to become the first black member of the Municipal Civil Service Commission. He remained a member of the commission until his retirement in 1948, and was its president, 1946–48.

MORTON, GEORGE (*b. Nottinghamshire, England, 1585; d. Plymouth, Mass., 1624*), Pilgrim father. Converted when very young by William Brewster, he was a member of the Scrooby congregation before their emigration, was one of the financial mainstays of the Pilgrims at Leiden, and was probably chief Pilgrim agent during the absence of Robert Cushman. He changed his name to George Mourt *ca.* 1619. Receiving the reports sent in the ship *Fortune* from Plymouth, 1622, he published them in London as *A Relation or Iournall of the Beginning and Proceedings of the English Plantation Setled at Plimoth in New England*, which is still the only contemporary account of the *Mayflower* voyage and the first months of the Plymouth colony. He settled at Plymouth, 1623.

MORTON, HENRY (*b. New York, N.Y., 1836; d. 1902*), scientist, Biblical archaeologist. Graduated University of Pennsylvania, 1857. As first president of Stevens Institute of Technology, 1870–1902, Morton developed the first curriculum in mechanical engineering in America. He was widely known as a research chemist and physicist.

MORTON, JAMES ST. CLAIR (*b. Philadelphia, Pa., 1829; d. Petersburg, Va., 1864*), military engineer. Son of Samuel G. Morton. Graduated West Point, 1851. Expert in fortification work, he served during the Civil War as chief engineer of the Army of the Ohio and the Army of the Cumberland; he was killed in action, June 17, 1864, while chief engineer of the IX Army Corps.

MORTON, JELLY ROLL.   *See* MORTON, FERDINAND JOSEPH.

MORTON, JOHN   (*b. Ridley, Pa., ca. 1724; d. 1777*), surveyor, farmer, Pennsylvania provincial legislator and jurist. Signer of the Declaration of Independence as a Pennsylvania delegate to the Continental Congress, 1774–77; active on a number of important congressional committees.

MORTON, JULIUS STERLING   (*b. Adams, N.Y., 1832; d. Lake Forest, Ill., 1902*), agriculturist, Nebraska politician. Raised in Michigan; removed to Nebraska, 1854, where he edited the *Nebraska City News* and became a leader in territorial affairs. He was secretary of Nebraska Territory, 1858–61, and was thereafter repeatedly a candidate for office on the Democratic ticket. His appointment as U.S. secretary of agriculture, 1893–97, was owing as much to his standing as a practical agriculturist as it was to his orthodox Democratic record. The annual celebration of Arbor Day was brought about at his suggestion.

MORTON, LEVI PARSONS   (*b. Shoreham, Vt., 1824; d. 1920*), banker. Congressman, Republican, from New York, 1879–81; U.S. minister to France, 1881–85; vice-president of the United States, 1889–93. Independent of party pressure while presiding over the Senate, he showed the same characteristic as governor of New York, 1895–97; a firm and moderate advocate of civil service reform, he consistently refused to accept the domination of Thomas C. Platt.

MORTON, MARCUS   (*b. Freetown, Mass., 1784; d. Taunton, Mass., 1864*), lawyer. Congressman, Democrat, from Massachusetts, 1817–21; lieutenant governor of Massachusetts, 1824–25; judge, Massachusetts Supreme Court, 1825–40. A perennial Democratic candidate for governor of Massachusetts, 1828–43, he was successful only in 1839 and 1842. An advocate of governmental economy, he was ahead of his time in his championship of the workingman, his distrust of overlarge corporations, and his advocacy of shorter working hours.

MORTON, MARCUS   (*b. Taunton, Mass., 1819; d. Andover, Mass., 1891*), jurist. Son of Marcus Morton (1784–1864). Held a number of Massachusetts judicial positions, 1858–90; was chief justice, Massachusetts Supreme Judicial Court, 1882–90.

MORTON, NATHANIEL   (*b. Leiden, Netherlands, 1613; d. Plymouth, Mass., 1685 o.s.*), Pilgrim father. Son of George Morton. Came to Plymouth, 1623; was reared in family of William Bradford, his uncle by marriage. As secretary of the colony and keeper of the records, 1647–85, Morton handled much of the routine work of government and probably drafted most of the colony's laws. Custodian of Bradford's papers after his death, Morton was an authority on Pilgrim history and was author-editor of *New Englands Memoriall* (printed at Cambridge, 1669).

MORTON, OLIVER PERRY   (*b. Salisbury, Ind., 1823; d. Indianapolis, Ind., 1877*), lawyer, politician. Rose rapidly to leadership of Wayne Co. bar, serving railway interests. Left Democratic party over Kansas-Nebraska Act and helped form the Republican party along national lines. As governor of Indiana, 1861–67, he was reputedly the ablest and most energetic of the Civil War state executives in the West, arousing the people of Indiana to enthusiastic support of the war and thwarting the plots of Copperhead elements by any means that worked. Elected to the U.S. Senate, 1867, he served there until his death as an uncompromising supporter of "thorough" Reconstruction. A contender for the Republican presidential nomination, 1876, he lost the nomination because of his tendency to favor soft money, his strict partisanship, and the state of his health (he had been a paralytic since 1865). Incorruptible in money matters, he was distinctly of

his time in his fanatical devotion to party and his intolerance of opposition.

MORTON, PAUL   (*b. Detroit, Mich., 1857; d. 1911*), businessman. Son of Julius S. Morton. Appointed U.S. secretary of the navy, 1904, he resigned, 1905, following exposure of his part in illegal rebate practices while an officer of the Santa Fe Railroad. Thereafter, he engaged in the rehabilitation of the Equitable Life Assurance Association, New York.

MORTON, SAMUEL GEORGE   (*b. Philadelphia, Pa., 1799; d. Philadelphia, 1851*), physician, naturalist. M.D., University of Pennsylvania, 1820; M.D., Edinburgh, 1823. Morton's research extended through the fields of medicine, geology, paleontology, zoology; his 1834 monograph describing fossils brought back by the Lewis and Clark Expedition has been called the starting point of all systematic work on American fossils. He was author of a number of other works, including *Human Anatomy* (1849), and exercised a marked influence upon Louis Agassiz.

MORTON, SARAH WENTWORTH APTHORP   (*b. Boston, Mass., 1759; d. Quincy, Mass., 1846*), poet. Her stilted and derivative didactic poems, which enjoyed great repute in their own time, appeared widely in American periodicals over her pseudonym "Philenia." Her published books included *Ouâbi¢R* (1790), *Beacon Hill* (1797), and *The Virtues of Society* (1799).

MORTON, THOMAS   (*fl. 1622–47*), adventurer. Came to Wessagusett (Massachusetts) probably in 1622; settled in limits of present Quincy, Mass., after a trip back to England and a return with the Wollaston Company. Established at "Merry Mount," he led a licentious and convivial life in the intervals of his work as fur trader. He was soon anathema to the Plymouth Pilgrims for this and also for selling guns to the Indians. Three times arrested and twice deported to England, he paid his compliments to New England in his satiric book *New English Canaan* (1637).

MORTON, WILLIAM JAMES   (*b. Boston, Mass., 1845; d. Miami, Fla., 1920*), neurologist. Son of William T. G. Morton. Made extensive investigations in electrotherapeutics; was one of first physicians in America to use X rays in treatment of skin disorders and cancerous growths, 1902–07.

MORTON, WILLIAM THOMAS GREEN   (*b. Charlton, Mass., 1819; d. New York, N.Y., 1868*), dentist. Practicing in Boston, Mass., 1842–44, Morton became acquainted with the Boston chemist and researcher Charles T. Jackson. In July 1844, at Jackson's suggestion, he employed ether in drops as a local anesthetic during the filling of a tooth. After testing the effect of inhalation of sulphuric ether on animal subjects and on himself, he made his first attempt to use it in the treatment of a human patient on Sept. 30, 1846. Public notice of the incident appeared in the *Boston Daily Journal* of Oct. 1. Other successful extractions followed. With the encouragement of Henry J. Bigelow and John C. Warren, ether was first used successfully in a surgical operation at the Massachusetts General Hospital, Oct. 16, 1846, when Warren removed a vascular tumor from a patient. The next day, again under Morton's supervision, Dr. George Hayward also operated with equal success. During the next two weeks a disagreement arose as to the advisability of continuing the procedure, since Morton was not a medical man and refused to tell the composition of his anesthetic agent. The difficulties were finally overcome and the discovery was first announced by Henry J. Bigelow on Nov. 18, 1846, in the *Boston Medical and Surgical Journal*.

Seeking at once to secure profit from his discovery, Morton applied for a patent to protect his rights, refusing to reveal that the anesthetic agent was sulphuric ether and designating it only by the name "letheon." Letters patent were issued to him (and to Charles T. Jackson, whom he had been forced to include by legal advisers) in November 1846, for a period of 14 years. Morton, however, adamantly insisted that the discovery was entirely his. A congressional appropriations bill to compensate him for the discovery was blocked by supporters of the claims of Jackson, Horace Wells, and Crawford W. Long; subsequent deliberations of congressional committees and subcommittees were drawn out for nearly two decades and the last 20 years of Morton's life brought him only honor without riches and the perpetual torment of controversy and litigation. Although others shared in the discovery, Morton's independent action, the experiments he made upon his own initiative, and his assumption of entire responsibility for the outcome make him the true discoverer of ether for surgical use. Important among his little-known writings are *Remarks on the Proper Mode of Administering Sulphuric Ether by Inhalation* (1847) and a brochure *On the Physiological Effects of Sulphuric Ether, and Its Superiority to Chloroform* (1850).

MORWITZ, EDWARD (*b. Danzig, Prussia, 1815; d. Philadelphia, Pa., 1893*), physician, publisher. Settled in Philadelphia, 1852, where he practiced, published several German-language newspapers, and organized the Newspaper Union, the most extensive German distributor of "patent-inside" material in the United States.

MOSBY, JOHN SINGLETON (*b. Edgemont, Va., 1833; d. Washington, D.C., 1916*), lawyer, Confederate ranger. A cavalry officer, Mosby operated in Virginia and Maryland under partisan ranger law, January 1863–April 1865; he rose to a colonelcy. Among his spectacular successes were the capture of General Stoughton at Fairfax Court House, March 1863; raids on Chantilly, April 1863; and Point of Rocks, Md., July 4, 1864; and the "greenback raid," Oct. 14, 1864, when he seized $168,000, dividing it among his men to buy new uniforms and equipment, as was his custom. Mosby personally never received any of the loot, but the Union forces regarded him and his men as robbers. After the war he joined the Republican party, was U.S. consul at Hong Kong, 1878–85, and an assistant attorney for the Department of Justice, 1904–10. He published *Mosby's War Reminiscences* (1887) and other works.

MOSCOSO DE ALVARADO, LUIS DE (*fl. 1530–43*), second in command under Hernando de Soto during conquest of Florida. After de Soto's death early in 1542, Moscoso led the survivors of the expedition back to Mexico City.

MOSELEY, EDWARD AUGUSTUS (*b. Newburyport, Mass., 1846; d. Washington, D.C., 1911*), lawyer, advocate of railway safety laws. Secretary, Interstate Commerce Commission, 1887–1911.

MOSER, CHRISTOPHER OTTO (*b. Dallas, Tex., 1885; d. 1935*), organizer of farm groups, scientific dairy farmer. Becoming interested in cotton cooperatives *ca.* 1920, he was responsible for organization of the American Cotton Growers Exchange and served it as president, 1925–30.

MOSES, ANNA MARY ROBERTSON ("GRANDMA") (*b. near Greenwich, N.Y., 1860; d. Hoosick Falls, N.Y., 1961*), folk painter. Farmed in Virginia and New York until 1930; at age seventy, she began making woolen embroideries, and in 1938 turned to painting on Masonite. First exhibited in New York in 1940; the charm, nostalgia, strong sense of design, and luminous color characteristic of her paintings, together with the esteem for the "primitive" in art that peaked in the 1940's, brought her immediate commercial success. Between 1941 and 1961 her paintings were widely exhibited in the United States; from 1950 to 1956 fifteen solo exhibitions were held in major European cities. Paintings include *Sugaring Off, Candle Dip Day, White Christ-*

mas, Applebutter Making at the Dudley Place, and *Shenandoah Valley.*

MOSES, BERNARD (*b. Burlington, Conn., 1846; d. 1930*), political scientist, historian. Pioneer in research study of Hispanic-American history. Graduated University of Michigan, 1870; Ph.D., Heidelberg, 1873. Taught at University of California, 1876–1930 (emeritus *post* 1910).

MOSES, FRANKLIN J. (*b. Sumter District, S.C., 1838; d. Winthrop, Mass., 1906*), lawyer, editor, Confederate soldier and official. Scalawag. Turning Republican, 1867, he entered on an opportunistic career of fraud and extravagance. A corrupt legislator and public official, he reached the climax of his unscrupulous course as governor of South Carolina, 1872–74. Turning state's evidence against former associates to save himself from prison, he slipped thereafter into obscurity.

MOSES, GEORGE HIGGINS (*b. Lubec, Maine, 1869; d. Concord, N.H., 1944*), journalist, politician. B.A., Dartmouth College, 1890; M.A., 1893. U.S. senator, Republican, from New Hampshire, 1918–33. Identified throughout his life with party regularity and the extreme conservative wing of the Republicans, he was tireless and vociferous in his opposition to all liberal policies and in his defense of the special interests of New Hampshire.

MOSES, MONTROSE JONAS (*b. New York, N.Y., 1878; d. 1934*), dramatic critic, editor. Graduated College of the City of New York, 1899. After serving as critic and editor on a number of periodicals, Moses devoted himself to free-lance writing *post* 1919. An authority on the history and traditions of the American theater, he edited the plays of Clyde Fitch, produced a number of valuable anthologies of American and foreign drama, and wrote several critical biographies of figures in the theater.

MOSESSOHN, DAVID NEHEMIAH (*b. Ekaterinoslav, Russia, 1883; d. 1930*), lawyer, businessman. Came to America as a child; was raised in Portland, Oreg. LL.B., University of Oregon, 1902. Practiced in New York City *post* 1918. Planned organization of Associated Dress Industries, 1918; was appointed its executive director, and *post* 1923 was its executive chairman. Distinguished as an impartial arbitrator in industrial disputes, Mosessohn was a leader in Jewish affairs and edited the *Jewish Tribune,* 1926–30.

MOSHER, ELIZA MARIA (*b. Cayuga Co., N.Y., 1846; d. Brooklyn, N.Y., 1928*), physician, educator, pioneer in physical education of women. M.D., University of Michigan, 1875. Professor of physiology and hygiene, Vassar College; professor of hygiene and first dean of women, University of Michigan, 1896–1902.

MOSHER, THOMAS BIRD (*b. Biddeford, Maine, 1852; d. Portland, Maine, 1923*), publisher of Mosher Books, beautifully printed, inexpensive editions of little known masterpieces.

MOSKOWITZ, BELLE LINDNER ISRAELS (*b. New York, N.Y., 1877; d. New York, 1933*), welfare worker, political leader, authority on factory legislation. Trusted adviser on social and economic problems of Alfred E. Smith.

MOSLER, HENRY (*b. New York, N.Y., 1841; d. New York, 1920*), genre painter. His *Le Retour* (1879) was the first painting by an American to be bought for the Luxembourg Museum, Paris.

MOSS, FRANK (*b. Cold Spring, N.Y., 1860; d. 1920*), lawyer, reformer. Counsel for Society for the Prevention of Crime *post* 1887. Associate of Howard Crosby and Charles H. Parkhurst in attacks against Tammany Hall and vice conditions in New York, he later acted as counsel to the Lexow and Mazet investigating committees and as an assistant district attorney under Charles Whitman, 1909–14.

MOSS, JOHN CALVIN (*b. near Bentleyville, Pa., 1838; d. 1892*), printer, pioneer commercial photoengraver. Perfected his process *ca.* 1870; worked in New York City, 1871–92.

MOSS, LEMUEL (*b. Boone Co., Ky., 1829; d. New York, N.Y., 1904*), Baptist clergyman, editor, educator. Taught at Bucknell University and at Crozer Theological Seminary; was president of (old) Chicago University, 1874, and of Indiana State University, 1875–84.

MOSS, SANFORD ALEXANDER (*b. San Francisco, Calif., 1872; d. Lynn, Mass., 1946*), mechanical engineer. A graduate of the University of California at Berkeley and of Cornell University's Sibley College of Engineering, Moss worked for the General Electric Co., 1903–38, serving thereafter as a consultant for that firm. He is distinguished for his successful development of the turbosupercharger for aircraft engines in 1939, after more than 20 years of research.

MOST, JOHANN JOSEPH (*b. Augsburg, Germany, 1846; d. Cincinnati, Ohio, 1906*), anarchist. Edited *Die Freiheit* from 1878. Expelled from the German Socialist party, 1880, for his extreme anarchist views, he came to New York City in 1882, where he continued to edit his paper and became leader of the most radical faction of the American anarchists. He dictated the declaration of principles adopted by the Pittsburgh convention of 1883 which became the doctrine of communist anarchism in America.

MOTLEY, JOHN LOTHROP (*b. Dorchester, Mass., 1814; d. England, 1877*), historian, diplomat. Attended Round Hill School, where George Bancroft was one of his teachers; graduated Harvard, 1831; made further studies in Germany and traveled in Great Britain and on the Continent. Returning to Boston, 1835, he worked at writing and published two novels: *Morton's Hope* (1839) and *Merrymount* (written *ca.* 1839, published 1849). After a brief service as secretary of legation at St. Petersburg, Russia, he decided *ca.* 1847 on the field of history that was to be his interest for the rest of his life, the attainment of independence by the Netherlands. Encouraged by W. H. Prescott, Motley entered on a lengthy research into his chosen subject and after numerous difficulties and disappointments, published *The Rise of the Dutch Republic* (London and New York, 1856). It had an immediate and great success, which it owed to its picturesque, dramatic narrative of a striking series of events and the enthusiasm which it showed for liberty; however, Motley's warm, partisan prejudices lessened the value of the work as history and it remains a brilliant personal interpretation of its subject. He next produced the *History of the United Netherlands* (1860, 1867, London; 1861, 1868, New York) and *The Life and Death of John of Barneveld* (1874), which completed his project but were lacking in the dramatic interest of the earlier work. Happy and reasonably successful as U.S. minister to Austria, 1861–67, Motley resigned under pressure from Washington occasioned by circumstances not of his making. Appointed U.S. minister to Great Britain, 1869, he was unsuccessful in pressing the *Alabama* claims. He was dismissed by President Grant in 1870, not so much for his failure as because he was a friend of Charles Sumner, with whom the president was at odds.

MOTLEY, WILLARD FRANCIS (*b. Chicago, Ill., 1909; d. Mexico City, Mexico, 1965*), novelist. Founded and edited, with Alexander Saxton, *Hull-House Magazine* (1939–40). Wrote *Knock on Any Door* (1947), which was praised by critics and remained on the *New York Times* best-seller list for ten months; in 1949 Columbia Pictures released a film version starring Humphrey Bogart. Reputation declined with the publication of *We Fished All Night* (1951), *Let No Man Write My Epitaph* (1958), and *Let Noon be Fair* (1966). Moved to Mexico in 1951. Critics praised his naturalistic sensibilities and derided a mawkish sentimentality they felt pervaded the later work. A black man, Motley defended himself against the criticism that his books dealt only tangentially with questions of race.

MOTON, ROBERT RUSSA (*b. Amelia Co., Va., 1867; d. Capahosic, Va., 1940*), black educational administrator. Graduated Hampton Institute, 1890. Served Hampton in many administrative capacities, 1890–1915; was principal, Tuskegee Institute, 1915–35.

MOTT, FRANK LUTHER (*b. What Cheer, Iowa, 1886; d. Columbia, Mo., 1964*), journalist, author, and educator. Studied at Simpson College, the University of Chicago, and Columbia University (Ph.D., 1924). Taught at Simpson (1919–21); and the University of Iowa (1921–25), where he was dean of the School of Journalism (1927–42) and coeditor (1925–33) of *Midland* magazine. Elected president of the American Association of Schools and Departments of Journalism in 1929. Editor of the *Journalism Quarterly* (1930–34). Dean of the University of Missouri School of Journalism (1942–51). Works include *History of American Magazines* (Pulitzer Prize, 1939), *American Journalism: A History, 1690–1940* (1941), and *Time Enough: Essays in Autobiography* (1962).

MOTT, GERSHOM (*b. Lamberton, N.J., 1822; d. 1884*), businessman, Union major general. Earned special recognition as a divisional commander in the battles of the Wilderness and Spotsylvania Court House, May–June 1864.

MOTT, JAMES (*b. North Hempstead, N.Y., 1788; d. Brooklyn, N.Y., 1868*), businessman, Quaker reformer, Abolitionist. Married to Lucretia Coffin Mott, 1811.

MOTT, JOHN R. (*b. Livingston Manor, N.Y., 1865; d. Orlando, Fla., 1955*), ecumenical pioneer and YMCA official. Received Ph.B. from Cornell (1888). Affiliated with the YMCA from 1886; senior student secretary (1890); director of the student volunteer movement. Founded the World's Student Christian Federation in 1895. Mott traveled widely throughout the world to recruit student members for his organization and to work for the YMCA. In 1915, he became the national executive for the American YMCA. During World War I, he donated the organization's resources both in the U.S. and abroad to the war relief effort. In 1921, he became the chairman of the International Missionary Council, and in 1926, president of the World YMCA. Influential in forming the World Council of Churches, he was honorary president in 1948. In 1946, along with Emily Green Balch, he received the Nobel Peace Prize.

MOTT, LUCRETIA COFFIN (*b. Nantucket, Mass., 1793; d. 1880*), reformer, Quaker preacher. Cousin of Isaac and John Coffin; married James Mott, 1811. Aligned, like her husband, with the liberal, or Hicksite, group of the Society of Friends, she traveled extensively to speak at Quaker meetings in different parts of the country. Her most notable work was connected with the questions of woman's rights and antislavery; with Elizabeth Cady Stanton, she was a chief promoter of the convention at Seneca Falls, N.Y., 1848, where the U.S. woman's rights movement was formally launched.

MOTT, VALENTINE (*b. Glen Cove, N.Y., 1785; d. New York, N.Y., 1865*), surgeon. M.D., Columbia, 1806; studied also in London and Edinburgh under Astley Cooper and other noted surgeons. Taught surgery at various times at Columbia, at Rutgers Medical College, at the New York College of Physicians and Surgeons, and at the University of the City of New York (New York

University). A bold, original surgeon of international repute, he was the first to tie the innominate artery, 1818, and successfully tied the common iliac artery, 1827, for an aneurism of the external iliac; he was also one of the first to perform a successful amputation of the hip joint, to excise the jaw for necrosis, and to resect and suture veins.

MOULTON, ELLEN LOUISIE CHANDLER (*b. Pomfret, Conn., 1835; d. Boston, Mass., 1908*), minor poet and author of juvenile stories.

MOULTON, FOREST RAY (*b. southern Mich., 1872; d. Wilmette, Ill., 1952*), astronomer and mathematician. Studied at Albion College, Michigan, and at the University of Chicago (Ph.D., 1899). Taught at the University of Chicago (1901–26). Co-developed the Chamberlin-Moulton hypothesis, "the planetesimal hypothesis" in 1904; the work attempted to explain the origins of the solar system and has largely been replaced by the Kant-Laplace hypothesis. Financial director of the Utilities Power and Light Corp. of Chicago (1926–36). Permanent secretary of the American Association for the Advancement of Science (1937–46).

MOULTON, RICHARD GREEN (*b. Preston, England, 1849; d. Tunbridge Wells, England, 1924*), educator, author. An enthusiastic and inspiring lecturer on literature, Moulton taught at the University of Chicago, 1892–1919.

MOULTRIE, JOHN (*b. Charleston, S.C., 1729; d. Shropshire, England, 1798*), physician, planter, lieutenant governor of East Florida, Loyalist. Brother of William Moultrie.

MOULTRIE, WILLIAM (*b. Charleston, S.C., 1730; d. 1805*), planter, Revolutionary general, South Carolina legislator. Brother of John Moultrie. A leader in the military affairs of South Carolina *post* 1762, Moultrie conducted a successful defense of the fort on Sullivan's Island, Charleston Harbor, June 28, 1776. Promoted brigadier general in the Continental service, he operated independently in South Carolina after the fall of Savannah in December 1778, and defeated a British force at Beaufort, February 1779. Took effective action that saved Charleston, S.C., from capture, May 1779, but was taken prisoner a year later with the garrison of that city when it fell. Exchanged, February 1782, he served till the end of the war, being made major general, October 1782. As governor of South Carolina, 1785–87, he worked for reestablishment of the state's credit, for better organization of the militia, and for improvement of internal navigation. Reelected governor, 1792, he retired to private life at the end of his term.

MOUNT, WILLIAM SIDNEY (*b. Setauket, N.Y., 1807; d. Stony Brook, N.Y., 1868*), genre and portrait painter, notable for the honesty and craftsmanship of his work. His genre pieces of country life on Long Island are valuable pictorial documents of his time.

MOURT, GEORGE. *See* MORTON, GEORGE.

MOUTON, ALEXANDER (*b. present Lafayette Parish, La., 1804; d. 1885*), planter, Louisiana legislator. U.S. senator, Democrat, from Louisiana, 1837–42; governor, 1843–46. Mouton put the state on a sound financial basis while governor; he was later a secessionist and sustained heavy loss by the Civil War.

MOWATT, ANNA CORA OGDEN (*b. Bordeaux, France, 1819; d. Twickenham, England, 1870*), actress, author. Granddaughter of Uzal Ogden. Raised and educated in New York City, she married James Mowatt, a New York lawyer, 1834. A write of verse and dramatic pieces since childhood, she published her first book *Pelayo* under the pseudonym "Isabel" in 1836, and attacked its critics in *Reviewers Reviewed*. After financial reverses she began

a career as a public reader of poetry at Boston, October 1841; obliged to give up work because of recurrent illness, 1842, she became a devotee of mesmerism and turned for financial support to general journalism and fiction writing. Her most important imaginative work was *Fashion: or, Life in New York*, a play first produced at the Park Theatre, New York, Mar. 24, 1845, and first published, 1850. It was a farce satirizing the pretensions of the New York nouveaux riches of its period. In September 1847, her *Armand*, a romantic historical play, was first produced in New York, where it met with favor, as it did later in London. It was first published in 1849. Meanwhile, Mowatt had made a highly successful debut as an actress in *The Lady of Lyons* (New York, 1845) and until 1853 acted in most important American cities and in England with E. L. Davenport as her leading man. Her *Autobiography of an Actress* appeared in 1854; in the same year, she made her final appearance on the stage in New York and (her husband having died, 1851) married William F. Ritchie, editor of the *Richmond Enquirer*. Active in her retirement as a writer and in the movement for the purchase and preservation of Mount Vernon, she separated from her husband, 1861, and lived abroad thereafter.

MOWBRAY, GEORGE MORDEY (*b. Brighton, England, 1814; d. North Adams, Mass., 1891*), pioneer oil refiner, inventor of explosives. Immigrated to America, 1854. Removed to Titusville, Pa., 1859, where he produced the first refined oil and was the first to use nitroglycerin for the shooting of dormant wells. *Post* 1866, he turned his attention to the manufacture of nitroglycerin and did valuable work in the development of celluloid.

MOWBRAY, HENRY SIDDONS (*b. Alexandria, Egypt, 1858; d. Washington, Conn., 1928*), figure and mural painter. Nephew and adopted son of George M. Mowbray. Made early success in Paris after study there in atelier of Léon Bonnat. Returning to the United States, 1886, he settled in New York City, removing to Washington, Conn., 1907. Recipient of many honors, Mowbray was most famous for his mural work in private mansions and public and commercial buildings. His most important and brilliant work was the decoration of the library of the University Club of New York.

MOWER, JOSEPH ANTHONY (*b. Woodstock, Vt., 1827; d. New Orleans, La., 1870*), Union major general. Entered army at outbreak of Mexican War as private of engineers; was commissioned second lieutenant, 1855, and had risen to rank of captain, 1861. His combat record during the Civil War was one rarely equaled in the American army. Twelve times cited for conspicuous bravery, in particular during the Vicksburg campaign, he was promoted major general of volunteers, August 1864. He headed a division under W. T. Sherman in Georgia and commanded the XX Corps in the Carolina campaign.

MOWRY, WILLIAM AUGUSTUS (*b. Uxbridge, Mass., 1829; d. 1917*), educator. As principal of the English and Classical School, Providence, R.I., he became a national authority on practical pedagogy and a leader in the Teachers' Institute movement.

MOXHAM, ARTHUR JAMES (*b. Neath, South Wales, 1854; d. Great Neck, N.Y., 1931*), steel manufacturer. Came to America, 1869. Organized Birmingham (Ala.) Rolling-Mill Co., 1878; removed to Johnson, Pa., *ca.* 1883, where, in partnership with Tom L. Johnson, he came to control a great part of the business in girder rails. After merging of his company in the U.S. Steel Corporation, 1901, Moxham was associated with the Du Pont Powder Co. He became president of the Aetna Explosives Co., 1914.

MOXOM, PHILIP STAFFORD (*b. Markham, Ontario, Canada, 1848; d. 1923*), Baptist and Congregational clergyman, prominent preacher. Held pastorates in Cleveland, Ohio, and Boston and Springfield, Mass.

MOYLAN, STEPHEN (*b. Cork, Ireland, 1737; d. Philadelphia, Pa., 1811*), merchant, Revolutionary soldier. Settled in Philadelphia, 1768. Recommended to George Washington by John Dickinson for patriotic zeal, he was appointed muster-master general of the army at Cambridge, Mass., August 1775, and served later as quartermaster general. He organized and commanded a regiment of light dragoons *post* April 1777, succeeded Casimir Pulaski in command of the American cavalry, March 1778, and retired in 1783 as brevet brigadier general.

MOZIER, JOSEPH (*b. Burlington, Vt., 1812; d. Faido, Switzerland, 1870*), sculptor. Resided and worked in Rome, Italy, *post* 1845.

MUDD, SAMUEL A. *See* BOOTH, JOHN WILKES.

MUDGE, ENOCH (*b. Lynn, Mass., 1776; d. Lynn, 1850*), Methodist clergyman. First native New Englander to enter the Methodist ministry, 1793, Mudge held many pastorates and as a member of the Massachusetts legislature, 1811–12 and 1815–16, aided in the passage of the religious freedom bill.

MUDGE, JAMES (*b. West Springfield, Mass., 1844; d. Malden, Mass., 1918*), Methodist clergyman. Great-nephew of Enoch Mudge. Missionary to India, 1873–83, and Massachusetts pastor.

MUHLENBERG, FREDERICK AUGUSTUS (*b. Lancaster, Pa., 1818; d. Reading, Pa., 1901*), Lutheran clergyman, educator. Great-grandson of Henry M. Mühlenberg. First president, Muhlenberg College, 1867–76.

MUHLENBERG, FREDERICK AUGUSTUS CONRAD (*b. Trappe, Pa., 1750; d. Lancaster, Pa., 1801*), Lutheran clergyman, politician. Son of Henry M. Mühlenberg; brother of John P. G. and Gotthilf H. E. Mühlenberg. A member of the Continental Congress and of the Pennsylvania Assembly, Muhlenberg presided over the Pennsylvania ratification convention, 1787. Congressman, Federalist, from Pennsylvania, 1789–97, he served as Speaker of the House of Representatives in the 1st Congress. Displaced in the 2nd Congress, he was reelected Speaker on organization of the 3rd Congress by the help of Democratic-Republican votes. He abandoned the Federalist party *ca.* 1799.

MUHLENBERG, GOTTHILF HENRY ERNEST (*b. Trappe, Pa., 1753; d. Lancaster, Pa., 1815*), Lutheran clergyman, botanist. Son of Henry M. Mühlenberg; brother of John P. G. and Frederick A. C. Mühlenberg. Pastor at Philadelphia, 1774–79; at Lancaster, Pa., 1780–1815. First president of Franklin College, 1787. Author of a number of valuable papers descriptive of his botanical fieldwork.

MÜHLENBERG, HENRY AUGUSTUS PHILIP (*b. Lancaster, Pa., 1782; d. 1844*), Lutheran clergyman, politician, diplomat. Son of Gotthilf H. E. Mühlenberg. Pastor at Reading, Pa., 1803–28. Congressman, Democrat, from Pennsylvania, 1829–38, a loyal, intelligent supporter of Andrew Jackson. First U.S. minister to Austria, 1838–40.

MUHLENBERG, HENRY MELCHIOR (*b. Einbeck, Hannover,[now Germany], 1711; d. New Providence [Trappe], Pa., 1787*), Lutheran clergyman, virtual founder of the Lutheran church in America. Graduated in theology at Göttingen, 1738; ordained, Leipzig, 1739. Offered a call to the United Congregations (Philadelphia, New Providence, New Hanover) in Pennsylvania, by G. A. Francke of the Halle Waisenhaus, where he had taught, 1738–39, Mühlenberg accepted the proposal. Rumors in Germany of Count von Zinzendorf's efforts at church union among the Germans in Pennsylvania prompted him to take the post. After conferring with Johann Martin Boltzius in Georgia, Mühlenberg arrived in Philadelphia, Nov. 25, 1742. He found his Philadelphia congregation split and his rural congregations known by the sinister vernacular names of Die Trappe and Der Schwamm. Received skeptically, he gradually won support of intelligent parishioners and was duly installed. Conflict with Zinzendorf, deplorable but inevitable, was fortunately brief. Mühlenberg saw his task, almost from the beginning, not as the serving of three isolated congregations but as the planting of a church, and to that great enterprise he brought high talents. His intellect was clear and vigorous, though not original; he had the necessary physical stamina to withstand long days in the saddle; his biblical and theological scholarship was sound; his personal religious life was mellowed by a mild type of Pietism. He was a good linguist, spoke Latin with ease, and learned to preach in English and Dutch with amazing rapidity. To his fundamental pastoral and missionary zeal he added a genius for organization. Nominally, he remained pastor of the United Congregations until almost the close of his life, but he soon made them the nucleus of an organization that spread rapidly wherever German Lutherans had settled in the middle colonies. Through his efforts, Lutheran congregations came to realize the need for closer organization and the first convention of the Evangelical Lutheran Ministerium of Pennsylvania was held at Philadelphia, Aug. 26, 1748. Mühlenberg remained the revered leader of a highly intelligent, constantly expanding Lutheran society in Pennsylvania. He formally resigned his rectorship of St. Michael's and Zion's in Philadelphia, 1779.

MUHLENBERG, JOHN PETER GABRIEL (*b. Trappe, Pa., 1746; d. Philadelphia, Pa., 1807*), Episcopal and Lutheran pastor, Revolutionary soldier, politician. Son of Henry M. Mühlenberg; grandson of John Conrad Weiser. Receiving Anglican orders from the bishop of London, 1772, he was pastor of the German Lutheran congregation at Woodstock, Va., until 1776; *post* 1774, he was associated with the leaders of the Revolutionary party and served in the House of Burgesses. Having raised and commanded a Virginia regiment composed of Shenandoah Germans, he was commissioned brigadier general in the Continental army, February 1777. Distinguished as a brigade commander at Brandywine, Germantown, and Monmouth, he supported Wayne in the assault on Stony Point, 1779, and served through 1780 as second in command to Baron von Steuben. On Oct. 14, 1781, he commanded the American brigade that stormed one of the two British redoubts at Yorktown. Leaving the army as brevet major general, he was elected to the Council of Pennsylvania, 1784, was vice president of the state, 1785–88, and was influential in securing early adoption of the U.S. Constitution. He served as representative at large, Democratic-Republican, 1789–91, and as congressman from Montgomery Co., Pa., 1793–95 and 1799–1801. Elected to the U.S. Senate, February 1801, he resigned a month later. He was collector of customs for Philadelphia, 1802–07.

MUHLENBERG, WILLIAM AUGUSTUS (*b. Philadelphia, Pa., 1796; d. New York, N.Y., 1877*), Episcopal clergyman, educator. Grandson of Frederick A. C. Mühlenberg. Graduated University of Pennsylvania, 1815; ordained, 1820; held pastorates at Lancaster, Pa., and Flushing, N.Y. Founded and headed Flushing Institute and St. Paul's College, which served as models for subsequent educational institutions under Christian auspices. Retiring from educational enterprises, 1843, he became rector of the Church of the Holy Communion, New York, 1846; among the philanthropic works which stemmed from this parish were the Episcopal Sisterhood of the Holy Communion and St. Luke's

Hospital, New York. The "Memorial" presented to the Episcopal bishops, 1853, requesting liturgical reform and other innovations, was drafted by Muhlenberg. Resigning his rectorship in 1858, he gave all his time thereafter to St. Luke's Hospital and to an experiment in Christian communal life on Long Island which was called St. Johnsland.

MUIR, CHARLES HENRY (b. *Erie, Mich., 1860; d. 1933*), army officer. Graduated West Point, 1885. Distinguished for gallantry in Spanish-American War; commanded 28th Division in France, 1918–19. Retired as major general, 1924.

MUIR, JOHN (b. *Dunbar, Scotland, 1838; d. Los Angeles, Calif., 1914*), naturalist, explorer, conservationist. Came to America as a boy; was raised in Wisconsin and attended the University of Wisconsin, where chemistry and geology were his major interests. After extensive travel on foot through the Midwest, he arrived in California, 1868. Six years of study and exploration in Yosemite Valley were followed by equivalent work in Nevada, Utah, the Northwest, and Alaska. On all his excursions, he kept a journal in which he noted his observations and illustrated them with sketches. After spending the decade, 1881–91, in securing a competence by fruit ranching, Muir devoted the rest of his life to travel and study. The principal objects of his interest were glaciers and forests; he was the first to demonstrate the origin of Yosemite Valley by glacial erosion and discovered and described many great glaciers in Alaska. The establishment of Yosemite National Park by Congress, 1890, was largely owing to propaganda written by him and Robert U. Johnson. A similar campaign based on Muir's observation of the wastage of the national forest resources and the general trend of his lecturing and writing, 1891–1903, played an influential part in securing conservation laws. Muir was author of, among other books, *The Mountains of California* (1894); *Stickeen* (1909); *The Yosemite* (1912); *The Story of My Boyhood and Youth* (1913); and *A Thousand Mile Walk to the Gulf* (1916).

MULDOON, WILLIAM (b. *Caneadea, N.Y., 1852; d. 1933*), wrestler, police officer, expert physical trainer.

MULFORD, CLARENCE EDWARD (b. *Streator, Ill., 1883; d. Fryeburg, Md., 1956*), writer. Self-educated, Mulford was the author of over a hundred Western novels, including the *Bar 20* series which became the basis for the popular hero, Hopalong Cassidy (portrayed by William Boyd), who was featured in sixty-six films. Awarded a laurette certificate for his novel *The Round-Up* (1933) by the Institute Littéraire et Artistique de France.

MULFORD, ELISHA (b. *Montrose, Pa., 1833; d. Cambridge, Mass., 1885*), Episcopal clergyman, educator. Author of *The Nation* (1870), in which he attempted to show that the nation is an organism responding in its total life to ethical ideals.

MULFORD, PRENTICE (b. *Sag Harbor, N.Y., 1834; d. Sheepshead Bay, N.Y., 1891*), journalist, comic lecturer. Creator of the system of popular philosophy known as "New Thought."

MULHOLLAND, ST. CLAIR AUGUSTIN (b. *Lisburn, Ireland, 1839; d. 1910*), Union major general. Came to America as a boy; was raised in Philadelphia, Pa. Fighting with distinction, 1861–65, he rose to brigade command and won the Congressional Medal of Honor for covering the withdrawal of the Army of the Potomac across the Rappahannock River after the battle of Chancellorsville. After the Civil War, he served as chief of police of Philadelphia, 1868–71, and as U.S. pension agent in the same city.

MULHOLLAND, WILLIAM (b. *Belfast, Ireland, 1855; d. Los Angeles, Calif., 1935*), engineer. Came to America ca. 1872; removed to California, 1877. Superintendent and chief engineer of the Los Angeles, Calif., waterworks, he provided water supply facilities keeping pace with that city's enormous growth.

MULLAN, JOHN (b. *Norfolk, Va., 1830; d. Washington, D.C., 1909*), explorer, army officer. Graduated St. John's College, Annapolis, 1847; West Point, 1852. Associated with I. I. Stevens in exploring railroad route from St. Paul to the Pacific, 1853–54; discovered Mullan Pass. Acting as chief of construction for a military road from Fort Benton on the Missouri to Walla Walla, Wash., he distinguished himself in battle with Indians at Four Lakes, September 1858, and elsewhere. After completion of the road, 1863, Mullan resigned from the army. Failing in several attempts at business, he was successful in practice of law at San Francisco, Calif., and Washington, D.C.

MULLANY, JAMES ROBERT MADISON (b. *New York, N.Y., 1818; d. 1887*), naval officer. Appointed midshipman, 1832, he retired as rear admiral, 1874, after a long and varied career; he won particular distinction in command of USS *Oneida* at battle of Mobile Bay, August 1864.

MULLANY, PATRICK FRANCIS. *See* AZARIAS, BROTHER.

MÜLLER, HERMANN JOSEPH (b. *New York, N.Y., 1890; d. Indianapolis, Ind., 1967*), founder of radiation genetics. Studied at Cornell Medical School and Columbia University (Ph.D., 1915). Professor, University of Texas at Austin (1921–32); University of Edinburgh (1938–40); Amherst (1940–45); and Indiana University (1945–67). In the Soviet Union, 1933–37, as guest investigator and corresponding member of the Soviet Academy of Sciences. Proposed theoretical interpretation of the gene as a molecule that reproduces or copies its errors. Achieved first artificial transmutation of the gene by X-rays in 1927; established that X-rays induce gene mutations in direct proportion to the dose received and that they also induce chromosome breakage that leads to structural rearrangements. Awarded the Nobel Prize in physiology and medicine in 1946.

MULLER, WILHELM MAX (b. *Gliessenberg, Bavaria, 1862; d. Wildwood, N.J., 1919*), orientalist, Egyptologist. Taught Hebrew and Greek at Reformed Episcopal Seminary, Philadelphia, Pa., *post* 1890; was later assistant professor of Egyptology at University of Pennsylvania.

MULLIGAN, CHARLES J. (b. *Co. Tyrone, Ireland, 1866; d. Chicago, Ill., 1916*), sculptor. Came to America ca. 1883; studied with Lorado Taft. Succeeded Taft as head of Department of Sculpture, Art Institute, Chicago.

MULLIKEN, SAMUEL PARSONS (b. *Newburyport, Mass., 1864; d. 1934*), chemist. Graduated Massachusetts Institute of Technology, 1887; Ph.D., Leipzig, 1890. Taught chemistry at Clark University and at Bryn Mawr and worked in private laboratory of Oliver W. Gibbs; *post* 1895, taught at Massachusetts Institute of Technology, specializing in courses in organic chemistry. He was author of the monumental work *A Method for the Identification of Pure Organic Compounds* (1904–22).

MULLINS, EDGAR YOUNG (b. *Franklin Co., Miss., 1860; d. Louisville, Ky., 1928*), Baptist clergyman, educator. President, Southern Baptist Theological Seminary, 1899–1928; president, Baptist World Alliance, 1923–28.

MULRY, THOMAS MAURICE (b. *New York, N.Y., 1855; d. New York, 1916*), contractor, banker, philanthropist. A leader in the Society of St. Vincent de Paul and in many other local and national charitable undertakings.

MUMFORD, JAMES GREGORY (*b. Rochester, N.Y., 1863; d. 1914*), surgeon, author. Practiced in Boston; was for many years on staff of Massachusetts General Hospital.

MUNCH, CHARLES (*b. Strasbourg, Alsace, 1891; d. Richmond, Va., 1968*), conductor. Assistant concertmaster of the Strasbourg Orchestra (1919–20); violin professor at the conservatory (1920–26). Concertmaster of Gewandhaus Orchestra in Leipzig, Germany (1926–32). Principal conductor of the Société Philharmonique de Paris (1935–38). Director and principal conductor of the Société des Concerts du Conservatoire de Paris (1938–46). Led the Orchestre National de la Radiodiffusion Française on U.S. tour (1948). As conductor of the Boston Symphony Orchestra, 1949–62, Munch presented 168 contemporary works and offered 39 world premieres. In 1956 the orchestra became the first American orchestra to play in the Soviet Union. Was also director of the Berkshire Music Center and the Tanglewood Music Festival in Lenox, Mass. (1951–62). After his return to Paris, became president of the École Normale de Musique (1963–67), and director of the Orchestre de Paris (1967–68).

MUNDÉ, PAUL FORTUNATUS (*b. Dresden, Germany, 1846; d. New York, N.Y., 1902*), physician. Came to America as a child. M.D., Harvard, 1866. After seven years' military and civilian practice in Europe, Mundé practiced in New York City, where, as teacher at New York Polyclinic and gynecologist to Mt. Sinai Hospital, he exerted a powerful influence on the course of the gynecological specialty in America.

MUNDELEIN, GEORGE WILLIAM (*b. New York, N.Y., 1872; d. Chicago, Ill., 1939*), Roman Catholic clergyman. Graduated Manhattan College, 1889; made theological studies at St. Vincent Seminary, Latrobe, Pa., and in Rome, where he was ordained. After 20 years of varied service in the Diocese of Brooklyn, N.Y., he succeeded as archbishop of Chicago, 1915. He was elevated to the cardinalate, 1924. Outspoken in his social views, Mundelein supported labor and the New Deal, opposed Hitler and the isolationist Rev. Charles E. Coughlin. Noted for his administrative talents, he initiated and supported much building on behalf of the church, in particular St. Mary of the Lake Seminary at Mundelein, Ill.

MUNFORD, ROBERT (*b. Prince George Co., Va., date unknown; d. Mecklenburg Co., Va., 1784*), Revolutionary soldier, dramatist. Nephew of Theodorick Bland, Sr. Author of *A Collection of Plays and Poems* (1798), which contains his excellent translation of the first book of Ovid's *Metamorphoses* and his satiric drama *The Candidates*, which includes what is probably the first black character in American drama.

MUNFORD, WILLIAM (*b. Mecklenburg Co., Va., 1775; d. 1825*), Virginia lawyer and legislator. Son of Robert Munford, whose poetic and dramatic works he edited, 1798. Studied law under George Wythe. Served as clerk of the House of Delegates, 1811–25; coreporter with W. W. Hening of the decisions of the Virginia Supreme Court of Appeals, 1806–10. After Hening's death, Munford continued as reporter until 1821. His literary works appeared as *Poems and Compositions in Prose* (1798); his blank-verse translation of Homer's *Iliad* was not published until 1846.

MUNGER, ROBERT SYLVESTER (*b. Rutersville, Tex., 1854; d. Birmingham, Ala., 1923*), inventor and manufacturer of cotton-gin machinery. The Munger system for pneumatic handling of cotton was a revolutionary improvement over the old system; first patented, 1892, it was quickly adopted throughout the cotton states and through the world generally.

MUNGER, THEODORE THORNTON (*b. Bainbridge, N.Y., 1830; d. 1910*), Congregational clergyman. After holding a number of pastorates, Munger served as minister of the United Church, New Haven, Conn., *post* 1885. He was author of a number of books, including *The Freedom of Faith* (1883) and *Horace Bushnell, Preacher and Theologian* (1899).

MUNI, PAUL (*b. Mehilem ["Muni"] Weisenfreund, Lemberg, Austria [now Lvov, USSR], 1895; d. Montecito, Calif., 1967*), actor. Immigrated to the United States in 1901; naturalized, 1923. Star of the Yiddish theater; with Weisenfreund's Pavilion Theatre in Chicago from 1908, and with the Yiddish Art Theatre in New York from 1919. Appeared in films *The Valiant* (1929), *Scarface* (1932), *I Am a Fugitive from a Chain Gang* (1932), *The Story of Louis Pasteur* (Academy Award, 1936), *The Good Earth* (1937), *The Life of Emile Zola* (1937), *Juarez* (1939), and *The Last Angry Man* (1958). Appeared on stage in the Broadway productions of *This One Man* (1930), *Key Largo* (1940), and *Inherit the Wind* (1955), and the London performance of *Death of a Salesman* (1949). A character actor, he achieved acclaim for his ability to transform himself into a variety of roles. The completeness and integrity of his impersonations owed much to his penchant for makeup. A cover article in *Time* (Aug. 16, 1937) proclaimed him the "first actor of the American screen."

MUNN, ORSON DESAIX (*b. Monson, Mass., 1824; d. 1907*), publisher. Joined Alfred E. Beach in purchase of *Scientific American*, 1846, and was associated with the publication and its correlative activities thereafter until his death.

MUÑOZ-RIVERA, LUIS (*b. Barranquitas,, Puerto Rico, 1859; d. Santurce, Puerto Rico, 1916*), poet, editor, Puerto Rican political leader. Elected resident commissioner from Puerto Rico to the United States, 1910.

MUNRO, DANA CARLETON (*b. Bristol, R.I., 1866; d. New York, N.Y., 1933*), historian. Graduated Brown, 1887; made graduate studies at Strassburg, Freiburg im Breisgau, and University of Pennsylvania. Taught medieval and European history at Pennsylvania and at University of Wisconsin; professor of medieval history, Princeton, 1915–33. Author of *The Middle Ages* (1902), Munro made his chief contribution in the incentive he gave others to produce work of high quality.

MUNRO, GEORGE (*b. West River, Nova Scotia, 1825; d. 1896*), publisher. Removed to New York City, 1856; clerked in firm of Beadle & Adams, dime-novel publishers. Prospered *post* 1866 as publisher of a number of cheap series, of which the most successful was the Seaside Library; he was also publisher of the *Fireside Companion*, a family paper, and of the manifold adventures of Old Sleuth and Old Cap Collier. The success of his reprints of British works on which no royalty was paid helped hasten passage of the international copyright law.

MUNRO, HENRY (*b. Scotland, 1730; d. Edinburgh, Scotland, 1801*), Presbyterian and Episcopal clergyman, army chaplain, Loyalist. Came first to America, 1757; worked as a Church of England missionary along the New York frontier, 1765–76; joined British forces in Canada, 1777. Munro married Eve, sister of John Jay, 1766.

MUNRO, WILLIAM BENNETT (*b. Almonte, Ontario, 1875; d. Pasadena, Calif., 1957*), educator. Studied at Queens College, Kingston, Ont., at Harvard (Ph.D., 1900), and at the universities of Edinburgh and Berlin. An expert in municipal government. Munro wrote *The Government of American Cities* in 1912 and *Municipal Administration* in 1934, as well as numerous other texts on political science. Taught at Williams College (1901–04); at Harvard (1904–1929); and at California Institute of Technology

(1929–45). Harvard Board of Overseers (1940–46); President, American Political Science Association (1927). Fellow, American Academy of Arts and Sciences.

MUNROE, CHARLES EDWARD (*b. East Cambridge, Mass., 1849; d. Forest Glen, Md., 1938*), chemist. Graduated Harvard, 1871. Taught at Harvard, at the U.S. Naval Academy, and at George Washington University. A pioneer in American chemical engineering, he was the outstanding explosives expert of his time; he was the discoverer of smokeless powder and of the so-called Munro effect.

MUNSELL, JOEL (*b. Northfield, Mass., 1808; d. Albany, N.Y., 1880*), printer, antiquarian. Edited and published at Albany, in addition to newspapers and periodicals, a number of important collections of historical source material relating to the early wars and settlements of America.

MUNSEY, FRANK ANDREW (*b. Mercer, Maine, 1854; d. New York, N.Y., 1925*), publisher, financier. Removed to New York City, 1882; began successful career in that year with the *Golden Argosy*, a magazine for boys and girls. Living for his business and for success alone, Munsey founded or purchased magazines and, later, newspapers with cold-blooded zeal, merging or destroying them if they failed to earn well. He was also a fortunate speculator in Wall St., was owner of a chain of grocery stores, and engaged in banking. Failing in his operations in the field of daily journalism more often than he succeeded, he kept his papers clean and respectable, if dull; his publications reflected the viewpoint of the average, prosperous American concerned with his own affairs and his own personal success. His career illustrated dramatically the trend toward consolidation, combination, and decreasing competition.

MUNSON, THOMAS VOLNEY (*b. near Astoria, Ill., 1843; d. Denison, Tex., 1913*), viticulturist, horticulturist. Gave hundreds of new horticultural varieties to the world by hybridization and selection experiments; was author of, among other outstanding works on grapes, *Foundations of American Grape Culture* (1909).

MUNSON, WALTER DAVID (*b. Cheshire, Conn., 1843; d. 1908*), shipowner. Founded the Munson Line, 1873 (incorporated 1899), which grew to be the largest freighting organization in the American coastal trade.

MÜNSTERBERG, HUGO (*b. Danzig, Germany, 1863; d. Cambridge, Mass., 1916*), psychologist. Studied under Wilhelm Wundt at University of Leipzig, where he graduated, Ph.D., 1885; he graduated also as M.D. at Heidelberg, 1887, and taught philosophy and psychology at Freiburg, 1887–97. On leave of absence from Freiburg, 1892–95, he headed the psychological laboratory at Harvard at the invitation of William James; associating himself permanently with Harvard, 1897, he taught there until his death.

Münsterberg paved the way for the more extensive use of psychology in industry, medicine, the arts, and education; he may justly be called one of the pioneers in the field of applied psychology. In philosophy, he was an idealist of the Fichte type. In psychology, he believed that the casual law held good for mental phenomena insofar as these were correlated with physiological processes. When, however, he considered the mental from the viewpoint of values, he believed in freedom. His chief contribution to theoretical psychology was probably his "action theory," which defined attention in terms of the openness of the nerve paths to the muscles of adjustment. His insistence upon the motor response as an essential factor of consciousness makes him a forerunner of modern behaviorism.

MURAT, ACHILLE (*b. Paris, France, 1801; d. Tallahassee, Fla., 1847*), author. Son of Joachim Murat and Caroline Buonaparte Murat, Achille became crown prince of Naples, 1808. With the fall of the French empire he came under suspicion in Europe and so went to New York, 1823, and settled near Tallahassee, Fla., 1827. His three books on the United States, if not as philosophic as the work of De Tocqueville, are often more graphic; of them, the most important is *Esquisse morale et politique des États-Unis* (1832).

MURCHISON, CLINTON WILLIAMS (*b. Athens, Tex., 1895; d. Athens, 1969*), oilman and industrialist. Developed oil and natural-gas deposits in Texas; founded partnership Fain and Murchison (1921); the Murchison Oil Company (1928); and the Southwest Drilling Company and the Southern Union Gas Company (1929). Formed Golding and Murchison Production (later the American Liberty Oil Company) in 1930. Organized and became president of, the Delhi Oil Corporation (1947), which merged with the Taylor Oil and Gas Company to form the Delhi-Taylor Oil Corporation in 1955. Developed oil fields in Venezuela from 1952. Diversified his holdings in the acquisition of as many as 115 companies, owned simultaneously. Personal fortune at time of death was estimated at $500 million.

MURDOCH, FRANK HITCHCOCK (*b. Chelsea, Mass., 1843; d. Philadelphia, Pa., 1872*), actor. Nephew of James E. Murdoch. Associated *post* 1861 with Mrs. Drew at Arch St. Theatre, Philadelphia; wrote *Davy Crockett* for Frank Mayo (produced Rochester, N.Y., 1872), the most popular of all the plays on this theme.

MURDOCK, JAMES (*b. Westbrook, Conn., 1776; d. Columbus, Miss., 1856*), Congregational clergyman, scholar, and author. Graduated Yale, 1797. Taught at University of Vermont, 1815–19; was professor of ecclesiastical history, Andover Theological Seminary, 1819–28.

MURDOCK, JAMES EDWARD (*b. Philadelphia, Pa., 1811; d. near Cincinnati, Ohio, 1893*), actor, lecturer, teacher of elocution. Excelled as a light comedian.

MURDOCK, JOSEPH BALLARD (*b. Hartford, Conn., 1851; d. 1931*), naval officer. Graduated Annapolis, 1870; specialized in the sciences, particularly in applied electricity. Promoted rear admiral, 1909, he commanded the Asiatic Fleet, 1911–12, and ably protected American interests during the Chinese upheavals of that period.

MURDOCK, VICTOR (*b. Burlingame, Kans., 1871; d. Wichita, Kans., 1945*), journalist, politician. Became a reporter for his father's newspaper, the *Wichita Daily Eagle*, at age 15; worked on Chicago *Inter Ocean*, 1891–94; was associated thereafter with the *Eagle* as managing editor and editor in chief. Elected to Congress as a Republican, 1903, he served until 1915 in a gradual rebellion against the established Republican leadership, becoming more and more insistent on reforms and the regulation of industry. He was a leader, with George W. Norris, of the "insurgents" who fought the successful fight of 1910 against Speaker Joseph G. Cannon. In 1912 he bolted the Republican party to support Theodore Roosevelt and was reelected to Congress that year as a Progressive. He became Progressive national chairman in 1915 and supported Woodrow Wilson in the 1916 presidential campaign. Appointed to the Federal Trade Commission in 1917, he served until 1924, a part of the time as chairman.

MUREL, JOHN A. *See* MURRELL, JOHN A.

MURFEE, JAMES THOMAS (*b. Southampton Co., Va., 1833; d. 1912*), Alabama educator. Graduated Virginia Military

Institute, 1853. Taught at University of Alabama *post* 1860; served as president, Howard College, 1871–1887; was superintendent, Marion (Ala.) Military Institute, 1887–1906.

MURFREE, MARY NOAILLES (*b. near Murfreesboro, Tenn., 1850; d. Murfreesboro, 1922*), novelist, short-story writer. Better known by pen name "Charles Egbert Craddock," she had a virile, robust, forthright style well suiting her masculine pseudonym. The Cumberland Mountains, where she spent many summers, were the scene of her first short stories, *In the Tennessee Mountains* (1884). The volume created a literary sensation and was followed until the mid-1890's by some 11 further collections of stories about the locale and its inhabitants. With simplicity, originality, graphic descriptions, and in a singularly rhythmical prose, she revealed the lonely, frustrated lives of mountaineers. *Post* 1900, she produced a quantity of historical fiction, which included *A Spectre of Power* (1903), *The Frontiersmen* (1904), and *The Amulet* (1906).

MURIETTA (MURIETA), JOAQUIN. *See* MURRIETA, JOAQUIN.

MURPHEY, ARCHIBALD DE BOW (*b. Caswell Co., N.C., 1777[?]; d. 1832*), North Carolina jurist, legislator, reformer. Advocated without success internal improvements and aids to navigation; also urged reform of the criminal code, abolition of imprisonment for debt, and colonization by free blacks. His *Report on Education* (1817) offered the first definite plan for public education submitted in North Carolina. A scholar and idealist, he was too advanced for his place and time.

MURPHY, CHARLES FRANCIS (*b. New York, N.Y., 1858; d. New York, 1924*), saloon-keeper, political boss. Tactful, shrewd, and reticent leader of Tammany Hall, 1902–24; brought that organization by the time of his death to its highest point of prestige and power.

MURPHY, DOMINIC IGNATIUS (*b. Philadelphia, Pa., 1847; d. Stockholm, Sweden, 1930*), government official. Served in Pension Office, Washington, D.C., *post* 1871; rose to commissioner of pensions, 1896. Secretary, Isthmian Canal Commission, 1904–05; was U.S. consul thereafter in numerous European posts, serving with particular distinction as consul general at Sofia, Bulgaria, 1915–19.

MURPHY, EDGAR GARDNER (*b. Fort Smith, Ark., 1869; d. 1913*), Episcopal clergyman. A strong liberal force in Montgomery, Ala., while a pastor there, he withdrew from the ministry, 1903, to serve as publicist for reform of race relations and improvement of education in the South and to secure child-labor legislation. Author of *Problems of the Present South* (1904) and other works.

MURPHY, FRANCIS (*b. Tagoat, Co. Wexford, Ireland, 1836; d. Los Angeles, Calif., 1907*), temperance reformer, evangelist.

MURPHY, FRANK (*b. Sand Beach, later Harbor Beach, Mich., 1890; d. Detroit, Mich., 1949*), lawyer, politician, justice of the U.S. Supreme Court. Christened William Francis Murphy. After attending the University of Michigan and receiving the LL.B. in 1914, he worked with a Detroit law firm. While working overseas, 1919, he was appointed first assistant U.S. attorney for the eastern district of Michigan. He was responsible for prosecuting violators of the Prohibition and narcotics statutes. In 1920 he was defeated when he sought election as the Democratic candidate in Michigan's First Congressional District. After resigning his federal job in 1922, Murphy joined a friend in private law practice. In 1924 he became a judge on Detroit's Recorder's Court. He won national attention with a 1925 report stemming from his one-man grand jury inquiry into irregularities in various city departments. In 1931

he was elected mayor of Detroit. He provided Detroit with a social-minded and clean government that was committed to free speech and maintained close ties with organized labor. He remained largely aloof from Democratic politics until the 1932 campaign, when he supported Franklin D. Roosevelt before his nomination for the presidency; consequently Murphy was appointed governor general of the Philippine Islands in 1933. When the Hare-Hawes-Cutting Act was rejected by the Filipinos, he aided the mission of Manuel Quezon to the United States in the negotiations that led to the Tydings-McDuffie Act of 1934, which provided for independence after a ten-year commonwealth status. When the Philippine Commonwealth was inaugurated in November 1935, Murphy became the U.S. high commissioner. He returned to Michigan in 1936 at Roosevelt's behest to run for governor. Murphy won the Democratic primary for governor, but it was the heavy Roosevelt majority that helped carry Murphy to victory in November.

Murphy played the crucial mediatory role in the negotiations that brought the General Motors strike to an end in 1937 on terms that amounted to a victory for the United Automobile Workers. As governor, he sought to bring the New Deal to Michigan and to strengthen and improve the state's administrative structure, but his ambitious plans for additional structural and social reforms were thwarted by his failure to win reelection in 1938, a major defeat for the New Deal. Selected by Roosevelt as attorney general, Murphy attracted attention as a crusader against crime and corruption, a role he played to the hilt. When he ascended to the Supreme Court in 1940, he lacked confidence in his qualifications for the post, but adjusted to his new life and began to take some satisfaction in his role. It is doubtful if there has ever been a more ardent defender of civil liberties on the Supreme Court than Justice Murphy. A firm believer in the "preferred position" of the First Amendment freedoms, he was a zealous advocate of freedom of religion and freedom of speech and of the press.

MURPHY, FRANKLIN (*b. Jersey City, N.J., 1846; d. Palm Beach, Fla., 1920*), varnish manufacturer, Union soldier. An early advocate of profit-sharing and pension systems for employees, he instituted numerous social, political, and administrative reforms as Republican governor of New Jersey, 1902–05.

MURPHY, FREDERICK E. (*b. near Troy, Wis., 1872; d. New York, N.Y., 1940*), newspaper publisher. Graduated Notre Dame, 1893. Long associated with the *Minneapolis Tribune*, Murphy served it as publisher and president *post* 1921. He was an authority on scientific agriculture and farm economics.

MURPHY, GERALD CLERY (*b. Boston, Mass., 1888; d. East Hampton, N.Y., 1964*), painter, businessman, and patron of the arts. Studied at Yale (graduated, 1912) and the Harvard School of Landscape Architecture. Worked for the Mark Cross Company established by his father in the 1890's, from 1912 to 1918; headed the company, 1933–56. Lived in France, 1921–33, and exhibited his paintings at the Salon des Indépendants (from 1924); works include *Razor* (1923), *Watch* (1925), *Doves* (1925), *Bibliothèque* (1926), and *Wasp and Pear* (1927). He and his wife, Sara, developed close relationships with prominent writers and artists of the period, and had a profound influence on the expatriate writers F. Scott Fitzgerald, John Dos Passos, Archibald MacLeish, and Ernest Hemingway.

MURPHY, HENRY CRUSE (*b. Brooklyn, N.Y., 1810; d. Brooklyn, 1882*), lawyer, politician, scholar. Graduated Columbia, 1830. Democratic mayor of Brooklyn, 1842; congressman, 1843–45 and 1847–49; U.S. minister to the Netherlands, 1857–61. He served with ability and integrity from 1861 to 1873 in the New York Senate, but his ambitions for higher office were blocked by the fact that he belonged to a minority faction of a minority party. He drafted and secured passage of the legislation necessary for building the Brooklyn Bridge; he was president of the private company which began the enterprise and of the corporation which succeeded it. Collector of a famous library of rare Americana, he edited, translated, and published important works relating to the early history of New Netherland.

MURPHY, ISAAC (*b. near Pittsburgh, Pa., 1802; d. Madison Co., Ark., 1882*), lawyer, Arkansas Unionist. As provisional governor and governor of Arkansas, 1864–68, Murphy avoided commitment to Radical Republican policies and gave the state an honest, economical government.

MURPHY, JAMES BUMGARDNER (*b. Morganton, N.C., 1884; d. Bar Harbor, Maine, 1950*), pathologist, cancer researcher. B.S., University of North Carolina, 1905; M.D., Johns Hopkins, 1909. He studied variations in the convolutions of the human brain and found no differences related to race. He also carried out experiments on sheep and goats to help elucidate the development of tetany after surgical removal of the parathyroid glandules. After taking the M.D. degree he joined the Pathological Institute of the New York State Hospitals on Ward's Island, New York City. At the end of a year there, he went to the Rockefeller Institute in New York City as an assistant pathologist. During these early years at the institute, Murphy worked on the cause of cancer and produced one of the earliest applications of lyophilization, a freezing and drying process. He also did research that helped elucidate the mechanism of the body's resistance to the grafting of foreign tissues and the role of lymphoid tissue in immunological reactions. In 1915 he was put in charge of cancer research and made an associate member of the Rockefeller Institute. From 1917 to 1919 he served in the Army Medical Corps with the rank of major.

Attached to the staff of the surgeon general in Washington, he directed the organization of mobile medical laboratories in France and the training of their personnel. A compilation of most of his pioneer research on the role of the lymphocyte in resistance to cancer, to tuberculosis, and to normal tissue transplantation appeared in 1926 in a Rockefeller Institute monograph. There followed a long series of papers on tumor inhibitors and on the cause of cancer. He was made a full member of the Rockefeller Institute in 1923. When in 1929 the American Society for the Control of Cancer was reorganized to meet these needs, Murphy became a member of the board of directors and its executive committee, serving until 1945. He also became a member of the advisory council of the National Cancer Institute, set up by the Cancer Act of 1937. He was also president of the American Association for Cancer Research, 1921–22. He was a member of the board of trustees of the Memorial Hospital of New York.

MURPHY, JOHN (*b. Omagh, Co. Tyrone, Ireland, 1812; d. Baltimore, Md., 1880*), publisher. Came to America as a boy. Founded John Murphy & Co., specializing in publication of Catholic books, 1837; engaged also in commercial printing and law-book publishing.

MURPHY, JOHN BENJAMIN (*b. near Appleton, Wis., 1857; d. Mackinac Island, Mich., 1916*), surgeon. Graduated Rush Medical College, 1879; made graduate studies in Vienna. Practicing in Chicago, he held teaching positions at Northwestern University and Rush Medical College; he served as chief of surgical staff, Mercy Hospital *post* 1895, and was an attending surgeon at Cook County Hospital. One of the first surgeons to investigate the cause and treatment of peritonitis following appendicitis, he produced the "Murphy button," 1892, a device which revolutionized gastrointestinal surgery; he also advanced surgical knowledge of every region of the abdomen. Later, devoting himself to study of surgery of the lungs, of the nervous system, and of bones and joints, he was

preeminent as a teacher of clinical surgery and was the recipient of many professional honors.

MURPHY, JOHN FRANCIS (*b. Oswego, N.Y., 1853; d. New York, N.Y., 1921*), landscape painter. Self-taught; opened New York City studio, 1875; enjoyed a career of gradually increasing popularity *post* 1880. The chief merit of his work is its poetic sentiment; his small early canvases are among his best productions.

MURPHY, JOHN W. (*b. New Scotland, N.Y., 1828; d. Philadelphia, Pa., 1874*), bridge engineer. Graduated Rensselaer Polytechnic, 1847. As assistant to Squire Whipple, he devised a modification of Whipple's truss bridge; he also developed a testing machine for determining elasticity of construction materials.

MURPHY, MICHAEL CHARLES (*b. Westboro, Mass., 1861; d. Philadelphia, Pa., 1913*), pioneer athletic trainer. Successful track coach and trainer at Yale and University of Pennsylvania; coached American Olympic teams of 1908 and 1912. Introduced crouching start for sprinters.

MURPHY, WILLIAM SUMTER (*b. South Carolina, 1796[?]; d. Galveston, Tex., 1844*), lawyer, Ohio militia officer. U.S. chargé d'affaires to Texas, 1843–44. An ardent annexationist, he acted mainly as an intermediary between Secretary of State Upshur and President Sam Houston.

MURPHY, WILLIAM WALTON (*b. Ernestown, Canada, 1816; d. 1886*), consular officer. Raised in Ovid, N.Y.; removed to Michigan, *ca.* 1835, where he became prominent in Free-Soil and Republican policies. As U.S. consul general in Frankfurt, Germany, 1861–69, Murphy skillfully blocked Confederate attempts at recognition and fund-raising.

MURRAY, ALEXANDER (*b. Chestertown, Md., 1754/5; d. near Philadelphia, Pa., 1821*), naval officer, Revolutionary privateersman, merchant. Appointed captain, July 1798, he served with credit in the naval war with France and later as commander of USS *Constellation* in the blockade of Tripoli. He was commanding officer at Philadelphia, 1808–21.

MURRAY, DAVID (*b. Bovina, N.Y., 1830; d. New Brunswick, N.J., 1905*), educator. Graduated Union, 1852; professor of mathematics and astronomy at Rutgers College, 1863–73; helped establish Japanese educational system as superintendent of educational affairs in Japan, 1873–79. Secretary, Regents of the University of the State of New York, 1880–89.

MURRAY, JAMES EDWARD (*b. near St. Thomas, Ontario, Canada, 1876; d. Butte, Mont., 1961*), U.S. senator. Studied at New York University (LL.M. 1900). Became a U.S. citizen in 1901 and established law practice in Butte, Mont. Chairman of the State Advisory Board of the Public Works Administration, 1933–34, and democratic senator, 1934–60. Promoted a number of far-reaching economic and social welfare measures, including the nation's first Medicare bill, which he introduced in the early 1950's. Also interested in western issues; chairman of the Interior and Insular Affairs Committees and of the Western Conference of Democratic Senators. Coauthored the first national wilderness bills.

MURRAY, JAMES ORMSBEE (*b. Camden, S.C., 1827; d. Princeton, N.J., 1899*), Presbyterian clergyman, educator. Raised in Ohio; graduated Brown, 1850, and Andover Theological Seminary, 1854. Held pastorates in Massachusetts and New York; taught English literature at Princeton, *post* 1875, and served as first dean of the Princeton faculty, *post* 1883.

MURRAY, JOHN (*b. near Lancaster, Pa., 1737; d. New York, N.Y., 1808*), Quaker merchant. Brother of Robert Murray, with whom he was in partnership in New York City, *post* 1753. President of New York Chamber of Commerce, 1798–1806. Murray, with Thomas Eddy, instituted movement for formation of a free school in New York, 1805.

MURRAY, JOHN (*b. Alton, England, 1741; d. Boston, Mass., 1815*), founder of Universalism in America. Bred up in strict Calvinism, Murray came first under the influence of Wesleyanism and then of George Whitefield. Convinced of the truth of James Relly's doctrine of universal redemption, he set forth for America, 1770, and began a two-year career of itinerant evangelism in New Jersey. Invited to New England, 1772, he won the admiration of prominent laymen and the hostility of the orthodox clergy. Befriended by Winthrop Sargent, a prosperous shipowner of Gloucester, Mass., Murray became minister of the Independent Church of Christ at Gloucester, 1779; after much persecution, he and his congregation finally obtained legal recognition as a church. He served as pastor of a Universalist society in Boston, 1793–1809.

MURRAY, JOHN GARDNER (*b. Lonaconing, Md., 1857; d. Atlantic City, N.J., 1929*), Episcopal clergyman. Ordained, 1894, he held pastorates in Birmingham, Ala., and Baltimore, Md.; elected bishop coadjutor of Maryland, he succeeded to the bishopric, 1911. In October 1925, he became presiding bishop of the Episcopal church, the first to hold this office through election.

MURRAY, JOSEPH (*b. Queen's Co., Ireland, ca. 1694; d. New York, N.Y., 1757*, lawyer. Immigrated to New York early in life, appearing at the bar there in 1718. He later attended the Middle Temple in London (admitted 1725). On his return to New York, *ca.* 1728, he appeared in most of the leading cases of his generation. He appears to have had a principal share in amending and completing the draft of the Montgomerie Charter and his "Opinion Relating to the Courts of Justice in the Colony of New York" (appended to William Smith's *Opinion*, published in 1734) is one of the few really important contributions to legal history written in the American colonies. He argued in this work against the claim that courts of law can be established only by statute and set forth the view that "fundamental courts" are a part of the constitution of England. Associated with the so-called DeLancey faction, Murray served as a New York delegate at the Albany Congress, 1754.

MURRAY, JUDITH SARGENT STEVENS (*b. Gloucester, Mass., 1751; d. near Natchez, Miss., 1820*), author. Wife of John Murray (1741–1815); sister of Winthrop Sargent. A contributor to Boston periodicals *post* 1784, Murray produced her most important work in the series of essays entitled "The Gleaner," which appeared in the *Massachusetts Magazine*, 1792–94. She was author also of two plays, *The Medium, or Virtue Triumphant* and *The Traveller Returned*, produced in Boston, 1795 and 1796, respectively. Her collected works were published by subscription at Boston as *The Gleaner* (1798); she also edited her husband's works.

MURRAY, LINDLEY (*b. present Dauphin Co., Pa., 1745; d. York, England, 1826*), grammarian. Son of Robert Murray. Studied law with John Jay in office of Benjamin Kissam; acquired extensive practice among Quakers; was successful as a New York merchant, 1779–83. Removing to England, 1784, he remained there until his death. Murray's fame rests on his school textbooks, of which the *English Grammar* (1795, fully revised, 1818) was definitive. He was author also of a number of miscellaneous works of a religious nature.

MURRAY, LOUISE SHIPMAN WELLES (*b. Athens, Pa., 1854; d. 1931*), archaeologist, local historian. Founder and director of Tioga Point Museum.

MURRAY, MAE (*b. Marie Adrienne Koening, Portsmouth, Va., 1889; d. Woodland Hills, Calif., 1965*), dancer and movie actress known as "The Girl With Bee-stung Lips." Began as a cabaret dancer in New York and Paris. Made film debut in *To Have and to Hold* (1916). Married director Robert Z. Leonard in 1918; with Leonard organized a production company, Bluebird (1917), at Universal Studios; made ten features for Universal, including two with Rudolph Valentino. With Leonard, formed Tiffany production company, in association with Metro; starred in eight films under this agreement. The epitome of the "glamorous" female film star, her best screen performance was in *The Merry Widow* (1925). Also starred in *The Masked Bride* (1926). She walked out on her MGM contract in 1926 and was blacklisted in the Hollywood film industry. Later, she appeared in several films and worked in radio and dance revues, but her popularity waned. In 1964 she was found, ill and destitute, in a St. Louis Salvation Army shelter.

MURRAY, PHILIP (*b. New Glasgow, Scotland, 1886; d. San Francisco, Calif., 1952*), labor leader. Immigrated to the U.S. in 1902. Joined the United Mine Workers in 1904; member of the UMW's executive board (1912); appointed vice president by John L. Lewis in 1920. Murray supported Lewis when the UMW split from the AFL in 1935 and formed the CIO. Murray was chairman of the Steel Workers' Organizing Committee in 1936; he was responsible for unionizing the U.S. Steel Company. Elected to the presidency of the CIO after Lewis' resignation in 1940, Murray guided that organization through World War II, working closely with President Franklin D. Roosevelt. Murray was a strong supporter of racial equality in the union ranks and led the CIO into international labor movements.

MURRAY, ROBERT (*b. Scotland, 1721; d. 1786*), Quaker merchant. Brother of John Murray (1737–1808). Brought to America as a child, Murray was raised in Dauphin Co., Pa.; he was engaged with his brother in general trade in New York *post* 1753 and represented the firm in England, 1767–75. Although he was a British sympathizer during the Revolution, his wife intentionally or unintentionally saved Putnam's division of Washington's army in September 1776 after the landing at Kip's Bay by delaying pursuing British officers at her country house ("Murray Hill").

MURRAY, THOMAS EDWARD (*b. Albany, N.Y., 1860; d. Southampton, N.Y., 1929*), consulting engineer, inventor. Associated in technical capacities *post* 1887 with utility companies operated by Anthony N. Brady, he removed to New York City, 1895, to consolidate and manage electric power properties in Brooklyn and Manhattan. As general director of the New York and Brooklyn Edison companies, Murray was responsible for the building of the principal power stations supplying New York City and was designer and builder of power plants in many other American cities. His inventive genius secured for him over 1,100 patents which touch upon almost every phase of industry. He held high corporate positions in the Edison companies and organized and directed several corporations of his own for the manufacture of devices invented by him.

MURRAY, THOMAS EDWARD (*b. Albany, N.Y., 1891; d. New York, N.Y., 1961*), engineer, business executive, and public official. Son of Thomas Edward Murray, inventor and president of the Metropolitan Engineering Company and the Murray Manufacturing Company. Studied at Yale University (graduated, 1911). Engineer for the New York Edison Company, 1911–13; for the Metropolitan Engineering and Murray Manufacturing companies, from 1913; president from 1929. Awarded more than 200 patents on electrical and welding devices. Appointed federal receiver of the bankrupt Interborough Rapid Transit company and of the Manhattan Railway Company in 1932. First engineer appointed to the U.S. Atomic Energy Commission (1950–57); fought for federal funds to develop both military and civilian uses of atomic energy and advocated vigorous development of nuclear technology.

MURRAY, WILLIAM HENRY DAVID (*b. Toadsuck, Tex., 1869; d. Oklahoma City, Okla., 1956*), lawyer and politician. Largely self-educated, Murray entered politics through activities with the Farmers' Alliance; he was admitted to the bar in 1897. A protégé of Texas governor James S. Hogg and to Chicasaw governor Douglas H. Johnston, Murray ran for Congress as a Democrat, serving in the House from 1912 to 1916. He helped found an agricultural colony in Bolivia in 1924. After returning to the U.S. in 1929, he became governor of Oklahoma from 1930 to 1934. He campaigned for the presidency in 1932 but was defeated at the convention by Roosevelt. A New Deal critic, an isolationist, and a racist, Murray was often thwarted in his attempt to maintain "constitutional" government and a dominant agrarian society.

MURRAY, WILLIAM VANS (*b. Cambridge, Md., 1760; d. near Cambridge, 1803*), diplomat. Studied law at the Middle Temple, London; began practice in Maryland, 1787; served as congressman, Federalist, from Maryland, 1791–97. Appointed U.S. minister to the Netherlands in 1797, he made The Hague the channel for restoring diplomatic negotiations with France after the XYZ affair, 1798. Appointed U.S. commissioner to treat with the French Directory, he and his fellow commissioners, Oliver Ellsworth and W. R. Davie, found themselves confronted with Napoleon Bonaparte, who had overthrown the Directory. After negotiating from February to October 1800, Murray and his fellows obtained a less than satisfactory convention, which, however, allayed previous misunderstandings and disputes. Resigning his post at The Hague, September 1801, Murray returned to the United States. He was author of *Political Sketches* (1787).

MURRELL, JOHN A. (*b. probably Tennessee, 1804; d. Pikesville, Tenn., post 1844*), outlaw, active in the Old Southwest, 1823–44. Beginning his career as a highway robber and horse thief, he created a criminal organization for disposition of spoils and later for slave stealing.

MURRIETA, JOAQUIN (*b. probably Sonora, Mexico, ca. 1832; d. near Tulare Lake, Calif., 1853*), brigand, most noted of California bandits, 1849–53. Strongly anti-American.

MURROW, EDWARD (EGBERT) ROSCOE (*b. Greensboro, N.C., 1908; d. Pawling, N.Y., 1965*), news and public affairs broadcaster. Studied at Washington State College at Pullman (graduated, 1930). With CBS radio network from 1935; European director from 1937. His eyewitness reports of the Battle of Britain and the German blitz against London brought the realities of World War II into American living rooms. A vice president and director of public affairs at CBS, 1946–47. Hosted weekly radio program "Hear It Now," which became "See It Now" on television, 1951–58, an informative and probing, as well as provocative, assay of American problems, policies, and personalities. Also hosted the television programs "Person to Person," 1953–59 and "Small World," 1958–60. Increasing disaffection with the industry led to his departure from broadcasting in 1958. Director of the U.S. Information Agency, 1961–64.

MURROW, JOSEPH SAMUEL (*b. Jefferson Co., Ga., 1835; d. Oklahoma, 1929*), Baptist clergyman. Missionary *post* 1857 to the Creek, Seminole, and Choctaw in Indian Territory (later Oklahoma).

MUSICA, PHILIP MARIANO FAUSTO (*b. New York, N.Y., 1884; d. Fairfield, Conn., 1938*), swindler. Under alias of "F. Donald Coster," he was the principal factor in the McKesson & Robbins fraud, 1930–38.

MUSIN, OVIDE (*b. near Liège, Belgium, 1854; d. Brooklyn, N.Y., 1929*), violinist, composer. After a notable career as a concert artist, he established a school of violin playing in New York City, 1908; his compositions were for the most part brilliant virtuoso pieces.

MUSMANNO, MICHAEL ANGELO (*b. McKees Rocks, Pa., 1897; d. McKees Rocks, 1968*), judge and writer. Earned seven academic degrees, including doctorates from American University and the University of Rome. Practiced law in Pittsburgh, Pa., in the 1920's. Member of the Pennsylvania House of Representatives (1928–32). Judge of the Allegheny County court (1932–34); of the Court of Common Pleas (1934–51); in the Nuremberg trials (1945–46) of Nazi war criminals; and of the Pennsylvania Supreme Court (1951–68). Author of *After Twelve Years* (1939), a vindication of Nicola Sacco and Bartolomeo Vanzetti; *Ten Days to Die* (1956), about his experience as a member of the team sent to determine whether Adolf Hitler had actually died; *The Story of the Italians in America* (1965); and *Columbus Was First* (1966).

MUSSEY, ELLEN SPENCER (*b. Geneva, Ohio, 1850; d. Washington, D.C., 1936*), lawyer, feminist, social reformer.

MUSSEY, REUBEN DIMOND (*b. Pelham, N.H., 1780; d. Boston, Mass., 1866*), surgeon. Graduated Dartmouth, 1803; M.B., Dartmouth, 1805; M.D., University of Pennsylvania, 1809. Taught medical subjects at Dartmouth and other eastern schools, 1814–38; professor of surgery, Medical College of Ohio, 1838–52; professor of surgery, Miami Medical College, Cincinnati, 1852–57. An early user of chloroform and ether as anesthetics; was particularly interested in temperance reform.

MUSTE, ABRAHAM JOHANNES (*b. Zierikzee, the Netherlands, 1885; d. New York, N.Y., 1967*), clergyman, labor leader and educator, and peace activist. Immigrated to Grand Rapids, Mich., 1891; naturalized, 1896. Studied at Hope College in Holland, Mich., the New Brunswick Theological Seminary in New Jersey, and Union Theological Seminary (B.D., 1913). Ordained a minister of the Dutch Reformed church in 1909. General secretary of the Amalgamated Textile Workers Union in Boston, from 1919. Faculty chairman at Brookwood Labor College, Katonah, N.Y., 1923–33. Cofounder and chairman of the Conference on Progressive Labor Action (CPLA) from 1929. Transformed CPLA into the American Workers Party (1933), which merged with the American Trotskyist Communist League of America to form the Workers Party in 1934. On staff of the Fellowship of Reconciliation (1936; 1938–53 as executive secretary). Director of the Presbyterian Labor Temple in New York City (1937). Cofounder of *Liberation* (1956). Embraced doctrine of radical pacifism; helped lead and inspire civil rights and antiwar movements throughout the 1950's and 1960's.

MUYBRIDGE, EADWEARD (*b. Kingston-on-Thames, England, 1830; d. England, 1904*), pioneer in motion photography. Came to America as a young man; was photographer for U.S. Coast and Geodetic Survey. Employed by Leland Stanford, Muybridge, by a series of photographs in silhouette made at Palo Alto, Calif., 1872, proved that at certain times all four feet of a running horse are off the ground. His book *The Horse in Motion* (1878) excited worldwide interest. Thereafter he worked in animal locomotion photography and developed the zoopraxiscope (1879), by which he successfully reproduced moving figures in large size on a screen. Results of his later experiments were published in 11 volumes as *Animal Locomotion* (1887).

MUZZEY, DAVID SAVILLE (*b. Lexington, Mass., 1870; d. Yonkers, N.Y., 1965*), historian and educator. Studied at Harvard (graduated, 1893), Union Theological Seminary, and Columbia (Ph.D., 1907). Professor, Barnard College (1905–23) and Columbia (1923–40). Wrote books on ethical culture, among them *Spiritual Heroes* (1902), *The Spiritual Franciscans* (1907), and *Ethics as a Religion* (1951). Also wrote controversial high-school text *An American History* (1911, later issued in 1939 as *History of Our Country*), a realistic account of American history surrounded by legends, and biographies of Thomas Jefferson and James G. Blaine.

MYER, ALBERT JAMES (*b. Newburgh, N.Y., 1829; d. Buffalo, N.Y., 1880*), army surgeon. Graduated Hobart, 1847; M.D., Buffalo Medical College, 1851. An enthusiastic experimenter in signal devices, he was appointed to organize and command the U.S. Army Signal Corps, June 1861. After extensive military field service in Virginia, he succeeded in securing the formal establishment of the Signal Corps, Mar. 3, 1863, together with his own appointment as chief signal officer and colonel. Friction with the War Department caused his relief in November 1863, but an act of Congress of July 1866, reorganized the Signal Corps and restored Myer to his post and rank, which he held until his death. Myer was responsible for the establishment of the U.S. Weather Bureau, under direction of the Signal Corps, February 1870. Two months before his death, he was promoted brigadier general.

MYERS, ABRAHAM CHARLES (*b. Georgetown, S.C., 1811; d. Washington, D.C., 1889*), soldier. Graduated West Point, 1833; served in the Seminole wars and with distinction in the Mexican War; thereafter, until 1861, he was stationed in the quartermaster service at various Southern posts. As quartermaster general of the Confederate army, 1861–63, he worked with personal honesty and efficiency in a situation of monumental difficulty. Unable to overcome the inefficiency of his subordinates, he was superseded.

MYERS, GUSTAVUS (*b. Trenton, N.J., 1872; d. New York, N.Y., 1942*), historian, reformer. Brother of Jerome Myers. A factory worker at 14, he was largely self-educated. After a period of employment on the *Philadelphia Record*, he moved to New York City to write for newspapers and magazines, and to pursue research into the causes of political corruption and economic evils. At first a Populist, he joined the Socialist party in 1907, but left it in 1912 because of what he considered its materialism and anti-individualism. By 1925 he had come to believe that America was progressively correcting social inequities, a view which was strengthened during the New Deal years; by 1939 he was convinced that the redistribution of wealth in America was nearly complete. The course of his thinking, based on detailed and tireless research in original sources, may be traced in his books, of which the following are representative: *History of Tammany Hall* (1901, 1917); *History of the Great American Fortunes* (1909–10 and later editions); *History of American Idealism* (1925); and *The Ending of Hereditary American Fortunes* (1939). His *History of Bigotry in the United States* was published posthumously in 1943.

MYERS, JEROME (*b. Petersburg, Va., 1867; d. New York N.Y., 1940*), painter. Studied at Cooper Union and the New York Art Students League. An associate of the New York realist school, Myers painted the everyday life of New Yorkers, particularly the residents of the lower East Side and Greenwich Village; after working in an early, rather dark impressionist manner, he developed a gay and sparkling method in his later work.

MYERSON, ABRAHAM (*b. Yanova, Lithuania, then Russia, 1881; d. Brookline, Mass., 1948*), neuropsychiatrist. Immigrated with his parents to Boston, Mass., as a boy. M.D., medical school of Tufts University, 1908. After internship and residencies at Boston City Hospital, Alexian Brothers Hospital (St. Louis, Mo.), and Boston Psychopathic Hospital, he was clinical director and pathologist at the Taunton (Mass.) State Hospital, 1913–17. He taught neurology at Tufts *post* 1918, becoming professor in 1921 and professor emeritus in 1940. He was director of research at Boston State Hospital in Mattapan, 1927–48, and clinical professor of psychiatry at Harvard, 1935–45. His early work and publications dealt primarily with classical neurology; his major contributions of this period were the popularization of the glabellar reflex ("Myerson's sign"), and his development of a technique for obtaining blood samples from both the internal carotid artery and the internal jugular vein as a way of studying brain metabolism. He later developed a major interest in psychiatry, to which his approach was physiological; he distrusted psychology as insufficiently scientific and was strongly anti-Freudian. He was author, among other works of *The Inheritance of Mental Diseases* (1925).

MYLES, JOHN (*b. probably Herefordshire, England, ca. 1621; d. Swansea, Mass., 1683*), pioneer Baptist clergyman. A leader among Welsh Baptists, Myles immigrated to New England in 1662 and became pastor of one of the earliest Baptist churches in America at Rehoboth in Plymouth Colony, 1663. He removed, with his church, to the present site of Swansea, 1667, where he was pastor with an interlude as acting pastor of the First Baptist Church in Boston.

MYRICK, HERBERT (*b. Arlington, Mass., 1860; d. Bad Nauheim, Germany, 1927*), editor and publisher of agricultural periodicals. Crusaded for post office improvement, farmers' cooperatives, federal farm legislation.

N

NACK, JAMES M. (*b. New York, N.Y., 1809; d. 1879*), poet. A deaf mute, Nack won celebrity for his work in the years 1827–60, principally because of his triumph over his physical handicap. Among his numerous books, imitative of Scott and Byron, were *The Legend of the Rocks* (1827) and *The Romance of the Ring and Other Poems* (1859).

NADAL, EHRMAN SYME (*b. Greenbrier Co., Va., now W. Va., 1843; d. Princeton, N.J., 1922*), journalist, essayist, public official.

NADELMAN, ELIE (*b. Warsaw, Poland, 1882; d. New York, N.Y., 1946*), sculptor. Child of Jewish parents, he attended the Academy of Arts in Warsaw. Giving up painting for sculpture, *ca.* 1903, he settled in Paris and was for a decade obsessed with the problem of demonstrating the formal principles that he assumed to be the basis of archaic Greek work; the sculptures executed between 1903 and his emigration to America in 1914, however, appear to be more a 20th-century version of neoclassism. Between 1903 and 1909 he produced a large number of works, which, when shown at the Galerie Druet in 1909, attracted a great deal of critical attention. His last showing in Paris was at Druet in 1913. He came to the United States in the fall of 1914 and began to prepare for his first New York exhibition, held at the Alfred Stieglitz Photo-Secession Gallery ("291"). His first large New York showing came in 1917 at the galleries of Scott Fowles and received high praise. Nadelman completed a prodigious number of works, the subjects of which were of three kinds: commissioned portraits elegantly stylized, concert and theatrical subjects whimsically conceived, and satirical references to drawing-room behavior. After his marriage in 1919 to a wealthy widow, Nadelman's career took a curious turn. His wife was then unwell, and she and the artist virtually retired from New York life to live in seclusion on an estate in the Riverdale section of the city. Here they amassed an important collection of American folk art numbering some 15,000 items.

NAGEL, CONRAD (*b. Keokuk, Iowa, 1897; d. New York, N.Y., 1970*), film, stage, radio, and television actor and director. Appeared in over one hundred movies, including *The Fighting Chance* (1919), *Fool's Paradise* (1921), and *Glorious Betsy* (1928), the first movie with spoken dialogue; and more than twenty theatrical productions, including *Forever After* (1918), and *The First Apple* (1933). Formed the Academy of Motion Picture Arts and Sciences with L. B. Mayer and Fred Niblo in 1927; president, 1932–33. Director and host of the Columbia Broadcasting System's radio drama series "Silver Theater," 1937–49. Host of the American Broadcasting Company's television show "Celebrity Time" in 1948.

NAIRNE, THOMAS (*b. probably Scotland, date unknown; d. South Carolina, 1715*), planter, South Carolina legislator, Indian agent. First mentioned in South Carolina records, 1698, as landowner on St. Helena Island, he acquired influence over the Indians that made him the most remarkable frontier figure of the South in the period of Queen Anne's War. Active in efforts to regulate the Indian trade among the Yamasee and to Christianize them, he became leader of the country party in the Assembly and clashed vigorously with Sir Nathaniel Johnson, the governor of the colony. Under the Indian Act, 1707, he served as the first provincial Indian agent. An active Carolina expansionist, he was burned at the stake after attempting a parley with the discontented Yamasee.

NAISMITH, JAMES (*b. Almonte, Canada, 1861; d. Lawrence, Kans., 1939*), professor of physical education, originator of basketball. Graduated McGill University, 1887; Presbyterian College, Montreal, 1890. While attending the Y.M.C.A. Training School in Springfield, Mass., Naismith invented the game of basketball in 1891 as a project to interest young athletes during the winter season. He taught in the physical education department, University of Kansas, 1898–1937.

NANCRÈDE, CHARLES BEYLARD GUÉRARD DE (*b. Philadelphia, Pa., 1847; d. Ann Arbor, Mich., 1921*), surgeon. Grandson of Paul J. G. de Nancrède. M.D., University of Pennsylvania, 1869; M.D., Jefferson Medical College, 1883. After successful practice in Philadelphia, Nancrède was appointed professor of surgery, University of Michigan, 1889, and held that position for the remainder of his life; he taught also during the summer months at Dartmouth Medical College *post* 1887.

NANCRÈDE, PAUL JOSEPH GUÉRARD DE (*b. near Fontainebleau, France, 1761; d. Paris, France, 1841*), soldier, teacher, bookseller, and printer. Served as a private in the Soissonnais regiment of Rochambeau's army, 1780–83. Returning to America, 1785, he was instructor in French at Harvard, 1787–98, and published the first French school text composed especially for use in American colleges, *L'Abeille Françoise* (1792). He published also a French newspaper, the *Courier de Boston*, 1789, and from 1796 to 1804 published a number of French and English books from his shop in Boston, mainly in the genre of Rousseau. After a residence in France, 1804–12, he returned to the United States and transferred his business from Boston to Philadelphia.

NANUNTENOO. *See* CANONCHET.

NAPTON, WILLIAM BARCLAY (*b. near Princeton, N.J., 1808; d. 1883*), jurist. Removed to Missouri, 1832; was judge of the state supreme court, 1839–51, 1857–61, 1873–80. A proslavery states'-rights Democrat, Napton made lasting contributions to the jurisprudence of commercial law, land titles, and equity.

NARVÁEZ, PÁNFILO DE (*b. Valladolid, Spain, ca. 1478; d. near Matagorda Bay, 1528*), Spanish conquistador. Came to West Indies early in the 16th century; served first in Jamaica. As chief captain of Diego Velásquez, Narváez participated ruthlessly in the pacifying and settling of Cuba. Commissioned by Velásquez to seize or kill Cortés and supersede him as captain general of Mexico, he was defeated by Cortés, May 23, 1520, lost an eye, and was imprisoned until 1521. Acquiring concessions in Florida, he sailed thence from Spain in June 1527. He arrived, accidentally and off-course, to the west of Tampa Bay and took possession of Florida for the King of Spain, April 16, 1528. Separated from his ships, he and 300 men trekked overland, fruitlessly hunting for riches amid the hostile Indians. Beset by great difficulties, he was drowned as his expedition was cruising in improvised boats along the Gulf Coast in search of Mexico.

NASBY, PETROLEUM V. *See* LOCKE, DAVID ROSS.

NASH, ABNER (*b. Amelia Co., Va., ca. 1740; d. New York, N.Y., 1786*), lawyer, Revolutionary patriot, North Carolina legislator. Prominent *post* 1774 in the movement toward revolution, Nash served as speaker of the first North Carolina House of Commons and as speaker of the state senate, 1779. As governor, 1780–81, he quarreled with the legislature over its usurpation of his executive powers; as a member of Congress, 1782–85, he advocated a strong federal government.

NASH, ARTHUR (*b. Tipton Co., Ind., 1870; d. Cincinnati, Ohio, 1927*), clergyman, clothing manufacturer. Originator of the "golden rule" plan of copartnership with workers. Author of *The Golden Rule in Business* (1923).

NASH, CHARLES SUMNER (*b. Granby, Mass., 1856; d. 1926*), Congregational clergyman. After pastoral and educational experience in the East, Nash removed to Oakland, Calif., 1891, as professor of homiletics and pastoral theology, Pacific Theological Seminary. He served the school as dean, 1906–11, as president, 1911–20, and as president emeritus until his death. Under his leadership, the Seminary became nondenominational, 1912, and in 1916, changed its name to Pacific School of Religion.

NASH, CHARLES WILLIAMS (*b. De Kalb County, Ill., 1864; d. Beverly Hills, Calif., 1948*), automobile manufacturer. Rose from laborer to general manager of the Durant-Dort Carriage Company in Flint, Mich., *post* 1891. In 1910–12 he took charge of the troubled Buick Motor Car Company and gave it sound and efficient management, restoring its stability; he performed a similar service for General Motors, as that company's president, 1912–16, but his cautious, conservative policies were not popular with the stockholders. He then formed the Nash Motors Company, one of the few consistently profitable independent car manufacturers, of which he was president until 1932 and chairman of the board thereafter. In 1937 he diversified his product by merging with the Kelvinator Company and moving into the home appliance field.

NASH, DANIEL (*b. present Great Barrington, Mass., 1763; d. Burlington, N.Y., 1836*), Episcopal clergyman. A successful missionary on the western New York frontier *post* 1797, Father Nash, as he was known, was the supposed prototype for "Reverend Mr. Grant" in J. F. Cooper's *The Pioneers.*

NASH, FRANCIS (*b. Amelia Co., Va., ca. 1742; d. Kulpsville, Pa., 1777*), Revolutionary soldier. Brother of Abner Nash. Mortally wounded in battle of Germantown, October 1777, while commanding Continental North Carolina brigade. Nashville, Tenn., was named in his honor.

NASH, FREDERICK (*b. New Bern, N.C., 1781; d. 1858*), North Carolina jurist and legislator. Son of Abner Nash. Graduated College of New Jersey (Princeton), 1799; commenced law practice in New Bern, 1801, but removed to Hillsboro, 1807. Served as state superior court judge, 1818–26, 1836–44; as state supreme court judge, 1844–58 (chief justice *post* 1852).

NASH, HENRY SYLVESTER (*b. Newark, Ohio, 1854; d. 1912*), Episcopal clergyman. *Post* 1882, taught literature and interpretation of the New Testament at Episcopal Theological School, Cambridge, Mass.

NASH, JOHN HENRY (*b. Woodbridge, Ontario, Canada, 1871; d. Berkeley, Calif., 1947*), fine printer. Settled in San Francisco, 1895. The technical excellence of his work as designer and producer of deluxe editions won him numerous Western patrons and considerable reputation. He headed his own firm between 1916 and 1938. Among his finest productions were editions of Dryden's play *All for Love* and Dante's *Divine Comedy,* both issued in 1929.

NASH, SIMEON (*b. South Hadley, Mass., 1804; d. Gallipolis, Ohio, 1879*), Ohio jurist. Author of *Pleadings and Practice under the Civil Code* (1856), a major contribution to the jurisprudence of his state.

NASON, ELIAS (*b. Wrentham, Mass., 1811; d. 1887*), Congregational clergyman, educator, lecturer. Author of a number of books and pamphlets principally on American colonial and religious history.

NASON, HENRY BRADFORD (*b. Foxboro, Mass., 1831; d. 1895*), educator. Graduated Amherst, 1855; Ph.D., Göttingen, 1857. Professor of natural history, Rensselaer Polytechnic Institute, 1858–66; professor of chemistry and natural science, 1866–95. An expert in analytic procedures, Nason introduced a number of improvements in the process of treating crude oil as adviser to the Standard Oil Co., 1880–90.

NASSAU, ROBERT HAMILL (*b. near Norristown, Pa., 1835; d. Ambler, Pa., 1921*), Presbyterian clergyman, linguist. Missionary in West Africa, 1861–1906. Author of a number of works dealing with African religion and society including *Fetichism in West Africa* (1904).

NAST, CONDÉ MONTROSE (*b. New York, N.Y., 1873; d. New York, 1942*), magazine publisher. Raised in St. Louis, Mo. A.B., Georgetown University, 1894; A.M., 1895. Graduated from law school of Washington University (St. Louis), 1897. Extraordinarily successful as advertising manager of *Collier's Weekly,* 1898–1907, he left to develop his own enterprises. Convinced that advertisers would be attracted to a "class" magazine that could guarantee a selective, high-income readership, he built up *Vogue* (which he bought in 1909) into the most prestigious fashion magazine in the United States; he later added overseas editions to his operation, also a pattern company, and *Vanity Fair,* a sophisticated magazine of general interest and fashionable tone. After bringing his various enterprises through the depression of the 1930's, he started a new magazine in 1939, *Glamour,* aimed at a relatively wide circulation among career girls.

NAST, THOMAS (*b. Landau, Germany, 1840; d. Guayaquil, Ecuador, 1902*), cartoonist. Brought to New York City as a child, he attended public schools and the National Academy of Design; he received much personal instruction from Alfred Fredericks. Engaged as a staff artist on *Frank Leslie's Illustrated Newspaper* at the age of 15, Nast left that paper in 1859 to join the *New York Illustrated News* as artist-correspondent. As a staff member and contributor to *Harper's Weekly,* 1862–86, he received a free hand in choice of subjects and method of treatment and vigorously advanced the art of political caricature. His Civil War period cartoons were vastly influential and made him, in Abraham Lincoln's words, "our best recruiting sergeant." Always a fierce partisan, Nast employed his art in support of the Radical Republicans; his attacks on the "Tweed Ring," 1869–72, contributed much to its overthrow. He made Horace Greeley ludicrous in the campaign of 1872, defended Hayes against Tilden, and forsook the Republicans only when James G. Blaine was nominated. He invented the symbolic Democratic donkey and Republican elephant, both becoming fixed in his pictures, 1874. Financially unfortunate in his later years, he died as U.S. consul at Guayaquil.

NAST, WILLIAM (*b. Stuttgart, Germany, 1807; d. 1899*), Methodist clergyman. Came to America, 1828. Active, *post* 1835, as missionary to Germans in Ohio and adjoining states; was a founder of German Wallace College, Berea, Ohio.

NATHAN, GEORGE JEAN (*b. Fort Wayne, Ind., 1882; d. New York, N.Y., 1958*), critic, editor, author. Graduated from Cornell University, B.A., 1904. Perhaps the most widely read drama critic of his time, Nathan began his career in 1905 as a reporter for the *New York Herald*. Wrote reviews for over twenty newspapers and magazines until the mid-1950's. Coeditor with H. L. Mencken of the magazine *Smart Set*, 1914–23; contributing editor of the *American Mercury*, 1924–30; and managing editor of the *American Spectator*, a magazine he founded with Theodore Dreiser and Eugene O'Neill, 1932–35. In 1934, he helped found the New York Drama Critics' Circle; president, 1937–39.

NATHAN, MAUD (*b. New York, N.Y., 1862; d. New York, 1946*), social reformer, feminist. Sister of Annie Meyer Nathan; cousin of Benjamin N. Cardozo. As a member of the Consumers' League of the City of New York *post* 1890, and its president, 1897–1917, she publicized the miserable working conditions for women employed in retail shops and factories, and applied pressure to correct them. She was also active in the movement for woman suffrage.

NATION, CARRY AMELIA MOORE (*b. Garrard Co., Ky., 1846; d. Leavenworth, Kans., 1911*), temperance agitator. An ignorant, unbalanced, and contentious woman of vast energies, afflicted with an hereditary paranoia, she was subjected to early hardships that fused all her great physical and emotional powers into a flaming enmity toward liquor and its corrupt purveyors. From her first saloon-smashing venture at Medicine Lodge, Kans., she carried her campaign to Wichita (1900), where her distinctive weapon, the hatchet, was first used, and then on to many of the principal American cities. Arrested thirty times for "disturbing the peace," she paid fines from sales of souvenir hatchets, lecture tours, and stage appearances. Her autobiography was published, 1904.

NAVARRE, PIERRE (*b. Detroit, Mich., 1790[?]; d. near Toledo, Ohio, 1874*), frontiersman. Pensioned for legendary exploits as scout of William Henry Harrison's army in campaigns of 1813–14; fur trader in Old Northwest.

NAZIMOVA, ALLA (*b. Yalta, Russia, 1878; d. Hollywood, Calif., 1945*), actress. Child of Jewish parents who had joined the Russian Orthodox Church, she was educated in Switzerland and in Odessa, Russia. In 1895 she entered the dramatic school of the Philharmonic Society of Moscow. Upon graduating in 1898 she was taken into the Moscow Art Theater. Here she studied Konstantin Stanislavski's techniques of training the actor to build a character internally as well as externally. In 1905 Nazimova immigrated to New York, where she appeared in *The Chosen People* (played in Russian) at the Herald Square Theater. After learning English, she appeared as Hedda in Ibsen's *Hedda Gabler* at the Princess Theater in 1906. Two months later she played Nora in Ibsen's *A Doll's House*. Although the Shuberts gave her other Ibsen roles—in *The Master Builder* (1907) and *Little Eyolf* (1910)—these were combined with inconsequential box-office plays. In 1918 she played a series of Ibsen dramas, and in 1923 the title role in *Dagmar*. She joined Eva Le Gallienne's Civic Repertory Theatre in New York in 1928 and gave a memorable performance as Madame Ranevsky in Chekhov's *The Cherry Orchard*. In 1930 Nazimova joined the Theatre Guild. She won

acclaim in Turgenev's *A Month in the Country* and particularly in Eugene O'Neill's *Mourning Becomes Electra* (1931). She earned enthusiastic praise once again in her final significant stage performance, as Mrs. Alving in Ibsen's *Ghosts* (1935). Returning to Hollywood, she played character roles in such films as *Escape* (1940), *Blood and Sand* (1941), *The Bridge of San Luis Rey* (1944), and *Since You Went Away* (1944).

NEAGLE, JOHN (*b. Boston, Mass., 1796; d. Philadelphia, Pa., 1865*), portrait painter. Studied with Bass Otis; was encouraged by Thomas Sully whose niece he married. Successful as a portraitist in Philadelphia, his picture "Pat Lyon the Blacksmith" (1826) added greatly to his reputation; his portrait of Gilbert Stuart is the best existing likeness of that artist.

NEAL, ALICE BRADLEY. *See* HAVEN, EMILY BRADLEY.

NEAL, DAVID DALHOFF (*b. Lowell, Mass., 1838; d. Munich, Germany, 1915*), painter. After study in Munich under von Piloty and other masters, he produced many popular historical canvases including "The First Meeting of Mary Stuart and Rizzio" and "Oliver Cromwell Visiting Mr. John Milton." The later years of his life were devoted to portrait work.

NEAL, JOHN (*b. Falmouth, now Portland, Maine, 1793; d. Portland, 1876*), author, editor. Resident in Baltimore, Md., 1815–23, Neal produced a prodigious amount of literary work, editing for brief periods the *Baltimore Telegraph* and the *Portico*, compiling a large part of *A History of the American Revolution* (1819) credited to Paul Allen, and publishing several narrative poems, a verse tragedy, and five novels which included *Logan* (1822), *Seventy-Six* (1823), and *Randolph* (1823). While resident in England, 1824–27, Neal was a contributor to the chief British periodicals. Among the most important of his works of this period were a critical appraisal of American authors entitled "American Writers" (in *Blackwood's Magazine*, September 1824–February 1825) and *Brother Jonathan* (published by Blackwood as a book, 1825). On his return to America, he settled in Portland, Maine, and was active in many fields, publishing three more novels and as a magazine editor encouraging young contributors, among them John G. Whittier and Edgar A. Poe. *Post* 1840, he devoted himself to business and civic interests but continued to write voluminously and to speak in behalf of numerous causes. His autobiography *Wandering Recollections* (1869) is invaluable as self-portraiture of this talented but hasty and over-enthusiastic man.

NEAL, JOSEPH CLAY (*b. Greenland, N.H., 1807; d. 1847*), Philadelphia journalist, humorist. Author of *Charcoal Sketches* (1838), *In Town and About* (1843), *Peter Ploddy, and Other Oddities* (1844), and *Charcoal Sketches: Second Series* (1848).

NEAL, JOSEPHINE BICKNELL (*b. Belmont, Me., 1880; d. New York, N.Y., 1955*), physician. Studied at Bates College and at Cornell University, M.D., 1910. Taught at Cornell University Medical School, 1914–20. Associated with the College of Physicians and Surgeons of Columbia University, 1922–55. Made most notable contributions to encephalitis research. Author of *Encephalitis: A Clinical Study* (1942).

NEALE, LEONARD (*b. near Port Tobacco, Md., 1746; d. Baltimore, Md., 1817*), Roman Catholic clergyman, Jesuit. As president of Georgetown College, 1799–1806, he transformed the school from an academy into an excellent classical college. Consecrated bishop coadjutor of Baltimore, 1800, he established a community of nuns in Georgetown which was affiliated in 1816 with the Visitation Order. Succeeding to the archbishopric of Baltimore, 1815, he served until his death.

NEEDHAM, JAMES (*b. England, date unknown; d. on the Yadkin River, near the Occaneechi Village, 1673*), explorer. Came to the southern Carolina settlement from Barbados, 1670; became a planter on the Ashley River. Exploring in search of a passage by water to the southwest from the present site of Petersburg, Va., 1673, Needham reached the main Cherokee village and was, so far as is known, the first Englishman to penetrate the country of the over-hill Cherokee.

NEEF, FRANCIS JOSEPH NICHOLAS (*b. Soultz, Alsace, 1770; d. New Harmony, Ind., 1854*), educator. Trained by Pestalozzi in Switzerland, Neef was persuaded to come to Philadelphia by William Maclure and arrived there, 1806. He established near Philadelphia the first Pestalozzian school in the United States *ca.* 1808, and maintained a school at Louisville, Ky., 1814–26. Neef conducted the educational program in the community at New Harmony from 1826 until the failure of that venture two years later.

NEELY, MATTHEW MANSFIELD (*b. Groves, W. Va., 1874; d. Washington, D.C., 1958*), politician, lawyer. Studied at West Virginia University, LL.B., 1902. Democratic congressman, 1913–20, 1944–46; U.S. Senator, 1922–28, 1930–41, 1948–58; governor of West Virginia, 1941–44. A colorful liberal, Neely was an ardent New Dealer who strongly supported the rights of labor, working ardently for the repeal of the Taft-Hartley Act. He was an outspoken critic of President Eisenhower and the Republican Administration.

NEELY, THOMAS BENJAMIN (*b. Philadelphia, Pa., 1841; d. 1925*), Methodist clergyman and bishop. A conservative, learned authority on Methodist polity and doctrine, Neely opposed Methodist unification, the granting of autonomy to the churches in mission lands, and other liberalizing tendencies.

NEF, JOHN ULRIC (*b. Herisau, Switzerland, 1862; d. Carmel, Calif., 1915*), chemist. Came to America as a boy; was raised in western Massachusetts. Graduated Harvard, 1884; Ph.D., Munich, 1886. Professor of chemistry at Purdue, 1887–89, and at Clark University, 1889–92; organized and headed department of chemistry, University of Chicago, 1892–1915. Author of much pioneer work in organic chemistry, Nef made outstanding researches on the structure of quinone.

NEGLEY, JAMES SCOTT (*b. East Liberty, Pa., 1826; d. Plainfield, N.J., 1901*), Union major general, horticulturist, railroad executive. A veteran of the Mexican War and long active in the Pennsylvania militia, Negley fought in the western campaigns of the Civil War with conspicuous skill and gallantry until Chickamauga, when he was relieved of command on charges of desertion and cowardice of which a court of inquiry cleared him. Entering business in Pittsburgh, Pa., he served as congressman, Republican, from Pennsylvania, 1869–75 and 1885–87.

NEHRLING, HENRY (*b. Herman, Wis., 1853; d. 1929*), ornithologist, horticulturist. Author of *North American Birds* (1889–93).

NEIDHARD, CHARLES (*b. Bremen, Germany, 1809; d. Philadelphia, Pa., 1895*), pioneer homeopathist. Stepson of Georg F. List. Came to America, 1825; after studies at the University of Pennsylvania, he completed his education at Leipzig and Jena. Returning to America, 1836, he practiced homeopathic medicine in Philadelphia and was a founder of the Hahnemann Medical College, 1839.

NEIGHBORS, ROBERT SIMPSON (*b. Virginia, 1815; d. Fort Belknap, Tex., 1859*), Texas pioneer, Indian agent. Removed to Texas, probably 1833. After holding a captaincy in the Texas army

and imprisonment by the Mexicans, 1842–44, his concern with the Indians began in 1845 when he became the Texas agent for the Lipan and Tonkawa tribes; he also treated with the Comanche and other wild tribes. Commissioned U.S. agent for the Texas Indians, 1847, he was instructed to keep the tribes peaceful, away from the settlements, and to prevent them from purchasing liquor. He was also responsible for keeping the white settlers from intruding onto Indian country. He performed his difficult task well in view of the inadequacy of the laws and the encroachments of the white settlers but he was removed from office, 1849. His reports constitute the most reliable information extant on Texas tribes, especially the Comanche, for the period of his activity. Reappointed in 1853, he served until his murder by an outlaw.

NEILL, EDWARD DUFFIELD (*b. Philadelphia, Pa., 1823; d. 1893*), Presbyterian clergyman, educator, historian. Brother of John and Thomas H. Neill. President, Macalester College, 1874–84. Author of studies on the colonization of Maryland and Virginia and of a *History of Minnesota* (1858). First superintendent of public instruction for Minnesota Territory, 1851–53.

NEILL, JOHN (*b. Philadelphia, Pa., 1819; d. Philadelphia, 1880*), surgeon, teacher of surgery. Brother of Edward D. and Thomas H. Neill. Distinguished organizer of military hospitals in Pennsylvania during the Civil War.

NEILL, THOMAS HEWSON (*b. Philadelphia, Pa., 1826; d. Philadelphia, 1885*), soldier. Brother of Edward D. and John Neill. Graduated West Point, 1847. Received brevet of major general of volunteers for services in eastern campaigns, 1861–65; after serving with the 6th Cavalry in Indian campaigns, 1870–75, he was commandant at West Point, 1875–79. Thereafter, until retirement in 1883, he was colonel, 6th Cavalry.

NEILL, WILLIAM (*b. near McKeesport, Pa., 1778 or 1779; d. 1860*), Presbyterian clergyman, educator. As pastor at Cooperstown, N.Y., 1805–09, Neill was tutor to James Fenimore Cooper; thereafter he served in a variety of pastorates, was president of Dickinson College, 1824–29, and was a director of Princeton Theological Seminary from its founding.

NEILSON, JOHN (*b. Raritan Landing, N.J., 1745; d. New Brunswick, N.J., 1833*), merchant, Revolutionary soldier, New Jersey jurist and legislator.

NEILSON, WILLIAM ALLAN (*b. Doune, Perthshire, Scotland, 1869; d. Northampton, Mass., 1946*), scholar, educator. M.A., Edinburgh University, 1891. Ph.D., Harvard, 1898. immigrated to Canada, 1891. Taught English at Bryn Mawr College, Harvard, and Columbia; professor of English at Harvard, 1906–17. President of Smith College, 1917–39.

NEILSON, WILLIAM GEORGE (*b. Philadelphia, Pa., 1842; d. Philadelphia, 1906*), mining engineer, locomotive builder. Pioneer in the bauxite industry *post* 1883. Helped establish Adirondack Mountain Reserve, 1888.

NELL, WILLIAM COOPER (*b. Boston, Mass., 1816; d. Boston, 1874*), black author, antislavery worker. First black to hold a federal government post (1861).

NELSON, CHARLES ALEXANDER (*b. Calais, Maine, 1839; d. 1933*), librarian, bibliographer, indexer. Graduated Harvard, 1860. Worked on catalogues of the New York Astor Library, the Howard Memorial Library of New Orleans, the Newberry Library of Chicago; was deputy librarian, Columbia University, 1898–1909.

NELSON, DAVID (*b. near Jonesboro, Tenn., 1793; d. Oakland, Ill., 1844*), Presbyterian clergyman, educator, Abolitionist.

Expelled from the state of Missouri, 1836, for antislavery preaching.

NELSON, DONALD MARR (*b. Hannibal, Mo., 1888; d. Los Angeles, Calif., 1959*), corporation executive, government official, diplomat. Graduated from the University of Missouri, B.S., 1911. Worked for Sears, Roebuck and Company from 1912 to 1942, becoming executive vice president and chairman of the executive committee (1939). As head of the War Production Board from 1942 to 1944, he helped convert the economy from civilian to war production. In 1944, he accompanied Major General Patrick Hurley to China and the Soviet Union as President Roosevelt's personal representative on economic matters with cabinet rank. Retired from government service in 1945.

NELSON, EDWARD WILLIAM (*b. Amoskeag, N.H., 1855; d. 1934*), naturalist. Made pioneer field studies *post* 1877 of the biology and ethnology of vast areas of country from arctic Alaska into Mexico; his work in Alaska was particularly notable. He was chief of the Bureau of Biological Survey, U.S. Department of Agriculture, 1916–27.

NELSON, HENRY LOOMIS (*b. New York, N.Y., 1846; d. New York, 1908*), journalist, teacher. *Post* 1878, Nelson was Washington, D.C., correspondent of the *Boston Post*, the New York *World*, and other papers; he was editor of *Harper's Weekly*, 1894–98. Wells Professor of Political Science at Williams College, 1902–08, he was a supporter of the gold standard, a free-trader, an anti-imperialist, and a fighter for civil-service reform.

NELSON, HUGH (*b. York Co., Va., 1768; d. Albemarle Co., Va., 1836*), planter, lawyer, Virginia legislator and jurist. Son of Thomas Nelson. Congressman, (Democrat) Republican, from Virginia, 1811–23. A close friend and adviser of Thomas Jefferson and James Monroe. U.S. minister to Spain, 1823–25.

NELSON, JOHN (*b. England, 1654; d. 1734*), New England merchant and statesman. Nephew and heir of Sir Thomas Temple who was proprietor and governor of Nova Scotia, 1656–70. Nelson came to Boston, Mass., *ca.* 1670 and engaged in fur trade in the Kennebec country. An opponent of Edward Randolph and Sir Edmund Andros and also of William Phips, he kept up a continuous propaganda with the Board of Trade in London for the expulsion of the French from North America.

NELSON, JULIUS (*b. Copenhagen, Denmark, 1858; d. 1916*), biologist, authority on oyster culture. Came to America as a child; was raised in Wisconsin. Graduated University of Wisconsin, 1881; Ph.D., Johns Hopkins, 1888. Served *post* 1888 as professor of biology at Rutgers and biologist of the New Jersey Agricultural Experiment Station.

NELSON, KNUTE (*b. Evanger, Norway, 1843; d. 1923*), lawyer, Union soldier, Wisconsin and Minnesota legislator. Congressman, Republican from Minnesota, 1883–89; governor of Minnesota, 1893–95; U.S. senator, 1895–1923. Nelson's Republican conservatism was modified by sympathy for a low tariff and for a federal income tax; among the more notable measures ascribed to him are the Nelson Bankruptcy Act (1898) and the act creating the Department of Commerce and Labor (1902).

NELSON, MARJORIE MAXINE (*b. Kansas City, Mo., 1909; d. San Francisco, Calif., 1962*), research anatomist and nutritional biochemist. Studied at the University of Washington at Seattle and the University of California at Berkeley (Ph.D., 1944). Lecturer and researcher from 1944 at Berkeley and the University of California Medical School in San Francisco. Studies using rats cataloged teratogenic effects of specific vitamin, mineral, and protein deficiencies in reproduction and development. Secretary-treasurer of the Teratology Society, 1960–62; president-elect, 1962.

NELSON, NELS CHRISTIAN (*b. near Fredericia, Jutland, Denmark, 1875; d. New York, N.Y., 1964*), anthropologist. Immigrated to the United States in 1892. Studied at the University of California at Berkeley (M.L., 1908); assistant curator at the Museum of Anthropology (1909–12); instructor in anthropology (1910–12). Assistant curator of prehistoric archaeology at the American Museum of Natural History in New York (1912–21); associate curator of North American archaeology (1921–23); associate curator of archaeology (1923–28); curator of prehistoric archaeology (1928–43); curator emeritus (1943–64). Contributed to the development of scientific standards of modern archaeology. Pioneer in the use of stratigraphic techniques in studies of prehistoric American Indians of the Southwest; his excavations verified that human culture diffuses outward from a center of origin.

NELSON, NELSON OLSEN (*b. Lillesand, Norway, 1844; d. 1922*), Union soldier, manufacturer, promoter of profit sharing. Came to rural Missouri as a child. Founded (1877) N. O. Nelson Manufacturing Co., St. Louis, Mo., makers of building and plumbing supplies, which became one of the largest concerns of its kind in the world. Long interested in problems of labor, he was arbitrator of the Gould railroad lines strike, 1886. After study of basic causes of industrial disharmony, he grew convinced of the practicability of profit sharing and introduced it into his own plant, 1886. Failing to understand that its success was more personal than institutional, he founded a model cooperative community, Leclaire, near Edwardsville, Ill., 1890, and later extended his ideas to a low-profit, cooperative grocery store chain, centered in New Orleans, La., which went bankrupt, 1918.

NELSON, RENSSELAER RUSSELL (*b. Cooperstown, N.Y., 1826; d. 1904*), lawyer, jurist. Son of Samuel Nelson. Removed to St. Paul, Minnesota Territory, 1850, where he served as associate justice, supreme court, 1857–58, and as U.S. district judge for Minnesota, 1858–96.

NELSON, REUBEN (*b. New York, N.Y., 1818; d. New York, 1879*), Methodist clergyman, educator. Principal, Wyoming Seminary, Kingston, Pa., 1844–71; thereafter, served as publishing agent, Methodist Book Concern, New York.

NELSON, ROGER (*b. Frederick Co., Md., 1759; d. Frederick, Md., 1815*), Revolutionary soldier. Fought with credit at battles of Camden, Guilford Court House, Eutaw Springs, and Yorktown. A practicing lawyer after the Revolution, he served in the Maryland legislature and as congressman, (Democrat) Republican, 1804–10.

NELSON, SAMUEL (*b. Hebron, N.Y., 1792; d. Cooperstown, N.Y., 1873*), jurist. Graduated Middlebury College, 1813; studied law in upstate New York. Appointed judge of the sixth New York circuit, 1823, he held this post until 1831, when he was appointed associate justice, New York supreme court; he acted as chief justice, 1837–45. Named an associate justice of the U.S. Supreme Court, 1845, Nelson served until his retirement, November 1872. He became one of the most useful and hard working members of the Court and a recognized authority on admiralty and maritime law, international law, patent law, and conflict of laws. His training as a common-law lawyer and judge made him somewhat less willing than some of his colleagues to blaze new trails in judicial review and constitutional interpretation. Unspectacular, he was logical, lucid, and brief. His unwillingness to play politics under the guise of constitutional interpretation was illustrated by his attitude in the Dred Scott case; in writing the first opinion, before the Court decided to widen the scope of the case,

Nelson denied the court's jurisdiction in the matter and omitted as irrelevant all consideration of the validity of the Missouri Compromise Act of 1820. During the Civil War, he was a conservative, loyal Democrat who doubted the constitutionality of coercing the Southern states, looked askance at what appeared to him to be unwarranted accretions of power to the executive and military branches of government, and was one of the original majority denying validity of the Legal Tender Acts. He was named a member of the Joint High Commission to negotiate settlement of the *Alabama* claims, 1871.

NELSON, THOMAS (*b. Yorktown, Va., 1738; d. Hanover Co., Va., 1789*), merchant, Revolutionary patriot, signer of the Declaration of Independence. Son of William Nelson (1711–1772). Governor of Virginia, 1781, the first conservative to hold that office. Nelson ruined his own personal fortune by his generosity in the American cause; he gave security for Virginia's loan of 1780 and financed equipment of the state troops.

NELSON, THOMAS HENRY (*b. near Maysville, Ky., ca. 1823; d. Terre Haute, Ind., 1896*), lawyer. Brother of William Nelson (1824–1862). Removed to Indiana, 1844; became a Whig leader, a friend of Abraham Lincoln, and a founder of the Republican party in the Middle West. Served ably as U.S. minister to Chile, 1861–66; to Mexico, 1869–73.

NELSON, WILLIAM (*b. near Yorktown, Va., 1711; d. Yorktown, 1772*), merchant, planter. Member of the Virginia Council, 1744–72; acting governor, October 1770-August 1771. Took leading part in opposing British pre-Revolutionary taxation policy.

NELSON, WILLIAM (*b. near Maysville, Ky., 1824; d. Louisville, Ky., 1862*), naval officer, Union soldier. Brother of Thomas H. Nelson. Appointed midshipman, 1840; served in Mexican War and with Mediterranean squadron. Commissioned brigadier general of volunteers, 1861, Nelson organized Unionist troops in Kentucky and fought with credit at Shiloh, at Corinth, and in the advance against Chattanooga, receiving promotion to major general, 1862. He was shot dead by Jefferson C. Davis while preparing the defenses of Louisville.

NELSON, WILLIAM (*b. Newark, N.J., 1847; d. Matamoras, Pa., 1914*), lawyer, New Jersey historian. Principal editor of *Archives of the State of New Jersey;* author of a number of works on the local history of that state.

NELSON, WILLIAM ROCKHILL (*b. Fort Wayne, Ind., 1841; d. 1915*), journalist. Owner-publisher *post* 1880 of *Kansas City Evening Star,* Nelson made his paper a family journal in the best sense, independent alike in politics and advertising policy. He and his paper were responsible for many Kansas City (Mo.) reforms and civic improvements.

NERINCKX, CHARLES (*b. Herffelingen, Belgium, 1761; d. Ste. Geneviève, Mo., 1824*), Roman Catholic clergyman. Came to America, 1804; joined Stephen T. Badin as a missionary in Kentucky, 1805, serving there with great zeal until 1824. He was founder of the Sisters of Loretto (Kentucky), 1812.

NESBIT, EVELYN FLORENCE (*b. Tarentum, Pa., 1884; d. Santa Monica, Calif., 1967*), entertainer. Early work as an artist's model for George Grey Barnard and Charles Dana Gibson, among others. Performed as a showgirl in the musicals *Floradora* (1901), *Wild Rose* (1902), and *Hello Ragtime* (1913). Married Harry K. Thaw in 1905; brought to national attention with his trial for murder of architect Stanford White, an admirer of Nesbit's, in 1906. Appeared in films, including *Threads of Destiny* (1914), *Judge Not* (1915); *Redemption* (1917); and *Woman, Woman; I*

Want to Forget; Her Mistake; My Little Sister; The Woman Who Gave; and *Thou Shalt Not* (all 1919). Worked in burlesque throughout the 1920's and 1930's. Technical adviser for the motion picture based on her life, *The Girl in the Red Velvet Swing,* in 1955.

NESBITT, JOHN MAXWELL (*b. Loughbrickland, Ireland, ca. 1730; d. Philadelphia, Pa., 1802*), merchant, Revolutionary patriot. Immigrated to Philadelphia, 1747. Cooperated with Robert Morris in sustaining of public credit, 1780. Director of the Bank of North America, 1781–92, and first president of the Insurance Company of North America, 1792–96.

NESMITH, JAMES WILLIS (*b. New Brunswick, Canada, 1820; d. 1885*), lawyer, Oregon pioneer and legislator. Removed as a youth to the Midwest; to Oregon, 1843. U.S. senator, Douglas Democrat, 1861–67, he sacrificed his career by his friendship for Andrew Johnson.

NESMITH, JOHN (*b. Londonderry, N.H., 1793; d. Lowell, Mass., 1869*), merchant, textile manufacturer, temperance reformer. Lieutenant governor of Massachusetts, 1862–63.

NESSLER, KARL LUDWIG (*b. Todtnau, Bavaria, 1872; d. Harrington Park, N.J., 1951*), developer of hair beauty treatments. Immigrated to the U.S. in 1915. Invented the permanent wave process for waving human hair. Founder of the Nestle (later Nestle-LeMur) Co., 1919.

NESTLE, CHARLES. *See* NESSLER, KARL LUDWIG.

NESTOR, AGNES (*b. Grand Rapids, Mich., 1880; d. Chicago, Ill., 1948*), labor leader. Led female glove workers in drive for union shop, Chicago, 1898; became president of all-female local, 1902. Elected a national vice president of the International Glove Workers Union, 1903, she continued to hold office in the union for the rest of her life, working as negotiator, speaker, organizer, and administrator. A progressive in opinion, and a skillful lobbyist for social legislation, particularly on behalf of working women and children, she was associated with the National Women's Trade Union League as an executive board member, and as president of the Chicago branch, 1913–48. She was also active in public service as a member of state and national boards and commissions.

NETTLETON, ALVRED BAYARD (*b. Delaware Co., Ohio, 1838; d. Chicago, Ill., 1911*), Union soldier, journalist. Publicity man for Jay Cooke in his Northern Pacific operations.

NETTLETON, ASAHEL (*b. Killingworth, Conn., 1783; d. East Windsor, Conn., 1844*), Congregational evangelist. Graduated Yale, 1809. A strict Calvinist, Nettleton evangelized eastern Connecticut, 1811–22, later working in Virginia and England. He was strongly opposed to the revival methods of Charles G. Finney.

NETTLETON, EDWIN S. (*b. near Medina, Ohio, 1831; d. Denver, Colo., 1901*), engineer. Joined the Greeley Colony, 1870; surveyed townsite of Greeley, Colo., and laid out its irrigation ditches. Later, working for private companies and for the state, he planned and built a number of irrigation systems in Colorado, Wyoming, and Idaho.

NEUBERGER, RICHARD LEWIS (*b. Portland, Oreg., 1912; d. Portland, 1960*), journalist, author, politician. Studied briefly at the University of Oregon. Worked as a reporter on the *Portland Oregonian;* in 1936, he was appointed *New York Times* correspondent for the Pacific Northwest. Served in the Oregon legislative assembly, 1940–42; U.S. Senator, 1954–58. Neuberger was a staunch conservationist and political reformer. His books include *Our Promised Land* (1938), *The Lewis and Clark Expedition* (1951), and *Adventures in Politics* (1954).

NEUENDORFF, ADOLPH HEINRICH ANTON MAGNUS (*b. Hamburg, Germany, 1843; d. New York, N.Y., 1897*), musician, conductor, impresario. Came to New York City as a boy; made debut as concert pianist, 1859. Pioneered in American productions of Wagner's operas.

NEUMANN, FRANZ LEOPOLD (*b. Kattowitz, Upper Silesia [now Katowice, Poland], 1900; d. Switzerland, 1954*), lawyer, political theorist. Studied at the universities of Breslau, Leipzig, Rostock, and Frankfurt, LL.D., 1923, and the London School of Economics, Ph.D., 1936. Immigrated to the U.S. in 1936. During the 1920's, legal adviser to the German Social Democratic party. Taught at the Institute of Social Research at Columbia University, 1937–42. Worked for the German Research section of the State Department, 1945–47. Professor of government at Columbia University, 1947–54. An expert on Nazism, he wrote *Behemoth: The Structure and Practice of National Socialism* (1942).

NEUMANN, JOHN NEPOMUCENE (*b. Prachatitz, Bohemia, 1811; d. Philadelphia, Pa., 1860*), Roman Catholic clergyman, Redemptorist. Ordained, New York City, 1836, after making studies in Europe; joined Redemptorists, 1840. After service as a missionary and as a pastor in Pittsburgh, Pa., and Baltimore, Md. (where he acted as vice-provincial of his order, 1847–51), Neumann was consecrated bishop of Philadelphia, 1852. Notable for his spiritual character and charity, he was declared venerable in 1896 and was beatified on Oct. 13, 1963.

NEUMANN, JOHN VON. *See* VON NEUMANN, JOHN.

NEUMARK, DAVID (*b. Szczerzec, Galicia, Austria, 1866; d. 1924*), Jewish philosopher, educator. Ph.D., Berlin, 1896; pursued scholarly and rabbinical career in Germany and Bohemia. Immigrated to Cincinnati, Ohio, 1907, to be professor of Jewish philosophy at Hebrew Union College and continued there for the remainder of his life. A daring and original thinker, he made the entire field of Hebrew learning his own, publishing a number of special studies and a work entitled *The Philosophy of the Bible* (1918). His great work, a history of medieval Jewish philosophy, was left incomplete at his death.

NEUTRA, RICHARD JOSEPH (*b. Vienna, Austria, 1892; d. Wuppertal, West Germany, 1970*), architect. City architect of Luckenwalde, Germany (1920). Collaborated on the remodeling of the Berliner Tageblatt Building and the Zehlendorf housing project with Eric Mendelsohn from 1921. Immigrated to the United States in 1923; naturalized, 1929. On staff of Holabird and Roche, Chicago, Ill., from 1924. Opened his own firm in Los Angeles in 1926. A modernist architect and leading exponent of the International Style; his basic structure was post-and-beam with cantilevered roof slabs extending into space. Wrote and lectured extensively on "bio-realism," that is, the psychological, physiological, and ecological dimension of architecture. Author of *Survival Through Design* (1954). Designs include the Jardinette Apartments (Hollywood, 1927); Lovell House (Hollywood Hills, 1929); the Vorona Avenue School (Los Angeles, 1935); Miller House (Palm Springs, 1937), Kaufman House (Palm Springs, 1946), Tremaine House (Montecito, 1948), the Los Angeles County Hall of Records and the American embassy in Karachi, Pakistan (with Robert Alexander); and the Channel Heights housing projects (1942).

NEVADA, EMMA (*b. near Nevada City, Calif., 1859; d. Liverpool, England, 1940*), operatic soprano. Stage name of Emma Wixom. Madame Nevada was celebrated in coloratura parts at all the leading opera houses, 1880–1910.

NEVILLE, JOHN (*b. near headwaters of Occoquan River, Va., 1731; d. near Pittsburgh, Pa., 1803*), Revolutionary soldier, western Pennsylvania landowner and legislator. A central figure in the Whiskey Rebellion, 1794, as "inspector of survey" for collection of the new tax.

NEVILLE, WENDELL CUSHING (*b. Portsmouth, Va., 1870; d. 1930*), U.S. Marine Corps officer. Graduated Annapolis, 1890; commissioned second lieutenant, U.S. Marine Corps, 1892; served in Cuba, China, the Philippines, and Nicaragua, 1898–1912. Decorated for his services at Veracruz, Mexico, 1914, he was stationed for two years in China; ordered to France, December 1917, he commanded the 5th Regiment of marines and later succeeded to command of the 4th Brigade (2nd Division). Promoted brigadier general, 1918, he was made major general, 1923, and was appointed commandant of the U.S. Marine Corps, 1929.

NEVIN, ALFRED (*b. Shippensburg, Pa., 1816; d. 1890*), Presbyterian clergyman, editor. Brother of Edwin H. Nevin; cousin of John W. Nevin.

NEVIN, EDWIN HENRY (*b. Shippensburg, Pa., 1814; d. 1889*), Presbyterian clergyman, educator. Brother of Alfred Nevin; cousin of John W. Nevin. President, Franklin College, Ohio, 1840–44. Author of a number of hymns and polemic tracts.

NEVIN, ETHELBERT WOODBRIDGE (*b. near Pittsburgh, Pa., 1862; d. New Haven, Conn., 1901*), composer. Son of Robert P. Nevin. Studied in Pittsburgh, Boston, and Berlin, Germany; made debut as concert pianist, Pittsburgh, 1886. As a composer, Nevin confined himself to the small instrumental and vocal forms; many of his compositions met with immediate and exceptional popularity. His *Sketch Book* (opus 2, 1888) contained several of his finest compositions; "Narcissus" from *Water Scenes* (1891) became a world favorite as did his setting of "The Rosary" (1898).

NEVIN, GEORGE BALCH (*b. Shippensburg, Pa., 1859; d. Easton, Pa., 1933*), composer, businessman. Published a great quantity of music principally for the church; among his larger works were the cantatas *The Adoration* and *The Gift of God*. He wrote also a number of anthems and secular songs.

NEVIN, JOHN WILLIAMSON (*b. Franklin Co., Pa., 1803; d. near Lancaster, Pa., 1886*), theologian, educator. Brother of Robert P. Nevin; cousin of Alfred and Edwin H. Nevin. Graduated Union, 1821; Princeton Theological Seminary, 1826. As instructor at Princeton, 1826–29, Nevin published *A Summary of Biblical Antiquities* (1828); while professor of biblical literature, Western Theological Seminary, Allegheny, Pa., 1830–40, he gradually departed from old-school Calvinist orthodoxy under influence of Neander. Elected professor at Mercersburg Seminary, Pa., 1840, he transferred his status from the Presbyterian to the Reformed Church and soon exercised great influence within that body, collaborating with Philip Schaff in development of what was known as the "Mercersburg theology." He was author of a number of books, of which the most important was *The Mystical Presence* (1846), and editor of the *Mercersburg Review*, 1849–53. Nevin acted as president of Marshall College from 1841, retiring because of ill health *ca.* 1853 from both his professorship and the presidency. He served later as the head of the combined Franklin and Marshall College, 1866–76.

NEVIN, ROBERT PEEBLES (*b. Shippensburg, Pa., 1820; d. near Pittsburgh, Pa., 1908*), journalist, pioneer oil refiner. Brother of John W. Nevin; father of Ethelbert W. Nevin.

NEVIUS, JOHN LIVINGSTON (*b. Seneca Co., N.Y., 1829; d. near Chefoo, China, 1893*), Presbyterian missionary in China, 1853–93.

NEW, HARRY STEWART (*b. Indianapolis, Ind., 1858; d. Baltimore, Md., 1937*), journalist, politician. Associated with the *Indianapolis Journal*, 1878–1903, New was active in Indiana Republican politics. A machine Republican, he served as U.S. senator from Indiana, 1917–23, and was U.S. postmaster general, 1923–29.

NEWBERRY, JOHN STOUGHTON (*b. Sangerfield, N.Y., 1826; d. 1887*), lawyer. Graduated University of Michigan, 1847; practiced law in Detroit. President, Michigan Car Co., 1863–80; partner with James McMillan *post* 1878 in financial operations involving railroad building, banking, and real estate investment in Detroit.

NEWBERRY, JOHN STRONG (*b. Windsor, Conn., 1822; d. New Haven, Conn., 1892*), geologist, paleontologist. Raised in Ohio; graduated Western Reserve College, 1846; made medical studies at Cleveland Medical School and in Paris. Newberry served on a number of government exploring expeditions in the West, including the coast division of the Pacific Railroad survey, 1855, and the Ives exploration of the Colorado River, 1857–58. After service with the U.S. Sanitary Commission throughout the Civil War, he was professor of geology and paleontology in the School of Mines, Columbia University, 1866–92. A general naturalist of the old school rather than a specialist, Newberry rarely touched upon broader tectonic problems. His reputation rests largely upon his reports made while state geologist of Ohio, 1869–74, on his studies of the fossils of New Jersey and the Connecticut valley, and on his *Paleozoic Fishes of North America* (1889).

NEWBERRY, OLIVER (*b. East Windsor, Conn., 1789; d. 1860*), merchant, shipbuilder. Brother of Walter L. Newberry. Settled in Detroit, Mich., 1826; was one of first to foresee future of Chicago, Ill. Beginning as the operator of a fleet of lake vessels, Newberry became a large holder of real estate and a promoter of industry in both Detroit and Chicago.

NEWBERRY, TRUMAN HANDY (*b. Detroit, Mich., 1864; d. Grosse Pointe Farms, Mich., 1945*), businessman, public official. Son of John Stoughton Newberry; succeeded him as head of the family business enterprises, 1887. Served as assistant secretary of the navy, 1905–08, and was secretary during the last three months of President Theodore Roosevelt's administration (1908–09). Defeated Henry Ford in contest for U.S. Senate seat, 1918, but was indicted with others in 1919 on a charge of conspiracy to violate the Corrupt Practices Act. Found guilty of excessive campaign expenses and sentenced to prison, he appealed and the conviction was overturned by a close decision of the U.S. Supreme Court in May 1921. Meanwhile, a U.S. Senate investigation into the matter had been taking place, and the Senate, early in 1922, voted a resolution expressing disapproval of the amount of money spent to obtain his election. He resigned from the Senate in November 1922.

NEWBERRY, WALTER LOOMIS (*b. East Windsor, Conn., 1804; d. at sea, 1868*), merchant, banker, philanthropist. Brother of Oliver Newberry. Settled in Detroit, Mich., 1826, where he prospered in the dry goods business. In association with his brother, with W. B. Astor and Lewis Cass, he invested in large tracts of land in Wisconsin, northern Michigan, and in the newly established town of Chicago, Ill. Removing to Chicago, 1833, he made that city his home for the rest of his life and played a great part in its progress. His business enterprises came to include banking and railroading; he also held many civic positions of trust and honor. Among his many charitable benefactions was his founding of the public library in Chicago which bears his name.

NEWBOLD, WILLIAM ROMAINE (*b. Wilmington, Del., 1865; d. Philadelphia, Pa., 1926*), philosopher, educator. Graduated University of Pennsylvania, 1887; Ph.D., 1891. Taught philosophy at University of Pennsylvania *post* 1889; served as dean of the Graduate School, 1896–1904. A many-sided scholar, Newbold made important contributions also in psychology and Oriental studies.

NEWBROUGH, JOHN BALLOU (*b. near Springfield, Ohio, 1828; d. 1891*), spiritualist. Founder of the Shalam Community, a communistic society in New Mexico.

NEWCOMB, CHARLES LEONARD (*b. West Willington, Conn., 1854; d. 1930*), mechanical engineer, inventor, and manufacturer of pumping machinery and fire-fighting equipment.

NEWCOMB, HARVEY (*b. Thetford, Vt., 1803; d. Brooklyn, N.Y., 1863*), Congregational clergyman. Author of a vast number of books of which the most important was his *Cyclopaedia of Missions* (1854).

NEWCOMB, JOSEPHINE LOUISE LEMONNIER (*b. Baltimore, Md., 1816; d. New York, N.Y., 1901*), philanthropist. Chief among her benefactions was the founding and support of the H. Sophie Newcomb College of Tulane University, New Orleans, La.

NEWCOMB, SIMON (*b. Wallace, Nova Scotia, 1835; d. Washington, D.C., 1909*), astronomer. Born of New England parents who had settled in Nova Scotia, Newcomb ran away from apprenticeship to a quack doctor *ca.* 1853 and roamed through Atlantic coastal cities until he settled to teach a country school in Maryland for several years. Aided by Joseph Henry and J. E. Hilgard, he was appointed computer in the Nautical Almanac Office, located then (1857) at Harvard, from which time he dated his "birth into the world of sweetness and light." He graduated B.Sc., Lawrence Scientific School, 1858. His important research, published 1860, demonstrated that orbits of minor planets of the solar system had never intersected and that their presumed origin in the disruption of a larger planet was impossible. Commissioned, 1861, professor of mathematics in the U.S. Navy, he continued at the Naval Observatory and the Nautical Almanac Office until retirement as captain, 1897.

Although he made many observations at the Naval Observatory, Newcomb was primarily a mathematical astronomer. In recognition of his fundamental investigations and tables of the orbits of Neptune and Uranus, he was made medalist of the Royal Astronomical Society, London, 1874. He began *ca.* 1868 his celebrated studies of the moon's motion, to which he thereafter devoted much attention. He pushed back a fairly exact knowledge of lunar positions from 1750 to *ca.* 1645, disclosing an unsuspected inadequacy of Hanson's tables of lunar motion. About this time, he became deeply concerned with question of the sun's parallax. His revision of the value of the solar parallax, published in *Washington Observations 1865*, (1867), was standard for many years, but was itself superseded by his newer revision, 1895. With assistance of A. A. Michelson, he redetermined velocity of light by the revolving-mirror method.

Internationally renowned, he was appointed (1877) superintendent of the American Ephemeris and Nautical Almanac and reformed the entire basis of fundamental data involved in computing the Ephemeris. The fundamental places of celestial bodies were to be redetermined, new tables computed to suit revised theory. For this he reviewed all worthwhile observations made since 1750, numbering several hundred thousands. In this highest type of practical mathematical research he was aided by George

William Hill. He published a catalogue of some 1,500 fundamental star positions (*Astronomical Papers*, VIII, 1898) and contributed many classic memoirs to the *Astronomical Papers*, including a corroboration of Leverrier's theory on the motion of Mercury that in recent years has supported Einstein's relativity theory; throughout numerous articles he masterfully treated almost every conceivable subject in astronomy. He also published several mathematical textbooks and sustained an avocational interest in political economy. He served as professor of mathematics and astronomy at Johns Hopkins, 1884–94 and 1898–1900.

NEWCOMER, CHRISTIAN (*b. Lancaster Co., Pa., 1749 o.s.; d. 1830*), a founder of the Church of the United Brethren in Christ. His "Journal," which records his organizational labors, 1795–1830, is an important historical document and was translated and published together with his *Life* in 1834. Elected bishop, 1813, he was five times re-elected between 1814 and 1829.

NEWEL, STANFORD (*b. Providence, R.I., 1839; d. St. Paul, Minn., 1907*), lawyer. U.S. minister to the Netherlands, 1897–1905.

NEWELL, EDWARD THEODORE (*b. Kenosha, Wis., 1886; d. New York, N.Y., 1941*), numismatist. B.A., Yale, 1907; M.A., 1909. Donor of an outstanding collection of Greek, Roman, and Byzantine coins to the American Numismatic Society (of which he had been president, 1916–41), he made a number of scholarly contributions to the literature of his subject. He was also an authority on Islamic and Indian coinages.

NEWELL, FREDERICK HAYNES (*b. Bradford, Pa., 1862; d. Washington, D.C., 1932*), civil engineer. Graduated Massachusetts Institute of Technology, 1885. Assistant hydraulic engineer, U.S. Geological Survey, 1888–1902; chief engineer, Reclamation Service, 1902–07, and director of that Service, 1907–14. Engaged in irrigation surveys and projects throughout the arid parts of the West, instituting construction of 25 irrigation projects in 18 different states. Author of a number of technical treatises, he headed the civil engineering department, University of Illinois, 1915–20.

NEWELL, PETER SHEAF HERSEY (*b. near Bushnell, Ill., 1862; d. Little Neck, N.Y., 1924*), cartoonist, illustrator. Largely self-taught, Newell was a regular contributor to the leading periodicals *post* 1893; his work as a book illustrator may be studied in *A House-Boat on the Styx* (1896) and *The Pursuit of the House-Boat* (1897) both by John K. Bangs. Inadequate as a draftsman, Newell was strongest in whimsical interpretation of nonsense.

NEWELL, ROBERT (*b. Muskingum Co., Ohio, 1807; d.. Lewiston, Idaho, 1869*), trapper, Oregon pioneer. Settled, along with Joseph L. Meek,, in the Willamette Valley, 1840; helped draw up Oregon constitution (ratified July 5, 1843) and was for two sessions speaker of the House of Representatives under the provisional government. "Doc" Newell held a uniquely important place in early Oregon history, maintaining leadership in the affairs of the colony for some years after the death of Ewing Young.

NEWELL, ROBERT HENRY (*b. New York, N.Y., 1836; d. Brooklyn, N.Y., 1901*), journalist, humorist. Wrote, under pen name "Orpheus C. Kerr," a number of satiric papers in the mock-heroic style for the New York *Sunday Mercury* and other journals. These satires enjoyed great contemporary popularity and were published in three volumes, 1862–65, but they possess now only a historical interest as a burlesque commentary on the Civil War.

NEWELL, WILLIAM AUGUSTUS (*b. Franklin, Ohio, 1817; d. Allentown, N.J., 1901*), physician, politician. Graduated Rutgers, 1836; M.D., University of Pennsylvania, 1839; practiced at Allentown, N.J. Congressman, Whig, from New Jersey, 1847–51; governor, Know-Nothing, 1857–60; congressman, Republican, 1865–67. Newell served also as governor of Washington Territory, 1880–84, and was a pioneer advocate of the U.S. life-saving service.

NEWELL, WILLIAM WELLS (*b. Cambridge, Mass., 1839; d. 1907*), scholar, editor. Graduated Harvard, 1859; Harvard Divinity School, 1863. A founder of the American Folk-Lore Society, 1888, Newell served thereafter as its permanent secretary and as editor of the *Journal of American Folk-Lore*. His major interest was in the Arthurian romances and kindred works of the medieval period.

NEWHOUSE, SAMUEL (*b. New York, N.Y., 1853; d. near Paris, France, 1930*), mine operator, financier. Projected and built the Argo (commonly called the Newhouse) Tunnel, Idaho Springs, Colo., 1894–1910; developed Utah copper properties. Did much to improve and beautify Salt Lake City.

NEWLANDS, FRANCIS GRIFFITH (*b. Natchez, Miss., 1848; d. 1917*), lawyer. Raised in Quincy, Ill.; after admission to the bar, removed to San Francisco, Calif., 1870, where he prospered in practice and in general business. Removing to Nevada, 1888, he became an advocate of free silver and served as congressman, Silver party and Republican, 1893–97; Democrat, 1897–1903. He was U.S. senator, Democrat, 1903–17. Newlands was among the ablest critics of Republican financial policy and was persistent in demanding that major problems of finance and reform should be solved by scientific services and administrative boards with delegated authority from Congress. He was a valuable member of the Senate committee on interstate commerce and an expert on problems of transportation and domestic trade.

NEWLON, JESSE HOMER (*b. Salem, Ind., 1882; d. New Hope, Pa., 1841*), educator. A.B., Indiana University, 1907. A.M., Teachers College, Columbia University, 1914. A proponent of progressive education, as conceived of in his time, he gave practical effect to his ideas on curriculum reform while he was superintendent of schools of Denver, Colo., 1920–27. He then served as professor of education at Teachers College and director of its experimental Lincoln School, as chairman of the division of instruction at Teachers College (1934–38), and as director of the division of foundations of education (1938–41).

NEWMAN, ALBERT HENRY (*b. Edgefield, S.C., 1852; d. Austin, Tex., 1933*), Baptist church historian, educator.

NEWMAN, ALFRED (*b. New Haven, Conn., 1900; d. Los Angeles, Calif., 1970*), Hollywood music director, composer, and conductor. Music director of United Artists (1930–38) and Twentieth Century–Fox (1940–60). A pioneer in the evolution of the grand symphonic style of movie music that prevailed in Hollywood from the mid-1930's to the mid-1950's. Scored and conducted more than 230 films; received forty-five Academy Award nominations and won nine Academy Awards for film scores of *Alexander's Ragtime Band* (1938), *Tin Pan Alley* (1940), *The Song of Bernadette* (1943), *Mother Wore Tights* (1947), *With a Song in My Heart* (1952), *Call Me Madam* (1953), *Love Is a Many-Splendored Thing* (1955), *The King and I* (1956), and *Camelot* (1967). Other film scores include *Stella Dallas* (1937), *Wuthering Heights* (1939), *How Green Was My Valley* (1941), *All About Eve* (1950), *The Robe* (1953), and *Airport* (1970).

NEWMAN, BARNETT (*b. New York, N.Y., 1905; d. New York, 1970*), painter and sculptor. Known for minimalist, reductivist compositions characterized by an almost uninflected expanse of a single color, traversed from top to bottom by one or more narrow stripes of contrasting hues. Stressed the importance of the subject in art, and allied himself with primitive artists. Works include *The Command* (1946), *Death of Euclid* (1947), *Onement I* (1948), *Be I* (1949), and *Stations of the Cross* (series, 1966). Also created freestanding sculptures related to his paintings, such as *Broken Obelisk* (1967).

NEWMAN, HENRY (*b. Rehoboth, Mass., 1670; d. England, 1743*), philanthropist. Graduated Harvard, 1687; removed to London, England, *ca.* 1703, where he was associated with Thomas Bray in a number of charitable activities. He served as secretary of the Society for Promoting Christian Knowledge, 1708–43, was a benefactor of both Harvard and Yale, and acted from time to time as colonial agent for New Hampshire.

NEWMAN, HENRY RODERICK (*b. Easton, N.Y., ca. 1843; d. Florence, Italy, 1918*), painter of architectural subjects and flower pieces. Resident in Europe *post* 1869, Newman became a friend and protégé of John Ruskin whom he aided in the illustration of the *Stones of Venice*.

NEWMAN, JOHN PHILIP (*b. New York, N.Y., 1826; d. Saratoga, N.Y., 1899*), Methodist clergyman. Notable as a preacher. Newman became a close friend of Ulysses S. Grant while pastor in Washington, D.C., 1869–72, and was extensively patronized by the president. He was elected bishop, 1888, with the active help of the Grant family, but was undistinguished as an administrator.

NEWMAN, ROBERT LOFTIN (*b. Richmond, Va., 1827; d. 1912*), figure painter. Profoundly influenced by the Barbizon school, Newman was highly esteemed by fellow-painters, but never attained popular success in his time. He was particularly noted for his delicate sense of color and the poetic feeling and suggestion of his work.

NEWMAN, SAMUEL PHILLIPS (*b. Andover, Mass., 1797; d. Andover, 1842*), Congregational clergyman, educator. Graduated Harvard, 1816. Taught a number of subjects at Bowdoin, 1818–39, serving also as acting president, 1830–33. He was author of widely used textbooks in rhetoric and political economy.

NEWMAN, WILLIAM H. (*b. Prince William Co., Va., 1847; d. New York, N.Y., 1918*), railroad official, traffic expert. President, New York Central, 1901–09.

NEWMAN, WILLIAM TRUSLOW (*b. near Knoxville, Tenn., 1843; d. 1920*), Confederate soldier, lawyer. City attorney of Atlanta, Ga., 1871–83; U.S. judge of the northern district of Georgia, 1888–1920. Father of Frances Newman (1883–1928), who won distinction as a writer and expressed the radical sentiment of a changing South in such works as *The Hard Boiled Virgin* (1926).

NEWPORT, CHRISTOPHER (*b. Bantam, East Indies, 1617*), mariner. Served on Drake's Cadiz expedition, 1587; commanded successful privateering expedition, West Indies, 1592. Entering service of the Virginia Company, 1606, he was given charge of its early voyages. His position between the colonists and the company was not easy. Commanding first voyage of *Susan Constant, Godspeed,* and *Discovery,* he with others selected the site of Jamestown, May 13, 1607, and explored the James to the fall line. Thereafter, he made several round-trip voyages, bringing out (1609) Sir Thomas Gates and Sir George Somers and surviving a Bermuda shipwreck. In 1611, he brought out Sir Thomas Dale and a new group of colonists. His last voyages (1613–17) were in service of the East India Company.

NEWSAM, ALBERT (*b. Steubenville, Ohio, 1809; d. near Wilmington, Del., 1864*), lithographer, a leader in that art, 1831–57.

NEWSOM, HERSCHEL DAVID (*b. near Columbus, Ind., 1905; d. Washington, D.C., 1970*), agricultural leader. Studied at Indiana University (graduated, 1925). Master of the Indiana Grange, 1937–50; master of the National Grange, 1950–68. Appointed to President Lyndon Johnson's Tariff Commission in 1968. An effective lobbyist for agricultural causes.

NEWTON, HENRY JOTHAM (*b. Hartleton, Pa., 1823; d. New York, N.Y., 1895*), piano manufacturer, pioneer in dry-plate photography, spiritualist.

NEWTON, HUBERT ANSON (*b. Sherburne, N.Y., 1830; d. New Haven, Conn., 1896*), mathematician. Graduated Yale, 1850; taught mathematics at Yale, 1853–96, and was an extensive contributor to scientific journals. Advocated use of metric system of weights and measures.

NEWTON, ISAAC (*b. Schodack, N.Y., 1794; d. New York, N.Y., 1858*), steamboat designer, associate of Daniel Drew in the People's Line. Introduced passenger-boat innovations such as the burning of anthracite coal and the double-decked grand saloon surrounded by galleries leading to state rooms.

NEWTON, ISAAC (*b. Burlington Co., N.J., 1800; d. 1867*), farmer. Long prominent as an advocate of a federal department of agriculture, Newton was appointed superintendent of the agricultural division of the Patent Office, 1861. When the division was established as a department by Act of May 15, 1862, Newton was appointed commissioner and with the aid of skilled technical assistance set up the new Department of Agriculture on solid foundations.

NEWTON, JOHN (*b. Norfolk, Va., 1823; d. New York, N.Y., 1895*), Union major general, engineer. Son of Thomas Newton (1768–1847). Graduated West Point, 1842. Commissioned in the engineers, he was engaged mainly in fortification and river and harbor work until the Civil War. He served in the war with exceptional brilliance, particularly at Fredericksburg, Chancellorsville, Gettysburg, and in the Atlanta campaign. The most notable of his achievements in later life was the removal of obstructions in the East River, New York City, 1876 and 1885.

NEWTON, JOSEPH FORT (*b. Decatur, Tex., 1876; d. Philadelphia, Pa., 1950*), clergyman, author. Ordained to the Baptist ministry, 1895, he left that communion in search of a more liberal affiliation and held pastorates in nonsectarian and Universalist churches, 1900–16. His fame as a preacher and lecturer brought him an invitation to the pulpit of the City Temple in London, England, where he was minister, 1916–19. He then served as pastor of the Church of the Divine Paternity (Universalist), New York City, 1919–25, resigning to accept ordination in the Episcopal priesthood, 1926. Thereafter, he was rector of churches in Overbrook and Philadelphia, Pa. In addition to his sermons, he was author of a syndicated newspaper column, a number of books on religious and patriotic subjects (including *Lincoln and Herndon,* 1910), and a history of Freemasonry.

NEWTON, RICHARD (*b. Liverpool, England, 1812; d. Philadelphia, Pa., 1887*), Episcopal clergyman. Came to America as a boy. Graduated University of Pennsylvania, 1836; attended General Theological Seminary, N.Y.; was ordained 1840. A leading evangelical, he held several Philadelphia pastorates and was famous for his success as a preacher to children.

NEWTON, RICHARD HEBER (*b. Philadelphia, Pa., 1840; d. East Hampton, N.Y., 1914*), Episcopal clergyman. Son of Richard Newton; brother of William W. Newton. Advocate of modern critical study of the Bible as minister of several churches in

Philadelphia and New York; resident preacher at Leland Stanford University, Calif., *post* 1902.

NEWTON, ROBERT SAFFORD (*b. near Gallipolis, Ohio, 1818; d. New York, N.Y., 1881*), eclectic physician, editor. Specialist in pathology and treatment of cancer.

NEWTON, THOMAS (*b. England, 1660; d. 1721*), New England colonial official, lawyer. Came to Boston, Mass., *ante* 1688; held a number of judicial and other appointments under the Crown, rising to attorney general of Massachusetts, 1720. Noted in his own time as a learned advocate, Newton behaved most unjudiciously as prosecutor in the trial of Jacob Leisler, 1691, and in the Salem witchcraft trials, 1692. His conduct of the trials has been called "morally criminal."

NEWTON, THOMAS (*b. Virginia, 1768; d. Norfolk, Va., 1847*), lawyer, Virginia legislator. Congressman, (Democrat) Republican, from Virginia, 1801–30, 1831–33. Active in support of the interests of the seacoast commercial classes, Newton vigorously supported the War of 1812 and all legislation which assisted American commerce.

NEWTON, WILLIAM WILBERFORCE (*b. Philadelphia, Pa., 1843; d. 1914*), Episcopal clergyman. Son of Richard Newton; brother of Richard H. Newton. Held a number of pastorates in New England; was markedly successful in preaching to children.

NEY, ELISABET (*b. Münster, Germany, 1833; d. 1907*), sculptor. Wife of Edmund D. Montgomery. Came to America, 1871, with a European reputation for eccentricity as well as artistic achievement; settled in Texas, 1873. Among the works of her American period were statues and busts of many Texan notables.

NEYLAND, ROBERT REESE, JR. (*b. Greenville, Tex., 1892; d. New Orleans, La., 1962*), football coach and army officer. Studied at the U.S. Military Academy (graduated, 1916). Served with the Army Corps of Engineers in Mexico, 1916–17, and with the Allied Expeditionary Force in France, 1917–18. Attended the Massachusetts Institute of Technology (B.S., 1921). At the University of Tennessee in Knoxville, head of the Reserve Officers Training Corps (1925–31); head coach of the football team (1926–35; 1936–41; 1946–53). With the Corps of Engineers in Panama (1935–36). Retired from the army, 1936. Recalled to active duty in 1941; stationed in Calcutta. Retired a brigadier general in 1946. His coaching legacy at Tennessee included 173 wins, 31 losses, 12 ties, 6 won or shared conference championships, and national recognition to Tennessee as a football power.

NG POON CHEW (*b. South China, 1866; d. San Francisco, Calif., 1931*), Chinese editor, lecturer. Came to California, 1881. After service as a Presbyterian missionary, 1892–99, he founded at San Francisco and edited the newspaper *Chinese Western Daily*. He lectured extensively to Americans on Chinese culture and to the Chinese on the material gifts of western civilization and was Chinese vice-consul in San Francisco, 1913–31.

NIBLACK, ALBERT PARKER (*b. Vincennes, Ind., 1859; d. Nice, France, 1929*), naval officer. Graduated Annapolis, 1880. After varied sea and shore service, he commanded the first squadron of battleships of the Atlantic Fleet, 1917, and *post* November of that year, ably directed the patrol force of the Atlantic Fleet based on Gibraltar. He retired as rear admiral, 1923.

NIBLACK, WILLIAM ELLIS (*b. Dubois Co., Ind., 1822; d. Indianapolis, Ind., 1893*), lawyer, jurist, Indiana legislator. Congressman, Democrat, from Indiana, 1857–61, 1865–75; judge,

state supreme court, 1877–89. Favored the Union but opposed radical Reconstruction and encroachments on states' rights.

NIBLO, WILLIAM (*b. Ireland, 1789; d. 1878*), New York hotel and theatre manager. Came to America as a youth, and *post* 1823 conducted hotels and concert gardens in New York City. By 1837, Niblo's Garden was a fashionable entertainment spot and offered musical, dramatic, and variety shows with great success until Niblo's retirement, 1861.

NICHOLAS, GEORGE (*b. Williamsburg, Va., 1754[?]; d. 1799*), Revolutionary soldier, Virginia legislator, Kentucky pioneer. Brother of John, Philip N., and Wilson C. Nicholas; son of Robert C. Nicholas. A leading supporter of Thomas Jefferson in the Virginia Assembly, Nicholas removed to Kentucky, 1790, where he served as that state's first attorney general; he was a member of the convention which drafted the first Kentucky constitution, 1792, and led in the framing and advocating of the Kentucky Resolutions, 1798. His association in land speculations with James Wilkinson and Harry Innes led him to involvement in the last phase of the Spanish Conspiracy, 1797.

NICHOLAS, JOHN (*b. Williamsburg, Va., 1756[?]; d. Geneva, N.Y., 1819*), lawyer. Brother of George, Philip N., and Wilson C. Nicholas; son of Robert C. Nicholas. As congressman, (Democrat) Republican, from Virginia, 1793–1801, he was an effective debater in support of this party's policies. Removing to Geneva, N.Y., 1803, he engaged in agriculture and served as a county judge.

NICHOLAS, PHILIP NORBORNE (*b. Williamsburg, Va., 1775[?]; d. 1849*), Virginia jurist and politician. Brother of George, John, and Wilson C. Nicholas; son of Robert C. Nicholas. Engaged *post* 1804 in banking in Richmond, Va.; judge, general court of Virginia, 1823–49; played powerful, though quiet, part in the triumph of Jacksonian ideas.

NICHOLAS, ROBERT CARTER (*b. probably Williamsburg, Va., 1728; d. Hanover Co., Va., 1780*), colonial official, Revolutionary patriot, lawyer. Active as a conservative in the Virginia Assembly *post* 1756, Nicholas gave reluctant assent to the various measures tending toward revolution. Alone, of all the important men in the Assembly, he opposed adoption of the Declaration of Independence. A man of almost puritanical austerity, he exposed fraud in high places and as treasurer of Virginia, 1766–76, served the colony with scrupulous honesty. Although he opposed most of the plans of the revolutionary party, he was trusted by the patriots to aid in carrying out the very policies against which he had argued. He was father of George, John, Philip N., and Wilson C. Nicholas.

NICHOLAS, WILSON CARY (*b. Williamsburg, Va., 1761; d. Albemarle Co., Va., 1820*), Revolutionary soldier, Virginia politician. Brother of George, John, and Philip N. Nicholas; son of Robert C. Nicholas. Influential Jeffersonian member of Virginia Assembly, 1784–89, 1794–99; U.S. senator, 1799–1804; congressman, 1807–09. As governor of Virginia, 1814–16, he worked on problems of internal improvement and education and collaborated with Jefferson in foundation of the University of Virginia. A heavy speculator, with his brother George, in Western lands, he involved Jefferson in his own financial collapse, 1819.

NICHOLLS, FRANCIS REDDING TILLOU (*b. Donaldsonville, La., 1834; d. near Thibodeaux, La., 1912*), Confederate brigadier general, lawyer. Nephew of Joseph R. Drake. Graduated West Point, 1855. After outstanding service under Stonewall Jackson in 1862, he was incapacitated for field duties by a severe wound at Chancellorsville. Resuming his law practice in Louisiana *post* 1865, he was elected governor of the state on the

Democratic ticket, 1876, defeated a Republican challenge of his election, and cleansed the state of Carpetbag rule before his retirement in 1880. Reelected governor for the term 1888–92, he destroyed the Louisiana Lottery. As chief justice of the supreme court of Louisiana, 1892–1904, and as associate justice, 1904–11, he molded Louisiana constitutional law in a series of lucid and elaborate opinions and reports.

NICHOLLS, RHODA HOLMES (*b. Coventry, England, 1854; d. Stamford, Conn., 1930*), artist, educator. Resided in the United States *post* 1884. Excelled as a water-colorist.

NICHOLS, CHARLES HENRY (*b. Vassalboro, Maine, 1820; d. New York, N.Y., 1889*), physician, psychiatrist. M.D., University of Pennsylvania, 1843. Planned, built, and was first superintendent of present St. Elizabeth Hospital, Washington, D.C., serving, 1852–77; designed and superintended *post* 1877 the Bloomingdale Asylum, New York, N.Y.

NICHOLS, CHARLES LEMUEL (*b. Worcester, Mass., 1851; d. 1929*), physician, bibliophile. Author of a number of scholarly monographs on American historical subjects and early printing.

NICHOLS, CLARINA IRENE HOWARD (*b. Townshend, Vt., 1810; d. Potter Valley, Calif., 1885*), woman's rights reformer, editor, Kansas pioneer.

NICHOLS, DUDLEY (*b. Wapakoneta, Ohio, 1895; d. Hollywood, Calif., 1960*), screenwriter, reporter. Attended the University of Michigan, majoring in electronics. After serving in the navy in World War I, Nichols became a reporter for various Philadelphia and New York newspapers. His fourteen filmscripts for director John Ford include *Men Without Women* (1930), *The Lost Patrol* (1934), *The Informer* (1935) for which he refused to accept the Academy Award, *The Plough and the Stars* (1936), and *The Long Voyage Home* (1940). Other filmscripts include his adaptation of Hemingway's *For Whom the Bell Tolls* (1943), *Sister Kenny* (1946), and O'Neill's *Mourning Becomes Electra* (1947), and *Heller in Pink Tights* (1960). Helped found the Screen Writers' Guild; president, 1938–39.

NICHOLS, EDWARD LEAMINGTON (*b. Leamington, England, 1854; d. West Palm Beach, Fla., 1937*), physicist. Graduated Cornell, 1875; Ph.D., Göttingen, 1879. After serving as a fellow at Johns Hopkins and as an assistant to Thomas A. Edison, Nichols taught at several Midwestern colleges. Returning to Cornell, 1887, as head of the department of physics, he remained there until his retirement, 1919. His principal research was done in the fields of color, physiological optics, and luminescence.

NICHOLS, ERNEST FOX (*b. Leavenworth, Kans., 1869; d. 1924*), physicist, educator. Graduated Kansas State College, 1888; made graduate studies at Kansas, Cornell, and in Germany. Taught physics at Colgate University, 1892–98; at Dartmouth, 1898–1903; at Columbia, 1903–09; and at Yale, 1917–20. He served as president of Dartmouth, 1909–16, and as president, Massachusetts Institute of Technology, for a very brief period in 1920; he engaged in laboratory research thereafter. With the aid of the Nichols's radiometer which he devised, he made a number of brilliant investigations of the unexplored region between the visible spectrum and the electro magnetic waves of Heinrich Hertz, a task which he successfully completed only on the day of his death. As a teacher, Nichols had the rare gift of inspiring students with a love of productive scholarship.

NICHOLS, GEORGE WARD (*b. Tremont, Maine, 1831; d. 1885*), journalist, Union soldier, promoter of art education and music in Cincinnati, Ohio.

NICHOLS, JAMES ROBINSON (*b. West Amesbury, now Merrimac, Mass., 1819; d. Haverhill, Mass., 1888*), manufacturing chemist, chemical journalist, inventor.

NICHOLS, MARY SARGEANT NEAL GOVE (*b. Goffstown, N.H., 1810; d. London, England, 1884*), water-cure physician, reformer. Married Thomas L. Nichols, 1848; advocated miscellaneous reforms including mesmerism, spiritualism, Fourierism, temperance, and dress reform.

NICHOLS, RUTH ROWLAND (*b. New York, N.Y., 1901; d. New York, 1960*), aviator. Graduated from Wellesley College, 1924. The first woman to receive a seaplane pilot's license by the Fédération Aéronautique Internationale (1922) and the second to receive a pilot's license from the American government, Nichols set speed, altitude, and duration records. She failed in her attempt to cross the Atlantic in 1931 when her plane crashed in New Brunswick. In the 1950's, she was active in charities, with UNICEF, and with the Save the Children Federation. With Amelia Earhart, Nichols was the leading pioneer American aviator.

NICHOLS, THOMAS LOW (*b. Orford, N.H., 1815; d. Chaumont-en-Vezin, France, 1901*), journalist, hydrotherapist, pioneer dietician. With his wife, Mary S.N.G. Nichols (married 1848), he wrote and published several books on health and other reforms and propagandized for a number of esoteric doctrines in *Nichols' Journal* and *Nichols' Monthly* (1853–57). Removing with his wife to England at the outbreak of the Civil War of which they disapproved, he concentrated for the rest of his active life on food reform.

NICHOLS, WILLIAM FORD (*b. Lloyd, N.Y., 1849; d. 1924*), Episcopal clergyman. Consecrated assistant bishop of California, 1890, he succeeded as bishop in 1893 and presided with notable success over the diocese until 1919, when he surrendered the heavier work to a coadjutor. He was first president of the Province of the Pacific, 1915–21.

NICHOLSON, ALFRED OSBORNE POPE (*b. Williamson Co., Tenn., 1808; d. Columbia, Tenn., 1876*), lawyer, jurist. Prominent in Tennessee railroad development and banking, he served with ability as a Democrat in both houses of the state legislature and was appointed to the U.S. Senate, 1840–42. He supported James K. Polk in 1844 and edited the *Nashville Union* in Polk's behalf. In 1848, he was the recipient of the famous "Nicholson Letter," in which Lewis Cass sought to explain his views on the Wilmot Proviso. At the Nashville Convention, he advocated acceptance of the compromise measures of 1850. Again in the U.S. Senate, 1859–61, he was expelled for support of the Confederacy; after disfranchisement by the Radicals, he was influential in the Tennessee constitutional convention (1870) that overthrew the Radical regime. He served as chief justice, Tennessee supreme court, 1870–76.

NICHOLSON, ELIZA JANE POITEVENT HOLBROOK (*b. near Pearlington, Miss., 1849; d. New Orleans, La., 1896*), poet, journalist. Coproprietor, New Orleans *Picayune*, 1876–96; author of *Lyrics by Pearl Rivers* (1873).

NICHOLSON, FRANCIS (*b. near Richmond in Yorkshire, England, 1655; d. England, 1728*), colonial official. Came first to America as captain of infantry under Sir Edmund Andros, 1686; in 1688 he was commissioned lieutenant governor of the Dominion of New England. Ineffective in his handling of the Leisler rebellion at New York, he returned to England but was immediately appointed lieutenant governor of Virginia where, until 1692, he conducted what was probably his most successful administration. Taking the broadest possible view of colonial affairs, he traveled in the interior to study frontier conditions, encouraged the establishment of postal services, and supported the foundation of the College of William and Mary. As governor of Maryland, 1694–98, he encouraged education and the Established Church and was largely responsible for removal of the capital to Annapolis. His second term as governor of Virginia, 1698–1705, was less successful than his first; he was, however, the leading spirit in the removal of the capital to Williamsburg and the improvement of finances and local administration. After four years of obscurity in England, he effected as brigadier general commanding British and colonial troops a bloodless conquest of Port Royal, Canada, October 1710, establishing British military supremacy in Acadia. In his last colonial governorship (South Carolina, 1720–25), he won the confidence of the colonists but gained the hostility of the Charleston merchants who petitioned for his recall. Nicholson's usefulness was seriously impaired by his high temper which made it difficult for others to work with him, yet his zeal and breadth of vision entitle him to high rank among colonial governors.

NICHOLSON, JAMES (*b. Chestertown, Md., ca. 1736; d. New York, N.Y., 1804*), Revolutionary naval officer. Brother of Samuel Nicholson; father-in-law of Albert Gallatin. Senior captain, Continental Navy, 1778–83; commanded frigates *Virginia*, *Trumbull*, and *Bourbon*.

NICHOLSON, JAMES BARTRAM (*b. St. Louis, Mo., 1820; d. Philadelphia, Pa., 1901*), bookbinder. Partner, 1848–90, in the Philadelphia firm of Pawson & Nicholson. Author of *Manual of the Art of Bookbinding* (1856).

NICHOLSON, JAMES WILLIAM AUGUSTUS (*b. Dedham, Mass., 1821; d. New York, N.Y., 1887*), naval officer. Grandson of Samuel Nicholson. Appointed midshipman, 1838; as lieutenant served under Matthew C. Perry in Japanese waters; helped in suppression of slave trade, 1857–60. During Civil War, Nicholson saw varied service with the Atlantic and Gulf blockade, commanding USS *Manhattan* at Mobile Bay. He later commanded the European station and retired as rear admiral, 1883.

NICHOLSON, JOHN (*b. Wales, [?]; d. Philadelphia, Pa., 1800*), financier, land-company promoter. Came to America at some time prior to the Revolution; was appointed comptroller general of Pennsylvania, 1782, and by use of extensive powers, brought order to the state's financial affairs. Resigning from this and other state offices, 1794, Nicholson became partner of Robert Morris in a number of land companies and did much to encourage settlement in western Pennsylvania, Georgia, and the new capital at Washington, D.C. (Federal City). Overextended like Morris, he was caught by the financial stringency of 1795–96 and was confined in debtors' prison, 1800.

NICHOLSON, JOSEPH HOPPER (*b. probably Chestertown, Md., 1770; d. Maryland, 1817*), lawyer, Maryland legislator. Nephew of James and Samuel Nicholson; son-in-law of Edward Lloyd (1744–1796). As congressman from Maryland, 1799–1806, he shared leadership in the House with Nathaniel Macon and John Randolph of Roanoke; he was a sponsor of many important measures and was one of the most formidable "Old Republicans" in public life. Serving as a judge of the Maryland court of appeals, 1806–17 (also chief judge, sixth judicial district), he displayed high ability. During the War of 1812, he raised at his own expense and commanded a company of artillery.

NICHOLSON, MEREDITH (*b. Crawfordsville, Ind., 1866; d. Indianapolis, Ind., 1947*), author, diplomat. Worked on Indianapolis *News*, 1885–97; published *Short Flights*, an undistinguished book of verse, 1891. Engaged in business in Denver, Colo., 1898–1901; returned to Indianapolis and began a long, successful career as popular novelist, essayist, lecturer, and "professional Hoosier." He was also active as a moderate reformer in Democratic party politics. He served as U.S. minister to Paraguay (1933–34), Venezuela (1935–38), and Nicaragua (1938–41). His best writing was in his essays (*The Hoosiers*, 1900; *The Provincial American*, 1912; and other collections). His novels, although plotted and developed according to convention and formula, contain much shrewd observation on the changes taking place in Midwestern society at the time they were written. They include *The Main Chance* (1903), *Zelda Dameron* (1904), *The House of a Thousand Candles* (1905), *A Hoosier Chronicle* (1912), *Otherwise Phyllis* (1913), and *Broken Barriers* (1922).

NICHOLSON, SAMUEL (*b. Maryland, 1743; d. Charlestown, Mass., 1811*), naval officer. Brother of James Nicholson. Commissioned captain in Continental Navy, 1776, he commanded the *Dolphin* and the frigate *Deane* on a number of successful cruises, 1777–83. Recommissioned captain, June 1794, Nicholson superintended construction of the frigate *Constitution* and commanded her at sea, 1798–99. *Post* 1801, he served as superintendent of the navy yard at Charlestown.

NICHOLSON, SAMUEL DANFORD (*b. Springfield, Prince Edward Island, Canada, 1859; d. 1923*), mining operator. Settled in Colorado, 1881, where he rose from mine laborer to president and manager of several mines. A successful prospector and an investor in business enterprises at Leadville and Denver, he was Populist mayor of Leadville, 1893–97. Returning to the Republican party, he was U.S. senator from Colorado, 1921–23.

NICHOLSON, SETH BARNES (*b. Springfield, Ill., 1891; d. Los Angeles, Calif., 1963*), astronomer. Studied at Drake University in Des Moines, Iowa, and the University of California at Berkeley (Ph.D., 1915). Instructor in astronomy at Berkeley (1913–15). On staff of the Mt. Wilson Observatory (1915–57). Discovered four Jovian satellites: Jupiter IX (1914); X and XI (1938); and XII (1951). Also studied solar spectra and surface features, and adapted the vacuum thermocouple to measure temperatures of astronomical bodies. President of the Astronomical Society of the Pacific (1935, 1960); editor of its *Publications* (1940–55).

NICHOLSON, TIMOTHY (*b. near Belvidere, N.C., 1828; d. 1924*), educator, bookseller, Quaker leader in Indiana *post* 1861. Outstanding in prison reform work.

NICHOLSON, WILLIAM JONES (*b. Washington, D.C., 1856; d. Washington, D.C., 1931*), soldier. Appointed second lieutenant, 7th cavalry, 1876, Nicholson served with that regiment against the Indians on the frontier and was an ordnance officer during the war with Spain. Promoted colonel, 1912, he commanded the 11th cavalry during the expedition after Villa into Mexico; he commanded the 157th Brigade of the 79th Division in France during World War I, winning distinction for the capture of Montfaucon.

NICHOLSON, WILLIAM THOMAS (*b. Pawtucket, R.I., 1834; d. Providence, R.I., 1893*), first manufacturer of machine-made files. Founded Nicholson File Co. in Providence, R.I., 1864.

NICOLA, LEWIS (*b. France or Ireland, 1717; d. Alexandria, Va., 1807*), merchant, editor, Revolutionary soldier, public official. Immigrated from Dublin, Ireland, to Philadelphia, Pa., *ca.* 1766. Entered business; edited *The American Magazine* (January–September 1769); helped form the American Philosophical Society. Author of three military manuals for American use (1776–77), Nicola was active as a recruiting officer and as commander of the Philadelphia home guard. He is noted for his proposal to George Washington in May 1782 that the government be changed to a monarchy with Washington as king.

NICOLAY, JOHN GEORGE (*b. Essingen, Bavaria, 1832; d. Washington, D.C., 1901*), journalist. Came to America as a child; was raised in Ohio, Indiana, Missouri, and Illinois; became editor-proprietor of the Pittsfield, Ill., *Free Press*, 1854. A friend of John Hay, Nicolay became Abraham Lincoln's private secretary (with Hay as assistant), 1860. Few men enjoyed Lincoln's confidence so fully as Nicolay. He served as U.S. consul at Paris, 1865–69, and as marshal of the U.S. Supreme Court, 1872–87, but he is principally famous for his collaboration with John Hay on *Abraham Lincoln: A History* (1890), a work of enduring importance.

NICOLET, JEAN (*b. Cherbourg, France, 1598; d. on St. Lawrence River, 1642*), French explorer. Came to New France with Samuel de Champlain; lived on Allumette Island on Ottawa River, 1618–20. Sent to live among the Nipissing, he was appointed their official interpreter, 1624; in 1633 he returned to Canada and became official interpreter for the colony with headquarters at Three Rivers. During a journey to the West, 1634, Nicolet was the first known white visitor to Lake Michigan and Wisconsin, but the extent of his explorations is still a matter of controversy.

NICOLL, DE LANCEY (*b. Shelter Island, N.Y., 1854; d. 1931*), lawyer. Graduated Princeton, 1874; Columbia Law School, 1876. Appointed assistant district attorney of New York County, 1885, he won immediate recognition as an outstanding prosecutor; he was elected district attorney on the Democratic ticket, 1890, served with success, but refused renomination. Thereafter, in private practice, he was counsel in a number of difficult cases, defending the New York *World* in the so-called Panama Libel case, and the American Tobacco Co. in antitrust proceedings. A supporter of genuine reforms, he despised demagogues and professional altruists.

NICOLL, JAMES CRAIG (*b. New York, N.Y., 1847; d. Norwalk, Conn., 1918*), marine painter, etcher.

NICOLLET, JOSEPH NICOLAS (*b. Cluses, Savoy, 1786; d. Washington, D.C., 1843*), explorer, mathematician. Immigrated to New Orleans, La., from France, 1832; removing soon to St. Louis, Mo., he was encouraged in his plan for exploration by the Chouteau family. He made a survey to the sources of the Mississippi River, 1836, and two surveys of the upper Missouri, 1838 and 1839. A report of his activities was published, 1843.

NICOLLS, MATTHIAS (*b. Plymouth, England, 1626; d. New York, 1687 or 1688*), lawyer. Came to America, 1664, as secretary to a royal commission sent to investigate conditions in New England. After the ousting of the Dutch from New York, August 1664, he was named secretary of that province and held the post until 1680 except for the time of Dutch reoccupation, 1673–74. He also held a number of other offices, and was chosen speaker, first N.Y. provincial assembly, 1683. He is best known as the reputed principal author of the "Duke's Laws," promulgated 1665.

NICOLLS, RICHARD (*b. Bedfordshire, England, 1624; d. in battle of Solebay, off coast of Suffolk, England, 1672*), colonial official. As first English governor of New York, 1664–68, Nicolls secured the bloodless surrender of New Amsterdam in August–September 1664 and supervised the transition to English rule with great ability and tact. In March 1665, he issued the celebrated "Duke's Laws," prepared to an indeterminate degree by the provincial secretary, Matthias Nicolls (to whom the governor was not related).

NICOLLS, WILLIAM (*b. England, 1657; d. 1723*), colonial lawyer and politician. Son of Matthias Nicolls by whom he was brought to New York as a child. A conservative, he became attorney general of the province, 1687. He was active in the opposition to Jacob Leisler, 1689–91, becoming thereafter a councillor and a large landholder in Suffolk Co., N.Y. Suspended from the Council in 1698 by the governor, the Earl of Bellomont, Nicolls returned to power as a member of the New York Assembly, 1701–23, ad was its speaker, 1702–18.

NIEBUHR, HELMUT RICHARD (*b. Wright City, Mo., 1894; d. Greenfield, Mass., 1962*), theologian and educator. Brother of theologian Reinhold Niebuhr. Studied at Eden Theological Seminary at Webster Groves, Mo.; Washington University; and Yale Divinity School (B.D., 1923; Ph.D., 1924). Ordained a minister of the German Evangelical Church (1916). Teacher of theology and ethics, Eden Seminary (1919–21; 1927–30); president of Elmhurst College (1924–27); professor, Yale University (1931–62). An analyst of American religious history; believed that ongoing interaction between God and humanity can redirect history. Advocated conversionist Christianity, in which Christ is seen as transforming culture; believed that to the degree that Christian communities made the "fitting response," they could spark a transformation that would bring the world closer to the kingdom of God. Works include *The Social Sources of Denominationalism* (1929), *The Kingdom of God in America* (1937), *The Meaning of Revelation* (1941), *Christ and Culture* (1951), and *Radical Monotheism and Western Culture* (1960).

NIEDRINGHAUS, FREDERICK GOTTLIEB (*b. Lübbecke, Westphalia, 1837; d. St. Louis, Mo., 1922*), tinplate manufacturer, protective tariff advocate.

NIEHAUS, CHARLES HENRY (*b. Cincinnati, Ohio, 1855; d. 1935*), sculptor. Studied in Cincinnati and at the Royal Academy, Munich. Executed many public commissions, all well designed and firmly modeled; among them, his memorial doors at Trinity Church, New York City, are especially noteworthy.

NIELSEN, ALICE (*b. Nashville, Tenn., 1870[?]; d. New York, N.Y., 1943*), operatic soprano, concert singer. Raised in Kansas City, Mo. Her greatest successes were in Victor Herbert's operettas, beginning with *The Serenade*, 1897; he wrote *The Fortune Teller* for her, 1898. She later sang in grand opera in Naples, London, and Boston, Mass., and made infrequent appearances with the Metropolitan Opera in New York.

NIEMAN, LUCIUS WILLIAM (*b. Bear Creek, Wis., 1856; d. Milwaukee, Wis., 1935*), newspaper editor, publisher. Served successively as printer, reporter, legislative correspondent, city editor, and managing editor on the *Milwaukee Sentinel*, 1871–80. After a brief period as managing editor of the *St. Paul Dispatch*, he purchased a half interest in the Milwaukee *Daily Journal*, 1882. Independent and consistent in his journalistic battles for reforms, Nieman combined business ability with essential editorial qualities as editor and publisher of the paper and raised it to a high place in the American press. The Nieman Fellowships at Harvard were founded by his widow in his memory.

NIEMEYER, JOHN HENRY (*b. Bremen, Germany, 1839; d. New Haven, Conn., 1932*), artist, teacher of drawing. Came to America as a child; was raised in Cincinnati, Ohio. Studied art in Paris, 1866–70, where he was a teacher of Augustus Saint-Gaudens. As professor of drawing, Yale Art School, 1871–1908, he came to be regarded as a great teacher and also won renown for the precision of line and perfection of modeling of his own paintings.

NIES, JAMES BUCHANAN (*b. Newark, N.J., 1856; d. Jerusalem, 1922*), Episcopal clergyman, archaeologist. Benefactor of the American School for Oriental Study at Jerusalem.

NIES, KONRAD (*b. Alzey, Rhenish Hesse, Germany, 1861; d. San Francisco, Calif., 1921*), journalist, German-language poet, educator.

NIEUWLAND, JULIUS ARTHUR (*b. Hansbeke, Belgium, 1878; d. Washington, D.C., 1936*), Roman Catholic clergyman, chemist, botanist. Came to America as a child; graduated Notre Dame, 1899. Entering the Congregation of the Holy Cross, he was ordained, 1903. Teacher of botany and chemistry at Notre Dame *post* 1904, Nieuwland engaged in extensive research in both his fields. Lewisite and neoprene (synthetic rubber) were produced on the basis of his discoveries.

NILES, DAVID K. (*b. Boston, Mass., 1892; d. Boston, 1952*), politician, government official. Entered government service, 1917, as aide to George W. Coleman, information director of the Department of Labor. A supporter of Franklin D. Roosevelt, Niles held several posts as a New Deal administrator, 1933–42, mostly in the field of labor relations under Harry Hopkins.

As administrative assistant to the president, 1942–51, was influential in persuading President Truman to support the founding of Israel and became the chief expert on that question. His memorandum of May 6, 1948, provided the substance of the recognition policy announced a week later by the administration.

NILES, HEZEKIAH (*b. Jefferis' Ford, Pa., 1777; d. Wilmington, Del., 1839*), printer, editor. Founded, edited, and published the *Weekly Register* (later, *Niles' Weekly Register*, 1811–36. This paper was the strongest and most consistent advocate of union, internal improvements, and protection to industry in the United States; its editor was probably as influential as any in the nationalist economic school which sponsored the American System *post* 1815. Originally a Jeffersonian Democrat, he differed with Andrew Jackson's policies and was a Whig *post* 1829. He favored the gradual abolition of slavery.

NILES, JOHN MILTON (*b. Windsor, Conn., 1787; d. Hartford, Conn., 1856*), lawyer, editor. Leader of the Jacksonian party in Connecticut; an independent and uncompromising Democrat. U.S. senator, 1835–39, 1843–49; U.S. postmaster general, 1840–41.

NILES, NATHANIEL (*b. South Kingston, R.I., 1741; d. Vermont, 1828*), preacher, Connecticut and Vermont legislator, (Democrat) Republican leader in Vermont. Congressman, from Vermont, 1791–95. As trustee of Dartmouth, 1793–1820, Niles was a vigorous opponent of President John Wheelock.

NILES, NATHANIEL (*b. Fairlee, Vt., 1791; d. New York, N.Y., 1869*), physician, diplomat. Son of Nathaniel Niles (1741–1828). Secretary of U.S. legation at Paris, 1830–33; special agent to Austria-Hungary, 1837–38, for negotiation on lowering tariffs against American commerce; negotiator of treaty of commerce with Sardinia, 1838. U.S. chargé d'affaires in Sardinia, 1848–50.

NILES, SAMUEL (*b. Block Island, R.I., 1674; d. Braintree, Mass., 1762*), Congregational clergyman, controversialist, historian. Minister of the Second Church at Braintree, 1711–62. Author, among other writings, of "A Summary Historic Narrative of the Wars in New England with the French and Indians," published in the *Collections of the Massachusetts Historical Society* (1837 and 1861).

NIMITZ, CHESTER WILLIAM (*b. Fredericksburg, Tex., 1885; d. Yerba Buena Island, Calif., 1966*), naval officer. Studied at the U.S. Naval Academy (graduated, 1905). On staff of Rear Admiral Samuel Robison, chief of the Submarine Force, Atlantic Fleet (1914–18; 1923–26). Promoted to commander (1921); captain (1927); and rear admiral (1938). Commander of Battleship Division One (1938–39). Headed the Bureau of Navigation (1939–41). Commanded U.S. Pacific Fleet (1941–45); commander in chief of the Pacific Ocean Area (1942–45). Nimitz' forces attained strategic victories in the Coral Sea and at Midway in 1942, and initiated the Central Pacific offensive in 1943. Promoted to five-star rank of fleet admiral in 1944. Chief of naval operations (1945–47). Retired, 1947. Established and headed Naval Reserve Officers Training Corps at the University of California (1926–29). Served as a roving goodwill ambassador with the United Nations (1949–52).

NIPHER, FRANCIS EUGENE (*b. Port Byron, N.Y., 1847; d. Kirkwood, Mo., 1926*), physicist. Graduated State University of Iowa, 1870; M.A., 1873. Taught physics at Washington University, St. Louis, Mo., 1874–1914. Contributed a number of important papers to the *Transactions* of the Academy of Science of St. Louis *post* 1882, which included investigations into magnetic measurements, the measurement of wind pressure on stationary and moving structures, the properties of photographic plates, and the nature of the electric discharge.

NISBET, CHARLES (*b. Haddington, Scotland, 1736; d. Carlisle, Pa., 1804*), Presbyterian clergyman, educator. Came to America, 1785, at invitation of Benjamin Rush and John Dickinson to serve as first president of Dickinson College. An animated and able teacher, Nisbet held the post until his death.

NISBET, EUGENIUS ARISTIDES (*b. Greene Co., Ga., 1803; d. Macon, Ga., 1871*), lawyer, Georgia legislator. Congressman, Whig, 1839–43; judge, supreme court of Georgia, 1845–53. Resuming his law practice in Macon, he became a leader of the Know-Nothing party and in 1861, drafted the Georgia ordinance of secession.

NITCHIE, EDWARD BARTLETT (*b. Brooklyn, N.Y., 1876; d. 1917*), teacher of the deaf. Author of *Self-Instructor in Lip-Reading* (1902), *Lessons in Lip Reading* (1905), and *Lip-Reading Principles and Practice* (1912).

NITSCHMANN, DAVID (*b. Zauchtenthal, Moravia, 1696; d. Bethlehem, Pa., 1772*), bishop of the Moravian Church. Consecrated bishop in 1735, Nitschmann visited Savannah, Ga., 1736, and also Pennsylvania. Returning to America in 1740, he founded the settlement at Bethlehem, Pa., and remained in charge of the American work until 1744. Thereafter, he traveled constantly to Europe and back seeking financial help, retiring at the age of 65 to live in Bethlehem.

NIXON, JOHN (*b. Framingham, Mass., 1727; d. Middlebury, Vt., 1815*), colonial and Revolutionary soldier. Served in the expedition against Louisbourg, 1745, and in the French and Indian War. After fighting at Lexington and Concord, April 1775, he was wounded at Bunker Hill; he participated in the siege of Boston. Commissioned colonel, 4th Continental Infantry, January 1776, he was elected brigadier general on Washington's recommendation in August of the same year. He commanded a brigade in the operations around New York, 1776, and at the defeat of Burgoyne, 1777. He resigned for reasons of health, 1780.

NIXON, JOHN (*b. Philadelphia, Pa., 1733; d. Philadelphia, 1808*), Revolutionary patriot, merchant, financier. Held a number of Pennsylvania civil and militia offices; was president of the Bank of North America, 1792–1808.

NIXON, JOHN THOMPSON (*b. Fairton, N.J., 1820; d. Stockbridge, Mass., 1889*), New Jersey jurist, legislator, and legal compiler. U.S. district judge in New Jersey, 1870–89.

NIXON, WILLIAM PENN (*b. Fountain City, Ind., 1833; d. 1912*), journalist. Managed, and for most of the period, edited the Chicago *Inter Ocean*, 1872–97; made his paper an unfaltering advocate of orthodox Republican policy.

NIZA, MARCOS DE (*b. Nice, Duchy of Savoy, [?]; d. Mexico City, 1558*), Franciscan missionary, author, explorer. Went to Santo Domingo, 1531, and from there to Peru; he is credited with having founded the Franciscan province of Lima. Appointed vice-commissary general of his order in New Spain, 1539, he was sent to New Mexico in that year to investigate reports brought by Nuñez Cabeza de Vaca concerning fabulous cities in present New Mexico and Arizona. His incorrect and enthusiastic account was the occasion of Coronado's expedition, 1540, on which Niza served as guide as far as Zuñi.

NIZZA, MARCOS DE. *See* NIZA, MARCOS DE.

NOAH, MORDECAI, MANUEL (*b. Philadelphia, Pa., 1785; d. 1851*), lawyer, playwright, journalist. U.S. consul to Tunis, 1813–15. Editor, N.Y. *National Advocate*, 1817–26; later edited N.Y. *Enquirer*, N.Y. *Evening Star*, and *Noah's Times and Weekly Messenger*. Attempted in 1825 to establish a colony for oppressed Jews of all nations on Grand Island in Niagara River. Author of a number of plays patriotic in character and of *Travels in England, France, Spain, and the Barbary States* (1819).

NOAILLES, LOUIS MARIE, VICOMTE DE (*b. Paris, France, 1756; d. Havana, Cuba, 1804*), French soldier. Served in the American Revolution; was at siege of Savannah, Ga., and took a distinguished part in the Yorktown campaign, 1781. Sought refuge from the French Revolution in Philadelphia, Pa., 1793–1800, where he made a moderate fortune in business and promoted the Asylum Company to provide a Pennsylvania refuge for French *émigrés*.

NOBILI, JOHN (*b. Rome, Italy, 1812; d. 1856*), Roman Catholic clergyman, Jesuit. Came to America as an associate of Pierre-Jean de Smet in the Rocky Mountain missions where he served, 1843–49. Assigned to San Francisco, Calif., 1849, he founded Santa Clara University (incorporated, 1855).

NOBLE, ALFRED (*b. Livonia, Mich., 1844; d. 1914*), civil engineer. C.E., University of Michigan, 1870. Long experienced in canal and bridge construction, Noble served on the Nicaragua Canal commission, 1895, on the Isthmian Canal commission, 1899–1903, and on the board of consulting engineers for the Panama Canal.

NOBLE, FREDERICK ALPHONSO (*b. Baldwin, Maine, 1832; d. 1917*), Presbyterian and Congregational clergyman. Principal pastorate at Union Park Church, Chicago, Ill., 1879–1901.

NOBLE, GLADWYN KINGSLEY (*b. Yonkers, N.Y., 1894; d. Englewood, N.J., 1940*), biologist, specialist in herpetology. Graduated Harvard, 1917; Ph.D., Columbia, 1922. Instituted and directed an extensive research program in experimental biology and animal behavior at the American Museum of Natural History, New York City.

NOBLE, JAMES (*b. Clarke Co., Va., 1783; d. Washington, D.C., 1831*), lawyer. Settled in Indiana *ca.* 1810; was prominent in organization of the new state. As U.S. senator from Indiana, 1816–31, he supported internal improvements and liberal land laws.

NOBLE, JOHN WILLOCK (*b. Lancaster, Ohio, 1831; d. St. Louis, Mo., 1912*), lawyer, Union brigadier general. Fought pension raids with some success as U.S. secretary of the interior,

1889–93; sponsored forest reserve sections in revised land laws of 1891, thus leading to National Park policy of later date.

NOBLE, SAMUEL (*b. Cornwall, England, 1834; d. 1888*), ironmaster, industrialist. Came to America as a child; removed to Georgia, 1855. Founder and general manager *post* 1872 of the Woodstock Iron Co., nucleus of that industry at Anniston, Ala. Progressive and intelligent, Noble typified in his success the new spirit of Southern industry operating with Northern capital. He envisioned Anniston as the "model city" of the South and engaged in much philanthropic work there.

NOCK, ALBERT JAY (*b. Scranton, Pa., 1870; d. Wakefield, R.I., 1945*), author, editor. After service in the Episcopal ministry, 1897–1909, Nock left his wife and family and became a journalist. A staff member of the muckraking *American Magazine*, 1910–14, he edited *The Freeman*, 1920–24; thereafter, he devoted himself to writing books and articles, receiving substantial financial support from a succession of admirers. Pacifist, antimaterialist, historical revisionist, disciple of Matthew Arnold in matters of taste and of Herbert Spencer in political science, romantic agrarian, and critic of "progressive" education, he is best summed up as one of the select company of American non-conformists whose function is to irritate men into thinking for themselves. Among his many books, his autobiography, *Memoirs of a Superfluous Man* (1943), seems likely to have a permanent place in American intellectual history.

NOEGGERATH, EMIL OSCAR JACOB BRUNO (*b. Bonn, Germany, 1827; d. Germany, 1895*), physician. Practiced and taught in New York, N.Y., 1857–85. One of the most talented physicians of his time, Noeggerath combined an acute sense of biological mechanism with an appreciation for the totality of the organism; he made extensive contributions to gynecology and obstetrics, particularly with relation to the infective power of gonorrhea; he also anticipated many of the later discoveries of the classical bacteriologists.

NOGUCHI, HIDEYO (*b. Inawashiro, Japan, 1876; d. Accra, Africa, 1928*), bacteriologist, parasitologist, immunologist. Raised in poverty, he learned medicine as apprentice to a surgeon and at Tokyo Medical College where he graduated in 1897. After hospital experience and field work in plague control, he worked at Kitasato's Institute, Tokyo. His American work was begun at Simon Flexner's laboratory of pathology, University of Pennsylvania, 1899. Assigned to study immunity against snake venoms, he painstakingly investigated problems relating to hemolysins and agglutinins of snake venom and the protective sera. In these and subsequent endeavors he demonstrated clarity of interest, technical skill, and prodigious industry, plus an extraordinary endurance for one physically frail. His brilliant study *The Action of Snake Venom upon Cold-blooded Animals* (1904) established his reputation. Transferring his work to the Rockefeller Institute, 1904, he devised a new, important method for diagnosis of syphilis that led into his most important researches upon methods for obtaining pure cultures of spiral organisms. He not only grew the syphilis spiral organism in pure culture but also obtained in pure culture a variety of pathogenic spiral organisms and many saprophytic spiral forms. He isolated *Treponema pallidum*, making possible the preparation of luetin, and demonstrated its role as the etiological agent in both general paresis and tabes dorsalis. In further experimentation, he applied his findings to cultivation of the globoid bodies in poliomyelitis, to the study of Rocky Mountain spotted fever, and to enrichment and purification of the virus of vaccinia. During the last ten years of his life, Noguchi directed his investigations to clearing up the etiology of yellow fever, of the Oroya fever of Peru, and of trachoma. The outstanding figure in microbiology since Pasteur and Koch, he succumbed to African yellow fever while studying that disease.

NOLAN, PHILIP (*b. probably Frankfort, Ky., ca. 1771; d. near present Waco, Texas, 1801*), contraband horse trader. A close associate of James Wilkinson, and his agent at New Orleans as early as 1790, Nolan traded into Texas *post* 1791; there, he was regarded by the Mexicans as a spy and was killed while resisting arrest. He was said to possess an exceptional knowledge of the Spanish frontier lands.

NOLEN, JOHN (*b. Philadelphia, Pa., 1869; d. Cambridge, Mass., 1937*), landscape architect, town and city planner.

NOLL, JOHN FRANCIS (*b. Fort Wayne, Ind., 1875; d. Fort Wayne, 1956*), bishop. Attended the seminary of Mount St. Mary's of the West in Cincinnati; ordained in 1898. Pastor of St. Mary's Church in Huntington, Ind., 1910–25; consecrated bishop of the diocese of Fort Wayne, 1925. Founded *Parish Monthly* (1908), which became *Family Digest*. *Our Sunday Visitor*, begun in 1912, reached a circulation of 400,000 in 1974, serving as the official publication for seven dioceses. Author of *Father Smith Instructs Jackson* (1913). Served on the board of the National Catholic Welfare Conference, 1930–47; helped found the Legion of Decency (1934), designed to rate the moral acceptability of motion pictures.

NOONAN, JAMES PATRICK (*b. St. Louis, Mo., 1878; d. Washington, D.C., 1929*), electric lineman. Able, respected president, International Brotherhood of Electrical Workers, 1919–29; American labor delegate to World Power Conference, London, 1924.

NORBECK, PETER (*b. Clay Co., Dakota Territory, 1870; d. Redfield, S.Dak., 1936*), businessman, South Dakota legislator. Progressive Republican governor of South Dakota, 1917–21; U.S. senator, 1921–36. An active and effective advocate of farm-relief legislation.

NORCROSS, ORLANDO WHITNEY (*b. Clinton, Maine, 1839; d. Worcester, Mass., 1920*), contractor, Union soldier. Associated with architect H. H. Richardson in many of his works; invented flat-slab construction of reinforced concrete; was a master of all phases of practical construction.

NORDBERG, BRUNO VICTOR (*b. Björneborg, Finland, 1857; d. Milwaukee, Wis., 1924*), mechanical engineer. Came to America, 1879, two years after graduation from University of Helsingfors. Beginning with E. P. Allis Co., Milwaukee, he entered the field of engine design, creating a blowing engine and a poppet valve cut-off governor to improve economy of slide-valve engines. He organized the Bruno Nordberg Co., 1886, which grew into the Nordberg Manufacturing Co., of which he was president and chief engineer. He designed and built governors, Corliss-valve and poppet-valve engines, also special compressors, pumps, blowing engines, mining hoists, condensers, and heaters. He held some 70 U.S. patents and developed the Nordberg generative cycle. His greatest achievement was the building of the pneumatic hoisting system for the Anaconda Copper Co. at Butte, Mont.

NORDEN, CARL LUKAS (*b. Semarang, Java, 1880; d. Zurich, Switzerland, 1965*), mechanical engineer and inventor. Studied at the Federal Institute of Technology in Zurich (graduated, 1904). Immigrated to the United States, 1904. On staff of the Sperry Gyroscope Company (1911–15); with Elmer Sperry, developed gyroscope for naval use; consultant to Sperry to 1917. Had own company from 1915; consultant to U.S. Navy. Worked on development of the Norden bombsight from 1921. With Theodore H. Barth and Frederick I. Entwhistle, formed Carl L. Norden, Inc., in 1928 (became Norden Laboratories Corporation in 1945). Produced first bombsight in 1927; by 1931, perfected it in form of the Mark XV. Designed numerous other military devices, including catapults and arresting gears for aircraft carriers, and the first hydraulically controlled aircraft landing gears.

NORDHEIMER, ISAAC (*b. Memelsdorf, Bavaria, 1809; d. New York, N.Y., 1842*), orientalist, grammarian. Ph.D., Munich, 1834. Came to America, 1835; taught at Union Theological Seminary, 1838–42, and at New York University. Published original, profound *Critical Grammar of the Hebrew Language* (1838–41).

NORDHOFF, CHARLES (*b. Erwitte, Prussia, 1830; d. San Francisco, Calif., 1901*), journalist. Came to America as a child. After working as a printer, he served in the U.S. Navy, 1844–47, and for several years thereafter in merchant ships. Managing editor, N.Y. *Evening Post*, 1861–71; Washington correspondent, *New York Herald*, 1874–90. Author of a number of books including *The Merchant Vessel* (1855), *Communistic Societies in the United States* (1875), and *The Cotton States, etc.* (1876).

NORDHOFF, CHARLES BERNARD. *See* HALL, JAMES NORMAN.

NORDICA, LILLIAN (*b. Farmington, Maine, 1859; d. Batavia, Java, 1914*), prima donna. Stage name of Lillian Norton. Made debut as soprano soloist in New York City with Patrick Gilmore's band *ca.* 1876; after studying in Milan, Italy, made operatic debut in Brescia in *La Traviata*, April 1879; first appeared as prima donna as Marguerite in *Faust*, Paris, July 1882. Famous for the richness of her tone, for a notable, coloratura range and consummate artistic ability; Nordica was outstanding in Wagnerian roles.

NORELIUS, ERIC (*b. Hassela, Sweden, 1833; d. Minnesota, 1916*), Swedish Lutheran clergyman. Came to America, 1850. Ordained, 1856, he entered upon a ministry at Vasa and Red Wing, Minn., which with interruptions he maintained until his death.

NORMAN, JOHN (*b. England, ca. 1748; d. Boston, Mass., 1817*), engraver, publisher. Came to America *ante* 1774; worked thereafter in Philadelphia, Pa., and Boston, Mass. Published the *Boston Magazine*, 1783–84, and the first *Boston Directory*, 1789. Low contemporary estimates of his engraving skill have been seconded by posterity.

NORRIS, BENJAMIN FRANKLIN (*b. Chicago, Ill., 1870; d. San Francisco, Calif., 1902*), journalist, novelist. Known generally as Frank Norris. After preliminary art studies in California and Paris, France, Norris attended the University of California where, under the influence of Zola, he adopted realism as his literary creed and began the first chapters of a story which was later completed and published as *McTeague* (1899). After an adventurous period in South Africa, 1895–96, he worked as a journalist in San Francisco; in 1898 he was a war correspondent for *McClure's Magazine*. Entering the employ of Doubleday, Page & Co., 1899, he continued literary work, soon becoming recognized as a novelist of unusual vigor and originality. *Moran of the Lady Letty* appeared as a book, 1898, followed in the next year by *Blix* and by *McTeague* which is considered by some critics his strongest work. His most ambitious undertaking was his "Epic of the Wheat," which, according to his plan, was to consist of *The Octopus* (published, 1901), *The Pit* (published, 1903), and *The Wolf*, the third volume of the trilogy, which was never written.

NORRIS, CHARLES GILMAN SMITH (*b. Chicago, Ill., 1881; d. Palo Alto, Calif., 1945*), editor, novelist. Brother of Frank Norris. Ph.B., University of California, 1903. Married Kathleen (Thompson) Norris, 1909. An exponent of naturalism, he wrote slowly and carefully, choosing currently controversial ethical and social problems for his themes. Among his books were *The Amateur* (1916), *Salt* (1918), *Brass* (1921), *Bread* (1923), *Pig Iron* (1925), and *Seed* (1930).

NORRIS, EDWARD (*b. possibly Gloucestershire, England, ca. 1584; d. Salem, Mass., 1659*), Congregational clergyman. Came to New England, 1639, and settled in the same year at Salem as assistant to Hugh Peter. An unusually tolerant clergyman, he was teacher of the Salem church from March 1640 until his death.

NORRIS, FRANK. *See* NORRIS, BENJAMIN FRANKLIN.

NORRIS, GEORGE WASHINGTON (*b. Philadelphia, Pa., 1808; d. 1875*), surgeon, medical author. Professor of clinical surgery, University of Pennsylvania, 1848–57; was also surgeon to the Pennsylvania Hospital, 1836–63.

NORRIS, GEORGE WILLIAM (*b. Sandusky County, Ohio, 1861; d. McCook, Nebr., 1944*), lawyer, independent politician, reformer. He attended Baldwin University (later Baldwin-Wallace College) in Ohio in 1877–78 and, after teaching school, entered Northern Indiana Normal School and Business Institute (later Valparaiso University), where he studied law, excelled in rhetoric and debate, and received the LL.B. degree in 1883. In 1885 he moved to Nebraska and opened a law office, at first in Beatrice and then in Beaver City.

Norris secured appointment to two unexpired terms as prosecuting attorney of Furnas County and then was elected in his own right in 1892. Three years later he won the first of two four-year terms as judge of the district court. From 1903 to 1913 he served in the U.S. House of Representatives. In 1910 he secured the passage of a resolution that wrested control from the speaker of the House, Joseph B. Cannon. Elected to the Senate in 1913, Norris was to serve in that body continuously for the next thirty years. On foreign affairs, he was highly critical of Wilson's Mexican policy and particularly of the American occupation of Vera Cruz in 1914. Believing that the United States was being led into the European hostilities by the nation's financial and commercial interests, he voted against the American declaration of war in April 1917. Although an advocate of international cooperation to ensure a permanent peace, he felt that the Versailles Treaty contained serious inequities.

During the Republican ascendancy of the 1920's, Norris was unrelentingly critical of the complacency and business domination of the Harding, Coolidge, and Hoover administrations. In 1924 he introduced the Norris-Sinclair Bill, a predecessor of the McNary-Haugen plan for government purchase and sale abroad of farm surpluses. He was the author of the Norris-La Guardia Anti-Injunction Act of 1932, which curbed the use of injunctions in labor disputes. He was also responsible for the 20th Amendment to the Constitution (the "Lame Duck" amendment). Braving the wrath of utility-company spokesmen, Norris became in the 1920's the leading figure in political life favoring the public production, transmission, and distribution of hydroelectric power. His loose ties to the Republican party continued to weaken during the 1920's. He endorsed the presidential candidacy of Franklin D. Roosevelt in 1932 and was a supporter of most New Deal measures. Still deeply committed to the public development of natural resources, he was the chief author of the act in May 1933 which created the Tennessee Valley Authority (TVA) to supervise the multipurpose development of the Tennessee River.

With the advent of the Second World War, Norris reluctantly concluded that totalitarian aggression could be met only by force or the threat of force. Although he opposed the establishment of compulsory military service in 1940, he did support a revision of the neutrality law to allow the Allies to buy American arms on a "cash and carry" basis; and in 1941 he endorsed the Lend-Lease Bill. Early in 1942 Norris was defeated for a sixth senatorial term. His autobiography, *Fighting Liberal* (written with the help of James E. Lawrence, a Nebraska newspaper editor and political associate), was completed in 1944.

NORRIS, ISAAC (*b. London, England, 1671; d. Germantown, Pa., 1735*), Quaker merchant, politician. Settled in Philadelphia, Pa., 1693; married a daughter of Thomas Lloyd, 1694. Soon successful in business, Norris held a number of Pennsylvania civic and judicial offices *post* 1699; he was an alderman of Philadelphia, 1708–24, and was elected mayor, 1724. Next to James Logan, Norris was chief representative of proprietary interests in Pennsylvania *post* 1708.

NORRIS, ISAAC (*b. Philadelphia, Pa., 1701; d. near Philadelphia, 1766*), Quaker merchant, party leader. Son of Isaac Norris (1671–1735), he also held a number of provincial offices; a member of the Pennsylvania Assembly, 1734–66, he acted as speaker, 1750–64. Norris was noted for the militant pacifism of his policies, especially during the French and Indian War. The celebrated inscription on the Liberty Bell was made at his suggestion.

NORRIS, JAMES FLACK (*b. Baltimore, Md., 1871; d. Boston, Mass., 1940*), chemist. Graduated Johns Hopkins, 1892; Ph.D., 1895. Taught chemistry at Massachusetts Institute of Technology, at Simmons College, and at Vanderbilt University; headed U.S. Army Chemical Warfare Service in England, 1917–19. Professor of organic chemistry and director of the research laboratory at Massachusetts Institute of Technology *post* 1919, Norris was author of several textbooks and was active in scientific societies.

NORRIS, JOHN FRANKLYN (*b. Dadeville, Ala., 1877; d. Keystone Heights, Fla., 1952*), clergyman. Studied at Baylor University and the Southern Baptist Theological Seminary (Th.M., 1905). Evangelist minister of the First Baptist Church of Fort Worth, 1909–52, and the Temple Baptist Church in Detroit, 1935–52. Acquitted of charges of burning his own church in 1912 and of murder charges in 1926 (for reasons of self-defense). Helped to organize the World Baptist Mission Fellowship, a coalition of fundamentalist churches that had missions in China until 1949 and supported the Bible Baptist Seminary in Fort Worth.

NORRIS, KATHLEEN THOMPSON (*b. San Francisco, Calif., 1880; d. San Francisco, 1966*), novelist. Called the "grandmother of the American sentimental novel." Wrote eighty-eight books, eighty-one of which are novels; sales of 10 million copies, in addition to earnings from other writing, totaled $9 million, making her the highest-paid writer of her day. Her work was characterized by honesty, directness, and clear-cut issues; domestic interiors convincingly rendered, blending sentiment and romance with sharply drawn characters. Wrote many serialized stories for magazines such as *Woman's Home Companion* and *Collier's*. Books include *Mother* (1911), *Certain People of Importance* (1922), and *Hands Full of Living: Talks with American Women* (1931).

NORRIS, MARY HARRIOTT (*b. Boonton, N.J., 1848; d. 1919*), author, educator. Graduated Vassar, 1870. First regularly elected dean of women of Northwestern University, 1898.

NORRIS, WILLIAM (*b. Baltimore, Md., 1802; d. 1867*), locomotive builder. Organized American Steam Carriage Co. with Stephen H. Long, 1832, for production of locomotives employing anthracite coal as fuel. After buying out Long's interest, Norris began construction of the "George Washington," a locomotive of his own design, completed, 1836, for the Philadelphia and Columbia Railroad. The success of this engine brought its designer and builder worldwide fame.

NORRIS, WILLIAM FISHER (*b. Philadelphia, Pa., 1839; d. 1901*), ophthalmologist. Son of George W. Norris. Graduated University of Pennsylvania, 1857; M.D., 1861. Made special studies in ophthalmology at Vienna; taught that subject at the University of Pennsylvania *post* 1870. He made many contributions to the literature of his subject, in particular (with an associate) *System of Diseases of the Eye* (1897–1900).

NORSWORTHY, NAOMI (*b. New York, N.Y., 1877; d. 1916*), psychologist, educator. Taught at Teachers College, Columbia, *post* 1901; excelled in classroom demonstration of the teaching of Thorndike and Dewey. Author of *The Psychology of Mentally Deficient Children* (1906).

NORTH, EDWARD (*b. Berlin, Conn., 1820; d. 1903*), educator, classicist. Professor of ancient languages at Hamilton College, 1843–1901; a skillful interpreter of Greek poetry. Nephew of Simeon North (1802–1884).

NORTH, ELISHA (*b. Goshen, Conn., 1771; d. 1843*), physician. Studied with Lemuel Hopkins and at University of Pennsylvania. Practicing at Goshen, 1795–1812, he removed in the latter year to New London, Conn., where he established the first eye dispensary in the United States. His *Treatise on . . . Spotted Fever* (1811) was the first published study of cerebrospinal meningitis.

NORTH, FRANK JOSHUA (*b. Ludlowville, N.Y., 1840; d. Columbus, Nebr., 1885*), scout, plainsman. Raised in Ohio; removed to Nebraska, 1856. Through association with the Pawnee, North learned their language and also Indian sign language; entering service as an army scout, 1864, under General S. R. Curtis, he continued to lead groups of Pawnee scouts and guides through six campaigns of the Indian wars until 1877. North had no superior as frontiersman and guide in his own time; he was probably the best revolver shot on the plains and was the only leader of Indian scouts thoroughly acquainted with the language and customs of the men he commanded. After the Pawnee scouts were mustered out of service, North and his brother were partners of William F. Cody in a Nebraska ranch; he was later the feature attraction in Cody's famous "Wild West" show.

NORTH, FRANK MASON (*b. New York, N.Y., 1850; d. Madison, N.J., 1935*), Methodist clergyman. Held a number of pastorates in the New York Conference; advocated interdenominational cooperation; pioneered in turning the mind of the Methodist Church from individualism to united social action.

NORTH, SIMEON (*b. Berlin, Conn., 1765; d. 1852*), mechanic, arms manufacturer. Produced pistols and rifles under government contracts, 1799–1852; made a repeating rifle capable of firing ten charges without reloading, 1825.

NORTH, SIMEON (*b. Berlin, Conn., 1802; d. 1884*), educator. Son of Simeon North (1765–1852). Graduated Yale, 1825. After a brief period as a tutor at Yale, North taught ancient languages at Hamilton College, 1829–39, and was president of the college, 1839–57.

NORTH, SIMON NEWTON DEXTER (*b. Clinton, N.Y., 1848; d. Wilton, Conn., 1924*), editor, statistician. Son of Edward North. Director, U.S. Census, 1903–09; was associated *post* 1911 with Carnegie Endowment for International Peace.

NORTH, WILLIAM (*b. Fort Frederick, Maine, 1755; d. New York, N.Y., 1836*), Revolutionary soldier, New York legislator. Aide-de-camp to Baron von Steuben and his lifetime friend. Federalist speaker of the New York Assembly, 1795–96 and 1810.

NORTHEN, WILLIAM JONATHAN (*b. Jones Co., Ga., 1835; d. Atlanta, Ga., 1913*), teacher, farmer, Georgia legislator, official in farm organizations. Democratic governor of Georgia, 1890–95.

NORTHEND, CHARLES (*b. Newbury, Mass., 1814; d. New Britain, Conn., 1895*), Connecticut school administrator, textbook writer.

NORTHROP, BIRDSEY GRANT (*b. Kent, Conn., 1817; d. 1898*), Congregational clergyman, educator. Agent for state boards of education in Massachusetts and Connecticut, 1857–83; advocate of Arbor Day and of Japanese-American amity.

NORTHROP, CYRUS (*b. near Ridgefield, Conn., 1834; d. Minneapolis, Minn., 1922*), lawyer, educator. Graduated Yale, 1857; Yale Law School, 1859. Professor of English at Yale, 1863–84; an outstanding administrator as second president of University of Minnesota, 1884–1911.

NORTHROP, LUCIUS BELLINGER (*b. Charleston, S.C., 1811; d. Pikesville, Md., 1894*), soldier. Graduated West Point, 1831. Studied medicine at Jefferson Medical College after permanent furlough for wound received in Seminole war, 1839; practiced in Charleston, 1853–61. Appointed Confederate commissary general, 1861, he was faced with the increasingly difficult task of providing food for the Southern armies and *post* 1862 for Northern prisoners. Generally unpopular and bitterly criticized, Northrop was supported by President Davis. Although General R. E. Lee had little patience with him and finally demanded his removal, he did not lose his office until February 1865. Despite the criticisms, Northrop seems to have been a good if routine executive who was badly hampered by the Confederate transportation system.

NORTON, ALICE PELOUBET. See NORTON, MARY ALICE PELOUBET.

NORTON, ANDREWS (*b. Hingham, Mass., 1786; d. Newport, R.I., 1853*), Unitarian theologian, Biblical scholar. Graduated Harvard, 1804. Appointed tutor at Harvard, 1811; librarian and lecturer on the Bible, 1813. Dexter Professor of Sacred Literature, Harvard Divinity School, 1819–30. A fastidious, independent, and solitary thinker, Norton was author, among a number of other books, of *Evidences of the Genuineness of the Gospels* (1837, 1844), one of the earliest studies of biblical literature from the critical point of view to be published in America.

NORTON, CHARLES ELIOT (*b. Cambridge, Mass., 1827; d. Cambridge, 1908*), editor, author, educator. Son of Andrews Norton. Graduated Harvard, 1846. After extensive travel abroad and a brief experience in business, Norton devoted his life chiefly to humanist studies. An intimate friend of the principal literary and artistic figures of his day in America and Europe, he conducted at Harvard from 1873 to 1897 at the invitation of his cousin, Charles W. Eliot, a course in the history of fine arts as related to society and general culture. The range of his activities in literature was great. Contributor to the *Atlantic Monthly*, a founder and supporter of *The Nation*, he edited Thomas Carlyle's correspondence and reminiscences (1883–91), the letters of James Russell Lowell (1894), the poetry of John Donne (1895 and 1905), and the poems of Anne Bradstreet (1897). His own book *Historical Studies of Church-Building in the Middle Ages* (1880) had considerable influence on architects. His critical judgments in art (as also his views on politics) were motivated by his belief that a strictly conceived but nonreligious *ethos*, derived from contemplation of the highest qualities of human nature, must be operative in both critic and statesman.

NORTON, CHARLES HOTCHKISS (*b. Plainville, Conn., 1851; d. Plainville, 1942*), mechanical engineer, machine tool designer. Associated with the Seth Thomas Clock Company, Brown and Sharpe Mfg. Company, and *post* 1800 with the Norton Company of Worcester, Mass., he developed the precision grinding machine from a light production tool of limited capability to a heavy special-purpose machine integral to modern industrial technology. He built his first heavy-production, cylindrical grinding machine in 1900, patenting it in 1904. He later designed and produced special machines for the automobile industry which progressively increased the machines' output and reduced the cost of car production.

NORTON, ELIJAH HISE (*b. near Russellville, Ky., 1821; d. near Platte City, Mo., 1914*), lawyer, Missouri Unionist and jurist. A stubborn opponent of secession, Norton was an outstanding member of the Missouri constitutional convention of 1875 and a leading formulator of the so-called "Norton Constitution" which it produced.

NORTON, JOHN (*b. Bishop's Stortford, England, 1606; d. Boston, Mass., 1663*), Puritan clergyman. M.A., Peterhouse, Cambridge, 1627; declined a benefice because of Puritan convictions. Came to New England, 1635, and became teacher of the church at Ipswich, Mass.; helped draft Cambridge Platform, 1648; succeeded John Cotton as pastor of First Church at Boston, 1652, but was not installed until 1656. Norton took a prominent part in the persecution of Quakers and failed as coagent with Simon Bradstreet in negotiations with Charles II, 1662. A learned man and prolific writer, Norton had a narrow and pedantic mind.

NORTON, JOHN NICHOLAS (*b. Waterloo, N.Y., 1820; d. 1881*), Episcopal clergyman, author. *Post* 1847, he ministered with great zeal in Frankfort and Louisville, Ky. He was author of a number of popular biographical studies and some fiction.

NORTON, JOHN PITKIN (*b. Albany, N.Y., 1822; d. Farmington, Conn., 1852*), agricultural chemist. Grandson of Timothy Pitkin. Made intensive studies of agriculture and included three years abroad at Edinburgh and Utrecht. Appointed professor of agricultural chemistry at Yale, 1846, he initiated with the younger Benjamin Silliman the department of scientific education at Yale which was later to become Sheffield Scientific School.

NORTON, MARY ALICE PELOUBET (*b. Gloucester, Mass., 1860; d. 1928*), teacher of home economics. Graduated Smith, 1882; was directed into her profession by Ellen H. Richards. Taught at a number of schools including University of Chicago and Indiana University.

NORTON, MARY TERESA HOPKINS (*b. Jersey City, N.J., 1875; d. Greenwich, Conn., 1959*), politician. Graduated from the Packard Business College, 1896. A protégé of Jersey City boss, Mayor Frank Hague, Norton was the first congresswoman from an eastern state and the first woman elected to the House of Representatives on the Democratic ticket (1924); served until her retirement in 1951. Norton was the first woman to chair a major congressional committee, the House Committee on the District of Columbia, 1932–37. An ardent New Dealer, she headed the House Labor Committee, 1937–47, backing all of Roosevelt's major labor proposals. Headed the House Administration Committee, 1949–51. Norton was the first woman to head a state party organization, as head of the New Jersey Democratic Committee, 1932–35 and 1940–44.

NORTON, WILLIAM EDWARD (*b. Boston, Mass., 1843; d. New York, N.Y., 1916*), marine painter.

NORTON, WILLIAM WARDER (*b. Springfield, Ohio, 1891; d. New York, N.Y., 1945*), book publisher. Attended Ohio State University and the New School for Social Research; founded People's Institute Publishing Company, 1923, for publication of the lecture courses given at the Institute (in Cooper Union, New York City) by Everett D. Martin and others. In 1926 he entered the general publishing field as W. W. Norton and Company.

NORWOOD, ROBERT WINKWORTH (*b. New Ross, Nova Scotia, 1874; d. 1932*), Episcopal clergyman. After holding a number of pastorates in Canada, he became rector of St. Paul's Church, Overbrook, Pa., 1917, and succeeded to the rectorship of St. Bartholomew's Church, New York City, 1925. A dramatic, poetic preacher, Norwood belonged to the liberal group in his denomination.

NOSS, THEODORE BLAND (*b. Waterloo, Pa., 1852; d. Chicago, Ill., 1909*), educator. Graduated Syracuse, 1880, Ph.D., 1884. A specialist in educational psychology, Noss won a national reputation as a progressive while principal of Southwestern State Normal School, California, Pa., *post* 1883.

NOTESTEIN, WALLACE (*b. Wooster, Ohio, 1878; d. New Haven, Conn., 1969*), historian and educator. Studied at the College of Wooster and Yale University (Ph.D., 1908). Assistant professor, University of Kansas (1905–14). Professor, University of Minnesota (1917–20); Cornell (1920–28); and Yale (1928–47). Works include *Commons Debates for 1629* (1921), *The Journal of Sir Simonds D'Ewes* (1923), *Commons Debates, 1621* (1935), *English Folk: A Book of Characters* (1938), *The Scot in History* (1946), *The English People on the Eve of Colonization, 1603–1630* (1954), and *Four Worthies* (1956). Devoting his academic career to the study of Elizabethan and Stuart England, he was a warm and enthusiastic teacher noted for his literary skill and personal charm.

NOTT, ABRAHAM (*b. Saybrook, Conn., 1768; d. Fairfield District, S.C., 1830*), lawyer, planter. Settled in South Carolina, 1789; was a Federalist member of Congress, 1799–1801. After serving as a law judge, 1810–24, he became head of the state court of appeals and held this post for the rest of his life.

NOTT, CHARLES COOPER (*b. Schenectady, N.Y., 1827; d. New York, N.Y., 1916*), jurist. Grandson of Eliphalet Nott. Graduated Union, 1848. After admission to the bar, 1850, he removed to New York City where he practiced until the outbreak of the Civil War. Serving with credit as a Union officer, 1861–65, he was appointed in the later year judge of the U.S. Court of Claims. Until his retirement, 1905, he helped greatly in the establishment of a system of jurisprudence under which claims of citizens against the federal government might be recognized and enforced. He also served as reporter to the Court, 1867–1914.

NOTT, ELIPHALET (*b. Ashford, Conn., 1773; d. Schenectady, N.Y., 1866*), Presbyterian clergyman, educator, inventor. Brother and pupil of Samuel Nott; M.A., Brown, *ca.* 1795. While pastor, First Presbyterian Church, Albany, N.Y., 1798–1804, he won repute as one of America's greatest pulpit orators; as president of Union College, Schenectady, N.Y., 1804–66, he successfully gained public support for a building program through lotteries, raised the instructional level, and introduced a scientific course as alternative to the classical curriculum. In public affairs, he opposed slavery, was active in educational associations and in the temperance movement. His research in the properties of heat resulted in some thirty patents, including the first base-burning stove for use of anthracite coal.

NOTT, HENRY JUNIUS (*b. Union District, S.C., 1797; d. at sea, off North Carolina coast, 1837*), educator. Son of Abraham Nott; brother of Josiah C. Nott. Graduated South Carolina College, 1814. Professor of criticism, logic, and the philosophy of language in South Carolina College, 1824–37; a frequent contributor to the *Southern Review*.

NOTT, JOSIAH CLARK (*b. Columbia, S.C., 1804; d. Mobile, Ala., 1873*), physician, ethnologist. Son of Abraham Nott; brother of Henry J. Nott. Graduated South Carolina College, 1824; M.D., University of Pennsylvania, 1827; practiced in Mobile *post* 1836. Nott is perhaps best known for his views on yellow fever, advanced in 1848 and 1854, in which he attributed the disease to a living organism.

NOTT, SAMUEL (*b. present Essex, Conn., 1754; d. present Franklin, Conn., 1852*), Congregational clergyman, educator. Graduated Yale, 1780; studied theology under the younger Jonathan Edwards. Pastor, *post* 1782, in the present town of Franklin, Conn., he made his home an educational institution where many young men were fitted for college; among them was his brother Eliphalet Nott.

NOTZ, FREDERICK WILLIAM AUGUSTUS (*b. Lehrensteinsfeld, Württemberg, 1841; d. Milwaukee, Wis., 1921*), educator. Ph.D., Tübingen, 1863, where he also made theological studies. Came to America, 1866. After holding several teaching positions, he became professor of Greek and Hebrew at Northwestern College, Watertown, Wis., 1872, and served until his retirement, 1912.

NOVARRO, RAMON (*b. José Ramón Gil Samaniegos, Durango, Mexico, 1899; d. Hollywood Hills, Calif., 1968*), motion-picture actor. To Los Angeles, 1916. Appeared regularly in movies as an extra from 1917; had prominent dance scenes in *Man, Woman, Marriage, A Small Town Idol*, and *The Concert* (all 1921). First minor acting role was in *Mr. Barnes of New York* (1922). Typecast in the Latin-lover mold of Rudolph Valentino in films such as *The Prisoner of Zenda* (1922), *Where the Pavement Ends* (1923), *Scaramouche* (1923), and *The Arab* (1924). With Metro-Goldwyn-Mayer (1925–34) made *Ben-Hur* (1926), *Mata Hari* (1932), and *The Barbarian* (1933). Wrote, produced, and directed the Spanish feature film *Contra la corriente* (1936). Other film appearances include *We Were Strangers* (1949), *The Outriders* (1950), and *Heller in Pink Tights* (1959). Two male prostitutes were charged with his murder.

NOVY, FREDERICK GEORGE (*b. Chicago, Ill., 1864; d. Ann Arbor, Mich., 1957*), microbiologist. Studied at the University of Michigan, Sc.D., 1890; M.D., 1891. Taught at that university, 1887–1953; dean of the medical school from 1935. The first to teach bacteriology at an American university (1888), Novy isolated the bacillus *Clostridium novyii* in 1894. In 1909 he discovered the spirochete *Spirocheta novyi*; in 1917, working with trypanosomes, he discovered reactions that led to the later production of histamines. Helped found the American Society of Bacteriologists; president, 1904. Elected to the National Academy of Sciences, 1934.

NOYAN, GILLES-AUGUSTIN PAYEN DE (*b. France, 1697; d. Louisiana, 1751*), French soldier, provincial legislator. Nephew of Bienville and Iberville; brother of Pierre-Jaques Noyan. Came to Louisiana, 1717 or 1718. Served in a number of military expeditions and was employed *post* 1732 in implementing Bienville's efforts to stiffen the resistance of the Choctaw against English-supported Chickasaw. Sitting frequently as a member of the Superior Council of Louisiana, he was acting governor, 1748.

NOYAN, PIERRE-JACQUES PAYEN DE (*b. Montreal, Canada, 1695; d. ca. 1763*), French-Canadian officer. Nephew of Bienville and Iberville; brother of Gilles-Augustin Noyan. Appointed commandant at Fort Frontenac, 1721, he was constantly active thereafter along the Great Lakes until 1758 in civil and military service. Among other policies which he urged on the French ministry were the better regulation of trade with the Indians, the establishment of permanent settlements, the growing of wheat to supply the trading posts, the building of boats on the Lakes, and the development of the copper and lead mines in the Lake region. As commandant at Detroit, 1739–42, he succeeded in keeping the Indians firmly attached to the French interest. Later holding command at Crown Point and at Three Rivers, he was sent to Fort Frontenac in 1758, where he surrendered in August to Col. John Bradstreet's attacking force.

NOYES, ALEXANDER DANA (*b. Montclair, N.J., 1862; d. New York, N.Y., 1945*), financial journalist. A.B., Amherst College, 1883. Financial editor of the New York *Evening Post*, 1891–1920; of the *New York Times*, 1920–45. Wrote extensively on currency problems, banking, and cognate subjects for the magazines, and was author of a number of books directed to a popular audience; an enlightened conservative, he prophesied the oncoming depression of 1929 as early as the fall of 1926.

NOYES, ARTHUR AMOS (*b. Newburyport, Mass., 1866; d. 1936*), chemist, educator, author. Graduated Massachusetts Institute of Technology, 1896; M.S., 1887. Ph.D., Leipzig, 1890, in physical chemistry. During many years of teaching at both Massachusetts and California Institutes of Technology, and by his influential textbooks, Noyes revolutionized the teaching of analytical and physical chemistry in the United States. He made important researches into the properties of solutions of electrolytes and in the rarer elements. He was founder (1895) of the presently titled *Chemical Abstracts*, held office in professional societies, and was acting chairman of the National Research Council, 1918.

NOYES, CLARA DUTTON (*b. Port Deposit, Md., 1869; d. Washington, D.C., 1936*), nurse, educator. Graduated Johns Hopkins Hospital, 1896. Demonstrating marked ability as administrator in several hospital positions, she became superintendent of training schools, Bellevue Hospital, N.Y., 1910. Appointed director of the American Red Cross military nursing bureau, 1916, she succeeded Jane A. Delano as director of the Red Cross nursing service, 1919, and held that post until her death.

NOYES, CROSBY STUART (*b. Minot, Maine, 1825; d. 1908*), journalist. Removed to Washington, D.C., 1847, where he worked on the *Washington News* and served as correspondent for several New England and New York papers. Employed *post* 1855 on the Washington *Star*, he purchased that paper with Alexander R. Shepherd, 1867, and served thereafter with great success as editor-in-chief.

NOYES, EDWARD FOLLANSBEE (*b. Haverhill, Mass., 1832; d. Cincinnati, Ohio, 1890*), lawyer, Union soldier. Graduated Dartmouth, 1857; practiced law *post* 1858 in Cincinnati, Ohio. Republican governor of Ohio, 1872–74, Noyes was a leading factor in the presidential nomination of Rutherford B. Hayes, 1876. He was U.S. minister to France, 1877–81.

NOYES, FRANK BRETT (*b. Washington, D.C., 1863; d. Washington, 1948*), newspaper publisher. Associated with the *Washington Star* as business manager and president; made noteworthy contribution to journalism as president of the Associated Press, 1900–38.

NOYES, GEORGE RAPALL (*b. Newburyport, Mass., 1798; d. 1868*), Unitarian clergyman. Professor of Oriental languages and biblical literature at Harvard, 1840–68, Noyes was an American pioneer in the critical study of the Bible. His most important work was his translation of the New Testament, published 1869. He graduated from Harvard in 1818 and from Harvard Divinity School in 1822.

NOYES, HENRY DRURY (*b. New York, N.Y., 1832; d. Mount Washington, Mass., 1900*), ophthalmologist. Graduated University of the City of New York (New York University), 1851; M.D., N.Y. College of Physicians and Surgeons, 1855. Associated *post* 1859 with development of the New York Eye and Ear Infirmary; was professor of ophthalmology and otology, Bellevue Hospital Medical College, 1868–92, and thereafter professor of ophthalmology alone.

NOYES, JOHN HUMPHREY (*b. Brattleboro, Vt., 1811; d. Niagara Falls, Canada, 1886*), social reformer. Graduated Dartmouth, 1830; studied law; attended Andover and Yale theological schools. Reacting against Calvinism, Noyes combined prevalent perfectionist and adventist beliefs in a personal theology *ca.* 1833. Persuading himself that he had attained a state of perfection or complete sinlessness, he developed a society known as Bible Communists at Putney, Vt. Among other doctrines which he promulgated for his followers *post* 1836 was free love or promiscuity within the bounds of the community; he also claimed miraculous powers of healing. Arrested on a charge of adultery, he broke bail and fled to central New York whither his Bible Communists followed him and established the Oneida Community, 1848. Noyes's organizing skill and dominating personality made this the most successful in a material way of the American utopias. After thirty years of undisturbed control, he sensed the imminent decline of his personal leadership and also the growing strength of outside opposition; permitting his followers to contract legal marriages, he immigrated to Canada and put himself beyond reach of legal action.

NOYES, LA VERNE (*b. Genoa, N.Y., 1849; d. Chicago, Ill., 1919*), inventor and manufacturer of farm machinery, notably steel windmills.

NOYES, WALTER CHADWICK (*b. Lyme, Conn., 1865; d. New York, N.Y., 1926*), lawyer. Practiced with Frank B. Brandegee at New London, Conn.; served 1895–1907 as judge of the court of common pleas. U.S. circuit judge of the second judicial circuit, 1907–13. Thereafter he resumed corporation practice in New York City.

NOYES, WILLIAM ALBERT (*b. near Independence, Iowa, 1857; d. Urbana, Ill., 1941*), chemist. B.A. and B.S., Iowa (later Grinnell) College, 1879; M.A., 1880. Ph.D., Johns Hopkins University, 1882. Ph.D., University of Munich, 1889. Taught at University of Minnesota (1882–83), University of Tennessee (1883–86), and Rose Polytechnic Institute (1886–1903); was first chief chemist of the U.S. Bureau of Standards, 1903–07. As chairman of the chemistry department at University of Illinois, 1907–26, he made it one of the most productive graduate departments in the nation. His own principal research was in organic chemistry. He was author of a number of textbooks, and editor of the *Journal* of the American Chemical Society, 1902–17; he was first editor as well of *Chemical Abstracts* (1907–10).

NOYES, WILLIAM CURTIS (*b. Schodack, N.Y., 1805; d. 1864*), lawyer. Practiced in Rome and Utica, N.Y., and in New York City *post* 1838; was famous for carefully researched briefs. He worked with Alexander W. Bradford and David D. Field on the codification of New York laws, 1857.

NUGENT, JOHN FROST (*b. LaGrande, Oreg., 1868; d. Washington, D.C., 1931*), lawyer. Raised in Idaho; was of defense counsel in prosecution of William D. Haywood et al. for murder of Governor Steunenberg. U.S. senator, Democrat, from Idaho, 1918–21; member of Federal Trade Commission, 1920–27.

NÚÑEZ CABEZA DE VACA, ALVAR (*b. Jerez de la Frontera, Spain, ca. 1490; d. Spain, probably in Seville, ca. 1557*), Spanish soldier, colonial official, explorer. Treasurer and *alguacil mayor* of Pánfilo de Narváez's expedition for the conquest of Florida, 1527, he advised the commander against abandonment of the ships on their reaching the Florida coast in April 1528. Overruled, he was assigned command of one of the rude boats fabricated after the fatal march to Apalache. Driven on an island off the Texas coast, he and other survivors were enslaved by hostile Indians; escaping in February 1530, he became resourceful and successful trader among friendly Indians. He began working his way westward in 1535 as a medicine man, accompanied by three companions. After traversing present southern Texas and northern Mexico, he arrived at Mexico City, July 23, 1536. His *La Relacion que Dio Alvar Nuñez, Cabeça de Vaca de lo Acaescido en las Indias* (1542) gave the first European account of the American opossum, the bison, and Texas Indians; it also prompted the expedition of Coronado. After his return to Spain, 1537, he led an extraordinary exploring expedition in the Rio de la Plata region of South America, 1540–44.

NUNÓ, JAIME (*b. San Juan de las Abadesas, Spain, 1824; d. Bayside, N.Y., 1908*), musician. After a successful career as a conductor in Spain, Cuba, and Mexico, Nunó came to the United States, 1856. He directed opera troupes and conducted here and abroad until 1869 when he settled in Buffalo, N.Y., as a teacher of singing and later as conductor of the Buffalo Symphony Orchestra. His outstanding composition was the Mexican national hymn (officially adopted, 1854).

NURSE, REBECCA (*b. Yarmouth, England, 1621; d. Salem, Mass., 1692*), victim of the Salem witchcraft delusion.

NUTHEAD, WILLIAM (*b. probably England, ca. 1654; d. St. Mary's City, Md., 1695*), printer. Nuthead appears for the first time in colonial records as an unlicensed printer in Virginia, 1683. Removing from Jamestown, where he had set up his press, to Maryland, he is mentioned in official records there as a printer of official documents and the like as early as 1686. Samples of his work are extremely rare.

NUTTALL, THOMAS (*b. Settle, Yorkshire, England, 1786; d. near Liverpool, England, 1859*), botanist, ornithologist. Immigrated to Philadelphia, Pa., 1808; Benjamin S. Barton introduced him to plant studies. Participated in explorations up Missouri River, 1809–11; along Arkansas and Red rivers, 1818–20; with Wyeth Expedition to mouth of Columbia River, 1834–35. Curator, Botanical Garden, Harvard, 1822–32. Wrote *Genera of North American Plants, etc.* (1818); was author also of the continuation (1842–49) of F. A. Michaux's *North American Sylva* and contributed numerous descriptions of new species to *Transactions of the American Philosophical Society*, Silliman's *Journal*, and others. Equally talented as ornithologist, he published *A Manual of Ornithology* (1832), which brought him great reputation. In geological observations on the Mississippi Valley, 1820, he made the first American attempt to correlate, by means of fossil remains, geological formations widely separated geographically, antedating work of S. G. Morton.

NUTTING, CHARLES CLEVELAND (*b. Jacksonville, Ill., 1858; d. Iowa City, Iowa, 1927*), ornithologist, marine zoologist. Traveled extensively as a field collector; was professor of zoology, State University of Iowa, *post* 1886. Author of an important series of reports, *American Hydroids* (1900–15), and other learned papers.

NUTTING, MARY ADELAIDE (*b. Frost Village, Quebec, Canada, 1858; d. White Plains, N.Y., 1948*), pioneer in nursing education. Graduated from Johns Hopkins Hospital training school for nurses, 1891; as superintendent of nurses and principal of the school, 1894–1907, she succeeded in transforming it from a hospital service adjunct into an educational institution, thus setting a pattern for other training schools. After conducting an experimental course in hospital economics at Teachers College, Columbia University, 1899–1907, she went there as full professor in 1907 and served as chairman of the department of nursing and health, 1910–25. Under her guidance the department became an international center for nursing education. She was author, among other works, of A *Statistical Report of Working Hours in Training Schools* (1895), *Educational Status of Nursing* (1912), and *History of Nursing* (1907–12, in collaboration with Lavinia Dock).

NUTTING, WALLACE (*b. Rockbottom, a village in the town of Marlborough, Mass., 1861; d. Framingham, Mass., 1941*), Congregational clergyman, antiquarian, photographer. Leaving the ministry in 1904 because of ill health, he turned his hobby of photography into a business and had great success in selling hand-tinted, platinum prints of rural New England scenes to a generation nostalgic for the past. A part of the same public, newly conscious of the merits of the older American craftsmanship, were customers for the reproductions of early furniture and metalwork which he began to manufacture in 1917. As early as 1912 he had begun to collect authentic period furniture and other antiques for use in four historic houses which he had bought and restored. Author of a number of books, notably his "States Beautiful" series in which his photographs were combined with an anecdotal text, he is best remembered for his three-volume *Furniture Treasury* (1928–1933), a comprehensive photographic archive of American furniture.

NYE, EDGAR WILSON (*b. Shirley, Maine, 1850; d. Arden, N.C., 1896*), journalist, humorist, better known as "Bill" Nye. Raised in Wisconsin, Nye drifted westward in 1876, settling at Laramie City, Wyo. After conducting the *Laramie Boomerang*, 1881–83, in which his reputation as a humorist was established, he moved east in 1886, was a staff writer for the N.Y. *World*, and enjoyed a great success as a lecturer. As a humorous writer, he belongs to the school of Artemus Ward and Mark Twain; his most ambitious books were *History of the United States* (1894) and *History of England* (1896); his shorter comic pieces were published in *Bill Nye and Boomerang* (1881) and later collections.

NYE, JAMES WARREN (*b. De Ruyter, N.Y., 1814; d. White Plains, N.Y., 1876*), lawyer. Territorial governor of Nevada, 1861–64; U.S. senator, Republican, from Nevada, 1864–73.

O

OAKES, GEORGE WASHINGTON OCHS (b. Cincinnati, Ohio, 1861; d. 1931), editor. Son of Julius Ochs; brother of Adolph S. Ochs. Served in several editorial capacities on the *Chattanooga Daily Times*, 1880–ca. 1888; after engaging in magazine work, returned to the *Times*, 1896, as general manager. A civic leader in Chattanooga, he served as mayor, 1893–97. *Post* 1900, he was employed in a number of editorial and managerial capacities on his brother's publications and others, including editorship of *Current History* and *The Times Mid-Week Pictorial*.

OAKES, THOMAS FLETCHER (b. Boston, Mass., 1843; d. Seattle, Wash., 1919), railroad executive. Director, 1881–88, president, 1888–93, and general receiver, 1893–95, of Northern Pacific Railroad.

OAKES, URIAN (b. probably London, England, ca. 1631; d. Massachusetts, 1681), Congregational clergyman, poet. Immigrated to New England as a boy; graduated Harvard, 1649. A dissenting minister and teacher in England, 1653–71, Oakes served thereafter as pastor of the church in Cambridge, Mass. A ringleader among those who drove Leonard Hoar out of the presidency of Harvard, he was acting president of the college *post* 1675 and received formal election as president in February 1679/80.

OAKLEY, ANNIE (b. Darke Co., Ohio, 1860; d. Greenville, Ohio, 1926), markswoman. A notable attraction in vaudeville and the circus, Annie Oakley starred in Buffalo Bill's "Wild West" show *post* 1885; the use of her name to denote punch-marked complimentary tickets derived from her ability to perforate a playing card with rifle bullets while it fluttered to the ground.

OAKLEY, THOMAS JACKSON (b. Beekman, N.Y., 1783; d. New York, N.Y., 1857), lawyer, politician, New York legislator. Congressman, Federalist, from New York, 1813–15; congressman, Clinton Democrat, 1827–28. In high repute as an advocate, Oakley was judge of the superior court of New York City, 1828–47, and chief justice of that court, 1847–57.

OATES, WILLIAM CALVIN (b. Bullock Co., Ala., 1835; d. Montgomery, Ala., 1910), Confederate soldier, lawyer, Alabama legislator. Congressman, Democrat, from Alabama, 1881–94; sound-money governor of Alabama, 1894–96.

OATMAN, JOHNSON (b. near Medford, N.J., 1856; d. Norman, Okla., 1922), gospel hymn writer.

OBER, FREDERICK ALBION (b. Beverly, Mass., 1849; d. Hackensack, N.J., 1913), ornithologist. Explored Lesser Antilles, 1876–78 and 1880, discovering 22 new species of birds.

OBERHOFFER, EMIL JOHANN (b. Munich, Bavaria, 1867; d. San Diego, Calif., 1933), musician. Immigrated to New York City, 1885; removed to Minnesota, 1897, where he taught music, conducted, and was one of the prime movers in the establishment of the Minneapolis Symphony Orchestra, 1903. *Post* 1923, he was active in the musical life of Los Angeles, Calif.

OBERHOLSER, HARRY CHURCH (b. Brooklyn, N.Y., 1870; d. Cleveland, Ohio, 1963), ornithologist. Attended Columbia and George Washington University (Ph.D., 1916). Began a career in government service with the Bureau of Biological Survey (now Fish and Wildlife Service) in 1895; retired as senior biologist in 1941. An expert identifier of birds, he reported 11 new families and subfamilies of birds, 99 new genera and subgenera, and 560 new species and subspecies. Taught at Biltmore Forest Summer School, 1904–10, and American University, 1920–35. Curator of ornithology at Cleveland Museum of Natural History, 1941–47.

OBERHOLTZER, ELLIS PAXSON (b. Cambria Station, Pa., 1868; d. Philadelphia, Pa., 1936), journalist, historian. Author, among other serious studies, of *History of the United States since the Civil War* (1917–37).

OBERHOLTZER, SARA LOUISA VICKERS (b. Uwchlan, Pa., 1841; d. Philadelphia, Pa., 1930), poet, advocate of school savings banks to promote thrift.

OBERNDORF, CLARENCE PAUL (b. New York, N.Y., 1882; d. New York, 1954), psychoanalyst. Studied at Cornell University, M.D., 1906. A pioneer analyst, Oberndorf helped to found the New York Psychoanalytic Society in 1911. Joined the American Psychoanalytic Association shortly thereafter; president, 1924 and 1936. Taught at Cornell medical school from 1914 to 1920, and at Columbia University, 1936–49. Helped to reorganize the American Psychoanalytic Association into a highly restricted group that set strictly Freudian standards in the training and practice of analysts. Published A *History of Psychoanalysis in America* (1953).

O'BRIEN, EDWARD CHARLES (b. Fort Edward, N.Y., 1860; d. Montevideo, Uruguay, 1927), merchant, public official, shipping expert. U.S. minister to Uruguay and Paraguay, 1905–09.

O'BRIEN, FITZ-JAMES (b. Co. Limerick, Ireland, ca. 1828; d. Cumberland, Md., 1862), journalist. Came to America ca. 1852. Sponsored by George P. Morris and others, he quickly became prominent in New York City's literary and Bohemian circles. Enlisting in the Union Army at the outbreak of the Civil War, O'Brien died of the effects of a wound. His *Poems and Stories* (posthumously published, 1881) reprints his best work of which "The Diamond Lens" is probably the best-known example.

O'BRIEN, FREDERICK (b. Baltimore, Md., 1869; d. Sausalito, Calif., 1932), journalist. Author of *White Shadows in the South Seas* (1919), *Atolls of the Sun* (1922), and other accounts of travel.

O'BRIEN, JEREMIAH (b. Kittery, Maine, 1744; d. Machias, Maine, 1818), Revolutionary patriot, naval officer. At the head of about forty volunteers, O'Brien seized the sloop *Unity* in the harbor of Machias and with her engaged and captured the armed schooner *Margaretta*, commanded by an officer of the Royal Navy, June 12, 1775. Thereafter he cruised with success in the service of the Massachusetts Navy until the fall of 1776, when he became a privateersman. Captured in 1780 with his vessel the *Hannibal*, he was imprisoned at New York and later in Mill Prison, England, whence he escaped; on returning to America, 1781, he commanded successively the *Hibernia* and the *Tiger*.

O'BRIEN, JUSTIN (*b. Chicago, Ill., 1906; d. New York, N.Y., 1968*), translator and scholar. Attended University of Chicago and Harvard (Ph.D., 1936). Taught at Harvard, 1929–31, and Columbia, 1931–65. Translated *Journals of André Gide* (1947–51) and wrote *Portrait of André Gide* (1953), the latter illustrating his ability to combine analysis with a sympathetic and intuitive understanding of a subtle and controversial writer. He had his greatest impact on English-language readers through his translation of Albert Camus's works.

O'BRIEN, MATTHEW ANTHONY (*b. Co. Tipperary, Ireland, 1804; d. Louisville, Ky., 1871*), Roman Catholic clergyman, Dominican missionary and provincial. Came to Canada, 1826; ordained in Kentucky, 1839. A magnetic preacher and able administrator.

O'BRIEN, MORGAN JOSEPH (*b. New York, N.Y., 1852; d. New York, 1937*), lawyer, jurist. Graduated, St. John's College (Fordham), 1872; Columbia Law School, 1875. Justice, New York supreme court, 1887–95; appellate division, 1895–1906. Resigning to reenter private practice, O'Brien rose in his profession and engaged in extensive public service; the 1936 New York City Charter revision was owing in great part to his efforts.

O'BRIEN, RICHARD (*b. Maine, ca. 1758; d. Washington, D.C., 1824*), mariner, privateersman. An Algerian captive, 1785–95, O'Brien served as U.S. consul general to Algiers, 1797–1803. Prior to this he had helped conclude treaties of peace with Algiers and Tripoli, 1796.

O'BRIEN, ROBERT LINCOLN (*b. Abington, Mass., 1865; d. Washington, D.C., 1955*), journalist, editor, tariff expert. Graduated from Harvard, B.A., 1891. Personal stenographer and executive clerk to President Grover Cleveland, 1892–95. Became Washington correspondent for the *Boston Evening Transcript*, 1895; editor, 1906–10. Editor of the *Boston Herald*, 1910–28. Head of the U.S. Tariff Commission, 1931–37; strongly endorsed the reciprocal tariff agreements of Secretary of State Cordell Hull.

O'BRIEN, THOMAS JAMES (*b. Jackson Co., Mich., 1842; d. Grand Rapids, Mich., 1933*), lawyer, Republican politician. U.S. minister to Denmark, 1905–07; ambassador to Japan, 1907–11; ambassador to Italy, 1911–13.

O'BRIEN, WILLIAM SHONEY (*b. Queen's Co., Ireland, ca. 1826; d. San Rafael, Calif., 1878*), capitalist, Nevada silver-mine operator. Came to America *ante* 1845; removed to California, 1849. Associated with John W. Mackay, James G. Fair, and others in highly successful mine operations.

O'BRIEN, WILLIS HAROLD (*b. Oakland, Calif., 1886; d. Hollywood, Calif., 1962*), film animator. He pioneered the use of pliable, miniature figures of clay over wood framing, exposing each film frame individually and then slightly altering the position of each model, thereby simulating movement. His first film, *The Dinosaur and the Missing Link* (1915), was purchased by the Edison Company, for whom he later worked (1916–17) on their "Conquest Programs." *The Lost World* (1925) combined animation and live action and is considered a cinema landmark. His best-known films were *King Kong* (1933) and *Mighty Joe Young* (1949); he received an Academy Award for the latter.

O'CALLAGHAN, EDMUND BAILEY (*b. Mallow, Ireland, 1797; d. 1880*), physician, historian. Removed to Albany, N.Y., from Canada, 1837; practiced medicine until 1848; devoted full time to editing early records of New York State, 1848–70. Among the important works which he produced were *History of New Netherland* (1846–48); *Documentary History of the State of New York* (1849–51); and *Documents Relative to the Colonial History of the State of New York* (Volumes I–XI, 1853–61).

O'CALLAGHAN, JEREMIAH (*b. Co. Cork, Ireland, 1780; d. Holyoke, Mass., 1861*), Roman Catholic clergyman, author. Ordained, 1805, in Ireland, O'Callaghan early became an opponent of the taking of interest on money loans, an anticapitalist position which involved him in difficulties with his ecclesiastical superiors for many years. Immigrating to America, 1823, he was unable to win acceptance in any diocese until 1830; at that time, accepted by the diocese of Boston, he was assigned to missionary and pastoral work in Vermont where he worked with great zeal and success. His book *Usury, or Interest, Proved . . . Destructive to Civil Society* (New York, 1824) went through several editions and had a strong influence on the English radical writer William Cobbett.

O'CALLAHAN, JOSEPH TIMOTHY (*b. Roxbury, Mass., 1905; d. Worcester, Mass., 1964*), Jesuit priest, educator, and navy chaplain. Attended Weston (M.A., 1929) and Georgetown. Taught at Boston College (1931), Weston (1936), and Holy Cross (1938–39, 1946–49). Enlisted in the navy in 1939 and in 1944 was assigned to the carrier *Franklin*, which was attacked by a Japanese dive bomber in March 1945. Fighting raging flames and without regard for his safety, although wounded by shrapnel, he organized and led firefighting crews and inspired crew members with his courage and faith in the face of almost certain death; he was awarded the Medal of Honor. He wrote *I Was Chaplain on the Franklin* (1956), which became a best-seller.

OCCIDENTE, MARIA DEL. *See* BROOKS, MARIA GOWEN.

OCCOM, SAMSON (*b. near New London, Conn., 1723; d. 1792*), Indian Presbyterian clergyman, missionary, First Indian to be trained (1743–47) by Eleazar Wheelock. Occom was ordained in 1759. He accompanied Nathaniel Whitaker to England to secure money for Wheelock's Indian Charity School, 1766–68. An active missionary among the New England tribes and the Oneida, he opposed as best he could the white encroachment upon Indian lands.

OCCONOSTOTA. *See* OCONOSTOTA.

OCHS, ADOLPH SIMON (*b. Cincinnati, Ohio, 1858; d. Chattanooga, Tenn., 1935*), newspaper publisher. Son of Julius Ochs. Began work, 1869, as office boy on the Knoxville, Tenn., *Chronicle*; tried various occupations in various places during his early youth but always came back to Knoxville and the newspaper business. Removing to Chattanooga, Tenn., at the age of 19, he began his publishing career by purchasing the *Chattanooga Times* with borrowed money, 1878. After developing the *Times* with great success as a newspaper "clean, dignified and trustworthy," he purchased the once-prosperous *New York Times*, 1896. He applied to his new purchase without compromise the principles he had practiced in Chattanooga; it was to be a strictly "news" paper in which editorial opinion was subordinate and the news was treated with freedom from personal and partisan bias. He also excluded advertising which seemed to him fraudulent or improper. Refusing to make any concessions to yellow journalism, Ochs brought the *Times* along slowly but steadily; after it began to succeed, he put most of his profits back into expansion of plant and services. From time to time he held interests in other papers, but came eventually to the conclusion that running the *Times* was job enough for any man. The excellence of the *Times*'s coverage of war news, 1914–18, raised the paper to preeminence. Ochs never held nor sought public office; in his later years, he gave much time to philanthropies and public causes.

OCHS, JULIUS (*b. Fürth, Bavaria, 1826; d. Chattanooga, Tenn., 1888*), merchant. Father of Adolph S. Ochs and George W. Oakes. Came to America, 1845. Resided successively in Kentucky, Ohio, and Tennessee; served in Union Army; was active in politics and civic affairs.

OCHSNER, ALBERT JOHN (*b. Baraboo, Wis., 1858; d. 1925*), surgeon. Graduated Rush Medical College, 1886; studied also in Vienna and Berlin. Practiced in Chicago *post* 1889; taught at Rush Medical College and at University of Illinois; was chief surgeon, Augustana Hospital, 1891–1925, and at St. Mary's Hospital, 1896–25.

OCKERSON, JOHN AUGUSTUS (*b. Skane Province, Sweden, 1848; d. St. Louis, Mo., 1924*), engineer. Came to America as a child; graduated University of Illinois, C.E., 1873. Associated *post* 1879 with the Mississippi River Commission, he became an international authority on river and harbor improvement and navigation. Among his individual achievements was the construction of levees (1910) to control flood waters of the Colorado River.

O'CONNELL, WILLIAM HENRY (*b. Lowell, Mass., 1859; d. Brighton, Mass., 1944*), Roman Catholic clergyman, archbishop and cardinal. Graduated Boston College, 1881; pursued theological studies at North American College, Rome; ordained to priesthood, June 1884. After service in parishes in Medford and Boston, Mass., he was rector of the North American College, 1895–1901. A strong proponent of papal authority, and of the autonomy of bishops within their dioceses, he was named bishop of Portland, Maine, 1901, and succeeded to the archbishopric of Boston in 1907. He was made a cardinal in 1911. In full control of the archdiocese until his death, he centralized its finances and all other institutional activities, imposing clear and firm policy guidelines on his clergy and on the administration of parishes and schools. Generally conservative on social issues, he strove consciously to improve relations between Roman Catholics and Protestants; he did not hesitate, however, to speak out on public issues which to his mind constituted a threat to Catholic interests. He gave encouragement to education, charitable activities, and the foreign missions, was frequently critical of errant politicians of his own faith, and took a lifelong interest in liturgical music.

O'CONNOR, EDWIN GREENE (*b. Providence, R.I., 1918; d. Boston, Mass., 1968*), novelist. Attended Notre Dame (B.A., 1939). Began a career as a radio announcer (1940) in Providence, R.I., and later worked at stations in Palm Beach, Fla.; Buffalo, N.Y.; and Boston, Mass. He left radio in 1946 to become a freelance writer. Under the name Roger Swift, he wrote for the *Boston Herald* and the *Atlantic Monthly*. His first novel, *The Oracle* (1951), shows his gift for satire, comedic insight into human folly, and the grace and humor of his objective style. *The Last Hurrah* (1956) was a best-seller and is called the best American novel on urban politics. *The Edge of Sadness* (1961) won a Pulitzer Prize. Other works include *I Was Dancing* (1964), *All in the Family* (1966), and *Benjy: A Ferocious Fairy Tale* (1957).

O'CONNOR, JAMES (*b. Cobh, Ireland, 1823; d. 1890*), Roman Catholic clergyman. Brother of Michael O'Connor. Came to America *ca.* 1839. Ordained in Rome, 1848, he served in the dioceses of Pittsburgh and Philadelphia until 1876 when he was consecrated vicar-apostolic of Nebraska. Appointed first bishop of Omaha, 1885, he served until his death.

O'CONNOR, MARY FLANNERY (*b. Savannah, Ga., 1925; d. Milledgeville, Ga., 1964*), novelist and short-story writer. Attended Georgia State College for Women and University of Iowa (M.F.A., 1947). Published her first story, "The Geranium," in *Accent* (1946); between 1946 and 1952 published stories and portions of her first novel, *Wise Blood* (1952), in *Accent, Sewanee Review, Mademoiselle*, and other magazines. "The Life You Save May Be Your Own" was selected for publication in *O. Henry Prize Stories* of 1954; later stories appeared regularly in that collection and others. Her work has been described as "southern gothic" and is in the grotesque tradition in American literature. O'Connor's writing was also influenced by her devout Catholicism.

O'CONNOR, MICHAEL (*b. near Cork, Ireland, 1810; d. Woodstock, Md., 1872*), Roman Catholic clergyman. Brother of James O'Connor. Educated in France and in Rome, Italy, he was ordained, 1833, and came to America *ca.* 1839 as rector of the Seminary of St. Charles, Philadelphia. Consecrated bishop of Pittsburgh, 1843, he served there with distinguished success until his resignation, 1860. Thereafter, having become a Jesuit, he traveled extensively throughout the United States as a missionary.

O'CONNOR, WILLIAM DOUGLAS (*b. Boston, Mass., 1832; d. Washington, D.C., 1889*), journalist, civil servant, friend and champion of Walt Whitman. Author of *The Good Gray Poet* (1866).

O'CONOR, CHARLES (*b. New York, N.Y., 1804; d. 1884*), lawyer. Admitted to the bar, 1824, he practiced with phenomenal success and appeared as counsel in most of the outstanding cases heard in his time. Among them were the Jumel Will case, the Roosevelt Hospital case, the Tilden-Hayes election contest, the Tweed case, and the Forrest divorce case. A Democrat, he ran unsuccessfully a number of times for public office; he was nominated for president of the United States by the "Straight-out" Democrats, 1872.

OCONOSTOTA (*d. 1785*), Cherokee Indian chief. Lived at Great Echota in present Monroe Co., Tenn. Imprisoned at Fort Prince George (S.C.), 1759, by Governor W. H. Lyttelton after proffering friendship, Oconostota was soon released; thereafter he devoted himself to repaying treachery with equal treachery. Unsuccessfully attempting to capture Fort Prince George, 1760, he led Cherokee in raids against the frontier settlements; later he commanded the Indians in the taking of Fort Loudoun and was responsible for the massacre of its defenders. Apparently reconciled to the superiority of the white forces, he led the Cherokee delegation at the treaty of peace with the Iroquois at Johnson Hall, 1768; he opposed sale of Cherokee lands at Sycamore Shoals, 1775. During the Revolution he fought for the British, resigning his leadership, 1782.

OCTACITE. *See* OUTACITY.

O'DANIEL, WILBERT LEE ("PAPPY") (*b. Malta, Ohio, 1890; d. Dallas, Tex., 1969*), businessman, radio musician, and politician. During a successful career in the flour-milling industry, organizing his own companies, he created, with Bob Wills, the radio program "Light Crust Doughboys" (1930); he wrote over 150 songs and programs on religion, families, morals, and Americanism. The song "Them Hillbillies are Politicians Now" resulted in a grass-roots letter campaign encouraging him to enter and later win the Texas gubernatorial race in 1938; he was reelected in 1940. A U.S. senator, 1942–48, he served without distinction; his election successes are often attributed to showmanship and radio.

ODELL, BENJAMIN BARKER (*b. Newburgh, N.Y., 1854; d. 1926*), businessman, New York State Republican politician and leader. Suggested Theodore Roosevelt's candidacy for governor, 1898; elected governor himself in 1900 and again in 1902, he served with efficiency and economy. A realist in politics, he was the first "machine" Republican to defy the rule of Thomas C. Platt.

ODELL, GEORGE CLINTON DENSMORE (*b. Newburgh, N.Y., 1866; d. New York, N.Y., 1949*), educator, theater historian. Brother of Benjamin B. Odell. B.A., Columbia University, 1889; M.A., 1890; Ph.D., 1892. Taught in English department at Columbia, 1895–1939; appointed professor of dramatic literature, 1924. Author of *Shakespeare from Betterton to Irving* (1920), and of the encyclopedic, fifteen-volume *Annals of the New York Stage* (1927–49).

ODELL, JONATHAN (*b. Newark, N.J., 1737; d. Fredericton, N.B., Canada, 1818*), Loyalist, physician, poet, Episcopal clergyman. Played important role in negotiations between Benedict Arnold and British headquarters in New York, 1779–80; was author of Tory satirical verses in Rivington's *Royal Gazette* and other newspapers; registrar and clerk of New Brunswick province, *ca.* 1784–1812.

ODENBACH, FREDERICK LOUIS (*b. Rochester, N.Y., 1857; d. Cleveland, Ohio, 1933*), Roman Catholic clergyman, Jesuit, meteorologist. Graduated Canisius College, Buffalo, N.Y., 1881; entered the Society of Jesus, 1881; made his subsequent studies in the Netherlands and England. Taught scientific studies at the present John Carroll University in Cleveland, 1892–1933, supervising and in large measure constructing the meteorological observatory there. He designed and built the first ceraunograph (an adaptation of the coherer to the detection and recording of static disturbances), 1899; in 1900, he began a seismological observatory and was the founder of Jesuit activity in that field in the United States.

ODENHEIMER, WILLIAM HENRY (*b. Philadelphia, Pa., 1817; d. Burlington, N.J., 1879*), Episcopal clergyman. Bishop of New Jersey, 1859–74, and of Northern New Jersey (later Newark), 1874–79.

ODETS, CLIFFORD (*b. Philadelphia, Pa., 1906; d. New York, N.Y., 1963*), dramatist, screenwriter, and actor. Acted on radio and in theater, 1923–30, including the Group Theatre, for which he wrote in 1935 *Waiting for Lefty, Awake and Sing!, Till the Day I Die,* and *Paradise Lost;* other plays for the Group were *Golden Boy* (1937), *Rocket to the Moon* (1938), and *Night Music* (1940). He later wrote the plays *The Big Knife* (1949), *The Country Girl* (1950), and *The Flowering Peach* (1954). His plays were sociological in theme and are distinguished by his concerns for individual loneliness in the modern world. Worked as a screenwriter in Hollywood (1936–38, 1943–47, 1955–61), writing *The General Died at Dawn* (1936) and *None But the Lonely Heart* (1944). Received Award of Merit Medal for Drama (1961) from the American Academy of Arts and Letters.

ODIN, JOHN MARY (*b. Ambierle, France, 1801; d. Ambierle, 1870*), Roman Catholic clergyman, Vincentian. Came to New Orleans, La., with Bishop Dubourg, 1822; served as missionary in Arkansas and Texas *post* 1923; consecrated vicar apostolic of Texas, 1842. Appointed bishop of Galveston, 1847, he was raised to the archbishopric of New Orleans, 1861.

O'DONNELL, THOMAS JEFFERSON (*b. Mendham Township, N.J., 1856; d. 1925*), lawyer. Removing to Denver, Colo., 1879, he spent the remainder of his life there in the practice of law and as a power in the Democratic party. Opposed to Grover Cleveland's financial policies, he was many times an unsuccessful seeker for public office.

O'DONOVAN, WILLIAM RUDOLF (*b. Preston Co., Va., now W. Va., 1844; d. New York, N.Y., 1920*), sculptor, painter, Confederate soldier.

O'DOUL, FRANCIS JOSEPH ("LEFTY") (*b. San Francisco, Calif., 1897; d. San Francisco, 1969*), baseball player and manager. Began professional career in baseball in 1917 with San Francisco Seals of the Pacific Coast League. During 1919–34, he was optioned or traded thirteen times by different major league clubs, first with the New York Yankees, 1919–22, and later the New York Giants, Boston Red Sox, Brooklyn Dodgers, and Philadelphia Phillies. Played in the first all-star game, 1933, and appeared in the 1933 World Series. Managed in the Pacific Coast League, 1935–57, and was a batting coach for the Giants in San Francisco. Among his protégés were Joe Di Maggio and Willie McCovey.

ODUM, HOWARD WASHINGTON (*b. near Bethlehem, Ga., 1884; d. Chapel Hill, N.C., 1954*), sociologist. Studied at Emory College; the University of Mississippi; Clark University, Ph.D., 1909; and Columbia University, Ph.D., 1910. Taught at the University of North Carolina, 1920–54. A scholar of folk cultures, especially black cultures, Odum wrote many works about black music. Urged government involvement in the social welfare programs that he espoused; in 1929, he joined William F. Ogburn in coordinating the study published as *Recent Trends In the United States* (1933), which marked a new departure in the relations between the federal government and the social sciences. A proponent of the concept of regionalism in the social welfare programs of his time, Odum sought unity through diversity. President of the American Sociological Society, 1930; president of the Southern Regional Council, 1944–46.

O'DWYER, JOSEPH (*b. Cleveland, Ohio, 1841; d. 1898*), physician. Graduated N.Y. College of Physicians and Surgeons, 1866; practiced thereafter in New York City. Successfully demonstrated value of intubation in treatment of diphtheria at New York Foundling Asylum *post* 1872; his findings, first attacked and later enthusiastically approved by the medical profession, were published first in the *New York Medical Journal,* Aug. 8, 1885. He was also among the first to recognize the value of diphtheria serum.

O'DWYER, WILLIAM (*b. Bohola, Co. Mayo, Ireland, 1890; d. New York, N.Y., 1964*), lawyer and mayor of New York City. Arrived in New York in 1910; became U.S. citizen, 1916, and next year joined New York City police force. Studied law in the evening at Fordham (LL.B., 1923). Following service in several city judicial positions, he was elected Kings County district attorney (1940) and smashed the crime ring "Murder, Inc." Elected mayor of New York City in 1945; reelected in 1949. A probe into gambling and police corruption led to his resignation in 1950, after he handed out $125,000 in raises to friends on the city's payroll. He appeared before the Senate Crime Committee, headed by Estes Kefauver, in 1951, while serving as U.S. ambassador to Mexico; although no charges of wrongdoing were made, it was evident that he had dealings with criminal elements; resigned as ambassador in 1952. The stereotype of the affable Irish politician, his rise in politics was due as much to hard work as to an understanding of machine politics. His accomplishments as mayor include bringing the United Nations headquarters to the city and the selection of Robert Moses as the city's construction coordinator.

OEHMLER, LEO CARL MARTIN (*b. Pittsburgh, Pa., 1867; d. Pasadena, Calif., 1930*), musician, piano teacher, composer. Teacher of Charles W. Cadman.

OEMLER, ARMINIUS (*b. Savannah, Ga., 1827; d. Savannah, 1897*), physician, agriculturist, Confederate soldier. Among the first to introduce scientific diversified farming into the South, Oemler anticipated by two years (1888) the German discovery of the presence of nitrogen-fixing bacteria in the nodules of leguminous plants. He started the first commercial oyster-packing plant in the South *ca.* 1883 and was thereafter a promoter of that industry.

OERTEL, JOHANNES ADAM SIMON (*b. Fürth, Bavaria, 1823; d. Vienna, Va., 1909*), Episcopal clergyman, artist. Came to America, 1848, after studying at Munich. Active in the ministry *post* 1867, he is remembered chiefly as the painter of the very popular "Rock of Ages," although he did much excellent work in church decoration and was a superior woodcarver.

O'FALLON, BENJAMIN (*b. probably Lexington, Ky., 1793; d. Jefferson Co., Mo., 1842*), Indian agent, trader. Son of James O'Fallon; nephew of William and George Rogers Clark; brother of John O'Fallon. As U.S. Indian agent at Prairie du Chien, O'Fallon made treaties with the Oto and Ponca, 1817. Appointed agent for the upper Missouri, 1819, he served until 1927 with great success owing to his honesty and courage and his remarkable knowledge of Indian customs, habits, and characteristics. He was a principal in the Missouri Fur Co.

O'FALLON, JAMES (*b. Ireland, 1749; d. 1794*), physician, Revolutionary soldier, adventurer. Immigrated to North Carolina, 1774; after the Revolution, removed to Charleston, S.C. Appointed general agent of the South Carolina Yazoo Company, he associated himself with James Wilkinson and with Esteban Miró in intrigues connected with the institution of an independent government for the West. A proclamation by President Washington, March 1791, proved disastrous to O'Fallon's plans. He married a sister of William and George Rogers Clark in 1791 and was the father of Benjamin and John O'Fallon.

O'FALLON, JOHN (*b. Louisville, Ky., 1791; d. St. Louis, Mo., 1865*), soldier, merchant. Son of James O'Fallon; nephew of William and George Rogers Clark; brother of Benjamin O'Fallon. After able army service at Tippecanoe and in the War of 1912, O'Fallon resigned his commission, 1818, and engaged in trade at St. Louis, Mo., where he became a wealthy and public-spirited citizen.

O'FERRALL, CHARLES TRIPLETT (*b. Frederick Co., Va., 1840; d. Richmond, Va., 1905*), lawyer. Confederate cavalry colonel, Virginia legislator. Congressman, Democrat, from Virginia, 1884–93. A strict constructionist and supporter of Grover Cleveland, O'Ferrall made a determined effort to wipe out lynching as governor of Virginia, 1894–98.

OFFLEY, DAVID (*b. Philadelphia, Pa.; d. Smyrna, Turkey, 1838*), merchant. Removing to Smyrna, 1811, he founded there the first American commercial house in the Levant. He served as consular commercial agent, 1823–32, and as U.S. consul, 1832–38.

OFTEDAL, SVEN (*b. Stavanger, Norway, 1844; d. 1911*), Lutheran clergyman, Minneapolis civic leader. Came to America, 1873. Professor of theology, 1873–1904, and president of trustees, 1874–1911, of Augsburg Seminary, Minneapolis.

OGBURN, WILLIAM FIELDING (*b. Butler, Ga., 1886; d. Tallahassee, Fla., 1959*), sociologist, statistician, educator. Studied at Mercer University and Columbia University, Ph.D., 1912. Professor of sociology at Columbia, 1919–27, and at the University of Chicago, 1927–51. Ogburn played a major role in converting the social sciences into quantitative empirical disciplines by introducing statistical techniques into research. Works include *Social Change: With Respect to Culture and Original Nature* (1922), in which he introduced the term, "cultural lag," and *Recent Social Trends in the United States* (1933). President of the American Association for the Advancement of Science, 1932; president of the Society for the History of Technology, 1959.

OGDEN, AARON (*b. Elizabeth, N.J., 1756; d. Jersey City, N.J., 1839*), Revolutionary soldier, lawyer, pioneer steamboat operator. Graduated College of New Jersey (Princeton), 1773. Entering practice after the Revolution, he became a leader of the New Jersey bar, served as U.S. senator, Federalist, 1801–03, and was elected governor of New Jersey in the fall of 1812 on a peace ticket. After commanding the New Jersey militia during the War of 1812, he undertook operation of a steamboat between Elizabeth and New York City which occasioned the legal conflicts concluded in the celebrated U.S. Supreme Court case of *Gibbons vs. Ogden*, 1824. Ruined by this litigation, he became collector of customs at Jersey City in 1829 and served until his death.

OGDEN, DAVID (*b. Newark, N.J., 1707; d. Whitestone, N.Y., 1798*), lawyer, New Jersey councilor and jurist, Loyalist.

OGDEN, DAVID BAYARD (*b. Morrisania, N.Y., 1775; d. Staten Island, N.Y., 1849*), lawyer. Son of Samuel Ogden. Practicing in New York City *post* 1803, Ogden's chief fame arose from the clarity of his presentations before the U.S. Supreme Court. The most celebrated of the many cases in which he participated was *Cohens vs. Virginia* (1821) in which he appeared for Cohens.

OGDEN, FRANCIS BARBER (*b. Boonton, N.J., 1783; d. Bristol, England, 1857*), engineer. Nephew of Aaron Ogden. A pioneer in designing steamboat engines, Ogden resided in England *post* 1830 where he served in several consular posts. He financed the work of John Ericsson and promoted his interests in England and in the United States.

OGDEN, HERBERT GOUVERNEUR (*b. New York, N.Y., 1846; d. Fortress Monroe, Va., 1906*), cartographer, topographer. Appointed an aid in the U.S. Coast and Geodetic Survey, 1863, Ogden remained with that service until his death, serving as cartographer and topographer and as director of publication of three editions of the *U.S. Coast Pilot* (1899, 1903, 1904). He also made original explorations in Alaska.

OGDEN, PETER SKENE (*b. Quebec, Canada, 1794; d. Oregon City, Oreg., 1854*), fur trader, explorer. Grandson of David Ogden. Entered employ of the North West Company *ca.* 1815. Transferred to the Columbia district beyond the Rockies *ca.* 1818, he spent the remainder of his life there. His work took him into almost every valley in southern Idaho and eastern Oregon and into Montana; he was one of the first white men to visit the Great Salt Lake region (Ogden, Utah, was named in his honor), and he was the first to traverse the Humboldt River valley in northern Nevada. Assigned to the Fraser River region *ca.* 1836, he was stationed at Fort Vancouver *post* 1844. A man of great cultivation and urbanity, he was author of *Traits of American Indian Life* (London, 1853).

OGDEN, ROBERT CURTIS (*b. Philadelphia, Pa., 1836; d. Kennebunkport, Maine, 1913*), merchant, promoter of education in the South.

OGDEN, ROLLO (*b. Sand Lake, N.Y., 1856; d. 1937*), Presbyterian clergyman, newspaper editor. Graduated Williams, 1877. Leaving the ministry, 1887, on conscientious grounds, Ogden joined the staff of the N.Y. *Evening Post*, 1891; he became editor-in-chief, 1903, and served until 1920, simultaneously controlling the editorial policy of the *Nation*. A champion of anti-imperialism, low tariffs, civil service reform, black rights, woman suffrage, and international action for peace, he at the same time opposed any wide expansion of governmental powers. Ogden served as associate editor of the *New York Times*, 1920–22, and as editor, 1922–37. Remaining a staunch internationalist, he approved of some parts of the New Deal but was hostile to its augmentation of federal power.

OGDEN, SAMUEL (*b. Newark, N.J., 1746; d. New York, N.Y., 1810*), iron founder, land promoter. Son of David Ogden.

OGDEN, THOMAS LUDLOW (*b. probably Morristown, N.J., 1773; d. 1844*), lawyer. Grandson of David Ogden; nephew of Samuel Ogden. Graduated Columbia, 1792; admitted to New York bar, 1796. Specializing in trusts and will and equity jurisprudence, Ogden became one of the most active corporation lawyers in New York City and was identified with many of its cultural and civic activities.

OGDEN, UZAL (*b. Newark, N.J., 1744; d. Newark, 1822*), Episcopal clergyman. Made theological studies under Thomas B. Chandler; was ordained in London, England, 1773. Rector of Trinity Church, Newark, 1788–1805, Ogden was elected first bishop of New Jersey, 1798, but was refused consecration. Suspended from the Episcopal ministry, 1805, as the final step in a long controversy over his broad views on order and doctrine, he became a Presbyterian.

OGDEN, WILLIAM BUTLER (*b. Walton, N.Y., 1805; d. New York, N.Y., 1877*), businessman. After early success as a land developer in New York, Ogden removed to Chicago, Ill., 1835, made a fortune in real estate operations there, and was elected the city's first mayor, 1837. After his term, he devoted himself to railroad construction east and west from Chicago; among the roads which he headed were the Galena & Chicago; the Pittsburgh, Fort Wayne & Chicago; the Chicago & Northwestern. He presided over the National Pacific Railway Convention, 1850, and was first president of the Union Pacific, 1862.

OGG, FREDERIC AUSTIN (*b. Solsberry, Ind., 1878; d. Madison, Wis., 1951*), political scientist, author, editor, educator. Studied at DePauw College (Ph.B., 1899), Indiana University, and Harvard, Ph.D., 1908. Taught history at Simmons College, 1909–14. Professor of political science at the University of Wisconsin, 1914–50. A pioneer in the field of political science, Ogg wrote many widely used texts: *Introduction to American Government* (1922) and *Essentials of American Government* (1932). Served on the editorial board of *American Political Science Review*, 1916–26; managing director, 1926–49. President of the American Political Science Association, 1941.

OGILVIE, JAMES (*b. Aberdeen, Scotland, date unknown; d. Aberdeen, 1820*), teacher, lecturer. An eccentric pseudo-philosopher, Ogilvie conducted several schools in Virginia *ante* 1809; thereafter, he became a wandering professor of oratory. Failing in his ambitions, he returned to Scotland where he committed suicide.

OGILVIE, JOHN (*b. probably New York, N.Y., 1724; d. New York, 1774*), Anglican clergyman. Graduated Yale, 1748. After ordination in London, England, 1749, Ogilvie returned to America with an appointment as missionary in Albany, N.Y., and to the Mohawk Indians. He served with zeal in this work, was a military chaplain, 1756–60, and in 1764 was appointed assistant minister of Trinity Church, New York City, where he served until his death.

OGLE, SAMUEL (*b. Northumberland Co., England, ca. 1702; d. Annapolis, Md., 1752*), British officer, colonial official. Proprietary governor of Maryland, 1732, 1733–42, and 1747–52, Ogle successfully resolved the question of the validity of English legal statutes in Maryland; he also regulated the tobacco trade.

OGLESBY, RICHARD JAMES (*b. Oldham Co., Ky., 1824; d. 1899*), lawyer, politician, Union major general. Republican governor of Illinois, 1865–69, also for a very brief period in 1873, and 1885–89; U.S. senator, 1873–79.

OGLETHORPE, JAMES EDWARD (*b. London, England, 1696; d. England, 1785*), soldier, philanthropist, founder of the colony of Georgia. Educated at Eton and Oxford; early gained military reputation in service under Prince Eugene against the Turks. Briefly involved in Jacobite activity abroad, he returned to England in 1719 to manage family estate. Entering Parliament as a mild High Tory, he held his seat, 1722–54, advocating naval preparedness, an expanding imperial commerce, improved penal conditions for debtors, and abolition of both impressment and slavery. He conceived the idea of sending newly freed and unemployed debtors to America at about the time when concern over the exposed position of Carolina to Indian and Spanish raids led the British government to seek expansion and defense of that colony by a buffer zone to the south. After a long period of many trials, Oglethorpe and 19 associates received a charter in 1732 to establish the colony of Georgia. His energetic publicity efforts and royal favor having brought both money and settlers for the venture, he landed at Charleston, 1733. Pursuing a conciliatory policy with the Indians, he secured a site at Savannah. Fortifications were at once erected and a rigorous system of military training established. Salzburger Lutherans were persuaded to migrate to the colony, 1734. Need for more money brought Oglethorpe back to England, 1734; he pressed successfully for new regulations banning sale of rum, prohibiting slavery, and setting up a licensing system for the Indian trade. Groups of Scotch Presbyterian and Moravian settlers were induced to join the colony between 1735 and 1738. Rumors of insurrection caused Oglethorpe to return to Georgia in 1735, accompanied by Charles and John Wesley, who did not find their stay congenial and soon left. An effective but expensive southern military outpost against the Spaniards, Fort Frederica, was founded in 1736.

Complaints by Carolina against the licensing of trade, Spanish resentment of Frederica, the tales reported to England by malcontent settlers, and increasing debts drew Oglethorpe back to London, 1736–37. Most difficulties were smoothed over, but trouble with Spain continued. Persisting in his efforts to strengthen the colony for both humanitarian and imperial reasons, Oglethorpe returned once more to Georgia in 1738, this time with a regiment of 700 men. Henceforth, a dragging war with Spain was his principal concern. Georgians attacked St. Augustine in 1740, and Frederica in turn was besieged by the Spanish in 1742. Oglethorpe borrowed heavily on his English holdings to conduct a successful defense of his colony, but internal discontents and serious charges by a subordinate forced his return to London in 1743. He was acquitted by a court martial but his administrative powers and vigor had diminished; his colonizing days were over and he lived uneventfully thereafter in England. He was promoted to the rank of full general, 1765.

O'GORMAN, THOMAS (*b. Boston, Mass., 1843; d. Sioux Falls, S.Dak., 1921*), Roman Catholic clergyman, Paulist, educator. Second bishop of Sioux Falls, 1896 = 1921; assisted William H. Taft in settlement of Philippine friar question, 1902.

O'HARA, JAMES (*b. Ireland, 1752; d. Pittsburgh, Pa., 1819*), Revolutionary soldier, manufacturer, land speculator. Early

Pittsburgh banker and glass manufacturer; associated with John H. Hopkins in Ligonier iron works.

O'HARA, JOHN HENRY (*b. Pottsville, Pa., 1905; d. Princeton, N.J., 1970*), novelist and short-story writer. American master of short fiction, began work as a reporter for the *New York Herald Tribune* in 1928, the year his first short story appeared in the *New Yorker*. Held a series of journalistic jobs, most of which he lost due to drinking. His novel *Appointment in Samarra* (1934) established his literary reputation. He practiced the novel of manners, and his principal themes were the cruelty of human conduct and the pain of loneliness. *The Doctor's Son* (1935) was his first short-story collection and led to his being credited with perfecting the sub-genre "the *New Yorker* story." *Butterfield 8*, his second novel (1935), led to work in Hollywood as a script polisher. His stories about "Pal Joey" began appearing in the *New Yorker* in 1938 and were collected in 1940, when the musical, for which he wrote the book, appeared on Broadway. During the 1940's he published stories, commuted to Hollywood, and wrote a column for *Newsweek*. *A Rage to Live* (1949) became a best-seller; other novels include *Ten North Frederick* (1955), *From the Terrace* (1958), and *Ourselves to Know* (1960). In the 1960's he wrote short stories and novellas for the *New Yorker* and published thirteen volumes of fiction.

O'HARA, THEODORE (*b. Danville, Ky., 1820; d. Guerryton, Ala., 1867*), soldier, journalist. Officer in both Mexican and Civil wars; author of "The Bivouac of the Dead," commemorating Kentuckians killed at Buena Vista.

O'HARE, KATE (RICHARDS) CUNNINGHAM (*b. Ottawa County, Kans., 1877; d. Benicia, Calif., 1948*), socialist lecturer and organizer. Apprenticed as a machinist; joined Socialist Labor party, 1899, leaving it for the Socialist party of America, 1901. Married F. P. O'Hare, 1902, with whom she worked as party organizer and as editor-publisher of the *National Rip-Saw* (later renamed *Social Revolution*). Imprisoned 1919 = 20 for opposition to U.S. involvement in World War I. With her husband, founded Commonwealth College in Leesville, La., 1922; removed with college to Mena, Ark., 1925. Divorced in 1928, she married C. C. Cunningham and resided thereafter in California, where she was active in prison reform and in support of Upton Sinclair's EPIC movement and his campaign for governor.

O'HIGGINS, HARVEY JERROLD (*b. London, Ontario, Canada, 1876; d. 1929*), novelist, journalist. Helped introduce literary use of psychoanalytic method in 1920's; was long associated with work of the Authors' League.

OHLMACHER, ALBERT PHILIP (*b. Sandusky, Ohio, 1865; d. Detroit, Mich., 1916*), physician, pathologist. M.D., Northwestern, 1890. Pioneered in study of the pathology of epilepsy.

O'KELLY, JAMES (*b. Ireland or America, ca. 1735; d. 1826*), Methodist preacher, opponent of slavery. Prominent as preacher in North Carolina and Virginia *post* 1778, he opposed authority, especially that of Bishop Francis Asbury, insisting that General Conferences should have a larger role in direction of church affairs. Seceding from the Methodist Episcopal Church, 1792, he set up his own group, called Republican Methodists and later simply "Christians." This group was congregational in policy and regarded the Scriptures as the only authority on faith and practice.

OKEY, JOHN WATERMAN (*b. Monroe Co., Ohio, 1827; d. Columbus, Ohio, 1885*), lawyer. Prominent common-pleas and supreme court jurist in Ohio. Co-author of *Digest of Ohio Reports* (1867) and *The Municipal Code of Ohio* (1869).

O'LAUGHLIN, MICHAEL. *See* BOOTH, JOHN WILKES.

OLCOTT, CHANCELLOR JOHN. *See* OLCOTT, CHAUNCEY.

OLCOTT, CHAUNCEY (*b. Buffalo, N.Y., 1860; d. Monte Carlo, Monaco, 1932*), actor, singer. Popular Irish-American tenor; wrote "My Wild Irish Rose."

OLCOTT, EBEN ERSKINE (*b. New York, N.Y., 1854; d. New York, 1929*), mining engineer. Graduated Columbia School of Mines, 1874. Pioneered development of Cerro de Pasco copper fields in Peru; managed Hudson River Day Line *post* 1895.

OLCOTT, HENRY STEEL (*b. Orange, N.J., 1832; d. 1907*), lawyer, president-founder of the Theosophical Society. Led a bizarre life as Helena Blavatsky's partner; was conciliator of Japanese and Ceylonese Buddhist sects, and editor of the *Theosophist.*

OLDEN, CHARLES SMITH (*b. near Princeton, N.J., 1799; d. Princeton, 1876*), businessman, farmer, New Jersey legislator and jurist. Anti-Democrat coalition governor of New Jersey, 1860–63.

OLDER, FREMONT (*b. near Appleton, Wis., 1856; d. near Stockton, Calif., 1935*), printer, editor, reformer. Removed to San Francisco, Calif., 1873; worked on a number of California and Nevada newspapers; settled in San Francisco, 1884, where he became managing editor of the *Bulletin*, 1895. He built up the paper's circulation and attracted national attention by journalistic crusades against the Southern Pacific Railroad, the Abraham Ruef political machine, and the domination of the state by special interests; he also worked for penal reform, encouraged labor unions, and demanded the acquittal of Thomas J. Mooney and others after the Preparedness Day bombings, 1916. Leaving the editorship of the *Bulletin*, he became editor of the San Francisco *Call*, 1918, and a loyal defender of his employer William R. Hearst. As an editor, he was forceful and successful; as a person, he was full of contradictions and difficult to analyze.

OLDFATHER, WILLIAM ABBOTT (*b. Urumiah, Persia, 1880; Homer Park, Ill., 1945*), classicist. Child of Presbyterian missionary parents. A.B., Hanover (Ind.) College, 1899. A.B., Harvard, 1901; A.M., 1902, Ph.D., University of Munich, 1908. Taught at Northwestern University, 1903–06, 1908–09; was associate professor and later professor of classics at University of Illinois, 1909–45. He headed the classics department at Illinois *post* 1926.

OLDFIELD, ("BARNEY") BERNA ELI (*b. near Wauseon, Ohio, 1878; d. Beverly Hills, Calif., 1946*), automobile racer. Known as "Barney" Oldfield. Began as a bicycle racer. Famous as the first man to break the one-minute mile, which he did driving Henry Ford's "999" at the Indiana State Fair, Indianapolis, June 15, 1903.

OLDHAM, JOHN (*b. probably Lancashire, England, ca. 1600; d. Block Island, R.I., 1636*), colonist, trader. Came to America, 1623; resided in both Plymouth and Massachusetts Bay colonies. His murder by Indians near Block Island helped to start Pequot War.

OLDHAM, WILLIAM FITZJAMES (*b. Bangalore, India, 1854; d. Glendale, Calif., 1937*), Methodist clergyman. A convert to Methodism, he was licensed to preach in India, 1876. After serving as pastor and teacher in the U.S., 1890–1904, he was bishop and supervisor of missions in southern Asia, 1904–12, and in South America, 1916–28.

OLDHAM, WILLIAMSON SIMPSON (*b. Franklin Co., Tenn., 1813; d. Houston, Tex., 1868*), Arkansas legislator and jurist. Removed to Texas, 1849. Confederate senator from Texas,

1861–65. Opposed both conscription and suspension of *habeas corpus* by Confederate government on states' rights grounds.

OLDS, IRVING SANDS (*b. Erie, Pa., 1887; d. New York, N.Y., 1963*), lawyer and corporation executive. Attended Yale and Harvard Law (graduated, 1910). Joined New York law firm White and Case (1911) and became a partner in 1917. Elected to the board and finance committee of U.S. Steel (1936); chairman of the board (1940–52). He expanded the company's facilities, breaking all production records during World War II. Despite severe postwar labor strife in the steel and coal industries, production exceeded records set during the war; his negotiation of a strike settlement in 1947 with United Steel Workers set an industrywide pattern for labor negotiations. Remained a director of U.S. Steel until 1960, then served as one of three voting trustees (1960–62) of TWA stock to protect the airline from bankruptcy.

OLDS, LELAND (*b. Rochester, N.Y., 1890; d. Bethesda, Md., 1960*), economist, public official. Studied at Amherst College, Harvard, Columbia, and the Union Theological Seminary. Industrial editor, 1922–29, for the Federated Press, a news service with an assortment of clients among labor journals. An expert in the field of public utilities, Olds was head of the New York State Power Authority, 1931–39. A member of the Federal Power Commission, 1939–49, he was involved in the controversial regulation of the natural gas industry. Appointed to a third term in 1949, he failed to receive ratification in the Senate. Attacked by such figures as Lyndon Johnson for his leftist writings in the 1920's and 1930's, Olds became a victim of the "red scare" of the Cold War.

OLDS, RANSOM ELI (*b. Geneva, Ohio, 1864; d. Lansing, Mich., 1950*), inventor, automobile manufacturer. Began as bookkeeper in his father's Lansing, Mich., machine shop, 1883; became a partner, 1885. Encouraged by his successful manufacture of a small engine heated by ordinary gasoline stove burners, Olds built a three-wheel self-propelled vehicle in 1887. Increasingly interested in the internal combustion engine, Olds adopted it for another vehicle, completed in 1896. The following year he formed the Olds Motor Vehicle Company and, to supersede the family machine shop, the Olds Gasoline Machine Works. In 1899 the assets of the motor vehicle company were incorporated into a new company, the Olds Motor Works, and operations transferred to Detroit. In 1904 Olds resigned and formed the Reo Motor Car Company (a name derived from his initials) in Lansing. To ensure a nearby and steady source of parts, he organized several subsidiary firms. He played a lesser role in Reo's affairs after 1915 and gave increasing time to other ventures, including the Ideal Power Lawn Mower Company to manufacture a mower he had invented, the Capital National Bank (forerunner of the Michigan National Bank), and R. E. Olds Company, an investment firm. His most ambitious project was Oldsmar, a Florida community on Tampa Bay.

OLDS, ROBERT EDWIN (*b. Duluth, Minn., 1875; d. Paris, France, 1932*), lawyer, Red Cross official. Assistant U.S. secretary of state, 1925–27; under secretary of state, 1927–28. A loyal and self-effacing subordinate to Frank B. Kellogg.

OLDSCHOOL, OLIVER. *See* SARGENT, NATHAN.

O'LEARY, DANIEL (*b. Clonakilty, Ireland, 1846[?]; d. Los Angeles, Calif., 1933*), pedestrian. Set many records for walking; twice winner of the Astley Belt.

OLIN, STEPHEN (*b. Leicester, Vt., 1797; d. Middletown, Conn., 1851*), Methodist clergyman, educator. President of Randolph-Macon College (1834–37) and Wesleyan University (1842–51); tried to prevent denominational split over slavery in 1840's.

OLIPHANT, HERMAN (*b. near Forest, Ind., 1884; d. Washington, D.C., 1939*), lawyer. Teacher of law at University of Chicago, 1914–21; at Columbia, 1921–28; at Johns Hopkins, 1928–33. U.S. treasury department adviser, 1933–39, he was influential in shaping New Deal fiscal policies.

OLIVER, ANDREW (*b. Boston, Mass., 1706; d. Boston, 1774*), Massachusetts provincial legislator. Brother of Peter Oliver. Graduated Harvard, 1724. Married Governor Thomas Hutchinson's sister-in-law, 1734, and thereafter consistently acted with Hutchinson in colonial policies. Appointed secretary of the province, 1756, he held this position until 1771 when he was appointed lieutenant governor. He was hated by the popular or patriot party because of his appointment as stamp officer under the Stamp Act, and the revelation in 1773 of letters which Governor Hutchinson and he had earlier written to England describing unsettled conditions in the colonies and prescribing remedies. On both occasions mobs threatened him and his family and attacked his home.

OLIVER, ANDREW (*b. Boston, Mass., 1731; d. Salem, Mass., 1799*), Massachusetts legislator and jurist, scientist. Son of Andrew Oliver (1706–1774). Graduated Harvard, 1749. His most significant scientific contribution was *An Essay on Comets* (1772).

OLIVER, CHARLES AUGUSTUS (*b. Cincinnati, Ohio, 1853; d. Philadelphia, Pa., 1911*), ophthalmologist. Coauthor with William F. Norris of *A Textbook of Ophthalmology* (1893) and *System of Diseases of the Eye* (1897–1900).

OLIVER, FITCH EDWARD (*b. Cambridge, Mass., 1819; d. Boston, Mass., 1892*), physician, historian. Edited diaries of Benjamin Lynde and William Pynchon; author of other studies of Massachusetts history.

OLIVER, GEORGE TENER (*b. Co. Tyrone, Ireland, 1848; d. Pittsburgh, Pa., 1919*), steel manufacturer, lawyer. Brother of business associate of Henry W. Oliver. Publisher of *Pittsburgh Gazette Times*; steadfast proponent of protective tariff; U.S. senator, Republican from Pennsylvania, 1909–17.

OLIVER, HENRY KEMBLE (*b. Beverly, Mass., 1800; d. Salem, Mass., 1885*), teacher, musician, cotton-mill superintendent. Massachusetts state treasurer, 1860–65; organized pioneer Massachusetts Bureau of Statistics of Labor, 1869, and headed it until 1873.

OLIVER, HENRY WILLIAM (*b. Co. Tyrone, Ireland, 1840; d. Pittsburgh, Pa., 1904*), ironmaster. Brother of George T. Oliver. Came to America as a child. Helped organize a firm in Pittsburgh to manufacture nuts and bolts, 1863; it grew steadily after the Civil War and was incorporated as the Oliver Iron & Steel Co., 1888. Oliver branched out into many phases of the ferrous metal industry; his chief distinction was in early (1892) recognizing the potential of Mesabi range iron ore. Organizing a mining company and building a feeder railroad, Oliver began the ore traffic from the lake ports to Pittsburgh.

OLIVER, JAMES (*b. Liddesdale, Scotland, 1823; d. South Bend, Ind., 1908*), cooper, foundryman, inventor. Came to America as a boy. Began experimenting with chilled iron for making hard-faced plows, *ca.* 1865; obtained two patents in 1868 for mould board processes. He went on to more important inventions, one (1869) to prevent castings from cooling too rapidly, others (1871–76) which guaranteed a hard, smooth surface on the face of the mould board. His Oliver Chilled Plow Works, employing his discoveries, was by the time of his death producing 200,000 plows annually.

OLIVER, JOSEPH (*b. in or near New Orleans, La., ca. 1885; d. Savannah, Ga., 1938*), cornetist, jazz composer, orchestra leader, known as "King" Oliver. A black, Oliver pioneered in bringing New Orleans jazz to a wide audience.

OLIVER, "KING."   *See* OLIVER, JOSEPH.

OLIVER, PAUL AMBROSE (*b. aboard ship in English Channel, 1830; d. 1912*), merchant. Union soldier. Raised in Germany; returned to America, 1849. Invented blasting powder manufacturing processes; headed powder plant in Wilkes-Barre, Pa., 1868–1903.

OLIVER, PETER (*b. Boston, Mass., 1713; d. Birmingham, England, 1791*), Loyalist, Massachusetts provincial jurist, and iron manufacturer. Brother of Andrew Oliver (1706–1774). Graduated Harvard, 1730. Judge of superior court, 1756–74; chief justice, 1771–74. Departed with British army to Halifax, N.S., 1776; later settled in England with a British pension.

OLMSTEAD, ALBERT TEN EYCK (*b. Troy, N.Y., 1880; d. Chicago, Ill., 1945*), orientalist, historian of the pre-Islamic civilizations of the Near East. A.B., Cornell University, 1902; A.M., 1903; Ph.D., 1906. Taught ancient history at University of Missouri, 1909–17; professor of history and curator of the Oriental Museum, University of Illinois, 1917–29; professor of oriental history, University of Chicago, 1929–45. Author of *Assyrian Historiography* (1916), in which he established the principles of source interpretation for the royal annals of Assyria; author also, among other works, of *History of Assyria* (1923) and *History of Palestine and Syria* (1931).

OLMSTEAD, GIDEON.   *See* OLMSTED, GIDEON.

OLMSTED, DENISON (*b. near East Hartford, Conn., 1791; d. New Haven, Conn., 1859*), scientist, inventor, teacher. Graduated Yale, 1813. Held chairs of mathematics and natural philosophy at Yale, 1825–59; won fame for meteor shower investigations; was author of widely used textbooks.

OLMSTED, FREDERICK LAW (*b. Hartford, Conn., 1822; d. Waverly, Mass., 1903*), landscape architect. Son of a prosperous merchant; attended Yale; studied engineering, 1837–40. An unhappy period in a New York dry goods importing firm was followed by a year's voyage to China, 1843. He next turned to farming on Staten Island acreage given him by his father and became friendly with Andrew J. Downing. During the 1850's he turned to writing noteworthy travel studies. His *Walks and Talks of an American Farmer in England* (1852) and articles in the *Horticulturist* were followed by a commission from the *New York Times* to report on economic and social conditions in the South. His travels through the Southeast and Texas and a lengthy journey from New Orleans to Richmond were recorded first in letters to the *Times*, then in separate volumes and finally in *The Cotton Kingdom* (2 vols., 1861). This work remains a classic picture and analysis of the planter-slavery system in the *ante bellum* South. His continuing interest in landscaping led to his appointment in 1857 as superintendent of Central Park in New York City; in 1858, he became the park's chief architect. Olmsted and a young English architect, Calvert Vaux, had entered a competition to provide a new design for the park. Their plan won and the two men set out to make the first American park not only a work of art but a successful municipal enterprise. Olmsted took leave of absence, 1861, to become general secretary of the U.S. Sanitary Commission, which he organized successfully. Political opposition in New York and failing health led Olmsted to go to California, 1863; there he

superintended John C. Frémont's Mariposa estate, led the move to make Yosemite a state reservation, and made designs for the grounds of the new University of California, Berkeley. Returning to New York, he resumed work on Central Park and set up with Vaux (1865) a firm for the practice of landscape architecture. For thirty years he did a richly varied business in city parks, city planning, private estates, historical sites, and university designs. Frequent visits to Europe and a succession of talented associates helped Olmsted to gain a towering reputation. His tenacity in seeking to protect quiet, sylvan retreats to be used by busy urban residents led to much political opposition. Central Park and Brooklyn's Prospect Park were his most spectacular New York City projects, but he also made the plans for the Riverside and Morningside parks. The Boston park system with the famed Arnold Arboretum, Chicago's South Park, Detroit's Belle Isle Park, and Mount Royal Park in Montreal were other major projects. Representative of his firm's varied designs were those for the Capitol grounds at Washington, D.C., and Albany, N.Y., for Stanford University, for the suburban development at Riverside near Chicago, the Niagara Reservation, George W. Vanderbilt's vast estate "Biltmore" near Asheville, N.C., and a crowning achievement, the design of the grounds of the "White City" at the 1893 Chicago World's Fair.

OLMSTED, FREDERICK LAW (*b. Staten Island, N.Y., 1870; d. Malibu, Calif., 1957*), landscape architect, planner, conservationist. Graduated from Harvard University, B.A., 1894. The son of America's most famous landscape architect, Frederick Olmsted, Sr., young Olmsted apprenticed with his father in laying out the plans for the campus of Stanford University and working on the grounds of the Vanderbilt estate, Baltimore, in Asheville, N.C. Landscape projects of the firm of Olmsted Brothers, founded in 1895, include Fort Tryon Park, the Cloisters, and Forest Hills Gardens in New York City; and the White House grounds, Lafayette Park, Washington Monument Gardens, the Jefferson Memorial, and Washington Cathedral. Helped found the American Society of Landscape Architects and the American Institute of Planners.

OLMSTED, GIDEON (*b. East Hartford, Conn., 1749; d. East Hartford, 1845*), sea captain, privateersman. Celebrated, but only nominally successful, as commander of various privateers, 1776–95. The case of the sloop *Active* resulted from one of his captures.

OLMSTED, JOHN CHARLES (*b. Geneva, Switzerland, 1852; d. Brookline, Mass., 1920*), landscape architect. Nephew, stepson, and pupil of Frederick L. Olmsted whose work he continued; first president of the American Society of Landscape Architects.

OLMSTED, MARLIN EDGAR (*b. Potter Co., Pa., 1847; d. New York, N.Y., 1913*), corporation lawyer. Orthodox Republican congressman from Pennsylvania, 1897–1913; chairman, Committee on Insular Affairs, *post* 1909. A master of parliamentary procedure.

OLNEY, JESSE (*b. Union, Conn., 1798; d. Stratford, Conn., 1872*), teacher, elementary school textbook writer. His *Practical System of Modern Geography* (1828) and *A New and Improved School Atlas* (1829) became standard works because of the simplicity and novelty of their method.

OLNEY, RICHARD (*b. Oxford, Mass., 1835; d. 1917*), lawyer, statesman. Graduated Brown, 1856; Harvard Law School, 1858. Practiced successfully in Boston as specialist in will cases and corporation law. Appointed U.S. attorney general, 1893, he took prompt action against seizure of trains by Coxey's Army (1894). In the summer of that year he enjoined the American Railway Union and its president, Eugene V. Debs, from interfering with the U.S mails by halting railroad operations as a gesture of sympathy with the Pullman Company strikers; in 1895, he directed the argument in the U.S. Supreme Court which successfully upheld his action and declared the union officials in contempt. Thereafter, however, he urged recognition of the rights of organized labor and supported the movement which brought about the arbitration act of 1898. As U.S. secretary of state, 1895–97, Olney drafted the famous threatening declaration to Great Britain in the Venezuela boundary dispute, arguing that "the United States is practically sovereign on this continent." Successful in securing arbitration, he then sought to persuade Spain to more humane measures in Cuba but resisted pressure to recognize Cuban rebels as belligerents.

OLSEN, JOHN SIGVARD ("OLE") (*b. Peru, Ind., 1892; d. Albuquerque, N.Mex., 1963*), and **JOHNSON, HAROLD OGDEN** (*"CHIC") b. Englewood, Ill., 1891; d. Las Vegas, Nev., 1962),* comedians and partners for nearly fifty years in vaudeville, on Broadway, in movies and nightclubs, and on radio and television. Teamed up as a vaudeville act in 1914 and starred in their own review, *Monkey Business*, in 1926. They made their Broadway debut in *Take a Chance* (1933), then began one-night stands when the vaudeville circuits began to disintegrate. Their most famous show, *Hellzapoppin*, opened in New York in 1938 and was a sellout, despite unenthusiastic reviews, winning over audiences with its zany antics; it closed in 1941 after 1,400 performances. Further productions included *Sons o' Fun* (1941), *Laffing Room Only* (1944), *Pardon Our French* (1950), and *Hellzasplashin* (1959), their last appearance as a team. Began a radio career in the late 1930's and presented "Comedy News" with limited success. Signed by NBC television as a summer replacement for Milton Berle (1949). Resumed a nightclub career in 1956, but the novelty of their act was gone.

OLSON, FLOYD BJERSTJERNE (*b. Minneapolis, Minn., 1891; d. Rochester, Minn., 1936*), lawyer, Farmer-Labor leader. Governor of Minnesota, 1931–36, he was more radical in his pronouncements than in his policies as an executive.

OLYPHANT, DAVID WASHINGTON CINCINNATUS (*b. Newport, R.I., 1789; d. Cairo, Egypt, 1851*), merchant. Engaged profitably in the China trade *post* 1820; supported and directed Presbyterian mission activity in China.

OLYPHANT, ROBERT MORRISON (*b. New York, N.Y., 1824; d. New York, 1918*), merchant. Son of David W. C. Olyphant. Engaged in China trade, 1844–73. Active in affairs of the Delaware & Hudson Co., he served as its president, 1884–1903.

O'MAHONEY, JOSEPH CHRISTOPHER (*b. Chelsea, Mass., 1884; d. Bethesda, Md., 1962*), journalist and U.S. senator. Attended Columbia and Georgetown (LL.B., 1920). Reporter and editor (1907–17), then practiced law in Cheyenne, Wyo., where he became active in Democratic politics. U.S. senator (1933–52, 1954–61); major assignments were to the Appropriations, Judiciary, and Interior committees, serving as chairman of the latter (1949–52). His greatest impact was as a crusading antimonopolist; he introduced the resolution that established the Temporary National Economic Committee (chairman, 1938–41), and cosponsored the Employment Act of 1946, which established the Joint Economic Committee (chairman for three congresses) and the Council of Economic Advisers.

O'MAHONY, JOHN (*b. Co. Cork, Ireland, 1816; d. New York, N.Y., 1877*), Fenian leader. Came to America, 1853. Headed American branch, Irish Republican Brotherhood, 1858–66 and 1872–77.

O'MALLEY, FRANK WARD (*b. Pittston, Pa., 1875; d. Tours, France, 1932*), journalist, author. Outstanding reporter on *New York Sun*, 1906–20.

OÑATE, JUAN DE (*b. Mexico, ca. 1549; d. Spain, ca. 1624*), colonizer of New Mexico. Son of a wealthy Spanish official in New Spain, he early engaged in military and mining operations in northern Mexico. Receiving an official contract to explore and colonize New Mexico, he led a well-equipped expedition up the Rio Grande, 1597–98. Establishing a capital at San Juan, he promoted missionary activities, and forced Indians of the upper Rio Grande pueblos to submit. He also sent expeditions to present-day Kansas (1601) and the Gulf of California (1605). After his resignation as chief of the colony, 1607, he returned to Mexico. Convicted of having mistreated his soldiers and the Indians, 1614, he was sentenced to banishment. He returned to Spain *ante* 1624.

ONDERDONK, BENJAMIN TREDWELL (*b. New York, N.Y., 1791; d. New York, 1861*), Episcopal clergyman. Brother of Henry U. Onderdonk. Consecrated bishop of New York, 1830. Suspended from office after a celebrated ecclesiastical trial, 1845.

ONDERDONK, HENRY (*b. Manhasset, N.Y., 1804; d. 1886*), teacher, local historian. Collected and published many valuable original documents of early Long Island history, especially Revolutionary War incidents.

ONDERDONK, HENRY USTICK (*b. New York, N.Y., 1789; d. 1858*), physician, Episcopal clergyman. Brother of Benjamin T. Onderdonk. Outstanding as a theological scholar and controversialist, he was consecrated assistant bishop of Pennsylvania, 1827, and succeeded as bishop, 1836. He was suspended at his own request from office and from the ministry for alcoholism (1844–56).

O'NEAL, EDWARD ASBURY (*b. Madison Co., Ala., 1818; d. Florence, Ala., 1890*), lawyer, Confederate officer, Democratic governor of Alabama, 1882–86.

O'NEAL, EDWARD ASBURY, III (*b. Florence, Ala., 1875; d. Florence, 1958*), agricultural leader. Studied at Washington and Lee University and at the University of Illinois. President of the Alabama chapter of the American Farm Bureau Federation; national vice president, 1924–31; president, 1931–46. A New Deal supporter, O'Neal helped Roosevelt draft the Agricultural Adjustment Administration legislation. Important during the transition of American agriculture from small family farms to modern scientific conglomerates.

O'NEALE, MARGARET L. (*b. Washington, D.C., 1796; d. Washington, 1879*). Daughter of a tavern-keeper, Peggy O'Neale led a varied, colorful, and dramatic life. First married to a navy purser, she charmed President Andrew Jackson's firm friend John H. Eaton, whom she met in 1818 and married soon after her husband's death in 1828. Washington society was scandalized. Jackson stood by his friend and newly appointed secretary of war, despite the consequent dramatic rift in Jackson's cabinet which led to mass resignation, 1831. After sharing her husband's position as governor of Florida and U.S. minister to Spain, Mrs. Eaton returned with him to Washington in 1840 where she resided thereafter.

O'NEALL, JOHN BELTON (*b. Newberry District, S.C., 1793; d. near Newberry, S.C., 1863*), South Carolina jurist and legislator. Held judicial posts, 1828–63. Chief justice of the state, 1859–63; opposed nullification and secession.

O'NEILL, EUGENE (*b. New York, N.Y., 1888; d. Boston, Mass., 1953*), playwright. Studied briefly at Princeton and Harvard. His first play, *Bound East for Cardiff* (1916), produced at

Provincetown, Mass., gave birth to the Provincetown Players and launched O'Neill's career. Awarded the Pulitzer Prize for *Beyond the Horizon* (1919) and *Anna Christie* (1920). His one-act play, *The Emperor Jones* (1920), was unique at the time for providing a serious dramatic role for a black actor. Other plays of this period include *The Hairy Ape* (1921), *The Great God Brown*, which used masks and monologues, and *Desire Under the Elms* (1924), based on themes from Greek tragedy.

Received third Pulitzer Prize for *Strange Interlude* (1926–27), which ran for several hours and brought O'Neill international fame. *Mourning Becomes Electra* (1929–31), was another long play based on the Orestes legend. *Ah! Wilderness* (1932), his only comedy, starred George M. Cohan and was made into a successful motion picture.

Stricken with a nervous disorder similar to Parkinson's disease, O'Neill had great problems writing in the years between 1935 and 1943. He produced his finest works during this period: *The Iceman Cometh* (1939); *Long Day's Journey Into Night* (1941), *A Touch of the Poet* (1942), and *A Moon for the Misbegotten* (1943).

O'Neill died almost forgotten. The posthumous productions of his plays restored his reputation as perhaps America's greatest playwright. *Long Day's Journey Into Night*, finally staged on Broadway in 1956, won O'Neill his fourth Pulitzer Prize. Awarded the Nobel Prize for Literature in 1936.

O'NEILL, JAMES (*b. Kilkenny, Ireland, 1849; d. New London, Conn., 1920*), actor. Came to America as a child. Early played varied roles; *post* 1882 was identified with "Edmond Dantes" in *Monte Cristo*, which he played more than 6000 times. Father of Eugene G. O'Neill.

O'NEILL, JOHN (*b. Co. Monaghan, Ireland, 1834; d. Omaha, Nebr., 1878*), Union soldier, Fenian leader. Immigrated to America as a youth. Attacked Canada three separate times (1866–71) with small forces which were easily repulsed.

O'NEILL, MARGARET L. *See* O'NEALE, MARGARET.

O'NEILL, ROSE CECIL (*b. Wilkes-Barre, Pa., 1874; d. Springfield, Mo., 1944*), illustrator, author. Creator of the Kewpie doll (patented March, 1913), which was based on her sketches in the *Ladies' Home Journal* and other magazines.

OPDYKE, GEORGE (*b. Hunterdon Co., N.J., 1805; d. 1880*), clothing merchant, municipal and currency reformer. Mayor of New York City during the Draft Riots (1863).

OPPENHEIM, JAMES (*b. St. Paul, Minn., 1882; d. 1932*), poet, novelist. Raised in New York City. Author, among other books, of *Songs for the New Age* (1914) and *The Golden Bird* (1923); edited *The Seven Arts*, 1916–17.

OPPENHEIMER, JULIUS ROBERT (*b. New York, N.Y., 1904; d. Princeton, N.J., 1967*), theoretical physicist. Attended Harvard; Cavendish Laboratory in Cambridge, England; and University of Göttingen (Ph.D., 1927). Taught at University of California and California Institute of Technology (1927–41, 1946–47); director of Institute for Advanced Study (1947–66), where under his leadership Princeton became the world center of theoretical physics. Played a major role in the emergence of an American school of physics by training outstanding members of a new generation. Although he predicted the positron in a 1930 paper (it was discovered in 1932) and in 1936 explained why electron-positron pairs required a new cosmic-ray particle (the meson was found the next year), no major breakthrough bears his name. Became involved in atomic bomb developments in 1941; in May 1942 appointed director of the central laboratory for bomb design and development at Los Alamos, N.Mex. Exhausted and deeply troubled in the aftermath of the bombings of Hiroshima

and Nagasaki, he resigned in 1945. Drafted a proposal (1946) for the U.S. State Department for the international control of atomic energy, which provided the tone and substance of the Acheson-Lilienthal plan. Served on numerous committees, most importantly the Atomic Energy Commission's General Advisory Committee, of which he was chairman. In late 1953 his security clearance was suspended; rather than accept the implication of disloyalty, he appeared before a secret appeals board in 1954, but despite testimony on his behalf from distinguished scientists and public servants, the board recommended against continuation of his clearance. Received the Enrico Fermi Award for outstanding contributions to atomic energy (1963).

OPPER, FREDERICK BURR (*b. Madison, Ohio, 1857; d. New Rochelle, N.Y., 1937*), pioneer comic strip artist. Creator of "Happy Hooligan" (1899), "Alphonse and Gaston," "Maude the Mule," and others; drew political cartoons for the Hearst newspapers.

OPTIC, OLIVER. *See* ADAMS, WILLIAM TAYLOR.

ORCUTT, HIRAM (*b. Acworth, N.H., 1815; d. Boston, Mass., 1899*), educator. Graduated Dartmouth, 1842. Won reputation as principal of Thetford (Vt.) Academy, 1843–55; thereafter headed a succession of New England academies; associate editor, *New England Journal of Education*.

ORD, EDWARD OTHO CRESAP (*b. Cumberland, Md., 1818; d. Havana, Cuba, 1883*), soldier. Graduated West Point, 1839. Served against Seminole Indians, also in California and Oregon. Appointed brigadier general of volunteers, Union army, 1861, he was promoted major general, 1862, after good service in Virginia. Assigned to the Army of the Tennessee, he distinguished himself at Iuka and Corinth; during the Vicksburg campaign, he commanded the XIII Corps. He directed the campaign against Staunton, Va., 1864, in association with General George Crook, and later headed the VIII and XVIII Corps in the operations before Richmond. In January 1865, he took command of the Army of the James. He retired as regular major general, 1880.

ORD, GEORGE (*b. probably Philadelphia, Pa., 1781; d. Philadelphia, 1866*), naturalist, philologist. Friend and associate of Alexander Wilson; completed Wilson's *American Ornithology* (volumes 8 and 9) and reissued the work, augmented, in 1824–25. Loyalty to Wilson caused attacks by Ord upon J. J. Audubon and the famous "Audubon-Wilson" controversy which began after Wilson's death. Ord accompanied Thomas Say and William Maclure on an extensive field trip through Georgia and Florida, 1818. He was a proud, reserved man of profound learning.

ORDRONAUX, JOHN (*b. New York, N.Y., 1830; d. Glen Head, N.Y., 1908*), lawyer, physician, teacher. First New York State commissioner in lunacy, 1874–82; specialist in medical jurisprudence.

ORDWAY, JOHN (*b. Bow, N.H., ca. 1775; d. probably Missouri, ca. 1817*), explorer, sergeant in Lewis and Clark Expedition. His important journal was first published in *Wisconsin Historical Collections* (Vol. 22, 1916).

O'REILLY, ALEXANDER (*b. Co. Meath, Ireland, 1722; d. Bonete, Spain, 1794*), Spanish lieutenant general. Joined Spanish army at age of ten. A leader in army reform and reorganization, he successfully put down the 1768 uprising against Ulloa, first Spanish governor of Louisiana, and swiftly integrated the colony into the Spanish colonial system. His regulations for administration of Louisiana were in effect until the end of Spanish rule.

O'REILLY, HENRY (*b. Carrickmacross, Ireland, 1806; d. 1886*), editor, pioneer telegraph line builder. Came to New York,

N.Y., as a boy. Became editor of the *Rochester* (N.Y.) *Daily Advertiser*, 1826, and was a leading citizen of that city. Agitated for enlargement and rebuilding of the Erie Canal; remained a leading exponent of the canal against railroad interests up to the Civil War. Entering into contract, 1845, with Amos Kendall and S. F. B. Morse for financing and construction of telegraph from Pennsylvania to St. Louis and the Great Lakes, he erected 8000 miles of line. Resulting litigation and money difficulties led him to abandon the enterprise.

O'REILLY, JOHN BOYLE (*b. near Drogheda, Ireland, 1844; d. Hull, Mass., 1890*), poet, editor. Came to America, 1869, after an adventurous career as an Irish rebel and consequent deportation to Australia. Became part owner and editor of the Boston *Pilot*, 1876. Author of *Songs, Legends and Ballads* (1878), *Moondyne* (1879), and other books.

O'REILLY, ROBERT MAITLAND (*b. Philadelphia, Pa., 1845; d. Washington, D.C., 1912*), surgeon general, U.S. Army, 1902–09. Personal physician to President Cleveland. Reformed medical corps practices after Spanish-American War and recommendations of Dodge Commission.

O'RIELLY, HENRY. *See* O'REILLY, HENRY.

ORMSBY, WATERMAN LILLY (*b. Hampton, Conn., 1809; d. Brooklyn, N.Y., 1883*), banknote engraver.

ORNE, JOHN (*b. Newburyport, Mass., 1834; d. Cambridge, Mass., 1911*), Orientalist, teacher. Graduated Amherst, 1855. Curator of Arabic manuscripts, Semitic Museum of Harvard University, 1889–1911.

ORR, ALEXANDER ECTOR (*b. Strabane, Ireland, 1831; d. 1914*), grain merchant. Came to New York, N.Y., 1851. Active in many civic and business organizations, Orr served as president, Rapid Transit Commission of New York City, 1894–1907. The first subways were efficiently built under his strict supervision. He reorganized the New York Life Insurance Co. after the Hughes Investigation, 1905.

ORR, GUSTAVUS JOHN (*b. Orrville, S.C., 1819 d. 1887*), educator. Graduated Emory, 1844. Reforming pioneer school commissioner of Georgia, 1872–87; agent for Peabody Fund in Georgia.

ORR, HUGH (*b. Lochwinnoch, Scotland, 1715; d. 1798*), toolmaker, Revolutionary patriot, manufacturer. Came to Massachusetts, 1740; settled in East Bridgewater and prospered as maker of edged tools. Produced first musket made in the colonies, 1748; during the Revolution, made great numbers of muskets and cannon, using advanced techniques, and produced quantities of cannon shot. Under state direction and encouragement, Orr induced English mechanics skilled in textile machine manufacture to immigrate to Massachusetts, but the sample machines produced by them in his shop (*ca.* 1786–87) were not practical.

ORR, JAMES LAWRENCE (*b. Craytonville, S.C., 1822; d. St. Petersburg, Russia, 1873*), lawyer, South Carolina legislator. Brother of Jehu A. Orr. Congressman, Democrat, from South Carolina, 1849–59; speaker of the House, 1857–59. Antisecessionist and supporter of Stephen A. Douglas's policies, Orr reversed himself in 1860, advocated secession, and served as a Confederate States senator, 1861–65. Espousing President Johnson's policies, he was elected governor of South Carolina and served 1866–68, advising the whites to accept the Reconstruction acts. Losing the confidence of the people, he joined the Radical party, 1868, and was elected to the circuit bench. He supported U.S. Grant in 1872, and was appointed U.S. minister to Russia after Grant's election.

ORR, JEHU AMAZIAH (*b. Anderson Co., S.C., 1828; d. Columbus, Miss., 1921*), Mississippi legislator, lawyer. Brother of James L. Orr. Moderate Democrat in Mississippi politics before and after Civil War.

ORRY-KELLY (*b. Orry George Kelly, Kiama, Australia, 1897; d. Hollywood, Calif., 1964*), costume designer. Designed sets and costume for the theater in the 1920's, including costumes for Ethel Barrymore and Katherine Hepburn. Hired by Warner Brothers as a costume designer; his first picture, *The Rich Are Always with Us* (1932), featured Bette Davis, and he continued to design for her for more than a decade. Other actresses he designed for were Ingrid Bergman (*Casablanca*, 1942), Rosalind Russell (*Auntie Mame*, 1958), and Marilyn Monroe (*Some Like It Hot*, 1959). He won Academy Awards for his costumes for *Les Girls* (1957) and *Some Like It Hot*, and shared the award for *An American in Paris*.

ORTH, GODLOVE STEIN (*b. near Lebanon, Pa., 1817; d. Lafayette, Ind., 1882*), politician, lawyer. Pursued long career in Indiana as Whig, Know-Nothing, and Republican legislator and congressman. U.S. minister to Austria-Hungary, 1875–76. Orth never hesitated to sacrifice principle for party solidarity; no unpopular measure ever received his vote.

ORTHWEIN, CHARLES F. (*b. near Stuttgart, Germany, 1839; d. St. Louis, Mo., 1898*), grain merchant. Immigrated to America, 1854; began grain commission business in St. Louis during Civil War. Sent first grain shipment to Europe via Mississippi River, 1866; worked generally to encourage St. Louis export trade.

ORTON, EDWARD FRANCIS BAXTER (*b. Deposit, N.Y., 1829; d. Columbus, Ohio, 1899*), geologist, educator. State geologist of Ohio, 1882–99; brought out last three volumes of state geological survey begun by John S. Newberry. Opposed reckless waste of natural gas and advocated conservation of state resources.

ORTON, HARLOW SOUTH (*b. Madison Co., N.Y., 1817; d. Madison, Wis., 1895*), lawyer, Wisconsin jurist and legislator. Dean of University of Wisconsin law school, 1869–74; justice of Wisconsin supreme court, 1878–94, and chief justice, 1894–95.

ORTON, HELEN FULLER (*b. near Pekin, N.Y., 1872; d. Queens, N.Y., 1955*), author. Orton's first book, *Prince and Rover of Cloverfield Farm* (1921), contained children's stories about farm and nature experiences. Wrote books about early American history, including *The Treasure in the Little Trunk* (1932), and mysteries for children, including *Mystery at the Little Red Schoolhouse* (1941).

ORTON, JAMES (*b. Seneca Falls, N.Y., 1830; d. Peru, 1877*), Presbyterian clergyman, zoologist, explorer, educator. Made three productive expeditions to the Amazon-equatorial Andes region (1867, 1873, and 1876); wrote *The Andes and the Amazons* (complete edition, 1876). Professor of natural history at Vassar *post* 1869.

ORTON, WILLIAM (*b. near Cuba, N.Y., 1826; d. 1878*), lawyer, telegraph executive. Instrumental in negotiations leading to creation of Western Union Telegraph Co. as a monopoly, 1866; served as its president, 1867–78.

ORTYNSKY, STEPHEN SOTER (*b. Galicia, Austria, 1866; d. Philadelphia, Pa., 1916*), Catholic prelate. Greek Catholic bishop for the United States *post* 1907; ministered to Americans of Ukrainian and Ruthenian extraction.

OSBORN, CHARLES (*b. Guilford Co., N.C., 1775; d. Porter Co., Ind., 1850*), Quaker minister, Abolitionist. Led abolition movements in Tennessee, Ohio, and Indiana; published the *Philanthropist* (Mt. Pleasant, Ohio), 1817–18.

OSBORN, CHASE SALMON (*b. Huntington County, Ind., 1860; d. Poulan, Ga., 1949*), journalist, prospector, politician. Attended Purdue University. Worked on newspapers in Lafayette, Ind.; Chicago, Ill.; and Milwaukee, Wis. Owned and edited a paper in Florence, Wis., 1883–87, at the same time prospecting for iron ore in the Menominee range. Settled in Sault Ste. Marie, Mich.; became wealthy through discovery of an iron deposit in Ontario, 1901; held half interest in the Saginaw, Mich., *Courier-Herald*, 1902–12. Early involved in Michigan politics as a Republican, he served on the state railroad commission, 1899–1903; his experience on the commission and his regard for Theodore Roosevelt made him progressive. Elected governor of Michigan, 1910, he instituted a strong program of reform, including a workmen's compensation act; in the presidential campaign of 1912 he supported Theodore Roosevelt. Pledged to a single term as governor, he did not seek reelection in 1912; he continued, however, to support liberal policies, backing Robert La Follette's candidacy in 1924 and Franklin D. Roosevelt's in 1940. He gave away much of his fortune to various institutions before his death.

OSBORN, HENRY FAIRFIELD (*b. Princeton, N.J., 1887; d. New York, N.Y., 1969*), naturalist and conservationist. Attended Princeton (B.A., 1909) and Trinity College, Cambridge. Following a career in business, from which he retired in 1935, he devoted his time and energy to his passion for animals. A trustee and member of the executive board of the New York Zoological Society from 1923, he became president of the organization in 1940. Under his direction the Bronx Zoo and the New York Aquarium developed new facilities for animals and promoted better opportunities for public education and scientific research. His work in conservation made his reputation; he warned of a depletion of forests, soils, and water resources that would threaten human existence and developed that argument in *Our Plundered Planet* (1948) and *The Limits of the Earth* (1953).

OSBORN, HENRY FAIRFIELD (*b. Fairfield, Conn., 1857; d. Garrison, N.Y., 1935*), paleontologist. Son of William H. Osborn. Graduated Princeton, 1877; made special studies in biological sciences at several New York City medical schools and also at Cambridge and London, England. Taught natural sciences at Princeton, 1881–91; organized department of biology at Columbia, 1891, and taught there until *ca.* 1907. Also in 1891, Osborn organized a department of mammalian paleontology for the American Museum of Natural History, New York. His connection with the museum continued for 45 years; he served as its president, 1908–33. During his association with it, the museum became a world leader, its collection of fossil vertebrates became second to none, and its displays, made under his direction, were effective in providing direct and interesting instruction for laymen. A prolific writer of papers and books, he popularized paleontology; among his more influential books were *The Age of Mammals* (1910) and *Men of the Old Stone Age* (1925). An evolutionary theorist, he originated a number of descriptive principles (such as that of "adaptive radiation") which were of value.

OSBORN, HENRY STAFFORD (*b. Philadelphia, Pa., 1823; d. Oxford, Ohio, 1894*), Presbyterian clergyman, mapmaker, metallurgist. Taught at Lafayette College and Miami University. Author, among other books, of *New Descriptive Geography of Palestine* (1877) and *Metallurgy, Iron and Steel* (1869).

OSBORN, LAUGHTON (*b. New York, N.Y., ca. 1809; d. New York, 1878*), poet, dramatist. Graduated Columbia, 1827. Prolific writer of limited talents and eccentric habits; spent much time attacking critics. Among his books were *The Vision of Rubeta* (1838) and *Arthur Carryl* (1841).

OSBORN, NORRIS GALPIN (*b. New Haven, Conn., 1858; d. New Haven, 1932*), editor, civil service and prison reformer. Influential editor of the *New Haven Evening Register* (1884–1907) and *New Haven Journal-Courier* (1907–32).

OSBORN, SELLECK (*b. Trumbull, Conn., ca. 1782; d. Philadelphia, Pa., 1826*), Democratic journalist, poet. Editor of *The Witness* (Litchfield, Conn.,) 1805–08; the *American Watchman* (Wilmington, Del.,) 1817–20; the *New York Patriot*, 1823–24. A collection of his poems was published in Boston, Mass., 1823.

OSBORN, THOMAS ANDREW (*b. Meadville, Pa., 1836; d. Meadville, 1898*), lawyer, businessman, Kansas legislator. Settled in Kansas, 1857. Republican governor of Kansas, 1873–77; U.S. minister to Chile and Brazil, 1877–85.

OSBORN, THOMAS OGDEN (*b. Jersey, Ohio, 1832; d. Washington, D.C., 1904*), Chicago lawyer, Union soldier. U.S. minister to Argentine Republic, 1874–85; helped adjust Patagonian boundary dispute with Chile (1881). Promoted South American railroads.

OSBORN, WILLIAM HENRY (*b. Salem, Mass., 1820; d. New York, N.Y., 1894*), merchant, railroad promoter and president, philanthropist. Controlled Illinois Central Railroad, 1855–82.

OSBORNE, JAMES WALKER (*b. Charlotte, N.C., 1859; d. New York, N.Y., 1919*), lawyer, reformer. Admitted to New York bar, 1885; was outstanding assistant district attorney, 1891–1902. Exposed seamy social and political conditions in Albany, N.Y., 1911; investigated abuses at Sing Sing prison, 1913.

OSBORNE, THOMAS BURR (*b. New Haven, Conn., 1859; d. New Haven, 1929*), biochemist. Grandson of Eli W. Blake. Graduated Yale, 1881; Ph.D., 1885. Staff member, Connecticut Agricultural Station, 1886–1928. Foremost expert on the proteins of plants. His first work was on proteins of the oat-kernel (1891), followed in the next decade by descriptions of the proteins in 32 other seeds. In 1906 he began a series of hydrolytic decompositions of purified proteins that led *post* 1909 to studies of their nutritive properties. He isolated and demonstrated dietary value of substance since known as vitamin A; later did similar work with what became known as vitamin B. His monograph *The Vegetable Proteins* (1909, extensively revised 1924) remains a biochemical classic.

OSBORNE, THOMAS MOTT (*b. Auburn, N.Y., 1859; d. Auburn, 1926*), prison reformer. Graduated Harvard, 1884; worked in, and later headed, father's prosperous agricultural machinery factory. Appointed chairman of the New York commission for prison reform, 1913, he began his tenure by "serving" a week's term in the Auburn prison, later recorded in his *Within Prison Walls* (1914). He pioneered in introducing a sense of corporate responsibility among prisoners with the Mutual Welfare League plan; he also founded the Welfare League Association (an aid society for discharged prisoners) and the National Society of Penal Information, which merged in the Osborne Association. He served as warden of Sing Sing, 1914–16, and as commandant of Portsmouth Naval Prison, 1917–20.

OSCEOLA (*b. among the Creek Indians on Tallapoosa River, Ga., ca. 1800; d. Charleston S.C., 1838*), leader in the Second Seminole War. Although not born to high rank or elected a chief, Osceola (also known as Powell) became influential among the Seminole and opposed the treaty of Payne's Landing (1832), at which some Seminole chiefs agreed to removal across the Mississippi. Vigorously rejecting all efforts to make the Seminole move from their land in 1835, he precipitated war, hiding Seminole women and children in the swamps and commencing effective harassing tactics against the U.S. forces sent to put down the uprising. Under a flag of truce, Osceola was treacherously arrested, October 1837, and imprisoned in Fort Moultrie where he died.

OSGOOD, FRANCES SARGENT LOCKE (*b. Boston, Mass., 1811; d. New York, N.Y., 1850*), poet. Prolific author of rather thin poetry; remembered mainly for love affair with Edgar Allan Poe, 1845.

OSGOOD, GEORGE LAURIE (*b. Chelsea, Mass., 1844; d. Godalming, England, 1922*), singer, composer, conductor, teacher. A leader in Boston musical life; organized and conducted Boston Singers' Society, 1890; author of a *Guide in the Art of Singing* (1874).

OSGOOD, HERBERT LEVI (*b. Canton, Maine, 1855; d. 1918*), historian. Graduated Amherst, 1877; studied also at Yale and Berlin; Ph.D., Columbia, 1889. Taught at Columbia *post* 1890. His seven-volume study of American colonial history (1904–24) was a pioneer scientific documentation of the struggle between British executive authorities and the colonial assemblies.

OSGOOD, HOWARD (*b. Plaquemines Parish, La., 1831; d. Rochester, N.Y., 1911*), Baptist clergyman, author. Learned, orthodox professor of Old Testament interpretation at Rochester Theological Seminary, 1875–1901.

OSGOOD, JACOB (*b. South Hampton, N.H., 1777; d. 1844*), founder of the Osgoodites. Opposed paid ministers, law courts, magistrates, abolitionists, and military training. Love of God and neighbor was the only theological principle accepted by Osgood and his sect.

OSGOOD, SAMUEL (*b. Andover, Mass., 1747/48; d. New York, N.Y., 1813*), Revolutionary soldier, Massachusetts and New York legislator. Able member of finance committees in Continental Congress, 1781–84; opposed Constitution as leading to excessive consolidation. First U.S. postmaster general, 1789–91; supported Jefferson *post* 1800.

OSGOOD, WILLIAM FOGG (*b. Boston, Mass., 1864; d. Belmont, Mass., 1943*), mathematician. A.B., Harvard, 1886; A.M., 1887. Studied at the University of Göttingen with Felix Klein; Ph.D., Erlangen, 1890. Joined department of mathematics at Harvard, 1890, where he remained until retirement in 1933 (professor *post* 1903); taught at National University of Peking, China, for two years after leaving Harvard. Devoted much of his research to the theory of functions; was author, among other works, of *Lehrbuch der Funktionentheorie* (Vol. 1, 1906–07; Vol 2, 1924–32).

O'SHAUGHNESSY, MICHAEL MAURICE (*b. Limerick, Ireland, 1864; d. San Francisco, Calif., 1934*), hydraulic engineer. Graduated Royal University, Dublin, 1884; immigrated to California, 1885. The most important of his many undertakings was the construction of the Hetch Hetchy water supply system, 1912–34.

O'SHAUGHNESSY, NELSON JARVIS WATERBURY (*b. New York, N.Y., 1876; d. Vienna, Austria, 1932*), diplomat. Entered U.S. diplomatic service, 1904. Made second secretary of the U.S. Embassy at Mexico City, 1911, he acted as chargé d'affaires, July 1913–April 1914, during the crisis of that period. He was later a severe critic of President Wilson's policy with respect to Huerta.

O'SHEA, MICHAEL VINCENT (*b. LeRoy, N.Y., 1866; d. Madison, Wis., 1932*), educator, author. Professor of education, University of Wisconsin, *post* 1897. Popular lecturer on educational techniques and practices; wrote *Newer Ways with Children* (1929).

OSLER, WILLIAM (*b. Bond Head, Upper Canada, 1849; d. Oxford, England, 1919*), physician. At the time of his death Osler was probably the greatest figure in the medical world. After attending grammar schools in Dundas and Barie, Ontario, he entered Trinity College School at Weston with the intention of becoming a minister. Influenced by teachers there, he decided to become a physician and entered the Toronto Medical School, 1868. After two years he went on to McGill Medical School where he graduated, 1872. At McGill he was particularly influenced by Dr. Robert Howard, a scholarly and thorough teacher by Edinburgh School methods. Osler next spent two years visiting the great clinics in England, Berlin, and Vienna; he gave much time to study of histology, physiology, and experimental pathology at University College Hospital, London. There he observed in circulating blood, before anyone else, the presence of what were later called "blood-platelets." In 1875 he was appointed professor of medicine at McGill. He took a wide interest in all medical activities in Montreal, writing for medical journals, delivering inspiring addresses, and enlivening interest in medical associations. He organized a demonstration course in pathology at the Montreal General Hospital, modeled on methods he had observed in Berlin. His continuing interest in clinical medicine while at Montreal led to a revolution in technique; patients were given little medicine but much encouragement and interest. A sharp rise in recoveries attended this method. By 1884 Osler had come to recognize the possibilities of medical school work on a university basis where teachers would be largely released from the harassment of practice. This recognition led him to leave Montreal and accept appointment as professor of clinical medicine in the University of Pennsylvania (1884), the beginning of a 21-year period of residence and work in the United States.

In Philadelphia, Osler's rare traits of personality together with thorough professional methods made him popular as teacher, clinician, and consultant. His many contributions to medical literature included *The Gulstonian Lectures on Malignant Endocarditis* (1885), and the Cartwright Lectures, *On Certain Problems of the Blood Corpuscles* (1886). In September 1888, Osler was appointed physician-in-chief to the new Johns Hopkins Hospital, Baltimore, and there he remained for 16 years, probably the most eventful and most influential period of his life. For the first four years Osler devoted much of his time to organizing the clinical staff and to the institutional work of the Johns Hopkins Medical School which opened in 1893. Organized upon the unit system with a graded resident staff as used in German universities, the school employed teaching methods which accorded with those in Great Britain and France. The teaching program included instruction of small groups of students who served in the wards as clinical clerks and surgical dressers, practical work in clinical laboratories, amphitheater clinics, and work in the outpatient clinics. Osler did everything he could to arouse in his students a love of thoroughness and orderliness, an appreciation of medical knowledge for its own sake, and a desire to make original contributions of their own. Through his pupils he may be said to have created an American school of internal medicine. In 1891 he published his classic *Principles and Practice of Medicine*. Although his main contribution in the Johns Hopkins period lay in his stimulation and insemination of the minds of others, Osler also did important research into typhoid fever, malaria, pneumonia, cardiovascular disease, and tuberculosis. Further, he found time to be an active propagandist in the field of public health, to make Johns Hopkins Hospital a place of refuge for the sick poor of Baltimore, to build up medical libraries there, and to deliver effective occasional addresses of lasting value, such as *Aequanimitas* (1889), which remains a powerful and affecting work, *The Master Word in Medicine* (1903), and *The Student Life* (1905).

Because he was slowly being overwhelmed by patients who came from near and far to seek his aid, and for reasons of health, Osler accepted the Regius Professorship of Medicine in the University of Oxford, 1905; he held it until his death. He became a curator of the Bodleian Library, helped develop the Oxford Medical School, and took an active part in setting up the Royal Society of Medicine and launching the *Quarterly Journal of Medicine.* Although Osler was a competent and productive investigator and researcher, most of his contemporaries placed highest emphasis upon his ability to inspire others, to lend friendly counsel, and to mediate disputes in the profession.

OSSOLI, MARGARET FULLER.   *See* FULLER, SARAH MARGARET.

OSTENACO.   *See* OUTACITY.

OSTEN SACKEN, CARL ROBERT ROMANOVICH VON DER   (*b. St. Petersburg, Russia, 1828; d. Heidelberg, Germany, 1906*), entomologist, diplomat. Came to America, 1856, as secretary to Russian legation; was consul general in New York City, 1862–71. Wrote a critical catalogue for the Smithsonian Institution of described diptera in North America (1858 and 1878); was coauthor of *Monographs of the Diptera of North America* (1862–73).

OSTERHAUS, PETER JOSEPH   (*b. Coblenz, Germany, 1823; d. Duisburg, Germany, 1917*), Union major general, U.S. consular official.

OSTERHOUT, WINTHROP JOHN VANLEUVEN   (*b. Brooklyn, N.Y., 1871; d. New York, N.Y., 1964*), physiologist. Attended Brown, Bonn, and University of California at Berkeley (Ph.D., 1899). His interest in biology led to his discovery that plants require sodium and the study of osmotic pressure of cells. Taught at Berkeley, Harvard (1909–29), and Rockefeller Institute. His *Experiments with Plants* (1905) is an excellent textbook. Cofounded the *Journal General of Physiology* (1928) and was editor for forty-five years. Elected to National Academy of Sciences (1919).

OSTROMISLENSKY, IWAN IWANOWICH   (*b. Moscow, Russia, 1880; d. New York, N.Y., 1939*), chemist. Came to America, 1922. Pioneer in development of polystyrene and synthetic rubber.

O'SULLIVAN, JOHN LOUIS   (*b. Gibraltar, 1813; d. New York, N.Y., 1895*), lawyer, journalist, diplomat. Helped found, and edited, *United States Magazine and Democratic Review* (1837–46), a leading Democratic and nationalist organ. Probably coined term "Manifest Destiny" (1845).

O'SULLIVAN, MARY KENNEY   (*b. Hannibal, Mo., 1864; d. West Medford, Mass., 1943*), labor organizer, reformer. Working as a bookbinder and bindery forewoman in Keokuk, Iowa, and Chicago, Ill., she was appalled by urban poverty and squalor and after organizing the Chicago Women's Bindery Workers' Union became a leader in the Chicago Trades and Labor Assembly. In 1892 she was appointed a national organizer by the American Federation of Labor, the first woman to hold such a post. After marriage to John F. O'Sullivan, labor editor of the *Boston Globe*, 1894, she continued to speak and organize; with William E. Walling she drafted the essential structure of the National Women's Trade Union League (1903), becoming its first secretary. Active in support of the Lawrence, Mass., textile workers' strike in 1912, she served as a factory inspector for the industrial safety division of the Massachusetts department of labor,

1914–34. A proponent of woman suffrage, international peace, and liberal politics, she never lost her commitment to reform.

OSWALD, LEE HARVEY   (*b. New Orleans, La., 1939; d. Dallas, Tex., 1963*), assassin of President John F. Kennedy. An unstable, violence-prone malcontent, he went to Moscow in 1959, where he renounced his U.S. citizenship and worked as a metalworker. He went to Texas in 1962 and in early 1963 purchased a rifle by mail, equipping it with a telescopic sight. He took a job at the Texas School Book Depository in Dallas, and on Nov. 22, from a window on the sixth floor of the depository, shot and killed Kennedy and wounded Gov. John B. Connally; less than an hour later, he shot and killed Patrolman J. D. Tippit, then was apprehended by police in the Texas Theater. On Nov. 24, as he was being transferred from city jail to county jail, he was shot and killed by Dallas nightclub operator Jack Ruby.

OTACITE.   *See* OUTACITY.

OTERMÍN, ANTONIO DE   (*fl. 1678–1683*), Spanish governor of New Mexico. Leader of settlers in retreat from Santa Fe to present Juárez (opposite El Paso, Texas) after Pueblo Indian uprising and massacre, 1680.

OTEY, JAMES HERVEY   (*b. Bedford Co., Va., 1800; d. Memphis, Tenn., 1863*), Episcopal clergyman. Consecrated bishop of Tennessee, 1834; served until his death. Helped found University of the South.

OTIS, ARTHUR SINTON   (*b. Denver, Colo., 1886; d. St. Petersburg, Fla., 1964*), psychologist. Attended Stanford (Ph.D., 1920). While working toward his doctorate, he helped devise the psychological tests used during World War I. In 1921 he became editor of tests and mathematics at World Book Company. His reputation rests on the development, publication, administration, and revision of various forms of the Otis Group Intelligence Scale, a test used in U.S. schoolbooks until 1963. During World War II he was a psychological consultant to the Navy Bureau of Aeronautics and then for the Civil Aeronautics Administration (1945–48).

OTIS, BASS   (*b. Bridgewater, Mass., 1784; d. Philadelphia, Pa., 1861*), portrait painter, engraver, pioneer in American lithography.

OTIS, CHARLES EUGENE   (*b. Barry Co., Mich., 1846; d. St. Paul, Minn., 1917*), Minnesota jurist.

OTIS, CHARLES ROLLIN   (*b. Troy, N.Y., 1835; d. Summerville, S.C., 1927*), inventor, elevator manufacturer. Son of Elisha G. Otis.

OTIS, ELISHA GRAVES   (*b. Halifax, Vt., 1811; d. Yonkers, N.Y., 1861*), mechanic, inventor. Engaged in constructing a bedstead factory at Yonkers, N.Y. 1852, Otis devised some unique features for an elevator in the structure, among them a safety appliance that prevented the elevator from falling if the lifting chain or cable broke. His invention attracted notice and he began a small manufactory at Yonkers. Orders came slowly, but in 1861 he established a firm foundation for his business by inventing and patenting a steam elevator; his sons carried on his work with great success.

OTIS, ELWELL STEPHEN   (*b. Frederick, Md., 1838; d. Rochester, N.Y., 1909*), lawyer, Union soldier. Established command school at Fort Leavenworth, 1881; commanded all American forces in Philippines at outbreak of Aguinaldo's insurrection, 1899; retired as major general, 1902.

OTIS, FESSENDEN NOTT   (*b. Ballston Springs, N.Y., 1825; d. New Orleans, La., 1900*), physician. Graduated N.Y. Medical College, 1852; taught at N.Y. College of Physicians and Surgeons, 1862–90. Concentrated on genitourinary diseases; first established curability of urethral stricture though his theory of cure is no longer accepted.

OTIS, GEORGE ALEXANDER (*b. Boston, Mass., 1830; d. Washington, D.C., 1881*), U.S. Army surgeon. Editor, *The Medical and Surgical History of the War of the Rebellion* (surgical volumes, 1870, 1876).

OTIS, HARRISON GRAY (*b. Boston, Mass., 1765; d. Boston, 1848*), lawyer, statesman. Nephew of James Otis and Mercy Otis Warren. Graduated Harvard, 1783; read law with John Lowell. Rose to leading place at the Boston bar and earned a large income, partly by successful land speculations in the decade 1785–95. Early became a leading Federalist politician through skill in oratory, and served in U.S. Congress, 1797–1801; supported President Adams in reconciliation with France, 1799. Represented Boston for many years in the Massachusetts legislature; helped plan, and was a leading figure at, the Hartford Convention in which he consistently threw his influence against proposals to force a break with the national government. U.S. senator from Massachusetts, 1817–22; mayor Boston, 1829–31. Deprecated the abolition movement but defended freedom of speech on the slavery question. A Whig in later life.

OTIS, HARRISON GRAY (*b. Marietta, Ohio, 1837; d. Hollywood, Calif., 1917*), Union soldier, journalist. Removed to California, 1876; active manager of the Times-Mirror Co. in Los Angeles, *post* 1886. A conservative Republican, of great influence in Southern California.

OTIS, JAMES (*b. West Barnstable, Mass., 1725; d. Andover, Mass., 1783*), politician, publicist. Born of a lawyer father, Otis prepared for Harvard with the minister in West Barnstable and graduated in 1743. Studying law under Jeremiah Gridley, he was admitted to the bar in Plymouth County, 1748, and two years later moved to Boson. He married Ruth Cunningham, well-dowered daughter of a Boston merchant, 1755. By painstaking study Otis became learned in the common, civil, and admiralty law and legal theory. A supple mind coupled with brilliant and captivating pleading made him early known in all parts of the province. This reputation led to his appointment by Governor Pownall as king's advocate general of the vice admiralty court at Boston, a lucrative post. In 1760, Pitt ordered the Sugar Act of 1733 to be strictly enforced. The royal customs collectors applied to the superior court of the province for writs of assistance in order to help them in searches for evidence of violation. Otis, in his official capacity, was expected to argue for the writs. Instead he resigned and undertook, for the Boston merchants, to oppose issuance. Circumstances were such as to cause his motives to be questioned. At this time, Otis's father was speaker of the House and had great influence among country members. When Chief Justice Stephen Sewall died in 1760, the elder Otis expected to be appointed to the court with the prospect of becoming chief justice. His ambition was thwarted, however, when Thomas Hutchinson was appointed to the chief justiceship. Since this occurred just before James Otis resigned his post and began to oppose issuance of the writs of assistance, many suggested that his actions stemmed from his father's disappointment. Otis vehemently denied the charge, but the Loyalists ever afterwards insisted that Otis's entire political course was determined by frustrated family ambition.

In February 1761, Otis argued the illegality of writs of assistance before the superior court. What he said is not precisely known, but his general line of attack was based upon the presumed existence of a fundamental law which embodied the principles of the natural law and was superior to acts of Parliament. The slogan "Taxation without representation is tyranny" appears in John Adams's 1820 expansion of his notes of the proceedings. Otis claimed that acts

against the Constitution and national equity should be declared void. He lost the case but Attorney General de Grey ruled in 1766 that the act of Parliament in question did not authorize writs of assistance in the colonies. Otis's speech, however, provided the base for continuing attacks upon acts of Parliament which regulated colonial commerce and taxation. Soon after his speech, Otis was elected one of Boston's representatives to the General Court where he helped to rouse sentiment against the Crown officials. In his first political pamphlet, A *Vindication of the Conduct of the House of Representatives* (1762), Otis summarized the rights of Englishmen. Later, in a notable speech in Faneuil Hall, he declaimed at length on the proposition that settlers in the colonies should enjoy all the rights, privileges, and duties of Englishmen living in the mother country and asserted that the difficulties of the time had been caused by illegal attempts to extend the royal prerogative.

From 1761 to 1769 Otis was the recognized political leader of Massachusetts Bay. Rumors of *rapprochement* with Governor Hutchinson often affected his standing with the popular party, but his speeches and pamphlets in these years indicate a consistent defense of the colonists' rights as against alleged royal and Parliamentary encroachments. His pamphlet *The Rights of the British Colonies Asserted and Proved* (1764) reasserted his position on natural rights as developed in the writs of assistance speech and defined the constitutional position of the colonies in the single commonwealth which he believed the British Empire to be.

One of three Massachusetts delegates to the Stamp Act Congress convened in New York City (1765), he was a leading figure there. The Congress accepted his constitutional position but rejected his argument in the *Rights* pamphlet that the colonies should have representation in Parliament. Otis, however, continued to urge his idea in another pamphlet, *Considerations on behalf of the Colonists, in a Letter to a Noble Lord* (1765). Otis's pamphlets had a profound effect in the colonies and in England, but he failed to see the possibility of a federal solution to the problem and never faced the choice between submission and revolution. He disapproved of violent action, recommending peaceful remonstrances. In 1768 Otis helped to adopt the Nonimportation declaration in the House as the colonial response to the Townshend Act. Struck on the head during an altercation with a Crown official, 1769, he was insane save for short intervals thereafter. His subsequent political opinions and actions are unimportant. He died as the result of a stroke of lightning.

OTT, ISAAC (*b. Northamptonn Co., Pa., 1847; d. Easton, Pa., 1916*), physician, neurologist. Credited with discovery of the hormone of milk secretion; demonstrated that injury in the corpus striatum causes body temperature rise.

OTT, MELVIN THOMAS ("MEL") (*b. Gretna, La., 1909; d. New Orleans, La., 1958*), baseball player. Right fielder and legendary batter for the New York Giants, 1926–47. Ott's lifetime average was .304; he hit 511 home runs, exceeded only by Babe Ruth and Jimmy Foxx. Manager of the Giants, 1941–48. Ott left baseball in 1955 but returned as broadcaster for the Detroit Tigers. Elected to the Baseball Hall of Fame, 1951.

OTTASSITE. *See* OUTACITY.

OTTENDORFER, ANNA BEHR UHL (*b. Würzburg, Germany, 1815; d. 1884*), journalist, philanthropist. Came to America *ca.* 1837; married Oswald Ottendorfer, 1859. Owner and manager *post* 1852 of the *New-Yorker Staats-Zeitung*, which she made prosperous and influential.

OTTENDORFER, OSWALD (*b. Zwittau [Moravia], Austria-Hungary, 1826; d. 1900*), journalist, philanthropist. Came to America, 1850; married Anna B. U. Ottendorfer, 1859. Editor of the *New-Yorker Staats-Zeitung*, *post* 1858; influential anti-Tammany Democrat and reformer.

OTTERBEIN, PHILIP WILLIAM (*b. Dillenburg, Prussia, 1726; d. Baltimore, Md., 1813*), clergyman. Educated for Reformed ministry in Germany; arrived in New York, 1752, to serve as missionary in Pennsylvania. Although he always considered himself a minister of the Reformed Church, he promoted a nonsectarian religious movement, which shortly before his death he made an independent denomination, the Church of the United Brethren in Christ. It was organized on the Wesleyan model with a strong evangelistic strain. Otterbein, a zealous and effective minister, labored to bring organized religion to scattered German settlements in Pennsylvania and Maryland.

OTTLEY, ROI (*b. New York, N.Y., 1906; d. Chicago, Ill., 1960*), author, journalist. Studied at St. Bonaventure College and at the University of Michigan. Worked for the *Amsterdam News* in New York (1932–37); joined the Federal Writers Project of the Works Progress Administration. Wartime and postwar correspondent for *Liberty* and the *Pittsburgh Courier*. Wrote feature articles for the *Chicago Defender*, *Ebony*, and the *Chicago Tribune*. Author of *New World A-Coming* (1943), *No Green Pastures* (1951), and *The Lonely Warrior* (1955).

OTTO, BODO (*b. Hanover, Germany, 1711; d. Reading, Pa., 1787*), physician. Came to America, 1755; practiced in New Jersey and Pennsylvania. Appointed senior surgeon of the Middle Department of the Continental hospitals, 1776, he served devotedly and effectively until 1782.

OTTO, JOHN CONRAD (*b. near Woodbury, N.J., 1774; d. Philadelphia, Pa., 1844*), physician. Grandson of Bodo Otto; pupil and friend of Benjamin Rush whom he succeeded as physician to the Pennsylvania Hospital, 1813–34. Gave first adequate description of hemophilia (1803) and noted its peculiar hereditary nature.

OTTO, WILLIAM TOD (*b. Philadelphia, Pa., 1816; d. Philadelphia, 1905*), Indiana jurist. Son of John C. Otto. Assistant U.S. secretary of the interior, 1863–71.

OUCONNASTOTE. *See* OCONOSTOTA.

OUIMET, FRANCIS DESALES (*b. Brookline, Mass., 1893; d. Newton, Mass., 1967*), golfer and stockbroker. Winner of the Greater Boston Interscholastic Championship at age sixteen and the U.S. Open in 1913, beating Harry Vardon and Ted Ray. He became a stockbroker in 1919. Other championships included U.S. Amateur (1914, 1931), French Amateur (1914), Massachusetts Amateur (1914, 1919, 1922, 1925), Western Amateur (1917), North and South Amateur (1920), St. George's Challenge Cup (1923), Crump Memorial (1924, 1927), and Massachusetts Open (1932). Played on or captained the U.S. Walker Cup Team from 1922 to 1949. First American elected captain of the Royal and Ancient Golf Club of St. Andrews (1951).

OURAY (*b. probably Taos, N.Mex., ca. 1833; d. Los Piños Reservation, Colo., 1880*), Ute Indian chief. Born of an Uncompahgre father and an Apache mother, Ouray spent much of his childhood among Mexican rancheros, from whom he learned to speak Spanish correctly. Became chief of the Uncompahgre, 1860; was appointed an interpreter at Los Piños Reservation, 1862; in 1863 signed a treaty by which he was recognized by the United States as head chief for all the Western Ute. Thereafter he helped put down occasional uprisings and negotiated with the government in defense of his tribe's interests.

OURSLER, (CHARLES) FULTON (*b. Baltimore, Md., 1893; d. New York, N.Y., 1952*), writer, editor. Self-educated, Oursler became editor for the publications of Bernarr Macfadden, the physical health popularizer, in 1922. Macfadden's companies published the magazines *Physical Culture, True Story, True Romance*, and *True Detective*. Author of *Behold This Dreamer!* (1924) and *The World's Delight* (1929). Best remembered for his religious stories, Oursler wrote *The Greatest Story Ever Told* (1949), *The Greatest Book Ever Written* (1951), and *The Greatest Faith Ever Known* (1953). Resigned from the Macfadden enterprises, 1942; became a senior editor of the *Reader's Digest*, 1944. Despite his involvement in the sensationalistic journalism of the Macfadden magazines, Oursler was a respected conservative, known for his piety and patriotism.

OUTACITY (*fl. 1756–1777*), Cherokee chief, known also as "Judd's Friend" and "Mankiller." Visited London, 1762, under tutelage of Henry Timberlake. He and his family were received by the King and sat for a Reynolds portrait.

OUTCAULT, RICHARD FELTON (*b. Lancaster, Ohio, 1863; d. Flushing, N.Y., 1928*), comic artist. Inaugurated the "funny paper" in November 1894 as cartoonist for the New York *World*. Created the "Yellow Kid" and "Buster Brown."

OUTERBRIDGE, ALEXANDER EWING (*b. Philadelphia, Pa., 1850; d. Philadelphia, 1928*), metallurgist, official of the U.S. Mint. Developed method for obtaining thin films of metal for microscopic studies, 1876; made notable studies of molecule mobility in cast iron, 1894–96.

OUTERBRIDGE, EUGENIUS HARVEY (*b. Philadelphia, Pa., 1860; d. 1932*), merchant. Brother of Alexander E. Outerbridge. In business in New York City *post* 1878, he is regarded as the "father of the Port of New York Authority."

OVERMAN, FREDERICK (*b. Elberfeld, Germany, ca. 1803; d. Philadelphia, Pa., 1852*), metallurgist, authority on metallurgy of iron. Came to America, 1842. Wrote *The Manufacture of Steel* (1851) and *A Treatise on Metallurgy* (1852).

OVERMAN, LEE SLATER (*b. Salisbury, N.C., 1854; d. 1930*), lawyer, North Carolina legislator. U.S. senator, Democrat, 1903–30. Vigorously supported Clayton Act (1914); is remembered for the 1918 Overman Law which widened the president's power to transfer functions of one government department to another.

OVERSTREET, HARRY ALLEN (*b. San Francisco, Calif., 1875; d. Falls Church, Va., 1970*), philosopher, social psychologist, and adult educator. Attended University of California (B.A., 1899) and Oxford (B.S., 1901). Ideologically interested in the working poor. Taught at University of California at Berkeley, 1901–11, City College of New York, 1911–39, and the continuing-education program of the New School for Social Research, 1924–36. Instrumental in the development of radio program "America's Town Meeting of the Air" (1938). His concern for the industrial worker was later supplemented by a solicitude for black Americans, victims of world hunger, and underprivileged children. By the end of the 1950's, he had become preoccupied with Communism as a domestic and foreign menace to American society. His first book was *Influencing Human Behavior* (1925). The pinnacle of his success was with *The Mature Mind* (1949), which discussed how the mature individual copes with the forces of politics, economics, family life, and religion.

OVERTON, JOHN (*b. Louisa Co., Va., 1766; d. Nashville, Tenn., 1833*), Tennessee jurist, politician. Early business partner and independent-minded political supporter of Andrew Jackson.

OWEN, DAVID DALE (*b. near New Lanark, Scotland, 1807; d. 1860*), geologist. Son of the British social reformer

Robert Owen; brother of Robert D. Owen. Immigrated to New Harmony, Ind., 1828; attended lectures in geology and chemistry in London, England, 1831–32; graduated Ohio Medical College, 1836. Began his career of geological surveying, 1836, with a trip through Tennessee; was state geologist of Indiana, 1837. Conducted for the federal government a geological survey of mineral deposits in the Dubuque, Iowa, and Mineral Point, Wisconsin, area, 1839. He followed this by extensive surveys in Wisconsin, Minnesota, and Iowa, which he described in a *Report* (1852), and he served successively thereafter as state geologist of Kentucky, Arkansas, and Indiana for each of which he published valuable survey reports.

OWEN, EDWARD THOMAS (*b. Hartford, Conn., 1850; d. Madison, Wis., 1931*), educator. University of Wisconsin teacher of Romance languages, 1878–1914. Pioneered in effort to rationalize grammar through a radical revision of method and nomenclature based on analysis of the antecedent psychological states that prompt expression.

OWEN, GRIFFITH (*b. near Dolgelly, Wales, ca. 1647; d. Philadelphia, Pa., 1717*), Quaker preacher, surgeon. Leader of the Welsh Quakers who settled (1684) in Lower Merion Township near Philadelphia. Member of Provincial Council, 1690–1717.

OWEN, ROBERT DALE (*b. Glasgow, Scotland, 1801; d. Lake George, N.Y., 1877*), social reformer, author. Son of Robert Owen, British industrialist and social reformer; brother of David D. Owen. Helped set up New Harmony community in Indiana, 1826–27; thereafter joined Frances Wright in a coterie known as the "Free Enquirers," formed to advocate liberal divorce laws, widespread industrial education, and a more nearly equal distribution of wealth. Owen continued to pursue these objectives long after the coterie disbanded. Resuming residence in Indiana *ca.* 1833, he served in the legislature (1836–38) and in the U.S. Congress (1843–47). A resolution introduced by him in 1844 became basis for solution of the Oregon boundary dispute. He also helped establish the Smithsonian Institution. Later he became an influential advocate of emancipation. His autobiography, *Threading My Way*, was published in 1874.

OWEN, ROBERT LATHAM (*b. Lynchburg, Va., 1856; d. Washington, D.C., 1947*), lawyer, politician. Graduated Washington and Lee University, 1877. Removed with his widowed mother (who was part Cherokee) to Salina, Indian Territory, 1879; there he became a citizen of the Cherokee Nation, served as secretary of the Cherokee board of education, studied law, and began practice in Tahlequah in 1880. He was federal agent for the Five Civilized Tribes, 1885–89, and thereafter represented the Choctaw and the Cherokee in several important court cases in Washington, D.C. He organized the First National Bank of Muskogee in 1890 and was its president until 1900. In 1901 he was influential in securing the congressional act that gave citizenship to Indians in the Territory. A leader in organizing the Democratic party in Indian Territory, he was elected to the U.S. Senate by the first legislature of the new state of Oklahoma, 1907, and served until 1925, declining to run again in 1924. Identified throughout his career with progressivism and popular democracy, he was one of the most consistent backers of Woodrow Wilson's "New Freedom" program; a money reformer, he was cosponsor with Carter Glass of the Federal Reserve Act (1913). He was also a champion of liberal labor laws, and cosponsor of the Palmer-Owen and Keating-Owen child labor bills. After leaving the Senate he resumed the practice of law in Washington, D.C.

OWEN, STEPHEN JOSEPH (*b. Cleo Springs, Okla., 1898; d. Oneida, N.Y., 1964*), football coach. Began professional football career with the Kansas City Cowboys, 1924–25. The 1926 season marked the beginning of a long career with the New York Giants: captained the 1927 team, which won the NFL championship; was made a player-coach in 1930; became permanent head coach in 1931; led the team to world championships in 1934 and 1938; resigned as coach in 1953. Coached the Philadelphia Eagles (1956–57) and in the Canadian Football League (1958–62). Rehired by the Giants as a scout (1963). Pioneer of the A formation, the "one-way" performer, and the "umbrella" defense; elected to the Pro Football Hall of Fame in 1966.

OWEN, THOMAS MCADORY (*b. Jefferson Co., Ala., 1866; d. Montgomery, Ala., 1920*), lawyer, archivist, historian. Established and later directed the Alabama Department of Archives, first state department of its kind, 1901.

OWEN, WILLIAM FLORENCE (*b. Limerick, Ireland, 1844; d. 1906*), actor. Made debut at Salem, Ohio, 1867; associated with Madame Modjeska, Augustin Daly, and Mrs. Fiske, he gained fame in such comic roles as "Falstaff" and "Touchstone."

OWENS, JOHN EDMOND (*b. Liverpool, England, 1823; d. near Baltimore, Md., 1886*), actor, theatrical manager. Came to America as a child; was raised in Philadelphia, Pa., where he made debut, 1840. Excelled in standard comic roles, particularly Yankee characters.

OWENS, MICHAEL JOSEPH (*b. Mason Co., Va., now W. Va., 1859; d. Toledo, Ohio, 1923*), inventor. Developed and perfected the first automatic bottle-blowing machine (patented 1895, 1904); was associated with Edward D. Libbey in glass manufacturing *post* 1888.

OWRE, ALFRED (*b. Hammerfest, Norway, 1870; d. 1935*), physician, dentist, educator. D.D.S., University of Minnesota, 1894. As professor and dean of the college of dentistry, University of Minnesota, *post* 1902, and as dean of the school of dentistry at Columbia, 1927–34, Owre fought for reforms in dental education which were bitterly opposed in his time but in many cases adopted after his death.

OWSLEY, FRANK LAWRENCE (*b. Montgomery County, Ala., 1890; d. Winchester, England, 1956*), historian. Studied at Alabama Polytechnic Institute and at the University of Chicago, Ph.D., 1924. Professor of history at Vanderbilt University, 1920–49, and at the University of Alabama, 1949–56. Defended and sought to correct many misconceptions about the Confederacy through such works as *State Rights in the Confederacy* (1925), *King Cotton Diplomacy* (1931), and *Plain Folk of the Old South* (1949).

OWSLEY, WILLIAM (*b. Virginia, 1782; d. near Danville, Ky., 1862*), Kentucky jurist, politician. Member and vigorous supporter of the "Old Court" in the dispute of the 1820's; Whig governor, 1844–48.

OXNAM, GARFIELD BROMLEY (*b. Sonora, Calif., 1891; d. White Plains, N.Y., 1963*), Methodist bishop, author, and social reformer. Attended University of Southern California (B.A., 1913), Boston (B.S.T., 1915), Harvard, and Massachusetts Institute of Technology. Ordained in Methodist Episcopal church (1916). Taught social ethics at USC (1919–23) and Boston University's School of Theology (1927–28); named president of DePauw University (1928). Elected bishop in 1936. The social creed he espoused was the solidarity of the human race, supremacy of the common good, and equal rights for all. A leader in postwar

Protestant ecumenism, he served on the Federal Council of Churches, the World Council of Churches, and the National Council of Churches. As bishop of Washington, D.C., he questioned the competence of the House Un-American Activities Committee and struck a crucial blow against Sen. Joseph McCarthy.

P

PACA, WILLIAM (*b. near Abingdon, Md., 1740; d. Talbot Co., Md., 1799*), Maryland legislator, signer of the Declaration of Independence, jurist. Active in political opposition to the proprietor of the colony. Elected to First and Second Continental Congresses (served 1774–79), Paca devoted his energy and much of his fortune to winning the Revolution. He participated in drawing up the first state constitution, served in the state senate, was elected three times governor of Maryland, 1782–85, and served as federal district judge, 1789–99.

PACE, EDWARD ALOYSIUS (*b. Starke, Fla., 1861; d. Washington, D.C., 1938*), Roman Catholic clergyman, educator. Graduated St. Charles College, Maryland, 1880; D.Th., Rome, 1886; Ph.D., Leipzig, 1891. A pioneer in scientific psychology and modern scholastic philosophy, he was professor of psychology, 1891–94, and of philosophy, 1894–1935, at Catholic University of America.

PACHECO, ROMUALDO (*b. Santa Barbara, Calif., 1831; d. Oakland, Calif., 1899*), California legislator and official, diplomat. Republican governor of California, 1875–76; performed valuable service in helping to unite native Californians with American settlers.

PACK, CHARLES LATHROP (*b. Lexington, Mich., 1857; d. New York, N.Y., 1937*), pioneer forest conservationist. Cofounder, National Conservation Association and American Tree Association; president, 1930–37, Charles Lathrop Pack Forestry Foundation.

PACKARD, ALPHEUS SPRING (*b. Chelmsford, Mass., 1798; d. Squirrel Island, Maine, 1884*), educator. Brother of Joseph Packard. Served in many academic capacities at Bowdoin, 1819–84.

PACKARD, ALPHEUS SPRING (*b. Brunswick, Maine, 1839; d. Providence, R.I., 1905*), entomologist, teacher. Son of Alpheus S. Packard (1798–1884); grandson of Jesse Appleton. Graduated Bowdoin, 1861; M.D., Maine Medical School, 1864. Early interested and trained in geology, Packard soon found his lifework in entomology and first gained notice as author of *Guide to the Study of Insects* (1869). An ardent evolutionist, Packard had taxonomic skills, but his principal contribution lay in the biological aspects of his field. His most important later publications were *Insects Injurious to Forest and Shade Trees* (1881), *Text-Book of Entomology* (1898), and his monumental *Monograph of the Bombycine Moths* (1895–1914), which was finished by T. D. A. Cockerell. At his death he was generally recognized as the most learned and accomplished entomologist in America. *Post* 1878, he taught at Brown University.

PACKARD, FREDERICK ADOLPHUS (*b. Marlboro, Mass., 1794; d. Philadelphia, Pa., 1867*), editor, writer. Editorial secretary of American Sunday School Union, 1828–67; persistently attacked exclusion of orthodox religion from public educational systems.

PACKARD, JAMES WARD (*b. Warren, Ohio, 1863; d. Cleveland, Ohio, 1928*), engineer, manufacturer, inventor. Graduating from Lehigh University, 1884, Packard worked as an engineer in an incandescent lamp company where he took out several patents for bulb manufacturing processes. After heading his own successful electrical company, 1890–1900, he began manufacture of Packard automobiles, 1900. Having little interest in the business side of the company, Packard spent most of his time inventing mechanical improvements, such as superior ignition and carburetion systems, braking mechanisms, and chassis construction methods.

PACKARD, JOHN HOOKER (*b. Philadelphia, Pa., 1832; d. Philadelphia, 1907*), surgeon. Son of Frederick A. Packard. Surgeon to the Pennsylvania Hospital, 1884–96; writer of medical treatises, including A *Hand-book of Operative Surgery* (1870).

PACKARD, JOSEPH (*b. Wiscasset, Maine, 1812; d. Virginia, 1902*), Episcopal clergyman, biblical scholar. Brother of Alpheus S. Packard (1798–1884). Professor, Theological Seminary of Virginia, 1836–95; dean, *post* 1874.

PACKARD, SILAS SADLER (*b. Cummington, Mass., 1826; d. 1898*), pioneer in business education. Founded Packard's Business College, New York City, 1858; successfully promoted training and use of women in office work.

PACKER, ASA (*b. Groton, Conn., 1805; d. Philadelphia, Pa., 1879*), carpenter, railroad builder, politician, philanthropist. Removed to Pennsylvania, 1822; began career by buying and operating a coal boat from Mauch Chunk to Philadelphia via the Lehigh Valley canal. Investing his earnings in coal land and contracting to construct canal locks, Packer added to his fortune by founding the Lehigh Valley Railroad Co., 1853, and by further purchases of coal lands; by the 1870's he was accounted the richest man in Pennsylvania. He established and endowed Lehigh University 1866.

PACKER, WILLIAM FISHER (*b. Centre Co., Pa., 1807; d. Williamsport, Pa., 1870*), editor, politician. Publisher of the *Lycoming Gazette*, 1829–36; joint publisher of the *Keystone*, 1836–41; Democratic governor of Pennsylvania, 1857–61.

PADDOCK, ALGERNON SIDNEY (*b. Glens Falls, N.Y., 1830; d. 1897*), lawyer. Secretary and acting governor of Nebraska Territory, 1861–67; U.S. senator, Republican, from Nebraska, 1875–81 and 1887–93. Fought excessive railroad freight rates.

PADDOCK, BENJAMIN HENRY (*b. Norwich, Conn., 1828; d. 1891*), Episcopal clergyman. Brother of John A. Paddock. As bishop of Massachusetts, 1873–91, he lessened the discord between High and Low Church factions.

PADDOCK, JOHN ADAMS (*b. Norwich, Conn., 1825; d. near Santa Barbara, Calif., 1894*), Episcopal clergyman. Brother of

Benjamin H. Paddock. Active in the Northwest *post* 1880 as missionary bishop of Washington Territory and bishop of Olympia.

PADILLA, JUAN DE (*b. Andalusia, Spain, ca. 1500; d. "Quivira," in northern Texas or Kansas, ca. 1544*), Franciscan missionary. Came to Mexico *ca.* 1528. Accompanied Coronado's expedition; established first mission in Southwest at Quivira; martyred attempting to extend his ministry to a hostile Indian tribe.

PAGE, CHARLES GRAFTON (*b. Salem, Mass., 1812; d. Washington, D.C., 1868*), physician, electrical pioneer. Graduation from Harvard, 1832, and medical studies in Boston preceded practice in Salem; Page, however, early devoted most of his time to electrical experiments. Starting with Joseph Henry's calorimotor, Page developed, 1836, an induction apparatus of greater intensity than Henry's; with Ruhmkorff's improvements, it is the induction coil of today. Page also discovered the superior effect of substituting bundles of iron wires for solid iron bars as cores in induction coils and invented a self-acting circuit breaker. He experimented with reciprocating electromagnetic engines, 1846, but failed in practical tests of his battery-powered locomotive, 1851. Page worked as examiner in the U.S. Patent Office from 1861 until his death.

PAGE, DAVID PERKINS (*b. Epping, N.H., 1810; d. 1848*), educator. Successful principal of first (1844) normal school in New York at Albany; author of *The Theory and Practice of Teaching* (1847).

PAGE, JOHN (*b. Gloucester Co., Va., 1743; d. Virginia, 1808*), Revolution patriot, planter, Virginia legislator. Grandson of Mann Page. Congressman, Democratic-Republican, from Virginia, 1789–97; governor of Virginia, 1802–05. Lifelong friend and political supporter of Jefferson.

PAGE, LEIGH (*b. South Orange, N.J., 1884; d. Randolph, N.H., 1952*), physicist and educator. Studied at Yale University (Ph.B., 1904; Ph.D., 1913), Yale faculty member from 1912 to 1952, he was professor of mathematical physics from 1922. Page's main contribution to physics was the emission theory of electromagnetism. Starting from a postulate regarding the emission of particles from charged bodies, he formulated the basic equations of electromagnetic theory from Einstein's relativity theory of 1905. Books include *An Introduction to Electrodynamics from the Standpoint of Electron Theory* (1922), and *Electrodynamics* (1940) written with N. I. Adams, Jr.

PAGE, MANN (*b. Virginia, 1691; d. 1730*), Virginia planter and councillor. Son-in-law of Robert Carter (1663–1732). Considered second largest landowner in Virginia; built huge, luxurious house, "Rosewell."

PAGE, ORAN THADDEUS ("LIPS") (*b. Dallas, Tex., 1908; d. New York, N.Y., 1954*), trumpet player, singer, and bandleader. Page began his career with the bands that accompanied such singers as "Ma" Rainey, Bessie Smith, and Ida Cox. From 1930 to 1935 he played with Bennie Moten's Kansas City Band; he later played with Count Basie, Artie Shaw, and the band that accompanied Ethel Waters. After playing at the Paris Jazz Festival in 1949, he worked New York as a single. His most famous recording was "Baby, It's Cold Outside," with singer Pearl Bailey in 1949.

PAGE, RICHARD LUCIAN (*b. Clarke Co., Va., 1807; d. Blueridge Summit, Pa., 1901*), Confederate naval and army officer. Nephew of "Light-Horse Harry" Lee. Commanded at Fort Morgan, Ala., 1864, during Union land and sea attack upon Mobile.

PAGE, THOMAS JEFFERSON (*b. Matthews Co., Va., 1808; d. Rome, Italy, 1899*), naval officer, explorer. Grandson of John Page and Thomas Nelson. Commanded a surveying and exploratory expedition, 1853–56, about which he wrote *La Plata: The Argentine Confederation and Paraguay* (1859). Commanded Confederate cruiser *Stonewall*, 1865.

PAGE, THOMAS NELSON (*b. "Oakland," Hanover Co., Va., 1853; d. Hanover Co., 1922*), diplomat, author, lawyer. Great-grandson of John Page, U.S. ambassador to Italy, 1913–19. *In Ole Virginia* (1887) established his reputation and helped establish (with his later books) the myth of a pre–Civil War feudal utopia in the South.

PAGE, THOMAS WALKER (*b. Albemarle Co., Va., 1866; d. Charlottesville, Va., 1937*), economist. Cousin of Thomas N. Page. Ph.D., Leipzig, 1896. Taught at universities of California, Texas, and Virginia. Member and vice-chairman, U.S. Tariff Commission, 1918–22; 1930–37.

PAGE, WALTER HINES (*b. Cary, N.C., 1855; d. Pinehurst, N.C., 1918*), journalist, diplomat. Educated at Trinity College (now Duke), Randolph-Macon, and Johns Hopkins. Successful as editor-director of *Forum* and *Atlantic Monthly*; became partner in Doubleday, Page and Co., 1899; founded *The World's Work*, a journal of politics and practical affairs, 1900. During these years Page campaigned for educational, agricultural, industrial, and sanitary improvements, particularly in the South. Appointed U.S. ambassador to Great Britain, 1913, Page pressed for immediate American intervention against Germany in World War I. Disappointed with Wilson's neutrality policy, he threatened to resign many times. *Post* 1917 Page worked effectively to cement the Allied powers into an effective partnership.

PAGE, WILLIAM (*b. Albany, N.Y., 1811; d. Tottenville, N.Y., 1885*), portrait painter. Pupil of James Herring and S. F. B. Morse; studied in Italy, 1849–60. Consciously imitated Titian.

PAINE, ALBERT BIGELOW (*b. New Bedford, Mass., 1861; d. New Smyrna, Fla., 1937*), journalist, biographer, writer of light fiction for children and adults. Literary executor of Mark Twain, whose authorized biography he published in 1912.

PAINE, BYRON (*b. Painesville, Ohio, 1827; d. 1871*), lawyer, states' rights advocate. Wisconsin Supreme Court judge, 1859–64 and 1867–71.

PAINE, CHARLES (*b. Williamstown, Vt., 1799; d. Waco, Tex., 1853*), woolen manufacturer, Vermont railroad promoter. Son of Elijah Paine; brother of Martyn Paine. Whig governor of Vermont, 1841–43.

PAINE, CHARLES JACKSON (*b. Boston, Mass., 1833; d. Weston, Mass., 1916*), Union brigadier general, capitalist, yachtsman. Brother of Robert T. Paine (1835–1910). Owned and successfully raced *Puritan, Mayflower*, and *Volunteer* in international competition.

PAINE, ELIJAH (*b. Brooklyn, Conn., 1757; d. 1842*), farmer, woolen manufacturer, Vermont legislator. Among first settlers of Williamstown, Vt., 1784. Justice of Vermont Supreme Court, 1791–93; U.S. senator, Federalist, from Vermont, 1795–1801.

PAINE, HALBERT ELEAZER (*b. Chardon, Ohio, 1826; d. 1905*), lawyer. Union officer. Early law partner of Carl Schurz. Congressman, Radical Republican, from Wisconsin, 1865–71; U.S. commissioner of patents, 1878–80. Wrote authoritative *Treatise on the Law of Elections to Public Offices* (1888).

PAINE, HENRY WARREN (*b. Winslow, Maine, 1810; d. Cambridge, Mass., 1893*), lawyer, leader of Boston, Mass., bar *post* 1854; lecturer, Boston University Law School, 1872–85.

PAINE, JOHN ALSOP (*b. Newark, N.J., 1840; d. Tarrytown[?], N.Y., 1912*), archaeologist, botanist.

PAINE, JOHN KNOWLES (*b. Portland, Maine, 1839; d. Cambridge, Mass., 1906*), composer, teacher, organist. Studied music, particularly the organ, in Germany, 1857–61; returning to America, he gave distinguished recitals and joined the Harvard faculty, 1862. Among his best compositions were his Symphony no. 2 (1880) and music for Sophocles' *Oedipus Tyrannus* (1881). As a teacher Paine developed at Harvard, 1862–1905, the first noteworthy music school in America, in which he stressed music as art and not as a trade.

PAINE, MARTYN (*b. Williamstown, Vt., 1794; d. New York, N.Y., 1877*), physician. Son of Elijah Paine; brother of Charles Paine. Graduated Harvard, 1813; Harvard Medical, 1816. Helped found, and taught at, University of the City of New York medical college; a leading professor of therapeutics, he advocated vivisection and wrote *Institutes of Medicine* (1847).

PAINE, RALPH DELAHAYE (*b. Lemont, Ill., 1871; d. Concord, N.H., 1925*), journalist, war correspondent. Author of excellent stories for boys and historical studies such as *The Old Merchant Marine* (1919) and *The Fight for a Free Sea* (1920).

PAINE, ROBERT (*b. Person Co., N.C., 1799; d. Aberdeen, Miss., 1882*), bishop of the Methodist Episcopal Church, South, 1846–82. Instrumental in peaceable division of Methodist church, 1844–45; strengthened his denomination's financial position during Reconstruction.

PAINE, ROBERT TREAT (*b. Boston, Mass., 1731; d. Boston, 1814*), signer of the Declaration of Independence, Massachusetts legislator and jurist. Graduated Harvard, 1749. After brief career in Congregational ministry, Paine settled in legal practice at Taunton, Mass., 1761. He early joined the patriot cause, acted as associate prosecuting attorney in the "Boston Massacre" trial, was elected to the legislature, and then served as delegate to Continental Congress, 1774–76. During the Revolution, Paine worked principally in Massachusetts, was elected the first state attorney general, 1777, and earned a lasting reputation as a zealous and effective patriot. Instrumental in suppressing Shays's Rebellion, Paine became a state supreme court justice, 1790. He continued active politics as a Federalist until his retirement from the bench in 1804.

PAINE, ROBERT TREAT (*b. Taunton, Mass., 1773; d. Boston, Mass., 1811*), editor, satirist, poet. Son of Robert T. Paine (1731–1814). Wrote "Adams and Liberty," 1798; edited the *Federal Orrery*, 1794–96. An early bohemian wit in proper Boston.

PAINE, ROBERT TREAT (*b. Boston, Mass., 1835; d. Waltham, Mass., 1910*), philanthropist. Brother of Charles J. Paine. Founder, and president, 1879–1907, of Associated Charities of Boston; a leading authority on philosophy and implementation of modern philanthropy.

PAINE, THOMAS (*b. Thetford, England, 1737; d. New York, N.Y., 1809*), pamphleteer, agitator, deist. Son of a Quaker corset maker, Paine attended school until he was 13 when poverty compelled his apprenticeship to the paternal trade. Serving briefly as a privateer, 1756, he returned to his home and spent the years 1757–74 working successively and in many towns as a corset maker, exciseman, schoolteacher, exciseman again, tobacconist, and grocer. He experienced two brief, childless marriages. He was

deeply, lastingly affected by the monotony of his occupation, the ugliness of his poverty, and the frustration produced by the gap, existing in his mind, between his abilities and his apparent destiny. However, he read widely in contemporary social, political, and scientific literature, and so educated himself.

Armed with letters of introduction from Benjamin Franklin, whom he had met in London when he was agitating to get salaries of excisemen increased, Paine immigrated to Philadelphia, arriving in October 1774. There he fell naturally into journalism, supporting himself largely by contributions to the *Pennsylvania Magazine* on a number of subjects, from recent inventions to slavery. Refreshed by what seemed the unlimited potentialities of the New World and deeply imbued with current rationalist theories on the nature of society, Paine quickly took up the patriot cause. His celebrated *Common Sense* was published as an anonymous pamphlet in Philadelphia on Jan. 10, 1776. It urged an immediate declaration of independence as the fulfillment of America's moral obligation to the world. The colonies, Paine reasoned, must fall away eventually. If they separated from a debasing monarchy while they were still uncorrupt, natural, and democratic, human destiny could be altered by their example, and America's mission would be served. The pamphlet enjoyed a phenomenal success; 120,000 copies were sold in three months and some 500,000 in all.

Paine joined Washington's army during the New Jersey retreat, November–December 1776, during which he wrote the first number of the *Crisis*. Beginning with the famous words "These are times that try men's souls," it appeared in the *Pennsylvania Journal* on Dec. 19, 1776, and in pamphlet form four days later. Eleven further numbers and four supernumerary ones appeared during the war. Urging vigorous action and sacrifice, they were widely read both in the army and the country at large. Appointed secretary of the congressional committee on foreign affairs, April 1777, Paine served efficiently, but was drawn into the Beaumarchais affair and engaged in public dispute with Silas Deane. Pressure from the French minister in Washington forced his resignation, whereupon he was appointed clerk to the Pennsylvania Assembly. After the war Paine lived in Bordentown, N.J., and in New York City, 1783–87; he was mildly lionized and worked on his cherished invention, an iron bridge. He had been given a confiscated Loyalist farm at New Rochelle, N.Y.

Despairing of getting his bridge adopted in America, Paine went to Europe in 1787, living in England and France and passing the time pleasantly as a favorite in liberal circles. Stirred by the onset of the French Revolution, he acted as self-appointed missionary of the world revolution, 1789–92. He hoped England would follow France's course, and after Edmund Burke published his quickly popular condemnation of events in France, 1790, Paine replied with the first part of his *Rights of Man* in 1791; the second part appeared in 1792. This pamphlet was a defense of specific measures taken by the French revolutionists and an exposition of the "natural rights" philosophy; Paine argued that man's rights to liberty, property, security, and resistance to oppression could only be guaranteed by a republican form of government with a written constitution, manhood suffrage, and an absence of artificial distinctions of birth and rank. Paine hoped his pamphlet would stimulate a revolution in England. Pitt's ministry suppressed it, however, and declared Paine, safe in France, an outlaw. Made a French citizen by the National Assembly and elected to the revolutionary convention in France (Pas de Calais Department, 1792), Paine served for a year, attaching himself to the moderate Gironde group. Imprisoned in December 1793 for being a national of a country at war with France, he was not released until the following November. Until 1802 he lived in Paris, supported in part by solicitous friends. His principal work of this period, *The Age of Reason* (1794, 1796), was a defense of deism and a rationalist attack upon literal acceptance of the Bible.

Before his return to America in 1802, Paine had become a central figure in the partisan dispute between Jeffersonians and Federalists, largely because Thomas Jefferson had commented favorably upon his deistic treatise and had offered Paine passage to America on a public vessel. The last seven years of his life were marked by poverty, declining health, and social ostracism, and were spent in Bordentown, in New York City, and in New Rochelle. He was buried in a corner of his New Rochelle farm, but in 1819 his bones were removed and taken to England by William Cobbett. In addition to the major works already cited, Paine was author of a number of minor pamphlets. A revolutionary by temperament and something of a professional radical, Paine was always pleading a cause; his books, lucid and studded with apt epithets, are arguments rather than expositions. He was essentially a propagandist through whom the ideas of more-original men were transmitted to the crowd.

PAINTER, GAMALIEL (*b. New Haven, Conn., 1743; d. 1819*), Revolutionary soldier, Vermont pioneer and legislator. Promoted settlement and development of Middlebury, Vt.; a founder of Middlebury College, and a fellow of the college, 1800–19.

PAINTER, WILLIAM (*b. Triadelphia, Md., 1838; d. Baltimore, Md., 1906*), engineer. Devised, patented (1892), and produced the "Crown Cork" single-use bottle cap, the basis of extensively used bottle sealers today.

PALEY, JOHN (*b. Russia, 1871; d. 1907*), editor, author. Came to America, 1888. Made the New York *Jewish Daily News* a powerful influence on Yiddish-speaking people as its editor *post ca.* 1893. His vigorous, conservative articles brought him a personal following and bitter abuse from the Yiddish socialist press.

PALFREY, JOHN CARVER (*b. Cambridge, Mass., 1833; d. Boston, Mass., 1906*), Union soldier, engineer. Son of John G. Palfrey. Graduated Harvard, 1853; West Point, 1857. Specialist in military fortifications; helped save Union gunboat fleet during Red River campaign, 1864, by raising level of the water, thus permitting passage over the rapids.

PALFREY, JOHN GORHAM (*b. Boston, Mass., 1796; d. Boston, 1881*), Unitarian clergyman, editor, historian. Graduated Harvard, 1815. Minister of Brattle Square Church, Boston, 1818–31; Dexter professor of sacred literature, Harvard, 1831–39. Contributed important articles to *North American Review*, and managed it between 1835 and 1843; served as congressman, Whig, 1847–49. Author of a number of books on religious topics which were largely made up of his successful public lectures. His most important work was his *History of New England* (5 vols., 1858–90), the product of vast research, painstakingly and accurately undertaken. It remained the standard work for decades afterward in spite of its bias in favor of New England Puritans and anti-English animus.

PALLADINO, LAWRENCE BENEDICT (*b. Dilecto, Italy, 1837; d. Missoula, Mont., 1927*), Roman Catholic missionary, Jesuit. Came to California, 1863; served in Montana area principally, 1867–1925. Author of *Indian and White in the Northwest* (1894).

PALLEN, CONDÉ BENOIST (*b. St. Louis, Mo., 1858; d. 1929*), editor, lecturer, author. Graduated Georgetown University, 1880; Ph.D., St. Louis University, 1885. A founder and managing editor, 1904–20, of the *Catholic Encyclopedia*.

PALMER, ALBERT MARSHMAN (*b. North Stonington, Conn., 1838; d. 1905*), theatrical manager. Managed Union Square Theatre, New York City, 1872–83; later managed Madison Square Theatre and Wallack's. Encouraged American authors to deal with native American material; helped found Actor's Fund, 1882.

PALMER, ALEXANDER MITCHELL (*b. Moosehead, Pa., 1872; d. Washington, D.C., 1936*), lawyer. Graduated Swarthmore, 1891; practiced law in Stroudsburg, Pa., *post* 1893. Congressman, progressive Democrat, from Pennsylvania, 1909–15; active supporter of Woodrow Wilson, 1912. As alien property custodian, 1917–19, he was widely criticized for his handling of some $600 million worth of enemy property; as U.S. attorney general, 1919–21, he was denounced in liberal circles for his onslaught on domestic radicalism, particularly his raids on private homes and deportation of aliens.

PALMER, ALICE ELVIRA FREEMAN (*b. Colesville, N.Y., 1855; d. Paris, France, 1902*), educator. Wife of George H. Palmer. Graduated University of Michigan, 1876; became head of Department of History at Wellesley College, 1879. Manifest administrative abilities led to her appointment, 1881–82, as president of Wellesley, which she developed into a first-rate women's college by the time of her resignation, 1888. In 1889 she was appointed to the Massachusetts Board of Education; she served as dean of women at the University of Chicago, 1892–95.

PALMER, ALONZO BENJAMIN (*b. Richfield, N.Y., 1815; d. 1887*), physician, teacher. Dean of medical department, University of Michigan, 1875–87. Wrote *Treatise on the Science and Practice of Medicine* (1882) and *Epidemic Cholera* (1866).

PALMER, BENJAMIN MORGAN (*b. Charleston, S.C., 1818; d. New Orleans, La., 1902*), Presbyterian clergyman. Pastor in New Orleans *post* 1856; helped found *Southern Presbyterian Review* and *Southwestern Presbyterian*.

PALMER, BERTHA HONORÉ (*b. Louisville, Ky., 1849; d. Osprey, Fla., 1918*), Chicago hostess and social leader. Married Potter Palmer, 1871.

PALMER, DANIEL DAVID (*b. near Toronto, Canada, 1845; d. Los Angeles, Calif., 1913*), founder of chiropractic. Started Palmer School of Chiropractic, Davenport, Iowa, 1898. Coauthor, *Science of Chiropractic* (1906); author, *Textbook of the Science, Art and Philosophy of Chiropractic* (1910).

PALMER, ELIHU (*b. Canterbury, Conn., 1764; d. Philadelphia, Pa., 1806*), militant deist. Graduated Dartmouth, 1787; served as Presbyterian and Universalist minister; practiced law. Founded formal deist organizations *ca.* 1795, known as the Philosophical Society (Columbian Illuminati) in New York City and as the Theophilanthropists in Philadelphia and Baltimore, Md.

PALMER, ERASTUS DOW (*b. Pompey, N.Y., 1817; d. Albany, N.Y., 1904*), cameo-cutter, sculptor. First American sculptor to exhibit lyric charm in his work; created *White Captive* (1858) and other ideal pieces; excelled as portraitist.

PALMER, GEORGE HERBERT (*b. Boston, Mass., 1842; d. Cambridge, Mass., 1933*), philosopher, teacher, man of letters. Married Alice E. F. Palmer, 1887. Graduated Harvard, 1864; Andover Theological Seminary, 1870. Appointed to the Harvard faculty, 1870, he continued to teach until retirement, 1913. Professor of philosophy *post* 1873, his professional interest was in the theory of ethics; a man of the middle ground, he criticized the extreme positions of Puritanism and Hegelianism. *The Odyssey of Homer* (1884), *The Field of Ethics* (1901), *The Problem of Freedom* (1911), and his edition of *The English Works of George Herbert* (3 vols., 1905) were among his best-known writings and indicate the range of his interests.

PALMER, HENRY WILBUR (*b. Clifford, Pa., 1839; d. Wilkes-Barre, Pa., 1913*), lawyer. Congressman, Republican, from Pennsylvania, 1901–07 and 1909–11. Often in controversy, he championed the established order, rugged individualism, and puritan reforms.

PALMER, HORATIO RICHMOND (*b. Sherburne, N.Y., 1834; d. Yonkers, N.Y., 1907*), musician, director of music. Dean of music at Chautauqua, 1877–91. Organized successful Church Choral Union, New York City, 1881; composed "Just for Today" and other popular hymns.

PALMER, INNIS NEWTON (*b. Buffalo, N.Y., 1824; d. Chevy Chase, Md., 1900*), soldier. Graduated West Point, 1846. Served with distinction in Mexican War; held Union army divisional command in Civil War, chiefly in North Carolina; commanded 2nd Cavalry in expanding West, 1865–79.

PALMER, JAMES CROXALL (*b. Baltimore, Md., 1811; d. Washington, D.C., 1883*), naval surgeon. Brother of John W. Palmer. Served with Wilkes Expedition, 1838–42; with West Gulf blockade squadron, 1863–65. Surgeon general of the navy, 1872–73.

PALMER, JAMES SHEDDEN (*b. New Jersey, 1810; d. St. Thomas, Virgin Islands, 1867*), naval officer. Led Union fleet in first passage of Vicksburg; succeeded in Farragut in command of Union forces on the Mississippi; commanded West Gulf squadron in fall, 1864; aided Virgin Islanders after earthquake, 1866.

PALMER, JOEL (*b. Ontario, Canada, 1810; d. Dayton, Oreg., 1881*), Oregon legislator and pioneer. Author of *Journal of Travels over the Rocky Mountains* (1847); successful and diligent superintendent of Indian affairs for Oregon Territory, 1853–57.

PALMER, JOHN MCAULEY (*b. Scott Co., Ky., 1817; d. Springfield, Ill., 1900*), lawyer, Union major general. Removed to Illinois, 1831; helped found Republican party there. Republican governor of Illinois, 1869–73. Palmer, a Democrat *post* 1872, served as U.S. senator, 1891–97. In 1896, he was the presidential nominee of the National, or "Gold," Democrats.

PALMER, JOHN MCAULEY (*b. Carlinville, Ill., 1870; d. Washington, D.C., 1955*), army officer. Graduated West Point, 1892. Served on the army general staff, 1911–12 and 1916–17. In 1917 he became Pershing's assistant chief of staff for operations for the American Expeditionary Force in France. Promoted brigadier general in 1922, he retired in 1926. Recalled during World War II as an adviser on reserve forces, he retired again in 1946. An advocate of universal military training during peacetime, he was the author of the National Defense Act of 1920 and helped frame the Selective Service Act of 1940.

PALMER, JOHN WILLIAMSON (*b. Baltimore, Md., 1825; d. Baltimore, 1906*), physician, author. Brother of James C. Palmer. Southern correspondent for *New York Tribune* during Civil War; wrote ballad "Stonewall Jackson's Way."

PALMER, JOSEPH (*b. Devonshire, England, 1716; d. Dorchester, Mass., 1788*), manufacturer, Revolutionary brigadier general. Immigrated to Massachusetts, 1746. Commanded unsuccessful attack on British at Newport, R.I., October 1777; lost most of his fortune during Revolution.

PALMER, NATHANIEL BROWN (*b. Stonington, Conn., 1799; d. San Francisco, Calif., 1877*), sea captain, explorer. In search of new seal rookeries in the South Atlantic, Palmer discovered Palmer Land on Antarctica, 1820. A respected packet and China clipper captain in later life, he made many valuable suggestions for improved clipper design.

PALMER, POTTER (*b. Albany Co., N.Y., 1826; d. Chicago, Ill., 1902*), Chicago merchant, real estate promoter. Removed to Chicago, 1852. Married Bertha H. Palmer, 1871. Founder of present Marshall Field stores, State Street business center, "Palmer system" of retailing, Palmer House hotel.

PALMER, MRS. POTTER. *See* PALMER, BERTHA HONORÉ.

PALMER, RAY (*b. Little Compton, R.I., 1808; d. Newark, N.J., 1887*), Congregational clergyman, hymnist. Author of "My Faith Looks Up to Thee" (*ca. 1831*); published *Hymns and Sacred Pieces* (1865), *Voices of Hope and Gladness* (1881), and other books.

PALMER, THOMAS WITHERELL (*b. Detroit, Mich., 1830; d. Detroit, 1913*), businessman, philanthropist. U.S. senator, Republican, from Michigan, 1883–89; U.S. minister to Spain, 1889–91. President, Chicago World's Fair Commission, 1892–93.

PALMER, WALTER LAUNT (*b. Albany, N.Y., 1854; d. Albany, 1932*), landscape, figure, and still-life painter. Son of Erastus D. Palmer. Studied with Frederick E. Church and, in Paris, with Carolus Duran. Achieved success and popularity with delicately shaded winter scenes.

PALMER, WALTER WALKER (*b. Southfield, Mass., 1882; d. Tyringham, Mass., 1950*), physician, medical educator. Graduated Amherst College, 1905. M.D., Harvard Medical School, 1910. His early research, much of it in collaboration with Lawrence J. Henderson at Harvard, was devoted to studies of acid-base balance in diabetes and nephritis; he continued this research as a staff member of the Rockefeller Institute, New York City, 1915–17, and also developed the first reliable quantitative method for hemoglobin determination. He later concerned himself principally with the physiology of the thyroid gland. He built up one of the world's renowned departments of internal medicine at Columbia University, where he served as associate professor, 1917–19, and Bard professor of medicine, 1921–47, and as director of the medical service at Presbyterian Hospital.

PALMER, WILLIAM ADAMS (*b. Hebron, Conn., 1781; d. Danville, Vt., 1860*), lawyer, Vermont legislator and jurist. U.S. senator, Democrat, from Vermont, 1818–25; anti-Masonic leader and governor 1831–35.

PALMER, WILLIAM HENRY (*b. England, ca. 1830; d. Philadelphia, Pa., 1878*), entertainer, known on stage as Robert Heller. Achieved success in America *post* 1864 with acts using magic, puppets, and piano numbers.

PALMER, WILLIAM JACKSON (*b. near Leipsic, Del., 1836; d. near Colorado Springs, Colo., 1909*), Union soldier, railroad executive. Served with distinction throughout the Civil War as a cavalry officer. After the war, he served as an official of the Union Pacific Railroad's Eastern Division, which became the Kansas Pacific and later merged into the Union Pacific. In 1870, he became first president of the Denver and Rio Grande and completed its line westward by 1883. During the 1880's, he organized and constructed Mexican railroads, two lines from Mexico City to the border being completed by 1890. He was an organizer and first president of the Colorado Coal and Iron Co. and helped develop Colorado Springs.

PALMORE, WILLIAM BEVERLY (*b. Fayette Co., Tenn., 1844; d. Richmond, Va., 1914*), clergyman of the Methodist

Episcopal Church, South. Owner-editor *post* 1890 of the influential *St. Louis Christian Advocate*.

PALÓU, FRANCISCO (*b. Mallorca*, ca. *1722*; *d. Mexico*, ca. *1789*), Franciscan missionary, historian. Accompanied Junípero Serra to Mexico, 1749; served as Serra's associate and independently on missions in Lower and Upper California; founded Mission Dolores (San Francisco), 1776. Author of monumental chronicles of the Franciscan work in California and a biography of Junípero Serra (1787).

PAMMEL, LOUIS HERMANN (*b. LaCrosse, Wis., 1862; d. Nevada, 1931*), botanist, educator, conservationist. Author of *The Grasses of Iowa* (1901), *Ecology* (1903), *Weed Flora of Iowa* (1913).

PANCOAST, HENRY KHUNRATH (*b. Philadelphia, Pa., 1875; d. Merion, Pa., 1939*), pioneer radiologist. Son of Seth Pancoast. M.D., University of Pennsylvania, 1898; headed Department of Radiology there *post* 1902.

PANCOAST, JOSEPH (*b. near Burlington, N.J., 1805; d. Philadelphia, Pa., 1882*), anatomist, surgeon. University of Pennsylvania, M.D., 1828; taught at Jefferson Medical College, 1838–74; accomplished spectacular surgical feats. Wrote *Treatise on Operative Surgery* (1844).

PANCOAST, SETH (*b. Darby, Pa., 1823; d. Philadelphia, Pa., 1889*), physician, anatomist, student of the occult.

PANGBORN, CLYDE EDWARD (*b. Bridgeport, Wash., 1894; d. New York, N.Y., 1958*), aviator. After studying briefly at the University of Idaho and receiving flight training in the army during World War I, Pangborn became a civilian aviator, working in flying circuses and barnstorming for a living. In 1931, with Hugh Herndon, he completed the first nonstop flight across the Pacific, flying from Japan to Washington state. In 1934, with Colonel Roscoe Turner, he flew a record flight from London to Australia.

PANOFSKY, ERWIN (*b. Hannover, Germany, 1892; d. Princeton, N.J., 1968*), art historian. Attended universities of Freiburg (Ph.D., 1914), Berlin, and Munich. Taught at University of Hamburg (1921–33), until dismissed by the Nazi regime, by which time he was well known for his theoretical and historical studies of medieval and Renaissance art. Immigrated to the United States in 1934 and taught at New York University (1934), Princeton (1934–46, 1948–68), Harvard (1947–48), and was a visiting member of the Institute for Advanced Study (1935). Called the most influential art historian of the twentieth century, he is best remembered as the deviser of an approach to analyzing works of visual art that depends on a well-thought-out theory of the relation of mind to world. His most frequently cited practical studies are *Albrecht Dürer* (1943), *Early Netherlandish Painting* (1947–48), *Renaissance and Renascences in Western Art* (1960), and *Problems in Titian, Mostly Iconographic* (1969). *Preface to Studies in Iconology* (1939) systematized his iconological method.

PANSY *See* ALDEN, ISABELLA MACDONALD.

PANTON, WILLIAM (*b. Aberdeenshire, Scotland*, ca. *1742*; *d. at sea near Nassau, Bahamas, 1801*), Indian trader. Immigrated to Charleston, S.C., *ca.* 1770; formed a trading partnership at Savannah, Ga.; spent most of 1775–84 in East Florida organizing trade relations with Creek Indians. His Loyalist sentiments led to confiscation of his Georgia property. From 1784 to 1801, he lived mostly in West Florida, where he carried on far-flung trading operations with the Creek, Choctaw, Chickasaw, and Cherokee; the Spanish authorities sponsored his operations in order to keep the Indians friendly to Spain. Trading as Panton, Leslie and Co. and successor firms, with headquarters at Pensacola, Panton

prospered until American companies began to cut into his business.

PAPANICOLAOU, GEORGE NICHOLAS (*b. Kyme, Greece, 1883; d. Miami, Fla., 1962*), anatomist and oncologist. Attended universities of Athens (M.D., 1904), Jena, Freiburg, and Munich (Ph.D., 1910). Arrived in the United States in 1913 and taught at New York Hospital (1913) and Cornell Medical College (1914–49); director of the Miami Cancer Institute (1961; later renamed Papanicolaou Cancer Research Institute). His systematic study of the cytology of human vaginal secretions and the observation of distinctive neoplastic cells in the vaginal fluid of women with cancer of the cervix led to the development of the Papanicolaou smear ("Pap" test), a means of cancer diagnosis; widespread application of the test was followed by a sharp reduction in the death rate from cancer of the uterus and cervix.

PARDEE, ARIO (*b. Chatham, N.Y., 1810; d. Ormond, Fla., 1892*), engineer, Pennsylvania coal operator, philanthropist. Benefactor and trustee of Lafayette College.

PARDEE, DON ALBERT (*b. Wadsworth, Ohio, 1837; d. Atlanta, Ga., 1919*), Union soldier, Louisiana jurist. Settled in legal practice at New Orleans, 1865. A Republican, yet respected in the South, Pardee was U.S. circuit court judge, fifth circuit, 1881–1919.

PARDOW, WILLIAM O'BRIEN (*b. New York, N.Y., 1847; d. 1909*), Roman Catholic clergyman, Jesuit educator. Provincial of Jesuit New York–Maryland province, 1893–97; widely known for pulpit eloquence.

PARIS, WALTER (*b. London, England, 1842; d. Washington, D.C., 1906*), architect, watercolor painter. Resident in America *post ca.* 1872; a founder of the Tile Club.

PARISH, ELIJAH (*b. Lebanon, Conn., 1762; d. Byfield, Mass., 1825*), Congregational clergyman. Pastor at Byfield *post* 1787; associate of Jedidiah Morse in authorship of geographies.

PARK, EDWARDS AMASA (*b. Providence, R.I., 1808; d. Andover, Mass., 1900*), Congregational clergyman, theologian. Last outstanding exponent of the "New England theology"; taught at Andover Theological Seminary, 1836–81; was an editor of *Bibliotheca Sacra*, 1844–84.

PARK, JAMES (*b. Pittsburgh, Pa., 1820; d. Allegheny, Pa., 1883*), iron and steel manufacturer. Encouraged introduction of new industrial processes, including Bessemer process; instrumental in increase of tariff schedules which gave steel a position of special privilege, 1882–83.

PARK, MAUD WOOD (*b. Boston, Mass., 1871; d. Melrose, Mass., 1955*), suffragist and social worker. Studied at Radcliffe College. After founding the College Equal Suffrage League in 1900, she toured the country and rallied college women to the cause of feminism. At the same time she was a social worker in Boston. In 1916 she joined the National American Woman Suffrage Association as head of the lobbying efforts for the right-to-vote amendment. After ratification in 1920, she headed the National League of Women Voters from 1920 to 1924. She established the Women's Joint Congressional Committee which brought about the right of independent citizenship for women in 1922. After her health failed she began to write plays about the women's movement.

PARK, ROBERT EZRA (*b. Harveyville, Pa., 1864; d. Nashville, Tenn., 1944*), sociologist. Raised in Red Wing, Minn. Ph.B., University of Michigan, 1887. After working as a journalist in Minneapolis, Detroit, Denver, and New York City, he was moved to resume studies in philosophy and psychology by his growing interest in the relation between "news" and social change. After receiving the M.A. from Harvard, 1899, he spent the next four years at the universities of Berlin, Strasbourg, and Heidelberg, which granted him the Ph.D., 1904. That same year he became secretary of the Congo Reform Association after his return to the United States; in the course of his work he met Booker T. Washington, for whom he acted as press agent, ghostwriter, and general assistant in the affairs of Tuskegee Institute. In 1913 he joined the sociology department at the University of Chicago, where he remained until 1929 (professor *post* 1923). After retirement he journeyed and lectured in the Orient, taught at University of Hawaii and at Yenching University, and was on the staff of Fisk University, 1935–37. Insistent on accuracy in data-gathering, and on the conduct of investigations with empathy as well as detachment, he excelled as a teacher of advanced students. He never produced a systematic treatise of sociology. In his widely used *Introduction to the Sciences of Sociology* (1921, with E. W. Burgess), he emphasized processes of social interaction rather than the study of institutions. Among his lasting contributions were his concepts of "collective behavior" and the "marginal man." He ranks with Franz Boas and William I. Thomas as a pioneer in the modern study of race and ethnic relations, but he was skeptical of the value of attempts to "engineer" social change.

PARK, ROSWELL (*b. Lebanon, Conn., 1807; d. Chicago, Ill., 1869*), educator, army officer, Episcopal clergyman. Established, and was first president of Racine College, Wisconsin, 1852–63.

PARK, ROSWELL (*b. Pomfret, Conn., 1852; d. Buffalo, N.Y., 1914*), surgeon, pathologist. Son of Roswell Park (1807–69). M.D., Northwestern, 1876. Popularized Lister's antiseptic technique; founded Institute for Malignant Diseases, New York; published *The Principles and Practice of Modern Surgery* (1907), and other works on the practice and history of medicine and surgery.

PARK, TRENOR WILLIAM (*b. Woodford, Vt., 1823; d. at sea, 1882*), lawyer, financier. Son-in-law of Hiland Hall. Removed to California, 1852; was land-title specialist in law firm of Henry W. Halleck and Frederick Billings, San Francisco. Sharp-trading manipulator of stocks in John C. Frémont's Mariposa estate, Vermont and Panama railroads, and the notorious Utah Emma mine.

PARK, WILLIAM HALLOCK (*b. New York, N.Y., 1863; d. New York, 1939*), bacteriologist, public health officer. Graduated College of the City of New York, 1883; M.D., New York College of Physicians and Surgeons, 1886. Began practice as a nose-and-throat specialist, simultaneously working on the bacteriology of diphtheria in New York City's Board of Health laboratory. Corroborating, supplementing, and applying the achievements of European scientists in isolating the diphtheria bacillus, developing an antitoxin and later an immunity test, Park pioneered in mass immunization. His program, widely followed in the United States and abroad, virtually eliminated diphtheria as a cause of death. As director of New York City's health laboratories, Park investigated many other infectious diseases and was a leader in milk sanitation.

PARKE, BENJAMIN (*b. New Jersey, 1777; d. Indiana, 1835*), soldier, jurist. Removed to Kentucky *ca.* 1797; settled to Vincennes, Ind., 1801. Negotiated treaty securing central Indiana for whites, 1818; served as a judge of the territorial court, 1808–17, and thereafter as U.S. district judge.

PARKE, JOHN (*b. Dover, Del., 1754; d. Kent Co., Del., 1789*), Revolutionary soldier, poet. Author of *Lyric Works of Horace . . . by a Native of America* (1786).

PARKE, JOHN GRUBB (*b. near Coatesville, Pa., 1827; d. Philadelphia, Pa., 1900*), Union soldier. Graduated West Point, 1849. A distinguished engineer officer and field commander, Parke served in almost all Civil War theaters, most notably at Vicksburg, 1863, and Fort Steadman, 1865. He retired as colonel, 1889.

PARKER, ALTON BROOKS (*b. Cortland, N.Y., 1852; d. New York, N.Y., 1926*), jurist. Graduating from Albany (N.Y.) Law School, 1873, Parker began practice at Kingston; thereafter he was elected and appointed to increasingly important judicial posts in the state, rising to chief justice, New York Court of Appeals, 1897. A consistent Democrat, Parker's judicial record, particularly on labor cases, was generally liberal. Party managers selected him to be Democratic presidential nominee, 1904, playing down his liberalism and presenting him as a safe, conservative candidate in contrast to Theodore Roosevelt. His campaign, accordingly, was colorless and he was badly defeated.

PARKER, ALVIN PIERSON (*b. near Austin, Tex., 1850; d. Oakland, Calif., 1924*), clergyman of the Methodist Episcopal Church, South. Missionary to China, 1875–1923; editor, *Chinese Christian Advocate*.

PARKER, AMASA JUNIUS (*b. Sharon, Conn., 1807; d. 1890*), New York lawyer, jurist. Active in Democratic politics and a founder of Albany (N.Y.) Law School, 1851.

PARKER, ARTHUR CASWELL (*b. Iroquois, N.Y., 1881; d. Naples, N.Y., 1955*), anthropologist, archaeologist, and museum administrator. Part Seneca, Parker fulfilled his lifelong interest in Indians and Indian affairs through the study of anthropology. He became ethnologist with the New York State Library at Albany in 1904; from 1906 to 1925 he was archaeologist for the New York State Museum; and from 1925 to 1946 he was director of the Rochester Municipal Museum (later the Rochester Museum of Arts and Sciences). Parker distinguished himself for the quantity of his writings about the Iroquois nation.

PARKER, CARLETON HUBBELL (*b. Red Bluff, Calif., 1878; d. 1918*), economist, labor conciliator. His report on the Wheatland, Calif., hop-field riot, 1912, became a model for similar injuries. He was author of *The Casual Laborer and Other Essays* (1920).

PARKER, CHARLIE ("BIRD") (*b. Kansas City, Kans., 1920; d. New York, N.Y., 1955*), jazz musician. An alto saxophonist, Parker was a leader in the development of improvisational jazz. He was a soloist with Jay McShann, Billy Eckstine, Red Norvo, Dizzy Gillespie, and accompanied Sarah Vaughan. In 1947 he formed the best of his small groups, the Quintet, with Max Roach and Miles Davis. One of the greatest jazz improvisors of his time, Parker, in the opinion of some critics, brought jazz to its highest level of achievement.

PARKER, CORTLANDT. *See* PARKER, JOHN CORTLANDT.

PARKER, DOROTHY ROTHSCHILD (*b. West End, N.J., 1893; d. New York, N.Y., 1967*), short-story writer, poet, dramatist, and critic. Hired by *Vanity Fair* in 1916, she became drama critic in 1918, but was fired in 1920 for an acerbic theater review. One of the Algonquin Wits, known for their puns, gibes, and gossip, she wrote a theater column for *Ainslee's Magazine*, and her essays, short stories, and character sketches appeared in *Saturday Evening Post*, *Ladies Home Journal*, *Everybody's*, and *Smart Set*. She collaborated with Elmer Rice on the play *Close Harmony, or The Lady Next Door* (1924); with Robert Benchley on the one-act play *Nero* (1924); with George S. Kaufman on her first filmscript, *Business is Business* (1925); and with her husband Alan Campbell on twenty-two filmscripts (1934−49). Unhappy in her personal life, she collected her sardonic poems in *Enough Rope* (1926), which became a best-seller. She also contributed occasionally to the *New Yorker* and began a weekly book-review column (1927−31). Her radical leftist activities in the 1930's led to her being blacklisted in Hollywood in 1949 for "un-American activities." Her best play during this difficult period was *The Ladies of the Corridor* (1953), written with Arnaud D'Usseau. In later years she taught at California State College at Los Angeles, wrote lyrics for Leonard Bernstein's musical *Candide* (1958), and wrote a book-review column for *Esquire* (1957−63).

PARKER, EDWIN BREWINGTON (*b. Shelbina, Mo., 1868; d. Washington, D.C., 1929*), Texas lawyer, international jurist. Priorities commissioner, War Industry Board, 1917−18. Chairman of the Liquidation Commission immediately following World War I, he was adjudicator in many war claims actions as Mixed Claims Commission umpire *post* 1923.

PARKER, EDWIN POND (*b. Castine, Maine, 1836; d. Hartford, Conn., 1920*), Congregational clergyman. Pastor of Second Church, Hartford, *post* 1860.

PARKER, EDWIN WALLACE (*b. St. Johnsbury, Vt., 1833; d. Naini Tal, India, 1901*), Methodist missionary and bishop. Active in development of Methodist church and educational enterprises in northern India, 1859−1901.

PARKER, ELY SAMUEL (*b. Indian Falls, N.Y., 1828; d. Fairfield, Conn., 1895*), Seneca sachem, engineer, Union brigadier general. Aided Lewis H. Morgan in research; attended Rensselaer Polytechnic Institute. As U. S. Grant's military secretary, 1864−65, Parker wrote the official copies of the surrender terms at Appomattox. After the Civil War, he rose rapidly in rank during service with the regular army. Commissioner of Indian affairs, 1869−71, he resigned after being unjustly accused of fraud; thereafter he made and lost a small fortune on Wall St.

PARKER, FOXHALL ALEXANDER (*b. New York, N.Y., 1821; d. Annapolis, Md., 1879*), naval officer. Brother of William H. Parker. Author of *The Naval Howitzer Afloat* (1866) and *Fleet Tactics Under Steam* (1870). Died as superintendent of the U.S. Naval Academy.

PARKER, FRANCIS WAYLAND (*b. Bedford, N.H., 1837; d. 1902*), educator. Introduced progressive classroom teaching *post* 1875 in Quincy, Mass., Boston, and Chicago schools; first director, School of Education, University of Chicago, 1901−02.

PARKER, GEORGE HOWARD (*b. Philadelphia, Pa., 1864; d. Cambridge, Mass., 1955*), zoologist. Studied at Harvard University (D.Sc., 1891). Taught at Harvard from 1894 until retirement. Director of the Harvard Zoological Laboratories, 1921−34. A specialist in the nervous systems of lower animals, Parker was elected to the National Academy of Sciences in 1913.

PARKER, HENRY TAYLOR (*b. Boston, Mass., 1867; d. 1934*), journalist. After experience on a number of newspapers, he served *post* 1905 as music and drama editor of the *Boston Transcript* and made the paper notable for care and originality in dealing with the arts.

PARKER, HORATIO WILLIAM (*b. Auburndale, Mass., 1863; d. Cedarhurst, N.Y., 1919*), musical composer, teacher, choral director. Received principal training in Munich, Germany, 1882−85, under Joseph Rheinberger. An accomplished organist, he wrote many compositions, principally works for orchestra and chorus, and collaborated in writing two operas. He was professor of music at Yale, 1894−1919. His style was marked by conservatism and a natural feeling for religion, both clearly present in his best-known work, *Hora Novissima* (1893).

PARKER, ISAAC (*b. Boston, Mass., 1768; d. 1830*), jurist. Graduated Harvard, 1786. Esteemed for decisions showing a broad social sensitivity while justice of Massachusetts Supreme Court, 1806−30 (chief justice, *post* 1814). Drew up plan for Harvard Law School, 1817, at which he was first Royall professor.

PARKER, ISAAC CHARLES (*b. Belmont Co., Ohio, 1838; d. Fort Smith, Ark., 1896*), lawyer. Congressman, Republican, from Missouri, 1871−75; federal judge, western district of Arkansas, 1875−96. A hard and fearless frontier jurist.

PARKER, JAMES (*b. Woodbridge, N.J., ca. 1714; d. Burlington, N.J., 1770*), printer, journalist. Apprenticed to William Bradford in New York, 1727; entered partnership with Benjamin Franklin, 1742, to carry on a New York printing business. As public printer of New York, 1743−60, Parker had a number of disputes with the government of the colony over printing antiadministration items. Parker published several New York newspapers and periodicals in addition to sermons, almanacs, and histories; he set up the first permanent printing office in New Jersey at Woodbridge, 1751, and entered also into partnerships for operation of other printing shops in New York and in New Haven, Conn.

PARKER, JAMES (*b. Hunterdon Co., N.J., 1776; d. 1868*), New Jersey landowner, official, and legislator. Father of John C. Parker. Originally a Federalist, he supported Andrew Jackson, 1824−37, thereafter becoming a Whig and finally a Republican. He was a principal factor in the promotion of the Delaware and Raritan Canal; served as congressman, 1833−37; and twice mayor of Perth Amboy; and was active in the cultural and religious life of his state.

PARKER, JAMES CUTLER DUNN (*b. Boston, Mass., 1828; d. Brookline, Mass., 1916*), composer, organist, music teacher. Nephew of Richard G. Parker. Organist, Trinity Church, Boston; teacher, New England Conservatory.

PARKER, JANE MARSH (*b. Milan, N.Y., 1836; d. Los Angeles, Calif., 1913*), author, essayist.

PARKER, JOEL (*b. Jaffrey, N.H., 1795; d. 1875*), jurist, legislator. Chief justice, New Hampshire superior court, 1838−48; Royall professor of Law, Harvard, 1848−68. Vigorously opposed Radical Republican tinkering with U.S. Constitution *post* 1862.

PARKER, JOEL (*b. Bethel, Vt., 1799; d. New York, N.Y., 1873*), Presbyterian clergyman. Vigorous and popular preacher; held prominent pastorates in New York City, New Orleans, Philadelphia, and Newark, N.J. President, Union Theological Seminary, New York, 1840−42.

PARKER, JOEL (*b. near Freehold, N.J., 1816; d. Philadelphia, Pa., 1888*), jurist, politician. Democratic governor of New Jersey, 1863−66 and 1872−75; state supreme court justice, 1880−88. Supported Civil War but defended states' rights against so-called "military necessities."

PARKER, JOHN (*b. Lexington, Mass., 1729; d. 1775*), Revolutionary soldier. Captain of the minuteman company which defended Lexington, Apr. 19, 1775.

PARKER, JOHN CORTLANDT (*b. Perth Amboy, N.J. 1818; d. Newark, N.J., 1907*), lawyer. Son of James Parker (1776−1868). Graduated Rutgers, 1836; studied law in Newark office of Theodore Frelinghuysen. President, American Bar Association, 1883−84, Parker was at the time of his death the acknowledged leader of the New Jersey bar. Prominent in organization of the New Jersey Republican party, he enthusiastically supported Lincoln in 1860 and 1864 and helped secure New Jersey's ratification of the 14th Amendment. He served on the U.S. commission to investigate Louisiana's electoral vote in 1876 and on various state legal commissions, but declined several high diplomatic appointments. His work as advisory master of the New Jersey Court of Chancery resulted in opinions which were landmarks in the state's corporate law.

PARKER, JOHN JOHNSTON (*b. Monroe, N.C., 1885; d. Washington, D.C., 1958*), jurist. Received LL.B. from the University of North Carolina, 1908. After practicing law in North Carolina and serving in Republican politics (member of the Republican National Committee, 1924), Parker was appointed appellate judge for the U.S. Court of Appeals for the Fourth Circuit in 1925 by President Coolidge; he served until his death. In 1930, President Hoover appointed him to the Supreme Court, but he failed to win ratification. As appellate judge, he heard more than 4,000 arguments and made over 1,500 decisions. He was against laissez-faire in economic matters, and heard many cases concerning race relations; his decision in *Briggs* v. *Elliott* (1951) ruled in favor of school segregation, later struck down by the Supreme Court in 1954. Parker was a member of the U.S. Judicial Conference from 1930 to 1958; in 1945, President Truman appointed him as alternate U.S. member of the International Military Tribunal at Nuremberg, Germany.

PARKER, JOHN MILLIKEN (*b. Bethel Church, Miss., 1863; d. Pass Christian, Miss., 1939*), cotton factor, leader in Progressive and Democratic parties. Democratic governor of Louisiana, 1920–24.

PARKER, JOSIAH (*b. Isle of Wight Co., Va., 1751; d. Isle of Wight Co., 1810*), Revolutionary soldier, politician. Antifederalist member of Congress from Virginia, 1789–1801.

PARKER, PETER (*b. Framingham, Mass., 1804; d. Washington, D.C., 1888*), Presbyterian medical missionary to China, 1834–40 and 1842–57. Served as secretary to Caleb Cushing in treaty negotiations, 1844; thereafter was ad interim U.S. representative in China at various times and U.S. minister, 1855–57.

PARKER, QUANAH. *See* QUANAH.

PARKER, RICHARD ELLIOT (*b. Westmoreland Co., Va., 1783; d. Clarke Co., Va., 1840*), War of 1812 soldier, Virginia legislator and U.S. senator. Judge of Virginia general court, 1817–36; judge, supreme court of appeals, 1837–40.

PARKER, RICHARD GREEN (*b. Boston, Mass., 1798; d. Boston, 1869*), Boston public school teacher, textbook writer.

PARKER, SAMUEL (*b. Ashfield, Mass., 1779; d. 1866*), Congregational clergyman, missionary, explorer. Selected sites for Oregon Indian missions during stay there, 1835–36; published *Journal of an Exploring Tour Beyond the Rocky Mountains* (1838).

PARKER, SAMUEL CHESTER (*b. Cincinnati, Ohio, 1880; d. Chicago, Ill., 1924*), educator. Graduated University of Cincinnati, 1901; a pupil also of John Dewey and E. L. Thorndike. Teacher of education, University of Chicago, 1909–24. His successful textbooks included *Methods of Teaching in High Schools* (1915).

PARKER, THEODORE (*b. Lexington, Mass., 1810; d. Florence, Italy, 1860*), theologian, Unitarian clergyman, publicist and author. Grandson of John Parker. Self-educated in the main, he graduated from Harvard Divinity School, 1836, and became minister in West Roxbury, Mass., 1837. Grown skeptical of orthodoxy, he believed that religious truths were drawn from individual intuition and feeling rather than from revelation. An immensely popular lecturer and essayist, Parker demanded a new theology based upon the immanence of God in nature and human experience. An associate of the Channings, F. H. Hedge, R. W. Emerson, and Bronson Alcott, he quickly became a figure of intense controversy in religious circles; resigning his pastorate, 1845, he became minister of a new free church in Boston. Here, he dealt largely with social questions, was a violent supporter of abolition, and exercised great influence on politics.

PARKER, THEODORE BISSELL (*b. Roxbury, Mass., 1889; d. Wellesley, Mass., 1944*), civil engineer. B.S., Massachusetts Institute of Technology, 1911. A specialist in waterway and hydroelectric engineering, he served with the U.S. Army Corps of Engineers and in civilian employment principally with Stone and Webster. Appointed state engineer and acting director for Massachusetts of the Federal Emergency Administration of Public Works, 1933, he was named chief engineer of construction of the Tennessee Valley Authority, 1935, and chief engineer in 1938. He resigned in 1943 to become professor of civil engineering and chairman of the department at MIT.

PARKER, THOMAS (*b. Wiltshire, England, 1595; d. Newbury, Mass., 1677*), minister at Newbury, 1635–77. An orthodox Calvinist in doctrine, he advocated the Presbyterian, rather than the Congregational, ecclesiastical polity.

PARKER, WILLARD (*b. Lyndeborough, N.H., 1800; d. 1884*), surgeon. Graduated Harvard, 1826; served medical apprenticeship with John C. Warren and S. D. Townsend in Boston; M.D., Harvard, 1830. Taught at a number of schools; was professor of surgery, New York College of Physicians and Surgeons, 1839–70. A courageous and successful operator, he pioneered in surgical techniques for appendicitis.

PARKER, WILLIAM HARWAR (*b. New York, N.Y., 1826; d. Washington, D.C., 1896*), naval officer, author. Brother of Foxhall A. Parker. Graduated U.S. Naval Academy, 1865.

PARKHURST, CHARLES (*b. Sharon, Vt., 1845; d. 1921*), Methodist clergyman. Edited *Zion's Herald*, 1888–1919; promoted temperance and reunion of Methodism, North and South.

PARKHURST, CHARLES HENRY (*b. Framingham, Mass., 1842; d. New York, N.Y., 1933*), Presbyterian clergyman, reformer. Graduated Amherst, 1866; held New York City pastorate, 1880–1918. Launched furious attack upon alliance between Tammany Hall and organized vice, 1892, which led to Lexow Investigation, 1894.

PARKHURST, JOHN ADELBERT (*b. Dixon, Ill., 1861; d. Williams Bay, Wis., 1925*), businessman, astronomer. Did valuable photometric research at Yerkes Observatory, particularly in determining magnitude ranges and color indices.

PARKINSON, THOMAS IGNATIUS (*b. Philadelphia, Pa., 1881; d. New York, N.Y., 1959*), lawyer and insurance executive. Received LL.B. from the University of Pennsylvania, 1902. Taught at the Columbia University Law School from 1917 to 1935. In 1933 Parkinson was offered the post of secretary of the treasury by Roosevelt; he declined and became a critic of the New Deal. In 1920 he joined the Equitable Life Insurance Company of America; serving as vice president, 1925–27, president, 1927–53, and chairman of the board, 1954 until his death.

PARKMAN, FRANCIS (*b. Boston, Mass., 1823; d. Boston, 1893*), historian. Son of a New England family of wealth, social standing, and culture, Parkman developed as a boy a taste for outdoor life and nature study; during college vacations, he took long trips through New England, partly on foot and partly by canoe. At Harvard, he excelled in subjects that interested him and gave much time to outside reading. After graduation in 1844, he entered Harvard Law School, received a law degree, but never bothered to take the bar examinations.

In 1846 Parkman set out from St. Louis, Mo., on a journey over the Oregon Trail to study the Indians and to improve his health. He returned in poor physical condition, but a result of the trip was his first major writing, *The California and Oregon Trail* (first published in *Knickerbocker* magazine, 1847; book publication, 1849). In 1848 he began to write the *History of the Conspiracy of Pontiac*; it was the first of a sequence of books detailing the history of the struggles between the English and the French for control of the North American continent which he had planned to be his life task. Parkman estimated that it would take about 20 years to finish his project, but because of serious and crippling physical ailments the work took much longer. He suffered from a malady affecting the nervous system; its symptoms were extreme weakness of sight, an inability to concentrate upon any intellectual pursuit for more than brief periods at a time, and continual exhaustion. For most of his historical research Parkman had to employ copyists and readers and to write with a special frame in which parallel wires were strung across the page to guide his hand. His prodigious research under these circumstances was a remarkable achievement. Parkman also found time to become an accomplished horticulturist, to help found the Archaeological Society of America, and to keep up an extensive and active social intercourse. He was author also of a negligible novel, *Vassall Morton* (1856).

His great series of historical works began with publication of the work on Pontiac's conspiracy (1851). Thereafter came *Pioneers of France in the New World* (1865); *The Jesuits in North America* (1867); *The Discovery of the Great West* (1869, better known as retitled in 1879, *La Salle and the Discovery of the Great West*); *The Old Régime in Canada* (1874); *Count Frontenac and New France Under Louis XIV* (1877); *Montcalm and Wolfe* (1884); and, to complete the series, *A Half-Century of Conflict* (1892). Long before ending his work, his fame as America's leading historian was well established. Parkman was a careful scholar, insisting upon working from original manuscript material, which he sought out at home and abroad, but he was equally an artist. Diligent scholarship was joined with a flowing and evocative prose style, a profound feeling for the wildness and spaciousness of the continent on which the struggle took place, and a poet's sense of the overarching drama of the conflict.

PARKS, WILLIAM (*b. probably Shropshire, England, ca. 1698; d. at sea, 1750*), printer, newspaper publisher. Public printer of Maryland, 1727–37; established and operated press at Williamsburg, Va., 1730–50. Founded the *Maryland Gazette*, 1727; also the *Virginia Gazette*, 1736. Distinguished as a typographer, Parks published a number of books of literary and historical importance.

PARLEY, PETER. *See* GOODRICH, SAMUEL GRISWOLD.

PARMENTIER, ANDREW (*b. Enghien, Belgium, 1780; d. Brooklyn, N.Y., 1830*), horticulturist, landscape gardener. Came to America, 1824; established a botanical garden and nursery in Brooklyn, N.Y., 1825; was an advocate of the naturalistic, rather than the formal, treatment of gardens.

PARMLY, ELEAZAR (*b. Braintree, Vt., 1797; d. New York, N.Y., 1874*), dentist. Beginning as student assistant to his eldest brother, Parmly practiced as an itinerant dentist in the Midwest, 1817–19; from 1819 to 1821 he studied and practiced in London and Paris. Returning to New York City, he began a lifelong practice there. Striving constantly to improve professional standards of dentistry, he helped found the New York Society of

Surgeon Dentists, 1834, and helped establish the *American Journal of Dental Science*, 1839. He became first president of the New York College of Dentistry, 1866.

PARR, SAMUEL WILSON (*b. Granville, Ill., 1857; d. Urbana, Ill., 1931*), chemist, inventor. Graduated University of Illinois, 1884; M.S., Cornell University, 1885. Professor of chemistry, University of Illinois, 1891–1926. Parr's principal scientific contributions were made with respect to the physical and chemical properties, classification, and utilization of coal. He developed three types of calorimeters for determining heat value of coal and other solids, and an alloy mixture, which he named "illium," for lining calorimeters. His method of low-temperature coking was another important contribution, as were his studies of the embrittlement of boiler plate.

PARRINGTON, VERNON LOUIS (*b. Aurora, Ill., 1871; d. Gloucestershire, England, 1929*), teacher, philologist, historian. Educated at College of Emporia (Kans.) and at Harvard (graduated, 1893). Taught English and French at Emporia and at University of Oklahoma; was professor of English at University of Washington, 1908–29. An effective teacher, he developed a notable and popular series of courses in the history of American literature and thought. He published *The Connecticut Wits* (1926) and *Sinclair Lewis, Our Own Diogenes* (1927); his fame rests, however, on his *Main Currents in American Thought* (1927–30), an original interpretation of American literature in its relation to the full life of the nation. His principal theme was the rise of the idea of democratic idealism and the struggle to make it prevail in every dimension of American society.

PARRIS, ALBION KEITH (*b. Hebron, Maine, 1788; d. 1857*), Maine legislator and jurist. Democratic governor of Maine, 1821–26; U.S. senator, 1827–28; Maine Supreme Court justice, 1828–36; second comptroller of federal treasury, 1836–49.

PARRIS, ALEXANDER (*b. Hebron, Maine, 1780; d. Pembroke, Mass., 1852*), builder, architect. Worked extensively *post* 1815 in Boston area; served as consultant to Loammi Baldwin and as superintendent of construction for Charles Bulfinch. Designed David Sears House, 1816; St. Paul's Church, 1819; and Faneuil Hall Market area, 1825.

PARRIS, SAMUEL (*b. London, England, 1653; d. Sudbury, Mass., 1719/20*), clergyman. Came to Massachusetts *ante* 1674; was pastor at Salem Village, 1689–96. Prominent in ferreting out and condemning "witches" during the delusion of 1692–93.

PARRISH, ANNE (*b. Philadelphia, Pa., 1760; d. Philadelphia, 1800*), philanthropist. Sister of Joseph Parrish. Founded Philadelphia school for poor girls, 1796, and House of Industry for employment of poor women, 1795.

PARRISH, CELESTIA SUSANNAH (*b. near Swansonville, Va., 1853; d. Clayton, Ga., 1918*), educator. Greatly advanced public education in Georgia, particularly among rural children and adult illiterates.

PARRISH, CHARLES (*b. Dundaff, Pa., 1826; d. Philadelphia, Pa., 1896*), coal operator. Managed a varied industrial and commercial empire around Wilkes-Barre *post* 1856. The Lehigh & Wilkes-Barre Coal Co. was his principal holding.

PARRISH, EDWARD (*b. Philadelphia, Pa., 1822; d. Fort Sill, Indian Territory [now Oklahoma], 1872*), pharmacist, teacher. Son of Joseph Parrish. A principal founder, and president, 1868–71, of Swarthmore College.

PARRISH, JOSEPH (*b. Philadelphia, Pa., 1779; d. Philadelphia, 1840*), physician, abolitionist, teacher. Brother of Anne

Parrish. M.D., University of Pennsylvania, 1805. Held numerous hospital staff appointments; was president of board of managers of Wills Eye Hospital, 1833–40.

PARRISH, MAXFIELD (*b. Philadelphia, Pa., 1870; d. Plainfield, N.H., 1966*), artist. Attended Haverford College, Pennsylvania Academy of Fine Arts, and Drexel Institute. Opened his own studio (1894) to pursue commercial illustration and received national recognition with a cover design for *Harper's Weekly* (1895). For the next several decades his work appeared on the covers of *Scribner's Magazine, Century Magazine, Ladies' Home Journal,* and *National Weekly.* Illustrated L. Frank Baum's *Mother Goose in Prose* (1897) and was established firmly as a master of fantasy and romance with illustrations for such children's classics as Eugene Field's *Poems of Childhood* (1904), *Arabian Nights* (1909), and Nathaniel Hawthorne's *Wonder Book and Tanglewood* (1910). He is best known for his color prints, which hung over the mantels of millions of middle-class homes. In the mid-1930's he retired from illustration to paint rural landscapes for calendars and greeting cards.

PARROTT, ENOCH GREENLEAFE (*b. Portsmouth, N.H., 1815; d. 1879*), naval officer. Cousin of Robert P. Parrott. Made first Union capture of a Confederate privateer, June 3, 1861; was senior officer during much of blockade off Charleston; commanded monitor *Monadnock* during attacks on Fort Fisher, 1864–65.

PARROTT, ROBERT PARKER (*b. Lee, N.H., 1804; d. Cold Spring, N.Y., 1877*), ordnance inventor, manufacturer. Graduated West Point, 1824. Resigning from the army, 1836, he became superintendent of Gouverneur Kemble's West Point Foundry at Cold Spring, N.Y., makers of ordnance. Parrott invented two important devices: a rifled cast-iron cannon in several calibers strengthened by wrought iron hoops around the breech (patented 1861) and an explosive projectile to fit his cannon's rifling. These were extensively used on land and at sea during the Civil War and were probably the most efficient and effective ordnance of their type in the world.

PARRY, CHARLES CHRISTOPHER (*b. Admington, England, 1823; d. Davenport, Iowa, 1890*), botanist. Came to America as a boy. Graduated Union College, 1842; M.D., Columbia, 1846. Settling in Davenport, Iowa, 1846; Parry began his lifelong study of flora in the western states, devoting his summers to wide exploration. As member of organized expeditions or on his own, he made many important contributions to knowledge *post* 1848; his studies of plants along the U.S.–Mexican border, of Alpine flora of the Colorado Rockies, of California chaparral and California manzanitas are particularly notable. He discovered hundreds of new plant forms, among them the *Lilium parryi,* the Lote bush, and the Ensenada buckeye.

PARRY, CHARLES THOMAS (*b. Philadelphia, Pa., 1821; d. Beach Haven, N.J., 1887*), locomotive builder. General superintendent in charge of construction at Baldwin Locomotive Works *post* 1855; partner *post* 1867. Introduced scientific management techniques and fair labor policies.

PARRY, JOHN STUBBS (*b. Lancaster Co., Pa., 1843; d. Jacksonville, Fla., 1876*), obstetrician, gynecologist. M.D., University of Pennsylvania, 1865. Made important studies of rachitis; reorganized obstetrical and gynecological departments at Philadelphia Hospital; wrote *Extra-Uterine Pregnancy* (1875).

PARSONS, ALBERT RICHARD (*b. Montgomery, Ala., 1848; d. Illinois, 1887*), printer, Confederate soldier, anarchist. Settled in Chicago, 1873; edited anarchist newspaper *The Alarm,* 1884–86; executed for alleged complicity in Haymarket Riot.

PARSONS, ALBERT ROSS (*b. Sandusky, Ohio, 1847; d. Mount Kisco, N.Y., 1933*), musician. Dean of New York piano teachers; ardent advocate of Wagner; wrote *The Science of Pianoforte Practice* (1886).

PARSONS, ELSIE WORTHINGTON CLEWS (*b. New York, N.Y., 1875; d. New York, 1941*), sociologist, anthropologist. Daughter of Henry Clews. Graduated Barnard College, 1896. M.A., Columbia University, 1897; Ph.D., 1899. Her early writings were much concerned with the role of women in society and the cramping effect of conventions; influenced by Franz Boas and Pliny E. Goddard, she devoted herself *post* 1915 to field research in ethnology, primarily among the Pueblo Indians of the Southwest. She interested herself also in folklore and the collection of folktales. Among her books were *Mitla, Town of the Souls* (1936), *Pueblo Indian Religion* (1939), and *Folk-Lore of the Antilles, French and English* (1933–43).

PARSONS, FRANK (*b. Mount Holly, N.J., 1854; d. Boston, Mass., 1908*), lawyer, teacher, political scientist. Urged currency and municipal government reforms in *Rational Money* (1898), *The City for the People* (1900), and other works; did pioneer work in vocational guidance.

PARSONS, JOHN EDWARD (*b. New York, N.Y., 1829; d. 1915*), corporation lawyer, advocate of industrial combination. Organized American Sugar Refining Co., 1891; successfully defended it in *U.S. v. E. C. Knight Co.*

PARSONS, LEWIS BALDWIN (*b. Perry, N.Y., 1818; d. Flora, Ill., 1907*), lawyer, railroad manager. Director of rail and river transportation for Union army in Department of the Mississippi 1861–64; for all departments, 1864–66. Received brevet of major general, 1866, for exceptional service.

PARSONS, LEWIS ELIPHALET (*b. Lisle, N.Y., 1817; d. Talladega, Ala., 1895*), lawyer, Alabama Unionist and legislator. Settled in Talladega *ca.* 1840. Provisional governor of Alabama, 1865; supported President Andrew Johnson; was Speaker of lower house in Alabama legislature, 1872–73.

PARSONS, SAMUEL BROWNE (*b. Flushing, N.Y., 1819; d. 1906*), horticulturist, nurseryman. Made first successful importation of Italian honeybees, 1860, and of Valencia oranges, 1870; specialized in Japanese maples and rhododendrons; wrote *The Rose: Its History, Poetry, Culture, and Classification* (1847).

PARSONS, SAMUEL HOLDEN (*b. Lyme, Conn., 1737; d. Big Beaver River, Ohio, 1789*), lawyer, Connecticut legislator, Revolutionary major general. Directed Connecticut's defense *post* 1778, after active service at Boston and Long Island and on the Hudson. A promoter and director of the Ohio Co., he served *post* 1787 as first judge of the Northwest Territory.

PARSONS, THEOPHILUS (*b. Byfield, Mass., 1750; d. Boston, Mass., 1813*), jurist. Graduated Harvard, 1769; was aided in study of law by Edmund Trowbridge; practiced in Newburyport, Mass., and *post* 1800 in Boston. Chief justice of the Massachusetts supreme court, 1806–13. In a pamphlet, *The Essex Result* (1778), Parsons outlined a plan for a government which greatly influenced John Adams' state constitution adopted in 1780. Leading member of the Essex Junto, a Federalist political clique in Massachusetts, Parsons enjoyed a towering reputation as lawyer and judge. He was instrumental in preserving the substance of common-law doctrines in American jurisprudence by restating them in intelligible form to suit American needs. In giving his decisions, he drew rules of general application from the English common law, much unwritten colonial law, and distinctive local usages.

PARSONS, THEOPHILUS (b. Newburyport, Mass., 1797; d. 1882), lawyer. Son of Theophilus Parsons (1750–1813). Professor at Harvard Law School, 1848–69; author of *The Law of Contracts* (1853-55), *A Treatise on Maritime Law* (1859), and many other treatises, both legal and philosophical.

PARSONS, THOMAS WILLIAM (b. Boston, Mass., 1819; d. Scituate, Mass., 1892), dentist, poet. Translated first ten cantos of Dante's *Inferno* (1843), the first extensive translation published in America. His able but incomplete version of the whole of the *Divine Comedy*, together with his original poems were issued in a collected edition, 1893.

PARSONS, USHER (b. Alfred, Maine, 1788; d. Providence, R.I., 1868), physician, surgeon. Commissioned surgeon's mate, July 1812, after private study of medicine, Parsons won fame for brilliant work in treating American wounded after battle of Lake Erie, 1813. He received M.D. degree from Harvard, 1818; in 1822 he became professor of anatomy and surgery at Brown University. An idealist in medicine and a scholar, he won the Bolyston Prize four times for professional writings.

PARSONS, WILLIAM BARCLAY (b. New York, N.Y., 1859; d. New York, 1932), engineer. Graduated Columbia, 1879; C.E., Columbia School of Mines, 1882. His early interest was in railway construction. As chief engineer of the New York City Transit Commission, 1894–98 and 1899–1904, he planned and oversaw construction of the first subway, developing lasting standards of design for such work. Thereafter he became engineering consultant on a wide range of projects, which included the Isthmian Canal Commission, the London Traffic Commission, and the Chicago Transit Commission. He designed the Cape Cod Canal, served with the United States Engineers during World War I, and designed the Detroit-Windsor vehicular tunnel.

PARTINGTON, MRS. *See* SHILLABER, BENJAMIN PENHALLOW.

PARTON, ARTHUR (b. Hudson, N.Y., 1842; d. Yonkers, N.Y., 1914), landscape painter. Followed traditional English practices as modified by Hudson River school.

PARTON, JAMES (b. Canterbury, England, 1822; d. Newburyport, Mass., 1891), journalist, biographer. Came to America as a child. Staff member of New York *Home Journal*, 1848–55. Thereafter highly successful as author of carefully researched and well-organized lives of Horace Greeley (1855), Aaron Burr (1857), Andrew Jackson (1859–60), and other major American figures.

PARTON, SARA PAYSON WILLIS (b. Portland, Maine, 1811; d. New York, N.Y., 1872), author. Daughter of Nathaniel Willis; sister of N. P. Willis; married James Parton, 1856. Under pen name of "Fanny Fern," Parton turned out quantities of frothy but popular chitchat on homey subjects.

PARTRIDGE, ALDEN (b. Norwich, Vt., 1785; d. Norwich, 1854), military educator. Originator of preparatory military academies of elementary and secondary grade; founded Norwich University (1819).

PARTRIDGE, JAMES RUDOLPH (b. Baltimore, Md., ca. 1823; d. Alicante, Spain, 1884), lawyer, politician, diplomat. Influential Maryland Unionist and Republican; U.S. minister to a number of Latin American countries, 1862–83.

PARTRIDGE, RICHARD (b. Portsmouth, N.H., 1681; d. London, England, 1759), merchant, colonial agent. Removed to England, 1701. Agent for New York, New Jersey, Massachusetts, and Pennsylvania at various times; was agent for Rhode Island, 1715–59, during which time he secured a favorable settlement of boundary questions; he served also as agent for Connecticut, 1750–59. He played an active part in making the Molasses Act, 1733, less offensive to New England interests.

PARTRIDGE, WILLIAM ORDWAY (b. Paris, France, 1861; d. New York, N.Y., 1930), sculptor. His equestrian General Grant in New York, 1896, and his marble Pietà in St. Patrick's Cathedral are perhaps his best-known works.

PARVIN, THEODORE SUTTON (b. Cedarville, N.J., 1817; d. 1901), lawyer, teacher, librarian. Raised in Cincinnati, Ohio; removed to Iowa, 1838, where he practiced law and held numerous judicial and civil offices. President, Iowa State Teachers' Association, 1867; principal founder, Masonic Library at Cedar Rapids.

PARVIN, THEOPHILUS (b. Buenos Aires, Argentina, 1829; d. Philadelphia, Pa., 1898), obstetrician, gynecologist. Grandson of Caesar A. Rodney. Graduated Indiana University, 1847; M.D., University of Pennsylvania, 1852. Wrote *Science and Art of Obstetrics* (1886).

PASCALIS-OUVERIÈRE, FELIX (b. France, ca. 1750; d. New York, N.Y., 1833), physician. Immigrated from Santo Domingo, 1793; practiced in Philadelphia, and after 1810, in New York. Author of accounts of yellow fever outbreaks in Philadelphia, 1796 and 1798.

PASCHAL, GEORGE WASHINGTON (b. Skull Shoals, Ga., 1812; d. Washington, D.C., 1878), jurist, author, journalist. Removed to Arkansas, 1837; to Texas, 1848. Prominent Texas Unionist. Compiled notable digest of Texas Supreme Court decisions (1872–75).

PASCO, SAMUEL (b. London, England, 1834; d. 1917), Florida politician. Came to America as a boy; was raised in Charlestown, Mass.; removed to Florida, 1859. A Democratic leader in Florida after service in Confederate army, he served as U.S. senator, 1887–99, and on the Isthmian Canal Commission, 1899–1904.

PASQUIN, ANTHONY. *See* WILLIAMS, JOHN.

PASSAVANT, WILLIAM ALFRED (b. Zelienople, Pa., 1821; d. Pittsburgh, Pa., 1894), Lutheran clergyman, editor. Devoted life to home missionary movement and establishing institutions of mercy; was responsible for introduction of Lutheran deaconesses into the United States, 1849.

PASTOR, ANTONIO (b. New York, N.Y., 1837; d. Elmhurst, N.Y., 1908), New York theater manager, actor, better known as "Tony Pastor." Played prominent role in developing vaudeville format and in encouraging young performers.

PASTORIUS, FRANCIS DANIEL (b. Franconia, Germany, 1651; d. Germantown, Pa., 1719/20), lawyer, author, schoolmaster. Laid out settlement of Germantown, 1683, as agent for colony of Quakers from Frankfurt am Main; signed first Quaker protest against slavery in America, 1688.

PASVOLSKY, LEO (b. Pavlograd, Russia, 1893; d. Washington, D.C., 1953), economist, journalist, foreign policy adviser. Studied at the College of the City of New York and at Columbia University. Wrote many books and articles about communism and economics in the Soviet Union, mainly under the auspices of the Institute of Economics (later the Brookings Institution), which he joined in 1922. Author of influential economic papers for the World Monetary and Economic Conference in London, 1932–33. Joined the Division of Trade Agreements of the Department of State, 1935. Appointed special assistant to Secretary of State Cordell Hull, 1936, and became his most trusted adviser;

forwarded the reciprocal trade agreements program and supplied memoranda on international questions. Became chief of the Division of Special Research and director of the Committee on Postwar Problems, 1941, and began his major work in formulating the concept and charter of the United Nations. At the San Francisco Conference, 1945, Pasvolsky was instrumental in negotiating many aspects of the organization's need for the veto in the Security Council and broad security provisions in the charter. As chairman of the Coordinating Committee, he was responsible for the final wording of the U.N. Charter. Explained the Charter to Congress and to national organizations, 1945. Attended the Bretton Woods Conference, 1945, before leaving the State Department to become director of international studies of the Brookings Institution.

PATCH, ALEXANDER MCCARRELL (*b. Fort Huachuca, Arizona Territory, 1889; d. San Antonio, Tex., 1945*), army officer. Raised in Pennsylvania. Graduated West Point, 1913; commissioned in the infantry. When the United States entered World War I, he went to France, where in 1917 his unit became a part of the new 1st Division. Machine guns were new to the division, and he was among the first Americans to be schooled by the British in their use. During the next two decades he alternated between regimental duty and assignments as a military student and instructor. In 1924 he attended the Command and General Staff School and in 1931 entered the Army War College. Six weeks after Pearl Harbor, General George C. Marshall selected Patch to command the task force destined to defend New Caledonia. On Mar. 1, 1944, Patch was given command of the U.S. 7th Army, which invaded southern France in concert with an Allied advance from a northern beachhead in Normandy. On Aug. 15 he began his landings along the Riviera. During January 1945 he met and repelled Hitler's last major offensive on the western front. Marshall ordered him home in June to ready the 4th Army for Pacific duty. When Japan capitulated, Patch headed a board to study the army's postwar structure. Posthumously, in 1954, he was made a general.

PATCH, SAM (*b. Rhode Island, ca. 1807; d. Rochester, N.Y., 1829*), daredevil. Gained national reputation diving into rivers from great heights, including Niagara River from ledge on Goat Island. Killed in a dive into the Genesee River.

PATE, MAURICE (*b. Pender, Nebr., 1894; d. New York, N.Y., 1965*), businessman and United Nations official. Attended Princeton (B.S., 1915). Following work with several U.S. relief agencies during World Wars I and II, he accompanied Herbert Hoover (1948) on a world food survey that helped spur the UN to establish its children's fund (UNICEF); he was appointed its first executive director, a post he held for life. Under his direction UNICEF provided emergency aid, then shifted its focus to the worldwide problem of chronic starvation and disease among children. In 1960 he refused to allow his nomination for the Nobel Peace Prize, claiming the honor belonged to UNICEF.

PATERSON, JOHN (*b. Wethersfield, Conn., 1744; d. Lisle, N.Y., 1808*), lawyer, Revolutionary brigadier general, public official. Helped organize the Ohio Co.; was a proprietor of the "Boston Purchase" in upper New York State.

PATERSON, WILLIAM (*b. Co. Antrim, Ireland, 1745; d. Albany, N.Y., 1806*), politician, U.S. Supreme Court justice. Taken to America as a child; was raised in New Jersey. Graduated to College of New Jersey (Princeton), 1763; studied law with Richard Stockton. Elected deputy to New Jersey Provincial Congress, 1775; served as attorney general of New Jersey, 1776–83. Appointed delegate to the Constitutional Convention, 1787, Paterson presented the "New Jersey Plan," which represented the

views of small states. U.S. senator, 1789, and governor of New Jersey, 1790–92, Paterson then became an associate judge of the U.S. Supreme Court and served until his death. He collected and collated the laws of New Jersey (published 1800) and also drafted remodeled rules for practice and procedure in the state courts which were adopted in 1799. Paterson, N.J., which he helped promote, bears his name.

PATILLO, HENRY (*b. Scotland, 1726; d. Dinwiddie Co., Va., 1801*), Presbyterian clergyman. Came to Virginia as a child. Removed to North Carolina, 1765; presided over first synod of the Carolinas; was an active patriot and delegate to North Carolina Provincial Congress, 1775.

PATON, LEWIS BAYLES (*b. New York, N.Y., 1864; d. 1932*), Congregational clergyman, Old Testament scholar, archaeologist. Taught at Hartford (Conn.) Theological Seminary, 1892–1932.

PATRI, ANGELO (*b. Piaggine, Salerno, Italy, 1876; d. Danbury, Conn., 1965*), educator and columnist. Attended City College of New York and Columbia (M.A., 1904). Teacher (from 1898) and principal (from 1908) in New York City public schools. His philosophy of liberal education promoted the teaching of subjects that promoted creative learning; developed a closer understanding between teachers and parents, and gained the participation of parents in school activities. He presented his ideas through radio, child guidance books, and his syndicated column, "Our Children." Author of *A Schoolmaster of the Great City* (1917) and books for children, such as *Pinocchio in Africa* (1911).

PATRICK, EDWIN HILL ("TED") (*b. Rutherford, N.J., 1901; d. New York, N.Y., 1964*), magazine editor. Copywriter for Young and Rubicam (beginning in 1928); writer for World Peaceways (mid-1930's), an organization of American businesses, publishers, and advertisers seeking to promote peace; with the Office of War Information (1942–44), then Compton Advertising (1944–46). He joined Curtis Publishing in 1946 and took over the editorship of the recently launched *Holiday* magazine. Under his direction the magazine became consistently profitable by attracting top authors and paying handsomely for articles; the inclusion of high-quality visual material; and "special issues" on individual countries. Elected chairman of the American Society of Magazine Editors and Magazine Publishers Association (both in 1963).

PATRICK, HUGH TALBOT (*b. New Philadelphia, Ohio, 1860; d. Chicago, Ill., 1939*), neurologist. M.D., Bellevue Hospital Medical School, 1884. Pioneered in neurology in the Middle West; was professor of nervous and mental diseases at Northwestern University and Chicago Polyclinic.

PATRICK, MARSENA RUDOLPH (*b. near Watertown, N.Y., 1811; d. 1888*), Union major general, agriculturist. Graduated West Point, 1835. After service in Seminole and Mexican wars, Patrick engaged in farming and agricultural education, 1850–61. During the Civil War, he held field commands up to Antietam (September 1862); he was provost marshal general for the Army of the Potomac until 1864 and thereafter for all Union armies operating against Richmond. He died while in command of the soldiers' home in Dayton, Ohio.

PATRICK, MARY MILLS (*b. Canterbury, N.H., 1850; d. Palo Alto, Calif., 1940*). First president of American College for Girls, Istanbul, Turkey, 1890–1924.

PATRICK, MASON MATHEWS (*b. Lewisburg, W.Va., 1863; d. Washington, D.C., 1942*), army officer. Graduated West Point, 1886; commissioned in the Corps of Engineers. After three decades of various and exemplary service, which included duty as chief engineer of the army of pacification in Cuba, he went to France in World War I as colonel commanding the 1st Engineers. He later had charge of all engineering construction for the American Expeditionary Forces in France. In May 1918, now a major general, he was assigned by General John J. Pershing to the task of bringing order out of confusion as commander of all Air Service units, which were plagued by bickering and poor organization. He returned to the United States in 1919 to resume his duties with the Corps of Engineers. Appointed chief of the Army Air Service in October 1921, he served until 1927; although convinced of the importance of air power, unlike his chief assistant, Col. William Mitchell, he was moderate in his approach to gaining some degree of autonomy for the Air Service. After retirement in 1927 he continued active and was public utilities commissioner for the District of Columbia, 1929–33.

PATTEN, GILBERT (*b. Corinna, Maine, 1866; d. Vista, Calif., 1945*), author. Christened George William Patten. In a 60-year career as a writer he published under his own name and a dozen pen names at least 1,500 works of fiction, principally for the dime-novel trade and the pulp magazines. Of these, more than 800 stories dealt with the fantastic career of "Frank Merriwell," a schoolboy and college athlete of impossible skill, strength, and virtue. Published as by "Burt L. Standish," the Merriwell stories appeared from 1896 until Patten abandoned the series in 1913.

PATTEN, JAMES A. (*b. Freeland Corners, Ill., 1852; d. Chicago, Ill., 1928*), grain merchant, capitalist. A successful speculator in grain futures, he held virtual corners in corn, oats, and wheat, 1908–09.

PATTEN, SIMON NELSON (*b. DeKalb Co., Ill., 1852; d. Brown's-Mills-in-the-Pines, N.J., 1922*), economist. Ph.D., Halle, 1878; was strongly influenced by German thought and economic example. Professor at University of Pennsylvania, 1888–1917, and an outstanding teacher, Patten was an economic optimist, holding that man by proper application of intelligence could better his economic condition. He opposed the gloomy view of the classical economists as being derived from an exploitative economic environment, contrasting with it the limitless social improvement which must follow on economic conservation. He believed that Americans were wasteful consumers and recommended a theory of prosperity based on a wisely managed consumption and on a philosophy of spending, rather than saving, in an era of growing abundance. *The Development of English Thought* (1899) and *The New Basis of Civilization* (1907) are representative of his writing but are no measure of his thought or influence.

PATTEN, WILLIAM (*b. Watertown, Mass., 1861; d. 1932*), zoologist, paleontologist. B.S., Harvard, 1883; Ph.D., Leipzig, 1884. Taught at University of North Dakota, and at Dartmouth *post* 1893.

PATTERSON, ALICIA (*b. Chicago, Ill., 1906; d. New York, N.Y., 1963*), editor and publisher. Raised in a journalistic family, she moved to New York where her father left the *Chicago Tribune* to launch the *New York Daily News*; she worked in the promotion department of the *Daily News* (1927–38) and later as literary critic (1932–43). Acquired the defunct *Nassau County Journal* on Long Island (1940) and renamed it *Newsday*. The newspaper won quick acceptance and was awarded the N. W. Ayer and Son award for excellence in typography, makeup, and printing (1955). Editorially, she supported internationlist positions in foreign affairs; called for the recognition of Communist China; and denounced Sen. Joseph McCarthy. A series of articles by Alan Hathway on corruption at racetracks received the 1954 Pulitzer Prize for meritorious public service.

PATTERSON, DANIEL TODD (*b. Long Island, N.Y., 1786; d. Washington, D.C., 1839*), naval officer. Conducted successful raid against Jean Laffite at Barataria Bay, La., 1814; provided Andrew Jackson with invaluable naval support on Lake Borgne in battle of New Orleans.

PATTERSON, ELEANOR MEDILL ("CISSY") (*b. Chicago, Ill., 1881; d. near Marlboro, Md., 1948*), newspaper editor and publisher. Granddaughter of Joseph Medill; sister of Joseph M. Paterson; niece of Robert S. McCormick. Served as editor-publisher of W. R. Hearst's Washington, D.C. *Herald*, 1930–37, doubling its circulation; leased the paper from Hearst, along with his evening paper, the *Times*, 1937, and in January 1939 exercised options to buy them. She then combined them into a single all-day paper with six editions, the *Washington Times-Herald*, which shortly had the largest circulation in the city and was as lively and spiteful as its owner.

PATTERSON, JAMES KENNEDY (*b. Glasgow, Scotland, 1833; d. 1922*), educator. Came to America as a boy; was raised in Indiana. President and ardent advocate of State College of Kentucky, later University of Kentucky, from 1869 to 1910.

PATTERSON, JAMES WILLIS (*b. Henniker, N.H., 1823; d. Hanover, N.H., 1893*), educator, politician. Graduated Dartmouth, 1848; taught there, 1852–65. Congressman, Republican, from New Hampshire, 1863–67; U.S. senator, 1867–73. Implicated in Crédit Mobilier scandals. State superintendent of education, New Hampshire, 1881–93.

PATTERSON, JOHN HENRY (*b. near Dayton, Ohio, 1844; d. 1922*), salesman, manufacturer. Bought a small, failing company, 1884, and built it into the highly successful National Cash Register Co., by using aggressive modern sales techniques and direct mail advertising.

PATTERSON, JOSEPH MEDILL (*b. Chicago, Ill., 1879; d. New York, N.Y., 1946*), newspaper publisher. Grandson of Joseph Medill; brother of Eleanor M. Patterson; nephew of Robert S. McCormick. B.A., Yale, 1901. Joined the *Chicago Tribune* staff as a reporter, rising to assistant editor; resigned on learning that his father had used the paper's influence to aid him in a successful campaign for election to the Illinois legislature, 1903. A nonconformist and a reformer, he joined the Socialist party and devoted himself to writing, 1906–10; in 1908 he published a novel, *A Little Brother of the Rich*. Disillusioned with socialism, he joined his cousin Robert M. McCormick as coeditor of the *Chicago Tribune*. More interested in reporting than editing, he personally covered the Mexican border incident, 1914, and the start of World War I in Europe. After serving with credit as an artillery officer in France, he returned home to bring out on June 26, 1919, in New York City, a mass-appeal tabloid, the *Illustrated Daily News* (soon called simply the *Daily News*, which under his close superintendence became the widest-selling newspaper in the United States.

PATTERSON, MORRIS (*b. Philadelphia, Pa., 1809; d. Philadelphia, 1878*), merchant, philanthropist. Pioneer in developing anthracite coal trade.

PATTERSON, RICHARD CUNNINGHAM, JR. (*b. Omaha, Nebr., 1886; d. New York, N.Y., 1966*), engineer, ambassador, and corporate executive. Attended Nebraska and Columbia (engineer of mines degree, 1912). Engineering inspector for New York City (1913) and secretary of the city's Fire Department (1917). With J. G. White Engineering (1920) and E. I. du Pont de Nemours (1921–27). As New York City's commissioner of corrections, 1927–32, he improved conditions in the city's eighteen prisons. Resigned to become executive vice president of the National

Broadcasting Company. Assistant U.S. secretary of commerce (1938–39); chairman of the board of R.K.O. (1939–45); and a trustee of the Import-Export Bank. Appointed ambassador to Yugoslavia (1944–47) and to Guatemala (1948–50); minister to Switzerland (1951–53). Head of New York City's Department of Commerce (1954–66).

PATTERSON, ROBERT (*b. near Hillsborough, Ireland, 1743; d. Philadelphia, Pa., 1824*), Revolutionary soldier, mathematician. Came to America, 1768. Professor of mathematics, University of Pennsylvania, 1779–1814; director of U.S. Mint, 1805–24.

PATTERSON, ROBERT (*b. Co. Tyrone, Ireland, 1792; d. Philadelphia, Pa., 1881*), soldier, industrialist. Came to America as a boy; served in War of 1812; was successful as a commission grocery merchant in Philadelphia. Major general of volunteers in the Mexican War, Patterson gained honors at Cerro Gordo and Jalapa. *Post* 1848 he became prominent in the Louisiana sugar industry, came to own 30 cotton mills in Pennsylvania, and was a promoter of the Pennsylvania Railroad. Made a major general of volunteers, 1861, he was given command of the military department composed of Pennsylvania, Delaware, Maryland, and the District of Columbia. His failure to check Confederate forces under General J. E. Johnston in July 1861 and his noncooperation with McDowell in first Bull Run led to much controversy and to his retirement from service.

PATTERSON, ROBERT MAYNE (*b. Philadelphia, Pa., 1832; d. Philadelphia, 1911*), Presbyterian clergyman, editor. Associate editor, *The Presbyterian*, 1870–80; editor, *The Presbyterian Journal*, 1880–93; authority on ecclesiastical law.

PATTERSON, ROBERT PORTER (*b. Glens Falls, N.Y., 1891; d. Elizabeth, N.J., 1952*), lawyer, judge, and statesman. Studied at Union College and Harvard University. He served in France during World War I, winning the Distinguished Service Cross. Practiced law in New York until 1930, when President Hoover appointed him judge of the U.S. District Court of the Southern New York District. President Roosevelt appointed him to the Second Circuit Court of Appeals in 1939; and in 1940, under secretary of war. During World War II he was influential in overseeing the military production necessary for winning the war. In 1945 he refused Truman's offer to appoint him to the Supreme Court, but accepted the appointment as secretary of war. He resigned in 1947 and returned to private law practice; serving as president of the Bar Association of New York City and of the Council on Foreign Relations.

PATTERSON, RUFUS LENOIR (*b. Salem, N.C., 1872; d. New York, N.Y., 1943*), inventor, businessman. Attended University of North Carolina; grandson of Francis Fries. Developed a machine for weighing, packing, stamping, and labeling smoking tobacco (patented March 1897) which brought him to the notice of James B. Duke. Becoming a close ally of Duke, he was made a vice president of the American Tobacco Co. in 1901, and was a founder of the American Machine and Foundry Co. President of that company *post* 1900 (chairman of the board, 1941–43), he was probably more responsible for the mechanization of the tobacco industry than any other individual. Under his guidance the company and its subsidiaries became the world's largest suppliers of tobacco manufacturing equipment, and expanded into many other fields.

PATTERSON, THOMAS HARMAN (*b. New Orleans, La., 1820; d. Washington, D.C., 1889*), naval officer. Son of Daniel T. Patterson. Served during Civil War on Union Atlantic blockade duty; retired as rear admiral, 1882.

PATTERSON, THOMAS MACDONALD (*b. Co. Carlow, Ireland, 1839; d. 1916*), lawyer, editor. Came to America as a boy; settled in Denver, Colo., 1872; was Democratic territorial delegate and congressman from Colorado, 1875–79. Controlled Denver *Rocky Mountain News*, 1892–1913; was a consistent friend of labor, reform, and popular control of government. U.S. senator, Populist Democrat, 1901–07.

PATTERSON, WILLIAM (*b. Co. Donegal, Ireland, 1752; d. Baltimore, Md., 1835*), merchant. Father of Elizabeth P. Bonaparte. Came to America, 1766. Imported supplies and munitions for patriot army and made fortune during Revolution; later a successful shipowner and industrialist, he was an incorporator and director of the Baltimore & Ohio Railroad and of the Canton Company.

PATTIE, JAMES OHIO (*b. Bracken Co., Ky., 1804; d. ca. 1850*), trapper, author. Published *Personal Narrative* (1831, 1833; ed. Timothy Flint), a dramatic, semifictional account of travels as far west as California.

PATTISON, GRANVILLE SHARP (*b. Glasgow, Scotland ca. 1791; d. New York, N.Y., 1851*), anatomist. Came to America, 1819; taught at University of Maryland, 1820–26. Brought great prestige to Jefferson Medical College as professor of anatomy, 1832–41; held chair of anatomy thereafter at University of the City of New York.

PATTISON, JAMES WILLIAM (*b. Boston, Mass., 1844; d. Asheville, N.C., 1915*), Union soldier, painter, lecturer on art. Popularized serious art and promoted art museums and schools in Illinois and Missouri, notably at Chicago and St. Louis; served for many years as secretary of the Chicago Municipal Art League.

PATTISON, JOHN M. (*b. near Owensville, Ohio, 1847; d. Milford, Ohio, 1906*), lawyer, insurance executive, Ohio legislator. Congressman, Democrat, 1891–93; Democratic governor of Ohio, 1906.

PATTISON, ROBERT EMORY (*b. Quantico, Md., 1850; d. Philadelphia, Pa., 1904*), lawyer, banker, politician. As Democratic governor of Pennsylvania, 1883–87 and 1891–95, stressed economy and reform; wrote distinguished minority report for U.S. Pacific Railway Commission (1887).

PATTISON, THOMAS (*b. Troy, N.Y., 1822; d. New Brighton, N.Y., 1891*), naval officer. Appointed midshipman, 1839. Retired as rear admiral, 1883, after varied and distinguished service.

PATTON, FRANCIS LANDEY (*b. Warwick, Bermuda, 1843; d. Bermuda, 1932*), Presbyterian clergyman, theologian. Graduated Princeton Theological Seminary, 1865; attained wide experience in New York and Chicago as pastor, lecturer, and writer for the religious press. He returned to Princeton Seminary as Stuart professor, 1881, teaching also in the College of New Jersey and specializing in Christian ethics. Patton was chosen president of the college (*post* 1896 called Princeton University), 1888. His administration was marked by financial success and academic progress; a trend toward appointing faculty members who had had formal graduate training in their subjects rather than men trained only as ministers was begun by him and he introduced electives to the curriculum. Patton retired in 1902, after nominating Woodrow Wilson as his successor. He continued, however, as professor of ethics, and as president of the Princeton Seminary until 1913.

PATTON, GEORGE SMITH (*b. San Gabriel, Calif., 1885; d. Heidelberg, Germany, 1945*), army officer. Great-grandson of John Mercer Patton; grandson and son of graduates of Virginia Military Institute. In 1903, after six years of study at Dr. Clark's Classical School for Boys in Pasadena, he entered the Virginia

Military Institute. The following year he transferred to the U.S. Military Academy at West Point. Upon graduation in 1909, he was commissioned a second lieutenant of cavalry. In 1912, he represented the United States in the Stockholm Olympic Games, where he placed fifth in the military pentathlon. The next year, he spent the summer at Saumur, France, studying instructional methods for the cavalry saber. As an unofficial aide to General John J. Pershing, Patton participated in the punitive expedition to Mexico in 1916. In 1917, now a captain and still on Pershing's staff, he sailed for France. Detailed to the Tank Corps, Patton attended courses at the French tank school and observed British training methods. As a major, he organized and directed the American Tank Center at Langres, France (later at Bourg), and formed the 304th Brigade of the Tank Corps. He participated in the Meuse-Argonne offensive with his brigade. Ending the war as a colonel, Patton was awarded the Distinguished Service Medal for his contributions to tank warfare and the Distinguished Service Cross. In 1932 he participated, under General Douglas MacArthur, in the forcible ejection from Washington of the "Bonus Army."

In July 1940 Patton took command of a brigade of the 2nd Armored Division at Fort Benning, Ga. In April 1941, as a major general, he became the division commander and, on Jan. 19, 1942, commanding general of the I Armored Corps. That October, in command of the Western Task Force, Patton sailed from Norfolk, Va. He directed the amphibious operations near Casablanca, French Morocco, Nov. 8.

In March 1943, after the Germans inflicted a severe defeat on American units at Kasserine Pass in Tunisia, Patton was appointed commanding general of the II Corps. On July 11, 1943, with Patton (now lieutenant general) in command of the U.S. 7th Army, the Allies invaded Sicily. The island was conquered in a lightning campaign of 38 days, and under Patton's leadership American combat performance was brought into maturity. On Aug. 10, 1943, while touring military hospitals in Sicily, he impetuously slapped and verbally abused two soldiers suffering from combat exhaustion; the incident incurred the wrath of his superiors and nearly ended his career. In March 1944, assigned to the European theater of operations and transferred to England, he trained the U.S. 3rd Army for its role as the major American follow-up force after the cross-channel invasion of Normandy.

When the Germans launched their Ardennes counteroffensive in December—the "Battle of the Bulge"—Patton, in one of the most remarkable movements in military history, took only a few days to turn his army from an eastward to a northward orientation and bring it into position to shore up the southern shoulder of the Bulge. When his troops linked up with the encircled defenders of Bastogne, the failure of the German offensive was sealed. The 3rd Army crossed the Rhine in March 1945 at Mainz and Oppenheim, and drove through the heart of Germany into Czechoslovakia and Austria. The discovery of Ohrdruf, the first of the Nazi concentration camps to be liberated, filled him with the deepest revulsion. In charge of the "denazification" program in Bavaria, he was upset by the wholesale dismissal of former Nazis from governmental positions, believing this would pave the way for a Communist coup. He also urged the employment of "more former members of the Nazi party in administrative jobs and as skilled workmen." For expressing these opinions he was removed from command of the 3rd Army and given command of the 15th Army, a largely paper force. Deeply religious yet often violently profane in his language, irascible yet given to mawkish sentimentality, identified by the ivory-handled pistols that became his trademark, "Blood and Guts" Patton was the outstanding American field commander of World War II.

PATTON, JOHN MERCER (b. *Fredericksburg, Va., 1797; d. Richmond, Va., 1858*), lawyer, Virginia legislator. Grandson of Hugh Mercer. Congressman, independent Democrat, from Virginia, 1830–38; coauthor, *Code of Virginia* (1849), a superior digest and revision of the civil and criminal codes.

PATTON, WILLIAM (b. *Philadelphia, Pa., 1798; d. New Haven, Conn., 1879*), Presbyterian and Congregational clergyman, author. A founder of Union Theological Seminary, New York, 1836.

PAUGER, ADRIEN DE (b. *France, date unknown; d. New Orleans, La., 1726*), engineer. Came to Louisiana, 1720, as assistant to Le Blond de la Tour; surveyed and laid out original town of New Orleans, 1721.

PAUL, ELLIOT HAROLD (b. *Malden, Mass., 1891; d. Providence, R.I., 1958*), novelist, journalist, and editor. Studied briefly at the University of Maine. As the literary editor of the European editions of the *Chicago Tribune* and the *New York Herald* in the 1920's and 1930's, Paul became an important figure in the literary world of Paris. He wrote the first serious evaluation of Gertrude Stein's work. In 1927 he founded the literary magazine *transitions*, publishing works by Stein and James Joyce. His many books include *The Life and Death of a Spanish Town* (1937) and *The Last Time I Saw Paris* (1942), both of which became minor classics.

PAUL, FATHER. *See* FRANCIS, PAUL JAMES.

PAUL, HENRY MARTYN (b. *Dedham, Mass., 1851; d. 1931*), astronomer, engineer, teacher. Graduated Dartmouth, 1873; C.E., 1875. Did important work at Washington Naval Observatory on variable stars and eclipses; professor of mathematics, U.S. Naval Academy, 1905–12.

PAUL, JOHN. *See* WEBB, CHARLES HENRY.

PAUL, JOSEPHINE BAY (b. *Anamosa, Iowa, 1900; d. New York, N.Y., 1962*), investment executive. Attended Colorado College (1916–17); later ran, with her sister, a flourishing greeting card business (1928–33). Following the death of her husband, wealthy broker and investor Charles Ulrick Bay (in 1955), she assumed many of his directorships and became chairman of American Export Lines, making her the first woman to control a major steamship company in the United States. Named president and chairman of the board of A. M. Kidder (1956), becoming the first woman to head a member firm of the New York Stock Exchange. Named woman of the year in business by Associated Press (1956).

PAULDING, HIRAM (b. *Westchester Co., N.Y., 1797; d. near Huntington, N.Y., 1878*), naval officer. Appointed midshipman, 1811; served as acting lieutenant aboard *Ticonderoga* in battle of Lake Champlain; graduated from Alden Partridge's military academy at Norwich, Vt., 1823. Paulding spent his entire active life on sea and shore duty, making frequent cruises in the Atlantic, Pacific, and Mediterranean. As captain, commanding the Home Squadron in the Caribbean, 1857, he seized William Walker with 150 filibusters at Grey Town, Nicaragua. President Buchanan, however, set Walker free and relieved Paulding of command. Head of the New York Navy Yard through much of the Civil War, Paulding, now rear admiral, did much to advance construction of Ericsson's monitors by advocating the design and expediting their actual building.

PAULDING, JAMES KIRKE (b. *Putnam Co., N.Y., 1778; d. near Hyde Park, N.Y., 1860*), author, naval official. Despite scanty schooling, he developed literary interests, an aesthetic appreciation of nature, and keen powers of social observation. Related by marriage to Washington Irving, he was associated with Irving in the first series of *Salmagundi*, 1807–08. Much of his subsequent writing was made up of caustic criticism of English ways and enthusiastic praise of his own homeland; his *Diverting History of John Bull and Brother Jonathan* (1812), *The United States and England* (1815), and *John Bull in America* (1825) were in this vein. Appointed secretary of the Board of Navy Commissioners, 1815, he became U.S. navy agent in New York, 1824. He served ably in Van Buren's cabinet as secretary of the navy, 1838–41. Liberal, tolerant in all but his view of the English, thoroughly American, Paulding was author of more than 70 short tales, a mass of miscellaneous prose (including a second series of *Salmagundi*, 1819–20), some unsuccessful efforts in verse (e.g., *The Backwoodsman*, 1818). The others were *Koningsmarke* (1823); *Westward Ho!* (1832); *The Old Continental* (1846); *The Puritan and His Daughter* (1849). Like the contemporaries, he wrote too much and revised too little, but the unsentimental tone of his stories in an age of sentiment and the versatility and range of his interests give him a place in American literary history.

Pavy, Octave (*b. New Orleans, La., 1844; d. 1884*), Arctic explorer. Physician and naturalist for A. W. Greely's Lady Franklin Bay expedition, 1881–84; died of exposure at Cape Sabine.

Pawnee, Bill. *See* Lillie, Gordon William.

Payne, Bruce Ryburn (*b. Mull's Grove, N.C., 1874; d. Nashville, Tenn., 1937*), educator. Graduated Duke, 1896; Ph.D., Teachers College, Columbia, 1904. President, George Peabody College for Teachers, 1911–37.

Payne, Christopher Harrison (*b. near Red Sulphur Springs, Va., 1848; d. St. Thomas, Virgin Islands, 1925*), Baptist clergyman, lawyer, black leader. U.S. consul, St. Thomas, Danish West Indies, 1903–17; thereafter a prosecuting attorney and a police judge.

Payne, Daniel Alexander (*b. Charleston, S.C., 1811; d. 1893*), bishop of the African Methodist Episcopal Church, educator. President of Wilberforce University, 1863–76; wrote history of his church.

Payne, Henry B. (*b. Hamilton, N.Y., 1810; d. Cleveland, Ohio, 1896*), lawyer, politician. Removed to Cleveland, 1833, where he practiced with great success and engaged also in railroad promotion. A leader in the Democratic party and a consistent supporter of business interests, he was congressman from Ohio, 1875–85, and U.S. senator, 1885–91.

Payne, Henry Clay (*b. Ashfield, Mass., 1843; d. Washington, D.C., 1904*), railroad and public utilities executive, politician. Settled in Milwaukee, Wis., 1863. Executive officer, Milwaukee Street Railway Co., 1890–95; receiver, Northern Pacific Railroad, 1893–95; U.S. postmaster general, 1902–04.

Payne, John Barton (*b. Pruntytown, Va. [now W.Va.], 1855; d. Washington, D.C., 1935*), lawyer. Winning reputation as lawyer and jurist in Chicago, Ill., *post* 1882, he was active in that city's civic affairs and held a number of national offices under the administration of President Wilson, including a brief period as U.S. secretary of the interior. He served as chairman of the American Red Cross *post* 1921 with great efficiency and without compensation.

Payne, John Howard (*b. New York, N.Y., 1791; d. Tunisia, 1852*), actor, dramatist, editor, diplomat. Produced first play, *Julia, or The Wanderer*, in New York, 1806. Made professional stage debut in *Douglas* at Park Theatre, New York, 1809; for two years was a theatrical sensation in New York and Boston; was first American to play Hamlet (Boston, 1809). Resided in Europe, principally in France and England, 1813–32, attaining occasional success as an actor and active playwright. *Charles the Second; or, The Merry Monarch* (1824), a play in which Washington Irving collaborated, won favor, as did others, but he was constantly in debt. Returning to America, he projected a number of unsuccessful schemes and was concerned, in an effort to obtain justice for the Cherokee, 1835. He served as U.S. consul in Tunis, 1842–45 and 1851–52. He is remembered principally today as author of the song "Home, Sweet Home!" which he had written for his operetta *Clari* (1823).

Payne, Oliver Hazard (*b. Cleveland, Ohio, 1839; d. 1917*), Union soldier, oil refiner, capitalist. Son of Henry B. Payne. Partner in notorious South Improvement Co. and treasurer of the Standard Oil Co. until 1884. Thereafter engaged in other industries, he was a dominant figure in American Tobacco Co. and influential in Tennessee Coal and Iron Co. He was a benefactor of Cornell Medical College and other institutions.

Payne, Sereno Elisha (*b. Hamilton, N.Y., 1843; d. Washington, D.C., 1914*), lawyer, Republican politician. Nephew of Henry B. Payne. Congressman from New York, 1883–87 and 1891–1914; chairman, House Ways and Means Committee, 1899–1914. A friend of high tariffs, he gave his name to the Payne-Aldrich Tariff, 1909.

Payne, William Harold (*b. Ontario Co., N.Y., 1836; d. Ann Arbor, Mich., 1907*), educator. Occupied first chair of education in the United States at University of Michigan, 1879–87 and 1901–04; wrote many textbooks.

Payne, William Morton (*b. Newburyport, Mass., 1858; d. Chicago, Ill., 1919*), teacher, translator, literary critic. Associate editor of the *Dial*, 1892–1915; wrote *American Literary Criticism* (1904) and *Leading American Essayists* (1910).

Payson, Edward (*b. Rindge, N.H., 1783; d. Portland, Maine, 1827*), Congregational clergyman. Son of Seth Payson. Pastor at Second Church, Portland, *post* 1811; an intense, unhealthily introspective preacher.

Payson, Seth (*b. Walpole, Mass., 1758; d. Rindge, N.H., 1820*), Congregational clergyman. Father of Edward Payson. Pastor at Rindge, *post* 1782; author of *Proofs of the Real Existence and Dangerous Tendency of Illuminism* (1802).

Peabody, Andrew Preston (*b. Beverly, Mass., 1811; d. 1893*), Unitarian clergyman, educator, author. Editor and proprietor, *North American Review*, 1853–63; Plummer professor of Christian morals, Harvard, 1860–81.

Peabody, Cecil Hobart (*b. Burlington, Vt., 1855; d. Boston, Mass., 1934*), educator. Son of Selim H. Peabody. Graduated Massachusetts Institute of Technology, 1877. After teaching in Japan and at the University of Illinois, he was associated *post* 1884 with his alma mater as teacher of steam engineering and *post* 1893 as head of the Department of Naval Architecture and Marine Engineering. He was author of pioneering textbooks such as *Thermodynamics of the Steam Engine* (1889) and *Naval Architecture* (1904). He retired as professor emeritus, 1820.

Peabody, Elizabeth Palmer (*b. Billerica, Mass., 1804; d. Jamaica Plain, Mass., 1894*), educator, author. Granddaughter of Joseph Palmer; sister-in-law of Nathaniel Hawthorne and Horace Mann. Conducted several private schools around Boston; acted as W. E. Channing's secretary, 1825–34; was A. Bronson Alcott's assistant in his Temple School, Boston. An early member of the Transcendental Club, she was friend of R. W. Emerson, Hawthorne, Thoreau. Her bookshop in Boston, opened 1839, carried a unique selection of European books and became a center for transcendentalists; plans for the Brook Farm community were drawn there, and she was publisher of Margaret Fuller's translations from the German, several of Hawthorne's books, and of the *Dial*, 1842–43. She established the first kindergarten in America, 1860, and published the *Kindergarten Messenger*, 1873–75.

PEABODY, ENDICOTT (*b. Salem, Mass., 1857; d. Groton, Mass., 1944*), Episcopal clergyman, educator. Great-grandson of Joseph Peabody; distantly related to George Peabody. Attended Cheltenham School in England; graduated Trinity College, Cambridge University, 1878. After returning to the United States, he spent three years in business and then began studies at the Episcopal Theological School in Cambridge, Mass. Ordained in 1884, he opened Groton School that same year as an Episcopal school for boys; he served as headmaster until 1940. Emphasizing hard work, physical fitness, self-discipline, and social responsibility, he strove to arouse a sense of moral leadership in his students, most of whom were from financially secure families.

PEABODY, FRANCIS GREENWOOD (*b. Boston, Mass., 1847; d. Cambridge, Mass., 1936*), Unitarian clergyman, writer. Professor of theology and Christian morals, 1881–1913, and founder of the Department of Social Ethics, Harvard Divinity School, 1906.

PEABODY, GEORGE (*b. South Danvers, Mass., 1795; d. London, England, 1869*), merchant, financier, philanthropist. Apprenticed at 11 to a Danvers grocer, he subsequently secured positions in Newburyport, Mass., and Georgetown, D.C. Made manager of a wholesale dry-goods warehouse, 1814, he moved to Baltimore with his employer, 1815, and became senior partner of the firm, Riggs & Peabody, 1829. In 1835 he negotiated in England without charge a loan of $8 million for the state of Maryland, then on the verge of bankruptcy; in 1836, as incorporator and president of the Eastern Railroad, he again demonstrated his talent for securing English funds for investment in America. He settled permanently in London, 1837, where he had previously established the firm of George Peabody & Co., specializing in foreign exchange and American securities in direct competition with the Barings and Rothschilds. In 1854 he took Junius S. Morgan into partnership. During the years 1837–41, when American credit in Europe was much shaken, Peabody used his name and funds to restore confidence. He made a gift of $15,000 to sponsor an American exhibit at the Crystal Palace exhibition, 1851; granted $10,000 to outfit an expedition to search for Sir John Franklin, the Arctic explorer; and gave elaborate Fourth of July dinners where English nobility met American visitors to England.

Peabody's philanthropic activities, however, were principally directed toward America. As his fortune mounted he made increasingly generous gifts to a wide range of projects. Notable among these were $1.5 million to found the Peabody Institute at Baltimore, which provided a free library, an academy of music, and an art gallery; $250,000 to found the Peabody Institute in Peabody, Mass., with its library and lecture fund; $150,000 to establish the Peabody Museum of Natural History at Yale; $140,000 to found the Peabody Academy of Science in connection with the Essex Institute, Salem, Mass.; and $3.5 million to the Peabody Education Fund for the promotion of education in the South. His foremost benefaction in England was a grant of $2.5 million for the erection of workingmen's tenements in London. After a funeral service in Westminster Abbey, his body was brought home for burial in Danvers, Mass.

PEABODY, GEORGE FOSTER (*b. Columbus, Ga., 1852; d. Warm Springs, Ga., 1938*), banker. Partner in Spencer Trask & Co., 1881–1906. An active philanthropist, he was especially interested in southern education.

PEABODY, JOSEPH (*b. Middleton, Mass., 1757; d. Salem, Mass., 1844*), Revolutionary privateersman, merchant ship-

owner. Became most prominent and wealthiest shipowner in Salem, employing about 7,000 seamen; traded principally with the Far East.

PEABODY, JOSEPHINE PRESTON (*b. Brooklyn, N.Y., 1874; d. 1922*), poet, dramatist. Her best-known plays, *The Piper* (1909), *The Wings* (1912) and *Harvest Moon* (1916), kept alive the tradition of poetic drama in America.

PEABODY, LUCY WHITEHEAD (*b. Belmont, Kans., 1861; d. Beverly, Mass., 1949*), leader in Baptist and interdenominational organizations for support of foreign missions. Served with first husband, Rev. Norman Waterbury, on Baptist mission to India, 1881–86; returned to the United States after his death and concerned herself with a great number of Protestant missionary enterprises. Married Henry W. Peabody, 1906.

PEABODY, NATHANIEL (*b. Topsfield, Mass., 1741; d. Exeter, N.H., 1823*), physician. Revolutionary patriot. Prominent member, New Hampshire Committee of Safety; organizer, New Hampshire Medical Society, 1791.

PEABODY, OLIVER WILLIAM BOURN (*b. Exeter, N.H., 1799; d. Burlington, Vt., 1848*), lawyer, Unitarian clergyman. Brother of William B. O. Peabody. Graduated Harvard, 1816; contributed to *North American Review*; supervised Boston, 1836, edition of Shakespeare's works. Pastor at Burlington, Vt., 1845–48.

PEABODY, ROBERT SWAIN (*b. New Bedford, Mass., 1845; d. Marblehead, Mass., 1917*), architect. Graduated Harvard, 1866; studied at École des Beaux Arts, Paris; partner in Peabody and Stearns *post* 1870. Designed State House at Concord, N.H., and (old) Union League Club, New York; worked mainly in Italian Renaissance style.

PEABODY, SELIM HOBART (*b. Rockingham, Vt., 1829; d. St. Louis, Mo., 1903*), educator. Graduated University of Vermont, 1852. Secured first legislature grant for Illinois Industrial University, which became University of Illinois in 1885; served there as regent (president), 1880–91.

PEABODY, WILLIAM BOURN OLIVER (*b. Exeter, N.H., 1799; d. Springfield, Mass., 1847*), Unitarian clergyman, man of letters. Brother of Oliver W. B. Peabody. Pastor at Springfield *post* 1820.

PEALE, ANNE CLAYPOOLE (*b. Philadelphia, Pa., 1791; d. 1878*), painter of miniatures. Daughter of James Peale; niece of Charles W. Peale; sister of Sarah M. Peale. Worked mainly in Philadelphia and Baltimore.

PEALE, CHARLES WILLSON (*b. Queen Anne Co., Md., 1741; d. Philadelphia, Pa., 1827*), portrait painter, naturalist, patriot. Peale's father, a native of Rutlandshire, England, became master of the Free School near Centerville, Md., 1740, and of the Kent County School at Chestertown, 1742; he died in 1750. Charles Peale received rudiments of schooling until his thirteenth year when he was apprenticed to a saddler. Released from his indenture, 1761, he set up his own saddlery, but his Loyalist creditors put him out of business when he joined the Sons of Freedom during the Stamp Act crisis. At this point he found that an amateur interest in portraiture could win him valuable commissions and he sought instruction, first from John Hesselius, then from John Singleton Copley in Boston. Several interested patrons advanced him money to obtain further training in England, where he studied under Benjamin West, 1767–69. On his return to Annapolis, Md., his work brought him recognition in several of the colonies; in 1776 he removed to Philadelphia, where he at once found subjects among delegates to the Continental Congress and distinguished visitors. Elected a first lieutenant in the city militia, he saw service during the engagements at Trenton and Princeton, and as a captain continued in active service during the campaign that resulted in the evacuation of Philadelphia. In 1779 he was elected one of Philadelphia's representatives to the General Assembly of Pennsylvania.

During his many encampments with the army he had painted miniatures of his fellow officers which served as nucleus of the portrait collection subsequently formed as his record of the war; after the Revolution he engraved mezzotint plates from this collection. An amateur naturalist, he decided to exhibit natural curiosities as well as paintings in his museum or gallery in Philadelphia, which he opened to the public and for which he was later granted use of rooms at the American Philosophy Society, 1794, and at Independence Hall, 1802. Subsequently, the collections were incorporated as the Philadelphia Museum, and managed after 1810 by his sons. Peale helped to found the Philadelphia Academy of Fine Arts, 1805, and left several notable writings, among them *An Essay on Building Wooden Bridges* (1797) and *Introduction to a Course of Lectures on Natural History* (1800). He married three times and raised 12 children, many of whom became distinguished painters or naturalists. (*See* entries for Raphael, Rembrandt, and Titian R. Peale.) He was brother of James Peale.

Peale's early portraits were large canvasses in the classic English style. His fingers were formally placed with the faces solidly and tightly painted, though the eyes were generally oversmall and the lips almost uniformly thin. He left scores of paintings depicting a wide cross section of the distinguished men and families of his day. He will always be known for his portraits of Washington, of which he painted 60 in all, 7 of them from life (one of the latter being the first portrait of him—a three-quarter length in uniform of a colonel of Virginia militia, 1772). The 6 other life studies generally accredited are a three-quarter length in Continental uniform (1776); a miniature on ivory (1777); a bust portrait begun at Valley Forge in 1777; a full-length portrait showing Washington with his left hand resting upon a cannon, with Nassau Hall, Princeton, and marching Hessian prisoners in the background (1779); a bust portrait painted during the Constitutional Convention in 1787; and a bust portrait of Washington when president (painted at Philadelphia, 1795). His representations of the first president, though perhaps uninspired, faithful to life.

PEALE, JAMES (*b. Chestertown, Md., 1749; d. Philadelphia, Pa., 1831*), Revolutionary soldier, portrait painter in miniature and oils. Brother of Charles W. Peale; father of Anne C. and Sarah M. Peale. His miniatures *post* 1795 are his best work.

PEALE, RAPHAEL (*b. Annapolis, Md., 1774; d. 1825*), painter. Son and pupil of Charles W. Peale; brother of Rembrandt and Titian R. Peale. Produced miniature portraits and still lifes which are adequate but undistinguished.

PEALE, REMBRANDT (*b. near Richboro, Bucks Co., Pa., 1778; d. Philadelphia, Pa., 1860*), portrait and historical painter. Son of Charles W. Peale; brother of Raphael and Titian R. Peale. Attended private schools in Philadelphia; early exhibited a talent for painting. Besides studying under his father and copying the paintings in his father's Philadelphia museum gallery, he practiced in the school of design which his father and others attempted to form in 1795; in that same year he made a portrait from life of Washington. Between 1796 and 1800, he worked in Charleston, S.C., and Baltimore, Md. When the elder Peale successfully recovered the skeletons of two mastodons, the son assisted in mounting them and was sent to Europe to exhibit one of the skeletons, 1802–03; while abroad, he studied under Benjamin West and had two portraits accepted for exhibition at the Royal Academy, 1803. Returning home, he was commissioned by his father to add further portraits to the Peale gallery and did several, the most noted being that of Thomas Jefferson. Study in France, 1808–10, was followed by an unsuccessful attempt to establish a museum and gallery of his own in Baltimore. After the failure of his Baltimore venture Peale established himself successively in New York, Philadelphia, and again in New York, where he was elected president of the American Academy of Fine Arts. *Post* 1828 he traveled in Italy and England, resided briefly in New York, and made his home in Philadelphia *post* 1834. His *Notes on Italy* (1831) and *Graphics: A Manual of Drawing and Writing* (1835) received some attention, and he lectured extensively. He became obsessed in later life with the idea of exploiting his 1823 portrait of Washington (a composite from his father's and his own sketches) as an "ideal" representation. He did his best painting in the period 1808–20, largely in encaustic, which presented a fine, enamel-like texture. His large canvas *The Court of Death* was exhibited *post* 1820 and brought favorable notice.

PEALE, SARAH MIRIAM (*b. Philadelphia, Pa., 1800; d. Philadelphia, 1885*), portrait painter. Daughter of James Peale; sister of Anna C. Peale.

PEALE, TITIAN RAMSAY (*b. Philadelphia, Pa., 1799; d. Philadelphia, 1885*), naturalist, artist, mechanician. Son of Charles W. Peale; brother of Raphael and Rembrandt Peale. Accompanied William Maclure on trip to Georgia and Florida to study and collect fauna, 1818; accompanied Stephen H. Long's expedition to the upper Missouri, 1819–20. Appointed assistant manager of the Philadelphia Museum, 1821, he built up its collection of Lepidoptera and published *Lepidoptera Americana* (1833). He contributed many colored plates to Charles Bonaparte's *American Ornithology* and Thomas Say's *American Entomology*. A member of the Wilkes Exploring Expedition to the South Pacific, 1838–42, Peale collected a notable selection of Polynesian ethnica for the Academy of Natural Sciences of Philadelphia. He was an examiner in the U.S. Patent Office, Washington, D.C., 1849–72.

PEARCE, CHARLES SPRAGUE (*b. Boston, Mass., 1851; d. Anvers-sur-Oise, France, 1914*), painter. Grandson of Charles Sprague. Studied in Paris; resided *post* 1885 in France.

PEARCE, JAMES ALFRED (*b. Alexandria, Va., 1805; d. Chestertown, Md., 1862*), lawyer, Maryland politician. Grandson of Elisha Dick. Congressman, Whig, from Maryland, 1835–39 and 1841–43; U.S. senator, 1843–62. An able and industrious committee worker of superior intelligence; urged reasonable settlement of the secession crisis.

PEARCE, RICHARD (*b. Cornwall, England, 1837; d. London, England, 1927*), metallurgist. Devised important and successful techniques for reduction of precious ores in Colorado and Montana, 1873–1902. President, American Institute of Mining Engineers, 1889. Retired to England, 1902.

PEARCE, RICHARD MILLS (*b. Montreal, Canada, 1874; d. 1930*), pathologist, medical educator. M.D., Tufts, 1894; M.D., Harvard, 1897; studied also at Leipzig. Professor of pathology at Albany Medical College and Bellevue Medical College, he went to University of Pennsylvania, 1910, appointed to the first U.S. chair or research medicine. His great contribution to medical education came during his directorship of the Division of Medical Education, Rockefeller Foundation, 1920–30. He collected data throughout the world on the state of medical education, directed expenditure of substantial sums in various medical centers, and established the annual publication *Methods and Problems of Medical Education* (1924).

PEARCE, STEPHEN AUSTEN (*b. Brompton, Kent, England, 1836; d. Jersey City, N.J., 1900*), musician, musical editor. D.Mus., Oxford, 1864. Settled in New York, N.Y., 1872; held position of organist at a number of city churches and was widely known as lecturer and recitalist.

PEARL, RAYMOND (*b. Farmington, N.H., 1879; d. Hershey, Pa., 1940*), biologist, statistician. Graduated Dartmouth, 1899; Ph.D., University of Michigan, 1902. Worked at University of Maine, 1907–18; at Johns Hopkins, 1918–40. Early exponent of the application of statistics to study of biology and medicine.

PEARSE, JOHN BARNARD SWEET (*b. Philadelphia, Pa., 1842; d. Georgeville, Canada, 1914*), metallurgist. Noted *post* 1870 for design and improvement of Bessemer steel plants and their products; wrote history of iron manufacture in America (1876).

PEARSON, DREW (*b. Evanston, Ill., 1897; d. Washington, D.C., 1969*), journalist. Attended Swarthmore (B.A., 1919). Foreign editor of the *United States Daily*, predecessor of *U.S. News and World Report* (1926–29), and diplomatic correspondent for the *Baltimore Sun* (1929–31). Coauthored anonymously with Robert S. Allen the best-selling *Washington Merry-Go-Round* (1931), a book containing Washington, D.C., gossip and attacks on President Herbert Hoover and Congress; it was followed by *More Merry-Go-Round* (1932), with indictments of Gen. Douglas MacArthur and the Supreme Court. These books displayed Pearson's unique style of slashing and partisan political observation mixed with titillating revelations about the private lives of Washington higher-ups. Began "Washington Merry-Go-Round," a syndicated column, in 1932, which became the most widely read daily newspaper column in the country, and had a weekly radio program on ABC (1938–55). His politics were liberal and left of center; he encouraged closer relations with the Soviet Union, and aimed at exposing corruption and incompetence in government and the private lives of public figures. He was the first to reveal that Germany was about to invade Russia in 1941 and that Gen. George Patton had slapped a soldier. His muckraking in the area of fiscal corruption led to the retirement of Congressman Adam Clayton Powell and Sen. Thomas J. Dodd; later, one of his targets was Sen. Joseph McCarthy. He was sued for libel scores of times, but lost only one lawsuit.

PEARSON, EDMUND LESTER (*b. Newburyport, Mass., 1880; d. New York, N.Y., 1937*), librarian, author. Notable for the literary distinction of his writing on crime in *Studies in Murder* (1924) and other books.

PEARSON, EDWARD JONES (*b. Rockville, Ind., 1863; d. Baltimore, Md., 1928*), engineer. Graduated Cornell University, 1883. As president, New York, New Haven & Hartford Railroad, 1917–28, restored it to sound financial and physical condition.

PEARSON, ELIPHALET (*b. Newbury, Mass., 1752; d. Greenland, N.H., 1826*), educator. Graduated Harvard, 1773. First principal, Phillips Academy, Andover, 1778–86; thereafter taught at Harvard, 1786–1806, and was instrumental in founding Andover Theological Seminary to combat Unitarianism.

PEARSON, FRED STARK (*b. Lowell, Mass., 1861; d. at sea aboard* Lusitania, *1915*), engineer. Graduated Tufts, 1883. Became an authority on design and construction of electrified street railway systems and electric power plants. His first major project, 1889–93, was electrifying the West End Street Railway in Boston, which required generators of unprecedented size. He went on to introduce electric streetcars in Brooklyn, N.Y., and to devise an underground conduit system for the Metropolitan Street Railway Co. of New York City. For the latter he constructed a power station of 70,000 horsepower, in 1896 the largest in the country. *Post* 1899, Pearson built large power plants for Mexico City, Rio de Janeiro, and Toronto.

PEARSON, LEONARD (*b. Evansville, Ind., 1868; d. Newfoundland, Canada, 1909*), veterinarian. Graduated Cornell University, 1888; D.V.M., University of Pennsylvania, 1890. Professor of veterinary medicine at University of Pennsylvania, *post* 1891. Learning of tuberculin studies of Koch and Gutmann whereby tuberculosis could be diagnosed in cattle before physical signs were apparent, he made the first tuberculin test in the western hemisphere, 1892; through speeches and writings he led in bringing about general acceptance of the test. As state veterinarian of Pennsylvania, he guided activities of the State Livestock Sanitary Board. His system of suppressing bovine tuberculosis became model for other states; his work in collaboration with associates on relation of bovine to human tuberculosis attracted worldwide attention. He was brother of Edward J. and Raymond A. Pearson.

PEARSON, RAYMOND ALLEN (*b. Evansville, Ind., 1873; d. Hyattsville, Md., 1939*), agricultural administrator, educator. Brother of Edward J. and Leonard Pearson. President, Iowa State A. & M., 1912–26; University of Maryland, 1926–35.

PEARSON, RICHMOND MUMFORD (*b. Rowan Co., N.C., 1805; d. Winston, N.C., 1878*), jurist. Chief justice, North Carolina Supreme Court, 1858–78; opposed conscription under Confederacy; supported Grant in 1868 campaign.

PEARSON, THOMAS GILBERT (*b. Tuscola, Ill., 1873; d. New York, N.Y., 1943*), ornithologist, wildlife conservationist. Raised in Indiana and Florida. Graduated Guilford (N.C.) College, 1896. B.S., University of North Carolina, 1899. Associated *post* 1902 with the Audubon Society movement, serving as secretary of the National Association of Audubon Societies from its incorporation in 1905, and as president, 1920–34. He campaigned successfully for protective measures and the maintenance of favorable environment for birds and other wildlife, both in the United States and abroad.

PEARSONS, DANIEL KIMBALL (*b. Bradford, Vt., 1820; d. 1912*), physician, financier, philanthropist. Removed to Chicago, Ill., 1860. Acquired great wealth as land agent and investor in Michigan pine lands; donated $5 million to educational institutions, especially Beloit College.

PEARY, JOSEPHINE DIEBITSCH (*b. Washington, D.C., 1863; d. Maine, 1955*), writer and arctic explorer. The wife of Robert E. Peary, Josephine Peary accompanied her husband on many of his expeditions to the arctic regions. In 1893 she was the first white woman to give birth in the Arctic. She wrote *My Arctic Journal* and *Snow Baby* about her experiences. In 1955 she was awarded the Gold Medal of the National Geographic Society.

PEARY, ROBERT EDWIN (*b. Cresson, Pa., 1856; d. Washington, D.C., 1920*), Arctic explorer. Graduated Bowdoin, 1877. Served in U.S. Coast and Geodetic Survey as a cartographic draughtsman, 1879–81; thereafter in U.S. Navy corps of civil engineers until his retirement as rear admiral, 1911. During the summer and fall of 1866 he made the first of his seven expeditions to the Far North, trudging with a Danish friend about 100 miles inland from the foot of the Greenland icecap. On his return home, he tried to win financial support for a larger expedition to cross the icecap, but his hopes of being the first to do so were blighted by Nansen's expedition in 1889. In 1891, however, he set out to explore the unknown northern extremity of Greenland, and in the next year became the first to reach the island's northeast coast. He also made important meteorological, tidal, and ethnological observations.

Peary next determined to explore north of the coast of Greenland and to reach the North Pole, if possible. Bad weather and ice conditions were encountered during the expedition of 1893–95 and the pole was not attained, but Peary was back on the west coast of Greenland for scientific work the next year. He published an account of his expeditions to this point, *Northward over the Great Ice* (1898). Failing in a dash for the pole, 1899, he remained in the Arctic until 1902, in the spring of that year reaching latitude 84°17′ N. With a new ship, the *Roosevelt*, Peary tried again in 1905–06, but reached only 87°6′ N. On his return, he published *Nearest the Pole* (1907) and made preparations for yet another expedition, which left New York in July 1908. By September the *Roosevelt* had reached 82°30′ N., a record for northern penetration by a vessel. Peary spent the next few months establishing his base camp at Cape Columbia on Ellesmere Island. Adopting Eskimo methods of dress and travel, he set out over the sea ice on Mar. 1, 1909, with 6 whites, a black, 17 Eskimos, 19 sledges, and 133 dogs. His plan was to let the trailblazing sledges gradually drop off and return to base, leaving the best dogs for the polar dash. Near the 88th parallel the last supporting party dropped off, leaving Peary, the black, 4 Eskimos, and 40 dogs. Nearly exhausted, Peary finally reached the North Pole on Apr. 6, 1909, spent 30 hours making astronomical observations, and then returned to camp under favorable conditions in 16 days. An ugly controversy at once broke out, however, when his cable announcing victory came 5 days after Dr. Frederick A. Cook's claim that he had reached the pole the preceding year. The American public generally sided with Cook, but careful scientific examination of data showed Cook's story to be false and Peary's substantiated.

PEASE, ALFRED HUMPHREYS (*b. Cleveland, Ohio, 1838; d. St. Louis, Mo., 1882*), pianist, composer. Prominent concert pianist; best remembered for songs "Hush Thee, My Baby" and "Stars of the Summer Night."

PEASE, CALVIN (*b. Suffield, Conn., 1776; d. Warren Ohio, 1839*), jurist. Brother-in-law of Gideon Granger, with whom he studied law. Removed to Ohio, 1800. Upheld right of jury trial against legislative act giving jurisdiction in civil suits to justices of the peace, 1806; state supreme court justice, 1816–30.

PEASE, ELISHA MARSHALL (*b. Enfield, Conn., 1812; d. Lampasas, Tex., 1883*), politician, lawyer. Removing to Texas, 1835, he was chosen secretary of the provisional government and helped draft the new republic's constitution. Thereafter he served the Texas government in a number of official positions. After Texas entered the Union he served in the legislature and was Democratic governor, 1853–57. During his administration the state debt was paid, a school fund of $2 million created, and an endowment for a state university established. A Unionist, Pease became a Republican and was provisional governor, 1867–70. His administration, though sane and moderate, arrayed a majority of Texans against him.

PEASE, JOSEPH IVES (*b. Norfolk, Conn., 1809; d. near Salisbury, Conn., 1883*), line engraver. Made charming and popular engravings for gift-book annuals and fashion plates for *Godey's Lady's Book.*

PEASLEE, EDMUND RANDOLPH (*b. Newton, N.H., 1814; d. New York, N.Y., 1878*), physician, gynecologist. Graduated Dartmouth, 1836; M.D., Yale, 1840. An esteemed teacher at many medical schools; wrote *Ovarian Tumors: Their Pathology, Diagnosis and Treatment, Especially by Ovariotomy* (1872).

PEATTIE, DONALD CULROSS (*b. Chicago, Ill., 1898; d. Santa Barbara, Calif., 1964*), botanist and writer. Attended University of Chicago and Harvard (B.A., 1922). Began work as a scientific botanist in the Bureau of Foreign Seed and Plant Introduction and became a free-lance writer in 1924. He established a wide readership for his mixture of history, biography, and description of nature through his column on the seasons in the *Washington Star* (1925–34); through the books *Almanac for Moderns* (1935), *Green Laurels* (1936), and *Prairie Grove* (1938); and as *Reader's Digest* roving editor (beginning in 1943). He also wrote the scientific study *Flora of the Indiana Dunes* (1930) for the Field Museum and fiction with his wife, including *Sons of the Martian* (1932), *Port of Call* (1932), and *A Wife to Caliban* (1934).

PEAVEY, FRANK HUTCHINSON (*b. Eastport, Maine, 1850; d. Chicago, Ill., 1901*), industrialist. Removed to Iowa, 1867. Built up a grain elevator empire centered in Minneapolis; organized Peavey Steamship Co., 1899, for freighting on Great Lakes.

PEAY, AUSTIN (*b. near Hopkinsville, Ky., 1876; d. Nashville, Tenn., 1927*), lawyer, Tennessee politician. Reform Democratic governor, 1923–27; grudgingly signed antievolution bill, which was basis for Scopes trial.

PECK, CHARLES HORTON (*b. Rensselaer Co., N.Y., 1833; d. Menands, N.Y., 1917*), pioneer mycologist. Graduated State Normal School, Albany, N.Y., 1852; Union College, 1859. Appointed to staff of New York State Cabinet of Natural History, 1867, he made a notable series of botanical studies, known as Peck's Reports (1868–1912) to the regents of the University of the State of New York. Appointed New York State botanist, 1883, he built up a state herbarium; he also made investigations of fungi native to America and Canada which resulted in descriptions of 2,500 species new to science, and wrote excellent synoptical studies of the agarics and other groups.

PECK, CHARLES HOWARD (*b. Newtown, Conn., 1870; d. 1927*), surgeon. M.D., New York College of Physicians and Surgeons, 1893; taught surgery there *post* 1900. Best known for gastrointestinal operations; senior consultant in general surgery, American Expeditionary Forces, 1918.

PECK, GEORGE (*b. Middlefield, N.Y., 1797; d. Scranton, Pa., 1876*), Methodist clergyman, editor, author. Grandfather of Stephen Crane.

PECK, GEORGE RECORD (*b. near Cameron, N.Y., 1843; d. Chicago, Ill., 1923*), Union soldier, railroad attorney. General solicitor, Santa Fe Railroad, 1882–84 and 1886–95; general counsel, Chicago, Milwaukee & St. Paul, 1895–1911.

PECK, GEORGE WASHINGTON (*b. Rehoboth, Mass., 1817; d. Boston, Mass., 1859*), lawyer, journalist, music critic. Author, among other books, of the California Gold Rush fantasy *Aurifodina* (under pseudonym "Cantell A. Bigly," 1849).

PECK, GEORGE WILBUR (*b. Henderson, N.Y., 1840; d. Milwaukee, Wis., 1916*), humorist, journalist. Raised in Wisconsin; founder-editor, Milwaukee *Sun*; Democratic governor of Wisconsin, 1891–95. Author of *Peck's Bad Boy and His Pa* (1883), *The Grocery Man and Peck's Bad Boy* (1883), and others.

PECK, HARRY THURSTON (*b. Stamford, Conn., 1856; d. 1914*), classical philologist, editor, literary critic. Taught Latin at Columbia University, 1882–1910; edited the *Bookman*, 1895–1902; headed staffs of encyclopedias and was prolific in literary journalism. Committed suicide after a long period of mental aberration.

PECK, JAMES HAWKINS (*b. present Jefferson Co., Tenn., ca. 1790; d. St. Charles, Mo., 1836*), jurist. As federal district judge in Missouri *post ca.* 1822, he was impeached but acquitted for alleged misuse of contempt powers, 1830–31.

PECK, JESSE TRUESDELL (*b.* *Middlefield, N.Y., 1811; d. 1883*), Methodist bishop, educator, author. Won notice for an antislavery speech at the 1844 General Conference which split the church; a founder of Syracuse University.

PECK, JOHN JAMES (*b.* *Manlius, N.Y., 1821; d. Syracuse, N.Y., 1878*), Union major general, railroad and insurance executive.

PECK, JOHN MASON (*b.* *Litchfield, Conn., 1789; d. Rock Spring, Ill., 1858*), Baptist clergyman. Missionary in Illinois, Indiana, and Missouri *post* 1817. Author of *Guide for Emigrants* (1831), *Gazetteer of Illinois* (1834), *The Traveller's Directory for Illinois* (1840), and other works.

PECK, LILLIE (*b.* *Gloversville, N.Y., 1888; d. New York, N.Y., 1957*), settlement-house leader. Attended Simmons College. Beginning in Boston settlement-house work, Peck helped found the International Federation of Settlements in 1922; served as president from 1947. Executive secretary of the National Federation of Settlements from 1930 to 1947, Peck organized an integrated conference of the National Settlements in the South in 1936, using TVA facilities. During the Berlin Blockade in 1949, she worked with the U.S. military authorities in setting up community centers in Berlin. She was the representative of International Settlements to the U.N. Economic and Social Council in 1952.

PECK, THOMAS EPHRAIM (*b.* *Columbia, S.C., 1822; d. Richmond, Va., 1893*), Presbyterian clergyman. Professor at Union Theological Seminary in Virginia, 1869–93; strictly orthodox interpreter of the Scriptures.

PECK, TRACY (*b.* *Bristol, Conn., 1838; d. Rome, Italy, 1921*), Latinist, scholar. Graduated Yale, 1861; taught Latin at Cornell University, 1871–80, and at Yale, 1880–1908. Devoted his profound learning to effective teaching rather than writing.

PECK, WILLIAM DANDRIDGE (*b.* *Boston, Mass., 1763; d. Cambridge, Mass., 1822*), naturalist. Graduated Harvard, 1782. Professor of natural history, Harvard, 1805–22; first teacher of entomology in U.S.; described bark beetles, lepidopterous borers, and other parasites in pioneer scholarly papers.

PECKHAM, GEORGE WILLIAMS (*b.* *Albany, N.Y., 1845; d. Milwaukee, Wis., 1914*), teacher, librarian, entomologist. With wife published valuable study, *On the Instincts and Habits of Solitary Wasps* (1898). Superintendent, public schools of Milwaukee, 1891–97; director, Milwaukee Public Library, 1897–1910.

PECKHAM, RUFUS WHEELER (*b.* *Albany, N.Y., 1838; d. near Albany, 1909*), U.S. Supreme Court justice. Brother of Wheeler H. Peckham. Judge, New York Supreme Court, 1883–86; New York Court of Appeals, 1886–95. Throughout his life as Democrat, Peckham often stood against his party organization but was unopposed by Democratic leaders when President Cleveland appointed him to the U.S. Supreme Court, 1896. Distinguished for learning and industry, he commanded the respect of fellow judges and lawyers. His opinions in *U.S. v. Trans-Missouri Freight Association*, *Addyston Pipe & Steel Co.* v. *U.S.*, and *Lochner* v. *New York* may especially be noted.

PECKHAM, STEPHEN FARNUM (*b.* *near Providence, R.I., 1839; d. 1918*), Union soldier, chemist, educator. Expert on petroleum and bitumens; wrote, among many other treatises, *Report on the Production, Technology, and Uses of Petroleum and Its Products* (1885); taught at a number of colleges in the East and Midwest.

PECKHAM, WHEELER HAZARD (*b.* *Albany, N.Y., 1833; d. New York, N.Y., 1905*), lawyer. Brother of Rufus W. Peckham. Prominent among prosecution counsel in conviction of William Tweed, 1873; a founder of New York City bar association, 1869.

PEDDER, JAMES (*b.* *Isle of Wight, England, 1775; d. Roxbury, Mass., 1859*), agriculturist, author. Came to America, 1832. Editor of the *Farmers' Cabinet*, Philadelphia, 1840–43, and the *Boston Cultivator*, 1848–59.

PEEK, FRANK WILLIAM (*b.* *Calaveras Co., Calif., 1881; d. Port Daniels, Canada, 1933*), electrical engineer. Graduated Stanford, 1905. Associated with General Electric Co. *post* 1906. Specialist in high-voltage generators and transmission; built a 10 million-volt lightning generator, 1931.

PEEK, GEORGE NELSON (*b.* *Polo, Ill., 1873; d. Rancho Santa Fe, near San Diego, Calif., 1943*), businessman, farm leader. Successful in the farm machinery business, he served on the War Industries Board, 1917–19, leaving federal service to become president of the Moline Plow Co. In an effort to lift the depression in agriculture which followed World War I, he and Hugh S. Johnson worked out a plan for federal help in removing price-depressing surpluses from the domestic market; resigning his business post in 1924, he gave all his time to organizing support for his farm relief program. His ideas were incorporated in the successive McNary-Haugen bills, which failed of enactment, 1924–28. Leaving the Republican party, he acted as adviser on farm problems to Franklin D. Roosevelt in the presidential campaign of 1932 and was named head of the Agricultural Adjustment Administration in May 1933. Immediately at odds with Secretary of Agriculture Henry A. Wallace over acreage restriction and other policy matters, he was shifted in December to a post as special adviser on foreign trade. Resigning two years later because he disapproved of the administration's reciprocal trade policies, he became a bitter and vocal critic of the New Deal.

PEERS, BENJAMIN ORRS (*b.* *Loudoun Co., Va., 1800; d. Louisville, Ky., 1842*), Episcopal clergyman, educator, advocate of Pestalozzi's principles. Acting president, Transylvania University, 1833–34; editor, *The Journal of Christian Education, post* 1838.

PEERSON, CLENG (*b.* *Norway, 1783; d. Bosque Co., Tex., 1865*), immigrant leader and organizer. Arrived in New York, 1821, as agent for Norwegian Quaker settlers and others; arranged land purchase and erection of houses near Rochester, N.Y.; guided first body of Norwegian immigrants to his settlement, 1825. Journeying west in 1833 to find a new site, he chose the Fox River Valley of Illinois to which he guided the first contingent of Norwegians to Illinois, 1834; many other Norwegian settlements in the West emanated therefrom. In 1850 he led settlers to Dallas and Bosque counties in Texas.

PEET, HARVEY PRINDLE (*b.* *Bethlehem, Conn., 1794; d. New York, N.Y., 1873*), educator of the deaf. Studied and worked with Thomas H. Gallaudet, 1822–30; director, New York Institution for the Instruction of the Deaf and Dumb, 1831–67.

PEET, ISAAC LEWIS (*b.* *Hartford, Conn., 1824; d. New York, N.Y., 1898*), educator of the deaf. Son and pupil of Harvey P. Peet; director, New York Institution for the Instruction of the Deaf and Dumb, 1867–92.

PEET, STEPHEN DENISON (*b.* *Euclid, Ohio, 1831; d. Salem, Mass., 1914*), Congregational clergyman, archaeologist. Pioneer student of ancient American Indian culture; editor, *American Antiquarian and Oriental Journal*, 1878–1910.

PEFFER, WILLIAM ALFRED (*b. Cumberland Co., Pa., 1831; d. Grenola, Kans., 1912*), journalist, politician. Settled successively in California, Indiana, Missouri, and Illinois, 1849–62. Having read law during Civil War service, he practiced in Tennessee, 1865–69. Removing to Kansas, he edited two small newspapers and became editor of the *Kansas Farmer*, 1881, later the most powerful farm journal in Kansas. First allied with the Republican party, he later sided with the conservative wing of the Farmer's Alliance. U.S. senator from Kansas, 1891–97, his odd appearance and dry, statistical speeches made him a symbol of Populism, if not a caricature. By 1900 he had drifted back to the Republicans.

PEGLER, WESTBROOK (*b. Minneapolis, Minn., 1894; d. Tucson, Ariz., 1969*), journalist. Worked for the United Press (1916–25) as a war correspondent and sportswriter, then for the *Chicago Tribune* as a sports editor (1925–33). His columns for the *Tribune* showed traits that later characterized his political columns: a cynical pose, a sustained irreverence toward national heroes and institutions, and a sure instinct for uncovering hypocrisy in the righteous. He wrote the column "Fair Enough" for Scripps-Howard newspapers (beginning 1933) and moved to the Hearst chain in 1944, where he wrote "As Pegler Sees It" until 1962. He won a Pulitzer Prize in 1941 for his articles on labor racketeering; later became an ardent supporter of Sen. Joseph McCarthy. Remembered after his death for hurling tirades and vituperative epithets at Franklin and Eleanor Roosevelt, Henry A. Wallace, Dwight D. Eisenhower, John F. Kennedy, the New Deal, and the Fair Deal.

PEGRAM, GEORGE BRAXTON (*b. Trinity, N.C., 1876; d. Swarthmore, Pa., 1958*), physicist. Studied at Trinity College (now Duke University) and at Columbia University (Ph.D., 1903). Taught at Columbia from 1905 until his death; dean of the School of Mines, Engineering and Chemistry, 1918–1930; chairman of the physics department, 1913–1945; vice president of the university, 1949–1950. Helped found the American Institute of Physics in 1931; secretary from 1938 to 1956. Remembered for his role in the development of atomic power, Pegram hired Enrico Fermi in 1938 and headed the Columbia division of the Manhattan Project. In 1941 he became head of the uranium section of the project under the Office of Scientific Research and Development. He was responsible for the assemblage and operations coordination of the staff and responsible for the engineering aspects of the Manhattan Project. Pegram was the main founder of the Brookhaven Laboratory, a direct outgrowth of the Manhattan Project.

PEIRCE, BENJAMIN (*b. Salem, Mass., 1809; d. 1880*), mathematician, astronomer. Father of Charles S. and James M. Peirce. While a student at the Salem Private Grammar School, Peirce came to know Nathaniel Bowditch, who stimulated him to undertake mathematical studies. He graduated from Harvard College in 1829; taught at Bancroft's Round Hill School, Northampton, Mass., for two years; and then joined the faculty at Harvard. He was professor of mathematics and astronomy from 1833 until his death. His first major work was revising and correcting Bowditch's translation of Laplace's work on celestial mechanics, 1829–39; he then undertook to write a series of textbooks on trigonometry, algebra, geometry, and calculus, creditable but hardly original works. A *System of Analytic Mechanics* (1855), however, included a masterly discussion of determinants and functional determinants. Pierce took an active part in founding the Harvard Observatory, and he made remarkably accurate computations of the general perturbations of Uranus and Neptune. From 1849 until 1867 he was consulting astronomer to

the *American Nautical Almanac* office established in Cambridge by Congress. In 1847 he was one of a committee of five appointed to organize the Smithsonian Institution. He was director of the longitude determinations of the U.S. Coast Survey, 1852–67, and superintendent of the survey, 1867–74. It was Peirce who determined upon extending coastal survey to a general geodetic survey, which would provide a general map of the country independent of local surveys. While superintendent, Peirce took personal charge of the American expedition to Sicily to observe a solar eclipse, 1870, and probably organized the two expeditions in 1874 to observe the transit of Venus. From his work with the survey he formulated in 1852 what is called "Peirce's criterion." His most original and able mathematical contribution was his *Linear Associative Algebra* (1870, 1881). About three-quarters of his published works related to questions in astronomy, geodesy, and mechanics, and one-quarter to pure mathematics. He was generally acknowledged to be the leading mathematician in America and exerted great influence upon the progress of mathematical science in the United States through encouragement of young and talented men and through his inspiring teaching at Harvard.

PEIRCE, BENJAMIN OSGOOD (*b. Beverly, Mass., 1854; d. Cambridge, Mass., 1914*), mathematician, physicist. Graduated Harvard 1876; Ph.D., Leipzig, 1879; studied with Weidemann and Helmholtz. As instructor and professor at Harvard *post* 1882, he helped develop a remarkable course on the Newtonian potential function and Fourier series, and taught graduate courses in pure mathematics and mathematical physics. His researches on the thermal conductivity of stone and its variation of temperature, and on magnetism were brilliant mathematical demonstrations. His most noteworthy publications were *Elements of the Theory of the Newtonian Potential Function* (1886, later expanded, 1902), *Short Table of Integrals* (1910), and *Mathematical and Physical Papers, 1903–1913* (1926).

PEIRCE, BRADFORD KINNEY (*b. Royalton, Vt., 1819; d. Newton Center, Mass., 1889*), Methodist clergyman, social worker. Wrote *A Half Century with Juvenile Delinquents* (1869); edited *Zion's Herald*, 1872–88.

PEIRCE, CHARLES SANDERS (*b. Cambridge, Mass., 1839; d. 1914*), philosopher, logician, scientist, founder of pragmatism. Son of Benjamin Peirce; brother of James M. Peirce. His father supervised his education with the hope of making him a mathematician. Young Peirce mastered Whately's *Elements of Logic* at age 13, and conducted quantitative analysis experiments in a laboratory which he set up. The elder Peirce trained his son in the art of concentration, encouraged in him the power of sensuous discrimination, and constantly presented him with mathematical problems, tables, and examples to the end that he discover the principles for himself. In spite of obvious brilliance, Peirce did poorly at Harvard, 1855–59. In 1861 he joined the U.S. Coast Survey staff, with which he remained for 30 years. He lectured at Harvard on the philosophy of science, 1864–65; gave the university lectures on philosophy, 1869–70; and worked as an assistant at the Harvard Observatory, where he did research leading to the only book he published during his lifetime, *Photometric Researches* (1878). For the Coast Survey, Peirce made important pendulum investigations and researches in gravity theory; he also made the first attempt to use the wavelength of a light ray as a standard unit of measure.

Peirce always called himself a logician and became the foremost logician in the United States, tending to see philosophy and other subjects almost entirely from a logical perspective. He first gained notice by bringing attention to the work of George Boole, the founder of modern logic, Peirce went on to make a number of vital and permanent improvements in Boole's system, many of them incorporated in a long series of technical papers completed between 1867 and 1885. Many of these papers were difficult and might never have been noticed if Ernst Schröder had not based a large part of his work on Peirce's contributions. Peirce modified, extended, and transformed the Boolean algebra, making it applicable to propositions, relations, probability, and arithmetic. Practically single-handedly, Peirce laid the foundations of the logic of relations, the instrument for the logical analysis of mathematics. He invented the copula of inclusion, the most important symbol in the logic of classes, two new logical algebras, and two new systems of logical graphs, and was the first to give the fundamental principle for the logical development of mathematics. Oddly, he never tried to get some of his most important logical papers published, though an elaborate work on logic was turned down by publishers as being too abstruse. Peirce published only a few important papers on pure mathematics. He clearly anticipated the method for the derivation and definition of number which Bertrand Russell and Alfred North Whitehead announced later. He showed too that every associative algebra can be represented by one whose elements are matrices. Further, Peirce made contributions to the theory of aggregates, transfinite arithmetic, and analysis situs.

Pragmatism, Peirce's creation, had its origin in the Cambridge discussions of a fortnightly "metaphysical club" founded in the 1870's and including among its members Oliver Wendell Holmes, Chauncey Wright, William James, and Nicholas St. John Green. Through his study of the history of logic, Peirce had discovered Duns Scotus and was by 1871 a convert to Scotist realism in opposition to Berkeley's nominalism. In a paper published that year in the *North American Review* (October 1871), in which Peirce criticized Berkeley, he outlined the pragmatic position, but his first definite statement of it was made in an article, originally written in French in 1877, which appeared in the *Popular Science Monthly* for January 1878 under the title "How to Make Our Ideas Clear." It was the second of a series of six articles on logic. In that article appeared this famous formula: "Consider what effects, which might conceivably have practical bearings, we conceive the object of our conception to have. Then, our conception of these effects is the whole of our conception of the object."

Peirce received no recognition for his work until William James in 1898 first publicly used the term "pragmatism" and acknowledged Peirce's priority. Peirce's pragmatism, however, was different from James's, having more in common with the idealism of Josiah Royce and the later views of John Dewey. Peirce, for example, believed in the idea of an absolute and in universals, but shared with the pragmatic school a belief in the dependence of logic on ethics, a critical attitude toward individualism and egoism, and a defense of the reality of absolute chance and the principle of continuity. He developed his own formulation of the last idea and considered it his main contribution to philosophy.

In spite of his formidable intellectual achievements, Peirce was given the opportunity to teach for only eight years of his life. He was a lecturer on logic at John Hopkins, 1879–84, and gave occasional lectures elsewhere in addition to his early Harvard career. His lectures were generally difficult, appealing only to the brightest students, but the chief hurdle was his general personality and personal habits. He was vain, sloppy in dress, forgetful, uncivil, highly emotional, and suffered socially and professionally from the circumstances of his divorce from his first wife in 1883. Having inherited some money, he retired in 1887 to a remote and wild section of Pennsylvania near Milford, where he wrote indefatigably on many subjects, and as poverty overtook him, eked out a living writing book reviews and articles for encyclopedias.

PEIRCE, CYRUS (*b. Waltham, Mass., 1790; d. West Newton, Mass., 1860*), Congregational clergyman, educator. Graduated Harvard, 1810; Harvard Divinity School, 1815. Principal of the first state normal school established in Massachusetts, at Lexington and West Newton, 1839–42 and 1844–49.

PEIRCE, HENRY AUGUSTUS (*b. Dorchester, Mass., 1808; d. San Francisco, Calif., 1885*), merchant, diplomat. As partner of James Hunnewell and Charles Brewer, made fortune in Pacific trade; U.S. minister to the Hawaiian Kingdom, 1869–77. Expansionist.

PEIRCE, JAMES MILLS (*b. Cambridge, Mass., 1834; d. Cambridge, 1906*), educator, mathematician. Son of Benjamin Peirce; brother of Charles S. Peirce. Graduated Harvard, 1853. Professor of mathematics at Harvard, *post* 1861; first dean of Harvard graduate school, 1890–95.

PEIRCE, WILLIAM (*b. probably England, ca. 1590; d. off New Providence, Bahamas, 1641*), shipmaster. Made many trips conveying emigrants to New England and Virginia, 1625–35; author of *An Almanac for . . . 1639. Calculated for New England* (Cambridge, Mass., printed by Stephen Day), the earliest almanac compiled in English America.

PEIXOTTO, BENJAMIN FRANKLIN (*b. New York, N.Y., 1834; d. 1890*), lawyer, diplomat, journalist. As consul to Romania, 1870–76, was influential in abating persecution of Jews there; founded (1886) and edited *The Menorah*, important Jewish periodical; was active official of B'nai B'rith.

PELHAM, HENRY (*b. Boston, Mass., 1748/9; d. Ireland, 1806*), painter, miniaturist, engraver, cartographer. Son of Peter Pelham; half brother of John S. Copley. A Loyalist, he removed to London, England, 1776.

PELHAM, JOHN (*b. present Calhoun Co., Ala., 1838; d. Kelly's Ford, Va., 1863*), Confederate soldier. Resigned from West Point, 1861, to join Confederate army. Became romantic hero in command of famed Stuart Horse Artillery; served brilliantly during Seven Days' Battles and at Antietam.

PELHAM, PETER (*b. England, ca. 1695; d. Boston, Mass., 1751*), limner, engraver. Learned mezzotint engraving in London and was well trained in portrait painting before he immigrated to Boston *ante* 1728. As the practice of his art did not produce a living for him, he opened a school in Boston at which he taught dancing, arithmetic, and other subjects. In 1748 he married Mary Singleton Copley, a widow, and it was in his household that John Singleton Copley was raised, as was Pelham's own son, Henry, who also became an engraver and painter.

PELHAM, ROBERT A. (*b. near Petersburg, Va., 1859; d. Washington, D.C., 1943*), journalist, politician, government official. Child of free black parents, he was raised in Detroit, Mich. Employed *post* 1877 by the *Detroit Post*, he and his brother Benjamin distributed the paper as independent contractors, 1884–91. They also published and edited (in association with others) a weekly, the *Plaindealer*, which soon became the leading newspaper under black management in the Midwest. Active in Republican politics, Robert Pelham gave up the management of the *Plaindealer* in 1891 to accept appointment as a special agent of the U.S. General Land Office. In 1900 he was appointed to the U.S. Census Bureau and removed to Washington, D.C.; serving until his retirement in 1937, he made important contributions as an inventor of tabulating machines for bureau use and as a statistician.

PELLEW, HENRY EDWARD (*b. Canterbury, England, 1828; d. Washington, D.C., 1923*), philanthropist. Brother-in-law of John Jay (1817–94); settled in the United States *post* 1873.

Helped organize Charity Organization Society in New York; aided tenement house reform and night refuge movements.

PELOUBET, FRANCIS NATHAN (*b. New York, N.Y., 1831; d. Auburndale, Mass., 1920*), Congregational clergyman, author. Pioneer in the American Sunday school movement and writer of widely used teaching aids for use with the International Lessons.

PELZ, PAUL JOHANNES (*b. Seitendorf, Silesia, 1841; d. Washington, D.C., 1918*), architect. Came to America, 1858; studied with Detlef Leinau. With John L. Smithmeyer, submitted winning design for the Library of Congress building, 1873.

PEMBERTON, BROCK (*b. Leavenworth, Kans., 1885; d. New York, N.Y., 1950*), theatrical producer, director. Cousin of Victor Murdock. B.A., University of Kansas, 1908. Worked as reporter and play reviewer on a number of newspapers, including the *Emporia Gazette* and the New York *Evening Mail*, *World*, and *Times*. He made his start as an independent producer with *Enter Madame* by Gilda Varesi and Dolly Byrne, 1920; after producing a number of artistic successes that lost money (including the first American performance of Luigi Pirandello's plays), he resolved to devote himself to plays that "would sell to an audience." Among these were *Strictly Dishonorable* (1929), *Personal Appearance* (1934), and *Harvey* (1944).

PEMBERTON, ISRAEL (*b. Philadelphia, Pa., 1715; d. 1779*), Quaker merchant, philanthropist. Brother of James and John Pemberton. One of the wealthiest merchants of his day; promoted friendly relations with Indians. Was imprisoned for refusing allegiance oath to Commonwealth of Pennsylvania, 1777.

PEMBERTON, JAMES (*b. Philadelphia, Pa., 1723; d. 1809*), Quaker, merchant, philanthropist. Brother of Israel and John Pemberton. A founder of Society for the Relief of Free Negroes, 1775; president, Pennsylvania Society for Promoting the Abolition of Slavery, 1790–1803.

PEMBERTON, JOHN (*b. Philadelphia, Pa., 1727; d. Pyrmont, Germany, 1795*), Quaker preacher. Brother of Israel and James Pemberton. Preached in Great Britain, 1750–53 and 1781–86; imprisoned in 1777–78 for opposing armed resistance to Great Britain.

PEMBERTON, JOHN CLIFFORD (*b. Philadelphia, Pa., 1814; d. Penllyn, Pa., 1881*), soldier. Great-grandson of Israel Pemberton. Graduated West Point, 1837. Served ably in Florida Indian wars in 1837–39, in the Mexican War, and in the West. Commissioned Confederate brigadier general, June 1861, he was made major general early in 1862, in charge of the southeastern department. He built Fort Wagner and Battery "B" for defense of Charleston during 1862. Appointed lieutenant general, October 1862, he commanded the department embracing Tennessee Mississippi, and eastern Louisiana. He took direct charge of the defense of Vicksburg against Grant, surrendering only when heavily outnumbered and totally without food on July 4, 1863.

PEÑALOSA BRICEÑO, DIEGO DIONISO DE (*b. Lima, Peru, ca. 1622; d. Paris, France[?], ca. 1687*), soldier. Governor of New Mexico, 1661–65; banished by the Inquisition from New Spain for misconduct, 1668; sold military information to England and France.

PENDER, WILLIAM DORSEY (*b. Edgecombe Co., N.C., 1834; d. Staunton, Va., 1863*), Confederate soldier. Graduated West Point, 1854. Commanded North Carolina brigade in General A. P. Hill's division from the Seven Days' Battles through Chancellorsville. Promoted major general, May 1863, he was mortally wounded while leading a division at Gettysburg.

PENDERGAST, THOMAS JOSEPH (*b. St. Joseph, Mo., 1872; d. Kansas City, Mo., 1945*), political boss. Resident in Kansas City *post* 1890, he succeeded his older brother as Democratic party leader in several of the city wards, 1910. By the mid-1920's he had secured political control of the entire city and of Jackson County, of which the city was a part, through manipulation of franchises, construction contracts, tax deductions to friends and other conventional, old-fashioned devices of city bosses. Grateful for the support of the Pendergast machine in the Democratic national convention, 1932, President Franklin D. Roosevelt put him in charge of considerable federal patronage in the state, which vastly implemented his power. A federal investigation conducted by a political enemy and the mobilization of public sentiment against the machine resulted in his trial and conviction for income tax evasion, 1939.

PENDLETON, EDMUND (*b. Caroline Co., Va., 1721; d. Caroline Co., 1803*), lawyer, jurist, Revolutionary patriot. Admitted to local bar, 1741, he was admitted to practice before the general court, 1745. Elected to the House of Burgesses, 1752, he was by 1765 a leader of the conservative Cavalier party, opposed to Patrick Henry and violent measures. On the approach of crisis, 1773, Pendleton emerged was one of Virginia's leading men. He represented Virginia in the first Continental Congress, was president of the two Virginia revolutionary conventions which met in 1775, presided over the Committee of Safety, and was president of the Virginia convention of 1776 which recommended a declaration of independence. He also helped draw up Virginia's constitution and was first Speaker of the Virginia House of Delegates, 1776. President of Virginia Supreme Court of Appeals, 1779–1803. He vigorously supported adoption of the federal Constitution.

PENDLETON, EDMUND MONROE (*b. Eatonton, Ga., 1815; d. 1884*), physician, agricultural chemist. Organized in Augusta, Ga., ca. 1867, a firm to manufacture commercial fertilizers on large scale, was among the first to use cotton seed for fertilizer.

PENDLETON, ELLEN FITZ (*b. Westerly, R.I., 1864; d. Newton, Mass., 1936*), educator. Graduated Wellesley, 1886; served on its staff thereafter, and was president, 1911–36.

PENDLETON, GEORGE HUNT (*b. Cincinnati, Ohio, 1825; d. Brussels, Belgium, 1889*), lawyer, Ohio legislator, diplomat. Congressman, Democrat, from Ohio, 1857–65; Democratic candidate for vice-presidency, 1864. Sponsored "Ohio idea" to pay U.S. bonds in greenbacks, 1867; served as U.S. senator from Ohio, 1879–85, and advocated civil service reform.

PENDLETON, JAMES MADISON (*b. Spotsylvania Co., Va., 1811; d. Bowling Green, Ky., 1891*), Baptist clergyman, editor. Strong Unionist as pastor at Bowling Green, Ky., and Murfreesboro, Tenn.

PENDLETON, JOHN B. (*b. New York, N.Y., 1798; d. New York, 1866*), lithographer. After study of process in Paris, and with aid of two French workmen, produced first commercial lithographs in United States at Boston, 1825.

PENDLETON, JOHN STROTHER (*b. Culpeper Co., Va., 1802; d. Culpeper Co., 1868*), lawyer, Virginia legislator. U.S. chargé d'affaires in Chile, 1841–44. Congressman, Whig, from Virginia, 1845–49. Concluded treaty of commerce, 1853, as U.S. chargé d'affaires to Argentine Confederation, 1851–54.

PENDLETON, WILLIAM KIMBROUGH (*b. Yanceyville, Va., 1817; d. Bethany, W.Va., 1899*), minister of the Disciples of Christ, educator. President, Bethany College, 1866–86; edited

Millennial Harbinger, 1865–70; superintendent, West Virginia public schools, 1873–80.

PENDLETON, WILLIAM NELSON (*b. Richmond, Va., 1809; d. Lexington, Va., 1883*), Episcopal clergyman, educator, Confederate soldier. Graduated West Point, 1830. Pastor of Grace Church, Lexington, Va., 1853–83. As brigadier general, 1862–65, he was distinguished chief of artillery in the Army of Northern Virginia.

PENFIELD, EDWARD (*b. Brooklyn, N.Y., 1866; d. Beacon, N.Y., 1925*), illustrator, painter, author. Inaugurator of the brief but golden age of American poster art; art editor for *Harper's Magazine*, *Weekly*, and *Bazar* (sic), 1890–1901.

PENFIELD, FREDERIC COURTLAND (*b. Wast Haddam, Conn., 1855; d. New York, N.Y., 1922*), journalist, diplomat. Able, tactful, U.S. ambassador to Austria-Hungary, 1913–17.

PENFIELD, WILLIAM LAWRENCE (*b. Dover, Mich., 1846; d. Washington, D.C., 1909*), jurist. As solicitor, U.S. Department of State, 1897–1905, Penfield made valuable contributions to U.S. policy and to promotion of international arbitration.

PENHALLOW, SAMUEL (*b. Cornwall, England, 1665; d. Portsmouth, N.H., 1726*), merchant, judge, historian. Immigrated to New England, 1686. Treasurer, province of New Hampshire, 1699–1726; chief justice, superior court, 1717; held numerous other offices. Author of *The History of the Wars of New-England* (1726), a valuable account of the Indian wars of 1702–25.

PENICK, CHARLES CLIFTON (*b. Charlotte Co., Va., 1843; d. Baltimore, Md., 1914*), Episcopal clergyman. Missionary bishop of Cape Palmas, Liberia, 1877–83.

PENINGTON, EDWARD (*b. Amersham, England, 1667; d. Philadelphia, Pa., 1701*), colonial official. Author of several tracts in defense of Quakers against attacks by Thomas Crisp and George Keith, 1695–96, he came to Pennsylvania as surveyor general, 1698, and served until his death.

PENINGTON, EDWARD (*b. Bucks Co., Pa., 1726; d. Philadelphia, Pa., 1796*), Quaker merchant. Grandson of Edward Penington (1667–1701). Member, Philadelphia Committee of Correspondence, 1774; delegate, first Continental Congress, 1774. Opposed armed resistance and independence.

PENN, JOHN (*b. England, 1729; d. Philadelphia, Pa., 1795*), Pennsylvania provincial official. Grandson of William Penn; brother of Richard Penn. Inherited life use of a quarter of the proprietary rights in Pennsylvania, 1771. A resident of the province and member of the provincial council, 1752–55, Penn attended the Albany Congress on Indian Affairs, 1754. He was again in residence as lieutenant governor of the province, 1763–71, and from 1773 to the end of proprietary rule on Sept. 26, 1776. He handled difficult boundary claims with Connecticut, Virginia, and Maryland, and tried to mediate between disgruntled Indians and revengeful frontiersmen. Yielding gracefully to the turn of events in 1776, he made his principal residence in or near Philadelphia until his death.

PENN, JOHN (*b. Caroline Co., Va., 1740; d. 1788*), lawyer, Revolutionary patriot. Removed to Granville Co., N.C., 1774. Member of the Continental Congress, 1775–77, 1778–80; signer, Declaration of Independence; member, North Carolina Board of War, 1780–81.

PENN, RICHARD (*b. England, 1735; d. England, 1811*), Pennsylvania provincial official. Grandson of William Penn; brother of John Penn (1729–95). Lieutenant governor of Pennsyl-vania, 1771–73; conveyed Congress's "olive branch" petition to the king, 1775; remained in England thereafter.

PENN, THOMAS (*b. Bristol, England, 1702; d. England, 1775*), Pennsylvania provincial official. Son of William Penn; uncle of John and Richard Penn. His father, on his death in 1718, left the proprietary interests in Pennsylvania to his widow as executrix for their four sons. Thomas acquired a one-fourth interest, 1727, and in 1746 an additional half interest. From 1732 to 1741 he managed the province's affairs in Philadelphia; thereafter, he lived in England and conducted business by correspondence. He was never well liked, either by colonists or Indians. The Indians were particularly incensed by his "Walking Purchase" of the forks of the Delaware in 1737. Penn was only a nominal Quaker for most of his life.

PENN, WILLIAM (*b. London, England, 1644; d. England, 1718*), Quaker statesman, founder of Pennsylvania. Son of Adm. Sir William Penn, a wealthy and influential Anglican, and Margaret Jasper Penn. Religiously inclined even in childhood, Penn came early under Puritan influences, which caused his expulsion in 1662, after two years' study, from Christ Church College, Oxford. Resident on the Continent for the next three years, he had a glimpse of naval service during the Dutch War of 1665, studied at Lincoln's Inn for about a year, and then, 1666, went to Ireland to take charge of several estates owned by his father. There came the great turning point of his life. Hearing the powerful preaching of Thomas Loe, an early Quaker apostle, he began to attend meetings of Friends and was soon in trouble with the authorities, who put him in jail for a time. Released, he was recalled to England by his father. He then became an avowed and active Friend, writing a number of powerful pamphlets—among them *The Sandy Foundation Shaken* (1668) and *No Cross, No Crown* (1669)—directed against luxury, economic oppression, and curbs on religious freedom and rights of free Englishmen. He was again imprisoned for his writings, but in 1670 won an outstanding legal victory for freedom of speech and juries by acting as his own pleader in the noted Bushell's Case. He made missionary tours through Holland, Germany, and England, 1670–80.

Meanwhile, by a series of transactions the American province of West Jersey had come into the hands of Friends, and Penn became one of the trustees to manage the property. The 200 settlers who arrived to found the town of Burlington, 1677, brought with them a statement of "Concessions and Agreements" for their government; this charter was written largely by Penn. It guaranteed the right of petition and jury trial, provided against imprisonment for debt, permitted no capital punishment, and guaranteed religious freedom. Further, it provided for fair treatment of the Indians; and it also announced itself as fundamental law, preeminent over subsequent statutes. The Assembly, which was to dominate the government, was to be freely elected by the settlers each year; its debates were to be public. The proprietors were to appoint the executive, but there was no provision for an executive veto.

Penn's next venture into practical politics was Pennsylvania. He had inherited from his father, besides a considerable fortune immediately available, a large claim for funds loaned to King Charles II. On petition, Penn received in payment, 1681, a great tract of land north of Maryland. The king insisted that it be called Pennsylvania in honor of the grantee's father. In 1682, Penn received from his friend the duke of York the territory of Delaware, which was first joined to Pennsylvania but later became a separate province. Penn called his new property a "Holy Experiment" and at once set to work to develop it. He sent over his cousin, William Markham, to act as his deputy, 1681, and himself followed the next year. He broadcast proposals to settlers, especially among his converts on the Continent. His terms for purchase or rental of land were very liberal and soon attracted many settlers. Penn's first

Frame of Government for his province was dated Apr. 25, 1682, and appended to it a few days later (May 5) were the Laws Agreed Upon in England. The government was not so strikingly democratic as that for West Jersey. Large powers were granted to the Governor's Council as compared with those given the Assembly, yet both were elective and the governor was assigned a rather minor place. Murder and treason were the only capital crimes and complete religious freedom was permitted. The preface stated, "Any Government is free to the People under it (whatever be the Frame) where the Laws rule, and the People are a Party to those Laws." The Pennsylvania Assembly soon became sensitive in claiming its rights. Penn usually acquiesced, though at times he became exasperated by the insistent claims. Penn's brightest record is that of his dealings with the Indians. He took stern measures to protect them against rum and the rapacity of white traders and to ensure fairness in land transactions. The Indians consequently were intensely loyal to him; not until his descendants and successors had betrayed and defrauded them did Pennsylvania know the terrors of frontier warfare. Tradition has fused his several treaties made with the Indians into one great one, "under the elm tree at Shackamaxon," as made famous by Benjamin West's painting. Penn's first stay in Pennsylvania lasted only from 1682 to August 1684, but he accomplished much, looking after affairs of government, superintending the laying out of Philadelphia, building his mansion at Pennsbury, visiting other colonies, preaching, trying to settle the difficult Maryland boundary dispute, and writing a memorable description of the colony (letter to the Free Society of Traders in England, August 1683).

Returning to England, Penn secured from King James II the release of 1,300 Friends from jail, and made a third missionary tour to Holland and Germany. His close friendship with James II made him suspect after the Revolution of 1688, and for the years 1692–94 his governorship of Pennsylvania was forfeited; it was restored when suspicions had abated. During these troubled years he continued to supervise his interests in the New World. He secured a partial settlement of his dispute with Lord Baltimore over boundaries and gave orders in 1689 for establishment of a public grammar school in Philadelphia (the William Penn Charter School). In 1697 he presented to the Board of Trade a plan for uniting the American colonies which included a central congress with limited powers.

Religious and governmental problems arose that demanded his presence in Pennsylvania. His second and last trip, 1699–1701, was marked by a change in the form of government, embodied in the Charter of Privileges, 1701. Separate legislatures were created for Pennsylvania and Delaware; the Council, made appointive, was to be practically an advisory board of the governor; the Assembly, annually elected on a wide suffrage, was to be unicameral legislature and was empowered to convene on its own call. After 1701, Penn, in spite of troubles and disappointments in his personal affairs and with his appointed officials, retained his active proprietorship until apoplexy rendered him incapable *ca.* 1712.

PENNELL, JOSEPH (*b. Philadelphia, Pa., 1857; d. Brooklyn, N.Y., 1926*), artist, etcher, lithographer. After study at Pennsylvania School of Industrial Art and the school of the Pennsylvania Academy (where he rebelled against the unsympathetic criticisms of Thomas Eakins), Pennell commenced *ca.* 1880 a long, colorful career as illustrator in Europe and the United States. By precept and example, he fought to raise standards of magazine and book illustration; his own expert draftsmanship and high artistic integrity lent authority to his waspish criticisms of shoddy work by others. Between 1884 and 1912, he was primarily engaged in familiarizing America with the picturesqueness of Europe; thereafter he interpreted the beauty of his own country, in particular the drama of skyscraper cities and great industrial enterprises. His

lithographs of the Panama Canal, done in 1912, were among his best work. Returning permanently to the United States in 1917, he pictured the industrial effort of World War I as he had previously lithographed the war work in British plants. His immense output comprised over 900 plates in etching and mezzotint, some 621 lithographs, and innumerable sketches and watercolors. He was the first to make the varied aspects of modern industry recognized subjects for art. He was also author as well as illustrator of a number of books, wrote treatises on illustration and lithography, and published a highly individual autobiography, *The Adventures of an Illustrator* (1925).

PENNIMAN, JAMES HOSMER (*b. Alexandria, Va., 1860; d. Philadelphia, Pa., 1931*), educator, textbook author, bibliophile. Donor of special educational reference libraries to Pennsylvania, Yale, and Brown universities.

PENNINGTON, JAMES W. C. (*b. Maryland, 1809; d. Jacksonville, Fla., 1870*), Congregational and Presbyterian clergyman, teacher. An escaped slave, he gained fame as a learned and eloquent preacher; he was author of *The Fugitive Blacksmith* (1849) and of works on black history.

PENNINGTON, WILLIAM (*b. Newark, N.J., 1796; d. Newark, 1862*), New Jersey lawyer and politician. Son of William S. Pennington. Whig governor of New Jersey, 1837–43; chief figure in Broad Seal War, 1838; congressman, and controversial Speaker of the House, 1859–61.

PENNINGTON, WILLIAM SANDFORD (*b. Newark, N.J., 1757; d. 1826*), lawyer, Revolutionary soldier. New Jersey legislator. Judge, state supreme court, 1804–13; Democratic-Republican governor, 1813–15; federal district judge, 1815–26.

PENNOCK, ALEXANDER MOSELY (*b. Norfolk, Va., 1814; d. Portsmouth, N.H., 1876*), naval officer. Won reputation for executive ability as commander of federal naval base at Cairo, Ill., 1862–64, serving Mississippi gunboat flotilla; promoted rear admiral, 1872.

PENNOYER, SYLVESTER (*b. Groton, N.Y., 1831; d. Portland, Oreg., 1902*), lawyer, businessman. As Democratic governor of Oregon, 1887–95, he advocated compulsory arbitration of labor disputes, a graduated income tax, and a general liberalization of government. He became a Populist in 1892, subsequent to his reelection, and bitterly opposed President Cleveland.

PENNYPACKER, ELIJAH FUNK (*b. Chester Co., Pa., 1804; d. 1888*), farmer. Pennsylvania legislator, abolitionist. President, state antislavery society; made his house near Phoenixville an important Underground Railroad station.

PENNYPACKER, GALUSHA (*b. Chester Co., Pa., 1844; d. Philadelphia, Pa., 1916*), Union soldier. Nephew of Elijah F. Pennypacker. Rose to major general of volunteers; won Congressional Medal for gallantry at Fort Fisher, 1865. Commanded U.S. 16th Infantry, 1869–83.

PENNYPACKER, SAMUEL WHITAKER (*b. Phoenixville, Pa., 1843; d. near Schwenksville, Pa., 1916*), lawyer, jurist, bibliophile, historian. Republican reform governor of Pennsylvania, 1903–07.

PENROSE, BOIES (*b. Philadelphia, Pa., 1860; d. Washington, D.C., 1921*), Pennsylvania Republican politician and legislator. Grandson of Charles B. Penrose; brother of Richard A. F. Penrose and Spencer Penrose. Graduated Harvard, 1881. After writing a scholarly treatise, *The City Government of Philadelphia* (1887), he commenced a long career as a tough, resourceful, often ruthless political boss in Pennsylvania, apparently motivated by a desire for power rather than money. Serving in the U.S. Senate from 1897 until his death, he was chairman of the Senate Finance Committee *post* 1911, and succeeded Matthew S. Quay as leader of the state Republican machine, 1904. He was a consistent supporter of a high protective tariff.

PENROSE, CHARLES BINGHAM (*b. Philadelphia, Pa., 1798; d. Harrisburg, Pa., 1857*), lawyer, politician. Anti-Masonic Whig state senator, 1833–41; solicitor, U.S. treasury, 1841–45; respected member of Philadelphia bar.

PENROSE, RICHARD ALEXANDER FULLERTON (*b. Philadelphia, Pa., 1863; d. Philadelphia, 1931*), geologist. Brother of Boies Penrose and Spencer Penrose. Graduated Harvard, 1884; Ph.D., 1886. Professor of economic geology, University of Chicago, 1892–1911; a founder of Commonwealth Mining and Milling Co. and of Utah Copper Co.

PENROSE, SPENCER (*b. Philadelphia, Pa., 1865; d. Colorado Springs, Colo., 1939*), Colorado mine operator, promoter, philanthropist. Brother of Boies and Richard A. F. Penrose.

PENTECOST, GEORGE FREDERICK (*b. Albion, Ill., 1842; d. Philadelphia, Pa., 1920*), Baptist clergyman, evangelist and author.

PEPPER, GEORGE SECKEL (*b. Philadelphia, Pa., 1808; d. Philadelphia, 1890*), philanthropist. Brother of William Pepper (1810–64). Benefactor of local cultural and charitable institutions; a legacy from his estate was first grant to Free Library of Philadelphia.

PEPPER, GEORGE WHARTON (*b. Philadelphia, Pa., 1867; d. Devon, Pa., 1961*), lawyer and U.S. senator. Attended University of Pennsylvania Law School (LL.B., 1889). For the next twenty-eight years he developed a successful law practice and taught at Pennsylvania while editing and writing legal material. U.S. senator, 1922–27, serving on the Military Affairs, Naval Affairs, and Foreign Relations committees and chairing the committees on Banking and Currency and the Library of Congress. Argued the congressional side in *Myers* v. *United States* (1926), involving the right of the president to remove a postmaster without the approval of Congress, and represented the defendants in *United States* v. *Butler* (1936), which resulted in the invalidation of the Agricultural Adjustment Act.

PEPPER, WILLIAM (*b. Philadelphia, Pa., 1810; d. 1864*), physician, teacher. Brother of George S. Pepper. M.D., University of Pennsylvania, 1832. Physician to the Pennsylvania Hospital, 1842–58, where he took prominent teaching role; professor of medicine, University of Pennsylvania, 1860–64.

PEPPER, WILLIAM (*b. Philadelphia, Pa., 1843; d. Pleasanton, Calif., 1898*), physician, educator, public benefactor. Son of William Pepper (1810–64). Graduated University of Pennsylvania, 1862; M.D., 1864. His early experience was as pathologist to the Pennsylvania Hospital. Beginning as a lecturer on morbid anatomy at the Medical School of the University of Pennsylvania, 1868, he continued to teach there until 1895, becoming professor of clinical medicine, 1876, and professor of the theory and practice of medicine, 1884. Through his efforts, there was founded at Pennsylvania, 1874, the first teaching hospital in the United States closely associated with a university medical school and in which the faculty acted as staff; in 1887 he founded the University Hospital nurses' training school. He outlined his principles of reform in medical education in two notable addresses delivered in 1877 and 1893. In honor of his father, he established and endowed the William Pepper Laboratory of Clinical Medicine, 1894, the first in America to

promote advanced clinical studies to the causation of disease. Pepper was one of the first to describe malarial parasites, to call attention to the involvement of the bone marrow in pernicious anemia, and to outline the modern therapeutics of tuberculosis. Among his better-known works were the editorship of *A System of Practical Medicine* (1885–86) and his *Text-Book of the Theory and Practice of Medicine* (1893–94).

In 1880 he was appointed provost of the University of Pennsylvania and soon showed administrative abilities of a high order. In 14 years he raised the university from a loosely organized group of schools to an integrated, modern university, highly esteemed in academic circles. He reorganized the faculties and curricula of the college, the dental school, the law school, and the Towne Scientific School. Further, he was instrumental in founding the Wharton School of Finance, the veterinary school, the school of architecture, the Wistar Institute of Anatomy and Biology, and the Bennett School for the graduate education of women. He built a new library, started departments of hygiene, biology, and physical education, and further developed the graduate school of philosophy. A notable contribution was his creation of the University Extension Lectures, a widely influential experiment in adult education.

PEPPER, WILLIAM (*b. Philadelphia, Pa., 1874; d. Philadelphia, 1947*), physician. Son of William Pepper (1843–98). B.A., University of Pennsylvania, 1894; M.D., 1897. Taught clinical pathology at the school of medicine, University of Pennsylvania, 1907–19; served with distinction and a special gift for harmonious leadership as dean of the school of medicine, 1912–45.

PEPPERRELL, SIR WILLIAM (*b. Kittery Point, Maine, 1696; d. 1759*), baronet, merchant, colonial official, soldier. Pepperrell's father, after apprenticeship to the captain of a fishing vessel sailing to the New England coast, became a merchant on the Isle of Shoals and later at Kittery Point. He prospered and took his son into partnership. Thereafter their business grew constantly; they built ships, engaged in trade with the Indies, the southern colonies, and the Mediterranean, and acquired extensive tracts of real estate in Maine, then part of Massachusetts. The younger Pepperrell spent much of his time in Boston managing business affairs, became known in the upper social circles, and married a granddaughter of Samuel Sewell, 1723. He was made colonel in charge of the Maine militia, 1726, became a lifelong member of the Governor's Council the next year, and for 18 years was its president. In 1730, Governor Jonathan Belcher appointed him chief justice of the province. When Governor William Shirley conceived the idea of attacking the French fortress at Louisbourg on Cape Breton, 1744, Pepperrell was chosen to command the expedition. Under protection of a British fleet, some 4,000 provincial troops arrived at Cape Breton on Apr. 30, 1745. Although Pepperrell had no experience investing a fortress, the troops landed in good style and the inefficient French garrison promptly gave up its main battery. The siege went on amidst much confusion and occasional merriment until the French surrendered on June 17. Pepperrell was acclaimed a hero, receiving a baronetcy in 1746, the first granted to an American. He raised troops during the French and Indian War, was made major general, 1755, and lieutenant general, 1759, but did not take part in any battles.

PERABO, JOHANN ERNST (*b. Wiesbaden, Germany, 1845; d. West Roxbury, Mass., 1920*), pianist, composer. Came to America as a child. Studied at Leipzig Conservatory, 1862–65. Especially noted for playing of Beethoven and Shubert, and as a teacher.

PERALTA, PEDRO DE (*b. Spain*, ca. *1584; d. Madrid, Spain, 1666*), colonial official. Appointed governor of New Mexico, 1609; founded the settlement of Santa Fe. Engaged in serious disputes with Franciscan missionaries. Returned to Mexico, *ca.* 1613.

PERCHÉ, NAPOLEON JOSEPH (*b. Angers, France, 1805; d. New Orleans, La., 1883*), Roman Catholic clergyman. Came to America, 1837, as missionary in Kentucky; served in New Orleans, La., from 1842; archbishop from 1870. Edited *Le Propagateur Catholique*, 1842–57.

PERCIVAL, JAMES GATES (*b. Kensington, Conn., 1795; d. Hazel Green, Wis., 1856*), poet, geologist. Graduated Yale, 1815; M.D., 1820. Regarded as the ranking American poet until Bryant's *Poems* appeared in 1832. After *Poems* (1821), Percival published *Clio I and II* (1822), *Prometheus Part II with Other Poems* (1822), *Clio III* (1827), and *The Dream of a Day, and Other Poems* (1843). In 1827–28 he aided Noah Webster in revising his dictionary. He was state geologist of Connecticut, 1835–38, and of Wisconsin, 1854–56, publishing reports of his work. Eccentric and impractical, he was one of the most learned men of his time.

PERCIVAL, JOHN (*b. West Barnstable, Mass., 1779; d. 1862*), merchant mariner, naval officer. Called "Roaring Jack." Sailing master of *Peacock* in victory over *Epervier*, 1813; commanded *Constitution* on world cruise, 1844–46.

PERCY, GEORGE (*b. England, 1580; d. England, 1632*), colonial official. Son of Henry Percy, 8th earl of Northumberland. Joined Virginia voyage of December 1606; incapacitated by illness as governor of Virginia, 1609–10; author of two accounts of early Virginia. He left the colony in April 1612.

PERCY, WILLIAM ALEXANDER (*b. Greenville, Miss., 1885; d. Greenville, 1942*), lawyer, planter, author. A representative of the traditional attitudes of enlightened white people in the South, he published, among other works, *Selected Poems* (1930) and an autobiography, *Lanterns on the Levee* (1941). His collected poems were issued posthumously in 1943.

PEREZ, LEANDER HENRY (*b. Plaquemines Parish, La., 1891; d. Plaquemines Parish, 1969*), politician and segregationist leader. Attended Louisiana State and Tulane Law School, and in 1919 was appointed judge of the Twenty-ninth Judicial District, comprising Plaquemines and St. Bernard parishes. Earned a lasting reputation as a flamboyant, ruthless partisan; elected district attorney for the two parishes (1924), using the post for thirty-six years to enrich himself, manipulate election returns, and perpetuate segregation. An early ally of Huey Long, he was chief defense strategist in Long's successful attempt to avoid impeachment. Broke with the Democratic party in 1948 to form the Dixiecrat party, and founded the White Citizens Council (1954), in the wake of the Supreme Court's desegregation decision, to thwart integration. He resigned in 1960, but continued to battle the civil rights movement as it gained momentum in the 1960's.

PERHAM, JOSIAH (*b. Wilton, Maine, 1803; d. East Boston, Mass., 1868*), showman, railroad executive. First to persuade railroads to issue cheap round-trip excursion fares; first, but unsuccessful, president of Northern Pacific Railroad, 1864.

PERIAM, JONATHAN (*b. Newark, N.J., 1823; d. 1911*), horticulturist, agricultural writer. Removed to Cook Co., Ill., 1838. Edited the *Prairie Farmer*, 1876–84 and 1887–93; wrote or compiled a number of farm reference books.

PERIN, CHARLES PAGE (*b. West Point, N.Y., 1861; d. New York, N.Y., 1937*), geologist, steel engineer. Chiefly associated, post 1902, with the Tata Iron and Steel Co., India's first modern steel plant.

PERKINS, CHARLES CALLAHAN (*b. Boston, Mass., 1823; d. near Windsor, Vt., 1886*), art critic, organizer of cultural activities. President, Boston Handel and Haydn Society, 1850–51 and 1875–86; largest subscriber toward Boston Music Hall and benefactor of Museum of Fine Arts.

PERKINS, CHARLES ELLIOTT (*b. Cincinnati, Ohio, 1840; d. Westwood, Mass., 1907*), railroad executive. Son of James H. Perkins; cousin of John Murray Forbes. President, Chicago, Burlington & Quincy Railroad, 1881–1901; added many subsidiary lines and strengthened the road financially.

PERKINS, DWIGHT HEALD (*b. Memphis, Tenn., 1867; d. Lordsburg, N.Mex., 1941*), architect, conservationist. Raised in Chicago, Ill. Attended Massachusetts Institute of Technology, 1885–86; served as instructor in architecture there before returning to Chicago in 1888 to join the firm of Burnham and Root; took charge of the office while Daniel Burnham was serving as chief of construction of the Chicago World's Fair, 1891–93. Opening his own office, 1894, he played a leading role in the movement known as the Chicago school of architecture. As architect to the Chicago Board of Education, 1905–10, he virtually created the modern style of architecture for educational buildings by applying to them the Chicago principles of functionalism and organic design. He continued to work with high distinction until his retirement from active practice in 1936; the most impressive of his later buildings was the Evanston Township High School, 1924.

PERKINS, ELI. *See* LANDON, MELVILLE DE LANCEY.

PERKINS, ELISHA (*b. Norwich, Conn., 1741; d. New York, N.Y., 1799*), medical quack. Invented curative "metallic tractors," which were pieces of metal to be drawn over affected areas of the body. "Perkinism" enjoyed international celebrity, 1795–1800.

PERKINS, FRANCES (*b. Boston, Mass., 1880; d. New York, N.Y., 1965*), labor reformer and secretary of labor. Attended Mount Holyoke, New York School of Philanthropy, and Columbia (M.A., 1910). Executive secretary of New York City Consumers' League (1910); executive secretary of the Committee on Safety of the City of New York (1912); and member of N.Y. Industrial Commission (1918–22) and N.Y. Industrial Board (1923–33). She scored a notable success in settling a violent strike of copper workers in Rome, N.Y. (1919), expanded the state's employment agencies, and made herself an expert on unemployment insurance. As U.S. secretary of labor (1933–45), she revived the somnolent Department of Labor, cleaned out the corrupt Bureau of Immigration, strengthened job-placement services, created the Division of Labor Standards to provide guidance to state labor departments, and played a crucial role in achieving the Social Security Act (1935) and Fair Labor Standards Act (1938). Her restraining hand prevented federal intervention in the San Francisco general strike of 1935, but the event gave rise to rumors linking her to radical leader Harry Bridges. The House Un-American Activities Committee launched a campaign to impeach her, but the House tabled the impeachment resolution after a unanimous report from the Judiciary Committee. During World War II she helped protect labor standards and defended her department's cost-of-living index against charges that it discriminated against labor. Her memoir (with Howard Taubman), *The Roosevelt I Knew* (1946) is an enduring contribution to Roosevelt scholarship. She served on the Civil Service Commission (1946–53) and was a visiting professor at the School of Industrial Relations, from 1957.

PERKINS, FREDERIC BEECHER (*b. Hartford, Conn., 1828; d. Morristown, N.J., 1899*), editor, author, and pioneer in library science. Librarian at Boston and San Francisco public libraries, among others.

PERKINS, GEORGE CLEMENT (*b. Kennebunkport, Maine, 1839; d. Oakland, Calif., 1923*), shipowner, banker, California legislator. Removed to California, 1855; incorporated Pacific Coast Steamship Co. Republican governor of California, 1880–83; U.S. senator, 1893–1915.

PERKINS, GEORGE DOUGLAS (*b. Holley, N.Y., 1840; d. 1914*), printer, newspaper publisher and editor. Associated with *Sioux City* (Iowa) *Journal*, 1869–1914; noted for his "lay sermons." Congressman, Republican, from Iowa, 1891–99.

PERKINS, GEORGE HAMILTON (*b. Hopkinton, N.H., 1836; d. Boston, Mass., 1899*), naval officer. Commanded monitor *Chickasaw* during forcing of Mobile Bay forts, successfully engaging Confederate ram *Tennessee*. Promoted commodore after retirement, 1891.

PERKINS, GEORGE HENRY (*b. Cambridge, Mass., 1844; d. 1933*), geologist, educator. Graduated Yale, 1867; Ph.D., 1869. Professor of natural sciences University of Vermont, 1869–1933; dean of the college, *post* 1907. State entomologist, 1880–95; state geologist, 1898–1933.

PERKINS, GEORGE WALBRIDGE (*b. Chicago, Ill., 1862; d. Stamford, Conn., 1920*), banker. Rose from office boy to first vice president of New York Life Insurance Co.; devised an improved agency system and extended firm's business in Europe. Joining J. P. Morgan & Co. in 1901, he took leading part in organizing International Harvester, International Mercantile Marine, Northern Securities Co., and U.S. Steel Corporation. Believed in cooperation and combination rather than competition of small business units. Leaving Morgan, 1910, he joined the Progressive party in 1912 and became chairman of its national executive committee. As chairman of a YMCA finance committee, he raised $200 million for World War I welfare work.

PERKINS, JACOB (*b. Newburyport, Mass., 1766; d. London, England, 1849*), inventor. Devised steel-plate method for printing bank notes, *ca.* 1805; successfully employed process in partnership in London with Gideon Fairman and others *post* 1819; produced first penny postage stamps, 1840. Perkins also patented an innovating high-pressure boiler and engine, and other devices for ships.

PERKINS, JAMES BRECK (*b. St. Croix Falls, Wis., 1847; d. Washington, D.C., 1910*), New York lawyer and politician, historian of France. Congressman, Republican, from New York, 1901–10. Author of a number of deservedly popular and useful surveys of 16th- and 17th-century French history.

PERKINS, JAMES HANDASYD (*b. Boston, Mass., 1810; d. near Cincinnati, Ohio, 1849*), Unitarian clergyman, author, social worker. Nephew of Thomas H. Perkins; father of Charles E. Perkins. Worked with poor of Cincinnati; president, Cincinnati Relief Union, 1841–49.

PERKINS, JAMES HANDASYD (*b. Milton, Mass., 1876; d. Mount Kisco, N.Y., 1940*), banker. Brother of Thomas N. Perkins. President, Farmers Loan and Trust Co., New York, and successor, 1921–33; board chairman, National City Bank, 1933–40.

PERKINS, JUSTIN (*b. Holyoke, Mass., 1805; d. Chicopee, Mass., 1869*), Congregational clergyman. Missionary to Persia *post* 1833; prominent Syriac scholar; author and translator.

PERKINS, MARION (*b. Marche, Ark., 1908; d. Chicago, Ill., 1961*), sculptor. In the late 1930's learned to use clay models, molds, and the mallet and chisel at the South Side Community Art Center in Chicago. Inspired by the art forms of Africa, he was an exponent of black pride through art. His most famous piece, *Man of Sorrows* (1950), is a powerful depiction of a black Christ; other sculptures include *John Henry* (1943), *Ethiopia Awaking* (1948), and *Jean Baptiste Point du Sable*. Although he gained fame from his sculpting, he was never able to support himself through his art, and had to continue working as a freight handler.

PERKINS, MAXWELL EVARTS (*b. New York, N.Y., 1884; d. Stamford, Conn., 1947*), editor. Grandson of Charles C. Perkins and of William Maxwell Evarts. Graduated Harvard, 1907. After work as a reporter on the *New York Times*, he joined the staff of Charles Scribner's Sons, publishers, as book advertising manager, 1910. As editor of the firm *post* 1914, he sponsored many of the talented writers who expressed the new spirit in American letters that followed on the close of World War I; he was particularly skillful in handling writers of fiction. Among those whom he encouraged and aided were F. Scott Fitzgerald, Ring Lardner, Ernest Hemingway, James Boyd, Marjorie Kinnan Rawlings, and Thomas Wolfe.

PERKINS, SAMUEL ELLIOTT (*b. Brattleboro, Vt., 1811; d. 1879*), jurist, legal writer. Justice, Indiana Supreme Court, 1847–64, 1876–79; wrote A *Digest of the Decisions of the Supreme Court of Indiana* (1858).

PERKINS, THOMAS HANDASYD (*b. Boston, Mass., 1764; d. Boston, 1854*), merchant, philanthropist, Massachusetts Federalist legislator. Commenced profitable trade chiefly with China *ca.* 1790; remained as principal partner in firm until 1838, extending ventures wherever a profit seemed likely. His public and private benefactions were numerous and generous.

PERKINS, THOMAS NELSON (*b. Milton, Mass., 1870; d. Westwood, Mass., 1937*), lawyer, public servant. Brother of James H. Perkins (1876–1940). Practiced in Boston as skilled adviser in corporate reorganizations; participant in formulation of the Dawes and Young plans.

PERLEY, IRA (*b. Boxford, Mass., 1799; d. Concord, N.H., 1874*), lawyer, jurist. Chief justice, New Hampshire Supreme Judicial Court, 1855–59 and 1864–69; wrote *Trial by Jury* (1867).

PERLMAN, PHILIP BENJAMIN (*b. Baltimore, Md., 1890; d. Washington, D.C., 1960*), attorney and government official. Studied at Johns Hopkins University and at the University of Maryland (LL.B., 1911). After serving in Maryland government as secretary of state and state attorney, Perlman was appointed U.S. solicitor general by President Truman in 1947, serving until 1952. He served briefly as U.S. attorney general in 1952. As solicitor general, Perlman argued sixty-one cases before the Supreme Court, winning forty-one. He represented the government in the dispute over Truman's seizure of the steel industry in 1952 (which the government lost) and many cases concerned with racial discrimination.

PERLMAN, SELIG (*b. Bialystok, Poland, 1888; d. Philadelphia, Pa., 1959*), labor economist. Immigrated to the U.S. in 1908. Studied at the University of Naples and the University of Wisconsin (Ph.D., 1915). Taught at the University of Wisconsin from 1919 to 1959. A student and protégé of John Rogers Commons, Perlman helped write sections of the *History of Labor in the United States* (1918). A theorist on the origins of the labor movement, Perlman believed that the greatest enemy of labor was manipulation by intellectuals. He wrote A *Theory of the Labor*

Movement in 1928, a work which established him as the leading labor scholar of his generation.

PERRIN, BERNADOTTE (*b. Goshen, Conn., 1847; d. Saratoga, N.Y., 1920*), classical scholar. Graduated Yale, 1869; Ph.D., 1873. Professor of Greek at Western Reserve, 1881–93; of Greek studies at Yale, 1893–1909; made excellent annotated translation of *Plutarch's Lives.*

PERRINE, CHARLES DILLON (*b. Steubenville, Ohio, 1867; d. Villa General Mitre, Argentina, 1951*), astronomer. Privately educated, Perrine became secretary of Lick Observatory in Mount Hamilton, Calif. in 1893; in 1895, assistant astronomer. He discovered nine comets between 1895 and 1902, and, in 1905, the sixth and seventh satellites of Jupiter. From 1909 to 1936 he was the director of the Argentine National Observatory at Córdoba. There he attempted to chart the positions of the stars in the southern skies. Although removed from the directorship of the Córdoba Observatory in 1936, his plans for Argentinian astronomy were eventually realized by the Argentinian government.

PERRINE, FREDERIC AUTEN COMBS (*b. Manalapan, N.J., 1862; d. Plainfield, N.J., 1908*), electrical engineer, consultant. Graduated Princeton, 1883; D.Sc., 1885. Organized Department of Electrical Engineering at Stanford as professor, 1893–1900. Designed first long 60-kilovolt transmission line.

PERRINE, HENRY (*b. Cranbury, N.J., 1797; d. Indian Key, Fla., 1840*), physician, U.S. consul, plant explorer. Introduced sisal and henequen from Mexico to southern Florida, 1833.

PERROT, NICOLAS (*b. France, 1644; d. ca. 1718*), explorer. Among first French fur traders to Algonquian tribes at Green Bay, Wis., 1668–70. Won great influence over western tribes and preserved their friendship for France; traded and built forts along the upper Mississippi, 1685–96. He has been called the ablest Indian diplomat of his time.

PERRY, ANTOINETTE (*b. Denver, Colo., 1888; d. New York, N.Y., 1946*), actress, stage director. Best remembered for her gifted and versatile stage direction, principally in association with the productions of Brock Pemberton, and for her encouragement of younger members of the profession. Among many other services, she was a founder and chairman, 1941–44, of the American Theatre Wing War Service and a trustee of the Actors' Fund. The annual "Tony" awards for distinguished work in the theater are made in memory of her.

PERRY, ARTHUR LATHAM (*b. Lyme, N.H., 1830; d. Williamstown, Mass., 1905*), economist, apostle of free trade, textbook writer. Graduated Williams, 1852; taught there, 1854–91.

PERRY, BENJAMIN FRANKLIN (*b. Pendleton District, S.C., 1805; d. 1886*), lawyer, South Carolina legislator, Unionist. Consistently opposed secession, 1832–60, but stood by his state, 1861–65. Appointed provisional governor, 1865, he effected many democratic reforms with tact and wisdom. *Post* 1866, he bitterly opposed congressional Reconstruction.

PERRY, BLISS (*b. Williamstown, Mass., 1860; d. Exeter, N.H., 1954*), professor, author, and editor. Studied at Williams College. Taught at Williams, 1881–1892; at Princeton University, 1893–1900. Editor of the *Atlantic Monthly*, 1900–1909. Professor at Harvard, 1909–1930. Remembered as one of Harvard's best literature teachers.

PERRY, CHRISTOPHER RAYMOND (*b. South Kingstown, R.I., 1761; d. Newport, R.I., 1818*), merchant mariner, naval officer. Father of Matthew C. and Oliver H. Perry.

PERRY, CLARENCE ARTHUR (*b. Truxton, N.Y., 1872; d. New Rochelle, N.Y., 1944*), social worker. B.S., Cornell University, 1899. After a decade of teaching and work with the U.S. Immigration Commission, he joined the staff of the Russell Sage Foundation in 1909. Appointed associate director of the foundation's Department of Recreation, 1913, he remained in that post (except for two years' army service during World War I) until his retirement in 1937. Believing that the public school should serve as a stimulus to neighborhood social cohesion and regeneration, he was active in the community center movement for after-hours use of the school plant for recreational, social, civic, and adult-educational purposes. His major contribution was in his promotion of the idea and his practice techniques for its implementation. *Post* 1921 he turned to housing and neighborhood unit planning as bases for encouraging cooperative citizenship and transcending the depersonalization of urban society. His ideas were expressed in his *The Neighborhood Unit: A Scheme of Arrangement for the Family Community* (1929).

PERRY, EDWARD AYLESWORTH (*b. Richmond, Mass., 1831; d. Kerrville, Tex., 1889*), lawyer, Confederate brigadier general, Democratic governor of Florida, 1885–89.

PERRY, EDWARD BAXTER (*b. Haverhill, Mass., 1855; d. Camden, Maine, 1924*), blind concert pianist, author. Studied with Clara Schumann and Liszt. Gave more than 3000 lecture recitals, 1885–1917.

PERRY, ENOCH WOOD (*b. Boston, Mass., 1831; d. New York, N.Y., 1915*), portrait and genre painter.

PERRY, MATTHEW CALBRAITH (*b. Newport, R.I., 1794; d. New York, N.Y., 1858*), naval officer. Son of Christopher R. Perry; brother of Oliver H. Perry. Entering the navy as midshipman, 1809, he served aboard the *President* and the *United States* during the War of 1812. After varied service, 1820–33, which included convoying settlers to Liberia, destroying pirates in the West Indies, and helping extinguish a conflagration at Smyrna, he was assigned to the Navy Yard at New York.

Serving chiefly ashore, 1833–41, he agitated for a naval apprenticeship system (adopted in 1837); organized, 1833, the U.S. Naval Lyceum to promote learning among naval officers; sponsored the *Naval Magazine*; and was a member of the board of examiners which established the first course of instruction at Annapolis. His continuing interest in better naval equipment led him to advocate steam warships; he is sometimes called the father of the steam navy. Promoted captain in 1837, he was given command of the *Fulton*, a pioneer naval steamship. Later he organized the naval engineer corps and in 1839–40 conducted aboard the *Fulton* at Sandy Hook the first U.S. naval school of gun practice. Perry commanded the American squadron sent to Africa to help suppress the slave trade, 1843, and the naval forces operating on the east coast of Mexico, 1846–47, sharing with General Winfield Scott credit for the capitulation of Veracruz, 1847.

Selected in January 1852, to negotiate a treaty with Japan, a country at that time closed to the West, Perry entered on his most famous work. State Department instructions included as objects of the mission protection of American seamen and property in Japan, and the opening of one or more Japanese ports to American commerce. Perry was requested first to use persuasion, but if this failed, to use "more vigorous methods." Provided with a letter from President Fillimore to the Emperor of Japan, he sailed from Norfolk on Nov. 24, 1852, and in late May 1853, arrived at Napa, Ryukyu Islands, which he made a base. He sailed for Edo (now Tokyo), the Japanese capital, on July 2, with his flagship *Susquehanna* and three other vessels. Deliberately surrounding himself with an aura of mystery, he refused to see a minor official at

Edo Bay, insisting upon delivering President Fillmore's letter to a representative of the highest rank. When directed to go to Nagasaki, where foreign business was ordinarily conducted, he refused and threatened to land with an armed force. Finally, on July 14, he delivered the letter and other documents to the princes Idzu and Iwami, representatives of the emperor. Perry said he would return later to receive a reply. The Japanese were conciliatory when he returned to Edo Bay in February 1854, and on Mar. 31 a treaty of peace and commerce was signed at Yokohama, which granted American trading rights at Hakodate and Shimoda. Perry later reported on the mission in *Narrative of the Expedition of an American Squadron to the China Seas and Japan* (1856).

PERRY, NORA (*b.* *Dudley, Mass., 1831; d. Dudley, 1896*), poet, journalist, author of juvenile stories. Best known for the poems "Tying Her Bonnet Under Her Chin" and "After the Ball."

PERRY, OLIVER HAZARD (*b. South Kingstown, R.I., 1785; d. Venezuela, 1819*), naval officer. Son of Christopher R. Perry; brother of Matthew C. Perry. Entered service as midshipman, April 1799; saw action during naval war with France aboard the *General Greene*, commanded by his father. During the war with Tripoli he served on the *Adams* and the *Constellation*. Promoted lieutenant, 1807, and master commandant, 1812, he requested duty on the Great Lakes under Commodore Isaac Chauncey. Ordered on Feb. 8, 1813, to proceed to Sackett's Harbor, N.Y., he was assigned to command the naval forces on Lake Erie. Making his own headquarters at Erie, Pa., Perry spent the spring and summer building, equipping, and manning a small fleet, an arduous task because many materials had to be brought overland from the seaboard. By August he was ready with a ten-ship fleet, the largest being two sister brigs of 480 tons, *Lawrence* and *Niagara*. The British naval force commander, Barclay, was blockading the harbor, but at one point relaxed surveillance and Perry escaped over the Erie bar, sailed up the lake, and made a base at a Put-in-Bay, north of Sandusky, Ohio. Barclay's force lay at a station at Amherstburg on the Detroit River. Deciding to force an action for control of Lake Erie, Barclay weighed anchor on Sept. 9; on the following day at sunrise he was sighted by Perry, who sailed from Put-in-Bay to engage the British fleet. Barclay's flagship, *Detroit*, was roughly comparable to Perry's *Lawrence*, and his other main ship, *Queen Charlotte*, to Perry's *Niagara*. The battle was joined late in the morning of Sept. 10. The weather gauge slightly favored Perry, whose fleet also enjoyed superiority in weight of metal. The fleets were roughly equal in number of effective men available. Perry's plan was for his flagship, the *Lawrence*, to engage the *Detroit*; the *Niagara*, the *Queen Charlotte*; and his smaller vessels, their opposite numbers in the British line. The *Lawrence* (flying a battle flag with the words "Don't give up the ship") bore the brunt of the battle for over two hours. When all its guns were disabled and 83 of her 103-man crew were casualties, Perry transferred his flag to the *Niagara*. After a brief further action, the British commander surrendered and Perry sent General W. H. Harrison the famous dispatch "We have met the enemy and they are ours." The victory secured control of Lake Erie, helped in the later invasion of Upper Canada, and also helped the United States to make good its claim to the Northwest at the Treaty of Ghent. Perry died while descending the Orinoco River after concluding negotiations with Venezuela.

PERRY, PETTIS (*b. Marion, Ala., 1897; d. Moscow, Soviet Union, 1964*), Communist party functionary. Forced to leave a life of deprivation and racial prejudice in the South (1917), he joined the Communist party in 1932. He rose steadily within the party, heading its National Negro Work Commission (1948) and being elected to its National Committee (1950). Arrested (1951) and tried and found guilty (1952) for attending Communist party

meetings, he resumed an active role in party activities after his release from prison (1955), but was never successful in recruiting a mass black following for the party. He died in Moscow while receiving medical treatment for a lung ailment and heart disease.

PERRY, RALPH BARTON (*b. Poultney, Vt., 1876; d. Cambridge, Mass., 1957*), philosopher. Educated at Princeton University and at Harvard (Ph.D., 1899). Perry taught at Harvard from 1902 until 1948. Remembered for his editing and scholarship on William James, Perry wrote *The Thought and Character of William James* (1935), for which he received the Pulitzer Prize in 1936. The author of some two dozen books and 200 essays, Perry is remembered as being one of the "Six Realists" in contemporary American philosophy. *The Approach to Philosophy* (1905), *General Theory of Value* (1926) and *Realms of Value*, (1954) are among his best-known works. From 1940 to 1945 Perry was chairman of the Committee of American Defense.

PERRY, RUFUS LEWIS (*b. Smith Co., Tenn., 1834; d. Brooklyn, N.Y., 1895*), Baptist clergyman, black leader, journalist. Editor of the *Sunbeam*, the *People's Journal*, the *American Baptist*, and the *National Monitor* (1872–95).

PERRY, STUART (*b. Newport, N.Y., 1814; d. 1890*), businessman, inventor. Patented, 1846, an improved noncompression gas engine using explosive rosin vapor within the engine cylinder, ignited by an incandescent platinum element.

PERRY, THOMAS SERGEANT (*b. Newport R.I., 1845; d. Boston, Mass., 1928*), author, scholar. Grandson of Oliver H. Perry.

PERRY, WALTER SCOTT (*b. Stoneham, Mass., 1855; d. Stoneham, 1934*), educator, artist. First director, Pratt Institute art school, Brooklyn, N.Y., 1887–1928.

PERRY, WILLIAM (*b. Norton, Mass., 1788; d. Exeter, N.H., 1887*), physician. Devised process for producing potato starch as substitute for imported cotton sizing and manufactured it *post* 1824.

PERRY, WILLIAM FLAKE (*b. Jackson Co., Ga., 1823; d. Bowling Green, Ky., 1901*), educator. First state superintendent of public education in Alabama, 1854–58; built efficient school organization, despite widespread indifference.

PERRY, WILLIAM STEVENS (*b. Providence, R.I., 1832; d. Iowa, 1898*), Episcopal clergyman, historiographer. Consecrated bishop of Iowa, 1876, he served until death. Author of *Historical Collections Relating to the American Colonial Church* (1870–78) and *History of the American Episcopal Church* (1885).

PERSHING, JOHN JOSEPH (*b. near Laclede, Mo., 1860; d. Washington, D.C., 1948*), soldier. Son of a small-town storekeeper, he spent his early childhood amid the alarms of the Civil War. Following graduation in 1886, he joined the 6th Cavalry at Fort Bayard, N.Mex., in the wake of Geronimo's capture, just in time for little skirmishes with a disappearing foe. In 1891 the 6th Cavalry joined in General Nelson A. Miles's campaign to prevent a great Sioux war; although not in the fight at Wounded Knee Creek, Pershing participated in mopping up after the battle. A brief stay at Fort Niobrara, Nebr., ended with his appointment, on Sept. 25, 1891, as professor of military science and tactics, commandant of the university battalion, and teacher of fencing at the University of Nebraska in Lincoln. He also used his time at the university to take a law degree in 1893.

Pershing went to West Point as instructor of tactics in June 1897. He became disliked as a "tac," or instructor, and the cadets nicknamed him "Black Jack." The epithet stemmed from his service with the black 10th Cavalry in Montana and his obvious devotion to the regiment. Unhappy at West Point, Pershing joined a regiment at Chickamauga, Ga., in 1898, and went with it to Cuba, where he took a prominent part in the battle of San Juan and Kettle hills and in operations around Santiago. Upon his return to the United States, he took charge of the Bureau of Insular Affairs, a new division within the War Department. He then served, 1899–1903, in the Philippines, commanding in the campaign against the Moros on Mindanao.

Called home for service with the General Staff, Pershing attended the Army War College in 1904–05. In February 1905 he was named military attaché in Japan and hence became official American observer of the Russo-Japanese War. In 1906 he was promoted to brigadier general, over more than 800 superiors in the army. Promotion took him again to the Philippines, where he remained, with some time out for home and European service, until 1914. As commander of the Department of Mindanao and governor of the Moro Province, he fought hard battles, but he also encouraged internal improvements and agricultural innovations. When he was recalled to permanent assignment in the United States in 1914, the Moros mourned his departure.

After being stationed briefly in San Francisco, Pershing was assigned to Fort Bliss, Tex., and became entangled in Mexican border problems. From Mar. 16, 1916, until Feb. 6, 1917, he led troops against Pancho Villa, who was never caught, but the relentless quest broke Villa's power. When the United States entered World War I, Pershing was made commander of the American Expeditionary Forces (AEF), with authority to use them as he saw fit, with one restriction: They were to constitute a separate American army. On Sept. 12, 1918, the U.S. 1st Army successfully launched an attack against the powerful Saint-Mihiel salient. Pershing then shifted his army to join the Allied offensive in the Meuse-Argonne—a logistical triumph. The Allied forces struggled on until the German line collapsed. With the armistice on Nov. 11, 1918, active fighting ended.

In September 1919 Pershing returned to the United States as America's most famous general. Rank had come swiftly (major general, Sept. 26, 1916; general, Oct. 6, 1917); on Sept. 3, 1919, he was named General of the Army. When, on July 1, 1921, he became chief of staff, his military achievements exceeded those of anyone before him. In 1931 he published *My Experiences in the World War*, which won the Pulitzer Prize for history.

PERSON, THOMAS (*b. Brunswick Co., Va., 1733; d. Franklin Co., N.C., 1800*), surveyor, landowner, North Carolina patriot and legislator.

PERSONS, WARREN MILTON (*b. West De Pere, Wis., 1878; d. Cambridge, Mass., 1937*), economist, statistician. Graduated University of Wisconsin, 1899; Ph.D., 1916. Taught at Wisconsin, Dartmouth, and Colorado, and at Harvard, 1919–28. Innovator in analysis and measurement of business fluctuations.

PETER, HUGH (*b. Cornwall, England, 1598; d. London, England, 1660*), clergyman, B.A., Trinity College, Cambridge, 1617/8; M.A., 1622. A Puritan in sympathy, he left England *ca.* 1629 and was associated with an English congregation at Rotterdam for which he drafted a covenant embodying Congregational principles. Leaving John Davenport in charge of his Rotterdam group, Peter immigrated to New England, 1635, and succeeded Roger Williams as pastor at Salem, Mass., December 1636. A firm supporter of nonseparating Congregationalism, he was active in public affairs and helped settle the differences between John Winthrop and Thomas Dudley. Concerned in the drafting of a legal code for the colony, 1636–37, and in the founding of Harvard, he was appointed one of the three agents from Massachusetts sent to further church reformation in England, 1641. Returning to England, he rose high in the councils of Parliament and

Cromwell, was active in the trial of King Charles I, and was executed after the Restoration.

PETER, JOHN FREDERICK (*b. Hernndyck, Holland, 1746; d. Bethlehem, Pa., 1813*), musician, schoolmaster, preacher. Trained as a Moravian minister in Holland, Peter also received instruction in music, including harmony and musical composition. Arriving at Nazareth, Pa., 1769, he served as a teacher, then became organist at the Brethren's House in Bethlehem, 1770. Leading organizer of musical activities there, he expanded the Collegium Musicum, where works of Mozart, Haydn, and Handel were performed with a full orchestra. He composed more than 30 anthems for chorus, solo, and orchestra which reflected Haydn and showed a tendency toward modern chromatic alteration. He was probably the first composer of serious concerted music in America. Under his direction, Haydn's *Creation* was first performed in full in America, 1811.

PETER, ROBERT (*b. Launceston, Cornwall, England, 1805; d. Winton, Ky., 1894*), physician, chemist. Came to America as a boy; attended the Rensselaer School, Troy, N.Y. Removed to Kentucky, 1832; became professor of chemistry at Morrison College, Lexington, 1833. In 1838 he was elected to the chair of chemistry and pharmacy at Transylvania University, which he held until 1857. As chemist of the Kentucky geological survey of 1854, Peter first noted that the productivity of the bluegrass soils was due to their high phosphorus content and gave excellent descriptions of the phosphatic limestone which underlies these soils. He was chemist also to David D. Owen's surveys of Arkansas and Indiana, and professor at Kentucky University, 1865–87.

PETER, SARAH WORTHINGTON KING (*b. Chillicothe, Ohio, 1800; d. Cincinnati, Ohio, 1877*), philanthropist. Daughter of Thomas Worthington. Converted to Catholicism, 1855, she brought many charitable groups, including Sisters of Mercy and Franciscan Sisters, to work in the Cincinnati area.

PETERKIN, GEORGE WILLIAM (*b. Clear Spring, Md., 1841; d. 1916*), Episcopal clergyman, Confederate soldier. First bishop of West Virginia, 1878–1916; established southern Brazil mission, 1893–99.

PETERKIN, JULIA MOOD (*b. Laurens County, S.C., 1880; d. Orangeburg, S.C., 1961*), writer. Attended Columbia (S.C.) College and Converse College (M.A., 1897). The wife of a plantation owner, she began to write sketches of plantation life that were published in H. L. Mencken's magazine *Smart Set* (1921) and Emily Clark's *Reviewer*. Her first book was *Green Thursday* (1924), a collection of sketches and short stories, and her first novel, *Black April* (1927), made her a leader in the southern literary renaissance. Her best novel, *Scarlet Sister Mary* (1928), won a Pulitzer Prize. After 1939 she devoted herself to the management of the family Lang Syne Plantation.

PETERS, ABSALOM (*b. Wentworth, N.H., 1793; d. New York, N.Y., 1869*), Presbyterian clergyman, editor. A principal founder of American Home Missionary Society, 1826, and of the Union Theological Seminary, New York.

PETERS, CHRISTIAN HENRY FREDERICK (*b. Coldenbüttel, Schleswig, 1813; d. 1890*), astronomer. Study at the University of Berlin and at Göttingen was followed by scientific work in Sicily and Turkey. Arriving in America in 1854, he became director of the observatory at Hamilton College and in 1867 professor of astronomy. There his solar observations were noteworthy, especially his descriptions of sun spots. While engaged in making comprehensive zodiacal charts he discovered 48 new asteroids. About 1876 he undertook to prepare a new edition of the star catalogue in Ptolemy's *Almagest*; it was published in 1915 by a collaborator, Edward Knobel.

PETERS, EDWARD DYER (*b. Dorchester, Mass., 1849; d. Dorchester, 1917*), mining and metallurgical engineer, physician, educator.

PETERS, JOHN ANDREW (*b. Ellsworth, Maine, 1822; d. Bangor, Maine, 1904*), lawyer, Maine legislator. Congressman, Republican, 1867–73; associate justice, state supreme judicial court, 1873–83; chief justice, 1883–1900. Noted for legal learning, fairness, and liberal decisions.

PETERS, JOHN CHARLES (*b. New York, N.Y., 1819; d. Williston, N.Y., 1893*), physician, medical writer. Became prominent homeopathist; was joint editor, *North American Journal of Homeopathy*, 1855–61; dramatically renounced the method, 1861.

PETERS, JOHN PUNNETT (*b. New York, N.Y., 1852; d. 1921*), Episcopal clergyman, archaeologist. Graduated Yale, 1873; Ph.D., 1876. Led University of Pennsylvania expedition to site of ancient Nippur, Babylonia, 1888–90; wrote *Nippur* (1897).

PETERS, MADISON CLINTON (*b. Lehigh Co., Pa., 1859; d. 1918*), clergyman. After holding Reformed, Baptist, and Presbyterian pastorates, he attempted *post* 1907 to reach unorganized religious-minded people in cities through lectures and syndicated newspaper articles.

PETERS, PHILLIS WHEATLEY. *See* WHEATLEY, PHILLIS.

PETERS, RICHARD (*b. Liverpool, England, ca. 1704; d. Philadelphia, Pa., 1776*), Church of England, clergyman, provincial official. Immigrated to Philadelphia *ca.* 1735; was secretary of province land office, 1737–60, and prospered in Indian trade. Served Pennsylvania's proprietors as provincial secretary, 1742/3–62, and as provincial councillor, 1749–76; attended Albany Congress, 1754, and Fort Stanwix conference, 1768. Rector of Christ and St. Peter's churches, 1762–75.

PETERS, RICHARD (*b. Philadelphia, Pa., 1744; d. Philadelphia, 1828*), lawyer, Revolutionary patriot, jurist, agriculturist. Nephew of Richard Peters (*ca.* 1704–76). Graduated College of Philadelphia, 1761. Elected secretary of the Board of War by the Continental Congress in June 1776, he served as a leading member of the board until 1781. He was Speaker of the Pennsylvania Assembly, 1789–90, and served in the state senate, 1791–92. As federal district judge for Pennsylvania, 1792–1828, Peters vigorously upheld the powers of the federal government, made important contributions to maritime law, and laid the legal foundations for suits for libel against those attacking the federal government before passage of the Sedition Act of 1798. Wrote *A Discourse on Agriculture: Its Antiquity* (1816), a plea for scientific farming.

PETERS, RICHARD (*b. Germantown, Pa., 1810; d. Atlanta, Ga., 1889*), civil engineer, railroad superintendent, agriculturist, financier. Grandson of Richard Peters (1744–1828). An early and successful promoter of Atlanta, Ga.; built a large flour mill and street railways in that city.

PETERS, SAMUEL ANDREW (*b. Hebron, Conn., 1735; d. New York, N.Y., 1826*), Anglican clergyman, Loyalist. Graduated Yale, 1757. Rector at Hebron, 1760–74. Forced to flee New England by Sons of Liberty, 1774, he resided in England, returning to America in 1805 as agent for land claims of heirs of Jonathan Carver. Author of *A General History of Connecticut* (1781), in which appeared his famous account of the "blue laws."

PETERS, WILLIAM CUMMING (*b. Woodbury, England, 1805; d. Cincinnati, Ohio, 1866*), music publisher, musician. Published Stephen Foster's "Susanna," "Old Uncle Ned," and others.

PETERSON, CHARLES JACOBS (*b. Philadelphia, Pa., 1819; d. Philadelphia, 1887*), editor, publisher, author. Cousin of Henry Peterson. Founded *Lady's World*, 1840 (known *post* 1848 as *Peterson's Magazine*, a successful imitator of *Godey's Lady's Book.*

PETERSON, HENRY (*b. Philadelphia, Pa., 1818; d. Germantown, Pa., 1891*), editor, publisher, poet. Cousin of Charles J. Peterson. Major owner and chief editor of *Saturday Evening Post*, 1848–73; increased its content of fiction and verse.

PETIGRU, JAMES LOUIS (*b. Abbeville District, S.C., 1789; d. Charleston, S.C., 1863*), lawyer, politician. Graduated South Carolina College, 1809; was admitted to the bar, 1812; served as state attorney general, 1822–30. An outstanding and eloquent opponent of secession and nullification, he remained all his life an intense nationalist and Unionist. Opposing John C. Calhoun's program by pamphlet and speech, he was by 1832 the leader of the Union party. Thereafter he held no judicial or political office (save a two-year term as federal district attorney, 1851–53), but as a superb advocate, he was undisputed head of the state bar. He opposed secession in 1860, but was grieved by Lincoln's policy of coercion. He has been described as "the greatest private citizen that South Carolina has ever produced."

PETRI, ANGELO (*b. Marseilles, France, 1883; d. San Francisco, Calif., 1961*), vintner and businessman. Arrived in the United States in 1895. While he served as president (1912–44) of the family-owned Petri Cigar Company, Marca Petri cigars became known nationally, and by the mid-1920's the firm was the largest cigar manufacturer west of Chicago. After Prohibition he began to revive the family's Petri Wine Company, established in the San Joaquin Valley, by acquiring several wineries in Napa Valley and selling his wine in bulk to bottlers. When his sons took over the two businesses, he acted mainly in an advisory capacity as chairman (until 1956). In 1949 Petri Wine acquired K. Arakelian, the second largest winery in the nation, and the firm was renamed United Vintners, which, with the Italian Swiss Colony label acquired in 1953, became the largest wine-making organization in the world.

PETTIGREW, CHARLES (*b. Chambersburg, Pa., 1743; d. Tyrrell Co., N.C., 1807*), Episcopal clergyman. Chief organizer and administrator of his church in North Carolina, 1775–1807; a leading founder of the University of North Carolina.

PETTIGREW, JAMES JOHNSTON (*b. Tyrrell Co., N.C., 1828; d. 1863*), lawyer. Confederate brigadier general. Grandson of Charles Pettigrew. Killed in action on retreat after Gettysburg, where he had succeeded to command of General Henry Heth's division.

PETTIGREW, RICHARD FRANKLIN (*b. Ludlow, Vt., 1848; d. 1926*), lawyer. Raised in Wisconsin. Settled in Sioux Falls, Dakota Territory, 1870; became a prominent member of the territorial legislature. Territorial delegate to Congress, 1881–83; he was U.S. senator from South Dakota, 1889–1901. A nonconformist Republican, he worked to reserve federal forest lands from sale; he also favored government ownership of railroads and telegraph lines, advocated unlimited silver coinage, and opposed annexation of Hawaii and the Philippines. He was indicted, but never tried, for opposing American entrance into World War I.

PETTIT, CHARLES (*b. near Amwell, N.J., 1736; d. Philadelphia, Pa., 1806*), merchant, New Jersey and Pennsylvania official, fiscal expert, patriot. Assistant quartermaster general, Continental army, 1778–81; instrumental in effecting Pennsylvania's adoption of U.S. Constitution; president, Insurance Co. of North America *post* 1796.

PETTIT, THOMAS MCKEAN (*b. Philadelphia, Pa., 1797; d. Philadelphia, 1853*), Pennsylvania jurist, Democratic politician. Grandson of Charles Pettit and Thomas McKean. Associate and presiding judge of district court for city and county of Philadelphia, 1833–45.

PETTUS, EDMUND WINSTON (*b. Limestone Co., Ala., 1821; d. Hot Springs, N.C., 1907*), lawyer, Confederate brigadier general, Alabama politician. U.S. senator, Democrat, from Alabama, 1897–1907.

PEW, JOSEPH NEWTON, JR. (*b. Pittsburgh, Pa., 1886; d. Philadelphia, Pa., 1963*), industrialist and political leader. Attended Cornell (engineering degree, 1908), then entered the family-owned business, Sun Oil Company, serving as vice president (1912–47) and chairman, and as president and chairman of Sun Shipbuilding and Dry Dock Company (from 1917). His contributions to those firms include the "custom blending" pump that delivered gas in nine octane ratings and a gyroscopic instrument that aided in achieving record drilling depths in oil exploration. Known outside the oil industry as a behind-the-scenes strategist of the conservative wing of the Republican party; his massive contributions to campaign funds gave him a major role in party affairs.

PEYTON, JOHN LEWIS (*b. near Staunton, Va., 1824; d. 1896*), lawyer, Confederate agent, author. North Carolina state agent in England, 1861–65, he was critical of Confederate foreign policy, expressing his views in several volumes of reminiscences.

PFAHLER, GEORGE EDWARD (*b. Numidia, Pa., 1874; d. Philadelphia, Pa., 1957*), radiologist. Studied at Bloomsburg State Normal School and at the Medico-Chirurgical College (later part of the University of Pennsylvania School of Medicine). Taught there from 1902. One of the first experimenters and practitioners of radiology in the U.S., Pfahler was the first president of the American College of Radiology, 1922–23.

PFISTER, ALFRED (*b. Zurich, Switzerland, 1880; d. New York, N.Y., 1964*), chemical manufacturer. Attended Chemical Institute of the University of Basel (Ph.D., 1903). With Jacques Wolf and Company in New Jersey (1914–32); under his presidency the company developed new lines of textile chemicals and captured a share of the lucrative U.S. market for synthetic organic chemicals. Started Pfister Chemical in 1932, producing chemicals for use in bactericides, fungicides, and cancer chemotherapy; during World War II produced napalm for the Chemical War Service.

PFUND, AUGUST HERMAN (*b. Madison, Wis., 1879; d. Baltimore, Md., 1949*), physicist. B.S., University of Wisconsin, 1901; Ph.D., Johns Hopkins University, 1906. Taught at Johns Hopkins *post* 1906; appointed professor, 1927; headed physics department from 1938 until his retirement in 1947. His innovative and exacting research established a firm foundation for the subsequent development of infrared technology.

PHELAN, DAVID SAMUEL (*b. Sydney, Nova Scotia, 1841; d. St. Louis, Mo., 1915*), Roman Catholic clergyman, journalist. Edited the *Western Watchman*, a militant newspaper published at St. Louis, 1868–1915; scored American Protective Association; upheld liberal point of view in politics and church polity; bluntly criticized hierarchy.

PHELAN, JAMES (*b. Queen's Co., Ireland, 1824; d. San Francisco, Calif., 1892*), merchant, capitalist. Came to America as a child; prospered in New York; established himself as general merchant in San Francisco, 1849. Organized First National Gold Bank, 1870, and other banks and insurance companies.

PHELAN, JAMES (*b. Aberdeen, Miss., 1856; d. Nassau, Bahamas, 1891*), lawyer, author. Ph.D., Leipzig, 1878. Published *Memphis Avalanche*, 1881–91; wrote *History of Tennessee* (1888). As congressman, Democrat, from Tennessee, 1887–91, Phelan opposed traditional Southern views on the tariff and black rights.

PHELAN, JAMES DUVAL (*b. San Francisco, Calif., 1861; d. Saratoga, Calif., 1930*), California politician, banker. Son of James Phelan (1824–92). Elected mayor of San Francisco in 1897 and reelected twice as a reform candidate, he vigorously attacked the corrupt board of supervisors and provided leadership in drafting and adopting a new city charter. He was also responsible for the beautifying of the city and for the "Burnham Plan," from which came San Francisco's present civic center. At his own expense he took steps to secure the city's water supply in the Hetch Hetchy Valley. As a Democrat in the U.S. Senate, 1915–21, he supported Wilson, but favored separation of the League of Nations Covenant from the Versailles Treaty.

PHELPS, ALMIRA HART LINCOLN (*b. Berlin, Conn., 1793; d. Baltimore, Md., 1884*), educator. Sister of Emma H. Willard. Author of popular elementary science textbooks, among them *Botany for Beginners* (1833) and *Lectures on Chemistry* (1837).

PHELPS, ANSON GREENE (*b. Simsbury, Conn., 1781; d. New York, N.Y., 1853*), metals merchant, philanthrophist. Senior partner of Phelps, Dodge & Co., *post* 1832; important in development of Pennsylvania iron and Lake Superior copper mines.

PHELPS, AUSTIN (*b. West Brookfield, Mass., 1820; d. Bar Harbor, Maine, 1890*), Congregational clergyman. Professor of sacred rhetoric and homiletics at Andover Seminary, 1848–79; aligned himself with conservatives at Andover.

PHELPS, CHARLES EDWARD (*b. Guilford, Vt., 1833; d. Baltimore, Md., 1908*), lawyer, jurist, Union soldier, Maryland congressman. Son of Almira H. L. Phelps. Judge of supreme bench of Baltimore, 1882–1908; wrote *Juridical Equity* (1894).

PHELPS, EDWARD JOHN (*b. Middlebury, Vt., 1822; d. New Haven, Conn., 1900*), lawyer. Graduated Middlebury College, 1840. Kent Professor of Law at Yale, 1881–85 and 1889–1900. U.S. ambassador to Great Britain, 1885–89; U.S. counsel in 1893 fur-seal arbitration with Great Britain.

PHELPS, ELIZABETH STUART. *See* WARD, ELIZABETH STUART PHELPS.

PHELPS, GUY ROWLAND (*b. Simsbury, Conn., 1802; d. Hartford, Conn., 1869*), physician. Founded Connecticut Mutual Life Insurance Co., 1846; did much to popularize mutual system of insurance.

PHELPS, JOHN SMITH (*b. Simsbury, Conn., 1814; d. 1886*), lawyer, Missouri legislator, Union soldier. Removed to Missouri, 1837. Congressman, Democrat, 1845–63; governor of Missouri, 1877–81. A consistent Unionist, and a faithful, honest public servant.

PHELPS, OLIVER (*b. Poquonock, Conn., 1749; d. Canandaigua, N.Y., 1809*), merchant Massachusetts legislator. Speculated on credit, 1788–96, in millions of acres of western lands, mostly in western New York. Partner of Nathaniel Gorham.

PHELPS, THOMAS STOWELL (*b. Buckfield, Maine, 1822; d. New York, N.Y., 1901*), naval officer. Made careful surveys of waterways preparatory to military operations during Civil War, especially of Potomac and York rivers and Pamlico Sound in 1861. Retired as rear admiral, 1884.

PHELPS, WILLIAM FRANKLIN (*b. Auburn, N.Y., 1822; d. St. Paul, Minn., 1907*), educator. Headed normal schools in New Jersey, Minnesota, and Wisconsin. First president, American Normal School Association, 1858–63.

PHELPS, WILLIAM LYON (*b. New Haven, Conn., 1865; d. New Haven, 1943*), educator, literary critic, lecturer. B.A., Yale, 1887; M.A., Harvard, 1891; Ph.D., Yale, 1891. As teacher of English literature at Yale, 1892–1933 (professor *post* 1901), he led the movement for informality and geniality in the classroom and for the inclusion of contemporary fiction and drama in the curriculum of study. An unashamed popularizer of literature, he championed the joys of reading in his courses of public lectures, his monthly essay column in *Scribner's Magazine* entitled "As I Like It," in a syndicated newspaper feature, and in radio addresses. Typical of his books, which were made up largely of his magazine essays and lectures, was *Essays on Modern Novelists* (1910).

PHELPS, WILLIAM WALTER (*b. Dundaff, Pa., 1839; d. Englewood, N.J., 1894*), lawyer. Congressman, Republican from New Jersey, 1873–75 and 1883–89. U.S. minister to Austria-Hungary, 1881; to Germany, 1889–93.

PHILIP (*d. Bristol, R.I., 1676*), Indian leader, known also as King Philip, Po-Metacom, and Metacomet. Son of Massasoit, he became sachem of the Wampanoag in 1662, and for nine years behaved peaceably. From 1671 to 1675 he was suspected of plotting against the settlers, and when the latter executed three Wampanoag for killing Sassamon, Philip's former secretary who had revealed his alleged plots, the conflict known as King Philip's War began in June 1675. With his allies, the Nipmuck, he killed many colonists and burned several towns after ineffectual resistance. He again fell upon the Massachusetts towns in 1676, but the colonial troops now turned to a policy of capturing Indian women and children, destroying India crops, and offering immunity to deserters. After the dwindling away of his forces, Philip sought refuge in a swamp near Mount Hope, where he was shot by an Indian serving under Capt. Benjamin Church.

PHILIP, JOHN WOODWARD (*b. Kinderhook, N.Y., 1840; d. 1900*), naval officer. Graduated U.S. Naval Academy, 1861. As captain of USS *Texas* during battle of Santiago Bay, 1898, he ordered, "Don't cheer, men, those poor devils are dying." Promoted rear admiral, 1899, he commanded the Brooklyn (N.Y.) Navy Yard at his death.

PHILIPP, EMANUEL LORENZ (*b. Sauk Co., Wis., 1861; d. 1925*), businessman, transportation expert. Served with distinction as governor of Wisconsin, 1915–21; although a "regular" Republican, he respected previous Progressive legislation.

PHILIPS, JOHN FINIS (*b. Boone Co., Mo., 1834; d. 1919*), lawyer, Union soldier. One of "Big Four" Democratic leaders of Missouri *post* 1874. Served as congressman, 1875–77 and 1880–81; as federal district judge, 1888–1910.

PHILIPS, MARTIN WILSON (*b. Columbia, S.C., 1806; d. Oxford, Miss., 1889*), Mississippi agriculturist, reformer. Urged introduction of fruit trees and use of improved agricultural implements.

PHILIPSE, FREDERICK (*b. Friesland, Holland, 1626; d. 1702*), merchant, New York colonial official. Immigrated to New Amsterdam, probably 1647. Acquired fortune through Indian trade, manufacture of wampum, importation of slaves, and Madagascar trade. Assembled extensive Hudson River landholdings, erected into manor of Philipsburgh, 1693.

PHILIPSON, DAVID (*b. Wabash, Ind., 1862; d. Boston, Mass., 1949*), rabbi, leader in American Reform Judaism. Raised in Dayton and Columbus, Ohio. Graduated University of Cincinnati, B.A., 1883; graduated in the same year from Hebrew Union College and was ordained a rabbi; D.D., Hebrew Union, 1886. Served at Har Sinai Temple, Baltimore, Md., 1884–88, and at Bene Israel, Cincinnati, Ohio, 1888–1938. A prolific writer, translator, and editor, he stressed two themes in his works and his ministry: liberal Judaism and Americanism. A man of ecumenical goodwill, he held the firm conviction that the bond of Judaism was religious, not political, national, or racial; he was strongly opposed to Zionism.

PHILLIPS, DAVID GRAHAM (*b. Madison, Ind., 1867; d. New York, N.Y., 1911*), novelist, journalist. Author of muckraking magazine exposés; also of a number of "problem" novels, of which the most ambitious was *Susan Lenox: Her Fall and Rise* (1917).

PHILLIPS, FRANCIS CLIFFORD (*b. Philadelphia, Pa., 1850; d. Ben Avon, Pa., 1920*), chemist. Professor of chemistry, Western University of Pennsylvania, 1875–1915; worked on standardization and improvement of methods of analysis.

PHILLIPS, FRANK (*b. Scotia, Greeley Co., Nebr., 1873; d. Atlantic City, N.J., 1950*), oil industry executive. Successful in both oil production and banking in and about Bartlesville, Okla., *post* 1903, he and his brother Lee E. Phillips organized and incorporated Phillips Petroleum Co., June 1917. Under his guidance as president (chairman of the board *post* 1938), the company pioneered in new production techniques and grew into the ninth largest oil corporation in the United States. He was a generous patron of educational institutions and the founder of the Woolaroc Museum.

PHILLIPS, GEORGE (*b. probably South Rainham, England, 1593; d. Watertown, Mass., 1644*), clergyman. An original settler of Watertown, 1630, he drafted covenant of the church there, and was pastor, 1630–44. First Massachusetts minister to practice congregational form of church polity.

PHILLIPS, HARRY IRVING (*b. New Haven, Conn., 1889; d. Milford, Conn., 1965*), journalist. Began as a cub reporter for New Haven Register; became a copy boy at the *New York Globe* (1917); and started a syndicated column (1918). The *Globe* was sold to the *New York Sun* (1923), and he became the *Sun's* star columnist (until 1950). His column was written with a gentle touch more typical of rural philosophers than the sophisticated cynicism of New York columnists. Evils, in his opinion, were the national debt, income taxes, fireside chats, and Eleanor Roosevelt. Prior to World War II, he wrote radio sketches, skits for Broadway musicals, and several books, including *The Globe Trotter* (1924) and *On White or Rye* (1941). During the war he introduced the character "Private Oscar Purkey," and the Purkey columns appeared in several book collections. Later he wrote for Bell McClure Syndicate.

PHILLIPS, HENRY (*b. Philadelphia, Pa., 1838; d. 1895*), numismatist, philologist, translator. Author of, among numerous other works, *Historical Sketches of the Paper Currency of the American Colonies* (1865) and *Continental Paper Money* (1866).

PHILLIPS, JOHN (*b. Andover, Mass., 1719; d. 1795*), land speculator, moneylender, philanthropist. Uncle of Samuel Phillips. Graduated Harvard, 1735. After making liberal gifts to Dartmouth College, he incorporated and endowed Phillips Exeter

Academy, 1781; it opened in 1783. Phillips patterned his new school after Phillips Academy, Andover, but reserved to himself much power over the school's affairs.

PHILLIPS, JOHN SANBURN (*b. Council Bluffs, Iowa, 1861; d. Goshen, N.Y., 1949*), magazine editor and publisher. Raised in Galesburg, Ill., B.A., Knox College, 1882; B.A., Harvard, 1885; studied also at University of Leipzig. Associated *post* 1886 with Samuel S. McClure as working editor and general manager of the McClure Syndicate, of *McClure's Magazine*, 1893–1906, and of the publishing firm of McClure, Phillips and Co., 1900–06. Differing over company policy with McClure, he left him in 1906 to join with various staff writers of *McClure's Magazine* in purchasing the *American Illustrated Magazine*, which was renamed the *American Magazine*. After its sale to the Crowell Publishing Co., 1911, he continued on as editor of the *American* until 1915, serving thereafter as consulting editor until 1938. Much of the success of *McClure's* was owing to Phillips' practical editorial talents and day-to-day thoroughness.

PHILLIPS, LENA MADESIN (*b. Nicholasville, Ky., 1881; d. Marseilles, France, 1955*), lawyer and women's organization leader. Studied at Women's College of Baltimore (later Goucher), at the University of Kentucky Law School (LL.B., 1917), and at New York University (LL.M., 1923). Founder of the National (1919) and International (1930) Federation of Business and Professional Women's Clubs. President of the national organization, (1926–29), and of the international, (1930–47). President of the National Council of Women, 1931–35. After World War II, she was consultant to the U.N. Economic and Social Council and chairwoman of the First International Conference on Public Information.

PHILLIPS, PHILIP (*b. Cassadaga, N.Y., 1834; d. Delaware, Ohio, 1895*), singing evangelist, composer, and compiler of hymns.

PHILLIPS, SAMUEL (*b. Northern Andover, Mass., 1752; d. Andover, Mass., 1802*), educator, public official. Nephew of John Phillips. Graduated Harvard, 1771. Delegate to Massachusetts Provincial Congress, 1775, and to state constitutional convention, 1779–80; served in state senate, 1780–1801. Securing financial aid from his uncle and father, he established, 1777, at Andover a unique endowed academy, controlled by a board of trustees, the majority of whom were laymen. The first object of Phillips Academy was "the promotion of true Piety and Virtue," that is, character, which emphasis showed the influence of John Locke and English nonconformist academies. The school opened in April 1778 with Eliphalet Pearson as principal.

PHILLIPS, THOMAS WHARTON (*b. near Mount Jackson, Pa., 1835; d. New Castle, Pa., 1912*), oil producer. Republican congressman, religious writer. Leading member of U.S. Industrial Commission, 1898–1902.

PHILLIPS, ULRICH BONNELL (*b. La Grange, Ga., 1877; d. 1934*), educator, historian. Graduated University of Georgia, 1897; Ph.D., Columbia, 1902. Taught history at Wisconsin, at Tulane, and at Michigan, 1911–29; thereafter, he was professor of history at Yale. Phillips's many articles and books were pioneering studies in the history of the South up to the Civil War; he was especially concerned with establishing the facts about the plantation system and slavery. His *Life and Labor in the Old South* (1929) was the first volume in a projected history of the South, which he did not live to complete.

PHILLIPS, WALTER POLK (*b. near Grafton, Mass., 1846; d. Vineyard Haven, Mass., 1920*), telegrapher, journalist. Devised Phillips Telegraphic Code for news transmission, 1879. Became managerial head of the United Press organization early in the 1880's; utilized independent wires, made alliances with foreign news agencies, and led the United Press forces during their "war" with the Associated Press, 1893–97. Thereafter, on the collapse of the United Press, he was prominent in the Columbia Graphophone Co.

PHILLIPS, WENDELL (*b. Boston, Mass., 1811; d. Boston, 1884*), lawyer, orator, reformer. Graduated Harvard, 1831. Becoming a rabid abolitionist, he first gained notice for a passionate speech in Faneuil Hall, 1837, at a meeting called to protest the murder of Elijah P. Lovejoy. A fairly consistent disciple of William L. Garrison, Phillips traveled extensively on the lyceum circuit. His language on the subject of slavery became increasingly intemperate through the 1840's and 1850's; he assailed the Constitution as a protector of reaction and ultimately called for secession by the North. After the Civil War he turned to a succession of other causes, among them prohibition and fair treatment for the Indians. His zeal for the labor movement led him to denounce the profit-and-wage system vehemently; he wrote *The Labor Question* (1884).

PHILLIPS, WILLARD (*b. Bridgewater, Mass., 1784; d. Cambridge, Mass., 1873*), lawyer, insurance executive, author. Zealous advocate of protective tariffs; wrote *Manual of Political Economy* (1828) and *Propositions Concerning Protection and Free Trade* (1850).

PHILLIPS, WILLIAM (*b. Beverly, Mass., 1878; d. Sarasota, Fla., 1968*), diplomat who served under every president from Theodore Roosevelt to Harry Truman. Attended Harvard (B.A., 1900) and Harvard Law. During a forty-four-year career, alternated between appointments in the Foreign Service and the State Departments; positions he held included ambassador to Belgium and Luxembourg (1924–27), Italy, (1936–40), and India (1942–44); resident director of the Office of Strategic Services; and ambassador to Supreme Headquarters, Allied Expeditionary Force (1940), working closely with Gen. Dwight Eisenhower. He officially retired in 1944. Assigned (1946) to the twelve-man Anglo-American Committee on Palestine, which reviewed the problem of Jewish refugees still detained in Europe. During a long retirement, wrote his memoir, *Ventures in Diplomacy* (1952).

PHILLIPS, WILLIAM (*b. Boston, Mass., 1750/1; d. Boston, 1827*), merchant, philanthropist, Federalist politician. Cousin of Samuel Phillips. Lieutenant governor of Massachusetts, 1812–23; generous benefactor of Phillips Academy, Andover; president, American Bible Society.

PHILLIPS, WILLIAM ADDISON (*b. Paisley, Scotland, 1824; d. 1893*), lawyer, Union soldier, journalist. Immigrated to Illinois as a boy. Won reputation as New York *Tribune* correspondent in Kansas, 1855; served in Kansas legislature. As Republican congressman from Kansas, 1873–79, he advocated then radical economic and reform policies.

PHINIZY, FERDINAND (*b. Oglethorpe Co., Ga., 1819; d. Athens, Ga., 1889*), cotton merchant, financier.

PHIPPS, HENRY (*b. Philadelphia, Pa., 1839; d. Great Neck, N.Y., 1930*), bookkeeper, steel manufacturer, philanthropist. From 1867 to 1901, Phipps was a close business associate of Andrew Carnegie, serving principally as a conservative financial adviser in Carnegie's operations.

PHIPPS, LAWRENCE COWLE (*b. Amityville, Pa., 1862 d. Santa Monica, Calif., 1958*), industrialist and politician. With only a high school education, Phipps went to work for the Carnegie Steel Company in 1879, rising eventually to vice president and treasurer. After the company was sold in 1901, Phipps took his earnings and moved to Colorado, becoming active in local Republican politics. He was elected to the U.S. Senate in 1918 and served until 1930. A conservative, Phipps supported President Coolidge, was for restrictive immigration and protective trade measures, and was chairman of the Committee on Education. He was forced from politics when it was learned that he received the support of the Ku Klux Klan.

PHIPS, WILLIAM (*b. Maine frontier of Massachusetts, 1650/1; d. London, England, 1694/5*), baronet, colonial official. Apprenticed early to a ship's carpenter in Boston, he followed that trade there. Successful in command of an expedition to raise a Spanish treasure ship off Haiti, he was knighted in 1687. *Post* 1688, he worked with Increase Mather for restoration of the old charter rule in the colony; in 1690, he won a spectacular victory over the French by capturing Port Royal in Nova Scotia. When William III granted a new charter to Massachusetts, Phips, on the nomination of Increase Mather, was made the first royal governor. Arriving at his post in May 1692, he abruptly halted the witchcraft trials. He alienated important political factions in the colony by high-handed actions, and the crown by refusing to enforce customs regulations and by failing to protect the colony's frontiers.

PHISTERER, FREDERICK (*b. Stuttgart, Germany, 1836; d. Albany, N.Y., 1909*), soldier. Immigrated to America, 1855; joined U.S. Army in that year. Rose from private to captain, winning fame at Stone's River, 1862. Resigning regular commission, 1870, he rose to brevet major general in New York National Guard.

PHOENIX, JOHN. *See* DERBY, GEORGE HORATIO.

PHYFE, DUNCAN (*b. Scotland, 1768; d. New York, N.Y., 1854*), cabinetmaker. After apprenticeship to a cabinetmaker in Albany, N.Y., he moved to New York City and was established in his own shop at 2 Broad St. by 1792. Combining the talents of an artist with those of a businessman, he soon built up a prosperous concern in which his sons eventually joined him as partners. Critics believe that he was the equal of the famous 18th-century English masters; his work in mahogany is unsurpassed. Starting with indebtedness to English contemporaries, he developed a unique style influenced strongly by the French Directoire and early Empire styles. Phyfe did his best work early in his career, afterward succumbing to the demand for so-called American Empire, which degenerated into heavy, commonplace forms called "butcher furniture" by Phyfe himself.

PHYSICK, PHILIP SYNG (*b. Philadelphia, Pa., 1768; d. 1837*), surgeon. Grandson of Philip Syng. Graduated University of Pennsylvania, 1785. Studied medicine with Adam Kuhn, in London with John Hunter, and at Edinburgh, M.D., 1792. Returning to Philadelphia, he slowly built a solid practice, helped by his close friendship with Benjamin Rush and Stephen Girard. Elected to the staff of Pennsylvania Hospital in 1794, he served there until 1816; he also lectured on surgery at the University of Pennsylvania, 1801–19. Among his advances in surgery were the invention of the needle forceps for tying deeply placed blood vessels, a snare for tonsillectomy, and new forms of catheters in surgery of the urinary tract.

PIATT, DONN (*b. Cincinnati, Ohio, 1819; d. near West Liberty, Ohio, 1891*), journalist, Union soldier. Founder and editor of the weekly *Capital*, published at Washington, D.C., 1871–80; exposed weaknesses and corruption of both Republicans and Democrats.

PIATT, JOHN JAMES (*b. James' Mills, Ind., 1835; d. Cincinnati, Ohio, 1917*), poet, U.S. consul, journalist. Coauthor with William Dean Howells of *Poems of Two Friends* (1860); author of a number of volumes of later work, 1866–97.

PIATT, SARAH MORGAN BRYAN (*b. Lexington, Ky., 1836; d. Caldwell, N.J., 1919*), poet. Wife of John J. Piatt.

PICCARD, JEAN FELIX (*b. Basel, Switzerland, 1884; d. Minneapolis, Minn., 1963*), organic chemist and aeronautical engineer. Attended University of Basel, Swiss Institute of Technology (D.Sc., 1909), and Munich. Taught at Munich, Lausanne, Chicago, and Massachusetts Institute of Technology, from 1914 to 1929. Formed Hercules Powder Company (1927); became head of the chemical service department (1929–32). Was naturalized in 1931. Interested in the scientific uses of balloons, and while at Bartol Research Foundation, he ascended over 57,000 feet, returning with data on radiation at various levels (1934). At the University of Minnesota (1936–52), he pioneered the use of blasting caps to sever mooring ropes and release ballast; developed the prototype of the "Skyhook" balloons (1946–47) used for meteorological research; and produced a frost-resistant window and a gas valve to prevent explosions of hydrogen gas.

PICK, LEWIS ANDREW (*b. Brookneal, Va., 1890; d. Washington, D.C., 1956*), army officer and engineer. Studied at Virginia Polytechnic Institute. Commissioned in the army during World War I, Pick remained in the Army Corps of Engineers until his retirement in 1953. He served in the Philippines, taught at various army colleges, and was appointed Missouri River engineer in 1942–43 and 1945–49. During World War II Pick gained international fame for constructing the famous Ledo Road from India into Burma, one of the great engineering feats of military history which enabled the Allies to reenter Burma.

PICKARD, SAMUEL THOMAS (*b. Rowley, Mass., 1828; d. Amesbury, Mass., 1915*), printer, author. Coeditor of *Portland* (Me.) *Transcript*, 1855–95; author of *Life and Letters of John Greenleaf Whittier* (1894).

PICKENS, ANDREW (*b. near Paxtang, Pa., 1739; d. Tomassee, S.C., 1817*), Revolutionary soldier. Defeated Loyalist force at Kettle Creek, Ga., 1779; took prominent part in battles of Cowpens and Eutaw Springs.

PICKENS, FRANCIS WILKINSON (*b. Colleton District, S.C., 1805; d. near Edgefield Court House, S.C., 1869*), lawyer, politician. Grandson of Andrew Pickens. Studied at Franklin College, Georgia, and South Carolina College. Passionately attached to Thomas Cooper's states' rights doctrines, he wrote extensively under pen names "Sydney" and "Hampden" urging South Carolina to implement nullification principles, 1827–30; he replied forcefully, 1832, to Jackson's nullification proclamation. As a congressman, Democrat, 1834–43, he led in protecting acceptance of abolitionist petitions. A leader of the secession movement growing out of dissatisfaction with the Compromise of 1850, he later became more moderate. After Lincoln's election, however, he urged immediate secession and served as Confederate governor of South Carolina, December 1860–1862.

PICKENS, ISRAEL (*b. near Concord, N.C., 1780; d. near Matanzas, Cuba, 1827*), lawyer. Congressman, Democrat, from North Carolina, 1811–17. Removed to Alabama, 1818, where he was anti-Crawford governor, 1821–25. First opposed, then tolerated, a state-owned banking system; helped found University of Alabama.

PICKENS, WILLIAM (*b. Anderson County, S.C., 1881; d. at sea, 1954*), educator and government administrator. Studied at Talladega College, Ala., at Yale University (B.A., 1904), where he was the first black elected to the Yale chapter of Phi Beta Kappa, and at Fisk University (M.A., 1908). After several years of teaching, he became dean and, later, vice president of Morgan State College, Baltimore, Md. Pickens was a member of the original Committee of 100 of the NAACP; in 1920, he became field director of the organization, a position he held until 1940. In 1941, he became chief of the Inter-racial Section of the Savings Bond Division of the U.S. Treasury. Although he was charged by Martin Dies as being a communist, he survived to become an effective head of the bond sales program. He retired in 1952.

PICKERING, CHARLES (*b. Susquehanna Co., Pa., 1805; d. 1878*), physician, naturalist. Chief zoologist, Wilkes South Seas Exploring Expedition, 1838–42; author of reports on geographical distribution of men, animals, and plants based on the expedition's findings and on later research.

PICKERING, EDWARD CHARLES (*b. Boston, Mass., 1846; d. 1919*), astronomer. Graduated Lawrence Scientific School, Harvard, 1865; taught physics at Massachusetts Institute of Technology, 1866–77. Director of the Harvard Observatory, 1877–1919, where he pioneered in using methods of physics to extend knowledge of stellar structure and evolution. Using Harvard's large instruments, Pickering developed the art of photometry, using the meridian photometer to establish the magnitudes of stars by instrumental rather than visual means. He thus catalogued the magnitudes of 80,000 stars and further compiled a photographic library of about 300,000 plates, which captured all stars down to the eleventh magnitude. He also pioneered in stellar spectroscopy.

PICKERING, JOHN (*b. Newington, N.H., ca. 1738; d. 1805*), New Hampshire legislator and jurist. Appointed U.S. district court judge for New Hampshire, 1795, he was impeached and removed in 1804 for partisan reasons, although actually suffering from mental collapse.

PICKERING, JOHN (*b. Salem, Mass., 1777; d. Boston, Mass., 1846*), lawyer, philologist. Son of Timothy Pickering. Graduated Harvard, 1796. Author of the first collection of American word usages (1816) and the outstanding *Comprehensive Lexicon of the Greek Language* (1826, 1829, 1846). Authority on American Indian languages.

PICKERING, TIMOTHY (*b. Salem, Mass., 1745; d. Salem, 1829*), soldier, administrator, politician. Graduated Harvard, 1763. An early supporter of the independence movement, he displayed great ability as a newspaper controversialist and pamphleteer. As colonel of Massachusetts militia, he took part in the operations of April 1775, was assigned to coast defense operations, then joined Washington's army in the 1776–77 campaign. He served as adjutant general of the army in 1777, was a member of the board of war, 1777–80, and quartermaster general, 1780–83. Much criticized for his work in the latter post, Pickering clearly served with energy and determination. After the Revolution, he engaged in mercantile business in Philadelphia, but in 1787 moved his family into the Wyoming Valley region of Pennsylvania, where he represented Pennsylvania's interest in the dispute with Connecticut settlers and demonstrated talent in negotiating with the Indians. A supporter of the federal Constitution, he was appointed agent to deal with the Seneca in 1790 and U.S. postmaster general in 1791. He continued to act as an Indian negotiator, supporting an enlightened policy. Appointed U.S. secretary of war, 1795, Pickering also had jurisdiction over naval affairs and pushed construction of the famous frigates that served so well in the War of 1812. He was a fervent Federalist and used his talents for controversy against fellow Federalists whom he suspected of deviation just as heartily as he used them against Jeffersonians. Alexander Hamilton was his special hero, and he came to believe that the French Revolution was the cause of all that was damnable in the world. On the resignation of Edmund Randolph, Pickering succeeded to the post of secretary of state in August 1795, serving until Adams dismissed him in 1800. As secretary, Pickering tried desperately to widen the breach with France and looked forward eagerly to hostilities. Frustration of these hopes, 1798–99, brought him to hate President Adams with a fine passion; he acted indiscreetly in corresponding with Adams' enemies and intriguing against him at every opportunity, thus helping to wreck his own party. Pickering later served in the U.S. Senate, 1803–11, and in the House of Representatives, 1813–17, where he continued to support "high-toned" Federalist principles and virulently opposed the War of 1812.

PICKET, ALBERT (*b. 1771; d. 1850*), teacher, author. Pupil of Noah Webster; taught in New York City *ca.* 1794–1826 and thereafter in Cincinnati, Ohio. Prepared widely adopted series of elementary English texts; edited early educational periodical, *The Academician*, 1818–20; formed Western Literary Institute and College of Professional Teachers, which was active from 1829 to 1845.

PICKETT, ALBERT JAMES (*b. Anson Co., N.C., 1810; d. 1858*), planter, historian. Removed to Autauga Co., Ala., as a child. Author of *History of Alabama and Incidentally of Georgia and Mississippi from the Earliest Period* (1851).

PICKETT, GEORGE EDWARD (*b. Richmond, Va., 1825; d. Norfolk, Va., 1875*), Confederate soldier. Graduated West Point, 1846. Went directly to the Mexican War, where he gained distinction at Contreras and Churubusco, and was first to cross the parapet of Chapultepec. After frontier service in the Northwest, he resigned from the U.S. Army, 1861, and was commissioned Confederate colonel. Made brigadier general in February 1862, he served gallantly at Seven Pines and Gaines's Mill and was given command of a Virginia division with rank of major general in October. At Gettysburg, Lee ordered Pickett with 4,500 effectives to assault the Union center on July 3, 1863. His command advanced half a mile, with parade precision, over ground raked by rifle and artillery fire; repulsed, a scant quarter of them returned from the charge. Pickett made the greatest fight of his career at Five Forks on Apr. 1, 1865.

PICKETT, JAMES CHAMBERLAYNE (*b. Fauquier Co., Va., 1793; d. Washington, D.C., 1872*), War of 1812 soldier, Kentucky legislator, diplomat. Arranged treaty with Republic of Ecuador, 1839 (proclaimed in 1842); negotiated convention with Peru, 1841.

PICKNELL, WILLIAM LAMB (*b. Hinesburg, Vt., 1853; d. Marbelhead, Mass., 1897*), landscape painter. Encouraged by George Innes; studied in Paris with J. L. Gérôme.

PICTON, THOMAS (*b. New York, N.Y., 1822; d. New York, 1891*), soldier of fortune, journalist. Served in Lopez' 1850–51 filibustering expedition against Cuba and William Walker's invasion of Nicaragua. Frequently wrote under pen name "Paul Preston."

PIDGIN, CHARLES FELTON (*b. Roxbury, Mass., 1844; d. Melrose, Mass., 1923*), statistician. Inventor of methods and instruments for mechanical tabulation of statistics. Author of best selling *Quincy Adams Sawyer* (1900) and other novels.

PIEPER, FRANZ AUGUST OTTO (*b. Carwitz, Germany, 1852; d. St. Louis, Mo., 1931*), Lutheran theologian. Came to America, 1870. Leader in Missouri Synod; president, Concordia Seminary, 1887–1931.

PIERCE, BENJAMIN (*b. Chelmsford, Mass., 1757; d. Hillsborough, N.H., 1839*), farmer, Revolutionary soldier, New Hampshire legislator. Father of Franklin Pierce. An avid Jeffersonian, he was elected governor of New Hampshire, 1827 and 1829, on basis of Revolutionary record and agrarian appeal.

PIERCE, EDWARD LILLIE (b. Stoughton, Mass., 1829; d. Paris, France, 1897), lawyer. Brother of Henry L. Pierce. Author of scrupulously honest *Memoir* of Charles Sumner (1877, 1893).

PIERCE, FRANKLIN (b. Hillsborough, N.H., 1804; d. Concord, N.H., 1869), lawyer, president of the United States. Son of Benjamin Pierce. Graduated Bowdoin, 1824. First elected to the New Hampshire lower house in 1829, he became Speaker in 1831 and 1832. He next served in the U.S. House of Representatives, 1833–37, and the U.S. Senate, 1837–42; he was a consistent, loyal Jacksonian Democrat. He respected southern rights and developed a settled antipathy for political abolitionists. During a decade of legal practice in New Hampshire, 1842–52, he gained a commanding reputation for effective jury pleading and was personally popular. From 1842 to 1847 he managed most of the local Democratic campaigns, enforcing strict party discipline. Enlisting for the Mexican War as a private, he rose to brigadier general, but did not participate in any battles. He took the lead in enforcing New Hampshire Democratic support for the Compromise of 1850, and his friends worked to secure for him the presidential nomination in 1852 as a compromise candidate. The convention, hopelessly deadlocked, turned to Pierce at last as a candidate who would satisfy the southern bloc. He carried all but four states in November, although his popular majority was less than 50,000.

Pierce selected his cabinet from all sections of the country and from among all factions that had supported him. He set his administration to a policy of complete respect for states' rights, economy, honesty, and a vigorous foreign policy aimed at acquiring more territory. One project dear to his heart was the acquisition of Cuba. American diplomats in Europe were working to this end, but news of their activity leaked prematurely and was publicized in the so-called Ostend Manifesto. Northern opposition followed and the project failed. Pierce succeeded in making the Gadsden Purchase of land from Mexico, 1853, and in persuading the British to agree to retire from Central America except Honduras. Pierce's chief political problem, however, was Kansas. Induced by a group of powerful Senate Democrats to support the Kansas-Nebraska Act in return for favorable action on his patronage appointments and his foreign policy program, he thereafter became engulfed in a political storm. Determined to enforce the act fairly, he selected appointees to office in the territories equally from the North and South, but his choice of men was generally unfortunate, notably in the case of Governor A. H. Reeder of Kansas. On the appearance of civil war in Kansas between Free-Soilers supporting a local government of their own choosing and Missouri forces threatening to disperse them by force, Pierce supported the technically legal proslavery government, a fact which further alienated Northern Democratic leaders. Pierce's second choice as Kansas governor, Wilson Shannon, proved ineffective, and not until the summer of 1856 were law and order restored under Governor John W. Geary. In his effort to be impartial an "legal," Pierce had helped to split his party and to lay the groundwork for organization of the Republican party. He had honestly tried to do his duty, but was without adequate experience or temperamental fitness and had failed utterly to estimate the depth of northern feeling against the South. Refused renomination in 1856, he became increasingly unpopular in New Hampshire and particularly so after later intemperate attacks upon Lincoln.

PIERCE, GEORGE FOSTER (b. Greene Co., Ga., 1811; d. Sparta, Ga., 1884), bishop of the Methodist Episcopal Church, South, educator. President, Emory College, 1848–54; appointed bishop, 1854.

PIERCE, GILBERT ASHVILLE (b. East Otto, N.Y., 1839; d. Chicago, Ill., 1901), lawyer, Union soldier, journalist, author. Dakota territorial governor, Republican, 1884–86; U.S. senator from North Dakota, 1889–91.

PIERCE, HENRY LILLIE (b. Stoughton, Mass., 1825; d. 1896), cocoa manufacturer, Massachusetts legislator, philanthropist. Brother of Edward L. Pierce. Managed and later owned Walter Baker and Co.; Boston mayor, 1872 and 1877; independent and liberal Republican congressman from Massachusetts, 1873–77. A man of outstanding integrity.

PIERCE, JOHN DAVIS (b. Chesterfield, N.H., 1797; d. Medford, Mass., 1882), Congregational clergyman, educator. Removed to Marshall Mich., 1831. Drafted plan for organization of primary schools and state university as Michigan superintendent of public instruction, 1836–41.

PIERCE, WILLIAM LEIGH (b. probably Georgia, ca. 1740; d. 1789), Revolutionary soldier, Savannah, Ga., businessman. As a delegate to the Constitutional Convention, 1787, he made notes on its debates and also wrote character sketches of fellow delegates which are especially useful for information on the less prominent persons present.

PIERPONT, FRANCIS HARRISON (b. near Morgantown, Va., [now W.Va.], 1814; d. Pittsburgh, Pa., 1899), lawyer, Virginia Unionist. Helped organize West Virginia and was provisional governor, 1861–63; served as governor of the "restored" state of Virginia (i.e., those counties under federal control but not included in West Virginia), 1863–65, and of Virginia, 1865–68.

PIERPONT, JAMES (b. Roxbury, Mass., 1659/60; d. New Haven, Conn., 1714), Congregational clergyman. Graduated Harvard, 1681. Pastor, First Church, New Haven, 1685–1714; leading founder and an original trustee of Yale College.

PIERPONT, JOHN (b. Litchfield, Conn., 1785; d. Medford, Mass., 1866), Unitarian clergyman, poet, reformer. Grandfather of John Pierpont Morgan. Minister of Hollis Street Church, Boston, 1819–45. Author of *Airs of Palestine* (1816); edited *American First Class Book* (1823) and *The National Reader* (1827).

PIERREPONT, EDWARDS (b. North Haven, Conn., 1871; d. New York, N.Y., 1892), New York lawyer, influential Union Democrat. U.S. attorney general, 1875–76; U.S. ambassador to England, 1876–77.

PIERSON, ABRAHAM (b. Yorkshire, England, 1609; d. Newark, N.J., 1678), clergyman. Graduated Trinity College, Cambridge, 1632. Strongly Puritan, he immigrated to Massachusetts, 1640, and became pastor of a group at Lynn who settled in December of that year at Southampton, Long Island. Believing strongly that church and state should act in unison and that only church members should be freemen, he opposed Southampton's union with Connecticut, 1644, and left in 1647 to organize a new church at Branford, New Haven Colony, where his views prevailed. There he remained pastor for 20 years. When New Haven in turn joined Connecticut, he departed with most of his congregation to found a new church at Newark, N.J., 1667.

PIERSON, ABRAHAM (b. Southampton, N.Y., ca. 1645; d. Killingworth [Clinton], Conn., 1707), Congregational clergyman. Son of Abraham Pierson (1609–78). Named one of ten trustees upon organization of Yale College; elected first rector of Yale, 1701.

PIERSON, ARTHUR TAPPAN (*b. New York, N.Y., 1837; d. Brooklyn, N.Y., 1911*), Presbyterian clergyman, promoter of missionary activities. Wrote *The Crisis of Missions* (1886); editor, *Missionary Review*, 1890–1911.

PIERSON, HAMILTON WILCOX (*b. Bergen, N.Y., 1817; d. Bergen, 1888*), Presbyterian clergyman, author. Served as traveling agent for American Bible Society; ministered to freedmen in Virginia and Georgia, 1863–69.

PIERZ, FRANZ (*b. near Kamnik, Carniola, Austria, 1785; d. Austria, 1880*), Roman Catholic missionary. Worked among Chippewa Indians in Michigan and Minnesota, 1835–71; promoted German settlement in Minnesota. Author of *Die Indianer in Nord-Amerika* (1855).

PIEZ, CHARLES (*b. Mainz, Germany, 1866; d. Washington, D.C., 1933*), manufacturer, engineer. Director of the Emergency Fleet Corp., 1917–19.

PIGGOT, ROBERT (*b. New York, N.Y., 1795; d. Sykesville, Md., 1887*), stipple engraver, Episcopal clergyman. Apprentice to David Edwin; partner of Charles Goodman. Held pastorates in Pennsylvania, Delaware, and Maryland *post* 1824.

PIGGOTT, JAMES (*b. Connecticut, ca. 1739; d. East St. Louis, Ill., 1799*), Revolutionary soldier, pioneer. Settled in Illinois, *ca.* 1780; served as judge of various courts at Cahokia during 1790's; organized ferry service at East St. Louis, 1797.

PIKE, ALBERT (*b. Boston, Mass., 1809; d. Washington, D.C., 1891*), lawyer, soldier, author, prominent Freemason. From 1833 to the Civil War, Pike lived principally in Arkansas, where he taught school, edited the *Arkansas Advocate*, 1835–37, and became one of the Southwest's most respected lawyers. He was the first reporter of the Arkansas Supreme Court, 1840–45, commanded a cavalry troop in the war with Mexico, was a prominent Whig, and later a promoter of the Know-Nothing party. Made brigadier general and commander of the Indian country west of Arkansas by the Confederate government in 1861, he recruited Indians into the army who committed some atrocities at Pea Ridge, 1862, for which Pike was unjustly accused. His quarrels with General T. C. Hindman, his superior, led to his arrest, 1863, and brief imprisonment. After the war he practiced law and directed the Southern Jurisdiction of Scottish Rite Masonry. His *Hymns to the Gods* were first published in *Blackwood's Magazine* for June 1839, and republished with additional poems in 1872 and subsequent editions. He was also author of *Prose Sketches and Poems* (1834), *Nugae* (1854), and Masonic writings.

PIKE, JAMES SHEPHERD (*b. Calais, Maine, 1811; d. Calais, 1882*), journalist, author. Wrote vivid and colorful accounts of official life in the capital as Washington correspondent of the *New York Tribune*, 1850–60. Served as U.S. minister to The Hague, 1861–66.

PIKE, MARY HAYDEN GREEN (*b. Eastport, Maine, 1824; d. Baltimore, Md., 1908*), novelist, abolitionist. Published *Ida May* (1854) and *Caste* (1856), melodramatic antislavery novels.

PIKE, NICOLAS (*b. Somersworth, N.H., 1743; d. 1819*), teacher, arithmetician. Graduated Harvard, 1766. Master for many years of the grammar school at Newburyport, Mass. His fame rests chiefly upon his well-organized and admirable treatise, *A New and Complete System of Arithmetick, Composed for the Use of the Citizens of the United States* (1788), and an abridgement thereof (1793). He was the first American arithmetician to attain wide popularity in the field of school textbooks.

PIKE, ROBERT (*b. Wiltshire, England, ca. 1616; d. 1708*), colonial official. Immigrated to New England, 1635; was an original settler of Salisbury, Mass., 1639; served almost continuously as a Massachusetts elected official, 1648–96. Denounced curtailing of rights of Baptists and Quakers; stressed invalidity of specter testimony in Salem witch trials.

PIKE, ZEBULON MONTGOMERY (*b. Lamberton, now part of Trenton, N.J., 1779; d. York, Canada, 1813*), soldier, explorer. Commissioned first lieutenant, U.S. Army, 1799; served on frontier; was ordered by General James Wilkinson, 1805, to lead party from St. Louis, Mo., to the headwaters of the Mississippi. He reached what he mistakenly thought was the river's source in the winter of 1805–06. Returning to St. Louis, he was sent to explore the source of the Arkansas and Red rivers and to reconnoiter the Spanish settlements in New Mexico. Setting out from St. Louis on July 15, 1806, he moved up the Arkansas and reached the site of the present Pueblo, Colo. Here on a side trip he attempted unsuccessfully to reach the summit of the peak which bears his name. Turning south, seeking the source of the Red River, he crossed the Sangre de Cristo Mountains and built a fort on the Conejos branch of the Rio Grande. The Spaniards, hearing of his incursion, sent a force to bring him to Santa Fe. He yielded without a struggle and was taken eventually to Chihuahua for questioning. Returning to the United States, he found his name coupled in some quarters with the Burr-Wilkinson scheme for erecting a separate empire in the Southwest. These charges were probably without foundation. Promoted major, 1808, and colonel, 1812, he was advanced in rank to brigadier general and put in command of troops attacking York (present Toronto), Canada, in April 1813. His mission was successful, but he was killed in the assault.

PILAT, IGNAZ ANTON (*b. St. Agatha, Austria, 1820; d. New York, N.Y., 1870*), landscape gardener. Came to America, 1848. Made comprehensive botanical survey of New York Central Park site; directed planting operations for Calvert Vaux and Frederick L. Olmsted.

PILCHER, JOSHUA (*b. Culpeper Co., Va., 1790; d. St. Louis, Mo., 1843*), fur trader, Indian agent. President, Missouri Fur Co., 1820–31; U.S. superintendent of Indian affairs, 1839–41.

PILCHER, LEWIS STEPHEN (*b. Adrian, Mich., 1845; d. 1934*), surgeon, Union soldier. Father of Paul M. Pilcher. Graduated University of Michigan, 1862; M.D., 1866. Practiced and taught in Brooklyn, N.Y., *post* 1872 until 1918. As editor of *Annals of Surgery*, from 1885, Pilcher exercised wide influence upon surgical thought in the English-speaking world.

PILCHER, PAUL MONROE (*b. Brooklyn, N.Y., 1876; d. 1917*), surgeon, urologist. Son of Lewis S. Pilcher. M.D., New York College of Physicians and Surgeons, 1900. Author of *Practical Cystoscopy and the Diagnosis of Surgical Diseases of the Kidneys and Urinary Bladder* (1911).

PILKINGTON, JAMES (*b. Cavendish, Vt., 1851; d. New York, N.Y., 1929*), New York policeman, contractor. Amateur champion boxer, wrestler, and oarsman during the 1880's.

PILLING, JAMES CONSTANTINE (*b. Washington D.C., 1846; d. Olney, Md., 1895*), ethnologist. Author of an outstanding bibliography of the languages of American Indian tribes.

PILLOW, GIDEON JOHNSON (*b. Williams Co., Tenn., 1806; d. Helena, Ark., 1878*), lawyer, politician, soldier. Close political friend of James K. Polk; served as general officer in Mexican War and attempted to exalt his own importance at expense of General Winfield Scott. A conservative opponent of extremist measures up to the Civil War, he accepted rank of Confederate brigadier general, 1861. Second in command at Fort Donelson, he escaped capture when the post was surrendered in February 1862, by passing his responsibility off on General Simon B. Buckner. He was given no important command during the remainder of the war.

PILLSBURY, CHARLES ALFRED (*b. Warner, N.H., 1842; d. Minneapolis, Minn., 1899*), flour miller. Nephew of John S. Pillsbury. Removed to Minneapolis, 1869; bought a share in a small local flour mill. Quick to recognize the importance of new technological advances, he installed the La Croix purifying process, which permitted use of Northwest spring wheat for high-grade bread flour, and later adopted the roller process. His firm, C. A. Pillsbury and Co., prospered, partly because of highly favorable railroad freight rates which he helped secure and maintain, partly because of his extensive system of grain elevators, and partly because of his effective advertising techniques based upon brand names. His incursions into the grain market were spectacular though not often profitable. *Post* 1889, he was managing director of Pillsbury-Washburn, Ltd.

PILLSBURY, HARRY NELSON (*b. Somerville, Mass., 1872; d. Frankford, Pa., 1906*), chess player. Among top international masters, 1894–1904; first American professional chess player; specialized in simultaneous blindfold play.

PILLSBURY, JOHN ELLIOTT (*b. Lowell, Mass., 1846; d. Washington, D.C., 1919*), naval officer, oceanographer. Graduated U.S. Naval Academy, 1867. Served with U.S. Coast Survey 1876–91; invented current meter; determined axis of Gulf Stream; wrote *The Gulf Stream* (1891).

PILLSBURY, JOHN SARGENT (*b. Sutton, N.H., 1828; d. Minneapolis, Minn., 1901*), flour miller, Minnesota legislator. Uncle of Charles A. Pillsbury. Settled in present Minneapolis, 1855. Partner in C. A. Pillsbury and Co. Republican governor of Minnesota, 1876–82; retrieved University of Minnesota from bankruptcy, 1864.

PILLSBURY, PARKER (*b. Hamilton, Mass., 1809; d. Concord, N.H., 1898*), reformer, Garrisonian abolitionist. Lecture agent, antislavery societies, 1840–61; edited *Herald of Freedom*, 1840 and 1845–46; ardent advocate of woman's rights.

PILMORE, JOSEPH (*b. Tadmouth, England, 1739; d. Philadelphia, Pa., 1825*), Episcopal clergyman. Trained by John Wesley, Pilmore went to America, 1769, and was first Methodist preacher in Philadelphia; he returned to England, 1774. Abandoning Methodism, 1784, he came back to America and was ordained, 1785, by Samuel Seabury. He served thereafter as rector in New York and the Philadelphia area.

PILSBURY, AMOS (*b. Londonderry, N.H., 1805; d. Albany, N.Y., 1873*), pioneer professional prison administrator.

PINCHBACK, PINCKNEY BENTON STEWART (*b. Macon, Ga., 1837; d. Washington, D.C., 1921*), Union soldier, politician. Son of a white father and a free black mother. Louisiana Radical legislator and official during Reconstruction.

PINCHOT, AMOS RICHARDS ENO (*b. Paris, France, 1873; d. New York, N.Y., 1944*), lawyer, politician, reformer. Brother of Gifford Pinchot. B.A., Yale, 1897. Served in Spanish-American War. Admitted to the New York bar after attending Columbia Law School and New York Law School, he devoted most of his time to managing the family estate until 1908, when he became active in politics as his brother's aide and adviser in the Ballinger controversy. Convinced that industrial monopolies were dictating national policy, he helped organize the Progressive party, 1912, and

aligned himself with its "radical nucleus" in favor of public ownership of forests, waterpower, and all sources of energy; he also advocated the breaking-up of private monopolies. Disillusioned with the Progressives' failure to press for reforms, he supported President Wilson's reelection in 1916 but soon opposed him because of domestic policies, especially curtailment of civil rights during World War I. In 1917 he helped found what was to become the American Civil Liberties Union, serving on its executive committee until his death. At first a supporter of Franklin D. Roosevelt, he broke with him in 1933 over monetary policy and the growth of federal power, which he considered as great a threat to the individual citizen as business monopolies.

PINCHOT, CORNELIA ELIZABETH BRYCE (*b. Newport, R.I., 1881; d. Washington, D.C., 1960*), social reformer. Socially prominent and the wife of two-time governor of Pennsylvania, Gifford Pinchot, Cornelia Pinchot advocated women's and children's rights in industry and the home. A colorful figure, her activities in support of important social legislation, her prolabor stands, and her positions on women's rights were widely reported in the press. She sought, but never attained, political office.

PINCHOT, GIFFORD (*b. Simsbury, Conn., 1865; d. New York, N.Y., 1946*), forester, conservationist, federal and state official. Member of a well-to-do New York merchant family, he was educated in a succession of private schools in New York and Paris and at Phillips Exeter Academy. He entered Yale University in 1885, determined to pursue a career in forestry. After receiving the B.A. degree in 1889, he enrolled for a year in the French National Forestry School at Nancy and then in 1892 took charge of the forests at Biltmore, the North Carolina estate of George W. Vanderbilt.

In 1896 Pinchot was appointed to the National Forest Commission of the National Academy of Sciences, created to make recommendations on the national forest reserves in the western states. The commission's study helped bring about passage of the Forest Management Act of 1897. In 1898 he was named chief of the tiny Division of Forestry in the U.S. Department of Agriculture. He induced Congress in 1905 to transfer the forest reserves from the General Land Office of the Interior Department to his own division in the Department of Agriculture. He quickly became a close companion and adviser in Roosevelt's select circle. In several ways Pinchot acted as a catalyst to the emerging conservation movement. In 1903 he served on the Committee of the Organization of Government Scientific Work. His work on the Public Lands Commission, which he initiated in 1903, led eventually to the systematic classification of the nation's natural resources by the U.S. Geological Survey, as well as to sweeping land-law reform. In 1908 the movement flowered in the proposals of the Inland Waterways Commission.

When Roosevelt was succeeded by William Howard Taft, who did not admit Pinchot to his inner circle of advisers, Taft appointed Richard A. Ballinger, onetime commissioner of the General Land Office, as secretary of the interior. Ballinger began to attack conservation policies on many fronts. He moved directly against the Forest Service. The struggle that developed between Ballinger and Pinchot split the Taft administration down the middle. In the end, Taft upheld Ballinger, and in 1910 Pinchot was dismissed from government service. The controversy contributed significantly to the estrangement between Taft and Roosevelt.

In January 1911, Pinchot helped found the National Progressive Republican League. He initially supported the presidential ambitions of Robert M. La Follette, but shifted his allegiance once Roosevelt became a candidate early in 1912. When the Republican party renominated Taft, Pinchot bolted and helped form the Progressive party, which nominated Roosevelt. Twice governor of Pennsylvania, 1923–27 and 1931–35, Pinchot drafted a new administrative code and grappled strenuously with economic problems caused by the Great Depression. Perhaps his most important accomplishment was the construction of thousands of miles of rural roads. He maintained his interest in forestry, serving as nonresident lecturer and professor at the Yale School of Forestry, established in 1900 by a grant from his father, and as a founder and president, 1900–08 and 1910–11, of the Society of American Foresters. Pinchot's autobiography, *Breaking New Ground*, was published posthumously in 1947.

PINCKNEY, CHARLES (*b. Charleston, S.C., 1757; d. 1824*), planter, lawyer, Revolutionary soldier. Second cousin of Charles C. and Thomas Pinckney. As congressman from South Carolina, 1784–87, he led in movement to amend the Articles of Confederation; a prominent delegate to the Constitutional Convention, 1787, he submitted a plan for a constitution (the "Pinckney draught") now known only in a reconstructed form. It is probable that he had an important share in determining the final form and content of the U.S. Constitution, but his egoistic claims for credit have made historians doubtful of his real achievements. He served as Federalist governor of South Carolina, 1789–92. Alienated from his party on personal and intellectual grounds, he became a Democratic-Republican and, as such, was governor in 1797–99 and 1807–09. While U.S. senator, 1799–1801, he was leader in attacks on the Adams administration and was the manager of Thomas Jefferson's campaign in South Carolina. Appointed U.S. minister to Spain, March 1801–1805, he succeeded in winning Spanish assent to the cession of Louisiana, but his attempt to secure a cession of the Floridas exceeded his instructions and failed. As congressman from South Carolina, 1819–21, he delivered one of his finest addresses in opposition to the Missouri Compromise.

PINCKNEY, CHARLES COTESWORTH (*b. Charleston, S.C., 1746; d. Charleston, 1825*), lawyer, Revolutionary soldier, statesman. Son of Elizabeth L. Pinckney; brother of Thomas Pinckney; second cousin of Charles Pinckney. Served in South Carolina colonial and state legislatures; was prominent as a delegate to Constitutional Convention, 1787. Between 1791 and 1795, he was offered and declined the command of the army, a seat on the U.S. Supreme Court, and the secretaryships of war and state. Accepting the post of U.S. minister to France, July 1796, he was refused official recognition by the Directory when he arrived at Paris in December. Appointed to serve with Elbridge Gerry and John Marshall on a special mission in France, 1797, he gave an indignant refusal to suggestions that a bribe to French officials might ease matters (the XYZ Affair). As major general, 1798–1800, he commanded all U.S. military posts and forces south of Maryland as well as those in Kentucky and Tennessee. A lifelong Federalist, he was his party's nominee for vice president in 1800 and for president in 1804 and 1808.

PINCKNEY, ELIZABETH LUCAS (*b. probably Antigua, ca. 1722; d. Philadelphia, Pa., 1793*), introducer of indigo into colonial South Carolina. Mother of Charles C. and Thomas Pinckney. Educated in England, she was brought to her father's plantation, "Wappoo," near Charleston in 1738 and left to manage the affairs of three plantations, her father returning to Antigua. Searching about for a profitable crop she experimented with indigo seeds, 1741; after three years' trial, she succeeded in raising a crop and, with help from a Montserrat man, prepared it for market. Her husband, Charles Pinckney, further developed the industry, which became a very profitable one. Upon the death of her husband in 1758, she again became manager of extensive plantation properties.

PINCKNEY, HENRY LAURENS (*b. Charleston., S.C., 1794; d. Charleston, 1863*), editor, South Carolina legislator and con-

gressman. Son of Charles Pinckney; brother-in-law of Robert Y. Hayne. Proprietor and principal editor of *Charleston Mercury*, 1823–32; made it the leading state daily and an uncompromising advocate of nullification. Mayor of Charleston, 1829 and 1837–39.

PINCKNEY, THOMAS (*b. Charleston, S.C., 1750; d. Charleston, 1828*), soldier, diplomat, politician. Son of Elizabeth L. Pinckney; brother of Charles C. Pinckney. Educated in England and called to the English bar in 1774, he returned to South Carolina, 1774. He served with credit, 1775–81, in the southern campaigns of the Revolution and was severely wounded at Camden. Entering successful legal practice at Charleston, he was governor of his state, 1787–89, and president of the South Carolina ratifying convention, 1788. He served fruitlessly as U.S. minister to Great Britain, 1792–95, but as special envoy to Spain he concluded the advantageous treaty of San Lorenzo, 1795. Unsuccessful candidate for the U.S. vice-presidency, 1796, he was a Federalist congressman from South Carolina, 1797–1801.

PINCUS, GREGORY GOODWIN ("GOODY") (*b. Woodbine, N.J., 1903; d. Boston, Mass., 1967*), biologist. Attended Cornell and Harvard (Sc.D., 1927). Taught at Harvard (1930–37), but later could not secure a regular academic position, believing himself to be a victim of scientific conservatism and anti-Semitism. Studied the effects of pH on mammalian sperm, the problems of developing in vitro fertilization and artificial parthenogenesis, and the role of hormones in embryonic maintenance. Founded (with Hudson Hoagland) the Worcester Foundation for Experimental Biology (1944), dedicated to biological engineering; he became a scientific entrepreneur and served as liaison between academic scientists and commercial interests. His most important achievement was the development of the first oral contraceptive, which was marketed in 1961. Elected to National Academy of Science (1965).

PINE, ROBERT EDGE (*b. London, England, 1730; d. Philadelphia, Pa., 1788*), portrait and subject painter. Came to America, 1784; painted many of the celebrities of the time (including Washington and members of his family). Proposed a series of paintings illustrative of the Revolution, but died before attempting more than one.

PIÑERO JIMÉNEZ, JESÚS TORIBIO (*b. Carolina, Puerto Rico, 1897; d. Canóvanas, Puerto Rico, 1952*), politician. Studied at Xavier College in Baltimore, Md., at the University of Puerto Rico, and the University of Pennsylvania. In 1937, with his friend Muñoz Marín, he formed the Popular Democratic Party of Puerto Rico; in 1940 he was elected to the legislature of Puerto Rico; in 1944 to the post of resident commissioner of Puerto Rico in the U.S. Congress. In 1946 President Truman appointed him the first native-born governor of Puerto Rico. He served until 1948, when he was succeeded by Marín.

PINGREE, HAZEN STUART (*b. Denmark, Maine, 1840; d. England, 1901*), manufacturer, Michigan politician, Union soldier. Settling in Detroit, 1865, he became partner in a shoe-manufacturing enterprise which prospered. Elected reform mayor of Detroit under Republican auspices, 1889, he found that a group of private vested interests controlled municipal affairs. After bitter fights he established a municipal power plant, removed toll gates, forced reductions in gas and telephone rates, and made the street railway monopoly give better service. During the panic of 1893 he inaugurated a plan of gardens for the unemployed ("Pingree's potato patches"). Elected governor of Michigan, 1896, he served until 1901. The chief target of his fight against special privilege while governor was the railroads, but his administration was only moderately successful.

PINKERTON, ALLAN (*b. Glasgow, Scotland, 1819; d. 1884*), detective. Settling in Illinois early in the 1840's, he first engaged in the cooper's trade. After uncovering a gang of counterfeiters, he was made deputy sheriff of Kane Co., Ill., 1846; he later held the same post in Cook Co. Named first detective of the Chicago police force, 1850, he established a private agency in the same year, one of the first in the United States. Successful in solving a number of train and express robberies, he learned through his operatives of a Southern plot against Abraham Lincoln's life, February 1861, and was responsible for the circuitous route followed by the president on his way to inauguration. Later in the year, on invitation of General George B. McClellan, Pinkerton organized a secret-service and counterespionage department for the army and conducted it until November 1862. Thereafter, he engaged in a wide variety of detective work, including antistrike activity and labor espionage; he was also author of a number of "real life" detective narratives based on his agency's experiences.

PINKERTON, LEWIS LETIG (*b. Baltimore Co., Md., 1812; d. 1875*), physician, Disciples of Christ clergyman, editor, educator. Prominent *post* 1839 in the activities and controversies of his denomination in Kentucky.

PINKHAM, LYDIA ESTES (*b. Lynn, Mass., 1819; d. Lynn, 1883*), reformer, manufacturer of patent medicine. Began producing her famous and widely advertised "Vegetable Compound" in 1875.

PINKNEY, EDWARD COOTE (*b. London, England, 1802; d. Baltimore, Md., 1828*), poet, lawyer, editor. Son of William Pinkney. His small but distinguished body of poetry appeared in *Rodolph* (1823) and *Poems* (1825); he edited *The Marylander*, a newspaper in support of J. Q. Adams' campaign for reelection, 1827–28.

PINKNEY, NINIAN (*b. Annapolis, Md., 1811; d. Easton, Md., 1877*), surgeon. Nephew of William Pinkney. Graduated St. John's, Annapolis, 1830; M.D., Jefferson Medical College, 1833. Served with distinction in U.S. Navy, 1834–73; was surgeon of the fleet in D. D. Porter's squadron, 1862–65.

PINKNEY, WILLIAM (*b. Annapolis, Md., 1764; d. Washington, D.C., 1822*), lawyer, Maryland legislator, diplomat. Father of Edward C. Pinkney. Studied law with Samuel Chase; was admitted to the bar, 1786. Pinkney rose rapidly to a commanding position in his profession and was considered the most talented advocate of his time, despite his personal affectations and the flamboyant character of his oratory. Inordinately vain, he wished to excel in everything and concealed his profound researches into precedents behind a screen of affected carelessness and haste of preparation. He appeared in 72 cases before the U.S. Supreme Court.

He served as joint commissioner with Christopher Gore in England, 1796–1804, working to adjust maritime claims under the seventh article of the Jay Treaty. Returning home, he was briefly attorney general of Maryland. Joint commissioner with James Monroe to treat with the British over reparations for ship seizures and impressment, 1806–07, he was concerned in the formulation of a proposed treaty which Jefferson angrily repudiated. He then engaged in frustrating and futile negotiations with the British over the *Leopard-Chesapeake* affair and the issue of the orders in council while serving as U.S. minister to Great Britain, 1807–11. He was an able U.S. attorney general, 1811–14; served in the militia, 1814; and sat in Congress from Maryland, 1815–16. Effective as U.S. minister to Russia, 1816–18, he became U.S. senator from Maryland in 1819 and served until his death. Here he performed his greatest work for his country as an interpreter of the Constitution. His speeches in

opposition to Rufus King during the debates over the Missouri Compromise were an important factor in bringing the compromise about. Meanwhile, he reached the heights of his forensic career in the Supreme Court in his arguments in *McCulloch* v. *Maryland* (1818–19) and *Cohens* v. *Virginia* (1821).

PINNEY, NORMAN (*b. Simsbury, Conn., 1804; d. New Orleans, La., 1862*), clergyman, educator. Organized the Mobile (Ala.) Institute, a classical school for boys, 1836, and headed it for many years.

PINO, JOSÉ.   *See* SON OF MANY BEADS.

PINTARD, JOHN (*b. New York, N.Y., 1759; d. New York, 1844*), merchant, philanthropist. Helped organize both the Massachusetts and New-York Historical societies; served as president of New York City's first savings bank, 1828–41.

PINTARD, LEWIS (*b. New York, N.Y., 1732; d. Princeton, N.J., 1818*), New York merchant. Served as American commissary for prisoners in New York City during most of the Revolution.

PINTO, ISAAC (*b. 1720, place unknown; d. New York, N.Y., 1791*), merchant, scholar, patriot. A Sephardic Jew, he appears first in New York records, 1740; he lived from time to time in various places including Charleston, S.C. He was best known as the translator into English of the first Jewish prayerbook printed in America, the *Evening Service of Roshashanah and Kippur* (1761), and *Prayers for Shabbath, Rosh-Hashanah, and Kippur* (1766). He was probably also translator of *The Form of Prayer . . . for a General Thanksgiving . . . for the Reducing of Canada* (1760) and may have been author of letters appearing under the pseudonyms "A.B." and "Philalethes" in New York newspapers, 1750–75.

PINZA, EZIO (*b. Rome, Italy, 1892; d. Stamford, Conn., 1957*), opera singer. Studied at the University of Ravenna and the Rossini Conservatory in Bologna. He made his debut as King Mark in *Tristan and Isolde* in Rome in 1920. After achieving success at Milan's La Scala, he came to the Metropolitan Opera in 1926 and was the reigning basso until his retirement in 1948. Operatic roles there include the title roles in *Don Giovanni*, *Faust*, *The Marriage of Figaro*, and *Boris Godunov*. After retirement he turned to Broadway where he succeeded in the role of Émile de Becque in *South Pacific* (1949).

PIPER, CHARLES VANCOUVER (*b. Victoria, British Columbia, Canada, 1867; d. 1926*), agronomist. Graduated University of Washington, 1885; Harvard, M.S., 1900. Taught botany and zoology at State College of Washington, 1893–1903; was employed thereafter by U.S. Department of Agriculture, having charge *post* 1905 of the Office of Forage Crops. His most important achievement was finding Sudan grass, a useful cousin of the Johnson grass of the South, which he discovered under a mistaken classification. He published *Sudan Grass, a New Drought-Resistant Hay Plant* (1913), which started culture of a commercially important product. He also wrote *Forage Plants and Their Culture* (1914) and other special studies.

PIPER, WILLIAM THOMAS (*b. Knapp Creek, N.H., 1881; d. Lock Haven, Pa., 1970*), oil company executive and airplane manufacturer. Attended Harvard (B.S., 1903). Founded (1914) Dallas Oil Company; bought C. G. Taylor aircraft (1931) and became dedicated to the idea of an inexpensive airplane for the average person. His Cub aircraft was licensed in 1931. Opened the Piper Aircraft Company (1937) and soon dominated the private-airplane industry. During World War II he sold 7,000 L-4's ("puddle jumpers") to the army; he began producing the SuperCub and Pacer in 1948; and the twin-engine Apache, the first all-metal Piper plane, went on the market in 1954. By 1970 the company was producing 12,000–15,000 planes a year.

PIPPIN, HORACE (*b. West Chester, Pa., 1888; d. West Chester, 1946*), artist. Wounded and partially disabled in World War I army service; began painting *ca.* 1929. After receiving enthusiastic critical praise for a showing of his work in 1937, he continued to paint with both critical and material success. He can properly be placed among the great "naive" painters, such as Henri Rousseau and Hector Hyppolite. Historically, he was the first black American to produce an important body of work not limited by defensive attitudes or emulation of supposedly "superior" models. His art conveyed a vision of the American scene—its history and folklore, its exterior splendors and interior pathos—which was uniquely his own.

PIRSSON, LOUIS VALENTINE (*b. Fordham, N.Y., 1860; d. 1919*), geologist. Graduated Sheffield Scientific School, Yale, 1882; studied also at Heidelberg and Paris. Became interested in igneous geology after serving with U.S. Geological Survey party in Yellowstone Park, 1889–90. Teacher at Yale *post* 1892, in 1893 he gave the first graduate course there in petrology. Associate editor of the *American Journal of Science*, 1899–1919, he was one of four authors of *Quantitative Classification of Igneous Rocks* (1903), a landmark in petrology. He was the sole author of *Rocks and Rock Minerals* (1908); and of Part 1 of the *Text Book of Geology* by Pirsson and Schuchert.

PISE, CHARLES CONSTANTINE (*b. Annapolis, Md., 1801; d. Brooklyn, N.Y., 1866*), Roman Catholic clergyman, author. Educated at Georgetown and at Mount St. Mary's, Emmitsburg, Md., he was ordained in 1825 and served parishes in Baltimore, Washington, D.C., New York City, and Brooklyn. He was the only Catholic priest ever to serve as chaplain to the U.S. Senate, 1832–33. Among his many books is the early novel *Father Rowland* (1829).

PITCAIRN, JOHN (*b. Dysart, Scotland, 1722; d. Boston, Mass., 1775*), British major of marines. Commanded British force at Lexington battle, April 1775; was mortally wounded at Bunker Hill.

PITCAIRN, JOHN (*b. near Paisley, Scotland, 1841; d. Bryn Athyn, Pa., 1916*), railroad executive, manufacturer, philanthropist. Came to the United States as a child. Helped organize Pittsburgh Plate Glass Co., 1883; was its president, 1897–1905.

PITCHER, MOLLY. *See* MCCAULEY, MARY LUDWIG HAYS.

PITCHER, ZINA (*b. near Fort Edward, N.Y., 1797; d. Detroit, Mich., 1872*), physician, naturalist. Settled in Detroit, 1836. Initiated medical department, University of Michigan, 1850; developed public schools while mayor of Detroit, 1840–41 and 1843.

PITCHLYNN, PETER PERKINS (*b. Noxubee Co., Miss., 1806, d. Washington, D.C., 1881*), Choctaw chief. Selected western lands for Choctaw resettlement, 1828; removed to Indian Territory after 1830 treaty; elected principal chief of tribe, 1860.

PITKIN, FREDERICK WALKER (*b. Manchester, Conn., 1837; d. Pueblo, Colo., 1886*), lawyer. Settled in Colorado, 1874. An able and honest Republican governor of the state, 1879–83, he was responsible for driving out the Ute and for suppressing the Leadville miners' strike, 1880.

PITKIN, TIMOTHY (*b. Farmington, Conn., 1766; d. New Haven, Conn., 1847*), lawyer, Connecticut legislator, historian. Grandson of William Pitkin (1694–1769). Congressman, Federalist, from Connecticut, 1805–19; author of an important statistical account of American commerce (1816).

PITKIN, WALTER BOUGHTON (*b. Ypsilanti, Mich., 1878; d. Palo Alto, Calif., 1953*), writer and educator. Studied briefly at the University of Michigan, at Hartford Theological Seminary, and at the universities of Munich and Berlin. Taught at Columbia University, 1905–43; professor in the School of Journalism from 1912. Editor of *Parents' Magazine* (1927–30), American editor of the *Encyclopaedia Britannica* (1927–28), and editorial director of the *Farm Journal* (1935–38). Pitkin's blend of iconoclasm and utopianism was part of the social history of the Great Depression; he wrote over thirty books that were optimistic in their appeal to the masses, including *The Psychology of Happiness* (1929), *Let's Get What We Want* (1935), and his most famous work, *Life Begins at Forty* (1932).

PITKIN, WILLIAM (*b. probably Marylebone, England, 1635; d. Hartford, Conn., 1694*), lawyer, jurist. Immigrated to Hartford, 1659. Became Connecticut's chief prosecutor, 1664; championed colony's right to control own militia and maintain independence of royal interference in local government.

PITKIN, WILLIAM (*b. Hartford, Conn., 1694; d. Hartford, 1769*), jurist, colonial administrator. Grandson of William Pitkin (1635–94). Member of committee to draw up confederation plan at Albany Congress, 1754; governor of Connecticut, 1765–69; held many other offices.

PITKIN, WILLIAM (*b. Hartford, Conn., 1725; d. Hartford, 1789*), jurist, manufacturer. Son of William Pitkin (1694–1769). Established first powder mill in Connecticut, 1776; judge of superior court, 1769–89; member, Revolutionary Council of Safety.

PITMAN, BENN (*b. Trowbridge, England, 1822; d. Cincinnati, Ohio, 1910*), phonographer. Came to America, 1852, to popularize his brother Isaac's system of shorthand; established Phonographic Institute in Cincinnati.

PITNEY, MAHLON (*b. Morristown, N.J., 1858; d. Washington, D.C., 1924*), New Jersey Republican legislator and congressman, U.S. Supreme Court justice. As associate justice, U.S. Supreme Court, 1912–22, he delivered a long series of painstaking opinions which were marked by conservatism and antilabor feeling.

PITTMAN, KEY (*b. Vicksburg, Miss., 1872; d. Reno, Nev., 1940*), lawyer. Began practice in Seattle, Wash., 1892. Moving to the Yukon, 1897, and to Nome, Alaska, 1899, he settled in 1901 in Tonopah, Nev. After a decade of mining, legal, and political activities, he was elected U.S. senator, Democrat, from Nevada, 1912. Unwaveringly loyal to mining interests, he won advantages by his abilities as a negotiator and by exploiting the bloc powers of the seven silver-mining states. The so-called Pittman Act, 1918; the silver agreement of the World Economic Conference, 1933; and the Silver Purchase Act, 1934, testify to his ingenuity in maintaining silver prices through large annual purchases by the U.S. government.

PITTOCK, HENRY LEWIS (*b. London, England, 1836; d. Portland, Oreg., 1919*), printer, newspaper publisher, paper manufacturer. Came to America as a child; removed from Pittsburgh, Pa., to Oregon *ca.* 1852. Published *Morning Oregonian post* 1861, Portland *Evening Telegram post* 1877, and *Sunday Oregonian post* 1881; enjoyed Portland newspaper monopoly by 1902.

PITTS, HIRAM AVERY (*b. ca. 1800; d. Chicago, Ill., 1860*), inventor. Raised in Maine; was blacksmith by trade. Patented chain-band for horsepower treadmill, 1834; improved thresher and fanning mill, 1837. Manufactured Chicago-Pitts threshers in Chicago *post* 1852.

PITTS, ZASU (*b. Parsons, Kans., 1898; d. Los Angeles, Calif., 1963*), actress. She used her fragile appearance, fluttering hands, wide-eyed countenance, and wistful demeanor to good effect in comedy and melodrama. Appeared opposite Mary Pickford in *The Little Princess* (1917) and reached the pinnacle of her art with *Greed* (1924) and *The Wedding March* (1928). She had a string of comedy hits in 1929–33 and made a memorable comic performance in *Ruggles of Red Gap* (1935). Appeared frequently on television (1954–63) and was best-known to television audiences for her role on "The Gale Storm Show" (1956–60).

PLACIDE, HENRY (*b. probably Charleston, S.C., 1799; d. Babylon, N.Y., 1870*), actor. Made debut in Augusta, Ga., 1808. After his first appearance in an important role at New York's Park Theatre, 1823, he occupied first rank in popularity as a comedian, ranging from dialect farce to high comedy, until his retirement from the stage, 1865. He played for 20 years at the Park; thereafter, he was a member of the company of Burton's Theatre and made extended tours throughout the United States. His brother and his three sisters all had stage careers.

PLAISTED, HARRIS MERRILL (*b. Jefferson, N.H., 1828; d. Bangor, Maine, 1898*), lawyer, Union major general by brevet. Commanded "Iron Brigade," 1863–65; was attorney general of Maine, 1873–75, and Republican congressman from Maine, 1876–77. Becoming a Greenbacker, 1879, he was elected Democrat-Greenback governor, 1880, but failed of reelection in 1883; thereafter he edited *The New Age* in support of bimetallism.

PLANT, HENRY BRADLEY (*b. Branford, Conn., 1819; d. 1899*), express company executive, railroad and steamship operator. Bought Atlantic and Gulf Railroad and Charleston and Savannah Railroad at foreclosure sales, 1879–80; using these as nucleus, he built up the "Plant System" of transportation lines along the southern Atlantic seaboard. He was also operator of several steamship lines and the builder of a number of hotels in the area served by his system. Providing Florida fruit growers a quicker and cheaper access to markets, he became rich and powerful as Florida and other states dependent on his roads grew in population and were developed. He was associated in the Plant Investment Co., holding company for his properties, with H. M. Flagler, M. K. Jesup, and W. T. Walters.

PLATER, GEORGE (*b. near Leonardtown, Md., 1735; d. 1792*), lawyer, Maryland colonial legislator, Revolutionary patriot. Member of Continental Congress, 1778–80; presided over Maryland ratifying convention, 1788; governor of Maryland, 1791–92.

PLATH, SYLVIA (*b. Boston, Mass., 1932; d. London, England, 1963*), poet. Attended Smith (A.B., 1955) where, despite publication of poems and short stories, suffered a nervous breakdown, attempted suicide, and underwent psychiatric treatment; those events form the material for her autobiographical novel, *The Bell Jar* (1963, 1971). Her poetry written while at Newnham College at Cambridge (B.A., 1957) appeared in her first published volume, *The Colossus* (1962). Taught at Smith (1957), then devoted herself entirely to writing; in 1959 received a fellowship to Yaddo, the writers' colony in Saratoga Springs, N.Y. Her best-known poems were published posthumously in *Ariel* (1965, 1966). She has been endowed with an unfortunate notoriety because of her suicide and the dark subjects of her poems.

PLATNER, SAMUEL BALL (*b. Unionville, Conn., 1863; d. 1921*), classical scholar. Graduated Yale, 1883; Ph.D., 1885. Taught Latin at Adelbert College, Western Reserve University,

post 1885; was author of a number of scholarly books, including *A Topographical Dictionary of Ancient Rome* (published posthumously, 1929).

PLATT, CHARLES ADAMS (*b. New York, N.Y., 1861; d. 1933*), architect, landscape architect, painter, etcher. Studied in New York and in Paris under Boulanger and Lefebvre; after publication of his *Italian Gardens* (1894), he moved into the practice of architecture. He designed the Freer Gallery, among other buildings in Washington, and is responsible for buildings at the University of Illinois, the University of Rochester, Dartmouth, Johns Hopkins, and the Deerfield, Mass., Academy. The Leader-News building, Cleveland, Ohio, is his most significant commercial structure. His most characteristic work, combining architecture and landscaping, is Phillips Academy, Andover, Mass.

PLATT, ORVILLE HITCHCOCK (*b. Washington, Conn., 1827; d. Meriden, Conn., 1905*), lawyer, Connecticut legislator. Pupil of Frederick W. Gunn; studied law under Gideon H. Hollister. After a short, early career in teaching and successful practice of law in Meriden, he won the hotly contested Republican nomination for U.S. senator, 1879; he served in the Senate thereafter until his death. In 1881 he became chairman of the Patents Committee (a position he held intermittently for ten years); his name became associated with practically every patent law passed during his long career. Advocate of liberal copyright relations with Europe, he was successful in securing an international copyright bill (passed 1891) which effectively ended literary piracy. Chairman of the Committee on Territories, 1887–93, he was associated with the admission of six Far West states. In fiscal and tariff legislation, however, he found his main interest. He believed in silver as a medium of exchange but opposed free coinage at 16-to-1 except under international agreement; his influence with the West led that section to accept the compromise Silver Purchase Act of 1890. In international relations Platt stood consistently with the administration in office. Cleveland received his support in the Venezuelan dispute with Great Britain; he was one of the props of the McKinley administration during the difficulties over Cuba. Almost overnight he became an expansionist in 1898, voting for the annexation of Hawaii and strongly urging the retention of the Philippines. As chairman of the Committee on Cuban Relations, he composed and introduced the famous Platt Amendment to the army appropriation bill, 1901. Following the death of McKinley, Platt became a valued supporter of Theodore Roosevelt. His last chairmanship was that of the judiciary committee. A "stand-pat" conservative, he was respected for his high character and unselfish service. He was several times mentioned for the vice presidential nomination, but his own political ambitions never went beyond the senatorship from Connecticut.

PLATT, THOMAS COLLIER (*b. Owego, N.Y., 1833; d. 1910*), businessman, politician. Began career as druggist in Owego; was elected county clerk on the Republican ticket, 1859, but soon returned to business as president of the Tioga County National Bank and a speculator in Michigan timberlands. He served on various state and county Republican committees during the 1860's, but his political career really began in 1870 when he became the close friend of Roscoe Conkling, helping to organize the "southern tier" counties against Horace Greeley and Senator Reuben E. Fenton. Thereafter he was consulted by Conkling on practically every phase of New York politics. As congressman from New York, 1875–79, Platt made little impression in the House, but remained an indispensable behind-the-scene "Stalwart" Republican worker in state politics. Deeply distrustful of James A. Garfield in 1880, he supported him for the presidency only in return for a promise of recognition and rewards if Garfield were elected. As chairman of the state committee, he did much to conciliate the outraged Senator Conkling and to organize the campaign in New York; his reward was election to the U.S. Senate in 1881. Having promised Chauncey M. Depew his unreserved support of the Garfield administration, Platt was faced with a dilemma when Garfield appointed a "Half-Breed," or reform, Republican as collector of the Port of New York. Both Platt and Conkling resigned their Senate seats in protest and were defeated when they sought reelection in the legislature. Conkling's active career was thus ended; Platt's was eclipsed for over six years. In 1888 Platt gave Benjamin Harrison his New York support for the presidential nomination in return for a supposed promise of the post of U.S. secretary of the treasury. When Harrison failed to fulfill his promise, Platt became angry; he also resented the starvation fare allotted him in federal patronage. His token support of Harrison was responsible for Grover Cleveland's sweep of New York in 1892. He continued, however, to perfect the New York Republican machine, to which he had fallen heir on Conkling's retirement. After the election of Levi P. Morton as governor, 1894, his power became almost irresistible; its chief agency was patronage, local, state, and federal. Year after year, New York State conventions carried out his preordained program, and the legislature docilely obeyed his commands. As Theodore Roosevelt's power grew, Platt's declined; he tried to shunt Roosevelt into obscurity as vice president in 1900, but found that with Roosevelt's accession as president and B. B. Odell's as New York's governor his power politics would no longer work. He continued to hold his seat in the Senate but was shorn of party authority. Industrious and patient, he was, however, the very type of ruthless, unprincipled party boss.

PLEASANTS, JAMES (b. *Goochland Co., Va., 1769; d. Goochland Co., 1836*), lawyer, Virginia legislator. Congressman, 1811–19; U.S. senator, 1819–22; governor of Virginia, 1822–25. A cousin of Thomas Jefferson, a Democrat and advocate of social reform, he opposed the rising dominance of Andrew Jackson.

PLEASANTS, JOHN HAMPDEN (b. *Goochland Co., Va., 1797; d. 1846*), journalist, Whig politician. Son of James Pleasants. Founder and editor of the Richmond *Whig*, 1824–46. Killed in a duel with Thomas Ritchie, Jr., an editor of the Richmond *Enquirer*.

PLEASONTON, ALFRED (b. *Washington, D.C., 1824; d. Washington, D.C., 1897*), Union major general, brilliant cavalry leader. Graduated West Point, 1844; was distinguished in Mexican War and in western and southern Indian campaigns. Averted complete disaster at Chancellorsville, 1863, by checking General T. J. Jackson's advance against the Union right flank; commanded all Union cavalry at Gettysburg; routed General Sterling Price near Marais des Cygnes River, Kansas, October 1864. Resigned commission in dispute over rank, 1868.

PLIMPTON, GEORGE ARTHUR (b. *Walpole, Mass., 1855; d. Walpole, 1936*), publisher, book collector. Graduated Amherst, 1876. Associated *post* 1877 with Ginn and Co. and its predecessor firms, he served as chairman of the firm, 1914–31, and greatly expanded its activities.

PLOTZ, HARRY (b. *Paterson N.J., 1890; d. Washington, D.C., 1947*), bacteriologist, physician. M.D., College of Physicians and Surgeons, Columbia University, 1913. After developing an antityphus vaccine, 1914–15, which involved him in controversy, he served in Europe with the American Red Cross Sanitary Commission, 1915–16, and as a major on the staff of the U.S. Army surgeon general, 1916–19. Medical adviser to the Jewish Joint Distribution Committee's relief expedition to eastern Europe

in 1921, he was with the Institut Pasteur in Paris from 1922 until 1940, becoming *chef de service* in 1931 and publishing extensively on bacteriologic, virologic, and immunologic subjects. In 1941 he rejoined the U.S. Army as lieutenant colonel and directed the division of virus and rickettsial diseases at the Army Medical Center, Washington, D.C., until 1945. Thereafter, he continued work as a consultant to the U.S. secretary of war until his death.

PLOWMAN, GEORGE TAYLOR (b. *Le Sueur, Minn., 1869; d. Cambridge, Mass., 1932*), architect, etcher.

PLUMB, GLENN EDWARD (b. *Clay, Iowa, 1866; d. Washington, D.C., 1922*), lawyer. Specialist in railroad law and traction problems. Advocated plan for cooperative government ownership of railroads, with operating managers and employees sharing in profits.

PLUMB, PRESTON B. (b. *Berkshire, Ohio, 1837; d. Washington, D.C., 1891*), journalist, Union soldier, lawyer. Established *Kanzas* (sic) *News*, 1857, at Emporia. Prominent as an independent Republican in Kansas politics, Plumb was U.S. senator from 1877 until his death. As chairman of the Public Lands Committee *post* 1881, he was responsible for the reforming land law of 1891 which inaugurated reclamation and conservation.

PLUMBE, JOHN (b. *Wales, 1809; d. Dubuque, Iowa, 1857*), railroadman, publicist, photographer. Came to America as a boy. Plumbe appears to have been the first (1836) responsible and effective advocate of a railroad to the Pacific, continuing his efforts to this end as late as 1851. Active as a photographer *post* 1840, he established studios and equipment shops in over a dozen cities. His special claim to distinction is his unpatented Plumbeotype process, a method for reproducing daguerreotypes on paper.

PLUMER, WILLIAM (b. *Newburyport, Mass., 1759; d. Epping, N.H., 1850*), lawyer. Served as a Federalist in the New Hampshire legislature at various periods, 1785–1800; was a Speaker of the House, 1791 and 1797. A member of the state constitutional convention of 1791–92, he was U.S. senator, 1802–07. The foreign policy difficulties of Jefferson's second administration led to Plumer's repudiation of Federalism and his support of Madison in 1808. Soon an active Democratic-Republican, he served as New Hampshire governor, 1812–13 and 1816–19, pressing for reforms, which included revising the Dartmouth College charter; this action led to a memorable controversy and Supreme Court action. After retirement he devoted himself to writing for the press.

PLUMER, WILLIAM SWAN (b. *Griersburg, now Darlington, Pa., 1802; d. Baltimore, Md., 1880*), Presbyterian clergyman, professor of theology, author. An "old school" leader, he was twice elected moderator of the General Assembly, 1838 and 1871.

PLUMLEY, FRANK (b. *Eden, Vt., 1844; d. Northfield, Vt., 1924*), jurist, Vermont Republican leader and congressman. Umpire for the Mixed Claims Commissions of British, Dutch, and French claims against Venezuela, 1903.

PLUMMER, HENRY (d. *Bannack, Mont., 1864*), bandit. Nothing is known of his early life. He began his public career in Nevada City, Calif., 1856, when he was elected town marshal. Convicted of murdering a man with whose wife he was involved, he escaped prison on the assumption that he was dying of tuberculosis, but lived to establish a record of seduction, brawling, murder, and jailbreaking for which he was never punished. Fleeing to Washington Territory, 1861, he soon removed to Lewiston, Idaho, where he led a gang of bandits. At the end of 1862, he settled in Bannack, where he managed to be elected sheriff and organized a band of outlaws who terrified all southern Montana and were responsible for killing over 100 men within a few months. His double life ended when the townspeople organized a committee of vigilantes who rounded up his gang, exposed him, and hanged him.

PLUMMER, HENRY STANLEY (*b.* Hamilton, Minn., 1874; *d.* Rochester, Minn., 1936), physician. M.D., Northwestern, 1898. A staff member of the Mayo Clinic *post* 1901, Plummer developed a number of mechanical aids to medical practice and on the basis of clinical observation proposed a new classification for thyroid diseases, which encouraged worldwide activity in their study. The Mayo concept of private group medical practice was greatly influenced by Plummer's thinking.

PLUMMER, JONATHAN (*b.* Newbury, Mass., 1761; *d.* Newburyport, Mass., 1819), peddler, ballad-monger. Poet laureate to "Lord" Timothy Dexter, 1793–1806.

PLUMMER, MARY WRIGHT (*b.* Richmond, Ind., 1856; *d.* Dixon Ill., 1916), librarian, teacher, poet. Headed library schools at Pratt Institute, 1894–1911, and New York Public Library; president, American Library Association, 1915–16.

PLUNKETT, CHARLES PESHALL (*b.* Washington, D.C., 1864; *d.* Washington, 1931), naval officer. Graduated Annapolis, 1884. Commanded batteries of 14-inch naval guns on railway mounts in Layon-Longuyon sector, Western Front, 1918; held important sea and shore commands until retirement as rear admiral, 1928.

POCAHONTAS (*b.* Virginia, ca. 1595; *d.* Gravesend, England, 1617), Indian "princess." Alternative name of Matoaka, daughter of Powhatan. Mentioned in Capt. John Smith's *True Relation* as a "child of ten" in 1607; saved Smith by her intervention when he was captured by Powhatan, 1608. The truth of this famous story is still a matter of controversy. In the spring of 1613 Pocahontas fell into the hands of Samuel Argall, who brought her to Jamestown, where she was received graciously by the acting governor, Sir Thomas Dale, and was subsequently converted to Christianity. Her marriage in April 1614 at Jamestown to John Rolfe, an English gentleman, acted as a bond between the English and the Indians and brought a peace which aided establishment of the colony. In 1616 she accompanied her husband to England, where she was received by the king and queen.

POE, EDGAR ALLAN (*b.* Boston, Mass., 1809; *d.* Baltimore, Md., 1849), poet, critic, short-story writer. Son of David and Elizabeth (Arnold) Poe, actors; brother of William H. L. Poe and Rosalie Poe. Orphaned in 1811, the Poe children were parceled out among foster parents; Edgar went to live with Mr. and Mrs. John Allan of Richmond, Va. In 1815, he was taken to Great Britain (where Allan, a merchant, planned to establish a branch of his firm), attended for a short period a school in Irvine, Scotland, and was later at the boarding school of the Misses Dubourg in Chelsea and at the Manor House School, Stoke Newington. On the failure of Allan's venture, 1820, they all returned to Richmond, where Poe attended the school of Joseph H. Clarke and began to write verse. Here he met Rob Stanard, to whose mother, Jane Stith Stanard, "To Helen" is addressed.

By 1824 the relation between John Allan and Poe was strained because of Poe's knowledge of Allan's infidelity to his wife. The young man, up to this point, had done well in school, read widely in contemporary literature, and was considered a very able swimmer. Secretly but transiently engaged to a neighbor's daughter, Sarah Elmira Royster, he was sent to the University of Virginia, 1826. He remained for only one term. Allan refused to pay his charges. In order to maintain himself Poe tried gambling, which got him heavily into debt; the situation was further complicated by Poe's drinking. It was plain, even at this time, that a very little

liquor was disastrous to him. Allan, refusing to pay the gambling debts, proposed that Poe take up the reading of law; Poe insisted on a literary career. The violent quarrel that ensued drove Poe from Allan's house to seek his fortune under an assumed name. Arriving in Boston sometime in April 1827, he published in that year his first volume, *Tamerlane and Other Poem*. The verse, although it gave hints of the poet's power, was undistinguished and went unnoticed. In desperate circumstances, he enlisted in the U.S. Army under the assumed name "Edgar A. Perry." Assigned to Battery H, 1st U.S. Artillery, at Fort Independence, Boston, he was ordered to South Carolina in October 1827 and served at Fort Moultrie until the end of 1828. Promoted sergeant major, he corresponded with Allan about going to West Point. Allan consented, partly because of Mrs. Allan's dying wishes, and Poe set off with letters of recommendation to the secretary of war in April 1829, requesting an appointment. It was not soon forthcoming. Proceeding in May to Baltimore, Md., he lived on a pittance sent him by Allan. He now first saw his blood relatives—his grandmother Mrs. David Poe, his aunt Mrs. Maria Clemm, and Mrs. Clemm's daughter Virginia, his future wife. For a time he lived with Mrs. Clemm and his elder brother William. His second volume of poetry, *Al Aaraaf, Tamerlane, and Minor Poems*, was published in Baltimore in December 1829. In January 1830 he returned to Richmond where he quarreled further with Allan. Receiving an appointment to West Point, he passed the examinations and entered the U.S. Military Academy on July 1, 1830.

Poe had hoped to win back his foster father's favor; however, a letter of his containing an unfortunate remark fell into Allan's hands, and Poe was definitely disowned. He now determined to leave the army and deliberately neglected his duties, for which he was dismissed in March 1831. His third volume, *Poems by Edgar A. Poe*, appeared in 1831; it contained three of his most famous lyrics, "To Helen," "Israfel," and "The Doomed City," but attracted little attention. Removing to Baltimore *ca.* March 1831, he took up residence with Mrs. Clemm and Virginia and stayed in that city until the summer of 1835. Beginning to write prose extensively, he first attracted notice in October 1833 on the publication in the *Baltimore Saturday Visiter* of "A MS. Found in a Bottle." An important outcome of this publication was the friendship of John P. Kennedy, who became his patron and introduced him to T. W. White, editor of the *Southern Literary Messenger*, to which Poe began to contribute. In midsummer of 1835 he joined the staff of the *Messenger* in Richmond and, through brilliant editing and critical writing, increased the circulation sevenfold. This success was offset by Poe's increased drinking, which caused a temporary separation between him and White. In September, Poe took out a license to marry his 13-year-old cousin Virginia; they were publicly married in Richmond, May 1836.

Discontented with the limited scope of the *Messenger*, Poe took his child bride and Mrs. Clemm to New York in January 1837. Unable to make a living there, in the summer of 1838 he moved to Philadelphia, where he edited a pirated textbook on conchology (1839), but supported himself mainly by free-lance writing. In May 1839 he was employed by William E. Burton as coeditor of Burton's *Gentleman's Magazine*, continuing in this capacity until June 1840. His prose *Narrative of Arthur Gordon Pym* had been published in book form, July 1838; the end of 1839 brought the publication of his sixth volume, *Tales of the Grotesque and Arabesque*. Quarreling with Burton, Poe set about the establishment of his own magazine in January 1841, but dropped the project to be literary editor of *Graham's Lady's and Gentleman's Magazine*. Once again Poe's talent increased the circulation as well as his own fame, but lapses into drink and general ill health ended this employment in May 1842. The remainder of Poe's sojourn in Philadelphia was a period of great poverty, visionary schemes to publish his own magazine (to be called "The Stylus"), and abortive attempts to obtain government employ. His wife was now advanced in tuberculosis, and only Mrs. Clemm's efforts kept the family together and alive. However, in 1843 Poe wrote and published "The Gold Bug" (*Dollar Newspaper*, June 21, 28), issued a pamphlet of stories (part of a proposed series) which contained "The Murders in the Rue Morgue," and composed the early version of "The Raven."

Poe left Philadelphia with Virginia and returned to New York in April 1844. "The Raven" was cast in final form and appeared first in the New York *Evening Mirror* (Jan. 29, 1845) to great applause; in June 1845, Poe found himself sole editor of the *Broadway Journal*. Later in that year, two more volumes of his work appeared: *Tales* and *The Raven and Other Poems*. Now famous, Poe through pressure of a number of circumstances gave up the *Broadway Journal*, January 1846. In the spring, he moved his family to Fordham, where he wrote a series of journalistic critical articles known as "The Literati of New York City" for *Godey's Lady's Book*. Virginia Poe died in January 1847 during a winter in which the family sounded the depths of misery. Poe now sought female sympathy ardently; among those whom he courted with an erratic, abnormal persistence were Mary Louise Shew, Sarah Helen Whitman, and Annie Richmond. During this time he published *Eureka: A Prose Poem* (1848) and composed some of his best-known lyrics: "The Bells," "Ulalume," "Annabel Lee," and "El Dorado." His time was occupied mainly in trips to Philadelphia, Richmond, and Fordham and by bouts of drinking. Arriving in Richmond almost dead in July 1849, he joined a lodge of teetotalers and began to court his old love Sarah Royster, now widowed. The marriage day was set, and Poe left Richmond to bring back Mrs. Clemm. Stopping in Baltimore five days before the election of 1849, Poe disappeared; he was found semiconscious in a tavern by an old friend, Dr. James E. Snodgrass, on Oct. 3. Four days later he died in great mental agony and was buried in the churchyard of the Westminster Presbyterian Church, Baltimore.

In the practical affairs of everyday life, in many of the common amenities, in the domestic circle, and in the general give-and-take of earthly existence, Poe was greatly lacking and frequently a complete failure. His relations with women, at least during the latter part of his life, were fantastic and nothing more. He certainly at various times resorted to opiates and he was the victim of alcohol. Combined with all this was an undoubted charm and fascination, a magnetism and reverse power of antagonism which caused him to be greatly loved by a few, hated by many, and memorable to everybody. He practiced literature in a time and place when what he had to say and his way of saying it were little appreciated, was constantly ground down by poverty and disappointments, and was victim of a succession of tragedies which cannot all be attributed to his own failings. All of this can be summed up by saying that as a man Poe was abnormal, and as a genius, unique.

His reputation as artist in the United States from 1845 on, contrary to the belief of foreign critics, has always been assured. At his death he was already in his native country a famous man. In France, owing largely to the early and brilliant translations of Baudelaire, Poe has exerted a very great literary influence. His fame rests on a small bulk of exquisite lyrical poetry, on a few of his stories, and on his contribution to the methods of writing certain types of short prose fiction. He is commonly considered to be the originator of the "detective story," or tale of logical deduction. His style in prose is a product of his own peculiar genius, unusually effective when used by him, but not to be imitated. His characters are either grotesques or the inhabitants of another world than this. As a critic there is much to be learned from him, but his dicta should be carefully compared with the sources from which he took them, principally Coleridge.

POE, ORLANDO METCALFE (*b. Navarre, Ohio, 1832; d. Detroit, Mich., 1895*), soldier, engineer. Graduated West Point, 1856. Commissioned brigadier general, 1862; received regular army brevet of that rank, 1865. A successful field officer, 1861–63, he was chief engineer under General W. T. Sherman, 1864–65. Thereafter he was active in railroad construction and in river and harbor improvement work in the Great Lakes region.

POINDEXTER, GEORGE (*b. Louisa Co., Va., 1779; d. Jackson, Miss., 1853*), lawyer. Removed to Mississippi, 1802; served as attorney general, delegate to Congress, and district judge of the territory; was congressman, Democrat, from Mississippi, 1817–19, and governor of the state, 1820–21. His able codification of the laws of Mississippi was published in 1824. As U.S. senator, 1830–35, he was an outspoken opponent of Andrew Jackson.

POINDEXTER, MILES (*b. Memphis, Tenn., 1868; d. Greenlee, Va., 1946*), lawyer, politician. Grandnephew of Joseph R. Anderson. LL.B., Washington and Lee University, 1891. Removed to the state of Washington, 1891, where he practiced law, first in Walla Walla and then in Spokane; entering politics as a Democrat, he was repelled by the populism of that party locally and became a Republican, 1897. After service as assistant prosecuting attorney for Spokane County, 1899–1904, and as judge of the superior court, 1904–08, he was elected to the U.S. House of Representatives, 1908. A progressive reformer and one of the "insurgent" group in Congress, he swept the Republican senatorial primary in 1910 and was elected to the U.S. Senate by the state legislature. Continuing his advocacy of reform during his first term, he was a member of the Progressive party, 1912–15, backed President Wilson's domestic policies, and was sympathetic to labor; by 1916, however, he had become critical of the president's international idealism and handling of foreign policy. Reelected in 1916 by popular vote, he strongly supported U.S. intervention in World War I, but was a bitter opponent of the Versailles Treaty and the League of Nations; during the postwar years he also opposed federal aid for farmers, which alienated his constituents and cost him election in 1922. He served as U.S. ambassador to Peru, 1923–28; thereafter, he practiced law in Washington, D.C.

POINSETT, JOEL ROBERTS (*b. Charleston, S.C., 1779; d. near Statesburg, S.C., 1851*), diplomat, statesman. Educated at Timothy Dwight's school, Greenfield Hill, Conn., and in England; studied law with Henry W. De Saussure; made extended tour of Europe and western Asia, 1801–08. Returning home hoping for high military appointment, he accepted in 1810 a post as special agent to Rio de la Plata (now Argentina) and Chile and supported the movement there to gain independence from Spain. On his return, 1815, he became interested in politics, served in the South Carolina legislature, and was congressman, Democrat, 1821–25. First U.S. minister to Mexico, 1825–30, he was recalled at request of the Mexicans for meddling in local politics. As U.S. secretary of war, 1837–41, he was distinguished for energy and ability. He was a strong Unionist. The poinsettia was developed by him from a Mexican flower.

POLAK, JOHN OSBORN (*b. Brooklyn, N.Y., 1870; d. Brooklyn, 1931*), obstetrician, gynecologist. Associated as consultant and teacher with many hospitals, in particular the Long Island College Hospital, from which he had graduated in 1891.

POLAND, LUKE POTTER (*b. Westford, Vt., 1815; d. Waterville, Vt., 1887*), Vermont jurist. U.S. senator, Republican, from Vermont, 1865–67; congressman, 1867–75. Chairman of House committees investigating Ku Klux Klan and Crédit Mobilier, he was also on committee which rejected the carpetbag régime in Arkansas, 1875. Poland was largely responsible for the revision of U.S. statutes, 1867–1875, as chairman of a House committee instituted for that purpose.

POLING, DANIEL ALFRED (b. Portland, Oreg., 1884; d. Philadelphia, Pa., 1968), Protestant minister and author. Attended Oregon's Dallas College (B.A., 1904) and was licensed to preach by the United Evangelical Church. A staunch prohibitionist, he was nominated by the Prohibition party for governor of Ohio (1912), drawing a record "dry" vote. He rejected pacifism and took a leading role by organizing a front-line Chaplain Corps in France during World War I. His wartime experiences were the basis for *Huts in Hell* (1918), his first popular book. In 1920 went to the New York Marble Collegiate Reformed Church and served as minister, 1923–30. Pastor of the Baptist Temple in Philadelphia (1936–48). Edited the *Christian Herald*, 1926–63, and in 1927 became head of the World's Christian Endeavor Union.

POLK, FRANK LYON (b. New York, 1871; d. New York, 1943), lawyer, diplomat, municipal, reformer. Son of William M. Polk. B.A., Yale, 1894; LL.B., Columbia University Law School, 1897. Resuming legal practice in New York City after service in the Spanish-American War, he also took on various civic and political responsibilities, including membership on the city board of education and the presidency of the Municipal Civil Service Commission. An independent Democrat, he effected a number of reforms in administration of the civil service and organized opposition to the Tammany Hall machine. A supporter of Woodrow Wilson in the presidential contest, 1912, Polk was appointed to the U.S. Department of State as second to Secretary Robert Lansing, 1915. In this post, he handled the diplomatic problems incident to the Mexican border crisis, advised on the problems of neutral rights arising out of World War I, and coordinated the intelligence gathering agencies of the federal government, 1917–18. In 1919 he was appointed first U.S. under secretary of state, a new position. He resigned in June 1920 and returned to the practice of law, but continued to act as adviser to Democratic governors and in general favored the New Deal.

POLK, JAMES KNOX (b. Mecklenburg Co., N.C., 1795; d. Nashville, Tenn., 1849), lawyer, eleventh president of the United States. Scotch-Irish in ancestry; moved in 1806 with his family to the valley of Duck River, Tenn. After preparation in Tennessee academies, he graduated from University of North Carolina with first honors in mathematics and classics, 1818. He read law in Tennessee with Felix Grundy; was admitted to the bar, 1820. Starting practice at Columbia, Tenn., in less than a year he was a leading practitioner. During two years in the state legislature he won notice as businessman and debater; he also became a friend of Andrew Jackson. He married Sarah Childress of Murfreesboro, 1824, a woman of ability and culture.

Entering the U.S. House of Representatives in 1825, he opposed the policies of President J. Q. Adams on political principle and because of loyalty to Jackson. After Jackson became president, 1829, Polk was a recognized leader of administration forces in the House. Owing to Polk, Jackson was able to triumph over the Bank of the United States. Polk, as a member of the House Ways and and Means Committee, submitted a strong minority report in favor of executive action when the bank issue was joined in 1832; as chairman of that committee *post* December 1833, he was chief defender of the president's action in withdrawing federal funds from the bank. Polk defeated John Bell for the speakership of the House in 1835, but was bitterly heckled and denounced as Jackson's "slave" during his brilliant four-year administration of the post. Contrary to his preferences he was drafted by the Democrats as candidate for governor of Tennessee and was

elected, 1839. His administration was satisfactory but uneventful; he was defeated for reelection in 1841 and again in 1843.

The Whigs had gained control of the federal government in 1840, but the Democrats began early to prepare for victory in 1844. Henry Clay would surely be the Whig candidate. Martin Van Buren was favored as the Democratic candidate, and Polk and Richard M. Johnson were being considered for the vice presidential nomination. Not until Van Buren wrote a letter in late April 1844 opposing the annexation of Texas was Polk's name suggested for the presidency. Jackson, as head of the Democratic party, declared that Van Buren had committed political suicide and directed Polk's nomination as a "dark horse." After the defeat of Clay in the election, Polk announced that his principles and policy were to be found in the Democratic platform and in his inaugural address. He advised prospective cabinet members to devote their time and energy to supporting his administration and not to possible candidacy as his successor. Politely but firmly, he made it clear that his decisions would be his own, although he would seek and accept advice from his party's elder statesmen.

Polk was younger than any of his predecessors, but few presidents have had more definite plans for their administrations, and none has been more successful in accomplishing his plans. In a conversation with George Bancroft, his secretary of the navy, a few days after inauguration he stated, "There are four great measures which are to be the measures of my administration: one, a reduction of the tariff; another, the independent treasury; a third, the settlement of the Oregon boundary question; and lastly, the acquisition of California." Before he left office in 1849, he had accomplished each of these measures. The Walker tariff law of 1846 placed import duties substantially on a revenue basis and substituted ad valorem for specific duties. The independent treasury bill of 1846 reestablished a financial system which continued, with slight modifications, until supplemented by the Federal Reserve system. The Oregon question was resolved also in 1846 by Polk's firmness in dealing with Great Britain and according to his own compromise plan of dividing the area between Alaska and California along the 49th parallel. Polk's plan for gaining California and New Mexico by forcing their cession as payment of Mexico's long-standing damage-claims debt to the United States led to the Mexican War. The charge that Polk wantonly provoked the war to extend slavery is unfounded. Polk was the first president to change the fundamental character of the Monroe Doctrine, opposing not only the use of foreign force but interference of any kind in American affairs. Opposed to "pork barrel" legislation, he indicated Clay's "American system" in his brilliant last annual message. Although a consistent party man, he had a supreme contempt for the spoils system. His expansion policy gave the United States a vast increase in territory and free access to the Pacific. He favored the course of extending the Missouri Compromise line to the Pacific and opposed all extremist views on the question of slavery; thus, he was disliked by both sides in that great controversy and has been given scant credit for his outstanding public services.

POLK, LEONIDAS (b. Raleigh, N.C., 1806; d. near Marietta, Ga., 1864), Episcopal clergyman, Confederate lieutenant general. Son of William Polk. Educated at University of North Carolina and West Point. Converted by Charles P. McIlvaine, he resigned his commission late in 1827, attended Virginia Theological Seminary, and was ordained in May 1831. Appointed missionary bishop of the Southwest, 1838, and bishop of Louisiana, 1841, he was a principal agent in the founding of the University of the South. Suspending his episcopal work, 1861, he accepted a commission as major general in the Confederate army and served conscientiously as a corps commander under Generals A. S. Johnston and Braxton Bragg. He fought bravely at Shiloh, Perryville, and Murfreesboro, but blundered at Chickamauga and was often in conflict with Bragg, whose removal he recommended to President Jefferson Davis. Meanwhile, he had been promoted to lieutenant general, October 1862. He was killed at Pine Mountain. An evangelical in his religious point of view, he was gifted as an executive; as a soldier, he was distinguished for organizing ability and as a disciplinarian.

POLK, LEONIDAS LAFAYETTE (*b. Anson Co., N.C., 1837; d. 1892*), farmer, newspaper editor, president of the National Farmers' Alliance and Industrial Union *post* 1889.

POLK, LUCIUS EUGENE (*b. Salisbury, N.C., 1833; d. Columbia, Tenn., 1892*), planter, Confederate officer. Nephew of Leonidas Polk. Valued subordinate to General P. R. Cleburne at Shiloh and later battles.

POLK, THOMAS (*b. Cumberland Co., Pa., ca. 1732; d. Charlotte, N.C., 1794*), Revolutionary soldier, North Carolina colonial legislator. Father of William Polk; great-uncle of James K. Polk.

POLK, TRUSTEN (*b. Sussex Co., Del., 1811; d. St. Louis, Mo., 1876*), lawyer, Confederate soldier. Governor, anti-Benton Democrat, of Missouri, 1856–57; U.S. senator, 1857–61. Responsible for education and tax reform in Missouri; prominent spokesman for Southern cause, 1861.

POLK, WILLIAM (*b. near Charlotte, N.C., 1758; d. Raleigh, N.C., 1834*), Revolutionary soldier, North Carolina businessman and legislator. Son of Thomas Polk. Unsuccessful Federalist gubernatorial candidate in several elections; later supported Andrew Jackson.

POLK, WILLIAM MECKLENBURG (*b. Ashwood, Tenn., 1844; d. Atlantic City, N.J., 1918*), Confederate soldier, gynecologist. Son of Leonidas Polk. Graduated New York College of Physicians and Surgeons, 1869. Dean, Cornell Medical School, 1898–1918.

POLK, WILLIS JEFFERSON (*b. near Frankfort, Ky., 1867; d. San Mateo, Calif., 1924*), architect. Studied with various architects, including Stanford White; entered Chicago office of Daniel H. Burnham and assisted in plan to adorn San Francisco, 1903. Practiced independently in San Francisco, *post* 1904; was chairman of architectural commission, Panama-Pacific Exposition, 1915. His buildings in San Francisco after the earthquake and fire of 1906 were mainly in a monumental, conservative style. Later buildings showed fresh handling of new materials and recognition of changes demanded by new functions, as in the Hallidie Building and the Central Pumping Station of Spring Valley Water Co. Restorer of the Mission Dolores, he is considered one of the creators of the "California style" of domestic architecture.

POLLAK, GUSTAV (*b. Vienna, Austria, 1849; d. Cambridge, Mass., 1919*), editor, critic. Came to America, 1866. Son-in-law of Michael Heilprin. Wrote on foreign politics and literary criticism for New York *Nation* and *Evening Post*; worked on encyclopedias.

POLLAK, WALTER HEILPRIN (*b. Summit, N.J., 1887; d. New York, N.Y., 1940*), lawyer. Son of Gustav Pollak; grandson of Michael Heilprin. Practicing in New York City, Pollak was active in the protection of the public interests and in defense of civil liberties, serving as counsel for Earl Browder, Benjamin Gitlow, and other individuals and groups of whose opinions he personally disapproved.

POLLARD, EDWARD ALFRED (*b. Albemarle Co., Va., 1831; d. Lynchburg, Va., 1872*), journalist, author. Edited *Daily Richmond Examiner*, 1861–67; was ablest and most prolific Southern writer of the period; bitterly opposed Jefferson Davis. Author of *The Lost Cause* (1866) and numerous other biased historical accounts of the Civil War.

POLLARD, JOSEPH PERCIVAL (*b. Greifswald, Pomerania, Germany, 1869; d. Baltimore, Md., 1911*), literary and dramatic critic. Reviewer for *Town Topics*, 1897–1911.

POLLOCK, CHANNING (*b. Washington, D.C., 1880; d. Shoreham, N.Y., 1946*), playwright, lecturer, reformer. Served as reporter, drama editor, and critic on Washington, D.C., newspapers, and as press agent for theatrical producers in New York City. After writing a successful dramatization of Frank Norris' novel *The Pit* (1903), he did a great deal of theatrical journeywork as playwright and librettist; in 1919, a melodrama by him, *The Sign on the Door*, was a success in both New York and London. He is best remembered for two subsequent plays that expressed Pollock's serious ethical and religious purpose as a writer: *The Fool* (1922) and *The Enemy* (1925).

POLLOCK, JAMES (*b. Milton, Pa., 1810; d. Lock Haven, Pa., 1890*), lawyer. Congressman, Whig, from Pennsylvania, 1844–49. As Whig and Know-Nothing governor, 1855–58, he materially reduced state debt by selling state-owned canals and railroads to Pennsylvania Railroad and other systems. Served as director of U.S. Mint at Philadelphia, 1861–66 and 1869–73; thereafter was its superintendent.

POLLOCK, OLIVER (*b. near Coleraine, Ireland, ca. 1737; d. Pinckneyville, Miss., 1823*), trader, planter, financier. Immigrated to Pennsylvania *ca.* 1760; removed to New Orleans, 1768. His generosity in feeding Alexander O'Reilly's army, 1769, gained him freedom of trade in Louisiana. He helped the American army get needed ammunition, 1776, through friendship with Unzaga, O'Reilly's successor as governor of Louisiana. By the close of 1777, Bernardo de Galvez, Unzaga's successor, had advanced to American frontier posts some $70,000 worth of ammunition and provisions, for which sum Pollock was personally responsible. George Rogers Clark's requests for aid were similarly financed by Pollock as U.S. commercial agent *post* 1778. His advances totaled $300,000. His credit exhausted, Pollock was imprisoned in 1783 but soon released. His claims against Virginia and the federal government were eventually paid.

POLLOCK, (PAUL) JACKSON (*b. Cody, Wyo., 1912; d. East Hampton, N.Y., 1956*), painter. The acknowledged master of the school of abstract expressionist painting, Pollock's training was with the academic painter Thomas Hart Benton at the Art Students League in New York. In the late 1930's, he came under the influence of European refugee painters. In 1942 he showed his first major painting, *Stenographic Figure*. His first one-man show was in 1943 and included the work *She Wolf*; from this time on, Pollock's works became less totemic and more abstract. In 1945, he moved to East Hampton, N.Y., where he immersed himself in developing his most innovative works of totally abstract, frequently large-scale, freely dripped, overall images that suggest limitless space. By 1950 he was called by many the greatest living American painter and the most influential.

POLOCK, MOSES (*b. Philadelphia, Pa., 1817; d. 1903*), publisher, rare-book dealer, bibliophile.

POMERENE, ATLEE (*b. Berlin, Ohio, 1863; d. Cleveland, Ohio, 1937*), lawyer, politician. Graduated Princeton, 1884. An active liberal Democrat and holder of local offices, Pomerene was elected lieutenant governor of Ohio, 1910, but was chosen almost immediately by the legislature as U.S. senator and served until 1923. A moderate progressive, he opposed woman suffrage, and in the debates over the League of Nations was one of the small group of Democrats willing to accept the Lodge reservations. He was cosponsor of the Bill of Lading Act, 1916, and the Webb-Pomerene Act, 1918. His best-known service was as special counsel, with Owen J. Roberts, to the prosecutor in the Teapot Dome scandal during the Harding administration. Appointed chairman of the Reconstruction Finance Corporation, July 1932, he did not receive Senate confirmation in the post. He later became one of Franklin D. Roosevelt's severest critics.

POMEROY, JOHN NORTON (b. Rochester, N.Y., 1828; d. California, 1885), legal author and educator. Associated *post* 1878 with Hastings College of Law. Among eight major treatises which he wrote, his *Equity Jurisprudence* (1881–83) was outstanding.

POMEROY, MARCUS MILLS (b. Elmira, N.Y., 1833; d. Brooklyn, N.Y., 1896), printer, newspaper editor and publisher, politician. Known as "Brick" Pomeroy. Gained national fame as editor of the La Crosse (Wis.) *Democrat, post* 1860. He engaged in railroad promotion and was an active "Greenbacker."

POMEROY, SAMUEL CLARKE (b. Southampton, Mass., 1816; d. Whitinsville, Mass., 1891), businessman, Kansas politician. As financial agent for New England Emigrant Aid Co., he went with the second group of settlers to Kansas in 1854; while chairman of public safety committee at Lawrence, 1856, he failed to prevent the town's ruin by "border ruffians." Delegate to the first Republican National Convention, he received eight votes for vice president. When Kansas was admitted to the Union, Pomeroy was elected to the U.S. Senate; serving 1861–73, he joined Radicals in opposition to Lincoln and was responsible for the "Pomeroy Circular," in favor of candidacy of Salmon P. Chase, 1864. His reelection to the Senate, 1867, was investigated by a committee of Kansas legislature which made charges of bribery against Pomeroy; the charges were repeated, 1873. Although cleared by a U.S. Senate committee, the incident ended his political career.

POMEROY, SETH (b. Northampton, Mass., 1706; d. Peekskill, N.Y., 1777), gunsmith, soldier. Fought in wars with French and Indians, 1745–59; distinguished at Lake George, September 1755. Raised and drilled troops in western Massachusetts, 1775–76; appointed first Continental brigadier general, June 1775.

PONCE DE LEÓN, JUAN (b. San Servos, Spain, ca. 1460; d. Cuba, 1521), Spanish explorer, discoverer of Florida. Said to have shipped with Columbus on second voyage to Hispaniola, 1493, where he fought under Nicolas de Ovando in conquest of Higuey and was made governor of that province. Learning from an Indian of gold in unexplored Puerto Rico, he subjugated that island and was made its governor, 1509, he was replaced by Diego Columbus, son of Christopher, 1512. Although now a rich man, enticed by Indian tales of gold and of a spring whose waters made the aged young again, he set forth in search of the island called Bimini, where all these were said to be found. Sailing from Puerto Rico in March 1513, he made the coast of Florida in true latitude 27°30′, explored the coast southward to the Tortugas, and made other explorations, returning to repacify Puerto Rico. On his second trip to Florida, 1521, he was wounded by an Indian arrow, which led to his death.

POND, ALLEN BARTLIT (b. Ann Arbor, Mich., 1858; d. Chicago, Ill., 1929), architect, humanitarian. Designer of Hull House group in Chicago; was long associated with its work.

POND, ENOCH (b. Wrentham, Mass., 1791; d. Bangor, Maine, 1882), Congregational clergyman, professor and official in Bangor Theological Seminary.

POND, FREDERICK EUGENE (b. Packwaukee, Wis., 1856; d. Brooklyn, N.Y., 1925), writer on field sports, better known by his pen name of "Will Wildwood."

POND, GEORGE EDWARD (b. Boston, Mass., 1837; d. Como, N.J., 1899), journalist. Editor-correspondent of *Army and Navy Journal*, 1864–68; at various times on staffs of *New York Times*, Philadelphia *Record*, and New York *Sun*.

POND, IRVING KANE (b. Ann Arbor, Mich., 1857; d. Washington, D.C., 1939), architect, structural engineer. Graduated University of Michigan, C.E., 1879. After working for several Chicago architectural firms, Pond established a partnership with his brother Allen B. Pond, 1886. Participating in Chicago's great architectural renaissance, the firm for nearly 50 years designed every kind of structure, most notably public and educational buildings. A conservative member of the Chicago group dominated by Louis Sullivan, Pond stressed structure and function but with strong emphasis on formal, plastic, and decorative elements.

POND, JAMES BURTON (b. Cuba, N.Y., 1838; d. 1903), lecture manager. Successful in managing celebrity tours. Among his clients were Henry Ward Beecher, Ann Eliza Young (nineteenth wife of Brigham), Mark Twain, and Henry M. Stanley.

POND, PETER (b. Milford, Conn., 1740; d. Boston, Mass., 1807), soldier, fur trader, explorer. Entered fur trade at Detroit, 1765; was one of first to explore the Athabaska. Made important maps, *ca.* 1784, of his travels through the Northwest.

POND, SAMUEL WILLIAM (b. New Preston, Conn., 1808; d. Shakopee, Minn., 1891), Congregational missionary to the Dakota Indians. Composed a Dakota grammar and dictionary; published various works for and about the Indians.

PONTIAC (d. 1769), Ottawa chief, identified through Francis Parkman's *The History of the Conspiracy of Pontiac* (1851) with the French and Indian War in the Old Northwest. Accounts of his early life are largely legendary. Parkman claims that he was born on the Maumee River in 1720 and that he influenced the Chippewa as well as the Ottawa tribes. He may have been the "Sachem of the Outawawas" encountered in Robert Rogers' *Concise Account of North America* (1765); he may also have been present at the conference between the Detroit Indians and Sir William Johnson on Sept. 3, 1761. Pontiac's claim to fame lies in his activities during the siege of Detroit in 1763–64, although his importance at that time was much less than Parkman supposed. He attempted to surprise the garrison by treachery, and during the long siege, he was the greatest local menace. When other tribes made offers of peace, Pontiac's group seemed bent on breaking the truce; yet copies exist of a letter dated Oct. 30, 1763, from Pontiac to Henry Gladwin suing for peace. He was probably not responsible for starting the 1764 uprising which Parkman named "Pontiac's conspiracy"; he merely took up opposition at Detroit. The other tribes involved came to terms, but Pontiac and his band held out until a conference at Fort Ontario in July 1766. Having accepted peace with the English, he abode by it thereafter. The accounts of his death in 1769 are contradictory. Instead of being a great organizer, Pontiac was more likely only a local villein. The reports of his resistance appealed to popular imagination, however, so that he gained, even during his own lifetime, a reputation more romantic than he deserved.

POOL, JOE RICHARD (b. Fort Worth, Tex., 1911; d. Houston, Tex., 1968), attorney and politician. Attended University of Texas and Southern Methodist (LL.B., 1937). Democratic representative in Texas legislature, 1952–58, and U.S. congressman, 1962–68. Opposed the programs of Presidents John Kennedy and Lyndon Johnson; in 1960 he recommended the creation of a lake near Dallas to control Mountain Creek (Joe Pool Lake was created after his death). He became a national figure in 1966 when he chaired a subcommittee that held hearings to make it a federal crime to aid anyone engaged in armed conflict against the United States; after tumultuous hearings, to which he subpoenaed leaders of organizations resisting the Vietnam War, the bill passed the House but died in the Senate.

POOL, JOHN (*b. Pasquotank Co., N.C., 1826; d. Washington, D.C., 1884*), lawyer, North Carolina legislator and Unionist. U.S. senator, Republican, from North Carolina, 1868–73. Instrumental in introducing national anti–Ku Klux Klan legislation.

POOL, MARIA LOUISE (*b. Rockland, Mass., 1841; d. Rockland, 1898*), writer of sketches of New England life.

POOLE, ERNEST COOK (*b. Chicago, Ill., 1880; d. New York, N.Y., 1950*), novelist, journalist, social critic. B.A., Princeton University, 1902. Author of a number of novels *post* 1906 which dealt with successive problems of the times and reflected both his own idealism and the too fast pace of change in American Life, he is remembered best for *The Harbor* (1915) and *His Family* (1917). The latter was awarded the first Pulitzer Prize offered in fiction. Poole had won distinction, meanwhile, as an investigative reporter and foreign correspondent for *McClure's* and other magazines. After the mid-1920's his novels declined in popularity; late in life he tapped with success a new vein of regional New England material in *The Great White Hills of New Hampshire* (1946) and *The Nancy Flyer* (1949).

POOLE, FITCH (*b. South Danvers, now Peabody, Mass., 1803; d. 1873*), journalist, humorist. Librarian of Peabody Institute *post* 1856. Author of witty satires published in newspapers of Peabody and Salem, Mass., 1836–71.

POOLE, WILLIAM FREDERICK (*b. Salem, Mass., 1821; d. Evanston, Ill., 1894*), librarian, historian. Graduated Yale, 1849. Served as assistant to John Edmands; expanded an indexing project of Edmands to later-titled *Poole's Index to Periodical Literature.* Served as assistant in Boston Athenaeum, as librarian of Boston Mercantile Library Association, and then as librarian of the Athenaeum, 1856–69. Helped establish libraries at U.S. Naval Academy and at Cincinnati. Librarian of Chicago Public Library, 1874–87; organized and headed the Newberry Library, Chicago, 1887–94. An outstanding leader in the progress of librarians to professional rank, he made pioneer contributions to the theory of library administration.

POOR, CHARLES HENRY (*b. Cambridge, Mass., 1808; d. Washington, D.C., 1882*), naval officer.

POOR, DANIEL (*b. Danvers, Mass., 1789; d. Mampy, India, 1855*), Congregational missionary.

POOR, ENOCH (*b. Andover, Mass., 1736; d. Paramus, N.J., 1780*), Revolutionary soldier. Settled in Exeter, N.H., *ca.* 1760. As colonel, 2nd New Hampshire, he served in the campaign of 1776 around Ticonderoga and in battles of Trenton and Princeton. Promoted brigadier general, 1777, he fought well at Saratoga and in Sullivan's expedition against the Six Nations.

POOR, HENRY VARNUM (*b. East Andover, Maine, 1812; d. Brookline, Mass., 1905*), railroad journalist, economist. Brother of John A. Poor. Author of many works on railways and economics, he was noted for compiling and publishing annual *Poor's Manual of Railroads* (first issued 1868).

POOR, JOHN (*b. Plaistow, N.H., 1752; d. York Haven, Pa., 1829*), educator. Graduated Harvard, 1775. Headed Young Lad-

ies' Academy, Philadelphia, Pa., 1787–1809, an important early venture in female education.

POOR, JOHN ALFRED (*b. East Andover, Maine, 1808; d. 1871*), lawyer, railroad official. Brother of Henry V. Poor. Projected railway lines connecting Portland, Maine, with Halifax, Nova Scotia, and Montreal; served as director, Atlantic and St. Lawrence Railroad Co. Published *American Railroad Journal* and was president of the York and Cumberland (later the Portland and Rochester) Railroad. He resigned these positions to devote himself to international railway expansion, securing the charter of the European and North American Railway Co. (completed in 1871), connecting Maine railroads with those of lower Canada. Poor was also author of *English Colonization in America: A Vindication of the Claims of Sir Ferdinando Gorges* (1862) and other works. He was a tireless promoter of Maine interests.

POORE, BENJAMIN PERLEY (*b. near Newburyport, Mass., 1820; d. 1887*), journalist, author. Noted as Washington, D.C., correspondent of *Boston Journal* and other papers *post* 1854; edited and published useful catalogues of U.S. public documents.

POPE, ALBERT AUGUSTUS (*b. Boston, Mass., 1843; d. Cohasset, Mass., 1909*), Union soldier, manufacturer. Pioneer maker of bicycles at Hartford, Conn., *post ca.* 1878; developed "Columbia" and "Hartford" brands. He popularized the bicycle, financing legal test cases over their use, advocating better-roads movement, and publishing *The Wheelman* and *Outing.* He began manufacturing electric phaetons and runabouts through the Columbia Electric Vehicle Co., 1896. Progressing to production of gasoline automobiles, he turned out the Pope-Toledo and the Pope-Hartford at Toledo, Ohio, and Hartford, Conn., respectively; the Pope-Waverly electric was made at a plant in Indianapolis, Ind. Decline in the bicycle trade and a lull in the development of the automobile forced his company into receivership.

POPE, FRANKLIN LEONARD (*b. Great Barrington, Mass., 1840; d. Great Barrington, 1895*), electrician, inventor, author. Active in development of telegraphy *post* 1865; partner of Thomas A. Edison, 1869–70; made practical adaptation of the railway block signal invented by Thomas S. Hall.

POPE, JAMES PINCKNEY (*b. Vernon, La., 1884; d. Alexandria, Va., 1966*), lawyer and U.S. senator. Attended Louisiana Polytechnic and University of Chicago (LL.B., 1909). Founded Pope and Barnes law firm (1910) and aligned himself with the Democratic party. Served in various positions in Boise, Idaho, including city attorney (1916–17) and mayor (1929–32). Leader of the progressive, "dry" segment of the state's party. U.S. senator, 1932–38, and an ardent supporter of the New Deal and President Franklin Roosevelt's "court-packing" plan. Cosponsored the second Agricultural Adjustment Act (1938). As one of three directors of the Tennessee Valley Authority (1939–51), he defended the agency from attacks by conservatives and private industry.

POPE, JOHN (*b. Louisville, Ky., 1822; d. Sandusky, Ohio, 1892*), soldier. Son of Nathaniel Pope. Graduated West Point, 1842; was assigned to topographical engineers. Served with General Taylor in Mexican War; performed survey work in Southwest and West. Commanded Army of the Mississippi under Halleck and opened up the river almost to Memphis, March–April 1862. Because of this success and efficiency in moves against Corinth, Miss., he was appointed in June to command of the (Union) Army of Virginia, ordered to protect Washington. His inept handling of personalities subsequent to his assumption of larger responsibilities on the failure of the Union peninsular campaign in July and his total failure at the second battle of Bull Run (Aug. 27–30, 1862), led to his removal and replacement by General G. B. McClellan. Pope was no longer employed in field operations, but distinguished himself as head of various military departments until his retirement, 1886.

POPE, JOHN RUSSELL (*b. New York, N.Y., 1874; d. New York, 1937*), architect. Graduated Columbia, School of Mines, 1894; attended the American School of Architecture (later the American Academy) in Rome, and the École des Beaux Arts in Paris. Practicing independently in New York *post* 1903, Pope set a new standard in domestic architecture, combining elegance, beauty, and livability with archaeological correctness in a variety of styles. Pope believed above all else in the reposeful serenity of the monumental classic. His monumental buildings, of which he designed more than any other architect of his generation, included the National Archives, the National Gallery of Art, and the Jefferson Memorial, all in Washington, D.C.

POPE, NATHANIEL (*b. Louisville, Ky., 1784; d. St. Louis, Mo., 1850*), territorial secretary, 1809–16, and delegate, 1816–18, from Illinois. Cousin of Ninian Edwards; father of John Pope. Influential in establishing laws, northern boundary, and educational policy of Illinois. U.S. district judge *post* 1819.

POPHAM, GEORGE (*d. Maine, 1608*), Maine colonist. Sailed from Plymouth, England, in May 1607 to colonize for Sir Ferdinando Gorges in "Northern Virginia"; settled, Aug. 18, on western side of mouth of Kennebec. The colony was abandoned soon after Popham's death in the following February.

PORCHER, FRANCIS PEYRE (*b. St. John's, S.C., 1825; d. Charleston, S.C., 1895*), physician, botanist. Practiced in Charleston. Author of, among other works, *The Resources of the Southern Fields and Forests* (1863).

PORMORT, PHILEMON (*b. Grimsby, England, ca. 1595; d. Boston, Mass., ca. 1656*), educator. Immigrated to New England, 1634; appointed master of first public school in Boston, 1635; an adherent of Anne Hutchinson.

PORTER, ALBERT GALLATIN (*b. Lawrenceburg, Ind., 1824; d. Indianapolis, Ind., 1897*), Indiana lawyer and congressman. Law partner of Benjamin Harrison. Republican governor of Indiana, 1881–85; U.S. minister to Italy, 1889–91.

PORTER, ALEXANDER (*b. Co. Donegal, Ireland, 1785; d. "Oak Lawn," St. Mary Parish, La., 1844*), Louisiana legislator, jurist, sugar planter. Came to America, 1801; settled in Louisiana, 1809. U.S. senator, Whig, 1833–37 and 1843.

PORTER, ANDREW (*b. Montgomery Co., Pa., 1743; d. Harrisburg, Pa., 1813*), teacher, Revolutionary artillery and ordnance officer, surveyor. Father of James M. and David R. Porter. Surveyor general of Pennsylvania, 1809–13.

PORTER, ARTHUR KINGSLEY (*b. Stamford, Conn., 1883; d. Ireland, 1933*), archaeologist. Graduated Yale, 1904. Taught history of art at Yale, 1915–19; professor of fine arts, Harvard, 1920–33. The leading American medieval archaeologist of his day, Porter was author of *Medieval Architecture: Its Origins and Development* (1909), *Lombard Architecture* (1915), *Romanesque Sculpture of the Pilgrimage Roads* (1923), *Spanish Romanesque Sculpture* (1928), and other works equally distinguished for originality and brilliance in research.

PORTER, BENJAMIN CURTIS (*b. Melrose, Mass., 1845; d. New York, N.Y., 1908*), portrait and figure painter.

PORTER, COLE (*b. Peru, Ind., 1891; d. Santa Monica, Calif., 1964*), composer and lyricist. Attended Yale (B.A., 1913), where he wrote more than 300 songs, some of which became Yale classics. His first major hit song, written for the Broadway musical *Paris*, was "Let's Do It, Let's Fall in Love" (1928), which like many of his songs elegantly combines graceful melody and rhyming ingenuity with a mixture of sexual innuendoes, offbeat humor, and colloquialisms. Hit songs came regularly after that: "What Is This Thing Called Love?" (1929), "You Do Something to Me" (1929), "Night and Day" (1932), and several from the Broadway musical *Anything Goes* (1934). Wrote the scores for numerous films, such as *High Society* (1956) and *Les Girls* (1957), and the scores for such Broadway shows as *Kiss Me, Kate* (1948), *Can-Can* (1953), and *Silk Stockings* (1955).

PORTER, DAVID (*b. Boston, Mass., 1780; d. near Constantinople, Turkey, 1843*), naval officer. Father of David D. Porter; foster father of David G. Farragut. Son of a Revolutionary naval officer, he saw service in the naval war with France, 1798–99, and was made prisoner aboard the *Philadelphia* at Tripoli. Commanding the *Essex*, 1811–13, he took her on a remarkable cruise in the Pacific, raiding British commerce. Captured by the British at Valparaiso, Chile, after a desperate defense, he was paroled and participated in the operations on the Potomac in September 1814. Appointed commissioner of Navy Board, 1815, he served until 1823. As commander of the West India Squadron, 1823–25, he suppressed piracy, but was court-martialed because of retaliation against Puerto Rico, where one of his officers had been mistreated. Resigning, he accepted command of the Mexican navy, 1826–29. He returned home, broken in health and fortune, and spent the remainder of his life in minor U.S. diplomatic posts.

PORTER, DAVID DIXON (*b. Chester, Pa., 1813; d. Washington, D.C., 1891*), naval officer. Son of David Porter; cousin of Fitz-John Porter. Served under father as midshipman in Mexican navy; appointed midshipman, U.S. Navy, 1829. Commanded merchant ships, 1849–55. Porter achieved great prominence during the Civil War. Promoted commander, 1861, he was responsible for the preliminary planning of the New Orleans expedition, 1862, and commanded the mortar flotilla which ably supported Farragut's fleet. Appointed to command of the Mississippi Squadron as rear admiral, October 1862, he received congressional commendation for his part in the surrender of Arkansas Post and Vicksburg; he received a similar compliment for his work in the reduction of Fort Fisher, 1864–65. He was superintendent of the U.S. Naval Academy, which he successfully reformed and expanded, 1865–69; he was named vice admiral, 1866. Appointed adviser to secretary of the navy, 1869, he virtually ran the department through 1870. Succeeding Farragut as full admiral, August 1870, he was head of the Board of Inspection *post* 1877.

PORTER, DAVID RITTENHOUSE (*b. near Norristown, Pa., 1788; d. Harrisburg, Pa., 1867*), iron manufacturer. Son of Andrew Porter. After long service in the Pennsylvania legislature, he served as Democratic governor, 1839–45; he opposed debt repudiation and upheld the state's credit, but was in conflict with his party's views on the protective tariff question.

PORTER, EBENEZER (*b. Cornwall, Conn., 1772; d. Andover, Mass., 1834*), Congregational clergyman. Graduated Dartmouth, 1792. A conservative in theology, he taught at Andover Theological Seminary *post* 1812 and was its president, 1827–34.

PORTER, EDWIN STANTON (*b. Connelsville, Pa., 1870; d. New York, N.Y., 1941*), pioneer motion-picture director. After working as a sign painter, telegraph operator, and, during a three-year hitch in the U.S. Navy, an electrician, he entered motion-picture work in 1896 as a projectionist. Soon after joining the Edison Co. in 1899, he took charge of production at Edison's New York studio, operating the camera, directing the actors, and editing the final print. During the next decade he became the most influential moviemaker in the United States and made a number of important innovations in technique, including the dissolve, the close-up, and side lighting, which were to become the basic modes of visual communication through film. His most important film was *The Great Train Robbery* (1903). He left Edison in 1909 and was one of the organizers of Rex, an independent company; he was chief director of Famous Players Film Co., 1912–16. Thereafter, he was concerned mainly with mechanical aspects of the industry.

PORTER, FITZ-JOHN (*b. Portsmouth, N.H., 1822; d. Morristown, N.J., 1901*), soldier. Cousin of David D. Porter. Graduated West Point, 1845. Assigned to the artillery, he served with credit in the Mexican War; he was an instructor at West Point, 1849–55, and was assistant adjutant general in the Mormon expedition, 1857–59. Becoming brigadier general of volunteers, 1861, he rose to command of the V Corps during the peninsular campaign, 1862. Blamed for the Union defeat in the second battle of Bull Run, August 1862, Porter was court-martialed and cashiered in January 1863. Claiming injustice, he continued to fight the case for many years and in 1886 was reappointed colonel of infantry and retired.

PORTER, GENE STRATTON (*b. Wabash Co., Ind., 1863; d. Los Angeles, Calif., 1924*), author. One of the most popular American novelists of the years 1903–24, Mrs. Porter produced, among other romances of idealism, sentimentality, nature lore and uplift, *Freckles* (1904), *A Girl of the Limberlost* (1909), *Laddie* (1913), and *The Keeper of the Bees* (1925).

PORTER, HOLBROOK FITZ-JOHN (*b. New York, N.Y., 1858; d. 1933*), engineer. Son of Fitz-John Porter. Graduated Lehigh, 1878. Highly reputed as a consulting engineer, Porter was interested as well in the social and humanitarian aspects of industry; while working with the Westinghouse Co., 1902–05, he installed the first shop committee with employee representation to function in the United States.

PORTER, HORACE (*b. Huntingdon, Pa., 1837; d. 1921*), Union brigadier general, railroad executive, diplomat. Son of David R. Porter. Graduated West Point, 1860. Served in Civil War as artillery and ordnance officer; received Congressional Medal for gallantry at Chickamauga; was aide-de-camp to General U. S. Grant, 1864–65, later serving as one of Grant's military secretaries until 1872. A noted orator and prominent figure in Republican politics, Porter was U.S. ambassador to France, 1897–1905; he served as a U.S. delegate to the Hague Conference, 1907.

PORTER, JAMES DAVIS (*b. Paris, Tenn., 1828; d. Paris, 1912*), lawyer, Confederate soldier, Tennessee jurist. Democratic governor of Tennessee, 1875–79; later served as an assistant U.S. secretary of state, and as U.S. minister to Chile, 1893–94. A principal factor in the founding of the George Peabody College for Teachers while governor, he served as president of the college, 1902–09.

PORTER, JAMES MADISON (*b. near Norristown, Pa., 1793; d. 1862*), Pennsylvania jurist and politician. Son of Andrew Porter; brother of David R. Porter. First president of the Lehigh Valley Railroad; principal founder of Lafayette College, 1826.

PORTER, JERMAIN GILDERSLEEVE (*b. Buffalo, N.Y., 1852; d. 1933*), astronomer. Director, Cincinnati Observatory, 1884–1930.

PORTER, JOHN ADDISON (*b. Catskill, N.Y., 1822; d. New Haven, Conn., 1866*), chemist. Graduated Yale, 1842; studied also in Germany. Taught chemistry at Yale *post* 1852; was first dean of Sheffield Scientific School.

PORTER, JOHN LUKE (*b. Portsmouth, Va., 1813; d. Portsmouth, 1893*), naval constructor. In Confederate service, 1861–65, Porter was associated with John M. Brooke in the design of the ironclad *Virginia* (*Merrimack*); he also designed a number of other ironclad steam sloops and rams, but was handicapped by lack of iron and adequate engines.

PORTER, NOAH (*b. Farmington, Conn., 1811; d. 1892*), Congregational clergyman, educator. Graduated Yale, 1831. A noted conservative scholar. After holding several pastorates he was associated with Yale *post* 1846 and served as president of the college, 1871–86. He succeeded Chauncey A. Goodrich as editor of Webster's *American Dictionary*.

PORTER, PETER BUELL (*b. Salisbury, Conn., 1773; d. Niagara Falls, N.Y., 1844*), lawyer, New York politician and congressman. Rose to major general of militia for effective service at Chippewa, Lundy's Lane, and Fort Erie in War of 1812. U.S. secretary of war, 1828–29. Influential in development of locality of present Buffalo, N.Y.

PORTER, ROBERT PERCIVAL (*b. Norwich, England, 1852; d. 1917*), journalist, statistician. Administered the eleventh census, 1889–93; *post* 1904, was associated as an editor of special supplements and as a correspondent with the London *Times*.

PORTER, RUFUS (*b. Boxford, Mass., 1792; d. New Haven, Conn., 1884*), inventor. Founded the *Scientific American*, August 1845.

PORTER, RUSSELL WILLIAMS (*b. Springfield, Vt., 1871; d. Pasadena, Calif., 1949*), Arctic explorer, architect, astronomer, telescope maker. A man of many talents, he assisted *post* 1928 in the design and construction of the great Palomar Mountain observatory and of the astrophysical laboratory at California Institute of Technology.

PORTER, SAMUEL (*b. Farmington, Conn., 1810; d. Farmington, 1901*), teacher of the deaf. Brother of Noah and Sarah Porter.

PORTER, SARAH (*b. Farmington, Conn., 1813; d. Farmington, 1900*), educator. Sister of Noah and Samuel Porter. Founded Miss Porter's School for Girls at Farmington, 1843.

PORTER, STEPHEN GEYER (*b. near Salem, Ohio, 1869; d. 1930*), lawyer. Raised in Pennsylvania, he served as a Republican congressman from that state, 1911–30; he became chairman of the House Committee on Foreign Affairs, 1919, and came to be one of the most influential figures in determination of American foreign policy.

PORTER, THOMAS CONRAD (*b. Alexandria, Pa., 1822; d. Easton, Pa., 1901*), German Reformed clergyman, botanist. Graduated Lafayette College, 1840; Princeton Theological Seminary, 1843. Taught science at Franklin and Marshall College and at Lafayette; did pioneer botanical work in the Rocky Mountains as aide to John M. Coulter and Joseph Leidy; wrote extensively on literature as well as the sciences.

PORTER, WILLIAM SYDNEY (*b. Greensboro, N.C., 1862; d. New York, N.Y., 1910*), short-story writer, better known by pseudonym "O. Henry." Left school at 15; worked in a drugstore; removed to Texas, 1882, settling in Austin. After holding various jobs, he was teller in a bank, 1891–94. After failure of a humorous weekly, the *Rolling Stone*, which he edited, Porter removed to Houston, 1895, where he wrote a column for the *Daily Post*. Accused of embezzlement of funds from the Austin bank in which he had been teller, he fled to New Orleans and thence to Honduras; returning to Austin, 1897, he was sentenced in March 1898 to five years in the federal penitentiary in Columbus, Ohio. Released July 1901 after reduction of his term for good behavior, Porter felt the disgrace intensely. Meanwhile, having written and published several stories while in prison under various pseudonyms, of which "O. Henry" eventually displaced all others, he went to New York City, 1902. Nowhere else in his varied experience of life had Porter encountered such a range and diversity of humanity as New York offered him, and he soon put this new material to work. Almost immediately successful as a writer for the magazines, he was essentially an observer and a teller of tales marked by compassion and irony. He employed a few formulas and introduced minor variations into them with great ingenuity, but his success owes less to his technique than to his view of life. His work was of uneven merit and was often trivial. Among the many collected volumes of his stories, *Cabbages and Kings* (1904), *The Four Million* (1906), *Heart of the West* (1907), and *The Gentle Grafter* (1908) are outstanding.

PORTER, WILLIAM TOWNSEND (*b. Plymouth, Ohio, 1862; d. Framingham, Mass., 1949*), physiologist. M.D., St. Louis Medical College (later Washington University School of Medicine), 1885; postgraduate studies at universities of Kiel, Breslau, and Berlin. Taught physiology at St. Louis Medical College, 1887–93; as professor of physiology at Harvard Medical School *post* 1893 (professor of comparative physiology, 1906–28), introduced use of laboratory experiments as part of instruction. He also established the Harvard Apparatus Co. to supply specialized laboratory equipment at minimum cost to educational institutions. In 1897 he founded the *American Journal of Physiology*, which he edited until 1914.

PORTER, WILLIAM TROTTER (*b. Newbury, Vt., 1809; d. New York, N.Y., 1858*), journalist, promoter of sporting literature. Established *Spirit of the Times*, New York, December 1831; was helped by the young Horace Greeley. Published *American Turf Register*, 1839–44. Losing ownership of *Spirit*, 1842, Porter continued in an editorial capacity until 1858. Sketches of southern and western life which had been contributed to the *Spirit* by various writers were gathered by Porter into *The Big Bear of Arkansas* (1845) and *A Quarter Race in Kentucky* (1847).

PORTIER, MICHAEL (*b. Montbrison, France, 1795; d. 1859*), Roman Catholic clergyman. Came to America as missionary, 1817; ordained at St. Louis, Mo., 1818. Consecrated vicar apostolic of Florida and Alabama, 1826; bishop of Mobile, 1829–59.

PORTOLÁ, GASPAR DE (*b. Balaguer, Spain*, ca. 1723; *d. post 1784*), soldier, first governor of Upper California. His contribution to U.S. history consists in his march, 1769–70, from Velicatá in Lower California to Monterey, Upper California, a distance of about 1,000 miles of untrod country, and in his founding of the missions and presidios of San Diego and Monterey. With the Portolá expedition were Juan Crespi (who kept a diary of the enterprise) and Junípero Serra.

PORY, JOHN (*b. Thompston, Norfolk, England, 1572; d. Sutton St. Edmund, England, 1635*), geographer, traveler. Secretary to the Virginia Council at Jamestown, 1619–21, and Speaker of the first Virginia Assembly, July 30, 1619.

POSEY, ALEXANDER LAWRENCE (*b. Eufaula, Okla., 1873; d. in North Canadian River near Eufaula, 1908*), Creek Indian journalist, poet. Influential in Indian affairs and delegate to virtually every convention called in Indian Territory in his time. Editor of the *Indian Journal*.

POSEY, THOMAS (*b. Fairfax Co., Va., 1750; d. Shawneetown, Ill., 1818*), soldier. Fought in Dunmore's War, and as officer in 7th Virginia Regiment during Revolution; was brigadier general, 1793, under Wayne. A Kentucky legislator *ca.* 1805–10, he was U.S. senator from Louisiana, 1812–13, and governor of Indiana Territory, 1813–16.

POST, AUGUSTUS (*b. Brooklyn, N.Y., 1873; d. New York, N.Y., 1952*), pioneer aviator and automobilist. Studied at Amherst College and at Harvard Law School. One of the first automobile owners in New York City, Post established the first public garage for autos. He founded in 1905 the Aero Club of America, which announced the intention of Raymond Orteig to award a $25,000 prize to the first person to cross the Atlantic in a heavier-than-air craft. The award went to Lindbergh in 1927. Post wrote *Problems of Flying at High Altitudes* with W. Kasperowicz; *Glenn Hammond Curtiss* (1912), and the *Curtiss Aviation Book* (1912) with Curtiss.

POST, CHARLES WILLIAM (*b. Springfield, Ill., 1854; d. Santa Barbara, Calif., 1914*), breakfast-food manufacturer, advertising expert. Producer of Postum. Waged fierce battles against trade unions.

POST, CHRISTIAN FREDERICK (*b. Conitz, East Prussia*, ca. 1710; *d. Germantown, Pa., 1785*), Moravian lay missionary. Came to Bethlehem, Pa., 1742. Evangelized Indians in New York, Wyoming Valley, and Ohio country; won Ohio Valley tribes to alliance with British, 1758, which resulted in French loss of Fort Duquesne. Later worked among Indians of Nicaragua.

POST, EMILY PRICE (*b. Baltimore, Md., 1873; d. New York, N.Y., 1960*), author and columnist. The social arbiter of the middle class in America, Emily Post wrote *Emily Price Post's Etiquette* in 1922; the book sold over 500,000 copies, and, along with her newspaper columns and her radio program, made Emily Post a household word on matters of etiquette. Post's guiding principle was the other person's comfort, not adherence to rigid rules of behavior. Other works include the novel *The Flight of a Mother* (1904), *The Personality of a House* (1930), and *Motor Manners* (1950).

POST, GEORGE ADAMS (*b. Cuba, N.Y., 1854; d. Somerville, N.J., 1925*), lawyer, journalist, manufacturer of railroad supplies.

POST, GEORGE BROWNE (*b. New York, N.Y., 1837; d. Bernardsville, N.J., 1913*), Union soldier, architect. Graduated New York University, 1858; studied in office of Richard M. Hunt. Interested primarily in the engineering side of architecture, he was uncritically eclectic in design. His first important work was the Williamsburgh Savings Bank, New York, 1874; among other important New York buildings which he designed were the Western Union Building, Produce Exchange, Cotton Exchange, original Times Building, Pulitzer Building, St. Paul Building, and the earlier buildings of the College of the City of New York. He was responsible for many of the largest residences of his time, was particularly effective in his plan for the Wisconsin State Capitol (begun in 1904), and was a pioneer in modern hotel design.

POST, GEORGE EDWARD (*b. New York, N.Y., 1838; d. 1909*), physician, missionary to Syria. Professor of surgery, Syrian Protestant College, Beirut, *post* 1868; later became dean of the medical school.

POST, ISAAC (*b. Westbury, N.Y., 1798; d. Rochester, N.Y., 1872*), abolitionist, spiritualist. Converted to spiritualism by Margaret Fox, 1848.

POST, LOUIS FREELAND (*b. near Danville, N.J., 1849; d. 1928*), lawyer, reformer, journalist. As leading protagonist of

Henry George's "single tax" philosophy; editor of the *Public*, Chicago, *post* 1898; assistant U.S. secretary of labor, 1913–21.

POST, MELVILLE DAVISSON (*b. near Clarksburg, W.Va., 1871; d. Clarksburg, 1930*), short-story writer, novelist, lawyer. Author of superior detective stories (*The Strange Schemes of Randolph Mason*, 1896; *The Nameless Thing*, 1912; and others) characterized by skill in plotting.

POST, TRUMAN MARCELLUS (*b. Middlebury, Vt., 1810; d. St. Louis, Mo., 1886*), educator, Congregational clergyman, Missouri Unionist. Taught at Illinois College, 1833–47; thereafter pastor in St. Louis of one of the first Congregational churches west of the Mississippi.

POST, WILEY (*b. near Grand Plain, Tex., 1899; d. northern Alaska, 1935*), aviator. Winner of Bendix Trophy race, 1930. Made record-breaking circumnavigation of the world, June 23–July 1, 1931, with Harold Gatty as navigator; flying solo, broke his own record, 1933. Died with Will Rogers in a crash while flying to the Orient by way of Siberia.

POST, WRIGHT (*b. North Hempstead, N.Y., 1766; d. 1828*), New York surgeon. Studied under Richard Bayley and in England. As professor of surgery at Columbia, 1792–1813, collected specimens for anatomical museum; was professor at New York College of Physicians and Surgeons *post* 1813 and its president, 1821–26. Did much to introduce Hunterian principles of surgical procedure in America.

POSTL, CARL. *See* SEALSFIELD, CHARLES.

POSTON, CHARLES DEBRILL (*b. Hardin Co., Ky., 1825; d. Phoenix, Ariz., 1902*), lawyer, explorer, author. First delegate from Arizona Territory to Congress, 1864–65; advocated irrigation works.

POTAMIAN, BROTHER (*b. Co. Cavan, Ireland, 1847; d. 1917*), Christian Brother, scientist. Name in religion of Michael Francis O'Reilly. Came to New York City as a child; entered congregation of Brothers of the Christian Schools at Montreal, 1859. Graduated University of London, D.Sc., 1883. After distinguished career as teacher and scientist in England and Ireland, he taught at Manhattan College, New York City, 1896–1917; he was particularly learned in electricity and magnetism.

POTT, FRANCIS LISTER HAWKS (*b. New York, N.Y., 1864; d. Shanghai, China, 1949*), Episcopal clergyman, missionary, educator. L.H.B., Columbia College, 1883; B.D., General Theological Seminary, New York City, 1886. President of St. John's College (later University) in Shanghai, 1888–1940.

POTT, JOHN (*b. England, date unknown; d. probably Virginia, ca. 1642*), physician. Came to Virginia, 1621. In course of a checkered career, was deputy governor of the colony, 1629–30.

POTTER, ALONZO (*b. Beekman, N.Y., 1800; d. San Francisco, Calif., 1865*), Episcopal clergyman. Brother of Horatio Potter. Graduated Union, 1818; taught mathematics and natural philosophy there. Ordained, 1824, he served as rector of St. Paul's Church, Boston, 1826–31, then as professor of philosophy at Union until 1845 when he was chosen bishop of Pennsylvania. Broad-minded and tolerant toward those of differing opinions, he upheld the doctrine of the Muhlenberg Memorial of 1853. He opposed slavery and wrote in confutation of the claim that it was justified by the Bible.

POTTER, CHARLES FRANCIS (*b. Marlboro, Mass., 1885; d. New York, N.Y., 1962*), clergyman. Attended Bucknell, Brown, and Newton Theological Seminary (S.T.M., 1916); ordained in

1908. While serving at the West Side Unitarian Church in New York City (1919–25), he emerged as the leading advocate of the modernist side in the fundamentalist-modernist conflict of the 1920's. He achieved national attention in a series of radio debates (1924) with John Roach Straton; served as Bible expert for Clarence Darrow's defense in the Scopes "monkey trial" (1925). Taught at Antioch (1925–27), then returned to the ministry as pastor of the Church of the Divine Paternity (1927–29), where he aligned himself with the Social Gospel movement. Wrote fifteen books, including *The Story of Religion* (1929) and *The Lost Years of Jesus Revealed* (1958). Campaigned against capital punishment and was an early advocate of birth control and euthanasia.

POTTER, EDWARD CLARK (*b. New London, Conn., 1857; d. New London, 1923*), sculptor. Studied with Daniel C. French and in Paris. Collaborated with French in work for Chicago World's Fair, 1893, and on numerous equestrian statues. Among his own best-known works are the celebrated New York Public Library lions and the Slocum statue at Gettysburg.

POTTER, ELIPHALET NOTT (*b. Schenectady, N.Y., 1836; d. Mexico City, 1901*), Episcopal clergyman, educator. Son of Alonzo Potter; grandson of Eliphalet Nott. Reorganized and expanded Union College as president, 1871–84; was president of Hobart College, 1884–97.

POTTER, ELISHA REYNOLDS (*b. South Kingston, R.I., 1811; d. 1882*), lawyer, Rhode Island legislator and congressman, writer. As state commissioner of public schools, 1849–54, he did much to promote efficient administration of education in Rhode Island. State supreme court justice, 1868–82.

POTTER, ELLEN CULVER (*b. New London, Conn., 1871; d. Philadelphia, Pa., 1958*), physician, social worker. Studied at the Women's Medical College of Pennsylvania (M.D., 1903). A public health official in Pennsylvania and New Jersey, Potter was secretary of welfare under Pennsylvania Governor Pinchot (1923–27), the first woman to serve on the state's cabinet. From 1930 to 1949, she was medical director and, from 1946, deputy commissioner of the New Jersey Department of Institutions and Agencies.

POTTER, HENRY CODMAN (*b. Schenectady, N.Y., 1835; d. Cooperstown, N.Y., 1908*), Episcopal clergyman. Son of Alonzo Potter. Rector of St. John's, Troy, N.Y., 1859–66, and Grace Church, New York City, 1868–83, he made his parishes centers for Christian work of every sort. In 1883 he was elected assistant bishop of New York, succeeding his uncle Horatio Potter. By training an evangelical, he adopted a moderate Broad Church position. As bishop he dealt wisely with many party disputes within the church, in particular the cases of R. Heber Newton, J. O. S. Huntington, and Charles A. Biggs; he also expanded the religious work of the diocese and was a strong force for civic reform. The Cathedral of St. John the Divine was begun by him.

POTTER, HORATIO (*b. Beekman, N.Y., 1802; d. 1887*), Episcopal clergyman. Brother of Alonzo Potter. Elected bishop of New York, 1854, he healed the breach in the church caused by the suspension of Bishop Benjamin T. Onderdonk and brought the diocese to flourishing condition before his virtual retirement in 1883.

POTTER, JAMES (*b. Co. Tyrone, Ireland, 1729; d. Pennsylvania, 1789*), farmer, Revolutionary soldier, one of the earliest settlers in Penn's Valley region of Pennsylvania (*ca. 1774*).

POTTER, LOUIS MCCLELLAN (*b. Troy, N.Y., 1873; d. Seattle, Wash., 1912*), sculptor. Studied in Paris. Interested in universal brotherhood of man, he did vividly realistic studies of primitive and exotic types, which were of ethnological rather than aesthetic interest.

POTTER, NATHANIEL (*b. Easton, Md., 1770; d. Baltimore, Md., 1843*), physician, surgeon. M.D., University of Pennsylvania, 1796. Practiced in Baltimore; taught at Maryland Medical College *post* 1807. Rendered great service as epidemiologist, particularly of yellow fever; established noncontagiousness of that disease, 1797–98.

POTTER, PAUL MEREDITH (*b. Brighton, England, 1853; d. 1921*), journalist, dramatist. Came to America *ante* 1876. Facile and competent adapter for the stage of successful novels such as Du Maurier's *Trilby* (1895).

POTTER, PLATT (*b. Galway, N.Y., 1800; d. Schenectady, N.Y., 1891*), jurist. Justice of New York Supreme Court, 1857–73.

POTTER, ROBERT (*b. Granville Co., N.C., ca. 1800; d. Texas, 1842*), lawyer, North Carolina legislator and Democratic congressman, Texas pioneer.

POTTER, ROBERT BROWN (*b. Schenectady, N.Y., 1829; d. 1887*), lawyer, Union major general. Son of Alonzo Potter; grandson of Eliphalet Nott. Displayed extraordinary skill and gallantry, notably at South Mountain and Antietam, 1862, as colonel of the 51st New York. He won equal distinction as a division commander at Knoxville, 1863, and at Petersburg, Va., 1864.

POTTER, WILLIAM BANCROFT (*b. near Northfield, Conn., 1863; d. 1934*), electrical engineer. Entered employ of Thomson-Houston Co., 1887, as machinist on electrical equipment; gained extensive experience in installation of electric traction and lighting systems; invented series-parallel controller for electric railway motors, 1892. Worked thereafter at General Electric Co. supervising operations of the railway department; held more than 130 patents.

POTTER, WILLIAM JAMES (*b. North Dartmouth, Mass., 1829; d. Boston, Mass., 1893*), clergyman, editor. Left Unitarian fold, 1867, to join in founding the Free Religious Association; was pastor in New Bedford, Mass., 1859–93.

POTTS, BENJAMIN FRANKLIN (*b. Carroll Co., Ohio, 1836; d. 1887*), Union brigadier general, lawyer. Territorial governor of Montana, Republican, 1870–83.

POTTS, CHARLES SOWER (*b. Philadelphia, Pa., 1864; d. 1930*), physician, neurologist, teacher.

POTTS, JONATHAN (*b. Colebrookdale, Pa., 1745; d. Reading, Pa., 1781*), physician, Revolutionary patriot. M.D., College of Philadelphia (University of Pennsylvania), 1768. Served as medical officer at Lake George, 1776; appointed deputy director general of the hospitals of the Northern Department, 1777; directed Middle Department hospitals as deputy, 1778–80.

POTTS, RICHARD (*b. Upper Marlborough, Md., 1753; d. Frederick, Md., 1808*), legislator, jurist. U.S. senator, Federalist, from Maryland, 1793–96.

POU, EDWARD WILLIAM (*b. Tuskegee, Ala., 1863; d. Washington, D.C., 1934*), lawyer, North Carolina official. Congressman, Democrat, from North Carolina, 1901–34. As chairman of the House Rules Committee, 1917–21 and 1933–34, he played a leading part in furthering the legislative programs of Presidents Wilson and F. D. Roosevelt.

POULSON, NIELS (*b. Horsens, Denmark, 1843; d. Brooklyn, N.Y., 1911*), architect, philanthropist, designer and manufacturer of ornamental metalwork. Came to America, 1864. Left fortune to American-Scandinavian Foundation.

POULSON, ZACHARIAH (*b. Philadelphia, Pa., 1761; d. Philadelphia, 1844*), printer, publisher, philanthropist. Edited the *American Daily Advertiser*, 1800–39.

POUND, CUTHBERT WINFRED (*b. Lockport, N.Y., 1864; d. Ithaca, N.Y., 1935*), jurist. Professor of law, Cornell University, 1895–1904. Judge, New York Supreme Court for 8th judicial district, 1906–15; associate judge, New York Court of appeals, 1915–34; (chief justice *post* 1932). A legal liberal and vigorous defender of civil liberties, Pound wrote the first American judicial opinion upholding validity of a workman's compensation act (*Ives v. South Buffalo Railway Co.*) and was author of a number of other opinions evidencing a broad tolerance of legislative discretion in cases involving constitutionality of statutes.

POUND, (NATHAN) ROSCOE (*b. Lincoln, Nebr., 1870; d. Cambridge, Mass., 1964*), law professor, jurist, and botanist. Attended University of Nebraska and Harvard Law. First developed an interest in botany, and his *Phytogeography of Nebraska* (1898) is considered a pioneering work. In the 1890's he practiced trial and appellate litigation; by 1899 botany became crowded out, and he channeled his energies into teaching law and the fusion of scholarship and "progressive" law reform. Taught at Nebraska Law School (1898–1907; dean, 1903–07), Northwestern (1907–09), Chicago (1909–10), Harvard Law (1910–47; dean, 1916–36), and University of California at Los Angeles (1949–53). Developed a theory of "sociological jurisprudence," stressing the dependency of legal rules on changing social conditions, and procedure, from which he developed a philosophy by which local rules were seen as embodiments of fundamental features of social organization. From this work came his famous 1906 address to the American Bar Association, "The Causes of Popular Dissatisfaction with the Administration of Justice," which launched his national career. The address combined traditional criticism of the legal profession and suggestions for reform. His rise was one of the most meteoric in the history of academic law. After 1910 he made his philosophy of professional reform more explicit; his approach, embodied in the phrases "sociological jurisprudence" and "social engineering," complemented his earlier work and expanded upon it. By 1916 he was regarded as the creator and architect of an approach to common-law decision making that favored the adjustment of legal principles and doctrines to the human condition they are to govern. He published at an extraordinary rate, including *Interpretations of Legal History* (1923) and *Law and Morals* (1924), but his scholarship eventually became repetitious and synthetic, and by 1936 he had lost his scholarly standing. Cultivating alumni who were anti-Communist and anti-Semitic, he gradually cast off the features of sociological jurisprudence: administrative agencies became a threat to private enterprise; social sciences, alien subjects; and academic freedom, invitation to Communism. His five-volume *Jurisprudence* appeared in 1959. He became opposed to curriculum reform and experimental research programs seeking to integrate law with social sciences; rejected the Realist movement in legal education, which had borrowed from his work; and rejected the New Deal, which he called the "service state."

POUND, THOMAS (*b. probably England, ca. 1650; d. Isleworth, England, 1703*), pirate, cartographer, captain in Royal Navy. Made first (*ca. 1691*) map of Boston harbor to be engraved and offered for sale.

POURTALÈS, LOUIS FRANÇOIS DE (*b. Neuchâtel, Switzerland, 1823; d. Beverly Farms, Mass., 1880*), marine zoologist. Associated with U.S. Coast Survey, 1848–73; pupil of J. L. R. Agassiz, whom he assisted in Switzerland *ante* 1846 and at Harvard *post* 1870. He specialized in collecting and studying animal life at great depths.

POWDERLY, TERENCE VINCENT (*b. Carbondale, Pa., 1849; d. Washington, D.C., 1924*), labor leader, government official. Machinist by trade, he joined the Machinists' and Blacksmiths' Union, 1871, and the Knights of Labor, 1874. Rising in the Knights through various official posts, he headed the organization, 1879–93, during the period of its rise and fall as a powerful labor group, showing himself an idealist and reformer, but not an aggressive leader. To him the Knights of Labor was a great educational organization, destined to reform the world by encouraging the working people to demand government ownership of public utilities, regulation of trusts and monopolies, reform of the currency and of the land system, and such measures as the abolition of child labor. Personally sober, he denounced drink as one of the great evils under which workingmen suffered. He opposed the trade form of organization because he believed skilled workers should assist the unskilled. He laid little stress on immediate demands, such as higher wages and shorter hours, and opposed strikes as an outmoded industrial weapon which should be superseded by arbitration. His ultimate ideal was the abolition of the wage system, not through revolution but through producers' cooperatives in which every man would be his own employer.

Before his retirement from the Knights of Labor he had begun to study law, and on Sept. 24, 1894, he was admitted to the bar in Lackawanna Co., Pa. In 1897 he was admitted to practice before the Pennsylvania Supreme Court and in 1901 before the U.S. Supreme Court. He served as U.S. commissioner general of immigration, 1897–1902, and as chief of the Division of Information of the Bureau of Immigration, 1907–21.

POWDERMAKER, HORTENSE (*b. Philadelphia, Pa., 1896; d. Berkeley, Calif., 1970*), anthropologist. Attended Goucher College and London School of Economics (Ph.D., 1928). Pioneer woman anthropologist who did fieldwork in exotic places: her data on the Bismarck archipelago village of Lesu helped update and further the ethnology of Melanesia (*Life in Lesu*, 1933); in Indianola, Miss. (1933–34) to study blacks and whites; in Hollywood (1946–47) to study the values and practices of the film industry (*Hollywood, the Dream Factory*, 1950); in Zambia (1953–54) to study culture change and the media (*Copper Town and Changing Africa*, 1962). Important works include *After Freedom* (1939), "The Channeling of Negro Aggression by the Cultural Process" (*American Journal of Sociology*, 1943), and *Probing Our Prejudices* (1944).

POWEL, JOHN HARE (*b. Philadelphia, Pa., 1786; d. Newport, R.I., 1856*), War of 1812 soldier, agriculturist, author. Brother of Robert Hare. Introduced improved breeds of Durham shorthorn cattle and Southdown sheep to America.

POWELL *See* OSCEOLA.

POWELL, ADAM CLAYTON, SR. (*b. Martin's Mill, Va., 1865; d. New York, N.Y., 1953*), clergyman. Studied at Wayland Seminary in Washington, D.C., and at the Yale Divinity School (1895–96). Pastor of the Abyssinian Baptist Church in New York from 1908 to 1937. Moved the church from midtown New York to Harlem in 1923. A founder of the Urban League and a member of the first board of directors of the NAACP. The father of congressman Adam Clayton Powell, Jr., Powell Sr. provided the political and cultural base for his son's political career.

POWELL, ALMA WEBSTER (*b. Elgin, Ill., 1874; d. Mahwah, N.J., 1930*), operatic soprano, singing teacher.

POWELL, EDWARD PAYSON (*b. Clinton, N.Y., 1833; d. Sorrento, Fla., 1915*), teacher, Congregational and Unitarian clergyman. Influenced by Darwinism; friend and associate of Jenkin L. Jones. Author of *Our Heredity from God* (1887).

POWELL, GEORGE HAROLD (*b. Ghent, N.Y., 1872; d. Pasadena, Calif., 1922*), horticulturist. Authority on preservation and transportation of perishable fruits; held important positions in U.S. Department of Agriculture, 1901–11, and with the California Fruit Growers' Exchange.

POWELL, JOHN BENJAMIN (*b. near Palmyra, Mo., 1886; d. Washington, D.C., 1947*), editor, correspondent, writer on Asia. Graduated from University of Missouri's school of journalism; rose to city editor of *Hannibal* (Mo.) *Courier-Post*, 1910–13; instructor in journalism, University of Missouri, 1913–16. Resident in China from 1917 until his repatriation after imprisonment by the Japanese during World War II, he represented, among other papers, the *Chicago Tribune*, the *Manchester Guardian*, and the London *Daily Herald*. He was also editor *post* 1917, and for many years proprietor, of *Millard's Review of the Far East* (renamed *China Weekly Review* in 1922), an English-language weekly report of developments in politics, economics, society, and religion, which strongly supported unification of China and gave early warning of Japanese aggressive designs.

POWELL, JOHN WESLEY (*b. Mount Morris, N.Y., 1834; d. Haven, Maine, 1902*), Union soldier, geologist, teacher. Under auspices of the Smithsonian Institution and with aid of appropriations from Congress, Powell first explored the gorges of the Green and Colorado rivers by boat, 1869, traversing the Grand Canyon; he continued his explorations of the Rocky Mountain region in 1871 and 1874–75. Appointed director of the U.S. Geological survey, 1880, after serving as director of its Rocky Mountain division *post* 1875, he administered the Survey with marked success until 1894. He was also director of the Bureau of Ethnology (under the Smithsonian), 1879–1902. He was especially notable for the quality of the reports made by him and issued under his supervision (in particular his *Explorations of the Colorado River of the West*, 1875) and for his encouragement of his subordinates to attain distinction on their own. He retired from the survey, partly for reasons of health, partly because of antagonism to his projects for forest preservation and irrigation.

POWELL, LAZARUS WHITEHEAD (*b. Henderson Co., Ky., 1812; d. near Henderson, Ky., 1867*), lawyer, planter. Democratic governor of Kentucky, 1851–55. As U.S. senator, 1859–65; he fought for neutrality of his state and was an advocate of the Crittenden propositions; throughout the Civil War, he opposed military interference in civic affairs.

POWELL, LUCIEN WHITING (*b. near Upperville, Va., 1846; d. Washington, D.C., 1930*), landscape painter. Student of Thomas Morgan; influenced strongly by the English artist J. M. W. Turner.

POWELL, MAUD (*b. Peru, Ill., 1868; d. Uniontown, Pa., 1920*), violinist. Niece of John W. Powell; daughter of William Bramwell Powell. Made studies in Chicago; also at the Paris Conservatory and in Leipzig. She then toured a year in England, playing before Queen Victoria. In 1885, after further study with Joseph Joachim, she made her debut with the Berlin Philharmonic. Returning to New York, she appeared with the New York Philharmonic, 1885, and made annual concert tours, 1886–92. Organizing the Maud Powell Quartet, 1894, she appeared with it until 1898. Thereafter, she continued as a successful solo artist in

America and Europe, winning praise for her technical mastery and deep interpretive insight.

POWELL, RICHARD EWING ("DICK") (*b. Mountain View, Ark., 1904; d. Hollywood, Calif., 1963*), actor. Beginning as a singer and musician in his teens, he was signed (1932) to a long-term contract by Warner Brothers and made more than thirty film musicals, including *42nd Street* (1933), *Broadway Gondolier* (1935), *On the Avenue* (1937), and *Going Places* (1940). A handsome, curly-haired tenor, he became the epitome of the actor-singer of the 1930's. Tired of musicals, he bought his release from Warners and won critical acclaim for serious roles in *Murder, My Sweet* (1945) and *Pitfall* (1948). In the 1950's he founded the Four Star Television Company.

POWELL, SNELLING (*b. Carmarthen, Wales, 1758; d. Boston, Mass., 1821*), actor, manager. Came to America, 1793. Prominent on the Boston stage as an actor *post* 1794, he was very successful as manager of the Boston Theatre, 1806–21.

POWELL, THOMAS (*b. England, 1809; d. Newark, N.J., 1887*), poet, dramatist, journalist. Came to America, 1849, after establishing himself as an industrious literary workman in London; was associated thereafter with the Frank Leslie publications. Author of a number of books, including the useful *Living Authors of England* (1849) and *Living Authors of America* (1850).

POWELL, THOMAS REED (*b. Richford, Vt., 1880; d. Boston, Mass., 1955*), constitutional lawyer. Studied at the University of Vermont, Harvard Law School (LL.B., 1904), and Columbia (Ph.D., 1913). Taught at Columbia (1906–25); at Harvard University (1925–49). Rejecting abstract and absolute principles, Powell concentrated on concrete criticisms and observations of the law; his special interest was the area of conflicts between national and state power in a federal system. His book *Vagaries and Varieties in Constitutional Law* was published posthumously in 1956.

POWELL, WILLIAM BRAMWELL (*b. Castile, N.Y., 1836; d. Mount Vernon, N.Y., 1904*), educator. Brother of John W. Powell; father of Maud Powell. Superintendent of schools in Peru and Aurora, Ill.; supervisor of District of Columbia schools, 1885–1900. Advocated progressive methods.

POWELL, WILLIAM BYRD (*b. Bourbon Co., Ky., 1799; d. Covington, Ky., 1866*), eclectic physician, phrenologist. Investigated relations between temperament and cranial conformation, evolving theory of phrenology—that human temperament could be read from examination of the cranium alone.

POWELL, WILLIAM HENRY (*b. New York, N.Y., 1823; d. New York, 1879*), historical and portrait painter. Pupil of James H. Beard and Henry Inman. Commissioned, 1847, to paint *De Soto* panel for rotunda in U.S. Capitol; painted *Battle of Lake Erie* for Ohio Capitol (completed 1863).

POWER, FREDERICK BELDING (*b. Hudson, N.Y., 1853; d. Washington, D.C., 1927*), pharmacist, chemist. Ph.D., Strassburg, 1800. Taught at Philadelphia College of Pharmacy and at University of Wisconsin; engaged in industrial research here and in England, 1892–1916; headed phytochemical laboratory, U.S. Department of Agriculture, 1916–27. Made major contributions to knowledge of plant constituents and distribution of organic compounds in plants; investigated chaulmoogra seeds and derivatives.

POWER, FREDERICK DUNGLISON (*b. Yorktown, Va., 1851; d. Washington, D.C., 1911*), Disciples of Christ clergyman. Pastor, *post* 1875, of Vermont Ave. Christian Church, Washington, D.C.

POWER, FREDERICK TYRONE (*b. London, England, 1869; d. California, 1931*), actor. Came to America as a boy; went on stage *ca.* 1886; was member of Augustin Daly's company. Later supporting Henry Irving. Mrs. Fiske, and others, he was famous in England and America for playing heroic and poetic roles in romantic drama.

POWER, JOHN (*b. Roscarberry, Ireland, 1792; d. 1849*), Roman Catholic clergyman. Came to America, 1819; served thereafter as pastor of St. Peter's Church, New York City, and was active in the social and political advancement of the Irish-Americans.

POWER, TYRONE. *See* POWER, FREDERICK TYRONE.

POWER, TYRONE (*b. Cincinnati, Ohio, 1914; d. Madrid, Spain, 1958*), actor. Self-trained, Power was a member of an old theatrical family. He began acting after high school, and after working in plays in Chicago, he was seen in *Romeo and Juliet* and *Saint Joan* (1936). That year, he signed a seven-year contract with Twentieth Century-Fox under the producer Darryl Zanuck. His first film was *Lloyd's of London* (1936); other films include *Suez* (1938), *The Rains Came* (1939), and *A Yank in the RAF* (1941). Power served in the marines during World War II and was discharged a first lieutenant. Other films include *The Razor's Edge* (1946), *The Sun Also Rises* (1957), and, his last film, *Witness for the Prosecution* (1958). He appeared on Broadway in the play *Mr. Roberts* (1950), and *John Brown's Body* (1953).

POWERS, DANIEL WILLIAM (*b. near Batavia, N.Y., 1818; d. Rochester, N.Y., 1897*), banker. Promoted civic and commercial interests of Rochester.

POWERS, HIRAM (*b. near Woodstock, Vt., 1805; d. Florence, Italy, 1873*), sculptor. Began career in Cincinnati, Ohio, *ca.* 1829, making wax figures of celebrities and mechanized monsters for a local "Chamber of Horrors"; worked briefly with Kirke Brown and Shobal Vail Clevenger. Removing to Washington, D.C., 1834, He made busts from life of such prominent figures as John Marshall, Andrew Jackson, John C. Calhoun, and Daniel Webster. Three benefactors—Nicholas Longworth, W. C. Preston, and John S. Preston—lent him the means of removing with his family to Florence, Italy, 1839, where he remained for the rest of his life. He was early befriended there by the sculptor Horatio Greenough. Soon after his arrival in Italy, he set up in clay a life-size figure called *Eve Before the Fall*, later carved in marble. This was a precursor of his *Greek Slave*, a nude female figure, finished in marble in 1843 and thereafter reproduced in at least six marble copies. It was without doubt the most celebrated single statue of its day, owing in part to the emotional appeal of the current Greek struggle for independence. Among others, Elizabeth Barrett Browning, Edward Everett, and Nathaniel Hawthorne wrote about it, and it received acclaim on exhibition at the Crystal Palace, London, 1851. In 1853 there was a movement to commission Powers to decorate the Capitol at Washington, but he declined to submit designs in competition with other artists. He made about 150 portrait busts, nearly all of men, which are now considered his strongest work. At the height of his successful career he built himself a fine house in Florence and there entertained many famous personages from America. The *Greek Slave* has historical importance as the first sculpture by an American to attract general public notice.

POWHATAN (*d. 1618*), Indian chief. His personal name was Wa-hun-sen-a-cawh or Wa-hun-son-a-cock, and he was chief, or "emperor," of the Powhatan federation, which at the beginning of the 17th century extended over Tidewater Virginia. His father was of a southern tribe, said to have been driven north by the Spaniards; upon his arrival in Virginia, he had conquered five of the local tribes. His son and successor, known to the Jamestown settlers at Powhatan, extended his sway over many more. He ruled with an iron hand, being excessively cruel to prisoners and malefactors. Despite frequent protestations of goodwill, he annoyed the English settlers by ambushing small parties, murdering workers in the field, and refusing to sell them corn when their provisions fell low, but with the marriage of his daughter Pocahontas to John Rolfe, he concluded a peace to which he steadily adhered thereafter. Powhatan died in April 1618 and was succeeded by his brother Itopatin, or Opitchapam.

POWNALL, THOMAS (*b. Lincolnshire, England, 1722; d. Bath, England, 1805*), colonial governor. Pownall deserves more than any other Englishman of his time to be called a student of colonial administration. He came to America in 1753 as secretary to Sir Danvers Osborn, governor of New York, who committed suicide two days after arrival. Pownall, however, remained in America as an observer for Lord Halifax and the Board of Trade until 1756, making the acquaintance of, among other notables, William Shirley and Benjamin Franklin. Appointed lieutenant governor of New Jersey in May 1755 to assist the aged Jonathan Belcher, he continued his close study of colonial trade and defense problems. Returning to England early in 1756, he presented a scheme for the unification of the military command of the colonies and stressed the importance of control of inland waterways. Offered the governorship of Pennsylvania, he declined it in order to accompany to America the new commander in chief, Lord Loudoun. He went back to England in October 1756 to present Loudoun's case against William Shirley, governor of Massachusetts. The favorable impression which he made on the newly formed Pitt ministry caused him to be offered the governorship of Massachusetts, which he accepted. He reached Boston on Aug. 3, 1757, and took up his work with vigor, using conciliation in order to get maximum cooperation in the war against the French and Indians. He defended the constitutional authority of the civil government against the war powers claimed by the military and was almost too able and too independent. The Board of Trade recalled him in November 1759, offering him several lucrative positions, which he declined. Pownall's chief claim to remembrance is his book *The Administration of the Colonies* (1764), in which he discussed the reorganization in administration, in law, and in the status of the colonies necessary to maintain the union with England. His policies were far ahead of the views of his contemporaries. Pownall never returned to America, but was in essential sympathy with the colonists until their final measures of resistance. As member of Parliament, he introduced in 1780 a bill favoring a conclusion of the war by royal negotiation, which was defeated.

POYDRAS, JULIEN DE LALANDE (*b. Rezé, near Nantes, France, 1746; d. Pointe Coupée Parish, La., 1824*), poet, public servant, planter, merchant, philanthropist. Came to New Orleans, 1768.

POZNANSKI, GUSTAVUS (*b. Storchnest, Poland, 1804; d. New York, N.Y., 1879*), Jewish religious leader and reformer. Came to America, 1831. Rabbi, Congregation Beth Elohim, Charleston, S.C., 1836–47. Instituted radical alterations in creed and ritual.

PRALL, DAVID WRIGHT (*b. Saginaw, Mich., 1886; d. Berkeley, Calif., 1940*), philosopher. Graduated University of Michigan, 1909; Ph.D., University of California, 1918. After teaching at Amherst and Harvard, he was on the faculty of the University of California, 1921–30. Again at Harvard *post* 1930, he became professor, 1938. A notable teacher, he was author of *A Study in the Theory of Value* (1921), *Aesthetic Judgment* (1929) and *Aesthetic Analysis* (1936).

PRANG, LOUIS (*b. Breslau, Prussian Silesia, 1824; d. California, 1909*), Boston lithographer. Immigrated to America, 1850. Publisher of prints and school drawing-books, he popularized "chromos," color reproductions of art.

PRANG, MARY AMELIA DANA HICKS (*b. Syracuse, N.Y., 1836; d. Melrose, Mass., 1927*), art teacher, author. Edited art manuals for the firm of Louis Prang, whom she later married.

PRATT, BELA LYON (*b. Norwich, Conn., 1867; d. Boston, Mass., 1917*), sculptor. Studied at Yale School of Fine Arts and Art Students League, New York City; served as assistant to Augustus Saint-Gaudens. Taught *post* 1893 at Boston Museum School. Excelled in decorative groups, portrait bas-reliefs, busts of noted men, ideal nudes of women and children, and youthful soldierly figures.

PRATT, CHARLES (*b. Watertown, Mass., 1830; d. Brooklyn, N.Y., 1891*), oil merchant, philanthropist. Foreseeing growth of petroleum industry upon discovery of oil in Pennsylvania, he established with Henry H. Rogers a refinery at Greenpoint, N.Y., 1867, and marketed Pratt's Astral Oil, a high-quality illuminant, which became world famous. Merging with Standard Oil, 1874, Pratt assumed a leading position in that firm and grew very wealthy. His philanthropies included a model tenement for workingmen and substantial gifts to Amherst College, University of Rochester, and Adelphi Academy, Brooklyn. He also founded Pratt Institute in Brooklyn, 1887, and the Pratt Institute Free Library.

PRATT, DANIEL (*b. Temple, N.H., 1799; d. 1873*), carpenter, cotton mill operator, industrialist. Removed to Georgia, 1819; to Alabama, 1833. Founded Prattville, Ala., 1838, where he engaged in cotton and wool milling. Financed Henry F. De Bardeleben in development of Birmingham, Ala., industries.

PRATT, DANIEL (*b. Chelsea, Mass., 1809; d. Boston, Mass., 1887*), vagrant. Under delusion that he had been elected president of the United States, he used to visit New England college campuses to "lecture" *post ca.* 1837.

PRATT, ELIZA ANNA FARMAN (*b. Augusta, N.Y., 1837; d. Warner, N.H., 1907*), writer of juvenile stories. Edited *Wide Awake*, 1875–93.

PRATT, ENOCH (*b. North Middleborough, Mass., 1808; d. 1896*), iron merchant, capitalist, philanthropist. Removed to Baltimore, Md., 1831; established firm of E. Pratt and Brothers in iron trade; later branched out into transportation, banking, and fire insurance. The most important of his philanthropies was the Enoch Pratt Free Library in Baltimore (opened 1886), which was first to embody idea of "branch" libraries. He was also greatly interested in the improvement of the condition of blacks and gave much to hospitals and educational institutions.

PRATT, FRANCIS ASHBURY (*b. Woodstock, Vt., 1827; d. 1902*), pioneer toolmaker, inventor. Began career as a machinist, eventually working at the Colt armory, Hartford, Conn., 1852–54. Here he met his future partner, Amos Whitney. Pratt and Whitney began doing machine work on their own, 1860; in 1864 both gave up positions with the Phoenix Iron Works to give full time to their own firm. Pratt was a promoter of the use of interchangeable parts, inaugurating that system in his own factory while making firearms during the Civil War. The establishment of a standard system of gauges for Europe and America was owing largely to Pratt's efforts.

PRATT, JAMES BISSETT (*b. Elmira, N.Y., 1875; d. Williamstown, Mass., 1944*), philosopher, student of Oriental religions. Graduated Williams College, 1898; studied at Columbia University Law School and at University of Berlin. Ph.D., Harvard, 1905. Taught philosophy at Williams College, 1905–43 (Mark Hopkins professor *post* 1917). Author of, among other works, *The Psychology of Religious Belief* (1907), *The Religious Consciousness* (1920), *Matter and Spirit* (1922), and *The Pilgrimage of Buddhism* (1928).

PRATT, JOHN (*b.* Unionville, S.C., 1831; *d.* ca. 1900), journalist. Patented the "ptereotype," 1866–68, forerunner of the Hammond typewriter.

PRATT, MATTHEW (*b.* Philadelphia, Pa., 1734; *d.* 1805), portrait painter. A friend and pupil of Benjamin West, Pratt painted many of the leading Americans of his time in a superior style; his color was refined and delicate, and he ranks with the best of his contemporaries as a technician.

PRATT, ORSON (*b.* Hartford, N.Y., 1811; *d.* Salt Lake City, Utah, 1881), Mormon leader. Brother of Parley P. Pratt. Converted by his brother, Orson rose rapidly in the Mormon hierarchy and was ordained one of the apostles of that church, 1835. He supported the Brigham Young faction on the death of Joseph Smith and was in the first company to enter the Salt Lake Valley, 1847. After a long career in missionary and administrative work both in the United States and in Europe, he was appointed historian of the church, 1874. He was also active in Utah politics and served seven terms as Speaker of the lower house of the territorial legislature. His philosophical vagaries occasionally irritated the more practical Brigham Young, but Pratt profoundly influenced Mormon theology.

PRATT, PARLEY PARKER (*b.* Burlington, N.Y., 1807; *d.* 1857), apostle of the Latter-Day Saints. Brother of Orson Pratt. Joined Mormons, 1830; ordained apostle, 1835. Author of an *Autobiography* (1874). Killed by the husband of a convert.

PRATT, RICHARD HENRY (*b.* Rushford, N.Y., 1840; *d.* San Francisco, Calif., 1924), soldier, Indian educator. Raised in Indiana. After Union army service in Civil War and regular army service in Indian campaigns, 1867–75, he had remarkable success as a teacher of Indian prisoners at Fort Marion, Fla., 1875–78. Continuing his work on a larger scale at Hampton Institute, 1878–79, he then founded the famous Indian school at Carlisle, Pa., and served as its superintendent until 1904. He was promoted to brigadier general shortly before his retirement.

PRATT, SERENO STANSBURY (*b.* Westmoreland, N.Y., 1858; *d.* Troy, N.Y., 1915), journalist, specialist in finance and commerce. Editor in chief, *Wall Street Journal*, 1905–08; author of *The Work of Wall Street* (1903); secretary, New York State Chamber of Commerce, 1908–15.

PRATT, SILAS GAMALIEL (*b.* Addison, Vt., 1846; *d.* Pittsburgh, Pa., 1916), pianist, composer.

PRATT, THOMAS GEORGE (*b.* Georgetown, D.C., 1804; *d.* 1869), lawyer, Maryland legislator. Restored state credit as Whig governor of Maryland, 1844–47; was U.S. senator, 1850–57. During Civil War period, he became a Democrat and was a strong Confederate sympathizer.

PRATT, THOMAS WILLIS (*b.* Boston, Mass., 1812; *d.* Boston, 1875), civil engineer, railroad construction and operation expert. Invented and patented the type of bridge and roof truss bearing his name, 1844; also patented improvements to steam boilers, ship hull construction, and the propulsion of ships.

PRATT, WALDO SELDEN (*b.* Philadelphia, Pa., 1857; *d.* Hartford, Conn., 1939), musicologist.

PRATT, WILLIAM VEAZIE (*b.* Belfast, Maine, 1869; *d.* Charleston, Mass., 1957), naval officer. Graduated from the U.S. Naval Academy in 1889. Pratt's early assignments included action in the Spanish-American War and the Philippine Insurrection; more routine was his teaching at the Naval Academy and the Naval War College. By 1921, he was promoted to the rank of rear admiral after serving as an assistant to Admiral William S. Benson, the Chief of Naval Operations during World War I. Pratt attended many international naval conferences including the Washington Conference (1921–22) and the London Conference in 1930, becoming an expert and proponent of naval limitations, a policy which he believed reduced the chances of war. By 1930, he was commander in chief of the U.S. Fleet. He retired in 1933 and during World War II was a naval specialist for *Newsweek*, a position he held until 1946.

PRATT, ZADOCK (*b.* Stephentown, N.Y., 1790; *d.* Bergen, N.J., 1871), tanner, New York Democratic legislator and congressman.

PRATTE, BERNARD (*b.* Ste. Genevieve, Mo., 1771; *d.* 1836), merchant, fur trader. Leading citizen of St. Louis, Mo., *post ca.* 1795.

PRAY, ISAAC CLARK (*b.* Boston, Mass., 1813; *d.* 1869), journalist, dramatist, actor. Graduated Amherst, 1833. Author of, among other works, *Prose and Verse from the Portfolio of an Editor* (1836) and *Memoirs of James Gordon Bennett* (1855).

PREBER, CHRISTIAN. *See* PRIBER, CHRISTIAN.

PREBLE, EDWARD (*b.* Falmouth, now Portland, Maine, 1761; *d.* Portland, 1807), naval officer. Shipped aboard a privateer, 1777; appointed midshipman, Massachusetts navy, 1779. *Post* 1783, served aboard merchant ships. Appointed lieutenant in the reorganized U.S. Navy, 1798, he was commissioned captain, 1799, and commanded the *Essex* on convoy duty. In the war with Tripoli, Preble sailed aboard the *Constitution* in command of the squadron which blockaded that state, 1803–04. In the face of numerous difficulties, Preble made an unsuccessful attempt to capture Tripoli in August–September 1804, and was soon after superseded as commodore by Samuel Barron. Preble was particularly effective as a trainer of the young officers who served under him, many of whom later distinguished themselves during the War of 1812.

PREBLE, GEORGE HENRY (*b.* Portland, Maine, 1816; *d.* 1885), naval officer, author. Nephew of Edward Preble. Appointed midshipman, 1835, he served in a variety of capacities until the Civil War when he was given command of the *Katahdin*. He fought under Farragut at New Orleans, and was actively engaged in operations up to Vicksburg. As commander of the sloop *Oneida*, he was severely censured for allowing the Confederate cruiser *Florida* (*Oreto*) to break through the blockade of Mobile, September 1862. Reinstated, he served thereafter with distinction and retired as rear admiral, 1878.

PREBLE, WILLIAM PITT (*b.* York, Maine, 1783; *d.* 1857), jurist, railroad executive. Active in achieving separation of Maine from Massachusetts. Aided Albert Gallatin in preparation of northeastern boundary case, 1828, and continued to act in this matter up to the Webster-Ashburton Treaty signing, 1842. He was associated with John A. Poor in the building of the Atlantic and St. Lawrence Railroad.

PREETORIUS, EMIL (*b.* Alzey, Rhenish Hesse, Germany, 1827; *d.* 1905), journalist. Settled in St. Louis, Mo., 1853. Early active in the Republican party, he was a friend and partner of Carl Schurz in the *Westliche Post*, editing it *post* 1864.

PRENDERGAST, MAURICE BRAZIL (*b. Roxbury, Mass., 1861; d. New York, N.Y., 1924*), painter. Studied in Boston and in Paris, France, 1887–89. Beginning as a painter of gay and sparkling studies of street life and holiday scenes, he changed his style radically *post* 1914 in the direction of a more abstract and purely decorative art, which won enthusiastic approval from contemporary critics.

PRENTICE, GEORGE DENNISON (*b. New London Co., Conn., 1802; d. 1870*), journalist. Removed to Kentucky, 1830, as editor of the *Louisville Daily Journal*. Within a short time he made his paper the most influential Whig organ in the South and West. A Unionist, he was largely responsible for Kentucky's refusal to secede. A collection of his witty editorials appeared as *Prenticeana* (1860).

PRENTICE, SAMUEL OSCAR (*b. North Stonington, Conn., 1850; d. 1924*), jurist. Graduated Yale, 1873; Yale School of Law, 1875. Connecticut superior court judge, 1889–1901; justice, supreme court of errors, 1901–20 (chief justice, 1913–20). Taught at Yale School of Law, 1896–1915.

PRENTIS, HENNING WEBB, JR. (*b. St. Louis, Mo., 1884; d. Lancaster, Pa., 1959*), business executive. Studied at the University of Missouri and the University of Cleveland. Prentis joined the Armstrong Cork Company in 1907, becoming vice president in 1926 and president in 1934. Under his leadership, Armstrong became one of America's leading corporations; through astute use of marketing and advertising, Prentis led the company to a prominent position by World War II. He was chairman of the National Association of Manufacturers in 1941.

PRENTISS, BENJAMIN MAYBERRY (*b. Belleville, Va., 1819; d. Bethany, Mo., 1901*), Union soldier, lawyer. Distinguished at Shiloh; promoted major general, 1862. Commanded at battle of Helena, Ark., July 1863, winning victory over superior force.

PRENTISS, ELIZABETH PAYSON (*b. Portland, Maine, 1818; d. Dorset, Vt., 1878*), writer of religious and juvenile fiction. Among her many books the most popular were *Stepping Heavenward* (1869) and the "Little Susy" books (1853 and later).

PRENTISS, GEORGE LEWIS (*b. West Gorham, Maine, 1816; d. 1903*), Congregational and Presbyterian clergyman, educator. Brother of Seargent S. Prentiss. Graduated Bowdoin, 1835. After holding a number of pastorates, he organized the New School Church of the Covenant, New York City, 1862, and served there until 1873. Taught a variety of subjects at Union Theological Seminary *post* 1871.

PRENTISS, SAMUEL (*b. Stonington, Conn., 1782; d. Montpelier, Vt., 1857*), Vermont jurist. U.S. senator, Federalist-Whig from Vermont, 1831–42; thereafter, U.S. judge, Vermont district.

PRENTISS, SEARGENT SMITH (*b. Portland, Maine, 1808; d. Natchez, Miss., 1850*), lawyer, orator, Whig congressman from Mississippi. Brother of George L. Prentiss. Removed to Mississippi *ca.* 1828; practiced at Natchez, Vicksburg, and, *post* 1845, New Orleans.

PRESBREY, EUGENE WILEY (*b. Williamsburg, Mass., 1853; d. California, 1931*), stage manager, dramatist. Successful as an adapter of popular novels into plays.

PRESCOTT, ALBERT BENJAMIN (*b. Hastings, N.Y., 1832; d. Ann Arbor, Mich., 1905*), chemist. M.D., University of Michigan, 1864. Taught at Michigan *post* 1865; took a major part in establishment of the university's school of pharmacy, serving as its dean, 1874–1905. Did notable work in sanitary and food chemistry and in toxicology; was author of influential treatises and papers.

PRESCOTT, GEORGE BARTLETT (*b. Kingston, N.H., 1830; d. New York, N.Y., 1894*), telegraph engineer. Chief electrician of Western Union, 1866–82; author of a number of works on the telegraph, the telephone, and other electrical subjects.

PRESCOTT, OLIVER (*b. Groton, Mass., 1731; d. Groton, 1804*), physician, Revolutionary soldier. Brother of William Prescott. Held a number of Massachusetts military and civic appointments.

PRESCOTT, SAMUEL (*b. Concord, Mass., 1751; d. Halifax, Nova Scotia, ca. 1777*), physician, Revolutionary patriot. Successfully completed the "midnight ride" of Apr. 18, 1775, after capture of Paul Revere; gave alarm at Concord. Died in prison after capture aboard a privateer.

PRESCOTT, SAMUEL CATE (*b. South Hampton, N.H., 1872; d. Boston, Mass., 1962*), bacteriologist. Attended Massachusetts Institute of Technology (S.B., 1894); joined the faculty (1895), retiring as dean of science (1942). Discovered the scientific method for making canned food entirely sanitary (1895–97) by boiling, which killed all microorganisms. Founded the Boston Biochemical Laboratory (1904) and directed a laboratory (1914–17) for United Fruit in Costa Rica. Chief of the U.S. Department of Agriculture dehydration division (1918–19), directing vital studies for the war effort. During and after World War II served as consultant to the government and various food industry corporations.

PRESCOTT, WILLIAM (*b. Groton, Mass., 1726; d. Pepperell, Mass., 1795*), farmer, Revolutionary soldier. Brother of Oliver Prescott. Colonel of minutemen, 1775; arrived too late for fight at Concord; appointed to council of war at siege of Boston. Ordered to fortify Bunker Hill, June 16, 1775, he decided after consultation with his officers to fortify Breed's Hill, since it commanded Boston more effectively. It is not known for certain whether he or Israel Putnam was in general command on the field of battle, June 17, but Prescott did command at a vital point in the line. He later took part in the evacuation of New York and the Saratoga campaign, but age and an injury forced him to retire from active service.

PRESCOTT, WILLIAM HICKLING (*b. Salem, Mass., 1796; d. Boston, Mass., 1859*), historian. Grandson of William Prescott; born to wealth and social position. Graduated Harvard, 1814. While in his junior year at college, a blow on his left eye permanently destroyed its sight; two years later an inflammation of the right eye impaired his vision, so that at periods he was practically blind. Deciding to follow a literary career despite these difficulties, he toured Europe, 1815–17; on his return to Boston he began an intensive study of the history and literature of the principal countries of western Europe with the aid of paid secretaries who read to him. He contributed reviews and articles to the *North American Review*, 1821–36, the best of which were collected as *Biographical and Critical Miscellanies* in 1845. At work since 1826 on the first of his masterpieces, he published *The History of the Reign of Ferdinand and Isabella the Catholic* late in 1837 (title-page date, 1838). The book was an immediate success, and Prescott was hailed on both sides of the Atlantic. The year after the publication of *Ferdinand and Isabella* was one of physical pain and enforced idleness, but he devoted much thought to the next of his endeavors—the history of the conquests of Mexico and Peru. He began research for the *History of the Conquest of Mexico* in April 1839; so well had he learned to handle his materials that he was able to publish the three volumes in 1843. The *History of the Conquest of Peru* was written at an even more rapid rate; two years apparently sufficed for actual composition, though the work was not published until March 1847. Despite the appearance of much new material, these books remain standard authorities on the two greatest achievements of the Spanish conquistadores in the New World. Prescott's fame was now so great that on a trip to England in 1850 he was entertained and honored as no other private American citizen. He had contemplated a history of the reign of Philip II as early as 1838; to this task he devoted the rest of his life. Only three of the projected ten volumes appeared, two in 1855 and the last in 1858. He also prepared a new edition of William Robertson's *History of the Reign of the Emperor Charles the Fifth* (1857).

Prescott's outstanding merit, in addition to courage, was the scrupulous care and integrity with which he used his materials, and it is a tribute to his skill as a historian that what was intended for the casual reader is now the material of the professional historical student. He was also a master of narrative. Although his inherited prejudices did not color his interpretation of facts to the extent displayed by J. L. Motley, they were dominant enough to deprive him of wholehearted sympathy with the 16th century. As a man, he possessed great gaiety and charm; his generosity was proverbial.

PRESSER, THEODORE (b. *Pittsburgh, Pa., 1848; d. Philadelphia, Pa., 1925*), music teacher and publisher, philanthropist, editor. Founded *Étude* magazine, 1883.

PRESSMAN, LEE (b. *New York, N.Y. 1906; d. Mount Vernon, N.Y., 1969*), lawyer. Attended New York University, Cornell, and Harvard Law (LL.B., 1929). Appointed assistant general counsel for the Agricultural Adjustment Administration (1933–35), then general counsel for relief programs and the Resettlement Administration. Joined the Communist party, then left in 1935, but did not reject its ideology. Hired in 1936 as general counsel for the Steelworkers Organizing Committee and later for the Congress of Industrial Organizations (CIO). Met frequently with Communists in the CIO, but at the 1940 convention, he dutifully moved for denouncing communism and fascism. His involvement with communism became an issue during the onset of the cold war, and he was forced to resign his position in the CIO in 1948.

PRESTON, ANN (b. *Westgrove, Pa., 1813; d. 1872*), physician. One of first (1852) graduates from Female Medical College of Pennsylvania, at which she became a professor. Helped found Woman's Hospital of Philadelphia.

PRESTON, HARRIET WATERS (b. *Danvers, Mass., 1836; d. Cambridge, Mass., 1911*), author. Noted for translations of Provençal and Roman classical poets.

PRESTON, JOHN SMITH (b. *near Abingdon, Va., 1809; d. Columbia, S.C., 1881*), lawyer, planter, orator. Brother of William C. Preston. Supported states' rights as South Carolina legislator; was effective superintendent, Confederate Bureau of Conscription, 1863–65.

PRESTON, JONAS (b. *Chester, Pa., 1764; d. Philadelphia, Pa., 1836*), physician, Pennsylvania legislator, philanthropist.

PRESTON, MARGARET JUNKIN (b. *Milton, Pa., 1820; d. Baltimore, Md., 1897*), poet. Daughter of George Junkin; sister-in-law of Thomas J. Jackson.

PRESTON, THOMAS SCOTT (b. *Hartford, Conn., 1824; d. 1891*), Roman Catholic clergyman, devotional and controversial writer. A convert from the Episcopal ministry, 1849, Monsignor Preston served in New York as chancellor of the diocese *post* 1855 and as vicar general, 1873–91. He was an uncompromising conservative.

PRESTON, WILLIAM (b. *near Louisville, Ky., 1816; d. 1887*), lawyer, soldier, Kentucky Whig legislator and congressman. A Democrat *post* 1854, he was U.S. minister to Spain, 1858–60; he returned to serve as Confederate brigadier general and minister to Mexico.

PRESTON, WILLIAM BALLARD (b. *Montgomery Co., Va., 1805; d. 1862*), lawyer, Virginia Whig legislator and congressman, U.S. secretary of the navy, 1849–50. Nephew of John Floyd. Opposed Virginia secession but presented secession ordinance; served as Confederate senator from Virginia, 1861–62.

PRESTON, WILLIAM CAMPBELL (b. *Philadelphia, Pa., 1794; d. Columbia, S.C., 1860*), lawyer, South Carolina legislator. Brother of John S. Preston; friend of Hugh S. Legaré and of Washington Irving. An intense advocate of states' rights and of slavery, Preston was elected to the U.S. Senate, 1833, as a Democrat from South Carolina. Opposing Jackson, he became a Whig and resigned from the Senate, 1842, rather than accept dictation from the legislature. He was president of South Carolina College, 1846–51.

PREUS, CHRISTIAN KEYSER (b. *Spring Prairie, Wis., 1852; d. 1921*), Lutheran clergyman. Taught at Luther College, Decorah, Iowa, *post* 1898; was president of the college *post* 1902.

PREVOST, FRANÇOIS MARIE (b. *Pont-de-Cé, France*, ca. *1764; d. Donaldsonville, La., 1842*), surgeon. Graduated in medicine at Paris; settled in Donaldsonville *ca.* 1800. Distinguished as one of the earliest successful performers of the cesarean section in the United States.

PRIBER, CHRISTIAN (b. *possibly Saxony, date unknown; d. Frederica, Ga., post 1744*), utopian community builder. Immigrated to South Carolina, *ca.* 1734; two years later, went to live among the Cherokee. Labored to draw all southern Indians into a great independent confederation which would be administered along communist lines, somewhat anticipating the doctrine of Saint-Simon.

PRICE, BRUCE (b. *Cumberland, Md., 1845; d. Paris, France, 1903*), architect. Began career in Baltimore, Md., 1869; removed to New York City, 1877. Price laid out Tuxedo Park, N.Y., 1885–86, and designed many of the individual houses there; his largest and most lavish domestic work was "Georgian Court," 1898–1900, at Lakewood, N.J. He also did a great deal of work in Canada, including the Château Frontenac at Quebec.

PRICE, ELI KIRK (b. *East Bradford, Pa., 1797; d. 1884*), Philadelphia lawyer, law reformer. Was responsible as Pennsylvania legislator for passage of Consolidation Act, 1854, giving Philadelphia a new charter and unifying that city.

PRICE, ELI KIRK (b. *Philadelphia, Pa., 1860; d. 1933*), lawyer, Philadelphia civic leader. Grandson of Eli K. Price (1797–1884). Devoted himself to the growth and development of Fairmount Park and to the construction of the Philadelphia Museum of Art.

PRICE, GEORGE EDWARD MCCREADY (b. *Havelock, New Brunswick, Canada, 1870; d. Loma Linda, Calif., 1963*), fundamentalist advocate and geologist. Attended Battle Creek College and taught in Canada (1897–1904), then taught nursing and medical students in the College of Medical Evangelists in California (1906–12), which granted him a B.A.; taught at other Adventist institutions (1912–38). Led a spirited crusade against evolution and advocated the "new catastrophism." In the mid-1920's he was described as the principal scientific authority of the fundamentalists. Wrote *The New Geology* (1923), his most comprehensive and systematic book.

PRICE, GEORGE MOSES (*b. Poltava, Russia, 1864; d. New York, N.Y., 1942*), physician, public health worker. Child of Jewish parents, he immigrated to the United States in 1882. After working as a New York City sanitary inspector and as an inspector for the Tenement Commission, he took his degree in medicine at New York University, 1895. Until 1913 he combined a career in private practice with continued activity in the field of public health. His major accomplishments came as an outgrowth of his association *post* 1910 with the International Ladies' Garment Workers Union; he served as director of the garment industry's Joint Board of Sanitary Control, 1910–25, and was responsible for investigations and legislation that corrected flagrant abuses in factory sanitary conditions and safety. After 1913 he gave his full professional time to the work of the Union Health Center, which he had founded; this was the first attempt by a trade union to provide medical services for its members and was a model for later union clinics. Price was author of, among other works, *The Modern Factory: Safety, Sanitation, and Welfare* (1914).

PRICE, HIRAM (*b. Washington Co., Pa., 1814; d. 1901*), banker, railroad builder. Removed to Davenport, Iowa, 1844. Congressman, Republican, from Iowa, 1863–69 and 1877–81; U.S. commissioner of Indian affairs, 1881–85.

PRICE, JOSEPH (*b. Rockingham Co., Va., 1853; d. Philadelphia, Pa., 1911*), physician, surgeon, gynecologist. M.D., University of Pennsylvania, 1877. After working as a ship's doctor, he began work at the Philadelphia Dispensary and made its clinic for women one of the best known and largest in the country. Working thereafter in three private hospitals in Philadelphia (among them the present Joseph Price Memorial), Price had vast influence as clinical teacher in the forming of gynecology and abdominal surgery as specialties. He revolutionized surgical practices in maternity and abdominal operations.

PRICE, RODMAN MCCAMLEY (*b. Sussex Co., N.J., 1816; d. 1894*), naval officer, politician. Played active role in U.S. occupation of California, 1846; as alcalde of Monterey, was said to be first American to exercise judicial authority in California. Congressman, Democrat, from New Jersey, 1851–53; governor, 1854–57.

PRICE, STEPHEN (*b. New York, N.Y., 1782; d. 1840*), theatrical manager. Purchased share in Park Theatre, New York City, 1808; became sole manager and lessee *ca.* 1815. Price began the practice of importing European stars for performances at his theater and for road tours under his direction.

PRICE, STERLING (*b. Prince Edward Co., Va., 1809; d. Missouri, 1867*), lawyer, farmer, Missouri legislator, soldier. Removed to Missouri *ca.* 1831; settled in Chariton Co. After rising to rank of brigadier general in the Mexican War, he was anti-Benton Democratic governor of Missouri, 1852–56. Chosen president of the Missouri convention of 1860 as a conditional Union man, he took command of the state troops by appointment of Governor C. F. Jackson after the convention adjourned. The aggressive policies of Unionists such as Frank P. Blair and Nathaniel Lyon drove him into support of the Southerners. Displaying high military ability at the battles of Wilson's Creek and Lexington, 1861, he retreated with his forces into Arkansas, where they joined the Confederate army, 1862. His subsequent campaigns in Mississippi and Arkansas, gave him great reputation and made him perhaps the leading secession figure west of the Mississippi.

PRICE, THEODORE HAZELTINE (*b. New York, N.Y., 1861; d. New York, 1935*), cotton merchant and broker. Founded and edited *Commerce and Finance*, 1912–35; compiled trade handbooks.

PRICE, THOMAS FREDERICK (*b. Wilmington, N.C., 1860; d. Hong Kong, China, 1919*), Roman Catholic clergyman, cofounder of Maryknoll. Graduated St. Charles College, Maryland, 1881; St. Mary's Seminary, Baltimore, Md. Ordained, 1886, the first native North Carolinian to become a Catholic priest, he worked in his own state and was editor of an apologetics magazine, *Truth*, 1896–1911. Together with Rev. James A. Walsh, Price established the Catholic Foreign Mission Society of America (Maryknoll), 1910–11.

PRICE, THOMAS LAWSON (*b. near Danville, Va., 1809; d. 1870*), businessman, railroad builder, politician. Removed to Missouri and settled in Jefferson City, 1831; was a leader in development of Missouri railroads. A pro-Benton Democrat and state officeholder, he became an unconditional Unionist and a War Democrat congressman, serving ably as an opponent of Radical measures through the year 1862. He was later prominent in the reorganization of the Democratic party in Missouri.

PRICE, THOMAS RANDOLPH (*b. Richmond, Va., 1839; d. 1903*), philologist, Confederate soldier. Taught Greek and English at University of Virginia, 1870–82; professor of English, Columbia University, 1882–1903.

PRICE, WILLIAM CECIL (*b. probably Russell Co., Va., 1818; d. Chicago, Ill., 1907*), lawyer. Removed as a young man to Missouri, where he held various offices and served as a Democratic legislator. For 20 years before the Civil War, he agitated for repeal of the Missouri Compromise and the removal of restrictions upon slavery. A fanatical secessionist, he served briefly in the Confederate army.

PRICE, WILLIAM THOMPSON (*b. Jefferson Co., Ky., 1846; d. 1920*), dramatic critic. Founded American School of Playwriting, New York, 1901; was regarded within the profession as an authority on dramatic construction.

PRIEST, EDWARD DWIGHT (*b. Northfield, Mass., 1861; d. 1931*), electrical engineer. Graduated present Worcester Polytechnic, 1884. Specialist in railway electrification problems; designed special type of motor for use on elevated railroads.

PRIESTLEY, JAMES (*b. probably Virginia, date unknown; d. Nashville, Tenn., 1821*), educator. Studied at Liberty Hall Academy (forerunner of Washington and Lee); was principal or director of a great number of academies and colleges *post* 1788, including Cumberland College at Nashville.

PRIESTLEY, JOSEPH (*b. near Leeds, England, 1733; d. Northumberland, Pa., 1804*), scientist, educator, Unitarian theologian. Attended a local grammar school where he learned Latin, Greek, and shorthand; studied Hebrew with John Kirkby, a Congregational clergyman. When ill health forced him to leave school, he taught himself modern languages, the rudiments of Chaldee, Syriac, Arabic, and also natural history. Entered Daventry, a dissenting academy, 1751, where his tendencies to Arianism took firm root. Unsuccessful as a pastor, 1755–61, he went as tutor in belles lettres to Warrington, the chief dissenting academy in England, where he found learned associates and adequate channels of expression for his many interests. He preached, wrote, and published, among others, *A Chart of Biography* (1765), for which he received a doctorate from Edinburgh. He was the first teacher to give formal instruction in modern history, and his teaching of the sciences was entirely new in secondary education. In 1767, because of his wife's poor health and his need for a larger salary, he took charge of the Mill Hill congregation in Leeds, which he held until 1772 when he became librarian to Lord Shelburne. In 1780 he removed to Birmingham and was minister of the New Meeting there until the 1791 riots when his expressed sympathies with the

French Revolution resulted in the burning of his house, his books, and all his effects. Deciding to immigrate to America, he arrived in New York City, June 4, 1794. His arrival caused much public comment and he was visited by the leading New York dignitaries; two weeks later in Philadelphia he again received public acclaim. Averse to the distractions of Philadelphia, he made his home in Northumberland, Pa., but made frequent trips to Philadelphia to address the American Philosophical Society and continued to write and perform scientific experiments.

Although his scientific interests had been manifested early, he had not begun active experimentation until 1766. In February 1767, he published *The History and Present State of Electricity*, to which he appended an account of experiments performed between June 1766 and the beginning of 1767. In this work he stated, but did not fully prove, the inverse-square law of electrostatics, explained the formation of the (Priestley) rings occurring as a result of electrical discharges on metallic surfaces, attempted to measure electrical resistance and impedance, and proposed an explanation of the oscillatory nature of the discharge from a Leyden jar. More important perhaps is his isolation of oxygen (before November 1771) and description of its basic properties (1774). His discovery was confirmed by Lavoisier, 1775. He also isolated and described eight other gases, including ammonia and carbon monoxide, and wrote a notable study of optics, *The History and Present State of Discoveries Relating to Vision, Light and Colours* (1772).

Priestley's versatility and his peculiar qualities of mind were more clearly manifested in his theological and political writings than in his science. He left Daventry Academy an Arian; by the time he went to Warrington he had rejected the Atonement and the inspiration of the sacred text. In 1775 he put forward the doctrine of the homogeneity of man, which brought upon him the charge of atheism. His principal theological works were written in America, and he was the chief protagonist of the Unitarian movement here. His books in this field include *A General History of the Christian Church* (1790–1802) and *A General View of the Arguments for the Unity of God . . .* (1793, 1812). In politics he was a utilitarian and a republican, but he prided himself on never having joined a political party. His *Essay on the First Principles of Government* (1768) strongly influenced Jeremy Bentham. In two anonymous pamphlets (1769 and 1774) he rebuked the British government for its treatment of the colonies. Prior to 1783 he was intimate with Edmund Burke, but Priestley's republican leanings estranged them, and their differences were brought to a dramatic climax by the French Revolution. Priestley's *Letters to the Right Honourable Edmund Burke* (1791) led more or less directly to the riots which destroyed his house in Birmingham. He was also opposed to slavery. In American politics he sided with the Democratic-Republicans against the Federalists. By 1797 or earlier he had become acquainted with Thomas Jefferson, who turned to him for counsel about the projected University of Virginia and wrote of his "affectionate respect" for Priestley.

PRIME, BENJAMIN YOUNGS (*b.* Huntington, N.Y., 1733 *o.s.; d.* Huntington, 1791), physician. Graduated College of New Jersey, 1751; M.D., University of Leiden, 1764; studied also in England and Scotland. Practiced *post* 1764 in New York City and in Huntington. Author of *The Patriot Muse* (London, 1764) and a number of writings in support of the American cause subsequent to the passage of the Stamp Act. His *Columbia's Glory; or British Pride Humbled* (1791) reviewed the events of the Revolutionary War.

PRIME, EDWARD DORR GRIFFIN (*b.* Cambridge, N.Y., 1814; *d.* New York, N.Y., 1891), Presbyterian clergyman. Grandson of Benjamin Y. Prime; brother of William C. and Samuel I. Prime.

PRIME, SAMUEL IRENAEUS (*b.* Ballston, N.Y., 1812; *d.* 1885), Presbyterian clergyman, author. Grandson of Benjamin Y. Prime; brother of Edward D. G. and William C. Prime. Assistant editor, *New York Observer*, 1840–49; editor in chief, 1851–85. During his editorship the *Observer* was a leading Presbyterian organ and a strong force in American life. He was author also of a number of popular books and was the conductor *post* 1853 of the "Editor's Drawer" in *Harper's Magazine*.

PRIME, WILLIAM COWPER (*b.* Cambridge, N.Y., 1825; *d.* New York, N.Y., 1905), journalist, educator. Grandson of Benjamin Y. Prime; brother of Edward D. G. and Samuel I. Prime. Graduated College of New Jersey (Princeton), 1843. After practicing law in New York City, 1846–61, Prime served as editor of the *N.Y. Journal of Commerce*, 1861–69, and remained a partner in the paper thereafter. An authority on numismatics and old porcelain, he was a principal promoter of the Metropolitan Museum of Art and was professor of the history of art at Princeton *post* 1884. He was author also of a number of books, including *Owl Creek Letters* (1848), *The Old House by the River* (1853), *Boat Life in Egypt and Nubia* (1857), and *Pottery and Porcelain* (1878).

PRINCE, FREDERICK HENRY (*b.* Winchester, Mass., 1859; *d.* Biarritz, France, 1953), investment banker and society figure. Studied at Harvard (1878–80). Prince turned a modest inherited fortune into a financial empire mostly through the acquisition of railroads. By the 1930's, he was worth $250 million. In 1933, Prince sponsored a plan to consolidate all major trunk lines in the nation into seven major lines; President Roosevelt was at first in favor of this plan, but was forced to back down because of the cost. After 1933, Prince concentrated on the meat packing industry in Chicago, acquiring the chairmanship of the executive committee of Armour and Company in 1934, and restoring that company to solvency. An avid sportsman. Prince remained active as a sailor and polo player into his seventies.

PRINCE, LE BARON BRADFORD (*b.* Flushing, N.Y., 1840; *d.* Flushing, 1922), lawyer, jurist. Son of William R. Prince. Prominent as a New York Republican politician, Prince served as chief justice of New Mexico Territory, 1879–82; he compiled and published *The General Laws of New Mexico* (1880). As governor of New Mexico, 1889–93, he was responsible for the adoption of the territory's first public school code and for the creation of the University of New Mexico.

PRINCE, MORTON (*b.* Boston, Mass., 1854; *d.* 1929), physician, psychologist. Graduated Harvard, 1875; Harvard Medical School, 1879. Becoming early interested in abnormal psychology, he made further studies at Vienna, Strasbourg, Paris, and Nancy, and was encouraged by S. Weir Mitchell to specialize in neurology and psychotherapy. From 1885–1913, he was physician for diseases of the nervous system at Boston City Hospital and taught at Harvard and at Tufts. He founded the *Journal of Abnormal Psychology*, 1906, and edited it up to the time of his death. Among his books the most famous is *The Dissociation of a Personality* (1906). He developed a psychology of the abnormal which integrates neurology, general psychology, and allied subjects effectively and with great benefit to them all. In addition to his professional work, he was active in civic projects in Boston.

PRINCE, THOMAS (*b.* Sandwich, Mass., 1687; *d.* Boston, Mass., 1758), theologian, scholar, bibliophile. Graduated Harvard, 1709. Became associate minister at Old South Church, Boston, 1718, and served in this connection until his death. An early collector and preserver of colonial documentary material, in particular the Mather papers, he was author of, among many other writings, *A Chronological History of New England in the Form of Annals* (1736), a pioneer attempt at accurate recording of the New

England past. A supporter of George Whitefield, Prince was a vital factor in sustaining the evangelist's popularity. He collected a remarkable library of Americana, which was left to Old South; some of the books were destroyed during the British occupation at Boston, but many of them are now preserved in Boston Public Library.

PRINCE, WILLIAM (*b. probably Flushing, N.Y., ca. 1725; d. Flushing, 1802*), nurseryman. American pioneer in selling budded or grafted stock and in breeding new varieties, particularly of the plum.

PRINCE, WILLIAM (*b. Flushing, N.Y., 1766; d. 1842*), nurseryman. Son of William Prince (*ca. 1725–1802*). Continued his father's work and introduced the Isabella grape *ca. 1816*, once important in New York wine culture.

PRINCE, WILLIAM ROBERT (*b. Flushing, N.Y., 1795; d. Flushing, 1869*), nurseryman. Son of William Prince (1766–1842). Associated with his father in business and coauthor with him of *A Treatise on the Vine* (1830) and *The Pomological Manual* (1831). He was author also of *Prince's Manual of Roses* (1846) and of many articles for gardening and horticultural publications.

PRING, MARTIN (*b. Devonshire, England, ca. 1580; d. Bristol, England, 1626*), naval commander, explorer. Made a successful trading voyage in command of the *Speedwell* and the *Discoverer* to the Cape Code area, 1603; made a chart of the coast of Virginia, 1606. Active in Far East waters, 1613–21, he was made a freeman of the Virginia Co. and given 200 acres of Virginia land, 1621.

PRINGLE, CYRUS GUERNSEY (*b. East Charlotte, Vt., 1838; d. 1911*), plant breeder and collector. Made important botanical explorations *post* 1880 in the Pacific states and Mexico. Built up herbarium at the University of Vermont.

PRINGLE, HENRY FOWLES (*b. New York, N.Y., 1897; d. Washington, D.C., 1958*), journalist and biographer. Studied at Cornell University. Through the 1920's, Pringle worked for various New York newspapers before turning to biography. In 1931, he published *Theodore Roosevelt*, which won the Pulitzer Prize. From 1932 to 1943, he taught at the School of Journalism at Columbia University. His other major work was *The Life and Times of William Howard Taft* (1939).

PRINGLE, JOEL ROBERTS POINSETT (*b. Georgetown Co., S.C., 1873; d. San Diego, Calif., 1932*), naval officer. Graduated Annapolis, 1892. Performed distinguished service as chief of staff to Admiral Sims, 1917–19, and as liaison with the British command at Queenstown, Ireland, having charge of destroyer refitting. After holding a number of other important appointments, he died while serving as commander, battleships, U.S. Fleet, with the rank of vice admiral.

PRINGLE, JOHN JULIUS (*b. Charleston, S.C., 1753; d. 1843*), lawyer, planter, South Carolina legislator and federal official. Attorney general of South Carolina, 1792–1808.

PRINTZ, JOHAN BJÖRNSSON (*b. Bottnaryd, Sweden, 1592; d. 1663*), soldier, colonial governor. After an adventurous career as a mercenary soldier and officer in the Swedish army, he was appointed governor of New Sweden, 1642, and arrived at Fort Christina (Wilmington, Del.), Feb. 15, 1643. He was handicapped from the outset by a shortage of men and supplies, and during the last five years of his administration, 1648–53, the Swedish government left him to shift for himself. Reputed to weigh 400 pounds and famous for severity and profanity, he was amply qualified for his work, making the colony a prosperous enterprise for his country. His harshness as a ruler, however, created conflicts between him and his settlers, which came to a head in July 1653, when a group of them petitioned to send two men to present their grievances to the home government. Printz regarded this move as rebellion and hanged the leader of the dissidents. Resigning the governorship to his son-in-law in September, he returned to Sweden.

PRITCHARD, FREDERICK JOHN (*b. Camanche, Iowa, 1874; d. Washington, D.C., 1931*), plant breeder. Graduated University of Nebraska, 1904. Did important work on the sugar beet and on disease-resistant tomatoes for the U.S. Department of Agriculture *post* 1910.

PRITCHARD, JETER CONNELLY (*b. Jonesboro, Tenn., 1857; d. 1921*), lawyer, legislator. U.S. senator, Republican, from Tennessee, 1894–1903. An able progressive, he became a U.S. circuit judge, 1904, and presiding judge of the circuit court of appeals (4th Circuit), 1913.

PRITCHETT, HENRY SMITH (*b. Fayette, Mo., 1857; d. Santa Barbara, Calif., 1939*), astronomer. Studied at the U.S. Naval Observatory under Asaph Hall; Ph.D., University of Munich, 1895. President, Massachusetts Institute of Technology, 1900–05; first president, Carnegie Foundation for Advancement of Teaching, 1905–30.

PROCTER, JOHN ROBERT (*b. Mason Co., Ky., 1844; d. Washington, D.C., 1903*), geologist, civil service reformer. Director of the Kentucky geological survey, 1879–93; U.S. Civil Service Commission member and president, 1893–1903.

PROCTER, WILLIAM (*b. Baltimore, Md., 1817; d. 1874*), pharmacist, teacher. Ran a drugstore in Philadelphia, Pa., *post* 1844. Professor at Philadelphia College of Pharmacy, 1846–66; editor, *American Journal of Pharmacy*, 1850–71; a founder of the American Pharmaceutical Association, 1852.

PROCTOR, FREDERICK FRANCIS (*b. Dexter, Maine, ca. 1851; d. Larchmont, N.Y., 1929*), vaudeville theater owner and manager.

PROCTOR, HENRY HUGH (*b. near Fayetteville, Penn., 1868; d. 1933*), Congregational clergyman, black leader. Graduated Fisk University, 1891; Yale Divinity School, 1894. Became prominent as pastor of First Congregational Church, Atlanta, Ga., 1894–1919; it became the first institutional church for blacks in the South and through its various agencies served some 10,000 persons. He was pastor of the Nazarene Congregational Church, Brooklyn, N.Y., *post* 1920. A pioneer in all interracial movements, he was elected moderator of the New York City Congregational Church Association, 1926.

PROCTOR, JOSEPH (*b. Marlboro, Mass., 1816; d. 1897*), actor, manager. Made professional debut at Boston, 1833; enjoyed early success playing principal character in *Nick of the Woods* (an adaptation of the novel by Robert M. Bird). Playing in support of many star actors in classic dramas, he was distinctly a "strong" actor of the Edwin Forrest school.

PROCTOR, LUCIEN BROCK (*b. Hanover, N.H., 1823; d. Albany, N.Y., 1900*), lawyer, writer of New York legal history and biography.

PROCTOR, REDFIELD (*b. Proctorsville, Vt., 1831; d. Washington, D.C., 1908*), businessman, lawyer, Union soldier. Republican governor of Vermont, 1878–80; able and efficient U.S. secretary of war, 1889–91; U.S. senator from Vermont, 1891–1908. Proctor was particularly interested as a senator in the committees on agriculture and military affairs. His speech on

Cuba, delivered in March 1898, helped condition the United States for the war with Spain.

PROCTOR, WILLIAM COOPER (*b. Glendale, Ohio, 1862; d. Cincinnati, Ohio, 1934*), soap manufacturer, philanthropist. President of Procter & Gamble *post* 1907. Instituted employee profit-sharing plans, stock ownership, and pensions; guaranteed employees 48 workweeks in each calendar year, 1923.

PROFACI, JOSEPH (*b. Villabati, Sicily, 1897; d. Bay Shore, N.Y., 1962*), organized crime leader. Came to the United States in 1921; by 1929 he controlled crime in Staten Island, N.Y., and by 1930 was head of one of New York City's five crime families, a position he retained for life. He used mob money from numbers, narcotics, and prostitution to establish about twenty legitimate businesses, including the importation of olive oil. Found guilty of obstructing justice (1957), but the conviction was overturned on appeal. His citizenship was revoked in 1958, a decision also reversed on appeal. Estimated revenues from his Brooklyn rackets were between $100 million and $200 million over a twenty-five-year period.

PROKOSCH, EDUARD (*b. Eger, Austria-Hungary, 1876; d. near New Haven, Conn., 1938*), Germanic philologist. Came to America, 1898. M.A., University of Chicago, 1901; Ph.D., University of Leipzig, 1905. Taught at University of Wisconsin, 1905–13; University of Texas, 1913–19; Bryn Mawr, 1920–27; New York University, 1927–28; and Yale, *post* 1929.

PROPHET   *See* TENSKWATAWA.

PROSSER, CHARLES SMITH (*b. Columbus, N.Y., 1860; d. Columbus, Ohio, 1916*), educator, geologist. After serving in a number of government and teaching positions, he was head of the Department of Historical Geology at Ohio State, 1901–16. His published work dealt mainly with the stratigraphy and paleontology of the Paleozoic formations of New York, Kansas, Maryland, and Ohio.

PROUD, ROBERT (*b. Yorkshire, England, 1728; d. Philadelphia, Pa., 1813*), educator, historian. Immigrated to Philadelphia, 1759; was master of the Friends Public School for many years. Author of *The History of Pennsylvania in North America* (1797–98), a valuable work based on original research.

PROUTY, CHARLES AZRO (*b. Newport, Vt., 1853; d. Newport, 1921*), lawyer. Member of Interstate Commerce Commission, 1896–1914; supported Theodore Roosevelt's railroad policy. *Post* 1914, he served as director of the commission's Bureau of Valuation, organizing it and shaping its policies and philosophy of value.

PROVOOST, SAMUEL (*b. New York, N.Y., 1742 o.s.; d. 1815*), Episcopal clergyman. Graduated King's College (Columbia), 1758; studied at Peterhouse, Cambridge; ordained in London, 1766. Returning to New York as assistant minister of Trinity Church, his Whig sympathies caused conflict with Loyalist members of the parish and he resigned, 1771. In 1784 he was chosen rector of St. Paul's, New York City, and served in the following year as chaplain of Congress. He was consecrated first bishop of New York, February 1787, by the Archbishop of Canterbury in the chapel of Lambeth Palace, London, and officiated until 1801 when private reasons caused him to offer his resignation. The resignation was refused, but thereafter the work of the diocese was done by a coadjutor. Bishop Provoost was chairman of the committee which drafted the constitution of the Episcopal church and was responsible for the necessary changes in the Book of Common Prayer following the creation of a distinctly American Episcopal church.

PROVOST, ETIENNE (*b. Canada, ca. 1782; d. St. Louis, Mo., 1850*), hunter, guide. Associated at times with William Ashley and the American Fur Co., he is supposed to have been the first white man to visit the Great Salt Lake and was possibly the discoverer of South Pass. He was guide for J. J. Audubon on his western expedition, 1843.

PROVOSTY, OLIVIER OTIS (*b. Pointe Coupée Parish, La., 1852; d. New Orleans, La., 1924*), jurist, Louisiana legislator. Justice, Louisiana Supreme Court *post* 1901; chief justice, 1922. He retired from public life at the end of 1922.

PRUDDEN, THEOPHIL MITCHELL (*b. Middlebury, Conn., 1849; d. 1924*), pathologist, bacteriologist. Graduated Sheffield Scientific School, Yale, 1872; Yale Medical School, 1875. Studied also in Heidelberg, Vienna, Berlin. Taught histology and pathology at New York College of Physicians and Surgeons. The first to make diphtheria antitoxin in the United States, he was for years adviser to Hermann M. Biggs of the New York health department. He was coauthor with Francis Delafield in the writing of the great standard textbook *Hand-book of Pathological Anatomy and Histology* (1885). In 1901, he became one of the scientific directors of the Rockefeller Institute.

PRUD'HOMME, JOHN FRANCIS EUGENE (*b. St. Thomas, Virgin Islands, 1800; d. Georgetown, D.C., 1892*), engraver, banknote designer. Came to New York City as a child. Long active in his profession, he was with the U.S. Bureau of Engraving and Printing, 1869–85.

PRUYN, JOHN VAN SCHAICK LANSING (*b. Albany, N.Y., 1811; d. Clifton Springs, N.Y., 1877*), lawyer. Official and general counsel of New York Central Railroad *post* 1853, he was directly or indirectly connected with many of the leading financial and railroad enterprises in the United States. Active also in politics and philanthropy, he was chancellor of the University of the State of New York, 1862–77, and was responsible for the establishment of the state board of charities.

PRUYN, ROBERT HEWSON (*b. Albany, N.Y., 1815; d. 1882*), lawyer. Graduated Rutgers, 1833. After service as a Whig New York State legislator and officeholder, he followed W. H. Seward into the Republican party and was commissioned U.S. minister resident in Japan, October 1861, serving in that post with great tact and ability until 1865.

PRYBER, CHRISTIAN.   *See* PRIBER, CHRISTIAN.

PRYOR, ARTHUR W. (*b. St. Joseph, Mo., 1870; d. West Long Branch, N.J., 1942*), musician. Member of a family of professional musicians, he was a master of the trombone. His rise to national fame began in 1892, when he became a featured soloist with John Philip Sousa's newly formed band. Forming his own band in 1903, Pryor was successful on tour, in seasonal engagements at resorts, and as a recording artist. Among his many compositions, the most popular was a novelty, "The Whistler and His Dog." He retired in 1933.

PRYOR, NATHANIEL (*b. probably Amherst Co., Va., ca. 1775; d. Osage Agency, Indian Territory, 1831*), soldier, trader. Sergeant in Lewis and Clark expedition; served with distinction in the battle of New Orleans.

PRYOR, ROGER ATKINSON (*b. near Petersburg, Va., 1828; d. New York, N.Y., 1919*), soldier, Confederate brigadier general, jurist. Graduated Hampden-Sydney College, 1845. Practiced law at Petersburg; was associated at various times with the *Southside Democrat*, the Washington *Union*, and the *Richmond Enquirer*; founded *The South*, 1857, as an ultrasouthern newspaper. Congressman, Democrat, from Virginia, 1859–61. Visiting Charleston, S.C., with other Virginians, 1861, he urged the attack on Fort Sumter, but declined the honor of firing the first shot in favor of Edmund Ruffin. After serving gallantly through the Civil War, he removed to New York City, September 1865, was admitted to the New York bar and practiced successfully. He was a justice of the New York Supreme Court, 1896–99.

PUGET, PETER RICHINGS.   *See* RICHINGS, PETER.

PUGH, ELLIS (*b. Dolgelley, North Wales, 1656; d. 1718*), Quaker preacher and writer. Resident in or near Philadelphia, 1687–1706, and *post* 1708. Author of *Annerch ir Cymru* (Philadelphia, 1721), the first book in Welsh known to have been printed in America.

PUGH, EVAN (*b. Jordan Bank, Pa., 1828; d. 1864*), chemist. Studied at Leipzig and Heidelberg; Ph.D., Göttingen, 1856; studied also in England. Organizer and president, Agricultural College of Pennsylvania (present Pennsylvania State College), 1859–64.

PUGH, GEORGE ELLIS (*b. Cincinnati, Ohio, 1822; d. Cincinnati, 1876*), lawyer, Ohio legislator. U.S. senator, Democrat, from Ohio, 1855–61. Opposed extreme Southern position; active in urging acceptance of Crittenden Compromise. Ran for lieutenant governor of Ohio on ticket with C. L. Vallandigham, 1863; assisted Charles O'Conor as defense counsel in case of Jefferson Davis.

PUJO, ARSÈNE PAULIN (*b. Calcasieu Parish, La., 1861; d. New Orleans, La., 1939*), lawyer. Congressman, Democrat, from Louisiana, 1903–13. An active member of the National Monetary Commission, 1908–12, Pujo in 1911 became chairman of the House Banking and Currency Committee, and in 1912 headed a subcommittee whose investigations of the money trusts (including J. P. Morgan & Co.) led to important reforms.

PULASKI, CASIMIR (*b. Podolia, Poland, ca. 1748; d. off Savannah, Ga., 1779*), Polish patriot, Revolutionary cavalry leader. Joined father in active rebellion against foreign domination of Poland, 1768; after defeat, fled to Turkey, 1772; arrived in Paris, France, 1775. Introduced by Benjamin Franklin and Silas Deane, Pulaski arrived in Boston, July 1777, and was recommended by George Washington to Congress for command of all the Continental cavalry. After service at Brandywine and Germantown, he commanded cavalry during the winter of 1777–78 and acted with General Anthony Wayne in foraging for the troops at Valley Forge. Refusing to serve under Wayne, he resigned his command, March 1778. After ill success with an independent cavalry corps of his own and guard service at Minisink on the Delaware River, he was ordered in February 1779 to South Carolina. Defeated in an attempt to block the British advance northward from Savannah, Ga., he joined forces with General Benjamin Lincoln in Georgia. During the siege of Savannah, he was mortally wounded while charging the enemy lines.

PULITZER, JOSEPH (*b. Mako, Hungary, 1847; d. in harbor of Charleston, S.C., 1911*), journalist. Obtained passage to America by enlisting in Union army at Hamburg, Germany; arrived in Boston, 1864; served for a year with the 1st New York (Lincoln) Cavalry. Removing to St. Louis, Mo., he performed all sorts of menial labor until he became in 1868 a reporter on the German daily *Westliche Post*. He soon became a prominent figure in local journalism and held important civic positions, 1869–72. He campaigned on behalf of Horace Greeley, 1872, and disappointment over the defeat of the Liberal Republican movement brought him to the Democratic party, to which he remained loyal for the rest of his life. In 1874 he bought the bankrupt St. Louis *Staats-Zeitung*, whose membership in the Associated Press he sold to the

St. Louis *Daily Globe* for a good profit. This gave him leisure to study law and he was admitted to the bar, 1876.

He settled finally on a career in journalism in 1878 when he bought the *St. Louis Dispatch* and merged it with the *Post*. The new daily, the *St. Louis Post-Dispatch*, was a huge success and a leader in fighting municipal and political corruption. In 1883 he bought the New York *World* from Jay Gould and converted it into a profitable venture and a great national political force. The program which Pulitzer announced on acquiring control made him immediately popular with labor. The *World* declared that it opposed the aristocracy of money, but that it wished to become the organ of the true American aristocracy, "the aristocracy of labor." Main items in its program were the taxation of luxuries, inheritances, large incomes, monopolies, and large and privileged corporations; the enactment of a tariff for revenue only; the reform of the civil service; the punishment of corrupt officials and purchasers of votes at elections; and the punishment of employers who coerced their employees at election times. Success was immediate, owing to this policy and to the sensational methods and "stunts" which Pulitzer employed. In 1887 he founded the *Evening World*.

Early in 1896 the morning *World* resorted to extreme "yellow journalism" in its rivalry with the rising dailies of William Randolph Hearst and was only redeemed by the personal supervision of Pulitzer, who had retired from direct management in 1887. Although ill and blind, he impressed upon the *World* its subsequent high character as an internationally minded, extremely well-informed daily, with a remarkably able editorial page, no longer an organ of the working classes but of all who favored liberal and democratic policies. The influence of the *World* upon the political life and the press of the country was very great after it abandoned its career of sensationalism and vulgarity. It opposed jingoism and special privilege; it was the fearless scourge of political corruption; it was completely free of domination by advertisers. After Pulitzer's death the papers passed to his sons, who failed to keep them profitable and sold them to the Scripps-Howard newspaper group. His will provided for the establishment of a school of journalism at Columbia University and for the annual awards known as the Pulitzer Prizes.

PULITZER, JOSEPH, JR. (*b. New York, N.Y., 1885; d. St. Louis, Mo., 1955*), newspaper editor and publisher. Studied at Harvard University (1904–06). Sent by his father as an apprentice to the *St. Louis Post-Dispatch* in 1906, Joseph Jr. acquired the newspaper in 1912. By expanding into radio (1922) and television (1947), the Pulitzer Publishing Co. became a major force in the communications industries. An ardent defender of the freedom of the press, Pulitzer often defended his reporters and cartoonists in court. He was conservative in politics and supported Landon and Dewey in their bids for the presidency. He stayed at the *Post-Dispatch* until his death.

PULITZER, RALPH (*b. St. Louis, Mo., 1879; d. New York, N.Y., 1939*), journalist, publisher. Son of Joseph Pulitzer. Graduated Harvard, 1900. Editor-publisher of the New York *World*, 1911–30, he gave primary attention to news and a liberal editorial policy.

PULLMAN, GEORGE MORTIMER (*b. Brocton, N.Y., 1831; d. 1897*), inventor, industrialist. Removed to Chicago, Ill., 1855, where he became a successful contractor. By 1858, he had brought his earlier-formulated idea for improved railroad sleeping accommodations to the point of remodeling several coaches of the Chicago & Alton Railroad into sleeping cars. On failure of railroads generally to adopt his cars, Pullman removed to Colorado, 1859, where he conducted a general store and worked on plans for improvement of his scheme. Returning to Chicago,

1863, he and an associate completed plans and secured a patent for the basic idea of a folding upper berth in April 1864 and a second patent covering the lower berth arrangement, September 1865. Their first car, *Pioneer*, was enthusiastically received. Pullman and his partner constructed a number of other similar cars and in 1867 organized the Pullman Palace Car Co. Pullman's business ability made it the greatest car-building organization in the world.

PULTE, JOSEPH HIPPOLYT (*b. Meschede, Westphalia* [*Prussia*], *1811; d. Cincinnati, Ohio, 1884*), homeopathic physician, author. M.D., University of Marburg, 1833; came to America, 1834. Practiced mainly in Cincinnati.

PUMPELLY, RAPHAEL (*b. Owego, N.Y., 1837; d. Newport, R.I., 1923*), geologist, explorer. Attended Royal School of Mines, Freiberg, Saxony. Began work as mining engineer in southern Arizona, 1859. Worked in Japan with William P. Blake, 1861–63, as government geologist; traveled in Asia until 1865. His reputation as a mining geologist rests chiefly on his work in association with Thomas B. Brooks in the copper and iron districts of Michigan and the Lake Superior area. Restlessly active, he served at various times as state geologist of Missouri, as head of the New England division of the U.S. Geological Survey, and in other professional assignments. In 1903 and 1904 under auspices of the Carnegie Institution, he organized and conducted expeditions into central Asia seeking traces of prehistoric civilization and evidences of geological and climatic changes. His most important technical achievements were his studies of the loess of China and his discovery of the secondary nature of the iron ores of Michigan, together with his work on the paragenesis of the copper deposits there.

PUPIN, MICHAEL IDVORSKY (*b. Idvor, Banat, Austria-Hungary, 1858; d. New York, N.Y., 1935*), physicist. Born of illiterate but highly intelligent Serbian parents, he received his early education in Idvor and Panchevo, a nearby town. He studied at schools in Prague and during a trip to Vienna was befriended by an American couple who stirred his desire to study in America. In 1874, he arrived at Castle Garden, New York City, with five cents capital. Working at odd jobs in New York, he spent his spare time in the library of Cooper Union. A German theological student taught him Greek and Latin as preparation for his admission to Columbia University. Passing the examinations with honor, 1879, he graduated in 1883 and secured his citizenship papers. He went to Cambridge University for study of physics and mathematics, and then on to Berlin to study under Helmholtz; he received the Ph.D. degree from Berlin, 1889. Returning to Columbia, 1889, as teacher of mathematical physics in the Department of Electrical Engineering, he was promoted to professor of electromechanics, 1901, a position which he held until his retirement in 1931.

His teaching brought him in contact with many practical engineering problems. Henry A. Rowland, for example, had reported distortions in an alternating current when it was magnetizing iron in electrical power apparatus. It consisted of addition of higher harmonics to the normal harmonic changes in current. Recollecting Helmholtz' work in analyzing complex sound waves by means of resonators, Pupin developed an analogous method for electrical waves and invented the electrical resonator, consisting of a circuit having a variable condenser and inductance akin to the tuning unit in a radio. When this direct method was applied to the current under study, its harmonics were readily obtained. Many later applications of this method were developed.

In 1894 he became interested in the theoretical problem of the propagation of waves in a vibrating string and applied his findings to solving the problem of attenuation of electrical currents in conveying speech in long-distance telephony. He had found that a disturbance set up in a string which was loaded with weights at equal intervals did not die out as quickly as in a string which was not loaded. Others had shown that transmission efficiency of long telephone or telegraph circuits could be improved by increasing the "uniformly distributed inductance," but no one had found a way of doing it. Pupin's study of the analogous string problem showed him the proper spacing for inductance coils along the telephone circuit. Coils inserted at about one for every four or five miles on overhead wires and at one to two miles in cables resulted in reduction of both attenuation and distortion. When the discovery of X rays was announced in 1895, Pupin constructed a tube and obtained the first X-ray photograph in America on Jan. 2, 1896. He also discovered secondary X-radiation.

After a long period of recuperation from the loss of his wife, 1896, and the effects of illness, he returned to Columbia to work on problems of radio transmission. E. H. Armstrong was one of his pupils. After World War I he ceased personal research; in 1919, he acted as an adviser to the Yugoslav delegation to the Paris Peace Conference.

An eloquent speaker with a poetic imagination, Pupin never failed to stress idealism in science and life. There is also much evidence of his deeply religious nature in his autobiography *From Immigrant to Inventor* (1923), which in 1924 received a Pulitzer Prize. Other of his works were a book on thermodynamics (1894), *Serbian Orthodox Church* (1918), *Yugoslavia* (1919), *The New Reformation* (1927), *Romance of the Machine* (1930), and 65 articles of scientific interest. He received 34 patents for his inventions.

PURCELL, JOHN BAPTIST (*b. Mallow, Ireland, 1800; d. 1883*), Roman Catholic clergyman. Came to America, 1818; attended the seminary at Mount St. Mary's College, Emmitsburg, Md., 1820–23; completed theological studies in Paris, where he was ordained, 1826. After a brief period as professor of moral philosophy and as president of Mount St. Mary's, Purcell was consecrated bishop of Cincinnati, 1833. An able and tactful administrator with a strong interest in education, he was, with the exception of John Hughes, the most influential figure in the American hierarchy of his time and was named archbishop, July 1850. His more than 50 years of distinguished service to the church were unfortunately shadowed in 1879 by the failure of a private bank for which he was nominally responsible and he was succeeded by his coadjutor, William H. Elder.

PURDUE, JOHN (*b. Huntingdon Co., Pa., 1802; d. Lafayette, Ind., 1876*), merchant, philanthropist. Principal benefactor of Purdue University.

PURDY, CORYDON TYLER (*b. present Wisconsin Rapids, Wis., 1859; d. Melbourne, Fla., 1944*), structural engineer. C.E., University of Wisconsin, 1886. Originally a designer of bridges, he was quick to see the possibilities of steel framing for high-building construction; in partnership with Lightner Henderson, 1893–1916 (*post* 1917 as chairman of the board of the corporation that succeeded the partnership), he displayed a mastery of the structural design of large and complex buildings. The first of his works with a frame constructed entirely of steel was the Marquette Building in Chicago, 1894; his best-known New York City skyscrapers were the Flatiron Building, 1903, and the Metropolitan Tower, 1909.

PURDY, LAWSON (*b. Hyde Park, N.Y., 1863; d. Port Washington, N.Y., 1959*), tax and zoning expert. Studied at Trinity College and New York Law School. Purdy achieved a national reputation while serving as secretary of the N.Y. Tax Reform Association (1896–1906); president of the N.Y. City Department of Taxes and Assessments (1906–17); vice president of the National Tax Association (1907–12); and president of the National

Municipal League (1916–19). His main achievement was the enactment of legislation for New York City that required publication of assessment rolls (1902) and the separate listing of land and total value of an assessed property (1906). Purdy was also involved in the enactment of the first comprehensive zoning law in 1916.

PURNELL, BENJAMIN (*b. Mayville, Ky., 1861; d. 1927*), founder of an eccentric religious sect, the House of David.

PURNELL, WILLIAM HENRY (*b. Worcester Co., Md., 1826; d. 1902*), lawyer, politician. Graduated Delaware College (present University of Delaware), 1846. Active in Maryland politics as a Whig and Know-Nothing, later as chairman of the Union party, 1864–66. President of Delaware College, 1870–85; served thereafter as principal of Frederick Female Seminary (present Hood College) and as president of New Windsor College.

PURPLE, SAMUEL SMITH (*b. Lebanon, N.Y., 1822; d. 1900*), physician, editor. Practiced in New York City *post* 1844; was a founder and benefactor of the New York Academy of Medicine, whose library was formed around the nucleus of books bequeathed to the academy by him.

PURRY, JEAN PIERRE (*b. Neuchâtel, Switzerland, 1675; d. ca. 1736*), colony promoter. Proposed settlement of European Protestants in Carolina, 1724–26; established Purrysburgh, S.C., with a group of Swiss immigrants, 1732–34.

PURSH, FREDERICK (*b. Grossenhain, Saxony, 1774; d. Montreal, Canada, 1820*), botanist, horticulturist, explorer. Came to America, 1799. Aided by Benjamin S. Barton, Pursh made two memorable journeys of botanical exploration in 1806 and 1807: the first through the mountains from western Maryland to the North Carolina border and back along the coast, the second across the Pocono region of Pennsylvania to central New York and thence east to the Vermont Green Mountains. He was author of *Flora Americae Septentrionalis* (1814), the first complete flora of America north of Mexico, and of a posthumously published journal of his explorations.

PURVIANCE, DAVID (*b. Iredell Co., N.C., 1766; d. Preble Co., Ohio, 1847*), frontier preacher and legislator in Tennessee, Kentucky, and Ohio. A founder of the so-called Christian denomination.

PURYEAR, BENNET (*b. Mecklenberg Co., Va., 1826; d. Madison Co., Va., 1914*), educator. Professor of chemistry, Richmond College (present University of Richmond), 1850–58 and 1865–95. A pioneer in applying chemistry to Virginia agriculture, he had a wide influence among farmers.

PUSEY, CALEB (*b. Berkshire, England, ca. 1650; d. Chester Co., Pa., 1727 o.s.*), miller, Pennsylvania provincial legislator, Quaker controversial writer. Immigrated to Pennsylvania, 1682; erected Chester Mills near Upland, 1683, which he managed until 1717.

PUSEY, WILLIAM ALLEN (*b. Elizabethtown, Ky., 1865; d. Chicago, Ill., 1940*), dermatologist, authority on syphilis. Graduated Vanderbilt University, 1885; M.D., New York University, 1888. Practiced in Chicago.

PUSHMATAHA (*b. probably present Noxubee Co., Miss., ca. 1765; d. Washington, D.C., 1824*), Choctaw chief. Opposed Tecumseh's efforts to form an Indian confederacy; led Choctaw warriors against the Creek in campaign under Andrew Jackson, 1813–14.

PUTNAM, ARTHUR (*b. Waveland, Miss., 1873; d. near Paris, France, 1930*), sculptor. Patronized by Willis Polk and E. W.

Scripps, he was particularly effective in bronzes of western animals.

PUTNAM, CHARLES PICKERING (*b. Boston, Mass., 1844; d. 1914*), physician. Brother of James J. Putnam; grandson of James Jackson. A noted specialist in pediatrics and orthopedics in Boston *post* 1871, he was also the most important leader in charitable and social work in that city *post* 1875.

PUTNAM, EBEN (*b. Salem, Mass., 1868; d. Wellesley Farms, Mass., 1933*), editor, genealogist, historian. Son of Frederic W. Putnam.

PUTNAM, FREDERIC WARD (*b. Salem, Mass., 1839; d. Cambridge, Mass., 1915*), archaeologist, naturalist. Strongly influenced by J. L. R. Agassiz while studying at Harvard, Putnam began his long career as a museum administrator at the Essex Institute. Influential in the founding of the Peabody Academy of Science, Salem, he served as its director, 1869–73. As curator of the Peabody Museum at Harvard *post* 1874, he revolutionized the methods of museum administration; *post* 1894, he served also as curator of anthropology, American Museum of Natural History, New York City. To these activities and many other advisory posts, Putnam added that of teaching, for he was appointed Peabody professor of archaeology at Harvard in 1887. In the rise and development of anthropology in America, Putnam played a leading, perhaps the foremost, part and was largely responsible for its acceptance as a university study.

PUTNAM, GEORGE HAVEN (*b. London, England, 1844; d. New York, N.Y., 1930*), Union soldier, publisher. Son of George P. Putnam, he succeeded his father as head of the firm of G. P. Putnam & Son, 1872, and remained its active head until 1930. He played a prominent part in securing the copyright act of 1909.

PUTNAM, (GEORGE) HERBERT (*b. New York, N.Y., 1861; d. Quissett, Mass., 1955*), librarian and lawyer. Studied at Harvard and at Columbia Law School. In 1884, he became head of the Minneapolis Athenaeum (later the Minneapolis Public Library). In 1895, he was appointed librarian of the Boston Library. In 1899, director of the Library of Congress in Washington. He remained in that position until 1939, when he became librarian emeritus. As chief of the Library of Congress, Putnam increased the collection sevenfold, added the annex, and acquired the funding for the Library of Congress Trust Fund (donated by Elizabeth Sprague Coolidge) which established the Library as a major center of chamber music, and raised the library to the level of one of the greatest centers of learning and research in the world. Putnam was president of the American Library Association in 1898 and 1904.

PUTNAM, GEORGE PALMER (*b. Brunswick, Maine, 1814; d. New York, N.Y., 1872*), publisher. Became partner in Wiley & Putnam, 1840; after a number of vicissitudes, established firm of G. P. Putnam & Son, 1866. Maintained close working relations with the British book trade; was an early advocate of international copyright.

PUTNAM, GIDEON (*b. Sutton, Mass., 1763; d. 1812*), developer of Saratoga Springs, N.Y., as a spa and resort, 1802–12.

PUTNAM, HELEN CORDELIA (*b. Stockton, Minn., 1857; d. Providence, R.I., 1951*), physician and health educator. Studied at Vassar College and the Women's Medical College of Pennsylvania (M.D., 1889). Practiced medicine in Providence, R.I. from 1892. Vice president of the American Academy of Medicine, 1894 and 1897; president, 1908. A specialist in child care, Putnam focused on physical education and sanitary conditions in schools. Helped found the American Association for the Study and Prevention of Infant Mortality; this became the Child Health Organization in 1923, and, later, the American Academy of Pediatrics.

PUTNAM, ISRAEL (*b. Salem Village, present Danvers, Mass., 1718; d. Brooklyn [earlier Pomfret, Conn.], 1790*), soldier. Served throughout French and Indian War with Connecticut forces and with Robert Rogers as one of his rangers; promoted major of colony forces, 1758, and lieutenant colonel, 1759. In 1764, he campaigned with Bradstreet's expedition in Pontiac's War. Active in the organization of the Sons of Liberty at the time of the Stamp Act troubles, he served in the General Assembly, 1766–67. After an exploring trip to the Gulf of Mexico and up the Mississippi River, 1773, he became chairman of the committee of correspondence of his home town, 1774, and in the same year was made lieutenant colonel of the 11th Regiment, Connecticut Militia. Appointed major general in the Continental army, 1775, he was a leading spirit in planning for the battle of Bunker Hill and was everywhere during the whole of that fight, although he seems not to have been in supreme command. Ordered to New York after the siege of Boston was ended in March 1775, he played a controversial part in the battle of Long Island and thereafter sunk steadily in the regard of George Washington and the other generals. His dilatoriness as commander of the forces in the Hudson Highlands brought him a sharp rebuke; a court of inquiry, however, exonerated him, but in December 1779 a stroke of paralysis ended his military career. Active, brave, and disinterested, he failed through incapacity in the superior commands to which his popularity advanced him.

PUTNAM, JAMES JACKSON (*b. Boston, Mass., 1846; d. 1918*), neurologist. Brother of Charles P. Putnam. Graduated Harvard, 1866; Harvard Medical School, 1870. After making special studies in Leipzig, Vienna, and London, he returned to Boston, where he practiced, and taught at Harvard Medical School, 1874–1912. In 1872, he started one of the first neurological clinics in the United States at Massachusetts General Hospital; he was the author of many important papers in the fields of structural and functional neurology.

PUTNAM, JAMES OSBORNE (*b. Attica, N.Y., 1818; d. 1903*), lawyer, Whig and Republican public servant and diplomat. Maintained a lifelong interest in the educational and cultural institutions of Buffalo, N.Y.; was a founder of University of Buffalo, 1846, and its chancellor, 1895–1902.

PUTNAM, NINA WILCOX (*b. New Haven, Conn., 1885; d. Cuernavaca, Mexico, 1962*), author. From the acceptance of a short story by *Ainslee's* magazine in 1907, she had continuing success as a popular author of romances, high comedy, and colloquial humor. Introduced her most popular character, Marie La Tour, in a story for *Saturday Evening Post*, where she published regularly for two decades. Wrote twenty-two books, including *In Search of Arcady* (1912), *Sunny Bunny* (1917), and *Paris Love* (1931). Wrote more than 1,000 short stories, and twelve were made into movies, including "Sitting Pretty" (1933). She wrote the syndicated column "I and George" for North American Newspaper Alliance (1928–38).

PUTNAM, RUFUS (*b. Sutton, Mass., 1738; d. 1824*), soldier, Ohio pioneer. Cousin of Israel Putnam. A self-taught surveyor and millwright, Putnam fought in the French and Indian War and rose to rank of brigadier general in the Continental service during the Revolution, serving with credit as an engineer and as a field commander. Active in the organization of the Ohio Co. Putnam became superintendent of the new colony and was with the first party of settlers to arrive at Marietta, April 1788. Commissioned brigadier general, U.S. Army, 1792, he made the Treaty of Vincennes, September 1792, with the lower Wabash tribes. As surveyor general of the United States, 1796–1803, he surveyed

the military tract (inaccurately). As delegate to the Ohio constitutional convention, 1802, he exerted strong influence against the admission of slavery.

PUTNAM, RUTH (*b. Yonkers, N.Y., 1856; d. Geneva, Switzerland, 1931*), author. Daughter of George P. Putnam; sister of George H. Putnam and Mary C. P. Jacobi. Specialist in the history of the Netherlands.

PUTNAM, WILLIAM LE BARON (*b. Bath, Maine, 1835; d. 1918*), jurist, diplomat, expert in equity. Judge, U.S. Circuit Court of Appeals (1st Circuit), 1892–1917.

PYE, WATTS ORSON (*b. near Faribault, Minn., 1878; d. 1926*), Congregational clergyman. As missionary to China *post* 1907, he directed pioneer activity in the provinces of Shansi and Shensi from headquarters at Fenchow.

PYLE, ERNEST TAYLOR (*b. near Dana, Ind., 1900; d. Ie Shima, Ryukyu Islands, Japan, 1945*), newspaper columnist, war correspondent. Popularly known as Ernie Pyle. Attended Indiana University. After serving in various capacities on several newspapers, he had risen by 1932 to be managing editor of the Washington, D.C., *Daily News*. In 1935 he was given an assignment as roving correspondent by the Scripps-Howard management and wrote a syndicated column of informal, chatty commentary, which was very well received. At the outbreak of World War II he went overseas. His reporting from the successive fronts was truthful and graphic, and had a special quality of sincerity that resulted from his concern with the combat infantryman whose perils and feelings he shared. After covering the liberation of Paris, he went home for a brief rest; he then returned to the battlefront, this time in the Pacific area, where he was killed by enemy machine-gun fire. In 1944 he had been awarded the Pulitzer Prize for his war correspondence.

PYLE, HOWARD (*b. Wilmington, Del., 1853; d. Florence, Italy, 1911*), artist, author, teacher. Educated in Quaker schools; studied art with a Flemish teacher (Van der Weilen) in Philadelphia and briefly at the Art Students League, New York City. Removing to New York, 1876, he developed his own style and technique through patient labor and experiment, encouraged by Edwin Abbey, A. B. Frost, F. S. Church, and others. Successful *post* 1878 as a magazine illustrator, he returned to Wilmington, where he set up his studio. Accurate in delineation of the characters and events of early American history, he was most effective in pen-and-ink work, but was one of the first in the field when the new process for reproducing pictures in color came into being. Important as are the illustrations which he did for the work of other men, his reputation really rests upon his own tales and the pictures he made for them. Outstanding among them are *The Merry Adventures of Robin Hood* (1883), *The Wonder Clock* (1888), *Otto of the Silver Hand* (1888), *Men of Iron* (1892), and *The Story of Jack Ballister's Fortunes* (1895); he also wrote and illustrated a variety of books which dealt with pirates, appealing as much to adults as to children. He taught illustration at Drexel Institute, Philadelphia, 1894–1900, and thereafter in his own school at Wilmington. By somewhat unorthodox methods of instruction, he developed such artists as Maxfield Parish, N. C. Wyeth, and Frank Schoonover.

PYLE, ROBERT (*b. London Grove, Pa., 1877; d. West Chester, Pa., 1951*), nurseryman and authority on roses. Studied at Swarthmore College. Pyle acquired his own mailorder nursery specializing in roses in 1907. One of the nation's leading authorities on roses, he was president of the American Rose Society from 1923 to 1932; founder of the American Association of Botanical Gardens and Arboretums; a member of the Advisory Council of the National Arboretum in Washington, D.C.; president of the American Horticultural Society from 1932 to 1935; and trustee and vice president of All-American Rose Selections. Trustee of Swarthmore College from 1910.

PYLE, WALTER LYTLE (*b. Philadelphia, Pa., 1871; d. 1921*), ophthalmologist, medical writer.

PYNCHON, JOHN (*b. Springfield, Essex, England, ca. 1626; d. 1702/3*), colonial industrialist, public servant. Son of William Pynchon. Came to New England with his father as a child. Conducted the family trading business *post* 1652 and exercised a controlling influence in and about Springfield, Mass.

PYNCHON, THOMAS RUGGLES (*b. New Haven, Conn., 1823; d. New Haven, 1904*), Episcopal clergyman. Graduated Washington College (present Trinity), Hartford, 1841; was professor of science there, 1855–77, and professor of moral philosophy, 1877–1902. President of the college, 1874–83.

PYNCHON, WILLIAM (*b. England, ca. 1590; d. near Windsor, England, 1662*), trader, colonial official. Immigrated from Springfield, Essex, England, 1630; settled first at Dorchester and started fur-trading operations at Roxbury, Mass., where he was first signer of the church covenant. He had brought considerable capital to the colony and served it as assistant, 1630–36, and as treasurer, 1632–34. Active in the immigration to the Connecticut River valley, he was appointed one of the commissioners to govern the new settlement, March 1635/6. He was at Springfield, May 1636, when, with seven others, he signed an agreement concerning land allotments and settling a minister. Falling out with Thomas Hooker, Pynchon severed connections with the River Colony and supported the claim of Massachusetts to Springfield, which took no further part in the Connecticut government after 1638. Largest landowner in Springfield, Pynchon virtually ruled the community and was successful as a trader, shipping furs direct to London down the Connecticut River. Reelected a Massachusetts assistant, 1642, he was elected annually thereafter until 1651. He returned to England probably in the spring of 1652 after deeding his property at Springfield to his son John Pynchon and to his sons-in-law. Shortly before his departure he had written a tract critical of the orthodox view of the Atonement which the Massachusetts clergy denounced as heretical.

Q

QUACKENBUSH, STEPHEN PLATT (*b. Albany, N.Y., 1823; d. Washington, D.C., 1890*), naval officer. Retired as rear admiral, 1885, after 45 years of valuable service, particularly with the Civil War blockade forces off Virginia and North Carolina.

QUANAH (*b. probably northern Texas, ca. 1845; d. near Fort Sill, Oklahoma, 1911*), Comanche chief. Son of a Kwahadi chief and a white captive, Cynthia Parker. Refusing to accept the Medicine Lodge treaty of 1867, he terrorized the frontier settlements in Texas until he was badly defeated at the fight at Adobe Walls in present Hutchinson Co., Texas, June 1874. Adapting himself to the white man's way after his surrender, 1875, he fostered building and agriculture among his tribesmen, popularized education, and discouraged extravagance.

QUANTRILL, WILLIAM CLARKE (*b. Canal Dover, Ohio, 1837; d. Louisville, Ky., 1865*), guerrilla chief. Settled in Kansas, 1857. Journeyed to Utah, 1858; worked as gambler. Returning to Kansas, he taught school in the winter of 1859–60, and thereafter engaged in horse-stealing, escaping arrest by fleeing to Missouri. Irregularly connected with the Confederate Army at the start of the Civil War, he soon appeared as the chief of a guerrilla band which operated in Missouri and Kansas, robbing mail coaches, raiding and sacking Unionist communities and farms. Formally outlawed in 1862, he mustered his troop into Confederate service and was given the rank of captain. In August 1863, he destroyed the town of Lawrence, Kans. Dissension arising among his followers, they broke up into smaller bands. He made a raid into Kentucky early in 1865 and in May of that year was fatally wounded near Taylorsville.

QUARTER, WILLIAM (*b. King's Co., Ireland, 1806; d. 1848*), Roman Catholic clergyman. Immigrated to Canada, 1822, where he was denied admission to seminaries because of his youth. Accepted by Dr. John Dubois at Mount St. Mary's, Emmitsburg, Md., he made his theological studies and was ordained, September 1829. After serving as a New York pastor, he was consecrated first bishop of Chicago, 1844.

QUARTLEY, ARTHUR (*b. Paris, France, 1839; d. New York, N.Y., 1886*), painter of seascapes. Came to New York as a boy; was taught to draw by his father, an engraver. Worked in Baltimore, Md., 1862–75, thereafter, in New York and in summers at Isle of Shoals, N.H.

QUAY, MATTHEW STANLEY (*b. Dillsburg, Pa., 1833; d. Beaver, Pa., 1904*), politician, lawyer, Union soldier. Rose to prominence in Pennsylvania politics by success in promoting gubernatorial campaign of Andrew G. Curtin, 1860. Reentering politics on his return from distinguished service in the Civil War, he served as secretary of Pennsylvania, 1872–78, and as recorder of Philadelphia; he was also chairman of the Republican state committee. Unable to gain control of the political machine in Philadelphia, he resigned the position of recorder and was again appointed commonwealth secretary, 1879, holding this position until 1882.

Elected state treasurer in 1885, from this time until his death he held undisputed political control of Pennsylvania and was U.S. senator *post* 1887 with the exception of a hiatus in 1899–1900. Quay's influence was decisive in matters connected with tariff legislation, but he is chiefly to be remembered for his genius as a political maneuverer. He always had a machine to work with, but he would build up a new one for each major contest and by aligning his enemies against one another was able to triumph over them all. His break with Benjamin Harrison and his failure to take an active part in the campaign of 1892 was a prime factor in the Democratic victory of that year. An educated man with a passion for literature, he displayed an utter contempt for ordinary political ideals and he was one of the best-hated men in politics.

QUAYLE, WILLIAM ALFRED (*b. Parkville, Mo., 1860; d. Baldwin, Kans., 1925*), Methodist clergyman, educator, bishop.

QUEEN, WALTER W. (*b. Washington, D.C., 1824; d. Washington, 1893*), naval officer. Retired as rear admiral, 1886, after varied sea and shore service, notably in Civil War blockade of North Carolina.

QUELCH, JOHN (*b. London, England, ca. 1665; d. Boston, Mass., 1704*), pirate. Unlawfully in command of the Boston brigantine *Charles*, Quelch plundered a number of Portuguese ships off the coast of Brazil, November 1703–February 1704. On the return of the *Charles* to Marblehead, Mass., Quelch and some of his crewmen were arrested, tried, and hanged on June 30. The speed and questionable procedures of the trial, together with the eagerness of Boston authorities to confiscate and divide the loot, have caused the case to be characterized as "judicial murder."

QUESNAY, ALEXANDRE-MARIE (*b. Saint-Germain-en-Viry, France, 1755; d. Saint-Maurice, France, 1820*), soldier, educator. Came to Virginia, April 1777; served as captain in Revolutionary army until autumn 1778. Taught school in Virginia, Philadelphia, New York, 1780–86. Returning to France, in the spring of 1787 he presented a plan for an Academy of the United States of America to Thomas Jefferson, then U.S. minister to France. His plan called for an extensive system of schools and universities throughout the United States centering around an establishment at Richmond. On Jefferson's statement that America was too poor to support such undertakings, the project failed.

QUEZON, MANUEL LUIS (*b. Baler, Tayabas [now Quezon Province], Luzon, Philippine Islands, 1878; d. Saranac Lake, N.Y., 1944*), lawyer, statesman. After serving as an officer in Emilio Aguinaldo's insurrection against the U.S. takeover in the Philippines, 1899–1901, he resumed his interrupted studies at the University of Santo Tomás (Manila) and received the LL.B. degree in 1903. Later that year he returned to his native province to practice. He was elected governor of Tayabas, 1906, running on a platform advocating immediate independence; the next year he was elected to the first Philippine Assembly, where he became floor leader of the majority party, the Nacionalista. By vote of the

Assembly, he served as one of the two Philippine resident commissioners to the United States, 1909–16. In public, a fiery partisan of independence, he realized that his people had much to gain in the material way from its postponement and so cooperated with the United States in many matters that might otherwise have become open issues. He helped draft the second Jones Bill, which provided for some autonomy but deferred independence until a stable government and economy had been well established. When the bill was passed in 1916, he returned to the Philippines as a national hero. Elected president of the new Philippine Senate, he shared leadership with Sergio Osmeña, speaker of the Assembly, rivaling him in building up a personal political machine or power bloc, as a process of Filipinization of government and industry got under way. The arrival of Leonard Wood as U.S. governor general in 1921 put a stop to Filipinization, and by opportunistic maneuvering Quezon put himself forward as the symbol of opposition to colonial status as reasserted by General Wood's governing policies. When his rivals Osmeña and Manuel Roxas on a mission in 1932–33 obtained from the U.S. Congress legislation that provided for Philippine independence after ten years, he saw to it that the proposal was rejected by the Philippine legislature. He then led a new mission to the United States and secured from Congress the Tydings-McDuffie Act (1934), which differed little from the previous legislation but which was ratified unanimously by his legislature. Forming a new coalition with Osmeña and his followers, Quezon was elected president of the Commonwealth—the transitional government that was to precede full independence—in 1935. Giving lip service to democratic forms and reforming principles, and hampered by agrarian and labor discontent, he steadily concentrated power in his own hands. In 1940 the Assembly granted him emergency powers and amended the constitution to permit his continuance in office. At the outbreak of war with Japan he went first to Corregidor, and then to the United States where, with Osmeña, he maintained a war cabinet.

QUICK, JOHN HERBERT (*b.* Grundy Co., Iowa, 1861; *d.* Columbia, Mo., 1925), lawyer, Iowa politician, author. His best work as a writer is contained in a trilogy of Iowa novels, *Vandemark's Folly* (1921), *The Hawkeye* (1923), and *The Invisible Woman* (1924), vivid, truthful pictures of pioneer life.

QUIDOR, JOHN (*b.* Tappan, N.Y., 1801; *d.* Jersey City, N.J., 1881), portrait and figure painter. Pupil of John W. Jarvis. Best known for paintings illustrative of scenes from the works of Washington Irving.

QUIGG, LEMUEL ELY (*b.* near Chestertown, Md., 1863; *d.* 1919), journalist, press agent, politician. Congressman, Republican, from New York, 1894–99; a political lieutenant of Thomas C. Platt. Ousted from Republican leadership of New York County by Benjamin B. Odell, 1900, he became a promoter of the traction interests of Thomas Fortune Ryan.

QUIGLEY, JAMES EDWARD (*b.* Oshawa, Canada, 1854; *d.* Rochester, N.Y., 1915), Roman Catholic clergyman. Raised in Rochester, N.Y.; graduated St. Joseph's College, Buffalo, N.Y., 1872; made theological studies in Buffalo, at the University of Innsbruck, and at Rome. Bishop of Buffalo, 1897–1903; archbishop of Chicago thereafter.

QUILL, MICHAEL JOSEPH (*b.* Kilgarvan, Co. Kerry, Ireland, 1905; *d.* New York, N.Y., 1966), labor leader. Immigrated to New York in 1926; worked for the Interborough Rapid Transit Company; in 1934 was a charter member of the Transport Workers Union at its founding and elected its president in 1935, a post he held for life. He was a militant unionist prone to theatrical gestures and extravagant rhetoric who won contracts for tens of thousands of workers in New York, Philadelphia, and Chicago.

Elected to New York City Council (1937–39, 1943–49) and vice president of the Congress of Industrial Organizations (1950); he was the only head of a major CIO union to oppose merger with the American Federation of Labor. Under his leadership, the TWU reached a membership of 135,000 by 1966. He led transit strikes in several cities and died shortly after a major strike against the New York City system in 1966, which paralyzed the city for twelve days.

QUIMBY, PHINEAS PARKHURST (*b.* Lebanon, N.H., 1802; *d.* Belfast, Maine, 1866), founder of mental healing in America. Trained as a clockmaker, he took up mesmerism, 1838, abandoning it in 1847 for mental healing which he practiced *post* 1859 in Portland, Maine. Mary Baker Eddy was a patient of his, 1862 and 1864, and derived her basic ideas from his teaching.

QUINAN, JOHN RUSSELL (*b.* Lancaster, Pa., 1822; *d.* Baltimore, Md., 1890), physician, medical historian. Practiced in Calvert, Co., Md., and in Baltimore.

QUINBY, ISAAC FERDINAND (*b.* Morris Co., N.J., 1821; *d.* Rochester, N.Y., 1891), soldier, professor of mathematics and natural science. Graduated West Point, 1843; served in Mexican War. He was associated with the University of Rochester, 1851–85, except for a period of distinguished Civil War service as colonel, 13th New York Volunteers, in 1861, and as a brigade and division commander under General U. S. Grant from March 1862 until resignation because of ill health in December 1863. He led the Yazoo Pass expedition, March 1863.

QUINCY, EDMUND (*b.* Boston, Mass., 1808; *d.* 1877), reformer, author. Son of Josiah Quincy (1772–1864). Graduated Harvard, 1827. An active associate of William L. Garrison and other Abolitionists, he held office in a number of radical antislavery societies but was personally devoid of fanaticism.

QUINCY, JOSIAH (*b.* Boston, Mass., 1744; *d.* at sea, off the harbor of Gloucester, Mass., 1775), lawyer, Revolutionary patriot. Graduated Harvard, 1763. Author, *post* 1767, of a number of essays strongly urging the patriot side in the difficulties with England; these were published in the Boston newspapers under several pseudonyms. He was associated with John Adams as counsel for the British soldiers on trial for the Boston massacre, 1770. Developing tubercular symptoms, he made a trip to Charleston, S.C., 1773, during which he met many of the prominent Southern patriots. In May 1774, he published his chief political work, *Observations of the Act of Parliament Commonly Called the Boston Port-Bill*. In the hope that he might present the case of the colonies correctly in England, he proceeded to London late in 1774 where he had interviews with Lord North, Lord Dartmouth, and other leading men without result.

QUINCY, JOSIAH (*b.* Braintree, now Quincy, Mass., 1772; *d.* Boston, 1864), politician, municipal reformer, educator. Son of Josiah Quincy (1744–1775); nephew of William Phillips. Graduated Phillips Andover in 1786; Harvard, 1790. Congressman, Federalist, from Massachusetts, 1805–13. Becoming a friend of John Randolph of Roanoke and minority leader in Congress, he opposed the Embargo and nonintercourse system as cowardly, futile, and unconstitutional. He also maintained that admission of any territory by majority vote without consent of all the original federators would virtually dissolve the Union. Advocating preparedness for war in the congressional session beginning November 1811 (hoping thereby to restore the Federalists to power by exposing the administration's supposed hypocrisy in this matter), he changed his position completely early in 1812 and opposed war legislation. After leaving Congress, he entered the Massachusetts senate where he continued his campaigns against the war, slave representation, and Southern dominance until 1820, when the Federalists dropped him for insurgency. Elected to the Massachusetts lower house and chosen its speaker, he resigned, 1821, to take a place on the Boston municipal bench. As mayor of Boston, 1823–27, he instituted a great program of city improvement and reform. His administration of Harvard as its president, 1829–45, was able and businesslike but not particularly distinguished for academic initiative, although he showed a genius for choosing good faculty members—among them, Jared Sparks, Henry Wadsworth Longfellow, and Benjamin Peirce. Deeply interested in the law school, he reformed it and made it into an academic professional school with the aid of Joseph Story. He was author of a number of books of which *The History of Harvard University* (1840) is probably best remembered.

QUINCY, JOSIAH PHILLIPS (*b. Boston, Mass., 1829; d. 1910*), author, historian. Grandson of Josiah Quincy (1772–1864). Graduated Harvard, 1850. Assisted his uncle Edmund Quincy in antislavery work; contributed fiction to periodicals; author of a variety of historical material in *Proceedings* of Massachusetts Historical Society.

QUINE, WILLIAM EDWARD (*b. St. Ann, Isle of Man, 1847; d. Chicago, Ill., 1922*), physician, educator. Came to America as a boy; graduated from Chicago Medical College, 1869. *Post* 1870, he taught with distinction at the Chicago Medical College and at the Chicago College of Physicians and Surgeons (*post* 1897 University of Illinois).

QUINN, ARTHUR HOBSON (*b. Philadelphia, Pa., 1875; d. Philadelphia, 1960*), educator, literary historian, biographer. Studied at the University of Pennsylvania (Ph.D., 1899); taught at the University of Pennsylvania (1894–1945). One of the first teachers of American literature and drama, Quinn was instrumental in making the study of native writers academically acceptable. His best work was a biography of *Edgar Allan Poe* (1941). Author of *A History of the American Drama from the Beginning to the Civil War* (1923) and *Literature of the American People* (1951).

QUINN, EDMOND THOMAS (*b. Philadelphia, Pa., 1868; d. New York, N.Y., 1929*), sculptor, painter. Studied at Pennsylvania Academy of Fine Arts under Thomas Eakins, and in France and Spain. Attained distinction as a portraitist and as a sculptor of ideal figures. Notable among his works are the reliefs for the battle monument at King's Mountain, S.C. (1908) and the statue of Edwin Booth as Hamlet in Gramercy Park, New York City.

QUINTARD, CHARLES TODD (*b. Stamford, Conn., 1824; d. 1898*), physician, Episcopal clergyman. Brother of George W. Quintard. After practicing medicine in Georgia and Tennessee, he was ordained in 1856 and became rector of Calvary Church, Memphis, Tenn., and a little later rector in Nashville. After distinguished service in the Confederate Army as chaplain and surgeon, he was elected bishop of Tennessee, 1865. As educator, his most important work was the "second founding" of the University of the South at Sewanee, 1866–72.

QUINTARD, GEORGE WILLIAM (*b. Stamford, Conn., 1822; d. New York, N.Y., 1913*), manufacturer of marine engines. Brother of Charles T. Quintard.

QUITMAN, JOHN ANTHONY (*b. Rhinebeck, N.Y., 1798; d. near Natchez, Miss., 1858*), lawyer, soldier. Settled in practice at Natchez, 1821. Quitman's activity as a Freemason contributed a great deal to his professional political progress. Chancellor of Mississippi, 1827–35, he became identified in 1834 with the political group known as "Nullifiers." Although the opinions of this group were not then popular in Mississippi, he was elected to the state senate, 1835, but was defeated in a campaign for Congress, 1836. Having recruited and led a company to the relief of the Texans (which took no part in the fighting), he was appointed brigadier general of Mississippi militia and served with ability in the Mexican War. As governor of Mississippi, 1850–51, he opposed the Compromise measures of 1850 and caused the legislature to protest their adoption by Congress. He was also concerned in a Cuban movement for independence which brought about his indictment at New Orleans by a federal grand jury. As congressman, 1855–58, he continued to act as a champion of the states' rights proslavery cause.

R

RABY, JAMES JOSEPH (*b. Bay City, Mich., 1874; d. near Midway, Ga., 1934*), naval officer. Graduated Annapolis, 1895. Commanded the cruiser *Albany*, June 1917–April 1918, escorting a larger number of ships in convoy to Europe than any other American naval vessel. Promoted rear admiral, 1927, he was for some time the only commissioned naval aviator in this grade. At the time of his death, he was commandant of all naval activities in the South.

RACHFORD, BENJAMIN KNOX (*b. Alexandria, Ky., 1857; d. Cincinnati, Ohio, 1929*), physiologist, pediatrician, philanthropist. M.D., Medical College of Ohio, 1882. After study at Berlin, he published a classic paper "The Influence of Bile on the Fat-Splitting Properties of the Pancreatic Juice" (*Journal of Physiology*, April 1891). Practicing in Cincinnati, Ohio, *post* 1894, he taught at the Medical College of Ohio (later University of Cincinnati), continued to make physiological experiments, and published several books on children's diseases. Elected director of pediatrics, Cincinnati General Hospital, 1897, he established a children's ward and one of the first outdoor wards in America for the treatment of tuberculosis of children. He initiated the Babies Milk Fund, 1909, and was associated with a number of other charities.

RACHMANINOFF, SERGEI VASILYEVICH (*b. estate of Oneg, near Novgorod, Russia, 1873; d. Beverly Hills, Calif., 1943*), composer, pianist, conductor. Cousin of Alexander Siloti. Studied at St. Petersburg Conservatory, 1882–85; at Moscow Conservatory, graduating as a pianist, 1891, and in composition, 1892. On the latter occasion he received the gold medal for his one-act opera *Aleko*, and in the same year composed his celebrated Prelude in C-sharp Minor. Earning his living as a piano teacher, he continued to compose; in 1901 he produced his very popular Second Piano Concerto. He turned next to conducting with outstanding success at the Moscow Bolshoi Theater, 1904–06. Desiring more time to compose, he lived for the next three years in Dresden, Germany. He made his American debut in the fall of 1909 at Smith College, and on Nov. 28 was soloist in the world premiere of his Third Piano Concerto in New York City. Residing in Moscow, 1910–17, he was conductor for part of that period of the Moscow Philharmonic Society orchestra. A steadfast opponent of the Soviet state, he left Russia at the time of the revolution and never returned. At this time, he deliberately set out on a career as a virtuoso pianist, traveling all over America and Europe and playing with incredible technical skill and startlingly original but convincing interpretation. He also continued to compose with great success and complete disregard of the work and theories of the musical revolutionaries of his time. He wrote four operas, one of which he left unfinished; three symphonies and two symphonic poems; a small but fine body of chamber music; impressive choral settings for the liturgy of the Russian Orthodox Church; more than seventy songs; and nearly a hundred piano pieces. Although he was at home in the United States, he remained loyal to the Czar; he did not become a U.S. citizen until 1943.

RADCLIFF, JACOB (*b. Rhinebeck, N.Y., 1764; d. Troy, N.Y., 1844*), lawyer, New York legislator and jurist. A founder (1804–05) of Jersey City, N.J. Federalist mayor of New York City, 1810 and 1815–17.

RADEMACHER, HANS (*b. Wandsbeck, Germany, 1892; d. Haverford, Pa., 1969*), mathematician and educator. Attended University of Göttingen (Ph.D., 1917). During 1917–19 published five papers on mathematical mapping and differentiability, including a paper that introduced the term "total differentiability." Taught at University of Berlin (1919–22), where he published a paper (1922) that introduced a type of orthogonal functions now known as Rademacher functions; at University of Hamburg (1922–25), where he turned his attention to number theory, a subject in which he made his most outstanding contributions; and at University of Breslau (1925–34), where he produced numerous studies in analytic number theory and mathematical functions. He achieved his most singular result at the University of Pennsylvania (1934–62): an expression for, and a means of calculating, the partition function $p(n)$, which enables one to determine in how many ways integers can be added together to yield a given integer. He became a naturalized citizen in 1943.

RADFORD, WILLIAM (*b. Fincastle, Va., 1809; d. 1890*), naval officer. Won particular distinction as commodore commanding ironclads in attacks on Fort Fisher, December 1864–January 1865; promoted rear admiral, 1866.

RADIN, MAX (*b. Kempen, Poland, 1880; d. Berkeley, Calif., 1950*), lawyer, philologist, educator. Son of a rabbi; came to the United States with parents, 1884. A.B., College of the City of New York, 1899. LL.B., New York University, 1902. Ph.D., Columbia University, 1909. Taught in the public schools of New York City, at the City College, and at Columbia, 1900–19. Professor of law, University of California at Berkeley, 1919–48, he was thereafter a member of the Institute for Advanced Study at Princeton. Author of a number of books and many contributions to journals, he is especially remembered for his historical and philosophical studies of the legal sources of the U.S. Constitution.

RADIN, PAUL (*b. Lodz, Poland, 1883; d. New York, N.Y., 1959*), anthropologist, linguist. Immigrated to the United States in 1884. Studied at the City College of New York and Columbia University (Ph.D., 1911). Taught at Mills College, the University of California, Oxford and Cambridge universities, and Black Mountain College. Studied primitive peoples, in particular the Indians of North America. Works include *Primitive Man As Philosopher* (1927), *Primitive Religion* (1937), and *The World of Primitive Man* (1953), and *The Trickster* (1956).

RADISSON, PIERRE ESPRIT (*b. France, 1636; d. ca. 1710*), explorer. Came to Canada *ca.* 1651; was captured by Iroquois, 1652, and adopted by them. Escaping, he returned to France, 1654, but came back to Canada in that same year. On westward journeys with his brother-in-law, the Sieur des Groseilliers, he became aware of the importance of the fur trade of inland North America and of the need to control either or both of the main exits for that trade—New York and Hudson's Bay. Angered by an injustice done them by the governor of Canada, Radisson and Groseilliers entered English service, and their reports led to the founding of the Hudson's Bay Co. (chartered 1670). Resuming his French connection, 1674, Radisson "passed over to England for good" *ca.* 1683. His own accounts of his voyages, valuable for vivid portrayal of the life of the early *coureurs de bois* in the north country, were edited as *Voyages of Peter Esprit Radisson* (Prince Society, 1885).

RAE, JOHN (*b. near Aberdeen, Scotland, 1796; d. Staten Island, N.Y., 1872*), economist, scientist. Immigrated to Canada, 1821. A wandering scholar, he resided thereafter in Canada, New York, Massachusetts, California, and the Hawaiian Islands His criticism of the doctrines of Adam Smith appeared as *Statement of Some New Principles on the Subject of Political Economy, etc.* (Boston, 1834). In the broad sense a collectivist, he was in the narrow sense a nationalist and protectionist; he worked out the time discount theory of interest long in advance of its better known expositors.

RAFFEINER, JOHN STEPHEN (*b. Walls, Tyrol, Austria, 1785; d. Brooklyn, N.Y., 1861*), Roman Catholic clergyman. Came to America, 1833, to be a missionary among German emigrants; served as vicar general for the Germans under Bishop John Hughes in New York and as vicar general of the Brooklyn diocese.

RAFINESQUE, CONSTANTINE SAMUEL (*b. near Constantinople, Turkey, 1783; d. Philadelphia, Pa., 1840*), naturalist. Of French and German parentage, he early showed a keen interest in natural history. Educated by private tutors, he never developed the orderly methods and mental attitudes of the trained scientist. Resident in Philadelphia, Pa., 1802–04, he worked in a merchant's counting-house but found time for considerable travel and made the acquaintance of President Jefferson and prominent scientists of the day. Journeying to Italy with his botanical collections, he lived at Palermo, was secretary to the U.S. consul, made an unhappy marriage, and conducted extensive research on the ichthyology of Sicilian waters. Engaging in the medical drug business, 1808, he set forth to settle in the United States, 1815, taking with him a stock of drugs and all his personal belongings. He arrived naked and penniless, for his ship was wrecked off Fisher's Island, and he narrowly escaped drowning. Befriended by Samuel L. Mitchill, he found work as a tutor in the Livingston family at Clermont. He then explored the Hudson Valley, Lake George, Long Island, and other regions, and in Philadelphia enjoyed the friendship of Zaccheus Collins, the Quaker naturalist. In 1818 he went to Lexington, Ky., to visit an old friend, John D. Clifford, through whose influence he was appointed professor of botany, natural history, and modern languages at Transylvania University. He traveled extensively in Kentucky and Tennessee and visited many points in Ohio, Indiana, and Illinois. After leaving Transylvania in 1826, he resided in Philadelphia but continued to make field trips.

No other American naturalist traveled so widely. He wrote and published incessantly but the eccentric manner in which he issued his works matched the general irregularity of his way of life. Botany and ichthyology continued to be his chief interests, but he wrote also on banking, economics, the Bible, and even produced verse. His descriptions of plants and fishes are often vague or inaccurate, and he had a passion for announcing new species. Behind this passion, however, lay the conviction, expressed more than once in his writings, that "every variety is a deviation which becomes a species as soon as it is permanent by reproduction. Deviations in essential organs may then gradually become new genera." He thus

had a glimpse, if no more than a glimpse, of the later development of biological thought. He was ahead of his generation in the United States, also, in advocating Jussieu's method of classification. During his last years he suffered from dire poverty, neglect, and ill-health, and some of his later schemes and activities indicate that he was not entirely sane, yet he was one of the great pioneers of natural science in America.

RAFTER, GEORGE W. (*b. Orleans, N.Y., 1851; d. Karlsbad, Austria, 1907*), civil engineer, specialist in water supply and control, and sewage disposal. Collaborated with William T. Sedgwick on a method of water analysis.

RAGUET, CONDY (*b. Philadelphia, Pa., 1784; d. Philadelphia, 1842*), lawyer, economist, U.S. consul and chargé d'affaires in Brazil, 1822–27. Active in journalism in Philadelphia and Washington, D.C., *post* 1827, he set forth acute analyses of tariff and currency questions in his *Free Trade Advocate, Banner of the Constitution,* and *The Examiner* which, with his other writings, give him a place among early students of the business cycle.

RAHT, AUGUST WILHELM (*b. Dillenburg, Germany, 1843; d. San Francisco, Calif., 1916*), metallurgist. Came to the United States, 1867; established a professional reputation in lead-silver smelting in Utah, Colorado, New Mexico, and Montana. He served as metallurgical expert for the Guggenheims, 1891–1910.

RAINES, JOHN (*b. Canandaigua, N.Y., 1840; d. Canandaigua, 1909*), lawyer, New York legislator, Union soldier. Congressman, Republican, from New York, 1889–93. As New York State senator, he was responsible for the "Raines Law" (1896) controlling the liquor traffic.

RAINEY, GERTRUDE MALISSA NIX PRIDGETT (*b. Columbus, Ga., 1886; d. Rome, Ga., 1939*), black blues singer, known as "Ma" Rainey. The first, and to some critics, the greatest of the blues singers, "Ma" Rainey sang what has come to be known as "country" blues.

RAINEY, HENRY THOMAS (*b. near Carrollton, Ill., 1860; d. St. Louis, Mo., 1934*), lawyer. Graduated Amherst, 1883. Congressman, Democrat, from Illinois, 1903–34, with the exception of the years 1921–23. A consistent progressive and ardent supporter of Presidents Wilson and F. D. Roosevelt, he was elected speaker of the House, March 1933, and pushed through the first New Deal measures with great efficiency.

RAINEY, JOSEPH HAYNE (*b. Georgetown, S.C., 1832; d. Georgetown, 1887*), first black to serve in the U.S. House of Representatives. Came into political prominence, 1867, as member of Republican executive committee in South Carolina. As congressman, 1870–79, he served with ability and tact and was particularly effective in speaking for civil rights. He later served as an agent for the U.S. Treasury Department.

RAINEY, "MA." *See* RAINEY, GERTRUDE MALISSA NIX PRIDGETT.

RAINS, CLAUDE (*b. London, England, 1889; d. Sandwich, N.H., 1967*), actor. Appeared in his first play at age eleven and by age eighteen was a stage manager set on an acting career. Performed in numerous productions in England, Australia, and the United States (1911–20), then began teaching at the Royal Academy of Dramatic Art. He achieved astounding success on Broadway in *The Constant Nymph* (1926) and signed with the Theatre Guild's repertory company. His first film was *The Invisible Man* (1933), one of many character roles in which he tended to be cast as madman or villain, such as the roguish prefect of police in *Casablanca* (1942). Signed a long-term contract with Warner

Brothers (1936) and played in numerous starring and supporting roles: *Anthony Adverse* (1936); *The Adventures of Robin Hood* (1938); *Mr. Smith Goes to Washington* (1939); *Mr. Skeffington* (1944); and *Notorious* (1946). Nominated for Academy Awards for *Mr. Smith*, *Casablanca*, *Mr. Skeffington*, and *Notorious*. Returned to the stage in 1950–51 and won six stage awards, including a Tony, for his role in *Darkness at Noon*.

RAINS, GABRIEL JAMES (*b. Craven Co., N.C., 1803; d. Aiken, S.C., 1881*), Confederate brigadier general. Brother of George W. Rains. Graduated West Point, 1827; served in the Seminole wars and in the war with Mexico. Commissioned in the Confederate Army, 1861, he served as explosives expert after holding field commands, 1861–62. He was particularly notable as the deviser of land mines and torpedoes and was engaged in much controversy over the ethics of their use.

RAINS, GEORGE WASHINGTON (*b. Craven Co., N.C., 1817; d. near Newburgh, N.Y., 1898*), soldier, Confederate munitions expert, inventor. Brother of Gabriel J. Rains. Graduated West Point, 1842; served with credit in the war with Mexico. Resigning from the army, 1856, he became president of an iron works at Newburgh, N.Y. Immediately upon his commissioning as major in the Confederate artillery, 1861, he was assigned to the procurement of gun powder and was placed in charge of all munitions operations, 1862, at Augusta, Ga. After the war, he was professor of chemistry and dean of the Medical College of Georgia until his retirement, 1894.

RAINSFORD, WILLIAM STEPHEN (*b. near Dublin, Ireland, 1850; d. New York, N.Y., 1933*), Episcopal clergyman. Ordained in England and beginning his ministry there, he became rector of St. George's Church, New York, N.Y., January 1883, and served there until 1904. Strongly individual, he built up St. George's as an "institutional church" with the constant support of his senior warden, J. Pierpont Morgan, who disagreed with Rainsford's increasing theological and political liberalism. He later developed a naturalistic theology of his own and in 1912 was released from the priesthood at his own request.

RÂLE, SÉBASTIEN (*b. Pontarlier, France, 1654 or 1657; d. Norridgewock, Maine, 1724*), Jesuit missionary. Ministered to Indians near Quebec, 1689–91; served on the mission to the Illinois, 1691–93. Recalled to Canada, he was sent to the Abenaki mission in what is now the state of Maine; he worked with success among that branch of the tribe which lived on the Kennebec River but on the outbreak of Queen Anne's War, 1702, his efforts to keep the Indians from ravaging the Massachusetts frontier were relatively ineffective. In 1705, an English expedition came up the Kennebec and burned the Abenaki village and its chapel. *Post* 1713, after the English claimed sovereignty over the region, the raiding was intensified and the English blamed Râle for inciting the Indians. The mission at Norridgewock was attacked again in 1721 by the English but Râle escaped. In 1724, he was shot down at the door of his house by a British war party and his scalp taken to Boston "to the great joy and exultation of the people of Massachusetts." He was an able missionary, a fine linguist, and a courageous champion of French policy.

RALPH, JAMES (*b. probably New Jersey, ca. 1695; d. Chiswick, England, 1762*), poet, political writer. Accompanied Benjamin Franklin to London, December 1724; was distinguished as a poet by Alexander Pope in the second edition of *The Dunciad*. Turning to work for the theatre, he produced (among other plays) *The Fashionable Lady* (1730), the first play by a born American to be produced in London, and was associated in management with Henry Fielding. Thereafter, he was employed as an able political writer in the interest of Frederick, Prince of Wales, and others, but renounced political writing *ca.* 1754 on receipt of a pension from the Pelham–Duke of Newcastle ministry. He aided Franklin in preparing for the press *An Historical Review of the Constitution and Government of Pennsylvania* (1759) and was author of an interesting essay, *The Case of Authors by Profession* (1758), a defense of professional writers.

RALPH, JULIAN (*b. New York, N.Y., 1853; d. 1903*), journalist, foreign correspondent. Made his reputation as one of Charles A. Dana's reportorial staff on the N.Y. *Sun*, 1876–95, and as correspondent in the Greco-Turk and Boer wars, 1897–1900.

RALSTON, SAMUEL MOFFETT (*b. near New Cumberland, Ohio, 1857; d. 1925*), lawyer. Began practice in Lebanon, Ind., 1886. Democratic governor of Indiana, 1913–17; U.S. senator, 1923–25. Refused possible Democratic presidential nomination, 1924.

RALSTON, WILLIAM CHAPMAN (*b. Wellsville, Ohio, 1826; d. 1875*), banker. Beginning as a clerk on a Mississippi River steamboat, 1842, he rose in eight years to be a steamship agent at Panama City for Garrison and Morgan, removing to San Francisco, Calif. (1854) as a partner in the firm. Quickly realizing the future of the city as a center of trade and finance, he was instrumental in the establishment of the banking firm of Garrison, Morgan, Fretz and Ralston, 1856; during the panic of 1857 his courage and ability won him the complete confidence of the business community of San Francisco. With D. O. Mills, he organized the Bank of California, 1864; it soon became the leading financial institution of the Far West and Ralston became its president, 1872. Meanwhile, having engaged himself in widespread and vast plans of imperial expansion, he used the resources of the bank to aid his enterprises, some of them of an extremely dubious character. Living lavishly and becoming further involved in a network of speculation, he was able to continue deceiving his directors and political supporters until August 1875 when the bank suspended payment. On August 27, when his resignation was demanded, he was found drowned.

RAMAGE, JOHN (*b. probably Dublin, Ireland, ca. 1748; d. Montreal, Canada, 1802*), painter of miniatures. Mentioned as a goldsmith and painter of miniatures in Boston as early as 1775. A Loyalist, Ramage followed the fortunes of the British arms, removing to Halifax in March 1776 and settling in New York City at some time in 1777. Remaining in New York after the British left, he was successful in his profession until 1794 when he removed to Montreal to escape involvement in debt. His miniatures are small, accurately painted in the line manner, delicately colored, and done with scrupulous care.

RAMBAUT, MARY LUCINDA BONNEY (*b. Hamilton, N.Y., 1816; d. Hamilton, 1900*), educator, reformer. Established Chestnut Street Female Seminary, Philadelphia, 1850; moved the school to Ogontz, Pa., 1883, changing its name to the Ogontz School.

RAMÉE, JOSEPH JACQUES (*b. Charlemont, France, 1764; d. near Noyon, France, 1842*), architect, landscape architect. Resident in America, 1811–16, Ramée did his most important American work on the layout and first buildings of Union College, Schenectady, N.Y. (1812–13).

RAMSAY, ALEXANDER (*b. in or near Edinburgh, Scotland ca. 1754; d. Parsonsfield, Maine, 1824*), anatomist. Came to America, 1801, and with the exception of the years, 1810–16, when he returned to Europe, led a wandering life as an itinerant lecturer and teacher. A man of immense learning, vanity, and ill-temper, he was constantly at odds with his contemporaries. He was author of *Anatomy of the Heart, Cranium and Brain* (1812; second edition, 1813).

RAMSAY, DAVID (*b. Lancaster Co., Pa., 1749; d. Charleston, S.C., 1815*), physician, Revolutionary patriot, South Carolina legislator, historian. Author of *History of the Revolution of South Carolina* (1785), *History of the American Revolution* (1789), *History of South Carolina* (1809), which are still of value for what they contain of his own eyewitness experience but were drawn to a large extent from the work of others.

RAMSAY, ERSKINE (*b. Six Mile Ferry, Pa., 1864; d. Birmingham, Ala., 1953*), mining engineer, inventor. Studied at St. Vincent's College (1882–83). Inventor, along with his father, Robert Ramsay, of most of the important inventions for coal-mining technology of the late nineteenth- and early twentieth-centuries. Holder of over 40 patents. Pioneer in the use of coal by-products. Founder of the Pratt Consolidated Coal Company, 1904, and the Alabama By-Products Corporation, 1924.

RAMSAY, FRANCIS MUNROE (*b. Washington, D.C., 1835; d. Washington, 1914*), naval officer. Served with great credit in the Mississippi River campaigns of the Civil War under David D. Porter. Promoted captain, 1877, he was superintendent of the U.S. Naval Academy, 1881–86. He retired as rear admiral, 1897.

RAMSAY, GEORGE DOUGLAS (*b. Dumfries, Va., 1802; d. 1882*), soldier. Graduated West Point, 1820. Assigned to the artillery, he became an expert in ordnance and was in command at numerous U.S. arsenals. Promoted brigadier general, 1863, he served as chief of ordnance of the Union army until September 1864 when he was retired for age.

RAMSAY, NATHANIEL (*b. Lancaster Co., Pa., 1741; d. Maryland, 1817*), lawyer, Revolutionary soldier. Served, 1776–81, with Maryland troops; won particular distinction at Monmouth, 1778, where he played a decisive part in checking the American retreat.

RAMSEUR, STEPHEN DODSON (*b. Lincolnton, N.C., 1837; d. Winchester, Va., 1864*), Confederate major general. Graduated West Point, 1860. Resigning from the U.S. Army, 1861, he commanded a North Carolina battery. Rising rapidly for conspicuous merit, he was wounded successively at Malvern Hill, Chancellorsville, and Spotsylvania. He was mortally wounded while rallying his men against Sheridan's counterattack at Cedar Creek.

RAMSEY, ALEXANDER (*b. near Harrisburg, Pa., 1815; d. 1903*), lawyer. Congressman, Whig, from Pennsylvania, 1843–47. Removing to Minnesota, 1849, as newly appointed territorial governor, he opened an immense area in the south of the territory to settlement by negotiating treaties with the Sioux, 1851. At the end of his term, 1853, he entered business in St. Paul, Minn., and served as governor of the state, 1859–63. As U.S. senator, Republican, from Minnesota, 1863–75, he made important contributions to postal reform. He was U.S. secretary of war, 1879–81, in President R. B. Hayes's cabinet.

RAMSEY, JAMES GETTYS McGREADY (*b. near Knoxville, Tenn., 1797; d. Knoxville, 1884*), physician, banker, railroad promoter. Author of *The Annals of Tennessee to the End of the 18th Century* (1853).

RAND, ADDISON CRITTENDEN (*b. Westfield, Mass., 1841; d. New York, N.Y., 1900*), manufacturer of rock drills. Organized Rand Drill Co., 1871; was leader in inducing mining companies to substitute rock drills and air compressors for handwork.

RAND, BENJAMIN (*b. Canning, N.S., Canada, 1856; d. Canning, 1934*), bibliographer, educator. Graduated Acadia University, 1875; Ph.D., Harvard, 1885. Associated thereafter with the Harvard philosophical department as instructor and librarian until 1933, Rand made his principal contribution as a painstaking bibliographer in the field of philosophy.

RAND, EDWARD KENNARD (*b. Boston, Mass., 1871; d. Cambridge, Mass., 1945*), classicist, medievalist. A.B., Harvard, 1894. Ph.D., University of Munich, 1900. Studied also at Harvard Divinity School, the Episcopal Theological School, and University of Chicago. Appointed instructor in Latin at Harvard, 1901, he was made professor in 1909 and held the Pope Professorship of Latin, 1931–42. He was author of many technical studies in Latin paleography and textual criticism, and of *Founders of the Middle Ages* (1928) and *The Building of Eternal Rome* (1943). He was a founder and first president of the Mediaeval Academy of America (1925), and first editor of *Speculum*.

RAND, EDWARD SPAGUE (*b. Newburyport, Mass., 1782; d. 1863*), merchant, New England woolen manufacturer, Massachusetts legislator.

RAND, JAMES HENRY (*b. Tonawanda, N.Y., 1859; d. North Falmouth, Mass., 1944*), inventor, businessman. Devised *ca.* 1880 a system of dividers and colored signal strips and tabs for organizing and indexing business files, which he later extended to include other devices for efficient record keeping. His firm, originally the Rand Ledger Company, enjoyed great success. *Post* 1925, when his son, James Henry Rand, Jr., became president and general manager, the Library Bureau and other firms were acquired and merged; after a merger with the Remington Typewriter Company, 1927, the firm was restyled the Remington-Rand Company.

RANDALL, ALEXANDER WILLIAMS (*b. Ames, N.Y., 1819; d. Elmira, N.Y., 1872*), lawyer. Removed to Wisconsin Territory, 1840. Originally a Whig, then a Free-Soil Democrat, he served as Republican governor of Wisconsin, 1857–61; his skill in mobilizing the state's resources for the Civil War was outstanding. As assistant postmaster general, he helped reelect Abraham Lincoln, 1864, and was U.S. postmaster general, 1866–69.

RANDALL, BENJAMIN (*b. New Castle, N.H., 1749; d. 1808*), founder and organizer of the Free Will Baptists.

RANDALL, BURTON ALEXANDER (*b. Annapolis, Md., 1858; d. Philadelphia, Pa., 1932*), ophthalmologist, otologist. Brother of Wyatt W. Randall. M.D., University of Pennsylvania, 1880. Practiced and taught in Philadelphia; coauthor of *American Text-Book of Diseases of the Eye, Ear, Nose and Throat* (1899).

RANDALL, CLARENCE BELDEN (*b. Newark Valley, N.Y., 1891; d. Ishpeming, Mich., 1967*), industrialist. Attended Harvard (LL.B., 1915); admitted to Michigan bar (1915). Joined Inland Steel Company (1925), becoming its president (1949) and chairman of the board (1953–56). Under his leadership the firm expanded its basic resources of iron and coal; in the area of labor relations, he believed in collective bargaining and that it was unfair for the federal government to intervene in dealing with the United Steelworkers. Steel consultant to the Economic Cooperation Administration in Paris (1948); member of the Department of Commerce Business Advisory Council (1951–57); and special assistant to the president on foreign economic policy (1956–61). Received the Presidential Medal of Freedom (1963).

RANDALL, HENRY STEPHENS (*b. Brookfield, N.Y., 1811; d. Cortland, N.Y., 1876*), agriculturist, educator. Author of numerous books and articles dealing with agricultural subjects and of *The*

Life of Thomas Jefferson (1858) for which he had the use of family manuscripts no longer accessible as a unit.

RANDALL, JAMES GARFIELD (*b. Indianapolis, Ind., 1881; d. Urbana, Ill., 1953*), historian and professor. Studied at Butler College and the University of Chicago (Ph.D., 1911). Taught at the University of Illinois, 1920–53. Authority on the Civil War and Lincoln biographer. Wrote *The Civil War and Reconstruction* (1937) and *Lincoln the President* (1945–55), which stresses the political, constitutional, and diplomatic developments, rather than the conventional military history of the Civil War.

RANDALL, JAMES RYDER (*b. Baltimore, Md., 1839; d. Augusta, Ga., 1908*), journalist, poet. Attended Georgetown College, Washington, D.C. Wrote "Maryland, My Maryland" on hearing of the attack on the 6th Massachusetts regiment as it marched through Baltimore, April 1861. The poem appeared first in the Sunday edition of the New Orleans *Delta* on April 26 and was immediately reprinted all over the South. Set to the music of an old German song, it became a battle song of the South. Randall's collected poems were published posthumously in 1910.

RANDALL, ROBERT RICHARD (*b. possibly New Jersey, ca. 1750; d. New York, N.Y., 1801*), merchant, privateersman, philanthropist. Bequeathed the bulk of his property to provide an asylum for seamen, Sailors Snug Harbor, Staten Island, N.Y. Moved in 1796 to Sea Level, N.C.

RANDALL, SAMUEL (*b. Sharon, Mass., 1778; d. 1864*), Rhode Island jurist, journalist. Graduated Brown, 1804. Notable for his authorship of two farces: *The Miser* and *The Sophomore*, both printed as pamphlets in Warren, R.I., 1812, but probably written by him while in college.

RANDALL, SAMUEL JACKSON (*b. Philadelphia, Pa., 1828; d. Washington, D.C., 1890*), businessman, politician. Congressman, Democrat, from Pennsylvania, 1863–90; speaker of the House, 1876–81; powerful chairman of the appropriations committee, 1883–87. Highly regarded by labor and small business, Randall gained national prominence during Reconstruction by uncovering scandals in the Grant administration and supplying the Democrats with the battle cry of "Retrenchment and Reform." In 1880 under his guidance the rules of procedure of the House were pruned and condensed. Falling out with President Cleveland in December 1887, Randall was deserted by his political friends and lost the federal patronage which had given him control of the Democrats in Pennsylvania.

RANDALL, SAMUEL SIDWELL (*b. Norwich, N.Y., 1809; d. 1881*), educator. Deputy superintendent of New York public schools, 1841–46, 1849–52; superintendent of New York City public schools, 1854–70. In a report to the legislature, Jan. 1, 1852, Randall made a series of recommendations for the control and financing of the public schools which were adopted and established public school education in New York State on a more efficient basis.

RANDALL, WYATT WILLIAM (*b. Annapolis, Md., 1867; d. Baltimore, Md., 1930*), chemist. Brother of Burton A. Randall. Graduated St. Johns, Annapolis, 1864; Ph.D., Johns Hopkins, 1890. Associated with the Maryland State Department of Health, 1911–30; taught biochemistry at Johns Hopkins, 1921–30. He was also consultant to the U.S. Department of Agriculture and to various agricultural associations.

RANDOLPH, ALFRED MAGILL (*b. near Winchester, Va., 1836; d. 1918*), Episcopal clergyman. Graduated William and Mary, 1855; Virginia Theological Seminary, 1858. After serving in several pastorates and as a Confederate chaplain, he was rector of Emmanuel Church, Baltimore, Md., 1867–83. A vigorous advocate of Low Church principles, he served as coadjutor bishop of Virginia, 1883–92, and as bishop of Southern Virginia, 1892–1918.

RANDOLPH, EDMUND (*b. near Williamsburg, Va., 1753; d. Clarke Co., Va., 1813*), lawyer, Virginia legislator, statesman. Grandson of Sir John Randolph; son of John Randolph (1727/8–84); nephew of Peyton Randolph. Briefly an aide-de-camp to George Washington, 1775, he became attorney general of Virginia, 1776, was a delegate to the Continental Congress, 1779–82, and in 1786, was elected governor of Virginia, holding that office until 1788. He was a delegate to the Annapolis Convention and to the Federal Convention of 1787 in which he proposed the Virginia Plan and also drew a draft (perhaps the first) of the work of the committee of detail of which he was a member. Declining to sign the finished Constitution because he thought it insufficiently republican, he wrote a *Letter . . . on the Federal Constitution* (1787) expressing his criticism. However, he advocated ratification in the Virginia ratification convention, 1788, on the grounds of practical expediency. First U.S. attorney general, 1789–93, he endeavored to remain nonpartisan in the conflict between Jefferson and Hamilton. Appointed U.S. secretary of state, Jan. 2, 1794, he was troubled by Hamilton's active interference in foreign affairs, but endeavored to maintain a truly American policy despite public inclination to sympathize either with France or Great Britain in the European struggle then raging. He approved sending a special envoy to Great Britain to clarify relations there, but opposed the appointment of John Jay and in particular opposed giving him the right to negotiate a commercial treaty. When Jay had accomplished his mission and when the contents of the so-called Jay Treaty were known, the French government protested that it violated treaty obligations of the United States to France. In fact, the treaty as negotiated by Jay came far short of carrying out the detailed instructions which had been given him and was unsatisfactory to the Senate and to Randolph unless it were modified. President Washington apparently supported Randolph's position in this matter up to the time when the British minister to the United States released some intercepted communications from Fauchet, the French minister at Philadelphia, to his home government. These seemed to imply that Randolph had made indiscreet revelations of information to him and appeared to suggest that French bribes would be welcome. Called to account by Washington under humiliating circumstances, Randolph resigned as secretary of state in August 1795. Later, Fauchet denied that he meant what had been said and Randolph himself wrote his own *Vindication*, published in 1795. Withdrawing to Richmond, Va., Randolph entered again upon the practice of law and became a leading legal figure; he was senior counsel for Aaron Burr in the famous treason trial of 1807.

RANDOLPH, EDMUND (*b. Richmond, Va., 1819; d. California, 1861*), lawyer. Grandson of Edmund Randolph (1753–1813). Settled in San Francisco, Calif., 1849, where he practiced with great success. He was leading counsel for the United States along with Edwin M. Stanton in the Alameden Quicksilver Mine case. A staunch defender of slavery, he somewhat inconsistently opposed secession and upheld the Union, yet his last public address (1861) was a stinging attack on President Lincoln.

RANDOLPH, EDWARD (*b. Canterbury, England, ca. 1632; d. 1703*), British commercial and political agent. Came to Boston, Mass., in June 1676, with orders requiring the colonial government to answer complaints of the Mason and Gorges heirs with respect to occupation of Maine and New Hampshire. Received with scant courtesy and informed that the laws of England did not apply to Massachusetts, he returned home and made a scathing report on the colonists. In consequence, Maine and New Hampshire were withdrawn from Massachusetts administration and the colony was ordered to enforce the navigation acts, to repeal all laws repugnant to English law, and to cease discrimination against non-church-members in public life. Appointed to take full charge of customs collections throughout New England, 1678, Randolph settled in Boston early in 1680; receiving no help in his task from the local government, he set himself to have the Massachusetts charter annulled. Commissioned secretary of the Dominion of New England, 1685, after the charter had been declared forfeit, he became a councilor in the government under Joseph Dudley and later under Sir Edmund Andros. Imprisoned on the fall of Andros, 1689, and sent to England, he was appointed surveyor of customs for all North America, 1691. Frequently returning to England to push his plans for reorganization of colonial administration, he was in America *post* 1702. He encountered everywhere a contempt for the laws of trade and was virtually powerless to enforce them in the face of constant opposition from local judges, juries, and governments. The British government acted absurdly in expecting one man to enforce the laws of trade, and Randolph's career illustrates the lack of understanding at home which eventuated in the final breakdown of imperial administration.

RANDOLPH, EPES (b. *Lunenberg, Va., 1856; d. Tucson, Ariz., 1921*), railroad executive. Early associated with Collis P. Huntington interests, especially Southern Pacific and Kentucky Central railroads; built and operated Pacific Electric Railway. Supervised Colorado River control project, 1905–07, which saved the Imperial Valley.

RANDOLPH, GEORGE WYTHE (b. *"Monticello," Virginia, 1818; d. "Edgehill," Virginia, 1867*), lawyer, Confederate brigadier general. Grandson of Thomas Jefferson; son of Thomas M. Randolph; brother of Thomas J. Randolph. Served as Confederate secretary of war, March to November, 1862; resigned because of ill health and Jefferson Davis's dominance in the department.

RANDOLPH, ISHAM (b. *New Market, Va., 1848; d. Chicago, Ill., 1920*), civil engineer. Highly reputed as consultant in railroad, canal, and land reclamation work. Supervised construction of Chicago Drainage Canal as chief engineer of Chicago Sanitary District, 1893–1907.

RANDOLPH, JACOB (b. *Philadelphia, Pa., 1796; d. 1848*), Philadelphia surgeon. M.D., University of Pennsylvania, 1817. A generally conservative operator and teacher, he introduced lithotripsy in America at the Pennsylvania Hospital.

RANDOLPH, SIR JOHN (b. *"Turkey Island," Henrico Co., Va., ca. 1693; d. 1736/7*), lawyer, scholar, Virginia legislator. Son of William Randolph; father of John Randolph (1727–84) and Peyton Randolph. Attended Gray's Inn, London; was called to bar, 1717. Clerk of the House of Burgesses, 1718–34; served as substitute for the Crown attorney general, 1727; represented the College of William and Mary and the Assembly on missions to King and Parliament, 1728 and 1732; was knighted, 1732. Speaker of the House of Burgesses, 1734–36/7. The most learned Virginia lawyer of his time.

RANDOLPH, JOHN (b. *Williamsburg, Va., 1727 or 1728; d. Brompton, England, 1784*), lawyer, Loyalist. Son of Sir John Randolph; brother of Peyton Randolph. Served as clerk of the House of Burgesses; succeeded his brother as attorney general for the Crown, 1766. After aiding Lord Dunmore in his struggle with the revolutionary party and seeking in vain to reconcile the differences between the King's government and the people, he fled to England, 1775, where he lived on a small pension.

RANDOLPH, JOHN (b. *"Cawsons," Prince George Co., Va., 1773; d. Philadelphia, Pa., 1833*), statesman, orator. Great-grandson of William Randolph; nephew of Theodorick Bland (1742–90). Best known as John Randolph "of Roanoke," after his residence in Charlotte Co., he adopted the designation *ca.* 1810, in order to distinguish himself from a detested distant kinsman. Capricious, thin-skinned, and passionate even as a boy, he received his early education under direction of his stepfather, St. George Tucker, and at schools in Orange Co. and Williamsburg. He attended the College of New Jersey (Princeton) for a brief period, studied for a short time in New York City, and in September 1790 went to study law with Edmund Randolph in Philadelphia. After several further desultory trials of formal education, he settled at "Bizarre," Cumberland Co., 1794, and distinguished himself mainly for horsemanship, restlessness, and impudent self-confidence.

From the outset of his career a Jeffersonian, or at least an opponent of the Federalists (above all things he cherished personal liberty), he was elected to Congress from Virginia in 1799. Attracting considerable attention for his extraordinary powers as a speaker and for his audacity in debate, he became chairman of the ways and means committee, 1801, and was in effect the administration leader of the House until 1805. Booted and spurred, whip in hand, he swaggered and sneered, but he was undeniably a tireless worker and a master parliamentarian. Somewhat inconsistently supporting the Louisiana Purchase, he returned to his character as a states' rights and strict construction man in the attack on the federal judiciary. He failed in his management of the impeachment of Justice Samuel Chase, however, and suffered a loss of reputation. Prior to this, he had become disillusioned with the administration's action in the Yazoo claims matter; by his fierce denunciation of all who favored compromise, he alienated Gallatin and Madison as well as the more unscrupulous of the party leaders. He came to a definite break with his party over Jefferson's secretive efforts to acquire Florida and ranged himself in open opposition with his "Decius" letters (beginning in the Richmond *Enquirer*, August 15, 1806).

A scrupulous precisian, unwilling to make the least concession of principle to suit the exigencies of politics, Randolph continued to pour out his scorn on his opponents in Congress until 1813. He opposed the Embargo; he opposed the War of 1812. However, with the appearance on the scene of Henry Clay, John C. Calhoun, and Daniel Webster, he ceased to be preeminent as an orator. Defeated for the 13th Congress by John W. Eppes, he returned to the House in 1815 and denounced the chartering of the second Bank of the United States, the tariff, and other nationalistic measures. Refusing to stand for the 15th Congress because of ill health, he served continuously from 1819 until 1825. With the rise of the Missouri question, he became a sectional leader, standing firmly on strict construction of the Constitution and opposing compromise as of old. He was hostile to John Q. Adams and suspicious of Henry Clay with whom he fought a duel in April 1826.

As a U.S. senator, 1825–27, he suffered from mental disorder during the first session and refrained from speaking during the second after John Tyler had been brought forward as a candidate against him. Returned to the House, 1827–29, he was leader of the opposition to John Q. Adams. As delegate to the Virginia convention of 1829–30, he opposed any significant constitutional change. Accepting appointment as U.S. minister to Russia, 1830, he was obliged to resign because of ill health when he had been less than a month at his post. After a long period of sickness and mental alienation, he died while waiting to take ship for England and was buried at "Roanoke" with his face to the West—to keep an eye on Henry Clay, it is said.

Randolph at the age of thirty already looked like an old man. He suffered from insomnia and rheumatism and died, probably, of tuberculosis. He was also impotent for the great part of his life. *Post* 1818, he was on several occasions clearly demented. A constitutional purist, a merciless hater of iniquity, a master of vituperation, and an incomparable orator, he comes down in history as a champion of lost causes, one of the most pathetic as well as one of the most brilliant figures ever to appear in our national public life.

RANDOLPH, PEYTON (*b. probably "Tazewell Hall," Williamsburg, Va., ca. 1721; d. Philadelphia, Pa., 1775*), lawyer, statesman. Son of Sir John Randolph; brother of John Randolph (1727–84). Educated at William and Mary; studied law in London at the Middle Temple; called to bar, 1744 n.s. Appointed King's attorney for Virginia in 1748; served in the House of Burgesses almost continuously, 1748–75. Resigning his post as King's attorney, 1766, he became speaker of the House and held office until the Revolution. A conservative by temperament, Randolph opposed Governor Dinwiddie on several occasions in the interest of the colonials and between 1765 and 1774 moved steadily with the current of Virginia rebel sentiment. He presided over every important Revolutionary assemblage, was appointed to the first Continental Congress, and served as its president in 1774 and 1775.

RANDOLPH, SARAH NICHOLAS (*b. Albemarle Co., Va., 1839; d. Baltimore, Md., 1892*), teacher, author. Daughter of Thomas J. Randolph. Wrote lives of Thomas J. (Stonewall) Jackson (1876) and of her great-grandfather (*Domestic Life of Thomas Jefferson*, 1871).

RANDOLPH, THEODORE FITZ (*b. New Brunswick, N.J., 1826; d. 1883*), industrialist. Conservative Democratic governor of New Jersey, 1869–72; U.S. senator, 1875–81.

RANDOLPH, THOMAS JEFFERSON (*b. "Monticello," Va., 1792; d. "Edgehill," Va., 1875*), planter, financier, Virginia legislator. Grandson of Thomas Jefferson; son of Thomas M. Randolph. Served as chief executor of his grandfather's estate; edited first published collection of his grandfather's writings, *Memoir, Correspondence, and Miscellanies from the Papers of Thomas Jefferson* (1829).

RANDOLPH, THOMAS MANN (*b. Goochland Co., Va., 1768; d. 1828*), Virginia planter and legislator. Son-in-law of Thomas Jefferson; father of Thomas J. Randolph and George W. Randolph. Brilliant but impractical and rash, he represented Virginia in Congress, 1803–07, and was governor of the state, 1819–22. He enjoyed some repute as a botanist.

RANDOLPH, WILLIAM (*b. Warwickshire, England, ca. 1651; d. 1711*), planter, merchant, colonial official. Father of Sir John Randolph; grandfather of John Randolph (1727–84) and Peyton Randolph. Came to Virginia ca. 1673. By 1705, he had acquired vast tracts of land and had become one of the leading planters in the colony. Among the many civil and military posts which he held were those of speaker of the House of Burgesses, 1696 and 1698, and attorney general for the Crown, 1694–98.

RANEY, GEORGE PETTUS (*b. Apalachicola, Fla., 1845; d. 1911*), lawyer, Confederate soldier, Florida Democratic legislator. State attorney general, 1877–85; associate justice, state supreme court, 1885–89, and chief justice, 1889–94.

RANGER, HENRY WARD (*b. Syracuse, N.Y., 1858; d. New York, N.Y., 1916*), landscape painter, of interest for his experiments with pigments and varnishes.

RANKIN, JEREMIAH EAMES (*b. Thornton, N.H., 1828; d. Cleveland, Ohio, 1904*), Congregational clergyman. Graduated

Middlebury College, 1848; Andover Seminary, 1854. President of Howard University, 1889–1903; author, among other hymns, of "God be with you till we meet again."

RANKIN, JOHN ELLIOT (*b. Bolanda, Miss., 1882; d. Tupelo, Miss., 1960*), congressman. Attended the University of Mississippi (LL.B., 1910). Democratic congressman from 1921 to 1952. Cosponsored the legislation that created the Tennessee Valley Authority (TVA) in 1933. He helped formulate the postwar G.I. Bill of Rights and served on the House Committee on Un-American Activities (1945–48). Closely identified with white supremacy, antisemitism, and union baiting.

RANKIN, MCKEE (*b. Sandwich, Ontario, Canada, 1844; d. 1914*), actor, theatrical manager. Played *post* 1865 with leading stock companies; was particularly effective in melodrama. Managed, and played leads to, Nance O'Neill.

RANKINE, WILLIAM BIRCH (*b. Owego, N.Y., 1858; d. 1905*), lawyer, "father of Niagara power." Gave full time *post* 1890 to the development of the Niagara Falls power project; was head executive of its operating department *post* 1897.

RANNEY, AMBROSE LOOMIS (*b. Hardwick, Mass., 1848; d. 1905*), physician. Graduated Dartmouth, 1868; M.D., University of the City of New York, 1871. Taught anatomy at his *alma mater* and at New York Post-Graduate. Author of authoritative papers on eye strain as the cause of functional nervous disease and other disorders.

RANNEY, RUFUS PERCIVAL (*b. Blandford, Mass., 1813; d. Cleveland, Ohio, 1891*), Ohio jurist, Democratic politician. State supreme court judge, 1851–56 and 1862–64.

RANNEY, WILLIAM TYLEE (*b. Middletown, Conn., 1813; d. West Hoboken, N.J., 1857*), historical and genre painter of the life of the American frontier, notably of the old Southwest.

RANSOHOFF, JOSEPH (*b. Cincinnati, Ohio, 1853; d. Cincinnati, 1921*), surgeon. M.D., Medical College of Ohio, 1874; studied also in England, France, and Germany and was made fellow of the Royal College of Surgeons, 1877. Taught at the Medical College of Ohio *post* 1877; was among first in America to operate on gall bladder and kidney; contributed prolifically to professional journals.

RANSOM, MATT WHITAKER (*b. Warren Co., N.C., 1826; d. 1904*), lawyer, Confederate soldier, North Carolina official and legislator. A Whig before the Civil War, he was a Democrat after it and served as U.S. senator from North Carolina, 1873–95. He was a leader in securing the compromise of 1876–77 by which the disputed presidential election was peacefully settled and in the defeat of the Lodge "Force Bill," 1890. As U.S. minister to Mexico, 1895–97, he arbitrated disputes between that country and Guatemala.

RANSOM, THOMAS EDWARD GREENFIELD (*b. Norwich, Vt., 1834; d. near Rome, Ga., 1864*), Union soldier, civil engineer. Removed to Illinois ca. 1851. At outbreak of Civil War he became lieutenant colonel, 11th Illinois Infantry, and brought the regiment to a high state of discipline and training; it served with particular distinction at Fort Donelson and Shiloh. Appointed brigadier general, he distinguished himself in the Vicksburg campaign and in an expedition against Natchez so as to win the particular praise of General Grant. After service in Texas and Arkansas, he was assigned to command the 4th Division, XVI Corps, under Sherman and was again outstanding in the Atlanta campaign. He died while in command of the XVII Corps, after pursuing the army of Confederate General John Hood across north Georgia. He was reputed one of the most capable volunteer soldiers developed in the Civil War.

RANSOME, FREDERICK LESLIE (*b. Greenwich, England, 1868; d. Pasadena, Calif., 1935*), geologist. Immigrated to California as a small child. Graduated University of California, 1893; Ph.D., 1896. An active staff member of the U.S. Geological Survey, 1897–1923, Ransome taught thereafter at the University of Arizona and at the California Institute of Technology. He was author of a veritable library of monographs on important mining districts and on problems of water control.

RANSON, STEPHEN WALTER (*b. Dodge Center, Minn., 1880; d. Chicago, Ill., 1942*), neurologist, anatomist. A.B., University of Minnesota, 1902. Ph.D., University of Chicago (under Henry H. Donaldson), 1905. M.D., Rush Medical College, 1907. Assistant in anatomy, Northwestern University Medical School, 1908–10; professor, and chairman of the department, 1911–24. After serving as professor of neuroanatomy and histology at Washington University Medical School, 1924–28, he returned to Northwestern to organize and direct the research of the Institute of Neurology and remained there for the rest of his life. Among other research he studied the degeneration and regeneration of nerve fibers, the structure of the vagus nerve, and the functional role of spinal ganglia; perhaps his most significant contributions were his studies of the function of the hypothalamus as control center for the sympathetic nervous system.

RANTOUL, ROBERT (*b. Salem, Mass., 1778; d. Beverly, Mass., 1858*), apothecary, public official, reformer. Father of Robert Rantoul (1805–52). Opposed the growth of corporations as inimical to liberty and equality; advocated temperance, international peace, and abolition of capital punishment.

RANTOUL, ROBERT (*b. Beverly, Mass., 1805; d. 1852*), lawyer, reformer. Son of Robert Rantoul (1778–1858). Graduated Harvard, 1826. A Jacksonian Democrat and a liberal Unitarian, he furthered a number of humanitarian causes as a Massachusetts legislator; these included the abolition of the death penalty, the extension of the public school system, and control of the liquor interests. The Massachusetts supreme court upheld in 1842 his reasoning in defense of journeymen bootmakers charged with unlawful conspiracy in organizing to compel collective bargaining (*Commonwealth v. Hunt and Others*); he also served as counsel for Rhode Islanders indicted in connection with the Dorr rebellion. Elected to Congress, 1851, by a coalition between Free-Soilers and Democrats, he was chosen to the U.S. Senate in the same year to fill out Daniel Webster's term. His early death was a great loss to the antislavery Democrats and to liberal reform.

RAPAPORT, DAVID (*b. Munkács, Hungary, 1911; d. Stockbridge, Mass., 1960*), psychoanalyst. Studied at the University of Budapest and the Royal Hungarian University (Ph.D., 1938). Immigrated to the United States in 1938. Director of research at the Karl Menninger Clinic at Topeka, Kans. (1940–48). Researcher at the Austin Riggs Center in Stockbridge, Mass., from 1948. Rapaport worked on systematizing psychoanalytic theory, in particular its metapsychology, the abstract level of theorizing in psychoanalysis, allegedly explanatory of its clinical theory. His works contain an extensive translation of psychoanalysis into the idiom of contemporary psychology. Works include *Emotions and Memory* (1942), *Diagnostic Psychological Testing* (1945–46), and *Organization and Pathology of Thought* (1951).

RAPHALL, MORRIS JACOB (*b. Stockholm, Sweden, 1798; d. 1868*), rabbi, author. Raised in Denmark and England; rabbi of Birmingham Hebrew Congregation, 1841–49. Came to New York, 1849, as preacher to Congregation B'nai Jeshurun and officiated until 1865. He was the first Jew to open a session of the House of Representatives with prayer (Feb. 1, 1860), and a champion of orthodox Judaism in America against the growing encroachments of reform.

RAPP, GEORGE (*b. Iptingen, Württemberg, 1757; d. Economy, Pa., 1847*), religious leader, founder of the Harmony Society. A student of the Bible and of the German mystics, Rapp became leader of a group of separatists in Germany which for a number of years was subject to much petty persecution. Purchasing unimproved land in Butler Co., Pa., 1803, Rapp and some of his followers built the town of Harmony where early in 1805 the rest of his group joined them. The Harmony Society was a communistic theocracy under Rapp as dictator; it was one of the most successful of the more than 200 communistic societies that have sprung up in the United States. Established at Harmony, Ind., 1814–24, the community returned to Pennsylvania and made their last settlement at Economy on the Ohio River below Pittsburgh.

RAPP, WILHELM (*b. Perouse, Württemberg, 1827; d. Chicago, Ill., 1907*), German language journalist. Came to America, 1852, after involvement in German revolutionary activity; worked as editor of several newspapers, notably of *Der Wecker*, Baltimore, Md., and the *Illinois Staats-Zeitung*.

RAREY, JOHN SOLOMON (*b. Groveport, Ohio, 1827; d. 1866*), horse tamer of international celebrity.

RASKOB, JOHN JAKOB (*b. Lockport, N.Y., 1879; d. near Centerville, Md., 1950*), financier, politician. Studied stenography and accounting. Beginning as secretary to Pierre S. du Pont, 1900, he worked closely with him and his cousins, A. I. and T. C. du Pont, in their expansion of E. I. du Pont de Nemours and Company *post* 1902, and pioneered in developing many useful techniques in modern corporate finance. Raskob was *de facto* treasurer of the firm *post* 1909, receiving the title officially in 1914. Interested in the General Motors Corporation as an investor, he worked with William C. Durant on the complicated finances of that firm and secured its financial control by the du Pont interests, resigning as treasurer of the Du Pont Company and becoming chairman of the finance committee of General Motors in March 1918. He introduced modern accounting and auditing practices and formed the General Motors Acceptance Corporation (1919); his funding of the firm's postwar expansion program, however, ran into difficulties during the business recession of 1920 and he had a relatively minor role in the massive reorganization that brought General Motors to its peak of success in a few years' time. Turning increasingly to outside investment and speculation, he also entered politics through his association and friendship with Alfred E. Smith. He resigned from General Motors to become national chairman of the Democratic party after Smith's nomination for the presidency in 1928. He continued to maintain a headquarters for the party's national committee in Washington, D.C., subsequent to Smith's defeat. With the aid of Charles Michelson and others, he kept President Herbert Hoover's administration under constant attack, 1929–32; hopeful of securing a renomination for Smith, he sought to block the candidacy of Franklin D. Roosevelt but was outmaneuvered at the 1932 Democratic national convention. He was replaced as national chairman by James A. Farley. In 1934 he helped found the American Liberty League, an anti-New Deal organization.

RASLE, SÉBASTIEN. *See* RÂLE, SÉBASTIEN.

RATHBONE, BASIL (*b. Johannesburg, South Africa, 1892; d. New York, N.Y., 1967*), actor. Began a career on the British stage in 1911, which he resumed after World War I. Appeared in New York in *The Czarina* (1922) and *The Dark* (1925), but embarked on a long film career in Hollywood in 1924. Tall and handsome, with finely chiseled features and an excellent profile, he made a vivid impression on the screen in about 150 films, ranging from classics to low-grade horror films: *Captain Blood* (1935), *A Tale of Two Cities* (1935), *The Adventures of Robin Hood* (1938), *Sons of Frankenstein* (1939), *The Mark of Zorro* (1940), *The Heiress* (1947), and *The Last Hurrah* (1958). Best remembered for his portrayal of Sherlock Holmes on radio and in thirteen films, the first being *The Hound of the Baskervilles* (1939).

RATHBONE, JUSTUS HENRY (*b. Deerfield, N.Y., 1839; d. Lima, Ohio, 1889*), teacher, government clerk. Founded fraternal order of the Knights of Pythias in Washington, D.C., 1864.

RATHBUN, RICHARD (*b. Buffalo, N.Y., 1852; d. 1918*), zoologist. Served on Geological Commission of Brazil and on U.S. Fish Commission; was on staff of National Museum and the Smithsonian. Rathbun wrote copiously on marine invertebrates and on the economic aspects of marine biology.

RATTERMANN, HEINRICH ARMIN (*b. near Osnabrück, Germany, 1832; d. 1923*), insurance executive, historian, man of letters. Came to Cincinnati, Ohio, as a boy. Established German Mutual Fire Insurance Co., 1858. Promoted musical and cultural activities in Cincinnati; became authority on pioneer German settlers in the United States.

RAU, CHARLES (*b. Verviers, Belgium, 1826; d. Washington, D.C., 1887*), archaeologist. Came to America, 1848; was associated *post* 1875 with the U.S. National Museum, acting as curator of the department of archaeology, 1881–87. Considered the foremost American archaeologist of his time, he was the first in America to recognize the importance of the study of aboriginal technology and was the author of many contributions to scholarly journals.

RAUCH, FREDERICK AUGUSTUS (*b. Kirchbracht, Prussia, 1806; d. Mercersburg, Pa., 1841*), philosopher, educator. Educated at Marburg, Giessen, and Heidelberg. Came to America as a political refugee, 1831; was ordained to German Reformed ministry, 1832; after seminary teaching at York, Pa., he was organizer and first president of Marshall College, 1836–41. Author of *Psychology or a View of the Human Soul* (1840), an important work.

RAUCH, JOHN HENRY (*b. Lebanon, Pa., 1828; d. Lebanon, 1894*), physician. M.D., University of Pennsylvania, 1849. Practiced in Iowa, 1850–56, and thereafter (excepting Civil War service) in Chicago. Promoted higher medical education and standards of practice as first president of Illinois State Board of Health and member, 1877–91.

RAUE, CHARLES GOTTLIEB (*b. near Loebau, Saxony, 1820; d. Philadelphia, Pa., 1896*), homeopathic physician.

RAULSTON, JOHN TATE (*b. Marion County, Tenn., 1868; d. South Pittsburg, Tenn., 1956*), lawyer, legislator, judge. Studied at Tennessee Wesleyan College and the University of Chatanooga. Practiced law until he was elected judge for the Eighteenth District in Tennessee (1918–26). Remembered as the presiding judge for the famed 1925 Scopes Trial in Dayton, Tenn., Raulston upheld the right of the state to determine the school curriculum. In 1926 Raulston resumed his law practice until his retirement in 1952.

RAUM, GREEN BERRY (*b. Golconda, Ill., 1829; d. Chicago, Ill., 1909*), Union soldier, lawyer, Illinois Republican congressman and politician.

RAUSCHENBUSCH, WALTER (*b. Rochester N.Y., 1861; d. Rochester, 1918*), Baptist clergyman, educator. Graduated University of Rochester, 1864; Rochester Theological Seminary, 1886. Pastor, Second German Baptist Church, New York City, 1886–97. Influenced by the sufferings of his parishioners during a time of depression and by the ideas of the Fabian socialists, he became an influential figure in the development in the United States of what has been called the "social gospel." Professor of New Testament interpretation at Rochester Seminary, 1897–1902, he was professor of church history thereafter until his death. Among his books, his *Christianity and the Social Crisis* (1907) was outstanding.

RAUTENSTRAUCH, WALTER (*b. Sedalia, Mo., 1880; d. Palisade, N.J., 1951*), industrial engineer, educator. Studied at the University of Missouri (M.S., 1903) and at Cornell University. Taught at Columbia University School of Engineering from 1906; headed the nation's first department of industrial engineering, 1919–45; professor emeritus from 1945. A disciple of Frederick W. Taylor's scientific management theories, he achieved fame through involvement with the technocracy movement of the early 1930's. Believed that social engineering, led by industrial engineers, could help rebuild society. Founded the Committee on Technocracy in 1932. In 1933 he resigned from the committee because of disenchantment; this signaled the end of the movement.

RAVALLI, ANTONIO (*b. Ferrara, Italy, 1811; d. 1884*), Roman Catholic clergyman, Jesuit missionary. Came to work among the Indians of the region that is now Montana, 1844, in response to an appeal of Father P.-J. De Smet. A skilled mechanic and builder as well as an artist, and also a physician, he worked until his death among the Indians and settlers of Montana with the exception of the years 1860–63.

RAVENEL, EDMUND (*b. Charleston, S.C., 1797; d. Charleston, 1871*), physician, planter, naturalist. M.D., University of Pennsylvania, 1819. Made a remarkable collection of marine shells of which he issued a catalogue, 1834, said to have been the first in the United States. Author of *Echinidae . . . of South Carolina* (1848) and other studies.

RAVENEL, HARRIOTT HORRY RUTLEDGE (*b. Charleston, S.C., 1832; d. Charleston, 1912*), author. Granddaughter of William Lowndes; married St. Julien Ravenel, 1851. Published *Eliza Pinckney* (1896), *Charleston, the Place and the People* (1906), and other works.

RAVENEL, HENRY WILLIAM (*b. Berkeley Co., S.C., 1814; d. Aiken, S.C., 1887*), planter, botanist, agricultural writer. Leading authority on American fungi; collected an extensive herbarium of fungi, mosses, and lichens.

RAVENEL, MAZYCK PORCHER (*b. Pendleton, S.C., 1861; d. Columbia, Mo., 1946*), bacteriologist, hygienist, public health authority. Graduated University of the South, 1881; Medical College of South Carolina, 1884. Studied hygiene at University of Pennsylvania with John S. Billings; studied also at the Pasteur Institute, Paris, and at the Institute of Hygiene in Halle, Germany. Taught bacteriology at the medical and veterinary schools, University of Pennsylvania, 1896–1904, serving also as bacteriologist of the Pennsylvania State Livestock Sanitary Board; made notable investigations of the relation of animal diseases to illness in man, especially bovine tuberculosis. As bacteriologist and assistant director of the Henry Phipps Institute (1904–07), and as professor of bacteriology, University of Wisconsin (1907–14), he continued his studies of tuberculosis, and made important investigations of typhoid fever, rabies, and diphtheria, largely in their public health aspects. *Post* 1914, he was professor of preventive medicine and bacteriology at University of Missouri, and director of its public health laboratory. He was editor of the *American Journal of Public*

Health, 1924–41, and author (among other works) of *A Half Century of Public Health* (1921).

RAVENEL, ST. JULIEN (*b. Charleston, S.C., 1819; d. 1882*), physician, Confederate soldier and surgeon, agricultural chemist. Nephew of Edmund Ravenel. Originated process for manufacture of ammoniated and acid fertilizers from phosphate deposits along Ashley and Cooper rivers, South Carolina, *ca.* 1867. Worked on soil-restoration problems.

RAVENSCROFT, JOHN STARK (*b. near Petersburg, Va., 1772; d. Raleigh, N.C., 1830*), planter, Episcopal clergyman. Ordained, 1817, after a late conversion; consecrated first bishop of North Carolina, 1823; built up a strong conservative body of clergy and laity before resigning his charge, 1828.

RAVOUX, AUGUSTIN (*b. Langeac, France, 1815; d. St. Paul, Minn., 1906*), Roman Catholic clergyman. Volunteered for mission work, 1838; came to Dubuque, Iowa, and was ordained there, 1840. Served Sioux missions on the St. Peter's (present Minnesota) River, 1841–44; was pastor for entire area on Mississippi River headwaters, 1844–51. Worked thereafter in many capacities in the diocese of St. Paul.

RAWLE, FRANCIS (*b. probably Plymouth, England, ca. 1662; d. Philadelphia, Pa., 1726/7*), merchant, political economist. After imprisonment as a Quaker, he immigrated to Pennsylvania, 1686. Member of the Assembly, 1704–09 and 1719–26/7, Rawle was a leader in the antiproprietary party. A mercantilist in theory, he was author of *Some Remedies Proposed for the Restoring the Sunk Credit of the Province of Pennsylvania* (1721) and *Ways and Means for the Inhabitants of Delaware to Become Rich* (1725).

RAWLE, FRANCIS (*b. Freedom Forge, Pa., 1846; d. 1930*), Philadelphia lawyer. Grandson of William Rawle. A founder of the American Bar Association, 1878; edited revisions of Bouvier's *Law Dictionary* (1883, 1897, 1914).

RAWLE, WILLIAM (*b. Philadelphia, Pa., 1759; d. Philadelphia, 1836*), lawyer, philanthropist. Great-grandson of Francis Rawle (*ca. 1662–1726/7*). A Loyalist, he studied law at the Middle Temple, London. Returning to Philadelphia after the Revolution, he served as U.S. attorney for Pennsylvania, 1791–99, and practiced in the city thereafter. He was active in many civic and cultural enterprises, advocated abolition of slavery, and was a devout Quaker; among his many writings, his *View of the Constitution of the United States* (1825) was outstanding. He was a member of the commission to revise the Pennsylvania statutes, 1830–34.

RAWLE, WILLIAM HENRY (*b. Philadelphia, Pa., 1823; d. 1889*), Philadelphia lawyer, Union soldier, legal author and editor. Grandson of William Rawle.

RAWLINGS, MARJORIE KINNAN (*b. Washington, D.C., 1896; d. St. Augustine, Fla., 1953*), novelist. Studied at the University of Wisconsin (B.A., 1918). Her books include *South Moon Under* (1933); *Golden Apples* (1935); *The Yearling* (1939), which won the Pulitzer Prize; *When the Whippoorwill* (1940); *Cross Creek* (1942); and *The Sojourner* (1953). Discovered by Scribners' Maxwell Perkins, she wrote with candid realism about poor whites in exotic settings. Work displays little of the prevailing pessimism and social consciousness of her time, or the naturalistic resort to sex, violence, and sensation. Her books give fresh expression to pastoral themes of central importance to the American cultural tradition.

RAWLINS, JOHN AARON (*b. Galena, Ill., 1831; d. Washington, D.C., 1869*), lawyer, Union soldier. Appointed aide-de-camp to General U. S. Grant, 1861, he remained constantly with him as principal staff officer and intimate adviser, exercising his influence with great tact and ability. Promoted brigadier general, 1863, he was made brevet major general and chief of staff of the army, 1865. Long in failing health, he served briefly as U.S. secretary of war, 1869.

RAWLINSON, FRANK JOSEPH (*b. Langham, England, 1871; d. Shanghai, China, 1937*), Baptist and Congregational clergyman. Immigrated to America, 1889. Graduated Bucknell, 1899; Rochester Theological Seminary, 1902. Missionary to China, 1902–22, as a Baptist. He served thereafter as a Congregational missionary at large and editor.

RAY, CHARLES BENNETT (*b. Falmouth, Mass., 1807; d. 1886*), Methodist and Congregational clergyman, pioneer black journalist, antislavery worker. Published and edited the *Colored American*, 1838–42; was Congregational pastor and missionary in New York City *post* 1846.

RAY, ISAAC (*b. Beverly, Mass., 1807; d. Philadelphia, Pa., 1881*), psychiatrist. M.D., Bowdoin, 1827. Headed Butler Hospital, Providence, R.I., 1846–66; practiced thereafter in Philadelphia. A leader in his specialty, he was author of *A Treatise on the Medical Jurisprudence of Insanity* (1838), *Mental Hygiene* (1863), and many other works.

RAYBURN, SAMUEL TALIAFERRO ("SAM") (*b. Roane County, Tenn., 1882; d. Bonham, Tex., 1961*), Democratic party leader and Speaker of the House of Representatives in every Democratic-controlled Congress from 1940 until his death. Attended Mayo Normal School (now East Texas State) and University of Texas; passed the state bar in 1908. Elected speaker of the Texas House in 1911. As U.S. congressman (1912–61) served on the Committee on Interstate and Foreign Commerce (chairman, 1930). He was a typical southern progressive of the period, devoted to free trade, aid to farmers, and states' rights and was indifferent to organized labor and hostile toward concentrated wealth. During the New Deal, he forged a close working relationship with President Franklin Roosevelt and helped develop and pilot through Congress some of the most significant New Deal legislation. Never an important influence in state politics after his election to Congress, he increasingly was only a revered symbol in the Texas Democratic party. He was among the foremost supporters of the internationalist-interventionist foreign policies of Roosevelt, Harry Truman, and Dwight Eisenhower, but was more comfortable with the moderate conservatism of Eisenhower in domestic affairs than with Truman's Fair Deal or John Kennedy's New Frontier. A quiet opponent of civil rights measures for most of his career, in 1957 and 1960 he finally lent his active support to civil rights legislation designed to facilitate exercise of the right to vote. During the 1950's he and Lyndon Johnson worked as a team with substantial control of Congress; they committed the Democratic party to a policy of "moderation" that fit both the requirements of their home constituency and what they perceived as the national mood. The Rayburn-Johnson approach drew heavy fire from liberal Democrats. Rayburn was vocal and consistent in his assertions that there could be no higher honor than leadership in what he considered the "popular branch" of the national government.

RAYMOND, ALEXANDER GILLESPIE (*b. New Rochelle, N.Y., 1909; d. Westport, Conn., 1956*), cartoonist. Studied at the Grand Central School of Art. Creator of strips such as "Flash Gordon" and "Jungle Jim" in 1934, he is considered the finest cartoonist of the golden age of the comics. Other series include "Secret Agent X-9" (1935), done in collaboration with writer Dashiell Hammett, and "Rip Kirby" (1946). Served in the Marines in World War II and was president of the National Cartoonists Society, 1950–51. Radio, film, comic book, and television series were made from most of his strips.

RAYMOND, BENJAMIN WRIGHT (*b.* Rome, N.Y., *1801; d. 1883*), Chicago merchant and capitalist. Removed to Chicago, Ill., 1836. As mayor, 1839 and 1842, he brought the city through effects of depression of 1837–39 and donated his salary to the unemployed. Active in many businesses *post* 1843, including real estate, railroad promotion and watch manufacturing, he laid out the town of Lake Forest.

RAYMOND, CHARLES WALKER (*b. Hartford, Conn., 1842; d. 1913*), military engineer. Brother of Rossiter W. Raymond. Graduated West Point, 1865; retired as brigadier general, 1904. Made survey and map of Yukon River, 1869; supervised many important river and harbor improvements; was chairman, board of engineers for constructing Pennsylvania Railroad tunnels under Hudson River.

RAYMOND, DANIEL (*b.* in or near New Haven, Conn., *1786; d. 1849[?]*), lawyer, economist. Studied law under Tapping Reeve. Settled in Baltimore, Md., *ca.* 1814; removed to Cincinnati, Ohio, *post* 1840. Author of *Thoughts on Political Economy* (1820, supplemented in the fourth edition, 1840, by *Elements of Constitutional Law, The Missouri Question* (1819), and *The American System* (1828). Opposing classical *laissez-faire* in principle, Raymond distinguished between individual wealth, i.e., the sum of individual riches, and national wealth which he considered the development of economic capacities; he believed that political economy was concerned less with property than with productive power and that national prosperity required a liberal measure of deliberate economic control. Convinced that social principles are always relative to place and time, he based his thought on the American economic environment; it is probable that Georg F. List and John Rae were influenced by him.

RAYMOND, GEORGE LANSING (*b. Chicago, Ill., 1839; d. 1929*), Presbyterian clergyman, educator. Son of Benjamin W. Raymond. Graduated Williams, 1862; Princeton Theological Seminary, 1865. Taught rhetoric at Williams; professor of aesthetics and oratory at Princeton, 1880–1905; professor of aesthetics at George Washington University, 1905–12. Author of a number of studies, issued in a uniform edition as *Comparative Aesthetics* (1909).

RAYMOND, HARRY HOWARD (*b. Yarmouth, N.S., Canada, 1864; d. 1935*), steamship line executive. Came to the United States, 1884; was long associated with the Mallory and Clyde companies and with the Atlantic, Gulf & West Indies lines.

RAYMOND, HENRY JARVIS (*b. Lima, N.Y., 1820; d. 1869*), editor, politician. Graduated University of Vermont, 1840. Removing to New York City, he worked for Horace Greeley on the *New Yorker* and became his chief assistant on the *New York Tribune*, 1841. Shifting to the *Morning Courier*, 1843, he grew in professional reputation. Also a Whig politician, he was elected to the N.Y. Assembly, 1849, and chosen speaker, 1851. His alignment with the Free-Soil group led by W. H. Seward and Thurlow Weed cost him his post with the *Courier*. In association with George Jones (1811–1891), with whom he had become friendly at the *Tribune*, he established the *New York Daily Times* (so-called until 1857). In its first issue (Sept. 18, 1851), he declared that "we do not mean to write as if we were in passion—unless that shall really be the case; and we shall make it a point to get into a passion as rarely as possible." This substitution of moderation and reason for intemperate partisanship brought the *Times* immediate success at the *Tribune's* expense. Through irked by the Whig refusal to face the realities of the slavery issue, Raymond could not bring himself to leave the party until 1856. Meanwhile his nomination

for lieutenant governor of New York, 1854, had mortally offended Greeley and made that formidable editor the political enemy of W. H. Seward.

Raymond wrote the Republican statement of principles at the founding of the national party, 1856; thereafter the *Times* was Republican. He discussed the crucial issues of 1860 in a notable series of open letters to W. L. Yancey (published as *Disunion and Slavery*) and was a steadfast supporter of Abraham Lincoln. As active in politics as in journalism, he was again speaker of the New York Assembly, 1862. In 1864 he played a chief part in Andrew Johnson's nomination for the vice presidency at Baltimore and was named Republican national chairman; he also ran for Congress and was elected.

As administration leader in the House, Raymond was a complete failure. Championing the moderate Reconstruction policies of President Johnson, he was completely outgeneraled by Thaddeus Stevens and the Radicals and acted with hesitation and inconsistency. When the president tried to organize a National Union coalition of conservative Republicans and War Democrats, Raymond supported its purposes in the *Times* but opposed formation of a new party as such. He attended the National Union Convention at Philadelphia, August 1866, pleading for harmony and intelligent action, but the Radicals carried the day and he was their first victim. Expelled from the national committee, he declined renomination for Congress. After the failure of an attempt by him and Weed to form a Union bloc of moderates in New York State, he ceased to struggle against the inevitable. In the campaign of 1868, the *Times* supported the Republicans but the tendency of the paper was increasingly less partisan. Raymond began the *Times* campaign (later brilliantly concluded by George Jones) against the "Tweed Ring" and advocated sound money, tariff reduction and civil-service reform.

Raymond's contribution to journalism was the substitution of decency for personal invective and fairness for black-and-white partisanship. He was one of the earliest and greatest of local reporters, with a prodigious speed and accuracy that became legendary. His editorials were lucid and persuasive, but they usually lacked the smashing force that some of his contemporaries derived from conviction of their own utter rightness and the wickedness of those who held divergent views. He once said that when he wrote a sentence he could not help seeing before he got to the end how only partially true it was. This trait and lack of a realistic appraisal of public opinion were his fatal weaknesses as a politician. His misfortune was not only that he was a temperamental nonpartisan in an age of bitter partisanship, but that he was a temperamental nonpartisan incurably addicted to party politics.

RAYMOND, JOHN HOWARD (*b. New York, N.Y., 1814; d. Poughkeepsie, N.Y., 1878*), educator. Graduated Union, 1832; Madison University (present Colgate) Seminary, 1838. Taught at Madison and at Rochester. First president, Brooklyn Polytechnic, 1855–64; thereafter president and academic organizer of Vassar College, for the success of which he was largely responsible.

RAYMOND, JOHN T. (*b. Buffalo, N.Y., 1836; d. Evansville, Ind., 1887*), comedian. Stage name of John O'Brien. Relied for effects on facial and physical eccentricities; was identified with role of Col. Mulberry Sellers in *The Gilded Age*, *post* 1873.

RAYMOND, MINER (*b. New York, N.Y., 1811; d. 1897*), Methodist clergyman, theologian. Principal of Wesleyan Academy (Wilbraham, Mass.), 1848–64; professor, Garrett Biblical Institute, Evanston, Ill., 1864–95. Author of *Systematic Theology* (1877).

RAYMOND, ROSSITER WORTHINGTON (*b. Cincinnati, Ohio, 1840; d. Brooklyn, N.Y., 1918*), mining engineer, editor. Brother of Charles W. Raymond. U.S. commissioner of mining statistics, 1868–76; was long associated with *American Journal of Mining* and with Cooper, Hewitt & Co. Secretary, American Institute of Mining Engineers, 1884–1911.

RAYNER, ISIDOR (*b. Baltimore, Md., 1850; d. Washington, D.C., 1912*), lawyer, legislator. Congressman, Democrat, from Maryland, 1887–89, 1891–95. After attracting national attention as counsel for Adm. W. S. Schley in the Santiago inquiry, he was U.S. senator from Maryland, 1905–12.

RAYNER, KENNETH (*b. Bertie Co., N.C., ca. 1810; d. 1884*), planter, North Carolina legislator and Whig congressman. An enthusiastic Know-Nothing in the middle 1850's, he verged from aggressive Unionism to whole-hearted secessionism between 1855 and 1861; by 1863, he was engaging in secret moves for peace. Removing to Tennessee, 1869, and later to Mississippi, he became a Republican. He was a judge of the *Alabama* claims commission, 1874–77, and solicitor of the U.S. treasury thereafter until his death.

REA, SAMUEL (*b. Hollidaysburg, Pa., 1855; d. Gladwyne, Pa., 1929*), civil engineer, expert in railroad construction and finance. President, Pennsylvania Railroad, 1913–25.

REACH, ALFRED JAMES (*b. London, England, 1840; d. Atlantic City, N.J., 1928*), baseball player, sporting-goods manufacturer.

READ, CHARLES (*b. Philadelphia, Pa., ca. 1713; d. Martinburg, N.C., 1774*), colonial New Jersey lawyer, land speculator, ironmaster, and official. A powerful figure in New Jersey, 1747–71, Read came on evil days and died as a small shopkeeper. He was notable as an agricultural experimenter and as a pioneer in the bog-iron industry and held a dominant position in New Jersey politics.

READ, CHARLES WILLIAM (*b. Yazoo Co., Miss., 1840; d. Meridian, Miss., 1890*), Confederate naval officer. Graduated U.S. Naval Academy, 1860; entered Confederate service, April 1861. As junior officer in Mississippi River campaigns, 1861–62, and as lieutenant commanding several commerce raiders, 1863–65, Read made a record of active service unsurpassed by any of his rank, North or South.

READ, CONYERS (*b. Philadelphia, Pa., 1881; d. 1959*), historian. Attended Harvard University (Ph.D., 1908), Oxford University (B.Litt., 1909). Taught at the University of Chicago, 1911 until World War I when he served with the Red Cross. After the war, Read worked in his family textile business until 1933. Professor at the University of Pennsylvania, 1934–51. An expert on Tudor history, Read wrote *Mr. Secretary Walsingham and the Policy of Queen Elizabeth* (1925), *Bibliography of British History, Tudor Period* (1933), and *The Tudors* (1936). Served as a British specialist for the Office of Strategic Services in World War II. President of the American Historical Association in 1949.

READ, DANIEL (*b. Rehoboth, present Attleboro, Mass., 1757; d. New Haven, Conn., 1836*), musician, composer. Partner in publishing business of Amos Doolittle. Author of *The American Singing Book* (1785), *An Introduction to Psalmody* (1790), *The Columbian Harmonist* (1793), and others; edited *The American Musical Magazine*, 1786–87, first periodical of its kind.

READ, DANIEL (*b. near Marietta, Ohio, 1805; d. Keokuk, Iowa, 1878*), educator. Graduated Ohio University, 1824. Taught at Ohio, Indiana State, and University of Wisconsin; modernized and expanded University of Missouri as president, 1867–76.

READ, GEORGE (*b. near North East, Md., 1733; d. 1798*), lawyer, statesman. Raised in New Castle, Del., where he practiced law *post* 1754; served as attorney general for the Lower Counties, 1763–74, and as a provincial assemblyman. A moderate Whig, much like his friend John Dickinson, he was a member of the First Continental Congress and of the Second Congress until 1777. Refusing to vote for the resolution of independence on July 2, 1776, he signed the Declaration and upheld it following its adoption. Dominant in the Delaware constitutional convention, 1776, he was elected to the legislative council and became its speaker and vice president of the state; he was acting president, November 1777 to March 1778. Resigning in 1779, he returned to the council, 1782–88. Jealous of the power that might be exerted by the larger states, he disapproved of some provisions of the Articles of Confederation; later, as a delegate to the federal convention, he was outspoken in defence of the rights of the smaller states. He finally accepted the compromise on representation, however, and largely through his efforts Delaware was the first state to ratify the U.S. Constitution. U.S. senator, Federalist, 1789–93, he was thereafter chief justice of Delaware.

READ, GEORGE CAMPBELL (*b. Ireland, 1787; d. Philadelphia, Pa., 1862*), naval officer. Served with credit aboard *Constitution* and *United States* in War of 1812; bombarded Quallah Battoo, Sumatra, 1838, in reprisal for plunder of an American merchant ship by the natives.

READ, GEORGE WINDLE (*b. Indianola, Iowa, 1860; d. Washington, D.C., 1934*), army officer. Graduated West Point, 1883. Showed marked abilities as a colonial administrator in Cuba and the Philippines; organized and commanded the II Army Corps in World War I; retired as major general, 1924.

READ, JACOB (*b. "Hobcaw," Christ Church Parish, S.C., 1752; d. Charleston, S.C., 1816*), Revolutionary soldier, lawyer, South Carolina legislator and congressman. Speaker of South Carolina House of Representatives, 1787–94; U.S. senator, Federalist, 1795–1801. One of the "midnight" judges of 1801.

READ, JOHN (*b. Fairfield, Conn., 1679/80; d. 1749*), lawyer. Graduated Harvard, 1697. After an early trial of the ministry, he was admitted to the Connecticut bar, 1708; he removed to Boston, Mass., 1721. Elected attorney general of the province repeatedly *post* 1721, he served only in 1723, 1726, and 1734 because of a dispute between governor and legislature over the right to appoint to this office. First lawyer to represent Boston in the General Court (1738) under the second charter, Read served on the Governor's Council, 1741–42. Outstanding as a counsel in his time, he had a great influence on the development of New England legal practices and in particular on the modernizing and simplifying of forms. He also engaged in extensive real-estate transactions.

READ, JOHN (*b. New Castle, Del., 1769; d. Trenton, N.J., 1854*), lawyer. Son of George Read; father of John M. Read (1797–1874). Practiced in Philadelphia *post* 1792; was active in the city's political and social life.

READ, JOHN MEREDITH (*b. Philadelphia, Pa., 1797; d. 1874*), jurist. Grandson of George Read; son of John Read; father of John M. Read (1837–96). U.S. district attorney for eastern Pennsylvania, 1837–41; attorney general of Pennsylvania, 1846; Pennsylvania supreme court justice, 1858–73 (chief justice, 1872–73). Opposed extension of slavery; was an early adherent of the Republican party.

READ, JOHN MEREDITH (*b. Philadelphia, Pa., 1837; d. Paris, France, 1896*), lawyer, diplomat. Son of John M. Read (1797–1874). U.S. consul general at Paris, 1869–73; U.S. minister resident in Greece, 1873–79.

READ, NATHAN (*b. Warren, Mass., 1759; d. Belfast, Maine, 1849*), iron manufacturer. Graduated Harvard, 1781; taught there, 1783–87. Settling as an apothecary in Salem, Mass., he conducted experiments on the application of the steam engine to land and water transportation. Having designed a multitubular steam boiler and an improved double-acting engine and also a form of paddle wheel, he petitioned Congress in 1790 for a patent on these plans for a steamboat, and also for a steam road carriage. In August 1791 he was granted a patent for the boiler and the engine and for a chain wheel method of propelling boats which he had added to his earlier application. Unable to secure financial help in building a vessel, he dropped his plans and engaged in iron manufacturing and farming.

READ, OPIE POPE (*b. Nashville, Tenn., 1852; d. Chicago, Ill., 1939*), author, humorist. After experience as a journalist in Tennessee, Arkansas, and Kentucky, Read founded the *Arkansaw Traveler* in Little Rock, 1882, a humorous weekly which became one of the most widely quoted papers in America. Relinquishing editorship, 1891, he concentrated on fiction, turning out some forty novels and collections of humorous stories and was in his later years a great favorite on the Chautauqua and lecture circuits. His work enjoyed great success, 1890–1900; one of his books, *The Jucklins* (1896), was said to have sold over a million copies.

READ, THOMAS (*b. Newcastle Co., Del., ca. 1740; d. Fieldsboro, N.J., 1788*), naval officer. Brother of George Read. Served with ability in both the Pennsylvania and the Continental navies, 1775–79, and as a privateer; sailed the frigate *Alliance* from Philadelphia to Canton, China, 1787–88, in a remarkably fast voyage by a new route.

READ, THOMAS BUCHANAN (*b. near Guthriesville, Pa., 1822; d. New York, N.Y., 1872*), painter, poet. Assisted Shobal V. Clevenger in Cincinnati, Ohio; worked as an itinerant portrait painter; was helped by Nicholas Longworth. Won success in Boston *post* 1841; removed to Philadelphia, 1846; resided in Florence, Italy, 1853–55, and in Rome, Italy, 1866–72. He published a number of volumes of verse which were extravagantly praised at the time, but his work was derivative and unpolished; of his shorter pieces, "Drifting" and "Sheridan's Ride" are alone remembered. His work as a painter was merely competent.

READE, EDWIN GODWIN (*b. Mount Tirzah, N.C., 1812; d. 1894*), lawyer, North Carolina supreme court justice, banker.

REAGAN, JOHN HENNIGER (*b. Sevier Co., Tenn., 1818; d. 1905*), surveyor, lawyer, Texas jurist, Confederate official. Congressman, moderate Democrat, from Texas, 1857–61. Member of the secession convention of Texas, 1861, and of the provisional Congress of the Confederacy, he was appointed Confederate postmaster general, March 1861, and served until the close of the Civil War. Advising Texans to accept the results of the war, acknowledge the extinction of slavery, and admit blacks to civil rights lest the state suffer the evils of military government, he lost political standing in the state but by 1875 had recovered his position and was returned to Congress. In the House of Representatives, 1875–87, he stood for orthodox Democratic policies and was for ten years chairman of the committee on commerce. He was U.S. senator, 1887–91, and in the latter year accepted the chairmanship of the Texas railroad commission which he held until 1903. His greatest service in Congress was the joint authorship and advocacy of the bill to establish the Interstate Commerce Commission (1887).

REALF, RICHARD (*b. Framfield, England, 1834; d. Oakland, Calif., 1878*), Abolitionist, Union soldier, journalist, poet. Came to America, 1854; was a newspaper correspondent in Kansas, 1856. Associated with John Brown (1800–1859), he was a promi-

nent member of Brown's convention at Chatham, Canada, May 1858, and was chosen secretary of state in the mysterious scheme of government which Brown hoped to establish. A tragic figure, he died a suicide; his poems were collected and published as a book in 1898.

REAM, NORMAN BRUCE (*b. Somerset Co., Pa., 1844; d. 1915*), capitalist. Settling in Chicago, Ill., 1871, he became a successful speculator in livestock and grain. Removing to New York City, 1895, he was an associate of the elder J. P. Morgan and others in corporate reorganizations and mergers, notably of the Baltimore & Ohio Railroad, the National Biscuit Co., and the Federal Steel Co.

RECORD, SAMUEL JAMES (*b. Crawfordsville, Ind., 1881; d. New Haven, Conn., 1945*), forester. B.A., Wabash College, 1903; M.A., 1906. Master of Forestry, Yale, as of 1905. Associated with the U.S. Forest Service, 1904–10, he then joined the Yale faculty as instructor in forestry; he was made professor in 1917, and dean of the School of Forestry, 1939. Early interested in study of the systematic anatomy of woods throughout the world, he was author, among other works, of *Identification of the Economic Woods in the United States* (1912), *The Mechanical Properties of Wood* (1914), and *Timbers of Tropical America* (1924, in collaboration with C. D. Mell).

RECTOR, HENRY MASSEY (*b. Louisville, Ky., 1816; d. 1899*), planter, lawyer. Removed to Arkansas *ca.* 1835 where he served in the legislature and as a judge of the supreme court. An active secessionist, he was Democratic governor of Arkansas, 1860–62.

RED CLOUD (*b. Blue Creek, Nebr., 1822; d. Pine Ridge, S.Dak., 1909*), chief of the Oglala Sioux. A noted warrior, Red Cloud took his band of hostile Sioux and Cheyenne on the war path, 1866, in protest against the opening of the Bozeman Trail and the building of forts along it in Sioux territory. He commanded the Indian forces at the Fetterman massacre, December 1866, and at the Wagon Box fight, August 1867. His able and resolute campaign induced the government to yield. The trail was closed by the treaty of 1868 and the three forts abandoned. Although a persistent critic of the government and of its Indian agents whom he charged with fraud, he was an advocate of peace thereafter.

RED EAGLE. *See* WEATHERFORD, WILLIAM.

RED JACKET (*b. probably Canoga, present Seneca Co., N.Y., ca. 1758; d. 1830*), Seneca chief. Indian name, Sagoyewatha. Skilled in oratory and political trickery, he played for popularity in his tribe, 1779–90, by attacking the unsuccessful policy of Cornplanter and other leaders and by haranguing against the whites and peace. Once his position as a chief among the Iroquois was assured, he worked for peace with the United States and avoidance of trouble with the British, hoping thus to maintain the independence of his people. Bitterly opposed to any encroachment of white civilization, he was at the height of his power, 1815–25. As the Christian party among the Seneca grew and because of his own increasing addiction to drink, he gradually lost influence.

RED WING (*b. probably near present Red Wing, Minn., ca. 1750; d. place unknown, ca. 1825*), chief of the Khemnichan band of Mdewakanton Sioux. Outstanding as a warrior, he adopted a policy of peace *post* 1814.

REDFIELD, AMASA ANGELL (*b. Clyde, N.Y., 1837; d. Farmington, Conn., 1902*), lawyer. Practiced *post* 1862 in New York City; was an authority on surrogate practice and on negligence. Author, among other works, of *Law and Practice of*

Surrogates' Courts (1875) and *A Treatise on the Law of Negligence* (with T. G. Shearman, 1869).

REDFIELD, ISAAC FLETCHER (*b. Weathersfield, Vt., 1804; d. Charlestown, Mass., 1876*), lawyer. Vermont supreme court justice, 1835–60 (chief justice, 1852–60). Author of *Practical Treatise upon the Law of Railways* (1858), *The Law of Wills* (1864–70), *The Law of Carriers* (1869), and other works. He was associated with Caleb Cushing, 1867–69, as a special U.S. counsel in Civil War claims cases against Great Britain.

REDFIELD, JUSTUS STARR (*b. Wallingford, Conn., 1810; d. Florence, N.J., 1888*), publisher. A successful printer and general publisher in New York City, 1841–60, he brought out collected editions of authors, among them W. G. Simms, and the 1850–56 edition of Edgar A. Poe.

REDFIELD, ROBERT (*b. Chicago, Ill., 1897; d. Chicago, Ill., 1958*), anthropologist. Attended the University of Chicago (Ph.B., 1920; Ph.D. in anthropology, 1928). Taught at the University of Chicago, 1927–53; dean of the Division of Social Sciences, 1934–46. His early research in Mexico helped develop social anthropology in Mexico and was a starting point of modern research on contemporary peasant societies. Works include *Tepoztlán* (1930), *The Folk Culture of Yucatán* (1941), *A Village that Chose Progress* (1950), and *The Primitive World and Its Transformations* (1953). Redfield's expertise was in the confrontation of primitive societies with the forces of technology. Was president of the American Anthropological Association in 1944.

REDFIELD, WILLIAM C. (*b. Middletown, Conn., 1789; d. New York, N.Y., 1857*), saddler, meteorologist, transportation promoter. Observing the "great September gale," 1821, in western Massachusetts, Redfield explained the nature of such storms in a meteorological classic "Observations on the Hurricanes and Storms of the West Indies and the Coast of the United States" (*American Journal of Science and Arts*, October 1833). This article and a previous one in the same periodical, 1831, were the first of any importance on their subject. He also proposed and put into successful operation between New York and Albany the tow method of conveying freight in barges and wrote a number of pamphlets advocating railroad construction.

REDFIELD, WILLIAM COX (*b. Albany, N.Y., 1858; d. New York, N.Y., 1932*), machinery manufacturer, statesman. Congressman, Democrat, from New York, 1911–13; U.S. secretary of commerce, 1913–19. A strong factor in Woodrow Wilson's election as president, 1912, Redfield reorganized and enlarged the commerce department, strengthened the Bureau of Standards, and, as a keen student of economic tendencies, was of great value in the cabinet during World War I.

REDMAN, BEN RAY (*b. Brooklyn, N.Y., 1896; d. Hollywood, Calif., 1961*), author, editor, and critic. Attended Columbia, 1914–15. Literary editor of the *Spur* (1922–29), managing editor of *Travel* (1923), and editorial and advertising manager for G. P. Putnam and Sons (1924–26). A prolific and diverse free-lance writer, his book reviews for the *New York Herald-Tribune* (1926–37) and the *Saturday Review of Literature* (1925–61) suggest the extensive and persistent influence he exerted on American literary taste. Also composed short stories, a volume of poetry (*Masquerade*, 1923), and several mysteries, including *The Bannerman Case* (1935) and *Sixty-Nine Diamonds* (1940).

REDMAN, JOHN (*b. Philadelphia, Pa., 1722; d. 1808*), physician. Studied medicine with John Kearsley; studied also at Edinburgh, London, and Paris and was graduated M.D., University of Leyden, 1748. An ardent follower of Boerhaave and Sydenham, he practiced and taught in Philadelphia, was a con-

sulting physician to the Pennsylvania Hospital, and was president of the College of Physicians of Philadelphia, 1786–1804. Among his pupils were John Morgan, Benjamin Rush, and Caspar Wistar.

REDPATH, JAMES (*b. Berwick-on-Tweed, Scotland, 1833; d. New York, N.Y., 1891*), journalist, editor. Immigrated to Michigan *ca.* 1850; became associated with the *New York Tribune*, 1852; attracted wide attention for articles on the political troubles in Kansas, slavery in the Southern states, and John Brown. An ardent abolitionist, he aided Haiti in securing recognition of its independence and helped ex-slaves to immigrate there from the United States. He established the Redpath Lyceum Bureau in Boston, 1868.

REDWOOD, ABRAHAM (*b. Antigua, W. I., 1709; d. 1788*), merchant, philanthropist. Brought to Philadelphia as a child; removed to Newport, R.I., 1726. Interested in the cultural and literary activity of colonial Newport, Redwood made the principal contribution towards the founding of a public library there, 1747.

REECE, BRAZILLA CARROLL (*b. Johnson County, Tenn., 1889; d. Bethesda, Md., 1961*), U.S. congressman from Tennessee (1920–30, 1932–46, 1950–61). Attended Carson-Newman College, New York University (M.A., 1916), and University of London. Emerged as one of the leading critics of the Roosevelt and Truman administrations, and by 1946 was considered to be the leading Republican politician in the South. Member of the House Rules, Interstate Commerce, and Military Affairs committees. Chairman of a special committee (1954) that issued a controversial report chastising large foundations for "directly supporting subversion" and dodging taxes on large fortunes. Was Republican national committeeman from Tennessee, 1939 until his death, and chairman of the Republican National Committee, 1946–48.

REED, DANIEL ALDEN (*b. Sheridan, N.Y., 1875; d. Washington, D.C., 1959*), congressman. Studied at Cornell University (LL.B., 1898). Elected as a Republican to the U.S. Congress from 1918. Served on the House Ways and Means Committee from 1933 and was chairman, 1953–54. An ardent advocate of tax-reduction legislation, he clashed with the Eisenhower administration. Resigned his chairmanship in 1955.

REED, DAVID (*b. Easton, Mass., 1790; d. 1870*), Unitarian clergyman. Founder, publisher, and editor of the *Christian Register*, 1821–66.

REED, DAVID AIKEN (*b. Pittsburgh, Pa., 1880; d. Sarasota, Fla., 1953*), lawyer, U.S. senator. Studied at Princeton University and the University of Pittsburgh law school. Practiced law in Pittsburgh, often appearing before the U.S. Supreme Court, before serving in the army in France during World War I. A protégé of Andrew Mellon, he was appointed to fill a vacancy in the U.S. Senate, 1922, and was elected later that year as conservative Republican. Author of the Reed-Johnson Immigration Act (1924), which sought to preserve the racial status quo by apportioning quotas to each "national stock" according to its representation in the population in 1920. This practice was especially prejudicial to the peoples of southern Europe and the Orient, while favoring the populations of northern Europe. The effects of this policy, especially on Japan, were considered one of many important factors leading to World War II. Lost his seat in the Senate, 1934, and returned to private law practice in Pittsburgh.

REED, EARL HOWELL (*b. Geneva, Ill., 1863; d. 1931*), author, etcher. Son of Elizabeth A. Reed; brother of Myrtle Reed.

REED, ELIZABETH ARMSTRONG (*b. Winthrop, Maine, 1842; d. 1915*), writer on Oriental literature. Mother of Earl H. and Myrtle Reed.

REED, HENRY HOPE (*b. Philadelphia, Pa., 1808; d. at sea, aboard steamer* Arctic, *1854*), educator. Grandson of Joseph Reed; brother of William B. Reed. Graduated University of Pennsylvania, 1825; was professor of rhetoric and English literature there, 1835–54. Author and editor of a number of works in belles lettres, Reed was the first American exponent of William Wordsworth and did more than anyone else to secure Wordsworth's fame in America.

REED, JAMES (*b. Woburn, Mass., 1722 o.s.; d. Fitchburg, Mass., 1807*), soldier in the French and Indian War and in the Revolution. Serving as colonel of the 2nd Continental regiment at Ticonderoga, July 1776, he was stricken with an illness that destroyed his sight; he retired in September as brigadier general. He was an original proprietor of Fitzwilliam, N.H.

REED, JAMES (*b. Boston, Mass., 1834; d. Boston, 1921*), minister of the Church of the New Jerusalem. Son of Sampson Reed. Graduated Harvard, 1855; ministered in Boston *post* 1860.

REED, JAMES ALEXANDER (*b. near Mansfield, Ohio, 1861; d. near Fairview, Mich., 1944*), lawyer, politician. Raised in Linn County, Iowa, was admitted to the bar, 1885; removed to Kansas City, Mo., 1887. Reed's first public post was city counselor (1897–98), followed by election as prosecuting attorney of Jackson County, which included Kansas City. He swept into the mayor's chair in 1900 as a reform candidate. Leading a consumers' war on street railway, electric, and telephone utilities, he won reelection in 1902. He was elected to the U.S. Senate in 1910, and was reelected by statewide vote, with increasing majorities, in 1916 and 1922.

In the Senate, Reed generally supported the Wilson administration's New Freedom legislation and its foreign policies, including the declaration of war against Germany in 1917. But he soon turned against wartime measures, especially economic controls. Reed's criticism of the conduct of the war paled beside his utterly uncompromising stand against the Versailles peace treaty and in particular against the covenant of the League of Nations. He likewise opposed the war's debt settlements and the four-power treaty proposed by the Washington Conference on arms limitation in 1921.

Reed made a serious bid for the Democratic presidential nomination in 1928, and consequently did not run for reelection to the Senate. Upon leaving Washington he resumed his law practice in Kansas City. Increasingly opposed to government "paternalism" and "socialist or regulatory schemes," he became a foe of the New Deal and of President Franklin D. Roosevelt. In 1936 he organized the National Jeffersonian Democrats and stumped for Alfred M. Landon; four years later he again supported the Republican nominee, Wendell L. Willkie.

REED, JAMES HAY (*b. Allegheny, Pa., 1853; d. Pittsburgh, Pa., 1927*), lawyer. Partner in practice of corporation law with Philander C. Knox until 1901, Reed was counsel to Andrew Carnegie, to the Vanderbilt interests in the Pittsburgh district, and to many other large business concerns.

REED, JOHN (*b. Hesse-Cassel, Germany, 1757; d. Cabarrus Co., N.C., 1845*), Hessian soldier, farmer, gold miner. Settling in Mecklenburg, present Cabarrus Co., N.C., after the Revolution, Reed began successful placer mining operations on his farm *ca.* 1803 which set off activity in an industry soon second in economic importance only to agriculture in the state. *Post* 1831, he worked his mine with shafts and steam power; the total yield between 1803 and 1845 has been estimated at ten million dollars.

REED, JOHN (*b. Portland, Oreg., 1887; d. Russia, 1920*), journalist. Graduated Harvard, 1910. His interest in the problems of society aroused *ca.* 1913 by Lincoln Steffens and Ida Tarbell, he took up a far more radical position than theirs. He joined staff of *The Masses* and engaged actively on behalf of the Paterson, N.J., silk strikers, 1914. Brilliant but biased articles on the Mexican revolution brought him national reputation as a war correspondent and he covered World War I successively with the armies of Germany, Serbia, Bulgaria, Romania, and Russia. His reports were published as *The War in Eastern Europe* (1916). An enthusiastic observer of the October revolution in Petrograd, 1917, Reed became a close friend of Lenin and wrote much of the Bolshevist propaganda dropped over the German lines. Returning to America, he published *Red Russia* and *Ten Days that Shook the World* (both in 1919) and was expelled with other left-wingers from the National Socialist Convention, August 1919. When the left-wing groups split into two bitterly hostile factions known as the Communist party and the Communist Labor party, Reed headed the latter. Indicted for sedition, he left America by means of a forged passport, was imprisoned briefly in Finland, and at last reached Russia where he died of typhus.

REED, JOSEPH (*b. Trenton, N.J., 1741; d. Philadelphia, Pa., 1785*), lawyer, Revolutionary soldier and statesman. Graduated College of New Jersey (Princeton), 1757; studied law with Richard Stockton and at the Middle Temple, London. Engaging in legal practice and also in the iron trade and real-estate business, he was appointed deputy secretary of New Jersey, 1767; he removed his practice to Philadelphia *ca.* 1770. Appointed a member of the committee of correspondence for Philadelphia, November 1774, he served as president of the second Provincial Congress early in 1775 and gradually shifted from a belief in accommodation with England to a feeling that independence was essential. On Washington's appointment as commander-in-chief, Reed became his military secretary and was later adjutant general of the Continental Army with the rank of colonel. He was of great service to Washington in the campaign of Trenton and Princeton and served with credit at the battles of Brandywine, Germantown and Monmouth. Delegate to the Continental Congress, 1777–78, he served on important committees, and in December 1778 was chosen president of the Supreme Executive Council of Pennsylvania, serving until 1781. The many attacks made on his reputation as a soldier and patriot were without foundation.

REED, LUMAN (*b. Austerlitz, N.Y., 1781; d. 1836*), New York merchant. Remembered as one of the earliest patrons of American painting, he encouraged, among others, A. B. Durand, Thomas Cole and W. S. Mount.

REED, MARY (*b. Lowell, Ohio, 1854; d. Chandag, Kumaon District, India, 1943*), Methodist Episcopal missionary to India *post* 1884. Headed the leper asylum at Chandag near Almora, 1891–1943.

REED, MYRTLE (*b. Norwood Park, Ill., 1874; d. 1911*), writer. Daughter of Elizabeth A. Reed; sister of E. H. Reed. Author of a number of deftly written and popular romances of which the most successful was *Lavender and Old Lace* (1902).

REED, RICHARD CLARK (*b. near Soddy, Tenn., 1851; d. Columbia, S.C., 1925*), Presbyterian clergyman, educator, author. Professor of church history, Columbia Theological Seminary, 1898–1925.

REED, SAMPSON (*b. West Bridgewater, Mass., 1800; d. Boston, Mass., 1880*), Swedenborgian writer, wholesale drug merchant. Author of several works of which *Observations on the Growth of the Mind* (1826) exerted great influence on R. W. Emerson.

REED, SIMEON GANNETT (*b. East Abington, Mass., 1830; d. 1895*), merchant, steamboat operator. Settled in Portland, Oreg., ca. 1852; was partner in the Oregon Steam and Navigation Co. and other successful enterprises. His fortune was used to found Reed College, opened 1911.

REED, THOMAS BRACKETT (*b. Portland, Maine, 1839; d. Washington, D.C., 1902*), lawyer, Maine legislator, parliamentarian. Graduated Bowdoin, 1860. As congressman, Republican, from Maine, 1877–99, Reed became famous for the sarcasm and invective which he employed in debate and in his committee work. Appointed to the committee on rules, 1882, he began a long fight for reform of the rules of the House, proposing that procedural checks be removed in order that the majority party might actually govern. Elected speaker, December 1889, he forced adoption in February of the famous "Reed Rules," whereby he was able to expedite passage of the Republican legislative program. He was also a noted exponent of protectionism. Replaced as speaker and his rules voided, 1891, he labored to rehabilitate the Republican party after its defeats in 1890 and 1892; he supported President Cleveland's sound-money policy but opposed all tariff reforms. Serving again as speaker, 1895–99, he brought about the return of the "Reed Rules." Resenting failure of the Republicans to nominate him for the presidency, 1896, he supported the McKinley administration until 1898 when he expressed bitter opposition to expansionism. Following the war with Spain and the annexation of Hawaii, Reed resigned in disgust and returned to the practice of law in New York City. His epigrams have become part of American political tradition. "A statesman," he once said, "is a successful politician who is dead."

REED, WALTER (*b. Belroi, Va., 1851; d. Washington, D.C., 1902*), physician, head of the U.S. Army Yellow Fever Commission. M.D., University of Virginia, 1869; M.D., Bellevue Hospital Medical College, New York City, 1870. Commissioned in the U.S. Army medical corps, 1875, he spent a number of years on frontier garrison duty. Requesting leave of absence for postgraduate work, 1890, he made specialized studies in bacteriology at Johns Hopkins Hospital; in 1893, he was detailed as professor of bacteriology and microscopy at the Army Medical School with James Carroll as assistant. Interested especially in the bacteriology of erysipelas and diphtheria, he served also as chairman of a committee to investigate causes and mode of transmission of typhoid fever. In 1900, having some experience with the problems involved, he was put at the head of a commission of U.S. Army medical officers to investigate cause and mode of transmission of yellow fever in Havana, Cuba. Reed was to have general superintendence of the investigation, James Carroll was bacteriologist, Jesse W. Lazear was entomologist, and other distinguished officers also served. The commission established by experimentation on human subjects (which resulted in the crippling of Dr. Carroll and the death of Dr. Lazear) that the disease was transmitted by mosquitoes, later definitely classified as the *Aëdes aegypti.* The commission worked from June 1900 to February 1901, and as a result of its findings and subsequent limitation of the carrier, yellow fever has virtually ceased to be a hazard in the United States.

REED, WILLIAM BRADFORD (*b. Philadelphia, Pa., 1806; d. New York, N.Y., 1876*), lawyer. Brother of Henry H. Reed; grandson of Joseph Reed. Originally a Whig, Reed became a Democrat in 1856, supported Buchanan in the campaign of that year, and was appointed U.S. minister to China. Serving in China from November 1857 until 1859, he concluded the treaty of Tientsin, 1858. His bitter and open opposition to the Civil War cost him his social and professional standing.

REEDER, ANDREW HORATIO (*b. Easton, Pa., 1807; d. 1864*), lawyer. Unsuccessful Democratic governor of Kansas Territory, 1854–55, Reeder became a Free State spokesman after his removal from the governorship for incapacity and land speculation.

REEDY, WILLIAM MARION (*b. St. Louis, Mo., 1862; d. San Francisco, Calif., 1920*), journalist. Editor of *Reedy's Mirror* (St. Louis), *post* 1893. Beginning as a society journal, the paper became under Reedy a link between the cultures of the East Coast and the Middle West and introduced in its pages many writers who became famous in the 1920's.

REES, JAMES (*b. Wales, 1821; d. 1889*), steamboat builder. Came to America as a child; was raised near present Wheeling, W. Va. Founder of a successful engine and boat-works at Pittsburgh, Pa., he popularized the "stern-wheeler" and invented a number of improvements in steamboat construction. He was an early advocate of the ten-hour day.

REES, JOHN KROM (*b. New York, N.Y., 1851; d. 1907*), geodesist, astronomer. Graduated Columbia, 1872; Columbia School of Mines, 1875. Director of the observatory at Columbia *post* 1881, he also taught astronomy; as secretary, American Meteorological Society, he advocated introduction of standard time.

REESE, ABRAM (*b. Llanelly, South Wales, 1829; d. Pittsburgh, Pa., 1908*), iron and machinery manufacturer. Brother of Isaac and Jacob Reese. Came to America as a child. Held a number of patents, issued *post* 1859, for perfection and improvement of machinery for rolling iron and steel; patented a universal rolling mill, 1892.

REESE, CHARLES LEE (*b. Baltimore, Md., 1862; d. Florida, 1940*), chemist. Graduated University of Virginia, 1884; Ph.D. Heidelberg, 1886. Chief chemist and director of research laboratory, Du Pont Company, 1902–31, he was one of the outstanding industrial chemists of his day.

REESE, ISAAC (*b. Llanelly, South Wales, 1821; d. Pittsburgh, Pa., 1908*), brick manufacturer. Brother of Abram and Jacob Reese. Came to America as a child. Among other inventions he produced the "Reese Silica Brick," 1882, which was capable of withstanding very high temperatures with practically no shrinkage or expansion.

REESE, JACOB (*b. Llanelly, South Wales, 1825; d. near Philadelphia, Pa., 1907*), metallurgist. Brother of Abram and Isaac Reese. Came to America as a child. Among a great number of inventions useful in the manufacture of iron and steel, Reese perfected the basic open-hearth steel process *ca.* 1877, although his claim as inventor was not favorably decided by the Patent Office until 1881.

REESE, JOHN JAMES (*b. Philadelphia, Pa., 1818; d. Atlantic City, N.J., 1892*), toxicologist. Graduated University of Pennsylvania, 1836; M.D., 1839. Author of *A Text Book of Medical Jurisprudence and Toxicology* (1884), a standard work.

REESE, LIZETTE WOODWORTH (*b. near Baltimore, Md., 1856; d. 1935*), poet, educator. Educated chiefly in private schools; taught for many years in the public schools of Baltimore. Her lyrics, intensely felt and inspired by a keen sense of the beauty of common things, were uninfluenced in technique by fashionable poetic fads. Her first volume, *A Branch of May*, appeared in 1887; after the appearance of her *Selected Poems* (1926), she published *Little Henrietta* (1927), *White April and Other Poems* (1930), and several other volumes both in verse and prose.

REEVE, TAPPING (*b. Brookhaven, N.Y., 1744; d. Litchfield, Conn., 1823*), jurist, teacher of law. Graduated College of New Jersey (Princeton), 1763. Admitted to the Connecticut bar, 1772, he settled in Litchfield where he began the practice of his profession. After teaching law informally for some time Reeve formally opened the Litchfield Law School in 1784. With exception of the department of law at William and Mary under George Wythe, it was the first school of its kind in the United States. Appointed a judge of the superior court, he associated James Gould with the school as a teacher. Under Gould's direction the school developed and flourished, numbering among its graduates some of the most prominent men in the public life of the next generation. Reeve was made chief justice of the supreme court of errors of Connecticut, 1814, and served until his retirement, 1816.

REEVES, ARTHUR MIDDLETON (*b. Cincinnati, Ohio, 1856; d. near Hagerstown, Ind., 1891*), philologist, historian, authority on Old Norse.

REEVES, JOSEPH MASON (*b. Tampico, Ill., 1872; d. Bethesda, Md., 1948*), naval officer. Graduated U.S. Naval Academy, 1894; served in Spanish-American War aboard USS *Oregon* as engineer; transferred to the line, 1899. After a number of varied assignments, including command of the battleship *North Dakota* (1921–23), he took command in 1925 of Aircraft Squadrons, Battle Fleet, based at San Diego, Calif., and in three years' hard training shaped them into an effective striking arm. Promoted rear admiral, 1927, he was responsible for the training of flight crews for the *Saratoga* and the *Lexington*, thus contributing to the evolution of the carrier task force. In 1933 he became commander, Battle Fleet, and then for two years before his retirement in 1936 was commander in chief, U.S. Fleet, conducting peacetime exercises with a realism never before attained. Recalled to duty, 1940, he served on the lendlease and munitions assignment boards.

REGAN, AGNES GERTRUDE (*b. San Francisco, Calif., 1869; d. Washington D.C., 1943*), educator, social reformer. Executive secretary, National Council of Catholic Women, *post* 1920; assistant director, National Catholic School of Social Service, *post* 1925; authority in the field of social legislation.

REHAN, ADA (*b. Limerick, Ireland, 1860; d. New York, N.Y., 1916*), actress. Came to America as a child; was raised in Brooklyn, N.Y. After making her stage debut at Newark, N.J., 1873, she joined the Arch St. company, Philadelphia. Although her name was properly Ada Crehan, she was billed by a printer's error as Ada C. Rehan for her Philadelphia debut and preserved the mistake throughout her subsequent career. Playing in support of Fanny Davenport, Edwin Booth, Lawrence Barrett, John T. Raymond, and others, she joined Augustin Daly's company, 1879, and remained under Daly's management until he died, 1899. The leading woman of his company, she was a popular idol in New York and London and was considered the perfect mistress of the classic, artificial style of playing. Famous in many parts, her performance as Katherine in Shakespeare's *Taming of the Shrew* is considered her outstanding role. Her last public appearance was at a New York benefit for Madame Modjeska, 1905.

REHN, FRANK KNOX MORTON (*b. Philadelphia, Pa., 1848; d. 1914*), artist, specialist in marines.

REICHEL, CHARLES GOTTHOLD (*b. Hermsdorff, Silesia, 1751; d. Niesky, Silesia, 1825*), Moravian bishop and educator. Principal of the academy at Nazareth, Pa., 1785–1801; bishop of the southern province, 1801–11, and of the northern province, 1811–18. He was sent to Germany, 1818.

REICHEL, WILLIAM CORNELIUS (*b. Salem, N.C., 1824; d. 1876*), Moravian clergyman, educator. Grandson of Charles G. Reichel. Author of a number of historical studies on the Moravian Church in America.

REICHENBACH, HANS (*b. Hamburg, Germany, 1891; d. Los Angeles, Calif., 1953*), educator, philosopher of science, logician. Studied at the Technische Hochschule of Stuttgart, and the universities of Berlin, Munich, and Göttingen. Taught at the Technische Hochschule of Stuttgart, 1920–25. One of the first students to attend Einstein's seminar on relativity at the University of Berlin. Taught at the University of Berlin, 1925–33. From 1933 to 1938, having fled Hitler, he taught at the University of Istanbul. Immigrated to the United States in 1938 and remained at the University of California at Los Angeles until his death. Reichenbach's detailed technical knowledge of mathematics and physics, combined with profound philosophical penetration, made him a seminal philosopher of science and the preeminent champion of empiricism in philosophy of science in the twentieth century. Works include *Philosophie der Raum-Zeit-Lehre* (1928), *Experience and Prediction* (1938), and *The Direction of Time* (1956).

REICK, WILLIAM CHARLES (*b. Philadelphia, Pa., 1864; d. 1924*), journalist. As city editor, *New York Herald*, 1889–1903, he became known as one of America's ablest journalists. Holding the presidency of the New York Herald Co., 1903–07, he resigned, and after working for the *New York Times* and the Philadelphia *Public Ledger*, bought a controlling interest in the N.Y. *Sun*, 1911. He was afterwards president of the company which published the *New York Journal of Commerce*.

REID, CHRISTIAN. *See* TIERNAN, FRANCES CHRISTINE FISHER.

REID, DAVID BOSWELL (*b. Edinburgh, Scotland, 1805; d. Washington, D.C., 1863*), chemist, educator, ventilation engineer. Resident in the United States, 1855–63.

REID, DAVID SETTLE (*b. Rockingham Co., N.C., 1813; d. 1891*), lawyer, North Carolina legislator. Congressman, Democrat, from North Carolina, 1843–47; governor, 1851–54; U.S. senator, 1854–59. A conservative pro-Southern man, Reid was considered the wisest and most resourceful Democratic leader in North Carolina between the day of Nathaniel Macon and the Civil War.

REID, GILBERT (*b. Laurel, N.Y., 1857; d. Shanghai, China, 1927*), Presbyterian clergyman, newspaper correspondent, missionary to China. Founded International Institute of China *ca.* 1897.

REID, HELEN MILES ROGERS (*b. Appleton, Wis., 1882; d. New York, N.Y., 1970*), newspaper executive. Attended Barnard (B.A., 1903), then was hired as social secretary to Elisabeth Mills Reid, wife of Whitelaw Reid, the owner of the *New York Tribune*. Married Ogden Mills Reid, their son, and became the *Tribune's* advertising director (1918); in her first two years the paper's advertising revenues more than doubled. As vice president of the paper (since 1922) she helped arrange the purchase of the *New York Herald* (1924); the expanded paper was renamed *Herald Tribune* and became one of the nation's best newspapers. Succeeded her husband as president (1947) and brought such noted columnists and writers as Walter Lippmann, Dorothy Thompson, and Clementine Paddleford to the paper. In the late 1930's the paper began to lose circulation and advertising revenues to the *New York Times* because of her higher advertising prices; she sold the paper in 1958. Trustee of Barnard (1914–56) and chairman (1947–70).

REID, IRA DE AUGUSTINE (*b. Clifton Forge, Va., 1901; d. Bryn Mawr, Pa., 1968*), sociologist and educator. Attended Morehouse College, universities of Chicago and Pittsburgh, and Columbia (Ph.D., 1939). As industrial secretary of the New York Urban League, 1925–28, he surveyed the living conditions of low-income black families. Gathered data for the National Interracial Conference (1928), which yielded the landmark *The Negro in American Civilization* (1930). Became director of research and investigations for the league (1928) and published one of the first reliable studies of blacks in the work force, *Negro Membership in American Labor Unions* (1930). Taught at Atlanta University (1934–44), New York University School of Education (1945–47), and Haverford College (1946–66).

REID, JAMES L. (*b. near Russellville, Ohio, 1844; d. 1910*), corn breeder. Raised in Illinois where, after a number of experiments, he produced the corn variety known as Reid's Yellow Dent *ante* 1880.

REID, JOHN MORRISON (*b. New York, N.Y., 1820; d. New York, 1896*), Methodist clergyman. President of Genesee College (nucleus of present Syracuse University), 1858–64; did valuable work as corresponding secretary, Methodist Missionary Society, 1872–88.

REID, MAYNE. *See* REID, THOMAS MAYNE.

REID, MONT ROGERS (*b. near Oriskany, Va., 1889; d. Cincinnati, Ohio, 1943*), surgeon. A.B., Roanoke College, 1908. M.D., Johns Hopkins, 1912. Worked at Johns Hopkins Hospital under William S. Halstead, becoming chief resident in surgery, 1918. Associate professor of surgery, University of Cincinnati, 1922–31, and chairman of the department thereafter, he made it one of the great U.S. training centers for surgeons. His chief research contributions were his experimental and clinical studies of surgery of the thyroid and of the large blood vessels, also his work in surgical treatment of angina pectoris and cancer.

REID, OGDEN MILLS (*b. New York, N.Y., 1882; d. New York, 1947*), newspaper editor and publisher. Son of Whitelaw Reid. B.A., Yale, 1904; LL.B., 1907. Joining the staff of the *New York Tribune*, 1908, he was named editor early in 1913 and held that post until his death. In 1924 he acquired the *New York Herald*; thereafter the combined papers were published as the *Herald Tribune*.

REID, ROBERT (*b. Stockbridge, Mass., 1862; d. Clifton Springs, N.Y., 1929*), portrait, figure and mural painter.

REID, SAMUEL CHESTER (*b. Norwich, Conn., 1783; d. New York, N.Y., 1861*), sea captain. Distinguished for his heroic conduct as commander of the privateer *General Armstrong*, 1814. Putting in at the harbor of Fayal (Azores) in September of that year, Reid defended his vessel against a series of attacks by armed boats from the British men of war *Carnation*, *Rota*, and *Plantagenet* which were en route to join the British forces concentrating at Jamaica against New Orleans. Reid eventually scuttled and abandoned his ship, but the delay he caused the British squadron indirectly aided Jackson's defense of New Orleans.

REID, THOMAS MAYNE (*b. Ballyroney, Ireland, 1818; d. London, England, 1883*), novelist, journalist. Came to America *ca.* 1838. After traveling widely in the South and West, hunting, trapping and trading with the Indians, he worked for a time as a tutor and at other occupations. Early in 1843 he went to Philadelphia where he lived for about three years, worked as a journalist and playwright, and established friendship with Edgar Allan Poe. He served with distinction as a U.S. Army officer in the Mexican War. Sailing from New York, 1849, to help in the German and Hungarian revolution, he found on arrival in Europe that they had collapsed and lived in England thereafter, with the exception of the years 1867–70 which he spent mainly in Newport, R.I., and New York City. Reid was author of more than seventy novels of romance and adventure; a number of these are based on his American experiences, notably *The Rifle Rangers* (London, 1850). His book *The Quadroon* (1856) was the basis for Dion Boucicault's sensational play *The Octoroon*.

REID, WHITELAW (*b. near Xenia, Ohio, 1837; d. London, England, 1912*), journalist, diplomat. Son-in-law of Darius O. Mills. Graduated Miami University, 1856; edited the *Xenia News* and was active in Republican politics. War correspondent of the *Cincinnati Gazette*, 1861–65, he showed marked ability although his combination of reserve with unusual ambition and self-assertiveness led some to regard him as a selfish careerist. After attempting to run cotton plantations in Louisiana and Alabama, 1865–67, he returned briefly to the *Cincinnati Gazette* and in the fall of 1868 joined the *New York Tribune* as Horace Greeley's editorial assistant; he became managing editor, 1869. Loyal in support fo Greeley's bid for the presidency as a Liberal Republican, 1872, Reid played as disinterested a part as could have been expected when Greeley's collapse brought about a crisis in the affairs of the *Tribune*. A brief struggle for the vacant editorship with Schuyler Colfax ended in Reid's victory and he became head of the most powerful newspaper in America. Maintaining the paper at a high level of competence, Reid increased the circulation of the daily, and though still devoted to Republican principles, fought the Grant administration and shared in exposing its corruption. After the election of James A. Garfield, a close friend, to the presidency, 1880, Reid encouraged the new president in measures which resulted in the resignation of Roscoe Conkling and the downfall of the "Stalwart" Republicans. Reid was the first to install the linotype in a newspaper composing room, believed in spending money liberally for talent, and, with E. L. Godkin, performed a valuable service to journalism by maintaining an important newspaper based on brains and character when others were depending upon sensationalism. An enthusiastic backer of James G. Blaine, Reid considered Cleveland's election a calamity. After stumping for Harrison in the campaign of 1888, he served as U.S. minister to France, 1889–92, and was nominated for the vice presidency, 1892. Generally supporting Grover Cleveland's chief policies during his second term, Reid gave early and ardent support to McKinley and vehemently denounced W. J. Bryan. He was an ardent expansionist and acted on his beliefs while serving as a member of the U.S. commission to negotiate peace with Spain, 1898. A first distrustful of Theodore Roosevelt, Reid soon warmed to him and was particularly pleased by his seizure of Panama. On his appointment as U.S. ambassador to Great Britain, 1905, he gave up active editorship of the *Tribune*.

REID, WILLIAM SHIELDS (*b. Chester Co., Pa., 1778; d. Lynchburg, Va., 1853*), Presbyterian clergyman, Virginia educator.

REID, WILLIAM WHARRY (*b. Argyle, N.Y., 1799; d. 1866*), surgeon. Graduated Union College, 1825. Practiced in Rochester, N.Y., 1828–ca. 1864; is credited with the first (1844) reduction of hip dislocation by flexion.

REIERSEN, JOHAN REINERT (*b. Vestre Moland, Norway, 1810; d. Prairieville, Tex., 1864*), journalist, editor. Traveled in the United States, 1843; published *Pathfinder for Norwegian Emigrants to the United North American States and Texas* (Norway, 1844). Established first Norwegian settlement in Texas at Brownsboro, 1845.

REIK, THEODOR (*b. Vienna, Austria, 1888; d. New York, N.Y., 1969*), psychoanalyst. Attended University of Vienna (Ph.D., 1912). Met Sigmund Freud in 1910 and began a professional and personal relationship that survived Reik's later deviations from Freud's teachings. Practiced psychoanalysis in Europe, 1918–38, then established a thriving practice in New York City (1938) and a clinic for people who could not afford the high fees of most psychoanalysts. Major themes in his work include the importance of intuition in psychoanalysis and the unconscious "duet" of patient and therapist. Disagreed with some orthodox Freudian emphases and criticized the sexual nature of the psychoanalytic view of human nature. His fullest exploration of psychoanalysis appeared in *Listening with the Third Ear* (1948).

REILLY, MARION (*b. Altoona, Pa., 1879; d. Philadelphia, Pa., 1928*), educator, suffrage leader, philanthropist. Dean of Bryn Mawr College, 1907–16.

REINAGLE, ALEXANDER (*b. Portsmouth, England, 1756; d. Baltimore, Md., 1809*), musician. Came to America, 1786; was successful as teacher and pianist and director of concerts in Philadelphia, New York City, and Baltimore. Served as musical director of the New Theatre, Philadelphia, from its opening in 1793 until 1809 and adapted many current English ballad operas to the American stage. His own four piano sonatas, written 1786–94, are the finest surviving American instrumental productions of the eighteenth century.

REINER, FRITZ (*b. Budapest, Hungary, 1888; d. New York, N.Y., 1963*), conductor. Attended Budapest Academy of Music (1898–1908). Began his music career as a coach at the Budapest Komishe Oper (1909) and was conductor and/or director of the Landestheater in Ljubljana, Yugoslavia (1910); the Budapest Volkoper (1911–13); State Orchestra in Dresden (1914–21); Cincinnati Symphony Orchestra (1922–30); Philadelphia Grand Opera (1934–35); San Francisco Opera (1936–38); Pittsburgh Symphony (1938–48); Metropolitan Opera (1949–53); and Chicago Symphony Orchestra (1953–62). Taught at the Curtis Institute of Music (1931–41). He became a U.S. citizen in 1928. His major contributions include the transmission of the best European conducting methods; his supreme musicianship that upgraded the quality of his orchestras; and his recordings of prominent classical and contemporary works.

REINHARDT, AD (*b. Buffalo, N.Y., 1913; d. New York, N.Y., 1967*), painter. Attended Columbia (B.A., 1915) and studied painting and art history at Teachers College, Columbia's Graduate School of Fine Arts, National Academy of Design, American Artists School, and New York University's Institute of Fine Arts. Eight of his paintings were shown at the 1939 New York World's Fair. Consistently nonobjective in his painting after 1940, he is grouped with the New York school of abstract expressionism, but by 1952 he was revolting against cubism, and his canvases appeared as monochrome color fields. His first one-man gallery exhibition was in 1944, and the first of many exhibitions at the Betty Parsons Gallery took place in 1946. Taught at Brooklyn College, 1946–67, and intermittently at California School of Fine Arts, University of Wyoming, Yale School of Fine Arts, and Syracuse.

REINHARDT, AURELIA ISABEL HENRY (*b. San Francisco, Calif., 1877; d. Palo Alto, Calif., 1948*), educator. B.Litt., University of California at Berkeley, 1898. Ph.D. in English, Yale, 1905. Dynamic and successful president of Mills College, 1916–43.

REINHART, BENJAMIN FRANKLIN (*b. near Waynesburg, Pa., 1829; d. 1885*), historical, genre, and portrait painter. Uncle of Charles S. Reinhart.

REINHART, CHARLES STANLEY (*b. Pittsburgh, Pa., 1844; d. 1896*), genre painter, illustrator. Nephew of Benjamin F. Reinhart. An excellent draftsman, he ranks high among American illustrators of his time.

REINSCH, PAUL SAMUEL (*b. Milwaukee, Wis., 1869; d. Shanghai, China, 1923*), political scientist, diplomat. Graduated University of Wisconsin, 1892; LL.B., 1894; Ph.D., 1898. Taught political science at Wisconsin, 1898–1913; was among first to develop systematic courses in world politics; wrote a number of books and articles opposing excessive nationalism and imperialism. As U.S. minister to China, 1913–19, he tried to obtain that country's entrance into World War I on the basis of specific guarantees of financial assistance and other aids.

REISINGER, HUGO (*b. Wiesbaden, Germany, 1856; d. Langenschwalbach, Germany, 1914*), import and export merchant. Resident in the United States *post* 1884, Reisinger collected and exhibited modern American and German art as a means of providing a cultural interchange between the countries.

REISNER, GEORGE ANDREW (*b. Indianapolis, Ind., 1867; d. Giza, Egypt, 1942*), Egyptologist. A.B., Harvard, 1889; Ph.D. in Semitics, 1893. In 1894 Reisner was appointed a scientific assistant in the Egyptian department of the Berlin Museum. He returned to Harvard in 1896–97 as an instructor in the Semitic department. In 1897 he went to Egypt as American member of an international commission designated to catalog the Khedivial Museum in Cairo. He began excavating in 1898 at Quft in Upper Egypt. In 1903 he excavated the valley temples and tombs near the great pyramids at Giza. In 1905 a Harvard University-Boston Museum of Fine Arts Egyptian Expedition was created, of which Reisner was director until his death in 1942. Although he left Egypt only infrequently, Reisner was a member of the Harvard faculty, as assistant professor of Semitic archaeology, 1905–10, assistant professor of Egyptology, 1910–1914, and professor of Egyptology, 1914–42. From 1910 to 1942 he was also curator of the department of Egyptian art of the Boston Museum of Fine Arts.

During the years 1908–10 Reisner was director of Harvard's Palestinian Expedition. At Giza he excavated progressively from 1899 to 1938 large portions of the cemetery west of the Great Pyramid; the entire royal family cemetery to the east, including the intact tomb of Queen Hetep-heres; and the temples of the Third Pyramid of Mycerinus. In 1907–09, during construction to raise the height of the Aswan Dam, Reisner was in charge of the Egyptian government's archaeological survey in Lower Nubia. He also worked extensively in the Sudan. Suffering from increasing blindness in the final years, he returned to the United States in 1939 to receive the honorary degree of Doctor of Letters from Harvard.

REITZEL, ROBERT (*b. Weitenau, Baden, Germany, 1849; d. Detroit, Mich., 1898*), German-American poet, editor. Immigrated to the United States, 1870. Issued the weekly *Der arme Teufel* at Detroit *post* 1884.

RELLSTAB, JOHN (*b. Trenton, N.J., 1858; d. Lake Placid, N.Y., 1930*), journeyman potter, New Jersey lawyer, official, and jurist. Judge of the U.S. district court for New Jersey, 1909–30.

REMEY, GEORGE COLLIER (*b. Burlington, Iowa, 1841; d. Washington, D.C., 1928*), naval officer. Graduated U.S. Naval Academy, 1859. Commanded naval base at Key West, Fla., during war with Spain, 1898; appointed rear admiral in that year, he commanded the Asiatic station, 1900, during the Philippine warfare and Boxer uprising in China.

REMINGTON, ELIPHALET (*b. Suffield, Conn., 1793; d. 1861*), iron forger, manufacturer. Father of Philo Remington. Founded celebrated firm for the manufacture of rifles, pistols, and agricultural implements at Ilion, N.Y., *ca.* 1828.

REMINGTON, FREDERIC (*b. Canton, N.Y., 1861; d. Ridgefield, Conn., 1909*), painter, sculptor, author, illustrator. Studied at Yale School of Fine Arts, 1878–80; studied also at the N.Y. Art Students League. Excelling as a delineator of outdoors men, preferably with horses, Remington is considered unsurpassed in his studies of Western Indians, cowboys and frontiersmen, soldiers in the field, and in general the human figure in action. In his later work, his ability to state by suggestion the character of land, the season of the year, and the state of the weather greatly improved. His sculpture was essentially illustration in bronze with his usual accent on character and action. His books include *Pony Tracks* (1895), *Crooked Trails* (1898), *Stories of Peace and War* (1899), *Done in the Open* (1902), and *The Way of an Indian* (1906). He wrote them in a fresh, journalistic style and illustrated them with the closest attention to accuracy of detail.

REMINGTON, JOSEPH PRICE (*b. Philadelphia, Pa., 1847; d. 1918*), pharmacist. Graduated Philadelphia College of Pharmacy, 1866; taught there *post* 1871 and was made dean, 1893. Author of *Practice of Pharmacy* (1885). Chairman of the committee to revise the *Pharmacopoeia of the Unites States*, 1901–18.

REMINGTON, PHILO (*b. Litchfield, N.Y., 1816; d. Silver Springs, Fla., 1889*), manufacturer. Son of Eliphalet Remington. President *post* 1865 of arms and agricultural equipment manufacturing firm founded by his father, he actively developed the pistol-making branch of the business, perfected the Remington breech-loader, marketed sewing machines, and introduced the Remington typewriter (developed from Sholes and Glidden prototype) in 1876.

REMINGTON, WILLIAM WALTER (*b. New York, N.Y., 1917; d. Lewisburg, Pa., 1954*), economist, federal government employee. Studied at Dartmouth College and at Columbia University (M.A., 1940). Economist with the National Resources Planning Board (1940–41); Office of Price Administration (1941–42); and War Production Board (1942–44). Appointed to the staff of the President's Council of Economic Advisers (1946–48). In 1948 he headed the division of the Department of Commerce that cleared export licenses to trade with Soviet bloc nations. Accused by Elizabeth Bentley in 1945 of having been a source for secrets during the war (Bentley had been a Communist courier). Subsequently accused of having belonged to the Communist party in 1937. In 1953 he was convicted of perjury and sentenced to prison, where he was murdered by two fellow inmates.

REMOND, CHARLES LENOX (*b. Salem, Mass., 1810; d. Boston, Mass., 1873*), black leader. The first black to address public gatherings on behalf of abolition, Remond was appointed agent of the Massachusetts Anti-Slavery Society, 1838, and achieved his greatest success on a lecture tour through Great Britain and Ireland, 1840–41.

REMSEN, IRA (*b. New York, N.Y., 1846; d. Carmel, Calif., 1927*), chemist, educator. Attended New York schools and the New York Free Academy (later College of the City of New York); M.D., N.Y. College of Physicians and Surgeons, 1867; Ph.D., University of Göttingen, 1870. A research student in organic chemistry under some of the best German authorities of the time, Remsen returned to America, 1872, won recognition for his *Principles of Theoretical Chemistry* (1877), and taught for a short time at Williams College. Chosen first professor of chemistry at Johns Hopkins, 1876, he soon surrounded himself with a group of brilliant students who in their later careers strongly influenced the development of chemistry in the United States. Also of great influence in the development of chemical research were the *American Chemical Journal* which Remsen established, 1879, and a series of notable textbooks which he wrote. Appointed president of Johns Hopkins, 1901, he served until 1913, meanwhile continuing his active direction of the department of chemistry.

RÉMY, HENRI (*b. Agen, France, ca. 1811; d. New Orleans, La., 1867*), Louisiana editor, lawyer. A political refugee from France, Rémy came to New Orleans *ca.* 1836 where he studied law in the office of Pierre Soulé. He was later an associate of William Walker in the seizure of Nicaragua, 1855–57.

RENICK, FELIX (*b. Hardy Co., Va., 1770; d. near Chillicothe, Ohio, 1848*), Ohio pioneer, cattleman. Settled in Ross Co., Ohio, 1801; became an outstanding agricultural leader in south central Ohio; improved cattle herd by importing English shorthorns, 1834–36.

RENO, JESSE LEE (*b. Wheeling, Va., present W. Va., 1823; d. 1862*), Union major general. Graduated West Point, 1846. After service in the Mexican War, he was active principally as an ordnance expert until the Civil War when he was commissioned brigadier general, 1861. Serving principally in General Burnside's commands, he was killed at the battle of South Mountain. The city of Reno, Nev., was named in his honor.

RENO, MILO (*b. Wapello Co., Iowa, 1866; d. Excelsior Springs, Mo., 1936*), farm leader. President (1921–30) of the Iowa Farmers' Union; organizer of the Farmers' Holiday Association, which struck in 1932 for higher farm prices and spurred remedial legislation.

RENWICK, EDWARD SABINE (*b. New York, N.Y., 1823; d. Short Hills, N.J., 1912*), engineer, patent expert. Son of James Renwick (1792–1863); brother of Henry B. and James Renwick (1818–1895). Among his many inventions the most important was a series of ten covering incubators and chicken brooders, 1877–86; he also patented a grain harvester and binder, 1851–53, from which he never profited commercially although his ideas were widely used by manufacturers of harvesting machinery after his patents expired.

RENWICK, HENRY BREVOORT (*b. New York, N.Y., 1817; d. New York, 1895*), engineer, patent expert. Son of James Renwick (1792–1863); brother of Edward S. and James Renwick (1818–1895).

RENWICK, JAMES (*b. Liverpool, England, 1792; d. New York, N.Y., 1863*), educator, engineer. Father of Edward S., Henry B. and James Renwick (1818–1895). Came to the United States as a child. Graduated Columbia, 1807; traveled abroad with Washington Irving; A.M., Columbia, 1810. Professor of natural philosophy and experimental chemistry at Columbia, 1820–53, Renwick was until his death a recognized authority on every branch of engineering of that day. Among many projects on which he was consultant was the Morris Canal for which he devised a system of inclined planes or railways for transporting boats; he served also as a commissioner for the survey of the Northeast Boundary, 1840. The more important of his original scientific works were *Outlines of Natural Philosophy* (1822–23) and *Treatise on the Steam-Engine* (1830).

RENWICK, JAMES (*b. New York, N.Y., 1818; d. 1895*), engineer, architect. Son of James Renwick (1792–1863); brother of Edward S. and Henry B. Renwick. Graduated Columbia, 1836; served on engineering staff of Erie Railroad and Croton Aqueduct.

Entirely self-trained in architecture, Renwick won a competition for design of Grace Church, New York City, 1843; thereafter he developed a large practice as an ecclesiastical and general architect. Working at first either in the Gothic or Romanesque style, he early accepted the trend towards eclecticism with sometimes incoherent results; technically, his work was not only careful but advanced, and he was full of imagination. Among his principal works were St. Patrick's Cathedral, New York City (1853–87), the Smithsonian Institution in Washington, D.C. (1846 and after), the Vassar College building (1865), and the Corcoran Gallery, Washington, D.C. An inspiring teacher, he trained among others William W. Root and Bertram G. Goodhue.

REPPLIER, AGNES (*b. Philadelphia, Pa., 1855; d. Philadelphia, 1950*), author, lecturer. Attended Eden Hall, a school conducted by the Sisters of the Sacred Heart, and a school in Philadelphia directed by Agnes Irwin; began to write professionally, 1871. Encouraged by the Rev. Isaac Hecker, she became a regular contributor to the *Catholic World* and later to the *Atlantic Monthly*, winning national prominence as a writer of essays on all manner of topics, marked by wit, irony, erudition, and stylistic distinction. Her books included *Books and Men* (1888); *The Fireside Sphinx* (1901); *A Happy Half-Century* (1908); an autobiography, *In Our Convent Days* (1905); and biographies of Père Marquette and Junipero Serra.

REQUA, MARK LAWRENCE (*b. Virginia City, Nev., 1865; d. Los Angeles, Calif., 1937*), mining engineer. Associate and political adviser of Herbert Hoover.

REQUIER, AUGUSTUS JULIAN (*b. Charleston, S.C., 1825; d. New York, N.Y., 1887*), poet, South Carolina and Alabama jurist, New York City lawyer.

RESE, FREDERICK (*b. Weinenburg, Hanover, Germany, 1791; d. Hildesheim, Germany, 1871*), Roman Catholic clergyman. After working as a journeyman tailor, he made theological studies in Rome and was ordained there, 1822. A volunteer for mission work, he came to Cincinnati, Ohio, *ca.* 1824, the first German priest in the old Northwest. Instrumental in founding the Leopoldine Society of Vienna and in bringing the Redemptorists to the United States, he was bishop of Detroit *post* 1833; he took no active part in the running of the diocese, however, subsequent to 1841.

RESOR, STANLEY BURNET (*b. Cincinnati, Ohio, 1879; d. New York, N.Y., 1962*), advertising executive. Attended Yale (B.A., 1901). Joined Proctor and Collier Advertising (1904), then became manager of the Cincinnati office of J. Walter Thompson (1908); moved to New York headquarters as vice president and general manager (1912); purchased the firm (1916); became its president (until 1955) and then chairman (until 1961). During his presidency the firm became the largest advertising agency in the world. He relied heavily on market research and the compilation of statistical data, and his chief accomplishment was to make advertising part of broader marketing strategies. Named Advertising Man of the Year (1948) by *Advertising and Selling* magazine.

RESTARICK, HENRY BOND (*b. Holcombe, England, 1854; d. 1933*), Episcopal clergyman. Immigrated to Canada *ca.* 1871; settled in Iowa, 1873. A rector for many years in San Diego, Calif., he served as bishop of the district of Honolulu, Hawaii, 1902–20.

REULING, GEORGE (*b. Romrod, Germany, 1839; d. 1915*), ophthalmologist. M.D., University of Giessen, 1865; studied also in Wiesbaden and at Vienna, Berlin, and Paris. Immigrated to Baltimore, Md., 1868; conducted Maryland Eye and Ear Infirmary *post* 1869. Professor of ophthalmology and otology at Washington University, Baltimore, and at Baltimore Medical College.

REUTER, DOMINIC (*b. Coblenz, Germany, 1856; d. Syracuse, N.Y., 1933*), Roman Catholic clergyman, Franciscan. Came to America as a child; entered Friars Minor Conventual at Syracuse, N.Y., 1875. Educated at St. Francis College, Trenton, N.J., and at the University of Innsbruck, he held a number of teaching and other positions in his order and served as minister general, 1904–10.

REUTERDAHL, HENRY (*b. Malmö, Sweden, 1871; d. Washington, D.C., 1925*), illustrator, painter, author. Settled in the United States, 1893. A specialist in depicting naval life and operations, he came to hold a semi-official status as artist to the U.S. Navy.

REUTHER, WALTER PHILIP (*b. Wheeling, W.Va., 1907; d. Pellston, Mich., 1970*), labor leader. Employed at the Ford automobile plant, 1927–32, then worked at Gorki auto works in the Soviet Union, 1933–35. Played a prominent role at the 1936 South Bend, Ind., convention of the United Auto Workers and was elected to the general executive board. Became president of UAW Local 174 and led a strike at Kelsey-Havers Corporation that started an influx of recruits into the local. Appointed director of UAW's General Motors Department (1939) and, through a series of strikes and pullouts, forced GM to recognize the UAW as the bargaining agent for the company's tool and die makers; reorganization of GM production workers quickly followed, as it did elsewhere in the industry. In 1940 he argued that auto plants could be converted to aircraft production, and a succession of other proposals established his reputation as the ablest of a new generation of trade-union leaders. Became UAW president (1946) and purged the union hierarchy of his opponents. He went on the offensive against Communists in the Congress of Industrial Organizations, of which the UAW was a member, and became a prominent figure in the anti-Communist left. A consistent supporter of Franklin Roosevelt, after Harry Truman's victory (1948) came to accept the Democratic party as the only viable instrument for labor politics in America. A brilliant practitioner of collective bargaining, his strategy was to single out one firm for strike actions and then to extend the gains achieved there to the rest of the industry. Became president of the CIO in 1952 and played a crucial part in the merger with the American Federation of Labor in 1955. He found himself increasingly at odds with AFL-CIO president George Meany, and the UAW left the AFL-CIO in 1968. Founded the Alliance for Labor Action (1969), which included only the UAW and the Teamster's Brotherhood, which Reuther had helped expel from the AFL-CIO in 1957 for corruption.

REVEL, BERNARD (*b. Pren, Russia, 1885; d. New York, N.Y., 1940*), Jewish scholar, educator. Came to America, 1906. As president, *post* 1915, of the Rabbi Isaac Elchanan Theological Seminary (the Yeshiva), New York, N.Y., Revel labored devotedly to develop it as a college of liberal arts and sciences which would produce enlightened rabbis, teachers, and laymen for the American Jewish community.

REVELL, FLEMING HEWITT (*b. Chicago, Ill., 1849; d. 1931*), publisher of religious books and Sunday-school materials. Brother-in-law of Dwight L. Moody.

REVELL, NELLIE MACALENEY (*b. Springfield, Ill., 1872; d. New York, N.Y., 1958*), journalist, publicist, radio personality. After working as a reporter for various midwestern and western newspapers, Revell became the first woman reporter for the *New York World* in the 1890's. She left journalism to become publicist for such notables as Al Jolson, Lillie Langtry, Lillian Russell, and Will Rogers, as well as for six circuses. In 1919 a paralyzing spinal ailment interrupted her career. She wrote several books about her illness. Upon partial recovery, she became an interviewer of stage, sports, and political personalities for NBC (1930–47).

REVELS, HIRAM RHOADES (*b. Fayetteville, N.C., 1822; d. Aberdeen, Miss., 1901*), Methodist clergyman, Mississippi legislator and educator. Of mixed African and Indian descent, Revels was U.S. senator, Republican, from Mississippi, 1870–71; thereafter, he served as president of Alcorn University. He was active in behalf of the Democrats in the 1875 campaign which led to the overthrow of the Carpetbag government.

REVERE, JOSEPH WARREN (*b. Boston, Mass., 1812; d. Hoboken, N.J., 1880*), naval officer, Union brigadier general. Grandson of Paul Revere. Appointed midshipman, 1828; served in a variety of capacities until 1845 when he was assigned to the Pacific and played a part in the conquest of California. Resigning from the navy, 1850, he became a rancher and trader, and in 1851 reorganized the artillery branch of the Mexican army. Removing to New Jersey, 1852, he became colonel of the 7th New Jersey Volunteers, 1861, and was promoted brigadier general, October 1862. Relieved of command and court-martialed and dismissed for his conduct at Chancellorsville, May 1863, he was reinstated by President Lincoln, 1864. He was author of *A Tour of Duty in California* (1849) and *Keel and Saddle* (1872).

REVERE, PAUL (*b. Boston, Mass., 1735; d. Boston, 1818*), patriot, silversmith, engraver. A successful craftsman, Revere came into close contact with John Hancock, Samuel Adams, and Joseph Warren through his leadership of the patriotic mechanic class of Boston. When the North End Caucus, most influential of all the patriotic political clubs, voted to oppose the selling of tea by the East India Co., Revere was one of three committeemen chosen to suggest a course of action and along with fifty other Boston workingmen shared in the famous Tea Party. Journeying to New York in the winter of 1773 to apprise the Sons of Liberty there of developments in Boston, he rode out again in the following spring to carry the news of the Boston Port Bill to New York and Philadelphia and to make an appeal for help. In September 1774 he rode to Philadelphia with the "Suffolk Resolves." He then was made official courier for the Massachusetts Provincial Assembly to Congress. Two days before his famous ride to Lexington, he rode with the important purpose of warning the patriots to move their military stores from Concord. On the 18th of April 1775, he rode again to warn Hancock and Adams that the British were out to capture them and to alert the countryside to the fact that the royal troops were on the march. Mounted on a stout work-horse, he eluded British patrols, reached Lexington, saw his two chiefs on the way, and then set out with William Dawes and Samuel Prescott to warn Concord. Stopped by British troopers, Revere was detained a little and then released to make his way back to Lexington without his horse. Anxious for action, he received no military command in the Continental Army. He designed and printed the first issue of Continental money; he made the first official seal for the colonies and the Massachusetts state seal. Learning the process of manufacturing gunpowder, he for a time directed a mill at Canton, Mass.; in 1779 he participated in the ill-fated Penobscot expedition. A master silversmith but a rather amateurish engraver of political cartoons, Revere later entered the foundry business and was the discoverer of a process for rolling sheet copper.

REYNOLDS, ALEXANDER WELCH (*b. Clarke Co., Va., 1817; d. Alexandria, Egypt, 1876*), Confederate brigadier general. Graduated West Point, 1838. Served in the Seminole War and on extensive Western frontier duty. After the Civil War, in which he was engaged principally in the Western campaigns, he removed to Egypt, took a commission in the Egyptian army and served as chief of staff to William W. Loring.

REYNOLDS, CHARLES ALEXANDER (*b. probably near Stephensburg, Ky., 1842[?]; d. near the Little Big Horn, Montana Territory, 1876*), Union soldier, hunter, scout, known as "Lonesome Charley." Generally ranked as the greatest of the Western scouts, Reynolds was raised in Illinois and Kansas. After Civil War service, he left home and became a hunter in the Dakota country, furnishing game to military posts. He served as a scout for the Yellowstone expedition under David S. Stanley, 1873, was the guide for Custer's Black Hills expedition, 1874, and in the following year was hunter and chief scout for, among other military expeditions, that of William Ludlow. Employed as a scout for the Big Horn expedition which left Fort Abraham Lincoln, May 17, 1876, he was assigned to Reno's battalion and was shot at the beginning of the retreat from the Little Big Horn valley.

REYNOLDS, EDWIN (*b. Mansfield, Conn., 1831; d. Milwaukee, Wis., 1909*), engineer. As plant superintendent for the Corliss Steam Engine Co., Providence, R.I., Reynolds built the giant engine displayed at the 1876 Exhibition. Associated *post* with the Edward P. Allis Co. and Allis-Chalmers, he incorporated many of his inventions and improvements in the machinery manufactured by those companies. He built the first triple expansion pumping engine for waterworks service in the United States, 1888, and in the same year patented a blowing engine for blast furnaces which was a radical departure from accepted design practice. In 1893 he designed and built a four-cylinder compound steam engine for the Manhattan Railway power house, New York, N.Y.

REYNOLDS, GEORGE McCLELLAND (*b. Panora, Iowa, 1865; d. Pasadena, Calif., 1940*), banker. Protégé of J. Ogden Armour, Reynolds served as president of the Continental National Bank of Chicago and its subsequent consolidations, 1906–33. He was associated with Nelson W. Aldrich in the investigations which produced the Aldrich Plan.

REYNOLDS, JOHN (*b. probably England, 1713; d. 1788*), British admiral, first royal governor of Georgia, 1754–57. In constant struggle with the Assembly over financial problems and procedures, Reynolds regarded the colonists as "lawless, antimonarchal people" who required government by military force.

REYNOLDS, JOHN (*b. Montgomery Co., Pa., 1788; d. Belleville, Ill., 1865*), lawyer, Illinois legislator, Democratic politician. Raised in Tennessee, and near Kaskaskia, Ill. Undistinguished as a lawyer but a glib and able cultivator of the electorate, Reynolds was governor of Illinois, 1830–34, and congressman from that state, 1834–37, 1839–43. He was author of a colorful autobiography, *My Own Times* (1855). He was later a strong Confederate sympathizer.

REYNOLDS, JOHN FULTON (*b. Lancaster, Pa., 1820; d. Gettysburg, Pa., 1863*), Union soldier. Graduated West Point, 1841. An artillery officer, he served with particular distinction in the Mexican War and in the Far West, 1854–60. Made brigadier general of volunteers, 1861, he was active in the Peninsular campaign, directed the Pennsylvania militia, and in November 1862 was promoted major general. He was most effective as the I Corps commander at Fredericksburg and Chancellorsville. Ordered to occupy Gettysburg on June 28, 1863, Reynolds set the I, III, and XI Corps in motion and arrived at the town on the morning of July 1. Marching at the head of the 2nd Wisconsin Regiment, he was killed by a sharpshooter.

REYNOLDS, JOSEPH JONES (*b. Flemingsburg, Ky., 1822; d. Washington, D.C., 1899*), Union soldier. Graduated West Point, 1843. Served as artillery officer with General Zachary Taylor's army in the Mexican War; taught at West Point, 1846–55;

resigned from the army, 1857. Appointed brigadier general, 1861, he served under General Rosecrans in western Virginia and on promotion to major general, 1862, commanded a division in the Army of the Cumberland. After the battle of Chickamauga, 1863, he became chief of staff of the Army of the Cumberland; *post* July 1864, he headed the XIX Corps. After postwar duty in Texas and Louisiana and in the Far West, he retired, 1877.

REYNOLDS, QUENTIN JAMES (*b. Bronx, N.Y., 1902; d. Travis Air Force Base, Calif., 1965*), author and war correspondent. Attended Brown and Brooklyn Law (LL.B., 1931). Obtained a job with the International News Service (1931) and was its feature writer in Berlin by early 1933. Returned to New York to work for *Collier's* (1933–48) and was sent to Europe as war correspondent in 1940, covering the fall of France and the Battle of Britain, after which he wrote *The Wounded Don't Cry* (1941), a best-selling book. His radio broadcasts for British Broadcasting and his risk-taking coverage of combat in Italy, North Africa, and the southwest Pacific helped establish his reputation as one of America's leading war correspondents.

REYNOLDS, RICHARD SAMUEL, SR. (*b. Bristol, Tenn., 1881; d. Richmond, Va., 1955*), aluminum executive. Studied briefly at Columbia University and at the University of Virginia Law School. Worked for the Reynolds family-owned tobacco company (1902–12), then resigned and formed his own business, the Reynolds Corporation. Founded the U.S. Foil Company in 1919, which became the Reynolds Metals Company in 1928. A pioneer in the manufacturer of aluminum, Reynolds guided the company through the Depression and World War II until it was the nation's second largest producer of aluminum in 1955. President of the Reynolds Metals Company until 1948; chairman of the board, 1948–55. Published *War Enthroned and Other Poems* (1936) and *Crucible: Poems* (1950).

REYNOLDS, ROBERT RICE (*b. Asheville, N.C., 1884; d. Asheville, 1963*), U.S. senator. Attended University of North Carolina (B.A., 1906) and its law school; began practicing law in 1909 and was elected prosecuting attorney for the state's Fifteenth Judicial District (1910–14). As U.S. senator (1932–45) advocated immigration restriction and opposed U.S. entry into World War II; created the Vindicators Association to further those causes in 1939. A colorful if uninfluential member of the Senate.

REYNOLDS, SAMUEL GODFREY (*b. Bristol, R.I., 1801; d. Bristol, 1881*), tanner, inventor of improved machinery for making nails, pins and spikes.

REYNOLDS, WILLIAM (*b. Lancaster, Pa., 1815; d. Washington, D.C., 1879*), naval officer. Brother of John F. Reynolds. Retired as rear admiral, 1877.

REYNOLDS, WILLIAM NEAL (*b. Patrick County, Va., 1863; d. Winston-Salem, N.C., 1951*), tobacco manufacturer, sportsman, philanthropist. Studied from 1882 to 1884 at Trinity College (now Duke University). Joined the family business, forming the R. J. Reynolds Tobacco Company in 1888; vice president and member of the board of directors (1889–1918); president (1918–24); chairman of the board (1924–31). His company produced the first modern mass-marketed cigarette, Camel, in 1913. Owner of one of the three largest tobacco companies in the nation, Reynolds was also an avid sportsman; he bred and raced horses. Endowed Wake Forest College, North Carolina State College, and was a trustee of Duke University.

REZANOV, NIKOLAI PETROVICH (*b. St. Petersburg, Russia, 1764; d. Krasnoyarsk, Siberia, 1807*), Russian civil service official, Alaskan colonizer. A founder of the Russian-American Co. for the exploitation of Alaska, Rezanov set out in 1803 to investi-gate the resources of the territory and to test the possibility of supplying the colonies there by sea. After many difficulties, he landed at New Archangel (Sitka), 1805; in search of food for the starving community, he visited the port of San Francisco, Calif., April–May 1806. He died on his way back to Russia.

RHEA, JOHN (*b. Co. Donegal, Ireland, 1753; d. 1832*), lawyer. Immigrated to America, 1769; settled in eastern Tennessee, 1778. Congressman, Democrat, from Tennessee, 1803–15, 1817–23; a friend and supporter of Andrew Jackson; opposed slavery.

RHEES, MORGAN JOHN (*b. Glamorganshire, Wales, 1760; d. 1804*), Baptist clergyman, reformer. Came to America, 1794. After traveling widely in the United States, Rhees collaborated with Benjamin Rush in land developments in central Pennsylvania where he also preached and organized Baptist churches among the Welsh settlers.

RHEES, RUSH (*b. Chicago, Ill., 1860; d. Rochester, N.Y., 1939*), Baptist clergyman, educator. Great-grandson of Morgan J. Rhees. Graduated Amherst, 1883; Hartford Theological Seminary, 1888. President, University of Rochester, 1900–35.

RHEES, WILLIAM JONES (*b. Philadelphia, Pa., 1830; d. Washington, D.C., 1907*), bibliographer, official and archivist of Smithsonian Institution.

RHETT, ROBERT BARNWELL (*b. Beaufort, S.C., 1800; d. Louisiana, 1876*), lawyer, statesman. Changed name from Smith to Rhett, 1837. Elected to the legislature, 1826, he quickly became prominent for his passionate and eloquent advocacy of an extreme states' rights doctrine; as congressman from South Carolina, 1837–49, he advanced to the forefront of the followers of J. C. Calhoun, accepting Calhoun's belief that the Constitution, rightly interpreted, would protect the South. After Calhoun's failure to secure the presidential nomination and the abandonment by Northern Democrats of the Southern position on the tariff, Rhett moved more and more towards secession, and *post* 1850 was its open advocate. Succeeding Calhoun as U.S. senator, 1850, he resigned his seat, 1852, when a South Carolina convention passed an ordinance merely declaratory of the right of secession which Rhett chose to regard as a "submission" to the Union over the Compromise of 1850. Continuing to work for his declared aim of Southern Confederacy, he met with William L. Yancey and other Southern radicals in 1858 but was forced with them to the conclusion that the only hope for secession lay in a Republican victory in 1860. Through his newspaper mouthpiece, the *Charleston Mercury*, Rhett worked to undermine Southern confidence in the Democratic party and was the principal architect of secession when the crisis arose in South Carolina in late 1860. At the Southern Congress in Montgomery, Ala., he failed to secure the Confederate presidency and was ignored in the cabinet appointments. Welcoming the Civil War because in his view it would stop any chance of a reconstruction of the Union, he was a vigorous critic of President Jefferson Davis's administration and opposed Davis's "usurpations" as vigorously as he had opposed the Union. He died still serenely confident in his faith that the South would be "separate and free." His character and the motivation of his career as well as his statesmanship are subjects on which historians are as little likely to reach agreement as were his contemporaries.

RHIND, ALEXANDER COLDEN (*b. New York, N.Y., 1821; d. New York, 1897*), naval officer. Son of Charles Rhind. Acquired a reputation for insubordination during his early years of service; performed a number of highly hazardous individual exploits during the Civil War, in particular at Charleston, S.C., April

1863, and at the first attack on Fort Fisher, 1864. Retired as rear admiral, 1883.

RHIND, CHARLES (*b. Aberdeen, Scotland, date unknown; d. probably New York, N.Y., post 1846*), merchant, diplomatic agent. Father of Alexander C. Rhind. First appears in New York City directory, 1810, as a ship chandler. U.S. commissioner with David Offley and James Biddle to negotiate treaty of commerce with Turkey, 1830.

RHOADS, CORNELIUS PACKARD (*b. Springfield, Mass., 1898; d. Stonington, Conn., 1959*), scientist, physician, administrator. Attended Bowdoin College (B.A., 1920), Harvard Medical School (M.D., 1924). Was an instructor at Harvard (1926); staff member of the Rockefeller Institute for Medical Research (1928–39). Became chief of the Medical Division of the Army Chemical Warfare Service during World War II. Rhoads is chiefly remembered as the country's foremost cancer researcher. Director of the newly formed Sloan-Kettering Institute for Cancer Research, from 1948. A proponent of chemotherapy in cancer treatment, he guided the foundation to international prominence.

RHOADS, JAMES E. (*b. Marple, Pa., 1828; d. Bryn Mawr, Pa., 1895*), physician, Quaker editor, philanthropist. President of Bryn Mawr College, 1883–94.

RHODES, EUGENE MANLOVE (*b. Tecumseh, Nebr., 1869; d. 1934*), cowboy, novelist. Raised in Kansas and New Mexico; worked as a cowpuncher and rancher, 1882–1906, with a short interval for study at the University of the Pacific. Author of a number of excellent fictional studies of the cattle kingdom which include *Good Men and True* (1910), *The Desire of the Moth* (1916), *West Is West* (1917), *Stepsons of Light* (1921), *Beyond the Desert* (1934), and *The Proud Sheriff* (1935). His books have been described as the only body of fiction devoted to the cattleman and his life that is both true to the subject and written by an artist in prose.

RHODES, JAMES FORD (*b. Cleveland, Ohio, 1848; d. Brookline, Mass., 1927*), businessman, historian. Brother-in-law of Marcus A. Hanna. Retiring from business, 1885, he wrote a *History of the United States from the Compromise of 1850* which is marked by good judgment and, for its day, notable fair-mindedness. Somewhat pedestrian in style, it still stands as a landmark in American historiography and is distinguished for the thoroughness and skill with which it handles vast materials. The first two volumes were published in 1893 and were greeted by competent critics with immediate and practically unanimous approval; five subsequent volumes (Vol. 3, 1895; Vol. 4, 1899; Vol. 5, 1904; Vols. 6 and 7, 1906) served to enhance the author's fame. He had originally intended to carry the history to 1855 but wisely decided to end it with the restoration of Southern home rule in 1877. He was author also of several other works, but his fame rests upon his major history and especially on the first five volumes.

RIBAUT, JEAN (*b. Dieppe, France, ca. 1520; d. Florida, 1565*), French mariner. A trusted captain under Admiral Coligny, Ribaut was chosen to establish a French colony and asylum for Huguenots on the coast of Florida, 1562. After making his landfall in late spring near St. John's River, he settled his colonists at the present Port Royal, S.C., which he called Charlesfort, and returned to France. Becoming embroiled there in the Wars of Religion, he fled to England where he was for a time imprisoned. After his release he set out with a reinforcement for his colony in 1565, but was taken prisoner by the Spaniards under Pedro Menéndez de Avilés and executed.

RICE, ALEXANDER HAMILTON (*b. Newton Lower Falls, Mass., 1818; d. Melrose, Mass., 1895*), paper manufacturer, Boston councilman and mayor. Congressman, Republican, from Massachusetts, 1859–67; governor of Massachusetts, 1876–78.

RICE, ALICE CALDWELL HEGAN (*b. Shelbyville, Ky., 1870; d. Louisville, Ky., 1942*), author. Married Cale Y. Rice, 1902. Author of numerous short stories and twenty novels, of which the first, *Mrs. Wiggs of the Cabbage Patch* (1901), was extraordinarily successful.

RICE, CALVIN WINSOR (*b. Winchester, Mass., 1868; d. New York, N.Y., 1934*), engineer. Promoter of national and international engineering societies.

RICE, CHARLES (*b. Munich, Bavaria, 1841; d. 1901*), chemist, philologist, Sanskrit scholar. Came to America, 1862. After service in U.S. Navy, was associated with the pharmacy department of Bellevue Hospital, New York City, and became eventually its superintendent. Chairman, revision committee, *U.S. Pharmacopoeia*, 1880–1901.

RICE, CHARLES ALLEN THORNDIKE (*b. Boston, Mass., 1851; d. New York, N.Y., 1889*), journalist. Publisher and editor, *North American Review, post 1876*, he made that moribund periodical a financial and literary success by persuading leaders of world opinion to write for it on contemporary public questions.

RICE, DAN (*b. New York, N.Y., 1823; d. Long Branch, N.J., 1900*), circus clown, showman. Remembered as one of the greatest of American clowns, Rice (born McLaren) was also famous as a crackerbox philosopher and commentator on public affairs.

RICE, DAVID (*b. Hanover Co., Va., 1733; d. 1816*), Presbyterian clergyman, active as a missionary and church organizer in Kentucky *post* 1783.

RICE, EDMUND (*b. Waitsfield, Vt., 1819; d. White Bear Lake, Minn., 1889*), lawyer, railroad executive, and promoter. Brother of Henry M. Rice. Settling in St. Paul, Minn., 1849, he was prominent in developing railroads of that state. Twice mayor of St. Paul, he was a Democratic member of Congress, 1887–89.

RICE, EDWIN WILBUR (*b. Kingsborough, present Gloversville, N.Y., 1831; d. 1929*), Congregational clergyman and missionary. Official of the American Sunday School Union.

RICE, EDWIN WILBUR (*b. La Crosse, Wis., 1862; d. 1935*), electrical engineer. Son of Edwin W. Rice (1831–1929). A longtime associate as pupil and assistant to Elihu Thomson, Rice served as technical director of the General Electric Co. and as its president, 1913–22. Patents issued to him cover practically the entire field of electrical operations; he was responsible for the addition of Charles P. Steinmetz to the company's staff.

RICE, ELMER (*b. New York, N.Y., 1892; d. Southampton, England, 1967*), playwright, director, and novelist. Attended New York Law School; admitted to the bar in 1913. His first play, *On Trial* (1914), was a sensation, and was followed by about fifty others, including *Wake Up Jonathan*, with Hatcher Hughes (1921); *The Adding Machine* (1923); *Close Harmony*, with Dorothy Parker (1924); *Street Scene* (1929), which won a Pulitzer Prize; *Counsellor-at-Law* (1931); and *Dream Girl* (1945). With other playwrights formed the Playwrights' Producing Company to produce and direct their own plays; in 1933 he directed Robert E. Sherwood's *Abe Lincoln in Illinois*. Also wrote three novels: *A Voyage to Purilia* (1930); *Imperial City* (1937); and *The Show Must Go On* (1949). One of the first dramatists to use the

American stage as a vehicle for social criticism, he had little impact on the American theater after World War II.

RICE, FENELON BIRD (*b. Greensburg, Ohio, 1841; d. Oberlin, Ohio, 1901*), music teacher. Grandson of David Rice. Graduated Boston Music School, 1863; studied also in Leipzig. Director of the school of music at Oberlin College, 1871–1901.

RICE, GEORGE SAMUEL (*b. Claremont, N.H., 1866; d. Takoma Park, Md., 1950*), mining engineer. Graduated School of Mines, Columbia University, 1887. After attaining marked success in private engineering practice, he began in 1908 a long crusade for mine safety, which brought him international reputation. He served as chief mining engineer, U.S. Bureau of Mines, 1910–37; during his tenure the Bureau became a world leader in research and promotion of safe mining techniques and procedures.

RICE, (HENRY), GRANTLAND (*b. Murfreesboro, Tenn., 1880; d. New York, N.Y., 1954*), sports journalist. Studied at Vanderbilt University (B.A., 1901). One of America's most famous sportswriters, Rice contributed to the *New York Tribune* (1914–30) and had nationwide distribution of his columns through syndication. Helped build the reputations of such figures as Babe Ruth, Red Grange, and Bobby Jones. Joined the North American Newspaper Alliance in 1930.

RICE, HENRY MOWER (*b. Waitsfield, Vt., 1816; d. San Antonio, Tex., 1894*), Indian trader, Minnesota pioneer. Brother of Edmund Rice. Resident in Minnesota *post* 1847, he was influential in establishment of the Territory, served as territorial delegate to Congress, and was U.S. senator, Democrat, from the State of Minnesota, 1858–63.

RICE, ISAAC LEOPOLD (*b. Wachenheim, Bavaria, 1850; d. 1915*), New York lawyer, financier, chess expert. Came to America as a child. LL.B., Columbia Law School, 1880. Prominent as a railroad lawyer and as a promoter of electrical inventions, he was also the inventor of the "Rice gambit" and was founder (1886) and chief proprietor of the *Forum*.

RICE, JOHN ANDREW (*b. Lynchburg, S.C., 1888; d. Silver Spring, Md., 1968*), educator. Attended Tulane (B.A., 1911), Oxford as a Rhodes Scholar (B.A., 1914), and University of Chicago. Taught at the University of Nebraska (1919–28), Rutgers (1928–30), New Jersey College for Women (1928–30), and Rollins College (1930–33), from which he was fired for his outspoken criticism of the curriculum system. With a few colleagues and little money, he founded Black Mountain College in rural North Carolina, where a steady stream of innovative faculty gave the school an unsurpassed reputation for creative work in literature and the arts; the college closed in 1956. Rice had resigned in 1940 and later contributed short stories to the *New Yorker* and *Saturday Evening Post*.

RICE, JOHN HOLT (*b. Bedford Co., Va., 1777; d. 1831*), Presbyterian clergyman, educator. Nephew of David Rice. Active in establishing the theological seminary at Hampden-Sydney, he served as professor of theology there *post* 1824; he was also a strong controversial writer and a promoter of Presbyterian missionary activities.

RICE, LUTHER (*b. Northboro, Mass., 1783; d. 1836*), Baptist clergyman and educational promoter. Devoted his life to the organization of American Baptists in support of missionary work and higher education for the clergy.

RICE, NATHAN LEWIS (*b. Garrard Co., Ky., 1807; d. Chatham, Ky., 1877*), Presbyterian clergyman, editor. Held numerous pastorates in the East and Middle West; helped influence Cyprus

H. McCormick to become patron of what is now known as McCormick Theological Seminary. President of Westminster College, Fulton, Mo., 1869–74, and professor of theology in Danville (Ky.) Seminary, 1874–77. He was most famous as a controversialist for his debates with Alexander Campbell in Kentucky, 1843.

RICE, RICHARD HENRY (*b. Rockland, Maine, 1863; d. 1922*), engineer. Graduated Stevens Institute of Technology, 1885. After wide experience as an engine and machine designer, Rice was associated with the General Electric Co. *post* 1903 for which he directed work on the development of the steam turbine. He designed the first turbo-blower for blast furnaces to be installed in America.

RICE, THOMAS DARTMOUTH (*b. New York, N.Y., 1808; d. New York, 1860*), father of the American minstrel show. Introduced the "Jim Crow" song and dance at the Southern Theatre, Louisville, Ky., 1828; as prepared for publication by William C. Peters, the song became a hit in America and England. In addition to making successful tours in the character of "Jim Crow," Rice wrote numerous extravaganzas known as "Ethiopian Opera." Although he was not the first blackface comedian, Rice, by his phenomenal success, created a vogue for them.

RICE, VICTOR MOREAU (*b. Mayville, N.Y., 1818; d. 1869*), educator. Graduated Allegheny College, 1841. First superintendent and organizer of the New York State Department of Public Instruction, 1854–57 and 1862–68. His most conspicuous accomplishment was abolition of the rate bill and final establishment of free schools on the principle that the property of the state should educate the children of the state.

RICE, WILLIAM MARSH (*b. Springfield, Mass., 1816; d. 1900*), merchant, philanthropist. Removed to Houston, Texas, 1838, where he prospered as a trader, investor, and landowner; left his large fortune for the foundation of Rice Institute, Houston.

RICE, WILLIAM NORTH (*b. Marblehead, Mass., 1845; d. Delaware, Ohio, 1928*), geologist. Graduated Wesleyan University, 1865; Ph.D., Yale, 1867. Professor of geology and natural history at Wesleyan, 1867–84; thereafter taught only geology. Promoted a reconciliation of science and religion in his writing and teaching.

RICH, ISAAC (*b. Wellfleet, Mass., 1801; d. 1872*), Boston fish merchant and real estate owner. A leading benefactor of Methodist educational institutions, Rich left practically his whole estate to Boston University.

RICH, OBADIAH (*b. Truro, Mass., 1783; d. London, England, 1850*), bibliographer, bookseller. After serving as U.S. consul at Valencia, Spain, 1816–ca. 1829, he moved to London, England, where he established himself as a bookseller and specialized in manuscripts and early printed books relating to America. His generosity with his stock and personal library won him the gratitude of such historians as Washington Irving, W. H. Prescott, George Bancroft, and others. He was author of a number of catalogues of items which he had for sale which are still useful in bibliographical research.

RICH, ROBERT (*b. Woolrich, Pa., 1883; d. Jersey Shore, Pa., 1968*), businessman and U.S. congressman. Attended Williamsport Commercial College and Dickinson College. Began work with the family-owned Woolrich Woolen Mills in 1896 and was its general manager by 1930. Appointed to complete a congressional term (1930), he was elected from that Pennsylvania district for the next six congresses. Vociferously opposed to the New Deal, he was alone among House Republicans to vote against extending the National Industrial Recovery Act. He called for the eradication of many New Deal agencies and was an arch-isolationist who opposed U.S. defense buildup and foreign assistance, including the Marshall Plan. Returned to Woolrich Mills in 1951 and was its chairman, 1964 to 1966.

RICHARD, GABRIEL (*b. Saintes, France, 1767; d. Detroit, Mich., 1832*), Roman Catholic clergyman, educator, Sulpician. Fleeing France during the Revolution, he came to Baltimore, June 1792, and was assigned by Bishop John Carroll to work among the French and Indians out of Kaskaskia and Cahokia. Settling in Detroit, June 1798, he succeeded as pastor of St. Anne's Church there and became vicar general of the region. A zealous, austere, and able man, he ministered to whites and Indians, fought the evils of liquor, and organized some of the earliest educational institutions in Detroit. Obtaining from Baltimore a printing press and a printer, he issued the first paper printed in Detroit, the *Essai du Michigan*, 1809, and also published a number of books. In an effort to stimulate local industry, he imported carding machines, spinning wheels, and looms. Imprisoned as an American during the War of 1812, on his return to Detroit he engaged in relief work there and together with John Monteith, a minister, founded the University of Michigania, 1817. Elected delegate to Congress, 1822, he served a single term. Returning to his church work in Detroit, he died ministering to victims of a cholera epidemic.

RICHARD, JAMES WILLIAM (*b. near Winchester, Va., 1843; d. 1909*), Lutheran clergyman, theologian, educator, Author of *The Confessional History of the Lutheran Church* (1909).

RICHARDS, CHARLES BRINCKERHOFF (*b. Brooklyn, N.Y., 1833; d. New Haven, Conn., 1919*), mechanical engineer. Trained as practical mechanic, Richards devised a steam-engine indicator which facilitated high-speed engine design. While an official at the Colt Armory, 1861–80, he devised the platform-scale testing machine for testing the strength of metals and became a recognized authority on heating and ventilation. He headed the department of mechanical engineering at Sheffield Scientific School, Yale, 1884–1909.

RICHARDS, CHARLES HERBERT (*b. Meriden, N.H., 1839; d. 1925*), Congregational clergyman, official of the Congregational Church Building Society, lecturer on ecclesiastical architecture.

RICHARDS, ELLEN HENRIETTA SWALLOW (*b. Dunstable, Mass., 1842; d. Jamaica Plain, Mass., 1911*), chemist, home economist. Graduated Vassar, 1870; B.S., Massachusetts Institute of Technology, 1873. Taught sanitary chemistry at Massachusetts Institute *post* 1884; was a leader in the home economics movement.

RICHARDS, JOHN KELVEY (*b. Ironton, Ohio, 1856; d. 1909*), jurist, Ohio legislator and official. U.S. solicitor general, 1897–1903; judge, U.S. circuit court (6th circuit), 1903–09. Gained high reputation for handling of Insular Cases and others before the U.S. Supreme Court, 1897–1903.

RICHARDS, JOSEPH WILLIAM (*b. Oldbury, England, 1864; d. 1921*), metallurgist. Came to America as a boy. Graduated Lehigh, 1866; Ph.D., the first to be granted by the university, 1893. An outstanding teacher at Lehigh *post* 1887, he was a recognized authority on the metallurgy of aluminum, electro-metallurgy, and metallurgical-chemical calculations.

RICHARDS, LAURA ELIZABETH HOWE (*b. Boston, Mass., 1850; d. Gardiner, Maine, 1943*), author. Daughter of Julia Ward Howe and Samuel Gridley Howe; married Henry Richards, an architect and paper mill manager, 1871. Author of more than seventy books, including jingles and nonsense verse (*Sketches & Scraps*, 1881, and others), humorous stories for children (*The Joyous Story of Toto*, 1885), and a number of books for young girls, of which the most popular was *Captain January* (1890). She also wrote juvenile biographies of famous people, and several books relating to her parents, collaborating with her sister on *Julia Ward Howe* (1915), which won a Pulitzer Prize.

RICHARDS, ROBERT HALLOWELL (*b. Gardiner, Maine, 1844; d. Natick, Mass., 1945*), mining engineer. Grandson of Robert Hallowell Gardiner. B.S., Massachusetts Institute of Technology, 1868. Appointed instructor in chemistry at M.I.T., he stressed laboratory work; in 1871 he organized the institute's mining and metallurgical laboratories, devising special equipment for practical illustration and testing of processes under actual mill conditions. He served as professor of mining engineering and head of that department, 1873–1914. He invented or improved a number of machines for ore dressing (which was his speciality) and was author of more than a hundred technical papers and of two books on ore dressing.

RICHARDS, THEODORE WILLIAM (*b. Germantown, Pa., 1868; d. Cambridge, Mass., 1928*), chemist. Son of William T. Richards. Graduated Haverford, 1885; Ph.D., Harvard, 1888. As a graduate student he came under the influence of Josiah P. Cooke who at the time was interested in atomic weights and because of his distrust of their current values had undertaken the revision of some of them. Cooke entrusted Richards with the experimental determination of the relation of the atomic weights of hydrogen and oxygen. In this extremely exacting problem Richards showed the qualities which made him the foremost experimental chemist of his time. After completion of his graduate work he spent one year as a traveling fellow in Europe. On his return he was appointed to the Harvard faculty, becoming a full professor in 1901 and obtaining the Erving Professorship of Chemistry in 1912. Richards always believed that only through measurements of precision was progress to be made in chemistry. Beginning with copper he redetermined the atomic weights of barium, strontium, and zinc, and, with the help of his students, twenty additional elements. In the course of his work many new analytical processes were devised and perfected. His determination of atomic weights brought to light many previous inaccuracies.

During the last half of his career his interest turned to various fields of physical chemistry, in particular, thermochemistry and thermodynamics. He devoted much energy to the perfecting of thermochemical measurements and devised the "adiabatic calorimeter." New and highly accurate data were obtained in this way, covering heats of solution of metals in acids, heats of combustion of organic substances, heats of neutralization, specific heats of liquids, specific heats of solids at low temperatures, and heats of evaporation of liquids. The study of the data thus obtained led Richards to the discovery that the magnitude of the difference between "total energy change" and "free energy change" depends upon change in heat capacity of a system during chemical change and that this difference gradually disappears as the absolute zero is approached. His work in thermochemistry led him into the field of thermometry and to the exact determination for the first time of the inversion temperatures of hydrated compounds for use as fixed points.

Richards's chief interest in the latter part of his life lay in the consideration of the relation between the physical properties of the various elements and their compounds, especially those connected with atomic volumes and compressibilities. He devised new forms of apparatus for determining exactly the compressibilities of the elements and their compounds, as well as certain related properties such as surface tension and heat of evaporation. This work led to the discovery of the periodicity of atomic volume and compressibility and the close parallelism between these properties, as well as to the fact that increase or decrease in volume during a chemical change depends on the one hand upon the compressibilities of the substances involved and on the other upon their chemical affinities. The latest aspect of this work was an attempt to compute from compressibilities and other data the actual internal pressures which hold matter together. Richards published nearly 300 papers covering a far wider field than indicated here. While many of the theoretical results which he reached have been and will be of the greatest importance, his contribution to the technique of precise physico-chemical investigation will undoubtedly always stand out as being equally important. Indeed he may well be said to have inaugurated a new era in the accuracy of analytical an physico-chemical experimentation. He received the Nobel prize of 1914 for his work on atomic weights.

RICHARDS, THOMAS ADDISON (b. *London, England, 1820; d. Annapolis, Md., 1900*), landscape painter, art teacher. Came to America as a boy. Studied at N.Y. National Academy of Design in which he became an associate and an official. His work as a painter belongs with the Hudson River school and his romantic enthusiasm for natural scenery may be considered the keynote of his career. He was professor of art in the present New York University, 1867–87. Among the books he wrote and illustrated were *The American Artist* (1838), *Georgia Illustrated* (1842), *American Scenery* (1854), and *Appletons' Illustrated Handbook of American Travel* (1857).

RICHARDS, VINCENT (b. *New York, N.Y., 1903; d. New York, 1959*), tennis player. Studied at Fordham University (1920–22), Columbia University (1922). Won twenty-seven national tennis titles in singles, doubles, and mixed doubles competition. Played and took the title in the national doubles championship with William Tilden in 1918. Represented the United States on five winning Davis Cup teams and won the men's singles and doubles titles at the 1924 Olympics. In 1927 he helped organize the Professional Lawn Tennis Association of the United States. Last title, again with Tilden, was the national professional doubles title in 1945. Was the first commissioner of the World Professional Tennis League, in 1947. Generally, he was instrumental in making professional tennis a successful sport.

RICHARDS, WILLIAM (b. *Plainfield, Mass., 1793; d. 1847*), Congregational clergyman, missionary to the Hawaiian Islands. Richards spent the great part of his life *post* 1838 as a Hawaiian government official and played a great but unobtrusive part in liberalizing the Hawaiian economic and political system.

RICHARDS, WILLIAM TROST (b. *Philadelphia, Pa., 1833; d. Newport, R.I., 1905*), painter. Father of Theodore W. Richards. Specialized in accurate, realistic seascapes.

RICHARDS, ZALMON (b. *Cummington, Mass., 1811; d. Washington, D.C., 1899*), educator. Graduated Williams, 1836. An organizer and first president (1857) of the National Teachers' Association which later became the National Education Association.

RICHARDSON, ALBERT DEANE (b. *Franklin, Mass., 1833; d. New York, N.Y., 1869*), journalist, Civil War correspondent for the *New York Tribune.* Author of two books immensely popular in their time, *The Secret Service* (1865) and *Beyond the Mississippi* (1866).

RICHARDSON, ANNA EURETTA (b. *Charleston, S.C., 1883; d. Washington, D.C., 1931*), home economist, educator.

RICHARDSON, CHARLES FRANCIS (b. *Hallowell, Maine, 1851; d. Sugar Hill, N.H., 1913*), educator. Graduated Dartmouth, 1871. Professor of English at Dartmouth, 1882–1911. Author, among other works, of two pioneer studies: *A Primer of American Literature* (1878) and *American Literature: 1607–1885* (1887, 1888). Despite their shortcomings, these works supplied a need and were for a time of considerable influence.

RICHARDSON, CHARLES WILLIAMSON (b. *Washington, D.C., 1861; d. Boston, Mass., 1929*), physician, specialist in diseases of the throat, nose, and ear.

RICHARDSON, EDMUND (b. *Caswell Co., N.C., 1818; d. Jackson, Miss., 1886*), cotton planter, factor, manufacturer. Removed to Mississippi, 1833, where he prospered as a merchant and plantation owner; he also engaged in factoring at New Orleans, La. Heavily in debt at the end of the Civil War, he rebuilt his fortune in a very short time, began the manufacture of cotton in addition to his other concerns, and was at the time of his death the largest cotton planter in the world.

RICHARDSON, HENRY HOBSON (b. *St. James Parish, La., 1838; d. Boston, Mass., 1886*), architect. Great-grandson of Joseph Priestley. Educated in Louisiana and at Harvard where he graduated, 1859. Accepted in the fall of 1860 at the École des Beaux Arts, Paris, he worked under L. J. André and got some of his first practical experience under French architects who were imbued with the doctrines of Néo-Grec rationalism. At the end of the Civil War, he was urged to remain in France where his brilliance had been widely recognized, but he returned to America and won his first recognition in an 1866 competition for design of the First Unitarian Church, Springfield, Mass. His American reputation grew swiftly. His success in the Brattle Street Church competition (Boston, 1870) was followed by his winning the competition for plans for Trinity Church, Boston, in 1872. He achieved a nationwide reputation for his Trinity design, and in 1876 shared with Leopold Eidlitz and Frederick L. Olmsted the work of completing the building and grounds of the New York State Capitol. Removing his home to Brookline, Mass., 1874, and his office there four years later, he continued on a successful course until his death, living well, enjoying life, and happy in his friendships.

The long list of Richardson's work includes buildings in Boston, Chicago, Pittsburgh, and Cincinnati. Beginning as an ecclesiastical architect, he turned increasingly to more modern problems; he is quoted as saying that he would have liked to have designed a grain elevator. His earlier churches are in a simplified Victorian Gothic style, but the Brattle Street Church tower strikes a new note, and in Trinity Church he first employed his own style of modified French and Spanish Romanesque. His larger houses betray a struggle between prevalent fashion and his own desire to be daringly new; his libraries, despite their Romanesque style, show the development of a rationalism not unlike that of the contemporary French. The Cincinnati Chamber of Commerce (1885) is grand in scale, but its roof shows the exaggeration into which the architect's gusto occasionally led him; his Pittsburgh Jail and Court House show his facility in handling materials and bringing out their special beauties, and achieve a grim, powerful magnificence that was new in American architecture. Richardson created outstanding innovations in his commercial buildings, notably in the Marshall Field Building, Chicago (1885). Almost equally revolutionary was the series of stations he designed in Massachusetts for the Boston & Albany Railroad.

Richardson's influence was enormous; he set an architectural fashion that dominated the eastern United States from 1880 until 1893. His imitators, however, copied his mannerisms only and failed to realize the deep foundations of his art. In consequence,

Richardson's style fell into disrepute soon after his death, although his care in handling materials, the brilliance of his planning, and his rationalism were all marked in the early work of Charles F. McKim and Stanford White who had served in his office. A lover of the decorative arts, he employed only the best men of his time in creating interior richness for his buildings, and his ideal of architecture and the sister arts as one unity persisted long after his death. A measure of his remarkable talents is the fact that to successive groups of architects from his own day to the present, each with varying demands, he has seemed to be the first great American example of the qualities that they each seek.

RICHARDSON, ISRAEL BUSH (b. Fairfax, Vt., 1815; d. Sharpsburg, Md., 1862), Union soldier. Graduated West Point, 1841. Served with great gallantry as an infantry officer in the Seminole and Mexican wars; after garrison duty in the Southwest, he resigned from the army, 1855. Organized and commanded the 2nd Michigan Regiment at the outbreak of the Civil War; covered Union retreat at first battle of Bull Run. Promoted brigadier general and major general, he led his division in the struggle for the "Bloody Lane" at Antietam and was mortally wounded there.

RICHARDSON, JAMES DANIEL (b. Rutherford Co., Tenn., 1843; d. Murfreesboro, Tenn., 1914), lawyer, Confederate soldier, Tennessee legislator, Masonic leader. Congressman, Democrat, from Tennessee, 1885–1905.

RICHARDSON, JOSEPH (b. Philadelphia, Pa., 1711; d. 1784), colonial silversmith. Member of the board of the Pennsylvania Hospital, 1756–70.

RICHARDSON, MAURICE HOWE (b. Athol, Mass., 1851; d. 1912), surgeon. Graduated Harvard, 1873; M.D., Harvard Medical School, 1877. Practiced in Boston; taught anatomy and surgery at Harvard Medical and served as Moseley Professor of Surgery, 1907–12. Wrote with great ability on the development of the operation for appendicitis (1892–98).

RICHARDSON, ROBERT (b. Pittsburgh, Pa., 1806; d. Bethany, W.Va., 1876), physician, educator. A notable convert to the Disciples of Christ, 1829, he was a close associate of Alexander Campbell.

RICHARDSON, RUFUS BYAM (b. Westford, Mass., 1845; d. 1914), Greek scholar and archeologist. Graduated Yale, 1869; Ph.D., 1878; B.D., 1883. Taught Greek at Yale, Indiana University, and Dartmouth; director, American School of Classical Studies at Athens, 1893–1903.

RICHARDSON, SID WILLIAMS (b. Athens, Tex., 1891; d. Saint Joseph's Island, Tex., 1959), oil executive, philanthropist. Studied briefly at Baylor University and Simmons College (now Hardin-Simmons University). Became an independent oil producer in 1919; owned his first oil field in 1932; by 1935 he was an established multimillionaire. A friend of President Dwight D. Eisenhower, Richardson assiduously shunned publicity. At his death he probably controlled more oil reserves than any other individual in the United States and more than several of the major petroleum companies. His philanthropic activities were kept from public view until after his death, when the Sid Richardson Foundation made numerous grants to educational and charitable institutions.

RICHARDSON, TOBIAS GIBSON (b. Lexington, Ky., 1827; d. New Orleans, La., 1892), surgeon. M.D., University of Louisville, 1848; was a private pupil of S. D. Gross. Taught anatomy and surgery at Louisville and Pennsylvania; professor of anatomy, University of Louisiana (now Tulane), 1858–62. After service on the Confederate medical staff, he returned to New Orleans and continued to teach anatomy at Tulane until 1872 when he became professor of surgery and so continued until 1889. He was also dean, 1865–85, and was elected president of the American Medical Association, 1877.

RICHARDSON, WILDS PRESTON (b. Hunt Co., Tex., 1861; d. Washington, D.C., 1929), army officer. Graduated West Point, 1884. Supervised building of Richardson Highway from Valdez to Fairbanks, Alaska; commanded U.S. forces in northern Russia, 1919; retired as colonel, Regular Army, 1920.

RICHARDSON, WILLARD (b. Massachusetts, 1802; d. 1875), journalist. Graduated South Carolina College, 1828; immigrated to Texas, 1837. As editor-owner of the Galveston News, post 1843, Richardson advocated states'-rights doctrines, remorselessly opposed Sam Houston, and was a Southern pioneer in independent journalism.

RICHARDSON, WILLIAM ADAMS (b. Tyngsborough, Mass., 1821; d. 1896), jurist. Graduated Harvard, 1843. After attending the law school and admittance to the bar, 1846, he practiced in Lowell, Mass., and was a probate judge. Accepting an assistant secretaryship of the U.S. treasury under G. S. Boutwell, 1869, he succeeded to the secretaryship, 1873. After a short term marked by weakness and ineptitude, he was made a judge of the Court of Claims, June 1874, and became chief justice of that court, 1885.

RICHARDSON, WILLIAM LAMBERT (b. Boston, Mass., 1842; d. 1932), obstetrician. Graduated Harvard, 1864; M.D., Harvard Medical School, 1867. Reopened the Boston Lying-In Hospital, 1873, and made it one of the outstanding hospitals of its type in the United States. Taught obstetrics at Harvard, 1871–1907, and was dean of the medical faculty post 1893.

RICHARDSON, WILLIAM MERCHANT (b. Pelham, N.H., 1774; d. 1838), jurist, congressman, New Hampshire official. As chief justice, New Hampshire superior court, 1816–38, he played a leading part in shaping the jurisprudence of that state.

RICHBERG, DONALD RANDALL (b. Knoxville, Tenn., 1881; d. Charlottesville, Va., 1960), lawyer, government official. Attended the University of Chicago (B.A., 1901), Harvard Law School (LL.B., 1904). Served as counsel for the Illinois Progressive Party, various labor unions, and the city of Chicago in a suit against public utilities. Member of the New Deal; was appointed general counsel to the National Recovery Administration (NRA) in 1933. President Franklin D. Roosevelt appointed him director of the Industrial Emergency Committee and of the National Emergency Council in 1934. The next year, when the Supreme Court found the NRA unconstitutional, Richberg's influence ended. Taught at the University of Virginia Law School from the late 1930's. Became an opponent of the New Deal and the welfare state; helped draft parts of the Taft-Hartley Act.

RICHINGS, PETER (b. probably London, England, 1798; d. Media, Pa., 1871), actor, opera singer. Immigrated to New York, 1821; made his debut there at the Park Theatre in September. Achieving success by hard work rather than outstanding talent, he remained active in the profession until 1867.

RICHMOND, CHARLES WALLACE (b. Kenosha, Wis., 1868; d. Washington, D.C., 1932), ornithologist. M.D., Georgetown University, 1897. Associated for much of his life with the U.S. National Museum in curatorial capacities, Richmond was a recognized authority in problems of avian nomenclature and bibliography.

RICHMOND, DEAN (b. Barnard, Vt., 1804; d. New York, N.Y., 1866), businessman, railroad president, political leader in New York State. Starting as a leader of the "Barnburner" movement, he was chairman of the New York State Democratic committee, 1850–66, and was a dominating factor in his party's councils. *Post ca.* 1852, he was a "Soft" Democrat, or favorer of compromise on the slavery issue; in 1860, he was a leader among the supporters of Stephen A. Douglas. With Thurlow Weed, he helped arrange the National Union Convention at Philadelphia, 1866, in an endeavor to unite Democrats and Conservative Republicans in opposition to the Republican Radicals.

RICHMOND, JOHN LAMBERT (*b. near Chesterfield, Mass., 1785; d. Covington, Ind., 1855*), Baptist clergyman, physician. Graduated Medical College of Ohio, 1822. While in practice at Newton, Ohio, he performed first successful Caesarean operation (1827) to be reported in the U.S. medical press.

RICHMOND, JOHN WILKES (*b. Little Compton, R.I., 1775; d. Philadelphia, Pa., 1857*), physician. Practiced in Providence, R.I., *post* 1815; is chiefly remembered for his endeavors to compel the payment of the Revolutionary War debt of Rhode Island after virtual repudiation in 1844.

RICHMOND, MARY ELLEN (*b. Belleville, Ill., 1861; d. 1928*), pioneer social worker, teacher. Beginning her career with the Charity Organization Society of Baltimore, 1889, she became general secretary of the Society for Organizing Charity in Philadelphia, 1900; *post* 1909, she was director of the Charity Organization Department, Russell Sage Foundation. Among her books were *Social Diagnosis* (1917) and *Marriage and the State* (with F. S. Hall, 1929).

RICHTER, CONRAD MICHAEL (*b. Pine Grove, Pa., 1890; Pottsville, Pa., 1968*), writer. His family's association with the Lutheran ministry influenced his writing and figures directly in two of his best novels: the National Book Award-winning *The Waters of Kronos* (1960) and *A Simple Honorable Man* (1962). Other novels include *The Sea of Grass* (1937) and the Pulitzer Prize-winning *The Town* (1950), which was the third part of the trilogy *The Awakening Land* (published as a set in 1966). His first acclaimed short story, "Brothers of No Kin," appeared in *Forum* (1914) and became the title piece of his first collection of stories (1924). In his work he employed quiet humor and clarity and economy of expression to depict what he called the "small authenticities" of daily life. Other collections include *Smoke Over the Prairie and Other Stories* (1947) and *The Rawhide Knot and Other Stories* (1948).

RICHTMYER, FLOYD KARKER (*b. Cobleskill, N.Y., 1881; d. Ithaca, N.Y., 1939*), physicist. Graduated Cornell, 1904; Ph.D., 1910. Taught physics at Cornell *post* 1906 and served *post* 1931 as dean of the graduate school. A pioneer in photometry and in the use of photoelectric cells, also in X-ray research.

RICKARD, GEORGE LEWIS (*b. Kansas City, Mo., 1871; d. Miami Beach, Fla., 1929*), gambler, prizefight promoter, better known as "Tex" Rickard.

RICKERT, MARTHA EDITH (*b. Dover, Ohio, 1871; d. Chicago, Ill., 1938*), philologist. Graduated Vassar, 1891; Ph.D., University of Chicago, 1899. Professor of English, University of Chicago, *post* 1924, Miss Rickert made her principal contribution to scholarship in association with John M. Manly as editor of the monumental *The Text of the Canterbury Tales* (1940). She was author also of a number of others works.

RICKETSON, DANIEL (*b. New Bedford, Mass., 1813; d. New Bedford, 1898*), poet, local historian. Friend and associate of H. D. Thoreau, R. W. Emerson, the Alcotts, and other leading literati.

RICKETTS, CLAUDE VERNON (*b. Greene County, Mo., 1906; d. Bethesda, Md., 1964*), naval officer. Graduated from U.S. Naval Academy (1929) and received his pilot's wings in 1932. Served as an officer aboard various vessels, beginning in 1938, and held key administrative posts in the navy. During World War II took part in the capture of the Gilbert, Marshall, and Marianas Islands and of Iwo Jima and Okinawa (1943–45). Promoted to rear admiral (1956) and full admiral (1961), then was made vice chief of naval operations.

RICKETTS, HOWARD TAYLOR (*b. Findlay, Ohio, 1871; d. Mexico City, Mex., 1910*), pathologist. Graduated University of Nebraska, 1894; M.D., Northwestern, 1897; studied also in Vienna and at the Pasteur Institute in Paris. Joining the department of pathology, University of Chicago, 1902, he began a program in the new field of immunology and in 1906 began his brilliant studies of Rocky Mountain spotted fever. In the course of his investigations, he discovered in the blood of patients and in the communicating ticks and their eggs a small organism which he rightly assumed to be the cause of the disease; this and related organisms responsible for many important diseases are now known as *Rickettsia* in the memory of the man who first identified them. Struck by the resemblance of Rocky Mountain fever to typhus, he undertook a successful investigation of that disease, demonstrating in a short time that the agent of transmission is chiefly the louse, and again finding micro-organisms which were later established as the true cause of the disease. He died of typhus himself in the midst of his successful work.

RICKETTS, JAMES BREWERTON (*b. New York, N.Y., 1817; d. Washington, D.C., 1887*), Union soldier. Graduated West Point, 1839. After service with the artillery in the Mexican War and in various posts throughout the United States, he was appointed brigadier general, 1862, and held divisional command at Cedar Mountain, second Bull Run, South Mountain, and Antietam. Disabled by many wounds, he left the field until March 1864 when he again commanded a division in the Wilderness campaign and under Sheridan in the Shenandoah Valley. He retired as major general in 1867.

RICKETTS, PALMER CHAMBERLAINE (*b. Elkton, Md., 1856; d. Baltimore, Md., 1934*), engineer, educator. Graduated Rensselaer Polytechnic, 1875. Engaged in engineering practice for many years, his reputation rests principally upon his educational work at Rensselaer and his development of that school materially and academically as teacher (*post* 1875), director (1892–1901), and president, 1901–34.

RICKEY, WESLEY BRANCH (*b. Lucasville, Ohio, 1881; d. Columbia, Mo., 1965*), major-league baseball executive. Attended Ohio Wesleyan and University of Michigan (LL.B., 1911). Played for the Cincinnati Reds (1904) and the St. Louis Browns (1905–07); became executive assistant to the Browns' owner (1913) and managed the team, reviving the farm system and enabling the Browns to compete with wealthy rivals in recruiting players. As manager and president of the St. Louis Cardinals (1916–42) he built a network of minor-league farm clubs; by 1940 he had over thirty teams in the chain, almost cornering the market in young players. Became president and general manager of the Brooklyn Dodgers (1942) and co-owner (1945). Won public support for admitting blacks to major-league baseball, selecting Jackie Robinson (1945) as a test case. Forced to sell his Dodgers stock, he became executive vice president of the Pittsburgh Pirates (1951–55). President (1959) of the Continental League, a rival league that, although it failed, forced major-league baseball to undertake continental expansion. Voted into the Baseball Hall of Fame (1967).

RICORD, FREDERICK WILLIAM (b. *Guadeloupe, French West Indies, 1819; d. Newark, N.J., 1897*), librarian, New Jersey public official and jurist. Nephew of Philippe Ricord.

RICORD, PHILIPPE (b. *Baltimore, Md., 1800; d. Paris, France, 1889*), physician, world-wide authority on venereal diseases. Uncle of Frederick W. Ricord. Removed to France, 1820, for medical study and practiced there, principally in Paris; his *Traité pratique des maladies vénériennes* (Paris, 1838) was an epical document in the history of medicine.

RIDDELL, JOHN LEONARD (b. *Leyden, Mass., 1807; d. 1865*), physician, botanist. M.D., Cincinnati Medical College, 1836. Professor of chemistry, Medical College of Louisiana (later Tulane), New Orleans, 1836–65. Author of a pioneer botany text, *Synopsis of the Flora of the Western States* (1835). Riddell was active in the medical and civic life of Louisiana, but is particularly noted for his invention of the binocular microscope which he devised in 1851, put in form in 1852, and displayed before the American Association for the Advancement of Science in July 1853.

RIDDER, HERMAN (b. *New York, N.Y., 1851; d. 1915*), newspaper publisher. Established the *Catholic News* (N.Y.), 1886. After managing the *New-Yorker Staats-Zeitung*, he bought it from Oswald Ottendorfer *post* 1890 and directed it until his death. Active in German-American affairs and as an independent Democrat, he also held office in trade associations and in the Associated Press.

RIDDLE, ALBERT GALLATIN (b. *Monson, Mass., 1816; d. Washington, D.C., 1902*), lawyer, Ohio legislator and congressman. A bitter anti-slavery Whig, Riddle issued the 1848 call for a mass meeting at Chardon which inaugurated the Ohio Free-Soil party.

RIDDLE, GEORGE PEABODY (b. *Charlestown, Mass., 1851; d. Boston, Mass., 1910*), actor, reader, able director of Greek play revivals.

RIDDLE, MATTHEW BROWN (b. *Pittsburgh, Pa., 1836; d. Edgeworth, Pa., 1916*), Reformed Dutch clergyman, biblical scholar. Taught New Testament exegesis at Hartford (Conn.) and Western Theological seminaries.

RIDDLE, SAMUEL DOYLE (b. *Glen Riddle, Pa., 1861; d. Glen Riddle, 1951*), sportsman. Graduated from Pennsylvania Military College (later Widener College) in 1879. Owner and trainer of the racehorse Man o' War, a famous American racehorse that broke track records almost every time he ran and set three world's records. Riddle bred some of the nation's most successful racehorses including War Admiral, Battleship, Crusader, War Glory, and Scapa Flow.

RIDEING, WILLIAM HENRY (b. *Liverpool, England, 1853; d. Brookline, Mass., 1918*), journalist, miscellaneous writer. Came to America, 1869. Associated *post* 1881 with editorial staff of *Youth's Companion*; also an editor of *North American Review*.

RIDEOUT, HENRY MILNER (b. *Calais, Maine, 1877; d. at sea, en route for Europe, 1927*), Harvard instructor, writer. Author of several textbooks in association with Charles T. Copeland, and of popular fiction.

RIDGAWAY, HENRY BASCOM (b. *Talbot Co., Md., 1830; d. 1895*), Methodist clergyman, theologian. Professor at Garrett Biblical Institute, 1882–95; president of the Institute *post* 1885.

RIDGE, MAJOR (b. *probably Hiwassee, in present Polk Co., Tenn., ca. 1771; d. near Van Buren, Okla., 1839*), Cherokee Indian leader. After first supporting John Ross in opposition to land cession, he signed a treaty at New Echota, Ga., December 1835, whereby all Cherokee lands east of the Mississippi were ceded and westward removal accepted. The tragic westward migration of the Cherokee followed, and Ridge was murdered in revenge for his part in causing it.

RIDGELY, CHARLES GOODWIN (b. *Baltimore, Md., 1784; d. Baltimore, 1848*), naval officer. Appointed midshipman, 1799. Saw varied service in the wars with the Barbary powers, the War of 1812, and in campaigns against the West Indian pirates.

RIDGELY, DANIEL BOWLY (b. *near Lexington, Ky., 1813; d. Philadelphia, Pa., 1868*), naval officer. Commended, 1865, for energetic action against Confederate blockade runners throughout the Civil War; promoted commodore, 1866.

RIDGELY, NICHOLAS (b. *Dover, Del., 1762; d. 1830*), Delaware legislator and jurist. State attorney general, 1791–1801; chancellor of Delaware, 1802–30.

RIDGWAY, ROBERT (b. *Mount Carmel, Ill., 1850; d. 1929*), ornithologist. A protégé of Spencer F. Baird, Ridgway assumed care of the bird collections of the Smithsonian Institution, and in 1880 was designated curator of birds, U.S. National Museum, in which post he continued until his death. He did important field work and was author of a number of books; among these were *Color Standards and Nomenclature* (1886), *The Birds of North and Middle America* (1901–19), and several works written in collaboration with Spencer F. Baird and Thomas M. Brewer. At the height of his career, Ridgway was considered the leading American ornithologist; his writings were models of accuracy.

RIDGWAY, ROBERT (b. *Brooklyn, N.Y., 1862; d. Fort Wayne, Ind., 1938*), civil engineer, expert in subway construction and deep tunnel work.

RIDPATH, JOHN CLARK (b. *Putnam Co., Ind., 1840; d. New York, N.Y., 1900*), educator, author of popular historical works.

RIEGER, JOHANN GEORG JOSEPH ANTON (b. *Aurach, Bavaria, 1811; d. Jefferson City, Mo., 1869*), German Evangelical missionary in Illinois, Iowa, and Missouri *post* 1836.

RIEGGER, WALLINGFORD (b. *Albany, Ga., 1885; d. New York, N.Y., 1961*), composer. Attended Cornell, Institute of Musical Art (now Juilliard), and Berlin Hochschule für Musik. Made conducting debut (1910) with the Blüthner Orchestra in Berlin. His first mature composition, *Trio in B minor* (1920), received the Paderewski Prize. His music was occasionally romantic, occasionally impressionistic, utilizing traditional harmonic and melodic procedures within formal structures. Broke with conservatism to embrace atonality with *Rhapsody for Orchestra* (1925). From atonality went on to the twelve-tone system: *Dichotomy* (1932), *String Quartet No. 1* (1938–39), and *Duos for Three Woodwinds* (1943). Taught at Drake University (1918–22), Institute of Musical Art (1924–25), Ithaca Conservatory (1926–28), and Metropolitan Music School (from 1936).

RIGDON, SIDNEY (b. *Piny Fork, Pa., 1793; d. Friendship, N.Y., 1876*), early Mormon leader. A Campbellite preacher in the Western Reserve *post* 1828, Rigdon announced a public conversion to Mormonism, 1830, and played an important role in the new movement until the death of Joseph Smith. Outmaneuvered in his attempt to be selected as "Guardian" of the church by Brigham Young and the other apostles, Rigdon was excommunicated at Nauvoo, 1844. In the following year, he was voted by a group of followers the president of a new sect. He was probably the author of the "Lectures on Faith," although Smith published them as his own.

RIGGE, WILLIAM FRANCIS (b. Cincinnati, Ohio, 1857; d. Omaha, Nebr., 1927), Roman Catholic clergyman, Jesuit, astronomer. Director of the observatory, Creighton University, 1896–1927. Author of *Harmonic Curves* (1926) and other contributions to the literature of mathematics and astronomy.

RIGGS, ELIAS (b. New Providence, N.J., 1810; d. *probably* Constantinople, Turkey, 1901), missionary in the Near East *post* 1832, linguist, author.

RIGGS, GEORGE WASHINGTON (b. Georgetown, D.C., 1813; d. Prince George's Co., Md., 1881), banker. Entered partnership with William W. Corcoran in Washington, D.C., 1840–48; purchased Corcoran's interest in Corcoran & Riggs, 1854. Thereafter he continued the firm as Riggs & Co. until his death.

RIGGS, JOHN MANKEY (b. Seymour, Conn., 1810; d. Hartford, Conn., 1885), dentist. Studied under Horace Wells. A strong advocate of hygienic care of the mouth, he gained wide repute as a specialist in treatment of pyorrhea. On Dec. 11, 1844, at Hartford, he performed an outstanding operation in the history of modern anesthesia, extracting a tooth from the mouth of Horace Wells while the latter was under the influence of nitrous oxide gas.

RIGGS, STEPHEN RETURN (b. Steubenville, Ohio, 1812; d. Beloit, Wis., 1883), Presbyterian clergyman. Missionary to the Sioux *post* 1837; authority on Siouan languages.

RIGGS, WILLIAM HENRY (b. New York, N.Y., 1837; d. 1924), art collector. Resident in Paris, France, *post ca.* 1857, Riggs made a remarkable collection of art and armor which he was influenced by his friend J. Pierpont Morgan to present to the Metropolitan Museum of Art.

RIIS, JACOB AUGUST (b. Ribe, Denmark, 1849; d. Barre, Mass., 1914), journalist, reformer. Immigrated to New York City, 1870; was employed as a police reporter on the *New York Tribune* and the *Evening Sun*. Offering evidence based on his personal observation of the degradation of the tenement districts of the city, Riis effected massive reforms in housing through his vivid writings and countless lectures. Opposed by politicians and landlords, he found a powerful friend and abettor in Theodore Roosevelt. Among his books were *How the Other Half Lives* (1890), *The Children of the Poor* (1892), *Out of Mulberry Street* (1898), and *The Making of an American* (1901).

RIIS, MARY PHILLIPS (b. Memphis, Tenn., 1877; d. New York, N.Y., 1967), stockbroker. As the widow of social reformer Jacob Riis, she was a lifelong supporter of the Jacob A. Riis Neighborhood House. She began selling bonds (1917) for Bonbright and Company, and in 1919 headed a Bonbright branch that specialized in serving women customers. She attributed her success in the securities business to her ability to evaluate facts unemotionally. Remained active as a broker until she was eighty, having evolved an investment philosophy that consisted of investing 20 percent of available funds in safe, income-oriented instruments, 60 percent in major growth stocks, and 20 percent in speculative capital gains.

RILEY, BENJAMIN FRANKLIN (b. near Pineville, Ala., 1849; d. Birmingham, Ala., 1925), Baptist clergyman, educator.

RILEY, BENNET (b. St. Mary's Co., Md., 1787; d. Buffalo, N.Y., 1853), soldier, Indian fighter. Entered U.S. Army as ensign of riflemen, 1813. After varied service in the War of 1812 and against the Western Indians, he became colonel of the 2nd Infantry at the outbreak of the Mexican War but was quickly advanced to brigade command. He received the brevet of major general for his outstanding charge at the battle of Contreras, August 1847. Transferred to California, 1848, he served as provisional governor and convened the assembly at Monterey, September 1849, which drew up the first constitution for California and applied for admission to the Union.

RILEY, CHARLES VALENTINE (b. London, England, 1843; d. 1895), entomologist. Immigrated to the United States *ca.* 1860; was associated with the *Prairie Farmer* (Chicago) as reporter and artist. Served as entomologist to the State of Missouri, 1868–77. His reports of his Missouri investigations established his reputation; many authorities date modern economic entomology from their publication. Through his efforts, the U.S. Entomological Commission was established, 1877, of which he became chief; he served as entomologist to the U.S. Department of Agriculture, 1878–79 and 1881–94. He was an able investigator and a prolific writer, his work showing an unusual sense of economic proportion combined with scientific accuracy.

RILEY, ISAAC WOODBRIDGE (b. New York, N.Y., 1869; d. 1933), philosopher, educator. Graduated Yale, 1892; Ph.D., 1902. Professor of philosophy, Vassar College, 1908–33. Author of the notable *American Philosophy: The Early Schools* (1907), *American Thought from Puritanism to Pragmatism* (1915), and other works.

RILEY, JAMES WHITCOMB (b. Greenfield, Ind., 1849; d. Indianapolis, Ind., 1916), poet. Leaving school at 16, Riley worked as a sign painter and as a small town journalist. His popularity dates from his employment on the *Indianapolis Journal*, 1877–85, during which time the verses which he contributed to the paper were widely copied. The series of verses signed "Benj. F. Johnson, of Boone" were particularly noticed and were published as a book in 1883 with the title *The Old Swimmin' Hole and 'Leven More Poems.* Riley was truly a Hoosier poet, for the whimsical and eccentric characters in his verses together with their dialect and the scene against which they moved were all drawn from his local observations. Oversentimental as he may be, he made an original contribution to American literature in portraying the special characteristics of his time and place. Among the long list of books, the most popular were *Afterwhiles* (1887), *Pipes o' Pan at Zekesbury* (1888), *Rhymes of Childhood* (1890), and *Poems Here at Home* (1893).

RILEY, WILLIAM BELL (b. Greene County, Ind., 1861; d. Golden Valley, Minn., 1947), Baptist clergyman, evangelist. B.A., Hanover (Ind.) College, 1885; M.A., 1888. Graduated Southern Baptist Theological Seminary, Louisville, Ky., 1888. Served small churches in Kentucky, Indiana, and Illinois; pastor of Calvary Baptist Church, Chicago, 1893–97, and of First Baptist Church in Minneapolis, Minn., 1897–1942. Founded Northwestern Bible Training School in Minneapolis, 1902; headed the World's Christian Fundamentals Association, 1919–29. A leader in the defense and propagation of fundamentalism.

RIMMER, WILLIAM (b. Liverpool, England, 1816; d. 1879), sculptor, painter. Came to Nova Scotia as a child; was raised in Hopkinton, Mass., and Boston. Worked at a number of trades and professions including shoemaking, medicine, and itinerant portrait painting; he was also a musician and a teacher of music. Encouraged to concentrate on sculpture *post* 1860, he won reputation but little income and was obliged to teach art anatomy in Boston and at Cooper Union, New York City. Unable to work with a group or with others at all, Rimmer was a man of extraordinary gifts, too widely lavished. However, William M. Hunt admired his genius and John La Farge and Daniel C. French were gladly his pupils.

RINDGE, FREDERICK HASTINGS (*b. Cambridge, Mass., 1857; d. Yreka, Calif., 1905*), philanthropist, California land developer. Donated a number of public buildings to Cambridge, Mass.

RINEHART, MARY ROBERTS (*b. Pittsburgh, Pa., 1876; d. New York, N.Y., 1958*), novelist, mystery writer. Graduated from the Pittsburgh Training School for Nurses in 1896. Married to a physician, Rinehart began selling stories in 1903 to help support her family. Her first mystery novel, *The Circular Staircase* (1908), was later made into a successful play, *The Bat*. As a European correspondent for the *Post*, she was the first woman to report from the front. Founded the publishing firm of Farrar and Rinehart. Immensely popular at the time, several of Rinehart's sixty-two books are still some of the finest mysteries in American literature.

RINEHART, STANLEY MARSHALL, JR. (*b. Pittsburgh, Pa., 1897; d. South Miami, Fla., 1969*), publisher. Attended Harvard (1915–17). Took a job in the advertising department of George H. Doran Company (1919) and, after buying an interest, eventually became director of the company. After the company merged with Doubleday, Page (1927), Rinehart, his brother Frederick, and John Farrar formed Farrar and Rinehart; in 1931 that company bought Cosmopolitan Book Corporation, acquiring such writers as Philip Wylie, Upton Sinclair, and Stephen Vincent Benét. The house's greatest success was with Hervey Allen's *Anthony Adverse* (1933), which sold over a million copies. As president of the firm, Rinehart exemplified the willingness of new young publishers to treat books as commodities. Rinehart bought out Farrar and established Rinehart and Company (1946), which published in the late 1940's Norman Mailer's *The Naked and the Dean* and Charles Jackson's *The Lost Weekend*. He sold the firm to Henry Holt and Company (1960), but stayed on as a director of Holt, Rinehart and Winston until 1963.

RINEHART, WILLIAM HENRY (*b. near Union Bridge, Md., 1825; d. Rome, Italy, 1874*), sculptor. Began work as a stonecutter and letterer in Baltimore, Md.; studied at the Maryland Institute. Under the patronage of several local merchants including W. T. Walters, Rinehart visited Italy, 1855–57. Finding it impossible to practice sculpture at home, he returned to Italy in 1858, and kept a studio in Rome for the rest of his life. Throughout his career, Walters remained his chief patron. Rinehart's best work was done in a sensitive and refined neo-classic style. Among his works his "Clytie" (Peabody Institute) is perhaps his masterpiece, but his massive seated figure of Roger B. Taney (Annapolis, Md.; copy in Baltimore) remains one of the most successful public monuments in the United States.

RINGGOLD, CADWALADER (*b. Washington Co., Md., 1802; d. New York, N.Y., 1867*), naval officer. Grandson of John Cadwalader. Appointed midshipman, 1819; promoted lieutenant, 1828, and commander, 1849. During this period he was employed against the pirates of the West Indies and cruised in the Mediterranean and the Pacific; he commanded the *Porpoise* in the Wilkes Exploring Expedition, 1838–42. Engaged in surveys on the California coast, 1849–50, he published *A Series of Charts . . . to the Bay of San Francisco* (1851) and subsequently commanded a surveying expedition in the North Pacific, 1853–54. Ordered home as insane by Commodore Matthew C. Perry, Ringgold resented the action bitterly, as a medical survey upon his return to America declared him fully competent. Promoted captain, 1857, he later served with great distinction in the Civil War and retired as commodore, 1864.

RINGLING, CHARLES (*b. McGregor, Iowa, 1863; d. Sarasota, Fla., 1926*), circus proprietor. Joined four of his brothers in a concert company, 1882. Organizing their first circus, 1884, the brothers by 1900 had one of the largest shows on the road and began absorbing other circuses; they acquired the Barnum & Bailey Circus, 1907. Charles Ringling was also a prominent factor in the real-estate developments along Florida's West Coast.

RIORDAN, PATRICK WILLIAM (*b. Chatham, N.B., Canada, 1841; d. 1914*), Roman Catholic clergyman. Raised in Chicago; graduated Notre Dame, 1858; studied for priesthood in North American College, Rome. Consecrated coadjutor to Archbishop Alemany of San Francisco, 1883, he succeeded almost immediately to the see and administered it prudently until his death.

RIPLEY, EDWARD HASTINGS (*b. Center Rutland, Vt., 1839; d. Rutland, Vt., 1915*), Union brigadier general, financier. Brother of Julia C. R. Dorr. Commanding the first federal infantry to enter Richmond, Va., 1865, he restored order, suppressed the mob, and extinguished the fire which was raging in the Confederate capital.

RIPLEY, EDWARD PAYSON (*b. Dorchester, Mass., 1845; d. Santa Barbara, Calif., 1920*), railroad executive. Notable in particular for his skill and integrity in restoring the Atchison, Topeka & Santa Fe Railway during his presidency, 1896–1920.

RIPLEY, ELEAZAR WHEELOCK (*b. Hanover, N.H., 1782; d. West Feliciana, La., 1839*), lawyer, soldier. Grandson of Eleazar Wheelock. Served in War of 1812 as colonel of the 21st (present 5th) Infantry and as brigadier general in the Niagara campaign. Resigning from the army, 1820, he practiced law at New Orleans, La., and was congressman, Democrat, from Louisiana, 1835–39.

RIPLEY, EZRA (*b. Woodstock, Conn., 1751; d. 1841*), Unitarian clergyman. Graduated Harvard, 1776. Pastor, First Church, Concord, Mass., 1778–1841. Abandoned Trinitarianism and orthodox Calvinism *ca.* 1772, but was a fervent evangelical.

RIPLEY, GEORGE (*b. Greenfield, Mass., 1802; d. 1880*), Unitarian clergyman, editor, reformer, literary critic. Graduated Harvard, 1823; Harvard Divinity School, 1826. Minister of Purchase Street Church, Boston, 1826–41. Ripley was strongly influenced by German theology, and with F. H. Hedge edited *Specimens of Foreign Standard Literature* (1838 and *post*), translations of Cousin, Jouffroy, Schleiermacher, and others which were of profound influence on New England intellectual life. He resumed a previous controversy with Andrews Norton over the philosophy of religion in 1839, defending his own views as well as those of R. W. Emerson in *Letters on the Latest Form of Infidelity* (1840). An associate of Emerson, Hedge, A. B. Alcott, Theodore Parker, Margaret Fuller, and others in the so-called "Transcendental Club," Ripley aided Fuller in editing the *Dial* (founded 1840) and assumed charge of the Brook Farm colony (1841) which was to be a practical application of what he and William E. Channing considered the New Testament social order. Although he disliked the regimentation involved in socialism, Ripley, as president, along with others of the group, accepted the new constitution which made Brook Farm a Fourierite Phalanx, January 1844, and edited the *Harbinger*, *post* 1845. Heavily involved in debt on the final collapse of Brook Farm, August 1847, Ripley removed to New York City and in 1849 succeeded Margaret Fuller as literary critic of the *New York Tribune*. For more than 20 years he labored to pay off the debts of Brook Farm. In his 31 years as critic for the *Tribune*, hardly a single important American book escaped his intelligent criticism. In 1850 he was a founder of *Harper's New Monthly Magazine* and edited its literary department. Success with *A Hand-Book of Literature and the Fine Arts* (edited with Bayard Taylor, 1852) was followed by a further success as editor (with Charles A. Dana) of the *New American Cyclopoedia* (1858–63).

RIPLEY, JAMES WOLFE (*b. Windham Co., Conn., 1794; d. Hartford, Conn., 1870*), soldier. Graduated West Point, 1814. After varied service in the artillery, 1814–33, Ripley transferred to the ordnance corps. In command of the armory at Springfield, Mass., 1841–54, he rebuilt and modernized the plant. Chief of ordnance, U.S. Army, 1861–63, he fought favoritism, fraud, and political influence.

RIPLEY, ROBERT LEROY (*b. Santa Rosa, Calif., 1893; d. New York, N.Y., 1949*), newspaper sports cartoonist and feature artist. Creator of the "Believe It or Not!" feature, which first appeared in the December 19, 1918, issue of the New York *Globe*. Widely syndicated, and the basis of movie shorts, radio programs, and a chain of museums of oddities, the feature made him a fortune.

RIPLEY, ROSWELL SABINE (*b. Worthington, Ohio, 1823; d. New York, N.Y., 1887*), soldier. Nephew of James W. Ripley. Graduated West Point, 1843. Author of *The War with Mexico* (1849). Resigning from the army, 1853, he engaged in business in South Carolina. As a state militia officer, he commanded and reconditioned Forts Moultrie and Sumter after their evacuation and fall, 1861. Thereafter, as a brigadier general in the South Carolina and Confederate forces, he was continually in disagreement with his superiors and subordinates although he was reputed an excellent officer and a wise, if unheeded, counselor.

RIPLEY, WILLIAM ZEBINA (*b. Medford, Mass., 1867; d. Boothbay, Maine, 1941*), economist. Graduated Massachusetts Institute of Technology, 1890, with degree in civil engineering. Ph.D., Columbia University, in political economy, 1893. Taught political science, sociology, and economics at M.I.T., 1893–1901; simultaneously taught physical geography, anthropology, and sociology at Columbia. Professor of political economy at Harvard, 1902–33. Author of early writings on anthropological topics, which gave support to nativists and advocates of immigration restriction, he devoted most of his time *post* 1900 to economics; he was an authority on transportation and undertook many public service assignments in this field. He was author, among other works, of *Railroads: Rates and Regulation* (1912); *Railroads: Finance and Organization* (1915); and *Main Street and Wall Street* (1927), a critique of contemporary developments in corporate practices, especially holding companies.

RISING, JOHAN CLASSON (*b. Risingé Parish, Östergötland, Sweden, 1617; d. 1672*), scholar, Swedish official. Succeeded Johan B. Printz as governor of New Sweden, 1654; surrendered Fort Christina to the Dutch under Peter Stuyvesant, August 1655.

RISTER, CARL COKE (*b. Hayrick, Tex., 1889; d. 1955*), historian. Studied at Hardin-Simmons and at George Washington University (Ph.D., 1925). Taught at Hardin-Simmons intermittently, 1919–29; and at the University of Oklahoma, 1929–51. Books include *The Southern Frontier* (1928), *The Greater Southwest*, with R. N. Richardson (1934), and *Oil! Titan of the Southwest* (1949).

RITCHEY, GEORGE WILLIS (*b. Tuppers Plains, Meigs County, Ohio, 1864; d. Azusa, Calif., 1945*), astronomer, optical expert. Attended University of Cincinnati; taught woodworking in Chicago Manual Training School; served as head of optical laboratory and superintendent of instrument construction at Yerkes Observatory. Superintended construction of Mount Wilson Observatory, 1904–09; headed the optical shop there, 1909–19. Thereafter, he held posts at the Paris Observatory and at the Naval Observatory, Washington, D.C. A perfectionist, Ritchey made important contributions to the design of large telescopes and to the development of celestial photography.

RITCHIE, ALBERT CABELL (*b. Richmond, Va., 1876; d. Baltimore, Md., 1936*), lawyer, Maryland public official. Great-grandson of William H. Cabell. Graduated Johns Hopkins, 1896; LL.B., University of Maryland, 1898. A strong fighter in the public interest against the public utility companies, Ritchie served as Maryland attorney general, 1915–19, and as governor of Maryland, 1919–34. A masterful tactician, he achieved many administrative reforms in the state and was frequently mentioned as a Democratic presidential prospect.

RITCHIE, ALEXANDER HAY (*b. Glasgow, Scotland, 1822; d. New Haven, Conn., 1895*), engraver, painter. Came to America, 1841. Engraved a number of popular reproductions of historical paintings, including "The Death of Lincoln" after one of his own paintings, and "The Republican Court" after Daniel Huntington.

RITCHIE, ANNA CORA. *See* MOWATT, ANNA CORA OGDEN.

RITCHIE, THOMAS (*b. Tappahannock, Va., 1778; d. 1854*), journalist, politician. Cousin of Spencer Roane. Published and edited the *Richmond Enquirer*, 1804–45, and the Washington *Union*, 1845–51. Making his newspaper the "Democratic Bible" of its time, he favored public schools and state internal improvements. Supporting the "Virginia principles of '98," he opposed Henry Clay and the divisive tactics of John C. Calhoun.

RITNER, JOSEPH (*b. Berks Co., Pa., 1780; d. 1869*), farmer, Pennsylvania legislator. Governor, Whig and anti-Mason, of Pennsylvania, 1835–39, Ritner contended as best he could against financial panic, canal and railroad lobbying, and antiabolitionist riots; he obtained a large increase in the permanent school appropriation and the number of common schools.

RITTENHOUSE, DAVID (*b. Paper Mill Run, near Germantown, Pa., 1732; d. 1796*), instrument-maker, astronomer, mathematician. Great-grandson of William Rittenhouse. Despite lack of formal schooling, Rittenhouse as a boy showed extraordinary mathematical and mechanical ability and by his own efforts acquired a sound knowledge of physical science. He opened an instrument shop on his father's farm chiefly for clock-making *ca.* 1751. His first public service was a province boundary survey to settle a dispute with Lord Baltimore, 1763–64. He designed his celebrated orrery which gave him much contemporary fame, 1767; he also experimented on the compressibility of water and invented a metallic thermometer. In 1768 he presented to the American Philosophical Society his calculations on the transit of Venus that was to occur in 1769. To observe that event, he built an observatory and its equipment, including a transit telescope now considered the first telescope made in America. His observations (aided by William Smith, 1727–1803, and others) are regarded as among the best that were made. Removing to Philadelphia, 1770, he continued to work at an observatory there and in 1785 invented the collimating telescope; he also made a plane transmission grating, 1786, anticipating Fraunhofer. In 1792, he solved the problem of finding the sum of the several powers of the sines by demonstration to the second power, by infinite series to the sixth, and by the law of continuation for higher powers. He was frequently engaged on boundary surveys and commissions for over half the British colonies in America and conducted canal and river surveys as well. As engineer of the Committee of Safety, 1775, he supervised the casting of cannon and the manufacture of saltpeter; in 1777, he was president of the Council of Safety, serving also as a member of the General Assembly and of the Board of War, and as state treasurer. Professor of astronomy at University of Pennsylvania, he was on the commission to organize the United States Bank and was appointed first director of the Mint, 1792, serving until 1795. He was president of the American Philosophical Society, 1791–96.

RITTENHOUSE, JESSIE BELLE (*b. Mount Morris, N.Y., 1869; d. Detroit, Mich., 1948*), poet, critic, lecturer. Active in the American poetic "renaissance" of the first third of the 20th century, she was editor of a number of influential and successful anthologies and was a major factor in the founding of the Poetry Society of America, 1910. Among her books were *The Younger American Poets* (1904); *The Little Book of Modern Verse* (1913); and an autobiography, *My House of Life* (1934).

RITTENHOUSE, WILLIAM (*b. Mülheim-am-Ruhr, Rhenish Prussia, 1644; d. Germantown, Pa., 1708*), Mennonite minister, pioneer paper manufacturer. Immigrated to America, 1688. In partnership with William Bradford (1663–1752) and others, he built the first paper mill to be erected in the colonies on Paper Mill Run near Wissahickon Creek (Roxborough Township, Pa.), 1690.

RITTER, FRÉDÉRIC LOUIS (*b. Strasbourg, Alsace, 1834; d. 1891*), musical composer and historian, educator. Came to America, 1856; founded Cecilia Society and Philharmonic Orchestra, Cincinnati, Ohio. Professor of music, Vassar College, 1867–91.

RITTER, JOSEPH ELMER (*b. New Albany, Ind., 1892; d. St. Louis, Mo., 1967*), Roman Catholic cardinal and reform leader. Attended St. Meinrad's seminary and was ordained in 1917. At the Cathedral of Saint Peter and Paul in Indianapolis, he began a lifelong career as diocesan administrator and leader. He was made bishop of Indianapolis (1934) and headed the see until 1946, serving the last two years as archbishop. He opened five catechetical centers for black children and ordered full integration of the parochial schools. Named archbishop of St. Louis (1946), he created a national stir by ordering the integration of its Catholic schools. Became a cardinal in 1961 and played a major role at Vatican II (1962–65); he authorized the first English-language mass, held in St. Louis in 1965.

RITTER, WILLIAM EMERSON (*b. near Hampden, Wis., 1856; d. Berkeley, Calif., 1944*), naturalist, science administrator. Graduated State Normal School at Oshkosh (Wis.), 1884. B.S., University of California, 1888. A.M., Harvard, 1891; Ph.D., 1893. Taught biology at University of California *post* 1891, becoming professor in 1902, and emeritus in 1923. With aid of E. W. Scripps and Ellen B. Scripps, he established three important institutions: the Scripps Institution of Oceanography at La Jolla; the Foundation for Population Research at Miami University in Ohio; and the news agency Science Service in Washington, D.C.

RIVERA, LUIS MUÑOZ. *See* MUÑOZ-RIVERA, LUIS.

RIVERS, LUCIUS MENDEL (*b. Gumville, N.C., 1905; d. Birmingham, Ala., 1970*), U.S. congressman. Attended College of Charleston and University of South Carolina Law School. Elected to South Carolina legislature (1933–36), then worked for the U.S. Department of Justice (1936–40). Elected U.S. congressman (1940); reelected fifteen times. The stereotype of the flamboyant southern politician, his unquestioning and unswerving support of the military brought him power and attention. He pressed for more sophisticated weapons and an expansion of the armed forces, but was an opponent of the all-volunteer army. One consequence of his power was the proliferation of military installations in his congressional district around Charleston.

RIVERS, THOMAS MILTON (*b. Jonesboro, Ga., 1888; d. New York, N.Y., 1962*), physician and virologist. Attended Emory and Johns Hopkins Medical School (M.D., 1915). At Johns Hopkins (1915–17, 1919) and at Rockefeller Institute for Medical Research, 1922–37, director, 1937–56. His work and that of his colleagues made Rockefeller Institute a leading center of virus research in the 1930's and 1940's. Chairman of the National Foundation for Infantile Paralysis committee on research (1933) and its vaccine advisory committee, which conducted the clinical trials of Jonas Salk's vaccine; medical director of the foundation (1956–58) and vice president for medical affairs (1958–62). Directed the formation of Naval Medical Research Unit Number 2 (1943), which conducted antivirus programs in the Pacific.

RIVERS, WILLIAM JAMES (*b. Charleston, S.C., 1822; d. Baltimore, Md., 1909*), educator. Professor of ancient languages at South Carolina College (later University of South Carolina), 1856–73. President of Washington College, Chestertown, Md., 1873–87. Author of the important *A Sketch of the History of South Carolina to the Close of the Proprietary Government, . . .* (1856).

RIVES, GEORGE LOCKHART (*b. New York, N.Y., 1849; d. Newport, R.I., 1917*), lawyer. Grandson of William C. Rives. Graduated Columbia, 1868; Trinity College, Cambridge, 1872. LL.B., Columbia Law School, 1873. Noted for his extensive and able public-service activity in New York City as trustee and officer of Columbia and of the Astor and Lenox libraries, as counsel and member of the Rapid Transit Commission, as president of the charter revision commission (1900), and in many other posts. Author, among other books, of *The United States and Mexico, 1821–1848* (1913).

RIVES, HALLIE ERMINIE (*b. Post Oak Plantation, Ky., 1876; d. New York, N.Y., 1956*), novelist. Wife of diplomat Post Wheeler, Rives wrote many popular novels including *Smoking Flax* (1897), *Hearts Courageous* (1902), with Patrick Henry as the hero, *Satan Sanderson* (1907), *The Kingdom of Slender Swords* (1910), and *The Magic Man* (1927). Writing was characterized by fast-moving narratives, vivid imagination, and shallow personalities. Although not a critical success, Rives achieved fame in the genre of romantic fiction.

RIVES, JOHN COOK (*b. probably Franklin Co., Va., 1795; d. 1864*), journalist. Partner of Francis P. Blair in management of the Washington *Daily Globe*, 1833–49; reported debates impartially in the *Congressional Globe*, 1833–64.

RIVES, WILLIAM CABELL (*b. Amherst Co., Va., 1793; d. "Castle Hill," near Charlottesville, Va., 1868*), Virginia political leader, diplomat. Grandson of William Cabell. Graduated William and Mary, 1809; was schooled in law and politics by Thomas Jefferson. Congressman, Jacksonian Democrat, from Virginia, 1823–29, U.S. minister to France, 1829–32. Elected to the U.S. Senate, 1832, he resigned in 1834 rather than obey instructions from the Virginia Assembly to take a stand against Jackson's removal of federal deposits from the U.S. Bank. Failing in a bid for the vice presidential nomination with Martin Van Buren, he was reelected to the Senate, 1836–39, replacing John Tyler. Heading the Virginia conservatives who insisted that federal money should be deposited in state banks, he came out squarely against Van Buren's sub-treasury system. Returning to the Senate, 1841, he stood with Tyler in his struggle with Henry Clay on the bank question; in 1844 he became a full-fledged Whig. On the expiration of his term, 1845, he retired to private life for several years, serving again as U.S. minister to France, 1849–53. In 1861, he opposed secession but declared that Virginia would join the Southern group if the government should attempt to coerce seceded states; he was a member of the peace convention which met in Washington that year at the insistence of Virginia. He sat as a member of the Confederate Provisional Congress and as a member of the first regular Confederate Congress.

RIVINGTON, JAMES (*b. London, England, 1724; d. New York, N.Y., 1802*), bookseller, printer, journalist. Came to America, 1760; opened book shops in Philadelphia, New York, and Boston, but confined his business interests to New York *post* 1766. Bankrupt several times through high living and free spending, he steadied himself *post* 1769 and his business prospered. On April 22, 1773, he put out the first regular issue of *Rivington's New-York Gazetteer*, a newspaper which proposed to print both sides of questions. The successful paper soon became offensive to the Sons of Liberty in New York because of its neutral policy, and in November 1775 a party of patriots from Connecticut destroyed Rivington's printing plant. Securing a new plant from abroad, he resumed publication in October 1777, this time in the Loyalist interest, and issued the paper through December 1783. Allowed to remain in the United States after the British departure, allegedly because of secret aid given to Washington's spies, Rivington failed to thrive and died poor.

RIX, JULIAN WALBRIDGE (*b. Peacham, Vt., 1850; d. New York, N.Y., 1903*), landscape painter, etcher. Became celebrated for his atmospheric renderings of California scenery; worked in Paterson, N.J., and New York, N.Y., *post* 1888.

ROACH, JOHN (*b. Mitchelstown, Co. Cork, Ireland, 1813; d. New York, N.Y., 1887*), shipbuilder. Came to America *ca.* 1829. Prospering as a foundryman and engine builder, Roach was among the first to recognize the importance of the shift from wooden to iron vessels and in 1868 began planning for development of an iron shipbuilding industry in the United States. Removing from New York to Chester, Pa., 1871, he launched 126 iron vessels there between 1872 and 1886 and was active in awakening public opinion in favor of an American merchant marine.

ROANE, ARCHIBALD (*b. Lancaster, present Dauphin, Co., Pa., 1759; d. 1819*), lawyer, Tennessee jurist. An associate of Andrew Jackson in pioneer eastern Tennessee, Roane became attorney general for the district of Hamilton when a territorial government was instituted, 1790. He served as Democratic governor of the State of Tennessee, 1801–03, and was twice a judge of the superior court of errors and appeals.

ROANE, JOHN SELDEN (*b. Wilson Co., Tenn., 1817; d. 1867*), planter, lawyer, Mexican War and Confederate officer. Removed as a young man to Arkansas, settling at Pine Bluff. Democratic governor of Arkansas, 1849–52.

ROANE, SPENCER (*b. Essex Co., Va., 1762; d. Warm Springs, Va., 1822*), jurist, Virginia legislator. Attended William and Mary; admitted to the bar, 1782, after attendance at the lectures of George Wythe. An admirer of the political thought of Patrick Henry and George Mason, Roane became a judge of the Virginia general court, 1789, and was elected to the supreme court of appeals, 1794. During his 27 years' service on this bench, his opinions were generally sound but inclined to the side of liberty rather than property; mindful of precedents, he was also alert to the public policies of his own time. A strict constructionist and supporter of Jefferson, he joined his cousin Thomas Ritchie in founding the *Richmond Enquirer* and contributed to it a series of articles (May and June 1819, May 1821) in opposition to what he regarded as the usurping tendencies of the U.S. Supreme Court under John Marshall. Heartily approved by Democratic-Republican leaders including Jefferson, these articles reinvigorated the extreme states' rights theory.

ROARK, RURIC NEVEL (*b. Greenville, Ky., 1859; d. Cincinnati, Ohio, 1909*), Kentucky educator.

ROBB, JAMES (*b. Brownsville, Pa., 1814; d. Cheviot, Ohio, 1881*), banker. Active in New Orleans, La., commerce, public utilities, and railroad promotion, 1838–59, and also subsequent to the Civil War.

ROBB, WILLIAM LISPENARD (*b. Saratoga, N.Y., 1861; d. Troy, N.Y., 1933*), electrical engineer, educator. Graduated Columbia, 1880; Ph.D., University of Berlin, 1883. Professor of physics, Trinity College, Hartford, Conn., 1885–1902; professor of electrical engineering and physics, Rensselaer Polytechnic, 1902–33.

ROBBINS, CHANDLER (*b. Lynn, Mass., 1810; d. Weston, Mass., 1882*), Unitarian clergyman, local historian. Pastor, Second Church, Boston, Mass., 1833–74.

ROBBINS, THOMAS (*b. Norfolk, Conn., 1777; d. Colebrook, Conn., 1856*), Congregational clergyman, antiquarian. Librarian, Connecticut Historical Society, 1844–54.

ROBERDEAU, DANIEL (*b. St. Christopher, British West Indies, 1727; d. Winchester, Va., 1795*), Philadelphia merchant, Revolutionary patriot. Father of Isaac Roberdeau.

ROBERDEAU, ISAAC (*b. Philadelphia, Pa., 1763; d. Washington, D.C., 1829*), engineer. Son of Daniel Roberdeau. Studied in London; assisted Pierre C. L'Enfant in work on the new city of Washington, 1791–92. Practicing as an engineer in Pennsylvania until 1812, he was appointed major in the newly organized topographical engineer corps of the U.S. Army, April 1813. He survived the temporary abolition of the corps in 1815, and in 1818 became its chief. He was given brevet rank of lieutenant colonel, 1823.

ROBERT, CHRISTOPHER RHINELANDER (*b. Suffolk Co., N.Y., 1802; d. Paris, France, 1878*), New York merchant, Presbyterian layman, philanthropist. Founded Robert College, Constantinople, Turkey, 1863.

ROBERT, HENRY MARTYN (*b. Robertville, S.C., 1837; d. Hornell, N.Y., 1923*), Union Army engineer, parliamentarian. Author of *Pocket Manual of Rules of Order* (1876), generally known as "Robert's Rules."

ROBERTS, BENJAMIN STONE (*b. Manchester, Vt., 1810; d. Washington, D.C., 1875*), railroad engineer, lawyer, inventor of a breech-loading rifle. Graduated West Point, 1835; resigned from army, 1839, to enter railroad work and assisted George W. Whistler in Russian railroad construction, 1842. Reentering the army, he gave distinguished service in the Mexican War and on the frontier. As a Union officer in the Civil War, he won brevets for gallantry in New Mexico and rose to rank of major general in later service in Virginia, Tennessee, and Louisiana.

ROBERTS, BENJAMIN TITUS (*b. Gowanda, N.Y., 1823; d. Cattaraugus, N.Y., 1893*), Methodist clergyman. An organizer and first general superintendent of the Free Methodist Church, 1860–93.

ROBERTS, BRIGHAM HENRY (*b. Warrington, England, 1857; d. 1933*), Mormon leader. Immigrated to Salt Lake City as a child. Author of *A Comprehensive History of the Church of Jesus Christ of Latter Day Saints* (1930).

ROBERTS, EDMUND (*b. Portsmouth, N.H., 1784; d. Macao, China, 1836*), merchant. As special agent of the United States, Roberts negotiated treaties of commerce with Siam and Muscat, 1833.

ROBERTS, ELIZABETH MADOX (*b. Perryville, Ky., 1881; d. Orlando, Fla., 1941*), author. Raised in Springfield Ky.; graduated from high school in Covington, Ky., 1900. Between 1900 and 1910 she conducted private classes at home in Springfield, and then taught in the public schools. Suffering from respiratory ailments including incipient tuberculosis, she spent much time after 1910 in Colorado. Verses that she composed to accompany photographs of mountain flowers by Kenneth Hartley appeared in a booklet issued in Colorado Springs for the tourist trade: *In the Great Steep's Garden* (1915). In 1917 she enrolled at the University of Chicago. She was elected to Phi Beta Kappa and in 1921 received the Ph.B. degree in English, with honors. The fruits of her college literary activity were published in *Under the Tree* (1922; enlarged edition, 1930). Roberts then returned to Springfield. Her first novel, *The Time of Man* (1926), won international acclaim; *My Heart and My Flesh* (1927) and *Jingling in the Wind* (1928) followed. Her second major success was *The Great Meadow* (1930), a re-creation of pioneer life in Kentucky during the period of the Revolutionary War. *A Buried Treasure* (1931) is Roberts' most vivid excursion into the life of the Kentucky folk. In 1932 she published her first collection of short stories, *The Haunted Mirror*. Her next novel, *He Sent Forth a Raven* (1935), was an allegorical work, the theme of which was the same as that in her next novel, *Black is My Truelove's Hair* (1938). A second volume of poems, *Song in the Meadow*, appeared in 1940, and a second volume of short stores, *Not by Strange Gods*, in 1941, shortly after her death. Although her novels are graphic portrayals of Kentucky life, they are most impressive for their timeless qualities. Her strongest characters have an authentic life on the soil, and her work is memorable for its depiction of the intimate relationships that exist between man and nature.

ROBERTS, ELIZABETH WENTWORTH (*b. Philadelphia, Pa., 1871; d. Concord, Mass., 1927*), painter, leader in work of the Concord (Mass.) Art Assn.

ROBERTS, ELLIS HENRY (*b. Utica, N.Y., 1827; d. Utica, 1918*), journalist, financier. Congressman, Republican, from New York, 1871–75; treasurer of the United States, 1897–1905. A "Half-Breed," a sound-money man, and a protectionist.

ROBERTS, GEORGE BROOKE (*b. near Bala, Pa., 1833; d. near Bala, 1897*), railroad executive, engineer. President of the Pennsylvania Railroad Co., 1880–97.

ROBERTS, HOWARD (*b. Philadelphia, Pa., 1843; d. Paris, France, 1900*), sculptor.

ROBERTS, ISSACHAR JACOB (*b. Sumner Co., Tenn., 1802; d. Upper Alton, Ill., 1871*), Baptist clergyman and missionary in China, 1837–52. Independent in status from 1852 until his return to America in 1866, he was deeply implicated in the Taiping Rebellion.

ROBERTS, JOB (*b. near Gwynedd, Pa., 1756; d. Gwynedd, 1851*), pioneer scientific agriculturist, inventor of farm machinery, leader in the Society of Friends.

ROBERTS, JONATHAN (*b. near Norristown, Pa., 1771; d. Montgomery Co., Pa., 1854*), farmer, Pennsylvania legislator. As congressman, (Democrat) Republican, from Pennsylvania, 1811–14, Roberts defended the policies of Albert Gallatin; as U.S. senator, 1814–21, and afterwards in the Pennsylvania legislature, he fought against Andrew Jackson and Jacksonian policies, later becoming a Whig.

ROBERTS, JOSEPH JENKINS (*b. Petersburg, Va., 1809; d. Monrovia, Liberia, 1876*), statesman. Born of free, colored parents, he migrated to Liberia, 1829, and became a merchant there. Appointed governor of Liberia, 1842, he mollified the hostile native chiefs, adjusted a difficult financial situation and, in 1847, called the conference at which the new republic of Liberia was proclaimed. Elected as first president, he served with wisdom and distinction through 1855; thereafter until his death he was president of the College of Liberia. Reelected to the presidency of the

republic, 1871, to quell a domestic crisis, he served until January 1876.

ROBERTS, KENNETH LEWIS (*b. Kennebunk, Maine, 1885; d. Kennebunkport, Maine, 1957*), novelist and journalist. Studied at Cornell University. The author of many historical novels, Roberts began his career as a journalist, working for the *Boston Post* and the *Saturday Evening Post* through World War I. In 1930, he published his first novel, *Arundel*, an apology of Benedict Arnold; other works include *Rabble in Arms* (1933), *Northwest Passage* (1937), *Oliver Wiswell* (1940), an apology for American Tories during the Revolution, and *Lydia Bailey* (1947). An iconoclast and disciplined historian, Roberts was often criticized for his unpopular historical views. His books received favorable criticism.

ROBERTS, MARSHALL OWEN (*b. New York, N.Y., 1814; d. Saratoga Springs, N.Y., 1880*), capitalist. Starting as a ship-chandler, Roberts came into prominence, 1847, when with George Law and others he took up a government contract for mail steamship service from New York to New Orleans and to the Isthmus of Panama. The California gold rush *post* 1849 tremendously increased business for their U.S. Mail Steamship Co. (incorporated April 1850), but later competition from Cornelius Vanderbilt and other factors ended the company's prosperity. Roberts's chartering and selling of steamships during the Civil War forms an interesting chapter in the history of profiteering; the success of his operations was in no way hindered by his activity in New York politics as an anti-Seward Whig and as a Republican. For many years president of the North River Bank in New York City, he was one of the group which financed Cyrus Field's cable venture, 1854.

ROBERTS, NATHAN S. (*b. Piles Grove, N.J., 1776; d. 1852*), civil engineer. Worked on surveys for the Erie Canal, 1816–22; had charge of construction from Lockport to Buffalo, 1822–25. Thereafter he served as consulting engineer for canals in New York, Pennsylvania, and elsewhere in the United States.

ROBERTS, ORAN MILO (*b. Laurens District, S.C., 1815; d. Austin, Tex., 1898*), lawyer. Admitted to the Alabama bar, 1837. Removing to Texas, 1841, he prospered in practice, served as district attorney and district judge, and was a justice of the Texas supreme court, 1857–61. Colonel of the 11th Texas Infantry, 1862–64, he was briefly chief justice of Texas under Confederate rule. Reappointed chief justice of the supreme court, 1874, he won repute for learning. Elected governor of Texas, 1878, while still chief justice, he was reelected, 1880, and during his terms improved the state's financial condition and established the University of Texas. Elected professor of law in the University, 1883, he served until 1893.

ROBERTS, OWEN JOSEPHUS (*b. Philadelphia, Pa., 1875; d. Chester Springs, Pa., 1955*), associate justice of the U.S. Supreme Court. Studied at the University of Pennsylvania; after receiving his law degree, he taught at the University of Pennsylvania until 1918, when he entered private practice. After serving as a special prosecutor to investigate the oil scandals of the Harding administration (the Teapot Dome scandals), Roberts was appointed to the Supreme Court by President Hoover in 1930; he served until retirement in 1945.

Along with Chief Justice Charles Evans Hughes, Roberts played a key role in the transition of a hands-off policy in government to the social service state. In the case of *Nebbia* v. *New York* (1934), he sustained a New York statute regulating the price of milk, helped cast aside Supreme Court-created limitations on the power to govern and furnished doctrinal foundations for legitimating the New Deal.

But in 1936, in the case of *U.S. v. Butler*, Roberts put New Deal legislation beyond the constitutional pale of the taxing and spending power in a case involving the Agricultural Adjustment Act (AAA). Roberts reasoned, going against his earlier decisions, that the Tenth Amendment places certain subject matter, including agriculture, absolutely beyond national control.

In 1937, Roosevelt, stymied by the Court's intransigence (in particular, that of Roberts) threatened to "pack" the court. Roberts then shifted his views and supported the minimum wage legislation of 1937—an obvious reversal of his decision in the AAA case. Roberts went on to support many other positions of the New Deal, including Social Security and eventually endorsing the Agricultural Adjustment Act of 1938.

Worried that the concept of precedent was being ignored in favor of instant decisions subject to the short-term needs of the times, Roberts became increasingly alienated from the other justices. He resigned in 1945.

ROBERTS, ROBERT RICHFORD (*b. Frederick Co., Md., 1778; d. Lawrence Co., Ind., 1843*), Methodist clergyman. Raised in frontier Westmoreland Co., Pa., he was one of the earliest settlers in present Mercer Co. (the Shenango settlement), 1797. A pastor and circuit rider *post* 1802, he was elected bishop, 1816, and served until his death, removing in 1819 to Indiana.

ROBERTS, SOLOMON WHITE (*b. Philadelphia, Pa., 1811; d. Atlantic City, N.J., 1882*), civil engineer, canal and railroad expert. Inspired construction of the first successful anthracite furnace for iron smelting in the Lehigh Valley, 1839–40.

ROBERTS, THEODORE (*b. San Francisco, Calif., 1861; d. Los Angeles, Calif., 1928*), actor, player of "heavy" roles on stage and in motion pictures.

ROBERTS, WILLIAM CHARLES (*b. Galltmai, Wales, 1832; d. Danville, Ky., 1903*), Presbyterian clergyman, educator. Immigrated to New York, N.Y., 1849. Graduated College of New Jersey (Princeton), 1855; Princeton Theological Seminary, 1858. President, Lake Forest College, Ill., 1886–93; Centre College, Danville, Ky., 1898–1903. Served many other colleges as trustee.

ROBERTS, WILLIAM HENRY (*b. Holyhead, Wales, 1844; d. Philadelphia, Pa., 1920*), Presbyterian clergyman. Came to America as a boy. Held a number of pastorates; served as stated clerk of the General Assembly *post* 1884. A dynamic administrator, he worked especially for unity among Presbyterians.

ROBERTS, WILLIAM MILNOR (*b. Philadelphia, Pa., 1810; d. Soledade, Brazil, 1881*), civil engineer, canal and railroad expert. Chief engineer, Northern Pacific Railroad, 1869–79; chief engineer of all public works in Brazil, 1879–81.

ROBERTS, WILLIAM RANDALL (*b. Mitchelstown, Ireland, 1830; d. New York, N.Y., 1897*), merchant, Fenian leader. Immigrated to New York, N.Y., 1849. Succeeded John O'Mahony as president of the Fenian Brotherhood, 1865; with T. W. Sweeny, organized invasion of Canada, 1866. Congressman, Democrat, from New York, 1871–75; U.S. minister to Chile, 1885–89.

ROBERTSON, ALICE MARY (*b. Tullahassee Mission, Indian Territory, 1854; d. 1931*), educator, social worker. Granddaughter of Samuel A. Worcester; daughter of William S. Robertson. Engaged *post* 1880 mainly in Indian education in Oklahoma, she served as member of Congress, Republican, from Oklahoma, 1921–23.

ROBERTSON, ARCHIBALD (*b. Monymusk, Scotland, 1765; d. probably New York, N.Y., 1835*), painter of miniatures. Studied in Edinburgh and at the Royal Academy in London. Came to America, 1791; with his brother, Alexander, opened the Columbian Academy of Painting in New York City, 1792; was associated with American Academy of Fine Arts *post* 1816. Author of *Elements of the Graphic Arts* (1802). He continued active as a painter until 1828. In addition to portraits, he executed many watercolor views of New York City.

ROBERTSON, ASHLEY HERMAN (*b. Ashmore, Ill., 1867; d. San Diego, Calif., 1930*), naval officer. Graduated Annapolis, 1888. Commanded battleships *California* and *Colorado*, 1914–16, and transport *Mount Vernon*, 1917. After holding a number of high and responsible commands *post* 1918, he died as vice admiral commanding the 11th Naval district.

ROBERTSON, GEORGE (*b. near Harrodsburg, Ky., 1790; d. Lexington, Ky., 1874*), Kentucky jurist and legislator. As congressman, Whig, from Kentucky, 1817–21, he initiated legislation passed in 1820 which liberalized the purchase of government land. Chief justice of the state court of appeals, 1829–43, he was an associate justice, 1864–70, and again chief justice, 1870–71. He was a Unionist during the Civil War.

ROBERTSON, JAMES (*b. Edinburgh, Scotland, 1740; d. probably Edinburgh, date of death unknown*), printer, journalist, Loyalist. Came to America *ante* 1766. Published *New-York Chronicle*, 1769; *Albany Gazette*, 1771–72; co-publisher of *Norwich Packet* (Conn.), 1773–76. Removing to New York City, 1776, Robertson and his brother published the *Royal American Gazette*, 1777–83, and also, in Philadelphia (March-May 1778), the *Royal Pennsylvania Gazette*. In Charleston, S.C., he published the *Royal South Carolina Gazette*, 1780–82. After the British evacuation of New York, he removed with his brother to Nova Scotia.

ROBERTSON, JAMES (*b. Brunswick Co., Va., 1742; d. Chickasaw Bluffs, Tenn., 1814*), Tennessee frontier leader, Indian fighter, and treaty negotiator.

ROBERTSON, JAMES ALEXANDER (*b. Corry, Pa., 1873; d. Annapolis, Md., 1939*), editor, librarian, historian. Graduated Adelbert College of Western Reserve, 1896. Expert in the collection and editing of documents, Robertson made many contributions to the history of the Hispanic world; he held research appointments at the U.S. Department of Commerce, Florida State Historical Society, and Stetson University, and was archivist of Maryland.

ROBERTSON, JEROME BONAPARTE (*b. Woodford Co., Ky., 1815; d. Tex., 1891*), physician, Texas pioneer, Confederate brigadier general. Graduated in medicine, Transylvania, 1835. Practiced in Washington Co., Texas, *post* 1838; succeeded John Hood in command of the Texas brigade, 1862.

ROBERTSON, JOHN (*b. near Petersburg, Va., 1787; d. Mount Athos, Va., 1873*), lawyer, Virginia legislator and official. Brother of Thomas B. and Wyndham Robertson. An uncompromising critic of Jackson, he was congressman, Whig, from Virginia, 1835–41. A justice of the Virginia circuit court *post* 1841, he urged moderation when the Civil War threatened, but became and remained an active supporter of the Confederacy after secession.

ROBERTSON, MORGAN ANDREW (*b. Oswego, N.Y., 1861; d. Atlantic City, N.J., 1915*), merchant seaman, author of sea stories. Among his books were *Where Angels Fear to Tread* (1899), *Shipmates* (1901), and *Sinful Peck* (1903); his work was distinguished for its adventurous spirit and fast-paced action.

ROBERTSON, THOMAS BOLLING (*b. near Petersburg, Va., 1779; d. White Sulphur Springs, Va., 1828*), lawyer, Louisiana official. Brother of John and Wyndham Robertson. Secretary of the territory of Orleans, 1807–12; congressman, (Democrat) Republican, from the state of Louisiana, 1812–18; governor of Louisiana, 1820–24; U.S. district judge for Louisiana, 1824–28.

ROBERTSON, WILLIAM HENRY (b. Bedford, N.Y., 1823; d. Katonah, N.Y., 1898), lawyer, New York politician and legislator. His appointment as collector of the port of New York by President Garfield precipitated the fight over federal appointments and patronage, 1880–81, which resulted in the resignation from the U.S. Senate of Roscoe Conkling and Thomas C. Platt.

ROBERTSON, WILLIAM JOSEPH (b. Culpeper Co., Va., 1817; d. Charlottesville, Va., 1898), Virginia lawyer and jurist, the leading corporation lawyer in his section post 1865.

ROBERTSON, WILLIAM SCHENCK (b. Huntington, N.Y., 1820; d. 1881), Presbyterian missionary to the Indians. Father of Alice M. Robertson. Worked as teacher among the Creeks at Tullahassee, Indian Territory, 1849–61 and post 1866.

ROBERTSON, WILLIAM SPENCE (b. Glasgow, Scotland, 1872; d. Urbana, Ill., 1955), historian. Studied at the University of Wisconsin and at Yale University (Ph.D., 1903). Taught at the University of Illinois (1909–45). An expert and pioneer in the field of South American history, Robertson wrote many books on his subject, concentrating on the wars for independence throughout Latin America: *Rise of the Spanish American Republics as Told in the Lives of Their Liberators* (1918), *The Life of Miranda* (1929), and *France and Latin-American Independence* (1939).

ROBERTSON, WYNDHAM (b. near Richmond, Va., 1803; d. Abingdon, Va., 1888), lawyer, Virginia legislator. Brother of John and Thomas B. Robertson. Whig governor of Virginia (acting), 1836–37. Opposed both secession and the coercion of seceded states.

ROBESON, GEORGE MAXWELL (b. Oxford Furnace, N.J., 1829; d. Trenton, N.J., 1897), lawyer, New Jersey official. As U.S. secretary of the navy, 1869–77, he was severely criticised for extravagance and favoritism. He was congressman, Republican, from New Jersey, 1879–83.

ROBIDOU, ANTOINE (b. St. Louis, Mo., 1794; d. St. Joseph, Mo., 1860), trapper, trader. Possibly traded to Taos, N.M., 1822; established home in New Mexico, 1828. Established, ca. 1832, Fort Robidou or Fort Uinta, famous trappers' rendezvous in northeastern Utah; removed his home to St. Joseph, Mo., 1845. Interpreter with General S. W. Kearny, 1846, he was badly wounded at the battle of San Pascual.

ROBINS, HENRY EPHRAIM (b. Hartford, Conn., 1827; d. Greenfield, Mass., 1917), Baptist clergyman, educator. President of present Colby College, 1873–82.

ROBINS, MARGARET DREIER (b. Brooklyn, N.Y., 1868; d. Hernando County, Fla., 1945), social reformer. Active in New York City and state reform movements post 1902, she removed to Chicago on her marriage in 1905 to Raymond Robins, who was head of the Northwestern University Settlement. Already engaged in the work of the National Women's Trade Union League, she served as its president, 1907–22; at her instigation the League established in 1914 a school to train working women for trade union leadership, a pioneering effort in the U.S. labor movement. She also worked for woman suffrage and for municipal reform.

ROBINS, RAYMOND (b. Staten Island, N.Y., 1873; d. near Brooksville, Fla., 1954), religious activist, social reformer, and politician. Received law degree from Columbian (now George Washington) Law School in 1896. Practiced law in San Francisco

until he went to Alaska to search for gold in 1897. He returned to the mainland and eventually settled in Chicago, becoming a reform worker in settlement houses and a member of the Chicago Board of Education (1906–09). A supporter of Theodore Roosevelt, he was chairman of the Bull Moose Convention of 1916; in 1917, he traveled to Russia with the Red Cross in an attempt to keep the Kerensky government in power and Russia in the war. He returned to Russia in 1933 and was instrumental in persuading Roosevelt to recognize the Soviet government.

ROBINSON, ALBERT ALONZO (b. South Reading, Vt., 1844; d. 1918), civil engineer. Brother of Stillman W. Robinson. Supervised development and construction of the Atchison, Topeka & Santa Fe Railroad, 1871–93, becoming chief engineer and general manager; was president, Mexico Central Railway Co., 1893–1906.

ROBINSON, BENJAMIN LINCOLN (b. Bloomington, Ill., 1864; d. Jaffrey, N.H., 1935), botanist. Brother of James H. Robinson. Graduated Harvard, 1887; Ph.D., University of Strassburg, 1889. As curator of the Gray Herbarium at Harvard post 1892, Robinson increased its endowment, housed it in a building of his own design, and maintained its high standards. He was editor of an additional volume of Asa Gray's *Synoptical Flora of North America* (1895–97), coeditor of the 7th edition of Gray's *Manual of the Botany of the Northern United States* (1908), and author of *Flora of the Galapagos Islands* (1902) and many other studies.

ROBINSON, BEVERLEY (b. Middlesex Co., Va., 1722 o.s.; d. England, 1792), landowner, New York colonial official. Brother of John Robinson; brother-in-law of Roger Morris. Wealthy through marriage to a Philipse heiress and through his own trading ventures, Robinson was an ardent Loyalist in the Revolution and served as colonel of the Loyal Americans and other Tory units; he was particularly effective as a director of British spy and intelligence work. He removed to England on the downfall of British rule.

ROBINSON, BILL (b. Richmond, Va., 1878; d. New York, N.Y., 1949), dancer, actor. Christened Luther; nicknamed "Bojangles." In 1891, at the age of twelve, he joined a traveling company in *The South Before the War*, and in 1905 he worked with George Cooper as a vaudeville team. Robinson began working as a solo act in nightclubs, and was featured in *Blackbirds of 1928*, a black revue for white audiences. From then on his public role was that of a dapper, smiling, plaid-suited ambassador to the white world, maintaining a tenuous connection with black show-business circles. After 1930 black revues waned in popularity, but he remained a vogue with white audiences for more than a decade in motion pictures. His most frequent role was that of an antebellum butler opposite Shirley Temple or Will Rogers in such films as *The Little Colonel*, *The Littlest Rebel*, and *In Old Kentucky* (all released in 1935). In a small vignette in *Hooray for Love* (1935) he played a mayor of Harlem modeled on his own ceremonial honors; in *One Mile From Heaven* (1937) he played a policeman; and in the war-time musical *Stormy Weather* (1943) he played a romantic lead. He appeared in one film for black audiences, *Harlem Is Heaven* (1931), a financial failure. In 1939 he returned to the stage in *The Hot Mikado*, a jazz version of the Gilbert and Sullivan operetta produced at the New York World's Fair. His next appearance, in *All in Fun* (1940), failed to attract audiences. His last theatrical project was to have been *Two Gentlemen From the South* with James Barton, but the show did not open.

ROBINSON, BOARDMAN (b. Somerset, Nova Scotia, 1876; d. Stamford, Conn., 1952), artist. Studied at the Massachusetts Normal Art School in Boston and at the École des Beaux Arts in

Paris. An illustrator for newspapers (*The New York Morning Telegraph*, 1907–10) and several magazines, Robinson turned to book illustration in the 1920's and 1930's, including *The Idiot, Moby Dick* and *Leaves of Grass*. He painted murals which included the fresco panels at the Department of Justice in 1937. Taught at the New York Art Students' League (1919–22 and 1924–30). Director of the Colorado Springs Fine Arts Center (1936–46). Works can be seen at the Metropolitan Museum of Art in New York, the Denver Art Museum, and the Detroit Institute of Art.

ROBINSON, CHARLES (*b. Hardwick, Mass., 1818; d. near Lawrence, Kans., 1894*), physician, California pioneer and legislator, agent of the New England Emigrant Aid Co. Cautious and calculating, Robinson was the balance wheel of the Free-State party in Kansas, 1855–59, and was a leader in uniting antislavery factions in the territory. An opponent of James H. Lane, he was elected governor of Kansas under the Topeka constitution, January 1856, but was soon indicted for usurpation and imprisoned by a proslavery grand jury. When the Republican party supplanted the Free-State organization, 1859, he was nominated for governor and elected, taking office on the admission of the state, 1861. His two years in office were filled with difficulties, including an attempt at impeachment because of alleged irregularities in sale of state bonds. Engaging in politics only sporadically thereafter, he was by turns a Liberal Republican, a Democratic candidate for Congress, and a Greenback-Populist-Democratic candidate for governor.

ROBINSON, CHARLES MULFORD (*b. Ramapo, N.Y., 1869; d. Albany, N.Y., 1917*), journalist, author, city planner. Professor of civic design, University of Illinois, 1913–17.

ROBINSON, CHARLES SEYMOUR (*b. Bennington, Vt., 1829; d. New York, N.Y., 1899*), Presbyterian clergyman, hymnologist, editor. Author of *Songs for the Sanctuary* (1865), *Laudes Domini* (1884), and other hymnals.

ROBINSON, CHRISTOPHER (*b. Providence, R.I., 1806; d. Woonsocket, R.I., 1889*), lawyer, diplomat, Rhode Island attorney general and congressman. U.S. minister to Peru, 1861–65.

ROBINSON, CLAUDE EVERETT (*b. Portland, Oreg., 1900; d. New York, N.Y., 1961*), public opinion research specialist. Attended University of Oregon and Columbia (Ph.D., 1932). As associate director of George Gallup's American Institute of Political Opinion (1936), he and Gallup were pioneers in the area of scientific public opinion research. He formed the Opinion Research Corporation (1938), serving as president until 1957 and chairman until 1960. Began *Public Opinion Index for Industry* (1943) and founded Gallup and Robinson, an advertising research company (1948).

ROBINSON, CONWAY (*b. Richmond, Va., 1805; d. Philadelphia, Pa., 1884*), lawyer. Brother of Moncure Robinson. Author of a number of scholarly works on history and legal institutions; worked with John M. Patton on revision of the Virginia codes, 1846–52.

ROBINSON, EDWARD (*b. Southington, Conn., 1794; d. New York, N.Y., 1863*), philologist, geographer. Husband of Therese A. L. von J. Robinson. Graduated Hamilton College, 1816; was influenced by Moses Stuart to specialize in Hebrew; studied in Germany, 1826–30. Professor of biblical literature at Andover Theological Seminary and later at Union Theological Seminary, New York City, Robinson was founder of the *American Biblical Repository*, 1831 (editor, 1831–35), and of the *Bibliotheca Sacra*, 1843. His principal book was *Biblical Researches in Palestine, Mount Sinai and Arabia Petraea* (London, 1841). His work is now recognized as marking an epoch in the development of historical geography and related fields.

ROBINSON, EDWARD (*b. Boston, Mass., 1858; d. New York, N.Y., 1931*), museum administrator, classicist. Associated with Boston Museum of Fine Arts, 1885–1905; director, Metropolitan Museum of Art, New York City, 1910–31.

ROBINSON, EDWARD MOTT (*b. Philadelphia, Pa., 1800; d. New York, N.Y., 1865*), New Bedford (Mass.) merchant. Father of Hetty H. R. Green.

ROBINSON, EDWARD STEVENS (*b. Lebanon, Ohio, 1893; d. New Haven, Conn., 1937*), psychologist. Graduated University of Cincinnati, 1916; Ph.D., University of Chicago, 1920. Taught at Chicago and Yale; made contributions to study of learning and memory, work and fatigue, and the development of a social psychology of the law.

ROBINSON, EDWARD VAN DYKE (*b. Bloomington, Ill., 1867; d. 1915*), economist. Graduated University of Michigan, 1890; Ph.D., University of Leipzig, 1895. Taught at University of Minnesota and at Columbia University.

ROBINSON, EDWIN ARLINGTON (*b. Head Tide, Maine, 1869; d. 1935*), poet. Descended collaterally from Anne Bradstreet, Robinson attended Harvard. His young manhood was clouded by family misfortunes. Unable to get magazine publication for his poems, he published them at his own expense in *The Torrent and the Night Before* (1896); with additional poems, they were republished in *The Children of the Night* (1897). After abortive attempts in Gardiner, Maine, and in Boston, Mass., to earn a living while remaining free to write, he removed to New York City, 1899. His *Captain Craig and Other Poems* (1902) received scant attention, but in 1905 his work was reviewed with intelligent praise in the *Outlook* by President Theodore Roosevelt. Thereafter, with the assistance of friends, he continued his career in more or less material security. His most distinguished early book *The Town Down the River* appeared in 1910; *The Man Against the Sky* (1916) won wide recognition. In 1917 he brought out *Merlin*, the first of his long poems on Arthurian themes. His *Collected Poems* (1921) was awarded the 1922 Pulitzer Prize; he received a second Pulitzer Prize for *The Man Who Died Twice* (1924), and a third for *Tristram* (1927). He was by this time in general critical esteem and *Tristram* enjoyed a large sale. Subsequent to *Avon's Harvest* (1921), he wrote a number of psychological studies in verse which included *Cavender's House* (1929), *Matthias at the Door* (1931), and *King Jasper* (1935); these had a mixed critical reception as contrasted with the general acclaim given his purely narrative and lyrical work.

A careful technician, particularly in blank verse, Robinson reflected himself in his poetry; like him, it was reticent, sincere, unposed, and rooted in essential New Englandism. Whether he wrote of Yankees or the dwellers in Camelot, he concentrated his insight on the fundamentals of human nature. His greatest defect was that of obscurity. In his Arthurian poems, however, his fusion of psychological insight with dramatic force and richness of language showed forth to greatest advantage. A well-worn story took on new life under his hands, as in *Tristram*, where the rush and passion of the tale itself simplified his thoughts and permitted his a perfect balance of intellect and feeling.

ROBINSON, EZEKIEL GILMAN (*b. S. Attleboro, Mass., 1815; d. Boston, Mass., 1894*), Baptist clergyman, educator. Graduated Brown, 1838; Newton Theological Institution, 1842. Professor of biblical theology. Rochester Theological Seminary, 1853–72, and its president *post* 1860, he became president of Brown University, 1872. His stern but efficient rule ended in

1889, leaving the University far richer in equipment and further advanced in educational policy.

ROBINSON, FREDERICK BYRON (*b. near Hollandale, Wis., 1855; d. 1910*), surgeon, anatomist. Graduated University of Wisconsin, 1878; M.D., Rush Medical College, 1882. Settling in Chicago, Ill., 1891, he taught gynecology and abdominal surgery at several Chicago medical schools and held a number of hospital staff posts. His chief claim to distinction rests upon his researches and voluminous writings in the field of the anatomy of the abdomen and pelvis.

ROBINSON, GEORGE CANBY (*b. Baltimore, Md., 1878; d. Greenport, N.Y., 1960*), physician and educator. Studied at Johns Hopkins University (M.D., 1903). Robinson's academic appointments included Washington University (1913–20), dean of the medical school from 1917; Vanderbilt University, dean (1920–28); and Cornell University Medical College, director (1928–34). Robinson's speciality was organizing medical departments. His books include *The Patient as a Person* (1939) and *Adventures in Medical Education* (1957).

ROBINSON, HARRIET JANE HANSON (*b. Boston, Mass., 1825; d. Malden, Mass., 1911*), woman suffrage leader. Wife of William S. Robinson.

ROBINSON, HENRY CORNELIUS (*b. Hartford, Conn., 1832; d. Hartford, 1900*), corporation lawyer, Connecticut Republican legislator and judicial reformer, leading Congregational layman.

ROBINSON, HENRY MORTON (*b. Boston, Mass., 1898; d. New York, N.Y., 1961*), author. Attended Columbia (M.A., 1924). Author of the novels *Children of Morningside* (1924), *The Perfect Round* (1945), and *The Cardinal*; the verse collections *Buck Fever* and *The Second Wisdom*; and the nonfiction works *John Erskine* (1928), *Science Versus Crime* (1935), and *Fantastic Interim* (1943). Contributed to *Century*, *Bookman*, and *North American Review* while teaching at Columbia (1924–27), and held three editorial positions with Reader's Digest (1935–45). He is remembered for his versatility as a teacher, editor, critic, essayist, scholar, novelist, and journalist.

ROBINSON, JAMES HARVEY (*b. Bloomington, Ill., 1863; d. New York, N.Y., 1936*), historian. Brother of Benjamin L. Robinson. Educated in the Bloomington public schools, and at the State Normal School where he developed a lifelong interest in biology, he traveled abroad and engaged in business before entering Harvard. Graduating in 1887, he took a master's degree the following year and received a doctorate from the University of Freiburg, 1890. He taught at University of Pennsylvania, 1891–95. Professor of European history at Barnard College and Columbia, 1895–1919, he helped found the New School for Social Research (New York City), 1919, and remained with it until 1921. Author of a best-selling work, *The Mind in the Making* (1921), which he had written in the hope of persuading the educated many to think critically about human behavior, he was author also of a number of textbooks and of *The New History* (1912) which advocated "totality" in historical study, viz., the employment of all the social and behavioral sciences in examining the record of man considered as an animal in a state of evolution. Filled with a sense of mission against organized Christianity, he rejected all forms of supernaturalism and considered that the principal task of the historian and his scientific allies must be to show ordinary men how to overcome the burden of the past and its precedents by understanding how that burden arose and grew. An outstanding teacher and lecturer, Robinson exercised great influence in shifting public secondary school teaching of history from its traditional

political emphasis to consideration of how human beings came to be what they are.

ROBINSON, JOHN (*b. Virginia, 1704; d. Virginia, 1766*), Virginia colonial legislator and official. Brother of Beverley Robinson. Speaker of the House of Burgesses and treasurer of Virginia, 1738–66. A report after his death, based on an investigation by Richard Henry Lee and others, showed his accounts short by more than 100,000 pounds.

ROBINSON, JOHN CLEVELAND (*b. Binghamton, N.Y., 1817; d. Binghamton, 1897*), soldier. Attended West Point, 1835–38, leaving to study law. After Mexican War service, he remained in the army and was engaged principally in Western frontier duty. Commanding Fort McHenry, Baltimore, Md., in April 1861, he discouraged any attempt on the part of rioters to attack the post. Thereafter in continuous service with the Army of the Potomac, he distinguished himself particularly at Gettysburg. He rose to rank of major general, retiring in 1869.

ROBINSON, JOHN MITCHELL (*b. Tuckahoe Neck, Caroline Co., Md., 1827; d. Annapolis, Md., 1896*), Maryland circuit and appeals court judge, *post* 1864; chief justice court of appeals, 1893–96.

ROBINSON, JOSEPH TAYLOR (*b. near Lonoke, Ark., 1872; d. Washington, D.C., 1937*), lawyer. Congressman, Democrat, from Arkansas, 1903–13, he was elected governor of Arkansas in 1912, but resigned to fill a seat in the U.S. Senate, where he served, 1913–37. Robinson became Senate Democratic leader in 1923 and received his party's vice presidential nomination in 1928. As Senate majority leader, 1933–37, he supported President F. D. Roosevelt on almost every issue, including the unpopular Supreme Court reorganization bill. An able parliamentarian and an effective behind-the-scenes worker, he played an important role in two progressive Democratic administrations.

ROBINSON, MONCURE (*b. Richmond, Va., 1802; d. Pennsylvania, 1891*), civil engineer. Brother of Conway Robinson. Built original line of Philadelphia & Reading Railroad, 1834–36.

ROBINSON, MOSES (*b. Hardwick, Mass., 1742; d. Bennington, Vt., 1813*), Revolutionary soldier, Vermont political leader. Chief justice of the supreme court, 1778–89; governor of Vermont, 1789–90; U.S. senator, 1791–96. Strongly opposed the Jay Treaty, 1794–95.

ROBINSON, ROWLAND EVANS (*b. Ferrisburg, Vt., 1833; d. Ferrisburg, 1900*). Author of a number of books of sketches in prose, depicting rural Vermont life and people.

ROBINSON, RUBY DORIS SMITH (*b. Atlanta, Ga., 1942; d. Atlanta, 1967*), civil rights activist. While attending Atlanta's Spellman College (1958–65), she joined the Student Nonviolent Coordinating Committee, participated in sit-ins and freedom rides, and became administrative secretary of SNCC in 1962. She visited Guinea in 1964 with other SNCC leaders and began to appreciate the economic as well as racial dimensions of exploitation. A hardworking, efficient, and determined volunteer, she was elected executive secretary of SNCC (1966) and endorsed the call for "black power"; she insisted that black women historically had to play strong roles for the survival of their families and formally protested the limited roles allotted to women in SNCC. Died of cancer.

ROBINSON, SOLON (*b. Tolland, Conn., 1803; d. Jacksonville, Fla., 1880*), Indiana pioneer, agriculturist, author. With James M. Garnett, Henry L. Ellsworth, and others, Robinson was advocating formation of a national agricultural society as early as 1838; his activities paved way for forming the U.S. Agricultural

Society, 1852. Writing in the *New York Tribune* (for which he was agricultural editor, 1853−*ca.* 1868), the *American Agriculturist*, and other journals, he produced a body of travel sketches which are trustworthy historical records of rural life of his time. He was author also of a number of books of more general interest which include *The Will: a Tale of the Lake of the Red Cedars* (1841) and *Hot Corn: Life Scenes in New York* (1854).

ROBINSON, STILLMAN WILLIAMS (*b. near South Reading, Vt., 1838; d. Columbus, Ohio, 1910*), engineer, educator. Brother of Albert A. Robinson. C. E., University of Michigan, 1863. Established department of mechanical engineering at present University of Illinois, where he taught from 1870−78; professor of physics and mechanical engineering at Ohio State, 1878−95. A pioneer in experimental instruction in engineering education, he was also author of several outstanding textbooks and the holder of a number of profitable patents.

ROBINSON, STUART (*b. Strabane, Ireland, 1814; d. Louisville, Ky., 1881*), Presbyterian clergyman, editor, educator. Came to America as a child. Pastor in Louisville *post* 1858; aggressive editor of denominational journals; Confederate sympathizer.

ROBINSON, THEODORE (*b. Irasburg, Vt., 1852; d. New York, N.Y., 1896*), artist. Passed early life in the Midwest and West; settled in New York City, 1874, where he was an organizer of the Art Students League whose name he suggested; studied in Paris, France, under Carolus-Duran and J. L. Gérôme *post* 1877. Returning home, he became a member of the Society of American Artists, 1881. During subsequent journeys to France, 1884−92, he came under influence of the Impressionists and subsequently was important as pioneer and spokesman for the new movement in America. His work occupies a unique and outstanding place in American painting.

ROBINSON, THERESE ALBERTINE LOUISE VON JAKOB (*b. Halle, Germany, 1797; d. Hamburg, Germany, 1870*), philologist, novelist, translator. Wife of Edward Robinson (1794−1863). Resided in America, 1830−37, 1840−63. Wrote scholarly works on a wide variety of subjects, also several novels; employed pen name "Talvj."

ROBINSON, WILLIAM (*b. Coal Island, Ireland, 1840; d. Brooklyn, N.Y., 1921*), engineer. Came to America as a child. Graduated Wesleyan University, 1865. Specializing in electrical work, Robinson was the inventor and basic patentee (1872) of the railroad block-signal; he also devised the bond wire system for connecting adjacent rails electrically, patented the radial car truck used on electric railways, and made important improvements in steam turbines.

ROBINSON, WILLIAM CALLYHAN (*b. Norwich, Conn., 1834; d. 1911*), legal educator and author. Graduated Dartmouth, 1854. Assisted in reorganization of Yale Law School, where he taught, 1869−96; thereafter headed department of law, Catholic University of America, Washington, D.C. Author of *Notes on Elementary Law* (1875, 1882, 1910), *Elements of American Jurisprudence* (1900), a scholarly edition of Horne's *Mirrour of Justices* (1903), and other works.

ROBINSON, WILLIAM ERIGENA (*b. Unagh, Ireland, 1814; d. Brooklyn, N.Y., 1892*), lawyer, journalist, politician. Immigrated to America, 1836. Graduated Yale, 1841; studied at Yale Law School. Contributed the "Richelieu" dispatches from Washington to the *New York Tribune*, 1844−48. An ardent Irish patriot, he held a number of minor federal offices in New York; he served as congressman, Democrat, from New York, 1867−69 and 1881−85.

ROBINSON, WILLIAM STEVENS (*b. Concord, Mass., 1818; d. Malden, Mass., 1876*), Massachusetts journalist, antislavery advocate. Whig, Free-Soil, and Republican political leader. Clerk of Massachusetts House of Representatives, 1862−73, he was known as the "Warwick" of state politics and successfully led opposition to Benjamin F. Butler's bids for the governorship.

ROBINSON-SMITH, GERTRUDE (*b. Mamaroneck, N.Y., 1881; d. New York, N.Y., 1963*), civic worker and music patron. President of the American Woman's Association (1911−28) and creator of the Ice Flotilla Committee, which provided ice-making machines for advance field hospitals in World War I. Organizer of the French Theater at the Barbizon Plaza Hotel in New York (1937). Formed the Berkshire Symphony Festival (1934) in Stockbridge, Mass., and was president until 1955. Convinced Serge Koussevitzky, conductor of the Boston Symphony, to bring the orchestra to Stockbridge in 1936, and donated her estate, "Tanglewood," to the festival. The Berkshire Music Center opened in 1940. Appointed to the advisory committee of the National Culture Center in Washington, D.C., in 1963.

ROBOT, ISIDORE (*b. Tharoiseau, France, 1837; d. Dallas, Tex., 1887*), Roman Catholic clergyman, Benedictine. Came to America, 1871; founded monastery at Sacred Heart, Okla., 1875; became prefect-apostolic of Indian Territory, 1876, and served until 1886.

ROBSON, MAY (*b. Wagga Wagga, New South Wales, Australia, 1858; d. Beverly Hills, Calif., 1942*), actress. Stage name of Mary Jeannette Robison. Raised in a suburb of Melbourne, Australia, and in England, she came to the United States on her marriage to C. L. Gore, 1877. Left destitute and with a son to support when her husband died in New York City, she turned on impulse to the stage. She made her debut in a character part at the Grand Opera House, Brooklyn, on Sept. 17, 1883, with great success; between 1884 and 1901 she was a member of three famous New York stock companies: A. M. Palmer's, Daniel Frohman's (Lyceum), and Charles Frohman's (Empire). A specialist in playing eccentrics, she won additional renown as a make-up expert. After leaving the Empire company, she played featured roles. She first starred in *The Rejuvenation of Aunt Mary* (1907), in which she toured for almost ten years. Experienced as a film actress since 1911, she resumed film work in the late 1920's; her greatest single success came in 1933, when she played "Apple Annie" in *Lady for a Day*.

ROBSON, STUART (*b. Annapolis, Md., 1836; d. New York, N.Y., 1903*), actor. Stage-name of Henry Robson Stuart. Partner of William H. Crane in a celebrated comedy team, 1877−89.

ROCHAMBEAU, JEAN BAPTISTE DONATIEN DE VIMEUR, COMTE DE (*b. Vendôme, France, 1725; d. Thoré, France, 1807*), French soldier. Entering the army as a junior officer of cavalry, 1740, he was given command of a troop, 1743, and by 1747 had risen to colonel. After a period of retirement in the Vendômois, 1749−56, he shared in the brilliant campaign against Minorca, and after distinguishing himself at Crefeld, June 1758, rose to command of an infantry regiment in the next year. His skill in maneuver and his personal bravery saved the French from a disaster at Klostercamp, October 1760; early in 1761 he was made brigadier general and inspector of cavalry. He was noted for his introduction of a number of tactical improvements and for his unusual interest in the welfare of his soldiers. Appointed to command the French expeditionary army in America, he sailed with his force from Brest on May 1, 1780, and arrived off Rhode Island on July 11. The splendid discipline of his army together with the tact and charm of the officers removed many old American prejudices against the French. Unwilling to make a major move until the French had command of the sea, he discouraged the idea of an attack on New York which was favored by Lafayette and Washington, requested reinforcement from France, and put his army into winter quarters in Rhode Island. Informed in May 1781 that no more troops were to be expected but that the French West India fleet under command of the Comte de Grasse would cooperate with him and with Washington, he held a conference with the American general at Wethersfield, Conn., May 21. Washington still favored an attempt against New York, but Rochambeau urged that combined operations be undertaken with the fleet against Cornwallis in Virginia. The French army then moved from Newport and united with Washington's troops near White Plains, N.Y. The Franco-American force now numbered some 10,000 men and awaited news from de Grasse before it determined on its next move. When it was learned on August 14 that the French fleet was sailing for the Chesapeake, Rochambeau once again advised a march southward against Cornwallis who was being harassed by Lafayette's force in Virginia. The march southward began on August 19; an army group under General Wm. Heath was left to threaten New York so as to deceive the British. Until August 29 the joint movement might well have been an attack in force on New York and so the British considered it; thereafter the speed with which the armies traveled to join Lafayette at Williamsburg, Va., was as extraordinary as the efficiency with which de Grasse (aided by the arrival of the French supporting fleet from Newport) repelled the efforts of the English fleet under Admiral Graves to prevent the sealing-off of the mouth of the Chesapeake. The combined armies arrived at Williamsburg, Va., on September 14 to find the British encamped at Yorktown in a hopeless position with no longer any chance of rescue by sea. After 17 days of formal siege, Yorktown was surrendered on Oct. 19, 1781. Rochambeau embarked for France, Jan. 11, 1783. Thereafter he held important district commands at home, commanded the northern military department in 1790–91, and was created a marshal of France, December 1791. Narrowly escaping death under the Terror, he was honored by Napoleon and received the Legion of Honor.

ROCHE, ARTHUR SOMERS (*b. Somerville, Mass., 1883; d. Florida, 1935*), popular novelist and storywriter. Son of James J. Roche.

ROCHE, JAMES JEFFREY (*b. Mountmellick, Ireland, 1847; d. Berne, Switzerland, 1908*), journalist. Immigrated as a child to Charlottetown, P.E.I.; removed to Boston, Mass., 1866. Assistant to John B. O'Reilly on the Boston *Pilot*, leading Irish Catholic journal in the United States, Roche became editor of the paper, 1890. He was U.S. consul at Genoa, Italy, 1904, and later at Berne.

ROCHESTER, NATHANIEL (*b. Westmoreland Co., Va., 1752; d. Rochester, N.Y., 1831*), merchant, Revolutionary soldier. After making several land purchases in the newly opened Genesee country of New York, he removed there from Hagerstown, Md., *post* 1803, and in 1818 settled in Rochester which had already been founded by him.

ROCK, JOHN (*b. Lauter, Hesse-Darmstadt, Germany, 1836; d. 1904*), nurseryman. Immigrated to New York City as a boy. Served in Union Army, 1861–65; removed to California, 1866, starting a nursery at Santa Clara. Established California Nursery Co. at Niles, 1884.

ROCKEFELLER, ABBY GREENE ALDRICH (*b. Providence, R.I., 1874; d. New York, N.Y., 1948*), philanthropist, art patron. Daughter of Nelson W. Aldrich; married John D. Rockefeller, Jr., Oct. 9, 1901. Shared in planning the restoration of Colonial Williamsburg and initiated the unique collection of American folk art housed there; was a founder and generous patron of the Museum of Modern Art, New York City. She was active as well in organizing and advancing numerous projects for social welfare.

ROCKEFELLER, JOHN DAVISON (*b. Richford, N.Y., 1839; d. Ormond, Fla., 1937*), industrialist, philanthropist. Brother of William Rockefeller. His father, a trader in lumber, salt, and other commodities, had a farm, first at Richford, later at Moravia, N.Y., where John first attended school. A year's further schooling at Owego, N.Y., and two years of high school in Cleveland, Ohio, where the family moved in 1853, comprised Rockefeller's formal education. After three-and-a-half years with a Cleveland firm of commission merchants, Rockefeller and a young Englishman, Maurice B. Clark, formed (1859) a successful partnership, dealing in grain, hay, meats, and miscellaneous goods. Inheriting his mother's religious bent, Rockefeller became the leading layman in the Erie Street Baptist Church, and began contributing at least a tenth of his modest income to charities. In 1864 he married Laura Celestia Spelman, by whom he had four children, Bessie, Alta, Edith, and John D., Jr.

In 1863 Rockefeller, sensing the commercial possibilities in the recent linking of Cleveland by a railroad to the new "Oil Regions" in northwestern Pennsylvania, had joined in building a refinery, which in two years was the largest in Cleveland. Buying out his partners, 1865, Rockefeller, his brother William, and one of his original partners, Samuel Andrews, built a second refinery, the Standard Works, and William went to New York to develop the export and eastern trade. Rockefeller's special talent for enlisting brains brought him Henry M. Flagler as a partner in 1867; Flagler undertook in the firm's behalf an expert negotiation of lower freight rates, then unstandardized. Rockefeller's efficiency and foresight in the intensely competitive oil business soon effected further economies in operation. The firm made its own barrels, built warehouses, obtained fleets of lighters and tankers. Meticulous about details, he instituted a cost-accounting system accurate to the third decimal. In 1870 the firm became a joint-stock corporation, the Standard Oil Company of Ohio. Rockefeller, now convinced that solvency depended upon organization to end or abate destructive competition, pressed forward to acquire all other Cleveland refineries, and then refineries in other cities. Ownership or control of pipelines was the next step, accompanied by the purchase or lease of oil-terminal facilities in New York, and the beginning of an elaborate marketing system. Within seven years Standard Oil, holding a position close to monopoly, dominated the American oil industry. A few years later it also dominated the foreign oil market.

The organization of this vast combination became perplexing. The Ohio company, nucleus of the group, had no legal right to own property or stock outside Ohio. The solution, in 1881, was the establishment of a board of trustees which took over all stock and issued certificates of interest in the trust estates. Thus was the modern "Trust" born, soon followed by antitrust laws as a result of public hostility against Standard Oil and similar trusts. Although it was never Rockefeller's intent to obtain absolute control of refining, the Standard's ruthless competitive practices gave great offense, and general American opinion refused to accept any excuses for monopoly. In 1892 Standard of Ohio's trust agreement was dissolved by court order. Management was subsequently controlled by interlocking directorates of various state companies and finally (1899) by a holding company, Standard Oil (New Jersey), which was disbanded after a federal suit and a dissolution decree in 1911.

Ironically, as public criticism of him rose to a climax, Rockefeller was only the nominal head of the combination. *Post* 1897 he was wholly occupied with the distribution of his vast fortune, but the "tainted money" controversy of 1905 threatened to interfere with acceptance of his benefactions. In philanthropy, however, as in business, he was a conspicuous innovator and organizer. By employing able publicity agents and mitigating his own policy of silence about his affairs, he effected an eventual change in public opinion. Frederick T. Gates, an able and imaginative Baptist clergyman whom Rockefeller had met when founding (1889) the University of Chicago, was his principal aide in philanthropy *post* 1891; he was joined in 1897 by John D. Rockefeller, Jr. The Rockefellers established four principal philanthropic institutions: the Rockefeller Institute for Medical Research (1901); the General Education Board (1902); the Rockefeller Foundation (1913), "to promote the wellbeing of mankind throughout the world"; and the Laura Spelman Rockefeller Memorial Foundation (1918), later absorbed by the Rockefeller Foundation. Rockefeller's benefactions during his lifetime totaled $550 million and the endowment of his foundations continued to multiply.

Rockefeller gained a preeminent place, both in industry and in philanthropy, as an organizing genius. Alike in rationalizing the chaotic oil industry as in exploring new fields in education, health, and social welfare, he contributed a powerful initial impulse, intense application to detail, great penetration in solving difficult problems, and a rare tact in welding together talented groups of men to implement his ideas. In industry he gave his associates the fullest latitude and in philanthropy a complete freedom, with the result that their loyalty never flagged. Rockefeller had neither great breadth of mind nor notable cultivation. His greatest failure was in public relations, which he never understood. His chief defect was his tardiness in comprehending the steady advance of business ethics and the necessity of squaring business practices with new demands by government. His dominant passion was neither money-getting nor power-seeking, but a hatred of disorder and waste.

ROCKEFELLER, JOHN DAVISON, JR. (*b. Cleveland, Ohio, 1874; d. Tucson, Ariz., 1960*), industrialist and philanthropist. Studied at Brown University. The heir of the Rockefeller Standard Oil fortune, Rockefeller's first major business experience was his adamant handling of a strike of the Colorado Fuel and Iron Co. in Ludlow, Colo. The strike ended in violence known as the Ludlow Massacre for which Rockefeller was blamed. Later Rockefeller became a champion of the rights of labor without abrogating his responsibilities to management. After World War I, he devoted his life to philanthropic pursuits: the endowment of Riverside Church, Rockefeller University in New York, Ft. Tryon Park, the restoration of Williamsburg, and the donation of the land for the permanent home of the United Nations. His major business venture turned out to be the development of Rockefeller Center in New York City.

ROCKEFELLER, WILLIAM (*b. Richford, N.Y., 1841; d. Tarrytown, N.Y., 1922*), financier, industrialist. Brother of John D. Rockefeller whom he assisted in his oil operations, managing Standard Oil's export selling functions in New York. An able salesman and commercial diplomat, he was active in bringing Henry H. Rogers, Charles Pratt, and others into the Standard Oil mergers and later, in association with Rogers and with James Stillman, carried on a number of adventurous speculations in Wall Street securities, chief of which was the Amalgamated Copper deal. *Post* 1911 and the dissolution of the Standard Oil trust, he withdrew from an active part in the oil industry and devoted himself to his investments.

ROCKHILL, WILLIAM WOODVILLE (*b. Philadelphia, Pa., 1854; d. Honolulu, Hawaii, 1914*), orientalist, diplomat. Educated in France; was official in American legations at Peking, China, and Seoul, Korea, 1884–87. Made scientific expeditions for the Smithsonian Institution in Mongolia and Tibet, 1888–89, 1891–92. Returning to the diplomatic service, 1893, he made his most notable contribution as special agent in China for settlement of the problems raised by the Boxer insurrection, 1900. He was also director of the International Bureau of the American Republics, 1899–1905, and thereafter U.S. minister to China and ambassador successively to Russia and Turkey. He presented a large library of rare Chinese works to the Library of Congress and was author of a number of important Far Eastern studies.

ROCKNE, KNUTE KENNETH (*b. Voss, Norway, 1888; d. southeast Kansas, 1931*), football coach. Came to America as a child; was raised in Chicago, Ill. Graduated Notre Dame, 1914. As head football coach at Notre Dame *post* 1918, Rockne developed colorful and highly trained teams whose play featured speed and deception. Many of the players trained by him became football coaches in colleges all over the country, further popularizing the so-called "Rockne System."

ROCKWELL, ALPHONSO DAVID (*b. New Canaan, Conn., 1840; d. 1933*), physician, Union Army surgeon. M.D., Bellevue Hospital Medical School, N.Y., 1864. In association with George M. Beard, Rockwell placed electrotherapeutics on a scientific and professional basis.

ROCKWELL, GEORGE LINCOLN (*b. Bloomington, Ill., 1918; d. Arlington, Va., 1967*), organizer and leader of the American Nazi party. Attended Brown University (1938–40) and Pratt Institute. Founded the fascist American Nazi Party (1958), whose membership probably never exceeded 100. A white supremacist, he advocated the sterilization or extermination of all Jews, who, he insisted, were responsible for the world-wide Communist movement. He also called for the deportation of all blacks to Africa and for the hanging of all "traitors," including former Presidents Harry Truman and Dwight Eisenhower and Chief Justice Earl Warren. He staged numerous provocative demonstrations, where his "storm troopers" were provided with Nazi uniforms and swastika armbands; his own presence at rallies often led to violence and arrests. He was shot to death by a former member of the party who had been expelled.

ROCKWELL, KIFFIN YATES (*b. Newport, Tenn., 1892; d. near Thann, Alsace, 1916*), aviator. Enlisted in French Foreign Legion, 1914; after pilot training, became member of Escadrille Lafayette, April 1916. Killed in action.

RODDEY, PHILIP DALE (*b. Moulton, Ala., 1820; d. London, England, 1897*), Confederate brigadier general, merchant. Developed great abilities as cavalry scout leader under Generals Braxton Bragg, Joseph Wheeler, and Nathan B. Forrest.

RODENBOUGH, THEOPHILUS FRANCIS (*b. Easton, Pa., 1838; d. New York, N.Y., 1912*), Union cavalry colonel, author. Awarded Congressional Medal of Honor for gallantry at Trevilian Station, Va., 1864.

RODES, ROBERT EMMETT (*b. Lynchburg, Va., 1829; d. Winchester, Va., 1864*), civil engineer, Confederate major general. Graduated Virginia Military Institute, 1848. Starting in the Civil War as colonel, 5th Alabama Infantry, he distinguished himself at first Bull Run, Fair Oaks, Gaines's Mill, South Mountain, and Antietam. Leading the flank march at Chancellorsville, his division launched the surprise attack which gave the Confederates the victory. Rodes was an outstanding officer in the Eastern campaigns, 1863–64, and died on the battlefield while counterattacking Union forces under General P. H. Sheridan.

RODGERS, CHRISTOPHER RAYMOND PERRY (*b. Brooklyn, N.Y., 1819; d. Washington, D.C., 1892*), naval officer. Son of George W. Rodgers (1787–1832). Served with high efficiency in Seminole, Mexican, and Civil wars; as superintendent, U.S.

Naval Academy, 1874–78, he attempted with fair success to raise standards of studies and behavior.

RODGERS, GEORGE WASHINGTON (*b. Cecil Co., Md., 1787; d. Buenos Aires, Argentina, 1832*), naval officer. Brother of John Rodgers (1773–1838); father of Christopher R. P. and George W. Rodgers (1822–1863). Warranted midshipman, 1804; served in War of 1812 aboard USS *Wasp* in engagement with HMS *Frolic* and later aboard USS *Macedonian*. Died while in command of the Brazil Squadron protecting American rights in present Argentina.

RODGERS, GEORGE WASHINGTON (*b. Brooklyn, N.Y., 1822; d. in action off Charleston, S.C., 1863*), naval officer. Son of George W. Rodgers (1787–1832); brother of Christopher R. P. Rodgers. Ordnance specialist.

RODGERS, JOHN (*b. Boston, Mass., 1727; d. New York, N.Y., 1811*), Presbyterian clergyman, Revolutionary chaplain, evangelist. Held pastorates for many years in New Castle Co., Del., and in New York City.

RODGERS, JOHN (*b. near present Havre de Grace, Md., 1773; d. Philadelphia, Pa., 1838*), naval officer. Father of John Rodgers (1812–1882); brother of George W. Rodgers (1787–1832). After merchant marine service in which he rose to master, Rodgers was appointed second lieutenant aboard the *Constellation*, March 1798, soon rising to first lieutenant and executive officer under Thomas Truxtun. Promoted captain a year later, he cruised in command of the *Insurgente* and later of the *Maryland*. Returning briefly to the merchant marine, 1801, he was recalled to the navy and served in the Mediterranean against the Barbary pirates, 1802–06. As senior officer under Commodores Morris and Barron, he commanded the blockading fleet off Tripoli with great success and played a great part in the treaty negotiations with Morocco, Tripoli, and Tunis. Commanding the northern division of coast defense, 1810–11, while cruising in the frigate *President* he engaged the British sloop *Little Belt* off Cape Henry, May 16, 1811. Ranking officer in active service in the War of 1812, Rodgers operated principally against British commerce, performing feats which although they were not as brilliant as some of the famous sea duels of the war were much more useful. On shore duty with a detachment of sailors and marines, he harassed the British on the retreat down the Potomac after the expedition against Washington, D. C. He also helped defend Baltimore, Md., when it was menaced by the enemy. He became senior naval officer, 1821, and in 1823 served briefly as U.S. secretary of the navy.

RODGERS, JOHN (*b. near Havre de Grace, Md., 1812; d. Washington, D.C., 1882*), naval officer. Son of John Rodgers (1773–1838). Appointed midshipman, 1828; was active in surveys, principally with the North Pacific Exploring and Surveying Expedition, 1852–56. He began his Civil War service at Cincinnati, Ohio, where he purchased and fitted out three small steamships, the nucleus of the Mississippi Flotilla. Aide to Admiral Du Pont in operations against South Carolina late in 1861 and later in actions on the James River, he became captain of the monitor *Weehawken*. He distinguished himself particularly in the attack on Fort Sumter, April 1863, and later against the Confederate ironclad *Atlanta*. At the time of his death he was senior rear admiral.

RODGERS, JOHN (*b. Washington, D.C., 1881; d. near Philadelphia, Pa., 1926*), naval officer. Great-grandson of John Rodgers (1773–1838). Graduated Annapolis, 1903. The second naval officer to be licensed as an aviator, Rodgers commanded the Naval Air Station, Pearl Harbor, Hawaii, 1922–25. He won particular notice for heroism as commander of the San Francisco–Hawaii flight, September 1925.

RODMAN, ISAAC PEACE (*b. South Kingston, R.I., 1822; d. near Sharpsburg, Md., 1862*), businessman, Rhode Island legislator, Union brigadier general. Commanding the 4th Division of the IX Corps, he was killed at the battle of Antietam.

RODMAN, THOMAS JACKSON (*b. near Salem, Ind., 1815; d. Rock Island, Ill., 1871*), soldier, ordnance expert. Graduated West Point, 1841. Invented process for casting cannon upon a hollow core, cooling inner surface by a flow of water so that each successive layer of metal was compressed by the shrinkage of outer layers; also developed an improved powder for artillery. His inventions were finally approved and adopted by the U.S. government, 1859, and were also adopted by the governments of Russia, Great Britain, and Prussia. During the Civil War, he commanded the arsenal at Watertown, Mass., where he supervised casting of the celebrated "Columbiad" and other heavy guns, both smoothbore and rifled, for use by the army and navy.

RODNEY, CAESAR (*b. near Dover, Del., 1728; d. Dover, 1784*), statesman, jurist. Brother of Thomas Rodney. Serving almost continuously, 1761–76, as Kent Co. delegate of the legislature at New Castle, Rodney was elected speaker in 1769, 1773–74, and 1775–76. He was an associate of Thomas McKean and George Read in patriotic activity and was a delegate to the First Continental Congress. Reelected to Congress, 1775, he was also made brigadier general of the Kent Co. militia. In the late afternoon of July 2, 1776, his vote committed the Delaware delegation to acceptance of independence and he also voted with McKean for the adoption of the Declaration. Rejected by the conservatives of Kent Co. because of his action, he failed to obtain any political office in the fall of 1776, but as a member of the Council of Safety busied himself in raising troops for Washington's army. In 1777 he was reelected to the Continental Congress, and in the spring of 1778 he was chosen president of Delaware; he served with ability until November 1781. He was regarded by his contemporaries as a man of wit and high courage.

RODNEY, CAESAR AUGUSTUS (*b. Dover, Del., 1772; d. Buenos Aires, Argentina, 1824*), lawyer, statesman, diplomat. Son of Thomas Rodney; nephew of Caesar Rodney. Congressman, (Democrat) Republican, from Delaware, 1803–05; was a House manager in impeachment proceedings against John Pickering and Samuel Chase. U.S. attorney general, 1807–11, he served in the Delaware militia during the War of 1812. After service, 1817–18, as a U.S. commissioner investigating the political status of the newly established South American republics, he was congressman again very briefly in 1821, and U.S. senator, 1822. Appointed first U.S. minister to the Argentine Republic, he arrived in Buenos Aires, November 1823, but soon fell dangerously ill and died in office.

RODNEY, THOMAS (*b. Kent Co., Del., 1744; d. Natchez, Miss., 1811*), farmer, Revolutionary soldier, jurist. Brother of Caesar Rodney; father of Caesar A. Rodney. Judge, supreme court of Delaware, 1802–03; U.S. judge for Mississippi Territory, 1803–11.

RODZINSKI, ARTUR (*b. Spalato, Dalmatia [now Split, Yugoslavia], 1892; d. Boston, Mass., 1958*), conductor. Studied at the University of Lvov and at the Vienna Academy of Music. While he was a conductor at the Teatr Wielki Opera House in Warsaw, he was heard by a touring conductor, Leopold Stokowski, and was hired as the assistant conductor of the Philadelphia Orchestra (1926–29). From 1929 to 1933, he was conductor of the Los Angeles Philharmonic; from 1933 to 1943, he directed the Cleveland Orchestra; from 1943 to 1947, the New York Philharmonic;

and from 1947 to 1948, the Chicago Symphony Orchestra. Remembered for his Wagner, Tchaikovsky, and Brahms interpretations, Rodzinski also championed twentieth-century composers such as Richard Strauss. In 1935, Rodzinski premiered Shostakovich's *Lady Macbeth of Mzensk* with the Cleveland Orchestra; in Florence, he conducted the Western premier of Prokofiev's *War and Peace*.

ROE, EDWARD PAYSON (*b. present New Windsor, N.Y., 1838; d. Cornwall-on-Hudson, N.Y., 1888*), Presbyterian clergyman, popular novelist. Author of *Barriers Burned Away* (1872), *A Knight of the Nineteenth Century* (1877), and other moralistic novels which were all best sellers.

ROE, FRANCIS ASBURY (*b. Elmira, N.Y., 1823; d. Washington, D.C., 1901*), naval officer. Performed outstanding Civil War service in the taking of New Orleans and later on the Atlantic Coast blockade where he commanded the *Sassacus* in action against the Confederate ironclad *Albemarle*, May 1864. He retired as rear admiral, 1885.

ROE, GILBERT ERNSTEIN (*b. Oregon, Wis., 1865; d. New York, N.Y., 1929*), lawyer, legal author. Political and legal adviser of Robert M. LaFollette. Practiced in New York, N.Y., *post* 1899.

ROEBLING, JOHN AUGUSTUS (*b. Mühlhausen, Germany, 1806; d. Brooklyn, N.Y., 1869*), engineer, bridge builder. Father of Washington A. Roebling. Graduated Royal Polytechnic Institute, Berlin; came to America, 1831. Settling in a German colony in Butler Co., Pa., Roebling soon abandoned his efforts to be a farmer and went to work for the State of Pennsylvania as an engineer on canal projects. Observing the greater utility of twisted wire cables over ropes made of hemp in hauling canal boats upon inclined planes, he designed machinery for fabrication of wire rope and in 1841 manufactured the first wire rope made in America. He moved his factory from Saxonburg, Pa., to Trenton, N.J., *ca.* 1848. Interested from youth in bridge-building, in 1844–45 he designed and built a wooden aqueduct for the Pennsylvania Canal, which was carried on two continuous wire cables; in 1846 he completed his first suspension bridge over the Monongahela River at Pittsburgh. Among his many successful bridge constructions thereafter, the most striking was his pioneer railroad suspension bridge at Niagara Falls, built 1851–55. As early as 1857, Roebling had suggested to the New York City authorities the possibility of a bridge over the East River between Manhattan and Brooklyn which would not interfere with navigation. Appointed chief engineer of the project ten years later, he perfected plans which were approved early in 1869. While making observations at the site of the proposed bridge in June 1869, he received the injury from which he died.

ROEBLING, WASHINGTON AUGUSTUS (*b. Saxonburg, Pa., 1837; d. Trenton, N.J., 1926*), civil engineer, industrialist. Son of John A. Roebling. Graduated Rensselaer Polytechnic Institute; served as assistant to his father until 1861. An officer of engineers in the Union Army, 1861–65, he received several commendations for gallant, efficient service, leaving the army as brevet colonel of volunteers. Returning to his post as assistant to his father, he succeeded the elder Roebling as chief engineer of the Brooklyn Bridge project in 1869 and saw it through to its successful conclusion, 1883. Seriously ill *post* 1872, Roebling had directed a great part of the work from his home, at the same time maintaining an active part in the family business at Trenton, John A. Roebling's Sons Co., of which he became president, 1876. He virtually retired from active professional work *ca.* 1888.

ROEDING, GEORGE CHRISTIAN (*b. San Francisco, Calif., 1868; d. 1928*), horticulturist, nurseryman. Established the Smyrna fig culture in California by demonstrating necessity of pollination by the Blastophaga wasp.

ROEMER, KARL FERDINAND (*b. Hildesheim, Germany, 1818; d. Breslau, Germany, 1891*), German geologist. Visited America, 1845, to study condition of German colonists in Texas and to report upon natural resources in the country. Three of his works resulted from this journey: *Texas Mit besondere Rücksicht . . .* (Bonn, 1849), *Die Kreidbildungen von Texas . . .* (Bonn, 1852), and a work on the fossils of western Tennessee published in 1860.

ROETHKE, THEODORE HUEBNER (*b. Saginaw, Mich., 1908; d. Bainbridge Island, Wash., 1963*), poet and teacher. Attended Harvard and University of Michigan (M.A., 1936). Known for his writing and public reading of poetry and brilliant teaching, his first significant publications were in *Commonweal* (1931), *New Republic*, and *Sewanee Review* (1932). Began to build his reputation as a teacher at Lafayette College (1931), while making headway as a poet, publishing in *Saturday Review of Literature*, *Nation*, and *Atlantic Monthly*. Taught (1935) at Michigan State College, where he suffered the first attack of a manic-depressive disorder that afflicted him periodically, and at Pennsylvania State College (1936–43). His work appeared in thirty American publications, including the *New Yorker*, *Harpers*, *Yale Review*, and the *American Scholar*. The poems in his first volume, *Open House* (1941), were exercises in traditional styles, forms, and rhymes. He reached a new peak in teaching at Bennington (1943–45), but also suffered his second major manic episode. Taught at the University of Washington (from 1947 until his death); given the title of poet in residence (1962). His major work was *The Lost Sea and Other Poems* (1949), in which traditional forms yielded to a rich experimentation in rhythms, line lengths, and groupings, and introduced the long poem, or "sequence," ranging between 50 and 175 lines, a continuing feature of his work. The new style continued with elaborations and variations in *Praise to the End!* (1951) and *The Waking* (1953), which won a Pulitzer Prize. He also received the Bollingen Prize (1958), the National Book Award (1959), and many other prizes.

ROGERS, CLARA KATHLEEN BARNETT (*b. Cheltenham, England, 1844; d. Boston, Mass., 1931*), opera and concert soprano. Made American debut in New York, 1871; settled in Boston. Professor of singing at New England Conservatory of Music *post* 1902.

ROGERS, EDITH NOURSE (*b. Saco, Mass., 1881; d. Boston, Mass., 1960*), politician. From experience she had in France during World War I, Rogers became interested in disabled veterans, becoming the personal representative of presidents Harding, Coolidge, and Hoover for veterans' affairs. She was elected as a Republican to Congress in 1925, filling her husband's seat; she served until her death. In the House, she was active in veterans' rights, being a prime supporter of the G.I. Bill of Rights. In 1942, she introduced legislation establishing the Women's Army Corps.

ROGERS, EDWARD STANIFORD (*b. Salem, Mass., 1826; d. 1899*), horticulturist, developer of the Rogers hybrid grape.

ROGERS, HARRIET BURBANK (*b. N. Billerica, Mass., 1834; d. 1919*), teacher of the deaf, pioneer in use of the oral method. Principal, Clarke School for the Deaf, 1867–86.

ROGERS, HENRY DARWIN (*b. Philadelphia, Pa., 1808; d. Glasgow, Scotland, 1866*), geologist, educator. Brother of James B., Robert E., and William B. Rogers. An early associate of Robert D. Owen, Rogers taught at the University of Pennsylvania, worked on surveys of New Jersey and Pennsylvania *ca.* 1835–*ca.* 1847, and was professor of natural history in the University of Glasgow *post* 1855. His report on the Pennsylvania survey (published, 1858) was a most important document, in particular for findings regarding the structures of the Appalachian Mountains.

ROGERS, HENRY HUTTLESTON (*b. Mattapoisett, Mass., 1840; d. New York, N.Y., 1909*), capitalist. Partner of Charles Pratt in oil refining, Rogers devised the machinery by which naphtha was first successfully separated from crude oil (patented, 1871). An executive of the Standard Oil Co. *post* 1874, he devoted much of his time to the Wall Street operations of that trust in association with William Rockefeller. Active in public utilities promotion and in such controversial deals as Amalgamated Copper (1899), he worked with E. H. Harriman in the latter's extensive railroad operations, and also in the insurance operations which led to the Mutual Life investigation, 1905. He was a friend and financial counselor of Mark Twain.

ROGERS, HENRY J. (*b. Baltimore, Md., 1811; d. Baltimore, 1879*), inventor, telegraph pioneer. An early associate of Samuel F. B. Morse.

ROGERS, HENRY WADE (*b. Holland Patent, N.Y., 1853; d. Pennington, N.J., 1926*), educator, jurist. Graduated University of Michigan, 1874. Professor of law, University of Michigan *post* 1882; dean of the law school, 1886–90. President of Northwestern University, 1890–1900. Professor, Yale Law School, 1901–21; dean, 1903–16. Judge, U.S. circuit court of appeals, sitting in New York City, 1913–26. Did outstanding work in raising standards at Yale Law School.

ROGERS, ISAIAH (*b. Marshfield, Mass., 1800; d. probably Cincinnati, Ohio, 1869*), architect. After apprenticeship to a carpenter, Rogers worked in the office of Solomon Willard and started his own practice *ca.* 1826. Called the father of the modern hotel, he planned the Tremont in Boston (1828–29) and Astor House in New York (1834–36); also Clinton Hall (1847) and the New York Merchants' Exchange (1836–42). He designed other important buildings throughout the country with great taste and success; these included the second St. Charles Hotel, New Orleans, La. (*ca.* 1851), and the Burnet House, Cincinnati, Ohio (1850). *Post* 1862, he was supervising architect of the U.S. Treasury Department.

ROGERS, JAMES BLYTHE (*b. Philadelphia, Pa., 1802; d. Philadelphia, 1852*), chemist, educator. Brother of Henry D., Robert E., and William B. Rogers. M.D., University of Maryland, 1822. Taught chemistry in many institutions and was associated with his brothers in their survey and other work; professor of chemistry, University of Pennsylvania, 1847–52.

ROGERS, JAMES GAMBLE (*b. Bryants Station, near Louisville, Ky., 1867; d. New York, N.Y., 1947*), architect. B.A., Yale, 1889. Began career in office of William Le B. Jenney, Chicago, Ill.; studied at École des Beaux Arts, Paris, 1893–99, and was awarded diploma *par excellence*. Practiced in Chicago and New York; founded his own firm in New York, 1908, and in the following quarter-century established himself as the leading U.S. designer of college and university buildings. A master of the modern collegiate Gothic style, he designed the principal buildings erected at Yale and at Northwestern universities between 1920 and 1932, as well as Columbia University's Butler Library and extensive parts of the campuses of Southern Baptist College, Colgate-Rochester Divinity School, and Sophie Newcomb College.

ROGERS, JAMES HARRIS (*b. Franklin, Tenn., 1856; d. Hyattsville, Md., 1929*), inventor. Among the many devices on which he held patents, probably the most valuable was his system of printing telegraphy (1887–94).

ROGERS, JAMES HARVEY (*b. Society Hill, S.C., 1886; d. Rio de Janeiro, Brazil, 1939*), economist. Studied at universities of South Carolina, Chicago, and Geneva (under Vilfredo Pareto), and at Yale (Ph.D., 1916). Taught at University of Missouri, at Cornell, and at Yale, 1931–39. Rogers combined a keen capacity for abstract mathematical analysis with concern for concrete social problems. One of President Franklin D. Roosevelt's early advisers, he undertook in 1933 with George F. Warren a revision of U.S. government fiscal policies. Among other recommendations, he urged that abandonment of the gold standard and devaluation of currency be accompanied by large-scale public works and expanded foreign lending and trade in cooperation with other governments. He was author of *Stock Speculation and the Money Market* (1927), *The Process of Inflation in France, 1914–1927* (1929), *America Weighs Her Gold* (1931), and *Capitalism in Crisis* (1938).

ROGERS, JOHN (*b. Milford, Conn., 1648; d. New London, Conn., 1721*), founder of the Rogerene sect.

ROGERS, JOHN (*b. Salem, Mass., 1829; d. New Canaan, Conn., 1904*), sculptor, creator of the "Rogers groups." While employed as a machinist, he spent leisure hours moulding in clay; he studied ways of reproducing clay groups in plaster form during a short stay in Rome, 1858–59. Conceiving the idea of producing statuary which told a story of immediate popular interest, he made a sensation in New York with his "Slave Auction," 1859. The sale of copies of his original models continued brisk until the 1890's by which time critics began to patronize his sincere and almost photographic renderings. His Civil War groups have historical importance and contain some of Rogers's best portraits, for example, the Abraham Lincoln in the "Council of War." His genre groups, most popular of his works, are often exquisite and catch something of the movement and mass of monumental sculpture.

ROGERS, JOHN ALMANZA ROWLEY (*b. Cromwell, Conn., 1828; d. Woodstock, Ill., 1906*), Congregational clergyman, antislavery advocate, one of the original founders of Berea (Ky.) College.

ROGERS, JOHN IGNATIUS (*b. Philadelphia, Pa., 1843; d. Denver, Colo., 1910*), Pennsylvania corporation and real-estate lawyer, professional baseball executive.

ROGERS, JOHN RANKIN (*b. Brunswick, Maine, 1838; d. Olympia, Wash., 1901*), druggist, farmer, Populist, writer, Washington legislator. Settled in the State of Washington, 1890. Liberal coalition governor of Washington, 1897–1901; author of the "Barefoot Schoolboy Law."

ROGERS, JOHN RAPHAEL (*b. Roseville, Ill., 1856; d. Brooklyn, N.Y., 1934*), inventor. Son of John A. R. Rogers. Patented a machine for making stereotype matrices (1888) and devised a double-wedge space band. After legal difficulties with Ottmar Mergenthaler, Rogers merged his own company with the Mergenthaler Linotype Co., 1895, and served the combined companies as engineer and chief of the experimental department thereafter. He patented more than 400 devices in the field of composing machines for printing.

ROGERS, MARY JOSEPHINE (*b. Roxbury, Mass., 1882; d. New York, N.Y., 1955*), religious worker. Studied at Smith College and Boston Normal School. In 1912, she joined the Catholic Foreign Mission Society of America, later known as Maryknoll, near Ossining, N.Y. Rogers became Mother Mary Joseph and was elected mother general from 1925 until her retirement in 1947. The Maryknoll Sisters opened their first mission in Los Angeles in 1920, an orphanage and school for

Japanese-American children. By the time of her death in 1955, there were 1,160 Maryknoll Sisters serving eighty-four missions in seventeen countries in Latin America, the Orient, Africa, the Pacific Islands, and the U.S.

ROGERS, MOSES (*b. New London, Conn., ca. 1779; d. Georgetown, S.C., 1821*), early steamboat captain. Commanded the *Phoenix*, 1809, in earliest ocean voyage of a steam vessel; fitted out the *Savannah*, 1818, and commanded her on her voyage to Liverpool, 1819.

ROGERS, RANDOLPH (*b. Waterloo, N.Y., 1825; d. Rome, Italy, 1892*), sculptor. Studied in Florence, Italy, 1848–51; resided principally in Rome, Italy, *post* 1855. A neo-classic whose modeling approaches realism, Rogers worked with great success and was an honored figure in his adopted Italian home. He is known principally for his "Columbus doors" of the U.S. Capitol at Washington, D.C., and for his heroic figure of "Michigan" on the top of the Detroit monument.

ROGERS, ROBERT (*b. Methuen, Mass., 1731 o.s.; d. London, England, 1795*), soldier. Reared on a farm near Rumford, present Concord, N.H. Raised recruits for Shirley's expedition to Nova Scotia, 1755; entered the New Hampshire regiment and became a captain on the Crown Point expedition. Noticed for his boldness and skill in scouting, he was appointed captain of an independent company of rangers, March 1756; he was promoted to be major of nine such companies, 1758. Famous in England and the colonies alike for rash courage, hardiness, and prankishness, he was constantly in the field; he was at Crown Point, 1759, when he destroyed the Saint Francis Indians in a daring raid, and in the final campaign about Montreal. Late in 1760, he went west as far as Detroit and Shawneetown to receive the surrender of all French posts. Unable to adjust to peace and civilization and quite lacking in principle in his dealings, he was a consistent failure in his employments, 1760–75. Returning to America from England, 1775, he courted both the Americans and the British and was imprisoned as a spy by Washington in 1776. Escaping to the British, he raised the Queen's American rangers but was soon deprived of his command. Employed thereafter in recruiting, his dishonesty and dissipation rendered him next to useless and in 1780 he returned to England. During a brief period as commander at Michilimackinac, 1766–67, he commissioned Jonathan Carver to undertake an exploratory journey into the present Minnesota. He was author of *A Concise Account of North America* and *Journals* (both London, 1765) and a crude tragedy *Ponteach* (1766), one of the first dramas written by a native New Englander.

ROGERS, ROBERT EMPIE (*b. Baltimore, Md., 1813; d. 1884*), chemist, educator. Brother of James B., Henry D., and William B. Rogers. M.D., University of Pennsylvania, 1836. Active with his brothers in research work. Professor of chemistry, University of Virginia, 1842–52; at medical school, University of Pennsylvania, 1852–77; at Jefferson Medical College, *post* 1877. He was also employed as a metals expert by the U.S. Mint.

ROGERS, ROBERT WILLIAM (*b. Philadelphia, Pa., 1864; d. near Chadds Ford, Pa., 1930*), Orientalist. A.B., University of Pennsylvania, 1886; A.B., Johns Hopkins, 1887; Ph.D., Haverford, 1890; Ph.D., Leipzig, 1895. Taught at Drew Theological Seminary and at Princeton. A student of Assyriology, Hebrew, and the Old Testament, Rogers made contributions to knowledge in all three fields. He was author, among other books, of *A History of Babylonia and Assyria* (1900, rewritten and reissued, 1915).

ROGERS, STEPHEN (*b. Tyre, N.Y., 1826; d. Valparaiso, Chile, 1878*), surgeon. Largely self-educated; M.D., New York Medical College, 1856. Practiced in Panama, 1849–55, and in Santiago, Chile, 1856–65, as surgeon to railroad companies.

Returned to Chile, 1875, after successful practice in New York City.

ROGERS, THOMAS (*b. Groton, Conn., 1792; d. New York, N.Y., 1856*), inventor, locomotive builder. Built the "Sandusky," first locomotive to operate west of the Allegheny Mountains, at Paterson, N.J., 1837, improving on English models. In 1842 he produced the "Stockbridge" with cylinders outside of the frame; in 1844 he designed and built the locomotive type which was subsequently adopted generally throughout the United States. This had two pairs of coupled driving wheels and was the first example of the use of equalizing beams between the drivers and the front swiveling truck. He also introduced the shifting link valve motion and was the first (1850) to apply the wagon top boiler.

ROGERS, WILL (*b. near Oologah, Indian Territory, present town of Claremore, Okla., 1879; d. near Point Barrow, Alaska, 1935*), humorist, actor, news commentator. Of Cherokee extraction on both his paternal and maternal side, he enjoyed a comfortable frontier youth on his father's ranch and became an expert roper of calves. After brief attendance at Kemper Military School 1897–98, he worked as a cowboy in Texas, traveled to the Argentine and to South Africa, worked as rope artist and rough rider with a Wild West show in Australia, and returned home in 1904. He made his New York debut at Madison Square Garden, April 1905, with Colonel Zach Maulhall's show; in the same year he discovered by chance that informal joking with the audience, often at the expense of his own skill with a lariat, improved his act. Projecting an essentially American image of a man playing his "natchell self," he rose to star rank in *Hands Up* (1915) and was a star of the *Ziegfeld Follies* in 1916–18, 1922, and 1924–25. Bringing news highlights into unexpected focus as part of his patter, he deflated rhetorical bunk and group smugness. A contributor of syndicated articles to newspapers *post* 1922, he began in 1926 a syndication of a single daily paragraph which dealt mainly with politics; ultraconservative at heart, he joked at whatever program, fad, or party was uppermost. He reached the height of his acting fame in a series of talking pictures, 1929–35, in which he played himself, whether the costume was top-hat, overalls, or medieval armor. A cowboy philosopher with a cool brain and a warm heart, he was held in popular affection as much for his personal qualities of decency and generosity as for his abilities as a performer. He was killed while attempting a flight north to the Orient with his fellow-Oklahoman, Wiley Post.

ROGERS, WILLIAM ALLEN (*b. Springfield, Ohio, 1854; d. Washington, D.C., 1931*), cartoonist, illustrator of stories by James Otis, Kirk Munroe, and other authors of children's books.

ROGERS, WILLIAM AUGUSTUS (*b. Waterford, Conn., 1832; d. 1898*), mathematician, astronomer, physicist. Graduated Brown, 1857. A teacher at Alfred and Harvard universities and at Colby College, Rogers made important researches on the value of the yard and the meter and changes therein. He was closely associated with Albert A. Michelson and Edward W. Morley in application of optical methods to determination of minute changes in length.

ROGERS, WILLIAM BARTON (*b. Philadelphia, Pa., 1804; d. Cambridge, Mass., 1882*), geologist, educator. Brother of Henry D., James B., and Robert E. Rogers. Educated at College of William and Mary, he served there as professor of natural history and chemistry, 1828–35; he was professor of natural philosophy, University of Virginia, 1835–53. State geologist of Virginia, 1835–42, he worked jointly with his brother Henry on theory of structure of the Appalachians. An early advocate of the founding of Massachusetts Institute of Technology, he was elected its first president, serving 1862–70 and 1878–81.

ROGERS, WILLIAM CROWNINSHIELD (*b. Salem, Mass., 1823; d. London, England, 1888*), sea captain. Grandson of Jacob Crowninshield. Master of the clipper *Witchcraft* on her record run from Rio to San Francisco, 1851; served in Union Navy during Civil War; occupied himself thereafter with finance.

ROHDE, RUTH BRYAN OWEN (*b. Jacksonville, Ill., 1885; d. Copenhagen, Denmark, 1954*), congresswoman, diplomat. The daughter of William Jennings Bryan, she studied at the Monticello Seminary and the University of Nebraska. Secretary-treasurer of the American Woman's Relief Fund in London, 1914–15. Became the first congresswoman from the Deep South, representing Florida's Fourth District as a Democrat, 1929–33. Nominated envoy extraordinary and minister plenipotentiary to Denmark and Iceland, 1933, she was the first woman to hold a post in the U.S. Foreign Service. Published *Look Forward, Warrior*, 1943, a plan for a United Nations of the World. Alternate to the American delegation to the U.N., 1949, and served as chairman of the executive committee of the Speakers Research Committee.

ROHÉ, GEORGE HENRY (*b. Baltimore, Md., 1851; d. New Orleans, La., 1899*), medical educator, psychiatrist. M.D., University of Maryland, 1873; studied also under Edward Wigglesworth. Taught and practiced in Baltimore principally; was active in modernizing treatment of the insane.

ROHEIM, GEZA (*b. Budapest, Hungary, 1891; d. New York, N.Y., 1953*), anthropologist and psychoanalyst. Studied at the University of Budapest (Ph.D., 1914). Taught at the University of Budapest from 1919; member of the Budapest Institute of Psychoanalysis. Immigrated to the U.S. in 1938. Roheim survives less as the author of specific works than as a controversial pioneer in the convergence of psychoanalysis and anthropology. In 1925, his study, *Australian Totemism*, based on the primal horde theory won the Freud Prize as the best work of applied psychoanalysis. Books include *The Origin and Function of Culture* (1943) and *The Eternal Ones of the Dream* (1945).

ROHLFS, ANNA KATHARINE GREEN (*b. Brooklyn, N.Y., 1846; d. 1935*), author. Graduated Green Mountain Junior College, 1866. Author of *The Leavenworth Case* (1878), pioneer work in modern detective fiction, and some thirty other mystery novels distinguished for technical skill.

ROLETTE, JEAN JOSEPH (*b. Canada, 1781; d. 1842*), fur trader. Worked out of Prairie du Chien along the Upper Mississippi and the Wisconsin, *post* 1806; was American Fur Co. agent *post* 1820. Served as chief justice of Crawford County, Wis., *post* 1830.

ROLFE, JOHN (*b. Heacham, Norfolk, England, 1585; d. probably Bermuda Hundred, Va., 1622*), colonist, Virginia official. Sailed in the *Sea Adventure*, 1609; settled in Virginia after stranding in Bermuda for some months; successfully adapted native tobacco to European taste. His marriage to Pocahontas in April 1614 brought an eight-year peace with the Indians in the neighborhood of Jamestown.

ROLFE, ROBERT ABIAL ("RED") (*b. Penacook, N.H., 1908; d. Gilford, N.H., 1969*), baseball player, manager, and coach. Graduated Dartmouth (B.A., 1931) and signed with the New York Yankees, playing in their minor leagues until 1934, when he established himself as one of the top third basemen in baseball. His best year was 1939, when he batted .329 and led the American League in runs scored (139), base hits (213), and doubles (46). Scored more than 100 runs in seven consecutive seasons. Selected for the American League all-star team (1937, 1939); retired after the 1942 season. After coaching at Yale (1943–46), he became supervisor of scouting for the Detroit

Tigers (1949), then field manager; he was voted manager of the year in 1950, but was fired in 1952. He returned to Dartmouth as athletic director, 1954–67.

ROLFE, WILLIAM JAMES (*b. Newburyport, Mass., 1827; d. Martha's Vineyard, Mass., 1910*), teacher, philologist, textbook author and editor. Introduced regular instruction in English literature into Massachusetts high-school curricula.

ROLLINS, ALICE MARLAND WELLINGTON (*b. Boston, Mass., 1847; d. Bronxville, N.Y., 1897*), author, book reviewer.

ROLLINS, EDWARD HENRY (*b. Rollinsford, N.H., 1824; d. Isles of Shoals, N.H., 1889*), Whig, Know-Nothing, and Republican politician. Elected to the lower house of the New Hampshire legislature, 1855, he became speaker in 1856; he took a vital part in the formation and subsequent success of the Republican party in his state. A congressman, 1861–67, he opposed reform in any guise and supported harsh measures of Reconstruction; thereafter he continued to operate the state Republican machine as its chairman, 1868–72. Treasurer of the Union Pacific Railroad, 1871–76 (with which he had been associated *post* 1869), he was U.S. senator from New Hampshire, 1877–83.

ROLLINS, FRANK WEST (*b. Concord, N.H., 1860; d. Boston, Mass., 1915*), banker. Son of Edward H. Rollins. Republican governor of New Hampshire, 1899–1901. Initiated "Old Home Week," 1898; promoted conservation.

ROLLINS, JAMES SIDNEY (*b. Richmond, Ky., 1812; d. 1888*), lawyer, Missouri legislator. Originally a Whig, Rollins served in Congress, from Missouri, as a Conservative-Unionist, 1861–65. Thereafter, as a member of the Missouri legislature, he assisted in the reorganization of the University of Missouri and opposed radical Republican policies. With Carl Schurz and Benjamin G. Brown, he was a leader in the Liberal Republican movement.

ROLLINSON, WILLIAM (*b. Dudley, England, 1762; d. 1842*), engraver. Came to America, 1789. Working thereafter in New York City in both line and stipple, he became eventually a bank-note engraver and made several improvements in the technique of bank-note manufacture.

ROLPH, JAMES (*b. San Francisco, Calif., 1869; d. Santa Clara Co., Calif., 1934*), businessman, public official. Successful in shipping and banking, Rolph served as nonpartisan mayor of San Francisco for 19 consecutive years *post* 1911 and dedicated himself to the expansion and physical improvement of the city. Elected governor of California as a Republican, 1930, he was ineffectual in dealing with the problems raised by the depression.

ROLSHOVEN, JULIUS (*b. Detroit, Mich., 1858; d. New York, N.Y., 1930*), painter. Studied at Cooper Union, New York City, and in Düsseldorf and Munich, Germany. Influenced by Frank Duveneck.

RÖLVAAG, OLE EDVART (*b. Island of Dönna, Helgeland, Norway, 1876; d. Northfield, Minn., 1931*), author, educator. Came to America, 1896. Graduated St. Olaf College, 1905; studied also at University of Oslo, Norway. Professor of Norwegian at St. Olaf College, *ca.* 1907–26, 1927–31. Among his many books, marked by creative realism and brooding imagination, *Giants in the Earth* (translated and published in America, 1927) achieved an outstanding artistic and popular success. It has been called the most powerful novel ever written about pioneer life in America.

ROMAN, ANDRÉ BIENVENU (*b. St. Landry Parish, La., 1795; d. probably New Orleans, La., 1866*), planter, Louisiana legislator. Outstanding Whig governor of Louisiana, 1831–35 and 1839–43; fostered efforts at flood control, public schools, internal improvements.

ROMANS, BERNARD (*b. Netherlands, ca. 1720; d. probably at sea, ca. 1784*), civil engineer, naturalist, cartographer, soldier. Came to America *ca. 1757*; appointed deputy surveyor of Georgia, 1766; ran surveys in East and West Florida, engaging also in botanical study. Variously active after journeying north in 1773, he was employed by the N.Y. committee of safety, 1775, to construct fortifications on the Hudson River. Resenting interference with his work, he resigned. Commissioned captain of Pennsylvania artillery, February 1776, he served under General Horatio Gates in part of the northern campaign. Ordered to South Carolina *ca. July 1780*, he was captured at sea and imprisoned in Jamaica until the end of the Revolutionary War. Among his books the most noted is *A Concise Natural History of East and West Florida* (Vol. I, New York, 1775, second edition, 1776; the second volume was never published). Maps made by him appear in a number of publications of the time.

ROMAYNE, NICHOLAS (*b. New York, N.Y., 1756; d. New York, 1817*), physician, medical educator. M.D., Edinburgh, 1780. Practiced and taught in New York; associated his private school with Queen's College, present Rutgers, 1792–93. After a somewhat checkered career *post 1794*, he returned to New York, 1806, and served as president and professor at the College of Physicians and Surgeons (later affiliated again with Queen's College) until 1816.

ROMBAUER, IRMA LOUISE (*b. St. Louis, Mo., 1877; d. St. Louis, 1962*), cookbook author. As a wife, mother, and hostess, she taught herself to cook by trial and error, using recipes and techniques from relatives, friends, and chefs, and culled from newspapers and books; she took copious notes on her successes and failures, recording precise weights and measurements, oven temperatures, and cooking times in a manner similar to that of a scientist. In 1922 she distributed copies of recipes to a cooking class, and in 1931 elaborated on the handout in the self-published book *The Joy of Cooking*. An enlarged edition was published by Bobbs-Merrill in 1936; rewritten in 1943, the book was a hefty tome that quickly became the best-selling cookbook in publishing history. The fourth edition, *The New Joy of Cooking*, appeared in 1951, with Rombauer's daughter cited as coauthor.

ROMBERG, SIGMUND (*b. Nagykanizsa, Hungary, 1887; d. New York, N.Y., 1951*), composer. Studied engineering briefly in Vienna. Immigrated to the U.S. in 1909. Composer of numerous operettas in the turn-of-the-century style of Vienna, including *Blossom Time* (1921), *The Student Prince* (1924), *The Desert Song* (1926), and *The New Moon* (1928). Discovered by the Shubert brothers, Romberg enjoyed enormous success on Broadway in the 1920's; his works include some of the best-known popular songs of the twentieth century.

ROMBRO, JACOB (*b. probably Zuphran, Russia, 1858; d. New York, N.Y., 1922*), editor, socialist leader, Yiddish author. Best known under pen name "Philip Krantz." Active here *post 1890*.

ROMEIKE, HENRY (*b. Riga, Russia, 1855; d. 1903*), originator of the press-clipping service. Resident in the United States *post ca. 1885*.

ROMMEL, EDWIN AMERICUS ("EDDIE") (*b. Baltimore, Md., 1897; d. Baltimore, 1970*), baseball pitcher and umpire. He began his nearly fifty years in professional baseball as a batboy for the Baltimore Orioles. His playing career started in the Peninsula and International leagues (1916–19), and in 1920 he signed with the Philadelphia Athletics. Known for his knuckle ball, he was with the Athletics when they won the 1929 and 1930 World Series

and the American League pennant in 1931. Released as a player in 1932, but remained until 1935 as a coach and batting-practice pitcher. He turned to umpiring and worked the 1943 and 1947 World Series and five all-star games. He retired from baseball in 1959.

RONDTHALER, EDWARD (*b. near Nazareth, Pa., 1842; d. 1931*), bishop of the Moravian Church. Held pastorates in Brooklyn, N.Y., Philadelphia, Pa., and Salem, N.C.; consecrated bishop, 1891. As Salem developed into Winston-Salem, largest industrial city in the state, Rondthaler played a leading part in its community life.

ROOD, OGDEN NICHOLAS (*b. Danbury, Conn., 1831; d. New York, N.Y., 1902*), physicist, specialist in physiological optics. Grandson of Uzal Ogden. Graduated College of New Jersey (Princeton), 1852; did post-graduate work at Sheffield Scientific School and at Berlin and Munich. Professor of physics, Columbia *post 1864*, he was a master at devising and improving physical apparatus and instruments. He was author of an influential book on the physics of color sensations, *Modern Chromatics* (1879); among other devices, he developed the flicker photometer.

ROONEY, PAT (*b. New York, N.Y., 1880; d. New York, 1962*), dancer, actor, and songwriter. With his wife, Marion Bent, they formed a memorable vaudeville and musical comedy dance team; in 1919 he introduced a waltz clog to the tune of "The Daughter of Rosie O'Grady" that identified him throughout his career. Teamed with Herman Timberg when Bent retired (1932), forming one of the popular Jewish-Irish pairs of vaudeville. Wrote several popular songs, including "You Be My Ootsie, I'll Be Your Tootsie," and appeared in the stage production of *Guys and Dolls* (1950).

ROOSA, DANIEL BENNETT ST. JOHN (*b. Bethel, N.Y., 1838; d. 1908*), physician. M.D., University of the City of New York (present New York University), 1860. Professor at his *alma mater* and also at the University of Vermont, he was responsible for the founding (1883) of the New York Post-Graduate Medical School and was its president, 1883–1908.

ROOSEVELT, (ANNA) ELEANOR (*b. New York, N.Y., 1884; d. New York, 1962*), humanitarian, United Nations diplomat, and social reformer. Niece of Theodore Roosevelt and wife of Franklin D. Roosevelt, whom she married in 1905. It was not until America's entry into World War I and her assumption of duties with the Red Cross that her organizational abilities found a public focus. She began to cultivate women associated with the trade unions, politics, and the successful suffrage movement. With the vote, women became more important in politics, and she was at her husband's side during his race for the vice-presidency in 1920. During the campaign she began to appreciate the qualities of Louis Howe, her husband's secretary, with whom she formed a deep and abiding friendship. She became her husband's proxy and surrogate in Democratic party politics after his polio attack in 1921 left his lower limbs useless. She began to define her identity as a publicist, politician, and organizer, and headed the women's division of the Democratic party when Franklin ran for governor of New York (1928). After Franklin became president (1932), her views and actions as first lady became as much a feature of New Deal Washington as her husband's. She took under her wing such New Deal projects as subsistence homesteads, the National Youth Administration, and services that involved women. She was adept on the radio and began to write the daily column "My Day" for United Features Syndicate (1935). Supported Franklin's efforts to rearm the nation at the time of the fall of France, and was cochairman of the Office of Civilian Defense (1941–42), which became the whipping boy of Congress and the press. During the war she toured Britain and the South Pacific, visiting field hospitals and front-line installations. Following Franklin's death in 1945, her public career entered a new phase. In December 1945 President Harry Truman appointed her one of five delegates to the first UN General Assembly in London and to the UN Human Rights Commission, whose first job was to draft an international bill of rights. As a UN delegate she vigorously advocated the establishment of a Jewish state; she resigned in 1952 and went to work for the American Association for the UN and was an unofficial ambassador at large, visiting the Middle East, Asia, and Europe. President John Kennedy named her to the U.S. delegation to the UN (1961); also giving up her forty-year opposition to the Equal Rights Amendment, she presided over the Commission on the Status of Women appointed by Kennedy. She wrote *This Is My Story* (1937), *Ladies of Courage* (1954), and *Tomorrow Is Now* (1963). She remained a political power within the Democratic party until her death.

ROOSEVELT, FRANKLIN DELANO (*b. Hyde Park, N.Y., 1882; d. Warm Springs, Ga., 1945*), thirty-second president of the United States. Roosevelt was the only son of James Roosevelt, the vice president of the Delaware and Hudson Railroad, and Sara Delano Roosevelt, a handsome strong-minded woman. In 1896, at fourteen, Franklin was plunged into the Spartan rigors of Groton School, Groton, Mass. He continued at Harvard, where he was president (editor) of the *Harvard Crimson*. He next entered the Columbia Law School. His work was fairly good, but after passing his bar examinations in the spring of the third year, he did not bother to finish his courses and take his LL.B. degree. In his final year at Harvard, Roosevelt had become engaged to Anna Eleanor Roosevelt, a distant cousin and the niece of Theodore Roosevelt. On Mar. 17, 1905, President Theodore Roosevelt came to New York City to give away his niece at her wedding. Franklin had long admired Theodore Roosevelt, and it was to a considerable extent the example of Theodore Roosevelt that impelled him toward politics and public service.

Roosevelt's entrance into politics came in 1910 when Democratic leaders in heavily Republican Dutchess County, where Hyde Park is located, invited him to run for the state senate. Despite the odds against him, he won the election. In the New York senate Roosevelt assumed leadership of Democratic insurgents blocking the election in the legislature of the Tammany Hall candidate for U.S. Senator, William F. Sheehan. Roosevelt, firmly established as a progressive on the basis of his opposition to Tammany, went on to champion the interests of the upstate farmers, conservationists, and advocates of good government. When he ran for reelection in 1912, typhoid fever kept him from campaigning. At this point, a newspaperman from Saratoga, Louis McHenry Howe worked for him so effectively that Roosevelt not only won but ran ahead of the Democratic candidates for president and governor.

Early in 1912 Roosevelt projected himself into presidential politics as a spokesman for New York progressive anti–Tammany Democrats who favored Woodrow Wilson, and he continued his strong advocacy both before and after the Democratic convention. His reward was an appointment, in March 1913, as assistant secretary of the navy. He was soon established in Washington as one of a handful of promising young progressive Democrats. In 1914, when Roosevelt campaigned for the nomination for U.S. Senator in the New York Democratic primary, Tammany easily defeated him. He learned his lesson. Thereafter, he and the Tammany leaders kept an uneasy peace. He managed to survive as assistant secretary and did much to help prepare the navy for war. During World War I he achieved a reputation as one of the most capable young administrators in the capital. He visited Europe in the winter of 1918–19 to supervise the disposal of navy property. In Paris he was able to observe the peace conference and he

returned on the *George Washington* with President Wilson, who transformed him into an ardent public supporter of the League of Nations.

Late in 1918 the Roosevelts underwent a serious family crisis. Eleanor Roosevelt discovered that her husband was romantically involved with her social secretary, Lucy Mercer. She offered him a divorce; he refused and, according to one account, told her not to be foolish. Although the Roosevelts remained married, their relationship was altered. Mrs Roosevelt, deeply and permanently hurt, developed a public and personal life of her own. In 1920 Roosevelt received the Democratic nomination for vice president as the running mate of Governor James M. Cox of Ohio. After a Republican landslide, Roosevelt became a vice president in New York City for a surety bonding concern, the Fidelity and Deposit Company of Maryland. He also entered into a law partnership in which he was not very active; in 1924 he left it to form a new partnership with Basil O'Connor. Suddenly, in August 1921, while vacationing at his summer home at Campobello Island, New Brunswick, Roosevelt fell ill with poliomyelitis. It was a severe attack which left him never again able to walk without braces and a cane. There followed grim years in which he doggedly worked at trying to regain the use of his legs and to remain a national political figure. Substantial recuperation began when he discovered the warm, buoyant mineral waters at Warm Springs, a rundown resort in Georgia which he first visited in the fall of 1924. Each year he spent part of his time at Warm Springs, gradually rebuilding muscles until in 1928 he could with difficulty walk with leg braces and two canes.

For Eleanor Roosevelt, a shy woman, Roosevelt's illness completed the transition she had already begun toward public activity. Whatever her personal feelings may have been, she remained intensely loyal to Roosevelt. When polio immobilized him, in order to keep him active in politics and thus bolster his morale, she began to act as his substitute at meetings. With the aid of Mrs. Roosevelt and Howe, Roosevelt succeeded in continuing without a break as a significant Democratic figure in both state and national politics. In New York he tied himself to the popular Alfred E. Smith, who had risen from the ranks of Tammany to become an outstanding governor. When Smith became a contender for the Democratic presidential nomination of 1924, he asked Roosevelt to manage his campaign. Smith regarded Roosevelt as attractive but ineffectual and wanted no more than his name and national contacts. Although Smith was not nominated at the 1924 convention, Roosevelt again made the speech nominating Smith at the 1928 convention; this time his candidate was chosen on the first ballot. Both before and after the nomination, Roosevelt peppered Smith with suggestions which were ignored. Roosevelt felt out of the campaign, and in September 1928 was at Warm Springs, trying to strengthen his leg muscles. Repeatedly Roosevelt had declined suggestions that he run for governor that year to strengthen Smith in New York, but during the state convention he unexpectedly gave in to Smith's pleas over the telephone. In high spirits Roosevelt undertook a four-week campaign for governor for New York. While Smith was losing New York by 100,000 votes, Roosevelt carried it by the narrow margin of 25,000 votes out of four-and-a-quarter million. Even before he took office, he was being discussed as a likely Democratic nominee for president in 1932.

Roosevelt undertook to become an outstanding governor in his own right. Cautiously he moved out from the shadow of Al Smith. In his first two-year term as governor he established himself as a moderate progressive, an effective administrator, and an extraordinarily able political leader. The Great Depression, which had steadily become more and more disastrous in the years after the stock market crash of 1929, had transformed both state and national politics. In response to it, Roosevelt gradually changed from a cautious progressive whose policies were scarcely distinguishable from those of President Herbert Hoover into a daring innovator, the prime challenger of the President. As governor, Roosevelt mobilized the resources of his state to provide at least minimum security for those in distress. Several of his proposals and agencies foreshadowed the New Deal. In August 1931 he obtained legislation establishing a Temporary Emergency Relief Administration, which under Harry Hopkins provided aid to 10 percent of the state's families. In 1930 he won reelection by an unprecedented plurality of 725,000 votes. Immediately the state Democratic chairman, James A. Farley, proclaimed that Roosevelt would be the next presidential nominee of his party. At the 1932 Democratic convention, a "stop Roosevelt" movement almost succeeded, as the combination of urban Smith followers and rural supporters of John Nance Garner, together with the delegates of "favorite sons," controlled more than one-third of the votes through three ballots. At that point Garner, realizing that continued deadlock would aid the urban forces rather than bring his own nomination, released his delegates, and Roosevelt was nominated on the fourth ballot.

Roosevelt campaigned cautiously in 1932 in order not to alienate any of the numerous groups of voters disillusioned with Hoover. Early in 1932 Roosevelt had assembled a group of campaign advisers and speech writers, for the most part Columbia University professors. Newspapermen labeled this group the "brain trust." Roosevelt not only assailed Hoover for deficit spending, but proposed familiar progressive solutions for recovery and reform. In the election of 1932 Roosevelt overwhelmingly defeated Hoover. Democrats also elected such substantial majorities to each house of Congress that Roosevelt could expect ready enactment of his recovery program. Carefully he set about planning administrative appointments and recovery and reform measures. Roosevelt for the first time appointed a woman to cabinet rank, Frances Perkins, who became secretary of labor. Four months of acute depression intervened before the new president could take office; the Norris "lame duck" amendment had not yet gone into effect, and Roosevelt was not to be inaugurated until Mar. 4. It was a time of bewilderment and despair. Industrial production was far below levels of the 1920's, a quarter of the wage earners were unemployed, and a quarter of the farmers had lost their land. While he was preparing to take office, tragedy almost intervened. In Miami on the night of Feb. 15, 1933, Roosevelt barely missed being shot by a would-be-assassin.

The effect of Roosevelt's powerful, positive inaugural address on Mar. 4, 1933, was in consequence electric. Speaking solemnly and forcefully, he sought to reassure the American people. "This great Nation will endure as it has endured, will revive and prosper," he declared. "So, first of all, let me assert my firm belief that the only thing we have to fear is fear itself." With few restraints upon him, Roosevelt asserted energetic leadership, and the nation was in a mood to follow. His overall plan was basically twofold. He hoped through a series of emergency measures to bring about rapid recovery. Next, through reforms he wished to eliminate the shortcomings and evils in the American economy that might bring future depressions.

The banking crisis forced Roosevelt to act even more speedily than he had planned. He issued a proclamation on Mar. 6, 1933, closing all banks and stopping gold transactions; and on Apr. 19, 1933, he officially took the nation off the gold standard. Economy had been a major theme of Roosevelt's campaign for election, and during his first few weeks in office he further gladdened conservatives with his insistence upon cutting governmental expenses.

Between March and May of 1933 Roosevelt sent to Congress in rapid succession a number of messages and draft bills. By June 16 Congress had enacted every one of these measures. The legislation of Roosevelt's "first hundred days" emphasized recovery and relief.

In the recovery program, the key measures were the farm recovery bill Roosevelt submitted to Congress on Mar. 16, leading to the Agricultural Adjustment Administration, and the industrial recovery bill of May 17, proposing the National Recovery Administration and the Public Works Administration. As he signed the National Industrial Recovery Act in June 1933, Roosevelt called it "the most important and far-reaching legislation ever enacted by the American Congress." It created the National Recovery Administration, rather analogous to the War Industries Board of World War I. The NRA sought to bring prosperity through limiting production and through placing a floor under prices. The NRA floundered during the first two years of the New Deal, suffering from the lack of purchasing power, the unwillingness of desperate businessmen to give up competitive undercutting, and the basic unenforceability of a multiplicity of code regulations. Roosevelt's achievement was more substantial through the Agricultural Adjustment Administration, which put into effect the crop restriction program that the Farm Bureau Federation had favored. He also succeeded in bringing a modicum of quick relief to millions who were hungry and in danger of losing their homes and farms. Congress in May 1933 created the Federal Emergency Relief Administration. Roosevelt appointed Harry Hopkins, who had been New York administrator, to head it; and Hopkins quickly funneled an initial half-billion dollars into state relief administrations.

Human erosion and loss of moral values among the unemployed worried Roosevelt. At the outset of the New Deal he persuaded Congress to establish the Civilian Conservation Corps to enlist unemployed men, mostly youths, in projects for forestation and flood control. This program was popular and continued through the New Deal. The devaluation of the dollar may have helped foreign trade; major competing nations had already devalued their currencies. It achieved little within the United States, and in January 1934 Roosevelt ended currency manipulation, setting the gold content of the dollar at 59.06 percent of its earlier level.

Through his first two terms in office, Roosevelt sought to reconcile two rather contradictory aims, to alleviate suffering and stimulate the economy through large-scale spending, and to prevent the federal deficit from soaring to dangerous heights. Of the two conflicting pressures upon Roosevelt, that from the dispossessed was the greater and the more sustained. Roosevelt responded to it with continued but cautious spending. The breakdown of Roosevelt's first economic recovery program by late spring of 1935 was forcing him into major readjustments. The NRA had not worked well, so in some respects the adverse Supreme Court decision to invalidate the NRA code system (May 1935) was a mercy killing. But while conservatives rejoiced, Roosevelt fumed, declaring to reporters that the Supreme Court was taking a horse-and-buggy view of the power of the government to regulate the economy. Yet what was most viable in the NRA program continued. Just before the court's decision, Roosevelt had finally accepted Senator Robert F. Wagner's bill establishing strong federal protection for collective bargaining, and in July this became the National Labor Relations Act.

Much of the failure of the earlier recovery program resulted, Roosevelt believed, from bad business practices and from the refusal of business to cooperate with the government. Increasingly he sought to reform business, in part as a means of achieving recovery. The Securities Exchange Act of 1934 had placed the stock market under federal regulation. In March 1935 Roosevelt proposed to Congress legislation prohibiting the pyramiding of public utility holding companies, and in June he recommended restructuring federal taxes to increase substantially the levies on wealthy individuals and corporations. The outcry against the holding company and tax bills further helped convince the underprivileged that Roosevelt was their champion. Nonetheless, national politics continued to be polarized sharply for and against Roosevelt. He was the lone issue in the 1936 campaign. The Republicans nominated Governor Alfred M. Landon of Kansas, who made constructive criticisms of the New Deal; but the result was a sweeping victory for Roosevelt, who received the electoral votes of every state except Maine and Vermont.

A single conservative bulwark seemed to stand between Roosevelt and his reform objectives—the Supreme Court. The Court had invalidated his initial industrial and agricultural recovery programs and several other New Deal measures. Without warning, in February 1937, he suddenly proposed to Congress an overhauling of the federal judiciary, purportedly to help the courts keep up with their growing dockets. At the heart of Roosevelt's bill was the proposal that he be empowered to name as many as six new Supreme Court justices. Roosevelt's plan shocked Congress and alarmed a large number of those who had voted for him in 1936. The Supreme Court itself affected the political battle when, by 5-to-4 decisions, it upheld both the National Labor Relations Act and the Social Security Act. There seemed no longer to be any need for Roosevelt's proposal, and in the end it was defeated.

Under the authority of the Reorganization Act of 1939, Roosevelt established the Executive Office of the President, placing within it the Bureau of the Budget and the National Resources Planning Board, and also providing for an office for emergency management, to be set up in the event of a national crisis. He was further empowered to appoint administrative assistants. Numerous pieces of legislation aided one or another group of Americans. For workers, there was the Fair Labor Standards Act of 1938, which made a start toward establishing minimum wages. For city people there was a beginning of slum clearance and public housing, through the Public Works Administration. In 1937 the New Deal seemed to be bringing such a substantial degree of recovery that Roosevelt feared a dangerous, unhealthy boom would result. Upon the advice of Secretary of the Treasury Morgenthau, he drastically cut back government spending, furloughing large numbers of WPA workers. Defenders of the status quo were alarmed not only by the increase in the national deficit, but also by the growing labor strife, as the rival C.I.O. and A.F. of L., under the protection of the Wagner Act, sought to organize mass production industries. The sit-down strikes of 1937, which many middle-class people regarded as labor preemption of employers' property, were especially frightening. Opponents placed the blame upon Roosevelt.

In the Congressional election of 1938, for the first time since 1932, the Republicans gained a number of seats in both houses of Congress. The election seemed to be another serious political setback for Roosevelt. Contrary to his earlier policy, he had openly intervened in several Democratic primaries in opposition to conservatives. By this time, 1939, Europe was on the brink of war, and increasingly Roosevelt was turning his attention toward foreign dangers and American defense.

Foreign affairs always interested Roosevelt, and even during the domestic crisis of the first month of his administration he had given a good bit of attention to them. His initial major decision in the realm of foreign affairs was a fundamental economic one: that the United States should seek recovery through a nationalistic program rather than one involving international economic cooperation. Before the end of 1933 Roosevelt recognized the Soviet Union, primarily in the hope of stimulating foreign trade, and in 1934 he gave his backing to a reciprocal trade program. Throughout the Western Hemisphere, Roosevelt projected himself as a smiling, benign "good neighbor." He and Secretary of State Cordell Hull pledged to Latin American nations that the United States would not intervene with armed force, and they held to the new policy even in 1938 when Mexico expropriated American oil

holdings. Gradually, as military threats became more serious in both Europe and East Asia, Roosevelt began to change the Good Neighbor program into a mutual security arrangement foreshadowing the post-World War II Pan-American pacts.

Toward Japan's expansionism in East Asia, Roosevelt brought some of the views he had acquired during his years in President Wilson's Navy Department. At one of his first cabinet meetings he discussed the possibility of war with Japan, and within several months he was channeling some of the public works funds into naval construction. In 1934 he obtained passage of a measure which began the rebuilding of the U.S. fleet.

Europe was another matter. There Roosevelt proceeded cautiously, and with good reason, since he could easily arouse acute criticism in Congress and among the electorate. Mussolini seemed to Roosevelt to have been a stabilizing force in Italy, and for several years the President looked upon him with favor. It was different with Hitler. He came into power a few months before Roosevelt, who in private immediately spoke of him as a menace. While the European dictatorships and Japan strengthened their armies and fleets and threatened weaker nations, Roosevelt long kept the nation on a neutral course. In 1935, as he saw Mussolini preparing to conquer Ethiopia, Roosevelt signed a Neutrality Act imposing restrictions. When the President proclaimed that a state of war existed, it became illegal for Americans to sell munitions to belligerents on either side, and Americans could travel on the vessels of belligerents only at their own risk. During the gathering crisis in Europe, Congress enacted, and Roosevelt signed, further neutrality measures.

In the fall of 1937, as the Japanese armies advanced into north China, Roosevelt made a first tentative proposal looking toward collective security, stating that peace-loving nations should act in concert to quarantine war as they would a contagion. Public sentiment was so opposed to a strong stand against Japan that at the end of 1937 when Japanese aviators sank the U.S. gunboat *Panay* in Chinese waters, Roosevelt quickly accepted Japanese offers of apology and indemnity. Throughout the Spanish Civil War he pursued a neutral course. Toward Hitler he shared with the leaders of France and England feelings of apprehension. When Hitler threatened war in 1938 over Czechoslovakia, Roosevelt urged him to accept a peaceful solution, but the President's message was not a factor of any significance in the Munich settlement. Apprehension turned to alarm during the next few months as Hitler began to put pressure upon Poland.

When war broke out in Europe in 1939, Roosevelt called Congress into special session and obtained modification of the Neutrality Act to allow belligerents to purchase arms on a "cash and carry" basis, an arrangement favoring the British and French. Hitler's triumphs in 1940 led Roosevelt to enlist the full backing of the United States, short of armed intervention, for the beleaguered British. With strong popular support, he moved the United States from neutrality to an active nonbelligerency. On June 10, 1940, as France was about to fall before Hitler's onslaught, Mussolini declared war on the French. Speaking that evening, Roosevelt bluntly declared, "The hand that held the dagger has struck it into the back of its neighbor."

There had been indications before the war crisis became intense that Roosevelt intended to retire at the end of his second term, in keeping with American tradition. In the national emergency following the fall of France, however, he accepted the Democratic nomination for a third term. Despite the repugnance of many Democratic politicians, Roosevelt insisted upon the nomination for vice president of Henry A. Wallace. The Republicans had responded to the national emergency by nominating the personable Wendell L. Willkie. It was a relatively close election, Roosevelt winning by 27 million votes to 22 million.

In the year between his reelection and Pearl Harbor, Roosevelt established defense organizations, stimulated the building of plants to produce enormous quantities of war matériel, gave massive aid to Britain, and tightened economic pressure upon Japan. Early in 1941, since the British were reaching the end of funds with which to buy munitions, Roosevelt pushed through Congress a new measure of aid, the Lend-Lease Act. This was a means of circumventing existing legislation prohibiting cash loans to nations which had not paid their World War I debts. Roosevelt proposed lending goods instead of money, and explained that the goods could be returned after the war. He met with Prime Minister Winston Churchill of England in the summer of 1941 and issued with him a statement of idealistic war aims, the Atlantic Charter. Step by step Roosevelt had moved toward war against Germany. When the attack came it was from Japan, not Germany. On Dec. 7 the Japanese launched their attack upon Pearl Harbor. It was an angry president addressing a united Congress and nation who called on Dec. 8 for a declaration of war against Japan. Three days later, Germany and Italy declared war on the United States. With the country fully involved in global war, Roosevelt assumed the role of commander in chief of the American nation and sought to head the coalition of nations arrayed against the Axis. As the war proceeded, Roosevelt also became increasingly the foe of colonialism and the advocate of a new world organization, the United Nations. The United States and its allies were to suffer one acute setback after another, yet even before hostilities began, the nation was well on its way toward winning the battle of production. To mobilize the country's resources, Roosevelt set up a variety of war agencies. In 1941 he established the Office of Price Administration, which set price ceilings and handled a rationing program for scarce commodities, and in January 1942, the War Production Board. Like President Wilson, Roosevelt tried to adjourn politics during the war. Congress voted the war measures Roosevelt wished, but he had to pay the price of acquiescing in the dismantling of several New Deal agencies, including the National Resources Planning Board. The electorate, now more prosperous and more conservative, in the 1942 election still further reduced the Democratic majorities in both houses.

At one press conference Roosevelt remarked that in place of "Dr. New Deal" he had brought in "Dr. Win-the-War," but it soon became apparent that with victory Roosevelt would bring back "Dr. New Deal." He continued to advocate long-range humane goals, even though during the war neither he nor Congress did much to implement them. For returning veterans, Congress did provide financing for further education, for a start in business or farming, or for the purchase of a house, through the Servicemen's Readjustment Act of 1944, popularly called the "G.I. Bill of Rights." The commander in chief varied from the president in little except that he was able to cloak many of his moves in wartime secrecy. He depended heavily upon his military commanders, especially General George C. Marshall and Adm. Ernest J. King. At a series of summit meetings to determine grand strategy, Roosevelt demonstrated his skill as a compromiser, making concessions first to the British and later to the Russians in order to hold together the alliance until final victory. In mid-January 1943 he and Churchill met, without Stalin, at Casablanca, Morocco, to plan the next stage in the war. Churchill again was persuasive. Roosevelt announced at a press conference that the Allied policy toward the Axis would be one of unconditional surrender. (Roosevelt had earlier broached the topic with Churchill.) By 1943 the balance of armed power had shifted perceptibly from Churchill to Roosevelt. At a conference in Washington they agreed upon May 1, 1944, as a tentative date for a cross-Channel invasion.

The key to postwar peace, Roosevelt believed, would be American-Russian amity. He long sought a face-to-face meeting with Marshal Stalin. The first such meeting came when Churchill, Stalin, and Roosevelt conferred at Teheran, Iran, in November 1943. Roosevelt tried to win over Stalin, and returned from the conference feeling that indeed he had done so. The 1944 invasion of France (on June 6) was a success, and when Stalin, Churchill, and Roosevelt met for a second time at Yalta, in the Crimea, early in 1945, the war was close to an end. In subsequent years Roosevelt has been harshly criticized for the agreements he made there with the Russians.

In his thinking about the postwar world, Roosevelt came to accept the concept of a United Nations as an international peace-keeping organization. His hope was that, within the framework of the United Nations, the Americans and the Russians could cooperate to maintain world order. At the time of his death he was preparing to go to San Francisco to address the opening session of the conference that would found the United Nations.

Even though the war was rapidly drawing to a close in Europe and Roosevelt was thinking seriously about peace-keeping, Japan was continuing its stubborn resistance. In the summer of 1939 Albert Einstein had sent a letter to Roosevelt warning him that German physicists had achieved atomic fission with uranium and might succeed in constructing such a device. After further warnings, Roosevelt authorized a small research program which in time became the mammoth Manhattan Project. By 1945 it was apparent that the Germans were not even close to producing a bomb but that the United States might soon have a workable one.

Despite deteriorating health, Roosevelt in 1944 ran for a fourth term as president and was reelected. Roosevelt accepted Senator Harry S. Truman of Missouri as his running mate. Roosevelt's Republican opponent was the youthful governor of New York, Thomas E. Dewey, who charged that the Roosevelt administration had "grown tired, old, and quarrelsome in office." At the end of September, Roosevelt threw himself into the campaign with his earlier zest, and by a popular vote of 25.6 million to 22 million he won the election. In the months after the 1944 election, Roosevelt's health continued to decline. He went to Warm Springs, Ga., for a vacation. It was there, on Apr. 12, 1945, that he died of a massive cerebral hemorrhage.

Many contemporaries and some later writers have considered Roosevelt an enigmatic, contradictory figure. He polarized American society; both ardent admirers and vehement haters were united in their feeling that they could not always understand him. Outwardly he was jovial, warm, and capable of seeming most indiscreet in his candor when he was not being indiscreet at all, and sometimes far from candid. He seldom talked about his thinking or his plans until he had firmly made up his mind. In not sharing his thought processes, he helped build an aura of mystery and authority, and he kept power firmly to himself. Roosevelt's merits as an administrator have also been frequently debated. On the surface he was haphazard in his handling of affairs. He liked to draw elaborate organization charts, but they seldom counted for much. His real interest was less in agencies than in men who could be loyal to him and effective. The surprising thing is how many administrators of widely varying views and talents, with little in common except their willingness to work for Roosevelt, continued over the years to render important service. Measured by these public servants and their contributions, Roosevelt ranks well as an administrator.

At the time of his death, Roosevelt was eulogized as one of the greatest figures of modern times. In the next few years, as conservatives in Congress sought to obliterate New Deal domestic programs and blamed the travail of the cold war upon Roosevelt's mistaken policies, his reputation declined. Despite adverse judgments concerning some of his policies and actions, he remains a major figure in modern history. The day before his death, he worked on the draft of a speech ending, "The only limit to our realization of tomorrow will be our doubts of today." Roosevelt added in his own hand, "Let us move forward with strong and active faith."

ROOSEVELT, HILBORNE LEWIS (*b. New York, N.Y., 1849; d. 1886*), organ builder, electrical experimenter. Cousin of Theodore Roosevelt.

ROOSEVELT, KERMIT (*b. Oyster Bay, L.I., N.Y., 1889; d. Alaska, 1943*), explorer, army officer, shipping executive. Son of Theodore Roosevelt (1858–1919). A.B., Harvard, 1912. Served in World War I with British forces in Mesopotamia, and with U.S. 1st Division in France; with brother Theodore, conducted exploring expeditions in eastern Turkestan (1925) and China (1928–29). In World War II, served with British army (1939–41), and as major in U.S. Army from April 1942 until his death.

ROOSEVELT, NICHOLAS J. (*b. New York, N.Y., 1767; d. Skaneateles, N.Y., 1854*), engineer. Operated an engine-building works at present Belleville, N.J., *post ca.* 1794. Entered partnership, 1797, with Robert R. Livingston and John Stevens to build a steamboat for which the engines were to be constructed at Roosevelt's works. The resulting vessel, *Polacca*, made a trial trip, 1798, attaining a speed of some three miles an hour under its own steam. Compelled to abandon his works because of financial difficulties, Roosevelt became associated with Robert Fulton, 1809, in introducing steamboats on Western rivers; in 1811 he built at Pittsburgh the steamboat *New Orleans* which descended the Ohio and Mississippi in 14 days. He also received a patent (1814) for the use of vertical paddle wheels.

ROOSEVELT, ROBERT BARNWELL (*b. New York, N.Y., 1829; d. Sayville, N.Y., 1906*), political reformer, conservation pioneer, author. Uncle of Theodore Roosevelt (1858–1919).

ROOSEVELT, THEODORE (*b. New York, N.Y., 1858; d. Sagamore Hill, Oyster Bay, N.Y., 1919*), statesman, author, president of the United States. Born in a well-to-do family long identified on the paternal side with mercantile pursuits in Manhattan, Roosevelt was on his mother's side a descendant of Archibald Bulloch of Georgia. Handicapped as a child by asthma, he built up his body by sheer determination, teaching himself to ride, box, and shoot; his early intellectual interests centered on natural history. Graduated Harvard, 1880. Finding that law failed to interest him, he turned to the writing of history, produced *The Naval War of 1812* (1882), and so entered on a literary career which made up one phase of his life and of which he never tired. As an independent Republican assemblyman for New York's 21st district, 1882–84, Roosevelt won acceptance in politics on his merits. An irritant to his elders and supposed betters, he attacked misconduct as he chose, saw to it that the newspapers had his side of every story, and zestfully supported laws for the relief of labor and for better government. After an experiment in ranching in Dakota Territory, and the untimely deaths in 1884 of his wife (he had married Alice Hathaway Lee in 1880) and of his mother, he threw himself into active work and in quick succession wrote *Hunting Trips of a Ranchman* (1885), *Thomas Hart Benton* (1886), *Gouverneur Morris* (1888), *Ranch Life and the Hunting-Trail* (1888), *Essays on Practical Politics* (1888), and the first two volumes of *The Winning of the West* (1889). Meanwhile he had returned to practical politics, running for mayor of New York (1886) in a hopeless contest against Abram S. Hewitt and Henry George. Marrying again (Edith Kermit Carow) in London, 1886, he continued active in Republican politics; he supported the winning presidential ticket in 1888 and was made a U.S. civil service commissioner, May 1889.

A firm believer in reform, Roosevelt brought a glare of happy publicity over civil service as the politicians tried to evade the specific requirements of the Pendleton Act of 1883. Happy in Washington, Roosevelt was accepted in the circle of Henry Adams and John Hay and made an on-the-spot study of high policy and backstage intrigue. Ethical to the core, Roosevelt wrote and spoke like a lay envangelist, keeping the crooks out of offices and protecting competent officeholders. Returning to New York City, 1895, he completed *The Winning of the West* (published 1894–96) and accepted the presidency of the board of police commissioners. Overzealous, he accomplished relatively little, but with Jacob A. Riis as his Boswell he studied the lowest levels of city life; observed the unholy alliance of graft, politics, and crime; and succeeded as before in turning his daily routine into pungent, front-page news. Laborious wire-pulling persuaded President McKinley to make Roosevelt assistant secretary of the navy, 1897, a post in which he served with his usual gusto until resigning in May 1898 to take active service in the field during the war with Spain.

As convinced as any jingo of the merits of war over Cuba, he and his friend Leonard Wood organized the first volunteer cavalry regiment (Rough Riders), equipped it, and secured its inclusion in the force mobilizing at Tampa. The Rough Riders, dismounted, took Kettle Hill before Santiago, July 1, 1898; when Wood was promoted to higher rank, Roosevelt became colonel. He later chronicled the unit's glories in *The Rough Riders* (1899), coming home an authentic hero of the war. His sudden popularity upset the plans of Republican Boss Thomas C. Platt for the approaching campaign for governor of New York. Roosevelt, nominated, campaigned with an escort of Rough Riders and was elected by a small majority. He pushed practical reforms as much as possible without breaking with Platt, but two years of him in Albany made Platt ready for promotion to any office outside the state. Unacceptable to President McKinley and Mark Hanna, Roosevelt was nevertheless nominated for the vice-presidency at Philadelphia in June 1900 and the *brio* of his campaign made it possible for McKinley to remain at home in dignity and safety. The Republican ticket was victorious.

Looking forward to a life on the political shelf as vice president, Roosevelt became 26th president of the United States through the assassination of McKinley; he took the oath of office in Buffalo, N.Y., Sept. 14, 1901. Sensing that there was a chance for a flexible president to place himself at the head of national movement for reorganization of the American pattern, and aware also that more was needed for reform than an ethical approach to government, Roosevelt bided his time and during his first term announced no change in administration doctrine. An able administrator, he brought a new virility to the job of president and a new technique to the office; red tape of any kind was abhorrent to him and with insatiable curiosity he strove for personal contact with as many kinds of human beings as was possible. Decisions flowed swiftly from his desk, more often right than wrong. The new sophistication in Washington, D.C., was marked abroad, and foreign nations altered the character of their diplomatic representatives in America, sending men of letters and wit rather than political factotums. Taking over the presidency in the midst of readjustments caused by the war with Spain, Roosevelt directed negotiation of the Hay-Herran Treat (ratified, 1903, but rejected by Colombia) in an effort to expedite building of the Panama Canal. Enraged at the tactics of Colombia, Roosevelt in effect encouraged the secession of the Panama territory from its mother country and its institution as a new republic which, within a month, agreed in its own name to the treaty that Colombia had rejected. Thereafter he guided every step in the construction of the canal. Acting with complete freedom in foreign affairs, he brought about settlement of a European intervention in Venezuela that bore on both the Monroe Doctrine and canal strategy in 1902. When the Dominican Republic was threatened with intervention because of a similar situation arising out of economic default, 1904, Roosevelt persuaded that country to invite him to set up a financial receivership with an American comptroller to collect and disburse its revenues. He also settled the old Alaska boundary dispute on his own terms, 1903, and his cautious pressure upon both Russia and Japan resulted in the Peace of Portsmouth, September 1905. As he did not recognize arbitration as any substitute for preparedness, he continued to encourage army reforms (which included formation of a general staff, 1903) and the strengthening of the navy. Subsequent to some difficulties with Japan over the social position of Orientals in the United States, he openly soothed that country and then sent the modernized battle fleet on a tour around the world (December 1907–February 1909), which was a triumph of administration and policy. "Speak softly," he liked to say, "and carry a big stick, you will go far." In Latin America, however, recent events seemed to have set a pattern of North American aggression inconsistent with the Monroe Doctrine. To explain away the illusion of a menace from the north, Elihu Root, now secretary of state after John Hay's death, was sent on tour among the southern neighbors.

Congress, meanwhile, resented these high-handed executive actions but was left no option but to pay the bills and to limit the president's reform activities at home. The "Ananias Club," numbering all those who had been called liars by the president, grew apace; Roosevelt's hard-hitting methods sometimes made it difficult for his friends to work with him and embittered his enemies more than was necessary. Behind these costly quarrels lay the fact that Roosevelt was trying to dominate a government of checks and balances in which the coordinate branches were as constitutional as he was himself. Since Thomas Jefferson, no president had ranged his mind over so broad a field; since Andrew Jackson, none had been so certain that he had a special mandate from the people. As Roosevelt appeared to be swerving cautiously towards the left, Republicans of the school of McKinley feared and fought him while radicals tried to steal his glory. The struggle involved a new hypothesis of the control of an industrial society in order to save individual economic freedom. There was no effective Democratic opposition in the Roosevelt congress, but the key positions were held by Republican conservatives who distrusted Roosevelt's applications of the "Square Deal." On the death of Marcus A. Hanna, 1904, the conservative Republicans were left leaderless. After renomination at Chicago without opposition, Roosevelt took over the Republican national committee, naming G. B. Cortelyou as chairman. Following his easy victory in the 1904 election, Roosevelt disclaimed a third term. Among specific domestic problems that confronted him, revision of the tariff was recognized as necessary but nothing was ever done about it. Anticipating the "muckrakers" in their attacks upon the trusts, Roosevelt had demanded at Pittsburgh, July 4, 1902, that trusts be subjected to public control, a policy popular in both parties. With the dissolution of the Northern Securities Co., 1904, the addition to the Cabinet of a secretary of commerce and labor, the Elkins Law, and the Expedition Act, further progress in trust control was made but there was more enthusiasm than certainty in the process. The Interstate Commerce Act was strengthened, 1906, and sweeping laws were passed for the protection of food and drug buyers. But by 1906 the fervor of the "muck-rake" period had begun to die out and the president was left unpopular with business and the Republican party stalwarts. The Wall Street panic of 1907 was called the Roosevelt panic. Among the most memorable of Roosevelt's national services were his efforts for conservation of national forest and land reserves; in these he was strenuously opposed by Congress on a number of grounds both worthy and unworthy.

When he sponsored his secretary of war, William H. Taft, for the presidential nomination in 1908, Roosevelt hoped that his administrative team would be held together, but Taft preferred to select his own Cabinet after his election. Out of office, Roosevelt worked at writing and engaged in extensive travels, returning to America in June 1910 and receiving a triumphant reception. It was not in his nature to abstain from political activity and he was dissatisfied with President Taft's favoring of conservative policies. By the summer or early autumn of 1911 he became completely estranged from the president. Having allowed himself to be persuaded that Roosevelt policies were lost unless he returned to politics, he entered the race for the nomination in 1912, but since the administration controlled the party machinery, the Republican convention renominated Taft. Roosevelt's delegation to the convention of 1912 became the nucleus of the Progressive party which met on August 5 and nominated Roosevelt for president and Hiram Johnson of California for vice president on a platform of liberal reform. His candidacy, however, only succeeded in providing opportunity for the victory of Woodrow Wilson. In 1914 Roosevelt went on an expedition to the Brazilian wilderness, where he discovered the "River of Doubt"; he returned with a tropical infection from which he never fully recovered. A neutral in World War I until his old suspicions of Germany were revived, he became an enthusiastic support of the Allies and denounced the diplomatic courses of President Wilson, seeking with tongue and pen to arouse the country. Disappointed of his wish for military command after the United States entered the war, he entertained hopes that he might run for the presidency again in 1920, but died peacefully in his sleep early in 1919. His career had personified America's recognition of a changing world; his flaws were on the surface but his human values were timeless.

ROOSEVELT, THEODORE (*b. Oyster Bay, L.I., N.Y., 1887; d. Cherbourg, France, 1944*), soldier, public official, businessman. Son of Theodore Roosevelt (1858–1919). A.B., Harvard, 1908. After distinguished service with the 1st Division, U.S. Army in France in World War I, he served in the New York Assembly (1919–21), and as assistant secretary of the navy, 1921–24. He ran as Republican candidate for governor of New York, 1924, and was defeated by Alfred E. Smith. With his brother Kermit, he conducted exploring expeditions in eastern Turkestan and the Yunnan and Szechuan provinces of China, 1925 and 1928–29. Returning to public life, he showed himself an able administrator and an intelligent reformer as governor of Puerto Rico (1929–32) and as governor general of the Philippines, 1932–33. An opponent of New Deal domestic policies, he supported he foreign policies of his kinsman Franklin D. Roosevelt. Returning to the army in 1941, he was promoted brigadier general and took part in the Tunisian and Italian campaigns of World War II; he led the 4th Division ashore on Utah Beach in the Normandy invasion, June 6, 1944. He died the next month of a heart attack while military governor of Cherbourg. Posthumously awarded the Medal of Honor, he held every combat decoration of the U.S. Army ground forces.

ROOT, AMOS IVES (*b. near Medina, Ohio, 1839; d. 1923*), apiarist, pioneer in commercial beekeeping.

ROOT, ELIHU (*b. Clinton, N.Y., 1845; d. New York, N.Y., 1937*), lawyer, statesman. Graduated Hamilton College, 1864; New York University Law School, 1867. Within a year he established his own law firm in New York City and began a career which made him the acknowledged leader of the American bar. His success was due to a phenomenal memory, capacity for hard work, mastery of detail, logical conciseness and clarity of argument, and ever-present wit. Court work was his specialty. No contemporary opprobrium attached to his serving (1873) as assistant to one of the defense counsel in the prosecution of Boss Tweed, or to later representation of large corporate interests, but these aspects of his practice were later magnified by his detractors, especially the Hearst press.

Active in local politics as a conservative, antimachine Republican, Root managed the N.Y. constitutional convention in 1894 and supported and advised Theodore Roosevelt during the latter's incumbency as New York City police commissioner and as governor of New York. Becoming President McKinley's secretary of war, 1899, Root made outstanding contributions in administration of Cuba and the new U.S. colonial possessions; he also effected a fundamental reorganization of the army. He created the Army War College and introduced the principle of the general staff; by requiring rotation from staff to line jobs, he discouraged entrenched military bureaucracy in Washington. In dealing with the problems of the former Spanish islands, Root sought for Puerto Rico a highly centralized system of government and exemption from the U.S. tariff. His fortunate selection of General Leonard Wood as military governor of Cuba resulted in a model regime of rehabilitation. In the Philippines, Root was responsible for a program that firmly guaranteed individual liberties and developed local institutions.

Root resigned his cabinet post in 1903 but returned in 1905 as U.S. secretary of state. Among his notable accomplishments (for which he received the Nobel Peace Prize, 1912) were the reestablishment of friendly relations with Latin America and Japan, and the conclusion of a series of arbitration treaties. He also settled the North Atlantic fisheries controversy and established the U.S. consular service on a career basis.

From 1909 to 1915 Root served as U.S. senator from New York. Committed to William H. Taft before Theodore Roosevelt "threw his hat in the ring," Root sorrowfully but doggedly presided over the 1912 Republican National Convention which led to the Bull Moose bolt and a lasting breach between him and Roosevelt. Critical of Wilson and neutrality, he wholeheartedly supported the Allied cause. His position in the League of Nations fight was that the treaty should be accepted with reservations; he believed Article X impracticable as a permanent commitment. Active in framing the statute for the Permanent Court of International Justice, he strongly advocated American membership in the Court. As friend and adviser of Andrew Carnegie, he helped establish a number of Carnegie benefactions and served as president or chairman of the board of the Carnegie Endowment for International Peace, the Carnegie Institution, and the Carnegie Corporation. Wise in counsel, skilled in advocacy, he was a distinguished elder statesman throughout his later years and remained active to the last in matters affecting the bar.

ROOT, ELISHA KING (*b. Ludlow, Mass., 1808; d. Hartford, Conn., 1865*), mechanic, inventor. As superintendent (later president) of the Colt Armory, 1849–65, Root designed and built the Armory as well as most of the machinery used in it. His drophammer (invented, 1853, 1858) put the art of die-forging on its modern basis.

ROOT, ERASTUS (*b. Hebron, Conn., 1773; d. New York, N.Y., 1846*), lawyer. Began practice at Delhi, N.Y.; served several terms in state legislature and was lieutenant governor of New York, 1823–24. Originally an anti-Clinton Democrat, he refused to support Andrew Jackson in 1832 and later became a Whig. He was congressman from New York, 1803–05, 1809–11, 1815–17, and 1831–33.

ROOT, FRANK ALBERT (*b. Binghamton, N.Y., 1837; d. 1926*), Kansas newspaper publisher. Author of *The Overland Stage to California* (with W. E. Connelley, 1901).

ROOT, FREDERIC WOODMAN (*b. Boston, Mass., 1846; d. Chicago, Ill., 1916*), music teacher, composer, organist. Son of George F. Root.

ROOT, GEORGE FREDERICK (*b. Sheffield, Mass., 1820; d. 1895*), music educator, composer. Father of Frederic W. Root. Established New York Normal Institute, 1853, to train music teachers; followed example of Lowell Mason in holding "musical conventions" to explain class instruction methods in singing. Removed to Chicago, 1859, where he engaged in music publishing until 1871 and continued teaching until his death. Among his many popular songs were "The Battle Cry of Freedom," "Tramp, Tramp, Tramp, the Boys are Marching," "Just Before the Battle, Mother," and "The Vacant Chair."

ROOT, JESSE (*b. Coventry, Conn., 1736 o.s.; d. Coventry, 1822*), Revolutionary soldier, Connecticut legislator and jurist. Member of the Continental Congress, 1778–82. Judge of the superior court of Connecticut, 1789–1807 (chief justice *post* 1798).

ROOT, JOHN WELLBORN (*b. Lumpkin, Ga., 1850; d. 1891*), architect. C.E., University of the City of New York (present New York University), 1869. Worked in office of James Renwick (1818–1895); at invitation of Peter B. Wight, became head draftsman in Chicago for Carter, Drake & Wight, 1871. Entered partnership with Daniel H. Burnham, 1873. The rise of the firm was rapid and owed much to Root's creative engineering mind; his designs, although superficially based on the popular Romanesque of H. H. Richardson, were all essentially personal and structurally true, especially his designs for business buildings. The Monadnock Building was a high point in his work. Appointed consulting architect for the World's Columbian Exposition, 1890, Root requested that his partner be included, an example of the superb cooperation between them throughout their careers. While Burnham deserves credit for the formation of the board of architects and the generalship of the work at the Exposition, to Root must go much of the credit for the final choice of site and the settlement of the basic plan.

ROOT, JOSEPH POMEROY (*b. Greenwich, Mass., 1826; d. Wyandotte, Kans., 1885*), physician, antislavery advocate, Kansas territorial legislator. Republican lieutenant governor of the State of Kansas, 1859–61, Root served in the Civil War as surgeon of the 2nd Kansas Cavalry. He was U.S. minister to Chile, 1870–73.

ROPER, DANIEL CALHOUN (*b. Marlboro County, S.C., 1867; d. Washington, D.C., 1943*), businessman, lawyer, public official. B.A., Trinity College (now Duke University), 1888. A Populist at heart who chose to remain within the Democratic party, he served briefly in the South Carolina legislature and held several federal appointments, of which the most important was with the Bureau of the Census, 1900–11. In course of this, he became an expert in the economics of the cotton trade. Active in support of President Woodrow Wilson's campaigns for the presidency, 1912 and 1916, he was appointed to high offices in the Post Office (1913–16), the U.S. Tariff Commission (1917), and was made Commissioner of Internal Revenue (1917–21). Chiefly engaged in the practice of law in Washington, 1921–32, he had a significant role in the nomination of Franklin D. Roosevelt, 1932. President Roosevelt named Roper to his cabinet as secretary of commerce, 1933, but despite his earlier liberalism, Roper was a generally conservative influence within the New Deal and resigned in 1938.

ROPES, JAMES HARDY (*b. Salem, Mass., 1866; d. 1933*), Congregational clergyman, New Testament scholar. Graduated Harvard, 1889; Andover Theological Seminary, 1893. After extensive further study in Europe, he taught at Harvard *post* 1895 and was Hollis Professor of Divinity *post* 1910. He is remembered principally for his work in reorganizing Phillips Academy, Andover, for his editorship of the *Harvard Theological Review* (1921–33), and for his scholarly work *The Text of Acts* (1926).

ROPES, JOHN CODMAN (*b. St. Petersburg, Russia, 1836; d. 1899*), Boston lawyer, military historian. Author, among other works, of *The Story of the Civil War* (1894–98).

ROPES, JOSEPH (*b. Salem, Mass., 1770; d. 1850*), merchant, War of 1812 privateersman.

RORER, DAVID (*b. Pittsylvania Co., Va., 1806; d. 1884*), lawyer. Removed to Little Rock, Ark., 1826; after practicing there and holding public office, he settled in pioneer Burlington, Iowa (then in Michigan Territory), 1836. Rorer plotted the town, drafted the charter, and suggested the name "Hawkeyes" for Iowans. He was for many years one of the most active members of the Iowa bar, especially in fugitive slave cases and railroad litigation.

RORIMER, JAMES JOSEPH (*b. Cleveland, Ohio, 1905; d. New York, N.Y., 1966*), art scholar and museum administrator. Graduated from Harvard (1927), then joined the Metropolitan Museum of Art. He was a central figure in the planning of the Cloisters, completed in 1938, which owed its authentically medieval architectural character to Rorimer. Became full curator of the Metropolitan's Department of Medieval Art in 1934 and director of the museum in 1955; among his notable acquisitions were Raphael's *Madonna of the Meadows* and Rembrandt's *Aristotle Contemplating the Bust of Homer*.

ROSA, EDWARD BENNETT (*b. Rogersville, N.Y., 1861; d. Washington, D.C., 1921*), physicist. Graduated Wesleyan University, 1886; Ph.D., Johns Hopkins, 1891. Taught physics at Wesleyan, 1891–1903; was in charge of electrical work of National Bureau of Standards *post* 1902. Jointly with Wilbur O. Atwater, Rosa devised apparatus and made measurements which showed that the physical law of conservation of energy also applied to animal processes, thus giving a scientific basis for study of nutrition problems. While with the Bureau of Standards, he did fundamental work on electrical measurements which included precise determination of the value of the ampere as measured by mechanical forces exerted between coils carrying current; he also determined relation between electrical units derived from magnetic effects and those derived from electrostatic forces. He later made studies of engineering problems arising in the operation and regulation of public-utility services.

ROSATI, JOSEPH (*b. Sora, Naples, 1789; d. Rome, Italy, 1843*), Roman Catholic clergyman, Vincentian. Came to America as volunteer for missions, 1816; worked in Kentucky; began St. Mary's Seminary, Perryville, Mo., 1818, teaching and also acting as pastor. Consecrated coadjutor to the bishop of Louisiana, 1824, he became bishop of St. Louis, 1827. Continuing to administer Lower Louisiana as well, he did not settle permanently in his own see until 1830. After attending the provincial Council of Baltimore, 1840, he proceeded to Rome whence he was sent as Apostolic Delegate to negotiate an agreement between the republic of Haiti and the Holy see.

ROSE, AQUILA (*b. England, ca. 1695; d. 1723*), printer, ferryman, poet. Immigrated to Philadelphia *ante* 1717. The best versifier that Philadelphia could show before the younger Thomas Godfrey, Rose produced translations from Ovid and other poems which appeared posthumously in *Poems on Several Occasions* (1740).

ROSE, BILLY (*b. New York, N.Y., 1899; d. Montego Bay, Jamaica, 1966*), producer, songwriter, and theater and nightclub owner. Published his first song, "Ain't Nature Grand," in 1921 and had his first hit, "Barney Google," in 1923. Of the nearly 400 songs for which he wrote lyrics, 41 were hits, including "Me and My Shadow" and "It's Only a Paper Moon." Founded the Songwriters Protective Association (1931) and became its first president. Owner of the Back Stage Club, which attracted underworld figures during and after Prohibition, he found it lucrative to work with mobsters. He managed the first theater-restaurant, the Casino de Paree, and his Billy Rose Music Hall for them, but he stopped being a front in 1934. His first musical, *Corned Beef and Roses* (1930) failed, but after some tinkering, it reopened (1931) as *Crazy Quilt* and was a success. Although *Jumbo* (1935) lost money, more than a million people saw the production, which brought the circus and the eponymous elephant to Broadway. In 1937 he coined the word "aquacade" for his first aquatic musical review; other aquacades he produced were for the 1939 New York World's Fair and the Golden State Exposition in San Francisco (1940). His most renowned nightclub, the Diamond Horseshoe (1939–52) became a top New York tourist attraction. Of the eleven Broadway shows he produced, *Carmen Jones* (1943) is the most memorable. Signed newspaper ads for that production and others evolved into his syndicated column, "Pitching Horseshoes" (1947–50). He organized the Billy Rose Foundation, to which he bequeathed almost all of his $54 million estate.

ROSE, CHAUNCEY (*b. Wethersfield, Conn., 1794; d. Terre Haute, Ind., 1877*), financier, railroad builder, philanthropist. Settled in Terre Haute, 1825. He was the principal benefactor of Rose Polytechnic Institute (formally opened, 1883).

ROSE, EDWARD (*fl. 1811–1834*), guide, interpreter. Child of a white trader and a part Cherokee and part black mother, Rose was engaged by Wilson P. Hunt at the Arikara village as hunter, guide, and interpreter, 1811; in May 1812, Rose joined Manuel Lisa's expedition to the upper Missouri. Living for some years among the Crow and the Arikara, in 1823 he was interpreter to William H. Ashley whom he vainly warned against the Arikara before the defeat of June 2. Rose was also interpreter to Henry Atkinson on his treaty-making expedition up the Missouri, 1825. In 1832, Zenas Leonard met him in a Crow village at the mouth of Stinking River where he ranked as a chief. Although Rose bore a bad reputation among his contemporaries, everything which is definitely known of him is creditable.

ROSE, ERNESTINE LOUISE SIISMONDI POTOWSKI (*b. Piotrkow, Russian Poland, 1810; d. Brighton, England, 1892*), reformer, advocate of woman's rights. Resided and worked in the United States, 1836–69.

ROSE, JOHN CARTER (*b. Baltimore, Md., 1861; d. Atlantic City, N.J., 1927*), Maryland jurist, reformer, member of Theodore Roosevelt's "tennis cabinet." U.S. district judge, 1910–22; judge, U.S. circuit court of appeals for the fourth circuit, *post* 1922.

ROSE, JOSEPH NELSON (*b. near Liberty, Ind., 1862; d. Washington, D.C., 1928*), botanist. Graduated Wabash College, 1885; Ph.D., 1889. Influenced in choice of a career by John M. Coulter, Rose served *post* 1888 as botanist in the U.S. Department of Agriculture, in curatorial posts in the National Herbarium (U.S. National Museum), and as a research associate of the Carnegie Institution of Washington. He was an authority on Mexican flora generally, and made particular studies of the *Crassulaceae* and *Cactaceae*.

ROSE, MARY DAVIES SWARTZ (*b. Newark, Ohio, 1874; d. Edgewater, N.Y., 1941*), nutritionist. Litt.B., Shepardson College, 1901. B.S., Teachers College, Columbia University, 1906. Ph.D. in physiological chemistry, Yale, 1909. Taught nutrition and dietetics at Teachers College, 1904–40 (professor of nutrition *post* 1923); author, among other works, of *Feeding the Family* (1916) and *The Foundations of Nutrition* (1927).

ROSE, URIAH MILTON (*b. Bradfordsville, Ky.,* 1834; *d.* 1913), Arkansas jurist, legal writer.

ROSE, WALTER MALINS (*b. Toronto, Canada,* 1872; *d. Los Angeles, Calif.,* 1908), legal annotator. Author, among other works, of an innovating 12-volume study *Notes on the U.S. Reports* (1899–1901) which treated cases reported from *2 Dallas* to *172 U.S.,* showing their value as authority by listing subsequent citations in state and federal courts.

ROSE, WICKLIFFE (*b. Saulsbury, Tenn.,* 1862; *d. Vancouver Island, Canada,* 1931), public health and educational administrator. After teaching at Peabody College for Teachers where he became dean, and at the University of Nashville, he served as general agent of the Peabody Education Fund, 1907–14. Director of the Rockefeller Commission for Education of Hookworm *post* 1910, he was made director of the International Health Board, 1913, and widened the scope of the enterprise to include malaria and yellow fever; the program later was expanded to a worldwide attack on all preventable disease. Retiring in 1923, he was made president of the General Education Board and of the International Education Board, supervising in the latter capacity a vast program of aid in the teaching of science and in fostering research.

ROSECRANS, SYLVESTER HORTON (*b. Homer, Ohio,* 1827; *d.* 1878), Roman Catholic clergyman. Brother of William S. Rosecrans. Influenced by his brother's conversion to Catholicism and by the instructions of Father John B. Lamy, he entered the Catholic Church and was graduated from St. John's (Fordham) College, N.Y., 1846. Ordained priest, 1852, he wa consecrated coadjutor bishop of Cincinnati, 1862, and made bishop of the new see of Columbus, Ohio, 1868.

ROSECRANS, WILLIAM STARKE (*b. Delaware Co., Ohio,* 1819; *d. near Los Angeles, Calif.,* 1898), soldier. Brother of Sylvester H. Rosecrans. Graduated West Point, 1842; was a convert to Catholicism while a cadet. After engaging in fortification work and four years' duty as instructor at West Point, he resigned his commission, 1854, and entered business as engineer-architect and head of an oil refining company. Volunteering for the Union Army at the outbreak of the Civil War, he was almost immediately commissioned regular brigadier general, commanded a brigade in McClellan's campaign in western Virginia, and won the battle of Rich Mountain, July 1861, one of the first battles of the war. Succeeding McClellan as commanding general, department of the Ohio, and later as chief of the department of western Virginia, he continued the operations which ended late that fall in complete expulsion of Confederate forces and formation of the State of West Virginia. He commanded the left wing of Pope's Army of the Mississippi, May 1862, during the movement upon Corinth and succeeded Pope in command a month later. After his defeat of the Confederate counterattack against Corinth under Price and Van Dorn, Oct. 3, 1862, he was promoted major general and ordered to relieve Buell in Kentucky. Reorganizing Buell's forces as the Army of the Cumberland, he advanced to Nashville.

In December, he moved against the Confederates under General Braxton Bragg who had concentrated at Murfreesboro. The two armies met on Stone River just west of Murfreesboro on Dec. 29, 1862; after a first Confederate success, Rosecrans established a new defensive line. Fighting continued, Bragg lost his nerve, and on Jan. 3, 1863, retreated to Shelbyville. For six months the armies engaged in only minor operations. On June 23 Rosecrans began to advance and in nine days maneuvered Bragg out of his positions at Shelbyville and Tullahoma back into Chattanooga. By

this time, Rosecrans' openly expressed resentment of interference from Washington had brought him into disfavor there. Prodded into advancing by General Halleck, Rosecrans on August 16 made a feint up the Tennessee River above Chattanooga, then crossed below that place, and maneuvered Bragg out of it. Owing to the overextension of his lines, Rosecrans was badly defeated in the bloody battle of Chickamauga on Sept. 19–20, 1863, when the reinforced Bragg turned to face him. Relieved of command on October 19, Rosecrans was assigned to command the department of the Missouri and was later detached to await orders. He resigned his commission in the regular army, March 1867. Generally regarded as an able officer, and even called the greatest strategist of the war, he was handicapped by a hot temper and a hasty tongue. In later life he was U.S. minister to Mexico, 1868–69, and a Democratic congressman from California, 1881–85.

ROSELIUS, CHRISTIAN (*b. near Bremen, Germany,* 1803; *d. New Orleans, La.,* 1873), lawyer, teacher of law. Immigrated to New Orleans, 1823; studied law in office of Auguste D'Avezac; attained first rank at the Louisiana bar, ranking with Pierre Soulé and Edward Livingston. Expert in the French civil law and its background, he taught for many years at the University of Louisiana (Tulane) and was dean of its law department.

ROSEN, JOSEPH A. (*b. Moscow, Russia,* 1878; *d. New York, N.Y.,* 1949), agronomist, resettlement expert. Came to the United States, 1903, after escape from exile to Siberia and residence for several years in Germany. Graduated Michigan Agricultural College, 1908; introduced high-yield Russian rye seeds to cultivation in Midwest; headed Baron de Hirsch Agricultural School in Woodbine, N.J. Believing that the emancipation of Russian Jews could be best achieved by their integration into the larger society of the nation, he joined Herbert Hoover's relief mission to Russia in 1921 as representative of the Joint Distribution Committee (J.D.C.) of the American Jewish Committee. Success in rehabilitating destroyed Jewish farms encouraged him to think that the mass of destitute, petit-bourgeois Jews could be transformed into a self-reliant peasantry through resettlement and special training. With financial aid from the J.D.C., he worked (1924–36) within the Russian socialist context and established a quarter-million Jews on farms in the Ukraine and in Crimea, which were models of productivity and organization. Returning to the United States, 1937, he worked on resettlement projects for German Jewish refugees.

ROSENAU, MILTON JOSEPH (*b. Philadelphia, Pa.,* 1869; *d. Chapel Hill, N.C.,* 1946), epidemiologist. Child of Jewish immigrant parents from Germany. M.D., University of Pennsylvania, 1889; studied at later periods in Berlin, Vienna, and at the Institut Pasteur, Paris. Associated with the present U.S. Public Health Service, 1890–1909 (director of its research laboratory, 1899–1909), he presided over the laboratory's rapid expansion and made important contributions to medicine. In collaboration with J. F. Anderson, he pioneered in the study of anaphylaxis; with Joseph Goldberger, he established the official unit for standardization of diphtheria antitoxin; he also made studies of the epidemiology of typhoid fever and acute respiratory infections; studies of malaria, botulism, and other diseases; and important contributions to milk supply sanitation. While professor of preventive medicine, Harvard Medical School, 1909–35, he was instrumental in establishing the first U.S. school for public health officers (1913); *post* 1922, he was its professor of epidemiology. Retiring from Harvard, 1935, he spent the rest of his life at the University of North Carolina, where he taught his specialty in the medical school and developed a school of public health.

ROSENBACH, ABRAHAM SIMON WOLF (*b. Philadelphia, Pa.,* 1876; *d. Philadelphia,* 1952); **ROSENBACH, PHILIP HYMAN** (*b.

Philadelphia, Pa., 1863; d. Los Angeles, Calif., 1953), antique and rare book dealers. Abraham studied at the University of Pennsylvania and received a Ph.D. in 1901; he then joined his brother Philip's antique business, introducing the selling of rare books, and the famed Rosenbach Co. was begun (1903). While Philip ran the antique business, his brother, Dr. Rosenbach, was in charge of the rare book division. One of the world's greatest collectors of rare books, the Dr. was responsible for the collection of the Widener family that became the Widener Memorial Library at Harvard. He also collected most of the volumes in the Huntington Library; the Folger Shakespeare Library; the collection given by the Harkness family to the Library of Congress; and the Elkins collection which went to the Free Library of Philadelphia.

Manuscripts include the Shakespeare First Folios, the Gutenberg Bible, first edition of Carroll's *Alice in Wonderland*, and Joyce's *Ulysses*.

ROSENBERG, ABRAHAM HAYYIM (*b. Karlin, Russia, 1838; d. 1925*), author, biblical scholar. A distinguished rabbi in Pinsk, Nikolayev, and Poltava, Rosenberg came to the United States in 1891. He was author of a number of works in both Hebrew and Yiddish which include his life-work *Ozar ha-shemoth*, a Hebrew cyclopedia of Biblical literature (published, 1898–99 and 1923).

ROSENBERG, ETHEL (*b. New York, N.Y., 1915; d. Ossining, N.Y. 1953*); **ROSENBERG, JULIUS** (*b. New York, N.Y., 1918; d. Ossining, N.Y., 1953*), spies. Julius studied at the City College of New York, graduating in 1939. He was employed as a junior engineer for the Army Signal Corps (1940–45). He was fired in 1945 for lying about his membership in the Communist party. Involved in a spy ring that included such figures as Claus Fuchs, a physicist employed at Los Alamos, and Ethel's brother, David Greenglass, also employed at Los Alamos. The Rosenbergs were arrested in 1950 during the "red scare" that was sweeping the nation. They were implicated by the testimonies of Greenglass and his wife, Ruth. Both were sentenced to be executed; the other members of the ring were all given prison terms. Despite numerous pleas for commutation of the sentences, the couple was executed at Sing Sing in 1953. Many arguments have been given as to their innocence, but none thus far that could clear their names of the charges brought against them. Their deaths stand as a monument even for many who accept their guilt, to the degree to which anti-Communist hysteria at the height of the Cold War prevented some Americans from tempering the demands of justice with an equally full measure of mercy.

ROSENBERG, HENRY (*b. Bilten, Switzerland, 1824; d. 1893*), merchant, banker. Immigrated to Galveston, Texas, 1843. Prospering there in the dry-goods business and many other enterprises, he was a benefactor of the city during life and on his death left a great part of his estate for charitable purposes in Galveston.

ROSENBERG, PAUL (*b. Paris, France, 1881; d. Paris, 1959*), art dealer and collector. Sharing art galleries in Paris with his father, and opening a gallery in London on his own, Rosenberg, after World War I opened a gallery in Paris that was to become the home of some of the most famous artists of this century: Picasso, with whom Rosenberg had an exclusive contract from 1918 to 1940, Braque, Léger, and Henri Matisse. Rosenberg fled the Nazis in 1940 and opened a gallery in New York where he remained the rest of his life, never reestablishing his business ties in France.

ROSENBLATT, BERNARD ABRAHAM (*b. Grodek, Poland, 1886; d. New York, N.Y., 1969*), Zionist leader. Arrived in the United States in 1892. Interested in Zionism as a youth, he organized the Zionist Literary Society for high school students (1902). At Columbia (M.A., 1908) he established the first Colum-

bia University Zionist Society; also attended Columbia Law (LL.B., 1909). In 1911 he served as honorary secretary of the Federation of American Zionists, thus moving into the inner circle of the small American Zionist movement. His efforts helped establish the nucleus of Hadassah, the American women's Zionist organization. His first book, *The Social Commonwealth* (1914), combined socialist ideals of cooperation and the regulation of economic life with the benefits of competition and a voluntary democracy. In 1915 he incorporated the American Zion Commonwealth to purchase land in Palestine for Jewish settlement. Attended the World Zionist Convention in 1920 and rallied behind Chaim Weizmann and his program of colonization in Palestine. During 1925–55, he divided his time between Haifa and New York. In the late 1930's organized a committee in Haifa to advocate partition and federation; the establishment of the state of Israel brought an end to his Zionist activity.

ROSENBLATT, JOSEPH (*b. Biélaya Tzerkov, near Kiev, Russia, 1882; d. Jerusalem, 1933*), cantor, concert tenor. Celebrated professionally in Europe, he came to America, 1912, where his natural vocal virtuosity and faultless pitch made him a musical celebrity. A concert artist exclusively *post* 1926, he died while on a visit to Palestine.

ROSENFELD, MORRIS (*b. Bokscha, Russian Poland, 1862; d. 1923*), tailor, poet. Immigrated to America, 1886. After a miserable existence in New York City sweatshops for some 14 years, Rosenfeld was enabled to devote himself entirely to literature and became editor and contributor to several Yiddish papers. He published his first collection of folk and revolutionary songs, *Die Glocke* (1888); other collections appeared in 1890 and 1917. His talent was made generally known by publication of *Songs from the Ghetto* in English (1898).

ROSENFELD, PAUL LEOPOLD (*b. New York, N.Y., 1890; d. New York, 1946*), critic of music, art, and literature. B.A., Yale, 1912. Litt.B., School of Journalism, Columbia University, 1913. Associated before World War I with the New York cultural circle that included Van Wyck Brooks, Leo Ornstein, Waldo Frank, and Randoph Bourne, he devoted himself to interpreting the modern movement in the arts to the American public. His first work appeared in the *New Republic* and *Seven Arts* (1916). He was music critic of the *Dial* and a regular contributor to the *Nation*, *Vanity Fair*, and other journals throughout the 1920's. Among his books were *Musical Portraits* (1920) and *Port of New York* (1924), a collection of essays on those of his contemporaries who, in his view, best represented the new art of the time.

ROSENTHAL, HERMAN (*b. Friedrichsstadt, Courland, Russia, 1843; d. 1917*), author. After establishing a literary reputation at home, Rosenthal came to America, 1881, and with Michael Heilprin became a pioneer in founding agricultural colonies of Russian Jews in this country. Employed as a statistician and economic surveyor for a time, he became chief of the Slavonic division, New York Public Library, 1898, and remained in this post until his death. He was an important member of the editorial board of the *Jewish Encyclopedia*.

ROSENTHAL, MAX (*b. Turck, Russian Poland, 1833; d. 1918*), lithographer, mezzotint engraver. Came to America, 1849, after apprenticeship in Paris, France; was engaged principally in chromolithography until about 1870. Thereafter, he won fame as an etcher and mezzotinter of portraits of distinguished Americans, principally of the colonial and Revolutionary War periods.

ROSENTHAL, TOBY EDWARD (*b. New Haven, Conn., 1848; d. Munich, Germany, 1917*), genre and portrait painter.

ROSENWALD, JULIUS (*b. Springfield, Ill., 1862; d. Chicago, Ill., 1932*), merchant, philanthropist. Associated with Sears, Roebuck & Co., *post* 1895, he was president of the company, 1910–25, and thereafter until his death, chairman of the board. After building up a great business through sensing the possibilities of mail-order, appreciating his own limitations, and surrounding himself with expert help, he turned to a wide range of philanthropies which transcended race, creed, and nationality. His benefactions were made principally through the Julius Rosenwald Fund which he created in 1917. His work for the advancement of the black was doubtless the outstanding feature of his philanthropy.

ROSEWATER, EDWARD (*b. Bukowan, Bohemia, Austria–Hungary, 1841; d. Omaha, Nebr., 1906*), Nebraska journalist and legislator, Union soldier. Came to the United States, 1854. Founded the *Omaha Daily Bee*, 1871, which he managed actively until shortly before his death.

ROSEWATER, VICTOR (*b. Omaha, Nebr., 1871; d. Philadelphia, Pa., 1940*), journalist, politician. Son of Edward Rosewater. Graduated Columbia, 1891; Ph.D., 1893. Associated with the *Omaha Bee* until 1920, he served it as managing editor, editor, and publisher. A dominant influence in the Republican party in Nebraska by 1908, he presided as chairman of the National Republican Committee over the stormy opening session of the convention of 1912. By ruling out of order a motion by Theodore Roosevelt's floor leader to substitute Roosevelt delegates for those approved by the committee, Rosewater made it possible for Elihu Root to become temporary chairman and was thus a major factor in Roosevelt's withdrawal from the convention.

ROSS, ABEL HASTINGS (*b. Winchendon, Mass., 1831; d. Port Huron, Mich., 1893*), Congregational clergyman, authority on the history and polity of that denomination.

ROSS, ALEXANDER (*b. Nairnshire, Scotland, 1783; d. present Winnipeg, Canada, 1856*), fur trader, explorer. Immigrated to Canada, 1804; worked as schoolteacher. Engaged by Wilson P. Hunt at Montreal, 1810, as a clerk in Astor's Pacific Fur Co., he sailed in September on the *Tonquin* and aided in the building of Fort Astoria and later of Fort Okanogan. He was a member of the expedition that founded Fort Walla Walla, July 1818, and remained in charge there until the fall of 1823. Starting east, he was persuaded to lead an expedition into the Snake River country, and in 1824 penetrated present Idaho as far as the mouth of the Boise River. In the spring of 1825, he started east again but halted at the Red River colony where he resided for the remainder of his life. He was author of important historical works of firsthand authority, *Adventures of the First Settlers on the Oregon or Columbia River* (London, 1849), *The Fur Hunters of the Far West* (1855), and *The Red River Settlement* (1856).

ROSS, ALEXANDER COFFMAN (*b. Zanesville, Ohio, 1812; d. Zanesville, 1883*), jeweler, song writer. Remembered principally for his authorship of the famous "Tippecanoe and Tyler, Too" for the presidential campaign of 1840.

ROSS, ARAMINTA. *See* TUBMAN, HARRIET.

ROSS, BETSY (*b. Philadelphia, Pa., 1752; d. 1836*), seamstress, upholsterer, legendary maker of the first United States flag.

ROSS, CHARLES GRIFFITH (*b. Independence, Mo., 1885; d. Washington, D.C., 1950*), journalist. Graduated University of Missouri, 1905. Rose to editorial rank on various newspapers in St. Louis, Mo., and elsewhere; taught at University of Missouri's school of journalism, 1908–18. Washington correspondent of the St. Louis *Post-Dispatch*, 1918–34, he was distinguished for thoroughness of investigation, accurate and lucid writing, and thoughtful analysis; he won the Pulitzer Prize for newspaper correspondence in 1932. After serving as editor of the editorial page of the *Post-Dispatch*, 1934–39, he returned to Washington as contributing editor and writer of a signed column of opinion. *Post* 1945, at considerable personal sacrifice, he was the widely respected press secretary of his friend and high school schoolmate, President Harry S. Truman.

ROSS, DENMAN WALDO (*b. Cincinnati, Ohio, 1853; d. London, England, 1935*), artist, educator. Graduated Harvard, 1875; did further work under Henry Adams and Charles E. Norton, receiving the doctorate, 1880, for a study of early German land tenure. Shifting his field to art, he taught at Harvard *post* 1899 in the departments of architecture and fine arts. His theories were set forth in *A Theory of Pure Design* (1907) and *On Drawing and Painting* (1912). Working with precise and clear-cut formulae, he cut at the root of Ruskinian vagueness and brought his master Norton's aesthetics to earth. Associated with Ernest Fenollosa, Edward S. Morse, and William S. Bigelow as a donor of Oriental art to the Boston Museum, he was also a benefactor of the Fogg Museum at Harvard.

ROSS, EDMUND GIBSON (*b. Ashland, Ohio, 1826; d. Albuquerque, N.Mex., 1907*), journalist, antislavery advocate, Union soldier. A free-state leader in Kansas *post* 1856, he edited and published the Topeka *Kansas Tribune*, and the Topeka *Kansas State Record*, 1857–62. He became editor of the Lawrence *Tribune*, 1865, and served as U.S. senator, Republican, from Kansas, 1866–71. Entering the Senate an intense radical and opponent of Andrew Johnson, he insisted that Johnson have a fair trial after the president's impeachment. His vote against conviction on grounds of lack of evidence destroyed his political career. Leaving the Republican party, 1872, because of his dislike of the protective system and of the character of Grant's administration, he continued active in Kansas journalism until 1882 when he moved to New Mexico. He was governor of that territory, 1885–89.

ROSS, EDWARD ALSWORTH (*b. Virden, Ill., 1866; d. 1951*), sociologist. Studied at Coe College in Iowa, and at Johns Hopkins (Ph.D. in political economy). Taught at Stanford University from 1893 to 1900; while there, he shifted his interests from economics to sociology. Widely acknowledged as a founder of American sociology, Ross coupled this discipline with an active interest in progressive politics and reform; as a result, he was asked to resign his tenured position at Stanford. Taught at the University of Nebraska from 1901 to 1906 and at the University of Wisconsin from 1906 until retirement in 1937.

Rejecting the prevalent philosophies of Darwinism and laissez-faire in social planning, Ross believed that a system of social control was possible that would enable Americans to keep the rugged individualism of the past as well as adapt to the corporate state they were creating for the future. His books include *Social Control: A Survey of the Foundations of Order* (1901), Ross's most creative contribution to social thought; *The Foundations of Sociology* (1905); *Social Psychology* (1908); and *The Principles of Sociology* (1920). Ironically, Ross was a racist, believing in the inferiority of the non-white races and working for a restricted immigration policy for the U.S.

ROSS, ERSKINE MAYO (*b. Belpré, Va., 1845; d. Los Angeles, Calif., 1928*), California jurist. Began practice in Los Angeles, 1868. Appointed judge, U.S. district court of the southern district of California, 1887, he was advanced in 1895 to the U.S. circuit court and served there until his resignation, 1925.

Ross, George (*b. New Castle, Del., 1730; d. Philadelphia, Pa., 1779*), Pennsylvania jurist, signer of the Declaration of Independence. Practiced at Lancaster, Pa., *post* 1750; member of provincial Assembly, 1768–75. A Tory as a member of the First Continental Congress, 1774, he became a Whig, 1775; as a member of the Second Continental Congress, he worked tirelessly for the patriot cause in Pennsylvania. Vice president of the Pennsylvania constitutional convention of 1776 and a strong factor in its deliberations, he was returned to Congress in July but withdrew because of illness in January 1777. Commissioned judge of the admiralty court of Pennsylvania, 1779, he defied Congress for attempting to review his judgment in the case of the sloop *Active*.

Ross, Harold Wallace (*b. Aspen, Colo., 1892; d. Boston, Mass., 1951*), publisher and editor. Founder of the *New Yorker* magazine in 1925. Self-educated, Ross began his editing work in Paris during World War I with the army newspaper *Stars and Stripes* and in New York, he edited the publication of the new American Legion. With the backing of a friend, Raoul Fleischmann, he founded the *New Yorker* and was its editor until his death in 1951. The magazine became a success and attracted such writers as Dorothy Parker, Robert Benchley, Corey Ford, E. B. White, James Thurber, John O'Hara, Jean Stafford, and John Cheever. Artists included Peter Arno, Alan Dunn, Whitney Darrow, Jr., and Charles Addams.

Ross, James (*b. near Delta, Pa., 1762; d. Allegheny City, Pa., 1847*), lawyer. Encouraged in his study of law by Hugh H. Brackenridge, he practiced at first in Washington Co., Pa., removing to Pittsburgh, 1795. A Federalist, he served as a commissioner to treat with the insurgents during the Whiskey Insurrection, 1794, and was largely responsible for the amicable settlement. He was U.S. senator from Pennsylvania, 1794–1803.

Ross, James Delmage McKenzie (*b. Chatham, Ontario, Canada, 1872; d. Rochester, Minn., 1939*), electrical engineer. Settled in Seattle, Wash., 1901; headed Seattle municipal power plant, 1911–39; was a principal architect of the public power program instituted during administrations of President F. D. Roosevelt.

Ross, John (*b. near Lookout Mountain, Tenn., 1790; d. Washington, D.C., 1866*), Cherokee chief. Indian name, Cooweescoowe. Son of a Scottish Loyalist and a mother of one-fourth Cherokee blood. Served under Andrew Jackson in War of 1812. President, National Council of the Cherokee, 1819–26; principal chief of the eastern Cherokee, 1828–39. A leader in the opposition to westward removal of his tribe, he led his people to present Oklahoma, 1838–39, and helped make the constitution of 1839 which united the eastern and western Cherokee under a single government. Chosen chief of the united nation, 1839, he held office until his death. Failing to keep the Cherokee nation neutral at the outbreak of the Civil War, he signed a treaty of alliance with the Confederacy in October 1861 which was repudiated two years later.

Ross, Lawrence Sullivan (*b. Bentonsport, Iowa, 1838; d. 1898*), planter, Texas legislator, Confederate brigadier general. Raised in Texas, Ross was captain of a ranger company operating against the Comanche, 1859–60. Entering Confederate service, 1861, he was particularly distinguished for skill in covering Van Dorn's retreat from Corinth, Miss., 1862. As Democratic governor of Texas, 1887–91, he led the legislature in passing laws which prohibited dealing in cotton futures and closed the sale of public lands to corporations. He was president, Agricultural and Mechanical College of Texas, *post* 1891.

Ross, Martin (*b. Martin Co., N.C., 1762; d. Bethel, N.C., 1827*), Revolutionary soldier, Baptist clergyman.

Rossen, Robert (*b. New York, N.Y., 1908; d. New York, 1966*), film writer, director, and producer. Attended New York University and began a career in the theater in 1930, acting in and directing off-Broadway and summer stock companies. Offered a contract by Warner Brothers (1936–43), his filmscripts include *Marked Woman* (1937), *The Sea Wolf* (1941), and *A Walk in the Sun* (1946). Became a film director with *Johnny O'Clock* (1947) and is best remembered for directing *Body and Soul* (1947). Established his own film-producing unit (1947), and in 1949 produced, directed, and wrote *All the King's Men*, which received the Academy Award for best picture. Blacklisted for a period because of his admission before the House Un-American Activities Committee (1951) of one-time membership in the Communist party, he later wrote *The Hustler* (1961) and *Lilith* (1964).

Rosser, Thomas Lafayette (*b. Campbell Co., Va., 1836; d. near Charlottesville, Va., 1910*), Confederate major general, engineer. Raised in Texas, Rosser attended West Point, 1856–61, resigning before graduation to enter Confederate service. A brilliant artillerist and cavalryman, Rosser served after the Civil War as chief engineer of the Northern Pacific Railroad and later of the Canadian Pacific, retiring in 1886 to become a gentleman farmer.

Rossiter, Clinton Lawrence, III (*b. Philadelphia, Pa., 1917; d. Ithaca, N.Y., 1970*), political scientist, historian, lecturer, and writer. Attended Cornell and Princeton (Ph.D., 1942); his thesis brought him wide professional acclaim when published as *Constitutional Dictatorship: Crisis Government in the Modern Democracies* (1948). Taught at University of Michigan (1946) and Cornell (1946–70). The award-winning *Seedtime of the Republic* (1953) established his reputation as a diligent and meticulous scholar. *The American Presidency* (1956) was an enormous success in both the scholarly world and popular paperback market. Before his death he had lectured or given seminars at fifty colleges or universities on every continent.

Rossiter, Thomas Prichard (*b. New Haven, Conn., 1818; d. Cold Spring, N.Y., 1871*), historical and portrait painter, associate of J. F. Kensett, J. W. Casilear, and Thomas Cole.

Rossiter, William Sidney (*b. Westfield, Mass., 1861; d. Concord, N.H., 1929*), official of the Census Bureau, statistician. Author of *A Century of Population Growth . . . 1790–1900* (1909). Managed and later headed the Rumford Press.

Rostovtzeff, Michael Ivanovitch (*b. Zhitomir, Ukraine, 1870; d. New Haven, Conn., 1952*), historian and archaeologist. Studied at the University of Kiev and the University of St. Petersburg (Ph.D., 1903). Immigrated to the U.S. in 1920 where he taught at the University of Wisconsin from 1920 to 1925. Professor of ancient history and archaeology at Yale University (1925–39), continuing as director of archaeological research until 1944. Recognized as one of the leading ancient historians of his time, Rostovtzeff placed emphasis on the social and economic histories in his interpretations of the ancient civilizations. Books published in this country include *A History of the Ancient World* (1926), *The Social and Economic History of the Roman Empire* (1926), and *The Social and Economic History of the Hellenistic World* (1941). President of the American Historical Society, 1935.

Rotch, Abbott Lawrence (*b. Boston, Mass., 1861; d. Boston, 1912*), meteorologist. Great-great grandson of William Rotch; grandson of Abbott Lawrence; brother of Arthur Rotch. Graduated Massachusetts Institute of Technology, 1884. Instituted and maintained the Blue Hill Observatory, 1884–1912; was a pioneer in American aeronautics. Coauthor of *Charts of the*

Atmosphere for Aeronauts and Aviators (1911), a first attempt at mapping conditions of the upper air.

ROTCH, ARTHUR   (*b. Boston, Mass., 1850; d. Beverly, Mass., 1894*), architect. Great-great-grandson of William Rotch; grandson of Abbott Lawrence; brother of Abbott L. Rotch. Graduated Harvard, 1871; studied architecture at Massachusetts Institute of Technology and at the École des Beaux Arts, Paris, France. Benefactor of architectural departments of M.I.T. and Harvard.

ROTCH, THOMAS MORGAN   (*b. Philadelphia, Pa., 1849; d. 1914*), pediatrician. Cousin of Abbott L. and Arthur Rotch. Graduated Harvard, 1870; Harvard Medical School, 1874; studied also in Berlin, Vienna, and Heidelberg. Began practice of pediatrics at Boston, 1876; founded and became medical director of the West-End Infants' Hospital, 1881. A teacher of pediatrics at Harvard Medical School *post* 1878, he was professor of pediatrics *post* 1893. Devising a "percentage" method of artificial feeding based on a careful estimation of the caloric value of milk, he placed the feeding of infants on a scientific basis. His book, *Pediatrics: the Hygiene and Medical Treatment of Children* (1896), was one of the first to be written on that branch of medicine.

ROTCH, WILLIAM   (*b. Nantucket, Mass., 1734 o.s.; d. 1828*), whaling merchant.

ROTHAFEL, SAMUEL LIONEL   (*b. Stillwater, Minn., 1881; d. New York, N.Y., 1936*), showman, motion-picture theatre operator. Better known as "Roxy," he was raised in Brooklyn, N.Y. He made his first innovations in showing of motion-pictures while manager of the Lyric Theatre, Minneapolis, Minn., 1912. Coming to New York in the following year, he became in a short time the most successful motion-picture theatre operator in the world, successively directing the Strand, Rialto, Rivoli, and Capitol theaters in New York City. His formula included presentation of an excellent orchestra, famous singers and musicians, and precision dancing, along with important feature films. He was a pioneer also in surrounding his productions with a luxurious décor. His radio program known as "Roxy and His Gang" was a popular feature in the mid- and late-1920's.

ROTHERMEL, PETER FREDERICK   (*b. Nescopeck, Pa., 1817; d. near Linfield, Pa., 1895*), artist. Painter, among much other somewhat photographic work, of "The Battle of Gettysburg" (1871), which now hangs in the Capitol at Harrisburg, Pa.

ROTHKO, MARK   (*b. Dvinsk, Russia, 1903; d. New York, N.Y., 1970*), painter. Arrived in the United States in 1913, and in the 1920's attended Yale and the Arts Students League. His early work consisted primarily of representational landscapes, still lifes, and nudes; participated in his first exhibition in 1928. During the following decade his subjects expanded to include cityscapes and genre scenes. Participated in the Works Progress Administration Federal Art Project (1936–37). One of "the Ten," a group that rebelled against the regional style prevailing in contemporary American art and that admired the innovative works of Milton Avery and European modernists. His work of the late 1930's reflects the social and political climate of the decade; a disquieting mood prevails in these works, coupled with a simplicity of composition. Explored ancient and Christian myths as subject matter for works, 1938–43. In 1944 he became interested in surrealists and painted Miró-like fantasies. By the mid-1940's his work was frequently included in major museum exhibitions. Began painting in a purely abstract style in 1947. By 1950 he was painting in the style for which he is best known; his brilliant-colored vertical canvases usually bore two or three frontally situated rectangles balanced one above the other. These works were primarily in red, orange, yellow, and violet. During the late 1950's and 1960's he worked primarily in a dark or muted palette; he reintroduced brilliant colors in his final works.

ROTHROCK, JOSEPH TRIMBLE   (*b. McVeytown, Pa., 1839; d. West Chester, Pa., 1922*), physician, Union soldier, botanist. M.D., University of Pennsylvania, 1867. After practicing at Wilkes-Barre, Pa., he served as botanist and surgeon to the government survey of Colorado, New Mexico, and California under Lt. G. N. Wheeler, describing many new plants in his report (published 1878). Professor of botany, University of Pennsylvania, 1877–1904, he was a leader in the forest conservation movement and the first Pennsylvania commissioner of forestry.

ROTHWELL, RICHARD PENNEFATHER   (*b. Oxford, Ontario, Canada, 1836; d. 1901*), mining engineer, editor. Worked in the United States *post* 1864 mainly as consultant to operators of anthracite mines; was a co-founder of the American Institute of Mining Engineers, 1871. Coeditor with Rossiter W. Raymond of the *Engineering and Mining Journal post* 1874 and sole editor *post* 1890.

ROULSTONE, GEORGE   (*b. Boston, Mass., 1767; d. 1804*), printer. Accompanied Governor William Blount to Tennessee; issued first number of the *Knoxville Gazette* at Hawkins Court House (Rogersville), Nov. 5, 1791, continuing publication (except for a brief period in 1798) until his death. As territorial and later state printer, Roulstone produced a number of volumes of official papers and a few general publications. His most important production was the *Laws of the State of Tennessee* (1803).

ROUND, WILLIAM MARSHALL FITTS   (*b. Pawtucket, R.I., 1845; d. Acushnet, Mass., 1906*), journalist, prison reformer. Corresponding secretary, Prison Association of New York, 1882–1900; introduced cottage system at Burnham Industrial Farm, Canaan, N.Y., as director *ca.* 1888.

ROUQUETTE, ADRIEN EMMANUEL   (*b. New Orleans, La., 1813; d. New Orleans, 1887*), Roman Catholic clergyman, missionary to the Choctaw, poet. Brother of François D. Rouquette. Author, among other works, of *Les Savanes* (1841) which won him the title of "the Lamartine of America," *La Thébaïde en Amérique* (1852), and *La Nouvelle Atala* (1879).

ROUQUETTE, FRANCOIS DOMINIQUE   (*b. Bayou Lacombe, La., 1810; d. Louisiana, 1890*), poet. Brother of Adrien E. Rouquette. An eccentric genius, he was author of a number of works of which *Meschacébéennes* (1839) and *Fleurs d'Amérique* (1856) received very high praise from notable French critics.

ROURKE, CONSTANCE MAYFIELD   (*b. Cleveland, Ohio, 1885; d. Grand Rapids, Mich., 1941*), folklorist, cultural historian. A.B., Vassar College, 1907. Taught English at Vassar, 1910–15; concentrated thereafter on research and writing in the areas of American folklore and social history. She was author, among other books, of *Trumpets of Jubilee* (1927), *Troupers of the Gold Coast* (1928), *American Humor* (1931), *Davy Crockett* (1934), *Audubon* (1936), and *The Roots of American Culture* (1942).

ROUS, FRANCIS PEYTON   (*b. Baltimore, Md., 1879; d. New York, N.Y., 1970*), medical researcher. Attended Johns Hopkins University and Medical School (M.D., 1905). Joined Rockefeller Institute for Medical Research (1909); became a full member of the institute (1920) and a member emeritus (1945). He published the findings of his most famous discovery—that a virus is the causative agent of a chicken sarcoma—in 1911; in 1966 he received the Nobel Prize in medicine for his discovery of tumor-inducing viruses. Editor of *Journal of Experimental Medicine* for almost fifty years. Elected to the National Academy of Sciences

(1927); received the Albert Lasker Award (1958), the National Medal of Science (1966), and other prestigious awards.

ROUSSEAU, HARRY HARWOOD (*b.* Troy, N.Y., 1870; *d. at sea, en route to Panama, 1930*), naval officer, engineer. Served on Isthmian Canal Commission under George W. Goethals, 1907–14, in special charge of design and construction of the Panama Canal terminals; later as rear admiral, held important navy administration posts and headed the shipyard division under the Shipping Board during World War I.

ROUSSEAU, LOVELL HARRISON (*b. near Stanford, Ky., 1818; d. New Orleans, La., 1869*), lawyer, Kentucky and Indiana legislator, Union major general. Received formal cession of Alaska from the Russians, 1867, as U.S. representative there.

ROVENSTINE, EMERY ANDREW (*b. Atwood, Ind., 1895; d. New York, N.Y., 1960*), physician and anesthesiologist. Studied at Wabash College, Indiana University (M.D., 1928), and at the University of Wisconsin. Taught at the University of Wisconsin from 1931 to 1935. Headed the anesthesia department at Bellevue Hospital and New York University from 1935. Instrumental in making anesthesiology a regulated speciality, Rovenstine helped found The American Board of Anesthesiology in 1937. Member of the National Research Council (1941–46). Full recognition for the legitimacy of anesthetists came with the creation of the American Board of Anesthesia in 1941.

ROWAN, JOHN (*b. near York, Pa., 1773; d. Louisville, Ky., 1843*), Kentucky jurist, legislator, and congressman. A liberal leader in the fight against the Kentucky judiciary, 1823–24, he served as U.S. senator, Democrat, 1825–31. He worked for reform of the federal judiciary and abolition of imprisonment for debt.

ROWAN, STEPHEN CLEGG (*b. near Dublin, Ireland, 1808; d. Washington, D.C., 1890*), naval officer. Raised in Ohio. Appointed midshipman, 1826; commended for gallant service in the Seminole War; was particularly distinguished in war with Mexico. Executive officer of the *Cyane*, he shared in the capture of Monterey, Calif., July 1846, and, in command of a battalion of seamen and marines, fought with the army in the retaking of Los Angeles and the relief of San José. His Civil War service was outstanding. In February 1862, he cooperated with General Burnside in the capture of Roanoke Island and later in the capture of New Bern, N.C. He performed outstanding service also at Charleston, S.C., July–September 1863. Promoted rear admiral, 1866, he retired as vice admiral, 1889.

ROWE, LEO STANTON (*b. McGregor, Iowa, 1871; d. Washington, D.C., 1946*), political economist, diplomat. Raised in Philadelphia, Pa. Ph.B., Wharton School, University of Pennsylvania, 1890. Ph.D., University of Halle, 1892. LL.B., University of Pennsylvania, 1895. While teaching political science at Pennsylvania, 1896–1917 (professor *post* 1904), he accepted a number of diplomatic assignments concerning U.S.-Latin American relations, culminating in his secretaryship of the U.S.-Mexico Mixed Claims Commission, 1916–17. Impressed with knowledge and tact, President Wilson appointed him to supervise Latin American affairs as assistant secretary of the treasury, 1917–19, and as chief of division in the State Department, 1919–20. Thereafter until his death, he was director general of the Pan American Union.

ROWE, LYNWOOD THOMAS (*b. Waco, Tex., 1912; d. El Dorado, Ark., 1961*), baseball pitcher. Signed by the Detroit Tigers (1932) and played in three World Series (1934, 1935, and 1940), winning the world championship in 1935. Sold to the Brooklyn Dodgers (1942), then to the Philadelphia Phillies (1943); in 1949 he asked for his release. Managed an Eastern League farm club at Williamsport, Pa. (1951), served as pitching coach for Detroit (1954–55), and in 1957 became a scout for Detroit.

ROWELL, CHESTER HARVEY (*b. Bloomington, Ill., 1867; d. Berkeley, Calif., 1948*), journalist, politician. Ph.B., University of Michigan, 1888; studied also at universities of Halle and Berlin; taught languages at several colleges and at University of Illinois between 1894 and 1898. Editor and manager of the *Fresno* (Calif.) *Republican*, 1898–1920; editor, 1932–35, and editorial columnist, 1935–47, of the *San Francisco Chronicle*. He was a leader in founding the Lincoln–Roosevelt League, 1907, and in the struggle to convert the California Republican party to progressivism and independence of the Southern Pacific Railroad. A close friend and adviser of Hiram Johnson, he parted company with him on the question of U.S. entry into the League of Nations, which Rowell favored.

ROWELL, GEORGE PRESBURY (*b. Concord, Vt., 1838; d. Poland Springs, Maine, 1908*), advertising agent. Devised the "list system" *ca.* 1865; founded *Printers' Ink*, July 1888.

ROWLAND, HENRY AUGUSTUS (*b. Honesdale, Pa., 1848; d. 1901*), physicist. Graduated Rensselaer Polytechnic, 1870. Taught science and physics at Wooster University and at Rensselaer; was chosen first professor of physics, Johns Hopkins, 1875. Rowland's principal contributions to physics were of three kinds: those which involved original concepts, those concerned with accurate measurement of physical constants, and those in which engineering talent was most conspicuous. His first important investigation resulted in "On Magnetic Permeability, and the Maximum of Magnetism of Iron, Steel, and Nickel" (*Philosophical Magazine*, August 1873) and provided the basis for subsequent study of both permanent and induced magnetization; it was the starting point for calculations for the design of dynamos and transformers. A second important experiment, performed during the winter of 1875–76, answered in the affirmative the question whether a moving charged conductor would have an effect upon a magnet similar to that of an electric current; this was of great significance in connection with the modern theory of electrons. For his study of spectra, he combined the principle of the grating with that of the concave mirror, eventually producing gratings ruled on concave surfaces thus obviating many of the difficulties inherent in the use of plane gratings. In order to produce gratings more accurate than any previously known, he designed a ruling machine which virtually eliminated errors. In the field of measurements, he obtained values for the mechanical equivalent of heat, the ohm, the ratio of the electric units, and the wave-lengths of various spectra. Teaching less by precept than by example, Rowland was a severe taskmaster in the laboratory.

ROWLAND, HENRY COTTRELL (*b. New York, N.Y., 1874; d. Washington, D.C., 1933*), physician, traveler and adventurer, author.

ROWLAND, THOMAS FITCH (*b. New Haven, Conn., 1831; d. New York, N.Y., 1907*), boat builder, engine designer. President of the Continental Iron Works *post* 1860, Rowland built the original *Monitor* for John Ericsson, and upon its completion built the monitors *Montauk*, *Catskill* and *Passaic* and also the double-turret monitor *Onondaga*.

ROWLANDS, WILLIAM (*b. London, England, 1807; d. Utica, N.Y., 1866*), Calvinistic Methodist clergyman, editor. Came to America, 1836; ministered mainly in New York City and in Oneida Co., N.Y. Founded and edited *Y Cyfaill*, influential Welsh language periodical (first number, January 1838).

ROWLANDSON, MARY WHITE (*b. probably England, ca. 1635; d. ca. 1678*), Indian captive, author. Daughter of one of the original proprietors of Lancaster, Mass., she was married to the minister there *ca.* 1656 and on Feb. 10, 1675/6, was carried into captivity when the Indians attacked and burnt Lancaster. Remaining in captivity for 11 weeks, she was ransomed and returned with her two surviving children; in 1677, she removed with her family to Wethersfield, Conn. Her narrative of her captivity entitled *The Soveraignty & Goodness of God, Together with the Faithfulness of His Promises Displayed, etc.* was first published in Cambridge, Mass., 1682, and became one of the most widely read pieces of 17th-century American prose.

ROWSE, SAMUEL WORCESTER (*b. Bath, Maine, 1822; d. Morristown, N.J., 1901*), painter, illustrator, lithographer. Gained wide reputation for his delicate, well-characterized crayon portraits of contemporary celebrities.

ROWSON, SUSANNA HASWELL (*b. Portsmouth, England,* ca. *1762; d. Boston, Mass., 1824*), novelist, actress, educator. Cousin of Anthony Haswell. Raised in Massachusetts, daughter of an English officer, she returned to England, 1778; her first novel, *Victoria,* was published, 1786, and received favorable London notice. Later in the year, she married William Rowson. Three works which she published in 1788 and 1789 added little to her reputation, but early in 1791 she produced, and published in London, a novel which was to make her famous—*Charlotte, a Tale of Truth.* Sentimental and didactic, supposedly based on an actual affair of Col. John Montrésor, the book captivated the American fancy when it was reprinted in Philadelphia, 1794; it became the chief American "best seller" before *Uncle Tom's Cabin.* On the business failure of her husband, 1792, the family turned for support to the stage and were recruited in England by Thomas Wignell for his Philadelphia company. They acted mostly in minor parts in Philadelphia, Baltimore and Annapolis, 1793–96, and Mrs. Rowson wrote and adapted plays for the company. The Rowsons went to the Federal Street Theatre, Boston, in 1796; in the spring of 1797, Mrs. Rowson left the stage to devote the rest of her life to conducting a school for girls in or near Boston. She served as editor of the *Boston Weekly Magazine,* 1802–05, and continued to write for its successor *The Boston Magazine;* she also wrote for *The Monthly Anthology* and *The New England Galaxy.* Among other books which she published were *Reuben and Rachel* (1798), *Miscellaneous Poems* (1804), *Sarah, the Exemplary Wife* (1813) and a sequel to *Charlotte* (*Temple*) entitled *Charlotte's Daughter* (1828).

"ROXY." *See* ROTHAFEL, SAMUEL LIONEL.

ROYALL, ANNE NEWPORT (*b. Maryland, 1769; d. Washington, D.C., 1854*), author. Of uncertain parentage, she was raised in the house of William Royall, an eccentric Virginia farmer and scholar who undertook her education and married her in 1797. Engaged in a long litigation over his property after his death, she started out to earn her own living in 1824 by traveling over the United States and publishing accounts of her journeys. Vigorous, straightforward, truly liberal in her reforming zeal but indiscreet and often amateurish, she made herself the terror of the national capital and was noted especially for her ability to uncover graft. Her attacks against Presbyterians led to her trial and conviction in 1829 on the trumped-up charge of being a common scold. Her paper *Paul Pry* ran from December 1831 to November 1836; *The Huntress* began in December 1836 and was continued until just before her death. Among her ten volumes of travel and comment were *Sketches of History, Life and Manners in the United States* (1826), *The Black Book* (1828–29), and *Mrs. Royall's Southern Tour* (1830–31). These and her other works deserve to survive as valuable sources for study of U.S. social history in her time.

ROYCE, JOSIAH (*b. Grass Valley, Calif., 1855; d. Cambridge, Mass., 1916*), philosopher, educator. Child of a pioneer California family, Royce was indebted to his mother for his early education, both religious and secular. The family settled in San Francisco ca. 1866, where he attended school and spent many of his leisure hours in the Mercantile Library. The intellectual and moral influence of the California environment was lifelong in him and was effective in two of his later books, *California . . . A Study of American Character* (1886) and *The Feud of Oakfield Creek* (1887). Shy and sensitive, he felt a wistful need of social relations. The belief that a man's fullest development can be found only in the life of the "community" became a major topic in his philosophizing. His philosophical development consists essentially in the interaction of his instinctive Protestantism and moral individualism with the pantheistic, aesthetic doctrines which he acquired from Lotze, Schelling, Schopenhauer, Fichte, and Hegel. Graduating from the University of California, 1875, he spent the next year mainly at Göttingen and Leipzig; in 1876 he was invited to be one of the first twenty fellows appointed at the new Johns Hopkins University. A fellow in literature, he received the Ph.D. degree, 1878, for study in the history of philosophy and German literature in the 18th and 19th centuries.

While teaching English literature at the University of California, 1878–82, he schooled himself in the technicalities of philosophy by continuous reading and thinking. He reexamined Kant and Hegel and made a study of contemporary writers such as William James, Charles S. Peirce, and the psychologists Wundt and Bain. In an article of January 1882 he announced his adhesion to the school of post-Kantian idealism. Encouraged by William James to venture into philosophy, Royce went to Harvard to substitute for James in the fall and winter term, 1882–83; he remained at Harvard during the balance of his days. Soon earning the good opinion of students, colleagues, and President Eliot, he became assistant professor, 1885, professor, 1892, and in 1914, received the Alford Professorship of Natural Religion and Moral Philosophy. During the earlier years of his career, Royce's development was greatly influenced by association with William James, and he did extensive work in psychology, publishing *Outlines of Psychology* (1903). Although his friendship with James was lifelong, Royce soon manifested a divergence of view from James. As early as 1883 Royce noted in his diary a criterion of truth which he often reaffirmed. A given statement is true, he said, when "the contradictory of this statement would involve this statement itself." The mind thinks what (if it is to think at all) it cannot avoid thinking without contradicting itself. Under this dialectical compulsion, the mind escapes the skepticism of the passing moment and the relativities of a merely human experience—all of which is widely removed from James both in matter and doctrine. Royce, as the protagonist of monism, and James, as the friend of pluralism, became symbolic of a good-humored philosophical controversy.

Royce's first major philosophical work was *The Religious Aspect of Philosophy* (1885), in which he set forth a religious view of the world which does not imply but is consistent with a positive creed. The method of the book is a variant of the method of doubt and the argument falls into two main parts. The first part is an appeal to the thinker to postulate what is not given in experience and asks why should religion not be permitted to postulate a goodness at the heart of things which satisfies the highest moral needs, as science postulates the simplicity and orderliness of nature. In the second part of the argument, Royce supports postulate by proof and arrives at his famous "Absolute," or universal knower. The general metaphysical implications are evident. They are idealistic and monistic. In *The Conception of God* (1897) Royce attempts to reconcile the human prerogatives of freedom and responsibility with his metaphysical Absolute by insisting that the principle of individuation is choice or preference, that the Absolute is an individual consisting ultimately in a sheer act of will, and that this Absolute Will is parceled out among human beings, each of which wills independently within its own province. In *The Spirit of Modern Philosophy* (1892), Royce treats his subject with humor and eloquence and handles his beloved Romanticists together with Kant, Hegel, and Schopenhauer with tenderness and insight. *The World and the Individual* (1900, 1901) is the most important of his systematic works. In the first volume Royce argues an unqualified idealism; the constructive portion of the book gives to this characteristic doctrine, however, a new and significant development. In *The Religious Aspect of Philosophy* Royce had used the term "thought" to designate the processes of the Absolute, while in *The Conception of God* the emphasis had been shifted to "will." In the present book the term "purpose" plays a mediating role. Thought is essentially purposive. The key to its nature is found in the double meaning of ideas. An idea's "internal meaning" consists of the universals or ideal possibilities which constitute *what* is judged; its "external meaning" consists in the particular object to which it refers, and which constitutes that which is judged *about*. This object, while it lies beyond the idea, is embraced within mind as the experience to which the idea points as its own "fulfilment." The second volume of *The World and the Individual* is devoted to cosmological and practical applications.

Post 1900, Royce's interests developed in opposite but complementary directions toward a more technical and specialized treatment of logic, and toward a more popular treatment of moral, social, and religious problems; he was one of the first Americans after Charles S. Peirce to enter the field of symbolic logic and the philosophical foundations of mathematics. In *The Philosophy of Loyalty* (1908) he outlines a basis for ethical action; in *The Problem of Christianity* (1913) he gives his final interpretation of the Christian faith and also his most thorough treatment of the subject of religion. He selected as the three central Christian ideas, the Pauline Church, the "lost" state of the natural man, and atonement. These ideas he interpreted in terms of the "community," as being the supreme object of the individual's loyalty, by estrangement from which man is lost, and by whose spirit and service he is restored. The effect of these ethical and religious studies was to bring the metaphysical Absolute into nearer relation to man. The Absolute assumes the form of a personified "Beloved Community," to which the individual man was bound by a sort of patriotic fervor, or blend of self-sacrifice and self-aggrandizement. Interpretations are triadic, involving a sign, an interpreter, and a second mind to which the interpretation is communicated. Thus, Royce argues, interpretation involved a *community* of two or more minds. Knowledge is creative of being, but knowledge is now construed as a social affair—a community of interpretation.

After the death of William James, Royce was the most influential American philosopher of his day and the leading exponent in America of post-Kantian idealism of which he represented the voluntaristic wing. He may be said to stand close to Fichte, but he was distinguished from German neo-Fichteans not only by his profound metaphysical passion but also by the English and American strains in his inheritance. Any mere doctrinal classification of Royce is inadequate, for he was a man of rich experience and varied talents. His defects as a thinker and writer flowed from a tendency to prolixity. His processes of mind were powerful, massive but laborious.

ROYCE, RALPH (*b. Marquette, Mich., 1890; d. Homestead Air Force Base, Fla., 1965*), U.S. Air Force officer. Graduated from the U.S. Military Academy (1913) and attended the Signal Corps Aviation School (1915–16). Assigned to the First Aero Squadron, assuming command of the squadron with U.S. entry into World War I; his dash and intrepidity during missions in France won him the Croix de Guerre. After the war he held several commands, and in 1941 became military attaché for air in London and was promoted to brigadier general. World War II commands included the Northeast Sector of the Allied Air Forces in Australia and U.S. Air Forces in the Middle East, headquartered in Cairo (1943); he was air officer aboard the cruiser *Augusta* on D day. He retired as a major general in 1946.

ROYE, EDWARD JAMES (*b. Newark, Ohio, 1815; d. at sea, off Liberia, 1872*), schoolteacher, businessman. Leading merchant of Liberia, *post ca.* 1848. Inaugurated fifth president of Liberia, January 1871, he was deposed in October on charges of mishandling a loan and boundary dispute with England.

ROYSTER, JAMES FINCH (*b. Raleigh, N.C., 1880; d. Richmond, Va., 1930*), philologist, educator. Graduated Wake Forest College, 1900; Ph.D., University of Chicago, 1907. Taught at Universities of North Carolina and Texas. Dean of college of liberal arts, University of North Carolina, 1922–25; dean of graduate school, 1925–29.

RUARK, ROBERT CHESTER (*b. Southport, N.C., 1915; d. London, England, 1965*), journalist and novelist. Attended University of North Carolina (B.A., 1935). Copyboy for the Washington, D.C., *Daily News* (1937), becoming assistant city editor by 1942. Washington correspondent for the Newspaper Enterprise Association Service (1942–45) and for Scripps-Howard Newspaper Alliance (1945). In 1946 he became a columnist for Scripps-Howard and United Feature Service in New York. Author of the novels *Something of Value* (1955), *The Old Man and the Boy* (1957), and *Uhuru* (1962).

RUBIN, ISIDOR CLINTON (*b. Vienna, Austria, 1883; d. London, England, 1958*), gynecologist. Studied at the City College of New York and at Columbia University (M.D., 1905). Working at New York's Mt. Sinai and Beth Israel Hospitals and teaching at Columbia and New York University, Rubin was the foremost gynecologist of his generation, specializing in fertility. He discovered that the ovum was conveyed to the uterus by the peristaltic waves of the fallopian tubes. In 1919, Rubin performed the first successful test to determine the patency of the fallopian tubes; this work brought him international fame.

RUBINOW, ISAAC MAX (*b. Grodno, Russia, 1875; d. New York, N.Y., 1936*), physician, social worker, economic statistician, Jewish leader. Came to America, 1893. Graduated Columbia, 1895; M.D., New York University, 1898. Practicing among the poor, Rubinow became convinced that ill health was as much an economic as a medical problem. In 1903 he gave up medical practice to become an expert in economics and statistics in the U.S. Department of Agriculture, the first of a succession of posts he held in the federal government. His report of European legislation on industrial accidents (1911) helped lay the foundation for state workmen's compensation laws passed, 1911–20. Leaving federal service, he worked for a time on studies of insurance for private companies and associations, but he is particularly remembered as a pioneer in the American social security movement. He was author of, among other books, *The Care of the Aged* (1931) and *The Quest for Security* (1934).

RUBINSTEIN, HELENA (*b. Cracow, Poland, 1870; d. New York, N.Y., 1965*), beauty expert and cosmetics manufacturer. Attended the medical school of the University of Cracow and was sent by her family to Australia in 1890. She took with her a supply of a special face cream that had long been used by her family and established (1902) the country's first beauty salon in Melbourne. Within a few years she amassed a small fortune from the sale of the cream; she subsequently invented and sold a wide variety of other preparations. In 1915 she moved to the United States and began to build a worldwide corporation. By the 1920's she had salons throughout Europe. World War II forced the closing of most European salons, and she contributed to the war effort by creating cosmetics for disfigured servicemen. In the 1940's she opened salons in Latin America, and in the 1950's, in Japan. She was also widely known as a collector of art, jewelry, and antiques.

RUBLEE, GEORGE (*b. Madison, Wis., 1868; d. New York, N.Y., 1957*), lawyer and statesman. Studied at Harvard University (LL.B., 1895). Rublee entered public life in 1913 as Louis D. Brandeis' liaison with Congress; in 1914, he wrote the key provision of the Federal Trade Commission Act which was a "decisive event in the history of the antitrust program." In 1918–19, President Wilson sent Rublee to the London Conference of the Allied Maritime Transport Council, which pooled and allocated shipping for war use. In 1938, Roosevelt appointed him director of the Intergovernmental Committee on Refugees. He served until 1939, when he resigned because of the unwillingness of governments to accept Jewish refugees.

RUBLEE, HORACE (*b. Berkshire, Vt., 1829; d. Milwaukee, Wis., 1896*), editor, diplomat. Raised in Wisconsin. Editorial writer and co-proprietor, *Wisconsin State Journal*, 1853–68, Rublee was active in the Republican party from its birth. After serving as U.S. minister to Switzerland, 1869–76, he returned to journalism, and was associated *post* 1881 with the *Daily Milwaukee Republican* and the *Milwaukee Sentinel*.

RUBY, JACK L. (*b. Chicago, Ill., 1911; d. Dallas, Tex., 1967*), assassin of Lee Harvey Oswald. A quick-tempered, disobedient, and incorrigible youth, he engaged in commercial ventures on Chicago streets until 1947, from which time until 1963 his main source of income was the operation of nightclubs and dance halls in Dallas. On Nov. 24, 1963, two days after Oswald assassinated President John Kennedy, as Oswald was being transferred to another jail, Ruby shot and killed him while a national television audience witnessed the event. Ruby maintained he shot Oswald to spare Mrs. Kennedy the ordeal of returning to Dallas to testify in a trial. He was convicted of murder and sentenced to death, but his conviction was reversed on appeal (1966); he died in jail while awaiting a second trial. Various theories attempted to link Ruby and Oswald with a conspiracy to kill President Kennedy, but none of several official investigations found any proof for these allegations.

RUCKER, GEORGE ("NAP") (*b. Crabapple, Ga., 1884; d. Crabapple, 1970*), major-league baseball player. First played professionally in 1904 with the Atlanta Crackers, then joined Augusta's South Atlantic League team (1905–06). He signed with the Brooklyn Dodgers in 1907 as a pitcher and quickly established himself as the best left-handed pitcher in the major leagues. Despite the weakness of the Dodgers of his time, he pitched a perfect game in 1908 and had thirty-eight shutouts in his career; his sixteen strikeouts against the Cardinals in 1909 was his greatest performance, giving him the National League's single-game strikeout record until 1933. He retired as a player in 1916, then became a Dodger scout.

RUCKSTULL, FREDERICK WELLINGTON (*b. Breitenbach, Alsace, France, 1853; d. New York, N.Y., 1942*), sculptor. Immigrated with parents to the United States, 1855; raised in St. Louis, Mo. Studied at Washington University art school, and in Paris with G. Boulanger and C. Lefèvre; had his studio in New York City *post* 1892. Dedicated to the neo-Baroque classicism of his time, he practiced with success and was especially gifted as an organizer and coordinator of large sculpture projects, e.g., the Dewey Arch in New York City, and the Appellate Court Building, also in New York.

RUDGE, WILLIAM EDWIN (*b. Brooklyn, N.Y., 1876; d. 1931*), printer, typographer. Influential in the encouragement of good design and fine printing *post* 1912.

RUDITSKY, BARNEY (*b. London, England, 1898; d. Los Angeles, Calif., 1962*), policeman and private detective. Joined New York City police force in 1921; promoted to detective in 1924. Working with Detective Johnny Broderick, they became leaders of a special antigangster squad assigned to combat organized crime in New York City. His exploits as a detective during Prohibition became the basis for the television series "The Lawless Years." Became a private detective after World War II and moved to Los Angeles (1948), where he worked for and against Hollywood stars. His most famous and bizarre episode involved his being hired by Joe Di Maggio to spy on his then-wife, Marilyn Monroe.

RUDKIN, MARGARET FOGARTY (*b. New York, N.Y., 1897; d. New Haven, Conn., 1967*), business executive. In 1937, after a doctor suggested that chemical additives in commercially baked goods were aggravating her son's asthmatic condition, she began baking her own whole wheat bread with stone-ground flour; when her son's condition improved, the allergist asked her to make the bread for other patients, which generated a sizable mail-order business. From that small beginning, she established Pepperidge Farm, a business that provided bakery products for people who wanted the quality of homemade goods and were willing to pay for them. Through favorable local and then national publicity, the business grew at a phenomenal rate; 1960 profits were $1.3 million on annual sales of $32 million. In 1960 she sold the company to Campbell Soup Company for $28 million in Campbell stock.

RUEF, ABRAHAM (*b. San Francisco, Calif., 1864; d. San Francisco, 1936*), lawyer. Graduated University of California, 1883; Hastings College of Law, 1886. Rose to political power through control of the Union Labor party *post* 1901 and became boss of his native city. Engaged in numerous corrupt practices, he was exposed by, among others, Fremont Older, Francis J. Heney, and James D. Phelan. After trial and conviction, he was in prison, 1911–15.

RUFFIN, EDMUND (*b. Prince George Co., Va., 1794; d. Amelia Co., Va., 1865*), agricultural experimenter and writer, farmer. After making trial of the use of marl on his worn-out fields (adopting a suggestion from Sir Humphrey Davy's *Elements of Agricultural Chemistry*, he concluded that soils once fertile but reduced by harmful cultivation had lost their power to retain manures. He believed that this condition could be corrected by the application of calcareous earths and that a fertility equal to or greater than the original could be acquired by the use thereafter of fertilizers, crop rotation, drainage, and good plowing. Presenting his theories and results in written form on several occasions, he issued them in 1832 in a volume entitled *An Essay on Calcareous Manures* which had wide influence. Active in the organization of agricultural societies, he became agricultural surveyor of South Carolina, 1842, publishing a report in the next year which became a landmark in the agricultural history of that state. He was a prolific writer on other topics as well as agriculture, especially in defense of slavery and states' rights. Originally a Whig, he became a Democrat as the struggle over states' rights developed and was one of the first secessionists in Virginia. He originated the League of United Southerners, was invited to sit in three secession conventions, and as a volunteer with the Charleston Palmetto Guard, fired the first shot from Morris Island against Fort Sumter. On the collapse of the Confederacy, he ended his own life.

RUFFIN, THOMAS (*b. King and Queen Co., Va., 1787; d. Hillsboro, N.C., 1870*), jurist. Graduated College of New Jersey (Princeton), 1805; studied law in Petersburg, Va., and in North

Carolina under Archibald D. Murphey; practiced in Hillsboro *post* 1808. After holding several minor court posts, he served as associate justice of the North Carolina supreme court, 1829–33, and as chief justice, 1833–52; in 1858 he was called back to the supreme court, but served for only one year. An ardent Unionist, he denied any constitutional right of secession, but after the failure of a compromise which he offered the North Carolina secession convention, he voted for the ordinance and supported the Confederate war effort. In constitutional law, the authorities rank him with John Marshall and Lemuel Shaw. He was equally noted in common law and equity.

RUFFNER, HENRY (*b. Shenandoah Co., Va., 1790; d. 1861*), Presbyterian clergyman, educator. Graduated Washington College, Lexington, Va., 1813. Taught at Washington College, 1819–48, at times acted as president, and was president in fact, 1836–48. In his *Address to the People of West Virginia* (1847), he argued for confinement of slavery to the region east of the Blue Ridge and its gradual abolition there on broad grounds of public policy.

RUFFNER, WILLIAM HENRY (*b. Lexington, Va., 1824; d. Asheville, N.C., 1908*), Presbyterian clergyman, educator. Son of Henry Ruffner. Graduated Washington College, 1842. As Virginia state superintendent of public education, 1870–82, Ruffner drew a school law which became a model for other Southern states and secured its enactment by the legislature. For his services to the schools, especially for his solution of the problem of the relation of church and state in the educational field, he has been called the "Horace Mann of the South."

RUGER, THOMAS HOWARD (*b. Lima, N.Y., 1833; d. Stamford, Conn., 1907*), lawyer, Union soldier. Graduated West Point, 1854. Commissioned colonel of the 3rd Wisconsin Infantry early in the Civil War, he distinguished himself at Antietam. Promoted brigadier general, 1862, he succeeded to divisional command at Gettysburg; in October 1863 he was transferred to brigade command in the West, took part in all of Sherman's operations, and won brevet of major general of volunteers for service at the battle of Franklin, November 1864. Remaining in the army, he was superintendent at West Point, 1871–76, and saw a variety of service in the West and Northwest. He retired as regular major general, 1897.

RUGG, ARTHUR PRENTICE (*b. Sterling, Mass., 1862; d. Sterling, 1938*), lawyer, jurist. Graduated Amherst, 1883. Appointed associate judge of the supreme judicial court of Massachusetts, 1906, he was made chief justice in 1911 and retained this position until his death. His almost 3,000 opinions were uniformly excellent and affected very nearly the entire body of the law of the commonwealth.

RUGG, HAROLD ORDWAY (*b. Fitchburg, Mass., 1886; d. Woodstock, N.Y., 1960*), educator and author. Studied at Dartmouth College and the University of Illinois (Ph.D., 1915). A social reconstructionist with a speciality in curriculum design, Rugg taught at Columbia University's Teachers College from 1920 to 1951. His major publications were fourteen pamphlets entitled "Man and His Changing Society" published between 1929 and 1945. Controversial, these works were critiques of American society that were termed subversive by 1940, and precipitated one of the most sensational cases of textbook censorship in American educational history.

RUGGLES, SAMUEL BULKLEY (*b. New Milford, Conn., 1800; d. Fire Island, N.Y., 1881*), lawyer, New York canal commissioner, 1839–58. Practiced in New York City *post* 1821; developed Gramercy Park, New York City, 1831, and was also active in promoting creation of Union Square. He was a strong

influence in the liberalization of Columbia College and its development into a university.

RUGGLES, TIMOTHY (*b. Rochester, Mass., 1711; d. Wilmot, N.S., Canada, 1795*), Massachusetts provincial legislator and jurist, soldier, Loyalist. Graduated Harvard, 1732. Rose to rank of brigadier general in the French and Indian War. Elected president of the Stamp Act Congress, 1765, over James Otis, Ruggles would not sign the petitions which were drawn up, alleging scruples of conscience. A supporter of Governor Thomas Hutchinson, he was made a Mandamus Councilor, 1774, and late in that year strove to form an association of Loyalists pledged not to acknowledge or submit to the pretended authority of any congress. Appointed to command three companies of Tory volunteers to be called the Loyal American Associators, November 1775, Ruggles was for a brief time with the British on Long Island. Banished from Massachusetts, 1778, his estates were confiscated and he removed to Nova Scotia, 1783.

RUHL, ARTHUR BROWN (*b. Rockford, Ill., 1876; d. Queens, N.Y., 1935*), journalist, foreign correspondent, dramatic critic. Author, among other books, of *White Nights and other Russian Impressions* (1917).

RUHRÄH, JOHN (*b. Chillicothe, Ohio, 1872; d. 1935*), pediatrician. Studied at present University of Maryland and at Johns Hopkins; practiced *post* 1894 in Baltimore, Md., and taught at University of Maryland, with intervals of study abroad. Made first collective investigation of actinomycosis in United States, 1899–1900; introduced use of soybean in infant dietetics, 1909. Author of *Pediatrics of the Past* (1925) and other works, he contributed articles on his specialty to most of the modern encyclopedias and systems of medicine.

RUMFORD, BENJAMIN THOMPSON, COUNT. *See* THOMPSON, BENJAMIN.

RUML, BEARDSLEY (*b. Cedar Rapids, Iowa, 1894; d. Danbury, Conn., 1960*), publicist. Studied at Dartmouth College and at the University of Chicago (Ph.D., 1917). Ruml successfully combined academic, business, and government service in his career. From 1921 to 1930, he was director of the Laura Spelman Rockefeller Memorial; from 1931 to 1934, he was dean of the social science division at the University of Chicago; and from 1934 to 1951, he was treasurer, chairman, and director of Macy's Department Store in New York while at the same time serving as director of the New York Federal Reserve Bank (1937–47). But Ruml is especially remembered for his "pay-as-you-go" income tax plan. Because of the difficulties most American servicemen encountered in paying taxes for their civilian earnings when they were earning minimal wages in the armed forces, Ruml devised what is essentially the withholding tax plan we know today, passed in 1943 as the Tax Payment Act.

RUMMEL, JOSEPH FRANCIS (*b. Steinmauern, Germany, 1876; d. New Orleans, La., 1964*), Roman Catholic archbishop. Attended St. Anselm's College, St. Joseph's Seminary ("Dunwoodie"), North American College in Rome, and Pontifical Urban University; ordained in 1902. Served as a curate, pastor, and vicar in various churches in New York State, 1903–28, when he was named ordinary of Omaha. Promoted to the New Orleans archbishopric (1935); his jurisdiction covered 13,200 square miles in twenty-three Louisiana parishes. He was a staunch defender of human rights, especially of racial justice, and was the first Catholic bishop to publicize a resolution upholding the Supreme Court decision in *Brown* v. *Board of Education* (1954).

RUMSEY, CHARLES CARY (*b. Buffalo, N.Y., 1879; d. 1922*), sculptor, polo player. Rumsey's bronzes depicting polo ponies and their riders were particularly effective; notable among his monumental works is an equestrian "Pizarro" now in the city of Lima, Peru. His compositions attained a rhythm and dynamic power which gave them individuality in spite of the evident influences of Rodin, Bourdelle, and Maillol.

RUMSEY, JAMES (*b. Bohemia Manor, Md., 1743; d. London, England, 1792*), inventor. Encouraged by George Washington and others in his efforts to produce a boat propelled by steam, Rumsey exhibited on the Potomac River in December 1787 a vessel propelled by streams of water forced out through its stern; the force pump was operated by a steam engine. He also developed an improved steam boiler, an improved grist mill and saw mill, and a plan for raising water by means of a steam engine. Securing English patents on his boiler and steamboat, and U.S. patents in 1791, he was unable to raise sufficient capital for manufacture.

RUMSEY, MARY HARRIMAN (*b. New York, N.Y., 1881; d. 1934*), leader in public welfare. Daughter of Edward H. Harriman; wife of Charles C. Rumsey. Graduated Barnard College, 1905. Conceived idea of organizing New York Junior League for public and social service, 1901; served five years as its president. Active as a cattle breeder, sportswoman, and art patron, she was also an advocate of cooperative movements and a worker for many civic and charitable enterprises, private and public.

RUMSEY, WILLIAM (*b. Bath, N.Y., 1841; d. 1903*), Union soldier, lawyer. Judge, New York State supreme court, 1880–1901. Author of one-time standard work on New York State practice.

RUNCIE, CONSTANCE FAUNT LE ROY (*b. Indianapolis, Ind., 1836; d. Winnetka, Ill., 1911*), composer, pianist. Niece of David and Robert D. Owen.

RUNKLE, JOHN DANIEL (*b. Root, N.Y., 1822; d. 1902*), mathematician, educator. Graduated Lawrence Scientific School, Harvard, 1851. Professor of mathematics, Massachusetts Institute of Technology, 1865–68, 1880–1902. Appointed acting president of the Institute, 1868, he held the title of president, 1870–78. He established the Lowell School of Practical Design, 1872, and was associated with the work of the *Nautical Almanac*, 1849–84.

RUNYON, DAMON (*b. Manhattan, Kans., 1880; d. New York, N.Y., 1946*), journalist, short story writer. After working on a number of small-town newspapers in Colorado, where he was raised, he became star reporter of the Denver *Rocky Mountain News*. Joining the staff of the *New York American*, 1911, he made a success as a writer of colorful sports news; thereafter, he was a war correspondent in Mexico and France, a reporter of crimes and trials, and the top feature writer of the Hearst organization. He is remembered in particular for a number of magazine short stories, written in and after 1929, of which *Guys and Dolls* (1931) was the first of several collections in book form. Well plotted and told in a special style of picturesque slang, they dealt with a cast of Broadway characters that never were in life but were wonderfully entertaining to read about. Many of the stories were adapted for the stage and screen.

RUPP, ISRAEL DANIEL (*b. Cumberland Co., Pa., 1803; d. Philadelphia, Pa., 1878*), schoolmaster, historian. Author of *History of Lancaster County* (1844) and other volumes devoted to the county history of Pennsylvania.

RUPP, WILLIAM (*b. Lehigh Co., Pa., 1839; d. 1904*), German Reformed clergyman, professor of theology, editor. Taught at his denomination's seminary in Lancaster, Pa., *post* 1894.

RUPPERT, JACOB (*b. New York, N.Y., 1867; d. New York, 1939*), brewer, New York Democratic congressman. Co-owner (1914–23) and sole owner thereafter of the New York Yankees baseball club.

RUSBY, HENRY HURD (*b. Franklin, present Nutley, N.J., 1855; d. Sarasota, Fla., 1940*), pharmacognosist, botanical explorer. M.D., New York University, 1884. Traveling as pharmacognosist for Parke, Davis & Co., 1884–88, Rusby made extensive investigations in North and South America and collected specimens of some 45,000 species of plants, many of them hitherto unknown to botany; among the new drugs which resulted was cocillana. Appointed professor of materia medica at New York College of Pharmacy, 1889, he became dean in 1901 and remained so until 1930 after the college was affiliated with Columbia University. He also taught at other institutions in New York and made further botanical collections in South America. By teaching, research, and writings, he established beneficial standards for pharmaceutical education and for American pharmacy at large. He was one of the foremost early exponents in America of the study of medicinal plants on a truly scientific basis and gave much knowledge and time to the formulation of legal standards for crude plant drugs.

RUSH, BENJAMIN (*b. Byberry, near Philadelphia, Pa., 1745 o.s.; d. Philadelphia, Pa., 1813*), physician, Revolutionary patriot. Graduated College of New Jersey (Princeton), 1760. Studied medicine with John Redman and attended first lectures of William Shippen and John Morgan at the College of Philadelphia; completing his medical education at the University of Edinburgh, he received its doctorate in 1768. Returning to Philadelphia, 1769, Rush began to practice medicine and to teach chemistry at the College of Philadelphia. He published the first American chemistry text, *A Syllabus of a Course of Lectures on Chemistry* (1770), and attracted attention by his unusual ability as practitioner of a new system of treatment taught by his Edinburgh master, the great William Cullen. He also wrote at length on medical, social, and political topics, and, as the quarrel between the colonies and the mother country mounted, he became the associate of patriot leaders like John Adams and Thomas Jefferson. Elected to the Continental Congress, 1776, he was a signer of the Declaration of Independence.

Appointed surgeon general of the Middle Department in the medical service of the Continental Army, 1777, he accused Dr. William Shippen, his superior, of maladministration and resigned when a decision was given against him. Association in the Conway Cabal and General Washington's recognition of his part in it (1778) ended Rush's military career and he returned to his practice in Philadelphia. Becoming a member of the staff of the Pennsylvania Hospital, 1783, he served in that capacity for the rest of his life. Sponsor of a number of ameliorative movements which were to remold America in the ensuing century, he was active against slavery and capital punishment and advocated temperance, an improved educational system, and prison reform. His ideas on social reform may be found in his *Essays, Literary, Moral and Philosophical* (1798). In the Pennsylvania convention for ratifying the new U.S. Constitution, he and James Wilson led the successful movement for adoption; in 1789, they inaugurated a campaign which secured a more liberal and effective state constitution for Pennsylvania. After the creation of the University of Pennsylvania, 1791, Rush became professor of the institutes of medicine and clinical practice in the university (1792) and in 1796 succeeded Dr. Adam Kuhn as professor of theory and practice as well. He was treasurer of the U.S. Mint, 1797–1813.

It is impossible to describe Rush's system of theory and practice briefly without oversimplification, but it might be called a logical extension of John Brown's reformulation (1788) of Cullen's theory. The essential principle was that all diseases were due to one "proximate" cause—a state of excessive excitability or spasm in the blood vessels. Hence, in most cases but one treatment was called for, namely, "depletion" through bleeding and purging. He confidently proclaimed his system when the initial volume of his *Medical Inquiries and Observations* was published in 1789, but critics declared that Rush's fondness for depletion led him to dangerous extremes in practice. In the epidemic of yellow fever which descended upon Philadelphia, 1793, Rush worked with desperation and devotion in the stricken city, but it was pointed out that there was an obvious correlation between increasing employment of Rush's treatment and an increasing mortality rate. Although Rush's treatment was not the only variable involved, yet it was impossible to reconcile his claims with the stark fact of the mortality tables, and he may be considered the victim of a credulity about diagnoses and cures which characterized much of his work. Also, his view that the "remote" cause of the epidemic was unsanitary conditions in the city antagonized many citizens. Despite all this, his published account of the epidemic and of those which followed it won him recognition both at home and abroad. His chief essay on the subject is *An Account of the Bilious Remitting Yellow Fever . . . 1793* (1794). Dr. Rush was an observant man but not a good observer. However, there is reason to believe that he was the pioneer worker in experimental physiology in the United States, and he was the first American to write on *cholera infantum* and the first to recognize focal infection in the teeth. His contributions to psychiatry were also notable, and his *Medical Inquiries and Observations upon the Diseases of the Mind* (1812) shows some appreciation of what would today be known as mental healing and even of psychoanalysis.

RUSH, JAMES (b. *Philadelphia, Pa., 1786; d. Philadelphia, 1869*), physician, psychologist. Son of Benjamin Rush; brother of Richard Rush. Graduated College of New Jersey (Princeton), 1805; M.D., University of Pennsylvania, 1809. Founder of the Ridgway Branch Library Company of Philadelphia.

RUSH, RICHARD (b. *Philadelphia, Pa., 1780; d. Philadelphia, 1859*), lawyer, statesman, diplomat. Son of Benjamin Rush; brother of James Rush. Graduated College of New Jersey (Princeton), 1798. Admitted to the Philadelphia bar, 1800, he grew in reputation as a speaker and made important political contacts as defense counsel for William Duane when Thomas McKean sued that editor for libel, 1808. An ardent Democratic-Republican, Rush became attorney general of Pennsylvania, 1811, and was appointed comptroller of the U.S. treasury in November of that year. Appointed U.S. attorney general, February 1814, he edited *Laws of the United States* (1815), and in a brief period as U.S. secretary of state just after the inauguration of President Monroe, negotiated the Rush-Bagot convention (April 1817) establishing limitation of naval armament on the Great Lakes. Appointed U.S. minister to Great Britain, October 1817, he was one of the most efficient and best-liked of American representatives in that post. Tactful, well-bred and with wide intellectual interests, he moved with ease in British society and succeeded in settling a number of disputes subsequent to the War of 1812. He negotiated a treaty of joint occupation of Oregon which served as a basis of understanding for nearly thirty years, and in 1819 handled wisely the issues raised by Andrew Jackson's invasion of Florida and the execution of Ambrister and Arbuthnot. Rush played a very important role in the preliminaries of the Monroe Doctrine, and his dispatches of August—September 1823 were an important factor in persuading President Monroe and John Quincy Adams to take a strong stand. Accepting the post of U.S. secretary of the treasury, 1825, he favored a mild protectionist policy. Candidate for vice president of the United States, 1828, he was badly defeated in the Jacksonian triumph. As a private citizen, he continued active in the public

interest, supported Andrew Jackson in the 1832 struggle over the Bank, and in 1835 served on a commission to settle the Ohio—Michigan boundary dispute. In 1836–38 he secured the Smithson bequest, then in chancery, which was used to establish the Smithsonian Institution. U.S. minister to France, 1847–49, he acted with his usual intelligence and tact during the revolutionary days of 1848 in Paris. Returning home, he continued interested in public affairs until his death. He was author of the important *Memoranda of a Residence at the Court of London* (1833, 1845) and *Occasional Productions . . .* (1860).

RUSH, WILLIAM (b. *Philadelphia, Pa., 1756; d. 1833*), carver of ship's figureheads, first native American sculptor. Worked in Philadelphia; co-founder, with Charles W. Peale and others, of the Pennsylvania Academy of the Fine Arts, 1805.

RUSK, JEREMIAH McCLAIN (b. *Morgan Co., Ohio, 1830; d. 1893*), farmer, businessman, Union soldier. Settled in Vernon Co., Wis., 1853. As Republican governor of Wisconsin, 1882–89, he gave the state a strong and effective government, earning the affectionate title "Uncle Jerry"; in quelling strike riots in Milwaukee, May 1886, he uttered a much-quoted remark, "I seen my duty and I done it." While U.S. secretary of agriculture, 1889–93, he secured inspection of all American meat exports and engaged the interest of the press in the activities and policies of his new department.

RUSK, THOMAS JEFFERSON (b. *Pendleton District, S.C., 1803; d. Nacogdoches, Tex., 1857*), Texas pioneer, soldier, jurist. Removed to Texas *ca.* 1835. Took active part in the convention of 1836, signed declaration of independence for Texas, aided in drafting of Texas constitution, and was elected secretary of war in the provisional government. Rusk fought at San Jacinto, commanding the Texas army after that battle. Appointed secretary of war in Sam Houston's cabinet, he soon resigned to practice law but led an active campaign against hostile Indians in East Texas Supreme Court, 1838, he presided over its first session, January—June 1840. A supporter of annexation of Texas to the United States, he served as U.S. senator, Democrat, *post* 1846, giving full support to the administration in the war with Mexico and working consistently for improvement of transportation. Choice of many delegates for the presidential nomination, 1856, he refused to have his name entered.

RUSS, JOHN DENNISON (b. *Essex, Mass., 1801; d. Pompton, N.J., 1881*), physician, penologist, pioneer teacher of the blind. Graduated Yale, 1823; M.D., Yale, 1825. Associated with Samuel G. Howe in support and relief of Greek revolutionaries, 1827–30; practiced in New York City *post* 1830. Cofounder of New York Institution for the Blind which he served as manager, 1832–35.

RUSSELL, ANNIE (b. *Liverpool, England, 1864; d. Winter Park, Fla., 1936*), actress, noted for ingenue roles. Made debut as a child actress in Montreal, Canada, 1872; made New York debut in a juvenile performance of *H.M.S. Pinafore* at the Lyceum Theatre, 1879; established herself in popular favor in title role of *Esmeralda*, 1881. Among her later important parts were the title role in *Hazel Kirke* and in Shaw's *Major Barbara*; she was effective also in Shakespearean repertory.

RUSSELL, BENJAMIN (b. *Boston, Mass., 1761; d. 1845*), journalist. Learned to set type in office of Isaiah Thomas to whom he was apprenticed. Founded *The Massachusetts Centinel* (first issued, March 24, 1784) which he edited and published until his retirement, 1828; *post* 1790 the paper was known as the *Columbian Centinel*. A vigorous writer, Russell took an active part in politics and made his Federalist paper the most enterprising and influential in Massachusetts. He held many public offices both honorary and elective.

RUSSELL, CHARLES EDWARD (*b. Davenport, Iowa, 1860; d. Washington, D.C., 1941*), journalist, socialist, reformer. Held various newspaper posts in the Midwest and New York City, including city editor of the New York *World* (1894–97), managing editor of the *New York American* (1897–1900), and publisher of the *Chicago American* (1900–02); he also lectured on free trade and worked for the Populists. Following a period of poor health, he wrote a series of articles on the Beef Trust for *Everybody's Magazine* (1905), which established him as a leading muckraker. He continued this line of activity in magazine articles and a number of books, exposing the evils of child labor, railroad finance, electoral frauds, and the concentration of wealth. Active in the right wing of the Socialist party, 1908–17, he was expelled from the party for his advocacy of U.S. participation in World War I, but continued to hold socialist views and lent his support to countless campaigns for social justice and civil liberties. An idealist, a gradualist, more interested in facts than in theories, and ever optimistic, he refused to be forced either into disappointed apathy or the advocacy of violence. Among his many books were *The American Orchestra and Theodore Thomas* (1927, a winner of the Pulitzer Prize) and an autobiography, *Bare Hands and Stone Walls* (1933).

RUSSELL, CHARLES ELLSWORTH ("PEE WEE") (*b. Maple Wood, Mo., 1906; d. Alexandria, Va., 1969*), jazz musician. Became a full-time professional clarinetist in 1922; for the next five years he worked as an itinerant player of a music that was increasingly being called "jazz." He apprenticed with numerous bands that included instrumentalists of major reputation of the burgeoning art form. In 1925 he often worked with Bix Beiderbecke and fell under the influence of what was later called the Chicago style of jazz. He emulated the tone of Frank Teschemaker, evident on Russell's first recording, "Ida," made with Red Nichols and His Five Pennies (1927). In the late 1930's he joined Louis Prima's band. From 1938 to 1950 he did his best-remembered work with the "Condon mob," a group of musicians who played for Eddie Condon. In 1950 he organized his own group, then rejoined Condon in 1955, remaining with him until 1961. He captured the *Downbeat* readers' poll for clarinet in 1942–44 and the critics' poll, 1962–68.

RUSSELL, CHARLES TAZE (*b. Pittsburgh, Pa., 1852; d. Tex., 1916*), religious leader. Commonly known as "Pastor Russell," founder of a millennial sect now known as Jehovah's Witnesses.

RUSSELL, CHARLES WELLS (*b. Wheeling, present W.Va., 1856; d. Washington, D.C., 1927*), lawyer, government official, diplomat. Prepared an important report on peonage in the South, 1907; was U.S. envoy extraordinary to Persia, 1909–14.

RUSSELL, DAVID ALLEN (*b. Salem, N.Y., 1820; d. Winchester, Va., 1864*), Union soldier. Graduated West Point, 1845. Commended for Mexican War service, he was active in Northwest Indian fighting until the outbreak of the Civil War. After hard and outstanding service in brigade command (notably at Rappahannock Station, Va., November 1863), he rose to divisional command, May 1864, and was killed in a critical moment of the battle of Winchester.

RUSSELL, HENRY NORRIS (*b. Oyster Bay, N.Y., 1877; d. Princeton, N.J., 1957*), astronomer. Studied at Princeton University (Ph.D., 1900), and at King's College, Oxford, England. Taught at Princeton from 1905; chairman of the astronomy department from 1912. Russell noted his own career could be briefly summed up: 1. The development of methods for calculating the orbits of eclipsing binary stars, and various practical applications. 2. The determination of dynamical parallaxes and the investiga-

tion of the masses of the binary stars. 3. The application of physical principles to the study of the spectra of the sun, sunspots, and stars. 4. The application of these principles to a quantitative analysis of the atmospheres of the sun and stars. 5. The term-analysis of complex atomic spectra. Known as "the dean of American astronomy," Russell had awesome power within the discipline. He spent summers working in various observatories, but preferred to return to Princeton and pursue theoretical studies.

RUSSELL, IRWIN (*b. Port Gibson, Miss., 1853; d. New Orleans, La., 1879*), poet. A pioneer in black dialect poetry, Russell was author of a single volume published posthumously, *Poems* (1888).

RUSSELL, ISRAEL COOK (*b. Garrattsville, N.Y., 1852; d. Ann Arbor, Mich., 1906*), geologist. Graduated in engineering, University of the City of New York (present New York University), 1872; attended Columbia School of Mines. After extensive field experience in government survey work under John J. Stevenson, G. K. Gilbert, and others, he served as professor of geology, University of Michigan, 1892–1906. An authority on North American geography, particularly that of Alaska and the Northwest, and a specialist in glaciology, Russell was author, among other works, of *Geological History of Lake Lahontan* (1885) which remains a classic of geological science.

RUSSELL, JAMES EARL (*b. near Hamden, N.Y., 1864; d. Trenton, N.J., 1945*), educator. A.B., Cornell University, 1887. After six years of experience as teacher and headmaster in secondary schools, he grew dissatisfied with their formalism and went abroad to study foreign educational systems and theories. His major studies were made in Germany; after work with Wilhelm Rein at Jena, he went to Leipzig and was awarded the Ph.D. there in 1894. He returned home, convinced that the subjects taught and the methods used in public education should reflect the underlying philosophy and pragmatic needs of a country; that in a democracy, education should assist all citizens to realize their highest intellectual and occupational capacities; and that a high degree of professional training was necessary and desirable for teachers. Achieving national reputation through his publications while professor of philosophy and pedagogy at University of Colorado, 1895–97, he became dean of Teachers College, Columbia University, late in 1897. When he retired in 1927, he had, with the aid of an outstanding faculty, made Teachers College the center of the progressive education movement in the United States and one of the most influential and successful university schools of education in the world.

RUSSELL, JAMES SOLOMON (*b. Palmer's Springs, Va., 1857; d. Lawrenceville, Va., 1935*), Episcopal clergyman, educator. Born of slave parents, he attended Hampton Institute and St. Stephen's School, Petersburg, Va.; he was ordained deacon in 1882 and priest, 1887. Principal and founder of St. Paul Normal and Industrial School (1888–1930), he was twice elected to the episcopal bench but declined to leave his school work.

RUSSELL, JOHN HENRY (*b. Frederick, Md., 1827; d. 1897*), naval officer. Graduated U.S. Naval Academy, 1848. Led force which burned the Confederate privateer *Judah*, Pensacola, Fla., September 1861; commanding *Kennebec*, he served ably in Admiral D. G. Farragut's operations at New Orleans and Mobile.

RUSSELL, JONATHAN (*b. Providence, R.I., 1771; d. Milton, Mass., 1832*), orator, diplomat, merchant. A prominent Democratic-Republican, Russell served as U.S. chargé d'affaires at Paris and London, and was U.S. minister to Sweden and Norway, 1814–18; in 1814 he was one of the peace commissioners at Ghent. Accused by John Quincy Adams of employing a false document against him, 1822, Russell retired from public life.

RUSSELL, JOSEPH (*b. Township of Dartmouth, Mass., 1719 o.s.; d. 1804*), New Bedford merchant, shipowner. A Russell vessel, the *Rebecca*, made the first whaling voyage around Cape Horn to the Pacific hunting grounds, 1791–93.

RUSSELL, LILLIAN (*b. Clinton, Iowa, 1861; d. Pittsburgh, Pa., 1922*), comic opera singer, internationally famous beauty. Stage name of Helen Louise Leonard. Raised in Chicago, Ill. After studying singing in New York under Leopold Damrosch, she made her first stage appearance, 1879, in the chorus of a company of *Pinafore*. In November 1880, she made her first appearance under her stage name at Tony Pastor's Theatre, New York. Beauty of face and figure, an excellent natural voice, and a great flair for publicity contributed to her success in a number of comic operas which featured her voice and appearance but required little dramatic ability.

RUSSELL, MOTHER MARY BAPTIST (*b. Newry, Ireland, 1829; d. California, 1898*), founder of the Sisters of Mercy in California. Name in religion of Katherine Russell. Raised in a family of remarkable distinction, Mother Russell joined the Institute of Mercy at Kinsale, 1848. As superior of a group of her order who had volunteered for work in San Francisco, Calif., she arrived there in December 1854 and established a convent and school. Early hostility to the nuns ended in gratitude after their work in the county hospital during an epidemic of cholera. Thereafter until her death she engaged in all works of charity, building and staffing hospitals, orphanages, homes for the aged, and schools throughout the state.

RUSSELL, OSBORNE (*b. probably Hallowell, Maine, 1814; d. Placerville, Calif., ca. 1865*), trapper, Oregon and California pioneer. Author of the important *Journal of a Trapper, Or Nine Years in the Rocky Mountains, 1834–1843* (published Boise, Idaho, 1914).

RUSSELL, SOL SMITH (*b. Brunswick, Mo., 1848; d. Washington, D.C., 1902*), actor. Nephew by marriage of Sol Smith. Celebrated throughout the country *post ca.* 1867 as a comedian, he had a dry, crackling manner that was irresistible in its appeal to contemporary audiences.

RUSSELL, WILLIAM (*b. Glasgow, Scotland, 1798; d. Lancaster, Mass., 1873*), educator. Immigrated to Georgia, 1817–18; taught at and conducted schools in many towns along the eastern seaboard. As principal of the New England Normal Institute, 1853–55, he made it an important center of Pestalozzianism in the United States. First editor of the *American Journal of Education* (1826), he was the author of a number of textbooks.

RUSSELL, WILLIAM EUSTIS (*b. Cambridge, Mass., 1857; d. St. Adelaide, Quebec, Canada, 1896*), lawyer, politician. Democratic governor of Massachusetts, 1891–94.

RUSSELL, WILLIAM HENRY (*b. Nicholas Co., Ky., 1802; d. Washington, D.C., 1873*), lawyer, Kentucky legislator, California pioneer. An associate of John C. Frémont in the early government of California, Russell later practiced law there. A large, expansive, bombastic man, he bore the nickname of "Owl" Russell.

RUSSELL, WILLIAM HEPBURN (*b. Burlington, Vt., 1812; d. Palmyra, Mo., 1872*), freighter, stagecoach operator. Joined Alexander Majors in partnership (December 1854) which later became Russell, Majors & Waddell. Persuaded the reluctant Majors to join him in operation of the Pony Express, starting April 1860. Involved with John B. Floyd, U.S. secretary of war, in a celebrated embezzlement scandal, Russell was indicted in January 1861, but action on the case was postponed because of the Civil War. Failure of the Pony express venture led to failure of Russell's firm, and he transferred his interest in the freighting part of it to Majors.

RUSSWURM, JOHN BROWN (*b. Port Antonio, Jamaica, B.W.I., 1799; d. Liberia, 1851*), educator, government official. Probably the first person of African descent to graduate from an American college (Bowdoin, 1826), Russwurm established one of the first newspapers for blacks in the United States, *Freedom's Journal*, 1827. Immigrating to Liberia, 1829, he served as superintendent of public schools and as colonial secretary. He was governor of the Maryland Colony at Cape Palmas, 1836–51.

RUST, JOHN DANIEL (*b. Necessity, Tex., 1892; d. Pine Bluff, Ark., 1954*), inventor. Studied briefly at Western College in Artesia, N.Mex. With his brother Mack, Rust invented the first cotton-picking machine in 1931. Because of the displacement their invention would cause in migrant workers, manufacture of the machine was put off until after World War II. John Rust established the World Foundation in 1944, which received the profits from the machine, then being manufactured by the Allis-Chalmers Manufacturing Company.

RUST, RICHARD SUTTON (*b. Ipswich, Mass., 1815; d. Cincinnati, Ohio, 1906*), Methodist clergyman, advocate of education for blacks.

RUTER, MARTIN (*b. Charlton, Mass., 1785; d. Tex., 1838*), Methodist clergyman, educator, missionary to Texas.

RUTGERS, HENRY (*b. near New York, N.Y., 1745; d. New York, 1830*), landowner, Revolutionary officer, philanthropist. A principal benefactor of New York educational institutions, Rutgers was a trustee of Princeton University and Queen's College; the latter institution changed its name to Rutgers in his honor.

RUTH, GEORGE HERMAN ("BABE") (*b. Baltimore, Md., 1895; d. New York, N.Y., 1948*), baseball player. Legally committed to St. Mary's Industrial Home for Boys, Baltimore, at age seven, he became the school's star baseball player. In 1914 Ruth joined the Baltimore club of the International League, but because of a financial squeeze, he was sold the same year to the major-league Boston Red Sox. With a brilliant overall record for 1914, his major-league career was launched. Over the next four years, as a regular Red Sox pitcher, Ruth helped Boston win three American League pennants and three World Series titles. Overall, his six years as a Boston pitcher showed eighty-nine victories and forty-six losses, a pace which, if continued, would surely have ranked him as one of baseball's greatest pitchers.

But Ruth's versatility ended his pitching. His exceptional abilities as a hitter prompted Boston manager Ed Barrow in 1918 to place him full-time in the outfield, where he played thereafter. In 1918 he batted .300 and hit eleven homers; a year later he astounded the baseball world by clubbing a record twenty-nine homers on a .322 batting average. In 1919 Ruth was sold to the New York Yankees. He was the dominant figure in American baseball from 1920 to 1935, leading the Yankees to seven league pennants and five World Series championships. In 1925, he was hospitalized and underwent surgery for an intestinal abscess. After engaging a trainer to help him lose weight, he effected a comeback and over the seasons of 1926–1928 led the Yankees to three straight pennants. In 1927, after hitting his all-time seasonal high of sixty homers, Ruth toured the Far West.

In a fifteen-year career as a Yankee, Ruth set many records. His overall performance was the more remarkable since he had spent a quarter of his big-league career as a pitcher. In 1935 the Yankees released him to the Boston Braves; disillusioned, Ruth quit in midseason. In 1936 he was elected a charter member of the Baseball Hall of Fame. Two years later he accepted a coaching offer from the Brooklyn Dodgers, but resigned before the end of the season. In 1948, shortly before his death, he saw himself portrayed in a Hollywood film, *The Babe Ruth Story*.

RUTHERFORD, JOSEPH FRANKLIN (*b. near Boonville, Mo., 1869; d. San Diego, Calif., 1942*), lawyer, second president of Jehovah's Witnesses. Succeeded Charles Taze Russell as president in January 1917.

RUTHERFORD, LEWIS MORRIS (*b. Morrisania, N.Y., 1816; d. 1892*), astrophysicist, pioneer in astronomical photography and spectroscopy. Great-grandson of Lewis Morris (1726–1798). Graduated Williams College; studied law under William H. Seward. Began serious work in science, 1856; secured first photographs of the moon, 1858. Following up observational work of Fraunhofer, he attempted a classification of stellar spectra which was published in the *American Journal of Science*, January 1863. Inventor of a number of devices for improving the efficiency of his work, he built during 1870 a machine with which he succeeded in ruling interference gratings superior to all others down to the time of Henry A. Rowland. Rutherfurd took a leading part in establishing the department of geodesy and practical astronomy at Columbia, 1881.

RUTLEDGE, EDWARD (*b. Charleston, S.C., 1749; d. Charleston, 1800*), lawyer, statesman. Brother of John Rutledge. Member of the First Continental Congress, 1774, and of the Second Continental Congress, 1775–76, he seconded the opinions of his brother. At first opposing independence, he influenced the South Carolina delegation to vote for it and was a signer of the Declaration. Returning home in November 1776 to serve in the defense of the state, he was taken prisoner at the fall of Charleston but was exchanged in time to take his seat in the legislature in January 1782. Although he drew up the bill proposing confiscation of Loyalist property, he was influential in moderating its effect. An active member of the legislature, 1782–98, he was a stiffly conservative Federalist. Elected governor, 1798, he served until his death.

RUTLEDGE, JOHN (*b. Charleston, S.C., 1739; d. 1800*), statesman, jurist. Brother of Edward Rutledge. After studying law at the Middle Temple, London, he was called to the English bar, 1760, and returned to an immediate and brilliant success in Charleston. A provincial legislator *post* 1761, he was sent as a delegate to the First Continental Congress in which, like Joseph Galloway, he favored maintaining self-government without breaking up the empire. In the Second Continental Congress, his efforts for establishment of regular governments in the colonies culminated in the advice of Congress to South Carolina (November 1775) to take such action if it should seem necessary. Returning to his native state, he was elected to the Council of Safety. He was one of the committee which wrote the South Carolina constitution of 1776 and served as president of the General Assembly until his resignation (1778) in protest against a revision of the state constitution which he considered dangerously democratic.

When the state faced invasion in January 1779, Rutledge was elected governor and worked tirelessly to support the efforts of American military forces during a calamitous period. Despite the fall of Charleston and the defeat at Camden, 1780, he did not despair and, while he begged Congress for help, encouraged Thomas Sumter, Francis Marion, and other partisans to wage detached warfare against the British. In August 1781 he set about a restoration of civil government, working to a large extent through the militia officers. Laying down his office at the end of the year, he reentered the legislature, served for a brief time in Congress, 1782–83, and in 1784 was elected to the South Carolina chancery court. Chairman of the committee of detail in the Federal Convention, 1787, he fought for wealth to be made part of the basis of representation, for assumption of state debts, and against restrictions on the slave trade; also for election of the president by Congress and of Congress by the legislatures. Elected chief justice of South Carolina, February 1791, he was offered the chief justiceship of the U.S. Supreme Court, 1795. His nomination was rejected by the Senate because of the bitterness of his attacks against Jay's Treaty. He embodied perhaps more perfectly than any other man of his time the ideas of the ruling class of 18th-century South Carolina.

RUTLEDGE, WILEY BLOUNT (*b. Cloverport, Ky., 1894; d. York, Maine, 1949*), legal educator, associate justice of the U.S. Supreme Court. B.A., University of Wisconsin, 1914. After a period of schoolteaching and of recovery from tuberculosis in New Mexico and Colorado, he took his LL.B. degree at University of Colorado, 1922. Associate professor of law at Colorado, 1924–26, he then became professor at Washington University (St. Louis, Mo.) law school, advancing to deanship of the school in 1931. In 1935 he became dean of the law school at the State University of Iowa; in 1939 he was appointed to the U.S. Court of Appeals for the District of Columbia, from which he was elevated to the Supreme Court four years later. Painstaking and unsparing of his time and energy, he was a "lawyer's judge," expert in disputed technical points. His opinions, which were not numerous, tended to be long and encyclopedic. He summarized his liberal philosophy in his book, *A Declaration of Legal Faith* (1947).

RYAN, ABRAM JOSEPH (*b. Hagerstown, Md., 1838; d. Louisville, Ky., 1886*), Roman Catholic clergyman, Confederate chaplain, poet of the Confederacy. Father Ryan's collected poems, including "The Conquered Banner" and "The Sword of Robert E. Lee," were published in book form, 1879.

RYAN, ARTHUR CLAYTON (*b. Grandview, Iowa, 1879; d. Scarsdale, N.Y., 1927*), Congregational clergyman, missionary to Turkey. General secretary, American Bible Society, *post* 1924.

RYAN, EDWARD GEORGE (*b. near Enfield, Ireland, 1810; d. Madison, Wis., 1880*), jurist. Came to America, 1830; settled in Milwaukee, Wis., 1848. Chief justice of Wisconsin, 1874–80, he ruled in important cases involving the power of the state legislature to regulate railway rates and to prescribe conditions upon which foreign corporations might do business in the state.

RYAN, HARRIS JOSEPH (*b. Matamoras, Pa., 1866; d. 1934*), electrical engineer. M.E., Cornell University, 1887. Taught at Cornell, 1888–1905; headed department of electrical engineering at Leland Stanford, 1905–31. Authority on power transmission at high voltages; a pioneer in engineering use of the cathode-ray tube.

RYAN, JOHN AUGUSTINE (*b. Vermillion Township, Minn., 1869; d. St. Paul, Minn., 1945*), Roman Catholic clergyman, economist, social reformer. Attended a school conducted by the Christian Brothers in St. Paul; entered St. Thomas Seminary (called after 1893 St. Paul Seminary), from which he graduated as valedictorian in 1892. Ordained to the priesthood in 1898, Ryan began graduate work in theology at the Catholic University of America in Washington, D.C., where he received his degree as S.T.B. and his licentiate in sacred theology (S.T.L.). He received his doctorate in sacred theology (S.T.D.) from Catholic University in 1906. His thesis, *A Living Wage: Its Ethical and Economic Aspects*, was published that same year. For thirteen years (1902–15) he taught at St. Paul Seminary. In 1909 he put together (and published in the *Catholic World*) a full program of social reform. Six years later he transferred to Catholic University, at first as associate professor of political science, then successively as associate professor of theology (1916), professor of theology (1917), and dean of the School of Sacred Sciences (1919). He published *Distributive Justice: The Right and Wrong of Our Present Distribution of Wealth* (1916). In 1917 he founded the *Catholic Charities Review*. When the bishops set up the National Catholic Welfare Council (later Conference) in 1919, Ryan was the obvious man to serve as the Washington director of its Social Action Department, created in 1920. In 1922 he was coauthor of the book *The State and the Church*, followed by the revised edition, *Catholic Principles of Politics* (1940). Ryan welcomed the New Deal as the triumphant realization of his lifetime struggle for social justice.

RYAN, JOHN DENNIS (*b. Hancock, Mich., 1864; d. New York, N.Y., 1933*), capitalist. Dominating figure *post* 1909 in the Anaconda Copper Mining Co. which he made one of the greatest industrial enterprises in the world; active also in public utilities and railroads.

RYAN, PATRICK JOHN (*b. Thurles, Ireland, 1831; d. 1911*), Roman Catholic clergyman. Immigrated to St. Louis, Mo., 1852, where he was ordained, 1853. A leading preacher and orator of his time, he was consecrated coadjutor bishop of St. Louis, 1872, and in 1884 succeeded to the see of Philadelphia.

RYAN, STEPHEN VINCENT (*b. near Almonte, Ontario, Canada, 1825; d. 1896*), Roman Catholic clergyman, Vincentian. Raised in Pennsylvania. Completed theological studies in Missouri and was ordained in St. Louis, 1849. Elected visitor general of his order in America, 1857, he was named against his will bishop of Buffalo, 1868, and served until his death. A strong liberal, Bishop Ryan found himself in continual disagreement with Bishop Bernard McQuaid of Rochester.

RYAN, THOMAS FORTUNE (*b. Lovingston, Va., 1851; d. 1928*), promoter, financier. Beginning as an errand boy in a Baltimore, Md., dry-goods commission house, Ryan removed to New York City, 1872, and prospered as a stockbroker, 1873–83. His first exploit in high finance was the organization of the New York Cable Railroad, 1883, a paper corporation with which, in association with William C. Whitney and Peter A. B. Widener, he eventually controlled practically every street railway line in New York City. His Metropolitan Traction Co., organized 1886, manipulated the securities of the various traction companies held by Ryan's syndicate and is considered to have been the first holding company in the United States. Threatened by the competition of the new subway system, 1905, Ryan bludgeoned the interests behind the Interborough Rapid Transit Co. into consolidating with his firm and engaging in a scheme of overcapitalization which left New York City traction in a state of financial collapse,

1906–07. Called "the most adroit, suave and noiseless man" in American finance, Ryan extended his power into banking, insurance, public utilities, and general industry by methods which were constantly under fire as prejudicial to the public interest.

RYAN, WALTER D'ARCY (*b. Kentville, N.S., Canada, 1870; d. Schenectady, N.Y., 1934*), illuminating engineer, developer of flood lighting and high-intensity streetlighting.

RYBNER, MARTIN CORNELIUS (*b. Copenhagen, Denmark, 1853; d. 1929*), composer, pianist, music teacher. Came to America as professor of music at Columbia University, 1904; resigned, 1919, to devote his time to composition and recital work.

RYDBERG, PER AXEL (*b. Odh, Sweden, 1860; d. New York, N.Y., 1931*), botanist. Came to America, 1882. Graduated University of Nebraska, 1891; Ph.D., Columbia, 1898. On staff of New York Botanical Garden *post* 1899; was author, among other books, of *Catalogue of the Flora of Montana* (1900), *Flora of Colorado* (1906), and *Flora of the Rocky Mountains* (1917, 1922).

RYDER, ALBERT PINKHAM (*b. New Bedford, Mass., 1847; d. Elmhurst, N.Y., 1917*), painter. Studied under William E. Marshall and at National Academy of Design. Living principally in New York City *post* 1868, and a virtual recluse not because of misanthropy but owing to his deep absorption in his work, Ryder produced hardly more than 150 pictures throughout his career. Not one of these is perfunctory and all are of the rarest kind of poetic painting; his best work was produced between 1873 and 1898, and his small marines are most representative of his highest technical and structural achievement. Ryder's work reveals a mastery of design and possesses a charm that is wholly spontaneous and original.

RYERSON, MARTIN ANTOINE (*b. Grand Rapids, Mich., 1856; d. 1932*), capitalist. Raised in Chicago, Ill., where he engaged in business until the early 1890's, Ryerson was identified with many philanthropies, notably as a benefactor to the Chicago Art Institute, the Field Museum, and the University of Chicago.

RYLAND, ROBERT (*b. King and Queen Co., Va., 1805; d. 1899*), Baptist clergyman, educator. Headed Virginia Baptist Seminary, Richmond, Va. (later Richmond College), from 1832 until the Civil War; thereafter was active in Kentucky education.

RYNNING, OLE (*b. Ringsaker, Norway, 1809; d. Iroquois Co., Ill., 1838*), immigrant leader. Immigrated to Beaver Creek region in Illinois, 1837; author of a remarkable guide book for Norwegians proposing to come to America (published at Christiania, 1838).

S

SAARINEN, EERO (*b. Kirkkonummi, Finland, 1910; d. Ann Arbor, Mich., 1961*), architect. Arrived in the United States in 1923. Graduated from Yale with honors (1934) and joined the architectural firm of his father, noted architect Eliel Saarinen, in Bloomfield Hills, Mich. Served as an instructor at Cranbrook (1939–49), a center of high culture and serious environmental thought. Collaborated with Charles Eames (1940) on the design of furniture using rubber-bonded plywood and metal and won first prize in the Organic Design Competition. Became a designer in the firm of Saarinen, Swanson and Associates (1941–47); his early works include the Kleinhans Music Hall in Buffalo (1938–40) and the Des Moines Art Center (1944–48). The firm reorganized as Saarinen, Saarinen and Associates and was commissioned for the General Motors Technical Center at Warren, Mich.; his technical innovations for that project included development of a thin, porcelain-faced "sandwich" panel serving as both exterior skin and interior finish and use of neoprene "zipper gaskets" for window glazing. Collaborated with Eames on a demonstration house sponsored as Case Study Houses by *California Arts and Architecture* (1945). Prepared plans for universities and colleges undergoing postwar expansion; many involved variations in a curtain-wall aesthetic, such as Noyes House at Vassar (1954–58) and the Kresge Auditorium and the interdenominational chapel at MIT (1953–56). His systematic, almost engineer-like insistence on analyzing the nature of a project suggested the possibility of an autonomous architecture for each building. He made dramatic use of mirror glass in the Bell Laboratories in New Jersey (1957–62) and self-rusting Cor-Ten steel at Deere and Company in Illinois (1957–63). Other projects were the U.S. embassy at Grosvenor Square, London (1955–60), the Gateway Arch in St. Louis (1959–64), the CBS Building in New York City (1960–64), and Dulles International Airport at Chantilly, Virginia (1958–62).

SAARINEN, GOTTLIEB ELIEL (*b. Rantalsami, Finland, 1873; d. Bloomfield Hills, Mich., 1950*), architect, educator, city planner. Studied at Polytechnic Institute, Helsinki. Pre-1914, his major works were the monumental Helsinki railroad station and his redesign of the city of Reval, Estonia. Through contacts made while teaching at the School of Architecture, University of Michigan, 1923, he was chosen to supervise the building of the school complex and academy of arts and crafts projected by George G. Booth for his estate at Cranbrook, Bloomfield Hills, Mich. He directed the academy until his death and was active in architectural practice as well as partner of his gifted son, Eero Saarinen.

SABATH, ADOLPH J. (*b. Zabori, Bohemia [now Czechoslovakia], 1866; d. Bethesda, Md., 1952*), congressman. Immigrated to the United States in 1881. Studied at Lake Forest University (LL.B., 1891). Elected Democratic congressman from Chicago's Fifth District, he served in the House until his death. A champion of immigrants' rights, Sabath was opposed to any restriction on immigration. He was a member of the Immigration and Naturalization Committee, chairman of the House Steering Committee (1936) and of the Rules Committee (1938). A liberal, Sabath was a supporter of Wilson, Roosevelt, and Truman. He backed the proposals of the New Deal, the formation of the State of Israel, and the Marshall Plan.

SABIN, CHARLES HAMILTON (*b. Williamstown, Mass., 1868; d. Shinnecock Hills, N.Y., 1933*), banker. President, Guaranty Trust Co., 1915–21; thereafter chairman of the board.

SABIN, FLORENCE RENA (*b. Central City, Colo., 1871 d. Denver, Colo., 1953*), anatomist. Studied at Smith College and at Johns Hopkins University. A member of the Johns Hopkins faculty, she became the first woman professor at the university in 1917. A specialist in the development of the lymphatic vessels in the embryo, and, later, of blood cells in embryos, Sabin made important contributions to anatomy. She was a researcher at the Rockefeller Institute from 1925 to 1938. In 1947, at age seventy-six, she was appointed the manager of the Department of Health and Welfare of the city of Denver. President of the American Association of Anatomists, 1924–26. Elected to the National Academy of Sciences in 1925, the first woman to be so honored.

SABIN, JOSEPH (*b. probably Braunston, Northamptonshire, England, 1821; d. 1881*), bookseller, bibliographer. Came to America, 1848. Dealer and cataloguer of rare books and prints in Philadelphia and New York, Sabin is particularly remembered as the compiler of *Dictionary of Books Relating to America* (1868–84, issued in parts), an outstanding reference work which he left unfinished. The work was brought to a conclusion by later scholars in the 19th and 20th centuries.

SABINE, LORENZO (*b. Lisbon, N.H., 1803; d. Boston Highlands, Mass., 1877*), historian, businessman, public official. Author of, among other works, the valuable *The American Loyalists* (1847; second and enlarged edition under title *Biographical Sketches of Loyalists*, 1864).

SABINE, WALLACE CLEMENT WARE (*b. Richwood, Ohio, 1868; d. 1919*), physicist. Graduated Ohio State, 1886; M.A., Harvard, 1888. Taught physics at Harvard *post* 1889; appointed dean of Lawrence Scientific School, 1906; dean, Harvard Graduate School of Applied Science, 1908–16. Authority on architectural acoustics and aerial warfare.

SACAGAWEA (*b. probably near present Lemhi, Idaho, ca. 1787; d. Fort Manuel, present N.Dak., 1812*), Shoshone woman, interpreter of the Lewis and Clark expedition. Sacagawea was of the greatest service to the explorers; without the aid she obtained for them from the Shoshone it is possible that the expedition could not have proceeded beyond the headwaters of the Salmon River. The details of her life are the subject of much controversy.

SACCO, NICOLA (*b. Torre Maggiore, Foggia, Italy, 1891; d. Massachusetts, 1927*), anarchist and a principal with Bartolomeo Vanzetti, who was a native of Piedmont, in a celebrated judicial controversy, 1920–27, which culminated in the execution of both men for murder. The mobilization of liberal and left-wing forces in favor of the defense lent emotional overtones to the case.

SACHS, BERNARD (*b. Baltimore, Md., 1858; d. New York, N.Y., 1944*), neurologist. Brother of Julius Sachs. B.A., Harvard, 1878. M.D., University of Strasbourg, 1882; studied also in Berlin, Vienna, Paris, and London. Practiced in New York *post* 1884; professor of mental and nervous diseases, New York Polyclinic, 1888–1905; served also as professor of clinical neurology at College of Physicians and Surgeons, Columbia University. Appointed consulting neurologist at New York's Mount Sinai Hospital, 1893, he was a major figure in the developing field of organic neurology. He published some 200 articles and several books, including *Nervous Diseases of Childhood* (1895). He was editor of the *Journal of Nervous and Mental Disease*, 1886–1911, and played a principal role in establishing international collaboration in the field of neurology. All through his career, he adhered to his belief in neuropsychiatry as a single practice; he was tolerant of Freudians, but viewed their generalizations with skepticism, particularly when made by people without training and experience in organic neuropathology, neurophysiology, and clinical medicine.

SACHS, HANNS (*b. Vienna, Austria, 1881; d. Boston, Mass., 1947*), psychoanalyst. An early associate of Freud. Came to the United States, 1932; practiced in Boston and taught at Harvard. Founded (1938) and edited *The American Imago*.

SACHS, JULIUS (*b. Baltimore, Md., 1849; d. 1934*), educator. Graduated Columbia, 1867; Ph.D., University of Rostock, 1871. Principal, Sachs Collegiate Institute, New York City, 1871–1901; professor of secondary education, Teachers College, Columbia, 1902–17; author of scholarly studies on Greek and educational topics.

SACHS, PAUL JOSEPH (*b. New York, N.Y., 1878; d. Cambridge, Mass., 1965*), art educator and philanthropist. Graduated from Harvard (1900) and joined the family firm of Goldman, Sachs and Company, investment bankers; elected a partner in 1904. Joined the Fogg Art Museum (1912) and became associate director (1923). Taught at Harvard's Fine Arts Department (1917–48). His most notable contribution as a teacher was his graduate seminar in museum administration (first offered in 1921). In 1948 he assumed a major administrative role in incorporating into Harvard two international research foundations: Dumbarton Oaks in Washington, D.C., and I Tatti at Settignano, near Florence, Italy. His publications include *Early Italian Engravings* (1915) and *Great Drawings* (1951).

SACHS, THEODORE BERNARD (*b. Dinaberg, Russia, 1868; d. Naperville, Ill., 1916*), physician, specialist in treatment of tuberculosis. Came to America *ca.* 1891. M.D., Chicago College of Physicians and Surgeons, 1895. Practicing in Chicago and vicinity, he was a leader in the establishment of the Chicago Municipal Tuberculosis Sanitarium, 1909–15.

SACHSE, JULIUS FRIEDRICH (*b. Philadelphia, Pa., 1842; d. Philadelphia, 1919*), businessman, antiquarian, photographer, writer on Pennsylvania German history.

SACK, ISRAEL (*b. Kaunas, Lithuania, 1883; d. Brookline, Mass., 1959*), antiques dealer. Immigrated to the U.S. in 1903. A cabinetmaker, Sack opened a shop in Boston in 1905. There he built a following for American antiques that was to culminate in his gathering the collection that became part of the permanent collection at the American Wing of the Metropolitan Museum of Art, given by Mrs. Russell Sage in 1924; in 1928, Sack was commissioned by John D. Rockefeller to furnish Colonial Williamsburg. Sack moved his business to New York in 1934 and remained active in the trade until 1955.

SACKETT, HENRY WOODWARD (*b. near Ithaca, N.Y., 1853; d. 1929*), lawyer, authority on libel, benefactor of Cornell University.

SADLIER, DENIS (*b. Co. Tipperary, Ireland, 1817; d. Wilton, N.Y., 1885*), book publisher. Came to America as a boy. Established with his brother the Catholic publishing firm of D. & J. Sadlier & Co. in New York City, 1836.

SADLIER, MARY ANNE MADDEN (*b. Cootehill, Ireland, 1820; d. Montreal, Canada, 1903*), author. Sister-in-law of Denis Sadlier. Immigrated to Montreal, 1844; resided in New York City *post* 1860. Writer of popular fiction for Catholic readers.

SADTLER, JOHN PHILIP BENJAMIN (*b. Baltimore, Md., 1823; d. Atlantic City, N.J., 1901*), Lutheran clergyman, educator. Graduated present Gettysburg College, 1842. Son-in-law of Samuel S. Schmucker. President, Muhlenberg College, 1877–85.

SADTLER, SAMUEL PHILIP (*b. Pinegrove, Pa., 1847; d. 1923*), chemist, educator. Son of John P. B. Sadtler; grandson of Samuel S. Schmucker. Graduated present Gettysburg College, 1867; S.B., Harvard, 1870; Ph.D., Göttingen, 1871. Taught chemistry at Gettysburg College, University of Pennsylvania and Philadelphia College of Pharmacy; chemical editor, *Dispensatory of the United States*, 1883–1923. Author of textbooks.

SAENDERL, SIMON (*b. Malgerzdorf, Bavaria, 1800; d. Gethsemane, Ky., 1879*), Roman Catholic clergyman, Redemptorist and Trappist. Came to America, 1832, as first Redemptorist superior in the United States; worked as a missionary in Wisconsin, Michigan, New York, and Pennsylvania. Entered the Trappists, 1852.

SAFFORD, JAMES MERRILL (*b. Zanesville, Ohio, 1822; d. Dallas, Tex., 1907*), geologist, educator. Graduated Ohio University, 1844. Taught sciences at Cumberland University, University of Nashville, and Vanderbilt; state geologist of Tennessee, 1854–60 and 1871–1900.

SAFFORD, TRUMAN HENRY (*b. Royalton, Vt., 1836; d. Newark, N.J., 1901*), astronomer, mathematician. A mathematical prodigy as a child, Safford graduated from Harvard, 1854. A staff member of Harvard Observatory, 1854–66, he taught at University of Chicago, 1866–71, and was professor of astronomy at Williams College, 1876–1901.

SAFFORD, WILLIAM EDWIN (*b. Chillicothe, Ohio, 1859; d. 1926*), ethnobotanist, ethnologist, philologist. Graduated U.S. Naval Academy, 1880; made postgraduate studies at Yale and Harvard. Resigning from the navy, 1902, he served thereafter as botanist in the U.S. Department of Agriculture. Among his many works, *The Useful Plants of the Island of Guam* (1905) is particularly notable. It established Safford's reputation as an ethnobotanist and was followed by a number of other important studies of food plants.

SAGE, BERNARD JANIN (*b. near New Haven, Conn., 1821; d. New Orleans, La., 1902*), lawyer, planter, Confederate agent. Author of *Davis and Lee* (London, 1865, later issued as *The Republic of Republics*, a defense of the Confederate leaders on the grounds of history and international law.

SAGE, HENRY WILLIAMS (*b. Middletown, Conn., 1814; d. Ithaca, N.Y., 1897*), merchant, lumber manufacturer, benefactor of Cornell University and Yale Divinity School.

SAGE, MARGARET OLIVIA SLOCUM (*b. Syracuse, N.Y., 1828; d. New York, N.Y., 1918*), philanthropist. Wife of Russell Sage. Inheriting practically the whole of her husband's fortune on his death in 1906, she distributed it over a wide range of charitable activities, including hospitals, social agencies, learned societies, museums, and 18 colleges. She established the Russell Sage Foundation, 1907.

SAGE, RUSSELL (*b. Oneida Co., N.Y., 1816; d. Long Island, N.Y., 1906*), financier, Whig congressman from New York. An associate in business of Jay Gould, Sage was one of the shrewdest and most conservative money manipulators of his time. Active *post* 1856 in railroad and other promotions, he was best known as a moneylender during the last quarter-century of his life. At his death his fortune was estimated at about $70 million. He is credited with invention of the Wall Street practice of "puts and calls."

ST. ANGE DE BELLERIVE, LOUIS (*b. Montreal, Canada, ca. 1698; d. St. Louis, Mo., 1774*), frontier soldier. Captain of the French post on the Wabash River, 1736–64; conducted evacuation of Fort Chartres, 1764–65. Commanded at St. Louis as acting governor of Upper Louisiana, 1765–70.

ST. CLAIR, ARTHUR (*b. Thurso, Scotland, 1736 o.s.; d. Chestnut Ridge, present Greensburg, Pa., 1818*), soldier. Appointed ensign in the British army, 1757, he served with Amherst in Canada, and in 1760 married a niece of James Bowdoin. Resigning from the army, 1762, he purchased an estate in western Pennsylvania and was the largest resident property-owner west of the mountains in that province. An enlightened agent of government in the frontier country, he opposed the influx of Virginians there, but was unable to prevent Virginia's domination of the Pittsburgh area. Member of the Committee of Safety of Westmoreland Co., he served as colonel in the retreat after the Canadian invasion, 1775, and was with Washington at Trenton and Princeton, 1776–77. Ordered to defend Fort Ticonderoga in the spring of 1777, he was obliged to surrender it and was recalled by Congress from service in the field. Active *post* 1778 in Pennsylvania politics, he was a delegate to the Confederation Congress, 1785–87, and president, 1787. Appointed governor of the Northwest Territory, 1787, he served until 1802. His attempts to maneuver the Indian tribes of the area into acceptance of the Treaty of Fort Harmar, 1789, led to a war in which he as major general and commander of the federal army was overwhelmingly defeated near present Fort Wayne, Ind., Nov. 4, 1791, by a confederated Indian army under Little Turtle. In governing the Northwest Territory he tried to enforce both the spirit and the letter of the Ordinance of 1787. Overbearing and paternalistic, he sought to prevent the Territory's progress to statehood and was removed from office by President Jefferson.

ST. DENIS (DENYS), LOUIS JUCHEREAU DE (*b. Beauport, Quebec, Canada, 1676; d. Natchitoches, La., 1744*), French explorer, colonizer. Accompanied Iberville on expedition for founding Louisiana; accompanied Bienville on exploration to Red River, 1700. Founded French trading post at Natchitoches, where he resided *post* 1719. A man of great influence with the Indians of Texas and Louisiana.

ST. DENIS, RUTH (*b. New Jersey, 1879; d. Hollywood, Calif., 1968*), modern-dance pioneer. Appeared with David Belasco's theatrical company (1900–04), then assembled a company of East Indian immigrants and choreographed the dance *Radha*, performed at the New York Theatre in 1906, which made her famous; *Radha* was a blend of exotic spectacle and morality tale and established the basic form, theme, and exotic trappings of her choreography. In 1915 she opened the Ruth St. Denis School of Dancing in Los Angeles with her husband and dance partner, Edwin Myers ("Ted") Shawn, and called it Denishawn. The Denishawn company toured the country (1915–29), creating an American audience for dance and pioneering a modern dance style. With the publication of her autobiography, *An Unfinished Life*, and the revival of her historical dances (both 1939), she created for herself a new role as matriarch of American modern dance. She made her last public dance appearance in 1966, at the age of eighty-seven.

SAINT-GAUDENS, AUGUSTUS (*b. Dublin, Ireland, 1848; d. Cornish, N.H., 1907*), sculptor. Of French and Irish descent, Saint-Gaudens was brought to America as an infant and raised in New York City. Trained as a cameo-cutter, he worked at his trade while studying at Cooper Union and at the National Academy of Design and also trusted to his trade for support during the decade he spent in France and Italy *post* 1867. At the Beaux-Arts in Paris he received a good grounding under Jouffroy, but he did not allow his talent to be fixed in any one mold either in Paris or, *post* 1870, in Rome. It is significant that he began his work in Rome not with an Apollo or a Venus but with a study of Hiawatha. He worked with great industry and in the highest spirits, drawing upon unusual stores of perseverance. The story of his success is not one of swift growth and facile triumph but one of persistent effort and study. Side by side with his gift for portraiture and taste for it ran his interest in imaginative design. The early *Hiawatha* in marble (Saratoga, N.Y.) and the *Silence* (Masonic Temple, New York City) attest to this. Commissioned *ca.* 1877 to do full-lengths of Admiral Farragut (Madison Square, New York City) and Captain Randall (Sailors' Snug Harbor, Staten Island, N.Y.), he returned to America and became a particular friend of John La Farge. The *Farragut*, unveiled 1881, was a landmark in Saint-Gaudens' life and in the history of American sculpture; it established him as a master. The subject was placed realistically before the world, a living embodiment, a public monument with the stamp of creative art on it. Stanford White designed the pedestal, and so began a long association with Saint-Gaudens.

Progressing in his line as interpreter of major American historical figures, Saint-Gaudens continued to reveal himself as a master of characterization and of plastic design. His research into the lives and backgrounds of his subjects and the long thought which he gave to his work account for its remarkable conviction much more than any supposed clairvoyance. *Sherman* (New York City) of 1903 is probably the greatest equestrian monument of modern times, and his two statues of Lincoln in Chicago, Ill., are eloquently expressive. His low reliefs show simple, charming composition and subtle modeling and were enhanced, as were all his works, by lettering which was made part of the design. Among his imaginative works, the *Amor Caritas* (1887); *Diana* (1892), which he made for the original Madison Square Garden; the Phillips Brooks monument; and the unfinished symbolic groups for the Boston Public Library are evidence of his deep sense that beauty must mean at least some goodness. Simplicity is the keynote to his art, even in his one essay in the grand style, the great Adams Monument in Rock Creek Cemetery, Washington, D.C. (1891). This enigmatic figure, displaying creative energy and originality, spiritual force, and the sure fusion of dramatic purpose with technical authority, is his bid for immortality. He played an important part in the general development of artistic matters. He was active in the National Academy of Design, was a founder of the Society of American Artists, and aided Charles F. McKim in establishing the American Academy in Rome; he also collaborated with Theodore Roosevelt in a proposed reform of American coinage. Generously appreciative of younger artists when he felt that they were on the right track, he never failed to stress the discipline of rigorous training; he was as devoted to craftsmanship as to beauty.

ST. JOHN, CHARLES EDWARD (*b. Allen, Mich., 1857; d. 1935*), astronomer, educator. Graduated Michigan Agricultural College, 1887; Ph.D., Harvard, 1896. Taught at University of Michigan and at Oberlin; served on staff of Mount Wilson Observatory *post* 1908, making special study of the sun. Probably his most important investigation was a test of the validity of Einstein's relativity theory through comparison of solar and terrestrial spectra (published in *Astrophysical Journal*, April 1928).

ST. JOHN, ISAAC MUNROE (*b. Augusta, Ga., 1827; d. White Sulphur Springs, W.Va., 1880*), civil engineer, Confederate brigadier general. Commissary general of the Confederate army, 1865.

ST. JOHN, JOHN PIERCE (*b. Brookville, Ind., 1833; d. Olathe, Kans., 1916*), prohibitionist, Union soldier. Republican governor of Kansas, 1879–83; presidential nominee, National Prohibition party, 1884.

ST. LUSSON, SIMON FRANÇOIS DAUMONT, SIEUR DE (*b. France, date unknown; d. probably Canada, 1674*), soldier, explorer. Served in Canada, 1663–68, 1670–73. While on an expedition to explore for mines near Lake Superior, St. Lusson presided over a formal ceremony of annexation to France of the Great Lakes area at Sault Ste. Marie, June 14, 1671.

SAINT-MÉMIN, CHARLES BALTHAZAR JULIEN FEVRET DE (*b. Dijon, France, 1770; d. Dijon, 1852*), artist, engraver. Resident in the United States, 1793–1814. Saint-Mémin produced more than 800 portraits of distinguished Americans of that time. Securing an exact profile of the sitter in crayon by means of a physionotrace, he reduced the profile with a pantograph to a miniature about two inches in diameter and recorded it directly on copper with graver and roulette. He also engraved topographical sketches of New York. A principal collection of his work is in the Corcoran Gallery, Washington, D.C.

SAINT-MÉRY, MOREAU DE. *See* MOREAU DE SAINT-MÉRY, MÉDÉRIC-LOUIS-ELIE.

ST. VRAIN, CERAN DE HAULT DE LASSUS DE (*b. near St. Louis, Mo., 1802; d. Mora, N.Mex., 1870*), pioneer merchant in the Southwest, soldier. Entered the fur trade at an early age; journeyed to Taos, N.Mex., 1824–25; traded out of Santa Fe, 1826. In partnership with Charles Bent, 1831–47, St. Vrain developed a business surpassed in importance only by the American Fur Co.; he also held large tracts of land under grant from the Mexican government. During the Mexican War, he organized and led a company of volunteers and later served against raiding Apache and Ute. Appointed colonel, 1st New Mexico Cavalry, 1861, he resigned because of age and was succeeded by Kit Carson.

SAJOUS, CHARLES EUCHARISTE DE MÉDICIS (*b. at sea, 1852; d. Philadelphia, Pa., 1929*), physician. Began medical studies at University of California; M.D., Jefferson Medical College, 1878. Practiced in Philadelphia and was lecturer and professor at several medical schools there, including Temple University and the postgraduate school of University of Pennsylvania. Authority on endocrinology and laryngology.

SAKEL, MANFRED JOSHUA (*b. Nadvorna, Austria* [now Nadvornaya, Ukrainian S.S.R.], *1900; d. New York, N.Y., 1957*), psychiatrist. Immigrated to the U.S. in 1936. Studied at the First State College in Brno and at the University of Vienna (M.D., 1925). Worked at the Lichterfelde Hospital in Berlin from 1927 to 1933. The first to use insulin coma therapy as a treatment for mental disorders, Sakel propagated his technique in the U.S. after immigration. Published *The Pharmacologic Shock Treatment of Schizophrenia* in 1938.

SALISBURY, ALBERT (*b. Lima, Wis., 1843; d. 1911*), educator, Union soldier. President, Whitewater (Wis.) Normal School, 1885–1911.

SALISBURY, EDWARD ELBRIDGE (*b. Boston, Mass., 1814; d. 1901*), orientalist, educator. Graduated Yale, 1932; made postgraduate studies there in Hebrew and cognate languages, and at Paris, Bonn, and Berlin. A pioneer teacher of Arabic and Sanskrit at Yale, 1843–56, Salisbury opened the field of Oriental studies in the United States. He was author of a number of learned studies published principally in *Journal of American Oriental Society*.

SALISBURY, JAMES HENRY (*b. Scott, N.Y., 1823; d. Dobbs Ferry, N.Y., 1905*), physician, chemist, plant pathologist. A precursor of the germ theory of disease in works published, 1862–68.

SALISBURY, ROLLIN D. (*b. Spring Prairie, Wis., 1858; d. 1922*), geologist, educator. Graduated Beloit College, 1881. Succeeded his mentor, Thomas C. Chamberlin, as professor of geology at Beloit, 1882–91. After teaching briefly at the University of Wisconsin, 1891, he became professor of geographic geology, University of Chicago, serving there as teacher (and dean of the Graduate School of Science *post* 1899) for the rest of his life. He was a leading authority on glacial and Pleistocene deposits.

SALMON, DANIEL ELMER (*b. Mount Olive, N.J., 1850; d. Butte, Mont., 1914*), veterinarian. Graduated Cornell, 1872; D.V.M., 1876. Outstanding as chief, Bureau of Animal Industry, U.S. Department of Agriculture, 1883–1905, he succeeded in bringing contagious pleuropneumonia and Texas fever among cattle under complete control. He also made investigations into the cause and prevention of fowl cholera, contagious diseases of swine, and nodular diseases of sheep. He was responsible for the inauguration of a nationwide system of meat inspection, for a quarantine system for imported livestock, and for inspection of export cattle and the ships which carried them.

SALMON, LUCY MAYNARD (*b. Fulton, N.Y., 1853; d. 1927*), educator. Graduated University of Michigan, 1876; M.A., 1883; fellow in history, Bryn Mawr, 1886–87. Taught history at Vassar, 1887–1927.

SALMON, THOMAS WILLIAM (*b. Lansingburg, N.Y., 1876; d. 1927*), physician, pioneer in mental hygiene.

SALM-SALM, AGNES ELISABETH WINONA LECLERQ JOY (*b. Franklin Co., Vt., or possibly Philipsburg, Quebec, 1840; d. Karlsruhe, Germany, 1912*), princess, adventuress. Princess Salm-Salm is principally remembered for her heroic role during the fall of Maximilian's regime in Mexico, 1867, when she attempted the emperor's rescue, and for her relief work with the German army, 1870.

SALOMON, HAYM (*b. Lissa, Poland, ca. 1740; d. Philadelphia, Pa., 1785*), merchant, Revolutionary patriot. An advocate of Polish independence, he fled to England, 1772, and thence to New York City, where he began business as a broker and commission merchant. Twice imprisoned by the British as an active Whig, 1776 and 1778, he removed to Philadelphia and within the next few years became a leading broker in that city. His liberal advances of cash to officers of the government and his equally liberal investments in Revolutionary paper, *ca.* 1780–84, constitute an outstanding example of devotion to the American cause; he contributed much in other ways to maintain the bankrupt government's credit.

SALTER, WILLIAM (*b. Brooklyn, N.Y., 1821; d. 1910*), Congregational clergyman. Removed to Iowa, 1843. At first an itinerant pastor, he served as minister of the First Church of Burlington,

1846–1910. He was author of a number of religious books and several works on Iowa history.

SALTER, WILLIAM MACKINTIRE (b. Burlington, Iowa, 1853; d. 1931), Ethical Culture lecturer, philosopher. Son of William Salter. Authority on the thought of Nietzsche.

SALTONSTALL, DUDLEY (b. New London, Conn., 1738; d. Mole St. Nicolas, Haiti, 1796), naval officer. Grandson of Gurdon Saltonstall. Served as a privateersman in the French and Indian War; commanded merchant ships before the Revolution. Given command of the *Alfred*, flagship of Commodore Esek Hopkins, 1775, he was in the expedition which captured New Providence, 1776. He is best remembered for his connection with the Penobscot expedition, 1779, during which he commanded the naval forces employed. He was dismissed from the navy for failure to support army operations against the fort and the British vessels which were protecting Castine (Bagaduce) harbor and for the eventual loss of his entire fleet. He was subsequently successful in privateering and afterward returned to the merchant service.

SALTONSTALL, GURDON (b. Haverhill, Mass., 1666 o.s.; d. 1724 o.s.), Congregational clergyman, colonial statesman. Great-grandson of Nathaniel Ward; grandson of Richard Saltonstall. Graduated Harvard, 1684. Ordained minister of the church at New London, Conn., 1691; became confidant and adviser of Fitz-John Winthrop. Closely associated with public affairs during Winthrop's governorship, 1698–1707, Saltonstall succeeded him as governor of Connecticut at the request of the Connecticut Assembly and was reelected annually until his death. His adroit and conservative management of the colony's affairs fully justified the confidence placed in him. He was a leader in the approval by the Assembly of the Saybrook platform of 1708 and was active in the permanent settlement of Yale College at New Haven.

SALTONSTALL, RICHARD (b. Woodsome, Yorkshire, England, ca. 1610; d. Hulme, Lancashire, England, 1694), Massachusetts colonist. Grandfather of Gurdon Saltonstall. Came with his father to Massachusetts Bay, 1630, where they established the settlement of Watertown. After studying law in England, 1631–35, he returned to New England and settled in Ipswich. His residence there was interrupted by three stays in England, 1649–63, 1672–80, and 1686–94. A colonial officeholder and magistrate, he served also in the militia and was a member of the liberal group which included Simon Bradstreet and Nathaniel Ward.

SALTUS, EDGAR EVERTSON (b. New York, N.Y., 1855; d. 1921), novelist, essayist. Author of *The Philosophy of Disenchantment* (1885) and other works expressive of rebellion against contemporary main currents in American literature, Saltus wrote in a style which strained after effect and was more bizarre than original. He is to be studied at his best in an account of the Roman emperors, *Imperial Purple* (1892); his fiction was marked by weakness of characterization and melodramatic situations.

SAMAROFF, OLGA (b. San Antonio, Tex., 1882; d. New York, N.Y., 1948), pianist, teacher. Christened Lucie Mary Olga Agnes Hickenlooper. Studied at Paris Conservatory, where in 1896 she was first American girl to win a scholarship; studied also in Berlin. Debut at Carnegie Hall, New York City, January 1905, as "Olga Samaroff," the name of a remote ancestor. Successful in European and American concert tours, she married Leopold Stokowski, 1911, from whom she was divorced in 1923. Taught at Juilliard School, New York City, *post* 1925, and at Philadelphia Conservatory of Music *post* 1928; organized Schubert Memorial, 1928, to provide debut opportunities for young American artists; created Layman's Music Courses, *ca.* 1930.

SAMPSON, MARTIN WRIGHT (b. Cincinnati, Ohio, 1866; d. 1930), educator, editor. Stimulating teacher of English composition and literature at University of Iowa, Stanford, Indiana, and Cornell, 1908–30.

SAMPSON, WILLIAM (b. Londonderry, Ireland, 1764; d. New York, N.Y., 1836), Irish patriot, lawyer. Imprisoned for activity with the United Irishmen at the end of the 18th century, Sampson was exiled in 1799 and settled in the United States, 1806. Admitted to the bar almost immediately, he won high rank through his eloquence and his advocacy of personal rights. He was counsel in one of the earliest American labor cases (the Journeymen Cordwainers Case in New York, 1809–10) and in 1813 was successful as amicus curiae in the Kohlmann Case. His *Memoirs* (1807) were in fact a denunciation of the British policy toward Ireland. He was also author of an early (1823) plea for the codification of American law.

SAMPSON, WILLIAM THOMAS (b. Palmyra, N.Y., 1840; d. Washington, D.C., 1902), naval officer. Graduated U.S. Naval Academy, 1861. After service with the Union naval forces, he performed several tours of duty as an instructor at Annapolis and was superintendent of the Naval Academy, 1886–90. As chief of the ordnance bureau, 1893–97, he was credited with making great advances in guns, explosives, and gunnery practice. President of the board of inquiry on the *Maine* disaster, he was selected to command the North Atlantic Squadron in the war with Spain; he supervised the entire blockade of Cuba and was responsible for cooperation with the army. His absence from the mouth of Santiago Harbor when the Spanish squadron issued forth to defeat on the morning of July 3, 1898, led to a celebrated controversy with Adm. Winfield S. Schley over credit for the victory. He was made permanent rear admiral, 1899.

SAMUELS, EDWARD AUGUSTUS (b. Boston, Mass., 1836; d. Fitchburg, Mass., 1908), ornithologist, sportsman, authority on the natural history of New England.

SAMUELS, SAMUEL (b. Philadelphia, Pa., 1823; d. Brooklyn, N.Y., 1908), master mariner. Celebrated for his 78 fast voyages as captain of the New York and Liverpool packet *Dreadnought*, 1854–62. Author of an interesting autobiography *From the Forecastle to the Cabin* (1887).

SANBORN, EDWIN DAVID (b. Gilmanton, N.H., 1808; d. New York, N.Y., 1885), educator. Graduated Dartmouth 1832. Taught Latin and Greek at Dartmouth, 1835–37, and in 1837 became professor of Latin. Removing to Washington University, St. Louis, Mo., 1859, he taught there until 1863; he then returned to Dartmouth as professor of oratory and belles lettres, resigning in 1882. A teacher of the old school, brimful of learning, he inspired generations of undergraduates with some measure of his own enthusiasm for letters.

SANBORN, FRANKLIN BENJAMIN (b. Hampton Falls, N.H., 1831; d. Plainfield, N.J., 1917), author, journalist, reformer. Graduated Harvard, 1855. Influenced by Theodore Parker and Ralph Waldo Emerson, he conducted a school at Concord, Mass., and was soon in the thick of the abolition movement. New England agent for John Brown, he was arrested in April 1860 for refusing to testify before the U.S. Senate on Brown's intentions, but was almost immediately released on a writ of habeas corpus. Thereafter he devoted the greater part of his time to newspaper work and to activity with the Massachusetts state board of charities. A lecturer at many schools and colleges, he joined with William T. Harris in establishing the Concord School of Philosophy. He had known intimately the men and women who had made Concord famous and served as their loyal, intelligent editor and biographer after their deaths. Among his books are *Henry D.*

Thoreau (1882), *The Life and Letters of John Brown* (1885 and later editions), *Ralph Waldo Emerson* (1901), and *Recollections of Seventy Years* (1909).

SANBORN, KATHERINE ABBOTT (*b.* Hanover, N.H., *1839; d. 1917*), teacher, lecturer, journalist. Daughter of Edwin D. Sanborn, she published most of her writing under the name of Kate Sanborn. Among her books are *Adopting an Abandoned Farm* (1891), *A Truthful Woman in Southern California* (1839), and *Memories and Anecdotes* (1915).

SANBORN, WALTER HENRY (*b.* Epsom, N.H., *1845; d. 1928*), jurist. Removed to St. Paul, Minn., *ca.* 1870. Judge, U.S. circuit court of appeals (8th Circuit), 1892–1928; presiding judge of the circuit *post* 1903. A man of deep learning, he was especially skilled in cases dealing with personal injury.

SANDBURG, CARL AUGUST (*b.* Galesburg, Ill., *1878; d. Flat Rock, N.C., 1967*), poet, biographer, journalist, and folklorist. Attended Lombard College in Illinois and published his first book of poems, *In Reckless Ecstasy*, in 1904. Was drawn into Chicago's radical circles, and in 1907 joined the Socialist party and became a professional organizer; but broke with the party in 1917. A number of his poems, including "Chicago," were published in *Poetry: A Magazine of Verse* in 1912, and their free verse in vigorous colloquial rhythms established him as an outstanding figure among Chicago writers. Published *Chicago Poems* (1916), *Cornhuskers* (1918), *Smoke and Steel* (1920), and *Slabs of the Sunburnt West* (1922). In 1918 he went to Stockholm, Sweden, to report on the Finnish Revolution for the Newspaper Enterprise and smuggled Lenin's "Letter to American Workingmen" into the United States. His first book for children was *Rootabaga Stories* (1922). He made frequent public appearances before college groups and literary audiences, and his platform appearances increased his popularity and the sale of his books. He brought together nearly 300 songs and ballads in *The American Songbag* (1927). His two-volume *Abraham Lincoln: The Prairie Years* (1926) won critical acclaim, and his four-volume *Abraham Lincoln: The War Years* (1939) won a Pulitzer Prize. His one novel *Remembrance Rock* (1948), and his *Complete Poems* (1950) won him another Pulitzer. He received the Presidential Medal of Freedom in 1964.

SANDE, EARL (*b.* Groton, S.Dak., *1898; d. Jacksonville, Oreg., 1968*), jockey and horse trainer. Began his professional career in 1918 in New Orleans and rode 158 winners that first season. He was the leading money-winning jockey in 1921, 1923, and 1927, winning the Kentucky Derby on Flying Ebony in 1925 and on Zev in 1927. He was suspended in 1927 for a foul at Pimlico, but was reinstated in 1928. Returned as a jockey in 1930 and rode Gallant Fox to the Triple Crown of racing; he rode thirteen winners in 1932, the year he retired. Was a trainer for Col. Maxwell Howard, 1932–44, then took over the Howard stable, and also trained for Clifford Mooers until 1949.

SANDEMAN, ROBERT (*b.* Perth, Scotland, *1718; d. Danbury, Conn., 1771*), preacher. Promoter in the American colonies of the sect which came to be known as Sandemanians, 1764–71. He and his followers were vigorously opposed by leading New England ministers for their rejection of the Covenant of Grace and of the doctrine of justification by faith as an act of regeneration. Sandeman taught that "every one who obtains a just notion of the person and work of Christ . . . is justified . . . simply by that notion."

SANDERS, BILLINGTON McCARTER (*b.* Columbia Co., Ga., *1789; d. Penfield, Ga., 1854*), Baptist minister. Graduated South Carolina College, 1809. First principal of Mercer Institute,

1832–39, he has been justly called the real founder of Mercer University.

SANDERS, CHARLES WALTON (*b.* Newport, N.Y., *1805; d. New York, N.Y., 1889*), educator. Author of elementary school textbooks in reading and spelling.

SANDERS, DANIEL CLARKE (*b.* Sturbridge, Mass., *1768; d. Medfield, Mass., 1850*), educator, Congregational clergyman. Graduated Harvard, 1788. First president of University of Vermont, 1800–14, Sanders managed its finances, supervised erection of its first building, and for some time carried the entire burden of instruction. Pastor of the First Church, Medfield, Mass., 1815–29.

SANDERS, DANIEL JACKSON (*b.* near Winnsboro, S.C., *1847; d. 1907*), Presbyterian clergyman, educator. Born in slavery, Sanders graduated from Western Theological Seminary, Allegheny, Pa., 1874. A leader in educational work and a pastor in Wilmington, N.C., he was editor of the *Africo-American Presbyterian*, *post* 1879, and president of Biddle (later Johnson C. Smith) University, *post* 1891.

SANDERS, ELIZABETH ELKINS (*b.* Salem, Mass., *1762; d. Salem, 1851*), author, reformer. Advocate of justice for the American Indian and opponent of foreign-mission activity.

SANDERS, FRANK KNIGHT (*b.* Batticotta, Ceylon, *1861; d. Rockport, Mass., 1933*), Congregational clergyman, biblical scholar. Son of missionary parents, he graduated Ripon College, 1882. Influenced by the teaching of William R. Harper at Yale Divinity School, he turned to graduate work in Semitic languages, Ph.D., 1889. Instructor and professor at Yale, 1889–1905, and dean of its Divinity School, 1901–05, he was active thereafter in church administrative positions and was author of a number of books.

SANDERS, GEORGE NICHOLAS (*b.* Lexington, Ky., *1812; d. 1873*), financial promoter, lobbyist, revolutionist. Grandson of George Nicholas. Led "Young America" movement, 1851–53, as means of furthering revolutionary republicanism in Europe. As U.S. consul in London, 1853, he plotted recklessly with Kossuth, Mazzini, and other exiled rebels and was refused Senate confirmation in the post. During the Civil War, he was a Confederate agent in Europe and Canada. Half-idealist, half-charlatan.

SANDERS, JAMES HARVEY (*b.* Union Co., Ohio, *1832; d. Memphis, Tenn., 1899*), agricultural journalist. Founded *Western Stock Journal*, May 1869, the first periodical devoted to animal husbandry; was a noted breeder of horses; wrote the *Norman Stud Book* (1876) and other studies in animal heredity.

SANDERS, THOMAS (*b.* South Danvers, Mass., *1839; d. Derry, N.H., 1911*), financier. Advanced money to Alexander Graham Bell for development of the telephone; later served as an official and director of the Bell Telephone Co.

SANDERS, WILBUR FISK (*b.* Leon, N.Y., *1834; d. 1905*), Montana pioneer lawyer. Nephew of Sidney Edgerton, with whom he removed to what was then eastern Idaho, 1863. An organizer of vigilantes and successful in his practice, he was a leader in the movement to form a separate territory from eastern Idaho. After organization of Montana Territory, 1864, he promoted the Republican party there, and on Montana's admission as a state, he was elected U.S. senator, serving January 1890–March 1893.

SANDERSON, EZRA DWIGHT (*b.* Clio, Mich., *1878; d. Ithaca, N.Y., 1944*), entomologist, rural sociologist. B.S., Michigan Agricultural College, 1897; B.S., Cornell University, 1898;

Ph.D., University of Chicago, 1921. Worked in the field of economic entomology in Maryland, Delaware, Texas, New Hampshire, and West Virginia; headed Department of Rural Sociology, Cornell University, 1918–43.

SANDERSON, JOHN (*b. near Carlisle, Pa., 1783; d. Philadelphia, Pa., 1844*), educator, author. Teacher of classical languages and English in Philadelphia, Sanderson was a popular contributor to periodicals and for a brief time edited the *Aurora* newspaper. He was author of *Sketches of Paris, by an American Gentleman* (1838), which was widely read, and with his brother published the first two volumes of the *Biography of the Signers to the Declaration of Independence* (1820, completed by Robert Waln, 1823–27).

SANDERSON, ROBERT (*b. England, 1608; d. Boston, Mass., 1693*), silversmith. Immigrated to America as a young man; was among first settlers in Hampton, N.H., 1638; resided in Watertown, Mass., 1639–53. Removed to Boston in 1653, after appointment (with John Hull) to manage the colony mint. A craftsman in the front rank of New England silversmiths, he was probably Hull's first teacher.

SANDERSON, SIBYL (*b. Sacramento, Calif., 1865; d. Paris, France, 1903*), dramatic soprano. Studied at Paris Conservatory, 1886–88. Made debut at The Hague in Massenet's *Manon*, 1888; made Paris debut at the Opéra Comique, 1889; created role of *Thaïs* at Paris, 1894. Despite her tremendous popularity on the Continent, she was received coldly in England and America.

SANDHAM, HENRY (*b. Montreal, Canada, 1842; d. London, England, 1910*), portrait painter, landscapist, illustrator. Worked in Boston, Mass., 1880–1901. Illustrated many books, including H. H. Jackson's *Ramona* (1900 ed.); painted several large historical studies, among them *The Dawn of Liberty*, now in Lexington, Mass., town hall.

SANDLER, JACOB KOPPEL (*b. Bialozerkove, Russia, 1856; d. 1931*), composer. Immigrated to New York City, 1888. After working as a shirtmaker and as a peddler, he became director of a synagogue choir and eked out a precarious living by acting also as chorus director in a Yiddish theater. As incidental music for a long-forgotten play, he composed the celebrated hymn "Eili, Eili"; it was first performed in April 1896 at the Windsor Theatre in the Bowery.

SANDOZ, MARI (*b. Sheridan County, Nebr., 1896; d. New York, N.Y., 1966*), historian and novelist. With only four and a half years of formal schooling, she taught in rural schools in Nebraska, 1913–22, then attended the University of Nebraska as a special student. *Old Jules* (1935), a biography of her father, a Swiss immigrant who had become a rancher and horticulturist, won the Atlantic Monthly Prize for nonfiction; it was the first book in her Trans-Missouri Series, which recounts the history of the Great Plains from the Stone Age to modern times. Taught fiction writing at Wisconsin, 1947–55. Her two highly regarded short novels on Indian themes are *The Horsecatcher* (1956) and *The Story Catcher* (1962). The best and least allegorical of her novels is *Miss Morissa* (1955).

SANDS, BENJAMIN FRANKLIN (*b. Baltimore, Md., 1812; d. Washington, D.C., 1883*), naval officer. Raised in Kentucky; entered navy as midshipman, 1828. After varied service, principally in survey and hydrographic work, he became chief of the Bureau of Construction and served, 1858–61. Promoted captain, 1862, he was senior officer on the North Carolina coast blockade until October 1864, when he was assigned to operations against Fort Fisher. Commander of the second division, West Gulf Squadron, 1865, he hoisted the flag at Galveston, Tex., on June 5 after receiving the surrender of the last Confederate troops. Super-

intendent of the Naval Observatory, 1867–74, he retired as rear admiral.

SANDS, COMFORT (*b. present Sands' Point, N.Y., 1748; d. Hoboken, N.J., 1834*), New York merchant, Revolutionary patriot and fiscal official. A founder of the Bank of New York, 1784, he was president of the New York Chamber of Commerce, 1794–98.

SANDS, DAVID (*b. present Sands' Point, N.Y., 1745; d. Cornwall-on-the-Hudson, N.Y., 1818*), Quaker preacher, abolitionist, merchant.

SANDS, JOSHUA RATOON (*b. Brooklyn, N.Y., 1795; d. Baltimore, Md., 1883*), naval officer. Nephew of Comfort Sands. Entering the navy, June 1812, he retired as rear admiral, 1872, after a career of active service which included the War of 1812, the Mexican War, and the Civil War.

SANDS, ROBERT CHARLES (*b. New York, N.Y., 1799; d. Hoboken, N.J., 1832*), journalist, author. Son of Comfort Sands. Graduated Columbia, 1815. Projected and edited minor literary periodicals; assisted William Cullen Bryant in editorship of *New York Review*, 1825–26; was on editorial staff of *New-York Commercial Advertiser*, 1827–32. Joined with Bryant and Gulian C. Verplanck in publication of *The Talisman*, an annual to which he contributed some of his best work. His collected writings were published, 1834, including his principal poetic work, *Yamoyden* (previously published, 1820).

SANDYS, GEORGE (*b. Bishopsthorpe, near York, England, 1577/8; d. Boxley Abbey, near Maidstone, Kent, England, 1643/4*), poet, Virginia colonist. A shareholder in the Virginia Co., he was appointed treasurer of the colony of Virginia, 1621. Removing to Virginia in the autumn of that year, he remained there until 1628 or later. An industrious and able administrator, he is best remembered for his verse translation of the *Metamorphoses* of Ovid which he completed in Virginia (1626; 2nd ed., 1632).

SANFORD, EDMUND CLARK (*b. Oakland, Calif., 1859; d. 1924*), psychologist, educator. Graduated University of California, 1883; Ph.D., Johns Hopkins, 1888. Taught at Clark University *post* 1889; president of Clark College, 1909–20; professor of psychology and education, Clark University, 1920–24.

SANFORD, EDWARD TERRY (*b. Knoxville, Tenn., 1865; d. 1930*), lawyer. Judge, U.S. district court in Tennessee, 1908–23; associate justice, U.S. Supreme Court, 1923–30. Considered slow in making decisions as a district judge, Sanford wrote a number of important opinions while on the Supreme Court. Probably his most important opinion was in what is known as the Pocket Veto Case, 1929.

SANFORD, ELIAS BENJAMIN (*b. Westbrook, Conn., 1843; d. 1932*), Congregational clergyman. A leader in the forming of the Federal Council of the Churches of Christ in America, he served it for many years as secretary and also wrote its history.

SANFORD, HENRY SHELTON (*b. Woodbury, Conn., 1823; d. Healing Springs, Va., 1891*), diplomat, developer of Sanford, Fla.

SANFORD, NATHAN (*b. Bridgehampton, N.Y., 1777; d. Flushing, N.Y., 1838*), lawyer, New York State legislator and public official. U.S. senator, Democrat, from New York, 1815–21 and 1826–31, he confined his attention to administration and to measures for improvement of government organization. He advocated creation of a department of the interior and expansion of the attorney general's office into a department of justice.

SANGER, CHARLES ROBERT (*b. Boston, Mass., 1860; d. Cambridge, Mass., 1912*), chemist. Son of George P. Sanger. Graduated Harvard, 1881; Ph.D., 1884. Associated in research work with Henry B. Hill, Sanger succeeded him as professor of chemistry at Harvard, 1903. His most important research was concerned with detection of arsenic and antimony and with the chemistry of pyromucic acid and its derivatives. His work confirmed the dangers suspected in the use of arsenic in wallpaper.

SANGER, GEORGE PARTRIDGE (*b. Dover, Mass., 1819; d. 1890*), Boston lawyer, Massachusetts public official. First president, John Hancock Mutual Life Insurance Co. (organized 1863).

SANGER, MARGARET HIGGINS (*b. Corning, N.Y., 1879; d. Tucson, Ariz., 1966*), birth control advocate. In 1911, professing the twin goals of sexual and political revolution, she joined the Socialist party, wrote articles for the Socialist *Call*, and participated in the Lawrence, Mass., textile mills strikes. As a visiting nurse on Manhattan's Lower East Side she encountered many women whose health had been broken by excessive childbearing or botched abortions. Began to publish *Woman Rebel* (1914), a belligerently radical sheet, but its postal privileges were almost immediately suspended for violating federal antiobscenity statutes. She fled to Europe to avoid prosecution, and remained there until 1915; charges were dropped in 1916. She opened the first birth control clinic in the United States in Brooklyn, N.Y., in 1916, and within weeks was arrested and served a thirty-day sentence. In 1917 she launched *Birth Control Review*, which served as link for birth control organizations springing up around the country. By the 1920's she had abandoned her radical associates and fallen in with upper-class woman reformers. Organized the first American Birth Control Conference and founded the American Birth Control League in 1921, over which she presided until 1928. She prodded the American Medical Association in 1937 to declare its support for prescribing contraception and for conducting research into improved contraceptive techniques; that research, with Sanger's quiet financial backing, led to the development of the birth control pill in the 1950's. In 1938 the American Birth Control League and her Clinical Research Bureau joined to form the Birth Control Federation of America, later the Planned Parenthood Federation of America.

SANGSTER, MARGARET ELIZABETH MUNSON (*b. New Rochelle, N.Y., 1838; d. Maplewood, N.J., 1912*), journalist. Editor of, among other periodicals, *Hearth and Home* and *Harper's Bazaar*; author of a number of volumes in prose and verse compiled from her magazine articles and of several novels, cheerful, practical, and religious in tone.

SANKEY, IRA DAVID (*b. Edinburg, Pa., 1840; d. Brooklyn, N.Y., 1908*), singing evangelist. Associated *post ca.* 1870 with the work of Dwight L. Moody. Collections of the songs used in the Moody and Sankey revivals gained almost worldwide popularity.

SANTAYANA, GEORGE (*b. Madrid, Spain, 1863; d. Rome, Italy, 1952*), philosopher and poet. Immigrated to the U.S. in 1872. Studied at Harvard (Ph.D., 1889) and Berlin. Taught at Harvard (1889–1912). Lived abroad after 1912. One of America's foremost philosophers, Santayana published many works: *Sonnets and Other Verses* (1894), *The Sense of Beauty* (1896), *Interpretations of Poetry and Religion* (1900), *The Life of Reason: or the Phases of Human Progress* (1905–06), *The Realm of Being* (1927–40), *Scepticism and Animal Faith* (1923), and a best-selling novel, *The Last Puritan* (1935). Santayana believed that nature is ultimately man's source and destiny and that nature manifests itself in man in his urge to make existence as reasonable and beautiful as possible. Man's moral task is to move towards reason and harmony through appreciation and action informed by critical and constructive effort.

SAPIR, EDWARD (*b. Lauenburg, Germany, 1884; d. New Haven, Conn., 1939*), anthropologist, linguist. Came to America as a child. Graduated Columbia, 1904; Ph.D., 1909. Influenced by Franz Boas, whose anthropological approach to the study of language opened up vistas for him, Sapir began the study of American Indian languages and cultures, the field in which much of his work was done. Chief of the anthropology division, Canadian National Museum, 1910–25, he was Sterling professor of anthropology and linguistics at Yale, 1925–39. A pioneer in the phonemic method of linguistic analysis, he was also much interested in general culture and its relation to personality. He was author of many specialized papers and of *Language* (1921).

SAPPINGTON, JOHN (*b. Maryland, 1776; d. 1856*), physician. Raised in Tennessee; removed to Missouri, 1817, where he practiced in Howard and later Saline counties. Soon after quinine (isolated 1820) became available in the United States, he strongly advocated its use in treatment of malaria without recourse to bleeding and purging. Author of *Theory and Treatment of Fevers* (1844), he distributed quinine wholesale, *post* 1832, as Dr. Sappington's Anti-Fever Pills.

SARDI, MELCHIORRE PIO VENCENZO ("VINCENT") (*b. San Marzano Oliveto, Italy, 1885; d. Saranac Lake, N.Y., 1969*), restaurateur. An adventurous boy, he worked on a coastal schooner and then in London gained experience as waiter in plush hotels. After arrival in New York (1907), he refined his skills in food service at several of the city's finest restaurants, such as Knickerbocker Hotel's dining room, the Palais Royale, and the Bartholdi Inn. In 1921 he opened Sardi's, a small forty-seat restaurant in the theater district; it soon attracted a steady stream of actors, producers, and writers. In 1926 he had to close to make way for the St. James Theater; he opened a new Sardi's in 1927 in the same area, but customers were slow in returning. He hired Alex Gard to do caricatures of his clientele, and soon hundreds of them covered the walls from floor to ceiling. By 1930's the restaurant was more popular than ever. Syndicated columnists, such as Walter Winchell, made the dining room their home base; following opening night performances on Broadway, it became a tradition to gather at Sardi's to wait for reviews. In 1946 Sardi's became the setting for the daily radio program "Luncheon at Sardi's." He retired in 1947.

SARG, TONY (*b. Coban, Guatemala, 1880; d. New York, N.Y., 1942*), illustrator, author, puppeteer. Son of a German coffee and sugar planter and his English wife; graduated Prussian military academy at Lichterfelde, 1899. Resigned army commission, 1905, and worked as an artist in England, 1905–15. Immigrated to New York City, 1915, where he worked as a designer and illustrator, and created highly original marionette shows, which toured with great success, 1920–30. Among his most notable creations were the giant animal balloons, featured in Macy's Thanksgiving Day parade in New York City.

SARGENT, AARON AUGUSTUS (*b. Newburyport, Mass., 1827; d. San Francisco, Calif., 1887*), printer, journalist, lawyer. Removed to California, 1849. Starting in politics as a Know-Nothing assemblyman, he was active in organization of the Republican party in California and served as congressman, 1861–63 and 1869–73. He was author, with Theodore D. Judah, of the first Pacific railroad bill to pass Congress. U.S. senator, 1873–79, he was U.S. minister to Germany, 1882–84. Closely identified with the railroad interests, he was a masterful machine politician.

SARGENT, CHARLES SPRAGUE (*b. Boston, Mass., 1841; d. 1927*), arboriculturist, Union soldier. Graduated Harvard, 1862. Professor of horticulture at Harvard, 1872–73; professor of arboriculture, 1879–1927. Directed the Arnold Arboretum *post* 1873. Author of *Report on the Forests of North America* (1884) and the notable *Silva of North America* (1891–1902), among other works. Advocated conservation and national parks.

SARGENT, DUDLEY ALLEN (*b. Belfast, Maine, 1849; d. 1924*), physician, physical culture expert. Developed programs of physical training at Bowdoin, Yale, and Harvard; organized a training school for physical education teachers at Cambridge, Mass., 1881.

SARGENT, EPES (*b. Gloucester, Mass., 1813; d. 1880*), journalist, poet, spiritualist. Brother of John O. Sargent. His numerous anthologies composed for school use gave him a wide contemporary celebrity. Among his plays, *Velasco* (published 1839) was the most successful; his best volume of verse was *Songs of the Sea* (1847), which contains the well-known "A Life on the Ocean Wave." *Post* 1865, he devoted most of his energy to the exposition of his new faith in spiritualism.

SARGENT, FITZWILLIAM (*b. Gloucester, Mass., 1820; d. Bournemouth, England, 1889*), ophthalmologist, surgeon. Practiced in Philadelphia, 1843–52; lived principally in Europe thereafter. Father of John Singer Sargent.

SARGENT, FRANK PIERCE (*b. East Orange, Vt., 1854; d. Washington, D.C., 1908*), labor leader. Headed Brotherhood of Locomotive Firemen, 1885–1902. As U.S. commissioner general of immigration *post* 1902, he helped initiate methods for the prevention of fraud against immigrants, for the exclusion of undesirable elements, and for the prevention of smuggling of Chinese across the borders.

SARGENT, FREDERICK (*b. Liskeard, England, 1859; d. Glencoe, Ill., 1919*), electrical engineer. Came to America, 1880. Consulting engineer for the Chicago Edison Co. and many other concerns, he was a specialist in the design and construction of central electric generating stations. He was among the first to recognize the advantages of the steam turbine.

SARGENT, GEORGE HENRY (*b. Warner, N.H., 1867; d. Warner, 1931*), journalist. City editor, *St. Paul* (Minn.) *Daily Pioneer Press*, 1890–95; staff member, *Boston Evening Transcript*, 1895–1931. Conducted "The Bibliographer" department for the *Transcript*.

SARGENT, HENRY (*b. Gloucester, Mass., ca. 1770; d. 1845*), painter. Brother of Lucius M. Sargent. Encouraged by John Trumbull, he studied in London with Benjamin West. Diligent and gifted, he fell short of genius; he is best represented by *The Tea Party* and *The Dinner Party* in the Boston Museum of Fine Arts.

SARGENT, HENRY WINTHROP (*b. Boston, Mass., 1810; d. 1882*), horticulturist, landscape gardener. Son of Henry Sargent.

SARGENT, JAMES (*b. Chester, Vt., 1824; d. 1910*), lock expert. Formed partnership of Sargent and Greenleaf in Rochester, N.Y., 1869, to manufacture the "nonpickable" lock which he had devised; perfected a time lock *ca.* 1873. He was also inventor and manufacturer of a number of other devices, including railway semaphore signals, automatic fire alarms, and glass-lined steel tanks.

SARGENT, JOHN OSBORNE (*b. Gloucester, Mass., 1811; d. 1891*), lawyer, journalist. Brother of Epes Sargent. Author of, among other works, the posthumous *Horatian Echoes* (1893).

SARGENT, JOHN SINGER (*b. Florence, Italy, 1856; d. London, England, 1925*), painter. Son of Fitz-William Sargent. Encouraged in art by his mother (who had been responsible for the family's expatriation to Europe shortly before his birth), Sargent received lessons at the Academy in Florence and continued to sketch from nature as the family wandered through southern Italy, France, and Germany. Beginning formal study at the Beaux-Arts in Paris, 1874, he acquired in the atelier of Carolus-Duran a facile and fluent technique quite suited to his temperament and a dexterity in seizing instantaneous effects. After a brief visit to the United States, 1876, he returned to France, where he painted his *Gitana* and *Rehearsal at the Cirque d'Hiver*; in 1877 he sent his first picture, a portrait of Miss Watts, to the Salon. Following productive visits to Italy, Spain, and Morocco, 1878–80, he entered on a period of activity to which belong some of his finest portraits, including the famous *Madame Gautreau*, which roused a tempest of abuse when it was first exhibited in Paris. The artist was entirely serious in his work and devoid of malice; he had depicted the lady in a costume of her own choosing and he was astonished and hurt at the outcry of disparagement. Removing from Paris to London, he encountered further harsh criticism from the press, his portraits of Mrs. White and the Misses Vickers being declared hard, tasteless, and raw in color. His exotic style and brilliance, however, offering a contrast to the academic manner of British portrait painters of the time, brought him all the patrons he could desire. Establishing himself in a studio in Tite St., London, 1885, he produced the first of a long series of pictures of children in which he revealed the most lovable side of his nature in work of remarkable delicacy and beauty. His *Carnation, Lily, Lily, Rose*, exhibited at the Royal Academy, 1887, was a great success.

Resident in Boston, Mass., 1887–88, Sargent was first accorded the American appreciation which was so great a source of satisfaction to him throughout his career. Henceforward, Boston became his American headquarters and the goal of a long series of visits. On his second trip to America, 1890, he painted *Carmencita*, considered his masterpiece by many critics, and portraits of Edwin Booth, Joseph Jefferson, and Lawrence Barrett. Commissioned by the trustees of the Boston Public Library to paint mural decorations for that building, he welcomed the change. Beginning preliminary work, 1891, he completed the first part, 1894, and went to Boston, 1895, to see to its emplacement. Meanwhile, his portrait work continued and culminated in the appearance of the Wertheimer family portraits (1898, 1901, 1902). Made a Royal Academician, 1897, he showed forth all the finest qualities of his art in his diploma picture, *A Venetian Interior* (1900). Crossing and recrossing the Atlantic almost every year, he enjoyed on these voyages the only real rest periods he ever allowed himself to take. In 1916 he returned to America to install the last of the Boston Public Library decorations, and that summer went sketching in the Canadian Rockies and Glacier National Park. On completion of the library decorations he undertook to decorate the rotunda of the Art Museum, Boston, and while preparing studies for this work went to the war front in France during 1918 to record impressions for the Imperial War Museum, London. The Sargent exhibition in New York, 1924, was harshly reviewed by the modernists and was indicative of the change of taste which was soon to depreciate Sargent's worth as an artist.

As a portrait painter Sargent ranks beneath the greatest masters but rates as the equal of the best painters of the British school, Reynolds and Gainsborough. His genre paintings are original, objective, and possess great charm of style, but he was not so effective in landscape. Much may be said pro and con about his mural paintings. As he violated the accepted canons which ban relief and perspective, his walls do not have the vertical aspect demanded by sound architectonic principles; also, the want of flatness of modeling is matched by overwhelming complexity of detail. His Boston Library work, however, presents a splendid effect. His fertility of invention is undeniable, and if his work has little of the impassioned conviction of the ages of faith, this can hardly be imputed to the artist as a serious fault, for he was of his own time.

SARGENT, LUCIUS MANLIUS (*b. Boston, Mass., 1786; d. Boston, 1867*), antiquary, temperance advocate. Brother of Henry Sargent. Author of *Hubert and Ellen* (1812), *The Temperance Tales* (1848), *Dealings with the Dead* (1856), and other works.

SARGENT, NATHAN (*b. Putney, Vt., 1794; d. 1875*), Whig and Republican journalist, lawyer. Washington correspondent under pseudonym "Oliver Oldschool" for many Northern newspapers *post* 1842.

SARGENT, WINTHROP (*b. Gloucester, Mass., 1753; d. near New Orleans, La., 1820*), Revolutionary soldier, Ohio pioneer. Graduated Harvard, 1771. A secretary of the Ohio Co., he aided Manasseh Cutler in the purchase of land and took an active part in the planning of the new colony at Marietta. Appointed by Congress the secretary of Northwest Territory, 1787, he assumed charge during the frequent, prolonged absences of Governor Arthur St. Clair and was acting governor of the territory after St. Clair's defeat by the Indians, November 1791. Resigning his secretaryship, 1798, he became the first governor of Mississippi Territory, but failed of reappointment in 1801. Unpopular because of his Federalism, he was a conscientious public servant and a man of wide intellectual interests.

SARGENT, WINTHROP (*b. Philadelphia, Pa., 1825; d. Paris, France, 1870*), author. Grandson of Winthrop Sargent (1753–1820). A talented historical researcher, Sargent was author of *The History of an Expedition Against Fort Du Quesne in 1755* (1855) and *Life and Career of Major John André* (1861); he also edited *The Loyal Verses of Joseph Stansbury and Doctor Jonathan Odell* (1860).

SARPY, PETER A. (*b. St. Louis, Mo., 1805; d. Plattsmouth, Nebr., 1865*), fur trader, probably first white resident of Nebraska. Headed trading post at Bellevue, Nebr., *post ca.* 1823; assisted the Mormons on their first expedition westward; played large part in negotiation of land-cession treaties with Omaha and Oto Indians, 1854.

SARTAIN, EMILY (*b. Philadelphia, Pa., 1841; d. Philadelphia, 1927*), painter, engraver, educator. Daughter of John Sartain; sister of Samuel and William Sartain. Principal of the School of Design for Women, Philadelphia, 1886–1919.

SARTAIN, JOHN (*b. London, England, 1808; d. Philadelphia, Pa., 1897*), engraver, publisher. Came to America, 1830. Executed engraved plates for the periodicals of the day and was associated, 1841–48, principally with *Graham's Magazine*. Published *Sartain's Union Magazine*, 1849–52, a literary and artistic success but a financial failure. A versatile artist in all types of work, Sartain was particularly distinguished for his facility in mezzotint. Of his eight children, Emily, Samuel, and William had distinguished careers. He was author of an autobiography, *Reminiscences of a Very Old Man* (1899).

SARTAIN, SAMUEL (*b. Philadelphia, Pa., 1830; d. Philadelphia, 1906*), engraver. Son of John Sartain.

SARTAIN, WILLIAM (*b. Philadelphia, Pa., 1843; d. 1924*), painter. Son of John Sartain. Studied with Christian Schüssele and in France with Léon Bonnat. Particularly effective as a landscape painter, he was also active as a teacher and in artists' associations.

SARTON, GEORGE ALFRED LÉON (*b. Ghent, Belgium, 1884; d. Cambridge, Mass., 1956*), historian of science. Studied at the University of Ghent (D.Sc., 1911). Founder of the history of science journal *Isis* (1912) and its companion journal *Osiris* (1936). Sarton immigrated to the U.S. in 1915. *Isis*, which included Poincaré, Arrhenius, Durkheim, and Ostwald on the editorial board, was to become the mainspring for the study and legitimation of the history of science. An associate at the Carnegie Institution in Washington, D.C., Sarton lived in Cambridge. He completed three volumes of his monumental, *Introduction to the History of Science* by 1948. *Isis* became the official journal of the History of Science Society in 1924. Sarton was elected to the American Philosophical Society in 1934. President, International Union of History of Science (1950–56). Considered the chief catalyst in America for the formation of history of science as a distinct discipline. Father of novelist May Sarton.

SARTWELL, HENRY PARKER (*b. Pittsfield, Mass., 1792; d. Penn Yan, N.Y., 1867*), physician, botanist. Author of, among other works, *Carices Americae Septentrionalis Exsiccatae* (1848–50).

SASLAVSKY, ALEXANDER (*b. Kharkov, Russia, 1876; d. San Francisco, Calif., 1924*), violinist, conductor. Studied in Kharkov and Vienna; came to America *ca.* 1893. A first violinist of the New York Symphony Society, 1893–1918, and concertmaster and assistant conductor *post* 1903, Saslavsky became concertmaster of the Philharmonic Orchestra of Los Angeles, 1919. Throughout his career he was important as a teacher and for his work in introducing chamber music to a larger public.

SASSACUS (*b. probably near Groton, Conn., ca. 1560; d. 1637*), chief sachem of the Pequot. Killed by the Mohawk while fleeing westward after defeat of Pequot by John Mason, 1637.

SATTERLEE, HENRY YATES (*b. New York, N.Y., 1843; d. 1908*), Episcopal clergyman. Graduated Columbia, 1863; studied at General Theological Seminary, New York. Minister at Wappinger Falls, N.Y., 1865–82; rector of Calvary Parish, New York City, 1882–96. Elected bishop of the diocese of Washington, D.C., 1896, he projected and outlined plans for the National Cathedral, which was later developed in accord with his vision of it.

SATTERLEE, RICHARD SHERWOOD (*b. Fairfield, N.Y., 1798; d. 1880*), army surgeon. Practiced in Seneca Co., N.Y., and in Detroit, Mich., 1818–22; entered the U.S. Army as assistant surgeon, 1822; served in Middle West frontier posts and in Seminole War. Senior surgeon of General Worth's division in the Mexican War, he supervised the general hospital in Mexico City after its fall. Appointed medical purveyor, 1853, he served in this capacity throughout the Civil War, retiring as lieutenant colonel, 1869.

SAUGANASH (*b. Canada, ca. 1780; d. near present Council Bluffs, Iowa, 1841*), Potawatomi subchief. Also known as Billy Caldwell or Englishman. An associate of Tecumseh, 1807–13, he swore allegiance to the United States *ca.* 1820 when he took up residence at present, Chicago, Ill. He migrated with his people to Iowa in 1836.

SAUGRAIN DE VIGNI, ANTOINE FRANÇOIS (*b. Paris, France, 1763; d. St. Louis, Mo., 1820*), physician, naturalist, philosopher. Visited the United States, 1787–88, when he became a friend of Benjamin Franklin. Resided in Gallipolis, Ohio, 1790–96; resided in St. Louis, *post* 1800, where he practiced, performed scientific experiments, and introduced the first smallpox vaccine virus brought there, 1809.

SAULSBURY, ELI (*b. Kent Co., Del., 1817; d. Dover, Del., 1893*), lawyer, Delaware legislator. Brother of Gove and Willard Saulsbury (1820–92). U.S. senator, Democrat, from Delaware, 1871–89.

SAULSBURY, GOVE (*b. Kent Co., Del., 1815; d. 1881*), physician, politician. Brother of Eli and Willard Saulsbury (1820–92). M.D., University of Pennsylvania, 1842. A recognized Democratic leader in the Delaware legislature, he became acting governor of the state in March 1865 and served until 1871. He opposed all constitutional amendments growing out of the Civil War and characterized Reconstruction as a flagrant usurpation of power.

SAULSBURY, WILLARD (*b. Kent Co., Del., 1820; d. 1892*), lawyer, politician. Brother of Gove and Eli Saulsbury; father of Willard Saulsbury (1861–1927). Attorney general of Delaware, 1850–55. As U.S. senator, Democrat, from Delaware, 1859–71, he supported the Crittenden Resolutions and later opposed military interference in elections and the suspension of the writ of habeas corpus by the administration. He was chancellor of Delaware, 1873–92.

SAULSBURY, WILLARD (*b. Georgetown, Del., 1861; d. Wilmington, Del., 1927*), lawyer, businessman. Son of Willard Saulsbury (1820–92). U.S. senator, Democrat, from Delaware, 1913–19. A leading supporter of Woodrow Wilson's policies and a useful member of the Committee on Foreign Relations, he gave special attention to Chinese affairs.

SAUNDERS, ALVIN (*b. near Flemingsburg, Ky., 1817; d. Omaha, Nebr., 1899*), businessman, Iowa legislator. Chairman of the Iowa delegation to the Republican convention, 1860, he was active during the campaign in behalf of Abraham Lincoln. Appointed governor of Nebraska Territory, 1861, he served with ability until March 1867 when Nebraska became a state. U.S. senator, Republican, from Nebraska, 1877–83, he was particularly interested in the development of inland waterways and Indian affairs.

SAUNDERS, CLARENCE (*b. Amherst County, Va., 1881; d. Memphis, Tenn., 1953*), merchant. Self-educated, Saunders founded the first modern supermarket, the Piggly Wiggly grocery store (1916), which grew into the chain. Saunders lost heavily in Wall Street maneuverings in the 1920's and never regained his early successes after many tries at new marketing techniques. Regarded as the inventor of modern supermarket stores.

SAUNDERS, FREDERICK (*b. London, England, 1807; d. 1902*), librarian, author, journalist. Came to America, 1837; made a pioneer appeal to Congress for protection of the copyright of English authors against American pirating. Failing in his effort, he remained in the United States, wrote a number of useful books, and was librarian of the Astor Library *post* 1859 and chief librarian, 1876–96.

SAUNDERS, PRINCE (*b. either Lebanon, Conn., or Thetford, Vt., date unknown; d. Port-au-Prince, Haiti, 1839*), black reformer, author. After teaching school in Boston, Saunders went to England, where he became concerned with William Wilberforce in educational plans for Haiti. Agent in London for Henri Christophe, emperor of Haiti, 1816–18, he lived for a while in Philadelphia and, after Christophe's overthrow, 1820, returned to Haiti. At the time of his death he was referred to as attorney general of the country.

SAUNDERS, ROMULUS MITCHELL (*b. Caswell Co., N.C., 1791; d. 1867*), lawyer, North Carolina legislator and official. Congressman, Democrat, from North Carolina, 1821–27 and 1841–45, Saunders was an active partisan and a tireless seeker after public office; John Quincy Adams said of him, "There is not a more cankered or venomous reptile in the country." Undistinguished as U.S. minister to Spain, 1846–49, he served as judge of the state superior court, 1852–67.

SAUNDERS, WILLIAM (*b. St. Andrews, Scotland, 1822; d. 1900*), horticulturist, landscape gardener. Came to America, 1848; formed partnership with Thomas Meehan in Philadelphia, 1854. Appointed superintendent of the experimental gardens of the U.S. Department of Agriculture, 1862, he designed the grounds of the department at Washington and had charge of their development until his death. He was designer of the national cemetery at Gettysburg and selected the site and designed the grounds for the Lincoln monument at Springfield, Ill. Organizer and director of the exhibits of the Department of Agriculture at numerous fairs and expositions, he was also a pioneer in the introduction of foreign plants to the United States. The Washington navel orange, brought by him from Brazil, 1871, became the leading commercial variety in California. Among his more than 3,000 published papers was the first bulletin of the Department of Agriculture (1862).

SAUNDERS, WILLIAM LAURENCE (*b. Raleigh, N.C., 1835; d. Raleigh, 1891*), lawyer, newspaper editor. Confederate soldier, Democratic politician. Edited and caused to be published *The Colonial Records of North Carolina* (1886–90).

SAUNDERS, WILLIAM LAWRENCE (*b. Columbus, Ga., 1856; d. Tenerife, Canary Islands, 1931*), engineer, inventor of rock-drill devices. President and chairman of the board, Ingersoll-Rand Co., *post* 1905, he was active as a Democrat in New Jersey politics.

SAUR, CHRISTOPHER. *See* SOWER, CHRISTOPHER.

SAUVEUR, ALBERT (*b. Louvain, Belgium, 1863; d. Boston, Mass., 1939*), metallographer, metallurgist. Graduated Massachusetts Institute of Technology, 1889. A teacher at Harvard, 1899–1935, Sauveur introduced metallography (the microscopic study of metal structure) into U.S. industrial practice.

SAVAGE, EDWARD (*b. Princeton, Mass., 1761; d. Princeton, 1817*), painter, engraver. Painted a celebrated portrait of George Washington, 1789–90; practiced his art in Boston, Philadelphia, and New York and was engaged, *post* 1809, in the manufacture of cotton at Lancaster, Mass.

SAVAGE, HENRY WILSON (*b. New Durham, N.H., 1859; d. 1927*), real estate operator, theatrical producer. Assumed management of Castle Square Theater, Boston, 1895, and organized there a famous light-opera company. He later produced, among other successes, *The Sultan of Sulu* (1902), *The Prince of Pilsen* (1903), *The College Widow* (1904), and *The Merry Widow* (1907).

SAVAGE, JAMES (*b. Boston, Mass., 1784; d. Boston, 1873*), antiquary, lawyer, civic worker. Author of *Genealogical Dictionary of the First Settlers of New England* (1860–62). Encouraged founding of Provident Institution for Savings, 1816, one of the first savings banks incorporated in the United States.

SAVAGE, JOHN (*b. Dublin, Ireland, 1828; d. near Spragueville, Pa., 1888*), journalist. Came to America, 1848. Engaging for a while in free-lance work, he became leading editorial writer for the Washington, D.C., *States*, 1857–61. He served in the Union army during the Civil War, worked for a brief time on the *New Orleans Times*, and in 1867 became chief executive of the Fenian Brotherhood in America.

SAVAGE, JOHN LUCIAN ("JACK") (*b. Cooksville, Wis., 1879; d. Englewood, Colo., 1967*), civil engineer. Attended University of Wisconsin (B.S., 1903). Worked for the newly created Bureau of Reclamation in Idaho, 1903–08, then joined Andrew J. Wiley's consulting practice (1908–16). Designed several important projects, including the Salmon River Dam, the Swan Falls Power Plant, and the Oakley Reservoir Dam. Rejoined the Reclamation Service in 1916 and was promoted in 1924 to chief designing engineer, a position he held until he retired from government work in 1945. Headed the design work on such massive dams as Hoover, Grand Coulee, Shasta, Parker, and Imperial, as well as hundreds of smaller engineering works. Retained by the TVA to help with designing the Norris, Wheeler, and Pickwick dams, and assisted in the design of the Madden Dam for the Panama Canal Zone.

SAVAGE, MINOT JUDSON (*b. Norridgewock, Maine, 1841; d. Boston, Mass., 1918*), Unitarian clergyman, lecturer. Principal pastorates at Church of the Unity, Boston, and the Church of the Messiah, New York City; author of *The Religion of Evolution* (1876).

SAVAGE, PHILIP HENRY (*b. North Brookfield, Mass., 1868; d. Boston, Mass., 1899*), poet. Son of Minot J. Savage. Graduated Harvard, 1893. Author of *First Poems and Fragments* (1895) and *Poems* (1898).

SAVAGE, THOMAS STAUGHTON (*b. present Cromwell, Conn., 1804; d. Rhinecliff, N.Y., 1880*), Episcopal clergyman, physician, naturalist. Graduated Yale, 1825; M.D., 1833. First missionary sent to Africa by his church, Savage served in Liberia and its neighborhood at intervals between 1836 and 1847; he wrote several pioneer papers on the behavior of chimpanzees.

SAVERY, WILLIAM (*b. place unknown, 1721; d. Philadelphia, Pa., 1787*), cabinetmaker. Father of William Savery (1750 o.s.–1804). Believed to have settled in Philadelphia *ca.* 1740, Savery worked there until his death. His designs reveal his indebtedness to English 18th-century design books, but his furniture displays his ability to naturalize and interpret his models in an original manner. There is considerable carving in his mahogany pieces, but for the most part his furniture has simple and pure lines. He excelled as a maker of chairs.

SAVERY, WILLIAM (*b. Philadelphia, Pa., 1750 o.s.; d. Philadelphia, 1804*), tanner, Quaker preacher in the United States and Europe. Son of William Savery (1721–87).

SAVILLE, MARSHALL HOWARD (*b. Rockport, Mass., 1867; d. New York, N.Y., 1935*), archaeologist. Trained in fieldwork by Frederic W. Putnam; was associated successively with the Peabody Museum, Harvard; the American Museum of Natural History; and the Museum of the American Indian, New York. First Loubat professor of American archaeology at Columbia University, designated 1903. Studied ruins at Copan, Honduras, 1891–92; secured important collections at Maya ruins of Palenque, Mexico, 1897; excavated at Mitla, Monte Albán, and Xochicalco, Mexico, 1899–1904; later extended collecting excursions to Colombia and Ecuador. Primarily interested in museum specimens, Saville was apt at securing patrons for his work and was an authority on the literature of his special field. He took no interest in theoretical anthropology nor did he greatly advance field-research technique.

SAWYER, LEICESTER AMBROSE (*b. Pinckney, N.Y., 1807; d. Whitesboro, N.Y., 1898*), Presbyterian and Independent clergyman, newspaper editor. Biblical scholar and exponent of the "higher criticism."

SAWYER, LEMUEL (*b. Camden Co., N.C., 1777; d. Washington, D.C., 1852*), lawyer, author. Congressman, Jefferson and Jackson Democrat, from North Carolina, 1807–13, 1817–23,

and 1825–29. Author of a number of works including *Blackbeard, A Comedy* (published, Washington, D.C., 1824; staged New York City, 1833); a novel, *Printz Hall: A Record of New Sweden* (1839); and *A Biography of John Randolph of Roanoke* (1844).

SAWYER, LORENZO (*b. Leray, N.Y., 1820; d. San Francisco, Calif., 1891*), California pioneer and jurist. Studied law in Columbus, Ohio, with Noah H. Swayne; removed first to Chicago, Ill., then to Wisconsin; removed to California, 1850. After terms as judge of the California district and supreme courts, Sawyer was named a U.S. circuit judge (9th Circuit), 1870, and served until his death; his best-known decision was in the case *In re Neagle* (1889). He was first president of the board of trustees of Leland Stanford University.

SAWYER, PHILETUS (*b. near Rutland, Vermont, 1816; d. Oshkosh, Wis., 1900*), lumberman, Wisconsin legislator. Removed to the vicinity of Oshkosh *ca.* 1847. Long a leader in Wisconsin Republican politics, he served as congressman, 1865–75, and as U.S. senator, 1881–93, contributing to the reputation of the Senate as a millionaire's club. Compelled, *ca.* 1891, to make good on bonds of Republican state treasurers who had failed to account for interest received on public deposits, he was also the principal target in the campaign against boss rule and corruption waged by Robert M. La Follette.

SAWYER, SYLVANUS (*b. Templeton, Mass., 1822; d. Fitchburg, Mass., 1895*), inventor of machinery for splitting and dressing rattan (patented 1849, 1851, 1854, 1855) and other mechanical devices.

SAWYER, THOMAS JEFFERSON (*b. Reading, Vt., 1804; d. 1899*), Universalist clergyman, editor, educator. Held principal pastorate at the Grand Street (Orchard St.) Universalist Society, New York City; professor of theology, Tufts Divinity School, 1869–92 (dean, 1882–92).

SAWYER, WALTER HOWARD (*b. Middletown, Conn., 1867; d. Auburn, Maine, 1923*), engineer, hydraulic and sanitary expert. Supervised waterpower development at Lewiston, Maine, and the Androscoggin River storage system *post* 1902; invented a number of devices for furthering this work.

SAWYER, WILBUR AUGUSTUS (*b. Appleton, Wis., 1879; d. Berkeley, Calif., 1951*), public health administrator. Studied at the University of California and at Harvard (M.D., 1906). After working for the California State Board of Health, Sawyer joined the International Health Board of the Rockefeller Foundation. As director of the West African Yellow Fever Commission (1926–27), he was responsible for the isolation of the yellow fever virus. Discovered methods of immunity by inoculation in 1931. Director of health for the U.N. Relief and Rehabilitation Administration from 1944.

SAXE, JOHN GODFREY (*b. Highgate, Vt., 1816; d. Albany, N.Y., 1887*), lawyer, humorist. Less a poet than a humorist using verse as his medium, Saxe enjoyed wide popularity in his time. He was author of, among other books, *Progress: A Satirical Poem* (1846), *The Money-King and Other Poems* (1860), and *Leisure-Day Rhymes* (1875).

SAXTON, EUGENE FRANCIS (*b. Baltimore, Md., 1884; d. New York, N.Y., 1943*), editor. B.A., Loyola College, Baltimore, 1904. Headed book editorial department, Harper & Brothers, *post* 1925, after earlier experience with Doubleday, Page & Co., 1910–17, and George H. Doran Co.

SAXTON, JOSEPH (*b. Huntington, Pa., 1799; d. 1873*), watchmaker, constructor of scientific apparatus, inventor. Curator of standard weighing apparatus, U.S. Mint, 1837–43; superintendent of weights and measures, U.S. Coast Survey, 1843–73.

Say, Benjamin (*b. Philadelphia, Pa., 1755; d. Philadelphia, 1813*), physician, apothecary, philanthropist. Father of Thomas Say.

Say, Thomas (*b. Philadelphia, Pa., 1787; d. New Harmony, Ind., 1834*), entomologist, conchologist. Son of Benjamin Say. Interested in natural history by William Bartram, his mother's uncle, Say devoted nearly all his time to its study *post* 1812. He visited Georgia and Florida with George Ord, William Maclure, and T. R. Peale, 1818. The next year, as zoologist, he accompanied Stephen H. Long's expedition to the Rocky Mountains; also as zoologist, he went with Long's second expedition, 1823, to the sources of the Minnesota River. Holder of a nominal curatorship at the American Philosophical Society, also nominally professor of natural history at the University of Pennsylvania, 1822–28, he worked on his *American Entomology* (planned and begun, 1816), bringing out the first two volumes in 1824 and 1825. In 1825 also he prepared for the press the first volume of Charles Bonaparte's *American Ornithology*. Resident in the community and village of New Harmony *post* 1825 (except for a visit to Mexico during late 1827 and early 1828), he continued to work industriously. In 1828 he completed the third volume of *American Entomology* and between 1830 and 1834 published the six numbers of his *American Conchology*. Say's work was almost wholly taxonomic and his writings were almost entirely descriptive. The excellence of his work was early acknowledged by European zoologists and nearly all his species have been recognized. His complete writings on entomology were edited by J. L. LeConte and published (1859) with a biographical memoir by George Ord.

Sayles, John (*b. Ithaca, N.Y., 1825; d. Tex., 1897*), lawyer. Removed to Texas, 1845. Practiced law at Brenham and Abilene; wrote extensively on Texas law and taught law at Baylor University.

Sayre, Lewis Albert (*b. present Madison, N.J., 1820; d. 1900*), orthopedic surgeon. M.D., New York College of Physicians and Surgeons, 1842. Practiced in New York City; played large part in organization of Bellevue Hospital Medical College, 1861, occupying there the first chair of orthopedic surgery in America. As resident physician of New York City, 1860–66, he bettered sanitary conditions in tenements. In his own specialty, he was acknowledged leader, developing among other techniques a treatment of lateral curvature that became known the world over as the Sayre method. He was father of Reginald H. Sayre.

Sayre, Reginald Hall (*b. New York, N.Y., 1859; d. 1929*), surgeon. Son of Lewis A. Sayre. Graduated Columbia, 1881. M.D., Bellevue Hospital Medical College, 1884. The trusted associate of his father, he became assistant to the professor of surgery at Bellevue, 1885, and afterward was lecturer and orthopedic surgeon there. He succeeded his father as clinical professor of orthopedic surgery at Bellevue, 1898, and served as consultant to numerous hospitals.

Sayre, Robert Heysham (*b. Columbia Co., Pa., 1824; d. South Bethlehem, Pa., 1907*), civil engineer, railroad official. Directing force in the building and development of the Lehigh Valley Railroad system, 1852–82 and 1885–98.

Sayre, Stephen (*b. Southampton, N.Y., 1736; d. "Brandon," Middlesex Co., Va., 1818*), merchant, banker, diplomatic agent. Graduated College of New Jersey (Princeton), 1757. Removing to London, he became a member of the mercantile firm of Dennys De Berdt and organized his own banking house in 1770. An outspoken friend of the colonies (author of *The En-*

glishman Deceived, 1768), Sayre was arrested and lodged in the Tower, 1775, charged with conspiracy to overthrow the government. Discharged for lack of evidence, he went to Paris and was appointed secretary to Arthur Lee in May 1777. Quarreling with Lee after Lee's Berlin mission failed, Sayre attempted to promote commercial treaties for the United States in Copenhagen and Stockholm but accomplished nothing. Returning home at the end of the Revolution, he became a partisan of the South American liberator Francesco Miranda.

Scammell, Alexander (*b. present Milford, Mass., 1747; d. Williamsburg, Va., 1781*), Revolutionary soldier. Staff officer under General John Sullivan at Boston and in the Long Island campaign. Promoted colonel, 3rd New Hampshire Continental Battalion, December 1776, he was at Ticonderoga and Saratoga. Appointed adjutant general of the Continental army, January 1778, he served through 1780, resigning to take command of the 1st New Hampshire Regiment.

Scammon, Jonathan Young (*b. Whitefield, Maine, 1812; d. Chicago, Ill., 1890*), lawyer, Chicago businessman and civic leader. Settled in Chicago, 1835; helped establish free schools there and was instrumental in founding many societies and charitable institutions, most of which he served as president. He founded, among other newspapers, the *Chicago Journal* (1844) and the *Inter Ocean* (1872).

Scanlan, Lawrence (*b. Co. Tipperary, Ireland, 1843; d. 1915*), Roman Catholic clergyman. Served in the diocese of San Francisco, Calif., after ordination in Ireland, June 1868; removed to Salt Lake City, 1873, as missionary to Utah and a great part of Nevada. Bishop of Salt Lake City, *post* 1891.

Scarborough, Dorothy (*b. Mt. Carmel, Tex., 1878; d. New York, N.Y., 1935*), educator, student of folklore. Graduated Baylor, 1896; Ph.D., Columbia, 1917. Taught at Baylor and Columbia; specialized in short-story technique and folk songs of the South.

Scarborough, Lee Rutland (*b. Colfax, La., 1870; d. Amarillo, Tex., 1945*), Southern Baptist clergyman, educator. B.A., Baylor University, 1892; B.A., Yale, 1896. Abandoned study of law for the ministry; held pastorates in Texas, 1896–1908. Professor of evangelism *post* 1908 and president, 1915–42, of Southwestern Baptist Theological Seminary.

Scarborough, William Saunders (*b. Macon, Ga., ca. 1852; d. 1926*), educator, author. Born in slavery, Scarborough attended Atlanta University and graduated from Oberlin, 1875. Appointed professor of classics, Wilberforce University, Wilberforce, Ohio, 1877, he remained there until his death, serving as president of the university, 1908–20. He had an unusual aptitude for the study of languages.

Scarbrough, William (*b. South Carolina, 1776; d. New York, N.Y., 1838*), planter, Savannah, Ga., merchant. In association with Moses Rogers and others, Scarbrough was backer of the pioneer transatlantic steamship *Savannah*, which voyaged to Europe and back in 1819.

Scattergood, Thomas (*b. Burlington, N.J., 1748; d. Philadelphia, Pa., 1814*), tanner, Quaker preacher, traveler. Displayed a quietist tendency reflecting the influence of John Woolman.

Schadle, Jacob Evans (*b. near Raunchtown, Pa., 1849; d. St. Paul, Minn., 1908*), laryngologist. M.D., Jefferson Medical College, 1881; did postgraduate study with Charles E. Sajous. Removing to St. Paul, Minn., 1887, he became the leading practitioner of laryngology in that section of the country and was professor of his specialty at the University of Minnesota. His chief professional interests were the investigation of the causes and treatment of hay fever and asthma and of the effects of postnasal adenoid growths upon the health of children.

SCHAEBERLE, JOHN MARTIN (*b. Württemberg, Germany, 1853; d. Ann Arbor, Mich., 1924*), astronomer. Taught at University of Michigan and served in the observatory there; was a member of original staff of the Lick Observatory.

SCHAEFFER, CHARLES FREDERICK (*b. Germantown, Pa., 1807; d. Philadelphia, Pa., 1879*), Lutheran clergyman, theologian, author. Son of Frederick D. Schaeffer; brother of David F. and Frederick C. Schaeffer. A conservative, he left his professorship at Gettysburg Theological Seminary to become professor and chairman of the faculty of the Philadelphia Seminary in 1864, and taught there until 1878.

SCHAEFFER, CHARLES WILLIAM (*b. Hagerstown, Md., 1813; d. Germantown, Pa., 1896*), Lutheran clergyman. Grandson of Frederick D. Schaeffer; nephew of Frederick C. Schaeffer. Held pastorates at Whitemarsh, Harrisburg, and Germantown; taught church history and pastoral theology at Philadelphia Seminary. Author of *Family Prayer for Morning and Evening* (1861) and other books.

SCHAEFFER, DAVID FREDERICK (*b. Carlisle, Pa., 1787; d. Frederick, Md., 1837*), Lutheran clergyman. Son of Frederick D. Schaeffer; brother of Charles F. and Frederick C. Schaeffer. Pastor at Frederick, Md., *post* 1808. An organizer of the Maryland Synod, 1820, he was also one of the most active in formation of the General Synod.

SCHAEFFER, FREDERICK CHRISTIAN (*b. Germantown, Pa., 1792; d. New York, N.Y., 1831*), Lutheran clergyman. Son of Frederick D. Schaeffer; brother of Charles F. and David F. Schaeffer. Pastor at Harrisburg, Pa., and New York City; organized St. James's Church in New York, *ca.* 1826, of which he was pastor until his death.

SCHAEFFER, FREDERICK DAVID (*b. Frankfurt am Main, Germany, 1760; d. Frederick, Md., 1836*), Lutheran clergyman. Father of Charles F., David F., and Frederick C. Schaeffer; grandfather of Charles W. Schaeffer. Came to America *ca.* 1774. Pastor at Carlisle, Pa., 1786–90; at Germantown, 1790–1812; at St. Michael's and Zion's, Philadelphia, 1812–34.

SCHAEFFER, NATHAN CHRIST (*b. near Kutztown, Pa., 1849; d. 1919*), educator, lecturer, German Reformed clergyman. Pennsylvania superintendent of public instruction, 1893–1919.

SCHAFF, PHILIP (*b. Chur, Grisons, Switzerland, 1819; d. New York, N.Y., 1893*), church historian. Studied at universities of Tübingen and Halle; was a pupil of Neander at the University of Berlin, 1840–41; made licentiate in theology, 1841. Invited by the Eastern Synod of the German Reformed church to succeed F. A. Rauch on the theological faculty at Mercersburg (Pa.) Seminary, 1843, he was ordained to the ministry, April 1844, and in July arrived in the United States. His inaugural address, *The Principle of Protestantism* (1845), portrayed the Reformation not as a revolution but as a development out of the good forces in the Catholic church and looked forward to the possibility of ultimate union of Protestantism and Catholicism. It was vigorously criticized, and during the years he remained at Mercersburg, he remained subject to opposition, which was strengthened by his association with John W. Nevin in development of the so-called Mercersburg theology. Schaff grew in reputation as a church historian and came to be recognized as the mediator between the theology of Germany and American scholarship. He was editor of A *Commentary on the Holy Scriptures* (1865–80, based on work of John P. Lange) and of the *Religious Encyclopaedia* (1882–84, based on work of Herzog, Plitt, and Hauck). Resigning his position at Mercersburg, 1865, he joined the faculty of Union Theological Seminary, New York City, 1870, transferring his denominational affiliation to the Presbyterian church. Active in ecumenical activities, he also rendered valuable service in the work revising the English Bible, 1881–85, arranging for the organization of the American committee, selecting its members, and acting as president. His most ambitious work was his *History of the Christian Church* (5th ed. rev., 1882–92).

SCHALK, RAYMOND WILLIAM ("CRACKER") (*b. Harvel, Ill., 1892; d. Chicago, Ill., 1970*), baseball player. Began his career as a catcher in 1911 with the class-D Illinois-Missouri League. In 1912 he signed with the Milwaukee Brewers, then the Chicago White Sox. His forte was defense; he revolutionized the art of major-league catching and was the first catcher to back up first and third base on infield ground balls. He caught four no-hitters, including a perfect game by Charley Robertson in 1922. He played in the World Series of 1917 and 1919, the latter being the series that involved the "Black Sox" scandal. Schalk was not part of the White Sox faction that threw the series, and he testified (1920) at a grand jury of the suspicious behavior of the defendants; he maintained a public silence about the scandal all his life and emerged from the episode unscathed. He was a player-manager for the White Sox (1927–29); a player-coach for the New York Giants (1929); coach and scout for the Chicago Cubs (1929–31); a minor-league manager (1932–40); and assistant baseball coach at Purdue (1947–63). Elected to the Baseball Hall of Fame (1955).

SCHALL, THOMAS DAVID (*b. near Reed City, Mich., 1877; d. 1935*), lawyer, politician. Beginning practice in Minneapolis, Minn., *ca.* 1904, after an early life of extreme difficulty, he became blind in 1907, but continued his career with his wife's aid. Congressman from Minnesota, at first Progressive and later Republican, 1915–25, he was U.S. senator thereafter until his death. A grim political fighter and a fluent, bombastic orator, he was a bitter critic of the New Deal.

SCHAMBERG, JAY FRANK (*b. Philadelphia, Pa., 1870; d. 1934*), dermatologist, authority on syphilis.

SCHARF, JOHN THOMAS (*b. Baltimore, Md., 1843; d. 1898*), Confederate soldier, lawyer, historian, collector of Americana. Among his numerous studies in local history, the most valuable is his *History of Maryland* (1879).

SCHAUFFLER, HENRY ALBERT (*b. Constantinople, Turkey, 1837; d. 1905*), Congregational clergyman. Son of William G. Schauffler. Graduated Williams, 1859. Ordained in Constantinople, 1865, he served as a Protestant missionary in Turkey and Austria and worked *post* 1882 among Slavic immigrants to the United States.

SCHAUFFLER, WILLIAM GOTTLIEB (*b. Stuttgart, Germany, 1798; d. 1883*), Congregational clergyman. Father of Henry A. Schauffler. Raised in southern Russia, he came to America, 1826, and received his ministerial education at Andover Theological Seminary. Ordained, 1831, in Boston, he worked thereafter as a missionary among the Jews in Turkey and elsewhere until 1856; thereafter he addressed himself to the Armenians and Turks.

SCHECHTER, SOLOMON (*b. Fokshan, Romania, 1850; d. 1915*), Hebraist, author. Studied at Lemberg, Vienna, and Berlin; removed to England, 1882; was appointed reader in Talmud and rabbinical literature at Cambridge University, 1890. Identifying a fragment of manuscript in 1896 as part of the lost original Hebrew of Ecclesiasticus, he attracted worldwide notice; shortly thereafter, excavating the Genizah at Cairo, he brought back to Cambridge some 50,000 Hebrew and Arabic manuscripts, among them many of the remaining chapters of Ecclesiasticus. He was author of *The Wisdom of Ben Sira* (1899), based on his findings. Unhappy in England, he welcomed appointment in 1901 as president of the Jewish Theological Seminary in New York and was within a short time the acknowledged leader of Jewish scholarship in America. He was author of a number of publications, some of them based upon the Cairo manuscripts, of which the most important was his *Documents of Jewish Sectaries* (1910). His *Some Aspects of Rabbinic Theology* (1909) was the first approach to a methodical presentation of Jewish theology.

SCHEEL, FRITZ (*b. Lübeck, Germany, 1852; d. 1907*), violinist, conductor. Came to America, 1893. First conductor of the San Francisco Symphony, he removed to Philadelphia, Pa., 1899, and in 1901 became conductor of the Philadelphia Orchestra Association, a post which he held until his death.

SCHELE DE VERE, MAXIMILIAN (*b. Wexiö, Sweden, 1820; d. Washington, D.C., 1898*), philologist. Holder of several German doctorates, he came to America, 1843, and served as professor of modern languages, University of Virginia, 1844–95. Inaugurator of systematic study of Anglo-Saxon, he also offered courses in comparative philology at a time when few American colleges recognized the value of the comparative method. He was author of a number of books, including *Americanisms: The English of the New World* (1871) and was associated with the work of the *Standard Dictionary* (1893–95).

SCHELL, AUGUSTUS (*b. Rhinebeck, N.Y., 1812; d. 1884*), lawyer, New York politician and businessman. An associate of Cornelius Vanderbilt (1794–1877) in his New York Central Railroad operations and in his fight for the Erie, Schell held numerous directorates in railroads, banks, and insurance companies. A heavy stock market operator, with Horace F. Clark and Jay Gould he engineered the post–Civil War corner in Chicago & Northwestern stock, which was one of Wall Street's notable episodes. Steadfast in support of the Tammany Democratic organization, he was collector of the Port of New York, 1857–61, and succeeded William M. Tweed as Grand Sachem of Tammany, 1872. Also in 1872 he served as Horace Greeley's financial banker and campaign manager. Interested in many of the clubs, societies, and institutions of New York City, he was twice president of the New-York Historical Society and a benefactor of the New York Institution for the Blind.

SCHELLING, ERNEST HENRY (*b. Belvidere, N.J., 1876; d. New York, N.Y., 1939*), pianist, conductor, composer. Studied with a long series of European masters, including Moszkowski and Paderewski. Successful as a concert artist and as composer of a number of piano and orchestral compositions, including *A Victory Ball* (1923), Schelling turned chiefly *post* 1925 to the conducting of children's orchestral concerts, at which he won his audiences over to music with an infectious enthusiasm.

SCHELLING, FELIX EMANUEL (*b. New Albany, Ind., 1858; d. Mount Vernon, N.Y., 1945*), educator, scholar. Brother of Ernest H. Schelling. B.A., University of Pennsylvania, 1881; LL.B., 1883; M.A., 1884. Taught English language and literature at Pennsylvania, 1886–1934 (professor *post* 1893), and was the principal creator of an English department in the modern sense at that university. Author of, among other works, *A Book of Elizabethan Lyrics* (1895); *Elizabethan Drama 1558–1642* (1908); *English Literature During the Lifetime of Shakespeare* (1910); and *The English Lyric* (1913).

SCHEM, ALEXANDER JACOB (*b. Wiedenbrück, Germany, 1826; d. Hoboken, N.J., 1881*), encyclopedia editor, statistician, journalist.

SCHENANDOA.   *See* SKENANDOA.

SCHENCK, FERDINAND SCHUREMAN (*b. Plattekill, N.Y., 1845; d. White Plains, N.Y., 1925*), Reformed Church clergyman, educator. Professor of theology, New Brunswick Theological Seminary, 1899–1924; lectured also at New York University, Rutgers, and Princeton Theological Seminary.

SCHENCK, JAMES FINDLAY (*b. Franklin, Ohio, 1807; d. 1882*), naval officer. Brother of Robert C. Schenck. Appointed midshipman, 1825; active in conquest of California, 1846; commended for excellence as division commander in Civil War attacks on Fort Fisher. Retired as rear admiral, 1869.

SCHENCK, NICHOLAS MICHAEL (*b. Rybinsk, Russia, 1881; d. Miami Beach, Fla., 1969*), motion-picture and theater executive. Immigrated to the United States in the early 1890's. With his brother Joseph offered vaudeville shows at Fort George in Manhattan, where around 1908 they established Paradise Park. Marcus Loew offered them partnerships in some of his theatrical ventures, beginning with the acquisition of the Lyric Theater in Hoboken, N.J.; in 1912 they established Palisades Amusement Park in Fort Lee, N.J., which they owned until 1935. Nicholas became president of Loew's, Inc. (1927), and its motion-picture subsidiary, MGM. After World War II the fortunes of Loew's and MGM declined, and for almost a decade Schenk delayed compliance with a 1946 court order requiring the division of Loew's into separate theatrical and motion-picture firms. He retired as president in 1955.

SCHENCK, ROBERT CUMMING (*b. Franklin, Ohio, 1809; d. Washington, D.C., 1890*), lawyer, Ohio legislator, Union major general. Brother of James F. Schenck. Congressman, Whig, from Ohio, 1843–51, he served as U.S. minister to Brazil, 1851–53. After two years' hard service in the Civil War, late in 1863 he returned, as a Republican, to the House of Representatives, where he distinguished himself by violent attacks on the Copperheads and by opposition to President Andrew Johnson. He was chairman of the Committee on Military Affairs and later of the Ways and Means Committee. Leaving Congress, 1871, he succeeded John L. Motley as U.S. minister to Great Britain. His connection with a fraudulent mine promotion in the West forced him to resign in 1876.

SCHERESCHEWSKY, SAMUEL ISAAC JOSEPH (*b. Tauroggen, Russian Lithuania, 1831; d. Tokyo, Japan, 1906*), Episcopal clergyman, a convert from Judaism. Came to America, 1854; served as a missionary in China and Japan for the greater part of his life *post* 1859; was Episcopal bishop of Shanghai, 1877–83. Naturally gifted as a linguist, he translated the Bible and the Book of Common Prayer into several forms of classical Chinese.

SCHERMAN, HARRY (*b. Montreal, Canada, 1887; d. New York, N.Y., 1969*), publishing entrepreneur. Moved to Philadelphia in 1889; attended Wharton School of Finance of the University of Pennsylvania. Worked in New York at newspaper jobs and various advertising agencies, specializing in writing copy for book publishers. With Max Sackheim and Albert and Charles Boni formed a partnership (1916) to publish inexpensive leather-bound literary classics; 48 million books were sold over eight years. He began the Book-of-the-Month Club in 1926; through his clever offers of bonuses and advertising, the club had more than 40,000 members by the end of the year. By 1931, was president of the BOMC and in 1950 became chairman of the board.

SCHEVE, EDWARD BENJAMIN (*b. Herford, Westphalia, Germany, 1865; d. Longmont, Colo., 1924*), musician. Came to America, 1888. Professor of music, Grinnell (Iowa) College, *post* 1906.

SCHEVILL, RUDOLPH (*b. Cincinnati, Ohio, 1874; d. Berkeley, Calif., 1946*), professor of Spanish. B.A., Yale, 1896; Ph.D., University of Munich, 1898. Taught French and German at Bucknell University, 1899–1900; German, French, and Spanish at Yale, 1900–10. Professor of Romance languages, University of California in Berkeley, 1910–19, and chairman of separate department of Spanish, 1919–44 (including Portuguese *post* 1931). Editor of complete works of Cervantes (1914–41, 18 vols.); author of studies of Cervantes and Lope de Vega.

SCHICKILLEMY. *See* SHIKELLAMY.

SCHIEREN, CHARLES ADOLPH (*b. Neuss, Germany, 1842; d. 1915*), leather-belting manufacturer. Came to America as a boy. Secured patents, 1887–88, for improvements in belting design for high-speed work. Reform mayor of Brooklyn, N.Y., 1893–95; rescued that city from bankruptcy.

SCHIFF, JACOB HENRY (*b. Frankfurt am Main, 1847; d. New York, N.Y., 1920*), financier, philanthropist. Coming to New York City, 1865, Schiff entered business as a broker and became an American citizen. After residence in Germany, 1872–74, he returned to the United States as a partner in Kuhn, Loeb & Co., and 1885 became head of that firm. He was concerned with financing important railroads in the East, in particular, the Pennsylvania Railroad and the Louisville & Nashville; in the great struggle for control of the Northern Pacific, he was allied with E. H. Harriman against J. J. Hill and J. P. Morgan & Co. He was also interested in the great insurance companies, particularly the Equitable. Schiff's philanthropies were many and varied and included the American Red Cross, hospitals, settlement houses, and libraries. He was benefactor of several Jewish seminaries and was one of the founders of the American Jewish Committee, 1906.

SCHILDKRAUT, JOSEPH (*b. Vienna, Austria, 1896; d. New York, N.Y., 1964*), actor. Studied at the American Academy of Dramatic Arts (1910–13). Appeared on the New York stage with the Theatre Guild (1920–24) and Eva Le Gallienne's Civic Repertory (1932–33); his several dozen plays include a memorable performance in *The Diary of Anne Frank* (1955). His first important movie was *Orphans of the Storm* (1921); others of his more than sixty films include *The King of Kings* (1927), *Tenth Avenue* (1928), *Show Boat* (1929), *Cleopatra* (1934), and *The Life of Emile Zola* (1937), for which he won an Academy Award for his portrayal of Captain Dreyfus. He appeared in more than eighty television productions and hosted his own series (1953–54).

SCHILLING, HUGO KARL (*b. Saalfeld, Germany, 1861; d. 1931*), philologist. Ph.D., Leipzig, 1885. Immigrating to America, 1886, he taught at Wittenberg College and at Harvard, and was professor of German at the University of California, 1901–29.

SCHILLINGER, JOSEPH (*b. Kharkov, Russia, 1895; d. New York, N.Y., 1943*), composer and musical theorist. Graduated Imperial Conservatory of Music, Petersburg, 1918. Taught at State Academy of Music, Kharkov, 1918–22, becoming dean; lectured thereafter at various institutions in Leningrad and was associated with modernist circles there. Came to the United States 1928, and settled in New York City, where he taught, and continued to develop his theories of modern composition. These found their most characteristic expression in his application of strict mathematical principles and formulas to the writing of music. His method was fully developed in two posthumous books: *The Schillinger System of Musical Composition* (1946) and *The*

Mathematical Basis of the Arts (1948). Several popular composers became his students, of whom the most famous was George Gershwin.

SCHINDLER, KURT (*b. Berlin, Germany, 1882; d. New York, N.Y., 1935*), musician, composer, music editor, authority on folk music. Came to New York, 1905. Assistant conductor at the Metropolitan Opera, 1905–08, he organized the MacDowell Chorus in 1909. Known as the Schola Cantorum *post* 1912, the organization remained under his direction until 1926 and became outstanding among choral groups. Schindler wrote a number of songs and choruses and edited 11 collections of Russian, Spanish and other music.

SCHINDLER, RUDOLPH MICHAEL (*b. Vienna, Austria, 1887; d. Los Angeles, Calif., 1953*), architect. Studied at the Imperial Institute of Engineering and at the Vienna Academy of Fine Arts. Came to the U.S. in 1914. Joined Frank Lloyd Wright (1917) to work on designs for the Imperial Hotel in Tokyo. Set up own firm in 1922. Schindler is remembered for his innovative styles of domestic architecture in California. He designed houses that were of a natural feeling—usually of wood and stucco and consisting of principal spaces oriented around outdoor living areas.

SCHINDLER, SOLOMON (*b. Neisse, Germany, 1842; d. 1915*), rabbi. Came to America, 1871. A radical reformer, Schindler held his principal pastorate in Boston, Mass., 1874–94, and was engaged thereafter in social work.

SCHINZ, ALBERT (*b. Neuchâtel, Switzerland, 1870; d. Iowa City, Iowa, 1943*), educator, scholar. Licentiate in both letters and theology, University of Neuchâtel; Ph.D., Tübingen, 1894; studied also at universities of Berlin and Paris. Immigrated to the United States, 1897. Taught French at University of Minnesota; Bryn Mawr College, 1899–1913; Smith College, 1913–28; and University of Pennsylvania, 1928–41. Author of a number of books and articles on many phases of French literature, he was a recognized authority on Jean-Jacques Rousseau; among his studies on this topic, *La Pensée de Jean-Jacques Rousseau* (1929) is probably the most important.

SCHIRMER, GUSTAV (*b. Königsee, Saxony, 1829; d. Eisenach, Germany, 1893*), music publisher. Came to America as a boy. Established the house of G. Schirmer in New York City, 1866; was among the original patrons of Bayreuth; encouraged native musical talent in America.

SCHIRMER, RUDOLPH EDWARD (*b. New York, N.Y., 1859; d. Santa Barbara, Calif., 1919*), lawyer, music publisher. Son of Gustav Schirmer, whom he succeeded as president of G. Schirmer, Inc.

SCHLATTER, MICHAEL (*b. St. Gall, Switzerland, 1716; d. Philadelphia, Pa., 1790*), German Reformed clergyman, educator. Came to Pennsylvania as a missionary, 1746; organized Reformed parishes throughout Pennsylvania, Maryland, Virginia, and New Jersey. Chaplain of the Royal American Regiment, 1757–59, and of the 2nd Pennsylvania Battalion in Bouquet's expedition, 1764, he was an ardent patriot during the Revolution.

SCHLESINGER, ARTHUR MEIER (*b. Xenia, Ohio, 1883; d. Cambridge, Mass., 1965*), historian. Attended Ohio State and Columbia (Ph.D., 1917). Taught at Ohio State (1912–19); University of Iowa (1919–24), where he offered what he believed to be the first course in the "social" and "cultural" aspects of U.S. history; and Harvard (1924–54). Published collections of his essays in *New Viewpoints in American History* (1922), *Paths to the*

Present (1949), and *The American as Reformer* (1950). Also wrote *The Political and Social History of the United States* (1925), with Homer C. Hockett; the provocative historical study of American etiquette books, *Learning How to Behave* (1946); and *Prelude to Independence: The Newspaper War on Britain, 1764–1776* (1957). Helped found the Social Science Research Council (1924) and was its chairman (1930–33); cofounder of the *New England Quarterly* (1928). His central importance to the writing of American history lies in his rejection of the unarticulated premises that had constricted much of the writing and teaching of that history to what had been "politically important." His "social history" was a liberating influence among American historians.

SCHLESINGER, BENJAMIN (*b. Krakai, Lithuania, 1876; d. Colorado Springs, Colo., 1932*), labor leader. Immigrated to Chicago, Ill., 1891; became a leading spirit in the Jewish labor movement. An able organizer and administrator, he was at various times business manager of the *Jewish Daily Forward* and president of the International Ladies' Garment Workers' Union.

SCHLESINGER, FRANK (*b. New York, N.Y., 1871; d. Old Lyme, Conn., 1943*), astronomer. B.S., College of the City of New York, 1890; M.A., Columbia University, 1897; Ph.D., 1898. The leading authority in his time on photographic astrometry, he was associated with the Yerkes Observatory, directed the Allegheny Observatory at University of Pittsburgh, 1905–20, and was director of the observatory at Yale University, 1920–41.

SCHLEY, WINFIELD SCOTT (*b. Frederick Co., Md., 1839; d. New York, N.Y., 1909*), naval officer. Graduated U.S. Naval Academy, 1860. After an active career on land and sea which included effective Civil War service, several tours of duty on the staff of the U.S. Naval Academy, and the command of the 1884 Arctic expedition to rescue the survivors of A. W. Greely's ill-fated party, Schley was selected to command the Flying Squadron at the opening of the Spanish-American War. After considerable friction with the commander of the Atlantic Squadron, William T. Sampson, Schley was in active command at the battle of Santiago, 1898, owing to Sampson's temporary absence from the station outside that port, a circumstance which left credit for the victory in doubt. Retiring as rear admiral, 1901, Schley demanded a court of inquiry to decide on the merits of the dispute. This was held late in 1901 and reached a judgment in general adverse to Schley, although Admiral George Dewey, on the question of command, rendered a minority opinion in his favor.

SCHMAUK, THEODORE EMANUEL (*b. Lancaster, Pa., 1860; d. Philadelphia, Pa., 1920*), Lutheran clergyman, historian. An uncompromising advocate of confessionalism, he was pastor at Lebanon, Pa., 1883–1920.

SCHMIDT, ARTHUR PAUL (*b. Altona, Germany, 1846; d. 1921*), music publisher. Immigrated to America *ca.* 1866; founded his own firm in Boston, Mass., 1876. Gave great encouragement to American composers by publishing works in larger forms which had no possibility of immediate commercial success.

SCHMIDT, CARL LOUIS AUGUST (*b. Brown County, S.Dak., 1885; d. Berkeley, Calif., 1946*), biochemist. B.S., University of California in Berkeley, 1908; M.S., 1910; Ph.D., 1916. Taught at University of California *post* 1915, becoming professor of biochemistry, 1924. Served as dean of the college of pharmacy, 1937–44, and as acting dean of the medical school, 1938–39. Principal research in the biochemistry of bile, the physical chemistry of proteins and amino acids, and applications of the data of biochemistry to immunology.

SCHMIDT, FRIEDRICH AUGUST (*b. Leutenberg, Germany, 1837; d. 1928*), Lutheran theologian, educator. Immigrated to

St. Louis, Mo., as a child. A graduate of Concordia Theological Seminary, 1857, he taught theology in a number of midwestern seminaries. He figured extensively in the predestination controversy during and after the 1880's as an opponent of what he considered the new Calvinism.

SCHMIDT, NATHANIEL (*b. Hudiksvall, Sweden, 1862; d. Ithaca, N.Y., 1939*), orientalist, historian. Professor of Semitic languages and Oriental history, Cornell University, 1896–1932.

SCHMUCKER, BEALE MELANCHTHON (*b. Gettysburg, Pa., 1827; d. near Phoenixville, Pa., 1888*), Lutheran clergyman. Son of Samuel S. Schmucker. A pastor in present West Virginia and Pennsylvania, Schmucker opposed his father's theological tendencies and became a leader of the extreme churchly party among Lutherans. He was distinguished as a liturgical scholar.

SCHMUCKER, JOHN GEORGE (*b. Michelstadt, Germany, 1771; d. Williamsburg, Pa., 1854*), Lutheran clergyman. Father of Samuel S. Schmucker. Came to Pennsylvania as a boy; was raised in western Virginia. Pastor at Hagerstown, Md., 1794–1809, and at York, Pa., and its neighborhood, 1809–52.

SCHMUCKER, SAMUEL SIMON (*b. Hagerstown, Md., 1799; d. 1873*), Lutheran clergyman, theologian. Son of John G. Schmucker. Graduated University of Pennsylvania, 1819; Princeton Theological Seminary, 1820. Pastor at New Market, Va., 1820–26. As a founder of, and professor at, Gettysburg Theological Seminary, 1826–64, he exercised a liberal, Americanizing influence and for many years led the thought of the General Synod. A classical school which he started at Gettysburg, 1827, became Pennsylvania College, 1832, and is now known as Gettysburg College; he served as its president, 1832–34. Author of *Elements of Popular Theology* (1834) and a number of other works. He precipitated the doctrinal battle between "American" and "Old" Lutheranism with the publication of his *Definite Platform . . . for Evangelical Lutheran District Synods* (1855). He was the father of Beale M. Schmucker.

SCHNABEL, ARTUR (*b. Lipnik, Austria, 1882; d. Axenstein, Switzerland, 1951*), pianist and composer. After studying privately in Vienna, Schnabel lived in Berlin from 1910 to 1933; taught at the High School for Music, 1925–33. The foremost interpreter of Beethoven of his time, Schnabel toured extensively in Europe and the U.S. (first U.S. tour, 1921); immigrated to the U.S. in 1939. An arch-conservative, traditional pianist, Schnabel played only eighteenth- and nineteenth-century composers— Beethoven, Schubert, Bach, Mozart, and Brahms. He composed many works of his own but refused to play them in public. The first pianist to record all of the Beethoven sonatas, 1931–35.

SCHNAUFFER, CARL HEINRICH (*b. Heimsheim, near Stuttgart, Germany, 1823; d. probably Baltimore, Md., 1854*), poet, editor. Influenced in Germany by Gustav Struve and Friedrich K. F. Hecker, Schnauffer fought in the Baden revolution, 1848–49. Immigrating to Baltimore, Md., 1851, he joined in the "Turner" movement and founded the *Baltimore Wecker*, 1851.

SCHNEIDER, ALBERT (*b. Granville, Ill., 1863; d. Portland, Oreg., 1928*), bacteriologist. M.D., Chicago College of Physicians and Surgeons, 1887; Ph.D., Columbia, 1897. Professor at Northwestern, University of California, University of Nebraska; also dean of pharmacy, North Pacific College, 1922–28.

SCHNEIDER, BENJAMIN (*b. New Hanover, Pa., 1807; d. Boston, Mass., 1877*), Presbyterian missionary to Turkey, 1834–*ca.* 1875.

SCHNEIDER, GEORGE (*b. Pirmasens, Rhenish Bavaria, 1823; d. Colorado Springs, Colo., 1905*), journalist, banker.

Came to America, 1849. As managing editor of the *Illinois Staats-Zeitung*, 1851–62, Schneider bitterly opposed Stephen A. Douglas and did much to consolidate the German vote in support of Abraham Lincoln. He was president, National Bank of Illinois, 1871–97.

SCHNEIDER, HERMAN (*b. Summit Hill, Pa., 1872; d. Cincinnati, Ohio, 1939*), engineer. Graduated Lehigh University, 1894. Taught engineering at Lehigh, 1899–1903; dean of College of Engineering at University of Cincinnati, 1906–39, serving for four years of this period also as president. Inaugurated at Cincinnati the "cooperative system" of technological education, in which theoretical studies were alternated with practical shop experience.

SCHNEIDER, THEODORE (*b. Geinsheim, Rhenish Palatinate, 1703; d. 1764*), physician, Roman Catholic clergyman, Jesuit. Highly distinguished as a professor at Liège and as rector of the University of Heidelberg, 1738–40, Schneider came to Philadelphia, 1741, assigned to act as missionary to German immigrants. He aided Robert Harding in eastern Pennsylvania and in New Jersey, founded a number of chapels, and built a large church at Goshenhoppen, Pa.

SCHNELLER, GEORGE OTTO (*b. Nürnberg, Germany, 1843; d. 1895*), inventor. Immigrated to America *ca.* 1860. Patented, 1880–1884, machinery for the manufacture and insertion of brass corset eyelets.

SCHNERR, LEANDER (*b. Gommersdorf, Baden, Germany, 1836; d. 1920*), Roman Catholic clergyman, Benedictine. Immigrated to Pittsburgh, Pa., as a child. Archabbot of St. Vincent's, Latrobe, Pa., *post* 1892.

SCHODDE, GEORGE HENRY (*b. Allegheny, Pa., 1854; d. 1917*), Lutheran clergyman, conservative biblical scholar. Professor at Capital University, Columbus, Ohio, *post* 1880.

SCHOENBERG, ARNOLD (*b. Vienna, Austria, 1874; d. Los Angeles, Calif., 1951*), composer. The most innovative and revolutionary of twentieth-century composers, Schoenberg's music evolved from a post-Romantic, Wagnerian style to the exploration of atonal and twelve-tone systems. His post-Romantic piece for orchestra and choruses, *Gurrelieder* (composed 1901; premiere 1913), was followed in 1907–08 by the String Quartet no. 2 in F-sharp Minor, the finale of which was the first piece of completely atonal music ever written. Dividing his time between Berlin and Vienna, Schoenberg was the leader of a school of composers that produced Alban Berg and Anton von Webern. Along with perfecting his use of the atonal medium, he introduced the concept of *Sprechstimme*, which became the fundamental use of the human voice in the new music. After World War I, he decided that atonalism gave anarchy instead of freedom and changed to the twelve-tone scale. His first entirely twelve-tone piece was the Suite for Piano (1924). Other works in this medium were the third and fourth String Quartets (1926; 1936), the Violin Concerto, (1936), and the opera *Moses und Aron* (1930–32).

Schoenberg immigrated to the U.S. in 1933; he taught at the University of California, Los Angeles, from 1936 to 1944. During this period, he returned to his Jewish origins for inspiration: *Kol Nidre* (1938), *A Survivor From Warsaw* (1947), and *Psalm 130* (1950).

SCHOENHEIMER, RUDOLF (*b. Berlin, Germany, 1898; d. Yonkers, N.Y., 1941*), biochemist. M.D., University of Berlin, 1922; studied at the University of Leipzig with Karl Thomas, 1923–26; worked in the Pathological Institute, University of Freiburg, 1926–33, becoming head of the Department of Pathological Chemistry and continuing his studies of sterols. Dismissed from his post because he was a Jew, he came to the United States in 1933 to teach in the biochemistry department of the College of Physicians and Surgeons, Columbia University. In addition to making a number of important further findings in his special field of research, he developed the methodology for use of isotopic tracers in the study of metabolic processes.

SCHOENHOF, JACOB (*b. Oppenheim, Germany, 1839; d. New York, N.Y., 1903*), lace merchant, free-trade advocate, economist. Immigrated to America, 1861. Author of, among other books, *The Industrial Situation and the Question of Wages* (1885) and *The Economy of High Wages* (1892), in which he forecast the doctrine later associated with the name of Henry Ford.

SCHOEPPEL, ANDREW FRANK (*b. Claflin, Kans., 1894; d. Bethesda, Md., 1962*), lawyer and politician. Attended universities of Kansas and Nebraska (LL.B., 1922); admitted to Kansas bar in 1923. As Kansas Republican governor (1942–47) he modernized the school systems, permitted the first executions of criminals since 1870, and launched an investigation that led to the state's repeal of prohibition (1949). Was U.S. senator, 1948–62, serving on the Interstate and Foreign Commerce, the Appropriations, and the Agricultural and Forestry committees.

SCHOFF, STEPHEN ALONZO (*b. Danville, Vt., 1818; d. Norfolk, Conn., 1904*), engraver. Employed professionally in bank-note work, Schoff produced, among other artistic plates, *Caius Marius on the Ruins of Carthage* after Vanderlyn, and *Bathers* after William M. Hunt.

SCHOFIELD, HENRY (*b. Dudley, Mass., 1866; d. 1918*), law teacher. Graduated Harvard, 1887; LL.B., 1890. Practiced principally in Chicago; was professor of law, Northwestern University *post* 1902. Authority on Chicago's relations to local traction systems. Author of a number of comments on important decisions which were later collected as *Essays on Constitutional Law and Equity* (1921).

SCHOFIELD, JOHN McALLISTER (*b. Gerry, N.Y., 1831; d. St. Augustine, Fla., 1906*), soldier. Graduated West Point, 1853. Commissioned in the artillery, he served as professor of natural philosophy at West Point, 1855–60. In Missouri at the outbreak of the Civil War, he became chief of staff to General Nathaniel Lyon and served until Lyon's death at the battle of Wilson's Creek, August 1861. Promoted brigadier general of volunteers in November, he was engaged in field operations in Missouri and later commanded the Department of the Missouri as major general. Assuming command of the XXIII Corps in February 1864, he took part in Sherman's Atlanta campaign as one of the three army commanders and badly shattered Hood's Confederate force at the fierce battle of Franklin, Tenn. Moving the XXIII Corps to the mouth of the Cape Fear River, he occupied Wilmington, N.C., and effected a junction with Sherman at Goldsboro, Mar. 23, 1865, for the final moves against General J. E. Johnston. After serving as confidential agent for the U.S. State Department in France, 1865–66, he commanded the Department of the Potomac, and in the spring of 1868 served briefly as U.S. secretary of war. Promoted major general, regular army, 1869, he commanded several departments successively and made the recommendations that led to the acquisition of Pearl Harbor, Hawaii, as a naval base. Superintendent at West Point, 1876–81, he became commanding general of the army, 1888, and retired as lieutenant general, 1895.

SCHOFIELD, WILLIAM HENRY (*b. Brockville, Ontario, Canada, 1870; d. Peterboro, N.H., 1920*), educator. Graduated Victoria College, 1889; Ph.D., Harvard, 1895. Expert in Scandinavian studies, Schofield taught English at Harvard, 1897–1906, and was thereafter professor of comparative literature.

SCHOLTE, HENDRIK PETER (*b. Amsterdam, Netherlands, 1805; d. Pella, Iowa, 1868*), Dutch Reformed and Independent clergyman, colonist. Seceding from the Netherlands state church, 1834, Scholte with other like-minded pastors urged emigration as a means of escape for their followers from persecution at home. Immigrating to the United States, 1847, he founded the settlement of Pella in Marion Co., Iowa, and was its principal citizen until his death.

SCHOMER, NAHUM MEIR (*b. Nesvizh, Russia, 1849; d. 1905*), Yiddish novelist and playwright. Prolific writer of popular works which helped develop the habit of reading among the Yiddish-speaking masses. Immigrated to New York City, 1889.

SCHOOLCRAFT, HENRY ROWE (*b. Albany Co., N.Y., 1793; d. 1864*), ethnologist. Attended Union and Middlebury colleges, where he favored the study of geology and mineralogy. Began explorations in 1817–18 with a trip which resulted in *A View of the Lead Mines of Missouri* (1819). A member of the Cass exploring expedition, 1820, he reported on it in *Narrative Journal of Travels through the Northwestern Regions of the United States . . . to the Sources of the Mississippi River* (1821). He described a later expedition to the sources of the Mississippi in his *Narrative of an Expedition . . . to Itasca Lake* (1834, 1855). Schoolcraft's wide acquaintance with the Indians led to his appointment as Indian agent for the Lake Superior tribes, 1822; he served as superintendent of Indian affairs for Michigan, 1836–41. A constant promoter of the study of Indian ethnology, he was author of *Algic Researches* (1839), which concerned Indian mental characteristics, and of other valuable works. His principal production was *Historical and Statistical Information Respecting the History, Condition and Prospects of the Indian Tribes of the United States* (six parts, 1851–57, illustrated with engravings from paintings by Seth Eastman).

SCHÖPF, JOHANN DAVID (*b. Wunsiedel, Germany, 1752; d. 1800*), physician, traveler. After service as a surgeon with a German regiment in the British service, 1777–83, Schöpf made a scientific tour from New Jersey to Florida before returning to his home in Bayreuth. He wrote a number of articles and monographs on his studies and an excellent travel book and historical source entitled *Reise durch einige der mittlern und südlichen vereinigten nordamerikanischen Staaten nach Ost-Florida und den Bahama-Inseln* (Erlangen, 1788; translated as *Travels in the Confederation*, 1911).

SCHOTT, CHARLES ANTHONY (*b. Mannheim, Germany, 1826; d. Washington, D.C., 1901*), geodesist. Came to America, 1848. Chief of computing division, U.S. Coast Survey, 1855–1900, Schott made his principal contributions to science in the fields of geodesy and terrestrial magnetism. He also wrote on meteorology and climatology, especially of the Arctic regions.

SCHOULER, JAMES (*b. present Arlington, Mass., 1839; d. 1920*), lawyer, historian. Son of William Schouler. Graduated Harvard, 1859. Schouler is principally remembered as the author of the *History of the United States of America Under the Constitution* (7 vols., 1880–1913). This was the first attempt to cover in a scholarly way the period from the Revolution to the Civil War. It appeared almost contemporaneously, however, with the work of John B. McMaster. Schouler's interpretation was primarily political and constitutional and was based on an industrious exploration of sources. To a large extent, his history and McMaster's supplement each other.

SCHOULER, WILLIAM (*b. near Glasgow, Scotland, 1814; d. 1872*), editor. Massachusetts legislator. Father of James Schouler. Came to America, 1816. Active as an editor of Whig and Republican papers in Massachusetts and Ohio, Schouler served as adjutant general of Massachusetts, 1860–66, revealing remarkable executive ability and winning the lasting admiration of Governor John A. Andrew. He was author of *A History of Massachusetts in the Civil War* (1868–71) and of personal reminiscences.

SCHRADIECK, HENRY (*b. Hamburg, Germany, 1846; d. Brooklyn, N.Y., 1918*), violinist, conductor, teacher. After a brilliant career in Europe, he came to America, 1883, and was a teacher in Cincinnati, Philadelphia, and New York City. Among his pupils were Maud Powell and Theodore Spiering.

SCHREMBS, JOSEPH (*b. Wurzelhofen, near Regensburg, Bavaria, Germany, 1866; d. Cleveland, Ohio, 1945*), Roman Catholic clergyman. Came to the United States, 1877; studied at St. Vincent's Archabbey, Latrobe, Pa., and at the Grand Séminaire, Montreal, Canada; ordained to the priesthood, June 1889. After service as curate and pastor of several parishes in the diocese of Grand Rapids, Mich., he was named auxiliary bishop in 1911; later that year he was appointed first bishop of Toledo, Ohio. An administrator of the National Catholic War Council, he played a crucial role in its continuation after 1920 as the National Catholic Welfare Council (Conference) and directed its department of lay organization. In 1921 he was appointed bishop of Cleveland, Ohio, and held that post until his death; *post* 1939, he had a personal title of archbishop.

SCHRIECK, LOUISE VAN DER (*b. Bergen op Zoom, Holland, 1813; d. Cincinnati, Ohio, 1886*), founder of the Sisters of Notre Dame de Namur in America. Came to Cincinnati, Ohio, 1840, as one of a group of volunteer nuns; was named superior of the convent, 1845. As superior provincial *post* 1848, she founded 26 convents of teaching sisters in Washington, D.C., Philadelphia, Pa., and through Ohio and Massachusetts.

SCHRIVER, EDMUND (*b. York, Pa., 1812; d. 1899*), soldier, railroad executive. Graduated West Point, 1833. Employed mainly in staff work, Schriver was brevetted major general, 1865, for effective service during the Civil War. Thereafter he served principally on inspection duty until retirement, 1881.

SCHROEDER, JOHN FREDERICK (*b. Baltimore, Md., 1800; d. 1857*), Episcopal clergyman. A skillful preacher, he was assistant at Trinity Church, New York City, 1823–39, having immediate charge of St. Paul's Chapel. He served thereafter as principal of a girl's school and as rector of several churches successively in Flushing, New York City, and Brooklyn, N.Y. He was a moderate evangelical.

SCHROEDER, RUDOLPH WILLIAM (*b. Chicago, Ill., 1886; d. Maywood, Ill., 1952*), pioneer aviator and aviation executive. One of the first men to enter the stratosphere, Schroeder successfully piloted a plane to an altitude of 33,113 ft. in 1920. A member of the Aviation Section of the Army Signal Corps (1916–20); special accident investigator for the Air Commerce Bureau (1933–37). Manager of operations and vice president of safety for United Air Lines (1937–42). A pioneer in aviation safety, Schroeder helped develop many devices for flight safety: night landing flares, instrument flying, and controllable pitch propellers.

SCHROEDER, SEATON (*b. Washington, D.C., 1849; d. 1922*), naval officer. Graduated Annapolis, 1868. An efficient officer of wide experience, Schroeder was author of treatises on torpedoes and torpedo boats, assisted in perfecting the Driggs-Schroeder gun, and retired as rear admiral, 1911. Earlier in his career he had assisted Henry H. Gorringe in transporting the Cleopatra's Needle obelisk, now in Central Park, from Egypt to New York City, 1879.

SCHUCHERT, CHARLES (*b. Cincinnati, Ohio, 1858; d. New Haven, Conn., 1942*), paleontologist. Assistant to Edward O. Ulrich, 1885–88, and to James Hall, 1889–91; worked with Newton H. Winchell on studies of Minnesota brachiopods; served as a preparator at Peabody Museum, Yale. Joining the U.S. Geological Survey, 1893, he became assistant curator of invertebrate paleontology at the National Museum, 1894. In 1904 he was appointed curator of geological collections at Peabody Museum, Yale, and professor of historical geology. He retired from teaching in 1925, but remained at the museum for the rest of his life. Highly effective as a teacher of graduate students, he made Yale an outstanding training ground for invertebrate paleontologists and stratigraphers.

SCHUESSELE, CHRISTIAN. *See* SCHUSSELE, CHRISTIAN.

SCHULTZ, DUTCH. *See* FLEGENHEIMER, ARTHUR.

SCHULTZ, HENRY (*b. Szarkowszczyzna, Russian Poland, 1893; d. near San Diego, Calif., 1938*), mathematical economist. Came to America as a boy. Graduated College of the City of New York, 1916; Ph.D., Columbia, 1925. Studied also at London School of Economics and at Galton Laboratory of University of London. Taught at University of Chicago, *post* 1926; was author of *The Theory and Measurement of Demand* (1938).

SCHULTZE, AUGUSTUS (*b. near Potsdam, Prussia, 1840; d. Bethlehem, Pa., 1918*), Moravian clergyman, editor, author. Professor of classics at Moravian College, Bethlehem, Pa., *post* 1870; president of the college, 1885–1918.

SCHUMANN-HEINK, ERNESTINE (*b. Lieben, near Prague, Bohemia, 1861; d. Hollywood, Calif., 1936*), singer. An outstanding contralto, she made her first professional appearance in Graz, Austria, 1876; after a somewhat difficult career with various German opera companies, she won success with the Hamburg Opera, 1888. Thereafter her European reputation grew and she was invited to join the Metropolitan Opera Co.; she made her American debut in Chicago, November 1898, in *Lohengrin.* Leaving the Metropolitan, 1903, to undertake work in concert and operetta, she returned to grand opera in 1905 and continued active on both sides of the Atlantic until *ca.* 1914. Displaying strong American patriotism during World War I, she made concert work her principal activity during the 1920's and the early 1930's; she also sang on the radio and in vaudeville. At its prime, her voice was remarkable for its compass as well as for its quality and power.

SCHUMPETER, JOSEPH ALOIS (*b. Triesch, Moravia, now Czechoslovakia, 1883; d. Cambridge, Mass., 1950*), economist. Educated at the University of Vienna. Precocious, with Napoleonic aspirations, and always a showman, he was a member of the Department of Economics at Harvard subsequent to his arrival in the United States, 1932. He brought with him a reputation as the enfant terrible of the Austrian school of economics; he had taught at Czernowitz and Graz, served as finance minister in the post–World War I socialist government of Austria, 1919–20, and occupied the chair of public finance at Bonn, 1925–32. It is probable, despite all his early brilliance, that the work he did in the last dozen years of his life is his most valuable contribution. He was author of, among other books, *Business Cycles* (1939), *Capitalism, Socialism and Democracy* (1942), *History of Economic Doctrines* (1951), and *History of Economic Analysis* (1954, incomplete and edited by his widow). A number of his earlier books have been translated from the German, e.g., *The Theory of Economic Development* (originally published in 1911).

SCHURMAN, JACOB GOULD (*b. Freetown, Prince Edward Island, Canada, 1854; d. New York, N.Y., 1942*), philosopher, educator, diplomat. Descended from New York Loyalists of Dutch extraction who had moved to Canada during the American Revolution. He attended the University of London, where he received a B.A. degree in 1877 from University College. He next studied philosophy for a year at Edinburgh, while simultaneously studying for an M.A. at London, and earned a D.Sc. with distinction in 1878. Schurman went to Cornell in 1886 for the professorship of Christian ethics and mental philosophy, recently endowed by Henry W. Sage. In 1890 Sage endowed the School of Philosophy at Cornell, with Schurman as its dean.

Schurman had already established himself as a philosopher of some distinction with *Kantian Ethics and the Ethics of Evolution* (1881), the first English-language critique of Kant's ethical system. He also wrote *The Ethical Import of Darwinism* (1888) and two books comprising his popular lectures, *Belief in God* (1890) and *Agnosticism and Religion* (1896). The objective idealism espoused by Schurman, who emphasized the totality of human experience in its social, historical, and institutional aspects, held sway at the Sage School of Philosophy. In 1892 the first general scholarly journal devoted to philosophy in America, the *Philosophical Review,* began publication at Cornell under his editorship. Schurman became president of Cornell in 1892. During his 28-year regime he created the Veterinary College, the College of Agriculture, the Medical College, and the ill-fated College of Forestry. Under his presidency Cornell changed from a privately endowed to a mixed public and private institution.

In the recently conquered Philippines, Schurman was chairman of a government commission to investigate local conditions, 1899. In 1902 he was publicly arguing (in his lecture and book *Philippine Affairs*) for Philippine independence. He also served as minister to Greece and Montenegro, 1912–13; minister to China, 1921–25, his most important diplomatic post; and ambassador to Germany, 1925–30.

SCHURZ, CARL (*b. Liblar, near Cologne, Germany, 1829; d. New York, N.Y., 1906*), German revolutionary, Union soldier, lawyer, diplomat, statesman. A leader of the student revolutionary movement at the University of Bonn, Schurz was profoundly influenced by Gottfried Kinkel and followed him in the abortive move upon Siegburg, May 1849. Thereafter he became a lieutenant and staff officer of the revolutionary army, fought in several engagements during June, and managed to escape from the fortress of Rastatt before its capture by the Prussians. After a brief refuge in Switzerland, he returned to Germany to rescue Kinkel, who had been sentenced to life imprisonment and was confined at Spandau. Achieving this purpose on the night of Nov. 6, 1850, he accompanied Kinkel to England. Thence, after a brief residence, he immigrated to the United States, August 1852. Settling on a small farm in Watertown, Wis., 1856, he espoused the antislavery cause and was drawn into Republican politics. Speaking in German, he campaigned for Frémont, 1856, and in 1858 spoke in Illinois for Abraham Lincoln. An able orator in both German and English, he was soon in demand for one campaign after another and was particularly effective during the campaign of 1860. His speech at Cooper Union, New York City, in September, a merciless criticism of Stephen A. Douglas, was regarded as his principal oratorical effort. Appointed U.S. minister to Spain by Lincoln, Schurz remained only a brief time in the post and returned to urge immediate emancipation of the slaves as a means of securing European sympathy for the North.

Appointed brigadier general of volunteers, June 1862, he took his military duties seriously. Commended as a division commander at the second battle of Bull Run, August 1862, he and his division were soon held up to scorn because of their flight during the battle of Chancellorsville. Schurz blamed the disaster on the improper placement of his division by General O. O. Howard and a long controversy ensued. Commanding the XI Corps at Gettysburg, Schurz was again unsuccessful in stemming an attack of the Confederates, and once again there were charges that his German troops had failed to stand their ground. Promoted to major general, Schurz and his corps were transferred to the west. After the battle of Chattanooga the depleted XI Corps was merged into a new unit and its general was appointed to an inactive post at Nashville. The end of the Civil War found Schurz serving as chief of staff to General Slocum in Sherman's army. Throughout his military service he had been in an anomalous situation because of his constant correspondence with President Lincoln; despite this, he won the regard of Sherman, Hancock, and other able Northern generals.

Traveling through the Southern states, July–September 1865, Schurz wrote a lengthy report on his observations which has value to this day, although President Johnson tried his best to suppress it. Briefly the Washington correspondent of the *New York Tribune* and the editor of the Detroit *Post*, he became coeditor, with Emil Preetorius, of the St. Louis *Westliche Post*, 1867. He delivered the keynote address at the Republican National Convention, 1868. As U.S. senator, Republican, from Missouri, 1869–75, Schurz soon found himself among the anti-Grant members; he opposed the president's spoils-loving and domineering partisans, introduced a bill to create a permanent civil service merit system, 1869, and made incessant attacks upon public corruption. Failing of reelection, he returned once again to journalism and lecturing. Having done more than any other leader to promote the Liberal Republican movement, he was permanent president of the Cincinnati convention, 1872, and was active in Horace Greeley's campaign. Supporting R. B. Hayes for the presidency, 1876, he served with enlightened ability as U.S. secretary of the interior, 1877–81. Coeditor of the New York *Evening Post* and the *Nation*, 1881–83, he resigned because of friendly differences over methods and policies with Edwin L. Godkin. He contributed the leading editorials to *Harper's Weekly*, 1892–98. Opposed to the war with Spain and later to expansionist policies, he held in his last years a unique position as a veteran statesman and political philosopher. Among his books are A *Life of Henry Clay* (1887) and *Reminiscences* (1907–08).

SCHUSSELE, CHRISTIAN (*b. Guebviller, Alsace, 1826; d. Merchantville, N.J., 1879*), painter, teacher, lithographer. Immigrated to Philadelphia, Pa., *ca.* 1849. Established reputation as a painter with *Clear the Track*, engraved by John Sartain, 1854. Among other of his well-known paintings are *Franklin Before the Lords in Council* (1856) and *Washington at Valley Forge* (1862). In the latter part of his life he served as professor of drawing and painting at the Pennsylvania Academy of the Fine Arts.

SCHUSTER, MAX LINCOLN (*b. Kalusz, Austria, 1897; d. New York, N.Y., 1970*), editor and publisher. Brought by his parents to New York City when he was several weeks old; attended Pulitzer School of Journalism at Columbia (B.Litt., 1917). In late 1923 he and Richard L. Simon started a publishing business and published their first project, a crossword puzzle book, in 1924. In 1926 they contracted Will Durant to write *The Story of Philosophy*, which sold over a half million copies. Many of their publications sold in the millions, including Dale Carnegie's *How to Win Friends and Influence People* (1938). In 1939 he, Simon, and Leon Shimkin joined Robert Fair De Graff in establishing Pocket Books, a company specializing in the publication of paperbound books; it soon became an outstanding success. Simon and Schuster and Pocket Books were sold to Field Enterprises in 1944, and until 1957 Schuster and Simon alternated as president and board chairman. In 1957 Shimkin and Schuster bought back the firm, and nine years later Schuster sold his interest to Shimkin.

SCHUTTLER, PETER (*b. Wachenheim, Hesse-Darmstadt, Germany, 1812; d. Chicago, Ill., 1865*), wagon maker. Came to America, 1834. In business in Chicago *post* 1843, Schuttler produced a lightweight easy-running wagon which displaced the old prairie schooner type for westward emigration.

SCHUYLER, EUGENE (*b. Ithaca, N.Y., 1840; d. Italy, 1890*), diplomat. Son of George W. Schuyler. Graduated Yale, 1859; Ph.D., 1861; LL.B., Columbia, 1863. A consular and diplomatic officer principally in Russia *post* 1867, Schuyler became widely known for a report on Turkish atrocities in Bulgaria (1876). Subsequently holding posts as diplomatic representative to Romania, Greece, Serbia, and Egypt, he was an outstanding figure during an era of mediocrity in the American foreign service. Among his literary works were translations from Turgenev and Tolstoy and a biography of Peter the Great (1884).

SCHUYLER, GEORGE WASHINGTON (*b. Stillwater, N.Y., 1810; d. 1888*), businessman, New York State official. Father of Eugene Schuyler. Author of *Colonial New York: Philip Schuyler and His Family* (1885).

SCHUYLER, JAMES DIX (*b. Ithaca, N.Y., 1848; d. Ocean Park, Calif., 1912*), hydraulic and railroad engineer, expert in dam building and water-supply systems.

SCHUYLER, LOUISA LEE (*b. New York, N.Y., 1837; d. 1926*), welfare-work leader. Great-granddaughter of Philip J. Schuyler and of Alexander Hamilton. Worked with U.S. Sanitary Commission through the Civil War; organized State Charities Aid Association, 1872; secured opening of nurses' training school at Bellevue Hospital, the first in America (*ca.* 1874).

SCHUYLER, MARGARITA (*b. Albany, N.Y., 1701; d. Albany, 1782*). Daughter-in-law of Peter Schuyler; aunt of Philip J. Schuyler. Celebrated as a hostess and as the subject of A. M. Grant's *Memoirs of an American Lady* (1808).

SCHUYLER, MONTGOMERY (*b. Ithaca, N.Y., 1843; d. New Rochelle, N.Y., 1914*), journalist, critic of architecture. Attended Hobart College. Served on the staff of the New York *World*, 1865–83; of the *New York Times*, 1883–1907. Meanwhile he had been managing editor, *Harper's Weekly*, 1885–87, and was a literary adviser to Harper & Brothers. He was author of *American Architecture: Studies* (1892), but the bulk of his writing on this topic is scattered through the files of periodicals, notably the *Architectural Record*, of which he was one of the founders, 1891.

SCHUYLER, PETER (*b. Beverwyck, present Albany, N.Y., 1657; d. 1724*), soldier and official of colonial New York. Elected first mayor of Albany, 1686, and head of the board of Indian commissioners, Schuyler acted with energy and efficiency as protector of the frontier against the French threat from Canada and possessed a remarkable influence over the Iroquois. Active in opposition to Jacob Leisler, he was made a judge of common pleas by Governor Sloughter, 1691, and appointed to the council in 1692 by Governor Fletcher. Acting governor of New York, July 1719–September 1720, he was removed from the council on the arrival of Governor Burnet, who feared him as a potential leader of the opposition. A trader and merchant, Schuyler owned numerous land grants, of which the most extensive was in the Saratoga patent.

SCHUYLER, PHILIP JOHN (*b. Albany, N.Y., 1733; d. Albany, 1804*), soldier, statesman, landowner. Commanded a company in the 1755 expedition against Crown Point; served in John Bradstreet's expedition to Oswego, 1756. Returned to service, 1758, as deputy commissary under Lord Howe and was again with Bradstreet at the taking of Fort Frontenac. Collected and forwarded provisions from Albany to Amherst's forces, 1759–60. Living as a country gentleman thereafter until the outbreak of the

Revolution, Schuyler developed his estates. Although he opposed the De Lancey-Colden royalist coalition, he withheld his sympathy from the radicals among the Sons of Liberty. Accepting membership in the New York delegation to the second Continental Congress, he was appointed on June 15, 1775, one of four major generals under Washington and assigned to command in northern New York. With only halfhearted support from New England he recruited and provisioned an army, strengthened garrisons at Ticonderoga and Crown Point, maintained the neutrality of the Iroquois, and organized the expedition of 1775–76 against Canada. Yielding the field command to General Richard Montgomery because of ill health, he was nevertheless held responsible for the failure of the expedition by New Englanders, who disliked him as a severe disciplinarian and as a symbol of the mutual antagonism between "Yorker" and "Yankee." Except for his indecision over defending Ticonderoga, which ended in St. Clair's abandonment of that fort, July 1777, Schuyler handled the difficult situation in northern New York with considerable skill. Retreating before the British in such a way as to permit levies of militia to harass the advancing General Burgoyne, he upset another part of the British strategy by relieving Fort Stanwix and so wrecking the efforts of the British general St. Leger to approach from the west. Congress, however, alarmed by the loss of Ticonderoga, superseded him with General Horatio Gates, Aug. 4, 1777. Demanding a court-martial, he was acquitted with honor, October 1778, and in the following spring resigned from the Continental service. He continued, however, to assist Washington with advice and served briefly in Congress, 1779–80. Holder of a number of public offices, 1780–98, Schuyler gave particular attention to problems of finance; he was a strong supporter of the movement which culminated in the Constitutional Convention of 1787 and served as U.S. senator, Federalist, from New York, 1789–91 and 1797–98. He was intimately associated with the career of his son-in-law, Alexander Hamilton.

SCHUYLER, ROBERT LIVINGSTON (*b. New York, N.Y., 1883; d. Rochester, N.Y., 1966*), historian, educator, and editor. Attended Columbia (Ph.D., 1909). Taught at Yale (1906) and Columbia (1910–51). Drew up the syllabus for the courses in American history and modern European history (1912–13). Author of *The Constitution of the United States* (1923); *Parliament and the British Empire* (1929), which demolished the old contention that the acts against which American colonists protested were without legal authority; *Josiah Tucker* (1931); and, his last major book, *The Fall of the Old Colonial System* (1945). Had a distinguished career as an editor, of *Political Science Quarterly* (1919–21), *Columbia Studies in History, Economics, and Public Law* (1923–29, 1944–48), and *American Historical Review* (1936–41), and the second supplement (1958) of the *Dictionary of American Biography.*

SCHWAB, CHARLES MICHAEL (*b. Williamsburg, Pa., 1862; d. New York, N.Y., 1939*), industrialist. Beginning work in the steel industry at the Carnegie-owned Edgar Thomson Steel plant as an engineer's helper, Schwab advanced swiftly, owing in great part to his genius in dealing with people and his open-mindedness toward technological, production, and laborsaving innovations. Appointed president of Carnegie Steel Co., 1897, he served as go-between in the sale of the Carnegie properties to the J. P. Morgan interests and in formation of the U.S. Steel Corporation, 1901. President of the new corporation, 1901–03, he built up the Bethlehem Steel Co., *post* 1904, into principal rival of U.S. Steel. To the operation of Bethlehem, Schwab brought daring, energy, and the skills of a great salesman. He set up an executive profit-sharing system, put essentially all wages on an incentive basis, and gave his associates a free hand. During World War I he was the principal factor in Bethlehem's success with war-contract

work and became in time a sort of senior spokesman for the steel industry. Dying insolvent because of unwise investment outside the steel industry and the effects of the Great Depression, he stands as an almost perfect specimen of the great entrepreneur in the heyday of American capitalism.

SCHWAB, JOHN CHRISTOPHER (*b. New York, N.Y., 1865; d. New Haven, Conn., 1916*), economist, librarian. Graduated Yale, 1886; Ph.D., Göttingen, 1889. Taught political economy at Yale *post* 1891. Author of *The Confederate States of America, 1861–1865: A Financial and Industrial History* (1901).

SCHWARTZ, DELMORE DAVID (*b. Brooklyn, N.Y., 1913; d. New York, N.Y., 1966*), writer. Attended University of Wisconsin, New York University (B.A., 1935), and Harvard. His masterpiece, "In Dreams Begin Responsibilities," appeared in *New Directions in Prose and Poetry* (1937). His first book (1938) was a collection of poetry and prose under that title and brought him instant critical attention and fame. Published the autobiographical play *Shenandoah* in 1941; the best of his short stories were collected in *The World Is a Wedding* (1948). *Summer Knowledge* (1959), which contains the best of his early work and his later, long-line poems, won the Bollingen Prize. Taught at Harvard (1940–47), Princeton (1949–50), Kenyon (1950), Indiana (1951), Chicago (1954), and Syracuse (1962–65). Editor of the *Partisan Review* (1943–55) and poetry editor and film critic for *New Republic* (1955–57). Suffered from paranoia and marital problems, and died in a seedy New York hotel. His life was depicted in Saul Bellow's novel *Humboldt's Gift* (1975).

SCHWARTZ, MAURICE (*b. Sudilkov, Russia, 1889; d. Tel Aviv, Israel, 1960*), actor. Born Avrom Moishe Schwartz. One of the leading figures in the Yiddish theater in America. Schwartz began acting with the Delancey Street Dramatic Club. By 1911, he was working in the David Kessler Theater on Second Avenue in New York. In 1920 took over the Yiddish Art Theater, dedicated to presenting plays of quality in Yiddish, including non-Jewish classics. The troupe included such actors as Paul Muni, Celia Adler, Lazar Fried, and Samuel Goldenberg. The repertory included works by Sholem Aleichem, Sholem Asch, and Osip Dymov, as well as Yiddish translations of Tolstoy, Ibsen, Chekhov, Molière, and Shaw. Schwartz is remembered as a great theater organizer as well as a fine actor. He was responsible for guiding the Yiddish theater to its heights.

SCHWARZ, EUGENE AMANDUS (*b. Liegnitz, Silesia, Germany, 1844; d. 1928*), entomologist. Came to America, 1872. In U.S. Department of Agriculture service *post* 1879, Schwarz was considered to be the most learned coleopterist of his time and also excelled as a field investigator.

SCHWATKA, FREDERICK (*b. Galena, Ill., 1849; d. Portland, Oreg., 1892*), explorer. Graduated West Point, 1871; M.D., Bellevue Hospital Medical College, New York, 1876. In association with William H. Gilder, Schwatka journeyed to the Arctic, 1878, and after a search of more than two years resolved all doubts concerning the fate of the famous expedition of Sir John Franklin. Resigning from the army, 1885, he devoted himself thereafter to travel and to writing and lecturing.

SCHWEINITZ, EDMUND ALEXANDER DE (*b. Bethlehem, Pa., 1825; d. 1887*), Moravian bishop, historian. Son of Lewis D. von Schweinitz.

SCHWEINITZ, EMIL ALEXANDER DE (*b. Salem, N.C., 1866; d. 1904*), biochemist. Grandson of Lewis D. von Schweinitz. Graduated University of North Carolina, 1882; Ph.D., 1885; Ph.D. in chemistry, Göttingen, 1886. Engaged *post* 1888 in research in the U.S. Department of Agriculture (*post* 1890 as chief of research in biochemistry, Bureau of Animal Industry), he specialized in the study of disease-producing bacteria and the production of means of immunity to them. In addition to his work for the government, he was dean and professor of chemistry at the medical school, present George Washington University.

SCHWEINITZ, GEORGE EDMUND DE (*b. Philadelphia, Pa., 1858; d. Philadelphia, 1938*), opthalmologist. Son of Edmund A. de Schweinitz; grandson of Lewis D. von Schweinitz. Graduated Moravian College, 1876; M.D., University of Pennsylvania, 1881. Taught ophthalmology at Philadelphia Polyclinic and at Jefferson Medical College; professor of ophthalmology, University of Pennsylvania, 1902–24, and at its Graduate School of Medicine thereafter. Long regarded as the American leader in his specialty, de Schweinitz was coauthor and editor of numerous textbooks and author of hundreds of articles; his principal work was *Diseases of the Eye* (1892), for many years the most admired textbook in its field.

SCHWEINITZ, LEWIS DAVID VON (*b. Bethlehem, Pa., 1780; d. Bethlehem, 1834*), Moravian clergyman, botanist, pioneer mycologist. Father of Edmund A. and grandfather of Emil A. and George E. de Schweinitz. Author of *The Fungi of Lusatia* (1805), *The Fungi of North Carolina* (1818), *A Synopsis of North American Fungi* (published in *Transactions* of the American Philosophical Society, 1834), and other works.

SCHWELLENBACH, LEWIS BAXTER (*b. Superior, Wis., 1894; d. Washington, D.C., 1948*), lawyer, politician. Raised in Spokane, Wash. LL.B., University of Washington, 1917. After World War I army service, he practiced in Seattle. Active in politics as a Democrat, he was elected to the U.S. Senate, 1934. A consistent supporter of the New Deal and especially interested in the problems of labor, he left the Senate in December 1940 to accept appointment as a federal judge for the eastern district of the state of Washington. In 1945 President Truman chose him to be U.S. secretary of labor, a post in which he served with considerable ability, despite increasing ill health.

SCHWIDETZKY, OSCAR OTTO RUDOLF (*b. Konitz, Germany [now Chojnice, Poland], 1874; d. Ramsey, N.J., 1963*), medical instrument maker. Immigrated to the United States in 1900 and became an importer of surgical supplies. Created the Ace bandage and invented devices to provide access to the bloodstream to control and fight disease, including the first glass-barrel and rubber-bulb syringe (1910), which evolved into the Asepto model; the standard syringe for injecting fluids into the genitourinary system (1916); the syrette syringe, used on wounded soldiers in World War 1 to inject morphine; and the caudal needle for the continuous administration of anesthesia into the spinal column. His lifelong association with Becton-Dickinson Company began in 1913.

SCHWIMMER, ROSIKA (*b. Budapest, Hungary, 1877; d. Winnetka, Ill.[?], 1948*), feminist, peace advocate, writer, lecturer. Conceived idea of Peace Ship, which Henry Ford underwrote, 1915; served as minister from Hungary to Switzerland during Mihály Károlyi's regime (November 1918–March 1919); center of controversy after her immigration to the United States, 1921, and denied right of citizenship. Her chief concern in later life was the establishment of an all-inclusive, democratic, nonmilitary federation of nations under a world government.

SCIDMORE, ELIZA RUHAMAH (*b. Madison, Wis., 1856; d. 1928*), journalist, traveler, lecturer.

SCOLLARD, CLINTON (*b. Clinton, N.Y., 1860; d. Kent, Conn., 1932*), poet. Author of *Pictures in Song* (1884) and of a number of other volumes of lyrics marked by painstaking care in versification.

SCOPES, JOHN THOMAS (*b. Paducah, Ky., 1900; d. Shreveport, La., 1970*), teacher and geologist. In 1925 the Tennessee legislature enacted a law making it a misdemeanor to teach evolution in the state's public schools, and the American Civil Liberties Union advertised that it would pay the expenses of anyone who would test the law's constitutionality. Scopes agreed to do so and was arrested for teaching evolution at Central High School in Dayton, Tenn. The case developed into the nation's biggest news story when William Jennings Bryan and Clarence Darrow volunteered to oppose each other in trying the case. At issue were the rights of religion and government to decide what should or should not be taught. The jury found Scopes guilty; Judge John Raulston fined him $100. Darrow argued the appeal before the Tennessee Supreme Court, which overturned the sentence, ruling that the jury, not the judge, should have set the fine. Scopes returned to teaching and relative obscurity. In 1960 he reemerged to promote the film version of the play *Inherit the Wind*, based on his trial.

SCOTT, ALLEN CECIL (*b. Omaha, Nebr., 1882; d. Omaha, 1964*), businessman. Developed the idea of a pilot chute that popped out of an individual parachute when the pilot pulled the ripcord and dragged the main chute free; the patent granted (1921) covered the packing of the main chute, the harness and release, and the pilot chute, which became the basic design of all later chutes.

SCOTT, AUSTIN (*b. Maumee, Ohio, 1848; d. Granville Centre, Mass., 1922*), educator. Graduated Yale, 1869; M.A., University of Michigan, 1870; Ph.D., Leipzig, 1873. Served as editorial assistant to George Bancroft. Taught history at Johns Hopkins, 1875–82, and at Rutgers College, *post* 1883, later becoming professor of political science. President of Rutgers, 1891–1906.

SCOTT, CHARLES (*b. present Powhatan Co., Va., ca. 1739; d. Clark Co., Ky., 1813*), colonial soldier. Revolutionary major general by brevet, Kentucky legislator. Removing to Kentucky, 1785, he served under General Josiah Harmar in the 1790 expedition against the Indians. In 1791 he led an expedition against the Indians on the Wabash River and was with General St. Clair at the disastrous defeat of Nov. 4. He led the mounted Kentucky volunteers at the battle of Fallen Timbers, August 1794. Governor of Kentucky, 1808–12.

SCOTT, COLIN ALEXANDER (*b. Ottawa, Canada, 1861; d. Boston, Mass., 1925*), psychologist, educational reformer. Author of *Social Education* (1908).

SCOTT, DRED (*b. in slavery, Southampton Co., Va., ca. 1795; d. St. Louis, Mo., 1858*). Nominal plaintiff in the famous legal process, 1846–57, which led to the Dred Scott decision by the U.S. Supreme Court.

SCOTT, EMMETT JAY (*b. Houston, Tex., 1873; d. Washington, D.C., 1957*), educator and publicist. Studied at Wiley University in Texas. In 1891, Scott became a reporter for the *Houston Post*; by 1894 he was the editor for the *Texas Freeman*, an influential black newspaper. It was as private secretary to Booker T. Washington (1897–1915) that Scott gained influence in black politics and social organization. In 1900, he helped Washington organize the National Negro Business League, serving as secretary until 1922. Secretary, Tuskegee Institute (1912–17), and secretary-treasurer (1919–38), Howard University. During World War I, was advisor to the secretary of war on black soldiers. Served on public relations staff of Republican national conventions

(1924–48); assistant publicity director, Republican National Committee (1939–42).

SCOTT, FRED NEWTON (*b. Terre Haute, Ind., 1860; d. San Diego, Calif., 1931*), educator. Taught at University of Michigan *post* 1889; headed departments of rhetoric and journalism. Author of a number of works on style, he was coauthor with C. M. Gayley of *An Introduction to the Methods and Materials of Literary Criticism* (1899).

SCOTT, GUSTAVUS (*b. probably Prince William Co., Va., 1753; d. Washington, D.C., 1800*), lawyer, Maryland legislator, Revolutionary patriot.

SCOTT, HARVEY WHITEFIELD (*near Groveland, Ill., 1838; d. Baltimore, Md., 1910*), journalist. Brother of Abigail J. S. Duniway. Editor of the Portland *Morning Oregonian*, 1866–72; editor and part owner, 1877–1910. A conservative Republican, he won national recognition for his newspaper and made it the strongest journal in the Pacific Northwest.

SCOTT, HUGH LENOX (*b. Danville, Ky., 1853; d. Washington, D.C., 1934*), army officer. Grandson of Charles Hodge. Graduated West Point, 1876. Served with cavalry, chiefly in the Dakotas and Oklahoma, 1876–97; became specialist in language, history, and "sign talk" of the Plains Indians. On staffs of General William Ludlow and General Leonard Wood in Cuba, 1899–1902, he was governor of Sulu Archipelago in the Philippines, 1903–06. Promoted colonel, he served as superintendent of West Point, 1906–10. As brigadier general, he commanded on the Mexican border, 1913–14. Appointed chief of staff, November 1914, he laid the basis for raising, training, and equipping the American forces in World War I. Retired as major general, 1917, he remained on active duty for two years and commanded the 78th Division at Camp Dix, N.J.

SCOTT, IRVING MURRAY (*b. Hebron Mills, Md., 1837; d. San Francisco, Calif., 1903*), shipbuilder, foundryman. Removed to San Francisco, 1860; was long associated with the Union Iron Works and its predecessor firm. Constructed U.S. warships *Charleston, Olympia, San Francisco, Oregon, Wisconsin,* and *Ohio,* 1889–1901.

SCOTT, JAMES BROWN (*b. Kincardine, Ontario, Canada, 1866; d. Wardour, Md., 1943*), international lawyer, foundation executive, advocate of international arbitration and conciliation. Raised in Philadelphia, Pa., B.A., Harvard, 1890; M.A., 1891; Doctor of Civil and Canon Law, Heidelberg, 1894. Organized Los Angeles Law School, serving as dean, 1896–99; dean, college of law of University of Illinois, 1899–1903; professor of law, Columbia University, 1903–06; solicitor (chief legal officer), U.S. Department of State, 1906–11; permanent secretary and director of the division of international law, Carnegie Endowment for International Peace, 1911–40. Influenced in his theories of international law by the work of Francisco de Vitoria and Hugo Grotius, he believed that warfare would give way to legal principles and practices if governments could be educated to accept an international tribunal for conciliation of disputes. Over the years, he continued to hold academic posts at George Washington University, Johns Hopkins, and Georgetown University.

SCOTT, JAMES WILMOT (*b. Walworth Co., Wis., 1849; d. New York, N.Y., 1895*), journalist. Associated with Chicago, Ill., newspapers *post* 1875, he made his *Chicago Herald* a conservative force for reform, 1881–95.

SCOTT, JOB (*b. Providence, R.I., 1751; d. Ballitore, Ireland, 1793*), Quaker preacher. An outstanding example of quietism,

Scott advanced views on biblical interpretation which anticipated modernist tenets.

SCOTT, JOHN (*b. probably Ashford, Kent, England, ca. 1630; d. England, 1696*), adventurer, swindling land speculator, spy. Nefariously active in New York and New England, 1654–64.

SCOTT, JOHN ADAMS (*b. Fletcher, Ill., 1867; d. Augusta, Mich., 1947*), classicist. Graduated Northwestern University, 1895; Ph.D., Johns Hopkins University, 1897. Taught Greek at Northwestern, 1897–1938 (professor *post* 1901; chairman of Department of Classical Languages *post* 1904); author of *The Unity of Homer* (1921), and other works.

SCOTT, JOHN MORIN (*b. New York, N.Y., ca. 1730; d. New York, 1784*), lawyer. Graduated Yale, 1746; studied law in office of William Smith (1697–1769). An active practitioner and a ready speaker, Scott was associated with William Livingston *post* 1752 in support of the Whig Presbyterian cause in New York and was an organizer of the New York Sons of Liberty. He was a leader of the radical party in the New York provincial congress, 1775–77, and ran against George Clinton for the governorship of New York, 1777. He was New York secretary of state, 1778–84, and was also a state legislator and a member of the Continental Congress. He served as brigadier general in the battle of Long Island, August 1776.

SCOTT, JOHN PRINDLE (*b. Norwich, N.Y., 1877; d. 1932*), composer, baritone, hymnist.

SCOTT, LEROY (*b. Fairmount, Ind., 1875; d. Chateaugay Lake, N.Y., 1929*), journalist, settlement worker. Author of *The Walking Delegate* (1905), *Counsel for the Defense* (1912), and other mediocre fiction; magazine writer on social questions and on crime and its detection.

SCOTT, ORANGE (*b. Brookfield, Vt., 1800; d. Newark, N.J., 1847*), Methodist clergyman, abolitionist. Led a secession from his church on the issue of slavery, 1841; presided over convention at Utica, N.Y., May 1843, at which the Wesleyan Methodist Connection of America was formed.

SCOTT, ROBERT KINGSTON (*b. Armstrong Co., Pa., 1826; d. Henry Co., Ohio, 1900*), businessman, Union major general by brevet. Chief, South Carolina branch of Freedmen's Bureau, 1865–68. As governor, Union Republican, of South Carolina, 1868–72, Scott was largely responsible for the scandals and disorder that characterized Republican rule in the state; his policies trebled the public debt, and he was leader in conspiracies to further fraudulent contracts and stock issues.

SCOTT, SAMUEL PARSONS (*b. Hillsboro, Ohio, 1846; d. Hillsboro, 1929*), lawyer. Hispanic scholar. Author of, among other works, *History of the Moorish Empire in Europe* (1904).

SCOTT, THOMAS ALEXANDER (*b. Fort Loudoun, Pa., 1823; d. near Darby, Pa., 1881*), railroad executive. Proposed plan for President-elect Lincoln's surreptitious entry into Washington, D.C., 1861; was assistant U.S. secretary of war in charge of government railways and transport, August 1861–June 1862; supervised removal of General Hooker's force from Virginia to Chattanooga, 1863. As first vice president of the Pennsylvania Railroad, 1860–74, Scott ably seconded the efforts of J. Edgar Thomson to strengthen the Pennsylvania system and continued that work as president, 1874–80.

SCOTT, THOMAS FIELDING (*b. Iredall Co., N.C., 1807; d. New York, N.Y., 1867*), Episcopal clergyman. Missionary bishop in Oregon and Washington Territory *post* 1854.

Scott, Walter (*b. Moffat, Scotland, 1796; d. Mason Co., Ky., 1861*), religious reformer, schoolteacher. Came to America, 1818. As a Disciples of Christ preacher *post* 1826, Scott established the evangelistic pattern and the form and method of propaganda to which the rapid growth of that sect was largely due.

Scott, Walter Dill (*b. Cooksville, Ill., 1869; d. Evanston, Ill., 1955*), applied psychologist and educator. Studied at Illinois State Normal University, Northwestern University, McCormick Theological Seminary, and the University of Leipzig (Ph.D., 1900). Taught at Northwestern (1900–16). Became the first professor of applied psychology in the nation at Carnegie Institute of Technology, 1916. During World War I, developed the first tests for personnel classification for the army. President of Northwestern (1920–39). Built the university into one of the leading institutions in the country, establishing several new departments and schools. A pioneer in the application of psychology in advertising.

Scott, Walter Edward (*b. Cynthiana[?], Ky., 1870[?]; d. Stovepipe Wells, Calif., 1954*), eccentric mining prospector. Performed at one time for "Buffalo Bill's Wild West" show. Known as "Death Valley Scotty," Scott perpetrated a series of hoaxes, claiming to have found a rich gold mine in Death Valley. A Chicago millionaire, A. M. Johnson, financed his escapades on a lark, building him a mansion, Scotty's Castle, in Death Valley in the 1920's. Scott ended his days showing tourists through the castle.

Scott, William (*b. Warrenton, Va., 1804; d. near Jefferson City, Mo., 1862*), jurist. Removed to Missouri, 1826. Appointed to the state circuit bench, 1835, he was advanced to the state supreme court, 1841; with the exception of a two-year interval, he served until his death. Conservative and competent, he wrote many opinions in cases involving master and slave, including those in the state actions in the Dred Scott Case. An ardent Democrat, he was an opponent of Thomas H. Benton and a sympathizer with the Confederate cause.

Scott, William Anderson (*b. Bedford Co., Tenn., 1813; d. San Francisco, Calif., 1885*), Presbyterian clergyman. Grew prominent as pastor at the First Presbyterian Church, New Orleans, La., 1842–54; formed Calvary Church, San Francisco, Calif., 1854, and St. John's Church in the same city, 1870. Helped found, 1871, and taught at, San Francisco Theological Seminary.

Scott, William Berryman (*b. Cincinnati, Ohio, 1858; d. Princeton, N.J., 1947*), geologist, paleontologist. Grandson of Charles Hodge; brother of Hugh Lenox Scott. B.A., College of New Jersey (Princeton), 1877; Ph.D., Heidelberg, 1880. Taught geology at Princeton, 1880–1930 (professor *post* 1884 and chairman of department *post* 1909). One of the most important vertebrate paleontologists of his era, he was preeminent in descriptive and taxonomic studies of fossil vertebrates and in the mammalian paleontology of the Tertiary period. Of his more than 170 publications, perhaps the most important was *A History of Land Mammals in the Western Hemisphere* (1913; 2nd. ed., 1937).

Scott, W(illiam) Kerr (*b. Haw River, N.C., 1896; d. Burlington, N.C., 1958*), politician. Studied at the North Carolina State College of Agriculture and Mechanic Arts (B.S., 1917). A Jeffersonian farmer who was active in agricultural affairs in North Carolina, Scott became state commissioner of agriculture (1936–48). Elected Democratic governor, 1948, he was instrumental in improving rural life through roadbuilding, electrification, and better health care facilities. He appointed first black to state board of education and first woman to the Superior Court. Elected to the U.S. Senate in 1954, Scott was an outspoken liberal—opposing Senator Joseph R. McCarthy and advocating equal rights for women.

Scott, William Lawrence (*b. Washington, D.C., 1828; d. 1891*), railroad and coal operator. Grandson of Gustavus Scott. A type of the individualistic capitalist of his time, he supervised his various and far-flung interests from home offices in Erie, Pa.

Scott, Winfield (*b. "Laurel Branch," in neighborhood of Petersburg, Va., 1786; d. West Point, N.Y., 1866*), soldier, statesman. Attended College of William and Mary; studied law in Petersburg. Commissioned captain of light artillery, May 1808, Scott recruited a company and embarked for New Orleans, La., arriving Apr. 1, 1809. Put on trial and suspended for a year from the army for stating that General James Wilkinson, his commander, had been as great a traitor as Aaron Burr, Scott rejoined his command, 1811, serving as a staff officer in New Orleans until February 1812. Promoted lieutenant colonel, he reported at Buffalo, N.Y., in October 1812, and was taken prisoner at the battle of Queenstown. Exchanged later in the year, he was sent to Philadelphia early in 1813 as adjutant general with rank of colonel.

Detailed for duty on the northern front, he planned and executed the successful attack on Fort George on the Niagara River in May 1813. Commanding an infantry battalion in the advance guard of General Jacob Brown's force, he defeated the British in an engagement on Uphold's Creek late in the year. Almost alone among American officers in the realization that adequate training and knowledge were prerequisites of victory, Scott was ordered by President Madison and Secretary Monroe to Albany, N.Y., to supervise preparations for another offensive on the Niagara, but, in fact, was left to supervise munitions at the arsenal. Promoted a regular brigadier general, March 1814, he returned to Buffalo, where he played the chief part in training the only American troops who gave a good account of themselves on land during the War of 1812. On July 4–5, he drove the enemy in a running fight for 16 miles to the Chippewa, and he and his brigade bore the brunt of the fighting at Lundy's Lane on July 25. He became overnight the idol of the United States and a hero abroad. Brevetted major general, he was prevented by wounds received at Lundy's Lane from joining Jackson at New Orleans.

Performing routine duties, 1815–32, Scott gave much of his time to study of military methods in Europe and to constructive writing. He headed the board which produced the first standard set of American drill regulations, 1815, and was the sole author of the revised *Infantry Tactics* (1835), which remained standard down to the Civil War. Passed over in favor of Alexander Macomb for appointment as commanding general of the army, 1828, Scott protested the appointment vainly. Employed briefly in the Black Hawk War, 1832, he was personally commissioned by President Jackson in that same year to watch the South Carolina nullifiers, and by his tact and wisdom did much to preserve the peace during the nullification crisis. Commissioned in 1835 to prosecute war against the Seminole and Creek Indians in Florida and adjacent states, he was denied adequate means for making a campaign and unreasonably relieved of the duty. Examined before a court of inquiry for his alleged failure, he was fully exonerated. During 1838 he performed with brilliance as a soldier-diplomat in settling difficulties raised by a rebellion in Canada, by the removal of the Cherokee Indians beyond the Mississippi, and by a dispute and a possible war with Great Britain over the Maine boundary question. Appointed general in chief of the army, 1841, he instituted reforms, outlawed cruel punishments for soldiers, and aided officers to become well schooled. *Post* 1839 he was mentioned as a possible Whig candidate for the presidency.

As war with Mexico approached, Scott endorsed the appointment of Zachary Taylor to command the army of occupation at Corpus Christi and supplied him with able officers as subordinates. When the fruitlessness of the campaign was demonstrated (despite the tactical victories which were gained), Scott proposed a strategic plan that would, as he put it, "conquer a peace." President Polk, inimical to anything that might advance Scott's political prestige, opposed it, but was forced to acquiesce in it by Secretary W. L. Marcy, Senator Thomas H. Benton, and others. Setting out with full powers for the seat of war, Scott managed by tireless effort to land 10,000 men below Veracruz, Mar. 9, 1847. Advised by senior officers to take the city by assault, he chose to invest it from the rear and took it Mar. 26 with less than 20 dead. No reinforcements were sent him, and it became plain that the administration was hedging on fulfillment of his plan; nevertheless, Scott pushed forward in April toward Mexico City. Winning a victory at Cerro Gordo, despite inefficiency on the part of his senior officers, he was halted at Jalapa when a large part of his force left in a body because of the expiration of their enlistments. His urgent demands for money and men brought him no response until midsummer. On Aug. 5, when his force had been raised by incoming recruits to about 10,000 effectives, he set off once more from Puebla. After a series of actions at Contreras, Churubusco, Molino del Rey, and Chapultepec, Scott marched into Mexico City on Sept. 14, and entered on the difficult task of putting his army to work at the government of an occupied territory. In this effort he was so successful that a deputation of Mexicans asked him to be their dictator. The administration at Washington, however, saw an opportunity to undercut the victorious general politically when his troublesome subordinate, Gideon J. Pillow, distributed his own personal version of Scott's battles to the newspapers at home. Scott protested Pillow's actions and also those of General Worth, but President Polk upheld the offenders and ordered the victorious commander himself before a handpicked court of inquiry. On Apr. 22, 1848, Scott returned to the United States. In the words of Robert E. Lee, an engineer officer on his staff, he had been "turned out as an old horse to die"; yet in the sequel, Scott was completely vindicated and received unprecedented honors from the people of New York and other cities. He ran as Whig candidate for the presidency in 1852 and was overwhelmingly defeated by Franklin Pierce after an exceptionally scurrilous campaign. In 1852, he was raised to rank of lieutenant general.

Foreseeing the Civil War, Scott pleaded with President Buchanan in October and December 1860, to reinforce the Southern forts and armories against seizure. In January 1861, with headquarters at Washington, he actively oversaw recruiting and training of the defenders of the capital and personally commanded Lincoln's bodyguard at the inauguration. Rendering all aid in his power to the president, he drew up a general plan for the conduct of the federal forces which might well have curtailed the war; it was disregarded on the ground he was too old to give advice. Retiring in November 1861, he continued active and in 1865 presented to General U. S. Grant, who had been one of his subalterns in the Mexican War, a gift bearing the inscription "from the oldest to the greatest general."

In his prime a bulky and immensely strong man, six feet, five inches in height, Scott possessed a whimsical egotism, was inclined to flourishes of unfortunate rhetoric, and was too outspoken for his own advancement; his exactness in dress and behavior won him the nickname "Fuss and Feathers." In his public career of nearly half a century he had been a main factor in ending two wars, in saving the country from several others, and in acquiring a large portion of its western territory.

SCOVEL, HENRY SYLVESTER (*b. Denny Station, Pa., 1869; d. Havana, Cuba, 1905*), engineer, journalist. Aggressive correspondent in Cuba for several U.S. newspapers, 1895–99.

SCOVEL, SYLVESTER. *See* SCOVEL, HENRY SYLVESTER.

SCOVELL, MELVILLE AMASA (*b. Belvidere, N.J., 1855; d. 1912*), agricultural chemist, educator. Patented processes for clarifying juice of sugar-producing plants and for manufacturing glucose, sugar, and syrup from sorghum; was director, Kentucky Agricultural Experiment Station *post* 1885; made notable contributions as chemist, agronomist, pure-food exponent, and administrator.

SCOVILLE, JOSEPH ALFRED (*b. Woodbury, Conn., 1815; d. New York, N.Y., 1864*), journalist. Secretary and biographer of John C. Calhoun. Scoville edited several New York newspapers *post* 1850 and is particularly remembered for his five volumes of commercial reminiscence entitled *The Old Merchants of New York City* (1863–66, published under pseudonym "Walter Barrett").

SCRANTON, GEORGE WHITFIELD (*b. Madison, Conn., 1811; d. Scranton, Pa., 1861*), iron manufacturer, railroad president, developer of transportation in the Lackawanna Valley. Founded city of Scranton, 1840.

SCREWS, WILLIAM WALLACE (*b. Jernigan, Ala., 1839; d. Coosada, Ala., 1913*), Confederate soldier, journalist. Editor-owner of the *Montgomery* (Ala.) *Advertiser*, 1866–1913, he led opposition to Reconstruction, fought the Farmers' Alliance, and directed the policies of the Democratic party in the state.

SCRIBNER, CHARLES (*b. New York, N.Y., 1821; d. Lucerne, Switzerland, 1871*), publisher. Father of Charles Scribner (1854–1930). Graduated College of New Jersey (Princeton), 1840. Gave up practice of law to found publishing firm of Baker & Scribner, 1846; on death of his partner, 1850, continued the firm in his own name.

SCRIBNER, CHARLES (*b. New York, N.Y., 1854; d. New York, 1930*), publisher. Son of Charles Scribner (1821–71); grandson of John I. Blair. Graduated College of New Jersey (Princeton), 1875. Entering the publishing house established by his father (known *post* 1878 as Charles Scribner's Sons), he served it as president, 1879–1928, and was thereafter chairman of the board. He was active also as a banker and as a benefactor of Princeton University and Skidmore College.

SCRIBNER, CHARLES (*b. New York, N.Y., 1890; d. New York, 1952*), publisher. Studied at St. Paul's School and at Princeton University (B.A., 1913). Joined the family publishing firm, Charles Scribner's Sons, in 1913; secretary, 1918; vice president, 1926; and president from 1932. Instrumental in the liberalization of the firm. Along with editor Maxwell Perkins, Scribner backed the publication of many of the century's most influential authors: F. Scott Fitzgerald, Ernest Hemingway, Thomas Wolfe, Taylor Caldwell, John Galsworthy, Alan Paton, Aubrey Menen, and James Jones. *Scribner's Magazine*, under the editorship of A. S. Dashiell, also included many leading authors but failed to make the transition from a conservative magazine to a more timely publication. Scribner expanded the reference book department, continuing the publication of the *Dictionary of American Biography*, begun by his father, and bringing out the *Dictionary of American History* in 1940. The children's book department was also expanded and many new children's authors attracted to the firm. Scribner also assisted the Princeton University Press, serving as president from 1940 until 1948.

SCRIPPS, EDWARD WYLLIS (*b. near Rushville, Ill., 1854; d. Monrovia Bay, Liberia, 1926*), newspaper publisher. Half brother of James E. and Ellen B. Scripps. Entering newspaper work in Detroit, Mich., 1872, he founded the Cleveland, Ohio, *Penny*

Press, 1878, first link of a chain of cheap daily papers extending from the Middle West to the Pacific. In partnership with Milton A. McRae *post* 1889, he organized, 1897, an independent news service to cover the field west of Pittsburgh; in 1907 it became known as the United Press Association, the first such agency to operate in connection with a chain of daily papers. He was also organizer of the NEA syndicate. Editorially, the Scripps papers were independent in politics, sympathetic with union labor, and liberal in their general attitude.

SCRIPPS, ELLEN BROWNING (*b. London, England, 1836; d. 1932*), journalist, philanthropist. Sister of James E. Scripps; half sister of Edward W. Scripps. Playing a large part in the success of the newspaper ventures of her brother and half brother, she also made a fortune in California real estate. Founded Scripps College at Claremont, Calif., and the present Scripps Institution of Oceanography.

SCRIPPS, JAMES EDMUND (*b. London, England, 1835; d. Detroit, Mich., 1906*), newspaper publisher. Brother of Ellen B. Scripps; half brother of Edward W. Scripps. Came to America as a boy; was raised near Rushville, Ill. Began newspaper career, 1857, as reporter on the Chicago *Democratic Press*; served as business manager and editor of *Detroit Tribune*; founded Detroit *Evening News*, August 1873. Helped finance founding of the Cleveland, Ohio, *Penny Press* by his half brother, Edward W. Scripps, 1878, and later joined with him in the formation of his chain of newspapers. Conservative in temperament, he disagreed with his partners over questions of management and gradually withdrew from the combination; by 1903 he had relinquished his holdings in all but the *Evening News*, later called the *Detroit News*. He purchased the *Detroit Tribune*, 1891.

SCRIPPS, ROBERT PAINE (*b. San Diego, Calif., 1895; d. near Santa Margarita Island, Magdalena Bay, Lower California, 1938*), newspaper publisher. Son of Edward W. Scripps. Headed the Scripps-Howard newspaper chain, 1926–38.

SCRIPPS, WILLIAM EDMUND (*b. Detroit, Mich., 1882; d. Oakland County, Mich., 1952*), newspaper publisher. Inheriting an interest in the *Detroit Evening News*, founded by his father, Scripps declined to accept the position of publisher, deferring to a relative. Instead he concentrated his energies on radio communications, aviation, and inventions. Eventually accepting the post of publisher in the 1930's he left the running of the paper to others and turned to agriculture, animal husbandry, conservation, and philanthropy.

SCRUGGS, WILLIAM LINDSAY (*b. near Knoxville, Tenn., 1836; d. Atlanta, Ga., 1912*), journalist, Tennessee Unionist, diplomat. Agent of Venezuela in the United States, 1894–98, during crisis over boundary difficulties with Great Britain.

SCRYMSER, JAMES ALEXANDER (*b. New York, N.Y., 1839; d. New York, 1918*), capitalist, Union soldier. Promoted and developed cable and telegraph lines to Cuba, Mexico, and Central and South American points.

SCUDDER, HORACE ELISHA (*b. Boston, Mass., 1838; d. Cambridge, Mass., 1902*), editor, author. Brother of Samuel H. Scudder. Graduated Williams, 1858. Editor with Houghton, Mifflin & Co. and its predecessor firms *post ca.* 1864; editor, *Riverside Magazine for Young People*, 1867–70; editor, *Atlantic Monthly*, 1890–98. Author of a number of books, which included eight juvenile "Bodley Books" of travel (1876–1884) and biographies of Noah Webster, Bayard Taylor, George Washington, and James Russell Lowell.

SCUDDER, JOHN (*b. Freehold, N.J., 1793; d. Wynberg, South Africa, 1855*), physician, Reformed Dutch clergyman. Missionary to Ceylon and India, 1819–42 and 1846–54.

SCUDDER, JOHN MILTON (*b. Harrison, Ohio, 1829; d. Daytona, Fla., 1894*), eclectic physician. Graduated Eclectic Medical Institute, Cincinnati, Ohio, 1856. Taught at his alma mater throughout his professional life and devoted much of his time and energy to its development and improvement. He served as dean *post* 1861 and as editor of the *Eclectic Medical Journal*, 1861–94.

SCUDDER, (JULIA) VIDA DUTTON (*b. Madura, India, 1861; d. Wellesley, Mass., 1954*), writer, professor, and Christian socialist. Studied at Smith College (B.A., 1884; M.A., 1889) and Oxford University. Taught English at Wellesley College (1887–1928). A member of the Socialist party, Scudder sought to reconcile Marxist theory with the Christian ideal of community. She founded the Women's Trade Union League in 1903 and helped establish a settlement house, Denison House, in Boston in 1890. Important works include *Social Ideals in English Letters* (1898).

SCUDDER, NATHANIEL (*b. either Huntington, N.Y., or near Freehold, N.J., 1733; d. near Shrewsbury, N.J., 1781*), physician, New Jersey Revolutionary patriot and colonel of militia. Member of Continental Congress, February 1778–December 1779. He was killed in a skirmish with Loyalist refugees three days before the surrender at Yorktown.

SCUDDER, SAMUEL HUBBARD (*b. Boston, Mass. 1837; d. Cambridge, Mass., 1911*), entomologist. Brother of Horace E. Scudder. Graduated Williams, 1857; studied at Lawrence Scientific School under Agassiz, whom he also served as assistant. Scudder's bibliography comprises 791 scientific titles. Outside the field of entomology he was author of *Catalogue of Scientific Serials . . . 1633–1876* (1879) and *Nomenclator Zoologicus* (1882–84), both important works. His true lifework, however, dealt with American diurnal Lepidoptera, the Orthoptera, and fossil insects. Among his numerous writings on butterflies, his *Butterflies of the Eastern United States and Canada, with Special References to New England* (1888–89) stands out as monumental. He was the greatest American orthopterist of his time, and his work on fossil insects was profound, extensive, and pioneer. His style of writing possessed great charm.

SCULL, JOHN (*b. Reading, Pa., 1765; d. near present Irwin, Pa., 1828*), newspaper editor. Partner with Joseph Hall in establishment at Pittsburgh, Pa., 1786, of the first newspaper published west of the Alleghenies, the Pittsburgh *Gazette*. Also a civic leader in Pittsburgh, he continued publication of the *Gazette* until 1816.

SCULLIN, JOHN (*b. near Helena, N.Y., 1836; d. St. Louis, Mo., 1920*), railroad builder, St. Louis street-railway operator, steel manufacturer. Contract or builder of many midwestern railroads, he constructed the major portion of the Missouri-Kansas-Texas system, 1869–74.

SEABURY, GEORGE JOHN (*b. New York, N.Y., 1884; d. New York, 1909*), chemist, pharmacist. Founded Seabury and Johnson, pioneer manufacturers of surgical dressings, of which he was president *post* 1885.

SEABURY, SAMUEL (*b. Groton, Conn., 1729; d. New London, Conn., 1796*), Episcopal clergyman, Loyalist, writer. Graduated Yale, 1748; studied medicine at University of Edinburgh; ordained by the bishop of London, 1753. Sent by the Society for the Propagation of the Gospel as missionary to New Brunswick, N.J., 1754, he was transferred to Jamaica, N.Y., 1757, and was inducted as rector at Westchester, N.Y., 1767. A leader in the campaign of the New York Anglican clergy to secure bishops for America, he was one of the authors of the articles "A Whip for the American Whig," published in Gaine's *New York Gazette*, April 1768–July 1769. Just before the outbreak of the Revolution, he produced several important pamphlets signed "A. W. Farmer" in which, with clear, homely language and arguments, he tried to convince Americans that their greatest freedom lay in submitting to the British government and securing desired change through peaceful appeals to that government. These pamphlets (which were answered by Alexander Hamilton) were *Free Thoughts on the Proceedings of the Continental Congress; The Congress Canvassed; A View of the Controversy Between Great Britain and Her Colonies* (published November and December 1774); and *An Alarm to the Legislature of the Province of New York* (January 1775). After entering actively into the Loyalist campaign to prevent election of delegates to provincial and Continental congresses, Seabury went into hiding, April 1775. In November, Connecticut soldiers under Isaac Sears took him prisoner at Westchester, and he suffered a brief confinement at New Haven, Conn. In the fall of 1776 he entered the British lines on Long Island, later serving as a guide to the British both on Long Island and in Westchester County. Holding several chaplaincies under the British, he lived comfortably in New York City throughout the Revolution. Presented by the Episcopal clergy of Connecticut as a candidate for consecration as bishop in the now independent colonies, 1783, he was refused consecration by Anglican authorities, who believed themselves legally debarred from performing the rite. He then proceeded to Scotland and, on Nov. 14, 1784, was consecrated by the nonjuring Scottish prelates. Returning to America in the early summer of 1785, he became rector of St. James's Church, New London, Conn., and served as bishop of Connecticut and Rhode Island until his death. Working strenuously to revive and reorganize the churches in his diocese, he stood for unity in essentials and liberty in nonessentials, but had little sympathy for the prevailing liberalizing ideas of his American brethren.

SEABURY, SAMUEL (*b. New London, Conn., 1801; d. 1872*), Episcopal clergyman. Grandson of Samuel Seabury (1729–96). A High Churchman of the old school, he served as editor of *The Churchman*, 1833–49, supporting Tractarianism and Bishop Benjamin T. Onderdonk. He served also as a teacher in the General Theological Seminary, and was rector of the Church of the Annunciation, New York, 1838–68.

SEABURY, SAMUEL (*b. New York, N.Y., 1873; d. New York, 1958*), lawyer, jurist, special investigator. Studied at New York Law School. Elected to city court of New York as judge, and from 1914 to 1916 served as judge on Court of Appeals. Defeated for governor in 1916 and returned to private practice. In 1930 appointed by Governor Franklin D. Roosevelt to conduct investigation of the magistrates' court. In 1931 formed the Joint Legislative Committee to Investigate the Affairs of the City of New York. Seabury became the symbol of the fight against corruption in New York County and the investigation resulted in the resignation of Mayor Jimmy Walker. Instrumental in the election of Fiorello H. La Guardia as mayor, he served as his advisor for twelve years.

SEAGER, HENRY ROGERS (*b. Lansing, Mich., 1870; d. Kiev, Russia, 1930*), economist. Graduated University of Michigan, 1890; Ph.D., University of Pennsylvania, 1894. Taught at Wharton School, 1894–1902, and at Columbia thereafter. A conservative and a believer in progress, Seager engaged in many meliorative activities with the purpose of bettering social conditions within the framework of laissez-faire. Among his works, *Principles of Economics* (1913) is the most considerable.

SEAGRAVE, GORDON STIFLER (*b. Rangoon, Burma, 1897; d. Namkham, Burma, 1965*), medical missionary. Attended Denison University and Johns Hopkins Medical School (M.D., 1921) and had additional surgical training at Columbia and Vienna universities. Appointed a missionary by the American Baptist Foreign Mission Society (1920). He was assigned to the Namkham Hospital in Burma (1922); his books on service in Burma are *Waste-Basket Surgery* (1930) and *Tales of a Waste-Basket Surgeon* (1938). In 1940 he ran a 400-bed hospital at Prome and jungle hospitals along the Burma Road and the Burma-China border. His Army Medical Corps unit of fifteen ran the only hospital for the remnants of Chiang Kai-shek's Fifth and Sixth armies (1942). He became famous with the publication of *Burma Surgeon* (1943). He amicably severed relations with the Baptist Foreign Mission Society in 1946; they retained ownership of the Namkham Hospital but leased it to Seagrave for $1 a year. His location embroiled him in Burma's civil war, and he was arrested in 1950, charged with treason, and sentenced to six years imprisonment. After appeals the High Court of Burma released him in 1951.

SEALSFIELD, CHARLES (*b. Poppitz, Moravia, Austria, 1793; d. near Solothurn, Switzerland, 1864*), novelist. Pen name of Karl Anton Postl, who abandoned the monastic life in Prague, fled Austria, and appeared as Charles Sealsfield in New Orleans, La., 1823. After traveling through the Southern states, Texas, and Mexico and a brief residence near Pittsburgh, he returned to Europe. His *The United States As They Are . . . by the Author of Austria As It Is* was published anonymously in English, 1828; it had appeared the previous year in German. After further travels and residence in the United States, the then Mexican Southwest and Mexico proper, he retired to Switzerland, 1832, where he continued to reside except for occasional visits to the United States. Sealsfield attempted to create a new type of fiction, the ethnographical novel in which a whole people figured as protagonist. He exemplified his theory in six books published in German and English between 1834 and 1843; in these the people of the United States and Mexico were portrayed in every possible social relation.

SEAMAN, ELIZABETH COCHRANE (*b. Cochran Mills, Pa., 1867; d. New York, N.Y., 1922*), journalist, known as "Nellie Bly." Famous for a tour around the world, 1889–90, in which she beat the time of Jules Verne's fictional "Phileas Fogg" by eight days.

SEARING, LAURA CATHERINE REDDEN (*b. Somerset Co., Md., 1840; d. San Mateo, Calif., 1923*), journalist. Civil War correspondent in Washington, D.C., for the *St. Louis (Mo.) Republican*; later on staff of New York City newspapers. Deaf and mute, she was taught speech by Alexander G. Bell.

SEARLE, ARTHUR (*b. London, England, 1837; d. Cambridge, Mass., 1920*), astronomer. Graduated Harvard, 1856. Associated with the Harvard Observatory *post* 1868, he became Phillips professor of astronomy, 1887, and was made emeritus, 1912; he also taught astronomy at Radcliffe, 1891–1912.

SEARLE, JAMES (*b. probably New York, N.Y., 1733; d. Philadelphia, Pa., 1797*), merchant, Revolutionary patriot. Prospering as a merchant in Philadelphia *post ca.* 1762, he took part in all early protests against British policy. Elected to the Continental Congress, November 1778, he allied himself with the radical group, seconding James Lovell and Richard H. Lee in their hostility to Silas Deane. Appointed special envoy to float Pennsylvania state loan in Europe, July 1780, he failed in his efforts at Paris, Amsterdam, and Lyons, and on his return *ca.* 1781 found that much of his fortune had been dissipated by unwise actions of his partners.

SEARLE, JOHN PRESTON (*b.* Schuylerville, N.Y., 1854; *d.* 1922), Dutch Reformed clergyman, educator. Graduated Rutgers, 1875; New Brunswick Theological Seminary, 1878. Held principal pastorate at Somerville, N.J. Professor of theology at New Brunswick Seminary *post* 1893, he served also as president of the faculty *post* 1902.

SEARS, BARNAS (*b.* Sandisfield, Mass., 1802; *d.* Saratoga, N.Y., 1880), Baptist clergyman, educator. Graduated Brown, 1825. Taught at Hamilton (N.Y.) Literary Institution, 1829–33 and 1835. Professor of theology, Newton Theological Institution, 1836–48; president Newton, 1839–48. Succeeding Horace Mann in 1848 as the secretary of the Massachusetts Board of Education, he gave permanence to Mann's reforms; in 1855 he left to become president of Brown University, remaining there until 1867. Thereafter, until his death, he was general agent of the Peabody Education Fund and the principal architect of its purpose and methods.

SEARS, EDMUND HAMILTON (*b.* Sandisfield, Mass., 1810; *d.* Weston, Mass., 1876), Unitarian clergyman. Held principal pastorates at Wayland, Mass., and Weston, Mass.; was author of a number of once-popular spiritual books and of the hymns "It Came Upon a Midnight Clear" and "Calm on the Listening Ear of Night."

SEARS, ISAAC (*b.* West Brewster, Mass., 1730; *d.* Canton, China, 1786), merchant, mariner, Revolutionary patriot. A leader of resistance to the Stamp Act in New York City, he was the head of nearly every mob demonstration in New York City *post* 1765, including the jettisoning of tea cargoes in 1774. After Lexington and Concord, he and his followers dispossessed the Loyalist leaders and officials and were virtually dictators in New York until the spring of 1776. Sears was especially noted for severe treatment of the Long Island Tories, January–August 1776. In Boston, 1777–83, he promoted privateering; after the war he resumed his general merchandise business in New York City, served in the state legislature, and died while promoting a business venture in China.

SEARS, RICHARD DUDLEY (*b.* Boston, Mass., 1861; *d.* Boston, 1943), businessman, tennis champion. Graduated Harvard, 1883. Won first U.S. national amateur lawn tennis championship at Newport, R.I., 1881; won also in succeeding years through 1887. Doubles champion (with James Dwight or Joseph S. Clark), 1882–87. First U.S. national court tennis champion, New York City, 1892.

SEARS, RICHARD WARREN (*b.* Stewartville, Minn., 1863; *d.* Waukesha, Wis., 1914), mail-order merchant, advertising expert. Beginning as a distributor of watches by mail order, 1886, he established the firm of Sears, Roebuck & Co., and served as its president and principal advertising writer until 1909. The company entered on its major phase of prosperity after its removal from Minneapolis to Chicago, 1893.

SEARS, ROBERT (*b.* St. John, New Brunswick, Canada, 1810; *d.* Toronto, Canada, 1892), printer, publisher. Resided in the United States *ca.* 1831–60. His illustrated Bibles and other works of reference had wide sale because of the excellence of their wood engravings. He was also editor and publisher of several gazetteers.

SEASHORE, CARL EMIL (*b.* Mörlunda, Sweden, 1866; *d.* Lewiston, Idaho, 1949), psychologist. His father, who came to the United States, 1869, and settled in Boone County, Iowa, an-glicized the family name from Sjöstrand. B.A., Gustavus Adolphus College, Minnesota, 1891; Ph.D., Yale, 1895. Taught at State University of Iowa, 1897–1937 (professor *post* 1902, chairman of Department of Philosophy and Psychology *post* 1905, dean of the Graduate College in 1908–37 and 1942–46). Built his department into one of the first large-scale psychology departments in the Midwest; developed methods for measurement of musical aptitude and talent. Author of, among other works, *The Psychology of Musical Talent* (1919) and *Psychology of Music* (1937).

SEATON, WILLIAM WINSTON (*b.* King William Co., Va., 1785; *d.* 1866), journalist. Brother-in-law of Joseph Gales (1786–1860), with whom he was associated as editor of the official administration newspaper, the *National Intelligencer*, Washington, D.C., *post* 1812. Gales and Seaton were exclusive reporters of the debates of Congress, 1812–29, Seaton covering the Senate. Their firm published the well-known *Annals of Congress* (1834–56) and the monumental *American State Papers* (1832–61). A civic leader in Washington, Seaton was mayor of the city, 1840–50, led the movement for the Washington Monument, and was treasurer of the Smithsonian Institution *post* 1846.

SEATTLE (*b.* in neighborhood of present Seattle, Wash., ca. 1786; *d.* 1866), chief of the Dwamish, Suquamish, and allied Indian tribes. A friend to the white settlers, he did not want his name to be given to their settlement.

SEAWELL, MOLLY ELLIOT (*b.* Gloucester Co., Va., 1860; *d.* Washington, D.C. 1916), author. A prolific and skillful writer, she produced a number of books for juvenile and adult readers, which include *Little Jarvis* (1890), *Midshipman Paulding* (1891), and *The Lively Adventures of Gavin Hamilton* (1899).

SEBASTIAN, BENJAMIN (*b.* ca. 1745, *place uncertain*; *d.* probably Grayson Co., Ky., 1834), lawyer, Revolutionary soldier. Removed to Kentucky from Virginia *ca.* 1784; was implicated as early as 1787 in the pro-Spanish intrigues of James Wilkinson. A judge of the state appellate court, 1792–1806, he served as intermediary in 1795 in F. L. H. de Carondelet's attempts to win over the Kentuckians and carried proposals of a seditious character to Harry Innes and George Nicholas. Exposed as a paid agent of Spain, 1804, he was forced to resign his office and was no longer a factor in political life *post* 1806.

SECCOMB, JOHN (*b.* Medford, Mass., 1708; *d.* Chester, Nova Scotia, Canada, 1792), Congregational clergyman, writer of humorous verse. Pastor at Harvard, Mass., 1733–63, he served thereafter as minister in Nova Scotia.

SEDDON, JAMES ALEXANDER (*b.* Fredericksburg, Va., 1815; *d.* Goochland Co., Va., 1880), lawyer. Congressman, Democrat, from Virginia, 1845–47 and 1849–51. An ardent follower of John C. Calhoun, he was later active in the secession movement in Virginia and was elected to the first Confederate Congress. He served as the somewhat dilatory Confederate secretary of war, November 1862–1865.

SEDELLA, ANTOINE. *See* ANTOINE, PÈRE.

SEDGWICK, ANNE DOUGLAS (*b.* Englewood, N.J., 1873; *d.* Hampstead, England, 1935), novelist. Resident chiefly in London and Paris *post* 1882, she married Basil de Sélincourt in 1908, residing thereafter in Oxfordshire. Primarily studies of character, her novels were based on intimate knowledge of British society and international contrasts. Winning wide readership first with *Tante* (1911), a study of feminine egotism, she produced a number of other successful books, including *Adrienne Toner* (1922), *The Little French Girl* (1924), and *Dark Hester* (1929).

SEDGWICK, ARTHUR GEORGE (*b. New York, N.Y., 1844; d. 1915*), lawyer, journalist. Son of Theodore Sedgwick (1811–59); brother-in-law of Charles E. Norton. Associated in editorial capacity with the *Nation,* 1872–1905, he was also author or editor of a number of legal treatises.

SEDGWICK, CATHARINE MARIA (*b. Stockbridge, Mass., 1789; d. West Roxbury, Mass., 1867*), author. Daughter of Theodore Sedgwick (1746–1813); sister of Theodore Sedgwick (1780–1839). A pioneer in the creation of the American domestic novel, she wrote because of her belief that the safety of the Republic depended upon the domestic virtues of its people and so tried to make unaffected goodness and wholesome living appear attractive. Her novels and tales, although marked by romanticism and her declared didactic purpose, also contain realistic presentations of domestic scenes and were extremely popular in their time. She was also author of a number of "self-help" books. Among her novels (which were praised by W. C. Bryant and Nathaniel Hawthorne) were *A New England Tale* (1822), *Redwood* (1824), *Hope Leslie* (1827), and *The Linwoods; or Sixty Years Since* (1835).

SEDGWICK, ELLERY (*b. New York, N.Y., 1872; d. Washington, D.C., 1960*), editor and publisher. Studied at Harvard (B.A., 1894). Owner and editor of the *Atlantic Monthly* from 1908 to 1938, Sedgwick moved the magazine from insolvency to one of the nation's most prosperous and respected periodicals. Published Ernest Hemingway, Robert Frost, Randolph Bourne, H. G. Wells, Felix Frankfurter, and William E. Ripley.

SEDGWICK, JOHN (*b. Cornwall Hollow, Conn., 1813; d. Spotsylvania, Va., 1864*), soldier. Graduated West Point, 1837. Commissioned in the artillery, he saw service in the Seminole and Mexican wars and was with the cavalry in the West and Southwest, 1857–60. Commissioned brigadier general of volunteers at the outbreak of the Civil War, Sedgwick held brigade and divisional command in the Army of the Potomac. Promoted major general, 1862, he took a prominent part in the battles of Antietam and Chancellorsville and led the V and VI Corps against Marye's Heights, Fredericksburg, Va. Distinguished also for his conduct at Gettysburg and in the operations at Mine Run, he was killed in action subsequent to the battle of the Wilderness. Although a strict disciplinarian, he was admired and trusted by his soldiers, who called him "Uncle John."

SEDGWICK, ROBERT (*b. Woburn, England, ca. 1613; d. Jamaica, British West Indies, 1656*), colonist, soldier. Settled in Charlestown, Mass., 1636. He was active in training the militia officers of the colony and was also successful in business; he was granted a monopoly of the colony's Indian trade, 1644. Deputy to the General Court from Charlestown and holder of a number of local offices, he was elected major general of the colony, 1652. After successfully harassing the French settlements in Maine and eastern Canada, he died while on a military expedition against Spain in the West Indies.

SEDGWICK, THEODORE (*b. West Hartford, Conn., 1746; d. Boston, Mass., 1813*), lawyer, Massachusetts jurist and legislator. Father of Catharine M. Sedgwick and Theodore Sedgwick (1780–1839). Practiced law in Berkshire Co., Mass., *post* 1766, first at Sheffield and later at Stockbridge. Early active in the struggle against Great Britain, he served as military secretary to General John Thomas in the invasion of Canada, 1776. An active legislator for most of the years 1780–88, he was Speaker of the Massachusetts House, 1788, and also sat in Congress, 1785–88. A strenuous opponent of Shays's Rebellion, he aided ratification by Massachusetts of the U.S. Constitution; while a Federalist member of Congress from Massachusetts, 1789–96, he was chairman of important committees. U.S. senator, June

1796–March 1799, he returned to the House of Representatives and was its Speaker, 1799–1801. In 1802 he was appointed for life to the supreme judicial court of Massachusetts.

SEDGWICK, THEODORE (*b. Sheffield, Mass., 1780; d. 1839*), lawyer, Massachusetts legislator, railroad advocate, reformer. Son of Theodore Sedgwick (1746–1813); brother of Catharine M. Sedgwick.

SEDGWICK, THEODORE (*b. Albany, N.Y., 1811; d. Stockbridge, Mass., 1859*), lawyer. Son of Theodore Sedgwick (1780–1839); nephew of Catharine M. Sedgwick; father of Arthur G. Sedgwick. Graduated Columbia, 1829. In extensive practice in New York City, 1834–50, he was hampered thereafter by ill health. A lifelong student of legal, judicial, and political problems, he wrote extensively on these subjects; his most important book was *A Treatise on the Measure of Damages* (1847), which was for years the only work in English on the subject.

SEDGWICK, WILLIAM THOMPSON (*b. West Hartford, Conn., 1855; d. Boston, Mass., 1921*), biologist, epidemiologist. Graduated Sheffield Scientific School, 1877; Ph.D., Johns Hopkins, 1881. Influences by Henry N. Martin, whom he served as an associate, 1881–83, Sedgwick was called in 1883 to teach biology at the Massachusetts Institute of Technology. Appointed full professor there in 1891, for the next 30 years he headed the departments of biology and public health. Among students trained by him were many of the leading sanitarians in the United States and abroad. He engaged also in extensive public service as consulting biologist to the Massachusetts State Board of Health. Among his works is the classic *Principles of Sanitary Science and the Public Health* (1902).

SEDLEY, WILLIAM HENRY. *See* SMITH, WILLIAM HENRY.

SEE, HORACE (*b. Philadelphia, Pa., 1835; d. New York, N.Y., 1909*), naval architect. Associated with William Cramp & Sons, 1870–89, he was designer and superintending engineer, 1879–89, and in that decade was responsible for the first vessels of the "New Navy." In private practice thereafter, he invented a great number of important devices for use in ship construction.

SEED, MILES AINSCOUGH (*b. Preston, England, 1843; d. Pelham, N.Y., 1913*), photographer, manufacturer of photography supplies. Came to America, 1865; settled in St. Louis, Mo. After perfecting process for manufacture of a photographic dry plate, he formed a company and began production, 1882. Overcoming prejudice against his revolutionary improvement by constant travel and personal demonstration, he opened up large markets. In 1902 the Eastman Kodak Co. purchased his business and formula.

SEEGER, ALAN (*b. New York, N.Y., 1888; d. near Belloy-en-Santerre, France, 1916*), poet. Graduated Harvard, 1910. Removing to Paris, France, in the autumn of 1912, he resided there until the beginning of World War I, at which time he enlisted in the French Foreign legion. He died in action. His best-known poem, "I Have a Rendezvous with Death," and other works were collected in *Poems* (1916).

SEELYE, JULIUS HAWLEY (*b. Bethel, Conn., 1824; d. 1895*), clergyman, educator. Brother of L. Clark Seelye. Graduated Amherst, 1849; Auburn Theological Seminary, 1852. After serving as pastor, First Dutch Reformed Church, Schenectady, N.Y., 1853–58, he became professor of philosophy at Amherst and began service there that lasted, except for one short interval, until his death. An exponent of the philosophical views of Laurens P. Hickock, he was an effective teacher and became acknowledged leader of an able faculty. Appointed president of Amherst, 1876, he devised the "Amherst Plan," a system of student self-government, doubled the college income, and raised academic standards.

SEELYE, LAURENUS CLARK (*b. Bethel, Conn., 1837; d. Northampton, Mass., 1924*), Congregational clergyman, educator. Brother of Julius H. Seelye. Graduated Union, 1857; studied theology at Andover, Berlin, and Heidelberg. After a brief pastorate in Springfield, Mass., he became professor of rhetoric at Amherst and served 1865–73. Thereafter, as president of Smith College until 1910, he carried that institution to success, despite an original poverty of means. The growth of the college in equipment and endowment was due more to his skillful management than to the generosity of outsiders.

SEEVERS, WILLIAM HENRY (*b. Shenandoah Co., Va., 1822; d. 1895*), Iowa legislator, jurist. Resident in Oskaloosa, Iowa, *post* 1846, he held a number of public offices and served as chief justice of the state supreme court, 1876, 1882, and 1887–88.

SEGHERS, CHARLES JEAN (*b. Ghent, Belgium, 1839; d. Yukon country, Alaska, 1886*), Roman Catholic clergyman, missionary. Served in British Columbia, 1863–78; was bishop of Victoria *post* 1873. Named coadjutor bishop of Oregon City (Portland), 1878, he succeeded to that see two years later as archbishop, but resigned in 1884 to resume his duties in British Columbia and to develop the missions in Alaska.

SEGUIN, EDOUARD (*b. Clamecy, France, 1812; d. 1880*), psychiatrist, pioneer in education of the retarded. Immigrated to America *ca.* 1850.

SEGUIN, EDWARD CONSTANT (*b. Paris, France, 1843; d. 1898*), neurologist. Son of Edouard Seguin. Came to America as a boy. M.D., New York College of Physicians and Surgeons, 1864; made special studies of nervous diseases in Paris under Brown-Sequard and Charcot. Ranking in his profession with S. W. Mitchell and William A. Hammond, he practiced in New York City until 1894 and taught diseases of the nervous system at the College of Physicians and Surgeons, 1868–87.

SEIBERLING, FRANK AUGUSTUS (*b. Summit County, Ohio, 1859; d. Akron, Ohio, 1955*), manufacturer, inventor, and promoter. Attended Heidelberg College in Ohio. Founded the Goodyear Tire and Rubber Co. in 1898; by 1915, it was the world's largest producer of automobile tires. The company prospered, acquiring railroads and foreign plants until the post–World War I recession. In 1921 Seiberling was forced to resign from Goodyear. He promptly founded the Seiberling Rubber Co. Helped reorganize Goodyear in 1927. Remained active until 1950.

SEIBOLD, LOUIS (*b. Washington, D.C., 1863; d. Washington, 1945*), journalist. A talented reporter, he was associated with the New York *World* through most of his working life; he was close to President Woodrow Wilson and gained a reputation as a launcher of the president's trial balloons of information on policy.

SEIDEL, GEORGE LUKAS EMIL (*b. Ashland, Pa., 1864; d. Milwaukee, Wis., 1947*), woodcarver, socialist politician. Raised in Prairie du Chien, Madison, and Milwaukee, Wis. Apprenticed at 13 after completing elementary school. Early interested in trade union activity, he was converted to the radical wing of socialist thought while resident in Germany, 1886–92. Returning to Milwaukee, he worked at his trade and was associated with Victor L. Berger, joining, 1897, the Milwaukee Branch of the Social Democracy of America formed by Berger and Eugene V. Debs. In 1904 and 1906 he was elected to the Milwaukee Common Council; in 1909 he became the first Social Democratic alderman-at-large. In 1910 he was elected mayor of Milwaukee by a wide margin, his party making a sweep of city elective offices and also winning control of the county board. The first socialist mayor of a principal American city, he stressed scientific methods of government, strict economy, and social service programs. For a variety of reasons, the Social Democrats lost public confidence, and Seidel was defeated for reelection in 1912 by a nonpartisan candidate. In 1912 also, he was the Socialist party's candidate for vice president of the United States, running on the ticket with Eugene V. Debs. He was again elected alderman-at-large in 1916, but failed in bids for the Wisconsin governorship, 1918, and for city treasurer of Milwaukee, 1920. From 1920 to 1923, as state secretary for his party, he toured Wisconsin in a vain effort to revive the prewar Socialist momentum. After a breakdown in health, he returned to public life as a member of the Milwaukee City Service Commission, 1926–32. Failing in his campaign for a U.S. Senate seat, 1932, he served once again on the common council, 1932–36.

SEIDENSTICKER, OSWALD (*b. Göttingen, Germany, 1825; d. Philadelphia, Pa., 1894*), philologist, historian of the Germans in Pennsylvania. Came to America, 1846. Taught German at University of Pennsylvania, 1867–94.

SEIDL, ANTON (*b. Pesth, Hungary, 1850; d. 1898*), musician. Studied at the Leipzig Conservatory; worked with Richard Wagner, 1872–78. Celebrated as a conductor of Wagnerian opera in Europe, he debuted at the Metropolitan Opera, New York City, 1885, and conducted there until German opera was temporarily dropped in 1891. Becoming conductor of the New York Philharmonic Society in succession to Theodore Thomas, he continued so for the rest of his life. resuming his work with German opera at the Metropolitan, 1895–97. Seidl exercised a great influence on American musical life and because of his association with Wagner was able to give a special authenticity to his interpretations of the Wagnerian music dramas.

SEILER, CARL (*b. Switzerland, 1849; d. Reading, Pa., 1905*), laryngologist. Began study of medicine in Vienna and Heidelberg; he received the M.D. degree at University of Pennsylvania, 1871, and was a special pupil and assistant of Jacob da Silva Solis Cohen. A teacher of his specialty at his alma mater, 1877–95, he was author of several books and the deviser of the widely used Seiler's tablets.

SEIP, THEODORE LORENZO (*b. Easton, Pa., 1842; d. Allentown, Pa., 1903*), Lutheran clergyman. Long a teacher at Muhlenberg College, he served with great ability as its president, 1885–1903.

SEISS, JOSEPH AUGUSTUS (*b. near Graceham, Md., 1823; d. Philadelphia, Pa., 1904*), Lutheran clergyman. Held chief pastorates in Baltimore and Philadelphia, notably at Church of the Holy Communion, Philadelphia, 1874–1904. An admired preacher and prolific author, he was one of the founders of the General Council of the Evangelical Lutheran Church in North America.

SEITZ, DON CARLOS (*b. Portage, Ohio, 1862; d. Brooklyn, N.Y., 1935*), journalist. On staff of *Brooklyn Eagle*, 1880–91. After a brief period as assistant publisher of the New York *Recorder*, he went with the New York *World*, of which he was first an editor, then advertising manager, and finally business manager from 1898 to 1923. A liberal and witty man of complete independence and fearlessness, he believed that a newspaper was an institution for public service; during his tenure, the *World* became one of the nation's powerful liberal voices; and he was in no way responsible for the decline and disappearance of the Pulitzer properties in New York. Retiring in 1926 from daily journalism, he served on the staffs of the *Outlook* and the *Churchman*. He was also author of many books, including biographies of John Paul Jones, Artemus Ward, Braxton Bragg, Joseph Pulitzer, and Horace Greeley.

SEIXAS, GERSHOM MENDES (*b. New York, N.Y., 1746; d. New York, 1816*). Chosen rabbi of the Spanish and Portuguese synagogue of New York (Shearith Israel), 1768, he was for many years New York's chief professor of Hebrew and through a great portion of his 50-year ministry one of the principal spokesmen of American Jewry. The first rabbi to preach sermons in English in an American synagogue, he constantly advocated the full participation by Jews in the life of the new democratic American state. He was, on the evidence of his public statements and prayers, a strong supporter of the American cause. He served as regent and trustee of Columbia College, 1784–1815.

SÉJOUR, VICTOR (*b. New Orleans, La., 1817; d. Paris, France, 1874*), dramatist. Born of black parents, Séjour was educated in New Orleans and Paris and in 1841 achieved celebrity with a heroic poem, *La Retour de Napoléon*. Influenced by Émile Augier, he became a writer of immediately popular dramatic spectacles; among his 21 plays which were produced in Paris, his greatest successes were *Richard III* (1852), *Les Noces Vénitiennes* (1855), *Le Fils de la Nuit* (1856), and *Les Volontaires de 1814* (1862). He died of tuberculosis after experiencing a decline in his fortunes.

SELBY, WILLIAM (*b. probably England, ca. 1739; d. Boston, Mass., 1798*), musician, composer. Immigrated to Boston *ante* October 1771; was at various times organist of King's Chapel. Three choral concerts organized and directed by him, 1782, 1786, and 1787, encouraged a taste for cantatas and oratorios in Boston and undoubtedly influenced the movement which led to formation of the Handel and Haydn Society more than 15 years after his death. Selby's only extant compositions are a few songs.

SELDEN, GEORGE BALDWIN (*b. Clarkson, N.Y., 1846; d. Rochester, N.Y., 1922*), patent attorney, inventor. After developing a lightweight high-speed three-cylinder gasoline compression engine employing hydrocarbon liquid fuels, 1877, Selden then designed a so-called road locomotive which was virtually an automobile. Having applied for a U.S. patent, May 1879, he tried without success to secure financial help in building his machine; he therefore delayed the issue of a patent to him until November 1895. Meanwhile, the automobile had made rapid strides, but the assignees of Selden's basic patent (who were obliged to pay him royalty) required all other persons manufacturing automobiles to pay for the privilege by licensing. The first successful action to compel payment was brought against the Winton Motor Co., 1900. A suit against the Ford Motor Co. initiated in 1903 came to final adjudication in January 1911 when it was held that Selden had a true and valid patent only with respect to the use of a two-cylinder type of engine as designated in the patent. Inasmuch as all manufacturers were by this time using a four-cycle engine, no further royalties were required to be paid.

SELDES, GILBERT VIVIAN (*b. Alliance, N.J., 1893; d. New York, N.Y., 1970*), journalist and critic. Graduated from Harvard (1914) and worked briefly as a reporter for the *Pittsburgh Sun* and as music critic and editorial writer for the *Philadelphia Evening Ledger* (1914–16); left for England as a free-lance war correspondent. Became associate editor (1919) of *Collier's Weekly*; managing editor (1919–23) and dramatic critic (1923–29) of *Dial*; and contributed reviews and critical essays to the *New Republic*, *Freeman*, and *Nation*. He regularly gave notice to art forms not generally considered serious, such as movies, vaudeville, and the popular theater of song and dance. Wrote *The Seven Lively Arts* (1924), a survey of nearly all the then-popular entertainment arts. His most ambitious social criticism of the

depression years was *Mainland* (1936). Columnist for the *New York Journal* (1931–37) and in the late 1950's for the *Village Voice*; also wrote for radio and television and was a program director for Columbia Broadcasting System (1937–45). Taught at and was dean of the Annenberg School of Communications (1959–63).

SELFRIDGE, THOMAS OLIVER (*b. Charlestown, Mass., 1836; d. 1924*), naval officer. Graduated U.S. Naval Academy, 1854. Cited for conspicuous gallantry during the Civil War. Surveyed Isthmus of Darien for an interoceanic canal, 1869–70; later surveyed the Amazon and Madeira rivers. Commissioned rear admiral, 1896, he retired, 1898.

SELIG, WILLIAM NICHOLAS (*b. Chicago, Ill., 1864; d. Los Angeles, Calif., 1948*), early motion-picture producer. Developed and marketed a projection machine (the Selig Polyscope, 1896) and other devices; gave his principal attention to film production after about 1904. Established in 1909 what has been called the first permanent motion-picture studio in the Los Angeles area, but soon removed to Edendale. Made and released several hundred pictures under the Diamond-S name, 1912–17; contracted with popular authors for story material, his 1914 film of Rex Beach's *The Spoilers* making him a small fortune. One of his early discoveries was the cowboy star Tom Mix.

SELIGMAN, ARTHUR (*b. Santa Fe, N.Mex., 1871; d. 1933*), merchant, banker, Democratic politician. Governor of New Mexico, 1931–33.

SELIGMAN, EDWIN ROBERT ANDERSON (*b. New York, N.Y., 1861; d. Lake Placid, N.Y., 1939*), economist. Son of Joseph Seligman; brother of Isaac N. Seligman. Graduated Columbia, 1879; LL.B., 1884; Ph.D., 1885. Beginning his teaching career at Columbia as a lecturer, he was promoted to full professor, 1891, and was the first McVickar professor of political economy, 1904–31. A unique combination of scholar and public figure, Seligman was author of *The Economic Interpretation of History* (1902) and *Principles of Economics, with Special Reference to American Conditions* (1905), two important and influential works; he was also editor in chief of the *Encyclopaedia of the Social Sciences* (1930–35) and was principally responsible for raising the funds needed for this monumental project. He was best known, however, for his pioneering achievements in public finance, in which field he was author of a number of significant books, which included *On the Shifting and Incidence of Taxation* (1892), *Progressive Taxation in Theory and Practice* (1894), *Essays in Taxation* (1895), and *The Income Tax* (1911). The theoretical core of his work was the marginal economics of which John Bates Clark was one of the leading formulators, yet Seligman allowed in his own work for considerable qualification in the theory. Conservative by nature, he was respected by enlightened members of the business community and frequently served the government as an adviser in matters of taxation; his writings and personal testimony helped shape the Transportation Act of 1920, and he was also active in the campaign for an effective central banking system that eventuated in the Federal Reserve Act. A worker for honest municipal government, for conservation of natural resources, and for a fair policy toward labor, Seligman was probably the first eminent American economist to advocate the doctrine of the living wage.

SELIGMAN, ISAAC NEWTON (*b. Staten Island, N.Y., 1855; d. New York, N.Y., 1917*), banker, civic leader. Son of Joseph Seligman. President of the family banking house of J. & W. Seligman & Co. *post* 1894.

SELIGMAN, JESSE (*b. Baiersdorf, Bavaria, 1827; d. Coronado, Calif., 1894*), banker, philanthropist. Brother of Joseph

Seligman. Immigrated to America as a boy; was in dry-goods business with a brother at Watertown, N.Y., 1848–50. Removing to California, he prospered as a merchant in San Francisco and served on the Vigilance Committee of 1851 and later on the Committee of Twenty-one. Removing to New York City, 1857, he joined his brother Joseph's clothing firm and later became a partner in the banking firm of J. & W. Seligman & Co. (organized 1862). He succeeded his brother Joseph as head of the firm, 1880, and was for a generation one of the leading financiers of the United States.

SELIGMAN, JOSEPH (b. *Baiersdorf, Bavaria, 1819; d. New Orleans, La., 1880*), financier, civic leader. Brother of Jesse Seligman; father of Isaac N. Seligman. Immigrating to America, 1837, he served for some time as secretary to Asa Packer. He founded a clothing firm with his brothers, including Jesse, 1857, which was transformed early in 1862 into the banking house of J. & W. Seligman & Co. Strong supporters of the Union, the Seligmans promoted large sales of U.S. bonds in Frankfurt at a time when it was almost impossible to sell the national securities in England or France. During the presidency of U. S. Grant, Joseph Seligman was one of his confidential financial advisers, and throughout the 1870's the firm figured prominently in the conversion and refunding of the obligations of the United States. Joseph Seligman was also active in New York City civic affairs and was a member of the Committee of Seventy, which ousted the Tweed Ring.

SELIJNS, HENRICUS (b. *Amsterdam, Holland, 1636; d. New York, N.Y., 1701*), Dutch Reformed clergyman, poet. Pastor in present Brooklyn, N.Y., 1660–64, and in New York City *post* 1682. A cultured and tolerant man and a popular preacher, he secured for the Dutch Reformed church the first church charter granted in the colony, 1696.

SELIKOVITSCH, GOETZEL (b. *Rietavas, Lithuania, 1863; d. 1926*), orientalist, journalist. Graduated École des Hautes Études, Paris, France, 1884. After traveling widely in the Near East and Africa, he came to America in 1887. Taking up Yiddish journalism as a profession, he served on the staff of the *Jewish Daily News* in New York City from 1901 until his death. He was author of a number of scholarly works in Hebrew and French.

SELLERS, COLEMAN (b. *Philadelphia, Pa., 1827; d. Philadelphia, 1907*), engineer. Grandson of Charles W. Peale. While chief engineer of William Sellers & Co., 1856–86, he patented a number of inventions, notably the Sellers coupling. Conducting a consulting practice thereafter, he was important in the design and construction of the hydroelectric power development at Niagara Falls.

SELLERS, ISAIAH (b. *Iredell, Co., N.C., ca. 1802; d. Memphis, Tenn., 1864*), pioneer steamboat pilot. An authority on Mississippi River navigation, he made a number of noteworthy record runs and was first to use the pseudonym "Mark Twain" in contributions to the New Orleans *Daily Picayune*.

SELLERS, MATTHEW BACON (b. *Baltimore, Md., 1869; d. Ardsley-on-Hudson, N.Y., 1932*), patent lawyer, pioneer in aerodynamics. Served on Naval Consulting Board, 1915–18 and *post* 1919. Patented a quadroplane, 1911, and secured other patents for airplane gear; was technical editor of *Aeronautics post* 1911.

SELLERS, WILLIAM (b. *Upper Darby, Pa., 1824; d. 1905*), machine-tool builder. President of William Sellers & Co. and predecessor firms in Philadelphia, Pa., *post* 1848; also headed Edge Moor Iron Co. *post* 1868, and Midvale Steel Co. *post* 1873. Sellers held about 90 U.S. patents for machine tools of all kinds; the most original of his inventions was the spiral geared planer,

patented 1862; he was one of the first designers to make the form of a machine follow the function to be performed. He was also author of the present system of standard screw threads (first proposed by him, 1864).

SELLSTEDT, LARS GUSTAF (b. *Sundsvall, Sweden, 1819; d. Buffalo, N.Y., 1911*), seaman, portrait painter, organizer and president of Buffalo Fine Arts Academy.

SELYNS, HENRICUS. *See* SELIJNS, HENRICUS.

SELZNICK, DAVID O. (b. *Pittsburgh, Pa., 1902; d. Beverly Hills, Calif., 1965*), movie producer. His early profitable and important films include *Dinner at Eight* (1933), *King Kong* (1933), *Viva Villa!* (1934), *David Copperfield* (1935), and *A Tale of Two Cities* (1935). In Hollywood since 1925, he introduced several great stars, such as Katharine Hepburn, Fred Astaire, Ingrid Bergman, and Joan Fontaine. Formed Selznick International Studios (1936), and some of the finest films in Hollywood history began to appear: *A Star Is Born* (1937), which received eight Academy Award nominations; *Gone With the Wind* (1939), which received ten Oscars; and *Rebecca* (1940), with eleven Oscar nominations. Further successes in the 1940's and 1950's include *I'll Be Seeing You* (1945) and *Spellbound* (1945) and several starring wife Jennifer Jones, such as *Duel in the Sun* (1947) and *A Farewell to Arms* (1958).

SEMBRICH, MARCELLA (b. *Wisnieczyk, Galicia, 1858; d. New York, N.Y., 1935*), soprano. Professional name of Praxede Marcelline Kochanska, who married Wilhelm Stengel, 1877. Urged by Franz Liszt to devote herself principally to singing, Sembrich was a versatile instrumentalist as well as a soprano of extraordinary range and brilliance. She made her début at Athens, Greece, in *I Puritani*, 1877; her début at the Metropolitan Opera, New York, 1883, was in the role of *Lucia*. After singing in the leading opera houses of Europe, she rejoined the Metropolitan, with which she sang, 1898–1909. *Post* 1917, she was active as a teacher.

SEMMES, ALEXANDER JENKINS (b. *Georgetown, D.C., 1828; d. New Orleans, La., 1898*), physician, Confederate surgeon, Roman Catholic clergyman. Cousin of Raphael Semmes; brother of Thomas J. Semmes. Served in the priesthood, principally in Georgia, *post* 1878.

SEMMES, RAPHAEL (b. *Charles Co., Md., 1809; d. Point Clear, Ala., 1877*), naval officer. Cousin of Alexander J. Semmes and Thomas J. Semmes. Appointed midshipman, 1826, he served in routine posts at sea until his promotion to lieutenant, 1837; thereafter, until the outbreak of the Mexican War, he was on survey duty on the southern coast and in the Gulf of Mexico. Commanding the brig *Somers* on the Mexican blockade, 1846, he lost the vessel in a tropical storm, but was exonerated of any blame. He served thereafter on shore at Veracruz and in the march to Mexico City, receiving several citations for gallantry. On awaiting-order status for a great part of the time, 1847–61, he practiced law, settling near Mobile, Ala., 1849. Promoted commander, 1855, he resigned from the U. S. Navy, 1861, and entered the navy of the Confederacy. He rebuilt and commissioned the *Sumter*, formerly a packet vessel, and took it to sea in June as a commerce raider. Highly successful in operations in Caribbean waters and off the South American coast, he sailed to Gibraltar, where he was blockaded by Union forces; laying up the *Sumter*, April 1862, he discharged its crew and sold it later to a British firm. Promoted captain and ordered to command the *Alabama*, nearing completion at Liverpool, England, he took the ship to the Azores, where he armed it and set about his old business of destroying Union commerce. He ranged from the Atlantic whaling grounds and the Grand Banks to the coast of Brazil, taking 44 merchantmen. Sailing for Africa, he arrived at Capetown, August 1863, and then went on a long cruise across the Indian Ocean and contiguous waters, returning up the Atlantic to Cherbourg, France, June 1864. He had by then captured a total of 82 merchantmen and had also defeated and sunk the USS *Hatteras*. At Cherbourg, awaiting French permission to overhaul, Semmes was challenged by the USS *Kearsarge*, which had appeared on the morning of June 19, 1864, and fought in a circle of less than one-half mile in diameter. Heavily battered by the Union man-of-war, the *Alabama* sank shortly after noon. Rescued by an English yacht from the water, Semmes was taken to England and returned to the Confederacy by way of Mexico. Assigned as rear admiral to command of the James River squadron, January 1865, he burned his ships on the evacuation of Richmond and turned his men into a naval brigade, which was surrendered at Greensboro, N.C., as part of General J. E. Johnston's army. Paroled, Semmes was arrested in December 1865 and held for a short time in prison but released by presidential order. Hounded out of one employment after another, he engaged in the practice of law at Mobile until his death. He was author of *Service Afloat and Ashore* (1851) and *Memoirs of Service Afloat During the War Between the States* (1869).

Semmes, Thomas Jenkins (*b. Georgetown, D.C., 1824; d. 1899*), lawyer, Louisiana legislator. Brother of Alexander J. Semmes; cousin of Raphael Semmes. Graduated Georgetown (D.C.), 1842; Harvard Law School, 1845. Removed to New Orleans, La., 1850, where he practiced thereafter. Attorney general of Louisiana, 1859–61; Confederate senator from Louisiana, 1862–65. The most notable part of his career followed the Civil War. He was a guiding influence in the Louisiana constitutional convention of 1879, and for years his name appeared as counsel in nearly every case before civil courts in the state. He was also professor of civil law at the University of Louisiana (later Tulane University).

Semple, Ellen Churchill (*b. Louisville, Ky., 1863; d. West Palm Beach, Fla., 1932*), anthropogeographer. Graduated Vassar, 1882; studied at Leipzig under Friedrich Ratzel. Taught at University of Chicago and at Clark University; was president of the Association of American Geographers, 1921, the only woman ever to hold that position. Among her books, all of which are outstanding, *Influences of Geographic Environment* (1911) was said to have shaped the whole trend and content of geographic thought in the United States.

Seney, George Ingraham (*b. Astoria, N.Y., 1826; d. New York, N.Y., 1893*), banker, art collector, philanthropist.

Senn, Nicholas (*b. Buchs, St. Gall, Switzerland, 1844; d. Chicago, Ill., 1908*), surgeon. Came to America as a boy. Graduated Chicago Medical College, 1868; M.D., University of Munich, 1878. Practiced principally in Milwaukee, Wis., 1874–93, and thereafter in Chicago, where he taught surgery at several schools, including Chicago Polyclinic and University of Chicago. He maintained a lifelong interest in military medicine.

Sennett, George Burritt (*b. Sinclairville, N.Y., 1840; d. Youngstown, Ohio, 1900*), manufacturer of oil-well machinery, ornithologist. Made prolonged and important studies in birdlife of the lower Rio Grande region of southern Texas. The materials gathered by him were utilized and described, however, by others.

Sennett, Mack (*b. Richmond, Quebec, Canada, 1880; d. Los Angeles, Calif., 1960*), film director, producer, and actor. Sennett, after an unsuccessful career on the stage, made his first film in 1908. In 1912, he formed the Keystone Film Co., and began making the comedies, with the famous Keystone Cops and Bathing Beauties, which remain standards for cinema comedy today. Using such talents as "Fatty" Arbuckle, Mack Swain, Gloria Swanson, Harry Langdon, and Ben Turpin, he was brilliantly successful during the era of silent films. When sound was introduced, he directed W. C. Fields and Bing Crosby. But his distributor and parent company, Paramount-Publix went bankrupt in the early 1930's, and Sennett, suffering great financial losses, retired from films in 1935.

Sequoyah (*b. Taskigi, Tenn., ca. 1770; d. possibly Tamaulipas, Mexico, 1843*), inventor of the Cherokee syllabary. Crippled for life in a hunting accident, he began his efforts to reduce his tribal language to characters *ca.* 1809 and, after much ridicule and opposition, completed his table of 85 or 86 characters in 1821. A tribal council approved his work and in a short time thousands of Cherokee had learned to read and write. Sequoyah has been called the ablest intelligence produced among the American Indians.

Sergeant, Henry Clark (*b. Rochester, N.Y., 1834; d. Westfield, N.J., 1907*), machinist. After securing a number of patents for useful inventions, 1854–68, he established a machine shop in New York City for development of crude ideas brought to him by other inventors. After working with Simon Ingersoll *ca.* 1870 in development of the idea of a rock drill, he was associated with Ingersoll in at least one patent and was responsible for the organization of the original Ingersoll Rock Drill Co., also adapting the device to use of compressed air rather than steam. Selling out his interest, 1883, he patented a new rock drill, 1884; after manufacturing it for a short time, he joined his company with the Ingersoll company. Among his other notable inventions of a later date were several types of valves for air compressors, the "tappet" drill, and the Sergeant release rotation.

Sergeant, John (*b. Newark, N.J., 1710; d. 1749*), Congregational clergyman, missionary to the Housatonic Indians. Graduated Yale, 1729. Entered permanently upon his work among Indians, 1735. Ministered principally in vicinity of present towns of Sheffield and Stockbridge, Mass.

Sergeant, John (*b. Philadelphia, Pa., 1779; d. 1852*), lawyer, Pennsylvania official. Son of Jonathan D. Sergeant; brother of Thomas Sergeant. Graduated College of New Jersey (Princeton), 1795; studied law with Jared Ingersoll. Practicing in Philadelphia *post* 1799, he became a leader of the bar and was a member of the intellectual group led by Joseph Dennie and Nicholas Biddle. Elected to Congress from Pennsylvania, he served in that body, 1815–23, 1827–29, and 1837–41, successively as a Federalist, as a National Republican, and as a Whig. A supporter of the "American system," he opposed the Missouri Compromise and was for many years the chief legal and political adviser to the Second Bank of the United States; he is credited with having had major influence in inducing Biddle to apply for renewal of the bank's charter. President of Pennsylvania constitutional convention, 1837–38, he took the lead in the fight over the judiciary. Sergeant's great strength was as a forensic legalist, less eloquent than intellectual. In his cases before the Supreme Court (*Osborn* v. *United States Bank*, *Worcester* v. *Georgia*, and the like) he advocated national powers as opposed to states' rights. His stature may be measured by the offices which he declined; these included a justiceship of the U.S. Supreme Court, a cabinet office under Harrison, and the embassy to England under Tyler.

Sergeant, Jonathan Dickinson (*b. Newark, N.J., 1746; d. Philadelphia, Pa., 1793*), lawyer, Revolutionary patriot. Nephew of John Sergeant (1710–49); grandson of Jonathan Dickinson. Graduated College of New Jersey (Princeton), 1762. As member of the New Jersey Provincial Congress, 1776, he led in forming a state constitution; he was also member of the Continental Congress, 1776–77, representing New Jersey. After removing to Pennsylvania, he engaged in politics there and was attorney general of that state, 1777–80. His zeal for democratic principles led him to support the French Revolution, and he was prominent during the Edmond Genêt episode as a friend of France. Among his children were John Sergeant (1779–1852) and Thomas Sergeant.

SERGEANT, THOMAS (*b. Philadelphia, Pa., 1782; d. 1860*), Pennsylvania official and jurist, legal author. Son of Jonathan D. Sergeant; brother of John Sergeant (1779–1852). Graduated College of New Jersey (Princeton), 1798; studied law under Jared Ingersoll; was associate justice, Pennsylvania Supreme Court, 1834–46. Strongly opposed amendment of state constitution, 1837–38, which provided for popular election of judges. Excelled as a legal writer.

SERRA, JUNÍPERO (*b. Petra, Mallorca, 1713; d. Mission San Carlos, near Monterey, Calif., 1784*), Roman Catholic clergyman, Franciscan. After winning early distinction as professor of philosophy and preacher, he volunteered for mission work and arrived in Mexico City with Francisco Palóu, January 1750. After mission work among Indians northeast of Querétaro and parish duties in the capital city, he was sent as *presidente* of the new Franciscan mission field in Lower California, 1767. Having engaged to cooperate with the government by founding missions in Upper California, Father Serra, with five companions, accompanied the expedition of Gaspar de Portolá northward and founded Mission San Diego in July 1769, the first of the 21 missions eventually erected on the California coast. During Father Serra's presidency, nine of these missions were founded: San Diego, San Carlos, San Antonio, San Gabriel, San Luis Obispo, San Francisco de Assisi, San Juan Capistrano, Santa Clara, and San Buenaventura. In his differences with the military authorities, no one could question his patriotism as a Spaniard or his sense of justice as a spiritual leader and protector of the rights of Indians. He traveled constantly on foot from mission to mission, aiding his associates by his counsel and encouragement.

SERRELL, EDWARD WELLMAN (*b. London, England, 1826; d. New York, N.Y., 1906*), civil and military engineer. Came to America as a child. An expert in railroad and bridge design and construction, Serrell organized and commanded the 1st New York Engineers at the outbreak of the Civil War; he later became chief engineer of the X Corps and chief engineer and chief of staff of the Army of the James. During the siege of Charleston, S.C., he devised and personally supervised construction of the famous "Swamp Angel" battery.

SERVICE, ROBERT WILLIAM (*b. Preston, England, 1874; d. Lancieux, France, 1958*), poet. After working in a bank in Scotland, Service immigrated to Canada and the U.S. in the mid 1890's. By the early 1900's, he was working in Dawson in the Yukon. It was there that he wrote his famous folk poems, published first in 1907 as *The Spell of the Yukon*, and, in 1909, as *Ballads of a Cheechako*. These books included his most famous poems. "The Shooting of Dan McGrew," and "The Cremation of Sam McGee." Other successful books include *Rhymes of a Rolling Stone* (1912) and *Rhymes of a Red Cross Man* (1916). He lived in France after 1913 except during World War II. Although only a popular poet, Service left his mark on the folklore of the North American frontier experience.

SERVOSS, THOMAS LOWERY (*b. Philadelphia, Pa., 1786; d. New York, N.Y., 1866*), merchant, shipowner. Active in trade at Natchez, Miss., and New Orleans, La., 1810–25, Servoss was representative of those northerners who made threefold profits in the cotton belt by selling northern goods, shipping back cotton in return, and transporting the goods in both directions. He operated a profitable line of sailing packet ships between New York and New Orleans, 1827–31, and later engaged in banking in New York.

SESSIONS, HENRY HOWARD (*b. Madrid, N.Y., 1847; d. Chicago, Ill., 1915*), railroad-car builder, inventor, 1887, of the passenger car "vestibule."

SESTINI, BENEDICT (*b. Florence, Italy, 1816; d. Frederick, Md., 1890*), Roman Catholic clergyman, Jesuit, mathematician, astronomer. Came to America, 1848. At the observatory of Georgetown University, Washington, D.C., he made observations of sunspots, 1850, which he sketched and which were later engraved and published, 1853. These are rated as among the best studies of the sun's maculae antedating the application of photography. Father Sestini was also an architect, and in 1866 founded the widely read Catholic publication *Messenger of the Sacred Heart*, which he edited until 1885.

SETCHELL, WILLIAM ALBERT (*b. Norwich, Conn., 1864; d. Berkeley, Calif., 1943*), botanist. B.A., Yale, 1887; Ph.D., Harvard, 1890. Taught biology at Yale, 1891–95; professor of botany, University of California at Berkeley, 1895–1934. For more than 40 years, the major subject of his research was the marine algal flora of the Pacific Coast, during much of the time in collaboration with Nathaniel L. Gardner. In one of his most significant investigations, he helped determine the role of algae in the formation of coral reefs. He was largely responsible for building his department at Berkeley into one of the world's principal botanical centers.

SETH, JAMES (*b. Edinburgh, Scotland, 1860; d. 1924*), philosopher. While professor of philosophy at Brown 1892–96, he completed his most important work, *A Study of Ethical Principles* (1894). In this work he sought to mediate between utilitarianism and the Kantian and other rationalistic systems, finding in "personality" a concept that unites the truth of both. Sage professor of moral philosophy at Cornell University, 1896–98, he returned to the University of Edinburgh as professor of moral philosophy and continued in that post until the end of his life. He was a strong force for social and other reforms in Scotland.

SETON, ELIZABETH ANN BAYLEY (*b. New York, N.Y., 1774; d. Emmitsburg, Md., 1821*), founder of the American Sisters of Charity, known as Mother Seton. Daughter of Richard Bayley, she was educated principally by her father and in 1794 married William Magee Seton, a New York merchant. In 1797, with Isabella M. Graham and others, she founded a society for relief of widows, the first charitable organization in New York City. Accompanying her husband to Italy, she made her first contact with Catholicism there, and on returning home after his death in December 1803, she became a convert in 1805. Estranged from her family and friends, she began a school for girls in Baltimore, Md., 1808, and there in the spring of 1809 with four companions formed a community which took the name Sisters of St. Joseph. Removing to Emmitsburg, Md., that summer, they took, with some modifications, the rule of the Daughters of Charity of St. Vincent de Paul; *post* 1812 they were known as the Sisters of Charity of St. Joseph and constituted the first native American religious community. Mother Seton served for the rest of her life as the first superior and, in spite of the poverty that threatened her community's existence, formed her associates into effective teachers and model religious. Her cause for canonization was introduced at Rome by Cardinal Gibbons *ca.* 1907. She was the grandmother of Robert and William Seton and the aunt of James R. Bayley.

SETON, ERNEST THOMPSON (*b. South Sheilds, Durham, England, 1860; d. near Santa Fe, N.Mex., 1946*), illustrator, author, naturalist, lecturer. Raised in Canada. Successful as writer and illustrator of a number of books about animals and nature, of which some were professedly scientific; his most popular works, however, were outdoor stories that depended for their effect on evocation of wonder and excitement and reader identification, rather than on accuracy or plausibility. He was a zealous propagandist for conservation, for the American Indian, and for preservation of woodcraft skill. Among his books were *The Birds of Manitoba* (1891); *Life Histories of Northern Animals* (1909); and *Lives of Game Animals* (1925–28)—which were representative of his work as a naturalist-scientist. His popular works included *Wild Animals I Have Known* (1898) and *Animal Heroes* (1905); he was author also of a number of books for children and of a Boy Scouts' *Handbook* (1910).

SETON, GRACE GALLATIN THOMPSON (*b. Sacramento, Calif., 1872; d. Palm Beach, Fla., 1959*), author and book designer. Studied at Packer Collegiate Institute. The wife of artist and naturalist Ernest Thompson Seton, Grace Seton wrote *A Woman Tenderfoot in the Rockies* (1900) and *Nimrod's Wife* (1907). She then designed her husband's books and managed publicity for his lectures and his business affairs. During World War I she directed the Women's Motor Unit of La Bienêtre du Blessé in France, for which she received three French decorations. In 1933 she organized a woman writers' conference at the Century of Progress Exhibition, which later became the core of the Biblioteca Feminina at Northwestern University. Other books include *A Woman Tenderfoot in Egypt* (1923), *Chinese Lanterns* (1924), and *Yes, Lady Saheb* (1925).

SETON, ROBERT (*b. Pisa, Italy, 1839; d. 1927*), Roman Catholic clergyman. Grandson of Elizabeth A. B. Seton; brother of William Seton. A brilliant student at several Roman colleges *post* 1857, he was ordained in 1865 and gave up the chance of a notable ecclesiastical career to serve as chaplain to St. Elizabeth's Convent near Madison, N.J., and as a pastor in Jersey City. Returning to Rome, 1902, he served until 1914 as an unofficial link between the Vatican and America. He passed the remainder of his life in virtual retirement, principally at Emmitsburg, Md., and Madison, N.J.

SETON, WILLIAM (*b. New York, N.Y., 1835; d. New York, 1905*), lawyer, Union soldier, author. Grandson of Elizabeth A. B. Seton; brother of Robert Seton.

SETTLE, THOMAS (*b. Rockingham Co., N.C., 1831; d. 1888*), politician, jurist. North Carolina legislator. Participated in meeting which organized the North Carolina Radical party, 1865, and introduced resolution which identified it with the Republican party. Associate judge, North Carolina Supreme Court, 1868–71 and 1872–76. He served also briefly as U.S. minister to Peru and was a U.S. district judge for Florida *post* 1877.

SEVERANCE, CAROLINE MARIA SEYMOUR (*b. Canandaigua, N.Y., 1820; d. 1914*), founder of women's clubs in Cleveland, Ohio, Boston, Mass., and Los Angeles, Calif.

SEVERANCE, FRANK HAYWARD (*b. Manchester, Mass., 1856; d. 1931*), Buffalo, N.Y., journalist, historian. Secretary, Buffalo Historical Society, *post* 1901; authority on the history of the Niagara frontier.

SEVERANCE, LOUIS HENRY (*b. Cleveland, Ohio, 1838; d. Cleveland, 1913*), capitalist. Engaged in oil production at Titusville, Pa., *post* 1864, he became associated with the Standard Oil Co. of Ohio and served as its treasurer, 1876–94. In association with Herman Frasch and others, he was a founder of the Union

Sulphur Co. His principal benefactions were made to the Presbyterian church and to its missions.

SEVIER, AMBROSE HUNDLEY (*b. Greene Co., Tenn., 1801; d. near Little Rock, Ark., 1848*), lawyer, Arkansas legislator, planter. Settled in Arkansas, 1821; became associated by marriage with a powerful, political family headed by Richard M. Johnson. Territorial delegate from Arkansas to Congress, Democrat, 1828–36, he took a prominent part in achieving statehood for Arkansas and served as U.S. senator, 1836–48. An expansionist, he warmly supported the Mexican War and served with Nathan Clifford in the conclusion of negotiations for peace under the Treaty of Guadalupe Hidalgo, 1848.

SEVIER, JOHN (*b. near present New Market, Va., 1745; d. Alabama, 1815*), pioneer, soldier. Immigrated to the remote frontier that is now East Tennessee, 1773. Continuing to move down the Holston River valley as settlement advanced, he lived on the Nolachucky River, 1783–90. *Post* 1790, he resided in or near Knoxville. An acknowledged leader of the backwoodsmen, he was a member of the local committee of safety, 1776, and a representative in the Provincial Congress of North Carolina. As an officer of the militia, he led a body of the Tennesseans across the Smokies to join in the victory over the British at King's Mountain, 1780, and later set out upon an expedition against the Cherokee. During 1781 and 1782 he continued raiding against the Indians. At the end of the Revolution he joined with William Blount and others in a project for colonizing at Muscle Shoals. At first opposing the movement for organization of a separate state of Franklin, he later put himself at the head of it and was elected governor. Concerting a military expedition against the Indians with the state of Georgia, he alienated many liberals among the pioneers and lost prestige when Georgia failed to give aid. The defeat of Sevier's faction in a so-called battle, February 1788, resulted in the virtual extinction of the state of Franklin. Denounced as a reckless disturber of the public peace, he sought refuge on the extreme frontier with a group of followers and sank to the level of a bushwhacker, defying the efforts of Congress and entering into dubious correspondence with Spanish agents. Taking advantage of a new trend in public affairs, Sevier came forth as an advocate of the new U.S. Constitution and with the aid of William Blount succeeded in winning a full pardon and election to the North Carolina Senate, 1789. After a brief term in Congress, 1789–91, he devoted most of his attention during the territorial period of Tennessee to his plantation and his business concerns; he took no part in the Genêt affair or in the conspiracies of Blount and Aaron Burr. Elected first governor of the state of Tennessee, he served 1796–1801 and 1803–09. Engaged in a bitter feud with Andrew Jackson from about 1796 to the end of his life, he served again in the state senate, 1809–11, and was a congressman, 1811–15, serving on several committees and supporting the administration.

SEWALL, ARTHUR (*b. Bath, Maine, 1835; d. near Bath, 1900*), shipbuilder. Brother of Frank Sewall; father of Harold M. Sewall. Launching the first of his 80 vessels, 1855, Sewall and his partners did much to keep the wooden sailing vessel alive in its period of decline. During the 1890's he built the *Rappahannock*, *Shenandoah*, *Susquehanna*, and *Roanoke*, largest and last of the great American full-rigged wooden ships.

SEWALL, FRANK (*b. Bath, Maine, 1837; d. Washington, D.C., 1915*), Swedenborgian clergyman, author, educator. Brother of Arthur Sewall. Made his chief contribution to the life of his church in the development of its forms of worship.

SEWALL, HAROLD MARSH (*b. Bath, Maine, 1860; d. New York, N.Y., 1924*), diplomat, Maine legislator. Son of Arthur Sewall. Opposed German coup d'état at Apia, Samoa, 1887, while U.S. consul general there. As U.S. minister to Hawaii, 1897–98, he received transfer of sovereignty of the islands and remained in Hawaii as U.S. special agent until establishment of regular territorial government, 1900.

SEWALL, JONATHAN (*b. Boston, Mass., 1728; d. St. John, New Brunswick, Canada, 1796*), lawyer, Loyalist. Graduated Harvard, 1748. Originally the intimate friend of John Adams, he became an adherent of the crown *ca.* 1761 because of opposition by James Otis to a request made by him to the Massachusetts General Court. Successively solicitor general and attorney general of Massachusetts, and *post* 1768 a judge of the vice admiralty court, he sailed for England early in 1775, whence he immigrated to Canada, 1788. A witty man, Sewall was a frequent and able contributor to the press.

SEWALL, JONATHAN MITCHELL (*b. Salem, Mass., 1748; d. Portsmouth, N.H., 1808*), lawyer, occasional poet. Grandnephew of Samuel Sewall. Author of *Miscellaneous Poems* (1801).

SEWALL, JOSEPH ADDISON (*b. Scarboro, Maine, 1830; d. 1917*), physician, educator. As first president of the University of Colorado, 1877–87, he developed that institution under most adverse conditions; he later taught at the University of Denver, where he was also dean of the school of pharmacy and acted as chemist for the city of Denver.

SEWALL, MAY ELIZA WRIGHT (*b. Milwaukee, Wis., 1844; d. 1920*), teacher, feminist. Principal for many years to the Girls' Classical School, Indianapolis, Ind., Sewall served as chairman of the executive committee of the National Suffrage Association and was a prominent figure in the International Council of Women. In 1889, when the Federation of Women's Clubs was formed, she became its first president.

SEWALL, SAMUEL (*b. Bishopstoke, England, 1652; d. Boston, Mass., 1730*), merchant, colonial magistrate. Born of New England parents, he returned with his family to Boston *ca.* 1661 and graduated from Harvard, 1671. Active in politics and the holder of many legislative and judicial offices in the colony throughout his life, he was particularly noteworthy for his service in 1692 as a special commissioner to try the cases of witchcraft at Salem. Sewall was the only one of the judges who ever publicly admitted that he had been in error in this matter; he made his confession of error in Old South Church, Boston, 1697. His tract *The Selling of Joseph* (1700) was one of the earliest appeals in the antislavery cause. He was also author of several tracts on religious subjects, on the Indians, and on politics, and wrote verses which circulated in manuscript form. As a writer he is remembered chiefly for his diary, which covers the period 1674–1729, with a gap at 1677–85. This work, which was first published in *Massachusetts Historical Society Collection* (1878–82), is an incomparable picture of the mind and life of a New England Puritan of the transition period. Sewall, as unwittingly portrayed by himself, emerges as mercenary, average in mentality, conventional, and introspective, yet also affectionate, honorable, strong, and fearless. Other American diaries possess higher importance from a political point of view, but none so vividly reproduces the diarist's entire world.

SEWALL, STEPHEN (*b. York, Maine, 1734; d. Cambridge, Mass., 1804*), classicist, Hebraist. Graduated Harvard, 1761. Succeeding Judah Monis as teacher of Hebrew at Harvard, 1761, he was first Hancock professor of Hebrew and Oriental languages, 1765–85. His interests also included science and politics, and he was an early supporter of the Revolution.

SEWARD, FREDERICK WILLIAM (*b. Auburn, N.Y., 1830; d. 1915*), journalist, diplomat, New York legislator. Son of William

H. Seward, served as his father's secretary and associate, 1849–72. Author-editor of *Autobiography of William H. Seward* (1877) and other works.

SEWARD, GEORGE FREDERICK (*b. Florida, N.Y., 1840; d. 1910*), diplomat. Nephew of William H. Seward. In the consular service, 1861–76, he was appointed U.S. minister to China, 1876; he resigned, 1879, after criticism of his record by the Democrats in Congress. He was president of Fidelity and Casualty Co., 1893–1910.

SEWARD, THEODORE FRELINGHUYSEN (*b. Florida, N.Y., 1835; d. East Orange, N.J., 1902*), musician, teacher, hymnologist. Studied in Boston, Mass., with Lowell Mason, George F. Root, and Thomas Hastings (1784–1872). Edited a collection of spirituals, *Jubilee Songs* (1872), and a number of other collections of songs and hymns; was coauthor with Lowell Mason of *The Pestalozzian Music Teacher* (1871). In helping to preserve spirituals, he made his most distinctive contribution.

SEWARD, WILLIAM HENRY (*b. Florida, N.Y., 1801; d. Auburn, N.Y., 1872*), statesman. Father of Frederick W. Seward; uncle of George F. Seward. Graduated Union College, 1820; was admitted to the bar, 1822; established himself in Auburn, N.Y., 1823. Moved by distrust of the Southern Jeffersonians and by his great interest in internal improvements, he supported DeWitt Clinton for governor and John Quincy Adams for president, 1824; the enthusiasm he then felt for Adams had a part in forming his political ideals. Drawn by expediency and conviction into the Anti-Masonic movement, he became a close friend of Thurlow Weed and through Weed's influence was elected to the New York State Senate, 1830. After four years' service he ran for governor as a Whig, but was defeated by William L. Marcy. Devoting himself to the practice of law, he acquired a small competence as agent for the Holland Land Co. in handling disputes with its settlers. Nominated, with Weed's assistance, by the Whigs for governor, 1838, he was forced for the first time to face the slavery issue and expressed a cautious opposition to that institution.

As governor of New York, 1839–43, he revealed an optimistic temper, strong humanitarian sympathies, impulsiveness, and a tendency to challenge majority opinion. Urging internal improvements upon the legislature in the midst of a depression, he brought about impairment of the state's credit. His declaration that the New York City public schools should be staffed by teachers of the same faith and racial extraction as the Catholic immigrant children brought down on him a nativist storm of criticism, and he was forced to retreat from this position. While he was governor, he took an advanced ground on the matter of slavery and won the support of the growing abolitionist element. In the belief that he was too far in advance of public opinion to prosper politically, he declined renomination in 1842 and returned to legal practice as a chancery court and patent specialist. He continued to take part in almost every campaign, however, and by championing the Irish cause won the support of Irish-American voters.

In 1848 he was elected to the U.S. Senate, many Democrats and all the Whigs in the legislature voted for him. In the debates over the proposed Compromise of 1850, Seward opposed all compromise and asserted that the Fugitive Slave Law was impossible to enforce in the North. In a speech of Mar. 11, 1850, he declared that the slave system would either be ended "by gradual voluntary effort and with compensation" within the framework of the Union, or the Union would be itself dissolved and a civil war ensue. In the same speech he used the famous phrase "a higher law than the Constitution," which was widely misunderstood as a threat of action outside the American charter. An intense Whig partisan, he had in common with Weed a great interest in party politics and party victory, so he curbed, for a time, his dislike of compromise and tolerated a party policy which would raise as few perplexing questions of principle as possible. Meantime, in the Senate, he expressed an ardent nationalism and republicanism with such recklessness as to lay him open to the charge of demagogy. He played a leading part in the welcome to Kossuth, protested against Russian intervention in Hungary, and once again championed the Irish cause. In the debates on the Kansas-Nebraska bill, Seward showed greater caution than in the discussions of 1850, although he spoke vigorously against the bill and warned the South of the conflict to which he felt it would inevitably give rise. *Post* 1854, the rise of the Republican party in the West and the Know-Nothing party in the East and South created embarrassment for him as a Whig party leader; however, with Weed, he was able to negate the efforts of the Know-Nothings and secure reelection to the Senate. After the merger of the old Whig party with the rising Republican organization in the fall of 1855, Seward's speeches on slavery became of the most forthright character, and from that time until 1860 he embodied the growing antislavery sentiment of the North as much as any man. He advocated admission of Kansas under the Topeka Constitution, denounced the Dred Scott decision as the product of a conspiracy, and in October 1858 made at Rochester, N.Y., the famous speech in which he declared that the slavery struggle was "an irrepressible conflict." Perhaps for tactical reasons, however, he supported the Douglas idea of decision by popular sovereignty in Kansas, 1858, and in a later speech minimized the effect of the "irrepressible conflict" speech by praising the moderation of the slaveholders and blaming the free Democrats of the North for the events of the past few years.

Passed over expediently in 1856 by the Republicans, who favored John C. Frémont, for the presidential nomination, he was undoubtedly the leading candidate when the Republican National Convention met in Chicago, June 1860. The hostility of Horace Greeley, the opposition of the Know-Nothings, and Seward's own radical utterances, however, conspired to deprive him of the nomination. With his usual outward calm and very real generosity, he campaigned for the Republican ticket throughout the North and, in the crisis following the election, employed conciliatory language and methods advocating, among other things, a constitutional convention to settle outstanding difficulties.

Appointed U.S. secretary of state by Lincoln, he accepted, although he was displeased at the choice of Salmon P. Chase and Blair for the cabinet. He took office believing that he would be the dominant figure in the administration, and during March and April 1861 conducted himself in a manner which hardly represented him at his best. His "Some Thoughts for the President's Consideration" of April 1861 advocated embroiling the United States with most of Europe and waging actual war on Spain and France as a means of preserving the Union; he also virtually suggested that the president abdicate his power to the secretary of state. He engaged in maneuvers behind Lincoln's back by which the reinforcement of Fort Pickens was delayed and the expedition to Fort Sumter weakened. His conduct of his office during the four years of war, however, deserves high praise, for he abandoned his early truculence toward other nations and expressed the views of the United States with dignity and force. His handling of the seizure of Mason and Slidell on board the *Trent* was masterly. He proved able to avert the possibility of European intervention in the Civil War and to check anti-Northern agitation in France and England by the self-confident optimism of his dispatches and the skillful use of the question of slavery. Seward's steady pressure (together with the diplomatic skill of Charles Francis Adams) led to British action against outfitting of Confederate cruisers in British ports. Seward was even more adroit in his management of the matter of French intervention in Mexico.

When the war was over, his strong instinct for expansionism revived. In 1867 he negotiated the cession of Alaska to the United States by Russia and secured prompt ratification of the treaty by the U.S. Senate. He was unsuccessful in maneuvers to acquire islands of the Danish West Indies. In addition to his normal duties, he served as a sort of political liaison officer, and his interest in patronage problems was continuous. After suffering serious injury in a carriage accident in the spring of 1865, he had been brutally attacked on the night of Lincoln's assassination; yet, despite the fact that he was partially crippled, he transacted the public business with as much skill and coolness as ever. In the administration of Andrew Johnson he was a central figure. He advocated a conciliatory policy toward the South, wrote some of Johnson's most important veto messages, and supported the president up to the very end, even though by so doing he lost both popularity and influence. Leaving office on President Grant's accession, he made a tour around the world and returned to his home in Auburn late in 1871.

SEWELL, WILLIAM JOYCE (*b. Castlebar, Ireland, 1835; d. Camden, N.J., 1901*), Union soldier, railroad executive, politician. Came to America, 1851. Prominent in management of the Pennsylvania Railroad system's New Jersey lines, Sewell became in time virtual Republican boss of New Jersey. He served in the state senate, 1872–81, and was U.S. senator, 1881–87 and 1895–1901.

SEYBERT, ADAM (*b. Philadelphia, Pa., 1773; d. Paris, France, 1825*), physician. Studied with Caspar Wistar; M.D., University of Pennsylvania, 1793. After continuing his studies at London, Edinburgh, and Göttingen, and making special studies in mineralogy in Paris, he returned to Philadelphia, 1797, where he practiced and ran an apothecary shop. An expert in the analysis of minerals, he also manufactured, it is claimed, the first mercurials in America. While a congressman, Democratic-Republican, from Pennsylvania, 1809–15 and 1817–19, he interested himself in government revenues and expenditure and was author of *Statistical Annals . . . of the United States* (1818). An active member and official of the American Philosophical Society, he was one of the leading pioneer American chemists and mineralogists.

SEYBERT, HENRY (*b. Philadelphia, Pa., 1801; d. Philadelphia, 1883*), mineralogist, philanthropist. Son of Adam Seybert. Endowed a chair of philosophy at the University of Pennsylvania; left a great part of his estate to Pennsylvania for relief of poor children.

SEYBERT, JOHN (*b. Manheim, Pa., 1791; d. near Bellevue, Ohio, 1860*), bishop of the Evangelical Association. Itinerant missionary among German immigrants in Pennsylvania and Ohio.

SEYFFARTH, GUSTAVUS (*b. near Torgau, Germany, 1796; d. New York, N.Y., 1885*), archaeologist, Lutheran theologian, classical and Oriental philologist. Opposed school of Champollion. Resigned professorship of archaeology at University of Leipzig, 1854; immigrated to America, 1856. Erudite, but afflicted with a speculative-dogmatic mentality, Seyffarth contended throughout his whole life that hieroglyphic signs were phonograms or syllabic writing and that Egyptian literature was based on ancient Coptic, related by him to Hebrew.

SEYMOUR, CHARLES (*b. New Haven, Conn., 1885; d. Chatham, Mass., 1963*), diplomat and historian. Studied at Kings College, Cambridge, England, and Yale (Ph.D., 1911). Joined the Yale faculty in 1911 and was president, 1937–50. His *Diplomatic Background of the War, 1870–1914* (1916) established his reputation as a diplomatic historian and expert on World

War I. Invited in 1917 by Col. Edward M. House, President Woodrow Wilson's adviser, to join the Inquiry, a group of "experts" who prepared background information for the forthcoming peace conference; after the war he accompanied Wilson to the Paris Peace Conference. Back at Yale he concentrated on writing the diplomatic history of the war and became editor of Colonel House's papers (published 1926–28).

SEYMOUR, GEORGE FRANKLIN (*b. New York, N.Y., 1829; d. Springfield, Ill., 1906*), Episcopal clergyman. An ardent Anglo-Catholic, he served as professor and dean at the General Theological Seminary, New York; he was consecrated bishop of Springfield, 1878

SEYMOUR, HORATIO (*b. Pompey Hill, N.Y., 1810; d. 1886*), lawyer, New York politician. Brother-in-law of Roscoe Conkling. Early a henchman of the Albany Regency, Seymour was a longtime political lieutenant of William L. Marcy. As a New York assemblyman, 1842 and 1844–45, he forced expansion measures of his famous "Report of the Committee on Canals" through the legislature against the strongest opposition and was elected Speaker of the assembly, 1845. His skill in effecting working compromises between the Democratic "Hunker" and "Barnburner" factions made him an important figure. Although an advocate *post* 1845 of "free soil" in any southwestern territory which might be gained from Mexico and opposed to federal meddling with slavery where it then existed, he expressed a strong dislike for both abolitionists and Southern extremists. A true Jeffersonian, he insisted on the supreme importance of local government. He served the first of his terms as governor of New York, 1853–55, showing himself industrious and conscientious, improving the penal system and opposing prohibition and anti-Catholicism. Defeated for reelection, he devoted himself for a while to private business. Considered a possible compromise candidate at the Charleston, S.C., Democratic convention, 1860, Seymour supported Stephen A. Douglas, but on Lincoln's election urged loyal acceptance of the constitutional fact and favored the Crittenden Compromise. Although he considered an armed conquest of the South unwise, he helped the Union war effort and, as governor, 1863–65, was tireless in supplying the state's army quotas. He found himself pushed, however, into a position as national leader of the opposition to the Republicans and was a constant critic of the extraconstitutional powers assumed by the Lincoln administration. Although he was denounced by Horace Greeley and others as a temporizing Copperhead during the draft riots in New York City, July 1863, the verdict of time has been in his favor. Defeated as Democratic candidate for the presidency after a vigorous campaign, 1868, he became an elder statesman of the party, assisted in driving Boss Tweed from power and lived to see his disciple, Grover Cleveland, in the White House. A man of dignity and integrity, he failed practically as a statesman, largely because of his gentlemanly scorn for extreme opinions.

SEYMOUR, HORATIO WINSLOW (*b. Cayuga Co., N.Y., 1854; d. New York, N.Y., 1920*), journalist. Raised in Wisconsin. Served as editor on *Milwaukee Daily News, Chicago Times, Chicago Herald, Chicago Chronicle,* and New York *World;* was noted for his innovating use of startling and effective headlines. A liberal Democrat, he opposed Republican money and tariff policies.

SEYMOUR, THOMAS DAY (*b. Hudson, Ohio, 1848; d. New Haven, Conn., 1907*), classicist. Grandnephew of Jeremiah Day. Professor of Greek at Western Reserve, 1872–80, and at Yale, 1880–1907. Chairman of managing committee, American School at Athens, 1887–1901; president, Archaeological Institute of America, 1903–07. Author of, among other books, *Life in the Homeric Age* (1907).

SEYMOUR, THOMAS HART (*b. Hartford, Conn., 1807; d. Hartford, 1868*), lawyer, Mexican War soldier. Congressman, Democrat, from Connecticut, 1843–45; governor of Connecticut, 1850–53; U.S. minister to Russia, 1854–58. A leader of the Connecticut Peace Democrats.

SEYMOUR, TRUMAN (*b. Burlington, Vt., 1824; d. Florence, Italy, 1891*), Union major general. Graduated West Point, 1846; served with artillery in Mexican War and against Seminoles. As brigade and later division commander during the Civil War, Seymour executed the decisive enveloping movement at the battle of South Mountain, and at Antietam led the advance of Hooker's corps in opening the battle. In continuous service thereafter, he was distinguished as a soldier but unaggressive in promotion of his own ambitions. He retired in 1876.

SEYMOUR, WILLIAM (*b. New York, N.Y., 1855; d. Plymouth, Mass., 1933*), actor, stage director, theater manager. Son-in-law of Edward L. Davenport. He was for many years associated with productions of Charles Frohman.

SHABONEE (*b. possibly near Maumee River, Ohio, ca. 1775; d. Grundy Co., Ill., 1859*), Potawatomi chief. An associate of Tecumseh, 1807–14, he later became a good but unrewarded friend of the settlers.

SHAFER, HELEN ALMIRA (*b. Newark, N.J., 1839; d. Wellesley, Mass., 1894*), educator. Graduated Oberlin, 1863. Professor of mathematics at Wellesley *post* 1877, she succeeded to the presidency of the college, 1888. She completely remodeled the curriculum, altered requirements for admission, and added many new courses of study.

SHAFROTH, JOHN FRANKLIN (*b. Fayette, Mo., 1854; d. Denver, Colo., 1922*), lawyer. Removed to Colorado, 1879. Congressman, Republican, Silver Republican, and Democrat, 1895–1904, he supported the Reclamation Act, a woman's suffrage amendment, and the abolition of lame-duck sessions. Democratic governor of Colorado, 1909–13, he forced adoption of the direct primary, initiative, and referendum. As U.S. senator, 1913–19, he supported President Wilson in the main, but clashed with him on conservation; his Senate speech, Mar. 21, 1914, is the classic statement of the western viewpoint of that subject.

SHAFTER, WILLIAM RUFUS (*b. Kalamazoo Co., Mich., 1835; d. near Bakersfield, Calif., 1906*), soldier. In service with the Union army, 1861–65, he received brevet of brigadier general of volunteers and the Medal of Honor for gallantry at Fair Oaks. Remaining in the army, he rose to colonel, 1st U.S. Infantry, 1879, and was made brigadier general, 1897. On outbreak of the war with Spain, he was promoted major general of volunteers. In command of the expeditionary force against Santiago de Cuba, he landed at Daiquiri, June 22, 1898, and took Santiago on July 17 in a campaign which was widely criticized because of high American mortality from malaria and yellow fever. Much of the criticism of Shafter may be more justly charged to the nation's general unpreparedness and ignorance of tropical diseases. Retiring from active service as brigadier general, 1899, he was advanced to the grade of major general retired, 1901.

SHAHAN, THOMAS JOSEPH (*b. Manchester, N.H., 1857; d. 1932*), Roman Catholic clergyman, educator. Educated at Sulpician College of Montreal and at the American College and the Propaganda in Rome, he was ordained, 1882; he studied later also at the universities of Paris and Berlin. Professor of church history, Roman law, and patrology at Catholic University, Washington, D.C., *post* 1891; rector of the university, 1909–28. He was consecrated titular bishop of Germanicopolis, 1914. A voluminous writer and an able executive, he was a founder and an editor of the *Catholic Encyclopedia* (1907–13).

SHAHN, BENJAMIN ("BEN") (*b. Kovno, Lithuania, 1898; d. New York, N.Y., 1969*), painter and graphic artist. Immigrated to the United States in 1906; attended New York University, City College of New York, National Academy of Design, Art Students League, Sorbonne, and Académie de la Grande Chaumière. Achieved wide acclaim with a series of paintings (1932) on the Sacco-Vanzetti case. Worked for several government agencies, 1934–43, creating paintings or murals for such buildings as the Social Security Building in Washington, D.C. While employed by the Farm Security Administration (1935–38), he took 6,000 photos portraying rural hardship; in 1942–43 designed posters for the Office of War Information. Taught at Boston Museum of Fine Arts and Brooklyn Museum Art School (1947–50); named Norton Professor of Poetry at Harvard (1956). He had several one-man shows and a major retrospective (1947) at the Museum of Modern Art. Foremost among the social-realist artists, he used art as a weapon for political and social change.

SHAIKEWITZ, NAHUM MEIR. *See* SCHOMER, NAHUM MEIR.

SHAKALLAMY. *See* SHIKELLAMY.

SHALER, NATHANIEL SOUTHGATE (*b. Newport, Ky., 1841; d. 1906*), Union soldier, geologist, educator. A favorite pupil of Agassiz, Shaler took a B.S. degree at Lawrence Scientific School, 1862. Returning to his alma mater after Union army service, he was assistant to Agassiz in paleontology; *post* 1868, he served as lecturer and professor of paleontology and geology. He was also dean of Lawrence Scientific School from 1891 until his death. As a teacher, he was concerned more with awakening the minds of his students than with imparting information; as dean, he revivified Lawrence and toward the end of his tenure fought its merger with Massachusetts Institute of Technology. A man of very wide interests, Shaler served also as state geologist of Kentucky, as a member of many Massachusetts state commissions, as a consultant in mining ventures, and as a supervising official of the U.S. Geological Survey. He was a prolific writer on many subjects, scientific and otherwise, displaying exceptional powers of observation and imagination.

SHALER, WILLIAM (*b. Bridgeport, Conn., ca. 1773; d. Havana, Cuba, 1833*), sea captain. Friend and partner of Richard J. Cleveland. Shaler held a number of U.S. consular offices, of which the most notable was the post of U.S. consul general at Algiers, 1815–28. He had previously served as U.S. commissioner with Stephen Decatur (1779–1820) in the arbitrary negotiation of the U.S.–Algiers treaty of 1815. He was author of *Sketches of Algiers* (1826).

SHANNON, FRED ALBERT (*b. Sedalia, Mo., 1893; d. Wickenburg, Ariz., 1963*), historian and art teacher. Attended Indiana State Teachers College and Indiana University (Ph.D., 1924). Taught at Iowa Wesleyan (1919–24), Iowa State Teachers (1924–26), Kansas State College of Agriculture (1926–39), and Illinois (1939–61). His first major work, *The Organization and Administration of the Union Army, 1861–1865* (1928), was a vividly written series of essays. *Economic History of the People of the United States* (1934) displayed his sympathies for the common man. He was part of the group that planned the nine-volume *Economic History of the United States*; his own volumes were *American Farmers' Movements* (1957) and *The Centennial Years* (1967).

SHANNON, WILSON (*b. Mount Olivet, Ohio Territory, 1802; d. 1877*), lawyer, public official. Democratic governor of Ohio, 1838–40 and 1842–44; inept and tactless U.S. minister to Mexico, 1844–45; undistinguished congressman from Ohio, 1853–55. Commissioned governor of Kansas Territory, August 1855, he became confidential with the Missouri party and accused the Free State group of a secret conspiracy to resist the laws. On outbreak of the so-called Wakarusa War in November, he was able to persuade both factions to disband their forces, but when guerrillas again assembled before the town of Lawrence in May 1856, he refused to intervene and contented himself after the pillaging of the town with a proclamation ordering armed bands to desist. On the invasion of the territory by James H. Lane (1814–66) and his army in August and the consequent attacks on proslavery areas, Shannon again played the role of peacemaker and effected a settlement. His resignation anticipated by an order for his removal, August 1856, he resumed the practice of law, becoming in time a leading member of the Kansas bar.

SHARKEY, WILLIAM LEWIS (*b. Holston Valley, East Tenn., 1798; d. Jackson, Miss., 1873*), lawyer, jurist. Removed to Mississippi as a young man; began practice at Warrenton, 1822. Chief justice, state court of errors and appeals, 1832–51. As president of Nashville Convention, 1850, he opposed Southern extremist efforts to dominate that body and up to 1861 was probably the most active antisecessionist in the state of Mississippi. Appointed provisional governor, June 1865, he served until the fall of that year. He was then chosen U.S. senator, but was denied his seat when Congress repudiated President Johnson's Reconstruction plan.

SHARP, DALLAS LORE (*b. Haleyville, N.J., 1870; d. Hingham, Mass., 1929*), educator, Methodist clergyman, naturalist. Author of *Wild Life Near Home* (1901) and some 20 more popular works on nature study, including *A Watcher in the Woods* (1903) and *Beyond the Pasture Bars* (1914).

SHARP, DANIEL (*b. Huddersfield, England, 1783; d. near Baltimore, Md., 1853*), Baptist clergyman. Highly influential in his principal pastorate at the Third Baptist Church, Boston, Mass., 1812–53.

SHARP, JOHN (*b. Clackmannanshire, Scotland, 1820; d. 1891*), Mormon pioneer and bishop, railroad contractor. Came to America, 1848; settled in Salt Lake City, 1850; served as superintendent of the church quarries. Principal subcontractor under Brigham Young in construction of Union Pacific roadbed from Echo Canyon to Ogden, he later undertook other contracts and developed the Utah Central Railroad, of which he was president *post* 1873.

SHARP, KATHARINE LUCINDA (*b. Elgin, Ill., 1865; d. Lake Placid, N.Y., 1914*), librarian. Graduated Northwestern University, 1885; New York State Library School, 1892. Director, Department of Library Science, Armour Institute (later at University of Illinois), 1893–1907; librarian, University of Illinois, 1897–1907. Author of *Illinois Libraries* (1906–08).

SHARP, WILLIAM GRAVES (*b. Mount Gilead, Ohio, 1859; d. Elyria, Ohio, 1922*), lawyer, industrialist. As congressman, Democrat, from Ohio, 1909–14, he became ranking member of Committee on Foreign Affairs; he was U.S. ambassador to France, 1914–19.

SHARPE, HORATIO (*b. near Hull, England, 1718; d. England, 1790*), British soldier, colonial governor of Maryland, 1753–69. Appointed governor, probably through family influence, he served as royal commander in chief during the French and Indian War, until replaced by Braddock. Defending the interests of Lord Baltimore, he quarreled with the legislature over its decision to tax the proprietor's revenue, though he opposed the retaliatory measure of quartering troops in Annapolis. Credited by some with first suggesting the Stamp Act, he warned the ministry that parliamentary taxation could be enforced only by troops. By 1760 he reached agreement with Virginia concerning the disputed boundary of the two colonies. Removed as governor in 1769, he returned to England in 1773.

SHARPLES, JAMES (*b. England, ca. 1751; d. New York, N.Y., 1811*), portrait painter, inventor. Came to America, 1793; worked as an itinerant painter through New England states and the South; settled in Philadelphia, 1796, and resided thereafter there or in New York except for the years 1801–09 when he returned to England. Noted for his ability to catch a likeness, he made many portraits of distinguished Americans, including George Washington and his wife, and of important foreign visitors. For his work in America he used pastels on a thick gray paper of soft grain. Because of the ability of his wife and children to duplicate his work in copies, there has been much confusion over authentication of works from his own hand.

SHARPLESS, ISAAC (*b. Chester Co., Pa., 1848; d. 1920*), Quaker leader and historian, educator. Graduated Harvard, 1873. Began a lifelong service at Haverford College as instructor in mathematics, 1875; president of Haverford, 1887–1917. He was one of the most eminent U.S. exponents of the small, efficient liberal arts college.

SHARSWOOD, GEORGE (*b. Philadelphia, Pa., 1810; d. 1883*), jurist. Judge of the district court of Philadelphia, 1845–68, he was president judge *post* 1848. Elevated to the state supreme court, he served until his retirement in 1882, and was chief justice *post* 1879. Noted for his learning, promptness of decision, and sound judgment, Sharswood was also a prolific legal writer and professor of law and dean of the law school at University of Pennsylvania.

SHATTUCK, AARON DRAPER (*b. Francestown, N.H., 1832; d. Granby, Conn., 1928*), portrait and landscape painter. Brother-in-law of Samuel Colman.

SHATTUCK, FREDERICK CHEEVER (*b. Boston, Mass., 1847; d. 1929*), noted Boston physician. Son of George C. Shattuck (1813–93); brother of George B. Shattuck. Jackson Professor of clinical medicine, Harvard Medical School, 1888–1912.

SHATTUCK, GEORGE BRUNE (*b. Boston, Mass., 1844; d. 1923*), Boston physician. Son of George C. Shattuck (1813–93); brother of Frederick C. Shattuck. Visiting physician for many years at Boston City Hospital, Shattuck was influential in establishing the Massachusetts State Board of Health, 1869, the first in the United States. He was editor in chief, *Boston Medical and Surgical Journal*, 1881–1912.

SHATTUCK, GEORGE CHEYNE (*b. Templeton, Mass., 1783; d. 1854*), physician, philanthropist. Father of George C. Shattuck (1813–93). Graduated Dartmouth, 1803; M.B., 1806; M.D., University of Pennsylvania, 1807. the leading physician of his time in Boston, Shattuck engaged in many philanthropies, including endowment of a professorship of anatomy at Harvard Medical School, foundation of the Shattuck lectures of the Massachusetts Medical Society, and assistance to authors such as James Thacher and John J. Audubon.

SHATTUCK, GEORGE CHEYNE (*b. Boston, Mass., 1813; d. 1893*), physician, philanthropist. Son of George C. Shattuck (1783–1854); father of Frederick C. and George B. Shattuck. Graduated Harvard, 1831; M.D., Harvard Medical School, 1835. During three years' postgraduate study in Europe he was influenced principally by P. C. A. Louis. Shattuck's report of studies differentiating typhoid from typhus fever, read in Paris, 1838, and published in America, 1840, was one of the early,

important contributions to the subject. Practicing with his father in Boston, *post* 1840, he gave much of his time to the improvement of medical education; with Oliver W. Holmes, Henry I. Bowditch, and James Jackson (1777–1867), he was a founder of the Boston Society of Medical Observation and succeeded Holmes as visiting physician to Massachusetts General Hospital, 1849. As professor at Harvard Medical School, and as dean *post* 1864, he woke the school out if its lethargy, extended the teaching into hospitals, and introduced clinical conferences. A leading Episcopal layman, he founded St. Paul's School, Concord, N.H., 1855.

SHATTUCK, LEMUEL (*b. Ashby, Mass., 1793; d. 1859*), merchant, statistician. Interested from an early period in the provision of precise vital statistics, Shattuck was a founder of the American Statistical Association, 1839, and of the New England Historic Genealogical Society. He was influential also in securing a state law requiring an effective system of registry of births, marriages, and deaths, 1842. Shattuck's census of the city of Boston, 1845, contained many innovations, and his services as consultant in the federal census of 1850 resulted in a marked advance in the amount and quality of information recorded. His *Report* (1850) as chairman of the commission to make a sanitary survey of Massachusetts was a milestone in the development of public health works; in it he anticipated almost all the public health measures later put into practice.

SHAUBENA.   *See* SHABONEE.

SHAUCK, JOHN ALLEN (*b. near Johnsville, Ohio, 1841; d. Columbus, Ohio, 1918*), jurist. Ohio circuit court judge, 1884–94; state supreme court judge, 1894–1913. A stern conservative, he held that it was the duty of courts to declare void all acts of state legislatures which were nongovernmental in nature even though not forbidden by constitutional provision.

SHAUGHNESSY, CLARK DANIEL (*b. St. Cloud, Minn., 1892; d. Santa Monica, Calif., 1970*), football coach. Attended Minnesota (B.A., 1914). Coached at Tulane (1915–28), Loyola of the South (1928–32); Chicago (1933–39); Stanford (1940–41), which won the 1941 Rose Bowl; Pittsburgh (1942–46), and Maryland (1947). Coached the professional Washington Redskins (1946) and Los Angeles Rams (1947–51) and was a technical adviser and vice president for the Chicago Bears. Most of his success was predicated on the use of the T formation.

SHAW, ALBERT (*b. present Shandon, Ohio, 1857; d. New York, N.Y., 1947*), journalist, reformer. B.A., Iowa (now Grinnel) College, 1879; Ph.D., Johns Hopkins University, 1884. Editorial writer, *Minneapolis Tribune*, 1884–91. Editor and publisher, *Review of Reviews*, 1892–1937.

SHAW, ANNA HOWARD (*b. Newcastle-upon-Tyne, England, 1847; d. Moylan, Pa., 1919*), physician, Methodist minister, woman suffrage and temperance reformer. Friend and associate of Susan B. Anthony, Shaw was a practiced orator and able publicist; she was president, National American Woman Suffrage Association, 1904–15.

SHAW, EDWARD RICHARD (*b. Bellport, N.Y., 1850; d. 1903*), educator. Graduated Lafayette College, 1881; Ph.D., New York University, 1890. Helped found pioneer school of education at New York University, 1890; served it as dean, 1894–1901.

SHAW, ELIJAH (*b. Kensington, N.H., 1793; d. 1851*), pioneer minister of the Christian Connection. An editor of the *Christian Journal*.

SHAW, HENRY (*b. Sheffield, England, 1800; d. St. Louis, Mo., 1889*), merchant. Succeeded in business in St. Louis, 1819–40. Advised by Asa Gray, George Englemann, and others, he established a garden for the scientific study of plants at St. Louis, 1857–60. Opened to the public, 1860, it was endowed by its founder as the Missouri Botanical Garden and continues to hold high rank among world botanical institutions.

SHAW, HENRY WHEELER (*b. Lanesboro, Mass., 1818; d. Monterey, Calif., 1885*), humorist. Better known by pseudonym "Josh Billings." Author of hundreds of once-popular bucolic aphorisms phrased in grotesque misspellings, Shaw was author of *Josh Billings, His Sayings* (1865) and a number of similar collections. His best work is in *Josh Billings' Farmer's Allminax,* published yearly from 1869 until 1880.

SHAW, HOWARD VAN DOREN (*b. Chicago, Ill., 1869; d. Baltimore, Md., 1926*), architect. Graduated Yale, 1890. Studied architecture at Massachusetts Institute of Technology and worked in office of William LeB. Jenney. Worked in a highly personal style, largely in the Middle West, where he became probably the best regarded practitioner of domestic and noncommercial architecture.

SHAW, JOHN (*b. Mountmellick, Ireland, 1773; d. Philadelphia, Pa., 1823*), naval officer, merchant mariner. Made brilliant record in command of schooner *Enterprise,* 1799–1800, as destroyer of French privateers. Prepared naval force in lower Mississippi to frustrate Aaron Burr's intrigues, 1807; after mainly shore service in the War of 1812, commanded the squadron stationed off Algiers to protect American interests, 1815–17.

SHAW, JOHN (*b. Annapolis, Md., 1778; d. at sea, 1809*), physician, naval surgeon, poet.

SHAW, LEMUEL (*b. Barnstable, Mass., 1781; d. 1861*), Massachusetts legislator and jurist. Father-in-law of Herman Melville. Graduated Harvard, 1800; studied law in Boston under David Everett. Practicing in Boston *post ca.* 1804, he became known as an adviser in important commercial enterprises; he drew up the first charter of the city, 1822. As chief justice of Massachusetts, 1830–60, he made much law on such matters as waterpower, railroads, and other public utilities; probably no other state judge has so deeply influenced commercial and constitutional law throughout the United States. The strength of his opinions lay in the entire solidity of their reasoning. Thorough and systematic, he had a remarkable ability to charge juries so that they understood the exact questions at issue before them.

SHAW, LESLIE MORTIER (*b. Morristown, Vt., 1848; d. Washington, D.C., 1932*), banker. Removed to eastern Iowa, 1869. Republican governor of Iowa, 1898–1902. Shaw's championing of the gold standard during the campaign of 1896 and his services as permanent chairman of the International Monetary Convention, 1898, led to his appointment as U.S. secretary of the treasury in 1902. He resorted to unprecedented expedients for dealing with stringency of credit, such as liberalizing security and waiving reserve requirements for government bank deposits, artificially stimulating gold importation, and regulating note issues by executive decree. A firm believer in high tariff protection and domestic laissez-faire, he retained office until 1907, despite President Theodore Roosevelt's uneasiness about him.

SHAW, MARY (*b. Boston, Mass., 1854; d. New York, N.Y., 1929*), actress. Made debut with Boston Museum Stock Co., 1879–80. A hardworking intellectual performer, she played ably in support of Helena Modjeska, Julia Marlowe, and other stars, but rarely won commercial success in her own vehicles. Among her own productions were Ibsen's *Ghosts* (produced, 1899 and later) and G. B. Shaw's *Mrs. Warren's Profession,* in which she appeared in New York, October 1905 and on later occasions.

SHAW, NATHANIEL (*b. New London, Conn., 1735; d. New London, 1782*), merchant, Revolutionary patriot. Naval agent for Connecticut, and agent and prize master for the Continental Congress *post* 1775.

SHAW, OLIVER (*b. Middleboro, Mass., 1779; d. Providence, R.I., 1848*), musician, composer. Organist of the First Congregational Church at Providence *post* 1807, he composed sacred music anticipatory of the work of Lowell Mason, but was equally important for his teaching and interest in the betterment of church music. His best known hymn tunes were "Taunton," "Bristol," and "Weybosset."

SHAW, PAULINE AGASSIZ (*b. Neuchâtel, Switzerland, 1841; d. 1917*), philanthropist, educational and social pioneer. Daughter of J. L. R. Agassiz. Gave early support to Boston kindergartens, to the manual-training movement during its experimental period, and to the Vocation Bureau of Boston for its pioneer work in vocational guidance, 1908–17.

SHAW, SAMUEL (*b. Boston, Mass., 1754; d. near Cape of Good Hope, 1794*), Revolutionary officer, merchant. Served with distinction in the Revolution as an artilleryman, for most of the war acting as aide-de-camp to General Henry Knox. Supercargo on the *Empress of China,* first American vessel to Canton, 1784–85, he served as first U.S. consul to China *post* 1786.

SHAW, THOMAS (*b. Philadelphia, Pa., 1838; d. Hammonton, N.J., 1901*), machinist, inventor. Patented almost 200 devices, including gas meters, pressure gauges, hydraulic pumps, engine governors, and iron and steel processes; among these, his spring-lock nut washer, 1868; his pile driver, 1868, 1870; and the Shaw gas tester, 1886–90, were outstanding.

SHAW, (WARREN) WILBUR (*b. Shelbyville, Ind., 1902; d. near Peterson, Ind., 1954*), automobile racer. Won the Indianapolis 500 in 1937, 1939, and 1940; national champion, 1937, 1939. President and general manager of the Indianapolis Speedway after the track was reopened after World War II. Killed in plane crash.

SHAW, WILLIAM SMITH (*b. Haverhill, Mass., 1778; d. Boston, Mass., 1826*), lawyer. Nephew of Abigail Adams. Helped found the Anthology Society, 1805; built up collections of the Boston Athenaeum as librarian, 1807–22.

SHAYS, DANIEL (*b. probably Hopkinton, Mass., ca. 1747; d. Sparta, N.Y., 1825*), Revolutionary soldier, insurgent. A brave and popular officer of the 5th Massachusetts Regiment, he resigned from the army, 1780, and settled in Pelham, Mass., being subsequently elected to various town offices. The acute economic depression which soon followed the peace of 1783 created grievances throughout the rural districts, particularly with reference to foreclosure for debt. On the failure of the legislature to help, the people of western Massachusetts resorted to force to compel legislative action, and Shays's prominence in this movement has caused his name to be given to the whole uprising. On Aug. 29, 1786, the insurgents prevented the sitting of the courts of common pleas and general sessions; the leaders, then fearing that indictments would be brought against them, moved to prevent the sitting of the supreme court at Springfield on Sept. 26. Militiamen under General William Shepard defended the court. A committee of which Shays was chairman drew up resolutions that the court should be allowed to sit, provided it dealt with no case involving indictments concerning insurgents or debts; on agreement, both the militia and the insurgents disbanded and court adjourned. The legislature of Massachusetts continuing to give offense, the insurgents rose again in January 1787 and moved against the arsenal at Springfield but were defeated by state troops under General Benjamin Lincoln. Pursuing the insurgents westward, Lincoln caught up with Shays's men at Petersham on the night of Feb. 2, 1787, and completely routed them. Shays fled to Vermont. At first condemned to death, he was pardoned in June 1788 and some time afterward removed to New York State. A man of little education and not much ability, he was honest and firmly convinced of the justice of his cause.

SHEA, JOHN DAWSON GILMARY (*b. New York, N.Y., 1824; d. Elizabeth, N.J., 1892*), historian, editor. Graduated Columbia Grammar School, 1837; was a Jesuit novice, 1848–52. Dedicating his life to the writing of American Catholic history, he received few material rewards for work of outstanding ability which won him many scholarly honors. Among his books of permanent value were *Discovery and Exploration of the Mississippi Valley* (1852), *History of the Catholic Missions Among the Indian Tribes of the United States* (1854) and the monumental *History of the Catholic Church in the United States* (1886–92); he was also editor of a number of works on Indian linguistics, of many additional Jesuit relations, and of an English translation of Charlevoix's *History and General Description of New France* (1866–72).

SHEAN, ALBERT (*b. Dornum, near Hannover, Germany, 1868; d. New York, N.Y., 1949*), actor. Stage name of Albert Schoenberg. Uncle of the Marx Brothers. Came to United States with parents *ca.* 1876. Burlesque and vaudeville comedian *post* 1884; teamed with Ed Gallagher and famous act of "Gallagher and Shean," 1910–14 and 1920–25, scoring greatest success in the second of these partnerships. Subsequent to the breakup of the team, Shean developed a solid reputation on stage and in films as an able and sensitive character actor.

SHEAR, THEODORE LESLIE (*b. New London, N.H., 1880; d. Newbury, N.H., 1945*), classical archaeologist. B.A., New York University, 1900; M.A., 1903; Ph.D., Johns Hopkins University, 1904. Studied also at American School of Classical Studies at Athens, and at University of Bonn. Taught Greek and Latin at Barnard College, 1906–10; moved to Columbia University as associate in classical philology, 1910, and thereafter spent much of his time in archaeological excavation. Appointed lecturer in the Department of Art and Archaeology at Princeton, 1920, he became professor of classical archaeology in 1928. He is especially remembered for his direction of large-scale excavations on various sites in ancient Greece, notably at Sardis, Corinth, and the Athenian Agora.

SHEARMAN, THOMAS GASKELL (*b. Birmingham, England, 1834; d. Brooklyn, N.Y., 1900*), lawyer, economist. Came to America as a boy. Employed by David D. Field to work with him on the civil code, 1860, Shearman became a partner of Field, 1868, and served as immediate legal adviser to James Fisk and Jay Gould during the Erie Railroad "war." Withdrawing from the partnership, 1873, Shearman continued to act as counsel for Gould and ably defended Henry Ward Beecher during his famous trial. Shearman was also counsel for a number of banks and railroads and for James J. Hill. By nature a reformer, he continued Field's work in pressing for codification of the law, argued for free trade, and in 1887 suggested the name "single tax" as definition of the measures proposed by Henry George, to which he had become a convert. He was author of *Natural Taxation* (1895).

SHECUT, JOHN LINNAEUS EDWARD WHITRIDGE (*b. Beaufort, S.C., 1770; d. 1836*), physician, botanist, novelist. Practiced in Charleston, S.C., *post ca.* 1790; studied medicine under David Ramsay.

SHEDD, FRED FULLER (*b. New Boston, N.H., 1871; d. Southern Pines, N.C., 1937*), journalist. After early editorial training on the *Haverhill* (*Mass.*) *Evening Gazette* and the *Boston Herald*, he served on the staff of the *Philadelphia Bulletin*, *post* 1911, and was its editor in chief, 1921–37.

SHEDD, JOEL HERBERT (*b. Pepperell, Mass., 1834; d. Providence, R.I., 1915*), hydraulic and sanitary engineer, inventor.

SHEDD, JOHN GRAVES (*b. near Alstead, N.H., 1850; d. Chicago, Ill., 1926*), merchant, philanthropist. Removed to Chicago, 1872, to enter employ of Field, Leiter & Co. as salesman. Rising rapidly in the firm, he became a partner of Marshall Field & Co., 1893, and served as its president, 1906–22.

SHEDD, WILLIAM AMBROSE (*b. Mount Seir, Persia, 1865; d. Sain Kala, Persia, 1918*), Presbyterian clergyman. The son of missionary parents, Shedd graduated from Marietta College, 1887, and from Princeton Theological Seminary, 1892. Serving thereafter as a missionary in Persia, he was active in relief work there during World War I.

SHEDD, WILLIAM GREENOUGH THAYER (*b. Acton, Mass., 1820; d. New York, N.Y., 1894*), Congregational and Presbyterian theologian. Graduated University of Vermont, 1839; Andover Theological Seminary, 1843. A professor at Union Theological Seminary, New York City, 1862–93, he was author of *Dogmatic Theology* (1888, 1894), a cogent defense of conservative Calvinism, and of a number of other books.

SHEEDY, DENNIS (*b. Ireland, 1846; d. Denver, Colo., 1923*), cattleman, merchant, capitalist. Came to America as an infant; removed to Lyons, Iowa, 1858. Active as a trader, miner, and freighter throughout the West, he was a rancher in Nevada, Texas, Nebraska, and Colorado, 1870–84. Foreseeing the end of the free range, he sold out his cattle interests and engaged in banking, smelting, and other activities in Colorado.

SHEELER, CHARLES R., JR. (*b. Philadelphia, Pa., 1883; d. Dobbs Ferry, N.Y., 1965*), artist and photographer. Trained at the Philadelphia School of Industrial Art (1900–03) and Pennsylvania Academy (1903–06). Six of his works were chosen for the 1913 Armory Show in New York, and one-man shows of his work were held at various galleries in the 1920's. A commercial photographer since 1912, he specialized in architecture during 1923–32. He was commissioned by Ford Motor Company to photograph their River Rouge Plant (1927) and his "portraits of machinery" further established his reputation. *Fortune* magazine commissioned six canvases on the theme of "Power" (1939–40). Was photographer-in-residence at the Metropolitan Museum of Art, 1942–55; during the 1950's he used his camera to interpret the architecture of Rockefeller Center and the United Nations.

SHEFFIELD, DEVELLO ZELOTES (*b. Gainesville, N.Y., 1841; d. Peitaiho, North China, 1913*), Union soldier, Presbyterian clergyman. Missionary to China, *post* 1869, he was active in educational work and in the translation of the Bible into classical Chinese.

SHEFFIELD, JOSEPH EARL (*b. Southport, Conn., 1793; d. New Haven, Conn., 1882*), merchant, financier, philanthropist. Successful as a dry-goods and naval stores merchant in New Bern, N.C., and as a cotton exporter in Mobile, Ala., 1813–35, he entered the fields of canal and railroad finance, in which he was equally successful. He was a principal benefactor of the scientific department of Yale. Given separate status in 1854, it was renamed Sheffield Scientific School in his honor, 1861.

SHEIL, BERNARD JAMES (*b. Chicago, Ill., 1886; d. Tucson, Ariz., 1969*), Roman Catholic bishop. Attended St. Viator's College and Seminary; ordained in 1910. After serving at Chicago's Holy Name Cathedral, he was named curate at St. Mel's in that city. Joined the staff of the chancery office (1923) and rose rapidly in the administration of the Chicago archdiocese. In 1924 he was consecrated an auxiliary bishop and titular bishop of Pege and was named vicar general of the archdiocese in 1928. Became a leader in liberal Catholic social action and supported non-Communist labor organizers in the 1930's. Served as pastor of St. Andrew's parish in Chicago, 1935–66; appointed titular archbishop of Selge (1959).

SHELBY, EVAN (*b. Tregaron, Wales, 1719; d. 1794*), frontier soldier, trader, landowner. Father of Isaac Shelby. Immigrating to America *ca.* 1734, he resided in Franklin Co., Pa., and, *post* 1739, in western Maryland. An officer of rangers in the French and Indian War, he was particularly distinguished in the Forbes campaign against Fort Duquesne, 1758. Removing to southwestern Virginia *ca.* 1773, he commanded the Fincastle Co. in Dunmore's War and at the close of the battle of Point Pleasant, October 1774, held the chief field command. Engaged against the Indians during the Revolution, he served later in the North Carolina legislature and was militia brigadier general of the Washington District of that state. He negotiated a truce with John Sevier in the troubles over the insurgent "State of Franklin," March 1787, and later declined the governorship of Franklin. Strong, blunt, fearless, and noted for truth-telling, he was prompt to act aggressively in any enterprise in which he engaged.

SHELBY, ISAAC (*b. near North Mountain, present Washington Co., Md., 1750; d. Kentucky, 1826*), soldier. Son of Evan Shelby. Removing to the Holston region of southwestern Virginia *ca.* 1773, he served under his father as a lieutenant in Dunmore's War, and in 1775 visited Kentucky as a surveyor for the Transylvania Co. During the Revolution he acted as commissary of supplies for militia detailed to frontier posts and also for the Continental army in its western field operations. A member of the Virginia legislature, colonel of the militia of Sullivan Co., N.C., and activist in patenting Kentucky lands, he joined Charles McDowell in operations against Tory forces in the South Carolina backcountry, 1780. He played a prominent part at King's Mountain and at Cowpens. After further military activity in 1781 and subsequent service in the North Carolina legislature, he removed to Kentucky, 1783, where he took part in achieving independence and statehood and was in 1792 a member of the convention which drafted the first Kentucky constitution. As first governor of Kentucky, 1792–96, he guided the state through a difficult formative period, holding it fast to the Union, despite contrary schemes and conspiracies. Retiring to private life, he emerged as governor again in 1812 and prosecuted vigorously the war against Great Britain. He led in person the Kentucky volunteers in W. H. Harrison's invasion of Canada, which resulted in British defeat at the battle of the Thames, October 1813. Offered the secretaryship of war by President Monroe in March 1817, he declined because of age. A man of great physical hardiness, Shelby was also an able executive and a wise judge and handler of men.

SHELBY, JOSEPH ORVILLE (*b. Lexington, Ky., 1830; d. Adrian, Mo., 1897*), Confederate soldier. Settled in Missouri, 1852, where he engaged in business. Commissioned a Confederate captain, 1861, he rose to the rank of brigadier general in the course of the Civil War, mainly operating as a cavalry leader in Arkansas and Missouri under General Sterling Price. Renowned for personal courage and mastery of cavalry tactics, he led his men into Mexico, July 1865, where their offer to assist Maximilian was rejected. He later returned to Missouri.

SHELDON, CHARLES MONROE (*b. Wellsville, N.Y., 1857; d. Topeka, Kans., 1946*), Congregational clergyman, author. Graduated Brown University, 1883; B.D., Andover Theological Seminary, 1886. Principal ministry at Central Congregational Church, Topeka, Kans., 1889–1919. Author of many inspirational works and editor in chief of the *Christian Herald*, 1920–25, he is remembered as the writer of *In His Steps* (1897), a novel that ranks among the all-time best-sellers.

SHELDON, EDWARD AUSTIN (*b. near Perry Center, N.Y., 1823; d. 1897*), educator, school superintendent in Oswego and Syracuse, N.Y. An advocate of free public schools, Sheldon was responsible for opening the Oswego Primary Teachers' Training School, the first city school of its kind in the United States, May 1861. He served it most successfully as principal, 1862–97.

SHELDON, EDWARD STEVENS (*b. Waterville, Maine, 1851; d. Cambridge, Mass., 1925*), philologist, lexicographer. Brother of Henry N. Sheldon. A specialist in Romance philology, in which he held a chair at Harvard, 1894–1921.

SHELDON, HENRY NEWTON (*b. Waterville, Maine, 1843; d. 1926*), jurist. Brother of Edward S. Sheldon. Judge of Massachusetts Superior Court, 1894–1905; of Massachusetts Supreme Judicial Court, 1905–15. Noted for legal scholarship and good judgment.

SHELDON, MARY DOWNING. See BARNES, MARY DOWNING SHELDON.

SHELDON, WALTER LORENZO (*b. West Rutland, Vt., 1858; d. 1907*), Ethical Culture leader in St. Louis, Mo., *post* 1886.

SHELDON, WILLIAM EVARTS (*b. Dorset, Vt., 1832; d. 1900*), educator, leader in progressive educational movements. Principal of several public high schools in Massachusetts, Sheldon was president of the National Education Association, 1887.

SHELEKHOV, GRIGORIĬ IVANOVICH (*b. Rylsk, Russia, 1747; d. Irkutsk, Siberia, 1795*), Russian merchant, fur trader. Father-in-law of N. P. Rezanov. Founded first Russian colony in America, on Kodiak Island, 1784; helped establish Russian dominion over Alaska.

SHELLABARGER, SAMUEL (*b. Washington, D.C., 1888; d. Princeton, N.J., 1954*), novelist, biographer, and educator. Studied at Princeton (B.A., 1909) and Harvard (Ph.D., 1917). Taught at Princeton (1919–23; 1927–29). Essentially a Victorian novelist, Shellabarger's early works were critically successful, but failed commercially. He wrote several mysteries under the pseudonym John Esteven. From 1938 to 1946, he was the headmaster of the Columbus (Ohio) School for Girls. While there, he published more novels under the name Peter Loring. Best remembered for the best-selling novels *Captain from Castile* (1945), *Prince of Foxes* (1947), *The King's Cavalier* (1950), and *Lord Vanity* (1953).

SHELTON, ALBERT LEROY (*b. Indianapolis, Ind., 1875; d. near Batang, China, 1922*), Disciples of Christ clergyman. Medical missionary in western China and Tibet, 1903–22.

SHELTON, EDWARD MASON (*b. Huntingdonshire, England, 1846; d. Seattle, Wash., 1928*), agriculturist. Came to America as a boy. Graduated Michigan Agricultural College, 1871. Professor of agriculture, Kansas State Agricultural College, 1874–90; government agricultural adviser in Australia, 1890–99; thereafter practiced horticulture in the state of Washington.

SHELTON, FREDERICK WILLIAM (*b. Jamaica, N.Y., 1815; d. 1881*), Episcopal clergyman. A rector for many years in New York State and Vermont, Shelton was author of, among other books, *The Trollopiad* (1837), a satire in verse, and of a number of sketches in the style of Washington Irving which he contributed to the *Knickerbocker* magazine, 1838–45.

SHEPARD, CHARLES UPHAM (*b. Little Compton, R.I., 1804; d. 1886*), mineralogist. Lecturer in science at Yale, South Carolina Medical College, and Amherst. His important collection of minerals and meteorites was acquired by Amherst.

SHEPARD, EDWARD MORSE (*b. New York, N.Y., 1850; d. Lake George, N.Y., 1911*), lawyer, political reformer. Ward of Abram S. Hewitt. Graduated College of the City of New York, 1869. Outstanding as counsel to the New York Rapid Transit Commission and to the Pennsylvania Railroad, Shepard devoted much of his time to reform of the New York Democratic organization from within, to the advocacy of civil service reform, and to the improvement of City College.

SHEPARD, FRED DOUGLAS (*b. Ellenburg, N.Y., 1855; d. Turkey, 1915*), physician, medical missionary to Turkey *post* 1882. An outstanding teacher and practitioner of medicine, Shepard died while combating an epidemic of typhus at Aintab.

SHEPARD, JAMES EDWARD (*b. Raleigh, N.C., 1875; d. Durham, N.C., 1947*), educator. Graduated in pharmacy, Shaw University, 1894. Engaged in various business and civic activities before service as field superintendent, International Sunday School Association, 1905–10. In 1910 he founded the National Religious Training School and Chautauqua to provide short, adult education courses for black ministers and teachers. This school, which he served as president until his death, was successively accredited as a state normal school, 1923, as the first state-supported liberal arts college for blacks, 1925, and is presently North Carolina Central University.

SHEPARD, JAMES HENRY (*b. Lyons, Mich., 1850; d. St. Petersburg, Fla., 1918*), chemist. B.S., University of Michigan, 1875, where he also did graduate work. Taught at South Dakota State College of Agriculture and was also director of its experiment station; won international reputation for researches on bleached flour and food adulterants.

SHEPARD, JESSE. *See* GRIERSON, FRANCIS.

SHEPARD, SETH (*b. Brenham, Tex., 1847; d. 1917*), jurist. Long active in Texas Democratic politics, he was appointed justice of the court of appeals of the District of Columbia, 1893, and served until 1917; he was chief justice *post* 1905.

SHEPARD, THOMAS (*b. Towcester, England, 1605; d. Cambridge, Mass., 1649*), New England theologian. A graduate of Emmanuel College, Cambridge, England, Shepard was silenced for nonconformity by Archbishop Laud, 1630. Removing to Boston, Mass., October 1635, he became pastor at Newtown (Cambridge). An orthodox Calvinist, he was active in the 1637 condemnation of the Antinomians; he defined Congregationalism as a middle ground between Brownism and Presbyterian polity. Concerned with education, he proposed a plan for the support of poor students; he also projected a plan of church government which was finally realized in the synod of 1647. A tireless preacher and writer, he was author of a number of tracts and books, including *These Sabbaticae* (1649) and the very popular *The Sincere Convert* (1641). His diary was first published in *Three Valuable Pieces* (1747) and issued as his *Autobiography* in 1832.

SHEPARD, WILLIAM (*b. Westfield, Mass., 1737; d. Westfield, 1817*), Revolutionary officer. Colonel of the 3rd Continental Infantry, he distinguished himself at the battle of Pell's Point, 1776. As major general of Massachusetts militia, 1786–87, he played an important part in the defense of Springfield against the insurgents during Shays's Rebellion. He served as congressman, Federalist, from Massachusetts, 1797–1803.

SHEPHERD, ALEXANDER ROBEY (*b. Washington, D.C., 1835; d. Batopilas, Mexico, 1902*), builder, politician, mine owner. As "boss" of District of Columbia and its territorial governor, 1873–74, he was largely responsible for the improvement of the capital city, although his financial recklessness and unscrupulous methods led to a congressional investigation and a change in the District's type of government.

SHEPHERD, WILLIAM ROBERT (*b. Charleston, S.C., 1871; d. Berlin, Germany, 1934*), historian. Graduated Columbia, 1893; Ph.D., 1896. Taught at Columbia all his life, becoming Seth Low professor of history, 1926. An expert in Latin American history and affairs, he was author of, among other books, *Historical Atlas* (1911) and *Atlas of Medieval and Modern History* (1932).

SHEPLEY, ETHER (*b. Groton, Mass., 1789; d. 1877*), Maine lawyer and jurist. U.S. senator, Democrat, from Maine, 1833–36, Shepley was a vigorous supporter of Andrew Jackson. Appointed judge of the Maine Supreme Court, 1836, he became chief justice, 1848, and retired at the close of 1855.

SHEPLEY, GEORGE FOSTER (*b. Saco, Maine, 1819; d. 1878*), lawyer. Son of Ether Shepley. Practiced in Bangor and Portland, Maine; was U.S. attorney for Maine, 1848–49 and 1853–61. Colonel commanding the 12th Maine Volunteers, Shepley became military commandant at New Orleans, La., May 1862, and in the next month was promoted brigadier general and made governor of Louisiana. An associate of Benjamin F. Butler (1818–93), he shares with him the responsibility for whatever dishonesty there may have been in the army administration of New Orleans. Assigned to command in eastern Virginia, May 1864, he became military governor of Richmond after the fall of that city. *Post* 1869, he was circuit judge of the U.S. court in Maine.

SHEPPARD, JOHN MORRIS (*b. near Wheatville, Tex., 1875; d. Washington, D.C., 1941*), lawyer, politician. B.A., University of Texas, 1895; LL.B., 1897; Master of Laws, Yale, 1898. Elected to fill his father's unexpired term as a member of Congress, 1902, he was a progressive Democrat in matters of policy and an able critic of the Republican party. Chosen to succeed J. W. Bailey in the U.S. Senate, 1913, he served until his death. Although he was an ardent supporter of President Woodrow Wilson's liberal program, he became best known as the author of the 18th (Prohibition) Amendment, which he continued to advocate after its repeal. He was Senate sponsor of the 1921 Sheppard-Towner Act, providing federal aid for maternal and infant health care, and a consistent favorer of help for farmers during the 1920's. A backer of most New Deal legislation, he himself sponsored the Federal Credit Union Act of 1934. He was the active and effective chairman of the Senate Committee on Military Affairs at the time of his death.

SHEPPARD, SAMUEL EDWARD (*b. Hither Green, Kent, England, 1882; d. Rochester, N.Y., 1948*), chemist. B.Sc., University College, London, 1903; D.Sc., 1906. Worked with Charles E. K. Mees in research in photographic processes; was coauthor with Mees of *Investigations on the Theory of the Photographic Process* (1907). With the aid of an 1851 Exhibition Scholarship, Sheppard continued his research in photochemistry at Marburg University in Germany and at the Sorbonne in Paris. At both institutions he studied the sensitizing action of dyes. He was the first to apply spectrophotometry to differentiating true and colloidal solutions. In 1910 he joined the photographic manufacturing firm of Wratten and Wainwright in Croydon, Surrey. Two years later he entered the School of Agriculture at Cambridge University in pursuit of an earlier interest in agricultural chemistry. The following year Sheppard joined the new Kodak Research Laboratory at Rochester, N.Y., as a colloid and physical chemist. He was to remain with the Kodak Laboratory until his retirement in 1948.

Sheppard's work can be grouped into nonphotographic and photographic categories. In the former, one of his notable contributions was the development of colloidal fuels during World War I. In 1921 he turned his attention to the electroplating of rubber and rubber compounds; his patents and processes were consolidated with those of others in the American Anode Co. Sheppard also developed concepts on the relationship between chemical constitution and colloidal behavior. In the photographic field he was responsible for elucidating the theory of the photographic process. In his first five years at the Kodak Laboratory, he was mainly concerned with the physicochemical properties of gelatin, the medium that contains the sensitive materials in photography. His research on the factors determining photographic sensitivity in silver halide–gelatin "emulsions" won him immediate recognition. Sheppard's later research dealt with a wide range of matters, including photovoltaic effects (the electrical response of silver halide to light), the physicochemical properties of film supports, the nature of development and of dye sensitizing, and absorption of dyes to crystals and their absorption spectra in relation to the resonance structure of the dyes. Alone or with coauthors he published nearly 200 scientific papers and nine books, beginning with *Photo-Chemistry* (1914), and took out more than 60 patents.

SHERIDAN, PHILIP HENRY (*b. Albany, N.Y., 1831; d. Nonquitt, Mass., 1888*), Union soldier. Raised in Somerset, Ohio, Sheridan graduated from West Point with the class of 1853. Assigned to the infantry, he served on frontier duty along the Rio Grande and in the Northwest. Promoted captain, he began Civil War service in the quartermaster department and was on H. W. Halleck's staff. Appointed colonel of the 2nd Michigan Cavalry, May 1862, he was raised to brigadier general in a little over a month for his victory at Booneville, Mo. His subsequent career was brilliant. Commanding infantry, he was successful at Perryville; at Stone River he practically saved the army of Rosecrans, for which he was made major general of volunteers, December 1862. Distinguished also at Chickamauga and at Missionary Ridge, he rose to high favor with U. S. Grant, who gave Sheridan command of all the cavalry of the Army of the Potomac. His brilliant and decisive raids on Confederate communications around Richmond in May 1864 caused great alarm and apprehension in the Confederate capital. In August, as commander of the Army of the Shenandoah, he effectively carried out Grant's orders to destroy all supplies in the valley. His army was surprised and almost routed at Cedar Creek on Oct. 9, while he was 20 miles away at Winchester, but he made his famous ride to the battlefield in time to rally his troops and to snatch victory from defeat. He was promoted to major general in the regular service, November 1864. Early in 1865 he severed Lee's communications with the South, turned the flank of the Confederate army, and forced Lee to begin the retreat to Appomattox. In the final operations of the war, Sheridan's troops cut off Lee from any further withdrawal and the Confederate surrender followed.

Sheridan administered the military division of the Gulf *post* 1865, and in 1867 was appointed military governor of Louisiana and Texas. His severely repressive measures in the interests of Reconstruction, though supported by Grant, incurred the disapproval of President Andrew Johnson. Transferred to the department of the Missouri, Sheridan compelled the hostile Plains Indians to settle upon their reservations. Promoted lieutenant general, March 1869, he commanded the division of the Missouri; in 1870–71 he visited the German armies during the Franco-Prussian War. Succeeding W. T. Sherman as commander in chief of the army, 1884, he received the highest military rank, that of general, on June 1, 1888. A few days before his death, he completed his *Personal Memoirs* (1888). Sheridan was a short man

of unprepossessing bearing, but endowed with a magnetic personality and a sincere concern for the welfare of his troops. Cool and self-possessed in battle, he was a dashing and brilliant leader of men, who acted according to two rules: to take the offensive whenever possible, and to wring the last possible advantage from a defeated army.

SHERMAN, FORREST PERCIVAL (*b. Merrimack, N.H., 1896; d. Naples, Italy, 1951*), naval officer. Graduated from the U.S. Naval Academy, 1917. A naval aviator, Sherman became captain of the carrier *Wasp* in 1942; the ship was sunk by the Japanese in the Pacific in 1942. Sherman then became chief of staff to Admiral John Towers in 1942; in 1943, head of the staff for the War Plans Division for Admiral Nimitz, commander in chief of the Pacific Fleet. As such, Sherman had "perhaps more influence on the strategy of [the Pacific] theater and its overall direction than any other air admiral." After the war, he commanded the Sixth Task Fleet in the Mediterranean. In 1949, he became chief of naval operations with the rank of full admiral.

SHERMAN, FRANK DEMPSTER (*b. Peekskill, N.Y., 1860; d. New York, N.Y., 1916*), poet, architect, mathematician, genealogist.

SHERMAN, FREDERICK CARL (*b. Port Huron, Mich., 1888; d. San Diego, Calif., 1957*), naval officer. Studied at the U.S. Naval Academy; commissioned in 1912. Through World War I Sherman had submarine and destroyer assignments. In 1936 he became a naval aviator. At the outbreak of World War II he was commander of the carrier *Lexington*, which saw battle at Rabaul, New Guinea, and the Battle of the Coral Sea in 1942. As commander of the Carrier Division 2 on board the *Enterprise*, Sherman saw action in the Solomon Islands; as commander of Division I, he saw action in the battles of Leyte Gulf, the Philippines, Iwo Jima, and Okinawa. He retired from the navy in 1947 with the rank of full admiral. Considered one of the ablest of commanders in World War II, Sherman contributed greatly to the concept of naval air tactics.

SHERMAN, HENRY CLAPP (*b. Ash Grove, Va., 1875; d. Rensselaer, N.Y., 1955*), food chemist. Studied at Maryland Agricultural College and at Columbia University (Ph.D., 1897). Taught at Columbia from 1899 to 1946. His research concerned the properties, activities, and purification of the digestive enzymes; the efficiency of proteins in the human diet; the protein requirements of man; the vitamin requirements of man; and man's need for calcium. His work on Vitamin D brought discovery of ways to induce and control rickets. President of the American Institute of Nutrition (1931–33, 1943–44); president of the American Society of Biological Chemists (1926). Wrote *Chemistry of Food and Nutrition* in 1911.

SHERMAN, JAMES SCHOOLCRAFT (*b. Utica, N.Y., 1855; d. 1912*), lawyer, businessman, politician, vice president of the United States. Congressman, Republican, from New York, 1887–91 and 1893–1909. A "regular," Sherman was not identified with important measures, preferring to give his time to parliamentary management, in which he was gifted. He was regarded as second only to Thomas B. Reed as presiding officer in the House. He served as U.S. vice president, 1909–12.

SHERMAN, JOHN (*b. Dedham, England, 1613; d 1685*), Puritan clergyman, mathematician. Immigrated to Massachusetts Bay, 1634. Renowned as a preacher, he ministered at Watertown, Mass., and at Wethersfield and other Connecticut settlements. Appointed pastor at Watertown, 1647, he remained in that post for the rest of his life. He was an occasional lecturer on mathematics at Harvard and held many honorary positions at the college.

SHERMAN, JOHN   (*b. Lancaster, Ohio, 1823; d. 1900*), statesman. Brother of William T. Sherman. Admitted to the bar, 1844, Sherman entered politics as a Whig and later became a hard-driving, effective worker for the rising Republican party. Elected to Congress from Ohio, 1854, he served in the House until 1861 when he became U.S. senator. Leaving the Senate in 1877, he was U.S. secretary of the treasury until 1881, when he regained his Senate seat and occupied it until 1897.

Sherman's moderate utterances on slavery and his party loyalty in Congress aided his rise to the chairmanship of the House Ways and Means Committee, 1859. As a senator, he served with realistic ability on the Finance Committee, becoming its chairman in 1867. Balked in his natural caution and conservatism by wartime necessity, he helped to give greenbacks the status of legal tender, but led in planning the national banking system, 1863, and advocated unsuccessfully a program of economy and rigorous taxation. Although favoring personally a moderate Reconstruction policy, his substitute for Thad Stevens' drastic military Reconstruction plan was hardly less rigorous. He voted for most of the Radical program, and although expressing sympathy for President Johnson, he voted to convict him. After the war, he dominated national financial policy. Privately opposed to the strong tide of inflationist sentiment, he was swayed by it. Thus, while seeing in the cancellation of greenbacks the most direct route to specie resumption, he opposed McCulloch's currency contraction policies of 1866–68. He believed that resumption was necessary to safeguard the national credit, but felt that it must be undertaken when political conditions permitted. His work on the Funding Act of 1870 reduced the burden of public interest and helped restore national credit. In 1873 he was largely responsible for the mint-reform bill which ended the coinage of silver dollars and was denounced as the chief agent of the "Crime of '73." Two years later he yielded his own excellent resumption plan for funding greenbacks in favor of the substitute scheme of George F. Edmunds.

Sherman's preeminence in financial matters caused President Hayes to appoint him secretary of the treasury in 1877. Ignoring the inflationist outcry, he strengthened the resumption act by declaring that he was empowered to issue bonds after, as well as before, resumption. He also convinced the bankers that the government would redeem its bonds in gold, thereby enhancing national prestige. The political difficulties of Hayes's administration, a depression, and the clamor for "free silver," all made it hard for him to attain his main purposes—the resumption of specie payments and the funding of the public debt. Humiliated by a congressional resolution declaring government bonds payable in silver, he was able to take advantage of divisions among the inflationists to defeat their extreme objectives. The Bland-Allison Act of 1878 stipulated only the limited coinage of silver, rather than free coinage. Encouraged by some favorable developments in trade, Sherman made his final preparations carefully, so that by Jan. 2, 1879, specie payments were smoothly resumed. As the end of his cabinet service approached, the United States stood firmly on the gold standard and the resumption policy was an admitted success.

In 1880, 1884, and 1888 Sherman sought the Republican presidential nomination, but his lack of popular appeal and strong inflationist opposition militated against him. During his second period of service in the Senate, his most significant contributions were his share in the Antitrust and Silver Purchase acts of 1890. Appointed U.S. secretary of state, 1897, he defended his antiexpansionist views when the cabinet decided for war with Spain, and resigned in protest. Prior to his resignation, he betrayed a growing loss of memory which incapacitated him for much beyond routine operations.

Economically, Sherman's point of view was that of the conservative creditor; politically, he understood very well the radical debtor psychology of his constituents. He carefully studied the attitudes of the Middle West and helped to stamp national legislation with the influence of that section.

SHERMAN, ROGER   (*b. Newton, Mass., 1721 o.s.; d. 1793*), lawyer, merchant, Connecticut colonial legislator and jurist, statesman. Settled in New Milford, Conn., 1743; resided in New Haven, *post* 1761. Serving, in addition to his many other public offices, as judge of the superior court of Connecticut, 1766–89, Sherman belonged to the conservative wing of the Revolutionary party; he was, however one of the first to deny the supremacy of Parliament in American affairs. Active in committee work in the Continental Congress, 1774–81 and 1783–84, he was a member of the committee appointed to draft the Declaration of Independence (which he signed) and of the committee on the Articles of Confederation. Described by John Adams as "an old Puritan, as honest as an angel and as firm in the cause of American Independence as Mount Atlas," Sherman fought attempts to weaken government credit by fiat currency or excessive loans and urged frequent levying of high taxes by Congress and by the states. Perhaps the most influential figure in Congress toward the end of the Revolution, he was hopeful that the Confederation might be strengthened and entered the Constitutional Convention, 1787, still disposed to patch up the old scheme of government. Soon aware of the need for creating a new system, he introduced the "Connecticut Compromise" in June 1787; he also favored an executive dominated by the legislature and made a stand for election of congressmen and senators by the state legislatures. A signer of the Constitution, he took a prominent part in the campaign for its ratification and contributed letters in support of it to the *New Haven Gazette* under the pseudonym "A Countryman," November and December 1787. Elected to Congress, 1789, he opposed amendments to the Constitution, urged use of western lands to extinguish the national debt, favored sale of public lands to settlers rather than speculators, and voted for Hamilton's measure for assumption. He served as U.S. senator from Connecticut, 1791–93. Illustrating at its best the Puritan combination of piety and a desire to succeed in practical affairs, he was honored by contemporaries for his ability and integrity, although his personal awkwardness and rusticity of manner were also remarked.

SHERMAN, STUART PRATT   (*b. Anita, Iowa, 1881; d. near Dunewood, on Lake Michigan, 1926*), literary critic, educator. Graduated Williams, 1903; took Ph.D. at Harvard, 1906, where he was influenced by Irving Babbitt. Taught English at Northwestern University; headed Department of English at University of Illinois, which he made one of the strongest in the Middle West. A frequent contributor to the *Nation*, 1908–18, he was in critical sympathy with its editor, Paul Elmer More. Author of *Matthew Arnold: How to Know Him* (1917), he applied Arnold's principles to the chief contemporary writers in his *On Contemporary Literature* (1917). In his belief that contemporary American writers had gone astray through failure to understand the national ideal, he became a standard-bearer of tradition against the modernist Crocean critics of the early 1920's, but later shifted his position to a greater sympathy with his opponents. *post* 1924, he was editor of the literary supplement of the *New York Herald Tribune*. Among his later books were *Americans* (1922), *Points of View* (1924), and *Critical Woodcuts* (1926).

SHERMAN, THOMAS WEST   (*b. Newport, R.I., 1813; d. Newport, 1879*), soldier. Graduated West Point, 1836. Assigned to the artillery, he served in the campaigns against the Florida Indians and rendered conspicuous service as a battery commander in the

Mexican War. After frontier duty largely in Minnesota and Kansas, he held brigade and division command during the Civil War in the Union army, distinguishing himself particularly in command of land forces at the taking of Port Royal, S.C., and Fernandina, Fla., 1861; also in the expedition against Port Hudson, La., May 1863. He retired as major general, 1871.

SHERMAN, WILLIAM TECUMSEH (*b. Lancaster, Ohio, 1820; d. New York, N.Y., 1891*), Union soldier. Brother of John Sherman (1823–1900). Losing his father as a young boy, Sherman was raised in the family of Thomas Ewing (1789–1871). On graduation from West Point, 1840, he was assigned to the artillery. He spent his leisure time in the study of law and in travel in the South. He saw little active service during the Mexican War, in which he was employed mainly as adjutant to Philip Kearny, Richard B. Mason, and Persifor F. Smith. In May 1850, he married Ellen Ewing, daughter of his guardian. Resigning his army commission, 1853, he was unsuccessful in a banking venture and as a lawyer in Leavenworth, Kans., but was very successful as superintendent of a military college at Alexandria, La., 1859–61.

Regarding, as he did, the Union and the Constitution with almost religious fervor, he also loved the South and its people; he considered it a duty to end the contest between the North and South as quickly and ruthlessly as possible, with the proviso that the peace terms be as lenient as the war was stern. Appointed colonel of the 13th Infantry, May 1861, he was assigned to brigade command in July and shared in the disaster of first Bull Run. Transferred to Kentucky as brigadier general of volunteers, he took on the thankless job of trying to hold that state in the Union with little more than raw home guards to work with. Anxiety preyed upon his mind, he overestimated the difficulties of his position, and his quarrels with the press over breaches of security encouraged newspapermen to report that Sherman's mind was giving way. Superseded, he was received at headquarters with suspicion and coldness. Joining U. S. Grant's army with a division of volunteers, he took prominent part in the battle of Shiloh and the advance to Corinth and was promoted major general of volunteers, May 1862. In July, Grant sent Sherman to Memphis, Tenn., where Sherman suppressed guerrillas, put civil authority on a firm basis, and made a push at Vicksburg, Miss., which was rendered hopeless when Grant's communications were cut and he had to withdraw from his part in the operation. Grant reorganized his forces and, with Sherman commanding the XV Corps, carried through the amphibious campaign which resulted in the surrender of Vicksburg on July 4, 1863.

On Grant's subsequent advance to supreme command in the West, Sherman was given command of the Army of the Tennessee. He participated in the relief of Chattanooga and Knoxville and destroyed the Confederate base at Meridian, Miss., in January 1864. Sherman succeeded to supreme command in the West after Grant's promotion to commander in chief of all the armies. By the combined plan of 1864, General George Meade was to advance against General R. E. Lee and Richmond, while Sherman advanced early in May against General J. E. Johnston and Atlanta. Concentrating about 100,000 men at Chattanooga, Sherman forced Johnston back to the Allatoona Pass–Kenesaw Mountain line, and then back to Peachtree Creek, by several flanking maneuvers. He swung around Atlanta and opened a siege, cutting the railroads to Montgomery and Macon. On Sept. 1, General Hood, who had replaced Johnston, evacuated Atlanta. Sherman, who had been promoted to major general in the regular army, ordered the removal of the civilian population from the city. With Grant's approval, he began the famous "march to the sea" through Georgia on Nov. 15. His purpose was to break the resistance of the South by cutting off the supply of its armies, for Georgia was the only untouched source of supply. His army lived off the country, destroying war supplies, public buildings, railroads, and manufacturing shops. By bringing the war home to the civilian population, Sherman believed that it could be terminated quickly; for his deliberate exploitation of this principle he has been called the first modern general. His activities made him the center of a bitter controversy, but he urged that it was better to destroy goods rather than life, that wanton destruction was prevented insofar as possible, and that there was no serious personal violence to noncombatants. It is obvious, however, that discipline in his army was not strict enough. After occupying Savannah on Dec. 21, 1864, he marched northward through the Carolinas, causing even more destruction than in Georgia. He occupied Columbia, S.C., and burned it, forced the evacuation of Charleston and then moved on Raleigh, N.C. Eight days after Lee's surrender on Apr. 9, 1865, General J. E. Johnston, Confederate commander in the Carolinas, surrendered to Sherman. The terms granted were liberal, but the Washington government, enraged by the assassination of Lincoln, repudiated them.

After the war Sherman commanded the Division of the Mississippi, aiding the construction of the transcontinental railway and controlling Indian hostility. In 1866 he was promoted to lieutenant general and was sent on a diplomatic mission to President Juarez of Mexico, as part of the pressure exerted on France for withdrawal of support to Maximilian. Three years later Sherman became general commanding the army and held the position until his retirement in 1883. He rejected repeated attempts to draw him into politics, especially in the Republican convention of 1884, when his positive veto prohibited a move for his nomination for the presidency. His *Memoirs* were first published in 1875.

SHERRY, LOUIS (*b. probably St. Albans, Vt., 1856; d. 1926*), restaurateur. Opened his first restaurant and confectionery at 38th St. and Sixth Ave., New York City, 1881. Removing to two successive locations on Fifth Ave. and Park Ave., he was highly successful as host and caterer to the wealthy.

SHERWIN, THOMAS (*b. Westmoreland, N.H., 1799; d. 1869*), educator. Graduated Harvard, 1825. As principal of the English High School, Boston, Mass., 1837–69, Sherwin made it the leading educational institution of its grade in the United States; he was active also in the establishment of the Massachusetts Institute of Technology.

SHERWOOD, ADIEL (*b. Fort Edward, N.Y., 1791; d. St. Louis, Mo., 1879*), Baptist clergyman, educator. Graduated Union, 1817. Removing to Georgia, 1818, he was active in the ministry there and as a teacher in several institutions; he was president of Shurtleff College, 1841–46, and later of Masonic and Marshall colleges.

SHERWOOD, ISAAC RUTH (*b. Stanford, N.Y., 1835; d. 1925*), journalist, Union soldier. Editor of a number of Ohio newspapers at various times, Sherwood served as congressman, Republican, from Ohio, 1873–75, but was refused renomination because of his greenback sympathies. As congressman, Democrat, from Ohio, 1907–21 and 1923–25, he was an aggressive advocate of veterans' pensions and an opponent of U.S. entry into World War I.

SHERWOOD, KATHARINE MARGARET BROWNLEE (*b. Poland, Ohio, 1841; d. 1914*), journalist, reformer. Wife of Isaac R. Sherwood.

SHERWOOD, MARY ELIZABETH WILSON (*b. Keene, N.H., 1826; d. New York, N.Y., 1903*), author. A prolific contributor to newspapers and periodicals and the writer of a number of books, Sherwood was principally renowned for her manuals of social life and etiquette, which were as popular as they were conservative.

SHERWOOD, ROBERT EMMET (*b. New Rochelle, N.Y., 1896; d. New York, N.Y., 1955*), writer and government official. Studied at Harvard University. Wrote book reviews for *Scribner's Magazine* and movie reviews for *Life*; wrote several screenplays and plays including *Idiot's Delight* (1936), *Abe Lincoln in Illinois* (1938), and *There Shall Be No Night* (1940)—all of which won the Pulitzer Prize. He wrote the screenplay, *The Best Years Of Our Lives* in 1946; the film won nine Academy Awards. In 1948 he published his book *Roosevelt and Hopkins: An Intimate History*, which also won the Pulitzer Prize. Sherwood wrote presidential addresses for President Roosevelt and served as director of the Overseas Branch of the Office of War Information from 1942 to 1944.

SHERWOOD, THOMAS ADIEL (*b. Eatonton, Ga., 1834; d. California, 1918*), jurist. Son of Adiel Sherwood. Judge of the Missouri Supreme Court, 1872–1902, was a strict constructionist and opponent of federal encroachment on state powers, but also an earnest defender of civil liberty and a proponent of both administrative and procedural judicial reform.

SHERWOOD, WILLIAM HALL (*b. Lyons, N.Y., 1854; d. Chicago, Ill., 1911*), pianist, teacher, composer. A pupil of William Mason (1829–1908) and others in America, he studied also with distinguished masters in Europe, including Franz Liszt. One of the first Americans to play with great European orchestras, he devoted himself to teaching and to concert work in America *post* 1876. He founded the Sherwood Music School in Chicago.

SHICK CALAMYS. *See* SHIKELLAMY.

SHIELDS, CHARLES WOODRUFF (*b. New Albany, Ind., 1825; d. Newport, R.I., 1904*), Presbyterian and Episcopal clergyman, educator. Graduated College of New Jersey (Princeton), 1844; Princeton Theological Seminary, 1847. A professor of philosophy and history for many years at Princeton, Shields devoted his life to the reconciliation of science with religion and to the reunion of Protestantism.

SHIELDS, GEORGE HOWELL (*b. Bardstown, Ky., 1842; d. St. Louis, Mo., 1924*), Missouri Republican politician and jurist.

SHIELDS, GEORGE OLIVER (*b. Batavia, Ohio, 1846; d. New York, N.Y., 1925*), journalist, author, pioneer in the conservation of wildlife.

SHIELDS, JAMES (*b. Altmore, Ireland, 1806; d. Ottumwa, Iowa, 1879*), soldier, politician. Immigrated to America *ca.* 1826; settled in Kaskaskia, Ill., where he studied and practiced law. As an Illinois legislator and state auditor, he helped correct that state's chaotic finances; he was judge of the Illinois Supreme Court, 1843–45. After brief service as commissioner of the U.S. General Land Office, he volunteered for the Mexican War and won a brevet of major general for gallantry in action. Resigning an appointment as governor of Oregon Territory, he served as U.S. senator, Democrat, from Illinois, 1849–55. Removing to Minnesota Territory, he did much to stimulate Irish settlement there and was U.S. senator from Minnesota, 1858–59. Removing to California and then to Mexico, he returned to the United States on the outbreak of the Civil War and was appointed brigadier general of volunteers, August 1861. Winning credit for his leadership at Kernstown and Port Republic, he resigned his commission, March 1863, and became a California railroad commissioner. Reentering politics in Missouri, 1866, he served in the legislature and as a railroad commissioner and finally as U.S. senator, Democrat, from Missouri, January–March 1879.

SHIELDS, JOHN KNIGHT (*b. near Bean's Station, Tenn., 1858; d. near Bean's Station, 1934*), Tennessee jurist. An irreconcilable isolationist and conservative as U.S. senator, Independent Democrat-Republican, 1913–25.

SHIELDS, THOMAS EDWARD (*b. near Mendota, Minn., 1862; d. 1921*), Roman Catholic clergyman, educator. Slow to develop mentally, Shields was ordained, 1891, after a rigorous course in self-education and graduation from St. Thomas Seminary; he received a Ph.D. in biology from Johns Hopkins, 1895. After teaching and pastoral work in St. Paul, Minn., he became an instructor at Catholic University, Washington, D.C., 1902, and was raised to professor of education and psychology, 1909. Constantly crusading against stereotypes in religious and general education, he was author of a number of books and founder of the *Catholic Educational Review*, which he edited *post* 1911. He was founder also of the Sisters College as an affiliated school of the university, 1911, and an innovator in providing summer courses for teaching sisters.

SHIKELLAMY (*b. Shamokin, Pa., 1748*), Oneida chief. Father of James Logan (*ca. 1725–80*). A sympathetic intermediary between the frontier whites and the Iroquois, he was influential in negotiating the treaties of 1736 and 1744 which greatly favored the Iroquois at the expense of the Delaware and Shawnee.

SHILLABER, BENJAMIN PENHALLOW (*b. Portsmouth, N.H., 1814; d. Chelsea, Mass., 1890*), journalist, humorist, printer. Edited the important weekly the *Carpetbag*, 1851–53, to which Artemus Ward and Mark Twain sent their first contributions. Creator of the character of "Mrs. Partington," Shillaber served as chief connecting link between the old school of American humor, which preceded the Civil War, and the new. Among his separately published works were *Life and Sayings of Mrs. Partington* (1854), *Knitting-Work* (1859), *Partingtonian Patchwork* (1872), and the "Ike Partington" juveniles.

SHINN, ASA (*b. New Jersey, 1781; d. Brattleboro, Vt., 1853*), Methodist clergyman, reformer. A founder of the Methodist Protestant church, 1830.

SHINN, EVERETT (*b. Woodstown, N.J., 1876; d. New York, N.Y., 1953*), painter and illustrator. Studied at the Pennsylvania Academy of Fine Arts. Member of the "Philadelphia Four" who formed the nucleus of a new wave of urban realism in American art; and of the dissident group, "the eight," who protested the academic strictures of art at the turn of the century. Theatrical in his style, his paintings include *The Docks, New York City* (1901) and *London Hippodrome* (1903). He did many illustrations for *Harper's Magazine*, and painted many murals, including those in the Oak Room at the Plaza Hotel in New York City. Elected to the American Academy of Arts and Letters in 1951.

SHIPHERD, JOHN JAY (*b. near Granville, N.Y., 1802; d. Olivet, Mich., 1844*), Congregational home missionary. Founder, with Philo P. Stewart and others, of Oberlin College, 1833.

SHIPLEY, RUTH BIELASKI (*b. Montgomery County, Md., 1885; d. Washington, D.C., 1966*), career civil servant. Joined the U.S. Patent Office in 1903; later worked in the Records Division of the State Department. As special assistant to second assistant secretary of state Alvey Adee (1919–21), she became one of the most able of her generation of bureaucrats. Appointed chief of the Passport Division in 1928, she turned it into a model of efficiency; upgraded passport fraud investigations, and her operatives later nabbed Communist party leader Earl Browder and Nazi spy Gunther Rumrich. After 1939, she was charged with preventing foreign travel rather than facilitating it; she invalidated all old passports, and with few exceptions, denied citizens passports to belligerent countries and combat zones. After the war her influence reached to the granting of visas and immigration; following passage of the McCarran Internal Security Act (1950), which gave the secretary of state the authority to deny passports to members of Communist oganizations, she took over the task of dealing with such cases and was criticized for blatant political bias. She retired in 1955.

SHIPMAN, ANDREW JACKSON (*b. Springvale, Va., 1857; d. 1915*), lawyer, Slavic scholar, philanthropist. Graduated Georgetown University, 1878. An able and successful lawyer in New York City, he maintained a lifelong interest in the welfare of Salvic immigrants, particularly in the religious rights of Catholics of the Eastern Rite.

SHIPP, ALBERT MICAJAH (*b. Stokes Co., N.C., 1819; d. Cleveland Springs, N.C., 1887*), Methodist clergyman, educator. Graduated University of North Carolina, 1840, where he taught history, 1849–59. President of Wofford College, 1859–75, and professor of exegetical theology at Vanderbilt, 1875–85.

SHIPP, SCOTT (*b. Warrenton, Va., 1839; d. 1917*), Confederate soldier, educator. Graduated Virginia Military Institute, 1859. After service in the West Virginia and Romney campaigns, 1861, he became commandant of cadets at VMI, 1862, and led his men into the field on five occasions; the famous charge of the cadets against the Union forces at New Market, May 1864, was made under his command. Resuming his work at VMI at the end of the war, he was promoted to its superintendency, 1890, and served in this capacity until 1907.

SHIPPEN, EDWARD (*b. Methley, England, 1639; d. Philadelphia, Pa., 1712*), Merchant, Pennsylvania colonial legislator. Immigrated to Boston, Mass., 1668. Joining the Society of Friends *ca.* 1671, he was severely persecuted until his removal to Philadelphia *ca.* 1694. Holder of many high provincial offices, he was mayor of Philadelphia, 1701–03, and acting governor of Pennsylvania, April 1703–February 1704.

SHIPPEN, EDWARD (*b. Philadelphia, Pa., 1728/9; d. Philadelphia, 1806*), jurist. Great-grandson of Edward Shippen (1639–1712); father-in-law of Benedict Arnold. A moderate Loyalist during the Revolution, Shippen held a number of judicial posts *post* 1784. An associate justice of the Pennsylvania Supreme Court, 1791–99, he was chief justice, 1799–1805.

SHIPPEN, WILLIAM (*b. Philadelphia, Pa., 1736; d. Philadelphia, 1808*), physician, medical educator. Great-grandson of Edward Shippen (1639–1712); cousin of Edward Shippen (1729–1806). Graduated College of New Jersey (Princeton), 1754. Studied medicine with his father and in London and at the University of Edinburgh, where he received the M.D. degree, 1761. Successful in practice in Philadelphia *post* 1762 and as a teacher of anatomy and midwifery, he was appointed professor of surgery and anatomy at the College of Philadelphia, 1765. During the Revolution, he served under various titles as director of several divisions of the Continental army hospital service. He was chief of the medical department of the Continental army, 1777–81, succeeding John Morgan, who charged him with bad faith. He was later court-martialed for alleged financial irregularities in office, but acquitted. A member of the staff of the Pennsylvania Hospital, 1778–79 and 1791–1802, he held the chair of anatomy, surgery, and midwifery at University of Pennsylvania *post* 1791.

SHIPSTEAD, HENRIK (*b. Burbank Township, Minn., 1881; d. Alexandria, Minn., 1960*), politician. Studied at Northwestern University School of Dentistry. Elected to the U.S. Senate on the Farmer-Labor ticket in 1922; he served in the Senate until 1946, switching to the Republican party in 1940. An ardent populist and isolationist, Shipstead served on the Senate Foreign Relations Committee, opposing U.S. involvement in the United Nations and wanting to limit U.S. defense commitments to the Western Hemisphere.

SHIRAS, GEORGE (*b. Pittsburgh, Pa., 1832; d. Pittsburgh, 1924*), jurist, U.S. Supreme Court justice. Brother of Oliver P. Shiras. Graduated Yale, 1853. Associate justice, U.S. Supreme Court, 1892–1903, he was widely criticized (perhaps unjustly) for his part in the nullification of the federal income tax statute in April 1895.

SHIRAS, OLIVER PERRY (*b. Pittsburgh, Pa., 1833; d. 1916*), jurist. Brother of George Shiras. Admitted to the Iowa bar, 1856, after graduation from Ohio University and Yale Law School, he practiced in Dubuque. As U.S. judge for the northern Iowa district, 1882–1903, he excelled in equity cases and enunciated, 1894, the concept of a national common law subject to independent application by the federal courts irrespective of state interpretation.

SHIRLAW, WALTER (*b. Paisley, Scotland, 1838; d. Madrid, Spain, 1909*), genre, portrait, and mural painter. Came to America as a child. Beginning his career as a bank-note engraver, he studied in Chicago and was a student in Munich, Germany, 1870–77. While in Germany, he painted his two best pictures, *Toning the Bell*, 1874, and *Sheep-Shearing in the Bavarian Highlands*, 1876. Returning to America, he became first president of the Society of American Artists, taught at the Art Students League in New York City and achieved a fair degree of professional success. His mastery of design may be studied in his ceiling painting *The Sciences*, in the Library of Congress, Washington, D.C.

SHIRLEY, WILLIAM (*b. Preston, Sussex, England, 1694; d. Roxbury, Mass., 1771*), colonial official, lawyer. Immigrated to Boston, Mass., 1731. As judge of admiralty and later advocate general, he upheld the imperial view of business matters, laboring faithfully to enforce the trade acts. Critical of Governor Jonathan Belcher's policies, Shirley succeeded Belcher as governor of Massachusetts in May 1741. Adroitly settling the land-bank controversy, Shirley persuaded the Massachusetts General Court to make appropriations for defense of the colony and had affairs in a good state of preparation by the time war was declared with the French in 1744. Aware of the economic importance of the French fortress of Louisburg on Cape Breton Island, he matured plans to capture it, despite discouragement from the English government; he won support of the General Court for the enterprise, in which the other New England colonies cooperated. The taking of weakly defended Louisburg in June 1745 proved to be the one great English victory of the war. From 1749 to 1753 Shirley participated in the negotiations held in Paris concerning the boundary line between French North America and New England. With the outbreak of the French and Indian War, which he had foreseen, he was appointed major general and given command of the campaign against Niagara. After General Braddock's death in July 1755, he succeeded to the supreme command of British forces on the American continent. Though his military plans were sound, they were unsuccessful, largely because of bickering among the colonies and their failure to lend adequate support. On the failure of the Niagara expedition, Shirley's enemies accused him of mismanagement, and suspicion was aroused in England that he was guilty of treasonable activity. Summoned to England early in 1756, he was threatened with court-martial, but charges were dropped for lack of evidence. Meantime, he had been removed as governor of Massachusetts. Named governor of the Bahama Islands, 1761, he resigned in 1767. As an executive Shirley showed ability and tact and became one of the most personally popular of colonial governors. Careless in his management of public finance, he was of unimpeachable personal integrity. More than any other contemporary governor, he had a broad grasp of the whole imperial problem.

SHOBONIER. *See* SHABONEE.

SHOLES, CHRISTOPHER LATHAM (*b. Mooresburg, Pa., 1819; d. 1890*), printer, journalist, inventor. Removing to Wisconsin *ca.* 1837, Sholes engaged in politics, held political appointments, and was editor of several Wisconsin newspapers, including the *Milwaukee News* and the *Milwaukee Sentinel.* Holder of a number of patents for mechanical devices, he devoted most of his life *post* 1867 to the perfection of the typewriter. Granted a basic patent, 1868, he patented improvements, 1871, but on failing to raise the means for making and marketing his machine, he sold his rights to the Remington Arms Co., March 1873. He continued to improve his typewriter until 1878, turning over his results to the Remington Co.

SHONTS, THEODORE PERRY (*b. Crawford Co., Pa., 1856; d. 1919*), railroad executive. Able president of a number of midwestern railroads; chairman, second Isthmian Canal Commission, 1905–07; president, Interborough Rapid Transit Co., New York City, *post* 1907. An efficient, adaptable manager.

SHOOK, ALFRED MONTGOMERY (*b. near Winchester, Tenn., 1845; d. Nashville, Tenn., 1923*), industrialist. As superintendent and general manager of the Tennessee Coal, Iron & Railroad Co., 1868–1901, Shook became a master of all phases of iron manufacture, greatly enlarged the business, and directed the company's engagement in steel manufacture at Ensley, near Birmingham, Ala. The opening of his company's steelworks in 1899 began a new era in southern industrial development.

SHOREY, PAUL (*b. Davenport, Iowa, 1857; d. Chicago, Ill., 1934*), classicist. Graduated Harvard, 1878. After attending the universities of Leipzig and Bonn and the American School at Athens, he received a Ph.D. from Munich in 1884. Professor of Latin and Greek at Bryn Mawr, 1885–92, he went to the University of Chicago as professor of Greek and served as head of the department, 1896–1927. An erudite and unusually effective teacher, he made his greatest contribution to scholarship in the field of Platonic studies; a founder of *Classical Philology,* he was its editor, 1908–34. Among his numerous books and monographs, *What Plato Said* (1933) is outstanding. Impatient with modern pedagogical methods, Shorey was a stout opponent of current prejudices against the classics in education.

SHORT, CHARLES (*b. Haverhill, Mass., 1821; d. New York, N.Y., 1886*), classical philologist. Graduated Harvard, 1846. After service as teacher and headmaster in several academies, he was president of Kenyon College, 1863–67. Succeeding Henry Drisler as professor of Latin at Columbia, 1867, he remained in that post for the rest of his life.

SHORT, CHARLES WILKINS (*b. Woodford Co., Ky., 1794; d. near Louisville, Ky., 1863*), physician, educator, botanist. Nephew of William Short; grandson of John C. Symmes. Graduated Transylvania University, 1810; M.D., University of Pennsylvania, 1815; made private studies with Caspar Wistar (1716–1818). Teacher and dean at Transylvania and later at the Medical Institute of Louisville, he is remembered principally as a collector and classifier of plants from the little-explored country west of the Alleghenies.

SHORT, JOSEPH HUDSON, JR. (*b. Vicksburg, Miss., 1904; d. Alexandria, Va., 1952*), journalist. Worked for many newspapers before joining the Associated Press in 1931; assigned to Washington, he remained there until 1941. From 1943 to 1950 he was a member of the Washington bureau of the *Baltimore Sun.* Appointed as presidential press secretary by President Truman in 1950, he covered many events for the president including the Korean War and the firing of General Douglas MacArthur.

SHORT, SIDNEY HOWE (*b. Columbus, Ohio, 1858; d. 1902*), electrical engineer, educator. Inventor of numerous important devices for arc-lighting and electric traction systems.

SHORT, WALTER CAMPBELL (*b. Fillmore, Ill., 1880; d. Dallas, Tex., 1949*), army officer. B.A., University of Illinois, 1901. Commissioned in U.S. Army, 1902; began service with 25th Infantry at Fort Reno, Okla. Served in Alaska and on Mexican punitive expedition, 1916–17; served with 1st Division in France during World War I and was decorated for forward reconnaissance work and for efficiency in training machine-gun units. After various peacetime assignments in which he rose to brigadier general, 1936, and divisional command, 1939, he was recognized as one of the army's best training specialists. In 1941 he took charge of the army's Hawaii department with rank of lieutenant general. Relieved of duty after the Japanese attack on Oahu, Dec. 7, 1941, he was accused of negligence by many at that time, but presented a reasonable public defense of his actions in hearings before an investigating committee of Congress, early in 1946.

SHORT, WILLIAM (*b. Surry Co., Va., 1759; d. 1849*), diplomat, planter, landowner. Graduated William and Mary, 1779. A founder of Phi Beta Kappa, Short served on the executive council of Virginia, 1783–84, and thereafter as Thomas Jefferson's private secretary and secretary of legation in Paris. Becoming chargé d'affaires, 1789, he served with ability until 1792 when he was appointed U.S. minister at The Hague. Named as joint commissioner with William Carmichael to negotiate a treaty with Spain, he went to Madrid in February 1793. Superseded by Thomas Pinckney, he loyally cooperated with Pinckney in securing the Pinckney Treaty, signed October 1795. Disappointed in his professional ambitions, he amassed a large fortune. He died probably in Philadelphia, Pa.

SHORTER, JOHN GILL (*b. Monticello, Ga., 1818; d. 1872*), jurist, Alabama legislator. An enthusiastic secessionist and strong supporter of Jefferson Davis, Shorter served in the provisional Confederate Congress, and was governor of Alabama, 1861–63.

SHOTWELL, JAMES THOMSON (*b. Strathroy, Ontario, Canada, 1874; d. New York, N.Y., 1965*), historian and internationalist. Attended University of Toronto and Columbia (Ph.D., 1903), taught history at the latter, 1905–42. He was an organizer and first chairman of the National Board for Historical Service following U.S. entry into World War I and accompanied President Woodrow Wilson to the Paris Peace Conference (1919). After the war he agreed to edit the 152-volume *Economic and Social History of the World War.* He became director of the Carnegie Endowment's Division of Economics and History (1924) and was president of the League of Nations Association (1935–39). In 1945 he became chairman of the consultants to the U.S. delegation to the United Nations Conference and became president of the Carnegie Endowment for International Peace (1949–50).

SHOUP, FRANCIS ASBURY (*b. Laurel, Ind., 1834; d. Columbia, Tenn., 1896*), Confederate brigadier general and artillerist, Episcopal clergyman, educator. Graduated West Point, 1855. Chief of artillery under Generals J. E. Johnston and John Hood in the Atlanta campaign, Shoup took orders after the war and was professor of mathematics at the University of Mississippi and at the University of the South.

SHOUP, GEORGE LAIRD (*b. Kittanning, Pa., 1836; d. Boise, Idaho, 1904*), businessman, Union soldier, Colorado and Idaho pioneer. Helped found Salmon, Idaho, 1866, where he made his home. Long active in Republican politics, he was territorial governor and governor of Idaho, 1889–90, and first U.S. senator from the state, 1891–1901.

SHOUSE, JOUETT (*b. Woodford County, Ky., 1879; d. Washington, D.C., 1968*), U.S. congressman. Attended University of Missouri (1895–98). In 1911 he became involved in Kansas politics and won a state senate seat (1912). As a U.S. congressman (1914–18), he was a member of the Banking and Currency Committee and active in developing the Federal Farm Loan Act (1916). Defeated for reelection in 1918, he became assistant secretary of the treasury, devoting his attention to the War Risk Bureau; resigned in 1920. Remained active in Kansas Democratic politics and led the Kansas delegation to the 1920 and 1924 national conventions; became chairman (1929) of the Executive Committee of the Democratic National Committee. He severed his connections with the Democratic party in 1932 and became more and more conservative. President of the American Liberty League (1934–40), an isolationist organization; later vigorously endorsed the campaigns of Thomas Dewey (1948) and Richard Nixon (1960).

SHOWERMAN, GRANT (*b. Brookfield, Wis., 1870; d. Madison, Wis., 1935*), classicist. Graduated University of Wisconsin, 1896; Ph.D., 1900. Professor at Wisconsin for the greater part of his life, he was expert in the history, literature, and art of Rome and an outspoken exponent of classical culture. Among his many books were *Eternal Rome* (1924) and *Rome and the Romans* (1931).

SHRADY, GEORGE FREDERICK (*b. New York, N.Y., 1837; d. 1907*), surgeon, medical journalist. M.D., College of Physicians and Surgeons, New York, 1858. Holder of many New York hospital staff appointments, he was a skillful, conservative operator, specializing mainly in plastic surgery. He made his principal contribution to medicine as editor of the *American Medical Times*, 1860–64, and of the *Medical Record*, 1866–1904, championing reforms in medical education and practice. He was father of Henry M. Shrady.

SHRADY, HENRY MERWIN (*b. New York, N.Y., 1871; d. 1922*), sculptor. Son of George F. Shrady. Mainly self-taught save for some technical instruction from Karl Bitter, Shrady did his finest work on the memorial group to General U. S. Grant, in Union Square, Washington, D.C. Winner of the competition for this work, 1902, he labored on it until 1922 and died two weeks before it was dedicated.

SHREVE, HENRY MILLER (*b. Burlington Co., N.J., 1785; d. St. Louis, Mo., 1851*), steamboat captain. Raised on the Pennsylvania frontier, Shreve began trading journeys by keelboat down the Monongahela and Ohio to the West, 1799. Initiator of the fur trade between St. Louis and Philadelphia via Pittsburgh, 1807, he then entered the lead trade between the upper Mississippi and New Orleans. Becoming a stockholder in the steamboat *Enterprise*, 1814, he freighted supplies for Andrew Jackson's army from Pittsburgh to New Orleans in the vessel and in May 1815 brought it successfully up to Louisville, Ky. He established the practicability of steam navigation on the Mississippi and Ohio route with his second steamboat, the *Washington*, 1816–17, and later broke the Fulton-Livingston monopoly which had been asserted against his operations in legal proceedings. As U.S. superintendent of western river improvements, 1827–41, Shreve designed the first steam snagboat and removed the famous Red River raft. Shreveport, La., was named for him.

SHREVE, THOMAS HOPKINS (*b. Alexandria, Va., 1808; d. Louisville, Ky., 1853*), journalist. Removing to Cincinnati,

Ohio, *ca.* 1830, he was associated there with such literary pioneers as William D. Gallagher and James H. Perkins; with Gallagher, he edited the *Cincinnati Mirror*, 1831–36. Active in business as well, he published essays and poems in the *Western Messenger*, the *Western Literary Journal*, the *Western Monthly Magazine*, the *Knickerbocker*, and others. He served as assistant editor of the *Louisville Daily Journal*, 1842–53.

SHUBERT, LEE (*b. Shirvinta, Russia, 1873[?]; d. New York, N.Y., 1953*), theatrical producer. Immigrated to the U.S. in 1883. With his brothers Samuel and Jacob, Lee Shubert began a career in theater ownership and production; by 1900, the brothers were producing plays in a leased theater in New York. In 1905 Lee Shubert became president of the Shubert Theatrical Corp. Over the next decade the Shubert brothers came to dominate American theatrical management and production; by 1925 they owned six London theaters, owned or controlled thirty-five New York theaters, and controlled seventy-five percent of all theater tickets sold, as well as owning many theaters in other American cities. The company suffered greatly during the Great Depression and underwent antitrust suits from the federal government. Shubert's last production of a play was in 1954; his earlier productions included Romberg's operettas, many reviews, and the play *Street Scene*, Elmer Rice's Pulitzer Prize winner of 1929. A theater in New York bears the Shubert name.

SHUBRICK, JOHN TEMPLER (*b. Bull's Island, S.C., 1788; d. 1815*), naval officer. Brother of William B. Shubrick. Appointed midshipman, 1806, he had an extraordinarily eventful career, serving in major actions aboard the *Constitution*, the *Chesapeake*, the *Hornet*, and the *Guerrière*. Returning home from Algiers, 1815, in command of the *Epervier*, he was lost at sea.

SHUBRICK, WILLIAM BRANFORD (*b. Bull's Island, S.C., 1790; d. 1874*), naval officer. Brother of John T. Shubrick. Appointed midshipman, 1806, he served for a time under Capt. James Lawrence and was shipmate with James Fenimore Cooper. Promoted lieutenant, 1813, he served aboard the *Constellation* and the *Constitution*, 1813–15. After some 30 years of routine ship and shore duty, he served on the Pacific Coast during the Mexican War. Chairman of the lighthouse board, 1852–71, he is chiefly remembered for his command of the expedition sent to settle difficulties with Paraguay, 1858–59. Retired as flag officer, 1861, he was raised to rear admiral (retired), 1862.

SHUCK, JEHU LEWIS (*b. Alexandria, Va., 1812; d. Barnwell Court House, S.C., 1863*), Baptist clergyman. Missionary to China, 1836–45 and 1847–51. He later served as a missionary among the Chinese in California.

SHUEY, EDWIN LONGSTREET (*b. Cincinnati, Ohio, 1857; d. 1924*), educator, advertising man, director of factory welfare work. Author of *Factory People and Their Employers* (1900).

SHUEY, WILLIAM JOHN (*b. Miamisburg, Ohio, 1827; d. 1920*), clergyman of the United Brethren in Christ. Able and energetic in the service of his church as minister, missionary, publishing agent, 1865–97, and seminary manager.

SHUFELDT, ROBERT WILSON (*b. Red Hook, N.Y., 1822; d. Washington, D.C., 1895*), naval officer. Appointed midshipman, 1839, he resigned, 1854, to engage in the merchant service and during the early years of the Civil War was consul to Cuba and a special agent to Mexico. Recommissioned commander, November 1862, he served with ability at sea and in miscellaneous postwar duties until 1878. The great achievement of his career was his negotiation of a treaty with China, 1882, which established diplomatic relations, extraterritoriality, and commercial privileges for the United States. He retired as rear admiral, 1884.

SHULL, GEORGE HARRISON (b. Clark County, Ohio, 1874; d. Princeton, N.J., 1954), plant geneticist. Studied at Antioch College, and the University of Chicago (Ph.D., 1904). Professor of botany and genetics at Princeton University, 1915–42. Responsible for the development of the hybridization of corn, 1908–09. By the beginning of World War II this development had increased American corn production by 20 percent. His methods of cross breeding were applied to other crops such as rice and wheat, and are said to be the most significant development in twentieth-century agriculture.

SHULZE, JOHN ANDREW (b. Berks Co., Pa., 1775; d. Lancaster, Pa., 1852), Lutheran clergyman, businessman, Pennsylvania legislator. Grandson of Henry M. Mühlenberg. As Democratic governor of Pennsylvania, 1823–29, he promoted canal construction and public elementary education.

SHUNK, FRANCIS RAWN (b. Trappe, Pa., 1788; d. 1848), educator, lawyer, public official. Restored Pennsylvania's financial credit and opposed concessions to corporate business interests as Democratic governor, 1845–48.

SHURTLEFF, NATHANIEL BRADSTREET (b. Boston, Mass., 1810; d. 1874), physician, antiquary. Democratic mayor of Boston, 1868–70. A thorough and conscientious editor of original Massachusetts records, he was author of A *Topographical and Historical Description of Boston* (1871).

SHURTLEFF, ROSWELL MORSE (b. Rindge, N.H., 1838; d. New York, N.Y., 1915), animal and landscape painter.

SHUSTER, W(ILLIAM) MORGAN (b. Washington, D.C., 1877; d. New York, N.Y., 1960), financier, lawyer, and publisher. Studied at Columbia University. Collector of customs in the Philippines, 1901–06; secretary of public instruction, 1906–09. A friend of President Taft, Shuster was asked to journey to Persia and help that nation out of its financial difficulties and reorganize the financial structure. In 1911 Shuster arrived in Teheran and began his work, which soon became embroiled in conflicts between British and Russian interests. After causing some military fighting and a possible international crisis between the two nations, he was dismissed and returned to Washington. In 1915 Shuster became president of Century, a publishing firm, later Appleton-Century (1933) and, still later, Appleton-Century-Crofts (1948). He was chairman of the board from 1952 until his death.

SHUTE, SAMUEL (b. London, England, 1662; d. England, 1742), British soldier. Shute's administration as colonial governor of Massachusetts Bay and New Hampshire extended from 1716 to 1727 and was one of the stormiest endured by any royal governor. Constantly at odds with the assembly over fiscal matters and questions of legislative privilege, he returned to England, 1723, to complain of his grievances and seek redress. As he was about to return to Massachusetts in the spring of 1727, his commission was vacated.

SIAMESE TWINS. See CHANG AND ENG.

SIBERT, WILLIAM LUTHER (b. Gadsden, Ala., 1860; d. near Bowling Green, Ky., 1935), military engineer. Graduated West Point, 1884. Commissioned in the engineers, he performed extensive river and harbor improvement work and distinguished himself in reconstruction of Philippine railways, 1899–1900. He supervised construction of the Atlantic Division of the Panama Canal, 1908–14. Promoted major general, May 1917, he organized the Chemical Warfare Service for the army in World War I.

SIBLEY, GEORGE CHAMPLAIN (b. Great Barrington, Mass., 1782; d. near St. Charles, Mo., 1863), Indian agent, explorer. Son of John Sibley; grandson of Samuel Hopkins (1721–1803). Served as factor and Indian agent at Fort Osage, Mo., 1808–26; explored the Grand Saline in present Oklahoma, 1811; was one of the commissioners to mark Santa Fe Trail from Council Grove to the Mexican boundary, 1825.

SIBLEY, HENRY HASTINGS (b. Detroit, Michigan Territory, 1811; d. 1891), fur trader, Minnesota pioneer. Settled at Mendota, 1834. Influential among the Sioux. He was delegate to Congress from Wisconsin Territory, 1848, and promoted the organization of Minnesota Territory, 1849, serving as its delegate, 1849–58. He was first governor of the state of Minnesota, 1858–60, elected as a Democrat. Commanding the Minnesota forces during the Sioux uprising of 1862, he relieved the frontier posts and fought the battle of Wood Lake. During 1863–64, he commanded punitive expeditions against the Sioux in the Dakota region, and in 1865–66 was one of the commissioners to negotiate peace treaties with the Sioux. Removing to St. Paul, Minn., he concerned himself with private business thereafter, but remained an important and influential figure in the life of the state.

SIBLEY, HIRAM (b. North Adams, Mass., 1807; d. Rochester, N.Y., 1888), businessman, promoter. A pioneer in the telegraph industry, he early reached the conclusion that there were too many small companies and that consolidation was demanded; in association with Ezra Cornell, he formed the Western Union Telegraph Co. (chartered 1856), which he served as president until 1866. An earnest advocate of a transcontinental telegraph line, he undertook the project first on his own account and amalgamated it with the Western Union in 1864. After his retirement from Western Union affairs, 1869, he invested in railroads and in agricultural enterprises with great success. He was one of the incorporators of Cornell University and a benefactor to it and to the University of Rochester.

SIBLEY, JOHN (b. Sutton, Mass., 1757; d. 1837), physician, Indian agent, Louisiana politician and planter. Father of George C. Sibley. Removed to Louisiana, 1802; served as contract surgeon to the U.S. Army at Natchitoches, 1803–05, and as Indian agent for Orleans Territory and Louisiana, 1805–14. He later prospered as a planter and salt manufacturer. His official reports to Governor Claiborne and to President Jefferson are important sources of information regarding Louisiana.

SIBLEY, JOHN LANGDON (b. Union, Maine, 1804; d. 1885), librarian. Graduated Harvard, 1825; Harvard Divinity School, 1828. Assistant librarian of Harvard, 1825–26 and 1841–56; librarian, 1856–77. He is remembered principally as author of the *Biographical Sketches of Graduates of Harvard University* (1873–85), covering the lives of graduates through the class of 1689.

SIBLEY, JOSEPH CROCKER (b. Friendship, N.Y., 1850; d. near Franklin, Pa., 1926), oil refiner. Congressman, Democrat-Populist-Prohibitionist, from Pennsylvania, 1893–95; congressman, Democrat, 1899–1901, and Republican, 1901–07. In addition to his activities in business and politics, he was an agriculturist and a stockbreeder.

SICALAMOUS. See SHIKELLAMY.

SICARD, MONTGOMERY (b. New York, N.Y., 1836; d. Westernville, N.Y., 1900), naval officer. Graduated U.S. Naval Academy, 1855. Distinguished as an ordnance expert, he developed the modern high-power naval guns installed before the war with Spain. Promoted rear admiral, 1897, he was superseded as commander of the North Atlantic Squadron because of medical reasons, March 1898, and retired for age later in that year.

SICKELS, FREDERICK ELLSWORTH (*b. Gloucester Co., N.J., 1819; d. 1895*), engineer. Patented first successful drop cutoff for steam engines devised in the United States, 1842; patented a steam-steering apparatus for ships, 1860, which failed to receive any financial support for its exploitation.

SICKLES, DANIEL EDGAR (*b. New York, N.Y., 1819; d. New York, 1914*), lawyer, Union major general, diplomat. Studied law under Benjamin F. Butler (1795–1858); was admitted to the bar, 1846. Active in politics as a Democrat, he served as New York City corporation counsel, as secretary of the U.S. legation at London, as a New York State senator, and as a congressman from New York, 1857–61. A spectacular figure in Washington, D.C., he killed the son of Francis S. Key in a duel, 1859, winning acquittal with an innovating plea of temporary mental aberration. Raising the New York Excelsior Brigade, 1861, he led it as brigadier general and was promoted major general early in 1863. Commanding the III Corps, he was an important factor in the Chancellorsville campaign and stopped Stonewall Jackson's advance. Criticized for a controversial maneuver at Gettysburg, July 2, 1863, he found his military career in the field at an end and served on diplomatic missions and as a military administrator until the end of 1867. Retiring from the army, 1869, he was a vigorous but undiplomatic U.S. minister to Spain, 1869–73. After living for a time abroad, he returned to New York, where he held state appointments, and served again in Congress, 1893–95.

SIDELL, WILLIAM HENRY (*b. New York, N.Y., 1810; d. New York, 1873*), civil engineer, Union brevet brigadier general. Graduated West Point, 1833. Performed effective service as provost and recruiting officer in Kentucky and Tennessee, 1861–65.

SIDIS, BORIS (*b. Kiev, Russia, 1867; d. Portsmouth, N.H., 1923*), psychopathologist. Came to America, 1887. Graduated Harvard, B.A., 1894; Ph.D., 1897; M.D., 1908. Author of *The Psychology of Suggestion* (1898), an attempt to explain the nature of the subconscious; *Psychopathological Researches: Studies in Mental Dissociation* (1902); *The Psychology of Laughter* (1913), and other works.

SIDNEY, MARGARET. *See* LOTHROP, HARRIET MULFORD STONE.

SIEBER, AL (*b. Baden, Germany, 1844; d. near Globe, Ariz., 1907*), soldier, scout. Came to America as a child; was raised in Pennsylvania and Minnesota. After Civil War service with the Union army, he went to the Far West, 1866, settling in Arizona *ca.* 1868. Winning repute as a leader in organizing the settlers to defend themselves against Indian attack, he was engaged, 1871, as an army scout. In command of the famous Apache scouts under General George Crook, he soon became recognized as the outstanding scout and Indian fighter of the Southwest. After service under a number of department commanders, he was discharged, 1890, by the agent of San Carlos Reservation for denouncing unfair treatment of the Apache, and engaged thereafter in construction work. Trusted absolutely by his men, he could match them in endurance and trail skills; he possessed a high sense of honor and was utterly fearless.

SIGEL, FRANZ (*b. Sinsheim, Germany, 1824; d. New York, N.Y., 1902*), Union soldier, editor. An associate of Friedrich K. F. Hecker in the Baden insurrection, 1848, Sigel acted for a short time as minister of war in the revolutionary government of Baden and, on the collapse of the movement, fled first to Switzerland and then to England. Immigrating to America, 1852, he worked as a teacher and interested himself in the New York militia. Resident

in St. Louis, Mo., when the Civil War broke out, Sigel became colonel of the 3rd Missouri Infantry, May 1861, and rose to divisional command during the struggle to hold Missouri in the Union. Promoted major general of volunteers, March 1862, he was transferred to the eastern theater of the war and was prominent as a corps commander until the spring of 1863. Considered unaggressive by the Washington authorities, he was removed from field command in the summer of 1864. Resigning his commission in May 1865, he worked as an editor of German-language newspapers in Baltimore, Md., and New York City, held several political appointments in New York, and was prominent as a lecturer. Although his military career was comparatively undistinguished, his prompt, ardent espousal of the Union cause united the German population of the North solidly behind the Union.

SIGERIST, HENRY ERNEST (*b. Paris, France, 1891; d. Pura, Switzerland, 1957*), medical historian. Immigrated to the U.S. in 1932. Studied at the University of Zurich (M.D., 1917), and at the Leipzig Institute for the History of Medicine, where he taught from 1925 to 1932. From 1932 to 1947 he taught at Johns Hopkins Institute of the History of Medicine. Major works include *Amerika und die Medizin* (1933), *Socialized Medicine in the Soviet Union* (1937), and the monumental *History of Medicine*, only one volume of which he was able to complete in 1951. A pioneer in the field of medical history, Sigerist was a believer in social problems and their solution as part of the responsibilities of modern medicine. Founded the *Bulletin of the History of Medicine* in 1933.

SIGMAN, MORRIS (*b. Costesh, Bessarabia, Russia, 1881; d. Storm Lake, Iowa, 1931*), labor leader, officer of the International Ladies' Garment Workers' Union.

SIGOURNEY, LYDIA HOWARD HUNTLEY (*b. Norwich, Conn., 1791; d. Hartford, Conn., 1865*), poet, essayist. Conventional and imitative, Sigourney held high reputation in her own time and was called "the American Hemans." She was author of 67 books whose theme, for the most part, was death.

SIGSBEE, CHARLES DWIGHT (*b. Albany, N.Y., 1845; d. 1923*), naval officer. Graduated U.S. Naval Academy, 1863. Distinguished principally for his services as a scientist and inventor, Sigsbee was associated with Alexander Agassiz in deep-sea explorations, principally in the Gulf of Mexico, and developed a number of devices which practically revolutionized deep-sea sounding and dredging. Chief hydrographer to the Navy Department, 1893–97, he was commissioned captain, March 1897, and was in command of the battleship *Maine* when it was blown up in the harbor of Havana, February 1898. During the war with Spain, he commanded the *St. Paul*; in 1905 he commanded the squadron which brought back the body of John Paul Jones to America. He retired as rear admiral, 1907.

SIKES, WILLIAM WIRT (*b. Watertown, N.Y., 1836; d. Cardiff, Wales, 1883*), journalist, consular officer, folklorist. Husband of Olive Logan.

SILCOX, FERDINAND AUGUSTUS (*b. Columbus, Ga., 1882; d. Alexandria, Va., 1939*), forester, labor relations counsel, conservationist. Chief of the U.S. Forest Service, 1933–39.

SILL, ANNA PECK (*b. Burlington, N.Y., 1816; d. Rockford, Ill., 1889*), educator. A pioneer in the education of women, she was a founder of the present Rockford College, 1849–51, and principal, 1851–84.

SILL, EDWARD ROWLAND (*b. Windsor, Conn., 1841; d. Cleveland, Ohio, 1887*), poet, educator. Raised in Ohio. Graduated Yale, 1861. Professor of English, University of California, 1874–82. A poet of metaphysical doubt and perplexity, Sill voiced a humane idealism in a simple classical style. Author of *The Hermitage and Other Poems* (1868), *The Venus of Milo and Other Poems* (1883), and *The Poems of Edward Rowland Sill*, a collected edition (1902).

SILLIMAN, BENJAMIN (*b. present Trumbull, Conn., 1779; d. New Haven, Conn., 1864*), chemist, geologist, naturalist. Graduated Yale, 1796. After studying law under Simeon Baldwin and David Daggett, he was admitted to the bar, 1802, but in September of that year accepted appointment to the professorship of chemistry and natural history at Yale. He retired in 1853 as professor emeritus with a reputation as the most prominent and influential scientific mind in America.

In order to prepare himself for his professorship, he made special studies for two years at the medical school in Philadelphia, worked in the laboratory of Robert Hare, and received much valuable advice on the teaching of science from Dr. John Maclean. He began his work at Yale in April 1804 with the first course of lectures in chemistry ever given there. While traveling abroad in 1805, he became the intimate friend of Sir Humphry Davy, Sir David Brewster, Dr. John Murray, and Dr. Thomas Hope and grew deeply interested in geology. He was able, by 1813, to begin a full course of illustrated lectures in mineralogy and geology, utilizing the famed mineral collection of his friend George Gibbs, which the college later purchased. Silliman acted as a leading member of the committee to organize Yale Medical School, opened in 1813. *Post* 1808, he won wide acclaim as a lecturer on science to the public in New Haven, New York, and other cities; lectures on geology before the Boston Society of Natural History, 1835, were especially notable. In 1839–40 he was invited to deliver the first series of Lowell Institute lectures; few series of scientific lectures ever aroused greater interest, and Silliman justly regarded them as the crowning success of his professional life. Realizing the need for advanced study and laboratory work in the sciences, and aided by his son Benjamin (1816–85) and by his son-in-law, James D. Dana, he persuaded Yale College to establish in 1847 the Department of Philosophy and the Arts, under which the natural and physical sciences could be studied intensively. From this modest beginning grew the Yale Scientific School, later called the Sheffield Scientific School.

In 1818 he had founded *The American Journal of Science and Arts*, devoted to the publication of original papers, notices, and reviews in the broad field of the natural and physical sciences. Under his management, it became one of the world's great scientific journals and brought him wide recognition; it is one of his most enduring monuments. In addition to editing two texts on chemistry and geology, he published his own excellent *Elements of Chemistry* (1830–31) and contributed numerous articles to scientific journals. He investigated gold deposits in Virginia and coal in Pennsylvania, and directed an investigation for the government on sugar culture. A member of the American Philosophical Society *post* 1805, he was elected in 1840 first president of the Association of American Geologists, forerunner of the American Association for the Advancement of Science. In 1863 he became an original member of the National Academy of Sciences.

Silliman exerted a profound influence on collegiate education by establishing science as a study on a basis of equality with the older disciplines. A sincerely religious man, he believed that to study science was to learn of the wonderful manifestations of God in the natural world, which it was man's duty to interpret reverently and by which it was his privilege to improve the conditions of his life. This combination of a superior scientific mind with deep religious conviction enabled him to exert so great an influence in the interests of science on a generation that itself was dominated by strong religious convictions.

SILLIMAN, BENJAMIN (*b. New Haven, Conn., 1816; d. New Haven, 1885*), chemist. Son of Benjamin Silliman (1779–1864). Graduated Yale, 1837. Began teaching as an assistant to his father, whom he succeeded as professor of chemistry at Yale, 1853; he taught also at the University of Louisville, 1849–54. In association with his father and later with his brother-in-law, James D. Dana, he was an editor of the *American Journal of Science, post* 1838. Author of several textbooks and a number of monographs on chemistry and mineralogy, he frequently acted as consultant on chemical and mining problems. In this capacity he made, 1855, a major contribution to the petroleum industry by showing that petroleum was essentially a mixture of hydrocarbons and that it could be separated, by fractional distillation and simple means of purification, into a series of distillations making up about 90 percent of the whole. He discovered the chief uses which were to be made of petroleum products for the next 50 years and outlined the principal methods of preparing and purifying those products.

SILLS, MILTON (*b. Chicago, Ill., 1882; d. Santa Monica, Calif., 1930*), actor. A forceful stage actor and a motion-picture star *post* 1916, he helped organize the Academy of Motion Picture Arts and Sciences.

SILOTI, ALEXANDER ILYITCH (*b. near Kharkov, Russia, 1863; d. New York, N.Y., 1945*), pianist, conductor. Cousin of Sergei Rachmaninoff. Graduated Moscow Conservatory, 1881; studied at Weimar with Franz Liszt, 1883–86. Winning fame as a concert artist, he was also renowned as a conductor; between 1903 and 1917 he organized and conducted in St. Petersburg the Siloti Concerts, introducing new works by contemporary composers, including Scriabin, Schoenberg, Stravinsky, Prokofiev, Ravel, Falla, and Enesco. Director of the Maryinsky Opera at the time of the Russian Revolution, he left Russia to reside for a time in England and Belgium. In 1922 he came to the United States, joining the faculty of the Juilliard School, New York City, 1924; from then until his retirement in 1942, he devoted his principal energies to teaching and editing.

SILSBEE, NATHANIEL (*b. Salem, Mass., 1773; d. Salem, 1850*), merchant mariner, shipowner, Massachusetts legislator. Congressman, Democratic-Republican, 1817–21, and U.S. senator, 1826–35, he was influential in maritime legislation and was chairman, Senate Committee on Commerce, 1833–35.

SILVER, ABBA HILLEL (*b. Sirvintus, Lithuania, 1893; d. Cleveland, Ohio, 1963*), rabbi and Zionist leader. Came to New York in 1902; attended University of Cincinnati and Hebrew Union College; ordained in 1915. From 1917 until his death he led "The Temple," the Tifereth Israel Reform congregation in Cleveland. Wrote several books, including *A History of Messianic Speculation in Israel* (1927), *Religion in a Changing World* (1930), and *The World Crisis and Jewish Survival* (1941); a collection of his Zionist speeches, *Vision and Victory*, appeared in 1949. Starting in the 1930's he spent more and more time involved in Zionist affairs; he was cochairman of the American Zionist Emergency Council (1943–44) and president of the World Zionist Organization (1945–48). After the establishment of the state of Israel in 1948, he was forced out of the Zionist leadership.

SILVER, GRAY (*b. White Hall, Va., 1871; d. 1935*), West Virginia farmer and legislator, spokesman for farm groups. Organized the nonpartisan farm bloc which dominated legislative activities of the 67th Congress, 1921–23.

SILVER, THOMAS (*b. Greenwich, N.J., 1813; d. New York, N.Y., 1888*), civil engineer, inventor. His marine engine governor, covered by patents between 1855 and 1866, was adopted for use by most of the naval authorities of the world, though not by the United States.

SILVERMAN, JOSEPH (*b. Cincinnati, Ohio, 1860; d. New York, N.Y., 1930*), rabbi. Graduated University of Cincinnati, 1883; Hebrew Union College, 1884; D.D., 1887. After serving in Texas for a short time, he became junior rabbi at Temple Emanu-El, New York City, 1888. Elected rabbi, 1897, he became emeritus in 1922. A liberal in religion, he was active in community affairs and became a strong supporter of Zionism toward the end of his life.

SILVERMAN, SIME (*b. Cortland, N.Y., 1873; d. Los Angeles, Calif., 1933*), editor and publisher of *Variety post* 1905. The success of this notable theatrical paper was owing entirely to Silverman's honesty, devotion to work, and imaginative editing. Much present-day slang originated in its pages.

SILVERS, LOUIS (*b. Brooklyn, N.Y., 1889; d. Hollywood, Calif., 1954*), composer and conductor. He composed the song "April Showers" for Al Jolson in 1921 (for the Broadway show, *Bombo*). Remembered for his compositions for films, Silvers wrote the music for *The Jazz Singer* (1927) which was the first all-talking motion picture, starring Al Jolson. Other films include *It Happened One Night* (1934) and *One Night of Love* (1934), which won Silvers an Academy Award.

SIMKHOVITCH, MARY MELINDA KINGSBURY (*b. Chestnut Hill, Mass., 1867; d. New York, N.Y., 1951*), settlement worker and housing reformer. Studied at Boston University, Radcliffe College, the University of Berlin, and Columbia University. Founded the settlement house, Greenwich House, in New York in 1902; head resident until 1946. The house became an important focal point for community life in the area of Greenwich Village, included John Dewey on the educational committee, and sheltered such figures as Frances Perkins, who became the first woman cabinet member. President of the National Federation of Settlements, 1917; vice-chairman of the N.Y. City Housing Authority, 1934–48. Convinced Secretary of the Interior Harold Ickes to include federal housing in the public works projects of the New Deal.

SIMMONS (SZYMANSKI), ALOYSIUS HARRY (*b. Milwaukee, Wis., 1903; d. Milwaukee, 1956*), baseball player. One of baseball's greatest outfielders and batters, Simmons played from 1924 to 1932 for the Philadelphia Athletics under the management of Connie Mack. His lifetime batting average was .334; his 1,827 runs batted in was the tenth best in baseball history. After 1932, he played for the Chicago White Sox and other teams before becoming a coach. He was elected to the Baseball Hall of Fame in 1953.

SIMMONS, EDWARD (*b. Concord, Mass., 1852; d. Baltimore, Md., 1931*), mural painter. A boyhood companion of H. D. Thoreau. He graduated from Harvard, 1874, and as a student of painting at the Boston Museum of Fine Arts was influenced by William Rimmer. Studied and worked in France and England, 1879–91, then returned home to execute a number of murals in public buildings and private residences. His murals were strong and direct, but lacked originality in composition and execution.

SIMMONS, FRANKLIN (*b. present Webster, Maine, 1839; d. Rome, Italy, 1913*), sculptor. A resident principally of Rome *post* 1867, he was author of many portrait busts, public monuments, and ideal figures, which at their best displayed power and a simple grace.

SIMMONS, FURNIFOLD McLENDEL (*b. near Polloksville, N.C., 1854; d. near New Bern, N.C., 1940*), lawyer, politician. Graduated Trinity College (later Duke University), 1873. Congressman, Democrat, from North Carolina, 1887–89. Simmons gradually established himself in control of the Democratic state machine *post* 1892 and employed "white supremacy" tactics and propaganda to recapture the radical whites who had been drawn away from the party by the Populists. U.S. senator from 1900 to 1930, Simmons continued to control North Carolina politics and maintained a parochial ultraconservative attitude toward legislation, except in matters which might assist the interests of North Carolina. Seniority and hard work as a committee member earned him national influence; however, a general restiveness under his control was aggravated by his opposition to Alfred E. Smith, 1928.

SIMMONS, GEORGE HENRY (*b. Moreton-in-Marsh, Gloucestershire, England, 1852; d. Chicago, Ill., 1937*), physician, medical editor and executive. Came to America, 1870, settling in the Middle West. M.D., Hahnemann Medical College, 1882. Contributed to raising medical education standards as secretary (later general manager) of the American Medical Association and editor of the association's *Journal*, 1899–1924.

SIMMONS, JAMES STEVENS (*b. Newton, N.C., 1890; d. Hartford, Conn., 1954*), bacteriologist, army medical officer, and university administrator. Studied at Davidson College, the University of North Carolina, the University of Pennsylvania (M.D., 1915), George Washington University (Ph.D., 1934), and at Harvard (Ph.D., 1939). U.S. Army Medical Reserve Corps (1917–46). During World War II, assigned to the Office of the Surgeon General of the Army, where he developed and directed a successful program to safeguard the health of American fighting men. Promoted to brigadier general in 1943. As a member of the National Research Council (1941–46) he researched the first widespread use of DDT to control the spread of insect-borne diseases. Dean of the Harvard School of Public Health (1946–54).

SIMMONS, ROSCOE CONKLING MURRAY (*b. Monroe County, Miss., 1878; d. Chicago, Ill., 1951*), orator, journalist, and politician. Studied at Tuskegee Institute. A black active in Republican politics, Simmons became columnist for the black newspaper the *Chicago Defender* in 1913, helping to make that paper, through his travels and orations, the largest black newspaper in the country. Chairman of the colored speaker's bureau of the Republican National Committee in the 1920's. Seconded the nomination of President Hoover at the national convention in 1932. Feature writer for the *Chicago Tribune* during the 1940's.

SIMMONS, THOMAS JEFFERSON (*b. Hickory Grove, Ga., 1837; d. 1905*), Confederate officer, Georgia legislator and jurist. A principal factor in the restoring of Georgia finances during the last years of Reconstruction, Simmons was elected to the state supreme court, 1887, became chief justice in 1894, and continued in that post until his death.

SIMMONS, WILLIAM JOSEPH (*b. Harpersville, Ala., 1880; d. Atlanta, Ga., 1945*), promoter, founder of the revived Ku Klux Klan. After riding circuit in rural Alabama and northern Florida as a minister of the Methodist Episcopal Church, South, 1899–1912, he left the ministry and became a successful organizer for various fraternal orders. On Thanksgiving night, 1915, atop Stone Mountain, near Atlanta, Ga., he held a ceremony at which he announced a formal revival of the post–Civil War secret society dedicated to the preservation of public morality and white supremacy. The new Ku Klux Klan made little progress, however, until 1920 when an Atlanta firm of publicity agents took over and devised for it a creed of militant opposition to Catholics, Jews, blacks, immigrants, bootleggers, and modernist theologians— among other categories. The Klan then grew at an astonishing rate, spreading into every part of the nation and engaging in numerous acts of terrorism. Simmons' power as "Imperial Wizard" dwindled as the society expanded. In 1924, after a legal struggle with various state leaders, he resigned from the Klan and surrendered all copyrights on Klan literature and paraphernalia in exchange for a cash settlement and the deed to the "palace" he occupied in Atlanta.

SIMMS, RUTH HANNA MCCORMICK (*b. Cleveland, Ohio, 1880; d. Chicago, Ill, 1944*), politician, rancher. Daughter of Marcus A. Hanna; niece of James F. Rhodes. Married Joseph M. McCormick, 1903 (deceased 1925); married Albert G. Simms, 1932. Early associated with progressivism and midwestern agrarian liberalism, and an effective lobbyist for labor reforms and woman suffrage, she was essentially a partisan Republican "regular." Delighting in her self-described role of "first woman ward politician," she served on state and national Republican committees, organized a network of active women's Republican clubs throughout Illinois, and in 1928 was elected congressman-at-large from Illinois on a platform of "no promises and no bunk." She thus became the first woman in the United States to win a statewide election. Defeated in her candidacy for the U.S. Senate, 1930, she devoted herself thereafter principally to her personal business, removing after her second marriage to New Mexico.

SIMMS, WILLIAM ELLIOTT (*b. near Cynthiana, Ky., 1822; d. 1898*), lawyer, Mexican War and Confederate soldier. Congressman, Democrat, from Kentucky, 1859–61. He abandoned his early neutral position and served as Confederate senator from Kentucky, 1862–65.

SIMMS, WILLIAM GILMORE (*b. Charleston, S.C., 1806; d. Charleston, 1870*), novelist, man of letters. Educated in public and private schools in his native city, he was at first apprenticed to a druggist, but studied law and was admitted to the bar, 1827. He wrote and published a good deal of verse and contributed articles to periodicals and newspapers; as editor of the Charleston *City Gazette* he took a vigorous, unpopular stand against nullification. In 1832, after the death of his wife and other private difficulties, he removed to the North, where, in New York, he formed a permanent friendship with William Cullen Bryant and wrote a crime story, *Martin Faber* (1833). On its favorable reception by the public, he followed it with *Guy Rivers* (1834) and *The Yemassee* (1835). As he did not feel at home in the North, he returned to Charleston.

Marrying the daughter of a Barnwell Co. plantation owner, 1836, he had much to do with the management of his father-in-law's property. He continued active as a writer, producing, among other books, *Richard Hurdis* (1838), *Border Beagles* (1840), *Beauchampe* (1842); his best work of this period was *The Partisan* (1835), *Mellichampe* (1836), and *The Kinsmen* (1841, later titled *The Scout*). Possessed of a strong bent toward public affairs and a warm local patriotism, Simms turned his pen to the defense of slavery, but more particularly to the upbuilding of a distinctively Southern image. By saving slavery, as he saw it, the South would be preserved in its essential quality. He undertook to do whatever a man of letters could do for South Carolina by compiling a history and a geography of the state, by delivering orations, and by writing biographies of figures either distinctively Southern or filled with the qualities which he believed to be those of his section. From 1842 to 1850 Simms wrote comparatively little fiction; he then issued *Katharine Walton* (1851), *The Sword and the Distaff* (1853, later titled *Woodcraft*), *The Forayers* (1855), *Eutaw* (1856), *Charlemont* (1856), *The Classique of Kiawah* (1859), and others. Ruined materially by the Civil War, during which he gave his sympathies entirely to the South, Simms could do nothing to restore himself and his defeated section but edit *The War Poetry of the South* (1867), busy himself with journalism, and write bad serials for magazines.

SIMON, RICHARD LEO (*b. New York, N.Y., 1889; d. North Stamford, Conn., 1960*), publisher. Studied at Columbia University. Founded, with Max Lincoln Schuster, the firm Simon and Schuster in 1924. The firm concentrated on publishing bestsellers; many "how-to" books were ordered by the publishers, and writers complied. Simon published books that reflected his interests such as music, bridge, and photography. In 1939, he published *A Treasury of Art Masterpieces* which became a model for art books in America. Simon wrote a column for *Publishers Weekly* entitled "From the Inner Sanctum" (1926–35). In 1939 the partners founded Pocket Books, Inc., and were instrumental in opening up the lucrative paperback market. In 1944, the firm was sold to Marshall Field Enterprises, with Simon remaining as executive; he retired in 1957.

SIMONDS, FRANK HERBERT (*b. Concord, Mass., 1878; d. Washington, D.C., 1936*), journalist, commentator on military events of World War I.

SIMONS, ALGIE MARTIN (*b. North Freedom, Wis., 1870; d. New Martinsville, W.Va., 1950*), socialist theorist, journalist, and politician; personnel management expert; medical economist. B.L., University of Wisconsin, 1895. Edited a number of socialist publications, 1899–1916; author of *Packingtown* (1899), a vivid description of Chicago stockyard conditions, and of *Social Forces in American History* (1911), the first Marxist attempt at an explanation of the American past. *Post* 1918, he was engaged in industrial personnel management and as an economist for the American Medical Association.

SIMONS, HENRY CALVERT (*b. Virden, Ill., 1899; d. Chicago, Ill., 1946*), economist. B.A., University of Michigan, 1920; graduate study of Columbia University and University of Chicago. Taught at the University of Iowa, 1920–27, and the University of Chicago, 1927–46. With Frank H. Knight, a major factor in formation of the Chicago school of economists. Author of, among other works, *Personal Income Taxation* (1938).

SIMONTON, CHARLES HENRY (*b. Charleston, S.C., 1829; d. Philadelphia, Pa., 1904*), Confederate officer, South Carolina legislator, lawyer. Judge, U.S. district court of South Carolina, 1886–93; circuit court of appeals (4th Circuit), 1893–1904.

SIMONTON, JAMES WILLIAM (*b. Columbia Co., N.Y., 1823; d. Napa, Calif., 1882*), journalist, Washington correspondent, newspaper publisher. General agent of the Associated Press, 1867–81, he was instrumental in exposing some of the corruption of President Grant's administration.

SIMPSON, ALBERT BENJAMIN (*b. Bayview, Prince Edward Island, Canada, 1843; d. 1919*), Presbyterian clergyman, independent evangelist. Founded the Christian Alliance, 1887 (*post* 1897, the Christian and Missionary Alliance), of which he served as president and general superintendent.

SIMPSON, CHARLES TORREY (*b. Tiskilwa, Ill., 1846; d. Miami, Fla., 1932*), naturalist, U.S. National Museum official, authority on mollusks.

SIMPSON, EDMUND SHAW (*b. England, 1784; d. New York, N.Y., 1848*), actor, manager. Made American debut at the Park Theatre, New York City, October 1809; became acting manager of the Park, 1812, and a partner in that theater *ca.* 1818. Successful for a number of years as manager and director. Simpson became sole lessee upon the death of Stephen Price, 1840, at a time when, for a number of reasons, the enterprise was tottering. After eight years of dogged struggle, he gave up his interest to others for a small annuity.

SIMPSON, EDWARD (*b. New York, N.Y., 1824; d. Washington, D.C., 1888*), naval officer. Son of Edmund S. Simpson. An ordnance expert and veteran of the Mexican and Civil wars,

Simpson held many important commands and retired as rear admiral, 1886.

SIMPSON, JAMES HERVEY (*b. New Brunswick, N.J., 1813; d. St. Paul, Minn., 1883*), soldier, explorer. Graduated West Point, 1832. Commissioned in the artillery, he transferred to the topographical engineers, 1838, and was engaged up to the Civil War in important survey work in the West and Southwest and also in Minnesota. After field service in the early days of the Civil War, he served as chief engineer, Department of the Ohio, 1862–63, and was in general charge of fortification and engineering projects in Kentucky, 1863–65, receiving the brevet of brigadier general. Chief engineer, Department of the Interior, 1865–67, he undertook general direction and inspection of the Union Pacific Railroad as well as of all government wagon roads and was promoted colonel, March 1867. Subsequently he engaged actively in engineering work in the South and the Middle West. Simpson was author of a number of interesting reports of great historical value, including *Report from the Secretary of War . . . of the Route from Fort Smith, Ark., to Santa Fe, N.Mex.* (1850) and *Journal of a Military Reconnaissance from Santa Fe, N.Mex., to the Navajo Country* (1852).

SIMPSON, JERRY (*b. Westmoreland Co., New Brunswick, Canada, 1842; d. Wichita, Kans., 1905*), farmer, rancher, politician. After working as a Great Lakes sailor, brief service in the Union army, and a short residence in Porter Co., Ind., Simpson settled in Kansas *ca.* 1879. Losing his savings and harassed by mortgages after the collapse of the boom times in Kansas, he drifted from the Republican party by various stages into the Populist movement and represented the seventh Kansas district in the U.S. House of Representatives, 1891–95. Reelected with Democratic help, he served again, 1897–99. Called "Sockless Jerry," he combined with the Populist doctrine a belief in the single tax. Although he delivered few speeches and proposed few bills in Congress, he directed his sharp, shrewd wit at insincerity and what he considered false doctrine. His belief in simple democracy and monetary reform were the two consistent threads through his career.

SIMPSON, JOHN ANDREW (*b. near Salem, Nebr., 1871; d. Washington, D.C., 1934*), farm leader, lawyer, Oklahoma legislator. Advocated legislation to guarantee cost of production plus reasonable profit to farmers for products consumed in the home market; also favored low farm-mortgage refinancing and free coinage of silver.

SIMPSON, MATTHEW (*b. Cadiz, Ohio, 1811; d. 1884*), Methodist clergyman, educator. President, present DePauw University, 1839–48, Simpson was elected bishop, 1852, and as a strong antislavery proponent became a friend and counselor of Salmon P. Chase, Edwin Stanton, and President Lincoln. He was public speaker of rare effectiveness and the most influential Methodist of his day in the United States.

SIMPSON, MICHAEL HODGE (*b. Newburyport, Mass., 1809; d. Boston, Mass., 1884*), capitalist, manufacturer, inventor of machinery for carpet-making and wool-burring.

SIMPSON, STEPHEN (*b. Philadelphia, Pa., 1789; d. Philadelphia, 1854*), periodical editor, reformer. Edited the *Portico*, Baltimore, Md., 1816–17; coproprietor of the *Columbian Observer*. A strong supporter of Andrew Jackson and the first man to run for Congress on a labor ticket in the United States, he was author of, among other books, *The Working Man's Manual: A New Theory of Political Economy on the Principle of Production the Source of Wealth* (1831). In this work he contended that labor should receive the whole of its production, denounced fund

holders and land monopolists, and advocated political divisions according to economic allegiance.

SIMPSON, WILLIAM DUNLAP (*b. Laurens District, S.C., 1823; d. 1890*), lawyer, South Carolina legislator, Confederate soldier and congressman. Democratic lieutenant governor of South Carolina, 1876–78; governor, 1878–80. Chief justice of South Carolina, 1880–90. Competent but not brilliant.

SIMPSON, WILLIAM KELLY (*b. Hudson, N.Y., 1855; d. 1914*), laryngologist. Associated with Joseph O'Dwyer in his work on intubation. Professor of laryngology, New York College of Physicians and Surgeons, 1904–14; served on many hospital staffs.

SIMS, CHARLES N. (*b. Fairfield, Ind., 1835; d. Liberty, Ind., 1908*), Methodist clergyman. Graduated present DePauw University, 1859. After an active ministry and a brief term as president of Valparaiso College, he served with great ability as chancellor of Syracuse University, 1881–93.

SIMS, JAMES MARION (*b. Lancaster Co., S.C., 1813; d. 1883*), gynecologist. Graduated South Carolina College, 1832; Jefferson Medical College, 1835. Settling in Mount Meigs, Ala., he attained his first local fame by urging an abdominal incision for an abscess after consultants had dismissed the patient with a diagnosis of cancer. Removing to Montgomery, Ala., 1840, he next won attention by the complete rectification of a cleft palate. Called to treat a woman in labor, June 1845, he found that impaction and extensive sloughing had resulted in a large bladder fistula which would render the patient unfit for all social relationships and which was considered incurable. Convinced that he could cure this and similar troubles by a new technique which accident had suggested to him, he began a long, drawn-out series of operations performed under the most difficult conditions. Successful in the late spring of 1849 with three patients, owing mainly to silver sutures which he had devised and to his own unparalleled skill, he wrote the history of his vesicovaginal fistula operation in full recognition of its importance and published it in the *American Journal of the Medical Sciences*, January 1852. Removing to New York City, 1853, he continued to perform fistula operations, instructed his fellow surgeons in his methods, and brought about institution of the Woman's Hospital, 1855. Removing to Europe for a rest, 1861, he was received everywhere with high praise and honor, performed a number of successful operations, and after a brief visit to America returned to Paris to practice, July 1862–1865. His *Clinical Notes on Uterine Surgery* (1866) was a factor in formation of the nascent specialty of gynecology. Resident principally in New York City after the Civil War, he performed volunteer service in France during the Franco-Prussian War, 1870. In 1876 he was president of the American Medical Association. His autobiography, *The Story of My Life*, appeared posthumously, 1884.

SIMS, WILLIAM SOWDEN (*b. Port Hope, Ontario, Canada, 1858; d. Boston, Mass., 1936*), naval officer, naval reformer. Son of Alfred W. Sims, an American civil engineer, and Adelaide (Sowden) Sims of Port Hope, he spent his youth in the United States and graduated from Annapolis, 1880. Six years at sea and a year of language study in Paris were followed by six more years at sea, including two on the China Station during the Sino-Japanese War; he then spent three years as naval attaché in France and, briefly, in Russia. His voluminous reports from Europe showed his awareness of the comparative backwardness of the U.S. Navy. By 1901 he was bombarding the Navy Department with problems of ship design and gunnery, enthusiastically advocating the new British technique of continuous-aim firing, and committing an insubordinate act by writing directly to President Theodore Roosevelt about the "very inefficient condition of the Navy." Ordered to Washington as inspector of target practice, 1902, he also served *post* 1907 as the president's naval aide. These were fruitful years for the naval reformers. By the end of the Roosevelt administration, American gunnery was second to none, and criticism of ship design and of navy bureaucracy had provoked congressional investigations, with, however, inconclusive results. In 1910 Sims made an effusively pro-British speech at the Guildhall in London, for which he was publicly reprimanded by President Taft. He served with distinction as commander, Atlantic Destroyer Flotilla, and as president, 1917, of the Naval War College. He won promotion to rear admiral, 1917, and to vice admiral, 1918, and was named commander, U.S. Naval Forces in European Waters, June 1918. Promoted full admiral in December, he spent the war in London supervising America's extensive overseas naval activity. Still agitating for Navy Department reorganization, Sims refused a decoration for wartime service. Retiring in 1922, he continued through speeches and articles to press for processes of reform. He later championed naval aviation and crusaded for legislation to keep America out of war. In the wider sense this highly competent officer represented the Progressive and muckraking movements, improbably situated within a military environment.

SIMS, WINFIELD SCOTT (*b. New York, N.Y., 1844; d. Newark, N.J., 1918*), inventor. First to apply electricity to torpedo propulsion, Sims also invented a pneumatic field gun, several dynamite guns, and a number of other ordnance devices.

SINCLAIR, HARRY FORD (*b. Wheeling, W.Va., 1878; d. Pasadena, Calif., 1956*), oil producer. Studied briefly at the University of Kansas. Sinclair became an oil broker in 1903; by 1905, he invested in the rich Kiowa Pool in Oklahoma. By 1916, he had founded one of the giants in American industry, the Sinclair Oil and Refining Company. The company prospered; in the 1920's, Sinclair was involved in the Teapot Dome Scandal and was called before a Senate investigating Committee. He later stood trial along with ex-secretary of the interior, Albert Fall. Sinclair refused to testify before the Senate and at his trial. While never convicted of the bribery charges brought against him, he did serve nine months in prison for contempt of court and of the Senate. An intensely private man, Sinclair retired from active life in his company in 1954.

SINCLAIR, UPTON BEALL, JR. (*b. Baltimore, Md., 1878; d. Bound Brook, N.J., 1968*), journalist and novelist. Attended City College of New York (B.A., 1897) and Columbia. In his earliest writings he exhibited the fluency of pen that enabled him to become one of the most prolific and widely read authors in American literary history. He joined the Socialist party in 1902; with Jack London he helped found the Intercollegiate Socialist Society in 1905. He was also an unsuccessful Socialist candidate for Congress and the California governorship in the 1920's and 1930's. The best of his early novels was *Manassas* (1904). *The Jungle* (1906) was an immediate and sensational best-seller; it depicted the lives of packinghouse workers and the unsanitary conditions in the meat-processing industry. With that work he became a "muckraker"; other muckraking books include *The Moneychangers* (1908), *King Coal* (1917), and *Oil!* 1927). He began a series of nonfiction works on the effects of capitalism in America seen from the socialist standpoint with *Profits of Religion* (1918). In 1940 he published the first of the eleven-volume Lanny Budd series; the third volume, *Dragon's Teeth* (1942), won a Pulitzer Prize. *What Didymus Did* (1954) was his farewell to fiction writing. His autobiography was published in 1962.

SINGER, ISAAC MERRIT (*b. Pittstown, N.Y., 1811; d. Torquay, England, 1875*), inventor. Developed the first practical domestic sewing machine (patented 1851, with improvement

patents thereafter until 1863) and brought it into general use through the manufacturing company which he founded and headed until 1863.

SINGER, ISRAEL JOSHUA (*b. Bilgoray, Poland, 1893; d. New York, N.Y., 1944*), Yiddish novelist, journalist. Brother of Isaac B. Singer. Son of a Hasidic rabbi, he rebelled against his religious and cultural traditions yet never could discover any values to replace them; in his work, he gives artistic expression to this sense of alienation and to the struggles which he observed and underwent. After a troubled career in Russia and Poland, he came to the United States in 1934. He was author of, among other works, *Yoshe Kalb* (1933, entitled in English *The Sinner*); *The Brothers Ashkenazi* (1936); *East of Eden* (1939); and *The Family Carnovsky* (1943). One volume of an unfinished autobiography, *Of a World That Is No More*, was published posthumously in 1946 (English translation, 1970).

SINGERLY, WILLIAM MISKEY (*b. Philadelphia, Pa., 1832; d. Philadelphia, 1898*), journalist. Editor-publisher of the *Philadelphia Record* (originally the *Public Record*) *post* 1877; Democratic political leader of Pennsylvania.

SINGLETON, ESTHER (*b. Baltimore, Md., 1865; d. Stonington, Conn., 1930*), editor, music critic. Author of, among other books, *The Furniture of Our Forefathers* (1900) and *Social New York Under the Georges* (1902).

SINGLETON, JAMES WASHINGTON (*b. Frederick Co., Va., 1811; d. Baltimore, Md., 1892*), Illinois lawyer, Civil War peace projector. Congressman, Democrat, from Illinois, 1879–83.

SINNOTT, EDMUND WARE (*b. Cambridge, Mass., 1888; d. New Haven, Conn., 1968*), botanist and geneticist. Attended Harvard (Ph.D., 1913), taught at Harvard Forestry School and Bussey Institution (1914–15), Connecticut Agricultural College (1915–28), Barnard (1928–39), and Columbia (1939); at Yale, beginning in 1940, he was Sterling Professor of Botany and director of the Osborn Botanical Laboratory, March Botanical Gardens, and, during 1946–56, the Sheffield Scientific School. Although a botanist, he approached the study of plants as a morphologist. In the 1920's and 1930's he published a series of articles that define how genes affect the shape of fruit, particularly squash. He became one of the leading plant geneticists in the United States and coauthored a book that became a standard work, *Principles of Genetics* (1925).

SIRINGO, CHARLES A. (*b. Matagorda Co., Tex., 1855; d. Hollywood, Calif., 1928*), cowboy, detective. Author of *A Texas Cowboy* (1885) and *A Cowboy Detective* (1912).

SITTING BULL (*b. on Grand River, S.Dak., 1834[?]; d. 1890*), Hunkpapa Sioux chief, medicine man. His camp in the buffalo country became the rallying point for Sioux, Cheyenne, and Arapaho Indians hostile to the whites; by the spring of 1876 he had gathered a force estimated at from 2,500 to 4,000 men. When General George A. Custer made his disastrous attack on the consolidated Indian village at the Little Bighorn in June, Sitting Bull did no fighting, but spent the time in "making medicine." Driven with his band across the Canadian border by the end of 1876, he surrendered at Fort Buford in 1881 and was settled on the Standing Rock Reservation. Arrested by Indian policemen for his part in the Messiah agitation, he was shot and killed in the fight that followed.

SIZER, NELSON (*b. Chester, Mass., 1812; d. 1897*), phrenologist. Pupil of J. G. Spurzheim; associated in practice with Orson Fowler and S. R. Wells; president, American Institute of Phrenology.

SKANIADARIIO (*b. Ganawaugus, N.Y., ca. 1735; d. Onondaga, N.Y., 1815*), Seneca sachem, religious leader. Claiming revelation from the Creator of Life, he propounded a new religion for the Iroquois called the Gaiwiio.

SKENANDOA (*b. 1706[?]; d. near Oneida Castle, N.Y., 1816*), Oneida chief. Converted to Christianity by Samuel Kirkland. During the Revolution, he helped keep the Oneida and Tuscarora from joining the British and later persuaded many members of these tribes to join the Americans.

SKENE, ALEXANDER JOHNSTON CHALMERS (*b. Fyvie, Scotland, 1837; d. 1900*), pioneer gynecologist. Came to America, 1856. M.D., Long Island College Hospital, 1863; served there for many years as teacher, dean, and president; was consultant to a number of hospitals; practiced in Brooklyn, N.Y. A founder and president of the American Gynecological Society and the International Congress of Gynecology and Obstetrics, he was author of more than 100 medical papers and of a number of books. His discovery, 1880, of what are now called Skene's urethral glands gave him an international reputation and an assured place in the history of gynecology. He also is known to have devised 31 surgical instruments.

SKIDMORE, LOUIS (*b. Lawrenceburg, Ind., 1897; d. Winter Haven, Fla., 1962*), architect. Attended Bradley Polytechnic in Illinois and Massachusetts Institute of Technology (1920–24). In 1929 he prepared drawings for the Chicago centennial celebration and was made chief of design of the fair, even though no design of his had yet been built. He succeeded in coordinating the design work to create the first coherent statement of modern architecture in the United States. In 1936 he opened an office in Chicago with his brother-in-law, Nathaniel Owings; John Merrill joined the firm in 1939, and Skidmore, Owings and Merrill began an innovative architectural practice. Skidmore headed the New York office, which had the bulk of the work and the prestige clients; its projects included designs for the 1939 New York World's Fair; the Fort Hamilton Veteran's Hospital (1939); the Community of Oak Ridge, Tenn., for the Manhattan Project (1942–45); Lever House in New York City (1952), and the U.S. Air Force Academy at Colorado Springs (1954–64). Skidmore retired in 1955 and was awarded the Gold Medal of the American Institute of Architects (1957).

SKILLERN, ROSS HALL (*b. Philadelphia, Pa., 1875; d. Philadelphia, 1930*), laryngologist, professor of laryngology in Medico-Chirurgical College of Philadelphia and University of Pennsylvania.

SKINNER, AARON NICHOLS (*b. Boston, Mass., 1845; d. Framingham, Mass., 1918*), astronomer. Associated with the U.S. Naval Observatory, 1870–1909.

SKINNER, ALANSON BUCK (*b. Buffalo, N.Y., 1886; d. near Tokio, N.Dak., 1925*), anthropologist, ethnologist. Associated with American Museum of Natural History, 1907–13; later with Milwaukee Museum and with Heye Foundation. Authority on material culture of Algonquian Indians and of Siouan tribes in contact with them.

SKINNER, CHARLES RUFUS (*b. Union Square, Oswego Co., N.Y., 1844; d. Pelham Manor, N.Y., 1928*), journalist. New York legislator and congressman. In state education department *post* 1886, he was state superintendent of public instruction, 1895–1904. He held several other state appointments thereafter, and was legislative librarian, 1915–25.

SKINNER, HALCYON (*b. Mantua, Ohio, 1824; d. 1900*), inventor of carpet-weaving machinery, notably a power loom for moquette carpets (patented 1877).

SKINNER, HARRY (*b. Perquimans Co., N.C., 1855; d. Greenville, N.C., 1929*), lawyer, North Carolina legislator. Congressman, Populist, from North Carolina, 1895–99. Claimed that his ideas formed basis of "subtreasury" plan for agricultural price-fixing as advocated by Populists.

SKINNER, JOHN STUART (*b. Calvert Co., Md., 1788; d. Baltimore, Md., 1851*), lawyer, public official, agricultural editor and writer. Companion of Francis Scott Key during bombardment of Fort McHenry, September 1814, he subsequently arranged to have "The Star-Spangled Banner" first printed. In 1819 he founded the *American Farmer*, the first continuous, successful agricultural periodical in the United States, which he published until 1830. In 1829 he started the *American Turf Register and Sporting Magazine*, the first magazine devoted to the improvement of American Thoroughbred horses. From 1845 to 1848 he edited the *Farmer's Library* in New York, and then established in Philadelphia *The Plough, the Loom, and the Anvil*, which he edited until his death. A member of leading agricultural organizations, he was an outstanding agricultural publicist.

SKINNER, OTIS (*b. Cambridge, Mass., 1858; d. New York, N.Y., 1942*), actor. While he worked as Hartford correspondent for the New York *Dramatic News* and editor of the *Hartford Clarion*, his thoughts constantly reverted to the theater. In 1877 a letter of recommendation from the showman P. T. Barnum, an acquaintance of his father's, helped Skinner obtain a position as "utility" actor. During his first season he played 92 roles. He spent the next season, 1878–79, with the more prosperous Walnut Street Theatre stock company in Philadelphia. In 1880 he played minor roles with a company formed around Edwin Booth, who became his revered friend and teacher. From 1881 to 1884 Skinner acted with Lawrence Barrett, but he left Barrett's troupe and toured with the comedy company of Augustin Daly. Barrett, as Booth's business manager, engaged Skinner for second leads in the combined tour of Booth and the Polish tragedienne Helena Modjeska, 1889–90.

In 1894 Skinner managed his own company, and over the next few years he enjoyed many successes in Shakespearean plays and 19th-century favorites. His most noteworthy appearances during this period were in *His Grace de Grammont* (1894); *Villon the Vagabond* (1895), written by Skinner and his brother Charles; *Hamlet* (1895); Sheridan's *The Rivals* (1899), on tour with Joseph Jefferson; *Prince Otto* (1900), Skinner's first New York success as a star; a revival of *Francesca da Rimini* (1901); a season of classic comedies with Ada Rehan (1903); and a poetic French drama, *The Harvester* (1904).

By 1904 Skinner was an established star on Broadway and in "the provinces." That year he went under the management of Charles Frohman, who presented him in Henri Lavedan's *The Duel* (1906) and in *The Honor of the Family* (1907), in which Skinner scored one of his biggest hits as the villain. After appearing as a hammy old actor in *Your Humble Servant* (1910), he went on to his greatest triumph, *Kismet* (1911). He played *Kismet* for three years (in New York and on tour) and made two films of the play. He continued his stardom as a deaf philanthropist in Jules Eckert Goodman's *The Silent Voice* (1914), as a lovable Italian organ-grinder in *Mister Antonio* (1916), as a bullfighter in *Blood and Sand* (1921), as Sancho Panza in the play of that name (1923), and as Falstaff in the Players Club revival of *Henry IV* (1926) and in the 1927 production of *The Merry Wives of Windsor* by Minnie Maddern Fiske. In the 1930's Skinner went on tour with Maude Adams, playing Shylock to her Portia, and appeared in several classic revivals presented by the Players. He retired from the stage in 1940. He was the father of the actress and author Cornelia Otis Skinner.

SKINNER, THOMAS HARVEY (*b. Harvey's Neck, N.C., 1791; d. New York, N.Y., 1871*), Presbyterian clergyman, professor of homiletics at Andover and Union Theological seminaries. An advocate of the "new school," he promoted broader theological views and closer interdenominational relations.

SKINNER, WILLIAM (*b. London, England, 1824; d. 1902*), silk manufacturer. Immigrated to America, 1843; did business at Holyoke, Mass., *post* 1874 after making start near Williamsburg, Mass., *ca.* 1874 after making start near Williamsburg, Mass., *ca.* 1849. Produced high-quality "Skinner's satin" lining.

SKOURAS, GEORGE PANAGIOTES (*b. Skourohorion, Greece, 1896; d. New York, N.Y., 1964*), theater executive. Arrived in the United States in 1911. Beginning in 1914 he and his brothers Charles and Spyros purchased entertainment properties in St. Louis, and by 1926 the Skouras chain included thirty-seven St. Louis–area theaters. Prior to the stock-market crash of 1929, the brothers had sold Skouras Brothers Enterprises to Warner Brothers, which became owner of one of the top theater circuits. Warners hired the brothers to head different divisions of its theater operations; George moved to New York City as general manager of the eastern section. In 1931 he became president of the new Skouras Circuit of fifty theaters in New York City area; in 1952 he was president of the United Artists Theatre Circuit. He founded the Magna Theatre Corporation (1953); its first product, *Oklahoma!* (1955), was shot in Todd-A-O and lost $4 million; he then guided Magna through the lucrative leasing of the Todd-A-O process to Twentieth Century-Fox for its highly profitable *South Pacific* (1958). He retired as head of Magna in 1963.

SLADE, JOSEPH ALFRED (*b. near Carlyle, Ill., ca. 1824; d. Virginia City, Mont., 1864*), freighter, wagon-train boss, stagecoach division agent, "bad man." Hanged by vigilantes.

SLADE, WILLIAM (*b. Cornwall, Vt., 1786; d. Middlebury, Vt., 1859*), lawyer, editor, public official, politician. Elected to Congress as Democrat in 1830, he served for 12 years and in that time became a Whig; he was a fierce opponent of slavery and a high-tariff advocate. As governor of Vermont, 1844–46, he reorganized the public school system. He served thereafter as agent of the Board of National Popular Education.

SLAFTER, EDMUND FARWELL (*b. Norwich, Vt., 1816; d. Hampton, N.H., 1906*), Episcopal clergyman, scholar. Graduated Dartmouth, 1840. Active in pastoral work and as an official of the American Bible Society, he was a valued member and officer of the New England Historic Genealogical Society and of the Prince Society (president, 1880–1906). He edited four Prince Society monographs, including *Voyages of Samuel de Champlain* (1878–82).

SLATER, JOHN FOX (*b. Slatersville, R.I., 1815; d. 1884*), cotton and woolen manufacturer, philanthropist. Founded John F. Slater Fund for black education, 1882.

SLATER, SAMUEL (*b. Belper, England, 1768; d. 1835*), founder of the American cotton-spinning industry. Apprenticed in 1783 to Jedediah Strutt, a partner of Richard Arkwright in development of cotton-manufacturing machinery, Slater immigrated by stealth to America in 1789. Having studied and memorized all details of making textile machinery (whose exportation from England was then forbidden by law), he contracted with Almy and Brown of Rhode Island to reproduce Arkwright's machine for that firm; in 1793 they built their first factory in

Pawtucket under the firm name of Almy, Brown and Slater. In 1798 he formed a family partnership known as Samuel Slater & Co. and undertook a variety of highly successful mill operations in Rhode Island, Connecticut, and Massachusetts.

SLATTERY, CHARLES LEWIS (*b. Pittsburgh, Pa., 1867; d. Boston, Mass., 1930*), Episcopal clergyman, author. Consecrated coadjutor bishop of Massachusetts, 1922; succeeded to the see, 1927. Made his principal contribution as pastor and scholar, in particular as chairman of commission to revise the Book of Common Prayer.

SLAUGHTER, PHILIP (*b. Culpeper Co., Va., 1808; d. 1890*), Episcopal clergyman, historian. Author of a number of Virginia parish histories and monographs.

SLEEPER, JACOB (*b. Newcastle, Maine, 1802; d. Boston, Mass., 1889*), merchant, philanthropist. One of the three founders of Boston University, 1869.

SLEMP, CAMPBELL BASCOM (*b. Turkey Cove, Lee County, Va., 1870; d. Knoxville, Tenn., 1943*), lawyer, politician. Chosen to complete his father's unexpired term as a Republican member of Congress from Virginia, 1907, he won reelection to seven consecutive terms. He voted consistently with the "Old Guard" of his party, and was one of its most influential southern members. He served as presidential secretary to President Calvin Coolidge, 1923–25.

SLICER, THOMAS ROBERTS (*b. Washington, D.C., 1847; d. New York, N.Y., 1916*), Unitarian clergyman. Principal pastorate at All Souls Church, New York City, *post* 1897. A prominent preacher and writer, he was best known as a militant leader of civic reform.

SLICHTER, SUMNER HUBER (*b. Madison, Wis., 1892; d. Boston, Mass., 1959*), economist. Studied at the University of Munich, Germany, at the University of Wisconsin, and at the University of Chicago (Ph.D., 1918). Taught at Cornell in the 1920's and at Harvard Business School from 1930. Believing that academic economists could have an important influence on the nation's economy, Slichter wrote *Union Policies and Industrial Management* in 1941, published by the Brookings Institution. Other books include *The Impact of Collective Bargaining on Management* (1960). Associate chairman of the Advisory Council on Social Security to the Senate Finance Committee (1947–48). President of the American Economic Association, 1941.

SLIDELL, JOHN (*b. New York, N.Y., 1793; d. Cowes, England, 1871*), lawyer, Louisiana politician, diplomat, Confederate agent. Brother of Alexander S. Mackenzie; brother-in-law of Matthew C. Perry. Graduated Columbia, 1810. Removing to New Orleans, La., 1819, he practiced successfully and entered politics as a Jackson Democrat. As congressman, 1843–45, he advocated tariff reductions, except for tariff on sugar; in the election of 1844, he helped secure a majority for Polk in Louisiana by maneuvering a "floater" vote. Appointed U.S. commissioner to Mexico to adjust Texas boundary and purchase New Mexico and California, 1845, he returned unsuccessful. As U.S. senator from Louisiana, 1853–61, he favored repeal of the Missouri Compromise and, as James Buchanan's campaign manager in 1856, materially promoted both his nomination for the presidency and election. During the first three years of the administration, he was the power behind the throne and recommended numerous cabinet and diplomatic appointments. He favored the Lecompton Constitution for Kansas, bitterly opposed Stephen A. Douglas, and supported the Breckinridge-Lane ticket in 1860. Breaking with Buchanan after the dismissal of John B. Floyd from the War Department, Slidell was chosen to represent the Confederacy in France and was apprehended with James M. Mason in the celebrated *"Trent* affair." He performed creditably enough at Paris, but was distrusted by other Confederate agents and won little more than lip service from Napoleon III. After the Civil War, he resided in Paris until the fall of the empire.

SLIPHER, VESTO MELVIN (*b. Mulberry, Ind., 1875; d. Flagstaff, Ariz., 1969*), astronomer. Attended Indiana (Ph.D., 1909). Began his career with the Lowell observatory in Flagstaff while attending college, becoming director in 1926 and retiring in 1954. His first task at the observatory was to install a new spectrograph; he discovered that the diffuse nebula in the Pleiades shone solely by reflected starlight, indicating the existence of interstellar dust. His most significant work involved the study of the velocity and rotation of spiral nebula; by 1912 he had obtained several exposures of the Andromeda nebula (M31) and announced in 1913 that the nebula was approaching earth at 300 kilometers per second. Over the next eighteen months, he calculated the radial velocities of fourteen other nebulae, finding that most were receding from the earth at velocities as great as 1,000 kilometers per second.

SLOAN, ALFRED PRITCHARD, JR. (*b. New Haven, Conn., 1875; d. New York, N.Y., 1966*), industrialist and philanthropist. Attended Brooklyn Polytechnic and Massachusetts Institute of Technology. In 1898 his father and an associate purchased the Hyatt Roller Bearing company and put Sloan in charge. He convinced the Olds Motor Company to use his bearing in the still-experimental horseless carriage; in 1916 he sold the company to William Durant, founder of General Motors, and received his share in United Motors stock, a collection of parts and accessories firms that supplied GM's several companies. Sloan was put in charge of United, and when it was incorporated into GM (1918), he became a member of the GM Executive Committee. He became president of GM (1923–37), then chairman (until 1946). By creating an administrative structure that became a model for the management of large-scale industrial enterprise, he transformed GM and the auto industry. He also developed the industry's first systematic trade-in policies; by 1929 GM surpassed its competitor Ford; by 1940 it was the largest motor vehicle manufacturer in the world. In the 1920's, with the demand for autos low, he embarked on a strategy of diversification; GM's success with the production of diesel locomotives made the steam locomotive obsolete in less than two decades. After 1946 he concentrated on philanthropy. He set up the Alfred P. Sloan, Jr., Foundation, which financed the Sloan-Kettering Institute for Cancer Research, and at MIT the Center for Advanced Engineering Study and the Fund for Basic Research in the Physical Sciences.

SLOAN, GEORGE ARTHUR (*b. Nashville, Tenn., 1893; d. New York, N.Y., 1955*), business executive, civic leader, music patron. LL.B., Vanderbilt University (1915). 1919–22, assistant to the chairman of the American National Red Cross, specializing in Chinese relief. President and chairman of the board of the Cotton and Textile Institute (1932–35); chairman of the Consumer Goods Industries Committee under the NRA. Commissioner of Commerce for New York after 1940; after World War II, chairman of the board of trustees of the International Chamber of Commerce. President of the Metropolitan Opera Association, 1940. Helped bring about the repeal of the federal admissions tax in 1951, saving the Met great sums of money.

SLOAN, HAROLD PAUL (*b. Westfield, N.J., 1881; d. Camden, N.J., 1961*), Methodist clergyman, editor, and author. Attended University of Pennsylvania and Crozer and Drew (B.D., 1908) seminaries; ordained in the Methodist Episcopal Church in 1908. Pastor of Haddonfield Methodist Church in New Jersey

(1924–33) and Wharton Methodist Church in Philadelphia (1941–53). He was the principal leader of the fundamentalist defense of the faith, but he rejected the term "fundamentalism" and disassociated himself from the premillenialism of organized fundamentalism, disavowed biblical literalism, and upheld the legitimacy of higher criticism. He personally rejected evolution, but felt that Christianity and evolution were compatible. In the late 1920's he grew increasingly alienated within Methodism by his attacks on the acceptance by liberal Methodists of naturalistic and behavioristic philosophy. Author of *The Child and the Church* (1916), *Historic Christianity and the New Theology* (1922), and *The Apostle's Creed* (1930); editor of Methodism's leading newspaper, the *New York Christian Advocate* (1936–41).

SLOAN, JAMES FORMAN (*b. Bunker Hill, Ind., 1874; d. Los Angeles, Calif., 1933*), jockey, popularly known as "Tod," Adopting a special seat whereby he revolutionized modern race-riding, Sloan became principal rider for William C. Whitney and the most celebrated jockey of the late 19th century. Riding principally in Europe *post* 1897, he was ruled off the turf in 1901 by the English Jockey Club.

SLOAN, JOHN FRENCH (*b. Lock Haven, Pa., 1871; d. Hanover, N.H., 1951*), painter, printmaker. A member of the "Philadelphia four," a group of modernist painters, and, later of the famous Ashcan school, a New York group of painters of urban scenes who dissented from the academic approach to art at the turn of the century. Their paintings, exhibited at the famed Armory Show in 1913, were influential in forming the school of realism in American art of the 1920's and 1930's, and influenced such painters as Edward Hopper and George Bellows. Sloan wrote *Gist of Art* (1939). His style was realistic and depicted scenes from everyday urban life. The painting *Dust Storm* was purchased by the Metropolitan Museum of New York in 1921.

SLOAN, MATTHEW SCOTT (*b. Mobile, Ala., 1881; d. New York, N.Y., 1945*), public utilities executive. B.S., Alabama Polytechnic Institute, 1901; M.S., 1902. After work with the General Electric Co. and its subsidiary, the Electric Bond and Share Co., he went in 1917 with the Consolidated Gas Co., New York City. This company, which controlled electric power distribution in the city through four subsidiary companies, was notoriously inefficient and dominated by local politicians. Successful in effecting reforms in administration and in modernizing plants while president of the Brooklyn Edison Co., 1919–28, he was chosen president and operating head of the several companies supplying power in and around New York when they were combined (later to be reorganized as Consolidated Edison Co.). After four years of struggle to achieve for the whole system what he had accomplished in Brooklyn, he made some progress in solving the technical problems involved; he was defeated, however, by labor and economic problems incident to the Great Depression and by pressure from the political enemies he had made. He was forced to resign in 1932. From 1934 to 1945 he was president and chairman of the board of the Missouri-Kansas-Texas Railroad and its related lines.

SLOAN, RICHARD ELIHU (*b. Preble Co., Ohio, 1857; d. Phoenix, Ariz., 1933*), lawyer, Arizona legislator and jurist. Republican governor of Arizona Territory, 1901–12.

SLOAN, SAMUEL (*b. Lisburn, Ireland, 1817; d. Garrison, N.Y., 1907*), railroad executive. Brought to America as an infant. After a successful career as a commission merchant in New York City, Sloan entered the railroad field as a director of the Hudson River Railroad, 1855, was chosen its president, and directed its rapid rise until 1864. As president of the Delaware, Lackawanna & Western Railroad, 1867–99, he transformed that road from a limited "coal road" into a profitable handler of general freight and passenger traffic.

SLOAN, TOD. *See* SLOAN, JAMES FORMAN.

SLOANE, ISABEL CLEVES DODGE (*b. Detroit, Mich., 1896; d. West Palm Beach, Fla., 1962*), racehorse owner and dog breeder. Her Brookmeade Stable in Virginia had its best year in horse racing in 1934, when it won more money than any other stable; its horse Cavalcade won the Kentucky Derby; and for the first time a woman headed the Thoroughbred-owner's list. In 1949 she was named outstanding breeder of the year by the New York Turf Writers Association; she also headed the owners' list in 1950. Her horse Sword Dancer was Horse of the Year in 1959. Brookmeade Kennels in Syosset, N.Y., did pioneering work with schnauzers and basset hounds, taking best of both breeds at the 1928 Westminster show.

SLOANE, WILLIAM MILLIGAN (*b. Richmond, Ohio, 1850; d. Princeton, N.J., 1928*), educator, historian. Graduated Columbia, 1868; Ph.D., Leipzig, 1876. Served as research assistant to George Bancroft, 1873–75; taught at Princeton and at Columbia, where he was Seth Low professor of history. Author of, among other books, *Life of Napoleon Bonaparte* (serialized in *Century Magazine,* published as book, 1896).

SLOAT, JOHN DRAKE (*b. near Goshen, N.Y., 1781; d. Staten Island, N.Y., 1867*), naval officer. Appointed midshipman, 1800; served in merchant marine, 1801–12, and on frigate *United States* in War of 1812. Received first command (schooner *Grampus*), 1823, and cruised against West Indian pirates; subsequently performed routine sea and shore services. Chosen commander of Pacific Squadron, 1844. He received secret and confidential orders dated June 1845 while based at Mazatlán, Mexico, directing what action he should take in the event of declaration of war by Mexico. Receiving word on June 7, 1846, that the Mexicans had invaded Texas, he sailed for California and arrived at Monterey on July 2. Five days later, overruling opinion of the U.S. consul there, Sloat landed a detachment and proclaimed the U.S. annexation of California; a little later he sent an officer to take possession of San Francisco. Turning over command to Commodore Robert F. Stockton on July 23, he returned to Washington. His conduct of affairs in the Pacific was both criticized and warmly commended. Put on the reserve list, 1855, he was promoted commodore, 1862, and rear admiral on the retired list, 1866.

SLOCUM, FRANCES (*b. Warwick, R.I., 1773; d. near present Peru, Ind., 1847*), Indian captive. Made prisoner near Wyoming, Pa., 1778, she was adopted by a Delaware Indian family, married in the tribe, and refused offers to return to her white relatives.

SLOCUM, HENRY WARNER (*b. Delphi, N.Y., 1827; d. New York, N.Y., 1894*), Union major general. Graduated West Point, 1852. Resigned from the army, 1856, to engage in the practice of law at Syracuse, N.Y. Appointed colonel, 27th New York Infantry, May 1861, he was soon promoted to brigadier general of volunteers and in July 1862 was promoted major general. An able division and corps commander, Slocum performed outstanding service at Chancellorsville and Gettysburg. He was later active in the campaigns in Tennessee, commanded the district of Vicksburg early in 1864, and with his troops was first to enter Atlanta. Thereafter he commanded the XIV and XX Corps under W. T. Sherman (later known as the Army of Georgia). Practiced law in Brooklyn, N.Y., *post* 1866, and was congressman, Democrat, from New York, 1869–73 and 1883–85.

SLOCUM, JOSHUA (*b. Wilmot Township, Nova Scotia, Canada, 1844; d. at sea,* ca. *1910*), mariner, lecturer. Sailed around the world alone in the sloop *Spray,* 1895–98. Author of *Sailing Alone Around the World* (1900) and various periodical writings.

SLOCUM, SAMUEL (*b. Canonicut Island, Newport Co., R.I., 1792; d. Pawtucket, R.I., 1861*), manufacturer. Inventor of, among other devices, a machine for sticking pins in paper so as to package them effectively for sale (patented 1841).

SLOSS, JAMES WITHERS (*b. Mooresville, Ala., 1820; d. 1890*), Alabama industrialist, railroad operator. Associated with H. F. De Bardeleben in development of coal and iron industry in the Birmingham district.

SLOSS, LOUIS (*b. Bavaria, 1823; d. San Rafael, Calif., 1902*), California capitalist, philanthropist. Immigrated to America, 1845; removed to California, 1849. Successful as a broker, leather merchant, and partner and official of the Alaska Commercial Co., Sloss engaged in systematic philanthropies and was an active supporter of almost every charity in San Francisco.

SLOSSON, EDWIN EMERY (*b. present Sabetha, Kans., 1865; d. Washington, D.C., 1929*), chemist, educator, writer of popular works on the sciences.

SMALL, ALBION WOODBURY (*b. Buckfield, Maine, 1854; d. Chicago, Ill., 1926*), sociologist. Graduated Colby College, 1876; Ph.D., Johns Hopkins, 1889. A teacher of history and political economy at Colby, 1881–88, he served Colby as president, 1889–91, and in 1892 became head of the Department of Sociology at University of Chicago, the first department of its kind. He served also as dean of the College of Liberal Arts there, and from 1904 until his retirement in 1924 was dean of the graduate school. Small was founder of the *American Journal of Sociology,* which he edited, 1895–1926. He was author of a number of books, which include *General Sociology* (1905) and *Between Eras: From Capitalism to Democracy* (1913).

SMALL, ALVAN EDMOND (*b. Wales, Maine, 1811; d. 1886*), homeopathic physician. Practicing and teaching at first in Pennsylvania, he removed to Chicago, Ill., 1856, where he was professor, dean, and president of the Hahnemann Medical College.

SMALLEY, EUGENE VIRGIL (*b. Randolph, Ohio, 1841; d. St. Paul, Minn., 1899*), journalist. Associated *post* 1883 with the advertising department of the Northern Pacific Railroad, he edited *The Northwest Illustrated Monthly Magazine.*

SMALLEY, GEORGE WASHBURN (*b. Franklin, Mass., 1833; d. London, England, 1916*), journalist, lawyer. Graduated Yale, 1853. After an outstanding career as war correspondent for the *New York Tribune,* November 1861–October 1862, Smalley served on the New York staff of the paper. As correspondent at the Austro-Prussian War, 1866, he sent what were probably the first of all cabled news dispatches, and in 1867 organized a London bureau for the coordination of all European news. Scoring a series of journalistic triumphs with the help of his correspondents during the Franco-Prussian War, 1870, he remained in charge of the *Tribune*'s European correspondence until 1895; he then served as U.S. correspondent of the London *Times,* 1895–1905.

SMALLS, ROBERT (*b. Beaufort, S.C., 1839; d. Beaufort, 1915*), black Union soldier, South Carolina politician. Smalls performed valuable service during the Civil War. He served in the legislature and was congressman, Republican, from South Carolina, 1875–79 and 1882–87.

SMALLWOOD, WILLIAM (*b. Charles Co., Md., 1732; d. Prince George's Co., Md., 1792*), Revolutionary soldier, Maryland colonial legislator. Commissioned colonel of the Maryland battalion, January 1776, Smallwood, who had had military experience during the French and Indian War, trained his command so effectively that the Maryland Line won high repute for valor through all the campaigns of 1776–77. Promoted major general, September 1780, he served with credit at Camden. Disliked for his constant complaints over lack of promotion and for his offensive attitude toward foreign officers, Smallwood performed his greatest service in the war as a drill master, a raiser of men and supplies, and a military administrator. He was governor of Maryland, 1785–88.

SMART, DAVID ARCHIBALD (*b. Omaha, Nebr., 1892; d. Chicago, Ill., 1952*), magazine publisher and promoter. Self-educated, Smart founded the David A. Smart Publishing Co. in Chicago in 1921; the first magazine of the company was *Gentlemen's Quarterly*; in 1933, he brought out the first edition of *Esquire: The Magazine for Men.* The magazine became successful and featured such writers as Ernest Hemingway, F. Scott Fitzgerald, H. L. Mencken, and John Dos Passos. The Magazine *Coronet* appeared in 1936 and became the nation's leading newsstand publication. Smart broke new ground in publishing standards, often running stories and articles (and cartoons) that were considered sexually and thematically bold for the time.

SMART, JAMES HENRY (*b. Center Harbor, N.H., 1841; d. 1900*), educator. After winning a reputation as an administrator of school systems in Indiana *post* 1865, he built up Purdue University and directed its emphasis toward engineering while he was president, 1883–1900.

SMEDLEY, AGNES (*b. Osgood, Mo.[?], 1894; d. Oxford, England, 1950*), journalist, propagandist for the Chinese Communist movement. Raised in Trinidad, Colo. After a grimly deprived childhood, adolescence, and early adult life during which she strove to educate herself, she had come to reject not only capitalism but all constituted authority, red or white. *Post* 1919, she resided mainly abroad. Her books on Chinese subjects contain little value to the historian, but her writings in general provide insight into the mentality of the American left wing in the 1930's and 1940's. She was author also of a fictionalized autobiography, *Daughter of Earth* (1929, rev. ed. 1935).

SMEDLEY, WILLIAM THOMAS (*b. Chester Co., Pa., 1858; d. Bronxville, N.Y., 1920*), portrait painter, illustrator. Expert in portraying the social characteristics of the genteel class.

SMIBERT, JOHN (*b. Edinburgh, Scotland, 1688; d. Boston, Mass., 1751*), painter. After employment as a coach-painter and as a copyist of pictures for dealers, he visited Italy, 1717–20, where he acquired a feeble Venetian technique and a facility at "face painting" in the grand manner; he also met at this time George Berkeley, later bishop of Cloyne. Practicing for a time as a portrait painter in London, Smibert accompanied Berkeley to Newport, R.I., 1729, as potential professor of art in Berkeley's proposed Bermuda college. Remaining in America after the failure of the project and Berkeley's return home, Smibert settled in Boston early in 1730 and, before the end of his professional career, painted likenesses of the "best" people in the Bay Colony. Despite his success in his profession, he found it necessary to earn additional income by conducting an art shop in his house in which he sold paints, brushes, prints, and copies of pictures in European galleries. He furnished the designs for Faneuil Hall (built 1742) and gave up painting *ca.* 1748 because of failing eyesight. Smibert's work is often awkward but important because of his precise and often grim records of New England worthies and because it served as an early link between the art of Europe and that of the colonies.

SMILEY, ALBERT KEITH (*b. Vassalboro, Maine, 1828; d. near Redlands, Calif., 1912*), educator. Graduated Haverford,

1849. Coproprietor with his brother of the celebrated Lake Mohonk resort in Ulster Co., N.Y., *post* 1870. A member of the Board of Indian Commissioners, 1879–1912, Smiley instituted the Lake Mohonk Conferences on Indian affairs in 1883 and another series of conferences for discussions of world peace, 1895.

SMILLIE, GEORGE HENRY (*b. New York, N.Y., 1840; d. Bronxville, N.Y., 1921*), landscape painter. Son of James Smillie; brother of James D. Smillie. Studied with his father and with James M. Hart.

SMILLIE, JAMES (*b. Edinburgh, Scotland, 1807; d. Poughkeepsie, N.Y., 1885*), engraver. Father of George H. and James D. Smillie. Settled in New York City, 1830. Assisted by Robert W. Weir and A. B. Durand, he became a successful banknote engraver and engraved the works of some of the leading figure painters and landscapists of his time. Among his important works were the series of plates after Thomas Cole's *Voyage of Life* and *The Rocky Mountains* after a painting of Albert Bierstadt.

SMILLIE, JAMES DAVID (*b. New York, N.Y., 1833; d. New York, 1909*), engraver, etcher. Son of James Smillie; brother of George H. Smillie. Studied with his father, with whom he collaborated in much of his work until 1864. Unsatisfied thereafter to confine his efforts to the mechanical phases of engraving, he employed himself in etching, dry point, aquatint, mezzotint, and lithography, and was foremost in the movement to promote painter-etching as an art. His work displayed technical mastery and great versatility.

SMILLIE, RALPH (*b. Pennsylvania, 1887; d. Essex Fells, N.J., 1960*), civil engineer. Studied at Yale and Columbia. From 1919 until 1927, he was the design engineer for the construction of the Holland Tunnel connecting New York and New Jersey. From 1933 to 1945 he worked on the construction of the Lincoln Tunnel for the Port of New York Authority, and from 1945 to 1950, he was chief of the New York Triborough Bridge and Tunnel Authority, completing work on the Brooklyn-Battery Tunnel. He retired and opened his own consulting firm in 1950.

SMITH, ABBY HADASSAH (*b. Glastonbury, Conn., 1797; d. 1878*), woman's rights advocate. Refusing, with her sister Julia Evelina Smith (1792–1886), to pay taxes unless given the right to vote, 1873, she continued to resist in this manner until her death, despite repeated sale of her livestock and other property for delinquent taxes. The sisters and their troubles gave publicity and an added impetus to the cause of woman's rights.

SMITH, ALBERT HOLMES (*b. Philadelphia, Pa., 1835; d. 1885*), obstetrician, gynecologist, advocate of recognition of women in medicine. Graduated University of Pennsylvania, 1853; M.D., 1856. Practiced in Philadelphia; devised the Smith-Hodge pessary and other obstetrical instruments.

SMITH, ALBERT MERRIMAN (*b. Savannah, Ga., 1913; d. Alexandria, Va., 1970*), journalist. Attended Oglethorpe University. Became a staff correspondent for United Press, first covering assignments in the South (1936–41), then as White House correspondent. He also wrote a column for UPI, "Backstairs at the White House," covering personal aspects of White House life. Accompanied presidents on many domestic and overseas trips, including Roosevelt's wartime conferences and the 1960 Kennedy-Khruschev summit. Author of five books on the presidency, including *Thank You, Mr. President* (1946). Won the Pulitzer Prize for his coverage of the Kennedy assassination. Awarded the Presidential Medal of Freedom (1969).

SMITH, ALEXANDER (*b. Edinburgh, Scotland, 1865; d. Edinburgh, 1922*), chemist. Taught at University of Chicago,

1894–1911; headed Department of Chemistry at Columbia University, 1911–19. Distinguished himself in physical chemistry; made important studies on the forms of sulfur and on vapor-pressure measurements at comparatively high temperatures.

SMITH, ALFRED EMANUEL (*b. New York, N.Y., 1873; d. New York, 1944*), politician, public official. The first Roman Catholic to be nominated for the presidency of the United States, Smith was born on the lower East Side of New York; his father was of German and Italian descent, his mother of Irish stock. At 14, a month before completing the eighth grade, he dropped out of school to work as an errand boy for a trucking firm. At 18 he became general clerk for Feeney and Co., a wholesale commission house in the Fulton Fish Market area. He changed jobs again at 20, this time working in a boiler manufacturing plant in Brooklyn.

In 1894 Smith opposed the man chosen by Tammany boss Richard Croker as the 4th District's congressional nominee. The insurgents failed to elect their own man, but helped defeat the Tammany candidate, and the vote in their district also helped elect as mayor a Republican reform candidate, William L. Strong. Early in 1895 Smith was appointed process server for the commissioner of jurors. In 1903 he was chosen as the Democratic nominee for state assemblyman. Nomination was equivalent to election, but Smith conducted an energetic campaign. Untrained in the law or in parliamentary procedure, he was at first ignored by both the Republican majority and the Tammany leaders, who instructed him how to vote but did not take him into their counsel. But slowly he learned assembly politics and state government. He was appointed to the Insurance Committee in 1906, a year of insurance company scandals, but he attracted little notice in the assembly until 1907, when, as a member of a special committee to revise the New York City charter, he defended home rule and the rights of the city's "plain people." In 1911, after a Democratic election sweep, Smith was selected by Charles F. Murphy, the head of Tammany, as majority leader of the assembly and chairman of the Ways and Means Committee. He became Speaker of the assembly in 1913.

In these years of his political emergence, Smith's energies were directed both to protecting the interests of Tammany and to achieving a variety of progressive reforms. He supported home rule for New York City (a favorite progressive issue), a state conservation department, and improvements in workmen's compensation. Indeed, the last issue would preoccupy Smith during most of his political career. Perhaps the most important single event in Smith's development as a reformer was the 1911 Triangle Shirtwaist Co. fire, a New York City disaster which took 146 lives, most of them working girls and women. His bill to establish a factory-investigating commission quickly passed the assembly, and the commission launched a statewide series of surveys and on-the-spot investigations of factory conditions. As its vice-chairman, Smith was thrown into a close working relationship with a remarkable group of independent and sometimes brilliant social workers and reformers. The commission's work continued until 1915, and Smith sponsored much of the social legislation it recommended. These reforms perhaps constitute Smith's greatest political achievement.

In 1915 he was elected to a two-year term as sheriff of New York City, and two years later won easy election as president of the board of aldermen. By 1918 the most popular man in the New York Democratic party, supported by Tammany, upstate politicians, and independent reform groups, Smith was the logical Democratic candidate for governor. Urging a broad reorganization of the state government, economy measures, and social legislation, especially the regulation of hours and wages for women and children, Smith won by only 15,000 votes.

The 1919–21 gubernatorial term set the pattern for Smith's later incumbencies. Most jobs went to deserving Democrats, but a few major appointments demonstrated the new governor's independence: a well-qualified Republican became the patronage-rich highway commissioner, and Frances Perkins, an independent, was appointed to the State Industrial Commission. Applying himself to crisis situations in city housing and milk distribution, two issues basic to tenement dwellers, Smith supported the temporary extension of wartime rent controls, tax incentives for the construction of low-cost housing, and price fixing of milk by a state commission. Normally prolabor, he utilized the State Industrial Commission to mediate labor differences, as in the Rome, N.Y., copper strike of 1919, when Frances Perkins initiated public hearings that led to negotiations and eventual recognition of the union. In a time of political reaction, Smith vetoed several antisedition bills that would have severely curtailed the civil liberties of Socialists. In 1923, during his second term, he pardoned an Irish revolutionary, Jim Larkin, imprisoned under the state sedition law; granted clemency to the Communist Benjamin Gitlow; and signed a bill virtually outlawing the Ku Klux Klan in the state. He supported the League of Nations; Wilsonianism evidently awakened in him an interest in international affairs that persisted into the 1920's.

In 1920, with an anti-Democratic current running nationally, Smith lost his bid for reelection by 75,000 votes. During the next two years, while serving as board chairman of the United States Trucking Corporation, he kept in close touch with politics. He was renominated in 1922, and in his campaign he again emphasized such welfare and reform issues as a 48-hour week, governmental reorganization, conservation, and the creation of a public hydroelectric power authority. His personal popularity, the continued support of his heterogeneous coalition, and a national business depression identified with the Republicans gave him a record plurality over the incumbent governor. Two more successful gubernatorial campaigns followed in 1924 and 1926.

In 1924 Smith was himself the most important Democratic leader in the state, and was thus freed from dependence upon bosses and machines. He supported James J. ("Jimmy") Walker for mayor of New York in 1925, but he did not reward Tammany heavily with political spoils. His welfare program included state support for low-cost housing projects, bond issues to develop an extensive park and recreation system, more funds for state education, and support for the State Labor Department in enforcing safety requirements and administering workmen's compensation. In short, in a decade little known for reform politics, Smith played an almost classic progressive role.

Smith's position and his record made him a serious presidential contender. Smith had strong support in the states with the largest electoral votes, but the 1924 Democratic convention was torn apart by a conflict between the rural-dry-Protestant forces and the urban-wet-Catholic representatives of the Northeast, and Smith withdrew after prolonging a deadlock. In April 1927 the *Atlantic Monthly* published an article by Charles C. Marshall, a prominent Episcopal layman, suggesting a basic conflict between Smith's loyalty to the Roman Catholic church and his allegiance to the U.S. Constitution. Smith's immediate reaction to Marshall's largely legalistic argument was, "I know nothing whatsoever about papal bulls and encyclicals." By 1928 Smith's candidacy could not be denied, and on the first ballot the Houston convention nominated him for the presidency. The campaign that followed has usually been interpreted as a victory for bigotry and narrow-minded rural prohibitionism. Yet, with Republican prosperity then reaching its zenith, the Democratic cause was all but hopeless. Smith and his running mate, Senator Joseph T. Robinson of Arkansas, received only 15 million votes to Herbert Hoover's 21.4 million; the electoral count was 444 to 87.

His hoped-for return to influence in Albany following Franklin D. Roosevelt's somewhat unexpected gubernatorial victory in 1928 was thwarted by Roosevelt's desire for independence. Instead, Smith entered business as president of the Empire State Building Corporation; he also served as chairman of a trust company. As he settled in a Fifth Avenue apartment and was lionized by New York's social and business circles, his conservatism hardened, and he drifted into an acrimonious feud with Roosevelt. Late in 1931, probably in an attempt to forestall Roosevelt, he launched an ill-organized campaign for the presidential nomination. He labeled "demagogic" Roosevelt's plea in April 1932 for the "forgotten man at the bottom of the economic pyramid," and throughout the next two years he expressed similar views in a monthly column of political opinion in the *New Outlook*, which he also served as editor. In the mid-1930's his close association with the moneyed classes and his genuine alarm at the New Deal led Smith to an active role in the right-wing, anti-Roosevelt American Liberty League. Smith's opposition to the Democratic ticket in 1936 and 1940 was largely ineffectual. Moreover, even in the private realm tranquility was not to be his. The stock-market crash had left two of his sons, a nephew, and several close friends deeply in debt, and Smith assumed heavy obligations on their behalf. The Empire State Building, completed in 1931, remained largely unoccupied, and only extreme efforts prevented bankruptcy. The approach of World War II partially mended the breach between Smith and Roosevelt. Smith supported the president's 1939 Neutrality Act amendments and actively backed the lend-lease program. Soon the two men were exchanging pleasantries, and Smith twice visited informally at the White House.

SMITH, ALFRED HOLLAND (*b. near Cleveland, Ohio, 1863; d. 1924*), railroad executive. President, New York Central Railroad, 1914–24.

SMITH, ANDREW JACKSON (*b. Bucks Co., Pa., 1815; d. 1897*), Union major general. Graduated West Point, 1838. Commissioned in the 1st Dragoons, Smith performed his early service mostly in the West. Becoming chief of cavalry under General Henry W. Halleck early in the Civil War, he served as such through the Corinth campaign and was appointed brigadier general of volunteers, March 1862. His important but unspectacular service, 1863–65, was highlighted by his defeat of General N. B. Forrest at Tupelo, Miss., 1864. Resigning from the army, 1869, he held several public offices at St. Louis, Mo.

SMITH, ARCHIBALD CARY (*b. New York, N.Y., 1837; d. Bayonne, N.J., 1911*), marine painter, naval architect. Designed well over a hundred yachts, of which the most notable were the *Vindex* (1871), *Mischief* (1879), *Meteor* (1902), and *Resolute* (1903).

SMITH, ARTHUR HENDERSON (*b. Vernon, Conn., 1845; d. Claremont, Calif., 1932*), Congregational clergyman. Missionary to China, 1872–1925. Author of a number of books, which included *Chinese Characteristics* (1890) and *China in Convulsion* (1901).

SMITH, ASA DODGE (*b. Amherst, N.H., 1804; d. Hanover, N.H., 1877*), Presbyterian clergyman, educator. Graduated Dartmouth, 1830; Andover Theological Seminary, 1834. A pastor in New York City, 1834–63, Smith served as president of Dartmouth College, 1863–77. He rebuilt the prestige of that institution and was responsible for the establishment of the Thayer School of Engineering and the New Hampshire College of Agriculture. A tactful and ultraconservative administrator, Smith was not particularly happy in matters of finance.

SMITH, ASHBEL (*b. Hartford, Conn., 1805; d. Tex., 1886*), physician, statesman, Confederate officer. Graduated Yale, 1824; M.D., 1828. Practicing at first in North Carolina, he removed to Texas, 1837, and became surgeon general of the Texas Republic. Texas minister to England and France, 1842–44, he became secretary of state of the Republic in February 1845 and negotiated with Mexico the Smith-Cuevas Treaty, acknowledging Texan independence. Cited during the Civil War for gallantry at Shiloh and Vicksburg, he later served actively in the defense of Texas. A leader in all educational movements in the state after the Civil War, he undertook the reorganizing of the University of Texas *post* 1881. He was author of *Reminiscences of the Texas Republic* (1876) and other works.

SMITH, AZARIAH (*b. Manlius, N.Y., 1817; d. Aintab, Armenia, 1851*), Presbyterian clergyman, medical missionary in Asiatic Turkey *post* 1843. Cousin of Judson Smith.

SMITH, BENJAMIN ELI (*b. Beirut, Syria, 1857; d. New Rochelle, N.Y., 1913*), editor. Son of Eli Smith. Managing editor of *The Century Dictionary and Cyclopedia* under William D. Whitney, 1882–94; editor in chief of the *Dictionary* and cognate enterprises, 1894–1911.

SMITH, BENJAMIN MOSBY (*b. Powhatan Co., Va., 1811; d. 1893*), Presbyterian clergyman. Professor at Union Theological Seminary, Virginia, *post* 1855.

SMITH, BESSIE (*b. Chattanooga, Tenn., 1894; d. near Clarksdale, Miss., 1937*), blues singer. An outstanding influence on jazz music, she achieved her greatest popularity between 1923 and 1929. Her singing had casual but great strength and a heartbreaking earthiness.

SMITH, BRUCE (*b. Brooklyn, N.Y., 1892; d. Southampton, N.Y., 1955*), police consultant and criminologist. Studied at Wesleyan University and Columbia (LL.B., 1916). Became the most prominent American authority on police administration and director of the Institute of Public Administration. Investigated police departments of New Orleans, St. Louis, and New York City. Most lasting contribution was the introduction of crime statistics, *The Uniform Crime Reports* first published in 1930. Wrote *Police Systems in the United States*.

SMITH, BUCKINGHAM (*b. Cumberland Island, Ga., 1810; d. New York, N.Y., 1871*), lawyer, diplomat, Florida Unionist, antiquarian. Smith is remembered particularly as an Americanist who stimulated study in the early history of Florida and the regions nearby. Among his many books and collections of documents were *The Narrative of Alvar Nuñez Cabeça de Vaca* (1851) and *The Narratives of the Career of Hernando de Soto in the Conquest of Florida, As Told by a Knight of Elvas* (first published as a whole, 1866).

SMITH, BYRON CALDWELL (*b. Island Creek, Ohio, 1849; d. Boulder, Colo., 1877*), philologist, educator.

SMITH, CALEB BLOOD (*b. Boston, Mass., 1808; d. Indianapolis, Ind., 1864*), lawyer. Studied law with Oliver H. Smith; began practice in Indiana, 1828. As an Indiana legislator *post* 1832, he promoted internal improvement projects; as congressman, Whig, from Indiana, 1843–49, he directed his principal efforts against annexation of Texas and war with Mexico. Later a leader in Indiana Republican politics, Smith seconded Lincoln's nomination at Chicago, 1860. U.S. secretary of the interior, 1861–62, he served thereafter as U.S. district judge from Indiana.

SMITH, CHARLES ALPHONSO (*b. Greensboro, N.C., 1864; d. Annapolis, Md., 1924*), educator. Friend and biographer of O. Henry. Graduated Davidson College, 1884; Ph.D., Johns

Hopkins, 1893. Taught English at Louisiana State University, 1893–1902; at University of North Carolina, 1902–09; at University of Virginia, 1909–17; at U.S. Naval Academy, 1917–24. A gifted, enthusiastic teacher and student of folklore.

SMITH, CHARLES EMORY (*b. Mansfield, Conn., 1842; d. Philadelphia, Pa., 1908*), journalist, diplomat. As editor of the Philadelphia *Press post* 1880, Smith enjoyed great political influence. He was U.S. minister to Russia, 1890–92, and U.S., postmaster general, 1898–1901.

SMITH, CHARLES FERGUSON (*b. Philadelphia, Pa., 1807; d. Savannah, Tenn., 1862*), Union soldier. Graduated West Point, 1825. Instructor and commandant of cadets at West Point, 1829–42, he received three brevets for gallant conduct in the Mexican War. After service in the Midwest and West and considerable administrative duty, he became brigadier general of volunteers, 1861. He was promoted major general, March 1862, for his decisive assault on Fort Donelson, which lodged federal troops within the defenses and was the immediate cause of the fort's surrender.

SMITH, CHARLES FORSTER (*b. present Greenwood Co., S.C., 1852; d. Racine, Wis., 1931*), classical philologist. Brother of James P. Smith. Taught at Williams College, Vanderbilt University, and University of Wisconsin. In addition to contributions to classical journals, he translated Thucydides for the Loeb Classical Library.

SMITH, CHARLES HENRY (*b. Lawrenceville, Ga., 1826; d. Cartersville, Ga., 1903*), journalist, humorist, Confederate soldier. Author of a number of sketches marked by genial satire and rustic philosophy, which he published under the pseudonym "Bill Arp."

SMITH, CHARLES HENRY (*b. Hollis, Maine, 1827; d. Washington, D.C., 1902*), Union major general, lawyer. An able but unspectacular cavalry commander with the Army of the Potomac, 1861–65, he returned to the regular service in 1866 and retired as colonel, 1891.

SMITH, CHARLES PERRIN (*b. Philadelphia, Pa., 1819; d. Trenton, N.J., 1883*), New Jersey politician, editor, genealogist.

SMITH, CHARLES SHALER (*b. Pittsburgh, Pa., 1836; d. St. Louis, Mo., 1886*), bridge engineer. Early associated with Albert Fink, Smith became a division engineer for the Louisville & Nashville Railroad and during the Civil War served as a Confederate captain of engineers. In 1866 he entered partnership with Benjamin H. and Charles H. Latrobe in the Baltimore Bridge Co. Smith produced his greatest engineering achievement in the Kentucky River bridge built for the Cincinnati Southern Railroad, 1876–77. The cantilever which he employed for this work had no precedent anywhere in the world but soon became the dominant type for long-span construction. His Lachine Bridge over the St. Lawrence River near Montreal, begun in 1880, was for many years the only continuous bridge of importance in America.

SMITH, CHARLES SPRAGUE (*b. Andover, Mass., 1853; d. 1910*), educator, professor of German at Columbia University. Founded the People's Institute at Cooper Union, New York City, 1897, as a community center for working-class education.

SMITH, CHAUNCEY (*b. Waitsfield, Vt., 1819; d. Cambridge, Mass., 1895*), lawyer. Successful as counsel to the Bell Telephone Co. in the great patent litigation of 1878–96.

SMITH, COURTNEY CRAIG (*b. Winterset, Iowa, 1916; d. Swarthmore, Pa., 1969*), educator. Attended Harvard (Ph.D., 1944) and Merton College, Oxford, as a Rhodes Scholar

(1938–39). Taught at Princeton (1946–53) and was president of Swarthmore College and American secretary of the Rhodes Scholarships (both 1953–69). He sought to improve Swarthmore by appointing faculty members with intellectual power and "character." He also challenged the students to reach his standards of intellect, character, and deportment; he was responsible for an increase in the number of black students, but was strongly committed to a system of merit. He reduced teaching loads, built a modern science center, and secured an excellent library.

SMITH, DANIEL (*b. Stafford Co., Va., 1748; d. Sumner Co., Tenn., 1818*), Revolutionary soldier, Tennessee official. Made the first map of Tennessee, published in Carey's *General Atlas for the Present War* (1794); wrote *A Short Description of the Tennessee Government* (1793). U.S. senator from Tennessee, 1798 and 1805–09.

SMITH, DANIEL B. (*b. Philadelphia, Pa., 1792; d. Germantown, Pa., 1883*), pharmacist, philanthropist. Long in business in Philadelphia, Smith was associated with establishment of Philadelphia College of Pharmacy, 1822, and served as its president, 1829–54. He was chosen first president of the American Pharmaceutical Association, 1852. From 1834 until 1846 he taught moral philosophy and chemistry at Haverford.

SMITH, DAVID EUGENE (*b. Cortland, N.Y., 1860; d. New York, N.Y., 1944*), educator, historian of science, Ph.B., Syracuse University, 1881; Ph.M., 1884; Ph.D., 1887. Taught mathematics at State Normal School, Cortland, N.Y., and at State Normal College, Ypsilanti, Mich.; principal, State Normal School, Brockport, N.Y., 1898–1901. Professor of mathematics, Teachers College, Columbia University, 1901–26. Author or coauthor of a number of widely used elementary and secondary school textbooks; active in U.S. mathematical associations, and in the International Commission on the Teaching of Mathematics. Instrumental in founding of the History of Science Society and its first president, 1927, he assembled a notable collection of rare books and manuscripts and of ancient mathematical and astronomical instruments. His best-known historical works were *Rara Arithmetica* (1908) and *History of Mathematics* (1923–25).

SMITH, DAVID ROLAND (*b. Decatur, Ind., 1906; d. Bennington, Vt., 1965*), sculptor. Attended Ohio University and Art Students League. First tentative experiments in sculpture (1931–34) were made with coral, wood, and metal, but he did not commit himself to sculpting until 1935, when he began a period of intensive experimentation in various styles derived chiefly from cubism and constructivism. Much of his sculpture of the 1930's uses human or other recognizable references, but very little expresses direct social commentary. His work of the 1940's shows a tendency toward larger pieces and more complex imagery, with an intensely felt and sometimes highly elaborate private symbolism. Two examples are *Home of the Welder* (1945) and *The Cathedral* (1950). He abandoned that style in the 1950's and by mid-decade achieved a commanding reputation among artists and critics of the avant-garde; a retrospective exhibit was held at the Museum of Modern Art in 1957. His work of the 1960's is characterized by a growing monumentality of scale and form; there are more and larger nonobjective arrangements of planes and cursive forms, culminating in the "Cubi," "Zig," and "Wagon" series.

SMITH, EDGAR FAHS (*b. York, Pa., 1854; d., Philadelphia, Pa., 1928*), chemist. Graduated present Gettysburg College, 1874; Ph.D., Göttingen, 1876. Taught at University of Pennsylvania, Muhlenberg College, and Wittenberg College. Headed Department of Chemistry, University of Pennsylvania, 1892–1920, and served as provost, 1911–20. Smith and his pupils at Pennsylvania carried out a great number of investigations into methods of electrochemical analysis, in which he was a pioneer; also investigated atomic weight determinations, compounds of the rarer metals, and complex salts of various inorganic acids. His research on tungsten led to its extensive use in scientific and artistic work. He was author of, among other books, *Electro-Chemical Analysis* (1890).

SMITH, EDMUND KIRBY. *See* KIRBY-SMITH, EDMUND.

SMITH, EDMUND MUNROE (b. Brooklyn, N.Y., 1854; d. 1926), educator. Nephew of Henry B. Smith. Graduated Amherst, 1874; LL.B., Columbia Law School, 1877; D.C.L., Göttingen, 1880. A teacher of history and political science at Columbia *post* 1880, Smith was professor of Roman law and comparative jurisprudence there, 1891–1924. From its establishment in 1886, he was for many years managing editor of the *Political Science Quarterly*. He was author of, among other studies, *The Development of European Law* (1928) and *A General View of European Legal History* (1927).

SMITH, EDWARD HANSON (b. Vineyard Haven, Mass., 1889; d. Falmouth, Mass., 1961), U.S. Coast Guard officer and oceanographer. Graduated from Coast Guard Academy and was commissioned an ensign in 1913; later attended Harvard (Ph.D., 1934). Assigned to the International Ice Patrol in the North Atlantic in 1920. Commanded the *Marion* expedition to the iceberg-producing areas of Greenland (1928), the most comprehensive oceanographic survey undertaken by the U.S. government. Promoted to rear admiral (1942). As commander of Task Force 24 of the Atlantic Fleet (1943), he was in charge of rescue ships on D day. Commandant of the Third Coast Guard District and captain of the port of New York (1945). Retired in 1950 and became director of Woods Hole Oceanographic Institution, until 1956.

SMITH, ELI (b. Northford, Conn., 1801; d. Beirut, Syria, 1857), Congregational clergyman. Father of Benjamin E. Smith. Missionary in the Near East for most of his life *post* 1826, Smith, with H. G. O. Dwight, was largely responsible for establishment of the American mission at Urumiah.

SMITH, ELIAS (b. Lyme, Conn., 1769; d. 1846), clergyman, healer. Rejecting the Calvinistic system held by the Baptists, he also denied the doctrine of the Trinity and founded a fundamentalist Bible church of his own at Portsmouth, N.H., *ca.* 1800. In 1818 he became a Universalist, but renounced that mode of thought in 1823. He was founder of the *Herald of Gospel Liberty*, September 1808, the first weekly religious newspaper published in the United States, which served as organ of the so-called Christian Connection. He was author of a number of controversial pamphlets and of several volumes of sermons and hymns.

SMITH, ELIHU HUBBARD (b. Litchfield, Conn., 1771; d. New York, N.Y., 1798), physician, editor, author. Graduated Yale, 1786; studied medicine with his father and with Benjamin Rush. As a student in Philadelphia, he became a friend of Charles B. Brown; as a practicing physician at Wethersfield, Conn., 1791–93, he was associated with the so-called Hartford Wits. A contributor to the *Echo* and editor of the earliest anthology of American poetry, *American Poems* (1793), he then settled in New York City, where he practiced until his death during a yellow fever epidemic. During his stay at New York, he was host to the Friendly Club, made up of, among others, William Dunlap, Samuel L. Mitchill, James Kent, and Samuel Miller (1769–1850). He projected the first American medical journal, the *Medical Repository*, and was coeditor of it, 1797–98. Just before his death he was planning to issue a literary magazine and review in association with Charles B. Brown.

SMITH, ELIZA ROXEY SNOW. *See* SNOW, ELIZA ROXEY.

SMITH, ELIZABETH OAKES PRINCE (b. North Yarmouth, Maine, 1806; d. North Carolina, 1893), novelist, lyceum lecturer, woman's rights reformer. Married Seba Smith, 1823. A contributor to popular periodicals.

SMITH, ELLISON DURANT (b. "Tanglewood," near Lynchburg, S.C., 1864; d. "Tanglewood," 1944), cotton planter, politician. Known as "Cotton Ed" Smith. Graduated Wofford College, 1889. Deeply affected by the ideology of the southern agrarian protest movement of the 1890's, he waged a lifelong battle against high tariffs, Wall St., big business, and hard money. Elected as a Democrat to the U.S. Senate, 1908, he represented South Carolina until his defeat in 1944; he died a few weeks before his last term expired. A consistent critic of the Taft Republicans and a reliable supporter of President Woodrow Wilson's policies, he opposed the tariff and fiscal policies of the Harding, Coolidge, and Hoover administrations and was an early backer of Franklin D. Roosevelt. Although he became chairman of the Senate Agricultural Committee, he had little influence in shaping the New Deal farm program and believed that the WPA, NRA, and other federal agencies for relief of the Great Depression threatened the South's social and economic structure. *Post* 1935, he was openly hostile to the administration and indulged in uncharacteristic tirades in the Senate against blacks; he opposed the regulation of wages and hours of labor, fought against the judiciary- and executive-reorganization bills of 1937, and in the World War II period was against selective service, lend-lease, and other wartime policies.

SMITH, ERASMUS DARWIN (b. De Ruyter, N.Y., 1806; d. 1883), jurist. As judge, New York Supreme Court, 1855–77, Smith tended to uphold legislative acts whenever possible and was unsympathetic in both law and equity cases toward artificial rules. His upholding of the Legal Tender Act as incident to the war powers of Congress, 1863, was said to be equal to a victory in the field for the cause of the Union. His best-known decision was in *People* v. *Albany & Susquehanna R.R.*, in which he settled the main point involved in the "Erie War."

SMITH, ERMINNIE ADELLE PLATT (b. Marcellus, N.Y., 1836; d. 1886), geologist, ethnologist. Authority on the language, customs, and myths of the Iroquois Indians.

SMITH, ERWIN FRINK (b. Gilberts Mills, N.Y., 1854; d. Washington, D.C., 1927), botanist, bacteriologist. Graduated University of Michigan, 1886; Sc.D., 1889. Thereafter, as a member of the scientific staff of the U.S. Department of Agriculture, he was a leader in development of the science of plant pathology and was unequaled in that field. He was author of a number of monographs and books, of which *Bacteria in Relation to Plant Diseases* (1905–14) was outstanding.

SMITH, EUGENE ALLEN (b. Washington, Ala., 1841; d. Tuscaloosa, Ala., 1927), geologist. Graduated University of Alabama, 1862; Ph.D., Heidelberg, 1868. Taught at universities of Mississippi and Alabama; was state geologist of Alabama, 1873–1927.

SMITH, FRANCIS HENNEY (b. Norfolk, Va., 1812; d. Lexington, Va., 1890), soldier, educator. Graduated West Point, 1833. Superintendent, Virginia Military Institute, 1840–89. Smith attacked the classical type of education prevalent in the antebellum South and emphasized a utilitarian approach.

SMITH, FRANCIS HOPKINSON (b. Baltimore, Md., 1838; d. New York, N.Y., 1915), engineer, artist, writer. Great-grandson of Francis Hopkinson. Successful in all three of his professions, Smith is remembered particularly for his best-selling works of fiction, which were marked by his own sunny temperament and by his special gift for observation of local color. Among his many books, *Colonel Carter of Cartersville* (1891) is outstanding; *The Fortunes of Oliver Horn* (1902) is in part autobiographical.

SMITH, FRANCIS MARION (*b. Richmond, Wis., 1846; d. Oakland, Calif., 1931*), capitalist. In 1872, at Columbus, Nev., he and his partner, William Tell Coleman, discovered in Teel's Marsh colemanite, from which borax is derived. These mines soon became the world's chief source of borax. The partners organized the Pacific Coast Borax Co. and succeeded in controlling the borax market for a long period. Later Smith acquired colemanite deposits in Death Valley, Calif. From there the product was hauled by mules to Mojave, Calif., and the "20-mule team" became a familiar borax trademark.

SMITH, FRANK LESLIE (*b. Dwight, Ill., 1867; d. Dwight, 1950*), businessman, banker, Illinois politician. Congressman, Republican, from Illinois, 1919–21. Chairman, Illinois Commerce Commission, 1921–26. He was denied admission to the U.S. Senate after election in November 1926, and appointment to fill out an unexpired term in December of the same year, on grounds that his victory in the primary had been gained by fraud and unlawful campaign expenditures.

SMITH, FRED BURTON (*b. near Lone Tree, Iowa, 1865; d. White Plains, N.Y., 1936*), lay evangelist, reformer, YMCA official.

SMITH, GEORGE (*b. Aberdeenshire, Scotland, 1806; d. London, England, 1899*), banker. Principally resident in America *ca.* 1834–60. Smith profited by the boom in Chicago, Ill., land values in 1835 and 1836. By influence in the Wisconsin legislature, he succeeded in evading antibanking laws by winning a charter for his Wisconsin Marine & Fire Insurance Co., 1839. Under a clause in this charter Smith was able to conduct a general banking business, of which Alexander Mitchell was the active manager. After making enormous profits, the company became a state bank in 1853. The rapid economic expansion of Wisconsin and Illinois in the 1840's would not have been possible without the trustworthy credit provided by Smith's company.

SMITH, GEORGE ALBERT (*b. Salt Lake City, Utah, 1870; d. Salt Lake City, 1951*), youth leader and leader of the Mormon Church. Studied briefly at the University of Deseret (later University of Utah). Worked with the Young Men's Mutual Improvement Association; general superintendent (1921–35). Member of the Council of the Twelve Apostles, the Mormon administrative body, from 1903 until his death. President of the Mormon Church (1945). He expanded Mormon programs to help American Indians and provided church property as a site for a state institute for the blind.

SMITH, GEORGE HENRY (*b. Knoxville, Tenn., 1873; d. Maplewood, N.J., 1931*), journalist, author of humorous juvenile stories.

SMITH, GEORGE OTIS (*b. Hodgdon, Maine, 1871; d. Augusta, Maine, 1944*), geologist. B.A., Colby College, 1893; Ph.D., Johns Hopkins University, 1896. A staff member of the U.S. Geological Survey *post* 1896, he served as its director, 1907–30, and was chairman of the Federal Power Commission, 1930–33.

SMITH, GERALD BIRNEY (*b. Middlefield, Mass., 1868; d. 1929*), theologian. Nephew of Judson Smith. Taught at the divinity school of University of Chicago. An empiricist, he bent his efforts "to find a vital religion which should not rest upon authoritative dogma" and sought to give his students a method of critical thinking rather than a body of conclusions.

SMITH, GERRIT (*b. Utica, N.Y., 1797; d. New York, N.Y., 1874*), reformer. Grandson of James Livingston; son of Peter Smith. Devoting his large fortune to what he considered the good of mankind, he experimented with systematic charity on a large scale. He also advocated strict Sunday observance, vegetarianism, total abstinence from liquor, reform of dress, prison reform, and woman's suffrage. Joining the antislavery movement in 1835, he became one of the best-known abolitionists in the United States and a backer of the aid societies for Kansas. A supporter of the use of force against proslavery adherents in Kansas, he backed John Brown enthusiastically, but later denied complicity in Brown's plot. During the Civil War he wrote and spoke in support of the Union cause, and in the Reconstruction period advocated moderation toward the Southern whites and supported black suffrage.

SMITH, GILES ALEXANDER (*b. Jefferson Co., N.Y., 1829; d. 1876*), Union major general. Brother of Morgan L. Smith. Distinguished himself particularly in command of the 2nd Division, XVII Corps, at the battle of Atlanta, July 1864.

SMITH, GUSTAVUS WOODSON (*b. Georgetown, Ky., 1822; d. New York, N.Y., 1896*), civil and military engineer, Confederate major general. Graduated West Point, 1842. After serving as actual commander of the army engineers during the Mexican War, Smith taught engineering at West Point and after his resignation from the army, 1854, was employed in important civil engineering work. Appointed major general in the Confederate army, 1861, he succeeded to command of Confederate forces in the Peninsular campaign between the wounding of General A. S. Johnston and General R. E. Lee's arrival. Resigning in 1863 after a series of quarrels with President Jefferson Davis, he returned to arms in June 1864 as major general of Georgia militia with the Army of Tennessee.

SMITH, HAMILTON (*b. near Louisville, Ky., 1840; d. Durham, N.H., 1900*), mining engineer, authority on hydraulics.

SMITH, HANNAH WHITALL (*b. Philadelphia, Pa., 1832; d. Iffley, England, 1911*), author, religious interpreter, reformer. Mother of Logan P. Smith.

SMITH, HAROLD BABBITT (*b. Barre, Mass., 1869; d. 1932*), electrical engineer, educator. M.E., Cornell University, 1891. Taught electrical engineering at University of Arkansas and Purdue; established and headed electrical engineering department at Worcester Polytechnic Institute, 1896–1931. A pioneer in electrical engineering education, Smith was also prominent as an industrial consultant and carried on extensive research in dielectric phenomena and electric stress distribution.

SMITH, HAROLD DEWEY (*b. near Haven, Kans., 1898; d. Culpepper, Va., 1947*), public administrator. As director of the federal Bureau of the Budget, 1939–46, he was forced to assume great additional responsibilities during World War II, which he did his best to handle with nonpartisan objectivity. On his resignation in mid-1946, he became vice president of the World Bank; in December 1946 he became its acting head.

SMITH, HARRY BACHE (*b. Buffalo, N.Y., 1860; d. Atlantic City, N.J., 1936*), operetta and musical comedy librettist, book collector. Raised in Chicago, Ill. Author of book and lyrics for a great number of successful shows, which included *Robin Hood* (music by Reginald de Koven), *The Fortune Teller* (music by Victor Herbert), *Gypsy Love* (music by Franz Lehar), and the *Ziegfeld Follies* of 1907, 1908, 1909, 1910, and 1912.

SMITH, HARRY JAMES (*b. New Britain, Conn., 1880; d. near Murrayville, British Columbia, Canada, 1918*), playwright, novelist. Author of a number of comedies of manners, of which *Mrs. Bumpstead-Leigh* (1910–11) and *A Tailor-Made Man* (1917) were the most successful.

SMITH, HENRY AUGUSTUS MIDDLETON (*b. Charleston, S.C., 1853; d. 1924*), South Carolina jurist, local historian.

SMITH, HENRY BOYNTON (*b. Portland, Maine, 1815; d. New York, N.Y., 1877*), Presbyterian clergyman. Professor of church history and later of theology at Union Theological Seminary, 1850–74. A representative of liberal orthodoxy, he edited the *American Theological Review*, 1859–74, and was the translator of several German theological works.

SMITH, HENRY JUSTIN (*b. Chicago, Ill., 1875; d. Evanston, Ill., 1936*), newspaper editor. Associated with the *Chicago Daily News*, 1899–1924, Smith returned to it as managing editor in 1926 and remained in that post until his death. Encourager of many later prominent journalists and writers who made their start under him, he was author of a number of books, including *Chicago: The History of Its Reputation* (with Lloyd Lewis, 1929) and *Oscar Wilde Discovers America* (1936).

SMITH, HENRY LOUIS (*b. Greensboro, N.C., 1859; d. Greensboro, N.C., 1951*), university president. Studied at Davidson College and the University of Virginia, Ph.D. in physics, 1891. President of Davidson College (1891–1912); during his tenure, the faculty, physical plant, student body, endowment, and annual income of the college approximately doubled. 1912–1930, president of Washington and Lee University. As president, Smith expanded the university, reestablished the school of journalism, and raised the admission requirements. Published *This Troubled Century* (1947).

SMITH, HENRY PRESERVED (*b. Troy, Ohio, 1847; d. Poughkeepsie, N.Y., 1927*), Presbyterian clergyman, biblical scholar. Brother of Richmond Mayo-Smith. A pioneer in the introduction of German higher criticism, he was suspended from the ministry after trial in November 1892 by the Presbytery of Cincinnati. He later taught at Amherst College and at Meadville Theological School, and was librarian at Union Theological Seminary, 1913–25. He was author of a number of books, including *A Critical and Exegetical Commentary on the Books of Samuel* (1899), *Samuel, Old Testament History* (1903), and *The Religion of Israel* (1914).

SMITH, HEZEKIAH (*b. Hempstead, N.Y., 1737; d. 1805*), Baptist clergyman. Pastor at Haverhill, Mass., *post* 1766, he frequently undertook missionary journeys into New Hampshire and Maine and served as a Revolutionary War chaplain. An associate with James Manning in the founding of Rhode Island College (Brown University), he devoted much of his time to the development of that institution.

SMITH, HIRAM (*b. Tinicum, Pa., 1817; d. 1890*), agriculturist. Removed to Sheboygan Falls, Wis., 1847, where he developed one of the outstanding dairy farms of the state. As a regent of the University of Wisconsin, he was responsible for establishment of the first U.S. dairy school there, 1890.

SMITH, HOKE (*b. Newton, N.C., 1855; d. 1931*), lawyer, newspaper publisher, Georgia politician. As U.S. secretary of the interior, 1893–96, Smith was an advocate of conservation of western natural resources and supported President Cleveland's effort to maintain the gold standard. A leader of liberal and reform elements in Georgia, Smith returned to politics in 1906, urging more effective control of the railroads and of elections, wherein fraud had been so great as to amount to disfranchisement of blacks. In his first term as governor, July 1907–July 1909, he accomplished more in extending the scope of social control in Georgia than any other governor in recent times; under his leadership, the assembly inaugurated the good-roads movement, established a department of commerce and labor, uprooted the convict-lease system, and curbed the state's public utilities companies. After a second brief term, July–November 1911, Smith became U.S. senator, Democrat, and served until 1921. His prime interest as a senator was in furthering the cause of education, especially vocational education. He disagreed with President Woodrow Wilson on a number of issues, particularly on the matter of the League of Nations. Throughout his long career he played an important part in the civic development of Atlanta, Ga.

SMITH, HOLLAND MCTYEIRE (*b. Hatchechubbee, Ala., 1882; d. San Diego, Calif., 1967*), Marine Corps officer. Attended Alabama Polytechnic and University of Alabama Law School. Commissioned a second lieutenant in 1905, and in 1906 was assigned to the first of various posts around the world. In France as a captain (1917–18), he became assistant operations officer with I Corps, First Army, and won the Croix de Guerre. Served with the occupation army in Koblenz, Germany, until 1919. Assistant Marine Corps commandant and director of operations and training (1937–39). Named assistant commandant in 1939 and promoted to brigadier general. Commander of the First Marine Brigade, Fleet Marine Force (1940); the First Marine Division (1941); all Marine Corps forces in the Central Pacific (1943–44); and Fleet Marine Force, Pacific (1944). Named commanding general of the Marine Training and Replacement Command in San Diego (1945–46), promoted to general, and retired.

SMITH, HOMER WILLIAM (*b. Denver, Colo., 1895; d. New York, N.Y., 1962*), physiologist. Attended University of Denver and Johns Hopkins (D.Sc., 1921). Chairman of the Department of Physiology, University of Virginia (1925–28) and professor at and director of the physiological laboratories at New York University College of Medicine (1928–61). His pioneer studies of the kidney and its function first involved refinement of the concept of renal clearance. Two of his books have had a profound influence in medicine: *The Physiology of the Kidney* (1937) and *The Kidney: Structure and Function in Health and Disease* (1951). Awarded the Presidential Medal of Freedom (1948), Lasker Award (1948), and Passano Award (1954) for his research.

SMITH, HORACE (*b. Cheshire, Mass., 1808; d. 1893*), inventor, arms manufacturer. In partnership with Daniel B. Wesson, he developed a revolver using a central-fire metallic cartridge (patented 1859, 1860), which was manufactured for the Union army in the Civil War and enjoyed large sales abroad.

SMITH, HORATIO ELWIN (*b. Cambridge, Mass., 1886; d. New York, N.Y., 1946*), professor of French. Graduated Amherst College, 1908; Ph.D., Johns Hopkins Chicago, 1912. Taught at Yale, 1911–18; at Amherst, 1919–25. Headed Romance language department, Brown University, 1925–36; headed French section of Romance language department, Columbia University, 1936–46. Editor of *Romantic Review*, 1937–46. Author of, among other works, *Masters of French Literature* (1937).

SMITH, HORTON (*b. Springfield, Mo., 1908; d. Detroit, Mich., 1963*), professional golfer. In 1928–29 began a meteoric rise to international recognition, winning eleven tournaments, including the French Open; then played on the U.S. Ryder Cup team for a decade. Won the Masters Tournament in 1934 and 1936 and continued to win tournaments through the 1930's. As president of the Professional Golfers' Association (1951–53) helped liberalize PGA policy with respect to black players. Elected to the PGA Hall of Fame (1958).

Smith, Israel (*b. Suffield, Conn., 1759; d. 1810*), lawyer. Raised in Vermont, Smith served in the Vermont legislature and was congressman, Democratic-Republican, from Vermont, 1791–97 and 1801–03; U.S. senator, March 1803–October 1807. He then became governor of the state for a single term.

Smith, James (*b. Northern Ireland, ca. 1719; d. Pennsylvania, 1806*), lawyer. Came to York Co., Pa., as a boy. Admitted to the bar, 1752. A backcountry leader during the Revolutionary era; member of the Continental Congress in 1776 and 1777; signer of the Declaration of Independence. A vigorous states' righter, he held but few political posts after his service in Congress and engaged chiefly in the practice of law.

Smith, James (*b. present Franklin Co., Pa., ca. 1737; d. 1814*), frontiersman, soldier, Kentucky pioneer. Author of *An Account of the Remarkable Occurrences in the Life and Travels of Col. James Smith, During His Captivity with the Indians, in the Years 1755, '56, '57, '58 & '59* (1799).

Smith, James (*b. Newark, N.J., 1851; d. Newark, 1927*), businessman, Democratic boss of New Jersey. Served as U.S. senator from New Jersey, 1893–99, without distinction; forced nomination of Woodrow Wilson for governor of New Jersey, 1910.

Smith, James Allen (*b. Pleasant Hill, Mo., 1860; d. 1924*), political scientist. Graduated University of Missouri, 1886; received Ph.D. at University of Michigan, 1894, after submitting a brilliant, controversial dissertation on the theory of money. In 1897 he became professor of political science at the University of Washington, remaining there until his death. His best-known work, *The Spirit of American Government* (1907), profoundly influenced Theodore Roosevelt, Robert La Follette, and many of the leading Progressives. Repeatedly denounced as a radical, he was in fact a Jeffersonian Democrat.

Smith, James Francis (*b. San Francisco, Calif., 1859; d. Washington, D.C., 1928*), soldier, lawyer, jurist. Graduated Santa Clara College, 1877. Commanded 1st California Volunteer Infantry in the Philippines, 1898; rose to rank of brigadier general and served as military governor of several subdistricts in the Philippines. After holding a number of high official positions in the administration of the islands, 1900–06, he served with great ability, and success as governor general, 1906–09. He was a judge, U.S. court of customs appeals, 1910–28.

Smith, James McCune (*b. New York, N.Y., 1813; d. Williamsburg, N.Y., 1865*), physician. The son of slave parents who had been emancipated, Smith graduated from the University of Glasgow, 1835, received his M.D. degree from Glasgow in 1837, and, after studying in clinics in Paris, France, returned to practice medicine in New York City. His chief claim to remembrance, however, rests upon his services, which were numerous and varied, on behalf of blacks. His writings show a high degree of scholarship.

Smith, James Perrin (*b. near Cokesbury, S.C., 1864; d. 1931*), paleontologist, geologist. Brother of Charles Forster Smith. Graduated Wofford College, 1884; M.A., Vanderbilt, 1886; Ph.D., Göttingen, 1892. Taught at Stanford *post* 1893; made special study of ammonite group; served as geologist in U.S. Geological Survey, 1906–24.

Smith, James Youngs (*b. Groton, Conn., 1809; d. 1876*), cotton manufacturer, philanthropist. Republican governor of Rhode Island, 1863–66.

Smith, Jebediah Strong (*b. Bainbridge, N.Y., 1798; d. near Cimarron River, Santa Fe Trail, 1831*), fur trader, explorer. Smith made the journeys on which his fame rests in the period 1826–30. Investigating the practicability of penetrating the Oregon country from California, he left Great Salt Lake in August 1826, passed through the territory of the Ute, Paiute, and the Mohave, and entered California from the desert in November. Restrained from any movement north by the governor of California, he proceeded east and north to the valley of King's River, where, in February 1827, he tried to cross the mountains and failed. He then moved north to the American River and with two companions crossed the mountains in May, making his way to Salt Lake over the unrelieved desert. Retracing his previous year's route from Salt Lake to Mission San Gabriel, he wintered in the Sacramento Valley; in April 1828 he headed northwest and in June reached the seacoast at the mouth of the Klamath River. After a hard journey to the Willamette, he reached Fort Vancouver, where Dr. John McLoughlin entertained him until March 1829. Smith then made his way on ground familiar to him to the rendezvous at Pierre's Hole. Retiring from the Rocky Mountain trade, he entered the Santa Fe trade and was killed on the trail by Comanche Indians. He was the first explorer of the Great Basin and the first American to make his way into California from the east and out of California from the west.

Smith, Jeremiah (*b. Peterborough, N.H., 1759; d. Dover, N.H., 1842*), lawyer. Congressman, Federalist, from New Hampshire, 1791–97. After service as U.S. attorney for the New Hampshire district, as a New Hampshire judge of probate, and as U.S. circuit judge, he was chief justice of New Hampshire, 1802–09. During this period he did more for the improvement of the jurisprudence of the state than any other man. After a single unsatisfactory term as Federalist governor of New Hampshire, 1809–10, he served again as chief justice, 1813–16. Retiring to private life, he was an associate counsel with Daniel Webster and Jeremiah Mason in celebrated Dartmouth College Case.

Smith, Jeremiah (*b. Exeter, N.H., 1837; d. St. Andrews, New Brunswick, Canada, 1921*), jurist, teacher of law. Son of Jeremiah Smith (1759–1842). Justice, New Hampshire Supreme Court, 1867–74; Story professor of law, Harvard, 1890–1910.

Smith, Jeremiah (*b. Dover, N.H., 1870; d. 1935*), lawyer, financial expert. Son of Jeremiah Smith (1837–1921). Practiced in Boston, Mass., *post* 1896. Successfully reorganized finances of Hungary under supervision of League of Nations, 1924–26; served as counsel to American financial experts in formulation of the "Young Plan."

Smith, Job Lewis (*b. Onondaga Co., N.Y., 1827; d. 1897*), physician. Brother of Stephen Smith. Graduated Yale, 1849; M.D., New York, College of Physicians and Surgeons, 1853. Author of one of the earliest American books to deal with the diseases of children as a specialty, Smith became one of America's leading pediatricians and was professor of the diseases of children at Bellevue Hospital Medical College, 1876–96.

Smith, Joel West (*b. East Hampton, Conn., 1837; d. Middletown, Conn., 1924*), educator of the blind.

Smith, John (*b. Willoughby, Lincolnshire, England, 1579/80; d. London, England, 1631*), adventurer, explorer, author. Apprenticed to a merchant, he soon left to seek adventure on the Continent and fought against the Turks in Transylvania. A prisoner and slave for some time among the Turks, he escaped, experienced further adventures, and returned to England, probably in 1604. Sailing with the colonists of the Virginia Co. of London late in 1606, he landed with them at Jamestown, 1607. During the troubled early days of the colony, Smith showed himself at his best in the expeditions he made among the Indians to procure food; taken prisoner on one of these trips, he was, according to his story in his *Generall Historie* (1624), condemned to death and saved by the intercession of Pocahontas. The story has been long in controversy, but there is nothing inherently improbable in it. Returning to Jamestown in January 1608, he found personal enemies in command of the turbulent colony and was arrested and condemned to be hanged. On the arrival, however, of Capt. Christopher Newport with new settlers from England, Smith was released and restored to a place in the colonial council, from which he had been ousted. Much more interested in exploring than in the administration of Jamestown, he settled down to governing the colony when elected president in the autumn of 1608. In October 1609, after much wrangling about authority, Smith returned to England, where he severely criticized the Virginia Co. and its methods. Despite the spectacular nature of his brief career in Virginia, his substantial contributions to the later founding of New England are possibly of more importance. Sent to New England by London merchants in March 1614, he brought back a valuable cargo of fish and furs and emphasized the value of the fisheries, continuing to the end of his life to proclaim the favorable prospects of New England for settlement. Among his numerous writings, *The True Travels, Adventures, and Observations of Captaine John Smith* (1630) and the *Generall Historie of Virginia, New-England, and the Summer Isles*, already cited, are considered the most important. His *Map of Virginia* (1612) and *Description of New England* (1616) were primary contributions to cartography.

SMITH, JOHN (*b. possibly Virginia, ca. 1735; d. present St. Francisville, La., ca. 1824*), Baptist clergyman, merchant. U.S. senator from Ohio, Democratic-Republican, 1803–07. Smith is best known for his association with Aaron Burr in the latter's western projects.

SMITH, JOHN AUGUSTINE (*b. Westmoreland Co., Va., 1782; d. 1865*), physician. Graduated William and Mary, 1800; received his medical education in London. A member of the first faculty of New York College of Physicians and Surgeons *post* 1807, he became president of the College of William and Mary, 1814. Returning to New York in 1825 after a most unsatisfactory tenure, he resumed his old duties as professor at the College of Physicians and Surgeons and, as its president *post* 1831, succeeded in broadening and improving the curriculum. He retired in 1843.

SMITH, JOHN BERNHARD (*b. New York, N.Y., 1858; d. 1912*), lawyer, entomologist. Appointed entomologist of the New Jersey state agricultural experiment station, 1889, he made his principal contribution in discovery of the breeding habits of the salt-marsh mosquito and the later institution of that insect's control. He served as professor of entomology, Rutgers College, 1889–1912.

SMITH, JOHN BLAIR (*b. Pequea, Pa., 1756; d. Philadelphia, Pa., 1799*), Presbyterian clergyman, educator. Nephew of Samuel Blair; brother of Samuel S. Smith. The leader of Presbyterian thought in Virginia in his time, he served as president of Hampden-Sydney College, 1779–89, and was made first president of Union College, 1795.

SMITH, JOHN COTTON (*b. Sharon, Conn., 1765; d. 1845*), lawyer, Connecticut legislator. A sturdy Calvinist and conservative, he served in Congress, sat on the state bench, and, as Federalist governor of Connecticut, 1813–17, was the last representative of the old "Standing Order" to hold the governor's chair. An opponent of the War of 1812, he urged Connecticut representation in the Hartford Convention and was an enemy of reform and of liberal revision of the Connecticut Charter.

SMITH, JOHN COTTON (*b. Andover, Mass., 1826; d. 1882*), Episcopal clergyman, author. Rector of the Church of the Ascension, New York City, *post* 1860. Active in support of foreign missions, reconciliation of theology and science, church union, and the solution of social problems, he was also a pioneer advocate of model housing and tenement-house reform.

SMITH, JOHN EUGENE (*b. Canton of Berne, Switzerland, 1816; d. Chicago, Ill., 1897*), soldier. Brought to America as an infant, Smith learned the jeweler's trade, which he followed in St. Louis, Mo., and Galena, Ill. Appointed colonel, 45th Illinois Infantry, July 1861, he rose to brigade and division command for brilliant services in the western campaigns and at Savannah, Ga. Commissioned colonel, 27th Infantry, regular army, in 1866, he served on the frontiers and helped quell the Sioux outbreak under Spotted Tail.

SMITH, JOHN GREGORY (*b. St. Albans, Vt., 1818; d. 1891*), railway organizer and executive, lawyer, Vermont legislator. Republican governor of Vermont, 1863 and 1864.

SMITH, JOHN JAY (*b. Burlington Co., N.J., 1798; d. Germantown, Pa., 1881*), editor, librarian. Grandnephew of Richard Smith; father-in-law of Hannah W. Smith; father of Lloyd P. Smith. Librarian of the Library Co. of Philadelphia, 1829–51; editor of *Waldie's Select Circulating Library* and briefly of *Littell's Museum*.

SMITH, JOHN LAWRENCE (*b. near Charleston, S.C., 1818; d. 1883*), chemist, mineralogist, authority on organic chemistry and meteorites.

SMITH, JOHN MERLIN POWIS (*b. London, England, 1866; d. New York, N.Y., 1932*), biblical scholar. Immigrated to Iowa, 1883. Ph.D., in Semitics, University of Chicago, 1899. After serving as assistant to William R. Harper, Smith taught at University of Chicago *post* 1908 and was also editor of the *American Journal of Semitic Languages*. He was author of a number of important works on Hebrew and on the Old Testament.

SMITH, JOHN ROWSON (*b. Boston, Mass., 1810; d. 1864*), painter. Son of John Rubens Smith. Employed as a painter of stage scenery, he produced a number of scenic panoramas which were exhibited on tour through the United States and in Europe. These included panoramas of Boston, the conflagration of Moscow, and the Mississippi Valley. The last of these has been credited with greatly stimulating immigration.

SMITH, JOHN RUBENS (*b. London, England, 1775; d. New York, N.Y., 1849*), engraver, painter, drawing master. Son of John Raphael Smith, an eminent English mezzotinter; father of John Rowson Smith. Immigrated to America *ante* 1809. As a teacher in Boston, Philadelphia, and New York, he was reputed able but quarrelsome; he engaged in a number of controversies with contemporary artists.

SMITH, JONAS WALDO (*b. Lincoln, Mass., 1861; d. New York, N.Y., 1933*), civil engineer, water-supply expert. Graduated Massachusetts Institute of Technology, 1887. Associated with Clemens Herschel in developing water supplies of Paterson, Passaic, and other New Jersey communities. Appointed chief engineer of the Aqueduct Commission of New York City, 1903, and of the New York Board of Water Supply, 1905, Smith performed the most important work of his life in creating and later extending the system for bringing water from the Catskill Mountains to New York City.

SMITH, JONATHAN BAYARD (*b. Philadelphia, Pa., 1742; d. 1812*), Philadelphia merchant, Revolutionary patriot and soldier, Continental congressman. Father of Samuel H. Smith.

SMITH, JOSEPH (*b. Hanover, Mass., 1790; d. 1877*), naval officer. Appointed midshipman, 1809; served with credit in War of 1812 and the war with Algiers. Held a number of important sea and shore commands, notably that of chief of the Bureau of Navy Yards and Docks, 1846–69; headed the naval board which decided on building the *Monitor*. Promoted rear admiral on the retired list, 1862.

SMITH, JOSEPH (*b. Sharon, Vt., 1805; d. Carthage, Ill., 1844*), Mormon prophet. While resident in Palmyra, N.Y., he experienced a series of visions, 1820–23, whereby he was led to believe that God had selected him to restore the church of Christ. In September 1827 he was permitted to take from their hiding place near Manchester, N.Y., certain golden plates which recorded the story of the "true" church on the American continent following its migrations from Jerusalem. After translating the history by miraculous means, he published the result at Palmyra in July 1830 as *The Book of Mormon*. Before its publication, Smith had founded the Church of Jesus Christ of Latter-Day Saints at Fayette, N.Y., April 1830, but the extraordinary growth of the sect did not begin until Sidney Rigdon became associated with it. A cooperative society ruled by an ecclesiastical oligarchy, Mormonism was a system excellently adapted to success on the far frontier, but it brought its members into continual conflict with neighbors in the communities they occupied during Smith's lifetime. Removing first to Kirtland, Ohio, 1831, and later to Missouri, 1838, Smith and his flock came in 1839 to Commerce, Ill., which Smith renamed Nauvoo. After five years of prosperity, during which Smith enjoyed power, publicity, and worship, he made formal announcement of his candidacy for the presidency of the United States, Feb. 15, 1844. However, the scandal of his business affairs, the general unpopularity of his sect, and the discovery by local non-Mormons of the practice of polygamy (foreshadowed *ca.* 1831, declared as revelation July 1843) brought about an uprising against the Mormons on the part of their neighbors. Smith and his brother were arrested and put in jail at Carthage, Ill., whence they were taken on June 27, 1844, and shot. He was the father of, among other children, Joseph Smith (1832–1914) and the uncle of Joseph F. Smith.

SMITH, JOSEPH (*b. Kirtland, Ohio, 1832; d. 1914*), Mormon prophet. Son of Joseph Smith (1805–44). President of the Reorganized Church of Jesus Christ of Latter-Day Saints *post* 1860; opposed polygamy, denying that his father had preached or practiced it.

SMITH, JOSEPH FIELDING (*b. Far West, Mo., 1838; d. 1918*), sixth president of the Utah branch of the Mormon Church. Nephew of Joseph Smith (1805–44). His chief contribution was the strengthening of the Mormon organization and the fostering of more friendly relations with non-Mormons.

SMITH, JULIA EVELINA. *See* SMITH, ABBY HADASSAH.

SMITH, JUNIUS (*b. Plymouth, Conn., 1780; d. New York, N.Y., 1853*), lawyer, merchant, "father of the Atlantic liner." Organized British & American Steam Navigation Co., 1836, to undertake establishment of regular transatlantic steamship service. The voyage of this company's vessel *Sirius* in 1838 was the first of its kind, beating the *Great Western* to New York by a few hours. Competition from the Cunard line and the loss of a new

vessel, the *President*, brought Smith's company to an end *ca.* 1842.

SMITH, JUSTIN HARVEY (*b. Boscawen, N.H., 1857; d. Brooklyn, N.Y., 1930*), historian, publisher, educator. Graduated Dartmouth, 1877. Taught modern history at Dartmouth, 1899–1908. Author of, among other books, *The Annexation of Texas* (1911) and *The War with Mexico* (1919), for which he was awarded the Pulitzer Prize and other honors.

SMITH, LILLIAN EUGENIA (*b. Jasper, Fla., 1897; d. Atlanta, Ga., 1966*), writer, editor, and civil rights advocate. Attended Piedmont College, Peabody Conservatory, and Columbia Teachers College. As music director at an American Methodist mission school in Huchow, China (1922–25), she embraced Chinese concepts of respect for human dignity, which gave her new perspectives on the South's social system. In 1935 launched the magazine *Pseudopodia*, devoted to southern issues; it used literary, cultural, and psychological criticism to indict caste and class in the South; it ceased publication in 1945. Her first novel, *Strange Fruit* (1944), depicting an ill-fated interracial love affair, was an immediate best-seller; it was declared obscene by the U.S. Post Office, which refused to allow it through the mails, but Eleanor Roosevelt got a White House order lifting the ban. Joined the Congress of Racial Equality, and in 1948–49 wrote a regular column for the *Chicago Defender*, in which she pressed for the abolition of segregation. Her second book, *Killers of the Dream* (1949), labeled racists as morally and psychologically unbalanced and evoked strong criticism from white southerners. Its companion volume was *The Journey* (1954). *Our Faces, Our Words* (1964), her last book, is a pictorial essay on the nonviolent civil rights movement.

SMITH, LLOYD LOGAN PEARSALL (*b. Millville, N.J., 1865; d. London, England, 1946*), author. Scion of a Quaker family, young Smith would have led the unruffled life of the son of a manufacturer had his father not experienced an ecstatic conversion to the Higher Life evangelical movement and become, with his wife, an international revivalist. When disillusionment with evangelical Christianity returned the family to their origins in Germantown, Pa., Smith entered the Quaker Penn Charter school, after which he attended Haverford College, 1881–84, and Harvard, 1884–85. He abandoned the family business in 1888 after a trial year and followed his sister Mary to England, entering Balliol College, Oxford, where he found in Walter Pater's aestheticism a way to reconcile his skepticism with his capacity for passionate attachment. The pursuit of artistic perfection became his lifelong concern. Smith persisted in his interest, moving first to Paris, where he met Whistler and produced a volume of stories entitled *The Youth of Parnassus* (1895), and then to a cottage in England. He published a few of his essays in *The Golden Urn* (1897–98) with his sister Mary and Bernard Berenson, later her husband, but waited until 1920 to assemble a collection, entitled *Trivia*. It was followed by *More Trivia* (1922) and the aphoristic *Afterthoughts* (1931); the three were united in *All Trivia* (1933) and supplemented in 1945 by *Last Words*.

Brought by his polished writing and his work on *The English Language* (1922) to the attention of the poet Robert Bridges, he joined with Bridges and others to form in 1913 the Society for Pure English, formally launched in 1919. Directing his sharpest attacks in his many tracts for the society against those who had confused pedantry with purity, compromising thereby the vitality and simplicity of the language, he presented numerous essays collected in his *Reperusals and Re-Collection* (1936). He enjoyed his greatest success with his autobiography, *Unforgotten Years* (1939). He was close to George Santayana, with whom he collaborated on *Little Essays* (1920), and to Henry James.

SMITH, LLOYD PEARSALL (*b. Philadelphia, Pa., 1822; d. 1886*), librarian, publisher, editor. Son of John Jay Smith, whom he succeeded as librarian of the Library Co. of Philadelphia, 1851. He was the first editor of *Lippincott's Magazine*, 1868–69, and the author of *On the Classification of Books* (1892), which was a pioneer discussion of that subject.

SMITH, LUCY HARTH (*b. Roanoke, Va., 1888; d. Lexington, Ky., 1955*), schoolteacher and administrator. Studied at Hampton Institute, Kentucky State College, and the University of Cincinnati (M.Ed., 1943). Teacher and principal at Booker T. Washington Elementary School in Lexington, Ky., from 1917 until her death. Only woman to serve as the president of the Kentucky Negro Education Association; regional vice president of the American Teachers' Association. Named one of the five outstanding black citizens of Kentucky by the *Louisville Defender* 1945. Smith traveled widely lecturing on black history and traditions. Her address on black music was published in the *Journal of Negro History* (1935).

SMITH, MARCUS (*b. New Orleans, La., 1829; d. Paris, France, 1874*), actor, better known as Mark Smith. Son of Solomon F. Smith. Superior in supporting roles, notably as an interpreter of old English gentlemen.

SMITH, MARGARET BAYARD (*b. 1778; d. Washington, D.C., 1844*), society leader, author. Daughter of John B. Bayard; wife of Samuel H. Smith. Writer of several novels and a contributor to the periodicals of her time, Smith is remembered for her letters, which form a record by a keen observer of social and political events from Jefferson's time to the administration of W. H. Harrison. Edited by Gaillard Hunt, they were published as *The First Forty Years of Washington Society* (1906).

SMITH, MARTIN LUTHER (*b. Danby, N.Y., 1819; d. Savannah, Ga., 1866*), Confederate major general. Graduated West Point, 1842. Helped plan and construct fortification of New Orleans and Vicksburg; served at various times as chief engineer of the Army of Northern Virginia and the Army of Tennessee.

SMITH, MELANCTON (*b. Jamaica, N.Y., 1744; d. New York, N.Y., 1798*), lawyer, merchant, Revolutionary patriot. Active in ferreting out Tories in New York, 1775–80, he served in the Continental Congress, 1785–88, and rendered his most conspicuous service as an Antifederalist debater in the New York convention for ratification of the U.S. Constitution.

SMITH, MELANCTON (*b. New York, N.Y., 1810; d. Green Bay, Wis., 1893*), naval officer. Grandson of Melancton Smith (1744–98). Entering the navy, 1826, he performed a variety of sea and shore duties up to the time of the Civil War, in which he won repute as a grim and dogged fighting commander. He served under Farragut in the campaign against New Orleans, 1862, and at Port Hudson, 1863. During 1864 he operated on the James River, and commanded a gunboat flotilla during efforts to destroy the ram *Albemarle*, May–June 1864. He was later commended for his part in the attacks against Fort Fisher. Promoted rear admiral, 1870, he retired, 1871.

SMITH, MERIWETHER (*b. Essex Co., Va., 1730; d. Essex Co., 1794*), Revolutionary patriot, Virginia legislator and congressman. Able, but erratic.

SMITH, MILTON HANNIBAL (*b. Greene Co., N.Y., 1836; d. Louisville, Ky., 1921*), railroad official. Associated principally with the Louisville & Nashville *post* 1866, he served as its chief executive, 1882–1921, under various titles. He made his road one of the more important transportation factors in the United States.

SMITH, MORGAN LEWIS (*b. Mexico, N.Y., 1821; d. Jersey City, N.J., 1874*), Union brigadier general. Brother of Giles A. Smith. Held brigade, division, and, for a brief time, corps command under U. S. Grant and W. T. Sherman, 1861–64; commanded District of Vicksburg, 1864–65. Celebrated for coolness under fire and for a remarkable ability to instill discipline and morale in raw troops.

SMITH, NATHAN (*b. Rehoboth, Mass., 1762; d. New Haven, Conn., 1829*), physician, medical educator. After apprenticeship to several physicians in Vermont, where he was raised, Smith began practice at Cornish, N.H., 1787. Realizing the inadequacy of his training, he studied at Harvard with John Warren and Benjamin Waterhouse, 1789–90, and then returned to his practice. Still unsatisfied with his education and desiring to teach, he made further studies in Europe, 1796–97, and in 1797–98 began work as professor of medicine at Dartmouth. In addition to his teaching he practiced generally in the area. Exasperated at lack of support of the medical school from the state legislature, he removed to Yale, where he became professor of the theory and practice of medicine, surgery, and obstetrics, 1813. In high repute as surgeon and teacher, he was one of the earliest to perform ovariotomy and in other ways showed an ability and resourcefulness which were unsurpassed in his day. The importance of his work for succeeding generations is to be found in the fresh and original manner in which he attacked problems in medicine and surgery, his essentially modern concept of disease, his distaste for theorizing, and his emphasis on the need for accurate observation. Among his writings *Practical Essay on Typhous Fever* (1824) has classic stature.

SMITH, NATHAN (*b. Woodbury, Conn., 1770; d. Washington, D.C., 1835*), lawyer. Brother of Nathaniel Smith. Active in the fight to disestablish Congregationalism in Connecticut, Smith held several judicial offices in the state and was U.S. senator, Whig, from Connecticut, 1832–35.

SMITH, NATHAN RYNO (*b. Cornish, N.H., 1797; d. Baltimore, Md., 1877*), surgeon, teacher of anatomy and surgery. Son of Nathan Smith (1762–1829). M.D., Yale, 1823. Taught at University of Vermont, at Jefferson Medical College, and at University of Maryland. Invented a new instrument for lithotomy; was a pioneer in extirpation of the thyroid gland.

SMITH, NATHANIEL (*b. Woodbury, Conn., 1762; d. 1822*), Connecticut jurist. Brother of Nathan Smith (1770–1835). Congressman, Federalist, from Connecticut, 1795–99; judge, state superior court, 1806–19. Attended Hartford Convention, 1814.

SMITH, OLIVER (*b. Hatfield, Mass., 1766; d. 1845*), businessman. Uncle of Sophia Smith. Bequeathed his very large fortune to several charitable enterprises under a will which was contested by his heirs at law. After a notable legal battle in which Rufus Choate and Daniel Webster were of counsel, the will was sustained. Among its present beneficiaries are the Smith Agricultural School and Northampton (Mass.) School of Technology.

SMITH, OLIVER HAMPTON (*b. Bucks Co., Pa., 1794; d. Indianapolis, Ind., 1859*), lawyer. Began practice at Versailles and Connersville, Ind., 1820. After service as a legislator and as prosecuting attorney, he was congressman, Democrat, from Indiana, 1827–29. As U.S. senator, Whig, from Indiana, 1837–43, he became chairman of the committee on public lands and was a leader in evolving a federal land policy in the interest of the actual settlers.

SMITH, ORMOND GERALD (*b. New York, N.Y., 1860; d. 1933*), publisher. Headed the firm of Street & Smith, publishers of dime novels and popular fiction, *post* 1887.

SMITH, PERSIFOR FRAZER (*b. Philadelphia, Pa., 1798; d. Fort Leavenworth, Kans., 1858*), soldier. Graduated College of New Jersey (Princeton), 1815. Removing to Louisiana, 1819, he practiced law in New Orleans and was active in the militia, serving in the Seminole War campaigns of 1836 and 1838. Commissioned colonel, U.S. Army, May 1846, he served with great distinction in the Mexican War as brigade commander under Zachary Taylor and during Scott's campaign against Mexico City. Breveted major general, he commanded several departments in the West, 1848–58. He was commissioned brigadier general, regular army, 1856. Gallant and efficient, he was noted particularly for the implicit trust which his men gave him.

SMITH, PETER (*b. near Tappan, N.Y., 1768; d. Schenectady, N.Y., 1837*), landowner. Father of Gerrit Smith. For a brief time a partner of John Jacob Astor in the fur trade, Smith acquired large tracts in Oneida and Onondaga counties, N.Y., by lease and purchase from the Indians.

SMITH, PRESERVED (*b. Cincinnati, Ohio, 1880; d. Louisville, Ky., 1941*), historian. Son of Henry Preserved Smith; nephew of Richmond Mayo-Smith. B.A., Amherst College, 1901; M.A., Columbia University, 1902; Ph.D., 1907. Granted a seven-year fellowship by Amherst, he studied in Berlin and Paris, but was incapacitated by tuberculosis, 1913–18. After lecturing at Harvard and Wellesley, he was appointed professor of history at Cornell University, 1922, a post he held until his death. He was author of, among other books, *Life and Letters of Martin Luther* (1911), *The Age of the Reformation* (1920), *Erasmus* (1923), and *History of Modern Culture* (1930–34).

SMITH, RICHARD (*b. Burlington, N.J., 1735; d. Natchez, Miss., 1803*), lawyer, land speculator. Smith's diary as a member of the Continental Congress from New Jersey, 1774–76, supplies much information not available from official sources concerning the proceedings in Congress. Another of his journals, covering his explorations of a tract of land which he owned on the upper Susquehanna River, was published as *A Tour of Four Great Rivers* (1906).

SMITH, RICHARD PENN (*b. Philadelphia, Pa., 1799; d. near Philadelphia, 1854*), lawyer, author, playwright. Grandson of William Smith (1727–1803). Author of 20 plays (1825–35), of which 15 were performed. Most of his work represented translations or adaptations from works by French and English authors; *The Deformed* (1830) and *Caius Marius* (1831) are considered his best works. He was author also of a novel, *The Forsaken* (1831), and of a number of tales, sketches, and verses.

SMITH, RICHARD SOMERS (*b. Philadelphia, Pa., 1813; d. 1877*), soldier, educator. Graduated West Point, 1834. Taught mathematics, drawing, and engineering at a number of schools, including West Point, 1840–55; Cooper Union; and the U.S. Naval Academy. Served in Union army, 1861–63; was president of Girard College, 1863–67.

SMITH, ROBERT (*b. possibly Glasgow, Scotland, ca. 1722; d. 1777*), Philadelphia architect and builder. Designed and built Nassau Hall at College of New Jersey (Princeton), 1754; St. Peter's Church, Philadelphia, 1758; also other Philadelphia churches. Planned obstructions in the Delaware River below Philadelphia for defense of that city, 1775–76. Smith handled the contemporary Georgian style with admirable dignity but tended to excessive plainness.

SMITH, ROBERT (*b. Worstead, England, 1732 o.s.; d. 1801*), Revolutionary patriot and chaplain, Episcopal clergyman. Came to Charleston, S.C., 1757, as assistant minister of St. Philip's Church; becoming rector, 1759, he continued so until his death. He was consecrated first bishop of South Carolina, 1795.

SMITH, ROBERT (*b. Lancaster, Pa., 1757; d. 1842*), lawyer, Maryland legislator. Brother of Samuel Smith, U.S. secretary of the navy, 1801–09, Smith ran his office with fair efficiency, although greatly criticized by Albert Gallatin. A member of the Senate cabal which included his brother, W. B. Giles, and Michael Leib, Smith continued his feud with Gallatin while acting as U.S. secretary of state, 1809–11. Forced to resign by President Madison, whose policies on commercial restrictions he opposed, Smith retired to private life.

SMITH, ROBERT ALEXANDER C. (*b. Dover, England, 1857; d. Southampton, England, 1933*), railroad and public utilities promoter, capitalist. As dock commissioner of New York City, 1913–17, Smith developed and provided for construction of the Hudson River piers, which greatly improved New York's standing among world seaports.

SMITH, ROBERT BARNWELL. *See* RHETT, ROBERT BARNWELL.

SMITH, ROBERT HARDY (*b. Camden Co., N.C., 1813; d. Mobile, Ala., 1878*), Alabama lawyer, member of the provisional Confederate Congress. Took active part in framing the permanent constitution of the Confederacy.

SMITH, ROBERT SIDNEY (*b. Bloomington, Ill., 1877; d. near Harvard, Ill., 1935*), comic-strip artist. Credited with being the first to use continuity in a comic strip, Smith began his successful "Andy Gump" series in 1917.

SMITH, ROSWELL (*b. Lebanon, Conn., 1829; d. New York, N.Y., 1892*), lawyer. publisher. Associated in publication of *Scribner's Monthly* with Josiah G. Holland, Charles Scribner, and Richard W. Gilder *post* 1870, he became sole proprietor, 1881. Thereafter, the periodical was known as the *Century*. Smith also proposed publication of *St. Nicholas* magazine, 1873, and conceived the idea of *The Century Dictionary*. He directed the publication activities of the Century Co. until his death.

SMITH, RUSSELL (*b. Glasgow, Scotland, 1812; d. Glenside, Pa., 1896*), painter. Came to America as a boy. Specialized *post* 1833 in painting scenery for theaters and opera houses.

SMITH, SAMUEL (*b. Carlisle, Pa., 1752; d. Baltimore, Md., 1839*), soldier, statesman. Brother of Robert Smith (1757–1842). Served throughout the Revolution and won particular distinction for commanding defense of Fort Mifflin, 1777. Growing wealthy in land speculation, he entered politics, serving as congressman from Maryland, 1793–1803; at first a Federalist, he soon became a supporter of Jefferson. Elected to the U.S. Senate, 1803, he remained a senator until 1815. During the War of 1812, as major general he headed the force which defended Baltimore. Returning to the House of Representatives, 1816, he served until December 1822, when he resigned to fill out a vacancy in the U.S. Senate. Reelected in 1826, he held office until 1833. A forceful debater, intelligent and ambitious, he made his influence felt both on the floor of Congress and behind the scenes, where he was much given to intrigue. One of the leaders in opposing the nomination of James Madison for the presidency, he also led the faction which fought Albert Gallatin as secretary of the treasury and obstructed Gallatin's financial program in Congress. Later, although he favored equalization of tariff duties, he fought bitterly against Henry Clay's "American system" and even suggested in 1832 that the Union be divided at the Potomac in order to escape it. His most constructive work was done in securing recovery of trade with the British West Indies, 1830.

SMITH, SAMUEL FRANCIS (*b. Boston, Mass., 1808; d. Boston, 1895*), Baptist clergyman, poet. Graduated Harvard, 1829. Author of the national hymn "America," which he wrote at the request of Lowell Mason, 1832.

SMITH, SAMUEL HARRISON (*b. Philadelphia, Pa., 1772; d. Washington, D.C., 1845*), journalist, banker. Son of Jonathan B. Smith; husband of Margaret B. Smith. Graduated University of Pennsylvania, 1787. Edited the *National Intelligencer*, official organ of the Jefferson administration, 1800–10; president, Washington Branch, Bank of the United States, 1828–36.

SMITH, SAMUEL STANHOPE (*b. Pequea, Pa., 1750; d. 1819*), Presbyterian clergyman, educator. Brother of John Blair Smith. Graduated College of New Jersey (Princeton), 1769. After pastoral work and missionary activity in western Virginia and periods of teaching at Princeton and at Hampden-Sydney, he became professor of moral philosophy at Princeton, 1779–1812. As acting president, 1795–1802, and as president, 1802–12, he contributed much to the physical and intellectual advancement of the college. Long interested in natural science himself, he raised money for scientific apparatus and called John Maclean to the college, 1795, to give the first undergraduate courses in chemistry and natural science in the United States. Although a popular teacher and preacher, he was subjected to much hostile criticism because of his supposed liberalism.

SMITH, SEBA (*b. Buckfield, Maine, 1792; d. 1868*), journalist, political satirist. Graduated Bowdoin, 1818. Husband of Elizabeth O. P. Smith. Founded *Portland Courier*, 1829, first daily paper to be issued in Maine, in which his celebrated "Major Jack Downing" letters appeared *post* January 1830. At first critical of the state legislature, Smith extended his satire to the administration and policies of President Andrew Jackson. Immediately popular and widely reprinted and imitated, the letters were published in book form as *The Life and Writings of Major Jack Downing of Downingville* (1833). Smith's rather mild ridicule of national leaders and party platforms is in contrast to the pointed wit of the "Jack Downing letters" written by Charles Augustus Davis, whose imitations of Smith's work received wide circulation. The creation of this Yankee type must, however, be credited to Seba Smith alone. After the success of Jack Downing, he held a number of editorial positions and was author of several other books, including 'Way Down East (1854) and a second series of Downing letters published as a book in 1859 under the title *My Thirty Years Out of the Senate*. The new pattern which he set for American humor was carried on by, among others, James Russell Lowell, Finley P. Dunne, and Will Rogers.

SMITH, SOLOMON FRANKLIN (*b. Norwich, N.Y., 1801; d. 1869*), comedian, theater manager, lawyer. Father of Marcus Smith. Better known as Sol Smith, he led a roaming life, 1818–35, associated at times with the itinerant companies of Samuel Drake and Noah M. Ludlow. At Mobile, Ala., 1835, he became junior partner with Ludlow in a theatrical firm which became one of the most important in the West. Operating theaters in St. Louis, Mo., Mobile, and New Orleans, the firm was successful until 1853, when it was dissolved. Thereafter Smith practiced law in St. Louis and served in the state convention which kept Missouri from secession.

SMITH, SOPHIA (*b. Hatfield, Mass., 1796; d. 1870*), founder of Smith College. Niece of Oliver Smith. Bequeathed her large fortune for the founding of Smith at the suggestion of the Congregational minister at Hatfield, John Morton Greene.

SMITH, STEPHEN (*b. near Skaneateles, N.Y., 1823; d. Montour Falls, N.Y., 1922*), surgeon, pioneer in public health. Brother of Job L. Smith. M.D., New York College of Physicians and Surgeons, 1851. An expert conservative surgeon and author of several valuable textbooks, Smith is remembered principally for his drafting of the Metropolitan Health Law for New York City, 1866, which became the basis of civic sanitation in the United States. He served as commissioner of the New York City Board of Health, 1868–75, and helped organize the American Public Health Association, 1871, of which he was first president.

SMITH, THEOBALD (*b. Albany, N.Y., 1859; d. 1934*), medical scientist. Ph.B., Cornell University, 1881; M.D., Albany Medical College, 1883. Organized Department of Bacteriology at present George Washington University, 1886, and taught there until 1895; taught also at Harvard Medical School, 1895–1915, and directed Massachusetts Board of Health pathological laboratory over the same period. Directed Department of Animal Pathology at the Rockefeller Institute for Medical Research *post* 1915. Smith, with Daniel E. Salmon, made important studies in the cause and prevention of swine plague; Smith later (1898–1902) wrote far-reaching studies on the relation between bovine and human tuberculosis. Between 1884 and 1893, Smith made classic investigations of Texas fever among cattle and showed for the first time how parasites may act as vectors of disease from animal to animal; he also made the first recorded observation of allergy. Author of more than 224 published works and studies, he ranks in American medical history in a place comparable to that of Pasteur in France and Koch in Germany.

SMITH, THEODATE LOUISE (*b. Hallowell, Maine, 1859; d. 1914*), genetic psychologist. Graduated Smith College, 1882; Ph.D., Yale, 1896; studied also at Clark University, where she was research assistant to Granville S. Hall, 1902–09. She was author of the interpretative *The Montessori System in Theory and Practice* (1912).

SMITH, THOMAS ADAMS (*b. Essex Co., Va., 1781; d. Saline Co., Mo., 1844*), soldier. Nephew of Meriwether Smith. Commissioned lieutenant of artillery, 1803, he served in command of infantry during War of 1812, rising to rank of brigadier general, 1814. Appointed commander of the territories of Missouri and Illinois, 1815, he resigned from the army, 1818, and was appointed receiver of public monies at Franklin, Mo. Resigning in 1826, he became a planter and a leader in Missouri public affairs. Fort Smith, Ark., was named in his honor.

SMITH, THOMAS VERNOR (*b. Blanket, Tex., 1890; d. Hyattsville, Md., 1964*), philosopher, political scientist, and politician. Attended University of Texas, Texas Christian, and University of Chicago (Ph.D., 1922). Taught at Texas Christian (1915–17), University of Texas (1919–21); University of Chicago (1921–48); and Syracuse University (1948–56). Published three books in 1934: *Beyond Conscience*, *Creative Sceptics*, and *Philosophers Speak for Themselves*. Elected to the Illinois State Senate (1934) and U.S. Congress (1938–40), on the Democratic ticket. Director of education for the Allied Control Commission in Italy (1944) and director of democratization for German prisoners of war.

SMITH, TRUMAN (*b. Roxbury, Conn., 1791; d. 1884*), lawyer. Nephew of Nathan Smith (1770–1835) and of Nathaniel Smith. Graduated Yale, 1815. Congressman, Whig, from Connecticut, 1839–43 and 1845–49, he was among the first Whig party leaders to promote Zachary Taylor's candidacy in 1848 and directed Taylor's campaign. As U.S. senator, 1849–54, he described the sectional crisis of the time as a matter requiring scientific settlement on the basis of the climate and topography of the regions into which it was proposed to extend slavery. In other legislative matters he followed the predominant views of his party and section.

Smith, Uriah (*b. West Wilton, N.H., 1832; d. Battle Creek, Mich., 1903*), Seventh-Day Adventist leader and editor, wood engraver.

Smith, Walter Bedell (*b. Indianapolis, Ind., 1895; d. Washington, D.C., 1961*), soldier and diplomat. Enlisted in the Indiana National Guard (1910); was commissioned a first lieutenant in the Regular Army in 1920. Advanced in rank slowly; he did not become a major until 1939. During interwar period he served with the Bureau of Military Intelligence and had staff assignments in various posts. Taught at the Infantry School (1935–37), where he caught the attention of Gen. George C. Marshall, who called him to Washington in 1939 to help build up the army. Promotions now came rapidly; by 1943 he was a lieutenant general and in 1951 a full general. In 1942 he was named secretary of the Joint Chiefs of Staff and U.S. secretary of the Combined Chiefs of Staff; became Gen. Dwight Eisenhower's chief of staff (1942–45). Ambassador to Russia (1946–49); commander of the First Army (1949); director of the Central Intelligence Agency (1950–52); and undersecretary of state (1953–54).

Smith, Walter Inglewood (*b. Council Bluffs, Iowa, 1862; d. Council Bluffs, 1922*), Iowa jurist. As congressman, Republican, from Iowa, 1900–11, he was an outstanding member of the Appropriations Committee; *post* 1911, he was judge, U.S. circuit court of appeals (8th Circuit).

Smith, William (*b. Newport-Pagnell, England, 1697; d. 1769*), jurist. Father of William Smith (1728–93). Immigrated to New York, 1715. Graduated Yale, 1719; studied law at home and at Gray's Inn. Practicing in New York City, Smith identified himself with the radical Presbyterian faction in provincial politics and was associated with leading cases seeking to curb the governor's prerogative. With James Alexander, he defended Rip Van Dam against claims of William Cosby, 1733, and also defended John Peter Zenger, 1735. Disbarred for criticism of Judge James DeLancey and an associate, Smith was readmitted to practice, 1737. He served as provincial attorney general, 1751, was a member of the Provincial Council, 1753–67, and was associate justice of the New York Supreme Court, 1763–69. Associated with the founding of the first New York public school, 1732, he was an incorporator of the College of New Jersey and a vigorous protester against the establishment of King's College (Columbia) under Anglican auspices.

Smith, William (*b. Aberdeen, Scotland, 1727; d. Philadelphia, Pa., 1803*), Episcopal clergyman, educator. M.A., University of Aberdeen, 1747. Immigrating to New York, 1751, he worked as a tutor on Long Island until 1753, during which time he wrote and published his plan for a college entitled *A General Idea of the College of Mirania* (1753). Invited by Benjamin Franklin and Richard Peters to associate himself with the Philadelphia Academy, he settled in Philadelphia in May 1754 and was the dominant influence in the academy's affairs until the Revolution. He taught logic, rhetoric, and natural and moral philosophy and, with Francis Alison, drew up a new charter, 1755, which established the academy on a collegiate basis. In the next year, Smith presented to the trustees a curriculum which was one of the most comprehensive educational schemes devised for any American school or college up to that time. An ambitious man, he made his influence felt in all the affairs of the province of Pennsylvania. Active in providing schools for the education of German immigrants, he favored the appointment of an American bishop and labored to that end; a leading supporter of the proprietary interest, he incurred Franklin's bitter enmity. During the French and Indian War he condemned the assembly for failure to adopt aggressive military measures and published several pamphlets on the subject; he established in 1757 *The American*

Magazine and Monthly Chronicle to support the interest of the British crown and of the Penn family. Arrested for libel, 1758, as a result of his association with William Moore (1699–1783), he was twice confined and jailed but later vindicated after an appeal to the king. Meanwhile, he had been provost of the College of Philadelphia since 1755 and had been very successful as a fund-raiser for the institution.

At the request of Henry Bouquet and from facts supplied by him, Smith prepared *An Historical Account of the Expedition Against the Ohio Indians in 1764* (1765), which remains an important historical source; he was also active in other intellectual activities, particularly the affairs of the American Philosophical Society. An opponent of the Stamp Act, Smith continued to oppose individual British measures, but was quite out of sympathy with independence and in a notable sermon preached before Congress, June 1775, and later in several pamphlets signed "Candidus," called for a liberal reconciliation with Great Britain. After a number of difficulties with the patriots and the voiding of the charter of the College of Philadelphia, November 1779, by the Pennsylvania Assembly, Smith withdrew to Chestertown, Md., where he established a school later known as Washington College. One of the leaders in the organization of the Protestant Episcopal church, he is said to have suggested its name; he failed, however, to attain the bishopric to which he aspired. On the restoration of the charter of the College of Philadelphia by the assembly, 1789, Smith resumed his position as provost, keeping it until 1791. Despite high positions which he held and the honors which he received, he never enjoyed the highest respect and confidence of his contemporaries, who variously described him as artful, haughty, self-opinionated, hypocritical, and bad-mannered. With all his faults, he was yet one of the ablest, most versatile, and most influential Pennsylvanians of his day. His service to what is now the University of Pennsylvania was incalculable, and in his editorship of the *American Magazine* he encouraged a notable group of young literary men, including Francis Hopkinson, Thomas Godfrey, and James Sterling.

Smith, William (*b. New York, N.Y., 1728; d. Quebec, Canada, 1793*), New York jurist, Loyalist, historian. Son of William Smith (1697–1769). Graduated Yale, 1745. After admission to the New York bar, 1750, he established himself as a leading practitioner in partnership with William Livingston; with Livingston, he published the first digest of the colony statutes in force, 1752. Counsel in very many important cases, Smith was, with his partner and with John Morin Scott, a contributor to the *Independent Reflector* and the *Occasional Reverberator*; with them, he was author also of a defense of William Shirley entitled *A Review of the Military Operations in North America* (1757). His chief literary contribution was *The History of the Province of New-York from the First Discovery to the Year M.DCC.XXXII* (London, 1757; repr. with additions, New York, 1829). An important continuation of this work still remains in manuscript. A justice of the province *post* 1763 and a councillor *post* 1767, he was a leader of the popular party and a founder of the Whig Club. However, he shifted to a "fence-sitting" role and refused commitment to either side after the outbreak of the Revolution. Although he was consulted in the drafting of the New York State constitution, he refused in 1777 to take the oath of allegiance to the state, withdrawing to New York City, which was in British hands. Appointed chief justice of New York, 1779, he never actually served, since the city was under military control. Removing to England, 1783, he immigrated to Canada, 1786, as chief justice, an office which he held until his death.

Smith, William (*b. probably Aberdeen, Scotland, ca. 1754; d. New York or Connecticut, 1821*), Episcopal clergyman, educator. Came to America *ante* 1785. A learned but unsuccessful man, Smith's chief claim to remembrance is that he contributed the "Office of Institution of Ministers" to the Episcopal Book of Common Prayer.

SMITH, WILLIAM (*b. possibly North Carolina, ca. 1762; d. Huntsville, Ala., 1840*), lawyer, statesman, South Carolina legislator and jurist. U. S. senator from South Carolina, 1816–23 and 1826–30. A Jeffersonian Democrat of the strictest sort, Smith was a lifelong defender of states' rights and slavery and an opponent of banks, internal improvements, tariffs, and capitalism. Allied with William H. Crawford in national politics, he won the enmity of John C. Calhoun, whom he detested. Disapproving of nullification, which he thought a remedy worse than the disease, he was refused reelection in 1830 and thereafter was identified with the Union party. *Post* 1833 he resided in Louisiana and Alabama and was a member of the legislature of the latter state.

SMITH, WILLIAM (*b. King George Co., Va., 1797; d. near Warrenton, Va., 1887*), lawyer, mail-coach operator, Virginia legislator and congressman. Democratic governor of Virginia, 1846–49 and 1864–65. He served with distinction as a Confederate brigadier general, in particular at Antietam and Fredericksburg.

SMITH, WILLIAM ANDREW (*b. Fredericksburg, Va., 1802; d. Richmond, Va., 1870*), Methodist clergyman, educator. President of Randolph-Macon College, 1846–66; of Central College, Missouri, 1868.

SMITH, WILLIAM FARRAR (*b. St. Albans, Vt., 1824; d. Philadelphia, Pa., 1903*), Union soldier, engineer. Graduated West Point, 1845, where he was assigned to teach mathematics. After hard service as brigade and division commander in the Army of the Potomac, Smith was author, with William B. Franklin, of an address of complaint to President Lincoln after the defeat at Fredericksburg. Transferred, he displayed extraordinary engineering skill in maintaining Union communications in the Chickamauga-Chattanooga campaigns, 1863, and was reappointed major general, March 1864. In constant controversy thereafter over credit for the opening of the "cracker-line," Smith went east with U. S. Grant. After participating in the action at Cold Harbor, he was once more moved to complain about the policies of his superiors and was relieved of command after failure in leading the attack on Petersburg in June 1864.

SMITH, WILLIAM HENRY (*b. Montgomeryshire, Wales, 1806; d. probably San Francisco, Calif., 1872*), actor, stage manager. Came to America, 1827, to make his debut at the Walnut Street Theatre, Philadelphia. Active thereafter in support of the elder Booth and with the Boston Museum company; during his latter years he was connected with the California Theatre, San Francisco.

SMITH, WILLIAM HENRY (*b. Austerlitz, N.Y., 1833; d. Lake Forest, Ill., 1896*), journalist, public official. General manager *post* 1882 of the combined New York Associated Press and Western Associated Press.

SMITH, WILLIAM LOUGHTON (*b. South Carolina, ca. 1758; d. 1812*), lawyer, pamphleteer. Son-in-law of Ralph Izard. Congressman, Federalist, from South Carolina, 1789–97; U.S. minister to Portugal, 1797–1801. A heavy speculator in government securities, Smith vigorously supported Hamilton's policy of assumption. He was author of several pamphlets in support of Federalism and attacking Thomas Jefferson, among which was *The Politicks and Views of a Certain Party, Displayed* (1792). He was also author, under the name "Phocion," of a series of letters in the *Charleston Daily Courier*, 1806, which defended the British point of view on topics then in dispute.

SMITH, WILLIAM NATHAN HARRELL (*b. Murfreesboro, N.C., 1812; d. 1889*), North Carolina legislator and jurist, Confederate congressman. Chief justice of the North Carolina Supreme Court *post* 1878.

SMITH, WILLIAM RUSSELL (*b. Russellville, Ky., 1815; d. 1896*), Alabama lawyer, legislator, and congressman. Raised in Alabama, Smith was active in politics, at first as a Whig and later as a Know-Nothing. Congressman from Alabama, 1851–57, he served in the Confederate House of Representatives, 1861–65. He wrote widely on legal and other subjects.

SMITH, WILLIAM SOOY (*b. Tarlton, Ohio, 1830; d. 1916*), civil engineer, Union brigadier general. Graduated West Point, 1853. Made first American use of pneumatic process for sinking foundations *ca.* 1859; later developed and improved the process. An expert in foundation work and bridge construction, he was one of the first to advocate carrying piers of high buildings down to rock and was foundation expert on nearly all large buildings constructed in Chicago, 1890–1910. He was father of Charles Sooysmith.

SMITH, WILLIAM STEPHENS (*b. New York, N.Y., 1755; d. Lebanon, N.Y., 1816*), Revolutionary soldier, lawyer, diplomat. As aide to Washington, he supervised evacuation of New York City by the British, 1783. Secretary of legation in London, 1785–88, he married Abigail, daughter of the then American minister, John Adams, 1786. Returning to the United States, he plunged heavily into land speculation and politics, held several federal offices, dabbled in South American filibustering activities, and was congressman, Federalist, from New York, 1813–16.

SMITH, WILLIAM WAUGH (*b. Warrenton, Va., 1845; d. 1912*), Confederate soldier, educator. President of Randolph-Macon College and of Randolph-Macon Woman's College and chancellor of the Randolph-Macon System of academies, Smith worked out new standards of secondary education for boys and of higher education for women which markedly influenced southern education.

SMITH, WINCHELL (*b. Hartford, Conn., 1871; d. 1933*), playwright, stage director. Rose to prominence as coproducer with Arnold Daly of a series of plays by George Bernard Shaw, 1904. An able theater craftsman, he was author of the stage version of *Brewster's Millions*, *The Fortune Hunter*, and *The Only Son*. The rest of his highly successful work was done in collaboration. Smith is also notable as creator of the fictitious "George Spelvin," a name to represent an actor who doubles in a part.

SMITH, XANTHUS RUSSELL (*b. Philadelphia, Pa., 1839; d. Edgehill, Pa., 1929*), painter of historical subjects and battles. Son of Russell Smith.

SMOHALLA (*b. ca. 1815; d. 1907*), Indian medicine man and prophet. Chief of the Wanapum, a small tribe which lived around Priest Rapids in present Yakima Co., Wash., Smohalla founded the so-called Dreamer religion *ante* 1872. He taught that Indians alone were real people and that the whites, the blacks, and the Chinese had been created to punish the Indians for their apostasy from ancient custom.

SMOOT, REED OWEN (*b. Salt Lake City, Utah, 1862; d. St. Petersburg, Fla., 1941*), businessman, apostle of the Church of Jesus Christ of Latter-Day Saints, politician. Raised in Provo, Utah. Graduated Brigham Young Academy (later University), 1879. Joining his father in extensive business enterprises, he amassed a considerable fortune; in 1900 he was ordained an apostle of his church, a position second only to its presidency. One of the earliest in Utah to become a member of the Republican party, he was elected to the U.S. Senate by the legislature in January 1903 and consistently reelected, serving until 1933. Named to the Senate Finance Committee in 1909, and its chairman, 1923–33, he was an indefatigable worker with a passion for economy and a magisterial grasp of facts and figures. A leading member of the standpat Republican group, he fought for efficiency in government, lower taxes, and high tariffs; he was cosponsor of the protectionist Smoot-Hawley Tariff Act of 1930. Defeated in the Democratic landslide of 1932, he returned to Utah and gave his full time to church affairs.

SMYTH, ALBERT HENRY (*b. Philadelphia, Pa., 1863; d. Germantown, Pa., 1907*), educator. Professor of English at Central High School, Philadelphia, Pa., *post* 1886. Smyth won recognition as a Shakespeare scholar, as the author of several useful essays in literary criticism on American subjects, and, in particular, as editor of the *Writings of Benjamin Franklin* (1905–07), which he undertook with the cooperation of the American Philosophical Society.

SMYTH, ALEXANDER (*b. Rathlin Island, Ireland, 1765; d. Washington, D.C., 1830*), lawyer, soldier. Came to Virginia as a child. Commissioned brigadier general, U.S. Army, 1812; attempted an invasion of Canada (at Black Rock, above Buffalo, N.Y., November 1812) which failed of success. He later served as a Virginia legislator and as a congressman, Democrat, from Virginia, 1817–25 and 1827–30.

SMYTH, EGBERT COFFIN (*b. Brunswick, Maine, 1829; d. 1904*), Congregational clergyman. Son of William Smyth; brother of Newman Smyth. Graduated Bowdoin, 1848; Bangor Theological Seminary, 1853. Brown professor of ecclesiastical history at Andover Theological Seminary *post* 1863, he was also a lecturer on pastoral theology, and was president of the faculty, 1878–96.

SMYTH, HERBERT WEIR (*b. Wilmington, Del., 1857; d. Bar Harbor, Maine, 1937*), Hellenist. Graduated Swarthmore, 1876; also attended Harvard, and received Ph.D. at Göttingen, 1884. Taught at Johns Hopkins, Bryn Mawr, University of California, and American School of Classical Studies in Athens; professor of Greek at Harvard, 1901–25. Author of outstanding studies in grammar, he is perhaps best known for *The Greek Melic Poets* (1900, 1906).

SMYTH, JOHN HENRY (*b. Richmond, Va., 1844; d. 1908*), lawyer, educator. Son of a slave father and a free black mother, Smyth was educated in Philadelphia, where he attended the Pennsylvania Academy of Fine Arts, taught school for a while, and considered studying for the stage under Ira Aldridge. Graduated from Howard University, 1872, he practiced law, engaged in Republican politics, and served as U.S. minister to Liberia, 1878–85. In 1897, he secured establishment of the Virginia Manual Labor School and headed it, 1899–1908.

SMYTH, JULIAN KENNEDY (*b. New York, N.Y., 1856; d. White Sulphur Springs, W.Va., 1921*), minister and official of the Church of the New Jerusalem.

SMYTH, NEWMAN (*b. Brunswick, Maine, 1843; d. New Haven, Conn., 1925*), Congregational clergyman. Son of William Smyth; brother of Egbert C. Smyth. Graduated Bowdoin, 1863; served in Union army; graduated Andover Theological Seminary, 1867. After holding pastorates in Maine and Illinois, he became pastor of the First Church, New Haven, Conn., 1882. Author of a number of liberal theological treatises, he was active in movements for church reunion. His nomination for the chair of theology at Andover in 1881 precipitated the well-known Andover controversy.

SMYTH, THOMAS (*b. Belfast, Ireland, 1808; d. 1873*), Presbyterian clergyman, author. Came to America, 1830; was minister and pastor at Second Presbyterian Church, Charleston, S.C., 1832–70.

SMYTH, WILLIAM (*b. Pittston, Maine, 1797; d. 1868*), mathematical textbook writer. Father of Egbert C. and Newman Smyth. Graduated Bowdoin, 1822. Beginning at Bowdoin as instructor in Greek, 1823, he was professor of mathematics there *post* 1828.

SNEAD, THOMAS LOWNDES (*b. Henrico Co., Va., 1828; d. New York, N.Y., 1890*), Missouri lawyer, Confederate officer. Practiced in New York City *post* 1866. Author of *The Fight for Missouri* (1886) and other studies of the Civil War.

SNELL, BERTRAND HOLLIS (*b. Colton, N.Y., 1870; d. Potsdam, N.Y., 1958*), businessman and politician. Studied at Amherst College. The owner of a paper and lumber company in upstate N.Y., Snell was elected as a Republican to the U.S. Congress in 1915; he served until his retirement in 1939. In the House, he was chairman of the House Rules Committee during the 1920's and House minority leader during the 1930's. An ardent foe of the New Deal, he was in favor of government spending for construction of the St. Lawrence Seaway in his own district.

SNELLING, HENRY HUNT (*b. Plattsburg, N.Y., 1817; d. St. Louis, Mo., 1897*), librarian, journalist. Son of Josiah Snelling; brother-in-law of George P. Putnam. Employed by E. & H. T. Anthony, dealers in photographic supplies, 1843–57, Snelling was author of *The History and Practice of the Art of Photography* (1849), a pioneer work. He founded and edited the *Photographic and Fine Art Journal*. A constant experimenter with photographic processes, he invented the enlarging camera, 1852, and at about the same time devised a ray filter.

SNELLING, JOSIAH (*b. Boston, Mass., 1782; d. Washington, D.C., 1828*), soldier. Commissioned as first lieutenant, 1808, and soon promoted captain, Snelling was made prisoner at Detroit during the War of 1812; after being exchanged, he took part in the Niagara campaign. Promoted colonel of 5th Infantry, 1819, he saw through to completion the building of Fort St. Anthony, adjacent to the present cities of St. Paul and Minneapolis. He remained in command there until 1828, the virtual ruler of a remote community completely isolated from civilization. The fort's name was changed to Fort Snelling in 1825.

SNELLING, WILLIAM JOSEPH (*b. Boston, Mass., 1804; d. Chelsea, Mass., 1848*), journalist. Son of Josiah Snelling. Author of, among other works, the verse satire *Truth: A New Year's Gift for Scribblers* (1831) and *Tales of the Northwest* (1830).

SNETHEN, NICHOLAS (*b. Glen Cove, N.Y., 1769; d. Princeton, Ind., 1845*), Methodist clergyman, a founder of the Methodist Protestant church.

SNIDER, DENTON JAQUES (*b. near Mt. Gilead, Ohio, 1841; d. St. Louis, Mo., 1925*), educator, philosopher. A disciple of William T. Harris and Henry C. Brokmeyer. Snider was one of the original members of the St. Louis Philosophical Society and, as a brilliant popular lecturer, did much to carry the idealism of the St. Louis movement to the intellectually starved cities of the Middle West. He was author of a number of critical works, of which those on Shakespeare and Goethe were possibly the best.

SNOW, CARMEL WHITE (*b. Dalkey, Ireland, 1887; d. New York, N.Y., 1961*), editor and fashion authority. Joined *Vogue* in 1921 as assistant fashion editor and was made American editor in 1929. Became fashion editor of *Harper's Bazaar* (1932) and made the magazine a "fortress of fashion opinion." As editor of *Harper's*

(1935–57), she changed the magazine into a literary as well as fashion medium. She attended all the Paris showings and is generally credited with bringing Christian Dior and Balenciaga to prominence in America.

SNOW, ELIZA ROXEY (*b. Becket, Mass., 1804; d. 1887*), Mormon leader and hymnist. Sister of Lorenzo Snow; polygamous wife of Joseph Smith, and later of Brigham Young.

SNOW, FRANCIS HUNTINGTON (*b. Fitchburg, Mass., 1840; d. Delafield, Wis., 1908*), educator, naturalist. An original faculty member of the University of Kansas, Snow specialized in entomology both as teacher and as state entomologist. He served as chancellor of the university, 1890–1901.

SNOW, JESSIE BAKER (*b. Nantucket, Mass., 1868; d. Great Neck, N.Y., 1947*), civil engineer, expert in compressed-air tunnel work. B.S., Union College, 1889. Served as supervisor or consultant on most tunnel construction for subways and under neighboring waterways, New York City, 1904–43. As chief engineer, Board of Transportation, New York City, was responsible for consolidation of subway lines after municipal ownership and for razing elevated railway structures.

SNOW, LORENZO (*b. Mantua, Ohio, 1814; d. 1901*), fifth president of the Utah branch of the Mormon Church. Brother of Eliza R. Snow.

SNOW, WILLIAM FREEMAN (*b. Quincy, Ill., 1874; d. Bangor, Maine, 1950*), public health administrator, leader in the social hygiene movement. B.A., Stanford University, 1896; M.A., 1897. M.D., Cooper Medical College, San Francisco, Calif., 1900. Taught hygiene at Stanford, 1902–09; secretary and executive officer, California State Board of Health, 1909–13. Director of American Social Hygiene Association *post* 1913. President, National Health Council, 1927–34.

SNOWDEN, JAMES ROSS (*b. Chester, Pa., 1809; d. Hulmeville, Pa., 1878*), numismatist, lawyer, Pennsylvania official. Director of U.S. Mint at Philadelphia, 1854–61.

SNOWDEN, THOMAS (*b. Peekskill, N.Y., 1857; d. 1930*), naval officer. Graduated Annapolis, 1879. Promoted rear admiral, 1917, after able, unspectacular service, he commanded a squadron of the battleship force of the Alantic Fleet through World War I and served with great ability as military governor of Santo Domingo, 1918–21.

SNYDER, EDWIN REAGAN (*b. Scottdale, Pa., 1872; d. San Jose, Calif., 1925*), educator, educational administrator, specialist in vocational training.

SNYDER, HOWARD MCCRUM (*b. Cheyenne, Wyo., 1881; d. Washington, D.C., 1970*), army physician. Received his M.D. from Jefferson Medical College (1905), then worked as an army contract surgeon at Fort Douglas, Utah; he was commissioned a first lieutenant in the medical corps of the Regular Army (1908) and held various assignments in the Philippines and United States (1909–17). During the 1920's he served at Fort Leavenworth, Kans., and the U.S. Military Academy. A medical adviser with the National Guard Bureau (1936–40), he pioneered cartilage surgery for the treatment of football injuries and supervised the training and facilities of National Guard medical personnel. Named assistant inspector general in 1940 and retired in 1945, but was recalled to active duty to serve as Dwight D. Eisenhower's personal physician (1945–48, 1951–60).

SNYDER, JOHN FRANCIS (*b. Prairie du Pont, Ill., 1830; d. Virginia, Ill., 1921*), physician, Confederate soldier, archaeologist.

SNYDER, SIMON (*b. Lancaster, Pa., 1759; d. 1819*), businessman, Pennsylvania legislator. A Jeffersonian Democrat, he served as governor of Pennsylvania, 1808–17, the first representative of German descent and of the backcountry farming class to be elected to that office.

SOBOLEWSKI, J. FRIEDRICH EDUARD (*b. Königsberg, East Prussia, 1808; d. 1872*), musician, author, composer. Immigrated to Milwaukee, Wis., 1859. Conductor, St. Louis Philharmonic, 1860–66. His opera *Mohega* produced in Milwaukee, October–November 1859, was probably the first operatic treatment of an episode from the American Revolution.

SOKOLSKY, GEORGE EPHRAIM (*b. Utica, N.Y., 1893; d. New York, N.Y., 1962*), author. Because of his early radical sympathies, left for Russia in 1917 and then wrote for English-language papers in Russia and China, 1917–31, and edited the *Far Eastern Review*. His knowledge of China enabled him to write for the *New York Times* (1931–33) and *New York Herald-Tribune* (1931–40). He also became a prominent spokesman for capitalism and wrote the column "These Days" for the *New York Sun* (1940–50). He promoted the cause of political conservatism through speeches and radio appearances, and his book *The American Way of Life* (1939) defended American capitalism against the attacks of consumer interests. He supported Sen. Joseph McCarthy's anti-Communist crusade and blamed the Truman administration for the triumph of the Chinese Communists.

SOLDAN, FRANK LOUIS (*b. Frankfurt am Main, Germany, 1842; d. St. Louis, Mo., 1908*), educator. Immigrated to America, 1863. Beginning as a teacher in the St. Louis public school system, 1868, he rose through a number of important assignments to be superintendent of instruction, 1895–1908. An able administrator, he also lectured frequently and was associated with William T. Harris and others in St. Louis cultural affairs.

SOLEY, JAMES RUSSELL (*b. Roxbury, Mass., 1850; d. 1911*), educator, lawyer, writer. Graduated Harvard, 1870. Appointed professor of ethics and English at Annapolis, 1871. He served as head of the department of English studies, history and law, 1873–82, supervised publication of Civil War naval records, 1882–90, and was commissioned in the naval corps of professors of mathematics, 1876–90. Resigning his commission, 1890, he served as assistant secretary of the navy until 1893 and practiced law thereafter in New York City. He was author of a number of books on naval history.

SOLGER, REINHOLD (*b. Stettin, Prussia, 1817; d. 1866*), scholar, lecturer, German revolutionary. Immigrated to Roxbury, Mass., 1853. Aided in securing support of German-Americans in the East for the Union cause.

SOLIS-COHEN, JACOB DA SILVA. *See* COHEN, JACOB DA SILVA SOLIS.

SOLOMONS, ADOLPHUS SIMEON (*b. New York, N.Y., 1826; d. Washington, D.C., 1910*), businessman, bookseller, philanthropist. Solomons was an inaugurator of a great number of charitable institutions, among them the American Red Cross, Mount Sinai and Montefiore hospitals in New York City, and the Jewish Theological Seminary of America.

SOMERS, RICHARD (*b. Somers Point, N.J., 1778; d. harbor of Tripoli, 1804*), naval officer. Volunteering to take the ketch *Intrepid* as a fireship into the harbor of Tripoli, Somers was killed in the premature explosion of the vessel, Sept. 4, 1804.

SOMERVELL, BREHON BURKE (*b. Little Rock, Ark., 1892; d. Ocala, Fla., 1955*), army engineer and business executive. Graduated West Point (1914). Studied at the U.S. Army Engineering

School (1922), the Command and General Staff School (1923), and at the Army War College (1926). Worked on various army engineering projects in Mexico and during World War I in action in France. As a lieutenant colonel on detached duty, he was chief of the WPA in New York City from 1936 to 1940, overseeing such projects as the construction of La Guardia Field. During World War II, as commanding general of the Services of Supply of the Operations Division under George C. Marshall; he was, in effect, Marshall's principal logistics adviser and operator. Retired a full general in 1946. President of the Koppers Co., a holding company in Pittsburgh, from 1946.

SONNECK, OSCAR GEORGE THEODORE (*b. Jersey City, N.J., 1873; d. 1928*), musician, librarian, historian. After extensive study in Germany, where he had been brought up, Sonneck returned to America, 1899, and thereafter became the principal scholar of American musical life in colonial and revolutionary times. As chief of the music division, Library of Congress, 1902–17, he made it one of the leading music libraries in the world. Among his most important books are *Early Concert-life in America* (1907), *The Star Spangled Banner* (1914), *Early Opera in America* (1915), and *Miscellaneous Studies in the History of Music* (1921). *Post* 1917 he worked for, and was an official of, the Schirmer music publishing company.

SONNICHSEN, ALBERT (*b. San Francisco, Calif., 1878; d. near Willimantic, Conn., 1931*), war correspondent, advocate of consumer's cooperatives.

SON OF MANY BEADS (*b. near Glenwood, N.Mex., ca. 1866; d. Ramah, N.Mex., 1954*), Navaho philosopher, leader, educator, and singer-curer. A Navaho schooled in the ceremonial intricacies of the Blessing Way and in the traditions and customs of the tribe, Son of Many Beads became famous among archaeologists and anthropologists who studied the Navahos, as the leading interpreter of the Navaho code of ethics. In 1951, Kluckhohn, an anthropologist, introduced Son of Many Beads to philosopher John Ladd, whose resulting book, *The Structure of a Moral Code* (1957) illuminates both Western and Navaho ethics through a detailed comparison of the two. Son of Many Beads became an important liaison for whites who wanted to learn from the Navaho.

SOOYSMITH, CHARLES (*b. Buffalo, N.Y., 1856; d. 1916*), civil engineer. Son of William S. Smith. Graduated Rensselaer Polytechnic Institute, 1876. Expert in foundation problems, he introduced to the United States the "freezing" process for excavation in unstable soils.

SOPHOCLES, EVANGELINUS APOSTOLIDES (*b. Tsangarada, Thessaly, ca. 1805; d. Cambridge, Mass., 1883*), classicist. Immigrated to Massachusetts *ca.* 1828. Teacher and professor of Greek at Harvard *post* 1842. Sophocles was author of a number of important works on Greek morphology, syntax, and cognate subjects, of which the most important was possibly his *Greek Lexicon of the Roman and Byzantine Periods* (1870).

SORENSEN, CHARLES (*b. Copenhagen, Denmark, 1881; d. Bethesda, Md., 1968*), automobile executive. Came to the United States in 1884. Began a forty-year career with the Ford Motor Company in 1904, becoming a vice president and member of the board in 1941. He helped work out the system of the moving assembly line at Ford (1909–13) and assisted Henry Ford and others in the design of the Model A of 1928. During World War II he was occupied with building and operating the Willow Run plant for the manufacture of B-24 Liberators; he was the scapegoat for the disappointing performances at the plant and resigned in 1944. He became president and vice-chairman of Willys-Overland, then retired in 1953.

SORGE, FRIEDRICH ADOLPH (*b. Bethau bei Torgau, Saxony, 1828; d. Hoboken, N.J., 1906*), socialist labor leader. Immigrated to New York City, 1852, where he worked as a music teacher. Active in radical activities in America *post* 1858, he came to be considered the authoritative American representative of Karl Marx.

SORIN, EDWARD FREDERICK (*b. Ahuillé, France, 1814; d. 1893*), Roman Catholic clergyman, educator. Ordained 1838, Sorin entered the Congregation of the Holy Cross, 1840, and immigrated to the neighborhood of Vincennes, Ind., as a missionary, 1841. Removing to a site near South Bend, Ind., 1842, he began to build a college there which was chartered in January 1844 as Notre Dame University; he served as president until 1865. He was also responsible for the establishment in the United States of the Sisters of the Holy Cross and in 1865 founded *Ave Maria* magazine. Elected superior general of his congregation, 1868, he supervised its activities in France, Canada, and Bengal, as well as in the United States.

SOTHERN, EDWARD ASKEW (*b. Liverpool, England, 1826; d. London, England, 1881*), actor. Father of Edward H. Sothern. Immigrating to America, 1852, he became associated *post* 1858 with the role of Lord Dundreary, in the play *Our American Cousin*, which he made the archetype of the British "silly ass."

SOTHERN, EDWARD HUGH (*b. New Orleans, La., 1859; d. New York, N.Y., 1933*), actor. Son of Edward A. Sothern. A leading man in Daniel Frohman's company at the New York Lyceum Theatre *post* 1886, Sothern built up a brilliant reputation as a light comedian and romantic actor in cloak-and-sword dramas; he was outstanding as Rudolf in *The Prisoner of Zenda*. From 1904 to 1907, under the management of Charles Frohman, he acted chiefly in Shakespeare with Julia Marlowe; these productions, carefully staged, were enormously popular. Among other plays in which he was successful were *The Sunken Bell, If I Were King*, and *When Knighthood Was in Flower*. He was author of an autobiography, *The Melancholy Tale of Me* (1916).

SOTHERN, JULIA MARLOWE.   *See* MARLOWE, JULIA.

SOTO, HERNANDO DE.   *See* DE SOTO, HERNANDO.

SOUCHON, EDMOND (*b. Opelousas, La., 1841; d. 1924*), surgeon, anatomist, sanitarian. After making his early medical studies in Paris, France, he returned to New Orleans and graduated, 1867, from the medical department of University of Louisiana (later Tulane). Professor of anatomy and clinical surgery at Tulane, 1885–1908, he was the author of outstanding monographs on aneurisms and shoulder dislocations.

SOULÉ, GEORGE (*b. Barrington, N.Y., 1834; d. 1926*), mathematician, pioneer in business education in the South. President of Soulé College, New Orleans, La., 1856–1926.

SOULE, JOSHUA (*b. Bristol, Maine, 1781; d. Nashville, Tenn., 1867*), Methodist clergyman and bishop, author of the constitution of the Methodist Episcopal church, 1807.

SOULÉ, PIERRE (*b. Castillon-en-Couserans, France, 1801; d. 1870*), Louisiana legislator and jurist, diplomat. Educated in France, Soulé was exiled for participation in republican plots, 1825, and came to Baltimore, Md., in October of that year. After travel in the interior of the United States, he settled in New Orleans, La., where he succeeded as a legal practitioner, orator, and financier. Active in Democratic politics, he served briefly as U.S. senator frm Louisiana early in 1847, and was elected for a full term with Whig support in 1848. As senator, he succeeded J. C. Calhoun as leader of the states' rights wing of the Southern Democrats, but, except for oratory, achieved no outstanding distinction. Appointed U.S. minister to Spain, April 1853, he made one error after another in his endeavors to secure acquisition of Cuba and resigned in December 1854 after the fiasco of the Ostend Manifesto. In this matter he was in fact a scapegoat for errors of the administration. Although opposed to secession, he went with his state, 1860, but was prevented by President Jefferson Davis' hostility from rising to any position of prominence in the Confederacy.

SOUSA, JOHN PHILIP (*b. Washington, D.C., 1854; d. Reading, Pa., 1932*), brandmaster, composer. Conductor of the U.S. Marine Band, 1880–92, and thereafter successful as conductor of his own band on concert tours, Sousa composed more than a hundred marches of outstanding merit. He was composer also of ten comic operas and a number of works in other musical forms. Among his best-known march tunes were "Washington Post March" (1889), "High School Cadets" (1890), "Semper Fidelis" (1888) and "Stars and Stripes Forever" (1897).

SOUTHACK, CYPRIAN *b. London, England, 1662; d. Boston, Mass., 1745*), mariner, pioneer New England cartographer. Came to Boston, 1685; served on coast guard duty against pirates and privateers; commanded the Province Galley in Benjamin Church's expedition against Maine and Nova Scotia, 1704. Issued charts of Boston harbor, the St. Lawrence River, the English colonies from the Mississippi's mouth to the St. Lawrence, and the New England seacoast; author of *New England Coasting Pilot* (*ca. 1720*).

SOUTHALL, JAMES COCKE (*b. Charlottesville, Va., 1828; d. 1897*), Virginia journalist, author. Edited the *Richmond Enquirer*, 1868–74; wrote *The Recent Origin of Man* (1875) and other works.

SOUTHARD, ELMER ERNEST (*b. South Boston, Mass., 1876; d. New York, N.Y., 1920*), neuropathologist, social psychiatrist. Graduated Harvard, 1897; M.D., 1901. Taught neuropathology at Harvard *post* 1904, becoming professor, 1909. As first director, Boston Psychopathic Hospital, 1912–19, he developed psychiatric social work as a profession and provided a program of training for such workers.

SOUTHARD, LUCIEN H. (*b. presumably Sharon, Vt., 1827; d. Augusta, Ga., 1881*), musician, composer, Union soldier. First director, music conservatory of the Peabody Institute, Baltimore, Md., 1868–71; composer of, among other works, an opera, *The Scarlet Letter* (1855).

SOUTHARD, SAMUEL LEWIS (*b. Basking Ridge, N.J., 1787; d. Fredericksburg, Va., 1842*), jurist, statesman. Associate justice, New Jersey Supreme Court, 1815–20; U.S. senator, Democrat, from New Jersey, 1821–23. As U.S. secretary of the navy, 1823–29, he advocated a naval academy, thorough charting of the coasts, and a more intelligent location of naval bases. He also acted ad interim as secretary of the treasury, March–July 1825, and as secretary of war, May–June 1828. Becoming a Whig, Southard served as attorney general of New Jersey and was governor of that state, 1832–33. Reelected to the U.S. Senate, he served from 1833 to 1842 and strongly opposed the policies of Andrew Jackson.

SOUTHGATE, HORATIO (*b. Portland, Maine, 1812; d. Astoria, N.Y., 1894*), Episcopal clergyman. A missionary and missionary bishop in Turkey, 1840–50, he later held a number of appointments as rector in Boston, New York City, and elsewhere. A moderate High Churchman, he was author of, among other works, a novel, *The Cross Above the Crescent* (1878).

SOUTHMAYD, CHARLES FERDINAND (*b. New York, N.Y., 1824; d. 1911*), lawyer. Beginning the study of law at the age of 12, Southmayd soon became proficient and served for some years as a partner of Alexander S. Johnson. He is particularly remembered as the "office" member of the celebrated firm of Evarts, Southmayd & Choate (formed 1851, Joseph H. Choate joining it *ca.* 1858). Southmayd's brief in the case of *Pollock* v. *Farmers' Loan and Trust* is said to have resulted in the Supreme Court's ruling against the income tax as imposed in the Wilson-Gorman Act.

SOUTHWICK, SOLOMON (*b. Newport, R.I., 1773; d. 1839*), printer, Albany (N.Y.) journalist, New York official.

SOUTHWORTH, EMMA DOROTHY ELIZA NEVITTE (*b. Washington, D.C., 1819; d. Georgetown, D.C., 1899*), novelist. Encouraged to write by John G. Whittier (to whom she suggested the story that later became the poem of Barbara Frietchie), Southworth was author of more than 60 sentimental and melodramatic novels, many of which appeared as serials in the *New York Ledger*. Among her works were *The Hidden Hand* (1859), *The Fatal Marriage* (1869), and *The Maiden Widow* (1870).

SOWER, CHRISTOPHER (*b. Laasphe, Germany, 1693; d. Germantown, Pa., 1758*), printer, publisher. Father of Christopher Sower (1721–84). Immigrated to Pennsylvania, 1724. Active *post* 1738 as a printer and publisher of German-language books and newspapers, Sower undertook his most ambitious task in issuing the Bible in German, 1743. Except for John Eliot's Indian version, this was the first American edition of the Bible.

SOWER, CHRISTOPHER (*b. Laasphe, Germany, 1721; d. Methacton, Pa., 1784*), printer, publisher, bishop of the Dunkers (German Baptist Brethren). Son of Christopher Sower (1693–1758). Brought to Pennsylvania by his parents, 1724, he succeeded to his father's publishing business, 1758. A political supporter of the proprietary party, he suffered considerable persecution and loss of property during the Revolution.

SOWER, CHRISTOPHER (*b. Germantown, Pa., 1754; d. Baltimore, Md., 1799*), printer, publisher, Loyalist. Son of Christopher Sower (1721–84); grandson of Christopher Sower (1693–1758). After seizure and condemnation of the family property, August 1778, Sower endeavored to establish Loyalist associations in Pennsylvania; he worked out of the British base in New York. Removing to England, 1783, he returned to America in 1785 as deputy postmaster general and king's printer of the province of New Brunswick.

SPAETH, ADOLPH (*b. Esslingen, Württemberg, 1839; d. Philadelphia, Pa., 1910*), Lutheran clergyman, author. Came to America, 1864, as assistant minister, St. Michael's and Zion's Church, Philadelphia; served later at St. Johannis Church and as a professor of New Testament exegesis in Philadelphia Lutheran Theological Seminary.

SPAETH, JOHN DUNCAN (*b. Philadelphia, Pa., 1868; d. Wayne, Pa., 1954*), educator. Studied at the University of Pennsylvania and the University of Leipzig (Ph.D., 1892). Preceptor at Princeton (1905–11); professor of English (1911–35); president of the University of Kansas City (Mo.) (1935–38). Wrote *Old English Poetry: Translations into Alliterative Verse With Introductions and Notes* (1921), an authoritative work on the subject which went into several printings.

SPAETH, SIGMUND (*b. Philadelphia, Pa., 1885; d. New York, N.Y., 1965*), musicologist. Attended Philadelphia Music Academy, Haverford, and Princeton (Ph.D., 1910). Music editor or reporter for several newspapers and magazines, including *New*

York Evening Mail (1914–18), *Boston Transcript* (1919–20), *McCall's* (1931–33), *Esquire* (1934), *Literary Digest* (1937–38), and *Music Journal* (1955–65). Published more than thirty books, including the widely read *The Common Sense of Music* (1924) and *The Art of Enjoying Music* (1933). In the late 1920's he began giving expert testimony in major music plagiarism cases, usually speaking for the defense. His radio program "At Home with Music" was cited by the Peabody Awards Committee (1949, 1950).

SPAHR, CHARLES BARZILLAI (*b. Columbus, Ohio, 1860; d. at sea in English Channel, 1904*), editor, economist, reformer.

SPAIGHT, RICHARD DOBBS (*b. New Bern, N.C., 1758; d. 1802*), North Carolina legislator, Revolutionary patriot. Nephew of Arthur Dobbs. Antifederalist governor of North Carolina, 1792–95; congressman, 1798–1801. Never a narrow partisan, he frequently voted independently of his party.

SPALDING, ALBERT (*b. Chicago, Ill., 1888; d. New York N.Y., 1953*), violinist. A friend of Saint-Saëns, Spalding was the first American violinist to achieve a major international reputation. American debut 1908 at Carnegie Hall with the New York Symphony led by Damrosch. He was the first American to sit on jury examinations at the National Conservatory of Music in Paris in 1923, and was invited to play at the Beethoven Centennial Festival in Hamburg in 1927. Taught at Juilliard (1933–1944).

SPALDING, ALBERT GOODWILL (*b. Byron, Ill., 1850; d. Point Loma, Calif., 1915*), professional baseball player, merchant. An outstanding pitcher with Harry Wright's Boston team and with the Chicago National League Club, Spalding was a founder, 1876, and for many years president of A. G. Spalding & Brothers, manufacturers of sporting goods.

SPALDING, CATHERINE (*b. Charles Co., Md., 1793; d. Louisville, Ky., 1858*), founder and mother superior of the Sisters of Charity of Nazareth, established in Bardstown, Ky., January 1813. Sister Catherine was for many years the guiding spirit of her community. She also established educational and charitable institutions in Louisville and elsewhere in Kentucky.

SPALDING, FRANKLIN SPENCER (*b. Erie, Pa., 1865; d. Salt Lake City, Utah, 1914*), Episcopal clergyman, missionary bishop of Utah, 1904–14. A prison reformer, a prohibitionist, and a pacifist he was known outside his own communion as "the socialist bishop."

SPALDING, JOHN LANCASTER (*b. Lebanon, Ky., 1840; d. 1916*), Roman Catholic clergyman. Nephew of Martin J. Spalding. Educated at Mount St. Mary's Seminary, Cincinnati, Ohio, and at Rome and Louvain. Bishop of Peoria, Ill., 1877–1908, he was associated with liberal movements in the church and was a prime factor in the founding of Catholic University of America. A prolific and profound writer on social, educational, and philosophical problems.

SPALDING, LYMAN (*b. Cornish, N.H., 1775; d. Portsmouth, N.H., 1821*), physician, surgeon. Studied medicine with Nathan Smith (1762–1829). M.B., Harvard, 1797. Practiced in Portsmouth, N.H., 1799–1812; taught at, and was president of, the College of Physicians and Surgeons of the Western District of New York, Fairfield, N.Y., 1813–16. Spalding's greatest achievement was his founding of the U.S. Pharmacopoeia (1820).

SPALDING, MARTIN JOHN (*b. Rolling Fork, Ky., 1810; d. 1872*), Roman Catholic clergyman. Uncle of John L. Spalding. Educated at Bardstown (Ky.) Seminary and at Rome, where he was ordained, August 1834, he then did pastoral work in Kentucky and won repute as a lecturer and writer. Consecrated coadjutor

bishop of Louisville, 1848, he succeeded to that see, 1850. A zealous administrator and builder of educational and charitable institutions, he proved a courageous leader during the Know-Nothing riots, 1855. He was one of the promoters of the North American College in Rome and of the American College at Louvain. Steadfastly neutral during the Civil War, he became archbishop of Baltimore, 1864, serving until his death. He took a leading part in the Vatican Council, 1870, where he was a strong supporter of papal infallibility.

SPALDING, THOMAS (*b. Frederica, Ga., 1774; d. Darien, Ga., 1851*), planter, Georgia legislator and congressman. Among the first to introduce sea-island cotton into the South, he was the first to grow sugar cane and to manufacture sugar in Georgia.

SPALDING, VOLNEY MORGAN (*b. East Bloomfield, N.Y., 1849; d. Loma Linda, Calif., 1918*), botanist. Graduated University of Michigan, 1873; Ph.D., Leipzig, 1894. Taught at Michigan, 1876–1904. Steadfast advocate of a rational policy of forest conservation, Spalding directed his interest in later years to ecology and the life relations of desert plants.

SPANGENBERG, AUGUSTUS GOTTLIEB (*b. Klettenberg-Hohenstein, Germany, 1704; d. Berthelsdorf, Saxony, 1792*), bishop and director of missions of the Moravian church. During the American periods of his very active career (at various times, 1735–62), he was the driving force in organization of Moravian work. Among his other achievements, he set up the "Economy" congregation at the Bethlehem, Pa., settlement and supervised the Moravian settlement in North Carolina, 1754–62.

SPANGLER, EDWARD. *See* BOOTH, JOHN WILKES.

SPANGLER, HENRY WILSON (*b. Carlisle, Pa., 1858; d. 1912*), engineer, educator. Graduated from engineer course, U.S. Naval Academy, 1878. Taught engineering at the University of Pennsylvania *post* 1881, and at the end of his career, head of the Department of Mechanical and Electrical Engineering there. He was author of standard textbooks on thermodynamics and other engineering subjects.

SPARGO, JOHN (*b. Stithians, England, 1876; d. Old Bennington, Vt., 1966*), socialist, reformer, museum director, and historian. Worked as a Methodist lay preacher in the 1890's and by 1899 was a well-regarded socialist intellectual. Immigrated to the United States in 1901. His best-selling *The Bitter Cry of the Children* (1906) was influential in the passage of child-labor and widows' pension laws. He wrote seven more books on socialism, notably *Karl Marx, His Life and Work* (1909). The socialism he espoused during those years was grounded in a faith in universal suffrage and democratic politics and remarkably tolerant of capitalist reforms. He resigned from the Socialist party in 1916, and by the mid-1920's had repudiated socialism and become a Republican. Founded and headed the Bennington Historical Museum (1926–54) and was president of the Vermont Historical Society (1926–38).

SPARKS, EDWIN ERLE (*b. near Newark, Ohio, 1860; d. 1924*), educator, historian, pioneer in university extension courses. President, Pennsylvania State College, 1908–20.

SPARKS, JARED (*b. Willington, Conn., 1789; d. Cambridge, Mass., 1866*), editor, historian. Graduated Harvard, 1815. After studying divinity and serving as science tutor at Harvard, 1817–19, Sparks was minister of the First Independent Church (Unitarian) of Baltimore, Md., 1819–23. His installation there occasioned the celebrated sermon by William Ellery Channing defining the precise position of the Unitarians. Successful as proprietor and editor of the *North American Review*, 1823–29, he became a leading social and literary figure in the Boston group which included Prescott, Ticknor, and the Everett. Meanwhile, he had undertaken collection and publication of *The Writings of George Washington* (1834–37) and published *The Life of Gouverneur Morris* (1832), *The Works of Benjamin Franklin* (1836–40), and *The Diplomatic Correspondence of the American Revolution* (1829–30); he was also editor and a contributor to *The Library of American Biography* (ser. 1, 1834–38). These formidable sets of printed letters and documents sold well and were pioneer works of their kind. However, Sparks's editorial methods were bad inasmuch as he treated historical documents as if they had been articles submitted to his magazine and used his editorial pencil entirely too freely. He was influenced thereto by a desire to spare the feelings of the descendants of great men and of those who had lent him documents. Famous and well off, he became McLean professor of history at Harvard in 1839. Although he began his work by setting forth an excellent and innovating plan for historical studies, he trained no disciples and his professorship proved a false dawn of the study of modern history in American universities. Chosen president of Harvard, 1849, he attacked the elective system of study in his inaugural address, proposing to substitute definite alternative programs for indiscriminate groupings of course units. The effect, however, was a reaction toward the rigidly prescribed course and the conditions prevalent at Harvard before the reforms associated with George Ticknor. Unhappy as president, Sparks resigned, 1853, and devoted his time thereafter to collecting material for a projected history of the Revolution, which was never written. Faulty as his methods may have been, his energetic search for original documents and his skill in selecting and annotating them, to say nothing of his success in getting them published, gave the American public a new conception of their history.

SPARKS, WILLIAM ANDREW JACKSON (*b. near New Albany, Ind., 1828; d. St. Louis, Mo., 1904*), lawyer, Illinois legislator. Congressman, Democrat, from Illinois, 1875–83, Sparks performed his most notable public service as commissioner of the General Land Office, 1885–87. Despite the hostility of Congress and the press, he succeeded in effecting extensive reforms.

SPARROW, WILLIAM (*b. Charlestown, Mass., 1801; d. Alexandria, Va., 1874*), Episcopal clergyman, educator. Principal and chief teacher of the theological seminary instituted at Worthington, Ohio, by Bishop Philander Chase, 1826, Sparrow was actual administrative head of the school as it developed into Kenyon College and Gambier Theological Seminary. Accepting a professorship in the Virginia Theological Seminary, 1841, he soon became dean and served there until his death. He was an evangelical Low Churchman.

SPAULDING, CHARLES CLINTON (*b. Columbus County, N.C., 1874; d. Durham, N.C., 1952*), insurance executive, bank president. Self-educated, Spaulding joined the newly founded North Carolina Mutual Life Insurance Co. in 1898. A black company, the North Carolina Mutual became the largest black business in the nation by the 1920's, expanding into banks, building and loan associations, and fire insurance companies. Spaulding became president of the company in 1923, and president of the Mechanics and Farmers Bank in 1922.

SPAULDING, EDWARD GLEASON (*b. Burlington, Vt., 1873; d. Princeton, N.J., 1940*), neorealist philosopher. B.S., University of Vermont, 1894; M.A., Columbia, 1896; Ph.D., Bonn, 1900. Taught at College of the City of New York, 1900–05. On the staff of Princeton University thereafter, he was named McCosh professor of philosophy, 1936. Author of, among other works, *The New Rationalism* (1918), in which he called for

the development of a constructive realism upon the basis of modern logic and science.

SPAULDING, ELBRIDGE GERRY (*b. Cayuga Co., N.Y., 1809; d. 1897*), Buffalo, N.Y., banker. A Whig congressman from New York, 1849–51, he returned to Congress as a Republican, 1859–63. Member of a subcommittee of the Committee on Ways and Means, he introduced into the House a bill for issuance of legal-tender treasury notes payable on demand, which became law, Feb. 25, 1862, and authorized the issue of the famous "greenbacks."

SPAULDING, LEVI (*b. Jaffrey, N.H., 1791; d. Uduvil, Ceylon, 1873*), Congregational clergyman. Missionary to Ceylon *post* 1820; distinguished as educator and Tamil linguist.

SPAULDING, OLIVER LYMAN (*b. Jaffrey, N.H., 1833; d. Georgetown, D.C., 1922*), lawyer, Union officer, government official. Special agent, U.S. treasury at Detroit, Mich., 1875–90; assistant secretary, U.S. treasury, 1890–93, 1897–1903; special agent, U.S. treasury in Washington, *post* 1903. Leading U.S. authority on customs law and administration.

SPEAKER, TRIS E. (*b. Hubbard, Tex., 1888; d. Lake Whitney, Tex., 1958*), baseball player. One of baseball's greatest hitters and fielders, Speaker finished his career standing third on the all-time list with 3,515 hits, sixth with 223 triples, and seventh with a .344 lifetime batting average. He played with the Boston Red Sox from 1907 to 1915; with the Cleveland Indians from 1915 to 1926, manager from 1919, and with the Philadelphia Athletics and Washington Senators for one year each. After retirement, he became a radio baseball announcer. Elected to the National Baseball Hall of Fame in 1937.

SPEAKS, OLEY (*b. Canal Winchester, near Columbus, Ohio, 1874; d. New York, N.Y., 1948*), singer, composer. Composed more than 200 songs and hymns, of which three attained great popularity: "On the Road to Mandalay" (1907, to words by Rudyard Kipling), "Morning" (1912), and "Sylvia" (1914).

SPEAR, CHARLES (*b. Boston, Mass., 1801; d. Washington, D.C., 1863*), Universalist clergyman. An opponent of capital punishment, he devoted himself to assistance of discharged prisoners; he was author of *Essays on the Punishment of Death* (1844), *A Plea for Discharged Convicts* (1846), and editor of the periodical *The Prisoners' Friend.*

SPEAR, WILLIAM THOMAS (*b. Warren, Ohio, 1834; d. Columbus, Ohio, 1913*), jurist. Graduated Harvard Law School, 1859; was law partner of Jacob D. Cox. Judge of the common pleas court, 1878–85, and of the Ohio Supreme Court, 1885–1912, he was considered one of the ablest and most conscientious of any who served on the Ohio bench.

SPECK, FRANK GOULDSMITH (*b. Brooklyn, N.Y., 1881; d. Philadelphia, Pa., 1950*), ethnologist, student of American Indian languages and cultures. B.A., Columbia University, 1904; M.A., 1905; Ph.D., University of Pennsylvania, 1908. Staff member, University Museum, University of Pennsylvania, 1908–11; taught anthropology at Pennsylvania *post* 1911 (chairman of anthropology department *post* 1925). Author of, among other works, *Naskapi: Savage Hunters of the Labrador Peninsula* (1935) and *Penobscot Man* (1940).

SPEED, JAMES (*b. Jefferson Co., Ky., 1812; d. near Louisville, Ky., 1887*), lawyer, Kentucky legislator. An uncompromising Union man, he was a principal adviser of Abraham Lincoln on Kentucky affairs. Appointed U.S. attorney general, 1864, he went along with the president's policy of moderation toward the Southern states until Lincoln's death, when he developed a strange fascination for the Radical policy. Favoring military commissions to try the Lincoln conspirators and other persons not protected by parole, he was an early advocate of black suffrage and a sharp critic of President Andrew Johnson. After his resignation, 1866, he was prominent in Radical Republican activities, but later altered his opinions and supported Grover Cleveland in 1884. He was party to the controversy with Joseph Hold over the alleged recommendation for mercy in the case of Mrs. Surratt.

SPEER, EMMA BAILEY (*b. Pottstown, Pa., 1872; d. Bryn Mawr, Pa., 1961*), association administrator. Attended Bryn Mawr (1888–90). An active volunteer for the Young Women's Christian Association (1898–1910), she was president of its National Board (1915–32). Under her leadership the YWCA helped young women cope with a changing world by providing residences, recreation, and practical education. She combined several programs for teen-age girls into the Girl Reserves (1918). During World War I she devoted herself to the cause of young women, particularly those who moved to cities seeking employment. She continued to be active in YWCA until the 1950's.

SPEER, EMORY (*b. Culloden, Ga., 1848; d. Macon, Ga., 1918*), jurist. After serving as Georgia solicitor general, 1873–76, Speer was elected to Congress as an independent Democrat and served, 1879–83. Affiliating with the Republicans in his second term, he was appointed a federal judge for the southern district of Georgia, 1885, and held that position until his death. He was also dean of the law school of Mercer University *post* 1893. He wrote pioneer decisions in many cases involving expansion of federal powers; his opinions in general were noted for lucidity and literary excellence, the most outstanding being *U.S.* v. *Greene and Gaynor.*

SPEER, ROBERT ELLIOTT (*b. Huntingdon, Pa., 1867; d. Bryn Mawr, Pa., 1947*), Presbyterian churchman and lay leader, foreign missions administrator. B.A., College of New Jersey (Princeton University), 1889; attended Princeton Theological Seminary, 1890–91. Secretary of Board of Foreign Missions of the Presbyterian Church in the USA, 1891–1937.

SPEER, WILLIAM (*b. New Alexandria, Pa., 1822; d. Washington, Pa., 1904*), Presbyterian clergyman. Organized first Presbyterian mission work in Canton, China, 1846–50. Later worked among Chinese immigrants to California, chiefly in San Francisco, and was secretary of the board of education of the Presbyterian church, 1865–76.

SPEIR, SAMUEL FLEET (*b. Brooklyn, N.Y., 1838; d. Brooklyn, 1895*), physician, Civil War surgeon. Graduated medical department, University of the City of New York (New York University), 1860; did European postgraduate study in ophthalmology and otology. Long a leader of the medical profession in Brooklyn, he was author of the notable *The Use of the Microscope in the Differential Diagnosis of Morbid Growths* (1871).

SPEISER, EPHRAIM AVIGDOR (*b. Skalat, Galicia, Austria-Hungary [now in the Soviet Union], 1902; d. Elkins Park, Pa., 1965*), archaeologist. Came to the United States in 1919, then attended University of Pennsylvania and Dropsie College (Ph.D., 1924). A concurrent Guggenheim fellowship (1926–28) and professorship at the American School of Oriental Research in Baghdad (1926–27) launched his career as an authority on the Sumerian, Akkadian, Babylonian, and Assyrian languages and the cultures of ancient Mesopotamia. Worked for the Office of Strategic Services as chief of the Near East section of the Research and Analysis Branch during World War II. Taught at the University of Pennsylvania (1931–65) and published *Mesopotamian Origins* (1930), *Introduction to Hurrian* (1941), and *The United States and the Near East* (1947).

SPELLMAN, FRANCIS JOSEPH (*b. Whitman, Mass., 1889; d. New York, N.Y., 1967*), Roman Catholic clergyman. Attended Fordham, the seminary for the Archdiocese of Boston, North American College in Rome, and the Urban College of Propaganda; he was ordained a priest in 1916. He first did parish work in Roxbury, Mass. (1916–18), then was assigned to the chancery staff (1922–25) and named archivist of the archdiocese (1924). In 1925 he accompanied a group of Boston pilgrims to Rome, where he developed friendships with prominent people, including Eugene Pacelli, later Pope Pius XII. In 1931 he smuggled Pope Pius XI's letter condemning fascism out of Italy to Paris, where it was printed and distributed by the Associated Press. Consecrated titular bishop of Sila (1932) and named auxiliary bishop of Boston (1932–39). In 1939 he was named archbishop of New York and vicar for the armed forces of the United States, using his dual position to gain national influence. During World War II he mobilized the Catholic war effort and became a symbol of Catholic patriotism. He was named a cardinal in 1946. Although frequently seen as the most powerful prelate in America, he never quite dominated the American hierarchy. He continually worked for the establishment of full diplomatic relations between the United States and the Holy See, and opposed the decreasing lack of censorship of American films; in a rare address from the pulpit, he struck out against the release of the film *Baby Doll* (1956). Socially, politically, and theologically, he was a conservative, but at Vatican II he was elected to the presidency of the council. After the council he became the object of increasing criticism for his stance in favor of U.S. involvement in the Vietnam War. He was perhaps the most powerful American Catholic churchman in the nation's history.

SPENCE, BRENT (*b. Newport, Ky., 1874; d. Fort Thomas, Ky., 1967*), U.S. congressman. Attended University of Cincinnati (LL.B., 1895); admitted to the Kentucky bar (1895). Elected to Kentucky State Senate (1904–08), later served as city solicitor of Newport (1916–24). U.S. congressman (1930–63); made chairman of the Committee on Banking and Currency in 1943, a position he held except for two Republican-led Congresses. A Democrat, he supported almost all New Deal and Fair Deal measures. Advocated requiring banks to divest themselves of real estate, insurance, and all nonbanking interests. Supported the International Monetary Fund, International Bank for Reconstruction and Development, and helped establish the Small Business Administration.

SPENCER, AMBROSE (*b. Salisbury, Conn., 1765; d. 1848*), New York legislator and jurist. Brother-in-law of DeWitt Clinton. Graduated Harvard, 1783. Admitted to the bar in New York, 1788, he served in the legislature as a Federalist, 1793–98, and as a Democratic-Republican, 1798–1802. From 1800 to 1820 Spencer was almost undisputed dictator of politics in New York State and, with DeWitt Clinton, dominated the scene by ruthless exploitation of the spoils system. Appointed judge of the state supreme court, 1804, he remained there until 1823, serving as chief justice *post* 1819. Dissatisfaction with his autocratic manner and his autocratic power found expression through Martin Van Buren in the constitutional convention, 1821, when extensive amendments were passed which limited Spencer's power. His great ability as a jurist has been obscured by the fury of his political activities; his dissents often gave first expression to what later became accepted doctrine in New York courts. He guided New York jurisprudence along lines he thought it should follow, and somewhat in the manner of John Marshall and Theophilus Parsons, he created judicial law largely by the sheer force of his own reasoning and authority. He was father of John C. Spencer.

SPENCER, ANNA GARLIN (b. *Attleboro, Mass., 1851; d. 1931*), journalist, independent clergyman, educator, woman's rights and peace reformer.

SPENCER, CHRISTOPHER MINER (b. *Manchester, Conn., 1833; d. Hartford, Conn., 1922*), machinist, inventor. Patented the Spencer self-loading, or repeating, rifle, 1860, which was immediately adopted by the U.S. government and used extensively in the Civil War. Patented a breech-loading gun, 1862, and a magazine gun, 1863. Successful in the manufacture of drop-forgings, he continued to work on inventions and patented, September 1873, a machine for turning metal screws automatically which included the automatic turret lathe. As this feature was overlooked by the patent attorney who made the application, Spencer could never claim patent rights to it. Organizing with others the Hartford Machine Screw Co., 1876, he laid the foundation of a very large industrial enterprise in Hartford, but later withdrew from it and in 1893 organized the Spencer Automatic Machine Screw Co. at Windsor, Conn.

SPENCER, CORNELIA PHILLIPS (b. *Harlem, N.Y., 1825; d. Cambridge, Mass., 1908*), author. Principally distinguished *post* 1866 for her efforts to rehabilitate the University of North Carolina.

SPENCER, ELIHU (b. *East Haddam, Conn., 1721; d. 1784*), Presbyterian clergyman. Brother of Joseph Spencer; grandfather of John and Thomas Sergeant; cousin of David and John Brainerd. Held principal pastorates at Elizabethtown, N.J., and Trenton, N.J. An ardent Revolutionary patriot, he was chaplain in the French and Indian War and the Revolution.

SPENCER, JESSE AMES (b. *Hyde Park, N.Y., 1816; d. 1898*), Episcopal clergyman, educator, author. A Broad Churchman, Spencer held a number of pastoral and teaching posts in New York and New Jersey. He was appointed custodian of the Standard Bible of the Church, 1883.

SPENCER, JOHN CANFIELD (b. *Hudson, N.Y., 1788; d. Albany, N.Y., 1855*), lawyer, New York official and legislator. Son of Ambrose Spencer. Graduated Union College, Schenectady, 1806. Admitted to the bar, 1809, in Albany, N.Y., he practiced in Canandaigua, N.Y., and with the help of his father rose rapidly in his profession and in politics. One of the ablest lawyers of his day, he served with John Duer and B. F. Butler on the committee to revise the New York statutes, 1827, and in 1829 was special prosecuting officer in the investigation of the murder of William Morgan. Joining the Whig party *ca.* 1838, he was appointed U.S. secretary of war, 1841, and served until March 1843; then appointed U.S. secretary of the treasury, he resigned in May 1844 because of opposition to the annexation of Texas. His son, Philip, suffered execution for attempted mutiny aboard the USS *Somers*, 1842, while serving under Alexander S. Mackenzie.

SPENCER, JOSEPH (b. *East Haddam, Conn., 1714; d. East Haddam, 1789*), Connecticut legislator and official, Revolutionary soldier. Brother of Elihu Spencer; cousin of David and John Brainerd. A militia officer *post* 1747, Spencer served in the colonial wars and was chosen brigadier general of Connecticut forces, 1775. Passed over in June of that year for promotion to major general in the Continental service, he left the army. Later reconciled, he served through the siege of Boston and in the New York campaign and was promoted major general, August 1776. Resigning 1778, he later served in the Continental Congress and in the Connecticut Assembly.

SPENCER, PITMAN CLEMENS (b. *Charlotte Co., Va., 1793; d. Petersburg, Va., 1860*), surgeon, lithotomist.

SPENCER, PLATT ROGERS (b. *East Fishkill, N.Y., 1800; d. Geneva, Ohio, 1864*), calligrapher, creator of the Spencerian handwriting. Developed his characteristic hand, a sloping, semiangular style with many embellishments, *ante* 1820. He issued copybooks *ca.* 1855 and thereafter brought out a whole series of textbooks.

SPENCER, ROBERT (b. *Harvard, Nebr. 1879; d. New Hope, Pa., 1931*), painter. Studied at National Academy of Design, New York, and at New York School of Art; worked with William M. Chase and Robert Henri.

SPENCER, SAMUEL (b. *Columbus, Ga., 1847; d. near Lawyers, Va., 1906*), railway engineer. Son-in-law of Henry L. Benning. After service with the Baltimore & Ohio Railroad and other roads, including a brief presidency of the B. & O., he became railroad expert for Drexel, Morgan and Co. and played an important part in the Morgan railroad reorganizations. He was highly efficient and successful as president of the Southern Railway, 1894–1906.

SPERRY, ELMER AMBROSE (b. *Cortland, N.Y., 1860; d. Brooklyn, N.Y., 1930*), engineer. Mainly self-taught, Sperry was first successful in developing and manufacturing improved dynamos and arc lamps and founded the Sperry Electric Co. at Chicago, Ill., 1880. In 1888 he organized a company to manufacture an electrically driven undercutting punching machine for soft-coal mining; he subsequently perfected a continuous chain undercutter and also electric mine-locomotives. Founding another company, 1890, for manufacture of his patented electric street-railway cars, he operated this concern with success until 1894 when he sold it and his patents to the General Electric Co. He was next engaged, 1894–1900, in manufacture of electric automobiles of his own design and his patented storage battery for their operation. In 1900 he established at Washington, D.C., a research laboratory wherein, with an associate, he evolved the so-called Townsend process for manufacture of caustic soda from salt and developed the chlorine process for recovering tin from scrap. Sperry's most distinctive inventions, however, were those which put to practical use the principle of the gyroscope. He began work on this project *ca.* 1896, and through long, expensive investigation successfully combined electrical and mechanical elements into gyroscopic compasses and stabilizers for ships and airplanes. His first compass was tried out on the USS *Delaware* at Brooklyn Navy Yard, 1910, and shortly after adopted by the U.S. Navy and by steamship lines generally. In 1918 he produced his high-intensity arc searchlight and, at his death, had just completed a device for detecting flaws in railroad rails. He was the holder of more than 400 patents and the recipient of many scientific honors.

SPERRY, NEHEMIAH DAY (b. *Woodbridge, Conn., 1827; d. New Haven, Conn., 1911*), contractor, businessman, Know-Nothing and Republican politician. Dominating Republican politics in Connecticut *post* 1856, Sperry served in Congress, 1895–1911, where he was an ardent protectionist. He also served as postmaster of New Haven, 1861–86 and 1890–94.

SPERRY, WILLARD LEAROYD (b. *Peabody, Mass., 1882; d. Cambridge, Mass., 1954*), clergyman, theologian, and essayist. Studied at Olivet College, Mich., as a Rhodes Scholar at Oxford University, and at Yale (M.A., 1908). From 1925 to 1953, he was professor and dean of the Harvard Divinity School. During his tenure, he liberalized the school's admissions policies to include students from a wide variety of denominations. He wrote *Religion in America* in 1946 at the request of Cambridge University Press as part of its series on American life and institutions.

SPEYER, JAMES JOSEPH (b. *New York, N.Y., 1861; d. New York, 1941*), financier, philanthropist. Scion of a great German

Jewish banking family, he was raised in Frankfurt am Main and attended schools there. In 1885 he joined the New York City branch of the family firm, Speyer and Co., becoming senior partner, 1899. Active in underwriting and distributing railroad securities and bonds of foreign governments, the firm ranked as one of the leading international banking houses of the time up to 1914. Adversely affected by its German connections on the outbreak of World War I and by the postwar fall in railroad stocks, Speyer and Co. declined in importance; the rise of the Nazis in Germany was the final blow. James Speyer formally retired in 1938 and the American firm was liquidated in 1939. His many philanthropies included the University Settlement, Teachers College, the Provident Loan Society, the Museum of the City of New York, and various political reform groups.

SPICKER, MAX (*b. Königsberg, Germany, 1858; d. 1912*), musician, conductor, composer. Came to New York City, 1882, after a successful career in Europe. Conductor of the Beethoven-Männerchor, 1882–88; director, Brooklyn Conservatory of Music, 1888–95; headed theory department, New York National Conservatory, 1895–1907; director of music, Temple Emanu-El, 1898–1910.

SPIER, LESLIE (*b. New York, N.Y., 1893; d. New Mexico, 1961*), anthropologist. Attended City College of New York and Columbia (Ph.D., 1920). Taught at University of Washington (1920–27, 1929–30), Yale (1933–39), and University of New Mexico (1939–55). Editor of *American Anthropologist* (1934–38) and the *Southwestern Journal of Anthropology* (1944–61). He was in the field for part of every year during 1916–35, studying North American Indians; his *Havasupai Ethnography* (1928) served as a model of ethnographic description, and *The Sun Dance of the Plains Indians* (1921) remains a classic of the historical method of anthropology.

SPIERING, THEODORE (*b. St. Louis, Mo., 1871; d. Munich, Germany, 1925*), violinist, conductor, music teacher. Studied in Cincinnati, Ohio, with Henry Schradieck; at Berlin with Joseph Joachim. Appreciated more in Europe than in America, Spiering organized and directed the Spiering Quartet, 1893–1905, taught for some years in Chicago, Ill., and was concertmaster of the New York Philharmonic, 1909–11, under Gustav Mahler.

SPILLMAN, WILLIAM JASPER (*b. Lawrence Co., Mo., 1863; d. 1931*), agricultural economist. Graduated University of Missouri, 1886. After serving on staff of Washington State College, Spillman acted for many years as an expert in the U.S. Department of Agriculture. He was also professor of commercial geography at Georgetown University, 1922–31. An innovator in development of scientific farm management, he was author of *Balancing the Farm Output* (1927).

SPILSBURY, EDMUND GYBBON (*b. London, England, 1845; d. New York, N.Y., 1920*), mining engineer, metallurgist. Trained in Belgium and Germany, Spilsbury came to America, 1870. Practicing for many years as a consultant, he was responsible for introduction of a number of European processes into the United States.

SPINGARN, JOEL ELIAS (*b. New York, N.Y., 1875; d. New York, 1939*), literary critic, reformer. Graduated Columbia, 1895; Ph.D., 1899. Strongly influenced by George E. Woodberry, Spingarn taught comparative literature at Columbia, 1899–1911. A man of many talents, activities, and enthusiasms, he was perhaps the leading American exponent of the principles of Benedetto Croce. He also interested himself in politics (liberal Republican), in the culture of flowers, and in securing justice for blacks. Among his books were *History of Literary Criticism in the Renaissance* (1899) and *Creative Criticism* (1917).

SPINK, JOHN GEORGE TAYLOR (*b. St. Louis, Mo., 1888; d. Clayton, Mo., 1962*), baseball publicist. Succeeded his father as publisher of *Sporting News*, a St. Louis-based weekly journal of baseball news, in 1914. Called the "Bible of Baseball," by 1942 the paper boasted a weekly circulation of 100,000 copies. Ancillary publications include *Sporting Goods Dealers* and yearbooks of baseball facts and statistics, including the *Baseball Register*, first published in 1940. After the postwar rise of rival sports and leisure publications, the paper became a lively tabloid and extended coverage to other sports.

SPINNER, FRANCIS ELIAS (*b. German Flats, N.Y., 1802; d. 1890*), banker. Congressman, antislavery Democrat, from New York, 1855–57, he served as a Republican, 1857–61. Honest and able as U.S. treasurer, 1861–75, his employment of young women in his department during the Civil War is said to have established the status of women in the civil service.

SPITZKA, EDWARD ANTHONY (*b. New York, N.Y., 1876; d. Mount Vernon, N.Y., 1922*), anatomist, criminologist. Son of Edward C. Spitzka. M.D., New York College of Physicians and Surgeons, 1902. Taught anatomy at Jefferson Medical College *post* 1906. Author of notable studies on the human brain, Spitzka edited the 18th American edition of Gray's *Anatomy* (1910).

SPITZKA, EDWARD CHARLES (*b. New York, N.Y., 1852; d. 1914*), neurologist, psychiatrist. Father of Edward A. Spitzka. Graduated medical department, University of the City of New York (New York University), 1873; made postgraduate studies in Leipzig and Vienna. Practiced in New York City *post* 1876 and gained nationwide reputation as a medicolegal expert in cases involving insanity; he also made many contributions to knowledge of the anatomy of the nervous system.

SPIVAK, CHARLES DAVID (*b. Krementchug, Russia, 1861; d. 1927*), physician, author. Came to America 1882; worked at first as a laborer in New York and New Jersey. M.D., Jefferson Medical College, 1890. An authority in the field of gastroenterology, he taught for many years at the medical school of the University of Denver and was founder of the Jewish Consumptives' Relief Society, 1904. From 1904 until his death he acted as secretary and gastroenterologist to the society's sanatorium near Denver, Colo.

SPOFFORD, AINSWORTH RAND (*b. Gilmanton, N.H., 1825; d. 1908*), bookseller, journalist. Appointed assistant in the Library of Congress, 1861, he became chief librarian, 1864, and directed the affairs of the library until 1897. Reverting then to the position of assistant, he continued in that post until his death. During his tenure the library made extraordinary progress.

SPOFFORD, HARRIET ELIZABETH PRESCOTT (*b. Calais, Maine, 1835; d. Deer Island, Maine, 1921*), author. Encouraged to write by Thomas W. Higginson, Spofford enjoyed a successful career as a miscellaneous writer, romantic novelist, and verse writer, 1860–1910.

SPOONER, JOHN COIT (*b. Lawrenceburg, Ind., 1843; d. New York, N.Y., 1919*), lawyer. Successful as counsel for railroads, Spooner was U.S. senator, Republican, from Wisconsin, 1885–91 and 1897–1907. Winning notice in his first term as an able debater and brilliant parliamentarian, he became a national figure during his second period in the Senate, sharing with Nelson W. Aldrich, W. B. Allison, and Orville H. Platt the confidence of Presidents McKinley and Roosevelt. A counselor rather than a leader in Republican politics, he belonged to the "stalwart" wing of the Wisconsin Republicans and was a principal target for attacks by the reform element. The decline of his faction in the state and the election of Robert M. La Follette as his colleague brought about Spooner's resignation. Thereafter he practiced law in New York City.

SPOONER, LYSANDER (*b. Athol, Mass., 1808; d. 1887*), lawyer, antislavery advocate, reformer. Author of, among other books, *Unconstitutionality of Slavery* (1845, 1847) and *Essay on the Trial by Jury* (1852).

SPOONER, SHEARJASHUB (*b. Orwell, Vt., 1809; d. Plainfield, N.J., 1859*), dentist, promoter of art. Author of, among other works, *A Biographical and Critical Dictionary of Painters, Engravers, . . .* (1853).

SPOTSWOOD, ALEXANDER (*b. Tangier, 1676; d. Annapolis, Md., 1740*), lieutenant governor of Virginia. Entering the British army, he fought in the War of the Spanish Succession, and in 1710 was appointed lieutenant governor of Virginia, under the nominal governor, the earl of Orkney. He undertook his new duties with a vigor rather disconcerting to a people inclined to reduce governmental activity to a minimum. He sought to regulate the fur trade, to maintain an enlightened Indian policy, to encourage actual settlers as opposed to mere land speculators, and to require inspection of tobacco designed for export or for use as legal tender. This last policy led to a violent quarrel with the House of Burgesses, 1715, particularly with two prominent members of his council, William Byrd and Philip Ludwell, who had little taste for the additional labors the governor thrust upon them. A struggle for power between the governor and the council ensued and harmony was not restored until 1720. From his arrival in Virginia, Spotswood was actively identified with the problems of the frontier. He made a number of explorations westward, of which the most famous was in 1716. He also attempted to protect the colony from Iroquois raids by establishing compact communities of friendly Indians, powerful enough to resist attack and convenient for the work of missionary and schoolmaster; he negotiated a treaty with the Iroquois whereby they were to keep north of the Potomac and west of the Blue Ridge. During the closing years of his administration his attitude toward colonial self-assertion mellowed perceptibly. Doubtless due in part to the conviction that it was futile to contend against what amounted to a Virginia nationalism, the change was natural in one who had decided to make America his permanent home. Removed from office in 1722, he engaged in the mining and smelting of iron. When war with Spain broke out in 1739, he set about to recruit a colonial regiment and was appointed major general of a proposed expedition against Cartagena. He died in the midst of his preparations for this service.

SPOTTED TAIL (*b. near Fort Laramie, Wyo., ca. 1833; d. 1881*), a head chief of the Lower Brulé Sioux. Uncle of Crazy Horse. Rising in tribal authority as a warrior, he opposed Red Cloud at the Fort Laramie council, 1866. He was a signer of the treaty of April 1868 providing for withdrawal of Indian opposition to railroad building and acceptance of a reservation in present South Dakota. Later removing to a reservation in northwestern Nebraska, he continued friendly to the whites and resisted efforts to bring his tribe to war in 1876. Sharp, witty, and affable in manner, he was considered one of the most brilliant of the Sioux leaders.

SPRAGUE, ACHSA W. (*b. Plymouth Notch, Vt., ca. 1828; d. 1862*), spiritualist, medium, mental healer.

SPRAGUE, CHARLES (*b. Boston, Mass., 1791; d. 1875*), banker, poet. Author of a number of odes and other minor poems which were published in a collected edition (1841).

SPRAGUE, CHARLES ARTHUR (*b. Lawrence, Kans., 1887; d. Salem, Oreg., 1969*), newspaper editor and governor of Oregon.

Graduated from Monmouth College (1910). Purchased the weekly *Journal-Times* of Ritzville (1915), a one-third interest in *Corvallis* (Oreg.) *Gazette-Times* (1925), and two-thirds interest in *Oregon Statesman* (1929), long the most influential paper in the state capital. As editor and publisher of the *Statesman* for the next forty years, he gained a national reputation as an articulate spokesman for small-town values, fiscal conservatism, and internationalism. As governor (1938–42) he improved the state's employment services, launched vocational-training programs to aid the jobless, modernized the school system, reduced the state debt by $12 million, and balanced the budget while increasing social welfare services. An early conservationist, he set up regulations for logging operations to ensure sustained-yield management of its forests. Described as the "conscience of Oregon," he was also an outspoken defender of civil liberties.

SPRAGUE, CHARLES EZRA (*b. Nassau, N.Y., 1842; d. New York, N.Y., 1912*), banker, Union soldier. Long employed by the Union Dime Savings Bank in New York City, he was its president, 1892–1912. One of the first to qualify as a certified public accountant, he was a leading spirit in establishment of the New York University School of Commerce, where he taught accountancy. He was author of a number of textbooks in accountancy and finance.

SPRAGUE, FRANK JULIAN (*b. Milford, Conn., 1857; d. 1934*), engineer, inventor. Graduated Annapolis, 1878. After naval service, 1878–83, during which he devoted himself to problems in electrical development, he joined the staff of Thomas A. Edison for a brief period, and then organized the Sprague Electric Railway & Motor Co. Winning repute in 1887 for adaptation of a constant-speed motor devised by him to use in street-railway service at Richmond, Va., he achieved rapid success. In 1892 he formed the Sprague Electric Elevator Co., which became part of the Otis Elevator Co. His system of "multiple unit" control for trains made up of motor cars was first tried out in 1897 and later generally adopted for subway, elevated, and suburban service. He was also a pioneer in design and production of miniature electric power units suitable for machine tools, printing presses, dentist's drills, and laborsaving conveniences in the home.

SPRAGUE, HOMER BAXTER (*b. South Sutton, Mass., 1829; d. 1918*), educator, Union soldier. Graduated Yale, 1852. After holding a number of important teaching and administrative posts in New York, Connecticut, and Massachusetts, Sprague served as president of Mills College, 1885–87, and of the University of North Dakota, 1887–91. He was founder of the Martha's Vineyard Summer Institute, 1879, said to be the first general summer school in the United States.

SPRAGUE, KATE CHASE (*b. Cincinnati, Ohio, 1840; d. Washington, D.C., 1899*), political hostess. Daughter of Salmon P. Chase; wife of William Sprague (1830–1915).

SPRAGUE, OLIVER MITCHELL WENTWORTH (*b. Somerville, Mass., 1873; d. Boston, Mass., 1953*), economist and professor. Studied at Harvard University (Ph.D., 1897). Taught at Harvard (1899–1905); at the Imperial University in Tokyo (1905–08); professor at the Harvard School of Business Administration (1913–41). From 1930 to 1933, he was chief economic advisor to the Bank of England, and also counseled the heads of the German Reichsbank, the Austrian Kreditsbank, the Bank of France, and the Bank for International Settlements. One of President Roosevelt's "brain trusters," Sprague was influential in government circles, but resigned in 1933 over differences in ways to achieve economic recovery. Wrote *Recovery and Common Sense* in 1934. President of the American Economic Association (1937).

SPRAGUE, PELEG (*b.* *Duxbury, Mass., 1793; d. Boston, Mass., 1880*), jurist. After serving in the first Maine legislature, 1821–22, and as congressman and U.S. senator from Maine, 1825–35, he found his true vocation when appointed U.S. district judge for Massachusetts, 1841. Sprague was outstanding on the bench until his retirement in 1865, despite constant weakness of the eyes which ended in total blindness. His decisions included a definitive statement on the doctrine of treason and the powers of the federal government to punish treason, March 1863.

SPRAGUE, WILLIAM (*b. Cranston, R.I., 1773; d. Cranston, 1836*), textile manufacturer, lumber merchant, stockbreeder.

SPRAGUE, WILLIAM (*b. Cranston, R.I., 1830; d. Paris, France, 1915*), textile manufacturer, Union soldier, politician. Grandson of William Sprague (1773–1836); husband of Kate C. Sprague. An inheritor of great wealth, he advanced easily in politics and was Democratic governor of Rhode Island, 1860–61. After Civil War service, he was reelected governor, 1862, but resigned to become U.S. senator from Rhode Island, serving 1863–75. Considered irresponsible by many of his constituents, almost beggared in the panic of 1873, and divorced in 1882 under scandalous circumstances, he lived in retirement *post* 1883.

SPRAGUE, WILLIAM BUELL (*b. Hebron, Conn., 1795; d. Flushing, N.Y., 1876*), Congregational clergyman, autograph collector, biographer. Held pastorates at West Springfield, Mass., and Albany, N.Y. Author of, among other works, lives of Timothy Dwight and Jedidiah Morse and of *Annals of the American Pulpit* (1857–69).

SPRECHER, SAMUEL (*b. Washington Co., Md., 1810; d. San Diego, Calif., 1906*), Lutheran clergyman, educator. President of Wittenberg College, 1849–74, he taught theology and philosophy there until 1884, thereafter bearing the title of professor emeritus.

SPRECKELS, CLAUS (*b. Lamstedt, Hannover, Germany, 1828; d. San Francisco, Calif., 1908*), sugar manufacturer, capitalist. Came to America, 1846; removed to San Francisco, 1856. Organized the California Sugar Refinery, 1867; held for many years a virtual monopoly of sugar manufacture and sale on the Pacific Coast; fought the Sugar Trust, 1888–89. Spreckels was also active in public utilities and in development of the sugar industry in Hawaii.

SPRECKELS, JOHN DIEDRICH (*b. Charleston, S.C., 1853; d. Coronado, Calif., 1926*), sugar merchant, capitalist. Son of Claus Spreckels.

SPRECKELS, RUDOLPH (*b. San Francisco, Calif., 1872; d. San Mateo, Calif., 1958*), industrialist and reformer. A bank founder and sugar industrialist, Spreckels was instrumental, along with San Francisco editor, Fremont Older, and muckraker Lincoln Steffens, in breaking the corrupt political ring of Abraham Ruef. The San Francisco Graft Prosecution (1906–10) successfully destroyed the political machine of the Union Labor Party whose officials were convicted of accepting bribes and payoffs from public utilities. Ruef went to prison, and Spreckels returned to private industry.

SPRING, GARDINER (*b. Newburyport, Mass., 1785; d. New York, N.Y., 1873*), Presbyterian clergyman. Son of Samuel Spring. Graduated Yale, 1805. After a brief practice of law, he attended Andover Theological Seminary and was called to the pastorate of the Brick Presbyterian Church, New York City, 1810, as colleague to John Rodgers (1727–1811). A thorough Calvinist and a conservative, he remained at the Brick Church until his death, building up a strong congregation and taking a commanding position in the life of New York City.

SPRING, LEVERETT WILSON (*b. Grafton, Vt., 1840; d. Boston, Mass., 1917*), Congregational clergyman, educator. Author of *Kansas: The Prelude to the War for the Union* (1885), the first nonpartisan account of the Kansas struggle. Served as Morris professor of rhetoric at Williams College, 1886–1909.

SPRING, SAMUEL (*b. Uxbridge, Mass., 1746 o.s.; d. 1819*), Congregational clergyman. Father of Gardiner Spring. Pastor at Newburyport, Mass., 1777–1819. Spring was identified with the "Hopkinsian" wing of the church and was a man of great influence. He was one of the founders of Andover Theological Seminary and of the American Board of Commissioners for Foreign Missions.

SPRINGER, CHARLES (*b. Louisa Co., Iowa, 1857; d. 1932*), lawyer, New Mexico cattleman and Republican politician. Brother of Frank Springer.

SPRINGER, FRANK (*b. Wapella, Iowa, 1848; d. 1927*), lawyer, paleontologist. Removing to New Mexico, 1873, he became one of the leading lawyers of that territory and state. Among other important cases in which he served as counsel was the case of the celebrated Maxwell Land Grant, which he fought in the U.S. courts for some 30 years and finally won. In association with Charles Wachsmuth, Springer did outstanding work in the study of fossil crinoids, publishing a series of volumes which have been called "the most magnificent monographs on invertebrate paleontology published in the United States."

SPRINGER, REUBEN RUNYAN (*b. Frankfort, Ky., 1800; d. 1884*), wholesale grocery merchant, financier, philanthropist. Remembered as a patron of music and art and as a benefactor of the Catholic church, he was largely responsible for providing his home city of Cincinnati, Ohio, with a music hall and a college of music.

SPRINGER, WILLIAM MCKENDREE (*b. New Lebanon, Ind., 1836; d. 1903*), lawyer, judge in Indian Territory. Congressman, Democrat, from Illinois, 1875–95, he was active on many committees and served as chairman of the committees on claims, territories, elections, ways and means, banking and currency. He introduced bills under which Washington, Montana, and the Dakotas were admitted into the Union as states. A strict parliamentarian, he seemed often more interested in the rules of procedure than in the issues involved.

SPROUL, WILLIAM CAMERON (*b. Octoraro, Pa., 1870; d. near Chester, Pa., 1928*), manufacturer, businessman. Republican governor of Pennsylvania, 1919–23, he actively promoted highway construction and reorganized several branches of the state government, but was criticized for his handling of the steel strike of 1919.

SPROULE, WILLIAM (*b. Co. Mayo, Ireland, 1858; d. San Francisco, Calif., 1935*), railroad executive. Immigrated to America *ca.* 1876. Entering employ of the Southern Pacific Railroad, 1882, he rose to post of freight traffic manager by 1898. Associated with other companies, 1906–11, he returned to the Southern Pacific as president, serving 1911–28.

SPROULL, THOMAS (*b. near Lucesco, Pa., 1803; d. 1892*), Reformed Presbyterian clergyman, educator. Pastor of the Old School Church at Allegheny (North Pittsburgh), Pa., 1834–68; taught thereafter at Allegheny Theological Seminary.

SPRUANCE, RAYMOND AMES (*b. Baltimore, Md., 1886; d. Pebble Beach, Calif., 1969*), naval officer. Graduated from U.S.

Naval Academy (1906) and circled the globe aboard the *Minnesota* as part of the Great White Fleet (1907–09). In Great Britain in 1917 to study fire-control techniques while serving as electrical officer at the New York Navy Yard. With the Office of Naval Intelligence (1928–29) and taught at the Naval War College (1931–32, 1935–37). Advanced to rear admiral in 1939 and assumed command of the Tenth Naval District in Puerto Rico (1940–41), then was transferred to the Pacific to command a division of heavy cruisers; he participated in the first carrier raids of the Pacific war (1942) and relieved Adm. William Halsey as commander of one of two carrier task forces assigned to stop the Japanese fleet. Took command of the Central Pacific Force, later designated the Fifth Fleet (1943), and directed the capture of numerous Pacific Islands. Made full admiral in 1944, he assumed command of the Pacific Fleet after Japan's surrender. President of the Naval War College (1946–48) and ambassador to the Philippines (1952–55).

SPRUNT, JAMES (*b. Glasgow, Scotland, 1846; d. 1924*), businessman, philanthropist, local historian. Immigrated to North Carolina as a boy; resident in Wilmington *post* 1854. One of the largest exporters of cotton in the country, Sprunt was active in civic affairs and was author of a number of valuable historical monographs, among them *Tales and Traditions of the Lower Cape Fear, 1661–1896* (1896) and *Chronicles of the Cape Fear River* (1914). He gave much financial assistance to Presbyterian church work and to hospitals.

SPURR, JOSIAH EDWARD (*b. Gloucester, Mass., 1870; d. Winter Park, Fla., 1950*), mining geologist. B.A., Harvard 1893; M.A., 1894. As staff member, Minnesota Geological Survey, he made the first geological map of the Mesabi iron range. While associated with U.S. Geological Survey, 1894–1906, he headed first expedition to Alaska, 1896, and reported on Yukon gold fields. Served as chief geologist, American Smelting and Refining Co., 1906–08. After conducting a private consulting practice, and service during World War I as chairman of the federal committee on mineral needs and resources, he was editor of *Engineering and Mining Journal*, 1919–27. He was author of two controversial treatises: *The Ore Magmas* (1923) and *Geology Applied to Selenology* (1944–49).

SQUANTO (*d. Chatham Harbor, Mass., 1622*), Pawtuxet Indian. Kidnapped at Pawtuxet (Plymouth) in 1615 by an English sea captain, he was sold in Spain as a slave. Escaping to England, he lived for a time in London. While serving as a pilot in an English expedition to the New England coast, 1619, he escaped and made his way home to Pawtuxet only to find himself the sole surviving member of his tribe. Introduced by Samoset to the Pilgrims, March 1621, he took Edward Winslow to Massasoit and acted as interpreter in concluding the treaty of Plymouth between that chief and the Pilgrims. He also showed the newcomers how to set corn and where to fish. After he had made himself obnoxious to the Indians by exploiting his friendship with the English, and notably by sounding a false alarm of impending treachery on the part of Massasoit, that chief demanded that the Pilgrims give him up for punishment. He later made his peace with Massasoit. In November 1622 he served as guide and interpreter on Bradford's expedition around Cape Cod.

SQUIBB, EDWARD ROBINSON (*b. Wilmington, Del., 1819; d. Brooklyn, N.Y., 1900*), physician, pharmacist, manufacturing chemist. M.D., Jefferson Medical College, 1845. A U.S. Navy surgeon, 1847–57, he established in 1852 a laboratory for preparation of high-grade pharmaceuticals for service use which he directed until 1857. Establishing his own manufactory in Brooklyn, N.Y., 1858, he continued to do pioneer work in manufacture of pure pharmaceuticals and was a leader in independent chemical research; he was also an authority on the U.S. *Pharmacopoeia*.

SQUIER, EPHRAIM GEORGE (*b. Bethlehem, N.Y., 1821; d. Brooklyn, N.Y., 1888*), journalist, archaeologist, diplomat. Considered in his time an authority on Central America, Squier held a number of consular and diplomatic posts in Latin America. He was coauthor with Edwin H. Davis of *Ancient Monuments of the Mississippi Valley* (1847) and author of *Aboriginal Monuments of the State of New York* (1851).

SQUIER, GEORGE OWEN (*b. Dryden, Mich., 1865; d. Washington, D.C., 1934*), soldier, engineer. Graduated West Point, 1887; Ph.D., Johns Hopkins, 1893. An expert in cable and radio communication, Squier did much important early experimental work in wireless telephony and multiple telephony; he was also a student of military aviation. He served as chief signal officer, U.S. Army, with the rank of major general, 1917–23.

SQUIERS, HERBERT GOLDSMITH (*b. Madoc, Canada, 1859; d. London, England, 1911*), soldier, diplomat. Outstanding as chief of staff in defense of legations at Peking, China, during the Boxer Rebellion, 1900; handled successfully the difficult post of U.S. minister to Cuba, 1902–05.

SQUIRE, WATSON CARVOSSO (*b. Cape Vincent, N.Y., 1838; d. Seattle, Wash., 1926*), lawyer, Union soldier, capitalist. Son-in-law of Philo Remington. Settling in Seattle, Wash., 1879, he was Republican governor of Washington Territory, 1884–87, and U.S. senator from the state of Washington, 1889–97.

STACY, WALTER PARKER (*b. Ansonville, N.C., 1884; d. Raleigh, N.C., 1951*), jurist and labor arbitrator. Studied at the University of North Carolina. Served on the Supreme Court of North Carolina from 1920 to 1951; chief justice (1925–51). Appointed by presidents Coolidge, Hoover, Roosevelt, and Truman to be a mediator on various labor boards specializing in railroad labor affairs, Stacy served with distinction. In 1932, headed a commission for the rewriting and modernizing of the Constitution of North Carolina.

STAGER, ANSON (*b. Ontario Co., N.Y., 1825; d. Chicago, Ill., 1885*), telegraph pioneer. Associated with the Western Union Telegraph Co. *post* 1856, he served as its general superintendent and later as superintendent of its Central Division; he was chief of U.S. military telegraphs, 1861–66. Leading western representative of the Vanderbilt interests, he helped found the Western Electric Manufacturing Co. and served as its president until shortly before his death.

STAGG, AMOS ALONZO (*b. West Orange, N.J., 1862; d. Stockton, Calif., 1965*), football coach. Attended Yale (B.A., 1888), Yale Divinity School, and International YMCA College at Springfield, Mass. Became director of physical culture and athletics at University of Chicago (1892), where he remained for forty-one years. An acknowledged leader in the development of football and most of its phases, he is credited with creating dozens of plays, formations, and strategies that have become standard, including the T formation and the forward pass. He originated the huddle, numbered uniforms, and lighted practice fields. His Chicago teams had five undefeated seasons and won six Western Conference (Big Ten) titles; the 1905 team was ranked first in the country. Became head coach at College of the Pacific (1933–46) and was named coach of the year in 1943. Became offensive coach at Susquehanna College (1947–53), then advisory coach at Stockton Junior College (1953–60). Elected to the Football Hall of Fame (1951) as both player and coach.

STAHEL, JULIUS (*b. Szeged, Hungary, 1825; d. 1912*), Union major general, U.S. consular officer, insurance executive. Veteran of the Hungarian revolution of 1848, Stahel immigrated to New York City, 1856. A volunteer at the outbreak of the Civil War, he rose to division command of cavalry and was awarded the Congressional Medal of Honor for gallantry in the Shenandoah Valley, June 1864.

STAHLMAN, EDWARD BUSHROD (*b. Güstrow, Germany, 1843; d. 1930*), railroad official, newspaper publisher. Came to America as a boy; settled in Nashville, Tenn., 1863. Becoming owner-publisher of the *Nashville Banner*, 1855, he built it into one of the best-known crusading journals in the South.

STAHR, JOHN SUMMERS (*b. near Applebachsville, Pa., 1841; d. 1915*), Reformed clergyman, educator. Graduated Franklin and Marshall College, 1867; studied theology under John W. Nevin. Taught *post* 1868 at his alma mater and was its president, 1890–1909. A linguist and a prolific writer in German and English, he was the last of the master exponents of the Mercersburg philosophy.

STALEY, CADY (*b. Montgomery Co., N.Y., 1840; d. Minaville, N.Y., 1928*), civil engineer, educator, sanitation expert. An able teacher and president of faculty at Union College and at the Case School of Applied Science.

STALLINGS, LAURENCE TUCKER (*b. Macon, Ga., 1894; d. Whittier, Calif., 1968*), writer. Attended Wake Forest (B.A., 1916). Severely wounded in France in 1918, his leg was amputated in 1922 and during his recuperation he wrote his autobiographical novel *Plumes* (1924). He became book reviewer for the *New York World* and collaborated with Maxwell Anderson on the play *What Price Glory?*, which was an instant success on stage in 1924; he achieved additional success with the film *The Big Parade* (1925). He worked for the *New York Sun* (1931) and adapted Ernest Hemingway's *A Farewell to Arms* to the screen (1932); he also worked on the films *Too Hot to Handle* (1938), *Northwest Passage* (1940), *A Miracle Can Happen* (1948), and *She Wore a Yellow Ribbon* (1949). Published *The Doughboys* (1963), a widely read history of U.S. participation in World War I.

STALLO, JOHANN BERNHARD (*b. Sierhausen, Oldenburg, Germany, 1823; d. 1900*), lawyer, philosopher of science, diplomat. Immigrated to America, 1839; practiced law in Cincinnati, Ohio, *post* 1849. An outstanding political liberal, he served as U.S. minister to Italy, 1885–89. Among his books and writings was the influential *The Concepts and Theories of Modern Physics* (1882).

STANARD, MARY MANN PAGE NEWTON (*b. Westmoreland Co., Va., 1865; d. Richmond, Va., 1929*), historian. Wife of William G. Stanard. Author of, among other works, *Colonial Virginia* (1917) and *Richmond, Its People and Its Story* (1923).

STANARD, WILLIAM GLOVER (*b. Richmond, Va., 1858; d. 1933*), editor, antiquarian. Husband of Mary M. P. N. Stanard. Secretary, Virginia Historical Society, and editor, *Virginia Magazine of History and Biography*, 1898–1933.

STANBERY, HENRY (*b. New York, N.Y., 1803; d. New York, 1881*), lawyer. Raised in Ohio. Law partner of Thomas Ewing, 1824–31. Practiced thereafter in Lancaster, Columbus, and Cincinnati, Ohio, and was in the first rank of the Ohio bar. A Whig and later a Republican, he served as U.S. attorney general, July 1866–March 1868. His able service as President Andrew Johnson's chief counsel during Johnson's impeachment cost him further political advancement.

STANCHFIELD, JOHN BARRY (*b. Elmira, N.Y., 1855; d. 1921*), lawyer. Graduated Amherst, 1876; studied law with David B. Hill, whose partner he became. Active in Democratic politics in New York State, he was celebrated as a courtroom pleader in a number of sensational cases, which included the trials of F. A. Heinze, Harry K. Thaw, and the Gould and Guggenheim family lawsuits.

STANDERREN, ANN LEES. *See* LEE, ANN.

STANDISH, BURT L. *See* PATTEN, GILBERT.

STANDISH, MYLES (*b. possibly Lancashire, England, ca. 1584; d. Duxbury, Mass., 1656*), Pilgrim father and military captain. A soldier of fortune in the Low Countries, he was hired by the Pilgrims to accompany them on the *Mayflower*, 1620. The only one with practical experience in camping, he was their mainstay in the first explorations of Cape Cod, and was one of the small party who made the first landing at Plymouth. He handled relations with the Indians expertly, designed and superintended the erection of a fort, and devised measures for defense. In 1625 he was sent to England to negotiate with the Merchant Adventurers and the Council for New England. There is no historical basis for the story of John Alden's proposal to Priscilla on Standish's behalf. He was a cofounder of Duxbury, 1631.

STANDLEY, WILLIAM HARRISON (*b. Ukiah, Calif., 1872; d. San Diego, Calif., 1963*), naval officer and diplomat. Graduated from U.S. Naval Academy (1895), Rising to prominence in the navy, he became chief of naval operations in 1933. His major task was to convince Congress of the need for modernizing and replacing ships in the midst of the Great Depression. Represented the United States at the naval disarmament conferences in 1934–35. Retired from the navy in 1937 and became naval adviser to President Franklin Roosevelt in 1939. Returned to active duty in 1941 and became a member of the Production Planning Board. U.S. ambassador to the Soviet Union (1942–43), then served with the Office of Strategic Services (1944–45).

STANFORD, AMASA LELAND (*b. Watervliet, N.Y., 1824; d. Palo Alto, Calif., 1893*), railroad builder. Admitted to the bar in New York State, 1848, he began practice at Port Washington, Wis., that same year. Encouraged by his brothers who had prospered as storekeepers in California, he removed there in 1852. After engaging in merchandising with some success in Placer County and at Sacramento, he was elected Republican governor of California in 1861. His success was due to his personal popularity and to his strong Union and Republican convictions, for he had had no opportunity to distinguish himself in public service. In 1863 he was not renominated, and he held no other public office until his election as U.S. senator in 1885. His chief task as governor was to hold California in the Union, and this he accomplished satisfactorily. He also approved several public grants to the transcontinental railroad—the enterprise which brought him wealth and upon which his reputation chiefly rests. Interested in the project by Theodore D. Judah's promotional activity, he subscribed money to finance the surveys which proved the feasibility of the proposed railroad line; he also helped finance organization of the Central Pacific Railroad in June 1861. As governor he signed four acts affording considerable assistance to the new enterprise. He had no scruples about taking official action where his private interests as railroad president were engaged, or he overcame such as may have occurred to him by reflecting upon the public importance of a railroad connection with the East. He was president and director of the Southern Pacific Co., 1885–90, and director of the Southern Pacific Railroad. At all times he was a shareholder in, and contributor to, the resources of the construction companies which built the railroads. The Central Pacific was built almost entirely with, or on the security of, public funds, so that Stanford and his friends risked less of their own capital in the undertaking than has sometimes been supposed.

From the great personal fortune he amassed, he was able to indulge his tastes in matters not strictly connected with his business. He maintained extensive vineyards and a large ranch where he bred fine racing stock. Out of his desire to raise a fitting memorial to his son, who died at the age of 15, grew Leland Stanford, Jr., University, founded in 1885. Entirely opposed to interference with the railroad business by public bodies, he asserted the railroad's right to protect itself by political action when attacked. Thus, he accepted election as U.S. senator in 1885, but he found himself in a field for which he had no proper training and for which his abilities were inadequate. It is not too much to say that his legislative record shows lack of interest or lack of capacity, probably both. His senatorship satisfied his vanity and increased his prestige in California, but it did not add to his reputation.

STANFORD, JOHN (*b. Wandsworth, England, 1754; d. 1834*), Baptist clergyman, humanitarian. Immigrated to America, 1786. Held pastorates in New York City and Providence, R.I., until 1801; thereafter preached in Baptist churches in New York, New Jersey, Pennsylvania, and Connecticut without a fixed pastorate. Appointed chaplain of the New York State Prison, 1812, he devoted his attention to the establishment of special reform institutions for youthful prisoners.

STANFORD, LELAND. *See* STANFORD, AMASA LELAND.

STANG, WILLIAM (*b. Langenbrücken, Baden, Germany, 1854; d. 1907*), Roman Catholic clergyman, educator. Served as curate, pastor, and chancellor of the diocese in Rhode Island, 1878–95 and 1899–1904, acting in the interim as vice-rector of the American College in Louvain. He was bishop of Fall River, Mass., 1904–07.

STANLEY, ALBERT AUGUSTUS (*b. Manville, R.I., 1851; d. Ann Arbor, Mich., 1932*), musician, educator. Professor of music, University of Michigan, 1888–1932, emeritus *post* 1921. He was author of a symphony and a number of choral compositions.

STANLEY, ANN LEE. *See* LEE ANN.

STANLEY, AUGUSTUS OWSLEY (*b. Shelbyville, Ky., 1867; d. Washington, D.C., 1958*), lawyer and politician. Studied at Centre College in Danville, Ky. Elected to the U.S. Congress as a Democrat (1903–15). In the House, the Stanley Committee's investigation of the U.S. Steel Corp. (1911–12), led to major regulations included in the Clayton Antitrust Act of 1914. From 1915 to 1919, Stanley was governor of Kentucky. In 1919, he was elected to the U.S. Senate as an antiprohibitionist. He served until 1924 when he was defeated. After some years in private law practice, he was appointed to the International Joint Commission which regulated American-Canadian waters; chairman from 1933; retired in 1954.

STANLEY, DAVID SLOANE (*b. Cedar Valley, Ohio, 1828; d. 1902*), soldier. Graduated West Point, 1852. A cavalry officer, Stanley served with ability on the western frontier. As major general of volunteers during the Civil War, he held corps command in the Mississippi and Tennessee campaigns and on Sherman's march through Georgia. Reverting in rank to colonel in the regular army, he showed himself a master in handling Indians while on service in the Yellowstone area and in Texas, 1866–92. He retired as regular brigadier general, 1892.

STANLEY, FRANCIS EDGAR (*b. Kingfield, Maine, 1849; d. 1918*), inventor, manufacturer. A portrait photographer, he organized with his brother a company for manufacture of dry plates according to his own formula, which he conducted successfully and sold to the Eastman interests, 1905. Meanwhile, having become interested in steam automobiles, he had begun early in 1897 a series of experiments which resulted in the production in that year of the first steam motorcar to be successfully operated in New England. In 1898 he began manufacture of the cars, but soon sold out to other interests. Repurchasing, 1902, their patents from what had become the Locomobile Co., Stanley and his brother organized the Stanley Motor Carriage Co., which they continued to operate until 1917.

STANLEY, HAROLD (*b. Great Barrington, Mass., 1885; d. Philadelphia, Pa., 1963*), investment banker and securities expert. Attended Yale (B.A., 1908). Joined the New York City bond house of J. G. White and Company (1910), then Guaranty Trust Company (1915), becoming vice president of the bond department (1916). Attracted Wall Street attention as a leading authority on the bond market and became a partner in J. P. Morgan and Company (1928). In 1935, with William Ewing and Henry S. Morgan, formed the independent bond house of Morgan, Stanley and Company, and became president of the new firm; he retired in 1955 but remained a limited partner.

STANLEY, HENRY MORTON (*b. Denbigh, Wales, 1841; d. London, England, 1904*), journalist, explorer. Brought up in an English workhouse and by unfeeling relatives, Stanley was known as John Rowlands until his adoption in December 1859 by Henry Morton Stanley, a New Orleans, La., merchant. After Civil War service in the Confederate army and in the Union army and navy, Stanley discovered his true vocation when he became a traveling newspaper correspondent, 1866. His early dispatches from the campaign of General W. S. Hancock against the western Indians brought him commissions from the *New York Herald*, 1868; his reports from Abyssinia, Crete, and Spain further established his reputation as a gifted correspondent. Sent by James Gordon Bennett (1841–1918) to find the Scottish missionary David Livingstone in the unexplored heart of Africa, he set off from Zanzibar in March 1871. After many hardships he discovered Livingstone in the native village of Ujiji on Nov. 10 and spoke a greeting which has passed into history: "Dr. Livingstone, I presume?" After further explorations in company with Livingstone along the northern shore of Lake Tanganyika, Stanley returned to London, where he was met with disbelief in his discoveries and much social scorn; however, he was soon vindicated after investigation of the proofs which he had brought back. On further expeditions, 1874–77, he made geographical studies of central Africa which were of the greatest importance, including exploration of the headwaters of the Nile, a complete survey of Lake Tanganyika, and a traverse of the Congo River. Between 1879 and 1884 he worked in the Congo, establishing 22 stations along the river, putting steamers in operation on it, and building roads; the Congo Free State was formed on the basis of his work. Thereafter he continued his restless, roving career in Africa and made lecture tours around the world until the failure of his health *ca.* 1899. First among African explorers by reason of the extent of his geographical discoveries, Stanley also possessed the vision and organizing ability of a pioneer. He believed that he was furthering Livingstone's fight against slavery by introducing European commerce to darkest Africa. A man of strong moral feeling, he was greatly disappointed over the later developments in the Congo, which he described as "a moral malaria." Generally successful in his dealings with the native peoples whom he encountered, he was completely lacking in tact at home in England and America; a lonely man, he was introspective and self-absorbed. He was author of a number of books descriptive of his travels and explorations; his unfinished *Autobiography* was published in 1909.

STANLEY, JOHN MIX (*b. Canandaigua, N.Y., 1814; d. Detroit, Mich., 1872*), painter. Apprenticed to a wagon maker as a boy, he removed to Detroit, 1834, where he painted portraits and landscapes. Resident in Chicago and Galena, Ill., 1838–39, he began painting portraits of the Indians near Fort Snelling. Between 1842 and 1852 he traveled widely in the West, painting wherever he went, and giving several exhibitions of Stephen W. Kearny to California. Much of his spirited, accurate work, of the greatest possible value to students of history and ethnology, was deposited in the Smithsonian Institution in 1852 and destroyed by fire there, 1865. In 1853 he served as artist of the U.S. expedition for exploration of the Pacific Railroad route from St. Paul, Minn., to Puget Sound.

STANLEY, ROBERT CROOKS (*b. Little Falls, N.J., 1876; d. Staten Island, N.Y., 1951*), metallurgist. Studied at Stevens Institute of Technology and at Columbia School of Mines. Employed by the Orford Copper Company, Bayonne, N.J. (1904–17). There he discovered and patented the white nickel-copper alloy Monel, used as roofing for Pennsylvania Station in New York. From 1918 to 1949, he was employed by International Nickel Company; vice president (1918–22); president (1922–49); chairman of the board, 1949 until his death. Stanley was responsible for the widespread peacetime uses of nickel, in particular by the automobile industry.

STANLEY, WILLIAM (*b. Brooklyn, N.Y., 1858; d. Great Barrington, Mass., 1916*), electrical engineer. Devised the multiple system of alternating-current distribution (patented 1887); in collaboration with others, worked out the "S.K.C." system of long-distance transmission of alternating current. Among his many other inventions were condensers, two-phase motors, generators, and an alternating-current watt-hour meter.

STANLY, EDWARD (*b. New Bern, N.C., 1810; d. San Francisco, Calif., 1872*), lawyer. Congressman, Whig, from North Carolina, 1837–43. Stanly was an extreme nationalist and a leader of his party in the House. After service in state offices and in the North Carolina legislature, he returned to Congress, 1849–53. Removing to California, 1854, he was successful in legal practice in San Francisco. Convinced that the secession of North Carolina from the Union had been the result of Democratic trickery, he accepted appointment by President Lincoln as military governor of the state in May 1862. He quickly discovered that his hope of restoring a civil government loyal to the Union was an illusion. Opposed to emancipation, he resigned in January 1863 and returned to California.

STANSBURY, HOWARD (*b. New York, N.Y., 1806; d. Madison, Wis., 1863*), soldier, civil engineer, explorer. Grandson of Joseph Stansbury. Entered the U.S. Army, July 1838, as lieutenant of topographical engineers. Among the many surveys which he undertook, the most outstanding was his expedition to the Great Salt Lake region, 1849, on which James Bridger acted as one of the guides. His report of this expedition was issued first as *Senate Executive Document* 3, 32 *Congress* (1852). It was several times reprinted, and is a classic of western Americana.

STANSBURY, JOSEPH (*b. London, England, 1742 o.s.; d. New York, N.Y., 1809*), Loyalist agent, merchant, satirist. Immigrated to Philadelphia, Pa., 1767. Transmitted Benedict Arnold's first proposals of treason to British headquarters and served thereafter as go-between for Arnold and the British. His witty satires were collected in *The Loyal Verses of Joseph Stansbury and Doctor Jonathan Odell* (edited, Winthrop Sargent, 1860).

STANTON, EDWIN MCMASTERS (*b. Steubenville, Ohio, 1814; d. Washington, D.C., 1869*), lawyer, public official. Admitted to the bar, 1836, he practiced at first in Cadiz and Steubenville, Ohio, and later in Pittsburgh, Pa., and Washington, D.C. Able and energetic, he soon won success; his work as counsel for the State of Pennsylvania (1849–56) against the Wheeling & Belmont Bridge Co., gave him a national reputation, and his masterly defense work in *McCormick* v. *Manny* deeply impressed one of his associates, Abraham Lincoln. Though his practice was chiefly in civil and constitutional law, he demonstrated in his defense of Daniel E. Sickles that he was no less gifted in handling criminal suits. In 1858, as special counsel for the U.S. government in combating fraudulent land claims in California, he won a series of notable victories. His services in this connection were the most distinguished of his legal career and won him the appointment of U.S. attorney general, December 1860. Although he disapproved of slavery, he accepted the Dred Scott decision and contended that all laws constitutionally enacted for the protection of slavery should be rigidly enforced. He had supported Breckinridge's candidacy for the presidency in 1860 in the belief that the preservation of the Union hung on the forlorn hope of his election.

During the early months of Lincoln's administration, Stanton, now in private life, was utterly distrustful and critical of the president and his cabinet. When Simon Cameron was removed from office in 1862, however, Stanton took his place as secretary of war. His appointment was well received as presaging a more honest and efficient management of War Department affairs and a more aggressive prosecution of the war. The department was reorganized, personnel increased, contracts investigated, those tainted with fraud revoked, and their perpetrators prosecuted. Stanton also put himself in active touch with generals, governors, and the congressional Committee on the Conduct of the War. Becoming impatient with General G. B. McClellan's slowness in achieving tangible results, Stanton joined with other members of the cabinet in seeking to have him deprived of any command. Quickness of decision, mastery of detail, and vigor in execution were among Stanton's outstanding characteristics as a war administrator, and he became annoyed when subordinates proved deficient in these qualities. He was frequently accused of meddling with military operations and was probably guilty of it on many occasions. His severe censorship of the press was also a source of much criticism in newspaper circles, and his exercise of the power of extraordinary arrest was often capricious and harmful. Soldiers and civilians alike found him arrogant, irascible, and often brutal and unjust.

At the request of President Andrew Johnson, Stanton retained his post after Lincoln's death and ably directed the demobilization of the Union armies. At the same time, he entered upon a tortuous course with respect to Reconstruction and related problems, which brought him into serious conflict with the president. It was soon suspected that Stanton was out of sympathy with the administration and was intriguing with the rising opposition. From the summer of 1865 onward, upon nearly every issue, he advised a course of action which would have played into the hands of the Radicals and which fostered a punitive Southern policy. By the beginning of August 1867, President Johnson could no longer tolerate his mendacious minister and was satisfied that Stanton had indeed plotted against him in the matter of Reconstruction legislation and had encouraged insubordination on the part of the commanders of the military districts. When called upon to resign, Stanton refused to do so until Congress reassembled, contending that the Tenure of Office Act had become law by its passage over the presidential veto. Dismissed in February 1868, he declared that he would not give up his post until expelled by force and was supported by the Senate. When the impeachment charges against President Johnson failed, Stanton accepted the inevitable and resigned the same day, May 26, 1868. He accepted President U. S. Grant's appointment to the U.S. Supreme Court, 1869, but death overtook him before he could occupy his seat. His defects of temperament and the disclosures of his amazing disloyalty and duplicity in his official relations detract from his stature as a public man, although his abilities as lawyer and administrator remain unquestioned. Whether he was motivated by egotism, mistaken patriotism, or a desire to stand well with the congressional opposition is difficult to determine.

STANTON, ELIZABETH CADY (*b. Johnstown, N.Y., 1815; d. New York, N.Y., 1902*), reformer, leader in the woman's rights movement. Daughter of Daniel Cady; granddaughter of James Livingston; cousin of Gerrit Smith. Married Henry B. Stanton, 1840, and insisted on omission of the word "obey" from the ceremony. Much influenced by Lucretia C. Mott, she joined with Mott and others in holding the celebrated women's rights convention at Seneca Falls, N.Y., 1848. *Post* 1851 she was closely associated in suffrage work with Susan B. Anthony, planning campaigns, appearing before legislative and congressional committees, and delivering speeches. President of the National Woman Suffrage Association, 1869–90, she also served as president of the National American Woman Suffrage Association subsequent to a merger of these organizations. Coauthor with Anthony of *History of Woman Suffrage* (1881–86), she was author also of many contributions to periodicals and newspapers and of an autobiography, *Eighty Years and More* (1898).

STANTON, FRANK LEBBY (*b. Charleston, S.C., 1857; d. 1927*), Georgia journalist, poet. Conducted one of the first newspaper columns in the *Atlanta Constitution* from 1889. He published a number of volumes of his poems, among them, *Up from Georgia* (1902) and *Little Folks Down South* (1904).

STANTON, FREDERICK PERRY (*b. Alexandria, Va., 1814; d. Stanton, Fla., 1894*), lawyer. Removing to Tennessee, 1835, he served as congressman, Democrat, from the Memphis district, 1845–55. As chairman of the Committee on Naval Affairs *post* 1849, he advocated useful reforms; in his last term he was chairman of the judiciary committee. Proslavery in his general opinions, he served as secretary and acting governor of Kansas Territory, March–May 1857, and as secretary thereafter until 1858, save for another brief period as acting governor after the resignation of Robert J. Walker. Although he apportioned delegates to the Lecompton Convention under an inequitable and incomplete census because of lack of experience, he and Walker later tried to ensure a fair vote for members of a legislature. After his removal from office for attempting to provide a referendum on the Lecompton Constitution, he became a Free-Soiler.

STANTON, HENRY BREWSTER (*b. Griswold, Conn., 1805; d. New York, N.Y., 1887*), lawyer, journalist, reformer, antislavery agent. Husband of Elizabeth Cady Stanton. Author of, among other books, *Random Recollections* (1887).

STANTON, RICHARD HENRY (*b. Alexandria, Va., 1812; d. 1891*), Kentucky congressman, jurist, legal writer.

STANWOOD, EDWARD (*b. Augusta, Maine, 1841; d. Brookline, Mass., 1923*), journalist, historian. After holding editorial posts on Maine and Boston, Mass., newspapers, Stanwood was for many years *post* 1883 managing editor and editor of the *Youth's Companion*. He was author of *A History of Presidential Elections* (1884), *American Tariff Controversies in the Nineteenth Century* (1903) and *James Gillespie Blaine* (1905).

STAPLES, WALLER REDD (*b. Stuart, Va., 1826; d. Montgomery Co., Va., 1897*), lawyer, Confederate congressman. Judge of the Virginia Supreme Court of Appeals, 1870–82, he gave his most notable opinion in the Coupon Case, 1878, which led to the forming of the Readjuster party and the partial repudiation of the state debt. Staples' dissenting opinion was later upheld. He served as a co-compiler of *The Code of Virginia* (1887).

STAPLES, WILLIAM READ (*b. Providence, R.I., 1798; d. 1868*), Rhode Island jurist, historian. Author of, among other works, *Annals of the Town of Providence* (1843) and *Rhode Island in the Continental Congress* (Reuben A. Guild, ed., 1870).

STARBUCK, EDWIN DILLER (*b. Bridgeport, now part of Indianapolis, Ind., 1866; d. 1947*), psychologist. B.A., Indiana University, 1890; M.A., Harvard, 1895; Ph.D., Clark University, 1897. Taught education at Stanford University, 1897–1903, and at Earlham College, 1904–06; professor of philosophy at State University of Iowa, 1906–30, and at University of Southern California, 1930–43. Author of *The Psychology of Religion* (1899), a pioneering work; innovator in character education.

STARIN, JOHN HENRY (*b. Sammonsville, N.Y., 1825; d. New York, N.Y., 1909*), freight agent. Operated *post* 1859 a general agency for the transport of freight around New York City by a system of lighters and tugs, which included his later invention of the car float. Owner and operator of the largest "harbor marine" in the United States, he also owned and operated passenger and freight lines on Long Island Sound.

STARK, EDWARD JOSEF (*b. Hohenems, Austria, 1858; d. 1918*), cantor, composer of synagogue music. Came to America as a boy; received musical education in New York City and abroad. Practicing his profession in Brooklyn, N.Y., and San Francisco, Calif., he was author of music which, by its successful combination of traditionalism and modernism, was particularly adapted for Reform Jewish temples.

STARK, JOHN (*b. Londonderry, N.H., 1728; d. 1822*), colonial and Revolutionary soldier. Saw extensive service with Rogers' Rangers in French and Indian War, attaining captaincy. Appointed colonel of a New Hampshire regiment on outbreak of the Revolution, he distinguished himself at Bunker Hill, on the retreat from Canada, 1776, and at Trenton and Princeton. Resigning his commission, March 1777, because Congress promoted junior officers over his head, he returned to the field as brigadier general, commanding New Hampshire troops for the defense of Vermont. He defeated a Hessian and Tory force at Bennington, August 1777, and later helped to effect Burgoyne's surrender by blocking his line of retreat. Promoted brigadier general in the Continental service, October 1777, he served with Gates in Rhode Island, 1779, participated in the battle of Springfield, N.J., 1780, and acted on the board of officers appointed to try Major André. He retired with the brevet of major general in 1783.

STARK, LOUIS (*b. Tibold Daracz, Hungary, 1888; d. New York, N.Y., 1954*), newspaper correspondent. Immigrated to the U.S. in 1890. Studied at the N.Y. Training School for Teachers. Reporter for the *New York Times* (1917–54); member of the editorial board (1951–54). Head of the labor correspondents of the Washington D.C. bureau (1933). Covered many significant New Deal legislative and executive programs, including the establishment of the NRA; also covered the split in the AFL which formed the CIO in 1935. Won the Pulitzer Prize for national reporting in 1942.

STARKS, EDWIN CHAPIN (*b. Baraboo, Wis., 1867; d. 1932*), ichthyologist. An authority on the osteology of fishes, Starks served on a number of important field expeditions under David S. Jordan, Charles H. Gilbert, and others. His principal academic post was at Stanford University, where he was curator of zoological collections *post* 1901. He retired as associate professor in the year of his death.

STARR, ELIZA ALLEN (*b. Deerfield, Mass., 1824; d. Durand, Ill., 1901*), author, lecturer on art. Settling in Chicago, Ill., *ca.* 1856, she became one of the first art teachers there and wrote and illustrated a number of books, devotional in character.

STARR, FREDERICK (*b. Auburn, N.Y., 1858; d. Tokyo, Japan, 1933*), anthropologist. Graduated Lafayette College, 1882; Ph.D., 1885. After teaching at a number of schools, he organized the work in anthropology at the University of Chicago, 1892, and in 1895 became associate professor there. He served as sole teacher of his subject until 1923. Author of a number of books and studies, he is chiefly remembered for the wide interest he created in anthropology through his teaching.

STARR, LOUIS (*b. Philadelphia, Pa., 1849; d. 1925*), physician, pediatrician. M.D., University of Pennsylvania, 1871. Author of *Hygiene of the Nursery* (1888), one of the first popular expositions of the subject.

STARR, MERRITT (*b. Ellington, N.Y., 1856; d. 1931*), corporation lawyer. Practiced in Chicago, Ill., *post* 1882; was active in Winnetka, Ill., civic affairs.

STARR, MOSES ALLEN (*b. Brooklyn, N.Y., 1854; d. 1932*), neurologist. Graduated Princeton, 1876; M.D., New York College of Physicians and Surgeons, 1880; made postgraduate studies in Heidelberg and Vienna. Taught at New York Polytechnic, 1884–89; was professor of mental and nervous diseases, New York College of Physicians and Surgeons, 1889–1915. An American pioneer in cerebral localization, he did valuable work on brain tumors. He was author of a great number of special articles on neurological subjects and of several books, including *Atlas of Nerve Cells* (1896) and *Organic and Functional Nervous Diseases* (1903). He was particularly noted as a teacher.

STARRETT, LAROY S. (*b. China, Maine, 1836; d. St. Petersburg, Fla., 1922*), engineer, architect, builder, financier. A partner and officer in Thompson-Starrett Co., engaged in skyscraper and factory construction, he was later associated with the George A. Fuller Co. and with Starrett Brothers and Eken. Completely oblivious to all city-planning values except the financial, he was essentially an executive and neither a designer nor a man of thought.

STARRETT, PAUL (*b. Lawrence, Kans., 1866; d. Greenwich, Conn., 1957*), builder. Studied briefly at Lake Forest University. A supervisor with the Fuller Company (1897–1922), Starrett was the builder of such notable American buildings as the Flatiron Building (1902), Pennsylvania Station (1906–10), General Post Office (1913), Metropolitan Life Insurance Tower (1909), and the Plaza Hotel (1907)—all in New York City. He founded his own firm in 1922 and constructed such buildings as the McGraw-Hill Building (1931) and the Empire State Building (1931).

STARRETT, WILLIAM AIKEN (*b. Lawerence, Kans., 1877; d. Madison, N.J., 1932*), engineer, architect, builder, financier. A partner and officer in Thompson-Starrett Co., engaged in skyscraper and factory construction, he was later associated with the George A. Fuller Co. and with Starrett Brothers and Eken. Completely oblivious to all city-planning values except the financial, he was essentially and executive and neither a designer or a man of thought.

STATLER, ELLSWORTH MILTON (*b. Somerset Co., Pa., 1863; d. New York, N.Y., 1928*), hotel owner and operator. Began his career as a bellboy in the McClure House, Wheeling, W.Va., and achieved success through his cardinal rule, "The guest is always right." At his death his hotel properties were the most extensive owned by one man.

STAUFFER, DAVID McNEELY (*b. Richland, Pa., 1845; d. Yonkers, N.Y., 1913*), civil engineer, editor, collector of prints and autographs. Author of *American Engravers upon Copper and Steel* (1907), the standard work in its field.

STAUGHTON, WILLIAM (*b. Coventry, England, 1770; d. Washington, D.C., 1829*), Baptist minister, educator. Came to America, 1793; held pastorates in Burlington, N.J., and Philadelphia, Pa. Helped establish Columbian College (present George Washington University); served as its president, 1822–29.

STAYTON, JOHN WILLIAM (*b. Washington Co., Ky., 1830; d. Tyler, Tex., 1894*), jurist. LL.B., Louisville University, 1856. Removed to Texas, 1856; served in the Confederate cavalry, 1861–65. Associate justice, Texas Supreme Court, 1881–88, he served as chief justice thereafter until his death.

STEAGALL, HENRY BASCOM (*b. Clopton, Ala., 1873; d. Washington, D.C., 1943*), lawyer, politician. Congressman, Democrat, from Alabama, 1914–43. A member of the bipartisan "farm bloc" during the 1920's, he frequently attacked Republican claims of national prosperity on the ground that farmers had no share in it. Named chairman of the House Banking and Currency Committee, 1930, he sought to cooperate with President Hoover in reviving the economy and had an important role in shaping the economic programs of the New Deal. He insisted on preserving the independence of state banks from the Federal Reserve System by provisions in the Glass-Steagall Act of 1933 and, with other inflationists, forced the Silver Purchase Act of 1934 on an unwilling administration. A cosponsor of the Wagner-Steagall National Housing Act of 1937, he grew increasingly skeptical of legislation exclusively benefiting labor and the urban poor and concentrated on agricultural issues in the last years of his career. During World War II he extended the number of basic crops to be subsidized (the "Steagall commodities"), and forced President Roosevelt to accept a bill providing that no price ceiling of less than 110 percent of parity would be placed on farm products.

STEARNS, ABEL (*b. Lunenberg, Mass., 1798; d. San Francisco, Calif., 1871*), California pioneer, stockraiser. Immigrated to Mexico *ca.* 1826; settled in Los Angeles, Calif., 1833. Joined in revolutions in favor of J. B. Alvarado, 1836, and against Manuel Micheltorena, 1844–45; remained neutral in hostilities during U.S. seizure of California.

STEARNS, ASAHEL (*b. Lunenberg, Mass., 1774; d. 1839*), lawyer. Cousin of Abel Stearns. Graduated Harvard, 1797. Practiced in present Lowell, Mass., and in Charlestown, Mass., served also in the legislature and as congressman for a single term, 1815–17. Professor of law, Harvard Law School, 1817–29, Stearns was author of *A Summary of the Law and Practice of Real Actions* (1824). Relatively unsuccessful as a law professor, he was an able lawyer and was a commissioner under Charles Jackson in making the first real revision of the Massachusetts statutes (adopted 1835).

STEARNS, EBEN SPERRY (*b. Bedford, Mass., 1819; d. 1887*), educator. Brother of William A. Stearns. Graduated Harvard, 1841. First president, State Normal School, Nashville, Tenn., *post* 1875, and chancellor of the University of Nashville, he proved himself an efficient administrator and was tireless in trying to raise educational standards in the South.

STEARNS, FRANK BALLOU (*b. Berea, Ohio, 1878; d. Cleveland, Ohio, 1955*), inventor and manufacturer. Studied briefly at Case School of Applied Science (now Case Institute of Technology). Founder of the F.B. Stearns Co. in 1898, makers of the Stearns-Knight cars; the company introduced the internal combustion engine in 1912. Stearns left the company in 1918 and concentrated on improvements in the diesel engine; he obtained sixteen patents and sold the engine to the Navy Department in 1935.

STEARNS, FRANK WATERMAN (b. Boston, Mass., 1856; d. Boston, 1939), dry-goods merchant. Partner in R. H. Stearns and Co., Boston, Mass., post 1880; resigned as president, 1919, retaining chairmanship of the board. Friend and backer of Calvin Coolidge.

STEARNS, FREDERIC PIKE (b. Calais, Maine, 1851; d. 1919), civil engineer, hydraulics expert. Planned improvement of Charles River Basin. As engineer for Massachusetts Board of Health, he designed and saw to completion the metropolitan water supply of Boston and its vicinity ca. 1895–1907. He later served as a consultant for many other municipal water supply projects and for the Panama Canal.

STEARNS, GEORGE LUTHER (b. Medford, Mass., 1809; d. New York, N.Y., 1867), abolitionist, manufacturer. A leader in the movement that put Charles Sumner in the U.S. Senate, he played a great part in the rise of the Republican party in Massachusetts. A friend and patron of John Brown, he financed Brown's proposed raid into Virginia and after his capture attempted his rescue. During the Civil War he recruited black troops for the Union army.

STEARNS, HAROLD EDMUND (b. Barre, Mass., 1891; d. Hempstead, N.Y., 1943), journalist, social critic. An expatriate in Paris, France, during the 1920's, he expressed the post–World War I alienation of many intellectuals in *America and the Young Intellectual* (1921) and in a symposium that he edited in 1922 entitled *Civilization in the United States*. Returning to the United States in 1932, he summed up the realities of the expatriate flight from responsibility in several books, including *The Street I Know* (1935, an autobiography) and *America: A Re-Appraisal* (1937).

STEARNS, HENRY PUTNAM (b. Sutton, Mass., 1828; d. 1905), physician, psychiatrist, Union army surgeon. Superintendent of Hartford (Conn.) Retreat for the Insane post 1874.

STEARNS, IRVING ARIEL (b. Rushville, N.Y., 1845; d. Wilkes-Barre, Pa., 1920), mining engineer. Graduated Rensselaer Polytechnic Institute, 1868. Managed coal interests of the Pennsylvania Railroad, 1885–97; made radical improvements in processes of mining and preparing anthracite coal. Thereafter he headed several coal and iron companies until his retirement from business, 1905.

STEARNS, JOHN NEWTON (b. New Ipswich, N.H., 1829; d. Brooklyn, N.Y., 1895), temperance reformer, author of much temperance propaganda.

STEARNS, OLIVER (b. Lunenberg, Mass., 1807; d. Cambridge, Mass., 1885), Unitarian clergyman. Nephew of Asahel Stearns. Graduated Harvard, 1826; Harvard Divinity School, 1830. After holding pastorates in Northampton and Hingham, Mass., he served as president of Meadville (Pa.) Theological School, 1856–63, and as professor at Harvard Divinity School, 1863–70. Appointed dean of that school on its reorganization, 1870, he served until 1878 and taught systematic theology and ethics. He was author of several interesting publications asserting that the progressive development of Christian doctrine is the story of intuitive reason interpreting revelation, but safeguarded against private error by an intention to seek truth in the light of the church.

STEARNS, ROBERT EDWARDS CARTER (b. Boston, Mass., 1827; d. Los Angeles, Calif., 1909), naturalist, early student of California fauna. Author of a number of articles on molluscan systematics and distribution. He served as paleontologist to the U.S. Geological Survey (appointed 1884) and as assistant curator of mollusks in the U.S. National Museum.

STEARNS, SHUBAL (b. Boston, Mass., 1706; d. 1771), Baptist clergyman. Brother-in-law of Daniel Marshall. Ordained, 1751, Stearns immigrated first to Virginia and then to Sandy Creek, N.C., where he served as pastor of the Separate Baptist church post 1755. He won high repute as a preaching evangelist in the Carolinas, Georgia, and Virginia.

STEARNS, WILLIAM AUGUSTUS (b. Bedford, Mass., 1805; d. Amherst, Mass., 1876), Congregational clergyman, educator. Brother of Eben S. Stearns. Graduated Harvard, 1827. After a long, successful pastorate at Cambridgeport, Mass., he was president of Amherst College, 1854–76.

STEBBINS, HORATIO (b. South Wilbraham, Mass., 1821; d. Cambridge, Mass., 1902), Unitarian clergyman. Graduated Harvard, 1848; attended Harvard Divinity School. After serving churches in Fitchburg, Mass., and Portland, Maine, Stebbins succeeded Thomas S. King as pastor of the Unitarian Church in San Francisco, Calif., 1864. For 35 years thereafter he was a force in the development of the state, particularly in its educational progress; he was a leader in the foundation of the University of California, Stanford University, and Lick Observatory. He resigned his pastorate, 1900.

STEBBINS, RUFUS PHINEAS (b. South Wilbraham, Mass., 1810; d. Cambridge, Mass., 1885), Unitarian clergyman. Cousin of Horatio Stebbins. Graduated Amherst, 1834; attended Harvard Divinity School. Pastor at Leominster, Mass., 1837–44, he became first president of the Meadville (Pa.) Theological School and served in that post until 1856. Thereafter he held various pastorates in Massachusetts and New York and served as president of the American Unitarian Association.

STECK, GEORGE (b. Cassel, Germany, 1829; d. New York, N.Y., 1897), piano manufacturer. Immigrated to New York City, 1853.

STEDMAN, EDMUND CLARENCE (b. Hartford, Conn., 1833; d. New York, N.Y., 1908), stockbroker, poet, critic. Son of Elizabeth C. D. S. Kinney. Author of a number of technically meritorious but imitative poems, Stedman exercised great influence on American letters of his period through his critical works and anthologies, among them, *Poets of America* (1885), *A Victorian Anthology* (1895), and *An American Anthology* (1900).

STEEDMAN, CHARLES (b. Santee, S.C., 1811; d. Washington, D.C., 1890), naval officer. On active service, principally at sea, post 1828, he retired as rear admiral, 1873. Remaining loyal to the Union during the Civil War, he served chiefly on blockade duty off the southeast coast and commanded the *Ticonderoga* during both attacks against Fort Fisher.

STEEDMAN, JAMES BLAIR (b. Northumberland Co., Pa., 1817; d. 1883), printer, Union major general, Ohio Democratic politician. Won his greatest distinction in the battle of Chickamauga, where he commanded a division of Granger's corps which came to the rescue of General George H. Thomas after the rest of the army had been swept away. He was active in journalism and civic affairs in Toledo, Ohio, post 1869.

STEELE, DANIEL (b. Windham, N.Y., 1824; d. Milton, Mass., 1914), Methodist clergyman, educator. Held a number of Massachusetts pastorates and was a strong reformer and a leader in Methodism. Professor of languages in Genesee College, 1862–69, and its acting president, 1869–71, he served briefly as professor of philosophy, vice president, and acting chancellor, 1871–72, after Genesee had become Syracuse University.

STEELE, FREDERICK (*b. Delhi, N.Y., 1819; d. San Mateo, Calif., 1868*), soldier. Graduated West Point, 1843. Commanded infantry with credit in Mexican War; *post* 1848, served in California, Minnesota, Nebraska, and Kansas. During the Civil War he rose to division command in Union army and the rank of major general of volunteers. Immediately after the surrender of Vicksburg, he was charged with completing the conquest of Arkansas, which he accomplished within a few months. He failed in an effort to assist General N. P. Banks in the Red River campaign, March–April 1864.

STEELE, JOEL DORMAN (*b. Lima, N.Y., 1836; d. 1886*), educator, author of science textbooks, Union soldier. Principal of the Elmira (N.Y.) Free Academy, 1866–72.

STEELE, JOHN (*b. Salisbury, N.C., 1764; d. 1815*), businessman, landowner. Congressman, independent Federalist, from North Carolina, 1789–93; comptroller of U.S. treasury, 1796–1802. Opposed to any extension of presidential or judicial powers.

STEELE, WILBUR DANIEL (*b. Greensboro, N.C., 1886; d. Essex, Conn., 1970*), writer. Attended University of Denver (B.A., 1907), Boston Museum School of Fine Arts, and Art Students League. His first story, "On the Ebb Tide," was published in *Success Magazine* (1910); other stories then appeared in *Atlantic Monthly, Scribner's Magazine,* and *Harper's.* His first story collection was *Land's End* (1918). Nine stories reappeared in the annual *Best Stories* volumes, 1915–26; during 1919–33 he received the O. Henry Memorial Award twelve times. His second collection of stories was *The Shame Dance* (1923). His novels include *Storm* (1914); *Isles of the Blest* (1924); and *Taboo* (1925), which treats the theme of incest, as did his story "When Hell Froze," which won first prize in Harper's 1925 Short Story Contest. Wrote the hit Broadway mystery-comedy *Post Road* (1935). During 1938 only a trickle of his works sold to mass-market magazines, and the novels he wrote after that were not well received.

STEENDAM, JACOB (*b. the Netherlands, 1616; d. Netherlands Indies, ca. 1672*), merchant, first poet of New Netherland. Resident on Long Island and in New Amsterdam, 1652–ca. 1662.

STEENWIJCK, CORNELIS VAN. *See* STEENWYCK, CORNELIS.

STEENWYCK, CORNELIS (*b. probably Haarlem, the Netherlands, date unknown; d. New York, N.Y., 1684*), colonial merchant. Came to New Amsterdam, 1651, as mate of a trading vessel. Prospering as a merchant, he held a number of civic posts under the Dutch rule and was a signer of the articles by which New Netherland was surrendered to the English. Mayor of New York, 1668–70, he became a member of Governor Francis Lovelace's council, continued influential during the brief restoration of Dutch rule, and survived the second English seizure of the colony sufficiently well to serve again as mayor of New York City, 1682–83. A wealthy man, he was reputed the best-dressed, most polite, and most popular man in the New York of his time.

STEERS, GEORGE (*b. Washington, D.C., 1820; d. 1856*), naval architect. Trained in his father's New York City shipyard, Steers introduced revolutionary changes in hull design. He was particularly renowned as builder of the famous yacht *America*, which he sailed in the memorable race of Aug. 22, 1851, around the Isle of Wight.

STEFANSSON, VILHJALMUR (*b. Arnes, Manitoba, Canada, 1879; d. Hanover, N.H., 1962*), Arctic explorer. In 1880 his family moved to Dakota territory. Attended University of North Dakota and Harvard (M.A., 1923). Spent the summers of 1904 and 1905 on archaeological expeditions to Iceland for the Peabody Museum and was selected a teaching fellow for the polar regions at Harvard (1905). Persuaded officials of the American Museum of Natural History to finance an Arctic expedition, with additional support from the Canadian government (1908–11), spending three years among the Eskimos of eastern Alaska. A second exploration was sponsored by the Canadian government to the Beaufort Sea and Coronation Gulf (1913–18). His two most influential books are *The Friendly Arctic: The Story of Five Years in Polar Regions* (1921) and *The Northward Course of Empire* (1922). During World War II he was a government consultant on Arctic matters.

STEFFENS, LINCOLN (*b. San Francisco, Calif., 1866; d. Carmel, Calif., 1936*), journalist, reformer. Reared in a prosperous family, Steffens graduated from the University of California, Ph.B., 1889, and made various studies in Germany, England, and France. After reportorial and editorial work on the New York *Evening Post* and the New York *Commercial Advertiser,* 1892–1901, he joined the staff of *McClure's Magazine* and found his true métier as writer of muckraking articles exposing civic corruption (collected as *The Shame of the Cities,* 1904). Continuing his investigations, he published *The Struggle for Self-Government* (1906) and *Upbuilders* (1909), in which he cited evidence of substantial reform gains achieved and expressed a growing belief in the need for firm leadership. Associated with Edward A. Filene in Boston reform efforts, 1909, he became convinced that exposure of evil was not enough to bring about reform and began to look about for some single principle as a solution. Disappointed in his belief in the Golden Rule, in his efforts to negotiate a settlement of the case of the McNamara brothers, and in his personal life as well, he sought a new panacea in violent social upheaval. From 1917 until his death, he was increasingly a partisan of the Soviet Union. *Post* 1929 he felt that Russia offered the only practical solution for the problems of progress and power. His *Autobiography* (1931), although manifestly self-serving in numerous passages, was written with skeptical humor and questioned social processes in a manner relevant to the Great Depression.

STEHLE, AURELIUS ALOYSIUS (*b. Pittsburgh, Pa., 1877; d. Pittsburgh, 1930*), Roman Catholic clergyman, Benedictine. Archabbot of St. Vincent Archabbey, 1920–30, he was founder of the Catholic University at Peking, China, 1924.

STEIN, EVALEEN (*b. Lafayette, Ind., 1863; d. 1923*), poet, writer of children's stories.

STEIN, GERTRUDE (*b. Allegheny, Pa., 1874; d. Neuilly-sur-Seine, France, 1946*), author. Her earliest memories were of Vienna, where her father, Daniel Stein, moved for business reasons in 1875, and then Paris. Her mother, Amelia (Keyser) Stein, figured only remotely in Gertrude's preadolescence. The family returned to America in 1879, settling the next year in Oakland, Calif. At Radcliffe College, which she attended from 1893 to 1897 (B.A., 1898), Gertrude's primary interest was the psychology of William James; his theory of consciousness forms the basis of her thought. To prepare for a career in psychology, she entered Johns Hopkins Medical School in 1897. Her research on the brain was solid, but she failed final examinations and preferred traveling abroad to retaking them. After a period in London at the British Museum systematically reading English narratives from the Elizabethans to the present, she joined her brother Leo in Paris in 1903 at 27 rue de Fleurus. Although he was never to succeed in translating his aesthetic intellections into tangible achievement, Leo was among the first to recognize the genius of postimpressionist painters. He and Gertrude began to cover their walls with masters of the Paris school, which Leo expounded to the uninitiated who streamed through their soon-famous flat. In her friendships, especially with Pablo Picasso, Juan Gris, and Francis Picabia, Gertrude promoted modern art.

Gertrude Stein's earliest fiction, *Q.E.D.*, completed in 1903, first appeared posthumously in 1950 under the title *Things As They Are*. Supposedly "forgotten," it was more probably withheld because of its homoeroticism. In "Melanctha," the last of three long stories published in 1909 as *Three Lives*, the central love affair is between a black doctor and a mulatto girl. Often cited as a minor classic, its racial clichés justified or denied, "Melanctha" is stylistically original but at the expense of fictional reality as created in the cruder *Q.E.D.* The book *The Making of Americans* (1925), probably written between 1903 and 1911, marked a stage in Stein's development parallel to cubism in its incorporation of random events and the process of completion itself. *Tender Buttons* (1914) was her work most resembling verbal collage. From this book onward, narrative, with its assumption of a causal ordering of events, mostly disappears.

Although in middle life she was still largely unpublished, Stein was sought after as a savant of the new. Her lectures given at Cambridge and Oxford in 1926 and published as *Composition As Explanation* represent one of her earliest efforts to elucidate her practice and formulate theoretical principles. Other important efforts are *Lectures in America* and *Narration* (both 1935) and *What Are Masterpieces* (1940). Through her influence on Sherwood Anderson and, more significantly, on Ernest Hemingway, she made a decisive contribution to modern American literature and prose style. Leo having left in 1913, and with Alice B. Toklas from 1909 as her companion and amanuensis, she enjoyed a Johnsonian eminence in her salon, where the roster of visitors was an index to the distinguished artists and intellectuals of her time. She created her own legend in *The Autobiography of Alice B. Toklas* (1933), using the persona of her friend to write about herself in a communicable style. The next year her esoteric opera *Four Saints in Three Acts*, with music by Virgil Thomson, was premiered with fanfare in Hartford, Conn., and moved to New York City. Of the other dramatic works produced with some critical success, the most notable are the ballet *A Wedding Bouquet* (1937), *Yes Is for a Very Young Man* (1946), and the opera *The Mother of Us All* (1947), in collaboration with Virgil Thomson.

After 30 years, Stein returned to America for a triumphant lecture tour in 1934. Her reacquaintance with the country led to insights into American character and landscape in *The Geographical History of America* (1936). Although she courted public success and effectively used her grasp of modern publicity techniques, being a headlined celebrity disturbed her sense of identity, as she revealed in *Everybody's Autobiography* (1937). Throughout World War II she lived in seclusion with Alice Toklas in occupied France. *Wars I Have Seen* (1945), beginning with the Spanish-American, had immediate journalistic appeal in its account of daily life during her last war.

STEIN, LEO DANIEL (*b. Allegheny, Pa., 1872; d. Settignano, Italy, 1947*), art critic, author. Brother of Gertrude Stein. Unable either to accept his limitations or to capitalize on his talents, he tried successively to be a historian, a scientist, a painter, and a writer. He achieved a critical success at last with his book *Appreciation: Painting, Poetry, and Prose* (1947), but he is remembered particularly as an early and discriminating collector of modern painting.

STEINBECK, JOHN ERNST, JR. (*b. Salinas, Calif., 1902; d. New York, N.Y., 1968*), writer. Attended Stanford, but did not pursue a degree. With the publication of *The Pastures of Heaven* (1932), *To a God Unknown* (1933), and the stories collected in *The Long Valley* (1938), he defined his primary subject matter—farm life in an enclosed California valley. He remained largely un-

known until *Tortilla Flat* (1935). The three great novels of his midcareer were *In Dubious Battle* (1936), *Of Mice and Men* (1937), and *The Grapes of Wrath* (1939), which won a Pulitzer prize and established his reputation as a major American writer. Following U.S. entry into World War II, he worked without pay for several government agencies, writing *The Moon Is Down* (1942) and, for the Army Air Corps, the nonfictional *Bombs Away*. Became a correspondent for the *New York Herald-Tribune* (1943) and was sent to the Mediterranean. In 1945 *Cannery Row* appeared, and then he worked on the script and filming of *The Pearl* (1948). Other works include *The Wayward Bus* (1947), *Burning Bright* (1950), *East of Eden* (1952), *The Winter of Our Discontent* (1961), and *Travels with Charley* (1962). He was awarded the Nobel Prize for literature in 1962. In 1966 he was in Vietnam as a correspondent for *Newsday*; his support for the Vietnam War alienated him from the liberal intellectual community. Few American writers have been the source of as much controversy. More of his works are on lists of books banned by schools and libraries than any other writer, but many of his novels are commonly taught in schools and colleges; *The Grapes of Wrath* remains one of the major American novels of the twentieth century.

STEINER, BERNARD CHRISTIAN (*b. Guilford, Conn., 1867; d. 1926*), educator, librarian, historian. Son of Lewis H. Steiner. Graduated Yale, 1888; Ph.D., Johns Hopkins, 1891. Taught at Williams College; was librarian of Enoch Pratt Free Library, Baltimore, Md., 1892–1926. He was author of a great number of monographs and books on the history of Maryland and Connecticut and on the history of education in America; he was also editor of Volumes 18 and 36–45 of the *Archives of Maryland*. Among his books, *Life and Correspondence of James McHenry* (1907), *Life of Reverdy Johnson* (1914), and *Life of Roger Brooke Taney* (1922) were of particular value.

STEINER, LEWIS HENRY (*b. Frederick, Md., 1827; d. 1892*), physician, librarian. Father of Bernard C. Steiner. A practicing physician and teacher of medicine, 1849–84, he served thereafter as first librarian of the Enoch Pratt Free Library of Baltimore, Md.

STEINERT, MORRIS (*b. Scheinfeld, Bavaria, 1831; d. 1912*), optician, merchant, collector of musical instruments. Immigrated to America *ca.* 1856; made his home in New Haven, Conn., *post* 1861. Founded Mathushek Piano Co. and New Haven Symphony Orchestra; donated his important collection of rare instruments to Yale University.

STEINHARDT, LAURENCE ADOLPH (*b. New York, N.Y., 1892; d. near Ottawa, Ontario, Canada, 1950*), lawyer, diplomat. After attending private schools, Steinhardt entered Columbia University, from which he received the B.A. degree in 1913 and the M.A. and LL.B. in 1915. He was admitted to the New York bar the following year. During World War I he served in the army field artillery and as a sergeant on the provost marshal general's staff. In 1920 he joined his uncle's law firm, Guggenheimer, Untermyer and Marshall. A liberal Democrat, Steinhardt became interested in politics and in 1932 joined the preconvention presidential campaign committee of Franklin D. Roosevelt. Following Roosevelt's election Steinhardt accepted an appointment in 1933 as U.S. minister to Sweden. He was the youngest chief of a diplomatic mission, and he negotiated one of the administration's first reciprocal trade agreements. He was named ambassador to Peru in 1937, and his efforts impressed Secretary of State Cordell Hull, who two years later recommended Steinhardt's appointment as ambassador to the Soviet Union.

Steinhardt arrived in Moscow on the eve of the Nazi-Soviet Nonaggression Pact of 1939. Grasping well the realities of Soviet policies, he stressed the solidarity of the agreement with Berlin and maintained that, for the time being at least, the two nations could not afford to quarrel. After the fall of France to the Germans in 1940, the United States sought to improve Soviet-American relations by granting unilateral concessions, despite Steinhardt's repeated warnings that America's prestige would be harmed by not demanding a quid pro quo. As the anticipated improvement in relations did not occur, Washington moved closer to Steinhardt's policy of reciprocity during the spring of 1941. Shortly after Pearl Harbor he was sent as ambassador to neutral Turkey, where he helped influence that country's decision not to fulfill its trade commitment with Germany.

Late in 1944 Roosevelt named Steinhardt ambassador to Czechoslovakia. After the announcement in 1947 of the Marshall Plan for the rebuilding of Europe, he successfully urged Washington to delay action on the Czech government's loan application until the campaign ended and American claims in Czechoslovakia were settled. As the Czech elections approached, Steinhardt saw the Communists' popularity declining, but he misjudged the party's ability, abetted by Moscow, to effect the coup d'état that took place in February 1948. In the summer of 1948 President Harry S. Truman appointed Steinhardt ambassador to Canada. Election to high office in New York State was Steinhardt's greatest ambition, although during his diplomatic career he did not court publicity. Early in 1950, while flying to New York to attend a political dinner, he was killed in a plane crash.

Steinitz, William (*b. Prague, Czechoslovakia, 1836; d. New York, N.Y., 1900*), champion chess player of the world, 1866–94. An American citizen *post* 1884, he wrote extensively on chess and was author of *The Modern Chess Instructor* (1889, 1895).

Steinman, David Barnard (*b. New York, N.Y., 1886; d. New York, 1960*), engineer. Studied at the City College of New York and at Columbia University (Ph.D., 1911). The designer of many of the world's most famous and spectacular bridges, Steinman taught at the University of Idaho from 1910 to 1915 before returning to New York to collaborate with Gustav Lindenthal in designing the Hell Gate Bridge over the East River in New York (1917). Other bridges designed through his company, Steinman, Boyton, Fronquist, and London, include the George Washington Bridge (1931), the Sidney Harbor Bridge in Australia (1932), the Thousand Islands International Bridge (1938), and the Mackinac Strait Bridge (1957).

Steinmetz, Charles Proteus (*b. Breslau, Germany, 1865; d. 1923*), mathematician, electrical engineer. Deformed from birth, he showed brilliance and a great capacity for study at the University of Breslau, which he attended, 1883–88. Having engaged in socialist journalism there, he was obliged to flee Germany to avoid arrest and never received the doctor's degree for which he had completed his work. Immigrating from Switzerland to the United States, 1889, he worked for Rudolf Eickemeyer, who before long established him in an experimental laboratory of his own.

Given the task of calculating and designing an alternating-current commutator motor, and wishing to calculate the hysteresis loss, he derived the law of hysteresis mathematically from existing data. He followed this with an elaborate series of tests to prove the law and simplify its application. In 1892, he read two papers on the subject before the American Institute of Electrical Engineers which at once established his reputation. His further studies of alternating electric current led him to develop a mathematical method of reducing alternating-current theory to a basis of practical calculation. His symbolic method is now universally used, although it required a process of elucidation by him in several books before it was generally understood. His third and last great

research undertaking had to do with lightning. He began a systematic study of the general equation of the electric current and of "transient electrical phenomena," as lightning is scientifically called. This work culminated in 1921 with dramatic experiments yielding man-made lightning in the laboratory. In addition to his work as consulting engineer for the General Electric Co., 1894–1923, he was professor of electrical engineering and electrophysics at Union University, Schenectady, N.Y. He received numerous honors, patented a great number of inventions, and wrote several books, including *Theory and Calculation of Transient Electric Phenomena and Oscillations* (1909) and *Theory and Calculation of Alternating Current Phenomena* (5th ed., 1916).

Steinmeyer, Ferdinand.   *See* Farmer, Father.

Steinway, Christian Friedrich Theodore   (*b. Seesen, Germany, 1825; d. Brunswick, Germany, 1889*), piano manufacturer. Son of Henry E. Steinway; brother of William Steinway. Resident in America, 1865–70, he made extensive experiments in application of modern science to the problems of piano-building.

Steinway, Henry Engelhard   (*b. Wolfshagen, Germany, 1797; d. New York, N.Y., 1871*), piano manufacturer. Father of Christian F. T. and William Steinway. Immigrated to New York City, 1851. Started his own business under his original name, Steinweg, 1853; introduced innovating square piano with overstrung strings and a full cast-iron frame, 1855. Thereafter he undertook the manufacture of grand pianos and uprights and built Steinway Hall (formally opened, 1867), which became a center of New York musical life.

Steinway, William   (*b. Seesen, Germany, 1835; d. New York, N.Y., 1896*), piano manufacturer. Son of Henry E. Steinway; brother of Christian F. T. Steinway. Immigrated to America with his family, 1851. Concerned mainly with the financial and sales departments of Steinway & Sons, he was a patron of music and won international standing for his firm by inducing foreign artists to play Steinway pianos. President of the firm, 1876–96, he was active also in civic affairs and was chairman of the New York City commission which planned the first subways.

Stejneger, Leonhard Hess   (*b. Bergen, Norway, 1851; d. Washington, D.C., 1943*), zoologist. Graduated in arts, 1870, philosophy, 1872, and law, 1875, University of Kristiania. Came to the United States, 1881, and, with help of Spencer F. Baird, was appointed to staff of the National Museum, Smithsonian Institution. Head curator of the museum's Department of Biology *post* 1911, he made substantial contributions to knowledge of the taxonomy and geographical distribution of North American and other birds, reptiles, and amphibians.

Stella, Joseph   (*b. Muro Lucano, near Naples, Italy, 1877; d. New York, N.Y., 1946*), painter. Came to the United States, 1896; studied for brief periods at Art Students League, New York City, and with William M. Chase. His drawings of immigrants (*Outlook* magazine, 1905) and of the persons and physical milieu of miners and steelworkers (Pittsburgh Survey in *Charities and the Commons*, 1908) rank among the best figure drawings ever produced in the United States. A student in Italy and France, 1909–12, he gave up his "old master" technique and was influenced by fauvism, cubism, and especially futurism. On his return to the United States, his semiabstract *Battle of Lights, Coney Island*, 1913, won him a leading place in the avant-garde. His most creative period followed World War I (*The Gas Tank*, 1918; *Brooklyn Bridge, ca.* 1919; *New York Interpreted*, 1920–22). He spent most of 1922–34 in Italy and France, abandoning abstraction for a primitivizing style. The few paintings of real merit which he did in the last decade of his life were produced on Barbados in 1938.

STELZLE, CHARLES (*b. New York, N.Y., 1869; d. New York, 1941*), Presbyterian clergyman. During apprenticeship as a machinist, he was distressed at the widening gap between workingmen and the church, and devoted himself to a special mission, interpreting the labor movement to the church and the church to working people. Ordained in 1900, was supported in his work by the Board of Home Missions and made a significant contribution to the spread of the Social Gospel movement; he was author of, among other works, *Christianity's Storm Center: A Study of the Modern City* (1907) and the founder of New York City's Labor Temple, 1910. In face of mounting conservative criticism, he resigned his special ministry in 1913 and set up an office and staff to undertake survey, publicity, and promotional services on behalf of social and religious causes.

STENGEL, ALFRED (*b. Pittsburgh, Pa., 1868; d. Philadelphia, Pa., 1939*), pathologist, medical educator. M.D., University of Pennsylvania, 1889; studied also at Berlin, Vienna, and London. A teacher of medicine at Pennsylvania *post* 1893, he served also as vice president of the university for medical affairs, 1931–39. As president of the American College of Physicians, 1925–27, he brought about its complete reorganization and made it the outstanding organization of internists in America.

STEPHENS, ALEXANDER HAMILTON (*b. Wilkes, later Taliaferro, Co., Ga., 1812; d. Atlanta, Ga., 1883*), statesman, lawyer. Half brother of Linton Stephens. Orphaned at an early age; graduated University of Georgia, 1832; began practice of law at Crawfordville, Ga., 1834. After effective service in the Georgia legislature *post* 1836 as an associate in the faction headed at various times by William H. Crawford and George M. Troup, he entered the U.S. House of Representatives as a Whig, 1843. His first notable speech was made at the beginning of 1845 on the Texas question. Annexation, he said, while tending to lessen the prosperity of the cotton states already in the Union, would give the South a greatly needed political weight and thus preserve a proper balance between the different sections of the nation. However, the next year, he denounced the sending of troops to the Rio Grande and the precipitation of war with Mexico. Deprecating the Democratic project of expansion, 1847, he censured the Wilmot Proviso, saying that if its policy were pursued, the Union must give place to a prospect of desolation, carnage, and blood. Growing more alarmed at what he considered the progressive erosion of states' rights and constitutional safeguards, he defied the North in August 1850 by stating, "Whenever this Government is brought in hostile array against me and mine, I am for disunion—openly, boldly and fearlessly, for revolution . . . seven millions of people fighting for their rights, their homes and their hearth-stones cannot be easily conquered." However, when Henry Clay's compromise measures were enacted, he hastened to Georgia to endorse the Union-saving legislation, provided that Congress and the North maintained it in letter and spirit. To improve the prospect of intersectional peace, he launched with Robert Toombs and Howell Cobb the Constitutional Union party, but the project collapsed for lack of support.

Rejecting Winfield Scott, the Whig candidate for president in 1852, Stephens abandoned the Whig party and shifted to the Democrats; he heartily denounced the Know-Nothing movement. Supporting the Kansas-Nebraska Act, he acted as House floor manager in its behalf. Convinced that the bill was admirable, he was proud of his maneuvers which resulted in its enactment. His essential concern, often and sincerely proclaimed, was the preservation of Southern security within a placid Union of all the states. In 1859 he gave up his seat in Congress, but continued his

interest in politics. In the campaign of 1860, he preferred the candidacy of R. M. T. Hunter, but supported Stephen A. Douglas. When Lincoln was elected, Stephens advised a policy of watchful waiting, with readiness for drastic action if Lincoln or Congress invaded Southern rights or violated the Constitution. At the convention summoned by the Georgia legislature which met in January 1861, he declared that he opposed "the policy of immediate secession," but if the majority voted for secession he would accept their decision. As a delegate to the convention of Southern states held at Montgomery, he proposed the formation of a union on the model of the United States. Under the quickly devised Provisional Constitution, Jefferson Davis was elected president of the Confederate States of America and Stephens vice president, February 1861.

As vice president, Stephens lent a hand in affairs where he could, but gradually drifted into the position of leader of the opposition. He disapproved of many of Davis' policies, and his fondness for principles, scruples, and constitutional restraint made him an unhappy member of a wartime government. War itself was keenly distressing to him, particularly the sufferings of the wounded and prisoners on both sides. Sent in 1865 to Hampton Roads as one of three commissioners to negotiate a peaceful settlement with Lincoln and W. H. Seward, he found that the maintenance of Confederate independence would be impossible. Shortly after the termination of the war he was arrested by federal troops, but was later released on parole. Elected to the U.S. Senate in 1866, he was excluded from that body along with all others from the "rebel" states.

In the Reconstruction period Stephens counseled self-discipline, patience, and forbearance from recrimination, and recommended support for President Johnson's policies. In hearings before a congressional committee on Reconstruction, he declared that Georgia acquiesced in the abolition of slavery but opposed granting the suffrage to blacks, and he denied the constitutional power of the federal government to impose conditions precedent to restoration of the late Confederate states to their functions in the Union. Congress proceeded with its drastic program, and Stephens accepted a publisher's invitation to write *A Constitutional View of the Late War Between the States* (published 1868, 1870). It is a tedious rationalization, obscuring the historic problem of slavery by refinements of doctrine on the sovereignty of the states. Dull as the book may be to readers in the 20th century, it was a sensation in its day, evoking attacks by Northern and Southern champions of causes upon which it impinged. In 1872 Stephens was elected to the House of Representatives and served for a decade. In 1882, after resigning from Congress, he was elected governor of Georgia but died a few months after inauguration.

STEPHENS, ALICE BARBER (*b. near Salem, N.J., 1858; d. Rose Valley, Pa., 1932*), illustrator. Studied at School of Design for Women, Philadelphia, Pa., where she later taught; worked under Thomas Eakins at Pennsylvania Academy. Excelled in pictures of quiet scenes and incidents from classical fiction, characterized by simplicity and technical assurance.

STEPHENS, ANN SOPHIA (*b. Derby, Conn., 1813; d. Newport, R.I., 1886*), editor, author. A prolific writer for the periodicals of her time, Stephens served in editorial capacities on the *Ladies' Companion*, *Graham's Magazine*, and *Peterson's Magazine*. She is particularly notable as author of the first of the celebrated Beadle "dime novels"—*Malaeska* (1860).

STEPHENS, CHARLES ASBURY (*b. Norway Lake, Maine, 1844; d. Norway Lake, 1931*), author of juvenile stories, experimenter in biology.

STEPHENS, EDWIN WILLIAM (*b. Columbia, Mo., 1849; d. Columbia, 1931*), editor-publisher of the *Columbia Herald*,

1870–1905, commercial printer. Chairman, Missouri State Capitol commission (completed 1918).

STEPHENS, HENRY MORSE (*b. Edinburgh, Scotland, 1857; d. 1919*), educator, historian. Graduated Balliol College, Oxford, B.A., 1882; studied also at Lincoln's Inn and at universities of Bonn and Paris. After achieving distinction in England as writer, librarian, and teacher, he served as professor of modern European history at Cornell University, 1894–1902, and was thereafter head of the Department of History at University of California. A rigorously scientific historian, he was author of, among other books, *History of the French Revolution* (1886, 1891). He was successful in obtaining for the University of California the collection of works relating to Spanish colonization and to the Pacific Coast which was gathered by H. H. Bancroft.

STEPHENS, JOHN LLOYD (*b. Shrewsbury, N.J., 1805; d. New York, N.Y., 1852*), lawyer, steamship and railroad promoter, traveler, author. After publishing several books on his travels in eastern Europe and the Near East, he investigated the Maya ruins in Honduras, Guatemala, and Yucatan, 1839–40, accompanied by an English artist, Frederick Catherwood, who was experienced in archaeology. Stephens aroused interest in the early Central American cultures by his *Incidents of Travel in Central America, Chiapas, and Yucatan* (illustrated by Catherwood, 1841). Returning for more intensive study of the subject in 1841, they published another collaborative work, *Incidents of Travel in Yucatan* (1843).

STEPHENS, LINTON (*b. near Crawfordville, Ga., 1823; d. Georgia, 1872*), Georgia legislator and jurist. Confederate soldier. Half brother of Alexander H. Stephens. A Whig legislator, he aided his half brother, Robert Toombs, and Howell Cobb in organizing the Constitutional Union party; he later returned to the Whigs and was a Democrat *post* 1856. After the Civil War he practiced law and refused to reenter politics, but militantly opposed Reconstruction.

STEPHENS, URIAH SMITH (*b. near Cape May, N.J., 1821; d. Philadelphia, Pa., 1882*), pioneer labor leader. A tailor by trade, he helped organize the Garment Cutters' Association of Philadelphia, 1862. Upon its dissolution in 1869, he and others founded the Noble Order of the Knights of Labor. The order, in which Stephens served for a time as "grand master workman," was based on the principles of secrecy, union of all trades, education, and cooperation. Stephens conceived of the Knights of Labor not simply as a trade union but as a nucleus for building a cooperative commonwealth. After a bitter struggle between Stephens and Terence V. Powderly, the principle of secrecy in the order was repudiated, 1881.

STEPHENSON, BENJAMIN FRANKLIN (*b. Wayne Co., Ill., 1823; d. Rock Creek, Ill., 1871*), physician, Union army surgeon, founder of the Grand Army of the Republic at Decatur, Ill., Apr. 6, 1866.

STEPHENSON, CARL (*b. Fayette, Ind., 1886; d. Ithaca, N.Y., 1954*), medievalist. Studied at DePauw University and at Harvard University (Ph.D., 1914); further study at the University of Ghent (1924). Taught at several universities including the University of Wisconsin (1920–30), and Cornell University (1930–54). An expert in the development of English urban settlements in the Anglo-Saxon period, he published *Borough and Town* (1933). A textbook was *Medieval History* (1935), which went into its fourth printing in 1962.

STEPHENSON, ISAAC (*b. Maugerville, New Brunswick, Canada, 1829; d. Marinette, Wis., 1918*), lumberman, politician. Removed to Milwaukee, Wis., 1845; settled at Marinette, 1858; was thereafter connected with many industrial operations in the Menominee River valley. A Republican member of the Wisconsin legislature and a congressman, 1883–89, he turned against the machine and financed Robert M. La Follette's campaign for governor, 1900. Elected U.S. senator, 1907, in succession to John C. Spooner, he was reelected in 1908. Attacked for his lavish expenditure of money in the campaign by both La Follette and the Progressives and also the "regular" Republicans, he was confirmed in his seat nevertheless and served out his term.

STEPHENSON, JOHN (*b. Co. Armagh, Ireland, 1809; d. New Rochelle, N.Y., 1893*), streetcar builder. Came to New York City as a child; was apprenticed to a coachmaker. Designed and built the first omnibus made in New York, 1831; also designed and built the first car for the first street railway in the world (Fourth Avenue line, New York & Harlem Railroad), 1832.

STEPHENSON, NATHANIEL WRIGHT (*b. Cincinnati, Ohio, 1867; d. 1935*), journalist, educator, historian. Taught principally at College of Charleston, 1903–20, and at Scripps College, 1927–35. Author of several novels, three successful textbooks in American history, and, among other historical studies, *An Autobiography of Abraham Lincoln* (1926) and *Nelson W. Aldrich* (1930). An able, thorough, and judicious writer, Stephenson was not distinguished for originality of research.

STERETT, ANDREW (*b. Baltimore, Md., 1778; d. 1807*), naval officer. Entered navy as a lieutenant, 1778; served as executive officer and first lieutenant of the *Constellation*, 1799–1800. Commanding the schooner *Enterprise*, he fought a brilliant engagement against a Tripolitan polacca in the Mediterranean, August 1801.

STERKI, VICTOR (*b. Solothurn, Switzerland, 1846; d. 1933*), physician, conchologist. Immigrated to America, 1883; practiced in New Philadelphia, Ohio. Made exhaustive studies of the smaller mollusks, in particular, the *Sphaeriidae*.

STERLING, GEORGE (*b. Sag Harbor, N.Y., 1869; d. San Francisco, Calif. 1926*), poet. Friend and disciple of Ambrose Bierce.

STERLING, JAMES (*b. Dowrass, Ireland, 1701[?]; d. Kent Co., Maryland, 1763*), Anglican clergyman, colonial customs official. Came to America, 1737; held several rectorships in Maryland. Author of *The Rival Generals* (1722), *The Parricide* (1736), and several volumes of lyric poetry before his immigration, Sterling expressed his conviction that the greatness of Britain was bound up with the development of its American colonies in a long poem *An Epistle to the Hon. Arthur Dobbs*. Written in Maryland, 1748, it was published in London and Dublin, 1752. A group of his later poems appeared in the *American Magazine*, 1757.

STERLING, JOHN WHALEN (*b. Blackwalnut, Pa., 1816; d. Madison, Wis., 1885*), educator. A graduate of the College of New Jersey (Princeton), 1840, and Princeton Theological Seminary, 1844, he became professor of mathematics, natural philosophy, and astronomy at University of Wisconsin in 1849. For some years he served as acting chancellor, dean, and vice-chancellor. In 1869 he was appointed vice president of the university and held the office until his death. Because of his devoted service, he is regarded as the chief builder and the guiding spirit of the university in its early years.

STERLING, JOHN WILLIAM (*b. Stratford, Conn., 1844; d. Grand Metis, Quebec, Canada, 1918*), lawyer, philanthropist. Graduated Yale, 1864; Columbia Law School, 1867. Employed in New York City office of David D. Field, he shortly became a junior partner in the firm of Field & Shearman, and was associated in the practice of law with Thomas G. Shearman, 1873–1900.

Counsel for Jay Gould, James Fisk, and other sensational clients, he acted also for the defense in the celebrated suit of Theodore Tilton against Henry Ward Beecher. Long active in a most lucrative corporation practice, Sterling left his estate to Yale University, providing thereby for erection of the Sterling Memorial Library and a number of other buildings. The receipt of this estate doubled Yale's resources.

STERLING, ROSS SHAW (*b. near Anahuac, Chambers Co., Tex., 1875; d. Fort Worth, Tex., 1949*), oilman, public official. President of Humble Oil Co. (later Humble Oil and Refining Co.), 1911–22; chairman of the board, 1922–25. A convinced "dry" and rigid advocate of honest government, he entered politics in opposition to the Texas dynasty of James E. Ferguson and his wife, "Ma" Ferguson. After serving with great ability as chairman of the Texas Highway Commission, 1926–30, he won the Democratic nomination for governor and was elected. Despite his honest intentions and public spirit, he could not cope with the double problems of the depression and ruinous overproduction in the East Texas oil field. Defeated in the 1932 primary by Ma Ferguson, he returned to private business.

STERN, JOSEPH WILLIAM (*b. New York, N.Y., 1870; d. Brightwaters, N.Y., 1934*), songwriter, music publisher. Author of, among other songs, with Edward B. Marks, his partner, "The Little Lost Child" (1894) and "My Mother Was a Lady" (1896). Became leading publishers of current hits *post* 1896.

STERN, KURT GUENTHER (*b. Tilsit, Germany, 1904; d. London, England, 1956*), biochemist. Studied at the Friedrich-Wilhelms University in Berlin (Ph.D., 1930). Immigrated to the U.S. in 1935. Taught at Yale University (1935–42); at the Overly Biochemical Research Foundation (1942–44); and at Brooklyn Polytechnic Institute (1944–56). Stern's work included study of the influences of heavy metals on the proteolytic action of tissue extracts on proteins; attempts at unraveling the Pasteur reaction (unsuccessful); and successful attempts to clarify the chemical and physical characteristics of catalase enzymes.

STERN, OTTO (*b. Sohrau, Upper Silesia, Germany, 1888; d. Berkeley, Calif., 1969*), physicist and physical chemist. Attended universities of Freiburg, Munich, and Breslau (Ph.D., 1912). Became an unpaid assistant to Albert Einstein in Prague, then accompanied him to Zurich as an unsalaried lecturer at Eidgenössische Technische Hochschule. In 1914 he transferred to the University of Frankfurt, but was drafted into the German army with outbreak of World War I. After the war he resumed his post at Frankfurt (until 1921) and began a series of investigations based on a dormant molecular-beam method, developing the technique into one of the most powerful research tools of modern physics; it was for the results of the series of experiments performed with this technique that he received the Nobel Prize for physics in 1943. His first experiment was the direct measurement of the distribution of the velocities in a gas at low temperature. His next result showed that individual atoms behave in a discontinuous or "jerky" manner instead of smoothly or continuously. At the University of Rostock (1921), the University of Hamburg (1922–33), and Carnegie Institute of Technology (1933–45), where he established a molecular-beam laboratory. He retired in 1945.

STERNBERG, CONSTANTIN IVANOVICH (*b. St. Petersburg, Russia, 1852; d. Philadelphia, Pa., 1924*), baron, pianist, composer, teacher. Having achieved a brilliant European reputation, he made a concert tour of the United States, 1880–81. He settled there in 1886, becoming an American citizen. He conducted the Sternberg School of Music in Philadelphia, Pa., *post* 1890; among his pupils were Olga Samaroff, Robert Armbruster, and George Antheil.

STERNBERG, GEORGE MILLER (*b. Hartwick Seminary, Otsego Co., N.Y., 1838; d. Washington, D.C., 1915*), bacteriologist, epidemiologist. M.D., New York College of Physicians and Surgeons, 1860. Appointed assistant surgeon, U.S. Army, May 1861, he was made prisoner at first battle of Bull Run, but escaped and participated in the early stages of the Peninsular campaign. Contracting typhoid, he passed the remainder of his Civil War service on hospital duty. After the war he served until 1879 at a number of army posts. While at Fort Barrancas, Fla., 1872–75, he noted the efficacy in treating yellow fever of removing inhabitants from an infected environment and successfully applied the method at the fort. Two articles in the *New Orleans Medical and Surgical Journal* (1875, 1877) gave him status as an authority upon that disease. On duty with the Havana Yellow Fever Commission, 1879–80, he studied its nature and the natural history of its cause; this involved microscopical examination of blood and tissues of yellow fever patients. In these investigations he was one of the first to employ the newly discovered process of photomicrography. In 1881 he reported that the so-called *Bacillus malariae* had no part in the causation of malaria. In the same year, simultaneously with Pasteur, he announced his discovery of the pneumococcus. He was the first in the United States to demonstrate the plasmodium of malaria, 1885, and the bacilli of tuberculosis and typhoid fever, 1886. His interest in bacteriology naturally led to an interest in disinfection; scientific disinfection had its beginning with his work and that of Koch.

Named surgeon general of the army with the rank of brigadier general in 1893, his nine years' tenure of that office saw the establishment of the Army Medical School, the organization of the Army Nurse Corps and the Dental Corps, the creation of the tuberculosis hospital at Fort Bayard, and of many general hospitals during the Spanish-American War. In 1898 he set up the Typhoid Fever Board, and in 1900, the Yellow Fever Commission. He was the first American bacteriologist to bring the fundamental principles and technique of the new science within the reach of American physicians. In 1892 he published A *Manual of Bacteriology*, the first exhaustive treatise on the subject published in the United States.

STERNE, MAURICE (*b. Libau, Latvia, 1878; d. Mount Kisco, N.Y., 1957*), artist. Studied at the National Academy of Design. The son of Jewish immigrants who came to the U.S. in 1889, Sterne won a grant to study in Paris in 1904. He was influenced by Cézanne and knew many leading art figures, including Gertrude Stein and Max Weber. After travel to Egypt, India, and Bali, Sterne had produced a great deal of work that brought him acclaim in America. In 1918, he founded an art school in Anticoli, Italy. Sterne's work is considered academic and conventional, though many pieces hang in major galleries throughout the world. In 1935, he was commissioned to paint murals for the library of the Department of Justice. In 1929, he was president of the Society of American Painters, Sculptors, and Engravers.

STERNE, SIMON (*b. Philadelphia, Pa., 1839; d. 1901*), lawyer, civic reformer. LL.B., University of Pennsylvania, 1859. Practiced in New York City *post* 1860, eventually specializing in cases involving common carriers. Secretary of the Committee of Seventy, which overthrew the Tweed Ring, he served on a number of commissions to secure improvement in New York State legislation and drafted a large body of legislation designed to regulate the activities of railroad companies. In the course of his practice, he secured important additions to the common law of New York with respect to the liability of railroad companies for obstructing passage of light and air, the responsibility of carriers to handle freight during a strike, and the analogy between telephone service and that rendered by a common carrier.

STERNE, STUART.   *See* BLOEDE, GERTRUDE.

STERRETT, JAMES MACBRIDE   (*b. Howard, Pa., 1847; d. 1923*), Episcopal clergyman, philosopher. Professor of philosophy at Seabury Divinity School, Minnesota, 1882–92; at Columbian (present George Washington) University, 1892–1909. Rector and associate rector at All Souls', Washington, D.C., *post* 1911. An adherent of the "St. Louis school" headed by William T. Harris, he devoted his thought to the philosophical principles which underlie the intellectual aspect of religion. By his several books and his teaching he helped give idealism a better standing in relation to the empirical pragmatic trend so pronounced in his time.

STERRETT, JOHN ROBERT SITLINGTON   (*b. Rockbridge Baths, Va., 1851; d. 1914*), archaeologist. Attended University of Virginia, 1868–71; studied at Leipzig, Berlin, and Munich, where he received the Ph.D., 1880. After service as professor of Greek at Miami University, University of Texas, and Amherst, he headed the Greek department at Cornell *post* 1901. His numerous published works include the data of his explorations and research in Asia Minor and Babylonia. Among other achievements, he identified the sites of scores of important ancient cities, among them the Lystra of St. Paul's travels.

STETEFELDT, CARL AUGUST   (*b. Holzhausen, Germany, 1838; d. Oakland, Calif., 1896*), metallurgist. Came to America, 1863. Invented and developed the Stetefeldt furnace, since superseded but in its time marking an advance in reducing sulphide ores containing gold and silver by the chlorination process.

STETSON, AUGUSTA EMMA SIMMONS   (*b. Waldoboro, Maine, ca. 1842; d. 1928*), Christian Science leader. Successful in developing Christian Science work in New York City *post* 1886, Stetson was formally excommunicated by Mary Baker Eddy in November 1909.

STETSON, CHARLES AUGUSTUS   (*b. Newburyport, Mass., 1810; d. Reading, Pa., 1888*), hotel proprietor. Manager and host of the Astor House, New York City, 1838–68.

STETSON, CHARLES WALTER   (*b. Tiverton Four Corners, R.I., 1858; d. Rome, Italy, 1911*), portrait painter, landscapist.

STETSON, FRANCIS LYNDE   (*b. Keeseville, N.Y., 1846; d. 1920*), lawyer. Graduated Williams, 1867; Columbia Law School, 1869. Expert in the organization and reorganization of corporations, Stetson became the personal counsel of J. Pierpont Morgan and, as such, took a leading part in creation of the U.S. Steel Corporation and other Morgan promotions. Active in Democratic politics, he was a friend and adviser of Grover Cleveland. He is to be credited with suggesting Cleveland's "sound money" policy; as Morgan's counsel, he attended the 1895 meeting at the White House at which the Morgan-Belmont syndicate offered to sell gold to the government to stem the drain on U.S. gold reserves. An extreme economic conservative, he joined with Joseph H. Choate and others in opposing the federal income-tax amendment to the Constitution.

STETSON, HENRY CROSBY   (*b. Cambridge, Mass., 1900; d. at sea, 1955*), geologist. Studied at Harvard (M.A., 1926). Taught at the Harvard Museum of Comparative Zoology (1927–55); worked at the Woods Hole Oceanographic Institution (1931–55). A specialist in paleontology and marine geology, Stetson devoted his life to research in these fields. He proposed theories on the nature of the continental shelves, maintaining that they were the products of sedimentation.

STETSON, JOHN BATTERSON   (*b. Orange, N.J., 1830; d. De Land, Fla., 1906*), hat manufacturer. Opened a one-man hat factory in Philadelphia, Pa., 1865, which grew through provision of a high-quality product into a vast industrial plant. Long a generous donor to Baptist churches and charities, Stetson was principal benefactor of the present John B. Stetson University at De Land.

STETSON, WILLIAM WALLACE   (*b. Greene, Maine, 1849; d. probably Auburn, Maine, 1910*), educator, public school administrator. Introduced extensive and constructive reforms as superintendent of Maine schools, 1895–1907.

STETTINIUS, EDWARD REILLY   (*b. Chicago, Ill., 1900; d. Greenwich, Conn., 1949*), corporation executive, public official. Son of Edward R. Stettinius (1865–1925). An Episcopalian, he considered becoming a minister, but was persuaded by John Lee Pratt, vice president of General Motors, to apply his humanitarian ideals to a business career. He began as a stockroom clerk at GM's Hyatt roller-bearing division and soon rose to employment manager. In 1926, as special assistant to Pratt, he instituted one of the automobile industry's first group insurance plans. He became assistant to GM president Alfred P. Sloan, Jr., in 1930 and, a year later, vice president in charge of industrial and public relations. In 1934 Stettinius moved to the U.S. Steel Corporation as a vice president, and the following year he became chairman of the board.

President Franklin D. Roosevelt appointed him to the Industrial Advisory Board in 1933 and chairman of the War Resources Board in 1939. The following year he was placed on the new National Defense Advisory Commission, at which point he resigned from U.S. Steel to devote full time to government service. He became director of priorities of the Office of Production Management in January 1941 and, nine months later, administrator of lend-lease.

In September 1943, Roosevelt appointed Stettinius undersecretary of state and charged him with the task of reorganizing the State Department. On Dec. 1, 1944, after the resignation of the ailing Cordell Hull, Stettinius was named secretary of state. His most notable contributions as secretary of state centered on his vigorous efforts to establish the United Nations. As undersecretary he had headed the American delegation to the seminal Dumbarton Oaks Conference in 1944. In February 1945 he accompanied Roosevelt to the Yalta Conference with Churchill and Stalin, at which it was decided to call a conference in San Francisco at the end of April to form the new organization. Stettinius subsequently attended the Inter-American Conference in Mexico City, which resulted in the Act of Chapultepec, which laid the foundation for the Organization of American States in 1948.

President Truman, who did not fully share Roosevelt's confidence in Stettinius, accepted his resignation as secretary of state at the close of the San Francisco Conference, but appointed him chairman of the U.S. delegation to the United Nations Preparatory Commission and, in January 1946, chairman of the American delegation to the first session of the UN General Assembly, as well as American representative on the Security Council. He resigned in June of that year.

STETTINIUS, EDWARD RILEY   (*b. St. Louis, Mo., 1865; d. Locust Valley, N.Y., 1925*), industrialist. Acting for J. P. Morgan & Co., Stettinius supervised contracts for, and production of, the war supplies purchased in the United States by the Allies, 1915–17. He continued his work after the entry of the United States into World War I, acting first as surveyor general of purchases and as an assistant secretary of war, 1918–19. Thereafter he was with the Morgan firm until his death.

STEUBEN, FRIEDRICH WILHELM LUDOLF GERHARD AUGUSTIN, BARON VON (*b. Magdeburg, Germany, 1730; d. Steuben, Oneida Co., N.Y., 1794*), baron, soldier. Son of a lieutenant of engineers in the army of Frederick William I of Prussia, Steuben spent his early childhood in Russia, where his father served for several years in the army of the Czarina Anne. Entering the officer corps of the Prussian army, he served with credit through the Seven Years' War as an infantry officer and later on the staff; he became a general staff officer, 1761, and soon thereafter was promoted captain. After a diplomatic mission to Russia, 1762, he served at the royal headquarters as one of the aides-de-camp to the king. His specific training for the experience in general staff duties, a military agency then little known outside Prussia, equipped him peculiarly for his career in the American Revolution. Discharged for obscure reasons from the army in the spring of 1763, he took employment as chamberlain at the court of the prince of Hohenzollern-Hechingen in 1764. There he attained the rank of baron. Financial difficulties caused him to seek employment in 1776, first with the French, then with the margrave of Baden, and finally, 1777, in the American army. In letters from Benjamin Franklin and others to Washington, he was introduced as a lieutenant general in the service of Prussia, although his actual rank was that of captain.

Well received in America because of the prestige of his supposed rank and his declaration that he wished no immediate compensation and would stake his fortunes upon the success of the Revolution, Steuben reported in February 1778 to Washington at Valley Forge. Prevailed upon to serve as acting inspector general and to undertake the training of the army, he was immediately successful. This involved serious difficulties, since he had to act through interpreters. He prepared brief drill instructions which were issued to the regiments from time to time as the drills progressed. He formed a model company of 100 selected men and undertook its drill in person. Progress of this company under his skilled instruction made an immediate appeal to the imagination of the whole army and drill became the fashion. In consequence, Washington recommended his regular appointment as inspector general with the rank of major general on Apr. 30. Thereafter, the Continental army proved itself, battalion for battalion, the equal in discipline of the best British regulars.

During the winter of 1778–79, Steuben prepared his *Regulations for the Order and Discipline of the Troops of the United States*, which became the military bible of the Continental army. He grew steadily in Washington's confidence; he was consulted upon all questions of strategic and administrative policy, and performed all of the essential functions of a modern general staff. In the autumn of 1780, when General Nathaniel Greene was sent to the Carolinas, Steuben accompanied him to assist in reorganizing the southern army. Greene, realizing that most of his replacements and supplies came from Virginia, left Steuben in command in that state. His efforts to make Virginia a base of supply for Greene's army were thwarted to a large extent by British forces, and with his limited troops, Steuben could offer slight resistance. Greene, however, appreciated Steuben's difficulties and acknowledged that his support had been indispensable to the success of the Carolina campaign. When Lafayette took command in Virginia in April 1781, Steuben served under his orders; at Yorktown, Steuben commanded one of the three divisions of the besieging army. In 1783 he assisted Washington in preparation of a plan for the future defense of the United States and in the arrangements for demobilizing the Continental army. When Washington relinquished command of the army, he deliberately made it his last official act to write a letter commending Steuben's invaluable services to the United States throughout the war. After retirement from the army, Steuben, a citizen of the United States since 1783, resided in New York and became one of the most popular figures in the social life of the city and state. In converting the American army into an effective and highly disciplined military force, he performed an essential service that none of his contemporaries in America was qualified to perform.

STEUBEN, JOHN (*b. Ukraine, Russia, 1906; d. Flemington, N.Y., 1957*), labor leader. Immigrated to the U.S. in 1923. In the early 1930's, Steuben became a full-time organizer for the Steel and Metal Workers Industrial Union, an affiliate of the Trade Union Unity League, the Communist-led union federation established in 1929. In 1936, he became an organizer for the Steel Workers Organizing Committee, which was actively trying to organize the Bethlehem, Republic, Inland, and Youngstown steel companies. The attempt ended in violence, and Steuben was purged because of his Communist affiliation. Steuben served in World War II, and was editor of the *March of Labor* from 1950 to 1954.

STEUER, MAX DAVID (*b. Homino, present Czechoslovakia, 1870[?]; d. Jackson, N.H., 1940*), lawyer. Came to New York City as a child. LL.B., Columbia Law School, 1893. Practicing in New York City *post* 1893, he became one of the outstanding trial lawyers of his time, skillful alike in commercial and criminal cases. Possessed of an unusual capacity for grasping a case as a whole, as the sum of all its parts, he also had great technical skill as a cross-examiner and was most dangerous when apparently checkmated.

STEVENS, ABEL (*b. Philadelphia, Pa., 1815; d. San Jose, Calif., 1897*), Methodist clergyman, editor. Author of *The History of the Religious Movement of the Eighteenth Century, Called Methodism* (1858–61) and *The History of the Methodist Episcopal Church in the United States* (1864–67), which take high rank among denominational histories.

STEVENS, ALEXANDER HODGDON (*b. New York, N.Y., 1789; d. 1869*), surgeon. Brother of John A. Stevens (1795–1874). Graduated Yale, 1807. Studied medicine with Edward Miller; M.D., University of Pennsylvania, 1811; studied also in London and Paris. Professor of surgery at present Rutgers and at New York College of Physicians and Surgeons, he was president of the latter institution, 1843–55. He maintained a large practice in New York City and held many honorary appointments.

STEVENS, ASHTON (*b. San Francisco, Calif., 1872; d. Chicago, Ill., 1951*), drama critic. Critic and writer for the Hearst paper *San Francisco Examiner* (1897–1906); for the *Chicago Examiner*, from 1910 until his death. A witty, restrained reviewer, Stevens was considered by many to be the dean of American theater reviewers.

STEVENS, BENJAMIN FRANKLIN (*b. Barnet, Vt., 1833; d. Surbiton, England, 1902*), bookman, antiquarian. Brother of Henry Stevens. Editor of a number of reprints of rare works and manuscripts of Americana.

STEVENS, CLEMENT HOFFMAN (*b. Norwich, Conn., 1821; d. 1864*), Confederate brigadier general. Grandson of Peter Fayssoux. Designed armored battery on Morris Island, Charleston, S.C. Recklessly gallant, he was mortally wounded near Peachtree Creek in the campaign against Atlanta, Ga.

STEVENS, DORIS (*b. Omaha, Nebr., 1892; d. New York, N.Y., 1963*), suffragist and feminist leader. Graduated from Oberlin (1911). Joined the suffrage crusade and became a member of the Congressional Union for Woman Suffrage (1914), which became the National Woman's Party in 1916. She was arrested for picketing the White House in 1917 and served three days of a sixty-day sentence; wrote *Jailed for Freedom* (1920) about the militant suffrage effort. Chaired the NWP's International Relations Committee (1923–29); led an NWP delegation to the Sixth Pan-American Conference (1928) to lobby for equal rights, which led to the creation of the Inter-American Commission of Women (which she chaired 1928–39); and was a member of the Women's Consultative Committee on Nationality for the League of Nations (1931–36). Later became an ardent champion of Sen. Joseph McCarthy.

STEVENS, EDWIN AUGUSTUS (b. Hoboken, N.J., 1795; d. Paris, France, 1868), engineer, financier. Son of John Stevens, whose business affairs he managed in great part; brother of Robert L. Stevens. Organized the Camden & Amboy Railroad, 1830, and managed it with great success until his death. Began experiments in construction of an armored or ironclad warship ca. 1814, which came to fruition in his vessel Stevens Battery 40 years later, but failed of acceptance by the government. He left land and money for the establishment of Stevens Institute of Technology in Hoboken.

STEVENS, EMILY (b. New York, N.Y., 1882; d. New York, 1928), actress. Cousin of Minnie Maddern Fiske. Adept in the performance of roles of beautiful and alluring women, she played for a number of years with her cousin's companies and scored her first great success in The Unchastened Woman, New York, 1915. She later won acclaim for her performance in Fata Morgana, 1924.

STEVENS, GEORGE BARKER (b. Spencer, N.Y., 1854; d. 1906), theologian. Graduated University of Rochester, 1877; Yale Divinity School, 1880; Ph.D., Syracuse, 1883; D.D., Jena, 1886. Professor of New Testament criticism, Yale Divinity School, 1886–95, and professor of systematic theology thereafter, he was author of a number of books which were concerned chiefly with the reinterpretation of religious truth in the light of modern scholarship.

STEVENS, GEORGE WASHINGTON (b. Utica, N.Y., 1866; d. 1926), educator, journalist. Revolutionized museum practice as director of the Toledo (Ohio) Museum of Art, 1903–26. Under his guidance the Toledo Museum was the first to enter on a policy of art education for all people, the first to maintain a free school of design, and among the first to give music an equal rank with the other arts.

STEVENS, HARRY MOZLEY (b. London, England, 1855; d. New York, N.Y., 1934), and STEVENS, FRANK MOZLEY (b. London, 1880; d. New York, N.Y., 1965), sports concessionaires and caterers. Starting with a concession to sell baseball scorecards at the Columbus, Ohio, park in 1887, Harry obtained other concessions over the next four years, including the New York Giants Polo Grounds in 1894, where he also sold snack food to fans. After 1900 he began selling peanuts, soda pop, and hot dogs. He built an army of hirelings to sell his food and expanded his enterprise into a profitable catering industry, catering to patrons of hotels, indoor shows, exhibitions, conventions, racetracks, and other public entertainments. Frank succeeded his father as head of Harry M. Stevens, Inc., having thirty-eight years experience with the firm. Although by the 1960's the firm had only two baseball concessions left, in 1962 it was estimated that it served about 30 million customers.

STEVENS, HENRY (b. Barnet, Vt., 1819; d. London, England, 1886), bookman. Brother of Benjamin F. Stevens. A pioneer in the collection of rare Americana, Stevens was also an authority on the bibliographical history of the English Bible. He was author of, among other works, Recollections of Mr. James Lenox (1886).

STEVENS, HIRAM FAIRCHILD (b. St. Albans, Vt., 1852; d. 1904), lawyer, Minnesota legislator. Removed to St. Paul, Minn., 1879, where he practiced until his death. A leader in starting the St. Paul College of Law, 1900, he served as its president thereafter.

STEVENS, ISAAC INGALLS (b. Andover, Mass., 1818; d. Chantilly, Va., 1862), soldier. Graduated West Point, 1839. Commissioned in the engineers, he served ably on fortification work in New England and was on General Winfield Scott's staff in the war with Mexico, winning brevets for gallantry in the capture of Mexico City. Executive assistant, U.S. Coast Survey, 1849–53, he showed high administrative talent; resigning from the army, he served as governor, Washington Territory, 1853–57. During this period he acted as director of exploration for the northern route of the Pacific Railway surveys. His term as governor was a controversial one since his Indian treaty policy brought about a number of uprisings among the tribes in the territory. Although much criticized, he was elected territorial delegate to Congress and served from March 1857 until the opening of the Civil War. Appointed colonel, 79th New York Volunteers, he was promoted, brigadier general, September 1861, and major general, July 1862. He was killed in battle.

STEVENS, JOHN (b. New York, N.Y., 1749; d. Hoboken, N.J., 1838), engineer, inventor. Grandson of James Alexander; father of Edwin A. and Robert L. Stevens. Graduated King's College (present Columbia), 1768. After Revolutionary War services, principally as a collector of money in New Jersey for the Continental army, he served as surveyor general for the eastern division of New Jersey, 1782–83, and then turned to the development of an estate in and around what is presently Hoboken, N.J. About 1788 his attention was drawn to the work of John Fitch and James Rumsey in the development of the steamboat; thereafter until his death he devoted himself to advancement of mechanical transport on water and on land. Concentrating on the use of steam, he began to work out designs of boilers and engines unique for the time. In 1791, having helped to bring about the framing of the act of 1790 establishing the first patent laws, he was among the first dozen citizens to receive U.S. patents; his inventions included an improved vertical steam boiler and an improved Savery-type steam engine, both intended for boat propulsion. He associated himself ca. 1797 with Nicholas I. Roosevelt and Robert R. Livingston in the project of building a steam engine and boat. Livingston obtained the exclusive privilege of steamboat operation on the waters of New York State, and with this incentive the partners set to work with added vigor. An experimental boat, the Polacca, proved unsuccessful in trials on the Passaic River, but experiments were continued and in 1800 a definite 20-year partnership agreement was consummated. Shortly after, Stevens became consulting engineer for the Manhattan Co., organized to furnish an adequate water supply to New York City. He convinced the directors that steam pumping engines should be used, and installed equipment of his own design, but it was not efficient, and a Boulton & Watt type of engine was later substituted. In 1803, after further experimentation, he secured a patent for a multitubular boiler. In the following year his small twin-screw steamboat Little Juliana traveled back and forth across the Hudson. Spurred to greater effort, Stevens determined to inaugurate an adequate steam ferry system between Hoboken and New York, and to operate a regular line of steamboats on the Hudson between New York and Albany. Before his Phoenix was completed, however, Fulton's Clermont made its successful voyage in 1807 to Albany and return. The achievement discouraged Stevens, since it was made under a monopoly granted to Livingston and Fulton, and he still considered himself bound by the earlier agreement with Roosevelt. He also had come to believe that any monopoly was unconstitutional.

Restricted by law from using the Hudson River, he sent the *Phoenix* to Philadelphia in 1809. It made the trip successfully and is considered the first seagoing steamboat in the world. Thereafter, plying between Philadelphia and Trenton, it served as a unit in the cross-state transportation system which was controlled and managed by Stevens' sons.

About 1810, he began giving greater attention to adaptation of the steam engine as motive power for railways. He induced the New Jersey Assembly in February 1815 to create a railway company. Eight years later, the Pennsylvania legislature authorized a railway company and empowered Stevens to build it. The necessary funds, however, could not be raised, although in 1825 he designed and built an experimental locomotive and operated it on a circular track on his estate in Hoboken to prove the feasibility of the scheme. This was the first American-built steam locomotive, though it was never used for actual service on a railroad. Stevens also proposed an armored navy, bridging the Hudson from New York to Hoboken, a vehicular tunnel under the Hudson, and an elevated railway system for New York City.

STEVENS, JOHN AUSTIN   (*b. New York, N.Y., 1795; d. New York, 1874*), banker. Brother of Alexander H. Stevens; father of John A. Stevens (1827–1910). President of the Bank of Commerce, New York City, 1839–66.

STEVENS, JOHN AUSTIN   (*b. New York, N.Y., 1827; d. Newport, R.I., 1910*), financier, author. Son of John A. Stevens (1795–1874). Founded the *Magazine of American History*, which he edited, 1877–81; author of *Colonial Records of the New York Chamber of Commerce* (1867), *The Burgoyne Campaign* (1877), *Albert Gallatin* (1884), and other works.

STEVENS, JOHN FRANK   (*b. near West Gardiner, Maine, 1853; d. Southern Pines, N.C., 1943*), civil engineer, railroad executive. Graduated State Normal School, Farmington, Maine, 1872. Removed to Minneapolis, Minn., 1873, where an engineer uncle helped him secure work as a rodman for the city engineer. Deciding to make a career in railroad work in 1875, he subsequently worked for the Sabine Pass & Northwestern Railroad; the Denver & Rio Grande Railroad; the Chicago, Milwaukee & St. Paul Railroad, 1881–82 and 1885–86; the Canadian Pacific Railroad, 1882–84; and beginning in 1886, the Duluth, South Shore & Atlantic Railroad.

Stevens next worked briefly as assistant engineer of the Spokane Falls & Northern Railway, where he gained valuable knowledge of the Pacific Northwest, and then began an important association with the Great Northern Railway and its president, James J. Hill. Hill was building an unsubsidized transcontinental railroad through the northernmost tier of states, and one of Stevens' first assignments was to explore the route west from Havre, Mont. He established the feasibility of the now famous Marias Pass, which provided the key passage across the Continental Divide. Sent next to Washington to explore the Columbia River and the Cascades for the final route down the western slopes of the Divide, he located another important pass, later named Stevens Pass, near Lake Wenatchee.

When the Pacific extension was completed in 1893, Stevens became assistant chief engineer on the Great Northern, with which he remained intermittently until 1903. During these years he supervised the planning and construction of more than a thousand miles of new track, much of it in Minnesota. Stevens left the Great Northern in 1903 to become chief engineer (in 1904, second vice president) of the Chicago, Rock Island & Pacific Railway. The following year he was named to the federal Philippine Commission, to head its railroad building program. Before he could serve, however, Secretary of War William Howard Taft

named Stevens, on Hill's suggestion, as chief engineer of the Isthmian Canal Commission.

When Stevens arrived at the Canal Zone in the early part of 1906, he found conditions chaotic. Drawing on his years of railroad experience, Stevens immediately set about reorganizing the work force and engineering staff. He also accepted the theory of the mosquito as the vector for yellow fever and malaria and aided Col. William C. Gorgas, head of the sanitation department, in implementing adequate sanitary and health measures. Construction was under way late in 1906, but Stevens, frustrated by political maneuvering in Washington, resigned a few months later.

Upon returning to the United States, Stevens became vice president of the New York, New Haven & Hartford Railroad, but in 1909 he accepted an offer to rejoin Hill in the building of a southward extension of the Hill lines from the Columbia River through central Oregon, the first step toward a connection with San Francisco; the new line was successfully completed in 1911. He then moved to New York City, where for several years he was a private consultant.

In 1917 Stevens was appointed by President Wilson as chairman of an advisory commission of American railway experts to study the Russian railway system. He went to Siberia later in 1917 as head of a second American commission, the Russian Railway Service Corps, and began reorganizing the Trans-Siberian and Chinese Eastern railways. In 1919 he was named president of the Technical Board of the Inter-Allied Railway Commission, an international body set up to supervise railways in those parts of Siberia and Manchuria where Allied troops were stationed. Upon his return to the United States in 1923, he became a member of the board of directors of the Baltimore & Ohio Railroad.

STEVENS, JOHN HARRINGTON   (*b. Brompton Falls, Quebec, Canada, 1820; d. 1900*), Minnesota pioneer, agricultural editor. After service in the Mexican War, Stevens settled *ca.* 1849 on a claim on the west banks of the Mississippi at the Falls of St. Anthony. His house was the first dwelling erected in the present city of Minneapolis.

STEVENS, JOHN LEAVITT   (*b. Mount Vernon, Maine, 1820; d. Augusta, Maine, 1895*), journalist, diplomat. Associated with James G. Blaine on the *Kennebec Journal* of Augusta, Maine. Stevens served as U.S. minister to Paraguay, Uruguay, Norway, and Sweden between 1870 and 1883. As minister resident to Hawaii and later as envoy extraordinary, 1889–93, he played a prominent part in the 1893 rebellion whereby Queen Liliuokalani was dethroned and a provisional government under Sanford B. Dole was installed.

STEVENS, ROBERT LIVINGSTON   (*b. Hoboken, N.J., 1787; d. Hoboken, 1856*), engineer, naval architect, inventor. Son of John Stevens; brother of Edwin A. Stevens. Assistant to his father in his steam propulsion experiments, he helped in the design and construction of the steamboat *Phoenix*, 1808, and with Moses Rogers took it on its pioneer sea voyage from New York to Philadelphia, 1809. Recognized in time as a leader in naval architecture, he designed and had built more than 20 steamboats and ferries which incorporated his successive inventions. Among these were the method of installing knees of wood and iron inside the ship's frame, a "cam-board" cutoff for steam engines, and balanced poppet valves. He also devised an improved type of walking beam, introduced a forced-draft firing system under boilers, and was first to perfect a marine tubular boiler. The split paddle wheel, "hog-framing" for boats, and the present type of ferry slip were also his inventions. He played an important part in managing the family transportation business in New Jersey and was president and engineer *post* 1830 of the Camden & Amboy

Railroad, for which he designed the T-rail, the hook-headed spike, and other rail devices. In November 1831, at the throttle of the locomotive *John Bull*, he inaugurated the first steam railway service in New Jersey at Bordentown. *Post* 1815, he worked for many years on problems of ordnance and the armoring of warships.

STEVENS, THADDEUS (*b. Danville, Vt., 1792; d. Washington, D.C., 1868*), lawyer, political leader. Lame and sickly from birth, Stevens grew up in the semifrontier atmosphere of Peacham, Vt., and early developed a strong sympathy for the poor and an intense dislike of caste in any form. Graduating from Dartmouth, 1814, he studied also at the University of Vermont. Beginning the study of law in Vermont, he continued his studies while teaching in an academy at York, Pa., and began practice at Gettysburg, Pa., 1816, engaging also *post* 1826 in the manufacture of iron. Seeing much of the slavery system as it operated in nearby Maryland, he became an extreme hater of the institution and defended numerous fugitive slaves without fee. Entering politics as a violent opponent of Andrew Jackson, he first became prominent at the Anti-Masonic Convention in Baltimore, Md., 1831, where he delivered a notable speech condemning secret orders. As a member of the Pennsylvania House, elected on the Anti-Masonic ticket, 1833–41, he became known as a brilliant advocate for the extension of free public education and as a defender of the protective tariff. At his retirement from the legislature, he was recognized as one of the strongest men in his state. Removing to Lancaster, Pa., 1842, he devoted himself for a while to his legal practice.

Elected to Congress on the Whig ticket, 1848, he took a leading place among the Free-Soilers, setting his face against any compromise with slavery in the territories and denouncing that institution as a national curse and crime with fierce invective. Disgusted with Whig moderation, he left Congress in March 1853. Playing a vigorous part in formation of the Republican party in Pennsylvania, he was reelected to Congress, 1858. Denouncing slavery and pleading for a protective tariff, he also warned the South to secede at its peril and called upon President Buchanan to exert the full federal authority against those who were flouting the national government. Passed over for a cabinet post on President Lincoln's election, he became chairman of the House Ways and Means Committee and exerted wide authority over measures dealing with the prosecution of the Civil War. Though in matters of finance he loyally supported the administration, his ideas of policy diverged sharply from Lincoln's, and he was a constant thorn in the side of the administration on matters concerning the conduct of the war. By 1864 he had become so far committed to stern measures as to speak of the necessity to exterminate the "rebels" and to desolate the South. He laid down the rule that the South was outside the Constitution and that the law of nations alone would limit the victorious North in determining the conditions of Southern restoration. He considered the Wade-Davis bill an inadequate measure for Reconstruction and was probably secretly hostile to Lincoln's 1864 candidacy. His almost fanatical fight to maintain Republican party supremacy in the government was motivated by economic as well as political considerations.

After Lincoln's assassination, Stevens prepared to give battle to Andrew Johnson on the question of reducing the South to a "territorial condition." To Stevens, it was a "conquered province"; he would make it choose between black suffrage and reduced representation. When Congress met in December 1865, a joint committee on Reconstruction was appointed on his motion; as chairman of the House group, Stevens was the dominant member of the committee. The first open rupture with President Johnson came in February 1866 on the Freedmen's Bureau bill, which Stevens belligerently pushed and Johnson vetoed. Stevens succeeded in passing the Civil Rights Act and a revised Freedmen's

Bureau Act over Johnson's veto, and in April 1866 the joint committee reported the 14th Amendment, which Congress adopted. A sweeping Republican victory in the congressional elections of 1866 gave Stevens the whip-hand over Johnson and the South. The first use he made of his triumph was to impose military Reconstruction and the 15th Amendment upon the South. When Johnson removed Edwin M. Stanton as U.S. secretary of war early in 1868, Stevens reported an impeachment resolution based on the president's supposed disregard of the Tenure of Office Act. Although a member of the committee to draft articles of impeachment and one of the managers to conduct the case before the Senate, Stevens took little part in the trial itself.

Shortly after Johnson's acquittal, Stevens died. An intense partisan, his career was marred by a harsh and vindictive temper, which in his last years made him frankly vengeful toward the South. His policy aroused fierce resentment, accentuated racial antagonism, cemented the Solid South, and postponed for many decades any true solution of the race problem. Had tolerance been added to his character, he might have been a brilliant, instead of a sinister, figure in American history.

STEVENS, THOMAS HOLDUP (*b. Charleston, S.C., 1795; d. probably Washington, D.C., 1841*), naval officer. Father of Thomas H. Stevens (1819–96). Appointed midshipman, 1809, he won distinction on the Niagara frontier in the War of 1812 and commanded the sloop *Trippe* in the battle of Lake Erie. He later served in a variety of ship and shore commands and was promoted captain, 1836.

STEVENS, THOMAS HOLDUP (*b. Middletown, Conn., 1819; d. Rockville, Md., 1896*), naval officer. Son of Thomas H. Stevens (1795–1841). Appointed midshipman, 1836. During the Civil War he served with great credit in blockade and other duties along the eastern coast and was the commander of the desperate night boat attack, Sept. 8, 1863, on Fort Sumter. He was later active in Union operations in the Gulf of Mexico. Promoted rear admiral, 1879, he retired, 1881.

STEVENS, WALLACE (*b. Reading, Pa., 1879; d. Hartford, Conn., 1955*), poet. Studied at Harvard, graduating in 1900, and at the New York University Law School (LL.B., 1903). Considered one of the twentieth century's major poets, Stevens never led the publicized life of a successful artist. He worked for the Hartford Accident and Indemnity Co. from 1916 until his death. From 1914 to 1922, he wrote poems for the magazines *Poetry* and *Others*. These poems were published by Alfred A. Knopf in 1923 under the title of *Harmonium*. The volume was reprinted in 1931, establishing Stevens as a leading poet of his generation. From 1923 to 1930, he wrote little. Volumes during the 1930's include *Ideas of Order* (1935), *Owl's Clover* (1936), and *The Man With the Blue Guitar* (1937). Other volumes include *Parts of the World* (1942), *Notes Toward a Supreme Fiction* (1942), *Esthetic du Mal* (1945), *Three Academic Pieces* (1947), *Transport to Summer* (1947), and *The Auroras of Autumn* (1950), which won the National Book Award. His *Collected Poems* (1954) won a second National Book Award, and in 1955, he won the Nobel Prize. After his death, the volume, *Opus Posthumous* was issued in 1957.

STEVENS, WALTER HUSTED (*b. Penn Yan, N.Y., 1827; d. Veracruz, Mexico, 1867*), Confederate brigadier general, military engineer. Graduated West Point, 1848. Served at various times as chief engineer, Army of Northern Virginia; supervised building of defenses of Richmond.

STEVENS, WILLIAM ARNOLD (*b. Granville, Ohio, 1839; d. 1910*), New Testament scholar. Graduated Denison University, 1862; studied also at Harvard, Newton Theological Institution, Leipzig, and Berlin. Taught Greek at Denison; was professor of

New Testament interpretation at Rochester Theological Seminary, 1877–1910. A scholarly theological conservative, he was author of, among other books, *A Harmony of the Gospels for Historical Study* (1894).

STEVENS, WILLIAM BACON (*b. Bath, Maine, 1815; d. 1887*), Episcopal clergyman, historian, physician. Brother-in-law of Henry Coppée. Assistant bishop of Pennsylvania, 1862–65, he succeeded to the see. He was instrumental in the founding of Lehigh University and was author of a number of scholarly works on religious and historical subjects, among them, *A History of Georgia from Its First Discovery* (1847, 1859).

STEVENSON, ADLAI EWING (*b. Christian Co., Ky., 1835; d. Chicago, Ill., 1914*), lawyer, U.S. vice president. Removed to Bloomington, Ill., 1852. Began practice of law at Metamora, Ill., 1858; practiced in Bloomington *post* 1868. Congressman, Democrat, from Illinois, 1875–77 and 1879–81, he served without particular distinction but made many friends. As first assistant postmaster general, 1885–89, he performed with extraordinary tact his unpleasant task of removing Republican postmasters to make way for deserving Democrats. As vice president of the United States, 1893–97, he presided gracefully over the Senate and did not embarrass the administration by pressing his well-known "soft money" views. In the campaign of 1900 he was William J. Bryan's running mate, and in 1908 ran unsuccessfully for the governorship of Illinois.

STEVENSON, ADLAI EWING, II (*b. Los Angeles, Calif., 1900; d. London, England, 1965*), politician and government official. Attended Princeton, Harvard Law, and Northwestern Law School (J.D., 1926); became a law clerk in the conservative Republican firm of Cutting, Moore and Sidley in Chicago. He then went to work for the Agricultural Adjustment Administration (1933), became chief attorney for the Federal Alcohol Control Administration (1934), rejoined his law firm and was made partner (1935), and was elected to the Chicago Council on Foreign Relations (1935). He became principal attorney for Secretary of the Navy Frank Knox, serving as speech writer and administrative assistant (1941–44). In 1945 he became special assistant to Secretary of State Edward Stettinius, Jr., his major task being to improve the public image of the State Department. He accompanied Stettinius to London for the Preparatory Commission of the United Nations (1945) and headed the delegation to the early General Assembly sessions of the UN. As governor of Illinois (1948–52) he achieved many improvements in state government, such as removing state police from political patronage, doubling aid to public schools, and launching the state's biggest road-building program. His Democratic presidential campaign in 1952 raised American political thinking to a high plane, and his campaign speeches became best-selling books at home and abroad. After his overwhelming defeat by Dwight D. Eisenhower, he devoted himself to rejuvenating the Democratic party; he played an important part in the successful campaign to elect a Democratic Congress in 1954. The Democratic candidate for president again in 1956, he raised issues that the Eisenhower administration had either ignored or handled inadequately; he advocated the suspension of nuclear testing in the atmosphere, reduction of tensions with the Soviet Union, end of the draft, and increased assistance to underdeveloped countries through the UN. Becoming the conscience of American politics, he urged Americans to live up to their ideals, spoke of the pressing necessity of improving race relations, and decried the destruction of natural resources for private profit. After his defeat, he was a prime mover in the founding of the Democratic Advisory Council, which became an effective instrument for issuing policy statements. As ambassador to the UN (1961–65), he wanted to make this

organization the center of U.S. foreign policy, a concept not acceptable to presidents John Kennedy or Lyndon Johnson. Repeated crises marked his tenure at the UN, requiring almost constant negotiations on his part: the Bay of Pigs; the Cuban missile crisis; UN forces in the Congo, on Cyprus, and on the Egypt-Israeli border; the wrangle with Portugal over its control of African colonies; the question of admitting Communist China to the UN; white racism in Rhodesia and South Africa; and the quest for disarmament. He died during UN Secretary General U Thant's overtures to the United States, Soviet Union, and Hanoi to discuss peaceful solutions to the Vietnam War.

STEVENSON, ANDREW (*b. Culpeper Co., Va., 1784; d. Albemarle Co., Va., 1857*), lawyer, Virginia legislator. Nephew of Lewis Littlepage. Congressman, Democrat, from Virginia, 1821–34, he was a member of the influential "Richmond Junto" and Speaker of the House, 1827–34. A Unionist during the nullification controversy, he later was a supporter of Martin Van Buren and served as U.S. minister to Great Britain, 1834–41. He was essentially a machine politician; his career lacks the stamp of a strong personality.

STEVENSON, CARTER LITTLEPAGE (*b. near Fredericksburg, Va., 1817; d. Caroline Co., Va., 1888*), Confederate major general, civil engineer. Nephew of Andrew Stevenson. Graduated West Point, 1838. Served principally in the western campaigns of the Civil War; commanded the right of the Confederate lines during the siege of Vicksburg. Taken prisoner there, he was later exchanged and fought in the Atlanta and Carolina campaigns.

STEVENSON, JAMES (*b. Maysville, Ky., 1840; d. New York, N.Y., 1888*), ethnologist, explorer. Employed in government engineering work *post* 1856, he became a member of the U.S. Geological Survey of the territories under Ferdinand V. Hayden, with whom he made explorations of the Missouri, Columbia, and Snake rivers; in 1871 he took an active part in the survey of the Yellowstone region. He climbed to the summit of the Grand Teton, 1872, and is believed to have been the first white man to do so. Continuing in the survey under the directorship of John W. Powell, he was in the service of the Bureau of Ethnology *post* 1879. Becoming interested in Indian language and customs, he collected a great deal of material on the Pueblo Indians and their former settlements, including large collections of culture material both ancient and modern, which he catalogued in bureau reports and which constitute a valuable and, in most respects, unique contribution to science.

STEVENSON, JOHN JAMES (*b. New York, N.Y., 1841; d. New Canaan, Conn., 1924*), geologist. Graduated present New York University, 1863; Ph.D., 1867. After teaching at West Virginia University and working on the geological surveys of Ohio and Pennsylvania and the Wheeler surveys in the West, he was professor of geology at New York University, 1881–1909. He was particularly interested in stratigraphic problems and those relating to coal.

STEVENSON, JOHN WHITE (*b. Richmond, Va., 1812; d. Covington, Ky., 1886*), lawyer, Kentucky legislator. Congressman, Democrat, from Kentucky, 1857–61, he was a moderate Confederate sympathizer during the Civil War. Elected lieutenant governor of Kentucky, 1867, he became governor in September of that year and served with ability and sanity until 1871. As U.S. senator, 1871–77, he was a close adherent of Jeffersonian principles.

STEVENSON, MATILDA COXE EVANS (*b. San Augustine, Tex., ca. 1850; d. 1915*), ethnologist. Wife and professional associate of James Stevenson. Author of an encyclopedic study on the Zuni Indians (*Twenty-third Annual Report of the Bureau of*

American Ethnology, 1901–02, published 1904) and other important works in her field.

STEVENSON, SARA YORKE (*b. Paris, France, 1847; d. 1921*), archaeologist. Raised and educated abroad, she resided in Philadelphia, Pa., *post ca.* 1867. Author of a number of papers on Egyptian archaeology and other subjects, she helped establish the Museum of the University of Pennsylvania and was literary editor of the Philadelphia *Public Ledger*, 1908–21.

STEWARD, IRA (*b. New London, Conn., 1831; d. Plano, Ill., 1883*), labor leader, proponent of eight-hour-day legislation. A believer in labor solidarity and an ultimate socialistic state, Steward, with George E. McNeill and George Gunton, joined with leading American members of the Marxian International Workingmen's Association to form the International Labor Union, 1878, for organization of unskilled laborers. In the realm of theory, Steward held that shorter hours of labor developed leisure-time wants and hence a demand for higher wages. Increased wages in turn would compel introduction of better techniques, which would make mass production possible. Mass production, to be stable, would need mass purchasing powers which must be protected against the down-drag of the unemployed by progressive shortening of hours of labor in accordance with an index of unemployment. Ultimately, the workers would be able to buy the capitalists out and so inaugurate socialism.

STEWARDSON, JOHN (*b. Philadelphia, Pa., 1858; d. near Philadelphia, 1896*), architect. Studied in Paris; was partner with Walter Cope *post* 1886. Primarily an artist, Stewardson specialized in English Gothic; his work at University of Pennsylvania, Bryn Mawr, and Princeton had great influence for good on American educational-building design.

STEWART, ALEXANDER PETER (*b. Rogersville, Tenn., 1821; d. Biloxi, Miss., 1908*), Confederate lieutenant general, educator. Graduated West Point, 1842. An artillery officer, Stewart rose to divisional command in the western campaigns of the Civil War and in the Atlanta campaign; at the end of the war, he was the commander of the Army of Tennessee. He was chancellor of the University of Mississippi, 1874–86.

STEWART, ALEXANDER TURNEY (*b. Lisburn, Ireland, 1803; d. 1876*), merchant. Immigrated to New York City *ca.* 1820; opened a small lace shop in New York, 1823. A canny observer of fashion and the market, he prospered in his own trade and made good profits by sale of stock bought at auction during the panic of 1837. By 1850 he had the largest dry-goods establishment in the city (operating in his own building at Broadway and Chambers St., built 1846), and in 1862 he opened at Broadway and Ninth St. what was then the largest retail store in the world. Profiting also by Civil War contracts, he acquired numerous other interests in the United States and abroad. Purchasing always for cash, he was a strict disciplinarian of his employees and his wage policy was poor even for his time. Garden City, N.Y., was built up by him as a "model town" for persons of moderate means.

STEWART, ALVAN (*b. South Granville, N.Y., 1790; d. 1849*), lawyer, abolitionist. Settled in Utica, N.Y., *ca.* 1832, where he practiced. Founder and first president of New York Anti-Slavery Society, he won by his vivid, erratic speeches the title of "humorist" of the antislavery movement. He advanced the argument that, since slaves were deprived of their freedom without due process, the institution of slavery was unconstitutional. With William L. Garrison, he was responsible for dissension in the national antislavery movement, 1840, and was presiding officer at the convention which organized the Liberty party.

STEWART, ANDREW (*b. Fayette Co., Pa., 1791; d. 1872*), lawyer, Pennsylvania legislator and official. Congressman, Democrat and National Republican, from Pennsylvania, 1821–29 and 1831–35; congressman, Whig, 1843–49. Ardent in support of protection and internal improvements, he was called "Tariff Andy."

STEWART, CHARLES (*b. Philadelphia, Pa., 1778; d. Bordentown, N.J., 1869*), naval officer. Trained in the merchant service, he was commissioned lieutenant, U.S. Navy, 1798, and in 1800 made a very successful cruise in command of the schooner *Experiment*. Capturing two armed French vessels and recapturing a number of American merchantmen, he also provided convoy protection. After further distinguished service in the troubles with the Barbary states, 1802–06, he was commissioned captain. He won further fame during the War of 1812, notably as commander of the *Constitution* from December 1813 to the end of the war. In varied service thereafter, he was made senior flag officer, 1859, and in 1862 became rear admiral on the retired list. He was the grandfather of Charles Stewart Parnell, the eminent advocate in the British Parliament of Irish home rule.

STEWART, EDWIN (*b. New York, N.Y., 1837; d. South Orange, N.J., 1933*), naval officer. Brother of John A. Stewart. Joining the U.S. Navy, September 1861, as assistant paymaster, he was associated with the business and supply activities of the service thereafter until his retirement, 1899. Largely instrumental in effecting the reform of naval purchase procedures and their centralization in a bureau of supplies and accounts, he was appointed paymaster general with rank of commodore, 1890, and retired as rear admiral. He distinguished himself particularly in his handling of navy supply problems during the Spanish-American War.

STEWART, ELIZA DANIEL (*b. Piketon, Ohio, 1816; d. Hicksville, Ohio, 1908*), schoolteacher, temperance advocate. Formed Woman's League in Osborne, Ohio, 1873, the first organization in the Women's Christian Temperance Union movement, and was a leader in the rapid extension of the work.

STEWART, GEORGE NEIL (*b. London, Ontario, Canada, 1860; d. Cleveland, Ohio, 1930*), physiologist. Raised in Scotland. Educated at University of Edinburgh, he received, among other degrees, M.A., 1883; D.Sc., 1887; and M.D., 1891. He also worked at Berlin on electrophysiology and was one of the group of investigators who worked at Cambridge under Sir Michael Foster. Stewart's investigations were chiefly on the velocity of blood flow, on temperature regulation, and on the cardiac nerves. Coming to America in 1893 as an instructor at Harvard, was professor of physiology at Western Reserve University, 1894–1903, and served as head of the Department of Physiology at the University of Chicago, 1903–07. *Post* 1907 he was director of the H. K. Cushing Laboratory of Experimental Medicine at Western Reserve. While in America, Stewart continued his investigations on circulation time and on the electric conductivity of the blood and hemolysis as an approach to the problem of cell permeability. From 1910 to 1915 he devised and applied a calorimetric method of measuring the blood flow suitable for clinical use. In association with J. M. Rogoff, he worked on the epinephrine output of the adrenal glands, 1916–23, and investigated the course of the removal of these glands, 1924–27, establishing the efficiency of extracts of adrenal cortex in clinical use.

STEWART, HUMPHREY JOHN (*b. London, England, 1854; d. San Diego, Calif., 1932*), organist, composer. Settled in San Francisco, Calif., 1886; was organist to a number of churches; served as municipal organist of San Diego *post* 1915.

STEWART, JOHN AIKMAN (*b. New York, N.Y., 1822; d. New York, 1926*), banker. Brother of Edwin Stewart. Planned organization of U.S. Trust Co., N.Y., 1852–53, and served as its president, 1864–1902, thereafter becoming chairman of the board. As senior trustee of Princeton University, he served as president pro tempore of Princeton, 1910–12.

STEWART, JOHN GEORGE (*b. Wilmington, Del., 1890; d. Washington, D.C., 1970*), architect of the U.S. Capitol. Attended University of Delaware (honorary B.S., 1958). Worked in his father's construction firm from 1911, becoming president in 1929; under his supervision the firm restored the original du Pont black powder plant at Hagley, Del., and constructed the museum house for Henry F. du Pont at Winterthur, Del. U.S. congressman (1934–37), then returned to the construction business. Was chief clerk of the Senate Committee on the District of Columbia (1947–51), then was named architect of the Capitol in 1954. Under his direction the new Senate (Dirksen) Office Building (1955–58) and the Rayburn House Office Building (1955–65) were built and the east front of the Capitol was extended (1958–60). The American Institute of Architects issued formal criticisms of his Capitol Hill work and projects, since many American architects had converted to modernism, and Stewart represented the old order of classical and traditional aesthetics.

STEWART, PHILO PENFIELD (*b. Sherman, Conn., 1798; d. Troy, N.Y., 1868*), Congregational missionary, inventor. Cofounder with John J. Shipherd of Oberlin College; received patent for his invention of the "Oberlin stove," 1834, which he deeded to that institution.

STEWART, ROBERT (*b. Sidney, Ohio, 1839; d. Sialkot, Punjab, India, 1915*), United Presbyterian clergyman, missionary to India.

STEWART, ROBERT MARCELLUS (*b. Truxton, N.Y., 1815; d. St. Joseph, Mo., 1871*), lawyer, Missouri legislator and railroad promoter. Anti-Benton Democrat governor of Missouri, 1857–61. Taking a middle ground on the secession issue at first, Stewart upheld the Crittenden Compromise, but later took a strong stand for the Union.

STEWART, WALTER WINNE (*b. Manhattan, Kans., 1885; d. New York, N.Y., 1958*), economist. Studied at the University of Missouri and taught there from 1913 to 1916, and at Amherst College from 1916 to 1922. Stewart was appointed director of the Division of Analysis and Research of the Federal Reserve Board in 1922; he served until 1926, when he joined the investment house of Case, Pomeroy and Company in New York. He was the first economic advisor to the Bank of England, 1928–30. From 1930 to 1938, he was chairman of the board of Case, Pomeroy and Company, and from 1938, he was professor of economics at the Institute for Advanced Study in Princeton, N.J. From 1953 to 1955, he served on President Eisenhower's Council of Economic Advisors.

STEWART, WILLIAM MORRIS (*b. Galen, N.Y., 1827; d. 1909*), lawyer. Raised in Ohio, he attended Yale College, 1848–50. Removing to California, 1850, he engaged in mining, studied law, and was admitted to practice, 1852. Author of the first rules and regulations for quartz mining in Nevada Co., 1853, he entered a law-partnership in San Francisco, 1854, with Henry S. Foote, whose daughter he married. Removing to Nevada, 1859, he came to the fore through his energy and knowledge of mining law; successful as counsel for the original claimants to the Comstock Lode, he was thereafter retained by some of the largest mining companies in the West. Chairman of the judiciary committee of the Nevada constitutional convention, he served as U.S. senator, Republican, from Nevada, 1864–75. Instrumental in

securing passage of the mining laws of 1866 and 1872. He advocated President Andrew Johnson's impeachment and voted for his conviction, and in 1869 was author of the 15th Amendment to the Constitution in the form in which it was finally adopted. Reelected to the U.S. Senate, 1887, he served continuously until 1905. Perhaps the first member of either House of Congress to propose federal aid for reclamation of arid lands in the West, but he directed his efforts mainly toward the remonetization of silver. His successful campaigns in 1893 and 1899 were conducted as a member of the Silver party. As senior counsel for the Roman Catholic prelates of California, he presented one of the winning arguments before the Hague Court in the controversy with Mexico over the Pious Fund, 1902. A lifelong friend and adviser of Leland Stanford, he was one of the first trustees of Stanford University.

STEWART, WILLIAM RHINELANDER (*b. New York, N.Y., 1852; d. New York, 1929*), capitalist, philanthropist. Appointed a commissioner of the New York State Board of Charities, 1882, he served the board as president, 1894–1903 and 1907–23. He organized the New York State Conference of Charities and Corrections, 1900, and a like New York City conference, 1910. He engaged also in many personal philanthropies and much civic work.

STICKNEY, ALPHEUS BEEDE (*b. Wilton, Maine, 1840; d. St. Paul, Minn., 1916*), lawyer, railroad builder. Removed to Minnesota, 1862; settled in St. Paul, 1869. Associated with a number of railroads as counsel and manager, he is remembered particularly for his connection with the Chicago Great Western and its antecedent lines. His original ideas on railroad finance and operation were set forth in his book *The Railway Problem* (1891).

STIEGEL, HENRY WILLIAM (*b. near Cologne, Germany, 1729; d. Charming Forge, near Womelsdorf, Pa., 1785*), ironmaster, glassmaker, known as "Baron" von Stiegel. Immigrated to Philadelphia, Pa., 1750; settled near Brickerville, Lancaster Co., Pa., ca. 1752. Acquired an iron manufactory, 1758, which he expanded and named Elizabeth Furnace; there he made all sorts of iron castings, including stoves, soap kettles, and sugar-making equipment and became by 1760 one of the most prosperous ironmasters in the country. In 1762 he laid out and promoted the town of Manheim, Lancaster Co.; there, early in 1764, he began building a glass factory, which by 1767 was in full operation and which was supplemented in 1769 by a second factory. The works produced, in addition to window and sheet glass, the beautiful Stiegel glassware now eagerly sought by collectors. A spendthrift and overambitious in business ventures, Stiegel began to suffer hard times in 1772 and by 1774 was obliged to sell his properties, becoming a bankrupt.

STIEGLITZ, ALFRED (*b. Hoboken, N.J., 1864; d. New York, N.Y., 1946*), photographer, art gallery proprietor, art patron. Son of German Jewish immigrant parents; brother of Julius Stieglitz. Raised in New York City. His father took the family to Germany in 1881. Alfred first enrolled at the Karlsruhe Realgymnasium and then, in 1882, entered the Technische Hochschule in Berlin as a student of mechanical engineering, but was diverted from this subject by a course he had elected in photochemistry taught by Hermann Wilhelm Vogel. Thereafter, Stieglitz gave most of his attention to photochemistry and photography, continuing his studies from 1887 to 1890 at the University of Berlin.

When Stieglitz returned to New York after eight years of study and travel in Europe, his father supported him in the photoengraving business, which he operated for five years without any great enthusiasm. Because Stieglitz had few customers, he was able to spend much of his time taking and exhibiting photographs. In the 1890's he became a frequent exhibitor in American and international photographic exhibitions and the editor of two influential journals, the *American Amateur Photographer*, 1893–96, and *Camera Notes*, 1897–1902, the organ of the Camera Club of New York.

Growing dissatisfied with the conservative policies of the Camera Club of New York, Stieglitz organized, in 1902, the Photo-Secession, a group of photographers who were sympathetic to his advanced ideas about creative "pictorial photography." To serve the ideals of the Photo-Secession, he established a quarterly magazine, *Camera Work*, which he issued from 1903 to 1917. From 1903 to 1905 he used *Camera Work* as his primary medium to promote the Photo-Secession. In 1905, however, he and his friend Edward Steichen discussed the prospect of converting the top floor of 291 Fifth Avenue, New York City, into a gallery for the Photo-Secession group. They agreed to work together on this project, and with Stieglitz' financial backing, Steichen redecorated three rooms to form the Little Galleries of the Photo-Secession, usually known simply as "291." The galleries opened in November 1905, with a show of photographs, and for more than a year the rooms were dedicated exclusively to the art of photography. But early in 1907 Stieglitz staged the first in a series of exhibitions of paintings, drawings, and sculptures; nonphotographic art gradually overshadowed photographic exhibitions, and in a year, 291 had become the most advanced center for the fine arts in America. Stieglitz here presented the first American exhibitions of such noted modern European artists as Matisse, 1908; Henri Rousseau, 1910; Cézanne, 1911; Picasso, 1911; Picabia, 1913; and Brancusi, 1914. It is safe to say that American painting would not have developed as it did without the exhibitions at 291. In his work as a gallery director lies much of Stieglitz' historical importance.

Stieglitz established himself quite early in his career as a vocal philosopher of art. Believing generally in progressive causes, he was antiacademic and antidescriptive in his views. By 1917, after 14 years of intense activity, he seemed to have exhausted himself. He closed the gallery in that year, and no further issues of *Camera Work* were published. His association with Georgia O'Keeffe, beginning in 1916, helped to renew his creative life. This talented painter, whom he married on Dec. 11, 1924, served as a model for a series of superb photographic portraits. Although Stieglitz closed 291 in 1917, his battle for modern art was not over. He continued to sell paintings and promote his circle of artists at the Intimate Gallery, 1924–29, and at An American Place, 1929–46.

STIEGLITZ, JULIUS (*b. Hoboken, N.J., 1867; d. Chicago, Ill., 1937*), chemist. Brother of the photographer Alfred Stieglitz. Ph.D., University of Berlin, 1889. A teacher of chemistry at University of Chicago *post* 1892 and chairman of the department, 1915–33, Stieglitz made important researches in four major fields of organic chemistry: molecular rearrangements, homogeneous catalysis, the theory of indicators, and stereochemistry in organonitrogen compounds. He is considered one of the founders of physicoorganic chemistry and was author of the important *The Elements of Qualitative Chemical Analysis* (1911). He played an important role in overcoming the lack of synthetics from Germany during World War I and served later as an adviser to the Chemical Foundation.

STIGLER, WILLIAM GRADY (*b. Newton, Indian Territory [now Oklahoma], 1891 d. Stigler, Okla., 1952*), congressman. Studied at Northeastern State College and the University of Oklahoma. Admitted to the bar in 1920; further study at the University of Grenoble, France, while serving with the U.S. Army during World War I. Part Choctaw Indian, Stigler was the national attorney for the tribe (1937–44). Elected to the Congress as a Democrat (1944–52). Served on the House Appropriations Committee and the Agricultural Appropriations Subcommittee; a champion of the rights of the American Indians.

STILES, CHARLES WARDELL (*b. Spring Valley, N.Y., 1867; d. Baltimore, Md., 1941*), medical zoologist, public health expert. Attended Wesleyan University, 1885–86; decided to continue his studies in Europe. After a few months in Paris and Göttingen, Stiles studied for two years at the University of Berlin. He then moved to the University of Leipzig to concentrate on zoology with Rudolph Leuckart. He received his Ph.D. degree in 1890. After an additional year spent at Robert Koch's laboratory in Berlin, at the Austrian Zoological Station in Trieste, at the Collège de France, and at the Pasteur Institute, Stiles returned to the United States in 1891 to begin work in Washington as principal zoologist in the Bureau of Animal Industry of the Department of Agriculture. In 1895 he was chosen a member of the five-man International Commission on Zoological Nomenclature, of which he subsequently served as secretary, 1898–1936.

At the Bureau of Animal Industry he investigated livestock disease caused by filth-ridden slaughterhouses in country towns. Stiles also became the focal point of the bureau's concern with trichinosis in pork. In 1900 and 1901, at the request of Representative Rudolph Kleberg, he went to Texas to investigate losses of cattle, sheep, and goats owing to parasitic worms. In 1902 Stiles transferred to the Hygienic Laboratory of the U.S. Public Health and Marine Hospital Service, where for the next 30 years he was chief of the division of zoology. He was also professor of medical zoology at Georgetown University from 1892 to 1906 and special lecturer in the subject at the Johns Hopkins University, 1897–1937.

Stiles's most dramatic and far-reaching contributions to public health were in connection with hookworm disease. In 1902 he discovered a variety of hookworm indigenous to the western hemisphere which he named *Uncinaria americana*, or *Necator americana*. In 1908 and 1909, as an expert on President Roosevelt's Country Life Commission, he was able to interest Walter Hines Page, Wallace Buttrick, and Frederick T. Gates in the problem of hookworm disease in the South. The result was the formation in 1909 of the Rockefeller Sanitary Commission, which conducted an extensive and highly successful campaign against hookworm disease through rural sanitation and education.

Stiles also investigated the health of cotton mill workers, mine sanitation, and other public health problems. Following World War I he directed experiments on soil pollution, which demonstrated how fecal matter and bacteria were spread by groundwater. An even larger project was his publication, with Albert Hassall, of the *Index-Catalog of Medical and Veterinary Zoology*. Their preparation of the first four volumes (1902–20) of this work, together with a series of supplemental *Key Catalogs* (of insects, parasites, protozoa, crustacea, and arachnoids), was a continuing task from the 1890's until the mid-1930's. After his formal retirement in October 1931, he continued some helminthological work at the Smithsonian Institution and taught zoology at Rollins College in Florida for several winters.

STILES, EZRA (*b. North Haven, Conn., 1727 o.s.; d. New Haven, Conn., 1795*), Congregational clergyman, scholar, educator. Graduated Yale, 1746. After further study of theology, he was licensed to preach, 1749, and in the same year appointed tutor at Yale. During his six years in this position he became noted as a public orator; he also engaged in electrical experimentation at the instance of his friend and correspondent Benjamin Franklin. Troubled in mind for some years as to the truth of Christian dogma, he made a long, patient study of the Bible and of Christian evidences before accepting ordination and installation as pastor of the Second Church of Newport, R.I., 1755. Extremely conscientious in his ministerial duties, he maintained a number of outside activities and a voluminous correspondence with outstanding people at home and abroad. Librarian of the Redwood Library, Newport, 1756–76, he was an ardent antiquarian, a very competent orientalist, and a scientific experimenter. Recognized as probably the most learned man in New England, he was made a member of the American Philosophical Society, 1768; meanwhile, in 1763, he had played an important part in the founding of Rhode Island College (present Brown University). He was a strong advocate of American rights and liberties and a supporter of the Revolution. Removing from Newport in March 1776, he lived in several towns before he accepted the offered presidency of Yale College, March 1778. Stiles carried Yale through a difficult period with reasonable success, teaching Hebrew, ecclesiastical history, philosophy, scientific subjects, and, for a time, theology, in addition to doing his administrative work. The most notable event of his administration was a change in the college charter whereby several of the state officials were made members of the corporation ex officio and certain financial aid from the state was secured. Although Stiles wrote much, he published very little. His manuscripts, edited by Franklin B. Dexter, have yielded two posthumous works of historical importance: *The Literary Diary of Ezra Stiles* (1901) and *Extracts from the Itineraries . . . of Ezra Stiles* (1916).

STILES, HENRY REED (*b. New York, N.Y., 1832; d. 1909*), physician, genealogist, local historian. Among his valuable studies of the history of early New England and New York were *The History of Ancient Windsor, Connecticut* (1859) and *A History of the City of Brooklyn* (1867–70). Intermittent in his practice of medicine, he conducted a sanitorium at Lake George, N.Y., *post* 1888.

STILL, ANDREW TAYLOR (*b. Jonesville, Va., 1828; d. Kirksville, Mo., 1917*), farmer, Union soldier, founder of osteopathy. Raised in Missouri, he resided in Kansas, 1853–75, where he entered on the practice of medicine and worked out his theory that "all the remedies necessary to health exist in the human body . . . they can be administered by adjusting the body in such condition that the remedies may naturally associate themselves together . . . and relieve the afflicted." Returning to Missouri, 1875, he settled at Kirksville, Mo., in 1892. In that year he incorporated the American School of Osteopathy, thereafter teaching at the school, writing, and practicing.

STILL, WILLIAM (*b. Burlington Co., N.J., 1821; d. Philadelphia, Pa., 1902*), black leader, reformer. Settling in Philadelphia, 1844, he became a clerk of the Pennsylvania Society for the Abolition of Slavery, 1847, remaining in that post until *ca.* 1861 when he went into business. Very active in the work of assisting runaway slaves to freedom, he was author of *The Underground Railroad* (1872), one of the best accounts available of that operation. Until the end of his life Still continued active in promoting the welfare of his race through legislation and charitable activity, displaying courage and independence.

STILLÉ, ALFRED (*b. Philadelphia, Pa., 1813; d. Philadelphia, 1900*), physician. Brother of Charles J. Stillé. M.D., University of Pennsylvania, 1836; studied also in Europe principally in Paris, France. Professor of the theory and practice of medicine, University of Pennsylvania, 1864–83, he received numerous professional honors. Author of *Elements of General Pathology* (1848), the first American book on the subject; he was also coauthor with John M. Maisch of the *National Dispensatory* (1879).

STILLÉ, CHARLES JANEWAY (*b. Philadelphia, Pa., 1819; d. Atlantic City, N.J., 1899*), educator, historian. Brother of Alfred Stillé. Graduated Yale, 1839. Outstanding worker for the U.S. Sanitary Commission during the Civil War. Accepted appointment in 1866 as professor of English in the University of Pennsylvania. As provost of the university, 1868–80, he showed unusual qualities as an educational leader and executive, arousing com-

munity interest in the university and opening new departments—among them, science, 1872; music, 1877; and dentistry, 1878. Removal of the university to its present site was accomplished by Stillé, and he secured a considerable extension of its endowment. Among his numerous books, *The Life and Times of John Dickinson* (1891) may be mentioned.

STILLMAN, JAMES (*b. Brownsville, Tex., 1850; d. New York, N.Y., 1918*), banker, capitalist. Raised in Connecticut and in New York City. A protégé of Moses Taylor, Stillman prospered first as a cotton trader, expanding his interests gradually into other industries. Named president of the National City Bank, 1891, he held that office until 1909 and was thereafter chairman of the board. Under his management the bank took a foremost place in serving the great industrial and financial combines that flourished at the end of the 19th century and in the first decade of the 20th; it had close contacts with the Standard Oil financiers headed by H. H. Rogers and William Rockefeller.

STILLMAN, SAMUEL (*b. Philadelphia, Pa., 1737 o.s.; d. Boston, Mass., 1807*), Baptist clergyman. Held principal pastorate at First Baptist Church, Boston, 1765–1807; was named among original trustees of Rhode Island College (present Brown University), 1764. Active and influential in the affairs of his denomination, he was noted as a preacher. His election sermon before the General Court, 1779, contained an interesting argument for the necessity of inserting a bill of rights in the constitution of Massachusetts and for separation of church and state.

STILLMAN, THOMAS BLISS (*b. Plainfield, N.J., 1852; d. 1915*), chemist, expert in water- and milk-supply problems. B.S., Rutgers, 1873; studied also in Germany. Noted as a consultant for industry, he also taught at Stevens Institute of Technology, where he was professor of analytical chemistry, 1886–1902, and head of the chemistry department, 1902–09. Author of *Engineering Chemistry* (1897) and of a number of articles in scientific journals. He held many patents for manufacturing processes and experimented in production of synthetic foods.

STILLMAN, THOMAS EDGAR (*b. New York, N.Y., 1837; d. France, 1906*), lawyer, specialist in admiralty and corporation law. Helped establish new principles of American maritime law in cases of the *Scotland*, the *Pennsylvania*, and the *Atlas*; in later years devoted much time to corporation management.

STILLMAN, WILLIAM JAMES (*b. Schenectady, N.Y., 1828; d. Surrey, England, 1901*), landscape painter, journalist, diplomat. A close friend of the celebrated English critic John Ruskin, Stillman had a varied career which included service as U.S. consul at Rome, 1862–65, and in Crete, 1865–68. Settling in London, England, he was employed for many years as a London *Times* special correspondent.

STILWELL, JOSEPH (*b. Palatka, Fla., 1883; d. San Francisco, Calif., 1946*), army officer. Raised in Yonkers, N.Y. Graduated West Point, 1904. Served for two years with 12th Infantry in the Philippines. Save for later regimental duty there and in Monterey, Calif., 1911–13, he spent the rest of the decade before World War 1 at West Point as an instructor. Upon promotion to captain, 1916, Stilwell joined the American Expeditionary Forces in France in December 1917. He played a major role in organizing G-2 operations for the American offensive at Saint-Mihiel, winning the Distinguished Service Medal and promotion to the temporary rank of colonel. His first postwar assignment was as the army's first language officer in China. The duty took him to Peking, 1920–23, where he learned to speak Chinese. After attending the army's Infantry and Command and General Staff schools, at Fort Benning and Leavenworth, he returned to China, 1926–29, as battalion commander and later executive officer of the 15th

Infantry, an American regiment stationed in Tientsin as a result of the Boxer Rebellion. His third China duty came in 1935–39, when he returned as U.S. military attaché.

From 1929 to 1933 Stilwell served as chief of the tactical section at the Infantry School, Fort Benning, Ga., under the direction of Col. George C. Marshall. At the Infantry School his unsparing and often acid critiques earned him the nickname "Vinegar Joe." In 1939 Marshall picked Stilwell for one of his first two promotions to brigadier general. By the time of Pearl Harbor, he had commanded the 3rd Infantry Brigade in Texas, 1939; the 7th Division in California, 1940; and the III Corps, 1940–41. He had been promoted to major general, September 1940. In February 1942 he was appointed commanding general of U.S. Army forces (at this time only air units) in the China-Burma-India theater, chief of staff to Generalissimo Chiang Kai-shek of China, and supervisor of lend-lease in the area.

Arriving at his new post in early March 1942, Stilwell took up the defense of Burma. When Burma fell to the Japanese, he lead an endangered remnant of 114 men on a 140-mile march across the mountains to India. He encountered further frustration in his subsequent program to train Chinese troops in India. His command status was further complicated in mid-1943 when, besides his other titles, he became deputy supreme Allied commander in Southeast Asia under Britain's Admiral Lord Louis Mountbatten. Yet Stilwell doggedly pressed construction of the Ledo Road (afterward named for him), which eventually linked up with the Burma Road to provide a land supply route from India to China; and in the first seven months of 1944 Stilwell led Chinese troops in the successful battle to retake northern Burma. But Stilwell's most enduring frustration was his long struggle to bring about a reform of the Chinese army, an effort doomed by the resistance of Chiang. Stilwell's persistence and his unconcealed contempt for the generalissimo caused three attempts by Chiang to bring about his recall. Although President Roosevelt sometimes wavered, Marshall, as chief of staff, steadfastly stood by Stilwell.

In 1944, when a renewed Japanese offensive in China made the situation desperate, Roosevelt, persuaded by Marshall, officially requested that Stilwell be appointed to command the Chinese armed forces. This proposal precipitated the final crisis, which culminated in Stilwell's recall in October 1944. His last command was of the 6th Army in charge of the Western Defense Command. Before his death, he was awarded the Combat Infantryman Badge, usually reserved for the enlisted foot soldier who has proved himself under fire. He had previously received the Distinguished Service Cross for action in Burma and the Legion of Merit for high command.

STILWELL, SILAS MOORE (*b. New York, N.Y., 1800; d. New York, 1881*), lawyer, banking reformer. New York legislator. Responsible as an assemblyman for passage of the Stilwell Act, 1831, abolishing imprisonment for debt in New York.

STILWELL, SIMPSON EVERETT (*b. Tennessee, 1849; d. Cody, Wyo., 1903*), army scout, peace officer. Raised in Missouri and Kansas, he became an army scout at Fort Dodge, 1867. While operating out of Fort Wallace with Maj. G. A. Forsyth's company in September 1868, Stilwell eluded a hostile Indian cordon to bring relief when the company was surrounded on the Arikaree Fork of the Republican River by Cheyenne and Sioux under Chief Roman Nose. He continued to serve irregularly as a scout under Custer, Miles, Mackenzie, and other army officers until 1881. He served thereafter as a deputy marshal at various places in Oklahoma.

STIMPSON, WILLIAM (*b. Roxbury, Mass., 1832; d. Ilchester, Md., 1872*), naturalist. Encouraged in his studies by Augustus A. Gould and J. L. R. Agassiz, he served as naturalist to the North

Pacific Exploring Expedition, 1852–56, and spent a number of years thereafter in classifying the material gathered in that time. His collections and works were destroyed in the Chicago fire of October 1871, together with much other scientific material which had been loaned to him for comparative study. He was author of many papers on mollusca and crustacea published mainly by the Smithsonian Institution.

STIMSON, ALEXANDER LOVETT (*b. Boston, Mass., 1816; d. Glens Falls, N.Y., 1906*), expressman. Author of, among other works, *History of the Express Companies: and the Origin of American Railroads* (1858).

STIMSON, FREDERIC JESUP (*b. Dedham, Mass., but possibly New York City or Dubuque, Iowa, 1855; d. Dedham, 1943*), lawyer, diplomat, author. A.B., Harvard, 1876; LL.B., 1878. Practiced in Boston, Mass., specializing in railroad law; was in partnership for a time with Francis C. Lowell and A. Lawrence Lowell. Originally a Republican, he became a mugwump and eventually a Democrat; he was an advocate of justice for the American Indian and for labor, an anti-imperialist, and opposed to governmental interference with individual liberty and property rights. In addition to a number of books on legal subjects, he was author of works of fiction (under pseudonym "J.S. of Dale"), including *Guerndale* (1882) and *King Noanett* (1896).

STIMSON, HENRY LEWIS (*b. New York, N.Y., 1867; d. "Highhold," Huntington, N.Y., 1950*), lawyer, statesman. Son of Lewis A. Stimson. A.B., Yale, 1888. Attended Harvard Law School, 1888–90. In 1891 he entered the law firm of Root and Clarke. Stimson started his exploration of politics in something smaller than a ward, an election district, and in time worked his way up to a seat on the powerful New York County Republican Committee. In 1899 he and Bronson Winthrop started their own partnership. They remained together for the rest of their lives. In 1906 Theodore Roosevelt appointed Stimson U.S. attorney for the Southern District of New York. Insufficiently staffed and badly managed at the time, the office was totally reconstructed by Stimson in the next two years. By his work in the Southern District, which ended in 1909, he gave one of the earliest demonstrations that the power of large corporations could be sensibly controlled by the action of a determined government.

His service as district attorney stirred up his concern over the dislocations produced in the society by the excesses of corporate enterprise. In 1910 he was persuaded to run for governor, in the hope that he might be able to put some of his ideas in effect from Albany. In the election, running behind most of his ticket, he was soundly defeated. In the following year, President William Howard Taft appointed him secretary of war. For two years thereafter he struggled to make a modern army out of a force that still was preparing itself. First, he obtained a "tactical reorganization" of the troop units. He also resolved the ancient immobilizing conflict between the staff and line. He left the War Department in 1913, but he returned to the army in 1914, to take an active part in the effort to prepare the country for the conflict. A persistent advocate of universal military service, he applied for active duty in 1917. That same year, he went to France as a lieutenant colonel in the field artillery to fight along the Chemin des Dames in Lorraine. In 1927, Stimson was sent to Nicaragua by President Calvin Coolidge. In a month of negotiation, he arranged a peace between two factions that were at civil war, but the day after he left the country, fighting broke out and continued for half a decade. In the next year, Coolidge sent Stimson to the Philippines as governor general. There, amid a population that was earnestly seeking independence, he sought to stabilize the precarious economy and restore the confidence of the people. But on his departure, agitation for independence began again, and in a few more years the great aim was actually achieved.

Stimson came home in 1929 to become secretary of state in President Herbert Hoover's cabinet. In each month of his tenure, it seemed, matters went from bad to worse. There was first the worldwide economic depression, and as the principal creditor, the United States had a considerable role to play. But nothing that was done by either Stimson or Hoover served to bring more than temporary relief; conditions steadily deteriorated. Then there was the effort to reduce tensions between nations by readjusting the structure of international armaments. At the London Naval Conference of 1930, Stimson was the principal negotiator for the United States; as such, he can be given much credit for the resulting agreement, which seemed on paper to eliminate "further naval competition" among the chief signatories. There was also the problem of how to get the Japanese out of Manchuria, which they had entered on Sept. 18, 1931; but the Japanese remained there, unresponsive alike to Stimson's structures and a later condemnatory finding by the League of Nations.

In 1933 Stimson returned to private life. When in 1939 World War II came, he spoke out increasingly for the support by all moral and material means of those nations opposing Germany and Italy. In June 1940 he was appointed the secretary of war by President Franklin Roosevelt. For the next five years he devoted himself to the discharge of the affairs of this office. In his first 15 months in office he surrounded himself with able, energetic, purposeful men and established a harmony of civil and military interests within the War Department that was without parallel in the direction of an American armed force in time of war.

The decisions that interested Stimson most had to do with military matters. In the first year of the war he tried to use radar-equipped army planes to assist in the fight against the German submarines. In this effort he was thwarted by the resistance of the navy. Stimson also did everything he could to convince Roosevelt and Churchill of an early landing in Europe from British bases. His objective was postponed by the landings in North Africa, but fulfilled in June 1944. Late in the war much of his time was taken up with the activities surrounding the development and manufacture of the atom bomb.

In those closing months of the war he searched increasingly for postwar settlements that would give some promise of extended peace, and in 1945 urged that the United States, England, and Russia share the secret of the atom so that they could act with a common sense of power and responsibility to stabilize by mutual action the postwar world. Soon after the coming of the peace, on Sept. 21, 1945, his seventy-eighth birthday, he retired.

STIMSON, JULIA CATHERINE (*b. Worcester, Mass., 1881; d. Poughkeepsie, N.Y., 1948*), leader in nursing. Niece of Lewis A. Stimson. B.A., Vassar, 1901. Graduated New York Hospital Training School for Nurses, 1908. Superintendent of nurses, Harlem Hospital, New York City, 1908–11; director of social service at hospitals of Washington University Medical School, St. Louis, Mo., 1911–13; directed training school for nurses at Washington University, 1913–17. Active also in Red Cross work, she served in France at No. 12 General Hospital, near Rouen, 1917–18, and at Paris, where, as World War I ended, she was appointed director of the Nursing Service of the American Expeditionary Forces. On her return to the United States, 1919, she served as dean of the Army School of Nursing until 1933 and as superintendent of the Army Nurse Corps until 1937. Chairman of the Nursing Council on National Defense, 1940–42, she returned to active army duty in 1942–43 as a recruiter of nurses. After full commissioned rank was authorized for nurses, she was promoted colonel on the retired list.

STIMSON, LEWIS ATTERBURY (*b. Paterson, N.J., 1844; d. Shinnecock Hills, N.Y., 1917*), surgeon. Graduated Yale, 1863; M.D., Bellevue Hospital Medical School, 1874. Practiced in New York City. Taught at medical college of the University of the City of New York (present New York University), 1883–98. Instrumental in founding Cornell University Medical College, he was professor of surgery there, 1898–1917. Author of *A Practical Treatise on Fractures and Dislocations* (1899), a classic in the subject, and other works.

STINE, CHARLES MILTON ATLAND (*b. Norwich, Conn., 1882; d. Wilmington, Del., 1954*), industrial chemist. Studied at Gettysburg College and Johns Hopkins University (Ph.D., 1907). Worked for E.I. du Pont de Nemours and Co. (1907–45); chemical director from 1924; member of the board of directors and vice president from 1930. One of the first organic chemists employed in American industry, Stine convinced the Du Ponts of the necessity of pursuing basic research in industry. He helped develop the first commercial TNT in the U.S., did extensive work in explosives and dyes, and directed the research that led to the discovery of nylon. Stine was the first du Pont official concerned with the atomic energy project, which was the company's largest single undertaking of World War II.

STINESS, JOHN HENRY (*b. Providence, R.I., 1840; d. 1913*), lawyer. Union soldier, expert in canon law. Judge, Rhode Island Supreme Court, 1875–1904, serving for four years as chief justice.

STIRLING, LORD WILLIAM. *See* ALEXANDER, WILLIAM.

STITH, WILLIAM (*b. Charles City Co., Va., 1707; d. Williamsburg, Va., 1755*), Anglican clergyman, educator, historian. B.A., Queen's College, Oxford, 1727/8. Appointed master of the grammar school at William and Mary, 1731, he served also as chaplain to the House of Burgesses. Rector of Henrico Parish, Henrico Co., 1736–1751/2, he was qualified as president of the College of William and Mary on Aug. 14, 1752, and served in that post uneventfully until his death. He is principally remembered for his *History of the First Discovery and Settlement of Virginia* (1747), the earliest important secondary account of the colony and one which has influenced most subsequent interpretations of the history of Virginia under the London Co.

STITT, EDWARD RHODES (*b. Charlotte, N.C., 1867; d. Bethesda, Md., 1948*), navy surgeon, educator. B.A., University of South Carolina, 1885. M.D.; University of Pennsylvania, 1889. Commissioned assistant surgeon, U.S. Navy Medical Corps, he spent much of 1890 serving in the eastern Atlantic and the Mediterranean. His interest in diseases of the tropics led to his selection as a medical member of the commissions formed to recommend possible routes for a canal across the isthmus of Central America.

In his first 20 years in the navy, Stitt spent all his available free time acquiring as much information as possible about tropical medicine and bacteriology. In 1902 he was appointed head of the departments of bacteriology, chemistry, and tropical medicine at the Navy Medical School, Washington, D.C. For the next 18 years, with the exception of two duty tours in the Philippines, he remained at the school. During this time he wrote two major books: *Practical Bacteriology, Hematology, and Animal Parasitology* (1908) and *Diagnostics and Treatment of Tropical Diseases* (1914). After 1916 he was made commanding officer of the Navy Medical School, and for his service in that capacity during World War I he won the Navy Cross. In 1917 he was promoted to the rank of rear admiral. In 1928 Stitt became inspector general of medical activities, West Coast, a position he held for the next two and a half years. Finally, on Aug. 1, 1931, he was obliged to retire from active duty.

STOBO, ROBERT (*b. Glasgow, Scotland, 1727; d. place unknown, ca. 1772*), soldier. Immigrated as a young man to Virginia. As a merchant, enjoyed patronage of Governor Dinwiddie. A captain in the Virginia militia, he was with George Washington at Fort Necessity, 1754, and was made a hostage. Escaping from prison in Quebec, he reached the British forces at Louisburg in the spring of 1759 and served ably in the expedition against Quebec. Commissioned captain in the 15th Regiment of Foot, he was in service until about 1770, at which time his name disappeared from the Army List. The *Memoirs of Major Robert Stobo* appeared posthumously in London (1800).

STOCK, FREDERICK AUGUST (*b. Jülich, near Cologne, Germany, 1872; d. Chicago, Ill., 1942*), orchestra conductor. A protégé of Theodore Thomas, he joined the Chicago Symphony Orchestra as a viola player, 1895. Succeeding Thomas as conductor, 1905, except for August 1918 to February 1919, he served until his death. Through special programs, children's concerts, and encouragement of musical education in the public schools, he made the orchestra an integral part of the community; it dominated the musical life of the Midwest by its brilliant performances and a repertory more catholic and extensive than that of any other American orchestra of his day.

STOCKARD, CHARLES RUPERT (*b. Stoneville, Miss., 1879; d. 1939*), biologist, anatomist. Graduated Mississippi A. & M. College, 1899, 1901; Ph.D., Columbia, 1907. A teacher at Cornell University Medical College *post* 1907, he became professor in 1911 and head of the anatomical laboratories. A lifelong student of the relative effects of environmental and hereditary factors upon the development of animals, Stockard was a codiscoverer of the method of timing the reproductive cycle of the female which later led to discovery of the ovarian hormones. Managing editor, *American Journal of Anatomy*, 1921–38, he served as president of the board of scientific directors of the Rockefeller Institute for Medical Research, 1935–39.

STOCKBRIDGE, HENRY (*b. Baltimore, Md., 1856; d. 1924*), jurist. Son of Henry S. Stockbridge; nephew of Levi Stockbridge. Prominent in Baltimore civic and legal affairs, he served as a judge of the supreme bench of Baltimore, 1896–1911, and as a judge of the Maryland Court of Appeals, 1911–23.

STOCKBRIDGE, HENRY SMITH (*b. North Hadley, Mass., 1822; d. Baltimore, Md., 1895*), lawyer, Maryland legislator. Brother of Levi Stockbridge; father of Henry Stockbridge. Originally a Whig, he early became a Republican and was a strong Unionist during the Civil War. A leader in the constitutional reform which abolished slavery in Maryland, he was active in support of black rights.

STOCKBRIDGE, HORACE EDWARD (*b. Hadley, Mass., 1857; d. Atlanta, Ga., 1930*), agricultural chemist and editor, educator. Son of Levi Stockbridge. Graduated Massachusetts Agricultural College, 1878; Ph.D., Göttingen, 1884. Taught at Massachusetts Agricultural College and in Japan; president of North Dakota Agricultural College, 1890–94. Associated with Florida Agricultural College, 1897–1902, he was editor of the *Southern Ruralist* and the *Southern Farm and Dairy*.

STOCKBRIDGE, LEVI (*b. Hadley, Mass., 1820; d. Amherst, Mass., 1904*), agriculturist, educator. Father of Horace E. Stockbridge; brother of Henry S. Stockbridge. Mainly self-educated and a pioneer in agricultural experiment, he served at various times in the Massachusetts legislature and was a member of the state board of agriculture. A shaper of the curriculum at

Massachusetts Agricultural College *post* 1867, he served there as professor of agriculture, 1869–80, and was president of the college, 1880–82. His investigations dealt primarily with plant feeding, and he published the first formulas for fertilizers for specific crops.

STOCKDALE, THOMAS RINGLAND (*b. Greene Co., Pa., 1828; d. Summit, Miss., 1899*), lawyer, Confederate soldier. Removed to Mississippi, 1856. As congressman, Democrat, from Mississippi, 1887–95, he employed a unique argument against tariffs, pointing out that much of the burden of protection fell upon blacks in agricultural work.

STÖCKHARDT, KARL GEORG (*b. Chemnitz, Saxony, 1842; d. St. Louis, Mo., 1913*), Lutheran clergyman. Disapproving of the state church in Saxony, Stöckhardt immigrated to St. Louis, Mo., where he served as pastor, 1879–1913, and as a professor in Concordia Theological Seminary. He had a strong influence on the teaching and preaching of the Missouri Synod.

STOCKTON, CHARLES G. (*b. Madison, Ohio, 1853; d. Buffalo, N.Y., 1931*), physician, specialist in internal medicine. M.D., University of Buffalo, 1878. Successful as a practitioner and consultant in Buffalo and as a professor *post* 1887 at his alma mater.

STOCKTON, CHARLES HERBERT (*b. Philadelphia, Pa., 1845; d. Washington, D.C., 1924*), naval officer. Graduated U.S. Naval Academy, 1865. A specialist in international law, Stockton retired as rear admiral, 1907, after long and varied service. First delegate at the Declaration of London Conference, 1908–09; served without salary as president of George Washington University, 1910–18.

STOCKTON, FRANK RICHARD (*b. Philadelphia, Pa., 1834; d. Washington, D.C., 1902*), author. Trained as a wood engraver. Stockton contributed to the *Riverside Magazine for Young People* the stories which were collected as *Ting-a-Ling Tales* in 1870; he was thereafter employed mainly as an editor and writer. Assistant editor of *St. Nicholas Magazine*, 1873–81, he was at the same time a frequent contributor to *Scribner's Monthly* and the *Century*. The popular success of *Rudder Grange* (1879) encouraged him to live entirely by his writing. Stockton's many novels and stories were worked out of a vein of absurd invention which he had discovered that he possessed and which the public liked. However circumstantial he might be in his stories, his imagination dealt with a world of cheerful impossibility, and his tales are in effect loose-knit comic operettas. Among them may be mentioned *The Casting Away of Mrs. Lecks and Mrs. Aleshine* (1886), *The Dusantes* (1888), *The Adventures of Captain Horn* (1895), and such classic short stories as "The Lady or the Tiger?" (first appearance, *Century Magazine*, November 1882) and "The Transferred Ghost" (1882). In addition to his fiction, Stockton was author of several volumes of local history, including *Buccaneers and Pirates of Our Coasts* (1898).

STOCKTON, JOHN POTTER (*b. Princeton, N.J., 1826; d. 1900*), lawyer, New Jersey politician and official. Son of Robert F. Stockton. Elected U.S. senator, Democrat, from New Jersey, March 1865, he became the center of a famous controversy over his right to be seated, which terminated adversely for him a year later. Elected to the U.S. Senate again, 1869, he served through 1875 and was New Jersey attorney general, 1877–97.

STOCKTON, RICHARD (*b. Princeton, N.J., 1730; d. Princeton, 1781*), lawyer, New Jersey provincial legislator, Revolutionary patriot. Father of Richard Stockton (1764–1828). Graduated College of New Jersey (Princeton), 1748; studied law under David Ogden. Successful in practice, he served as a provincial councillor, 1768–75, and was regarded as a moderate in his opposition to crown policy. Elected to the Continental Congress, June 1776, he heard the closing debate on the Declaration of Independence, of which he was a signer; he also served on several important congressional committees in the summer and fall of 1776. Betrayed to the British by Loyalists late in the year, he was imprisoned at Perth Amboy and New York. In shattered health on his release, he returned to find his estate, "Morven," pillaged. He remained an invalid until his death.

Stockton, Richard (*b. near Princeton, N.J., 1764; d. near Princeton, 1828*), lawyer, farmer, politician. Son of Richard Stockton (1730–81). U.S. senator, Federalist, from New Jersey, 1796–99; congressman, Federalist, 1813–15. Conspicuous in opposition to the War of 1812. He approved highly of the U.S. Constitution, but felt that it had not been improved by a single one of its amendments. He was the father of Robert F. Stockton.

Stockton, Robert Field (*b. Princeton, N.J., 1795; d. 1866*), naval officer. Son of Richard Stockton (1764–1828). Appointed midshipman, 1811, he served with credit under Commodore John Rodgers in the War of 1812; he also distinguished himself later in the war with Algiers and on duty in the Mediterranean, 1816–20. After further duty in suppressing slave traders and pirates, he engaged in private business while on furlough, 1828–38. Promoted captain, 1838, and returning to active service, he interested himself in application of steam power in the U.S. Navy and was commander of the USS *Princeton*, 1843–45.

As war with Mexico was imminent, he was ordered to proceed in USS *Congress* to the Pacific and reinforce the U.S. squadron there. When he arrived at Monterey, Calif., July 1846, war had already begun. Relieving Commodore J. D. Sloat on July 23, he began military operations for the seizure of California. Entering Los Angeles in August, he issued a proclamation declaring California a territory of the United States and organized a civil and military government, assuming for himself the title of governor and commander in chief. Forced to abandon further ambitious plans because of the recapture of Los Angeles by the Mexicans, he joined with the forces of General S. W. Kearny early in January 1847, repossessed Los Angeles and ended the war on California soil. Superseded soon thereafter, he resigned from the navy, May 1850. As U.S. senator, Democrat, from New Jersey, 1851–53, he urged several naval reforms, including the abolition of flogging.

Stockton, Thomas Hewlings (*b. Mt. Holly, N.J., 1808; d. Philadelphia, Pa., 1868*), Methodist clergyman, notable pulpit orator.

Stockwell, John Nelson (*b. Northampton, Mass., 1832; d. 1920*), mathematical astronomer. Raised in Ohio, Stockwell was mainly self-educated and came to notice first as editor of an almanac. Employed as a computer with the U.S. Coast Survey and the U.S. Naval Observatory; taught at Case School of Applied Science, 1881–88. His chief contributions, made over a period of 70 years, dealt with the theory of the moon's motion and with the computation of eclipses.

Stoddard, Amos (*b. Woodbury, Conn., 1762; d. near present Maumee, Ohio, 1813*), lawyer, soldier. An artilleryman in the Revolution, Stoddard returned to the U.S. Army in 1798 after practicing law and service as a Massachusetts official and legislator. Commissioned captain in the 2nd Artillery, 1798, he was promoted major, 1807, and died during the siege of Fort Meigs. Meanwhile, he had served as first civil and military commandant of Upper Louisiana, 1804, receiving the cession of that territory early in March and acting as governor until the end of September. He was author of *Sketches, Historical and Descriptive, of Louisiana* (1812).

Stoddard, Charles Warren (*b. Rochester, N.Y., 1843; d. 1909*), author. Removed to San Francisco, Calif., 1855; published verses in the *Golden Era*, 1861–63, which were collected in *Poems* (Bret Harte, ed., 1867). Converted to Catholicism, 1867, he traveled widely during the succeeding 20 years and was for a short time secretary to Mark Twain in London. After teaching English for a time at Notre Dame and Catholic universities, he lived in Monterey, Calif., *post* 1906. As a writer he is remembered chiefly for *South-Sea Idyls* (1873).

Stoddard, David Tappan (*b. Northampton, Mass., 1818; d. Seir, Persia, 1857*), Congregational clergyman. Nephew of Arthur and Lewis Tappan. Missionary among the Nestorians in Persia, 1843–48 and 1851–57.

Stoddard, Elizabeth Drew Barstow (*b. Mattapoisett, Mass., 1823; d. New York, N.Y., 1902*), novelist, poet. Married Richard H. Stoddard, 1851. Encouraged by her husband, she became a contributor to periodical publications of her day. She wrote fiction praised for its realism by Nathaniel Hawthorne and others, although she lacked skill in plotting and her work showed a morbid strain. Among her books were *The Morgesons* (1862), *Two Men* (1865), and *Temple House* (1867).

Stoddard, John Fair (*b. Greenfield, N.Y., 1825; d. Kearny, N.J., 1873*), educator, mathematician, author of a number of superior textbooks in mathematics.

Stoddard, John Lawson (*b. Brookline, Mass., 1850; d. near Meran, Tyrol, Austria, 1931*), lecturer, writer. Highly successful as a travel lecturer, he was author of, among other books, the *John L. Stoddard's Lectures* (1897–98, with later supplements).

Stoddard, John Tappan (*b. Northampton, Mass., 1852; d. Northampton, 1919*), chemist. Nephew of David T. Stoddard. Graduated Amherst, 1874; Ph.D., Göttingen, 1877. Taught physics and chemistry at Smith College *post* 1878 and was chairman of Department of Chemistry there *post* 1897.

Stoddard, Joshua C. (*b. Pawlet, Vt., 1814; d. Springfield, Mass., 1902*), inventor, apiarist. Invented and patented, 1855, a steam calliope which he later manufactured; also devised and patented hayraking machines (1861, 1870, and 1871).

Stoddard, Richard Henry (*b. Hingham, Mass., 1825; d. New York, N.Y., 1903*), poet, critic, editor. Husband of Elizabeth D. B. Stoddard. An iron moulder by trade, Stoddard won reputation as a writer *post* 1845 and did much worthy, if derivative and ephemeral, work. Personally popular among writers of his time, he achieved an important position in criticism, and with his wife turned his home into a center of New York literary life. Among his numerous volumes of collected verse, *Poems* (1851), *Abraham Lincoln: An Horatian Ode* (1865), and *Poems* (1880) may be cited.

Stoddard, Solomon (*b. Boston, Mass., 1643; d. Northampton, Mass. 1728/9*), Congregational clergyman. Grandfather of Jonathan Edwards (1703–58) and progenitor of a long line of distinguished persons. Graduated Harvard, 1662; was first librarian of Harvard, 1667–74. Pastor at Northampton, Mass., *post* 1672, Stoddard accepted the Half-Way Covenant and introduced in his church *ante* 1677 the practice called "Stoddardeanism," which allowed many of the privileges of full church membership to professing Christians even when they were not certain they were in a state of grace. Although most of the churches in western Massachusetts accepted Stoddard's view, his grandson, Jonathan Edwards, rejected it and was therefore dismissed from his pastorate at Northampton, in which he had succeeded Stoddard.

STODDARD, THEODORE LOTHROP (*b. Brookline, Mass., 1883; d. Washington, D.C., 1950*), author, foreign policy student, publicist of nativism. Son of John Lawson Stoddard, B.A., Harvard, 1905; M.A., 1910; Ph.D., 1914. Also studied law at Boston University and was admitted to Massachusetts bar, 1908. Achieved contemporary reputation for four books and numerous articles on race relations, which dramatized the theories of Madison Grant and other white supremacists and proponents of eugenics. The first and most successful of his books was *The Rising Tide of Color* (1920).

STODDARD, WILLIAM OSBORN (*b. Homer, N.Y., 1835; d. Madison, N.J., 1925*), author, inventor. Graduated University of Rochester, 1858. As editor of an Illinois newspaper, 1858–60, Stoddard was a strong supporter of Abraham Lincoln, whom he served as secretary, 1861–63. He was author of over a hundred books, among them, *Inside the White House in War Times* (1890) and 76 excellent stories for boys.

STODDART, JAMES HENRY (*b. Barnsley, England, 1827; d. Sewaren, N.J., 1907*), actor. Immigrated to New York City, 1854; was associated with the companies of James W. Wallack, Laura Keene, Joseph Jefferson, and Albert M. Palmer. His most successful role was in Maclaren's *Beside the Bonnie Briar Bush* from 1901.

STODDART, JOSEPH MARSHALL (*b. Philadelphia, Pa., 1845; d. Elkins Park, Pa., 1921*), editor, publisher. First American publisher and representative in America of Gilbert and Sullivan and of Oscar Wilde.

STODDERT, BENJAMIN (*b. Charles Co., Md., 1751; d. 1813*), Revolutionary soldier, merchant. Served with great ability as first secretary of the U.S. Navy, 1798–1801. Supervised plans for new vessels; established and located navy yards.

STOECKEL, CARL (*b. New Haven, Conn., 1858; d. Norfolk, Conn., 1925*), philanthropist, patron of music. Originated and sponsored the Norfolk Music Festival, presented, 1900–23.

STOEK, HARRY HARKNESS (*b. Washington, D.C., 1866; d. Urbana, Ill., 1923*), mining engineer, editor, educator. Organized Department of Mining Engineering at University of Illinois, which he headed, 1909–23. Wrote a number of technical articles on coal mining which changed that occupation from a rule-of-thumb trade to an engineering science; maintained lifelong interest in vocational education of miners.

STOESSEL, ALBERT FREDERIC (*b. St. Louis, Mo., 1894; d. New York, N.Y., 1943*), violinist, conductor, composer. Studied at Hochschule für Musik, Berlin, 1910–13; made debut as solo violinist with Blüthner Orchestra in Berlin, November 1914. American debut with St. Louis Symphony, November 1915. After World War I army service, he made concert tours and served as assistant to Walter Damrosch in direction of the New York Oratorio Society; in 1921 he succeeded Damrosch as director. Stoessel also directed the music at Chautauqua (*post* 1928) and was director of the Worcester (Mass.) Music Festival *post* 1925. He organized and directed the music department at New York University, 1923–30, and headed the orchestra and opera department at Juilliard Graduate School, New York City, *post* 1927. In addition to these duties, he appeared as guest conductor with leading symphony orchestras and composed, among other works, an opera *Garrick* (1936).

STOEVER, MARTIN LUTHER (*b. Germantown, Pa., 1820; d. Philadelphia, Pa., 1870*), educator. Principal of the Academy at Gettysburg, 1842–51; professor of history and Latin, Gettysburg College, 1844–70. Secretary for a number of years of the General Synod, Evangelical Lutheran Church, he was an editor of the *Evangelical Review*, 1857–61, and sole editor, 1862–70.

STOKES, ANSON PHELPS (*b. New York, N.Y., 1838; d. New York, 1913*), merchant, banker, civic reformer. Brother of William E. D. and Olivia E. P. Stokes.

STOKES, ANSON PHELPS (*b. Staten Island, N.Y., 1874; d. Lenox, Mass., 1958*), educator and clergyman. Studied at Yale University and the Episcopal Theological Seminary in Cambridge, Mass. Secretary of Yale University from 1899 to 1921, where he was instrumental in shaping Yale into an international center of learning of the highest standards. From 1924 to 1938, Stokes was the canon residentiary of the National Cathedral (Episcopal) in Washington, D.C. An outspoken critic of the practice of racial bigotry, Stokes was a trustee of Tuskegee Institute. After retirement, he wrote a monumental study, *Church and State in the United States* (1950), regarded as essential for understanding religion in America.

STOKES, CAROLINE PHELPS. *See* STOKES, OLIVIA EGLESTON PHELPS.

STOKES, FREDERICK ABBOT (*b. Brooklyn, N.Y., 1857; d. New York, N.Y., 1939*), publisher. Became partner in White & Stokes, 1881; later published over imprint of White, Stokes & Allen; Frederick A. Stokes & Brother; and Frederick A. Stokes Co.

STOKES, ISAAC NEWTON PHELPS (*b. New York, N.Y., 1867; d. Charleston, S.C., 1944*), architect, housing reformer. Son of Anson P. Stokes. Following his graduation from Harvard in 1891, Stokes acceded to his father's demand that he enter the banking business. But after two years he decided to study architecture, enrolling first at Columbia University and then in 1894 at the École des Beaux Arts in Paris. He returned to the United States in 1897, and that year, with John Mead Howells, submitted the winning design for the University Settlement building. Encouraged by this success, the pair opened an architectural office in Manhattan, a partnership which lasted until 1917. Among their more noteworthy designs were the Baltimore Stock Exchange, the headquarters for the American Geographical Society in New York, and the Bonwit Teller department store in New York.

In 1898 Stokes helped organize the Charity Organization Society's Tenement House Committee. He was chiefly responsible for the preparation of the committee's tenement architecture competition and exhibition, which led in 1900 to the establishment by Governor Theodore Roosevelt of the New York State Tenement House Commission. Appointed to the commission in 1901, Stokes focused on the city's ubiquitous dumbbell tenements. Though Stokes helped set minimum standards for air, light, and sanitation, he soon lost faith in this type of legislation. Convinced that detailed codes inhibited the architectural experimentation necessary for the development of low-cost housing, Stokes resigned in 1912 from the Tenement Housing Committee because of its emphasis on restrictive legislation. He now believed that the solution to the housing problem lay entirely in the development of more economical designs; thereafter, as president, 1911–24, and secretary, 1924–37, of the Phelps-Stokes Fund, which had been established by Caroline Phelps Stokes in 1911, he concentrated on technical problems to lower the cost of construction.

Beginning in 1908, when his historical imagination was fired by the Hudson-Fulton celebration in New York, Stokes collected prints of old Manhattan as a hobby. Eventually his collection took the form of the monumental published compilation *The Iconography of Manhattan Island, 1498–1909* (6 vols., 1915–28), a full record of the physical evolution of the island.

STOKES, MAURICE (*b. Pittsburgh, Pa., 1933; d. Cincinnati, Ohio, 1970*), basketball player. Attended St. Francis College

(B.A., 1955), where he achieved stardom on the basketball court; he was named to the All-American Basketball team in his sophomore, junior, and senior years. He was a first-round choice of the Rochester Royals in 1955 and was chosen NBA Rookie of the Year. In his second season the Royals moved to Cincinnati, and he led the NBA in rebounds. A serious fall in his third season (1958) left him in a coma for six months, after which he was paralyzed and confined to a wheelchair.

STOKES, MONTFORT (*b. Lunenburg Co., Va., 1762; d. Fort Gibson, Indian Territory, 1842*), planter, North Carolina public official and legislator. Uncle of Joseph M. Street. U.S. Senator, Democrat, from North Carolina, 1816–23; governor of North Carolina, 1830–32; U.S. Indian commissioner and agent, 1833–42.

STOKES, OLIVIA EGLESTON PHELPS (*b. New York, N.Y., 1847; d. Washington, D.C., 1927*), philanthropist. Sister of Anson P. and William E. D. Stokes. Active in many charitable activities with her sister, Caroline P. Stokes; chief patron of the Phelps-Stokes Fund, which Caroline had endowed prior to her death in 1909.

STOKES, ROSE HARRIET PASTOR (*b. Russian Poland, 1879; d. Frankfurt am Main, Germany, 1933*), agitator. Immigrated to America as a young girl; married a son of Anson P. Stokes, 1905; was long associated with left-wing Socialist and Communist activity.

STOKES, THOMAS LUNSFORD, JR. (*b. Atlanta, Ga., 1898; d. Washington, D.C., 1958*), journalist. Studied at the University of Georgia. Stokes left Georgia in 1920 to assume a position as reporter for United Press in Washington. In 1933, he became Washington correspondent for the New York *World Telegram*, and in 1936, he became a national correspondent for the Scripps-Howard Newspaper Alliance. In 1938, though a backer of Roosevelt, Stokes investigated charges of political use of the Works Progress Administration in Kentucky. He uncovered widespread corruption. His stories led to a Senate investigation that resulted in the passing of the Hatch Act in 1938 and won Stokes the Pulitzer Prize for journalism. Stokes continued to write his columns until retirement.

STOKES, WILLIAM EARL DODGE (*b. New York, N.Y., 1852; d. New York, 1926*), capitalist, real estate operator. Brother of Anson P. and Olivia E. P. Stokes.

STOLBERG, BENJAMIN (*b. Ninich, Germany, 1891; d. New York, N.Y., 1951*), labor journalist. Immigrated to the U.S. in 1908. Studied at George Washington University, Harvard University, and the University of Chicago (M.A., 1919). A socialist, Stolberg was labor reporter for the *Nation*, the *New Republic*, and *The New York Evening Post*; after 1933, he supported himself entirely as a free-lance journalist. An ardent critic of the New Deal and the CIO, Stolberg was anti-Stalin, favoring instead the thinking of Leon Trotsky; he was a member of the commission of inquiry, headed by John Dewey, that exonerated Trotsky in 1937. Wrote *Economic Consequences of the New Deal* in 1935.

STONE, ABRAHAM (*b. Russia, 1890; d. New York, N.Y., 1959*), physician and birth control activist. Attended New York University (M.D., 1912). A urologist, he practiced in New York as well as taught at the New School for Social Research and other institutions. In 1921, he attended with his wife, Hannah, the First International Birth Control Congress in New York and met Margaret Sanger. He and his wife, who was a gynecologist, devoted much of their lives to educating the public about birth control. He was director of the Margaret Sanger Research Center from 1941. Books include *A Marriage Manual* and *Practical Birth-Control Methods*. Stone was vice president of the Planned Parenthood Federation and of the International Planned Parenthood Federation.

STONE, AMASA (*b. Charlton, Mass., 1818; d. 1883*), capitalist, railroad builder. Brother-in-law of William Howe; father-in-law of John Hay and Samuel Mather. A carpenter by trade, Stone prospered as holder of the rights to the Howe truss bridge. Contracting with others to build the Cleveland Columbus & Cincinnati Railroad in 1849, he became its superintendent and president and made his residence in Cleveland. He played a great part in the industrial development of the Cleveland area. As managing director of the Lake Shore & Michigan Southern, he cooperated with the Rockefeller interests by allowing them preferential shipping rates. He was a principal benefactor of Western Reserve University.

STONE, BARTON WARREN (*b. near Port Tobacco, Md., 1772; d. Hannibal, Mo., 1844*), frontier evangelist, leader in the Christian denomination in Kentucky and Ohio.

STONE, CHARLES AUGUSTUS (*b. Newton, Mass., 1867; d. New York, N.Y., 1941*) and **WEBSTER, EDWIN SIBLEY** (*b. Roxbury, Mass., 1867; d. Newton, Mass., 1950*), electrical engineers, founders of the firm of Stone & Webster. The two men first met in 1884, when taking the entrance examinations for the Massachusetts Institute of Technology. Upon graduating in 1888, they planned to go into partnership as electrical engineers. After their plan was discouraged, Stone worked first as an assistant to Elihu Thomson at the Thomson Electric Welding Co. of Lynn, Mass., and then as the agent for the C & C Motor Co. in Boston. Webster spent several months touring Europe, and then worked at Kidder, Peabody & Co. Yet their idea persisted, and in November 1889, Stone and Webster launched a consulting engineering company in Boston.

Their first major project provided New England with one of its earliest high-voltage power transmission facilities. During the next few years they built small electric light plants, reported on the operations of existing facilities, and gained support for their laboratory by testing electrical materials. During the depression of 1893, electrical manufacturers had taken securities of operating power companies in partial payment for equipment. In the panic that followed, banks demanded reduction on loans to manufacturers, and General Electric had to run unseasoned and unsalable securities over to a syndicate, which engaged Stone & Webster to examine and report upon them. On the advice of the elder J. P. Morgan, they invested in one of the most promising of the properties, the Nashville (Tenn.) Electric Light and Power Co. They later gained a controlling interest in the Nashville company, extended and developed it, and within a few years sold it for a staggering profit. Until 1905 they were the only partners, but by 1912 there were seven.

Meanwhile, the need for capital to improve and extend the utilities they managed had led the partners to establish, in 1902, a securities department to act as fiscal agent in floating securities for the utility companies under their management. In 1906 they formed the Engineering Corporation to systematize design and construction and to relate these to management and finance. The Massachusetts Institute of Technology had the firm build the limestone-faced buildings of its new campus on the Charles River esplanade, 1913–15. In 1913 the company also completed construction of the Keokuk hydroelectric station at Des Moines Rapids on the Mississippi River.

In 1920 the partnership was incorporated in Massachusetts; Webster became vice-chairman in 1930 and succeeded to the chairmanship after Stone's death in 1941. Subsidiary firms were set up to manage the company's various functions; in 1927, Stone,

Webster & Blodget (later Stone & Webster Securities Corporation), to handle securities sales; in 1928, Stone & Webster Engineering Corporation, to assume the engineering and construction work; and in 1929, the Stone & Webster Service Corporation, to take over the development and operation of public utility properties.

Despite changes in the organization of the firm, Charles Stone and Edwin Webster in their later years saw their company continue to provide services along the lines they had established. Both served on the executive committee of MIT for many years and were directors of numerous organizations.

STONE, CHARLES POMEROY (*b. Greenfield, Mass., 1824; d. New York, N.Y., 1887*), Union brigadier general. Blamed and imprisoned for the Union defeat at Ball's Bluff, Oct. 21, 1861, he was later exonerated and served in the Port Hudson and Red River campaigns. He served in the Egyptian army, 1870–83, becoming chief of staff and lieutenant general.

STONE, DAVID (*b. near Windsor, N.C., 1770; d. Wake Co., N.C., 1818*), planter, lawyer, North Carolina governor and jurist. Congressman, Democratic-Republican, from North Carolina, 1799–1801; U.S. senator, 1801–07 and 1813–14. Lost prestige with the electorate during his second term as senator for opposing administration measures for the War of 1812.

STONE, DAVID MARVIN (*b. Oxford, Conn., 1817; d. Brooklyn, N.Y., 1895*), editor, publisher. Associated with the New York *Journal of Commerce* from 1849, he became its editor in chief in 1866 and held that post until 1893. He was also president of the New York Associated Press, 1869–*ca.* 1894.

STONE, ELLEN MARIA (*b. Roxbury, Mass., 1846; d. Chelsea, Mass., 1927*), Congregational missionary in Bulgaria, 1878–1902. Her seizure and captivity by brigands, 1901–02, attracted worldwide attention.

STONE, GEORGE WASHINGTON (*b. Bedford Co., Va., 1811; d. Montgomery, Ala., 1894*), jurist. Raised in Tennessee; admitted to the Alabama bar, 1834. Judge of Alabama circuit court, 1843–49; associate justice, Alabama Supreme Court, 1856–65 and 1876–84. *Post* 1884 he served as chief justice, at first by appointment and afterward by election. An earnest advocate of judicial reform, Stone labored to raise the standards of his court, which had been demoralized by war and Reconstruction.

STONE, HARLAN FISKE (*b. Chesterfield, N.H., 1872; d. Washington, D.C., 1946*), lawyer, chief justice of the United States. Attended Massachusetts Agricultural College; graduated Amherst College, 1894. While teaching science at the high school in Newburyport, Mass., he became interested in the law and entered Columbia Law School, New York City, 1895. After graduation in 1898, Stone combined law school teaching at Columbia with a clerkship in the firm of Sullivan and Cromwell. A year later he shifted to Wilmer and Canfield. He resigned his professorship in March 1905 for a full-time partnership at Wilmer and Canfield. In 1906, however, he accepted an invitation to return as professor and dean at Columbia, with the understanding that he would enjoy freedom in choosing the law faculty. Soon the authoritarian president and the staunchly independent dean clashed. Again, Stone resigned, evoking a concerted drive by students, faculty, and trustees on his behalf. The upshot was his unanimous appointment as dean, effective July 10, 1910. The years 1910–16 were marked by efforts to raise academic standards and improve the curriculum. Stone himself set an example by continuing to teach, write, and maintain a nominal law practice at Wilmer, Canfield, and Stone. As a practicing lawyer, his career was brief—1905–10 and about six months in 1923–24. In later

years, he rated his teaching more enduring than anything he did as a judge.

An Anglophile and strong interventionist, Stone anxiously observed the course of World War I. He lamented his ineligibility for active service, but doubted the wisdom of coerced conformity at the cost of conscience. His essay "The Conscientious Objector" (1919) is recognized as a classic. Stone resigned as dean on Feb. 21, 1923. On Apr. 1, 1924, President Coolidge named Stone attorney general. In trying to brighten the tarnished Justice Department, Stone's primary goal was recruitment of personnel unsullied by alliance with the underworld. William J. Burns was dismissed as head of the Federal Bureau of Investigation and replaced by 29-year-old J. Edgar Hoover on Dec. 19, 1924. Eliminating political plums for congressional protégés, accustomed to serving as counsel for the government in cases before the Supreme Court, Stone revived the tradition of arguing cases himself. He campaigned for Coolidge in 1924, and was nominated to the Supreme Court on Jan. 5, 1925. Stone was overwhelmingly confirmed on Feb. 5, 1925, and sworn in on Mar. 2. The ideas Stone expounded in a series of lectures (later published as *Law and Its Administration*, 1915) at Columbia University have been regarded as conservative, even reactionary. But when, as a Supreme Court justice, he harshly attacked judicial distrust of social legislation, he was hailed as a liberal. The notion, vigorously advanced in certain quarters, that Holmes and Brandeis were the "pacemakers" and Stone a sort of judicial "me-too" is not borne out by the record. Without minimizing the contributions of Holmes and Brandeis, Stone was the one who, in both the old Court (before 1937) and the new (after 1937), carried the Holmes-Brandeis tradition to fulfillment.

In *United States* v. *Carolene Products Co.* (1938), Stone suggested in the text of the opinion that the Court would not go so far as to say that no economic regulation would violate constitutional restraints, but he did indicate that henceforth the Court's role in this area would be strictly confined. Attached to this proposition is what is considered to be the most famous footnote in the Court's history, suggesting special judicial scrutiny in three areas: legislative encroachment on 1st Amendment freedoms; government action impeding or corrupting the political process; and official conduct adversely affecting the rights of racial, religious, or national minorities.

Stone considered judicial review to be one of the auxiliary precautions envisioned by the founding fathers against abuse of power. He believed that unless the Court invokes its authority to preserve the rights deemed fundamental, especially the crucial preliminaries of the political process—speech, press, assembly— no free government can exist. On June 2, 1941, Chief Justice Hughes resigned at the age of 79. Speculation concerning Hughes's successor centered on Attorney General Robert H. Jackson and Associate Justice Stone. The choice of Stone seemed a fitting reward for the uphill battle he had waged, despite his strong misgivings, on behalf of the New Deal's constitutionality. Refuting the charge that he made party loyalty the primary qualification for appointment to the Supreme Court, Roosevelt passed over his popular attorney general and sent Stone's name to the Senate on June 12, 1941. Stone's chief justiceship, however, was unimpressive. The bench Stone headed was the most frequently divided, the most openly quarrelsome in history.

As chairman of the board of trustees of the National Gallery, Stone played an important role in expanding its collections and rescuing European art treasures during World War II. He also served on committees of the Smithsonian Institution and the Folger Library. Stone's charm made him a favorite companion of President Hoover, with whom he sometimes went fishing; he was also a member of the intimate group known as the Medicine Ball Cabinet.

STONE, HORATIO (*b. Jackson, N.Y., 1808; d. Carrara, Italy, 1875*), sculptor, physician, Union army surgeon.

STONE, JAMES KENT (*b. Boston, Mass., 1840; d. 1921*), educator, Roman Catholic clergyman, Passionist. Son of John S. Stone. Graduated Harvard, 1861. After service in the Union army, he became a teacher of Latin at Kenyon College, took orders in the Protestant Episcopal church and was president of Kenyon, 1867. President of Hobart College, 1868–69, he resigned and became a Catholic in December 1869. Joining the Paulists, he was ordained in the Catholic priesthood, 1872, but withdrew in 1876 to join the more severe Congregation of the Passion, wherein he took the name in religion of Father Fidelis. Thereafter he achieved high distinction in his order, holding a number of administrative offices and founding its work in South America.

STONE, JOHN AUGUSTUS (*b. Concord, Mass., 1800; d. Philadelphia, Pa., 1834*), playwright, actor. Author of a number of plays and adaptations which are no longer extant, he wrote his most important play, *Metamora*, for Edwin Forrest. It was first produced at the Park Theatre, N.Y., December 1829, and provided Forrest with one of his most popular parts.

STONE, JOHN MARSHALL (*b. Milan, Tenn., 1830; d. Mississippi, 1900*), politician, Confederate officer. As Democratic governor of Mississippi, 1876–82 and 1890–96, Stone reorganized the state government on the basis of control by whites, tempered the extravagances of the recent carpetbag administrations, and, in his second administration, provided for the perpetuation of white control by the provisions of the 1890 state constitution. He served briefly before his death as president of Mississippi A. and M. College (present Mississippi State). He was an able administrator and of high personal character.

STONE, JOHN SEELY (*b. West Stockbridge, Mass., 1795; d. Cambridge, Mass., 1882*), Episcopal clergyman, educator. Father of James K. Stone. An eloquent preacher and a leader in the evangelical school, he held a number of pastorates, taught theology in the Philadelphia Divinity School, 1862–67, and was dean and professor of theology at Episcopal Theological School, Cambridge, Mass., 1867–76.

STONE, JOHN STONE (*b. Dover, Va., 1869; d. San Diego, Calif., 1943*), telephone and radio engineer. Son of Charles Pomeroy Stone. Studied at School of Mines, Columbia University, 1886–88, and at Johns Hopkins University, 1888–90. Worked in Boston laboratory of American Bell Telephone Co.; unsuccessful in attempt to manufacture and market his own inventions; was associate engineer at large for American Telephone and Telegraph Co., 1920–34. A pioneer in radio telegraphy and telephony, unlike most of the other pioneer experimenters, he was a theoretician who relied almost wholly on mathematical analysis to test the validity of his concepts. His system of loosely coupled tuned circuits for radio transmission and reception (patented 1902) anticipated Marconi's similar system; the priority was established by the U.S. Supreme Court shortly after Stone's death. He made important contributions also in the field of high-frequency wire transmission and to shortwave and ultrahigh-frequency radio.

STONE, JOHN WESLEY (*b. Wadsworth, Ohio, 1838; d. Lansing, Mich., 1922*), lawyer, jurist. Removed to Michigan *ca.* 1856. Held state and federal offices in Michigan; served as a state circuit judge; was congressman, Republican, from Michigan, 1877–81. Elected to the state supreme court 1909, he served with ability until his death.

STONE, LUCY (*b. near West Brookfield, Mass., 1818; d. Dorchester, Mass., 1893*), reformer, pioneer in the woman's rights movement. Graduated Oberlin, 1847. An ardent abolitionist, she lectured widely on this subject *post* 1848, losing no opportunity at the same time to lecture on the inferior position of her sex. She led in calling the first national woman's rights convention, Worcester, Mass., 1850. On her marriage to Henry B. Blackwell, 1855, she gained notoriety by insistence on keeping her maiden name as a symbol of equality. Thereafter, with the aid of her husband, she continued and extended her labors and helped form the American Woman Suffrage Association, which concentrated on gaining the suffrage by states. With her husband, she edited the *Woman's Journal* from 1872.

STONE, MELVILLE ELIJAH (*b. Hudson, Ill., 1848; d. New York, N.Y., 1929*), journalist. Coproprietor, *Chicago Daily News*, 1875–88, he sold out his interest to his partner, Victor F. Lawson, and after several years of travel, engaged for a while in banking. On becoming general manager of Associated Press of Illinois, 1893, he secured exclusive right for use of Reuter's news in the United States and continued to head the Associated Press after its reorganization in New York, 1900, until his retirement, 1921. A man of constructive mind, executive powers, and engaging personality, he fostered the cooperative principle on which the Associated Press was based, kept its news free of partisanship and bias, and opposed sensationalism. He was also active in persuading official European news sources to deal fairly with American correspondents and played a part behind the scenes in settlement of the Russo-Japanese War by treaty at Portsmouth, N.H., 1905.

STONE, ORMOND (*b. Pekin, Ill., 1847; d. Clifton Station, Va., 1933*), astronomer. Brother of Melville E. Stone. Director of Cincinnati Observatory, 1875–82; of University of Virginia McCormick Observatory, 1882–1912. Founded *Annals of Mathematics*, 1884.

STONE, RICHARD FRENCH (*b. near Sharpsburg, Ky., 1844; d. Indianapolis, Ind., 1913*), physician. Author of, among other works, *Biography of Eminent American Physicians and Surgeons* (1894, 1898).

STONE, SAMUEL (*b. Hertford, England, 1602; d. Hartford, Conn., 1663*), Puritan clergyman. Immigrated to Massachusetts with Thomas Hooker and John Cotton, 1633. Removing to the Connecticut settlement, he selected the site of Hartford, negotiated its purchase from the Indians and settled there, 1636. After Hooker's death in 1647, he remained sole minister of the church at Hartford until his own death. Although his idea of church government approached Presbyterianism more than Independency, he was steadfastly supported by a majority of his congregation.

STONE, THOMAS (*b. Charles Co., Md., 1743; d. Alexandria, Va., 1787*), lawyer, planter, Maryland legislator. As member of the Continental Congress for the greater part of the period 1775–78, he was a signer of the Declaration of Independence and did important work on the committee which framed the Articles of Confederation.

STONE, WARREN (*b. Saint Albans, Vt., 1808; d. New Orleans, La., 1872*), physician, surgeon. M.D., Berkshire Medical Institution, Pittsfield, Mass., 1831. In practice at New Orleans *post ca.* 1833, he served on the staffs of several hospitals, founded one of the earliest private hospitals in the United States, 1839, and taught at the Medical College of Louisiana (later Tulane), 1834–72. During the Civil War, he was surgeon general of Louisiana. Among his professional achievements were the first resection of part of a rib to secure permanent drainage in cases of empyema, the first successful cure for traumatic vertebral aneurism by open incision and packing, and the first use of silver wire for ligation of the external iliac.

STONE, WARREN SANFORD (*b. near Ainsworth, Iowa, 1860; d. Cleveland, Ohio, 1925*), trade-union official. Headed Brotherhood of Locomotive Engineers, 1903–25. Led in struggle to secure better wages and shorter hours by dealing with railway managers through regional groups, thereby finishing one contest before taking up another; favored cooperative ownership of railways and independent political action by labor.

STONE, WILBUR FISK (*b. Litchfield, Conn., 1833; d. Denver, Colo., 1920*), Colorado pioneer and jurist. Raised in the Midwest; removed to Nebraska, 1859, and to Colorado, 1860. Holder of both federal and state offices, he was active in railroad promotion. From 1877 until 1889 he was judge of the state supreme court and of the criminal court of Denver, and from 1891 until 1904 he sat on a unique court appointed to determine Spanish and Mexican land titles in the Southwest.

STONE, WILLIAM (*b. Northamptonshire, England, ca. 1603; d. Charles Co., Md., ca. 1660*), planter, Maryland colonial official. Immigrated to Virginia *ante* 1628. Appointed proprietary governor of Maryland, 1648, he was engaged in a continuous struggle with the Puritan element of the colony, which climaxed in his defeat in the battle of the Severn, Mar. 25, 1655.

STONE, WILLIAM JOEL (*b. Madison Co., Ky., 1848; d. 1918*), lawyer. Congressman, Democrat, from Missouri, 1885–91, and a moderate reformer, he served with tact and ability as governor of Missouri during the troubled period 1893–97. U.S. senator from Missouri *post* 1903, he was a disciple of William J. Bryan and an orthodox Democratic partisan; however, on becoming chairman of the Foreign Relations Committee, 1914, he invited criticism by his steadfast opposition to the U.S. involvement in World War I.

STONE, WILLIAM LEETE (*b. New Paltz, N.Y., 1792; d. New York, N.Y., 1844*), journalist. After experience on a number of newspapers and periodicals, he became a proprietor of the *New York Commercial Advertiser*, 1821. He was an influential Federalist editor, but is remembered principally for his efforts to arouse interest in the preservation and historical use of the state archives and for several of his works in local history, including *Life of Joseph Brant* (1838), *Life and Times of Red Jacket* (1841), and *Border Wars of the American Revolution* (1843).

STONE, WILLIAM LEETE (*b. New York, N.Y., 1835; d. 1908*), journalist. Son of William L. Stone (1792–1844); nephew of Francis Wayland. Graduated Brown, 1858. Editor and compiler of a number of valuable source works on the history of the American Revolution, notably on the Saratoga campaign.

STONE, WILLIAM OLIVER (*b. Derby, Conn., 1830; d. Newport, R.I., 1875*), portrait painter. Studied with Nathaniel Jocelyn. A prolific and successful portraitist of prominent persons; worked in New York City *post* 1854.

STONE, WITMER (*b. Philadelphia, Pa., 1866; d. Philadelphia, 1939*), naturalist, museum curator and director. Associated *post* 1888 with Academy of Natural Sciences in Philadelphia; editor, *The Auk*, 1912–36. Author of, among other works, *Bird Studies at Old Cape May* (1937), regarded as one of the best all regional bird books.

STONEMAN, GEORGE (*b. Busti, N.Y., 1822; d. Buffalo, N.Y., 1894*), soldier. Graduated West Point, 1846. A cavalryman, he served mainly in the Southwest prior to the Civil War. Chief of cavalry, Army of the Potomac, under General George B. McClellan, he was assigned to command the 1st Division, III Corps, and succeeded to command of the corps as major general, November 1862. When General Joseph Hooker took command of

the Army of the Potomac, he put Stoneman in charge of the separate corps of cavalry. While in this post Stoneman made a famous raid toward Richmond, Va., April–May 1863, as part of the Chancellorsville campaign. Transferred to the western armies, he commanded the cavalry corps of the Army of the Ohio in the Atlanta campaign, but suffered defeat and capture at Clinton, Ga., early in August 1864. Exchanged, he returned to duty, making another cavalry raid with considerable success into southwestern Virginia in December 1864 and later acting in cooperation with Sherman in the Carolinas. After his retirement from the army for disability, 1871, he settled near Los Angeles, Calif. As Democratic governor of California, 1883–87, he opposed the increasing power of the railroads in state affairs and in business, and favored legislation encouraging irrigation projects.

STONG, PHIL(IP DUFFIELD) (*b. Pittsburg, Iowa, 1899; d. Washington, Conn., 1957*), author. Studied at Drake University and Columbia University. Author of forty books, two anthologies, and many magazine stories and articles. Stong's best-known work was *State Fair* (1932), a novel which was filmed three times. Other works include *Week-End* (1935) and *Career* (1936, filmed 1939). Children's books include *The Hired Man's Elephant* (1939), which won the *New York Herald Tribune* Award in 1939.

STORER, BELLAMY (*b. Cincinnati, Ohio, 1847; d. Paris, France, 1922*), lawyer, diplomat. Nephew of David H. Storer. Graduated Harvard, 1867; law school of Cincinnati College, 1869. Married Maria Nichols, widow of George W. Nichols, 1886. Congressman, Republican, from Ohio, 1891–95, he helped William McKinley in the campaign of 1896 and was appointed U.S. minister to Belgium, 1897. Becoming U.S. minister to Spain, 1899, he successfully handled problems incident to the Spanish-American War, and in 1902 was made U.S. ambassador at Vienna. Popular and successful, he was summarily removed in March 1906 after a dispute with President Theodore Roosevelt.

STORER, DAVID HUMPHREYS (*b. Portland, Maine, 1804; d. Boston, Mass., 1891*), Boston obstetrician, naturalist, collector of rare fishes and shells. Graduated Bowdoin, 1822; Harvard Medical School, 1825; served apprenticeship with John C. Warren (1776–1856). As a practitioner and as a teacher at Harvard Medical School (dean, 1854–64), he did much to advance obstetrics in the United States; he was also regarded as expert in medical jurisprudence. He was father of Francis H. and Horatio R. Storer and uncle of Bellamy Storer.

STORER, FRANCIS HUMPHREYS (*b. Boston, Mass., 1832; d. Boston, 1914*), chemist. Son of David H. Storer; brother of Horatio R. Storer. Studied at Lawrence Scientific School; served as assistant to Josiah P. Cooke, and was chemist with U.S. North Pacific exploring expedition, 1853–54. Chemist of the Boston Gas Light Co., *ca.* 1858–71, he was associated also in research projects with Charles William Eliot, with whom he collaborated on several textbooks and whose sister he married. On Eliot's appointment to the presidency of Harvard, 1869, he appointed Storer professor of agricultural chemistry at the Bussey Institution. Becoming dean of the institution, 1871, he held both posts until 1907. During this period he performed important research on soils, fertilizers, forage crops, cereals, vegetables, and other products, publishing the results in the *Bulletin of the Bussey Institution*. He was author also of *Agriculture in Some of Its Relations with Chemistry* (1887) and various manuals and textbooks.

STORER, HORATIO ROBINSON (*b. Boston, Mass., 1830; d. Newport, R.I., 1922*), gynecologist, numismatist. Son of David H. Storer; brother of Francis H. Storer. Graduated Harvard, 1850; M.D., Harvard Medical School, 1853; studied also in Paris,

London, and Edinburgh. Among the early American specialists in gynecology, he wrote and lectured extensively against abortion. After his retirement from practice, 1872, he became a world authority on medallions of medical interest and a notable collector of them.

STOREY, MOORFIELD (b. Roxbury, Mass., 1845; d. Lincoln, Mass., 1929), lawyer. Graduated Harvard, 1866. As assistant to Charles Sumner, 1867–69, he was closely connected with the attempt to impeach President Andrew Johnson. Winning an international reputation in the practice of commercial law in Boston *post* 1871, he became a crusader against political corruption, attacking Benjamin F. Butler and James G. Blaine, and leading the Mugwump Republicans during the presidential campaign of 1884. An anti-imperialist and a defender of the rights of blacks and Indians, he wrote prolifically in support of his opinions. Earnest and courageous, he won little gratitude or popularity by his activity.

STOREY, WILBUR FISK (b. near Salisbury, Vt., 1819; d. Chicago, Ill., 1884), journalist. Gaining experience on newspapers in New York, Indiana, and Michigan, he made the *Detroit Free Press* one of the leading Democratic newspapers in the West as co-owner and owner, 1853–61. Purchasing the *Chicago Times*, 1861, he was its active head until 1878, making it one of the most prosperous of the Chicago dailies despite a brief suppression for alleged "copperhead" proclivities in 1863 and the destruction of its plant in 1871. Not a writer, but rather a directing executive, Storey emphasized the importance of news and attacked men and issues with vigor and fearlessness.

STORROW, CHARLES STORER (b. Montreal, Canada, 1809; d. Boston, Mass., 1904), engineer. Born of American parents and raised in Boston and in Paris, France, Storrow graduated from Harvard, 1829. He studied engineering with Loammi Baldwin and in Paris. Construction engineer and manager, Boston & Lowell Railroad, 1832–45, he then became engineer for the Essex Co. and, as such, planned, laid out, and built the industrial town of Lawrence, Mass. He was father of James J. Storrow.

STORROW, JAMES JACKSON (b. Boston, Mass., 1837; d. Washington, D.C., 1897), lawyer. Son of Charles S. Storrow; grandson of James Jackson. Graduated Harvard, 1857. Devoting himself to patent law, he was associated with Chauncey Smith in the long litigation over validity of the Bell Telephone patents, showing himself a master in clear analysis of evidence. He was author of the brief on behalf of Venezuela, 1895–96, which brought about British consent to submit the boundary controversy to arbitration.

STORRS, RICHARD SALTER (b. Longmeadow, Mass., 1787; d. Braintree, Mass., 1873), Congregational clergyman. Pastor, First Church, Braintree, 1811–73, he was a conspicuous defender of orthodoxy and active in home missionary work. He was father of Richard S. Storrs (1821–1900).

STORRS, RICHARD SALTER (b. Braintree, Mass., 1821; d. Brooklyn, N.Y., 1900), Congregational clergyman. Son of Richard S. Storrs (1787–1873). Pastor, Church of the Pilgrims, Brooklyn, N.Y., *post* 1846, he was active in Brooklyn's civic, philanthropic, and cultural affairs, and won great popularity as a lyceum lecturer.

STORY, ISAAC (b. Marblehead, Mass., 1774; d. Marblehead, 1803), poet, miscellaneous writer. Cousin of Joseph Story. A contributor to the *Farmer's Museum* and the *Columbian Centinel* and other papers, he was author of essays modeled on Joseph Dennie's "Lay Preacher" papers and of a number of satirical and serious poems. His best-known verses were published in *A Parnassian Shop . . . By Peter Quince, Esq.* (1801).

STORY, JOSEPH (b. Marblehead, Mass., 1779; d. Cambridge, Mass., 1845), lawyer, jurist, U.S. Supreme Court justice. Father of William W. Story. Graduated Harvard, 1798; studied law in office of Samuel Sewall, later chief justice of the supreme court of Massachusetts. Began practice at Salem, Mass., 1801. Although he was an avowed follower of Jefferson in a Federalist community, he did well in his profession and was elected to the state legislature, where, among other reforms, he made an unsuccessful effort to establish a state court of chancery. He served briefly as a member of Congress, 1808–09, opposing administration policies on the Embargo of 1807 and naval affairs. Reelected to the Massachusetts legislature, he served as Speaker of the House in January and May 1811. On Nov. 18, 1811, he was appointed an associate justice of the U.S. Supreme Court.

Supreme Court judges at this time also exercised circuit court jurisdiction, and Story's circuit took in Maine, New Hampshire, Massachusetts, and Rhode Island. A pioneer in outlining and defining the field of admiralty law for the United States, Story, by his decisions, first put the admiralty jurisdiction of the federal courts on a sound basis. Many of his opinions are still impressive for their breadth of learning, but in some there is a tendency to range beyond the facts and law necessary for judgment in a particular case. However, not a few of his opinions had important legal and constitutional results. His opinion in *Martin* v. *Hunter's Lessee* (1816) has been called the keystone of the arch of federal judicial power, holding as it did that appellate jurisdiction of the Supreme Court could rightfully be exercised over the state courts. In the case of the *Thomas Jefferson*, Story's opinion allayed a mounting feeling in some of the inland states that the federal courts were menacing state common-law jurisdiction over inland waters. Story spoke for the court in the case of the *Amistad*, a slaverunner, holding that the human cargo should be freed and sent back to Africa; he also wrote the opinion in the Girard will case. Daniel Webster considered Story's ablest opinion his dissent in *Charles River Bridge* v. *Warren Bridge*, in which he upheld the sanctity of contracts. The facts disprove the often-quoted charge that Story was dominated by John Marshall, whom he failed to succeed as chief justice, in part because Andrew Jackson disliked him and considered him dangerous.

Together with the vast amount of work he performed on the bench, Story was professor of law at Harvard, *post* 1829, and may be regarded in a very real sense as a founder of the Harvard Law School. The method of teaching which he devised later resulted in his famous *Commentaries* on bailments, the Constitution, conflict of laws, equity jurisprudence and pleading, agency, partnership, and bills and notes, which were published in quick succession between 1832 and 1845. He was author also of a number of other legal treatises and, by his writing, has provided an example of industry and legal scholarship hardly to be equaled. The success of the *Commentaries* was widespread and immediate and provided the author of a handsome income and an international reputation. Together with Chancellor James Kent, Story will be remembered as the founder of the equity system in the United States. He drew up the rules of equity practice for the U.S. Supreme Court and the circuit courts in 1842, and among his *Commentaries* those on equity jurisprudence and pleading remain outstanding. A Unitarian, a great lover of conversation, poetry, and music, his favorite novelist was Jane Austen.

STORY, JULIAN RUSSELL (b. Walton-on-Thames, England, 1857; d. Philadelphia, Pa., 1919), portrait painter. Son of William W. Story.

STORY, WILLIAM EDWARD (*b. Boston, Mass., 1850; d. 1930*), mathematician. Graduated Harvard, 1871; Ph.D., Leipzig, 1875. After teaching at Harvard and at Johns Hopkins, where he was associated with J. J. Sylvester, Story was professor of mathematics at Clark University, 1889–1921.

STORY, WILLIAM WETMORE (*b. Salem, Mass., 1819; d. Vallombrosa, Italy, 1895*), sculptor, author. Son of Joseph Story. Graduated Harvard, A.B., 1838; LL.B., 1840. Practiced law with, among others, his brother-in-law, George T. Curtis, and wrote two long-standard legal textbooks; devoted himself in his spare time to painting, sculpting, and music. After completing a statue of his late father for Mount Auburn Cemetery and also composing his father's biography, he settled in Rome, Italy, 1856, and thereafter devoted his chief efforts to sculpture and travel in Europe. He revisited his own country only occasionally. Intimate friend of Robert and Elizabeth Barrett Browning, Nathaniel Hawthorne, and many other distinguished literary and artistic figures, Story led a happy life but one of artistic unfulfillment. His approach to his conceptions was fundamentally intellectual and deficient in intensity. Among his numerous books, *Roba di Roma* (1862) may still be read as an outstanding appreciation of the spirit of Italy.

STOTESBURY, EDWARD TOWNSEND (*b. Philadelphia, Pa., 1849; d. Chestnut Hill, Pa., 1938*), banker. Entering employ of Drexel & Co. as a clerk, 1866, he rose in successive promotions to senior partner, 1904. Partner also in Drexel's New York City affiliate, the then J. P. Morgan & Co., he was active in the railroad reorganizations and securities underwriting which were responsible for the success of both firms.

STOTT, HENRY GORDON (*b. Orkney Island, 1866; d. probably New Rochelle, N.Y., 1917*), electrical engineer. Came to America, 1891. As engineer for Buffalo (N.Y.) Light & Power Co., he constructed its conduit system and major power plant; *post* 1901 he superintended power plants and transmission lines for the Manhattan Railway Co. and the Interboro Rapid Transit, New York City.

STOUFFER, SAMUEL ANDREW (*b. Sac City, Iowa, 1900; d. New York, N.Y., 1960*), sociologist, statistician. Educated at Morningside College, Iowa; Harvard University, and the University of Chicago (Ph.D., 1930). Taught at the University of Chicago (1930–31 and 1935–46), at the University of Wisconsin (1932–35), and at Harvard University (1946–60). Stouffer was a reformist in purpose and empiricist in approach, insisting on verified evidence for the advancement of social science and the solution of social problems. He introduced and developed the system of sample surveys for the gathering of social data. From 1941 to 1946, he directed the Research Branch Information and Education Division of the U.S. Army, gathering social data on over half a million servicemen. Stouffer was chairman of the joint committee of the National Research Council and the Social Science Research Council, for which he did a survey in 1954 on the effects of McCarthyism.

STOUGHTON, EDWIN WALLACE (*b. Springfield, Vt., 1818; d. New York, N.Y., 1882*), lawyer. Practiced in New York City *post* 1840; won reputation in patent suits, including the Goodyear rubber, the Wheeler & Wilson sewing machine, and Corliss steam-engine cases. Originally a War Democrat, he became a Republican and served on the commission which investigated the Louisiana vote in the election of 1876; he later spoke in behalf of the Republican position before the Electoral Commission. He was U.S. minister to Russia, 1877–79.

STOUGHTON, WILLIAM (*b. probably England, 1631; d. Dorchester, Mass., 1701*), colonial official. Graduated Harvard, 1650; M.A., New College, Oxford, 1653. Ejected from his Oxford fellowship, 1660, he returned to Massachusetts, 1662, where he held a number of offices and became a political henchman of Joseph Dudley. Named lieutenant governor of the colony, 1692, under Sir William Phips, he became acting governor, 1694, and except for a brief period, 1699–1700, continued to head the government until his death. As chief justice of oyer and terminer during the Salem witchcraft cases, 1692, he was largely responsible for the tragic aspect they assumed, because of his insistence on the admission of "spectral evidence" and by his overbearing attitude.

STOVALL, PLEASANT ALEXANDER (*b. Augusta, Ga., 1857; d. Savannah, Ga., 1935*), Georgia journalist and legislator, diplomat. Graduated University of Georgia, 1875. Editor, *Savannah Press* from 1891; U.S. minister to Switzerland, 1913–20.

STOW, BARON (*b. Croydon, N.H., 1801; d. 1869*), Baptist clergyman, editor. A powerful evangelical preacher, he held his principal pastorates at the Second Baptist Church, Boston, Mass., 1832–48, and at the Rowe Street Baptist Church, 1848–67.

STOWE, CALVIN ELLIS (*b. Natick, Mass., 1802; d. 1886*), educator. Graduated Bowdoin, 1824. Taught at Dartmouth, Lane Theological Seminary, Bowdoin, and Andover Theological Seminary; author of a celebrated *Report on Elementary Instruction in Europe* (1837). Husband of Harriet E. B. Stowe.

STOWE, HARRIET ELIZABETH BEECHER (*b. Litchfield, Conn., 1811; d. Hartford, Conn., 1896*), author. Daughter of Lyman Beecher; sister of Catharine E., Edward, and Henry Ward Beecher; wife of Calvin E. Stowe. A true member of her family in her earnestness, intelligence, and devotion to the antislavery cause, Stowe developed an early taste for writing. She was influenced in choosing an antislavery subject for her pen by current discussions of the Fugitive Slave Law and also by her brother Edward and his wife. While tending her newly born seventh child, she began work on what was to be *Uncle Tom's Cabin, or Life Among the Lowly*, which was first published as a serial in the *National Era*, June 5, 1851–Apr. 1, 1852; it was brought out as a book in two volumes by John P. Jewett on Mar. 20, 1852. Within a year of publication the sales of the book had mounted to 300,000; however, Stowe received surprisingly little remuneration for her work. She, as well as her novel, became the center of violent controversy, and she was attacked on the grounds of inaccuracy, literary quality, and motive. As a picture of American manners, however, *Uncle Tom's Cabin* deserves high rank and at times its style rises to eloquence. The influence of her work in England and on the Continent was very great, winning enormous favor for the antislavery cause. Exceedingly industrious as a writer, she continued to pour forth a steady stream of fiction, despite distractions of family life, trips to Europe, and the like. Over nearly 30 years she wrote, on the average, almost a book a year, including *Dred: A Tale of the Great Dismal Swamp* (1856), *The Minister's Wooing* (1859), and *Oldtown Folks* (1869), which is considered perhaps the richest and raciest of her works. It has been lately said of her that "as the historian of the human side of Calvinism she tempered dogma with affection" and also "the creative instinct was strong in her but the critical was wholly lacking."

STRACHEY, WILLIAM (*b. fl. 1606–18*), first secretary of the Virginia colony, historian. A grantee under the second charter to the London Co. of Virginia, he sailed for that colony, 1609, with Sir Thomas Gates, reaching Jamestown after shipwreck, 1610; he returned to London late in 1611. His fame rests principally on his letter of 1610 descriptive of the colony (first printed by Samuel Purchas in his *Pilgrimes*, 1625, but previously circulated in manuscript), on his production of the first written code of laws for

Virginia, and on *The Historie of Travaile into Virginia Britannia* (written in 1613). This last work is the most ably written of the contemporary accounts of the region and is a highly authoritative and valuable historical source. It was first printed and published in 1849.

STRAIGHT, WILLARD DICKERMAN (*b. Oswego, N.Y., 1880; d. Paris, France, 1918*), diplomat, financier. Son-in-law of William C. Whitney. Graduated in architecture, Cornell University,, 1901. After working in the Chinese customs service and as a newspaper correspondent, he held consular offices in the Far East and served briefly in the U.S. Department of State. He then served as a representative of various banking groups in China, 1909–12. Thereafter resident in the United States, he engaged in promoting American capital investments in foreign countries. With his wife he financed publication of the weekly *The New Republic* (1914).

STRAIN, ISAAC G. (*b. Roxbury, Pa., 1821; d. Aspinwall, present Colón, Panama, 1857*), naval officer, explorer. Conducted exploration of the Isthmus of Darien, 1853, which determined impracticability of a ship-canal route there.

STRANAHAN, JAMES SAMUEL THOMAS (*b. Peterboro, N.Y., 1808; d. Saratoga, N.Y., 1898*), capitalist. Assisted Gerrit Smith in promotion of his Oneida Co., N.Y., properties; was successful as a railroad contractor in New Jersey. *Post* 1844, transferring his activities to Brooklyn, N.Y., he developed the Atlantic Basin there, invested in the East River ferries, and came to be known as a principal civic leader. He was largely responsible for the creation of Brooklyn's Prospect Park and for the consolidation of Brooklyn into the city of New York.

STRANG, JAMES JESSEE (*b. Scipio, N.Y., 1813; d. Voree, Wis., 1856*), Mormon leader, founder of the sect known by his name.

STRANGE, MICHAEL (*b. New York, N.Y., 1890; d. Boston, Mass., 1950*), actress, writer. Christened Blanche Oelrichs. Married Leonard M. Thomas, 1910 (divorced, 1919); John Barrymore, 1921 (divorced, 1928); Harrison Tweed, 1929 (divorced, 1942).

STRATEMEYER, EDWARD (*b. Elizabeth, N.J., 1862; d. Newark, N.J., 1930*), juvenile fiction writer, creator of the "Rover Boys" and other series.

STRATEMEYER, GEORGE EDWARD (*b. Cincinnati, Ohio, 1890; d. Orlando, Fla., 1969*), U.S. Army and Air Force officer. Graduated from the U.S. Military Academy (1915) and the Army War College (1939). Earned his Air Force wings in 1917, and in 1920 was transferred to the Army Air Service. In 1941 he became executive officer for the Chief of Air Corps and, in 1942, chief of the Air Staff. In August 1943 he was assigned to the China-Burma-India Theater; his responsibilities included command of the Tenth Air Force in India-Burma and the theater's Air Service Command; supply and maintenance of the Fourteenth Air Force; protection of the Hump route to China; and coordination of Air Transport Command's theaterwide operations. Was also air adviser to the theater's commander, Gen. Joseph Stilwell. Became deputy commander of the American and British air forces in 1943 and exercised operational control of all Southeast Asia Command air forces. In the spring of 1945 he was given command of all U.S. air forces in the China theater. During the Korean War, he persuaded Gen. Douglas MacArthur, Far East commander, to extend U.S. air operations into North Korea, and within a month his air forces, with navy carriers and Marine Corps aviation, had driven the North Korean air force from the skies. He retired in 1951.

STRATON, JOHN ROACH (*b. Evansville, Ind., 1875; d. Clifton Springs, N.Y., 1929*), Baptist clergyman, fundamentalist leader, sensational preacher. Held pastorates in Chicago, Ill., Baltimore, Md., and Norfolk, Va.; *post* 1918 was pastor of Calvary Baptist Church, New York City.

STRATTON, CHARLES SHERWOOD (*b. Bridgeport, Conn., 1838; d. Middleboro, Mass., 1883*), midget, the celebrated "General Tom Thumb" of P. T. Barnum's museum.

STRATTON, SAMUEL WESLEY (*b. Litchfield, Ill., 1861; d. 1931*), physicist. B.S., University of Illinois, 1884. Taught mathematics and physics at Illinois; assistant professor of physics, University of Chicago, 1892–1901. After preparing the plan of a proposed Bureau of Standards, 1900, he drafted the bill authorizing the establishment of the bureau and won acceptance for the bill which was passed in 1901. As first director of U.S. Bureau of Standards, 1901–23, he made it a great research center and secured for it an international reputation. He served as president, Massachusetts Institute of Technology, 1923–30.

STRATTON-PORTER, GENE. *See* PORTER, GENE STRATTON.

STRAUS, ISIDOR (*b. Otterberg, Rhenish Bavaria, 1845; d. at sea, aboard the* Titanic, *1912*), merchant, philanthropist. Brother of Nathan and Oscar S. Straus. Immigrated with family to Georgia, 1854. Prospered in crockery and glassware business; with brother Nathan, became owner of R. H. Macy and Co., New York City, 1896, developing it subsequently into the largest department store in the world. He also developed the Brooklyn, N.Y., store of Abraham & Straus. An enthusiastic Democrat, he served briefly in Congress and twice refused nomination for mayor of New York City.

STRAUS, JESSE ISIDOR (*b. New York, N.Y., 1872; d. New York, 1936*), merchant, diplomat. Son of Isidor Straus; nephew of Nathan and Oscar S. Straus. Associated with the family business of R. H. Macy & Co. *post* 1896, he took over its supervision in 1912 and acted as its president *post* 1919. An active Democrat, Straus served with success as U.S. ambassador to France, 1933–36. He was a benefactor of New York University and Harvard.

STRAUS, NATHAN (*b. Otterberg, Rhenish Bavaria, 1848; d. New York, N.Y., 1931*), merchant, philanthropist. Brother of Isidor and Oscar S. Straus. Immigrated to Georgia with his family, 1854. A partner in the family crockery and glassware business, and later associated with his brother Isidor in the ownership of R. H. Macy and Co., Nathan Straus is particularly remembered as a pioneer in public health, a strong supporter of Zionism, and an active worker in innumerable campaigns for the relief of primary needs to which he devoted a great part of his fortune. During the last 15 years of his life he concentrated his efforts on supplying educational and social agencies for relief in Palestine.

STRAUS, OSCAR SOLOMON (*b. Otterberg,, Rhenish Bavaria, 1850; d. New York, N.Y., 1926*), lawyer, diplomat. Brother of Isidor and Nathan Straus. Immigrated with his family to Georgia, 1854. Graduated Columbia, 1871; Columbia Law School, 1873. *Post* 1881 a partner in the family crockery and glassware business, he is chiefly remembered as a diplomat. Prominent in the Democratic party, he served as U.S. minister to Turkey, 1887–89, 1898–1900, and 1909–10, distinguishing himself each time by his tact and success in negotiation. In 1902 he was appointed a member of the Hague Court and was subsequently reappointed in 1908, 1912, and 1920. He was U.S. secretary of commerce and labor, 1906–09, having become at this time a progressive Republican because of opposition to William J. Bryan. At the Paris Peace Conference, 1918–19, he continued a lifelong career of activity in behalf of his fellow Jews by striving to provide for safeguarding of the rights of Jewish minorities in Europe.

STRAUS, PERCY SELDEN (*b. New York, N.Y., 1876; d. New York, 1944*), department store executive, philanthropist. Son of Isidor Straus; brother of Jesse I. Straus. A.B., Harvard, 1897. Associated *post* 1897 with the family firm of R. H. Macy and Co., New York City, he was its president, 1933–39. An expert in the technique of store management, he was among the first in industry to use objective testing in the hiring and placement of employees and a leader in the introduction of formal training programs for clerks and executives.

STRAUS, ROGER W(ILLIAMS) (*b. New York, N.Y., 1891; d. Liberty, N.Y., 1957*), industrialist. Studied at Princeton University. The husband of Gladys Guggenheim, Straus entered the Guggenheim interests by becoming the family's representative at the American Smelting and Refining Co. before World War I. After the war, he became assistant to the president of the company, and president himself in 1941. Straus diversified the company by developing independent processing capabilities. In 1928, he helped found and finance the National Conference of Christians and Jews.

STRAUS, SIMON WILLIAM (*b. Ligonier, Ind., 1866; d. New York, N.Y., 1930*), banker. President S. W. Straus & Co., 1898–1928. Promoted building of skyscrapers; originated financing of building projects by sale of real estate bonds, 1909.

STRAUSS, JOSEPH BAERMANN (*b. Cincinnati, Ohio, 1870; d. Los Angeles, Calif., 1938*), bridge engineer, C.E., University of Cincinnati, 1892; assistant to Ralph Modjeski, 1899–1902. Originated and developed the Strauss trunnion bascule bridge and the Strauss lift bridge. Designer and builder of well over 400 bridges of all types, including his important modifications of the bascule, he is best known as chief engineer for the Golden Gate Bridge at San Francisco (completed 1937).

STRAWBRIDGE, ROBERT (*b. near Carrick-on-Shannon, Ireland, date unknown; d. near Towson, Md., 1781*), Methodist preacher. Immigrated between 1759 and 1766 to Maryland where he was the first apostle of Methodism, preaching in his home colony and also in neighboring Virginia, Delaware, and Pennsylvania.

STRAWN, JACOB (*b. Somerset Co., Pa., 1800; d. Illinois, 1865*), farmer, livestock dealer. Active *post* 1831 as a grazer and fattener of cattle on pasture tracts in Morgan, Sangamon, and LaSalle counties, Ill.

STRAWN, SILAS HARDY (*b. near Ottawa, Ill., 1866; d. Palm Beach, Fla., 1946*), corporation lawyer, businessman. Practiced in Chicago, with firm of Winston, Strawn, Black, and Towner; held office in local, state, and national bar associations and in U.S. Chamber of Commerce.

STREET, ALFRED BILLINGS (*b. Poughkeepsie, N.Y., 1811; d. 1881*), lawyer, poet, librarian of the New York State Library.

STREET, AUGUSTUS RUSSELL (*b. New Haven, Conn., 1791; d. New Haven, 1866*), businessman. Graduated Yale, 1812. A notable benefactor of Yale, Street endowed professorships in ecclesiastical history, modern languages, and the arts; he was also donor of Street Hall and endowed, in part, the Yale School of Fine Arts.

STREET, JOSEPH MONTFORT (*b. Lunenburg, Co., Va., 1782; d. near present Agency City, Iowa, 1840*), frontier journalist, Indian agent. Nephew of Montfort Stokes. Edited controversial Federalist *Western World* in Frankfort, Ky., in 1806–07, and for a time thereafter; on losing libel suit brought against him by Harry Innes, 1812, he removed to Shawneetown, Ill., where he was active in local politics. Appointed agent to the Winnebago tribe, he sought unsuccessfully to protect his wards from encroaching settlement and from frauds.

STREETER, GEORGE LINIUS (*b. Johnstown, N.Y., 1873; d. Gloversville, N.Y., 1948*), embryologist. Graduated Union College, 1895. M.D., College of Physicians and Surgeons, Columbia University, 1899. To prepare himself for practice in the diseases of the nervous system he studied in Germany, 1902–03, with the anatomist Ludwig Edinger at Frankfurt and the embryologist Wilhelm His at Leipzig. Strongly attracted by embryological research, upon his return to the United States, Streeter gave up the practice of medicine and joined the Department of Anatomy of the Johns Hopkins University School of Medicine, 1904. He was assistant professor of anatomy at the Wistar Institute, Philadelphia, 1906–07. He was professor of human anatomy at the University of Michigan, 1907–14, where he continued work on the development of the human brain, nerves, and auditory system. His chapter on the development of the major structures of the brain in the *Handbook of Human Embryology*, edited by Franz Keibel and Franklin P. Mall (1910), remains the most authoritative account of this complicated subject.

In 1914 Streeter joined the Department of Embryology of the Carnegie Institution of Washington, located at the Johns Hopkins Medical School, as a research associate; three years later he became director. During his directorship its publications filled 22 volumes of the *Contributions to Embryology of the Carnegie Institution*, one of the most distinguished American scientific publications. A notable early publication was a set of charts (in *Contributions to Embryology*, Vol. 2, 1920) relating the principal dimensions of human embryos and fetuses to their developmental age. This is still the standard quantitative record of human prenatal growth. Streeter participated with Chester H. Heuser and Carl G. Hartman in a masterly study of the early embryology of the rhesus monkey, 1925–41. He contributed also to the pathology of the embryo and fetus, notably by a revolutionary explanation of defects in which the loss of a limb (intrauterine amputation) or similar damage is associated with adhesions of the amnion at the site of injury. After his retirement in 1940, Streeter devoted himself to the compilation of a series of papers entitled "Developmental Horizons in Human Development" (1942–51), a descriptive and pictorial classification of the stages of embryonic development.

Streeter was elected to the National Academy of Sciences, 1931, and the American Philosophical Society, 1943. He was also a fellow of the Royal Society of Edinburgh, 1928. He was president of the American Association of Anatomists, 1926–28.

STRIBLING, THOMAS SIGISMUND (*b. Clifton, Tenn., 1881; d. Florence, Ala., 1965*), novelist and short-story writer. Attended Southern Normal College, Florence Normal College, and University of Alabama Law School (LL.B., 1905). Wrote fiction for Sunday-school magazines and adventure stories for such magazines as *Youth's Companion* and *American Boy* until 1917. His first novel, *Birthright*, was serialized in *Century Magazine* (1921–22) and gained wide attention; it was one of the first novels by a southerner to treat racial problems in a serious way. The novel *Teeftallow* (1926) firmly established his reputation. His most ambitious work was a trilogy: *The Forge* (1931); *The Store* (1932), which won the Pulitzer Prize in 1933; and *The Unfinished Cathedral* (1934). He frequently published short stories in the *Saturday Evening Post*, 1935–42, and mysteries in *Ellery Queen*, after 1945.

STRICKLAND, WILLIAM (*b. Philadelphia, Pa., ca. 1787; d. Nashville, Tenn., 1854*), architect, engineer, engraver. Studied under Benjamin H. Latrobe. An outstanding exponent of the Greek revival in America, he designed a number of Philadelphia buildings, including the U.S. Custom House, 1819; the Bank of the United States, completed 1824 (later the Custom House); and the Merchants' Exchange, 1834. At the time of his death he was engaged on the state capitol at Nashville, Tenn. Concurrently with his architectural work, he engaged in engineering work for the Chesapeake and Delaware Breakwater and made several railroad surveys.

STRINGFELLOW, FRANKLIN (*b. Culpeper Co., Va., 1840; d. Louisa Co., Va., 1913*), Episcopal clergyman, chief of scouts in the Army of Northern Virginia, 1864–65.

STRINGHAM, SILAS HORTON (*b. Middletown, N.Y., 1797; d. Brooklyn, N.Y., 1876*), naval officer. Appointed midshipman, 1809. Served in War of 1812 on frigate *President*; served against Algiers and in suppression of slave trade; commanded *Ohio* in Mexican War. Commodore in 1861, he was a valued adviser of Gideon Welles and, as commander of the Atlantic blockade fleet, planned and executed the expedition against forts at Hatteras Inlet, N.C., August 1861. Irked by criticism, he requested release in September; promoted rear admiral, 1862, he commanded the Boston navy yard until 1865.

STRINGHAM, WASHINGTON IRVING (*b. Yorkshire Center, present Delevan, N.Y., 1847; d. Berkeley, Calif., 1909*), mathematician. Graduated Harvard, 1877, influenced by Benjamin Peirce. Ph.D., Johns Hopkins, 1880. Author of a number of professional papers of high quality, he was professor of mathematics, University of California, 1882–1909.

STRITCH, SAMUEL ALPHONSUS (*b. Nashville, Tenn., 1887; d. Rome, Italy, 1958*), Roman Catholic prelate. Studied at St. Gregory's Preparatory Seminary and at the American College in Rome; he earned doctorates in philosophy (1906) and theology (1910) and was ordained on special dispensation from Pope Pius X in 1910. Consecrated bishop of Toledo, Ohio, he served there from 1921 to 1930; from 1930 to 1940, he was archbishop of Milwaukee; and, from 1940 to 1958, Archbishop of Chicago. In 1946, he became a Cardinal. In 1958, shortly before his death, he was appointed pro-prefect of the Sacred Congregation for the Propagation of the Faith in the Rome Curia, the first American to head a Rome Curia department. Remembered for his work with the poor, especially during the Depression years, Stritch was often called the Cardinal of the Poor.

STROBEL, CHARLES LOUIS (*b. Cincinnati, Ohio, 1852; d. Chicago, Ill., 1936*), civil engineer, specialist in steel-framed structures. As consultant for Burnham & Root and for Adler & Sullivan, he helped devise the steel-skeleton construction of many early skyscrapers. Active in standardization of the design and manufacture of steel structural shapes, he was originator of the Z-bar and designer of standard I-beam sections. He was author of *A Pocket Companion . . . to the Use of Wrought Iron for Engineers, Architects and Builders* (1881).

STROBEL, EDWARD HENRY (*b. Charleston, S.C., 1855; d. Bangkok, Thailand, 1908*), diplomat. Entering the U.S. diplomatic service, 1885, as secretary of legation at Madrid, Spain, he held posts thereafter at Washington, D.C., and in Ecuador and Chile. Appointed Bemis professor of international law, Harvard Law School, 1898. Became a general adviser to the then Siamese government with rank of minister plenipotentiary, 1903, and effected numerous reforms before his death.

STROHEIM, ERICH VON. *See* VON STROHEIM, ERICH.

STROMME, PEER OLSEN (*b. Winchester, Wis., 1856; d. 1921*), Lutheran clergyman, Norwegian-American journalist and author.

STRONG, ANNA LOUISE (*b. Friend, Nebr., 1885; d. Beijing, China, 1970*), radical journalist and lecturer. Attended Oberlin, Bryn Mawr, and University of Chicago (B.A. from Oberlin, 1905). Moved to New York City in 1909, and her circle of radical and bohemian friends widened to include most of the city's left-wing intellectuals. In Seattle in 1916 she made friends with unionists and members of the Industrial Workers of the World. She began to write for the IWW's *Seattle Daily Call*, then for the *Seattle Union Record*, a paper run by the Seattle branch of the American Federation of Labor. She traveled to Moscow in 1921 to report on the Soviet famine. During 1921–49 she traveled often to Russia and China and recounted events in those countries in such works as *China's Millions* (1928) and *The Soviets Conquer Wheat* (1931). Also wrote an autobiography, *I Change Worlds! The Remaking of an American* (1935). Founding editor of the *Moscow Daily News*, an English-language paper (1930–46); she was arrested in Moscow in 1949 and expelled "for spying activities." In 1957 she moved to China, her chief activity being the writing of the newsletter *Letters from China* (1961–70).

STRONG, AUGUSTUS HOPKINS (*b. Rochester, N.Y., 1836; d. 1921*), Baptist clergyman, theologian. Graduated Yale, 1856; Rochester Theological Seminary, 1859. Pastor, First Baptist Church, Haverhill, Mass., 1861–65; First Baptist Church, Cleveland, Ohio, 1865–72. President and professor of biblical theology, Rochester Theological Seminary, 1872–1912; thereafter, president emeritus. Author of, among other works, *Systematic Theology* (1886, 1907–09) and *Philosophy and Religion* (1888). Influenced his onetime parishioner John D. Rockefeller in founding a university under Baptist auspices, an idea which eventuated in refounding of University of Chicago.

STRONG, BENJAMIN (*b. Fishkill-on-Hudson, N.Y., 1872; d. New York, N.Y., 1928*), banker. Official in Bankers' Trust Co., New York; first governor, Federal Reserve Bank of New York, 1914–28.

STRONG, CALEB (*b. Northampton, Mass., 1745; d. Northampton, 1819*), lawyer, Federalist statesman, Massachusetts legislator and official. Graduated Harvard, 1764; studied law under Joseph Hawley; was admitted to Massachusetts bar, 1772. Served on committee for drafting Massachusetts constitution, 1779. Represented Massachusetts in Constitutional Convention of 1787, advocating annual elections of representatives and choice of a president by Congress and making the successful motion that the House alone should originate money bills, although the Senate might amend them. U.S. senator from Massachusetts, 1789–96, he formed, with Oliver Ellsworth and Rufus King, the bulwark of the administration in the Senate. As Federalist governor of Massachusetts, 1800–07, he was responsible, fair-minded, and an able administrator; during his second period as governor, 1812–16, he was in continuous opposition to the national administration and the War of 1812. He approved both the calling of the Hartford Convention in December 1814 and its subsequent report.

STRONG, CHARLES AUGUSTUS (*b. Haverhill, Mass., 1862; d. Fiesole, Italy, 1940*), psychologist, philosopher. Son of Augustus H. Strong; son-in-law of John D. Rockefeller. Graduated University of Rochester, 1884; A.B., Harvard, 1885; studied also in Germany. Influenced by William James and George Santayana. Strong taught briefly at Cornell, Clark, and University of Chicago; he was lecturer in psychology, Columbia University, 1896–1903, and professor of psychology, 1903–13. Author of a number of books, he belonged to the group known as the critical realists.

STRONG, CHARLES LYMAN (*b. Stockbridge, Vt., 1826; d. 1883*), mining engineer. First superintendent of Gould & Curry mine at Virginia City, Nev. (Comstock Lode), 1860–64.

STRONG, HARRIET WILLIAMS RUSSELL (*b. Buffalo, N.Y., 1844; d. near Whittier, Calif., 1926*), horticulturist, civic leader. Wife of Charles L. Strong. Raised in California. Pioneered in California walnut industry; was an early advocate of flood control for irrigation; patented device for impounding debris and water in hydraulic mining, 1893.

STRONG, JAMES (*b. New York, N.Y., 1822; d. Round Lake, N.Y., 1894*), biblical scholar, businessman. Professor of exegetical theology, Drew Theological Seminary, 1868–93. A learned, conservative scholar.

STRONG, JAMES HOOKER (*b. Canandaigua, N.Y., 1814; d. Columbia, S.C., 1882*), naval officer. Appointed midshipman, 1829. Distinguished for Civil War service as commander of USS *Monongahela*, notably at Mobile Bay, August 1864, where he put the Confederate ram *Tennessee* out of action. He retired as rear admiral, 1876.

STRONG, JAMES WOODWARD (*b. Brownington, Vt., 1833; d. Northfield, Minn., 1913*), Congregational clergyman, educator. Brother of William B. Strong. President, Carleton College, 1870–1903.

STRONG, JOSIAH (*b. Naperville, Ill., 1847; d. 1916*), Congregational clergyman, social reformer. A pioneer, with Washington Gladden and Walter Rauschenbusch, in the Social Gospel movement. Strong was author of two influential books, *Our Country* (1885) and *The New Era* (1893), analyzing the social and economic ills of his day and calling for the creation of an ideal society upon earth. Founder of the League for Social Service (later the American Institute for Social Services), 1898, he initiated the Safety First movement and was active participant in the establishment of the Federal Council of Churches.

STRONG, MOSES McCURE (*b. Rutland, Vt., 1810; d. Mineral Point, Wis., 1894*), surveyor, lawyer, Wisconsin legislator and official. Settled at Mineral Point, 1836.

STRONG, RICHARD PEARSON (*b. Fortress Monroe, Va., 1872; d. Cambridge, Mass., 1948*), public health physician, educator, expert on tropical medicine. Ph.B., Sheffield Scientific School, Yale, 1893; M.D., Johns Hopkins, 1897. Served as assistant surgeon, U.S. Army, during Spanish-American War; from 1899 to 1901 he established and directed the work of the Army Pathological Laboratory and served as president of the Board for the Investigation of Tropical Diseases in the Isthmus of Panama. In 1901 he went to the Philippines. Leaving the army while in Manila, he became director of the Biological Laboratories Bureau of Science, 1901–13; professor of tropical medicine at the College of Medicine and Surgery at University of the Philippine Islands, 1907–13, and chief of medicine at the Philippine Islands General Hospital, 1910–13.

Strong joined the faculty of medicine of Harvard University in 1913 as the first professor of tropical medicine, a post he held until his retirement in 1938. During these years he led numerous expeditions to study tropical diseases in their natural habitat. Many publications by Strong and his associates resulted from these expeditions, notably his monograph on onchocerciasis in Africa and America in 1934 and his two volumes in Liberia. In 1938 he assumed responsibility for the foremost textbook in his field, Edward Stitt's *Diagnosis and Treatment of Tropical Disease*, which he rewrote after his retirement from Harvard.

In 1915 Strong directed the Rockefeller Institute's expedition to Serbia to combat a typhus epidemic. Joining the American Expeditionary Forces in 1917 as a member of the chief surgeon's staff, he and his group demonstrated that trench fever was transmitted by a louse. Rejoining the Medical Reserve Corps as a colonel in 1941, he served as director of tropical medicine at the Army Medical School in Washington through World War II.

STRONG, THEODORE (*b. South Hadley, Mass., 1790; d. 1869*), mathematician, educator. Graduated Yale, 1812. Professor of mathematics and natural philosophy at Hamilton College, 1816–27; at Rutgers College, 1827–61.

STRONG, WALTER ANSEL (*b. Chicago, Ill., 1883; d. 1931*), journalist. Associated *post* 1905 with the *Chicago Daily News*, he served as its publisher, 1925–31. He was active also in many national publishing organizations and in local civic affairs.

STRONG, WILLIAM (*b. Somers, Conn., 1808; d. 1895*), jurist, U.S. Supreme Court justice. Graduated Yale, 1828. Admitted to the Philadelphia, Pa., bar, October 1832, he began practice in Reading, Pa. Congressman, Democrat, from Pennsylvania, 1847–51; outstanding justice, Pennsylvania Supreme Court, 1857–68. Appointed associate justice of the U.S. Supreme Court, 1870, he was concerned with Joseph P. Bradley in the 1871 reversal of a previous Supreme Court decision which had held the Legal Tender Act of February 1862 unconstitutional. This action led to the charge that President Grant, by appointing Strong, had "packed" the Court in order to ensure such a decision. Strong's position, however, was wholly consistent with his previous record and views on the subject. Until his resignation, December 1880, he remained a power on the Supreme Court bench and generally regarded as one of the truly great judges of the Court. He has been compared for integrity of character to John Jay.

STRONG, WILLIAM BARSTOW (*b. Brownington, Vt., 1837; d. Los Angeles, Calif., 1914*), railroad official. Brother of James W. Strong. Transformed the Atchison, Topeka & Sante Fe Railroad into a system of national importance as its general manager *post* 1877 and its president, 1881–89.

STRONG, WILLIAM LAFAYETTE (*b. Richland Co., Ohio, 1827, d. 1900*), merchant. Removed to New York City, 1853, where he became wealthy in the dry-goods business. An ardent Republican, he served as reforming mayor of New York City, 1894–97. Appointed Theodore Roosevelt police commissioner.

STROTHER, DAVID HUNTER (*b. Martinsburg, Va. [now W.Va.], 1816; d. Charles Town, W.Va., 1888*), Union soldier, author, illustrator. A valued contributor to *Harper's New Monthly Magazine*, he produced a number of illustrated articles dealing with life in Virginia which were collected as *Virginia Illustrated, by Porte Crayon* (1857). He was author and illustrator of other superior magazine series which were not reprinted. A Unionist, he served on staff duty throughout the Civil War, receiving brevet of brigadier general at its close. He was U.S. consul general at Mexico City, 1879–85.

STRUBBERG, FRIEDRICH ARMAND (*b. Cassel, Germany, 1806; d. Gelnhausen, Germany, 1889*), novelist, physician. Resident in frontier America, 1826–29 and *ca.* 1840–54, he used his experiences in Texas and Arkansas as materials for more than 50 volumes of fiction, written in German under the pen name "Armand."

STRUDWICK, EDMUND CHARLES FOX (*b. near Hillsboro, N.C., 1802; d. Hillsboro, 1879*), physician, surgeon. M.D., University of Pennsylvania, 1824. The best type of "country doctor," he practiced at Hillsboro *post* 1826.

STRUNSKY, SIMEON (*b. Vitebsk, Russia, 1879; d. Princeton, N.J., 1948*), journalist, essayist. Brought at age seven to the

United States by Jewish immigrant parents, he grew up on New York City's Lower East Side. A.B., Columbia College (University), 1900. Employed first as an encyclopedia editor, he was a member of the editorial staff of the *New York Evening Post*, 1906–24 (chief editorial writer *post* 1920), and editorial writer and columnist on the *New York Times*, 1924–48. A humorist and a prose stylist, he was author of, among other books, *The Patient Observer and His Friends* (1911), *Belshazzar Court* (1914), and *No Mean City* (1944).

STRUVE, GUSTAV (*b. Munich, Bavaria, 1805; d. Vienna, Austria, 1870*), publicist, revolutionary agitator. Union soldier. A lawyer and jurist in his native Germany, he was active in the events which led up to the Revolution of 1848 and was associated with F. K. F. Hecker and Franz Sigel in the abortive republic of Baden. Resident in the United States, 1851–63, he wrote without much success, edited the socialist periodical *Die sociale Republik*, and worked for cooperation of labor groups in New York and Philadelphia. A 19th-century disciple of Rousseau and Robespierre, he combined noble intentions with opinionated impracticability.

STRUVE, OTTO (*b. Kharkov, Russia, 1897; d. Berkeley, Calif., 1963*), astronomer. Attended Kharkov University and then, after arriving in the United States in 1921, University of Chicago (Ph.D., 1923). Joined the Yerkes Observatory of the University of Chicago in 1921, becoming director in 1932 and editor of the *Astrophysical Journal*. He mastered observing techniques in spectroscopic stellar astronomy, but rapidly advanced into modern astrophysics. He drafted a plan whereby the universities of Chicago and Texas joined forces in the construction of McDonald Observatory (1935–36) in west Texas. Chairman of the Department of Astronomy at the University of California at Berkeley (1950–59), then director of the National Radio Astronomy Observatory in West Virginia (1959–62). His many projects included spectroscopic observations of double stars and studies of novae, surface brightness of bright and dark nebulae, and general radiation of the interstellar medium.

STRYKER, LLOYD PAUL (*b. Chicago, Ill., 1885; d. New York, N.Y., 1955*), attorney. Studied at Hamilton College. Called "the most celebrated American criminal lawyer since Clarence Darrow," by the *New York Times*, Stryker won fame for his work in two trials: the defense of James J. Hines, a Tammany Hall leader indicted for conspiring to protect an illegal daily lottery who was prosecuted by district attorney Thomas E. Dewey; and the defense of Alger Hiss in his first perjury trial. Both men were later convicted, but Stryker's defense gained him a national reputation. He wrote *Courts and Doctors* (1932) and *The Art of Advocacy* (1954).

STRYKER, MELANCTHON WOOLSEY (*b. Vernon, N.Y., 1851; d. Rome, N.Y., 1929*), Presbyterian clergyman, hymnologist. President of Hamilton College, 1892–1917, he improved that institution in all departments, procuring large additions to its funds.

STUART, ALEXANDER HUGH HOLMES (*b. Staunton, Va., 1807; d. 1891*), lawyer, Virginia legislator. Son of Archibald Stuart. Graduated University of Virginia, 1828. A follower of Henry Clay, he served in the U.S. Congress, 1841–43. As U.S. secretary of the interior, 1850–53, he proved himself a successful organizer of his department. Active in the Know-Nothing party, he opposed secession as long as opposition was practicable. He was prevented by age from taking any active part in the Civil War, but was sympathetic with his section. After the war he played a large part in securing restoration of home rule to Virginia. He was rector of the University of Virginia, 1876–82 and 1884–86, and served for some years as a trustee of the Peabody Fund.

STUART, ARCHIBALD (*b. near Staunton, Va., 1757; d. 1832*), Revolutionary soldier, Virginia legislator and jurist. Father of Alexander H. H. Stuart. For many years a prominent leader of the conservative wing of Virginia Democratic-Republicans, he was judge of the general court of Virginia, 1800–32.

STUART, CHARLES (*b. Jamaica, British West Indies, 1783; d. Lake Simcoe, Canada, 1865*), abolitionist, mentor of Theodore D. Weld. Settled in Canada *ca.* 1814. Author of, among other antislavery tracts, *The West India Question* (1832), a widely circulated and influential statement of abolitionist principles.

STUART, CHARLES BEEBE (*b. Chittenango Springs, N.Y., 1814; d. Cleveland, Ohio, 1881*), engineer, Union soldier. Active in New York State railroad construction, 1833–49; proposed railway suspension bridge over Niagara River below the Falls (completed 1855); supervised construction of navy dry docks, 1849–53. Thereafter a successful businessman and consulting engineer, he was author of, among other works, *The Naval and Mail Steamers of the United States* (1853) and *Lives and Works of Civil Military Engineers of America* (1871).

STUART, CHARLES MACAULAY (*b. Glasgow, Scotland, 1853; d. La Jolla, Calif., 1932*), Methodist clergyman, educator, editor. Energetic and successful president of Garrett Biblical Institute, 1911–24.

STUART, ELBRIDGE AMOS (*b. near Greensboro, N.C., 1856; d. Los Angeles, Calif., 1944*), businessman, cattlebreeder. Raised in Indiana. Cofounder, president, 1899–1932, and chairman of the board, 1932–44, of the Carnation Co., producers of milk products "from contented cows."

STUART, FRANCIS LEE (*b. Camden, S.C., 1866; d. Essex Falls, N.J., 1935*), civil engineer, specialist in railroad and transportation problems.

STUART, GILBERT (*b. North Kingstown Township, Kings [later Washington] Co., R.I., 1755; d. Boston, Mass., 1828*), painter. Growing up in Newport, R.I., Stuart early showed talent for drawing and, *ca.* 1769, became pupil of a Scottish artist, Cosmo Alexander, then working in Newport. Traveling to Edinburgh with Alexander, who died there in August 1772, Stuart failed in an attempt to support himself by his art and is said to have worked his way home in 1773 or 1774 on a collier bound for Nova Scotia. After busying himself at home in painting and the study of music, he sailed for London in June 1775 as conditions in pre-Revolutionary America were adverse to the practice of art as a profession. After about a year of privation, he wrote to Benjamin West (1738–1820) asking help; receiving an immediate, friendly response, he became West's pupil and later (probably summer 1777) became a member of his household and remained with him for nearly five years. By 1781 he had become an exhibitor at the Royal Academy exhibitions, and his work was attracting favorable notice from London critics. In 1782 his *Portrait of a Gentleman Skating* brought him prominently before the public and he received many commissions.

By 1787, Stuart had become one of the leading portrait painters of London, sharing honors with J. Reynolds, G. Romney, and Gainsborough. He was also living in a very lavish style and, because of his lifelong unconcern with business details, came in danger of imprisonment for debt. Accordingly, he left England for Ireland, probably early in the summer of 1787, and scored success all over again in Dublin. Here, too, however, he lived injudiciously, fell in debt, and late in 1792 or early in 1793 sailed for New York City hopeful of making enough money to pay off his English and Irish creditors. He also had in mind to make a fortune by painting portraits of George Washington and to profit through the sale of prints of a Washington portrait. After practicing in New

York, he removed to Philadelphia in November 1794, and opened a studio on the southwest corner of Fifth and Chestnut streets. As always immediately successful in securing commissions from leaders of intellect and fashion, he completed in Philadelphia a brilliant series of portraits of women, and there painted his first two life portraits of Washington. The first, a bust showing the right side of the face and known as the Vaughan Type, was painted in the late winter of 1795. Beginning in April 1796, Washington sat for Stuart for a second life portrait, a life-size standing figure showing left side of face and with right hand outstretched, which is known as the Landsdowne Type. Stuart removed to Germantown, Pa., in the summer of 1796 and during the early fall made a third life portrait of the president, a bust showing the left side of the face, eyes front. This is the well-known "Athenaeum Head," unfinished as to the stock and coat; it is highly idealized.

Stuart followed the seat of government to Washington in 1803. He opened a studio there at F and Seventh streets and there painted Jefferson, Madison, Monroe, and many other contemporary leaders. Removing to Boston, Mass., in the summer of 1805, he lived there for the remainder of his life. Successful as usual, he was overrun with commissions, but chronically out of money owing to his indifferent business habits. *Post* 1825, although symptoms of paralysis developed in his left arm, he continued to paint, but with difficulty.

Stuart had in his manners much of the formality of the old school, yet his dress was usually disordered, and he took snuff from a tin box holding perhaps half a pound, which he used up in a single day. A witty man with a keen sense of the ridiculous, he was celebrated for his gifts as a talker and for his extensive knowledge of the art masters of all ages, on whom he could discourse with great charm and learning. A procrastinator, he would only paint when in the mood, was quick to take offense, and impatient of any criticism of his work. Benjamin West is quoted as having said, "It's no use to steal Stuart's colors; if you want to paint as he does you must steal his eyes." Stuart's mastery of the use of what may be called transparent color gave his portraits their lifelike and luminous effect, and it is this quality which ranks them supreme among American portrait paintings.

STUART, GRANVILLE (*b. Clarksburg, Va. [now W.Va.], 1834; d. Missoula, Mont., 1918*), Montana pioneer. Raised in Illinois and Iowa. After prospecting in California, September 1852–June 1857, Stuart, on a return journey east with some companions, turned north before reaching Great Salt Lake and entered Beaverhead Valley in present Montana. Proceeding to Deer Lodge Valley in spring 1858, Stuart and a brother, with others, found gold. After further prospecting and varying success he settled permanently in Deer Lodge Valley, 1867, took a leading part in community affairs, and served in the territorial council and legislature. He organized and managed the stock-raising firm of Davis, Hauser and Stuart Co., 1879, and was successful for a time in operations of the Judith Basin. Overstocking of the range and losses in the winter of 1886–87 brought the firm to disaster. He served thereafter as state land agent, as U.S. minister to Uruguay and Paraguay, and as librarian of the Butte city library. A student and an observer, he was instrumental in founding many of the civic and cultural organizations in Montana. He was author of *Montana As It Is* (1865), and his journals, together with those of his borther James, were published in part as *Forty Years on the Frontier* (1925).

STUART, HENRY ROBSON. *See* ROBSON, STUART.

STUART, ISAAC WILLIAM (*b. New Haven, Conn., 1809; d. Hartford, Conn., 1861*), local historian, orator. Son of Moses Stuart.

STUART, JAMES EWELL BROWN (*b. Patrick Co., Va., 1833; d. Richmond, Va., 1864*), soldier. Graduated West Point, 1954. Commissioned in the cavalry, he served briefly in Texas. He was in Kansas with the 1st Cavalry for the most part of 1855–61, rising to rank of captain. Resigning from the U.S. Army on learning of the secession of Virginia, he was commissioned lieutenant colonel of Virginia infantry, May 10, 1861, and captain of Confederate cavalry, May 24, 1861. At the first battle of Bull Run, he protected the Confederate left with the 1st Virginia Cavalry and contributed to the victory. Promoted brigadier general, September 1861, he brought his cavalry command to high efficiency and showed himself outstanding in outpost duty. His spectacular sweeps around the Union army during the fighting in northern Virginia won him General R. E. Lee's praise as the "eyes of the army"; skillful though not original in tactics, he was defective in strategic sense, but had the rare gift of winning the goodwill of men as dissimilar as Stonewall Jackson and Longstreet. Dressed like a beau and always alive to the dramatic, Jeb Stuart was often accused by other officers (some of them in his own corps) of selfish disregard of the achievements of subordinates, of consciously parading himself for admiration, and of claiming credit that belonged to others. However, he confounded his critics at Fredericksburg and held the line of the Rappahannock with much skill during the winter of 1862–63. He was also extremely effective in the Confederate victory at Chancellorsville, commanding the II Corps after the wounding of Stonewall Jackson and the incapacitation of A. P. Hill. Meanwhile, he had been promoted major general and confirmed in that grade, September 1862.

The Gettysburg campaign represents the most disputable chapter in Stuart's career. Expected to play his usual role of screening the army's movements and collecting information and provisions, he engaged in a raid which achieved little in itself and which left Lee groping in the dark at a time when accurate information of the enemy was of the essence. Although he rejoined the main Confederate army on the afternoon of July 2 and was ceaselessly active through the rest of the campaign, it has been asserted that he cost Lee the victory by his actions. This matter is still a subject of controversy. Thereafter he served with ability and zeal at his principal task of keeping his commander informed of hostile movements and engaged in a number of lesser battles, very often employing his cavalrymen as infantry. He covered with skill Lee's operations subsequent to Grant's crossing of the Rapidan, May 4, 1864, but was mortally wounded a week later as he endeavored to intercept General P. H. Sheridan's drive on Richmond at Yellow Tavern.

STUART, JOHN (*b. Scotland, ca. 1700; d. Pensacola, Fla., 1779*), colonial Indian agent. Immigrated to America *ca.* 1748; settled in South Carolina. Superintendent of Indian affairs for the southern district *post* 1762, Stuart fled to Florida, 1775, after his arrest was ordered by the South Carolina assembly on the charge of attempting to incite the Catawba and the Cherokee in the British interest. Thereafter until his death he strove to raise Loyalist companies and secure Indian cooperation with the British, but died under censure for his failures and for the enormous amount of money he had spent.

STUART, JOHN LEIGHTON (*b. Hangchow, China, 1876; d. Washington, D.C., 1962*), missionary, university president, and ambassador. Son of missionary parents, arrived in the United States in 1887. Attended Hampden-Sidney College (1893–96; D.D., 1913) and Union Theological Seminary; ordained a Presbyterian minister in 1902. Settled in the Hangchow area of China in 1904 as professor at Nanking Theological Seminary (1908–19). Wrote *Essentials of New Testament Greek in Chinese* (1916) and a *Greek-Chinese-English Dictionary of the New Testament* (1918). Became the first president of Yenching University in Beijing in

1919; when Japan invaded China in 1937 and captured the capital, he refused to fly the flag of the puppet government and in 1939 was interned by the Japanese in a house in Beijing; he was freed in 1945 and resumed the presidency of the university. Appointed U.S. ambassador to China in 1946, but returned to the United States in 1949. Wrote his memoirs, *Fifty Years in China* (1954).

STUART, JOHN TODD (*b. near Lexington, Ky., 1807; d. 1885*), Illinois lawyer, legislator, and congressman. Cousin of Mary Todd Lincoln. Practiced law in Springfield, Ill., *post* 1828. Friend, political mentor, and first law partner (Springfield, Ill., 1837–41) of Abraham Lincoln, he remained an old-line Whig and opposed the Republican party. Although a strong Unionist, he actively opposed Lincoln's administration, whose emancipation policy he decried.

STUART, MOSES (*b. Wilton, Conn., 1780; d. 1852*), Congregational clergyman, educator, biblical scholar. As professor at Andover Theological Seminary, 1810–48, he was outstanding for insistence on investigation of German scholarly literature and was author of some 40 books and monographs. He was the father of Isaac W. Stuart and the father-in-law of Austin Phelps.

STUART, ROBERT (*b. Callander, Perthshire, Scotland, 1785; d. Chicago, Ill., 1848*), fur trader. Immigrated to Canada, 1807; through Wilson P. Hunt, became partner in J. J. Astor's Pacific Fur Co., 1810. Sailing in that year on the *Tonquin* to the Columbia River, he was active in affairs of the Astoria colony; he journeyed eastward overland, 1812–13, with Ramsay Crooks and others over what was largely a new route. He later served as a traveling agent for Astor in the East and as Crooks's assistant at Mackinac, succeeding him *ca.* 1820 and remaining as head of the American Fur Co. for the upper Great Lakes region until 1834. Settling in Detroit, Mich., 1835, he engaged in business and civic affairs and was superintendent of Indian affairs for Michigan, 1841–45. His journal of the journey from Astoria appears in *The Discovery of the Oregon Trail* (P. A. Rollins, ed., 1935); it was summarized in Washington Irving's *Astoria*.

STUART, ROBERT LEIGHTON (*b. New York, N.Y., 1806; d. 1882*), sugar refiner, philanthropist. A generous benefactor to Presbyterian institutions and charities.

STUART, RUTH McENERY (*b. Marksville, La., 1849; d. 1917*), short-story writer, editor. Raised in New Orleans, which was her principal residence until her removal to New York City *ca.* 1892. Her stories and sketches, published in more than 20 volumes after periodical publication, were humorous, sentimental, and optimistic; however, she was the first to describe the post–Civil War black in his own social environment, and possessed an extraordinary skill in rendering dialect.

STUB, HANS GERHARD (*b. Muskego, Wis., 1849; d. St. Paul, Minn., 1931*), Lutheran clergyman, celebrated principally for his services in merging several synods into the Norwegian Lutheran Church of America, 1917. He served as president of this new body, 1917–25, and was emeritus thereafter.

STUBBS, WALTER ROSCOE (*b. near Richmond, Ind., 1858; d. Topeka, Kans., 1929*), railroad contractor, Kansas legislator, stockman. Raised in Douglas Co., Kans. Progressive Republican governor of Kansas, 1909–13, he failed of further political advancement after his support of Theodore Roosevelt, 1912.

STUCK, HUDSON (*b. London, England, 1863; d. Fort Yukon, Alaska, 1920*), Episcopal clergyman. Came to America, 1885; was employed at first as a public school principal in Texas. Ordained, 1892, he held several rectorates in Texas; *post* 1904 he

served as archdeacon of the Yukon. Author of several books descriptive of his travels and his mission work, he was one of the party which made the first complete ascent of Mount McKinley, 1913.

STUCKENBERG, JOHN HENRY WILBRANDT (*b. Bramsche, Hannover, Germany, 1835; d. London, England, 1903*), Lutheran clergyman, educator, sociologist. Immigrated to Pittsburgh, Pa., as a child; was raised in Cincinnati, Ohio. Graduated Wittenberg College, B.A., 1857; theology degree, 1858; studied also at universities of Halle, Göttingen, Tübingen, and Berlin. Held pastorates in several midwestern states and was pastor of the American Church in Berlin, Germany, 1880–94. A pioneer in the field of sociology, he was author of a number of studies, of which *Sociology, the Science of Human Society* (1903) was outstanding.

STUDEBAKER, CLEMENT (*b. Pinetown, Pa., 1831; d. 1901*), wagon and carriage manufacturer. Raised in Ashland Co., Ohio. Established with a brother the firm of H. & C. Studebaker at South Bend, Ind., 1852, which became the largest manufacturer of horsedrawn vehicles in the world. In 1897 he began experiments with self-propelled vehicles, and the company began their manufacture soon after his death.

STUHLDREHER, HARRY A. (*b. Massillon, Ohio, 1901; d. Pittsburgh, Pa., 1965*), college football player, coach, and athletic director. Attended Notre Dame (B.A., 1924), where he played football under coach Knute Rockne. One of the members of the "Four Horsemen" backfield, his Notre Dame teams won two national championships, had an undefeated season in 1924, and won the 1925 Rose Bowl game against Stanford. Named to Walter Camp's 1924 All-America team. Was football coach and athletic director at Villanova (1925–36), then at the University of Wisconsin (1936–50), after which he joined the industrial relations division of the United States Steel Company.

STURGES, PRESTON (*b. Chicago, Ill., 1898; d. New York, N.Y., 1959*), playwright, film director, and producer. Sturges was educated in Europe, served in the U.S. Army during World War I, and worked in his family's cosmetic firm before turning to writing. His first play, *Strictly Dishonorable* (1929) was a hit on Broadway; after other plays, Sturges went to Hollywood as a screenwriter. Films include *Diamond Jim* (1935), *If I Were King* (1939), and *The Great McGinty* (1940), which Sturges also directed and which won an Academy Award for the best screenplay.

STURGIS, RUSSELL (*b. Baltimore, Md., 1836; d. New York, N.Y., 1909*), architect, critic. Graduated present College of the City of New York, 1856; studied in office of Leopold Eidlitz and at Munich. Practiced in association with Peter B. Wight, 1863–68, and by himself until about 1880. A competent architect in the Greek revival and Victorian Gothic styles, he was more celebrated as a connoisseur and Ruskinian critic of art and architecture. As writer in the *Nation* and *Scribner's Magazine* and author of a number of books, he was perhaps the most important single factor in the artistic reawakening of the American people in the early years of the 20th century. His most ambitious work was *A History of Architecture* (1906–15, left unfinished).

STURGIS, SAMUEL DAVIS (*b. Shippensburg, Pa., 1822; d. St. Paul, Minn., 1889*), soldier. Graduated West Point, 1846. After service in the Mexican War, he performed duty in the West with the 1st Dragoons and the present 4th Cavalry. Commanding at Fort Smith, Ark., 1861, he brought off his troops in safety, together with most of the government property at the post, although menaced by hostile militia. He succeeded General Nathaniel Lyon in command at the battle of Wilson's Creek. Promoted brigadier general, August 1861, he commanded Union cavalry divisions for the rest of the Civil War, particularly distinguishing himself at Antietam, but suffering a severe defeat at Guntown, Miss., June 1864.

STURGIS, WILLIAM (b. Barnstable, Mass., 1782; d. Boston, Mass., 1863), Boston merchant in the China trade, Massachusetts legislator. Author of *The Oregon Question* (1845).

STURTEVANT, BENJAMIN FRANKLIN (b. Norridgewock, Maine, 1833; d. Jamaica Plain, Mass., 1890), inventor and manufacturer of shoemaking machinery. Patented a rotary exhaust fan, 1867, which he adapted for use in pressure blowers, ventilating fans, pneumatic conveyors, and the like, thereby virtually creating a new industry.

STURTEVANT, EDWARD LEWIS (b. Boston, Mass., 1842; d. 1898), agricultural scientist. Graduated Bowdoin, 1863; M.D., Harvard Medical School, 1866. Developed an experimental farm near South Framingham, Mass., where he made important studies of the physiology of milk and of the history of edible plants. First director, New York Agricultural Experiment Station at Geneva, 1882–87, he outlined broad plans of operation, which were largely followed in other stations established under the Hatch Act. He was author of a number of books and monographs.

STURTEVANT, JULIAN MONSON (b. Warren, Conn., 1805; d. Jacksonville, Ill., 1886), Congregational clergyman, educator. Graduated Yale, 1826. A member of the "Yale Band" pledged to further religion and education in the West, he taught *post* 1830 at Illinois College and served it as president 1844–76.

STUTZ, HARRY CLAYTON (b. Ansonia, Ohio, 1876; d. Indianapolis, Ind., 1930), automobile manufacturer, machinist. As engineer and manager of the Marion Motor Car Co., 1906–10, he designed for it the first "underslung" pleasure car. In 1911, he became a partner in the Ideal Motor Car Co., organized to manufacture a car designed by Stutz. In 1913 he consolidated this company with another under the name of the Stutz Motor Car Co. and served as president until 1919. His automobile gained its greatest reputation in the period 1913–19. *Post* 1919 he engaged principally in the manufacture of taxicabs and airplane engines.

STUYVESANT, PETRUS (b. Friesland, the Netherlands, date given variously from 1592 to ca. 1610; d. New York, N.Y., 1672), colonial governor and statesman. After early military service and a term as governor of Curaçao and adjacent islands (during which he lost his right leg subsequent to an expedition against the island of St. Martin), he was commissioned director general of New Netherland, July 28, 1646. Sailing from the Texel on Christmas Day, 1646, he stopped first at Curaçao and thence went on to New Amsterdam, arriving May 11, 1647, "like a peacock, with great state and pomp." Active and able, he set himself to promote good order in the colony by somewhat stern measures; he promoted intercolonial relations with the English, drove the Swedes from the Delaware, increased commerce, and set his face resolutely against assertions of the popular will in government. Despite his efforts, the people of New Amsterdam won independent municipal government in February 1653 after making a "remonstrance" to the States-General. Much to his disgust, Stuyvesant was obliged to surrender New Netherland to the English in the late summer of 1664 and thereafter withdrew from public affairs. After journeying to the Netherlands, 1665, to defend his official conduct, he returned to New York, where he lived on his farm until his death.

SUBLETTE, WILLIAM LEWIS (b. Lincoln Co., Ky., 1799[?]; d. Pittsburgh, Pa., 1845) fur trader, merchant. One of five brothers conspicuous in the early fur trade, he removed with his family to St. Charles, Mo., ca. 1818. He joined the expedition of William H. Ashley to the Rocky Mountains, 1822. He was with Ashley in the Arikara fight, June 1823, and served under Col. Henry Leavenworth in the attack on the Arikara villages in August. In his own business financed by Ashley, Sublette made a fortune, and, with Jedediah S. Smith and another partner, finally bought Ashley out. They continued to trade successfully as a firm until 1832, when Sublette formed a partnership with Robert Campbell which continued for some ten years; their principal trading posts were on the Platte at the mouth of the Laramie and on the Missouri near Fort Union.

SULLAVAN, MARGARET (b. Norfolk, Va., 1909; d. New Haven, Conn., 1960), actress. Studied at the E. E. Clive Dramatic School in Boston. Sullavan worked first for the University Players Guild where she met and married Henry Fonda. Her Broadway debut was *A Modern Virgin* (1931) and was followed by a series of bad plays but good personal reviews. In 1933, she took over a role in *Dinner at Eight* which won her a contract with Universal Pictures. Her first film won her stardom, *Only Yesterday*. Other films include *Three Comrades* (1938), *The Shining Hour* (1938), *The Shop Around the Corner* (1940), and *Back Street* (1941). Other Broadway roles include *Stage Door* (1936), *The Voice of the Turtle* (1942), considered her best role, and *Sabrina Fair* (1953).

SULLIVAN, GEORGE (b. Durham, N.H., 1771; d. Exeter, N.H., 1838), lawyer, New Hampshire legislator and congressman. Son of John Sullivan. Graduated Harvard, 1790. A Federalist, he opposed President Madison's foreign policies and the War of 1812. As New Hampshire attorney general, 1815–35, he served with ability but was said to rely too little on his preparation and too much upon his oratory.

SULLIVAN, HARRY STACK (b. Norwich, N.Y., 1892; d. Paris, France, 1949), psychiatrist. M.D., Chicago College of Medicine and Surgery, 1917. Best known for his work with schizophrenics, his theory of interpersonal relations, and his labors to bring about a fusion of psychiatry and social science.

SULLIVAN, JAMES (b. Berwick, District of Maine, 1744; d. probably Boston, Mass., 1808), lawyer, Massachusetts patriot, legislator and jurist. Brother of John Sullivan; father of William Sullivan. Practicing at first in Maine and *post* 1783 in Boston, Mass., he became one of the most prominent lawyers in the state and was a leader of the Democratic-Republicans there. A promoter of historical studies, he was author of several legal and historical treatises and served as governor of Massachusetts, 1807–08. During his term he engaged in a celebrated controversy with Timothy Pickering over the Embargo of 1807.

SULLIVAN, JAMES EDWARD (b. New York, N.Y., 1860; d. 1914), journalist, publisher, athlete. A zealot for the preservation of amateurism in sports, he was a founder of the Amateur Athletic Union of the United States, 1888, and American director of the Olympic Games.

SULLIVAN, JAMES WILLIAM (b. Carlisle, Pa., 1848; d. Carlisle, 1938), printer, trade unionist, advocate of the initiative and referendum. For many years a trusted lieutenant of Samuel Gompers in the American Federation of Labor.

SULLIVAN, JOHN (b. Somersworth, N.H., 1740; d. Durham, N.H., 1795), Revolutionary general, statesman. Brother of James Sullivan; father of George Sullivan. An able if somewhat litigious lawyer, generous, oversensitive, and a born political organizer, he was early engaged on the patriot side in the American Revolution. A New Hampshire delegate to the First Continental Congress, September–December 1774, he returned home to lead in the seizure of Fort William and Mary in Portsmouth harbor. After taking his seat in the second Continental Congress, he received appointment as brigadier general, June 1775. Serving through the siege of Boston, he was ordered to join the forces retreating from Canada after Montgomery's defeat at Quebec; he succeeded to their command on the death of General John Thomas. Superseded by General Horatio Gates in July 1776, he offered his resignation, but withdrew it and was promoted major general in August. Taken prisoner at the battle of Long Island, he was exchanged after serving as the bearer of Lord Howe's peace overtures to Congress and rejoined the American army in Westchester Co., N.Y. He shared in the retreat across New Jersey in the late fall of 1776, led the right column at Trenton, and pursued the British at Princeton. Embroiled with Congress because of his protests against undue favor given newly arrived foreign officers, he found his conduct in various engagements through 1777, including the battle of the Brandywine, called into question, but after investigation he was exonerated. He always had the strong support of George Washington. Once again unfortunate in his operations around Newport, R.I., in the summer of 1778, principally because of the failure of support from a French fleet, Sullivan was highly successful in a punitive expedition through western Pennsylvania and New York against the Iroquois Indians in the spring and summer of 1779, in association with General James Clinton. His health impaired, he resigned from the army, November 1779. Thereafter, he served briefly in Congress, was a New Hampshire legislator and attorney general, and was president (governor) of New Hampshire, 1786–87 and 1789. Appointed U.S. district judge for New Hampshire, 1789, he held that post until his death.

SULLIVAN, JOHN FLORENCE.   *See* ALLEN, FRED.

SULLIVAN, JOHN LAWRENCE   (*b. Boston, Mass., 1858; d. West Abington, Mass., 1918*), pugilist, the "Great John L." Defeated the American champion Paddy Ryan by a knockout in the ninth round at Mississippi City, Miss., Feb. 7, 1882; dominated the American prize ring for the next decade; ended his career in defeat by James Corbett, Sept. 7, 1892.

SULLIVAN, LOUIS HENRI   (*b. Boston, Mass., 1856; d. Chicago, Ill., 1924*), architect. Attended course in architecture at Massachusetts Institute of Technology under William R. Ware, 1872–73, but was irked by academic study; admired work of Henry H. Richardson; was encouraged by Richard M. Hunt. Removed to Chicago, where he worked for a time in office of William Le B. Jenney; studied at the École des Beaux Arts, Paris (atelier Vaudremer), 1874–75. Returning to Chicago, he won a reputation in several offices as a skillful draftsman, and in 1879 began to work with Dankmar Adler, becoming a partner in May 1881. The firm of Adler and Sullivan rose rapidly, but there is little in Sullivan's work done at this time to back his claim that he attempted a radical departure from contemporary work. However, on the completion of the Auditorium Building, Chicago, 1886–90, the firm received international recognition, not only for a demonstrated mastery of the problem of acoustics but for a definite break with tradition so far as the interior design was concerned. Accepting with enthusiasm the revolutionary principle of skeleton construction as demonstrated by Holobird and Roche, Sullivan then designed a series of important buildings expressing his own principles. Notable among these are the Wainwright Building, St. Louis, Mo.; the sensational Transportation Building at the World's Fair of 1893; and the Gage Building, Chicago. After the death of Adler in 1900, Sullivan's opportunity to do work on a large scale ceased and his material fortunes declined, yet he continued to fight for his major principle that "form follows function." In his writings and in what work he did, he stressed the essentially modern function of the skyscraper and the proper form for its expression, attacking the triumphant eclecticism of the post-1893 period. Known as the founder of the

"Chicago school," Sullivan is father of modernism in architecture and more than any man helped to make the skyscraper America's greatest contribution to the art. His style of architectural ornament, although too personal and complicated for popular acceptance, was a distinct contribution, and he will be remembered also for the philosophy he set forth in *The Autobiography of an Idea* (1924).

SULLIVAN, LOUIS ROBERT   (*b. Houlton, Maine, 1892; d. 1925*), physical anthropologist. Author of a number of important studies of race, describing geographical distribution and physical characteristics of anthropological types.

SULLIVAN, MARK   (*b. Avondale, Pa., 1874; d. Avondale, Pa., 1952*), journalist. Studied at West Chester Normal School and Harvard University (LL.B., 1903). A noted "muckraker," Sullivan was a journalist for *Collier's Weekly* from 1906 to 1917; editor from 1914. From 1919 to 1923 he was Washington correspondent for the *New York Evening Post*. From 1923 until his death he wrote a syndicated column for the *New York Tribune* (later the *Herald-Tribune*). A personal friend of Herbert Hoover, Sullivan was a champion of the nineteenth-century ideals of individualism; he saw the New Deal as a threat to these ideals and became increasingly conservative in his political views. Wrote *Our Times*, a popular history of the United States from 1900 to 1925.

SULLIVAN, TIMOTHY DANIEL   (*b. New York, N.Y., 1862; d. near Eastchester, N.Y., 1913*), politician, known as "Big Tim." A saloonkeeper and vaudeville entrepreneur, Sullivan raised himself to leadership of the Tammany Democracy in New York City's Third Assembly District and was uncrowned king of the lower East Side, 1892–1912. An efficient organizer of graft and a magnetic machine boss, Sullivan played a strong role in New York State politics, 1900–10. He served as congressman, Democrat, from New York, 1903–07.

SULLIVAN, WILLIAM   (*b. Biddeford, Maine, 1774; d. 1839*), lawyer, Massachusetts legislator. Son of James Sullivan. Author of, among other works, *Familiar Letters on Public Characters and Public Events* (1834; repr., 1847, as *The Public Men of the Revolution*).

SULLIVAN, WILLIAM HENRY   (*b. Port Dalhousie, Canada, 1864; d. 1929*), lumberman. Organized and directed, *post* 1906, the vast lumbering operations and factory complex at Bogalusa, La.; helped build lumber industry in Louisiana along intelligent and conservationist lines.

SULLIVANT, WILLIAM STARLING   (*b. Franklinton, Ohio, 1803; d. 1873*), botanist, bryologist. Graduated Yale, 1823. Among his several pioneering and important works, his *Icones Muscorum* (1864) is considered outstanding; he also assisted in the amplification of Gray's *Manual*, 1856, and was associated in studies with Leo Lesquereux and others. His contribution to Gray's *Manual*, also published separately, laid the foundation for subsequent bryological studies in the United States.

SULLY, DANIEL JOHN   (*b. Providence, R.I., 1861; d. Beverly Hills, Calif., 1930*), cotton speculator, dominant in the New York City market, 1902–04.

SULLY, THOMAS   (*b. Horncastle, Lincolnshire, England, 1783; d. Philadelphia, Pa., 1872*), painter. Came to America, 1792; was raised in Charleston, S.C. Encouraged in his artistic tastes by Charles Fraser and by his elder brother, Lawrence Sully, a painter of miniatures. He removed to Virginia *ca.* 1799 and lived and studied with his brother in Richmond and Norfolk until 1803. In May 1801, Thomas Sully painted his first miniature portrait from life and continued to work industriously, but with little remuneration, until his removal to New York City in November 1806. There, with the aid of Thomas A. Cooper, Sully received a number of profitable commissions. Encouraged by a brief interview with Gilbert Stuart at Boston in 1807, Sully went to Philadelphia and made that city his permanent home in 1808. Although much of his early work ranks among his best, he was dissatisfied with his own skill. With the aid of friends, he visited England, July 1809–March 1810. There, Benjamin West (1738–1820) suggested that he make a serious study of anatomy and osteology, which Sully did; he also made the acquaintance of Sir Thomas Lawrence and the Kemble family of actors. After his return to Philadelphia he attempted several historical subjects and grew in reputation as a portraitist. After the deaths of Charles W. Peale, 1827, and Gilbert Stuart, 1828, Sully had no formidable rivals in his art. When he made a second visit to England, 1837, and painted the young Queen Victoria, he reached the summit of his fame, receiving a number of commissions from distinguished English people and achieving also a social success. During his career he produced more than 2,600 works. Although occasionally his draftsmanship was defective, he was always a master of color and his works have a characteristic warmth and beauty. Sometimes called "the Sir Thomas Lawrence of America," he was especially happy in delineation of women and children, yet some of his portraits of men, such as that of Dr. Samuel Coates, are marked by an admirable firmness.

SULZBERGER, ARTHUR HAYS (*b. New York, N.Y., 1891; d. New York, 1968*), newspaper publisher. Attended Columbia (B.S., 1913). In 1917 he married the daughter of *New York Times* publisher Adolph S. Ochs and began work with the *Times* in 1918 as assistant to the executive manager with unspecified duties. By the late 1920's he had worked his way up to a vice-presidency. His role in managing the paper grew in the 1930's, and he succeeded Ochs as president of the company and publisher of the paper in 1935. Under his leadership the *Times* experienced gradual and steady change and improvement in news coverage, newspaper content, and technical progress. In his twenty-five years as publisher, the advertising linage more than tripled, daily circulation increased by 40 percent, and Sunday circulation nearly doubled. After retiring as publisher in 1961, he became chairman of the board.

SULZBERGER, CYRUS LINDAUER (*b. Philadelphia, Pa., 1858; d. New York, N.Y., 1932*), textile merchant, leader in Jewish affairs, philanthropist.

SULZBERGER, MAYER (*b. Heidelsheim, Germany, 1843; d. Philadelphia, Pa., 1923*), jurist, Hebrew scholar. Cousin of Cyrus L. Sulzberger. Came as a child to Philadelphia, where he practiced law *post* 1865 after study in office of Moses A. Dropsie. He served as judge of the court of common pleas, 1895–1916, and was president judge *post* 1902. He was also active in Jewish welfare work and the promotion of higher Jewish learning.

SULZER, WILLIAM (*b. Elizabeth, N.J., 1863; d. New York, N.Y., 1941*), lawyer, politician. Attended Cooper Union; admitted to New York bar, 1884. A member of Tammany Hall, he represented an East Side district in the state assembly, 1890-94, serving as Speaker, 1893, and minority leader the following year. During nine terms in the House, Sulzer compiled a creditable record of support for progressive measures, including the graduated income tax and direct election of U.S. senators. As chairman of the House Foreign Affairs Committee after 1910, he opposed American intervention in Mexico and was responsible for the resolution abrogating the 1832 treaty of commerce with Russia. He advocated Cuban independence and supported the Boers' struggle in South Africa.

Although a product of Tammany Hall, Sulzer was a reformer independent enough to be opposed by the machine in one of his congressional races. When Tammany boss Charles F. Murphy finally accepted him as the organization's choice for governor in 1912, he campaigned as the "unbossed" candidate; after he won he promised that he would be "his own" governor, "the people's governor." As governor, Sulzer irritated Murphy by denying patronage to Tammany and by ordering investigations which revealed vast corruption, inefficiency, and maladministration in state departments. Resentful legislators, seeking to discredit him, uncovered evidence that he had diverted unreported campaign contributions to speculation in the stock market. Impeachment proceedings began, and on Oct. 17, 1913, in his tenth month as governor, Sulzer was found guilty.

Sulzer was again elected to the state assembly, this time for one term on the Progressive ticket. Defeated in the Progressive gubernatorial primary in 1914, he ran unsuccessfully as the American-Prohibition candidate. His political career ended ingloriously in 1916 when the Prohibitionists refused to make him their presidential candidate and he declined the American party nomination.

SUMMERALL, CHARLES PELOT (*b. Blount's Ferry, Fla., 1867; d. Washington, D.C., 1955*), soldier and educator. Graduated West Point in 1888. Saw action in the Spanish-American War, the Philippines, the Boxer Rebellion, and in France during World War I. An expert on the uses of artillery, Summerall made important contributions in the uses of these weapons. As commander of the Hawaiian Dept., he was criticized by Col. William Mitchell; later, Summerall sat on the court-martial of Mitchell. Appointed chief of staff by President Coolidge, 1926–30. Retired a four-star general in 1930. From 1931 to 1953, president of The Citadel, a military college in South Carolina, making that institution into one of the leading military colleges in the nation.

SUMMERS, EDITH. *See* KELLY, EDITH SUMMERS.

SUMMERS, GEORGE WILLIAM (*b. Fairfax Co., Va., 1804; d. Charleston, W.Va., 1868*), lawyer, Virginia legislator and congressman. Originally a Whig, he was an active Unionist and strong opponent of secession.

SUMMERS, THOMAS OSMOND (*b. near Corfe Castle, Dorsetshire, England, 1812; d. Nashville, Tenn., 1882*), Methodist clergyman, editor. Immigrated to New York, N.Y., 1830. After ministry, 1835-40, in Maryland, he became a founder of the Texas and Alabama conferences and was secretary to the 1844 convention at Louisville, Ky., which organized the Methodist Episcopal Church, South. He served thereafter as secretary of its conferences until his death. He was dean and professor of systematic theology at Vanderbilt University, 1876–82.

SUMNER, CHARLES (*b. Boston, Mass., 1811; d. Washington, D.C., 1874*), statesman. Son of an independent-minded antislavery lawyer and Massachusetts public official, Charles Sumner attended Boston Latin School, 1821–26, and Harvard College, 1826–30; at Harvard Law School, 1831–33, he was the pupil and friend of Joseph Story. Reacting against practical politics and finding the routine of legal practice little to his liking, he became a lecturer in the Harvard Law School, a contributor to the *American Jurist* and a reviser of legal textbooks. Francis Lieber and William E. Channing exercised a profound influence upon him. During two years of travel and observation in Europe *post* 1837, he learned French, German, and Italian and became acquainted with many literary and political figures; he also studied European governments and jurisprudence. Ambitious for distinction on the intellectual side of his profession, he produced an annotated edition of Vesey's *Reports of Cases . . . in the High Court of Chancery* (1844-45).

He reached a turning point in his career when he delivered the Boston Independence Day oration in 1845. Powerful of voice and skillful in oratory, he denounced war and, although bringing considerable odium on himself, discovered at the same time that he could thrill and sway great audiences. For years thereafter he was a successful lyceum lecturer. Loudly championing peaceful arbitration in public disputes and denouncing the Mexican War, he increased the antipathy of the conservative Whigs of Boston toward him, but was elected to the U.S. Senate by a coalition of Free-Soilers and Democrats, taking his seat, Dec. 1, 1851. Although the compromise measures of the previous year had apparently been accepted as final, Sumner rose toward the end of his first session to arraign the Fugitive Slave Law in a tremendous speech, Aug. 26, 1852, and moved an amendment that no allowances be permitted for expenses incurred in executing the law. The Southern senators heaped angry derision upon the amendment, and it received only four votes in its favor. Sumner, however, continued outspoken in opposition, particularly to the Kansas-Nebraska Act, which brought him into greater disfavor with the Boston press and society. In the debate on the right of petition, Southern senators charged Sumner with repudiating his oath of office and urged his expulsion, but could not muster the requisite two-thirds vote for this. Sumner's answer was that he had sworn to support the Constitution as he understood it, and his courage won admirers for him. Boldly denouncing the Know-Nothing party and scorning its support, he had a large part in organization of the Republican party.

During the hot debate in the Senate over the struggle for Kansas, Sumner delivered his famous "crime against Kansas" speech, May 20, 1856, denouncing the Kansas-Nebraska Act as "in every respect a swindle" and arraigning Andrew P. Butler and Stephen A. Douglas in bitter terms, thrilling antislavery forces throughout the North. Two days later he was assaulted at his desk in the Senate by Preston S. Brooks of South Carolina, a kinsman of Senator Butler. Seriously injured, Sumner went abroad in search of health and did not return to the Senate for three and a half years. Meantime, he had been reelected by almost unanimous vote of the Massachusetts legislature. Announcing his determination to assault American slavery all along the line, he set forth in a speech "the barbarism of slavery" (delivered during the debate on the bill for the admission of Kansas) a social, moral, and economic attack on the institution as well as a political one; widely distributed, the speech had great influence in the presidential election of 1860.

During the months following Lincoln's victory, Sumner refused to support the Crittenden Compromise. In October 1861, at the Massachusetts Republican convention, he became the first statesman of prominence to urge emancipation and thereafter never ceased to press for it. Appointed chairman of the Senate Committee on Foreign Relations, 1861, he rendered invaluable service to the Union in many ways, notably in effecting a peaceful solution of the problems raised by the seizure of Mason and Slidell and in bringing about the defeat or suppression of Senate resolutions which would have involved the United States in war with France and Great Britain. As early as the second year of the Civil War, he began a struggle to secure absolute equality of civil rights for all United States citizens. In February 1862, he announced the extravagant doctrine that the seceding states had abdicated all their rights under the Constitution and remained insistent that initiation and control of Reconstruction should be by Congress, not by the president.

During the administration of President Andrew Johnson, Sumner and Thaddeus Stevens headed, respectively, in the Senate and the House opposition to Johnson's Reconstruction policy. Sumner's persistence led the Senate to add to the requirements for readmission of seceded states the insertion in their constitution of a provision for equal suffrage for blacks and whites.

Prominent in the move to impeach President Johnson, Sumner descended to lurid and furious invective and showed himself at his worst in the opinion which he filed in support of his vote for conviction.

Antipathetic to President U.S. Grant, Sumner became antagonistic soon after the new administration began. Among other clashes, the most violent developed over the president's project of acquiring Santo Domingo. Sumner's committee brought in an adverse report on treaties negotiated by Grant's personal envoy, 1869. The administration retaliated against Sumner's friends and by bringing about his demotion from the chairmanship of the Foreign Relations Committee. The administration was influenced in this action also by fears that Sumner's excessive views on U.S. claims against Great Britain for wartime losses might jeopardize plans already under way for settlement of these claims. Among other legislation which Sumner introduced before his sudden death was a bill (introduced in session beginning December 1872) which provided that the names of Civil War battles should not be perpetuated in the Army Register or placed on regimental colors, an irenic gesture which brought him official censure.

Unlike Abraham Lincoln, Charles Sumner outlived his best days; his later years brought domestic sorrows, illness, and ceaseless struggle over problems of Reconstruction. Through many years in the Senate he strove for "absolute human equality" and judged every man and every measure by reference to that goal, becoming progressively intolerant not only of opposition but even of dissent. Diligent in the routine work of a senator, he commanded respect in discussions of money and finance, the tariff and copyright; he also introduced an intelligent bill for civil service reform. His great work, however, was not in the framing of laws but rather in the kindling of moral enthusiasm and the overthrow of injustice. A major force in the struggle that put an end to slavery, he also attempted to hold in check barbarous attempts at retaliation during wartime and maintained peace with European nations when war with them would have meant the end of the Union.

Sumner, Edwin Vose (*b.* Boston, Mass., 1797; *d.* Syracuse, N.Y., 1863), soldier. Commissioned lieutenant in infantry, 1819; appointed captain in 1st Dragoons, 1833. Served on the frontier and in the Mexican War with great credit; was for a time military commandant of New Mexico. Promoted colonel, 1st (present 4th) Cavalry, 1855, he campaigned along the Oregon Trail and was commander at Fort Leavenworth, 1856, acting with discretion to keep order during the struggle for Kansas. He assumed command of the Department of the West, 1858, with headquarters at St. Louis, Mo. A loyal Union man, Sumner accompanied the president-elect to Washington, D.C., 1861, and during the Civil War rose to rank of major general of volunteers for gallant service at Fair Oaks. He commanded the right grand division at Fredericksburg, but was soon after relieved of duty with the Army of the Potomac at his own request.

Sumner, Francis Bertody (*b.* Pomfret, Conn., 1874; *d.* La Jolla, Calif., 1945), zoologist. B.S., University of Minnesota, 1894; Ph.D., Columbia University, 1901. Taught biology at College of the City of New York, 1899–1906; directed laboratory of U.S. Fish Commission at Woods Hole, Mass., 1903–11; naturalist on the Bureau of Fisheries marine research ship *Albatross*, 1911–13. Associated thereafter with Scripps Institution at La Jolla, he became professor of biology there in 1926. Made important researches in the biology of fishes; demonstrated by breeding experiments with field mice that the accumulation of minor adaptive characteristics was a major factor in the evolution of the various geographic races.

SUMNER, INCREASE (*b. Roxbury, Mass., 1746; d. Roxbury, 1799*), jurist. Graduated Harvard, 1767; began practice of law at Roxbury, 1770. A Massachusetts legislator during the Revolution, he was appointed a justice of the Supreme Judicial Court of Massachusetts, 1782, winning repute as an able judge and a warm supporter of the new national government. Federalist governor of Massachusetts, 1797–99, he followed middle-of-the-road policy, allayed partisan bitterness, and gave special attention to improving the state's military defenses.

SUMNER, JAMES BATCHELLER (*b. Canton, Mass., 1887; d. Buffalo, N.Y., 1955*), biochemist. Studied at Harvard University (Ph.D., 1914). Around 1915, joined the faculty of Cornell University Medical College at Ithaca, N.Y.; full professor from 1929. Discovered that enzymes were proteins; successfully isolated the enzyme urease in 1926. Awarded the Nobel Prize for chemistry in 1946. Retired from Cornell in 1955.

SUMNER, JETHRO (*b. Nansemond Co., Va., ca. 1733; d. Warren Co., N.C., 1785*), planter, Revolutionary brigadier general. Fought in French and Indian War; removed to North Carolina, 1764. Among the foremost of North Carolina patriots in the Revolution, he distinguished himself in the defense of Charleston, 1776, with Washington's army in the campaigns of 1777–78, and in the defense of North Carolina against Cornwallis' invasion, 1780. He was also outstanding at the battle of Eutaw Springs, 1781.

SUMNER, WALTER TAYLOR (*b. Manchester, N.H., 1873; d. Portland, Oreg., 1935*), Episcopal clergyman. Attracted nationwide attention for activities in behalf of reform and social betterment as a minister in Chicago, 1904–15. Active and public-spirited bishop of Oregon, 1915–35.

SUMNER, WILLIAM GRAHAM (*b. Paterson, N.J., 1840; d. Englewood, N.J., 1910*), educator, social scientist. Graduated Yale, 1863. After study abroad in preparation for the ministry, he returned home and was tutor at Yale, 1866–69. Ordained priest of the Protestant Episcopal church, 1869, he remained in the ministry until 1872, also helping to establish, and editing, *The Living Church*. Because his interests turned increasingly to social and economic questions, he accepted the chair of political and social science at Yale in 1872 and spent the remainder of his life at that institution. A man of prodigious industry, he made his influence felt widely beyond the university, serving as a New Haven alderman and as a member of the Connecticut Board of Education. He wrote extensively, expressed his views on public questions, and engaged in extended research into the origin of social institutions which ranks him among the foremost students in this field. Skilled in all the social sciences, he had a working knowledge of at least a dozen languages.

A respected teacher and a most effective one, he made everyday affairs his textbook for the examination of social facts and principles. Rebelling against the conservatism of Yale, he labored against opposition to broaden the curriculum. Through public addresses and periodical essays he carried on a warfare against economic and political evils, treating practically every social question of his day in an unsentimental and critical fashion. He was an outstanding advocate of a sound monetary system and opposed all inflationary expedients, yet he also fought protectionism. Deploring the agitation against "big business" and regarding the evolution of the trusts as a natural phenomenon, he opposed with vigor any government interference upon the industrial field, maintaining that state remedies would be worse than the disease. He believed that social conditions can be improved, but only by scientific procedure carried on by thoroughly informed individuals. In his use of the term "the Forgotten Man" in an 1883 lecture, he meant the self-supporting person who has to bear the cost of political bungling and social quackery. Finding himself less and less satisfied by the traditional boundaries of political economy and political science, he became preoccupied with the concept of a general science of society which should incorporate religion, marriage customs, and all other examples of the human experience which might provide the facts for a scientific induction. Attempting a treatise on this subject, he became convinced that he must begin it with an analysis of custom and from this conviction developed his classic book *Folkways* (1907). His data and outline for the projected treatise appeared as *Science of Society* (reclassified and revised by Albert G. Keller, 1927). Sumner was author also of a number of other books on banking, finance and currency, three biographies, and several volumes of essays.

SUMNERS, HATTON WILLIAM (*b. Boons Hill, Tenn., 1875; d. Dallas, Tex., 1962*), lawyer and U.S. congressman. Admitted to the Texas bar in 1897; elected county attorney (1900–02, 1904–06) and U.S. congressman (1912–46). He was named to the Judiciary Committee in 1918; he appeared in four cases before the Supreme Court as spokesman for Congress and managed the impeachment trials of three federal judges (1926–36). A Democrat, he tolerated the New Deal in its early years, but was a central participant in defeating President Franklin Roosevelt's "court-packing" plan.

SUMTER, THOMAS (*b. near Charlottesville, Va., 1734; d. near Statebury, S.C., 1832*), Revolutionary officer, South Carolina partisan leader and legislator. After military experience in the campaigns of Braddock and Forbes and in fighting against the Cherokee, he settled as a storekeeper near Eutaw Springs, S.C., ca. 1765. A provincial congressman and for a time lieutenant colonel in the Continental service, he is remembered principally for his leadership of partisan troops against British and Tory forces in the Carolinas, 1780 and 1781–82. Feared by the enemy and called the "Gamecock of the Revolution," he played a role whose importance was out of all proportion to the small numbers he commanded. His campaigns were of material assistance to the later American victory at Yorktown.

SUNDAY, WILLIAM ASHLEY (*b. Ames, Iowa, 1862; d. 1935*), evangelist, popularly known as "Billy" Sunday. A member successively of the Chicago White Sox and the Pittsburgh and Philadelphia teams, 1883–91; he was associated thereafter until 1896 with activities of the Chicago YMCA and was assistant to the evangelist J. Wilbur Chapman. Beginning his independent career, 1896, he was ordained by the Chicago Presbytery, 1903. Soon becoming widely known, he held meetings in the largest cities of the United States. A vivid and unconventional preacher, he proclaimed a crude version of ultraconservative evangelical theology and instituted the practice of "hitting the sawdust trail," so called from the fact that the floors of the places in which he preached were covered with sawdust. Earnest and sincere, he preached the divine wrath rather than divine love.

SUNDERLAND, ELIZA JANE READ (*b. near Huntsville, Ill., 1839; d. Hartford, Conn., 1910*), educator, reformer. Active generally for human betterment, especially the promotion of temperance, the improvement of education, and the advancement of women, during long residences in Chicago, Ill., and Ann Arbor, Mich.

SUNDERLAND, LA ROY (*b. Exeter, R.I., 1804; d. 1885*), abolitionist. Originally a Methodist clergyman, but later a "faddist" and finally an infidel, he was responsible for organization of the first antislavery society in the Methodist church and was the first editor of *Zion's Watchman*, 1836.

SURRAT, JOHN H. *See* BOOTH, JOHN WILKES.

SURRAT, MARY. *See* BOOTH, JOHN WILKES.

SUTHERLAND, EDWIN HARDIN (*b. Gibbon, Nebr., 1883; d. Bloomington, Ind., 1950*), sociologist, criminologist. Graduated Grand Island (Nebr.) College, 1904; Ph.D., University of Chicago, 1913. Taught sociology at William Jewell College, University of Illinois, University of Minnesota, University of Chicago; professor of sociology and chairman of that department, Indiana University, 1935–50. Author of *Criminology* (1924, and subsequent editions), *The Professional Thief* (1937), and *White Collar Crime* (1949).

SUTHERLAND, GEORGE (*b. Stony Stratford, Buckinghamshire, England, 1862; d. Stockbridge, Mass., 1942*), lawyer, justice of the U.S. Supreme Court. His father was a Mormon convert who immigrated in 1863 to Utah. Young George left school at the age of 12, but in 1879 entered the new Brigham Young Academy in Provo. He left the academy in 1881 to take a job for the contractors building the Denver & Rio Grande Western Railroad, but the next year enrolled as a law student at the University of Michigan. Within a year he was admitted to the Michigan bar and to that of Utah.

For three years Sutherland practiced law in Provo with his father; he then entered a partnership with other young attorneys. Although an Episcopalian, he acted as counsel for the Mormon church. In politics he first joined the non-Mormon Liberal party and was its candidate for mayor of Provo in 1890; but by 1892, when he ran unsuccessfully for territorial delegate to Congress, he had become a Republican. In 1893 he moved to Salt Lake City, where he joined a leading law firm and rose rapidly through railroad and other corporate cases. With the admission of Utah to the Union in 1896, he was elected to the first state senate, 1897–1901, and in 1900 to Utah's sole congressional seat. He did not seek reelection, but returned to Utah in 1903 and, by speaking at patriotic and civic gatherings, began to muster support for a seat in the U.S. Senate. In January 1905 he won the first of two consecutive terms.

Despite his basic conservatism, as senator Sutherland yielded to the progressive sentiments of the day and supported much of Theodore Roosevelt's reform program. Defeated for reelection in the Democratic year of 1916, Sutherland took up law practice in Washington, D.C. He was president of the American Bar Association in 1916–17. During the presidential campaign of 1920 he was a prominent adviser to his friend and former Senate colleague Warren G. Harding. Sometimes called "the Colonel House of the Harding administration," Sutherland served as chairman of the advisory committee for the Washington Arms Conference, 1921.

On Sept. 5, 1922, Harding appointed Sutherland to the Supreme Court. He was often aligned with the Court's other conservative justices in effective opposition to federal and state regulatory legislation and appeals under the Bill of Rights. Yet he occasionally took positions that were surprising for their liberality. During the 1920's many of Sutherland's opinions reflected his commitment to the limitation of political authority, as well as to the survival of "dual federalism," the balance between state and federal power. He led the majority that found unconstitutional much of the legislation of Franklin D. Roosevelt's New Deal and curtailed the activities of New Deal agencies. On Jan. 6, 1938, six months after the defeat of President Roosevelt's plan to enlarge the Supreme Court, Sutherland announced his retirement.

SUTHERLAND, JOEL BARLOW (*b. Clonmel, N.J., 1792; d. 1861*), physician, lawyer, Pennsylvania legislator. Congressman, Democrat, from Pennsylvania, 1827–37. Brilliant but shallow, he began as an enthusiastic Jacksonian but became a protectionist.

SUTHERLAND, RICHARD KERENS (*b. Hancock, Md., 1893; d. Washington, D.C., 1966*), army officer. Attended Yale (B.A.,

1916). Served on the Mexican border in a federalized National Guard unit, then became a second lieutenant in the Regular Army. Joined the Second Infantry Division in France in 1918, and tours of duty during 1919–37 included various school, troop, and staff assignments. From 1938 to 1946, when he retired, he was closely associated with Gen. Douglas MacArthur, becoming his chief of staff in 1939. He oversaw MacArthur's staff activities during the latter's various commands and acted as liaison between MacArthur and senior field officers. In 1943 Sutherland coordinated the rapid buildup of Southwest Pacific Area forces, but he and MacArthur had an angry clash at Tacloban and they were never close again, although he continued to serve as chief of staff for MacArthur's new commands: U.S. Army Forces, Pacific, and Supreme Commander for the Allied Powers, Japan.

SUTRO, ADOLPH HEINRICH JOSEPH (*b. Prussia, 1830; d. San Francisco, Calif., 1898*), mining engineer. Immigrated to America, 1850; settled in San Francisco, 1851. Established quartz-reducing mill in Nevada, 1860, where he conceived idea of driving a tunnel into Mount Davidson from Carson River to the Comstock Lode as a more efficient means of transporting men and materials to and from the mines. After great difficulty in securing financing, Sutro brought the tunnel to completion, 1878; it proved immediately and immensely profitable. Selling out his interest, 1879, he returned to San Francisco, where he made profitable real estate investments and served as Populist mayor, 1894–96.

SUTTER, JOHN AUGUSTUS (*b. Kandern, Baden, 1803; d. Washington, D.C., 1880*), soldier, California colonizer. Officially a Swiss citizen, Sutter immigrated to America, 1834, journeyed to St. Louis, Mo., and in 1835 and 1836 accompanied trading parties to Santa Fe. Removing overland to Oregon, 1838, he reached California by way of Honolulu, Hawaii, and Sitka, Alaska, on July 1, 1839. Receiving large grants from the Mexican governor of California, he set up the colony of Nueva Helvetia on the American River at its junction with the Sacramento. Virtual sovereign ruler of his domain, he assisted early American settlers in his neighborhood. After the conquest of California by the United States he seemed secure in his fortunes, but discovery of gold on his estate, Jan. 24, 1848, marked the beginning of his ruin. Squatters settled upon his lands, his herders and workmen deserted the colony, and by 1852 he was bankrupt. He spent the rest of his life fruitlessly petitioning Congress for redress.

SUTTON, WILLIAM SENECA (*b. Fayetteville, Ark., 1860; d. Austin, Tex., 1928*), Texas educator.

SUZZALLO, HENRY (*b. San Jose, Calif., 1875; d. Seattle, Wash., 1933*), educator. Graduated Stanford University, 1899; Ph.D., Columbia, 1905. Taught in San Francisco public school system, at Stanford, and at Teachers College, Columbia, where he was professor of educational sociology. As president, University of Washington, 1915–26, he successfully coordinated the services of the university with the needs of the state. After supervising preparation of the report of the National Advisory Committee on Education (published 1931), which led to reforms in government educational services, he served as president of the Carnegie Foundation for the Advancement of Teaching, 1930–33. He was author also of a study of higher education in the state of California (1932).

SVERDRUP, GEORG (*b. near Bergen, Norway, 1848; d. Minneapolis, Minn., 1907*), Lutheran theologian, educator. Professor of theology, Augsburg Seminary, Minneapolis, 1874–1907. An opponent of state-dominated churches, he championed congregationalist ideas.

SWAIN, CLARA A. (*b. Elmira, N.Y., 1834; d. Castile, N.Y., 1910*), pioneer woman medical missionary in India, 1869–76 and 1879–85. A graduate of the Woman's Medical College, Philadelphia, 1869, she worked in India under Methodist auspices.

SWAIN, DAVID LOWRY (*b. Buncombe Co., N.C., 1801; d. 1868*), lawyer, North Carolina legislator and jurist. Whig governor of North Carolina, 1832–35, he pressed for tax reform and improved public education; he also induced the legislature to call the constitutional convention of 1835, at which he favored every liberal reform proposed. A constructive figure of the first rank, he did not believe in secession, but accepted it as a necessity and later advised President Andrew Johnson on plans of reconstruction. As president of the University of North Carolina *post* 1835, he built up that institution financially and scholastically, kept it open during the Civil War by heroic efforts, and until his death continued his efforts in its behalf. Appointed state agent for the collection of historical material, 1854, he began the work which resulted years later in the publication of the North Carolina *Colonial and State Records.*

SWAIN, GEORGE FILLMORE (*b. San Francisco, Calif., 1857; d. Holderness, N.H., 1931*), engineer. B.S., Massachusetts Institute of Technology, 1877. Teacher of civil engineering at MIT *post* 1881, he served as professor and head of the department, 1887–1909; he was McKay professor of civil engineering at Harvard, 1909–29. A well-known consultant on engineering projects, he had a profound influence on methods of teaching and of interpreting technology in the practice of structural engineering.

SWAIN, JAMES BARRETT (*b. New York, N.Y., 1820; d. 1895*), journalist, New York Republican politician and officeholder.

SWALLOW, GEORGE CLINTON (*b. Buckfield, Maine, 1817; d. Evanston, Ill., 1899*), geologist. Graduated Bowdoin, 1843. As state geologist, Swallow made important surveys in Missouri, 1853–61, and in Kansas, 1865. He was professor of agriculture at University of Missouri, 1870–82, and later a journalist in Montana.

SWALLOW, SILAS COMFORT (*b. near Wilkes-Barre, Pa., 1839; d. 1930*), Methodist clergyman, reformer. Holder of many pastoral charges in central Pennsylvania, he was a bitter and persistent enemy of the Republican machine in that state. As presidential nominee of the Prohibition party, 1904, he polled better than a quarter-million votes.

SWAN, JAMES (*b. Fifeshire, Scotland, 1754; d. Paris, France, 1830*), Massachusetts legislator and official speculator. Immigrated to Boston, 1765. Removing to France, 1787, with the help of Lafayette he won contracts to furnish the French with marine stores. In 1795, by a complicated series of transactions and as agent for the French Republic, he transformed the American foreign debt outstanding to France into a domestic one at considerable profit to himself. Failing in later French mercantile ventures, he remained in debtor's prison in Paris, 1808–30, refusing to permit his debt to be paid, because he considered it unjust.

SWAN, JOSEPH ROCKWELL (*b. Westernville, N.Y., 1802; d. Columbus, Ohio, 1884*), Ohio jurist, legal writer, abolitionist. Celebrated for a classic opinion on state and federal court jurisdiction in the case of *Ex Parte Bushnell*; author of among other works, *A Treatise on the Law Relating to the Powers and Duties of Justices of the Peace . . . in the State of Ohio* (1837).

SWAN, TIMOTHY (*b. Worcester, Mass., 1758; d. Northfield, Mass., 1842*), composer and compiler of psalms. Author of,

among other music, the very popular "China," composed in 1790 and first publicly sung in 1794.

SWANK, JAMES MOORE (*b. Westmoreland Co, Pa., 1832; d. Philadelphia, Pa., 1914*), statistician. Associated in a managerial capacity with the American Iron and Steel Association, 1873–1912, he was an outstanding propagandist for protection.

SWANN, THOMAS (*b. Alexandria, Va., ca. 1806; d. 1883*), lawyer, businessman. Rose to prominence as able president of Baltimore & Ohio Railroad, 1848–53, extending the line to the Ohio River. Know-Nothing mayor of Baltimore, 1856–60. Swann was a strong Unionist during the Civil War, and Union party governor of Maryland, 1866–68. Opposing Radical Reconstruction, he succeeded in restoring the franchise to former Southern sympathizers. Congressman, Democrat, from Maryland, 1869–79, he rose to be chairman of the Committee on Foreign Relations, thereafter retiring to his estate near Leesburg, Va.

SWANSON, CLAUDE AUGUSTUS (*b. near Danville, Va., 1862; d. near Criglersville, Va., 1939*), lawyer, statesman. Graduated Randolph-Macon College, 1885; LL.B., University of Virginia, 1886. As congressman, Democrat, from Virginia, 1893–1906, he fought to secure rural free delivery service and was an able member of the House Ways and Means Committee. A progressive and successful governor of Virginia, 1906–10, he became U.S. senator in the latter year and served until 1933. A consistent supporter of Woodrow Wilson's policies and a "big navy" advocate, he was active also on the Senate Foreign Relations Committee. He was U.S. secretary of the navy, 1933–39, continuing his support of the navy although hampered by ill health.

SWANTON, JOHN REED (*b. Gardiner, Me., 1873; d. Newton, Mass., 1958*), anthropologist and folklorist. Studied at Harvard University (Ph.D., 1900). Member of the staff of the Bureau of American Ethnology, Smithsonian Institution, 1900–44. An expert on American Indians, especially on the Southeast, Swanton conducted mostly field work, collecting records, artifacts, and legends from his sources. Not an anthropological theorizer, he was content to let his materials speak for themselves. Works include *Myths and Tales of the Southeastern Indians* (1929), *Indians of the Southeastern United States* (1946), and *Source Material on the History and Ethnology of the Caddo Indians* (1942).

SWARTWOUT, SAMUEL (*b. Poughkeepsie, N.Y., 1783; d. New York, N.Y., 1856*), merchant, speculator, politician. A close associate of Aaron Burr (1756–1836), Swartwout delivered the famous cipher letter from Burr to James Wilkinson, October 1806, which produced such a strong impression of Burr's treason. Arrested as an accomplice, he served as an important witness against Burr. Later an active supporter of Andrew Jackson, he was collector of the Port of New York, 1829–38, achieving notoriety for misappropriation of more than a million dollars of public money.

SWASEY, AMBROSE (*b. Exeter, N.H., 1846; d. Exeter, 1937*), mechanical engineer, manufacturer, philanthropist. With W. R. Warner, entered machine-tool manufacturing business, 1880, in Chicago, removing to Cleveland, Ohio, 1881. Successful specialists in manufacture of hand-operated turret lathes, Warner and Swasey achieved greatest distinction for a sideline, the making of precision astronomical and other scientific instruments.

SWAYNE, NOAH HAYNES (*b. Frederick Co., Va., 1804; d. New York, N.Y., 1884*), jurist, U.S. Supreme Court justice. Father of Wager Swayne. Reaching high rank at the Ohio bar *post* 1823, he was appointed justice of the U.S. Supreme Court, 1862, and served until 1881. A satisfactory judge but not a brilliant one, he gave his principal opinions in *Gelpcke* v. *City of Dubuque* and *Springer* v. *U.S.* He was regarded as the most nationalistic-minded member of the Court in his time.

SWAYNE, WAGER (b.Columbus, Ohio, 1834; d. 1902), Union major general, lawyer. Son of Noah H. Swayne. Winner of the Medal of Honor for gallantry at Corinth, Miss., October 1862, Swayne did valuable service in Alabama with the Freedmen's Bureau. He was later successful in the practice of law in New York City in partnership with John F. Dillon and others.

SWEENEY, MARTIN LEONARD (b. Cleveland, Ohio, 1885; d. Cleveland, Ohio, 1960), lawyer and politician. Studied at Baldwin-Wallace College (LL.B., 1914). Elected to the House of Representatives, 1931–42. A Democrat and supporter of Roosevelt, Sweeney was pro-labor but was not a New Dealer. He was known for his ardent isolationism; was against Lend-Lease and did not want America involved in the war. Re-elected many times without party endorsement, Sweeney was defeated in 1942 and returned to private law practice in Cleveland.

SWEENY, PETER BARR (b. New York, N.Y., 1825; d. Lake Mahopac, N.Y., 1911), lawyer, politician. Considered the guiding intelligence of the Tweed Ring in New York City *ca.* 1861–71.

SWEENY, THOMAS WILLIAM (b. Co. Cork, Ireland, 1820; d. Astoria, N.Y., 1892), Union brigadier general, Fenian leader of the ill-starred raid on Canada in 1866.

SWEET, JOHN EDSON (b. Pompey, N.Y., 1832; d. Syracuse, N.Y., 1916), mechanical engineer, educator. Headed the Straight Line Engine Co. *post* 1880; received John Fritz Medal, 1914, for pioneer work in construction and development of high-speed steam engines.

SWENSON, DAVID FERDINAND (b. Kristinehamn, Sweden, 1876; d. Lake Wales, Fla., 1940), philosopher. Came to America as a child. Graduating University of Minnesota, 1898, he taught philosophy and psychology there until the end of his life. He was noted as the pioneer American authority on work of Søren Kierkegaard and as a sharp, effective critic of current symbolic logics.

SWENSSON, CARL AARON (b. Sugargrove, Pa., 1857; d. Los Angeles, Calif., 1904), Swedish Lutheran clergyman, educator. Long associated with the congregation at Lindsborg, Kans., he was instrumental in founding Bethany College there, 1881.

SWETT, JOHN (b. near Pittsfield, N.H., 1830; d. near Martinez, Calif., 1913), California public school administrator, opponent of political influence in the schools.

SWIFT, GUSTAVUS FRANKLIN (b. near Sandwich, Mass., 1839; d. 1903), meatpacker. Established himself in Chicago, Ill., as a cattle buyer, 1875; sought to avoid waste by shipping already dressed beef to eastern markets, 1877. Conceived of the railroad refrigerator car as aid to year-round shipping. A pioneer in development of by-products from animal parts previously thrown away, Swift extended his business successfully to foreign markets; before his death, Swift & Co. (incorporated 1885) was capitalized at $25 million.

SWIFT, JOHN FRANKLIN (b. Bowling Green, Mo., 1829; d. Japan, 1891), lawyer, California legislator. Practiced in San Francisco, Calif., *post* 1857; was outstanding as an opponent of monopolistic corporations. A U.S. commissioner, 1880, to negotiate modifications of the Burlingame Treaty with China, he was later counsel for California in sustaining constitutionality of the Chinese Exclusion Act, 1888. U.S. minister to Japan, 1889–91.

SWIFT, JOSEPH GARDNER (b. Nantucket, Mass., 1783; d. Geneva, N.Y., 1865), military engineer. Brother of William H. Swift. Graduated West Point, 1802, in the first class. Chief engineer of the U.S. Army, 1812–18, he resigned because of conflict over appointment of Simon Bernard and worked thereafter on railroad and harbor improvement projects. An engineer of distinction, he exerted influence over George W. Whistler, William G. McNeill, and other, younger professionals.

SWIFT, LEWIS (b. Clarkson, N.Y., 1820; d. Marathon, N.Y., 1913), astronomer, businessman.

SWIFT, LINTON BISHOP (b. St. Paul, Minn., 1888; d. New York, N.Y., 1946), social welfare administrator. Practiced law in St. Paul, 1910–17; following service in France during World War I, decided to devote himself to social work. After experience in St. Paul and in Louisville, Ky., 1920–25, he removed to New York City as executive secretary of the Family Service Association of America. In this position, which he held for the rest of his life, he was chief spokesman for a federation of 230 family welfare agencies in the United States and Canada. Throughout his career he insisted on a differentiation of social work from both psychiatry and social activism.

SWIFT, LOUIS FRANKLIN (b. Sagamore, Mass., 1861; d. Chicago, Ill., 1937), meatpacker. Son of Gustavus F. Swift. Official of Swift & Co. *post* 1885 and its president, 1903–31. With aid of brothers, he made the firm one of the world's greatest food processing and distributing businesses. He also pioneered in employee-welfare activities.

SWIFT, LUCIUS BURRIE (b. Orleans Co., N.Y., 1844; d. 1929), lawyer, civil service reformer. Practiced in Indianapolis, Ind., *post* 1879; edited and published the *Civil Service Chronicle*, 1889–96.

SWIFT, WILLIAM HENRY (b. Taunton, Mass., 1800; d. New York, N.Y., 1879), soldier, engineer. Brother of Joseph G. Swift. Attended West Point, 1813–18; accompanied Stephen H. Long to the Rocky Mountains and was commissioned in the artillery, 1819. After employment in railroad and canal work, he was made captain of topographical engineers, 1838, and was principal assistant in the topographical bureau at Washington, D.C., 1843–49. Resigning from the army, he was successively president of the Philadelphia, Wilmington & Baltimore and the Massachusetts Western railroads, a director of many corporations, and a financial adviser of Baring Brothers.

SWIFT, ZEPHANIAH (b. Wareham, Mass., 1759; d. Warren, Ohio, 1823), Connecticut legislator and jurist. Congressman, Federalist, from Connecticut, 1793–97; secretary to Oliver Ellsworth on mission to France, 1800. Author of the first American law text, *A System of the Laws of the State of Connecticut* (1795, 1796), he was a judge of the state superior court, 1801–19, serving for a time as chief justice. Deprived of office as a Federalist, he retired to legal researches and writing.

SWING, DAVID (b. Cincinnati, Ohio, 1830; d. Chicago, Ill., 1894), Presbyterian and independent clergyman. Pastor, Fourth Church, Chicago, *post* 1866, he was cited for heresy, 1874, and served *post* 1875 as minister of Chicago's Central Church.

SWING, RAYMOND EDWARDS (GRAM) (b. Cortland, N.Y., 1887; d. Washington, D.C., 1968), foreign correspondent and news commentator. Attended Oberlin and became a cub reporter for the *Cleveland Press* in 1906; for the next six years he worked for newspapers in Ohio and Indiana. In Berlin in 1912, he became foreign correspondent for the *Chicago Daily News*. In 1919 he became correspondent for the *New York Herald* in Berlin, and was admitted to Moscow in 1921. In 1922 he became London correspondent for the *Wall Street Journal* and during 1924–33 was with the foreign-news service of the *Philadelphia Public Ledger* and the *New York Post*. He returned to Washington to write for the *Nation*, *London News-Chronicle*, and Britain's *Economist*. In 1935–45 he was the American end of a weekly exchange of broadcasts with Britain undertaken by the BBC. During World War II the exchange became one between two Americans, Swing and London-based Edward R. Murrow. In 1951 he became the first political commentator for Voice of America, then joined Murrow in writing the latter's daily radio commentaries until 1959, when he returned to Voice of America. He retired in 1963.

SWINTON, JOHN (*b. near Edinburgh, Scotland, 1829; d. Brooklyn, N.Y., 1901*), journalist, social reformer. Brother of William Swinton. Raised in Canada; worked as journeyman printer in the South and Middle West *post* 1853; was active in free-state movement in Kansas, 1856. Employed by the *New York Times* and *Sun* from *ca.* 1860, Swinton was an outstanding labor sympathizer and edited *John Swinton's Paper*, 1883–87.

SWINTON, WILLIAM (*b. near Edinburgh, Scotland, 1833; d. Brooklyn, N.Y., 1892*), journalist, educator. Brother of John Swinton. Resident in the United States *post ca.* 1863, he served as Civil War correspondent for *New York Times*, wrote several books about the war, and in 1869 became professor of English, University of California. Resigning in 1874 because of differences with Daniel C. Gilman, Swinton became a successful writer of school textbooks.

SWISSHELM, JANE GREY CANNON (*b. Pittsburgh, Pa., 1815; d. Swissvale, Pa., 1884*), teacher, antislavery and woman's rights reformer. Founded and edited the *Pittsburgh Saturday Visiter* (1847–57), the *St. Cloud Visiter*, the *Reconstructionist* (Washington, D.C.), and other waspishly written journals.

SWITZLER, WILLIAM FRANKLIN (*b. Fayette Co., Ky., 1819; d. Columbia, Mo., 1906*), Missouri legislator and journalist. Editor of the *Missouri Statesman*, 1842–85, he was active in Democratic politics, supported the Union during the Civil War, and subsequently held several federal offices. One of the best-informed men of his time in the history of his state, he published, among other works, *Early History of Missouri* (1872).

SWOPE, GERARD (*b. St. Louis, Mo., 1872; d. New York, N.Y., 1957*), engineer and business executive. Studied at the Massachusetts Institute of Technology. Swope began working with Western Electric in 1895; in 1919 he was International General Electric's first president; in 1922 he became president of General Electric. Remembered as an organizational genius, Swope's main accomplishments included reorganizing Western Electric's foreign interests and, later, those of General Electric; during World War I, he overhauled the Army Supply Service. Along with Owen D. Young, Swope was associated with the "new capitalism," especially with corporate welfare and employee representation programs, mass marketing of durables, and the recognition of managerial responsibility to workers, customer, and the industry as a whole. The famous "Swope Plan" of 1931 was adopted by the National Industrial Recovery Act of 1933. He retired from General Electric in 1939, but returned during World War II.

SWOPE, HERBERT BAYARD (*b. St. Louis, Mo., 1882; d. New York, N.Y., 1958*), newspaper editor. After working as a reporter for several midwestern and New York papers, Swope joined the Staff of the *New York World* in 1909. He was executive editor from 1920 to 1928. At the *World*, Swope's reporting won the Pulitzer Prize (the first for reporting) in 1917 for a series of articles on Germany before and during World War I. As executive editor he

introduced the concept of the "Op Ed" page, now widely used by leading papers. Influential in politics, Swope was a backer of Al Smith in 1928, and later supported Roosevelt.

SYDENSTRICKER, EDGAR (*b. Shanghai, China, 1881; d. New York, N.Y., 1936*), social and economic investigator, public health statistician. Brother of Pearl S. Buck. Author of, among other works, *Conditions of Labor in American Industries* (with W. J. Lauck, 1917) and *Health and Environment* (1933).

SYDNOR, CHARLES SACKETT (*b. Augusta, Ga., 1898; d. Biloxi, Miss., 1954*), historian. Studied at Hampden-Sydney College and Johns Hopkins University (Ph.D., 1923). Taught at Hampden-Sydney College, 1923–36; at Duke University, 1936–54; chairman of the history department from 1952; dean of the Graduate School of Arts and Sciences from 1952. An expert in southern history, his works include *Slavery in Mississippi* (1933) and volume 5 in the *History of the South*, entitled *The Development of Southern Sectionalism, 1819–1848*, in 1948.

SYKES, GEORGE (*b. Dover, Del., 1822; d. Fort Brown, Tex., 1880*), Union major general. Graduated West Point, 1842. An excellent tactician on the defense, Sykes commanded the V Corps at Gettysburg, defending the Round Tops successfully, but suffering criticism for his failure to counterattack.

SYLVESTER, FREDERICK OAKES (*b. Brockton, Mass., 1869; d. 1915*), painter, art teacher. Employed in the St. Louis, Mo., public school system, 1892–1914, he produced many highly regarded canvases of scenes on the Mississippi River.

SYLVESTER, JAMES JOSEPH (*b. London, England, 1814; d. probably Oxford, England, 1897*), mathematician, educator. A brilliant student at St. John's College, Cambridge, 1831–33 and 1836–37, he was barred as a Jew from taking his degree or receiving a fellowship. Professor of natural philosophy at University College, London, 1837–41. He taught mathematics at the University of Virginia, 1841–42, but because of problems of discipline resigned and returned to London. Engaged there in actuarial work, 1844–56, he also studied law; he was professor of mathematics, Royal Military Academy at Woolwich, 1855–70. Invited to serve as professor of mathematics at Johns Hopkins University, 1876, he brought there a reputation as one of the greatest mathematicians of his time and an infectious eagerness for intellectual endeavor. Setting new standards for mathematical research in America and inspiring scores of students, he acted also as editor of the *American Journal of Mathematics*, 1878–84. Resigning his chair, December 1883, he became Savilian professor of geometry at Oxford, in which position he remained for the rest of his life. He devoted his attention as a scholar to the theory of numbers; to higher algebra; and to the theory of invariants, a subject in which he was recognized as preeminent. Many of his contributions to learned journals were issued in a collected edition, edited by H. F. Baker (1904–12).

SYLVIS, WILLIAM H. (*b. Armagh, Pa., 1828; d. 1869*), labor leader. An official of an iron-moulders' union, organized in Philadelphia, Pa., 1855, he signed the call for the first convention of the Iron-Moulders International Union, Philadelphia, 1859. His address at the convention became the preamble to the constitution of the new union, of which he was elected treasurer, 1860, and president, 1863. Active in calling the Labor Congress at Baltimore, Md., 1866, he was elected president of the National Labor Union, 1868. An opponent of strikes in theory, in practice he led some of the first great struggles of the American trade unions. Although he urged affiliation with the First International, he was influenced more personally by the English cooperative movement.

SYMMES, JOHN CLEVES (*b. Southold, N.Y., 1742; d. Cincinnati, Ohio, 1814*), Revolutionary patriot, New Jersey legislator and jurist, Ohio pioneer. Becoming interested in western colonization as a member of Congress from New Jersey, 1785–87, Symmes applied for a large tract between the two Miamis on the Ohio. In October 1788 he was given a definite contract for 1 million acres, the so-called Miami Purchase. Early in 1789 he founded a settlement at North Bend, but was unable to make collections for sales of his land in time to meet the payments due under his contract with the government. Aided by Jonathan Dayton and Elias Boudinot, he received a patent in September 1794 for the acreage which he had actually paid for. A persevering man with qualities of leadership, he was also exceedingly careless as a businessman and lost control of much of his property; however, he had planted an important colony. Its chief settlement, Cincinnati, was perhaps the most important military and commercial outpost in the early West.

SYMONS, GEORGE GARDNER (*b. Chicago, Ill., 1865; d. Hillside, N.J., 1930*), landscape painter specializing in winter scenes.

SYMONS, THOMAS WILLIAM (*b. Keeseville, N.Y., 1849; d. Washington, D.C., 1920*), military engineer. Graduated West Point, 1874. Served on survey expeditions under George M. Wheeler, 1876–79, and with the Mississippi River Commission and other government agencies; had charge of construction of the Buffalo, N.Y., breakwater; advocated construction of New York State Barge Canal.

SYMS, BENJAMIN (*b. probably England, ca. 1591; d. Virginia, ca. 1642*), Virginia planter. Resident in Virginia *post* 1624, Syms executed a will on Feb. 12, 1634/5 bequeathing property for establishment of a free school, thus becoming probably the first inhabitant of any North American colony to provide the means for such a purpose.

SYNG, PHILIP (*b. Cork, Ireland, 1703; d. 1789*), Philadelphia silversmith. Grandfather of Philip S. Physick. Immigrated to Maryland, 1714; was established in Philadelphia by 1720. An outstanding craftsman, Syng was a member of Benjamin Franklin's Junto, an electrical experimenter, and an original trustee of the College of Philadelphia (later University of Pennsylvania).

SZELL, GEORGE (*b. Budapest, Austria-Hungary, 1897; d. Cleveland, Ohio, 1970*), orchestra conductor. Conducted for the first time in 1913 with the Vienna Konzertvereins-Orchester in Bad Kissingen. Engaged as a conductor at the Berlin Royal Opera (1915–17), Municipal Theater in Strassburg (1917–18), German Opera in Prague (1919–21), Darmstadt Court Theater (1921–22), Municipal Theater in Düsseldorf (1922–24), and Berlin State Opera (1924–29). His first American concert was with the St. Louis Symphony Orchestra (1930). He fled to Western Europe in 1937 and simultaneously served as conductor for the Scottish Orchestra in Glasgow and the Residentie Orchestra in The Hague (1937–39). In 1939 he became a teacher at the Mannes School of Music and a director of an opera workshop at the New School for Social Research, both in New York City. Appeared with Toscanini's NBC Symphony Orchestra in 1941, and debuted with the Metropolitan Opera in 1942, where he remained until 1946. Appeared with the New York Philharmonic (1943–70) and became music director of the Cleveland Orchestra (1946–70).

SZILARD, LEO (*b. Budapest, Hungary, 1898; d. La Jolla, Calif., 1964*), physicist. Attended Budapest Institute of Technology, Technische Hochschule at Charlottenburg, and University of Berlin (Ph.D., 1922). He collaborated with Albert Einstein in developing a pumping system for liquid metals and filed a patent (1928) for a prototype cyclotron, or particle accelerator. Fled to England in 1933 and during 1934–38 initiated research on the problem of controlling and sustaining an artificial chain reaction. At Columbia in 1935 it became clear to him that a controlled nuclear chain reaction could become the basis for a bomb of enormous destructive force. He joined forces with Enrico Fermi in 1939, and they persuaded Einstein to write to President Franklin Roosevelt on the probability of developing nuclear weapons. He was a leading member of the Manhattan Project; at the University of Chicago, he and Fermi directed construction of a uranium-graphite reactor, which in 1942 sustained the first controlled nuclear reaction. Became a U.S. citizen in 1943. After the war he and Fermi received patent rights to the world's first nuclear fission reactor. When the war ended he became more concerned about control of atomic energy in the postwar world and lobbied for the creation of the Atomic Energy Commission. His endeavors to achieve international arms control were mostly negated by the Cold War; but one result of his efforts was the Pagwash Conference on Science and World Affairs, a disarmament forum.

SZOLD, BENJAMIN (*b. Nemiskert, Hungary, 1829; d. Berkeley Springs, W.Va., 1902*), rabbi. A moderate in his religious views and an outstanding scholar, he served as rabbi of Congregation Oheb Shalom, Baltimore, Md., 1859–92, and was thereafter emeritus.

SZOLD, HENRIETTA (*b. Baltimore, Md., 1860; d. Jerusalem, Palestine [now Israel], 1945*), Zionist leader. Daughter of Benjamin Szold. Taught at a private school in Baltimore; helped found, 1889, and managed an evening school for immigrants; aided her father in his research and writing; made a public espousal of Zionism, 1895. Editor of the Jewish Publication Society, 1893–1916. A member of the executive council of the Federation of American Zionists *post* 1899, she became its secretary and displayed unusual executive and public-speaking abilities. In 1912 she founded and became president of Hadassah, serving as president until 1926 and as honorary president thereafter. In 1920 she left for Palestine to help Isaac M. Rubinow in the administration of the American Zionist Medical Unit. Elected a member of the newly formed Jewish Agency Executive in Jerusalem, 1929, and elected in 1931 to the national council sanctioned under the British mandate, she was responsible for education and health programs and instituted a modern system of social service. In 1933 she was appointed director of the Youth Aliya Bureau and took a leading role in the rescue of European Jewish children and their settlement in Palestine. A democrat and a pacifist, she advocated Arab-Jewish binationalism; for her, there was no necessary antagonism between Jewish hopes and Arab rights.

SZYK, ARTHUR (*b. Łodz, Russian Poland, 1894; d. New Canaan, Conn., 1951*), miniaturist and cartoonist. Studied at the Académie Julien in Paris. Immigrated to the U.S. in 1937. Remembered for his miniature book illustrations, Szyk's works include the *Song of Songs* (1917), *The Last Days of Shylock* (1931), *George Washington and His Times* (1931)—the originals of which President Roosevelt had hung in the White House—and *The Arabian Nights* (1952). During World War II Szyk published many anti-Nazi political cartoons.

T

TABB, JOHN BANISTER (b. Amelia Co., Va., 1845; d. 1909), Confederate dispatch carrier, Roman Catholic clergyman, poet. A convert to Catholicism, 1872, Father Tabb was ordained in December 1884, and taught at St. Charles' College, Md., thereafter for the rest of his active life. His work, epigrammatic and somewhat cryptic, appeared in Poems (1894), Lyrics (1897), and other volumes. Calling himself an "unreconstructed rebel," he had a rich and paradoxical nature.

TABER, JOHN (b. Auburn, N.Y., 1880; d. Auburn, 1965), lawyer, U.S. congressman. Attended Yale University (B.A., 1902) and New York Law School in Albany, from which he graduated in 1904. Began his congressional career in 1923 when he was elected to the House of Representatives. A conservative Republican, Taber was a leading anti-New Dealer during the 1930's. After the 1946 elections he became chairman of the Appropriations Committee, as well as the first chairman of the Joint Congressional Committee on the Budget. These two positions made him one of the most influential members of government. Such was his zeal for fiscal conservatism that the expression "Taberizing" became a synonym for dismissal or cutback. His chairmanship of the Appropriations Committee ended in 1949, by which time he claimed to have saved the federal government over $6 billion. He regained the chairmanship briefly (1953–54), and continued to serve in the House until 1963.

TABOR, HORACE AUSTIN WARNER (b. Holland, Vt., 1830; d. Denver, Colo., 1899), prospector, mineowner, merchant. One of the "rushers" to Pike's Peak in 1859. Tabor, a storekeeper, grubstaked the discoverers of the Little Pittsburgh Mine (1878) of which he became a one-third owner. Prosperous for a time, he spent the returns of the great silver lode with a lavish hand; among other benefactions he built an opera house at Leadville, Colo., and Tabor Grand Opera House in Denver. At first he invested in real estate, but soon turning to less conservative operations, he was brought to bankruptcy by the decline in the price of silver and the crash of 1893. His second wife was the celebrated "Baby Doe."

TAFT, ALPHONSO (b. Townshend, Vt., 1810; d. California, 1891), lawyer. Father of Charles P. and William H. Taft. Graduated Yale, 1833. Successful at the bar in Cincinnati, Ohio, post 1839, he was interested also in railroad development in the Middle West and in Cincinnati traction lines. Judge of the Cincinnati superior court, 1865–72, he served briefly as U.S. secretary of war in 1876 and as U.S. attorney general, 1876–77. Politically a conservative, originally a Whig and later a Republican, he was U.S. minister to Austria-Hungary, 1882–84, and to Russia, 1884–85.

TAFT, CHARLES PHELPS (b. Cincinnati, Ohio, 1843; d. 1929), lawyer, publisher, philanthropist. Son of Alphonso Taft; half brother of William H. Taft. Graduated Yale, 1864; LL.B., Columbia, 1866; studied also at Heidelberg and at the Sorbonne. In the practice of law in Cincinnati, 1869–79, he acquired a controlling interest in the Cincinnati Times, 1879. He consoli-

dated it in 1880 with the Star. Editor and ultimately sole proprietor, he built the Times-Star into a profitable newspaper property, made notable contributions to the aesthetic life of Cincinnati, and played a large part in shaping the career of William H. Taft.

TAFT, HENRY WATERS (b. Cincinnati, Ohio, 1859; d. New York, N.Y., 1945), lawyer, civic leader, philanthropist. Son of Alphonso Taft; brother of William H. Taft; half brother of Charles P. Taft. B.A., Yale, 1880. Admitted to New York bar, 1882, he became a partner in the firm of Strong & Cadwalader, 1899 (post 1914, Cadwalader, Wickersham & Taft).

TAFT, LORADO ZADOC (b. Elmwood, Ill., 1860; d. Chicago, Ill., 1936), sculptor. Graduated University of Illinois, 1879; attended École des Beaux Arts, Paris, France, 1880–83. The outstanding "art missionary" of his time, Taft lectured widely, served on city, state, and federal fine arts commissions, and worked unceasingly for public school art education. He wrote History of American Sculpture (1903), Modern Tendencies in Sculpture (1921), and hundreds of articles. At the Chicago Art Institute (1886–1906), he pioneered in new methods of instruction. A competent and essentially conservative sculptor, he was one of the early workers in group composition and monumental fountains ("Columbus Fountain," 1912, Washington, D.C.; "Thatcher Memorial Fountain," 1917, Denver; "Fountain of the Great Lakes," 1913, "Fountain of Time," 1922, both Chicago).

TAFT, ROBERT ALPHONSO (b. Cincinnati, Ohio, 1889; d. New York, N.Y., 1953), lawyer, politician. Graduated from Yale University and Harvard Law School, 1913. During World War I, served under Herbert Hoover for the U.S. Food Administration and worked on relief programs in Europe. Entered Ohio politics, becoming the Republican speaker of the assembly in the Ohio legislature, 1925. The son of President William Howard Taft, he was a conservative advocate of big business, an isolationist, and an outspoken critic of Roosevelt and the New Deal, which he termed socialistic. Served in the U.S. Senate, 1938–53. Tried unsuccessfully to win the Republican nomination for the presidency, 1940.

By 1944, Taft was the leading Republican in the Senate and an influential spokesman for the bipartisan conservative bloc that ruled Capitol Hill. For the next eight years he was one of the most powerful senators in modern American history. Author of the Taft-Hartley Act, which placed curbs on union abuses, he emerged as a leading contender for the presidency; he was defeated in 1948 by Thomas E. Dewey and in 1952 by Eisenhower. He was a defender of Senator Joseph McCarthy, was against the Marshall Plan and NATO, and opposed the U.N. At the end of his career, he was known as "Mr. Republican."

TAFT, WILLIAM HOWARD (b. Cincinnati, Ohio, 1857; d. Washington, D.C., 1930), lawyer, jurist, president and chief justice of the United States. Son of Alphonso Taft; half brother of Charles P. Taft. Graduated Yale, 1878; Cincinnati Law School, 1880. A large, good-natured young man with a tendency toward sloth, Taft early showed a weakness for procrastination which he never quite overcame. Entering Republican party politics, he served as assistant prosecutor of Hamilton County, his first public office, but in 1882, after appointment as collector of internal revenue for Cincinnati, resigned because he refused to conform to the prevalent spoils system. Resuming the practice of law, he became judge of the superior court of Ohio in March 1887. Happy in his work as a jurist, he served until 1890, attracting unwelcome labor criticism for his exhaustive opinion in the case of *Moores & Company* v. *The Bricklayers' Union, No 1.* Appointed U.S. solicitor general, he assumed office in February 1890 and served with great credit until March 1892 when he became a federal circuit court judge.

A man of scholarly tastes and abilities, Taft found his new post ideal, but continued to win the enmity of organized labor for rulings in major cases. Although his own position on the right of labor to organize was in advance of the existing legal opinion of the day, he refused to win an easy popularity by seeking for reasons to support illegal acts by labor, especially in matters of attempted boycotts. Taft, however, ruled in favor of labor in cases involving attempts of employers to evade responsibility for negligence; in the Addyston Pipe Case, 1898, he ruled that a combination of manufacturers was in restraint of trade and enjoined them. He became president of the Philippine Commission, 1900, resigning from the bench at the request of President William McKinley. He served as civil governor of the islands, 1901–04, devoting himself with great tact and energy to the solution of several thorny problems which were legacies of the Spanish-American War and the insurrection, and also to the improvement of the economic status of the Philippines. Accepting office as U.S. secretary of war, 1904, at the request of President Theodore Roosevelt, he soon became a close adviser of the president whose impulsive qualities he balanced with his own easygoing conservatism. He became in effect the "trouble shooter" of the administration. His nomination for the presidency on the Republican ticket in 1908 was owing to his unusual talents as administrator and conciliator and also to Roosevelt's backing; Taft, however, had to be urged to run, as he stated that he had no taste for the office.

After his election over William Jennings Bryan by an electoral vote of 321 to 162, he took office in March 1909 and was troubled and harassed almost from the start. Taft's troubles were owing to certain specific mistakes but principally to his erroneous belief that the Republican party could continue in power without giving ground to its liberal wing. He was also hampered by his stolid, plodding honesty of purpose; he had no part of his predecessor's genius for guiding and (when he chose) confusing public opinion. Bringing unpopularity on himself by his courageous attempt to secure tariff revision (which Roosevelt had zealously refrained from attempting), he then found himself threatened by the insurgents in his own party such as Senators LaFollete, Dolliver, Borah and others, and by the growing strength of the Democratic party which won the House in November 1910. At odds with his sponsor, Theodore Roosevelt, because of a number of incidents, notably Roosevelt's resentment over the dismissal of Gifford Pinchot, Taft turned more and more to the conservative members of his cabinet and his party. Despite this, he proposed and achieved "trust-busting" and other reform activities much more efficiently than Roosevelt. Renominated at Chicago in June 1912 by a convention whose behavior threw Roosevelt into opposition as a candidate of the Bull Moose party, Taft received only 8 electoral votes in the election of 1912 as against 88 for Roosevelt and 435 for Woodrow Wilson.

Unique among presidents in that he did not want the office and surrendered it gladly, Taft retired to Yale in March 1913 as Kent Professor of Constitutional Law. Named chief justice of the United States in June 1921, he achieved his heart's desire. In many ways his work as administrator and reformer of the Supreme Court's procedure was more important than any of his decisions; among the best of his accomplishments was the so-called Judges' Bill, February 1925. Generally conservative in his decisions, he made his most important dissent in the case of *Adkins* v. *Children's Hospital* (261 *U.S.*, 525), holding that a minimum wage law for women was constitutional because sweatshop wages did just as much to impair health and morals as did long hours. In so far as Taft sanctioned control of commerce and industry, his decisions show that he believed that supervision by the federal government was superior to that by the states, but he was, in contrast, an advocate of broad federal powers under the commerce clause of the Constitution. One of his most important contributions to constitutional law is said to have been his ruling in *Myers* v. *U.S.* (272 *U.S.*, 52) sustaining the presidential power to remove executive officers. A coordinator and conciliator all his life rather than an advocate, Taft was not a leader of judicial thought in the sense that Justice O. W. Holmes or Justice Brandeis was a leader. Retiring from the bench, February 1930, because of ill health, he died a month later.

TAGGARD, GENEVIEVE (*b. Waitsburg, Wash., 1894; d. New York, N.Y., 1948*), poet. Raised in the Hawaiian Islands, where her parents were missionaries; graduated University of California at Berkeley, 1920; removed to New York City, where she was associated with the *New Masses* and a variety of left-wing causes; taught at Mt. Holyoke College (1929–30), Bennington College (1932–35), and Sarah Lawrence College (1935–46).

TAGGART, THOMAS (*b. Co. Monaghan, Ireland, 1856; d. Indianapolis, Ind., 1929*), Indiana politician, hotel proprietor, banker. Immigrated to America as a child. Long a power in state and national Democratic politics, he served with ability as mayor of Indianapolis, 1895–1901, and was U.S. senator from Indiana, March–November 1916.

TAGLIABUE, GIUSEPPE (*b. Como, Italy, 1812; d. Mt. Vernon, N.Y., 1878*), instrument maker. Settled in New York, N.Y., 1831, after apprenticeship in the family business of thermometer making. For years he supplied instruments used by the U.S. Geodetic Survey; he also patented improvements on the hydrometer, a mercurial barometer, and other scientific devices.

TAIT, AUTHUR FITZWILLIAM (*b. near Liverpool, England, 1819; d. Yonkers, N.Y., 1905*), landscape and animal painter. Immigrated to New York, N.Y., 1850. A skillful academic painter, Tait produced many pictures which had wide contemporary circulation as popular lithographs and are of present value as documents of phases of the life of his time.

TAIT, CHARLES (*b. Louisa Co., Va., 1768; d. Alabama, 1835*), lawyer. Cousin of Henry Clay. Admitted to the Georgia bar, 1795, he practiced in association with William H. Crawford and was a prominent figure in the faction which opposed the Yazoo sales. U.S. senator, Democrat, from Georgia, 1809–19, he was untiring in efforts on behalf of the navy, and aided in formation of Alabama as a territory and its later admission to the Union. Removing to Claiborne, Ala., 1819, he served as U.S. judge of the district of Alabama, 1820–26. He was also known for his scientific accomplishments.

TAKAMINE, JOKICHI (*b. Takaoka, Japan, 1854; d. 1922*), chemist, industrialist. Graduated University of Tokyo, 1879; studied at Glasgow University. Headed Japanese patent bureau and also division of chemistry in Japanese department of agriculture. Resident *post* 1890 in the United States and long associated with Parke, Davis & Co., Takamine developed the starch-digesting enzyme known as takadiastase and in 1901 succeeded in isolating adrenalin from the suprarenal gland. Among other industries, he aided in the development in Japan of dyes, aluminum, the electric furnace, and nitrogen fixation.

TALBOT, ARTHUR NEWELL (*b. Cortland, Ill., 1857; d. Chicago, Ill., 1942*), civil engineer, engineering educator. B.S., Illinois Industrial University (later the University of Illinois), 1881. Taught engineering at University of Illinois, 1885–1926 (professor of municipal and sanitary engineering *post* 1890); a pioneer in application of scientific research to engineering, in particular to railway construction and the use of reinforced concrete.

TALBOT, EMILY FAIRBANKS (*b. Winthrop, Maine, 1834; d. Holderness, N.H., 1900*), teacher, philanthropist. Wife of Israel T. Talbot. Was active in promoting organizations of university women and higher education for women.

TALBOT, ETHELBERT (*b. Fayette, Mo., 1848; d. Tuckahoe, N.Y., 1928*), Episcopal clergyman. Consecrated missionary bishop of Wyoming and Idaho, 1887, he served with ability until 1897, recounting his experiences in *My People of the Plains* (1906). Bishop of central Pennsylvania, 1898–1904, he continued as bishop of Bethlehem (after the division of the original diocese) until 1927. He was presiding bishop of the Protestant Episcopal Church, 1924–26.

TALBOT, FRANCIS XAVIER (*b. Philadelphia, Pa., 1889; d. Washington, D.C., 1953*), Roman Catholic priest, writer. Studied at Woodstock (Md.) College. A Jesuit, Talbot prepared at the Society of Jesus at St. Andrew-on-the-Hudson; ordained in 1921. As literary editor for the Catholic weekly *America*, 1924–44, and editor in chief of *America* and *Catholic Mind*, 1936–44, he introduced leading Catholic writers and thinkers and was responsible for broad coverage of poetry, literature, and drama. President of Loyola College, Baltimore, 1947–50. Author of several books about Catholic missionaries and contributor to the *Encyclopaedia Britannica*.

TALBOT, HENRY PAUL (*b. Boston, Mass., 1864; d. 1927*), chemist. Graduated Massachusetts Institute of Technology, 1885; studied organic and physical chemistry at Leipzig (Ph.D., 1890). Taught *post* 1890 at the Massachusetts Institute of Technology, rising to head of department of chemistry and chemical engineering, 1902, and acting as dean of students, 1921–27.

TALBOT, ISRAEL TISDALE (*b. Sharon, Mass., 1829; d. Hingham, Mass., 1899*), physician. Husband of Emily F. Talbot. A leader in homeopathic medicine, he was appointed dean and professor of surgery at Boston University School of Medicine on its establishment, 1873.

TALBOT, JOHN (*b. Wymondham, England, 1645; d. Burlington, N.J., 1727*), Anglican clergyman. Assistant to George Keith on missionary travels in America, Talbot arrived in Boston, Mass., 1702. Rector of St. Mary's Church, Burlington, N.J., *post* 1704, he made numerous trips to England on behalf of an American episcopate and engaged in many controversies both in America and England. Losing his missionary status because of alleged disaffection toward the government, 1724, he was described by a defender as "a man universally beloved, even by the dissenters."

TALBOT, SILAS (*b. Dighton, Mass., 1751; d. New York, N.Y., 1813*), Revolutionary soldier, naval officer. Trained in the merchant service, he was commissioned captain in the Continental Army, 1775, was at the siege of Boston, and later commanded a fireship in the attempt to burn the British warship *Asia* at New York. Prominent in the defense of the Delaware River forts and in the 1778 Rhode Island campaign, he was made captain, Conti-

nental Navy, 1779, but put to sea in an unsuccessful privateer, was captured and underwent many hardships. A farmer after the war in New York State, he was chosen captain in the reorganized navy, 1794, and superintended building of the frigate *President*. He resigned from the navy, September 1801, after service as commander of the Santo Domingo station.

TALBOTT, HAROLD ELSTNER (*b. Dayton, Ohio, 1888; d. Palm Beach, Fla., 1957*), business executive, government official. Studied at Yale University. A member of the "Dayton group" of industrialists, Talbott was active in the aviation industry, organizing the Wright Aeroplane Co. before World War I, and from 1932, chairman of the board of the North American Aviation concern. Involved in the campaigns of Wendell Willkie, Thomas Dewey, and Eisenhower. Secretary of the air force, 1952–55; resigned over alleged conflicts of interest.

TALCOTT, ANDREW (*b. Glastonbury, Conn., 1797; d. Richmond, Va., 1883*), soldier, engineer. Graduated West Point, 1818. After varied service he resigned his commission, 1836, and served as chief engineer of a number of railroads. He undertook his most important work in locating and building the railroad from Veracruz to the city of Mexico, 1857–67. He devised the so-called "Talcott's method" of determining terrestrial latitudes.

TALCOTT, ELIZA (*b. Vernon, Conn., 1836; d. Kobe, Japan, 1911*), Congregational missionary to Japan *post* 1873.

TALCOTT, JOSEPH (*b. Hartford, Conn., 1669; d. 1741*), Connecticut colonial legislator, soldier, and jurist. Governor of Connecticut, 1724–41, he was the first of the colony's governors to have been native born.

TALIAFERRO, LAWRENCE (*b. King George Co., Va., 1794; d. Bedford, Pa., 1871*), soldier. Indian agent at Fort Snelling (Minn.), 1819–39, he set himself to keep peace between the Sioux and their enemies the Chippewa and other neighbors, an endeavor in which he was often successful because the Indians trusted him. He engaged, however, in almost constant strife with the traders whose efforts to bribe or oust him failed.

TALIAFERRO, WILLIAM BOOTH (*b. Gloucester Co., Va., 1822; d. "Dunham Massie," Gloucester Co., Va., 1898*), lawyer, farmer, Confederate major general. Won high reputation as one of Stonewall Jackson's lieutenants; served with great ability in the defense of Charleston, S.C., *post* 1863. As a Virginia legislator, 1874–79, he opposed repudiation of the state debt.

TALLMADGE, BENJAMIN (*b. Brookhaven, N.Y., 1754; d. Litchfield, Conn., 1835*), Revolutionary officer, businessman. Graduated Yale, 1773. In service as a major during most of the Revolution, Tallmadge won distinction as a field officer (notably in the capture of Fort St. George, Long Island, November 1780) and as principal director of Washington's secret service, 1778–83. Congressman, Federalist, from Connecticut, 1801–17, he served on many committees and was for a time chairman of the military affairs committee. He won a son-in-law of William Floyd.

TALLMADGE, JAMES (*b. Stanford, N.Y., 1778; d. New York, N.Y., 1853*), lawyer, New York politician and militia officer. As congressman, Democrat, from New York, 1817–19, he introduced in February 1819 an amendment to the Missouri admission bill which was designed to prohibit further introduction of slaves into that state and to provide for gradual emancipation of those born there after admission. The amendment precipitated a nationwide controversy. Lieutenant governor of New York, 1825–27, he concerned himself thereafter with nonpolitical activities and was a founder of the present New York University.

TALMADGE, EUGENE (*b. Forsyth, Ga., 1884; d. Atlanta, Ga., 1946*), lawyer, politician. LL.B., University of Georgia, 1908. Following a year of law practice in Atlanta, where he made excellent political connections, Talmadge moved to Ailey in Montgomery County. In 1912 the family moved to Telfair County, where for the next fourteen years he engaged in farming and the law. His only involvement in politics during these years was on the local level; as solicitor for the McRae city court (1918–20) and as county attorney (1920–23).

Talmadge began his statewide political career in 1926 when he defeated the "machine" candidate for the office of commissioner of agriculture. He was reelected in 1928 and 1930, but his tenure was marked by controversy. In 1932 he was elected governor, after defeating a field of nine in the Democratic primary; he was reelected two years later. Talmadge took office as governor at the same time that Franklin D. Roosevelt became president. Delighted at first by the Democratic sweep and Roosevelt's leadership, he gradually became a bitter foe of the New Deal. The chief objects of his attack were agricultural policies of acreage and poundage reduction and the WPA minimum-wage level. Determined to consolidate his authority, he suspended the entire Public Utilities Commission (1933) and declared martial law to "subjugate" the Highway Commission (1933). A determined foe of organized labor, Talmadge called out the National Guard to break strikes during attempts to unionize the state's textile mills in 1934. By 1936 he was solidly in the "stop-Roosevelt" camp, and called a "Grass Roots" convention at Macon, Ga., which formed the "Constitutional Jeffersonian Democratic" party and nominated Talmadge for president. The movement soon collapsed, and the fiasco, together with his opposition to the Agricultural Adjustment Act, temporarily cost Talmadge the support of the farmers. Ineligible to run again in 1936 for governor, he made an unsuccessful attempt to unseat incumbent U.S. Senator Richard B. Russell, Jr. A similar attempt against Walter G. George in 1938 also failed. Between 1936 and 1940 Talmadge practiced law in Atlanta, continued to run his farms, and published the *Statesman*, a weekly newspaper that he founded in 1932.

Talmadge was returned to the governor's chair in 1940. He wisely refrained from attacking Roosevelt, but embroiled himself in a feud with the University of Georgia while attempting to return a political favor. The episode was largely responsible for Talmadge's defeat by Ellis G. Arnall when he ran for a four-year term in 1942. He was nonetheless again elected governor in 1946; but before assuming office he died.

TALMADGE, NORMA (*b. Jersey City, N.J., 1897; d. Las Vegas, Nev., 1957*), film actress. First appeared in *The Household Pest* (1910), in which only the back of her head was seen. Her first lead was in *Under the Daisies* (1913). Her reputation was established in *The Battle Cry of Peace* (1915). Founded her own film company and appeared in *Panthea* (1917), *Smilin' Through* (1922), *Secrets* (1924), and *Kiki* (1926). Retired from films in 1930, having failed to make the transition from silent films to talkies. Second in popularity only to Mary Pickford, Talmadge was considered an accomplished actress.

TALMAGE, JAMES EDWARD (*b. Hungerford, England, 1862; d. 1933*), geologist, Mormon theologian. Immigrating to Utah as a boy, he was educated at the present Brigham Young University, Lehigh, Johns Hopkins, and Illinois Wesleyan. Professor of geology, University of Utah, he served as its president, 1894–97. Appointed an Apostle, 1911, he occupied himself in the service of the Mormon Church thereafter.

TALMAGE, JOHN VAN NEST (*b. Somerville, N.J., 1819; d. Boundbrook, N.J., 1892*), Dutch Reformed missionary to China, 1847–89. Brother of Thomas De W. Talmage.

TALMAGE, THOMAS DE WITT (*b. near Boundbrook, N.J., 1832; d. 1902*), Dutch Reformed clergyman, lecturer. Brother of John Van N. Talmage. Achieving notice for his sensational style of preaching while pastor of the Second Church in Philadelphia, Pa., 1862–69, he was called to the Central Presbyterian Church, Brooklyn, N.Y., and there drew the largest audiences of any contemporary minister in America. His sermons preached in the Brooklyn Tabernacle, which was built specially for him, were published in some 3,500 newspapers each week. Pastor in Washington, D.C., 1894–99, he devoted himself thereafter to conducting the *Christian Herald*.

TALVJ. *See* ROBINSON, THERESE ALBERTINE LOUISE VON JAKOB.

TAMARKIN, JACOB DAVID (*b. Chernigov, Russia, 1888; d. Washington, D.C., 1945*), mathematician. Graduated University of St. Petersburg, 1910; taught there, and also at the School of Communications, and the Electro-Technical School; spent 1920–22 at the University of Perm; returned to his professorships at St. Petersburg (Petrograd). A Menshevik, he had to flee Russia in 1924 and came to the United States, 1925. After two years as visiting lecturer at Dartmouth College, he joined the faculty of Brown University (professor *post* 1928) and brought Brown's mathematics department to a front-rank position. His early research was in number theory and boundary value problems; he was one of the contributors to the theory of functional analysis and did much to make the new theory appreciated.

TAMARÓN, PEDRO (*b. La Guardia, Spain, date uncertain; d. Bamoa, Sinaloa, Mexico, 1768*), Mexican ecclesiastic. Immigrating to Venezuela when quite young, he was named bishop of Durango, Mexico, 1758. His diary of his episcopal tours to the most remote provinces of his diocese includes a valuable record of New Mexico in 1760.

TAMIRIS, HELEN (*b. New York, N.Y., 1903; d. New York, 1966*), dancer, choreographer. She studied Italian ballet with Rosina Galli and Russian ballet with Michel Fokine, then performed with several theatrical companies. One of the leaders of the revolt against traditional dance, Tamiris abandoned mimed stories, theatricality, and atomospheric staging. In her School of the American Dance (1929), she emphasized the innate ability of each student to be expressive, but developed no identifiable style of her own. She helped form the Dance Repertory Theatre (1930–31). Formed her Group and created the *Walt Whitman Suite* (1934), *Cycle of Unrest* (1935), and *Momentum* (1936). Choreographed works for the Federal Dance Theater, 1936–39; choreographed, staged, and directed dances in eighteen Broadway musicals (1945–57), receiving an Antoinette Perry Award for *Touch and Go* (1948). With husband Daniel Nagrin she formed the Tamiris-Nagrin Dance Company (1960–63).

TAMMANY (*fl. 1683–1698*), Delaware Indian chief. A legendary figure in Pennsylvania history, he is known principally in tradition and by presence of his name on several documents and in minutes of conferences. Not a principal chief of his tribe, he was believed to be a strong friend of the white settlers. As years went by, he was gradually invested with the noblest attributes and came to be regarded as a symbol of American resistance to British tyranny and to aristocracy in general.

TAMMEN, HARRY HEYE. *See* BONFILS, FREDERICK GILMER.

TANEY, ROGER BROOKE (*b. Calvert Co., Md., 1777; d. Washington, D.C., 1864*), jurist, statesman. Brother-in-law of Francis S. Key. Descended through his mother from the old Catholic landed aristocracy of Maryland, Taney graduated from Dickinson College, 1795, was admitted to practice law in 1799, and served as a Federalist legislator, 1799–1800. Practicing in Frederick, Md., 1801–23, he attained considerable professional success. Breaking with the leading Federalists in 1812 over the conduct of the war with England, he became a leader of the faction called the "Coodies," and exerted a liberal influence as a state senator, 1816–21. Removing to Baltimore, Md., 1823, he soon became recognized as a leader at the bar. A master of procedural technicalities, he had a simple, direct style of delivery which was highly effective in contrast to contemporary florid eloquence. A supporter of Andrew Jackson *post* 1824, he served as attorney general of Maryland, 1827–31, and in July 1831 was appointed attorney general of the United States, assuming also for a short time the duties of secretary of war. In the controversy over the renewal of the charter of the second Bank of the United States, Taney, who from experience as counsel to a state bank had concluded that definite limitations should be put on the national Bank's powers, opposed rechartering and helped draft President Jackson's veto message. After Jackson's reelection, 1832, and the revelation of the Bank's activities during the campaign, Taney with others advised the president to withdraw government deposits from the Bank of the United States and place them in selected state banks. Appointed U.S. secretary of the treasury, September 1833, to implement this policy, he did so, setting up a system of government depositories which continued to function despite the opposition of all the friends of the Bank. Far from being the pliant instrument of the president, Taney was actually putting into effect long-held opinions of his own; however, the enmity of the friends of the Bank in the Senate effected his retirement to private life in June 1834.

Rejected in January 1835 as a nominee for an associate justiceship of the U.S. Supreme Court, Taney was confirmed over Whig opposition as chief justice in March 1836. His appointment reversed certain trends which are characterized as the work of his predecessor, John Marshall. Speaking for the majority in *Charles River Bridge* v. *Warren Bridge* (36 U.S., 420), Taney held that rights not specifically conferred by a corporation charter could not be inferred from the language of the document. "While the rights of private property are sacredly guarded," he declared, "we must not forget that the community also have rights, and that the happiness and well being of every citizen depends on their faithful preservation." However, this decision did not mean that Taney meant to devitalize the obligation of the contract clause of the Constitution or that his decisions would always be uncompromisingly against corporations. In *Bank of Augusta* v. *Earle* (38 U.S., 519) he asserted the important principle that although a state might specifically exclude from its borders the corporations of other states, the courts, in the absence of specific legislation to that effect, would observe the rule of comity and hold that it had not done so. In effect Taney stood for a modification of the assumption that unchecked centralization of federal power and unqualified judicial benevolence toward private wealth and power always work for the good of the country. Taney felt that the commerce clause of the Constitution should be interpreted narrowly when the issue involved a mere arbitrary use to defeat state laws; he opposed use of the Constitution to prevent state regulation where regulation otherwise would not exist. He apparently had little sympathy for the laissez-faire regime which was being enforced upon the states under color of Constitutional necessity. Yet in dealing with the extension of admiralty laws to inland waters and the jurisdiction of federal courts over cases arising there, he asserted a breadth of federal power which had not been claimed even by Marshall.

Taney had been brought up in a Southern agrarian atmosphere and, although he personally assisted in several plans for the amelioration of slavery he was convinced that white and black could not satisfactorily live together in large numbers as equals. He was also convinced that the solution of the problem was to be arrived at only by the people who were in immediate contact with it, and not by emotional Northern abolitionism. In general he believed that the courts should scrupulously guard the sovereignty of the states from federal encroachment because that part of the population dominated by Northern culture and interests was gaining rapidly over the population of the South and must in time come to control the federal government without reference to the principles of the Constitution. Accepting the challenge which circumstances presented to him in the case of *Dred Scott* v. *Sandford* (60 U.S., 393), he consented to discuss in his opinion several sectional issues which might easily have been avoided. He argued that a black could not possess the rights of citizenship which entitled him to sue in a federal court, and that the lower court, in the case at hand, had erred in taking jurisdiction. Since doubt had been expressed, however, as to whether this phase of the question of jurisdiction could now legitimately be determined by the Supreme Court, he sought to strengthen his position by another argument in proof of the contention that the lower court had been in error in taking jurisdiction. It was admitted that Dred Scott had been born a slave. Taney sought to demonstrate that he was still a slave and that he had not, as contended, become free because of residence in territory made free by act of Congress—because Congress had never had the constitutional power to exclude slavery from the territories. Thus, under cover of a discussion of jurisdiction, Taney ruled on questions which were basic in the bitter controversy between North and South. Attacked with extreme bitterness by Republicans and Abolitionists for deciding, as they said, unnecessarily that Congress had no such power and attacked also for what were called his *obiter dicta*, Taney found that his well-meant attempt to protect the Southern culture against Northern aggression had hastened rather than retarded the ultimate downfall of the South. He wrote two other major opinions on sectional issues: the masterly analysis of the relations between the state and national governments in *Ableman* v. *Booth* (62 U.S., 506); and also the defense of the rights of civilians in wartime contained in *Ex parte Merryman* (Federal Cases No. 9,487). He had a complete lack of sympathy with the national government in the conduct of the Civil War and believed that force should not have been used to prevent the South from leaving the Union. Hence it was that when he died he was scorned by the war-frenzied masses. His character and motives have come more and more to be understood, however, and he is regarded today as a great chief justice.

TANGUAY, EVA (*b. Marbleton, Quebec, Canada, 1878; d. Hollywood, Calif., 1947*), singer, vaudeville star. First sang her trademark song, "I Don't Care," in *The Chaperones*, a 1903 musical show. A headliner in vaudeville, 1906–ca. 1925, she owed her success primarily to her brash, publicity-wise personality, and a flouting of conventions that foreshadowed the attitudes of succeeding generations of women.

TANNEBERGER, DAVID (*b. Berthelsdorf, Saxon Lusatia, 1728; d. York, Pa., 1804*), organ builder. Immigrated to Bethlehem, Pa., 1749. He worked there and in its neighborhood for the remainder of his life, building organs for use in such distant points as Albany, N.Y., Salem, N.C., and Baltimore, Md.

TANNER, BENJAMIN (*b. New York, N.Y., 1775; d. Baltimore, Md., 1848*), engraver. Brother of Henry S. Tanner. Worked in Philadelphia, Pa., *post* 1799, where he was for a time partner with Francis Kearny and Cornelius Tiebout in banknote engraving.

TANNER, BENJAMIN TUCKER (*b. Pittsburgh, Pa., 1835; d. 1923*), bishop of the African Methodist Episcopal Church, 1888–1908.

TANNER, HENRY OSSAWA (*b. Pittsburgh, Pa., 1859; d. Paris, France, 1937*), painter. Son of Benjamin T. Tanner. Studied under Thomas Eakins at Pennsylvania Academy of the Fine Arts. A black, Tanner worked in the United States without success, eking out a bare living as a photographer. A student in Paris, France, under Benjamin Constant and J. P. Laurens, 1891, he made his home abroad thereafter and won prestige as a painter on religious themes.

TANNER, HENRY SCHENCK (*b. New York, N.Y., 1786; d. New York, 1858*), cartographer, statistical geographer. Brother of Benjamin Tanner. Author of a number of maps, atlases, guide books and geographical compendia, Tanner was principally notable for his *A New American Atlas* (five parts, 1818–23), a work of extraordinary merit which was founded on primary source material. In 1829 he published a map of the United States, 64 by 50 inches in size, on the scale of about 32 miles to the inch, practically twice as detailed as Melish's map of 1816.

TANNER, JAMES (*b. Richmondville, N.Y., 1844; d. Washington, D.C., 1927*), Union soldier, pension lobbyist, known as "Corporal Tanner." Inept U.S. commissioner of pensions, March–August 1889.

TANSILL, CHARLES CALLAN (*b. Fredericksburg, Tex., 1890; d. Washington, D.C., 1964*), historian. Attended Catholic University of America (B.A., 1912; M.A., 1913; Ph.D., 1915) and Johns Hopkins University (Ph.D., 1918). Joined the Department of History at American University in Washington as assistant professor (1919) and was promoted to full professor two years later. His most influential book, *America Goes to War* (1938), challenged the orthodox view that the United States entered World War I solely to defend its neutral rights. Tansill was a fine scholar and popular teacher, but his isolationism and anti-British bias prompted him to praise Hitler, and he was forced to resign his professorship at American University in 1937. Later he taught at Fordham University (1939–44) and Georgetown University (1944–58). After World War II he became obsessed with anti–communism and served as an adviser to Sen. Joseph Mc-Carthy.

TAPPAN, ARTHUR (*b. Northampton, Mass., 1786; d. New Haven, Conn., 1865*), New York City silk merchant, Abolitionist. Brother of Benjamin and Lewis Tappan. Founded *New York Journal of Commerce*, 1827; aided free church movement of Charles G. Finney; assisted Kenyon College, Oberlin College, Auburn Theological Seminary. Helped support William L. Garrison's *Liberator* from 1830; active in launching the *Emancipator*, 1833; first president, American Anti-Slavery Society, from which he withdrew, 1840, to help form American and Foreign Anti-Slavery Society. Convinced that slavery could be destroyed under the Constitution by political action, he supported the Liberty Party and helped establish the *National Era*. Oblivious of threats and unpopularity, he was a major financier of the abolitionist movement.

TAPPAN, BENJAMIN (*b. Northampton, Mass., 1773; d. Steubenville, Ohio, 1857*), Ohio legislator and jurist, antislavery leader. Brother of Arthur and Lewis Tappan; father of Eli T. Tappan. Studied law with Gideon Granger; settled in present Portage Co., Ohio, 1799; practiced in Ravenna and Steubenville, and was later a partner of Edwin M. Stanton. A Jacksonian Democrat, he opposed slavery but was not an Abolitionist; he served as U.S. senator from Ohio, *post* 1838. He refused to follow instructions of the Whig legislature to oppose Texas annexation, 1845, yet he was active in free-soil affairs and cast his last presidential vote for Frémont, 1856.

TAPPAN, ELI TODD (*b. Steubenville, Ohio, 1824; d. 1888*), lawyer, educator. Son of Benjamin Tappan. Taught mathematics at Ohio University; president of Kenyon College, 1869–75; lifelong champion of common schools.

TAPPAN, EVA MARCH (*b. Blackstone, Mass., 1854; d. Worcester, Mass., 1930*), teacher, author of anthologies, textbooks and stories for children.

TAPPAN, HENRY PHILIP (*b. Rhinebeck, N.Y., 1805; d. probably Switzerland, 1881*), Congregational clergyman, philosopher. Graduated Union, 1825; Auburn Theological Seminary, 1827. Taught at University of the City of New York, 1832–37. As president, University of Michigan, 1852–63, he strove to give that institution a university status according to ideas expressed in his *University Education* (1851).

TAPPAN, LEWIS (*b. Northampton, Mass., 1788; d. Brooklyn, N.Y., 1873*), merchant, Abolitionist. Brother of Arthur and Benjamin Tappan. Proprietor of *New York Journal of Commerce*, 1828–31. Established "the Mercantile Agency," 1841, the first commercial-credit rating agency in the United States; retired from business, 1849, to devote himself to antislavery work and other humanitarian labors. As did his brother Arthur, Lewis Tappan repudiated William L. Garrison when the latter proposed to attach other reforms to the abolition cause; he took a leading part in the American and Foreign Anti-Slavery Society and later in the Abolition Society.

TAPPEN, FREDERICK DOBBS (*b. New York, N.Y., 1829; d. Lakewood, N.J., 1902*), banker. President of the Gallatin National Bank (1868–1902), he was invariably chosen by the other New York banks as dictator-chairman to direct their united policy in times of financial panic.

TAPPER, BERTHA FEIRING (*b. Christiania, Norway, 1859; d. Boston, Mass., 1915*), painter, music teacher. Graduated Leipzig Conservatory of Music, 1878. Immigrating to America 1881, she played with the Kneisel Quartet and was an outstanding teacher at the New England Conservatory of Music and at the New York City Institute of Musical Art.

TARBELL, EDMUND CHARLES (*b. West Groton, Mass., 1862; d. New Castle, N.H., 1938*), painter. Trained as a lithographer, he studied at the Museum of Fine Arts, Boston, and in Paris under Boulanger and J. J. Lefebvre. Teacher of drawing and painting at the Boston Museum, 1889–1913, he was one of the group known as "The Ten" *post* 1898, and was celebrated for his solid craftsmanship, particularly in portraits of outstanding men. He was principal, Corcoran School of Art, Washington, D.C., 1918–26.

TARBELL, FRANK BIGELOW (*b. West Groton, Mass., 1853; d. New Haven, Conn., 1920*), archaeologist. Graduated Yale, 1873; Ph.D., 1879. Among the first American to achieve distinction in classical archaeology, he taught Greek at Yale and Harvard, served as director and secretary of the American School at Athens, and was professor of archaeology at the University of Chicago, 1893–1918.

TARBELL, IDA MINERVA (*b. Hatch Hollow, near Wattsburgh, Pa., 1857; d. Bridgeport, Conn., 1944*), writer. Graduated Allegheny College, 1880. Interested in biology, she discovered that science offered no such opportunity for a woman, and she took a post as preceptress at a seminary in Poland, Ohio. She found her teaching burdens oppressive and left at the end of two years. Returning to Meadville, Pa., she went to work in the editorial offices of the *Chautauquan* and found her calling as a journalist in an environment heady with aspirations to improvement. In 1891 she departed for Paris, where she divided her time between lectures at the Sorbonne, research at the Bibliothèque Nationale on the role of women in the French Revolution, and writing topical columns for a group of midwestern American newspapers. The editor S. S. McClure found her in Paris in 1892 and thus began a connection with *McClure's Magazine* that lasted for twelve years. On her return to the United States in 1894 McClure hired Tarbell to write a serial biography of Napoleon Bonaparte. The success of the Napoleon series led her next to Abraham Lincoln, a subject she revered and one to which she would return repeatedly over the next forty years.

In 1901, spurred on by the creative enthusiasm of McClure, she set to work on the most important assignment of her career, her famous inquiry into the oil interests of John D. Rockefeller. The project lasted five years, ran to nineteen articles in *McClure's*, and appeared as a two-volume history in 1904. What began as a careful exposure of the oil trust as a national economic fact ended as a studied ethical indictment of corporate arrogance, dishonesty, and secret privilege. The age of muckraking journalism produced no document more substantial than *The History of the Standard Oil Company*.

In 1906 the staff at *McClure's* blew apart in controversy over S. S. McClure's ambitious managerial policies and erratic personal behavior. Tarbell was intimately involved in the struggle against him. The dispute ended in her resignation and departure, along with John S. Phillips, Ray Standard Baker, and Lincoln Steffens. This group, soon joined by Finley Peter Dunne and William Allen White, promptly acquired control of the *American Magazine*, where by the end of 1906 Tarbell had launched her major series on the tariff.

The limits of her reformist zeal were revealed in her journalistic inquiry into the status of women. Sensitive to criticism of her failure to support the suffrage cause, she privately characterized the movement as "part of what seems to me the most dangerous fallacy of our times— and that is that we can be saved morally, economically, socially by laws and systems." The judgment reflected her growing distrust of politics and group militance as ways to human progress. To her mind the suffragists shared with the urban boss and the trade union leader a mistaken reliance on coercion to get what they wanted. She was more sympathetic with the settlement house work and peace activities of Jane Addams.

Henry Ford helped convert her to welfare capitalism, or what she called "the Golden Rule in Industry." From 1912 to 1915 she traveled widely to examine factory conditions, and was awestruck by Ford's mass-production methods, his wage policy, and his "sociological" treatment of his work force. Similarly, she came to place great confidence in the scientific management plans of Frederick W. Taylor as an antidote for industrial strife and inefficiency. Once more her conclusions startled some who had tagged her as a radical muckraker and who felt her newfound faith in corporate "fair play" was platitudinous. After she ended her connection with the *American Magazine* in 1915, Tarbell remained a prolific writer and lecturer.

TARBELL, JOSEPH (b. *probably Massachusetts*, ca. *1780*; d. *Washington, D.C., 1815*), naval officer. Appointed midshipman, 1798, he served in the naval war with France, and also with distinction in the attacks on Tripoli in 1804. On June 20, 1813, as commander of a gunboat flotilla, he engaged three British frigates indecisively in Hampton Roads. He was promoted captain, 1813.

TARBOX, INCREASE NILES (b. *East Windsor, Conn., 1815*; d. *West Newton, Mass., 1888*), Congregational clergyman, genealogist. A founder and an original editor (1849–51) of the *Congregationalist*, he served as secretary of the American Education Society, 1851–84.

TARKINGTON, BOOTH (b. *Indianapolis, Ind., 1869*; d. *Indianapolis, 1946*), novelist, playwright. Christened Newton Booth Tarkington. Nephew of Newton Booth. His ambition was to become a writer and an illustrator, and he cultivated both skills at Phillips Exeter Academy, Purdue University (1890–91), and Princeton University (1891–93). For five years he made little progress as a free-lance writer and illustrator. In 1899 he published his successful first novel, *The Gentleman From Indiana*; followed it the next year with the popular historical romance *Monsieur Beaucaire*; and was launched on a career as novelist and playwright. His books ultimately totaled more than forty-five.

Tarkington's great public and critical successes belonged to the decade 1914–24, when he wrote his best-known books of childhood and adolescence, *Penrod* (1914), *Penrod and Sam* (1916), *Seventeen* (1916), and *Gentle Julia* (1922); his two Pulitzer Prize novels, *The Magnificent Ambersons* (1918) and *Alice Adams* (1921); and two other mature novels, *The Turmoil* (1915) and *The Midlander* (1924). A 1921 *Publishers' Weekly* poll of booksellers named him the most significant of contemporary authors. In a *Literary Digest* contest in 1922 he was voted the greatest living American writer, and a *New York Times* poll of the same year put him on a list of the ten greatest contemporary Americans. Tarkington's work, however, has ill survived the test of time; half a century later, his serious novels were scarcely read at all and even his juvenile entertainments were out of favor.

Tarkington wrote some twenty plays, including such successes as *The Man From Home* (first performed in 1907), *The Country Cousin* (1917), and *Clarence* (1919). A number of these plays Tarkington wrote in collaboration with Harry Leon Wilson; for *The Country Cousin* his coauthor was Julian Street. Even in the best of his novels, the fine *Alice Adams*, Tarkington takes up a position above and slightly to the right of his characters, and as he manipulates them, however gently, one detects the strings of the puppet master.

TARR, RALPH STOCKMAN (b. *Gloucester, Mass., 1864*; d. *Ithaca, N.Y., 1912*), geologist, geographer. Studied at Lawrence Scientific School, Harvard, and worked under Alpheus Hyatt and Spencer F. Baird, and with the U.S. Geological Survey. Taught geology at Cornell University *post* 1892; headed department of physical geography *post* 1906. Author of a number of widely used textbooks and coauthor of *Alaskan Glacier Studies* (1914), he made important contributions to glaciology.

TASHRAK. *See* ZEVIN, ISRAEL JOSEPH.

TASHUNCA-UITCO. *See* CRAZY HORSE.

TATE, GEORGE HENRY HAMILTON (b. *London, England, 1894*; d. *Morristown, N.J., 1953*), mammalogist. Immigrated to the U.S. in 1912. Studied at Columbia University, B.S., 1927, and the University of Montreal, Ph.D., 1938. Staff member of the American Museum of Natural History from 1921; associate curator of mammals, 1942; curator of mammals, 1946. An expert on South American mammals and on Asian and Australian wildlife, he published *Mammals of the Pacific World* (1945) and *Mammals of Eastern Asia* (1947).

TATE, JOHN TORRENCE (b. *Lenox, Iowa, 1889*; d. *Minneapolis, Minn., 1950*), physicist. B.S., University of Nebraska, 1910; M.A., 1912. Ph.D., University of Berlin, 1914. Taught physics at University of Nebraska; and at University of Minnesota, 1916–50 (professor *post* 1920). An outstanding teacher and active in professional associations; managing editor of *Physical Review*, 1926–50; helped found American Institute of Physics and served as its chairman, 1936–39. Dean of College of Science, Literature, and the Arts, University of Minnesota, 1937–44. Chief of Division 6 (on subsurface warfare), National Defense Research Committee,

1941–45. His research work at Minnesota developed out of his interest in electron collision and ionization phenomena first stimulated by Franck at Berlin; studies by him and his students led to the refinement of such precision experimental techniques as those of mass spectroscopy and yielded much specific information on the structure and internal force fields of numerous gaseous molecules and compounds.

TATHAM, WILLIAM (*b. Hutton-in-the-Forest, England, 1752, d. near Richmond, Va., 1819*), civil engineer, geographer. A brilliant but eccentric man, Tatham lived for long periods *post* 1769 in Virginia and on the North Carolina and Tennessee frontiers, engaging in a bewildering number of occupations. He was author of, among other works, *A Topographical Analysis of the Commonwealth of Virginia* (1791). He made a pioneer survey of Atlantic Coast from Cape Fear to Cape Hatteras *post* 1805, was the friend and correspondent of Thomas Jefferson, and collaborated with Robert Fulton in the field of canalization.

TATLOCK, JOHN STRONG PERRY (*b. Stamford, Conn., 1876; d. Northampton, Mass., 1948*), medievalist, educator. B.A., Harvard, 1896; M.A., 1897; Ph.D., 1903. Taught English at University of Michigan, 1897–1901, 1903–15. Professor of English at Stanford University, 1915–25; at Harvard, 1925–29; and at University of California at Berkeley, 1929–46. Among his major publications were *The Development and Chronology of Chaucer's Works* (1907); *A Concordance to the Complete Works of Geoffrey Chaucer*, etc. (1927, with A. G. Kennedy); and *The Legendary History of Britain: Geoffrey of Monmouth's Historia Regum Britanniae and Its Early Vernacular Versions* (1950).

TATTNALL, JOSIAH (*b. near Savannah, Ga., 1795; d. Savannah, 1871*), naval officer. Appointed midshipman, 1812, he served aboard the *Constellation* and was in the engagement at Craney Island, Va., June 1813. Assigned to the *Epervier*, he was in the war with Algiers, 1815. Thereafter until the war with Mexico he engaged in routine duties, rising to the rank of commander; during that war he engaged in the operations on the east coast of Mexico and was promoted to captain, 1850. Although opposed to secession, he was loyal to his native state and in March 1861 was commissioned captain in the Confederate Navy, commanding the naval defenses of Georgia and South Carolina. He succeeded Franklin Buchanan as commander in Virginia waters, March 1862. On the abandonment of Norfolk, he again commanded the Georgia naval defense, particularly at Savannah.

TATUM, ART (*b. Toledo, Ohio, 1910; d. Los Angeles, Calif., 1956*), jazz pianist. Blind in one eye, Tatum began his career as a child star on a radio program. In 1932, he became singer Adelaide Hall's accompanist; traveled with her to New York, where he made his first recordings and played in leading nightclubs. Played at clubs in Chicago, returning to New York in 1943 with his own jazz trio. He continued to give concerts and play in clubs until his death. Greatly influenced by Fats Waller, Tatum's intricate and varied style is considered by many to be the greatest of jazz piano.

TAUSSIG, FRANK WILLIAM (*b. St. Louis, Mo., 1859; d. Cambridge, Mass., 1940*), economist. Son of William Taussig. Educated at Harvard (A.B., 1879; Ph.D., 1883; LL.B., 1886); served there, 1882–1935, as a profoundly influential teacher of economics. As editor of the *Quarterly Journal of Economics*, 1896–1937, though essentially conservative, he introduced many new and unorthodox writers. He served as first chairman of the federal Tariff Commission, 1917–19, and as a member of the Paris Peace Conference. His writings include a famous textbook *Principles of Economics* (1911), *Tariff History of the United States* (1888), *Wages and Capital* (1896), *Investors and Money Makers* (1915),

International Trade (1927), and, with C. S. Joslyn, a sociological study of American business leaders (1932).

TAUSSIG, FREDERICK JOSEPH (*b. Brooklyn, N.Y., 1872; d. Bar Harbor, Maine, 1943*), gynecologist, advocate of legalized abortion. B.A., Harvard, 1893. Graduated Washington University Medical School, St. Louis, Mo., 1898. Practiced in St. Louis; professor of clinical obstetrics and gynecology, Washington University Medical School *post* 1911. Author of, among other works, *Abortion, Spontaneous and Induced: Medical and Social Aspects* (1936).

TAUSSIG, JOSEPH KNEFLER (*b. Dresden, Germany, 1877; d. Bethesda, Md., 1947*), naval officer. Cousin of F. W. Taussig. Born abroad of American parents from St. Louis, Mo. Graduated U.S. Naval Academy, 1899. Wounded while on duty in Boxer Rebellion, China; commanded first division of destroyers to go overseas in World War I (May 1917). Opposed policies of Franklin D. Roosevelt (then assistant secretary of the navy), 1919. On duty at Naval War College (except for three years in commands at sea), 1920–31, he rose to rank of rear admiral. Held high staff positions, 1931–36, but only minor assignments thereafter until retirement, 1941. Recalled to active duty, 1943, he served until 1946 as chairman of the naval clemency board.

TAUSSIG, WILLIAM (*b. Prague, Bohemia, 1826; d. St. Louis, Mo., 1913*), physician, businessman, civic leader. Immigrated to America, 1847; practiced medicine in and near St. Louis, Mo., *post* 1850. Turning to the banking profession, 1866, he served as manager, and later president, of the company organized to bridge the Mississippi River at St. Louis and of its successor companies until his retirement in 1896.

TAWNEY, JAMES ALBERTUS (*b. near Gettysburg, Pa., 1855; d. Excelsior Springs, Mo., 1919*), lawyer, Minnesota legislator. Settled in Winona, Minn., 1877. Congressman, Republican, from Minnesota, 1893–1911, he rose to the chairmanship of the committee on appropriations and was one of the clique, along with Joseph G. Cannon, John Dalzell, and others, which dominated the House for a number of years. He was a consistent protectionist and orthodox Republican.

TAYLOR, ALFRED ALEXANDER (*b. Happy Valley, Tenn., 1848; d. near Johnson City, Tenn., 1931*), lawyer, Tennessee legislator and Congressman. Brother of Robert L. Taylor. Republican governor of Tennessee, 1921–23, he attributed his political success and that of his brother to the fact that "We played the fiddle, were fond of dogs, and loved our fellow men."

TAYLOR, ARCHIBALD ALEXANDER EDWARD (*b. Springfield, Ohio, 1834; d. Columbus, Ohio, 1903*), Presbyterian clergyman. An Old School minister, he held pastorates in Kentucky, Iowa, the District of Columbia, and Columbus, Ohio; he also served as president of University of Wooster, 1873–83.

TAYLOR, BAYARD (*b. Kennett Square, Pa., 1825; d. Germany, 1878*), traveler, author, diplomat. A printer by trade, Taylor attracted the notice of Rufus W. Griswold and was encouraged by him to publish *Ximena* (1844), a first volume of verse. Commissioned by several periodicals and newspapers (including the N.Y. *Tribune*) to contribute letters descriptive of his travels, he spent two years in Europe and on his return published the successful *Views Afoot* (1846). Thereafter until 1860 he continued to travel and tell about his travels and also lectured widely. He represented to the home-keeping Americans of that time an enviable adventurer's image. Among his numerous books of this period, *Eldorado* (1850) still has value as an early picture of California. During the Civil War he served for a time as Washington correspondent for the N.Y. *Tribune*, and was U.S. secretary of legation at St. Petersburg, Russia, 1862–63. Subsequent to his return he continued to pour out hackwork and labored on his translation of Goethe's *Faust* (published, 1870–71). Meanwhile, increasingly ambitious for reputation as poet and man of letters, he published a great quantity of mediocre verse and three undistinguished novels. Immensely renowned in his own time, the brilliant activity of his life blinded people to the low quality of his actual achievement. Appointed U.S. minister to Germany, 1878, he died late in that year at his post. His outstanding work, his translation of *Faust*, has been extravagantly praised for its fidelity but it is, when all is said and done, a rendering in second-rate English verse.

TAYLOR, BENJAMIN FRANKLIN (*b. Lowville, N.Y., 1819; d. Cleveland, Ohio, 1887*), journalist, lecturer, poet. Associated with the Chicago *Daily Journal*, 1845–65, he won national reputation for his realistic Civil War battle reports. A collected edition of his popular verses was published in 1886.

TAYLOR, BERT LESTON (*b. Goshen, Mass., 1866; d. Chicago, Ill., 1921*), newspaper columnist. Employed principally on newspapers in Chicago, Ill., *post* 1899, he was author of the "A Line o' Type or Two" column which set a standard for such work that has been the inspiration and despair of many other journalists. He was noted also as a writer of highly polished satirical verse.

TAYLOR, CHARLES ALONZO (*b. Greenfield, Mass., 1864; d. Glendale, Calif., 1942*), dramatist. Author of blood-and-thunder melodramas (e.g., *The Queen of the White Slaves*; *The Child Wife*). Married Laurette Taylor, 1901, whose first successful vehicle was *From Rags to Riches* (1903), which he wrote for her.

TAYLOR, CHARLES FAYETTE (*b. Williston, Vt., 1827; d. Los Angeles, Calif., 1899*), orthopedic surgeon. M.D., University of Vermont, 1856. In practice in New York City, 1857–*ca.* 1882, Taylor devised a method for eventual cure of the spinal lesion known as Pott's disease by giving protection to the diseased vertebrae through the principle of fixed points for adequate support. He also devised many other appliances for chronic bone, joint, and muscle lesions, and was instrumental in establishing the New York Orthopedic Dispensary.

TAYLOR, CHARLES HENRY (*b. Charlestown, Mass., 1846; d. 1921*), Union soldier, journalist. Publisher of the *Boston Daily Globe, post* 1873, Taylor successfully developed his paper as a reflection of New England life and thought.

TAYLOR, CHARLOTTE DE BERNIER (*b. Savannah, Ga., 1806; d. Isle of Man, 1861*), entomologist. Daughter of William Scarbrough. A naturalist rather than a laboratory scientist, she was author of a number of early and important articles stressing the agricultural significance of entomological studies. These appeared principally in *Harper's New Monthly Magazine* during the late 1850's.

TAYLOR, CREED (*b. probably Cumberland Co., Va., 1766; d. 1836*), Virginia legislator and jurist, law teacher. Political sponsor of John Randolph of Roanoke. Conducted *post* 1821 at "Needham," his Cumberland Co. estate, a law school at which many Virginia attorneys received their training and which was recommended by Thomas Jefferson, James Madison, and John Marshall.

TAYLOR, DAVID WATSON (*b. Louisa Co., Va., 1864; d. Washington, D.C., 1940*), naval officer, naval constructor. Graduated Randolph-Macon College, 1881; U.S. Naval Academy, 1885; made advanced studies at Royal Naval College, Greenwich, England. An early advocate of the need of scientific research in naval architecture, Taylor designed and constructed the navy's

experimental model basin and remained in charge of it from 1899 until 1914 when he was appointed chief naval constructor. Promoted rear admiral in 1916, he retired from active duty, 1923, but continued active in naval aviation research and ship design. He was author of *The Speed and Power of Ships* (1910) in which he proposed the "standard series method" of estimating propulsion power. He supervised the naval building program during World War I and was one of the pioneers in development and production of naval aircraft of all types.

TAYLOR, EDWARD (*b. Leicestershire, England, ca. 1645; d. 1729*), Puritan clergyman, poet. Immigrated to Boston, Mass., 1668. Graduating from Harvard, 1671, he served as minister at Westfield, Mass., until his death. He was a strict supporter of the Congregational way. Writing in the style of the early 17th-century "concettist" poets of England, Taylor produced a number of poems marked by intensity, metrical variety and skill, and freshness of imagery—all in all perhaps the finest single poetic achievement in America before the 19th century. His works remained in manuscript virtually unknown until 1937; they were first published as *The Poetical Works of Edward Taylor* (edited by T. H. Johnson, 1939) and have received much subsequent critical attention.

TAYLOR, EDWARD THOMPSON (*b. Richmond, Va., 1793; d. Boston, Mass., 1871*), mariner, peddler, Methodist clergyman. Known as "Father Taylor." Minister of the Boston (Mass.) Seamen's Bethel *post* 1830, Father Taylor was reputed one of the greatest American preachers of his generation. The sermon of Father Mapple in Herman Melville's *Moby Dick* is a portrayal of Taylor's manner and method. He was highly respected for his charitable character and noted for his epigrams; he described Daniel Webster as the "best bad man he ever knew."

TAYLOR, FRANCIS HENRY (*b. Philadelphia, Pa., 1903; d. Worcester, Mass., 1957*), museum director. Studied at the University of Pennsylvania, the Sorbonne, the universities of Paris and Florence, and at Princeton. Director of the Worcester Art Museum in Massachusetts, 1931–39 and 1955–57. Director of the Metropolitan Museum of Art in New York, 1939–54. An innovative museum director, Taylor introduced the techniques of modern display and community participation in museum affairs. Instituted international loan programs for the Metropolitan after World War II. Author of *The Taste of Angels* (1948).

TAYLOR, FRANK BURSLEY (*b. Fort Wayne, Ind., 1860; d. Fort Wayne, 1938*), geologist, specialist in glacial history of the Great Lakes region.

TAYLOR, FRANK WALTER (*b. Philadelphia, Pa., 1874; d. Ogdensburg, N.Y., 1921*), book and magazine illustrator, painter, portraitist.

TAYLOR, FRED MANVILLE (*b. Northville, Mich, 1855; d. Pasadena, Calif., 1932*), economist. Graduated Northwestern University, 1876; Ph.D., University of Michigan, 1888. Taught economics at Michigan, 1892–1929. An authority on currency and banking, he was author of the influential *Principles of Economics* (1911, and subsequent editions).

TAYLOR, FREDERICK WINSLOW (*b. Germantown, Pa., 1856; d. Philadelphia, Pa., 1915*), mechanical engineer, inventor, efficiency expert. Learned trades of pattern maker and machinist; graduated M.E., Stevens Institute of Technology, 1883. Noted for design and construction of large machines and for his joint discovery of the Taylor-White process of heat treatment of tool steel. Taylor evolved over years of observation a theory that by scientific study of every operation in a manufacturing plant, a fair and reasonable estimate of the production capacities of both man and machine could be made. Application of the data found would, he felt, abolish the antagonism between employer and employee and thus bring about increased efficiency. In addition, he worked out a system of analysis, classification, and symbolization to be used in the study of every type of manufacturing organization. Applying his theory with success for, among other clients, the Bethlehem Steel Co., he devoted his life *post* 1901 to expounding his principles. He published *The Principles of Scientific Management* in 1911 and was author of a number of technical papers.

TAYLOR, GEORGE (*b. probably northern Ireland, 1716; d. 1781*), ironmaster, Pennsylvania colonial legislator. Immigrated to Pennsylvania *ca.* 1736; operated furnaces in Bucks Co., Pa., *post ca.* 1754. A moderate radical, he served as member of the Continental Congress, July 1776–*ca.* February 1777. He was a signer of the Declaration of Independence.

TAYLOR, GEORGE BOARDMAN (*b. Richmond, Va., 1832; d. Rome, Italy, 1907*), Baptist clergyman. Son of James Barnett Taylor. Served as a Baptist missionary in Italy *post* 1873.

TAYLOR, GRAHAM (*b. Schenectady, N.Y., 1851; d. Ravinia, Ill., 1938*), Dutch Reformed and Congregational clergyman, civic reformer. After ministerial and teaching experience elsewhere, he served as head of the department of Christian sociology at Chicago Theological Seminary, 1892–1924; he was also founder of the Chicago Commons, a settlement house, 1894. In the fall of 1903, with Charles R. Henderson, he offered the first course for social workers in Chicago which developed through various changes of title into the Graduate School of Social Service Administration at the University of Chicago.

TAYLOR, HANNIS (*b. New Bern, N.C., 1851; d. 1922*), lawyer, scholar. Practiced at Mobile, Ala., 1870–92, and in Washington, D.C., *post* 1898; able U.S. minister to Spain, 1893–97; author of *The Origin and Growth of the English Constitution* (1889, 1898).

TAYLOR, HARRY (*b. present Tilton, N.H., 1862; d. Washington, D.C., 1930*), soldier. Graduated West Point, 1884. Chief engineer of the AEF in France, 1917–18, he planned port facilities, bases, and training camps, supervised their construction, and took over operation of necessary French railroads, all with remarkable efficiency and speed. He also planned and constructed water systems, electrical supply, and roads for frontline troops. Promoted major general, 1924, he retired in 1926 as chief of engineers of the U.S. Army.

TAYLOR, HENRY OSBORN (*b. New York, N.Y., 1856; d. New York, 1941*), historian. B.A., Harvard, 1878. LL.B., Columbia Law School, 1881. Studied Roman law at University of Leipzig. Admitted to the New York bar, 1884, he devoted himself to scholarship and was author among other works of *The Classical Heritage of the Middle Ages* (1901) and *The Mediaeval Mind* (1911).

TAYLOR, JAMES BARNETT (*b. Barton-upon-Humber, England, 1804; d. Richmond, Va., 1871*), Baptist clergyman. Father of George B. Taylor. Brought to New York, N.Y., as an infant, he was raised in Virginia; he held pastorates *post* 1826 in or near Richmond. He was active in mission work and in the movement to establish Richmond College.

TAYLOR, JAMES BAYARD. *See* TAYLOR, BAYARD.

TAYLOR, JAMES MONROE (*b. Brooklyn, N.Y., 1848; d. 1916*), Baptist clergyman. Graduated University of Rochester, 1868; Rochester Theological Seminary, 1871. As president of Vassar College, 1886–1914, he strove for a proper endowment, carried a heavy teaching load, improved the faculty, and was largely responsible for setting and maintaining high academic standards.

TAYLOR, JAMES WICKES (*b. Starkey, N.Y., 1819; d. Winnipeg, Canada, 1893*), lawyer, journalist, government official. Practiced law in Cincinnati, Ohio, and St. Paul, Minn.; served as special U.S. treasury agent, 1859–69; was effective U.S. consul at Winnipeg, 1870–93.

TAYLOR, JOHN (*b. Fauquier Co., Va., 1752; d. 1835*), Baptist preacher, farmer. Organized and served churches in the Virginia frontier settlements; removed to Kentucky, 1783, where he continued his work. Author of *A History of Ten Baptist Churches* (1823), a fine picture of religion on the frontier.

TAYLOR, JOHN (*b. either Orange or Caroline Co., Va., 1753; d. Caroline Co., 1824*), Revolutionary soldier, Virginia legislator, agriculturist, political philosopher. Generally known as "John Taylor of Caroline." Raised by his cousin Edmund Pendleton, he attended the College of William and Mary, read law in Pendleton's office, and was licensed to practice in 1774. He married a daughter of John Penn, 1783.

Early identified with the democratic group led by Thomas Jefferson, Taylor was prominent in forwarding land legislation for the advantage of actual settlers and favored a wider franchise and a more equal system of representation. He opposed the Federal Constitution, along with Patrick Henry and George Mason, on the ground that the rights of the individual and of the states were not sufficiently protected by it; he later roundly condemned Alexander Hamilton's financial measures. In December 1798 he introduced into the Virginia legislature the famous resolutions in support of the doctrine of delegated powers and the right of states to interpose in cases of "deliberate, palpable and dangerous exercise of other powers." U.S. senator from Virginia, 1792–94, 1803, and 1822–24, he remained a strong supporter of Jefferson and Jeffersonian principles both as public man and as writer. Among his numerous pamphlets, books, and contributions to newspapers, his *An Inquiry into the Principles and Policy of the Government of the United States* (published, 1814, first conceived in 1794) deserves rank among the two or three historic contributions to political science produced in the United States. In this work he denied the existence of a natural aristocracy, and condemned the idea of a permanent debt with taxes and a banking system to support it. He proposed shortening terms of both president and senators and checking their patronage. He contended that the American government was one of divided powers, not classes and that its agents were responsible to the people alone; in a later work he denied validity of appeals from state courts to the U.S. Supreme Court. In 1820 and 1822 he launched powerful attacks against the right of Congress to dictate to Missouri on the question of slavery, and also against the protective tariff system. His important contributions to scientific agriculture were collected in *The Arator* (1813). Champion of local democracy and state rights, he was one of America's greatest philosophers of agrarian liberalism.

TAYLOR, JOHN (*b. Milnthorpe, Westmoreland, England, 1808; d. Kaysville, Utah, 1887*), journalist, Mormon Apostle. Third president of the Utah branch of the Mormon Church, 1880–87.

TAYLOR, JOHN LOUIS (*b. London, England, 1769; d. Raleigh, N.C., 1829*), North Carolina jurist, legal writer. Justice of the state superior court, 1798–1818 (chief justice *post* 1811); chief justice, state supreme court, 1819–29.

TAYLOR, JOHN W. (*b. Charlton, N.Y., 1784; d. Cleveland, Ohio, 1854*), lawyer, New York legislator, antislavery leader. Congressman, National Republican and later Whig, from New York, 1813–33; speaker of the House, 1820–21, 1825–27. Seconded James Tallmadge's amendment to the Missouri bill. Delivered early antislavery speeches in Congress (1819–21) in support of his proposal prohibiting introduction of slavery into territories north of 36°30'.

TAYLOR, JOSEPH DEEMS (*b. New York, N.Y., 1885; d. New York, 1966*), composer, author, editor, music critic. Attended New York University (B.A., 1906). Created one of his most celebrated works, *Through the Looking Glass*, in 1917. He was a humor columnist for the *New York Press*, the music critic of the *New York World* (1921–25), the editor of *Musical America* (1927–29), and the music critic of the *New York American* (1931–32). Wrote music for the Broadway theater and four operas: *The King's Henchman* (1927), *Peter Ibbetson* (1931), *Ramuntcho* (1942), and *The Dragon* (1958). Broadcast a series of radio talks on opera and was intermission commentator (1936–43) for national broadcasts of the New York Philharmonic Orchestra. Books include *Of Men and Music* (1937), *The Well-Tempered Listener* (1940), *Music to My Ears* (1949), and *Some Enchanted Evenings: The Story of Rodgers and Hammerstein* (1953). Served as president of American Society of Composers, Authors, and Publishers, 1942–48, and as a director of the society, 1933–66.

TAYLOR, JOSEPH WRIGHT (*b. Monmouth Co., N.J., 1810; d. 1880*), physician, leather merchant. Founded Bryn Mawr College, purchasing land for it in 1878 and supervising construction of buildings *post* 1879; virtually the whole of his estate was left to the college.

TAYLOR, LAURETTE (*b. New York, N.Y., 1884; d. New York, 1946*), actress. Christened Loretta Cooney. Married Charles Alonzo Taylor, 1901, and acted in his melodramas until 1908; divorced him, 1910. After attracting favorable notices in mediocre Broadway plays, she rose to stardom in *Peg O' My Heart*, 1912, written especially as a vehicle for her by John Hartley Manners whom she married. Unfortunately the public insisted on her appearance in similar parts, and her efforts to break her image as a "lovable" personality failed of financial success although critics applauded them. At a low personal and professional ebb after Manners died in 1928, she made a triumphant comeback in 1945, presenting one of the great performances in American theatrical history as Amanda Wingfield in Tennessee Williams' *The Glass Menagerie*.

TAYLOR, MARSHALL WILLIAM (*b. Lexington, Ky., 1846; d. New Orleans, La., 1887*), Methodist clergyman, editor of *Southwestern Christian Advocate* and other church publications.

TAYLOR, MOSES (*b. New York, N.Y., 1806; d. 1882*), banker, capitalist. Starting as an importer and sugar broker, he became president of the City Bank, N.Y., 1855. *Post* 1857, he owned a controlling interest in the Delaware, Lackawanna & Western Railroad. Active also in many other public utilities, he was treasurer of the first Atlantic Cable Co.

TAYLOR, MYRON CHARLES (*b. Lyons, N.Y., 1874; d. New York, N.Y., 1959*), financier, diplomat. Graduated from Cornell University, LL.B., 1894. Practiced law in New York before becoming a financier. Gained directorships of the First National Bank of New York, the New York Central, and the Atchison, Topeka, and Santa Fe. Chairman of the finance committee of U.S. Steel, 1927–32. As chairman of the board, 1932–38, guided the company through periods of low production; in 1937, he signed a labor contract with the CIO—making U.S. Steel the first great steel company to do so. An ardent supporter of the New Deal, Taylor was appointed special representative with ambassadorial rank to the Vatican in 1939. The position occasioned great controversy from parties afraid of church ties. Forced to leave Rome in 1942; returned in 1944 and served until 1949.

TAYLOR, NATHANIEL WILLIAM (*b. New Milford, Conn., 1786; d. New Haven, Conn., 1858*), theologian, educator. Graduated Yale, 1807; studied theology with Timothy Dwight whom he served as secretary. Installed as minister of the First Church, New Haven, 1812, he was appointed Dwight Professor of Didactic Theology at Yale Divinity School, 1822, and continued in this post until the end of his life. A bold, original thinker, Taylor broke through the confines of the orthodox Calvinism of his day, asserting that the freedom of the will to choose is a reality and consists in the power to distinguish between motives. To induce men to turn from evil, an appeal must be made to man's natural desire for happiness which, in a regenerated mind, becomes identical with an unselfish love of God. Debate over Taylor's opinions became a principal theological reason for the disruption of the Presbyterian Church in 1838.

TAYLOR, RAYNOR (*b. England, ca. 1747; d. Philadelphia, Pa., 1825*), musician. Immigrating to America, 1792, and settling soon afterwards in Philadelphia, Taylor produced a number of entertainments featuring burlesques and parodies also known as "olios." He also composed hymns, songs, and music for the theater.

TAYLOR, RICHARD (*b. near Louisville, Ky., 1826; d. New York, N.Y., 1879*), Louisiana sugar planter and legislator, Confederate lieutenant general. Son of Zachary Taylor. Commanding at various times under T. J. Jackson in the Valley, under Lee before Richmond, and in Louisiana, Mississippi, and Alabama, Taylor performed his most notable service in stopping General N. P. Bank's Red River campaign in April 1864 by decisive battles against odds at Pleasant Hill and Sabine Crossroads. He surrendered the last Confederate Army east of the Mississippi at Citronelle, Ala., May 4, 1865. Author of the important *Destruction and Reconstruction* (published 1879).

TAYLOR, RICHARD COWLING (*b. England, 1789; d. Philadelphia, Pa., 1851*), geologist. Immigrated to America, 1830, after winning high professional repute in England. Taylor made numerous surveys of the Pennsylvania coal regions and of many other mineral districts, ranging from Canada to Central America. He was author of the monumental *Statistics of Coal* (1848).

TAYLOR, ROBERT (*b. Spangler Arlington Brugh, Filley, Nebr., 1911; d. Santa Monica, Calif., 1969*), actor. Attended Doane College and Pomona College (graduated in 1933). He was given the name Robert Taylor by Louis B. Mayer, head of Metro-Goldwyn-Mayer (MGM). Taylor stayed with MGM from 1934 until 1958, a record for a major star to remain with one studio. He became a star in 1935 with *Magnificent Obsession*. Other films included *Small Town Girl* (1936), *Camille* (1937), *A Yank at Oxford* (1938), and *Waterloo Bridge* (1940). In the late 1940's his box office appeal waned, and he was thereafter cast in expensive costume dramas such as *Quo Vadis* (1951). He left MGM to form his own company, Robert Taylor Productions, appearing in eleven films, 1959–67. Starred in the television series "The Detectives" (1959–61), and served as host, narrator, and occasional star of "Death Valley Days."

TAYLOR, ROBERT LOVE (*b. Happy Valley, Tenn., 1850; d. 1912*), lawyer, lyceum lecturer, politician. Brother of Alfred. A. Taylor. Outstanding as a conciliator and a reformer of local abuses, he served as Democratic governor of Tennessee, 1887–91 and 1897–99. U.S. senator, 1907–12. A favorite of the plain people, he was unpopular with the party leaders who could not control him.

TAYLOR, ROBERT TUNSTALL (*b. Norfolk, Va., 1867; d. Baltimore, Md., 1929*), physician. B.A., Johns Hopkins, 1889; M.D., University of Virginia, 1891. In large part responsible for creation of the orthopedic department in University of Maryland medical school, he taught there until his death; he was also responsible for the founding and growth of the present Kernan Hospital and Industrial School, Baltimore.

TAYLOR, SAMUEL HARVEY (*b. Londonderry, N.H., 1807; d. Andover, Mass., 1871*), educator. Graduated Dartmouth, 1832; Andover Theological Seminary, 1837. Principal, Phillips Academy, Andover, 1837–71. A stern, able Puritan.

TAYLOR, STEVENSON (*b. New York, N.Y., 1848; d. New York, 1926*), marine engineer, machinery designer. Established high standards for the American Bureau of Shipping as president, 1916–26; served as president of the Webb Institute of Naval Architecture *post* 1899.

TAYLOR, WILLIAM (*b. Rockbridge Co., Va., 1821; d. Palo Alto, Calif., 1902*), Methodist clergyman and evangelist. After traveling and preaching literally all over the world, 1847–84, he was elected missionary bishop for Africa in which post he served until 1896. Developed "Pauline" system of self-supporting missions.

TAYLOR, WILLIAM CHITTENDEN (*b. San Francisco, Calif., 1886; d. Corning, N.Y., 1958*), industrial chemist. Graduated from the Massachusetts Institute of Technology, B.S., 1908. A chemist with the Corning Glass Works, 1908–54, Taylor became director of manufacturing and engineering in 1947. Contributed to the transformation of the glass industry from a hand-blown to a totally automated industry. Instrumental in introducing and developing borosilicate glass, marketed in 1915 by Corning under the Pyrex trademark. It revolutionized not only home baking, but all of industry and was used in laboratories, in electronics, and for the construction of the 200-inch mirror of the Mt. Palomar Observatory.

TAYLOR, WILLIAM LADD (*b. Grafton, Mass., 1854; d. 1926*), book and magazine illustrator.

TAYLOR, WILLIAM MACKERGO (*b. Kilmarnock, Scotland, 1829; d. New York, N.Y., 1895*), Congregational clergyman. Coming to America, 1871, he served as pastor of Broadway Tabernacle, New York City, 1872–92, and ranked as a preacher with Richard S. Storrs and Henry W. Beecher.

TAYLOR, WILLIAM ROGERS (*b. Newport, R.I., 1811; d. Washington, D.C., 1889*), naval officer. Son of William V. Taylor. Appointed midshipman, 1828. After service in Mexican War, he engaged in ordnance work at Washington. Promoted captain, 1862, he commanded blockade vessels off Charleston, S.C., and was captain of USS *Juniata* in the first attack on Fort Fisher, December 1864. Promoted rear admiral, 1871, he retired, 1873.

TAYLOR, WILLIAM VIGNERON (*b. Newport, R.I., 1780; d. Newport, 1858*), naval officer. Father of William R. Taylor. Supervised rigging and arming of Oliver H. Perry's squadron before battle of Lake Erie, September 1813; served as sailing master of flagship *Lawrence* in the battle. Promoted captain, 1841, he commanded USS *Ohio* in the Mexican War. He was put on the reserved list, 1855.

TAYLOR, ZACHARY (*b. Montebello, Orange Co., Va., 1784; d. Washington, D.C., 1850*), soldier, president of the United States. Father of Richard Taylor. Nicknamed "Old Rough and Ready." Raised in Kentucky, he was appointed first lieutenant in the 7th Infantry in 1808, was promoted captain in 1810, and in 1812 won brevet of major for defense of Fort Harrison, Indiana Territory, against Indians. During the War of 1812 he assisted in defense of the frontier from Indiana to Missouri. Appointed

lieutenant colonel of the 4th Infantry, 1819, he performed arduous but uneventful service on the Southwestern and Western frontiers until 1832 when he was promoted colonel and given command of the 1st Regiment stationed at Fort Crawford (Prairie du Chien). He commanded regular troops under General Henry Atkinson in the Black Hawk War and was brevetted brigadier general for his defeat of the Seminoles at Lake Okeechobee, December 1837. Unsuccessful in a two-year campaign against the Seminoles, he returned to the Southwest, 1840, where he served at Fort Gibson and Fort Smith, Ark.

Ordered to Fort Jesup on the Louisiana frontier, 1844, he prepared for action that might be necessary in view of the annexation of Texas. Collecting an army of about 4000 men at Corpus Christi, he advanced to the Rio Grande early in 1846 and established a base at Point Isabel and entrenchments opposite Matamoros. On May 8, 1846, he met the Mexicans at Palo Alto and defeated them principally with artillery; he was again successful the following day at Resaca de la Palma. Despite distrust of him in Washington, Taylor was promoted major general by brevet and designated commander of the Army of the Rio Grande. With about 6,000 men, half regulars and half volunteers, he moved against Saltillo in September, attacking Monterey on September 21. After three days of skirmishing, the Mexican army asked for and received an eight weeks' armistice which brought Taylor more criticism from Washington. Taylors' letters attacking the administration for lack of support increased the tension between him and President Polk. Evading cooperation with General Winfield Scott, Taylor disobeyed orders to remain on the defensive and advanced southward, defeating the Mexicans under Santa Anna at Buena Vista, Feb. 22–23, 1847, and so ending the war n the northern provinces. Taylor ascribed most of his success against superior Mexican forces to his regular artillery. At the end of the war he had achieved a great personal popularity.

A lifelong Whig in his opinions, he was a logical candidate for the presidential nomination of that party in 1848. Endorsed by Thurlow Weed and J. J. Crittenden, he asserted that he would accept nomination only if the people drafted him, that he would not be the candidate of a party, nor would he reach the office through any agency of his own. Too outspoken to please the politicians, Taylor expressed himself on many issues, urging in particular that the executive office should return to its proper position of a coordinate government branch. He also expressed dislike for extremists on the subject of slavery, both in the North and South. Nominated on the first ballot at the Whig Convention in Philadelphia, June 1848, over Henry Clay, Winfield Scott, and Daniel Webster, he expressed the politics he proposed to implement in the so-called second "Allison" letter, once again promising a nonpartisan administration. Successful in November over Lewis Cass, the Democratic candidate, Taylor delivered a noncommittal inaugural address expressive of basic Whig principles. His cabinet was harmonious and industrious but inferior. Headed by John M. Clayton of Delaware as secretary of state, it made no effort to conciliate a fractious and sensitive Congress. Dissension soon sprang up among party leaders, and although Taylor had declared for nonpartisanship, he concluded by May 1849 that all offices must be filled with his own partisans. Before his nomination he had described the Wilmot Proviso as negligible, but it now became apparent that Taylor would not veto the Proviso should a bill containing it be presented to him. Hoping to prevent sectional agitation of the question of the further extension of slavery (which he had assured the North would not take place), he encouraged California and New Mexico to apply for statehood, recommending in his message to Congress, December 1849, that both be admitted to the Union if they presented governments which were republican in form. Southern representatives led by Alexander H. Stephens filibustered to prevent a vote on the admission of California and to insist on the combination into a single measure of all proposals affecting the Mexican cession. Facing the open hostility of the Southern Whigs for his plan to admit California and New Mexico and also for his hostile attitude toward Texas, Taylor remained obstinate despite threats of secession. He died before the separate legislative acts which were devised to alleviate the situation and which are known as the Compromise of 1850 were passed. His brief experience with foreign relations was not particularly happy; the most significant achievement of the administration was the Clayton-Bulwer Treaty.

Lacking political skills and experience, Taylor displayed practical wisdom, common sense, and resolution of purpose during his brief public career; these, however, were not enough for the kind of leadership demanded by the crisis of 1850.

TAZEWELL, HENRY (*b. Brunswick Co., Va., 1753; d. Philadelphia, Pa., 1799*), Virginia legislator and jurist, Revolutionary patriot. Father of Littleton W. Tazewell. Probably the most popular Virginian of his day, he served his state as U.S. senator, Democratic-Republican, 1794–99.

TAZEWELL, LITTLETON WALLER (*b. Williamsburg, Va., 1774; d. Norfolk, Va., 1860*), lawyer, Virginia legislator, statesman. Son of Henry Tazewell. A pupil of George Wythe, he graduated from the College of William and Mary, 1791, and was licensed to practice law, 1796. An individualist, of high intellectual powers but cold and lacking in human sympathy, Tazewell enjoyed a great contemporary reputation but has left no lasting mark on history. In principle an anti-Federalist, he opposed as legislator many important policies of Jefferson's administration and later opposed the War of 1812. As U.S. senator, 1824–32, he led in opposition to President J. Q. Adams, but after supporting Andrew Jackson for the presidency, opposed Jackson's coercion policy as strongly as he opposed nullification. Elected governor of Virginia, 1834, he resigned in March 1836.

TCHELITCHEW, PAVEL (*b. Moscow, Russia, 1898; d. Rome, Italy, 1957*), painter, stage designer. A leader of the "neoromantic" school of the 1920's and 1930's, Tchelitchew had one-man shows in London and Paris, before his first show in New York in 1934. Immigrated to the U.S. in 1938. Important paintings include *Phenomena* (1936–38) and *Hide and Seek* (1940–42). His ballet designs include works for Balanchine, Diaghilev, and others: *Ode* (1929), *L'Errante* (1933), *Ondine* (1939), and *Balustrade* (1941).

TEAGARDEN, WELDON LEO ("JACK") (*b. Vernon, Tex., 1905; d. New Orleans, La., 1964*), trombonist, bandleader. Started playing the trombone at the age of seven. During 1921–27 played with several bands, including Peck Kelley's Bad Boys and Doc Ross' Jazz Bandits. Moved to New York (1927) where he became one of the most highly regarded trombonists in white jazz. Played in Paul Whiteman's orchestra (1933–38). The popularity of swing induced him to form "Jack Teagarden and His Orchestra," which he led 1939–46. Performed in the film *Birth of the Blues* with Bing Crosby (1941) and made many recordings. Played with Louis Armstrong's All Stars, 1947–51, then appeared with his own All Stars until 1956.

TEALL, FRANCIS AUGUSTUS (*b. Fort Ann, N.Y., 1822; d. Bloomfield, N.J., 1894*), printer, journalist. A learned and conscientious proofreader, he did outstanding work on the *American Cyclopaedia* and on the *Century Dictionary*.

TEASDALE, SARA (*b. St. Louis, Mo., 1884; d. New York, N.Y., 1933*), lyric poet. Author, among other volumes, of *Sonnets to Duse* (1907), *Flame and Shadow* (1920), and *Dark of the Moon* (1926).

TECUMSEH (*b. probably near present Oldtown, Ohio, ca. 1768; d. near present Thamesville, Ontario, Canada, 1813*), Shawnee chief. Brother of Tenskwatawa, the Prophet. A brave warrior, remarkable for humanity and trustworthiness, Tecumseh and his brother and their followers were forced by pressure of white settlers into present Indiana, 1808. They settled on the Wabash near the mouth of the Tippecanoe at a place later known as Prophet's Town. Tecumseh there developed a program of action that threatened to stop westward movement of American settlement. He maintained that no Indian land sale or cession could be valid without consent of all the tribes assembled, since the Indians owned land in common. He pointed out also that the United States had given an implied assent to this point of view under the treaty of Greenville in 1795. Seeking to combine the tribes into a confederacy to prevent further land cessions and to reform abuses which contact with the whites had brought, he visited widely among the tribes and brought more and more of them under his influence. His program was not necessarily a warlike one; he hoped that (if unmolested by the whites) his people might in time adapt to civilization and escape decadence. Led to expect help by the British officials in Canada who wished to see an Indian buffer state set up in the Old Northwest, Tecumseh defied Governor W. H. Harrison at Vincennes in August 1810. While absent in the south on a speaking tour, Tecumseh's chance of success was lost by the action of his brother, the Prophet, who allowed himself to be tricked into the battle of Tippecanoe, November 1811. Commissioned brigadier general by the British, Tecumseh fought in the War of 1812 with great courage and fell at the battle of the Thames.

TEDYUSKUNG (*b. in vicinity of Trenton, N.J., ca. 1700; d. Wyoming, Pa., 1763*), Delaware chief, largely responsible with Christian F. Post for British success at Fort Duquesne, 1758.

TEEPLE, JOHN EDGAR (*b. Kempton, Ill., 1874; d. New York, N.Y., 1931*), chemist, educator, practicing chemical engineer. Among his many achievements in designing and directing chemical plants was his notable success in developing potash production at Searles Lake, Calif., *post* 1919. He is credited with building up the American potash industry almost single-handed.

TEGGART, FREDERICK JOHN (*b. Belfast, Ireland, 1870; d. Berkeley, Calif., 1946*), librarian, historian, sociologist. Settled near San Diego, Calif., 1889. B.A., Stanford University, 1894. Librarian at Stanford, at San Francisco's Mechanics Mercantile Library, and at Bancroft Library, University of California. A teacher of history at California *post* 1905, he became associate professor in 1916; in 1919 he founded the department of social institutions at Berkeley, which he headed until academic retirement, 1940. He was author of a number of books and articles on his theory of a science of society, which was to be based on concrete historical materials employed free of the conventionalized framework of unilinear, narrative, history writing. His major effort to apply his theories of comparative history and change was his book *Rome and China* (1939).

TELFAIR, EDWARD (*b. Scotland, ca. 1735; d. 1807*), merchant, Georgia colonial legislator, Revolutionary patriot. Came to Virginia ca. 1758; settled in Georgia ca. 1766, identifying himself with the city of Savannah and its trade. Member of the Continental Congress, 1777–83, he also held a number of state appointments. Elected governor of Georgia for 1786, he acted with vigor in dealing with the Indians and in the boundary dispute with South Carolina. As governor of Georgia, 1791–94, he was in conflict with the federal government, in particular over the case of *Chisholm v. Georgia*. He brought about by his actions the passage of the Eleventh Amendment. He was also reckless in his dealings with the state's public lands.

TELLER, HENRY MOORE (*b. Allegany Co., N.Y., 1830; d. Denver, Colo., 1914*), lawyer. In practice *post* 1861 at Central City, Colo., he became a leading figure in that territory and served as U.S. senator, Republican, 1877–82. After appointment as U.S. secretary of the interior, 1882–85, he returned to the Senate and served there until 1909. He was elected for his first two terms as a Republican, the third as an Independent Silver Republican, and the fourth as a Democrat. Outspoken as an advocate of silver remonetization, he tended more and more (as his career proceeded) to align himself with the weaker groups in society and to support woman's suffrage, income taxes, and government regulation of big business. The Teller Resolution which pledged the United States to an independent Cuba was named for him. He strongly opposed United States policy in the Philippines (1899–1902) as well as President Theodore Roosevelt's policy toward Panama.

TEMPLE, OLIVER PERRY (*b. near Greenville, Tenn., 1820; d. 1907*), Knoxville, Tenn., lawyer and Unionist, author.

TEMPLE, WILLIAM GRENVILLE (*b. Rutland, Vt., 1824; d Washington, D.C., 1894*), naval officer. Appointed midshipman, 1840. Performed valuable Civil War service on Union blockade duty and was recommended for promotion for conduct in both attacks on Fort Fisher, December 1864 and January 1865. Retired as rear admiral, 1884.

TEMPLETON, ALEC ANDREW (*b. Cardiff, Wales, 1910; d. Greenwich, Conn., 1963*), pianist, musical satirist. Attended the Royal Academy of Music (licentiate degree, 1931) and the Royal College of Music (1932–34). Blind from birth, Templeton was a musical prodigy who created his first musical composition by the age of four. At eleven, he was employed by the British Broadcasting Company to present a musical program that remained popular for twelve years. Made his American debut in 1935 and decided to remain in the United States, becoming a naturalized citizen in 1941. Got his own national network radio show, "Alec Templeton Time," in 1939, and achieved fame chiefly for his ironic improvisation of operatic themes and on-the-spot creation of melodies. His compositions include *Concertina Lirico* (1942) and *Gothic Concerto* for piano and orchestra (1954).

TEN BROECK, ABRAHAM (*b. Albany, N.Y., 1734; d. 1810*), New York colonial legislator, Revolutionary soldier. Brother-in-law of Philip Livingston. Albany County judge, 1781–94; mayor of Albany, N.Y., 1779–83, 1796–99.

TEN BROECK, RICHARD (*b. Albany, N.Y., 1812; d. near Menlo Park, Calif., 1892*), horseman. Early a partner of William R. Johnson in racing on Southern tracks, he was the owner, among other horses, of Lexington, Prioress, and Starke. He was the first (1856) American horseman to race successfully on the English turf.

TENÉ-ANGPÓTE. *See* KICKING BIRD.

TENNENT, GILBERT (*b. Co. Armagh, Ireland, 1703; d. Philadelphia, Pa., 1764*), Presbyterian clergyman. Son of William Tennent (1673–1746); brother of William Tennent (1705–77). Immigrated to America as a boy. Assisted father at newly established "Log College"; was ordained at New Brunswick, N.J., 1726; was friendly with and influenced by Theodorus J. Frelinghuysen. A zealous evangelical, Tennent soon became known as a vivid preacher, and with his clerical associates in the New Jersey area prepared the way for the Great Awakening. Intimate of George Whitefield in 1739–40, he continued with great force in New England and elsewhere, and attacking his conservative Presbyterian associates with great virulence as religious formalists. Reproved by the Synod of 1741 for disregarding its authority and for

other disturbing actions, Tennent and members of the New Brunswick Presbytery withdrew and caused a division of the Presbyterian Church which lasted 17 years. During his later years as pastor in Philadelphia he showed evidence of regret for his earlier contentiousness and worked for a reunion of the Presbyterian Church.

TENNENT, JOHN (*b. England, ca. 1700; d. place unknown, ca. 1760*), physician. Active in Virginia *ca.* 1725–39, he was author of *Essay on the Pleurisy* (Williamsburg, Va., 1735), an enthusiastic account of his experience in the therapeutic use of rattlesnakeroot.

TENNENT, WILLIAM (*b. Ireland, 1673; d. Neshaminy, Pa., 1746*), Presbyterian clergyman, founder of the "Log College." Father of Gilbert and William Tennent (1705–77). Immigrated to Philadelphia, Pa., *ca.* 1717. Pastor at Neshaminy, Pa., *post* 1726, where he trained for the ministry and filled with his own evangelical spirit an outstanding group which included his sons and also Samuel Blair and Samuel Finley. He erected his famous "Log College," 1736. At his death, its supporters united with others in organizing the College of New Jersey.

TENNENT, WILLIAM (*b. Co. Armagh, Ireland, 1705; d. Freehold, N.J., 1777*), Presbyterian clergyman. Son of William Tennent (1673–1746); brother of Gilbert Tennent. Pastor at Freehold, N.J., *post* 1733, he was a friend of George Whitefield, a promoter of revivals, and celebrated as a peacemaker and counselor.

TENNEY, CHARLES DANIEL (*b. Boston, Mass., 1857; d. Palo Alto, Calif., 1930*), Congregational clergyman, missionary and educator in China, U.S. consular and diplomatic official in China.

TENNEY, EDWARD PAYSON (*b. Concord, N.H., 1835; d. 1916*), Congregational clergyman, educator. President of Colorado College, 1876–84.

TENNEY, TABITHA GILMAN (*b. Exeter, N.H., 1762; d. Exeter, 1837*), novelist. Author, among other works, of *Female Quixotism* (1801), a satire on the prevailing literary taste of her time, and in particular on the American fondness for foreign romantic sentimentality.

TENNEY, WILLIAM JEWETT (*b. Newport, R.I., 1811; d. Newark, N.J., 1883*), editor. Graduated Yale, 1832. A convert to Catholicism, Tenney was an important member of the staff of D. Appleton & Co., 1853–83. He served as editor of *Appleton's Annual Cyclopaedia* (1861–83) and collaborated on Jefferson Davis's *Rise and Fall of the Confederate Government* (1881).

TENSKWATAWA (*b. present Oldtown, Ohio, ca. 1768; d. place unknown, possibly Kansas, ca. 1834*), Shawnee Indian, known as "The Prophet." Brother of Tecumseh whose plans for an Indian confederacy he upset by allowing himself to be maneuvered into the battle of Tippecanoe, November 1811. He was known to his contemporaries as a vain, boastful man who gave a false impression of ability and power.

TERESA, MOTHER (*b. Ireland, ca. 1766; d. Georgetown, D.C., 1846*), founder of the Visitation Order in the United States. Name in religion of Alice Lalor. Immigrated to Philadelphia, Pa., 1795, where with two friends she lived in an unofficial religious community under the direction of Father Leonard Neale. Removing with her community to Georgetown, D.C., 1799, she conducted a school. In December 1816, she and her associates took vows as Visitation nuns.

TERHUNE, ALBERT PAYSON (*b. Newark, N.J., 1872; d. Pompton Lakes, N.J., 1942*), author. Son of Mary V. H. Terhune. B.A., Columbia University, 1893. On staff of New York *Evening World*, 1894–1916. Author of a great number of magazine short stories and serials, but achieved reputation for stories about dogs, in particular collies. These were collected in *Lad, a Dog* (1919) and later volumes.

TERHUNE, MARY VIRGINIA HAWES (*b. Dennisville, Va., 1830; d. New York, N.Y., 1922*), author, writer on household management. Better known as "Marion Harland," she was author among many other works of *Common Sense in the Household* (1871), one of the most successful books of its kind.

TERMAN, LEWIS MADISON (*b. Johnson County, Ind., 1877; d. Palo Alto, Calif., 1956*), psychologist. Studied at Central Normal School, Danville, Ind., and at Clark University, Ph.D., 1905. Taught at Stanford University, 1910–43; chairman of the psychology department from 1922. Author of the Stanford-Binet intelligence test, which he standardized for use in this country. President of the American Psychological Association and member of the National Academy of Sciences. Author of *The Measurement of Intelligence* (1916) and *Genetic Studies of Genius* (1925–56).

TERRELL, EDWIN HOLLAND (*b. Brookville, Ind., 1848; d. San Antonio, Tex., 1910*), lawyer. Practiced in San Antonio, Texas *post* 1877. Active in Texas Republican politics, he served as U.S. minister to Belgium, 1889–93.

TERRELL, MARY ELIZA CHURCH (*b. Memphis, Tenn., 1863; d. Annapolis, Md., 1954*), civil rights advocate, feminist. Graduated from Oberlin College, 1884. The daughter of slaves, Mary Terrell helped form the National Association of Colored Women in 1896 and was its first president. A charter member of the NAACP and the first black woman to serve on the Washington, D.C., school board, 1895–1901. Published *A Colored Woman in a White World* (1940), with foreword by H.G. Wells. In 1953, she won a civil rights suit before the Supreme Court.

TERRY, ALFRED HOWE (*b. Hartford, Conn., 1827; d. New Haven, Conn., 1890*), lawyer, soldier. Commissioned colonel of the 2nd Connecticut Militia, 1861, he soon became colonel of the 7th Connecticut Volunteers and was promoted brigadier general in April 1862. After outstanding service in the operations against Charleston, S.C., 1863, and those against Richmond and Petersburg, Va., 1864, he commanded in the attacks against Fort Fisher, N.C., December 1864–January 1865, achieving success in concert with fleet action under Adm. D. D. Porter. Promoted brigadier general in the regular army, January 1865, and major general of volunteers three months later, he remained in service after the Civil War. During the Indian troubles in the Dakotas in the 1870's, he commanded that Department. Becoming involved in controversy over the Custer Massacre (June 1876), Terry refused to make a statement with respect to Custer's conduct, preferring to accept criticism rather than create an issue. Promoted major general, 1886, he retired in 1888. A student of the science of war, Terry was also noted for his ability to work harmoniously with others.

TERRY, DAVID SMITH (*b. Todd Co., Ky., 1823; d. Lathrop, Calif., 1889*), Mexican War and Confederate soldier, California jurist and political leader. Raised in Texas, Terry settled in California, 1849, where he practiced law and was active in Know-Nothing party activities. He became a judge of the California supreme court in 1855, and was raised to chief justice in 1857. Affiliated *post* 1859 with the Gwin Democrats, he engaged David Broderick in a duel, Sept, 13, 1859, which resulted in Broderick's death. Prior to the duel, Terry had resigned judicial office.

Returning to California, 1869, after service in the Confederate Army and a short exile in Mexico, Terry resumed practice of law. He was shot dead by a bodyguard of Justice Stephen J. Field whose life Terry had threatened after the rendering of a judgment adverse to him.

TERRY, ELI (*b. East Windsor, Conn., 1772; d. Plymouth, Conn., 1852*), inventor, pioneer clock manufacturer. Set up first clock factory in America at Plymouth, Conn., *ca.* 1800; became partner of Seth Thomas and another, 1807. Devised popular "pillar scroll top" wood clock, 1814; also built brass clocks of high quality, and tower clocks.

TERRY, MARSHALL ORLANDO (*b. Watervliet Center, N.Y., 1848; d. Coronado, Calif., 1933*), physician, Florida real-estate developer. As surgeon general of New York State National Guard, he made a valuable critical study of care of New York troops in federal camps at the time of the Spanish-American War, with special reference to the high incidence of typhoid fever.

TERRY, MILTON SPENSER (*b. Coeymans, N.Y., 1840; d. Los Angeles, Calif., 1914*), Methodist clergyman, educator. Advocated the higher criticism as head of department of Hebrew and Old Testament and professor of Christian doctrine at the Garrett Biblical Institute, *post* 1884.

TESLA, NIKOLA (*b. Smiljan, Croatia [then part of Austria-Hungary], 1856; d. New York, N.Y., 1943*), inventor, electrical engineer. As a child Tesla had shown a precocious talent for mental arithmetic and a fascination with mechanical problems. He entered the Joanneum at Graz, at the age of nineteen, and during the next four years acquired a sound knowledge of mathematics, physics, and mechanics—as well as a brief fondness for gambling, billiards, and chess. In 1879 he enrolled in the philosophical faculty of the University of Prague, but his father's death required him to become self-supporting and he left without a degree.

While at Graz, Tesla had become preoccupied with the problem of eliminating the useless sparks produced at the commutators and brushes of early direct-current electric motors. During his years in Budapest he conceived the idea of the spatially rotating electric field to make possible the efficient use of alternating-current electricity, a principle that underlies the design of all later polyphase induction motors. His attempts to exploit his invention in Europe proved unsuccessful, and in 1884 he sailed to New York, armed with a letter of introduction to Thomas A. Edison, who rejected Tesla's ideas but gave him a job designing direct-current components. Tesla resigned in 1885 after a disagreement over compensation. He then formed a company to develop an arc lamp for streets and factories, but he was eased out of the company.

Tesla then formed his living by day labor, but by 1887 he had formed the Tesla Electric Company and had set up a laboratory to develop his idea for an alternating-current motor. He sold his patents for a polyphase induction motor to George Westinghouse and joined the staff of the Westinghouse Company. He resigned after a year because of conflicts with the company's engineers and because he realized that for creative work he required complete independence.

The next few years were a period of great affluence for Tesla. His work on arc lights, which produced an objectionable hum at low frequencies, led him to become interested in the generation of high-frequency currents. He constructed machines with output frequencies up to 25,000 cycles per second. Although similar machines were to play a part in the development of radiotelegraphy, he foresaw their limitations and turned his attention to other high-frequency circuits and components, of which the Tesla coil, a resonant air-core transformer, is the best known. He also designed or conceived apparatus for the high-frequency heating of dielectrics, which anticipated diathermy and induction heating. His high-frequency devices brought him worldwide scientific fame and made him a social celebrity. After his mother's death he resolved to withdraw from social life and to concentrate on what he believed to be his true destiny, the discovery of new scientific principles, and he adopted an increasingly solitary and eccentric pattern of living.

The 1893 Chicago World's Fair buildings and grounds were illuminated by means of his polyphase alternating-current system and the following year he received honorary doctorates from Columbia and Yale. In 1896 Tesla saw one phase of his work come to impressive fruition with the completion of the Niagara Falls project: the world's first hydroelectric generating plant and a network for transmitting and distributing the electric power, both in Niagara Falls and in Buffalo, twenty-two miles away. The project used Tesla's polyphase alternating-current system, his greatest achievement. Tesla forecast the possibility of transmitting electricity without wires, not merely for communication but as a means of sending large amounts of power from one place to another. In 1897 he successfully demonstrated his wireless communications system over a distance of twenty-five miles. His methods were not well conceived, and radio ultimately developed along quite different lines.

In 1898 Tesla patented and then built a model of a radio-controlled ship, the ancestor of all remotely guided craft. The next year he built and successfully tested a high-voltage transmission system and experimented with the production of artificial lightning. In the last four decades of his life Tesla experienced increasing poverty and produced few realizable ideas, although he continued to conceive startling new devices. In spite of his genius, his personality imposed severe handicaps. In 1912, despite his need for funds, he refused to be corecipient with Edison of the Nobel Prize in physics. Because others had consistently exploited his work, Tesla increasingly concealed the details of his new concepts and insisted on working in complete independence. As he gradually withdrew from society he developed a fondness for pigeons, which he fed in the New York parks and harbored in his hotel room.

Tesla remained in the public eye for many years and made several predictions of remarkable prescience. Besides his earlier forecast of radio, a prediction he made in 1917 described several features of pulsed radar nearly twenty years before it was realized, although Tesla suggested electromagnetic propagation through water, not through air. Tesla's predictions were not invariably fulfilled; a careful study of his later writings would doubtless reveal more bad guesses than good. On his seventy-eighth birthday, he announced that he had invented a powerful "death ray," but the claim was never substantiated.

Tesla was granted more than a hundred patents, but his fame rests almost entirely on the discoveries he made before he was thirty-six. A complete recluse in his later years, he was almost wholly dependent on a yearly gift of $7,200 from the Yugoslavian government.

TESTUT, CHARLES (*b. France, ca. 1818; d. New Orleans, La., 1892*), Louisiana journalist, physician, poet. Active in French-language journalism in New Orleans *post ca.* 1844; indefatigable founder of unsuccessful newspapers.

TEUSLER, RUDOLF BOLLING (*b. Rome, Ga., 1876; d. Japan, 1934*), surgeon, Episcopal medical missionary. Worked in Japan *post* 1900; founded St. Luke's Hospital, Tokyo; was pioneer in public-health methods in Japan.

TEVIS, LLOYD (*b. Shelbyville, Ky., 1824; d San Francisco, Calif., 1899*), lawyer, capitalist. Removed to California, 1849. Entered law and business partnership with James Ben Ali Haggin,

1850, at Sacramento; moved office to San Francisco, 1853. Identified with some of California's greatest business undertakings, Tevis was an early projector of telegraph lines, a promoter of the Southern Pacific Railroad and briefly its president, an organizer of the Pacific Express Co., and president of Wells, Fargo & Co., 1872–92. He was a partner in mining ventures with, among others, George Hearst and Marcus Daly.

THACHER, EDWIN (*b. De Kalb, N.Y., 1839; d. New York, N.Y., 1920*), civil engineer, bridge constructor. Graduated Rensselaer Polytechnic Institute, 1863. Invented Thacher cylindrical slide rule, 1881; devised the "Thacher bar" used in reinforced concrete construction.

THACHER, GEORGE (*b. Yarmouth, Mass., 1754; d. Biddeford, Maine, 1824*), lawyer. Settled at Biddeford, Maine, 1782. Congressman from the District of Maine, Federalist, 1789–1801; associate judge, Massachusetts Supreme Judicial Court, 1801–24.

THACHER, JAMES (*b. Barnstable, Mass., 1754; d. Plymouth, Mass., 1844*), physician, Revolutionary Army surgeon, historian. Author, among other works, of the valuable *A Military Journal during the American Revolutionary War* (1823, and many subsequent editions) and of the *American Medical Biography* (1828), a chief source book for the medical history of his time.

THACHER, JOHN BOYD (*b. Ballston Spa, N.Y., 1847; d. Albany, N.Y., 1909*), businessman, New York State public servant, book collector.

THACHER, PETER (*b. Salem, Mass., 1651; d. Milton, Mass., 1727*), Congregational clergyman, theologian. Graduated Harvard, 1671; held principal pastorate at Milton *post* 1681.

THACHER, PETER (*b. Milton, Mass., 1752; d. Savannah, Ga., 1802*), Congregational clergyman, Revolutionary patriot. Great-grandson of Peter Thacher (1651–1727). Graduated Harvard, 1769. Held pastorates in Malden, Mass., and at Brattle Street Church, Boston, Mass.; served as chaplain to the General Court *post* 1776. An outstanding orator on the patriot side, he was a founder of the Massachusetts Historical Society, 1790–91.

THACHER, SAMUEL COOPER (*b. Boston, Mass., 1785; d. Moulins, France, 1818*), Unitarian theologian. Son of Peter Thacher (1752–1802). Graduated Harvard, 1804. A friend and pupil of William E. Channing (1780–1842), he served as pastor of the New South Church, Boston, Mass., *post* 1811.

THACHER, THOMAS ANTHONY (*b. Hartford, Conn., 1815; d. 1886*), classicist. Graduated Yale, 1835. Taught at Yale *post* 1838, becoming eventually professor of Latin and performing much of the work which a modern dean would do. Active in the administration of the college, he and Theodore D. Woolsey were the first advocates at Yale of graduate instruction in nontechnical fields; he played a larger part in the building of modern Yale than any of his contemporaries there.

THACHER, THOMAS DAY (*b. Tenafly, N.J., 1881; d. New York, N.Y., 1950*), lawyer, jurist, civic leader. Grandson of Thomas A. Thacher. B.A., Yale, 1904; attended Yale Law School. Admitted to the New York bar, 1906, he entered the office of his father's firm, Simpson, Thacher & Bartlett, and became a partner, 1914. He devoted a great part of his time to municipal reform and public service. Among the posts he held were U.S. district court judge, Southern District of New York (1925–30); solicitor general of the U.S. (1930–33); New York City corporation counsel, 1943; justice of the New York State Court of Appeals, 1943–48.

THALBERG, IRVING GRANT (*b. Brooklyn, N.Y., 1899; d. Santa Monica, Calif., 1936*), motion picture producer and studio executive. Began career as secretary to Carl Laemmle *ca.* 1918 and rose to be head of studio of Universal Pictures Corp. Associated with Louis B. Mayer *post* 1923, he headed the production department of the subsequent Metro-Goldwyn-Mayer studio, 1924–32, thereafter limiting his activity because of progressive ill health. He was noted for his skill in casting and taste in production.

THANET, OCTAVE. *See* FRENCH, ALICE.

THATCHER, BENJAMIN BUSSEY (*b. Warren, Maine, 1809; d. Boston, Mass., 1840*), lawyer, philanthropist, advocate of African colonization as solution of slavery question. Author, among other works, of *Indian Biography* (1832), the first work of its kind to seek accuracy in handling the subject.

THATCHER, GEORGE. *See* THACHER, GEORGE.

THATCHER, HENRY KNOX (*b. Thomaston, Maine, 1806; d. Boston, Mass., 1880*), naval officer. Grandson of Henry Knox. Appointed midshipman, 1823; rose to commodore, 1862. After service on the North Atlantic blockading squadron, 1863–64, he was commended for his part as a division commander under Adm. David D. Porter in the reduction of Fort Fisher, N.C., December 1864–January 1865. He succeeded Adm. D. G. Farragut in command of the West Gulf blockade squadron, January 1865, and aided in the reduction of Mobile, Ala. He retired as rear admiral, 1868.

THATCHER, MAHLON DANIEL (*b. New Buffalo, Pa., 1839; d. 1916*), pioneer Colorado merchant and banker. Removed to Pueblo, Colo., 1865, where with his brother he ran a general store. Turning to professional banking, 1871, he founded the First National Bank of Pueblo, of which he was president *post* 1889. Active in stock-raising and other businesses, he came in time to have holdings in nearly forty banks.

THATCHER, ROSCOE WILFRED (*b. Chatham Center, Ohio, 1872; d. Amherst, Mass., 1933*), agricultural chemist. Graduated University of Nebraska, 1898. Conducted experiment stations and taught at Washington State College and University of Minnesota; served as director, New York State agricultural experiment station, 1921–27; president, Massachusetts Agricultural College, 1927–32.

THAW, HARRY KENDALL (*b. Pittsburgh, Pa., 1871; d. Miami Beach, Fla., 1947*), notorious character. Married Evelyn Nesbit, April 1905. Shot and killed Stanford White, June 25, 1906; escaped death penalty on grounds of insanity.

THAW, WILLIAM (*b. Pittsburgh, Pa., 1818; d. Paris, France, 1889*), Pennsylvania capitalist, freighting and transportation executive. Benefactor of the present University of Pittsburgh.

THAXTER, CELIA LAIGHTON (*b. Portsmouth, N.H., 1835; d. Appledore, Isles of Shoals, N.H., 1894*), poet. Mother of Roland Thaxter. Author, among other works, of *Poems* (1872), *Among the Isles of Shoals* (1863), and *Driftweed* (1879).

THAXTER, ROLAND (*b. Newtonville, Mass., 1858; d. 1932*), botanist. Son of Celia L. Thaxter. Graduated Harvard, 1882; Ph.D., 1888. Taught cryptogamic botany at Harvard, 1891–1919. Renowned as a research scholar, he specialized in mycology, publishing many excellent studies. His greatest work is his *Contribution Towards a Monograph of the Laboulbeniaceae* in *Memoirs of the American Academy of Arts and Sciences* (1896–1931).

THAYER, ABBOTT HANDERSON (*b. Boston, Mass., 1849; d. Monadnock, N.H., 1921*), painter. Grandson of Gideon F.

Thayer. Early skilled as a painter of animals, he attended art classes in Boston and New York and studied in Paris, France, at the atelier of J. L. Gérôme. Returning to New York City, 1879, he was chosen president of the Society of American Artists. In 1901 he was elected an Academician, but at about that time he removed to New Hampshire and adopted a hermitlike habit of life. Winner of many important distinctions, Thayer painted varied subjects and in varied techniques but ideal figures and landscapes supplied his masterpieces. Chief among these are "Caritas" in the Boston Museum of Fine Arts and "Winter Sunrise, Monadnock" in the Metropolitan Museum, New York City. Idealizing women, Thayer realized his figures on the canvas directly and sincerely, and originality was the very basis of his style. He was free from the control of French technique. Almost mystically conscious of his artistic mission, he tried to make visible the beauty of spirit he saw in a person or natural object. To gain monumentality he exaggerated light and shadow and placed his colors in large, simple masses. His color range was limited but his whites—sometimes luminous, sometimes flat, but always suggestive. A large part of his later career was taken up with experiments in the protective coloration of animals and the promotion of what is called "Thayer's Law" of coloration.

THAYER, ALEXANDER WHEELOCK (*b. South Natick, Mass., 1817; d. 1897*), lawyer, journalist, U.S. consular officer. Author of the standard biography of Ludwig van Beethoven, first published in Berlin (Volume 1, 1866; Volume 2, 1872; Volume 3, 1879) and issued in an English version, edited by Henry E. Krehbiel, in 1921.

THAYER, AMOS MADDEN (*b. Mina, N.Y., 1841; d. 1905*), Union soldier, Missouri jurist. Admitted to the bar in St. Louis, Mo., 1868. Judge of the St. Louis circuit court, 1876–87, he served as federal judge for the eastern district of Missouri, 1887–94, and as federal circuit judge for the eighth circuit *post* 1894. He delivered notable opinions in cases involving the law of conspiracy in 1897 and 1903; the second of these in *U.S. v. Northern Securities Company* had great economic significance.

THAYER, ELI (*b. Mendon, Mass., 1819; d. 1899*), Massachusetts educator, legislator, and congressman. Principal of the Oread Collegiate Institute, Worcester, Mass. Thayer originated and was principal promoter of the New England Emigrant Aid Co., chartered, February 1855, as a means of financing organized free-soil immigration to Kansas.

THAYER, EZRA RIPLEY (*b. Milton, Mass., 1866; d. 1915*), legal educator. Son of James B. Thayer; brother of William S. Thayer. Graduated Harvard, 1888; Harvard Law School, 1891. Practiced with Boston law firm of Louis D. Brandeis and with other firms. Dean, Harvard Law School, 1910–15.

THAYER, GIDEON FRENCH (*b. Watertown, Mass., 1793; d. Keene, N.H., 1864*), Massachusetts educator, businessman. Grandfather of Abbott H. Thayer. Founded Chauncy-Hall School in Boston, Mass., 1828.

THAYER, JAMES BRADLEY (*b. Haverhill, Mass., 1831; d. Cambridge, Mass., 1902*), legal educator. Father of Ezra R. and William S. Thayer. Graduated Harvard, 1852; attended Harvard Law School, 1854–56. Practiced in Boston; served as editor (with Oliver W. Holmes, Jr.) of Kent's *Commentaries* (12th edition, 1873). Professor at Harvard Law School *post* 1874, he cooperated with C. C. Langdell, J. C. Gray, and James B. Ames in promoting the case system of study. A prolific writer of treatises and textbooks, he became recognized as a leading scholar in constitutional law and the law of evidence.

THAYER, JOHN (*b. Boston, Mass., 1758; d. Limerick, Ireland, 1815*), Roman Catholic clergyman. A convert to Catholicism, 1783, Thayer studied theology in Paris where he was ordained, 1787. Returning to Boston, Mass., 1790, he worked there with dedicated but tactless zeal. Replaced as pastor in 1792, he served courageously as a roving missionary through the New England towns, in Virginia, and on the Kentucky frontier until 1803 when he retired to work in Ireland.

THAYER, JOHN MILTON (*b. Bellingham, Mass., 1820; d. Lincoln, Nebr., 1906*), lawyer, Union major general. Settled in Omaha, Nebr., 1854, where he practiced law and was commissioned first brigadier general of the territorial militia. After distinguished service in the Western campaigns of the Civil War, he was U.S. senator, Republican, from Nebraska, 1867–71. An active Radical, he did his best work in Indian Affairs. Governor of Wyoming Territory, 1875–79, he returned to Nebraska and served as Republican governor of that state, 1887–92.

THAYER, JOSEPH HENRY (*b. Boston, Mass., 1828; d. 1901*), Congregational clergyman, New Testament scholar. Graduated Harvard, 1850; Andover Theological Seminary, 1857. Taught sacred literature at Andover, and at Harvard Divinity School where he was Bussey Professor of New Testament, 1884–1901. Editor-reviser of *Greek-English Lexicon of the New Testament* (adapted from Grimm and Wilke, 1887).

THAYER, NATHANIEL (*b. Lancaster, Mass., 1808; d. Boston, Mass., 1883*), financier, philanthropist, benefactor of Harvard.

THAYER, SYLVANUS (*b. Braintree, Mass., 1785; d. Braintree, 1872*), military engineer, educator. Graduated West Point, 1808. Called the "Father of the Military Academy," Thayer served at West Point as superintendent, 1817–33. He instituted many needed reforms and established an efficient organization for military and academic training including an able and distinguished faculty. From 1833 until his retirement as brevet brigadier general, 1863, he was engineer in charge of fortifications at Boston Harbor entrance and of the improvement of harbors on the New England coast. He established (1867) and endowed the Thayer School of engineering at Dartmouth.

THAYER, THOMAS BALDWIN (*b. Boston, Mass., 1812; d. Roxbury, Mass., 1886*), Universalist clergyman. Pastor in Lowell, Mass., 1833–45, 1851–59; in Boston, Mass., 1859–67. Editor, *Universalist Quarterly*, 1864–86.

THAYER, TIFFANY ELLSWORTH (*b. Freeport, Ill., 1902; d. Nantucket, Mass., 1959*), novelist, actor, advertising scriptwriter. Acted in the Midwest, 1918–22, before becoming an advertising copywriter in New York in 1926. The first of his more than twenty novels, *Thirteen Men* (1930), was a bestseller. His works were described as smutty, and he never achieved critical success. Other works include *Call Her Savage* (1931), *An American Girl* (1933), and *The Old Goat* (1937). Published the first three volumes of a projected series on the Italian Renaissance, *Mona Lisa: The Prince of Taranto* (1959).

THAYER, WHITNEY EUGENE (*b. Mendon, Mass., 1838; d. Burlington, Vt., 1889*), organist, music teacher, composer.

THAYER, WILLIAM MAKEPEACE (*b. Franklin, Mass., 1820; d. Franklin, 1898*), Congregational clergyman. Author of a number of "rags-to-riches" biographies which included *The Poor Boy and Merchant Prince* (1857), *The Bobbin Boy* (1860), and *The Pioneer Boy and How He Became President* (1863).

THAYER, WILLIAM ROSCOE (*b. Boston, Mass., 1859; d. Cambridge, Mass., 1923*), journalist, editor, historian. Graduated Harvard, 1881; M.A., 1886. Editor, *Harvard Graduates'*

Magazine, 1892–1915. Author of *The Dawn of Italian Independence* (1893) and the outstanding *Life and Times of Cavour* (1911), among other works.

THAYER, WILLIAM SYDNEY (*b. Milton, Mass., 1864; d. Washington, D.C., 1932*), physician. Son of James B. Thayer; brother of Ezra R. Thayer. Graduated Harvard, 1885; Harvard Medical School, 1889. After further study in Berlin and Vienna, he served on the staff of Johns Hopkins Hospital under William Osler; he later became professor of clinical medicine in Johns Hopkins Medical School and professor of medicine and physician-in-chief to the hospital. He made numerous contributions to knowledge of the circulatory system and investigated the condition of blood in leukemia, typhoid fever, and malaria.

THÉBAUD, AUGUSTUS J. (*b. Nantes, France, 1807; d. New York, N.Y., 1885*), Roman Catholic clergyman, Jesuit educator. In America *post* 1838, he held various teaching and administrative appointments at institutions of his order in Kentucky, New Jersey, New York, and Canada; he was three times rector of the present Fordham University. Distinguished as a preacher and lecturer, he made studies of immigration and social problems and wrote widely for Catholic magazines.

THEOBALD, ROBERT ALFRED (*b. San Francisco, Calif., 1884; d. Boston, Mass., 1957*), naval officer. Graduated from the U.S. Naval Academy, 1907; commissioned in 1908. Following routine assignments through World War I, Theobald became a popular instructor at the Naval War College and, in 1924, head of the Postgraduate School. Served on the staff of the War Plans Division, 1931–35, and by 1940 was an admiral in command of a destroyer flotilla that was destroyed at Pearl Harbor. Commander of the North Pacific Forces (1942); because of friction between commanders of other branches of the armed forces, he was reassigned to the Boston Navy Yard in 1943. Author of *The Final Secret of Pearl Harbor* (1954), which accused Roosevelt of purposely failing to alert the fleet because he wanted the U.S. in the war.

THEOBALD, SAMUEL (*b. Baltimore, Md., 1846; d. 1930*), ophthalmologist. Grandson of Nathan R. Smith, by whom he was raised. M.D., University of Maryland, 1867; studied also in Vienna and London. Practicing in Baltimore *post* 1871, he was founder of the Baltimore Eye, Ear, and Throat Charity Hospital and professor of his specialty at Johns Hopkins School of Medicine. Among other contributions, he invented lachrymal probes and introduced use of boric acid in ophthalmology.

THEUS, JEREMIAH (*b. probably Switzerland, ca. 1719; d. 1774*), painter. Immigrated *ca.* 1739 to Orangeburg Co., S.C.; by 1740 had begun his successful career as portraitist in Charleston. Painter of many men and women of the Southern colonies, he was celebrated for true if somewhat stiff and formal likenesses.

THIERRY, CAMILLE (*b. New Orleans, La., 1814; d. Bordeaux, France, 1875*), Louisiana poet. In part of black ancestry, Thierry resided in France *post* 1855. His popular poems were published in collected form at Bordeaux as *Les Vagabondes* (1874).

THILLY, FRANK (*b. Cincinnati, Ohio, 1865; d. 1934*), philosopher, educator. Graduated University of Cincinnati, 1887; studied also at Berlin and Heidelberg. Taught philosophy at Cornell, University of Missouri, and Princeton; professor at Sage School, Cornell, *post* 1906. Dean, College of Arts and Sciences, Cornell, 1915–21. Adhered in principle to the so-called tradition of idealism.

THOBURN, ISABELLA (*b. St. Clairsville, Ohio, 1840; d. Lucknow, India, 1901*), Methodist missionary and educator.

Sister of James M. Thoburn. Associated in mission work with Clara A. Swain, she conducted schools in India, 1870–80, 1882–86, and *post* 1891.

THOBURN, JAMES MILLS (*b.* St. Clairsville, Ohio, 1836; *d.* Meadville, Pa., 1922), Methodist clergyman. Brother of Isabella Thoburn. Missionary in India for the greater part of the years 1859–88; missionary bishop for India (later Southern Asia), 1888–1908; acknowledged missionary leader in his denomination.

THOMAS, ALLEN (*b.* Howard Co., Md., 1830; *d.* Waveland, Miss., 1907), lawyer, Louisiana planter, Confederate brigadier general. U.S. minister to Venezuela, 1895–97.

THOMAS, AMOS RUSSELL (*b.* Watertown, N.Y., 1826; *d.* Philadelphia, Pa., 1895), homeopathic physician. Taught anatomy in Philadelphia Academy of the Fine Arts, 1856–70. Professor of anatomy, Hahnemann Medical College of Philadelphia, 1867–95. He served also as dean of the college *post* 1874.

THOMAS, AUGUSTUS (*b.* St. Louis, Mo., 1857; *d.* Nyack, N.Y., 1934), dramatist. Author or adapter of nearly seventy plays. Thomas was a master of conventional stage technique and the painstaking use of local color, but displayed little dramatic interest in what lay below the surface of his situations. His work was important in its day in helping to free the American stage from bondage to Europe and in regularizing and professionalizing the craft of dramatist in America. Outstanding among his plays were *Alabama* (produced, 1891), *In Mizzoura* (1893), *Arizona* (1899), *The Witching Hour* (1907), *As a Man Thinks* (1911), and *The Copperhead* (1918).

THOMAS, CALVIN (*b.* Lapeer, Mich, 1854; *d.* 1919), German scholar. Graduated University of Michigan, 1874. Taught Germanic studies at Michigan and at Columbia University. An authority on Goethe, he produced a remarkable edition of *Faust* (1892–97) and was author of *Goethe* (1917), along with many other scholarly contributions in his field.

THOMAS, CHARLES SPALDING (*b.* near Darien, Ga., 1849; *d.* Denver. Colo., 1934), lawyer. Removed to Denver, Colo., 1871, where he won success in practice and was a partner of Thomas M. Patterson for a number of years. A nonconformist in politics as in other matters, he was elected governor of Colorado by the Silver Fusionists in 1898, serving until 1901. As U.S. senator, Democrat, 1913–21, he opposed the League of Nations, the soldiers' bonus, and what he considered extreme demands by both capital and labor.

THOMAS, CHRISTIAN FRIEDRICH THEODORE (*b.* Esens, Germany, 1835; *d.* Chicago, Ill., 1905), musician. Immigrated to New York City, 1845. Pupil of his father, Thomas early won reputation as a violinist. He was elected to the Philharmonic Society, 1854, and in the next year joined William Mason (1829–1908) in the first of the long famous series of Mason-Thomas chamber music concerts given at Dodworth's Hall. First conducting at the N.Y. Academy of Music, December 1860, Thomas entered on a new career as a kind of musical missionary, taking a series of orchestras on tours under his direction and developing the taste for symphonic music in the United States. Throughout a career filled with practical difficulties, he showed himself a shrewd program maker, seeking to elevate public taste progressively and gradually rather than immediately. He served as conductor of the Chicago Symphony Orchestra, 1891–1905. Often a storm center because of his artistic integrity, he was an important figure in the growth of American culture.

THOMAS, CYRUS (*b.* Kingsport, Tenn., 1825; *d.* 1910), ethnologist, entomologist, pioneer in Mayan studies, authority on the Mound Builders.

THOMAS, DAVID (*b.* Pelham, Mass., 1762; *d.* Providence, R.I., 1831), Revolutionary soldier, New York State politician. Congressman, Democratic-Republican, from New York, 1801–08, and treasurer of New York State, 1808–10, 1812, he was a prominent supporter of DeWitt Clinton. Indicted and acquitted for attempted bribery of a legislator, 1812, he retired from politics and removed to Rhode Island.

THOMAS, DAVID (*b.* Glamorganshire, Wales, 1794; *d.* Catasauqua, Pa., 1882), iron manufacturer. An expert in the hot-blast method of smelting iron ore, Thomas came to Pennsylvania, 1839, and constructed the first American anthracite iron manufacturing plant at Catasauqua, Pa. (operational, July 1840).

THOMAS, EDITH MATILDA (*b.* Chatham, Ohio, 1854; *d.* 1925), poet, editor. Resident in New York City *post* 1887, she was author, among other works, of *A New Year's Masque* (1885), *Lyrics and Sonnets* (1887), and *The Flower from the Ashes* (1915). Her remote, unimpassioned, classical verses were marked by painstaking craftsmanship.

THOMAS, ELBERT DUNCAN (*b.* Salt Lake City, Utah, 1883; *d.* Honolulu, Hawaii, 1953), political scientist, politician. Studied at the University of Utah, A.B., 1906, and the University of California. Professor of history and political science at the University of Utah, 1924–32. Democratic senator from Utah, 1932–50. A liberal, Thomas was an administration spokesman, championing the New Deal, the formation of the U.N., and labor rights. Urged retainment of the Japanese emperor after World War II to prevent anarchy. High commissioner of the U.S. Trust Territory of the Pacific Islands, 1951–53.

THOMAS, FRANCIS (*b.* near Petersville, Md., 1799; *d.* 1876), lawyer, Maryland legislator. Congressman, Democrat, from Maryland, 1831–41, he was chairman of the judiciary committee, an able and eloquent parliamentarian, and a friend and defender of Andrew Jackson. As governor of Maryland, 1841–44, he preserved the state from repudiation of its debt. Retiring from politics because of a personal scandal, he emerged at the outbreak of the Civil War as a strong Unionist; while congressman, 1861–69, he supported the extreme Radicals. He was U.S. minister to Peru, 1872–75.

THOMAS, FREDERICK WILLIAM (*b.* Providence, R.I., 1806; *d.* Washington, D.C., 1866), journalist, author, friend and correspondent of Edgar Allan Poe.

THOMAS, GEORGE (*b.* Antigua, British West Indies, ca.1695; *d.* London, England, 1774). Appointed deputy governor of Pennsylvania and the Lower Counties, he served from 1738 until 1747. In bitter controversy with the Assembly over financial and military affairs for the greater part of his term, he was successful in his dealings with the Indians. Advised by Conrad Weiser, he secured the neutrality of the Iroquois, thus permitting settlement of the back country.

THOMAS, GEORGE ALLISON (*b.* on the Onondaga Reservation, south of Syracuse, N.Y., 1911; *d.* Syracuse, 1968), Onondaga Indian chief and spiritual leader. Promoted Iroquoian culture and the spiritual welfare of the Iroquois's Six Nations for much of his life. Succeeded his father as chief and spiritual leader in 1957. Led protests against the St. Lawrence Seaway (1954–59), the Niagara Power Project (1957–61), and the Kinzua Dam (1957–66) because Iroquois lands were expropriated for their construction.

THOMAS, GEORGE CLIFFORD (*b. Philadelphia, Pa., 1839; d. Philadelphia, 1909*), banker, philanthropist. Partner in Jay Cooke's banking house, 1866–73, he was active *post* 1883 in Drexel & Co. and its Morgan affiliates.

THOMAS, GEORGE HENRY (*b. Southampton Co., Va., 1816; d. San Francisco, Calif., 1870*), soldier. Graduated West Point, 1840; was commissioned in the 3rd Artillery. Served in the Florida War, in several Southern garrisons and throughout Taylor's campaign in the war with Mexico. Instructor in artillery and cavalry at West Point, 1851–54. Promoted to major, 1855, he was assigned to the 2nd (later the 5th) Cavalry, a regiment officered by men almost all of whom rose to high rank, both Union and Confederate, during the Civil War. He served with this unit in Texas and on exploration duty until 1860. Remaining loyal to the Union, Thomas commanded a brigade in the opening operations in the Shenandoah Valley, 1861, rising to brigadier general in August. Commanding the 1st Division, Army of the Ohio, he won a decisive action at Mill Springs, January 1862, and later took part in Buell's advance to Nashville and to Pittsburg Landing. Promoted major general, April 1862, he commanded the right wing of Halleck's army in the march against and capture of Corinth. Reassigned to Buell's army, he served during the campaign against Bragg in Kentucky; he was second in command to Buell in the Perryville operations in October. Under Rosecrans, Thomas commanded the XIV Army Corps at Stone River, and in the Tullahoma campaign of June and July 1863. In September, Thomas reached his highest pitch of fame at the battle of Chickamauga, maintaining the field with his corps despite the rout of the rest of the Union forces. After General U.S. Grant ordered concentration of federal forces on Chattanooga, Thomas succeeded Rosecrans in command of the Army of the Cumberland, holding Chattanooga under great difficulties until Grant was ready to undertake a general offensive. In the battle that followed, Thomas was in general command during the seizure of Lookout Mountain and Missionary Ridge (November 1863).

Thomas's Army of the Cumberland made up over half of General W. T. Sherman's force during the Atlanta campaign and was constantly engaged; units of it were first to enter Atlanta. While Sherman was marching to the sea with his main force, Thomas was designated to command a new army, based in Nashville, which would oppose Confederate forces under General John Hood in the West. After a delaying action, the federal field force took position at Franklin, Tenn., checked Hood's advance there on Nov. 30, 1864, and then withdrew into Nashville. Although Grant insisted on an immediate offensive by Thomas, the latter refused to move until he was ready. When he did attack (December 15–16), he vindicated his judgment by crushing Hood's army so severely that it played no further important part in the war. Promoted major general in the regular army for this victory, he also received the thanks of Congress. He remained in command in the Nashville area for the rest of the war and for a few years after it. In June 1869, he assumed command of the Division of the Pacific at San Francisco. Studious, deliberate but decided in action, Thomas was respected by his superiors and loved by his subordinates. General U.S. Grant said of him that his military dispositions were always good and that he could not be driven from a point he was given to hold.

THOMAS, ISAIAH (*b. Boston, Mass., 1749 o.s.; d. Worcester, Mass., 1831*), printer, historian of the press. After apprenticeship to a Boston printer (Zechariah Fowle), and early journeyman work in Halifax, Nova Scotia, and Charleston, S.C., he became Fowle's partner in July 1770. Establishing the *Massachusetts Spy*, a fearless and successful Whig newspaper, in that same year, he soon bought out his partner. Removing his printing establishment to Worcester, Mass., April 1775, he continued to publish his newspaper and served as official printer for the patriots of the colony. Despite difficulties, by the end of the Revolutionary War his business was on a firm footing. The leading book and periodical publisher of his day, he conducted branches of his business in Boston, Newburyport, Baltimore, Albany, and in other towns. Notable for good typography, he published more than 400 books which included a folio Bible, a number of school textbooks, reprints of the best English literature of his day, and the first edition of *The Power of Sympathy* (1789), attributed to William H. Brown and the first novel by a native American. He was also famous for a long list of children's books, among them the first American issues of *Mother Goose's Melody* (1786) and *The History of Little Goody Two-Shoes*, and illustrated editions of the *New England Primer*. He was publisher also of the *Royal American Magazine*, 1774–75, and of the *Massachusetts Magazine*, 1789–96. Retiring from personal control of his business, 1802, he devoted the rest of life to scholarship. His *History of Printing in America* (1810) is still a recognized authority on the subject. In 1812 he founded and incorporated the American Antiquarian Society of which he became first president.

THOMAS, JESSE BURGESS (*b. Shepherdstown, present W. Va., 1777; d. Mount Vernon, Ohio, 1853*), lawyer, Indiana and Illinois politician. Removing to Indiana Territory *ca.* 1803, he served as speaker of the territorial legislature, 1805–08. As territorial delegate to Congress, 1808–09, he worked successfully to secure independent territorial status for Illinois. Federal judge in Illinois, 1809–18, he was president of the Illinois constitutional convention, 1818, and served as U.S. senator, Democrat, from the state of Illinois, 1818–29. During the debate over the admission of Missouri, 1820, he introduced an amendment prohibiting slavery north of the line 36°30' except for the area of the proposed state of Missouri. This was embodied in the "Missouri Compromise."

THOMAS, JESSE BURGESS (*b. Illinois, 1832; d. Brooklyn, N.Y., 1915*), Baptist clergyman. Brooklyn, N.Y., pastor; professor of church history at Newton Theological Institution. Grandnephew of Jesse B. Thomas (1777–1853).

THOMAS, JOHN (*b. Marshfield, Mass., 1724; d. near Chambly, Canada, 1776*), physician, Revolutionary major general. Practiced at Kingston, Mass., served as military surgeon in French and Indian War, also as soldier. Commissioned general officer of Massachusetts troops, February 1775, he was elected brigadier general of Continentals, June 1775. Commanded at Roxbury during siege of Boston, 1775–76; commanded occupation of Dorchester Heights, March 1776. Promoted major general and ordered to command in Canada after the failure of Montgomery, he died of smallpox on the retreat from Quebec.

THOMAS, JOHN CHARLES (*b. Meyersdale, Pa., 1891; d. Apple Valley, Calif., 1960*), baritone. Studied at the Peabody Conservatory of Music. Appeared in light opera; made his opera debut in 1925 at the Washington Opera. Appeared in *Salome* at the San Francisco Opera, 1930; and Metropolitan Opera debut in *La Traviata*, 1934. Made numerous recordings; made farewell concert tour in 1952–53.

THOMAS, JOHN JACOBS (*b. Ledyard, N.Y., 1810; d. Union Springs, N.Y., 1895*), pomologist. Brother of Joseph Thomas. A pioneer fruit grower and nurseryman in central New York, he was editor of several agricultural papers, and an outstanding associate editor of the *Country Gentleman*, 1853–94. Inventor of several farm implements, among them the smoothing harrow. Author of *The Fruit Culturist* (1846, expanded edition, 1849) which marks the beginning of systematic pomology in America.

THOMAS, JOHN PARNELL (*b. John Parnell Feeney, Jr., Jersey City, N.J., 1895; d. St. Petersburg, Fla., 1970*), businessman, U.S. congressman. Attended the University of Pennsylvania (1914–16) and New York University Law School (1916–17). Joined the Paine Webber Company after World War I and stayed there until 1941. In 1920 he changed his name from Feeney to Thomas in the belief he would achieve greater recognition and business under his mother's maiden name. In 1936 he won the first of six successive terms in the U.S. House of Representatives where he specialized in ferreting out Communists and liberals. He became chairman of the House Un-American Activities Committee (HUAC) after the elections of 1946. Under his leadership HUAC investigated the movie industry in 1947 and conducted the Hiss-Chambers hearings in 1948. Indicted for padding his congressional payroll (1948), he resigned from the House in 1950 and served nearly nine months in prison before being paroled by President Truman.

THOMAS, (JOHN WILLIAM) ELMER (*b. near Greencastle, Ind., 1876; d. Lawton, Okla., 1965*), politician, businessman. Attended Central Normal College (teaching certificate, 1897) and DePauw University (Ph.D., 1900). Moved to the Oklahoma Territory in 1900 where he practiced law and worked for a real estate company. Elected senator to Oklahoma's first legislature (1907). A leader in the state Democratic party, he was elected to the House of Representatives in 1922 and served two terms. Elected to the U.S. Senate in 1926, he supported the interests of farmers and the free coinage of silver. Was reelected to the Senate in 1932, 1938, and 1944, but was narrowly defeated for his party's nomination in 1950.

THOMAS, JOHN WILSON (*b. near Nashville, Tenn., 1830; d Nashville, 1906*), Tennessee railroad executive, President of the Nashville, Chattanooga & St. Louis Railway *post* 1884.

THOMAS, JOSEPH (*b. Ledyard, N.Y., 1811; d. Philadelphia, Pa., 1891*), physician, lexicographer, educator. Brother of John J. Thomas. Compiler and editor of a number of reference books for J. B. Lippincott and Co. Long associated with Swarthmore College, he was an authority in his day on etymology and pronunciation.

THOMAS, LORENZO (*b. New Castle, Del., 1804; d. Washington, D.C., 1875*), soldier. Graduated West Point, 1823. A staff officer for many years, Thomas became adjutant general of the U.S. Army in 1861, ranking as brigadier general. Criticized as inadequate, he was relieved in March 1863 and assigned to other duties. Reappointed adjutant general in February 1868, he lost reputation for his foolish actions as *ad interim* secretary of war during contest for control of the War Department between President Andrew Johnson and Edwin M. Stanton.

THOMAS, MARTHA CAREY (*b. Baltimore, Md., 1857; d. Philadelphia, Pa., 1935*), educator. Niece of Hannah W. Smith. Graduated Cornell, 1877. Studied Greek at Johns Hopkins with Basil Gildersleeve and made further philological and linguistic studies abroad, winning her doctorate at University of Zurich, 1882. Appointed dean and professor of English at Bryn Mawr, 1884, she influenced the formation of its curriculum and served as its president, 1894–1922. Active in the fight for woman's suffrage and for international peace, she was also a successful fund-raiser for the Johns Hopkins Medical School, giving her assistance on condition that women be admitted there.

THOMAS, NORMAN MATTOON (*b. Marion, Ohio, 1884; d. Huntington, N.Y., 1968*), reformer, socialist. Attended Bucknell University, Princeton University (B.A., 1905), and Union Theological Seminary (B.D., 1911). An ordained Presbyterian minister, Thomas joined the Socialist party in 1918. In 1917 he helped establish the Civil Liberties Bureau, which later became the American Civil Liberties Union. Became head of the Socialist party in1 1926. Every four years during 1928–48 he ran for the presidency of the United States. As a pacificst, Thomas ardently opposed U.S. entry into World War I and World War II; after Pearl Harbor, however, he gave "critical support" to the war effort. Spoke out against the interning of Japanese-Americans and the dropping of the atomic bomb on Japan. Worked tirelessly to promote world peace through international cooperation and eloquently defended unpopular people and causes throughout his life.

THOMAS, PHILIP EVAN (*b. Montgomery Co., Md., 1776; d. Yonkers, N.Y., 1861*), Baltimore merchant, banker. Active in securing the charter for the Baltimore and Ohio Railroad, 1827, Thomas became its first president. He resigned in 1836 after the road had reached Harpers Ferry and its chief mechanical problems had been resolved under his direction.

THOMAS, PHILIP FRANCIS (*b. Eastern, Md., 1810; d. 1890*), lawyer, Maryland legislator and congressman. Democratic governor of Maryland, 1847–50; U.S. secretary of the treasury, 1860 (for one month). A Confederate sympathizer, he was denied the post–Civil War seat in the U.S. Senate to which he had been chosen.

THOMAS, RICHARD HENRY (*b. Baltimore, Md., 1854; d. Baltimore, 1904*), physician, Quaker minister, author. Developed and preached an interpretation of Christianity which met challenges of contemporary science and higher criticism.

THOMAS, ROBERT BAILEY (*b. Grafton, Mass., 1766; d. West Boylston, Mass., 1846*), founder, editor, and publisher of the *Farmer's Almanack*, 1792–1846.

THOMAS, ROLAND JAY (*b. East Palestine, Ohio, 1900; d. Muskegon, Mich., 1967*), labor organizer. Attended Wooster (Ohio) College (1919–21). Took a welding job at a Detroit Chrysler auto plant (1929), and in 1934 was elected employee representative of his plant to the Automobile Labor Board. Two years later he became plant president and overall vice-president of the Automotive Industrial Workers of America, an independent union that joined the UAW in 1936. Made a UAW vice-president (1937), he was placed in charge of all bargaining with the Chrysler Corporation. Elected UAW-CIO president, 1939. In 1941 under his leadership UAW successfully organized the Ford Motor Company. Defeated by Walter Reuther for the UAW presidency in 1946, Thomas was active in the CIO for the rest of his career.

THOMAS, SETH (*b. Wolcott, Conn., 1785; d. Plymouth, present Thomaston, Conn., 1859*), pioneer clock manufacturer. Joined Eli Terry and another in partnership at Plymouth, Conn., 1807; began clock production on his own, 1812; purchased manufacturing rights for Terry's shelf clock, 1814. Organized Seth Thomas Clock Co., 1853.

THOMAS, THEODORE. *See* THOMAS, CHRISTIAN FRIEDRICH THEODORE.

THOMAS, THEODORE GAILLARD (*b. Edisto Island, S.C., 1831; d. Thomasville, Ga., 1903*), obstetrician, gynecologist. Graduated Medical College of South Carolina, 1852; studied also in Paris and Dublin. Practiced in New York City *post* 1855; professor of obstetrics (later of gynecology) at N.Y. College of Physicians and Surgeons, 1865–90. Inventor of many surgical instruments, he originated, among many other new techniques, the operation of laparoelytrotomy and suggested and used an incubator as early as 1867. He was author of the classic *Practical Treatise on the Diseases of Women* (1868).

THOMAS, WILLIAM ISAAC (*b. Russell County, Va., 1863; d. Berkeley, Calif., 1947*), sociologist. B.A., University of Tennessee, 1884; Ph.D., 1886. Studied at Göttingen and Berlin, 1888–89. Professor of English, Oberlin College, 1889–95. Redirecting his interests, he became one of the first graduate students in the department of sociology, University of Chicago, and was awarded the doctorate, 1895. He then taught sociology at University of Chicago until 1918 (professor *post* 1910), when he was arrested for violation of the Mann Act and dismissed. Thereafter, he was engaged primarily in research projects sponsored by private organizations, and occasional visiting university appointments. His core concerns in his work were social control and the process of social change; his achievement in linking theoretical and empirical research set a model for subsequent sociological investigations. His principal book was his comparative study, *The Polish Peasant in Europe and America* (1918–19).

THOMAS, WILLIAM WIDGERY (*b. Portland, Maine, 1839; d. 1927*), lawyer, U.S. consular office, Maine legislator. Helped establish Swedish settlement in Aroostook Co., Maine, 1870. He was U.S. minister to Sweden and Norway, 1883–85, 1889–94, and 1897–1905.

THOMES, WILLIAM HENRY (*b. Portland, Maine, 1824; d. 1895*), mariner, journalist, California pioneer, Boston (Mass.) publisher. Author of a number of tales of the "dimenovel" variety, and of the vivid and accurate work on pioneer California entitled *On Land and Sea* (1883).

THOMPSON, ALFRED WORDSWORTH (*b. Baltimore, Md., 1840; d. Summit, N.J., 1896*), landscape, figure, and historical painter.

THOMPSON, ARTHUR WEBSTER (*b. Erie, Pa., 1875; d. Pittsburgh, Pa., 1930*), civil engineer, railroad and utilities executive. Associated with the Baltimore and Ohio, 1899–1919, he was president of the Philadelphia Co., 1919–26, and of the United Gas Improvement Co. thereafter.

THOMPSON, BENJAMIN (*b. Woburn, Mass., 1753; d. Auteuil, France, 1814*), scientist, philanthropist, better known as "Count Rumford." Early apt at mathematics and drafting, he was apprenticed to a merchant in Salem, Mass., 1766, but gave much of his time to reading, and scientific experimentation and discussion with Loammi Baldwin (1744–1807). After studying medicine and teaching school for a short time, he married a wealthy widow, 1772. By exercising his lifelong gift for promoting his own interests, he rose high in favor of Governor Wentworth of New Hampshire. Ambivalent in his sympathies at the outbreak of the Revolution, he definitely chose the British side in the fall of 1775. After the British evacuation of Boston, he removed to England, where he again exercised his art of pleasing the great, was appointed to a sinecure and became a fellow of the Royal Society, 1779. Commissioned a British lieutenant colonel for service in America, 1781, he engaged in action near Charleston, S.C., March 1782; he then served on Long Island until late spring 1783 when he returned to England and was put on half pay. Touring in Europe, he entered the service of the Elector of Bavaria in which he was made major general, councilor of state, and head of the war department. Already holder of a British knighthood, he was made a Count of the Holy Roman Empire, 1791. Famous for his efficient reforms in Bavaria, he returned to England, 1795, where he published the first volume (1796) of his *Essays, Political, Economical, and Philosophical.* He introduced improvements in heating and cooking equipment, and established (1796) a fund for the Rumford Medal of the Royal Society and the Rumford prize of the American Academy of Arts and Sciences. Returning to Bavaria as head of the council of regency, he performed important diplomatic services and supervised the department of police. Refused recognition as Bavarian minister to Great Britain, 1798, he remained for a time in London where, at his suggestion, The Royal Institution was incorporated in January 1800. He personally supervised construction of its building and secured for it the services of Humphry Davy. After helping plan the Bavarian Academy of Arts and Sciences, 1801, he settled permanently on the continent of Europe, 1802, and in 1805 married the widow of Lavoisier, the chemist, from whom he later separated. Continuing the scientific investigations he had long conducted on the transmission of heat, the absorption of moisture by various substances and the like, he developed a calorimeter and photometer, made improvements in lamps and illumination, and in his essay *Of the Excellent Qualities of Coffee* (1812) described the drip coffee pot. He contributed papers to the meetings of the Institute of France and to the Royal Society, and in 1802 published *Philosophical Papers* (projected as a two-volume work of which only one volume was issued). He is remembered best as a tireless encourager of scientific and humanitarian activities, and for his demonstration by experiment that a hot body cooling in air loses much of its heat by radiation, also that heat is a mode of motion.

THOMPSON, CEPHAS GIOVANNI (*b. Middleboro, Mass., 1809; d. New York, N.Y., 1888*), painter. Brother of Jerome B. Thompson; brother-in-law of Anna C. O. Mowatt. A successful portraitist and social figure in New York City *post* 1837, he became an intimate friend of Nathaniel Hawthorne while resident in Rome, Italy, 1852–59.

THOMPSON, CHARLES OLIVER (*b. East Windsor Hill, Conn., 1836; d. Terre Haute, Ind., 1885*), engineer. Graduated Dartmouth, 1858. Introduced shop practice in engineering teaching at present Worcester Polytechnic Institute while principal, 1868–82. President, Rose Polytechnic Institute *post* 1883.

THOMPSON, DANIEL PIERCE (*b. Charlestown, Mass., 1795; d. 1868*), lawyer, Vermont historical novelist. Raised in frontier Vermont, Thompson graduated from Middlebury College, 1820, and practiced law in Montpelier *post ca.* 1823. Active in politics as successively a Democrat, a member of the Liberty party, and a Republican. He was author of a number of novels of romantic adventure of which *The Green Mountain Boys* (1839) and *Locke Amsden* (1847) are considered the best.

THOMPSON, DAVID (*b. London, England, 1770; d. Canada, 1857*), fur trader, explorer, geographer. Served for many years *post ca.* 1785 as a Hudson's Bay Company apprentice and surveyor in western Canada, retiring from field service in 1812. Publication (1916) of some of his journals and field notes have won him recognition as one of the greatest land geographers of the English race. Among his achievements were the survey of the most northerly source of the Mississippi (1798), discovery of the source of the Columbia River (1807) and a survey of the Columbia from source to mouth (1811).

THOMPSON, DAVID P. (*b. Cadiz, Ohio, 1834; d. 1901*), contractor, banker, Oregon legislator and public official. Removed to Oregon, 1853. Beginning his career as a U.S. deputy surveyor, he prospered in numerous enterprises and was a leader of the Republican party in Oregon. Among other public offices, he was mayor of Portland, 1879 and 1881.

THOMPSON, DENMAN (*b. near Girard, Pa., 1833; d. West Swanzey, N.H., 1911*), actor, playwright. Star of one of the best-known and most successful dramas to appear on the American stage, *The Old Homestead.* Developed from a brief sketch which was first produced in Pittsburgh, Pa., 1875, the play was expanded first to three acts (produced as *Joshua Whitcombe,* Chicago, Ill.,

1877) but did not appear in its final and most successful form until the production of April 1886 at Boston, Mass.

THOMPSON, DOROTHY (*b. Lancaster, N.Y., 1893; d. Lisbon, Portugal, 1961*), journalist. Attended the Lewis Institute (A.A., 1912) and Syracuse University (B.A., 1914). In 1920 she sailed to Europe where she became a highly successful journalist. In 1925 she was named to head the Berlin bureau of the *New York Evening Post* and the *Public Ledger*. Married novelist Sinclair Lewis in 1928. Expelled from Germany in 1934 because of her anti-Nazi sentiments, she returned to the United States. Beginning in 1936 she wrote a thrice-weekly public-affairs column, "On the Record," for the *New York Herald Tribune*; it was eventually carried by 170 newspapers. Moved to the Bell Syndicate after the presidential elections of 1940. In 1941 she founded the Ring of Freedom to prepare the United States for war and became the second president of Freedom House, a liberal internationalist organization. She and Lewis were divorced in 1942, but she wrote a tribute to him in a highly praised article in *Atlantic Monthly* (November 1960). After World War II she supported the cause of Palestinian Arabs and anti-Zionist organizations.

THOMPSON, EDWARD HERBERT (*b. Worcester, Mass., 1856; d. Plainfield, N.J., 1935*), explorer, archaeologist, U.S. consular official in Mexico. A pioneer scientific investigator of Mayan antiquities, Thompson is associated in particular with the work done at Chichen-Itza.

THOMPSON, EGBERT (*b. New York, N.Y., 1822; d. Washington, D.C., 1881*), naval officer. Nephew of Smith Thompson. Appointed midshipman, 1837. After service with the Wilkes Exploring Expedition, 1838–42, and aboard the brig USS *Somers* at the time of the famous alleged mutiny, Thompson engaged in routine duty up to the Civil War, during which he was engaged principally in service with the Union flotillas on the Mississippi River. He was balked of advancement because of alleged tardiness in supporting land operations after running the Confederate batteries at Island No. 10 with the gunboat *Pittsburg*, April 1862. He was retired as captain in 1874.

THOMPSON, HUGH MILLER (*b. Londonderry, Ireland, 1830; d. Jackson, Miss., 1902*), Episcopal clergyman. Came to America as a boy. Held a number of pastorates in the Midwest, in New York City, and in New Orleans, La. Editor, *American Churchman*, 1860–71, he subsequently edited the *Church Journal*. Elected coadjutor bishop of Mississippi, 1882, he became diocesan bishop, 1887, and served until 1902.

THOMPSON, HUGH SMITH (*b. Charleston, S.C., 1836; d. New York, N.Y., 1904*), educator. Nephew of Waddy Thompson. Brilliantly successful as South Carolina superintendent of education, 1877–82, he served efficiently as Democratic governor of that state, 1882–86. Subsequently an assistant secretary of the U.S. treasury and a member of the civil service commission, he was comptroller of the New York Life Insurance Co., 1892–1904.

THOMPSON, JACOB (*b. Leasburg, N.C., 1810; d. Memphis, Tenn., 1885*), lawyer. Removed to Mississippi, 1835. Congressman, Democrat, from Mississippi, 1839–51, he was for a time chairman of the committees of public lands and Indian affairs. Efficient as U.S. secretary of the interior, 1857–61, he resigned because of his states' rights views. Serving in the Confederate Army until the fall of Vicksburg, he fomented trouble in Canada *post* 1864 as a secret Confederate agent. After a brief post–Civil War exile in Europe, he returned to America and settled permanently in Memphis.

THOMPSON, JAMES MAURICE (*b. Fairfield, Ind., 1844; d. Crawfordsville, Ind., 1901*), Confederate soldier, civil engineer, lawyer, authority on archery. Author, among other works, of the best-selling historical romance *Alice of Old Vincennes* (1900).

THOMPSON, JEREMIAH (*b. Rawdon, Yorkshire, England, 1784; d. New York, N.Y., 1835*), merchant, shipowner. Organizer (1817, with Benjamin Marshall and others) of regular American packet-ship sailings between New York and Liverpool.

THOMPSON, JEROME B. (*b. Middleboro, Mass., 1814; d. Glen Gardner, N.J., 1886*), painter. Brother of Cephas G. Thompson. He won success as a painter of rustic scenes and other subjects which were widely reproduced by lithography.

THOMPSON, JOHN.   *See* THOMSON, JOHN.

THOMPSON, JOHN.   (*b. present Peru, Mass., 1802; d. 1891*), broker, commercial publisher, banker. President, First National Bank, New York City, 1863–77; cofounder of the Chase National Bank, New York City, 1877.

THOMPSON, JOHN BODINE (*b. Readington, N.J., 1830; d. Trenton, N.J., 1907*), Reformed Church clergyman, educator, liberal theologian.

THOMPSON, JOHN REUBEN (*b. Richmond, Va., 1823; d. New York, N.Y., 1873*), editor, poet. Edited *The Southern Literary Messenger*, 1847–60. While assistant secretary of Virginia during the Civil War, he helped edit *Richmond Record* and *Southern Illustrated News* and also contributed to the *Index*, spokesman of the Confederacy in England. After the war he served as literary editor of the N.Y. *Evening Post*. His collected poems were first published in 1920.

THOMPSON, JOSEPH PARRISH (*b. Philadelphia, Pa., 1819; d. Berlin, Germany, 1879*), Congregational clergyman, editor. Father of William G. Thompson. Held principal pastorate at Broadway Tabernacle, New York City, 1845–71; helped edit the *Independent*, 1848–62; was a leader in home missionary work.

THOMPSON, JOSIAH VAN KIRK (*b. near Uniontown, Pa., 1854; d. Uniontown, 1933*), Pennsylvania coal operator, banker.

THOMPSON, LAUNT (*b. Queens Co., Ireland, 1833; d. Middletown, N.Y., 1894*), sculptor. A pupil of Erastus D. Palmer, Thompson was celebrated in his time for his ideal medallion heads and for portrait busts and statues.

THOMPSON, MALVINA CYNTHIA (*b. Bronx, N.Y., 1893; d. New York, N.Y., 1953*), personal secretary. As secretary and companion to Eleanor Roosevelt, 1932–53. Thompson edited columns, advised, and traveled with the first lady. A constant companion, she often issued statements to the press in Mrs. Roosevelt's name.

THOMPSON, MARTIN E. (*b. place uncertain, ca. 1786; d. Glen Cove, N.Y., 1877*), architect. Described in the 1816 New York City directory as a carpenter, he designed (1822–23) the second Bank of the United States on Wall Street, New York City, and also the remarkable Merchants' Exchange (1824), destroyed in the great fire of 1835. Briefly a partner of Ithiel Town, Thompson became a convert to the Greek Revival Style. Little or nothing of the work which he did subsequently has survived in New York City, although it is supposed by some that he was the architect of the dignified houses built in the northern part of Greenwich Village, 1840–60.

THOMPSON, MAURICE.   *See* THOMPSON, JAMES MAURICE.

THOMPSON, OSCAR LEE (*b. Crawfordsville, Ind., 1887; d. New York, N.Y., 1945*), journalist, music critic. Nephew of James Maurice Thompson. Edited newspapers in Seattle and Tacoma,

Wash.; removed to New York City, 1919, to join staff of *Musical America*, of which he was editor, 1936–43. Concurrently, he served as music critic successively of the New York *Evening Post*, *Times*, and *Sun*. He was author, among other books, of *Practical Music Criticism* (1934) and *The International Cyclopedia of Music and Musicians* (1939).

THOMPSON, RICHARD WIGGINTON (*b. Culpeper Co., Va., 1809; d. Terre Haute, Ind., 1900*), lawyer, Whig and Republican politician, Indiana legislator. Resident in Indiana *post ca.* 1832, Thompson remained continuously active in politics and was throughout his life a figure of controversy. Secretary of the navy, 1877–81, he was frequently attacked for unethical conduct.

THOMPSON, ROBERT ELLIS (*b. near Lurgan, Ireland, 1844; d. Philadelphia, Pa., 1924*), Reformed Presbyterian clergyman, educator. Immigrated to Philadelphia as a boy. Graduated University of Pennsylvania, 1865; taught social science there, 1871–92, and was first dean of Wharton School of Finance, 1881–83. A follower of Henry C. Carey, he was author of, among other books, *Social Science and National Economy* (1875) and *Protection to Home Industry* (1866). He represents in his career the unsuccessful struggle of the national economic optimists against the rising tide of reformers, mainly socialists, who preached class cleavage instead of a harmony of economic interests. *post* 1894 he served with great success as president of the Philadelphia Central High School.

THOMPSON, ROBERT MEANS (*b. Corsica, Pa., 1849; d. Fort Ticonderoga, N.Y., 1930*), naval officer, lawyer, financier. Graduated U.S. Naval Academy, 1868; Harvard Law School, 1874. Successful in practice and as an official of the International Nickel Co., Thompson was a benefactor of the Naval Academy and the first president of the American Olympic Association.

THOMPSON, SAMUEL RANKIN (*b. South Shenango, Pa., 1833; d. New Wilmington, Pa., 1896*), educator and physicist. Pioneer in public educational organization and normal school work in Nebraska, Pennsylvania, and West Virginia.

THOMPSON, SEYMOUR DWIGHT (*b. Will Co., Ill., 1842; d. East Orange, N.J., 1904*), Union soldier, Missouri jurist. Principal editor, *American Law Review*, *post* 1883, he was distinguished chiefly for his many widely read legal treatises which included *A Treatise on Homestead and Exemption Laws* (1878), *A Treatise on the Law of Trials* (1889), and *Commentaries on the Law of Private Corporations* (1895–99).

THOMPSON, SLASON (*b. Fredericton, N.B., Canada, 1849; d. Lake Forest, Ill., 1935*), journalist. A newspaper editor of wide experience and one of the first important industrial press agents in the United States, Thompson is remembered particularly as the friend, publisher, and biographer of Eugene Field.

THOMPSON, SMITH (*b. Amenia, N.Y., 1768; d. Poughkeepsie, N.Y., 1843*), jurist. Graduated College of New Jersey (Princeton), 1788; studied law under James Kent. Allied by marriage with the Livingston family, he was appointed a justice of the New York supreme court, 1802, and was made chief justice, 1814. U.S. secretary of the navy, 1819–23, he accepted appointment as an associate justice of the U.S. Supreme Court and served, 1823–43. One of the group which had already begun to pull away from John Marshall's strong nationalism, he dissented in *Brown* v. *Maryland* (1827) and in the same year helped overrule Marshall in *Ogden* v. *Saunders*; he later (1830) dissented from Marshall's decision in *Craig* v. *Missouri*. Although personally a bitter opponent of slavery, he upheld the federal Fugitive Slave Act. The most notable case in which Thompson spoke for the Court was *Kendall* v. *U.S.* (1838). His opinion in this case

contained a paragraph vigorously rejecting the theory attributed to Andrew Jackson that the president, under his power to see that laws are faithfully executed, may enforce his own interpretation of the Constitution by extending protection to subordinates when they violate acts of Congress or mandates of the courts. This paragraph delivered orally was expunged from the written opinion at the request of the attorney general who denied that the theory had been urged in argument.

THOMPSON, THOMAS LARKIN (*b. present Charleston, W. Va., 1838; d. Santa Rosa, Calif., 1898*), California editor and congressman. Removed to California, 1855, where he was active in journalism and Democratic politics. Tactful and efficient as U.S. minister to Brazil, 1893–97.

THOMPSON, WADDY (*b. Pickensville, S.C., 1798; d. Tallahassee, Fla., 1868*), lawyer, South Carolina legislator. Uncle of Hugh S. Thompson; brother-in-law of Andrew and Pierce M. Butler. An ardent nullifier, he was congressman, Whig, from South Carolina, 1835–41, and served with success as U.S. minister to Mexico, 1842–44. Too honest to trim sails to the popular breeze, disapproving the war with Mexico and doubting the expediency of secession, he retired to private life.

THOMPSON, WILEY (*b. Amelia Co., Va., 1781; d. near Fort King, Fla., 1835*), Georgia soldier and legislator, Indian agent. Congressman, Democrat, from Georgia, 1821–33, he rose to chairmanship of the military affairs committee and was a bitter opponent of protection. Approving Andrew Jackson's Indian removal policy, he accepted appointment as agent to supervise removal of the Seminoles under treaties of Payne's Landing and Fort Gibson. Beginning work, 1834, Thompson was opposed by a group of chiefs under Osceola's leadership and in 1835 attempted to remove Osceola and other chiefs. Overruled by President Jackson and condemned as tyrannical by the press, he made further efforts to break Osceola's power but was ambushed and slain by the chief and some of his followers.

THOMPSON, WILL LAMARTINE (*b. Beaver Co., Pa., 1847; d. New York, N.Y., 1909*), song writer and hymnist. Composer of "Softly and Tenderly Jesus Is Calling."

THOMPSON, WILLIAM (*b. Ireland, 1736; d. Carlise, Pa., 1781*), Revolutionary brigadier general. Commanded Pennsylvania riflemen (1st Continental Infantry) at siege of Boston. Made prisoner at attack on Three Rivers, Canada, June 1776, he was paroled and later exchanged for Baron Riedesel.

THOMPSON, WILLIAM BOYCE (*b. Virginia City, Mont., 1869; d. 1930*), mine operator, financier. Founded present Boyce Thompson Institute for Plant Research, 1919.

THOMPSON, WILLIAM GILMAN (*b. New York, N.Y., 1856; d. 1927*), physician. Son of Joseph P. Thompson; nephew of Daniel C. Gilman. Graduated Yale, 1877; M.D., N.Y. College of Physicians and Surgeons, 1881. Practiced in New York City; taught at medical schools of present New York University and Cornell University; served as director of the Loomis Laboratory *post* 1888. Best known for his work in reeducation in connection with war and industrial diseases, he was the founder of the N.Y. Reconstruction Hospital.

THOMPSON, WILLIAM HALE (*b. Boston, Mass., 1867; d. Chicago, Ill., 1944*), politician, demagogue. He attended a select preparatory school in Chicago until he was fourteen when he left for the West and worked as a ranch hand. He spent the winters in Chicago attending a business college. His wealthy family brought him a 3,800-acre ranch in Nebraska, but he returned to Chicago on the death of his father. He devoted most of his time to sporting pasttimes until 1899 when he ran for and was elected alderman. His political career was undistinguished, and he returned to private life and his sporting pursuits until 1915 when he was elected mayor. His administration was run by political boss Fred Lundin, who encouraged Thompson to run for the senate in 1918. He was defeated in the primary but was narrowly reelected mayor in 1919. He launched a large program of public works. Race riots and the indictment of his mentor Lundin for fraud caused his withdrawal from politics. He returned to politics in 1927 and with the support of Al Capone was elected mayor. He then embarked on a campaign to purge "pro-British" elements from the school board and school libraries of books favorable to Britain. He became the object of nationwide ridicule, and his alleged gangland connections cost him reelection in 1931. Isolationist, xenophobic, he was perhaps the most famous of America's urban demagogues.

THOMPSON, WILLIAM OXLEY (*b. Cambridge, Ohio, 1855; d. 1933*), Presbyterian clergyman. Graduated Muskingum College, 1878; Western Theological Seminary, 1882. President, Miami University, Oxford, Ohio, 1891–99; Ohio State University, 1899–1925.

THOMPSON, WILLIAM TAPPAN (*b. Ravenna, Ohio, 1812; d. Savannah, Ga., 1882*), journalist, humorist. Founder and editor of the *Savannah Morning News*, 1850–82. Author, among other works, of a series of humorous letters originally published in a Georgia periodical and later collected as *Major Jones's Courtship* (1843), *Major Jones's Chronicles of Pineville* (1843), and *Major Jones's Sketches of Travel* (1848).

THOMPSON, ZADOCK (*b. Bridgewater, Vt., 1796; d. Burlington, Vt., 1856*), educator, naturalist, mathematician. Author, among other works, of *History of Vermont, Natural, Civil and Statistical* (1842).

THOMSON, CHARLES (*b. Co. Derry, Ireland, 1729; d. near Philadelphia, Pa., 1824*), Philadelphia teacher and merchant. Secretary of the Continental Congress, 1774–89. Came to America as a boy; prospered in trade and was active in Pennsylvania provincial politics. Described as "the life of the cause of liberty" in Philadelphia, Thomson performed his task of minuting the birth records of the nation with fidelity and zeal. Disappointed in not receiving office under the new federal government, he retired to his estate, 1789, and devoted many years to biblical scholarship and translation.

THOMSON, EDWARD (*b. Portsea, England, 1810; d. Wheeling, W.Va., 1870*), physician, Methodist clergyman. Came to America as a boy; was raised in Ohio. First president, Ohio Wesleyan University, 1842–60, he was active also as an editor and in mission work. Elected bishop, 1864, he served until his death.

THOMSON, EDWARD WILLIAM (*b. Toronto, Canada, 1849; d. Boston, Mass., 1924*), Union soldier, Canadian and American journalist, poet.

THOMSON, ELIHU (*b. Manchester, England, 1853; d. Swampscott, Mass., 1937*), scientist, inventor. Came to America as a child. Graduated Philadelphia Central High School, 1870; taught chemistry, physics, and electricity there, 1870–76, and began a partnership with Edwin J. Houston. Their success in devising an efficient and salable arc-lighting system led to the formation (1883) of the Thomson-Houston Electric Co. at Lynn, Mass., with Thomson as chief engineer. The company soon dominated the industry. In 1892 it merged with the Edison General Electric Co. to form the General Electric Co. Thomson, remaining in Lynn as a consultant, pursued investigations in many fields; he obtained nearly 700 patents. The foremost scientist in the electrical manufacturing field, he was one of the first to recognize the importance of research to industrial progress.

THOMSON, FRANK (*b. Chambersburg, Pa., 1841; d. Merion, Pa., 1899*), railroad executive. Associated *post* 1858 with the Pennsylvania Railroad, he served as assistant to Thomas A. Scott during the Civil War in directing military transport. Elected president of the Pennsylvania, 1897, he served until his death.

THOMSON, JOHN (*b. Petersburg, Va., 1776; d. 1799*), lawyer, orator, political writer. A leader among Virginia Jeffersonians and close friend of John Randolph of Roanoke.

THOMSON, JOHN (*b. Fochabers, Scotland, 1853; d. Brooklyn, N.Y., 1926*), patent attorney, inventor. Came to America as an infant; was raised in Wayne Co., N.Y. Obtained basic patent for disk water meter, December 1887; held a number of other patents for improvements in watchmaking, printing presses, and zinc refining. Headed the Thomson Meter Co.

THOMSON, JOHN EDGAR (*b. Delaware Co., Pa., 1808; d. Philadelphia, Pa., 1874*), civil engineer, railroad executive, financier. A pioneer in railroad engineering, he served with the Georgia Railroad, 1832–47, and won high reputation for his work on the grades of the Pennsylvania Railroad, 1847–54. Elected president of the road, 1852, Thomson purchased a variety of lines projected by the state of Pennsylvania (1857), and by consolidation of other lines west of Pittsburgh extended his system to Chicago. In 1870–71 the Pennsylvania Co., one of the first of the holding companies, was created to control these additional parts of the system. Continuously engaged up to the time of his death in important projects that were to render the Pennsylvania safe from competitive attack, Thomson also insisted on high standards of operating practice.

THOMSON, MORTIMER NEAL (*b. Riga, N.Y., 1831; d. New York, N.Y., 1875*), journalist, humorist, known as "Q. K. Philander Doesticks." Author, *post* 1854, of humorous letters vivid with slang and terse, vigorous phrases which appeared first in the *Detroit Daily Advertiser*, the *New York Tribune*, and the *N.Y. Spirit of the Times*. Thomson served as a staff reporter for the *Tribune* during the Civil War and afterwards continued his successful career as a humorous lecturer.

THOMSON, SAMUEL (*b. Alstead, N.H., 1769; d. Boston, Mass., 1843*), botanic physician, originator of the "Thomsonian system" of treatment by vegetable remedies and the vapor bath.

THOMSON, WILLIAM (*b. possibly Pennsylvania, 1727; d. Sweet Springs, Va., 1796*), Revolutionary soldier. Raised in South Carolina, Thomson traded with the Indians, was an indigo planter, and was active in civic affairs and the militia. During the Revolution he rendered his greatest service at Fort Moultrie in June 1776, when, with his Rangers, he blocked the British attempt to land on Sullivan's Island.

THOMSON, WILLIAM McCLURE (*b. Spring Dale, Ohio, 1806; d. Denver, Colo., 1894*), Presbyterian clergyman, missionary in Syria. Author, among other books, of the widely selling *The Land and the Book* (1858, enlarged edition in 1880–85), a work which greatly increased knowledge of Palestine in English-speaking countries.

THORBURN, GRANT (*b. near Dalkeith, Scotland, 1773; d. New Haven, Conn., 1863*), seedsman, author. Immigrated to New York City, 1794. Beginning trade as a seedsman *ca.* 1803, he issued the first American seed catalogue, 1812. After the Scottish novelist John Galt told his life story in *Lawrie Todd* (1830), Thorburn assumed that title as a pen name for his numerous contributions to newspapers and magazines.

THOREAU, HENRY DAVID (*b.* *Concord, Mass.,* *1817; d.* *Concord, 1862*), essayist, poet, transcendentalist. Thoreau most resembled his Scotch maternal ancestors; on his father's side, the family derived from the Isle of Jersey and remotely from the French city of Tours. Delighting as a boy in hunting, fishing, and country sports, the young Thoreau took a passionate interest in nature; during his early maturity his journal entries on the subject were characterized by the ecstasy of pantheism, but in later life his observations became more objective and scientific. As an undergraduate at Harvard, 1833–37, he entered little into college life, went to chapel in a green coat "because the rules required black" and solaced himself in the college library with the writings of the 17th-century English poets. He began keeping a journal in 1834 and continued the practice until the end of his life. At college he was particularly influenced by Edward T. Channing and Jones Very. After graduation he taught in the Concord town school and helped his father in what had become the family industry of pencil making; with his brother John he conducted a private school at Concord, 1838–41.

In September 1839, he and his brother made a thirteen-day voyage down the Concord River and up the Merrimack, immortalized later by Henry in his first book. After the closing of their school because of John's bad health, Henry lived for two years with R. W. Emerson, so beginning their long friendship; he also began meeting the group now known as the Transcendental Club and became acquainted with F. H. Hedge, A. Bronson Alcott, James F. Clarke, George Ripley, Margaret Fuller, and Elizabeth P. Peabody. While employed as a tutor on Staten Island, N.Y., in the home of William Emerson from spring 1843 to spring 1844, he came to know William H. Channing, Lucretia Mott, Henry James, Sr., and Horace Greeley, meanwhile seeking unsuccessfully to sell articles to the magazines.

Between July 4, 1845, and Sept. 6, 1847, he lived in a small house on Emerson's land on the northwest shore of Walden Pond, Concord, which he regarded as a retreat suitable for philosophic meditation and the practice of a simple, healthy life. During the summer of 1845 he was arrested for nonpayment of poll tax as a gesture of "civil disobedience" in protest against slavery and the Mexican War. After one night in jail he was released, the tax being paid by one of his aunts; the incident underlay his essay "Resistance to Civil Government" (later called "Civil Disobedience") first published in Elizabeth Peabody's *Aesthetic Papers* (1849) and retold in *Walden.* Thoreau regarded his two-year experiment in simple living as a success since it gave him leisure to think and write. On coming back to Concord village and his father's house in the autumn of 1847, he brought with him the first draft of his book *A Week on the Concord and Merrimack Rivers,* notes on life and literature gleaned from his journals and strung on a thread of narrative. He brought back also new journals to be used in the preparation of *Walden* six years later. He resided in Emerson's house through 1848 and published *Week on the Concord* at his own risk in the spring of 1849. Slightly over 200 copies were sold, and in 1853 three-quarters of the original thousand copies came back to the author. Early in 1849 he returned to live in his father's house and resided there during the rest of his life, participating in the family business and sharing in its delightful social life. Late in 1849 he toured Cape Cod, in 1850 he spent a week in Canada and in 1853 went on his second journey into Maine. From these expeditions derive in part his *Excursions* (1863), *The Maine Woods* (1864), *Cape Cod* (1865), and *A Yankee in Canada* (1866), all posthumous.

Between 1847 and 1851 he took keen delight in daily walks about Concord and thought of himself happily as a poet. However, he grew involved in the slavery question once again in October 1851, and showed a growing distrust also of the rising New England industrialism with its concomitant problems of labor.

These new concerns and his new critical attitude are found in *Walden, or Life in the Woods* (finished during 1853 and published Aug. 9, 1854). Seemingly parochial in its comment on the society of Concord, it had universal social criticism in it and struck blows at all the superficialities of society and government. At first blush a harmless study of nature, it was at once disarming and devastating. Subsequent to *Walden's* publication, Thoreau's life was anticlimactic and he became more the scientific observer than the poet of nature. He made his last trip to Cape Cod in 1855 and a last journey to Maine in 1857. Tuberculosis began to ravage him. Among friends whom he made in this period were John Brown of Osawatomie (met in Emerson's house, March 1857) and Walt Whitman whom he had met in New York the previous autumn. Thoreau's life burned out in a great enthusiasm, the defense of John Brown after his arrest in October 1859. He was the first American to make public utterance in defense of Brown, speaking at Concord on October 30 and in Boston on November 1. To him the John Brown affair was a touchstone which had tested and exposed the true nature of the American government.

Thoreau made a long journey to Minnesota seeking health in the spring of 1861, but returned home weaker than when he had left; his last days were spent feverishly editing manuscripts which he left for his sister, Sophia, to publish. The posthumous books already mentioned were drawn from this huge mass of manuscript material. His journal which had already served as quarry for himself was later the source for *Early Spring in Massachusetts* (1881), *Summer* (1884), *Winter* (1888), and *Autumn* (1892). Collected editions of his work were published in 1894 and 1906.

Thoreau's influence upon later literature, both English and American, is due in great part to his effective, usually staccato, although often poetically rhythmic, style. His ideas were presented with the pith and force of a man who is more concerned with incisive thought than with sustained argument and cares more for his sentences than for his essays as a whole. He is a master of the single vivid image. At his best, he is among the finest of American prose writers, but he is most impressive when he is read in excerpts. Of all his books, only *Walden* is really organized; the other books are material from his Journals, either padded out with reflections or left in their original leanness. His observations of nature are characterized not so much by their accuracy as by a tension that gives them at their best a splendid force, for he was always deeply perceptive of spirit manifest in form. *Walden* is his greatest achievement. It is a complete report of an experiment in thinking and living whose purpose is to argue for true values against false and to show that civilized man can escape the evils of competition and be independent of commercialism and industrialism. Although Thoreau has been called anarchistic or antisocial, it would be more accurate to describe him as one who, urging conscience above government and determined to rely upon himself before relying upon others, proposed to obey a set of laws which he regarded as more fundamental than those enforced by his particular state. His essay on civil disobedience is a classic of individualism in its inevitable conflict with government, but by no means proposes to do away with fundamental laws whose existence supports what is noblest and most worthily human. Essentially a man of letters with a touch of the prophet, Thoreau belongs with Walt Whitman as one who having put his own definition upon morality exhorted to the moral life. Both men are at the heart of the persistent American tradition of perfectibility, although Thoreau leans to the pessimistic, Whitman to the optimistic view of the matter.

THOREK, MAX (*b.* *Hungary, 1880; d.* *Chicago, Ill, 1960*), surgeon. Immigrated to the U.S. in 1897. Studied at the University of Chicago, and at Rush Medical College, M.D., 1904. Founded the American Hospital (now the Thorek Hospital and Medical Center) in Chicago, 1911. A controversial figure, Thorek was interested in mammoplasty, surgical reconstruction of the female body, and gonadal transplantation. Author of *The Human Testis* (1924) and *Plastic Surgery of the Breast and the Abdominal Wall* (1942). Founded the International College of Surgeons in Geneva in 1935.

THORNDIKE, ASHLEY HORACE (*b. Houlton, Maine, 1871; d. 1933*), educator, scholar. Brother of Edward L. and Lynn Thorndike. Graduated Wesleyan University, 1893; Ph.D., Harvard, 1898. Taught English at Boston University, Western Reserve, and Northwestern; professor of English, Columbia, 1906–33. An authority on the Elizabethan drama, he was author, among other works, of *Tragedy* (1908), *Shakespeare's Theatre* (1916), and *English Comedy* (1929). He was coeditor of "The Tudor Shakespeare," 1913–15.

THORNDIKE, EDWARD LEE (*b. Williamsburg, Mass., 1874; d. Montrose, N.Y., 1949*), educational psychologist. Brother of Ashley H. and Lynn Thorndike. B.A., Wesleyan University, 1895. B.A. Harvard, 1896; M.A., 1897. Influenced by William James, he began graduate work in psychology, pioneering in the use of animals for psychological research. In 1897–98 a fellowship brought Thorndike to Columbia, where he worked primarily under James McKeen Cattell and Franz Boas; he derived from both a lifelong interest in the quantitative treatment of psychological data. He completed work for the doctorate in 1898 with his thesis, "Animal Intelligence," which inaugurated the scientific study of animal learning and laid the foundation for a dynamic psychology emphasizing stimulus-response connections (known as "S-R bonds") as the central factors in all learning. After a year at the College for Women of Western Reserve University, Thorndike came to Teachers College, Columbia University, in 1899 as instructor in genetic psychology and remained there for the rest of his life, earning the title adjunct professor in 1901, professor in 1904, and professor emeritus in 1941.

From the beginning, Thorndike's work was precise, systematic, and original; and it quickly came to symbolize his generation's commitment to developing a true science of education. Out of his experiments came a new theory of learning and a series of "laws" founded on that theory. The theory maintained that learning involves the joining of a specific stimulus to a specific response through a neural bond, so that the stimulus regularly calls forth the response. From this followed Thorndike's primary law of learning, the "law of effect," namely, that a satisfactory outcome of any response tends to "stamp out" the bond or connection. Thorndike was able to avoid the age-old problem of defining mind by simply eliminating it as a separate entity. He also discarded the biblical, Rousseauean, and Lockean views of human nature arguing that human nature is nothing more or less than a mass of "original tendencies" in man, as these are subsequently modified by learning. He emphasized activity as the basic pedagogical principle. His work lent strong support for more individualized and utilitarian approaches to education and thus served the cause of reformers who were seeking to introduce greater flexibility into education.

Thorndike may well have been the most influential educational theorist of the early twentieth century. He developed some of the earliest and most widely used American tests of aptitude and achievement. He prepared a series of arithmetics, and his *Teacher's World Book* (1921) was the foundation for the most important series of school readers to appear between the two world wars. (He also compiled a set of dictionaries for school use.) More generally, his laws of learning led to a fundamental rethinking of the entire school curriculum and affected everything from organization of course content to techniques for appraising student progress. His studies of adult learning, after 1925, opened up the field of adult education.

THORNDIKE, ISRAEL (*b. Beverly, Mass., 1755; d. Boston, Mass., 1832*), Revolutionary privateersman, merchant, Massachusetts legislator. An early participant in post–Revolutionary American trade with the Orient.

THORNDIKE, LYNN (*b. Lynn, Mass., 1882; d. New York, N.Y., 1965*), medieval historian, historian of science. Attended Wesleyan University (B.A., 1902) and Columbia (M.A., 1903; Ph.D., 1905). Taught at Northwestern University (1907–09) and Western Reserve University (until 1924) before accepting a professorship of history at Columbia University in 1924; he remained at Columbia for twenty-six years, training many American medievalists at his seminar. His *History of Medieval Europe* (1917; second revision 1949) was, in its earliest form, one of the most popular textbooks of its day. But his international reputation rests chiefly on A *History of Magic and Experimental Science* (1923–58), a masterly eight-volume exploration of the relationship between magic and science. Other major contributions to medieval scholarship include A *Catalogue of Incipits of Mediaeval Scientific Writings in Latin* (1937; rev. and enl., 1963). He helped organize the History of Science Society in 1924 and was elected to the Mediaeval Academy of America in 1926.

THORNE, CHARLES ROBERT (*b. New York, N.Y., ca. 1814; d. San Francisco, Calif., 1893*), actor, theatrical manager. Father of Charles R. Thorne (1840–1883).

THORNE, CHARLES ROBERT (*b. New York, N.Y., 1840; d. New York, 1883*), actor. Son of Charles R. Thorne (*ca. 1814–1893*). Popular for many years in heroic roles in domestic melodrama.

THORNTON, HENRY WORTH (*b. Logansport, Ind., 1871; d. New York, N.Y., 1933*), railroad executive. Efficient in management of several American railroads and of the Great Eastern Railway of England. Thornton served with great ability in the British military transport service during World War I and was the directing genius and president of the Canadian National Railways, 1922–32.

THORNTON, JESSY QUINN (*b. near Point Pleasant, present W. Va., 1810; d. Salem, Oreg., 1888*), lawyer, Oregon pioneer. Removed to Oregon, 1846; was associated with Joseph L. Meek in urging (at Washington, D.C., 1848) the establishment of a territorial government for Oregon. Author of *Oregon and California in 1848* (1849).

THORNTON, JOHN WINGATE (*b. Saco, Maine, 1818; d. Scarboro, Maine, 1878*), Boston lawyer, historian, antiquary. A founder of the New England Historic Genealogical Society and of the Prince Society, he had a part in the rediscovery of the manuscript of Bradford's history "Of Plimoth Plantation" and obtained the Trelawny papers for the Maine Historical Society. He was author, among other works, of *The Landing at Cape Ann* (1854) and *The Pulpit of the American Revolution* (1860).

THORNTON, MATTHEW (*b. Ireland, ca. 1714; d. Newburyport, Mass., 1803*), physician, Revolutionary patriot, New Hampshire legislator. Came to America as a boy. Began to practice medicine in Londonderry, N.H., ca. 1740. Prominent in pre-Revolutionary activity and president of the New Hampshire provincial congress of 1775, Thornton continued active as legislator and jurist during the Revolution. Elected to the Continental Congress, 1776, he was a signer of the Declaration of Independence; he served about one year.

THORNTON, WILLIAM (*b. Jost van Dyke, V.I., 1759; d. Washington, D.C., 1828*), architect, inventor, public official. Studied medicine at Edinburgh and Aberdeen. Coming to America, 1787, he became a citizen and a resident of Philadelphia, Pa. An architect by avocation, he was associated with John Fitch in steamboat experimentation and was designer in 1789 of the Library Company of Philadelphia building on Fifth St. He is remembered chiefly as the successful competitor for the design of the U.S. Capitol, Washington, D.C., and for his defense of the design against the efforts of other architects and structural superintendents to alter it. He was also designer of the "Octagon House" (1798–1800) in Washington, of Tudor Place in Georgetown, D.C., and of Brentwood in the District of Columbia, all of which show a plastic and spatial variety and mastery rarely found in America before their time. Pavilion VII at the University of Virginia was built from a sketch by Thornton. Appointed superintendent of patents, 1802, he served in that post until his death. Among other activities in which he engaged were the education of the deaf, the work of the American Colonization Society and the liberation of the Spanish colonies in South America.

THORNWELL, JAMES HENLEY (*b. Marlboro District, S.C., 1812; d. Columbia, S.C., 1862*), Presbyterian clergyman, educator. A teacher at South Carolina College for the greater part of the years 1837–51, he served as its president, 1851–55. Thereafter, professor of theology at the Presbyterian Seminary at Columbia, he was a leading spirit in organization of the Presbyterian Church in the Confederate States.

THORP, JOHN (*b. probably Rehoboth, Mass., 1784; d. North Wrentham, Mass., 1848*), machinist. Obtained first patent in March 1812 for a hand and water loom; patented a power loom, October 1816. In November and December 1828 he received the basic patents for the continuous method of spinning, covering improvements in spinning and twisting cotton, now called "ring spinning." He also patented a netting machine (1828) and a narrow fabric loom (1829).

THORPE, JAMES FRANCIS (*b. Prague, Indian Territory [now Oklahoma], 1888; d. Lomita, Calif., 1953*), athlete. Studied at Carlisle Indian School in Pennsylvania. Considered by many to be the greatest football player and one of the greatest athletes in modern history. Played football for Carlisle, 1908–09, helping that college defeat the University of Pennsylvania and Harvard. Won four out of five possible events at the 1912 Olympics but, because of his having played professional baseball, was disqualified as an Olympic athlete and returned his honors. Played on the New York Giants baseball team, 1913–16. Helped found the National Football League, 1922.

THORPE, ROSE ALNORA HARTWICK (*b. Mishawaka, Ind., 1850; d. San Diego, Calif., 1939*), poet, author of children's books. Her most celebrated work "Curfew Must Not Ring Tonight" was first published in the Detroit (Mich.) *Commercial Advertiser*, 1870; a collection of her poems was published in 1912.

THORPE, THOMAS BANGS (*b. Westfield, Mass., 1815; d. New York, N.Y., 1878*), artist, humorist. Resident in Louisiana *ca.* 1836–53, Thorpe won reputation as a painter of prairie life and as a portraitist. *Post* 1853 he resided principally in New York City, contributed to periodicals, and held public offices. He is remembered particularly today for his realistic sketches in prose of Southern frontier life; of these the most important was the "Big Bear of Arkansas," first published in the N.Y. *Spirit of the Times*, Mar. 27, 1841. A tall tale, and the first great piece of genuinely "Western" humor, it appeared in book form in the anthology edited by William T. Porter, *The Big Bear of Arkansas* (1845). Other specimens of his work were collected in *Mysteries of the Backwoods* (1846) and *The Hive of the Bee-Hunter* (1854). Thorpe was author also of a number of works of contemporary journalistic appeal.

THRASHER, JOHN SIDNEY (*b. Portland, Maine, 1817; d. Galveston, Tex., 1879*), journalist, adventurer. Noted as a proslavery protagonist of the purchase of Cuba, Thrasher was also concerned in several attempts at armed intervention there, among them the activities of John A. Quitman in 1852 and after.

THROOP, ENOS THOMPSON (*b. Johnstown, N.Y., 1784; d. 1874*), lawyer, New York jurist and politician. Uncle of Montgomery H. Throop. Elected lieutenant governor of New York (Democrat) 1828, he became acting governor in March 1829 and after election in 1830 held the post until 1833.

THROOP, MONTGOMERY HUNT (*b. Auburn, N.Y., 1827; d. Albany, N.Y., 1892*), lawyer, legal writer. Nephew of Enos T. Throop and also of Ward Hunt. Partner at various times of his uncle Hunt and of Roscoe Conkling, Throop was a strong Democrat and opposed coercion of the South during Reconstruction. Chairman of a commission to revise the New York statutes, he was principal author of the 1877 *Code of Civil Procedure* and thereafter devoted most of his time to legal authorship.

THULSTRUP, BROR THURE (*b. Stockholm, Sweden, 1848; d. New York, N.Y., 1930*), artist, illustrator. After military training and service in Sweden and with the French Foreign Legion, he immigrated to Canada in the early 1870's, but soon removed to the United States where he was successful for many years as a painter of military subjects.

THUMB, TOM. *See* STRATTON, CHARLES SHERWOOD.

THURBER, CHARLES (*b. East Brookfield, Mass., 1803; d. Nashua, N.H., 1886*), teacher, inventor, manufacturer. Received a U.S. patent in August 1843 for a hand printing machine which was the first invention that approximated the modern typewriter.

THURBER, CHRISTOPHER CARSON (*b. Norwich, Conn., 1880; d. Greece, 1930*), social worker. Performed heroic service for the Near East Relief organization in Turkey and Greece *post* 1921.

THURBER, GEORGE (*b. Providence, R.I., 1821; d. Passaic, N.J., 1890*), botanist, horticulturist. Served as botanist on Mexican Boundary Survey, 1850–53; editor, *American Agriculturist*, 1863–85. One of the earliest exponents of agricultural botany, he was a specialist in study of the grasses.

THURBER, JAMES GROVER (*b. Columbus, Ohio, 1894; d. New York, N.Y., 1961*), writer, cartoonist. Attended Ohio State University. Began his journalistic career as a reporter on the Columbus *Evening Dispatch* (1920). In 1927 he met E. B. White, who introduced him to *New Yorker* editor Harold Ross, and Thurber then joined the magazine's staff. In 1929 White and Thurber collaborated on *Is Sex Necessary?*. This was followed by *The Seal in the Bedroom* (1932), a book of Thurber cartoons, and *My Life and Hard Times* (1933). Further establishing his reputation as an illustrator and humorist were "The Secret Life of Walter Mitty" (*New Yorker*, March 18, 1939), *Fables for Our Time* (1940), and *My World—and Welcome to It* (1942). Later in his career he experimented with fantasy and fairy tale, as typified by *The 13 Clocks* (1950) and *The Wonderful O* (1957). In 1960 he appeared on Broadway in *A Thurber Carnival*, based on his literary sketches and cartoon captions.

THURBER, JEANNETTE MEYER (*b. New York, N.Y., 1850; d. Bronxville, N.Y., 1946*), patron of music. Founded National Conservatory of Music, 1885; American Opera Company, 1886. Sought to secure federal support for the Conservatory as a national institution.

THURE DE THULSTRUP. *See* THULSTRUP, BROR THURE.

THURMAN, ALLEN GRANBERRY (*b. Lynchburg, Va., 1813; d. Columbus, Ohio, 1895*), lawyer, Ohio jurist. Studied law with his uncle William Allen (1803–1879), and with Noah H. Swayne. Long active in Democratic politics in Ohio, he served in the U.S. House of Representatives, 1845–47, and was chief justice of the supreme court of Ohio, 1854–56. Opposing federal interference in the question of slavery in the territories, he was a leader of the "Peace Democrats" during the Civil War although an opponent of the doctrine of secession. Serving as U.S. senator, 1867–79, he was a partisan Democrat of the school of Jefferson, a valuable member of the judiciary committee and chairman of that committee in the 46th Congress. He is best remembered as author of the Thurman Act relating to the Pacific railroads; he ran unsuccessfully for vice president on the Democratic ticket, 1888.

THURSBY, EMMA CECILIA (*b. Brooklyn, N.Y., 1845; d. New York, N.Y., 1931*), singer, voice teacher. One of the first American singers to win international fame and a noted interpreter of Mozart, she was teacher, among others, of Geraldine Farrar.

THURSTON, HOWARD (*b. Columbus, Ohio, 1869; d. Miami, Fla., 1936*), magician. Influenced in choice of his profession by example of Alexander Herrmann, Thurston played for many years with trifling success until a triumphant engagement at Tony Pastor's theater in New York City, 1899. Attractive in his personality and a fine showman who contrived his effects regardless of expense, Thurston was a leading performer in vaudeville, 1908–30, thereafter playing principally in motion-picture theaters.

THURSTON, LORRIN ANDREWS (*b. Honolulu, Hawaii, 1858; d. 1931*), lawyer, Hawaii official. Grandson of Lorrin Andrews. A leader in the movement to overthrow the native Hawaiian government and annex the islands to the United States, Thurston drafted the 1893 proclamation of the provisional government and headed the commission sent to Washington to secure annexation. He was prominent thereafter in industry and the tourist business and was owner-editor of the *Honolulu Advertiser.*

THURSTON, ROBERT HENRY (*b. Providence, R.I., 1839; d. Ithaca, N.Y., 1903*), engineer, educator. Son of Robert L. Thurston. Graduated Brown, 1859. Rose to rank of first assistant engineer, U.S. Navy, during Civil War service; headed department of natural and experimental philosophy, U.S. Naval Academy, 1866–71. Devised pioneer four-year course of instruction in mechanical engineering (including both a mechanical laboratory and shop courses) which became basis for curriculum at Stevens Institute of Technology where he served as professor of mechanical engineering, 1871–85. Developer of further innovating courses and techniques of instruction, he was author also of textbooks (notably *The Materials of Engineering,* 1883–84), manuals, and technical papers in many fields. Director of Sibley College, Cornell University, 1885–1903, he worked tirelessly to develop the college and its department of experimental engineering; he himself taught the courses in thermodynamics and steam engineering.

THURSTON, ROBERT LAWTON (*b. Portsmouth, R.I., 1800; d. 1874*), pioneer manufacturer of steam engines. Father of Robert H. Thurston. Partner, *post* 1830, in the Providence Steam Engine Co. and successor firms, he was first manufacturer of engines to employ the Sickels "drop cut-off" and to build a standard form of expansion steam engine.

THURSTONE, LOUIS LEON (*b. Chicago, Ill., 1887; d. Chapel Hill, N.C., 1955*), psychologist. Graduated from Cornell University and the University of Chicago, Ph.D., 1917. Taught at the Carnegie Institute of Technology, 1915–24; and at the University of Chicago, 1924–52. Established a psychometric laboratory in 1930. President of the American Psychological Association, 1932–33. A specialist in developing and applying mathematical means of measuring mental activity, Thurstone developed many tests for the army and the American Council of Education. At Chicago, he worked on the measurement of intelligence, approaching it as a problem in multiple correlation. Wrote *The Vectors of Mind* (1935) and *Multiple-Factor Analysis* (1947). Also did work in the measurement of mental stimulation. Founded a psychometric laboratory at the University of North Carolina, 1952.

THWAITES, REUBEN GOLD (*b. Dorchester, Mass., 1853; d. Madison, Wis., 1913*), journalist, librarian, editor. Removed to Wisconsin, 1866. Managing editor of the *Wisconsin State Journal,* 1876–86, he became a friend and protégé of Lyman C. Draper who recommended him in 1886 for the post of secretary of the Wisconsin State Historical Society. Taking office in 1887, he built up the Society's manuscript collections (in 1891 adding the Draper Manuscripts) and generally made the Society a great center for historical research. During his tenure he produced a yearly volume of the Society's *Proceedings* and a biennial volume of *Collections* and did a vast amount of other editorial work. Among projects supervised by him were the *Jesuit Relations and Allied Documents* (73 vols., 1896–1901), *Original Journals of the Lewis and Clark Expedition* (8 vols., 1904–05), *Early Western Travels* (32 vols. of annotated reprints, 1904–07). He was author also of a number of works including *France in America* (1905) and *Wisconsin* (1908).

THWING, CHARLES FRANKLIN (*b. New Sharon, Maine, 1853; d. Cleveland, Ohio, 1937*), Congregational clergyman, educator. Graduated Harvard, 1876; Andover Theological Seminary, 1879. Presided ably over great expansion of Western Reserve University while president, 1890–1921, establishing schools of law, dentistry, pharmacy, applied social science and also a graduate school in liberal arts. He also affiliated the university with the city in developing the Cleveland School of Education. He was a prolific writer on educational and historical subjects.

THYE, EDWARD JOHN (*b. Frederick, S.Dak., 1896; d. near Northfield, Minn., 1969*), governor of Minnesota, U.S. senator. Attended the American Business College (1914–16). A farmer for his entire life, Thye achieved statewide political prominence in 1938 when Harold Stassen, the governor of Minnesota, appointed him deputy commissioner of agriculture. He was elected Minnesota's lieutenant governor in 1942, succeeding Stassen as governor when the latter resigned to serve in the Navy in 1943. Thye was elected to a full term as governor in 1944; in 1947 he was elected to the U.S. Senate, serving there until 1959, but always remaining close to his farm roots. He was defeated for a third term in the Senate by Eugene J. McCarthy.

TIBBETT, LAWRENCE MERVIL (*b. Bakersfield, Calif., 1896; d. New York, N.Y., 1960*), baritone. American-trained, Tibbett made his Metropolitan Opera debut in 1923 in *Boris Godunov*; received tremendous acclaim in 1925, substituting in the role of Ford in Verdi's *Falstaff.* Sang with the Metropolitan until 1950, performing 559 times. A superb singer, Tibbett was one of the first Americans to achieve an international reputation. Helped found the American Guild of Musical Artists in 1936; president, 1940–52; honorary president, 1952–60.

TIBBLES, SUSETTE LA FLESCHE. *See* BRIGHT EYES.

TIBBLES, THOMAS HENRY (*b. Washington Co., Ohio, 1838; d. Omaha, Nebr., 1928*), journalist, social reformer, friend of the Indians, Populist leader.

TICHENOR, ISAAC (*b. Newark, N.J., 1754; d. Bennington, Vt., 1838*), lawyer, Vermont legislator and jurist. U.S. senator, Federalist, from Vermont, 1796–97. Served with tact and intelligence as governor of his state, 1797–1807, 1808–09. Once again U.S. senator, 1815–21, he played no prominent part in national affairs.

TICHENOR, ISAAC TAYLOR (*b. Spencer Co., Ky., 1825; d. Atlanta, Ga., 1902*), Baptist clergyman, Confederate chaplain, educator. Held principal pastorate in Montgomery, Ala.; first president, Alabama State Agricultural and Mechanical College, 1872–82; secretary, Southern Baptist Home Missionary Board.

TICKNOR, ELISHA (*b. Lebanon, Conn., 1757; d. Hanover, N.H., 1821*), Boston, Mass., educator and merchant. Father of George Ticknor. Urged improvement in public school system, especially establishment of free schools for children under 7 years of age.

TICKNOR, FRANCIS ORRAY (*b. Fortville, Ga., 1822; d. 1874*), physician, poet. Long in practice in rural Georgia, Ticknor was author of a number of poems including the Confederate heroic ballad "Little Giffen" and possibly "The Barefooted Boys." An incomplete collected edition of his work appeared as *Poems of Frank D. Ticknor, M.D.* (ed. Kate M. Rowland, 1879).

TICKNOR, GEORGE (*b. Boston, Mass., 1791; d. Boston, 1871*), educator, author. Son of Elisha Ticknor. Graduated Dartmouth, 1807. A man of independent means, Ticknor abandoned practice of the law for a career as a scholar. Between 1815 and 1819 he traveled widely in Europe, calling on leading scientists, scholars, and men of letters and pursuing formal studies mainly at the University of Göttingen. One of the first students from the United States to attend German institutions of learning for the expressed purpose of obtaining a university training more advanced than that to be had at home, Ticknor at first devoted himself to Greek philology. On appointment to the Smith professorship of French and Spanish at Harvard with an added professorship of *belles lettres* (accepted by him, November 1817), he made special studies in France, Italy, and Spain. In August 1819 he was inducted into the professorship which he was to hold until 1835. A leader in efforts to broaden the stereotyped curriculum at Harvard, he proposed a division of the college into departments which would handle related subjects of study. He succeeded, however, only in making this method of organization official for his own modern language courses and resigned in favor of Henry W. Longfellow. After further travel in Europe and a long process of research, he published in 1849 his classic *History of Spanish Literature*, the first truly scholarly survey ever produced of the whole range of Spanish letters and a seminal work in later Hispanic studies. He was an active benefactor of the Boston Public Library and was author also of a number of other books, but his reputation rests on his pioneer work in Spanish literature.

TICKNOR, WILLIAM DAVIS (*b. Lebanon, N.H., 1810; d. Philadelphia, Pa., 1864*), publisher. Cousin of George Ticknor. Headed the leading New England publishing firm of its time (in which James T. Fields early became a junior partner) known successively as Allen and Ticknor (1832–33), William D. Ticknor and Co. (1833–49), Ticknor, Reed and Fields (1849–54), and Ticknor and Fields. Publisher of the *Atlantic Monthly* and of many of the leading contemporary writers of England and America. Ticknor was a close friend of Nathaniel Hawthorne.

TIDBALL, JOHN CALDWELL (*b. Ohio Co., present W. Va., 1825; d. 1906*), Union major general of volunteers by brevet. Graduated West Point, 1848. An artillery expert, he served principally with the Army of the Potomac during the Civil War and showed outstanding skill in management of artillery in support of cavalry as well as in siege work. He retired as colonel, regular army, 1889.

TIEBOUT, CORNELIUS (*b. New York, N.Y., 1777; d. New Harmony, Ind., ca. 1832*), line and stipple engraver. Apprenticed to a goldsmith in New York City, Tiebout received training in London, 1793–96. After working in New York City, 1796–99, he removed to Philadelphia where he remained active until about 1825 and was in partnership, 1817–22, with Benjamin Tanner and Francis Kearny in banknote engraving. In 1826, he removed with William Maclure to New Harmony, where he taught in the community school.

TIEDEMAN, CHRISTOPHER GUSTAVUS *b. Charleston, S.C., 1857; d. Buffalo, N.Y., 1903*), professor of law, writer of legal treatises and textbooks. Taught at University of Missouri and present New York University; dean, University of Buffalo Law School, 1902–03.

TIERNAN, FRANCES CHRISTINE FISHER (*b. Salisbury, N.C., 1846; d. Salisbury, 1920*), novelist, author. Devoted to the Confederacy and to her Catholic religion, she was author of some fifty now-forgotten novels including *Valerie Aylmer* (1870, under pseudonym of Christian Reid) and *Carmela* (1891).

TIERNEY, RICHARD HENRY (*b. Spuyten Duyvil, N.Y., 1870; d. New York, N.Y., 1928*), Roman Catholic clergyman, Jesuit, journalist. Liberal and aggressive editor of the weekly *America*, 1914–25.

TIFFANY, CHARLES LEWIS (*b. Killingly, Conn., 1812; d. Yonkers, N.Y., 1902*), jeweler. Opened a stationery and notion store in New York City, 1837, which through successive partnerships became the famous Tiffany & Co., 1853. Thenceforward until his death he was considered leader of the jewelry trade in America.

TIFFANY, KATRINA BRANDES ELY (*b. Altoona, Pa., 1875; d. New York, N.Y., 1927*), civic worker, social reformer. Daughter-in-law of Louis C. Tiffany. Graduated Bryn Mawr, 1897. A leader in charitable work, the suffrage movement, and the New York League of Women Voters.

TIFFANY, LOUIS COMFORT (*b. New York, N.Y., 1848; d. New York, 1933*), painter, glassmaker, philanthropist. Son of Charles L. Tiffany. Studied with George Inness and Samuel Colman; later studied in Paris. Organized Society of American Artists, 1877, with John La Farge, Augustus Saint-Gaudens, and others. Possessed of an oriental love of color, he began experiments with stained glass, 1875, and devised a process of his own for production of what he called "Favrile glass" which brought him great popular reputation. His largest work in this medium was the curtain for the National Theatre, Mexico City; he was also a designer of jewelry, rugs, and textiles and a patron of other artists.

TIFFANY, LOUIS MCLANE (*b. Baltimore, Md., 1844; d. 1916*), surgeon. Grandson of Louis McLane. M.D., University of Maryland, 1868; studied in office of Nathan R. Smith. A teacher at Maryland, 1869–1902, he was a pioneer in many fields; he is credited with performing the first nephrolithotomy in America and the first successful gastroenterostomy in Baltimore (October 1892). For many years he dominated surgical thought and practice in Maryland.

TIFFIN, EDWARD (*b. Carlisle, England, 1766; d. probably Chillicothe, Ohio, 1829*), physician, Ohio legislator and jurist, public official. Immigrated to present Jefferson Co., W. Va., 1784; attended Jefferson Medical College, Philadelphia, Pa.; removed to Chillicothe, Ohio, 1798. A leader of Ohio (Democrat)

Republicans, he served as the first governor of Ohio, 1803–06, and as U.S. senator, 1807–09. As commissioner of the General Land Office, 1812–14, he brought order out of its chaotic records and surveys. Thereafter until death, he served as surveyor general of the Northwest.

TIGERT, JOHN JAMES (*b. Louisville, Ky., 1856; d. Tulsa, Okla., 1906*), clergyman of the Methodist Episcopal Church, South, educator and editor.

TIGERT, JOHN JAMES (*b. Nashville, Tenn., 1882; d. Gainesville, Fla., 1965*), professor, U.S. commissioner of education, and university president. Attended Vanderbilt University (B.A., 1904) and Oxford University (B.A. in jurisprudence, 1907; M.A., 1915). The grandson of the first president of Vanderbilt, Tigert began his academic career as professor of philosophy and psychology at Central College in Fayette, Mo. (1907). Became president of Kentucky Wesleyan College (1909), then joined the University of Kentucky as professor of philosophy and psychology (1911). Appointed U.S. commissioner of education in 1921, the youngest man to have held that office. In 1928 became president of the University of Florida at Gainesville, a post he held for nineteen years. Under Tigert, the university conferred its first Ph.D. degrees (1934). His greatest curriculum innovation was creating the General College to provide general arts and sciences instruction for all freshmen and sophomores.

TIKAMTHI. *See* TECUMSEH.

TILDEN, SAMUEL JONES (*b. New Lebanon, N.Y., 1814; d. Yonkers, N.Y., 1886*), lawyer, statesman. Acquainted as a boy with Martin Van Buren, Silas Wright, William L. Marcy, and other Democratic leaders of the time, Tilden grew up in frail health and received a somewhat sporadic formal education. He attended Yale for one term in 1834 and then attended the University of the City of New York (present New York University) but concerned himself mainly for several years with writing political treatises for newspapers in support of Van Buren's policies. After attending the law school of the University of the City of New York, 1838–41, and simultaneously clerking in the office of John W. Edmonds, he was admitted to the bar and began practice in New York City, 1841. He soon became a commanding figure in the New York Democracy and a leader of the free-soil opposition group called "Barnburners." Divorced from practical leadership in the party because of the resultant split of the Democratic factions, he turned his energies to the development of his law practice and was conspicuously successful in many complex cases, showing a peculiar genius for railroad reorganization and refinancing. In this way, and through acquisition of mining interests, he laid the foundation of his later enormous fortune.

Tilden opposed Lincoln's election and disapproved of the Civil War from the beginning, but at the declaration of war advised E. M. Stanton to call out immediately the full military strength of the North and so crush the rebellion by a swift stroke. Thereafter, he encouraged the Democratic party in its "constitutional opposition" to the powerful centralized Washington government. He favored President Andrew Johnson's liberal policy of Reconstruction. As chairman of the New York State Democratic committee, 1866–74, he performed the great service of ousting William M. Tweed and his "ring," leading the battle for adequate legislation with which to fight the situation in New York City and aiding in the production of the necessary judicial proof. He was responsible also at this time for reforming and purifying the state judiciary. As governor of New York, 1875–77, he continued his efforts for reform, brought about a substantial reduction in state taxes and expenses, and broke the so-called "Canal ring," a bipartisan group of thieving politicians who had battened on the repair and extension of the state canal system.

Having fired the imagination of the country by his reform activities, he was nominated by the Democrats for the presidency at St. Louis, Mo., June 1876; Thomas A. Hendricks ran with him for vice president. After a campaign of exceptional bitterness, Tilden received a majority of the popular vote, but lost the election when the doubtful states of Oregon, Louisiana, South Carolina, and Florida were claimed by the Republican managers for their candidate, Rutherford B. Hayes. A controversy followed which was resolved by creation of an Electoral Commission containing a majority of one in favor of the Republicans. By a strict party vote, the Commission declared in favor of Hayes's claim. Tilden acquiesced in the decision only as an escape from a renewal of civil war. Remaining to the end of his life a significant figure in national politics, Tilden left the bulk of his estate in trust for establishment of a free library for New York City. Unimpressive in appearance and plagued through life by ill health, Tilden was secretive and dilatory, yet he possessed great power of concentration when he chose, had a marvelous memory and was indebted for his success to intellect rather than personality.

TILDEN, WILLIAM TATEM ("BIG BILL"), II (*b. Philadelphia, Pa., 1893; d. Los Angeles, Calif., 1953*), tennis player. Studied at the University of Pennsylvania. Won the U.S. championship seven times and in 1920 was the first American to win the men's singles at Wimbledon; won again in 1921 and 1930. As a professional player, Tilden continued to dominate the sport. He wrote a syndicated column and appeared in several films and stage plays. Persecuted as a homosexual, he served two prison terms in the 1940's and died penniless. In 1949, the Associated Press named him the greatest tennis player of the first half of the twentieth century.

TILESTON, THOMAS (*b. Boston, Mass., 1793; d. New York, N.Y., 1864*), printer, merchant, shipowner, financier. Removing to New York City, 1818, he entered the successful shipping partnership of Spofford & Tileston. President of the Phoenix Bank, 1840–64, he was also a founder (1829) and director of the Atlantic Insurance Co.

TILGHMAN, EDWARD (*b. Wye, Md., 1750/51; d. Philadelphia, Pa., 1815*), lawyer. Cousin of William and Tench Tilghman. Practicing in Philadelphia *post* 1774, he was a powerful advocate and was recognized as an authority in the field of contingent remainders and executory devices.

TILGHMAN, MATTHEW (*b. Queen Anne Co., Md., 1718; d. Talbot Co., Md., 1790*), landowner, Maryland colonial legislator and jurist, Revolutionary patriot. Headed Maryland delegation to Continental Congress, September 1774–December 1776; served as president of the Annapolis convention in August 1776 which drafted the first state constitution.

TILGHMAN, RICHARD ALBERT (*b. Philadelphia, Pa., 1824; d. 1899*), chemist. Grandson of Edward Tilghman. Graduated University of Pennsylvania, 1841; gained practical experience in laboratory of James C. Booth. His paper "On the Decomposing Power of Water at High Temperatures" (*Proceedings, American Philosophical Society*, IV, 1847) was the first systematic study of hydration. Employed for much of his time in Scotland and England, he was the developer of many industrial processes including those for manufacture of potassium dichromate, for the manufacture of paper pulp by sulphite process, and for the "sand blast" process for shaping objects out of hard, brittle materials.

TILGHMAN, TENCH (*b. Talbot Co., Md., 1744; d. Baltimore, Md., 1786*), merchant, Revolutionary soldier. Grandson of Tench Francis; brother of William Tilghman; cousin of Edward Tilghman. Trusted and able aide-de-camp to General George Washington, August 1776–83. He rose to rank of lieutenant colonel and was selected to carry the news of the surrender of Cornwallis to the Continental Congress.

TILGHMAN, WILLIAM (*b. Talbot Co., Md., 1756; d. Philadelphia, Pa., 1827*), Maryland legislator. Pennsylvania jurist. Brother of Tech Tilghman; grandson of Tench Francis; cousin of Edward Tilghman. Graduated College of Philadelphia, 1772; read law in office of Benjamin Chew. A Loyalist during the Revolution, he served 1788–93 in the Maryland Assembly and Senate. Removing to practice in Philadelphia, 1793, he held several Pennsylvania judicial appointments before becoming chief justice of the Pennsylvania supreme court, 1806. He served in this post until his death.

TILGHMAN, WILLIAM MATTHEW (*b. Fort Dodge, Iowa, 1854; d. Cromwell, Okla., 1824*), outstanding peace officer in Kansas and Oklahoma *post* 1877.

TILLICH, PAUL (*b. Starzeddel, East Prussia, Germany [now in Poland], 1886; d. Chicago, Ill., 1965*), theologian, philosopher. Attended the University of Berlin, the University of Breslau (Ph.D., 1910), the University of Breslau (Ph.D., 1910), and the University of Halle (licentiate in theology, 1912). Son of a Lutheran pastor, Tillich was ordained a minister of the Evangelical Lutheran Church in 1912. Served as field chaplain on the western front (1914–18), an experience that transformed both his theology and his life. In his first public lecture on his own thought before the Kant Society (1919), he introduced his now-famous dictum: "Religion is the substance of culture; culture is the form of religion." Was associate professor of theology at the University of Marburg (1924), professor of philosophy and religious studies at Dresden's Institute of Technology (1924–29), and professor of philosophy at the University of Frankfurt (1929–33). His first book, *The Religious Situation* (1925), challenged Karl Barth's exclusion of cultural problems from theology, while his second, *The Socialist Decision* (1933), so provoked the Nazis that he was suspended from the University of Frankfurt. In December 1933 he came to the United States, becoming a U.S. citizen in 1940. Visiting lecturer in philosophy at Columbia University and visiting professor of theology at Union Theological Seminary. His twenty-two years at Union saw the publication of some of his most significant English works: *The Protestant Era* (1948), the *Courage to Be* (1952), and volume I of the *Systematic Theology* (1951). In 1955 Tillich was appointed to Harvard as university professor. Here he published volume II of the *Systematic Theology*, *Existence and the Christ* (1957), a work that aroused concern about his orthodoxy. Upon retiring from Harvard (1962), he became Nuveen Professor of Theology at the University of Chicago Divinity School. The third volume of *Systematic Theology*, cumulatively his greatest contribution to theology, appeared in 1963. An unrivalled "major mentor" of systematic theologians, Tillich was probably the most famous American theologian of the century.

TILLMAN, BENJAMIN RYAN (*b. Edgefield Co., S.C., 1847; d. 1918*), farmer, politician. A blunt, irascible, unmannerly representative of rural interests in his state *post* 1885, he forced South Carolina to undertake a system of agricultural education, served as Democratic governor, December 1890–1894, and was for many years complete master of South Carolina politics. Organizing an uprising of the farmers against the long-powerful aristocratic element, he dictated a new constitution for the state in 1895, meanwhile equalizing taxes, reapportioning legislative representation, and virtually disfranchising the blacks. He also implemented the powers of the state railroad commission, increased expenditures for public education, and established a public monopoly (1893) over the sale of liquor. Elected U.S. senator, 1894, he served until his death and won national notoriety as an extreme champion of southern agrarianism, becoming known as

"Pitchfork Ben." A violent and unscrupulous enemy of Presidents Cleveland and Theodore Roosevelt, he was exposed by the latter as a user of influence in land purchases, and his power in South Carolina declined. His most constructive act as a senator was the steering of the Hepburn Bill through the Senate. A defender of the use of force in disfranchising the black and an advocate of repeal of the Fifteenth Amendment, Tillman grew more conservative as his personal ambitions were gratified.

TILNEY, FREDERICK (*b. Brooklyn, N.Y., 1875; d. Oyster Bay, N.Y., 1938*), neurologist. Graduated Yale, 1897; M.D., Long Island College Hospital, 1903; Ph.D., Columbia, 1912. Taught at N.Y. College of Physicians and Surgeons *post* 1915. Medical director, Neurological Institute, 1935–38.

TILSON, JOHN QUILLIN (*b. Clear Branch, Tenn., 1866; d. New London, N.H., 1958*), lawyer, politician. Studied at Carson-Newman College and at Yale University, LL.B., 1893. Practiced law and participated in Connecticut state politics. Republican Congressman, 1909–13, and 1915–31; majority leader, 1925–31. Author of *Manual of Parliamentary Law and Procedure* (1935).

TILTON, EDWARD LIPPINCOTT (*b. New York, N.Y., 1861; d. Scarsdale, N.Y., 1933*), architect. Designed U.S. immigrant station on Ellis Island (completed, 1900); was especially notable for contributions to modern public library design.

TILTON, JAMES (*b. Kent Co., Del., 1745; d. near Wilmington, Del., 1822*), army surgeon. Graduated College of Philadelphia, B.M., 1768, and M.D., 1771. A regimental and hospital surgeon during the Revolution, he served also as surgeon general of the U.S. Army, 1813–15. He was author of two important treatises: *Economical Observations on Military Hospitals* (1813) and *Regulations for the Medical Department* (1814).

TILTON, JOHN ROLLIN (*b. Loudon, N.H., 1828; d. Rome, Italy, 1888*), landscape painter. Resident in Italy *post* 1852; he specialized in pictures of places famous for their historical associations.

TILTON, THEODORE (*b. New York, N.Y., 1835; d. Paris, France, 1907*), journalist. Managing editor of the *Independent*, a Congregationalist journal, 1856–70, he was a close associate of Henry Ward Beecher and prominent in the antislavery movement and as a post–Civil War Republican partisan. At first attempting to suppress knowledge of alleged adulterous relations between his wife and Beecher, he brought suit against the minister. The trial began Jan. 11, 1875, in Brooklyn, N.Y., lasted 112 trial days, and resulted in a hung jury and a division of public opinion over Beecher's culpability that still persists. Ruined in fortune and reputation, Tilton left the United States, 1883, never to return.

TILYOU, GEORGE CORNELIUS (*b. New York, N.Y., 1862; d. 1914*), amusement park owner and inventor. Laid out Coney Island's famous "Bowery"; founded Steeplechase Park, 1897. Tilyou originated most of the fun-devices used in his enterprises.

TILZER, HARRY VON (*b. Detroit, Mich., 1872; d. New York, N.Y., 1946*), composer and publisher of popular songs. Born Harry Gumm, son of German Jewish parents; adopted his mother's maiden name (with an added "Von"), *ca.* 1887. After work as a tumbler in the circus, in a traveling repertory company, and in burlesque, he came to New York City, 1892, and began writing songs for vaudeville performers. His first great success was "My Old New Hampshire Home" (1898); two years later, he wrote and published "A Bird in a Gilded Cage," which won him wealth and fame. Perhaps his most productive year was 1905, when he wrote (among others) "On a Sunday Afternoon," "Down Where the Wurzburger Flows," "Wait 'til the Sun Shines, Nellie," and "Where the Morning Glories Twine Around the Door." Later successes were "I Want a Girl Just Like the Girl That Married Dear Old Dad" (1911) and "That Old Irish Mother of Mine" (1920).

TIMBERLAKE, GIDEON (*b. Charlottesville, Va., 1876; d. St. Petersburg, Fla., 1951*), physician, urologist. Studied at the University of Virginia, M.D., 1902, and at Johns Hopkins University. Taught at the University of Maryland Medical School, 1910–17. Persuaded the army to establish a school of urology; became chief of the department of urology at Walter Reed Hospital in Washington. Left the University of Maryland in 1926 and entered private practice in Greenville, S.C. and in St. Petersburg, Fla., 1928.

TIMBERLAKE, HENRY (*b. Hanover Co., Va., 1730; d. London, England, 1765*), soldier. Served in French and Indian War; was distinguished for mission (accompanied by Thomas Sumter) to the Cherokees, November 1761–62. Accompanied Outacity and two warriors to England on state visit, 1762. Author of a valuable volume of *Memoirs* (London, 1765) recording his war experiences and observations of the customs and ceremonies of the Cherokee.

TIMBY, THEODORE RUGGLES (*b. Dutchess Co., N.Y., 1822; d. Brooklyn, N.Y., 1909*), inventor. Filed a *caveat,* January 1843, covering a revolving gun turret for use on land or water, a device unrecognized until used by John Ericsson as a feature of his first *Monitor,* 1861–62.

TIMKEN, HENRY (*b. near Bremen, Germany, 1831; d. San Diego, Calif., 1909*), wagon maker, manufacturer. Immigrated to Missouri as a boy. Patented a successful carriage spring, 1877, which he manufactured with profit; patented the Timken tapered roller bearing, June 1898.

TIMM, HENRY CHRISTIAN (*b. Hamburg, Germany, 1811; d. Hoboken, N.J., 1892*), musician, conductor. Immigrated to New York City, 1835. An accomplished organist and pianist, he was an early member of the New York Philharmonic Society and its president, 1848–63.

TIMME, WALTER (*b. New York, N.Y., 1874; d. St. Petersburg, Fla., 1956*), physician, neurologist, endocrinologist. Graduated from the City College of New York and Columbia University, 1897. Member of the staff of the Neurological Institute of New York, 1910–37; professor of clinical neurology at Columbia University, 1929–37. First publicly described the Timme syndrome in 1918: ovarian and adrenal insufficiency leading to compensatory hypopituitarism. Founded and was first president of the Association for Research in Nervous and Mental Diseases, 1920.

TIMON, JOHN (*b. Conewago, Pa., 1797; d. 1867*), Roman Catholic clergyman, Vincentian. Ordained, 1825, at St. Louis, Mo., he served in the missions of the Southwest, held administrative posts in his Order, and came to be one of the best-known priests in the Mississippi Valley. Consecrated first bishop of Buffalo, N.Y., 1847, he served with great ability until his death. He was especially noted for his interest in charitable and educational institutions.

TIMOTHY, LEWIS (*b. France or Holland, date unknown; d. Charleston, S.C., 1738*), printer. Immigrated to Philadelphia, Pa., October 1731. First an employee and later a partner of Benjamin Franklin, Timothy conducted a printing business at Charleston, 1734–38, as successor to Franklin's former partner there. His publication *The Laws of the Province of South-Carolina*

(1736) was the most ambitious production of the South Carolina colonial press.

TIMROD, HENRY (*b. Charleston, S.C., 1828; d. Columbia, S.C., 1867*), educator, poet. The most gifted Southern poet of his time (with exception of Sidney Lanier), Timrod possessed high artistic integrity and a crystalline style. He surpassed most of his poetical contemporaries in knowledge of his craft, in taste, and in sheer lyrical power, despite the restricted range and the small body of his production. A lifelong friend of Paul H. Hayne and a literary associate of William G. Simms, he brought out a small collection of his poems in 1860, which was lost sight of in the coming of civil war. The passionate war poems which brought him notice as the "laureate of the Confederacy" showed a ripening of his powers; however, after discharge from the Confederate Army because of his incipient tuberculosis, he suffered one calamity after another and was reduced to abject poverty. Despite his misfortunes, he continued to compose, producing what is perhaps his most perfect composition, the "Magnolia Cemetery Ode," shortly before his death. In 1873 his friend Hayne edited *The Poems of Henry Timrod,* prefacing them with a sympathetic memoir of the author. In his ideals, his fancy, his spirituality, and his high-mindedness, Timrod was characteristic of the finest qualities of his section; it is an irony of American literature that so gentle a spirit should have been the outstanding poet of the Confederacy at war.

TINCKER, MARY AGNES (*b. Ellsworth, Maine, 1831; d. Dorchester, Mass., 1907*), novelist, teacher. A convert to Catholicism, 1851, she contributed to periodicals and was author of 11 novels and books of sketches; among them the most popular was *Signor Monaldini's Niece* (1879). Her work received much contemporary praise.

TINGEY, THOMAS (*b. London, England, 1750; d. Washington, D.C., 1829*), naval officer. Trained in the British navy and later a merchant captain, he resided in the United States *post* 1783. Made captain in the U.S. Navy, September 1798, he served with credit during the naval war with France and in 1800 was appointed to lay out and command the new Washington, D.C., navy yard. He remained in charge of this yard under various titles until his death. Thomas T. and Tunis A. M. Craven were his grandsons.

TINGLEY, KATHERINE AUGUSTA WESTCOTT (*b. Newbury, Mass., 1847; d. Sweden, 1929*), theosophist leader.

TINKHAM, GEORGE HOLDEN (*b. Boston, Mass., 1870; d. Cramerton, N.C., 1956*), politician. Graduated from Harvard, 1894. Practiced law and participated in Massachusetts state politics. As a Republican Congressman, 1915–43, he was a strict isolationist, a foe of Prohibition, a staunch supporter of civil rights, and an opponent of the New Deal.

TIPTON, JOHN (*b. Baltimore Co., Md., 1730; d. near Jonesboro, Tenn., 1813*), Virginia legislator, Revolutionary soldier, frontier politician. Uncle of John Tipton (1786–1839). Removed to Watauga settlements, 1783. A bitter opponent of John Sevier, he served *post* 1793 in the Tennessee legislature.

TIPTON, JOHN (*b. Sevier Co., Tenn., 1786; d. Logansport, Ind., 1838*), Indiana soldier, legislator, and land speculator. Nephew of John Tipton (1730–1813), U.S. senator, Democrat, from Indiana, 1831–39.

TISQUANTUM. *See* SQUANTO.

TITCHENER, EDWARD BRADFORD (*b. Chichester, England, 1867; d. 1927*), experimental psychologist. B.A., Brasenose College, Oxford, 1890; Ph.D., Leipzig, 1892; D.Sc., Oxford, 1906. Taught psychology at Cornell *post* 1892; was author of

Experimental Psychology (1901–05), a milestone in the progress of that science. Leader of the "structuralist" school, he opposed the fashionable rage for applied psychology, educational psychology, and mental testing that threatened to obliterate study of the science in its pure form in America.

TITCOMB, JOHN WHEELOCK (*b. Farmington, N.H., 1860; d. Hartford, Conn., 1932*), fish culturist, conservationist.

TITTLE, ERNEST FREMONT (*b. Springfield, Ohio, 1885; d. Evanston, Ill., 1949*), Methodist clergyman. B.A., Ohio Wesleyan, 1906. B.D., Drew Theological Seminary, 1908. Ordained in 1910, he held several pastorates in Ohio before serving in France as a YMCA secretary during World War I. From 1918 until his death, he was pastor of the First Methodist Episcopal Church of Evanston, Ill. A preacher of great distinction, he became the recognized leader of Methodism's liberal ministers. He was dedicated to the social gospel, an absolute pacifist, a foe of racial discrimination, and an incisive critic of unfettered capitalism.

TOBANI, THEODORE MOSES (*b. Hamburg, Germany, 1855; d. Jackson Heights, N.Y., 1933*), composer of semiclassical music. Came to America as a boy. His most popular work "Hearts and Flowers," long in use as incidental music to pathos in the theater, was first published as a piano piece, 1893.

TOBEY, CHARLES WILLIAM (*b. Roxbury, Mass., 1880; d. Bethesda, Md., 1953*), politician. Self-educated. New Hampshire state senator, 1924–28; governor, 1928–30; U.S. Congressman (Republican), 1932–38; U.S. Senator, 1938–53. At first an ardent nationalist and isolationist, Tobey became a backer of more internationalist positions. He opposed the policies of Senator Joseph McCarthy, supported many of the programs of Truman, and was a backer of Eisenhower.

TOBEY, EDWARD SILAS (*b. Kingston, Mass., 1813; d. Brookline, Mass., 1891*), Boston merchant, capitalist. Prominent in many organizations for public safety, welfare, and the propagation of religion.

TOBIAS, CHANNING HEGGIE (*b. Augusta, Ga., 1882; d. New York, N.Y., 1961*), civic and religious leader, YMCA executive. Attended Paine College (B.A., 1902) and Drew Theological Seminary (B.D., 1905). Ordained a minister in the Colored Methodist Episcopal Church (1900). In 1911 he became student secretary of the International Committee of the Young Men's Christian Association (YMCA) and senior secretary of the colored men's department in 1923. Served as director of Paine College, the National Association for the Advancement of Colored People, the Council on Race Relations, and many other groups. Became the first black director of the Phelps-Stokes Foundation (1946–53). In 1946 President Harry S Truman appointed him to the Committee on Civil Rights. He was one of the authors of *To Secure These Rights* (1947), the committee's report, which many consider a major document on the treatment of minority groups.

TOBIN, DANIEL JOSEPH (*b. County Clare, Ireland, 1875; d. Indianapolis, Ind., 1955*), labor leader. Immigrated to the U.S. in 1889. Affiliated with Boston Local 25 of the Team Drivers' International Union (1900). Helped found the International Brotherhood of Teamsters, Chauffeurs, Warehousemen and Helpers of America (IBT), 1903; president, 1907–52. American Federation of Labor executive treasurer, 1917–28; member of the AFL executive council and vice president of the building trades department from 1933. Chairman of the Labor Bureau of the Democratic National Campaign Committee, 1932–44.

TOBIN, MAURICE JOSEPH (*b. Roxbury, Mass., 1901; d. Scituate, Mass., 1953*), politician. Studied briefly at Boston College. Democratic member of the Massachusetts House of Representatives, 1926–28; mayor of Boston, 1937–44; governor of Massachusetts, 1944–46. As governor, he introduced a bill that ended discrimination in employment practices based on race, creed, color, and national origin. As secretary of labor, 1948–52, Tobin set up the Federal Safety Council in the Bureau of Labor Standards (1950), supported an increase in the minimum wage law, and strengthened child labor regulations.

TOD, DAVID (*b. near Youngstown, Ohio, 1805; d. 1868*), lawyer, coal and iron operator, railroad executive. Son of George Tod with whom he studied law. Removed *ca.* 1802 to chairman, Democratic presidential convention of 1860, after withdrawal of Caleb Cushing; was Union party governor of Ohio, 1862–64. Refused secretaryship of the U.S. treasury, 1864.

TOD, GEORGE (*b. Suffield, Conn., 1773; d. near Youngstown, Ohio, 1841*), jurist. Brother of John Tod; father of David Tod. Graduated Yale, 1795; studied law under Tapping Reeve. Removed to Youngstown, Ohio, 1800. Served as state supreme court judge, 1806–10, establishing by decision in 1809 the doctrine of judicial review in Ohio. After two terms in the legislature and War of 1812 military service, he was presiding judge of the 3rd district circuit court of appeals, 1816–29.

TOD, JOHN (*b. Suffield, Conn., 1779; d. Bedford, Pa., 1830*), lawyer, Pennsylvania legislator and jurist. Brother of George Tod with whom he studied law. Removed *ca.* 1802 to Bedford, Pa., where he practiced with success; served as a congressman, Democrat, 1821–24. As chairman of the House committee on manufactures, he strove for higher tariffs and extension of the protective list.

TODD, CHARLES STEWART (*b. near Danville, Ky., 1791; d. Baton Rouge, La., 1871*), lawyer, War of 1812 soldier, diplomat. Son of Thomas Todd; son-in-law of Isaac Shelby. Appointed U.S. diplomatic agent in Columbia, 1820, Todd handled U.S. affairs there during a critical period with great integrity and tact; he was U.S. minister to Russia, 1841–45.

TODD, ELI (*b. New Haven, Conn., 1769; d. Hartford, Conn., 1833*), physician. An American pioneer in the humane and intelligent treatment of mental illness and alcoholism, he was superintendent of the Connecticut Retreat at Hartford, 1824–33.

TODD, HENRY ALFRED (*b. Woodstock, Ill., 1854; d. New York, N.Y., 1925*), Romance philologist. Graduated College of New Jersey (Princeton), 1876; studied at Paris, Berlin, Rome and Madrid; Ph.D., Johns Hopkins, 1885. Taught at Johns Hopkins and at Stanford; professor Romance philology, Columbia University, 1893–1925. A founder and editor of *Modern Language Notes* (1886) and an organizer of the Modern Language Association (1883), he was editor of a number of Old French works and in 1909 helped found the *Romantic Review*.

TODD, JOHN (*b. Rutland, Vt., 1800; d. Pittsfield, Mass., 1873*), Congregational clergyman. A Calvinist of the school of Jonathan Edwards, he held his principal pastorate at the First Church in Pittsfield, and was author of a number of once-popular books including *The Student's Manual* (1835).

TODD, MABEL LOOMIS (*b. Cambridge, Mass., 1856; d. Hog Island, Maine, 1932*), author. Undertaking to prepare the poems of Emily Dickinson for publication *ca.* 1886, she was editor (with Thomas W. Higginson) of *Poems* (first series, 1890; second series, 1891) and was sole editor for the third series of *Poems* (1896). She was also collector and editor of the *Letters of Emily Dickinson*

(1894). A conscientious editor, she endeavored, not always with success, to keep Higginson from "correcting" what the poet had written; alienation from the Dickinson family *post* 1895 prevented her from completing her work as planned.

Todd, Mike (*b. Minneapolis, Minn., 1909; d. Grants, N.Mex., 1958*), theatrical and motion picture producer. Worked as a builder and real estate operator before becoming radio writer and vaudeville producer. Produced *The Hot Mikado* (1939), *Star and Garter* (1942), *Something for the Boys* (1943), *Mexican Hayride* (1944), and *Up in Central Park* (1945). The main founder of the cinematic process called Cinerama; later developed, along with the American Optical Company, the process called Todd-AO, used for *Oklahoma* and Todd's own *Around the World in 80 Days*, winner of the Academy Award for best film, 1956.

Todd, Sereno Edwards (*b. near Lansingville, N.Y., 1820, d. near Orange, N.J., 1898*), journalist, agriculturist, author of works on systematic and economical farm management.

Todd, Thomas (*b. near Dunkirk, Va., 1765; d. 1826*), lawyer, Kentucky public official and jurist. Father of Charles S. Todd. Removed to Danville, Ky., 1786, where he made his home with Harry Innes and studied law. Judge of the state court of appeals, 1801–06, and chief justice, 1806–March 1807, he rendered many opinions basic to Kentucky land law. Appointed associate justice of the U.S. Supreme Court, March 1807, he served until his death. A consistent supporter of John Marshall in cases involving constitutional doctrine (except in the Dartmouth College case), he devoted most of his time and strength to traveling the western circuit. His judgment, especially on cases involving land laws, was highly regarded by his colleagues.

Todd, Thomas Wingate (*b. Sheffield, England, 1885; d. Cleveland, Ohio, 1938*), anatomist, physical anthropologist. Educated at Manchester University (England), he also taught there until 1912. Todd served thereafter as professor of anatomy at the medical school of Western Reserve University and as director of its Hamann Museum of comparative anthropology and anatomy. He was a pioneer in growth studies based on skeletal development.

Todd, Walter Edmond Clyde (*b. Smithfield, Ohio, 1874; d. Rochester, Pa., 1969*), ornithologist, museum curator. Attended college for a few weeks in 1891 but withdrew to accept an apprenticeship in the Division of Ornithology and Mammalogy in the Department of Agriculture. In 1899 he became curator of birds at the Carnegie Museum in Pittsburgh, an association that lasted seventy years. As curator, he classified large collections of neotropical birds in the museum's collections. In 1901 he made the first of eighteen expeditions to northern Canada—the resulting *The Birds of the Labrador Peninsula and Adjacent Regions: A Distributional List* appeared in 1943. In 1940 he published his exhaustive *Birds of Western Pennsylvania*.

Toklas, Alice Babette (*b. San Francisco, Calif., 1877; d. Paris, France, 1967*), writer. Attended the music conservatory at the University of Washington, and after 1897 was the housekeeper of an extended household of her grandparents. Journeyed to Paris in 1907 where she met Gertrude Stein and became her secretary. Their salon was one of the centers of intellectual life in Paris for nearly four decades. With the publication of Stein's *The Autobiography of Alice B. Toklas* (1933), both women became celebrities. After Stein's death in 1946, Toklas launched her own writing career; her first published book was *The Alice B. Toklas Cookbook* (1954), with its famous recipe for hashish fudge. In *What Is Remembered* (1963), she recalled her early days in San Francisco and Seattle and her life in Paris.

Toland, Hugh Huger (*b. Guilder's Creek, S.C., 1806; d. San Francisco, Calif., 1880*), surgeon. Graduated in medicine from Transylvania University, 1828; made special studies in Paris, France, 1830–33. Practiced in Columbia, S.C., until 1852 when he removed to California. Widely known for his skill in lithotomy and plastic surgery, he founded Toland Medical College in San Francisco, 1864, and served as its professor of surgery until his death. In 1873 he placed the institution unconditionally in charge of the University of California, of which it became a part.

Tolley, Howard Ross (*b. Howard County, Ind., 1889; d. Alexandria, Va., 1958*), agricultural economist. Graduated from Indiana University, 1910. Active in government agricultural offices from 1915, Tolley worked for the Bureau of Agricultural Economics, 1923–30, and was director, 1938–46. Known as the "soil wizard," Tolley directed the Giannini Foundation for Agricultural Economics at the University of California, 1930–36; was the assistant administrator of the Agricultural Adjustment Administration; and chief of the Program Planning Division, 1933–35. The author of the quota system for planting specific crops and of federal cash grants to farmers for restricting the planted acreage, Tolley was a leader in shaping the agricultural policies of the nation as they exist today. Tolley worked in organizing food and agricultural programs at the U.N. and was head of the Ford Foundation office in Washington, 1951–54.

Tolman, Edward Chace (*b. West Newton, Mass., 1886; d. Berkeley, Calif., 1959*), psychologist. Graduated from the Massachusetts Institute of Technology, B.S., 1911, and Harvard University, Ph.D., 1915. Taught at Northwestern University, 1915–18, and at the University of California at Berkeley, 1918–54. Through a series of experiments with white rats, Tolman laid the foundations for the interest in cognitive psychology that became prominent in the U.S. after his death. Author of *Purposive Behavior in Animals and Men* (1932).

Tolman, Herbert Cushing (*b. South Scituate, Mass., 1865; d. Nashville, Tenn., 1923*), Greek and Indo-Iranian scholar, Episcopal clergyman. Graduated Yale, 1888; Ph.D., 1890. Taught at University of Wisconsin and University of North Carolina; was professor of Greek at Vanderbilt, 1894–1923, and dean of its College of Arts and Sciences, 1913–23.

Tolman, Richard Chace (*b. West Newton, Mass., 1881; d. Pasadena, Calif., 1948*), physical chemist, mathematical physicist. Upon graduation from M.I.T. in 1903, Tolman studied at the Technische Hochschule in Berlin and then at an industrial chemical laboratory at Crefeld. He returned to M.I.T. as a graduate student and shortly thereafter joined Arthur Amos Noyes's new Research Laboratory of Physical Chemistry. He received the Ph.D. in 1910. Tolman taught briefly at the University of Michigan and the University of Cincinnati. With Earl Osgerby he made a series of measurements on the electromotive force produced by the acceleration of electrolytes. With T. Dale Stewart, he made the first laboratory determination of the inertial mass of electrons in metals (1916).

In the closing days of World War I Tolman served as chief of the Dispersoid Section of the Chemical Warfare Service. At the close of the war he joined the Fixed Nitrogen Research Laboratory (associate director, 1919–20; director, 1920–22), supervising research in the chemistry of nitrogen pentoxide, the cyanamide and arc process of nitrogen fixation, the separation of helium from natural gases, the theory of catalysis, and the rate of chemical reaction. He also worked on a modified method of measuring the mass of the electric carrier in conductors. In 1922 he joined the faculty of the new California Institute of Technology as professor of physical chemistry and mathematical physics. Tolman became dean of the graduate school as well (1922–46).

Starting from first principles in statistical mechanics, Tolman analyzed completely the problem of accounting for the rate at which chemical reactions occur. His theoretical treatment of monomolecular thermal and photochemical reaction rates underscored the need to clarify the meaning of the loosely defined concept of the energy of activation. This done, Tolman turned to the decomposition of nitrogen pentoxide as a check on the then-current proposed mechanisms of chemical reaction. He showed that the simple radiation theory of reaction did not adequately account for known rates of reaction. These studies reveal Tolman's consuming interest in using statistical mechanics in dealing with quantum mechanical phenomena. His *Principles of Statistical Mechanics* (1938) remains a classic in its field.

From its inception in 1905, Tolman followed closely the development of relativity theory and its application to the problems of cosmology. With Gilbert N. Lewis he published the first American account of Einstein's special theory of relativity (1909). This early interest led to a series of studies on the applications of the general theory to the overall structure and evolution of the universe. His pioneering work on the thermodynamics and behavior of radiation in nonstatic cosmological models of the universe drew public attention, because it challenged the pessimistic view required by classical thermodynamics. In particular, he derived relativistic expressions for the first two laws of thermodynamics and found that reversible processes could take place both at a finite rate and without increase in entropy. In his comprehensive treatise *Relativity, Thermodynamics, and Cosmology* (1934), Tolman presented the model of a universe expanding and contracting rhythmically.

During World War II he served on the National Defense Research Committee, as scientific adviser on the Manhattan Project, and as adviser to the Combined Policy Committee.

TOME, JACOB (*b. York Co., Pa., 1810; d. 1898*), Maryland merchant, banker, philanthropist. Founded Tome School for Boys at Port Deposit, Md. (incorporated 1889, opened 1894).

TOMKINS, FLOYD WILLIAMS (*b. New York, N.Y., 1850; d. 1932*), Episcopal clergyman. A zealous evangelical preacher, he performed his most notable work as rector of the Church of the Holy Trinity, Philadelphia, Pa., 1899–1932.

TOMLIN, BRADLEY WALKER (*b. Syracuse, N.Y., 1899; d. New York, N.Y., 1953*), painter. Studied at Syracuse University, B.A., 1921, and the L.C. Tiffany Foundation in Oyster Bay, L.I. Until 1939, his work was largely realistic, consisting mainly of idealized portraits; he then painted cubistic still lifes. After 1945, influenced by Jackson Pollock, Robert Motherwell, and Philip Guston, his style became completely abstract. Works include *Number 20* (1949) and *Number 9* (1950), New York Museum of Modern Art; *Number 1* (1952), Whitney Museum of Art; *Number 2* (1952–53), Hirshhorn Museum and Sculpture Garden, Washington, D.C. Although he never received great public recognition, Tomlin is considered a leader in the abstract school of painting.

TOMLINS, WILLIAM LAWRENCE (*b. London, England, 1844; d. Delafield, Wis., 1930*), teacher of music. Came to America, 1870. Achieving distinction in America as conductor of the Apollo Club, Chicago, Ill., *post* 1875, he later was notably successful in training children for choral singing and as an instructor of public school music teachers. His system became known as "The Tomlins Idea."

TOMLINSON, EVERETT TITSWORTH (*b. Shiloh, N.J., 1859; d. Elizabeth, N.J., 1931*), Baptist clergyman and missionary executive. Author of over 100 historical stories for boys, including *Three Colonial Boys* (1895), *The Fort in the Forest* (1904), and *Mad Anthony's Young Scout* (1908).

TOMOCHICHI (*b. possibly Apalachicola, in present Alabama, ca. 1650; d. Georgia, 1739*), Creek Indian chief. Leader of a few Creek and Yamassee, he settled at Yamacraw on the Savannah River *post* 1721, where he resided when the first Georgia colonists landed in 1733. Signer of a formal treaty with James E. Oglethorpe, May 1733, he helped negotiate a treaty with the other Creek tribes and accompanied Oglethorpe to England on a visit, 1734.

TOMPKINS, ARNOLD (*b. near Paris, Ill., 1849; d. Menlo, Ga., 1905*), educator, leader in normal school work. Author of *The Philosophy of Teaching* (1893), *The Philosophy of School Management* (1895), and other works once widely used in teacher training schools.

TOMPKINS, DANIEL AUGUSTUS (*b. Edgefield Co., S.C., 1851; d. Montreat, N.C., 1914*), engineer. Graduated Rensselaer Polytechnic Institute, C.E., 1873. After training with Alexander L. Holley and John Fritz in steel and iron making, he began practice in Charlotte, N.C., 1882. Preaching the gospel of northern industrial development to the South, he promoted, designed, and built cottonseed-oil mills throughout the South, and by speeches and newspaper articles popularized the concept that manufactures must supplement agriculture in the section. He next waged a successful campaign in favor of his plan for community financing and founding of cotton manufacturing plants. Realizing that the economic recovery of the South required improved education, he helped found textile schools in both the Carolinas and in Mississippi and Texas. Author of a number of books and pamphlets, he was also chief owner for many years of the *Charlotte Daily Observer* which served him as a means of propagating his ideas.

TOMPKINS, DANIEL D. (*b. Scarsdale, N.Y., 1774; d. Staten Island, N.Y., 1825*), lawyer, New York legislator. Graduated Columbia, 1795. Beginning practice in New York City, he was elected to Congress as a (Democrat) Republican in 1804 but resigned almost at once to accept appointment as a justice of the New York supreme court. Elected governor of New York, 1807, he served through 1817. His administration was marked by liberal and popular reform measures in the school system, the militia and in the criminal code, and also by the complete abolition of slavery in the state. Handicapped during the War of 1812 by lack of money and a hostile Assembly as well as by the incompetence of the U.S. command, he handled the defense of the state as successfully as any man could have done, pledging his personal credit for much of the necessary money. He served as vice president of the United States, 1817–25, without particular distinction. For many years he was DeWitt Clinton's most able antagonist in New York State politics.

TOMPKINS, SALLY LOUISA (*b. Mathews Co., Va., 1833; d. Richmond, Va., 1916*), philanthropist. Fitted up and maintained the Robertson Hospital for Confederate wounded in Richmond, 1861–65. Commissioned captain in the Confederate service, September 1861, she was the only woman ever to receive such an honor and was known to the end of her life as "Captain Sally."

TOMPSON, BENJAMIN (*b. present Quincy, Mass., 1642; d. 1714*), teacher, physician. Graduated Harvard, 1662. Taught at present Boston Latin School, also in Charlestown, Braintree and Roxbury. Author of a number of topical poems which were published as broadsides and in *New Englands Crisis* (Boston, 1676; also as *New-Englands Tears for Her Present Miseries*, London in the same year).

TONDORF, FRANCIS ANTHONY (*b. Boston, Mass., 1870; d. Washington, D.C., 1929*), Roman Catholic clergyman, Jesuit, seismologist. A professor of the sciences principally at Georgetown University *post* 1904, he founded the seismological observatory at Georgetown and served it as director, 1909–29.

TONE, STANISLAS PASCAL FRANCHOT (*b. Niagara Falls, N.Y., 1905; d. New York, N.Y., 1968*), actor. Attended Cornell University (B.A., 1927). Originally intending to teach, Tone instead succumbed to a passion for the theater. He made his Broadway debut in 1928 and played his first starring role in *Green Grow the Lilacs* (1931). In 1932 he made his screen debut in *Wiser Sex*; the same year he was signed to a five-year contract by Metro-Goldwyn-Mayer (MGM). He turned in one of his best performances in Paramount's *The Lives of a Bengal Lancer* (1935) and was nominated for an Academy Award as best actor for his role in *Mutiny on the Bounty* (1935). After his MGM contract expired in 1939, Tone returned to the New York stage, occasionally free-lancing as a film actor.

TONER, JOSEPH MEREDITH (*b. Pittsburgh, Pa., 1825; d. Cresson, Pa., 1896*), physician. Graduated Vermont Medical College, 1850; M.D., Jefferson Medical College, 1853. A leading practitioner in Washington, D.C., *post* 1855, he was best known as a medical historian and as the collector of a remarkable library of American medical history which he presented to the Library of Congress. He was the author of *The Medical Men of the Revolution* (1876) among other books, and editor of the early journals of George Washington.

TONTY, HENRY DE (*b. probably Paris, France, 1650; d. near present Mobile, Ala., 1704*), explorer, soldier. Cousin of Daniel Greysolon Duluth; son of the originator of the Tontine form of life insurance. Known as "Iron Hand" because of an artificial right hand with which he had replaced one lost in service with the French army. Tonty became lieutenant to Robert Cavelier, Sieur de la Salle, in 1678, and accompanied La Salle to Canada. He was his chief's principal assistant in the exploration of the Great Lakes and the Illinois country. He commanded at Fort Crèvecoeur, 1680, escaping with great difficulty with five companions after the Iroquois raid on that post. Going first to Green Bay and then to Michilimackinac, he rejoined La Salle at the latter place in June 1681. Cobuilder with La Salle of Fort St. Louis on the Illinois, he joined his chief in the spring of 1682 for the famous exploration of the Mississippi River and the claiming of the Mississippi Valley for France. Left in charge in Illinois, Tonty made an unsuccessful attempt to find La Salle in 1686, and even as late as March 1689 was still unaware of La Salle's death. On learning of it in September of that year, he attempted to find the colonists which La Salle had left in lower Louisiana but was unsuccessful. In 1700, after a decade of able, honest management of the Illinois settlements, he joined the new colony made by Pierre le Moyne, Sieur d'Iberville, near the mouth of the Mississippi, and for the last four years of his life gave valuable service to Louisiana. A great explorer and an able administrator, he succeeded where La Salle failed, was respected and trusted by the Indians and by the settlers, and was particularly noted for his courtesy and consideration. He wrote two brief memoirs of his experiences, one covering the years 1678–83, the other covering the years 1678–91, which remained unpublished until late in the 19th century. Earlier publications credited to him are considered spurious.

TOOLE, EDWIN WARREN (*b. Savannah, Mo., 1839; d. Helena, Mont, 1905*), lawyer. Brother of Joseph K. Toole. Removed to Denver, Colo., 1863, and thence to Montana Territory where he settled in Virginia City; in 1865 he moved to Helena which was thereafter his home. An outstanding lawyer with a varied practice, he is particularly remembered for his representation of the state of Montana in *Barden* v. *Northern Pacific Railroad* (154 *U.S.*, 288–349) which maintained the state's right to mineral lands reserved in the Congressional grant of land to the railroad. He was also successful in defending constitutionality of the "apex" law.

TOOLE, JOSEPH KEMP (*b. Savannah, Mo., 1851; d. 1929*), lawyer, Montana legislator. Brother of Edwin W. Toole. Removed to Helena, Mont., 1869; became his brother's law partner, 1872. Territorial delegate to Congress from Montana, Democrat, 1885–89, he was influential and active in the movement for statehood and was a member of the 1889 convention that drafted the Montana constitution. Elected first governor of the state of Montana, he served November 1889–January 1893 and January 1901–April 1908. A successful administrator, he fostered public education and supported many political and social reforms.

TOOMBS, ROBERT AUGUSTUS (*b. Wilkes Co., Ga., 1810; d. Washington, Ga., 1885*), lawyer, planter, Georgia statesman and legislator. Friend and associate of Alexander H. Stephens. Graduated Union College, 1828. Displaying high ability as a Whig member of the Georgia legislature, Toombs was elected to Congress and took his seat at the close of 1845. A careful student of public finance and robustly eloquent, he soon became popular and influential. Shocked out of his faith that the welfare of the South would be safe in Whig hands by the events which led to the crisis of 1850, he became a leader in the aggressive defense of his section. However, he was satisfied with the Compromise finally adopted and with Alexander H. Stephens and Howell Cobb canvassed Georgia to procure its ratification. He then led in the launching of the Constitutional Union party, pledged to maintain the Compromise measures. After dissolution of the party because of lack of response in other states, he reluctantly joined the Democrats. As U.S. senator, 1853–61, he approved the Kansas-Nebraska Act. He sought to end the ensuing disorders by an 1856 bill of his own providing for prompt admission of Kansas with whatever constitution a new convention might adopt after a thoroughly policed election of delegates. His bill was adopted by the Senate but died in the House. Convinced that control of the government by the Republicans would menace the security of the South, Toombs strove for harmony among the Democrats; after the split in 1860 he supported the Breckinridge ticket. Upon the failure of the Crittenden Compromise which he supported, he publicly urged secession and resigned from the Senate. Author of the address which the Georgia secession convention adopted to justify its acts, he was chosen one of the Georgia delegates sent to launch a Southern confederacy at Montgomery, Ala. Accepting the office of Confederate secretary of state with some reluctance, he discovered that his excellent advice on financial and other matters was little regarded. Growing contemptuous of Jefferson Davis, he resigned and took command in July 1861 of a brigade on the Virginia front. Restless under the defensive policy of his superiors, he censured their inaction and was disliked by them. Wounded at Antietam where his brigade held the stone bridge, Toombs demanded promotion and on its refusal resigned his commission. Thereafter he continued to criticize the government, especially its continued reliance upon credit, and served briefly in arms during Sherman's advance against Atlanta. Briefly a fugitive at the end of the Civil War, he returned home in 1867 and rebuilt a large law practice. Between 1867 and 1880 he fought to overthrow the rule of the Radicals. He dominated the constitutional convention of 1877 which repudiated the carpetbag bonds, curbed black suffrage, improved the judiciary, and provided for the control of corporations.

TOPLIFF, SAMUEL (*b. Boston, Mass., 1789; d. 1864*), dealer in foreign news. Operated Merchants' Reading Room and associated news-gathering services at Boston, 1814–42.

TORBERT, ALFRED THOMAS ARCHIMEDES (*b. Georgetown, Del., 1833; d. at sea, off Florida coast, 1880*), soldier, diplomat. Graduated West Point, 1855. After frontier service with infantry he became colonel, 1st New Jersey Volunteers, September 1861. Following extensive service with the Army of the Potomac, he was promoted brigadier general, 1862. As a cavalry division commander *post* April 1864, Torbert served with great ability under General Philip Sheridan, winning particular honors at the battles of Winchester and Cedar Creek.

TORRENCE, FREDERICK RIDGLEY (*b. Xenia, Ohio, 1874; d. New York, N.Y., 1950*), poet, editor, playwright. Attended Miami University and Princeton. Friend of Edwin Arlington Robinson, Robert Frost, and William V. Moody. Poetry editor of the *New Republic* (1920–33). Author of *The House of a Hundred Lights* (1899), *Hesperides* (1925), and *Poems* (1941); also of dramas in verse and prose, of which the most important were three one-act plays of black life published as *Plays for a Negro Theatre* (1917).

TORRENCE, JOSEPH THATCHER (*b. Mercer Co., Pa., 1843; d. Chicago Ill., 1896*), engineer, Chicago iron manufacturer and businessman.

TORREY, BRADFORD (*b. Weymouth, Mass., 1843; d. Santa Barbara, Calif., 1912*), ornithologist, editor. A faithful and accurate field observer, Torrey was author of *A Rambler's Lease* (1889), *The Foot-path Way* (1892), and other volumes of essays on birds; he served also as editor of the journal of Henry D. Thoreau (Walden edition, 1906).

TORREY, CHARLES CUTLER (*b. East Hardwick, Vt., 1863; d. Chicago, Ill., 1956*), Bible scholar, Semitist. Studied at Bowdoin College, at Andover Theological Seminary, and at the University of Strassburg, Ph.D., 1892. Taught at Andover Seminary, 1892–1900; professor at Yale University, 1901–32. Founded and was the first director of the American School of Archaeology in Jerusalem, 1900–01. Works include controversial interpretations of texts and theological results of the Scriptures and biblical history: *Ezra Studies* (1910), *Pseudo-Ezekiel and the Original Prophecy* (1930), and *The Jewish Foundation of Islam* (1933).

TORREY, CHARLES TURNER (*b. Scituate, Mass., 1813; d. Maryland, 1846*), Congregational clergyman, anti-Garrison abolitionist.

TORREY, JOHN (*b. New York, N.Y., 1796; d. New York, 1873*), botanist, chemist. Inspired with interest in science by Amos Eaton, Torrey graduated M.D., N.Y. College of Physicians and Surgeons, 1818. In medical practice in New York City, Torrey maintained his interest in mineralogy and botany, and served as reporter and classifier of plant specimens sent to him by a long series of government-sponsored Western exploratory expeditions. He was professor of chemistry, mineralogy and geology at West Point, 1824–27, and professor of chemistry at N.Y. College of Physicians and Surgeons, 1827–55; concurrently with his New York professorship he taught chemistry and natural history at the College of New Jersey (Princeton). On his retirement from teaching, he served for the rest of his life as U.S. assayer in New York City. Torrey's great contribution was in pioneer work on the findings of the aforesaid government exploring expeditions (thereby first describing many plants native to North America) and by his lifelong encouragement of young botanists, including Asa Gray. He was also largely instrumental in establishing the New York Botanical Garden. Among his many books and monographs are the following: *A Catalogue of Plants . . . Within Thirty Miles of the City of New York* (1819); *A Flora of the Northern and Middle Sections of the United States* (1823); *A Compendium of the Flora of the Northern and Middle States* (1826); *Flora of North America* (with Asa Gray, seven parts, 1838–43); *Flora of the State of New*

York (1843); and contributions to the official reports of almost every important survey expedition between 1820 and 1860.

TOSCANINI, ARTURO (*b. Parma, Italy, 1867; d. New York N.Y., 1957*), conductor. Graduated from the Parma Conservatory (1885). Made professional conducting debut conducting *Aida* in Rio de Janeiro (1886) substituting for an ill conductor. Conducted the world premieres of Leoncavallo's *I Pagliacci* (1892) and Puccini's *La Bohème* (1896). Principal conductor at La Scala, Milan (1898–1903 and 1906–08); artistic director (1920–29). Introduced many operas by German, French, and Russian composers; led the world premiere of Puccini's *Turandot* (1926). Associate conductor of the New York Philharmonic (1927–33) and musical director (1933–36). As conductor of the NBC Orchestra (1937–54), elevated it into one of the best orchestras of its day.

Toscanini was a literalist, determined to carry out every demand of a score as strictly and meticulously as he could. Fortunately, he lived in the age of musical recordings and many of his interpretations are preserved.

TOTTEN, GEORGE MUIRSON (*b. New Haven, Conn., 1809; d. 1884*), engineer. A specialist in canal and railroad work, he served for many years *post* 1850 as chief engineer of the Panama Railroad and was an adviser to the French company which first attempted the Panama Canal.

TOTTEN, JOSEPH GILBERT (*b. New Haven, Conn., 1788; d. 1864*), military engineer. Nephew of Jared Mansfield. Graduated West Point, 1805. Highly effective as chief engineer on the Niagara frontier, War of 1812, he served thereafter in coast defense and river and harbor improvement work. Promoted colonel, he became chief engineer of the U.S. Army and inspector of West Point in 1838, holding both posts until his death. During the Mexican War he planned the operations at Veracruz. Thereafter he won high repute in lighthouse work, and during the Civil War as brigadier general supervised the defensive works around Washington, D.C.

TOU, ERIK HANSEN (*b. near Stavanger, Norway, 1857; d. Napoleon, S.Dak., 1917*), Lutheran clergyman. Immigrated to Minneapolis, Minn., 1881. A graduate of Augsburg Seminary, 1886 and 1889, he served as a missionary in Madagascar, 1889–1903.

TOUCEY, ISAAC (*b. Newtown, Conn., 1792; d. Hartford, Conn., 1869*), lawyer, Connecticut legislator and public official. Congressman, Democrat, from Connecticut, 1835–39; governor of Connecticut, 1846–47; U.S. attorney general, June 1848–March 1849. As U.S. senator, 1852–57, he condemned the "higher law" theory of W. H. Seward and was a supporter of the Kansas-Nebraska bill. During his term as U.S. secretary of the navy, 1857–61, he was criticized for a sympathetic attitude toward the South but conducted his department with efficiency and economy.

TOULMIN, HARRY (*b. Taunton, England, 1766; d. Alabama, 1823*), clergyman, educator, jurist. Immigrating to America with Joseph Priestley, 1794, he served briefly as president of Transylvania University, and was secretary to the Commonwealth of Kentucky, 1796–1804. As secretary, he compiled several collections of Kentucky laws. Appointed judge of the superior court for the eastern district of Mississippi Territory, 1804, he opposed filibusters into Spanish territory; he strove to thwart the designs of Aaron Burr (1807) and the later activities of Reuben Kemper. Retaining his judgeship until 1819 he did much to straighten out the land claims in the region, was prominent in the convention that formed the constitution for Alabama, and was editor of *The Statutes of the Mississippi Territory* (1807) and *A Digest of the Territorial Laws of Alabama* (1823).

TOULMIN, HARRY THEOPHILUS (*b. Mobile Co., Ala., 1838; d. Toulminville, Ala., 1916*), Confederate officer, Alabama jurist. Grandson of Harry Toulmin. Alabama state circuit judge, 1874–82; U.S. district judge, southern district of Alabama, 1887–1916.

TOUMEY, JAMES WILLIAM (*b. Lawrence, Mich., 1865; d. 1932*), forester, teacher. Graduated Michigan Agricultural College, 1889. Taught botany at Michigan Agricultural College and University of Arizona, taught at Yale School of Forestry *post* 1900 and served as its dean, 1910–22.

TOURGÉE, ALBION WINEGAR (*b. Williamsfield, Ohio, 1838; d. Bordeaux, France, 1905*), Union soldier, lawyer, North Carolina carpetbag jurist, U.S. consular officer. Author of a number of books, he is remembered chiefly for his novel *A Fool's Errand* (1879), an early literary picture of Reconstruction.

TOURJÉE, EBEN (*b. Warwick, R.I., 1834; d. Boston, Mass., 1891*), musician. Cofounder (1867) of the New England Conservatory of Music.

TOUSARD, ANNE LOUIS DE (*b. Paris, France, 1749; d. Paris, 1817*), French army artillery officer. An active and efficient aide to Lafayette, 1777–78, Tousard later had a colorful career in Santo Domingo and during the first years of the French Revolution. Immigrating to America *ca.* 1793, he was reinstated in the U.S. Army, 1795, and performed useful service as engineer and artillery officer until 1802 when he returned to France. He served as a French consular officer in several America cities, 1805–16.

TOUSEY, SINCLAIR (*b. New Haven, Conn., 1815; d. New York, N.Y., 1887*), news agent. Merged his own news agency and book distribution business with other similar companies into the American News Co., 1864, which he served as president until his death.

TOWER, CHARLEMAGNE (*b. Philadelphia, Pa., 1848; d. Philadelphia, 1923*), lawyer, financier. Graduated Harvard, 1872. U.S. minister to Austria-Hungary, 1897–99; U.S. ambassador to Russia, 1899–1902; U.S. ambassador at Berlin, 1902–08.

TOWER, ZEALOUS BATES (*b. Cohasset, Mass., 1819; d. Cohasset, 1900*), soldier, engineer. Graduated West Point, 1841. Won distinction in the Mexican War for skill in reconnoitering as an engineer on staff of General Winfield Scott. Helped organize defenses of Fort Pickens, Fla., 1861. As Union brigadier general of volunteers, he commanded a brigade with distinction until his serious wounding at the second battle of Bull Run. After brief service as superintendent of West Point, he performed brilliantly as engineer in charge of the field defenses of Nashville, Tenn., his work proving of great service to General George Thomas in the destruction of General Hood's Confederate army (December 1864).

TOWERS, JOHN HENRY (*b. Rome, Ga., 1885; d. New York, N.Y., 1955*), naval aviator. Graduated from the U.S. Naval Academy, 1906. A pioneer in aviation, Towers volunteered for flight training in 1911; in 1912, he set a record for flight endurance. In the battle to win acceptance by the navy of air power, Towers was often involved in squabbles. During the 1930's, he became a key figure in the fleet air modernization as the country anticipated World War II. Worked at the Bureau of Aeronautics as assistant chief, 1938, and chief, 1939–42. In 1942, he became a vice admiral and Commander Air Force Pacific Fleet, developing the fleet's aviation logistics and tactics. As deputy fleet commander for Admiral Nimitz, 1944, Towers played a key role in victory over

Japan. After retirement as a full admiral in 1947, he became an assistant vice president of Pan American World Airways.

TOWLE, GEORGE MAKEPEACE (*b. Washington, D.C., 1841; d. Brookline, Mass., 1893*), Boston journalist, lecturer, and author.

TOWLER, JOHN (*b. Rathmell, Yorkshire, England, 1811; d. Orange, N.J., 1889*), educator. Came to America, 1850; taught at Hobart College and was dean of Geneva Medical College; was also in the U.S. consular service. Editor of *Humphrey's Journal of Photography*, 1862–70, he was author of a number of technical photographic manuals, including the important *The Silver Sunbeam* (1864).

TOWN, ITHIEL (*b. Thompson, Conn., 1784; d. New Haven, Conn., 1844*), architect. Studied in Boston, Mass., with Asher Benjamin. His first important work was the Center Church on New Haven Green; he was next commissioned (1814) to design and build Trinity Church, also on the Green at New Haven. His reputation established, he designed many more public buildings in a number of cities, including the New York Custom House on Wall St. and the state capitols in Indianapolis, Ind., and Raleigh, N.C. He entered partnerships with Martin E. Thompson (1827–28) and Alexander J. Davis (*ca.* 1829–43). Patentee of a truss bridge (1820), he was thereafter celebrated also as a bridge builder. A collector of books on architecture and the fine arts and author of various miscellaneous pieces, he was a founder of the National Academy of Design.

TOWNE, BENJAMIN (*b. Lincolnshire, England, date unknown; d. Philadelphia, Pa., 1793*), printer, journalist. Appeared as a journeyman printer in Philadelphia, 1766. Opening a press of his own, 1774, he published the *Pennsylvania Evening Post*, 1775–84, the first evening newspaper printed in Philadelphia and the only newspaper that continued to be published in that city throughout the Revolutionary War.

TOWNE, CHARLES ARNETTE (*b. Oakland Co., Mich., 1858; d. Tucson, Ariz., 1928*), lawyer. In practice at Duluth, Minn., 1890–1901, and thereafter in New York City, Towne was a Republican congressman from Minnesota, 1895–97. Becoming recognized as leader of the Silver Republicans, he was chairman of their national committee, 1897–1901, and closely associated with William J. Bryan. He served as congressman, Democrat, from New York, 1905–07.

TOWNE, CHARLES HANSON (*b. Louisville, Ky., 1877; d. Earlville, N.Y., 1949*), editor, essayist. Attended College of the City of New York. Held editorial positions successively on *Cosmopolitan* magazine, *Smart Set* (1901–07), *The Delineator, Designer, McClure's Magazine* (1915–20), and *Harper's Bazaar* (1926–29).

TOWNE, HENRY ROBINSON (*b. Philadelphia, Pa., 1844; d. New York, N.Y., 1924*), engineer, manufacturer. Son of John H. Towne. Joined with Linus Yale, 1868, in manufacture of locks at Stamford, Conn.; served as president of Yale Lock Mfg. Co. and its successor corporation, 1868–1916, and was thereafter chairman of its board. Towne was also the pioneer builder of cranes in the United States.

TOWNE, JOHN HENRY (*b. Pittsburgh, Pa., 1818; d. Paris, France, 1875*), engineer, heavy machinery builder, philanthropist. Father of Henry R. Towne. Endowed Towne Scientific School, University of Pennsylvania.

TOWNLEY, ARTHUR CHARLES (*b. Browns Valley, Minn., 1880; d. Makoti, N.Dak., 1959*), political organizer. A farmer in Beach, N.Dak., Townley helped organize and found the Nonpartisan League, 1915; the group espoused the state control to help the farmers and endorsed candidates. The League succeeded in electing the state governor in 1916 and had a clean sweep of the state offices the following year. The group spread to Minnesota and was the father of the Farmer-Labor party. Townley lost all influence in 1921–22, when the League folded because of internal dissension.

TOWNS, GEORGE WASHINGTON BONAPARTE (*b. Wilkes Co., Ga., 1801; d. Macon, Ga., 1854*), lawyer, Georgia legislator and congressman. As Democratic governor of Georgia, 1847–51, he secured amelioraton of the slave code, adoption of the *ad valorem* system of taxation, and completion of the Western and Atlantic Railroad; he also worked to improve public education. Becoming an extreme "fire eater" by 1849, he opposed the Wilmot Proviso and called the convention which adopted the "Georgia platform," later the position taken by the entire South on further invasion of states' rights.

TOWNSEND, EDWARD DAVIS (*b. Boston, Mass., 1817; d. Washington, D.C., 1893*), soldier. Grandson of Elbridge Gerry. Graduated West Point, 1837. Originally an artilleryman, Townsend served for many years in the adjutant general's department, heading it as adjutant general 1862–80 (formal appointment in 1869) with extraordinary tact and efficiency. Collection of material for *War of the Rebellion: Official Records* was owing to him.

TOWNSEND, FRANCIS EVERETT (*b. Fairbury, Ill., 1867; d. Los Angeles, Calif., 1960*), physician. Graduated from Omaha Medical College, 1899. Moved to California in 1919, where he practiced in obscurity and great financial deprivation. Conceived his Old Age Revolving Pension Plan, 1933, designed to distribute $200 per month to every citizen over the age of sixty; the money had to be spent within thirty days to bolster the economy. The plan grew in appeal, and Townsend became a national hero. He joined forces with other reformers in the Union Party. The political force of his plan was felt in Washington, but was undermined by Roosevelt's Social Security Act (1935). Convicted of contempt of Congress, 1937, for refusing to answer questions; President Roosevelt commuted the sentence.

TOWNSEND, GEORGE ALFRED (*b. Georgetown, Del., 1841; d. New York, N.Y., 1914*), journalist, Civil War correspondent. Distinguished for vivid reportorial work for the *New York Herald* and the New York *World*, 1861–65, and also for his work as a Union propagandist in England, he contributed a wise and often satirical series of Washington letters to a great number of newspapers, 1867–*ca.* 1907. This Washington correspondence appeared under the signature of "Gath" and although mainly occupied with politics often dealt with the social life of the time. Among his many books, a novel *The Entailed Hat* (1884) ranks as the best.

TOWNSEND, JOHN KIRK (*b. Philadelphia, Pa., 1809; d. Washington, D.C., 1851*), ornithologist. Traveled to Oregon, 1834, on an expedition with Nathaniel J. Wyeth; visited Hawaii, 1835; served as post surgeon at Fort Vancouver, 1835–36. Described Oregon birds in *Journal of the Academy of Natural Sciences of Philadelphia* (1837, 1839); supplied material on mammals of Oregon and elsewhere for picturing by J. J. Audubon and John Bachman in *Viviparous Quadrupeds of North America* (1845–49). Author of *Narrative of a Journey across the Rocky Mountains to the Columbia River* (1839) and *Ornithology of the United States of America* (one part, 1840; now one of the rarest works on this subject).

TOWNSEND, LUTHER TRACY (*b. Orono, Maine, 1838; d. Brookline, Mass., 1922*), Union soldier, Methodist clergyman. A popular apologist for traditional evangelical theology, he taught church history, classic languages, and theology at present Boston University School of Theology, 1868–93.

TOWNSEND, MARY ASHLEY (*b. Lyons, N.Y., 1832; d. Galveston, Tex., 1901*), New Orleans, La., journalist and poet.

TOWNSEND, MIRA SHARPLESS (*b. Philadelphia, Pa., 1798; d. Philadelphia, 1859*), philanthropist. Founded the Rosine Association and Home for reform of fallen women (Philadelphia); also founded the Temporary Home, a transient residence for unemployed women and destitute children.

TOWNSEND, ROBERT (*b. Albany, N.Y., 1819; d. off the China coast, 1866*), naval officer. Appointed midshipman, 1837. After both army and navy service in the Mexican War, he resigned from the navy, 1851. Returning to the service during the Civil War, he rose to rank of commander on Atlantic blockade duty and in operations *post* 1863 on the Mississippi River. Promoted captain, 1865, he commanded the *Wachusett* of the East India squadron.

TOWNSEND, VIRGINIA FRANCES (*b. New Haven, Conn., 1836; d. Arlington, Mass., 1920*), teacher, magazine editor, writer of popular stories for girls.

TOWNSEND, WILLARD SAXBY, JR. (*b. Cincinnati, Ohio, 1895; d. Chicago, Ill., 1957*), labor leader. Studied at the University of Toronto and the Royal College of Science in Toronto. Organized and was first president of the International Brotherhood of Red Caps, 1936, renamed the United Transport Service Employees (1940). In 1942, Townsend was the first black to obtain a seat on the executive council of the CIO. Appointed to the Committee to Abolish Racial Discrimination, 1942. Earned a degree from the Blackstone Law School, 1951.

TOY, CRAWFORD HOWELL (*b. Norfolk, Va., 1836; d. 1919*), orientalist, educator. Graduated University of Virginia, 1856; studied also in Berlin. Taught biblical interpretation at Southern Baptist Seminary, 1869–79; was Hancock Professor of Hebrew and Oriental languages at Harvard, 1880–1909. Author, among other scholarly studies, of *Introduction to the History of Religions* (1913).

TRACY, BENJAMIN FRANKLIN (*b. near Owego, N.Y., 1830; d. 1915*), lawyer, New York legislator, Union brigadier general by brevet. An able U.S. attorney for the New York eastern district, 1866–73, he later served as one of defense counsel for Henry Ward Beecher and briefly as a judge of the New York court of appeals. U.S. secretary of the navy, 1889–93, he instituted a number of reforms in administration and began work on rebuilding a powerful naval force of the most modern type.

TRACY, JOSEPH (*b. Hartford, Vt., 1793; d. Beverly, Mass., 1874*), Congregational clergyman, editor. Secretary of the Massachusetts Colonization Society, 1842–74, and director of the American Colonization Society *post* 1858, he was active in the founding of Liberia College and made other outstanding contributions to the colonization movement.

TRACY, NATHANIEL (*b. present Newburyport, Mass., 1751; d. Newbury, Mass., 1796*), merchant, Revolutionary patriot. Uncle of Charles and Patrick T. Jackson, and of James Jackson (1777–1867). Graduated Harvard, 1769. Operated privateers and merchant vessels out of Newburyport, 1775–83; after initial success he was reduced to virtual bankruptcy through loss of a number of vessels and other business misfortunes.

TRACY, SPENCER BONAVENTURE (*b. Milwaukee, Wis., 1900; d. Beverly Hills, Calif., 1967*), actor. Attended Ripon College (1921–22) and the American Academy of Dramatic Arts

(1922–23). Originally intending to become a doctor, Tracy decided to become an actor after appearing in Ripon's dramatic productions. His first speaking part on Broadway was in *A Royal Fandango* (1923), but he did not achieve a critical and popular breakthrough until 1930, in *The Last Mile*. His performance attracted the attention of film director John Ford, who cast him in *Up the River* (1930), a comedy about prison life. Fox signed Tracy to a five-year contract in 1931, releasing him in 1935. Immediately thereafter he signed with Metro-Goldwyn-Mayer, where he was cast in the three roles that raised him to stardom: *San Francisco* (1936), *Fury* 1936), and *Libeled Lady* (1936). He received his first Academy Award as best actor for *Captains Courageous* (1937) and his second for *Boys Town* (1938). In 1941 he began a professional and personal association with Katharine Hepburn; they made nine films together. His later films include *Father of the Bride* (1950), *The Old Man and the Sea* (1958), *Inherit the Wind* (1960), and *Judgment at Nuremberg* (1961). He received two Oscars and nine best-actor nominations; to many of his contemporaries, he was the greatest screen actor of his generation.

Tracy, Uriah (*b. present Franklin, Conn., 1755; d. Washington, D.C., 1807*), lawyer, Connecticut legislator and official. Congressman, Federalist, from Connecticut, 1793–96; U.S. senator, 1796–1807. A shrewd partisan politician.

Traetta, Filippo. *See* Trajetta, Philip.

Train, Arthur Cheney (*b. Boston, Mass., 1875; d. New York, N.Y., 1945*), lawyer, author. A.B., Harvard, 1896; LL.B., Harvard Law School, 1899. Assistant district attorney, New York County, New York City, 1901–08 and 1913–15, he won reputation as a skillful prosecutor and gained the experience that he employed in his best remembered stories—the courtroom adventures of lawyer "Ephraim Tutt," an ideal character embodying the virtues of Robin Hood, Abraham Lincoln, and Uncle Sam. Mr. Tutt appeared for the first time in a story in the *Saturday Evening Post*, June 1919, and in some eighty stories thereafter. *Mr. Tutt at His Best* (1961, with an introduction by Judge Harold Medina) is a representative selection.

Train, Enoch (*b. probably Weston, Mass., 1801; d. Saugus, Mass., 1868*), Boston merchant, shipowner. Father of Adeline D. T. Whitney. Established a line of sailing packets between Boston and Liverpool, 1844; commissioned a number of vessels from Donald McKay. Made notable success by importing Irish immigrants *post* 1846, serving also as an immigrant agent and banker.

Train, George Francis (*b. Boston, Mass., 1829; d. New York, N.Y., 1904*), Boston merchant, shipowner, champion of eccentric causes.

Trajetta, Philip (*b. Venice, Italy, ca. 1776; d. probably Philadelphia, Pa., 1854*), musician, composer, Italian revolutionary. Resided and worked in a number of American cities *post* 1799; composed operas, oratorios, and cantatas.

Trask, James Dowling (*b. Astoria, L.I., N.Y., 1890; d. Chicago, Ill., 1942*), pediatrician, medical researcher. Ph.B., Yale, 1913. M.D., Cornell Medical College, 1917. After World War I service with U.S. Army Medical Corps, he worked at Rockefeller Institute, New York City, 1919–21, on determination of the cause of measles; thereafter, he taught at Yale Medical School and carried out important studies on pneumonia, scarlet fever, and streptococcal infections. Appointed to two commissions of the U.S. Army's epidemiological board, 1941, he contracted a fatal disease while investigating an outbreak of streptococcal infection at Chanute Field, Illinois.

Traubel, Horace L. (*b. Camden, N.J., 1858; d. Bon Echo, Ontario, Canada, 1919*), journalist. A close friend of Walt Whitman, Traubel served as one of his literary executors and was author of *With Walt Whitman in Camden* (1906–14), a valuable diary of his association with the poet beginning March 1888. He was also active in the American Socialist movement and edited a monthly paper, the *Conservator*, 1890–1919.

Trautwine, John Cresson (*b. Philadelphia, Pa., 1810; d. Philadelphia, 1883*), engineer, mineralogist. Trained in office of William Strickland, Trautwine was employed mainly in railroad work in the United States until 1844. Between 1849 and 1853 he worked on surveys for the Panama Railroad in association with George M. Totten and explored the Isthmus of Panama in search of a possible route for an interoceanic ship canal. He was author, among other works, of the celebrated *Engineers' Pocket Book*, first published in 1871.

Travers, Jerome Dunstan (*b. New York, N.Y., 1887; d. East Hartford, Conn., 1951*), amateur golfer. Dominated American amateur golf from 1907 to 1915. Won the U.S. Amateur in 1907, 1908, 1912, and 1913. Won the U.S. Open in 1915. One of the first members of the Golf Hall of Fame, 1940.

Travis, Walter John (*b. Maldon, Australia, 1862; d. Denver, Colo., 1927*), champion amateur golfer of the United States, 1900, 1901, 1903; British amateur champion, 1904.

Travis, William Barret (*b. near Red Banks, S.C., 1809; d. The Alamo, San Antonio, Tex., 1836*), lawyer, leader in the Texas revolution. Raised in Alabama, Travis removed to Texas, 1831, where he practiced first at Anahuac and later at San Felipe. Active in local politics and in opposition to Mexican rule, Travis was commissioned lieutenant colonel of cavalry late in 1835. Ordered to reinforce the Alamo which the Texans had taken, he assumed joint command of the post with James Bowie, Feb. 13, 1836, and was in full command subsequent to Feb. 24. He died with his men in the final massacre.

Traylor, Melvin Alvah (*b. Breeding, Ky., 1878; d. Chicago, Ill., 1934*), banker, lawyer. Beginning his career in Texas, he was active in Chicago banking circles *post ca.* 1914 and held the presidency of the First National Bank *post* 1925. A liberal man, he was active in drought relief and other civic affairs and represented the United States in the organization of the Bank for International Settlements.

Treadwell, Daniel (*b. Ipswich, Mass., 1791; d. Cambridge, Mass., 1872*), inventor, Rumford Professor at Harvard. Apprenticed to a silversmith, he gave much of his time to experiments with machinery and patented a power printing press (March 1826) which became widely used in book and newspaper printing. Between 1831 and 1835 he secured basic patents for a hemp-spinning machine which attained worldwide use. A popular lecturer on the steam engine and other practical subjects, he also devised a system of turnouts for railroad operation and a method of manufacturing steel cannon out of rings welded together and reinforced by bands. Internationally honored, he was active in many learned societies.

Treat, Robert (*b. Pitminster, England, ca. 1622; d. Milford, Conn., 1710*), Connecticut colonial official. Settled at Wethersfield, Conn., by 1639, he soon removed to Milford and by 1653 was deputy from Milford to the General Court. A holder of various town offices, he actively opposed absorption of New Haven Colony by Connecticut and was leader of the group from New Haven which settled Newark, N.J. He represented Newark in the East Jersey Assembly, 1667–72. Returning to Milford, he was active in military affairs, commanding the Connecticut troops operating against King Philip, 1675, and in later Indian skirmishes. Elected deputy governor of Connecticut, 1676, he advanced to the governorship in 1683 and held that office until 1687. After the overthrow of Andros's government, 1689, Treat became governor again and served until 1698, maintaining the conservative traditions of the colony. He was deputy governor, 1698–1708.

TREAT, SAMUEL (*b. Portsmouth, N.H., 1815; d. Rochester, N.Y., 1902*), Missouri jurist, teacher of law. Removing to St. Louis, Mo., 1841, he became influential in Democratic politics and was judge of the St. Louis court of common pleas, 1849–57. Appointed U.S. district judge for eastern Missouri, 1857, he served until 1887 and was one of the organizers of the law school at Washington University. He was expert in admiralty law.

TREAT, SAMUEL HUBBELL (*b. Plainfield, N.Y., 1811; d. 1887*), Illinois jurist. Admitted to the New York bar, 1834, he removed to Springfield, Ill., where he soon had an extensive practice. State circuit court judge, 1839–41, and state supreme court judge, 1841–55, he served thereafter as U.S. judge for the southern district of Illinois. He was coeditor and annotator of *The Statutes of Illinois* (1858).

TREE, LAMBERT (*b. Washington, D.C., 1832, d. New York, N.Y., 1910*), lawyer, diplomat. Practiced in Chicago, Ill., *post* 1855; served as a reforming judge of Cook Co. circuit court, 1870–75. A Democrat, he was U.S. minister to Belgium, 1885–88, and U.S. minister to Russia briefly in 1888.

TRELEASE, WILLIAM (*b. Mount Vernon, N.Y., 1857; d. Urbana, Ill., 1945*), botanist. B.S., Cornell University, 1880; made graduate studies at Harvard, receiving the S.D. degree in 1884. Taught botany at University of Wisconsin, 1881–85; headed Shaw School of Botany, Washington University, St. Louis, Mo., and was director of the Missouri Botanical Garden, 1889–1912. Professor of botany, University of Illinois, 1913–26. Author of some three hundred papers and extensive monographs, marked by unusual bibliographic thoroughness.

TREMAIN, HENRY EDWIN (*b. New York, N.Y., 1840; d. 1910*), Union officer, New York City lawyer and legal editor. Medal of Honor winner for gallantry at Resaca.

TREMAINE, HENRY BARNES (*b. Brooklyn, N.Y., 1866; d. Washington, D.C., 1932*), manufacturer of mechanical musical instruments, developer of the player piano. President, Aeolian Co., 1898–1930.

TRENCHARD, STEPHEN DECATUR (*b. Brooklyn, N.Y., 1818; d. 1883*), naval officer. Appointed midshipman, 1834. Served throughout the Civil War principally on blockade duty; won particular distinction in the second attack on Fort Fisher. Commissioned captain, 1866, he retired as rear admiral, 1880.

TRENHOLM, GEORGE ALFRED (*b. Charleston, S.C., 1807; d. Charleston, 1876*), cotton broker, South Carolina legislator, financier. Rendered important but unspectacular aid to the Confederacy through financial relations abroad and blockade running. Confederate secretary of the treasury, June 1864–65.

TRENT, WILLIAM (*b. probably Philadelphia, Pa., 1715; d. Philadelphia, ca. 1787*), Indian trader, land speculator. In partnership with George Croghan, *ca.* 1749–*ca.* 1755. Trent along with others suffered loss from French and Indian raids along the Ohio in 1754 and later during Pontiac's uprising, 1763. In compensation, he and his associates, including Samuel Wharton and George Morgan, got from the Iroquois a grant of a tract along the upper Ohio known as "Indiana," Accompanying Wharton to England, 1769, he remained there until 1775, endeavoring to obtain royal confirmation of this grant and of another larger project known as Vandalia. Failing to do so, he returned home and continued to present unsuccessful memorials to the Virginia Assembly and to Congress in the hope of securing validation of title.

TRENT, WILLIAM PETERFIELD (*b. Richmond, Va., 1862; d. Hopewell Junction, N.Y., 1939*), educator, historian. Graduated University of Virginia, 1883; A.M., 1884. Made postgraduate studies in history at Johns Hopkins where he was deeply influenced by Herbert B. Adams. As professor at University of the South, Sewanee, Tenn., 1888–1900, he changed his field from history to literature, and in 1900 began a long career at Columbia University as professor of English literature, Barnard College. Professor also in the graduate school of the university, he remained active in teaching until 1927. A prodigious worker, Trent was editor of a number of texts and author of many books. Among his early works, his *William Gilmore Simms* (1892) was condemned by southern critics for its unfair criticism of the environment in which Simms lived and wrote. A principal editor of the *Cambridge History of American Literature* (1917–21) and editor-in-chief of the Columbia edition of *The Works of John Milton* in the earlier stages of its development, Trent devoted many years of research to a monumental work on Daniel Defoe which remains unpublished. As a teacher he insisted always on appreciation of literature for its own sake subordinating philology and literary history to aesthetic understanding.

TRESCA, CARLO (*b. Sulmona, Italy, 1879; d. New York, N.Y., 1943*), labor agitator, journalist. A revolutionary activist in the 19th-century, romantic tradition, he came to the United States in 1904. Associated at various times with the socialists, the communist anarchists, the I.W.W., and the communist wing of the socialists, he was a consistent and truculent enemy of totalitarianism *post ca.* 1937. A man with many enemies, he was murdered on January 11, 1943, as he left his office in New York City; his murderer was never discovered.

TRESCOT, WILLIAM HENRY (*b. Charleston, S.C., 1822; d. Pendleton, S.C., 1898*), lawyer, South Carolina Confederate legislator, U.S. diplomatic agent, historian. After winning repute as a public speaker and for a number of valuable historical works which included *The Position and Course of the South* (1850), *Diplomacy of the Revolution* (1852), and *The Diplomatic History of the Administrations of Washington and Adams* (1857), he was appointed assistant U.S. secretary of state, 1860. On South Carolina's secession in December of that year, he resigned but stayed in Washington until February 1861 as unofficial adviser of the South Carolina authorities, playing an important part in the negotiations over the Charleston forts and endeavoring to postpone a crisis by preventing reinforcements of the forts by the federal government. After valuable services to the Confederacy, he worked *post* 1865 in Washington as South Carolina agent for recovery of lands seized and taxes levied under the direct tax act of Congress. He also served as a special diplomatic agent of the United States in missions to China, Chile, and Mexico.

TREVELLICK, RICHARD F. (*b. St. Mary's, Scilly Islands, England, 1830; d. Detroit, Mich., 1895*), ship's carpenter, seaman, labor leader. Immigrating to New Orleans, La., 1857, and settling in Detroit, 1861, he became president of the ship carpenters' and caulkers' union and also first president of the Detroit Trades' Assembly. He was president of the National Labor Union, 1869, 1871–72. In 1868, at his own expense, he led one of the first successful labor lobbies, pushing an eight-hour-day act for federal mechanics and laborers through Congress; he also upheld the unpopular idea of abolishing the color line in unions. Active in the Greenback party and convinced of the need for combined industrial and political labor activity, he was one of the first great labor agitators of America.

TRIMBLE, ALLEN (*b. Augusta Co., Va., 1783; d. Hillsboro, Ohio, 1870*), agriculturist, Ohio legislator. Raised near Lexington, Ky.; settled in present Highland Co., Ohio, 1805. Acting governor of Ohio, 1822. National Republican governor of Ohio, 1826–30, he was a supporter of Henry Clay's policies and continued after retirement to be an active Whig.

TRIMBLE, ISAAC RIDGEWAY (*b. Culpeper Co., Va., 1802; d. Baltimore, Md., 1888*), soldier, engineer. Raised in Kentucky. Graduated West Point, 1822. Resigning from the army, 1832, he engaged in railroad surveys and management, and was general superintendent of the Baltimore and Potomac Railroad, 1859–61. Commissioned Confederate brigadier general, he served with distinction under Ewell and T. J. Jackson in the Army of Northern Virginia, notably at the second battle of Bull Run in which he was seriously wounded. Commissioned major general, 1862, he was again badly wounded at Gettysburg and taken prisoner. He was not exchanged until just before Appomattox.

TRIMBLE, ROBERT (*b. Augusta Co., Va., 1777; d. Paris, Ky., 1828*), Kentucky jurist. Studied law under George Nicholas and James Brown; practiced at Paris, Ky., *post* 1800. An outstanding lawyer of his section, he was U.S. district judge for Kentucky, 1817–26. Appointed a justice of the U.S. Supreme Court, 1826, he served until his untimely death, supporting John Marshall on constitutional doctrine in most cases but differing with him in *Ogden* v. *Saunders* (12 *Wheaton*, 121), wherein Trimble wrote one of his ablest opinions.

TRIPP, BARTLETT (*b. Harmony, Maine, 1842; d. Yankton, S.Dak., 1911*), jurist, diplomat. Practiced in Dakota Territory *post ca.* 1869; presided over first territorial constitutional convention, 1883; chief justice, territorial supreme court, 1885–89. As U.S. minister to Austria-Hungary, 1893–97, he secured Austrian consent to a ruling that its administrative officers must accept American passports as *prima facie* evidence of American citizenship. He was chairman of the Samoan commission, 1899.

TRIPP, GUY EASTMAN (*b. Wells, Maine, 1865; d. New York, N.Y., 1927*), industrialist. An associate and officer of Stone & Webster, 1897–1911, he became chairman of the board of Westinghouse Electric & Manufacturing Co. in 1912 and held that post until his death. During World War I, as brigadier general he gave important assistance to the chief of ordnance, U.S. Army.

TRIPPE, JOHN (*b. Dorchester Co., Md., 1785; d. Havana, Cuba, 1810*), naval officer. Appointed midshipman, 1799, he is particularly remembered for his single combat with a Tripolitan ship captain during a boarding mission off Tripoli, Aug. 3, 1804.

TRIST, NICHOLAS PHILIP (*b. Charlottesville, Va., 1800; d. Alexandria, Va., 1874*), diplomat, lawyer. Attended West Point; studied in law office of Thomas Jefferson whose granddaughter, Virginia Jefferson Randolph, he later married. A man of high integrity, Trist served as U.S. consul to Havana, Cuba, 1833–41. Appointed chief clerk of the U.S. State Department, 1845, he went as special agent to negotiate a treaty of peace with Mexico, 1847. Exceeding his instructions, he was recalled in November 1847, possibly as part of a U.S. government maneuver to exact severer terms. Trist, however, considered it his duty to proceed with the work and on Feb. 2, 1848, signed a treaty in strict compliance with his original instructions, thereby ending his diplomatic career.

TROLAND, LEONARD THOMPSON (*b. Norwich, Conn., 1889; d. California, 1932*), psychologist, scientist, inventor.

B.S., Massachusetts Institute of Technology, 1912; Ph.D., Harvard, 1915. A teacher of psychology at Harvard, 1916–29, and noted for his researches in physiological optics, Troland was chief engineer and director of research for the Technicolor Motion Picture Corp. *post* 1918. He invented and perfected the modern multicolor process for colored motion pictures in all its details.

TROOST, GERARD (*b. Bois-le-Duc, Holland, 1776; d. Nashville, Tenn., 1850*), geologist. Educated at the universities of Leyden and Amsterdam, Troost practiced as a pharmacist and served in the Netherlands army; he traveled in Europe making collections of minerals for the King of Holland, 1807–09. Sailing from Paris, Troost arrived in America early in 1810. Resident in Philadelphia, Pa., 1810–25, he established a pharmaceutical and chemical laboratory; a founder of the Academy of Natural Sciences in Philadelphia, 1812, he served it for five years as its first president. Joining William Maclure, Thomas Say, Robert D. Owen, and others in the community at New Harmony, Ind., 1825, he removed in 1827 to Nashville, Tenn., and was professor of sciences at the University of Nashville, 1828–50. He was also state geologist of Tennessee *post* 1831.

TROTT, BENJAMIN (*b. probably Boston, Mass., ca. 1770; d. probably Baltimore, Md., ca. 1841*), portrait painter, miniaturist. Trott was self-taught save for experience gained making miniatures after the portraits of Gilbert Stuart. His best work (done *ca.* 1805) is excelled only by that of Malbone and is distinguished by fine clear color, a talent for characterization, elimination of any but the most necessary costume details, and a characteristic elongation of the neck line and collar.

TROTT, NICHOLAS (*b. England, 1662/63; d. Charleston, S.C., 1739/40*), colonial jurist and official. Came to Charleston, S.C., in May 1699 as attorney general of that part of the Province of Carolina which lay south and west of Cape Fear. An English lawyer of great learning (not to be confused with Nicholas Trott, governor of the Bahamas, his cousin), he became a member of the Commons House and its speaker and was an aggressive leader of the ruling faction in the province until *ca.* 1720. Appointed chief justice, 1702/03, he continued to claim that office as late as 1729. He was author, among other works, of *The Laws of the Province of South Carolina* (1736).

TROUP, GEORGE MICHAEL (*b. McIntosh's Bluff, on Tombigbee River, present Alabama, 1780; d. Montgomery Co., Ga., 1856*), lawyer, Georgia legislator. Graduated College of New Jersey (Princeton), 1797. Congressman, Democratic-Republican, from Georgia, 1807–15, he opposed the Yazoo claims and recharter of the federal bank; he was a consistent supporter of the Jeffersonian program. U.S. senator, 1816–18, he was Crawford Democrat governor of Georgia, 1823–27, in which time he vigorously defended the rights of the state to Creek lands in defiance of President John Q. Adams. Again U.S. senator, 1829–33, he upheld the right of nullification but considered it unwise; he urged legislative action and southern nonconsumption as remedies against tariff pressures from Washington. After his formal retirement from political office, he continued active as a strong states' rights Democrat.

TROUP, ROBERT (*b. probably New York, 1757; d. New York, N.Y., 1832*), Revolutionary soldier, New York jurist and land agent. Interested in land speculation *post* 1794, he was successful as agent for the Pulteney interests in western New York State, 1801–32, and closely connected with settlement of the Genesee country.

TROW, JOHN FOWLER (*b. Andover, Mass., 1810; d. Orange, N.J., 1886*), printer, bookseller, publisher. In business in New

York City *post* 1833, he is best remembered for his publication of *Trow's New York City Directory*, post *ca.* 1852.

TROWBRIDGE, AUGUSTUS (b. *New York, N.Y., 1870; d. Taormina, Sicily, 1934*), physicist. Attended Columbia University; Ph.D., Berlin, 1898. Taught physics at universities of Michigan and Wisconsin; was professor of physics at Princeton, 1906–33. An able administrator and research scholar in the field of radiation, he was dean of the graduate school at Princeton, 1928–32.

TROWBRIDGE, EDMUND (b. *Cambridge, Mass., 1709; d. Cambridge, 1793*), jurist. Graduated Harvard, 1728. Massachusetts attorney general, 1749–67, he served as judge of the superior court from 1767 until the Revolution with great ability and impartiality. A moderate conservative and an expert in real property law, he presided over the Boston Massacre trial with fairness and courage. Among his pupils in the law were Theophilus Parsons and Francis Dana, his nephew.

TROWBRIDGE, JOHN (b. *Boston, Mass., 1843; d. Cambridge, Mass., 1923*), physicist, educator. S.B., Lawrence Scientific School, Harvard, 1865. A teacher of physics at Harvard and Massachusetts Institute of Technology for many years, he was Rumford Professor of Science, 1888–1910, and director of the Jefferson Physical Laboratory. A proponent of original research by students, Trowbridge was largely responsible for modernizing methods of teaching science at Harvard and development of improved laboratory facilities there. He was author of a number of research papers in spectrum analysis and the conduction of electricity through gases.

TROWBRIDGE, JOHN TOWNSEND (b. *Monroe Co., N.Y., 1827; d. Arlington, Mass., 1916*), journalist, novelist, poet. Author of a number of works of which the most popular and successful were stories for older boys.

TROWBRIDGE, WILLIAM PETIT (b. *Troy, N.Y., 1828; d. New Haven, Conn., 1892*), engineer, educator. Graduated West Point, 1848. Engaged for a number of years in coast survey work and geodetic surveys, he performed valuable services for the Union Army during the Civil War, taught engineering at Yale, 1871–77, and thereafter was professor of engineering in the School of Mines, Columbia University.

TROYE, EDWARD (b. *near Geneva, Switzerland, 1808; d. Georgetown, Ky., 1874*), Artist whose paintings (*post* 1835) of celebrated American blood horses have much historical and artistic value.

TRUDE, ALFRED SAMUEL (b. *New York, N.Y., 1847; d. 1933*), lawyer. Removed to Chicago, Ill., *ca.* 1864; practiced there *post* 1871; one of the most successful trial lawyers of his time in both civil and criminal cases.

TRUDEAU, EDWARD LIVINGSTON (b. *New York, N.Y., 1848; d. Saranac Lake, N.Y., 1915*), physician, pioneer in tuberculosis research. After early education in France and study at Columbia College, Trudeau graduated at New York College of Physicians and Surgeons, 1871. Stricken with pulmonary tuberculosis, 1873, he moved to the Adirondacks where he lived quietly until 1880 when he resumed medical practice in that region. His work led him to the study of both early diagnosis of tuberculosis and the cure of tubercular patients. In 1884 he founded what became Trudeau Sanatorium, the first American institution of its type; he also built a laboratory (eventually the Saranac Laboratory) where the first tuberculosis immunity experiments in America were performed.

TRUE, ALFRED CHARLES (b. *Middletown, Conn., 1853; d. 1929*), leader in agricultural education. Brother of Frederick W. True. Educated at Wesleyan and Harvard, True taught classic languages for some years before joining the staff of the office of experiment stations, U.S. Department of Agriculture, 1889. He became director of the office in 1893 and expanded its function greatly, supervising research and publication in agricultural education, home economics, irrigation and drainage, and also directing experiment stations in the territories. True's influence was furthered by leadership in what became the Association of Land Grant Colleges and Universities.

TRUE, FREDERICK WILLIAM (b. *Middletown, Conn., 1858; d. 1914*), zoologist. Brother of Alfred C. True. *Post* 1881 an executive of the Smithsonian Institution and ultimately curator of the National Museum, he combined administrative functions with scholarly research on whales and other mammals.

TRUEBLOOD, BENJAMIN FRANKLIN (b. *Salem, Ind., 1847; d. 1916*), educator, professional pacifist worker. Secretary, American Peace Society, 1892–1915.

TRUETT, GEORGE WASHINGTON (b. *near Hayesville, N.C., 1867; d. Dallas, Tex., 1944*), Southern Baptist clergyman. Ordained, 1890. Graduated Baylor University, 1897. Principal pastorate at First Baptist Church, Dallas, 1897–1944. A great preacher and revivalist.

TRUMAN, BENJAMIN CUMMINGS (b. *Providence, R.I., 1835; d. Los Angeles, Calif., 1916*), journalist, federal official, author. A brilliant Civil War correspondent, he observed conditions in the South, 1865–66, reporting them in letters to the *New York Times* and also in *Senate Exec. Doc. No. 43*, 39th Congress, 1st Session.

TRUMBAUER, HORACE (b. *Philadelphia, Pa., 1868; d. Philadelphia, 1938*), architect. Began his own practice in Philadelphia, 1892; became preferred architect for activities of Peter A. B. Widener and his financial allies, the Elkins family. Working principally in the style of the French Renaissance, he excelled in persuading his clients that their magnificent incomes could find best expression in magnificence of building. His firm's work is best represented in Philadelphia and New York and the areas about those cities, but it was also responsible for the plans for the entire campus of Duke University at Durham, N.C. Among the designers whose work contributed to Trumbauer's success were Frank Seeburger, William O. Frank, and Julian Abele.

TRUMBULL, BENJAMIN (b. *Hebron, Conn., 1735; d. 1820*), Congregational clergyman, historian. Pastor *post* 1760 at North Haven, Conn., he is remembered for his valuable chronicle of Connecticut history from the beginnings to 1764 (first volume, 1797; extended edition, 1818).

TRUMBULL, HENRY CLAY (b. *Stonington, Conn., 1830; d. Philadelphia, Pa., 1903*), Congregational clergyman, Union chaplain in Civil War, Sunday School missionary and writer. Brother of James H. Trumbull.

TRUMBULL, JAMES HAMMOND (b. *Stonington, Conn., 1821; d. Hartford, Conn., 1897*), Connecticut public official, bibliographer, philologist. Brother of Henry C. Trumbull. Historian of New England Indians, particularly those of Connecticut; edited Connecticut colonial records; catalogued library of George Brinley.

TRUMBULL, JOHN (b. *Westbury, Conn., 1750 o.s.; d. Detroit, Mich., 1831*), poet, Connecticut jurist. Descendant of Solomon Stoddard; second cousin of John (1756–1843), Jonathan (1740–1809), and Joseph Trumbull. Passed Yale entrance examination at age of 7 but did not in fact matriculate until 13. As student, he was critical of a curriculum which neglected *belles lettres* in favor of theology, linguistics, and mathematics. Achieving more than local reputation for poems both satirical and classic and for prose essays, he graduated in 1767 but continued his studies at Yale and was awarded the M.A., 1770. While a Yale tutor, 1772–73, he composed and published a satire on college studies, *The Progress of Dulness*; he was also author of a series of essays published under pen name "The Correspondent" in *The Connecticut Journal* (1770 and 1773). Removing to Boston, Mass., 1773, he continued legal studies under John Adams and published a poem on national affairs. *An Elegy on the Times* (1774). He practiced law at New Haven, Conn., 1774–77, and *post* 1781 at Hartford. Meanwhile he had written the first canto of his *M'Fingal* which was published early in 1776 bearing a 1775 imprint; after the Revolution he divided this canto into two and wrote two additional ones, publishing the entire work for the first time at Hartford, 1782. A Hudibrastic, loose narrative of the troubles of a Tory squire, the poem constitutes a comprehensive review of the blunders of pro-British leaders, and took rank *post* 1783 as an important contribution to American literature; it was the most popular American poem of its length before Longfellow's *Evangeline*. Although regarded as literary leader of the "Hartford Wits," 1785–1800, Trumbull did little to sustain his reputation and showed an increasing interest in law and politics. A strong Federalist, he held state office and served in the legislature; he was judge of the state superior court, 1801–19, and judge of the state supreme court of errors, 1808–19. *The Poetical Works of John Trumbull*, a collected edition, appeared in 1820.

TRUMBULL, JOHN (*b. Lebanon, Conn., 1756; d. New York, N.Y., 1843*), painter of the Revolution. Son of Jonathan Trumbull (1710–85); brother of Jonathan (1740–1809) and Joseph Trumbull; second cousin of John Trumbull (1750–1831). Showed early talent for drawing, but was given little opportunity for study, either during years at Harvard (graduated 1773) or during intermittent military service in the Revolution. At one time an aide-de-camp of George Washington, Trumbull resigned his commission in 1777. He served as a volunteer in the Rhode Island campaign, 1778, but devoted the years 1777–79 mainly to the study of art in Boston. In 1780 he went abroad, settling in England where he became a pupil of Benjamin West. Imprisoned on suspicion of treason and released, he went to Amsterdam and there painted a full-length portrait of Washington which was engraved and published (1781) as the first authentic likeness of the General issued in Europe. Returning to America, he engaged in commercial activities but in 1783 was back in West's London studio. Here he produced his first paintings of the Revolution, *The Battle of Bunker Hill* and the *Death of General Montgomery in the Attack of Quebec* (completed, 1786). Engravings were arranged for, though not published for twelve years.

The years 1786–89, spent in London mainly, were his most productive. He began his 8 years' labors on his *Declaration of Independence*, the most important visual record of the heroic period of American history. (Of its 48 portraits, 36 were from life, the rest from portraits by others or from memory; 13 signers were not represented and 4 non-signers were included.) Other paintings of this period include the *Surrender of Lord Cornwallis at Yorktown* and *Capture of the Hessians at Trenton*. Declining Thomas Jefferson's offer of the post of private secretary in the American Legation in Paris, he returned to America, 1789. He painted portraits, took records of "heads" for his planned historical compositions, and solicited subscriptions for engravings, but the results did not meet his expectations. As John Jay's private secretary, 1793–94, he was successful in diplomatic duties connected with Jay's Treaty; he was unsuccessful in prosecution of various commercial ventures on his own account, 1795–97.

Appointed a commissioner to oversee execution of the seventh article of Jay's Treaty, he served with distinction, 1796–1804.

Trumbull married an Englishwoman in 1800 and returned with her to America in 1804, settling in New York City where he had indifferent success as a painter and art dealer. A rapid painter, he averaged five sittings to a head for which he charged $100. His style had deteriorated from disuse, however, and commissions were infrequent; in 1808 he returned to London where he was no more fortunate. In 1815 he was back in New York and two years later secured a congressional commission, over the opposition of many younger painters, to do four panels on Revolutionary subjects for the Rotunda of the U.S. Capitol at Washington. D.C. These heavy-handed, chalky, oversized reworkings of his earlier masterful paintings were unsuccessful despite seven years' effort. Other troubles were added to a steady decline in reputation and income. In 1824 his wife died. In 1826 the founding of the National Academy of Design by S. F. B. Morse and others deprived Trumbull of influence he had wielded as president of the American Academy of Fine Arts. A serious financial crisis was probably averted in 1832 by a military pension and the establishment of the Trumbull Gallery at Yale, the earliest art museum in America connected with an educational institution, which took over the artist's unsalable pictures. In his prime, Trumbull was handsome and courtly, frank and abstemious, excitable and exceedingly sensitive. As an old and disappointed man he became irritable and uncompromising. He published his *Autobiography* in 1841.

Far as he is from America's greatest painter, he is an important part of the national cultural heritage. His 250 to 300 faithful representations, drawn from life, of the principal actors and actions of the Revolution make him the chief, the most prolific, and the most competent visual recorder of that heroic time.

TRUMBULL, JONATHAN (*b. Lebanon, Conn., 1710; d. 1785*), merchant, Connecticut legislator and jurist. Father of John (1756–1843), Jonathan (1740–1809), and Joseph Trumbull. Graduated Harvard, 1727. A candidate for the ministry, he became his father's business associate when his elder brother died, 1731. His commercial ventures flourished for many years, but in 1766 he suffered a reverse for reasons not entirely clear. Meanwhile he had entered politics. First elected to the Connecticut Assembly in 1733, he served in that body or as assistant in the Council almost continually until 1766. In that year Trumbull became deputy governor, holding concurrently the post of chief justice of the superior court. In 1769 he was named governor by the Assembly (and served until his retirement in 1784). A constant supporter of colonial rights, he was the only colonial governor to take the radical side when the Revolution began. During the war Trumbull's chief contribution lay in making Connecticut a principal source of supplies for Washington's army. Though he and Washington frequently differed over details, Washington subsequently acknowledged the great importance of Trumbull's services. When the war ended, Trumbull's expressed wish for a stronger central government made him unpopular in Connecticut; this and other political complications caused his voluntary retirement.

TRUMBULL, JONATHAN (*b. Lebanon, Conn., 1740; d. 1809*), merchant, Connecticut legislator, Revolutionary soldier. Son of Jonathan Trumbull (1710–85); brother of John (1756–1843) and Joseph Trumbull. Graduated Harvard, 1759. Paymaster of the forces, New York department, Continental Army, 1775–78; first comptroller of the U.S. treasury, November 1778–April 1779; secretary to General George Washington, 1781–83. Congressman, Federalist, from Connecticut, 1789–94; was chosen speaker of the House in October 1791. U.S. senator, March 1795–June 1796, he resigned to become deputy governor of Connecticut. He succeeded to the governorship, December

1797, and was annually reelected to that post for the remainder of his life. He refused to employ the Connecticut militia in enforcement of the Embargo, 1809.

TRUMBULL, JOSEPH (*b. Lebanon, Conn., 1737; d. Lebanon, 1778*), merchant, Connecticut legislator, Revolutionary soldier. Son of Jonathan Trumbull (1710–85); brother of John (1756–1843) and Jonathan Trumbull (1740–1809). Graduated Harvard, 1756. Serving as commissary general of Connecticut troops at the siege of Boston, he showed so much efficiency that Congress at General George Washington's request appointed him commissary general of the Continental Army with the rank of colonel, July 1775. Bringing order out of chaos, he served with great ability until his resignation in 1777 over a proposal by Congress to reorganize his department. "Few armies if any," wrote Washington, "have been better and more plentifully supplied than the troops under Mr. Trumbull's care."

TRUMBULL, LYMAN (*b. Colchester, Conn., 1813; d. Chicago, Ill., 1896*), Illinois jurist. Grandson of Benjamin Trumbull. Began practice of law in Belleville, Ill., 1837. Originally a Democrat, he became a Republican after election to the U.S. Senate (1854) as a Free-Soiler. He had Abraham Lincoln's support. As senator, he opposed Douglas on Kansas. He helped Lincoln during the Civil War but resisted executive encroachments on congressional authority. After aiding the Radicals against President Andrew Johnson, he opposed impeachment and later Radical actions as legally excessive. He gave support to Horace Greeley as a Liberal Republican before retiring from the Senate, 1873. He was counsel for Samuel J. Tilden in the contest over the 1876 election. An able statesman and scholarly constitutionalist, he missed fame because of a colorless personality.

TRUTEAU, JEAN BAPTISTE (*b. Montreal, Canada, 1748; d. St. Louis, Mo., 1827*), Indian trader, explorer. Schoolmaster in St. Louis *post* 1774; leader and diarist of exploring expedition on upper Missouri, 1794–95.

TRUXTUN, THOMAS (*b. near Hempstead, N.Y., 1755; d. Philadelphia, Pa., 1822*), naval officer, merchant mariner. A successful privateersman during the Revolution, he took out the first Philadelphia ship to China, the *Canton*, in 1786. Made captain in the U.S. Navy, 1794, he published several important service manuals. During the naval war with France, as commodore of a squadron operating in the West Indies, he served aboard the *Constellation*, winning actions against the French frigates *Insurgente* and *La Vengeance*, 1799–1800. Energetic and a strict disciplinarian, he set high and enduring standards for the young navy.

TRUXTUN, WILLIAM TALBOT (*b. Philadelphia, Pa., 1824; d. Norfolk, Va., 1887*), naval officer. Grandson of Thomas Truxtun. Appointed midshipman, 1841, he saw extensive service at sea up to the Civil War. During that conflict he held several commands on Atlantic blockade duty, winning the commendation of Adm. D. D. Porter. Engaged in navy-yard administration *post-bellum*, he retired as commodore, 1886.

TRYON, DWIGHT WILLIAM (*b. Hartford, Conn., 1849; d. 1925*), landscape painter, art teacher. Self-taught, Tryon worked first in the manner of John F. Kensett or William T. Richards. After study and work abroad, 1876–81 (principally in France under a disciple of Ingres), he achieved his own mature manner. Conservative in style, refined but somewhat lacking in color, Tryon's work won the admiration of Homer Martin and J. A. M. Whistler for its quality of exquisiteness and its rendering of tiny differences of tone at dusk. He painted few pictures but took great pains with them and sold them well; Charles L. Freer was a principal patron and friend. Tryon was visiting professor of art at Smith College, 1885–1923.

TRYON, GEORGE WASHINGTON (*b. Philadelphia, Pa., 1838; d. Philadelphia, 1888*), businessman, conchologist. Long active in Academy of Natural Sciences of Philadelphia; author of a number of studies on mollusks, and of the *Manual of Conchology, Structural and Systematic* (12 vols., 1879–88).

TRYON, WILLIAM (*b. Surrey, England, 1729; d. London, England, 1788*), colonial governor. After an early career in the British army, Tryon was appointed lieutenant governor of North Carolina in 1764. He became governor in 1765 and was involved immediately in the crises caused by deteriorating colonial-British relations. He strongly supported the naval and customs officers during the Stamp Act controversy, but lacking military force was unable to compel compliance with the law. When the Regulator movement broke out in the frontier counties, 1768, he restored order by force and a drastic riot act, culminating his exertions with a crushing military defeat of the Regulators at the Alamance in 1771. Transferred to the governorship of New York, 1771, he encountered frontier disturbances in the Vermont area, caused by conflicting claims between New York and New Hampshire, and also difficulties over land purchases from the Mohawk Valley Indians. Returning from an official trip to England (April 1774–June 1775), he found the Revolution in progress and his civil functions necessarily limited. Active in his preferred role of soldier, he performed his chief feats of arms in raids upon Connecticut which were successful in destroying supplies and in diverting some of Connecticut's energies from support of Washington's army to home defense. Illness ended his career in 1780 and forced his return to England. Loyal to the Crown and prone to use force, Tryon was an able if somewhat vain administrator.

TSCHERINOFF, MARIE VAN ZANDT. *See* VAN ZANDT, MARIE.

TUBMAN, HARRIET (*b. Dorchester Co., Md., ca. 1821; d. Auburn, N.Y., 1913*), fugitive slave, Abolitionist, leading figure in the Underground Railroad. Author of memoirs issued as *Scenes in the Life of Harriet Tubman* (1869); revised and reissued in 1886 as *Harriet the Moses of Her People*.

TUCK, AMOS (*b. Parsonfield, Maine, 1810; d. 1879*), lawyer. Practiced in Exeter, N.H., *post* 1838. Congressman, independent Democrat-Whig, from New Hampshire, 1847–53, he acted with Joshua R. Giddings and John G. Palfrey as a nucleus of antislavery sentiment and was influential in the formation of the Republican party. He was naval officer for Boston district, 1861–65.

TUCKER, ALLEN (*b. Brooklyn, N.Y., 1866; d. New York, N.Y., 1939*), architect, painter. Graduated Columbia, 1888. While a draftsman with Richard M. Hunt, he studied painting at the Art Students League, 1891–95; the teacher who most influenced him was John H. Twachtman. Devoting all his effort to painting *post* 1904, he developed his style from impressionism into an expressionism at first influenced by Van Gogh. The work of the final decade of his life was marked by a vigorously personal maturity of style best observed in *The Pale Horse* (1928), *The Review* (1931), and a *Crucifixion* (1936).

TUCKER, BENJAMIN RICKETSON (*b. South Dartmouth, Mass., 1854; d. Monaco, 1939*), radical reformer. Attended Massachusetts Institute of Technology, 1870–73. Converted to individualist anarchism, 1872, through Josiah Warren and others, he became an authority on the work of Pierre Joseph Proudhon. He is remembered principally for his publication *Liberty*, issued regularly at Boston, 1881–92, and at New York, 1892–1908. At first an organ for publicizing the views of European anarchists in general, *Liberty* in its later days came more and more to reflect the outlook of Max Stirner.

TUCKER, GEORGE (*b. Bermuda, 1775; d. Albemarle Co., Va., 1861*), political economist, author. Removed to Virginia as a boy. There he studied and practiced law and served in the state legislature before election to Congress as a Democrat, 1819–25. In 1825 he became professor of moral philosophy at the University of Virginia, probably at the suggestion of James Madison, whom he knew intimately. During twenty years at Virginia he produced, among other works, his *Life of Thomas Jefferson* (1837). Based on extensive research and many conferences with Madison, this was an impartial and on the whole a successful contribution to early American history. Tucker's more important writings were in economics, among them, *The Laws of Wages, Profits and Rent Investigated* (1837) and *The Theory of Money and Banks Investigated* (1839). After his retirement from Virginia in 1845, he continued his scholarly activities, beginning a four-volume *History of the United States* and producing *Political Economy for the People* in 1859. Although a pragmatist in insisting that economic scholarship should lead to recommendations for public policy, Tucker was a conservative and pessimistic adherent of classical French and English economics, apparently learning nothing from the prodigious economic developments going on around him, or from such contemporaries as Henry C. and Matthew Carey. Admiring Adam Smith, he disagreed with David Ricardo in many details. He was impressed with Malthus's principle of population and used it as a basis for predicting the eventual extinction of slavery as unprofitable. His opposition to slavery was unmistakable but his criticism was never outspoken, ranging from discreetly academic statements to strong but anonymous ridicule. It dwindled to mere feeble mention in his work published on the eve of the Civil War.

TUCKER, GILBERT MILLIGAN (*b. Albany, N.Y., 1847; d. Albany, 1932*), editor of the *Country Gentleman*, 1897–1911. Son of Luther Tucker.

TUCKER, HENRY HOLCOMBE (*b. near Camak, Ga., 1819; d. Atlanta, Ga., 1889*), lawyer, Baptist clergyman. Grandson of Henry Holcombe. A professor at Mercer University, and its president, 1866–71, he was chancellor of the University of Georgia, 1874–78. Thereafter he was proprietor and editor of the *Christian Index.*

TUCKER, HENRY ST. GEORGE (*b. "Matoax," Chesterfield Co., Va., 1780; d. Winchester, Va., 1848*), Virginia legislator, congressman and jurist. Son of St. George Tucker; brother of Nathaniel B. Tucker (1784–1851); half brother of John Randolph of Roanoke (1773–1833); father of John R. (1823–97) and Nathaniel B. Tucker (1820–90). Virginia chancery judge, 1824–31; president of supreme court of appeals of Virginia, 1831–41; professor of law, University of Virginia, 1841–45. Author, among other works, of *Commentaries on the Laws of Virginia* (1836–37).

TUCKER, HENRY ST. GEORGE (*b. Winchester, Va., 1853; d. Lexington, Va., 1932*), lawyer, legal educator. Son of John R. Tucker (1823–97). Congressman, Democrat, from Virginia, 1889–97, 1922–32. A liberal during his first service in Congress, *post* 1922 he was an ardent exponent of states' rights and a strict constructionist, opposing the social and economic legislation of that period.

TUCKER, HENRY ST. GEORGE (*b. Warsaw, Va., 1874; d. Richmond, Va., 1959*), Episcopal minister and bishop. Studied at the University of Virginia and at the Theological Seminary of Virginia, D.D., 1899. Missionary to Japan, 1899–1923. Became bishop of Virginia, 1927; presiding bishop of the Protestant Episcopal Church of America, 1941; president of the Federal Council of the Churches of Christ in America, 1942. Retired in 1946.

TUCKER, JOHN RANDOLPH (*b. Alexandria, Va., 1812; d. Petersburg, Va., 1883*), naval officer. Appointed midshipman, 1826, he rose after extensive general service to rank of commander, 1855. Entering the Confederate service, 1861, he commanded the Charleston Squadron and was promoted captain, 1863. Forming his crews into a naval brigade on evacuation of Charleston in February 1865, he distinguished himself with his command at the battle of Sailor's Creek in April. He served for a time after the war as rear admiral in the Peruvian navy.

TUCKER, JOHN RANDOLPH (*b. Winchester, Va., 1823; d. 1897*), lawyer, teacher of law, Virginia official and congressman. Son of Henry St. G. Tucker (1780–1848); brother of Nathaniel B. Tucker (1820–90); father of Henry St. G. Tucker (1853–1932). A strict-constructionist states' rights logician, he advocated tariff reform, the repeal of the internal revenue system, and sound money. He was eminently successful in his practice of law, serving in such diverse actions as the trial of Jefferson Davis and the case of the Chicago anarchists before the U.S. Supreme Court.

TUCKER, LUTHER (*b. Brandon, Vt., 1802; d. Albany, N.Y., 1873*), printer, agricultural journalist. Proprietor of *Rochester Daily Advertiser* (N.Y.), 1826–39; established *Genesee Farmer*, 1831, which he merged with the *Cultivator* in 1839. In 1846 he established the *Horticulturist*; edited by Andrew J. Downing, it became an outstanding journal. Beginning issue of the *Country Gentleman*, 1853, he consolidated it with his *Cultivator*, 1866, thereafter publishing under the title *Cultivator and Country Gentleman*. Leader and model of agricultural journalists in his time, he was succeeded as editor-proprietor by his sons, 1873; among them was Gilbert M. Tucker.

TUCKER, NATHANIEL BEVERLEY (*b. "Matoax," Chesterfield Co., Va., 1784; d. Winchester, Va., 1851*), professor of law, southern rights publicist. Son of St. George Tucker; brother of Henry St. G. Tucker (1780–1848); half brother of John Randolph of Roanoke (1773–1833). Professor of law at College of William and Mary *post* 1834, he reflected in his numerous letters, books, and lectures the theories of his colleague Thomas R. Dew. A lifelong advocate of secession and aristocratic government, he was author, among other works, of *George Balcombe* (published anonymously, 1836) and *The Partisan Leader* (1836, but bore fictitious date of 1856). The second of these titles attempted a fictional prophecy of what would follow as a result of the Jacksonian policies and was reprinted as propaganda by both sides during the Civil War.

TUCKER, NATHANIEL BEVERLEY (*b. Winchester, Va., 1820; d. 1890*), planter, journalist, Confederate agent. Son of Henry St. G. Tucker (1780–1848); brother of John R. Tucker (1823–97).

TUCKER, ST. GEORGE (*b. Port Royal, Bermuda, 1752 o.s.; Nelson Co., Va., 1827*), Revolutionary soldier, Virginia jurist. Father of Nathaniel B. (1784–1851) and Henry St. G. Tucker (1780–1848); stepfather of John Randolph of Roanoke (1773–1833). Judge of the general court of Virginia and professor of law in the College of William and Mary, he was elected to the state supreme court of appeals, 1803, and served until 1811. Appointed U.S. district judge for Virginia, 1813, he resigned shortly before his death. He was author of a number of works, notably an annotated edition of *Blackstone's Commentaries* (1803), one of the most important law texts of its day. His minor poetry included *The Probationary Odes of Jonathan Pindar* (2 pts., 1796), once attributed to Philip M. Freneau.

TUCKER, SAMUEL (*b. Marblehead, Mass., 1747; d. Bremen, Maine, 1833*), merchant mariner, naval officer. Commanded army warships *Franklin* and *Hancock*, 1776, capturing valuable prizes off Boston. As captain in the navy *post* March 1777, he commanded frigate *Boston* and performed important services until capture of the vessel at Charleston, S.C., 1780. Retiring from active naval service, 1781, he sailed for a while on merchant ships and later became a farmer.

TUCKER, SOPHIE (*b. somewhere on a road leading to the Baltic Sea, Russia, 1887; d. New York, N.Y., 1966*), singer, actress. Arrived in the United States as a newborn, with her mother; entered show business in 1906. A headliner in vaudeville, Tucker amused audiences around the country with songs like "There's Company in the Parlour, Girls, Come on Down." In 1914 she "played the Palace," the epitome of success for vaudeville performers. She toured England, 1922 and 1924, and was a sensation. At the Palace in 1928 she was billed as "The Last of the Red Hot Mamas," a title that remained with her for the rest of her career. When vaudeville faded in popularity, she performed at nightclubs and for television. She established the Sophie Tucker Foundation (1945) and the Sophie Tucker Chair of Theater Arts at Brandeis University (1955).

TUCKER, STEPHEN DAVIS (*b. Bloomfield, N.J., 1818; d. London, England, 1902*), printing machinery inventor. Associated with R. Hoe & Co. *post* 1834, he retired as its senior partner, 1893.

TUCKER, WILLIAM JEWETT (*b. Griswold, Conn., 1839; d. 1926*), Congregational clergyman, educator. Graduated Dartmouth, 1861; Andover Theological Seminary, 1866. Distinguished for development of sociology courses at Andover and for settlement work in Boston, Mass., Tucker was a figure in the so-called "Andover controversy," 1886–92. As president of Dartmouth, 1893–1909, he strengthened the college, reforming many archaic attitudes, reorganizing finances, and modernizing the plant.

TUCKERMAN, BAYARD (*b. New York, N.Y., 1855; d. 1923*), scholar, writer. Author, among other works, of *Life of General Lafayette* (1889), *William Jay and the Constitutional Movement for the Abolition of Slavery* (1894), and *Life of General Philip Schuyler* (1903). Editor of *Diary of Philip Hone* (1889).

TUCKERMAN, EDWARD (*b. Boston, Mass., 1817; d. Amherst, Mass., 1886*), botanist, leading authority on American lichenology. Brother of Frederick G. Tuckerman. B.A., Union College, 1837; B.A., Harvard, 1847; also studied at Harvard Law and Divinity schools and at Upsala in Sweden. Professor of botany, Amherst College, *post* 1858. Author of many studies of lichens including his principal work, *Genera Lichenum* (1872).

TUCKERMAN, FREDERICK (*b. Greenfield, Mass., 1857; d. 1929*), comparative anatomist, naturalist. Son of Frederick G. Tuckerman.

TUCKERMAN, FREDERICK GODDARD (*b. Boston, Mass., 1821; d. Greenfield, Mass., 1873*), poet. Father of Frederick Tuckerman; brother of Edward Tuckerman.

TUCKERMAN, HENRY THEODORE (*b. Boston, Mass., 1813; d. New York, N.Y., 1871*), critic, essayist. Nephew of Joseph Tuckerman; cousin of Edward and Frederick G. Tuckerman. Author of a number of works, once widely read, which were typical of the romantic approach to travel, literature, and art. He produced several books of lasting value which include *Book of the Artists: American Artist Life* (1867) and *America and Her Commentators* (1864).

TUCKERMAN, JOSEPH (*b. Boston, Mass., 1778; d. Havana, Cuba, 1840*), Unitarian clergyman, philanthropist. Uncle of Edward, Frederick G., and Henry T. Tuckerman. Pastor in Chelsea, Mass., 1801–26, he was an original member of the Anthology Society; removing to Boston, 1826, he began a city mission for the poor which served as a model for similar institutions in England and France.

TUCKEY, WILLIAM (*b. Somersetshire, England, ca. 1708; d. Philadelphia, Pa., 1781*), organist, choirmaster, composer. Developed choir of Trinity Church, New York City, *post* 1753; conducted first American rendering of Handel's *Messiah* in New York, 1770. Author of a number of original compositions of which only the hymn called "Liverpool" survives.

TUDOR, FREDERIC (*b. Boston, Mass., 1783; d. Boston, 1864*), businessman. Brother of William Tudor. Conceived idea of shipping ice from Boston to tropical cities *ca.* 1804; made first shipment to Martinique, 1806. Thereafter, with great ingenuity and complete ruthlessness, he developed his trade to worldwide proportions.

TUDOR, WILLIAM (*b. Boston, Mass., 1779; d. Rio de Janeiro, Brazil, 1830*), merchant, Massachusetts legislator, U.S. consular officer, author. Brother of Frederic Tudor. Founder and first editor (1815–17) of the *North American Review*; helped found Boston Athenaeum. A keen critic of contemporary manners, he was author, among other works, of *Letters on the Eastern States* (1820), *The Life of James Otis* (1823), and *Gebel Teir* (1829, anonymously).

TUFTS, CHARLES (*b. present Somerville, Mass., 1781; d. 1876*), farmer, brickmaker, Universalist leader. Donated land for the building site of Tufts College, 1852.

TUFTS, COTTON (*b. Medford, Mass., 1732; d. Weymouth, Mass., 1815*), physician, Revolutionary patriot. Nephew of John Tufts. Graduated Harvard, 1749. After study of medicine with a brother, began practice in Weymouth, 1752. A close friend of John Adams, Tufts was long associated with scientific, cultural, and political affairs in Massachusetts.

TUFTS, JAMES HAYDEN (*b. Monson, Mass., 1862; d. Berkeley, Calif., 1942*), philosopher. Graduated Amherst College, 1884. B.D., Yale Divinity School, 1889. Ph.D., University of Freiburg, 1892. Taught philosophy at University of Michigan, 1889–91; at University of Chicago, 1892–1930 (chairman of the department *post* 1905). Shared in the rise of the "Chicago School" of instrumentalist philosophy; made contributions to pragmatic moral theory; active in civic and social reform. Coauthor with John Dewey of *Ethics* (1908); author, among other books, of *America's Social Morality* (1933). Editor, *International Journal of Ethics*, 1914–34.

TUFTS, JOHN (*b. Medford, Mass., 1689; d. Amesbury, Mass., 1752*), Congregational clergyman. Minister in West Newbury, Mass., 1714–38. Notable for influence exerted upon American music by his *A Very Plain and Easy Introduction to the Art of Singing Psalm Tunes* (ca. 1715) which was considered "a daring and unjustifiable innovation" and aroused much controversy.

TULANE, PAUL (*b. near Princeton, N.J., 1801; d. Princeton, 1887*), New Orleans, La., merchant, philanthropist. Successful in trade and real estate operations in New Orleans, 1822–73, Tulane donated property whose income made possible the conversion of the University of Louisiana, a state institution, into the independent Tulane University, 1884.

TULLY, WILLIAM (*b. Saybrook Point, Conn., 1785; d. Springfield, Mass., 1859*), physician. Graduated Yale, 1806;

studied medicine with, among others, Nathan Smith (1762–1829) and Eli Ives. In practice thereafter in many locations, Tully was considered the most learned and scientific physician of his time in New England. An authority on *Materia medica*, he was a prolific writer on medical topics and a teacher for many years at the medical school at Castleton, Vt., and at Yale.

TUMULTY, JOSEPH PATRICK (*b.* *Jersey City, N.J., 1879; d. Baltimore, Md., 1954*), politician. Graduated from St. Peter's College, 1899. Adviser to Woodrow Wilson in his gubernatorial campaign in New Jersey, 1910. As secretary to Wilson, 1913–21, Tumulty advised on both domestic and foreign affairs, losing favor with his support of anti-Prohibitionists. Retired to private law practice in Washington, D.C.

TUPPER, BENJAMIN (*b.* *Stoughton, Mass., 1738; d. 1792*), Revolutionary officer, Massachusetts legislator, Ohio pioneer. Associated with Rufus Putnam in formation of the Ohio Company, he went with the original settlers to Marietta, 1788, and was practically sole administrator of local justice along the Muskingum until his death.

TUPPER, HENRY ALLEN (*b.* *Charleston, S.C., 1828; d. 1902*), Baptist clergyman, Confederate chaplain. Corresponding secretary, Board of Foreign Missions, Southern Baptist Convention, 1872–93.

TURELL, JANE (*b.* *Boston, Mass., 1708; d. Medford, Mass., 1735*), poet. Daughter of Benjamin Colman. Her religious verses and others appeared in *Reliquiae Turellae* (Boston, 1735; published under another title in London, 1741).

TURKEVICH, LEONID IERONIMOVICH. *See* LEONTY, METROPOLITAN.

TURNBULL, ANDREW (*b.* *Scotland, ca. 1718; d. Charleston, S.C., 1792*), colonizer, physician. Securing a grant in East Florida, 1766, he endeavored unsuccessfully to develop the colony of New Smyrna by settlement of Greek, Italian, and Minorcan immigrants. He was the father of Robert J. Turnbull.

TURNBULL, ROBERT JAMES (*b.* *New Smyrna, Fla., 1775; d. 1833*), South Carolina planter, writer. Son of Andrew Turnbull. Obsessed by fears of national consolidation under the doctrine of implied constitutional power, he advocated the compact theory of the Union and extreme state sovereignty. He took a leading part in the nullification convention of 1832, writing its *Address*. Author, among other works, of *The Crisis: or, Essays on the Usurpations of the Federal Government* (1827, originally published in *Charleston Mercury* over pen name "Brutus"), he strongly influenced the thinking of Robert B. Rhett.

TURNBULL, WILLIAM (*b.* *Philadelphia, Pa., 1800; d. 1857*), soldier, engineer. Grandson of Charles Nisbet. Graduated West Point, 1819. Long active in topographical and other engineering work, he is particularly remembered for his design and construction of the Potomac Aqueduct, and for his services as chief topographical engineer on General Winfield Scott's staff during the Mexican War.

TURNER, ASA (*b.* *Templeton, Mass., 1799; d. Oskaloosa, Iowa, 1885*), Congregational clergyman, educator. Brother of Jonathan B. Turner. A home missionary in Illinois and Iowa, Turner promoted establishment of numerous churches and several colleges and academies, including Illinois College at Jacksonville and Iowa College at Davenport.

TURNER, CHARLES YARDLEY (*b.* *Baltimore, Md., 1850; d. New York, N.Y., 1918*), mural painter.

TURNER, DANIEL (*b.* *probably Richmond, S.I., N.Y., 1794; d. Philadelphia, Pa., 1850*), naval officer. Appointed midshipman, 1808, he commanded the *Caledonia* in the battle of Lake Erie, September 1813. After a long and varied career on sea and land, he was promoted captain, 1835. His last post was as commandant at Portsmouth navy yard.

TURNER, EDWARD (*b.* *Fairfax Co., Va., 1778; d. near Natchez, Miss., 1860*), Mississippi legislator and jurist. Raised in Kentucky, he settled in Mississippi, 1801, where he prospered in the law. He also held a number of judicial posts including chief justice of the supreme court and chancellor, and was a member of the committee that drafted the first Mississippi constitution. A practical, hardworking man, he was distinguished for his integrity and good manners.

TURNER, EDWARD RAYMOND (*b.* *Baltimore, Md., 1881; d. 1929*), historian. Graduated St. John's College, Annapolis, 1904; Ph.D., Johns Hopkins, 1910. Professor at University of Michigan, Yale, and Johns Hopkins, he devoted his research to English constitutional history. Author of, among other works, *The Privy Council of England, etc.* (1927–28) and *The Cabinet Council of England, etc.* (1930–32).

TURNER, FENNELL PARRISH (*b.* *Danielsville, Tenn., 1867; d. Santa Cruz, Calif., 1932*), missionary executive. Secretary, Student Volunteer Movement for Foreign Missions, 1897–1919; secretary for missionary education, Methodist Episcopal Church, 1928–30.

TURNER, FREDERICK JACKSON (*b.* *Portage, Wis., 1861; d. Pasadena, Calif., 1932*), historian. Educated at University of Wisconsin, A.B., 1884; M.A., 1888. Ph.D., Johns Hopkins, 1890. Assistant professor of history, University of Wisconsin, 1889–91; professor of history, 1891–92; professor of American history, 1892–1910. Professor of history, Harvard, 1910–24. Familiar from his college days with the unique archival materials collected by Lyman C. Draper and housed in the Wisconsin State Historical Society, Turner was attracted to a scientific investigation of American life at its beginnings; he never strayed far from this theme. Invited to present a brief paper at a meeting of the American Historical Association to be held at the Chicago World's Fair, he assembled data for an essay on "The Significance of the Frontier in American History" which he read on July 12, 1893. First printed in *Proceedings of the State Historical Society of Wisconsin . . . 1893* (1894), it was reprinted in the *Annual Report of the American Historical Association* (1894). In this essay he set forth a new hypothesis and opened a new period in the interpretation of the history of the United States. Beyond this important seminal study Turner wrote little, concentrating his energies on his classroom and university work.

Turner's frontier hypothesis was an attempt to account for the fact that emigrants to the United States from western Europe and their descendants had brought into being a nation so variant from any of those from which they came. He accounted for this on the ground that people who came from an environment in which they were unable to own land into an open continent where there was little to impede their free access to good land were thereby subjected to an influence unusual in history and perhaps formative in shaping American culture. Many of Turner's followers who took up his hypothesis dogmatically went far beyond their master in applying it. Turner himself was content to point out the possibility that human nature in a free environment might behave differently from the same nature under social and economic pressure; that equality of opportunity might have something to do with democracy in politics; that isolation on a new frontier might encourage the survival of the robust and the opinionated; that the necessity of repeatedly setting up social and governmental institutions brought about a "laboratory process' in which nonessentials dropped out while tested principles survived; and finally that the relationship between frontiersmen and government led naturally to an intense nationalism. He also pointed out that by 1893 the influence of the frontier was about to terminate. He regarded the frontier less as a place than as a continuous process sweeping the continent, and regarded the region where it might be temporarily operating as a section with aspects and interests deriving from its cultural state. For the rest of his creative life Turner tested his hypothesis, applying it at times to microscopic examination of limited regions and periods, and trying at other times to reconcile it with larger views of American development.

TURNER, GEORGE (b. Edina, Mo., 1850; d. Spokane, Wash., 1932), lawyer. Practiced in Alabama, 1870–85; led Republican party in Alabama. Appointed a justice of the supreme court of Washington Territory, 1885, he resigned in 1888 and began practice in Spokane. Successful in mine development and reputed an able constitutional lawyer, Turner served as U.S. senator from Washington, 1897–1903; he was elected on a fusion ticket made up of Silver Republicans, Democrats, and Populists. He later served as a member of the Alaska Boundary Tribunal and as counsel for the United States in a number of actions before international commissions.

TURNER, GEORGE KIBBE (b. Quincy, Ill., 1869; d. Miami, Fla., 1952), journalist, editor, author. Graduated from Williams College (B.A., 1890). As a writer for *McClure's Magazine*, 1906–16, Turner was one of the most effective muckrakers of the time. He concentrated on municipal government and his articles on political support of the white slave traffic led to passage of the so-called Mann Act in 1910. His many novels include *The Last Christian* (1914) and *Red Friday* (1919).

TURNER, HENRY MCNEAL (b. near Abbeville, S.C., 1834; d. Windsor, Ontario, Canada, 1915), bishop of the African Methodist Episcopal Church. The first black to be appointed an army chaplain (1863), Turner was active in Georgia Republican politics during Reconstruction. He was bishop of his church for Georgia, 1880–92, and for many years chancellor of Morris Brown College in Atlanta.

TURNER, JAMES MILTON (b. St. Louis Co., Mo., 1840; d. Ardmore, Okla., 1915), black leader, educator. An important figure in Missouri Republican politics, he was a benefactor of present Lincoln University and served ably as U.S. minister resident and consul general to Liberia, 1871–78.

TURNER, JOHN WESLEY (b. near Saratoga, N.Y., 1833; d. St. Louis, Mo., 1899), Union soldier, St. Louis, Mo., businessman. Graduated West Point, 1855. Served as chief of artillery, chief commissary, and chief of staff at various times in many theaters of the Civil War, rising to rank of brevet major general. He was outstanding as a division commander in the Army of the James and chief of staff in that army, 1864–65.

TURNER, JONATHAN BALDWIN (b. Templeton, Mass., 1805; d. Jacksonville, Ill., 1899), educator, agriculturist. Graduated Yale, 1833. Taught at Illinois College, 1833–47, serving for the most part as professor of rhetoric. An early leader in the movement for public schools in Illinois, he was largely responsible for the free school law of 1855 and the establishment of the first normal school in Illinois in 1857. Between 1850 and 1867 he conducted a remarkable campaign for establishment of a state university which would be supported by congressional appropriation of public lands. Through Turner's urgings, the Illinois legislature of 1867 took advantage of the Morrill Act to establish the present University of Illinois.

TURNER, JOSIAH (b. Hillsboro, N.C., 1821; d. near Hillsboro, 1901), lawyer, North Carolina legislator and editor. As editor of the Raleigh *Sentinel*, 1868–76, he worked to discredit and defeat the carpetbag government of North Carolina, displaying a single-minded gift for ridicule and sarcasm.

TURNER, NAT (b. Southampton Co., Va., 1800; d. Jerusalem, Va., 1831), black preacher and leader. A precocious child, Nat Turner received the rudiments of an education and early developed a fanatical religious conviction that he had been chosen to lead his fellow slaves out of bondage. Settling upon Aug. 21, 1831, as the great day of deliverance, he and some associates plotted a slave insurrection; as a first step they murdered Nat Turner's master and all his family. Securing arms and horses and enlisting other slaves, they killed in all 51 white persons in a single day and night. However, the rebellion collapsed at the first sign of armed resistance and on August 25 Nat Turner went into hiding. Discovered by accident six weeks later, he was at once tried and hanged. This revolt, following closely on slave insurrections in the West Indies, sent a profound shock through the slaveholding states and brought about a great increase in severity of the slave codes; it also dealt a death blow to the flourishing emancipation movement in the South.

TURNER, RICHMOND KELLY (b. East Portland, Oreg., 1885; d. Monterey, Calif., 1961), naval officer. Attended the U.S. Naval Academy (1904–08). After a series of assignments on air, land, and sea, in which he steadily advanced in his naval career, Turner became director of war plans in the Office of Naval Operations (1940–42). He was promoted to rear admiral (1941). In 1942 he headed the amphibious forces in the attack on Guadalcanal and Tulagi and soon became an expert in this complex type of warfare. Later he presided over the invasions of many Japanese-held islands, most notably Okinawa, where more than 1,000 ships were under his command. Promoted to vice admiral in 1944 and admiral in 1945, he ended the war as commander of amphibious forces, Pacific Fleet. He retired in 1947.

TURNER, ROSS STERLING (b. Westport, N.Y., 1847; d. Nassau, Bahamas, 1915), painter, teacher of art. Associated in his studies at Munich with Frank Duveneck and other young American artists, he was also familiar with Whistler at Venice. *Post* 1882 a popular teacher of art in the Boston, Mass., area, Turner was distinguished as a watercolorist and as one of the few modern exponents of the art of illumination of manuscripts.

TURNER, SAMUEL HULBEART (b. Philadelphia, Pa., 1790; d. New York, N.Y., 1861), Episcopal clergyman, educator. Professor of biblical learning and interpretation at General Theological Seminary, New York City, *post* 1822, he was also professor of Hebrew at Columbia for many years *post* 1830. A conservative scholar both in his teaching and his writings, he was moderately opposed to the contemporary influence of the Oxford Movement.

TURNER, WALTER VICTOR (b. Epping Forest, England, 1866; d. Wilkinsburg, Pa., 1919), engineer. Came to America, 1888, as a textile expert. Taking employment with the Santa Fe Railroad, 1897, he became an expert on air brakes; *post* 1903 he directed engineering operations for the Westinghouse Air Brake Co. and won the reputation of being the foremost pneumatic engineer in the world. Among his more than 400 patents, the "K" triple valve (patented, October 1904) and his later electropneumatic brake were outstanding contributions to transportation efficiency.

TURNER, WILLIAM (b. Kilmallock, Ireland, 1871; d. Buffalo, N.Y., 1936), Roman Catholic clergyman, educator. Graduated Royal University of Ireland, 1888; studied at North American

College, Rome; was ordained, 1893. A seminary professor at St. Paul, Minn., 1894–1906, he became professor of logic and the history of philosophy at Catholic University of America, and also editor of the *American Ecclesiastical Review* and other learned journals. Consecrated bishop of Buffalo, N.Y., 1919, he served there until his death, continuing his scholarly interests as far as his administrative duties permitted. He was author of, among other works, an outstanding *History of Philosophy* (1903).

TURNEY, PETER (*b.* Jasper, Tenn., 1827; *d.* Winchester, Tenn., 1903), lawyer, Tennessee secessionist and Confederate soldier. Justice of Tennessee supreme court, 1870–93; chief justice, 1886–93. Conservative Democratic governor of Tennessee, 1893–97.

TURPIN, BEN (*b.* New Orleans, La., ca. 1869; *d.* Santa Monica, Calif., 1940), slapstick comedian. Raised in New York City; roamed the country for some five years as a hobo; entered show business as a burlesque and vaudeville comedian in Chicago, Ill., *ca.* 1891. Toured for many years in the stage character of "Happy Hooligan." Entering the movies *ca.* 1907, and capitalizing on his cross-eyed appearance and on his skill as a clown-acrobat, he was by 1914 one of Essanay Studio's leading comics. Under the direction of Mack Sennett at the Keystone Studio in California, Turpin reached his height of fame in comedy-parodies of contemporary starring vehicles.

TUTHILL, WILLIAM BURNET (*b.* New York, N.Y., 1855; *d.* 1929), architect. Studied in office of Richard M. Hunt; began practice, 1877, in New York City. Principally celebrated for building Carnegie Hall, New York City (1891, in association with Dankmar Adler and Louis H. Sullivan), Tuthill also designed a number of other buildings on a broadly eclectic basis. The acoustic success of Carnegie Hall led him to be called in as consultant for many churches and concert halls.

TUTTLE, CHARLES WESLEY (*b.* Newfield, Maine, 1829; *d.* 1881), astronomer, lawyer, antiquarian. An assistant at the Harvard Observatory, 1850–54, Tuttle made his most important contribution to science by explaining the "dusky" ring of Saturn. A successful Boston lawyer *post* 1856, he was author of a number of scholarly articles on New England history and of *Capt. John Mason* (1887).

TUTTLE, DANIEL SYLVESTER (*b.* Windham, N.Y., 1837; *d.* St. Louis, Mo., 1923), Episcopal clergyman. Graduated Columbia, 1857; General Theological Seminary, New York, 1862. Missionary bishop of Montana, with jurisdiction in Utah and Idaho, 1867–86, he served thereafter as bishop of Missouri. *Post* 1903 he was presiding bishop of his church.

TUTTLE, HERBERT (*b.* Bennington, Vt., 1846; *d.* Ithaca, N.Y., 1894), journalist, educator, historian. Graduated University of Vermont, 1869. After employment on the *Boston Daily Advertiser* as a correspondent in Washington, D.C., and in Paris, France, he was Berlin correspondent of the London *Daily News*, 1873–79. Encouraged by Andrew D. White, Tuttle began an academic career as lecturer in international law at University of Michigan and Cornell, 1880–83. *Post* 1883 he taught the history of politics and modern European history at Cornell. Among other works he was author of an unfinished *History of Prussia* (1884, 1888, 1896).

TUTWILER, HENRY (*b.* Harrisonburg, Va., 1807; *d.* Greene Springs, Ala., 1884), educator. Graduated University of Virginia, 1829. Professor of ancient languages, University of Alabama, 1831–37. Headed Greene Springs School for Boys, 1847–84, an institution unusual in its time for its emphasis on the sciences and its respect for the individual student.

TUTWILER, JULIA STRUDWICK (*b.* Greene Springs, Ala., 1841; *d.* Birmingham, Ala., 1916), Alabama educator, social reformer. Daughter of Henry Tutwiler. Studied at Vassar; tutored by faculty at Washington and Lee; spent three years in advanced study in France and Germany. A teacher in Alabama *post* 1876, she was responsible for founding of Alabama Normal College, and was its co-principal and principal, 1883–1910. Through her efforts vocational training for women was established in Alabama, 1896.

TWACHTMAN, JOHN HENRY (*b.* Cincinnati, Ohio, 1853; *d.* Gloucester, Mass., 1902), painter. Studied drawing at Ohio Mechanics' Institute and at University of Cincinnati; went to Munich with Frank Duveneck, 1875, and studied there and at Venice until 1878. After a brief stay in America, he painted, studied, and traveled abroad until 1884. Thereafter he resided principally in New England and was for many years an instructor of the antique class at the Art Students League, New York. Twachtman's work falls into three distinct periods. His early work (1875–81) is characterized by strong contrast of values in subdued variations of brown and black, by vigorous brush work, and by direct rendering from nature. His second period is marked by a reaction against the dark tones of the Munich tradition; the color is in variations of silver grays and greens, the pigment is applied thinly with a delicate but precise technique and the composition is restricted to very simple themes. *Post* 1889 his work shows the obvious influence of impressionism. From subdued hues the color changes to the higher key of sunlight or the ethereal and pallid harmony of winter landscape. He seems striving for the sensitive rather than the striking and for the subtle rather than the obvious, displaying a mastery of nuance. He openly declared the decorative intention of his work at this time. Twachtman found his interest in the expressive organization of form and the harmonic relation of line and color; his art therefore relates to the doctrine of Whistler; his appreciation of light and color is owing to Monet.

TWAIN, MARK. *See* CLEMENS, SAMUEL LANGHORNE.

TWEED, BLANCHE OELRICHS. *See* STRANGE, MICHAEL.

TWEED, HARRISON (*b.* New York, N.Y., 1885; *d.* New York, 1969), lawyer, bar association officer. Attended Harvard (B.A., 1907) and Harvard Law School (LL.B., 1910). After service as a captain in World War I, he joined one of the predecessor firms to Milbank, Tweed, Hadley, and McCloy, where he remained as a partner for the rest of his life, drafting wills and trust agreements and administering estates. He became chairman of the legal aid committee of the Association of the Bar of the City of New York (1932), and zealously espoused the cause of providing competing legal services for all. He served as president of the Legal Aid Society of New York (1936–45) and of the National Legal Aid and Defender Association (1949–55). In 1945 he was elected president of the New York City bar association, which he transformed into a strong force for public service. In 1947 he became president of the American Law Institute (ALI) and chairman of the ALI-American Bar Association joint committee on continuing legal education. He was interim president of Sarah Lawrence College for a year (1959–60). In 1963 became cochairman of the Lawyers' Committee for Civil Rights Under Law.

TWEED, WILLIAM MARCY (*b.* New York, N.Y., 1823; *d.* New York, 1878), saddler, bookkeeper, political boss. Rising in New York City politics through his influence as officer of a volunteer fire company (Americus No. 6), Tweed was elected an alderman, 1851. Among aldermanic associates who were known in their time as "The Forty Thieves," Tweed soon displayed a capacity for grafting which rendered further honest toil unnecessary for him. He served as congressman, Democrat, from New York, 1853–55, but found that he preferred municipal politics. Defeated for alderman in 1855, Tweed, with Peter B. Sweeny and Richard B. Connolly (later his chief partners in the "Tweed Ring"), set up a faction in Tammany Hall to oppose Fernando Wood. Successful in disposing of Wood, Tweed secured membership for himself on several key boards and commissions, had his friend Sweeny nominated for district attorney, and placed other allies in strategic positions. Made chairman of the Democratic central committee of New York County, 1860, he maneuvered another satellite, A. Oakey Hall, into the district attorney's post and was thereafter dictator of his party in New York.

Reaching out his tentacles of graft in every direction and levying toll on all who did business with the city or in the city, Tweed was doubtless a millionaire by 1867. In 1868 he practically secured control of New York State by dictating the nomination of John T. Hoffman as governor. Tweed, elected a state senator in 1867, ran everything from his seven-room hotel suite in Albany; it was there in 1869 that the members of his "Ring" decided that all bills thereafter rendered against New York City and County must be 50 percent. fraudulent. The proportion was later raised to 85 percent. Bogus naturalization of immigrants and repeating at elections were now carried to hitherto unknown lengths. Tweed was also a partner with Jay Gould and James Fisk in the plundering of the Erie Railroad. By this time *Harper's Weekly*, with Thomas Nast as cartoonist, began a campaign against Tweed and his friends and against the new (1870) city charter which riveted the rule of the "Ring" more firmly on the city. In September 1870 the *New York Times*, directed by George Jones, began attacks on Tweed. In the spring of 1871 two discontented county officials turned over to the *Times* proofs of the swindling by the "Ring." The evidence was published in July, and in September at a mass meeting in Cooper Union a Committee of Seventy was formed to take action. This committee, made up of prominent citizens including Samuel J. Tilden, was prompt to act. By December, Tweed had been arrested and Sweeny and others had fled the jurisdiction. Convicted at his second trial in November 1873, Tweed was sentenced to twelve years in prison and a fine, but the sentence was reduced by the court of appeals. Rearrested in January 1875 on leaving prison, Tweed escaped from custody late in the year and went to Spain. Returned to America in November 1876 by Spanish officials, Tweed was committed to prison until he made payment under a judgment in a civil suit brought to recover the 'Ring's' thefts. After giving extensive testimony about many of his crooked transactions, he died in jail. The amount which the "Tweed Ring" stole from the city has been variously estimated at between $30 million and $200 million.

TWICHELL, JOSEPH HOPKINS (*b. Southington, Conn., 1838; d. 1918*), Congregational clergyman. Graduated Yale, 1859; Andover Theological Seminary, 1865. Pastor, Asylum Hill Church, Hartford, Conn., *post* 1865, he was a leader in the city's religious and civic affairs and a member of the literary group that included Charles D. Warner, the Stowes, and Mark Twain. He was Mark Twain's companion on the trip described in *A Tramp Abroad* and one of the humorist's most intimate friends.

TWIGGS, DAVID EMANUEL (*b. Richmond Co., Ga., 1790; d. 1862*), soldier. Rose to rank of major in War of 1812; promoted lieutenant colonel of the 4th Infantry, 1831, and colonel of the 2nd Dragoons, 1836. Distinguished for dogged perseverance and bravery rather than intelligence while serving under both General Zachary Taylor and General Winfield Scott in the Mexican War, he rose to brigadier general and brevet major general. In command of the Department of Texas at the outbreak of the Civil War, he surrendered all the forces and stores under his control to the Confederate General McCulloch and was dismissed from the U.S. Army. Made a Confederate major general, May 1861, he

was given command of the district of Louisiana. Too old to take the field, he resigned and soon died, probably near Augusta, Ga.

TWINING, ALEXANDER CATLIN (*b. New Haven, Conn., 1801; d. New Haven, 1884*), engineer, astronomer, educator. Graduated Yale, 1820. Taught at Yale and at Middlebury College, Vermont; served for many years as a consulting engineer to railroads. His most important invention was an application of the absorption process for the manufacture of ice on a commercial scale (patented 1853).

TWITCHELL, AMOS (*b. Dublin, N.H., 1781; d. Keene, N.H. 1850*), pioneer New Hampshire surgeon. Graduated Dartmouth, 1802; studied medicine with Nathan Smith (1762–1829). Practiced principally at Keene, N.H., performing many operations with exceptional skill. In 1807 he tied the carotid artery with success; he was also one of the first in the United States to perform extensive amputations for malignant disease, tracheotomy, and trephining of the long bones for suppuration.

TYDINGS, MILLARD EVELYN (*b. Havre de Grace, Md., 1890; d. near Havre de Grace, 1961*), lawyer, U.S. Senator. Attended Maryland Agricultural College (B.S., 1910) and the University of Maryland (LL.B., 1913). Elected to the Maryland House of Delegates (1916), the Maryland State Senate (1922), and the U.S. House of Representatives (1924). Elected in 1926 to the U.S. Senate where he achieved prominence as a conservative Democratic opponent of President Franklin D. Roosevelt's New Deal. He bitterly opposed Roosevelt's plan to pack the Supreme Court in 1937. After World War II Tydings battled for nuclear disarmament. In 1950, as chairman of a special Senate Foreign Relations Committee subcommittee, he labeled Sen. Joseph R. McCarthy's charges of Communist influence on American foreign policy "contemptible." A McCarthy-backed candidate defeated Tydings' bid for a fifth term in 1950.

TYLER, BENNET (*b. Middlebury, Conn., 1783; d. 1858*), Congregational clergyman, educator. Graduated Yale, 1804. Pastor in South Britain, Conn., 1808–22; president of Dartmouth College, 1822–28. Pastor in Portland, Maine, until 1834 when he became president and professor of theology at present Hartford Theological Seminary. An ardent conservative Calvinist, Tyler opposed the innovations of Nathaniel W. Taylor and the "New Divinity," holding throughout his career to the Calvinist system as modified by Jonathan Edwards and later by Timothy Dwight. He resigned his presidency of the seminary in 1857.

TYLER, CHARLES MELLEN (*b. Limington, Maine, 1832; d. Scranton, Pa., 1918*), Congregational clergyman, Union Army chaplain, educator. Graduated Yale, 1855. Professor of history and philosophy of religion at the Sage School, Cornell University, 1891–1903, and emeritus thereafter.

TYLER, DANIEL (*b. Brooklyn, Conn., 1799; d. New York, N.Y., 1882*), soldier, industrialist. Attended West Point and was commissioned lieutenant of artillery, 1819; studied later at the artillery school at Fortress Monroe, Va., and in the French army artillery school at Metz. Exposed shoddy conditions at Springfield Arsenal, 1830–32. Resigning from the army, 1834, he began a highly successful career as engineer and financier of railroads and canals both North and South. Commissioned Union brigadier general, 1861, Tyler commanded a division during the first Bull Run campaign, but through his failure to attack at the proper time must bear some of the blame for the disaster of that battle. His later Civil War career was not notable. In association with Samuel Noble he began exploitation of the iron deposits of eastern Alabama, 1872, and was largely responsible for successful operations at Anniston thereafter.

TYLER, GEORGE CROUSE (b. *Circleville, Ohio, 1867; d. Yonkers, N.Y., 1946*), theatrical manager and producer. A printer by trade, he worked in various capacities in and out of the theater before forming a partnership with Theodore A. Liebler (Liebler and Company), 1897, for play production. Thanks to Tyler's flair and Liebler's financing, the firm produced or managed over 300 superior attractions in New York City and on tour before its bankruptcy in 1914; among their successes were *The Christian* (1898); tours by Mrs. Patrick Campbell, Eleonora Duse, Madame Réjane, and the Abbey Theatre Company; and their management of Arnold Daly's Shaw productions. Tyler staged some of his most elaborate shows while manager of the New Theater (Century), 1911–14. After a period of producing plays with the backing of Klaw and Erlanger, he became an independent manager in 1918; outstanding Tyler productions before his last (*For Valor*, 1935), were *Clarence* (1919); an early version of O'Neill's *Anna Christie*; *Dulcy* (1921, the first collaboration of Marc Connelly and George S. Kaufman); Gordon Craig's *Macbeth* (1928); and a series of all-star revivals.

TYLER, JOHN (b. *York Co., Va., 1747; d. Charles City Co., Va., 1813*), Revolutionary patriot, Virginia legislator and jurist. Father of John Tyler (1790–1862). Studied law with Robert C. Nicholas. A friend of Thomas Jefferson and a follower of Patrick Henry, Tyler held a number of judicial posts in Virginia and was active in the House of Delegates where he served for a time as speaker. An opponent of the Federal Constitution, he became an ardent Democratic-Republican. Elected governor of Virginia, 1808, he held that post until 1811 when he became U.S. judge for the district of Virginia.

TYLER, JOHN (b. *Charles City Co., Va., 1790; d. 1862*), lawyer, Virginia legislator, president of the United States. Son of John Tyler (1747–1813); father of Robert Tyler. Educated at College of William and Mary; read law with his father; began practice *ca.* 1809. Elected to the House of Delegates, 1811, he served until 1816, loyally supporting the Madison administration and indicating a preference for strict constuctionism. A man of great charm and a gifted speaker, Tyler was elected to the U.S. Congress as a Democrat in 1816 and served until 1821. He favored revocation of the charter of the Bank of the U.S., voted against Calhoun's "bonus bill" for internal improvements, against a protective tariff, and against adoption of the Missouri Compromise in 1820. Consistent in opposition to the slave trade, he trusted to time and climate for the abolition of the whole institution of slavery. He supported William H. Crawford for president in the campaign of 1824 and had little use for Andrew Jackson. As governor of Virginia, 1825–27, he strove for the development of roads and schools. Elected to the U.S. Senate, 1827, as an anti-Jackson Democrat, he voted against the "tariff of abominations," 1828, and supported Jackson for the presidency as a choice of evils. Although he approved Jackson's opposition to the recharter of the Bank of the U.S., he supported the resolutions which condemned the president for removing federal deposits. Personally opposed to nullification, Tyler considered Jackson's nullification proclamation a violation of the Constitution and cast the single vote recorded in the Senate against the Force Bill. However, it was he who first formulated a plan of conciliation and brought Calhoun and Clay together to agree upon the compromise tariff of 1833. A member of the southern states' rights group in Congress which acted with the National Republicans within the now-forming Whig party, Tyler did not accept the nationalist doctrines of Clay and his following. Reelected to the Senate, 1833, he resigned in 1836 in protest against direction by the Virginia legislature to vote for expunging the resolutions censuring Jackson for removal of the Bank deposits. Losing the contest for a Senate seat to William C. Rives in 1839, Tyler was nominated for the vice presidency on the Whig ticket with William H. Harrison, 1840. Elected, he succeeded Harrison who died within a month of inauguration and became president by right of succession, the first ever to do so.

Henry Clay and the Whig nationalists were soon at odds with the president on matters of fundamental principle although Tyler had retained Harrison's cabinet as a gesture of conciliation. A crisis between the president and the Whigs was brought on by the bank question. Tyler had made it clear that he would not sanction a measure which permitted a national bank to establish branches in the states without their previous consent, and he had devised a plan known as the "exchequer system" which would have avoided this difficulty. Congress passed a bill chartering a U.S. bank along lines desired by Clay, and Tyler promptly vetoed it. A revised bill was presented and passed which Tyler also vetoed. At Clay's urging, the original cabinet then resigned with the exception of Daniel Webster, the secretary of state. A president without a party, Tyler nevertheless made a remarkable record as administrator and negotiator. He was responsible for a reform and reorganization of the navy which included encouragement of scientific work; he ran the government with a minimum of waste and extravagance. He brought the Seminole War to an end, and withheld federal interference from Dorr's Rebellion in Rhode Island. A treaty was negotiated with China which opened the doors of the Orient for the first time, and the Monroe Doctrine was enforced in the cases of Texas and Hawaii. The greatest achievements of Tyler's administration were the negotiation of the Webster-Ashburton treaty and the annexation of Texas, in which the president played an inconspicuous but considerable part.

Although he was supported for reelection in 1844 by a strong element in many states, he withdrew his name in favor of James K. Polk and retired to private life in Virginia. On the outbreak of the Civil War he proposed a convention of the border states to consider compromises which might save the Union, and acted as chairman of the convention which was called for this purpose by the Virginia Assembly and met in Washington, February 1861. A member of the Virginia secession convention, Tyler declared for separation after all compromise measures had failed. He served in the provisional Congress of the Confederacy and was elected to the Confederate House of Representatives but died before he could take his place. An intelligent, approachable, courteous man, Tyler has failed of his due because of a lack of appreciation among historians for a record of courageous consistency and integrity.

TYLER, LYON GARDINER (b. *Charles City Co., Va., 1853; d. Charles City Co., 1935*), lawyer, educator, Virginia legislator, historian. Son of John Tyler (1790–1862). A.B., University of Virginia, 1874; A.M., 1875. A representative of Richmond in the House of Delegates, he sponsored bill reopening College of William and Mary, 1888, and served thereafter as its president until 1919. Author, among other works, of *Parties and Patronage in the United States* (1891); *History of Virginia, Federal Period* (1924); and *The Cradle of the Republic* (1900).

TYLER, MOSES COIT (b. *Griswold, Conn., 1835; d. Ithaca, N.Y., 1900*), Congregational and Episcopal clergyman, reformer, educator, historian. Raised in Detroit, Mich., Tyler attended the University of Michigan and graduated from Yale, 1857. After a few years in the ministry and a period of ardent preoccupation with reform movements (including a crusade for physical culture), he became professor of English at the University of Michigan, 1867, and taught there with success until 1881. He then became professor of American history at Cornell University, the first man to hold such a post in the country. Among other activities, he introduced German methodology into graduate instruction and helped found the American Historical Association (1884). He was generally recognized as a leader in the cause of "critical" as opposed to "patriotic" history. Tyler's permanent reputation is owing to his authorship of *A History of American Literature during the Colonial Time, 1607–1765* (1878), a biography of *Patrick Henry* (1887), *The Literary History of the American Revolution, 1763–1783* (1897), and *Three Men of Letters* (1895). Based on profound research of an original nature and written with clarity and sanity, Tyler's histories of literature in the colonial period have become by common consent the standard account of early American literary development.

TYLER, RANSOM HUBERT (*b. Franklin Co., Mass., 1815; d. Fulton, N.Y., 1881*), lawyer, New York jurist. Author of *American Ecclesiastical Law* (1866) and a number of subsequent texts and treatises on various aspects of civil law which were valuable for their wealth of material but poorly organized.

TYLER, ROBERT (*b. Charles City Co., Va., 1816; d. Montgomery, Ala., 1877*), lawyer, politician, editor. Son of John Tyler (1790–1862) whom he served as private secretary, 1841–44. Thereafter he took a leading part in Philadelphia politics and became a political friend of James Buchanan, influencing Virginia support of Buchanan at the convention of 1856. Removing to the South at the outbreak of the Civil War, Tyler served as register of the Confederate Treasury, and was editor *post* 1867 of the Montgomery (Ala.) *Mail and Advertiser*.

TYLER, ROBERT OGDEN (*b. Hunter, N.Y., 1831; d. Boston, Mass., 1874*), soldier. Nephew of Daniel Tyler. Graduated West Point, 1853. Commissioned in the artillery, he served against the Indians on the frontiers. Appointed colonel, 1st Connecticut Heavy Artillery, September 1861, he served his guns with great distinction during the Peninsular campaigns and was promoted brigadier general, November 1862. At Gettysburg he commanded the artillery reserve which was so effective in stopping Pickett's charge. Serving as infantry, his artillerymen distinguished themselves at Spotsylvania and Cold Harbor. Reverting to lieutenant colonel in the Regular Army, he served in a number of capacities and died as a belated result of war wounds.

TYLER, ROYALL (*b. Boston, Mass., 1757; d. Brattleboro, Vt., 1826*), playwright, novelist, jurist. Graduated Harvard, 1776; studied law with Francis Dana. After brief service in the Revolution, began practice of law, 1780, in present Portland, Maine. A successful lawyer in Boston, 1785–91, and thereafter in Vermont where he held, among other public offices, the post of chief justice of the supreme court, 1807–13, Tyler is remembered principally as author of *The Contrast*. This play, produced April 1787 in New York City and immediately successful, was the first comedy to be written by a native American and produced by a professional company. A satire on city affectation, *The Contrast* contained the character "Jonathan," the prototype of a long succession of stage Yankees. Tyler was author also of a comic opera, *May Day in Town* (produced in New York City, May 1787), and several other plays which have not survived in print. In 1794 he entered into a literary mock-partnership with Joseph Dennie, writing prose and verse under the pseudonym of "Spondee" for various publications. The best of these are contained in *The Spirit of the Farmer's Museum* (1801). He was author also of a picaresque novel *The Algerine Captive* (1797) and of the *Yankey in London* (1809).

TYLER, ROYALL (*b. Quincy, Mass., 1884; d. Paris, France, 1953*), historian, League of Nations official, United Nations official. Studied at Harrow and Oxford. Served in the U.S. delegation to the Versailles Peace Conference, 1919, and on the Reparations Commission, 1919–23. Appointed to the Financial Committee of the League of Nations, 1924, and served in Budapest as deputy commissioner general for Hungary, 1924–28. Tyler was also a member of the Greek Refugee Settlement Committee, 1927, and financial adviser to the Hungarian government, 1932–38. During World War II, he worked for the League of Nations in Geneva. Served in Beirut as chief financial adviser to U.N. Economic Survey mission, 1949.

TYLER, SAMUEL (*b. Prince Georges Co., Md., 1809; d. Georgetown, D.C., 1877*), lawyer, writer. An authority on pleading and procedure. Author, among other works, of *Memoir of Roger Brooke Taney* (1872), an authorized biography and a useful source.

TYLER, WILLIAM (*b. Derby, Vt., 1806; d. 1849*), Roman Catholic clergyman. A convert to Catholicism, Tyler studied theology with Benedict J. Fenwick and at Montreal. Ordained 1829, he served as curate in Boston and as a missionary through New England. Consecrated first bishop of Hartford, Conn., 1844, he established his see at Providence, R.I., where he erected a cathedral and laid sound foundations for his church in an unfriendly region.

TYLER, WILLIAM SEYMOUR (*b. Harford, Pa., 1810; d. 1897*), Congregational clergyman, educator. Graduated Amherst, 1830. Professor of classics at Amherst, 1836–93 (*post* 1847 Williston Professor of Greek), Tyler served as president of the trustees of several schools including Mount Holyoke and Smith colleges. He was author, among other works, of *The History of Amherst College* (1873, 1895).

TYNDALE, HECTOR (*b. Philadelphia, Pa., 1821; d. Philadelphia, 1880*), glass merchant, authority on ceramics, Union major general by brevet. Tyndale was particularly outstanding as a soldier at the battles of Antietam and Missionary Ridge.

TYNG, EDWARD (*b. Boston, Mass., 1683; d. Boston, 1755*), merchant, outstanding officer in the colonial Massachusetts navy. Cruised with success against French and Spanish privateers, 1741–44; later commanded frigate *Massachusetts*.

TYNG, STEPHEN HIGGINSON (*b. Newburyport, Mass., 1800; d. Irvington-on-Hudson, N.Y., 1885*), Episcopal clergyman. Graduated Harvard, 1817; studied theology with Alexander V. Griswold. Held pastorates in Maryland and in Philadelphia, Pa., rector of St. George's Church, New York City, 1845–78. A dogmatic Low Churchman, Tyng was considered one of the greatest preachers of his time and was one of the first Episcopal clergyman to stress the importance of Sunday Schools.

TYSON, GEORGE EMORY (*b. Red Bank, N.J., 1829; d. Washington, D.C., 1906*), whaling captain. Assistant navigator and very capable second-in-command under Charles F. Hall on the *Polaris* expedition to the Arctic, 1871–73. Hero of a remarkable six-months' drift on an ice floe.

TYSON, JAMES (*b. Philadelphia, Pa., 1841; d. 1919*), physician. Graduated Haverford College, 1861; M.D., University of Pennsylvania, 1863. After Civil War service as surgeon, he practiced in Philadelphia. A teacher of various medical subjects at Pennsylvania *post* 1868, he held the chair of medicine there, 1899–1910, and for several years was dean of medical faculty. A staff member of many hospitals, he was author of a number of successful texts.

TYSON, JOB ROBERTS (*b. in or near Philadelphia, Pa., 1803; d. 1858*), Philadelphia lawyer, reformer. An authority on the history of Pennsylvania, he was instrumental in providing for the printing of the Pennsylvania Archives and did pioneer service in criticizing the exaggerated claims made by the New England historians for their section as the primary source of American freedom.

TYSON, LAWRENCE DAVIS (*b. near Greenville, N.C., 1861; d. Philadelphia, Pa., 1929*), soldier, lawyer, Tennessee legislator and publisher. Graduated West Point, 1883; LL.B., University of Tennessee, 1894. Served in frontier campaigns, 1883–91, and in the Spanish-American War. As brigadier general, National Army (commissioned 1917), he commanded the 59th Brigade of the 30th Division in France during its outstanding service in breaking the Hindenburg line, 1918. Publisher thereafter of the Knoxville *Sentinel*, he was active in Democratic politics and served as U.S. senator from Tennessee, 1925–29. He was interested also in coal companies and textile mills.

TYSON, STUART LAWRENCE (*b. Pennllyn, Pa., 1873; d. New York, N.Y., 1932*), Episcopal clergyman, author, lecturer. Graduated Nashota House, Wisconsin, 1895; studied for a number of years at Oxford, England, from which he received the degrees of M.A., B.D., and D.D. Returning to America, 1907, he taught at Western Theological Seminary and the University of the South and served later on the staffs of several New York churches. Moving from an early conservative position, Tyson became an aggressive liberal and modernist; in 1925 after a divorce he left the Episcopal Church and entered the Congregational ministry, presiding thereafter over a Summit, N.J., church composed principally of Unitarians. He was particularly notable during his later career for his defense of clergymen accused of heresy.

TYTUS, JOHN BUTLER (*b. Middletown, Ohio, 1875; d. Cincinnati, Ohio, 1944*), inventor. B.A., Yale, 1897. After working in his family's paper mill, and for a bridge builder, he became interested in steelmaking and in 1904 took a job as laborer in the Middletown, Ohio, plant of the American Rolling Mill Company (Armco). He thus learned steelmaking firsthand. Remembering the machines that produced an unending sheet of paper, Tytus began to study the possibility of designing analogous machinery for the steel industry.

Tytus took on increasing responsibilities in the operation of Armco, which before World War I was beginning various expansion programs. In 1906 he became superintendent of the company's new plant in Zanesville, Ohio; and in 1909, as operations chief at Middletown, he planned a new mill in that city. Meanwhile, he continued to work at designing a continuous process. Armco's acquisition in 1921 of blast furnaces and open hearth furnaces gave Tytus his opportunity. His revolutionary plant began operation in January 1924. The continuous mill won almost immediate acceptance within the steel industry.

U

UDDEN, JOHAN AUGUST (b. Uddabo, Sweden, 1859; d. Tex., 1932), geologist. Came to America as a child; was raised in Minnesota. Graduated Augustana College, 1881; M.A., 1889. A teacher at Augustana, 1888–1911, and associated thereafter with the Bureau of Economic Geology of the University of Texas, Udden was eminent as a research geologist and was author of many important papers in his field. His investigations included stratigraphic and areal geology, till in the upper Mississippi Valley, clastic sediments, and related subjects. He was one of the first in America to stress the value of seismograph observations for locating geologic structure and devised a pioneering technique for examining subsurface material. His work in Texas contributed much to the economic development of that state.

UHLER, PHILIP REESE (b. Baltimore, Md., 1835; d. 1913), entomologist, librarian of the Peabody Institute. A world authority on entomology specializing in *Hemiptera*, Uhler taught at Harvard, 1864–67, and was associate in natural history at Johns Hopkins, 1876–1913.

ULLOA, ANTONIO DE (b. Seville, Spain, 1716; d. probably Spain, 1795), Spanish naval officer, colonial administrator. Celebrated for several reports on conditions in Spanish America (1748–49) which were translated into other languages and widely read, Ulloa became governor of Louisiana in 1766. Given no support by his government and obliged to let the last French governor of the province continue to rule it in the name of the Spanish king, he was recalled in 1768 in the midst of a Creole uprising and was succeeded by Alejandro O'Reilly.

ULRICH, EDWARD OSCAR (b. Cincinnati, Ohio, 1857; d. Washington, D.C., 1944), geologist, paleontologist. His work with fossils at the Cincinnati Society of Natural History, and with the Illinois and Minnesota geological surveys, brought him in 1900 a permanent appointment with the U.S. Geological Survey. He was soon recognized as the Survey's leading stratigrapher, and became the principal authority on the early Paleozoic formations and fossils in the eastern United States.

UNANGST, ERIAS (b. Easton, Pa., 1824; d. Hollidaysburg, Pa., 1903), Lutheran clergyman. Missionary in India for the greater part of the years 1858–95.

UNCAS (b. ca. 1588; d. ca. 1683), sachem of the Mohegan Indians. Son-in-law of Sassacus, chief sachem of the Pequot, against whom he lead a number of rebellions. On his final revolt the Pequot territory was divided, and Uncas became ruler of the western part, called Moheag, his tribe becoming known as the Mohegans. He courted the favor of the English, and in May 1637, with the Narragansett, joined them in a war against the Pequot. Known during his career for being untrustworthy and dissolute. He appears to have been tolerated by the English in Connecticut and Massachusetts because of his enmity to the Narragansett, and because his presence served as a divisive force among the other Indian tribes.

UNDERHILL, FRANK PELL (b. Brooklyn, N.Y., 1877; d. New Haven, Conn., 1932), pharmacologist, toxicologist. Graduated Yale, 1900; Ph.D., 1903. Taught thereafter at Yale, serving as professor of pathological chemistry, 1912–18, of experimental medicine, 1918–21, and of pharmacology and toxicology post 1921. His early researches dealt with the physiologic action of proteins and tartrates, and with the effects of chemical substances on the behavior of sugars, salts and water within the body. He was active in organization of the U.S. Army Chemical Warfare Service and made investigations of the effects of lethal gases on the animal body. He also investigated the effects of fluid administration in treating burns and made studies of pellagra.

UNDERHILL, JOHN (b. probably Warwickshire, England, ca. 1597; d. Oyster Bay, N.Y., 1672), colonial military leader, magistrate. Trained as a soldier in the Netherlands, Underhill moved to Boston, 1630, as captain and organizer of the Massachusetts Bay militia. Associated with the Connecticut forces in the defeat of the Pequot, 1637, he was disfranchised and discharged from military service by Massachusetts in that same year because of his alliance with the Antinomian. In England during the winter of 1637–38, he published *Nevves from America* (1638), a classical account of the Pequot troubles. On his return to Boston he was banished in September 1638 and fled to Dover, N.H., where he secured the governorship and opposed the claims of Massachusetts upon the region. Losing support at Dover, he returned to Massachusetts where he made a public confession of various crimes, 1640, but was considered insincerely repentant and was excommunicated. In September 1640, however, he was reinstated in the church and in the following year his sentence of banishment was repealed. He now moved to Stamford, Conn., which he represented in the assembly of New Haven, 1643. Soon afterwards, being employed by the Dutch to fight Indians, he moved to Long Island where he held office; in 1653 he denounced Peter Stuyvesant's government for its unjust taxation and dealings with the Indians. In the same year, commissioned as a privateer at Providence, he seized the property of the Dutch West India Company at Hartford. After helping reduce the New Amsterdam Dutch to English control, 1664–65, he held several public offices under the English government of New York before retiring from public life, 1666/67.

UNDERWOOD, BENJAMIN FRANKLIN (b. New York, N.Y., 1839; d. Westerly, R.I., 1914), Union soldier, journalist, freethinker. One of the earliest and most zealous American supporters of the theory of evolution, Underwood lectured widely on this and other subjects. He wrote a number of pamphlets which expressed his philosophic position, roughly that of orthodox materialism. Post 1897 he was editor of the Quincy (Ill.) Journal, retiring in 1913.

UNDERWOOD, FRANCIS HENRY (b. Enfield, Mass., 1825; d. Edinburgh, Scotland, 1894), lawyer, author, consular official. Conceiving the idea of a magazine which should enlist the literary forces of New England in a crusade against slavery, 1853, he was successful in persuading Phillips, Sampson & Co. to undertake the project in 1857. It was issued as the *Atlantic Monthly* (first issue, November 1857), but Underwood was relegated to the routine post of editorial assistant to James Russell Lowell. Subsequent to his leaving the *Atlantic* in 1859, he engaged in a number of activities before his service as U.S. consul at Glasgow, Scotland, 1886–89, and at Leith *post* 1893. A talented man, he contributed much to the fame of others but won little credit for himself. As Francis Parkman observed, he was "neither a Harvard man nor a humbug" and so was a victim of his own merit.

UNDERWOOD, FREDERICK DOUGLAS (*b. Wauwatosa, Wis., 1849; d. New York, N.Y., 1942*), railroad executive. Associated *post* 1867 with the Chicago, Milwaukee & St. Paul Railroad, the Soo Line, and the Baltimore & Ohio successively, he achieved his greatest success in rehabilitating the Erie Railroad. As president of the Erie, 1901–26, he made it an efficient and profitable freight-service road, a strong competitor of the larger Eastern trunk lines.

UNDERWOOD, HORACE GRANT (*b. London, England, 1859; d. Atlantic City, N.J., 1916*), Dutch Reformed clergyman. Presbyterian missionary to Korea *post* 1885.

UNDERWOOD, JOHN CURTISS (*b. Litchfield, N.Y., 1809; d. Washington, D.C., 1873*), lawyer. A planter in Clarke Co., Va., *post* 1839, Underwood was a Free-Soiler in politics and was virtually driven from Virginia for his attacks on slavery during the presidential campaign of 1856. A Republican officeholder during the Civil War, he became a U.S. district court judge in Virginia, 1864. In this capacity he asserted the right of the United States to confiscate property of persons in rebellion and treated Jefferson Davis with great harshness during and after Davis's indictment for treason at Norfolk, Va., 1866. He presided over the Virginia constitutional convention which met at Richmond, December, 1867.

UNDERWOOD, JOHN THOMAS (*b. London, England, 1857; d. Wianno, Mass., 1937*), typewriter manufacturer. Brother of Horace G. Underwood. Came to America 1873, and engaged with his father in the pioneer manufacture of typewriter supplies. Purchasing the rights to the Wagner "front-stroke" typewriting machine (patented, 1893), Underwood marketed the first typewriters under his own name in 1897. His product was superior in design to its competitors and was soon highly successful.

UNDERWOOD, JOSEPH ROGERS (*b. Goochland Co., Va., 1791; d. 1876*), Kentucky legislator and jurist. Grandfather of Oscar W. Underwood. Practiced at Glasgow, Ky., 1813–23, and at Bowling Green thereafter. Justice, Kentucky court of appeals, 1828–35; congressman, Whig, from Kentucky, 1835–43; U.S. senator, 1847–53. An orthodox Whig in his political opinions and actions, he supported Southern views on slavery short of secession. A Unionist during the Civil War, he became a Democrat, 1864, and was instrumental in reorganizing that party in Kentucky.

UNDERWOOD, LORING (*b. Belmont, Mass., 1874; d. 1930*), landscape architect. Graduated Harvard, 1897; studied at Bussey Institution and in Paris. Practiced his profession in Boston, Mass., *post* 1900. Author of *The Garden and Its Accessories* (1906).

UNDERWOOD, LUCIEN MARCUS (*b. New Woodstock, N.Y., 1853; d. Redding, Conn., 1907*), botanist. Graduated Syracuse University, 1877; Ph.D., 1879. Taught at Illinois, Wesleyan, Syracuse, De Pauw, and Alabama Polytechnic; professor of botany, Columbia, 1896–1907. Authority on ferns and hepaticae. Took leading part in initiating (1905) publication of the *North American Flora*.

UNDERWOOD, OSCAR WILDER (*b. Louisville, Ky., 1862; d. 1929*), lawyer, statesman. Grandson of Joseph R. Underwood. Admitted to the bar, 1884, after study at the University of Virginia. Practiced briefly in Minnesota; removed to Birmingham, Ala. Congressman, Democrat, from Alabama, 1895–96 and 1897–1915; U.S. senator, 1915–27. A man of high character and unflagging industry, Underwood made a lifelong study of the tariff and was a strong opponent of tariffs for protection. He served as Democratic floor leader in the House, 1911–15, and was chairman of the ways and means committee. A supporter of W. H. Taft's reciprocity program, Underwood at the same time took the lead in revising many tariff schedules downward; when the legislation advanced by him was vetoed by President Taft, the outstanding issue of the campaign of 1912 was created. Underwood showed such conspicuous ability in Congress that he was among the leading contenders for the Democratic presidential nomination in 1912 and again in 1924. A loyal supporter of President Woodrow Wilson, Underwood efficiently carried out Wilson's legislative program. His work in framing the tariff bill which bears his name, and in support of the Federal Reserve Act, was especially noteworthy. In the Senate *post* 1915 he continued his support of Wilson's policies, although in the fight over the League of Nations he was of the opinion that the president should have agreed to certain mild reservations. His uncompromising hostility to the Ku Klux Klan and to national prohibition alienated the South and cost him presidential nomination by the Democrats in 1924. A devout follower of Thomas Jefferson, he was strongly averse to all extensions of the federal authority.

UNTERMYER, SAMUEL (*b. Lynchburg, Va., 1858; d. Palm Springs, Calif., 1940*), lawyer. Graduated Columbia Law School, 1878. Celebrated during his early career as a trial lawyer in important suits of every type, he grew wealthy as an organizer of large industrial combinations. Moved by growing doubts about the virtues of the corporate combinations he had helped to create, he slowly became known as an enemy of corporate abuses. In 1911 he delivered a series of addresses calling for government action to break up or regulate the trusts. During 1912–13 he served without pay as counsel to the Pujo investigation instituted by Congress to look into the operations of the leading financiers of the country. The recommendations of the Pujo Committee contributed to passage of the Federal Reserve Act, the Federal Trade Commission Act, and the Clayton Anti-Trust Act; in each of these Untermyer had some part. He served again without pay as counsel to the New York Joint Legislative Committee on Housing, 1919–20, investigating conspiracies to profiteer in the building trades; thereafter, he devoted much time, without compensation, to New York City transit problems. An early advocate of a graduated income tax and of public ownership of public utilities, he was a lifelong Democrat and an ardent supporter of the New Deal. In Jewish matters he was a moderate Zionist.

UPCHURCH, JOHN JORDAN (*b. Franklin Co., N.C., 1820; d. Steelville, Mo., 1887*), railroad mechanic. Founder of the Ancient Order of United Workmen, 1868, a lodge which began as an opponent of trade unions and strikes and which became in time the prototype for subsequent fraternal benefit societies.

UPDEGRAFF, DAVID BRAINARD (*b. Mount Pleasant, Ohio, 1830; d. Mount Pleasant, 1894*), Quaker preacher, editor. Considered an innovator and a controversial figure within the Society of Friends, he represented an intense form of evangelical thought and practiced a dramatic style of preaching.

UPDIKE, DANIEL (*b. North Kingstown, R.I., ca. 1693; d. Newport, R.I., 1757*), lawyer. Attorney general of Rhode Island, 1722–32, 1743–57; attorney general for Kings Co., R.I., 1741–43.

UPDIKE, DANIEL BERKELEY (*b. Providence, R.I., 1860; d. Boston, Mass., 1941*), scholar-printer. His incomplete formal education was acquired in private schools in Providence. After a winter as an assistant in the Providence Athenaeum, he went to Boston in 1880 to the publishing firm of Houghton, Mifflin & Company. His first published work (except for a few anonymous articles in the *Atlantic Monthly*) was *On the Dedications of American Churches* (1891). In 1892 he collaborated with Bertram Grosvenor Goodhue in designing and decorating an edition of the Book of Common Prayer.

In 1893 he struck out on his own as a "typographic adviser." This was the beginning of the Merrymount Press, a name adopted in 1896. The variety and ingenuity of his designs is best seen in the many books that he privately printed for his Boston friends, and in the work that he did for the Club of Odd Volumes, the Grolier Club, and the Limited Editions Club. His masterpiece is the folio edition of the 1928 revision of the Book of Common Prayer that he completed in 1930 for J. Pierpont Morgan.

During the years 1911–16 Updike gave a course at the Harvard Business School on the technique of printing that he eventually recast into the two scholarly volumes of *Printing Types, Their History, Forms, and Use* (1922). He also published an autobiography, *Notes on the Merrymount Press & Its Work* (1934).

UPHAM, CHARLES WENTWORTH (*b. St. John, N.B., now Canada, 1802; d. Salem, Mass., 1875*), Unitarian clergyman, Massachusetts legislator, historian. Graduated Harvard, 1821. Minister in Salem, Mass., 1824–44. After engaging in politics as a Whig and later a Republican, 1848–61, Upham turned to historical research producing, among other works, his *Salem Witchcraft* (1867). He is considered the prototype of "Judge Pyncheon" in *The House of the Seven Gables* by Nathaniel Hawthorne.

UPHAM, SAMUEL FOSTER (*b. Duxbury, Mass., 1834; d. 1904*), Methodist clergyman. A popular and witty preacher as pastor of a number of New England churches, Upham was professor of practical theology at Drew Theological Seminary, 1881–1904.

UPHAM, THOMAS COGSWELL (*b. Deerfield, N.H., 1799; d. New York, N.Y., 1872*), Congregational clergyman, metaphysician. Graduated Dartmouth, 1818; Andover Theological Seminary, 1821. Professor of philosophy at Bowdoin College, 1824–67, he was author, among other books, of *A Philosophical and Practical Treatise on the Will* (1834), an original contribution to modern psychology.

UPHAM, WARREN (*b. Amherst, N.H., 1850; d. St. Paul, Minn., 1934*), glacial geologist, archeologist. Graduated Dartmouth, 1871. After employment on the geological surveys of New Hampshire and Minnesota and service with the U.S. Geological Survey, he was librarian-secretary of the Minnesota Historical Society, 1895–1914, and the society's archeologist thereafter. His principal field in science was glacial geology, and his best-known monograph is "The Glacial Lake Agassiz" (*U.S. Geological Survey Monographs*, Vol. 25, 1896). After changing his major field to archaeology and history *ca.* 1905, he published a number of important essays on the history of Minnesota and its area.

UPJOHN, RICHARD (*b. Shaftesbury, England, 1802; d. Garrison, N.Y., 1878*), architect. Trained as a cabinet-maker, Upjohn Immigrated to America, 1829, and settled in New Bedford, Mass., 1830. At first a draftsman and teacher of drawing, he began to practice as an architect and removed to Boston, Mass., 1834, where he worked with Alexander Parris. In 1837 he completed St. John's Church, Bangor, Maine, his first Gothic church. Chosen architect for the new Trinity Church, New York City, he removed to New York in 1839; Trinity Church, begun in 1841 and consecrated in 1846, won him immediate fame. Upjohn did a great deal of important work, making a careful and sensitive use of the precedents of English Gothic; his influence in the United States was in many ways similar to the contemporary influence in England of Pugin. Among his outstanding buildings were the Church of the Pilgrims, Brooklyn, N.Y.; St. Paul's in Brookline, Mass.; and his own favorite work, Trinity Chapel on W. 25th St., New York City. He also designed a number of houses and civic buildings. He was a founder and first president of the American Institute of Architects, 1857–76, and many famous architects were trained in his office or worked for him.

UPJOHN, RICHARD MICHELL (*b. Shaftesbury, England, 1828; d. Brooklyn, N.Y., 1903*), architect. Son of Richard Upjohn. Came to America as a child. Trained in his father's office, he practiced with him *post* 1853 and exercised a growing influence on the elder man's design. Although he designed a great number of churches, his work was less dominantly ecclesiastical than his father's. His most famous building was the State Capitol at Hartford, Conn. (1885), for which drawings were begun in 1872.

UPSHAW, WILLIAM DAVID (*b. Coweta County, Ga., 1866; d. Glendale, Calif., 1952*), writer, politician, evangelist. Studied briefly at Mercer College. Democratic Congressman from Georgia, 1918–26. An ardent Prohibitionist, Upshaw was against the rights of blacks and was an avowed anti-Communist; failed to win reelection because of his connections with and defense of the Ku Klux Klan. Presidential candidate of the Prohibition party, 1932. Vice president of the Southern Baptist Convention in the late 1930's. Vice president of Linda Vista Baptist College and Seminary in San Diego, 1949–52.

UPSHUR, ABEL PARKER (*b. Northampton Co., Va., 1791; d. aboard battleship Princeton, 1844*), Virginia legislator and jurist. A judge of the Virginia supreme court, 1826–41, he associated himself in politics with the extreme states' rights proslavery group. U.S. secretary of the navy, 1841–43, he succeeded Daniel Webster as U.S. secretary of state. He was killed by the explosion of a gun on the *Princeton* while cruising on the Potomac. A strong conservative, Upshur was opposed to numerical majorities, democratic conceptions, and the nationalistic theory of the Constitution; he rejected almost entirely the natural rights philosophy.

UPSHUR, JOHN HENRY (*b. Eastville, Va., 1823; d. Washington, D.C., 1917*), naval officer. Nephew of Abel P. Upshur. Entering the navy as midshipman, 1841, he retired as rear admiral, 1885, after varied world-wide service which included the Union North Atlantic blockade.

UPTON, EMORY (*b. near Batavia, N.Y., 1839; d. San Francisco, Calif., 1881*), Union soldier, expert in tactics. Graduated West Point, 1861. Commissioned in the artillery, Upton had a notable career during the Civil War, serving in the infantry and cavalry as well as his own arm and participating in a great number of engagements. He won promotion to brigadier general on the field of Spotsylvania, May 1864, and held divisional command at the battle of Winchester in September. In April 1865 he led in the capture of Selma, Ala., and its arsenal. He was an outstanding commandant of cadets at West Point, 1870–75, and was author of a system of infantry tactics which bears his name. An incomplete but important work by him was published as *The Military Policy of the United States* (ed. J. P. Sanger, 1904).

UPTON, GEORGE BRUCE (*b. Eastport, Maine, 1804; d. Boston, Mass., 1874*), merchant, capitalist, Massachusetts Whig legislator. Author of a public letter (March 23, 1870) charging the British with being responsible for Confederate commerce raiders and with having operated them in the Civil War.

UPTON, GEORGE PUTNAM (*b. Roxbury, Mass., 1834; d. Chicago, Ill., 1919*), journalist, music critic. Associated with Chicago, Ill., newspapers *post* 1855, Upton served on the staff of the *Chicago Daily Tribune* for 57 years *post* 1861. His local reputation was established by his writings as a music critic under the pseudonym "Peregrine Pickle"; he was author also of a number of books in the field of musicology.

UPTON, WINSLOW (*b. Salem, Mass., 1853; d. 1914*), astronomer, meteorologist. Graduated Brown, 1875; M.A., University of Cincinnati, 1877. Professor of astronomy at Brown, 1883–1914, and director of the Ladd Observatory, 1890–1914.

URBAN, JOSEPH (*b. Vienna, Austria, 1872; d. New York, N.Y., 1933*), architect, stage designer. Worked principally in the United States *post* 1911; introduced the new stage art of Europe to this country and to a great degree made possible the introduction of "modern" design concepts. Employing a style which owed much to the Secessionists and to *art nouveau*, he designed furniture, motor cars, clubs and public buildings, as well as the settings for the *Ziegfeld Follies* for which he was famous.

U'REN, WILLIAM SIMON (*b. Lancaster, Wis., 1859; d. Portland, Oreg., 1949*), political reformer. After a rootless childhood in Nebraska, Colorado, and Wyoming, he left home at age seventeen to work in the mines of Colorado and later became a blacksmith in Denver, attending business college at night. He read law for two years and in 1881 was admitted to the bar. In 1888, ill with tuberculosis, he went to Hawaii, where he worked on a sugar plantation. He then settled in Oregon. After reading Henry George's *Progress and Poverty* he became a convert to the single tax. In 1893 he helped organize and became the secretary of a joint committee on direct legislation, and embarked on a campaign to pledge candidates for the legislature to vote for the initiative and referendum.

U'Ren had meanwhile helped organize the Populist party in Oregon and was secretary of its state committee. In 1896 he was elected to the Oregon house of representatives. In 1902 the initiative and referendum amendment was ratified by popular vote. U'Ren then moved toward the next step in the series of measures that became known as the "Oregon System." In 1903 he organized the Direct Primary Nomination League to secure the nomination of candidates for office by primary election. The direct-primary amendment passed in 1904. It included a provision that in effect made possible the direct election of U.S. senators.

In 1905 U'Ren organized the People's Power League. League measures that were enacted included recall of state officers, a corrupt practices law, and one prohibiting railroads from giving free passes. Woodrow Wilson, earlier critical of direct democracy, allowed himself to be tutored by U'Ren on its principles after his election as governor of New Jersey in 1910. U'Ren felt the time was ripe to enact the single tax, and in 1914 ran for governor as an independent; but he and the single tax were soundly defeated.

URSO, CAMILLA (*b. Nantes, France, 1842; d. New York, N.Y., 1902*), violinist. Came to America as a child prodigy, 1852; played on concert tours with Henriette Sontag and Marietta Alboni. Outstanding in concert work, 1862–95, she devoted her last years to teaching.

USHER, JOHN PALMER (*b. Brookfield, N.Y., 1816; d. Philadelphia, Pa., 1889*), lawyer. Began practice in Terre Haute, Ind., 1840. Early active in the Republican party, he became assistant U.S. secretary of the interior *ca.* February 1862 and was appointed head of the department, January 1863. Resigning in May 1865, he removed to Lawrence, Kans., and became chief counsel for the Union Pacific Railroad, a post which he held for the rest of his life.

USHER, NATHANIEL REILLY (*b. Vincennes, Ind., 1855; d. probably Potsdam, N.Y., 1931*), naval officer. Nephew of John P. Usher. Graduated U.S. Naval Academy, 1875. Promoted rear admiral in 1911 after varied service which included the Greely Relief Expedition and command of the torpedo boat *Ericsson* in the Spanish-American War, he performed outstanding service as commandant of the Brooklyn Navy Yard during the period of World War I. Owing principally to his energy and organizing ability, the Port of New York was able to ship the greater part of all supplies and 80 percent of all the men that the United States sent to France. On his retirement, 1919, he was described as a principal factor in the successful incorporation of the Naval Reserve into the regular machine of the naval service.

UTLEY, GEORGE BURWELL (*b. Hartford, Conn., 1876; d. Pleasant Valley, Conn., 1946*), librarian. Ph.B., Brown University, 1899. Held library posts in Hartford, Baltimore, Md., and Jacksonville, Fla.; effectively guided development of American Library Association as its executive secretary, 1911–20; librarian of the Newberry Library, Chicago, Ill., 1921–42.

V

VACA, ALVAR NÚÑEZ CABEZA DE. *See* NÚÑEZ CABEZA DE VACA, ALVAR.

VAIL, AARON (*b. L'Orient, France, 1796; d. Pau, France, 1878*), U.S. state department official. Secretary of legation at London, England, 1831–32, he served as chargé d'affaires, 1832–36, with great success. While chief clerk of the U.S. State Department, 1838–40, he acted on numerous occasions as secretary of state; he was chargé d'affaires at Madrid, Spain, 1840–42.

VAIL, ALFRED (*b. Morristown, N.J., 1807; d. Morristown, 1859*), telegraph pioneer. Cousin of Theodore N. Vail. Graduated University of the City of New York, 1836. Became associated with Samuel F. B. Morse as constructor of instruments, 1837, and aided in financing early telegraph experiments. As chief assistant to Morse *post* 1843, Vail received the famous first test message "What hath God wrought!" at Baltimore, Md., May 24, 1844.

VAIL, ROBERT WILLIAM GLENROIE (*b. Victon, N.Y., 1890; d. Albuquerque, N.Mex., 1966*), librarian, bibliographer, historian. After receiving a B.A. from Cornell (1914), started his career at the New York Public Library where he became interested in completing a bibliographic record (initiated in the 1850's) of all the titles in American history and literature. World War I and other employment, including his editorship of the final twelve volumes of the *Memorial Edition of the Works of Theodore Roosevelt,* interrupted his work on the bibliography, but he returned to the New York Public Library as its coeditor (1928). In 1930 he was appointed sole editor and completed *Bibliotheca Americana* in 1936 while working as librarian for the American Antiquarian Society. Served as director of New-York Historical Society (1944–60) where he discovered the original document authorizing the Louisiana Purchase.

VAIL, STEPHEN MONTFORT (*b. Union Vale, N.Y., 1816; d. Jersey City, N.J., 1880*), Methodist clergyman, U.S. consular official, educator. Graduated Bowdoin, 1838; Union Theological Seminary, New York City, 1842. Professor of Hebrew at Methodist Biblical Institute, Concord, N.H., 1847–69. A vigorous advocate of theological training for Methodist clergymen and an active abolitionist.

VAIL, THEODORE NEWTON (*b. near Minerva, Ohio, 1845; d. Baltimore, Md., 1920*), telephone and utilities executive. Cousin of Alfred Vail. Raised in New Jersey where he became a telegrapher; resided in Iowa and Nebraska, 1866–73. Entering service of the Post Office Department, Vail devised a number of improvements in the railway mail service. He became assistant general superintendent of that service, 1874, and general superintendent, 1876. At the urging of Gardiner G. Hubbard, he became general manager of the new Bell Telephone Co. in 1878. When he resigned in 1887 he had been responsible for organizing the expanding telephone system into a series of efficient companies properly financed, and he had provided for future technical development and more economical manufacture of telephone apparatus. He had also arranged for a long-distance telephone system by connecting numerous operating companies, for which purpose he had incorporated the American Telephone & Telegraph Co., 1885. Retiring for several years to a Vermont farm, he engaged between 1894 and 1907 in financing and developing vast utility projects in Argentina. Chaotic conditions in the telephone industry followed on the expiration of the Bell patents in 1893 and 1894, and the Bell Company directors persuaded Vail to reenter the telephone industry, electing him president of the American Telephone & Telegraph Co., May 1907. By a policy of cooperation with the independent telephone companies, he achieved a second unification of the industry; meanwhile he pushed forward scientific research and technical improvement. In January 1915 the first transcontinental telephone line was opened, and in the same year telephone engineers under John J. Carty developed radio telephone into a practical means of communication. In 1919 Vail resigned the presidency of the American Telephone & Telegraph Co., becoming chairman of the Board of Directors.

VAILLANT, GEORGE CLAPP (*b. Boston, Mass., 1901; d. Devon, Pa., 1945*), archaeologist. Graduated Harvard, 1922; Ph.D., 1927. Associated with the American Museum of Natural History, New York City, *post* 1927, he made a series of excavations in the Valley of Mexico which, with subsequent studies, placed Mexican archaeology on a firm scientific footing and corrected earlier theories of the duration of the preclassic period. His major work, *The Aztecs of Mexico,* was published in 1941, and in that same year he became director of the University Museum, University of Pennsylvania. During 1943–44, he served as senior cultural relations officer in the U.S. embassy in Peru.

VALENTINE, DAVID THOMAS (*b. East Chester, N.Y., 1801; d. New York, N.Y., 1869*), New York City official, antiquarian. Clerk of the common council of New York, 1842–68, Valentine is particularly remembered for his supervision and publication of the *Manual of the Corporation of the City of New York* (1841–67) which included with the customary statistical information a vast amount of pictorial and documentary historical material of the greatest interest. The *History of the City of New York* (1853), which bears his name, was chiefly the work of W. I. Paulding.

VALENTINE, EDWARD VIRGINIUS (*b. Richmond, Va., 1838; d. Richmond, 1930*), sculptor. Studied in Paris with Thomas Couture and François Jouffroy, and in Berlin with August Kiss. Executed a number of portrait busts of Southern leaders, including the figure of Robert E. Lee for the Lee Mausoleum at Washington and Lee University.

VALENTINE, MILTON (*b. near Uniontown, Md., 1825; d. 1906*), Lutheran theologian, educator. A teacher *post* 1866 at the Lutheran Theological Seminary, Gettysburg, Pa., and a vigorous defender of General Synod Lutheranism, he served as president of the seminary, 1868–84.

VALENTINE, ROBERT GROSVENOR (*b. West Newton, Mass., 1872; d. 1916*), public official, founder of the profession of industrial counselor. Graduated Harvard, 1896. Retiring from business, 1904, he served as assistant to Francis E. Leupp and was head of the U.S. Indian Office, 1909–12. Becoming a consulting adviser to corporations, labor unions, and public officials *post* 1912, Valentine devised a system of "industrial audits" which would bear the same relation to the social health of an industry or community that a financial audit bore to its solvency.

VALLANDIGHAM, CLEMENT LAIRD (*b. New Lisbon, Ohio, 1820; d. 1871*), lawyer, Ohio legislator, politician. Of Southern stock, Vallandigham idealized the Southern character; he strove for the suppression of Abolitionists and a return to Jeffersonian states' rights principles. As congressman, Democrat, from Ohio, 1858–63, he denounced sectionalism on both sides, opposed disunion sentiment and, although disliking the popular sovereignty views of Stephen A. Douglas, supported him for the presidency in 1860. Proclaiming that the Southern "fire-eaters" would vanish if the Republican party were destroyed, he expressed his intention never to vote as a congressman for any measure in support of a civil war. His strong and able opposition to all measures for national defense proposed in the House brought him the intense hatred of the Republicans. Many Northerners were sympathetic with his pleas for restoration of peace and freedom of speech. After his defeat for reelection to Congress, 1862, he was regarded as a leader of the Peace Democrats or "Copperheads" in his section. For defiance of General A. E. Burnside's General Order Number 38 (1863), Vallandigham was arrested in Dayton, Ohio, and tried in Cincinnati for treason. He was condemned to imprisonment in Boston harbor, but President Lincoln shrewdly banished him to the Confederacy. Running the blockade, he made his way to Windsor, Canada. Defeated in a candidacy for governor of Ohio, 1863, he returned to his native state in June 1864. His influence in the framing of the national Democratic platform helped bring about a Democratic defeat in November. Thereafter he continued active in politics but failed of election to office. Shortly before his death he was instrumental in beginning the movement of reconciliation which took shape later in the Liberal Republican party.

VALLEJO, MARIANO GUADALUPE (*b. Monterey, Calif., 1808; d. Sonoma, Calif., 1890*), soldier, California politician. Supported J. B. Alvarado in the rebellion that led to proclamation of a free California, 1836; on estrangement from Alvarado, made himself a semi-independent chief at Sonoma. A powerful agent in securing submission of California to the United States, Vallejo was elected to the constitutional convention of 1849 and to the first state senate.

VALLENTINE, BENJAMIN BENNATON (*b. London, England, 1843; d. New York, N.Y., 1926*), journalist, playwright. Immigrated to New York City, 1871. A founder of *Puck*, 1877, he served as its managing editor until 1884, contributing the "Fitznoodle" letters which remain his principal achievement.

VALLIANT, LEROY BRANCH (*b. Moulton, Ala., 1838; d. Greenville, Miss., 1913*), lawyer, Confederate officer. Judge of the circuit court of St. Louis, Mo., 1886–98; judge of Missouri supreme court, 1898–1912.

VAN ALLEN, FRANK (*b. Dubuque, Iowa, 1860; d. Melur, Madura, India, 1923*), Congregational clergyman, medical missionary in India *post* 1888. Built and administered an outstanding hospital in Madura City.

VAN ALSTYNE, FANNY CROSBY. *See* CROSBY, FANNY.

VAN AMRINGE, JOHN HOWARD (*b. Philadelphia, Pa., 1835; d. Morristown, N.J., 1915*), educator. Graduated Columbia, 1860. Taught mathematics at Columbia *post* 1860, resigning in 1910 as professor emeritus. A unique figure in the history of Columbia and a promoter of its alumni association, he served as dean of the college *post* 1894 and as acting president of Columbia University, 1899.

VAN ANDA, CARR VATTEL (*b. Georgetown, Ohio, 1864; d. New York, N.Y., 1945*), journalist. Attended Ohio University at Athens, Ohio; rose from printer to editor on Cleveland newspapers; was night editor of Baltimore *Sun*, 1886–88, and of *New York Sun*, 1893–1904. As managing editor of the *New York Times*, 1904 until retirement in 1925 (retaining the title, however, until 1932), he had charge of the newsroom and it was his skill, intuitive sense of news values, and capacity for leadership that won the *Times* its reputation as the foremost news operation in the country.

VAN BEUREN, JOHANNES (*b. Amsterdam, the Netherlands, ca. 1680; d. New York, N.Y., 1755*), physician. A pupil of Boerhaave, Van Beuren came to New York *ca.* 1702 and built up a large practice both in the city and in the town of Flatbush on Long Island. Appointed first medical director of the New York almshouse hospital, 1736, he held the position until his death. This hospital was the beginning of the present Bellevue Hospital.

VAN BRUNT, HENRY (*b. Boston, Mass., 1832; d. Milton, Mass., 1903*), architect. Graduated Harvard, 1854; studied in office of Richard M. Hunt. After Civil War service, formed a partnership with William R. Ware, 1863–83. Working *post* 1883 under firm name of Van Brunt & Howe, he designed a great number of Western railroad stations, shops, and houses. The firm became the most important architectural organization west of Chicago and was domiciled in Kansas City, Mo. Van Brunt was an eclectic. His most important contribution to architecture was in his writings, of which some appear in *Greek Lines and Other Architectural Essays* (1893).

VAN BUREN, JOHN (*b. Kinderhook, N.Y., 1810; d. at sea en route to New York from England, 1866*), lawyer, New York politician and official. Son of Martin Van Buren, he was known as "Prince John." Constantly active in politics in his father's interest *post* 1834, he was influential in organizing the "Barnburners" and espoused free-soil doctrines with evangelistic fervor. Later returning to more moderate views, he supported popular sovereignty in Kansas, denounced Lincoln for precipitancy in calling for troops, and in 1864 supported George B. McClellan for president.

VAN BUREN, MARTIN (*b. Kinderhook, N.Y., 1782; d. Kinderhook, 1862*), lawyer, president of the United States. Father of John Van Buren. After serving as law clerk to William P. Van Ness, he practiced at Kinderhook *post* 1803, handling the cases of small landholders and becoming an adherent of the Clinton-Livingston faction among the Democratic Republicans. Attorney general of New York, 1816–19, and a state senator, 1812–20, he gradually turned against his early political associates in his rise to leadership in Democratic state politics. His wit and charm combined with a clear, realistic intelligence in effecting his rise. His enemies thought him hypocritical, intriguing, and selfish. He was, indeed a political manipulator, but he was honest and serious in both private and public relations and steadfast in his adherence to principle and faithful public service. At the state constitutional convention, 1821, he brought extreme radicals and conservatives together in successful opposition to the old Council of Appointment, thereby securing a distribution of the power to appoint state officers among local authorities, the legislature, and the governor.

Elected to the U.S. Senate, February, 1821, by the "Bucktail" faction, he continued to have a deep interest in New York politics and headed the influential "Albany Regency" which included W. L. Marcy, Benjamin F. Butler (1795–1858), and others. Formidable in their solidarity, Van Buren and his group were sincere as well as shrewd and faithfully performed the duties of the important offices they obtained. A supporter of William H. Crawford for president, 1824, he opposed the movement which gave John Q. Adams the presidency and remained in opposition to Adams's policies throughout that president's term. By 1828 he was a leading supporter of Andrew Jackson and assumed an important role in the campaign of that year. Elected governor of New York, he resigned the office to become Jackson's secretary of state in 1829 and the most influential member of the Jackson cabinet. He urged on the administration the introduction of the political spoils system which had been operated with such success by the Albany Regency. Wholly in Jackson's confidence, Van Buren resigned his post, April 1831, in a move which enabled the president to effect a reorganization of his cabinet and thus eliminate the supporters of John C. Calhoun. His appointment as U.S. minister to Great Britain was refused confirmation by the Senate in January 1832, whereupon he accepted nomination for vice president. He had done well as secretary of state, displaying unusual tact and high administrative ability. In addition to other achievements he settled the old dispute over the West Indian trade between Great Britain and the United States, secured an agreement with France for the payment of claims dating back to the Napoleonic wars, negotiated a favorable trade treaty with Turkey, and made an attempt to buy Texas from Mexico.

Following his nomination for the vice presidency, he aided Jackson in defeating a bill to recharter the Bank of the United States and joined in the president's opposition to nullification. Contrary to opinion, he did not disagree with Jackson over removal of the government's Bank deposits, but he was doubtful about the expediency of their removal at that time. A fair and able presiding officer of the Senate during his vice presidency, he was nominated for the presidency in May 1835 at Baltimore, Md., as Jackson's protégé.

Elected on a platform of opposition to recharter of the Bank, opposition to distribution of the Treasury's surplus, and opposition to improvement of rivers above ports of entry, he also conveyed the impression that his distaste for the extension of slavery did not extend to any meddling with the right of slave-holding states to control the institution within their boundaries. Striving throughout his term to hold together the Northern and Southern wings of his party, he was much plagued by Abolitionist agitators as well as by those who would compel them to silence. But his chief problems were economic. During the panic of 1837 he held to Jackson's specie circular and properly said that the panic was the result of over-expansion of credit and rashness in business. Determined to divorce the "money power" from the federal government, he urged establishment of an independent Treasury and recommended withholding of the distribution of the Treasury surplus to the states, suggesting a temporary issue of Treasury notes to meet the pressing needs of government. His foresighted efforts were generally unsuccessful and alienated conservative Democrats, especially in New York and Virginia, while at the same time he was denounced by the Whigs for his heartlessness in not undertaking measures of relief. In foreign affairs he continued his wise policy of conciliation during troubles with Canada and Mexico. Despite an enlightened and able administration, he could not maintain popular approval in the face of the prevailing bad times and was overwhelmingly defeated by William H. Harrison in the campaign of 1840.

In retirement he continued to be a leading Democrat but made public announcement that he would take no step to secure another nomination. In the well-known "Hammet letter" of April 1844, he courageously said that the annexation of Texas would mean war with Mexico and that he saw no need for immediate action; this stand probably cost him the Democratic nomination in 1844. Bitter opposition to President James K. Polk soon developed in New York State, and the introduction of the Wilmot Proviso in 1846 provided a rallying point for discontent and for the antislavery feeling that had been steadily increasing. Author in part of the address of the "Barnburner" Democrats in the New York legislature, February 1848, Van Buren accepted the Free-Soil party nomination for the presidency that summer. Although like many Northern Democrats he had grown impatient with the "slavocracy," he accepted the nomination reluctantly and ran unsuccessfully although his candidacy helped to defeat Lewis Cass. After supporting the 1850 compromise measures, he returned to the Democrats in 1852 to find himself successively disillusioned by Pierce and Buchanan. Shocked deeply by the Civil War, he expressed himself confident in the abilities of Abraham Lincoln but died in the summer of 1862 despondent over the situation of the Union armies.

VAN BUREN, WILLIAM HOLME (*b. Philadelphia, Pa., 1819; d. New York, N.Y., 1883*), physician, surgeon. Descendant of Johannes Van Beuren; son-in-law of Valentine Mott. M.D., University of Pennsylvania, 1840. After service as army surgeon, Van Buren practiced in New York City *post* 1845. A member of the staff of Bellevue and other hospitals, he taught in the medical department of the University of the City of New York, 1851–66, and was thereafter professor of surgery in Bellevue Hospital Medical College.

VANCE, AP MORGAN (*b. Nashville, Tenn., 1854; d. Louisville, Ky., 1915*), orthopedic surgeon. M.D., University of Louisville, 1878. Practicing in Louisville *post* 1881, he was the first exclusive practitioner of surgery in Kentucky. His greatest contribution was his improvement of the operation of osteotomy for correction of deformity of long bones in the extremities; he also improved the procedure of tenotomy for the treatment of congenital clubfoot.

VANCE, ARTHUR CHARLES ("DAZZY") (*b. Orient, Iowa, 1891; d. Homosassa Springs, Fla., 1961*), baseball pitcher. Began his pitching career with Superior and Red Cloud in the Nebraska League in 1912. Played with minor league teams until 1922 when he was traded to the Brooklyn Robins. For seven consecutive seasons he led the National League in strikeouts, and ended his career with 2,045. His best year was 1924, when he led the league with 28 victories, 262 strikeouts and a 2.16 earned run average. That year he won fifteen consecutive games. First winner of the National League's Most Valuable Player Award (1924). Traded to St. Louis Cardinals (1933), but returned to Brooklyn where he pitched the 1935 season before retiring. He left baseball with 197 wins, 140 losses, and a 3.24 earned run average. Elected to Baseball Hall of Fame (1955).

VANCE, HAROLD SINES (*b. Port Huron, Mich., 1890; d. Washington, D.C., 1959*), industrialist, executive, government official. Began his career as a mechanic's assistant for the Everitt-Metzger-Flanders Co. in 1910; in 1912, the company was absorbed by the Studebaker Corporation. Became vice president in charge of manufacturing in 1926; chairman of the board in 1933; and president, 1948–52; the company merged with Packard in 1954. Served as a consultant to the Office of Defense Mobilization, 1952–55, and as a member of the Atomic Energy Commission, 1955–59.

VANCE, LOUIS JOSEPH (*b. Washington, D.C., 1879; d. New York, N.Y., 1933*), popular novelist. Author, among other works, of *The Brass Bowl* (1907), *The Lone Wolf* (1914), and many magazine serials.

VANCE, ZEBULON BAIRD (*b. Buncombe Co., N.C., 1830; d. Washington, D.C., 1894*), lawyer, Confederate soldier, politician. Entered politics as a Whig. On the dissolution of that party he became a Know-Nothing; as congressman from North Carolina, 1858–61, he supported Union measures. Winning reputation as a masterly stump speaker for the Bell-Everett ticket, 1860, he continued to campaign against secession until Lincoln's call for troops whereupon he reversed his position. As a Conservative party governor of North Carolina, 1862–65, he was often at odds with the Confederate government at Richmond, although he pressed the Confederate war effort with as much zeal as the disturbed and unwillng attitude of North Carolina would permit. He tried in vain to explain to President Davis that his execution of conscription laws was not willful obstruction but was dictated by a regard for legality and realism. Opposing the efforts of W. W. Holden to make peace by separate state action, Vance held North Carolina to the support of a cause which many of its citizens felt was now contrary to their real interests. After a brief imprisonment, 1865, he was released on parole and resumed practice of law. As Democratic governor, 1877–79, he stimulated railroad enterprises, agriculture, and industry, improved the public schools, and repudiated the fraudulent state bonds issued during the Reconstruction period. His regime marked the beginning of a new era in North Carolina. Elected to the U.S. Senate, 1879, he served there until his death and was for many years minority leader on the finance committee. He opposed the internal revenue system as a source of political corruption, and during Cleveland's two administrations opposed the president on civil service reform and on the money question.

VAN CORTLANDT, OLOFF STEVENSZEN (*b. probably the Netherlands, 1600; d. New York, 1684*), merchant. Came to New Amsterdam, March 1638, as a soldier of the Dutch West India Company. Successful as a trader and purchaser of real estate, he held many public offices including those of city treasurer (1657, 1659–61, and 1664) and burgomaster (mayor) (1655–60 and 1662–63). Rated at his death as the fourth richest person in the colony, he was founder of one of the most prominent families in the American colonies and father, among other children, of Stephanus Van Cortlandt.

VAN CORTLANDT, PHILIP (*b. New York, N.Y., 1749; d. Croton, N.Y., 1831*), landowner, New York legislator, Revolutionary officer. Son of Pierre Van Cortlandt. Colonel of the 2nd New York Regiment in the Revolution, he served principally in New York State and cooperated effectively with the Sullivan-Clinton expedition, 1779. He received brevet of brigadier general, 1783, for conspicuous bravery at Yorktown. As congressman from New York, 1793–1809, he was a loyal Democratic-Republican and punctilious in performance of his committee duties.

VAN CORTLANDT, PIERRE (*b. New York, N.Y., 1721; d. Croton, N.Y., 1814*), landowner, New York colonial legislator, Revolutionary patriot and soldier. Grandson of Stephanus and father of Philip Van Cortlandt. Presided over New York constitutional convention, 1777. Elected lieutenant governor, 1777, he served until 1795 as a loyal follower of George Clinton (1739–1812). He was a regent of the University of the State of New York, 1784–95, and a patron of the work of the early Methodists.

VAN CORTLANDT, STEPHANUS (*b. New Amsterdam, 1643; d. 1700*), merchant, colonial official. Son of Oloff S. Van Cortlandt. An officer in the colonial militia and a councilor of the province *post* 1674, he was appointed first native-born mayor of the City of New York, 1677, a position to which he was again

appointed in 1686–87. Mistreated by Jacob Leisler and forced to flee for his life during Leisler's usurpation of the New York government, he returned to the Council under Governor Henry Sloughter and, with the support of Frederick Philipse and Nicholas Bayard, vigorously pressed Leisler's prosecution on the charge of treason. Associated throughout his career with several of the provincial courts, he became a judge of the supreme court, 1691, and was raised to the post of chief justice a month before his death. He was an important adviser to the provincial governors on Indian relations. A large purchaser of Indian land tracts and a patentee of province lands, he erected his holdings into the manor of Cortlandt by royal patent dated June 17, 1697.

VAN CURLER, ARENT (*b. Nykerk, the Netherlands, 1620; d. Perou Bay, Lake Champlain, N.Y., 1667*), colonial trader and official. Came to New Netherland *ca.* 1638 as a clerk at Rensselaerswyck; soon became *commis*, or resident manager. Famous for his enduring influence over the Indian tribes in the province, Van Curler made the first settlement of Schenectady and was the rescuer of Father Isaac Jogues. A humane man and a peacemaker, he was long remembered by the Indians who called all subsequent governors of New York "Corlaer" in memory of him.

VAN DAM, RIP (*b. Fort Orange, present Albany, N.Y., ca. 1660; d. 1749*), New York merchant, colonial politician. Roused to political activity by actions of the Jacob Leisler party, Van Dam became a member of the governor's Council in 1702 and served until 1736. As president of the Council he became acting governor of the province, 1731, and for 13 months received the salary of the office. Refusing to divide this salary with Governor William Cosby on the new governor's arrival, Van Dam lost a law suit to Cosby and was suspended from the Council in November 1735. He refused to recognize his removal in March 1736 until dispatches from England certified to the validity of George Clarke's appointment as president of the Council. Thereafter he took part in the struggle for popular rights and against prerogative, acting as a leader in this movement with William Smith and James Alexander.

VAN DE GRAAFF, ROBERT JEMISON (*b. Tuscaloosa, Ala., 1901; d. Boston, Mass., 1967*), physicist, inventor. Studied at the Sorbonne (1924) and was awarded a Rhodes Scholarship at Oxford (1925) where he got a B.S. degree in physics (1926) and a Ph.D. (1928). Invented the Van de Graaff generator, a device that accelerates electrons, protons, or heavier atomic nuclei to high energies (1931). The machine is considered one of the classic "atom smashers." During World War II Van de Graaff directed a project to develop X-ray machines for the nondestructive testing of naval ordnance. Formed a corporation to manufacture a more compact and powerful Van de Graaff accelerator in 1946. In 1960, he resigned his professorship at the Massachusetts Institute of Technology, a position he had held since 1934, to devote all his time to developing the commercial applications of his invention.

VAN DEMAN, ESTHER BOISE (*b. South Salem, Ohio, 1862; d. Rome, Italy, 1937*), archaeologist. Graduated University of Michigan, 1891; Ph.D., University of Chicago, 1898. Taught Latin at Wellesley, Mount Holyoke, and Goucher. *Post* 1906 she worked at the American School in Rome. Projected methods of determining the date of ancient building construction; published a preliminary study of her work in *American Journal of Archaeology*, 1912.

VANDENBERG, ARTHUR HENDRICK (*b. Grand Rapids, Mich., 1884; d. Grand Rapids, 1951*), journalist, U.S. senator. Studied at the University of Michigan. Appointed to the Senate, 1928, and served, as a Republican, until his death. Opposed most New Deal legislation and was one of the most effective of the die-hard isolationists. On the Senate Foreign Relations Committee from 1929, he became chairman in 1946. During World War II, abandoned his isolationist position and helped draft the Connally Resolution providing for U.S. membership in the future United Nations. Subsequently became a leading proponent of the United Nations and was instrumental in rallying Republican support in the Senate. Appointed to the delegation to the U.N. Conference on International Organization in San Francisco, 1945, and helped draft Articles 51–54 of the Charter, which allowed for regional defense agreements; was instrumental in securing Senate ratification of the Charter, 1945. Appointed delegate to the first two U.N. General Assemblies, 1946–47. Was adviser to Secretary of State James F. Byrnes at the Big Four foreign ministers' conferences in Paris and New York.

Became a chief advocate of a bipartisan foreign policy; helped persuade the Senate to approve the Marshall Plan, and drafted the Vandenberg Resolution, 1948, which became the basis for the U.S. leadership in the formation of the North Atlantic Treaty Organization.

VANDENBERG, HOYT SANFORD (*b. Milwaukee, Wis., 1899; d. Washington, D.C., 1954*), aviator, soldier. Graduated from West Point, 1923. Served in the Army Air Service, 1924–34; graduated from the Army War College, 1939. Chief of staff of the Twelfth Air Force (1942), charged with supporting the North African campaign. Commanded the Ninth Air Force (1944), which gave air support to General Omar Bradley's advance into Germany. Chief of staff of the newly created U.S. Air Force, 1948–53, which during his tenure bore the brunt of the Berlin airlift, the Korean War, and the expansion of the force into a major defense arm.

VANDENHOFF, GEORGE (*b. Liverpool, England, 1813; d. Brighton, England, 1885*), actor, lawyer, public reader. Made his American debut at New York City's Park Theater, 1842, as Hamlet. Toured extensively in the United States and England until 1858, when he undertook practice of law in New York City, but continued his popular public readings from the works of classic writers. Vandenhoff was a scholarly actor with a restrained, elevated style.

VAN DEPOELE, CHARLES JOSEPH (*b. Lichtervelde, Belgium, 1846; d. Lynn, Mass., 1892*), scientist, inventor. Immigrated to America, 1869, settling in Detroit, Mich., where he became a successful manufacturer of church furniture and at the same time continued his early experimental interest in electricity. He developed an improved arc-lighting system, 1870–79, and in 1880 tested an electric tramcar on which he had been working since 1874. In September 1883 at Chicago, he gave the first practical demonstration of a spring-pressed under-running trolley; in November 1885 his overhead current feed system was put into operation in South Bend, Ind. After success in developing his trolley-car system, he sold his patents to the Thomson-Houston Electric Co. in 1888 and became electrician of that company. In all, he filed 444 applications for patents, of which some 249 were granted to him under his own name. In addition to his electric railway patent (October 1883) and his patent for an overhead conductor (August 1885) were the following: a carbon commutator-brush which revolutionized motor construction (1888); an alternating-current reciprocating engine (1889); a multiple-current pulsating generator (1890) and a telpher system in the same year; a coal-mining machine (1891); and a gearless electric locomotive (1894). He also made experiments in electric refrigeration.

VANDERBILT, ARTHUR T. (*b. Newark, N.J., 1888; d. 1957*), lawyer, jurist. Studied at Wesleyan University and Columbia University Law School, LL.B., 1912. Taught at New York Uni-versity Law School, 1914–48, dean from 1943. Vanderbilt was a leading legal reformer, chairing the New Jersey Judicial Council (1930–40) and the National Conference of Judicial Councils (1933–37). President of the American Bar Association, 1937. Chief Justice of the New Jersey Supreme Court, 1948–57.

VANDERBILT, CORNELIUS (*b. Port Richmond, N.Y., 1794; d. 1877*), financier, steamship and railroad promoter. Father, among other children, of William H. Vanderbilt; grandfather of Cornelius (1843–99), George W., and William K. Vanderbilt. Began business *ca.* 1810 as a freight and passenger ferryman between Staten Island and New York City. Taking advantage of expanded opportunities during the War of 1812, he built up a small fleet of schooners for the Hudson River and coastal trade but disposed of his sailing ships in 1818 to become a ferry captain in the employ of Thomas Gibbons. A strong and tough ally to Gibbons in his fight against the steam-navigation monopoly which existed in New York waters, Vanderbilt turned what was a losing venture into a profitable one within a year. After fighting Gibbons' battles and expanding his business for some 11 years, Vanderbilt entered the steamboat business on his own, 1829. With characteristic zest for conflict, he fought for a share of the Hudson River trade by cutting prices and for the first time came into conflict with a later antagonist, Daniel Drew. His opponents finally paid him to withdraw from competition for ten years, and he then set up lines running on Long Island Sound to Providence and Boston. As he took pleasure in making his ships fast, safe, and comfortable, he did much to promote an advance in steamboat design.

A wealthy man by 1846 "Commodore" Vanderbilt, as he had come to be known, was loud and coarse in speech—a big, bumptious, hardheaded man who was at the same time courageous, constructive, frank, and faithful to a bargain once he had made it. He was also a man of broad vision for his time. When traffic to California reached important proportions with the 1849 gold rush, he conceived the idea of starting a line of his own via Nicaragua to California. He constructed a fleet of new steamers to make the first part of the journey from New York to Nicaragua, and also built roads and other installations in that country to facilitate the overland part of the journey. His aggressive competition reduced the length of time for the New York-San Francisco trip and also greatly reduced the passenger fare. While on an extensive vacation during 1853 he committed the management of his Nicaragua line to Charles Morgan and Cornelius K. Garrison. During his absence they manipulated the stock and secured control of the company; later, as Vanderbilt struggled to win it back, Morgan and Garrison persuaded the filibuster William Walker, who was then temporarily in control of the Nicaraguan government, to void Vanderbilt's operating charter and issue a new one to them. Rising to the challenge, Vanderbilt thereupon set about to oust Walker, which he succeeded in doing early in 1857. Once again in control of his line, he bludgeoned the Pacific Mail Steamship Co. into buying it out. He then entered competition for the Atlantic trade against the Cunard and Collins lines. This, however, was an unprofitable venture.

Vanderbilt had begun buying stock of the New York & Harlem Railroad in 1862; in 1863 he induced the New York City council to let him extend the line by streetcar tracks to the lower part of the city. He also took over the presidency of the road. When Daniel Drew, with the aid of members of the council, attempted a "bear raid" on the stock of the company, Vanderbilt outwitted him and forced a settlement by which many of the plotters were ruined. At about this time he put his son William H. Vanderbilt into the post of vice president of the Harlem Railroad, and thereafter his son was his closest aide. The Harlem's competitor, the Hudson River Railroad, was then acquired, and Vanderbilt sought permission of the New York legislature to combine the two. Again Daniel Drew plotted a raid, this time by legislative bribery, and again the old

Commodore was victorious over his enemies. By careful management and by following his lifelong policy of improving the equipment and service of his lines, he presently had them on a paying basis. After another financial and political struggle in which Drew was involved, he succeeded in gaining control of the New York Central in 1867, improved it, and by 1872 had consolidated three inefficient roads into a single excellent line. Meanwhile Drew, Jay Gould, and James Fisk, by a series of spectacular and reprehensible maneuvers, had defeated his attempt to control the Erie Railroad in 1868.

By the addition to his holdings of the Lake Shore & Michigan Southern Railroad (1873) and the Michigan Central and Canada Southern roads (1875), Vanderbilt created one of the great American systems of transportation. During the last years of his life he exerted a strong, stabilizing influence on national finance. He engaged in no philanthropies until late in his life when he gave $1 million to Vanderbilt University (previously Central University) at Nashville, Tenn., of which he is regarded as the founder.

VANDERBILT, CORNELIUS (*b. near New Dorp, N.Y., 1843; d. New York, N.Y., 1899*), financier, philanthropist. Son of William H. Vanderbilt; grandson of Cornelius Vanderbilt (1794–1877); brother of George W. and William K. Vanderbilt. A favorite of his grandfather, he became assistant treasurer of the New York & Harlem Railroad *ca.* 1867 and served as its president from 1886 until his death. *Post* 1885 he acted as the head of the Vanderbilt family and was the director, with his brother William K. Vanderbilt, of its investments. A conscientious worker and a director of many corporations, he was a trustee and benefactor of the N.Y. College of Physicians and Surgeons, of Columbia University, of the N.Y. General Theological Seminary, and of many other public institutions.

VANDERBILT, GEORGE WASHINGTON (*b. near New Dorp, N.Y., 1862; d. Washington, D.C., 1914*), capitalist, agriculturist, forestry pioneer. Son of William H. Vanderbilt; grandson of Cornelius Vanderbilt (1794–1877); brother of Cornelius (1843–99) and William K. Vanderbilt. Studious and caring little for finance, he built up a very large property in the vicinity of Asheville, N.C., where he planned and built the finest country home in America, working with Richard M. Hunt and Frederick L. Olmsted. At his estate, which he named "Biltmore," he practiced scientific farming and stockbreeding, founded and conducted the Biltmore Nursery, and also founded the Biltmore School of Forestry. Gifford Pinchot was his first superintendent of forests. The stimulus which his example gave to agricultural reforms in the South has been called beyond estimate.

VANDERBILT, GLORIA MORGAN (*b. Lucerne, Switzerland, 1904; d. Los Angeles, Calif., 1965*), socialite. Daughter of an American career diplomat, Gloria Morgan and twin Thelma became society's darlings when newspaper columnist "Cholly Knickerbocker" chronicled their activities. In 1923 Gloria consolidated her social celebrity by marrying Reginald Claypoole Vanderbilt, twenty-four years her senior. Gave birth to a daughter, Gloria, in 1924. Following her husband's death in 1925, Gloria Morgan Vanderbilt, "the world's most beautiful widow," became the toast of two continents but neglected her child. In 1934, after a sensational trial, the courts awarded custody of the girl to Vanderbilt's sister-in-law, Gertrude Vanderbilt Whitney. In 1958 Gloria and Thelma wrote of their past in *Double Exposure*.

VANDERBILT, GRACE GRAHAM WILSON (*b. New York, N.Y., 1870; d. New York, 1953*), society leader. Privately educated, Grace Wilson married the heir to the New York Central Railroad, Cornelius Vanderbilt III, in 1896. Succeeded Mrs. Astor as New York social arbiter; famous for her parties in Newport; entertained European nobility as well as several presidents.

VANDERBILT, WILLIAM HENRY (*b. New Brunswick, N.J., 1821; d. New York, N.Y., 1885*), financier, railroad executive. Son of Cornelius Vanderbilt (1794–1877); father of Cornelius (1843–99), George W., and William K. Vanderbilt. Alienated for some years from his father, he was returned to favor *ca.* 1863 after he had achieved success on his own as a farmer and railroad executive. Appointed to high positions in the Vanderbilt railroads, he served as his father's principal aide until *ca.* 1876, showing great ability in management, in the improvement of track and equipment, in regulating rates, and in conciliating labor. After the death of his father, William Henry Vanderbilt became president of all the affiliated New York Central network corporations. Within a few years he bought control of the Chicago & Northwestern and a large interest in the Cleveland, Columbus, Cincinnati & Indianapolis Railroad. He also exercised effective control over the New York, Chicago & St. Louis line and in 1885 leased the West Shore. Like his father a constructive man who prized efficiency, he greatly improved his properties and increased his own fortune. Recognizing the unpopularity of unified and monopoly control, he disposed in 1879 of a large block of his own shareholdings in the roads. He designed all his railroad presidencies in May 1883, ordering that members of the family should be chairmen of the boards of directors thereafter, but that presidents should be practical, working executives. Temperate and simple in his personal habits, he was fond of horses and driving, and made a number of philanthropic benefactions during his lifetime.

VANDERBILT, WILLIAM KISSAM (*b. near New Dorp, N.Y., 1849; d. Paris, France, 1920*), capitalist, sportsman. Son of William H. Vanderbilt; grandson of Cornelius Vanderbilt (1794–1877); brother of Cornelius (1843–99) and George W. Vanderbilt. An executive in the family railroads *post ca.* 1869 and, with his brother Cornelius, for many years a manager of the family investments, William K. Vanderbilt voluntarily permitted the executive direction of the New York Central system to pass the Rockefeller-Morgan-Pennsylvania combination in 1903. He continued, however, as a board member of many railroads until his death and aided in increasing the size of the Vanderbilt fortune. An enthusiastic yachtsman and turfman, he was also active in the affairs of the Metropolitan Opera and in theatrical matters, and was a collector of paintings.

VANDERBURGH, WILLIAM HENRY (*b. Vincennes, Ind., ca. 1798; d. on an affluent of the Jefferson River, present Montana, 1832*), fur trader. Worked for Missouri Fur Co. *post ca.* 1818; was later a partner in the American Fur Co. and in charge of the Rocky Mountain trappers *post ca.* 1828. Ambushed and killed by Blackfeet Indians while on a trapping expedition.

VAN DER DONCK, ADRIAEN (*b. Breda, North Brabant, the Netherlands, 1620; d. New Netherland, ca. 1655*), colonist, lawyer. Studied law at the University of Leyden. Came to America as *schout* (justice officer) at Rensselaerswyck, 1641. Dismissed from office *ca.* 1644 because of enmity of Arent Van Curler, he remained in the colony and established a settlement at the present site of Yonkers, N.Y. Appointed secretary of the Board of Nine Men, 1649, he wrote the famous "Remonstrance" of 1650, which set forth the people's grievances against their rulers, and was one of three men sent to The Hague to present it to the States-General. This gained him the enmity of Peter Stuyvesant. Detained at home by the government, he wrote the description of New Netherland entitled *Beschrijvinge van Nieuvv Nederlant* (written in 1653, published 1655 at Amsterdam). He returned to America late in 1653 with permission to give legal advice but not to appear before the courts since there was no lawyer in the colony competent to contend with him.

VANDERGRIFT, JACOB JAY (*b. Allegheny, Pa., 1827; d. Pittsburgh, Pa., 1899*), riverboat captain. Settling at Oil City, Pa., early in 1861, he became a shipper of oil and later a dealer. In association with John Pitcairn and others, he established the Imperial Refinery, 1872. Although not the builder of the first oil pipe line, he is said to have been the first to make one profitable. With Pitcairn he also laid what was probably the first natural gas line of any importance.

VANDERGRIFT, MARGARET. *See* JANVIER, MARGARET THOMSON.

VAN DER KEMP, FRANCIS ADRIAN (*b. Kampen, the Netherlands, 1752; d. 1829*), clergyman, Dutch revolutionary leader, scholar. Long a friend and correspondent of John Adams, Van der Kemp immigrated to New York, 1788, settling first near Kingston and later by Oneida Lake. At the request of DeWitt Clinton, he translated the Dutch colonial records of New York into English.

VANDERLIP, FRANK ARTHUR (*b. near Aurora, Ill., 1864; d. New York, N.Y., 1937*), journalist, banker, public official. Entering journalism as city editor of his hometown newspaper, he went to the *Chicago Tribune*, 1889, where he soon rose to be financial editor. Associate editor of *The Economist* (Chicago, Ill., 1894–97), he further developed his reputation as a financial authority, and was appointed (1897) private secretary to Lyman J. Gage, U.S. secretary of the treasury. Soon becoming an assistant treasury secretary, he won national repute handling the Spanish War loan of 1898. Joining the National City Bank of New York in 1901 as vice president, he brought that institution into the investment field, developed foreign and domestic branches, and, as president, 1909–19, made the bank the largest in the United States. He maintained a lifelong interest in public affairs, denouncing the scandals of the Harding administration, opposing the growing isolationism of the United States, and advocating abandonment of the gold standard, 1933.

VANDERLYN, JOHN (*b. Kingston, N.Y., 1775; d. Kingston, 1852*), historical and portrait painter. Patronized by Aaron Burr, Vanderlyn took his first lessons in drawing from Archibald Robertson and later studied under Gilbert Stuart. A student in Paris, 1796–1801, he returned briefly to America. Between 1803 and 1815 he worked in Europe where, at Rome, he met and became a friend of Washington Allston. His painting *Marius Amid the Ruins of Carthage* (Rome ca. 1806) made a great stir and he received a number of honors abroad. His *Ariadne* of 1812 made a greater sensation than the *Marius*. After his return to New York in 1815 Vanderlyn painted a number of portraits of eminent men, engaged in a controversy with John Trumbull over the paintings for the rotunda of the U.S. Capitol, and executed panoramas of Paris, Versailles, Athens, and Mexico for exhibition. His popularity early waned and he died in poverty.

VAN DER STUCKEN, FRANK VALENTIN (*b. Fredericksburg, Tex., 1858; d. Hamburg, Germany, 1929*), musical composer, conductor. Raised in Belgium, he studied music in Antwerp and Brussels and at Leipzig. Winning repute abroad, he succeeded Leopold Damrosch as conductor of the Arion Society chorus (1884–95) and appeared frequently as an orchestral conductor. *Post* 1895 he was conductor of the Cincinnati Symphony Orchestra and director of the Cincinnati Conservatory until 1907 and 1903 respectively. *Post* 1908 he resided principally in Europe. Early in his conducting career he adopted a policy of presenting all-American programs at which the works of American musicians were played exclusively.

VANDER VEER, ALBERT (*b. Root, N.Y., 1841; d. 1929*), Union Army surgeon, medical educator. M.D., Columbia College (present George Washington University), 1863. A practitioner in Albany, N.Y.; taught at Albany Medical College, 1869–1915, and served as dean, 1897–1904. He was a regent of the University of the State of New York, 1895–1927, and its chancellor, 1921–22.

VANDER WEE, JOHN BAPTIST (*b. Antwerp, Belgium, 1824; d. Baltimore, Md., 1900*), educator, provincial of the Xaverian Brothers. Known in religion as Brother Alexius, he joined the Xaverian Brothers, 1845, and helped establish the congregation in England, 1848. Sent to America, 1872, he was named provincial of the congregation in 1875. From beginnings of desperate poverty he labored to extend the work of the Brothers, building several schools and colleges, and conducting St. Mary's Industrial School in Baltimore which served as a model to later institutions for the training of boys.

VAN DEVANTER, WILLIS (*b. Marion, Ind., 1859; d. Washington, D.C., 1941*), lawyer, justice of the U.S. Supreme Court. He attended Indiana Asbury (later DePauw) University, 1875–78, and the Cincinnati Law School, LL.B., 1881. He then practiced law in his father's office in Marion for three years.

In July 1884 Van Devanter moved to Cheyenne, Wyo., where he was drawn into public service and Republican politics. He served as commissioner to revise the Wyoming statutes (1886), Cheyenne city attorney (1887–88), as a member of the territorial legislature and chairman of its judiciary committee (1888), and as chief justice of Wyoming (1889–90). Thereafter his political involvement was chiefly as a party manager. His strenuous efforts for William McKinley in 1896 came to the attention of Mark Hanna, and with McKinley's accession to the presidency, Van Devanter entered federal office. In 1897 he became assistant attorney general in charge of Indian and public lands cases. Theodore Roosevelt raised him in 1903 to a judgeship on the federal circuit court of appeals. William Howard Taft made him associate justice of the Supreme Court in 1911.

Van Devanter's outlook was formed on the last frontier. He believed in property rights, in "economic freedom," and in the philosophy that that government governs best which governs least. A consummate lawyer and subtle negotiator, he wielded an important influence. Among Van Devanter's opinions, a number, such as *Evans* v. *Gore* and *Indian Motorcycle Company* v. *United States* have been overridden. But the judgment upholding the Federal Employers' Liability Act speaks in more modern tones. Other notable opinions were *National Prohibition Cases*, sustaining the constitutionality of the Eighteenth Amendment; *Pennsylvania* v. *West Virginia*, applying the commerce clause of the Constitution to prevent a state from reserving its natural resources for use exclusively within its internal commerce; *McGrain* v. *Daugherty* affirming the Congressional power to investigate; and *New York ex. rel. Bryant* v. *Zimmerman et al.*, upholding a state statute under which the Ku Klux Klan was required to disclose its membership. An opinion displaying Van Devanter's mastery of the law affecting the Supreme Court's jurisdiction is *Dahnke-Walker Milling Company* v. *Bondurant*. One of his rare dissents, *Herndon* v. *Lowry*, argued the validity under the Fourteenth Amendment of a conviction of a black Communist organizer for violating a Georgia anti-insurrection statute.

Van Devanter was a firm member of the group of five justices who declared key New Deal measures unconstitutional. He announced his retirement when the Senate Judiciary Committee was voting on the "court packing" bill, thus probably contributing to the bill's defeat.

VAN DE VELDE, JAMES OLIVER (*b. near Termonde, Belgium, 1795; d. Natchez, Miss., 1855*), Roman Catholic clergyman, Jesuit. Recruited for the American missions by Charles

Nerinckx, 1817, he was ordained in 1827. Ordered to St. Louis University, 1831, he served there as vice president (1833) and as president (1840–43). Vice provincial of Missouri, 1843–48, he fostered the Jesuit missions of the Far West. Consecrated bishop of Chicago, 1849, he had a brief and unhappy tenure and was transferred at his own request to the diocese of Natchez, 1853.

VAN DE WARKER, EDWARD ELY (*b. West Troy, present Watervliet, N.Y., 1841; d. 1910*), Union Army surgeon, gynecologist. M.D., Albany Medical College, 1863. Practiced with great success at Syracuse, N.Y., *post* 1870.

VAN DINE, S. S. *See* WRIGHT, WILLARD HUNTINGTON.

VAN DOREN, CARL CLINTON (*b. Hope, Ill., 1884; d. Torrington, Conn., 1950*), literary critic, biographer. B.A., University of Illinois, 1907. In September 1908 Van Doren left home to attend Columbia University, Ph.D., 1911. He became an influential figure as literary editor (1919–22) of the *Nation*. The "new," "modern" writers were now coming into their own, and Van Doren was one of their great supporters and was a great friend to writers he admired. He was not a bold or venturesome critic, and all his life thought of himself as a novelist *manqué*. Yet his most successful narrative writing was his best-selling biography of Benjamin Franklin (1938), which won the Pulitzer Prize. Van Doren was a superb professional writer, gifted, yet never quite fulfilled. He was an indispensable part of American literary opinion in the vital years after World War I, which saw the triumph of modern American literature.

VAN DOREN, EARL (*b. near Port Gibson, Miss., 1820; d. Spring Hill, Tenn., 1863*), soldier. Graduated West Point, 1842. As an infantry officer, he served with credit in the war with Mexico and against the Seminole Indians (1849–50); thereafter he served with the then 2nd Cavalry in Texas and Indian Territory. Resigning from the army, 1861, he was appointed brigadier general of Mississippi troops and rose to major general in the Confederate army in the same year. Commander of the trans-Mississippi district, 1862, he was defeated at Pea Ridge in March, and later at Corinth, Miss., after transfer there. In charge of the cavalry during the defense of Vicksburg, he made a brilliant raid on Holly Springs in December 1862, effectively crippling General Ulysses S. Grant's projected campaign. He was shot and killed by a personal enemy while in camp.

VAN DOREN, IRITA BRADFORD (*b. Birmingham, Ala., 1891; d. New York, N.Y., 1966*), literary editor. In 1912 married Carl Van Doren, who went on to become a prominent literary critic and biographer. Joined editorial staff of the *Nation* where her husband was literary editor in 1919, succeeding him as book editor in 1923. Became literary editor of the *Herald Tribune* (1926) and won recognition as a leading literary figure and editor during her thirty-seven years of running the paper's literary supplement. Was divorced in 1935 and in 1937 became romantically involved with Wendell L. Wilkie, the Republican candidate for president in 1940. Collaborated with him on his best-selling *One World* (1943). Retired from the *Herald Tribune* (1963), then was literary consultant to the publishing company William Morrow.

VAN DRUTEN, JOHN WILLIAM (*b. London, England, 1901; d. Indio, Calif., 1957*), playwright. Became a U.S. citizen in 1944. Studied at the University College School and the University of London, LL.B., 1923. Taught English law and legal history at University College, Wales, 1923–26. His first produced play, *Young Woodley*, opened on Broadway in 1925. Other works include *Leave Her to Heaven* (1940), *The Voice of the Turtle* (1943), *I Remember Mama* (1944), *Bell, Book and Candle* (1950), and his dramatization of Isherwood's Berlin stories, *I Am a*

Camera (1951). Films include *Night Must Fall* (1937) and *Gaslight* (1944). Directed *The King and I* (1951).

VAN DYCK, CORNELIUS VAN ALEN (*b. Kinderhook, N.Y., 1818; d. 1895*), medical missionary, Arabic scholar, author of scientific textbooks in modern Arabic. A graduate of Jefferson Medical College in 1839, he served in Syria and Lebanon, 1840–65 and 1867–95. A master of the Arabic language, he continued and completed the translation of the Bible into Arabic which had been begun by Eli Smith.

VAN DYKE, HENRY (*b. Germantown, Pa., 1852; d. Princeton, N.J., 1933*), Presbyterian clergyman, author, educator, diplomat. Brother of Paul Van Dyke. Graduated Princeton, 1873; Princeton Theological Seminary, 1877. Pastor at Newport, R.I., 1879–83; minister of Brick Presbyterian Church, New York City, 1883–99, 1902, 1911. Murray Professor of English Literature, Princeton University, 1899–1923, thereafter emeritus. U.S. minister to the Netherlands and Luxembourg, 1913–16. An eloquent preacher and able administrator, Van Dyke was as competent as he was versatile. Active in the fight against political corruption while a New York pastor, he stood for a positive evangelical Christianity during the doctrinal controversies that shook the Presbyterian Church of his time. Equally versatile as a writer, Van Dyke's outdoor essays are in the tradition of Thoreau, Burroughs, and Muir, although his deep religious faith pervades his work at all times. Although changing standards of taste have diminished his reputation, he was master of a lucid style beautifully adapted to his purposes. Among his principal books are *The Poetry of Tennyson* (1899); *Little Rivers* (1895); *Fisherman's Luck* (1899); *The Story of the Other Wise Man* (1896); *The First Christmas Tree* (1897); *The Blue Flower* (1902); and *Out-of-doors in the Holy Land* (1908).

VAN DYKE, JOHN CHARLES (*b. New Brunswick, N.J., 1856; d. New York, N.Y., 1932*), art critic, educator. Grandson of Theodore Strong. A librarian at the New Brunswick Theological Seminary *post* 1878, Van Dyke was also a lecturer on art at Rutgers College, and served as professor of the history of art there, 1891–1929. Author of a number of careful, scholarly works on art and also of several distinguished volumes of nature study (such as *The Desert*, 1901, and *The Mountain*, 1916), Van Dyke was possessed of an almost microscopic acuteness of vision. He employed this in effecting a severe and controversial revision of attributions to the artist in his *Rembrandt and His School* (1923).

VAN DYKE, JOHN WESLEY (*b. near Mercersburg, Pa., 1849; d. Philadelphia, Pa., 1939*), oil company executive. Associated with various Standard Oil companies, 1873–1911, he was president of the Atlantic Refining Co., 1911–27, and chairman of the board until his death. Among his patented inventions were mechanical improvements for the sulfur-eliminating process devised by Herman Frasch, and improvements on railroad tank cars. Probably his most important invention (developed with W. W. Irish) was the tower still which enabled refiners to improve the separation of fractions, to eliminate some refining processes, and to reduce costs.

VAN DYKE, NICHOLAS (*b. New Castle, Del., 1738; d. New Castle Co., Del., 1789*), lawyer, Delaware legislator. Father of Nicholas Van Dyke (1770–1826). A moderate Whig *post* 1774, he served in the Continental Congress, 1777–82, but was more interested in his work as a Delaware councilor. While president (governor) of Delaware, 1783–86, he strove to improve commerce and to put the state finances on a sound basis.

VAN DYKE, NICHOLAS (*b. New Castle, Del., 1770; d. New Castle, 1826*), lawyer, statesman. Son of Nicholas Van Dyke (1738–1789); brother-in-law of Kensey Johns (1759–1848). A moderate in politics like his father, he served as attorney general of Delaware, 1801–06, and as a Federalist congressman, 1807–11. A U.S. senator, 1817–26, he voiced the traditional states' rights sentiments, and although personally opposed to slavery, refused to vote against the admission of Missouri on the ground that Congress had no authority to impose restrictions on slavery.

VAN DYKE, PAUL (*b. Brooklyn, N.Y., 1859; d. Washington, Conn., 1933*), historian. Brother of Henry Van Dyke. Graduated Princeton, 1881; Princeton Theological Seminary, 1884. A Presbyterian pastor for some years at Geneva, N.Y., and at Northampton, Mass., he was an instructor in church history at Princeton Seminary, 1889–92, and professor of modern history in Princeton University, 1898–1928. His most important book, *Catherine de Medicis* (1922), won international recognition as a history of the religious wars in France.

VANE, SIR HENRY (*b. probably Debden, Essex, England, 1613; d. London, England, 1662*), Puritan statesman. Immigrated to Massachusetts, 1635. Attempted with Hugh Peter to reconcile the factions of former governors John Winthrop and Thomas Dudley. Elected governor of Massachusetts, May 1636, he served with tact and energy, but his career was soon wrecked by his support of Anne Hutchinson during the great controversy over her religious opinions. At the election of 1637 he sailed for England. An honest and generous man, he was later outstanding during the struggle of King and Parliament in England. He was instrumental in securing the condemnation of the Earl of Strafford and Archbishop Laud, but he had no part in the trial and condemnation of King Charles I, and after the dissolution of the Long Parliament he retired from public life. Excepted from the act of indemnity at the Restoration, he was tried for treason, found guilty, and executed.

VAN FLEET, WALTER (*b. Piermont, N.Y., 1857; d. Miami, Fla., 1922*), physician, naturalist, horticulturist. M.D., Hahnemann Medical College, 1880. Taking up plant breeding as his main vocation, 1891, he gave distinguished service as an expert in the bureau of plant industry, U.S. Department of Agriculture, *post* 1909. His work covered a wide range and included experiments on production of nonblighting chestnuts and the development of many new varieties of plants. He is most famous for his work with the rose, especially the climbing and pillar varieties.

VAN HISE, CHARLES RICHARD (*b. Fulton, Wis., 1857; d. Milwaukee, Wis., 1918*), geologist, educator. Graduated in engineering, University of Wisconsin, 1879; Ph.D., 1892. Taught metallurgy and mineralogy at Wisconsin *post* 1879 and was professor of geology, 1892–1903; he also served with the U.S. Geological Survey. He was president of the University of Wisconsin *post* 1903. Trained in geology under Roland D. Irving, he collaborated with Irving in much research work for the Geological Survey, and was coauthor of several monographs on the iron-bearing districts of the Lake Superior region; he later collaborated with C. K. Leith in the writing of several more general treatises on the subject. As president of the university he developed its research activities and its extension department and engaged actively in public service. He contributed to the conservation movement what has been called its most valuable book, *The Conservation of Natural Resources in the United States* (1910). He was later an enthusiastic supporter of the League of Nations concept.

VAN HOOK, WELLER (*b. Greenville, Ind., 1862; d. Coopersville, Mich., 1933*), Chicago, Ill., surgeon and medical teacher. Did pioneer work in surgery of the genitourinary tract; devised *ante* 1896 the Van Hook-Mayo operation for correction of hypospadias and the repair of epispadias.

VAN HORN, ROBERT THOMPSON (*b. East Mahoning, Pa., 1824; d. Kansas City, Mo., 1916*), Union soldier, journalist, Missouri legislator. Trained as a printer, he removed to Kansas City, 1855, where he was editor-publisher of the *Journal* (published daily, 1858–97). Originally a conservative Democrat, he became a Republican at the outbreak of the Civil War and served as a loyal partisan in Congress, 1865–71, 1881–83, and 1895–97. Several times mayor of Kansas City, he played a leading role in making that place the principal railroad center west of Chicago.

VAN HORNE, WILLIAM CORNELIUS (*b. Will Co., Ill., 1843; d. Montreal, Canada, 1915*), railroad executive. Starting as a telegraph operator with the Illinois Central Railroad *ca.* 1857, he rose by outstanding merit to the superintendency of the Chicago, Milwaukee & St. Paul Railroad. Impressing James J. Hill with his abilities during an 1880 controversy, Van Horne was recommended by Hill to the directors of the Canadian Pacific Railway as the man best qualified to supervise its construction. He began work at Winnipeg at the end of 1881 and carried the project through to completion in 1886. President of the Canadian Pacific, 1888–99, thereafter he developed important railroads in Cuba and Guatemala. A naturalized citizen of Canada *ante* 1890, he was knighted, 1894.

VAN ILPENDAM, JAN JANSEN (*b. Leyden, the Netherlands, ca. 1595; d. probably Amsterdam, the Netherlands, 1647*), Dutch colonial official. Commissary at Fort Nassau on the Delaware *ca.* 1637–45. Opposed English efforts to settle on the Schuylkill, 1641, and on the Delaware, 1644.

VAN LENNEP, HENRY JOHN (*b. Smyrna, Asiatic Turkey, 1815; d. Great Barrington, Mass., 1889*), Congregational clergyman. Graduated Amherst, 1837. Missionary in Turkey, 1839–69; author, among other works, of *Travels in Little-Known Parts of Asia Minor* (1870).

VAN LENNEP, WILLIAM BIRD (*b. Constantinople, Turkey, 1853; d. Philadelphia, Pa., 1919*), surgeon. Son of Henry J. Van Lennep. Graduated Princeton, 1876; Hahnemann Medical College, 1880; made postgraduate studies in London, Paris, and Vienna. A faculty member of Hahnemann College *post* 1886 and dean *post* 1910.

VAN LOON, HENDRIK WILLEM (*b. Rotterdam, the Netherlands, 1882; d. Old Greenwich, Conn., 1944*), author, illustrator. Came to the United States, 1902. A.B., Cornell University, 1905. Ph.D., University of Munich, 1911. Failing to gain a foothold in the academic world, he became an itinerant lecturer on modern European history, illustrating his talks with maps and sketches which he made as he was speaking. After publishing five books with comparatively little success, he became a best-selling author in 1921 with *The Story of Mankind*, addressed to a juvenile audience, and followed up his first success with similar generalized, panoramic narratives about the Bible, the lives of great men, the story of geography, and the arts. His anecdotal style, personal approach to his subjects, and the drawings with which he illustrated his books brought him popularity and prestige with a loyal and large body of admirers, if not with scholars.

VAN METER, JOHN BLACKFORD (*b. Philadelphia, Pa., 1842; d. Baltimore, Md. 1930*), Methodist clergyman, educator. Associated with John F. Goucher in founding Woman's College of Baltimore (president Goucher); served there as a faculty member, 1888–1914, and as dean, 1892–1910. Largely responsible for the educational policy of the college, he served it also as acting president, 1911–13.

VAN NAME, ADDISON (*b. Chenango, N.Y., 1835; d. New Haven, Conn., 1922*), philologist, librarian. Brother-in-law of Josiah W. Gibbs (1839–1903). Graduated Yale, 1858. Appointed librarian of Yale, 1865, he served until his retirement as emeritus, 1905. He built up the collection of Oriental literature and supervised the library during a period of extraordinary growth.

VAN NESS, WILLIAM PETER (*b. Claverack, Columbia Co., N.Y., ca. 1778; d. 1826*), politician, jurist. Graduated Columbia, 1797; studied law in office of Edward Livingston. Began practice in New York City, 1800, as protégé of Aaron Burr. A loyal follower of Burr in politics, Van Ness defended his patron in *An Examination of the Various Changes Exhibited against Aaron Burr* (1803, under pseudonym "Aristides") and served him as second in his duel with Alexander Hamilton, 1804. Subsequently an associate of Martin Van Buren, he served as U.S. judge for the Southern District of New York, 1812–26. He was coeditor of the annotated *Laws of the State of New York* (1813) and wrote several other works.

VAN NEST, ABRAHAM RYNIER (*b. New York, N.Y., 1823; d. New York, 1892*), Dutch Reformed clergyman. After holding several New York pastorates he resided abroad, 1863–78, and organized American chapels in Paris, Rome, Florence, and Geneva. Returning to the United States, he was pastor of Third Reformed Church of Philadelphia, Pa., 1878–83.

VAN NOSTRAND, DAVID (*b. New York, N.Y., 1811; d. 1886*), bookseller, publisher, student of military engineering. Opened a New York City bookstore *ca.* 1848, specializing in books on military and naval science. Venturing into publishing, he made his firm the largest American publishers of scientific, technical, and military works, also issuing for many years *Van Nostrand's Engineering Magazine*.

VAN OSDEL, JOHN MILLS (*b. Baltimore, Md., 1811; d. Chicago, Ill., 1891*), carpenter, architect. Employed by William B. Ogden to plan and erect a house for him in Chicago, 1837, Van Osdel removed to Chicago and has the honor of being that city's first professional architect. He was particularly active in the restoration of the city after the great fire of 1871.

VAN QUICKENBORNE, CHARLES FELIX (*b. Peteghem, East Flanders, 1788; d. Portage des Sioux, Mo., 1837*), Roman Catholic clergyman. Jesuit. Assigned to the Jesuit Maryland mission, 1817, he taught at Georgetown and served as professor at the seminary at Whitemarsh. He was renowned for charitable service among the poor and especially the blacks. Named first superior of the Missouri Province, 1823, he instituted its work at Florissant; in 1828 he established St. Louis College, later incorporated as St. Louis University. A zealous missionary among the Osage, Potawatomi, Kickapoo, and other tribes, he traveled extensively through Missouri, Illinois, and Iowa, and served as the pioneer of Catholicism on those frontiers. He was also responsible for the training of such celebrated Jesuits as Christian Hoecken, Pierre De Smet, and Peter Verhaegen.

VAN RAALTE, ALBERTUS CHRISTIAAN (*b. near Zwartsluis, the Netherlands, 1811; d. 1876*), nonconformist Dutch Reformed clergyman. Founded Dutch settlement at Holland, Mich., 1847, and served as its preacher and physician.

VAN RENSSELAER, CORTLANDT (*b. Albany, N.Y., 1808; d. Burlington, N.J., 1860*), Presbyterian clergyman. Son of Stephen Van Rensselaer. Graduated Yale, 1827. Rendered conspicuous service as corresponding secretary and chief executive officer of the Presbyterian Board of Education, 1846–60, furthering the development of parochial schools, Presbyterian academies, and synodical colleges.

VAN RENSSELAER, MARIANA GRISWOLD (*b. New York, N.Y., 1851; d. New York, 1934*), art critic, author. A leader and expositor of the new interest in art that was current in the educated America of the 1880's and 1890's, Van Rensselaer wrote a number of books which included *American Etchers* (1886), *Henry Hobson Richardson and His Works* (1888, the first important monograph on a modern American architect), and *English Cathedrals* (1892). Her best-known work is her authoritative *History of the City of New York in the Seventeenth Century* (1909).

VAN RENSSELAER, MARTHA (*b. Randolph, N.Y., 1864; d. 1932*), teacher, home economist. An early leader in the education of country women, particularly through her extension work at Cornell University *post* 1900.

VAN RENSSELAER, NICHOLAS (*b. Amsterdam, North Holland, 1636; d. 1678*), Dutch Reformed and Anglican clergyman. Son of the first patroon of the Manor of Rensselaer, he became a close associate of Charles II of England during the king's exile on the continent of Europe. In England *post* 1662, he received Anglican orders and came to New York with Sir Edmund Andros who tried to force him on the congregation at Albany as minister. Rejected, he complained to the governor and the dispute was brought before the Council, September–October 1675. On his promise to conform to the rites of the Dutch Church, he was finally installed at Albany but was deposed by the governor, 1677.

VAN RENSSELAER, SOLOMON (*b. Rensselaer Co., N.Y., 1774; d. 1852*), soldier, public official. Entered U.S. Army as cornet of cavalry 1792; served under Anthony Wayne, 1794, and was wounded at Fallen Timbers; honorably discharged as major, 1800. Appointed aide-de-camp to his cousin General Stephen Van Rensselaer, 1812, he commanded the advance party of militia at Queenstown, Canada, Oct. 13, 1812, and was severely wounded while successfully carrying out his part of the operation. As congressman, probably Federalist, from New York, 1819–22, he opposed the Missouri Compromise. He was postmaster at Albany, N.Y., 1822–39 and 1841–43.

VAN RENSSELAER, STEPHEN (*b. New York, N.Y., 1764; d. 1839*), soldier, New York legislator, eighth patroon of the Manor of Rensselaer. Grandson of Philip Livingston. Graduated Harvard, 1782. Married Margaret, daughter of General Philip Schuyler, June 1783. A Federalist legislator, 1789–95, and lieutenant governor of New York, 1795–1801, he ran unsuccessfully for governor against George Clinton in the latter year. Thereafter at various times a member of the New York legislature and an active improver of his great estates, he was called on in 1812 (as a major general in the New York militia) to command the entire northern frontier of the state. Assembling a force based at Lewiston, he was hampered by the refusal of General Alexander Smyth of the regular army to take orders from him. Venturing to attack Queenstown, Canada, in October 1812 without Smyth's support, he suffered a severe defeat and resigned his command. As congressman from New York, 1823–29, he cast the deciding vote for John Q. Adams, 1825, when the choice of a president was thrown into the House of Representatives. Van Rensselaer's chief services to New York were economic and educational. He was an early advocate of a canal to connect the Hudson with the Great Lakes and served on both Erie Canal commissions; he was president of the second *post* 1825. He was instrumental in creating the state's first board of agriculture and paid the costs of the first state geological survey by Amos Eaton. He established in 1824–26 the present Rensselaer Polytechnic Institute and gave generously to other educational institutions.

VAN SANTVOORD, GEORGE (*b. Belleville, N.J., 1819; d. East Albany, N.Y., 1863*), lawyer, New York legislator. A proponent of the civil law as against the "churlish and exclusive spirit" of the common law. Author, among other works, of *A Treatise on the Principles of Pleading in Civil Actions under the New-York Code* (1852) and *Sketches of the Lives . . . of the Chief Justice of the United States* (1854).

VAN SCHAACK, HENRY CRUGER (*b. Kinderhook, N.Y., 1802; d. 1887*), antiquarian, lawyer. Son of Peter Van Schaack. Author, among other works, of a life of his father (1842) which was the first attempt to present a justificatory memoir of a Tory in the Revolution.

VAN SCHAACK, PETER (*b. near Kinderhook, N.Y., 1747; d. Kinderhook, 1832*), lawyer, Loyalist. Graduated King's College (Columbia), 1766; studied law with William Smith (1728–93). A member of several pre-Revolutionary New York committees of protest against the British government's treatment of the colonies, he attempted to maintain neutrality after the outbreak of fighting. His several refusals to take the oath of allegiance to the State of New York caused him to be banished to England in 1778. Returning to Kinderhook, 1785, he was readmitted to the bar but took no active part in politics.

VAN SCHAICK, GOOSE (*b. Albany, N.Y., 1736; d. Albany, 1789*), Revolutionary patriot and soldier. An officer in the New York provincial militia *post* 1756, he was commissioned colonel of the 1st New York Regiment at the outbreak of the Revolution, and saw constant service during the war in defense of New York's northern and western frontiers. His most famous exploit was a punitive expedition against the Onondaga tribe (April 1779) which was preliminary to the better-known campaign of General John Sullivan later that summer.

VAN SLYKE, LUCIUS LINCOLN (*b. Centerville, N.Y., 1859; d. 1931*), agricultural chemist. Graduated University of Michigan, 1879; Ph.D., 1882. Chief chemist, New York State agricultural experiment station, Geneva, N.Y., 1800–1929; professor of dairy chemistry, Cornell University, 1920–29. He is remembered for pioneer work in dairy chemistry which included basic research on the chemical constituents of milk and their relation to one another. His researches on milk casein led to improvement on cheese-making and were of immense scientific value in contributing to knowledge of the nature and behavior of colloids.

VAN SWERINGEN, MANTIS JAMES (*b. Wooster, Ohio, 1881; d. 1935*), real estate operator, railroad manager, and speculator. Working in close partnership with his brother, Oris P. Van Sweringen, he developed the suburb of Shaker Heights, Cleveland, Ohio, *post* 1900. The brothers later acquired stock control of a vast railroad system, which at its peak included the Nickel Plate, the Chesapeake & Ohio, the Erie, the Pere Marquette, and the Missouri Pacific railroads. In 1935 their holding company pyramid showed signs of weakening, and after the death of the brothers their empire disintegrated.

VAN TWILLER, WOUTER (*b. Gelderland, present the Netherlands, ca. 1580; d. ca. 1656*), colonial official. Nephew of Kiliaen Van Rensselaer, the first patroon of Rensselaerswyck. Arrived at New Amsterdam, 1633, as director general of New Netherland. His foresighted desire to build up the agricultural potential of the colony, rather than produce an immediate profit by trade, was thwarted by a lack of colonists and by the enmity of David P. De Vries and Everardus Bogardus. Popular with the Indians because of his just treatment of them, he was relieved of his post by Willem Kieft in 1637. Returning to the Netherlands, 1639, he justified his actions before the West India Company and was later a manager of his uncle's properties.

VAN TYNE, CLAUDE HALSTEAD (*b. Tecumseh, Mich., 1869; d. 1930*), educator, historian. Graduated University of Michigan, 1896; Ph.D., University of Pennsylvania, 1900. A professor of history at Michigan *post* 1903 and later head of the department of history there, Van Tyne was a stimulating and exacting teacher. He was author, among other scholarly publications, of *The Loyalists in the American Revolution* (1902), *The Causes of the War of Independence* (1922), and *The War of Independence, American Phase* (1929) for which he was awarded a Pulitzer Prize.

VANUXEM, LARDNER (*b. Philadelphia, Pa., 1792; d. Bristol, Pa., 1848*), geologist. Graduated École des Mines, Paris, 1819. Taught chemistry at South Carolina College. Made geologic surveys in Mexico, New York, Ohio, Kentucky, Tennessee, and Virginia; made studies also of the Third District iron- and salt-bearing formations for the New York State Geological Survey *post* 1836. Author of *Geology of New York, Part III* (1842), he was instrumental in effecting a uniform system of nomenclature for American geology, a cooperative task which led to the later founding of the American Association for the Advancement of Science.

VAN VECHTEN, ABRAHAM (*b. Catskill, N.Y., 1762; d. 1837*), lawyer, Federalist New York legislator, and public official. Studied law with John Lansing; was first lawyer admitted to practice under the New York constitution, 1785; practiced in Albany, N.Y. Held leading position at New York constitutional convention, 1821. Gave notable opinion in *Gibbons* v. *Ogden* (9 *Wheaton*, 1) in which he was sustained by Chief Justice Marshall.

VAN VECHTEN, CARL (*b. Cedar Rapids, Iowa, 1880; d. New York, N.Y., 1964*), music and dance critic, novelist, photographer. Attended the University of Chicago (Ph.B., 1903), then moved to New York in 1906 and worked as music and arts critic for the *New York Times* and *New York Press*. Met Gertrude Stein (1913) and championed her work for decades, serving as her literary executor after her death. Books of essays hailing works of experimental composers and artists he considered neglected include *Music After the Great War* (1915), *In the Garret* (1919), and *Red* (1925). Also wrote seven novels during 1922–30. Turned to documentary photography in the 1930's; his first show was part of the "Leica Exhibition" in New York City in 1935. Personal reminiscences include *Sacred and Profane Memories* (1932) and *Fragments from an Unwritten Autobiography* (1955).

VAN VLECK, EDWARD BURR (*b. Middletown, Conn., 1863; d. Madison, Wis., 1943*), mathematician. A.B., Wesleyan University, 1884; did graduate work at Johns Hopkins, 1885–87; Ph.D., University of Göttingen, 1893. Taught at University of Wisconsin, 1893–95; at Wesleyan, 1895–1906. Professor of mathematics, University of Wisconsin, 1906–29, and for many years chairman of the department. A conscientious teacher, clear and meticulous in his presentation, he showed the profound influence of his mentor, Felix Klein, in his own mathematical work, especially in its earlier period. This was typified by a broad approach to problems, using both analytical and geometrical methods, together with a keen sense for the relationship between different fields.

VAN WINKLE, PETER GODWIN (*b. New York, N.Y., 1808; d. Parkersburg, W.Va., 1872*), lawyer. Removed to Parkersburg as a young man and practiced law there *post* 1835. Prominent in the creation of the present State of West Virginia, he had much to do with the framing of its constitution (1861–62) and was a member of its first legislature. U.S. senator, Republican, from West Virginia, 1863–69, he showed courage and independence, especially in his refusal to vote for conviction of President Andrew Johnson.

VAN WYCK, CHARLES HENRY (*b. Poughkeepsie, N.Y., 1824; d. Washington, D.C., 1895*), lawyer, Union brigadier general, New York and Nebraska legislator. Congressman, Republican, from New York, 1859–63, 1867–71, he removed to the vicinity of Nebraska City, Nebr., 1874. In the Nebraska legislature, and as U.S. senator, 1881–87, he was a supporter of tariff reform, railroad regulation, protection of the public lands, and direct popular election of senators. He was active in the Farmer's Alliance and in the Populist movement in Nebraska.

VANZETTI, BARTOLOMEO. *See* SACCO, NICOLA.

VARDAMAN, JAMES KIMBLE (*b. near Edna, Tex., 1861; d. 1930*), lawyer, newspaper editor, politician. Raised in Mississippi, he rose in politics and was speaker of the Mississippi House, 1894. Denied nomination for the governorship by the ruling clique in the Mississippi Democratic party, he managed by his powers as a stump speaker to establish popularity with the poor-white farming group and fractured his party along class lines. Among other arguments, he asserted that the education of the black person was threatening white supremacy. Elected governor, he served 1904–08. Although charged with extending the spoils system, he attacked the custom of leasing out state convicts to private employers. As U.S. senator, 1913–19, he opposed President Wilson's war policies and was one of the "little group of willful men" who filibustered against the Armed Neutrality Bill. He was defeated in the election of 1918 after a specific request for his ouster was made by the president to the Mississippi voters.

VARDILL, JOHN (*b. New York, N.Y., 1749; d. probably England, 1811*), Anglican clergyman, British spy. A graduate of King's College (Columbia), 1766, and later a tutor there, he was elected professor of natural law, 1773. Meantime he had come into public notice for essays he had written in connection with the controversy between William Livingston and Thomas B. Chandler over an American episcopate. He was author also of essays signed "Poplicola" against the nonimportation agreement, 1773. Ordained at London in April 1774, he was elected assistant minister of Trinity Church, New York, in December, but remained in England and continued writing for periodicals in defense of the government. Between 1775 and 1781 he was a Crown agent spying on American sympathizers in England. His greatest feat was in securing the theft from Silas Deane of the whole confidential correspondence between the American commissioners and the French Court from March to October 1777.

VARE, WILLIAM SCOTT (*b. South Philadelphia, Pa., 1867; d. Atlantic City, N.J., 1934*), contractor, Pennsylvania legislator and official. Established with aid of his brothers a Republican political machine in Philadelphia which by 1917 dominated that city. A congressman, 1912–23, 1923–27, Vare climaxed his career in the primary elections of 1926 when he was successful candidate for the Republican nomination to the U.S. Senate. Rejected by the Senate after a special senatorial committee investigation for expenditures in the primary, Vare continued active in politics and aided in the nomination of Herbert Hoover for the presidency, 1928. Although he maintained his organization largely by spoils and political charity, he was a man of high personal reputation and throughout his career opposed child labor and supported liberal social reform bills.

VARELA Y MORALES, FÉLIX FRANCISCO JOSÉ MARÍA DE LA CONCEPCIÓN (*b. Havana, Cuba, 1788, d. St. Augustine, Fla., 1853*), Roman Catholic clergyman, Cuban patriot, author. An educational reformer as professor of philosophy at the College of San Carlos in Havana, Varela was a liberal in politics and served

as a delegate from Cuba to the Spanish Cortes, 1822–23. Fleeing to New York on the return of the absolute monarchy in Spain, 1823, he served until 1851 as an exemplary pastor at various churches in New York City. He was twice named an administrator of the diocese and was a vicar general *post* 1839.

VARÈSE, EDGARD (*b. Paris, France, 1883; d. New York, N.Y., 1965*), composer. Studied music in Paris (at the Schola Cantorum, Paris Conservatory, and Conservatoire de Musique et Déclamation). First public performance of his work took place in Berlin in 1910. Came to the United States in 1915. Helped found the International Composers' Guild (ICG) in 1921; during his six years with the ICG he conducted works by the most advanced composers of the day and presented his own new pieces: *Offrandes* (1921), *Hyperprism* (1922), *Octandre* (1923), *Integrales* (1924), and *Arcana* (1925–27). Became a U.S. citizen in 1927. While in Paris, 1928–32, he completed *Ionisation* (1931). *Ecuatorial* (1934) was the first piece in which he used an electronic instrument. Interpolated taped sounds into an orchestral work, *Déserts*, first performed in 1954 in Paris.

VARICK, JAMES (*b. near Newburgh, N.Y., ca. 1750; d. 1828*), Methodist clergyman. A founder of the African Methodist Episcopal Zion Church, 1799, Varick was chairman of the committee which drew up a discipline after secession of his church from the Methodist Episcopal organization, 1820. Elected bishop in 1822, he served as such until his death.

VARICK, RICHARD (*b. Hackensack, N.J., 1753; d. Jersey City, N.J., 1831*), Revolutionary soldier, public official. Military secretary to General Philip J. Schuyler; deputy commissary general of musters, 1776–80; aide to General Benedict Arnold at West Point, 1780. Cleared of any complicity in Arnold's treason, Varick was selected by General Washington as secretary to arrange, classify, and copy all headquarters records of the Continental Army; he completed his task in 1783 with the greatest skill and success. Appointed recorder of New York City, 1784, he worked with Samuel Jones on the codification of the New York statutes (published 1789). Speaker of the New York Assembly, 1787–88, and state attorney general, 1788–89, he served as Federalist mayor of New York City, 1789–1801.

VARNUM, JAMES MITCHELL (*b. Dracut, Mass., 1748; d. Marietta, Ohio, 1789*), lawyer, Revolutionary soldier. Brother of Joseph B. Varnum. Commissioned colonel of the 1st Rhode Island Infantry (9th Continental), he was promoted brigadier general, February 1777, and conducted a gallant though unsuccessful defense of Forts Mercer and Mifflin on the Delaware River. He later took part in the campaigns around Newport, R.I., and was made commander of the Department of Rhode Island early in 1779. Elected to the Continental Congress, 1780, he served at intervals until 1787. A director of the Ohio Company, Varnum was appointed U.S. judge for the Northwest Territory and took up duties at Marietta, Ohio, June 1788.

VARNUM, JOSEPH BRADLEY (*b. Dracut, Mass., 1750/1; d. 1821*), Revolutionary soldier, Massachusetts legislator. Brother of James M. Varnum. Congressman, Anti-Federalist, from Massachusetts, 1795–1811, he favored a militia as against a standing army, opposed building naval vessels, and was an early opponent of slavery and the slave trade; he served as speaker of the House, 1807–11. U.S. senator, 1811–17, he was associated with the "war hawks" of the Southwest and was a strong supporter of the War of 1812. In 1813 he was president *pro tempore* of the Senate and acting U.S. vice president.

VASEY, GEORGE (*b. near Scarborough, England, 1822; d. Washington, D.C., 1893*), physician, botanist. Immigrated to central New York State as a child. Removed to northern Illinois,

1848, where he practiced his profession and continued botanical studies of the regional flora. After accompanying John W. Powell on an exploring expedition to Colorado, 1868, he served in several posts before his appointment (1872) as botanist of the U.S. Department of Agriculture and curator of the U.S. National Herbarium. A distinguished specialist on grasses, he published several outstanding monographs on this subject.

VASILIEV, ALEXANDER ALEXANDROVICH (*b. St. Petersburg, Russia, 1867; d. Washington D.C., 1953*), Byzantine scholar. Studied at the University of St. Petersburg, Ph.D., 1902. Taught at the university, 1912–25. Immigrated to the U.S. in 1925. Professor at the University of Wisconsin, 1925–39. Lectured at Columbia University and at Oberlin College; senior scholar at the Dumbarton Oaks Center for Byzantine Studies, 1944–53. Introduced the study of Byzantine culture to the U.S. Author of *Justin the First* (1950) and *History of the Byzantine Empire* (1917–25; English translations, 1928–29).

VASSALL, JOHN (*b. Stepney, Middlesex Co., England, 1625; d. 1688*), colonist, merchant. Immigrated to New England as a boy; was a resident of Scituate, Mass. With an English cousin and others he attempted establishment of a colony at Cape Fear in present North Carolina, 1664. After the failure of the colony, 1667, he removed first to Virginia and later to Jamaica, B.W.I., where he prospered in trade. His great-grandson was the builder of the "Craigie-Longfellow" house in Cambridge, Mass.

VASSAR, MATTHEW (*b. East Tuddingham, England, 1792; d. Poughkeepsie, N.Y., 1868*), brewer, merchant. Came to America as a small boy; was successful as a brewer and in other enterprises at Poughkeepsie, N.Y. Founder of Vassar College.

VATTEMARE, NICHOLAS MARIE ALEXANDRE (*b. Paris, France, 1796; d. Paris, 1864*), ventriloquist, impersonator. Made U.S. debut at the Park Theater, New York City, October 1839. Impressed by the number of duplicate books and art objects in libraries and museums, he evolved the idea of an exchange system for which he won some support in Europe and enthusiastic aid in the United States. Between 1841 and 1851 his system was successful, and his propaganda resulted in the establishment of several free libraries and museums, including the Boston Public Library.

VAUCLAIN, SAMUEL MATTHEWS (*b. Port Richmond, Pa., 1856; d. Rosemont, Pa., 1940*), locomotive manufacturer. Associated *post* 1883 with the Baldwin Locomotive Works, he served as president of the company, 1919–29, and thereafter as chairman of the board. One of the world's leading authorities on locomotive design and inventor of a number of important improvements in locomotives, he ran his business autocratically and fought against any attempt at labor organization.

VAUDREUIL-CAVAGNAL, PIERRE DE RIGAUD, MARQUIS DE (*b. Canada, 1704; d. Paris, France, 1778*), Canadian soldier and public official. Winning honors as a soldier, as governor of Trois Rivières, and as governor of the colony of Louisiana in 1743–53, he was then appointed governor of Canada. Taking up his duties, June 1755, he found the colony on the brink of war with England. Allowing himself to be drawn into the corrupt ring of politicians that surrounded the intendant Bigot, he refused support to Montcalm who had been seen to conduct the war for France; he has been held responsible for the defeat on the Plains of Abraham, September 1759. A year later he capitulated at Montreal and, by so doing, cost France her last chance to hold Canada. Arriving in France, December 1760, he was arrested and thrown into the Bastille; at his trial he was acquitted of dishonesty and pensioned. Jealous of better soldiers than himself, he talked more than was prudent and failed to check the corruption that went on all around him.

VAUGHAN, BENJAMIN (*b. Jamaica, British West Indies, 1751; d. Hallowell, Maine, 1835*), lawyer, physician, merchant, diplomat, agriculturist. Brother of Charles Vaughan. An active propagandist for the American cause during the Revolution, Vaughan was employed in confidential matters by the Earl of Shelburne. He was co-editor with Benjamin Franklin of the latter's *Political, Miscellaneous and Philosophical Pieces* (1779). He did his most important work in connection with the Anglo-American peace negotiations of 1782, helping to promote confidence between the American commissioners and Shelburne and to reconcile conflicting points of view. In 1789 he published *A Treatise on International Trade*, a plea for free trade. He was sympathetic with the French Revolution and fled to France during an official investigation of the activities of English political enthusiasts, May 1794. Imprisoned by the French, he was later released and retired to Switzerland. Removing to Hallowell, Maine, 1796, he remained retired from active politics but was a correspondent and adviser of the first six presidents and a member of many scientific and literary societies. He published a second collection of Franklin's works in London, 1793, and was probably author of much work which still remains unidentified.

VAUGHAN, CHARLES (*b. London, England, 1759; d. Hallowell, Maine, 1839*), merchant. Brother of Benjamin Vaughan. Immigrated to New England, 1785. He then engaged in a long and generally unsuccessful attempt to improve the "Kennebec Purchase" in Maine of which his maternal grandfather, Benjamin Hallowell, had been an original proprietor; in this effort he built a settlement just below Augusta at Hallowell and tried to establish a seaport at Jones Eddy near the mouth of the Kennebec. Establishing himself as a merchant in Boston, 1791, he was a promoter, with Charles Bulfinch and William Scollay, of Boston's first brick block, the Franklin or Tontine Crescent. Later bankrupted, he retired to Hallowell where he devoted himself to the development of Maine agriculture.

VAUGHAN, DANIEL (*b. near Killaloe, Ireland, ca. 1818; d. Cincinnati, Ohio, 1879*), astronomer, mathematician, chemist. Immigrated to America, 1840; served as a tutor and schoolmaster in Kentucky and in Cincinnati, Ohio. Celebrated as a lecturer on scientific subjects, he was made a fellow of the American Association for the Advancement of Science for his work in experimental physiology. In 1852 he anticipated by many years the demonstration made by J. E. Keeler of the nature of the rings of Saturn. A gentle genius, he died in poverty.

VAUGHAN, THOMAS WAYLAND (*b. Jonesville, Tex., 1870; d. Washington, D.C., 1952*), geologist, paleontologist, oceanographer. Studied at Tulane University and Harvard, Ph.D., 1903. A leader in the study of coral and the larger Foraminifera, Vaughan was affiliated with the U.S. National Museum as custodian of the madreporarian corals, 1903–23, and as a paleontologist, 1936–47. Worked at the Dry Tortugas biological laboratory of the Carnegie Institution of Washington, 1907–18. Wrote *The Recent Madreporaria of the Hawaiian Islands and Laysan* (1907). Studied the coastal plains of the U.S. and became an authority on American Tertiary stratigraphy. Headed the Scripps Institution in La Jolla, Calif., 1924–36, turning that institution into a leading marine laboratory.

VAUGHAN, VICTOR CLARENCE (*b. near Mt. Airy, Mo., 1851; d. Richmond, Va., 1929*), biochemist, hygienist, medical teacher. M.S., University of Michigan, 1875; Ph.D., 1876; M.D., 1878. For many years a lecturer and professor at Michigan, he served as director of the hygienic laboratory, 1887–1909, and as dean of the medical school, 1891–1921. While dean he put Michigan in a prominent place in the movement to elevate American medical education. After studying at Berlin with Robert

Koch, Vaughan and an associate set up one of the earliest laboratories in the United States for the systematic teaching of bacteriology. His work upon ptomaines with F. G. Novy influenced improvement of methods of food preservation. He developed early in his career the interest in public health and education of the public in preventive medicine for which he is best known. Among his many writings were the classic *Report on the Origin and Spread of Typhoid Fever in the U.S. Military Camps* (1904) and *Epidemiology and Public Health* (1922–23) of which he was coauthor.

VAUX, CALVERT (*b. London, England, 1824; d. New York, N.Y., 1895*), landscape architect. Came to America, 1850, as assistant to Andrew J. Downing at Newburgh, N.Y.; removed to New York City *ca.* 1857. Submitted winning design for New York's Central Park in collaboration with Frederick L. Olmsted, 1857; was associated in practice with Olmsted for a number of years, their work including Prospect Park in Brooklyn, N.Y., and South Park in Chicago, Ill. Vaux was landscape architect to the New York City department for parks, 1881–83 and 1888–95.

VAUX, RICHARD (*b. Philadelphia, Pa., 1816; d. 1895*), lawyer, public official. Son of Roberts Vaux. Practicing in Philadelphia *post* 1839, Vaux held a number of local and federal offices. Carrying out his father's theories of penology, he served as a governor of the Eastern Penitentiary, 1839–92, and was president of its board *post* 1852.

VAUX, ROBERTS (*b. Philadelphia, Pa., 1786; d. Philadelphia, 1836*), philanthropist. Son-in-law of Thomas Wistar; father of Richard Vaux. Associated throughout his life with almost every worthy public and private activity for social welfare in Philadelphia, he was a leader in creation of the free public school system, was active in hospital work and the work of learned societies, advocated temperance, and was outstanding as a prison reformer. He drafted legislation for administration of the Eastern Penitentiary and was an advocate of separate confinement of prisoners.

VAWTER, CHARLES ERASTUS (*b. Monroe Co., present W. Va., 1841; d. 1905*), Confederate soldier, educator. Graduated Emory and Henry College, 1866, and taught mathematics and Hebrew there, 1868–78. Built, organized, and headed the Miller Manual Labor School of Albemarle Co., Va., *post* 1878; promoted development of industrial education in the nation's public schools; aided J. M. McBryde in shaping policies of Virginia Polytechnic Institute.

VEATCH, ARTHUR CLIFFORD (*b. Evansville, Ind., 1878; d. Port Washington, N.Y., 1938*), geologist. Attended Indiana and Cornell universities. Began professional career with the Louisiana State Geological Survey; served with U.S. Geological Survey, 1902–10; worked thereafter for various corporations and as a consultant. Specialist in the geology of petroleum and the direction of foreign oil explorations.

VEAZEY, THOMAS WARD (*b. Cecil Co., Md., 1774; d. Cecil Co., 1842*), Maryland legislator, planter. Whig governor of Maryland, 1836–38; directed a reform of state constitution by amendments, 1836.

VEBLEN, OSWALD (*b. Decorah, Iowa, 1880; d. Brooklin, Me., 1960*), mathematician. Studied at the State University of Iowa and at the University of Chicago, Ph.D., 1903. Taught at Princeton University, 1905–32, and at the Institute for Advanced Study, 1932–50. Responsible for assembling the faculty of the Institute, Veblen also helped to relocate many foreign scholars after Hitler's rise to power. Author of *Introduction to Infinitesimal Analysis* (1907), *Analysis Situs* (1922), *Invariants of Quadratic Differential Forms* (1927), and *Geometry of Complex Domains* (1936).

VEBLEN, THORSTEIN BUNDE (*b. Cato Township, Manitowoc Co., Wis., 1857; d. Palo Alto, Calif., 1929*), economist, social theorist. Raised in a Minnesota farm community made up mainly of Norwegian immigrants, Veblen graduated from Carleton College, 1880. Carrying on graduate studies under great difficulties at Johns Hopkins and at Yale, he was granted the doctorate of philosophy at Yale in 1884 but returned to a Minnesota farm when he found that no teaching post was available. After seven miserable years as a farmer he obtained a special fellowship at Cornell University through the aid of J. Laurence Laughlin, 1891, and in the same year published his first essay, "Some Neglected Points in the Theory of Socialism" (*Annals of the American Academy of Political and Social Science*, November 1891), which contained many germs of his later theories.

Following Laughlin to the University of Chicago, Veblen taught political economy there, made private studies of anthropology and psychology, and was managing editor of the *Journal of Political Economy* (University of Chicago, 1895–1905). He achieved overnight prominence on publication in 1899 of *The Theory of the Leisure Class* into which he poured all the acidulous ideas and fantastic terminology that had been simmering in his mind for years. It was a savage attack upon the business class and their pecuniary values, half concealed behind an elaborate screen of irony and polysyllabic learning. *The Theory of Business Enterprise* (1904) contained Veblen's basic economic theory and dealt with the effects of the machine process, the nature of corporate promoting, the use of credit, the distinction between industry and business, and the influence of business ideas and pressures upon law and politics. Obliged to leave Chicago for reasons of personal conduct, he became associate professor at Leland Stanford, 1906, but further difficulties with women brought about his departure in December 1909. While lecturer at the University of Missouri, 1911–18, he brought his course in "Economic Factors in Civilization" to its classic form. Viewing all history and all cultures, the course was omniscient and rambling; his classroom manner was casual and inarticulate. The content of this course is most nearly approximated in his *The Instinct of Workmanship* (1914) which stresses the thesis that proper craftsmanship, an instinct deeply ingrained in man since savage times, has been thwarted throughout history by the piling up of predatory and pecuniary institutions.

Removing to New York City, 1918, he became first an editor of the *Dial* and then, in 1919, a member of the faculty of the New School for Social Research. To this period belong his more revolutionary writings. In *An Inquiry into the Nature of Peace* (1917) Veblen described patriotism and business enterprise as useless to the community at large and as the principal obstructions to a lasting peace; in *The Higher Learning in America* (1918) he leveled a bitter and direct attack on the conduct of universities by businessmen. In *The Vested Interests and the State of the Industrial Arts* (1919) he pointed out with savagery that the aim of business was to maximize profits by restricting or sabotaging production, and defined a vested interest as "a marketable right to get something for nothing." In *The Engineers and the Price System* (1921) he sketched out a technique of revolution through organization of a soviet of technicians who would take over and carry on the productive processes of the nation. Greatly lionized by liberal intellectuals, he declined gradually both in health and mental powers. Six months before his death he remarked that "Naturally there will be other developments right along, but just now communism offers the best course that I can see." Veblen's thinking does not fall easily into the accepted categories of liberalism and radicalism; his intellectual attitudes and methods are those of liberalism, but his criticism of capitalist society is, at least in its implications, revolutionary. Relatively unaffected by other American writers, he drew his material largely from European sources. His influence was crucial in weakening the hold of neoclassical theory, but his most powerful effect was on economic opinion and policy. He was in no small measure responsible for the trend toward social control in an age dominated by business enterprise.

VEDDER, EDWARD BRIGHT (*b. New York, N.Y., 1878; d. Washington, D.C., 1952*), physician, army officer. Studied at the University of Rochester and the University of Pennsylvania, M.D., 1902. Graduated from the Army Medical College, 1904. Specialist in tropical medicines and diseases; studied beriberi and scurvy, contributing to the discovery, by others, that ascorbic acid is a vitamin. Chief of medical research of the Edgewood, Md., Arsenal, 1922–25; studied the effects of chemical warfare. Commandant of the Army Medical College, 1930–31. Professor of experimental medicine at George Washington University, 1933–42.

VEDDER, ELIHU (*b. New York, N.Y., 1836; d. Rome, Italy, 1923*), figure and mural painter, illustrator. Began study of art by himself as a boy; worked for a time with Tompkins H. Matteson. Resided in Florence, Italy, and elsewhere in Europe, 1856–61; *post* 1867 made his home in Rome. Vedder's workmanship is heavy and his color is not remarkable, but his work has rare imaginative power; in his penetration of the realm of abstract ideas he ranks with Albert P. Ryder. Among his best works are his outstanding illustrations for the Rubáiyát of Omar Kháyyam (1884).

VEDDER, HENRY CLAY (*b. De Ruyter, N.Y., 1853; d. 1935*), Baptist clergyman, journalist, and church historian. Served on staff of the *Examiner*, a leading Baptist newspaper in New York, 1876–94; professor of church history, Crozer Theological Seminary, 1895–1926. Author of a number of works on the history of his own sect and on Christianity in general which were marked by a strong social approach.

VEILLER, LAWRENCE TURNURE (*b. Elizabeth, N.J., 1872; d. New York, N.Y., 1959*), social worker, housing expert. Studied at the City College of New York. One of the nation's first housing experts, Veiller, under the auspices of the Charity Organization Society of New York, established the Tenement House Committee in 1898 and directed it until 1907. Founded the National Housing Association (1911) and was director, 1911–36. Opposed to public financing of housing, Veiller sought to improve American housing through legislation. His legislative efforts led to the passage of the New York State Tenement House Law of 1901 and the Standard Zoning Law of the U.S. Department of Commerce in 1921. Works include *Housing Reform: A Hand-Book for Practical Use in American Cities* (1910).

VENABLE, CHARLES SCOTT (*b. Prince Edward Co., Va., 1827; d. 1900*), mathematician, Confederate soldier, educator. Graduated Hampden-Sydney, 1842; studied also at University of Virginia. Professor of mathematics at Hampden-Sydney and later at South Carolina College, he served in the Civil War as aide on the staff of General Robert E. Lee. He was professor of mathematics at University of Virginia, 1865–96, and was largely responsible for the development there of schools of applied chemistry and engineering, astronomy, biology, and agriculture.

VENABLE, FRANCIS PRESTON (*b. Prince Edward Co., Va., 1856; d. 1934*), educator. Son of Charles S. Venable. Graduated University of Virginia, 1879; Ph.D., Göttingen, 1881. Professor of chemistry at the University of North Carolina *post* 1881; president of the university, 1900–14. A frequent contributor to learned journals; author of a number of books on chemical subjects.

VENABLE, WILLIAM HENRY (*b. near Waynesville, Ohio, 1836; d. 1920*), educator, textbook writer. Taught English in Cincinnati, Ohio, schools *post* 1862. Author of *Beginnings of Literary Culture in the Ohio Valley* (1891).

VERBECK, GUIDO HERMAN FRIDOLIN (*b. Zeist, the Netherlands, 1830; d. Tokyo, Japan, 1898*), Dutch Reformed clergyman. Immigrated to America, 1852. Ordained, 1859, he served thereafter as a missionary and public official in Japan.

VERBECK, WILLIAM (*b. Nagasaki, Japan, 1861; d. 1930*), educator, inventor, New York State militia officer. Son of Guido H. F. Verbeck. Headmaster, St John's School, Manlius, N.Y., *post* 1888; pioneer in the Boy Scout movement.

VERBRUGGHEN, HENRI (*b. Brussels, Belgium, 1873; d. Northfield, Minn., 1934*), violinist, conductor. Director of the Minneapolis Symphony Orchestra, 1922–32.

VERENDRYE, PIERRE GAULTIER DE VARENNES, SIEUR DE LA. *See* LA VERENDRYE, PIERRE GAULTIER DE VARENNES, SIEUR DE.

VERHAEGEN, PETER JOSEPH (*b. Haecht, Flanders, 1800; d. St. Charles, Mo., 1868*), Roman Catholic clergyman, Jesuit. Came to America, 1821, to enter novitiate at Whitemarsh, Md. Accompanied band of Jesuits led by Charles Van Quickenborne to Missouri, 1823. Ordained, 1825, he became rector of the present St. Louis University, 1829. Named superior of the Indian missions, 1836; became provincial of the Maryland Province of the Society of Jesus, 1844. President of St. Joseph's College, Bardstown, Ky., 1847–50. Thereafter a pastor at St. Charles, Mo.

VERITY, GEORGE MATTHEW (*b. East Liberty, Ohio, 1865; d. Middletown, Ohio, 1942*), steel manufacturer. President, American Rolling Mill Company (Armco), *post* 1899; backed John B. Tytus's plan for a continuous mill; was a pioneer in welfare capitalism, and active in many projects involving the health, education, and recreation of his employees and the community.

VERMILYE, KATE JORDAN. *See* JORDAN, KATE.

VERNON, SAMUEL (*b. Narragansett, R.I., 1683; d. 1737*), silversmith. Cousin of Edward Winslow (1669–1753). Produced work notable for craftsmanship, novelty, and variety of design at his shop in Newport, R.I.; engraved first Rhode Island bank bills. Served as a Rhode Island legislator and judge *post* 1729.

VERNON, WILLIAM (*b. Newport, R.I., 1719; d. 1806*), merchant. Son of Samuel Vernon. Active in the "triangular trade" out of Newport and in privateering. Performed invaluable work for the infant American Navy as a member of the so-called Eastern Navy Board during the Revolution.

VEROT, JEAN MARCEL PIERRE AUGUSTE (*b. Le Puy, France, 1805; d. St. Augustine, Fla., 1876*), Roman Catholic clergyman, Sulpician. Came to Maryland, 1830. A teacher at St. Mary's Seminary and a pastor in Maryland, he was named vicar-apostolic of Florida *ca.* 1858. Identified with the cause of the Confederacy during the Civil War, he was transferred to the see of Savannah, Ga., 1861, with Florida continued under his care. Active after the war in restoration of his diocese, he disinterestedly returned to Florida, 1870, becoming bishop of St. Augustine when it was made a see.

VERPLANCK, GULIAN CROMMELIN (*b. New York, N.Y., 1786; d. New York, 1870*), lawyer, New York legislator, author. Grandson of William Samuel Johnson. Graduated Columbia, 1801; studied law with Josiah O. Hoffman. Practicing in New York City *post* 1807, he organized (with Issac Sebring and Richard

Varick) the Washington Benevolent Society as a Federalist answer to the Tammany Society. A principal with Hugh Maxwell in the Columbia College commencement riot of 1811, Verplanck became an enemy of De Witt Clinton who had presided over his trial and conviction. Among the products of the pamphlet war in which both men engaged, Verplanck was responsible for *A Fable for Statesmen and Politicians* (1815) and *The State Triumvirate* (1819). A professor in the General Theological Seminary, New York City, 1821–24, he was author of *Essays on the Nature and Uses of the Various Evidences of Revealed Religion* (1824), one of the earliest American works influenced by the Scottish school of common-sense philosophy. Congressman, Democrat, from New York, 1825–33, he was chairman of the ways and means committee, 1831–33, and was chiefly instrumental in obtaining the 1831 law improving authors' copyrights. Becoming estranged from the Democrats, he lost in a run as Whig candidate for mayor of New York City, 1834. As a state senator, 1838–41, he outlined plans for reform of the judiciary system which had effect in the state constitutional changes of 1846 and 1868. Editor of a scholarly edition of Shakespeare's plays (1847), he was editor also of the *Talisman* (in association with Robert C. Sands and William Cullen Bryant, 1828–30). Some of his thoughtful and learned essays were collected in *Discourses and Addresses on Subjects of American History, etc.* (1833).

VERRILL, ADDISON EMERY (*b. Greenwood, Maine, 1839; d. Santa Barbara, Calif., 1926*), zoologist. B.S., Lawrence Scientific School, Harvard, 1862. While an undergraduate, assisted J. R. L. Agassiz, Alpheus Hyatt, and N. S. Shaler. Taught zoology at Yale, 1864–1907; taught also in the Sheffield Scientific School, and at University of Wisconsin (1868–70). Wide-ranging in his interests and investigations, he performed the greater part of his work in the study of marine invertebrates. A patient, painstaking investigator, he held firmly to a belief in the value of taxonomical work as a basis for scientific investigations. Among his many collateral activities were work (1871–87) with the U.S. Commission of Fish and Fisheries, the curatorship of the Peabody Museum at Yale, and an editorship of the *American Journal of Science* (1869–1920).

VERRILL, ALPHEUS HYATT (*b. New Haven, Conn., 1871; d. Chiefland, Fla., 1954*), author, illustrator, naturalist, explorer. Studied at the Yale School of Fine Arts. Illustrator of the natural history section of *Webster's International Dictionary*, 1896. Invented the autochrome process of natural-color photography, 1902. Under the auspices of the Museum of the American Indian, Heye Foundation, New York, he explored much of the ancient civilations of the Western Hemisphere and did studies of wildlife and fauna.

VERWYST, CHRYSOSTOM ADRIAN (*b. Uden, the Netherlands, 1841; d. Bayfield, Wis., 1925*), Roman Catholic clergyman, Franciscan, Indian linguist. Came to America as a boy; was raised in Wisconsin. Ordained, 1865. He served as a missionary in the Lake Superior region for many years and was an authority on the language of the Chippewa.

VERY, JONES (*b. Salem, Mass., 1813; d. Salem, 1880*), poet, transcendentalist. Graduated Harvard, 1836. Encouraged by Elizabeth P. Peabody and R. W. Emerson, Very produced a number of sonnets (first published in the *Western Messenger*, March–April 1839; later published in *Essays and Poems*, 1839) which received wide contemporary praise and were distinguished by sincere religious emotion.

VERY, LYDIA LOUISA ANN (*b. Salem, Mass., 1823; d. Salem, 1901*), teacher, poet. Sister of Jones Very. Author, among

other works, of *Poems* (1856) and *An Old-fashioned Garden* (1900).

VESEY, DENMARK (*b. ca. 1767; d. Charleston, S.C., 1822*), rebel. Purchasing his freedom in 1800, Vesey (a mulatto) prospered as a carpenter in Charleston. Between the years 1818–22 he laid the foundation for an uprising of slaves against their masters by quoting scripture with powerful effect, identifying the black slaves with the Israelites. He interpreted the debate over the Missouri Compromise to mean that blacks were being held by their masters in defiance of law. Exempt from slave restrictions, he carried his message to the plantations from the Santee to the Euhaws. His conspiracy was betrayed to the city authorities in June 1822, and he was tried, convicted on the testimony of informers, and hanged. The true extent of his conspiracy is not known for he and his aides died without making any revelations.

VESEY, TÉLÉMAQUE. *See* VESEY, DENMARK.

VESEY, WILLIAM (*b. Braintree, Mass., 1674; d. New York, N.Y., 1746*), Anglican clergyman. Graduated Harvard, 1693. Ordained by the bishop of London, 1697, he served thereafter with great ability as rector of Trinity Church, New York City, until his death. An extreme conservative, he engaged in many controversies with the royal governors over the rights vested in Trinity and its rector.

VEST, GEORGE GRAHAM (*b. Frankfort, Ky., 1830; d. Sweet Springs, Mo., 1904*), lawyer, Missouri legislator. Removed to Missouri, 1854. Elected to the Missouri legislature, 1860, he was author of the "Vest Resolutions" denouncing coercion of the South, and was probably the author of the "Ordinance of Secession" adopted by the Southern wing of the legislature at Neosho, fall of 1861. A member of the Confederate Congress, 1862–65, he resumed practice of law in Missouri after the Civil War. His career as U.S. senator, Democrat, from Missouri, 1879–1903, was characterized by a disinclination to recognize new developments and new issues in American life, and by outstanding opposition to high protective tariffs. He was a leading exponent of the theory that it was unconstitutional for the United States to hold and govern Spanish territory permanently as colonies after cession *post* 1898.

VETCH, SAMUEL (*b. Edinburgh, Scotland, 1668; d. England, 1732*), colonial soldier, trader. Immigrating to Central America, 1698, as captain in the military force accompanying the Scotch colony at Darien, he came to New York in 1699 after the failure of the venture. Marrying the daughter of Robert Livingston, 1700, Vetch engaged in the Indian trade out of Albany, N.Y. He moved to Boston *ca.* 1702, where he traded with Acadia and Canada and was tried and fined in 1706 by the General Court for furnishing arms and ammunition to the French and Indians. Appealing the case in England, he won favor by suggesting to the authorities there a plan for conquering the French in America. In it he proposed an attack on Montreal by way of Lake Champlain and a complete investment of Quebec by land and sea. Dispatched by the Whig ministry in March 1709 to carry out this enterprise, Vetch was given powers to enlist colonial assistance from Pennsylvania northward and was accompanied by Francis Nicholson as a volunteer assistant. Mustering three New England regiments at Boston while at the same time Nicholson prepared a force with boats to proceed up Lake Champlain, Vetch was ready to execute his plan early in the summer but an expected British auxiliary force failed to appear and the scheme was dropped. On the arrival of British aid late in 1710, however, Nicholson was able to make an easy conquest of Port Royal and Acadia, and Vetch was appointed military governor of Annapolis Royal and Nova Scotia. Taking a part in the 1711 expedition against Canada, he shared in the disaster which befell the English forces at the mouth of the St. Lawrence River. Pursued by the enmity of Nicholson, who was civil governor of Nova Scotia, Vetch fled to England in 1714. He succeeded in displacing Nicholson in January 1715 only to lose his place two years later. After further misfortunes he died in debtor's prison.

VETHAKE, HENRY (*b. British Guiana, 1792; d. Philadelphia, Pa., 1866*), economist. Came to America as a boy. Graduated Columbia, 1808. Taught mathematics and philosophy at a number of institutions; was a professor and an official at the University of Pennsylvania, 1836–59. An orthodox classical economist, he opposed practically every form of governmental interference in economic life, also trade unions and statutory shortening of hours of labor. Author of *The Principles of Political Economy* (1838, 1844).

VEZIN, HERMANN (*b. Philadelphia, Pa., 1829; d. London, England, 1910*), actor. Made debut at the Theatre Royal, York, England, 1850, and remained active on the British stage until his death. Scholarly and intellectual in his impersonations, he had a somewhat formal manner of delivery.

VIBBARD, CHAUNCEY (*b. Galway, N.Y., 1811; d. Macon, Ga., 1891*), railroad executive, capitalist. Rose to post of general superintendent of the Utica & Schenectady Railroad, 1836–49; prepared the first railroad timetable ever followed in New York State; increased the comfort of passenger travel and was an innovator in use of safety appliances. Urged Erastus Corning to take the lead in creating the consolidation of small lines which was known as the New York Central, of which Vibbard was general superintendent, 1853–65. After Civil War service in Congress and as a railroad expert, he devoted his time to various private business interests.

VICK, JAMES (*b. Chichester, England, 1818; d. Rochester, N.Y., 1882*), printer, seedsman, publisher. Immigrated to America, 1833; settled in Rochester, N.Y., 1837, where he edited the *Genesee Farmer* and the *Rural New Yorker*. An importer and producer of seeds for his own amusement *post* 1848, he began to sell them by mail. He made this activity his principal business *post* 1862. As a merchant of flower seeds and as publisher of an annual catalogue and also a magazine, Vick exercised great influence on the horticulture of the United States. Among the products of his crossbreeding were the white double phlox, the fringed petunia, white gladiolus, and others.

VICKERY, HOWARD LEROY (*b. Bellevue, Ohio, 1892; d. Palm Springs, Calif., 1946*), naval officer, director of merchant marine shipbuilding during World War II. Graduated U.S. Naval Academy, 1915. M.S. in naval architecture, Massachusetts Institute of Technology, 1921. Assigned to naval construction and repair work; was director of shop, supply, and transportation work for government of Haiti (1925–28), and technical adviser on shipping to the governor general of the Philippines (1929–33). As assistant to Adm. Emory S. Land on the U.S. Maritime Commission *post* 1937, and vice chairman of the Commission, 1942–45, he was responsible for all U.S., maritime construction preceding and during World War II. Under his innovative supervision, the moribund shipbuilding industry of the 1930's became the world's fastest, most efficient, and foremost producer of vessels. By the time of his resignation for reasons of health as vice admiral (December 1945), some seventy shipyards turned out almost 40 million gross tons of vessels, including the famous Liberty and Victory ships.

VICTOR, FRANCES FULLER (*b. Oneida Co., N.Y., 1826; d. Portland, Oreg., 1902*), author. Sister-in-law of Orville J. Victor. Removed to Oregon, 1865, where she became the most compe-

tent authority on the region of the Pacific Northwest and its history. She was a member for a number of years of H. H. Bancroft's staff and wrote a great part of the histories of Oregon, Washington, Idaho, Montana, Nevada, Colorado, and Wyoming which appeared under his name. She was author also of Volumes 6 and 7 of the *History of California* (1890).

VICTOR, ORVILLE JAMES (*b. Sandusky, Ohio, 1827; d. Hohokus, N.J., 1910*), author, publisher. Married Metta Victoria Fuller, sister of Frances F. Victor, 1856, and was thereafter associated with a number of New York publishing houses specializing in the production of cheap popular books and magazines. For many years he was chief editor of the enterprises of Erastus F. Beadle and is regarded as the editorial projector of the American dime novel (1860).

VIEL, FRANÇOIS ÉTIENNE BERNARD ALEXANDRE (*b. New Orleans, La., 1736; d. France, 1821*), Roman Catholic clergyman, Oratorian. Educated in France, Viel was the first native-born Louisianian to take holy orders and taught for many years at the Academy of Juilly. A parish priest in Louisiana, 1792–1812, he returned to France to aid in the reestablishment of the Oratorians. He was a classical Latin scholar of the highest distinction, and a poet.

VIELE, AERNOUT CORNELISSEN (*b. New Amsterdam, 1640; d. ca. 1704*), trader, Indian interpreter and negotiator. Skilled in Indian languages and oratory, Viele was highly effective as a diplomat to the Iroquois and other tribes *post* 1680. He helped extend the New York colony's trade into the country north of the Great Lakes and to the southwest.

VIELE, EGBERT LUDOVICUS (*b. Waterford, N.Y., 1825; d. 1902*), soldier, engineer. Graduated West Point, 1847; served in the Mexican War and on the southwest frontier. Resigning his commission, 1853, he worked as a civil engineer in New York City, and was chief engineer of the New York Central Park, 1856–57; in 1860 he was engineer of Prospect Park, Brooklyn. After Civil War service with the Union Army as brigadier general of volunteers, 1861–63, he resumed engineering practice in New York. He made a plan for the "Arcade" railway, a precursor of the later subways, *ca.* 1868, and was author of a *Topographical Atlas of the City of New York* (1874). One of his sons was educated in France and attained distinction there as a poet under the name Francis Vielé-Griffin.

VIERECK, GEORGE SYLVESTER (*b. Munich, Germany, 1884; d. Holyoke, Mass., 1962*), writer, propagandist. Came to the United States in 1897 and began a lifetime of work on newspapers and magazines. Published his first volume of poetry in 1904; graduated from the College of the City of New York (B.A., 1906). Staff member and editor of several German–language publications. During World War I served as an apologist for German politics. Suspected of receiving money to aid Germany's war effort, he was vilified as a traitor, but was not formally prosecuted. He continued as a controversial journalist, interviewing, among others, Adolf Hitler (1923). During the 1930's he defended the Nazi regime. Arrested for violating the Foreign Agents Registration Act (1941), he was sentenced to prison in 1943. Released in 1947, he wrote two novels and a memoir of his prison years, *Men Into Beasts* (1952).

VIGNAUD, HENRY (*b. New Orleans, La., 1830; d. near Paris, France, 1922*), journalist, diplomat, historian. Taken prisoner while serving as a Confederate soldier, 1862, he escaped to Paris and never returned to the United States. After working with the Confederate mission to France under John Slidell, and service for a number of years in various occupations, he was appointed second secretary of the U.S. legation in Paris, 1875. He was promoted to first secretary, 1885. Until his retirement in 1909 he was an indispensable member of the Paris mission. He was distinguished also for his researches into the career of Columbus and for studies of aboriginal America and of the earliest European contacts with America.

VIGO, JOSEPH MARIA FRANCESCO (*b. Mondoví, Piedmont, Italy, 1747; d. Vincennes, Ind., 1836*), soldier, merchant. Came to Louisiana in youth as a member of a Spanish regiment; prospered in the fur trade and gained influence with French settlers and Indians. Established headquarters at St. Louis, 1772. Shares credit with George Rogers Clark for conquest of the Northwest in 1778–79, because of information, personal influence, and financial aid which he put at Clark's disposal.

VILAS, WILLIAM FREEMAN (*b. Chelsea, Vt., 1840; d. 1908*), statesman. Raised in Madison, Wis., where he was admitted to the bar, 1860; won professional distinction as a law teacher and official of University of Wisconsin and as reviser of the state statues. A leader in the Democratic party and a counselor and friend of Grover Cleveland, Vilas served as postmaster general, March 1885–January 1888, and as U.S. secretary of the interior, January 1888–March 1889. U.S. senator from Wisconsin, 1891–97, he retired to private life in Madison and was active thereafter in rebuilding the University of Wisconsin.

VILLAGRÁ, GASPAR PÉREZ DE (*b. Puebla de los Angeles, Spain, ca. 1555; d. at sea, en route to Guatemala, 1620*), Spanish soldier and colonial official. An officer in Juan de Oñate's expedition to New Mexico, 1598, he served subsequently at various times in New Mexico until *ca.* 1608. Villagrá was author of *Historia de la Nueva Mexico* (Alcalá de Henares, 1610), an epic poem which lauds Oñate's achievements in 1598–99. It has the distinction of being the first published history of any American commonwealth.

VILLARD, FANNY GARRISON. *See* VILLARD, HELEN FRANCES GARRISON.

VILLARD, HELEN FRANCES GARRISON (*b. Boston, Mass., 1844; d. Dobbs Ferry, N.Y., 1928*), reformer. Daughter of William L. Garrison; wife of Henry Villard. Among the many philanthropies and social reforms to which Villard lent her services were woman suffrage, pacifism, and the work of the National Association for the Advancement of Colored People.

VILLARD, HENRY (*b. Speyer, Rhenish Bavaria, 1835; d. Dobbs Ferry, N.Y., 1900*), journalist, railway promoter, financier. Educated in Germany, Villard changed his name from Ferdinand H. G. Hilgard before immigrating to America, 1853; this move was dictated by disagreement with his father over the younger man's republican sympathies. Settling eventually in Illinois, he studied English and, as a special correspondent for the New York *Staats-Zeitung*, reported the Lincoln-Douglas debates and made the acquaintance of Abraham Lincoln. Becoming correspondent for the *Cincinnati Commercial*, he covered the Pike's Peak gold rush, and later the Republican convention at Chicago, 1860. After Lincoln's election he became correspondent at Springfield, Ill., for the *New York Herald*.

A Civil War correspondent for the *Herald* and also the *New York Tribune*, 1861–63, he organized a news agency to compete with the New York Associated Press, 1864. Secretary of the American Social Science Association, 1868–71, he then traveled abroad to restore his health. Becoming a member of a committee of bondholders of the Oregon & California Railroad in Germany, 1873, he went to Oregon in 1874 as their representative and there perfected a plan for efficient operation of that railroad and other local transportation agencies. He became president of the Oregon & California, and of the Oregon Steamship Co., 1876. Named

the receiver of the Kansas Pacific Railway, 1876, he achieved an important financial success and laid the foundation of his later fortune. With the idea of building a railway empire in the Far Northwest, he organized with associates the Oregon Railway & Navigation Co., 1879, and built a road eastward from Portland, Oreg., along the south bank of the Columbia River. His plan was to make this line the Pacific Coast outlet for any Northern transcontinental road which might be built, so concentrating the trade of the Northwest in Portland. Clashing with the Northern Pacific, whose objective was an outlet on Puget Sound, Villard with his supporters bought a controlling interest in the Northern Pacific. He was made president, 1881, and completed its line in 1833. His control of transportation in the Northwest did not last long, as a huge deficit forced Villard's resignation from the presidency early in 1884. In 1893 he ended his connections with Northwest transportation. Meanwhile, however, he had helped found the Edison General Electric Co. and had acquired a controlling interest in the New York *Evening Post*. The most important railway promoter in the United States between 1879 and 1883, Villard displayed fairness and breadth of view in dealing with the people of the region which his railroad served. As newspaper proprietor, he permitted complete independence of policy to such editors as Horace White, E. L. Godkin, Carl Schurz, and his son O. G. Villard.

In 1866 he married Helen Frances Garrison, the daughter of W. L. Garrison.

VILLARD, OSWALD GARRISON (*b. Wiesbaden, Germany, 1872; d. New York, N.Y., 1949*), editor, reformer, author. Son of Henry Villard; grandson of William Lloyd Garrison. Born while his parents were on a trip abroad, he was raised in New York City and Dobbs Ferry, N.Y. Received B.A., Harvard, 1893; M.A., 1896. His apprenticeship on the *Philadelphia Press* was cut short at the urging of his father, and he joined the elder Villard's *New York Evening Post* in May 1897. The *Post* came out in opposition to war with Spain, the first of three major Villard stands against involvement in war. Villard was also against U.S. involvement in World War I and World War II. His consistent pacifism cost him the newspaper, but he retained the other Villard-controlled publication, the *Nation*, and proceeded to develop it into what was probably the foremost liberal voice of the 1920's and 1930's. Villard's pacifism led to loss of control of the *Nation* also and social ostracism from his family.

Villard had supported woman's rights as early as his Harvard days, and another area of lasting interest was the status of the blacks in the United States. He prepared the call for a national interracial conference as observance of Lincoln's centennial in 1909. Out of that meeting of black and white social critics and reformers came the organization of the National Association for the Advancement of Colored People. Villard criticized Booker T. Washington and W. E. B. Du Bois; but he worked with virtually every black leader to remove racial discrimination. As chairman of the National Association for the Advancement of Colored People, he obtained an interview with Woodrow Wilson at which he proposed the appointment of a national commission to study black education, health, housing, employment, income, legal rights, and civic participation. Wilson was seemingly sympathetic but found himself "absolutely blocked by the sentiment of Senators." He became increasingly critical of Wilson as a result.

In 1915 Villard went to Washington as the *Evening Post's* capital correspondent and sought to arrest the drift toward war with editorials, cartoons, and interpretive news reports. Liberal issues in which Villard became involved over the years seemed limitless in number, but the subject on which he was preeminently qualified was the press, and he spoke as both high-level practitioner and informed observer in editorials, columns, magazine articles, books, and lectures. His views, presented in part in *Newspapers* and *Newspaper Men* (1923) were expanded in *The Disappearing Daily* (1944) and in his autobiography, *Fighting Years* (1939). Three of Villard's books were about Germany: *Germany Embattled* (1915), *German Phoenix* (1933), and *Within Germany* (1940). In *Prophets True and False* (1928) he sketched and evaluated twenty-seven public figures of the time; he was the owner of the *Nautical Gazette* from 1918 to 1935, and he founded *Yachting* magazine in 1907.

VILLERÉ, JACQUES PHILIPPE (*b. near New Orleans, La., 1761; d. 1830*), planter. An efficient and conscientious governor of Louisiana, 1816–20, he was the first Creole to hold that position.

VINCENNES, FRANÇOIS MARIE BISSOT, SIEUR DE (*b. Montreal, Canada, 1700; d. on headwaters of Tombigbee River, present Mississippi, 1736*), French colonial soldier and official. Son of Jean B. B. de Vincennes. At request of the governor of Louisiana, Vincennes built a fort in 1731 or 1732 on the site of the Indiana city that now bears his name.

VINCENNES, JEAN BAPTISTE BISSOT, SIEUR DE (*b. Canada, 1668; d. site of present Ft. Wayne, Ind., 1719*), French colonial soldier, explorer. Father of François M. B. de Vincennes. Commanded among the Miami Indians, 1696; accompanied Henry de Tonty to the West, 1698. Principal factor in keeping the Miami Indians loyal to France.

VINCENT, FRANK (*b. Brooklyn, N.Y., 1848; d. Woodstock, N.Y., 1916*), world traveler, collector of Orientalia. Author, among other works, of *The Land of the White Elephant* (1874).

VINCENT, GEORGE EDGAR (*b. Rockford, Ill., 1864; d. New York, N.Y., 1941*), educator, sociologist, foundation executive. Son of John Heyl Vincent. B.A., Yale, 1885. Associated with his father thereafter in the work of the Chautauqua Institution, he served as its president, 1907–15. Ph.D., University of Chicago, 1896; taught there from 1895 to 1911. In 1900, he became dean of the junior colleges at Chicago, and in 1907 dean of the faculties of arts, literature, and science. His success as an administrator led to his appointment as president of the University of Minnesota in 1911. Serving until 1917, he reanimated the professional schools and gave full support to development of graduate study in the arts and sciences. From 1917 to 1929, when he retired, he was president of the Rockefeller Foundation.

VINCENT, JOHN HEYL (*b. Tuscaloosa, Ala., 1832; d. 1920*), Methodist clergyman and bishop, educational leader. Introduced uniform Sunday School lessons in Chicago, Ill., 1864, an innovation later followed in Protestant Sunday Schools throughout the world. Founded, 1874, a national training institute for Sunday School teachers at Lake Chautauqua, N.Y., in association with Lewis Miller; out of this developed the so-called Chautauqua movement for popular education. Vincent's plan of prescribed readings over a four-year term mark the beginning of directed home study and correspondence schools in America. A tolerant man, widely read, Bishop Vincent became the advocate of an intellectual and spiritual evangelism which relied on education rather than emotion.

VINCENT, MARVIN RICHARDSON (*b. Poughkeepsie, N.Y., 1834; d. Forest Hills, N.Y., 1922*), Methodist and Presbyterian clergyman. Graduated Columbia, 1854. Professor of sacred literature, Union Theological Seminary, New York, 1887–1916. Author, among other works, of *Word Studies in the New Testament* (1887–1900).

VINCENT, MARY ANN (*b. Portsmouth, England, 1818; d. Boston, Mass., 1887*), actress. Made American debut at Boston,

November 1846. As a member of the stock company of the Boston Museum *post* 1852, Mrs. Vincent became its leading comedienne and later its leading old lady. A Boston institution, she is commemorated by a hospital founded there in her memory and by the Vincent Club which raises funds for the hospital's support by annual amateur theatricals.

VINER, JACOB (*b. Montreal, Canada, 1892; d. Princeton, N.J., 1970*), economist. Attended Harvard (M.A., 1915; Ph.D., 1922), then became leading figure in the University of Chicago economics department; promoted to full professorship at the age of thirty-four. In *Canada's Balance of International Indebtedness, 1900–13* (1923), he was one of the first to subject balance-of-payments theory to an empirical test. Other important works include *Studies in the Theory of International Trade* (1937), *The Customs Union Issue* (1950), and *International Trade and Domestic Development* (1952). Also an authority on the social philosophy of Adam Smith. Moved to Princeton in 1946. Served as special assistant to the U.S. Treasury (1934–39) and as consultant to the State Department (1943–52).

VINSON, FRED(ERICK) MOORE (*b. Louisa, Ky., 1890; d. Washington, D.C., 1953*), lawyer, politician. Studied at Kentucky Normal College and Centre College in Danville, Ky., LL.B., 1911. As Democratic member of Congress, 1924–29 and 1931–38, Vinson was an expert on federal taxation and a New Deal "regular" who supported Roosevelt's major policies. Member of the House Ways and Means Committee. Associate justice of the U.S. Circuit Court of Appeals for the District of Columbia, 1938–43. Director of the Office of Economic Stabilization, 1943–45. As secretary of the treasury, 1945–46, oversaw the negotiations of the British loan and lend-lease settlements; supervised the beginnings of the International Bank for Reconstruction and Development and the International Monetary Fund.

Chief justice of the U.S. Supreme Court, 1946–53. Three major themes characterized Vinson's judicial career: a reliance on precedent and a refusal to "make law" where precedent was unclear; deference to the government when the issue of government power was in question; and a corollary tendency to justify alleged governmental infringements of individuals' civil liberties.

Vinson's three opinions on race relations all spoke for a unanimous court. Upheld governmental power over individual claims in more than 80 percent of civil liberties cases involving state governments and more than 90 percent involving the federal government. In two major cases involving the rights of American Communists to proselytize, Vinson upheld government encroachments on free speech, supporting the Taft-Hartley Act's anticommunist affadavit requirements and the Smith Act's anti-free-speech provisions. Vinson enthusiastically supported presidential authority to intervene in the economy and upheld presidential power to seize industry in alleged emergencies. In 1953, he voted with the majority against a stay of execution for the Rosenbergs in an extraordinary special session.

Vinson's approach as chief justice was to avoid public controversy, to seek a low profile, and to minimize the Supreme Court's role as a policy-making and power body. He proved to be neither the intellectual nor the social leader of the Court, and did not in any major sense control its direction.

VINTON, ALEXANDER HAMILTON (*b. Providence, R.I., 1807, d. Philadelphia, Pa., 1881*), Episcopal clergyman, physician. Brother of Francis Vinton. M.D., Yale, 1828. A rector in Boston, Philadelphia, and New York, he was prominent in the evangelical group of his church and ranked among its leading preachers.

VINTON, FRANCIS (*b. Providence, R.I., 1809; d. Brooklyn, N.Y., 1872*), soldier, Episcopal clergyman. Brother of Alexander H. Vinton. Graduated West Point, 1830. Resigning from the army, 1836, he was ordained deacon, 1838, and advanced to priest, 1839. An ardent evangelical and a fluent preacher, he ministered with zeal and success in several Rhode Island parishes and also in Brooklyn, N.Y., and at Trinity Church, New York City. He was professor of canon law in the General Theological Seminary, New York, 1869–72.

VINTON, FRANCIS LAURENS (*b. Fort Preble, Portland Harbor, Maine, 1835; d. Leadville, Colo., 1879*), Union soldier, mining engineer. Nephew of Alexander H. and Francis Vinton. Graduated West Point, 1856; studied at École des Mines, Paris, France, 1856–60. Rising to brigade command in the Civil War, he received disabling wounds in the battle of Fredericksburg. First professor of civil and mining engineering at Columbia School of Mines, 1864–77, he was thereafter a consulting engineer in Colorado.

VINTON, FREDERIC (*b. Boston, Mass., 1817; d. 1890*), librarian. Graduated Amherst, 1837. As assistant librarian, Boston Public Library, 1856–65, he aided in preparation of its printed catalogues; as first assistant librarian, Library of Congress, 1865–73, he continued his specialization in catalogue work. First full-time librarian of the College of New Jersey (Princeton), 1873–90, he produced for it a subject catalogue in 1884 which was considered one of the most scholarly and useful publications of the sort up to that time. He was one of the founders of the American Library Association, 1876.

VINTON, FREDERIC PORTER (*b. Bangor, Maine, 1846; d. Boston, Mass., 1911*), portrait painter. Encouraged by William M. Hunt. Studied drawing at Lowell Institute; studied also in Paris under Léon Bonnat and J. P. Laurens. Practiced his art with great success in Boston *post* 1878, specializing in portraits of men.

VINTON, SAMUEL FINLEY (*b. South Hadley, Mass., 1792; d. Washington, D.C., 1862*), lawyer. Began practice in Gallipolis, Ohio, *ca.* 1816. Congressman, National Republican and Whig, from Ohio, 1823–37, 1843–51, he was at various times a member of committees on public lands, roads, canals, and the judiciary; he was chairman of the ways and means committee during the war with Mexico. Vinton was especially interested in the survey and sale of public lands so as to prevent speculation; also in internal improvements, in the imposition of a protective tariff and the proper apportionment of representatives. He opposed the annexation of Texas and any direct tax for prosecution of the war with Mexico. He reported out the bill providing for establishment of the U.S. Department of the Interior, February 1849.

VISSCHER, WILLIAM LIGHTFOOT (*b. Owingsville, Ky., 1842; d. Chicago, Ill., 1924*), journalist, actor. Starting in journalism as secretary to George D. Prentice, he served, 1875–95, as editorial writer for some of the most important Western newspapers and was author of much journalistic verse.

VITALE, FERRUCCIO (*b. Florence, Italy, 1875; d. 1933*), landscape architect. Came first to America as military attaché to the Italian embassy, 1898. After resignation from the army and study of landscape architecture, he practiced that profession in New York City *post* 1904. Designer of many private estates, towns, and suburbs, he worked to strengthen the position of his profession as one of the fine arts.

VIZCAÍNO, SEBASTIÁN (*b. Spain, ca. 1550; d. ca. 1628*), merchant, explorer. Went to Mexico *ca.* 1585. Engaged in the China trade, he lost a good part of his fortune when the galleon *Santa Ana* was destroyed off Lower California, 1587. Commissioned by the viceroy of New Spain, he sailed from Acapulco in June 1596 for an exploration of the Gulf of California. This expedition was fruitless, but a voyage undertaken in 1602 to explore the outer

coast of California as far as Cape Mendocino was more successful. Leaving Acapulco on May 5, 1602, Vizcaíno explored the coast of Lower California and reached San Diego Bay in November; in mid-December he discovered Monterey Bay. He reached Cape Mendocino on Jan. 12, 1603, missing San Francisco Bay in the bad weather. Returning southward he arrived at Mazatlán, Feb. 18, 1603. This expedition, the first to make a scientific exploration of the west coast, furnished the first maps of that coast and did much to explode the myth of the Northwest Passage.

VIZETELLY, FRANK HORACE (*b. London, England, 1864; d. New York, N.Y., 1938*), lexicographer, etymologist. Member of a family which had been engaged in the printing trades and journalism in England ever since 1725, he came to New York City, 1891, and was associated with the staff of Funk & Wagnalls thereafter until his death. His principal work was done on the various editions of the *Standard Dictionary of the English Language*. He was author also of a column in the *Literary Digest*, which dealt with the complications of grammar, usage, and word derivations, and provided the material for nearly a dozen books on these subjects.

VLADECK, BARUCH CHARNEY (*b. near Minsk, Russia, 1886; d. New York, N.Y., 1938*), Socialist and Jewish leader. Coming to America, 1908, he undertook lecture tours for three years and became manager of the Philadelphia edition of the New York *Jewish Daily Forward* in 1912. A leader in the American Socialist party, he became the *Forward's* city editor, 1916, and moved to New York. An opponent of the Communist wing of the Socialist party *post* 1919, he was associated in party affairs with Louis Waldman. Appointed a member of the New York City Housing Authority, 1934, he began, after election to the city council, one of the first municipal slum-clearance projects in the United States. Vladeck's career is interesting as an example of the transformations wrought by American institutions on a European-shaped radicalism.

VLADIMIROFF, PIERRE (*b. St. Petersburg, Russia, 1893; d. New York, N.Y., 1970*), ballet dancer. Graduated from Imperial School of Ballet in St. Petersburg (1911). In 1912 joined Sergei Diaghilev's Ballets Russes for its tour of western Europe. As premier danseur at the Maryinsky Theater (from 1915) he created roles in Fokine's *Francesca da Rimini* and *Eros*. His repertoire also include *Paquita, Raymonda*, and *Giselle*. Escaped from Russia in 1920 and joined Diaghilev's company in 1921 but left the following year. Joined Anna Pavlova's company in 1928 and danced as her partner. After her death in 1931 he stopped performing. Taught at the School of American Ballet in New York City (1934–67), providing a link to the Russian tradition of pure classical dance.

VOGRICH, MAX WILHELM KARL (*b. Hermannstadt, Transylvania, 1852; d. New York, N.Y., 1916*), pianist, composer. Came to America, 1878. Toured the country as accompanist to August Wilhelmj and was also associated with Eduard Reményi. A resident in New York, 1886–1902 and 1914–16, he composed much music in various forms and was an adviser to the publishing firm of G. Schirmer.

VOLCK, ADALBERT JOHN (*b. Augsburg, Bavaria, 1828; d. Baltimore, Md., 1912*), dentist, caricaturist. Immigrated to America, 1849. A graduate of the Baltimore College of Dental Surgery, 1852, he practiced with success in Baltimore, but is principally remembered as author of a series of caricatures favorable to the South under the pseudonym "V. Blada." The most important collection of his work is *Confederate War Etchings* (n.d.) and *Sketches from the Civil War in North America* (1863, bearing a possibly false London imprint).

VOLK, LEONARD WELLS (*b. Wellstown, present Wells, N.Y., 1828; d. Osceola, Wis., 1895*), sculptor. Removed to St. Louis, Mo., 1848, where he taught himself drawing and modeling. Aided by Stephen A. Douglas, he studied in Rome, Italy, 1855–57, and thereafter practiced his art in Chicago, Ill. He organized the first art exhibition held there (1859) and was a founder of the Chicago Academy of Design, 1867. He produced the colossal Douglas monument at Chicago, statues of Lincoln and Douglas in the Illinois State Capitol, and other portraits of Lincoln which are valuable historic mementos. His talent lay in faithful portraiture.

VOLSTEAD, ANDREW JOHN (*b. near Kenyon, Minn., 1860; d. Granite Falls, Minn., 1947*), lawyer. Attended St. Olaf College; graduated Decorah (Iowa) Institute, 1881; admitted to Minnesota bar, 1884. Congressman, Republican, from Minnesota's 7th District, 1903–23. As chairman of the House Judiciary Committee, 1919, he personally drafted the Volstead Act to enforce the 18th Amendment and became for most Americans the personification of prohibition. In fact his legislative record was on the whole progressive; he was especially proud of his authorship of the Capper-Volstead Act (1922) which exempted farmers' cooperatives from the antitrust laws. Opposed to big business, big labor, and every kind of monopoly, he supported woman's suffrage, a federal antilynching law, and other liberal measures.

VON HOLST, HERMANN EDUARD. *See* HOLST, HERMANN EDUARD VON.

VON KÁRMÁN, THEODORE. *See* KÁRMÁN, THEODORE (TODOR) VON.

VON MOSCHZISKER, ROBERT (*b. Philadelphia, Pa., 1870; d. Philadelphia, 1939*), jurist. Admitted to the Philadelphia bar, 1896, he won reputation as an assistant district attorney, and as judge of the court of common pleas in Philadelphia Co., 1903–09. Elected an associate justice of the Pennsylvania supreme court, 1909, he became chief justice in 1921 and resigned in 1930.

VON NEUMANN, JOHN (*b. Budapest, Hungary, 1903; d. Princeton, N.J., 1957*), mathematician, physicist, economist. Studied at the University of Berlin; the Technische Hochschule in Zurich, Ph.D., 1926; and the University of Budapest, Ph.D., 1926. Immigrated to the U.S. in 1930; taught at Princeton University, 1930–33; member of the Institute for Advanced Study, 1933–57. Began to study and work on atomic weapons in 1940; advisor to the U.S. Department of Defense and chairman of the nuclear weapons committee of the U.S. Air Force. Worked at Los Alamos (1943–45), where his ideas of using converging shock waves to detonate the nuclear explosive proved decisive. Made important contributions to the advancement of computers. Member of the U.S. Atomic Energy Commission, 1954–57. A founder of econometrics.

VONNOH, ROBERT WILLIAM (*b. Hartford, Conn., 1858; d. Nice, France, 1933*), portrait and landscape painter. An able and conscientious craftsman, he was a teacher, among others, of W. J. Glackens and Maxfield Parrish.

VON RUCK, KARL (*b. Constantinople, Turkey, 1849; d. 1922*), physician. M.D., University of Tübingen, 1877; M.D., University of Michigan, 1879. After practice at Norwalk, Ohio, he began a specialization in tuberculosis and founded the Winyah Sanitorium, Asheville, N.C., 1888. By long laboratory research and clinical application, he produced (1912) an anti-tuberculosis vaccine which was widely used in treatment of the disease, although designed primarily for the protective immunization of those exposed to tuberculous infection. Though he was in con-

stant controversy with his fellow-workers in the field, his work and many of his ideas have received general acceptance.

VON STERNBERG, JOSEF (*b. Vienna, Austria-Hungary, 1894; d. Los Angeles, Calif., 1969*), motion-picture director. Came to the United States in 1901 and settled with his parents in New York City. After World War I, worked as a cutter, editor, title writer, and assistant director in New Jersey, New York, Austria, and England before moving to Hollywood in 1923. In 1924 he wrote, produced, and directed *The Salvation Hunters*, chosen by one critic as one of the ten best films of the year. During 1927–35 directed fourteen films for Paramount—including *The Last Command* (1928), starring the eminent German actor Emil Jannings. At Jannings' behest, a German production company with ties to Paramount engaged von Sternberg to film *The Blue Angel* (1930), his most famous film and the first of seven pictures in which he established Marlene Dietrich as the screen's ultimate *femme fatale*. After leaving Paramount in 1935, he made a few films and spent most of the 1950's and 1960's teaching and appearing at retrospectives of his work around the world.

VON STROHEIM, ERICH (*b. Vienna, Austria, 1885; d. Maurepas, Seine-et-Oise, France, 1957*), film director, actor. Studied at the Mariahilfe Military Academy. Immigrated to the U.S. in 1909. An extra in D. W. Griffith's *The Birth of a Nation*; became an assistant to director John Emerson and also acted in Griffith's *Intolerance* and *Hearts of the World*. Directed, wrote, and appeared in *Blind Husbands* (1918). Directed and acted in *Foolish Wives* (1922), his first lavish spectacle. *Greed* (1924), released in a truncated version, was a failure but is now considered his finest work. Other films include *The Wedding March* (1928) and *Queen Kelly*. Von Stroheim failed to make the transition as a director from silent to sound films. He returned to acting, most notably in *Great Gabbo* (1929), in Jean Renoir's *Grand Illusion* (1938), in which he gave an unforgettable performance as a disabled German soldier. Often cast as the quintessential German or Prussian officer, he played Rommel in *Five Graves to Cairo* in 1943. His greatest performance was in *Sunset Boulevard* (1950), in which he played opposite Gloria Swanson as her ex-director who was now her butler.

Remembered for his realism and frank treatment of sex, Von Stroheim broke much important ground for the art of cinema. His films were poetic and had a touch of surrealism that prompted director Sergei Eisenstein to cite him as "The Director."

VON TEUFFEL, BLANCHE WILLIS HOWARD. *See* HOWARD, BLANCHE WILLIS.

VON WIEGAND, KARL HENRY (*b. Hesse, Germany, 1874; d. Zurich, Switzerland, 1961*), foreign correspondent. Immigrated with his family to Iowa when he was a year old. Began journalistic career in 1899 in Arizona, thereafter moving to California, where he covered the 1906 San Francisco earthquake. After he began working in Europe for United Press (1911), except for brief visits, he never lived in the United States again. World War I made his by-line famous. Moved to the Pulitzers' *New York World* in 1915 and thence in 1917 to the Hearst newspapers where he became chief foreign correspondent, retaining the title until his death. He never wrote a book and his reputation has proved to be quite evanescent.

VOORHEES, DANIEL WOLSEY (*b. Butler Co., Ohio, 1827; d. Washington, D.C., 1897*), lawyer. Raised in Indiana, he settled in practice at Terre Haute, 1857. Opposed equally to abolition and secession, he served as congressman, Democrat, from Indiana, 1861–66, and was a virulent critic of administration policies. After a second term in the House of Representatives, 1869–73, he was U.S. senator from Indiana, 1877–97. At first a typical

Democrat of his era in his ideas, he became less strictly agrarian and supported President Grover Cleveland in the various questions that divided the Democrat party during Cleveland's terms. As chairman of the committee on finance, he led the fight for repeal of the Sherman silver purchase act, 1893. He was unrivaled as a stump speaker.

VOORHEES, EDWARD BURNETT (*b. Minebrook, N.J., 1856; d. 1911*), agriculturist. Graduated Rutgers, 1881. Assistant chemist of the New Jersey State Experiment Station, 1883–88, at which time he became chief chemist. Professor of agriculture at Rutgers, 1890–1911. Director, New Jersey Experiment Station *post* 1893. Founded short agricultural courses for working farmers. Author of *Fertilizers* (1898) and many other works.

VOORHEES, PHILIP FALKERSON (*b. New Brunswick, N.J., 1792; d. Annapolis, Md., 1862*), naval officer. Appointed midshipman, 1809. While commanding frigate *Congress* September 1844, as reprisal for Argentine attacks on an American brig, he captured the entire Argentine squadron which was blockading Montevideo. Court-martialed for his action, June 1845, he was at first suspended from duty, but was reinstated by President Polk in 1849.

VOORSANGER, JACOB (*b. Amsterdam, the Netherlands, 1852; d. San Francisco, Calif., 1908*), rabbi. Came to America, 1873. After occupying several pulpits in the East and in Texas, he served at Temple Emanu-El, San Francisco, *post* 1886. He was professor of Semitic languages and literature, University of California *post* 1894. A moderate member of the reform school of Judaism, he was a gifted journalist and in time was considered the foremost rabbi on the Pacific Coast. He was chairman of relief during the San Francisco earthquake and fire of 1906.

VOPICKA, CHARLES JOSEPH (*b. Dolni Hbity (Bohemia), Austria-Hungary, 1857; d. Chicago, Ill., 1935*), brewer, diplomat. A leader among the Czechs in Chicago, he was active in civic matters there. He served as U.S. minister to Romania, Serbia, and Bulgaria, 1913–20, representing the interests of many of the warring nations as well as those of the United States, and strongly concerning himself with the welfare of prisoners of war.

VORIS, JOHN RALPH (*b. Franklin, Ind., 1880; d. Duarte, Calif., 1968*), minister and social reformer. Received B.D. from the University of Chicago's School of Divinity (1906). Exchanged pastoral for social work after responding to an urgent request to administer programs for army recruits during World War I. During and after the war he served as general secretary of the YMCA, as director of the Inter-church World Movement, and as an officer for the Near East Relief Program. He co-founded the Save the Children Foundation in 1932, guiding it until his retirement in 1952. Thereafter, he formed Seniors in Philanthropic Service. Honored by British and French foreign governments for his international relief work.

VORSE, MARY HEATON (*b. New York, N.Y., 1874; d. Provincetown, Mass., 1966*), author, journalist, labor activist. A prolific writer for popular magazines, she specialized in sketches of family life. Although she published several books of fiction in addition to her magazine work, she is chiefly remembered for her work on behalf of organized labor. Her reporting of labor's crucial struggles, as well as books like *Men and Steel* (1920) and *Labor's New Millions* (1938), helped make organized labor and the right to strike part of American life. Her last major article, on union corruption on the New York City waterfront, appeared in *Harper's* in 1952. In addition, she helped found the Provincetown Players, which revitalized the American theater in the early twentieth century.

VOSE, GEORGE LEONARD (*b. Augusta, Maine, 1831; d. Brunswick, Maine, 1910*), engineer, specialist in railroads. Professor of civil engineering, Bowdoin, 1872–81; Massachusetts Institute of Technology, 1881–86. Author of *Handbook of Railroad Construction* (1857), *Manual for Railroad Engineers and Engineering Students* (1873), and a number of other useful works.

VOUGHT, CHANCE MILTON (*b. New York, N.Y., 1890; d. Southampton, N.Y., 1930*), aircraft designer and manufacturer. Studied engineering at Pratt Institute, New York University and University of Pennsylvania. Learned to fly *ca.* 1910 under instruction of the Wright brothers. Designed and built an advanced training plane for the British in World War I, 1914. As chief engineer of the Wright Company, he produced the Model V military biplane, 1916. Forming his own company, 1917, he made it in very short time an outstanding factor in the aircraft industry, developing new designs practically alone and directing their realization in the shop. Among his designs were the Vought VE-7 (1919), the Vought UO-1 (1922–25) and the Vought O2U Corsair. Vought worked above all for tactical flexibility in naval aircraft and maintained unsurpassed standards of workmanship. He merged his firm in the United Aircraft & Transport Corp., 1929, but continued to head the Chance Vought unit until his death.

VROOM, PETER DUMONT (*b. Somerset Co., N.J., 1791; d. Trenton, N.J., 1873*), lawyer, New Jersey legislator. Graduated Columbia, 1808. Democratic governor and chancellor of New Jersey, 1829–32, 1833–36; congressman, 1839–41. U.S. minister to Prussia, 1854–57. An opponent of secession, he was a member of the futile peace conference which met at Washington, February 1861. He was reporter of the New Jersey supreme court, 1865–73.

W

WABASHA (*b. probably near present Winona, Minn., ca. 1773; d. ca. 1855*), Mdewakanton Sioux chief. First prominent through conferences with Zebulon M. Pike on upper Mississippi, 1805; was conspicuous at council at Prairie du Chien, August 1825; supported Americans during Black Hawk War, 1832. A wise, honorable, and prudent chief, Wabasha won general respect and was a skillful orator.

WACHSMUTH, CHARLES (*b. Hanover, Germany, 1829; d. probably Burlington, Iowa, 1896*), paleontologist. Came to America, 1852; settled in Burlington, Iowa, *ca.* 1854. Prospering in the grocery business, he retired in 1865 and devoted his time to collecting and studying fossils. After a brief period of work with Louis Agassiz in Cambridge, Mass., he returned to Burlington and worked in a general partnership with Frank Springer *post* 1873. Attempting a personal critical examination of all the collections of crinoids throughout the world, Wachsmuth and Springer continued work until the former's death when it was carried on alone by Springer. They were authors of *North American Crinoidea Camerata* (1897) and a number of other memoirs.

WACKER, CHARLES HENRY (*b. Chicago, Ill., 1856; d. 1929*), brewer, real estate operator, city planner. Chairman of the Chicago Plan Commission, 1909–26, he was a principal factor in the improvement and beautification of that city.

WADDEL, JAMES (*b. Newry, Ireland, 1739; d. near Gordonsville, Va., 1805*), Presbyterian clergyman. Immigrated to southeast Pennsylvania as an infant; was educated in Samuel Finley's "Log College." Pastor in Northumberland and Lancaster counties, Va., 1762–77; pastor of congregations at Tinkling Spring and Staunton, Va., 1777–85. Established a number of churches in Orange, Louisa, and Albemarle counties.

WADDEL, JOHN NEWTON (*b. Willington, S.C., 1812; d. Birmingham, Ala., 1895*), Presbyterian clergyman, educator. Son of Moses Waddel. Graduated present University of Georgia, 1829. Removed to Alabama, 1837, and thence to Mississippi where he established Montrose Academy, 1842, and took a leading part in founding University of Mississippi at Oxford. A teacher at the University of Mississippi and pastor, 1848–57, he served as teacher and president at the Presbyterian College, La Grange, Tenn., until the Civil War when he became a chaplain in the Confederate Army. A leader in organization of the Southern Presbyterian Church, 1861, he held numerous high official positions in that church. Chancellor of University of Mississippi, 1865–74; of Southwestern Presbyterian University, 1879–88.

WADDEL, MOSES (*b. present Iredell Co., N.C., 1770; d. Athens, Ga., 1840*), Presbyterian clergyman, teacher. Father of John N. Waddel. Educated by James Hall; graduated Hampden-Sydney, 1791. Conducted schools in Columbia Co., Ga., and Willington, S.C., where he educated among others John C. Calhoun, William H. Crawford, Hugh S. Legaré, George

McDuffie, A. B. Longstreet, and James L. Petigru. President of Franklin College (present University of Georgia), 1819–29.

WADDELL, ALFRED MOORE (*b. Hillsboro, N.C., 1834; d. 1912*), lawyer, Confederate soldier. A moderate conservative and an opponent of post–Civil War sectionalism as congressman, Democrat, from North Carolina, 1871–79. He was a leading citizen of Wilmington, N.C., and its mayor, 1899–1905.

WADDELL, HUGH (*b. Lisburn, Ireland, ca. 1734; d. 1773*), North Carolina colonial soldier and legislator. Immigrated to North Carolina, 1754, where he became clerk of the council of Governor Arthur Dobbs. Built and commanded at Fort Dobbs on the Rowan County frontier, 1755–57; served as major commanding three companies in the expedition of John Forbes against Fort Dunquesne, 1758; defended Fort Dobbs against Indian attacks, 1760. A principal leader in the colony's defiance of the Stamp Act, he yet remained on good terms with Governor Tryon and helped pacify the back country during the Regulator troubles, 1771.

WADDELL, JAMES IREDELL (*b. Pittsboro, N.C., 1824; d. Annapolis, Md., 1886*), Confederate naval officer. Great-grandson of Hugh Waddell. Appointed midshipman, 1841, he served with credit during the Mexican War and in routine naval duties until 1862 when he resigned and was commissioned lieutenant in the Confederate Navy. After shore service, 1862–March 1863, he went to Paris, and in October 1864 took command at the Madeira Islands of the Confederate raider *Shenandoah*. Thereafter, until he learned in August 1865 of the Confederate defeat, he made havoc among the New England whaling ships in the Pacific. Fearing treatment as a pirate, he surrendered the *Shenandoah* in Liverpool, England, on November 6, still flying the only Confederate flag that ever sailed round the world.

WADDELL, JOHN ALEXANDER LOW (*b. Port Hope, Ontario, Canada, 1854; d. New York, N.Y., 1938*), civil engineer. Graduated Rensselaer Polytechnic Institute, 1875. After work in Canada as a government draftsman and several years of teaching at Rensselaer, he was professor of civil engineering at the Imperial University of Tokyo, 1882–86. In practice at Kansas City, Mo., 1886–*ca.* 1920, and thereafter in New York City, he became one of the best-known bridge engineers in the United States, and was designer or consultant on many of the major bridge construction operations in his time. His most important contribution was an originator of the modern vertical-lift bridge. Although European developments anticipated his, Waddell independently invented and successfully introduced the large-scale high-clearance vertical-lift bridge, the first of his many structures of this type being the South Halsted Street Bridge, Chicago, Ill., 1893.

WADE, BENJAMIN FRANKLIN (*b. near Springfield, Mass., 1800; d. Jefferson, Ohio, 1878*), lawyer, Ohio legislator, and jurist. Removed to Andover, Ohio, 1821. Admitted to the Ohio bar *ca.* 1827, he attained a successful practice in partnerships with J. R. Giddings and R. P. Ranney. President-judge, third state judicial circuit, 1847–51, he was elected to the U.S. Senate by the Whigs in the Ohio legislature and served, 1851–69. Rough in manner, coarse and vituperative in speech, yet intensely patriotic, he became a leader of the antislavery group in Congress, a close cooperator with Simon Cameron and Zachariah Chandler in resisting Southern aggressions. A Republican *post* 1856, he voted against the Crittenden Compromise and on the outbreak of the Civil War became one of the most belligerent men in Congress. A sharp critic of General George B. McClellan, he was one of those who set up the Committee on the Conduct of the War, and as its chairman made it a violently partisan agency. Working closely with the secretary of war, E. M. Stanton, Wade, like other of the Radical Republicans, seemed incapable of understanding President Lincoln and deplored his cautious conservative policies. He himself favored drastic measures against the South, including confiscation of the property of Confederate leaders and the emancipation of their slaves, nor was he burdened with constitutional scruples. Finding Lincoln's policy of Reconstruction (announced in December 1863) particularly obnoxious, he and Henry W. Davis tried to counteract it by the so-called Wade-Davis bill; on its veto by the president in July 1864 they issued the fierce claim of congressional supremacy known as the Wade-Davis Manifesto. Previous to this, Wade had joined with others in planning to replace Lincoln with Salmon P. Chase, yet he supported Lincoln in the closing weeks of the campaign of 1864. At first believing that he and his group could bend President Andrew Johnson to support of their measures, Wade later turned on him and his policies. *Post* December 1865, along with Charles Summer, Thaddeus Stevens, and others, he waged a persistent campaign against Johnson and seemed ready to resort to any extremity in order to carry through the congressional program. Chosen president *pro tempore* of the Senate, March 2, 1867, he would, according to the custom of that time, have succeeded to the presidency in the event of Johnson's removal. In the ensuing impeachment of Johnson, Wade voted for the president's conviction, despite the fact that he was an interested party. He was so expectant of success that he began the selection of his cabinet before the impeachment trial was ended. Thwarted by Johnson's acquittal and failing of reelection to the Senate, Wade resumed the practice of law in Ohio.

WADE, DECIUS SPEAR (*b. near Andover, Ohio, 1835; d. near Andover, 1905*), lawyer. Nephew of Benjamin F. Wade. As chief justice of Montana, 1871–87, he shared in the formulation of the mining and irrigation law of that state and was a member of the commission which drafted the state code adopted by the legislature in 1895.

WADE, JEPTHA HOMER (*b. Romulus, N.Y., 1811; d. 1890*), portrait painter, financier. Organized and built a number of Midwest telegraph lines *post* 1847 which were consolidated with those of Royal E. House, 1854. After a further combination into the Western Union Telegraph Co., 1856, Wade served the new company as general agent, and was president, 1866–67. He was organizer also of the California State Telegraph Co. and the Pacific Telegraph Co. *Post* 1867 he engaged in varied businesses in Cleveland, Ohio.

WADE, JEPTHA HOMER (*b. Cleveland, Ohio, 1857; d. Thomasville, Ga., 1926*), financier, philanthropist. Grandson of Jeptha H. Wade (1811–1890). An incorporator of the Cleveland Museum of Art, 1913, he was its president *post* 1920, and also one of its most liberal benefactors. He was a large contributor to many charities.

WADE, MARTIN JOSEPH (*b. Burlington, Vt., 1861; d. Los Angeles, Calif., 1931*), Iowa jurist and Democratic congressman. LL.B., University of Iowa, 1886; taught law there. Justice of the

state district court, 1893–1902; U.S. district judge, southern district of Iowa, 1915–27.

WADSWORTH, ELIOT (*b. Boston, Mass., 1876; d. Washington, D.C., 1959*), financier, philanthropist, and government official. Studied at Harvard (B.A., 1898). Combined a lifelong connection with the Red Cross and government activity. Vice-chairman of the War Council during World War I, assistant secretary of the Treasury (1921–26); Loyalty Review Board, Civil Service Commission (1950–53). Member of the Harvard Board of Overseers for twelve years, becoming president in 1929.

WADSWORTH, JAMES (*b. Durham, Conn., 1768; d. Geneseo, N.Y., 1844*), landowner, community builder. Graduated Yale, 1787. As agent with his brother for the Phelps-Gorham Purchase in western New York State, James Wadsworth removed to the neighborhood of the Genesee River, 1790, and settled near the present town of Geneseo. Acquiring large quantities of land and prospering both as land agents and agriculturists, the Wadsworths had unequaled influence in the development of the Genesee country. Except for business, James Wadsworth's chief interest was in public education.

WADSWORTH, JAMES SAMUEL (*b. Geneseo, N.Y., 1807; d. Virginia, 1864*), lawyer, landowner. Son of James Wadsworth. Volunteering as an aide to General Irvin McDowell, 1861, he was commissioned brigadier general of volunteers in August. After two years spent in gaining experience in handling and training men, he took command of the 1st Division, I Corps, December 1862. Highly effective in the Union victory of Gettysburg, Wadsworth was appointed commander of the 4th Division of the V Corps, 1864. He died of wounds received on the second day of the battle of the Wilderness.

WADSWORTH, JAMES WOLCOTT, JR. (*b. Geneseo, N.Y., 1877; d. Washington, D.C., 1952*), politician and farmer. Dominant force in New York State Republican politics for 25 years. Graduated Yale University (1898). Served New York State Assembly (1904–10); U.S. Senate (1914–26). Chairman, Senate Military Affairs Committee; author of National Defense Act of 1920. Lost senate seat to Robert F. Wagner because of anti-Prohibitionist stand. Elected to House of Representatives (1933–51). Ardent opponent of New Deal. Principal architect of National Selective Service Act of 1940. As a member of the House Rules Committee, was a mainstay of the coalition of southern Democrats and Republicans that blocked much of Truman's Fair Deal legislation.

WADSWORTH, JEREMIAH (*b. Hartford, Conn., 1743; d. Hartford, 1804*), merchant mariner, Connecticut legislator, Revolutionary soldier. Grandson of Joseph Talcott. Outstanding as commissary general, at first to the Connecticut forces, and then to the Continental Army, 1778–79, Wadsworth served briefly as a Federalist in Congress where he was a strong advocate of assumption. A man of varied business interests, he was a founder of the Bank of North America, a director of the U.S. Bank, and president of the Bank of New York.

WADSWORTH, PELEG (*b. Duxbury, Mass., 1748; d. Hiram, Maine, 1829*), schoolmaster, farmer, trader, Revolutionary general. Grandfather of Henry Wadsworth Longfellow and Samuel Longfellow. Graduated Harvard, 1769. As engineer officer, 1775, he laid out the American lines at Roxbury and Dorchester Heights during siege of Boston. Briefly aide to Artemas Ward, he then saw service at New York and in 1778 in Rhode Island. He was second-in-command of the ill-fated American attack on Castine, Maine, 1779. Removing to present Portland, Maine, *ca.* 1782, he was a congressman from that district, 1793–1807.

WAESCHE, RUSSELL RANDOLPH (*b. Thurmont, Md., 1886; d. Bethesda, Md., 1946*), Coast Guard officer. Attended Purdue University; graduated U.S. Revenue Cutter Service cadet school (forerunner of U.S. Coast Guard Academy), 1906. After formation of U.S. Coast Guard, 1915, he served in a number of line and staff capacities, at sea and on land, before his appointment as commandant in 1936 with rank of rear admiral. As commandant, he streamlined the administration of the service, upgraded its educational facilities, and presided over its expansion during World War II to a multi-purpose force of more than 171,000 men and women. He was promoted to admiral in 1945.

WAGENER, JOHN ANDREAS (*b. Sievern, Hanover, Germany, 1816; d. Walhalla, Oconee Co., S.C.,1876*), businessman, South Carolina legislator, Charleston civic leader. Settled in Charleston S.C., 1833, where he led in movements for the economic and social improvement of German immigrants to that state.

WAGGAMAN, MARY TERESA MCKEE (*b. Baltimore, Md., 1846; d. 1931*), writer of fiction, principally for Catholic magazines.

WAGNER, CLINTON (*b. Baltimore, Md., 1837; d. Geneva, Switzerland, 1914*), laryngologist. M.D., University of Maryland, 1859. An outstanding medical officer in the U.S. Army, 1859–69, he was cited for notable services at Gettysburg where he established a field hospital near Little Round Top. Practicing his speciality in New York City *post* 1871, he became known as a surgeon of extraordinary technical skill and a brilliant teacher; he established the Metropolitan Throat Hospital, the first U.S. special hospital of its kind, and was founder of the New York Laryngological Society, 1873. First professor of laryngology at New York Post-Graduate Medical School, he was author of a number of studies, including the pioneer *Habitual Mouth-Breathing* (1881).

WAGNER, JOHN PETER ("HONUS") (*b. Mansfield (now Carnegie), Pa., 1874; d. Carnegie, Pa., 1955*), baseball player. Played for the Pittsburgh Pirates from 1900 to 1917; coach from 1933 to 1951. Beginning in 1897, Wagner hit .300 or better in seventeen consecutive seasons; led the National League in hitting in 1900, 1903, 1904, 1906–09, and 1911, a record that still stands. A shortstop, Wagner was elected as one of the first members of the National Baseball Hall of Fame in 1936. One of the greatest players of all time, he was also one of the most popular.

WAGNER, ROBERT FERDINAND (*b. Nastätten, Germany, 1877; d. New York, N.Y., 1953*), politician. Immigrated to the U.S., 1896. After studying at the City College of New York (1898) and New York Law School (1900), Wagner became a Tammany politician. He served ably in the New York State Assembly and Senate, championing safety standards in industry, child labor statutes, and the minimum wage. Elected to the First District Supreme Court in 1918, and to the U.S. Senate as a Democrat (1926–53).

As a senator, Wagner was a leader in social legislation and a strong backer of Franklin D. Roosevelt and the New Deal. He sponsored and had a major role in drafting the National Industrial Recovery Act, Social Security legislation, the Railroad Retirement Act, and bills for unemployment insurance, low-cost public housing, and federal health programs. In 1935, the "Wagner Act"—the National Labor Relations Act which created the National Labor Relations Board (NLRB)—had a profound impact on the nation's working classes. He supported the formation and recognition of the State of Israel in 1948; his last major legislative achievement was the Public Housing Act of 1949.

WAGNER, WEBSTER (*b. Palatine Bridge, N.Y., 1817; d. Spuyten Duyvil, N.Y., 1882*), carpenter, New York Republican legislator. Designed and operated sleeping-cars and drawing-room cars for operation on the New York Central Railroad *post* 1858; was involved for years in litigation with G. M. Pullman.

WAGNER, WILLIAM (*b. Philadelphia, Pa., 1796; d. Philadelphia, 1885*), merchant, philanthropist. Apprenticed to Stephen Girard; engaged in business on his own account, 1818. Retiring, 1840, he devoted himself to studies in geology and mineralogy and founded the Wagner Free Institute of Science, 1855.

WAHL, WILLIAM HENRY (*b. Philadelphia, Pa., 1848; d. 1909*), scientific journalist, metallurgist. Graduated Dickinson College, 1867; Ph.D., Heidelberg, 1869. Principally distinguished as secretary of the Franklin Institute and as editor *post* 1882 of its *Journal*. The most important of his contributions to science was his discovery and application of aluminum as an energetic oxidizing agent for creation of high temperatures in metallurgical operations, the basis of what is known as the "thermit process."

WAIDNER, CHARLES WILLIAM (*b. near Baltimore, Md., 1873; d. 1922*), physicist. A.B., Johns Hopkins, 1896; Ph.D., 1898. Headed the division of heat and thermometry, National Bureau of Standards, *post* 1901; established standard scale of temperature in collaboration with others. Participated anonymously in many of the important activities of his division.

WAILES, BENJAMIN LEONARD COVINGTON (*b. Columbia, Co., Ga., 1797; d. Mississippi, 1862*), surveyor, planter, scientist. Made extensive studies of the plant and animal life and the soil and fossils of Mississippi; supplied information and specimens of the natural history of his region to many individual scientists and to institutions.

WAINWRIGHT, JONATHAN MAYHEW (*b. Walla Walla, Wash., 1883; d. Ft. Sam Houston, Tex., 1953*), military officer. Graduated West Point, 1906. After serving in various posts in the First Cavalry (seeing action in the Philippines) he was sent to France during World War I. Commander of the Philippine Division (1941). Remembered for his valiant leadership during the Japanese invasion, Wainwright was forced to surrender his forces to the Japanese at the battles of Bataan and Corregidor. He was a prisoner of war from 1942 to 1945, when he was rescued by parachutists and brought to Tokyo in time to witness the Japanese surrender on the USS *Missouri*. Promoted to four-star general, Wainwright was given command of the Fourth Army.

WAINWRIGHT, JONATHAN MAYHEW (*b. Liverpool, England, 1792; d. New York, N.Y., 1854*), Episcopal clergyman. Grandson of Jonathan Mayhew. Graduated Harvard, 1812. After his ordination in 1817, he served as minister in Hartford, Conn., and Boston, Mass., but was principally identified with Grace Church and Trinity Parish, New York City. His consecration as bishop of New York, 1852, ended a long controversy in the diocese caused by doctrinal differences and the suspension of Bishop B. T. Onderdonk. A founder of the present New York University, he was active also as a writer and was chief working member of the committee which prepared the standard edition of the *Book of Common Prayer*.

WAINWRIGHT, JONATHAN MAYHEW (*b. New York, N.Y., 1821; d. off Galveston, Tex., 1863*), naval officer. Son of Jonathan M. Wainwright (1792–1854). Appointed midshipman, 1837. After varied sea and shore service, he began duty in the Civil War with the Atlantic Blockading Squadron. Given command (1862) of the *Harriet Lane*, he played a leading role in the reduction of the Confederate forts on the lower Mississippi and the taking of New Orleans. He was killed in action defending his ship against boarders after the recapture of Galveston.

WAINWRIGHT, RICHARD (*b. Charlestown, Mass., 1817; d. Donaldsonville, La., 1862*), naval officer. Appointed midshipman, 1831; served mainly with the U.S. Coast Survey and on ordnance duty until the Civil War. Commanded the USS *Hartford*, flagship of Admiral Farragut, at the taking of New Orleans and later in the passage of the batteries at Vicksburg.

WAINWRIGHT, RICHARD (*b. Washington, D.C., 1849; d. Washington, 1926*), naval officer. Son of Richard Wainwright (1817–1862). Graduated U.S. Naval Academy, 1868. Performed a variety of duties, notably with the hydrographic office, the U.S. Coast Survey, and the bureau of navigation until 1896 when he became chief of intelligence. Appointed executive officer of the USS *Maine*, 1897, he helped in recovery of the bodies and in preliminary examinations of the ship's hull after its sinking in Havana harbor, Feb. 15, 1898. In command of the USS *Gloucester* (formerly J. P. Morgan's yacht *Corsair*), he performed brilliantly in the battle of Santiago Bay, July 3, 1898, attacking and destroying the Spanish ships *Furor* and *Pluton* and helping in the rescue of Admiral Cervera and other of the Spanish seamen. He retired as rear admiral, 1911.

WAIT, SAMUEL (*b. White Creek, N.Y., 1789; d. Wake Forest, N.C., 1867*), Baptist clergyman. Active *post* 1827 in the organization of the Baptists in North Carolina, he raised funds for the Wake Forest Manual Labour Institute and served as its principal *post* 1834. On its becoming Wake Forest College, 1838, Wait was its president until 1846; he was also president of Oxford Female College, 1851–56.

WAIT, WILLIAM (*b. Ephratah, N.Y., 1821; d. Johnstown, N.Y., 1880*), lawyer. Studied law in office of Daniel Cady; was admitted to the New York bar, 1846. Wait is principally remembered for his legal writings, including a number of useful compilations and manuals of procedure. Among his works were *The Law and Practice in Civil Actions* (1865); *A Table of Cases Affirmed, Reversed, or Cited* (1872, one of the earliest manuals for quick search); *The Practice at Law, in Equity, and in Special Proceedings, etc.* (1872–80, a standard authority on New York adjective law); and *A Treatise upon Some of the General Principles of the Law* (1877–79, a topical digest which was in effect a *corpus juris* for students of that day).

WAIT, WILLIAM BELL (*b. Amsterdam, N.Y., 1839; d. 1916*), educator of the blind. Graduated Albany Normal College, 1859. Starting as superintendent of the New York Institution for the Blind in New York City, 1863, he remained in the service of the Institution until his death. A leader in advancing education of the blind to the status of a profession and in the provision of full intellectual development for blind students, Wait was inventor of the New York Point System (a variant of Braille), 1868, and other learning devices.

WAITE, HENRY MATSON (*b. Toledo, Ohio, 1869; d. Washington, D.C., 1944*), civil engineer, public administrator. Grandson of Morrison R. Waite. B.S., Massachusetts Institute of Technology, 1890. Employed in railroad maintenance and supervision, 1890–1909; chief engineer, Clinchfield Coal Corporation, 1909–12; chief engineer of Cincinnati, Ohio, 1912–14; efficient city manager of Dayton, Ohio, 1914–18. After World War I service in Europe, he practiced in New York City until 1927, when he became chief of planning and construction for the Cincinnati Union Terminal. On its completion in 1933, he served for a year as deputy administrator of the federal Public Works Administration; from 1934 to 1937 he directed a regional unemployment survey in Cincinnati. Thereafter until his death,

he combined private practice with a variety of advisory public service appointments.

WAITE, MORRISON REMICK (*b. Lyme, Conn., 1816; d. 1888*), jurist. Graduated Yale, 1837. Admitted to the Ohio bar, 1839, he practiced *post* 1850 at Toledo, becoming a recognized authority in the law of real estate and the status of legal titles. Active in Whig and Republican politics, he was a leader in his locality in support of the Union cause during the Civil War. After serving, 1871–72, with Caleb Cushing and William M. Evarts, as American counsel in the Geneva Arbitration, he became president of the Ohio constitutional convention of 1873. Named and confirmed as chief justice of the United States, January 1874, he immediately assumed a large share of the work of the U.S. Supreme Court and in his 14 years of tenure gave the Court's opinion in more than a thousand cases. He contributed substantially to clarification of Reconstruction legislation and the constitutional amendments arising out of the Civil War. He reaffirmed the doctrine of the Slaughterhouse Cases in *Minor* v. *Happersett*. Upholding the right of a state to deny the vote to women, he held that suffrage was not a privilege of U.S. citizenship and that the Fourteenth Amendment did not add to the privileges and immunities of citizens. In *U.S.* v. *Reese* he demolished the Radical plan of protecting the black by direct federal action, holding sections three and four of the Civil Rights Act of May 31, 1870, unconstitutional. In *U.S.* v. *Cruikshank*, he held that the Fourteenth Amendment did not authorize Congress to legislate affirmatively for the protection of civil rights and did not add to the rights of one citizen against another. In *Munn* v. *Illinois*, he upheld the power of the state to regulate the charges of grain elevators and public warehouses—businesses that were "clothed with a public interest." Here and in other Granger cases the Court upheld state laws fixing maximum rates on all railroads operating within the state, and by its action profoundly affected the course of American social and economic development. The due process clause was narrowly interpreted while the power of the states was necessarily enlarged. However, it was Waite himself who laid the foundation for the modern interpretation of due process as a limitation on state power. He issued a famous dictum in *Stone* v. *Farmers Loan and Trust Co.*: "From what has been said it is not to be inferred that this power . . . of regulation is itself without limits . . . It is not a power to destroy . . . The State cannot do that which . . . amounts to a taking of private property . . . without due process of law." Upon this and other dicta rested the decision of the rate cases in 1890 after Waite's death, which made the Supreme Court the final judge in matters of rates. His interpretation of the contract clause constitutes another major contribution to constitutional development. In various decisions he modified profoundly the decision of the doctrine of vested rights as established in the Dartmouth College Case and indicated his willingness to allow the states to exercise wide regulatory power over corporate enterprises in matters pertaining to the "public interest." He strongly upheld the power of Congress to regulate commerce and broadened the sense of that term to include the transfer of intangibles such as telegraphic communications. He scanned very closely the claims of individuals as against the state, even interpreting the Bill of Rights strictly. A skillful and courteous administrator, Waite possessed a style which was eminently judicial, terse, vigorous, and clear. Among other quotable dicta was his statement that "No legislature can bargain away the public health or the public morals."

WAKELEY, JOSEPH BURTON (*b. Danbury, Conn., 1809; d. New York, N.Y., 1875*), Methodist clergyman. Author, among other contributions to the history of early Methodism, of *Lost Chapters Recovered* (1858) and *The Bold Frontier Preacher* (1869).

WALCOT, CHARLES MELTON (*b. London, England, ca. 1816; d. Philadelphia, Pa., 1868*), actor, dramatist. Father of Charles M. Walcot (1840–1921). Immigrated to Charleston, S.C., *ca.* 1837. Celebrated *ca.* 1840–60 as a light and eccentric comedian and as the author of a number of topical burlesques.

WALCOT, CHARLES MELTON (*b. Boston, Mass., 1840; d. New York, N.Y., 1921*), actor. Son of Charles M. Walcot (*ca.* 1816–1868). Made debut at Charleston, S.C., 1858. Played with companies of Edwin Booth, Laura Keene, and Charlotte Cushman; appeared with his wife *post* 1863 in a number of stock companies, including that of the Walnut Street Threatre, Philadelphia, Pa. They joined the Lyceum Company in New York City, 1887, and remained with it until about the turn of the century.

WALCOTT, CHARLES DOOLITTLE (*b. New York Mills, Oneida Co., N.Y., 1850; d. 1927*), paleontologist. Early interested in the collection of fossils and minerals, Walcott was employed by James Hall (1811–98), the New York State geologist, 1876. He was appointed a field assistant with the U.S. Geological Survey, 1879. Gradually advancing in rank with the Survey, he became chief geologist, 1893, and succeeded John W. Powell as director, 1894. Serving in this post until 1907, he developed and strengthened the Survey along lines already laid down, also taking an active part in the work which led to the establishment of the U.S. Forest Service and the Bureau of Mines. As secretary of the Smithsonian Institution, *post* 1907, he handled its affairs with high executive ability and was influential in founding the Freer Gallery, the Carnegie Institution, the National Research Council, and the National Advisory Committee for Aeronautics. Continuing his field work along with his administrative tasks, he was author of 222 papers of which 110 dealt with the Cambrian formations. Among these works, the most considerable was his *Cambrian Brachiopoda* (1912). The most striking of his field discoveries was that of the Middle Cambrian Burgess shale of British Columbia.

WALCOTT, HENRY PICKERING (*b. Hopkinton, Mass., 1838; d. Cambridge, Mass., 1932*), physician. Graduated Harvard, 1858; M.D., Bowdoin, 1861. After further studies in Vienna and Berlin, he practiced in Cambridge, Mass. Chairman of the Massachusetts State Board of Health, 1886–1915, he widened the Board's influence by giving it advisory power over public water supplies, sewerage, and the protection of the purity of inland waters. He was chairman of the commission which recommended the building of the Charles River Basin, 1893, and planned the metropolitan water supply system of Boston. The most important man in the field of public health in his day, he expressed in his annual reports germinal ideas which have deeply influenced the public health movement in America.

WALD, LILLIAN D. (*b. Cincinnati, Ohio, 1867; d. Westport, Conn., 1940*), public health nurse, settlement house founder. Graduated New York Hospital 1891; studied also at Women's Medical College, New York City. Asked to organize a course of instruction in home nursing for immigrant families on New York's lower East Side, 1893, she soon discovered at first hand the need for reform of conditions under which the immigrants were living. Going to live with an associate in an East Side tenement, she secured financial support from a number of benefactors, notably Jacob H. Schiff, and founded the Nurses' Settlement (*post* 1895 at 265 Henry St.). The settlement house and visiting nurse services which were developed at Henry St. were pioneering innovations. Miss Wald largely originated the concept of public health nursing and the public school nursing system. At her suggestion, several life insurance companies undertook nursing service for their policyholders. Visiting the sick in their homes had revealed many social needs which Wald moved to meet; these included instruc-

tion in cooking and sewing, programs in music and art, and the organization of clubs for boys' and girls' recreation. She was also influential in efforts to obtain better housing, to regulate sweatshops, and to abolish child labor. Declining health caused her to retire as head worker at Henry St., 1933.

WALDEN, JACOB TREADWELL (*b. Walden, N.Y., 1830; d. Boston, Mass., 1918*), Episcopal clergyman, author. A rector at various times in Philadelphia, Pa., Indianapolis, Ind., Boston, Mass., and Minneapolis, Minn., he aided in the liberalizing movement by which the broad church group evolved.

WALDEN, JOHN MORGAN (*b. near Lebanon, Ohio, 1831; d. 1914*), Free-soil journalist in Illinois and Kansas, Methodist clergyman. Active in the Cincinnati Conference, 1858–68; able executive of the Western Methodist Book Concern *post* 1868; elected bishop, 1884. Worked for the improvement of the condition of blacks.

WALDERNE, RICHARD (*b. Alchester, Warwickshire, England, ca. 1615; d. Cochecho, present Dover, N.H., 1689*), pioneer. Immigrated to New England, *ca.* 1640. Settled at present Dover, N.H., where he engaged in lumbering and Indian trade and filled at various times practically all important local offices. Member of the Massachusetts General Court, 1654–74 and 1677; appointed to the president's Council of New Hampshire, 1860. Killed by Indians in reprisal for treacherous seizure of refugee tribesmen and their subsequent sale into slavery.

WALDO, DAVID (*b. Clarksburg, present W.Va., 1802; d. Independence, Mo., 1878*), physician, banker, merchant. Removed to Missouri, 1820, and to Taos in present New Mexico *ante* 1829. Becoming a citizen of Mexico, 1830, he amassed a great fortune in the Santa Fe trade, and served as a captain in the regiment commanded by A. W. Doniphan during the Mexican War. Maker and loser of several fortunes in the overland trade, Waldo later executed provision contracts for the U.S. Army and engaged in banking.

WALDO, SAMUEL (*b. Boston, Mass., 1695; d. near present Bangor, Maine, 1759*), merchant, capitalist, land speculator. Attempted for many years to develop wild lands on the Maine coast between the Muscongus and Penobscot rivers (known *post ca.* 1731 as the Waldo Patent). Served as brigadier general and second-in-command of the Massachusetts forces in the Louisburg campaign of 1745. At first a close friend and associate of William Shirley, he had become a bitter enemy of Shirley by the 1750's.

WALDO, SAMUEL LOVETT (*b. Windham, Conn., 1783; d. New York, N.Y., 1861*), portrait painter. Mainly self-taught, Waldo met with his first success in Charleston, S.C., 1804–06. In England, 1806–09, he settled in New York City on his return, where he worked diligently, *post* 1820 in partnership with William Jewett. The firm produced a great number of excellent if somewhat literal likenesses.

WALDO, SAMUEL PUTNAM (*b. Pomfret, Conn., 1779; d. Hartford, Conn., 1826*), lawyer, miscellaneous writer. Author of a number of biographies of great contemporaries in which his formula was a pound of rhetoric to an ounce of fact. Compiled the very popular *Journal Comprising an Account of the Loss of the Brig Commerce . . . by Archibald Robbins* (1817).

WALDRON, RICHARD. *See* WALDERNE, RICHARD.

WALES, JAMES ALBERT (*b. Clyde, Ohio, 1852; d. 1886*), cartoonist. Trained as a wood engraver, he began to draw political cartoons for the *Cleveland Leader*; removing to New York, N.Y., 1873, he worked, among other papers, for *Frank Leslie's Illustrated Newspaper.* Resident for a short time in London, he became a staff member of *Puck*, 1877, and established his reputation by a series of full-page political portraits entitled "Puck's Pantheon." Less vindictive in satire than Thomas Nast but more of a realist than Joseph Keppler, Wales had a decided gift for portraiture.

WALES, LEONARD EUGENE (*b. Wilmington, Del., 1823; d. Wilmington, 1897*), jurist. Associate justice, Delaware superior court, 1864–84; U.S. judge for the district of Delaware, 1884–97.

WALGREEN, CHARLES RUDOLPH (*b. near Galesburg, Ill., 1873; d. Chicago, Ill., 1939*), pharmacist, drugstore chain founder. Organized C. R. Walgreen & Co. in Chicago, 1909. A leader in modernization of the drugstore, he popularized the lunch counter, open-display merchandising, and attractive decoration in his shops.

WALKE, HENRY (*b. Princess Anne Co., Va., 1808; d. Brooklyn, N.Y., 1896*), naval officer. Raised in Ohio. Appointed midshipman, 1827. Evacuated Union garrison and others from Pensacola Navy Yard, January, 1861, after its seizure by the South. In service with Foote's flotilla on the upper Mississippi, 1861–63, he won high distinction as captain of the *Carondelet* in the actions at Fort Henry and Fort Donelson. His most celebrated exploit was the running of the batteries at Island No. 10, an operation which he alone favored in the preliminary council, volunteered for, and executed successfully on the night of Apr. 4, 1862. He was later conspicuous in engagements with Confederate forces above Fort Pillow and in a running fight with the ram *Arkansas* in the Yazoo River, July 15. Commanding the ironclad *Lafayette*, he shared in the reduction of Vicksburg. He was later active against Confederate raiders in the Atlantic. Promoted rear admiral, 1870, he retired, 1871.

WALKER, ALEXANDER (*b. Fredericksburg, Va., 1818; d. Fort Smith, Ark., 1893*), New Orleans lawyer and journalist. Removed to New Orleans, La., 1840; edited and managed at various times the Democratic *Jeffersonian*, the *Daily Delta*, the *New Orleans Times*, the *Herald*, and the *Daily Picayune*. A firm believer in "manifest destiny," he was one of the supporters of the filibuster William Walker, and backed the expedition of General Narciso Lopez to Cuba, 1851.

WALKER, AMASA (*b. Woodstock, Conn., 1799; d. 1875*), Boston businessman, Massachusetts legislator and congressman, economist. Father of Francis A Walker. Especially interested in the monetary system, he was author of, among other works, *The Nature and Uses of Money and Mixed Currency* (1857) and *The Science of Wealth* (1866).

WALKER, ASA (*b. Portsmouth, N.H., 1845; d. Annapolis, Md., 1916*), naval officer. Graduated U.S. Naval Academy, 1866. An expert navigator, he was author of *Navigation* (1888), long used as a textbook at the Naval Academy. Walker commanded the USS *Concord* under Admiral Dewey at the battle of Manila Bay, winning high commendation. Commissioned rear admiral, 1906, he retired, 1907.

WALKER, MADAME C. J. *See* WALKER, SARAH BREEDLOVE.

WALKER, DAVID (*b. Wilmington, N.C., 1785; d. 1830*), black leader. A free black, Walker traveled widely in the South as a youth, and was established as a clothing dealer in Boston, Mass., *ante* 1827. He is best known as author of *Walker's Appeal* (1829 and later editions) in which he called upon blacks to rise against their oppressors if the slaveholders refused to let their victims go. At the same time he pleaded with the slaveholders to repent of their past actions for fear of God's wrath. A violent reaction to this pamphlet was immediate in the South, and a price was set on the author's head.

WALKER, DAVID (*b. present Todd Co., Ky., 1806; d. 1879*), jurist, Arkansas legislator. Cousin of David S. Walker. Settled in Fayetteville, Ark., *ca.* 1831. Justice, supreme court of Arkansas, 1848–67, 1874–78. Originally opposed secession as president of Arkansas convention, 1861, but followed the general sentiment in his state after bombardment of Fort Sumter.

WALKER, DAVID SHELBY (*b. near Russellville, Ky., 1815; d. Tallahassee, Fla., 1891*), jurist, Florida legislator. Cousin of David Walker (1806–79). Removed to Tallahassee, 1837. Register of public lands and *ex-officio* state superintendent of schools, 1850–59, he was influential in securing passage of the basic school law of 1853. Justice, Florida supreme court, 1859–65, he opposed Florida secession and confined himself to judicial duties during the Civil War. As governor of Florida, 1866–67, he opposed bringing immigrants to Florida, contending that the blacks had the right to furnish the labor supply. He ranks generally among the best of his state's governors. He served as judge of the second state judicial *circuit post* 1879.

WALKER, FRANCIS AMASA (*b. Boston, Mass., 1840; d. 1897*), lawyer, Union soldier, educator, economist. Son of Amasa Walker. Graduated Amherst, 1860. Rising from private to brevet brigadier general in the Civil War, he became a deputy to David A. Wells, commissioner of the revenue, 1869, and chief of the Bureau of Statistics. He reorganized the Bureau along scientific lines and struggled to free it from dependence upon political appointments and special interests. His experience in superintending the census of 1870 without adequate authority was useful to him later as superintendent of the tenth census (1879–81), for which he appointed his own staff of tellers and in which he established his reputation as a statistician. Meanwhile he had served as commissioner of Indian affairs, November 1871–December 1872, with great ability, and, as professor of political economy in Sheffield Scientific School of Yale, 1873–81, had become a leading figure in a new inductive and historical school of economics.

Of first importance was his attack upon the wages-fund theory. He showed that wages were not wholly dependent upon the amount of preexisting capital, but also, and more particularly, upon the current productivity of labor. According to his theory of distribution, which aroused controversy, interest was regulated by a general principle of supply and demand, the profits of the entrepreneur were like rent, and the laborer was left "as the residual claimant to the remaining portion of the product." He believed competition to be the fundamental basis of economic life but recognized that perfect competition is not attained in practice. He defined money to include bank notes and everything serving as a medium of exchange. He asserted that the government had the right to declare irredeemable paper legal tender, adding that governments were not yet wise enough to avoid over-issue and effectively exposing the inflation fallacy. He held throughout his life to the doctrine of international bimetallism and lectured widely in its behalf. Opposed to any blind acceptance of *laissez-faire*, he advocated a limited reduction of hours of labor from fourteen to ten for increased efficiency; he thought unemployment was due chiefly to the effects of worldwide division of labor. Relations between labor and capital seemed to him in 1888 to have reached an equilibrium which could not be disturbed without threat to the public welfare. His influence extended into England (markedly), Italy, and France, but not far into Germany, and as a theoretical economist he stood higher abroad than at home. A freetrader, he was attacked by other freetraders because he was willing to concede that the protectionists had at least a claim to a hearing.

As president of Massachusetts Institute of Technology, 1881–97, he won public recognition for technical education and extended the physical plant of the Institute. Among the educational reforms which he championed were an insistence on the laboratory method in order to maintain the interest of students of mechanical trend as well as those of retentive memory, and also the inclusion of studies in history and political science in technical schools. He opposed absorption of the Institute by Harvard because he believed that technical schools should maintain a separate identity in order to keep free of the arrogance of the classical disciplines. He was author, among other works, of *The Indian Question* (1874), *The Wages Question* (1876), *Money* (1878), *Land and Its Rent* (1883), and *International Bimetallism* (1896).

WALKER, FRANK COMERFORD (*b. Plymouth, Pa., 1886; d. New York, N.Y., 1959*), lawyer and government official. Grew up in Butte, Mont. Studied at Gonzaga University and at Notre Dame (LL.B., 1909). After practicing law in Butte and serving in state legislature, Walker moved to New York. Became active in Democratic politics in 1928. A backer of Roosevelt and a strong fund raiser among Catholics for the president, he was appointed treasurer of the Democratic National Committee in 1932; chairman 1943–44. Director, National Emergency Council (1933–35). Postmaster general (1940–45). Tenure marked by censorship of *Esquire* magazine as being obscene, which was overturned by the courts. Public career based on personal loyalty to Roosevelt rather than a dedication to politics.

WALKER, GILBERT CARLTON (*b. Cuba, N.Y., 1832; d. New York, N.Y., 1885*), lawyer. After practice in Owego, N.Y., and Chicago, Ill., he removed to Norfolk, Va., 1865, where he engaged in business and banking. After the Virginia constitutional convention of 1867, he helped to secure federal approval of the new constitution without a provision for disfranchisement of Confederates who had held office under the United States. Elected governor of Virginia as a "Conservative" Republican with Democratic support, he served from 1869 through 1874. Successful in restoring Virginia to the Union and in enforcement of law and order, he pursued a fiscal policy which was unworkable and by which, it was believed, he profited personally. His funding of the state's debt was done on very hard terms, and Virginia's interests in transportation companies were diverted to private hands. After service in Congress, 1875–79, he returned to New York State.

WALKER, HENRY OLIVER (*b. Boston, Mass., 1843; d. Belmont, Mass., 1929*), painter. Studied in Paris, France, under Léon Bonnat, 1879–82; worked in Boston, 1883–89; removed to New York City *ca.* 1889. A portraitist and painter of ideal figures, he made a special mark as a muralist. His *Joy and Memory* and *Lyric Poetry* in the Library of Congress are among the most decorative of the many mural works there. He painted other effective works for the Massachusetts State House and the Appellate Court House, New York City.

WALKER, JAMES (*b. present Burlington, Mass., 1794; d. Cambridge, Mass., 1874*), Unitarian clergyman. Graduated Harvard, 1814. Pastor, Harvard Church, Charlestown, Mass., 1818–39; Alford Professor of Natural Religion, etc., Harvard, 1839–53; president of Harvard, 1853–60. A man of erudite but not original mind, he derived almost his entire thought from the Scotch Realists and was the preeminent expounder of the metaphysics of early 19th-century Unitarianism—a common-sense rationalism combined with a simple piety and a lofty ethical tone. His administration of Harvard was competent but uneventful.

WALKER, JAMES BARR (*b. Philadelphia, Pa., 1805; d. Wheaton, Ill., 1887*), Presbyterian and Congregational clergyman, antislavery journalist in Ohio and Illinois. Author of *The Philosophy of the Plan of Salvation* (published anonymously, 1841), a widely popular treatise on Christian apologetics. Professor of philosophy and belles lettres, Wheaton College, Wheaton, Ill., 1870–84.

WALKER, JAMES JOHN (*b. New York, N.Y., 1881; d. New York, 1946*), lawyer, politician, son of a lumberyard owner who was active in local Democratic politics. An indifferent and undisciplined student, he dropped out of the College of St. Francis Xavier (New York City) after a year and out of business school after three months. He enrolled at the New York Law School in 1902 and graduated two years later, but almost a decade passed before he became a member of the New York bar. He spent the intervening time in Tin Pan Alley, grinding out lyrics for popular ballads. In 1905 he scored a minor success with the lyrics for "Will You Love Me in December as You Do in May?" On Apr. 11, 1912, he married Janet Frances Allen, a musical comedy singer and vaudeville performer.

At thirty Walker quit songwriting for politics. His style and values, however, remained those of a man who had started out in show business, and he continued to frequent the world populated by celebrities and characters of the type chronicled by Damon Runyon. In 1909 Walker received the Democratic nomination for the safe state assembly seat from Greenwich Village. He was elevated to the state senate in 1914 and was leader of his party in that body from 1921 to 1925. In 1925 Al Smith and other party leaders picked Walker as an attractive contrast to the blundering incumbent mayor of New York. Walker won the election by more then 400,000 votes. Four years later he won reelection by an even wider margin against Fiorello La Guardia.

Walker introduced many innovations in New York City but the major reason for his popularity was that he embodied qualities that so many of his contemporaries admired during the Jazz Age. An official investigation began to uncover graft and incompetence in his administration, and in 1931 the legislature appointed a committee to investigate the city government in general. Walker failed to give a satisfactory explanation of either the chaos of his administration or the unorthodoxy of his personal finances. His resignation on Sept. 1, 1932, ended one of the more colorful careers in American politics.

WALKER, JOHN BRISBEN (*b. near Pittsburgh, Pa., 1847; d. 1931*), iron manufacturer, rancher, journalist. As publisher and editor of the *Cosmopolitan Magazine*, 1889–1905, he made it one of the leading American illustrated magazines of that time. Of a restless and adventurous turn of mind, he engaged in political activity and urged economic and other reforms. An enthusiast for aviation, automobiles, and good roads, he offered a prize in 1896 for the automobile showing the greatest speed, safety, and ease of operation at low cost which was won by the Duryea car. In 1898 he bought the Stanley Automobile Co. and began the manufacture of Locomobile steam cars.

WALKER, JOHN GRIMES (*b. Hillsboro, N.H., 1835; d. near Ogunquit, Maine, 1907*), naval officer. Nephew of James W. Grimes. Graduated U.S. Naval Academy, 1856; rose to rank of commander for his Civil War service under Adm. D. D. Porter in Mississippi River operations. Recognized as the most influential officer in the navy during his later career, he was chief of the Bureau of Navigation, 1881–89, held important sea commands, and was in charge of the North Pacific Squadron, 1894, during establishment of the Hawaiian Republic. Retired as commodore, 1897, he served as president of the Isthmian Canal Commission,

1899–1904. He headed the reorganized Commission which administered the Canal Zone until 1905.

WALKER, JONATHAN HOGE (*b. near Hogestown, Pa., 1754; d. Natchez, Miss., 1824*), lawyer. Father of Robert J. Walker. Began practice in Northumberland Co., Pa., 1790, where he was an associate in politics of Robert Whitehill and Thomas Cooper. President judge of the fourth Pennsylvania district, 1806–18; U.S. judge, district of western Pennsylvania, *post* 1818.

WALKER, JOSEPH REDDEFORD (*b. probably Virginia, 1798; d. Contra Costa Co., Calif., 1876*), trapper, explorer, guide. Raised in Roane Co., Tenn.; removed to vicinity of Independence, Mo., 1819. After trading and trapping out of Independence, he joined Bonneville's company which left Fort Osage for the mountains, May 1832. In July 1833, from the Green River rendezvous, he set off westward, first to Great Salt Lake, then to the Humboldt River, and on to what has since been known as Walker Lake. Scaling the Sierra Nevada with great difficulty, he and his group reached Monterey, Calif. in November, and were probably the first whites to cross the Sierra from the East, and also, it is believed, the first to see the Yosemite Valley. On his return east in February 1834, Walker crossed the mountains farther south by what is now known as Walkers Pass and rejoined Bonneville in the present Utah in the early summer. Remaining in the mountains for some nine years, he joined J. B. Chiles' emigrant company at Fort Bridger, August 1843, and led a part of it by way of Walkers Pass to the coast. Overtaking John C. Frémont's second expedition on its return journey, he accompanied it to Bent's Fort. He was the guide to Frémont's third expedition (1845–46) to California. Resident for a short time in Jackson Co., Mo., he reached California among the first of the Forty-niners. He led a company to Arizona 1861, an discovered rich placers on the site of present Prescott, 1862. His knowledge of the geography of the West was outstanding.

WALKER, LEROY POPE (*b. Huntsville, Ala., 1817; d. Huntsville, 1884*), Alabama lawyer, legislator, and jurist. Identified with the secessionist wing of the Democratic party by 1860, he was chairman of the Alabama delegation to his party's convention of that year at Charleston, S.C., and as such announced the withdrawal of the delegation. He was delegate also to the Richmond convention and was sent by the Alabama secession convention as special commissioner to induce Tennessee to secede. Recommended by W. L. Yancey, he was appointed Confederate secretary of war, February 1861. Utterly inexperienced, he resigned in September and served thereafter in several area commands and as judge of a military court until 1865.

WALKER, MARY EDWARDS (*b. Oswego, N.Y., 1832; d. near Oswego, 1919*), physician. Certified by Syracuse Medical College, 1855, Dr. Walker was a lifelong campaigner for woman's rights. Early in her career she adopted men's dress. After service in the Union Army medical corps, 1861–65, she practiced in Washington, D.C. She was principally famous as a lecturer in favor of dress reform, woman suffrage, the abolition of capital punishment, and other reforms, but her consuming egotism is said to have alienated similarly-minded persons.

WALKER, PINKNEY HOUSTON (*b. Adair Co., Ky., 1815; d. 1885*), jurist. Admitted to the Illinois bar, 1839. A judge of the Illinois circuit court, 1853–58, he served thereafter as a justice of the state supreme court. He was chief justice, 1864–67 and 1874–75. Author during his judicial career of about 3000 opinions, he was known for integrity, fairness, and clarity of reasoning. Among his most important opinions were *Starkweather* v.

American Bible Society and *Ruggles* v. *People*. He concurred in the opinion in *Munn* v. *Illinois*.

WALKER, REUBEN LINDSAY (*b. Logan, Va., 1827; d. Virginia, 1890*), Confederate brigadier general, civil engineer. Great-grandson of Thomas Walker. Graduated Virginia Military Institute, 1845. Served throughout the Civil War without a day's leave of absence, principally in command of the artillery of A. P. Hill's division (later corps). After the war he engaged in farming and in railroad and contracting work.

WALKER, ROBERT FRANKLIN (*b. Florence, Mo., 1850; d. Jefferson City, Mo., 1930*), Missouri legal official and jurist. As judge of the supreme court of Missouri *post* 1912, he did his most important work in criminal appeals and tactfully mitigated the older Missouri doctrine that all error presumes prejudice against the defendant.

WALKER, ROBERT JOHN (*b. Northumberland, Pa., 1801; d. Washington, D.C., 1869*), lawyer, public official. Son of Jonathan H. Walker. Admitted to the bar in Pittsburgh, Pa., 1821, he soon became a leader of the Democratic party in the state, but removed to Natchez, Miss., 1826. Successful in practice and as a land speculator, he posed as the friend of the squatter and small farmer and was a follower of Andrew Jackson. As U.S. senator from Mississippi, 1836–45, he was identified with the anti-Bank and repudiating party in his state. He spoke often in favor of preemption, lower land prices, and the independent treasury plan; he opposed distribution of the surplus, the protective tariff, and abolition. His service as senator is chiefly memorable for his activities in connection with the annexation of Texas. He was author of the resolution of January 1837 calling for recognition of Texan independence, and was one of President Tyler's foremost allies in efforts to add Texas to the Union, 1843–45.

Walker appears to have been at the center of the manipulations which resulted in the rejection of Martin Van Buren and the nominations of James K. Polk, 1844. After drafting the compromise resolutions which resolved the Senate deadlock over annexation of Texas, February 1845, he became secretary of the treasury. A hardworking secretary, he secured establishment of the independent treasury system for handling public money and financed the conduct of the Mexican War on favorable terms and without scandal. His report of 1845 on the state of the finances became a classic of free-trade literature and remains a very able state paper. He also established the government warehousing system for the handling of imports, and was mainly responsible for creation of the Department of the Interior in 1849. An advocate of seizure of the whole of Mexico, 1847, Walker is believed to have lobbied for the rejection of the Trist treaty, February 1848.

Between 1849 and 1857 Walker lived in Washington, D.C., attending to his speculative interests. Appointed governor of Kansas Territory, March 1857, he had an understanding with President Buchanan that the bonafide residents of Kansas should choose their social institutions by a fair vote. His inaugural address contained the thesis that climatic conditions would be the ultimate determinant of the location of slavery and aroused a storm of protest in the South. Despite his attempts to conciliate the free-state party in Kansas and his own conviction that Kansas would be free state, he failed in his attempts to settle the Kansas difficulties because of the failure of the administration to support him. He resigned in December 1857 when he was unable to persuade Buchanan that the so-called ratification of the Lecompton Constitution was unacceptable. Himself a Free-soiler as early as 1849 and said to have freed his slaves in 1838, Walker was a Unionist in the Civil War and was active in the sale in Europe of federal bonds. After the war he aided in putting the Alaska purchase bill through

Congress and was hopeful of annexing Nova Scotia to the United States.

WALKER, SARAH BREEDLOVE (*b. Delta, La., 1867; d. Irvington-on-Hudson, N.Y., 1919*), pioneer black businesswoman, philanthropist. Known throughout later life as Madame C. J. Walker. Educated in public night schools of St. Louis, Mo., Mrs. Walker discovered in 1905 the formula of a hair preparation for blacks which she sold by mail with great success. Settling her business in Indianapolis, Ind., 1910, she manufactured various cosmetics and maintained a training school for agents and beauty culturists. One of her most original ideas was the organization of her agents into clubs for business, social, and philanthropic purposes. She willed two-thirds of her estate to educational institutions and charities.

WALKER, SEARS COOK (*b. Wilmington, Mass., 1805; d. Cincinnati, Ohio, 1853*), mathematician, astronomer. Brother of Timothy Walker (1802–56). Graduated Harvard, 1825. Founded one of earliest astronomical observatories in the United States, 1827, in connection with the Philadelphia High School. Associated *post* 1845 with the U.S. Naval Observatory, Washington, D.C., and with the U.S. Coast Survey, he made important researches in the orbit of the planet Neptune, 1847. He originated the telegraphing of transits of stars and application of the graphic registration of time-results to the registry of time-observations for general astronomical purposes.

WALKER, STUART ARMSTRONG (*b. Augusta, Ky., 1880; d. Beverly Hills, Calif., 1941*), playwright, theatrical producer, film director. Graduated in engineering, University of Cincinnati, 1903. Devoted to the theater from boyhood, he worked for David Belasco as actor, play reader, and director, 1909–14, and for a year as director for Jessie Bonstelle. Eager to make imaginative drama of high quality available to people in every part of the nation, he organized the "Portmanteau Theater" (1915–17), an innovative traveling repertory company, which expressed the best elements in the "little theater" movement's challenge to the mediocrity of the commercial stage. In 1917, he became resident director of the Indianapolis Repertory Company; from 1922 to 1931, he directed the Cincinnati Repertory; in both posts, he continued his previous success in experimental theater and the training of young actors. Thereafter, he was employed as screen writer, acting coach, and director in Hollywood.

WALKER, THOMAS (*b. King and Queen Co., Va., 1715; d. present Albermarle Co., Va., 1794*), physician, soldier, explorer. Studied medicine at Williamsburg, Va., and practiced in Fredericksburg. Joined company of land speculators who explored the southern end of the valley of Virginia, 1748; became chief agent for Loyal Land Company, 1749. Explored westward in 1750 to examine land claims, becoming first white man to have made a recorded expedition to the Kentucky country (as established by his journal, published 1888). Commissary general to Virginia troops serving under George Washington, 1755, he was charged with misconduct for entering partnership with Andrew Lewis in the supply business. Acted as guardian for Thomas Jefferson. Represented Virginia at treaty of Fort Stanwix, 1768; thereafter took important part in Revolutionary movement. A member of the executive council of Virginia and of the House of Delegates, he was typical of the men of action who explored and exploited the early frontier.

WALKER, THOMAS BARLOW (*b. Xenia, Ohio, 1840; d. 1928*), Minnesota lumber magnate, founder of the Walker Art Gallery, Minneapolis.

WALKER, TIMOTHY (*b. Woburn, Mass., 1705; d. Concord, N.H., 1782*), Congregational clergyman. Father-in-law of Benjamin Thompson. Graduated Harvard, 1725. Pastor in present Concord, N.H., 1730–82. He acted as agent for the settlers there in securing a Crown decision which validated their titles to the lands after transfer of the township from Massachusetts to New Hampshire sovereignty. To this end he traveled to England in 1753, 1755, and 1762.

WALKER, TIMOTHY (*b. Wilmington, Mass., 1802; d. Cincinnati, Ohio, 1856*), Ohio lawyer, legal writer, jurist, and law teacher. Brother of Sears C. Walker. Practiced and taught law in Cincinnati *post* 1831. Author of the influential *Introduction to American Law* (1837), a statement of the elementary principles of American jurisprudence.

WALKER, WALTON HARRIS (*b. Belton, Tex., 1889; d. near Seoul, Korea, 1950*), army officer. Graduated West Point, 1912; commissioned in infantry. Served with distinction in World War I; during the 1920's, graduated from the Field Artillery School, the Infantry School, and the Command and General Staff College. Also during the 1920's, he served as instructor at the Infantry and Coast Artillery schools and as a tactical officer at West Point. From 1930 to 1933 he was on railroad patrol in Tientsin, China. After a series of promotions and commands in the United States, Walker became head of the XX Corps, which entered combat in France in August 1944. Walker's troops captured Angers, Chartres, and Rheims. After crossing the Rhine, the so-called Ghost Corps captured Kassel and liberated Buchenwald. In the Korean War, Walker further distinguished himself and commanded all ground troops. Driving into North Korea he captured the capital, Pyongyang. He was killed in a jeep accident.

WALKER, WILLIAM (*b. Nashville, Tenn., 1824; d. Trujillo, Honduras, 1860*), adventurer, greatest of American filibusters. Graduated University of Nashville, 1838; M.D., University of Pennsylvania, 1843; after studying law, was admitted to the bar in New Orleans, La. Failing to succeed as lawyer and journalist, he removed to California, 1850, where he practiced at Marysville. Invading the Mexican province of Lower California with an armed expedition, 1853, he proclaimed himself president of an independent republic there, but was forced to return to the United States. He was acquitted after trial for violation of the neutrality laws. Invited by the leader of a revolutionary faction in Nicaragua, Walker led a small, armed band there in 1855. With the help of the Accessory Transit Co., an American concern, he seized control of Nicaragua and, after recognition of his regime by the United States in May 1856, had himself inaugurated as president. Ambitious to unite the Central American republics into a single military empire, he planned an interoceanic canal and attempted to reintroduce African slavery. Undertaking to double-cross Cornelius Vanderbilt in a struggle for control of the Accessory Transit Co., he was driven from his presidency after a coalition of neighboring republics was formed against him with Vanderbilt's aid. Returning to the United States, 1857, he attempted an invasion of Nicaragua late in the year, but was arrested on landing by Commodore Hiram Paulding of the U.S. Navy and sent back to the United States. Arrested by British authorities after a landing in Honduras, 1860, he was condemned to death by a court-martial of Honduran officers and shot. A small man, extremely shy and reticent, he was yet able to maintain iron discipline and something like personal devotion among his desperate followers. He was author of *The War in Nicaragua* (1860).

WALKER, WILLIAM HENRY TALBOT (*b. Augusta, Ga., 1816; d. near Atlanta, Ga., 1864*), soldier. Graduated West Point, 1837. Commissioned in the infantry, he served in the Florida Indian War and in the Mexican War. Badly wounded at Molino del Rey, 1847, he undertook minor duties and went on sick leave for a great part of the time until 1860 when he resigned his commission. In service mainly with Georgia state troops, 1861–63, he entered the Confederate service as a brigadier general and was appointed major general, January 1864. Active in the western campaigns, he was with the Army of Tennessee during the northern Georgia campaign and was killed in a sortie out of Atlanta.

WALKER, WILLIAM JOHNSON (*b. Charlestown, Mass., 1790; d. 1865*), physician, financier. A successful practitioner at Charlestown *post* 1816, he accumulated a large fortune in railroad and manufacturing stocks which he devoted to the endowment of Amherst, Tufts College, the Boston Society of Natural History, and Massachusetts Institute of Technology.

WALKER, WILLISTON (*b. Portland, Maine, 1860; d. 1922*), church historian. Graduated Amherst, 1883; Hartford Theological Seminary, 1886; Ph.D., Leipzig, 1888. Taught church history at Hartford, 1889–1901; at Yale, 1901–22. Provost of Yale *post* 1919. A teacher of great ability, Walker made his major contributions to scholarship in the field of New England Congregational history; he was actively concerned in work for Christian unity and for missions.

WALLACE, CHARLES WILLIAM (*b. Hopkins, Mo., 1865; d. Wichita Falls, Tex., 1932*), educator, Shakespeare scholar. Graduated University of Nebraska, 1898; did graduate work at Nebraska and at University of Chicago; Ph.D., Freiburg im Breisgau, 1906. Taught English at University of Nebraska *post* 1901. Applied proceeds of successful work as oil operator in Texas to furtherance of research in history of the early English stage.

WALLACE, DAVID (*b. Pennsylvania, 1799; d. Indianapolis, Ind., 1859*), lawyer. Father of Lewis Wallace. Raised on Ohio and Indiana frontiers. Graduated West Point, 1821. Admitted to the Indiana bar, 1824, he succeeded in practice and was one of the Whig leaders in Indiana. Lieutenant governor, 1831–37, and governor of Indiana, 1837–40, he lost the state millions in money through procuring loans for public improvements from Eastern speculators. Whig congressman, 1841–43, he returned to the practice of law in Indianapolis and died while a judge of the court of common pleas.

WALLACE, HENRY (*b. near West Newton, Pa., 1836; d. 1916*), United Presbyterian clergyman, editor and writer on agricultural subjects. Father of Henry C. Wallace. A pastor in Illinois and Iowa, 1863–76, he took up farming as a way of recovering his health and soon entered agricultural journalism. With his son, he began publishing *Wallace's Farmer*, 1895, and was its editor until his death. He was president of the National Conservation Congress, 1910.

WALLACE, HENRY AGARD (*b. Orient, Iowa, 1888; d. Danbury, Conn., 1965*), agricultural scientist, editor, government official, and politician. Attended Iowa State (B.S., 1910). Experimented with various strains of corn and produced the first hybrid corn suitable for commercial use; wrote for and edited *Wallaces' Farmer*, a family-owned newspaper, assuming the editorship in 1921. U.S. secretary of agriculture (1932–40), concentrating on drafting and securing approval of legislation to assist farmers; he implemented the domestic allotment plan, whereby farmers were eligible to receive support payments for decreasing output; authorized paying cotton and hog farmers for plowing up 10 million acres of growing cotton and for slaughtering 6 million pigs (1933); promoted efforts to find markets abroad for American goods; and staunchly advocated reciprocal trade agreements to lower trade barriers and increase world commerce. The institution of support payments for crop control, soil conservation, food stamp distribution, and government-operated warehouses for storing surpluses helped alleviate the distress of farmers during the Great Depression. Elected vice president (1940) and made goodwill tours to Mexico, Latin America, Soviet Asia, and China. His appeals for responsible American leadership to foster lasting peace and global prosperity in the postwar world commanded wide attention. His pronouncements about postwar policies made him the leading spokesman for liberal opinion in the country and a target for conservatives. President Franklin Roosevelt's tepid endorsement of him for a second term in 1944 doomed his chances for renomination. Named secretary of commerce after the election; he called for extension of the 1934 Trade Agreements Act as one way to promote international economic cooperation and world peace and supported federal programs to provide full employment and higher standards of living. He became increasingly outspoken in calling for U.S. policies to ease tensions with Russia, including economic assistance as well as international control of atomic energy. A public uproar in response to one of his speeches prompted President Harry Truman to dismiss him in 1946. By late 1947 his views had alienated him from the overwhelming majority of Americans, including most liberals.

WALLACE, HENRY CANTWELL (*b. Rock Island, Ill., 1866; d. Washington, D.C., 1924*), agricultural journalist. Son of Henry Wallace; father of Henry A. Wallace. Graduated Iowa State Agricultural College, 1892. Associated with his father in publishing *Wallace's Farmer post* 1895, he became its editor, 1916. As U.S. secretary of agriculture, 1921–24, he emphasized that department's role in the adjustment of production to the needs of consumption, and opposed transfer of its marketing functions to the Department of Commerce. He was a champion of conservation, supported the principles of the McNary-Haugen Bill, established the bureau of agricultural economics and the bureau of home economics in his department, and inaugurated radio market reports.

WALLACE, HORACE BINNEY (*b. Philadelphia, Pa., 1817; d. Paris, France, 1852*), lawyer, literary, art, and legal critic. Brother of John W. Wallace. Graduated College of New Jersey (Princeton), 1835. Author of a novel *Stanley, or the Recollections of a Man of the World* (issued anonymously, 1838), and of two collections of critical and philosophical essays published posthumously. Editor, with J. I. C. Hare, of J. W. Smith's *A Selection of Leading Cases*, and also of *Select Decisions of American Courts* (1847, revised in 1857 as *American Leading Cases*). Auguste Comte recognized Wallace as his leading American disciple.

WALLACE, HUGH CAMPBELL (*b. Lexington, Mo., 1863; d. Washington, D.C., 1931*), financier, diplomat. Identified *post* 1887 with the commercial development of Tacoma, Wash., Wallace became one of the most influential financiers of the Northwest and was a leader of the Democratic party in that region. A trusted adviser to President Woodrow Wilson, he served as U.S. ambassador to France, 1919–21, exercising considerable private influence after the withdrawal of the American delegation to the Peace Conference.

WALLACE, JOHN FINDLEY (*b. Fall River, Mass., 1852; d. Washington, D.C., 1921*), civil engineer, outstanding executive of Midwestern and Western railroads. First chief engineer of the Panama Canal, 1904–05, he continued as such after reorganization of the Canal Commission in April 1905, but resigned in June of that year because of inadequate authority given him and thereby precipitated a bitter controversy. He later served as president of Westinghouse, Church, Kerr & Co. and was an officer and consultant for many other concerns.

WALLACE, JOHN HANKINS (*b. Allegheny Co., Pa., 1822; d. 1903*), cattle breeder, expert on the trotting horse. Published *Wallace's American Stud Book*, 1867; began publication of

Wallace's Year-Book of Trotting and Pacing, 1886; also published *Wallace's Monthly*, a magazine devoted to the interest of the trotting horse. Author of *The Horse of America* (1897).

WALLACE, JOHN WILLIAM (*b. Philadelphia, Pa., 1815; d. 1884*), legal scholar, author. Brother of Horace B. Wallace. Graduated University of Pennsylvania, 1833; studied law with his father and with John Sergeant. Librarian of the Law Association of Philadelphia, 1841–60. Succeeded his brother as coeditor of *American Leading Cases* and edited a number of other legal compilations; was author of *The Reporters, Chronologically Arranged* (1844). He served as reporter of the U.S. Supreme Court, 1863–75. He was president of the Historical Society of Pennsylvania, 1868–84.

WALLACE, LEWIS (*b. Brookville, Ind., 1827; d. Crawfordsville, Ind., 1905*), lawyer, Indiana legislator, Union soldier, diplomat, author. Son of David Wallace, he was commonly known as "Lew" Wallace. A student of law under his father, he served briefly in the Mexican War and began practice of law in Indianapolis, Ind., 1849. Resident in Crawfordsville *post* 1853, he became adjutant general of Indiana and colonel of the 11th Regiment, 1861. Promoted brigadier general in September, and major general in March 1862 after the capture of Fort Donelson, he won the enmity of General H. W. Halleck who twice attempted to bar him from a command. Among Wallace's outstanding exploits during the Civil War were his saving of Cincinnati, Ohio from capture in 1863 by Confederate General E. Kirby-Smith; also his holding action against Confederate General Jubal Early at the Monocacy, July 1864, for which he was highly commended by General Grant. After the war he spent some time in Mexico and then returned to practice law at Crawfordsville. Republican governor of New Mexico, 1878–81; U.S. minister to Turkey, 1881–85. Wallace is best remembered as a man of letters and as author of, among other books, *The Fair God* (1873), a story of the conquest of Mexico; *Ben Hur* (1880), which had extraordinary success; and of *The Prince of India* (1893). A man of simple, democratic tastes, he disliked the law, had no aptitude for politics, and was disinclined to the military life except when his country required his services. Art, music, and literature were his most vital interests.

WALLACE, LURLEEN BURNS (*b. Tuscaloosa, Ala., 1926; d. Montgomery, Ala., 1968*), governor of Alabama. Graduated from the Tuscaloosa Business College (1942). In 1943 she married George Wallace, who was elected to the state legislature in 1946 and became governor of Alabama in 1962. Forbidden by Alabama's constitution from succeeding himself in office, he asked his wife to run. Lurleen Wallace was elected governor in 1966, becoming only the third woman to be elected a governor in the United States. She proceeded to carry on her husband's programs, which included maintaining segregated public schools. Poor health cut short her tenure in office.

WALLACE, WILLIAM (*b. Manchester, England, 1825; d. 1904*), wire manufacturer, inventor. Immigrated to America as a boy. Established firm of Wallace & Sons with his father and brothers, 1848, locating their plant at Ansonia, Conn., 1850. With Moses G. Farmer, he constructed dynamos based on Farmer's patent of 1872, one of which was used to light the Centennial Exhibition at Philadelphia, 1876. His firm built dynamos for use with the plate-carbon arc lamp, patented by Wallace, December 1877, and believed to be the first commercial arc light made in the United States. Wallace was the first to demonstrate operation of arc lights in series. He also constructed an electroplating plant at Ansonia.

WALLACE, WILLIAM ALEXANDER ANDERSON (*b. near Lexington, Va., 1817; d. near Devine, Tex., 1899*), frontiersman, popularly known as "Bigfoot." Removed to Texas, 1837. As private in a ranger company under John C. Hays, 1840–44, he fought on the Salado and was taken prisoner in the futile Mier expedition. After further service as a ranger and with the Mounted Rifle Volunteers in the Mexican War, he raised a company of volunteers for frontier service under his own command, 1850. A legendary figure in Texas history, he sallied out from his Medina River farm time and again with a hastily gathered band of neighbors to protect life and property from Indian raiders. He was also responsible for the delivery of the mail between San Antonio and El Paso. He had no sympathy with the Civil War and took no part in it.

WALLACE, WILLIAM JAMES (*b. Syracuse, N.Y., 1837; d. Jacksonville, Fla., 1917*), jurist. LL.B., Hamilton College, 1857. U.S. district judge, northern district of New York, 1874–82; U.S. judge, second circuit court, 1882–91; presiding judge, circuit court of appeal, second circuit, 1891–1907.

WALLACE, WILLIAM ROSS (*b. Lexington or Paris, Ky., 1819; d. New York, N.Y., 1881*), lawyer, poet. Practiced in New York City *post* 1841; was a friend of Samuel Woodworth, G. P. Morris, and other New York literati, and of Edgar A. Poe whose memory he defended against John Neal. A frequent contributor to the periodicals of the day, he was author of *The Battle of Tippecanoe* (Cincinnati, 1837) and of *Meditations in America* (1851), which contains his best-known work. He was author of the famous lines, "And the hand that rocks the cradle, Is the hand that rules the world."

WALLACK, HENRY JOHN (*b. London, England, 1790; d. New York, N.Y., 1870*), actor. Brother of James W. Wallack (*ca. 1795–1864*); father of James W. Wallack (*1818–1873*). Made American debut at Baltimore, Md., 1819, and was known thereafter as a versatile player in a most extensive repertoire, both in America and in England.

WALLACK, JAMES WILLIAM (*b. London, England, ca. 1795; d. New York, N.Y., 1864*), actor. Brother of Henry J. Wallack; father of Lester Wallack. Made American debut at the Park Theatre, New York City, as Macbeth, September 1818, after achieving early success on the British stage. An actor of the school of J. P. Kemble, he played with a nervous, exuberant vitality; he alternated appearances between several American cities and England. The most distinguished member of a notable theatrical family, he was manager of the National Theatre in New York, 1837–39, and of the old Brougham's Lyceum in New York, 1852–61. With his son Lester, he opened the third of the Wallack theaters in New York City at Broadway and 13th St., 1861.

WALLACK, JAMES WILLIAM (*b. London, England, 1818; d. near Aiken, S.C., 1873*), actor. Son of Henry J. Wallack; nephew of James W. Wallack (*ca. 1795–1864*). Came to America as an infant; made stage debut in Philadelphia, Pa., 1822. After learning his trade at the Bowery Theater, New York City, and with English provincial companies, he became leading juvenile with his uncle's company, 1837, and for many years played with success both in America and England. *Post* 1855 he remained in the United States. At his best in tragedy or romantic drama, he joined his cousin Lester Wallack's stock company, 1865, and scored one of his greatest successes in the part of Fagin in *Oliver Twist*, 1867.

WALLACK, JOHN LESTER. *See* WALLACK, LESTER.

WALLACK, LESTER (*b. New York, N.Y., 1820; d. near Stamford, Conn., 1888*), actor, dramatist. Son of James W. Wallack (*ca. 1795–1864*). Educated in England and trained in the English provincial theatres, he made his American debut at the Broadway Theatre, New York City, 1847; in 1848 he made a sensation in the part of Don César de Bazan, and also as Edmond Dantès in *The Count of Monte Cristo.* Soon becoming the matinee idol of New York in comic or romantic parts, he assisted his father in the management of the Wallack theatres and was their actual manager *post* 1861. After a great run of success in his own plays and others, he opened the new Wallack Theatre at Broadway and 30th St., New York City, 1882, which he managed until his retirement, 1887.

WALLER, EMMA (*b. England, ca. 1820; d. New York, N.Y., 1899*), actress. Made American debut at Walnut Street Theatre, Philadelphia, Pa., October 1857, as Ophelia to her husband's Hamlet. Thereafter, often with her husband as her principal associate, she starred as an emotional actress throughout the United States for some twenty years. After her retirement she gave public readings and was a teacher of elocution.

WALLER, FATS. *See* WALLER, THOMAS WRIGHT.

WALLER, FREDERIC (*b. Brooklyn, N.Y., 1886; d. Huntington, N.Y., 1954*), inventor, motion picture producer, and manufacturer. Developed first automatic printer and timer for motion pictures, and first optical printer. Inventor of Cinerama. Released first commercial Cinerama picture, *This Is Cinerama,* in 1952. Won an Academy Award for his invention in 1954.

WALLER, JOHN LIGHTFOOT (*b. Woodford Co., Ky., 1809; d. Louisville, Ky., 1854*), Baptist clergyman. Engaged in controversy with Alexander Campbell. Edited *Baptist Banner and Western Pioneer;* founded *Western Baptist Review* (later called *Christian Repository*), 1845. A capable and militant leader under whom the Baptists in Kentucky made notable advances in education and missionary work.

WALLER, THOMAS MACDONALD (*b. New York, N.Y., ca. 1840; d. Ocean Beach, Conn., 1924*), lawyer, Connecticut legislator and official. Democratic mayor of New London, Conn., 1873–79; governor of Connecticut, 1883–85. U.S. consul general at London, England, 1885–89. Uncompromising leader of the "Gold Democrats" in Connecticut, 1896–1900.

WALLER, THOMAS WRIGHT (*b. New York, N.Y., 1904; d. near Kansas City, Mo., 1943*), musician, composer, jazz pianist. Known as "Fats" Waller. Child of a musical family, he was a professional at age fifteen and attracted the attention and assistance of established Harlem jazz musicians such as James P. Johnson. By 1922, he was recording for the Okeh label and had begun to compose, which he did with remarkable ease and speed. His first big success was "Ain't Misbehavin" (1929). More important musically than his hit songs were his many piano solos. Despite his public image as a humorous entertainer, he was a deeply committed musician; he continually developed his art, studying with Carl Bohm at the Juilliard School and briefly with Leopold Godowsky. After 1934, he spent most of his professional time on the road, touring in the United States, the British Isles, and continental Europe, maintaining a crushing schedule without regard for his failing health. He died on a train, en route from Hollywood to New York.

WALLER, WILLARD WALTER (*b. Murphysboro, Ill., 1899; d. New York, N.Y., 1945*), sociologist. B.A., University of Illinois, 1920. M.A., University of Chicago, 1925. Ph.D., University of Pennsylvania, 1929. Taught at University of Nebraska, Pennsylvania State College, and Barnard College; drew on personal experience for iconoclastic views of the social psychology of marriage and the family.

WALLGREN, MON(RAD) C(HARLES) (*b. Des Moines, Iowa, 1891; d. Olympia, Wash., 1961*), U.S. representative, senator, and governor. Elected U.S. congressman from Washington State (1933–40); his greatest legislative achievement was a bill to create Olympic National Park. U.S. senator (1941–44) who investigated national defense contracts and uncovered defects in aircraft engines and Liberty ships. Governor of Washington (1945–48); enacted the nation's most liberal unemployment compensation law. Chairman of the Federal Power Commission (1950–51).

WALLING, WILLIAM ENGLISH (*b. Louisville, Ky., 1877; d. Amsterdam, the Netherlands, 1936*), Socialist, labor reformer. Grandson of William H. English. Graduated University of Chicago, 1897. Devoting his energies to the labor movement *post ca.* 1900, Walling was a founder of the National Women's Trade Union League, 1903, and presided over a series of meetings (*ca.* 1908) out of which grew the National Association for the Advancement of Colored People. He was a sympathizer with contemporary Russian revolutionary movements and opposed the conservative element in the Socialist party, 1909. In 1917 he supported entry of the United States into World War I and was critical of the Socialist pacifists. After the war he worked full-time for the American Federation of Labor. The conservatism of his later career was brought about largely by the anti-libertarian character of the Communist revolutions.

WALLIS, SEVERN TEACKLE (*b. Baltimore, Md., 1816; d. 1894*), lawyer. Graduated St. Mary's College, Baltimore, 1832; studied law in office of William Wirt. A Whig in early life, he became a Democrat upon the disintegration of the Whig party, but remained, above all, a reformer, never surrendering his personal independence of opinion. Considered for many years the leader of the Maryland bar, he exercised a strong influence in Baltimore and in the state and was an eloquent speaker. Sympathetic with the Confederacy but opposed to secession, he argued against the doctrine of military necessity in 1861, and was imprisoned for 14 months. His letters to the press during the campaign of 1875, when he supported the Reform ticket, are among the choicest of Maryland polemics.

WALN, NICHOLAS (*b. Fair Hill, near Philadelphia, Pa., 1742; d. 1813*), lawyer, Quaker preacher. Cousin of Robert Waln (1765–1836). Withdrawing from the practice of law, *ca.* 1772, he gave himself up thereafter to the service of the Society of Friends in which he exercised a great influence both here and abroad. He took a leading part in the proceedings of Meeting in its handling of the "Free Quakers" at the time of the Revolutionary War.

WALN, ROBERT (*b. Philadelphia, Pa., 1765; d. 1836*), merchant, textile and iron manufacturer. Cousin of Nicholas Waln; father of Robert Waln (1794–1825). Active as a Federalist in the Pennsylvania legislature, and as a member of Congress, 1798–1801, he became an ardent protectionist and was identified with the high tariff acts of 1816, 1824, and 1828. He was author of *An Examination of the Boston Report* (1828), which was considered a crushing and final argument against the free traders. An orthodox Quaker, he entered into the controversy with Elias Hicks.

WALN, ROBERT (*b. Philadelphia, Pa., 1794; d. Providence, R.I., 1825*), businessman. Son of Robert Waln (1765–1836). A contributor to current periodical literature; editor of Volumes III through VI of Sanderson's *Biography of the Signers to the Declaration of Independence* (1823–24); author of *The Hermit in America* (1819, 1821) and other satires.

WALSH, BENJAMIN DANN (*b. London, England, 1808; d. near Rock Island, Ill., 1869*), businessman, entomologist. A fellow and M.A. of Trinity College, Cambridge, England, Walsh immigrated to Henry Co., Ill., *ca.* 1838, where he engaged in farming and was later a lumber dealer in Rock Island. Retiring from business, *ca.* 1858, he devoted the rest of his life to entomology, publishing a number of excellent papers in which his breadth of knowledge and accurate prophesy of the future of economic entomology were outstanding. He was the first to show that American farmers were planting crops in ways which facilitated the multiplication of insects, and was among the first to suggest introduction of foreign parasites for the control of pests. In 1868, with Charles V. Riley, he founded and edited the *American Entomologist.* An associate of Charles Darwin in England, he attacked the anti-evolutionary views of Agassiz and Dana.

WALSH, BLANCHE (*b.* New York, N.Y., 1873; *d.* Cleveland, Ohio, 1915), actress. Entering her profession in the company of Marie Wainwright, 1889, she played with most of the principal American stock companies of her time and took over in 1899 the repertory of Sardou plays in which Fanny Davenport had long starred. She made the greatest success of her career as Maslova in the dramatization of Tolstoy's *Resurrection*, 1903.

WALSH, DAVID IGNATIUS (*b.* Leominister, Mass., 1872; *d.* Boston, Mass., 1947), lawyer, politician. A.B., Holy Cross College, 1893. LL.B., Boston University, 1897. Rising in Massachusetts Democratic politics by ability as an orator and by refusal to identify himself with the Boston bosses of his party, he was elected governor of Massachusetts in 1913 and 1914, the first non-Yankee to serve as the state's chief executive. Aided by a coalition of Democrats, Progressives, and working-class Republicans in the legislature, he instituted a number of reforms, including improvement of the labor code and inauguration of state-supported university extension courses for wage-earning students. As U.S. senator, 1919–25 and 1927–47, he opposed the League of Nations but was otherwise liberal in his views during the 1920's and the earlier years of the New Deal. He opposed Franklin D. Roosevelt's Supreme Court reform bill, his acceptance of a third term, and all the moves that brought the United States closer to involvement in World War II. He was defeated for reelection in 1946.

WALSH, EDMUND ALOYSIUS (*b.* Boston, Mass., 1885; *d.* Washington, D.C., 1956), Roman Catholic clergyman, educator, and author. Novitiate of the Society of Jesus, student at Woodstock College, at the Universities of Dublin and London, and at Georgetown University (Ph.D., 1920). Dean of the Georgetown University College of Arts and Sciences from 1918, vice president from 1924. Founded School of Foreign Service in 1919 (regent until 1952) and Institute of Languages and Linguistics in 1949. In 1922, Walsh led a Papal delegation to oversee famine relief in Russia and as Vatican representative for the Church's interests; he returned an ardent anticommunist. In 1945–46, he was civilian consultant to the American counsel at the Nuremberg trials. Works include *Total Power* (1949) and *Total Empire* (1951). Widely influenced American foreign policy through his lectures, writings, and the school that he founded.

WALSH, EDWARD AUGUSTINE ("BIG ED") (*b.* Plains, Pa., 1881; *d.* Pompano Beach, Fla., 1959), baseball player. Pitcher for the Chicago White Sox, 1906–17, Walsh was a successful practitioner of the spitball. Won 194 games for the White Sox, forty of them in the 1908 season. His earned run average of 1.82 was a record.

WALSH, FRANCIS PATRICK (*b.* St. Louis, Mo., 1864; *d.* New York, N.Y., 1939), lawyer, public official. Raised in Kansas City, Mo., Walsh was admitted to the Missouri bar, 1889, and quickly became an outstanding trial lawyer. Associated with many reform movements in Kansas City, he served with ability as chairman of the U.S. Commission on Industrial Relations, 1913–18, doing

much to arouse public sympathy for labor's side in industrial disputes. Active also in work for preservation of civil liberties, he was counsel for Tom Mooney during the long litigation over Mooney's conviction for murder. *Post* 1919 he acted as counsel for many labor organizations in important cases. A worker for Irish freedom and for a number of liberal causes, he served as chairman of the New York State Power Authority after his removal to New York City *ca.* 1928, and with his friend George W. Norris was influential in shaping Franklin D. Roosevelt's ideas on public power. First president of the National Lawyers Guild, he resigned in protest over its failure to take a position against Communist dictatorships.

WALSH, HENRY COLLINS (*b.* Florence, Italy, 1863; *d.* Philadelphia, Pa., 1927), journalist, explorer, magazine editor. Grandson of Robert Walsh.

WALSH, JAMES ANTHONY (*b.* Cambridge, Mass., 1867; *d.* Maryknoll, N.Y., 1936), Roman Catholic clergyman. Attended Boston College and Harvard; ordained, 1892, after study at St. John's Seminary, Brighton, Mass. Interested in foreign missions from his seminary days, he worked for the establishment of an American foreign mission society and with Thomas F. Price founded the Catholic Foreign Mission Society of America (Maryknoll) which received official approval, June 1911. Elected Maryknoll's first superior general, 1929, Father Walsh became a bishop, 1933. Before his death, the mission activities of Maryknoll had extended to China, Korea, Japan, Manchuria, the Philippines, and Hawaii.

WALSH, MICHAEL (*b.* near Cork, Ireland, *ca.* 1815; *d.* New York, N.Y., 1859), printer, journalist, politician. Immigrated to America as a child. Resident in New York City *post* 1839, he recruited the young laboring men of the city into the Spartan Association as a workingman's protest against Tammany control of the local Democratic organization. Through the efforts of this association the organized gang became a new feature in political practice. Continuing his efforts on behalf of labor, Walsh founded a paper, the *Subterranean*, 1843, and briefly collaborated with George H. Evans in the National Reform program. When the New York Democrats split over the free-soil controversy, Walsh joined the Hunker faction, denouncing the Abolitionists who neglected the wage slaves of the North for the cause of the black. After service in the New York legislature and a single term in Congress (1853–55), he gradually fell into intemperance.

WALSH, ROBERT (*b.* Baltimore, Md., 1784; *d.* Paris, France, 1859), journalist, man of letters. Attended St. Mary's College, Baltimore, and the present Georgetown University; studied law with Robert G. Harper; traveled and studied in France and the British Isles, and for a while served as secretary to William Pinkney. Returning to the United States, 1809, he served as editor of a number of reviews and miscellanies, and in 1811 founded the first American quarterly, *The American Review of History and Politics.* He was professor of English, University of Pennsylvania, 1818–28. Among his books, which were influential in their time, were *A Letter on the Genius and Dispositions of the French Government* (1810); *An Appeal From the Judgments of Great Britain Respecting the United States of America* (1819); and *Didactics: Social, Literary and Political* (1836). Settling permanently in Paris, 1837, he founded there what was probably the first American salon and was U.S. consul general, 1844–51.

WALSH, THOMAS (*b.* Brooklyn, N.Y., 1871; *d.* Brooklyn, 1928), poet, critic, editor. Graduated Georgetown University, 1892; Ph.D., 1899. Distinguished as a student and translator of Hispanic literature, Walsh engaged also in general editorial work, and was assistant editor of the *Commonweal*, New York City,

1924–28. A selection of his original poems and translations appeared in 1930; he was editor of the *Hispanic Anthology* (1920) and of *The Catholic Anthology* (1927, 1932).

WALSH, THOMAS JAMES (b. *Two Rivers, Wis., 1849; d. on a train en route to Washington, D.C., 1933*), lawyer, statesman. LL.B., University of Wisconsin, 1884. Beginning practice in Dakota Territory, he removed to Helena, Mont., 1890, where he won a reputation in copper litigation and as a constitutional lawyer. He was U.S. senator, Democrat, from Montana, 1913–33. Invariably on the liberal side in debates, he advocated woman suffrage and the child-labor amendment, and also the protection of farm organizations and trade unions from suit under the Sherman Act. He was a loyal follower of the policies of President Woodrow Wilson. His greatest fame derived from his services as counsel and director of the investigation of leases of naval oil reserves in Wyoming and California to private individuals, an investigation brought about by a resolution introduced in the Senate by Robert M. LaFollette, April 1922. After 18 months' study of the evidence, Walsh began public hearings in October 1923 and disclosed with calm precision and unemotional clarity the whole sordid story of Teapot Dome and Elk Hills. The leases were in consequence voided and the public officials responsible for them were discredited. Selected as U.S. attorney general in the cabinet of President F. D. Roosevelt, Walsh died suddenly before Roosevelt's inauguration.

WALSH, THOMAS JOSEPH (b. *Parkers Landing, Pa., 1873; d. South Orange, N.J., 1952*), Roman Catholic clergyman. Studied at St. Bonaventure College (B.A., 1896) and Seminary (ordained, 1900). Secretary to the bishop of Buffalo (1900–15) and chancellor (1900–18). Received doctorates in theology and canon law from Apollinaris Seminary in Rome (1908). Bishop of Trenton, N.J., 1918–28; of Newark, N.J., 1928–37. In 1937 he was appointed archbishop of the archdiocesan see of New Jersey. Known as the Bishop of Charity and Education, Walsh helped found the Mount Carmel Guild while in Buffalo (and which he transplanted to all his later assignments); the Guild was organized to aid immigrants and the needy. He helped found Caldwell College and stimulated the growth of Seton Hall University.

WALTER, ALBERT G. (b. *Germany, 1811; d. Pittsburgh, Pa., 1876*), surgeon. M.D., University of Königsberg; studied also in Berlin and in London. Immigrated to America, ca. 1835, and practiced in Pittsburgh, Pa., *post* 1837. An American pioneer in orthopedic surgery and a versatile general surgeon, Walter performed an epoch-making laparotomy for the relief of a ruptured bladder, January 1859. He was author, among other medical writings, of *Conservative Surgery . . . in Cases of Severe Traumatic Injuries of the Limbs* (1867).

WALTER, BRUNO (b. *Berlin, Germany, 1876; d. Beverly Hills, Calif., 1962*), conductor. First conducted with several German opera companies and state theaters, in Hamburg, Breslau, Berlin, and Munich; became musical director of the Berlin Municipal Opera (1925–29) and director of the Leipzig Gewandhaus Orchestra (1929–33), then moved to Austria. He conducted in Europe and the United States until 1936, when he became principal conductor and artistic adviser for the Vienna State Opera. Immigrated to America in 1939, having made his debut with the New York Symphony in 1923; he made his Metropolitan Opera debut in 1941. He was a guest conductor with several U.S. orchestras, but mainly for the New York Philharmonic, serving as its musical adviser and principal conductor from 1947 to 1949.

WALTER, EUGENE (b. *Cleveland, Ohio, 1874; d. Hollywood, Calif., 1941*), journalist, playwright. Author of a number of "well made" plays, of which *Paid in Full* (1908) and *The Easiest Way* (1909) were outstanding successes. In the latter of these, his use of an unhappy ending in which vice triumphed over virtue won him extravagant contemporary acclaim as a great realist, an "American Ibsen." After 1929, he worked as a contract writer for movie studios.

WALTER, FRANCIS EUGENE (b. *Easton, Pa., 1894; d. Washington, D.C., 1963*), U.S. congressman and lawyer. Attended Lehigh, George Washington, and Georgetown Law School (LL.B., 1919). U.S. congressman from Pennsylvania, 1933–63; his main specialties while in Congress after World War II were immigration laws and investigations of un-American activities. As chairman of the Judiciary Subcommittee on Immigration and the Immigration and Naturalization Subcommittee, he backed laws that retained quotas favoring northern European countries and limiting the number of immigrants from most other countries. Became chairman of the House Un-American Activities Committee, 1955; his search for Communist infiltration covered the fields of entertainment, education, religion, and government.

WALTER, THOMAS (b. *Roxbury, Mass., 1696; d. Roxbury, 1725*), Congregational clergyman. Nephew of Cotton Mather. Assistant pastor at Roxbury *post* 1718, he engaged in a controversy with John Checkley, but is principally remembered as author of *The Grounds and Rules of Musick Explained* (1721). This was an effort, scientifically and artistically conceived, to correct the "horrid medley of confused and disorderly sounds" which passed for singing in the New England churches.

WALTER, THOMAS (b. *Hampshire, England, ca. 1740; d. South Carolina, 1789*), planter, botanist. Immigrated to eastern South Carolina as a young man. Author of a work of lasting scientific importance—*Flora Caroliniana* (London, 1788), the first tolerably complete account of the flora of any definite portion of eastern North America in which an author used the so-called binomial system of nomenclature.

WALTER, THOMAS USTICK (b. *Philadelphia, Pa., 1804; d. 1887*), architect. A master bricklayer, Walter studied architecture under William Strickland and others at the Franklin Institute. After entering practice in 1830, he designed the Moyamensing Prison, Philadelphia, and also Girard College (1833), which marked the climax and at the same time sounded the knell of the Greek Revival in America. He had charge of the extension of the U.S. Capitol at Washington, 1851–65, adding the wings of the present structure, the dome, and also projecting a center extension. Among his other works in Washington were the completion of the Treasury Building begun by Robert Mills, St. Elizabeth's Hospital, and the design for the interior of the State, War, and Navy Building. He also assisted Nicholas Biddle in the design of "Andalusia" and designed churches, banks, and private houses in Philadelphia, Baltimore, Richmond, and elsewhere. He helped organize the American Institute of Architects, 1857, and served as its president, 1876–87.

WALTERS, ALEXANDER (b. *Bardstown, Ky., 1858; d. 1917*), bishop of the African Methodist Episcopal Zion Church. An active minister *post* 1877 in a number of cities throughout the United States, he became pastor of "Mother Zion" in New York City, 1888, and was elected bishop, 1892. He was an organizer of the Afro-American League and later president of the National Afro-American Council. He was author of *My Life and Work* (1917).

WALTERS, HENRY (b. *Baltimore, Md., 1848; d. New York, N.Y., 1931*), capitalist, art collector. Son of William T. Walters, whom he assisted and succeeded in the development of the Atlantic Coast Line Railroad and other large operations. Adding extensively to his father's collections of art, he established the Walters Art Gallery and bequeathed it, with an endowment, to the City of Baltimore.

WALTERS, WILLIAM THOMPSON (*b. Liverpool, Pa., 1820; d. 1894*), merchant, railroad executive, art collector. Father of Henry Walters. Played an important part in the railroad development of the South by consolidating a number of small roads and coordinating their service. After the interruption of his plans by the Civil War, Walters renewed his activities when efficient through service by rail to the North was demanded by development of truck farming in eastern North Carolina and Virginia. In 1889 he incorporated the holding company, later known as the Atlantic Coast Line Co., which, under his son, became the means of effecting consolidation of roads from Washington to Florida and the Gulf ports, and also to Memphis and St. Louis. He was an eager collector of objects of art and a patron of artists; he was also a breeder of fine stock and brought the Percheron horse to America.

WALTHALL, EDWARD CARY (*b. Richmond, Va., 1831; d. Washington, D.C., 1898*), Confederate major general, lawyer. Raised in Mississippi where he began practice at Coffeeville, 1852. An officer of unusual bravery and steadiness, he fought with tenacity at Chickamauga, at Lookout Mountain, and at Missionary Ridge where his brigade covered the Confederate retreat. After sharing in the fighting about Atlanta, he served under Hood in Tennessee. A friend of Lucius Q. C. Lamar, he helped overthrow the Carpetbag government in Mississippi, and was U.S. senator, Democrat, 1885–94, 1895–98. Like Lamar, he was an advocate of conciliation and strove to lessen sectional animosity.

WALTHALL, HENRY BRAZEAL (*b. Shelby Co., Ala., 1878; d. Monrovia, Calif., 1936*), motion picture actor. Grandnephew of Edward C. Walthall. A successful stage player, Walthall was persuaded to try the new medium of motion pictures by David W. Griffith *ca.* 1909. His greatest role while under Griffith's direction was that of Benjamin Cameron in *The Birth of a Nation*, 1915. A leader in the effort to produce motion pictures that would attract educated audiences, he failed to thrive after leaving Griffith *ca.* 1915 and faded from notice until the coming of talking pictures gave him the chance of a new start.

WALTHER, CARL FERDINAND WILHELM (*b. near Waldenburg, Saxony, 1811; d. St. Louis, Mo., 1887*), Lutheran clergyman. Immigrated to America, 1839; settled as pastor in Perry Co., Mo. With three associates, he founded a school at Altenburg in December 1839 which was moved to St. Louis, 1850, and became Concordia Theological Seminary. Pastor in St. Louis *post* 1841, he became professor of theology in Concordia Seminary, 1850. Meanwhile, in 1844 he issued the first number of *Der Lutheraner*, and was organizer of the Missouri Synod which he served as president, 1847–50, 1864–78. Walther dominated every activity in the synod and directed it with strict efficiency. An exponent of confessional Lutheranism, he engaged in a number of controversies with other theologians in which he displayed immense learning, considerable intolerance, and a strong belief in his own inerrancy. His influence has been greater than that of any other American Lutheran clergyman of the 19th century.

WALTON, GEORGE (*b. near Farmville, Va., 1741; d. "College Hill," near Augusta, Ga., 1804*), lawyer, Revolutionary patriot and soldier. Removed to Savannah, Ga., 1769. Served on Revolutionary committees; was secretary of the Georgia Provincial Congress and president of the Council of Safety. Elected to the Continental Congress, February 1776, he served until 1778 and from 1779 until September 1781. A signer of the Declaration of Independence, he was a member of a number of important committees. He advocated an equal vote for all states and urged

that the Indian trade be made a monopoly and that its control be vested in Congress. In January 1777, with George Taylor, he negotiated a treaty with the Six Nations at Easton, Pa. A conservative Whig and opponent of the radicals led by Button Gwinnett, he was governor of Georgia from November 1779 to January 1780. Chief justice of Georgia, 1783–89, he was again governor, 1789–90. This second term was marked by the establishment of a new state constitution, the location of the state capital at Augusta, and by pacification of the Creek Indians. He was several times a judge of the superior court of Georgia between 1790 and his death, and was U.S. senator, Federalist, from Georgia, 1795–99.

WALTON, LESTER AGLAR (*b. St. Louis, Mo., 1882; d. New York, N.Y., 1965*), diplomat and journalist. Editor of *New York Age* (1908–14, 1932) and writer for the *New York World* (1922–31) and *New York Herald Tribune* (1931). Publicity director for the National Negro Business League (1926–35) and the black division of the Democratic National Committee during the 1924, 1928, and 1932 presidential campaigns. Appointed envoy extraordinary and minister plenipotentiary to Liberia, 1935–46. Adviser to Liberia's United Nations delegation, 1948–49.

WALWORTH, CLARENCE AUGUSTUS (*b. Plattsburgh, N.Y., 1820; d. 1900*), Roman Catholic clergyman, Paulist. Son of Reuben H. Walworth. Graduated Union, 1838. After beginning the practice of law, he attended the General Theological Seminary, New York City. On becoming a Catholic in 1845, he went with Isaac T. Hecker and J. A. McMaster to study theology at St. Trond in Belgium and entered the Redemptorist Order. Ordained, 1848, he preached as a missionary in England, and returned to America, 1851, where he preached missions until 1858. With Hecker and others he helped found the Congregation of St. Paul the Apostle (Paulists), 1858. After further missionary service, he was pastor at St. Mary's Church, Albany, N.Y. *post* 1866. Among his books is a notable study, *The Oxford Movement in America* (1895).

WALWORTH, JEANNETTE RITCHIE HADERMANN (*b. Philadelphia, Pa., 1837; d. New Orleans, La., 1918*), Southern novelist. Author, among much negligible work, of *Southern Silhouettes* (1887), a series of post–Civil War sketches.

WALWORTH, REUBEN HYDE (*b. Bozrah, Conn., 1788; d. 1867*), jurist. Father of Clarence A. Walworth. Admitted to the New York bar, 1809, he began practice at Plattsburgh. During the War of 1812 he served as adjutant general of the state militia, distinguishing himself in the land battles at Plattsburgh, Sept. 6 and 11, 1814. Congressman, Democrat, from New York, 1821–23, he was circuit judge of the supreme court for the fourth judicial district of New York, 1823–28. Succeeding James Kent as chancellor of New York, 1828, he made important contributions to the system of equity jurisprudence which had been erected by Kent. He filled numerous gaps in the law of evidence and in equity pleading and practice by his decisions; he also added materially to the law relating to injunctions, to arbitration in equity matters, and the adoption of statutes in the Northwest Territory. A number of appeals were taken from his decisions to the court of errors, and in about one-third of these cases he was reversed. Given to biting sarcasm on the bench, he won a host of enemies, and the abolition of the court of chancery under the New York constitution in 1846 has been attributed in great measure to the desire of the bar to retire Walworth to private life. He thus contributed by indirection to an important legal reform, the merger of the courts of law and equity. Upon retirement in 1848, he was Democratic candidate for governor, but lost to Hamilton Fish. He then retired from political life.

WAMBAUGH, SARAH (*b. Cincinnati, Ohio, 1882; d. Cambridge, Mass., 1955*), internationalist and authority on plebiscites. Studied at Radcliffe College (B.A., 1902; M.A., 1916), the University of London School of Economics, and Oxford University. Prepared *Monograph on Plebiscites, With a Collection of Official Documents*, for the Paris Peace Conference (1920). Working for the League of Nations, she was adviser for the plebiscites on the Saar and the free city of Danzig; and for the Peruvian government in administering the Tacna-Arica plebiscite. For the United Nations, she observed elections in Greece (1945–46) and helped arrange plebiscites in Jammu and Kashmir in 1949. First Woman lecturer at the Academy of International Law at The Hague in 1927; also taught at Radcliffe and Wellesley. Wrote and lectured widely on the importance of the League of Nations and the United Nations.

WANAMAKER, JOHN (*b. Philadelphia, Pa., 1838; d. near Philadelphia, 1922*), merchant, pioneer in development of the modern department store. Beginning as an errand boy, he became a salesman of men's clothing. Between 1857 and 1860 he was secretary of the YMCA in Philadelphia, the first paid secretary of that organization. Opening a men's clothing shop in Philadelphia with his brother-in-law, 1861, Wanamaker conducted the business successfully and in 1876, with characteristic showmanship, opened a huge dry goods and clothing store in the former freight depot of the Pennsylvania Railroad at 13th and Chestnut Sts. In March of the next year he inaugurated his "new kind of store," a collection of specialty shops under one roof, with which he had extraordinary success. In 1896 he bought the New York City store of Alexander T. Stewart and continued it as Wanamaker's. An innovator and even a gambler, he began in 1865 a policy of guaranteeing their money back to dissatisfied customers; he was also a master of the art of publicity, notably newspaper advertising. He provided an employee's mutual-benefit association (1881), training classes for clerks, and other educational and recreational features. A consistent Republican, he was U.S. postmaster general, 1889–93. Although he instituted several technical improvements in the Post Office, he was denounced by reformers for his use of the spoils system.

WANAMAKER, LEWIS RODMAN (*b. Philadelphia, Pa., 1863; d. Atlantic City, N.J., 1928*), merchant. Son of John Wanamaker. Graduated College of New Jersey (Princeton), 1886. A member of the Wanamaker firm *post* 1902, and sole owner and director *post* 1922, he was responsible for the emphasis on the sale of antiques and other art objects which became an integral part of the business. A collector of rare musical instruments, he instituted public concerts in both the New York and Philadelphia stores. He was also an enthusiast for aviation and financed several expeditions among the Indian tribes of the West for the purpose of study.

WANAMAKER, REUBEN MELVILLE (*b. North Jackson, Ohio, 1886; d. Columbus, Ohio, 1924*), Ohio jurist, reformer of Ohio criminal jurisprudence.

WANER, PAUL GLEE (*b. Harrah, Okla., 1903; d. Sarasota, Fla., 1965*), baseball player. Began his career in 1924 with the Pacific Coast League, then was purchased in 1925 by the Pittsburgh Pirates for the then-unprecedented sum of $100,000. One of the most successful hitters of doubles in the game, he won the National League batting crown in 1927, 1934, and 1936. Named the National League's most valuable player in 1927. From 1940 to 1944 played as a reserve outfield and pinch hitter for the Boston Braves, New York Yankees, and Brooklyn Dodgers. Elected to Baseball Hall of Fame, 1952.

WANGER, WALTER (*b. Walter Feuchtwanger, San Francisco, Calif., 1894; d. New York, N.Y., 1968*), theater and motion-picture producer. Studied at Dartmouth, then worked in New York City as an assistant to the producer Harley Granville-Barker,

and later joined Elisabeth Marbury agency (1915–17). In 1919 was hired by Jesse L. Lasky to be general manager of Paramount Pictures' Long Island studios; supervised all of Paramount's productions (1923–31), became an executive producer at Metro-Goldwyn-Mayer in 1931, then returned to Paramount as an independent producer. In the late 1930's he was with United Artists, and in 1941 he set up his own production company allied with Universal Pictures. He was president of the Academy of Motion Picture Arts and Sciences (1939–45). He produced more than sixty pictures, and his erudition and love of innovation made him a leader in the industry.

WANLESS, WILLIAM JAMES (*b. Charleston, Ontario, Canada, 1865; d. Glendale, Calif., 1933*), Presbyterian medical missionary. Active in service in India, 1889–1930, principally at Miraj, he received knighthood (1928), for extraordinary work as hospital builder and medical teacher.

WANTON, JOSEPH (*b. Newport, R.I., 1705; d. Newport, 1780*), merchant, colonial governor of Rhode Island, 1769–75. A partial sympathizer with the Revolutionary movement in America, he opposed independence and retired from public life shortly after the outbreak of hostilities at Lexington.

WARBASSE, JAMES PETER (*b. Newton, N.J., 1866; d. Woods Hole, Mass., 1957*), surgeon and sociologist. Studied at Columbia College of Physicians and Surgeons (M.D., 1889) and at Göttingen and Vienna. Founder and first president of the Cooperative League of America (1916). An early advocate of socialized medicine. His liberal views, considered radical by his conservative colleagues, often put him at odds with his profession, and he withdrew from medicine to pursue interests in sociology. In 1939, he offered the first course in medical sociology at Long Island College of Medicine. Books include *Surgical Treatment* (1918–19), *Cooperative Democracy* (1923), and *Cooperative Medicine* (1936).

WARBURG, FELIX MORITZ (*b. Hamburg, Germany, 1871; d. New York, N.Y., 1937*), financier, philanthropist. Brother of Paul M. Warburg; son-in-law of Jacob H. Schiff. Came to America, 1894; became partner in Kuhn, Loeb & Co., 1897. Although he was the senior partner of this banking firm at the time of his death, Felix Warburg was primarily a humanitarian and lent his support to innumerable charitable, educational, and cultural organizations. A member of the New York City Board of Education and trustee of a number of schools including Teachers College at Columbia University, he also worked closely with Lillian D. Wald in her settlement work and was a leader in the establishment and management of the Federation for Support of Jewish Philanthropic Societies. Never a Zionist, he became increasingly associated *post* 1917 with the work of the Zionists in relocating displaced Jews and in securing a peaceful settlement of the Arab-Jewish problem in Palestine.

WARBURG, JAMES PAUL (*b. Hamburg, Germany, 1896; d. Greenwich, Conn., 1969*), financier, author, and government official. Moved with his parents to the United States in 1901. Studied at Harvard (B.A., 1917), then worked in several financial corporations. In 1933 joined President Franklin D. Roosevelt's first "brain trust" as a financial adviser, but soon resigned and criticized Roosevelt in a series of books, including *The Money Muddle* (1934), *It's Up to Us* (1934), *Hell Bent for Election* (1935), and *Still Hell Bent* (1936). As a free-lance originator of industrial financing, Warburg made a fortune by helping to find financing for Edwin H. Land, the inventor of the Polaroid process. He became a leading spokesman for the Committee to Defend America by Aiding the Allies and wrote *Peace in Our Time* (1940) and *Our War and Our Peace* (1941). During World War II he worked for the Office of Coordinator of Information and the Office of War Information. He became a critic of the Truman Doctrine and the idea of the United States as a global policeman. He opposed containment and favored accommodation with the Soviet Union and Communist China in the interest of peace. In 1961 he was appointed to assist John McCloy, who was forming a new Arms Control and Disarmament Agency and was negotiating with the Soviet Union.

WARBURG, PAUL MORITZ (*b. Hamburg, Germany, 1868; d. New York, N.Y., 1932*), banker. A partner in Kuhn, Loeb & Co., New York City, *post* 1902, Warburg was an authority on the central banking system employed in the principal European countries. After the panic of 1907 he joined with those urging a fundamental reform in the American banking system, and had a large part in the plan for a proposed national reserve association submitted by Senator Nelson W. Aldrich in 1911. Although the Federal Reserve law of 1913 was not wholly to his liking, Warburg served with great ability as a member of the first Federal Reserve Board, 1914–18. Thereafter he devoted himself chiefly to the organization and operation of the International Acceptance Bank. He received nationwide notice in March 1929 because of his plain warning of the disaster threatened by the wild stock speculation of that period; he predicted that unless speculation were brought under control, a general depression would ensue. After the panic of October 1929 and the succeeding commercial depression, he was quick to condemn emotional prophecies of ruin just as vigorously as he had warned against the delusions of the period of speculation. In analyzing the causes of the depression, he stressed the bad effects of efforts to maintain high prices by tariff barriers and other artificial expedients in the face of constantly accelerated mass production. He was the brother of Felix M. Warburg.

WARD, AARON MONTGOMERY (*b. Chatham, N.J., 1843; d. Highland Park, Ill., 1913*), mail-order merchant. As a salesman traveling out of St. Louis, Mo., Ward became aware of the difficulties of people in rural areas who were obliged to sell their own produce at low prices determined by competition, but had to make their own retail purchases at high cost without competition. He then conceived the idea of buying goods in large quantities for cash from the manufacturer and selling for cash by mail to the farmer. He began operations with his partner, G. R. Thorn, in Chicago, Ill., 1872; the firm's first stock was a small selection of dry goods, the first catalogue a single price sheet. By shrewd purchasing and a policy of permitting the return of goods if unsatisfactory, Ward succeeded from the very outset. By 1876 the Montgomery Ward catalogue had 150 pages with illustrations; at the time of his death, annual sales amounted to $40 million. Owing to a prolonged legal battle which he carried on in the Illinois courts, Chicago's lake frontage was preserved as a heritage for the people of that city.

WARD, ARCH BURDETTE (*b. Irwin, Ill., 1896; d. Chicago, Ill., 1955*), sportswriter and promoter. Notre Dame University's first athletic publicity director at the behest of Knute Rockne. Sportswriter for the *Chicago Tribune* from 1925 until his death. From 1937 wrote the column "In the Wake of the News," the oldest continuous sports column in American journalism. Conceived of and founded the all-star baseball series (1933) and the all-star football series (1934).

WARD, ARTEMAS (*b. Shrewsbury, Mass., 1727; d. Shrewsbury, 1800*), storekeeper, Massachusetts colonial legislator, Revolutionary general. Graduated Harvard, 1748. Holder of a number of offices in Worcester Co., Ward rose to colonel in the provincial militia during the French and Indian War. Active in opposition to royal authority, he became a member of the Council, 1770–74, despite disapproval of the royal governor. A member of the first and second Massachusetts provincial congresses, he took command of the forces besieging Boston, April 1775, and in May was formally commissioned general and commander in chief of Massachusetts troops. Reduced to second-in-command with the rank of major general after the appointment of George Washington to supreme command, he viewed his successor without cordiality and offered his resignation to Congress soon after the fall of Boston, March 1776. He remained, however, in command at Boston after the withdrawal of the main army to New York until relieved by William Heath, March 1777. Thereafter, he served as a councillor of Massachusetts, as a legislator, and as a member of the Continental Congress. As congressman, Federalist, from Massachusetts, 1791–95, he was assigned to committees dealing with military affairs.

WARD, ARTEMUS. *See* BROWNE, CHARLES FARRAR.

WARD, CHARLES ALFRED (*b. Elyria, Ohio, 1883; d. New York, N.Y., 1951*), marine architect. Studied at Webb's Academy and Home for Shipbuilders (now Webb Institute of Naval Architecture), graduating in 1904. Supervisor of early designs of submarines, Ward is remembered for his designs of commercial ships, notably the United States Lines' *America* (1938) and the *United States* (1952), holder of the record of the fastest transatlantic crossing.

WARD, CHARLES HENSHAW (*b. Norfolk, Nebr., 1872; d. New Haven, Conn., 1935*), teacher. A.B., Pomona College, 1896; A.M., Yale, 1899. Taught English at the Taft School, Watertown, Conn., 1903–22. Wrote a number of elementary textbooks of grammar and English and several popular expository works on the sciences.

WARD, CYRENUS OSBORNE (*b. western New York State, 1831; d. Yuma, Ariz., 1902*), machinist, labor journalist, and lecturer. Brother of Lester F. Ward. Author, among other works, of *A Labor Catechism of Political Economy* (1878) and *A History of the Ancient Working People* (1889, later published as *The Ancient Lowly*). He urged working people to refrain from violence and to achieve a socialistic state by political methods.

WARD, ELIZABETH STUART PHELPS (*b. Boston, Mass., 1844; d. 1911*), writer. Daughter of Austin Phelps; granddaughter of Moses Stuart. Married Herbert D. Ward, 1888. Interpreter of the intellectual, oversensitive people of New England and their compulsion to do "the painful right," she was the author of the phenomenally successful *The Gates Ajar* (1869) and of many works of fiction, including *The Silent Partner* (1871), *The Madonna of the Tubs* (1886), and *A Singular Life* (1894).

WARD, FREDERICK TOWNSEND (*b. Salem, Mass., 1831; d. Tzeki, China, 1862*), adventurer, soldier. After a number of years at sea, and in military service with William Walker in Nicaragua and with the French in the Crimea, he appeared in Shanghai, China, 1859. Developing an army of well-drilled Chinese soldiers which came to be called the "Ever Victorious Army," he opposed the Taiping rebels and recaptured Sungkiang. His force later cooperated effectively with the Anglo-French forces near Shanghai and Ning-po. He was mortally wounded in battle. The celebrated British general Charles "Chinese" Gordon later achieved success in quelling the rebellion with the military instrument that Ward had created.

WARD, GENEVIEVE (*b. New York, N.Y., 1838; d. London, England, 1922*), singer, actress. After success in opera in Paris, she made her American debut at the Academy of Music, New York City, November 1862, in *La Traviata* as Violetta. On the failure of her singing voice, she studied for the dramatic stage and played with success at both Drury Lane and the Comédie-

Française, 1875–77. Thereafter she was professionally active in the United States and abroad, scoring her greatest success in *Forget-Me-Not* by Herman Merivale. An intellectual player, she was described as of the school of Ristori.

WARD, GEORGE GRAY (*b. Great Hadham, England, 1844; d. New York, N.Y., 1922*), telegrapher, cable engineer. Came to America *ca.* 1876 as U.S. superintendent of a new cable company which broke the existing monopoly of the Anglo-American Telegraph Co. Served as general manager of the Commercial Cable Co. *post* 1884. Ward was primarily responsible for the diplomatic and engineering aspects of the work that resulted in the first cable across the Pacific. It was laid to Honolulu in 1902, to Manila in 1903, and to China and Japan in 1906.

WARD, HARRY FREDERICK (*b. Brentford, England, 1873; d. Palisades, N.J., 1966*), religious educator, author, and social critic. Immigrated to the United States in 1891. Studied at the University of Southern California, Northwestern (B.A., 1897), and Harvard (M.A., 1898). A disciple of the Social Gospel, he was accredited as a Methodist minister in 1902 and served several churches in the Chicago area. In 1907 drafted "The Social Creed of the Churches," a landmark church program for the benefit of the workers. This led to the formation in 1907 of the Methodist Federation for Social Service (later, Social Action). Ward served the federation as editor (1907–11) and general secretary (1911–44). Taught at Boston University's School of Theology (1913–18) and Union Theological Seminary (1918–41). He was chairman of the national board of the American Civil Liberties Union (1920–40) and national chairman of the American League Against War and Fascism (after 1936 the League for Peace and Democracy) (1934–40). His books include *The Labor Movement* (1917), *The New Social Order* (1919), *Our Economic Morality* (1929), *Which Way Religion?* (1931), and *In Place of Profit* (1933).

WARD, HENRY AUGUSTUS (*b. Rochester, N.Y., 1834; d. Buffalo, N.Y., 1906*), naturalist. Assisted in his efforts by the family of James S. Wadsworth, Ward worked under Agassiz at Cambridge, Mass., and later studied at the School of Mines in Paris, France. Professor of natural science in the University of Rochester, 1861–76, he is principally remembered for his founding of Ward's Natural Science Establishment for the preparation and sale of scientific materials to colleges and other institutions. Engaged chiefly in this work *post* 1864, he made a number of outstanding collections, including the natural history exhibit at the World's Columbian Exposition in 1893 which was bought by Marshall Field and was the nucleus of the Field Museum of Natural History.

WARD, HENRY BALDWIN (*b. Troy, N.Y., 1865; d. Urbana, Ill., 1945*), zoologist, parasitologist. Son of Richard Halsted Ward. A.B., Williams College, 1885. After graduate study abroad, in particular at University of Leipzig with Rudolph Leuckart, he entered the graduate school at Harvard (1890) and received the Ph.D. degree in 1892. He taught zoology briefly at University of Michigan, and then at University of Nebraska, 1902–09. As head of the department of zoology, University of Illinois, 1909–33, he established one of the first research laboratories in the United States to offer graduate work in parasitology. In 1914, he founded the *Journal of Parasitology*, which he continued to edit until 1932. Besides his papers on parasites, he was coauthor of *Fresh-Water Biology* (1918, with George C. Whipple).

WARD, HENRY DANA (*b. Shrewsbury, Mass., 1797; d. Philadelphia, Pa., 1884*), reformer, Episcopal clergyman. Grandson of Artemas Ward. Active in the Anti-Masonic movement and party *post* 1828, and in William Miller's Adventist movement, he was

ordained to the Episcopal ministry, 1844. Thereafter he devoted most of his time to teaching in New York City and Flushing, N.Y.

WARD, HERBERT DICKINSON (*b. Waltham, Mass., 1861; d. Portsmouth, N.H., 1932*), author. Son of William H. Ward; husband of Elizabeth S. P. Ward.

WARD, JAMES EDWARD (*b. New York, N.Y., 1836; d. Great Neck, N.Y., 1894*), shipowner and operator. Originally a ship chandler and manager of a general freighting business to Cuba, Ward instituted direct passenger and mail service to Havana by steamship, 1877, as the Ward Line. The firm was incorporated, 1881, as the New York & Cuba Mail Steamship Co.

WARD, JAMES HARMON (*b. Hartford, Conn., 1806; d. off Matthias Point, Va., 1861*), naval officer. Appointed midshipman, 1823. One of the most scholarly officers in the service and a recognized authority on ordnance and naval tactics, he was author of *An Elementary Course of Instruction on Ordnance and Gunnery* (1845) and of *A Manual of Naval Tactics* (1859). He served as first commandant of midshipmen at the U.S. Naval Academy, 1845–47. Commanding a flying flotilla which he had proposed for use on Chesapeake Bay and the Potomac River in the Civil War, he silenced Confederate batteries at Aquia Creek, June 1, 1861, and was killed in action about three weeks later.

WARD, JAMES WARNER (*b. Newark, N.J., 1816; d. Buffalo, N.Y., 1897*), teacher. Appointed librarian of the Grosvenor Library in Buffalo, 1874, he served until 1896, and brought the library to a position of eminence.

WARD, JOHN ELLIOTT (*b. Sunbury, Ga., 1814; d. Dorchester, Ga., 1902*), lawyer, Georgia legislator and official. Having held, among other offices, the posts of acting lieutenant governor of the state and mayor of Savannah, he presided over the Democratic Convention at Cincinnati, Ohio, 1856, which nominated James Buchanan. As U.S. minister to China, 1859–60, he was successful in exchanging ratifications of the new American treaty with China and in settling outstanding American claims. Opposed to the secession of Georgia, he took no part in the Civil War. *Post* 1866 he practiced law in New York City.

WARD, JOHN QUINCY ADAMS (*b. near Urbana, Ohio, 1830; d. New York, N.Y., 1910*), sculptor. Began career as student assistant to Henry Kirke Brown *ca.* 1849. Winning notice for bust portraits of Alexander H. Stephens, John P. Hale, and other statesmen in Washington, D.C., 1857–59, he opened a studio in New York City, 1861. His "Indian Hunter" was among the first statues to be placed in New York's Central Park; conceived as a statuette in 1857, it was sited, 1868. Meanwhile, along with "The Freedman" it had been shown in the Paris Exposition of 1867. These works, and also his statue of Matthew C. Perry and his 7th Regiment Memorial in Central Park, showed his characteristic technical mastery, but his finest work was still to come. Winning further fame for his equestrian monument to General G. H. Thomas (1878) and his statue of William G. Simms (1879), he touched the heights in his "Lafayette" (Burlington, Vt.) and his "George Washington" (Wall St., New York City, Sub-treasury Building), both of 1883. Among other outstanding works by Ward were his *Pilgrim*, placed in Central Park, 1885; his *Horace Greeley* in City Hall Park, New York; the James A. Garfield monument in Washington; and the Henry Ward Beecher Monument, Borough Hall, Brooklyn, N.Y. Ward was at his best in realistic rather than in idealized representation and preferred masculine themes. He was the first native sculptor to create without benefit of foreign training an impressive body of good work. Bringing a primitive Ohio vigor to what he did, he showed himself wholly out of sympathy with the mid-Victorian pseudoclassic ideals fostered in

Florence and Rome. In the final decade of his life he produced, among other works, the pediment of the New York Stock Exchange and the equestrian statue of General Hancock, Fairmount Park, Philadelphia, both in collaboration with Paul Bartlett. A generous man, he gave his support to every worthy enterprise in art.

WARD, JOSEPH (*b. Perry Centre, N.Y., 1838; d. 1889*), Congregational clergyman. Graduated Brown, 1865; attended Andover Theological Seminary. Began his ministry at Yankton, Dakota Territory, 1869. Opened a private school there which became the Yankton Academy, 1872, and was eventually made the Yankton High School, earliest in the territory. Principal founder of Yankton College, 1881, he served there as president and professor of philosophy until his death. The education law of South Dakota was almost wholly his work, and he played a great part in keeping the school lands of the territory safe from speculators.

WARD, LESTER FRANK (*b. Joliet, Ill., 1841; d. Washington, D.C., 1913*), Union soldier, sociologist. Brother of Cyrenus O. Ward. Raised in Illinois and Iowa. After Civil War service, he worked in the U.S. Treasury Department at Washington, D.C., 1865–81, meanwhile receiving from Columbian College (present George Washington University) the A.B. degree in 1869, the LL.B. in 1871, and the A.M. in 1872. Joining the staff of the U.S. Geological Survey, 1881, he was appointed geologist, 1883, and paleontologist, 1892. He was professor of sociology at Brown University, 1906–13. Ward made valuable studies in the natural sciences, but he is best known because of his leadership in the field of American sociology. He became a pioneer of evolutionary sociology in the United States through the publication of *Dynamic Sociology* (1883), *Outlines of Sociology* (1898), *Pure Sociology* (1903), and other works in which he sought to give a strongly monist and evolutionary interpretation to social development. He argued that the emotional, willing aspects of the human mind have produced ambitious aspirations for individual and social improvement, and that the intellect, when rightly informed with scientific truth, enables the individual or the social group to plan for future development. The mind will become "telic," enabling mankind to pass from passive to active evolutionary processes, and from natural to human or social evolution. This ability will usher in an age of systematic planning for human progress in which government will stress social welfare and democracy will pass into "sociocracy." Accepting the fact of wide differences in human heredity and racial aptitudes, he argued that latent talent can be called forth by a stimulating social environment and a general education in the sciences. Governments, therefore, should aim to abolish poverty and develop national systems of general education, suited in one aspect for genius, in another, for ordinary minds. He was author also of a "mental autobiography," *Glimpses of the Cosmos* (1913–18).

WARD, LYDIA ARMS AVERY COONLEY (*b. Lynchburg, Va., 1845; d. Chicago, Ill., 1924*), author, Chicago civic leader. Wife of Henry A. Ward.

WARD, MARCUS LAWRENCE (*b. Newark, N.J., 1812; d. 1884*), businessman, philanthropist. Republican governor of New Jersey, January 1866–January 1869; congressman from New Jersey, 1873–75. Established Civil War welfare institutions in Newark; secured passage of reform legislation as governor.

WARD, MONTGOMERY. *See* WARD, AARON MONTGOMERY.

WARD, NANCY (*fl. 1776–1781*), Cherokee leader, known as "Beloved Woman." A resident of Great Echota in present Monroe Co., Tenn., she was a strong advocate of peace and a friend of the white frontier settlers. On several occasions during the Revolution she warned the settlers in the Watauga and Holston valleys in time to save themselves from raids and exercised her tribal right of sparing prisoners.

WARD, NATHANIEL (*b. Haverhill, England, ca. 1578; d. Shenfield, England, 1652*), lawyer, clergyman, author. A.B., Emmanuel College, Cambridge, 1599; A.M., 1603. After practicing law for some time in England, he entered the ministry *ca.* 1619 and was chaplain to the British merchants at Elbing, Prussia. Returning to England, 1624, he was successively curate of St. James's, Piccadilly, London, and rector of Stondon Massey. Dismissed for nonconformity, 1633, he immigrated to Massachusetts Bay, 1634, and served briefly as a colleague minister at Agawam (Ipswich). Resigning his ministry, he was appointed by the General Court in 1638 to help prepare a legal code for Massachusetts, the first code of laws to be established in New England. According to John Winthrop, these laws (enacted 1641) were composed by Ward. The code was known as the "Body of Liberties" and was in effect a bill of rights, setting one of the cornerstones in American constitutional history. In 1645 Ward completed *The Simple Cobler of Aggawam in America* (London, 1647, under pseudonym "Theodore de la Guard"). The book was a protest against toleration, amusingly digressive and satirical; through it runs the prophecy of Presbyterianism. Ward expressed a strong opposition to "polypiety" in the church; in the state he would restore the old order with king, lords, and commons. Several other works in defense of tradition have been attributed to him. He was minister at Shenfield *post* 1648.

WARD, RICHARD (*b. Newport, R.I., 1689; d. 1763*), merchant, Rhode Island colonial legislator and official. Father of Samuel Ward (1725–76). Elected deputy governor of Rhode Island, May 1740, he became governor a few months later and continued in office three years. A conservative, he supported colonial defense efforts, unsuccessfully opposed excessive issue of paper money, supported Rhode Island in a boundary controversy with Massachusetts, and protested against invasion of charter rights by the British.

WARD, RICHARD HALSTED (*b. Bloomfield, N.J., 1837; d. 1917*), physician, microscopist. Graduated Williams, 1858; M.D., N.Y. College of Physicians and Surgeons, 1862. *Post* 1863 he practiced in Troy, N.Y., and taught botany and other scientific subjects at Rensselaer Polytechnic Institute, 1867–92. One of the first to demonstrate by the microscope the difference in cellular structure of blood from various animals, he was also an authority on adulteration of foods and medicines. He perfected a number of accessories for the microscope, notably an iris illuminator for the binocular instrument.

WARD, ROBERT DECOURCY (*b. Boston, Mass., 1867; d. 1931*), educator, climatologist. Graduated Harvard, 1889; A.M., 1893. Taught physical geography and meteorology at Harvard *post* 1890, becoming professor of climatology, 1910, the first in the United States. Author of *Practical Exercises in Elementary Meteorology* (1899), *The Climate of the United States* (1925), and other works.

WARD, SAMUEL (*b. Newport, R.I., 1725; d. Philadelphia, Pa., 1776*), farmer, Rhode Island colonial legislator. Son of Richard Ward. Conservative opponent of Stephen Hopkins in pre-Revolutionary politics. Governor of Rhode Island, 1762, 1765, and 1766, Ward signed the charter of the present Brown University, of which he was an original trustee. He vigorously opposed the Stamp Act. Elected a delegate to the First and Second Continental Congresses, Ward served as chairman of the Committee of the Whole, 1775, and proposed the appointment of George Washington as commander in chief of the colonial forces.

WARD, SAMUEL (*b. Westerly, R.I., 1756; d. New York, N.Y., 1832*), Revolutionary soldier, New York City merchant. Son of Samuel Ward (1725–76); father of Samuel Ward (1786–1839).

WARD, SAMUEL (*b. Warwick, R.I., 1786; d. New York, N.Y., 1839*), banker. Son of Samuel Ward (1756–1832); father of Samuel Ward (1814–84) and Julia Ward Howe. Became partner in the New York banking house of Prime & Sands, 1808; later became head of the firm, then known as Prime, Ward & King. Prevented repudiation of financial obligations by New York State in the panic of 1837; helped restore specie payments by New York banks in 1838. Helped found and became president of the Bank of Commerce in New York, 1839.

WARD, SAMUEL (*b. New York, N.Y., 1814; d. Pegli, Italy, 1884*), financier, lobbyist, author. Son of Samuel Ward (1786–1839); brother of Julia Ward Howe; uncle of Francis Marion Crawford. Graduated Columbia, 1831; made studies in France and Germany; worked briefly in his father's banking house of Prime, Ward & King. Having lost his fortune by 1849, he joined the gold rush to California, where he adapted himself with great success to the rough environment. He became the confidant of James R. Keene, who helped him with financial advice. After journalistic and other activities, he lived in Washington, D.C., during the closing years of the Civil War and through the administrations of Andrew Johnson and U. S. Grant, acting as a lobbyist in the employ of financiers and gaining a reputation for the entertainments which he offered to public officials. Among the intimates of the "King of the Lobby," as he was known, were W. H. Seward, Charles Sumner, James A. Garfield, William M. Evarts; he was also a friend of W. M. Thackeray and Henry W. Longfellow. Described as having "a vagueness concerning all points of morality, which would have been terrible in a man less actively good," Ward was author of *Lyrical Recreations* (1865, 1871) and is believed today to have been the author of "The Diary of a Public Man" (*North American Review*, August–November 1879).

WARD, SAMUEL RINGGOLD (*b. Maryland, 1817; d. Jamaica, British West Indies, ca. 1866*), black abolitionist and orator, Baptist and Congregational clergyman. Agent of the American and the New York State Anti-Slavery societies and of the Anti-Slavery Society of Canada. Spoke extensively and successfully in Great Britain, 1853–54.

WARD, THOMAS (*b. Newark, N.J., 1807; d. 1873*), physician, poet, playwright. Author of, among other works, *Passaic, a Group of Poems* (1842, under pseudonym "Flaccus") and *War Lyrics* (1865). Produced amateur operettas for charity in a theater attached to his New York City house, 1862–72.

WARD, THOMAS WREN (*b. Salem, Mass., 1786; d. 1858*), Boston merchant. Becoming American agent for the London, England, banking establishment of Baring Brothers through influence of his friend, Joshua Bates, Ward held that post from 1830 to 1853. Supervising operations which annually involved several million pounds sterling, he was regarded as one of the soundest financiers in the United States. He succeeded in bringing the firm through the crisis of 1837–42 with unimpaired reputation and credit.

WARD, WILLIAM HAYES (*b. Abington, Mass., 1835; d. 1916*), editor, orientalist. Father of Herbert D. Ward. Graduated Amherst, 1856; Andover Theological Seminary, 1859. Associated in editorial capacities with the *New York Independent*, 1868–1916. One of the earliest Assyriologists in the United States, he became the leading authority in the world on Assyrian and Babylonian seals. An exploring expedition conducted by him, 1884–85, resulted in the uncovering of ancient Nippur, 1888–1900. He was author, among other works, of *The Seal Cylinders of Western Asia* (1910).

WARDE, FREDERICK BARKHAM (*b. Deddington, England, 1851; d. Brooklyn, N.Y., 1935*), actor. Making his American debut in New York at Booth's Theatre, 1874, he subsequently played Shakespearean roles in support of Edwin Booth, Charlotte Cushman, Madame Janauschek, and others. At his death, he represented the last of the old school of tragedians. *Post* 1907 he lectured on Shakespeare and other topics connected with the drama, displaying scholarship and taste.

WARDEN, DAVID BAILIE (*b. near Greyabbey, Ireland, 1772; d. France, 1845*), teacher, diplomat, collector of Americana. A.M., University of Glasgow, 1797. Immigrated to America, 1799, after his arrest for association with the United Irishmen. Becoming a U.S. citizen, 1804, he went to Paris as private secretary to General John Armstrong and was later consul at Paris. After his removal from office, 1814, he spent the rest of his life in France, but gave a great deal of his time to the dissemination of information concerning America. He wa author, among other works, of *On the Origin . . . of Consular Establishments* (1813), *A Statistical, Political and Historical Account of the United States of North America* (1819), and several annotated catalogues of his book collections.

WARDEN, ROBERT BRUCE (*b. Bardstown, Ky., 1824; d. Washington, D.C., 1888*), Ohio jurist and supreme court reporter. Author of biographies of Salmon P. Chase and Stephen A. Douglas.

WARDER, JOHN ASTON (*b. Philadelphia, Pa., 1812; d. 1883*), physician. Associated as a boy with John J. Audubon, François Michaux, and Thomas Nuttall. M.D., Jefferson Medical College, 1836. Practiced in Cincinnati, Ohio, 1837–55. Thereafter a farmer at North Bend, Ohio, he was active in the state and national horticultural and pomological societies as officer and editor. He served as president of the American Forestry Association, 1875–82, and was an organizer of its successor, the American Forestry Congress. Among his books were *Hedges and Evergreens* (1858) and *American Pomology: Apples* (1867).

WARDMAN, ERVIN (*b. Salt Lake City, Utah, 1865; d. 1923*), journalist. Graduated Harvard, 1888. On staff of *New York Tribune*, 1889–95, he was briefly managing editor of *New York Press* and its editor in chief, 1896–1916. He made the paper an aggressive organ of liberal Republicanism and in the late 1890's coined the term "yellow journalism." *Post* 1916 he was publisher of the New York *Sun*. As an editorial writer his chief field was labor economics.

WARE, ASHUR (*b. Sherborn, Mass., 1782; d. 1873*), editor, jurist. Nephew of Henry Ware (1764–1845). Graduated Harvard, 1804; studied law in office of Loammi Baldwin. Removed to Portland, Maine, 1817, mainly to edit the *Eastern Argus*, and was an active force in Maine's home-rule politics and in the Democratic party. Becoming Maine's secretary of state, 1820, he served as U.S. district court judge in Maine, 1822–66. He was, in the opinion of Judge Story, perhaps the ablest American authority in the field of maritime law.

WARE, EDMUND ASA (*b. North Wrentham, Mass., 1837; d. 1885*), Congregational clergyman, educator. Graduated Yale, 1863. Appointed superintendent of education for Georgia by General O. O. Howard, 1867, Ware was a founder of Atlanta University (chartered 1867, opened 1869) and served as its president until his death. His idealism and courage were important factors in the university's success.

WARE, HENRY (*b. Sherborn, Mass., 1764; d. Cambridge, Mass., 1845*), Unitarian clergyman, theologian. Graduated Harvard, 1785. Pastor, First Church, Hingham, Mass., 1787–1805. His election as Hollis Professor of Divinity at Harvard in 1805 marked a new era in the history of Congregationalism and gave rise to a controversy between members of the liberal and orthodox parties. In 1820 the liberal Ware engaged in pamphlet argument with Dr. Leonard Woods (1774–1854), known as the "Wood'n Ware Controversy." In 1811 Ware began a course of instruction for ministerial candidates from which developed the Harvard Divinity School (organized, 1816), with Ware as professor of systematic theology and evidences. He resigned as Hollis Professor, 1840, but continued to teach in the Divinity School. He was father of Henry (1794–1843), John, and William Ware.

WARE, HENRY (*b. Hingham, Mass., 1794; d. Framingham, Mass., 1843*), Unitarian clergyman, author. Son of Henry Ware (1764–1845); brother of John and William Ware; father of John F. W. Ware and William R. Ware. Graduated Harvard, 1812. Pastor of the Second Church (Unitarian), Boston, 1817–*ca*. 1829, he served as editor of the *Christian Disciple* and was a leader in the establishment of the American Unitarian Association. He was professor of pulpit eloquence and pastoral care in Harvard Divinity School, *ca*. 1830–42.

WARE, JOHN (*b. Hingham, Mass., 1795; d. 1864*), physician, editor. Son of Henry Ware (1764–1845); brother of Henry (1794–1843) and William Ware. Graduated Harvard, 1813; M.D., Harvard Medical School, 1816. Practicing in Boston, he served as editor of several publications and was author in 1831 of the first important work on *delirium tremens* to appear in America. After succeeding James Jackson as Hersey Professor at Harvard Medical School, 1836, Ware was author of a number of scientific papers which included important discussions of croup and hemoptysis.

WARE, JOHN FOTHERGILL WATERHOUSE (*b. Boston, Mass., 1818; d. Milton, Mass., 1881*), Unitarian clergyman. Son of Henry Ware (1794–1843); half brother of William R. Ware. Principal pastorates at Fall River and Cambridgeport, Mass., and at Church of the Saviour, Baltimore, Md.; pastor of Arlington Street Church, Boston, *post* 1872.

WARE, NATHANIEL A. (*b. Massachusetts or South Carolina, date uncertain; d. near Galveston, Tex., 1854*), land speculator, public official. Secretary of Mississippi Territory, 1815–17, he lived thereafter in a number of places both North and South. He is best remembered for *Notes on Political Economy . . .* (1844, under pseudonym "A Southern Planter"), a work often echoing Henry C. Carey. Ware was a protectionist, almost unique in a Mississippian of that period, and an advocate of a balanced economy for the South.

WARE, WILLIAM (*b. Hingham, Mass., 1797; d. Cambridge, Mass., 1852*), Unitarian clergyman. Son of Henry Ware (1764–1845); brother of Henry (1794–1843) and John Ware. Graduated Harvard, 1816. Pastor of the first Unitarian Church to be established in New York City, 1821–36, he resigned the ministry and became noted thereafter as an author. Among his works, which were very popular in their time, were *Letters of Lucius M. Piso from Palmyra* (1837, entitled in subsequent editions *Zenobia: or, the Fall of Palmyra*); *Probus: or, Rome in the Third Century* (1838, published afterwards under the title *Aurelian*); *Julian: or, Scenes in Judea* (1841); and *Lectures on the Works and Genius of Washington Allston* (1852).

WARE, WILLIAM ROBERT (*b. Cambridge, Mass., 1832; d. Milton, Mass., 1915*), architect. Son of Henry Ware (1794–1843); half-brother of John F. W. Ware. Graduated Harvard, 1852; S.B., Lawrence Scientific School, 1856; studied in offices of Edward C. Cabot and Richard M. Hunt. Successful in practice in Boston with Henry Van Brunt, Ware and his partner experimented with an atelier for students in their own office, 1863–65. Appointed head of a proposed school of architecture in the Massachusetts Institute of Technology, 1865, Ware studied professional education abroad, and on his return brought with him Eugène Létang to take charge of the work in design at the new school. In 1881 Ware was called to New York to found a school of architecture at Columbia University where he remained until his retirement as professor emeritus, 1903. He may be called the founder of American architectural education in a very real sense. To him the architect was more than a mere technician—he was a an artist, an exponent of a traditional cultural history, and a member of society as a whole. In order to develop the creative side of his students, he borrowed from France the idea of teaching design by projects to be solved under criticism. His ideals of education appear in *An Outline of a Course of Architectural Instruction* (1866) and in a paper "On the Condition of Architecture and of Architectural Education in the United States" (*Papers*, Royal Institute of British Architects, 1866–67). He was author also, among other works, of *Modern Perspective* (1883); *The American Vignola* (1902–06); and *Shades and Shadows* (1912–13).

WARFIELD, BENJAMIN BRECKINRIDGE (*b. near Lexington, Ky., 1851; d. Princeton, N.J., 1921*), Presbyterian clergyman. Grandson of Robert J. Breckinridge. Graduated College of New Jersey (Princeton), 1871; Princeton Theological Seminary, 1876; studied also at University of Leipzig. Professor of New Testament in Western Theological Seminary, Pittsburgh, 1879–87, he was professor of theology at Princeton Seminary thereafter. Editor of the *Presbyterian and Reformed Review* (1890–1903), he was author of some twenty books on biblical and theological subjects. An orthodox Calvinist, he continued without concessions the theological tradition established at Princeton by the Hodges.

WARFIELD, CATHERINE ANN WARE (*b. Natchez, Miss., 1816; d. 1877*), writer. Daughter of Nathaniel A. Ware. Educated in Philadelphia, Pa., and a resident of Kentucky *post* 1833, Mrs. Warfield was author of minor verse and of the novel *The Household of Bouverie* (1860) and much other fiction. Her work was melodramatic and written in a cheerless, pedantic style.

WARFIELD, DAVID (*b. San Francisco, Calif., 1866; d. New York, N.Y., 1951*), actor. After years of playing burlesque and vaudeville, Warfield, known for his dialects, appeared in the David Belasco play *The Auctioneer* in 1900. The role of Simon Levi, a Russian Jewish exile on New York's Lower East Side, became Warfield's stock character. His next play, Belasco and Klein's *The Music Master*, opened in 1904, followed by Belasco's *The Grand Army Man* (1907), *The Return of Peter Grimm* (1911), and the Belasco production of Shakespeare's *The Merchant of Venice* (1922), in which Warfield played Shylock. He retired from the stage after the failure of the latter. Early investments in Loew's Incorporated made Warfield a millionaire.

WARFIELD, SOLOMON DAVIES (*b. near Mount Washington, Md., 1859; d. 1927*), Maryland manufacturer and financier. Postmaster of Baltimore, Md., 1894–1905. Organized and became president of Continental Trust Co., 1898, which was the agency of his later operations in railroads, public utilities, and cotton manufacturing. Among his successful operations were the organization and reorganization of the Seaboard Air Line Railway, and the merging of Baltimore utilities in the Consolidated Gas, Electric Light & Power Co.

WARING, GEORGE EDWIN (*b. Pound Ridge, N.Y., 1833; d. New York, N.Y., 1898*), agriculturist, sanitary engineer. Studied agricultural chemistry under James J. Mapes; managed Horace Greeley's farm at Chappaqua, N.Y.; drainage engineer of Central Park, New York City, 1857–61. After Civil War service in the Union Army, he managed the Ogden Farm near Newport, R.I., and then engaged as a professional expert in sanitary drainage of houses and towns. He made a notable success as a reforming and efficient streetcleaning commissioner of New York City, 1895–98.

WARING, JULIUS WATIES (*b. Charleston, S.C., 1880; d. New York, N.Y., 1968*), lawyer, federal judge, and civil rights activist. Studied at the College of Charleston (B.A., 1900), then built a thriving law practice in Charleston. Was assistant U.S. attorney (1914–21) and corporate counsel of Charleston (1933–42). In 1938 he directed the senatorial campaign of the notorius racist "Cotton" Ed Smith. While serving as a federal district judge (1942–52), he changed his racial views and handed down a series of liberal civil rights decisions, opposing, for example, the disfranchisement of blacks and segregation in public schools. Ostracized, even by relatives, he moved to New York City following his retirement, lending his hand to many civil rights causes.

WARMAN, CY (*b. near Greenup, Ill., 1855; d. Chicago, Ill., 1914*), railroadman, Colorado journalist. Author of many short stories and novels depicting the romance of the frontier and, in particular, of the pioneer railroads. Among his books were *Tales of an Engineer with Rhymes of the Rail* (1895) and *The Last Spike and Other Railroad Stories* (1906).

WARMOTH, HENRY CLAY (*b. MacLeansboro, Ill., 1842; d. Louisiana, 1931*), Union soldier, lawyer. Opened law office in New Orleans, La., 1865, for practice before military commissions and government departments. Outraged all factions by his attempts to harmonize interests of both blacks and whites while Republican governor of Louisiana, 1868–72. Engaged thereafter in sugar planting and refining near New Orleans.

WARNER, ADONIRAM JUDSON (*b. Wales, N.Y., 1834; d. Marietta, Ohio, 1910*), teacher, Union officer. Settled in Marietta, Ohio, 1865; bought and developed oil and coal lands and built two short-line railroads. A vehement opponent of the demonetization of silver in 1873, he introduced unsuccessful free-coinage bills while congressman, Democrat, from Ohio, 1879–81 and 1883–87. Remaining active in the fight for free silver, he served as president of the American Bimetallic League and later of the American Bimetallic Union. He spent the latter part of his life in industrial activity, for the most part in Georgia.

WARNER, AMOS GRISWOLD (*b. Elkader, Iowa, 1861; d. Las Cruces, N.Mex., 1900*), sociologist. Graduated University of Nebraska, 1885; Ph.D., Johns Hopkins, 1888. Taught economics at Nebraska and at Leland Stanford. Served as superintendent of charities for District of Columbia, 1891–93. Author of the standard work *American Charities* (1894).

WARNER, ANNA BARTLETT (*b. New York, N.Y., 1827; d. Highland Falls, N.Y., 1915*), author of children's books. Sister of Susan B. Warner.

WARNER, ANNE RICHMOND (*b. St. Paul, Minn., 1869; d. England, 1913*), popular novelist. Resided principally abroad *post* 1901. Author of many magazine serials and other works of fiction, of which the best known were *Susan Clegg and Her Friend Mrs. Lathrop* (1904) and four other books dealing with the same principal character.

WARNER, CHARLES DUDLEY (*b. Plainfield, Mass., 1829; d. Hartford, Conn., 1900*), journalist, essayist. Graduated Hamilton College, 1851. After attempting surveying, general business, and the law, Warner became assistant to Joseph R. Hawley on the Hartford, Conn., *Evening Press*, 1860, and was editor of the paper *post* 1861. After consolidation of the *Press* with the *Hartford Courant*, 1867, Warner remained identified with the *Courant* for the rest of his life. A friend of Mark Twain (with whom he collaborated on *The Gilded Age*, 1873) and other notable literary men of the period, Warner was author of a number of travel books, three novels, and two biographies, but he was at his best in the essay form. *My Summer in a Garden* (1871), *Backlog Studies* (1873), *Being a Boy* (1878), and other collections all bear the impress of the work of Charles Lamb and have something of his mellowness and grace. Warner was also a contributing editor to *Harper's New Monthly Magazine* and was a coeditor of *The Library of the World's Best Literature* (1896–97).

WARNER, EDWARD PEARSON (*b. Pittsburgh, Pa., 1894; d. Duxbury, Mass., 1958*), aeronautical engineer and civil servant. Studied at Harvard University and at the Massachusetts Institute of Technology. In 1919–20 he was chief physicist for the National Advisory Committee for Aeronautics. Warner taught at M.I.T. from 1920 to 1926, when he was appointed assistant secretary of the navy for aeronautics (1926–29). From 1929 to 1934 he was the editor of the magazine *Aviation*. From 1934 to 1935 he was vice-chairman of the Federal Aviation Commission and from 1938 to 1945 he was a member and vice-chairman of the Civil Aeronautics Authority (later Board). After World War II Warner became head of the International Civil Aviation Organization (1947–57), and was instrumental in standardizing flight rules and procedures for international commercial flights. Books include *Airplane Design* (1927).

WARNER, FRED MALTBY (*b. Hickling, Nottinghamshire, England, 1865; d. Orlando, Fla., 1923*), businessman, Michigan legislator. Brought to America as an infant, he was raised in Farmington, Mich. Successful in the cheese-making industry, farming, and banking, he appeared thoroughly conservative in background when elected Republican governor of Michigan in 1904. However, during his term (1905–11) he undertook a sturdy fight for liberal reforms, including a general primary law, heavier taxation and lower rates on railroads, stricter control of public utilities and insurance companies, conservation of natural resources, and curbing of stock manipulation.

WARNER, GLENN SCOBEY ("POP") (*b. Springville, N.Y., 1871; d. Palo Alto, Calif., 1954*), football coach. Football coach at Carlisle Indian School, Pa. (1899–1903; 1907–14). Experimented with new rules and forms of the game including the forward pass, the single wingback attack, and the double wingback formation. With All-American halfback Jim Thorpe on his 1912 team, Warner gained national recognition when the team beat Harvard, Dartmouth, the University of Pennsylvania, and the University of Chicago. From 1914 to 1925 he coached at the University of Pittsburgh; from 1925 to 1932 at Stanford University; and from 1932 to 1939 at Temple University. All of these teams enjoyed great success. Along with Knute Rockne of Notre Dame, he dominated college football coaching.

WARNER, HARRY MORRIS (*b. Krasnosielce, Poland, 1881; d. Bel Air, Calif., 1958*), motion picture executive. Immigrated to the U.S. in the late 1880's. Harry Warner was the financial manager of Warner Brothers Pictures, Inc., founded in 1923. A distributing company founded in 1903 by four Warner brothers and a sister, the firm was, by 1930, the second largest film company in Hollywood. Through early expansion into theaters and sound pictures, the company was financially successful from the beginning. Famous for musicals and gangster films. Harry Warner was president of the company from 1923 until 1951 and chairman of the board until his death.

WARNER, HIRAM (*b. Williamsburg, Mass., 1802; d. Atlanta, Ga., 1881*), Georgia jurist and legislator. Chief justice of the state supreme court, 1867–68 and 1872–80.

WARNER, JAMES CARTWRIGHT (*b. Gallatin, Tenn., 1830; d. 1895*), industrialist. A prime factor in the revival and modernization of the charcoal iron industry in Middle Tennessee *post* 1868.

WARNER, JONATHAN TRUMBULL (*b. Hadlyme, Conn., 1807; d. California, 1895*), California pioneer and legislator. Employed by Jedediah Smith, 1831, as clerk of a trading expedition to New Mexico, Warner reached Santa Fe early in July; he then joined a trading expedition to California, arriving in Los Angeles in December. Employed for a time by Abel Stearns, he opened a store of his own in 1836. He became a Mexican citizen, 1843, and began acquisition of Warner's Ranch, southeast of Los Angeles, 1844. Later losing the bulk of his property, he yet remained one of the most widely esteemed of the American pioneers. He was coauthor of *An Historical Sketch of Los Angeles County* (1876).

WARNER, JUAN JOSÉ. *See* WARNER, JONATHAN TRUMBULL.

WARNER, LANGDON (*b. Cambridge, Mass., 1881; d. Cambridge, 1955*), art historian. Graduated Harvard, 1903. Taught at Harvard, 1915–17, when he became director of the Philadelphia Museum of Art (1919–23). Returned to Harvard where he remained until his death. Offered the first courses in Oriental art in the U.S. The leading Orientalist in the U.S., Warner was technical consultant to General Douglas MacArthur on arts and monuments in occupied Japan. His books include *Japanese Sculpture of the Suiko Period* (1923), *The Long Old Road in China* (1926), *Buddhist Wall Paintings* (1936), and *The Enduring Art of Japan* (1951). Responsible for at least four new departments of Asian art in leading museums and trained a generation of teachers, curators, experts, and collectors.

WARNER, OLIN LEVI (*b. Suffield, Conn,., 1844; d. 1896*), sculptor. Originally self-taught, he studied in Paris under Jouffroy and J. B. Carpeaux, *ca.* 1869–1872. He gradually gained fame *post* 1876 as a sculptor of portrait busts which were truly classic in feeling and profound in their interpretation of character. Among his outstanding works were portrait studies of a number of Northwest Indian chiefs including Chief Joseph; William L. Garrison on Commonwealth Avenue, Boston, Mass.; and the figure of Charles Devens in front of the Boston State House. He also designed and modeled the door of the Library of Congress, Washington D.C., entitled "Oral Tradition."

WARNER, SETH (*b. present Roxbury, Conn., 1743; d. Roxbury, 1784*), Revolutionary soldier. Removed to Bennington, Vt., 1763, where, with Ethan Allen and others, he resisted assertion of authority over Vermont by the province of New York. During the Revolution he aided Allen and Benedict Arnold in the surprise of Ticonderoga on May 10, 1775, and himself captured Crown Point on the following day. Commanding a regiment of Green Mountain Boys, he served under Montgomery in Canada. In 1777, during the advance of Burgoyne, he commanded the rear guard of St. Clair's army and fought an action at Hubbardton on July 7. The timely arrival of his regiment in the latter part of the battle of Bennington (August 16, 1777) is said to have turned the tide in favor of the Americans.

WARNER, SUSAN BOGERT (*b. New York, N.Y., 1819; d. Highland Falls, N.Y., 1885*), novelist. Sister of Anna B. Warner. Author, among other works, of the best-selling *The Wide, Wide World* (1850, under pseudonym "Elizabeth Wethrell") and *Queechy* (1852). Her description of the emotions of her characters (which found expression in tears on almost every page) compensated in the minds of contemporary readers for the absence of action in her stories.

WARNER, WILLIAM (*b. Shullsburg, Wis., 1840; d. 1916*), lawyer. Union soldier. In practice in Kansas City, Mo., *post* 1865, he was U.S. attorney for the western district of Missouri, 1882–84, 1898, and 1902–05. Republican congressman from Missouri, 1885–87, 1889–91, and U.S. senator, 1905–11, he was strongly conservative and seldom rose above the level of complacent mediocrity.

WARNER, WILLIAM LLOYD (*b. Redlands, Calif., 1898; d. Chicago, Ill., 1970*), social anthropologist. Studied at Berkeley (B.A., 1925), then worked in Australia under Alfred Radcliffe-Brown (1926–29), where his work was one of the earliest efforts to understand the linkages between social-structural and cultural-symbolic phenomena. His dissertation is the classic *A Black Civilization: A Social Study of an Australian Tribe* (1937). At Harvard (1929–35) Warner worked with Elton Mayo on the Hawthorne Western Electric plant and the Yankee City studies. The latter were published in six volumes, 1941–59. He took a position at the University of Chicago in 1935 and became involved with the Committee on Human Development. In 1946 Warner and Mary Gardner formed Social Research, Inc., a consulting firm. While teaching at Michigan State (1959–70), he wrote *The American Federal Executive* (1967), a study of corporate executives.

WARNER, WORCESTER REED (*b. near Cummington, Mass., 1846; d. Eisenach, Germany, 1929*), manufacturer. Partner with Ambrose Swasey in making turret lathes and other special machinery, 1881–1911, Warner devoted most of his leisure to astronomy and the engineering of telescopes. Among others which he and Swasey designed, built, and installed were those at the Lick Observatory, the Yerkes telescope, and the 72-inch telescope for the Dominion of Canada.

WARREN, CHARLES (*b. Boston, Mass., 1868; d. Washington, D.C., 1954*), constitutional authority and historian. Graduated Harvard Law School, 1892. Appointed assistant U.S. attorney general (1914–18) by Woodrow Wilson; author of the Espionage and Trading With the Enemy Acts of 1917. In private practice in Washington, *post* 1918. His three-volume *The Supreme Court in United States History* (1922) won the Pulitzer Prize for history in 1923, and is often cited by the justices of the court in their rulings and by presidents in their uses of presidential powers.

WARREN, CYRUS MOORS (*b. West Dedham, Mass., 1824; d. Manchester, Vt., 1891*), tar-roofing manufacturer, chemist. B.S., Lawrence Scientific School, Harvard, 1855. Studied also in Paris, at Heidelberg under Bunsen, at Munich under Liebig, and elsewhere abroad. Made important researches on the hydrocarbon constituents of tars; developed improved process of "fractional condensation" (*ca.* 1865) which was afterwards applied to study of the hydrocarbons in Pennsylvania petroleum; invented processes of purification for asphalt. Warren's petroleum investigations may be said to mark the beginning of modern exact research in this field.

WARREN, FRANCIS EMROY (*b. Hinsdale, Mass., 1844; d. 1929*), Union soldier, Wyoming pioneer, cattle- and sheep-raiser. Republican governor of Wyoming Territory, 1885–86, 1889–90. Elected first governor of the state of Wyoming, he resigned immediately to become U.S. senator, serving 1890–93 and 1895–1929. He was at various times chairman of the Senate committee on military affairs and of the committee on appropriations; he was particularly interested in the reclamation of arid lands.

WARREN, GEORGE FREDERICK (*b. near Harvard, Nebr., 1874; d. probably Ithaca, N.Y., 1938*), agricultural economist. Graduated University of Nebraska, 1897; Ph.D., Cornell University, 1905. *Post* 1906 a teacher of agricultural subjects at Cornell, and ultimately head of the department of agricultural economics there, Warren made his chief contribution by originating farm cost-accounting and by promotion of efficiency through statistical analysis of the income of individual farms and groups of farms. The agricultural surveys introduced at Cornell became the basis of surveys conducted at other land-grant colleges and by the U.S. Department of Agriculture. A frequent adviser to the government both on the state and federal level, he advocated the "commodity" or "compensated" dollar, a government-managed currency whose purchasing power in terms of commodities would be kept uniform by manipulating the price of gold through government purchases of that metal. In October 1933 President F. D. Roosevelt devalued the dollar in accordance with the Warren plan and, though the results failed to live up to Warren's predictions as a remedy for depression, Warren continued for several years to act as a consultant on monetary policy to the Roosevelt administration.

WARREN, GOUVERNEUR KEMBLE (*b. Cold Spring, N.Y., 1830; d. Newport, R.I., 1882*), soldier, engineer. Graduated West Point, 1850. Assigned to the Topographical Engineers. Made surveys in Mississippi River Delta and on other river-improvement projects; assisted A. A. Humphreys as compiler of maps and reports for Pacific Railroad exploration; made maps and reconnaissances in Dakota and Nebraska territories. A gallant and highly effective Union Army brigade, division, and corps commander during the Civil War, he rendered his most distinguished service at Gettysburg, July 1863. Making a reconnaissance of the Union left, he discovered that Little Round Top was undefended and improvised a force for its defense, an action which saved the Union Army from repulse. Commanding the V Corps at Five Forks, April 1, 1865, he clinched the victory but was summarily relieved of command by General P. H. Sheridan. Returning to river and harbor work, he continued to apply for a board of inquiry into the causes of his relief at Five Forks, but did not receive vindication until after his death.

WARREN, HENRY CLARKE (*b. Cambridge, Mass., 1854; d. 1899*), orientalist, authority on Pali and the sacred books of southern Buddhism.

WARREN, HENRY ELLIS (*b. Boston, Mass., 1872; d. Ashland, Mass., 1957*), inventor. Studied at Massachusetts Institute of Technology (B.S., 1894). Inventor of the synchronous electric clock in 1914. Later devised master clock for General Electric to control power frequencies at generating stations.

WARREN, HENRY WHITE (*b. Williamsburg, Mass., 1831; d. University Park, near Denver, Colo., 1912*), Methodist clergyman. Brother of William F. Warren. Pastor in several Massachusetts towns and in Philadelphia, Pa., and New York City. Elected bishop, 1880, he took up residence at Atlanta, Ga., and later in the neighborhood of Denver, Colo. Among his numerous writings was *The Lesser Hymnal* (1875), which he prepared with Eben Tourjée.

WARREN, HERBERT LANGFORD (*b. Manchester, England, 1857; d. 1917*), architect. The son of an American Swedenborgian missionary, Warren came to America in 1876 and studied at the Massachusetts Institute of Technology, 1877–79.

He served as assistant in the office of Henry H. Richardson, 1879–84. After practicing for a time, he became an instructor at Harvard in 1893 and the school of architecture there formed itself about him. Elected professor of architecture, 1899, he became first dean of the independent faculty of architecture, 1914. Gifted in the interpretation of great architecture and its principles, he was author, among other works, of *The Foundations of Classic Architecture* (1919, augmented by Fiske Kimball).

WARREN, HOWARD CROSBY (*b. Montclair, N.J., 1867; d. 1934*), psychologist. Graduated College of New Jersey (Princeton), 1889; M.A., 1891; studied also at Leipzig, Berlin, and Munich. Early a believer in a deterministic interpretation of mental processes, he was influenced by Spencer and the psychology of the British Associationists. A teacher of psychology at Princeton *post* 1893, and first chairman of a separate department of psychology *post* 1920, he expressed in his writings and in his textbook *Elements of Human Psychology* (1922) a conservatively behavioristic point of view. He was joint editor of the *Psychological Bulletin*, 1904–34, and editor of the *Psychological Review*, 1916–34.

WARREN, ISRAEL PERKINS (*b. present Bethany, Conn., 1814; d. 1892*), Congregational clergyman. Editor of publications, American Tract Society at Boston, Mass., 1859–70; editor and publisher, the *Christian Mirror* at Portland, Maine, *post ca.* 1876.

WARREN, JAMES (*b. Plymouth, Mass., 1726; d. 1808*), merchant, farmer, Massachusetts legislator. Graduated Harvard, 1745. Married Mercy Otis Warren, 1754. A friend and trusted adviser of John and Samuel Adams, he figured in his own community as an organizer of the radicals and served on the local revolutionary committees. President of the Provincial Congress of Massachusetts, 1775, he became speaker of the state House of Representatives in the new General Court in 1776. Pursued by the enmity of John Hancock, he failed of reelection to the legislature, 1778, and did not return to political power until Shays's Rebellion, 1786, when he plainly showed sympathy to the insurgents. Elected speaker of the Massachusetts House, 1787, he boldly criticized the government's handling of the insurrection and adopted a very unorthodox stand on the question of the currency. He opposed with ability any ratification of the Federal Constitution without a bill of rights. Defeated as candidate for lieutenant governor, he retired to scientific farming.

WARREN, JOHN (*b. Roxbury, Mass., 1753; d. 1815*), surgeon. Father of John C. Warren (1778–1856). Graduated Harvard, 1771; studied medicine with his brother, Joseph Warren, and with Edward A. Holyoke. After Revolutionary War service, 1775–77, he began practice in Boston, Mass., and was soon the leading surgeon there. His private course of anatomical lectures in 1780–81 led to the establishment of a medical department at Harvard College, November 1782. Warren began service there as professor of anatomy and surgery in 1783. A bold and skillful operator, Warren performed one of the first abdominal operations recorded in America and was a pioneer in amputation at the shoulder joint; he also did much to promote adoption of cowpox vaccination *post* 1800. His most notable contribution to medical literature was *A View of the Mercurial Practice in Febrile Diseases* (1813).

WARREN, JOHN COLLINS (*b. Boston, Mass., 1778; d. 1856*), surgeon. Son of John Warren. Graduated Harvard, 1797; studied medicine with his father and in London, Edinburgh, and Paris. Practiced in Boston *post* 1802. Adjunct professor of anatomy and surgery at Harvard Medical School *post* 1809, he became full professor on the death of his father, serving 1815–47. With James

Jackson, he revolutionized medical education and practice and was a prime mover in the erection of the Massachusetts General Hospital. First surgeon in the United States to operate for strangulated hernia, he was operator also in the famous trial of anesthesia by ether at Massachusetts General, Oct. 16, 1846 (the ether administered by W. T. G. Morton). He was author, among other works, of *Surgical Observations on Tumours* (1837), a landmark in the history of this subject.

WARREN, JOHN COLLINS (*b. Boston, Mass., 1842; d. 1927*), surgeon. Grandson of John C. Warren (1778–1856). Graduated Harvard, 1863; Harvard Medical School, 1866. Returning from further study abroad in 1869, he began practice in Boston and soon associated himself with the Harvard Medical School as a teacher of surgery; he was Moseley Professor, 1899–1907. Author, among other works, of *Surgical Pathology and Therapeutics* (1895), a notable accomplishment based on bacteriology. His principal interest was in medical progress and education.

WARREN, JOSEPH (*b. Roxbury, Mass., 1741; d. Breed's Hill, outside Boston, Mass., 1775*), physician, Revolutionary patriot. Brother of John Warren. Graduated Harvard, 1759. Practicing in Boston, Warren became a friend of John Adams and an ardent Whig; he was a member of the North End Caucus and of other revolutionary clubs and committees. He delivered the anniversary speeches of the Boston Massacre in 1772 and 1775, served on the local Committee of Safety, and drafted the "Suffolk Resolves." On Apr. 18, 1775, he sent William Dawes and Paul Revere to warn Hancock and Adams of their danger of capture. Chosen president *pro tempore* of the Provincial Congress, August 23, he was killed rallying troops during the battle of Bunker Hill.

WARREN, JOSIAH (*b. Boston, Mass., ca. 1798; d. Charlestown, Mass., 1874*), musician, inventor, American pioneer of philosophical anarchy. An extreme individualist, he was author, among other works, of *Equitable Commerce* (1846), *True Civilization an Immediate Necessity* (1863), and the posthumous *True Civilization* (1875).

WARREN, LEONARD (*b. New York, N.Y., 1911. d. New York, 1960*), operatic and concert singer. One of the world's greatest Verdi baritones, Warren won the Metropolitan Opera Auditions of the Air in 1938 after studying at the Greenwich House Music School. He then studied in Italy before making his Metropolitan Opera debut in 1939 as Paolo in Verdi's *Simon Boccanegra*. Sang 25 roles at the Metropolitan in 633 performances. Died on the stage at the Metropolitan during a performance of *La Forza del Destino*.

WARREN, MERCY OTIS (*b. Barnstable, Mass., 1728; d. 1814*), poet, dramatist, historian. Sister of James Otis; wife of James Warren; aunt of Harrison G. Otis (1765–1848). A talented woman, Mercy Warren became an early laureate of the patriot cause and was later its historical apologist. Among other works, she was author of *The Adulateur* (1773) and *The Group* (1775), satires; and *Poems Dramatic and Miscellaneous* (1790). Her *History of the Rise, Progress and Termination of the American Revolution* (1805) reveals expert knowledge of public affairs and is a caustic analysis of the motives of those "malignants" who opposed American freedom.

WARREN, MINTON (*b. Providence, R.I., 1850; d. Cambridge, Mass., 1907*), classicist. Graduated Tufts College, 1870; did graduate studies at Yale, Leipzig, Bonn; Ph.D., Strasbourg, 1879. Inaugurated Latin Seminary at Johns Hopkins while professor there, 1879–99; taught Latin at Harvard *post* 1899 and was appointed Pope Professor, 1905. A master in the idiom of Latin comedy.

WARREN, SIR PETER (*b. Warrenstown, Ireland, 1703; d. Dublin, Ireland, 1752*), British vice admiral. On duty in America, 1730–47, he made his residence in New York City where he acquired title to the "Warren Farm," now known as Greenwich Village, and bought a large tract in the Mohawk Valley of which his nephew, Sir William Johnson, became manager. In 1731 he married Susannah, sister of James and Oliver De Lancey. In 1745 he cooperated with William Shirley in the attack on Louisburg, Cape Breton Island, later receiving appointment as governor. On May 3, 1747, he was the outstanding hero of the British naval victory over the French off Cape Finisterre. Thereafter, he changed his residence from New York City to London, was knighted, and served in the British Parliament.

WARREN, RICHARD HENRY (*b. Albany, N.Y., 1859; d. South Chatham, Mass., 1933*), organist, composer. Remembered principally as organist at St. Bartholomew's Church and at the Church of the Ascension, both in New York City, 1886–1921.

WARREN, RUSSELL (*b. Tiverton, R.I., 1783; d. Providence, R.I., 1860*), architect. A devotee of the Greek Revival, he designed a number of luxurious houses for ship captains and merchants in Bristol, R.I., *ca.* 1805–25, and thereafter practiced in Providence. He is said to have devised the Warren truss used in steel bridge construction. Several of his finest productions were erected in New Bedford, Mass., among them his masterpiece, the J. A. Parker house (1834).

WARREN, SAMUEL PROWSE (*b. Montreal, Canada, 1841; d. 1915*), organist, composer. Held principal posts as organist at Grace Episcopal Church, New York City, 1868–74 and 1876–94, and at the First Presbyterian Church, East Orange, N.J., 1895–1915. His choral settings for the Epsicopal service are of very high merit.

WARREN, WILLIAM (*b. Bath, England, 1767; d. Baltimore, Md., 1832*), actor, theatre manager. Father of William Warren (1812–1888). Came to America, 1796, to act with Thomas Wignell's company; played and managed theaters almost exclusively in Baltimore and Philadelphia, Pa. Celebrated for the dignity and rich humor of his "old man" roles. He was founder, through his son and the marriages of his daughters, of a celebrated American theatrical family.

WARREN, WILLIAM (*b. Philadelphia, Pa., 1812; d. Boston, Mass., 1888*), actor. Son of William Warren (1767–1832). Made debut, Oct 27, 1832, at Arch Street Theater, Philadelphia, Pa. After obtaining his professional schooling in a number of migratory troupes and lesser companies, he was associated with the stock company at the Boston Museum from 1847 until his retirement from the stage in 1883. A skillful comedian, whose acting was marked by high intelligence and faithful study, he was also a leading citizen of Boston and the friend, among others, of Oliver W. Holmes, Henry W. Longfellow, and Mr. and Mrs. James T. Fields.

WARREN, WILLIAM FAIRFIELD (*b. Williamsburg, Mass., 1833; d. Brookline, Mass., 1929*), Methodist clergyman, educator. Brother of Henry W. Warren. Graduated Wesleyan University, 1853; studied at Andover Theological Seminary and at the universities of Berlin and Halle. A professor of theology in Germany, 1861–66, he became president of the Boston Theological School, 1867, serving as such until 1873. A founder of Boston University and the guiding spirit in its development, he served it as president, 1873–1903, continuing his work as professor at the theological school throughout his term and as late as 1920. Basing his plan for the university upon a fusion of English emphasis on the humanities grounded in the classics with German thoroughness in research, he also insisted on the maintenance of comparative independence by the professional and technical schools. He was zealous in providing international educational opportunities for the university's students. Under his leadership the theological school was the first to require sociology and the study of missions in the course leading to a degree. He was author, among many other works, of a celebrated address published in 1886 under the title *A Quest for a Perfect Religion.*

WARRINGTON, ALBERT POWELL (*b. Berlin, Md., 1866; d. Ojai, Calif., 1939*), lawyer, Theosophical leader.

WARRINGTON, LEWIS (*b. Williamsburg, Va., 1782; d. 1851*), naval officer. Appointed midshipman, 1800. In active and varied service thereafter, Warrington is remembered for his victory of Apr. 29, 1814, off Cape Canaveral, when he captured the British brig *Epervier,* himself commanding the sloop-of-war *Peacock. Post* 1842 he was chief of the bureau of yards and docks, briefly secretary of the navy in 1844, and chief of the bureau of ordnance.

WARTHIN, ALDRED SCOTT (*b. Greensburg, Ind., 1866; d. 1931*), clinical pathologist, investigator of syphilis.

WASHAKIE (*b. probably Montana, ca. 1804; d. Fort Washakie, Wyo., 1900*), Shoshone chief. Part Shoshone and part Umatilla, he became chief of the eastern band of Shoshone during the 1840's. Friendly to the whites and of great assistance to the overland immigrants, he ranked high as a warrior in many small defensive wars which he fought against more powerful neighboring tribes. His band, originally ranging over the lower valley of the Green River, was settled on the present Shoshone reservation in the Wind River country at the Fort Bridger council of 1868.

WASHBURN, ALBERT HENRY (*b. Middleboro, Mass., 1866; d. Vienna, Austria, 1930*), lawyer, diplomat. Graduated Cornell University, 1889. Entering the U.S. consular service, he served at Magdeburg, Germany, 1890–93. While private secretary to Henry Cabot Lodge, 1893–96, he studied law and was engaged for some years in federal and private practice, becoming a specialist in customs cases. As U.S. minister to Austria *post* 1922, he aided in the financial rehabilitation of the country and the restoration of its credit.

WASHBURN, CADWALLADER COLDEN (*b. Livermore, Maine, 1818; d. Eureka Springs, Ark., 1882*), lawyer, land agent, Union major general, industrialist. Brother of Elihu B. Washburne, Israel Washburn, and William D. Washburn. Removing to the West in 1839, he began practice of law at Mineral Point, Wis., 1842, but gradually abandoned the law for banking and land operations. As congressman, Republican, from Wisconsin, 1855–61, 1867–71, he achieved no great prominence, nor was his term as governor of Wisconsin (1872–73) particularly outstanding. Engaging in vast industrial enterprises, he acquired water-power rights at the Falls of St. Anthony (Minneapolis, Minn.), which enabled him to become one of the nation's foremost manufacturers of flour. He was one of the first to adopt the "new process" of milling which created a demand for Northwest spring wheat and completely revolutionized the U.S. flour industry. He was an organizer in 1877 of Washburn, Crosby & Co.

WASHBURN, CHARLES GRENFILL (*b. Worcester, Mass., 1857; d. 1928*), lawyer, wire manufacturer, Massachusetts legislator. As congressman, Republican, from Massachusetts, 1906–11, he performed his principal service with the committees on insular affairs and patents and copyrights. His advice to Chief Justice White in 1911 helped establish a reaffirmation by the U.S.

Supreme Court of the application of the "rule of reason" to the Sherman Law.

WASHBURN, EDWARD ABIEL (*b. Boston, Mass., 1819; d. New York, N.Y., 1881*), Episcopal clergyman. Principal rectorate at Calvary Church, New York, N.Y., *post* 1865. Next to Phillips Brooks, he was in his day the leading representative of broad churchmanship in the Episcopal ministry.

WASHBURN, EDWARD WIGHT (*b. Beatrice, Nebr., 1881; d. 1934*), chemist, educator. B.S., Massachusetts Institute of Technology, 1905; Ph.D., 1908. His paper on the iodometric determination of arsenious acid (1908) was the result of a study of particular significance inasmuch as it prompted the first thermodynamic treatment of "buffer" solutions so important in later work on indicators. He made the first accurate measurement of true transference numbers and of the relative hydration of aqueous ions. Professor of chemistry at the University of Illinois and editor (1922–26) of the *International Critical Tables of Numerical Data: Physics, Chemistry and Technology,* he became head of the division of chemistry at the National Bureau of Standards in 1926. There he initiated a program of thermochemical research, instituted and directed an extensive project on petroleum research, was responsible for the isolation of the first crystals of rubber. In December 1931 he made his most notable discovery—the fractional electrolysis of water with respect to the isotopes of hydrogen.

WASHBURN, ELIHU BENJAMIN. *See* WASHBURNE, ELIHU BENJAMIN.

WASHBURN, EMORY (*b. Leicester, Mass., 1800; d. Cambridge, Mass., 1877*), lawyer, Massachusetts legislator. Graduated Williams, 1817. Admitted to the Massachusetts bar, 1821, he practiced principally in Worcester, achieving great success and reputation. After an uneventful term as Whig governor of Massachusetts, 1854–55, he joined the staff of the Harvard Law School and served as Bussey Professor until 1876. He was author of treatises on real property and easements which were greatly valued in their day.

WASHBURN, GEORGE (*b. Middleboro, Mass., 1833; d. 1915*), Congregational clergyman, educator. Graduated Amherst 1855. Son-in-law of Cyrus Hamlin, Washburn became a missionary at Constantinople, Turkey, 1863, and also taught at Robert College. *Post* 1871 he was director and professor of philosophy at Robert; between 1878 and 1903 he served as its president, steadily increasing its enrollment, its physical plant, and its prestige. He was a consultant on Near Eastern affairs to James G. Blaine, John Hay, and President Theodore Roosevelt.

WASHBURN, ICHABOD (*b. Kingston, Mass., 1798; d. Worcester, Mass., 1868*), blacksmith, manufacturer. Partner in a firm which made wool-spinning machinery, 1823–34, Washburn then began the manufacture of wire and became the leader of that industry in the United States; the firm was known as Washburn & Moen *post* 1850. He introduced the galvanized iron telegraph wire once so extensively used, and developed the first continuous method of tempering and hardening wire in 1856.

WASHBURN, ISRAEL (*b. Livermore, Maine, 1813; d. Philadelphia, Pa., 1883*), lawyer. Brother of Elihu B. Washburne, Cadwallader C. and William D. Washburn. Admitted to the Maine bar, 1851–61, he was a leader in the formation of the Republican party in Washington, D.C., and is considered by some to have been the first to suggest the name "Republican." On May 9, 1854, ten weeks after the original meeting at Ripon, Wis., he called a meeting of about thirty anti-slavery representatives in Washington which undertook further steps toward organizing the new party. As governor of Maine, 1861–63, he ranks among the leading war governors of the North. He was collector of the port at Portland, Maine, 1863–78.

WASHBURN, MARGARET FLOY (*b. New York, N.Y., 1871; d. Poughkeepsie, N.Y., 1939*), experimental psychologist. Graduated Vassar, 1891; Ph.D., Cornell, 1894. Taught at Wells College, Sage College, and at University of Cincinnati; headed psychology work at Vassar, 1903–37. Author of *The Animal Mind* (1908) and *Movement and Mental Imagery* (1916), she made Vassar one of the most active psychological centers in America, employing a unique system of collaboration in experimental research between student and professor on problems of feasibly limited scope.

WASHBURN, NATHAN (*b. Stafford, Conn., 1818; d. Stafford Springs, Conn., 1903*), iron founder. Patented an improved cast-iron railroad-car wheel in April 1849 which soon displaced every other pattern of wheel; later that year he founded a firm for the manufacture of the wheel and also textile machinery. During the Civil War, Washburn perfected a process of puddling pig iron whereby he produced a superior gun barrel.

WASHBURN, WILLIAM DREW (*b. Livermore, Maine, 1831; d. Minneapolis, Minn., 1912*), lawyer, mill owner. Brother of Elihu B. Washburne and of Cadwallader C. and Israel Washburn. Graduated Bowdoin, 1854; studied law with his brother Israel and with John A. Peters. Removing to the West, 1857, he settled in Minnesota for the practice of law, served for some time as agent for his brother Cadwallader, and was federal surveyor for Minnesota, 1861–65. Thereafter, a resident of Minneapolis, he engaged in lumbering, real estate operation, and flour manufacture. In 1878, after a brief association with his brother in Washburn, Crosby & Co., he founded the milling firm of W. D. Washburn & Co. He was congressman, Republican, from Minnesota, 1879–85, and U.S. senator, 1889–95, but his principal importance was as a major figure in the financial and business life of his community.

WASHBURNE, ELIHU BENJAMIN (*b. Livermore, Maine, 1816; d. 1887*), lawyer, diplomat. Brother of Cadwallader C., Israel and William D. Washburn. After admission to the Massachusetts bar, he removed to the West, 1840, and settled at Galena, Ill. Moderately successful in practice, he made careful investments in Western lands and became a wheel-horse of the local Whig party. As congressman, Whig and Republican, from Illinois, 1853–69, he was a fierce opponent of lobbyists and treasury raiders, and was one of the first of a long succession of "watchdogs of the treasury" while chairman of the committee on appropriations. Active in furthering the career of Ulysses S. Grant, Washburne was a member of the joint committee on reconstruction and a violent attacker of President Andrew Johnson. Continuing his sponsorship of Grant through the campaign of 1868, he served less than two weeks as U.S. secretary of state, 1869, and was then U.S. minister to France, 1869–77. A capable diplomat, he was the only official representative of a foreign government to remain in Paris throughout the siege and the Commune, 1871; his *Recollections* (1887) contain a valuable account of those exciting days.

WASHINGTON, BOOKER TALIAFERRO (*b. Hale's Ford, Franklin Co., Va., 1856; d. Tuskegee, Ala., 1915*), black educational leader. Born in slavery, he was taken by his mother soon after emancipation to Malden, W.Va., where he worked for a time in a salt furnace. Studying at night and later attending regular classes after his work, he was encouraged by the wife of his employer to fulfill his ambition to attend Hampton Institute. Working his way through Hampton, which he attended, 1872–75, he won the

regard of General Samuel C. Armstrong whom he later served as secretary. After graduation in 1875, he taught in a black school at Malden, W. Va., and between 1879 and 1881 had charge of the night school at Hampton Institute. In May 1881 General Armstrong recommended Washington as principal to a black normal school at Tuskegee, Ala., for which a charter had just been secured. He opened the institution with forty students in a dilapidated shack and thereafter labored incessantly for the good of Tuskegee. Acting on the theory of first things first, he taught his students the dignity of efficient labor and how to live "on the farm off the farm." He also stressed the values of cleanliness and a proper diet. By the time of his death Tuskegee had grown to remarkable strength in plant, endowment, faculty, and reputation. Washington also started many forms of rural extension work and established the National Negro Business League and a number of conferences for self-improvement. In great demand throughout the country as a lecturer, he stressed the necessity of providing an education useful in life, the need of keeping close to nature and of cultivating the respect of one's neighbors. A remarkable address at the Cotton States Exposition, Atlanta, Ga., September 1893, brought him national recognition.

Booker Washington's views were opposed by black intellectuals who felt that he did not sufficiently emphasize political rights and that his stress on industrial education might result in keeping the black in virtual bondage. However, he was more interested in the immediate improvement of his race from a material point of view and in making it worthy of the franchise. He opposed agitation. In view of the general public opinion of his day, which he hoped to influence, he would appear to have adopted the only policy which could be then really effective. A man of high character and devoted to spiritual values, he made a number of memorable observations, including his characteristic saying, "No man, black or white, from North or South, shall drag me down so low as to make me hate him." He was author, among other works, of *The Future of the American Negro* (1899), *Up From Slavery* (1901), *Frederick Douglass* (1907), and *My Larger Education* (1911).

WASHINGTON, BUSHROD (*b. Westmoreland Co., Va., 1762; d. Philadelphia, Pa., 1829*), Revolutionary soldier, lawyer. Nephew of George Washington. Graduated William and Mary, 1778; studied law after the Revolution in the office of James Wilson. A devoted student of the law, he was appointed an associate justice of the U.S. Supreme Court in 1798 and served until his death. Slow of mind, but thorough in reasoning, he excelled as a *nisi prius* judge. Following John Marshall on constitutional matters, he rendered a number of important opinions in admiralty and commercial cases.

WASHINGTON, DINAH (*b. Tuscaloosa, Ala., 1924; d. Detroit, Mich., 1963*), singer and pianist known as the "Queen of the Blues" and "Queen of the Jukeboxes." Beginning at age fifteen, she performed in several Chicago nightclubs. Sang with the Lionel Hampton band, 1943–45, and made her first solo recordings. The preeminent female rhythm and blues singer of the day, her more than twenty-five best-selling discs include "Baby Get Lost" (1949), "Cold, Cold Heart" (1951), "Wheel of Fortune" (1952), "Unforgetable" (1952), and, with Brook Benton, "Baby, You've Got What It Takes" (1960). Her biggest hit was a revival of the ballad "What a Diff'rence a Day Makes" (1960).

WASHINGTON, GEORGE (*b. Westmoreland Co., Va., 1732; d. "Mount Vernon," Fairfax Co., Va., 1799*), planter, soldier, first president of the United States. Born on his father's estate which lay between Bridges Creek and Popes Creek and was later known as Wakefield, George Washington was the eldest son of Augustine Washington and his second wife, Mary Ball (1708–1789). He was descended from Lawrence Washington of

Sulgrave, Northamptonshire, England, whose descendant John immigrated to Virginia in 1657–58. Augustine Washington lived in Westmoreland until 1735 when he removed to Little Hunting Creek on the Potomac and thence to Ferry Farm in King George County. Augustine died in 1743, and for the next six years George Washington lived with relatives in Westmoreland and the Chotank region, at Ferry Farm, and at Mount Vernon, home of his elder half brother, Lawrence Washington. His principal, if not his only, teachers appear to have been his father and Lawrence; the extent of his mother's influence upon Washington cannot be accurately appraised. His training in mathematics extended to trigonometry and surveying, and he had a natural talent for mapmaking. His accounts show purchases of books dealing with military affairs, agriculture, history, biography, and a fair number of the outstanding novels of his day such as *Tom Jones* and *Humphry Clinker.* Quotations sprinkled through his correspondence indicate his familiarity with the works of Pope and Addison, and he made extensive use of biblical allusions.

Washington learned the courtly manners and customs of the best English culture at Mount Vernon. Connected by marriage through his half-brother with the Fairfax family, he owed the first important adventure of his career to Lord Fairfax, who permitted him to go along on a survey of Fairfax lands in the Shenandoah, 1748. A year later, appointed county surveyor for Culpeper Co., Washington explored more wild country and received an insight into the importance of land ownership. He interrupted his work to accompany his half-brother to Barbados on a health-seeking voyage. Lawrence Washington returned to Virginia to die in July 1752, bequeathing the Mount Vernon estate in such a way that it shortly became the property of George. Appointed district-adjutant for the southern district of Virginia, 1752, he was soon transferred to that of the Northern Neck and Eastern Shore. His military ambitions, first stimulated during his half-brother's service with Adm. Edward Vernon, were now reawakened. In 1753 he accepted Governor Dinwiddie's appointment to carry an ultimatum to the French forces encroaching on English lands in the Ohio country. This mission, although one of hardship and danger, appealed to Washington as a road to possible honor and glory. Instructed to warn off the French, and to strengthen the friendship of the Six Nations with the English, he left Wills Creek in the middle of November 1753, but on arrival at the forks of the Ohio a week after discovered that the French had withdrawn for the winter. After holding a council at Logstown with certain of the chiefs of the Six Nations at which he accomplished little, he traveled farther into the wilderness to reach the next French post. Arriving at Venango, he was directed by the officer there to carry his message to the commandant at Fort Le Boeuf. Proceeding another hundred miles through winter-clogged swamps nearly to the shores of Lake Erie, he reached the fort only to receive in writing a refusal to heed Dinwiddie's ultimatum. Guided by Christopher Gist, he was several times in danger of death on his return journey. His report to the governor was printed as *The Journal of Major George Washington . . .* (1754) and created a stir in England as well as America.

Washington had noted a position at the forks of the Ohio (present site of Pittsburgh) as the best place for an outpost, and the governor had dispatched a small force to forestall the French in building a fort there. Commissioning Washington a lieutenant colonel, Dinwiddie ordered him to reinforce the forks with the militia then assembling at Alexandria. After setting out with 150 men on April 2, 1754, Washington was met on the ways by news that the French had taken the British outpost and renamed it Fort Duquesne. Nevertheless, he advanced to the Ohio Company trading post at Red Stone about forty miles from the forks, and began to build a road which would facilitate the later attempt at recapture which Dinwiddie would be obliged to make. He also

fortified a camp (Fort Necessity) at Great Meadows, Pa. Informed by friendly Indians of the approach of the French scouting party, he marched out to intercept it. On May 27 he surprised and defeated the French party; their leader, Jumonville, was killed. As the French advanced in force out of Fort Duquesne, Washington fell back to Great Meadows since he feared an attack at some less defensible place. After a ten-hour siege of the camp, the French proposed terms which Washington accepted, unwittingly signing an admission that Jumonville had been "assassinated." Dinwiddie's mismanagement of military affairs having left Washington in the position of being commanded by officers junior to himself, he therefore resigned toward the end of the year 1754.

When the British sent an expedition of regular troops under General Braddock against Fort Duquesne in 1755, Braddock offered Washington a post as aide. Falling sick on the march to Duquesne, he rejoined Braddock the day before the action on the Monongahela, during which he strove to carry out Braddock's orders before being swept from the field in the resultant panic after the French and Indians struck. As his appointment as aide ended with the general's death, he returned to Mount Vernon and made ready the militia of his district. Appointed colonel and commander in chief of all Virginia forces in the fall of 1755, he was responsible for the defense of about 300 miles of mountainous frontier with about 300 men. Averaging two engagements with raiding Indians a month, Washington acquired the habit of thinking and acting for the welfare of a people, and also a skill in conducting military operations over an extensive range of territory. His difficulties at this time closely parallel those he was later to meet in the Revolution. In order to settle a dispute over his rank and right to command, Washington rode from Winchester, Va., to Boston, Mass., in 1756. His journey had a secondary but important effect in broadening his viewpoint in respect to the character of the people of the other colonies. Returning to his duty in defense of the frontier, he managed reasonably well despite lack of money, clothes, shoes, powder, and even at times food. His efforts to win the cooperation of Maryland and Pennsylvania in supporting a Virginian attack on Fort Duquesne were unsuccessful. Joining the British expedition under General John Forbes against Fort Duquesne in 1758, Washington commanded the two Virginia regiments with the title of brigadier. His suggestion that the expedition use an open-order method of marching and fighting was ignored by the British officers. The British found, on their approach to Fort Duquesne, November 1758, that it had been abandoned by the French, and Washington resigned soon thereafter from military service.

On Jan. 6, 1759, he married Martha (Dandridge) Custis, a widow, and settled down to the life of a gentleman-farmer at Mount Vernon. He was active in local affairs and a generous contributor to educational organizations. He took a seat in the House of Burgesses, 1759. Appreciative of music and the theatre, he also enjoyed card playing, billiards, horseracing, dancing, fishing, hunting, and, indeed, all the usual sports of a gentleman of his time. However, his pleasant, busy life at Mount Vernon was not without its annoyances, mainly on the head of British commercial restrictions and the sharp practice of the English factors without whose services no Virginia planter could transact business with the English markets. Washington's disillusion with British military efficiency, as evidenced during the campaigns against Fort Duquesne, now revived and merged into a subconscious antagonism against the mother country which had been inspired by senseless difficulties thrown in his way as he endeavored to improve his estates. A faithful attendant at the sessions of the legislature, he clarified his view of the handicaps imposed on America by the British colonial system. At the time of the Stamp Act he expressed the general American attitude toward the claims of Parliament, saying that it "hath no more right to put their hands into my pocket, without my consent, than I have to put my hands into yours for money." Another major grievance was the British prohibition of colonial paper money. Since the balance of trade was always against them, the colonists required paper money. Acting as agent for the officers and men he had formerly commanded, he traveled down the Ohio and up the Great Kanawha rivers in 1770 to locate the bounty lands allotted to men who had served. This journey revived his interest in the west and provided him with a personal knowledge which was later useful in developing his western land policy when he was president.

Washington supported the device of nonimportation as a check to British political and economic aggression, yet prophesied that blood would be spilt if the British ministers continued to be stubborn. He was one of the burgesses who met in the Raleigh Tavern at Williamsburg on May 27, 1774, after the Assembly had been dissolved by the governor; he signed the proceedings of that important meeting. On July 18 he acted as chairman of a meeting in Alexandria at which the Fairfax Resolutions were adopted. A Virginia delegate to the First Continental Congress, he was also chosen to command the independent militia companies of several Virginia counties. As delegate to the Second Continental Congress beginning May 1775, he served on the committee for drafting army regulations and planning the defense of New York City. Elected to command the American armies, June 15, 1775, as the result of a compromise between the northern and southern factions in Congress, he refused all pay for the employment, asking only that he be reimbursed for necessary expenses.

On taking command of the army at Cambridge, Mass., on July 3, 1775, Washington found it little better than a loosely organized mob of New England militia whose terms of service were to expire at the end of the year or sooner. Hampered in his efforts to obtain legislation for creation of an efficient army by the widespread belief that some accommodation might still be made with the British, he was also thwarted in establishing discipline by a too-democratic spirit among the troops. Scarcity of powder as well as insufficiency of men kept Washington back from any major operation until 1776. At the first opportunity, however, he seized and fortified Dorchester Heights, so threatening the besieged British in Boston with bombardment and putting the British fleet in jeopardy. As a result, the city was evacuated on March 17, 1776.

As it was obvious that the next logical base of operations for the British would be New York City, Washington set out for that place with his army of newly enlisted troops. On his arrival he found that he was partially committed to a plan of defense already mapped out by Major General Charles Lee and others. Faced with the decree that New York must be defended, although the place was virtually indefensible, he was further handicapped by a lack of experienced officers and by the three-to-one superiority which the British soon massed against him. His concept of duty compelled him to obey the orders of Congress, despite his personal opinion of them, and he deferred scrupulously to the views of subordinates in cases where he believed that his knowledge and experience were inadequate. When Sir William Howe, the British commander, chose Long Island as his point of attack, Washington sent a large part of his force to reinforce the defensive works at Brooklyn, meanwhile holding a strong body on Manhattan to oppose a possible attack by the British fleet. After the American forces on Long Island had been outflanked and defeated on Aug. 27, 1776, Washington withdrew the remnant of the forces on Long Island over to Manhattan on the night of Aug. 29, a retreat which is considered a military masterpiece. Following on the British landing at Kips Bay, Sept. 15, Washington was obliged to give up his footing on Manhattan, retreating to a strong natural position at White Plains, N.Y., where the British were held in a sharp engagement. The fall of Fort Washington and Fort Lee in November resulted from the same misplaced deference to the opinions of his generals which

has been noted previously, yet both these disasters were blessings in disguise. They freed Washington and the Continental Army from responsibility for fixed fortifications and made it into a mobile force of maneuver which Washington could handle in accordance with his own ideas. The general principle on which he preferred to wage the war was the avoidance of a general action unless compelled to undertake it by necessity. Until Congress created a permanent army, this was the only way in which inexperienced troops always inferior in numbers to the enemy could survive. Survival was all-important to Washington, for his belief in the moral rightness of the American fight for liberty was based on his sense of the injustice of the British course. Having scrupulously determined on a course of rebellion and a change of allegiance, he considered that any turning back was unthinkable. The fortitude with which he met his difficulties was based upon his faith.

As the British pushed forward into New Jersey, Washington, with a steadily dwindling force, fell back before them, but contrived to give his enemy the impression that they might encounter a strong opposition at any point. After he had apparently taken refuge with an army of barely 5000 men behind the Delaware River, the British settled into winter quarters in a series of outposts along the Delaware at and near Trenton, N.J., and in a line across New Jersey to Amboy.

Meanwhile, as Congress had left Philadelphia and the protection of that city had become relatively unimportant in his judgment, Washington fixed his eye on Morristown, N.J., as the base of operations most threatening to the British. Crossing the Delaware on Christmas night, 1776, he took the outpost at Trenton and captured its Hessian garrison, so dislocating the British arrangements. Finding it impossible to drive to Morristown (as had been his first intention) through failure of two supporting detachments, he returned across the river. A few days later he again crossed into Jersey and began to move northward. After a stubborn engagement at Assunpink Creek, he outwitted the British by a night march and attacked their line at Princeton. Victorious there, he was soon at Morristown, where his position presented such a strategic threat that the British abandoned their whole line and retreated to Brunswick. Meanwhile, Washington had been assigned by Congress a grant of extraordinary powers in order that he might wage war with more efficiency, but was severely criticized when he endeavored to use these powers. However, *post* 1777, he could enlist troops for a period of three years or the duration of the war, and he then began to build a permanent military machine. He continued to be forced to rely upon militia for swelling his forces to a respectable total at times of crisis; this was a constant annoyance to him for he held and expressed a very low opinion of militia troops.

Slowly shaping and disciplining his army at Morristown, he managed to contain the enemy during the spring of 1777 and convinced Sir William Howe that the risk of marching across New Jersey to take Philadelphia was too great. On Howe's transport of his forces to Chesapeake Bay by sea, Washington marched south and on Sept. 11, 1777, engaged the British at Brandywine Creek. Defeated, he refused to withdraw and delayed the British entry into Philadelphia for two weeks. Although he continued to act with great deference to the civil power as expressed by Congress, he complained of a lack of information on political matters. His surprise attack on the British at Germantown, Oct. 3–4, 1777, failed through no fault of plan, damaged the British forces and also Sir William Howe's confidence in himself, and is to be credited with great influence in the decision of France to aid the United States. During the winter encampment at Valley Forge which followed, a continuing intrigue to supplant Washington in command of the army reached its crisis in the events of the so-called Conway Cabal. The victory of Horatio Gates at Saratoga, Oct. 17,

1777, gave Washington's enemies in Congress a chance to draw invidious comparisons. The whole plot was at bottom a culmination of a continuous effort by Massachusetts ever since 1775 to regain control of the war. The exposure of the Cabal and of Gates's share in it aroused resentments in Congress and effectually destroyed congressional support for Washington's replacement as commander. True to his nature, he did not allow this episode to interfere with more important matters, nor was he troubled by any vulgar desires for popularity. In the spring of 1778 the Continental Army emerged from its trials at Valley Forge, drilled to a high standard of efficiency by Baron von Steuben, and heartened by the news of the French alliance which had come in March. A determining factor in the securing of French support had been the character and purpose of George Washington as certified to Vergennes, the French foreign minister, and to Louis XVI by Gerard, the French acting minister in America. Once convinced by Washington's example that the Americans would not compromise with Great Britain, the French moved effectively.

An early proof that the Continental Army had become efficient and a new demonstration of Washington's skill as a general were provided at the battle of Monmouth, N.J., June 28, 1978. In this battle the Americans struck at the British army as it was retreating from Philadelphia across New Jersey to New York City. Washington turned the confusion brought about by the debatable conduct of General Charles Lee into an obstinate and successful holding action from which the British were glad to make good their withdrawal. A new problem, however, arose in the lethargy which seized upon Congress and the states after the announcement of the French alliance. Lacking troops, supplies, and even powder in the summer of 1779, Washington was unable to make a major move, yet succeeded in mounting an expedition under General John Sullivan into New York State which broke the power of the Six Nations and freed the frontier from Indian warfare. After the arrival of a French army under Rochambeau at Rhode Island in July 1780, Washington was still unable to attempt a major campaign because of his own lack of supplies and men and frankly confessed this fact to the French general. At a conference with Rochambeau in Wethersfield, May 21–22, 1781, it was decided to attempt an attack on New York, and both French and American forces closed in on the northern defenses of that city. The availability of the French West India fleet under Adm. De Grasse providing the chance for a combined operation, Washington changed his plans and determined on a move against Cornwallis in Virginia. Organizing his march with remarkable skill, Washington brought the French and American armies on schedule before Yorktown, Va., where Cornwallis had fortified himself and where he had been cut off from an escape by sea by the French fleet. After a short siege, Yorktown fell and Cornwallis was taken. Rochambeau took his army into winter quarters in Virginia, and Washington led his troops back to the Hudson River, making headquarters at Newburgh.

The states now became even more supine than before, and Washington's arguments for the necessity of a continued effort had no effect. He remained patient while an orgy of profiteering broke out, even to the extent of a clandestine trade with the British, which he and the army were unable to stop. For two more dreary years the war dragged on, although no military events of importance took place. The Continental soldiers were restless because of neglect of their services and lack of pay; their dissatisfaction took form in a proposal to make Washington a king by military force. Shaken to his depth by the realization that the men on whom he relied were ready to support him in a monstrous treason for personal power, he replied to the proposal on May 22, 1782, with a blast that ended the whole affair. Continuing unrest and a prospect of mutiny were met by him with tact and wisdom; he urged Congress to take action on the petitions addressed by the soldiers

and their officers, and also addressed a circular letter to the states, pleading with them for justice to the personnel of the fast-disbanding Continental Army. Revealing how close to his heart was the national principle for which he had fought, he stated that four things were essential to respectable national existence: (1) an indissoluble union of the states under one federal head; (2) a sacred regard to public justice; (3) the adoption of a proper national defense; (4) a spirit of cooperation and the suppression of local prejudices. Hostilities ended on April 19, 1783, the anniversary of the battle of Lexington, and Washington then entered New York City at the head of those troops which still remained in service, just as the British evacuated it. He bade farewell to his officers at Fraunces Tavern and resigned his commission to Congress at Annapolis.

Washington's financial condition at the close of the war was unsatisfactory. Mount Vernon was now not even self-supporting; however, he continued his usual unostentatious charities. During the autumn of 1784 he went on a horseback journey of exploration in the west in furtherance of his favorite project of opening a route to the western country from tidewater Virginia by connecting the Potomac and Ohio rivers. Discouraged by the inefficiency of slave labor, he grew convinced that the gradual abolition of slavery by legislative authority would prevent much future mischief. Although he had more slaves than he could profitably employ, he refused on principle to sell any of them. Absorbed in the management of Mount Vernon and in the affairs of the Potomac Company, he considered himself as a retired man, writing to Lafayette that he would "move gently down the stream of life, until I sleep with my fathers." This philosophic calm was interrupted in 1786 by Shay's Rebellion in Massachusetts, which only added to his conviction that the Articles of Confederation would have to be revised in the interest of a strong central government. Serving as president of the Federal Convention, he lent the great authority of his reputation to its deliberations. Admitting that the Constitution as written had imperfections, he maintained that it was the best obtainable at that time and that, since a workable machinery had been provided for amending it, it should be first adopted and then altered.

Repelling the suggestion that he should be first president when it was made to him, he opposed it wherever he decently could, saying that he had no "wish beyond that of living and dying an honest man on my own farm." He accepted the presidency with diffidence, dreading the possibility that he would appear incompetent. Believing that the success of the Revolution was owing to Providence, and content with the thought that he had played an honorable part in a great popular movement, he was doubtful of his ability to administer a government. Driven by the sense of duty that always actuated him, he accepted the post, although he was compelled to borrow money to pay his traveling expenses to his inauguration, Apr. 30, 1789, in New York City. Declining a salary, he accepted the later offer of Congress of $25,000 annually for expenses; in his case, his expenses exceeded this sum. Cautious in his organization of the governmental machine and his appointment of officials, he faced a number of pressing problems, both domestic and foreign. At home it was essential that the nation be made financially stable and that manufacturing and commerce be encouraged; the retention of military posts in the west by Great Britain constituted the major foreign problem.

Unsympathetic with those divergent theories of government which almost immediately proved the basis of a struggle between Alexander Hamilton and Thomas Jefferson within the circle of his first cabinet, he thought of these differences of opinion as purely personal and as willful obstacles to the task of establishing the government firmly. He could not understand differences on the basis of theory, although he acted with great forbearance toward both Jefferson and Hamilton on the grounds that their talents were essential to success. The gradual emergence of Federalist and Democratic-Republican points of view in government influenced him in his decision to serve a second term. He was strongly influenced by the disturbed foreign situation and adamant in his belief that the European powers must be convinced that Americans acted for themselves and not for others. At first sympathetic with the revolution in France, he grew speedily sick of the excesses which it produced and desired a strict American neutrality as between the French and their principal opponent, Great Britain. Although unopposed in his election to a second term, he was roundly criticized for his neutrality policy and was subjected to an abuse which went beyond the bounds of decency. Continuing firm in his belief that twenty years of peace would make the United States strong enough to bid defiance "in a just cause to any power whatever," he could not comprehend emotional attitudes at home which could put any other problem ahead of this. He gradually came to regard the French sympathizers in the United States as virtual traitors. When, after the recall of the French envoy Edmond Genêt, the political frenzy in the United States subsided, Washington attempted a settlement of United States difficulties with Great Britain by appointing John Jay to negotiate a treaty with the British, 1794. In this same year the resistance to the excise tax in Pennsylvania known as the Whiskey Rebellion seemed to Washington to prove that the same indifference of the states to the national welfare which had plagued him in the Revolution must still be reckoned with. Acting with decision against the rebels, he was heartened by the prompt response of the militia to his call. On the collapse of the rebellion, he again displayed his broad understanding by avoiding any harsh reprisal measures.

Offsetting the optimism brought about by the signing of the Pinckney Treaty, 1795, which secured the navigation of the Mississippi River and established the southern boundary of the United States, came an outburst of criticism over Jay's Treaty. Denounced as a base surrender to the British, it yet seemed to Washington the best treaty that could be obtained at the time, and he withstood the storm of opposition just as he had withstood previous ones, confident of his integrity of purpose and likening the attacks to a cry against a mad dog.

In 1796 he set about to prepare an address which would announce to the people of the United States his determination to retire from public life. His Farewell Address is partly an explanation of his course as president, with main emphasis upon the need for a firm union and a strong central government, and it is also a solemn warning against the spirit of party. Political parties, as Washington had observed them, seemed devoted to a usurpation of power for personal ends and would logically result in a loss of liberty. He urged morality and education as necessities for the people's happiness and prosperity, counseled good faith and justice toward all nations but favors to none, and warned against the wiles of foreign influence. On his retirement from the presidency, the nation was well on the road to international importance. Washington had given it dignity; he had demonstrated its power crushing the Indians in the west (at Fallen Timbers, 1794, the army commanded by Anthony Wayne); he had seen its credit firmly fixed through the efforts and policy of Alexander Hamilton. Treaties with Spain and with Great Britain had amicably settled the questions of navigation on the Mississippi and also the Florida and the eastern boundaries. Having sacrificed his personal inclination throughout his life to his sense of duty, he now looked forward to a quiet and fruitful old age at Mount Vernon. However, when trouble with France brought about a war situation in 1798, he was brought out of retirement by President John Adams to command a provisional army of defense with the rank of lieutenant general. As changing conditions in France reduced the chance of conflict, Washington never personally commanded the army and allotted a greater and greater part of his time to the management of Mount Vernon. He never brought his farms to the point of efficiency which he had planned, although he did work out a scheme of rotation of crops in his fields. He died on Saturday, Dec. 14, 1799, with high courage. Used to driving himself unsparingly and often beyond his strength, he had neglected a cold which developed into a malignant cynanche trachealis.

WASHINGTON, HENRY STEPHENS (*b. Newark, N.J., 1867; d. 1934*), petrologist. Graduated Yale, 1886; made extensive travels, studying especially the volcanic islands of the Greek and Turkish archipelagoes; Ph.D., Leipzig, 1893. Associated with Joseph P. Iddings, L. V. Pirsson, and W. Cross in formulating a systematic classification of igneous rocks based primarily upon chemical composition; published *Manual of the Chemical Analysis of Rocks* (1904), *Chemical Analyses of Igneous Rocks* (revised edition, 1917). A research worker *post* 1912 at Geophysical Laboratory of the Carnegie Institution of Washington, D.C., he issued a number of publications which established him as the most learned student of igneous rocks of his time.

WASHINGTON, JOHN MACRAE (*b. Stafford Co., Va., 1797; d. at sea, off the mouth of the Delaware River, 1853*), soldier. Graduated West Point, 1817. Commissioned in the artillery, he served principally in Florida and in the South; in 1838–39 he aided General Winfield Scott in the removal of the Cherokee to Oklahoma. After further duty with Scott in quelling disturbances along the Canadian border, he returned to routine duty, 1842. As a battery commander in the Mexican War, he was the chief factor in securing victory at the battle of Buena Vista, Feb. 22, 1847, repelling Mexican attacks on the first day and on the second day holding a key point after a rout of the American militia. He served later as governor of Saltillo and as civil and military governor of New Mexico.

WATERHOUSE, BENJAMIN (*b. Newport, R.I., 1754; d. Cambridge, Mass., 1846*), physician. Apprenticed in medicine to a Newport physician, he studied also in London and Edinburgh, 1775–78, and at the University of Leyden, 1778–ca. 1782. Returning to America, he became professor of the theory and practice of medicine in the medical department of Harvard, 1783. On reading Edward Jenner's 1798 essay on vaccination with cowpox, Waterhouse sent to England for the vaccine and immediately after its receipt (July 8, 1800) tested it successfully on his own son and on another child. Continuing to vaccinate others with cowpox with equally good results, he published A *Prospect of Exterminating the Small Pox* (Aug. 18, 1800). As the news of his work spread, vaccination was administered improperly by a number of unqualified persons using impure vaccine. A number of people died and there was a general resentment against Waterhouse. After a committee of physicians had investigated the affair and approved Waterhouse's practice, 1802, he continued to publicize vaccination and to insist on maintaining the purity of vaccine. He opposed the moving of the Harvard Medical School from Cambridge to Boston and also the suggestion that the instruction given be more clinical in character. After the failure of his attempt to open a rival medical school and his publication of a number of libels on his colleagues, he was forced to resign from Harvard, 1812. Medical superintendent of New England army posts, 1813–20, he gave considerable time thereafter to general literature as well as the practice of his profession.

WATERHOUSE, FRANK (*b. Cheshire, England, 1867; d. Seattle, Wash., 1930*), capitalist. After immigrating to Canada as a young man, he settled in Tacoma, Wash., ca. 1893. Soon removing to Seattle, he became general manager of the Pacific Navigation Co., 1895, and was thereafter highly successful in shipping enterprises and other business interests in the Pacific Northwest.

WATERHOUSE, SYLVESTER (*b. Barrington, N.H., 1830; d. St. Louis, Mo., 1902*), educator, civic leader. Professor of Greek at Washington University, St. Louis, Mo., 1864–1901, he was an outstanding publicist for the Middle West, advocating Mississippi River improvement, encouraging immigration to Missouri, and endeavoring to stimulate trade.

WATERMAN, ALAN TOWER (*b. Cornwall, N.Y., 1892; d. Washington, D.C., 1967*), physicist and federal scientific administrator. Studied at Princeton (B.A., 1913; M.A., 1914; Ph.D., 1916), then taught at the University of Cincinnati. He taught at Yale (1919–48), where much of his work centered on the conduction of electricity through solids. In 1942 he went to Washington to work with the National Defense Research Committee, soon renamed the Office of Scientific Research and Development, which mobilized science and technology for World War II. During the war Waterman was deputy to Karl T. Compton in the Office of Scientific Research and Development. He assisted Compton in directing the development and application of radar from the original British work in that field. Appointed deputy chief of the Office of Field Service in 1943, he succeeded Compton as chief of the Office of Scientific Research and Development (1945–46). Waterman was appointed deputy chief of the Office of Naval Research in 1946 and rose to chief by 1951. He became the first director of the National Science Foundation in 1951, where he made "basic science" the foundation's policy and its public ideology in national politics.

WATERMAN, LEWIS EDSON (*b. Decatur, N.Y., 1837; d. Brooklyn, N.Y., 1901*), book agent, life insurance salesman, inventor. Obtained his first patent for an efficient fountain pen, 1884; established the Ideal Pen Co. in New York to manufacture it. Incorporated his successful business as the L. E. Waterman Co., 1887, and served the firm thereafter as president and manager.

WATERMAN, ROBERT H. (*b. Hudson, N.Y., 1808; d. San Francisco, Calif., 1884*), sea captain. A mate and master aboard packets of the Black Ball line and ships owned by Howland & Aspinwall, Waterman made a series of remarkable passages to China with the *Natchez*, 1842–45. As master of the clipper *Sea Witch*, he made a record run between Hong Kong and New York, 1849. Accepting command of the new clipper *Challenge*, he sailed it from New York to San Francisco in a passage which has frequently been cited as a classic voyage in a "hell ship." An attempted mutiny and the death of several members of the crew resulted in an attempt to lynch Waterman when he arrived in California, Oct. 29, 1851. Subsequently tried for murder, he was exonerated by the testimony of both crew and passengers.

WATERMAN, THOMAS WHITNEY (*b. Binghamton, N.Y., 1821; d. 1898*), lawyer, writer of digests and legal treatises. Admitted to the bar, 1848, he began practice in New York City, making his residence in Binghamton again *post* 1862. He was author of a great number of works on phases of law which were rapidly changing. Although ephemerally useful and successful, his writings have not noticeably affected the later development of law.

WATERS, DANIEL (*b. Charlestown, Mass., 1731; d. Malden, Mass., 1816*), naval officer. Commanded the schooner *Lee* under John Manley in warfare on British communications off Boston, 1776. Appointed captain in the Continental Navy, March 1777, he commanded several small ships of war on Atlantic cruises and was in command of the Massachusetts ship *General Putnam* in the expedition against Castine, Maine. His most famous exploit came on Dec. 25, 1779, when he defeated the British privateers

Governor Tryon and *Sir William Erskine* while captain of the Boston privateer *Thorn*.

WATERS, WILLIAM EVERETT (*b. Winthrop, Maine, 1856; d. 1924*), classicist. Graduate Yale, 1878; Ph.D., 1887. An enthusiastic and able teacher of Greek at several schools and colleges, including Chautauqua summer and correspondence courses, he held the presidency of Wells College, 1894–1900. He was associate professor and professor of Greek at New York University, 1901–23.

WATIE, STAND (*b. near site of present Rome, Ga., 1806; d. 1871*), Cherokee leader planter, Confederate brigadier general. Brother of Elias Boudinot (*ca. 1803–1839*). Joined his brother, his uncle Major Ridge, and John Ridge in signing the treaty of New Echota, 1835, whereby the Georgia Cherokee surrendered their lands and removed to what is now Oklahoma. Bitterly attacked for his part in the treaty, Watie later became leader of the minority, or treaty, party of his tribe. Appointed colonel of the Cherokee Mounted Rifles, 1861, he was promoted brigadier general, 1864. During the entire Civil War he was active as a raider and cavalry leader, taking part in many engagements in Indian Territory and along its borders. He was one of the last Confederate officers to surrender (June 23, 1865).

WATKINS, GEORGE CLAIBORNE (*b. Shelbyville, Ky., 1815; d. St. Louis, Mo., 1872*), Arkansas jurist. As chief justice of the Arkansas supreme court, 1852–54, he handed down an early decision holding that the United States had exclusive admiralty jurisdiction over navigable streams (in *Merrick* v. *Avery*, 14 *Ark.*, 370).

WATKINS, JOHN ELFRETH (*b. Ben Lomond, Va., 1852; d. New York, N.Y., 1903*), engineer, museum curator. Built up collections pertaining to the transportation industry at U.S. National Museum, Washington, D.C., 1884–92; curator of mechanical technology and superintendent of buildings of the Museum *post* 1895. Authority on the history of engineering and the mechanical arts.

WATSON, ANDREW (*b. Oliverburn, Scotland, 1834; d. Cairo, Egypt, 1916*), United Presbyterian clergyman. Immigrating to America *ca.* 1848, he was raised near Sussex, Wis. Ordained, 1861, he served thereafter as a missionary in Egypt.

WATSON, CHARLES ROGER (*b. Cairo, Egypt, 1873; d. Bryn Mawr, Pa., 1948*), United Presbyterian clergyman, missionary, educator. Child of missionary parents. Graduated Princeton University, 1894; Princeton Seminary, 1899. Ordained in 1900. After a brief pastorate in St. Louis, Mo., he served as corresponding secretary of the United Presbyterian Board of Foreign Missions, 1902–16. He was a founder of Cairo Christian University (American University in Cairo), and its president, 1920–45.

WATSON, DAVID THOMPSON (*b. Washington, Pa., 1844; d. Atlantic City, N.J., 1916*), lawyer. Practiced successfully in Pittsburgh, Pa., *post* 1868. Gained widest prominence as one of counsel for the United States in Alaskan Boundary controversy with Great Britain, 1903.

WATSON, ELKANAH (*b. Plymouth, Mass., 1758; d. 1842*), merchant, promoter, agriculturist. Apprenticed to John Brown (*1744–80*) of Providence, R.I., *ca.* 1774, he remained in the employ of the Browns after he came of age. Embarking for France to carry money and dispatches to Benjamin Franklin, 1779, he entered business on his own at Nantes, and for a time was very successful. Failing in 1783, he returned to America and made an unsuccessful attempt to raise capital for establishment of an American canal system. After a second failure in business at

Edenton, N.C., he settled in Albany, N.Y., 1789, organized the Bank of Albany, and became a leading citizen of that community. Continuing to urge his plans for canals, he persuaded several prominent New Yorkers to join him in a tour of central New York, 1791, during which he projected a plan for a canal in that region. Retiring from active business *ca.* 1802, he moved to Pittsfield, Mass., where he devoted himself to scientific agriculture. He staged the "Cattle Show" (1810) which preceded incorporation of the Berkshire Agricultural Society, sponsor of the first county fair in America. He thereafter helped make the county fair an American institution. He was author of *Men and Times of the Revolution* (1856).

WATSON, HENRY CLAY (*b. Baltimore, Md., 1831; d. Sacramento, Calif., 1867*), journalist. Trained as a printer and newspaper editor in Philadelphia, Pa., he settled in Sacramento, Calif., 1861, where he became editor of the *Daily Union* and won considerable local fame as an editorial writer during the Civil War. He was author also of a number of historical stories and studies for young people.

WATSON, HENRY COOD (*b. London, England, 1818; d. New York, N.Y., 1875*), journalist, music critic. Immigrated to New York, N.Y., 1841. Founded the *Musical Chronicle*, 1843, which later became the *American Musical Times*; was associated with C. F. Briggs and Edgar Allan Poe on the *Broadway Journal*. Later served as an editor of *Frank Leslie's Illustrated Newspaper* and as music critic for the *New York Tribune*. In 1842 he was one of the group that founded the Philharmonic Society of New York.

WATSON, JAMES CRAIG (*b. near Fingal, Ontario, Canada, 1838; d. 1880*), astronomer. Graduated University of Michigan, 1857. Directed the observatory at Michigan and taught physics there, 1859–79; served thereafter as director of the Washburn Observatory, University of Wisconsin. Discovered 22 asteroids; worked with Benjamin Peirce on lunar theory; was author of *Theoretical Astronomy* (1868), a complete compilation and digest of the theory and method of orbital determination.

WATSON, JAMES ELI (*b. Winchester, Ind., 1864; d. Washington, D.C., 1948*), lawyer, politician. Graduated De Pauw University, 1886. Congressman, Republican, from Indiana, 1895–97, 1899–1909; U.S. senator, 1916–33. A member of the "Old Guard," he labored faithfully in Congress for the railroads, the banks, and the corporations; he supported high tariffs and isolationism and believed in the rigid restriction of immigration. As majority leader in the Senate, he blocked President Hoover's attempt to revise the tariff. A skillful "horse trader," he was gifted principally in the political arts of survival and party loyalty.

WATSON, JAMES MADISON (*b. Onondaga Hill, N.Y., 1827; d. Elizabeth, N.J., 1900*), teacher, textbook salesman, and writer.

WATSON, JOHN BROADUS (*b. near Greenville, S.C., 1878; d. New York, 1958*), psychologist. Studied at Furman University and the University of Chicago (Ph.D., 1903). Taught at the University of Chicago (1903–08) and Johns Hopkins University (1908–20). One of the founders of the school of behaviorist psychology which stressed stimulus-response patterns and objective observation. President (1915), American Psychological Association. Watson was forced to resign from Johns Hopkins because of a scandal surrounding his marriage. Left psychology to work in advertising in New York City until his retirement in 1945.

WATSON, JOHN CRITTENDEN (*b. Frankfort, Ky., 1842; d. Washington, D.C., 1923*), naval officer. Graduated U.S. Naval Academy, 1860. Promoted master, 1861, he was navigating officer in the *Hartford* during the 1862 operations against New

Orleans and Vicksburg and the 1863 operations against Port Hudson and Grand Gulf. He later served as flag lieutenant on the staff of Adm. D. G. Farragut. Promoted commodore, 1897, he commanded the North Cuban Blockade Squadron and the Eastern Squadron during the Spanish-American War. Promoted rear admiral, 1899, he retired in 1904.

WATSON, JOHN FANNING (*b. Batsto, N.J., 1779; d. 1860*), businessman, antiquarian. Successively a publisher, a banker, and a railroad executive, Watson is remembered as author of studies of pioneer days in Pennsylvania and New York based on the methodical collection of memories of old inhabitants and authentic documents. Among his works were *Annals of Philadelphia* (1830, and subsequent editions), *Historic Tales of Olden Time* (1832); and *Annals and Occurrences of New York City and State* (1846).

WATSON, JOHN WILLIAM CLARK (*b. Albermarle Co., Va., 1808; d. Holly Springs, Miss., 1890*), lawyer, Mississippi jurist, Confederate senator.

WATSON, SERENO (*b. East Windsor Hill, Conn., 1826; d. Cambridge, Mass., 1892*), botanist. Graduated Yale, 1847. Failing in various occupations, he removed to California, 1867, and found employment as a volunteer aide with Clarence King's exploration of the Great Basin. Soon afterwards he was commissioned to collect plants and secure data regarding them, thus by chance undertaking the work in which he was to attain distinction. His *Botany* (1871), the fifth volume in the report of the King survey, was virtually a flora of the Great Basin and contained phytogeographic material in advance of its time. Settling in Cambridge, Mass., Watson became assistant in the Gray Herbarium, 1873, and was its curator *post* 1874. He was author, among other works, of the *Botany of California* (1876, 1880); *Bibliographical Index to North American Botany* (1878); and of many outstanding monographs. He completed the *Manual of the Mosses* begun by Leo Lesquereux and T. P James, and in 1889, with the assistance of John M. Coulter, revised Gray's *Manual of Botany*.

WATSON, THOMAS AUGUSTUS (*b. Salem, Mass., 1854; d. Passagrille Key, Fla., 1934*), telephone pioneer, shipbuilder. *Post* 1874 he assisted Alexander G. Bell during the experimental period of the telephone, and was given an interest in the business in 1877 on formation of the first telephone organization. He was the first research and technical head of the Bell Telephone Co. Resigning in 1881, he first attempted farming, but soon began to build engines and ships. In 1896 his firm undertook contracts for the USS *Lawrence* and *Macdonough*; these were followed by the Cape Hatteras lightship and the cruiser USS *Des Moines*. Watson's shipyard was incorporated as the Fore River Ship & Engine Co., 1901. In 1904 he resigned, retired from business, and gave himself up to the special interests in geology and literature which he had cultivated during his business career.

WATSON, THOMAS EDWARD (*b. near Thomson, Ga., 1856; d. 1922*), lawyer, politician. Attended Mercer University; began successful career as a criminal lawyer, 1880. Brought early under the personal influence of Robert Toombs and Alexander H. Stephens, Watson entered politics as an agrarian reformer, hostile to the new order in the South and nostalgic for the imagined glories of the period before the Civil War. As a young member of the Assembly, he fought against the Georgia Democratic machine which was dominated by capitalist-industrialists, and entered Congress, 1891, as a supporter of the Farmers' Alliance and a Populist. Introducing many reform bills and supporting advanced labor legislation, he was defeated for reelection in 1892 and 1894, but continued to sway thousands of his followers with his denunciations of the trusts, capitalist finance, and Democratic policies. Nominated for the vice presidency of the United States by the Populist convention, 1896, he received a very small vote. Embittered, he retired from public life and turned to writing, producing, among other books, biographies of Napoleon and Thomas Jefferson. As the Populist candidate for president in 1904, he polled only a small vote but gained considerable attention from reformers. In 1905 he founded *Tom Watson's Magazine* which featured his reform editorials; he later established *Watson's Jeffersonian Magazine*.

As new issues overshadowed the conflict between industrialists and agrarians, Watson took up and prosecuted a number of sensational crusades against Catholics, Jews, blacks, Socialists, and foreign missionaries. Shifting his followers from one Democratic faction to another, he virtually dictated state politics. He conducted a campaign against American intervention in World War I and against conscription. Although he lost the state presidential primary in 1920, he was elected that same year to the U.S. Senate by a large vote on the same platform, namely, restoration of civil liberties and the defeat of the League of Nations.

WATSON, THOMAS JOHN (*b. East Campbell, N.Y., 1874; d. New York, N.Y., 1956*), business executive. Studied at the Miller School of Commerce, Elmira, N.Y. Founder of the International Business Machines Corporation in 1924; president and chairman of the board until 1956. Watson began his career with the National Cash Register Company in 1895; he served as salesman and sales manager until 1913, when he was convicted on charges of conspiracy in restraint of trade; the conviction was later overturned. He joined the Computing-Tabulating-Recording Co. and became president in 1914; this was the organization that became IBM. During the Depression and the necessary accounting procedures demanded by the expanded bureaucracies of the New Deal programs, Watson and IBM prospered; during World War II, the firm produced about forty military ordnance items; profits went from $41 million in 1939 to $142 million in 1945. Watson emphasized sales and distribution instead of original research and despite IBM's strong research ties with universities Sperry-Rand marketed the first commercial computer. However, IBM—after Watson had relinquished control to his sons, Thomas Jr., and Arthur—soon gained preeminence in the computer field.

WATSON, WILLIAM (*b. Nantucket, Mass., 1834; d. 1915*), engineer, educator. Graduated Lawrence Scientific School, Harvard, 1857; Ph.D., University of Jena, 1862. While abroad, he collected information on technical instruction which in 1864 was used as basis in planning organization of the Massachusetts Institute of Technology. He served at the Institute as its first professor of mechanical engineering and descriptive geometry, 1865–73. Thereafter he devoted himself to private studies, and was recording secretary of the American Academy of Arts and Sciences, 1884–1915.

WATTERSON, HARVEY MAGEE (*b. Beech Grove, Tenn., 1811; d. 1891*), lawyer, Tennessee legislator. Father of Henry Watterson. Congressman, Democrat, from Tennessee, 1839–43, and for several years thereafter in the diplomatic service, Watterson became proprietor of the *Nashville Daily Union*, 1849. Removing to Washington, D.C., as editor of the *Washington Union*, 1851, he gave up the post because he would not support administration policy in regard to the repeal of the Missouri Compromise. An opponent of the extension of slavery and of secession, he was a Unionist throughout the Civil War. After the war, he engaged in law practice at Washington, D.C.

WATTERSON, HENRY (*b. Washington, D.C., 1840; d. Jacksonville, Fla., 1921*), journalist, statesman. Son of Harvey M. Watterson. Beginning his career as journalist, 1858, he worked briefly in New York and then became a reporter for the Washington, D.C., *Daily States*. By conviction a Unionist, but a secessionist and Confederate soldier because of sectional sympathies. He became editor of the *Cincinnati Evening Times*, 1865, but withdrew to Nashville, Tenn., 1866. After service on the Nashville *Republican Banner*, he went to Louisville, Ky., to help edit the *Daily Journal* (from November 1868, the *Courier-Journal*). As editor of the *Courier-Journal* from November 1868, Watterson struggled for the restoration of Southern home rule, agitating for complete civil and legal rights for blacks in exchange for the return of the South to its own people. Associated with Carl Schurz, Murat Halstead, and Samuel Bowles, he formed the famous "Quadrilateral" (which later included Whitelaw Reid and Horace White) at the Liberal Republican convention of 1872. A powerful advocate of the candidacy of Samuel J. Tilden for nomination and election, 1876, Watterson served in Congress from the summer of 1876 through part of the winter of 1877 as Tilden's floor leader during the contest that ended with the certification of Hayes.

Never again did Watterson express more than a temporary fealty to any Democratic presidential nominee or White House incumbent. He was editorially critical of Grover Cleveland, and a fiery opponent of William J. Bryan in 1896; his stand against Bryan produced a Republican victory in Kentucky and nearly ruined the standing of his newspaper in that state. As late as 1913 Watterson deplored Bryan's appointment as U.S. secretary of state, assailing him as an impractical dreamer. Before this, however, he had made a national sensation with a series of philippics against Theodore Roosevelt, whom he called a potential dictator. Failing to prevent the nomination of Woodrow Wilson in 1912, Watterson remained critical of Wilson until the issues raised in 1916 by Charles E. Hughes and Theodore Roosevelt ranged him on Wilson's side. He once again parted company with the president over the League of Nations. Selling his control of the *Courier-Journal* in 1918, he retired to private life.

Celebrated as a public speaker and lecturer, Watterson had amazing zest, a great gift for conversation, and the ability to set other editors chattering over what he wrote. He belonged to the time when journalism was personal and editorial writing often had immediate and dynamic effect. He died convinced that civilization was facing a crisis because of prevalent godlessness. He was rendered pessimistic more immediately, however, by the triumph of national prohibition and woman suffrage, championed by those whom for many years he had attacked as "red-nosed angels," "silly-sallies," and "crazyjanes." He was author of, among other books, an autobiography, *Marse Henry* (1919).

WATTERSTON, GEORGE (*b. New York, N.Y., 1783; d. Washington, D.C., 1854*), lawyer, librarian. After practicing law in Hagerstown, Md., and Washington, D.C., he served as librarian of Congress, 1815–29, and was thereafter editor of the Washington *National Journal*. He was author of a number of works including novels, poems, guidebooks, statistical digests, and a comedy. He began the movement to build the Washington Monument, 1833, and remained as secretary of the Washington National Monument Society until his death.

WATTS, FREDERICK (*b. Carlisle, Pa., 1801; d. Carlisle, 1889*), lawyer, farmer, Pennsylvania jurist and supreme court reporter, railroad executive. As U.S. commissioner of agriculture, 1871–77, he obtained an appropriation for a forestry investigation that was the beginning of the Agriculture Department's division of forestry. Throughout his busy life he engaged in farming and in the activities of state and county agricultural societies.

WATTS, THOMAS HILL (*b. near present Greenville, Ala., 1819; d. Montgomery, Ala., 1892*), lawyer, Alabama legislator, confederate soldier. A Whig and later a Know-Nothing, he was a strong Unionist until Lincoln's election and its alleged threat to state rights. Confederate attorney general, 1862, he was governor of Alabama, 1863–65. During his term he fought against invasion of his state by the North and also opposed encroachments on state rights by the Confederate government at Richmond. After the Civil War, he practiced law in Montgomery.

WATTSON, LEWIS THOMAS. *See* FRANCIS, PAUL JAMES.

WAUGH, BEVERLY (*b. Fairfax Co., Va., 1789; d. Baltimore, Md., 1858*), Methodist clergyman. Elected assistant book agent of the Church, 1828, he became principal book agent, 1832, and served with efficiency and success until 1836 when he was elected bishop. He refused to be influenced in the conduct of his duties by either the proslavery or the antislavery groups among Methodists. After endeavoring to prevent the schism of 1844, he remained identified with the Northern wing of the Church and was senior bishop *post* 1852.

WAUGH, FREDERICK JUDD (*b. Bordentown, N.J., 1861; d. Provincetown, Mass., 1940*), painter. Studied with Thomas Eakins at Pennsylvania Academy of the Fine Arts and in Paris. A versatile artist, Waugh is known principally to the public as a talented marine painter whose many seascapes were marked by picturesque realism.

WAXMAN, FRANZ (*b. Königshütte, Upper Silesia, Germany, [now Chorozów, Poland], 1906; d. Los Angeles, Calif., 1967*), composer and conductor. Studied at the Dresden Music Academy and the Berlin Conservatory. He orchestrated and conducted Friedrich Hollaender's music for *The Blue Angel* (1930). His first major original score was for Fritz Lang's *Liliom* (1933). Moving to Hollywood, Waxman composed an original score for *The Bride of Frankenstein* (1935). He was briefly the music director of Universal studios, where he scored *Magnificent Obsession* (1935). For Metro-Goldwyn-Mayer he did scores for *Captains Courageous* (1937), *Three Comrades* (1938), *Rebecca* (1940), *The Philadelphia Story* (1940), *Dr. Jekyll and Mr. Hyde* (1941), *Suspicion* (1941), *Objective, Burma!* (1945), and *Humoresque* (1947). Waxman received Academy Awards for his scores for *Sunset Boulevard* (1950), and *A Place in the Sun* (1951). His other major works of the 1950's include scores for *The Silver Chalice* (1954), *Rear Window* (1954), *Crime in the Streets* (1956), *Sayonara* (1957), *Peyton Place* (1957), *The Spirit of St. Louis* (1957), and *The Nun's Story* (1959). His concert compositions include the *Carmen* Fantasie (1947), the Sinfonietta for Strings and Timpani (1955), the oratorio *Joshua* (1959), the song cycle *The Song of Terezin* (1965), and an unfinished opera based on his film music for *Dr. Jekyll and Mr. Hyde.*

WAYLAND, FRANCIS (*b. New York, N.Y., 1796; d. 1865*), Baptist clergyman, educator. Father of Francis Wayland (1826–1904). Graduated Union, 1813; was influenced at Andover Theological Seminary by Moses Stuart. Chosen president of Brown University, 1827, he gave that school a dynamic administration until his retirement, 185. Standards were generally raised; an analytic method of study succeeded the old memorization of textbooks; the curriculum was extended and enriched. He was author of a number of textbooks in moral philosophy, political economy, and other subjects. His reforming views on education were expressed in *Thoughts on the Present Collegiate System in the United States* (1842) and *Report on the Condition of the University* (1850). Instrumental in devising a school system for the city of Providence, R.I., he was author of the plan for free Rhode Island public schools (1828) and served as first president of the American Institute of Instruction, 1830.

WAYLAND, FRANCIS (*b. Boston, Mass., 1826; d. New Haven, Conn., 1904*), lawyer. Son of Francis Wayland (1796–1865). Graduated Brown, 1846; studied law at Harvard. Practiced in Worcester, Mass., until 1857. Thereafter a resident of New Haven, he taught at Yale Law School *post* 1871 and served as dean, 1873–1903. A conservative in legal education, he was responsible for much material progress at the school but damaged its prestige by refusing to adopt modern methods of study as instituted at Harvard by C. C. Langdell and others.

WAYMACK, WILLIAM WESLEY (*b. Savanna, Ill., 1888; d. Des Moines, Iowa, 1960*), journalist and government official. Studied at Morningside College in Iowa (B.A., 1911). Reporter and editor for the *Sioux City Journal* (1911–18). From 1918 until 1946, he was editor (1918–1929), and director of publishing (1931–1946), of the Cowles papers, *The Register* and *Tribune*, in Des Moines. An advocate of reform in agriculture, Waymack wrote against "farm tenancy" during the 1920's and the Depression. An internationalist in a time of national isolation, Waymack gained a national reputation for his editorials. From 1946 to 1948, he was a member of the Atomic Energy Commission. Trustee of the Carnegie Endowment for International Peace (1941–59); director of the Twentieth Century Fund (1942–60). He also served as director of the Federal Reserve Bank of Chicago.

WAYMAN, ALEXANDER WALKER (*b. Caroline Co., Md., 1821; d. Baltimore, Md., 1895*), bishop of the African Methodist Episcopal Church. Born a freeman, he was mainly self-educated. His principal pastorates until his election as bishop (1864) were in Washington, D.C., and Baltimore. As bishop, he organized and supervised conferences throughout the United States.

WAYMOUTH, GEORGE (*b. Devonshire, England, date unknown; d. place unknown, post 1612*), navigator, explorer. Commanded East India Company's expedition of 1602 in search of the Northwest Passage. Commanded ship *Archangel* on the 1605 voyage of exploration to Virginia sponsored by the Earl of Southampton, Lord Wardour, and Sir Ferdinando Gorges, during which he explored and traded along the coast to present Maine. Captured Indians whom he brought back to England later served as pilots to Martin Pring, George Popham, and other explorers. Waymouth was author of several treatises on navigation and shipbuilding.

WAYNE, ANTHONY (*b. Waynesboro, Pa., 1745; d. Presque Isle, now Erie, Pa., 1796*), surveyor, tanner, soldier. An active committeeman during the early Revolutionary movement, he served in the provincial assembly, 1775, and was commissioned colonel of a Pennsylvania regiment by Congress, January 1776. Impetuous and brave, he was often at odds with commanding officers but won credit for covering the retreat of Montgomery's army from the mouth of the Sorel to Ticonderoga, 1776. Commissioned brigadier general, February 1777, he joined Washington at Morristown, N.J., and took command of the Pennsylvania line. At Brandywine, September 1777, he held the center of the defense against the British at their main point of crossing; nine days later (September 20), he was surprised and badly defeated at Paoli. In the battle of Germantown (October 4), he led an almost victorious attack but was obliged to fall back when the rest of the American force became confused and retreated. He wintered with Washington at Valley Forge and led the advance attack at Monmouth, June 1778. Leading a separate corps of Continental light infantry, he took the British outpost of Stony Point on the Hudson River, July 1779. When Benedict Arnold tried to surrender West Point, September 1780, Wayne prevented British occupation of that post. At the end of the same year he helped quell a mutiny of the Pennsylvania line and secured from Congress a correction of the grievances that had caused it. Serving under Lafayette in the Yorktown campaign, he further distinguished himself at Green Spring, Va., July 1781. During the next year he campaigned successfully against the Creek Indians in Georgia, negotiating treaties with Creek and Cherokee, 1782–83.

Unsuccessful as a rice planter in Georgia after the Revolution, he engaged in conservative politics both in Pennsylvania and Georgia and was strongly in favor of the new Constitution. After the defeats of Generals Harmar and St. Clair by the confederated Indians of the Wabash and Maumee regions, 1790–91, Washington named Wayne as major general to rehabilitate the American army and move against the Indians. Carefully training and organizing his forces, and employing great tact in denying the British any excuse to lend official aid to the Indians, he won a complete victory at Fallen Timbers (near present Toledo, Ohio), Aug. 20, 1794. Pacification and submission of the Indians was secured by Wayne a year later at the treaty of Greenville, where he convinced them of the hopelessness of further resistance. He died on his return from the occupation of the post at Detroit, surrendered under the terms of Jay's Treaty.

WAYNE, ARTHUR TREZEVANT (*b. Blackville, S.C., 1863; d. 1930*), ornithologist. An indefatigable field worker in South Carolina and Florida. Author, among other works, of *Birds of South Carolina* (1910) and *A List of Avian Species for Which the Type Locality is South Carolina* (1917). Added about 45 birds to fauna of South Carolina; discovered breeding grounds of white ibis, 1922.

WAYNE, JAMES MOORE (*b. Savannah, Ga., ca. 1790; d. Washington, D.C., 1867*), lawyer, Georgia legislator, official and jurist. Graduated College of New Jersey (Princeton), 1808. As congressman, Democrat, from Georgia, 1829–35, he supported President Jackson's major policies and rose to chairmanship of the committee on foreign relations. Appointed a justice of the U.S. Supreme Court, 1835, he served until his death and was particularly effective in cases involving admiralty problems and the acquisition of lands from foreign countries. He was a Unionist in the Civil War.

WEARE, MESHECH (*b. Hampton Falls, N.H., 1713; d. 1786*), New Hampshire colonial legislator and jurist, Revolutionary patriot. Graduated Harvard, 1735. President of the New Hampshire Council and chairman of the committee of safety, 1776–84; chief justice, 1776–82. Elected president of the state of New Hampshire (governor), 1784, he resigned because of ill health in 1785. He was a cautious, temperate man, influential because of his shrewdness and honesty.

WEATHERFORD, WILLIAM (*b. probably in present Elmore Co., Ala., ca. 1780; d. 1824*), Creek Indian chief, known also as Red Eagle. Roused to war against the whites by the visit of Tecumseh in 1811, he took up arms after Tippecanoe, ignorant that his cause was already hopeless. Responsible for the massacre at Fort Mims, Aug. 30, 1813, he was a leader with Menewa of the force defeated at Horseshoe Bend, 1814. After his surrender to Andrew Jackson, he settled as a planter in Monroe Co., Ala. Accused, possibly falsely, by the whites of extreme personal dissoluteness, he was admitted to be eloquent and courageous.

WEAVER, AARON WARD (*b. Washington, D.C., 1832; d. Washington, 1919*), naval officer. Appointed midshipman, 1848; graduated U.S. Naval Academy, 1854. Served with distinction in Union campaigns on the lower Mississippi River, 1862–64, and with the South Atlantic blockade, 1864–65. Retired as rear admiral, 1893.

WEAVER, JAMES BAIRD (*b. Dayton, Ohio, 1883; d. Colfax, Iowa, 1912*), lawyer, Union soldier, Populist. Raised in Michigan and Iowa; practiced law in Iowa. Volunteering for the Union Army, 1861, he served in the western campaigns and rose to rank of brevet brigadier general. Utterly incorruptible, he held post of internal revenue assessor in Iowa, 1867–73, but lost favor with the Republican party to which he belonged because of his objection to its currency policy and his denunciations of predatory corporations. As a Greenbacker, he was elected to Congress from Iowa, 1878, ran for president in 1880, was defeated for Congress in 1882, but won again in 1884 and 1886. Identifying himself with the Farmers' Alliance, he took a leading part in transforming it into the Populist party. No advocate of unlimited inflation, nor of repudiation of debt, he held to the quantity theory of money and opposed what he considered the systematic efforts of creditors to appreciate the purchasing power of the dollar. As Populist candidate for the presidency, 1892, he campaigned with force and dignity; he received a popular vote of over a million, and 22 electoral votes. An advocate of the fusion of all soft-money forces, he helped bring about Populist endorsement of William J. Bryan in 1896.

WEAVER, PHILIP (*b. North Scituate, R.I., 1791; d. Attica, Ind., ante 1861*), cotton manufacturer. Removed to Spartanburg District, S.C., 1816, where with his brothers and others he set up and operated one of the earliest cotton mills in the region.

WEAVER, WILLIAM DIXON (*b. Greensburg, Pa., 1857; d. Charlottesville, Va., 1919*), electrical engineer, editor of technical journals, organizer of professional societies in his field.

WEBB, ALEXANDER STEWART (*b. New York, N.Y., 1835; d. Riverdale, N.Y., 1911*), soldier, educator. Son of James W. Webb. Graduated West Point, 1855; was commissioned in the artillery. Outstanding in his distinguished Civil War service with the Union Army was his command of the 2nd Brigade, Second Division, II Corps, 1863–64. Webb's brigade occupied the "bloody angle" at Gettysburg and bore the brunt of Pickett's charge. Severely wounded at Spotsylvania, May 1864, he returned to duty the next year as chief-of-staff to General Meade. Resigning with the rank of lieutenant colonel, Regular Army, he served as president of the College of the City of New York, 1869–1902. Serving also as professor of political philosophy, he maintained the standards of the college but made no significant advance in the scope of its work.

WEBB, CHARLES HENRY (*b. Rouse's Point, N.Y., 1834; d. New York, N.Y., 1905*), journalist, Civil War correspondent. Active on California journals, 1863–66, he became a close friend of Bret Harte and of Mark Twain. He founded, and was first editor of, the *Californian*, 1864. Working in New York City *post* 1866, he was the sponsor and publisher of Mark Twain's first book, *The Celebrated Jumping Frog of Calaveras County* (1867). His "John Paul" letters for the *New York Tribune* were collected in 1874 as *John Paul's Book*. He was author also of other parodies and satires.

WEBB, CLIFTON (*b. Indianapolis, Ind., 1893; d. Beverly Hills, Calif.; 1966*), singer, dancer, and actor. Appeared in a number of children's plays, operas, and musical comedies. He became a popular ballroom dancer and established his own private studio. He appeared in *Love o' Mike* (1917), *Listen, Lester* (1918), *As You Were* (1920), *Jack and Jill* (1923), *Meet the Wife* (1923), *Sunny* (1925), *She's My Baby* (1928), *Treasure Girl* (1928), the first *Little Show* (1929), *Three's a Crowd* (1930), *Flying Colors* (1932), *As Thousands Cheer* (1933), *And Stars Remain* (1936), *The Importance of Being Earnest* (1939), *Burlesque* (1939), *The Man Who Came to Dinner* (1940), and *Blithe Spirit* (1942). His early films include *Polly with a Past* (1920), *New Toys* (1925), and *The Heart of a Siren* (1925). In 1944 he began a long career with Twentieth Century–Fox, appearing in *Laura*, which earned him an Oscar nomination for best supporting actor. He also appeared in *The Dark Corner* (1946), *The Razor's Edge* (1946), *Sitting Pretty* (1948), for which he received an Oscar nomination for best actor, *Mr Belvedere Goes to College* (1949), *Cheaper by the Dozen* (1950), *For Heaven's Sake* (1950), *Mr. Belvedere Rings the Bell* (1951), *Dreamboat* (1952), *Titanic* (1953), and *Mister Scoutmaster* (1953).

WEBB, DANIEL (*b.* England, ca. 1700; *d.* 1773), British soldier. Rising in the regular service to be colonel of the 48th Foot (November 1755), he was selected early in 1756 to command in North America under Lord Loudoun and James Abercromby. A temporary major general after the fall of Oswego, he went up the Mohawk River to make a stand against the expected French attack on the forts there. Stricken with panic by Indian rumors, he destroyed the forts and retreated, leaving the colonists unprotected. As Loudoun had no one else to leave in command in New York during 1757, he continued Webb in his post despite that officer's illness and incapacity. During the siege of Fort William Henry in August he made no attempt at its relief. Recalled in December 1757, he later served with ability in Germany.

WEBB, GEORGE JAMES (*b.* near Salisbury, England, 1803; *d.* Orange, N.J., 1887), musician, composer. Came to Boston, Mass., 1830; was appointed organist of Old South Church. Associated with Lowell Mason in his educational projects, Webb organized an orchestra at the Boston Academy of Music and was important in other ways in the development of music in Boston.

WEBB, HARRY HOWARD (*b.* San Francisco, Calif., 1853; *d.* Montecito, Calif., 1939), mining engineer. Associated with the development of gold and diamond mines in South Africa, 1895–1916, he was later active in development of the potash and borax deposits near Death Valley, Calif.

WEBB, JAMES WATSON (*b.* Claverack, N.Y., 1802; *d.* New York, N.Y., 1884), journalist, diplomat. Father of Alexander S. Webb. Commissioned a second lieutenant in the U.S. Army, 1819, he served principally with infantry in the Midwest, won a reputation as a duellist, and resigned from the army, 1827. Acquiring the N.Y. *Morning Courier*, he merged the *Enquirer* with it in 1829 and continued to edit the *Courier and Enquirer* until 1861. Originally a Jacksonian, he later was a chief prop of the Whigs and a Free-Soiler. He was effective, if rash, as U.S. minister to Brazil, 1861–69, and gave useful aid to the Union cause by his personal friendship and contact with Napoleon III.

WEBB, JOHN BURKITT (*b.* Philadelphia, Pa., 1841; *d.* Glen Ridge, N.J., 1912), engineer, educator, inventor. C.E., University of Michigan, 1871; studied also at Heidelberg, Göttingen, Berlin, and Paris. Professor of civil engineering, University of Illinois, 1871–79; professor of applied mathematics, Cornell, 1881–86; professor of mathematics and mechanics, Stevens Institute of Technology, 1886–1908. Invented the floating dynamometer, 1888, and other devices for power measurement.

WEBB, THOMAS (*b.* England, ca. 1724; *d.* Bristol, England, 1796), British army officer, Methodist preacher. A wounded veteran of the French and Indian War, Webb became a Methodist in England, 1764. Returning to America, 1766, he assisted Philip Embury in preaching to the original New York City congregation of Methodists. He aided in the building of Wesley Chapel, 1768, and continued to evangelize until his return to England at some time during the Revolution.

WEBB, THOMAS SMITH (*b.* Boston, Mass., 1771; *d.* 1819), printer, founder of the American system of chapter and encampment Masonry. Author of *The Freemason's Monitor* (1797). He

was a founder and first president (1815) of the Handel and Haydn Society of Boston.

WEBB, WALTER PRESCOTT (*b.* Panola County, Tex., 1888; *d.* San Antonio, Tex., 1963), historian. Attended University of Texas (Ph.D., 1932). Appointed instructor to train secondary teachers at University of Texas 1918, remaining at that university as a professor from 1933 until his death. Beginning with his dissertation, he continued research on the Texas Rangers until 1931, when he published the highly acclaimed *The Great Plains*, which argued that the environment of the West caused dramatic alterations in institutions and technology and brought forth the Colt revolver, barbed-wire fences, and windmills. He returned to his first interest and published *The Texas Rangers* (1935). He also wrote *Divided We Stand: The Crisis of a Frontierless Democracy* (1937), an indictment of the corporate structures of the Northeast, and *The Great Frontier* (1952). President of the Mississippi Valley Historical Association (1955) and American Historical Association (1958).

WEBB, WILLIAM HENRY (*b.* New York N.Y., 1816; *d.* New York, 1899), shipbuilder. Working at his New York City yard on the East River between 5th and 7th Sts., 1843–69, Webb showed remarkable versatility in design and construction of vessels. He designed and built a number of notable packets and pre-clippers, and ranked high among the builders of regular clippers. Among his products were the *Sword Fish* (1851), the *Challenge* (1851), *Young America* (1853), and *Black Hawk* (1857). He also constructed hulls for a number of steamships and was the constructor of the Pacific Mail ships *California, Panama, Golden Gate, San Francisco,* and *Yorktown.* Among the warships which he built were the cutter *Harriet Lane* (1857) and several vessels for the Russian and Italian navies. His masterpiece was the ironclad ram *Dunderberg* (1865) which was sold to the French navy and sailed as the *Rochambeau.* He established and endowed Webb's Academy, New York, N.Y. (opened, May 1894).

WEBB, WILLIAM ROBERT (*b.* near Mount Tirzah, N.C., 1842; *d.* Bellbuckle, Tenn., 1926), Confederate soldier, educator. Graduated University of North Carolina, 1867. Founder (1870) and headmaster of a celebrated preparatory school at Culleoka, Tenn., which he removed to Bellbuckle, 1886.

WEBBER, CHARLES WILKINS (*b.* Russellville, Ky., 1819; *d.* Nicaragua, 1856), journalist, explorer. After serving in the Texas war for independence, he studied medicine and also theology, but became a journalist in New York City, 1844. He projected several abortive exploring expeditions in the Southwest and in 1855 joined the filibuster commanded by William Walker in Nicaragua. He was killed there in the battle of Rivas. Excelling in the description of wild border life, he was author, among other works, of *Old Hicks the Guide* (1848); *The Gold Mines of the Gila* (1849); *The Hunter-Naturalist* (1851); *Tales of the Southern Border* (1852); and *Wild Scenes and Song Birds* (1854).

WEBBER, HERBERT JOHN (*b.* Lawton, Mich., 1865; *d.* Riverside, Calif., 1946), plant physiologist. B.S., University of Nebraska, 1889; M.A., 1890. Ph.D., Washington University (St. Louis, Mo.), 1901. Associated with the U.S. Department of Agriculture, 1892–1907, he made notable contributions to the study of citrus fruit culture and cotton breeding. As professor of plant biology (1907–08) and head of the department of experimental plant biology (1908–12) at Cornell University, he undertook important research in corn and timothy. He was director of the Citrus Experiment Station and dean of the Graduate School of Tropical Agriculture, University of California at Riverside, 1912–20; after holding a number of posts elsewhere, he returned to Riverside in 1926 and was professor of subtropical horticulture until 1936 when he was made emeritus.

WEBER, ALBERT (*b. Bavaria, 1828; d. New York, N.Y., 1879*), musician, piano-maker. Came to New York City *ca.* 1844; began business as a piano manufacturer, 1851. Weber did not create anything new in piano construction, but was a thorough craftsman and made a quality product.

WEBER, GUSTAV CARL ERICH (*b. Bonn, Germany, 1828; d. Willoughby, Ohio, 1912*), physician. Immigrated to America *ca.* 1849. Graduated Beaumont Medical College, St. Louis, Mo., 1851; made further studies in Vienna, Amsterdam, and Paris. Practiced surgery and taught at several medical schools in Ohio, 1856–70; was professor of clinical surgery and dean of medical department of Wooster University, 1870–81; also dean of medical department, Western Reserve University, 1881–94. U.S. consul at Nuremberg, 1897–1902.

WEBER, HENRY ADAM (*b. Franklin Co., Ohio, 1845; d. Columbus, Ohio, 1912*), chemist. Studied at Otterbein College and in Germany. Chemist, Ohio Geological Survey, 1869–74; professor of chemistry, University of Illinois, 1874–82; professor of agricultural chemistry, Ohio State University *post* 1884. In addition to his academic work, Weber collaborated with M. A. Scovell in the manufacture of sugar from sorghum and was active in the work of the state board of agriculture and the state board of health. He was a pioneer in the national pure-food movement initiated by Harvey W. Wiley.

WEBER, JOSEPH MORRIS (*b. New York, N.Y., 1867; d. Los Angeles, Calif., 1942*), and **FIELDS, LEWIS MAURICE** (*b. New York, N.Y., 1867; d. Los Angeles, Calif., 1941*), dialect and burlesque comedians, theatrical producers. The famous comedy team met while in school on New York's Lower East Side. They began their collaboration at age nine and after a long apprenticeship had fully developed their act, which consisted of blackface, song-and-dance, dialect, and outrageous slapstick routines. The zenith of their career came with a seven-year series of travesties on more serious plays and musicals. The partnership was dissolved in 1904, but in 1912 they were reunited. Taste had changed, however, and the two comedians turned their talents to musical comedy, vaudeville, and motion pictures. They retired in 1930.

WEBER, MAX (*b. Bialystok, Russia, 1881; d. Great Neck, N.Y., 1961*), artist. Attended Pratt Institute and taught construction drawing and manual training in Lynchburg, Va., public schools, the University of Virginia (1901–03), and State Normal School in Duluth, Minn. (1903). Studied in Europe (1905–09), including at the Académie Julien in Paris, meeting such influential artists as Henri Rousseau, Henri Matisse, and Pablo Picasso. He became the contact between the Paris school and American modern painting. He was among the pioneers of cubism and futurism and was considered by some as responsible for the entry of American art into the mainstream of twentieth-century art. His first one-man show was at Gallery Haas (1909) and showed at Alfred Steiglitz's Gallery 291 (1911). Taught at the White School of Photography in New York (1914–18) and the Art Students League (1920–21, 1926–27). The Museum of Modern Art honored him in 1930 with a retrospective exhibit.

WEBSTER, ALICE JANE CHANDLER (*b. Fredonia, N.Y., 1876; d. 1916*), author, known as Jean Webster. Graduated Vassar, 1901. A grandniece of Mark Twain, she was author of *When Patty Went to College* (1903) and other Patty stories, and of the extraordinarily successful *Daddy-Long-Legs* (1912).

WEBSTER, ARTHUR GORDON (*b. Brookline, Mass., 1863; d. 1923*), physicist. Graduated Harvard, 1885; Ph.D., University of Berlin, 1890. Taught physics at Clark University *post* 1890, succeeding Albert A. Michelson as head of the department, 1892. His course of lectures on mathematical physics was unsurpassed in scope and thoroughness; at the same time he continued his work in experimental physics. He was outstanding in the development of various gyroscopic instruments and in sound investigations; during World War I he established and conducted a school of ballistics at Clark. He was author, among other works, of *The Theory of Electricity and Magnetism* (1897); *The Dynamics of Particles and of Rigid, Elastic and Fluid Bodies* (1904); and *The Partial Differential Equations of Mathematical Physics* (published posthumously, 1927).

WEBSTER, DANIEL (*b. Salisbury, N.H., 1782; d. Marshfield, Mass., 1852*), lawyer, statesman. A boy of delicate health, he early displayed a precocious mind and a strongly emotional nature. While a student at Phillips Exeter in 1796, he made rapid headway with his studies, but was shy and sensitive about his unfashinoble clothes and clumsy manners. At Dartmouth, he was outstanding in one of the college debating societies. After his graduation in 1801, he began the study of law in a desultory way, but gave up his studies to teach in the Fryeburg Academy in order to help his elder brother complete a college course. Returning to the study of law, September 1802, he varied the monotony of legal treatises with extensive readings in history and the classics. Removing to Boston, he became a clerk in the office of Christopher Gore and was admitted to the Boston bar, March 1805. After practicing for a short time at Boscawen, N.H., he removed to Portsmouth in September 1807 and practiced there with distinction until 1816.

A rival of Jeremiah Mason at the bar, he improved his style of speaking by conscious imitation of Mason and also learned from him the importance of a most careful preparation of arguments. Temperamentally a conservative, he had inherited from his father strong Federalist convictions and strove by Fourth of July orations and occasional political pamphleteering to assist the revival of Federalism after the Jeffersonian triumph of 1800. A champion of New England shipping interests, he was author of *Considerations on the Embargo Laws* (1808). A vigorous critic of the national administration for having led the nation into an unjustifiable war, 1812, he renounced the idea of resistance or insurrection, advocating "the peaceable remedy of election." His famous Rockingham Memorial was a forceful statement of his anti-war views.

Webster's national political career began with his election to Congress in 1812. A member of the committee on foreign relations, he introduced a number of resolutions designed to embarrass the administration, eloquently denouncing the government's draft bill and favoring repeal of the Embargo Act. He even suggested the expedient of state nullification of a federal law in the debate over conscription, but continued to repudiate any thought of disunion and advised New Hampshire against sending delegates to the Hartford Convention. Reelected to Congress, 1814, he urged the provision of adequate safeguards for financial stability in any reestablishment of the United States Bank. In discussion of the tariff, he announced himself as opposed to any "hotbed" treatment of manufactures and opposed the high duties of the tariff of 1816. Removing to Boston, August 1816, he devoted himself to legal work. The so-called Dartmouth College case, a suit in which the college trustees sought to defend their rights against acts of the New Hampshire legislature which changed the character of the institution and its governing body, made Webster, in the opinion of many people, the foremost lawyer of the time. Placed in charge of the case before the U.S. Supreme Court, he drew on the notes and briefs of his colleagues for most of his materials, but was himself responsible for their brilliant presentation. On Feb. 2, 1819, the Supreme Court by its decision completely upheld the college and its counsel. Three weeks after his victory, he appeared for the Bank of the United States in *McCulloch* v. *Maryland* and soon thereafter played an important part in three other important constitutional cases, *Gibbons* v. *Ogden*; *Osborn* v. *Bank of the United States*; and *Ogden* v. *Saunders*. He also delivered a number of outstanding orations on public occasions, notably his commemoration of the landing of the Pilgrims, December 1820, and his address at the laying of the cornerstone of the Bunker Hill Monument, June 1825.

Returning to Congress, 1823–27, he was made chairman of the judiciary committee. In April 1824 he challenged Henry Clay's arguments for a protective tariff, attacking the proposed tariff bill and its principles and refusing to vote for it. Although he shared the distrust of the New England Federalists for John Q. Adams, he gave Adams his vote during the contest over the presidency in the House, and influenced others over in the same direction. As party lines reshaped themselves under the new administration, Webster became an increasingly loyal Adams supporter. Elected to the U.S. Senate from Massachusetts, June 1827, he was soon in the thick of the fight over the tariff act of 1828. An associate of the mill-owners of his state and an investor in the Merrimack Manufacturing Co., he was frank to state that New England must consider protection as a determined national policy. Since the tariff bill with all its "abominations" granted protection to woolens, he supported it and helped accomplish its passage. Henceforward, he was an aggressive champion of protection.

Webster rose to the height of his oratorical abilities in the famous debate of January 1830 with John C. Calhoun's mouthpiece, Robert Y. Hayne, over the issue of state rights and nullification. Webster declared that the Union, in origin, preceded the states. He insisted that the Constitution was framed by the people not as a compact, but to create a government sovereign within the range of the powers assigned to it, with the Supreme Court as the only proper arbiter of the extent of these powers. Nullification could result only in violence and civil war. He was for "Liberty *and* Union, now and forever, one and inseparable." Webster supported President Jackson in his defiance of the nullifiers, 1832–33. When the "Compromise Tariff" was enacted in March 1833, Webster voted with the opposition.

As soon as all those with a common interest in vested rights began to combine in the Whig party, Webster joined the new coalition. He was further persuaded to oppose President Jackson because of Jackson's war on the Bank of the United States which Webster supported both on principle and as a client. Reelected to the Senate, 1833, he spoke constructively in the debates over the removal of deposits from the Bank and the resolution of censure then adopted by the Senate. Named as the Massachusetts Whig candidate for the presidency, 1836, he received only the electoral vote of his own state. Having given so much of his time and energy to the public, he found himself in a poor financial condition which was aggravated by his ill-timed investments during the 1830's in midwestern lands. Harassed by his creditors, he was saved from disgrace only by the loans of wealthy friends. After the panic of 1837, he returned to the special session of Congress and took a brilliant part in the Whig fight against Van Buren's subtreasury plan; he also clashed with Calhoun over slavery and the right of petition. Reelected to the Senate once again in 1839, he campaigned for William H. Harrison in the presidential race of 1840. Named U.S. secretary of state, he remained in office under President John Tyler after Harrison's death. After the resignation of Tyler's cabinet over the president's veto of Whig measures for reestablishing a United States Bank, Webster, suspicious of Henry Clay's leadership, continued in office in order to bring to a conclusion the negotiations over the boundary of Maine; these he carried through to a successful adjustment in the Webster-Ashburton Treaty of 1842. Eminently successful in the State Department, he conducted negotiations also with Portugal and Mexico and undertook the preliminaries to the opening of diplomatic relations with China. Resigning in May 1843 from the only office which had ever allowed him reasonable satisfaction and scope for his talents, he returned to his law practice.

Reelected to the U.S. Senate once again in 1845, he announced that it was his special business to look to "the preservation of the great industrial interests of this country" from Democratic free-trader propensities. He joined in the Whig policy of condemning the war with Mexico, but held that supplies should be appropriated for the war so long as it was not connected with territorial aggrandizement or the dismemberment of Mexico. In the dispute over the disposition of the territories acquired from Mexico after the war, Webster voted consistently for the Wilmot Proviso, but preferred the "no territory" basis that would prevent a controversy from arising over slavery, which he considered "a great moral and political evil." Once again disappointed of hope for the presidency by the election of Zachary Taylor, he grew alarmed over the sectional controversy which seemed likely to result in a Southern separatism. He was also disturbed over the obstacle presented by a continued discussion of slavery to Whig efforts at tariff revision. Increasingly annoyed at the militant intransigence of the Abolitionists and anti-slavery men, he declared himself in favor of Henry Clay's compromise measures. On March 7, 1850, he delivered a famous speech designed to "beat down the Northern and Southern follies now raging in equal extremes." No evil was so great as disunion, he said; there could be no peaceful secession. A congressional prohibition of slavery in the territories was useless since a law of nature had settled that slavery cannot exist in California or New Mexico. Conservatives approved his speech, but the antislavery forces denounced him as a fallen star. Serving once again with skill as U.S. secretary of state, 1850–52, he was denied a presidential nomination, 1852. Repudiating the candidacy of General Winfield Scott, he prophesied the downfall of the Whig party, and died before the election.

Forty years in politics revealed in Webster two seemingly contrasting but naturally allied forces. An eloquent champion of the Union, he was also a special advocate for the new industrial interests then forging to the front in the national economy. In behalf of the masters of capital, he sacrificed the popular following that stood ready to rall around a great democratic chieftain. The logic and eloquence of his oratory, the magnetic quality of his personality, did little to bring him the support of workingmen. A great constitutional lawyer, he found his equals or betters among his contemporaries. His victories were never on a par with his ambitions. Even his personal fortunes failed to bring him any sense of security and life was for him a series of great frustrations. However, no other Northern man left so strong an impress upon the political life of the "middle period" or more substantially contributed to the preservation of the Union in the supreme test of the 1860's.

WEBSTER, EDWIN SIBLEY. *See* STONE, CHARLES AUGUSTUS.

WEBSTER, HAROLD TUCKER (*b. Parkersburg, W. Va., 1885; d. Stamford, Conn., 1952*), comic artist. Syndicated political and cultural cartoonist, Webster was the creator of Caspar Milquetoast, one of the best-known of all comic strip characters. The term immediately became part of the language.

WEBSTER, JEAN. *See* WEBSTER, ALICE JANE CHANDLER.

WEBSTER, JOHN WHITE (*b. Boston, Mass., 1793; d. 1850*), physician, educator. A teacher of chemistry at Harvard, 1824–49, Webster is principally remembered as the murderer of George Parkman (uncle of Francis Parkman), Nov. 23, 1849. After a sensational trial, Webster was convicted and hanged.

WEBSTER, JOSEPH DANA (*b. Hampton, N.H., 1811; d. Chicago, Ill., 1876*), soldier, engineer. Graduated Dartmouth, 1832. Served as an officer in the topographical engineers, 1838–54, resigning to enter business in Chicago. During the Civil War he served as chief-of-staff to General U. S. Grant in 1862 and part of 1863, rising to rank of brigadier general. In charge of all military railways before, during, and after the Vicksburg campaign, he then became chief-of-staff to General W. T. Sherman. He resigned from the army, 1865, as brevet major general.

WEBSTER, NOAH (*b. West Hartford, Conn., 1758; d. New Haven, Conn., 1843*), educator, lexicographer, editor. Graduated Yale, 1778. While teaching at Goshen, N.Y., 1782, he composed an elementary spelling book, Part I of *A Grammatical Institute of the English Language* (Hartford, Conn., 1783), which he supplemented with a grammar (1784) and a reader (1785). In preparing the series, he strove to correct the neglect of the American scene in the then current textbooks, and in the introduction to his speller issued a literary declaration of independence. Of the three books, the speller was the outstanding success and under various titles continued to be issued well into the 20th century. Its use had much to do with the standardization of spelling and, to some degree, of pronunciation in the United States along lines differing somewhat from those that prevailed in England. Neither the reader nor the grammar had the vogue of the speller, but the grammar (Part II of the *Institute*) was interesting because it was based on an objective study of the actual phenomena of English speech. Aroused by piracies of his work, he began an agitation which in time led to provision of American copyright; this activity took him into politics and made him an ardent Federalist. His efforts to promote copyright legislation in the 13 states involved travel over most of the country and drew from him several political pamphlets in support of a strong central government. Encouraged by Benjamin Franklin, he became an advocate of spelling reform, but was unable to effect any substantial changes.

Between 1787 and 1798, he served as editor of several newspapers in New York and was editor of the *American Magazine*, 1787–88. Removing to New Haven, 1798, he gave up journalism for good in 1803. Meanwhile, he had produced a number of interesting works including *The Prompter* (1791, informal essays), several treatises in economics, a work on epidemic diseases which was standard in its time, and much political writing. He edited John Winthrop's *Journal* in 1790, and was author of a pioneer American essay in physical science, *Experiments Respecting Dew* (begun 1790, printed 1809). After issuing a preparatory study, *A Compendious Dictionary of the English Language* (1806), Webster devoted twenty years to a larger work which was published in 1828 under the title *An American Dictionary of the English Language*. It took first place at once among English dictionaries on its merits. In it the author freely recorded non-literary words and based definitions upon the usage of American as well as British writers. In defining a word, he proceeded from what he considered its original or primary meaning and as far as possible derived the other meanings from the primary one. The great weakness of Webster's dictionary lay in its etymologies, but it was on the whole a scholarly achievement of the first order.

WEBSTER, PELATIAH (*b. Lebanon, Conn., 1726; d. 1795*), Congregational clergyman, Philadelphia merchant, political economist. Graduated Yale, 1746. Author of a number of papers urging support of the Revolution by taxation rather than by loans, and suggesting curtailment of paper money issues, Webster later (1791) gathered these studies together in a volume entitled *Political Essays on the Nature and Operation of Money, etc.* His *Dissertation on the Political Union and Constitution of the Thirteen United States* (1783) helped educate the people to the need of a new form of government, and he ably supported the Federal

Constitution in several pamphlets published during the struggle in Pennsylvania over its adoption, 1787.

WEBSTER-POWELL, ALMA.   *See* POWELL, ALMA WEBSTER.

WEDDELL, ALEXANDER WILBOURNE (*b. Richmond, Va., 1876; d. near Sedalia, Mo., 1948*), diplomat, philanthropist. LL.B., George Washington University law school, 1908. A protégé of Maurice F. Egan, Weddell served in the U.S. consular service, 1910–28; as U.S. ambassador to Argentina, 1933–39; and as U.S. ambassador to Spain, 1939–42.

WEED, LEWIS HILL (*b. Cleveland, Ohio, 1886; d. Reading, Pa., 1952*), anatomist and medical administrator. Studied at Yale and Johns Hopkins universities (M.D., 1912). Taught at Johns Hopkins (1914–39); chair of anatomy, (1917); dean of the medical school (1923); director of the medical school (from 1929). From 1939 to 1950, chief of the medical division of the National Research Council of the National Academy of Sciences and vice-chairman of the Office of Scientific Research. Did major medical research for the wartime efforts of the nation. Trustee of the Carnegie Institution of Washington and the Institute for Advanced Study, Princeton.

WEED, THURLOW (*b. Greene Co., N.Y., 1797; d. 1882*), printer, journalist, New York politician and legislator. Began as publisher-editor of upstate New York newspapers supporting DeWitt Clinton, 1817–22; served as editorial writer on the *Rochester Telegraph*, which he purchased, 1825. A supporter of John Q. Adams in 1824, Weed became an active Anti-Mason. Elected to the New York Assembly, 1829, he took over editorship of the *Albany Evening Journal*, March 1830. Becoming a Whig, he fought the dominant "Albany Regency" in his state, drilled his new party through the campaigns of 1834 and 1836, and helped create the Whig victories that made William H. Seward governor of New York in 1838 and W. H. Harrison president in 1840. Although he was charged with dominating Seward, his great personal friend, actually he was content for others to formulate the principles while he secured the votes. He considered bribery and legislative favors legitimate party instruments, but was personally not corrupt. A sincere antislavery man, he had nothing but scorn for Abolitionists and other extremists; while recognizing the power of Horace Greeley, he was dubious about Greeley's efforts at social reform. Discouraged at first by the Whig failures in 1842 and 1844, he early recognized the possibilities of a presidential candidacy by General Zachary Taylor, but was again disappointed in his hopes for Whig unity when Taylor died soon after election. Slow to join the new Republican party, he devoted his energies *post ca.* 1854 to the furtherance of his friend Seward's candidacy for the presidency, but was again unsuccessful. Consulted by Abraham Lincoln during the latter's campaign and after, he had considerable influence on appointments, but was distrustful of Abolitionist influences on Lincoln. Preferring an active War Democrat as Union candidate in 1864, he was held in the Republican ranks because of the nomination of George B. McClellan. As the Radical Republicans gained strength after Lincoln's death, Weed's influence declined. He became editor of the N.Y. *Commercial Advertiser*, 1867, but had to abandon editorial work because of failing health and sight. A generous man, good-natured and charming of manner, Weed was described by Henry Adams as "the model of political management and patient address—a complete American education in himself."

WEEDEN, WILLIAM BABCOCK (*b. Bristol, R.I., 1834; d. Providence, R.I., 1912*), woolen manufacturer, social historian. Author, among other works, of *Indian Money as a Factor in New England Civilization* (1884) and the *Economic and Social History of New England* (1890).

WEEKS, EDWIN LORD (*b. Boston, Mass., 1849; d. Paris, France, 1903*), painter, specializing in Oriental subjects.

WEEKS, JOHN ELMER (*b. Painesville, Ohio, 1853; d. San Diego, Calif., 1949*), ophthalmologist. Worked as a painter and repairman in a railroad shop; then read medicine with a local physician. M.D., University of Michigan, 1881. Studied at Ophthalmic and Aural Institute (New York City), 1882. After six months' study in Berlin (1885), he began a two-year internship at the Ophthalmic and Aural Institute where he established and taught the first systematic course in bacteriology given in New York City. In 1886, he isolated the causative organism of the acute epidemic conjunctivitis known as "pink eye," thereafter known as the Koch-Weeks bacillus. Maintained a private practice and was surgeon and pathologist at New York Eye and Ear Infirmary (1890–1920). He held teaching appointments at Women's Medical College, New York University, and Bellevue Hospital Medical College.

WEEKS, JOHN WINGATE (*b. near Lancaster, N.H., 1860; d. Lancaster, 1926*), stockbroker. Graduated Annapolis, 1881. Entered brokerage business in Boston, Mass., 1888, becoming a partner in Hornblower & Weeks. Congressman, Republican, from Massachusetts, 1905–13; U.S. senator, 1913–19. U.S. secretary of war, 1921–25. An able, hard-working, orthodox Republican.

WEEKS, JOSEPH DAME (*b. Lowell, Mass., 1840; d. 1896*), technical journalist. Long associated in an editorial capacity with the *American Manufacturer* (Pittsburgh, Pa.), he was responsible for the first wage scale offered by the manufacturers to the Amalgamated Association of Iron and Steel Workers. He subsequently presided over a number of wage conferences and other essays in labor arbitration. He is credited with conducting the experiments that led to the first use of gas in a puddling furnace; he was also responsible for assembly of petroleum, coke, gas, and other statistics for the Census and for various state and federal bureaus.

WEEKS, STEPHEN BEAUREGARD (*b. Pasquotank Co., N.C., 1865; d. Washington, D.C., 1918*), historian, federal educational official. Graduated University of North Carolina, 1886; Ph.D., 1888. Ph.D., Johns Hopkins, 1891. Author of, among other works, *Southern Quakers and Slavery* (1896) and of the *Index to the Colonial and State Records of North Carolina* (1909–14).

WEEMS, MASON LOCKE (*b. near Herring Bay, Md., 1759; d. Beaufort, S.C., 1825*), Episcopal clergyman, subscription book agent, author. One of the first candidates to receive Anglican ordination for service in the United States (1784), Weems served Maryland parishes, 1784–92. Passionate in his faith in the value of good books, he journeyed (*post* 1794 as agent for Mathew Carey) up and down the Eastern coast from New York to Savannah, acting as book salesman and occasional preacher until his death. Author of a number of moralizing tracts, he is remembered for what may be called his masterpiece, *The Life and Memorable Action of George Washington* (*ca.* 1800), in whose fifth edition (1806) the hatchet and cherry-tree story first appeared in book form.

WEEMS, TED (*b. Pitcairn, Pa., 1901; d. Tulsa, Okla., 1963*), orchestra leader and composer. After playing trombone with Paul Specht's band in the early 1920's, he and his brother Art formed their All-American Band, which went on the road and gravitated toward Chicago, where radio broadcasts helped widen the band's popularity. In the 1930's the band performed on radio with Jack Benny. Their first hit record was "Somebody Stole My Gal"

(1924); other successes were "My Gal Sal," "You're the Cream in My Coffee," and "Heartaches" (1938).

WEGMANN, EDWARD (*b. Rio de Janeiro, Brazil, 1850; d. Yonkers, N.Y., 1935*), engineer. C.E., New York University, 1871. He was particularly notable for his thirty years of service with the water-supply system of New York City (1884–1914) during which he made studies for design of the Croton Dam, supervised much of the work on the Croton Aqueduct, and continued in service on the maintenance of the Croton water system. He was author of authoritative works on the design of dams and of *The Water Works of the City of New York: 1658–1895* (1896).

WEHLE, LOUIS BRANDEIS (*b. Louisville, Ky., 1880. d. New York, N.Y., 1959*), lawyer, author, and public servant. Studied at Harvard (LL.B., 1904). Wehle practiced law in Kentucky until World War I, when he joined the legal committee of the General Munitions Board. In June 1917, he was special assistant to the secretary of war, negotiating labor contracts for wartime construction. A personal friend of Franklin D. Roosevelt, during the New Deal he was a member of the White House Conference on Power Pooling. He practiced law in Washington and New York until his death.

WEIDENMANN, JACOB (*b. Winterthur, Switzerland, 1829; d. 1893*), landscape architect. Trained in Munich, he settled in America *ca.* 1861. Superintendent of parks in Hartford, Conn., 1861–68, he was later employed in a number of important projects, sometimes alone and sometimes in collaboration with Frederick L. Olmsted. He was a pioneer in the modern park type of cemetery.

WEIDENREICH, FRANZ (*b. Edenkoben, Germany, 1873; d. Westwood, N.J., 1948*), physical anthropologist. Studied at universities of Munich, Kiel, and Strasbourg; M.D., Strasbourg, 1898. Professor at University of Heidelberg, 1921–35. His early research was concerned largely with human blood and lymph systems; pursuing the relationships of hematology with various tissue systems, he made the structure, functions, and evolution of the human skeleton his dominant scientific interest. Concerned with the Nazi perversion of anthropological data, he wrote extensively against racism; he resigned from Heidelberg, 1935. As professor at Peking Union Medical School, 1935–41, he continued the research already begun on the fossil human remains discovered at Chou Kou Tien, producing a series of major studies of Peking Man. He continued his work *post* 1941 at the American Museum of Natural History, New York City.

WEIDIG, ADOLF (*b. Hamburg, Germany, 1867; d. Hinsdale, Ill., 1931*), musician, composer. Studied at the Hamburg and Munich conservatories. Came to America, 1892; played with Chicago Symphony Orchestra as a first violin; taught at American Conservatory of Music, Chicago, *post* 1893. A conservative modernist as a composer, he was author of songs, chamber music, and large orchestral works, notably "Drei Episoden" (*Opus* 38, 1908). He was author also of a treatise, *Harmonic Material and Its Uses* (1923).

WEIDNER, REVERE FRANKLIN (*b. Center Valley, Pa., 1851; d. Tangerine, Fla., 1915*), Lutheran theologian. Graduated Muhlenberg, 1869; Lutheran Theological Seminary, Philadelphia, 1873. Professor of dogmatics, Augustana Seminary, 1882–91; first president, Chicago Lutheran Seminary *post* 1891.

WEIGEL, GUSTAVE (*b. Buffalo, N.Y., 1906; d. New York, N.Y., 1964*), theologian. Attended the Jesuit novitiate at St. Andrew-on-Hudson, Woodstock College, and Pontifical Gregorian University in Rome (S.T.D., 1937); assigned to teach dogmatic theology at Catholic University in Chile, 1937–48;

became dean of the theological faculty, 1942–48. In 1948 he became the specialist in Protestant theology for *Theological Studies* and professor of ecclesiology at Woodstock in 1949. A pioneer in the promotion of ecumenism in the United States, he served as a consultant to the Secretariat for the Promotion of Christian Unity, 1960–62. During the Second Vatican Council, 1962–65, he served as interpreter for the English-speaking ecumenical observer-delegates.

WEIGHTMAN, WILLIAM (*b. Waltham, England, 1813; d. 1904*), chemist. Immigrated to America *ca.* 1829; was long associated with Powers & Weightman and its antecedent firms. Weightman was the first to manufacture quinine sulphate and popularize the use of the cheaper alkaloids of cinchona as substitutes. His firm is also credited with introducing and perfecting the manufacture of citric acid in the United States. He was also an extensive holder of real estate in Philadelphia and director of a number of banks.

WEIL, RICHARD (*b. New York, N.Y., 1876; d. Macon, Ga., 1917*), physician. Graduated Columbia, 1896; M.D., New York College of Physicians and Surgeons, 1900; studied also in Vienna and Strasbourg. Teacher of experimental pathology and therapeutics at Cornell Medical College, 1905–15, he became head of the department of experimental medicine, 1916. Working *post* 1906 at the Loomis Laboratory, he gained international reputation in the field of the serology of cancer and general problems of immunity. He established the *Journal of Cancer Research*, 1915, and was its managing editor until his death in military service during World War I.

WEILL, KURT (*b. Dessau, Germany, 1900; d. New York, N.Y., 1950*), musician, composer. Child of Jewish parents who were both musical; studied with Albert Bing, briefly at the Berlin Hochschule für Musik, and with Ferruccio Busoni, 1921–24. His first compositions were in the "modernist" tradition of European art music; his own inclinations, and the success of several operas which he wrote in jazz and other popular idioms, convinced him that he should write for the popular theater. Working in collaboration with Berthold Brecht, he produced a number of contemporary versions of the traditional German *Singspiel*, satirical, ideologically motivated, and technically adroit; of these, the most celebrated was *The Threepenny Opera* (1928), adapted from John Gay's 18th century satire *The Beggar's Opera*. Fleeing Germany in 1933, he lived for a time in France and in England; in 1935, he came to the United States to write music for Max Reinhardt's production *The Eternal Road*. He was highly successful as a composer of musical shows for Broadway: *Knickerbocker Holiday* (1938); *Lady in the Dark* (1941); *One Touch of Venus* (1943); and *Lost in the Stars* (1949).

WEIR, ERNEST TENER (*b. Pittsburgh, Pa., 1875. d. Philadelphia, Pa., 1957*), business executive. Self-educated. Weir was able to buy a bankrupt tinplate mill in 1905, which by 1918 had become the Weirton Steel Company, and by 1929, with consolidation with other small firms, the National Steel Company, the nation's fifth largest steel manufacturer. Violently opposed to unions and an espouser of right-wing causes, Weir conducted a colorful but losing battle to keep his company out of the hands of the unions; he succumbed in the mid-1930's. In 1940, he became chairman of the Republican National Finance Committee. He was active in his company until his death, uncompromising in his political and economic beliefs.

WEIR, JOHN FERGUSON (*b. West Point, N.Y., 1841; d. Providence, R.I., 1926*), artist. Son of Robert W. Weir; brother of Julian A. Weir. Studied with his father and at the National Academy of Design, New York. Grouped with the "Hudson River School," he painted genre, landscapes, portraits, and flowerpieces; his early studies of industry were important and include his masterpiece, *Forging the Shaft*, now in the Metropolitan Museum of Art. He taught painting and design at Yale *post ca.* 1869 and was first director of the School of Fine Arts at Yale.

WEIR, JULIAN ALDEN (*b. West Point, N.Y., 1852; d. New York, N.Y., 1919*), painter. Son of Robert W. Weir; brother of John F. Weir. Studied with his father, at the N.Y. National Academy of Design, and in the atelier of Gérôme in Paris; was influenced by Bastien-Lepage. He settled in New York City *ca.* 1883 after nearly ten years of intermittent foreign travel and study. Friend of most of the outstanding painters of his time, he was also a wise adviser to art collectors in the purchase of contemporary works. His own early painting is somewhat eclectic, marked by skilled craftsmanship and highly developed technique. Deeply influenced by the French Impressionists, he was not an Impressionist in the limited sense; his art is more directly related to that of Whistler, and to the decorative methods of the Japanese. A versatile craftsman in varied media, he never aspired to the grand manner. His conception was expressed in terms of spatial arrangement, simplification of form, and harmonization of tone. In all his work there is reflected his own restraint, sincerity, and reasonableness, together with subtlety of observation and delicacy of feeling. In his ultimate style, the color is subdued, marked by neutralized hues of closely related values; the form is manifested by a universal lighting that eliminates strong contrasts.

WEIR, ROBERT FULTON (*b. New York, N.Y., 1838; d. 1927*), surgeon. Nephew of Robert W. Weir. Graduated present College of the City of New York, 1854; M.D., N.Y. College of Physicians and Surgeons, 1859. After service with the Union Army, he practiced in New York City where he held a number of hospital appointments. He taught surgery at the College of Physicians and Surgeons, 1883–1903. A brilliant operator, he was notable for work in connection with surgery of the joints and intestines. He was among the first to recognize duodenal ulcer as an entity, and to adopt Lister's method. He also made important modifications of the Murphy button for use in gastroenterostomy.

WEIR, ROBERT WALTER (*b. New Rochelle, N.Y., 1803; d. New York, N.Y., 1889*), painter, teacher. Father of John F. and Julian A. Weir. Mainly self-taught, he was enabled by a patron to make studies in Florence and Rome. Teacher of drawing at the U.S. Military Academy, West Point, 1834–76, he also executed portraits, illustrations, and genre paintings. *The Embarkation of the Pilgrims* in the rotunda of the U.S. Capitol, Washington, D.C., was painted by him, 1836–40. A contemporary critic described him as showing "considerable skill of manipulation and detail, facility of composition, and those composite qualities which make up an accomplished rather than an original man."

WEISENBURG, THEODORE HERMAN (*b. Budapest, Hungary, 1876; d. 1934*), neurologist. Came to the United States as a child. M.D., University of Pennsylvania, 1899. Practiced and taught in Philadelphia; was associated in much of his work with Charles K. Mills. Professor of neurology, Graduate School of Medicine, University of Pennsylvania *post* 1917. A contributor to professional journals, *post* 1920 he was best known as editor of the *Archives of Neurology and Psychiatry*.

WEISER, JOHANN CONRAD (*b. near Herrenberg, Württemberg, 1696; d. Womelsdorf, Pa., 1760*), Indian interpreter and agent. Settled in New York, 1710, where he became expert in the Mohawk language and farmed near Schoharie. On his removal to Tulpehocken, Pa., 1729, he renewed his friendship with the chief, Shikellamy, and was responsible for the Philadelphia conferences (1731 and 1736) which won the Iroquois to the interests of the Penns. He made the Iroquois alliance binding by the treaty of 1742, and in 1743 averted war between the Iroquois and Virginia. Through his influence, the Lancaster Treaty of 1744 marked a shift to the direction of Indian affairs from New York to Pennsylvania and a reduction of the power of Sir William Johnson. With George Groghan, he won over the Western tribes at the treaty of Logstown, 1748, thereby extending Pennsylvania trade to the Mississippi.

Superseded in the formulation of policy *post* 1748, he continued active in local politics and was first president-judge of Berks Co., Pa., 1752–60. Weiser is also celebrated for his religious activities. Born a Lutheran, he became a follower of John P. Miller in the German Reformed Church and formed with Miller a Baptist group, 1735. Baptized by Johann C. Beissel, Weiser removed his family to Ephrata and became a member of the cloister there under the name of Brother Enoch. After several quarrels with Beissel, he ended his connection with Ephrata *ca.* 1743. Thereafter, he was successively a Lutheran again and a member of the Reformed Church. Throughout his early career, he assisted the Moravian missions to the Indians.

WEISS, EHRICH. *See* HOUDINI, HARRY.

WEISS, JOHN (*b. Boston, Mass., 1818; d. Boston, 1879*), Unitarian clergyman. Pastor at various times in Watertown and New Bedford, Mass., he is remembered principally for his efforts to introduce German literature to New England readers through translations of Schiller and Goethe. He was author also of the *Life and Correspondence of Theodore Parker* (1863).

WEISS, SOMA (*b. Bestercze, Hungary, 1899; d. Cambridge, Mass., 1942*), professor of medicine, researcher in pharmacology and physiology. Studied physiology and biochemistry at Royal Hungarian University, Budapest. Came to United States, 1920. A.B., Columbia University, 1921. M.D., Cornell University Medical School, 1923. After internship at Bellevue Hospital, New York City, he moved to Boston, 1925, as research fellow at Harvard Medical School and assistant at Thorndike Laboratory of Boston City Hospital. There, with associates he made classic studies of velocity of human blood flow and contributed greatly (among other subjects of investigation) to knowledge of pathophysiology of left ventricular failure and acute pulmonary edema, also to relation between cardiovascular disturbances and vitamin deficiencies. Winning rapid advancement at Harvard Medical School, he was appointed Hersey Professor of Physics in 1939, and left the Thorndike Laboratory in that same year to become physician-in-chief at Peter Bent Brigham Hospital.

WEITZEL, GODFREY (*b. Cincinnati, Ohio, 1835; d. Philadelphia, Pa., 1884*), soldier, engineer. Graduated West Point, 1855. After service as engineer in several theaters of the Civil War, he was promoted brigadier general, 1862, and commanded a brigade and provisional division during Union Army operations in Louisiana, 1862–63. Chief engineer of the Army of the James, June–September 1864, he returned to troop duty, commanding first the XVIII and later the XXV Corps. Cited for gallantry at the capture of Fort Harrison, Va., 1864, he was promoted major general and served under General Benjamin Butler in the first expedition against Fort Fisher. His command took possession of Richmond upon its evacuation, April 3, 1865. He was distinguished as a corps commander and for his success with black troops. Returning to the engineer service after the Civil War, he was active in river- and harbor-improvement works of which the most important were the ship canals at the falls of the Ohio and at Sault Sainte Marie, Mich.

WELBY, AMELIA BALL COPPUCK (*b. St. Michaels, Md., 1819; d. Louisville, Ky., 1852*), verse writer. Author of the once-celebrated *Poems* (1845) by "Amelia," a book filled with echoes of her greater contemporaries.

WELCH, ADONIJAH STRONG (*b. East Hampton, Conn., 1821; d. Pasadena, Calif., 1889*), educator. Graduated University of Michigan, 1846. As first principal (1852–65) of Michigan State Normal School at Ypsilanti, he conducted teachers' institutes and aided in organizing the state teachers association. Chosen first president of Iowa State Agricultural College at Ames, he served, 1869–83, and later taught history and psychology there. A defender of industrial education, he based his courses in agriculture and mechanic arts on study of fundamental and applied sciences. He also encouraged systematic experimentation in stock raising and farm products at his college some seven years before the federal act providing for experiment stations.

WELCH, ASHBEL (*b. Nelson, N.Y., 1809; d. Lambertville, N.J., 1882*), civil engineer. Studied at Albany Academy under Joseph Henry. Associated with the Delaware & Raritan Canal of which he was made chief engineer in 1835, he engaged in a variety of engineering work in the field of transportation and developed a large consulting practice. He aided John Ericsson in designing the *Princeton*, and supervised the naval gunnery experiments begun by Commodore R. F. Stockton. After beginning the work of designing and constructing the Chesapeake & Delaware Canal, he was active *post* 1854 in work with the New Jersey railroads, notably the Camden & Amboy for which he planned what is regarded as the earliest (1865) installation of the block signaling system.

WELCH, CHARLES CLARK (*b. Jefferson Co., N.Y., 1830; d. Jacksonville, Fla., 1908*), Colorado miner, railroad builder, and capitalist.

WELCH, JOHN (*b. Harrison Co., Ohio, 1805; d. Athens, Ohio, 1891*), lawyer, Ohio jurist and legislator, Whig and Republican politician. Justice of the Ohio supreme court, 1865–78; expert in cases involving real property.

WELCH, JOSEPH NYE (*b. Primghar, Iowa, 1890; d. Hyannis, Mass., 1960*), lawyer. Graduated Grinnell College (1914); Harvard Law School (1917). Attended Army Officer Candidate School and served with the legal division of the U.S. Shipping Board. Headed the trial department of the Boston firm of Hale and Dorr. In April 1954 Welch was called to serve as special counsel to the Department of the Army in its confrontation with Senator Joseph R. McCarthy. He had never been politically active but showed his acumen nonetheless. His probing questions, general demeanor, and deft thrusts proved to be the senator's undoing. In 1956 Welch was narrator of a much-praised series of "Omnibus" programs on the constitutional history of the nation. Appearances on other shows followed, and in 1959 he played the judge in the movie *Anatomy of a Murder*.

WELCH, PHILIP HENRY (*b. Angelica, N.Y., 1849; d. Brooklyn, N.Y., 1889*), journalist, humorist. Employed on the staffs of newspapers in Rochester, N.Y., and Philadelphia, Pa., he was, *post* 1884, a member of the staff of the N.Y. *Sun*. He is remembered principally for anonymous "question and answer" jokes and satires which he contributed to the *Sun* and also to most of the periodicals of his time. He was author of *The Tailor-Made Girl* (1888, reprinted from *Puck*). Some of his characteristic jokes were published posthumously as *Said in Fun* (1889).

WELCH, WILLIAM HENRY (*b. Norfork, Conn., 1850; d. Baltimore, Md., 1934*), pathologist, medical educator. Son of William W. Welch. Graduated Yale, 1870; studied chemistry at Sheffield Scientific School. M.D., N.Y. College of Physicians and Surgeons, 1875. As a student at Strasbourg, Leipzig, and Breslau, 1875–78, he worked with some of the greatest men of the time, among them Ludwig, Julius Cohnheim, Paul Ehrlich, and von Recklinghausen. He also studied briefly in Paris and London. Commencing work as a pathologist in New York, 1878, he was associated with Bellevue Hospital and with the Woman's Hospital until 1883 when he accepted an invitation to become professor of pathology at Johns Hopkins University. After further study in Europe under Koch and his pupils, he organized a pathological laboratory at Johns Hopkins, 1885, heading a group of men which included William T. Councilman, William S. Halsted, and Franklin P. Mall. His work at this time later resulted in the publication of his *Thrombosis and Embolism* (1899). Devoting himself then to the study of diphtheria and pneumonia, he also discovered and described in detail the gas-producing bacillus known by his name, which was the cause of "gas gangrene" in wounded soldiers during World War I. When the Johns Hopkins hospital opened in 1889, he suggested William Osler and William S. Halsted as department heads; later, in the organization of the school of medicine, he was responsible for the choice of Mall and other outstanding men. He himself served as the first dean for several years and founded and edited the *Journal of Experimental Medicine*, 1896–1906.

Influential in determining the character of the Johns Hopkins medical school, he turned his attention *post* 1900 to the general advance of medical education throughout the country. The Rockefeller Institute of Medical Research was founded in a way largely based upon his counsel; *post* 1901, he was chairman of its board of scientific directors. *Post* 1906, he was associated in a similar advisory capacity with the activities of the Carnegie Foundation and was active in many scientific and medical associations. As president of the Maryland board of health, 1898–1922, he was frequently consulted by the Baltimore municipal authorities on matters of public health, and during World War I he served actively with the surgeon general of the army. Throughout all these busy years of administration his interest in the problems of pathology and bacteriology remained intense. Among the topics to which he devoted attention were adaptation in pathological processes, morbid conditions caused by the *aerogenes capsulatus*, and immunity. On the opening of the school of hygiene and public health at Johns Hopkins, 1918, Welch, who had resigned his professorship of pathology, was appointed director. His skill in the choice of men and his profound interest in the work were responsible for the success of this school and its far-reaching influence. He resigned in 1926 and entered upon a third career as professor of the history of medicine which he continued until his retirement in 1931.

His keenness of judgment and extraordinary organizing ability were as effective in his research work as in his work of administration. His fame rests on his appreciation of the significance of the epochal developments in pathology and bacteriology which he had witnessed in Europe, and in his introduction to America, not only of the practical results of his investigations, but of the whole spirit of these medical advances. The consequent reform in American medical education, and the development of public health studies for which he was responsible, set up an influence which was felt and treasured in many other countries as well as the United States.

WELCH, WILLIAM WICKHAM (*b. Norfolk, Conn., 1818; d. Norfolk, 1892*), physician, Connecticut legislator. Father of William H. Welch.

WELD, ARTHUR CYRIL GORDON (*b. Jamaica Plain, Mass., 1862; d. West Point, N.Y., 1914*), musician, composer. Achieved greatest distinction as conductor of musical comedy orchestras and composer of incidental music for the theater. He was musical director for productions of Henry W. Savage.

WELD, THEODORE DWIGHT (*b. Hampton, Conn., 1803; d. Hyde Park, Mass., 1895*), Abolitionist. Raised in western New York State. Influenced by Charles Stuart and Charles G. Finney, Weld worked while a young man as an evangelist and as a temperance speaker. Converted to the antislavery cause by Stuart, he lent his principal efforts to this work *post* 1830; his own first converts to emancipation were Arthur and Lewis Tappan. Commissioned by the Tappans to find a site for a Western theological seminary, Weld traveled widely, 1831–34, advocating antislavery at every opportunity. Among his later converts were James G. Birney, Elizur Wright, Beriah Green, Harriet and Henry Ward Beecher, and Gamaliel Bailey. Organizing students at Lane Theological Seminary and training them as agents for the American Anti Slavery Society, Weld continued to preach emancipation with extraordinary success in the then West and part of New England. In 1838 he married Angelina Grimké.

Post 1836, with an augmented group of agents, he consolidated the antislavery movement throughout the North. He employed anonymous pamphlets and tracts in this work with great effect; most of the tracts were written by himself. When congressional insurgents in the House of Representatives broke with the Whigs on the slavery issue, Weld assisted their leader, John Q. Adams, and actively directed the insurgent movement through the sessions of 1841–43. He then withdrew from public life, but his Washington lobby was continued by Lewis Tappan. The greatest of the Abolitionists, Weld has remained largely anonymous in history, in part owing to his almost morbid modesty. He accepted no office, attended no conventions, published nothing under his own name, and would permit neither his speeches nor his letters to be printed.

WELD, THOMAS (*b. Sudbury, England, 1595; d. London, England, 1660/61*), Puritan clergyman, colonial agent. Deposed for nonconformity as vicar at Terling, Essex, 1631, he immigrated to Boston, Mass., 1632, and became first pastor of the church at Roxbury. Opposed the Antinomians. With John Eliot and Richard Mather, was author of the "Bay Psalm Book" (*The Whole Booke of Psalmes* 1640). Sent to England by the General Court to seek financial aid for the colony, 1641, he was associated in this work with Hugh Peter until Peter's involvement in work of the Parliament. He was coeditor with Peter of *New England's First Fruits* (London, 1643). Weld secured Harvard's first scholarship fund, but failed to prevent issuance of a patent for the Narragansett territory to Roger Williams. Poor bookkeeping and misapplication by the General Court of funds collected led to charges of embezzlement against Weld and Peter; they were later vindicated. Weld, like Peter, became involved in English affairs and was induced by the Presbyterians there to edit with additions John Winthrop's manuscript account of the Antinomian troubles. Publication of this book emphasized Congregational intolerance and put Weld in a bad position from which he recovered by publishing *A Brief Narration of the Practices of the Churches in New England* (London, 1645). Thereafter he was an active supporter of the Commonwealth and an unpopular rector in several parishes until the Restoration.

WELKER, HERMAN (*b. Cambridge, Idaho, 1906; d. Washington D.C., 1957*), lawyer and politician. Studied at the University of Idaho (LL.B., 1929). After practicing law in Idaho and California, Welker entered politics, serving as a Republican in the state legislature in Boise. In 1950 he ran for the U.S. Senate and defeated his opponent, using a "soft on Communism" technique popular in the nation at the time. In the Senate, Welker served on the Internal Security Subcommittee led by Sen. Joseph R. McCarthy. An ardent conservative, he backed McCarthy's persecution of alleged Communists and attempted to halt the censure by the Senate, which led to his being defeated for reelection.

WELLER, JOHN B. (*b. Montgomery, Ohio, 1812; d. New Orleans, La., 1875*), lawyer. Congressman, Democrat, from Ohio, 1839–45. Colonel of Ohio militia in the Mexican War; chairman of commission to run boundary line between Mexico and the United States, 1849–50. Practicing in San Francisco, Calif., *post* 1850, he was U.S. senator, Union Democrat, from California, 1851–57, and governor of California, 1858–60. After service as U.S. minister to Mexico, December 1860—March 1861, he engaged in a variety of activities in various parts of the United States before settling in New Orleans, 1867.

WELLES, (BENJAMIN) SUMNER (*b. New York, N.Y., 1892; d. Bernardsville, N.J., 1961*), diplomat. Attended Harvard (B.A., 1914). Took the Foreign Service exam in 1915 and was assigned as third secretary in the embassy at Tokyo; his principal assignment, 1915–17, was inspection of camps in which German and Austrian prisoners of war were being held. Became second secretary in Buenos Aires, 1917–20; assistant chief of the Division of Latin American Affairs of the State Department, 1920–22; and commissioner to devise plans for the withdrawal of U.S. troops and the military government from the Dominican Republic (accomplished in 1924). Assistant secretary of state in 1933, he was the leading proponent of the Good Neighbor policy. In 1934 he undertook negotiations of a treaty with Panama designed to rectify some of the inequities of the 1903 Canal Treaty. Appointed undersecretary of state in 1937, and, after the outbreak of war in Europe, represented the United States at a special inter-American meeting in Panama, at which a neutrality zone was declared around the continent south of Canada; he also assisted in drafting the Atlantic Charter, 1941. He resigned in 1943.

WELLES, GIDEON (*b. Glastonbury, Conn., 1802; d. 1878*), journalist, Connecticut legislator and official. Attended present Norwich University, 1823–25. Editor of the *Hartford Times*, 1826–36, he was a devoted Jeffersonian Democrat. As a member of the legislature, 1827–35, he led fights against imprisonment for debt, property and religious qualifications for voting, grants of special privilege, and religious tests for witnesses in court. He was the father of Connecticut's general incorporation law which became a model for other states. An adviser and supporter of President Andrew Jackson, Welles held several state offices *post* 1835, and was postmaster of Hartford, 1836–41. He was chief of the bureau of provisions and clothing for the U.S. Navy, 1846–49. Leaving the Democratic party on the slavery question, he helped organize the Republican party and *post* 1856 was a chief political writer for the Republican *Hartford Evening Press*. He also contributed an important series of articles on the slavery question to the *New York Evening Post* and to the *National Intelligencer*. Unsuccessful candidate for the governorship of Connecticut, 1856, he headed Connecticut's delegation to the Republican Chicago convention, 1860.

Welles was U.S. secretary of the navy, 1861–69. Foreseeing the Civil War would be a long one, he reorganized his department and created a navy overnight. Although he was accused of undue deliberateness and extravagance, he succeeded in building an adequate navy from nothing with surprising speed. No other Civil War enterprise was conducted so economically. When scandals developed in navy affairs, he was the first to investigate them and punish the offenders. No other department was more free from political favoritism. His masterly rebukes of delinquent officers made him enemies but improved the efficiency of the service. Although it is hard to determine how much of the credit for supervision of actual naval warfare belonged to him and how much to Gustavus V. Fox and other officers, Welles supervised matters closely and followed all new developments with intelligence. He was an early sponsor of ironclads and supported John Ericsson in building the *Monitor*. He also encouraged development of heavy ordnance, improved steam machinery, and armored cruisers. The navy under Welles's direction was a very important factor in the crushing of the Confederacy.

His contribution to the general policies of the government was as important as his administration of the Navy Department. He distrusted Edwin M. Stanton and suspected the motives of W. H. Seward, yet he did not intrigue against either. He protested against Salmon P. Chase's depreciation of the currency, 1862–63, opposed the admission of West Virginia as unconstitutional, and deplored the suspension of the writ of *habeas corpus*, 1863. He also had doubts whether immediate universal emancipation might not be as injurious to the freed slaves as to the masters. Contending throughout the war that it was fought against rebellious individuals and not against states, he backed Lincoln's moderate program of Reconstruction and later supported the policy of President Andrew Johnson. Returning to the Democratic party, 1868, he became a Liberal Republican in 1872, and in 1876 not only supported Samuel J. Tilden, but wrote attacks against the decision of the Electoral Commission.

Between his retirement in 1869 and his death he published a number of articles in the *Galaxy* magazine which are important documents on the history of his time; one of these was expanded as *Lincoln and Seward* (1874). He kept a painstaking diary which is a storehouse of data, although in its published form (*Diary of Gideon Welles*, 1911), there was no warning to the reader that it was corrected and revised by the diarist in later years. A New England conscience, a keen sense of duty, and a methodical mind made Welles a dependable public servant. Throughout the stormy days of the Civil War he maintained a poise and calmness that often encouraged, but equally irritated, his associates. Realism and unusual common sense prevented too great disappointment on his part when men fell short of his standards.

WELLES, NOAH (*b. Colchester, Conn., 1718; d. 1776*), Congregational clergyman, Revolutionary patriot. Graduated Yale, 1741. Pastor at Stamford, Conn., 1746–76, he was widely known as an advocate of resistance to British oppression, as a defender of the validity of Presbyterian ordination, and as an opponent of episcopacy. He is now generally credited with the authorship of the anonymous *The Real Advantages Which Ministers and People May Enjoy . . . by Conforming to the Church of England* (1762); he was author also of other works of controversy.

WELLES, ROGER (*b. Newington, Conn., 1862; d. 1832*), naval officer, explorer. Graduated Annapolis, 1884. Served in the North Pacific on the cruise of the *Thetis* under W. H. Emory; made three successive voyages into the Polar regions. In 1891 he ascended the Orinoco River to a point farther than any white man had reached before and brought back an important ethnological collection. Director of naval intelligence during World War I, he was promoted rear admiral, 1919, and retired, 1926.

WELLING, JAMES CLARKE (*b. Trenton, N.J., 1825; d. Hartford, Conn., 1894*), journalist, educator. Graduated College of New Jersey (Princeton), 1844. Literary editor of the *Daily National Intelligencer* of Washington, D.C., 1850–56, he became the chief editor of the newspaper and conducted it as a conservative Unionist organ until 1865. A strong legalist, he questioned the validity of the Emancipation Proclamation and joined his friend Edward Bates in declaring trials by military commissions to be irregular. After short terms as president of St. John's College, Annapolis, Md., and as professor of English at Princeton, he served as president of Columbian College (present George Washington University), 1871–94.

WELLING, RICHARD WARD GREENE (*b. North Kingstown, R.I., 1858; d. New York, N.Y., 1946*), lawyer, political and educational reformer. B.A., Harvard, 1880. Attended Harvard

Law School; admitted to New York bar, 1883. Active throughout his life in municipal reform movements and organizations, and in educational efforts to increase the sense of civic responsibility in public school students.

WELLINGTON, ARTHUR MELLEN (*b. Waltham, Mass., 1847; d. 1895*), civil engineer, engineering trade journalist. Author of a classic treatise, *The Economic Theory of the Location of Railways* (1877 and later editions).

WELLMAN, SAMUEL THOMAS (*b. Wareham, Mass., 1847; d. Stratton, Maine, 1919*), engineer, inventor. After directing the building of Siemens regenerative gas furnaces in various parts of the United States, 1867–73, he designed and built the Otis Steel Works of Cleveland, Ohio, where he remained as chief engineer, 1873–89. During this time he began invention of machinery and other equipment for the manufacture of iron and steel for which he was granted nearly 100 patents. Of these, the most outstanding were the electric open-hearth charging machine (*ca.* 1885) and an electromagnet for handling pig iron and scrap steel (patented, December 1895). *Post* 1890 Wellman was associated as president or chairman of the board with a number of engineering companies specializing in the manufacture of iron and steel.

WELLMAN, WALTER (*b. Mentor, Ohio, 1858; d. 1934*), journalist, aeronaut. Founded *Cincinnati Post*, 1879; was Washington correspondent of *Chicago Herald* and *Record-Herald*, 1884–1911. After several Arctic expeditions by boat and sledge (1894 and 1898–99), he was commissioned in 1906 to attempt a trip to the Arctic by air. He took off for the North Pole from Spitzbergen, September 1907, but was defeated by weather conditions. He made a second abortive attempt in August 1909, but abandoned further efforts to reach the Pole by air after the success of Robert E. Peary. Wellman's most ambitious undertaking was his attempt to cross the Atlantic in the airship *America*, 1910. The *America* was 228 feet long and had a speed of 25 miles an hour; below the hydrogen-filled bag of silk and cotton hung a car of steel tubing, a gas tank, a lifeboat, and an equilibrator which was also a fuel supply. Taking off from Atlantic City, N.J., Wellman and five companions exchanged messages by wireless with the shore (a pioneer feat), but were compelled by motor failure to come down and were rescued some 375 miles off Cape Hatteras after covering a distance of 1008 miles in 72 hours.

WELLONS, WILLIAM BROCK (*b. near Littleton, Va., 1821; d. Suffolk, Va., 1877*), clergyman, educator, leader of the Christian Connection in the Southern states.

WELLS, DAVID AMES (*b. Springfield, Mass., 1828; d. Norwich, Conn., 1898*), economist. Graduated Williams, 1847; Lawrence Scientific School, 1851. Published *The Annual of Scientific Discovery*, 1850–66; made important improvements in textile manufacture; wrote several popular works on science and science textbooks. Wells came into wide prominence in 1864 through publication of *Our Burden and Our Strength*. In this pamphlet he reassured foreign investors and the people of the North concerning the ability of the government to pay its mounting debts by demonstrating the dynamic character of Northern economic life, stressing its rapid accumulation of capital and constant introduction of labor-saving devices. Chairman of the national revenue commission, 1865–66, he served as a special commissioner of the revenue, 1866–70, and was responsible for setting up the bureau of statistics under Francis A. Walker. Originally a protectionist, Wells was converted to free trade and was to the end of his life a leading advocate of abolition of the tariff. While chairman of the New York State tax commission, 1870–76, he was author of *Local Taxation* (1871), the earliest competent study of the subject. He served later as a receiver and trustee in the reorganization of several

railroads including the Erie (1875), and in 1878 became a member of the board of arbitration of the Associated Railways. Wells was author of a large number of books, pamphlets, and articles, each based on a current problem; his chief interests were the tariff, the theory of money and the currency question, and taxation. An expositor of the nature and consequences of the "machine age," he felt that the new economics of production required abolition of protective tariffs in order to furnish wide markets, and he was convinced that industrial depressions, with falling prices, were due not to insufficient circulating media but to sudden and rapid increase in commodities. Some of his best writing was in opposition to fiat money or depreciated monetary standards. He was among the earliest to appreciate the importance of what is now known as "technological unemployment." A foe of the general property tax as applied to intangibles, he accepted the diffusion theory of taxation, and his opposition to the faculty theory led him to fight against income taxes. An out-and-out apostle of *laissez faire*, he missed the later implications of many of the tendencies in American economic life which he discovered and expounded. Among his works were *Robinson Crusoe's Money* (1876, 1896); *True Story of the Leaden Statuary* (1874); *The Silver Question* (1877); *A Primer of Tariff Reform* (1884); and *The Theory and Practice of Taxation* (1900).

WELLS, ERASTUS (*b. near Sacketts Harbor, N.Y., 1823; d. near St. Louis, Mo., 1893*), St. Louis street-railway builder and utilities executive. Active in his city's political and civic life, he was congressman, Democrat, from Missouri, 1869–77 and 1879–81. His principal legislative concerns were the improvement of the Mississippi River and the development of the Southwest. He was ahead of his time in regard to both, however, and few of his projects resulted in legislative action.

WELLS, HARRIET SHELDON (*b. Brooklyn, N.Y., 1873; d. New York, N.Y., 1961*), woman suffragist. Treasurer of the Woman's Suffrage Party of New York City and named chairman of its Woman Voter Subcommittee, 1915. A trusted lieutenant of Carrie Chapman Catt, she and others of the party sought to dissociate themselves from the militant tactics used by zealous suffragists. After New York State enacted woman suffrage (1917), she worked for passage of a federal suffrage amendment.

WELLS, HARRY GIDEON (*b. Fair Haven, Conn., 1875; d. Chicago, Ill., 1943*), pathologist. Ph.B., Sheffield Scientific School, Yale, 1895. M.D., Rush Medical College, 1898. Ph.D., University of Chicago, 1903. Studied also at University of Berlin with Ernst Salkowski and Emil Fischer. Within a decade of his return to Chicago in 1905, he had become the leading U.S. authority on the chemical aspects of pathology and immunology; he also continued his affiliation with the medical faculty of the University of Chicago (begun in 1901), becoming professor of pathology, 1913. He retired in 1940. As director of the Sprague Memorial Institute, Chicago, 1911–40, he stimulated and supported research in many fields, including the chemotherapy of tuberculosis and the role of heredity in cancer. His most notable publication was his classic *Chemical Pathology* (1907).

WELLS, HENRY (*b. Thetford, Vt., 1805; d. Glasgow, Scotland, 1878*), expressman. Began as operator of an express service between Albany and Buffalo, N.Y., *ca.* 1843; later extended his activities into New England and the Midwest. Removing to New York City, 1846, to handle the eastern and transatlantic phases of the business, he served as president of the American Express Co. (a merger of three older companies), 1850–68. In 1852 he organized Wells, Fargo & Co. under the presidency of Edwin B. Morgan for business to California; in 1857 the California service and the business east of the Missouri were linked by award of the overland mail contract to John Butterfield, who represented Wells, Fargo interests. The company prospered, despite heavy competition, until the completion of the transcontinental railroad. Wells retired after a further consolidation within the American Express Co., 1868, traveled widely, and devoted himself to local affairs in Aurora, N.Y. In 1868 he founded Wells Seminary, the present Wells College.

WELLS, HORACE (*b. Hartford, Vt., 1815; d. New York, N.Y., 1848*), dentist, anesthetist. Successful in practice at Hartford, Conn., *post* 1836, Wells was the teacher, and for a short time a partner, of William T. G. Morton. Interested in the narcotic effects of nitrous oxide inhalation, Wells suggested its use as a pain-deadener in tooth extraction as early as 1840. In December 1844 Wells, with the aid of G. Q. Colton, acted as the subject for a successful nitrous oxide extraction by John M. Riggs, and was taught by Colton how to make and administer the gas. He followed up this early trial by extracting several teeth without pain, and although familiar with the similar effects of ether, discarded its use because he considered nitrous oxide less likely to do injury. Traveling to Boston early in 1845, he was enabled through Morton to speak before a medical class of John C. Warren, but failed in a subsequent exhibition of his process. Wells's claim to discovery of anesthesia first appeared in print in the *Hartford Courant*, Dec. 7, 1846, nearly two months after W. T. G. Morton had demonstrated the use of ether. Claiming priority in the discovery and asserting that he had used ether as well as nitrous oxide in his own experiments, Wells published statements in several journals and in a pamphlet entitled *A History of the Discovery of the Application of Nitrous Oxide Gas, Ether, and Other Vapors, to Surgical Operations* (1847). After the general recognition of the superiority of ether over nitrous oxide in protracted operations, Wells, who had removed to New York City, committed suicide in discouragement.

WELLS, JAMES MADISON (*b. near Alexandria, La., 1808; d. 1899*), planter, Louisiana Unionist. Elected lieutenant governor of Louisiana in February 1864, he succeeded as governor upon the resignation of Michael Hahn in March 1865. He was elected in his own right as a National Democrat the following November. An advocate of general black suffrage, he became unpopular and was threatened with impeachment. Removed from office, June 1867, by General Philip Sheridan, he continued to be prominent in state politics and was chairman of the Louisiana returning board during the dispute over the election of 1876.

WELLS, JOHN (*b. Cherry Valley, N.Y., ca. 1770; d. New York, N.Y., 1823*), lawyer. Graduated College of New Jersey (Princeton), 1788. Editorial associate of William Coleman on the N.Y. *Evening Post*, he edited *The Federalist*, bringing out the fifth edition of the papers in 1802. *Post* 1804, he shared with Thomas A. Emmet the bulk of the commercial law practice which had hitherto gone to Alexander Hamilton and Aaron Burr; he was frequently engaged as special counsel by the City of New York. His argument in the celebrated case of *Gibbons* v. *Ogden* (1819), that the grant by the State of New York of a monopoly of the navigation of its waters by steam was unconstitutional since Congress alone had the right to regulate commerce, was unsuccessful. However, Daniel Webster and William Wirt, pursuing the same argument on appeal to the U.S. Supreme Court, secured a reversal of the original decision, 1824.

WELLS, ROBERT WILLIAM (*b. Winchester, Va., 1795; d. Bowling Green, Ky., 1864*), Missouri legislator and jurist. State attorney general, 1826–36; U.S. district judge for Missouri (*post* 1857 of the western district only), 1836–64. Interested in legal reform, he opposed jury trial in civil cases and advocated simplification of pleading. He was a Civil War Unionist.

WELLS, SAMUEL ROBERTS (*b. West Hartford, Conn., 1820; d. New York, N.Y., 1875*), tanner, phrenologist, and publisher. Partner with Orson S. Fowler and brother in phrenological publishing firm; faddist reformer.

WELLS, WILLIAM CHARLES (*b. Charleston, S.C., 1757; d. London, England, 1817*), physician, physicist, Loyalist. Apprenticed to Alexander Garden (*ca.* 1730–1791), Wells fled to England on the outbreak of the Revolution and studied at the University of Edinburgh and in London; he took the M.D. degree at Edinburgh, 1780. Resident in America, 1781–84, he practiced thereafter in London, England. His most significant contribution to science was contained in a paper read before the Royal Society, 1813, and published with other papers in *Two Essays: One Upon Single Vision . . . The Other on Dew* (1818) in which Wells assumed a biological evolution of human species and clearly explained the principle of a natural selection in the struggle for existence. Darwin, originally unfamiliar with this essay, acknowledged its importance in the fourth (1866) edition of his own *Origin of Species.*

WELLS, WILLIAM HARVEY (*b. Tolland, Conn., 1812; d. 1885*), educator, writer on English grammar. After an outstanding career in New England as teacher, principal, assistant to Henry Barnard in conducting teachers institutes, and normal-school work, Wells was chosen superintendent of public schools in Chicago, Ill., 1856. There he organized the city's first high school and introduced a graded system of schools with a course of study which was widely imitated throughout the United States. He was author, among other works, of *The Graded School* (1862).

WELLS, WILLIAM VINCENT (*b. Boston, Mass., 1826; d. Napa, Calif., 1876*), merchant mariner, adventurer, California journalist. Great-grandson of Samuel Adams. Author, among other works, of *Walker's Expedition to Nicaragua* (1856), and of the *Life and Public Services of Samuel Adams* (1865). Inclusion of family records in the latter book has maintained its importance as a historical source.

WELSH, JOHN (*b. Philadelphia, Pa., 1805; d. 1886*), Philadelphia merchant, philanthropist. Helped develop Fairmount Park system; managed finances of Philadelphia Centennial Exhibition, 1876. U.S. ambassador at London, 1877–79.

WEMYSS, FRANCIS COURTNEY (*b. London, England, 1797; d. New York, N.Y., 1859*), actor, theater manager. American debut at Chestnut Street Theatre, Philadelphia, Pa., 1822. Wemyss later played with success in New York and was for a time manager in Philadelphia, Pittsburgh, and Baltimore; *post* 1841 he was active in a number of New York City theaters. Conspicuous for good taste and integrity, he helped found and administer the theatrical fund for the benefit of needy actors. He was also editor of a number of volumes of the *Acting American Theatre* and was author of *Twenty-Six Years of the Life of an Actor and Manager* (1847).

WENDE, ERNEST (*b. Millgrove, N.Y., 1853; d. Buffalo, N.Y., 1910*), dermatologist, health official. Brother of Grover W. Wende. M.D., University of Buffalo, 1878; M.D., University of Pennsylvania, 1884; made special studies at Berlin and Vienna. Practiced and taught in Buffalo, N.Y., *post* 1886; won national repute for extensive sanitary reforms as Buffalo health commissioner, 1892–1905.

WENDE, GROVER WILLIAM (*b. Millgrove, N.Y., 1867; d. Buffalo, N.Y., 1926*), physician, dermatologist. Brother of Ernest Wende. M.D., University of Buffalo, 1889; made graduate studies at Pennsylvania and in Prague, Vienna, and Paris. Practiced with his brother; served as professor of dermatology at University of

Buffalo; was a staff member of many hospitals. A leader in his specialty and an exceedingly accurate observer, he was author of a number of monographs on the rarer skin diseases.

WENDELL, BARRETT (*b. Boston, Mass., 1855; d. 1921*), educator, man of letters. Graduated Harvard, 1877. Appointed a teacher of English composition at Harvard, 1880, he remained associated with that university thereafter, and was celebrated as a teacher for his powers of generalization, his ready control of the background of events and ideas, and his profuse and well-chosen literary illustrations. In 1898 he became the first teacher at Harvard to offer American literature as an object of systematic study, and *post* 1902 served on several occasions as an exchange professor in England and France. Steadily enlarging his field of thought, he moved gradually into the field of comparative literature, striving in all his work "so to increase our sympathetic knowledge of what we study that we may enjoy it with fresh intelligence and appreciation." Literature was, in his opinion, a vital concern—"the best record that human beings have made of human life." He was author, among other books, of *English Composition* (1891); *Cotton Mather, the Puritan Priest* (1891); *William Shakespeare* (1894); *A Literary History of America* (1900); *The Temper of the Seventeenth Century in English Literature* (1904); *The France of Today* (1907); and *The Traditions of European Literature, from Homer to Dante* (1920).

WENDTE, CHARLES WILLIAM (*b. Boston, Mass., 1844; d. Berkeley, Calif., 1931*), Unitarian clergyman, hymn-writer. Removing to San Francisco, Calif., 1861, he became a protégé of Thomas S. King. A graduate of Harvard Divinity School, 1869, he held a number of ministerial posts, and served as general secretary of the International Council of Liberal Religious Thinkers and Workers, 1900–20. In this capacity he organized a number of foreign congresses in the interest of rational, ethical theism.

WENLEY, ROBERT MARK (*b. Edinburgh, Scotland, 1861; d. 1929*), philosopher, educator. Sc.D., University of Edinburgh, 1891; Ph.D., University of Glasgow, 1895. Succeeding John Dewey in the department of philosophy at University of Michigan, 1896, he taught there the rest of his life. He was author of a number of works setting forth his own particular form of Green-Caird-Bosanquet Hegelianism which included *The Life and Work of George Sylvester Morris* (1917).

WENNER, GEORGE UNANGST (*b. Bethlehem, Pa., 1844; d. New York, N.Y., 1934*), Lutheran clergyman. Graduated Yale, 1865; Union Theological Seminary, 1868. Pastor at Christ Lutheran Church, New York City, 1868–1934. A pioneer in weekday religious education and a liturgical scholar, Wenner was a conservative Lutheran in theology, but a recognized leader in interdenominational enterprises. His sixty-six-year pastorate is possibly the longest on record in the United States.

WENTWORTH, BENNING (*b. Portsmouth, N.H., 1696; d. Little Harbor, N.H., 1770*), merchant, New Hampshire colonial official. Uncle of John Wentworth (1737–1820). Graduated Harvard, 1715. Wentworth labored to make New Hampshire independent of Massachusetts, and was first royal governor of New Hampshire province, 1742–67. A tactless man, determined to uphold the royal prerogative, he engaged in bitter controversies with the Assembly and was roundly criticized for appointing relatives to office and favoring them in grants of land; he was also accused of having grown rich through pre-empting choice land in each township. Other complaints were made of his exercise of the office of surveyor of the King's Woods. However, he gave vigorous support to colonial defense against the French and the province prospered materially under his administration.

WENTWORTH, CECILE DE (*b. New York, N.Y., date uncertain; d. Nice, France, 1933*), portrait painter. A student in Paris of Alexandre Cabanel and Edouard Detaille, Madame Wentworth, as she was known, lived abroad for the greater part of her life and was regarded in France as one of the outstanding portraitists of her time.

WENTWORTH, GEORGE ALBERT (*b. Wakefield, N.H., 1835; d. Dover, N.H., 1906*), teacher, author of textbooks in mathematics. Graduated Harvard, 1858. For many years a teacher at Phillips Exeter Academy, he headed the department of mathematics there *ca.* 1861–91. His outstanding texts included *Elements of Geometry* (1878), *Elements of Algebra* (1881), and *College Algebra* (1888).

WENTWORTH, JOHN (*b. Portsmouth, N.Y., 1737; d. Halifax, Nova Scotia, Canada, 1820*), merchant, landowner. Nephew of Benning Wentworth. Graduated Harvard, 1755. Resident in England, 1763–66, he came to know, among other influential Englishmen, the Marquis of Rockingham, and was appointed an agent for New Hampshire. Succeeding his uncle as governor of New Hampshire, 1767, he served with ability and a sincere desire to further the welfare of his native province; he was particularly active in protecting the integrity of the King's Woods and preventing the private cutting of timber. He was responsible for the survey on which the 1784 map of New Hampshire was based and was a supporter and benefactor of Dartmouth College. As the Revolutionary movement grew in force, he did his best to prevent cooperation between New Hampshire and the other colonies, but was obliged to take refuge in Boston, Mass., 1775. Accompanying the British to Halifax, March 1776, he later lived for a time in England, returning to Halifax, 1783. Becoming lieutenant governor of Nova Scotia (in effect governor), 1792, he held that office until 1808.

WENTWORTH, JOHN (*b. Sandwich, N.H., 1815; d. Chicago, Ill., 1888*), editor. Graduated Dartmouth, 1836; settled in Chicago, Ill., in the same year. Beginning as editor of the weekly *Chicago Democrat*, he soon became its owner and in 1840 started the *Daily Democrat*, which he made the leading paper of the Northwest. As congressman, Democrat, from Illinois, 1843–51, 1854–55, he advocated free homestead legislation and favored Western railway land grants. Leaving the Democratic party over the slavery issue, he was elected mayor of Chicago, 1857, on a Republican Fusion ticket; he was elected again in 1860 and also served as police commissioner during the Civil War. One of Chicago's principal owners of real property and a leading figure in the city's civic life, he served again in Congress as a Republican, 1865–67, where he urged immediate resumption of specie payments.

WENTWORTH, PAUL (*b. date and place of birth unknown, but probably New Hampshire; d. Surinam, Dutch Guiana, 1793*), British spy. Described by Governor John Wentworth of New Hampshire as "my near relation," he was a man of education and talents who made his living principally as a stock jobber and served briefly as New Hampshire agent in London in the early 1770's. Becoming one of the important members of the British secret intelligence on the Continent, he recruited Edward Bancroft for the service and was the agent by which Bancroft's reports were transmitted to the British government. He failed in a bold attempt to halt the treaty negotiations between France and the United States, December 1777—January 1778.

WERDEN, REED (*b. Delaware Co., Pa., 1818; d. Newport, R.I., 1886*), naval officer. Appointed midshipman, 1834. Held varied commands in Civil War including post of fleet captain, East

Gulf Squadron, 1864–65. Commanded South Pacific Squadron, 1875–76, retiring as rear admiral, 1877.

WERGELAND, AGNES MATHILDE (*b. Christiania, Norway, 1857; d. Laramie, Wyo., 1914*), historian, educator. Ph.D., University of Zürich, 1890. Immigrated to America, 1890. Chairman, department of history, University of Wyoming, 1902–14.

WERNWAG, LEWIS (*b. Württemberg, Germany, 1769; d. Harpers Ferry, Va., 1843*), pioneer bridge builder. Came to Philadelphia, Pa., *ca.* 1786. Chiefly remembered as a designer and builder of wooden bridges and for early (1811) use of the cantilever. His beautiful "Colossus of Fairmount," built in 1812 across the Schuylkill River at Philadelphia, was the greatest single-arch span (340 feet) then in America. The canal of the Schuylkill Navigation Co. was partially constructed by him in 1817, and the Fairmount water works and dam at Philadelphia were erected in accordance with his plans.

WERTENBAKER, CHARLES CHRISTIAN (*b. Lexington, Va., 1901; d. Ciboure, France, 1955*), author and editor. Studied at the University of Virginia, 1925. Wrote his first novel, *Boojum,* a satire on life at the University of Virginia, in 1928. Correspondent and editor for the Luce publications of *Time* and *Fortune,* 1931–47. Other novels include *Write Sorrow on the Earth* (1947), a novel of the French resistance during World War II; and *The Barons* (1950) and *The Death of Kings* (1954), novels about American corporate power modeled after Luce and his empire.

WERTENBAKER, THOMAS JEFFERSON (*b. Charlottesville, Va., 1879; d. Princeton, N.J., 1966*), historian. Studied at the University of Virginia (B.A., M.A., 1902; Ph.D., 1910). His dissertation, *Patrician and Plebian in Virginia; or The Origin and Development of the Social Classes of the Old Dominion,* was published at his own expense. Wertenbaker taught at Princeton (1910–47). He wrote *Virginia Under the Stuarts* (1914), *The Planters of Colonial Virginia* (1922), *The American People: A History* (1926), *The First Americans, 1607–1690* (1927), *Norfolk: Historic Southern Port* (1931), *The Middle Colonies* (1938), *Torchbearer of the Revolution: The Story of Bacon's Rebellion and Its Leader* (1940), *The Golden Age of Colonial Culture* (1942), *The Old South* (1942), *Princeton, 1746–1896* (1946), *The Puritan Oligarchy* (1947), *Father Knickerbocker Rebels: New York City During the Revolution* (1948), *Bacon's Rebellion: 1676* (1957), and *Give Me Liberty: The Struggle for Self-Government in Virginia* (1958). Internationally recognized, he taught at the University of Göttingen in 1931 and from the 1940's on received a number of honorary degrees. In 1947 was president of the American Historical Association.

WERTHEIMER, MAX (*b. Prague, Bohemia, 1880; d. New Rochelle, N.Y., 1943*), psychologist, founder of the Gestalt movement. Began his university education at the Charles University, Prague, as a student of law; studied psychology subsequently at Berlin, and at Würzburg, Ph.D., 1904. While working at Frankfurt am Main, he became associated with Kurt Koffka and Wolfgang Köhler, and it was from Frankfurt in 1912 that he published the paper on the perception of movement that marks the official beginning of Gestalt psychology. On the seizure of power in Germany by Hitler, he left his professorship at Frankfurt and moved with his family to Czechoslovakia; in September 1933, he joined the faculty of the New School for Social Research, New York City.

WESBROOK, FRANK FAIRCHILD (*b. Brant Co., Ontario, Canada, 1868; d. Vancouver, British Columbia, Canada, 1918*), pathologist, educator. Graduated University of Manitoba, B.A., 1887; M.D.C.M., 1890; studied also at Cambridge University and at Marburg; received further training at London, Dublin, and

Hamburg. Appointed director of laboratories, Minnesota State Board of Health, 1895; became professor of pathology and bacteriology, University of Minnesota Medical School, 1896, and dean, 1906. Won world reputation as coauthor of "Varieties of Bacillus diphtherias" (1900). A leader in medical education and an authority on problems of public health and sanitation, he was chosen president of University of British Columbia, 1913.

WESSELHOEFT, CONRAD (*b. Weimar, Germany, 1834; d. Boston, Mass., 1904*), homeopathic physician, educator. Came to America as a child. M.D., Harvard Medical School, 1856. A founder of Boston University Medical School, 1873, and associated with it until his death, he was professor of materia medica and pathology and therapeutics. Elected president of American Institute of Homeopathy, 1879. Attempted to formulate principles of homeopathy in accordance with modern science. Published his translation of Samuel Hahnemann's *Organon,* 1876; coeditor, *Homoeopathic Pharmacopoeia of the United States* (1914).

WESSELHOEFT, WALTER. *See* WESSELHOEFT, CONRAD.

WESSON, DANIEL BAIRD (*b. Worcester, Mass., 1825; d. Springfield, Mass., 1906*), inventor and manufacturer of firearms. Formed partnership with Horace Smith for manufacture of a rim-fire metallic cartridge at Norwich, Conn., 1853; with Smith, patented a pistol (1854) whose entirely new repeating action was later adapted to rifles and was an essential factor in the success of the famous Winchester. Again in partnership with Smith, he developed and manufactured *post* 1857 the Smith & Wesson revolver, the only one made with an open cylinder and using a metallic cartridge. He introduced numerous improvements in it, and *ca.* 1887 devised the "hammerless" safety revolver.

WEST, ALLEN BROWN (*b. Reedsburg, Wis., 1886; d. near Stafford Springs, Conn., 1936*), historian. Graduated Milton (Wis.) College, 1907; was Rhodes scholar at Oriel, Oxford; Ph.D., University of Wisconsin, 1912. Principal teaching post, professor of classics and ancient history, University of Cincinnati *post* 1927. West's particular interest lay in the history of imperial Athens. His studies of the financial records of the Athenian Empire in collaboration with Benjamin D. Meritt instituted a revolution in Greek epigraphic scholarship.

WEST, ANDREW FLEMING (*b. Allegheny, Pa., 1853; d. Princeton, N.J., 1943*), classicist, university official. A.B., College of New Jersey (Princeton), 1874. After teaching Latin in Ohio high schools, he became principal of Morris Academy, Morristown, N.J., 1881. Two years later, he was appointed Giger professor of Latin at Princeton. His role became more and more that of an administrator and educational controversialist than of a teacher. He defended the study of the classics without compromise, and attacked the unrestricted elective system of studies and the assignment of academic credit for study of utilitarian subjects. The aim of education, as he saw it, was to discipline the mental faculties and to develop moral character. In 1913, he suffered curtailment of his extensive powers as dean of the graduate school when it lost its autonomous status. He retired in 1928.

WEST, BENJAMIN (*b. Rehoboth, Mass., 1730; d. Providence, R.I., 1813*), almanac-maker, astronomer. Entirely self-educated, West taught mathematics and astronomy at Rhode Island College (later Brown University), 1788–99. He brought out *The New-England Almanack, or Lady's and Gentleman's Diary* 1765–1781; this, and others which he prepared, achieved an excellent reputation in New England for accuracy. He collaborated with Joseph and Moses Brown on observation of transit of Venus, 1769, and published astronomical papers.

WEST, BENJAMIN (*b. near Springfield, Pa., 1738; d. London, England, 1820*), painter. Showing an early aptitude for art, he was assisted by several local patrons, including William Henry. Removing to Philadelphia, Pa., at the invitation of William Smith (1727–1803), he painted portraits and inn signs, continued to practice and study, and by chance made an independent discovery of the principle of the camera obscura. Journeying to Italy in 1760, apparently the first American to study art there, he attracted wide attention and was aided by the then-celebrated painter Anton Fafael Mengs. After traveling about Italy and making special studies of the work of Titian and Raphael, he arrived in England, August 1763, and remained there until his death.

West's agreeable manners and romantic history won him entrance to the highest English circles; among his friends were Sir Joshua Reynolds, the great Samuel Johnson, Edmund Burke, and Dr. Robert H. Drummond, archbishop of York, who became his most powerful patron. Employing Titianesque colors, delicacy of stroke, and subtlety of blended tone, he marked a departure from the robustness of the English school and his work took the public fancy. Admired and liked by George III, he was extensively patronized by that monarch and by the king's appointment was made a charter member of the Royal Academy, founded 1768. *Post* 1772, when he was appointed historical painter to the king, he devoted almost all his time to executing the king's orders for paintings for the royal palaces, including many portraits of the royal family. In his *Death of Wolfe*, exhibited in the Royal Academy, 1771, he represented his heroes in contemporary military costume, a departure from the classic conventions of the day. After approval of this effort at realism by Sir Joshua Reynolds, the picture brought about a new direction in English historical painting. Succeeding Reynolds as president of the Royal Academy, 1792, West devoted much time to teaching young artists, impressing on them the formation of a good palette, truthfulness of design, and a sound technique. Among his American pupils were Matthew Pratt, Charles W. Peale, Gilbert Stuart, John Trumbull, Robert Fulton, Thomas Sully, S. F. B. Morse, and Charles R. Leslie. His generosity to young artists was unfailing.

Post 1801, West's favor at court began to decline and he set himself to work upon a series of religious pictures for public sale. One of these, *Christ Healing the Sick* (1801), was among his most successful, and *Christ Rejected* (*ca.* 1815) and *Death on the Pale Horse* (1817) were also much admired. At his death on March 11, 1820, his body lay in state at the Royal Academy, and he was buried with great honor in St. Paul's Cathedral. Fitted to the ideals of his time by character, by training, and by many small personal traits, he was a painter of little genuine power. His works are formal and uninspired. His important position in the history of English and American painting is owing largely to the help and encouragement he gave so freely to other artists. One of the best of his works, *Penn's Treaty with the Indians*, hangs in Independence Hall, Philadelphia.

WEST, FRANCIS (*b. probably Hampshire, England, 1586; d. probably Virginia, 1634*), governor of Virginia. Brother of Thomas, Lord De La Warr. Immigrating to Virginia, 1608, he was one of those who quarrelled with Captain John Smith and in September 1609 deposed him in favor of George Percy and a council, of which West became a member. He succeeded Percy as commander at Jamestown, 1612, was commissioned master of the ordnance, 1617, and became one of the most influential of "ancient planters." Governor of Virginia, 1627–March 1629.

WEST, GEORGE (*b. near Bradninch, Devonshire, England, 1823; d. 1901*), paper manufacturer, New York legislator. Immigrated to America *ca.* 1849; settled, 1861, in Saratoga Co., N.Y. By 1878 he owned nine mills whose total output was estimated to exceed that of any other paper maker in the United States and Europe. Manufacture of manila wrapping and grocer's bags was the basis of his fortune. A thoroughgoing protectionist, he was congressman, Republican, from New York, 1881–83 and 1885–89.

WEST, HENRY SERGEANT (*b. Binghamton, N.Y., 1827; d. Sivas, Turkey, 1876*), missionary physician. M.D., N.Y. College of Physicians and Surgeons, 1850. Served in Northern Armenian (later the West Turkey) Mission of the American Board, 1859–76. Besides engaging in extensive and far-reaching practice, West trained native students and doctors.

WEST, JAMES EDWARD (*b. Washington, D.C., 1876; d. New Rochelle, N.Y., 1948*), lawyer, social worker. Chief executive, Boy Scouts of America, 1911–43; editor of *Boys' Life*, 1922–43. One of the outstanding child welfare workers of the 20th century.

WEST, JOSEPH (*b. England, date unknown; d. New York, ante 1692*), South Carolina colonial official. As agent and store-keeper for the proprietors of Carolina (1669), he commanded the three vessels sent out to make a settlement after the first attempt by John Yeamans failed. Having assisted William Sayle, the first governor, to make a settlement at Albemarle Point on the Ashley, West succeeded Sayle as governor, 1671, and directed the colony through a trying year of scarcity. Superseded by Yeamans, 1672, he returned to the governorship in 1674 and held the post until 1682. During his administration the center of settlement was moved to New Charles Town (late Charleston) at the junction of the Ashley and Cooper rivers. Again removed from office, 1682, he was reinstated in 1684, but left the province the next year.

WEST, OSWALD (*b. Guelph, Ontario, 1873; d. Portland, Oreg., 1960*), politician and lawyer. West entered Oregon politics in 1903 as state land agent. In 1910 he was elected governor and served until 1914. One of that state's most progressive governors, West was an early conservationist, an advocate of women's suffrage (women won the right to vote in Oregon in 1912), and an opponent of capital punishment. He was a member of the Democratic National Committee from 1926 to 1930. He then returned to private law practice.

WEST, ROY OWEN (*b. Georgetown, Ill., 1868; d. Chicago, Ill., 1958*), cabinet member and party leader. Studied at De Pauw University (LL.B., 1890). West practiced law in Chicago and became involved in Republican politics. He was chairman of the Republican State Committee, 1904–14, a member of the National Committee, 1912–16 and 1928–32; and National Committee secretary, 1924–28. In 1928 he was appointed secretary of the interior by President Coolidge. President of the board of trustees of De Pauw University from 1924 to 1950.

WEST, SAMUEL (*b. Yarmouth, Mass., 1730; d. Tiverton, R.I., 1807*), Congregational clergyman, author. Graduated Harvard, 1754. Pastor at Dartmouth (later New Bedford), Mass., 1761–1803. As Revolutionary War chaplain, he deciphered for General George Washington the famous treasonable code letter sent by Dr. Benjamin Church, 1775, to the British at Newport, R.I. Arminian in doctrine, he was author of *Essays on Liberty and Necessity* (1793), the most thorough and persuasive reply to Jonathan Edwards's *Freedom of the Will*. West was a member of the committee to frame the Massachusetts constitution and is credited with persuading John Hancock to vote for the Federal Constitution.

WEST, WILLIAM EDWARD (*b. Lexington, Ky., 1788; d. Nashville, Tenn., 1857*), portrait painter. Studied in Philadelphia, Pa., under Thomas Sully. In Europe, 1822–40, he won renown for portraits of Lord Byron and Countess Guiccioli, among other celebrities, and exhibited at the Royal Academy,

London, 1826–33. He worked in New York City, 1840–50, and 1852.

WESTCOTT, EDWARD NOYES (*b. Syracuse, N.Y., 1846; d. 1898*), author, banker. Remembered for his best-selling novel *David Harum* (1898), dramatized in 1900 and played by William H. Crane.

WESTCOTT, THOMPSON (*b. Philadelphia, Pa., 1820; d. Philadelphia, 1888*), lawyer, journalist. Despite Philadelphia indifference to Sunday journalism, he successfully edited the strong, independent *Sunday Dispatch* there, 1848–84. He is remembered principally as coauthor with J. T. Scharf of *History of Philadelphia* (1884), the most comprehensive account of the city up to that time.

WESTERGAARD, HARALD MALCOLM (*b. Copenhagen, Denmark, 1888; d. Belmont, Mass., 1950*), civil engineer. Graduated Royal Technical College, Copenhagen, 1911; studied also at universities of Göttingen and Munich. Ph.D., University of Illinois, 1916. Taught theoretical and applied mechanics at Illinois, 1916–36 (professor *post* 1927). Gordon McKay professor of civil engineering at Harvard, 1936; dean of the Graduate School of Engineering, Harvard, 1937–46, returning thereafter to full-time academic and research work. Made notable contributions in the areas of stress analysis, particularly of plates and slabs; was deeply learned in engineering mechanics and the mathematical theory of elasticity.

WESTERMANN, WILLIAM LINN (*b. Belleville, Ill., 1873; d. 1954*), ancient historian. Studied at the University of Nebraska and at the University of Berlin (Ph.D., 1902). Taught at the University of Wisconsin, 1908–20; Cornell University, 1920–23; Columbia University, 1923–48; lectured at the University of Alexandria, 1953–54. An expert on the economics of the ancient world, he published a book-length article, "Sklaverei," in German in 1935; the same material appeared posthumously as *Slave Systems of Greek and Roman Antiquity* (1955).

WESTERN, LUCILLE (*b. New Orleans, La., 1843; d. probably Brooklyn, N.Y., 1877*), actress. A trouper from early childhood with her sister, Helen, she became famous *post* 1863 for emotional acting in roles such as Camille, Lucretia Borgia, Queen Gertrude in *Hamlet*, and Nancy in *Oliver Twist*. A wayward genius, she achieved her effects by temperament rather than art.

WESTERVELT, JACOB AARON (*b. Tenafly, N.J., 1800; d. 1879*), shipbuilder. Apprenticed to Christian Bergh, 1817–20, he was Bergh's silent partner, 1822–35. They built several of the best transatlantic packets of the day at their East River (New York City) yard. Westervelt turned out 247 packets, clippers, steamers, and other vessels before his retirement in 1868. His most important steamships were the 1700-ton *Washington* and *West Point* (1847). During the golden years of clipper construction he built, among others, the N.B. *Palmer*, *Golden Gate*, and *Resoulte*. He was Democratic mayor of New York City, 1853–54.

WESTINGHOUSE, GEORGE (*b. Central Bridge, N.Y., 1846; d. New York, N.Y., 1914*), Union soldier, inventor, manufacturer. After service in both the Union Army and Navy, he worked in his father's agricultural implement factory and in October 1865 obtained his first patent for a rotary steam engine. In the same year he patented a device for putting derailed freight cars back on the track and later developed a type of railroad frog. In April 1869 he took out his first air-brake patent, incorporating the Westinghouse Air Brake Co. six months later for its manufacture. He was subsequently awarded more than twenty further patents on the device as its automatic features were developed. This invention was of revolutionary importance as it made high-speed railroad travel safe. Moreover, by making all air-brake apparatus standardized and interchangeable, Westinghouse was one of the first industrialists to apply modern techniques of production. In 1880 he began to purchase signal and interlocking-switch patents which he combined with his own inventions into a complete signal system. Interest in developing electrical control of signals manufactured by his Union Switch & Signal Co. led Westinghouse to a more general interest in electrical processes and inventions and to the organization of the Westinghouse Electric Co. Between 1880 and 1890 he took out more than 125 patents in such diverse fields as air-brakes, signals, natural-gas production and control, and electrical power transmission. He developed a pressure system of transmission for natural gas which effectively reduced accidents. Having learned (1885) of French and German methods of transmitting single-phase alternating currents at high voltage over very small wires, and then, by means of transformers, stepping the current down to lower voltages for local distribution, he purchased test apparatus in Europe and set a team of electrical engineers, including William Stanley, to the task of adapting transformers to American conditions. Late in 1885 the Stanley "shell-type" transformer was ready for manufacture, but the system met with much opposition on the ground that high-tension current transmission was dangerous. In order to employ the new alternating-current system in industry, Westinghouse set his assistants to work on development of an induction motor and a two-phase system satisfactory for both lamps and motors. A successful experiment in the practical use of high-tension transmission was conducted by William Stanley at Great Barrington, Mass., in 1886, where a number of dwellings and shops were lighted; a later successful experiment was conducted in a Pittsburgh suburb. From 1893, in which year the Westinghouse Electric Co. contracted to light the Chicago World's Columbian Exposition and to develop the power of Niagara Falls, down through 1907, the Westinghouse interest flourished, but in 1907 the founder lost control of his companies. On reorganization, he continued as president with greatly limited power until retirement, 1911. He served (1905–10) as a trustee of the Equitable Life Assurance Society in the reorganization of that company. After his retirement, he continued experiments with the steam turbine and reduction gear and with an air-spring for automobiles until the failure of his health in 1913.

WESTLEY, HELEN (*b. Brooklyn, N.Y., 1875; d. Franklin Township, N.J., 1942*), actress. Christened Henrietta Remsen Meserole Manney. Studied at Academy of Dramatic Arts, New York City, and at Emerson School of Oratory, Boston. Married actor John Westley, 1900; divorced, *ca.* 1912. A member of the Washington Square Players, 1915–18; a founder, member of the board of managers, and leading actress of the Theatre Guild, 1918–36; thereafter, highly successful as a character actress in films.

WESTON, EDWARD (*b. near Wolverhampton, England, 1850; d. Montclair, N.J., 1936*), electrical engineer, industrialist. After receiving his medical diploma in England, 1870, he immigrated to New York City. Organizing the Weston Dynamo Electric Machine Co., 1877, he soon became the leading manufacturer of electroplating dynamos in the United States. He failed in efforts to develop an arc-lighting system and an incandescent lighting system, although he made important contributions to the technology of both. He achieved great success as designer and manufacturer of precision electrical measuring instruments *post* 1888.

WESTON, EDWARD HENRY (*b. Highland Park, Ill., 1886; d. Carmel, Calif., 1958*), photographer. Studied at the Illinois College of Photography. One of the earliest of the "straight" photographers, Weston moved to California and in 1911 opened a photography shop in Glendale, specializing in soft-focus pictures of Hollywood celebrities. He changed his style to realism, strongly influenced by Alfred Stieglitz, Paul Strand, and Charles Sheeler. Further experiences in Mexico, where he was influenced by the Mexican painters Orozco, Rivera, and Siquieros, developed his style further. In 1930 and 1931 he had one-man shows in New York and San Francisco. In 1937 he was the first photographer to be granted a Guggenheim Fellowship. In 1946 a major retrospective of his work was held at the Museum of Modern Art in New York. A victim of Parkinson's disease, Weston took his last photograph in 1948.

WESTON, EDWARD PAYSON (*b. Providence, R.I., 1839; d. 1929*), long-distance walker. Made first professional venture in 1867, walking from Portland, Maine, to Chicago, Ill. (1326 miles) in 26 days. Participated thereafter in many types of walking races, winning the Astley Belt at London, England, 1879. In 1910, he walked from San Francisco to New York in about 70 days.

WESTON, NATHAN AUSTIN (*b. Champaign, Ill., 1868; d. 1933*), economist. B.L., University of Illinois, 1889; Ph.D., Cornell, 1901; studied also at Berlin. Taught at University of Illinois *post* 1900; *post* 1920 he devoted himself entirely to graduate-school teaching. Especially interested in development of the quantity theory of money, he was an outstanding American student of orthodox classical economics.

WESTON, THOMAS (*b. ca. 1575; d. Bristol, England, ca. 1644*), ironmonger, merchant adventurer. Served as agent of the London syndicate which underwrote the sailing of the Pilgrims to Plymouth, 1620; secured the patent for the colony from the Virginia Company and hired the *Mayflower*, but was unable to secure signature of the Separatists to the articles of agreement drawn up by him and Robert Cushman. This document remained unsigned until 1621. Weston later made an attempt to settle at the site of present Weymouth and engaged in trade up and down the New England coast and in Virginia. A roving, resourceful, and generally unsuccessful man, he is of significance only for his connection with the Pilgrims.

WESTON, WILLIAM (*b. probably in or near Oxford, England, ca. 1752; d. London, England, 1833*), civil engineer. Came to America early in 1793 as engineer of Schuylkill and Susquehanna Canal. Planned Middlesex Canal for elder Loammi Baldwin, 1794. At request of George Washington, 1795, reported on locks at Great Falls of Potomac. Served as adviser (1796–97) to Western Inland Lock Navigation Co., New York State, on the precursor of the Erie Canal. In 1799 he made an examination of future New York City water supply; he suggested the Bronx River as source, purification by artificial filters, and use of 24-inch cast-iron water pipe. His deep coffer dam for the "Permanent Bridge," Philadelphia, Pa., was the first in America. He removed to England *ca.* 1800. Weston commanded large fees and was highly respected by such public figures as Washington, Robert Morris, and Philip Schuyler. He taught native engineers how to design and build lock canals and published, among other reports, *An Account of the Rise, Progress and Present State of the Canal Navigation in Pennsylvania* (1795).

WETHERILL, CHARLES MAYER (*b. Philadelphia, Pa., 1825; d. Bethlehem, Pa., 1871*), chemist. Cousin of Samuel Wetherill (1821–1890). Graduated University of Pennsylvania (where he studied under A. D. Bache and J. F. Frazer), 1845; studied also in laboratory of James C. Booth and Martin H. Boyé and in Paris. Ph.D., University of Giessen, 1848. Published well-known treatise *The Manufacture of Vinegar* (1860). Appointed chemist of the U.S. Department of Agriculture, 1862, he was the first scientist of the department; his *Report on the Chemical*

Analysis of Grapes (1862) was the department's first scientific bulletin. Made studies of munitions for the War Department, 1862 and 1863. As chemist of the Smithsonian Institution, 1863–66, he made an important investigation upon ventilation of the Capitol. Professor of chemistry, Lehigh University, 1866–71.

WETHERILL, SAMUEL (*b. near Burlington, N.J., 1736; d. 1816*), pioneer American manufacturer of white lead and other chemicals, Philadelphia civic leader. He was cut off from the Society of Friends, 1777, for supporting the cause of the colonies and the use of weapons in its defense. He then joined in forming the sect of Free, or Fighting, Quakers before whom he preached regularly until his death.

WETHERILL, SAMUEL (*b. Philadelphia, Pa., 1821; d. Oxford, Md., 1890*), inventor, Union soldier, industrialist. Great-grandson of Samuel Wetherill (1736–1816). Graduated University of Pennsylvania, 1845. Invented (1852) process for deriving white zinc oxide direct from ore; founded Lehigh Zinc Co., 1853. He was the father of John P. Wetherill (1844–1906), inventor of the Wetherill furnace and Wetherill magnetic concentrating process for treatment of refractory ores.

WETZEL, LEWIS (*b. probably Lancaster Co., Pa., 1764; d. probably near Natchez, Miss., 1808[?]*), Indian fighter, scout. Raised near present Wheeling, W.Va. Served on a number of war expeditions, notably against Indian village on site of present Coshocton, Ohio, 1781. An implacable Indian hater.

WEXLER, IRVING (*b. New York, N.Y., 1888; d. Alcatraz Prison, San Francisco, Calif., 1952*), criminal. Under the name of Waxey Gordon, Wexler was a leading bootlegger and trafficker in narcotics during the 1920's and 1930's. Sentenced to a ten-year prison term for income tax evasion, he was released in 1940. Sentenced in 1951 for selling heroin, Wexler died in Alcatraz. He had been brought West to testify at the trial of a nationwide narcotics ring.

WEYERHAEUSER, FREDERICK EDWARD (*b. Rock Island, Ill., 1872; d. St. Paul, Minn., 1945*), lumberman, financier. Assumed control of his family's widespread business interests after his father's death in 1914.

WEYL, HERMANN (*b. Elmshorn, Germany, 1885; d. Zurich, Switzerland, 1955*), mathematician. Studied at the University of Göttingen (Ph.D., 1908). Taught at the Federal Institute of Technology in Zurich, 1913–30; at the University of Göttingen, 1930–33. Immigrated to the U.S. in 1933 and became a member of the Institute for Advanced Study in Princeton, N.J., 1933–55; emeritus after 1951. Published *The Concept of a Riemann Surface* (1913), *Space, Time, Matter* (1918), his account of Einstein's theory of relativity, and *The Classical Groups, Their Invariants and Representations* (1939). Member of the National Academy of Sciences and a fellow of the Royal Society of London.

WEYMOUTH, FRANK ELWIN (*b. Medford, Maine, 1874; d. San Marino, Calif., 1941*), hydraulic engineer. B.S. in civil engineering, University of Maine, 1896. On staff of Isthmian Canal Commission, 1899–1903; associated with U.S. Reclamation Service, 1903–24 (chief engineer *post* 1920). After a few years in private practice, and in irrigation projects for the Mexican government, he crowned his career as chief engineer and general manager of the Colorado River Aqueduct (1929–41).

WHALEN, GROVER ALOYSIUS (*b. New York, N.Y., 1886; d. New York, 1962*), businessman and city official. Attended Packard Commercial College and New York Law School. Began work with Wanamaker Department Store in New York City in 1914, and was general manager, 1924–34. In 1918 he was named secretary to

Mayor John F. Hyland and became a member of the New York and New Jersey Bridge-Tunnel Commission (1919–23) and chairman of New York's Board of Purchasing (1919–24). He was also appointed chairman of the Mayor's Committee for the Reception of Distinguished Guests (1919), becoming the city's official greeter. Appointed police commissioner (1928–29) and established the Police Academy and originated a crime-prevention bureau. President of a nonprofit corporation to organize the 1939 World's Fair; he enlisted foreign countries to participate and transformed 1,216 acres of wasteland into a magnificent exhibition grounds. Chairman of Schenley Products (1934–37) and Coty (1941) and president of Transcontinental Industries (1956) and the Fifth Avenue Association (1957).

WHALLEY, EDWARD (*b. Nottinghamshire, England, date unknown; d. probably Hadley, Mass., 1674 or 1675*), regicide. Father-in-law of William Goffe; cousin of Oliver Cromwell. Rose to colonel in English civil war, 1645; answered to Parliament for escape of the King from Hampton Court. As member of High Court of Justice he signed Charles I's death warrant. Appointed major general, 1655; became member of Cromwell's House of Lords. Condemned at the Restoration, he fled to New England with Goffe, 1660, and resided at various places in Massachusetts and Connecticut thereafter.

WHARTON, ANNE HOLLINGSWORTH (*b. Southampton Furnace, Pa., 1845; d. Philadelphia, Pa., 1928*), writer. An authority on genealogy and American colonial social history, she was author of, among other books and articles, *Through Colonial Doorways* (1893), *Heirlooms in Miniature* (1898), *Social Life in the Early Republic* (1902), and *English Ancestral Homes of Noted Americans* (1915).

WHARTON, CHARLES HENRY (*b. St. Mary's Co., Md., 1748; d. Burlington, N.J., 1833*), Episcopal clergyman. Educated in Jesuit schools in France and Belgium; ordained a Catholic priest, 1772. Served as chaplain to Roman Catholics at Worcester, England, where he underwent a change in his religious views. Returning to Maryland, 1783, he published a justification of his conversion to Protestantism, 1784, which was answered by Rev. John Carroll. Thereafter, one of the leading Episcopal clergymen of the United States, he served as rector of St. Mary's Church, Burlington, N.J., 1798–1833.

WHARTON, EDITH NEWBOLD JONES (*b. New York, N.Y., 1862; d. St. Brice-sous-forêt, near Paris, France, 1937*), author. Descended from several families of the small, tightly-knit group which dominated the business and social life of New York City before the Civil War, Edith Jones grew to maturity in a somewhat restricted world which attempted to maintain its stratified codes of behavior and its tradition of elegance against the threats of the new industrialism. Her family circle was predominantly masculine and communicated a masculine temper to her mind. As Henry James, her friend of later years, remarked, in her novels the "masculine conclusion" tended "to crown the feminine observation." Educated by governesses and tutors and by her own wide reading, she resided abroad for long periods with her family and grew fluent in French, German, and Italian. In 1885 she married a wealthy Bostonian, Edward Wharton. The couple divided the year between residence in New York City and Newport, R.I.; later Newport was replaced by Lenox, Mass., where Mrs. Wharton drew about herself a small, distinguished circle of intimates. As her husband began to decline in health, the Whartons spent more and more time abroad in England or Italy; in 1907 they established themselves in Paris. They were divorced in 1913. During World War I, Mrs. Wharton applied her talents for organization and her boundless sympathies to support of the Allied cause and to relief work in France. With Walter Berry, an international jurist and an old friend of her youth who possessed a marked influence over her opinions, she spent much time during and after the war visiting hospitals and serving on many committees. She was the first woman to receive an honorary LL.D. from Yale University (1923) and was the recipient of many other civic and literary honors.

Although she had issued a privately printed volume of verses in Newport, R.I., 1878, Mrs. Wharton did not publish her first book until 1897; it was *The Decoration of Houses* written in collaboration with Ogden Codman, Jr. Her first collection of stories was *The Greater Inclination* (1899). In 1902 she published *The Valley of Decision*, a long historical novel set in 18th-century Italy. However, it was not until *The House of Mirth* appeared in 1905 that Edith Wharton found a wide public and her major subject—the depiction of an individual who wishes to escape from the inhibitions of a rigid society, but is unable to do so because he has been molded beyond change by its values and standards. The tragedy of Lily Bart in this novel is a tragedy of unfulfilled possibilities. As Mrs. Wharton later said of her own purpose in adopting such a subject, "A frivolous society can acquire dramatic significance only through what its frivolity destroys. Its tragic implications lie in its power of debasing people and ideals." Her criticism of society, however, did not blind her to the vulgarities of the "new" people who challenged it. In *The Custom of the Country* (1913) she lashed out at the selfishness and arrogance of a money-dominated society.

In *The Age of Innocence* (1920; awarded the Pulitzer Prize in 1921), she continued her study in depth of the aristocratic-plutocratic struggle at the point of its early beginnings. Under the common title of *Old New York* (1924) she published four novelettes which examine the same theme of values in conflict throughout the latter two-thirds of the 19th century. Of these *The Old Maid* is the best known but is by no means superior to the others in the group, notably *False Dawn*. A group of her later novels published *post* 1925 deal generally with this theme as well. Written in the tradition of George Eliot and Gustave Flaubert and of her American predecessor, Henry James, these novels had in them a prophetic vein and a high moral vision. Other works, while partaking of her central theme, touched the international theme first developed by Henry James—the contrast of foreign and domestic manners. Outstanding examples were *Madame de Treymes* (1907) and *The Reef* (1912); however, where Henry James probed the contrasts in manners ever more deeply on psychological level, Wharton remained close to the actual data she observed. Her two novels of New England, *Ethan Frome* (1911) and *Summer* (1917), are distinct from her other work in background and method, but not in underlying theme. The first, realistic and grim, tells of a large nature harnessed to a mean spirit and doomed to a life of physical and spiritual confinement. The second of these novels is a tightly told story of a girl who cannot rise above her environment, and is an outstanding piece of work. These, together with a briefer tale, "The Bunner Sisters" (in *Xingu*, 1916), illustrate the author's broad sympathies with individuals outside her own environment. She was author, in all, of more than fifty books, including collections of short stories and travel books such as *Italian Villas and Their Gardens* (1904) and *Italian Backgrounds* (1905). She published several collections of her verse and a critical study, *The Writing of Fiction* (1925).

Wharton's writings fall into two distinct periods. Most critics agree that her best work was done during the years preceding 1914 and that her later work is largely an echo of it; a number of reasons have been assigned for this decline in her powers, but none is wholly satisfactory. She was a friend of many distinguished men, among whom may be mentioned Charles E. Norton, Theodore Roosevelt, and Bernard Berenson. The influence upon her work of her friend Henry James has been perhaps exaggerated, although she was in certain respects (choice of theme, moral attitude, interest in technique) one of his disciples. A *Backward Glance* (1934) contains autobiographical material.

WHARTON, FRANCIS (*b. Philadelphia, Pa., 1820; d. Washington, D.C. 1889*), lawyer, Episcopal clergyman, government official, educator. Son of Thomas I. Wharton. Graduated Yale, 1839. Admitted to Pennsylvania bar, 1843. An authority on criminal and international law, he wrote, among other works, *A Treatise on the Criminal Law of the United States* (1846) and *Treatise on the Conflict of Laws* (1872). Professor of history and literature, Kenyon College, 1856–63. Active as a religious writer, editor, and lay preacher, he was ordained in 1862, and served as rector, St. Paul's Episcopal Church, Brookline, Mass., 1863–71. Professor at Episcopal Theological Seminary, Cambridge, Mass., 1871–81, he was a leader of the Low Church school. Wharton was examiner of claims, legal division, Department of State, *post* 1885. He compiled *A Digest of the International Law of the United States* (1886, 1887; largely incorporated by J. B. Moore in *A Digest of International Law* 1906).

WHARTON, GREENE LAWRENCE (*b. near Bloomington, Ind., 1847; d. Calcutta, India, 1906*), Disciples of Christ clergyman. Missionary in India, 1882–99, 1904–06.

WHARTON, JOSEPH (*b. Philadelphia, Pa., 1826; d. 1909*), manufacturer, philanthropist. Studied chemistry at laboratory of Martin H. Boyé in Philadelphia. As manager of Lehigh Zinc Co. from 1853 to 1863, he was responsible for the first commercially successful production of spelter in the United States. For many years the only producer of refined nickel in America, he succeeded in 1875 in manufacturing a pure, malleable nickel. Wharton exerted strong political influence, particularly as a leading spokesman for a high protective tariff. He was a founder of Swarthmore College and established the Wharton School of Finance at the University of Pennsylvania.

WHARTON, RICHARD (*b. England, date unknown; d. England, 1689*), merchant, promoter. Immigrating to New England early in the Restoration Period (*post* 1660), he associated himself with a group of imperialistic recent settlers and with Puritan descendants who wished monopolistically to expand commerce, invest capital, and develop natural resources. Successive marriages to members of the Higginson and Winthrop families aided his business success. He involved New England in a trade war with the Dutch and urged recapture of New Netherland in order to develop American commerce on a unified plan with the port of New York as center. Advocating a remodeling of government so as to eliminate church power over the state, Wharton was influential in establishing the Dominion of New England, 1686. An importer, owning his own wharves and vessels, he aspired to a landed proprietorship and was associated in the Atherton Company and the Million Purchase; alone, he undertook the large Pejepscot Purchase in Maine. The New England Puritan governments and Governor Edmund Andros disapproved of these large projects, preferring a more democratic distribution of land. While in England to further his projects at court and to build opposition to Andros, he died suddenly, leaving his vast estate bankrupt.

WHARTON, ROBERT (*b. Philadelphia, Pa., 1757; d. 1834*), flour merchant. Half brother of Samuel Wharton. Elected mayor of Philadelphia, 1798, he was re-elected, 1799, and served subsequently, 1806–07, 1810, 1814–18, and 1820–24. An avid sportsman, he was for many years governor of the Schuylkill Fishing Company.

WHARTON, SAMUEL (*b. Philadelphia, Pa., 1732; d. near Philadelphia, 1800*), merchant, land speculator. Half brother of Robert Wharton. Associated *post* 1763 with George Morgan in trading firm of Baynton, Wharton & Morgan. Obtained "Indiana Grant," 1768. In England, 1769, he organized the Grand Ohio Company (Walpole Company) and petitioned for a grant to the proposed "Vandalia" colony of 20,000,000 acres between the Alleghanies and the upper Ohio. The Revolution ended this scheme.

WHARTON, THOMAS (*b. Chester Co., Pa., 1735; d. Lancaster, Pa., 1778*), merchant, Revolutionary patriot. First cousin of Robert and Samuel Wharton. Advocate of Whig policies, he served on the provincial Committee of Safety, 1775, and was president of the Council of Safety, 1776–77. He was in constant touch with General George Washington and was the principal figure in ordering out the Pennsylvania militia and encouraging enlistments. Elected president of the Supreme Executive Council of Pennsylvania, March 1777, he issued bills of credit to carry on the war, passed laws to punish the disloyal, and organized the new state's courts and military defenses.

WHARTON, THOMAS ISAAC (*b. Philadelphia, Pa., 1791; d. 1856*), lawyer, author. Nephew of William Rawle and Samuel Wharton; cousin of Thomas Wharton. Graduated University of Pennsylvania, 1807. Practiced in Philadelphia; was authority on real property and profoundly learned in other legal fields. A member of Joseph Dennie's Tuesday Club and a contributor to the *Port Folio*, he succeeded Washington Irving in 1815 as editor of *Analectic Magazine*. In 1830 he was appointed with William Rawle and Joel Jones to codify civil statute law of Pennsylvania.

WHARTON, WILLIAM H. (*b. Albemarle Co., Va., 1802; d. 1839*), lawyer, leader in Texas revolution. Settled in Texas *ca.* 1828. Wrote petition for repeal of law prohibiting foreign colonization in Texas at San Felipe convention, Oct. 1, 1832. Favored complete separation of Texas from Mexico. Accompanied S. F. Austin and B. T. Archer to the United States on mission for aid and support to Texas revolution, 1835–36. Minister to the United States to negotiate for recognition and annexation of Texas, 1836–37.

WHATCOAT, RICHARD (*b. Quinton, England, 1736; d. Dover, Del., 1806*), Methodist clergyman. Came to New York with Thomas Coke in 1784, at request of John Wesley, to organize American Methodists; was itinerant preacher and elder, and traveling companion of Bishop Asbury on episcopal tours. Elected bishop at the General Conference, 1800.

WHEATLEY, PHILLIS (*b. Africa, ca. 1753; d. Boston, Mass., 1784*), poet. A slave, purchased as a child by John Wheatley of Boston, Mass., she rapidly mastered English and read extensively in Greek mythology, Greek and Roman history, and contemporary English poetry. Her verses, influenced by Pope and Gray, won her reputation in Boston and London, and were published as *Poems on Various Subjects, Religious and Moral* (London, 1773).

WHEATLEY, WILLIAM (*b. New York, N.Y., 1816; d. New York, 1876*), actor, theater manager. Made debut with Macready at Park Theatre, New York City, 1826; by 1834 had become principal "walking gentleman" at the Park. Active as a player and manager in Philadelphia, Pa., Washington, D.C., and New York, he was most successful at Niblo's Garden, New York, 1862–68, where he presented sumptuous productions of romantic dramas with star actors. In 1866 he introduced the extravagant ballet spectacle to America with his production of *The Black Crook*.

WHEATON, FRANK (*b. Providence, R.I., 1833; d. Washington, D.C., 1903*), soldier. Appointed first lieutenant, 1st U.S. Cavalry, 1855. As lieutenant colonel, 2nd Rhode Island Infantry, he fought at first Bull Run and was cited by General Burnside. Made brigadier general late in 1862, he commanded a brigade in the VI (Sedgwick's) Corps and played a prominent part in the Wilderness campaign, 1864. Commanding a division, he repelled a threatened attack on Washington, D.C., by General J. A. Early, July 1864, and was rewarded by brevet of major general. Successful in the assault on Petersburg, Va., Apr. 2, 1865, he continued in the army after the Civil War and, among other duties, ably commanded the campaign against the Modoc Indians, 1872. He retired as major general, 1897.

WHEATON, HENRY (*b. Providence, R.I., 1785; d. Dorchester, Mass., 1848*), jurist, diplomat, authority on international law. Graduated Brown, 1802. After studying law in his native city, he made a special study of civil law at Poitiers, France, 1805–06. Practicing in Providence, 1806–12, he removed to New York City where he was editor of the *National Advocate*, a (Democrat) Republican newspaper, until 1815. Justice of the New York City marine court, 1815–19, he was also reporter of the U.S. Supreme Court, 1816–27. A member also of the New York Assembly for one term and a commissioner to revise the New York laws (1825–27), he was author of a number of legal works and of a life of William Pinkney. His published reports of the decisions of the U.S. Supreme Court during his incumbency as reporter were distinguished for the excellence and extent of his notes. Appointed chargé d'affaires to Denmark, 1827, he brought about agreement on a treaty of indemnity (signed, March 1830) for seizures of American vessels during the Napoleonic wars which served as the prototype of similar treaties negotiated later with France and Naples. While in Denmark, he learned the language and studied the history of the Scandinavian peoples; in 1831 he published his *History of the Northmen*. Appointed chargé d'affaires at Berlin at the request of the Prussian authorities, March 1835, he was raised in rank to minister to Prussia, 1837, indirectly as a result of publication of his celebrated *Elements of International Law* (1836). In 1844 he secured signature of a treaty with Prussia which arranged for reciprocal tariff reductions; the treaty, however, was rejected by the U.S. Senate. Among other treaties negotiated by Wheaton and put into effect were those providing for the abrogation of taxes imposed on emigrants to the United States from Hanover, Württemberg, Hesse-Cassel, Saxony, Nassau, and Bavaria. Resigning at the request of President Polk, 1846, Wheaton returned to the United States the next year.

Notable as were Wheaton's accomplishments in a number of fields, his most distinguished achievement was his work as an expounder and historian of international law. His *Elements* (previously mentioned) was an immediate success both at home and in Europe and encouraged Wheaton to further literary efforts which included his *History of the Law of Nations in Europe and America* (Leipzig, 1841; New York 1845). He is regarded by competent critics as standing with John Marshall, Judge Story, and Chancellor Kent among the greatest of American legal writers.

WHEATON, NATHANIEL SHELDON (*b. Marbledale, Conn., 1792; d. Marbledale, 1862*), Episcopal clergyman, educator. Graduated Yale, 1814. As rector, Christ Church, Hartford, Conn., 1821–31, he assisted Ithiel Town in design of its new (1827) edifice, said to be first truly Gothic church in America. President, Washington College (present Trinity), Hartford, 1831–37. While rector, Christ Church, New Orleans, 1837–44, he lost his health in heroic ministry during a yellow fever epidemic.

WHEDON, DANIEL DENISON (*b. Onondaga, N.Y., 1808; d. Atlantic City, N.J., 1885*), Methodist clergyman, editor, teacher. Graduated Hamilton College, 1828. Converted by Charles G. Finney. Professor of classics, Wesleyan (Conn.) College, 1833–43. A strong controversialist, he opposed the radical

abolitionist movement in his church, but was also opposed to extension of slavery; he defended Wesleyan Arminianism. Professor of logic, rhetoric, and philosophy of history, University of Michigan, 1845–51. Editor, *Methodist Quarterly Review*, 1856–84. Author, among other works, of *Commentaries* on the Bible (1860–1884), which were widely popular.

WHEELER, ANDREW CARPENTER (*b. New York, N.Y., 1835; d. 1903*), journalist, playwright, drama and music critic. Entered journalism on staff of *New York Times* 1857; local editor, *Milwaukee Sentinel*, 1859–62; served as Civil War correspondent. *Post ca.* 1867, he wrote dramatic criticism under pseudonym "Trinculo" for *New York Leader*; as "Nym Crinkle," his weekly music and drama reviews for the New York *World* attracted wide attention for caustic humor and breadth of information.

WHEELER, ARTHUR LESLIE (*b. Hartford, Conn., 1872; d. Princeton, N.J., 1932*), classical scholar. Graduated Yale, 1893; Ph.D., 1896. Taught classical languages at Yale; headed department of classics at Bryn Mawr, 1900–25; headed department of classics at Princeton thereafter. Made special studies of the types of poetry as they developed in Latin literature, particularly of the Roman elegy.

WHEELER, BENJAMIN IDE (*b. Randolph, Mass., 1854; d. Vienna, Austria, 1927*), educator. Graduated Brown, 1875. Ph.D., Heidelberg, 1885. Professor of philology and Greek, Cornell University, 1886–99; taught also at Brown, American School of Classical Studies in Athens (1895–96), and University of Berlin (1909–10). Through his efforts as president of the University of California, 1899–1919, students and faculty increased four-fold; twenty new departments were added as well as divisions for special research; the summer session, extension division, and material equipment were expanded; and student self-government was instituted. Relieved from active conduct of the university, 1918, because of German sympathies, he retired (1919) as "Professor of Comparative Philology and President Emeritus."

WHEELER, EVERETT PEPPERRELL (*b. New York, N.Y., 1840; d. 1925*), lawyer, civil service reformer. Cousin of James R. Wheeler. Graduated present College of the City of New York, 1856; LL.B., Harvard, 1859. Admitted to the New York bar, 1861, he practiced there until his death. Specialist in admiralty law, he was a founder of the New York Bar Association, 1869. Devoted to civil service reform and better government, he aided in drafting of revised Pendleton Bill, 1881, and with Edward M. Shepard wrote New York State civil service bill, 1883. He was active in reform politics and in the Citizen's Union which he helped found.

WHEELER, GEORGE MONTAGUE (*b. Hopkinton, Mass., 1842; d. New York, N.Y., 1905*), topographical engineer. Graduated West Point, 1866. Supervised survey of territory west of 100th meridian, 1871–88, commonly known as the "Wheeler Survey." His 14 field trips, 1871–79, in deserts and among mountain peaks entailed hardships which broke Wheeler's health. The survey's definitive *Report* was published in a number of volumes between 1875 and 1889, and Wheeler devoted the years 1879–88 to supervising their publication. He retired in 1888 with major's rank and pay awarded by act of Congress.

WHEELER, (GEORGE) POST (*b. Oswego, N.Y., 1869; d. Neptune, N.J., 1956*), diplomat and writer. Studied at Princeton University (D.Litt., 1893), at the Sorbonne, and the University of Pennsylvania. The first American career diplomat, Wheeler passed his State Department examination in 1906 and was sent as secretary to the embassy in Tokyo, 1906–09; to St. Petersburg, 1909–11; to Rome, 1912–13; and to Tokyo again from 1914 to 1916. He was counselor in London, Madrid, and Rio de Janeiro, and was minister to Albania from 1933 until his retirement in 1934. Books include *Russian Wonder Tales* (1912), *Dragon in the Dust* (1946), and his autobiography, written with his wife, novelist Hallie Rives, *Dome of Many-Colored Glass* (1955).

WHEELER, GEORGE WAKEMAN (*b. Woodville, Miss., 1860; d. Bridgeport, Conn., 1932*), jurist, law reformer. A.B., Yale, 1881; LL.B., 1883. Judge, Connecticut superior court, 1893–1910. In 1910 he was appointed associate justice, supreme court of errors; he served as chief justice, 1920–30. Influential in procuring uniform state bar admission standards. As chairman, Connecticut judicial council, 1927–30, he was mainly responsible for the rule of summary judgment and other innovations.

WHEELER, JAMES RIGNALL (*b. Burlington, Vt., 1859; d. 1918*), classicist, archaeologist. Cousin of Everett P. Wheeler. Graduated University of Vermont, 1880; Ph.D., Harvard, 1885. Studied also at American School of Classical Studies, Athens, 1882, and was closely identified with it for many years. Taught at Johns Hopkins, Harvard, and University of Vermont; professor of Greek literature and archaeology, Columbia University *post* 1895. Dean, faculty of fine arts, Columbia, 1906–11.

WHEELER, JOHN HILL (*b. Murfreesboro, N.C., 1806; d. Washington, D.C., 1882*), lawyer, diplomat, historian, North Carolina legislator and politician. As U.S. minister to Nicaragua, 1854–57, he recognized the insurrectionist government of William Walker, thereby exceeding instructions, and was forced to resign by Secretary of State W. L. Marcy. Wheeler's historical works abound in error, but aroused interest in local history in North Carolina and other Southern states.

WHEELER, JOHN MARTIN (*b. Burlington, Vt., 1879; d. Underhill Center, Vt., 1938*), ophthalmologist. Graduated University of Vermont, 1902; M.D., 1905. Long associated with the New York Eye and Ear Infirmary, he was head of ophthalmic service at New York's Bellevue and Presbyterian hospitals and consultant to a number of other hospitals. A teacher of his specialty at Cornell Medical College and at New York University, he was professor at N.Y. College of Physicians and Surgeons *post* 1928. He directed the Institute of Ophthalmology at Columbia-Presbyterian Medical Center from 1933 until his death. An operator of exquisite dexterity, he was skilled also in the field of plastic surgery.

WHEELER, JOSEPH (*b. near Augusta, Ga., 1836; d. Brooklyn, N.Y., 1906*), soldier. Graduated West Point, 1859; resigned commission, 1861. Colonel, 19th Alabama Infantry, he was given command in July 1862 of the cavalry of the Army of Mississippi. Rising by merit eventually to rank of Confederate lieutenant general, he led all cavalry in the Civil War western theater; he took a most prominent part in the Murfreesboro and Chickamauga campaigns. After Rosecrans's retirement to Chattanooga, Wheeler executed a masterly raid on Union communications. His cavalry provided the main obstacle to Sherman's march to the seas after Atlanta. R. E. Lee bracketed Wheeler with J. E. B. Stuart as one of the two outstanding Confederate cavalry leaders. Congressman, Democrat, from Alabama, 1881–83, 1885–1900, he was ranking Democrat of the ways and means committee; he fought for low tariff, and was instrumental in congressional rehabilitation of Fitz-John Porter. His chief public contribution was untiring advocacy of reconciliation between North and South. Appointed by President McKinley as major general of volunteers in Cuba, 1898, he commanded cavalry in General Shafter's Santiago expedition.

WHEELER, NATHANIEL (*b. Watertown, Conn., 1820; d. Bridgeport, Conn., 1893*), manufacturer, inventor, Connecticut legislator. Manufactured new rotary-hook sewing machine of Allen B. Wilson (patented 1851), adding four-motion feed in

1854. Invented and patented a wood-filling compound (1876, 1878) and a home ventilating system (1883).

WHEELER, ROYALL TYLER (*b. Vermont, 1810; d. Washington Co., Tex., 1864*), jurist. Studied law in Delaware, Ohio. Removed to Texas, 1839. In 1844 he became a district judge. Appointed to the state supreme court, 1845, he became chief justice, 1858. A strong advocate of secession, he upheld and enforced the Confederate conscription law.

WHEELER, SCHUYLER SKAATS (*b. New York, N.Y., 1860; d. New York, 1923*), inventor, engineer, manufacturer. A founder with Francis B. Crocker, 1888 (and president *post* 1889) of the Crocker-Wheeler Co., soon prominent in manufacture of motors. With Crocker, he published *Practical Management of Dynamos and Motors* (1894). He was inventor of an electric fire-engine system, an electric elevator (both patented 1885), and an electric fan.

WHEELER, WAYNE BIDWELL (*b. near Brookfield, Ohio, 1869; d. 1927*), lawyer, professional Prohibitionist. Superintendent, Anti-Saloon League of Ohio, 1904–15; general counsel, Anti-Saloon League of America, *post* 1915; also legislative superintendent. Successfully lobbied for national prohibition; favored extreme measures of enforcement.

WHEELER, WILLIAM (*b. Concord, Mass., 1851; d. 1932*), engineer, educator. Graduated Massachusetts Agricultural College, 1871. Professor of mathematics and civil engineering, Imperial Agricultural College of Sapporo, Japan, 1876–77; president, 1877–80. Began wide consulting practice in Boston, Mass., 1880, and became a national authority on water works.

WHEELER, WILLIAM ADOLPHUS (*b. Leicester, Mass., 1833; d. Boston, Mass., 1874*), lexicographer, bibliographer. Graduated Bowdoin College, 1853. Assisted J. E. Worcester in preparing *Dictionary of the English Language* (1860); supervised unabridged quarto and other editions of the Webster dictionary for Merriam Company. Assistant superintendent, Boston Public Library, from 1868 until his death. Author, among other reference works, of *Dictionary of the Noted Names of Fiction* (1865).

WHEELER, WILLIAM ALMON (*b. Malone, N.Y., 1819; d. 1887*), lawyer, banker, New York legislator. Admitted to the bar, 1845; practiced successfully in Malone, N.Y. Independent Republican congressman from New York, 1861–63, 1869–77, he stood out among his contemporaries as a man of scrupulous integrity. His "Wheeler adjustment" of a Louisiana disputed election, 1874, averted collapse of the state's government. Nominated for the U.S. vice-presidency, 1876, to secure a balance of sectional elements in the party, he was elected and served as a good presiding officer but cared little for the office.

WHEELER, WILLIAM MORTON (*b. Milwaukee, Wis., 1865; d. Cambridge, Mass., 1937*), zoologist, entomologist. Educated at Englemann German Academy, Milwaukee; worked under Henry A. Ward at Rochester, N.Y. Continuing his studies while teaching in Milwaukee, he became a research fellow at Clark University, 1890, where he received the Ph.D., 1892. His "A Contribution to Insect Embryology" (*Journal of Morphology*, 1893) achieved classic status. After teaching at the universities of Chicago and Texas, 1893–1903, he became a curator of invertebrate zoology at the American Museum of Natural History, New York City. In 1908 he became professor of entomology at the Bussey Institution, Harvard, and remained at Harvard until his retirement, 1934. Although most of his more than 450 publications are concerned with insects, a large number deal with problems of evolution, ecology, and behavior; among his books was *Social Life among the Insects* (1923).

WHEELOCK, ELEAZAR (*b. Windham, Conn., 1711; d. 1779*), Congregational clergyman, first president of Dartmouth. Father of John Wheelock. Graduated Yale, 1733. Pastor of Second Church, Lebanon, Conn., 1735–70. A popular emotional preacher during the Great Awakening, he founded a school at Lebanon primarily to convert and educate Indians to be missionaries and teachers for their tribes. Dissatisfied with the progress of the mission work and recruiting, and desiring to enlarge his educational program, Wheelock founded Dartmouth College, Hanover, N.H. (chartered 1769), maintaining it during the Revolutionary turmoil until his death.

WHEELOCK, JOHN (*b. Lebanon, Conn., 1754; d. 1817*), Revolutionary soldier, educator. Son of Eleazar Wheelock. Graduated Dartmouth College, 1771. As president of Dartmouth, 1779–1815, he established salaried professorships, built Dartmouth Hall and a chapel, revived in 1800 the educational program for the Indians, and secured the financing of the college and of Moor's Charity School. The last twelve years of his term were embittered by his struggles with the trustees, resulting in Wheelock's removal and a public controversy. The case was brought before the Supreme Court (*Trustees of Dartmouth College v. Woodward, 4 Wheaton, 518*), and was won for the college in 1819 by Daniel Webster.

WHEELOCK, JOSEPH ALBERT (*b. Bridgetown, N.S., Canada, 1831; d. 1906*), editor. Removed to Minnesota Territory, 1850. Edited *St. Paul Daily Press*, 1861–75; edited *St. Paul Daily Pioneer-Press* as an influential Republican paper *post* 1875. Opposed Republican party on Reconstruction and tariff; fought faction led by Ignatius Donnelly. His editorials in the 1890's helped keep Minnesota in the gold ranks.

WHEELOCK, LUCY (*b. Cambridge, Vt., 1857; d. Boston, Mass., 1946*), educator. Founded Wheelock School (later College) for training of kindergarten teachers, 1888, and headed it until 1940. Active in professional and other organizations, she strove to maintain the best aspects of the traditional kindergarten while preserving an open mind with respect to significant current educational theories.

WHEELWRIGHT, EDMUND MARCH (*b. Roxbury, Mass., 1854; d. Thompsonville, Conn., 1912*), architect. Studied architecture at Massachusetts Institute of Technology and in Paris; worked in offices of Peabody & Stearns and McKim, Mead & White. In 1888 he formed a Boston partnership which in 1910 became Wheelwright, Haven and Hoyt. As city architect for Boston, 1891–95, and consultant thereafter, he set a new high level for American municipal architecture. Perhaps his most widely known buildings are the subway entrances at Park St. corner of Boston Common. In 1900 he was chief designer of the Cambridge bridge. Among other works, Wheelwright designed Horticultural Hall (1900) and the Boston Opera House (1908). He sought the monumental, classic solution; stylistically he was catholic, even erratic. His later work tended toward a rational simplicity.

WHEELWRIGHT, JOHN (*b. probably Saleby, Lincolnshire, England, ca. 1592; d. Salisbury, N.H., 1679*), clergyman. B.A., Sidney College, Cambridge, 1614/15; M.A., 1618. For some years vicar of Bilsby (England), he was deprived for nonconformity, 1633, and immigrated to Boston, Mass., 1636. Pastor at Mount Wollaston (now Quincy), Mass., he and John Cotton alone among the clergy supported Anne Hutchinson, Wheelwright's sister-in-law, in the Antinomian controversy. Publicly denouncing the majority (which now included Cotton), 1637, he was disfranchised and banished from Massachusetts colony by the General Court. After organizing a community at present Exeter, N.H., he served there as pastor until Massachusetts asserted jurisdiction, when he removed to present Wells, Maine. Recanting his opinions, 1643, he secured reversal of his sentence in May 1644.

WHEELWRIGHT, MARY CABOT (*b. Boston, Mass., 1878; d. Sutton's Island, Maine, 1958*), anthropologist. With scanty formal education but of independent means, Mary Wheelwright became, at the age of forty, an eminent amateur anthropologist. She founded the Museum of Navajo Ceremonial Art in Santa Fe, N.M., in 1936. Her study of symbolism in primitive religions around the world was published by the Peabody Museum at Harvard University in 1956.

WHEELWRIGHT, WILLIAM (*b. Newburyport, Mass., 1798; d. England, 1873*), merchant mariner, promoter of Latin American enterprises. Became U.S. consul at Guayaquil in 1824. Removing to Valparaiso *ca.* 1830, he built port facilities, provided gas and water works, and also secured British charter for Pacific Steam Navigation Co. (1840) of which he became chief superintendent. Between 1849 and 1852, he built the first railroad in Chile; in 1850 he gave Chile the first South American telegraph line. He also promoted the Grand Central Argentine Railway (opened 1870), a part of his projected trans-Andean railway (completed, 1910). He created the port of La Plata and completed the railroad linking it with Buenos Aires, 1872.

WHELPLEY, HENRY MILTON (*b. Battle Creek, Mich., 1861; d. Argentine, Kans., 1926*), pharmacist, drug-trade editor, teacher. Graduated St. Louis (Mo.) College of Pharmacy, 1883. Professor of microscopy, 1886–1922, at his *alma mater*; professor of pharmacognosy, materia medica, and physiology, 1915–26; dean, 1904–26. From 1890 to 1909 he also served as professor of these subjects at a number of other Missouri institutions.

WHERRY, ELWOOD MORRIS (*b. South Bend, Pa., 1843; d. Indiana, Pa., 1927*), Presbyterian clergyman. Graduated Princeton Theological Seminary, 1867. Served in missions to India, 1867–89, and 1898–1922. Among other works, he published a monumental *Comprehensive Commentary of the Quran* (1882–84).

WHERRY, KENNETH SPICER (*b. Liberty, Nebr., 1892; d. Washington, D.C., 1951*), politician. Studied at the University of Nebraska and at Harvard University, 1915–16. Elected to the U.S. Senate as a Republican in 1942, he served until his death. An isolationist and conservative, Wherry was opposed to the policies of the New and Fair Deals, all foreign aid, federal aid to education and housing, and the Office of Price Administration. Too conservative to be a party policymaker, he was an efficient party member.

WHETZEL, HERBERT HICE (*b. near Avilla, Ind., 1877; d. Ithaca, N.Y., 1944*), phytopathologist, mycologist. Graduated Wabash College, 1902. Graduate study at Cornell University with George F. Atkinson. Headed department of plant pathology at Cornell *post* 1906, resigning the chairmanship in 1922 to devote himself to his research and teaching as professor. A dynamic and innovative teacher, he concentrated in his early research on practical problems of plant disease control; later, he devoted more and more time to mycology. His researches on the family *Sclerotiniaceae* were a major contribution to the field of plant pathology.

WHIPPLE, ABRAHAM (*b. Providence, R.I., 1733; d. Marietta, Ohio, 1819*), naval officer. Brother-in-law of Stephen and Esek Hopkins. In 1772 he led party which burned British schooner *Gaspée* near Pawtucket, R.I., sometimes regarded as the first overt act of the Revolution. Appointed Rhode Island commodore, 1775, he captured the British frigate *Rose*, first prize taken by an official American vessel. In 1779, commanding flagship *Providence* as commodore of a Continental squadron, he brought back eight East-Indiamen, one of the richest captures of the war. Entrusted with naval defense of Charleston, S.C., 1779, he was made prisoner when the city was taken.

WHIPPLE, AMIEL WEEKS (*b. Greenwich, Mass., 1816; d. Washington, D.C., 1863*), soldier, topographical engineer. Graduated West Point, 1844–49; on survey of boundary between United States and Mexico, 1849–53; and on Pacific Railroad surveys, 1853–56. As chief topographical engineer, he served with Union forces at Bull Run. Promoted brigadier general, April 1862, he was active in the defense of Washington until October when he was assigned command of the third division of the III (Stoneman's) Corps. He was mortally wounded on the second day of Chancellorsville (May 3, 1863).

WHIPPLE, EDWIN PERCY (*b. Gloucester, Mass., 1819; d. Boston, Mass., 1886*), broker, lyceum lecturer, literary critic. Published, among other works, *Essays and Reviews* (1848–49), *Lectures on Subjects Connected with Literature and Life* (1850), *Recollections of Eminent Men* (1887), and *American Literature and Other Papers* (1887) with an introduction by Whittier, his intimate friend. Popular as a lyceum lecturer, he enjoyed a considerable contemporary reputation as a reviewer and critic, exhibiting logical analysis, imagination, discrimination, and sensitive love of beauty.

WHIPPLE, FRANCES HARRIET. *See* GREEN, FRANCES HARRIET WHIPPLE.

WHIPPLE, HENRY BENJAMIN (*b. Adams, N.Y., 1822; d. Faribault, Minn., 1901*), Episcopal clergyman, reformer of U.S. Indian system. Ordained priest, 1850; rector, Zion Church, Rome, N.Y., until 1857 except for 1853–54. Built up and administered Holy Communion parish, south side of Chicago, 1857–59. Consecrated first bishop of Minnesota, October 1859, he opposed the U.S. government's Indian policy. During the 1862 uprising of the Minnesota Sioux, which began the series of Indian wars he had predicted, Whipple appealed on behalf of the Indians to the outraged settlers and to President Lincoln who forbade execution of many condemned Sioux. His proposed reforms of the reservation system, and his suggestions of land-ownership by Indians, adequate schools, and inspection, were largely adopted under President Grant. During the next two decades he exposed frauds, built up missions among the Minnesota Chippewa, traveled widely, and made eloquent addresses in America and abroad for support of his work. In 1897 he attended the fourth Lambeth Conference as presiding bishop of the American Church. Author of an autobiography, *Lights and Shadows of a Long Episcopate* (1899).

WHIPPLE, SHERMAN LELAND (*b. New London, N.H., 1862; d. Brookline, Mass., 1930*), Boston, Mass., lawyer. Graduated Yale Law School, 1884. Celebrated as a plaintiff's attorney in personal injury and will cases.

WHIPPLE, SQUIRE (*b. Hardwick, Mass., 1804; d. Albany, N.Y., 1888*), civil engineer, author, inventor. A.B., Union College, 1830. Devised (*ca.* 1846) a widely used truss of trapezoidal form which placed him among American pioneers in development of the pure truss bridge. Whipple's chief contribution to bridge engineering was publication of *A Work on Bridge Building* (1847), the first notable attempt to present the subject on a scientific basis and the first thorough treatment of modern methods of computing stresses and designing parts to meet them.

WHIPPLE, WILLIAM (*b. Kittery, Maine, 1730; d. 1785*), merchant, revolutionary patriot, New Hampshire legislator. Promi-

nent in early provincial congresses as a close associate of John Langdon. Member of the Continental Congress, 1776–79, with interludes for militia commands, he was a signer of the Declaration of Independence. An active committee member, he urged effective naval operations and strong measures against speculators and Tories. He advocated also the spread of the burden of the struggle over the entire people by means of adequate taxation. He served as a justice, state supreme court, from 1782 until his death.

WHISTLER, GEORGE WASHINGTON (*b. Fort Wayne, Ind., 1800; d. St. Petersburg, Russia, 1849*), soldier, engineer. Father of James A. M. Whistler. Graduated West Point, 1819. Commissioned second lieutenant of artillery, he was assigned to topographical duty. In 1828 he assisted in location and construction of the Baltimore and Ohio Railroads, subsequently supervising construction of other roads. Resigned from army, 1833. As chief engineer, Western Railroad of Massachusetts (now Boston & Albany), 1840–42, he located section between Springfield and Pittsfield through the Berkshires under especially difficult conditions. This resulted in appointment by the Czar of Russia as consulting engineer for a railroad between St. Petersburg and Moscow which was completed in 1850. He also supervised construction of fortifications and docks at Cronstadt, and of the iron bridge of the Neva.

WHISTLER, JAMES ABBOTT MCNEILL (*b. Lowell, Mass., 1834; d. London, England, 1903*), painter, etcher, author. Son of George W. Whistler; nephew of William G. McNeill. A bright boy, somewhat delicate in health but precociously able as a draftsman, Whistler resided in Russia and England, 1843–49. Although his mother was offered a place for him in the Russian imperial school for pages after his father's death, she brought him and her other children back to America in 1849. A West Point cadet, 1851–54, he was dismissed for deficiency in chemistry. "Had silicon been a gas," he is reported to have said, "I would have been a major general." He retained from his military education his insistence upon the point of honor, his erect carriage, and probably his lifelong proclivity for fighting. After a brief engagement as a draftsman of maps in the U.S. Coast Survey at Washington, D.C., during which he learned much about the mechanics of etching, he departed to study in Paris, 1855.

He never returned to his native country probably because he found more congenial conditions of life abroad and friends with whom he was instinctively at home. Entering the atelier of Charles Gleyre, a competent painter in the tradition of Ingres, Whistler conducted himself in dress and manner as a Bohemian of the Bohemians. He had the gift of dramatizing his own every movement and adopted originality as a career, not because he was a *poseur*, but because he couldn't help it; he was invincibly an individual in his life as in his work. Among his friends of this period were many artists later to become famous—among them, George Du Maurier, Henri Fantin-Latour, and Alphonse Legros. Resisting contemporary French art influences with the exception of that of Gustave Courbet, Whistler sought beauty in truth but subjected truth to his very personal conception of beauty. Among his early paintings, *The Music Room*, with its decisively decorative motive, foreshadows the essential Whistler. He published his first group of etchings in Paris, November 1858. His painting *The White Girl*, rejected at the Paris Salon in 1863, later made a sensation in the Salon des Refusés.

After the 1850's, Whistler oscillated between Paris and London, with London becoming more and more the field of his labors. His mother came to live in England, 1863, and it was there that he painted the celebrated portrait of her first shown in 1872 and now in the Louvre. In London, between 1872 and 1877, he painted those other portraits which won him so much reputation—notably his *Carlyle*, and *Miss Alexander*. Also of London ancestry are his

Nocturnes and the Thames set of etchings. Harshly criticized by John Ruskin for work shown in the Grosvenor gallery exhibition of 1877, Whistler sued the critic (November 1878), winning a nominal verdict. He later described the affair in his book *The Gentle Art of Making Enemies* (1890). The episode served to dramatize the fact that Whistler had created something new and strange in art, something beyond the comprehension of the contemporary British mind which had been nurtured on the sentimental "subject" picture or painted anecdote. "Take the picture of my mother," he said, "exhibited at the Royal Academy as an 'Arrangement in Grey and Black.' Now that is what it is. To me it is interesting as a picture of my mother; but what can or ought the public to care about the identity of the portrait?" Again, in regard to one of his Nocturnes, he said "My picture of a 'Harmony in Grey and Gold' is an illustration of my meaning—a snow scene with a single black figure and a lighted tavern. I care nothing for the past, present, or future of the black figure, placed there because the black was wanted at that spot. All that I know is that my combination of grey and gold is the basis of the picture."

Sensitive to the appeal of Japanese art, he acquired from Japan a feeling for pattern as pattern. His admiration for Velásquez was great, but Whistler was by no means a disciple of the great Spaniard. Each painter strove for perfection, which probably explains Whistler's admiration; but each did so in his own specific way. Velásquez was first and last constrained to record the fact before him, but Whistler, although properly regardful of the fact, was constrained to produce a distinctively Whistlerian pattern or "harmony." The many Nocturnes and Symphonies by Whistler do more than even his original and distinguished portraits to bring out the artist's singularity and creative power. He was not a great designer as Raphael was, nor was his craftsmanship equal to that of Velásquez. He gave us no high imaginative conceptions and attempted no emotional interpretation of life. However, he is very rich in sheer beauty, partly through the simplicity characterizing his design and his arrangement of color, and partly through the play of mysterious and elusive feeling. His contribution to art was inimitable. He has had no followers, as he had had no predecessors, in painting.

On the other hand, Whistler has had a widespread influence upon etching, and it is a paradox in his career that the draftsmanship which worried him so much when he was using a brush was ever ready to his hand when he used an etcher's needle. He was already a master of line and style in the French set of etchings which date from 1858; the Thames set (1860) discloses the same technical authority and grasp of composition. By the time he went to Venice in the 1870's and in later years, he more and more practiced elimination of intrusive detail, employing a lighter, more broken line in work of great beauty and distinction. His lithographs, as well as his etchings and paintings, express his distinctive artistic qualities and are equally models of conscientious craft. A prodigious worker, absorbed in his art, he often presented himself to the public as a dilettante, discharging airy shafts of wit against critics, artists, functionaries, or any others who appeared to him either bad at their work or scornful of his aesthetic principles. His gifts of sarcasm, as well as his inexhaustible gaiety, are to be found in *The Gentle Art of Making Enemies* (1890) in which he also expresses his philosophy of art. Much of what it contains had already appeared in pamphlets, exhibition catalogues, and letters to the press.

Prosperous *post* 1885, admired and imitated by the rising generation of young artists, he moved a good deal in society and served briefly but effectively as president of the Society of British Artists and of the International Society of Sculptors, Painters and Gravers. Subsequent to the early 1890's, he lived mainly in Rue du Bac, Paris, and gave some of his time to teaching in the short-lived Académie Carmen. After the failure of his health *ca.* 1901, he traveled for a time in Africa and Corsica before returning to London where he died.

WHITAKER, ALEXANDER (*b. Cambridge, England, 1585; d. near Henricopolis, Va., 1616/17*), Anglican clergyman. Came to Virginia as a volunteer minister, 1611. Helped to form and strengthen Virginia's attitude of welcome toward Puritan ministers and lay people, and to establish the colony's characteristic tradition of low churchmanship. Instructed and baptized Pocahontas in Christian faith. Author of *Good News from Virginia* (1613).

WHITAKER, CHARLES HARRIS (*b. Woonsocket, R.I., 1872; d. Great Falls, Va., 1938*), architectural editor and critic. A strong influence on modern architecture as editor-in-chief of the *Journal of the American Institute of Architects*, 1913–27; author of *Rameses to Rockefeller: The Story of Architecture* (1934).

WHITAKER, DANIEL KIMBALL (*b. Sharon, Mass., 1801; d. Houston, Tex., 1881*), editor, writer. South Carolina planter, lawyer. B.A. Harvard, 1820. Organized, edited, and contributed to Southern periodicals including *Southern Quarterly Review*, New Orleans, La., 1842–47, which encouraged such well-known writers as William G. Simms.

WHITAKER, NATHANIEL (*b. Huntington, N.Y., 1730; d. Hampton, Va., 1795*), Presbyterian clergyman, Revolutionary patriot. Conducted a tour in the British Isles with Samson Occom, 1766, which raised £12,000 for Moor's Charity School for Indians and effected the grant of the Dartmouth College charter, 1769. D.D., St. Andrew's University, 1767. Minister, Third Church, Salem, Mass., 1769–84; Presbyterian Church, Skowhegan, Maine, 1785–90. An ardent patriot, active in practical matters, his fondness for controversy brought him many enemies.

WHITCHER, FRANCES MIRIAM BERRY (*b. Whitesboro, N.Y., 1814; d. Whitesboro, 1852*), author. Her popular humorous sketches satirizing smalltown society appeared in Joseph C. Neal's *Saturday Gazette and Lady's Literary Museum*, 1846–50, and in *Godey's Lady's Book*. They were published as *The Widow Bedott Papers* (1856) and *Widow Spriggins, Mary Elmer, and Other Sketches* (1867).

WHITCOMB, JAMES (*b. Rochester, Vt., 1795; d. New York, N.Y., 1852*), lawyer, Indiana legislator. Father-in-law of Claude Matthews. Raised near Cincinnati, Ohio. Prosecuting attorney at Bloomington, Ind., 1826–29. Commissioner, General Land Office, 1836–41. Established successful law practice at Terre Haute, Ind., 1841. As governor of Indiana (the first Democrat to defeat a Whig), 1843–48, he contributed decisively toward adjustment of staggering indebtedness incurred by previous internal improvements, promoted popular education and developed state benevolent institutions. An ardent supporter of the national administration in war with Mexico. U.S. senator from Indiana, 1849–52. Author of *Facts for the People* (1843), one of the most effective arguments ever written against a protective tariff.

WHITCOMB, SELDEN LINCOLN (*b. Grinnell, Iowa, 1866; d. 1930*), educator, writer. A.B., Grinnell, 1887; A.M., Columbia, 1893. A notable teacher, he was professor of English, Grinnell College, 1895–1905; professor of comparative literature, University of Kansas, 1905–30. Author of poems, essays on nature, and studies in literature which include *Chronological Outlines of American Literature* (1894).

WHITE, ALBERT SMITH (*b. Blooming Grove, N.Y., 1803; d. near Stockwell, Ind., 1864*), lawyer, jurist, railroad builder. Settled in Tippecanoe Co., Ind., 1829. Congressman, Whig, from Indiana, 1837–39; U.S. senator, 1839–45. As congressman, Republican, from Indiana, 1861–63, he introduced a resolution for a plan for gradual indemnified emancipation of slaves in the border states which was supported by President Lincoln. Judge, U.S. District Court for Indiana, 1864.

WHITE, ALEXANDER (*b. Frederick Co., Va., ca. 1738; d. 1804*), lawyer, Virginia legislator. Began practice in Virginia, 1765. Served in state House of Burgesses, 1772; later championed allegedly Loyalist Quakers. In state assembly, 1782–86, 1788, 1799–1801, he was one of James Madison's ablest lieutenants. Successful leader in northwestern Virginia for ratification of U.S. Constitution, 1788. Congressman, Federalist, from Virginia, 1789–93. A commissioner to lay out city of Washington, D.C., 1795–1802.

WHITE, ALEXANDER (*b. Elgin, Scotland, 1814; d. 1872*), pioneer merchant, art collector. Immigrated to America, 1836. Settled in Chicago, Ill., 1837; prospered as merchant in paints, oils, glass, and dyestuffs and *post* 1857 in real estate. His collection of notable European contemporary and American paintings constituted the first private art gallery in Chicago. Sold at auction, New York, 1871, it was considered the best in America at that time.

WHITE, ALFRED TREDWAY (*b. Brooklyn, N.Y., 1846; d. Orange Co., N.Y., 1921*), pioneer in housing reform. Built model tenements in Brooklyn, N.Y., *post* 1876; also Riverside Tower and Homes Building, 1890, and others. His outstanding success spurred enactment of New York's tenement-reform legislation of 1895 and later. Published, among other books, *Better Homes for Workingmen* (1885). As commissioner of city works (appointed 1893), he set new standards of efficiency and economy.

WHITE, ALMA BRIDWELL (*b. Lewis County, Ky., 1862; d. Zarephath, N.J., 1946*), schoolteacher, evangelist, founder of the Pillar of Fire Church.

WHITE, ANDREW (*b. London, England, 1579; d. London, 1656*), Jesuit missionary, "Apostle of Maryland." A proscribed recusant, he was ordained at Douai (now France), *ca.* 1605, and joined the Society of Jesus, 1609. While a secret priest in England, he corresponded with George Calvert, first Baron of Baltimore, and composed the *Declaratio Coloniae Domini Baronis de Baltimore* (revised and published by Cecil Calvert as *Conditions of Plantation*). Headed mission to Baltimore's immigrant group which sailed on the *Ark* and the *Dove*, landing in the lower Chesapeake, March 25, 1634. Missionary to the white colonists and Indians for ten years, he was author of *Relatio Itineris in Marilandiam*. He arranged a scheme of manors for the support of the Catholic organization in the palatinate. After William Claiborne's Puritan insurrection, 1644, White was shipped in irons to London, tried for treason, and exiled.

WHITE, ANDREW DICKSON (*b. Homer, N.Y., 1832; d. Ithaca, N.Y., 1918*), educator. Graduated Yale, 1853; studied briefly at Paris and Berlin. Served as an attaché to the U.S. legation at St. Petersburg, Russia, 1854–55. After a year of graduate study again at Yale, he became professor of history in the University of Michigan, 1857. While winning distinction as an inspiring and original teacher, he matured his early concept of a state university for New York which would be as scholarly and free as the universities which he had observed in his travels abroad. In writing for help to his friend Gerrit Smith, he described the university of his dream as "excluding no sex or color, battling mercantile morality and tempering military passion . . . it should afford an asylum for science where truth shall be sought for truth's sake." In command of considerable wealth after the death of his father in 1860, he continued to propagandize in favor of his university, but was obliged to seek rest abroad late in 1862.

Returning to America late in 1863, he found that he had been elected *in absentia* to the New York State senate. As chairman of the senate committee on education, 1864, he played a large part in codifying New York's school laws and creating its new normal schools. Employing the endowment of land given New York under the Morrill Act, together with the benefactions of Ezra Cornell whom he won over to his own plans, White worked with Cornell to draw the charter of a new university at Ithaca, N.Y., which should bear Cornell's name. The educational clauses of the charter were written by White and ensured instruction not only in agriculture and the mechanic arts as the Morrill Act directed, but also provided for instruction in "such other branches of science and knowledge as the trustees may deem useful and proper." After a sharp struggle with rivals the charter was validated, April 1865. The most novel elements in the new institution were: (1) its democracy of studies—the humanities, sciences, and technical arts taught commonly; (2) its parallel courses, open to free choice and leading to varying but equal degrees; (3) its equal rank for modern languages and literatures and for history and political science with classics; (4) its large use of eminent scholars as "nonresident professors;" (5) its treatment of the students as men, not boys.

As Cornell would not go on with the project unless White served as president, White resigned his position at Michigan, and set about gathering a faculty and equipment, reserving the chair of European history for himself. At the opening of the university in 1868, its resident faculty was young, although among the non-residents were Louis Agassiz and J. R. Lowell, George W. Curtis, James Hall, and Bayard Taylor. In addition to teaching, White busied himself in defending the university and its founder against attacks on its method; he also coped with financial crises brought about by a failure of working capital. He continued to struggle with his burdens until 1885 when he was succeeded as president by Charles K. Adams. Meanwhile, he had spent several years abroad in travel and had served as U.S. minister to Germany, 1879–81; in 1884 he had helped found the American Historical Association, becoming its first president.

After seeking to recruit his health again in travel, 1885–89, he resumed his research work and lectured widely. Among the many honorable posts which he held thereafter were U.S. minister to Russia, 1892–94; U.S. ambassador to Germany, 1897–1902; and a trusteeship of the Carnegie Institution of Washington under the presidency of his old friend Daniel C. Gilman *post* 1902. He considered the greatest event of his diplomatic career his headship of the American delegation to the Hague Conference, 1899. He was author, among other works, of *History of the Warfare of Science with Theology* (1896) and an *Autobiography* (1905).

WHITE, BENJAMIN FRANKLIN (*b. Whitevale, Ontario, 1873; d. Orlando, Fla., 1958*), driver, breeder, and trainer of harness horses. The trainer and driver of more winners of major harness races than anyone in history, White drove in nineteen Hambletonians, winning four; he also won seven Kentucky Futurities, six Matron Stakes, and four Review Futurities. His success earned him the title "Dean of Colt Trainers." Famous horses he trained and drove include Lee Worthy, Volga, Rosalind, and Volo Song.

WHITE, CANVASS (*b. Whitesboro, N.Y., 1790; d. St. Augustine, Fla., 1834*), civil engineer. Benjamin Wright's principal assistant *post* 1818 on Erie Canal construction; was chief expert in designing the locks and their equipment; supervised Glens Falls feeder. Obtained patent for waterproof cement (1820). Chief engineer, Delaware & Raritan Canal, New Jersey, and Lehigh and Union canals in Pennsylvania. Characterized as possessing "the most strict engineering mind . . . of his time."

WHITE, CHARLES ABIATHAR (*b. North Dighton, Mass., 1826; d. Washington, D.C., 1910*), geologist, paleontologist, naturalist, physician. Raised near Burlington, in Territory of Iowa. His large collections of fossils, including the famous Burlington crinoids, served to introduce his work to James Hall, F. B. Meek, A. H. Worthen, and other geologists of the time. Graduated Rush Medical College, 1864. From 1866 to 1870 he served as Iowa state geologist; he was also professor of geology, Iowa State University, 1867–74. Employed successively, 1875–79, by G. M. Wheeler's survey west of 100th meridian, by J. W. Powell's survey of Rocky Mountain region, and by F. V. Hayden's geological survey of the Territories, he published important reports and paleontological studies. Curator, invertebrate fossils, National Museum, Washington, D.C., 1879–82; organized paleontologic collections. Geologist, U.S. Geological Survey, 1882–92. White's major scientific contributions were in invertebrate paleontology and stratigraphy, particularly of the Mesozoic.

WHITE, CHARLES IGNATIUS (*b. Baltimore, Md., 1807; d. Washington, D.C., 1878*), Roman Catholic clergyman. Ordained to secular priesthood, Nôtre Dame Cathedral, Paris, France, 1830. Influential and scholarly rector, St. Matthew's Church, Washington, D.C., 1857–78, where he did notable social work. A founder and editor (1842) of *Religious Cabinet* (later *U.S. Catholic Magazine* and *Metropolitan Magazine*, 1853.

WHITE, CLARENCE CAMERON (*b. Clarksville, Tenn., 1880; d. New York, N.Y., 1960*), violinist, composer, and educator. Studied at the Oberlin Conservatory of Music. Taught at the Washington Conservatory of Music, 1903–08; at West Virginia State College, 1924–30; and at the Hampton Institute, 1932–35. Major works include many pieces about black life in America and the Caribbean: *Forty Negro Spirituals* (1927), *Traditional Negro Spirituals* (1940), and the opera *Ouanga* (1932), first performed in 1949. Other works include *Elegy* (1954), *Fantasie* (1954), and *Heritage* (1959), with text by poet Countee Cullen. A major black composer, White's works for violin have been performed by Fritz Kreisler and Albert Spalding, among others.

WHITE, DAVID (*b. near Palmyra, N.Y., 1862; d. Washington, D.C., 1935*), paleobotanist, geologist. B.S., Cornell University, 1886. Associated thereafter with the U.S. Geological Survey, he performed most of his research in the period before 1912, at which time he was made chief geologist of the Survey and became active in the National Academy of Sciences. He was curator of paleobotany, U.S. National Museum, 1903–35. He resigned the post of chief geologist, 1922, to return to research, but his administrative duties continued to be heavy.

In such works as *Fossil Flora of the Lower Coal Measures of Missouri* (1899) and *Flora of the Hermit Shale, Grand Canyon, Arizona* (1929), White brought to his work an unusually keen mind; he was never content with a mere description of fossils, but interpreted them in terms of their chronology and environment, particularly their climatic significance and the part which they took in the foundation of coal and petroleum. His methodology consisted essentially in employment of a much greater precision than had been used by earlier scientists and in the discrimination of slight differences, particularly if such differences could be shown to occur at different stratigraphic horizons. His success demanded a combination of work in the field with personal office studies of the resulting collections. His method provided a disproof of prevailing opinions on the constitution of the Appalachian coal basin; he was also able to show that coals should be classified according to a standard in which the degree of deoxygenation served as an index of coal evolution; this in turn led to the generalization announced in 1915 (commonly known as the "carbon-ratio" hypothesis) which enables the determination of the rank of a coal, and also limits the extent of liquid and gaseous hydrocarbons. A few years later the economic importance of this brilliant idea was universally recognized in petroleum exploratory work. White's theory, amplified and clarified, was stated in his "Metamorphism of Organic Sediments and Derived Oils" (*Bulletin of the American Association of Petroleum Geologists*, May 1935).

WHITE, EDWARD DOUGLASS (*b. Maury Co., Tenn., 1795; d. New Orleans, La., 1847*), lawyer, planter, political leader. Father of Edward D. White (1845–1921). Studied law in office of Alexander Porter. Congressman, Whig, from Louisiana, 1829–34 and 1839–43. As governor of Louisiana, 1835–39, he effectively vetoed bill to charter Farmers' Bank in panic of 1837.

WHITE, EDWARD DOUGLASS (*b. Parish Lafourche, La., 1845; d. Washington, D.C., 1921*), lawyer, Confederate soldier, planter, jurist. Son of Edward D. White (1795–1847). Left the present Georgetown University to serve in the Confederate Army; studied law after the Civil War with Edward Bermudez. Admitted to the Louisiana bar, 1868, he entered politics and served in the Louisiana senate; he was also a justice of the state supreme court, 1879–80. Early identified with the anti-lottery movement, he was elected to the U.S. Senate as a Democrat and served, 1891–94. Appointed to the U.S. Supreme Court, 1894, he was raised to the post of chief justice, 1910.

During his years on the bench, Justice White wrote opinions in more than 700 cases. It is difficult to characterize his decisions as a whole. He was sometimes found with the so-called liberals as, for example, when he dissented in the case of *Lochner* v. *New York* (1905) and when he wrote the majority opinion in *Wilson* v. *New* upholding the Adamson Act. On the other hand, while he concurred in the New York Central case (243 *U.S.*, 188) upholding the New York workmen's compensation act, he dissented in the Mountain Timber Co. case (243 *U.S.*, 219) which upheld the Washington compensation law. Many other examples of an apparent inconsistency could be cited. *Wilson* v. *New* was probably the most important decision he ever wrote even though the reasoning he employed left much to be desired, but he is doubtless best known for the "rule of reason" laid down in the Standard Oil and the American Tobacco cases (221 *U.S.*, 1, 106) interpreting and applying the Anti-trust Act. He had earlier announced this rule in a dissent. It must be said, however, that by applying the rule he wrote into the law something which Congress had not put there, and that he did it by a sophistical course of reasoning.

An untiring worker, courteous and devoted to the public service, he unwittingly gave an approximation of his own philosophy in a 1916 address on the death of Joseph R. Lamar. It could be said of him, as he said of Lamar, that he appreciated keenly the duty to adjust between conflicting activities so as to preserve the rights of all by protecting the rights of each, and that it was his duty to uphold and sustain the authority of the Union as to the subjects coming within the legitimate scope of its power as conferred by the Constitution. He believed that no thought of expediency, no mere convictions about economic problems, and no personal belief that the guarantees of the Constitution were becoming obsolete should sway his purpose to uphold and protect those constitutional guarantees.

WHITE, EDWARD HIGGINS, II (*b. San Antonio, Tex., 1930; d. Cape Kennedy, Fla., 1967*), U.S. Air Force officer and astronaut. Graduated from the U.S. Military Academy (1952) and received a master's degree from the University of Michigan (1959). He was accepted into the astronaut program by the National Aeronautics and Space Administration in 1962, and he was the pilot on *Gemini IV* in 1965. In 1966 he was named to the crew of the first Apollo flight. With Virgil Grissom and Roger Chaffee he was killed in a fire in the Apollo spacecraft during a preflight ground test.

WHITE, ELLEN GOULD HARMON (*b. Gorham, Maine, 1827; d. St. Helena, Calif., 1915*), Seventh-day Adventist leader. Embracing Advent faith of William Miller in the 1840's, she exerted great influence on Adventists, most of whom accepted her visions and messages as from God. Her husband, Rev. James White, managed Adventist publishing work *post* 1849. They founded the Western Health Reform Institute, Battle Creek, Mich., 1866, and promoted Battle Creek College (founded 1874). Mrs. White also helped found College of Medical Evangelists, Loma Linda, Calif., 1909.

WHITE, EMERSON ELBRIDGE (*b. Mantua, Ohio, 1829; d. 1902*), educator. Influential as editor and proprietor, *Ohio Educational Monthly*, 1861–75; as commissioner of common schools, 1863–65, he codified Ohio school laws. President, Purdue University, 1876–83. Superintendent, Cincinnati, Ohio, public schools, 1886–89. President, among other school organizations, of National Council of Education, 1884, which he helped found. Author of widely used *White's New School Register Containing Forms for Daily, Term and Yearly Records* (1891), and of a number of textbooks.

WHITE EYES (*d. 1778*), Delaware chief. Became chief sachem of the Delaware nation, 1776. Held his people neutral in early stages of the Revolution because of false representations by agent George Morgan; was deceived into signing treaty with the American states, 1778. Murdered while guiding American troops against Detroit.

WHITE, GEORGE (*b. Charleston, S.C., 1802; d. 1887*), writer, teacher, Episcopal clergyman. Self-educated, White settled in Savannah, Ga., 1823, where he established an academy and night school. He was ordained, 1833. Helped organize Georgia Historical Society, 1839. Published *Statistics of the State of Georgia* (1849), a work of great merit; also an account of the Yazoo Fraud (1852), and *Historical Collections of Georgia* (1854), a classic in Georgia bibliography. Among other church assignments, he served as rector of Calvary Church, Memphis, Tenn., 1859–85.

WHITE, GEORGE (*b. New York, N.Y., 1890; d. Los Angeles, Calif., 1968*), producer, director, actor, librettist, and lyricist. Danced in Bowery saloons, then teamed up with Benny Ryan. They appeared on Broadway in *The Echo* (1910). On his own, White appeared in the 1911 *Ziegfeld Follies*, *Vera Violetta* (1911), in which he helped to popularize the turkey trot, *The Red Widow* (1912), *The Whirl of Society* (1912), *The Pleasure Seekers* (1913), *The Midnight Girl* (1914), and the 1915 *Ziegfeld Follies*. During 1919–39 White produced thirteen editions of his musical revues called the *Scandals*. He also produced and directed *Runnin' Wild* (1923), in which the Charleston was introduced, *Manhattan Mary* (1927), *Flying High* (1930), *George White's Music Hall Varieties* (1932, 1933), and *Melody* (1933). He wrote, produced, directed, and performed in film versions of the *Scandals* (1934, 1935, 1945), and he appeared as himself in the film *Rhapsody in Blue* (1945).

WHITE, GEORGE LEONARD (*b. Cadiz, N.Y., 1838; d. Ithaca, N.Y., 1895*), conductor of Jubilee Singers of Fisk University, music teacher, self-educated, White was a choir leader in Ohio. He became instructor of vocal music at Fisk University, Nashville, Tenn., 1867, and subsequently a trustee and treasurer. To help maintain Fisk, White took a choir of his newly emancipated students on highly successful concert tours (1871–78) in America,

Great Britain, and the Continent, spreading understanding and respect for the freedmen.

WHITE, HENRY (*b. Maryland, 1732; d. England, 1786*), Loyalist, New York city merchant. Appointed to the Province Council, 1769; opposed Stamp and Townshend acts. Agent and attorney for Governor Tryon, 1774. A signer of the Loyal Address to the Howes, he served the British by equipping Tory provincial regiments and as agent for selling prizes. By Act of Attainder, 1779, his property was confiscated and he later removed to London.

WHITE, HENRY (*b. Baltimore, Md., 1850; d. Pittsfield, Mass., 1927*), diplomat. Son-in-law of Lewis M. Rutherfurd. Began career as secretary, Vienna legation, 1883; was second, then first, secretary in London, 1883–93; Richard Olney's unofficial agent in clearing up Venezuelan dispute. Resuming his London post, 1897, he served brilliantly for eight years under Ambassadors John Hay and Joseph Choate in furthering Anglo-American cooperation. Ambassador to Italy *post* March 1905, and to France, 1907–09, he was President Roosevelt's agent at the Algeciras Conference, 1906, and aided in preventing a war-menacing rupture. Head of American delegation, fourth Pan-American Conference, Buenos Aires, 1910. Appointed by President Wilson to Peace Commission, November 1918, he accompanied Wilson to Paris and strongly advocated America's entrance into the League of Nations. White might be called the first professional American diplomatist.

WHITE, HENRY CLAY (*b. Baltimore, Md., 1848; d. Athens, Ga., 1927*), chemist, educator. Graduated University of Virginia, 1870. Appointed professor of chemistry at University of Georgia, 1872; served as president, Georgia State College of Agriculture and the Mechanic Arts, 1890–1907. State chemist of Georgia, 1880–90, and vice-director, Georgia Experiment Station, 1890–1913. Organized Farmers' Institutes of Georgia.

WHITE, HORACE (*b. Colebrook, N.H., 1834; d. 1916*), journalist, economist. Raised in Beloit, Wis. Reported on Lincoln-Douglas debates, 1858, for *Chicago Tribune*, becoming friend of Lincoln and Henry Villard; was *Tribune's* Washington correspondent, 1861–65, and served as its editor-in-chief, 1865–74. Managed financial and economic policies of *New York Evening Post* and the *Nation* from *ca.* 1883; was editor in chief of the former, 1899–1903, succeeding E. L. Godkin. A free-trader and Manchester-school liberal, he threw himself into the *Evening Post's* opposition to Hawaiian annexation; he also opposed America's attitude in the Venezuelan imbroglio with England (1895), the war with Spain, and the Philippine conquest. His paper's editorial page was one of the most distinguished in American journalism. Author of *Money and Banking* (1985) and other works.

WHITE, HUGH LAWSON (*b. Iredell Co., N.C., 1773; d. near Knoxville, Tenn., 1840*), Tennessee legislator and jurist. Son of James White. Secretary to William Blount, 1793. Judge, superior court of Tennessee, 1801–07. Chosen presiding judge, supreme court of errors and appeals, 1809, he served until 1815. President, Bank of the State of Tennessee, 1812–27. U.S. senator, Democrat, from Tennessee, 1825–40. A strict constructionist, a Jeffersonian and Jacksonian Democrat, he opposed J. Q. Adam's administration. As chairman of the committee on Indian affairs, he was active in planning for Indian removal westward. President Jackson, to promote Martin Van Buren's political fortunes, attempted to force acceptance of the U.S. secretaryship of war on White, 1831; in refusing, White broke with Jackson. With John Tyler as his running mate and the support of the Whigs, he ran for the U.S. presidency in 1836 and was defeated. He favored Henry Clay for the presidency in 1840 and promised him support after

Clay's pledge not to push his nationalist program and to oppose Texas annexation. White resigned from the Senate, January 1840, when instructed by the Tennessee legislature to vote for the sub-treasury bill. Strict of conscience, he was entirely disinterested as a public servant.

WHITE, ISRAEL CHARLES (*b. Monongalia Co., present W.Va., 1848; d. Baltimore, Md., 1927*), geologist. Graduated West Virginia University, 1872; studied also at Columbia University. Held chair of geology at West Virginia, 1877–92; from 1897 until his death was superintendent of geological survey of West Virginia which he largely established; was assistant geologist on U.S. Geological Survey, 1884–88. He was author of "Stratigraphy of the Bituminous Coal Field of Pennsylvania, Ohio, and West Virginia" (1891), said to be the foundation for later work in this field. His most important work, ranking him foremost among petroleum geologists of the world, was his "anticlinal theory" of oil and gas, formulated *ca.* 1883. In it he drew the conclusion that a direct relation existed between gas territory and disturbance in rocks caused by their upheaval into arches. Successful dealings in "wildcat" leases proved his theory. His White House address "The Waste of Our Fuel Resources" (May 1908) greatly influenced the subsequent conservation movement.

WHITE, JAMES (*b. Rowan, present Iredell, Co., N.C., 1747; d. Knoxville, Tenn., 1821*), Revolutionary soldier, pioneer, North Carolina and Tennessee legislator. Father of Hugh L. White. Laid out town of Knoxville, Tenn., 1792; directed its defense against Indians, 1793. Served in 1796 convention which drew up Tennessee constitution; supported policies of William Blount and John Sevier; represented Tennessee in first treaty of Tellico, 1798. Made brigadier general, Tennessee militia, in late 1790's; he served in the Creek War, 1813.

WHITE, JAMES CLARKE (*b. Belfast, Maine, 1833; d. 1916*), dermatologist, reformer of medical education. Graduated Harvard, 1853; M.D., Harvard Medical School, 1856; did postgraduate work in Vienna. Adjunct professor of chemistry, Harvard Medical School, 1866–71; held chair of dermatology, 1871–1902. Established with B. J. Jeffries first dermatological clinic in America *ca.* 1860. President, Sixth International Dermatological Congress, 1907.

WHITE, JAMES WILLIAM (*b. Philadelphia, Pa., 1850; d. Philadelphia, 1916*), surgeon. Nephew of Samuel S. White. M.D. and Ph.D., University of Pennsylvania, 1871. Professor of clinical surgery at Pennsylvania, 1887–1900; Barton Professor of Surgery, 1900–11, becoming professor emeritus. Author, with Edward Martin, of *Genito-Urinary Surgery and Venereal Diseases* (1897), his most important work. An editor of *Annals of Surgery*, 1892–1916.

WHITE, JOHN (*fl. 1585–93*), artist, cartographer. Sent by Sir Walter Raleigh to Roanoke Island on the expedition of 1585, White painted a series of sketches in water color depicting the flora and fauna of America as well as the appearance of the native Indians. These first scientific and careful studies are primary historical sources. They were later adapted in engravings by Theodore de Bry for the 1590 edition of Thomas Hariot's *A Briefe and True Report of Virginia*. It is possible that he was the John White who served as governor of Raleigh's "second colonie," Roanoke, Va., *post* 1587.

WHITE, JOHN BLAKE (*b. near Eutaw Springs, S.C., 1781; d. ca. 1859*), artist, dramatist, lawyer. Studied under Benjamin West, 1800–03. Settled in Charleston, S.C., 1804, where he remained for most of his life. Between 1804 and 1840 he produced historical pictures (four in the U.S. Capitol) and portraits; also painted miniatures. Among his plays were *Foscari* (1806) and *The Triumph of Liberty, or Louisiana Preserved* (1819).

WHITE, JOHN DE HAVEN (*b. near New Holland, Pa., 1815; d. Philadelphia, Pa., 1895*), dentist. Practiced in Philadelphia *post* 1837. Graduated Jefferson Medical College, 1844. Teacher of Thomas W. Evans and Samuel S. White. An organizer of Philadelphia College of Dental Surgery, he was professor of anatomy and physiology and of operative dental surgery and special dental physiology, 1854–56. Author of numerous professional papers.

WHITE, JOHN WILLIAMS (*b. Cincinnati, Ohio, 1849; d. Cambridge, Mass., 1917*), Hellenist. Graduated Ohio Wesleyan, 1868; Ph.D., Harvard, 1877. Taught Greek at Harvard, 1874–1909. Aided President C. W. Eliot in expansion of the college into a university. Broke from older teaching methods by insisting on wide and rapid reading in his courses on Greek authors; was expert in Greek meters. Founded with J. B. Greenough and helped edit the *Harvard Studies in Classical Philology*; with C. E. Norton and W. W. Goodwin, organized Archaeological Institute of America, 1879. Influenced James Loeb; helped establish Loeb Classical Library.

WHITE, JOSEPH MALACHY (*b. New York, N.Y., 1891; d. New York, 1959*), composer and singer. One of the first recording artists and radio singers, White was an Irish tenor. He became famous while performing with the B.F. Goodrich Silvertown Orchestra on radio from 1924 to 1930. Known as "The Silver-Masked Tenor," White sang on radio and in vaudeville until 1943, when his leg had to be amputated because of an accident. Songs he composed include "Maureen Mavourneen," "In Flanders," and "Drifting in the Moonlight."

WHITE, JOSH (*b. Greenville, S.C., 1915; d. Manhasset, N.Y., 1969*), guitarist and folksinger. He also performed as Tippy Barton, Pinewood Tom, and the Singing Christian. From the age of seven wandered the streets of southeastern cities and Chicago, leading a series of blind street singers and learning their songs. He recorded Blind Joe Taggart and Blind Lemon Jefferson. He performed in New York City with Clarence Williams' "Southernaires" and in 1939 formed the Josh White Singers. White appeared on Broadway in *John Henry* (1940), *Blue Holiday* (1945), and *A Long Way from Home* (1948). He recorded and appeared with Leadbelly and became a favorite performer of President Roosevelt, entertaining frequently at the White House. His best-known songs include "Ball and Chain Blues," "Delia," "Hard Times Blues," "Jim Crow Train," "Silicosis Blues," "Uncle Sam Says," and "Welfare Blues." Described as "a pre-Belafonte black sex idol," he was a major contributor to the blues and to American folk music.

WHITE, LEONARD DUPEE (*b. Acton, Mass., 1891; d. Chicago, Ill., 1958*), political scientist. Studied at Dartmouth College and at the University of Chicago (Ph.D., 1921). Taught at the University of Chicago, 1920–56, chairman of the political science department, 1940–48. An expert in public administration and the civil service, White was a member of the Committee on Social Trends from 1929. From 1934 to 1936 he was commissioner of the U.S. Civil Service Commission; and from 1939 to 1941 he was a member of Roosevelt's Committee on Civil Service Improvement. Major works include histories of the American civil service and public administration: *The Federalists* (1948); *The Jeffersonians* (1951); *The Jacksonians* (1954); and *The Republican Era, 1869–1901* (1958), which won him the Pulitzer Prize in 1959. President of the American Political Science Association in 1944.

WHITE, PEARL (*b. Greenridge, Mo., 1889; d. Paris, France, 1938*), motion picture actress, star of *The Perils of Pauline* (1914) and other popular serial motion pictures.

WHITE, RICHARD GRANT (*b. New York, N.Y., 1821; d. New York, 1885*), writer. Graduated present New York University, 1839. Won distinction as musical critic of *Morning Courier and New-York Enquirer*. Wrote extensively for *Putnam's Magazine*, *Galaxy*, *Atlantic Monthly*, and London *Spectator*. Author, among other works, of *The New Gospel of Peace* (anonymous, 1863–66), *Words and Their Uses* (1870), and *Studies in Shakespeare* (1886). An acute Shakespeare scholar, he edited *The Works of William Shakespeare* (1857–66). He was father of Stanford White.

WHITE, SAMUEL (*b. Kent Co., Del., 1770; d. Wilmington, Del., 1809*), lawyer. Admitted to the Delaware bar, 1793. U.S. senator, Federalist, from Delaware, 1801 until his death.

WHITE, SAMUEL STOCKTON (*b. Hulmeville, Pa., 1822; d. Paris, France, 1879*), dental supplies manufacturer, dentist. Credited with important improvements in porcelain teeth; also introduced new or improved dental appliances and instruments.

WHITE, STANFORD (*b. New York, N.Y., 1853; d. New York, 1906*), architect. Son of Richard G. White. Worked in firm of Gambrill & Richardson as close associate of H. H. Richardson *post ca.* 1872; was associated with Charles F. McKim and W. R. Mead and others in McKim, Mead & White *post* 1880. A friend of Augustus Saint-Gaudens, White designed the pedestal for Saint-Gaudens' statue of Farragut in Madison Square, New York City (unveiled, 1881), for which he received much praise. Operating on the theory that all things intrinsically good can be brought into harmony, White worked with great skill in a number of styles; he planned luxurious city and country houses, designed furniture, ransacked Europe for interior decorations, designed magazine covers, gravestones, and jewelry. The splendid success of McKim, Mead & White was aided by the rapid contemporary increase in wealth in America and the desire of the traveled wealthy for a share in Old World art and culture. White was notably successful among his partners in impressing wealthy clients with a respect for the beautiful even though they might fail to understand it, and was aptly called the protagonist of popular art in New York City. Among the number of churches which he designed, the Judson Memorial in Washington Square, New York City, remains as an example. He was designer also of a number of clubs including the Metropolitan Club, New York City, his supreme achievement in Renaissance architecture. His work has been described as graceful and charming rather than imposing; among his most enduring achievements are the Washington Arch (New York City) and the Prison Ship Martyrs Monument, Brooklyn, N.Y. His business buildings included the one-time Gorham and Tiffany buildings on Fifth Avenue, New York City, and he was the designer (1889) of the original Madison Square Garden. There he met his death, murdered by Harry K. Thaw.

WHITE, STEPHEN MALLORY (*b. San Francisco, Calif., 1853; d. Los Angeles, Calif., 1901*), lawyer. Admitted to the bar, 1874, he began successful practice in Los Angeles, Calif. U.S. senator, Democrat, from California, 1893–99. Favored free coinage of silver, opposed imperialism, and championed the "country" voters against monopolistic aggression. Defeated C. P. Huntington's plans to divert federal funds from San Pedro to harbor site desired by Southern Pacific Railroad.

WHITE, STEPHEN VAN CULEN (*b. Chatham Co., N.C., 1831; d. 1913*), banker, lawyer. Raised in Illinois. Practiced law in Iowa, 1856–64, and was acting U.S. district attorney for Iowa, 1864. Became member of New York Stock Exchange, 1869,

where he was soon known as a daring manipulator, especially in shares of Delaware, Lackawanna & Western Railroad. Congressman, Republican, from New York, 1887–89. He was a friend of Henry Ward Beecher and long the treasurer of Plymouth Church.

WHITE, STEWART EDWARD (*b. Grand Rapids, Mich., 1873; d. San Francisco, Calif., 1946*), author. Traveled widely as a child and youth in the wilder parts of the West and Canada, which lent verisimilitude to his action-filled, romantic stories. A lover of adventure and the outdoors, he worked at various times as trapper and lumberjack; in later life, he traveled and explored in East Africa. Among his books (which included novels, travel books, juveniles, and collections of essays and short stories) were: *The Westerners* (1901); *The Blazed Trail* (1902); *Arizona Nights* (1907); his carefully researched fictional history of California in *Gold* (1913); *The Gray Dawn* (1915); *The Rose Dawn* (1920); *The Leopard Woman* (1916); and *The Long Rifle* (1932).

WHITE, THOMAS WILLIS (*b. Williamsburg, Va., 1788; d. New York, N.Y., 1843*), printer. Established successful printing business in Richmond, Va., ca. 1817. Founded (1834) the *Southern Literary Messenger*, of which Edgar Allan Poe was editor, 1835–37.

WHITE, WALTER FRANCIS (*b. Atlanta, Ga., 1893; d. New York, N.Y., 1955*), civil rights leader. Studied at Atlanta University. Member of the NAACP, 1918–55; assistant secretary of the national staff, 1918–31; from 1931, executive secretary. Only one-fourth black and fair-complexioned, White wrote a novel *Flight* (1926) telling of experiences of passing for white. In 1929, he wrote *Rope and Faggot; A Biography of Judge Lynch*, a study of the complex forces behind lynching. Under White's leadership, the NAACP embarked on its most important legal battles: antilynching legislation, the press for equality in public conveniences, education, and the professions, and the battle for equality in elections and voting rights. In 1946 he led a delegation to the White House and persuaded President Truman to establish the President's Committee on Civil Rights which led to the controversial civil rights platform in the 1948 Democratic campaign. In 1945 he published *A Rising Wind*, an exposé of discrimination against black soldiers which led to Truman's 1948 executive order desegregating the armed forces. In spite of friction within the NAACP, White remained a leader of the organization until his death.

WHITE, WILLIAM (*b. Philadelphia, Pa., 1748 n.s.; d. Philadelphia, 1836*), Episcopal clergyman. Graduated College of Philadelphia, 1765; ordained deacon in London, England, 1770, and priest, 1772. Principal rectorate at Christ Church, Philadelphia. Largely devised plan for organization of Protestant Episcopal Church in the United States (1785–89) on principle that laity should have an equal part with clergy in all legislation; drafted original constitution of Church and secured its adoption. With William Smith, he was chiefly responsible for the American revision of the Book of Common Prayer. Consecrated bishop of Pennsylvania in England, 1787, he served with tact and ability and was presiding bishop *post* 1796. Noted for active promotion of Sunday School work; trained, among other clergyman, W. A. Muhlenberg and J. H. Hobart. Long chaplain of Congress, he published, among other works, *Comparative Views of the Controversy between the Calvinists and the Arminians* (1817) and *Memoirs of the Protestant Episcopal Church in the United States of America* (1820).

WHITE, WILLIAM ALANSON (*b. Brooklyn, N.Y., 1870; d. Washington, D.C., 1937*), psychiatrist, hospital administrator. M.D., Long Island College Hospital, 1891. Influenced by Boris

Sidis while at Binghamton (N.Y.) State Hospital. Superintendent of the present St. Elizabeth's Hospital, Washington, D.C., *post* 1903, he established a psychological laboratory there, developed department of internal medicine, and was an early exponent of psychoanalysis. Under his leadership the hospital became one of the leading centers of psychiatric care and training in the United States. A professor at Georgetown and George Washington universities, he also taught in the army and navy medical schools; he was president of the first International Congress on Mental Hygiene, Washington, D.C., 1930. Among his many publications was *The Outlines of Psychiatry* (1907).

WHITE, WILLIAM ALLEN (*b. Emporia, Kans., 1868; d. Emporia, 1944*), newspaper editor, author. Raised in Eldorado, Kans., son of a physician-druggist, he was accustomed to hear public issues debated at home and so learned a lifelong tolerance for contrary views. Taught to honor the Puritan conscience, he attended Sunday schools and camp meetings, but did not join the Congregational Church until he was an adult. His father died in the midst of financial reverses when White was in high school. He attended the College of Emporia (1884–86) and the University of Kansas, 1886–90, but did not graduate. After a series of newspaper jobs, White borrowed $3,000 in 1895 and bought the daily *Emporia Gazette*. His lively, conversational editorial style soon made him the most celebrated person in town and his Aug. 15, 1896, editorial entitled "What's the matter with Kansas?" made him nationally famous. Republican editors in Chicago and new York reprinted it, and in the year of the campaign against William Jennings Bryan and free silver, the Republican national chairman, Marcus A. Hanna, distributed more than a million copies over the country. For *McClure's* he wrote a series of boyhood stories later collected as *The Court of Boyville* (1899). A group of fictionalized articles on politics for *Scribner's Magazine*, published in 1901 as *Stratagems and Spoils*, reflected his Republican conservatism.

By 1901 his political outlook had begun to change. On his first trip east, in 1897, he met Theodore Roosevelt, who quickly became his political hero. White began to see a need for government regulation of business and such reforms as the direct primary. He also met S. S. McClure and formed friendships with Lincoln Steffens and Ray Stannard Baker. When in 1906 Steffens, Baker, Ida M. Tarbell, and others took over the *American* magazine, White joined them as an Emporia-based editorial associate. His articles for the *American* and *Collier's* now expounded progressive ideas. In Kansas he worked to build up a reform-minded antirailroad wing of the Republican party. White helped found the National Progressive Republican League in 1911 and was an early supporter of Robert M. La Follette for president. The next year he followed Roosevelt into the Progressive party.

After the Progressive spell broke, White returned, disheartened, to the Republican fold. He praised Wilson's progressivism in 1913, and during the war years he backed the government's control of prices, wages, and the railroads and vigorously supported the League of Nations. A mission to inspect Red Cross services took him overseas in 1917, and in 1919 he reported the Paris Peace Conference.

As a member of the platform committee of the Republican national conventions of 1920 and 1928 he sought, with little success, to commit the party to more progressive policies. He supported the unions in the 1922 railroad strike, during which he was briefly under arrest for displaying a pro-union poster in the window of the *Gazette* office. His editorial during the controversy received a Pulitzer Prize. He was an uncompromising foe of the Ku Klux Klan. When in 1924 he could not persuade either candidate for governor of Kansas to oppose the Klan, he ran as an independent, delighting in the opportunity to speak out against intolerance. Yet White shared a small-town dislike of the cities and their way of life that, together with his strong prohibitionism,

led him to attack Alfred E. Smith in the campaign of 1928 with a severity that distressed even members of his family.

White's attitude toward the New Deal was ambivalent. He did not wholly trust Franklin D. Roosevelt and criticized many of his specific proposals. White's efforts to liberalize the Republican platform in 1936 were again unsuccessful, and his backing of his fellow Kansan Alfred M. Landon was less than enthusiastic. White was most consistent in his endorsement of Roosevelt's foreign policies. After the outbreak of World War II he became a leading advocate of supplying Britain and France with arms and war materials. For nearly a half-century the sage of Emporia was nationally recognized as a spokesman and interpreter of rank-and-file, first-name, commonsense, God-fearing, good-neighbor, small-town, Main Street America.

WHITE, WILLIAM NATHANIEL (*b. Longridge, Conn., 1819; d. 1867*), horticulturist, editor. Settled in Georgia, 1847. Authority on pomology, horticulture, and rural economy, he became editor (1863) and owner (1865) of the *Southern Cultivator*. Author of *Gardening for the South* (1856), a standard work.

WHITEFIELD, GEORGE (*b. Gloucester, England, 1714 o.s.; d. Newburyport, Mass., 1770*), clergyman, evangelist. The son of a tavern keeper, but descended from a line of clergymen, Whitefield as a boy was impetuous and emotional, but his own picture of his youthful depravity is doubtless over-colored. Admitted as a servitor to Pembroke College, Oxford, 1732, he made the acquaintance of Charles and John Wesley. Adopting a rule of life and engaging in charitable activities, he behaved with such fanatical zeal that he became seriously ill late in the spring of 1735. Experiencing a "new birth" at this time, he was filled with a sense of the pardoning love of God and became convinced that such an experience was indispensable to all individuals in search of religious conviction. While recovering from his illness, he converted some of his friends and formed a religious society; he devoted a part of each day to corporal works of mercy. Returning to Oxford, March 1736, he was admitted to deacon's orders in Gloucester Cathedral in June. The powerful effect of his first sermon upon his fellow townsmen was prophetic of the power over audiences which he was to exhibit later. In July he was graduated as B.A. from Oxford and, as the Wesleys were now in Georgia, he became leader of the few Methodists left at the university. Taking every opportunity offered to preach his idea of the "new birth," he soon achieved extraordinary prominence in several provincial cities and in London, incidentally collecting large sums of money for the Georgia mission of the Wesleys and for charity schools. Soon attacked by conservative churchmen, he left for Georgia on Dec. 30, 1737, accompanied by friends, one of whom was James Habersham.

Undiscouraged by the unsatisfactory experiences of the Wesley brothers in Georgia, Whitefield landed at Savannah on May 7; during a four-months' stay, he began services, started several schools, and determined to establish an orphanage. Returning to England in September 1738, he was ordained priest in January 1739, but encountered further bitter opposition at home and was denied use of churches for preaching. Accepting the use of halls and other meeting places, he continued his preaching work, delivering his first open-air sermon on Feb. 17, 1739, to a group of colliers near Bristol; soon he was preaching at many of the public resorts of the London populace. Accused of ignorance and Pharisaism (with considerable justification), he persevered in his work as an itinerant preacher to constantly increasing audiences, and won the patronage of several members of the aristocracy, notably the Countess of Huntingdon.

Departing once again for America, August 1739, he remained there for more than a year, although his parish at Savannah saw little of him. He spent most of his time in further itinerant preaching which awakened religious excitement all the way from

Georgia to Massachusetts; encouraged by the Presbyterians and Congregationalists, he was opposed by clergy of the Church of England. Among his supporters among the Presbyterians were William and Gilbert Tennent. During a brief stay in Savannah, he began construction of the orphanage which he had planned, giving it the name Bethesda, but he soon made himself disliked by his general attitude of censoriousness and his abuse of fellow clergymen. Setting out once again to visit the North, he preached with great effect in Philadelphia and in New York; among his triumphs was the securing of a donation for his orphanage from Benjamin Franklin. Summoned before an ecclesiastical court in Charleston, S.C., June 1740, because of irregularities in doctrine and practice, he denied the court's jurisdiction, failed to appear and was suspended, but did not cease his activities. Journeying to New England, he produced there the same great religious awakening that he had already produced in the Middle Colonies. On his leisurely return southward he stopped in many places, visiting Jonathan Edwards at Northampton, Mass., and when in New Brunswick, N.J., persuading Gilbert Tennent to go to Boston and further the revival which was in progress there. He sailed for England in January 1741, and almost four years elapsed before he was once again in America.

Whitefield had by now become a rigid Calvinist and engaged in a unpleasant controversy with John Wesley. His admirers had built the Tabernacle for him in London, but he continued his wanderings and his field-preaching in all parts of the British Isles. In Wales he was made moderator of the first Calvinistic Methodist Conference. Married in Wales, November 1741, he left England for America with his wife in August 1744, landing at the present York, Maine. Since his first visit to New England, a spirit of opposition to him had arisen in many of the Congregational leaders, foremost among whom was Charles Chauncy (1705–1787). Yet he had strong supporters and his preaching continued to draw large audiences. Removing to Georgia at the end of 1745, he spent part of the next two years there and in evangelistic journeys; in 1748 he went to Bermuda and returned to England during that same summer to become domestic chaplain to the Countess of Huntingdon. He also continued his preaching in London and throughout the British Isles.

His activities in Great Britain were broken by four more visits to America. In 1751–52 he spent some seven months in Georgia and the Carolinas; in 1754–55 he spent about the same period of time on a preaching itinerary that included Philadelphia, New York, Virginia, and parts of New England. Returning in September 1763, he remained until *ca.* 1765, traveling and preaching as always, and also petitioning Georgia for a grant of land for establishment of a college at Bethesda; this failed because of opposition in England. In September 1769 he left England for the last time, arriving in Charleston, S.C., in November, and proceeding to Bethesda. In the spring of 1770 he entered on a most strenuous itinerary, preaching in Pennsylvania, New York, and New England, during which he met his death at Newburyport, Mass.

A man of middle stature, graceful, although somewhat fleshy in his later years, he had a fair complexion and small, keen dark-blue eyes in one of which was a noticeable squint. When speaking, he used many gestures; his voice was strong and musical and his mastery of it was perfect; his histrionic gifts would have made him one of the immortals of the stage and he was a master of pathos. He followed a simple and orderly manner of life. Easily irritated, he was as easily placated. His influence in America, quite apart from that which he exerted in Great Britain, was far-reaching. He stimulated a religious awakening which had already begun and by his preaching added thousands to the churches. The doctrinal discussions which arose in his wake resulted in a definitely American contribution to theology. He gave impetus to education and to philanthropic work. It is fair to say that because he made the

denominations intercolonial and encouraged his followers to ignore parish and sectional lines, he made a very real contribution to the creation of a distinct Americanism among the colonies. His work also encouraged limitation of ecclesiastical and political authority and advocated freedom of conscience and individual liberty; his weakening of the Church of England in the South loosened one of the closest links between the colonies and the mother country. In these and other respects the Great Awakening prepared the way for revolution and independence.

WHITEHEAD, ALFRED NORTH (*b. Ramsgate, Isle of Thanet, Kent, England, 1861; d. Cambridge, Mass., 1947*), philosopher. Son of an Anglican clergyman, who had been headmaster of a private school; educated at home until age fourteen, when he was sent to school at Sherborne in Dorset. He was outstanding there in mathematical studies and rugby; in his last year, he was head prefect and captain of games. In 1880 he matriculated at Trinity College, Cambridge (B.A., 1884). In October of that year he was elected a fellow of Trinity (his dissertation was on Clerk Maxwell's theory of electricity and magnetism) and appointed an assistant lecturer in mathematics, becoming the senior lecturer in 1903. He earned the D.Sc. in 1905.

Whitehead wrote few papers in mathematics, although he taught that subject for thirty-nine years. He was most interested in those newer branches that went beyond the traditional notion of what mathematics was—quaternions, the Boolean algebra of logic, and Grassmann's calculus of extension. The first volume of his *Treatise on Universal Algebra* (1898) secured his election to the Royal Society in 1903. He abandoned a second volume to collaborate with Bertrand Russell on *Principia Mathematica*, which is generally considered one of the great intellectual monuments of all time. In January 1901 Russell secured Whitehead's collaboration on the second volume of his *Principles*. Russell always deplored the tendency of scholars to give him the major credit for *Principia Mathematica*. Most of the work was done by 1909, and the three huge volumes were published in 1910–13. Whitehead began a fourth volume, but he never finished it.

In 1910 Whitehead resigned his lectureship and moved to London. In this year he wrote *Introduction to Mathematics*. University College in 1911 made him lecturer in applied mathematics and mechanics and in 1912 appointed him reader in geometry. In 1914 Whitehead was elected to the chair of applied mathematics at the Imperial College of Science and Technology, where he remained until 1924. If the fourth volume of *Principia Mathematica* had been finished, it would have presented a complete theory of geometry, conceived as the first chapter of natural science. The development of Whitehead's thought went into three books on the foundations of natural science: *An Enquiry Concerning the Principles of Natural Knowledge* (1919), *The Concept of Nature* (1920), and *The Principle of Relativity* (1922).

In a memoir published by the Royal Society in 1906, Whitehead had expressed the classical concept of the material world (as composed of particles occupying points of space at instants of time) and some theoretical alternatives to it. The main purpose of the *Enquiry* was to replace the classical concept, with its unperceivable points and instants, by a coherent set of meanings defined in terms logically derived from the kinds of data and of relationships that are given in every external perception. The *Enquiry* was highly original, but it was too philosophical and the paths to the required definitions were too intricate to influence physicists. His principle of relativity was explored by a few mathematical physicists but could not compete with Einstein's.

Whitehead was more successful with philosophers, and *The Concept of Nature*, a nonmathematical companion to his *Enquiry*, made a great impression. In 1924 Harvard offered him a five-year appointment, as professor of philosophy. Whitehead had made a point of excluding metaphysics from his work on the basic concepts of natural science; now he felt his way into a metaphysical position that would embody that work and satisfy his convictions about value and existence. He emphasized the continuing disastrous effect on Western culture of "scientific materialism." The most striking thing here was Whitehead's appeal to his favorite poets, Wordsworth and Shelley, against the extrusion of values from nature. He held that philosophic theory must not defy, but elucidate, the unsophisticated intuitive experience of mankind and that the deepest expression of these institutions is found in great poetry.

In 1926 Whitehead published *Religion in the Making*. He argued that religion needs a metaphysics and makes its own contribution to metaphysics. His discussions of religious experience and expression and of the use and misuse of dogmas were short and pointed. He attempted a compressed presentation of his metaphysical system at the University of Edinburgh in June 1928. Because of its complexity and the new terminology required, the lectures were a fiasco, but their publication in 1929 was an important event in the history of metaphysics.

The central notion in Whitehead's speculative philosophy was that of a process, or becoming, and it was handled in an original way. No one before Whitehead had produced a full-fledged non-Hegelian theory of process. As Whitehead was aware (although not in detail), some Buddhistic philosophies long ago had made process ultimate; but they sought intuitive, not intellectual, understanding of it. Whitehead's concept of becoming was based on his analysis of an occasion of human experience, considered in its entirety and not as limited to what we are conscious of. In *Symbolism: Its Meaning and Effect* (1927) he argued that a vague, but insistent, perception of casual efficacy underlies all our sensory impressions. In *Process and Reality*, he developed the thesis that an experience is fundamentally a process of absorbing the past and making ourselves different by actualizing some value-potentialities and rejecting others.

In an experience-event, so conceived, consciousness, thought, and sense perception may be absent. The basic pattern could be ascribed to an amoeba and even to the inanimate—not to rocks, but to their molecules or to subatomic particles—by permitting novelty to be negligible or limited to alternation. Whitehead fashioned a conceptual matrix for all levels of existence with his speculative hypothesis: the ultimate units of the entire temporal world ("actual occasions") are becomings, each an individual process of appropriating (prehending) into its perspective the infinity of items ("reality") provided by the antecedent universe of finished becomings and by God, the abiding source of new potentialities. As each becoming is the achievement of an organic unity, Whitehead called his metaphysics "the philosophy of organism." According to it, living things are those organizations of becoming that show a marked degree of coordinated initiative in their reactions to the pressures of their environments, and any object that we meet in everyday life or in science is a group of interdependent series ("societies") of becomings that maintain a certain character for a certain time. The various sciences of course use their own concepts of process; Whitehead's hope was that these (e.g., wave transmission of energy, nutrition, communication) could be placed under his metaphysical theory, in accordance with the special abstractions that each science makes in delimiting its topic, and he made some suggestions toward this end. As for our laws of nature, Whitehead thought it parochial to suppose them eternal; they only express average regularities that prevail in what he called "our present cosmic epoch."

The many principles that appear in Whitehead's formal statement of his speculative hypothesis presuppose three notions implicit in that of becoming: "many," "one," and "creativity." Whitehead tried to fashion and interweave his concepts in such a way as to bridge every traditional dualism. Whitehead would not allow anything in his universe the possibility of existing in independence of other things. His metaphysics is a unified monadology, much richer than Leibniz's.

The originality of Whitehead's theism stems from his way of conceiving of God and the temporal world as mutually dependent and of both as "in the grip of the ultimate metaphysical ground, the creative advance into novelty." This conception of a growing God has become the most favored and most discussed part of Whitehead's metaphysics. In *Adventures of Ideas* (1933) Whitehead used his lifetime of reading in history to bring out the humanistic and sociological side of his philosophy. It was the third and last of his major American books, and the best for most readers.

Whitehead's published writings do not show that his metaphysics was implicit in the work he did while a mathematician; they do exhibit the same imaginative mind seeking, in each area it dealt with, a precision and a generality beyond that of familiar terms. Whitehead was a speculative thinker—indeed, one of the greatest—with a great respect for facts and a healthy disrespect for their compartmentalization and conventional expression. The rarity of such disrespect in his readers accounts for the frequency with which his philosophical writing is called deliberately obscure. Harvard revised the terms of his appointment and did not retire him until 1937.

Whitehead, Wilbur Cherrier (*b. Cleveland, Ohio, 1866; d. at sea, 1931*), bridge expert. Author of *Whitehead's Conventions of Auction Bridge* (1914) and *Auction Bridge Standards* (1921). Contributed a complete tabulation of conventions of play and desirable leads and a complete bidding system. A founder and first president of the Cavendish Club.

Whitehead, William Adee (*b. Newark, N.J., 1810; d. 1884*), historian. Collector of the port of Key West, Fla., 1813–38, and also mayor. A leading organizer of the New Jersey Historical Society, 1845, and its secretary until his death, he published, among other works, *East Jersey Under the Proprietary Governments* (1846); *The Papers of Lewis Morris* (1852); and *Documents Relating to the Colonial History of the State of New Jersey* (1880–85).

Whitehill, Clarence Eugene (*b. Marengo, Iowa, 1871; d. New York, N.Y., 1932*), opera singer. Studied in Paris, 1896, at urging of Melba and Campanari. Made debut, 1899, as Friar Lawrence in *Romeo and Juliet* at Théâtre de la Monnaie, Brussels. Leading baritone, Cologne Opera House, 1903–08. Well known for Wagnerian roles, he sang at Metropolitan Opera House, N.Y., 1909–11, 1915–32.

Whitehill, Robert (*b. Lancaster Co., Pa., 1738; d. near Harrisburg, Pa., 1813*), Pennsylvania legislator and official. Played an important part in drafting the state constitution (1776) and was principal aide of George Bryan. A strong anti-Federalist and democrat, he was one of the group which set up a vehement opposition in the Pennsylvania back country, whose suspicions of central government he reflected in the Pennsylvania convention to ratify the Federal Constitution. Congressman, Democratic-Republican, from Pennsylvania, 1805 until his death.

Whitehouse, Frederic Cope (*b. Rochester, N.Y., 1842; d. New York, N.Y., 1911*), lawyer, archeologist. Chiefly interested in Egyptology, he was author, among other writings, of *Lake Moeris: Justification of Herodotus* (1885), *Memorandum on the Raiyan Project and the Action of Her Majesty's Government* (1891), and *The Assuan Reservation and Lake Moeris* (1914). Devoted many years to promotion of plan for irrigation of lower Egypt by impounding surplus Nile flood-waters.

WHITEMAN, PAUL SAMUEL ("POPS") (*b. Denver, Colo., 1890; d. Doylestown, Pa., 1967*), bandleader. Played with the symphony orchestras in Denver and San Francisco. In 1919 he formed the "original" Paul Whiteman orchestra. In concert in 1924 he performed the number that became most associated with him, *Rhapsody in Blue*, with the composer, George Gershwin, playing the piano part. Known as the "King of Jazz," Whiteman starred in numerous radio programs beginning in the mid-1920's. In 1929 he hired the vocalist Mildred Bailey. In 1943 he became musical director of the Blue Network, later known as the American Broadcasting Company. He was a vice president of the ABC network (1947−55). Also appeared in films and television.

WHITESIDE, ARTHUR DARE (*b. East Orange, N.J., 1882; d. New York, N.Y., 1960*), executive. Studied at Princeton University. As president of National Credit from 1912, Whiteside succeeded in incorporating National Credit, R.G. Dun and the Bradstreet Company, into Dun and Bradstreet, Inc., (1933). He served as president until 1952, and served on the board of directors until his death. The company became the nation's leading credit reporting bureau.

WHITFIELD, HENRY (*b. near London, England, 1597; d. Winchester, England, 1657/8*), nonconformist clergyman, settler. Friend of George Fenwick. Came to New Haven Colony, 1639; returned to England, 1650. Founded, with William Leete and others, the town of Guilford, Conn.; preached to Indians and aided John Eliot in work of conversion. Cotton Mather spoke of the "marvelous majesty and sanctity" of his preaching.

WHITFIELD, OWEN (*b. Jamestown, Miss., 1892; d. Cape Girardeau, Mo., 1965*), Baptist minister and union organizer. Attended Okolona College, and by the 1930's had become pastor of a number of rural churches. Joined the Southern Tenant Farmers Union (1937) and became one of the union's best organizers. In January 1939 he organized a massive roadside demonstration in Missouri to protest mass evictions of croppers and tenant farmers (a device common to the civil rights protests of the 1950's and 1960's). The demonstration did not produce radical changes in farm policy, and he again became minister of several churches.

WHITFIELD, ROBERT PARR (*b. New Hartford, N.Y., 1828; d. Troy, N.Y., 1910*), draftsman, paleontologist. Became chief illustrator, New York State geological survey, 1856; for twenty years, made highly finished drawings of fossils for reports of James Hall. Curator of geology, American Museum of Natural History, New York City, 1877−1909, he identified and classified the James Hall fossil collection and others; prepared and published a catalogue of museum's 8,000 types and figured specimens; helped establish museum's *Bulletin*.

WHITING, ARTHUR BATTELLE (*b. Cambridge, Mass., 1861; d. Beverly, Mass., 1936*), pianist, teacher, composer. Nephew of George E. Whiting. Studied in Boston with William H. Sherwood and George W. Chadwick; in Munich with Josef Rheinberger and Ludwig Abel. Best known for his "university concerts" of chamber music at many Eastern colleges and universities, he was a composer in the classic spirit whose high musical ideals and severity of judgment limited his output of composition. His most admired work was a Fantasy for Piano and Orchestra (1897).

WHITING, CHARLES GOODRICH (*b. St. Albans, Vt., 1842; d. Otis, Mass., 1922*), journalist. Literary editor, *Springfield Republican*, 1874−1910; associate editor, 1910−19. Author of *The Saunterer* (1886) and *Walks in New England* (1903).

WHITING, GEORGE ELBRIDGE (*b. Holliston, Mass., 1840; d. Cambridge, Mass., 1923*), organist, composer, organ teacher. Head of organ and composition department, College of Music, Cincinnati, Ohio, 1878−82; organist and music director, Church of the Immaculate Conception, Boston, Mass., 1882−1910. Principal instructor of organ, New England Conservatory of Music, 1876−78 and 1882−98.

WHITING, WILLIAM (*b. Concord, Mass., 1813; d. Roxbury, Mass., 1873*), lawyer, public official. Graduated Harvard, 1833; LL.B., 1838. Eminent in his own field of patent law, he served during the Civil War as a special counselor of the U.S. War Department, and as its solicitor, 1863−65. He was author of two useful tracts, *The War Powers of the President, etc.* (1862) and *Military Arrests in Time of War* (1863), together with other works.

WHITING, WILLIAM HENRY CHASE (*b. Biloxi, Miss., 1824; d. Governors Island, N.Y., 1865*), Confederate major general. Graduated West Point, 1845. As chief engineer of General J. E. Johnston's Army of the Shenandoah, he arranged transfer of troops to Manassas, 1861, where he was promoted brigadier general by order of President Davis. At Gaines's Mill the conduct of his division was characterized by General T. J. Jackson as a "matchless display of valor." Assumed command (November 1862) of the military district of Wilmington, N.C., which he guarded for two years, making Cape Fear River the best haven in the South for blockade runners. Developed Fort Fisher into the most powerful defensive work of the Confederacy. Heroically aided Colonel Lamb in defense of Fort Fisher, 1865.

WHITLOCK, BRAND (*b. Urbana, Ohio, 1869; d. Cannes, France, 1934*), writer, diplomat. A journalist in Toledo, Ohio, 1887−90, and in Chicago, Ill., 1891−93, he was admitted to the Illinois bar, 1894. Mayor "Golden Rule" Jones's legal adviser in Toledo, he succeeded Jones as mayor of Toledo (1905−13) on a home-rule, nonpartisan, anti-monopoly platform. Became U.S. minister to Belgium, 1913. Remaining in Brussels after the outbreak of World War I, he helped organize non-resistance and relief projects. Highly honored by the Belgian government, he held advanced rank of ambassador to Belgium, 1919−22. Author of, among other books, *Forty Years of It* (1914), the record of his adventures in liberalism; *Turn of the Balance* (1907), his most considered novel; and *Belgium: A Personal Record* (1919), his best-known work. His fiction is concerned in great part with the technique and problems of justice administration.

WHITMAN, ALBERY ALLSON (*b. Hart Co., Ky., 1851; d. Atlanta, Ga., 1901*), poet, clergyman of African Methodist Episcopal Church. Born in slavery, he was associated with Wilberforce University and was influential in establishing many churches. Author of, among other books, *Leelah Misled* (1873) and *An Idyl of the South* (1901). Whitman's poetry is essentially derivative, yet it is fluent and shows a real, unforced love of nature. He is the most considerable black poet before Paul L. Dunbar.

WHITMAN, CHARLES OTIS (*b. North Woodstock, Maine, 1842; d. Chicago, Ill., 1910*), biologist. Graduated Bowdoin, 1868; Ph.D., Leipzig, 1877. Taught at Imperial University of Japan, Harvard, and Clark; headed zoology department, University of Chicago *post* 1892. Directed Marine Biological Laboratory, Woods Hole, Mass., from its foundation in 1888 until 1908. His main scientific contributions were in embryology, comparative anatomy, taxonomy, evolution, heredity, and animal behavior. Introduced European scientific zoology into America, founding in 1887 the *Journal of Morphology* and establishing new standards for American scientific publication.

WHITMAN, CHARLES SEYMOUR (*b. Hanover, Conn., 1868; d. New York, N.Y., 1947*), lawyer, politician, public official. Graduated Amherst College, 1890. LL.B., New York University, 1894. Active in New York City Republican politics while he was building a private practice; he was appointed to a place in the corporation counsel's office in 1902 and made a magistrate in 1903. Whitman was the compromise choice for chief of the city's Board of Magistrates in March 1907 and almost immediately set about making headlines by conducting a drive against payoffs to local police by bail bondsmen and the keepers of after-hours saloons. In 1909 he was the successful reform candidate for district attorney of New York County. During this period he established a mutually convenient alliance with Herbert Bayard Swope, a young reporter for the *New York World*. Whitman began to feed Swope stories about what was going on in the district attorney's office, and, in return, Swope headlined Whitman's role as a demon crime fighter. In a sensational investigation into ties between the police and gambling interests touched off by a gangland killing, Whitman successfully prosecuted the alleged killers and was elected governor of New York on the strength of his fame as a crime fighter. Whitman paid little attention to his duties in Albany and trained his sights on the presidency. His defeat by Al Smith in the 1918 governor's race put an end to his political career.

WHITMAN, EZEKIEL (*b. present East Bridgewater, Mass., 1776; d. East Bridgewater, 1866*), jurist, Maine legislator. Admitted to Plymouth Co., Mass., bar, 1799; practiced successfully in New Gloucester, Maine, until 1807, and thereafter in Portland. Congressman, Democrat, from Maine, 1809–11 and 1817–June 1822. Judge, court of common pleas, 1822–41; chief justice, Maine Supreme Court, 1841–48.

WHITMAN, MARCUS (*b. Rushville, N.Y., 1802; d. near present Walla Walla, Wash., 1847*), physician, missionary, pioneer. M.D., College of Physicians and Surgeons at Fairfield, N.Y., 1832. Accompanied Samuel Parker on Oregon reconnaissance for Congregational missions, 1835; in 1836, with Rev. Henry H. Spalding and others, journeyed as missionary to Fort Walla Walla. Opened wagon road between Fort Hall and Fort Boise; established himself at mission at Waiilatpu, while the Spaldings took charge at Lapwai in present Idaho. After early success at missions, dissensions arose and Whitman made his famous "winter ride" east in 1842–43 to settle difficulties at mission headquarters in Boston, Mass. Successful, he returned to Oregon, 1843, accompanying the great immigration of that year. A continuing series of misfortunes at the mission climaxed in the murder of Whitman, his wife, and others by Cayuse Indians.

WHITMAN, ROYAL (*b. Portland, Maine, 1857; d. New York, N.Y., 1946*), orthopedic surgeon. M.D., Harvard Medical School, 1882. After starting practice in Boston, Mass., he went to England in the late 1880's, studied at Cook's School of Anatomy (London), and became a member of the Royal College of Surgeons. As a member of the staff of New York City's Hospital for the Ruptured and Crippled, 1889–1929, he originated several techniques for treatment of disorders of the foot and hip which quickly became standard. Professor also at College of Physicians and Surgeons, Columbia University, and at New York Polyclinic, he exerted important influence through his clinical teaching and through his textbook *A Treatise on Orthopaedic Surgery* (1901, and subsequent editions).

WHITMAN, SARAH HELEN POWER (*b. Providence, R.I., 1803; d. Providence, 1878*), poet. Chiefly remembered as fiancée of Edgar A. Poe, 1848, and the subject of his "To Helen." Praised by Poe and others, her work has grace and sincerity, but little originality or vigor. Author of *Hours of Life and Other Poems* (1853), *Edgar Poe and His Critics* (1860), and *Poems* (1879).

WHITMAN, WALT (*b. West Hills, town of Huntington, N.Y., 1819; d. Camden, N.J., 1892*), poet. Whitman's parents were of predominantly Dutch and English stock, and inclined to Quaker tenets; his father was a farmer and carpenter-builder; his mother, an uneducated woman, but "perfect in understanding and sympathy." The family moved to Brooklyn, N.Y., *ca.* 1823, and there the poet spent a few years in the public schools. In the summers he went visiting in Huntington and in other places on Long Island and was subsequently to believe that the knowledge thus gained of life on farm and seashore was one of the few important influences upon his work. At the age of eleven he was an office boy and an avid reader of the *Arabian Nights* and the works of Sir Walter Scott; in his thirteenth year he became a printer's devil in the office of the *Long Island Patriot*, whence he went to the *Long Island Star*. This was the beginning of a long career on newspapers in which during three decades he was to be identified with a bewildering number of editorial offices. While working as a journeyman compositor in Brooklyn and New York, he made occasional contributions to the papers for which he worked and got his first taste of the theater and the opera. Between 1836 and 1841 he taught in a number of schools on Long Island and edited the *Long Islander* at Huntington in 1838–39. His writings in this and other local papers were conventional and youthfully sentimental; he impressed people at this time as a dreamy, impractical person, indolent, morose, and untidy. According to his own later testimony, he was beginning to read at this time the Bible, Shakespeare, Ossian, the Greek tragic poets, Dante, and others; he was also interested in Democratic politics.

Of the ten or more newspapers or magazines with which Whitman was associated, 1841–48, the most important were the *Democratic Review*, to which he contributed melodramatic stories after the manner of Hawthorne and Poe, and the *Brooklyn Eagle* which he edited, 1846–January 1848. He provided the *Eagle* with an enlightened and well-written editorial page supporting most contemporary reforms. Moving rapidly in the Free-Soil direction on the question of slavery, he was dismissed as editor for protesting against the failure of the Democrats to face the issue of slavery in the new states. The few poems which he published during this period were competent, conventional verse exercises on routine subjects. He was author also of a temperance novel, *Franklin Evans; or, The Inebriate*, issued as an "extra" of the *New World*, 1842. In his leisure hours he made himself familiar with the varied life of New York, sauntering about the streets, haunting the ferries and omnibuses, strolling off to the beaches, and attending the theater and the opera regularly.

Engaged to write for the New Orleans *Crescent*, he spent three months in that city. The romantic legends which have grown up about this stay are doubtful; however, the city charmed him and provided him with new visual experiences. On his return to Brooklyn he resumed journalism, moving like a nomad from paper to paper, editing the *Brooklyn Times*, 1857–59, and publishing a long series of articles on early Brooklyn history in the *Standard*. He also assisted his father in house-building operations.

At about the year 1848, he entered on the period which came to its end and climax with the publication in 1855 of *Leaves of Grass*. The many attempts to analyze the poet's character in terms of these poems have not been particularly successful, and the theory that he passed through some mystical experience shortly before he wrote the twelve poems which make up the first edition of *Leaves of Grass* is more conjecture than logical deduction. Whitman's sudden full apprehension of himself dates back before 1848. If there was a sudden illumination, it would appear to have been a discovery not of his own nature, which he already knew too well, but of a way in which that nature might be presented to the world and so justified. So far he had managed to be little more than a knockabout journalist in life, which was unsatisfactory to him;

also, and more importantly, he had been forced to realize how unlike the rest of the world he was inwardly. He insisted always that his book had no other value than the celebration of himself as an "average man," yet he was anything but average. Early and late his writings testify to his sense of isolation; the theme of separateness is constantly evident. Well before 1850 he must have recognized that his impulses were extraordinary. He has been called autoerotic, erethistic, and homosexual, and some such extremes of nomenclature are necessary to explain certain passages in the "Song of Myself." Although tall and heavy, he was fastidious in his habits and precise in details of his dress, even after he had adopted the rough workmen's clothes which he affected after his return from New Orleans. It is true that love for his own sex is the only kind of love about which he is ever personal or convincing. All this, of course, has nothing to do with his being a great poet, but it has much to do with the state of mind out of which *Leaves of Grass* grew with such slow and conscious effort—an effort made in order that the poet might become an artist and so free himself from the slavery of self-contemplation. It is likely that the immediate influences in this process came through intellectual contact with contemporaries. Goethe's autobiography, the works of Thomas Carlyle and Emerson provided him with an example, and Emerson's work in particular provided him with a style. He learned from Emerson a fundamental lesson, that a man could accept and celebrate himself in cosmic language, transferring his vision from the unique self to the general. He was also encouraged by his then faith in phrenology. Ambitious at this time, and later, to go forth among the American people and astonish them with fresh and forceful utterances, he gave considerable time to the practice of oratory and the planning of lectures; some of the style of his poetry can best be explained in terms of this apprenticeship.

Leaves of Grass was a failure with the public. It was incomprehensible to some readers and shocking to others. Part of the public bafflement may be attributed to Whitman's insistence on being first of all a prophet and only secondly a poet, but the book did strike home here and there. Emerson responded to Whitman's gift of a copy with the famous and generous letter containing the phrase, "I greet you at the beginning of a great career." Thoreau and Bronson Alcott visited Whitman as did William Cullen Bryant, and there were a few favorable reviews, but for the most part the book fell dead from the press despite three rhapsodical reviews of it which Whitman himself wrote for several journals. In 1856 he issued a second edition of *Leaves of Grass* which contained 21 new poems and bore the quotation from Emerson stamped in gold on the cover. This edition was even more unfavorably received, principally because of exploitations of the sexual theme such as "Spontaneous Me." Before the issue of the third edition of 1860, which was published in Boston and contained two new sections, "Children of Adam" and "Calamus," Whitman engaged again in newspaper work and associated with the "Bohemians" who met at Pfaff's rathskeller in New York City. This latest edition of his work contained "Out of the Cradle Endlessly Rocking," one of the high points of the poet's achievement which had previously appeared in the *Saturday Press*. Henceforward, the principal themes which he was to treat were love and death—love as longing and death as the satisfaction of longing. In "Children of Adam" he celebrated what he called "amativeness," or the love of men and women; in "Calamus" he celebrated what he termed "adhesiveness," or the love of men for men. The edition of 1860–61 sold better than either of the others, and on Whitman's visit to Boston in connection with its printing he met William D. O'Connor, later his greatest champion. However, the Civil War reduced his Boston publishers to bankruptcy and the book became the prey of literary pirates; furthermore, the war itself produced an incalculable effect on Whitman's life, influencing and modifying

his every thought and constituting the occasion of his last great burst of poetry.

Journeying to Washington, D.C., in December 1872, in search of a soldier brother who had been wounded with the Union Army in Virginia, Whitman found his brother recovered but saw enough of the misery of war to realize that his life must somehow be involved with it. Residing in Washington and earning a little money by copying documents, he devoted himself to the wounded soldiers in the various hospitals about the city (a work described in *Memoranda During the War*, 1875). He worked entirely on his own, going about the wards to talk with the soldiers or read to them, and bringing gifts of fruit, jelly, and candy; on occasion he would write letters which they dictated to their families; now and then, he assisted at wound-dressing. Through the O'Connor family, with whom he lived, he met Edmund C. Stedman and was sought out in 1863 by John Burroughs. Although he does not appear ever to have met Abraham Lincoln, the president's death, occurring a few weeks after Whitman had secured a clerkship in the Department of the Interior, was the occasion for the poet's masterpiece, "When Lilacs Last in the Dooryard Bloom'd" (printed as a supplement to *Drum Taps*, 1865). Henceforth, Whitman's work is mellower, less egocentric, less raw; henceforth, it makes much of religion and the spiritual problems of society. In successive editions of *Leaves of Grass* the poems are tempered and shorn of excesses. The war and advancing age completed the process in Whitman whereby his private nature was lost sight of in the gray, kindly figure of legend.

Soon dismissed from his position in the Department of the Interior, he was given another post in the attorney general's office. Since he had been dismissed ostensibly because he was the author of a scandalous book, his friends attempted his defense: O'Connor published *The Good Gray Poet* (the first published volume about Whitman) in 1866, and John Burroughs published *Notes on Walt Whitman* (1867), at least half of which was written by Whitman himself. Meanwhile, *Leaves of Grass* was finding European admirers, and an expurgated London edition was issued by W. M. Rossetti in 1868. Publication in England led to the poet's long correspondence and friendship with Mrs. Anne Gilchrist, the widow of William Blake's biographer. Whitman's Washington period came to a close in January 1873 when he suffered a stroke of paralysis and removed to a residence in Camden, N.J. The death of his mother soon thereafter was a blow from which he never recovered; henceforth his life ran gradually downhill. He was dependent for his living upon his brother George, upon the contributions of friends, and upon the sale of his books which he conducted partly from his own house, receiving orders and filling them with his own hand.

Between 1865 and 1873 he had published two new editions of *Leaves of Grass* (1867 and 1871), *Passage to India* (1871), and the prose *Democratic Vistas* (1871). *Democratic Vistas*, written more or less in answer to Carlyle's *Shooting Niagara*, frankly discusses the shortcomings of American democracy and shows that the reference of Whitman's idealism is now to the future in which he still has faith. Constantly at work on revisions, he issued before his death five new editions of *Leaves of Grass* (1876, 1881–82, 1882, 1888–89, 1891–92) and published three collections which contained new poems: *Two Rivulets* (1876), *November Boughs* (1888), and *Good-Bye, My Fancy* (1891). His war *Memoranda*, already published, was included in *Specimen Days and Collect* (1882–82) which with *Democratic Vistas* represented him in prose until his earlier work began to be republished long after his death. His friends Burroughs and O'Connor were usually within his reach, although he was estranged from O'Connor, 1872–82. Visitors arrived for interviews, many of them from abroad, and as time went on Whitman found himself surrounded by a group of disciples, among them his later literary executor Horace Traubel and Richard M. Bucke, a Canadian physician who wrote the first official biography of Whitman in 1883. The poet's fame continued to grow steadily, although some earlier admirers (notably A. C. Swinburne) lost their enthusiasm. Whitman's tendency to bask in adoration and surround himself with inferior champions is pardonable but pitiable. He mellowed perceptibly as he grew older, especially with respect to his view of other American poets; his mature appraisals of Longfellow, Poe, Bryant, and Emerson are valuable contributions to criticism.

With the passage of years, a saner criticism and a more scientific approach to his biography have improved Whitman's image. The claims originally made for him as a prophet and moralist are less often made, and he is today judged as he should be—as a poet. He has never been popular or accepted by the democracies as he had hoped, nor has he been often imitated by other poets. But as his isolation grows more apparent, it grows more impressive, so that his rank among the poets of his country and his century is higher than it has ever been before. His work survives as certainly the most original work yet done by any American poet. As a maker of phrases, a master of rhythms, a weaver of images—indeed, as an architect of poems—he is often beyond the reach of criticism. His diaries of the war, his prefaces to *Leaves of Grass*, his *Democratic Vistas* are a permanent part of American prose.

WHITMER, DAVID (*b. near Harrisburg, Pa., 1805; d. Richmond, Mo., 1888*), Mormon leader. One of the "The Three Witnesses" to the *Book of Mormon* whose translation was completed in the Whitmer House, 1829. Made president of the "High Council of Zion" to manage Mormon interests in Missouri, 1834; excommunicated, 1838, for so-called neglect of moral and religious obligations to the church. Author of *An Address to All Believers in Christ by a Witness to the Divine Authenticity to the Book of Mormon* (1887), a straightforward account of events at the beginning of Mormonism.

WHITMORE, FRANK CLIFFORD (*b. North Attleboro, Mass., 1887; d. State College, Pa., 1947*), organic chemist. B.A., Harvard, 1911; Ph.D., 1914. Taught at Williams College, Rice Institute, and University of Minnesota; professor of organic chemistry, Northwestern University, 1920–29. Appointed dean of the School of Chemistry and Physics, Pennsylvania State College, 1929, he remained there until his death, becoming research professor of organic chemistry, 1937. His earliest research interests were summed up in his *Organic Compounds of Mercury* (1921); he devoted himself *post* 1929 chiefly to discovering the nature of intramolecular rearrangements of organic molecules, formulating in 1932 an electronic theory of rearrangement that gained wide acceptance. He was author also of *Organic Chemistry* (1937).

WHITMORE, WILLIAM HENRY (*b. Dorchester, Mass., 1836; d. 1900*), merchant, antiquarian. Boston common councilman, 1874–86; appointed a record commissioner, 1875, and city registrar, 1892. Under his supervision many volumes of invaluable local records were edited and issued, and manuscript copies of vital Boston church records were collected. He was author-editor of a number of works on genealogy and colonial history, including *The Andros Tracts* (1868–74) and the diary of Samuel Sewall. Much of his printed work, although good for its time, requires careful checking.

WHITNEY, ADELINE DUTTON TRAIN (*b. Boston, Mass., 1824; d. 1906*). Daughter of Enoch Train. Author of *Boys at Chequasset* (1862), *Faith Gartney's Girlhood* (1863), *The Gayworthys* (1865); also of the Real Folks Series and collections of verse. Her books for girls dealt largely with New England, her later stories with domestic life.

WHITNEY, ALEXANDER FELL (*b. Cedar Falls, Iowa, 1873; d. Bay Village, Ohio, 1949*), railway brakeman, labor leader. Joined Brotherhood of Railroad Trainmen, 1896; served as chairman of its grievance committee (1901–07), as a vice president (1907–28), and as president of the union *post* 1928. Aggressively liberal in his labor philosophy and devoted to the interests of the rank-and-file, he never hesitated to confront Congress or the president of the United States in defense of what he believed to be legitimate labor claims.

WHITNEY, ANNE (*b. Watertown, Mass., 1821; d. Boston, Mass, 1915*), sculptor, poet. Studied anatomy and modeling with William Rimmer and in Rome, Paris, and Munich. Established studio in Boston, Mass., 1872. Executed, among other portrait busts and ideal figures, the heroic marble statue of Samuel Adams (commissioned *ca.* 1873) in Statuary Hall, U.S. Capital, Washington, D.C.

WHITNEY, ASA (*b. Townsend, Mass., 1791; d. Philadelphia, Pa., 1874*), inventor, manufacturer. Superintendent, Mohawk & Hudson Railroad, *ca.* 1833–39; canal commissioner of New York State, 1839–42. Granted patent for a locomotive steam engine (1840). Removed to Philadelphia, Pa., 1842, and entered partnership with Matthias W. Baldwin; developed sound management system for the firm, also a system of locomotive classification. Resigned, 1846, to work on improvement of cast-iron car wheels (patented, 1847–48). Formed Asa Whitney & Sons, the largest and most successful car-wheel works in America. President, Philadelphia & Reading Railroad, 1860–61.

WHITNEY, ASA (*b. North Groton, Conn., 1797; d. 1872*), dry goods merchant, railroad promoter. Favored and unsuccessfully promoted (1844–51) an American transcontinental railroad from Lake Michigan via the South Pass of the Rockies to the Pacific Ocean. Author of, among other pamphlets, *A Project for a Railroad to the Pacific* (1849).

WHITNEY, CASPAR (*b. Boston, Mass., 1861; d. New York, N.Y., 1929*), journalist, sports writer. Originated idea of the All-American football team, 1889, whose members he and Walter Camp chose together for some ten years. Served as war correspondent in Cuba for *Harper's Weekly*, 1898. Later editor of *Outing* magazine and others, he was correspondent for the *New York Tribune* in Europe, 1917–19, protesting vigorously and practically against wartime censorship regulations.

WHITNEY, CHARLOTTE ANITA (*b. San Francisco, Calif., 1867; d. San Francisco, 1955*), suffragist and political activist. Studied at Wellesley College (1889). President of the California College Equal Suffrage League (1911) and second vice president of the National American Woman Suffrage Association. Member and supporter of the Communist Labor party (renamed the Communist party); she was arrested under the antisyndicalism laws in Oakland in 1919 and sentenced to prison; she served only a few days because of health. National chairman of the Communist party, 1936; Communist candidate for the U.S. Senate from California in 1950.

WHITNEY, COURTNEY (*b. Takoma Park, Md., 1897; d. Washington, D.C., 1969*), army officer. While in the Army Air Corps he studied at the National University in Washington (LL.B., 1923). As a civilian, he established a lucrative law practice in Manila, Philippines. In 1940 he returned to active duty, and in 1943 became the head of the Philippine Regional Section. He soon became General Douglas MacArthur's confidant, and in 1945 moved to Japan with MacArthur and became chief of the Government Section, which was largely responsible for drafting Japan's constitution of 1946. When the Korean War erupted, Whitney was named military secretary of the United Nations

Command, headed by MacArthur. He retired as a major general in 1951 to become MacArthur's personal secretary. When the latter became board chairman of Remington Rand in 1952, Whitney was employed as an executive by the firm.

WHITNEY, ELI (*b. Westboro, Mass., 1765; d. New Haven, Conn., 1825*), inventor. Disinclined to study as a boy, he showed a marked proficiency for mechanical work; he made and repaired violins, worked in iron, and at the age of 15 began the manufacture of nails in his father's shop. On making up his mind to acquire a college education (at the age of 18), he taught school to obtain the necessary money and entered Yale in May 1789. Graduating in 1792, he set out for Savannah, Ga., to serve as a tutor while he studied law. Disappointed of the position he had expected, he took up residence on the plantation of General Nathanael Greene's widow in Georgia, began law studies, and showed his appreciation for Mrs. Greene's hospitality by making and repairing all manner of things about the house and the plantation.

During the following winter he learned that many unprofitable areas of land in the South could be made profitable if the green seed cotton which could be raised on them could be cleansed of seeds by some mechanical device. Encouraged by Mrs. Greene, Whitney turned his mind to the problem and within ten days designed a cotton gin and completed an imperfect model. After further experiment, he built by April 1793 a larger, improved machine with which one man could produce fifty pounds of clean cotton a day. Entering into partnership with Phineas Miller, the plantation foreman, to patent and manufacture the new device and also to maintain a monopoly of its use, Whitney obtained his patent, Mar. 14, 1794, but soon found that a monopoly was impossible because of almost universal infringement of his patent by rival machines. Whitney obtained a court decision in his favor in 1807 after a long series of infringement suits; meanwhile Miller had died. On Whitney's application to Congress for a renewal of his patent in 1812, his request was refused. All in all he received practically no return for an invention which let loose tremendous industrial forces in the nation and the world.

Prior to this, on Jan. 14, 1798, he had obtained from the U.S. government a contract to manufacture and deliver 10,000 stand of arms. He proposed to make the guns by a new method, his aim being to make the same parts of different guns (for example, the locks) as much like each other as the successive impressions of a copper-plate engraving. This was perhaps the first suggestion of the system of interchangeable parts which has played so great a part in industrial development and mass production. Raising the necessary capital in New Haven, Conn., he built a factory in present Whitneyville and began design and construction of the machine tools required to carry out his schemes. He worked against great difficulties, having no experienced workmen to aid him and having to make himself practically every tool required. Completing the contract in some eight years instead of two, he nevertheless accomplished all which he had set out to do. Workmen with little or no experience could operate his machinery and turn out the various parts of a musket with so much precision that they were readily interchangeable. In 1812 he received a second contract from the U.S. government for the manufacture of firearms and also a similar contract from the state of New York. Thereafter, his unique manufactory yielded him a just reward.

WHITNEY, GEORGE (*b. Boston, Mass., 1885; d. New York, N.Y., 1963*), banker. Attended Harvard (B.A., 1907). Organized Markoe, Morgan and Whitney, a brokerage house, in 1909, and in 1915 left to join J. P. Morgan and Company, working in the division that was the U.S. purchasing agents for Great Britain and France's massive war purchases. Became a partner in 1919, and in the 1920's worked on several major European reconstruction and currency stabilization loans. Following the 1929 stock market

crash, he directed salvage operations for Morgan, and in 1932 headed the bankers' group that devised the financial rescue plan that saved New York City from bankruptcy. When the firm incorporated as a bank and trust company, he served as president and chief executive officer (1940–50), board chairman (1950–55), and then as a director until 1959, when the bank merged to form the Morgan Guaranty Trust Company of New York.

WHITNEY, GERTRUDE VANDERBILT (*b. New York, N.Y., 1875; d. New York, 1942*), sculptor, art patron. Daughter of Cornelius Vanderbilt (1843–99). Married Harry Payne Whitney, 1896. Recognized internationally for her work in sculpture, she is especially remembered for her many efforts to encourage art in the United States and to aid artists less fortunate than herself. These included the establishment of galleries to show and sell the work of innovating artists to whom the conventional galleries were unfriendly (Whitney Studio Club; Whitney Studio Galleries), and the Whitney Museum of American Art (opened in November 1931), which was committed to purchase only the work of living American artists.

WHITNEY, HARRY PAYNE (*b. New York, N.Y., 1872; d. 1930*), financier, sportsman. Son of William C. Whitney (1841–1904), who trained him to he his business successor. Developed silver, lead, and copper interests with Daniel Guggenheim, 1902. Director, Guggenheim Exploration Co., Guaranty Trust Co., and other banking, mining, and railroad concerns. Organizer and captain of American "Big Four" polo team. His polo tactics were adopted by the British and be became one of the few "ten-goal" players. Maintained distinguished racing stables. Financed Whitney South Sea Expedition, 1921–22.

WHITNEY, JAMES LYMAN (*b. Northampton, Mass., 1835; d. Cambridge, Mass., 1910*), bookseller, librarian. Half brother of William D. and Josiah D. Whitney. Graduated Yale, 1856. Chief of catalogue department, Boston Public Library, 1874–99; librarian, 1899–1903. His great contribution to library technique was the building up of the card-catalogue system at Boston. Compiler and editor of *Catalogue of the Spanish Library and of the Portuguese Books Bequeathed by George Ticknor to the Boston Public Library* (1879) and of many other special catalogues.

WHITNEY, JOSIAH DWIGHT (*b. Northampton, Mass., 1819; d. Lake Sunapee, N.H., 1896*), geologist, chemist. Brother of William D. Whitney; half brother of James L. Whitney. Graduated Yale, 1839. Studied chemistry and mineralogy under Benjamin Silliman and Robert Hare; also in Paris, Berlin, and Giessen. Engaged by C. T. Jackson (1847) to aid in survey of mineral lands of northern Michigan, he completed the survey in 1849 and issued its report, 1850–51. In practice as a mining consultant, 1850–55, he served as chemist and mineralogist, 1855–58, on the geological survey of Iowa; he also investigated lead regions of Wisconsin. As state geologist of California, 1860–74, he undertook an elaborate survey, introducing topographical mapping by triangulation and issuing a number of notable reports, some of which were published at his own expense. Founder of a school of mines at Harvard, 1868, he was Sturgis-Hooper Professor at Harvard from 1875 until his death. He was author, among other writings, of *Metallic Wealth of the United States* (1854), *Auriferous Gravels of the Sierra Nevada of California* (1880), and *Climatic Changes of Later Geological Times* (1882). His work stimulated later scientific study of ore deposits.

WHITNEY, MARY WATSON (*b. Waltham, Mass., 1847; d. 1921*), astronomer, educator. Graduated Vassar, A.B., 1868, A.M., 1872. Succeeded Maria Mitchell as director of Vassar Observatory, 1888–1910, and as professor of astronomy.

WHITNEY, MYRON WILLIAM (*b. Ashby, Mass., 1836; d. Sandwich, Mass., 1910*), oratorio and operatic basso. Considered by critics an unequaled artist in oratorio, Whitney was active as a concert, church, and stage singer, 1852–90.

WHITNEY, WILLIAM COLLINS (*b. Conway, Mass., 1841; d. 1904*), financier, sportsman. Son-in-law of Henry B. Payne; father of Harry P. Whitney. Graduated Yale, 1863; attended Harvard Law School, 1863–64; admitted to the bar, 1865. A success in New York law and politics, he gained the confidence of Samuel J. Tilden, helped in action against the "Tweed Ring," and (1875–82) effectively reorganized the New York City corporation counsel's office. Identified with New York City utilities, notably street-railways, and other large corporate activities, he won great wealth and a prominent place in society. As U.S. secretary of the navy, 1885–89, he fought successfully against outmoded concepts of ship design, modernized procedures, and supported aims of the Naval War College. A member of Grover Cleveland's inner circle, he played a significant role in Cleveland's second nomination and election, 1892, and fought Free Silver at the 1896 Democratic convention. *Post* 1899 he devoted himself to horse-racing activities.

WHITNEY, WILLIAM DWIGHT (*b. Northampton, Mass., 1827; d. 1894*), Sanskrit scholar, linguistic scientist. Brother of Josiah D. Whitney; half brother of James L. Whitney. Graduated Williams, 1845. Beginning his career as a natural scientist, he turned to the study of linguistics after a chance reading of Franz Bopp's Sanskrit grammar. After a year's study of Sanskrit at Yale under Edward E. Salisbury (1849), Whitney went to Germany where he continued his studies at Berlin and Tübingen. Elected professor of Sanskrit at Yale, 1854, he remained active there in teaching and research until his death. He devoted himself principally to Sanskrit, linguistic science, modern languages, and lexicography, and his bibliography numbers some 360 titles. Editor-author of a number of texts and translations in his special field, he did his most important work in his *Sanskrit Grammar* (Leipzig, 1879, later revised and supplemented). His method was essentially descriptive and statistical and marks a transition in the history of Sanskrit study; he subordinated to the technique of modern linguistic science the classifications, rules, and terms of the ancient and medieval Hindu grammarians. His work in linguistics antedated many recent developments, and his books still may serve as a valuable introduction to the science. He had considerable influence upon the modern trend, especially in his recognition of the distinction of linguistic science from philology and in his conception of linguistics as a historical, and not a physical or natural, science. When the Sheffield Scientific School was established, he organized its modern language department and became its head; out of this subsidiary activity grew a long list of publications in modern languages, including series of annotated German texts, a reader and a grammar and a dictionary; also, French and English grammars which show the same clarity and insight that mark his Sanskrit work. The last decade of his life was given largely to *The Century Dictionary* (1889–91), of which he was editor in chief. An outstanding interest in Whitney's life was the American Oriental Society which he served for many years as librarian, editor of publications, and secretary; he was president of the Society, 1884–90. Outstanding among his works (in addition to those already mentioned) are *Language and the Study of Language* (1867), *The Life and Growth of Language* (1875), and *Oriental and Linguistic Studies* (1873, 1874).

WHITNEY, WILLIS RODNEY (*b. Jamestown, N.Y., 1868; d. Schenectady, N.Y., 1958*), chemist and research director. Studied at the Massachusetts Institute of Technology and the University of Leipzig (Ph.D., 1896). Taught at MIT from 1896 to 1904. From 1900 until retirement in 1954, he was associated with the General Electric Company in Schenectady, N.Y., director of the research laboratories from 1904 to 1932, vice president from 1928. Whitney himself held over forty patents and helped in the development of the GEM lamp filament, the modern X-ray tube, and the "gas-filled" lamp.

WHITON, JAMES MORRIS (*b. Boston, Mass., 1833; d. 1920*), Congregational clergyman, educator, author. A popular preacher and able controversialist; held pastorates at Lynn, Mass., 1865–75, and in Newark, N.J., and New York City.

WHITSITT, WILLIAM HETH (*b. near Nashville, Tenn., 1841; d. Richmond, Va., 1911*), Baptist minister, church historian. Accepted chair of ecclesiastical history, Southern Baptist Theological Seminary, Greenville, S.C., 1872; served as president, 1895–99. Precipitated "the Whitsitt controversy" over succession of Baptist churches by article in *Johnson's Universal Encyclopaedia* (1896). Professor of philosophy, Richmond College, Richmond, Va., 1900–10.

WHITTELSEY, ABIGAIL GOODRICH (*b. Ridgefield, Conn., 1788; d. Colchester, Conn., 1858*), editor, author. Sister of Charles A. and Samuel G. Goodrich. Editor and contributor, *Mother's Magazine*, 1833–47 and 1848–49.

WHITTEMORE, AMOS (*b. Cambridge, Mass., 1759; d. West Cambridge, Mass., 1828*), inventor, gunsmith. Patented (1797) a machine for making cotton and wool cards which reduced card manufacture to a series of rapid, entirely automatic operations.

WHITTEMORE, THOMAS (*b. Boston, Mass., 1800; d. Cambridge, Mass., 1861*), Universalist clergyman, editor, railroad president, financier, Massachusetts legislator. Editor-owner, *Trumpet and Universalist Magazine*, 1828–61.

WHITTEMORE, THOMAS (*b. Cambridge, Mass., 1871; d. Washington, D.C., 1950*), archaeologist. Grandson of Thomas Whittemore (1800–61). B.A., Tufts College, 1894. Taught English and the history of art at Tufts; engaged in archaeological excavation in Egypt, 1911–15. Organized a relief program for Russian refugees, 1916, and directed its activities within Russia, 1916–18; thereafter until about 1927, he worked to provide education as well as relief for Russian youths in exile. Taught history of art at New York University, 1927–30. In 1930, he organized the Byzantine Institute as a means of educating the public in the Christian art of the East; his greatest achievement was the uncovering of the mosaics in Santa Sophia and other Byzantine churches in Constantinople.

WHITTIER, JOHN GREENLEAF (*b. Haverhill, Mass., 1807; d. Hampton Falls, N.H., 1892*), poet, abolitionist. Raised on a farm, the son of Quaker parents, Whittier improved a limited formal education by wide reading. His earliest attempts at verse were inspired by the work of Robert Burns. Publication of "The Exile's Departure" in the Newburyport *Free Press*, June 1826, brought Whittier to the attention of editor William Lloyd Garrison, who was to be a leading influence in the poet's life. Further publication of poems in the *Free Press* and the *Haverhill Gazette* made Whittier's work widely known in his locality. After a brief time at Haverhill Academy, he became editor with Garrison's help of *The American Manufacturer* (Boston), serving from January 1829 through the summer of that year. This was the first of many editorial positions which he was to hold. Succeeding George D. Prentice as editor of the *New England Weekly Review*, June 1830, Whittier held that post until 1832; meanwhile in February 1831 he published his first book, *Legends of New England in Prose and Verse*. Converted to abolitionism in the spring of 1833, he devoted himself for the next thirty years to the antislavery cause, as a poet and as an active agent, lobbyist, and editor. From March 1838 to February 1840 he edited the *Pennsylvania Freeman*. Sympathetic with the political-action party of the abolitionists to which Garrison was opposed, Whittier became a member of the American and Foreign AntiSlavery Society, and in the fall of 1842 ran for Congress on the Liberty Party ticket. After working as an editor of several minor journals, he became corresponding editor of the *National Era* of Washington, D.C., January 1847, and to it he contributed most of his poems and articles for the next 13 years. He remained active in politics, attacking the administration bitterly for the Mexican War, and in the famous poem "Ichabod" (*National Era*, May 2, 1850) he poured out scorn on Daniel Webster for the "Seventh of March" speech. He encouraged and furthered the career of Charles Sumner and was one of the first to suggest formation of the Republican party.

Whittier's life was uneventful *post* 1861 although his fame as a poet increased by reason of his many contributions to the *Atlantic Monthly* (in the founding of which he had a part) and to the *Independent*. However, he reached the summit of his poetic career in the decade of the 1860's during which appeared *Home Ballads* (1860); *In War Time and Other Poems* (1864, containing "Barbara Frietchie"); *Snow-Bound* (1866); *The Tent on the Beach* (1867); and *Among the Hills* (1869). In the summer of 1876 he settled in Danvers, Mass., which he made his place of abode almost to the time of his death, with occasional visits to his previous residence at Amesbury which continued to be his legal residence. He was the recipient of numerous honors and was surrounded by friends. Among the more important poetical volumes of his later years were *Miriam and Other Poems* (1871), *The Vision of Echard* (1878), and *At Sundown* (1890).

Whittier sacrificed much and endured much abuse in his devotion to the antislavery cause. He was in general tolerant and keenly sympathetic with all persecuted persons. He had a fine sense of humor and was adept at telling amusing stories. Radical though he might be in his views of slavery, he was extremely conservative on all industrial and economic questions, and as a means of settling economic difficulties recommended simple obedience to the golden rule and saving of money. Greatly admired as a poet in his own day and ranked with Longfellow and Bryant, he is today regarded as possessing mastery only in the poems inspired by the contest over slavery. These appeared in many of the volumes of poems which he issued *post* 1831 and were published collectively under the title *Voices of Freedom* in 1846. The best of his early work will be found in *Lays of My Home and Other Poems* (1843), *Songs of Labor* (1850), *The Chapel of the Hermits* (1853), and *The Panorama and Other Poems* (1856). Many of his religious poems have found a permanent place in the hymns of various denominations. In spite of the modern exaltation of the merits of his antislavery poems, *Snow-Bound* is still usually considered his masterpiece.

WHITTINGHAM, WILLIAM ROLLINSON (*b. New York, N.Y., 1805; d. Orange, N.J., 1879*), Episcopal clergyman. Graduated General Theological Seminary, New York City, 1824. Ordained to priesthood, 1829. Rector of St. Luke's Church, New York, 1831–36; professor of ecclesiastical history, General Theological Seminary, 1836–40. Consecrated bishop of Maryland, 1840, he upheld Union sentiments, 1857–65. A statesman-like and scholarly ecclesiastic, he was highly valued by his contemporaries in the House of Bishops.

WHITTREDGE, WORTHINGTON (*b. Springfield, Ohio, 1820; d. Summit, N.J., 1910*), painter. Studied in Europe, 1849–59, principally in Düsseldorf. A landscapist of the Hudson River School, Whittredge painted pictures which, despite their over-emphasis on detail, possess their own individuality and charm. He was Emanuel Leutze's model for Washington in *Washington Crossing the Delaware*.

WHITWORTH, GEORGE FREDERIC (*b. Boston, England, 1816; d. 1907*), Presbyterian clergyman, educator. Graduated New Albany Theological Seminary (later McCormick Theological Seminary), 1847. Helped found churches in Portland, Oreg., 1853, and in Olympia, Wash., 1854. Successful as a businessman and civic leader in Seattle, Wash. President of University of Washington, Seattle, 1866–67 and 1875–76. Whitworth College, Spokane, Wash., was named in his honor.

WHORF, BENJAMIN LEE (*b. Winthrop, Mass., 1897; d. Wethersfield, Conn., 1941*), chemical engineer, anthropological linguist. B.S., Massachusetts Institute of Technology, 1918. Associated all his life with the Hartford Fire Insurance Company as an expert in industrial fire prevention, his fame rests on his avocational work in linguistic theory. Encouraged by Edward Sapir, he made intensive studies of the Hopi language, and evolved chiefly from this investigation his theory of linguistic relativity; i.e., that the structure of the particular language a person speaks influences his patterns of thought and action.

WHYTE, WILLIAM PINKNEY (*b. Maryland, 1824; d. Baltimore, Md., 1908*), lawyer, Maryland legislator. Grandson of William Pinkney. Admitted to the Maryland bar, 1846. Long active in Democratic politics, an opponent of the Know-Nothings and later a Confederate sympathizer, Whyte served as governor of Maryland, 1872–74. He was U.S. senator, Democrat, from Maryland, 1868–69, 1875–81, and 1906. He also served as mayor of Baltimore, 1881–83; attorney general of Maryland, 1887–91; and city solicitor of Baltimore, 1900–03.

WICKARD, CLAUDE RAYMOND (*b. near Flora, Ind., 1893; d. near Delphi, Ind., 1967*), U.S. secretary of agriculture. Studied at Purdue (B.S., 1915), then took over management of his father's farm. He was elected to the Indiana State Senate in 1932 as a Democrat, and the next year he was called to Washington, D.C., to become an assistant in the Corn-Hog Section of the Agricultural Adjustment Administration. In 1940 he became secretary of agriculture, and in 1942 he took on the added post of food administrator. Was also administrator of the Rural Electrification Administration (1945–53).

WICKERSHAM, GEORGE WOODWARD (*b. Pittsburgh, Pa., 1858; d. New York, N.Y., 1936*), lawyer, public servant. After studying civil engineering and serving briefly as secretary to Matthew S. Quay, he graduated from the law school of the University of Pennsylvania and was admitted to the bar, 1880. In 1883 he joined the firm of Strong and Cadwalader in New York City and became a partner, 1887; he was considered one of the leading corporation experts of the New York State bar. Active in the local Republican party, he was chosen U.S. attorney general, 1909, and over the next four years initiated more actions against the nation's leading corporations under the Sherman Antitrust Law than the preceding administration had begun in seven years. So vigorously did he drive against the trusts that many representatives of industrial and financial circles demanded his resignation. He was one of the closest advisers of President William H. Taft during this period, drew up the original draft of the Mann-Elkins Act, and helped with the corporation tax provision in the Payne-Aldrich Tariff Act. Continuing his interest in public affairs in New York State *post* 1913, he was an internationalist and supported disarmament moves and the World Court. Appointed chairman of the so-called Wickersham Committee, 1929, he undertook an extensive inquiry into the entire federal system of jurisprudence and reported the committee's findings in 14 separate reports. Unfortunately, the major work of the committee was overlooked because of the confusion of its report on the enforcement of the 18th (Prohibition) Amendment.

WICKERSHAM, JAMES PYLE (*b. Chester Co., Pa., 1825; d. Lancaster, Pa., 1891*), educator, Union soldier. Appointed principal, Lancaster County Normal School, Millersville, Pa., 1856; under his administration it became the first state normal school in Pennsylvania 1859. Appointed state superintendent of common schools, 1866, he held that post until 1881; by 1874 he had succeeded in having a school established in every Pennsylvania district. Editor and part owner, *Pennsylvania School Journal*, 1870–81.

WICKES, LAMBERT (*b. Kent Co., Md., 1735[?]; d. at sea, off Newfoundland, 1777*), Revolutionary naval officer. In autumn 1774 he distinguished himself by refusing to ship tea from London in his vessel *Neptune*. Given command of the Continental armed ship *Reprisal*, April 1776, he was victorious in several actions with the British and captured valuable prizes. In October 1776 he carried Benjamin Franklin to France. The *Reprisal* was the first American ship of war and Wickes was the first American naval officer to appear in European waters after the Declaration of Independence.

WICKES, STEPHEN (*b. Jamaica, N.Y., 1813; d. Orange, N.J., 1889*), physician, historical writer. M.D., University of Pennsylvania, 1834. Practiced in Troy, N.Y., and Orange, N.J. Author of, among other works, *History of Medicine in New Jersey, and of Its Medical Men, from the Settlement of the Province to A.D. 1880* (1879). Edited *Transactions of the Medical Society of New Jersey*, 1861–82.

WICKHAM, JOHN (*b. Southold, N.Y., 1763; d. 1839*), lawyer. Began practice in Williamsburg, Va.; removed to Richmond, 1790, where he became celebrated as a pleader. In the case of *Ware* v. *Hylton* (1793), Wickham's contention that by the U.S. Constitution all treaties were a part of the law of the land and all state legislation inconsistent therewith was invalid was sustained on appeal by the Supreme Court. In 1809 he represented plaintiff in *Hunter* v. *Fairfax's Devisee*, which established doctrine that the Supreme Court has appellate jurisdiction over decisions of state courts. Wickham's argument, as counsel for the defense, that Aaron Burr had committed no overt act of treason was accepted by Chief Justice Marshall, who so instructed the jury during Burr's celebrated trial, 1807.

WICKLIFFE, CHARLES ANDERSON (*b. near Springfield, Ky., 1788; d. near Ilchester, Md., 1869*), lawyer, Kentucky legislator. Father of Robert C. Wickliffe; cousin of Ben Hardin. Congressman, Democrat, from Kentucky, 1823–33; became chairman, Committee on Public Lands, 1829. Whig lieutenant governor of Kentucky, 1836–39; governor, 1839–40. Postmaster general of the United States, 1841–45. Rejoining the Democrats on the issue of Texas annexation, he later opposed the secession movement and served in Congress, 1861–63, as a Union Whig.

WICKLIFFE, ROBERT CHARLES (*b. Bardstown, Ky., 1819; d. 1895*), lawyer, planter, Louisiana legislator. Son of Charles A. Wickliffe. Removed to Louisiana, 1846. Democratic governor of Louisiana, 1856–60.

WICKSON, EDWARD JAMES (*b. Rochester, N.Y., 1848; d. Berkeley, Calif., 1923*), horticulturist. Graduated Hamilton, 1869. Removing to California, 1875, to join staff of *Pacific Rural Press*, he encouraged founding or reorganizing of state agricultural organizations and taught a variety of subjects in the agricultural school of the University of California. In 1905 he was appointed dean of the school and professor of horticulture, and became director of the university agricultural experiment station, 1907.

Author of, among other books, *The California Fruits and How to Grow Them* (1889) and *The California Vegetables in Garden and Field* (1897). Editor in chief, *Pacific Rural Press*, 1898–1923.

WIDENER, HARRY ELKINS (*b. Philadelphia, Pa., 1885; d. at sea, aboard the* Titanic, *1912*), rare-book collector. Grandson of P. A. B. Widener and William L. Elkins. Graduated Harvard, 1907.

WIDENER, PETER ARRELL BROWN (*b. Philadelphia, Pa., 1834; d. 1915*), financier, philanthropist. After early success as a butcher and Union army meat supplier during the Civil War, he served as Philadelphia city treasurer, 1873–74, in which post he made a large amount of money in fees. *Post* 1875 he was associated with W. L. Elkins and others in street-railway ownership and operation in Philadelphia, Pittsburgh, Baltimore, and Chicago; their properties totaled a greater mileage than any similar syndicate. Widener helped in consolidation of the Philadelphia Rapid Transit Co. and was an organizer of the U.S. Steel Corporation and the American Tobacco Co. He had large investments in many corporations, including the Pennsylvania Railroad Co. Widener's collections of art and Chinese porcelains were considered among the finest in America. He was a generous benefactor to Philadelphia institutions.

WIDFORSS, GUNNAR MAURITZ (*b. Stockholm, Sweden, 1879; d. Grand Canyon, Ariz., 1934*), artist. Studied at Institute of Technology, Stockholm, Sweden, 1896–1900. Settled in the United States, 1921. Called the "painter of the National Parks," he excelled in studies of the Grand Canyon, recording its moods in watercolor and oil. Widforss reproduced nature with remarkable feeling and accuracy.

WIDNEY, JOSEPH POMEROY (*b. Miami Co., Ohio, 1841; d. Los Angeles, Calif., 1938*), physician, civic leader. M.D., Toland Medical College, San Francisco, Calif., 1866. In practice in Los Angeles *post ca.* 1869, he was a principal factor in the development of the Los Angeles area. He helped found the institution chartered in 1880 as the University of Southern California, serving as dean of the medical school and as president of the university itself, 1892–95.

WIECHMANN, FERDINAND GERHARD (*b. Brooklyn, N.Y., 1858; d. 1919*), scientist, author. Chief chemist, Havemeyer and Elder Sugar Refining Co., Brooklyn, N.Y., 1887–1909. Author of, among other books, *Sugar Analysis* (1890).

WIELAND, GEORGE REBER (*b. Boalsburg, Pa., 1865; d. West Haven, Conn., 1953*), paleontologist. Studied at Pennsylvania State College, Göttingen, and Yale (Ph.D., 1900). Associated with the Osborn Botanical Laboratory at Yale (1906–35). Collector and cataloguer of fossils, especially cycadlike plants. Published *American Fossil Cycads* (1906–16) and *Cerro Cuadrado Petrified Forest* (1935), a description of early Mesozoic conifers from Patagonia. Wieland bought land in South Dakota's Black Hills in 1916 and attempted to obtain federal assistance for the preservation of the region as a park for cycadophyte localities; the area was made a national monument in 1922 but was disestablished in 1957. Wieland's ideas are not now the basis for any significant paleobotanical theories.

WIENER, LEO (*b. Bialystok, Poland, 1862; d. Belmont, Mass., 1939*), Slavic scholar, philologist, cultural historian. A teacher of languages after his immigration to the United States, 1882, he was appointed to the staff of Harvard University through the influence of Francis J. Child and Archibald C. Coolidge, becoming instructor in Slavic languages and literature, 1896. He remained at Harvard, rising through the academic grades and becoming professor emeritus, 1930. In the latter part of his career he abandoned research in the Slavic field and gave much time to investigations of Arabic, Germanic, African, and American Indian culture. He was author of, among other works, *Anthology of Russian Literature* (1902–03) and *History of Yiddish Literature in the Nineteenth Century* (1899).

WIENER, NORBERT (*b. Columbia, Mo., 1894; d. Stockholm, Sweden, 1964*), mathematician. Attended Tufts, Cornell, and Harvard (Ph.D., 1913), and universities of Göttingen and Cambridge (1913–14). Taught at Harvard, University of Maine, and in 1919 joined the Massachusetts Institute of Technology. He began work on integration in function spaces, which led to his greatest achievements, the first of which was differential space. He also studied harmonic analysis, Fourier transforms, and Tauberian theorems, work that established him as a mathematician of the first rank. His 1930 paper "Generalized Harmonic Analysis" was probably his finest contribution. After the outbreak of World War II in Europe, he worked on the control of antiaircraft guns, which led him to investigate the problem of estimating the future position of an airplane on the basis of a finite number of (not perfectly accurate) measurements. His book *Cybernetics* (1948) propelled him to a position of instant fame and popularized several important aspects of communication theory.

WIGFALL, LOUIS TREZEVANT (*b. near Edgefield, S.C., 1816; d. Galveston, Tex., 1874*), lawyer, Texas legislator, Confederate brigadier general. Favored secession of South Carolina, 1844. Settled in Texas, 1848. During crisis of 1849–50, he again declared for separation of South from North. Elected to Texas Senate, 1856, he led "Southern-rights" Democrats. As U.S. senator from Texas, 1860–61, he urged secession, justifying it on the compact theory; he was one of those Southerners whose abstention from voting brought about defeat of the Crittenden Compromise. Remaining in the Senate until March 1861, he aided the Confederacy by confidential advice. Commanded "Texas Brigade" in Virginia, resigning February 1862 to enter Confederate Senate. Bitterly opposed President Jefferson Davis' conduct of the war; led movement making R. E. Davis' conduct of the war; led movement making R. E. Lee general in chief of Confederate armies. After the war he escaped from Galveston, Tex., to England, returning to the United States, 1872.

WIGGER, WINAND MICHAEL (*b. New York, N.Y., 1841; d. 1901*), Roman Catholic clergyman. Studied in Genoa and Rome; ordained, 1865; D.D., University of the Sapienza, Rome, 1869. After holding pastorates in Madison, Summit, and Orange, N.J., he was consecrated third bishop of Newark, N.J., 1881. Notable for work on behalf of German and Italian immigrants.

WIGGIN, ALBERT HENRY (*b. Medfield, Mass., 1868; d. Greenwich, Conn., 1951*), banker. Entering banking after graduation from high school, Wiggin worked his way up through a succession of jobs in Boston and New York until he became vice president of Chase National Bank (1904); president (1911); chairman of the board (1917); chairman of the governing board (1930–32), when he retired. Wiggin built the Chase into the world's largest bank through a series of mergers (the bank absorbed seven major New York banks) and expansion with the foundation of the Mercantile Trust Co., 1917, and the Chase Securities Corp. After retirement, a Senate investigation disclosed that Wiggin used his position for his own profit. He settled a stockholders suit out of court.

WIGGIN, JAMES HENRY (*b. Boston, Mass., 1836; d. 1900*), Unitarian clergyman, editor. Graduated Meadville Theological School, 1861; ordained, 1862. Held pastorates in Massachusetts, 1861–75. An agnostic by 1881, he devoted himself thenceforth to literary pursuits. The great popularity of Mary Baker Eddy's

Science and Health dated from his revision (16th ed.), done at her request, 1885. He was associated with Mrs. Eddy for some years thereafter.

WIGGIN, KATE DOUGLAS (*b. Philadelphia, Pa., 1856; d. Harrow, England, 1923*), author, pioneer kindergarten worker. Trained by Emma J. C. Marwedel, she was selected in 1878 to organize in San Francisco the Silver St. Kindergarten, first free kindergarten west of the Rocky Mountains. She established the California Kindergarten Training School, 1880, with Nora A. Smith, her sister and collaborator in teaching and kindergarten writings. Author of, among many other books, *The Birds' Christmas Carol* (1887), typical of her work in its brevity, wide range of characterization, broad humor, and Dickensian pathos; *Polly Oliver's Problem* (1893); and *Rebecca of Sunnybrook Farm* (1903).

WIGGINS, CARLETON (*b. Turner, N.Y., 1848; d. Old Lyme, Conn., 1932*), landscape and animal painter. Studied at National Academy of Design, 1870, and under George Inness. Elected member of the academy, 1906.

WIGGLESWORTH, EDWARD (*b. Malden, Mass., ca. 1693; d. 1765*), educator, theologian. Son of Michael Wigglesworth. Graduated Harvard, 1710; appointed first Hollis professor of divinity at Harvard, 1722. D.D., University of Edinburgh, 1730. A leader among the antievangelical clergy, Wigglesworth's gradual compromise between Arminian and Calvinistic extremes heralded later Unitarianism. Author of, among other works, *A Letter to the Reverend Mr. George Whitefield* (1745) and *The Doctrine of Reprobation Briefly Considered* (1763).

WIGGLESWORTH, EDWARD (*b. Cambridge, Mass., 1732; d. 1794*), educator, theologian. Son of Edward Wigglesworth (*ca.* 1693–1765); grandson of Michael Wigglesworth. Graduated Harvard, 1749. Succeeded his father as Hollis professor of divinity at Harvard, 1765. Author of, among other works, *Calculations on American Population* (1775).

WIGGLESWORTH, EDWARD (*b. Boston, Mass., 1840; d. 1896*), dermatologist. Graduated Harvard, 1861; M.D., Harvard Medical School, 1865; studied in Europe, 1865–70. Practicing in Boston, Mass., he inaugurated and maintained Boston Dispensary for Skin Diseases, 1872–77. Headed Department of Diseases of the Skin, Boston City Hospital, taught at Harvard Medical School.

WIGGLESWORTH, MICHAEL (*b. probably Yorkshire, England, 1631; d. 1705*), Congregational clergyman, author. Father of Edward Wigglesworth (*ca.* 1693–1765). Came to America as a boy. Graduated B.A., Harvard, 1651; served as fellow and tutor at Harvard, 1652–54, and was a fellow *post* 1697. Minister at Malden, Mass., *post ca.* 1655, he also practiced medicine. He was author of, among other works, *The Day of Doom* (1662), a long edificatory poem in ballad meter. Its picture of the Judgment Day has occasional dramatic flashes and possesses a real if undeveloped poetic power. The work has been criticized for the alleged inhumanity of its theological doctrines; however, *The Day of Doom* is merely a dramatized version of tenets commonly held at the time.

WIGHT, FREDERICK COIT (*b. New London, Conn., 1859; d. 1933*), musician, composer of marches.

WIGHT, PETER BONNETT (*b. New York, N.Y., 1838; d. Pasadena, Calif., 1925*), architect. Graduated present College of City of New York, 1855. Began practice in Chicago, Ill. Won 1862 competition for National Academy of Design building, Fourth Ave. and 23rd St., New York City, notable for Italian Gothic facades. Subsequently he designed the Brooklyn Mercantile Library building and was commissioned to design the Yale School of Fine Arts. Associated with Russell Sturgis, 1863–68. *Post* 1872 his Chicago firm of Drake & Wight (formerly Carter, Drake and Wight) engaged in commercial and domestic work and became a training ground for young architects. Wight devoted himself to development of terra-cotta structural tile, 1881–91. He was responsible for the 1897 Illinois law requiring examination and licensing of architects.

WIGMORE, JOHN HENRY (*b. San Francisco, Calif., 1863; d. Chicago, Ill., 1943*), legal scholar and educator. B.A., Harvard, 1883; M.A. and LL.B., 1887. Practiced in Boston for two years; taught law at Keio University, Tokyo, Japan, 1889–92. Appointed professor of law at Northwestern University, 1893, he was made dean of the law school in 1901 and retained that position until his retirement in 1929. An advocate of the case method of teaching law, he led in the movement to modernize and systematize U.S. legal education. A founder of the *Harvard Law Review*, he became one of the most respected legal writers in the country, publishing the classic *Treatise on the System of Evidence in Trials at Common Law* (1904–05), *Principles of Judicial Proof* (1913), and A *Panorama of the World's Legal Systems* (1928).

WIGNELL, THOMAS (*b. England, ca. 1753; d. Philadelphia, Pa., 1803*), comedian, theatrical manager. Came to America, 1774, to join the American Co. managed by his cousin Lewis Hallam; removed with the company immediately to Jamaica, British West Indies. First appeared in the United States, November 1785, with the American Co. at New York. The best comedian seen in America up to that time, he soon became a favorite and was noted for his intelligence and taste. One of his most popular roles was Joseph Surface in Sheridan's *The School for Scandal*. In 1791 he became partner of Alexander Reinagle and opened the Chestnut St. Theatre, Philadelphia, 1794. In 1796 he brought Ann B. Merry and Thomas A. Cooper from England to join the company. The succeeding Philadelphia seasons were the most brilliant of their time. He opened the first theater in Washington, D.C., 1800.

WIKOFF, HENRY (*b. probably Philadelphia, Pa., ca. 1813; d. Brighton, England, 1884*), author, adventurer. Made the grand tour of Europe, 1834–40; was a transatlantic commuter, 1840–50. It was said that no American of the period knew so many European notables or more important unwritten political history. Served in various diplomatic capacities; was ballerina Fanny Elssler's manager, 1840; spent 15 months in jail at Genoa, Italy, for abducting an heiress *ca.* 1852–53. Author of, among other writings, *Napoleon Louis Bonaparte, First President of France* (1849), *My Courtship and Its Consequences* (1855), and *The Reminiscences of an Idler* (1880).

WILBUR, CRESSY LIVINGSTON (*b. Hillsdale, Mich., 1865; d. Utica, N.Y., 1928*), vital statistician. Ph.B., Hillsdale College, 1886; Ph.M., 1889. Appointed chief of Division of Vital Statistics, Michigan State Department of Health, 1893. Chief statistician for vital-statistics, U.S. Census Bureau, 1906–14. In charge of Division of Vital Statistics, New York State Department of Health, 1914–16. Wilbur's outstanding contribution was the fostering of a model vital statistics law that led to establishment of uniform and effective registration in all states.

WILBUR, CURTIS DWIGHT (*b. Boonsboro (now Boone), Iowa, 1867; d. Palo Alto, Calif., 1954*), jurist and government official. Graduated U.S. Naval Academy (1888) but never commissioned. Studied law and began practicing in Los Angeles. Elected to the county court in 1902; appointed to the California Supreme Court in 1918. Appointed secretary of the navy in 1924 by Calvin Coolidge after Teapot Dome scandals. Attempted to build the

navy's forces but was hampered by an economy-minded Congress. An advocate of naval air power, he established the first course in aviation at the Naval Academy. Adamantly opposed to a separate air force. Served on Ninth Federal Circuit Court of Appeals in San Francisco (1929–45).

WILBUR, HERVEY BACKUS (*b. Wendell, Mass., 1820; d. Syracuse, N.Y., 1883*), pioneer educator of the retarded, physician. Graduated Berkshire Medical Institution, Pittsfield, Mass., 1843. Established Institute for Idiots at Barre, Mass., *ca.* 1848, the first school of its kind in the United States; was associated with New York State Asylum for Idiots *post* 1851. His system of training became basis for every similar institution in the United States, Canada, and many European countries; he was also an authority on care of the insane. Author of, among other writings, *Aphasia* (1867) and *Report on the Management of the Insane in Great Britain* (1876).

WILBUR, JOHN (*b. Hopkinton, R.I., 1774; d. Hopkinton, 1856*), Quaker preacher, antievangelical leader. Opposed movement led by Joseph J. Gurney; was expelled from Society of Friends, 1843. His followers separated from meeting in 1845. They were popularly known as Wilburites and officially as the New England Yearly Meeting of Friends.

WILBUR, RAY LYMAN (*b. Boonesboro, Iowa, 1875; d. Palo Alto, Calif., 1949*), physician, educator, public official. Raised in Dakota Territory and Riverside, Calif. B.A., Stanford University, 1896; M.A., 1897; M.D., Cooper Medical College, 1899. During his freshman year at Stanford University, he met Herbert Hoover, with whose career he was often intertwined over the next 40 years. After practicing medicine in San Francisco he returned to Stanford as professor and in 1916 became president of the university. He promoted his old friend Hoover as wartime food administrator and served as his assistant. At Stanford his reorganization plans for the university were only partially successful because of recalcitrant alumni.

When Hoover became president, Wilbur became his secretary of the interior and served in Washington for four years. As secretary he was moderately conservationist, but was generally opposed to strong government intervention. His chief contribution seems to have been his personal support for Hoover. He returned to Stanford in 1933 and in 1943 became chancellor.

WILBUR, SAMUEL (*b. England, ca. 1585; d. Boston, Mass., 1656*), Rhode Island merchant and colonist. Immigrated to America some time before 1633; was one of the buyers of Boston Common from William Blackstone, 1634. A purchaser and settler of the island of Aquidneck (now Rhode Island), he was a signer of the Portsmouth Compact. He later returned to Massachusetts.

WILCOX, CADMUS MARCELLUS (*b. Wayne Co., N.C., 1824; d. Washington, D.C., 1890*), Confederate major general. Graduated West Point, 1846. Distinguished himself in Mexican War, notably at Chapultepec. Accepted colonelcy, 9th Alabama Infantry, Confederate army, 1861. With General R. E. Lee's army in nearly every great battle, Wilcox was one of the best subordinate commanders of the South. Published *Rifles and Rifle Practice* (1859), first American textbook on the subject.

WILCOX, DELOS FRANKLIN (*b. near Ida, Mich., 1873; d. 1928*), franchise and public utility expert. Ph.D., Columbia, 1896. Chief of Bureau of Franchises, Public Service Commission, New York City, 1907–13; deputy commissioner of Department of Water Supply, Gas and Electricity, New York City, 1913–17; thereafter a consultant on utility problems. Author of, among other works, *Municipal Franchises* (1910–11), *Analysis of the Electric Railway Problem* (1921), *Depreciation in Public Utilities* (1925), and *The Administration of Municipally Owned Utilities*

(1931). Revised R. A. Whitten's *Valuation of Public Service Corporations* (1928). Inclined always to the side of the public in controversies.

WILCOX, ELLA WHEELER (*b. Johnstown Center, Wis., 1850; d. Short Beach, Conn., 1919*), writer of inspirational verse. *Poems of Passion* (1883, her first success) was followed by 20 volumes mainly in verse. She wrote a daily poem for a newspaper syndicate and contributed frequent essays to *Cosmopolitan* and other magazines. All her later work shows influence of "New Thought." Defending herself against criticism of sentimentality, she maintained that her poems "comforted" millions.

WILCOX, REYNOLD WEBB (*b. Madison, Conn., 1856; d. 1931*), physician. M.D., Harvard Medical School, 1881. Practiced in New York City. Professor of medicine, New York Post-Graduate Medical School and Hospital, 1886–1908. Edited William Hale-White's *Materia Medica* (1892). Author of, among other works, *Treatment of Disease* (1907). Therapeutic editor of *American Journal of Medical Sciences* for many years.

WILCOX, STEPHEN (*b. Westerly, R.I., 1830; d. Brooklyn, N.Y., 1893*), inventor, engineer. Secured a patent for a safety water-tube boiler with inclined tubes, 1856, and a steam generator, 1867; formed Babcock, Wilson & Co., 1867, with George H. Babcock. The Babcock & Wilcox boiler and stationary steam engine were used in the first central stations (power plants) in America and were of significant value in electric lighting developments.

WILCZYNSKI, ERNEST JULIUS (*b. Hamburg, Germany, 1876; d. Denver, Colo., 1932*), mathematician, educator. Immigrated to America as a child; raised in Chicago, Ill. Ph.D., University of Berlin, 1897. Taught at universities of California and Illinois; professor of mathematics, University of Chicago, 1914–26. Eminent as a projective differential geometer, a field of geometry he largely created.

WILDE, GEORGE FRANCIS FAXON (*b. Braintree, Mass., 1845; d. 1911*), naval officer. Graduated U.S. Naval Academy, Newport, R.I., 1864. Commanded new steel cruiser *Dolphin* on world cruise, 1886–89; commanded ram *Katahdin* on North Atlantic patrol, 1898. Commanded cruiser *Boston*, 1898–99, and battleship *Oregon*, 1899–1901, during Philippine Insurrection. Commandant of Philadelphia navy yard, February–May 1904; thereafter at Boston navy yard. Retired as rear admiral, 1905.

WILDE, RICHARD HENRY (*b. Dublin, Ireland, 1789; d. New Orleans, La., 1847*), lawyer, poet. Immigrated to Baltimore, Md., 1797; was raised in Georgia. Became attorney general of Georgia, 1811. Congressman, Democrat, from Georgia, 1815–17 and 1827–35. Traveled extensively in Europe, 1835–40; discovered Giotto's portrait of Dante in the Bargello at Florence, Italy. Removed to New Orleans, La., 1843; was appointed professor of constitutional law, University of Louisiana (present Tulane), 1847. Author of "My Life Is Like the Summer Rose" (composed *ante* 1815), *Conjectures and Researches Concerning . . . Torquato Tasso* (1842), and *Hesperia: A Poem* (1867).

WILDER, ALEXANDER (*b. Verona, N.Y., 1823; d. 1908*), physician, eccentric philosopher. M.D., Syracuse Medical College, 1850. Removed to New York City, 1857, where for 13 years he worked on New York *Evening Post*, becoming financial expert and political journalist. President of the Eclectic Medical College, 1867–77; professor of physiology, 1873–77. Professor of psychology, United States Medical College, 1878–83. Author of, among other books, *New Platonism and Alchemy* (1869), *Vaccination a Medical Fallacy* (1875), and *History of Medicine* (1901).

WILDER, HARRIS HAWTHORNE (*b. Bangor, Maine, 1864; d. 1928*), zoologist. B.A., Amherst, 1886; Ph.D., University of Freiburg, 1891. Professor of zoology, Smith College *post* 1892. Made important contributions to knowledge of vertebrate anatomy, friction-ridge patterns of the skin, and descriptive anthropology.

WILDER, JOHN THOMAS (*b. Hunter Village, N.Y., 1830; d. Jacksonville, Fla., 1917*), Union brigadier general, industrialist. "Wilder's Lightning Brigade" of Indiana and Illinois volunteers acquitted itself with particular brilliance at Chickamauga, 1863. Resigning from the army, October 1864, Wilder settled in Chattanooga. A developer of Tennessee's natural resources, he founded the Roane Iron Works, 1867, and built at Rockwood one of the first blast furnaces in the South; he was also active in railroad and coal lands development.

WILDER, LAURA INGALLS (*b. Pepin, Wis., 1867; d. Mansfield, Mo., 1957*), author. Self-educated. Wilder began writing novels at the age of sixty-five. Her *Little House* books for children describe life as a pioneer and settler in the American West. *Little House on the Prairie* (1935) and *These Happy Golden Years* (1943) are typical of the books, which have sold over two million copies. In 1974, *Little House on the Prairie* was successfully adapted for a television series.

WILDER, MARSHALL PINCKNEY (*b. Rindge, N.H., 1798; d. 1886*), agriculturist, merchant, Massachusetts legislator. Removed to Boston, Mass., 1825; was known for many years as its chief citizen. A founder of the Constitutional Union party, 1860. Vice president, Massachusetts Institute of Technology, 1865–70, of which he was a founder. President, Massachusetts Horticultural Society, 1840–48. Helped found American Pomological Society, 1848, and was president for 38 years. Helped establish, 1852, and directed Massachusetts Board of Agriculture, and the U.S. Agricultural Society. Led in formation of Massachusetts Agricultural College, one of the first in any state. His proposed reformation in nomenclature of American fruits, 1883, was later adopted. He also developed many important flower and fruit varieties.

WILDER, RUSSELL MORSE (*b. Cincinnati, Ohio, 1885; d. Rochester, Minn., 1959*), medical clinician. Studied at the University of Chicago (Ph.D., 1912), and at Rush Medical College (M.D., 1912). An expert in diabetes and its treatment, Wilder worked at the Mayo Clinic from 1919 to 1950. He was one of the first to use insulin as a treatment for diabetes. In 1921, he published, along with colleagues, *A Primer for Diabetic Patients*, which did much to educate victims of the disease to the possibilities of treatment and to the uses of insulin.

WILDMAN, MURRAY SHIPLEY (*b. Selma, Ohio, 1868; d. Stanford, Calif., 1930*), banker, economist. Ph.D., University of Chicago, 1904. Taught at University of Missouri and Northwestern. As secretary of the National Citizen's League for the Promotion of a Sound Banking System, 1911–12, he contributed to the establishment of the Federal Reserve System. In 1912 he became head of the Department of Economics, Stanford University, and was dean of the school of social sciences *post* 1925. Author of *Money Inflation in the United States* (1905).

WILDWOOD, WILL. *See* POND, FREDERICK EUGENE.

WILEY, ALEXANDER (*b. Chippewa Falls, Wis., 1884; d. Philadelphia, Pa., 1967*), studied at Augsburg College, the University of Michigan, and the University of Wisconsin Law School (LL.B., 1907). He practiced law and was district attorney for Chippewa County, Wisconsin (1909–15). He served as a Republican in the U.S. Senate (1939–63), becoming a leader of the party's internationalist wing. Was member of Foreign Relations and Senate Judiciary committees, and U.S. delegate to the United Nations General Assembly (1952–53).

WILEY, ANDREW JACKSON (*b. New Castle Co., Del., 1862; d. Monrovia, Calif., 1931*), irrigation engineer. Graduated Delaware College, 1882. Associated with private irrigation projects in Idaho and Montana *post* 1883, he later extended his field of work over most of the West. Consultant to U.S. Bureau of Reclamation *post* 1902, he worked on practically all major government dam projects of recent times, including the Shoshone, Arrowrock, Roosevelt, and Boulder dams. He was also consultant for other federal departments on the Coolidge and Madden dams, Canal Zone power plant, and the Columbia River Basin and other projects.

WILEY, CALVIN HENDERSON (*b. Guilford Co., N.C., 1819; d. Winston, N.C., 1887*), educator, North Carolina legislator. Graduated University of North Carolina, 1840. Effective first superintendent, North Carolina common schools, 1853–65. Established, 1856, and edited *North Carolina Journal of Education*; organized Educational Association of North Carolina; promoted Normal College, 1852–59. Author of, among other works, *The North-Carolina Reader* (1851), a standard text.

WILEY, DAVID (*b. probably Pennsylvania, date uncertain; d. possibly North Carolina, ca. 1813*), Presbyterian clergyman. Graduated College of New Jersey (Princeton), 1788; ordained by presbytery of Carlisle, Pa., 1794. Became principal of Columbian Academy, Georgetown, D.C., 1801. Best remembered as secretary of the Columbian Agricultural Society (organized 1809) and as editor of the *Agricultural Museum* (first number, July 1810), probably the first agricultural journal published in the United States.

WILEY, EPHRAIM EMERSON (*b. Malden, Mass., 1814; d. 1893*), Methodist clergyman, educator. Graduated Wesleyan University, 1837. Professor of ancient languages and literature, 1838–52; president, 1852–79; and treasurer and financial agent, 1886–93, at Emory and Henry College, Virginia. President, Martha Washington College, Virginia, 1881–86. Leader of the Holston Conference, he adhered to the Methodist Episcopal Church, South, after the schism of 1844.

WILEY, HARVEY WASHINGTON (*b. Kent, Ind., 1844; d. Washington, D.C., 1930*), chemist, author, pure-food reformer. M.D., Medical College of Indiana, Indianapolis, 1871; B.S., Harvard, 1873. Professor of chemistry, Purdue University, 1874–83, serving also as state chemist of Indiana. Studied at University of Berlin, 1878. As chief chemist, U.S. Department of Agriculture, 1883–1912, he made a chemical study of sugar and syrup crops and devised new apparatus and procedures for agricultural chemical analyses. His most important work, however, was his campaign against food adulteration and his securing (despite prolonged opposition) of the passage of the Pure Food and Drugs Act, 1906. Thereafter until 1912 he administered the enforcement of the act with tenacity and success. Professor of agricultural chemistry, George Washington University, 1899–1914. Director of Bureau of Foods, Sanitation and Health, *Good Housekeeping*, 1912–30. Successful as a lyceum and Chautauqua lecturer, he was author of, among other books, *Principles and Practice of Agricultural Analysis* (1894–97), *Foods and Their Adulteration* (1907), *History of a Crime Against the Food Law* (1929), and an autobiography (1930).

WILKES, CHARLES (*b. New York, N.Y., 1798; d. 1877*), naval officer, explorer. Appointed midshipman, 1818; studied under F. R. Hassler. Appointed to head U.S. Navy Depot of Charts and Instruments, Washington, D.C., 1833. From August 1838 until July 1842, he commanded the flagship *Vincennes* and five other

vessels on an extended exploring expedition, surveying the Antarctic coast, the islands of the Pacific Ocean, and the American Northwest coast. *Narrative of the United States Exploring Expedition* (1844) and three of the expedition's scientific reports were his work. In command of *San Jacinto*, he halted the British mail steamer *Trent*, 1861, removing two Confederate agents by force and causing the *"Trent"* affair." Commanding a special squadron in the West Indies and Bahamas against Confederate commerce destroyers, 1862–63, his actions brought protests of neutrality violations. Further conflicts with the Navy Department led to his court-martial, 1864. He was commissioned rear admiral, retired, 1866.

WILKES, GEORGE (*b. New York, N.Y., 1817; d. New York, 1885*), journalist. Cofounded *National Police Gazette*, 1845. Removed to California, 1849, as aide to David C. Broderick, whose fortune he inherited. Bought *Spirit of the Times*, 1856, renaming it *Porter's Spirit of the Times*; it appeared later as *Wilkes' Spirit of the Times*. Its political articles were influential, and Wilkes reported major Civil War engagements as if they were sporting events. He introduced pari-mutuel betting system to America and promoted famous prizefights. Author of, among other books, *Project for a National Railroad from the Atlantic to the Pacific Ocean* (1845), *The Great Battle Fought at Manassas* (1861), and *Shakespeare from an American Point of View* (1877).

WILKESON, SAMUEL (*b. Carlisle, Pa., 1781; d. Kingston, Tenn., 1848*), boat-builder, contractor, New York legislator. Removed to Lake Erie, near present Westfield, N.Y., 1809. Settling in Buffalo, N.Y., 1814, he engaged successfully in almost all its early business enterprises and constructed an artificial harbor at the mouth of Buffalo Creek for western terminus of the Erie Canal, 1820. Appointed first judge of common pleas, Erie County, 1821; became mayor of Buffalo, 1836. Assisted immigration of freed blacks to Liberia.

WILKIE, FRANC BANGS (*b. West Charlton, N.Y., 1832; d. Norwood Park, Ill., 1892*), journalist. Chief correspondent of *New York Times* in Civil War campaigns in the West and Southwest; assistant editor, *Chicago Times*, 1863–81 and 1883–88. Author of, among other books, *Personal Reminiscences of Thirty-five Years of Journalism* (1891).

WILKINS, ROSS (*b. Pittsburgh, Pa., 1799; d. 1872*), lawyer. Nephew of William Wilkins. Territorial judge of Michigan, 1832–37; U.S. judge, eastern district of Michigan, 1837–70.

WILKINS, WILLIAM (*b. Carlisle, Pa., 1779; d. 1865*), lawyer, businessman. Uncle of Ross Wilkins. President, Bank of Pittsburgh, Pa., 1814–19. President judge, 5th district of Pennsylvania, 1820–24; judge, U.S. district court for western Pennsylvania, 1824–31. U.S. senator, Democratic and Anti-Masonic, 1831–34; U.S. minister to Russia, 1834–36; U.S. secretary of war, 1844–45. A supporter of Andrew Jackson's policies and an expansionist.

WILKINSON, DAVID (*b. Smithfield, R.I., 1771; d. Caledonia Springs, Ontario, Canada, 1852*), inventor, manufacturer. Patented machine for cutting screw threads, incorporating slide rest, 1798. It was widely adopted, particularly in U.S. government firearms manufacture. In 1788–89, he constructed iron parts for Samuel Slater's cotton machinery; he later made patterns and cast wheels and racks for locks of the Charlestown, Mass., canal. Cofounded, *ca.* 1800, David Wilkinson & Co., iron and textile machinery manufactory, at Pawtucket, R.I. Perfected, among other machines, a mill to bore cannon by waterpower.

WILKINSON, JAMES (*b. Calvert Co., Md., 1757; d. Mexico City, Mexico, 1825*), soldier. Brother-in-law of Clement Biddle.

Commissioned a captain in the Continental army, 1776, he served at the siege of Boston, joined Benedict Arnold at Montreal, and accompanied Arnold during the retreat to Albany; in December, he was appointed aide-de-camp to General Horatio Gates. After serving at Trenton and Princeton and a promotion to lieutenant colonel, he rejoined Gates and was appointed deputy adjutant general for the northern department, May 1777. Although he dallied on his way to report the victory at Saratoga to Congress, he was given a brevet of brigadier general and in January 1778 became secretary of the Board of War. A gifted intriguer, he shared in the Conway Cabal against George Washington and was forced to resign his posts. Appointed almost immediately clothier general to the army, he rendered defective accounts and was obliged to give up the assignment in March 1781. He then took up farming in Bucks Co., Pa., and in 1783 was elected to the state assembly.

Engaging in trade westward in 1784, he supplanted George Rogers Clark as a leader in the rapidly growing Kentucky region. The success of two memorials which he wrote advocating immediate separation from Virginia (August 1785) gave him the idea of turning prevalent discontent in the area to his own financial gain. Making approaches through the Spanish authorities in upper Louisiana, he went on a trading voyage to New Orleans, 1787, where he won the favor of Governor Esteban Miró and received an exclusive trading monopoly. He received this in part because he had persuaded the Spaniards that he was working toward disunion in the West. Active in the Kentucky convention of November 1788 as a moderate, he managed to convince Miró that he had achieved much for Spain. On a second journey to New Orleans in the summer of 1789 he composed and presented to the governor a second memorial or report on disunion sentiment and added to it a list of prominent westerners to whom, he suggested, the Spanish government might profitably grant pensions. After receiving a pension himself, together with a so-called loan, he was temporarily upset by a decree of the Spanish government which opened up the river trade on the Mississippi and so rendered his monopoly valueless. Meanwhile, he had also endeavored to worm his way into the confidence of the Yazoo land speculators, only to betray them to the Spaniards. In financial straits because of Kentucky land speculations, he returned to the army, leaving his business affairs to be settled by Harry Innes.

After leading a force of volunteers against the Indians north of the Ohio in March 1791, Wilkinson was commissioned lieutenant colonel in the regular army and in March 1792 was made brigadier general under General Anthony Wayne. A disloyal subordinate to Wayne whom he attempted to discredit, he continued his tenuous connection with the Spaniards and revealed to Baron Carondelet the filibustering activities of George Rogers Clark. In 1796 he took over Detroit from the British, but soon departed for Philadelphia to intensify his lobbying against Wayne. Becoming the ranking officer of the army after Wayne's unexpected death, he returned to Detroit, 1797, where he was extremely unpopular.

Transferred to command on the southern frontier in 1798, he was criticized for his friendship with the Spaniards and for personal land deals and speculations in army contracts. He also schemed to become governor of Mississippi Territory. Following the Democratic-Republican victory of 1800, Aaron Burr helped him keep his place in the army, and Jefferson commissioned him to treat with the various southern Indian tribes, a task that kept him traveling a year and a half. In 1803, after sharing with William C. C. Claiborne the honor of taking possession of the Louisiana Purchase, he invested a great part of a new bribe which he had received from the Spanish boundary commissioner in sugar, and then sailed for New York City. He then began his spectacular relations with Aaron Burr in the so-called Burr Conspiracy. He conferred frequently with Burr in Washington, D.C., during the winter of 1804–05, and again in the following June at the mouth of the Ohio, whence Wilkinson furnished Burr with conveyance to New Orleans and letters of introduction. Public opinion at this time associated the two in a possible invasion of Mexico.

In the spring of 1805, Wilkinson assumed the governorship of Louisiana Territory with headquarters at St. Louis. He was engaged with R. A. Chouteau in the fur trade and at this time dispatched the famous expedition under Zebulon M. Pike to open up a feasible military route to New Mexico. This activity was generally believed to have a connection with the mysterious movements of Burr. Soon as unpopular in St. Louis as he had been at Detroit, he was ordered again to the southern frontier in May 1806 and ultimately removed from the governorship. Aroused by the threat to himself in Joseph Street's current exposures concerning Burr's purposes, Wilkinson, from his headquarters at Natchitoches, covered himself by warning President Jefferson that a plot was afoot to disrupt the Union and to invade Mexico. He suggested that he should meet this peril by transferring troops to New Orleans. After making these dispositions, he sent a messenger to inform the viceroy of Mexico of the peril of armed invasion which threatened the Spanish dominions and asked for a sum of money for his efforts to avert it. He declared martial law at New Orleans, embargoed vessels, and arrested and imprisoned without regard to law all whom he chose to regard as agents of Burr. Unaware of the hostile reception which Wilkinson had planned, Burr with some 60 men arrived in Mississippi Territory, where he was arrested.

When Burr was put on trial for treason in Richmond, Va., Wilkinson assumed the role of chief witness against him, but narrowly escaped indictment by the grand jury. Suspected by everyone, with the possible exception of Thomas Jefferson, he was deserted by his friends and business associates, caricatured, denounced, and publicly insulted. He was brought before a court of inquiry, which acquitted him after six months of deliberation. President Jefferson now ordered him to New Orleans and empowered him to confer on the way with the Spanish officials at Havana and Pensacola regarding a proposed alliance. Failing in this pioneer attempt at Pan-Americanism, he was once again investigated and in July 1811 was court-martialed by order of President James Madison. The "not guilty" verdict of this court, December 1811, was so worded that the president approved it with regret.

Restored to command at New Orleans, Wilkinson occupied Mobile early in 1813 and later that year was commissioned major general and ordered to the Canadian frontier. There he made a fiasco of the campaign against Montreal. Relieved from regular duty and ordered to Washington, he provoked a quarrel with John Armstrong (1758–1843) which led to yet another inquiry and acquittal, but he was not reinstated in the service. For some years thereafter he lived on a plantation below New Orleans, but Mexico once more claimed his attention in 1821 and he went there in pursuit of a Texas land grant. In time he obtained an option on lands in Texas, but before he could fulfill the conditions of the grant, he died. His *Memoirs of My Own Times*, three confused volumes of documents which are as significant for what they omit as for what they contain, were published in 1816.

WILKINSON, JEMIMA (*b.* Cumberland, R.I., 1752; *d.* 1819), religious leader. Sister of Jeremiah Wilkinson. Influenced by George Whitefield's sermons and by the example of Ann Lee, she announced, *ca.* 1775, her conviction that her body was inhabited by a prophetic spirit. Assuming the name Public Universal Friend, she preached with great success in her part of Rhode Island and won a number of followers. After considerable opposition and several removes, she founded the colony of Jerusalem in Yates Co., N.Y., 1789–90, presiding over it until her death.

WILKINSON, JEREMIAH (*b. Cumberland, R.I., 1741; d. Cumberland, 1831*), forge-master, farmer, inventor. Brother of Jemima Wilkinson. Perfected a number of devices to expedite his manufacture of wool-cards; drew wire by horsepower *ante* 1776; made first experiments in nail manufacture from cold iron, *ca.* 1776.

WILKINSON, JOHN (*b. Norfolk, Va., 1821; d. Annapolis, Md., 1891*), naval officer *post* April 6, 1861, he was highly successful as commander of the blockade-runners *Giraffe* (later named *Robert E. Lee*), *Chickamauga*, and *Chameleon*. He also led an abortive 1863 attempt to release Confederate prisoners confined on Johnson's Island in Lake Erie. Author of *Narrative of a Blockade-Runner* (1877).

WILKINSON, ROBERT SHAW (*b. Charleston, S.C., 1875; d. 1932*), educator. Son of free black parents, A.B., Oberlin, 1891. Professor of Greek and Latin, State University, Louisville, Ky., 1891–96. Appointed professor of science at State Agricultural and Mechanical College, Orangeburg, S.C., 1896, he served the college as president *post* 1911 with remarkable success. He raised standards in every particular and emphasized a balanced curriculum of industrial and literary instruction.

WILKINSON, THEODORE STARK (*b. Annapolis, Md., 1888; d. Virginia, 1946*), naval officer. Graduated U.S. Naval Academy, 1909. M.S., George Washington University, 1912. Awarded Medal of Honor for leadership in landing at Veracruz, Mexico, 1914. Served in Bureau of Ordnance during World War I; rose to rank of rear admiral in various duties, 1919–41. Director, Office of Naval Intelligence, Oct. 1941–July 1942; commander, Battleship Division 2, Aug. 1942–Jan. 1943; deputy commander, South Pacific Force, Jan.–July 1943; commander, 3rd Amphibious Force, July 1943–45. A leading advocate and practitioner of the "leapfrogging" strategy, whereby U.S. forces in the Pacific theater bypassed and isolated enemy strong points, concentrating on the capture of weaker targets. Promoted vice admiral, 1944.

WILL, ALLEN SINCLAIR (*b. Antioch, Va., 1868; d. New York, N.Y., 1934*), journalist, educator. On *Baltimore Sun* staff, 1889–1912; city editor, 1905–12. Associate editor and editorial writer, *Baltimore News*, 1912–14; news editor, *Philadelphia Public Ledger*, 1914–16; assistant editor, *New York Times*, 1917–24. Director, Department of Journalism, Rutgers University, *post* 1926. Author of, among other works, *Life of Cardinal Gibbons, Archbishop of Baltimore* (1922), and *Education for Newspaper Life* (1931).

WILLARD, DANIEL (*b. North Hartland, Vt., 1861; d. Baltimore, Md., 1942*), railroad executive. From a section hand on the Vermont Central Railroad, Willard rose to a division superintendency on the Minneapolis, St. Paul and Sault Ste. Marie (Soo Line), 1879–99. From 1899 to 1901, he was assistant general manager of the Baltimore & Ohio; from 1901 to 1904, first vice president and general manager of the Erie; from 1904 to 1910, operating vice president of the Chicago, Burlington & Quincy. Returning to the Baltimore & Ohio as president in 1910, he served until 1941, when he became chairman of the board. His rebuilding program produced a major increase in B & O traffic and revenues during the 1920's; during the depression years, his economical management kept the road from receivership. President of the board of trustees of Johns Hopkins University, 1926–41.

WILLARD, DE FOREST (*b. Newington, Conn., 1846; d. Lansdowne, Pa., 1910*), physician, pioneer in orthopedic surgery. Studied under Joseph Pancoast and Samuel D. Gross at Jefferson Medical College; graduated in medicine, University of Pennsylvania, 1867. Taught at Pennsylvania *post* 1867; was clinical professor of orthopedic surgery, 1889–1903, and professor thereafter.

General surgeon at the Presbyterian Hospital, Philadelphia, and consultant at many others, he was surgeon in chief of the Widener Memorial Industrial Training School for Crippled Children, which he had helped to plan.

WILLARD, EMMA HART (*b. Berlin, Conn., 1787; d. 1870*), educator. Encouraged by her parents to read widely and to do her own thinking, she attended the district school and Berlin Academy. Becoming a teacher, she was unusually successful as head of the Female Academy, Middlebury, Vt., 1807–09. Opening a school for girls in her own home at Middlebury, 1814, she experimented with plans for improving female education and proved that such subjects as mathematics and philosophy could be mastered by girls without costing them their health, refinement, or charm. Despite the support of New York's Governor DeWitt Clinton and others, she failed in a pioneer campaign, 1818, for establishment with state aid of schools in which women would be given the same educational advantages as men; she then removed to New York State and in 1821 founded the Troy Female Seminary with the aid of local citizens. As it grew in reputation and influence, she continued her policy of adding higher subjects to the curriculum, especially mathematics. She retired from active management, 1838. Subsequently she worked with Henry Barnard and others for improvement of the common schools. While active at Troy, she evolved new methods of teaching and published widely used textbooks in geography and history. She was author also of a number of mediocre poems, including "Rocked in the Cradle of the Deep."

WILLARD, FRANCES ELIZABETH CAROLINE (*b. Churchville, N.Y., 1839; d. New York, N.Y., 1898*), teacher, reformer. Raised in pioneer Wisconsin. Graduated Northwestern Female College, Evanston, Ill., 1859. Evanston became her permanent home. Joining the temperance crusade, 1874, she was elected president of the National Woman's Christian Temperance Union, 1879. She enlisted her society in the cause of woman's suffrage, helped organize the Prohibition party, 1882, and devoted her life to furthering the cause with tongue and pen. In 1891 she was elected president of the World's Woman's Christian Temperance Union. Temperance, in her opinion, was basically a measure for the protection of home life and therefore an ideal which demanded personal sacrifice.

WILLARD, FRANK HENRY (*b. Anna, Ill., 1893; d. Los Angeles, Calif., 1958*), cartoonist. Studied briefly at the Chicago Academy of Fine Arts. After World War I, Willard settled in New York and by 1923 was producing the cartoon "Moon Mullins," begun for the *New York Daily News*. This strip, along with "Kitty Higgins" insured his fame as a cartoonist. At the time of Willard's death, "Moon Mullins" was appearing in over 250 newspapers.

WILLARD, JAMES FIELD (*b. Philadelphia, Pa., 1876; d. 1935*), historian, medievalist. Graduated University of Pennsylvania, 1898; Ph.D., 1902. Professor and head of the Department of History. University of Colorado *post* 1906. He was author of a number of important studies in medieval history and also edited several volumes of important source materials on the history of the American West.

WILLARD, JOSEPH (*b. Biddeford, Maine, 1738; d. New Bedford, Mass., 1804*), Congregational clergyman, educational leader. Great-grandson of Samuel Willard (1639/40–1707). Graduated Harvard, 1765. Pastor at Beverly, Mass. For many years corresponding secretary and vice president of the American Academy of Arts and Sciences (of which he was a founder, 1780), he was well known for work in astronomy, mathematics, and the classics. President of Harvard, 1781–1804, he repaired ravages of the Revolution, raised entrance requirements, broadened instruction, and founded the medical school.

WILLARD, JOSEPH (*b. Cambridge, Mass., 1798; d. 1865*), lawyer, historian. Son of Joseph Willard (1738–1804); brother of Sidney Willard. LL.B., Harvard Law School, 1820. Clerk, court of common pleas, Suffolk County, *post* 1841. Officer of Massachusetts Historical Society, 1833–64. Author of, among other works, *Sketches of the Town of Lancaster* (1826).

WILLARD, JOSEPH EDWARD (*b. Washington, D.C., 1865; d. New York, N.Y., 1924*), diplomat, lawyer, Virginia legislator. Practiced at Richmond, Va., bar. Gained statewide reputation as soldier in Spanish-American War. Democratic lieutenant governor of Virginia, 1902–06. Served as U.S. ambassador to Spain, 1913–21.

WILLARD, JOSIAH FLINT (*b. Appleton, Wis., 1869; d. 1907*), writer on vagrancy and criminology, better known under the pen name "Josiah Flynt." Nephew of Frances E. Willard. Author of, among other works of sociological value, *Tramping With Tramps* (1899), *The Powers That Prey* (1900), and *The World of Graft* (1901).

WILLARD, MARY HATCH (*b. Jersey City, N.J., 1856; d. New York, N.Y., 1926*), businesswoman, social worker. Established, *ca.* 1890 in New York City, the successful Home Bureau, for supply of food for invalids; later added a trained nurses' registry service. In World War I, led huge emergency movement to supply hospitals on western front with surgical dressings. Associated for many years with State Charities Aid Association of New York.

WILLARD, SAMUEL (*b. Concord, Mass., 1639/40; d. 1707*), Congregational clergyman, controversialist. Son of Simon Willard (1605–76 o.s.). Graduated Harvard, 1659. Pastor of Groton, Mass., 1664–78; of Old South Church, Boston, Mass., *post* 1678. He was conservative in theology, liberal in practice. Like his friends the Mathers, he was an opponent of the methods used in the witchcraft trials, 1692. Vice president of Harvard University, 1700–07, he in fact headed the institution. A voluminous writer, he made one of the best psychic investigations in the literature of the witchcraft delusion (*Massachusetts Historical Society Collections*, 4 ser. VIII, 1868). His *Compleat Body of Divinity* was published in 1726.

WILLARD, SAMUEL (*b. Petersham, Mass., 1775; d. Deerfield, Mass., 1859*), Congregational and Unitarian clergyman, educator, hymnist. Brother of Solomon Willard. Graduated Harvard, 1803. Pastor at Deerfield, Mass., 1807–29. The controversy over his ordination was the first sign in western Massachusetts of the liberal theological opinions which led to Unitarian-Congregational split. As superintendent of Deerfield schools, he wrote and published numerous textbooks, he was author also of hymnals, including the *Deerfield Collection of Sacred Music* (1814).

WILLARD, SIDNEY (*b. Beverly, Mass., 1780; d. 1856*), educator, writer, Massachusetts legislator. Son of Joseph Willard (1738–1804); brother of Joseph Willard (1798–1865). Graduated Harvard, 1798. Hancock professor of Hebrew and Oriental languages at Harvard, 1806–*ca.* 1830; professor of Latin, 1827–31. Established and edited *American Monthly Review*, 1831–33, and was a contributor to, or otherwise associated with, almost all Massachusetts magazine ventures in his time. Mayor of Cambridge, Mass., 1848–50.

WILLARD, SIMON (*b. probably Kent, England, 1605; d. Charlestown, Mass., 1676*), colonist, fur trader. Father of Samuel Willard (1639/40–1707). Cofounder, with Peter Bulkeley, of Concord, Mass., 1635; was one of the leading men on the Merrimac frontier. Represented Concord in the General Court, 1636–54 with exception of 1643, 1647, and 1648; chosen assistant, 1654, he served until his death. Assisted John Eliot among Merrimac tribes, 1646 and afterward. In charge of Merrimac defenses during King Philip's War, his relief of Brookfield, Mass., Aug. 4, 1675, was a notable feat.

WILLARD, SIMON (*b. Grafton, Mass., 1753; d. Roxbury, Mass., 1848*), clockmaker, inventor. Established clock factory at Roxbury, Mass., between 1777 and 1780; retired from business, 1839. Built up enviable reputation specializing in church, hall, and gallery timepieces. He is especially renowned for the "Willard Patent Timepiece," or "banjo clock" (patented 1802). President Jefferson was one of his patrons.

WILLARD, SOLOMON (*b. Petersham, Mass., 1783; d. Quincy, Mass., 1861*), sculptor, architect. Brother of Samuel Willard (1775–1859). Executed wood and marble carvings primarily for Boston, Mass., churches and public buildings. His sculpture included the eagle on old Boston Customs House, 1809, and many ship figureheads from *ca.* 1813. Made wooden model of completed U.S. Capitol for Charles Bulfinch. He designed, among other buildings, the Doric U.S. Branch Bank, Boston (1824), and the Boston Court House (1832). Famous chiefly as architect of Bunker Hill Monument, 1825–42, he supervised construction, published *Plans and Section of the Obelisk . . .* (1843) and discovered and worked the Quincy granite quarries.

WILLCOX, LOUISE COLLIER (*b. Chicago, Ill., 1865; d. Paris, France, 1929*), essayist, critic, editor. Sister of Hiram P. Collier. Studied and traveled in Europe; resident in Norfolk, Va., *post* 1887. Editorial writer for *Harper's Weekly* and *Harper's Bazar*; wrote also for the *Delineator*. Member of editorial staff, *North American Review*, 1906–13. Reader and adviser for Macmillan Co., 1903–09; for E. P. Dutton & Co., 1910–17. Translator of contemporary French and German books.

WILLCOX, ORLANDO BOLIVAR (*b. Detroit, Mich., 1823; d. Coburg, Ontario, Canada, 1907*), soldier. Graduated West Point, 1847. First lieutenant of artillery in campaigns against Seminole Indians, 1856–57; commissioned colonel, 1st Michigan Infantry, 1861. Brigadier general of volunteers assigned to Burnside's IX Corps, 1862, he commanded a division, and sometimes the corps, with marked distinction at Antietam, Fredericksburg, and Knoxville, and in campaigns from the Wilderness to Petersburg. Breveted major general of volunteers, 1864, brigadier general and major general in regular army, 1867. Commanded Department of Arizona, March 1878–September 1882, operating notably against the Apache. Commanded Department of Missouri, October 1886–April 1887.

WILLEBRANDT, MABEL WALKER (*b. Woodsdale, Kans., 1889; d. Riverside, Calif., 1963*), lawyer. Attended University of Southern California (LL.B., 1916; LL.M., 1917). Started a private practice and volunteered her services as assistant public defender in police courts. Assistant U.S. attorney general, 1921–29; her major responsibilities included the administration of the Bureau of Federal Prisons, supervision of federal tax cases, and prosecution of cases arising under the National Prohibition Act. By 1925 she was responsible for more than 45,000 criminal prosecutions in the federal courts. Counsel to the Screen Directors' Guild, 1936–57.

WILLET, WILLIAM (*b. New York, N.Y., 1867; d. Philadelphia, Pa., 1921*), artist in stained glass. Studied at New York Mechanics' and Tradesmen's Institute, 1884–85, and under William M. Chase and John La Farge. Resided in Pittsburgh, Pa., *ca.* 1898–1913. Possessing a vivid color sense and high artistic integrity, he challenged popular taste in his speciality after traveling in Europe, 1902. Among his works are the chancel window, Calvary Church, Pittsburgh, 1907; the sanctuary window of West Point Chapel, 1910, called the symbol of a regenerated craft in America; and the great west window, Princeton University Graduate School (1913).

WILLETT, HERBERT LOCKWOOD (*b. Ionia, Mich., 1864; d. Winter Park, Fla., 1944*), Disciples of Christ clergyman, educator, biblical scholar. B.A., Bethany College, 1886. Ordained, 1890. While engaged in various pastoral activities, he pursued graduate studies at University of Chicago and received the Ph.D., 1896. Joining the staff of the Semitics department at Chicago on completion of his graduate work, he remained there until retirement in 1929 (professor of Oriental languages and literature *post* 1915). He endeavored to popularize liberal biblical scholarship within his own denomination and beyond it, and was widely known as a lecturer. A supporter of ecumenism, he held pastorates in Chicago and Kenilworth, Ill.

WILLETT, MARINUS (*b. Jamaica, N.Y., 1740; d. Cedar Grove, N.Y., 1830*), merchant, Revolutionary soldier. An outstanding Son of Liberty and leader of radical patriots in New York City. After service in Montgomery's invasion of Canada, 1775, he was commissioned lieutenant colonel, 3rd New York Regiment, 1776, commanding at Fort Constitution. As second-in-command under Col. Peter Gansevoort at Fort Schuyler, 1777, he distinguished himself during British attack by Col. Barry St. Leger. He fought under Washington at Monmouth and took part in the Sullivan-Clinton expedition against the Iroquois, 1779. Appointed lieutenant colonel commandant, 5th New York Regiment, 1780. Led regiment of levies on Tryon frontier, 1781, in successful battle of Johnstown. Sheriff of New York City and county, 1784–88 and 1792–96. Obtained treaty with Creek Indians, 1790. Appointed mayor of New York City, 1807.

WILLEY, SAMUEL HOPKINS (*b. Campton, N.H., 1821; d. 1914*), California clergyman, educator. Graduated Dartmouth, 1845; Union Theological Seminary, N.Y., 1848. On behalf of American Missionary Society, he went as minister to Monterey, Calif., 1849. Removed to San Francisco, 1850; established and became pastor of Howard Presbyterian Church, resigning 1862. Helped found College of California, Berkeley, 1855; served as vice president and acting president, 1862–69. Held pastorates in Santa Cruz and Benicia, 1870–89; was president of Van Ness Seminary, 1889–96. Author of, among other historical writings, *Thirty Years in California* (1879) and *A History of The College of California* (1887).

WILLEY, WAITMAN THOMAS (*b. near present Farmington, W.Va., 1811; d. Morgantown, W.Va., 1900*), lawyer, politician. Opposed Virginia's secession, 1861, at state convention, but checked radical movement for immediate West Virginia statehood. U.S. senator from Virginia, July 1861–63, from West Virginia, 1863–71. As senator, he was instrumental in Congress's acceptance of West Virginia's constitution and in ratification of the "Willey Amendment" for gradual abolition of slavery. First a Whig, he became a Republican, 1864. Later, as a Radical Republican, he voted for impeachment of President Andrew Johnson.

WILLIAMS, ALPHEUS STARKEY (*b. Saybrook, Conn., 1810; d. Washington, D.C., 1878*), lawyer, soldier. Practiced in Detroit, Mich., *post ca.* 1837; served in Mexican War; postmaster of Detroit, 1849–53. A Union brigadier general of volunteers, 1861, he commanded a division in the Shenandoah Valley campaign, 1862, and a division of the XII Corps in battle of South Mountain. Lee's famous "lost order" was brought to his headquarters. Succeeding to command of Mansfield's Corps at Antietam,

he later led his own division with conspicuous ability at Chancellorsville and Gettysburg. Served with 1st Division of new XX Corps in Army of the Cumberland in Atlanta campaign. Commanded XX Corps in Sherman's march to the sea and during Carolinas campaign. Mustered out, 1866. U.S. minister resident to Salvador, 1866–69. Congressman, Democrat, from Michigan, 1875–78.

WILLIAMS, AUBREY WILLIS (*b. Springville, Ala., 1890; d. Washington, D.C., 1965*), social worker, federal official, and civil rights advocate. Attended Maryville and University of Cincinnati (B.A., 1920). Executive director of the Wisconsin Conference on Social Work, 1922–32, gaining a national reputation as an effective proponent of rationally administered public assistance programs. Field representative for the American Public Welfare Association, 1932–33, to ensure that relief loans from the Reconstruction Finance Corporation reached those in need. A fervent New Dealer, he became deputy administrator of the Works Progress Administration. His outspoken liberalism made his career stormy; he infuriated conservatives by blaming social injustice on "arrogant aggregates of concentrated economic power." Head of the National Youth Administration, 1935–43. Returned to the South and purchased the *Southern Farmer*, a monthly, and continued to be one of the most vigorous white southern spokesmen for civil rights. Became president of the Southern Conference Education Fund in 1947, putting him very much out of step with the white South's determination to preserve segregation.

WILLIAMS, BARNEY (*b. Cork, Ireland, 1823; d. New York, N.Y., 1876*), actor. Stage name of Bernard Flaherty. In 1849, married Maria Pray, with whom he costarred thereafter throughout the United States. Williams was an infectiously humorous entertainer in broad Irish character.

WILLIAMS, BEN AMES (*b. Macon, Miss., 1889; d. Brookline, Mass., 1953*), novelist and short-story writer. Studied at Dartmouth College (1906). Between 1917 and 1941, he published 179 stories, serials, and articles in the *Saturday Evening Post*, and all together, more than 400 pieces in other magazines and journals. His stories usually concerned the people of a fictionalized town, Searsmont, in Maine. Novels include *House Divided* (1947), an epic Civil War novel that became a best seller, *The Strange Woman* (1941), and *Leave Her to Heaven* (1944); the last two were made into successful motion pictures.

WILLIAMS, BERT (*b. New Providence, Bahamas, ca. 1876; d. New York, N.Y., 1922*), comedian, songwriter. Stage name of Egbert Austin Williams. Formed successful vaudeville team with George Walker, 1895. In 1903 they produced the musical comedy *In Dahomey* with an all black cast in New York and London; similar pieces such as *Abyssinia* and *Bandanna Land* followed. Leading comedian in the Ziegfeld Follies *post* 1909, Williams' skits and such songs as "Jonah Man" were often the best things in the show. A pioneer in assuring talented blacks a place in the American theater, he was himself a performer of rare gifts.

WILLIAMS, CATHARINE READ ARNOLD (*b. Providence, R.I., 1787; d. Providence, 1872*), poet, novelist, biographer. Author of, among other works, *Original Poems, on Various Subjects* (1828), *Tales, National and Revolutionary* (1830), and *The Neutral French, or the Exiles of Nova Scotia* (1841), whose theme anticipated Longfellow's *Evangeline*. Her vigorous, didactic books were popular in her day.

WILLIAMS, CHANNING MOORE (*b. Richmond, Va., 1829; d. Richmond, 1910*), Episcopal clergyman. Graduated William and Mary, 1852; Theological Seminary, Alexandria, Va., 1855. Ordained priest, 1857. Sent to Japan, 1859, by board of missions of the Protestant Episcopal church; he supervised erection of the first

Protestant church building there. Consecrated in New York, 1866, as bishop of China with jurisdiction in Japan. Named bishop of Tokyo, 1874, he resigned 1889.

WILLIAMS, CHARLES DAVID (b. Bellevue, Ohio, 1860; d. 1923), Episcopal clergyman. Graduated Kenyon, 1880; ordained, 1884. Dean of Trinity Cathedral, Cleveland, Ohio, 1893–1906. Consecrated bishop of Michigan, 1906. A liberal, Williams was the leading exponent in his communion of the Social Gospel. He believed the church, by engendering a worldwide fellowship, should help bring about a new social order by proclaiming principles of industrial democracy, not by recommending economic and political programs. Author of, among other books, *The Christian Ministry and Social Problems* (1917), *The Prophetic Ministry for Today* (1912), and *The Gospel of Fellowship* (1923), all of which set forth his social views.

WILLIAMS, CHARLES RICHARD (b. Prattsburg, N.Y., 1853; d. Princeton, N.J., 1927), editor, author. Son-in-law of William H. Smith (1833–96). A.B., College of New Jersey (Princeton), 1875. Editor in chief, *Indianapolis News*, 1892–1911. The correctness of style and nicety of language of the *News* set a high standard in the Midwest. Author of, among other books, *The Life of Rutherford Birchard Hayes* (1914); edited Hayes's *Diary and Letters* (1922–26).

WILLIAMS, DANIEL HALE (b. Hollidaysburg, Pa., 1858; d. Idlewild, Mich., 1931), surgeon. M.D., Chicago Medical College, 1883. Organized Provident Hospital, Chicago, Ill., 1891, with first black nurses' training school in the United States. Surgeon in chief, Freedmen's Hospital, Washington, D.C., 1893–98. Appointed professor of clinical surgery, Meharry Medical College, Nashville, Tenn., 1899. Performed first successful surgical closure of a wound of the heart and pericardium, 1893; perfected suture for arrest of hemorrhage from the spleen. Charter member of American College of Surgeons, 1913. The most gifted surgeon and most notable black medical man in U.S. history.

WILLIAMS, DAVID ROGERSON (b. Robbin's Neck, S.C., 1776; d. Williamsburg district, S.C., 1830), planter, South Carolina legislator, pioneer manufacturer. Congressman, Democratic-Republican, from South Carolina, 1805–09 and 1811–13. Supported the Embargo of 1807, espoused cause of war hawks, and was chairman of House Committee on Military Affairs. Governor of South Carolina, 1814–16. Opposing nullification, he advocated development of southern domestic manufactures and engaged in making cotton yarns, hats and shoes, and cottonseed oil. Opposition to John C. Calhoun was the consuming purpose of his later life.

WILLIAMS, EDWARD THOMAS (b. Columbus, Ohio, 1854; d. Berkeley, Calif., 1944), Disciples of Christ clergyman, missionary and diplomat in China, educator. Graduated Bethany College, 1875. Held pastorates in Springfield, Ill., Denver, Colo., Brooklyn, N.Y., and Cincinnati, Ohio. A missionary in China, 1887–96, he left the ministry and became translator at the U.S. consulate general in Shanghai. For the next quarter-century, he served in a number of diplomatic capacities in China and in Washington, D.C., concluding as chief of the Far East division in the U.S. Department of State, 1914–18, and as a consultant at the Washington Conference, 1921. From 1918 until his retirement in 1927, he was Agassiz professor of Oriental languages and literature, University of California, Berkeley. He was author of *China Yesterday and Today* (1923) and *A Short History of China* (1928).

WILLIAMS, EDWIN (b. Norwich, Conn., 1797; d. New York, N.Y., 1854), New York City journalist, miscellaneous writer. Author of, among other works, *The Statesman's Manual* (1846–58).

WILLIAMS, EGBERT AUSTIN. *See* WILLIAMS, BERT.

WILLIAMS, ELEAZAR (b. possibly Sault St. Louis, Canada, ca. 1789; d. Hogansburg, N.Y., 1858), Episcopal Indian missionary. A half-breed, he led Oneida chiefs to Green Bay, Wis., 1821, where they negotiated a treaty with the Menominee and Winnebago and were ceded land on the Fox River. In 1822 Williams led a number of Oneida to Wisconsin, becoming their missionary. Repudiated by the Indians, he became well known for hypocrisy, indolence, and desire for notoriety. *Post* 1839 he maintained that he was Louis XVII of France. Published, among other writings, *Good News to the Iroquois Nation* (1813).

WILLIAMS, ELISHA (b. Hatfield, Mass., 1694; d. Wethersfield, Conn., 1755), Congregational clergyman, Connecticut colonial legislator. Half brother of Israel Williams. Graduated Harvard, 1711. Gained high repute as teacher in Wethersfield, 1716–19, where he instructed a part of the Yale student body, among them, Jonathan Edwards. Pastor at Wethersfield, 1722–26, he was rector of Yale College, 1726–39. Represented Wethersfield in Connecticut General Assembly, 1717–19, 1740–49, and *post* 1751; several times chosen Speaker. Judge, Connecticut Superior Court, 1740–43. As army chaplain, he was present at capture of Louisburg, Cape Breton Island, 1745. Delegate at Albany Congress, 1754.

WILLIAMS, ELISHA (b. Pomfret, Conn., 1773; d. probably Waterloo, N.Y., 1833), lawyer, politician. Admitted to the New York bar, 1793; practiced in Spencertown and Hudson, N.Y.; displayed brilliant oratorical gifts. Elected to New York Assembly for Columbia County, 1800; he served at nine sessions down to 1828. A Federalist leader, he was strongly antidemocratic in the New York constitutional convention in 1821. In 1815 he founded Waterloo, Seneca Co., N.Y.

WILLIAMS, ELKANAH (b. near Bedford, Ind., 1822; d. Hazelwood, Pa., 1888), ophthalmologist. M.D., University of Louisville, 1850; influenced by S. D. Gross. Studied in Europe, 1852–55. Returning to Cincinnati, Ohio, 1855, he became the pioneer ophthalmologist in the Midwest. As professor of opthalmology and aural surgery, Miami Medical College *post* 1865, he was first in the United States to hold a chair in this specialty. One of first in America to use the ophthalmoscope.

WILLIAMS, EPHRAIM (b. Newton, Mass., 1714 n.s.; d. near Crown Point, N.Y., 1755), colonial soldier. Settled in Stockbridge, Mass., 1739. Commissioned captain, 1745, commanding forts and posts along northern boundary of Massachusetts from Northfield to the New York border. Commissioned colonel of a regiment to aid William Johnson in expedition against Crown Point, 1755, he was killed in ambush while reconnoitering in force with Chief Hendrick. His estate was employed in founding the school which became Williams College.

WILLIAMS, FANNIE BARRIER (b. Brockport, N.Y., 1855; d. Brockport, 1944), Afro-American civic leader. Graduated State Normal School, Brockport, 1870; studied also at New England Conservatory of Music and at School of Fine Arts, Washington, D.C. Married S. Laing Williams, a lawyer, 1887, and settled in Chicago, Ill. Having experienced race discrimination for the first time while she was a teacher in the South during the late 1870's, she became a militant and persuasive advocate of equal rights for black people; she made her public debut in 1893 when she delivered a widely acclaimed address before a women's congress at the Chicago World's Fair. During the next ten years, she traveled extensively, speaking to women's clubs and church groups on various aspects of Afro-American life; she also worked to develop an organizational and institutional life in the black community and urged black women to take a leading part in the woman suffrage movement.

WILLIAMS, FRANCIS HENRY (*b. Uxbridge, Mass., 1852; d. Boston, Mass., 1936*), physician. Son of Henry W. Williams. Graduated Massachusetts Institute of Technology, 1873; M.D., Harvard Medical School, 1877. Distinguished in practice in Boston, Mass., and as a faculty member at Harvard Medical School, he is remembered as a pioneer in the use of X rays. Shortly after their discovery by Roentgen in December 1895, Williams began using them to study cases of thoracic lesions, and as early as April 1896 delivered a paper on the use of X rays in medicine, illustrating it with X-ray photographs. He was author of, among other works, *The Roentgen Rays in Medicine and Surgery* (1901). He was also an early experimenter with the therapeutic use of beta rays from radium.

WILLIAMS, FRANK MARTIN (*b. Durhamville, N.Y., 1873; d. Albany, N.Y., 1930*), civil engineer. State engineer and surveyor of New York, 1909–10 and 1915–22, he supervised construction of a barge canal to supersede Erie Canal. Consultant for, among other projects, the Holland Vehicular Tunnel and Sacandaga Reservoir.

WILLIAMS, FREDERICK WELLS (*b. Macao, 1857; d. New Haven, Conn., 1928*), writer, teacher. Son of Samuel W. Williams. Graduated Yale, 1879. Taught Oriental history at Yale, 1893–1925. *Post* 1901 he was associated with Yale-in-China. Author of *The Life and Letters of Samuel Wells Williams* (1889) and *Anson Burlingame and the First Chinese Mission to Foreign Powers* (1912).

WILLIAMS, GAAR CAMPBELL (*b. Richmond, Ind., 1880; d. Chicago, Ill., 1935*), cartoonist. Studied at Art Institute of Chicago; began work on staff of *Chicago Daily News*. Editorial cartoonist, *Indianapolis News*, 1909–21; special cartoonist, *Chicago Tribune* thereafter. Author of the celebrated single-panel series "Just Plain Folks" and the Sunday feature "Among the Folks in History," which were widely syndicated.

WILLIAMS, GARDNER FRED (*b. Saginaw, Mich., 1842; d. 1922*), mining engineer. Graduated College of California, 1865; studied also at Freiberg. Consultant in western mining regions, 1875–83. Manager, under Cecil Rhodes, of De Beers Mining Co., South Africa, 1887–1905. His improved working methods made possible worldwide regulation of diamond prices. Author of *The Diamond Mines of South Africa* (1902).

WILLIAMS, GEORGE HENRY (*b. New Lebanon, N.Y., 1820; d. 1910*), jurist, politician. Iowa district judge, 1847–52; chief justice, Oregon Territory, 1853–57. Leading member of Oregon constitutional convention, 1857; delegate to Union state convention, 1862. As U.S. senator, Republican, from Oregon, 1865–71, he was a member of joint committee on reconstruction; introduced Tenure of Office Act, December 1866, and Military Reconstruction Act, February 1867; voted "guilty" in President Johnson's impeachment trial. He was U.S. attorney general, 1871–75. His nomination as chief justice of U.S. Supreme Court, 1873, was withdrawn after inquiry revealed his connection with Oregon election frauds. He served with Lew Wallace as examiner of the Florida vote, 1876, so "saving the state" for Hayes. He was mayor of Portland, Oreg., 1902–05.

WILLIAMS, GEORGE HUNTINGTON (*b. Utica, N.Y., 1856; d. 1894*), mineralogist, petrologist, teacher. Grandson of William Williams (1787–1850). A.B., Amherst, 1878; Ph.D., Heidelberg, 1882. Taught at Johns Hopkins *post* 1883; professor of inorganic geology, 1891–94. Author of, among other works, *The*

Greenstone Schist Areas of the Menominee and Marquette Regions of Michigan (1890, *Bulletin* 62 of U.S. Geological Survey).

WILLIAMS, GEORGE WASHINGTON (*b. Bedford Springs, Pa., 1849; d. Blackpool, England, 1891*), Baptist clergyman, Union colonel. Studied law under Alphonso Taft. Born the child of an interracial union. He held federal offices and served in the Ohio legislature following the Civil War. U.S. minister to Haiti, 1885–86. Made critical survey writings of conditions in Congo Free State. Author of, among other writings, *A History of the Negro Troops in the War of the Rebellion* (1888).

WILLIAMS, HARRISON CHARLES (*b. Avon, Ohio, 1873; d. Bayville, L.I., 1953*), utilities executive. Beginning in 1906 with the foundation of the American Gas and Electric Co., Williams built one of the largest financial empires in the nation's history. Through the subsequently outlawed practice of pyramiding, he added to his holdings such companies as Central States Electric Co., the Cleveland Illuminating Co., and the North American Co; under the top holding company, New Empire Corporation, his stock in Central States reached a high of $680 million in 1929; after the Crash, his fortune was reduced. In the 1930's and 1950's, he struggled in endless litigations and antitrust suits under the provisions of the Public Utility Holding Company Act of 1935. In 1952, a $12 million decision was handed down, one of the largest decisions ever brought against an individual; the decision was later reversed and Williams' lawyers settled for $800,000 against his estate in 1959.

WILLIAMS, HENRY SHALER (*b. Ithaca, N.Y., 1847; d. Havana, Cuba, 1918*), paleontologist. Ph.B., Sheffield Scientific School, Yale, 1868; Ph.D., Yale, 1871. Taught paleontology at Cornell University, 1879–92; Silliman professor at Yale, 1892–1904. Returning to teach at Cornell, 1904, he became professor emeritus, 1912. Williams was an authority on the American Devonian and developed the now-common photographic method of fossil illustration. He was also associated with the U.S. Geological Survey from 1883 until his death. Author of, among other works, *Geological Biology* (1895); associate editor of the *Journal of Geology*, 1893–1918, and of *American Journal of Science*, 1894–1918.

WILLIAMS, HENRY WILLARD (*b. Boston, Mass., 1821; d. Boston, 1895*), ophthalmologist. One of the founders of ophthalmology in America, Williams studied in Paris, London, and Vienna, and graduated from Harvard Medical School, 1849. In 1871 he became the first professor of ophthalmology at Harvard Medical School. He was ophthalmologic surgeon, Boston City Hospital, 1864–91. Author of, among other valuable writings, *The Diagnosis and Treatment of the Diseases of the Eye* (1881), the best book of its day on the subject.

WILLIAMS, (HIRAM) HANK (*b. Mt. Olive, Ala., 1923; d. Oak Hill, W.Va., 1953*), songwriter, singer. One of the nation's most famous and talented country and western singer, Hank Williams began recording in Nashville for Sterling Records in 1946. Later, for MGM records, he released such songs as "Lovesick Blues," "Cold, Cold Heart," "Kaw-liga," "Jambalaya," "Half as Much," "Your Cheatin' Heart," and "Take These Chains From My Heart." Williams appeared on the "Grand Ole Opry" and "Louisiana Hayride." He died at the age of twenty-nine from alcohol and drugs.

WILLIAMS, ISRAEL (*b. Hatfield, Mass., 1709; d. Hatfield, 1788*), farmer, land speculator, Massachusetts official, Loyalist. Half brother of Elisha Williams (1694–1755). Active in effecting dismissal of his cousin Jonathan Edwards from Northampton church, 1750. Made colonel of Hampshire Co. militia, 1748; conducted defense of western Massachusetts throughout French and Indian War. Judge, Hampshire Co. court of common pleas, 1758–74; Massachusetts legislator, 1733–73. Lost early paramount influence in his county to his radical cousin Joseph Hawley. The leading Loyalist in western Massachusetts *post* 1774, he was the model for the mobbed Tory squire in Trumbull's *M'Fingal*. As executor of the will of Ephraim Williams, he helped found Williams College.

WILLIAMS, JAMES (*b. Grainger Co., Tenn., 1796; d. Graz, Austria, 1869*), journalist, Confederate diplomat, Tennessee legislator. Aided Confederate propaganda by articles in the London *Times, Standard,* and *Index,* 1861–64; served as Confederate contact with Maximilian of Mexico. He kept John Slidell and James M. Mason posted on his activities, but carried on secret, perhaps more detailed, correspondence with President Jefferson Davis. Author of *Letters on Slavery from the Old World* (1861), enlarged and published in London as *The South Vindicated.*

WILLIAMS, JAMES DOUGLAS (*b. Pickaway Co., Ohio, 1808; d. Indianapolis, Ind., 1880*), farmer, miller, Indiana legislator. As congressman, Democrat, from Indiana, 1875–77, he was chairman of the Committee on Accounts. Insistent on cutting expenses, he became known as "Blue Jeans Williams." Defeating Benjamin Harrison in a famous campaign for governor of Indiana, 1876, he served with ability and independence, 1877–80.

WILLIAMS, JESSE LYNCH (*b. Westfield, N.C., 1807; d. 1886*), civil engineer. Chief engineer, Wabash & Erie Canal, 1832–35 and 1847–76, and of many other transportation projects in Indiana. His report on the Union Pacific to the secretary of the interior, 1862, led to the Crédit Mobilier investigation.

WILLIAMS, JESSE LYNCH (*b. Sterling, Ill., 1871; d. Herkimer Co., N.Y., 1929*), novelist, playwright, editor. Grandson of Jesse L. Williams (1807–86). B.A., Princeton, 1892. Author of, among other fiction and drama, *Princeton Stories* (1895), the Pulitzer Prize play *Why Marry?* (1917), and the novel *She Knew She Was Right* (1930).

WILLIAMS, JOHN (*b. Roxbury, Mass., 1664; d. Deerfield, Mass., 1729*), Congregational clergyman, author. Ordained first pastor at Deerfield, Mass., 1688. Following sacking of the town by French and Indians, 1703/4, he was held captive for two years in Canada. He later prepared with Cotton Mather's help *The Redeemed Captive Returning to Zion* (1707), a testimony of Congregational fortitude against "Popish Poisons." Returned to Deerfield, 1707. Served as chaplain on 1711 expedition against Port Royal and as commissioner to Canada for return of English prisoners, 1713–14.

WILLIAMS, JOHN (*b. London, England, 1761; d. Brooklyn, N.Y., 1818*), satirist, dramatic critic, miscellaneous writer. Under the pseudonym "Anthony Pasquin," he was author of the *Hamiltoniad* (Boston, preface dated 1804), a savage Antifederalist poem, more important for its extensive notes than for its verse. Called "a common libeller" and "polecat," he had been driven in disgrace from England *ca.* 1797 and died destitute in America.

WILLIAMS, JOHN (*b. Surry Co., N.C., 1778; d. Knoxville, Tenn., 1837*), soldier, lawyer, Tennessee legislator. Brother-in-law of Hugh L. White. As colonel of volunteers in War of 1812 he operated against the Seminole in Florida. Colonel, 39th U.S. Infantry in the Creek campaign, he helped bring about Andrew Jackson's victory in battle of Horseshoe Bend, 1814. U.S. senator from Tennessee, 1815–23. Denied renomination because of identification with the Crawford wing of the Democrats, he insisted on running for reelection, thus compelling Jackson to run against him and defeat him in a bitter campaign.

WILLIAMS, JOHN (*b. Old Deerfield, Mass., 1817; d. Middletown, Conn., 1899*), Episcopal clergyman. Graduated present Trinity College, Hartford, Conn., 1835; ordained priest, 1841; while in England, 1840–41, he grew acquainted with the Oxford Movement leaders. President and also Hobart professor of history and literature, Trinity College, 1848–53; chancellor, *post* 1865. In 1851 he was elected bishop coadjutor of Connecticut, succeeding to the see in 1865. Dean and professor of theology and liturgies, Berkeley Divinity School, Middletown, Conn., *post* 1854, presiding bishop of the Protestant Episcopal church *post* 1887.

WILLIAMS, JOHN ELIAS (*b. Merthyr-Tydfil, Wales, 1853; d. Streator, Ill., 1919*), coal miner, industrial mediator. Came to America, 1864; settled in Streator, Ill. Chairman, arbitration board for Hart, Schaffner & Marx and United Garment Workers of America, *post* 1912. One of the first advocates of union-management cooperation, he believed industrial democracy could come through trades organization and continuous collective bargaining; he was instrumental in introducing new devices, including a compromise between closed and open shop called the preferential shop. His procedure and philosophy of mediation created a precedent for board chairmen and influenced so-called progressive unions.

WILLIAMS, JOHN ELIAS (*b. Coshocton, Ohio, 1871; d. Nanking, China, 1927*), Presbyterian missionary to China. Working in China *post* 1899, he helped found, and became vice president of, the University of Nanking, 1911. His murder by a Chinese Communist, 1927, began the "Nanking Incident."

WILLIAMS, JOHN FLETCHER (*b. Cincinnati, Ohio, 1834; d. Rochester, Minn., 1895*), journalist, librarian. Removed to St. Paul, Minn., 1855. Secretary and librarian, Minnesota Historical Society, 1867–93.

WILLIAMS, JOHN FOSTER (*b. Boston, Mass., 1743; d. Boston, 1814*), naval officer. His Revolutionary commands included the state vessels *Republic, Massachusetts,* and *Hazard,* in which he took several prizes, 1778–79, and compelled surrender of British brig *Active,* March 1779. He commanded *Protector,* largest ship in the Massachusetts navy, 1780–81. From 1790 until his death he was captain of the revenue cutter *Massachusetts.*

WILLIAMS, JOHN JOSEPH (*b. Boston, Mass., 1822; d. 1907*), Roman Catholic clergyman. Graduated Sulpician college, Montreal, Canada, 1841; studied theology at St. Sulpice, Paris, where he was ordained, 1845. Named rector of Cathedral of the Holy Cross, Boston, 1855; pastor of St. James Church and vicar general of the diocese, 1857. Consecrated bishop of Boston, 1866, and archbishop, 1875; retired in 1906.

WILLIAMS, JOHN SHARP (*b. Memphis, Tenn., 1854; d. 1932*), planter, lawyer. Educated at universities of the South, Virginia, and Heidelberg. Admitted to the bar, 1877; practiced in Yazoo City, Miss., 1878–93. As congressman, Democrat, from Mississippi, 1893–1909, he became an effective minority leader, 1903. Temporary chairman of the 1904 Democratic National Convention, he upheld conservative views in the fight over the platform and continued to champion moderation in reform through 1912. Entering the U.S. Senate, 1911, after a victory over J. K. Vardaman, he served on the Finance and Foreign Relations committees and consistently supported Woodrow Wilson's policies as president. Disgusted with the trends in public life *post* 1920, he retired in 1923. The most consistent Jeffersonian Democrat of his day, he wrote *Thomas Jefferson, His Permanent Influence on American Institutions* (1913).

WILLIAMS, JOHN SKELTON (*b. Powhatan Co., Va., 1865; d. near Richmond, Va., 1926*), financier, public official. Developed the Seaboard Air Line Railway; served it as president, 1899–1903. Appointed assistant U.S. secretary of the treasury, 1913, he was comptroller of the currency, 1914–21, and an ex officio member of the committee which established the Federal Reserve System. He was also U.S. director of finances and purchases for the railroads, 1917–19. Attacked concentration of banking control "in the hands of a dozen men;" praised Federal Reserve System as means of decentralization; antagonized national banks by charges of usury. His later accusations against the Federal Reserve Board formed basis of congressional investigations which sustained some of the charges. *Post* 1921, he was board chairman of the Richmond Trust Co.

WILLIAMS, JOHN WHITRIDGE (*b. Baltimore, Md., 1866; d. 1931*), physician, obstetrician. M.D., University of Maryland, 1888; studied also in Vienna, Berlin, and Leipzig. Taught at Johns Hopkins *post* 1896, becoming professor of obstetrics and obstetrician in chief to the hospital, 1899. Dean of the Medical School, 1911–23. Author of, among a number of treatises on bacteriology, pathology and obstetrics, an authoritative *Textbook of Obstetrics* (1903).

WILLIAMS, JONATHAN (*b. Boston, Mass., 1750; d. 1815*), merchant, army officer. Sent to London, 1770, to complete business training under his uncle Benjamin Franklin. Employed by commissioners of Continental Congress, 1776, as Nantes agent to inspect arms and supplies, he became unwittingly involved in the controversy between Silas Deane and Arthur Lee. Although vindicated of false charges made by Lee, he left public service, remaining in business in Europe until he returned with Franklin to America, 1785. Williams then settled in Philadelphia as a well-to-do merchant. In 1796 he became associate judge of the court of common pleas and later acquired reputation as scientist. Named by President Jefferson in 1801 as inspector of fortifications and superintendent at West Point with rank of major, he soon became first superintendent of the U.S. Military Academy. Laboring under many handicaps, he resigned, 1803. Reappointed in 1805 as lieutenant colonel of engineers with complete authority over all cadets at the institution, he was now hampered in his efforts to create a first-rate military school by many extra engineering duties which took up most of his time and by the antagonism of Secretary of War, William Eustis. He resigned from the army, 1812, embittered because of failure at West Point and because he was not given command of the New York fortifications. During the War of 1812 he served as brevet brigadier general of New York militia.

WILLIAMS, LINSLY RUDD (*b. New York, N.Y., 1875; d. 1934*), physician. M.D., New York College of Physicians and Surgeons, 1899. Director, Rockefeller Commission for the Prevention of Tuberculosis in France, 1919–22. Directed National Tuberculosis Association, 1922–28; thereafter developed and directed New York Academy of Medicine.

WILLIAMS, MARSHALL JAY (*b. Fayette Co., Ohio, 1837; d. Columbus, Ohio, 1902*), lawyer, Ohio legislator. Judge, Ohio 2nd circuit court, 1884–86, and first chief justice; judge, Ohio Supreme Court, 1887–1902; dean, College of Law, Ohio State University, 1891–93. Conservative in constitutional law, liberal in tort law on questions of negligence and liability.

WILLIAMS, NATHANAEL (*b. Boston, Mass., 1675; d. 1737/8*), physician, schoolmaster. Father-in-law of John Smibert. Graduated Harvard, 1693. Succeeded Ezekiel Cheever as headmaster, Boston Latin School, 1708; resigned from the school, 1733.

WILLIAMS, OTHO HOLLAND (*b. Prince Georges Co., Md., 1749; d. Miller's Town, Va., 1794*), Revolutionary officer. After good service at siege of Boston and with a Maryland-Virginia rifle regiment, he was made prisoner at the fall of Fort Washington, November 1776. Exchanged, January 1778, he began duties as colonel of the 6th Maryland Regiment. Deputy adjutant general under Horatio Gates, 1780, and adjutant under Nathanael Greene; commanded rear guard during Greene's retreat across North Carolina and distinguished himself in battles of Guilford Court House, Hobkirk Hill, and Eutaw Springs. Promoted brigadier general, 1782. Elected naval officer, Baltimore district, 1783; appointed federal collector of the port, 1789.

WILLIAMS, REUEL (*b. present Augusta, Maine, 1783; d. Augusta, 1862*), Maine legislator. Inherited a practice, 1812, including administration of Kennebec Purchase and Bowdoin College timberlands; prospered in many business ventures. In Maine legislature, 1812–29, as a Federalist; 1832 and 1848, as Democrat. U.S. senator, Democrat, from Maine, 1837–43. Actively supported Maine in the boundary dispute, 1832–42. With Thomas Hart Benton, fought against Webster-Ashburton Treaty in 1842.

WILLIAMS, ROBERT (*b. probably England, ca. 1745; d. near Suffolk, Va., 1775*), pioneer Methodist preacher. Appointed as missionary to America, he worked in New York City and Maryland, 1769–71. His reprinting of John Wesley's sermons alerted American Methodists to the value of a religious press. Extending his work to Virginia, he led a great religious revival, 1773; in Petersburg; he organized Brunswick circuit, 1774. Williams was the first Methodist traveling preacher to come to America, the first to publish a book, and the first to settle here.

WILLIAMS, ROGER (*b. London, England, ca. 1603; d. Providence, R.I., 1682/3*), clergyman, president of Rhode Island. A protégé of Sir Edward Coke, Williams was educated at Charterhouse and at Pembroke College, Cambridge (B.A., 1627). He took orders *ante* 1629 and served as chaplain to a Puritan family in Essex; in December 1629 he married Mary Barnard.

Already friendly with John Cotton and Thomas Hooker, Williams took ship aboard the *Lyon* with his wife in December 1630 and was welcomed at first in Massachusetts as "a godly minister." His open criticism of the Puritan system of government soon made him enemies, for he declared that civil government had no power to enforce the religious injunctions of the Ten Commandments. Denied a post as teacher of the church at Salem, he went to Plymouth, and after two years there returned to Salem as assistant minister. In August 1634 he was accepted as full minister at Salem in defiance of the General Court. He continued to work for a more democratic church system, also attacking land claims under the royal charter as a violation of Indian rights and denouncing the oath by which the Massachusetts oligarchy was trying to keep the lower orders of settlers in strict submission. Found guilty on Oct. 9, 1635, of propagating new and dangerous opinions, he was ordered banished by the General Court. Learning that Williams was trying to organize his Salem followers for a colony in Narragansett, the magistrates, who feared the existence of a radical community on their southern border, sent to arrest him. Warned, he escaped and made his way to the friendly Indians at Sowams. After suffering privations, he gathered enough followers to found Providence, the earliest Rhode Island settlement, 1636.

Grown skeptical of the claims of the existing churches, he became, 1639, a Seeker—one who accepts no creed, although professing belief in the fundamentals of Christianity. Frontier influences and Williams' own liberalism produced local institutions in Rhode Island which marked a radical advance over the Puritan colonies. Town government was at first a primitive democracy; all heads of families had an equal voice. Heads of families were to share alike in the distribution of land. Religious liberty and complete separation of church and state were provided for. By 1643, four settlements had sprung up in the Narragansett area, and the need of a charter was becoming evident. The Puritan colonies were organizing the New England Confederation and taking steps to end the independent existence of nonconforming settlements. Massachusetts invaded Rhode Island, carried off Samuel Gorton and the Warwick settlers to prison, and began negotiating in London for a Narragansett patent. Williams sailed for England, and with the aid of Sir Henry Vane, circumvented the Bay authorities and secured a patent for the whole area; this charter for the Providence Plantations was issued in March 1644.

While in England, Williams opposed attempts there by the Puritans to establish a national church and a compulsory uniformity. In *The Bloudy Tenent of Persecution* (1644), his most celebrated work, he held that all individuals and religious bodies were entitled to religious liberty as a natural right. He also attacked the undemocratic character of contemporary governments and declared that the foundation of civil power was in the people, who might establish whatever form of government seemed to them "most meete."

After Williams' return to Rhode Island, William Coddington, the dominant figure at Newport, delayed organization of the Rhode Island settlement until 1647; in 1651 he obtained a commission from England splitting the colony and making him governor of Aquidneck for life. Williams traveled to England, accompanied by John Clarke, and succeeded in getting Coddington's commission rescinded. During this second visit Williams continued his propaganda for democracy and religious liberty, publishing among other works *The Bloody Tenent Yet More Bloody* (1652). After his return to Rhode Island, he reunited the colony, became its president, and served three terms; during his presidency Jews and Quakers found a safe harbor in the colony, despite the protests and threats of Massachusetts. The latter years of his life were darkened by controversy and by Indian wars. In 1659 Williams defended the Narragansett tribe against an attempted fraud which would have deprived them of much of their lands, yet during King Philip's War the Narragansett cast in their lot with the other Indians and ended their old-time friendship with the Rhode Island settlements. Williams served as one of the captains in command of the Providence forces during the war and remained active in town affairs to the end of his life. Colonial thinker, religious liberal, and earliest of the fathers of American democracy, he owes his enduring fame to his humanity and breadth of view and to his long record of opposition to privilege and self-seeking.

WILLIAMS, SAMUEL MAY (b. *Providence, R.I., 1795; d. Galveston, Tex., 1858*), Texas pioneer, banker. Became private secretary to Stephen F. Austin, 1824, and a partner in his great colonization project; he kept and preserved the colony's records. *Post* 1834 Williams became unpopular because of land speculations. His mercantile firm of McKinney & Williams (organized 1836) served as financial backer of the Republic of Texas and opened the Commercial and Agricultural Bank, Galveston, 1847, the first chartered bank of Texas.

WILLIAMS, SAMUEL WELLS (b. *Utica, N.Y., 1812; d. 1884*), missionary, diplomat, sinologue. Son of William Williams (1787–1850); father of Frederick W. Williams. Removed to China, 1833. Directed the Canton press for the American Board of Commissioners for Foreign Missions and helped edit the *Chinese Repository*. Accompanied the Perry expedition to Japan as interpreter, 1853–54. Became secretary and interpreter of the American legation to China, 1856. Associated with the legation until 1876, he helped negotiate treaties. Author of, among other writings, *The Middle Kingdom* (1848, 1883) and *A Syllabic Dictionary of the Chinese Language* (1874). Became professor of

Chinese language and literature at Yale, 1877. Williams was the outstanding American sinologist of his time.

WILLIAMS, STEPHEN WEST (b. *Deerfield, Mass., 1790; d. Laona, Ill., 1855*), medical historian. Practiced in Deerfield. Lectured on medical jurisprudence at Berkshire Medical Institution, 1823–31; at Willoughby University, Ohio, 1838–53; at Dartmouth Medical School, 1838–41. Author of, among other works, *A Catechism of Medical Jurisprudence* (1835) and *American Medical Biography* (1845).

WILLIAMS, TALCOTT (b. *Abeih, Turkey, 1849; d. 1928*), journalist. Nephew of Samuel W. Williams. Joined New York *World*, 1873; became night editor. An outstanding political reporter, he was editorial writer for the *Springfield Republican*, 1879–81, and on staff of the Philadelphia *Press*, 1881–1912, becoming associate editor. Became first director, Columbia School of Journalism, 1912; served as professor emeritus *post* 1919. Williams combined cultural courses with practical newspaper training in the curriculum at Columbia and largely originated reporting of scientific news. His greatest contribution to journalism was his ideal of the scholar-journalist.

WILLIAMS, THOMAS SCOTT (b. *Wethersfield, Conn., 1777; d. 1861*), jurist. Connecticut legislator. Nephew of William Williams (1731–1811); son-in-law of Oliver Ellsworth. Studied law under Tapping Reeve and Zephaniah Swift. Congressman from Connecticut, 1817–19; mayor of Hartford, 1831–35. Associate justice, Connecticut Supreme Court of Errors, 1829–34; chief justice, 1834–47. Distinguished for lifelong interest in civic and charitable affairs.

WILLIAMS, WALTER (b. *Boonville, Mo., 1864; d. 1935*), journalist, educator. Distinguished for his editorship of the *Columbia* (Mo.) *Herald*, he was appointed a member of the board of curators of the University of Missouri, 1899, and served as chairman of its executive committee for many years. Becoming first dean of the school of journalism at the University of Missouri, 1908, he organized an educational program which aimed to reproduce as nearly as possible the apprentice experience obtained in a good newspaper office. This school was the first to place journalistic training on a professional level and its plan vastly influenced other schools and departments, as did also Williams' idealistic views on the responsibilities of the press to society. He served also as president of the University of Missouri, 1930–35.

WILLIAMS, WILLIAM (b. *Lebanon, Conn., 1731; d. Lebanon, 1811*), businessman, Revolutionary patriot, signer of the Declaration of Independence, Connecticut official and legislator. Son-in-law of Jonathan Trumbull (1710–85). Graduated Harvard, 1751. Gave heavy financial aid to the Revolutionary movement, helped compose many of Governor Trumbull's state papers. Occupied many Connecticut public offices and was a member of the Continental Congress, 1776–78 and 1783–84; assisted in framing Articles of Confederation and served on the board of war.

WILLIAMS, WILLIAM (b. *Framingham, Mass., 1787; d. Utica, N.Y., 1850*), printer, publisher, soldier. Father of Samuel W. Williams. Became partner in Utica, N.Y., printing firm, 1807, and published many almanacs, music collections, and anti-Masonic books. Managed bookstore which by 1820 was the largest west of Albany, N.Y.; owned, printed, and sometimes edited Utica newspapers, notably the *Patriot* and the *Patrol*.

WILLIAMS, WILLIAM CARLOS (b. *Rutherford, N.J., 1882; d. Rutherford, 1963*), poet and physician. Attended University of Pennsylvania Medical School and interned in New York City (1906–09); he began a general practice in Rutherford in 1910. His first book was a collection of twenty-six poems, entitled *Poems* (1909), printed at his own expense. Wrote numerous essays on the arts, collected in *A Recognizable Image* (1978). The startling range of his achievement is evident in works published in the 1920's: *Kora in Hell: Improvisations* (1920) and *The Great American Novel* (1923), both prose experiments in randomness and discontinuity; *Spring and All* (1923), his most ambitious and successful early book; *The American Grain* (1925), both prose studies of figures in American History; and *A Voyage to Pagany* (1928), a novel. Throughout his career he addressed what he believed to be the American writer's need to discard European precedents. In 1924 he and his wife went to France for six months, where they associated with James Joyce, Ford Madox Ford, Gertrude Stein, Ernest Hemingway, and many other writers and artists. His verse was collected in *The Complete Collected Poems of William Carlos Williams, 1906–38* (1939). His major writings of the 1930's were fiction: *The Knife of the Times and Other Stories* (1932) and *Life Along the Passaic River* (1938). His epic poem *Paterson* appeared in five books (1946, 1948, 1949, 1951, 1958); during the years he was writing *Paterson*, he also produced a substantial number of short lyrics—*The Desert Music* (1954) is considered one of his finest long poems. His reputation grew steadily in the last fifteen years of his life; he received the first National Book Award for poetry (1950), the Bollingen Prize (1953), and (posthumously) the Pulitzer Prize in poetry (1963).

WILLIAMS, WILLIAM R. (*b. New York, N.Y., 1804; d. 1885*), Baptist clergyman, author. Practiced law in New York City, 1825–30. Influential, scholarly pastor of Amity St. Baptist Church, New York City, *post* 1832. Helped found Rochester Theological Seminary. Author of, among other writings, *The Conservative Principles in Our Literature* (1844).

WILLIAMS, WILLIAM SHERLEY (*b. probably Kentucky, date uncertain; d. probably north of Taos, N.Mex., 1849*), trapper, guide. Better known as Bill, or Old Bill, Williams. A member of Joseph C. Brown's surveying party which marked Santa Fe Trail, 1825–26. In 1833–34, he was with the California expedition led by Joseph R. Walker; he then trapped the Utah-Colorado country. Set out in 1843 on a two-year journey to the Columbia River, the Great Basin, and Santa Fe; joined the disastrous fourth expedition of John C. Frémont as guide, 1848. Probably killed by Ute. The most eccentric of the "mountain men," Williams has lent his name to numerous western landmarks. The queer jargon which he affected became standard in fictional treatments of the West as true trapper talk.

WILLIAMSON, ANDREW (*b. possibly Scotland, ca. 1730; d. near Charleston, S.C., 1786*), Revolutionary soldier, planter. Came to America as a child. Was influential Whig in South Carolina backcountry. As major of militia, he took part in the 1775 fighting around Ninety-Six and led an expedition against the Cherokee, 1776. Promoted colonel, he commanded South Carolina troops in a second campaign which subdued the Cherokee. Made brigadier general, 1778, he commanded South Carolina militia in Howe's Florida expedition. Accused of treason after the fall of Charleston, 1780, he went into the British lines there and was denounced as "the Arnold of Carolina." He is credited, however, with later supplying Whigs with valuable information through Col. John Laurens.

WILLIAMSON, CHARLES (*b. Balgray, Scotland, 1757; d. at sea, 1808*), British officer, secret agent, New York legislator. As a land promoter in western New York, 1791–1802, he administered and developed for a British syndicate headed by Sir William Pulteney a tract of 1.2 million acres acquired from Robert Morris. He became a citizen and was elected to various offices; he also built roads and bridges and a hotel at Geneva, N.Y. Serving *post* 1803 as a volunteer adviser to the British cabinet on American affairs, he reverted to British citizenship. After an 1806 visit to the United States, he advised a policy directed at overthrow of the "Frenchified" Jeffersonian regime and considered Aaron Burr as a possible agent in this endeavor.

WILLIAMSON, HUGH (*b. West Nottingham, Pa., 1735; d. New York, N.Y., 1819*), physician, statesman, scientist, North Carolina legislator. Graduated College of Philadelphia (University of Pennsylvania), 1757, where he taught mathematics. In 1764 he studied medicine at Edinburgh, London, and Utrecht, receiving M.D. at University of Utrecht. Practicing in Philadelphia, he continued scientific studies. While in England, 1773–76, seeking aid for a proposed school, he obtained by a trick the Hutchinson-Oliver letters from Massachusetts and delivered them to Benjamin Franklin. He also collaborated with Franklin in electrical experiments. Settling in Edenton, N.C., 1777, he built up a large trade with the French West Indies and served as surgeon general of the state troops. Member of the Continental Congress, 1782–85 and 1787–88. At the Federal Convention, 1787, he was the most active North Carolina delegate and played a large part in securing the compromise on representation. He signed the U.S. Constitution and worked for its ratification. After serving in Congress from North Carolina, 1789–93, he devoted the rest of his life to literary and scientific pursuits in New York City. Williamson's work on climate brought him his greatest reputation as a scientist. He showed originality as an economist and was a sound scholar; his historical work was poor. Author of, among other writings, "An Essay on Comets" (1771); "Letters of Sylvius" (*American Museum*, August 1787); and *Observations on the Climate in Different Parts of America* (1811).

WILLIAMSON, ISAAC HALSTED (*b. Elizabethtown, now Elizabeth, N.J., 1767; d. Elizabeth, 1844*), lawyer. Democratic governor and chancellor of New Jersey, 1817–29. Williamson's lasting reputation came through his work in the dual office of chancellor, wherein he increased the dignity and effectiveness of the chancery court and laid the foundations of its unique position in New Jersey. His 1822 code of rules of practice clarified the then confused situation of mortgages.

WILLIAMSON, WILLIAM DURKEE (*b. Canterbury, Conn., 1779; d. Bangor, Maine, 1846*), lawyer, historian, Massachusetts and Maine legislator. Postmaster of Bangor, Maine, 1809–20. Advocated separation of Maine from Massachusetts, 1820. Acting governor of Maine, May–December 1821; congressman, Democrat, from Maine, 1821–23. Judge of probate, Penobscot Co., Maine, 1824–40. Author of *History of the State of Maine* (1832; repr., 1839).

WILLIE, ASA HOXIE (*b. Washington, Ga., 1829; d. Galveston, Tex., 1899*), jurist. Removed to Texas, 1846; admitted to the bar, 1849. Elected to the Texas Supreme Court in 1866, he was removed after 15 months by the federal military authorities. Congressman-at-large from Texas, 1873–75; chief justice of Texas Supreme Court, 1882–88.

WILLING, THOMAS (*b. Philadelphia, Pa., 1731 o.s.; d. Philadelphia, 1821*), banker, Pennsylvania official and legislator. Father of Anne Willing Bingham. Became partner in father's countinghouse, 1751; formed Willing, Morris & Co. with Robert Morris, eventually the leading Philadelphia mercantile firm. Engaged in many public activities; elected mayor of Philadelphia, 1763. Justice, Pennsylvania Supreme Court, 1767–77. President of first Provincial Congress of Pennsylvania, 1774; member of second Continental Congress, 1775–76. Voted against Richard Henry Lee's resolution for independence, July 1776. During British occupation declined taking oath of allegiance to the king.

President of the Bank of North America, 1781–1807. Supported movement for new constitution of 1787 and Alexander Hamilton's fiscal measures. President, first Bank of the United States, 1791–97.

WILLINGHAM, ROBERT JOSIAH (*b. Beaufort District, S.C., 1854; d. 1914*), Baptist clergyman. Highly effective secretary of the Foreign Mission Board of the Southern Baptist Convention, 1893–1914.

WILLIS, ALBERT SHELBY (*b. Shelbyville, Ky., 1843; d. Honolulu, Hawaii, 1897*), lawyer, Kentucky official, diplomat. Congressman, Democrat, from Kentucky, 1877–87; chairman, Committee on Rivers and Harbors. As envoy extraordinary and minister plenipotentiary to Hawaii, 1893–97, he was unsuccessful in effecting President Cleveland's policy of restoring prerevolutionary status after uprising of 1893.

WILLIS, BAILEY (*b. Idlewild, near Cornwall, N.Y., 1857; d. Palo Alto, Calif., 1949*), geologist. Son of Nathaniel Parker Willis. Took degrees in mechanical and civil engineering, Columbia University, 1878 and 1879. Assisted Raphael Pumpelly in surveys for the tenth federal census and for the projected Northern Pacific Railroad. Associated with U.S. Geological Survey, 1884–1915; headed Department of Geology, Stanford University, 1915–22, and retained close connection with Stanford for the rest of his life. Made important studies in California geology, especially of faulting, seismology, and earthquake hazards. Author of, among other works, *Index to the Stratigraphy of North America* (1912, and collaborated on the accompanying map); *Living Africa* (1930); *A Yanqui in Patagonia* (1947).

WILLIS, HENRY PARKER (*b. Elmira, N.Y., 1874; d. Oak Bluffs, Mass., 1937*), economist, educator. Raised in Racine, Wis. Graduated University of Chicago, 1894; Ph.D., 1897. A teacher at Washington and Lee University, 1898–1905, he served also as editorial writer on the New York *Evening Post* and was briefly Washington correspondent for the New York *Journal of Commerce* and the *Springfield Republican*. He collaborated with J. Laurence Laughlin in *Reciprocity* (1903). Removing to Washington, D.C., 1905, he continued to work as a correspondent and also served as professor of finance at George Washington University until 1912. He then removed to New York City as associate editor of the *Journal of Commerce*. He served as editor in chief of the *Journal*, 1919–31, and was professor of banking at Columbia University *post* 1917. Active as an adviser to congressional committees *post* 1910, Willis helped to draw up the Underwood Tariff Act of 1913 and later contributed to the drafting of the Federal Reserve Act. He was the first secretary of the Federal Reserve Board, 1914–18, and served as the board's director of analysis and research, 1918–22. In his *Journal of Commerce* editorials he called attention to the dangers inherent in the Republican high-tariff policy and in the overextension of credit during the 1920's; he was among the first to foresee a stock-market collapse and a business depression. His chief interest lay in his academic work; at Columbia he organized a banking seminar which played an important role in the university and in the banking life of New York. An old-fashioned political liberal, Willis defended individual and constitutional rights, advocated the competitive enterprise system, and fought against all monopolies, whether in business or labor. He was author of a number of books in the field of banking, including his legislative history entitled *The Federal Reserve System* (1923).

WILLIS, NATHANIEL (*b. Boston, Mass., 1780; d. Boston, 1870*), editor, journalist. Father of Nathaniel P. Willis. Established the *Eastern Argus* at Portland, Maine, 1803, in opposition to the Federalist party; sold the paper, 1809. Removed to Boston, Mass., 1812. Began publication, 1816, of the *Recorder* (*Boston Recorder*), claiming it to be the world's first religious newspaper. *Youth's Companion*, his greatest contribution to journalism, originated as a department in the *Recorder* and appeared in separate covers, 1827. Willis served as editor until 1857.

WILLIS, NATHANIEL PARKER (*b. Portland, Maine, 1806; d. near Tarrytown, N.Y., 1867*), journalist, author. Son of Nathaniel Willis. Won celebrity as a poet while still an undergraduate at Yale; entered journalism on graduation, 1827. As editor of the Boston *American Monthly Magazine*, 1829–31, he posed in print as a dandy and aesthete, attracting envy and criticism, but achieving a reasonable success. Removing to New York City, he became associated with George P. Morris and went abroad as foreign correspondent for the *New-York Mirror*. Resident in Europe until May 1836, he had a great social success, notably in England, but was guilty of considerable indiscretion in the articles which he sent back to the *Mirror* (collected as *Pencillings by the Way*, 1835 and later editions).

Although one of the best paid of American periodical writers after his return to the United States, he also attempted the drama and was author of, among other plays, *Bianca Visconti* (1839; produced in New York, 1837) and *Tortesa* (1839). He continued to write for the *Mirror* and was a cofounder of the weekly *Corsair*, 1839–40, for which he engaged W. M. Thackeray as a correspondent. *Post* 1840 he was associated with G. P. Morris as an editor of the *New Mirror* and the *Evening Mirror* (a daily paper); in 1846 he joined Morris in publication of the *Home Journal*, their final and most prosperous undertaking. A colorful and lighthearted commentator on the day-to-day life of New York City and the nation, Willis was a generous friend to many less fortunate writers, including Edgar Allan Poe, whom he defended against later calumnies. Modern critics have given him a place of importance in the development of the American short story. Among his many books, which were almost wholly made up from his magazine pieces, were (in addition to those already cited) *A l'Abri; or, The Tent Pitch'd* (1839); *Letters from Under a Bridge* (1840); *Dashes at Life with a Free Pencil* (1845); and *Fun Jottings* (1853). He published a number of volumes of his verses, and almost all his works were reprinted in England.

WILLIS, OLYMPIA BROWN. *See* BROWN, OLYMPIA.

WILLIS, WILLIAM (*b. Haverhill, Mass., 1794; d. 1870*), historian, lawyer. Portland, Maine, official. Graduated Harvard, 1813. Became law partner of William Pitt Fessenden, 1835. For 50 years a "subtantial citizen" of Portland, Maine, he was mayor of Portland and president of the Maine Central Railroad. His chief works were *The History of Portland* (1831–33; 2nd ed., 1865) and *A History of the Law, the Courts, and the Lawyers of Maine* (1863). He edited first six volumes of Maine Historical Society's *Collections* (1831–59).

WILLISTON, SAMUEL (*b. Easthampton, Mass., 1795; d. Easthampton, 1874*), philanthropist, businessman. Best known as a promoter of religious and charitable enterprises; founded Williston Seminary, Easthampton, 1841; benefactor of Amherst and Mount Holyoke.

WILLISTON, SAMUEL (*b. Cambridge, Mass., 1861; d. Cambridge, 1963*), lawyer and educator. Attended Harvard Law (LL.B., 1888). Practiced law on and off throughout his life, but found its scholarly aspects more appealing than its practice. Taught at Harvard Law, 1890–1938, proving to be one of the most capable and popular men ever to teach there. Wrote or edited eighteen casebooks and more than fifty articles; his five-volume *Law of Contracts* (1920–22) became the standard text in the field. Served as Massachusetts commissioner for uniform state laws,

1910–29, and prepared a draft statute covering the law of sales that five years later became the Uniform Statute on Sales. After leaving Harvard he taught at the University of Texas and Catholic University in Washington. He returned to Harvard during World War II, and was still an able and popular teacher as an octogenarian.

WILLISTON, SAMUEL WENDELL (*b. Roxbury, Mass., 1852; d. 1918*), paleontologist, physician, dipterist. Graduated Kansas State College, 1872; M.D., Yale Medical School, 1880; Ph.D., Yale, 1885. Employed by Othniel C. Marsh as collector, preparator, and writer, 1873–85; worked in western Kansas, and in dinosaur-bearing beds in Colorado and Montana. Taught anatomy at Yale, 1886–90; taught geology, paleontology, vertebrate anatomy, and physiology at University of Kansas, 1890–1902, serving also for a time as dean of the school of medicine. Headed Department of Vertebrate Paleontology at University of Chicago, *post* 1902. His many papers on the reptiles of the Cretaceous include the classic work on the mosasaurs (in Vol. 4 of *The University Geological Survey of Kansas*, 1898). A pioneer dipterist, he wrote *Manual of North American Diptera* (1908) and was author of, among other works, *American Permian Vertebrates* (1911) and *Water Reptiles of the Past and Present* (1914). W. K. Gregory edited his *Osteology of the Reptiles* (1925). His contributions to paleontology were fundamental and of lasting influence.

WILLISTON, SETH (*b. Suffield, Conn., 1770; d. Guilford Center, N.Y., 1851*), Congregational clergyman, home missionary. Graduated Dartmouth, 1791; appointed to missionary service in New York State by Connecticut Missionary Society, 1798. A follower of Samuel Hopkins (1721–1803), his preaching evoked the revival of 1799–1800 in central and western New York. While pastor at Lisle, N.Y., 1801–10, he continued to preach widely and to establish churches. He removed, 1810, to Durham, N.Y., where he served 18 years as pastor before returning to his missionary travels.

WILLKIE, WENDELL LEWIS (*b. Elwood, Ind., 1892; d. New York, N.Y., 1944*), lawyer, public utility executive, presidential candidate. Both his father and mother were practicing lawyers. In 1913 he received the B.A. degree from Indiana University. To earn money for law school, he next taught history at the Coffeyville, Kans., high school, but in 1914 resigned to take a more remunerative job as a chemist in a Puerto Rican sugar factory. He entered the Indiana University law school in 1915 and a year later received his LL.B. After graduation he joined his parents' law firm; but on the outbreak of World War I, he volunteered for military duty and gained a commission as first lieutenant. After his discharge from the army in 1919, Willkie joined the legal staff of the Firestone Tire and Rubber Co. He resigned at the end of 1920 to enter a private law firm in Akron. Willkie's firm was counsel for a subsidiary of the Commonwealth & Southern Corporation. In 1933 he became president and chief executive officer, and supplied the company with effective leadership during the Great Depression. He also gained national attention as the most articulate opponent of two New Deal projects—the Public Utility Holding Act and the Tennessee Valley Authority.

Willkie's winning of the Republican presidential nomination at Philadelphia in 1940 was an event unparalleled in American history. A liberal Democrat in early life, he had largely withdrawn from politics after serving as a delegate to the party's disastrous national convention in 1924, and his change of party affiliation in 1939, inspired by his distaste for Roosevelt and his policies, was hardly known even to his friends. Moreover, he did not seriously consider trying for the nomination until early in 1940. He was, however, well known to the business community and had the

support of the publishers Henry Luce and John and Gardner Cowles. But it was his personal warmth and magnetism, along with his forthright stand for aid to Britain after the shock of Hitler's easy conquest of western Europe, that created the wave of popular enthusiasm on which he was swept to a sixth-ballot victory.

In the contest with Franklin Roosevelt, who was seeking a third term, Willkie waged a vigorous campaign. He alienated many Republicans by supporting the Selective Service Act and Roosevelt's policy of aid to Britain. At the same time, he accused the president of deliberately leading the country toward war and, on the domestic front, attacked Roosevelt's seeming acceptance of the idea of a closed economy rather than an expanding one, although the issues were sometimes obscured by reckless invective on both sides. Willkie polled a larger popular vote than any other Republican candidate before Eisenhower, but lost in the electoral college by a wide margin.

During the next year Willkie devoted himself to unifying the country behind a policy of increasing military aid to Britain, to which country he paid a dramatic visit during the intense German bombings early in 1941. Again he earned support of Roosevelt's lend-lease proposal, as well as by his continued crusade against isolationism. After Pearl Harbor, Willkie turned to two concerns that dominated the closing years of his life: the creation of an international organization to preserve world peace and the defense of civil liberties, with an increasing emphasis on black rights. His book *One World* (1943) sold millions of copies in a few months. His main theme was the desire of the awakening colonial peoples to join the West in a global partnership based on economic, political, and racial justice.

A related notion, the urgent need for postwar harmony between the United States and the Soviet Union, was in part responsible for his unsparing attacks on the State Department's reliance on former Fascist leaders in French North Africa and Italy. Conservatives in both parties were further enraged when Willkie successfully defended before the Supreme Court a naturalized citizen, William Schneiderman, whose citizenship the Justice Department was trying to revoke because he was an admitted Communist.

Late in 1943 Willkie embarked on a strenuous campaign to win the 1944 Republican presidential nomination, but his hopes were crushed in the Wisconsin primary, and he withdrew from the race.

WILLOUGHBY, WESTEL WOODBURY (*b. Alexandria, Va., 1867; d. Washington, D.C., 1945*), political scientist, adviser to the Chinese government. A.B., Johns Hopkins University, 1888; Ph.D., 1891. A founder of political science as a U.S. academic discipline, he taught at Johns Hopkins, 1895–1933; most of his doctoral students became themselves eminent in the field. He was a leader in organizing the American Political Science Association, 1903, and editor of the *American Political Science Review*, 1906–16. During World War I, he served in Peking as constitutional adviser to the Chinese republic, 1916; he counseled the Chinese government on later occasions as well, including service as legal adviser in the League of Nations debate on the Manchuria crisis, 1931.

WILLS, CHILDE HAROLD (*b. Fort Wayne, Ind., 1878; d. Detroit, Mich., 1940*), automotive designer, manufacturer, metallurgist. An early associate of Henry Ford in motorcar design, Wills acted as chief engineer and factory manager of the Ford Motor Co. *post* 1903, helping to design every Ford car, including the Model T. Shifting his interest to the study of metals, he adapted vanadium steel and other alloys to Ford use and eventually developed molybdenum steel for use in auto parts subject to stress. Disagreeing with Ford over basic policies, he left the company in March 1919 and began to manufacture the Wills–St. Claire motor car. The new car introduced molybdenum steel, four-wheeled brakes, and other features, and was highly regarded, but production of it was abandoned in 1926 because Wills spent too much time and money on changes.

WILLS, HARRY (*b. New Orleans, La., 1889[?]; d. New York, N.Y., 1958*), boxer. Beginning in 1910, Wills officially fought one-hundred and two times, winning sixty-two, forty-five by knock-outs, and losing only eight. A longtime contender for the heavyweight boxing title, Wills was refused a bout with champion Jack Dempsey because Wills was a black. Wills' most important match in terms of earnings and prestige was against Argentinian Luis Angel Firpo in 1924, officially a draw. Wills retired in 1932 and went into the real estate business in New York. He was elected to the Boxing Hall of Fame in 1970.

WILLSON, AUGUSTUS EVERETT (*b. Maysville, Ky., 1846; d. Louisville, Ky., 1931*), lawyer, politician. Junior partner in Louisville office of John M. Harlan, 1874–79. Unsuccessful Republican candidate for Congress from Kentucky, 1884–92. As governor of Kentucky, 1907–11, he was checkmated by a hostile Democratic legislature and aroused criticism for allegedly partisan executive acts during the night-rider troubles in Kentucky.

WILLYS, JOHN NORTH (*b. Canandaigua, N.Y., 1873; d. 1935*), industrialist. A successful bicycle manufacturer in Elmira, N.Y., he began the sale of Pierce motorcars, 1901, and took over the handling and sale of the entire output of the Overland Co., 1906. Securing control of the Pope-Toledo plant at Toledo, Ohio, he installed the Overland Co. there and produced great numbers of the Willys-Overland between 1908 and 1916. He also invested heavily in concerns making automobile parts. After World War I, the Willys-Overland declined in popularity and faced strong competition; these factors and a strike at the plant, together with Willys' inability to control costs, brought about the liquidation of Willys' overall holding corporation, but left him a principal stockholder and manager of the main manufacturing concern. A heavy contributor to the Republican campaign fund in 1928, he served as U.S. ambassador to Poland, 1930–32, after providentially disposing of his stock in Willys-Overland just before the 1929 crash. He returned to the management of Willys-Overland *post* 1932 as receiver and later president.

WILMARTH, LEMUEL EVERETT (*b. Attleboro, Mass., 1835; d. 1918*), painter, teacher. Studied at Pennsylvania Academy of the Fine Arts, Philadelphia; also at Munich Academy and in Paris under J. L. Gérôme. Began exhibiting genre paintings at the National Academy in New York City, 1866. Taught at the National Academy of Design school, 1870–89; headed it, 1871–87.

WILMER, JAMES JONES (*b. Kent Co., Md., 1749/50; d. Detroit, Mich., 1814*), clergyman. Served as rector of four Maryland parishes, 1779–89. Became leader of Baltimore group which founded in 1792 the first New Church (Swedenborgian) Society in America. Reinstated as Episcopal clergyman, 1799, he held charges in Delaware, Maryland, and Virginia. A chaplain of Congress, 1809–13, he became a U.S. Army chaplain, 1813. Author of, among other writings, *Consolation, Being a Replication to Thomas Paine* (1794) and *The American Nepos* (1805).

WILMER, JOSPEH PÈRE BELL (*b. 1812; d. New Orleans, La., 1878*), Episcopal clergyman. Nephew of William H. Wilmer. Graduated Theological Seminary, Virginia, 1834; ordained, 1838. Served as chaplain, U.S. Navy, 1839–44; rector, St. Mark's Church, Philadelphia, Pa., 1849–61. Consecrated bishop of Louisiana, 1866, he was identified with the High Church party and noted as an orator.

WILMER, RICHARD HOOKER (*b. Alexandria, Va., 1816; d. Mobile, Ala., 1900*), Episcopal clergyman. Son of William H. Wilmer (1782–1827). Graduated Yale, 1836; Theological Seminary, Virginia, 1839. Ministered in rural Virginia parishes, 1840–61; in 1843 was minister, St. James Church, Wilmington, N.C. Consecrated bishop of Alabama, March 1862, he helped organize the Protestant Episcopal Church in the Confederate States, returning to union, 1865. Notable as a preacher, he proved an able administrator during Reconstruction.

WILMER, WILLIAM HOLLAND (*b. Kent Co., Md., 1782; d. 1827*), Episcopal clergyman. Father of Richard H. Wilmer. Ordained, 1808, he became rector of St. Paul's Church, Alexandria, Va., 1812; he was a leader of the convention which effected the election of Bishop R. C. Moore, 1814. Zealous in his denomination's revival in Virginia and in ministerial education, he was appointed a deputy to every meeting of the General Convention from 1814 until his death. Established in Washington, D.C., 1819, the *Theological Repertory*, which he edited until 1826. In 1823, with others, he organized the Theological Seminary at Alexandria, Va. Became president, College of William and Mary, and rector, Bruton Parish, Williamsburg, Va., 1826. Author of, among other works, *The Episcopal Manual* (1815).

WILMER, WILLIAM HOLLAND (*b. Powhatan Co., Va., 1863; d. Washington, D.C., 1936*), ophthalmologist. Son of Richard H. Wilmer. M.D., University of Virginia, 1885; worked with Emil Gruening at Mount Sinai Hospital, New York City; studied also in Europe. Practiced in Washington, D.C., *post* 1889, where he won repute as a diagnostician and surgeon of the highest order and served as professor in the medical school of Georgetown University. *Post* 1925, he directed the Wilmer Ophthalmological Institute at Johns Hopkins until his retirement in 1934. During World War I he directed researches in depth perception, muscular fatigue, and other factors influencing the abilities of flyers.

WILMOT, DAVID (*b. Bethany, Pa., 1814; d. 1868*), lawyer, politician. Congressman, Democrat, from Pennsylvania, 1845–51; U.S. senator, Republican, 1861–63. A leader among the Free-Soilers *post* 1848 and a founder of the Republican party, he served as president judge, 13th judicial district of Pennsylvania, 1851–61. He is principally famous for his addition of the Wilmot Proviso in the bill which appropriated funds for making peace with Mexico, 1846. Passed by the House but defeated in the Senate, the Proviso was intended to impede the growth of Southern power by prohibiting slavery in any territory which might be acquired with the money thus appropriated.

WILSON, ALEXANDER (*b. Renfrewshire, Scotland, 1766; d. Philadelphia, Pa., 1813*), weaver, poet, ornithologist. Immigrating to New Castle, Del., 1794, he engaged in teaching in New Jersey and Pennsylvania. Association with the naturalist William Bartram inspired him to attempt a large-scale study of the birds of the United States. He began at once to observe and to collect specimens, setting himself to learn how to draw and paint them. Engaging Alexander Lawson to prepare engraved plates from his drawings, he devoted ten years to *American Ornithology* (Vol. 1, 1808; Vols. 2–7 published by 1813). George Ord completed the work from Wilson's manuscripts after the author's death and later published two new editions of it. Wilson's reputation rests wholly upon this original and accurate contribution to science. He covered only the eastern United States north of Florida; during the next hundred years, however, only 23 indigenous land birds were added to his list. His *The Foresters* (1805) is a versified account of a walking tour from Philadelphia to Niagara Falls. Wilson's poetry is undistinguished, but the prose essays in his *Ornithology* are outstanding in American nature literature.

WILSON, ALLEN BENJAMIN (*b. Willet, N.Y., 1824; d. Woodmont, Conn., 1888*), inventor. A journeyman cabinet-maker, he patented a sewing machine featuring a double-pointed shuttle, 1850, but sold his interests in the patent to E. Lee & Co. of New York. He then devised a rotary hook and bobbin (patented 1851) as a substitute for the double-pointed shuttle and entered partnership with Nathaniel Wheeler to make and market his improved machine. In 1854 he obtained a patent for a four-motion feed used on all later machines. Thereafter, he invented cotton-picking machinery and devices for photography and for illuminating-gas manufacture.

WILSON, AUGUSTA JANE EVANS. *See* EVANS, AUGUSTA JANE.

WILSON, BIRD (*b. Carlisle, Pa., 1777; d. New York, N.Y., 1859*), Episcopal clergyman, Pennsylvania jurist. Son of James Wilson (1742–98). Ordained priest, 1820; professor of systematic divinity, General Theological Seminary, N.Y., 1821–50; a moderate Anglican. Secretary, House of Bishops, 1829–41. Author of, among other writings, *Memoir of the Life of the Rt. Rev. William White* (1839).

WILSON, CHARLES ERWIN (*b. Minerva, Ohio, 1890; d. Norwood, La., 1961*), auto executive and secretary of defense. Attended Carnegie Institute (E.E., 1909). An engineer for Westinghouse Electric (1910–21) who designed their first starting motor for autos (1912) and was put in charge of all Westinghouse auto electrical products (1916). Became factory manager of Remy Electric (1921), a subsidiary of General Motors, and a vice president of GM (1928) in charge of the accessory-producing subsidiaries. In 1929 he became vice president for manufacturing with responsibility for approving any proposal for expansion by a GM division or subsidiary. He subsequently assumed charge of labor relations. The settlement of the 1937 strike by the United Auto Workers was historic; it ended the open-shop policy that had dominated the auto industry. He became president of GM in 1941. Through the war years he supervised the enormous volume of military production turned out by GM; by the end of 1943 all GM war contracts were in production and on schedule. In 1952 he was nominated as secretary of defense and was confirmed only after he agreed to sell his GM holdings. He had a stormy term of office (until 1953); he cut the defense budget by $5 billion and the civilian staff by 40,000. He antagonized part of the military establishment by attempting to curtail conventional forces in favor of reliance on massive nuclear retaliation. Even after leaving government, he was attacked as having left the nation exposed to nuclear threats from the Soviet Union by creating a "missile gap."

WILSON, CLARENCE TRUE (*b. Milton, Del., 1872; d. Portland, Oreg., 1939*), Methodist clergyman. Elected president of the Oregon Anti-Saloon League, 1906, he spent his life thereafter in the prohibition movement. Chosen general secretary of the (later-named) Board of Temperance, Prohibition, and Public Morals of the Methodist Episcopal Church, 1910, he gave it an aggressive leadership and, along with men such as Wayne B. Wheeler, was instrumental in securing much church support for national prohibition. After the 18th Amendment had been adopted in 1919, he continued his efforts to secure its full enforcement, giving much time to political action and employing extravagant lobbying and other tactics which brought upon him much bitter criticism.

WILSON, EDITH BOLLING (*b. Wytherville, Va.; d. Washington, D.C., 1961*), wife of President Woodrow Wilson who became one of her husband's most trusted advisers. After Wilson suffered a paralyzing stroke in 1909, she acted as a shield for the president. With the backing of his doctor, no one was allowed to enter the president's sickroom or to communicate with him without her consent. It was charged that she usurped the authority of the presidency, but later evidence shows that she made no policy decisions by herself. After Wilson's death in 1924, she was a mainstay of the Woodrow Wilson Foundation.

WILSON, EDMUND BEECHER (*b. Geneva, Ill., 1856; d. New York, N.Y., 1939*), biologist, experimental embryologist and cytologist. Ph.B., Yale, 1878; Ph.D., Johns Hopkins, 1881. A student of William K. Brooks at Johns Hopkins, Wilson spent some time at the universities of Cambridge and Leipzig and worked for almost a year at the Zoological Station at Naples, Italy. After teaching at Williams, Massachusetts Institute of Technology, and Bryn Mawr, he went to Columbia University in 1891 as adjunct professor in the Department of Zoology; he later became full professor and chairman of the department. His monograph on the development of the colonial jellyfish *Renilla* (1883) established him as a scientist, and he became one of the outstanding pioneers of "cell lineage." He then took up the problems presented by the organization of the individual cell, and for a number of years engaged in experiments on various regions of the egg or of different cleavage cells; this aspect of his work was signalized in *The Cell in Development and Inheritance* (1896 and later editions). From 1900 to 1905 his research on germinal localization ran side by side with his investigations of the cellular phenomena that are correlated with artificial parthenogenesis. After 1905 he turned his attention to the problem of sex determination and, in a series of brilliant cytological studies on sex chromosomes, reached the high point of his research labors. He prepared the ground for the sensational series of genetic discoveries made *post* 1910 by Thomas H. Morgan and his associates in the Columbia laboratories.

WILSON, ERNEST HENRY (*b. Chipping Campden, England, 1876; d. near Worcester, Mass., 1930*), botanist. As a plant collector for the Arnold Arboretum, Harvard University, he went to the Far East, Africa, Australia, and New Zealand, 1907–10 and 1914–22, and introduced to cultivation more than a thousand plant species. He became assistant director of the Arnold Arboretum, 1919, and keeper, 1927.

WILSON, FRANCIS (*b. Philadelphia, Pa., 1854; d. 1935*), actor. Began his career *ca.* 1880 as comedian in a number of musical comedies. He became famous in the role of Cadeaux in *Erminie* (1886) and continued as a musical-comedy star until 1904 when he became a "legitimate" actor. His principal vehicle was *The Bachelor's Baby*, which he wrote himself; it opened in Baltimore, Md., 1909, ran for three years, and made Wilson a fortune. Elected president of Actors Equity Association, 1913, he devoted much of his time to its affairs until 1921 when he resigned as president. The victory of the actors in the famous strike of 1919 was in great measure his victory. Wilson had a genius for friendship; among his many friends were Joseph Jefferson and Eugene Field.

WILSON, GEORGE FRANCIS (*b. Uxbridge, Mass., 1818; d. East Providence, R.I., 1883*), chemical manufacturer, inventor. Established (with Eben N. Horsford) George F. Wilson & Co., later known as the Rumford Chemical Co., at East Providence, R.I., which he headed until his death. Benefactor of Brown University and Dartmouth College.

WILSON, GEORGE GRAFTON (*b. Plainfield, Conn., 1863; d. Cambridge, Mass., 1951*), professor of international law, author, and editor. Studied at Brown University (Ph.D., 1891). Taught at Brown (1891–1907) and at Harvard (1907–36). Professor at the U.S. Naval War College (1900–37). Special counsel to the U.S. Maritime Commission (1941–51). Wrote *Elements of International Law*, an annotated version of Richard Henry Dana's edition of Henry Wheaton's work (1936). Founder of the American

Society of International Law and editor of the *American Journal of International Law* (1924–43). Founder of and professor at the Fletcher School of Law and Diplomacy at Tufts University (1933).

WILSON, HALSEY WILLIAM (*b. Wilmington, Vt., 1868; d. Yorktown Heights, N.Y., 1954*), publisher, bibliographer. Studied intermittently at the University of Minnesota. Owned a bookshop in Minneapolis; founded a bibliographical publishing company. Issued the *Cumulative Book Index* (1898); *Readers' Guide to Periodical Literature* (1901), which is the standard periodical index; *Book Review Digest* (1905); and the *Wilson Library Bulletin* (1914). In 1917 his H. W. Wilson Company was transferred to the Bronx, N.Y., and a plant for all aspects of publishing was set up.

WILSON, HARRY LEON (*b. Oregon, Ill., 1867; d. Carmel, Calif., 1939*), novelist, playwright. Began literary career as a contributor to *Puck*, 1887; served on that magazine as assistant to Henry C. Bunner, 1892–96, and as editor in chief, 1896–1902. After writing several serious novels, including *The Spenders* (1902), he achieved in *The Boss of Little Arcady* (1905) for the first time that adroit mingling of burlesque and realism which marked his later work. A collaborator with Booth Tarkington for several years in writing plays (among them the hit *The Man from Home*, 1907), Wilson became a regular contributor of fiction to the *Saturday Evening Post*. Outstanding among his later works were *Bunker Bean* (1913), *Ruggles of Red Gap* (1915), and *Merton of the Movies* (1922).

WILSON, HENRY (*b. Farmington, N.H., 1812; d. Washington, D.C., 1875*), shoemaker, lawyer, Massachusetts legislator and statesman, vice president of the United States. Born Jeremiah Colbath of poverty-stricken parents, he was indentured to a farmer as a boy; he had his name legally changed to Henry Wilson *ca.* 1833. His formal education was never more than meager. With minimum capital, he established a shoe factory which was a moderate success. Elected to the Massachusetts House of Representatives as a Whig in 1840, he served in the state legislature for most of the next 12 years. Disaffected at the 1848 Whig convention because it took no stand on the Wilmot Proviso, he and a small group withdrew and launched the Free Soil party at a Buffalo, N.Y., convention. An ardent opponent of slavery, he edited the *Boston Republican* (the Free Soil organ), 1848–51, and aligned himself with the American (Know-Nothing) party, mistakenly believing it would be an important force in freedom's cause. When its 1855 convention adopted a platform which was evasive on the slavery issue, he revolted and withdrew, thereby foiling the party's first attempt to control national politics. Elected to fill a Massachusetts vacancy in the U.S. Senate, 1855, he aligned himself with the abolitionists, was vehement in the debate over Kansas, and supported the Republican campaign in 1860. At the outset of the Civil War, he was chairman of the Senate Military Affairs Committee and threw his tremendous energy into the task of framing, explaining, and defending legislative measures necessary for enlisting, organizing, and provisioning a vast army. (*Post* 1852, he had served with his state's militia, attaining a brigadier generalship.) He constantly urged Lincoln to declare emancipation as a war measure, and he shaped the bills which brought freedom to many slaves in the border states before the 13th Amendment was ratified.

After the war, Wilson as senator at first bitterly opposed President Johnson's Reconstruction policy and attitude toward Congress, but he later became more conciliatory. He favored federal legislation to aid education and homesteading in the impoverished South, through which he had made long tours. His name on the Republican ticket as vice presidential candidate in 1872 contributed to its victory, and he made a highly efficient and acceptable presiding officer in the Senate until his death. Independent of

mind, he never lost sympathy with the working people and promoted legislation in their behalf.

WILSON, HENRY LANE (*b. Crawfordsville, Ind., 1857; d. Indianapolis, Ind., 1932*), lawyer, diplomat. Brother of John Lockwood Wilson. Practiced in Spokane, Wash., 1884–96. As U.S. minister to Chile, 1897–1904, he was instrumental in averting trouble between Chile and Argentina, 1900. U.S. minister to Belgium, 1905–09. As ambassador to Mexico, 1909–13, he unsuccessfully urged presidents Taft and Wilson to recognize the Huerta government.

WILSON, HENRY PARKE CUSTIS (*b. Workington, Md., 1827; d. Baltimore, Md., 1897*), surgeon, gynecologist. Beginning practice in Baltimore, Md., 1851, he was first in the state to remove uterine appendages by abdominal section and the second to perform successful ovariotomy, 1866. Said to be second in the world to remove an intrauterine tumor by morcellation. Cofounder of Hospital for the Women of Maryland, 1882; consultant at Johns Hopkins and other Baltimore hospitals.

WILSON, HUGH ROBERT (*b. Evanston, Ill., 1885; d. Bennington, Vt., 1946*), diplomat. B.A., Yale, 1906. After study at the École Libre des Sciences Politiques, Paris, and brief service as secretary to the U.S. minister in Lisbon, he returned to the United States, passed the Foreign Service examination, 1911, and was appointed secretary of the U.S. legation in Guatemala, 1912. Thereafter, he held a number of posts before appointment as U.S. minister to Switzerland, 1927. Returning to Washington, D.C., in August 1937, he served briefly as assistant secretary of state and then as U.S. ambassador to Germany, 1938–39 (recalled in November 1938 to protest against Nazi anti-Jewish policies). Resigning from the Foreign Service at the end of 1940, he was with the World War II Office of Strategic Services, 1941–45. Belonging to the "realist" rather than the "messianic" school of U.S. diplomats, he was one of the first career men to achieve ambassadorial rank.

WILSON, JAMES (*b. Carskerdo, Scotland, 1742; d. Edenton, N.C., 1798*), jurist, U.S. Supreme Court justice. Described by James Bryce as "one of the deepest thinkers and most exact reasoners" in the Federal Convention of 1787, and as one whose works "display an amplitude and profundity of view in matters of constitutional theory which place him in the front rank of the political thinkers of his age." Immigrated to America, 1765. Better educated than most immigrants of the time, he quickly obtained a position as Latin tutor in the College of Philadelphia. After studying law with John Dickinson, he began practice in Reading, Pa., 1768. Soon removing to Carlisle, Pa., he was very successful in cases involving land disputes. By 1773 he had begun borrowing capital for speculative land purchases, a lifelong activity of his.

Active in the early Revolutionary movement, he was elected to the first Continental Congress and distributed to its members his pamphlet *Considerations on the Nature and Extent of the Legislative Authority of the British Parliament* (1774), a work which denied to Parliament the least authority over the colonies. This able statement of the extreme American position was widely read in both England and America. Wilson also spoke to the same effect before the provincial conference of January 1775 and introduced a resolution on the Boston Port Act which presaged the doctrine of judicial review.

From his position on the extreme left in 1774, Wilson moved steadily thereafter to the right. As a Continental congressman, 1776–77, he aided in delaying moves toward independence during June 1776, but on July 2 was one of three out of seven Pennsylvania delegates who voted for independence. Active in executing burdensome committee assignments, he was among the first to urge relinquishment of the claims of the states to western lands, to advocate taxation powers for Congress, and to try to strengthen the national government. He also urged that representation in Congress should be based on free population. However, he fought bitterly against the 1776 Pennsylvania Constitution, a democratic product of the frontier. Leaving Congress in September 1777, he engaged in corporation practice in Philadelphia after a brief stay at Annapolis, Md. Acting as counsel for Loyalists and engaging in privateering and land-jobbing schemes, he widened the breach between himself and the people, and soon became personally unpopular. He served again in Congress, 1782 and 1785–87, but was chiefly concerned with his multiplying business interests. In 1785 he published *Considerations on the Power to Incorporate the Bank of North America*, an able argument in which he foreshadowed John Marshall's doctrine of inherent sovereignty.

Wilson's greatest achievement in public life was his part in the establishment of the U.S. Constitution. With the possible exception of James Madison, no member of the 1787 convention was better versed in the study of political economy, none grasped more firmly the central problem of dual sovereignty, and none was more farsighted in his vision of the future of the United States. Wilson kept constantly in view the idea that sovereignty resided in the people, favoring popular election of the president and of members of both houses of Congress. He clearly stated that the national government was not "an assemblage of States, but of individuals for certain political purposes." He opposed the idea of equal representation in the Senate. He was a member of the committee of detail which prepared the draft of the U.S. Constitution, and after signing it, he fought for its adoption. He was author of the Pennsylvania state constitution of 1790, which represented the climax of his 14-year fight against the earlier democratic constitution. Although he expected appointment as chief justice, he accepted the post of associate justice of the U.S. Supreme Court, September 1789. Also appointed to the chair of law in the College of Philadelphia, 1789, he delivered a series of lectures in December in which he departed from Blackstone's definitions and, discovering the residence of sovereignty in the individual, postulated as the basis of law the consent of those whose obedience the law requires. He also set forth clearly the implications of the U.S. Supreme Court for judicial settlement of international disputes and for the administration of international law. Commissioned to make a digest of the laws of Pennsylvania, he began the task and also recommended himself to President Washington as being willing and able to establish a body of theoretical principles for future judicial and legislative interpretation of the U.S. Constitution—especially with respect to the problems of federal and state relations. He was unsuccessful in his application, however, as the attorney general urged on the president the impropriety of any single person determining such principles for future guidance. Wilson now plunged further into vast land speculations, involving the Holland Land Co. in unwise purchases, 1792–93, and buying an interest in one of the Yazoo companies, 1795. These and other speculative enterprises in which he engaged brought on him much severe criticism, and he died amid talk of impeachment and while endeavoring to escape from creditors. His most noted decision on the bench was that in *Chisholm* v. *Georgia*, in which he positively affirmed the doctrine that the people of the United States formed a nation.

WILSON, JAMES (*b. Ayrshire, Scotland, 1836; d. 1920*), farmer, Iowa legislator. Settled in Iowa, 1855. Congressman, Republican, from Iowa, 1873–77 and 1883–85; known as "Tama Jim," he was a member of the Agricultural and Rules committees. Appointed professor of agriculture and head of experiment station at Iowa State College, 1891, he helped place instruction on both a scientific and practical basis. As U.S. secretary of agriculture, 1897–1913, he established many new experiment stations and

began farm demonstration work in the South; he also began cooperative extension work in agriculture and home economics, promoted world agricultural information, and initiated much helpful legislation.

WILSON, JAMES FALCONER (*b. Newark, Ohio, 1828; d. Fairfield, Iowa, 1895*), lawyer, Iowa legislator. Studied law under William B. Woods; began practice in Iowa *ca.* 1852; was influential delegate in state constitutional convention, 1857. Known as "Jefferson Jim," he was congressman, Republican, from Iowa, 1861–69; as chairman of the House Judiciary Committee, he forwarded the Union program and introduced the original resolution for an abolition amendment. During Reconstruction, he was one of the ablest leaders among the legalistic Radicals. He introduced important amendments to the resolution for repudiation of Confederate debt, an amendment repealing appellate jurisdiction of the Supreme Court under the Habeas Corpus Act of 1867, and the final form of the Civil Rights Act. Advocate of the Pacific railroad, he was a government director of the road under Presidents Grant and Hayes. Attacked for alleged financial improprieties in this connection, he was closely questioned during the House investigations of the railroad, 1873. He was undistinguished as U.S. senator, Republican, from Iowa, 1883–95.

WILSON, J(AMES) FINLEY (*b. Dickson, Tenn., 1881; d. Washington, D.C., 1952*), newspaperman, politician. Studied at Fisk University. A black, Wilson founded, edited, and published the *Washington Eagle* (originally the *Sun*). Joined lodges of the Improved Benevolent and Protective Order of Elks of the World in 1903; was the Grand Exalted Ruler from 1922. Wilson organized and expanded black Elk programs in civil liberties, education, and health. Raised money for legal battles such as the Scottsboro trial. A friend of Franklin D. Roosevelt, he worked for cooperation between the Elks and the National Recovery Administration (NRA). President of the Colored Voters League of America, 1933. Ran unsuccessfully for the New York State Senate as a Republican in 1946.

WILSON, JAMES GRANT (*b. Edinburgh, Scotland, 1832; d. 1914*), editor, Union soldier. Son of William Wilson (1801–60). Came to America as an infant. Removed to Chicago, Ill., 1856, where he edited and published periodicals, including the *Chicago Record*, April 1857–March 1862. Colonel, 4th U.S. Colored Cavalry, 1863; brevetted brigadier general of volunteers, 1865. Settled in New York City, 1865. He was a prolific writer of military and literary biographies and an editor of church and local histories. His most extensive work was as coeditor (with John Fiske) of *Appleton's Cyclopaedia of American Biography* (1886–89; rev. ed., 1898–99).

WILSON, JAMES HARRISON (*b. near Shawneetown, Ill., 1837; d. Wilmington, Del., 1925*), engineer, Union cavalryman, author. Graduated West Point, 1860. Chief topographical engineer on Port Royal expedition; volunteer aide to General G. B. McClellan at South Mountain and Antietam. Named inspector general, Army of Tennessee, 1863, he was active in Vicksburg's siege and capture. Advanced to brigadier general of volunteers, October 1863, he was chief engineer of the Knoxville relief expedition and was made chief of the Washington cavalry bureau, January 1864. Commanding the 3rd Division of General P. H. Sheridan's cavalry corps, Army of the Potomac, he led the advance across the Rapidan, covered General U. S. Grant's passage to the Chicahominy, formed part of Sheridan's first Richmond expedition. Appointed chief of cavalry, Military Division of the Mississippi, with brevet rank of major general, October 1864, he defeated General N. B. Forrest in several engagements, enabling General J. M. Schofield to repulse Confederate General John

Hood and contributing to Hood's defeat by General G. H. Thomas at Nashville. On April 2, 1865, Wilson took Selma, Ala., by assault in one of the most brilliant actions of the Civil War. He then moved on through Montgomery, Ala., took Columbus, Ga., and reached Macon, Ga., on April 20. After the war he superintended navigation improvements, resigning from the army in 1870. As senior major general in the Spanish-American War, he served in Puerto Rico and Cuba; in the Boxer Rebellion in China, he was second in command to General A. R. Chaffee. He was advanced to major general, retired, 1915.

WILSON, JAMES SOUTHALL (*b. Bacon's Castle, Va., 1880; d. Charlottesville, Va., 1963*), educator, editor, and author. Attended William and Mary, University of Virginia, and Princeton (Ph.D., 1906). Taught at William and Mary (1906–18) and the University of Virginia (1919–51), where he helped secure the Ingram collection of Edgar Allan Poe memorabilia. Founded (1925) and edited (until 1930) the *Virginia Quarterly*. Prepared an edition of Poe's *Tales* (1927) and wrote *An Appreciation of Edgar Allan Poe* (1923).

WILSON, JOHN (*b. Windsor, England, ca. 1591; d. 1667*), clergyman, verse writer. Immigrated to Massachusetts, 1630. Served the First Church in Boston, Mass., from 1635 until his death, sharing the pulpit with John Cotton until 1652. A spokesman of orthodoxy and a constant counselor of the magistrates, Wilson was zealous for conversion of the Massachusetts Indians and was ranked among the most influential of the Massachusetts clergy.

WILSON, JOHN FLEMING (*b. Erie, Pa., 1877; d. Santa Monica, Calif., 1922*), journalist, author of sea stories.

WILSON, JOHN LEIGHTON (*b. near Salem, S.C., 1809; d. near Salem, 1886*), Presbyterian clergyman. Graduated Columbia (S.C.) Seminary; ordained, 1833. Went to Liberia, 1834; established missions in western Africa at Cape Palmas and Gabon. Returned to America, 1852. Elected secretary of the Board of Foreign Missions, 1853; edited *Home and Foreign Record*, 1853–61; founded *The Missionary*, 1866, which he edited for nearly 20 years. Supervised foreign missions of the Presbyterian Church in the Confederate States of America (later in the United States) *post* 1861; also its home missionary projects, 1863–72. Author of encyclopedic *Western Africa: Its History, Conditions, and Prospects* (1856).

WILSON, JOHN LOCKWOOD (*b. Crawfordsville, Ind., 1850; d. Washington, D.C., 1912*), lawyer, publisher. Brother of Henry L. Wilson. Receiver, federal land office at Colfax, Washington Territory, 1882–87. Republican representative-at-large in Congress from Washington, 1889–95. Promoted Pacific Northwest river and harbor development; sponsored effective lieu land bill; secured passage of bill creating Mount Rainier National Park. U.S. senator, 1895–99. In 1899 he purchased a controlling interest in the *Seattle Post-Intelligencer*, which he managed until his death.

WILSON, JOSEPH MILLER (*b. Phoenixville, Pa., 1838; d. 1902*), civil engineer, architect. Son of William H. Wilson. C.E. Rensselaer Polytechnic Institute, 1858. Engineer of bridges and buildings, Pennsylvania Railroad, 1865–86. Organized Wilson Bros. & Co., consulting civil engineers and architects, 1876. The firm's projects included stations and shops for the Ninth and Third Avenue lines of the New York Elevated Railway and for a number of other railroads; also, buildings for the Drexel Institute, Philadelphia, Pa., and other institutions there. Wilson himself designed and built, among others, the Susquehanna and Schuylkill bridges, the original Broad St. Station in Philadelphia, and the main exhibition building and machinery hall at the Philadelphia Centennial Exhibition, 1876. He did important later consulting work and wrote on scientific and engineering subjects.

WILSON, JOSHUA LACY (*b. Bedford Co., Va., 1774; d. Cincinnati, Ohio, 1846*), Presbyterian clergyman, educator. Father of Samuel R. Wilson. Called to the First Presbyterian Church, Cincinnati, Ohio, 1808, he served there until his death. An "old school" theologian, his defense of Calvinism led him into many controversies; he opposed the "New England theology" and the "Plan of Union" and prosecuted Lyman Beecher for heresy before the presbytery and synod.

WILSON, LOUIS BLANCHARD (*b. Pittsburgh, Pa., 1866; d. Rochester, Minn., 1943*), pathologist, medical educator. Graduated State Normal School at California, Pa., 1886. While teaching high school in St. Paul, Minn., he attended the medical school of the University of Minnesota and received the M.D. degree, 1896. He then became assistant to Frank Wesbrook of the state board of health, who furthered his interest in bacteriology. In 1905, he was invited to join the staff of the Mayo Clinic in Rochester, Minn., to establish laboratories for pathologic and bacteriologic studies. Although he made a number of important contributions to laboratory technique and pathology, he made his most enduring mark as director of the Mayo Graduate School of Medicine, 1915–37.

WILSON, MORTIMER (*b. Chariton, Iowa, 1876; d. New York, N.Y., 1932*), composer, conductor, teacher. Headed theoretical courses, music department, University of Nebraska, 1901–08; revived and conducted the Lincoln Symphony Orchestra. Studied in Leipzig under Max Reger and Hans Sitt, 1908–10. Conducted Atlanta, Ga., symphony orchestra, and directed Atlanta Conservatory of Music, 1913–14. Arranged and wrote music for motion pictures. His compositions included symphonies, suites, sonatas, and numerous short pieces and songs; they displayed fluency and inventiveness in counterpoint.

WILSON, PETER (*b. Banff, Scotland, 1746; d. New Barbadoes, N.J., 1825*), philologist, educator, New Jersey legislator. Educated at University of Aberdeen. Immigrated to New York City, 1763. Principal of Hackensack (N.J.) Academy; of Erasmus Hall Academy, Flatbush, N.Y., ca. 1792–1805. Professor of Greek and Latin, Columbia College, 1789–92; of Greek and Latin and Grecian and Roman antiquities, 1797–1820. Wrote treatises on prosody and edited classic texts.

WILSON, ROBERT BURNS (*b. near Washington, Pa., 1850; d. Brooklyn, N.Y., 1916*), painter, poet, novelist. Author of the poem "Remember the Maine" (*New York Herald*, April 17, 1898), which supplied the slogan for the Spanish-American War.

WILSON, SAMUEL (*b. West Cambridge, now Arlington, Mass., 1766; d. Troy, N.Y., 1854*), meatpacker; original of "Uncle Sam" as symbolic figure for the United States. Furnished beef to the army's supply center at Troy, N.Y., during War of 1812. The "U.S." on the casks was humorously defined as standing for "Uncle Sam's" monogram.

WILSON, SAMUEL GRAHAM (*b. Indiana, Pa., 1858; d. Tabriz, Persia, 1916*), Presbyterian clergyman. Missionary to Persia and Armenia *post* 1880. Distinguished as an educator and relief worker among Armenian refugees from Turkey, 1916. Author of, among other works, *Persian Life and Customs* (1895).

WILSON, SAMUEL MOUNTFORD (*b. Steubenville, Ohio, ca. 1823; d. 1892*), lawyer. Admitted to the Ohio bar, 1844; removed to San Francisco, Calif., 1853, after practicing in Galena, Ill. Restricted his work to civil suits; took leading part in nearly all noted California land law cases. Outstanding as counsel for hydraulic mining companies, 1880–86, against farming interests on debris question (*People of California* v. *Gold Run Ditch and Mining Company*). Also in high repute for will cases, notably for his successful defense of David Broderick's will. A fluent, direct speaker, he depended for success on a complete mastery of the matters at issue. He served as chairman of the judiciary committee of the Californian constitutional convention, 1878–79, opposing radical demands of Denis Kearney.

WILSON, SAMUEL RAMSAY (*b. Cincinnati, Ohio, 1818; d. Louisville, Ky., 1886*), Presbyterian clergyman. Son of Joshua L. Wilson. Graduated Princeton Theological Seminary, 1840. Pastor, First Presbyterian Church, Cincinnati, Ohio, 1846–61; First Presbyterian Church, Louisville, Ky., 1865–79. A Southern sympathizer, he opposed the Reconstruction policy of the majority of the "old school" Presbyterian church and drew up the "Declaration and Testimony," adopted by the Louisville Presbytery in protest against the General Assembly's position.

WILSON, SAMUEL THOMAS (*b. London, England, 1761; d. Kentucky, 1824*), Roman Catholic clergyman. Dominican. Ordained priest in Belgium, 1786. Served as vicar provincial of the Dominican community at Bornhem, Belgium, during the French Revolution. A missionary in Kentucky *post* 1805, he was named provincial in 1807 and was responsible for building the Church of St. Rose and College of St. Thomas Aquinas near Springfield, Ky. Founded first American convent of Sisters of the Third Order of St. Dominic, 1822.

WILSON, THEODORE DELAVAN (*b. Brooklyn, N.Y., 1840; d. Boston, Mass., 1896*), ship constructor. Served in Union navy, 1861–63, as ship's carpenter at sea; worked in navy yard at New York, 1863–65. Rose to rank of naval constructor, 1873, after service at Pensacola and Philadelphia yards and as instructor at Annapolis. Chief, Navy Bureau of Construction and Repair, 1882–93, he supervised transition of the navy from wooden vessels to steel, surmounting innumerable problems of material and design.

WILSON, THOMAS WOODROW. *See* WILSON, WOODROW.

WILSON, WARREN HUGH (*b. near Tidioute, Pa., 1867; d. New York, N.Y., 1937*), Presbyterian clergyman, educator. Graduated Oberlin, 1890; Union Theological Seminary, New York, 1894. Ph.D., Columbia University, 1908. After studying the operation of new social forces on rural America while a pastor, he became secretary of the Church and Country Life Department of the Presbyterian Board of Missions, 1908, and held that post until his death. His scientific rural surveys in every major region of the United States became standard documents for the developing rural-life movement and exposed the problems and deficiencies of rural education. His chief contributions to rural sociology were the application of the theory of marginal utility to rural social life and, as early as 1919, the development and application of the concept of regionalism to rural social conditions. He taught rural sociology at Teachers College, Columbia, 1914–23.

WILSON, WILLIAM (*b. Loudoun Co., Va., 1794; d. White Co., Ill., 1857*), jurist. Began practice in White Co., Ill., 1817. Justice, Illinois Supreme Court, 1819–24; chief justice, 1824–48. Rendered decision in *Field* v. *State of Illinois ex rel. McClernand*, 1839, in which the governor's power to remove a secretary of state appointed by his predecessor was denied on the ground that the state constitution did not expressly place any limitation upon the duration of the term of office.

WILSON, WILLIAM (*b. Crieff, Perthshire, Scotland, 1801; d. 1860*), bookseller, publisher. Father of James G. Wilson.

Conducted business at Poughkeepsie, N.Y., *post* 1834; author of unoriginal verse, collected in *Poems* (1869).

WILSON, WILLIAM BAUCHOP (*b. Blantyre, Scotland, 1862; d. Savannah, Ga., 1934*), labor leader. Immigrated to Arnot, Pa., as a boy; worked as a miner; was active in early union organization. Secretary-treasurer, United Mine Workers of America, 1900–08. As congressman, Democrat, from Pennsylvania, 1907–13, he was outstanding as chairman of the Committee on Labor. He sponsored investigation of mine safety conditions and influenced organization of federal Bureau of Mines, 1810; in 1912 he secured passage of Seamen's Act, for protection of merchant marine seamen. As first U.S. secretary of labor, 1913–21, he thoroughly reorganized the Bureau of Immigration and Naturalization; developed agencies for mediating and adjusting industrial disputes (probably his most significant work); and set up the U.S. Employment Service.

WILSON, WILLIAM DEXTER (*b. Stoddard, N.H., 1816; d. Syracuse, N.Y., 1900*), Episcopal clergyman, educator. Graduated Harvard Divinity School, 1838. A convert from Unitarianism, 1842, he taught moral and intellectual philosophy at Geneva (later Hobart) Divinity School, 1850–68, and was briefly acting president. Professor of moral and intellectual philosophy, Cornell University, 1868–86, he served also as registrar and was active in university organization and administration. Became dean, St. Andrew's Divinity School, Syracuse, N.Y., 1887.

WILSON, WILLIAM HASELL (*b. Charleston, S.C., 1811; d. 1902*), civil engineer. Grandson of William H. Gibbes; father of Joseph M. Wilson. Principal assistant engineer, Philadelphia & Reading Railroad, 1835–36. Engaged in general practice, 1837–57; served as consultant to the Pennsylvania Railroad in westward extensions; appointed resident engineer, Philadelphia & Columbia Railroad, 1857. Given charge of maintenance of way and new construction for the Pennsylvania Railroad "main line" between Philadelphia and Pittsburgh, 1859, he held title of chief engineer, 1862–74. Constructed works of Altoona Gas Co., of which he was president, 1859–71. Headed real estate department of the Pennsylvania Railroad, 1874–84; thereafter, served as president and director of several Pennsylvania-leased railroads.

WILSON, WILLIAM LYNE (*b. Middleway, Va., now W.Va., 1843; d. 1900*), Confederate soldier, lawyer, educator. Graduated Columbian College, Washington, D.C., 1860; LL.B., 1867. Assistant professor of ancient languages, Columbian College, 1865–71. Successfully practiced law in Charles Town, W.Va., 1871–ca. 1883. President, West Virginia University, September 1882–June 1883. As congressman, Democrat, from West Virginia, 1883–95, his most important work was in tariff reform. He supported the Morrison bills and, as a member of the Ways and Means Committee, helped frame the Mills bill. He first reached national prominence in the 1888 debate on this measure. He was a principal opponent of the McKinley bill, 1890. As chairman of the Ways and Means Committee, 1893, he led in framing the Wilson bill; his moderate reform measures were vitiated by Senate amendments in 1894. U.S. postmaster general, 1895–97, he inaugurated rural free delivery and enlarged classified civil service. A staunch believer in the gold standard, Wilson fought the Democratic stampede to free coinage of silver in 1895–96. After the Democratic convention of 1896, he condemned Bryan and was considered for the presidential nomination by the Gold Democrats. He was president of Washington and Lee University, Lexington, Va., *post* 1897.

WILSON, WOODROW (*b. Staunton, Va., 1856; d. Washington, D.C., 1924*), educator, statesman, president of the United States. Christened Thomas Woodrow Wilson, he came of Scottish ancestry and was the son of a Presbyterian minister. In his second year the family removed to Augusta, Ga.; in 1870 Wilson's father became professor at the theological seminary at Columbia, S.C., and pastor of the First Presbyterian Church; in 1874 the family moved to Wilmington, N.C., where the father held a pastorate. The young Wilson was the personal and intellectual companion of his father, acquired much learning at home, and lived a youth largely separated from those of his own age. He retained an indelible impression of the horror produced in him as a child by the Civil War.

After attending Davidson College, 1873–74, he entered the College of New Jersey (Princeton), from which he graduated, 1879. As an undergraduate he was a leader in debating and devoted much study to the lives of British statesmen. Aspiring to a career in public life, he attended the law school of the University of Virginia, where he took more interest in the study of political history than in the formal law courses. In 1882 he began practice of law in Atlanta, Ga., but failed largely because of his repugnance to the purely commercial side of practice. Entering the graduate school of Johns Hopkins, 1883, he worked under Herbert B. Adams, but rebelled against German methods of postgraduate work. However, his newly stimulated literary powers won him a fellowship in the history department, and he published his important *Congressional Government* (1885), a beautifully written analysis of American legislative practice, with emphasis on the evils that come from the separation of the legislative and executive branches of government and from the consequent power of congressional committees. This served also as his thesis for his Ph.D. degree, 1886. In 1885 he married Ellen L. Axson, who was profoundly sympathetic with his ideals and influenced him strongly. After teaching history at Bryn Mawr, 1885–88, and at Wesleyan University, 1888–90, he joined the Princeton faculty as professor of jurisprudence and political economy.

Wilson cared little for scholarly distinction acquired by intensive research; his broad reading and intense intellectual curiosity, however, made him influential among faculty and undergraduates. He was soon a leader of the younger liberals on the faculty. He labored over his literary style and exercised a rigid self-criticism. He also engaged in lecture tours, thereby winning confidence in his ability to interest and dominate general audiences.

Elected president of Princeton, June 1902, he embarked on an already formulated program of academic reform. Convinced that the object of a university is simply and entirely intellectual, he proposed to revolutionize Princeton's attitude toward college life, giving the serious scholar the prestige he had rightly earned and reducing the social and athletic sideshows to a subordinate place. He undertook a structural reorganization of the university by means of the preceptorial system and the quad plan (providing for more intensive individual instruction and for a democratization of the student body by housing it in small nonexclusive units like the English colleges), and he brought to the faculty a group of new scholars who were prepared to undertake the duties of preceptors to small groups. Wilson hoped to break the hold of the already existing and exclusive undergraduate clubs on the social life of the university, but the quad plan was opposed bitterly, and he was asked by the board of trustees to withdraw this part of his program.

By a stroke of irony this academic defeat served to bring Wilson before the American public as a champion of the underprivileged and as a supporter of democratic principles. However, he received another setback in a controversy which had arisen over the location of the new graduate college. Wilson saw in the refusal of the trustees to give him their entire support a block to the development of his ideal of a democratic coordinated university; he was also disappointed at the manifestation of bitter personal feeling incident to these struggles. At this juncture his early admirer Col. George B. M. Harvey urged Wilson upon the state Democratic

organization as an ideal candidate for governor in 1910. The doubtful machine politicians allowed themselves to be persuaded to nominate Wilson; after resigning the presidency of Princeton, October 1910, he was elected governor of New Jersey in November.

Regarded by the machine politicians as a naive theorist and suspected by the reformers as a tool of the machine politicians, he speedily disillusioned both groups. Driving forward reform measures with vigor; by the end of the first session of the legislature he had secured enactment of the most important proposals of his campaign—a primary-election law, an invigorated public utilities act, a corrupt-practices act, and an employers' liability act. New Jersey was now studied by reformers as a practical example of possibilities, and Wilson began to attract national attention. Through the efforts of his friend Col. Edward M. House, who believed that Wilson was a man of genius and a Democrat untouched by "Bryanesque heresies," and also because of the admiration of people in general for the eloquence and power of his public addresses, Wilson was nominated by the Democrats for the presidency at Baltimore, Md., in the summer of 1912.

The political split between Republican progressives and conservatives and the personal quarrel between Theodore Roosevelt and W. H. Taft made the Democratic nomination in 1912 tantamount to election. Wilson was victor in November with 435 electoral votes as against 88 for Roosevelt and 8 for Taft; it was the largest electoral majority ever achieved up to that time, although it represented a popular minority. Wilson presented himself to the public as champion of what he called the "New Freedom." He was to be a conservative reformer, eager to return to the common people an equality of opportunity which had been threatened by the "interests" of industry, finance, and commerce. Distrustful of radical remedies, he believed that the first essential to government at Washington was to render it sensitive to public opinion. His campaign speeches had embodied his program; they were a series of magnificent manifestos and established him as the leader of American liberalism. Aware of the tremendous influence still exercised in the United States by William J. Bryan, Wilson named him secretary of state; the other members of the Wilson cabinet proved to be of more than adequate administrative ability. Determined at the outset to establish a closer working connection between the executive and the legislature, he appeared in person before both houses of Congress in April 1913 to deliver his first message, thus reviving a custom that had lapsed since Jefferson's time. He soon began to use the large Democratic majority in Congress to win extraordinary legislative triumphs; of these, the most important were the Underwood Tariff and the Federal Reserve Act. The third major aspect of his program took form in creation of the Federal Trade Commission and in the Clayton Antitrust Act, which was designed to prevent interlocking directorates and declared that labor organizations should not be held, or construed to be, illegal combinations in restraint of trade. The aim of this legislation was to liberalize the industrial system and to eliminate special privilege, destroy monopoly, and maintain competition. Influential industrialists and the wilder reformers among the Democrats were equally opposed to the president, but he was able to control Congress through judicious use of the political patronage. However, the chief factor in Wilson's early success was his own genius for leading public opinion and mobilizing it against opposition. There were many, however, who said that he was too restless and wanted to go too fast.

Another irony in Wilson's career soon manifested itself. The president, primarily interested in solution of domestic problems, was soon forced to give major attention to international affairs. A determined pacifist, he was to be compelled to lead his country in a great war. Attempting to eliminate the traditional Latin American jealousy of the United States by a policy of goodwill and accommodation, he was thwarted by conditions in Haiti, Central America, and Mexico. Problems occasioned by the Huerta-Carranza struggle in Mexico led to "incidents" and the necessity of military action in defense of United States rights at Tampico and Veracruz. Subsequent to the partial solution of these difficulties by the mediation of Argentina, Brazil, and Chile, a new set of troubles developed because of guerrilla raids across the border into New Mexico. In 1916 Wilson was forced to send a small force under General John J. Pershing across the Mexican border in pursuit of Pancho Villa, and the National Guard was mobilized for protection of the border. He was, however, able to project the essential articles of an agreement to provide for international security of the western hemisphere which forecast the later Covenant of the League of Nations. This matter was discussed with Latin American statesmen, but was soon merged in Wilson's more comprehensive plan for a world organization built upon a similar model. Wilson also engaged in diplomatic efforts through Colonel House to create a closer Anglo-American understanding, which might later be developed by the inclusion of Germany and so end the mutual distrust among nations which was poisoning Europe.

After the sudden outbreak of World War I, the general favor given the cause of the Allies by people of the eastern states was shared by the president; he was determined, however, that this should in no way affect a policy of complete neutrality. Soon, both Allied regulation of neutral maritime trade and the German submarine campaign challenged the neutral policy which Wilson favored. The United States issued a formal protest against Allied maritime control in December 1914, but difficulties with the Allies were at once alleviated by the German decree of February 1915, declaring the waters around the British Isles a war zone and threatening to sink all belligerent merchant ships, with a further intimation that neutral ships might also be sunk. Reacting against such blind destruction of property as was entailed in the German threat, Wilson was further disturbed by the threat to life, for which no adequate compensation could ever be made. On Feb. 10 he warned Germany that destruction of an American vessel or American lives would be regarded as a violation of neutral rights and a matter of strict accountability. Soon "accidents" began to happen. On May 7 the *Lusitania* was sunk; among the victims were 128 Americans. Wilson's firmness in demanding that Germany give up the ruthless submarine campaign led to the resignation of William J. Bryan in June; Bryan saw the danger of war in Wilson's insistence on the preservation of traditional neutral rights. However, the president's combination of patience and firmness triumphed temporarily. Following the sinking of the *Arabic* in August 1915, the German ambassador to the United States announced his government's promise that passenger liners would not be attacked without warning. A later comprehensive agreement to abandon ruthless submarine warfare was extracted from Germany by the threat of a diplomatic rupture, which Germany hoped to avoid. "My chief puzzle is to determine where patience ceases to be a virtue," Wilson wrote to Colonel House in September 1915. He continued to act, however, on the principle that the people of the United States counted on him to keep them out of the war and that it would be a world calamity if the United States should be actively drawn into the conflict and so deprived of disinterested influence over the peace settlement. His policy toward Germany continued to receive confirmation from Congress right up to the national election of 1916.

At a disadvantage because of domestic dislike of his reform legislation and because of the revived solidarity of the Republican party, Wilson was reelected in November 1916 over the Republican candidate, Charles E. Hughes, by a very narrow margin (277 to 254). Indeed, he at first thought that he had been defeated, and it was not until the full returns from the West came in that Republican majorities in the East were wiped out. He now began to make a

determined move for peace, following along lines which he had pursued since the early autumn of 1914, despite constant rebuffs. The failure of the Allies to respond to intimations of a possible settlement from Germany and from Wilson now influenced the Germans to plan resumption of unrestricted submarine warfare; on Jan. 31, 1917, the German government told the United States that its earlier pledges would no longer be observed. Wilson decided immediately to give the German ambassador his passports.

Wilson believed that by upsetting the tentative movements for peace then in progress, however unlikely of success they might be, the Germans had morally condemned themselves. He still refused to believe, however, that a diplomatic rupture meant war. His hand was forced very soon by the publication of the notorious "Zimmermann telegram," suggesting that a German-Mexican-Japanese alliance was in prospect, and by the sinking of more American ships. On April 2, 1917, he appeared before Congress to ask for a declaration of war; the resolution was voted on April 6. It represented an all but unanimous sentiment of the American people, who appeared to share the president's conviction that imperial Germany was an international criminal.

Once the United States was at war, Wilson mustered the full national strength and concentrated on victory. The nation was inadequately prepared for war, yet the president's war leadership was particularly distinguished in that he inspired a general conviction that it was a people's war and that every citizen should make individual sacrifices. He made wise choices of the men who were to occupy vital administrative and military posts, and he let them alone to do their jobs. His own supreme contribution to a victory lay in his formulation of war aims—aims which he had publicized well before the conflict. Embodying the principle of the Monroe Doctrine to the entire world, he demanded a concert of the powers capable of maintaining international peace and the rights of small nations. However, even during the war it became obvious that Wilson's aims were not those of the Allies. Subsequent to the Russian Revolution a restatement of aims became necessary, and on Jan. 8, 1918, the president delivered before Congress the speech of the Fourteen Points. This was not intended as a public international charter but as a diplomatic weapon to meet the Bolshevik drive for peace and to strengthen the morale of the Allied liberals. It contained six general points which repeated ideals already enunciated by Wilson: open diplomacy, freedom of the seas, removal of trade barriers, reduction of armaments, impartial adjustment of colonial claims, a league of nations. There were also eight special points dealing with immediate political and territorial problems.

By this speech the president committed himself to participation in the general world problem of preserving the peace and also to an interest in certain local problems peculiar to Europe which might disturb the peace. When the Germans recognized early in the autumn of 1918 that they would be defeated, they seized upon this speech as a general basis of peace negotiations and turned to Wilson as their savior from political and economic annihilation. Although his interchange of notes with the Germans at this point ran counter to public sentiment in the United States and irritated the Allies, it contributed to securing an early armistice by encouraging the existing demand for peace among the German people. When Wilson offered the Allies Germany's acceptance of an armistice on Oct. 23, 1918, the Allies were free to refuse it if they chose. Likewise, although the Germans later complained that they had been lured into a peace without guarantees, they were more than eager at the time to accept the undefined Fourteen Points rather than lose a chance at peace. After compelling the Allied leaders to accept the Fourteen Points by a threat to expose their intransigent attitude to Congress, the president sent Germany a qualified Allied acceptance of the basic conditions of peace and an armistice was signed on Nov. 11, 1918.

Now at the height of his influence, Wilson was the greatest single force in the world, yet the difficulties of capitalizing on the victory were far greater than those which had been involved in winning it. The sense of common interest in war soon evaporated, and Wilson's political ideals could not readily be transplanted to Europe. Also, at this critical moment Wilson made three mistakes. He asked for a heavy Democratic vote in the November elections as a sign of confidence in him and his policies, thus abdicating the national leadership by assuming the role of a party leader; Democratic defeats in the election therefore gave the appearance of a national repudiation. His second mistake lay in his failure to appoint to the Peace Commission a single member who truly represented either the Republican party or the U.S. Senate; he thus forfeited the chance of winning support from his domestic opponents. His third and greatest mistake lay in his decision to attend the Peace Conference in person, since by lowering himself to haggle at the conference table he lost his commanding position as first citizen of the world. He did succeed at the very beginning of the conference in forcing an acceptance of the League of Nations Covenant as an integral part of the treaty of peace. At later sessions he was shaken by the discovery that in their application his principles were sometimes at variance with each other, and he was compelled to compromise—a series of adjustments which left liberals disappointed and the Germans bitter. However, the need for compromise is apparent from the fact that the Allied nationalists were equally disappointed. He could congratulate himself, however, on the adoption of the League of Nations Covenant, through which, as he believed, all errors and omissions could later be rectified.

There now remained the problem of winning the approval of the U.S. Senate for the Versailles Treaty. Wilson had solved many more difficult problems during the negotiations, and there seemed little chance of an upset; public opinion generally favored the League of Nations and cared little about the treaty details. Even Wilson's chief opponent, Senator Henry C. Lodge, hoped only to add amendments or reservations, not to defeat the treaty and the covenant. Even a few conciliatory gestures by the president would have won the two-thirds vote necessary for ratification, but Wilson's attitude was not conciliatory. He would permit no changes, and as opposition developed, his tone became more unyielding. As the debate continued it shifted from the merits of the case to the question of the respective authority of president and Senate and even to personal differences between the president and Senator Lodge, chairman of the Senate Committee on Foreign Relations. Setting forth on Sept. 3, 1919, on a countrywide speech-making tour on behalf of the treaty, the president fell gravely ill at Pueblo, Colo., Sept. 25, and was brought back hurriedly to Washington. He was thereafter incapable of transacting official business. Had Wilson died then, his successor might have made the compromises which the Senate considered necessary for ratification of the covenant; had Wilson recovered sufficiently, he might have made them himself. Isolated from the situation, he could do no more than maintain his earlier position. Despite the efforts of many in both the United States and Europe, the treaty and the covenant were rejected by only seven votes. The rest of his life was spent in invalidism and anticlimax.

Woodrow Wilson was by taste and inheritance designed for a quite life. He was always dependent upon the help and encouragement he received from his domestic circle. Mrs. Wilson died in 1914 and a year later he married Edith B. Galt, who survived him. He never capitalized fully on his personal and intellectual gifts in his public life. To those who worked closely with him he displayed a genial, humorous, and considerate personality, but he was incapable of unbending with men whom he did not like or did not

trust. He was handicapped in meeting the simplest problem of political tactics because he carried the attitude of a private citizen into public life; he refused to make many of the sacrifices of taste demanded by the rough game of politics. He was a man of strong prejudices, often ill founded, and he would not yield them; because of this, he alienated important leaders in the world of business and journalism. Although pictured in the public mind at the end of his career as a self-willed and arbitrary egoist, he was actually highly considerate of the feelings and interests of those around him and a man who was unsparing in self-criticism. Sharply sensitive to the sympathies and advice of those for whom he cared, he had little respect for the arguments of personal or political enemies. The public force of his speeches resulted in part from clarity of expression and fine phrasing; they were equally characterized by strong and effective moral fervor. Wilson strove consciously to measure everything by spiritual rather than material values and the great masses of the people recognized this fact. His political philosophy was simple; he was a liberal individualist, insistent upon the rights of unprivileged persons and small nations. Possessed of a noble vision, he was not able to transform that vision into fact, but he will remain in history as an eminent prophet of a better world.

WILTZ, LOUIS ALRED (*b. New Orleans, La., 1843; d. 1881*), businessman, Confederate soldier, Louisiana legislator. An active and able Democratic leader and New Orleans official, Wiltz presided over the legislature as Speaker in 1875 and was elected lieutenant governor, 1876. He served as president of the state constitutional convention, 1879, and was elected governor that same year. He died in office.

WIMAR, CARL (*b. Siegburg, near Bonn., Germany, 1828; d. St. Louis, Mo., 1862*), painter of Indians and the frontier. Immigrated to St. Louis, 1843. Apprenticed to a painter of decorations for carriages and steamboats. Studied in Düsseldorf, 1852–57, with, among others, Emanuel Leutze. On returning to America, Wimar made several trips to the trading posts on the upper Missouri and the Yellowstone to sketch Indians in their natural habitat and gave much attention to details of costume, weapons, and the western scene. Among his outstanding paintings are *Attack on an Emigrant Train* and *Buffalo Hunt by Indians*; his four historical panels in the St. Louis courthouse were his last work and have been spoiled by inexpert renovation.

WIMMER, BONIFACE (*b. Thalmassing, Bavaria, 1809 d. 1887*), Roman Catholic clergyman, Benedictine. Christened Sebastian Wimmer; ordained priest at Regensburg, 1831; took solemn vows at monastery of Metten, 1833. Influenced by Peter H. Lemke to act on a plan to found a Benedictine monastery in America for ministry to immigrant Germans, he erected St. Vincent's Abbey in Westmoreland Co., Pa., 1946. He was appointed first abbot, 1855, and raised to archabbot, 1883. His foundation marked the beginning of the Benedictine Order in the United States; from it, many other abbeys and priories were established throughout the nation.

WINANS, ROSS (*b. Sussex Co., N.J., 1796; d. 1877*), inventor, mechanic. Father of Thomas De Kay Winans. Devised, 1828, a model "rail wagon" which had friction wheels with outside bearings, thereby setting the distinctive pattern for railroad car wheels. While engineer of the Baltimore & Ohio, 1829–30, he assisted Peter Cooper with his *Tom Thumb* engine. Employed an improvement of railroad machinery for the Baltimore & Ohio, 1834–60, Winans planned the first eight-wheel car for passenger purposes and is credited with innovating the mounting of a car on two four-wheeled trucks. In 1842, he constructed the *Mud-Digger* locomotive with horizontal boiler, and in 1848, the first powerful "camelback" locomotive. He developed, 1859, with his son, the "cigar-steamer," whose hull shape has been adopted in modern ocean liners.

WINANS, THOMAS DE KAY (*b. Vernon, N.J., 1820; d. Newport, R.I., 1878*), engineer, inventor. Son of Ross Winans. Associated with Joseph Harrison in firm of Harrison, Winans and Eastwick, St. Petersburg, Russia, which supplied locomotives and other rolling stock for the railroad from St. Petersburg to Moscow and cast the iron for the first permanent bridge over the Neva River. Director, Baltimore & Ohio Railroad. Devised, 1859, with his father a cigar-shaped hull for high-speed steamers.

WINANS, WILLIAM (*b. Chestnut Ridge, Pa., 1788; d. Amite Co., Miss., 1857*), Methodist clergyman, outstanding figure in Mississippi Methodism *post* 1820. Championed status quo of Methodist policy and doctrine at General Conferences, 1824–44; actively opposed abolition. At the General Conference, 1844, he defended Bishop J. O. Andrew and was a member of the "Plan of Separation" committee. Elected to General Conferences, Methodist Episcopal Church, South, 1846, 1850, and 1854.

WINANT, JOHN GILBERT (*b. New York, N.Y., 1889; d. Concord, N.H., 1947*), teacher, reform politician, diplomat. Reared in a well-to-do-family, he attended private schools in New York City and St. Paul's School, Concord, N.H. Winant entered Princeton University, but did poorly in his studies. He accepted a standing offer from the rector of St. Paul's School to join its faculty; in 1911 he became an instructor in history there. During his years at St. Paul's he was active in local Republican politics, and in 1916 he was elected to the New Hampshire legislature. He quickly challenged the reactionary Republican politicians and industrial interests that dominated the state. He interrupted his political and academic career in 1917 and joined the American Air Service.

Appointed second vice-rector, he returned to St. Paul's and remained there until 1920, when he won election to the state senate. Two years later, despite a Democratic trend, he was again elected to the lower house. In 1924 he was elected governor, but failed of reelection in 1926. He returned to state politics in 1930 and won reelection as governor (and again in 1932). Winant's reputation as a friend of labor led to his appointment by President Franklin D. Roosevelt in 1934 to head an emergency board of inquiry into a nationwide textile strike.

Upon leaving office in January 1935, Winant, with the help of Roosevelt, was appointed assistant director of the International Labor Organization in Geneva. Within four months, however, Roosevelt brought him back to head the newly created Social Security Board. Spoken of for the Republican presidential nomination in 1936, he was never a serious candidate, and when the party's nominee, Alfred M. Landon, attacked social security, Winant resigned from the Social Security Board so that he could defend the act, thus destroying any future possibility of winning Republican support for a national office. Winant returned to his ILO post in 1937, and two years later became the director. As the European war intensified, he transferred a reduced ILO staff to Canada in mid-1940.

In late 1940 Roosevelt appointed Winant ambassador to the Court of St. James's. Winant was one of the planners of the 1943 Three-Power Foreign Ministers Conference in Moscow, which paved the way for the later summit conference at Teheran. In 1946 he was named by President Truman as the U.S. representative to the Economic and Social Council of the United Nations; he resigned his ambassadorship in March 1946.

WINCHELL, ALEXANDER (*b. Northeast, N.Y., 1824; d. 1891*), educator, geologist. Brother of Newton H. Winchell. Graduated Wesleyan University, 1847. Held chairs in geology, zoology, and botany at University of Michigan, 1855–73; in geology and paleontology *post* 1879. Director of Michigan state geological survey, 1859–61 and 1869–71. Took advanced stand on evolution and helped reconcile supposed conflict between science and religion. Author of, among other popular works, *Sketches of Creation* (1870), *The Doctrine of Evolution* (1874), *Sparks from a Geologist's Hammer* (1881), and *World Life* (1883).

WINCHELL, HORACE VAUGHN (*b. Galesburg, Mich., 1865; d. 1923*), geologist, mining engineer. Son of Newton H. Winchell; nephew of Alexander Winchell. Prepared reports and maps of Mesabi range *ante* 1892, predicting its importance. Associated with Anaconda Copper Mining Co. *post* 1898, he headed its geological department but also maintained a consultant practice. A leading authority on the "apex law;" did pioneer work in origin of ore deposits. Author of *The Iron Ores of Minnesota* (1891), a standard reference work.

WINCHELL, NEWTON HORACE (*b. Northeast, N.Y., 1839; d. Minneapolis, Minn., 1914*), geologist, archaeologist. Father of Horace V. Winchell; brother of Alexander Winchell. Graduated University of Michigan, 1866. Minnesota state geologist, 1872–1900; professor of geology, University of Minnesota, 1874–1900. Did valuable geological studies on recession of St. Anthony's Falls, Minneapolis. A founder and editor of the *American Geologist*, 1888–1905. Author of *The Aborigines of Minnesota* (1911).

WINCHESTER, CALEB THOMAS (*b. Montville, Conn., 1847; d. 1920*), teacher, editor of texts in English literature. A.B., Wesleyan University, 1869. Professor of rhetoric and English literature at Wesleyan *post* 1873. Author of, among other works, *Some Principles of Literary Criticism* (1899).

WINCHESTER, ELHANAN (*b. Brookline, Mass., 1751; d. Hartford, Conn., 1797*), Baptist and Universalist clergyman. Moved in his theology from open-communion Baptist tenets to strict Calvinism; accepted doctrine of universal restoration *ca.* 1787. Preached in London, England, 1787–94, where he made many friends, among them John Wesley and Joseph Priestley. Probably the ablest and the most intellectual of early American Universalists, he was author of a number of books, which included a refutation of Thomas Paine's *Age of Reason*.

WINCHESTER, JAMES (*b. Carroll Co., Md., 1752; d. Tennessee, 1826*), planter, soldier, Tennessee legislator. After service in the Revolution, he settled in the then Mero District of North Carolina, 1785; as brigadier general of the district, he won fame as an Indian fighter. On admission of Tennessee, 1796, he was elected state senator and Speaker of the Senate. Appointed U.S. brigadier general, 1812, he was surprised and badly defeated by the British on the River Raisin in southeast Michigan, Jan. 22, 1813. Exchanged after imprisonment in Canada, he commanded the Mobile District until 1815. He was a founder of the city of Memphis, Tenn.

WINCHESTER, OLIVER FISHER (*b. Boston, Mass., 1810; d. New Haven, Conn., 1880*), manufacturer. Invented and patented a new method of shirt manufacture, 1848, in which he was successful at New Haven, Conn. Organized New Haven Arms Co. (later Winchester Repeating Arms Co.), 1857, for manufacture of pistols and rifles under patents of Tyler Henry, D. B. Wesson, and others. Began production of Henry repeating rifle using new rimfire copper cartridge, 1860; it was widely used by state troops during the Civil War, but was not adopted by the federal government. The improvement of a method of loading the magazine through the gate in the frame was made in 1866. Patented features of the Spencer rifle were added later. Winchester also acquired and produced the bolt-action inventions of B. B. Hotchkiss and the single-shot mechanism invented by John M. Browning.

WINCHEVSKY, MORRIS (*b. Yanovo, Lithuania, 1856; d. 1932*), poet, essayist, miscellaneous writer. Changed name from Lippe Benzion Novachovitch. Resident in London, England, after expulsion as socialist propagandist from Prussia and Denmark, he founded in 1884 the first Yiddish socialist periodical *Der Polischer Yidel*. Immigrating to the United States, 1894, he became the most representative contributor to the Yiddish daily *Forward* after its establishment in 1897; he was associated also with many other socialist periodicals. His proletarian poems dwell with sympathy on the sordid aspects of the life of laborers.

WINDER, JOHN HENRY (*b. Rewston, Md., 1800; d. Florence, S.C., 1865*), Confederate soldier. Son of William H. Winder. Graduated West Point, 1820. An artilleryman, he won brevet of lieutenant colonel in Mexican War. Appointed Confederate brigadier general, 1861, he held the thankless post of commander of military prisons, at first in Richmond, where he was also provost marshal, and later in Alabama and Georgia. The extent of his responsibility for bad conditions in the Southern prison camps is still in dispute. He was defended by Jefferson Davis, Samuel Cooper, and James A. Seddon. Also, his task was made an impossible one by the refusal of the Northern authorities to continue exchanges and by a general lack of food, clothing, and medicines.

WINDER, LEVIN (*b. Somerset Co., Md., 1757; d. Baltimore, Md., 1819*), farmer, Revolutionary soldier, Maryland legislator. Federalist governor of Maryland, 1813–15. On failure of the federal government to provide adequate defense of Maryland against British attacks in the War of 1812, Winder rallied and equipped the state forces and frustrated the enemy's operations against North Point, Fort McHenry, and elsewhere.

WINDER, WILLIAM HENRY (*b. Somerset Co., Md., 1775; d. Baltimore, Md., 1824*), Baltimore lawyer, soldier. Father of John H. Winder. Served on northern frontier as colonel of infantry, 1812; promoted brigadier general, March 1813. Commanded at battle of Bladensburg, Md., August 1814, and was blamed for the disgraceful defeat there which laid the city of Washington open to spoil by the British. The degree of his responsibility for the defeat is still a matter of dispute.

WINDOM, WILLIAM (*b. Belmont Co., Ohio, 1827; d. New York, N.Y., 1891*), lawyer, politician. Settled in Minnesota, 1855. Congressman, Republican, from Minnesota, 1859–69; voted with the Radicals; was chairman of committee on Indian affairs. Appointed U.S. senator, 1870, he served also 1871–83, interrupted by a term as U.S. secretary of the treasury, March–November 1881. He was probably most notable as a chairman of a special committee on transportation routes to the seaboard. He was also chairman of the Committee on Appropriations, 1876–81, and chairman of the Committee on Foreign Relations *post* 1881. Urged a liberal railroad policy; supported homestead legislation; was a strong nationalist and high-tariff man. He served again with competence as U.S. secretary of the treasury, 1889–91.

WINEBRENNER, JOHN (*b. near Walkersville, Md., 1797; d. Harrisburg, Pa., 1860*), clergyman. Ordained, 1820, by General Synod of the German Reformed Church; dropped from the synod, 1828, because of extravagant revivalistic methods. Founded the General Eldership of the Churches of God in North America, 1830, a sect based on a medley of primitive Methodist and Baptist doctrines.

WINES, ENOCH COBB (*b. Hanover, N.J., 1806; d. Cambridge, Mass., 1879*), prison reformer, educator, Congregational clergyman. Father of Frederick H. Wines. Secretary, Prison Association of New York, *post* 1861. With Theodore W. Dwight, prepared monumental *Report on the Prisons and Reformatories of the United States and Canada* (1867); stimulated widespread movement toward prison reform and encouraged such experimenters as Zebulon R. Brockway at Detroit, Mich. With Franklin B. Sanborn, promoted adaptation of Irish-Crofton system in the United States. Called national prison reform convention at Cincinnati, Ohio, 1870. Secretary of National Prison Association, *ca.* 1870–77.

WINES, FREDERICK HOWARD (*b. Philadelphia, Pa., 1838; d. Springfield, Ill., 1912*), social reformer, Presbyterian clergyman. Son of Enoch C. Wines. Influential secretary, Illinois state board of public charities, 1869–92 and 1896–98. Secretary, National Prison Association, 1887–90. Author of *Punishment and Reformation* (1895), long a standard work. Brought from England the idea of the Kankakee State Hospital plan for care of insane; in early 1890's was among the first to urge use in America of "pathological research" and hydrotherapy. Appointed assistant director of the 12th Census, 1897, he was given major responsibility for *Report on Crime, Pauperism and Benevolence in the United States* (1895–96). Became statistician, Illinois Board of Control, 1909.

WING, JOSEPH ELWYN (*b. Hinsdale, N.Y., 1861; d. Marion, Ohio, 1915*), Ohio farmer, agricultural journalist. Became first strong propagandist for alfalfa culture in central and eastern states. Staff correspondent for the *Breeder's Gazette* from 1898, he lectured widely and was a national figure in agricultural journalism. Author of, among other books, the authoritative *Alfalfa Farming in America* (1909).

WINGATE, PAINE (*b. Amesbury, Mass., 1739; d. Stratham, N.H., 1838*), Congregational clergyman, New Hampshire legislator and jurist. Brother-in-law of Timothy Pickering. Graduated Harvard, 1759. Pastor at Hampton Falls, N.H., 1763–71; *post* 1776, a farmer at Stratham. Delegate to state constitutional convention, 1781; elected to last Congress under the Confederation, 1787. U.S. senator, Federalist, from New Hampshire, 1789–93; U.S. congressman, 1793–95. Opposed Hamilton's funding scheme. As judge of the New Hampshire Superior Court, 1798–1809, he served usefully, although ignorant of legal technicalities and procedure.

WINGFIELD, EDWARD MARIA (*fl. 1586–1613*), soldier. An original grantee of the Virginia charter, 1606, he came with the first settlers and served as president of the Virginia colony, April–September 1607. Removed from office, he was sent back to England in the spring of 1608. Author of "A Discourse of Virginia," a spirited defense of himself and an account of the colony from June 1607 to his departure, first published by Charles Deane in 1860 (*Transactions and Collections of the American Antiquarian Society*, Vol. 4).

WINKLER, EDWIN THEODORE (*b. Savannah, Ga., 1823; d. 1883*), Baptist clergyman, Confederate chaplain, author. Executive secretary, Southern Baptist Publishing Society, 1852–54; edited *Southern Baptist*. Principal pastorates included First Baptist Church, Charleston, S.C., 1854–61, and Citadel Square Baptist Church, Charleston, 1865–72. Editor of *Alabama Baptist*, from 1874. For ten years he was president of Home Missionary Board, Southern Baptist Convention. Deeply interested in the welfare of blacks.

WINLOCK, HERBERT EUSTIS (*b. Washington, D.C., 1884; d. Venice, Fla., 1950*), Egyptologist, museum director. Grandson of Joseph Winlock. B.A., Harvard, 1906. On staff of Metropolitan Museum of Art, New York City, *post* 1906, he served as assistant curator of Egyptian art, 1909–22; associate curator, 1922–29; and curator, 1929–39. Until 1932, he spent the greater part of his time excavating in Egypt; he became director of field work officially in 1928. The most important site at which he worked was the area of Deir al-Bahri on the western side of Thebes; one of his major contributions was the excavation of the royal tombs at Thebes of the periods preceding and following the Middle Kingdom. Concurrently with his Egyptian curatorship, he was director of the Metropolitan Museum, 1932–39.

WINLOCK, JOSEPH (*b. Shelby Co., Ky., 1826; d. Cambridge, Mass., 1875*), astronomer, mathematician. Graduated Shelby College, Kentucky, 1845. Superintendent at various times of the *American Ephemeris;* headed mathematics department, U.S. Naval Academy, 1859–61. Became director, Harvard College observatory and Phillips professor of astronomy, 1866 (later also professor of geodesy), serving in these positions until his death.

WINN, RICHARD (*b. Fauquier Co., Va., 1750; d. Duck River, Tenn., 1818*), Revolutionary soldier, planter, South Carolina legislator. As captain in command, made spectacular defense of Fort McIntosh, Ga., 1777. Served under Thomas Sumter and took distinguished part in skirmish at Fishdam Ford and in the battle of Blackstock. Promoted major general of militia, 1800. Lieutenant governor of South Carolina, 1800–02. Congressman, Democratic-Republican, from South Carolina, 1793–97 and 1803–13. Removed to Tennessee, 1813.

WINNEMUCCA, SARAH (*b. near Humboldt Lake, Nev., ca. 1844; d. Monida, Mont., 1891*), Indian teacher, lecturer. Daughter of a Paiute chief. Mediator between the Paiute and the whites, she served as "guide and interpreter" to General O. O. Howard during the Bannock War of 1878, performing many daring acts. Author of *Life Among the Paiute: Their Wrongs and Claims* (Mary T. P. Mann, ed., 1883).

WINSHIP, ALBERT EDWARD (*b. West Bridgewater, Mass., 1845; d. 1933*), editor, educator, Congregational clergyman. Editor, *Journal of Education*, Boston, Mass., 1886–1933; also edited the *American Teacher* (*post* 1896, the *American Primary Teacher*). Played important part in building National Education Association; was a pioneer in conducting community classes for adult education, 1876–83.

WINSHIP, BLANTON (*b. Macon, Ga., 1869; d. Washington, D.C., 1947*), army officer. B.A., Mercer University, 1889; LL.B., University of Georgia, 1893. Commissioned first lieutenant in Judge Advocate's Department, 1899, after volunteer service in Spanish-American War. Served in Philippines and in Cuba; had charge of civilian administration of Veracruz, Mexico, after 1914 occupation. Commanded 110th Infantry, 28th Division, in Aisne-Marne, St.-Mihiel, and Champagne-Marne actions of World War I. He directed Army Claims Settlement Commission, 1918–19; and was judge advocate of the Army of Occupation in Germany and on the Reparations Commission. He was promoted colonel in 1920. Named judge advocate general with rank of major general, 1931, he retired from active duty in 1933. As governor of Puerto Rico, 1934–39, he reacted to the growing discontent on the island with a strict insistence on public order, which led to controversial acts by the insular police and an attempt on his own life in 1938. Recalled to active duty in World War II, he served until 1944 as coordinator of the Inter-American Defense Board.

WINSHIP, GEORGE PARKER (*b. Bridgewater, Mass., 1871; d. 1952*), bibliographer, librarian. Studied at Harvard University (M.A., 1894). From 1895 to 1915, librarian of the private collection of pre-1800 Americana of John Carter Brown in Providence. Librarian of the Harry Elkins Widener Collection at Harvard, 1915–26. From 1926 to his retirement in 1936, he was assistant librarian of Harvard College in charge of the Treasure Room. An expert in Spanish Americana, he published *The Coronado Expedition* (1896) and *Cabot Bibliography* (1900).

WINSLOW, CAMERON MCRAE (*b. Washington, D.C., 1854; d. Boston, Mass., 1932*), naval officer. Graduated Annapolis, 1875. Commanded cruiser *Nashville*'s launches in cable-cutting operation of Cienfuegos, Cuba, 1898; performed extensive staff duty. Promoted rear admiral, 1911, he commanded successively the 2nd, 3rd, and 1st Atlantic Fleet divisions, 1911–13, and the Special Service Squadron off Mexico, 1914. Commanded the Pacific Fleet, September 1915–July 1916; inspector of Atlantic Coast naval districts, 1917–19. Excelled in navigation and ship handling.

WINSLOW, CHARLES-EDWARD AMORY (*b. Boston, Mass., 1877; d. New Haven, Conn., 1957*), bacteriologist and public health expert. Educated at Massachusetts Institute of Technology (M.S., 1899). Taught at MIT, 1899–1910; College of the City of New York, 1910–14; Yale University, from 1915 until retirement. Curator of public health at the American Museum of Natural History in New York (1910–22). Director of publicity and health education for the New York State Department of Public Health in 1915. First editor of *Journal of Bacteriology* (1916), and of *American Journal of Public Health*, 1944–54. President of the American Public Health Association, 1926. In the 1950's he was consultant to the World Health Organization. Winslow wrote numerous books, articles, and gave countless lectures. A pioneer in public health and preventive medicine, he championed national health insurance, advocated health measures through better housing. Studied the effects of ventilation and bacteriology on health.

WINSLOW, EDWARD (*b. Droitwich, England, 1595; d. at sea, en route from Jamaica, British West Indies, to England, 1655*), Pilgrim father, author. Joined the Separatist congregation at Leiden *ca.* 1617. Sailed on *Speedwell,* 1620, transshipping to *Mayflower;* landed at site of Plymouth, Mass., Dec. 11/21, 1620. Chosen envoy to greet Massasoit, 1621, he made the colonists' first treaty with the Indians. Next to Myles Standish, Winslow was the Pilgrim's most important man in dealing with the Indians throughout his career in America. He became the most active explorer and trader of the colony, setting up valuable posts in Maine, on Cape Ann, at Buzzard's Bay, and on the Connecticut River. In 1629, he was made the colony's agent. He was assistant nearly every year from 1624 to 1646, and governor in 1633, 1636, and 1644. He aided the organization of the New England Confederation and was Plymouth's representative. Active in reorganizing the colonial and local governments, 1636, and in drafting the new code of laws, he was also called on to travel to England on several occasions to defend both Plymouth and the Bay Colony against their enemies at home. Going to England in 1646 to refute the charges of Samuel Gorton, he never returned to Plymouth, but was employed by Cromwell's government on several important missions. Winslow was author of four narratives of explorations in A *Relation or Iournall of the beginning and proceedings of the English Plantation setled at Plimoth in New England* (printed by George Morton, London, 1622) and *Good News . . . at the Plantation of Plymouth . . . Written by E.W.* (1624), the first accounts of the colony and the only contemporary record to be published which had been written in America. He was author also of *Hypocrisie Unmasked by the True Relation of the Proceedings of the Governor and Company of the Massachusetts Against Samuel Gorton* (1646) and *The Glorious Progress of the Gospel Among the Indians in New England* (1649), which led to the founding that year of the Society for the Propagation of the Gospel in New England.

WINSLOW, EDWARD (*b. Boston, Mass., 1669; d. Boston, 1753*), silversmith, Boston public official. Grandnephew of Edward Winslow (1595–1655); cousin of Samuel Vernon.

WINSLOW, EDWARD FRANCIS (*b. Augusta, Maine, 1837; d. Canandaigua, N.Y., 1914*), Union soldier, railroad builder. Removed to Iowa, *ca.* 1856. Served in 4th Iowa Cavalry. Promoted colonel, July 1863, at Vicksburg, he was chief of cavalry of the XV Corps; his force took Jackson, Miss. Thereafter, he succeeded to command of a cavalry brigade and distinguished himself at Brice's Cross Roads, June 1864. He took part in the expedition against Selma, Montgomery, Columbus, and Macon in the spring of 1865, capturing Columbus by assault. After the Civil War he returned to railroad building, constructing part of the St. Louis, Vandalia & Terre Haute and the St. Louis & South-Eastern. Subsequently he held high executive posts in several midwestern railroads and was president of the New York, Ontario & Western; he was also general manager for a time of the Manhattan Elevated Railway in New York City.

WINSLOW, HUBBARD (*b. Williston, Vt., 1799; d. Williston, 1864*), Congregational clergyman. Brother of Miron Winslow; father of William C. Winslow. Principal pastorate at Bowdoin St. Church, Boston, Mass., 1832–44; conducted Mount Vernon School for Young Ladies, Boston, 1844–53. A frequent contributor to periodicals.

WINSLOW, JOHN (*b. Marshfield, Mass., 1703; d. Hingham, Mass., 1774*), colonial soldier, Massachusetts legislator. Grandson of Josiah Winslow. Began career as captain of a Massachusetts company in the West Indian expedition under Edward Vernon, 1740; subsequently, as a British soldier he served at Cartagena and in Nova Scotia until 1751. Sent to build Fort Western (present Augusta) and Fort Halifax (later Winslow). In 1755, he commanded the New England battalions in the force under Robert Monckton which took forts Beauséjour and Gaspereau. The task of expelling the French inhabitants from Nova Scotia fell largely on Winslow. Assigned to command the provincial army raised in New England and New York, 1756, for the reduction of Crown Point, he cooperated with the British troops, but was held inactive by orders of Lord Loudoun. He never received adequate compensation for his services and continued to the end of his life to put in fruitless claims for pay or preferment to the colonies and to Great Britain.

WINSLOW, JOHN ANCRUM (*b. Wilmington, N.C., 1811; d. Boston Highlands, Mass., 1873*), naval officer. Became midshipman before his sixteenth year. Acquired reputation for gallantry in Mexican War. An abolitionist, he viewed the Civil War as a holy cause and was openly critical of its conduct on the Mississippi, 1862. Promoted captain, July 1862, he was given the USS *Kearsage* and served on patrol from the Azores to the English Channel, 1863–64. Encountering the Confederate cruiser *Alabama* off Cherbourg on June 19, 1864, Winslow won a complete victory and was promoted commodore. Promoted rear admiral, 1870, he commanded the Pacific fleet, 1870–72.

WINSLOW, JOHN BRADLEY (*b. Nunda, N.Y., 1851; d. 1920*), jurist. LL.B., University of Wisconsin, 1875; practiced in Racine, Wis. State circuit court judge, 1883–91; state supreme court justice *post* 1891, becoming chief justice in 1907 by virtue of seniority. An excellent administrator and a profound student of jurisprudence, he won a national reputation for his opinions. His abilities are well represented in *Nunnemacher v. State* and in the *Income Tax Cases*. In his greatest opinion, *Borgnis v. Falk Co.*, he laid the foundation for much of the so-called progressive legislation in Wisconsin and the nation while dealing with the constitutionality of the workmen's compensation law.

WINSLOW, JOHN FLACK (*b. Bennington, Vt., 1810; d. Poughkeepsie, N.Y., 1892*), industrialist. Associated with Erastus Corning in the firm of Corning & Winslow, 1837–67. In time the largest producers of railroad and other iron in the United States, the firm delegated Alexander L. Holley to purchase the American rights to the Bessemer steel process, 1863, and began operation of the first Bessemer plant in America at Troy, N.Y., 1865. Winslow manufactured the machinery and iron-plating for the original *Monitor* and also financed the undertaking.

WINSLOW, JOSIAH (*b. Plymouth, Mass., ca. 1629; d. 1680*), colonial soldier and legislator. Son of Edward Winslow (1595–1655). Studied at Harvard, but left without taking a degree. Served as a militia officer; as an assistant, 1657–73; as Plymouth commissioner for the United Colonies, 1658–72. Succeeded Myles Standish as commander in chief of the colony, 1659, after a three-year vacancy of that post. Captured Alexander, the son and successor of Massasoit, 1662, thus ending danger of Indian uprising. Becoming governor of New Plymouth, 1673, he established the first public school there in 1674. Elected commander in chief of the forces of the United Colonies when Indian uprisings began in 1675, he thus became the first native-born commander of an American army and won a decisive battle against the Narragansett, December 1675. He was succeeded by Benjamin Church, the actual effective commander of the force, in February 1676. Liberal and tolerant, Winslow showed his statecraft in his handling of Edward Randolph in 1677, when he converted Randolph from a suspicious investigator into a friend of the Pilgrims. At the time of his death, Winslow was negotiating with the authorities in London to secure a crown charter for Plymouth.

WINSLOW, MIRON (*b. Williston, Vt., 1789; d. Capetown, South Africa, 1864*), Congregational clergyman, educator, translator. Brother of Hubbard Winslow. Missionary at Oodooville, Ceylon, 1819–33, working among the Tamils. Residing in Madras *post* 1836, he was responsible for the final edition of the *Comprehensive Tamil and English Dictionary of High and Low Tamil* (1862) and helped revise the Tamil Bible.

WINSLOW, SIDNEY WILMOT (*b. Brewster, Mass., 1854; d. Beverly, Mass., 1917*), manufacturer, capitalist. Joining Gordon McKay and the Goodyear Co., he formed the United Shoe Machinery Co., 1899, becoming president. Instituted monopolistic lease system for his product, with "tying clause" in contracts. Prominent in New England financial affairs, he was a principal owner of the *Boston Herald* and *Boston Traveller*.

WINSLOW, WILLIAM COPLEY (*b. Boston, Mass., 1840; d. Boston, 1925*), Episcopal clergyman, archaeologist. Son of Hubbard Winslow. Founded and supported the American branch of the Egypt Exploration Fund; procured notable Egyptian collection for Boston Museum.

WINSOR, JUSTIN (*b. Boston, Mass., 1831; d. 1897*), historian, cartographer, librarian. Granted Harvard College degree as of class of 1853; studied in Paris and Heidelberg, 1852–54. A linguist and man of letters, Winsor contributed criticism, poetry, and fiction to periodicals, 1854–68. Librarian, Boston Public Library, 1868–77; he served thereafter as librarian at Harvard College. Winsor was a founder of the *Library Journal* and of the American Library Association (first president, 1876–85, and 1897). He was editor of *The Memorial History of Boston* (1880–81), characterized as the best work of its kind produced up to that time, and of the *Narrative and Critical History of America* (1884–89), to which he contributed outstanding bibliographies. He was author of, among other writings, *The Reader's Handbook of the American Revolution* (1880), an important bibliographical manual;

Christopher Columbus (1891); *Cartier to Frontenac* (1894); *The Mississippi Basin* (1895); and *The Westward Movement* (1897).

WINSTON, JOHN ANTHONY (*b. Madison Co., Ala., 1912; d. 1871*), planter, Alabama legislator, Confederate soldier. A leader of Southern-rights Democrats in Alabama, he served as governor, 1853–57. By vetoing state aid to railroads, he saved Alabama from a burden of debt. At the Democratic convention at Charleston, S.C., 1860, he prevented any compromise with Northern Democrats and insisted on withdrawal of the Alabama delegation in accordance with its instructions; during the ensuing presidential campaign, he supported Stephen A. Douglas. Elected U.S. senator for the term 1867–73, he refused to take the oath of allegiance and was denied the post.

WINSTON, JOSEPH (*b. Louisa Co., Va., 1746; d. 1815*), Revolutionary soldier, North Carolina legislator and public official. Cousin of Patrick Henry. Commanded part of right wing of patriot army at battle of King's Mountain, 1780. Congressman, Democratic-Republican, from North Carolina, 1793–95 and 1803–07. Winston (now Winston-Salem), N.C., was named for him.

WINTER, WILLIAM (*b. Gloucester, Mass., 1836; d. 1917*), dramatic critic, historian of the stage, essayist, poet. After beginning his career as a reviewer on the *Boston Transcript*, Winter removed to New York City shortly before the Civil War and served for a time as assistant editor to Henry Clapp, Jr., on the *Saturday Press*. At this time he associated with the bohemian group which met in the cellar of Pfaff's café on Broadway near Bleecker St.; his account of this group in *Old Friends* (1909) is perhaps as accurate as any that exists. While dramatic critic of the *New York Tribune*, 1865–1909, he at first enjoyed a national reputation, but had the misfortune to live into a time in the theater for which he had neither appreciation nor liking. Author of a number of volumes of essays, verse, and critical studies, he is remembered particularly for a series of accurate biographical studies of actors, which include *The Jeffersons* (1881); *Henry Irving* (1885); and *Ada Rehan* (1891). He was an excellent judge of the technicalities of the actor's art. His *Shakespeare on the Stage* (1911–15) is a record of the "traditional" interpretations employed by actors in Shakespearean roles, a number of whom Winter had observed.

WINTHROP, FITZ-JOHN. *See* WINTHROP, JOHN (1638–1707).

WINTHROP, JAMES (*b. probably Cambridge, Mass., 1752; d. Cambridge, 1821*), scholar, librarian, Massachusetts jurist. Son of John Winthrop (1714–79). Graduated Harvard, 1769. Librarian at Harvard, 1770–87, he was concurrently for a part of this time register of probate for Middlesex Co.; in 1779 he was considered as a successor to his father in the Harvard chair of mathematics and natural philosophy, but was passed over. The next year, he encouraged the students at Harvard in the revolution which deposed President Samuel Langdon. He was a founder of the Massachusetts Historical Society, a miscellaneous writer on a number of subjects, and a judge of common pleas for Middlesex Co. *post* 1791.

WINTHROP, JOHN (*b. Edwardstone near Groton, Suffolk, England, 1587/8 o.s.; d. Boston, Mass., 1649*), lawyer, colonial statesman, first governor of Massachusetts Bay. Father of John Winthrop (1605/6 o.s.–1676). The son of a Suffolk landowner who held the manor of Groton, John Winthrop attended Trinity College, Cambridge, and later studied at Gray's Inn. Early in life he adopted Puritan habits of living. At first successful in the practice of law (he was admitted to the Inner Temple, 1628), he encountered financial difficulties in and after 1629. A Puritan of the type of John Milton, he was much concerned for the future of religion and morals in England. He became interested in the

Company of the Massachusetts Bay, which had been chartered in March 1629, and made up his mind, despite family opposition, to immigrate with his immediate family to New England. Entering into the executive work of the new corporation, which was distinguished from earlier colonial ventures by the intention of its settlers to remain permanently in America, he was chosen governor of the proposed colony on Oct. 20, 1629. The decision had already been reached by the Company to transfer itself with its General Court and its charter to America.

Winthrop sailed from Southampton in the *Arbella* on Mar. 22, 1630; he reached John Endecott's settlement at Salem on June 12. From 600 to 700 persons had taken passage in the *Arbella* and other vessels of the little fleet which accompanied it; 200 or 300 more arrived almost simultaneously, and another 1,000 soon afterward. These numbers and the fact that, owing to the transfer of the charter and the Company organization to America, the entire management was local, gave Winthrop a position very different from that held by governors of any of the other early plantations. Soon settling in Boston, which appeared to offer a better site for the center of government of the colony than Charlestown, which had earlier been considered, he threw himself into the work of forming the new community.

The term of governor was one year, and he was elected in 1631, 1632, and 1633. In April 1634, however, at the spring meeting of the General Court, the freemen (that is, the members of the Company) of the town requested to be shown the colony charter. Finding that under the charter the General Court was the only body entitled to legislate, they wanted to know why some of its powers had been usurped by the leaders or magistrates. They then refused Winthrop's suggestion that the General Court should permanently abrogate some of its powers in order that authority might be concentrated in the hands of the leaders. John Cotton, the principal clergyman in the colony, in a sermon before the General Court, May 14, 1634, declared that a magistrate ought to be reelected continually unless there was sufficient reason that he should not and that officials had a vested interest in their offices. The freemen replied by turning Winthrop out of the governorship and electing Thomas Dudley. Late in 1635, Hugh Peter and Henry Vane began an investigation into the causes of dissent in Massachusetts. Early the next year Winthrop, who had continued to serve as a magistrate, was called before a meeting of investigators, including John Cotton, and was accused of having been too lenient in discipline and judicial decisions. The united clergy of the colony agreeing with this charge, Winthrop promised to adopt a stricter course in future, and so another step was taken toward clerical domination. Also in 1636 the General Court adopted a plan whereby certain magistrates should be chosen for life or good behavior. Winthrop and Dudley allowed themselves to be chosen the first two members of this unconstitutional life council, which was always unpopular and lasted only a few years.

Winthrop, as deputy governor, took a part in the antinomian controversy over the teachings of Anne Hutchinson, which began to rock the colony at about this time. Passion was running so high at the 1637 election that the General Court held its meeting at Newton instead of Boston and elected Winthrop governor in place of Henry Vane. Grown much more narrow and severe since his rebuke by the clergy for leniency, Winthrop executed the law with rigor against the followers of Hutchinson and drove many from the colony. He wrote an account of the controversy, which was incorporated by Thomas Welde in *A Short Story of the Rise, Reign, and Ruine of the Antinomians* (1644). Elected governor again in 1638, Winthrop protected the colony charter from attacks upon it at home in an able letter to the Lords Commissioners for Plantations. Reelected in 1639, he learned at this time of serious financial losses in England which had resulted from the dishonesty of his agent there; for the rest of his life he was in financial straits.

A member of the Court of Assistants, 1640–41, he was again elected governor in 1642. During this term he engaged in the famous controversy over the veto power of magistrates, which led to the separate sitting of the magistrates and the deputies as two houses. Still governor in 1643, Winthrop headed the Massachusetts commissioners for framing the articles for the United Colonies and was first president of the confederation after it was formed. At this time he came under heavy criticism for giving military aid to French officials in Acadia without consulting the General Court. Deputy governor in 1644, he wrote a discourse called "Arbitrary Government Described and the Government of the Massachusetts Vindicated from That Aspersion." It was an attempt to justify the older principles under which the colony had operated and served only to show that Winthrop was losing touch with his people. Regaining his popularity in 1645, however, he was elected governor thereafter annually until his death, although the contentions over Robert Childe and Samuel Gorton, and Winthrop's severity in dealing with them, aroused active opposition to his rule.

A refined and sensitive man, affectionate in his nature, Winthrop lacked aggressiveness. As a writer he had an excellent English prose style, and his journal (published in part as A *Journal of the Transactions and Occurrences in the Settlement of Massachusetts . . . 1630 to 1644*, 1790; supplemented with further manuscript materials, 1825–26) is a sourcebook of the greatest importance. Winthrop had no faith in democracy, believing that, once chosen, representatives should govern according to their own best judgment. His own integrity was always beyond question.

WINTHROP, JOHN (*b. Groton, Suffolk, England, 1605/6 o.s.; d. Boston, Mass., 1676*), lawyer, soldier, colonial statesman. Son of John Winthrop (1587/8 o.s.–1649). Immigrated to Boston, Mass., 1631. Elected an assistant, 1632, he was one of the founders of Ipswich, 1633. Returning to England late in 1634, he accepted the governorship of the plantation in Connecticut which his father's friends Lord Say and Sele and Lord Brooke were undertaking. Arriving at Boston in October 1635, he sent an advance party to build a fort at Saybrook, the defense of which was entrusted to Lion Gardiner. Winthrop resided in Connecticut from March until autumn of 1636. After settling again at Ipswich, he appears to have moved to Salem in 1639. His father's financial difficulties having put a burden upon him, he began the manufacture of salt and tried to interest English capital in the erection of ironworks. The General Court granted him 3,000 acres of land for the encouragement of iron-making, 1644, and he set up a furnace at Lynn and another at Braintree; in the same year, he was given leave to found a settlement for a similar purpose in Connecticut in the Pequot country (later New London). Retaining his public offices in Massachusetts, he made frequent journeys between the two colonies. Deciding after his father's death in 1649 to remain permanently in Connecticut, he was admitted a freeman of that colony, 1650, and elected an assistant, 1651. While developing ironworks in the New Haven Colony, he was elected chief executive of Connecticut, 1657, and removed to Hartford. Elected lieutenant governor, 1658, he was annually elected governor from 1659 until his death. The most important of his many services to the colony was his mission to England to obtain a charter, 1661–63. Gaining the favor of Charles II, he returned to New England with the most liberal charter that had yet been granted to any colony, making Connecticut almost independent and including within it the former colony of New Haven. One of the most engaging New Englanders of his day and probably the most versatile, he cultivated scientific interests, was skilled in medicine and chemistry, and was elected a member of the Royal Society, 1663—the first member resident in America. He was ahead of his

time in his belief that New England's future lay in manufacturing and commerce rather than in agriculture.

WINTRHOP, JOHN (*b. Ipswich, Mass., 1638; d. Boston, Mass., 1707*), colonial soldier and official. Son of John Winthrop (1605/6 o.s.–1676); commonly known as Fitz-John Winthrop. Commissioned in the English parliamentary army, he served in the Scottish campaigns and entered London with General Monk, 1660. Returning from England to Connecticut, 1663, he made his home in New London. He commanded the Connecticut troops which defended Southold, N.Y., 1673, against the Dutch, and served with distinction in the Indian wars of 1675–76. Thereafter spending a large part of his time in Boston, he was appointed to the Governor's Council of Massachusetts by Joseph Dudley in 1686 and served on the council of Sir Edmund Andros. Returning to Connecticut after Andros' defeat, he helped reestablish the government and was elected assistant in Connecticut, 1689. As major general commanding a New York and Connecticut force under orders to invade Canada, 1690, he abandoned the attempt at a point north of Albany on finding himself without the provisions and munitions promised him by Jacob Leisler. Successful in a mission to King William III to request confirmation of the Connecticut charter, 1693, Winthrop was elected governor of Connecticut five years later and reelected annually until his death.

WINTHROP, JOHN (*b. Boston, Mass., 1714; d. Cambridge, Mass., 1779*), astronomer, physicist, mathematician. Father of James Winthrop; descendant of John Winthrop (1587/8 o.s.–1649) and John Winthrop (1605/6 o.s.–1676). America's first astronomer and Newtonian disciple, he graduated from Harvard, 1732; LL.D., University of Edinburgh, 1771, and Harvard, 1773. Elected Hollis professor of mathematics and natural philosophy at Harvard, 1738. The results of his forty years' research, mainly in astronomy, were all published in *Philosophical Transactions of the Royal Society*. His other publications include *Relation of a Voyage from Boston to Newfoundland, for the Observation of the Transit of Venus* (1761) and *Two Lectures on the Parallax and Distance of the Sun* (1769). He made a series of sunspot observations, April 19–22, 1739, which were the first in the colony; he also studied transits of Mercury over the sun, April 21, 1740, Oct. 25, 1743, and Nov. 9, 1769. He established at Harvard, 1746, the first laboratory of experimental physics in America and demonstrated with a series of lectures the laws of mechanics, light, heat, and the movements of celestial bodies according to Newtonian doctrines; these lectures were attended by Count Rumford. Winthrop introduced to Harvard's mathematical curriculum the elements of fluxions (differential and integral calculus), 1751. In 1759, he predicted the return of Halley's comet of 1682; he later organized expeditions to Newfoundland for study of transits of Venus. He carried on magnetic and meteorological observations and was the main support of Benjamin Franklin in his theories relative to his electrical experiments. An ardent patriot, he was counselor and friend of Washington, Franklin, and other founders of the Republic.

WINTHROP, ROBERT CHARLES (*b. Boston, Mass., 1809; d. 1894*), lawyer, Massachusetts legislator, orator. Graduated Harvard, 1828; studied law in office of Daniel Webster. Congressman, Whig, from Massachusetts, 1840–42, 1842–50; Speaker of the House, 1847–49. Appointed to the U.S. Senate on the resignation of Daniel Webster, 1850, he was defeated for reelection by Charles Sumner, 1851, because of alleged reluctance to oppose slavery. He was often called upon for orations and addresses on notable occasions, served for 30 years as president of the Massachusetts Historical Society, and was later in life chairman of the board of the Peabody Education Fund.

WINTHROP, THEODORE (*b. New Haven, Conn., 1828; d. Big Bethel, Va., 1861*), lawyer, author, Union soldier. Nephew of Theodore D. Woolsey. Graduated Yale, 1848. Engaged in a number of occupations. Traveled in Europe, across the plains, in the Far West, and in Central America. Enlisting in the 7th New York Regiment, 1861, he remained at the front subsequent to his regiment's return after a short term of service and was killed leading the advance in a skirmish on June 10. Winthrop is remembered for a number of books of marked originality, all published posthumously, which enjoyed a great popularity in their time. They include the novels *Cecil Dreeme* (1861) and *John Brent* (1862); also, *The Canoe and the Saddle* (1863) and *Life in the Open Air* (1863).

WINTON, ALEXANDER (*b. Grangemouth, Scotland, 1860; d. 1932*), pioneer automobile manufacturer. Immigrated to New York City *ca.* 1880. After working as a marine engine builder and as assistant engineer on an ocean steamship, he settled in Cleveland, Ohio, 1884, where he began a bicycle-repair business. Inventor of a number of improvements in bicycle mechanisms, he began the manufacture of bicycles, 1890, as the Winton Bicycle Co. As early as 1893 he began experimenting in gasoline engine design for automotive use; he built a gasoline motor bicycle, 1895, and completed his first gasoline motorcar, September, 1896. Forming the Winton Motor Carriage Co., March 1897, he made a nine-day trip in one of his cars from Cleveland to New York in July of that year—the first reliability run in the history of the American automobile. On Mar. 24, 1898, he sold one of his cars for $1,000, the first sale in America of a gasoline automobile made according to set manufacturing schedules. By the end of 1898 he was successfully producing more cars, all constructed under his patent, granted him September 1898. Energetic and progressive, Winton designed, built, and raced cars both in the United States and abroad; his "Bullet No. 1" established a record of a mile in 52.2 seconds at Daytona Beach, Fla., 1902. *Post* 1904 all his cars were equipped with four-cylinder engines; *post* 1907 all had six-cylinder engines. He was the first in America to experiment with straight-eight-cylinder engines, 1906; as early as 1902 he had designed external and internal brakes on the same brake-drum. Although he gave his major interest *post* 1912 to design and manufacture of diesel engines and other activities, he continued to act as president of his automobile company, maintaining the Winton car in the front rank of American automobiles until February 1924.

WIRT, WILLIAM (*b. Bladensburg, Md., 1772; d. Washington, D.C., 1834*), lawyer, author. Admitted to the Virginia bar *ca.* 1792, he began practice in Culpeper Co., Va. After a modest success, he removed to Richmond, Va., *ca.* 1800; his name first came prominently before the public when he served as counsel for James T. Callender in a famous trial under the Alien and Sedition Acts. After brief service as a chancellor, 1802–03, he removed his residence to Norfolk. His literary career began with the serial publication of *The Letters of the British Spy* in the Richmond *Argus*; published anonymously, they purported to be contemporary observations of an English traveler and were, in fact, shrewd social commentary in essay form. First published as a book, 1803, the letters went through numerous editions. Removing to Richmond, 1806, Wirt appeared for the prosecution in the trial of Aaron Burr and gained much professional prestige. After publication of another series of essays, which did not acquire the popularity of the *British Spy*, Wirt published *Sketches of the Life and Character of Patrick Henry* (1817), his most serious literary effort. Although his material was acquired largely from men who had

known Henry, he presented it in a most ornate and strained manner. Also in 1817 he was appointed U.S. attorney general and held that post for 12 consecutive years. He was the first holder of that office to organize its work and to make a systematic practice of preserving his official opinions so that they might serve as precedents. He returned to private life in 1829 on the accession of President Andrew Jackson, but was later an unwilling candidate of the Anti-Masons for the presidency, 1832.

WIRT, WILLIAM ALBERT (*b. Markle, Ind., 1874; d. Gary, Ind., 1938*), school administrator. Graduated DePauw University, 1898; Ph.D., 1916. A leading exponent of progressive education, he first attracted public attention while superintendent of schools at Bluffton, Ind., 1899–1907. As school superintendent of Gary, Ind., *post* 1907, he devised the "platoon" or "work-study-play" system of organization of activities, which attracted nationwide attention before World War I and was widely copied. Although his specific program did not maintain its popularity, his emphasis on including vocational and recreational subjects in the curriculum has had a lasting effect on American education.

WISE, AARON (*b. Erlau, Hungary, 1844; d. New York, N.Y., 1896*), rabbi. Immigrated to America, 1874. Rabbi of Temple Rodeph Sholom, New York, an influential, conservatively reformed congregation, *post* 1875. A founder of the Jewish Theological Seminary of New York, 1886. Edited new prayer book, *The Temple Service* (1891); editor, New York *Jewish Herald* and Boston *Hebrew Observer*.

WISE, DANIEL (*b. Portsmouth, England, 1813; d. Englewood, N.J., 1898*), Methodist clergyman, editor. Immigrated to America, 1833. Held various Massachusetts and Rhode Island pastorates. Editor, *Sunday School Messenger*, 1838–44; *Zion's Herald*, 1852–56. Corresponding secretary and editor of publications of the Sunday School Union, 1856–72; also editor of the Tract Society *post* 1860. Author of religious works, biographies, and moralistic tales for young people.

WISE, HENRY ALEXANDER (*b. Drummondtown, Va., 1806; d. Richmond, Va., 1876*), lawyer, Confederate general. Congressman, Jacksonian Democrat, from Virginia, 1833–44; chief antagonist of John Quincy Adams in effort to repeal "gag rule" against antislavery petitions. Breaking with President Jackson on the Bank of the United States, Wise went over to the Whigs. A close friend of President John Tyler, he led the Tyler adherents in Congress. U.S. minister to Brazil, 1844–47. An outspoken defender of slavery, he was liberal and progressive in other matters; in the Virginia constitutional convention, 1850–51, he played an important part in securing compromise suffrage and taxation reforms. Influential in transferring the Virginia delegation's support to Franklin Pierce at the Democratic convention of 1852, he helped secure the presidential nomination for Pierce. As Democratic candidate for governor, he conducted an exciting campaign against a Know-Nothing opponent; his victory broke the force of the Know-Nothing wave in the South. As governor, 1856–61, he was active in quelling John Brown's raid and advocated internal improvements. He was largely responsible for James Buchanan's nomination at the Democratic convention, 1856. Delegate to the Virginia convention, 1861, he became a fiery advocate of the Confederacy. Made brigadier general, 1861, he served throughout the Civil War and was promoted major general by General Robert E. Lee, 1865. Wise was one of the last great individualists in Virginia history.

WISE, HENRY AUGUSTUS (*b. Brooklyn, N.Y., 1819; d. Naples, Italy, 1869*), naval officer. Appointed midshipman, 1834. Served with credit in the Mexican War. Appointed assistant in the U.S. Navy Bureau of Ordnance, July 1862, he headed the bureau with great energy and ability, 1863–68. He was author (under pseudonym "Harry Gringo") of a number of books, which included *Los Gringos* (1849) and *Tales for the Marines* (1855).

WISE, ISAAC MAYER (*b. Steingrub, Bohemia, 1819; d. Cincinnati, Ohio, 1900*), rabbi. Studied in Prague and Vienna; named rabbi, 1842. Immigrated to America, 1846. Rabbi of the Jewish congregation, Albany, N.Y., 1846–54; of Bene Yeshurun congregation, Cincinnati, Ohio, *post* 1854. Espoused cause of liberal Judaism; published weekly newspaper, the *Israelite* (later the *American Israelite*). His three great projects were organization of the Union of American Hebrew Congregations, 1873; founding of Hebrew Union College, 1875, which he served as president until his death; organization of the Central Conference of American Rabbis at Detroit, Mich., 1889, of which he was president until his death. In his day the foremost figure in American Jewish religious life, he preached the universalistic interpretation of Judaism and a welding of the spirit of Judaism with the free spirit of America. A prolific writer, he was author of, among other works, *The Cosmic God* (1876), *History of the Hebrews' Second Commonwealth* (1880), and *Reminiscences* (1901).

WISE, JOHN (*b. Roxbury, Mass., 1652; d. 1725*), Congregational clergyman. Graduated Harvard, 1673. Minister of the church at Chebacco in Ipswich, Mass., *post* 1680, he was active and influential in civil and ecclesiastical affairs throughout his life. Having led his fellow townsmen in resistance to a provincial tax levied by Sir Edmund Andros, he was tried and fined in October 1687, but was soon restored to his ministerial post. He served as chaplain of the expedition against Quebec, 1690. In the belief that a movement initiated by the Mathers and others to establish associations of clergy was the beginning of a reactionary revolution, Wise attacked the movement in *The Churches Quarrel Espoused* (1710). In 1717 he published *A Vindication of the Government of New-England Churches*, in which he considered the fundamental ideas of civil as well as religious government from what has been described as a fully democratic point of view. Wise was an extremely forceful and brilliant writer, standing almost alone among the writers of his time for the blending of a racy humor with impassioned earnestness. The two pamphlets were reprinted in 1772 as a body of democratic doctrine suitable for use in the controversy then raging with England.

WISE, JOHN (*b. Lancaster, Pa., 1808; d. by drowning in Lake Michigan, 1879*), balloonist. A scientific aerostatic pioneer, Wise made important contributions to safety of balloons, including the invention of the rip panel. He set a long-distance record of 804 miles in balloon travel, 1859. Author of *A System of Aeronautics* (1850) and *Through the Air* (1873).

WISE, JOHN SERGEANT (*b. Rio de Janeiro, Brazil, 1846; d. near Princess Anne, Md., 1913*), lawyer, politician, Confederate soldier, author. Son of Henry Alexander Wise. Graduated in law, University of Virginia, 1867. Practiced in Richmond; won notoriety for opportunism in politics and as a leader in the William Mahone machine. Congressman-at-large, Republican-Coalition, from Virginia, 1883–85. Removed to New York City, 1888; became leading counsel in important litigation between street railways and other companies; an international authority on law in field of electricity. Author of, among other works, *Diomed* (1897); *The End of the Era* (1899); and *The Lion's Skin* (1905).

WISE, STEPHEN SAMUEL (*b. Budapest, Hungary, 1874; d. New York, N.Y., 1949*), rabbi, Zionist leader, reformer. Son of Aaron Wise. Brought to New York City as a baby. Deciding early in life to enter the rabbinate, he began Jewish studies with his father, continuing them with Alexander Kohut and Gustav Gottheil. Concurrently, he attended the College of the City of New York and in 1892 graduated from Columbia University, to which he had transferred in 1891. He then pursued rabbinic studies with Adolph Jellinek, chief rabbi of Vienna, and received ordination in 1893. On his return to New York City, 1893, he was appointed assistant rabbi at Congregation B'nai Jeshurun and soon assumed full responsibility, at the age of 19. He resumed his graduate studies at Columbia University, Ph.D., 1901.

Wise involved himself in social causes early in his career. In 1895 during a transit strike in Brooklyn, he announced his prolabor sympathies from the pulpit of B'nai Jeshurun. After he moved to Portland, Oreg., in 1899 to become rabbi of Temple Beth El, his involvement in social justice became a dominant motif in his ministry. Wise achieved national recognition in 1906 when he rebuffed offers to become the rabbi of the prestigious Temple Emanu-El in New York City, after having been refused his demand of a free pulpit. The next year, he founded the Free Synagogue, which served as Wise's principal forum in New York for the next 43 years.

Wise became ever more prominently identified with the cause of labor, and he consistently supported demands for improved working conditions and better pay. In the realm of politics, Wise fought government corruption. Wise's most ambitious attack on the Tammany wigwam came in 1930 with his assault against Mayor Jimmy Walker, which led to the mayor's resignation. Wise was a cofounder of the National Association for the Advancement of Colored People in 1909 and of the American Civil Liberties Union in 1920. Closer to his Jewish concerns were his battles against the Ku Klux Klan and his support in 1924 and 1926 for liberal immigration laws. Wise made an important contribution to the training of rabbis in 1922 as founder of the Jewish Institute of Religion, which in 1948 was merged with the Hebrew Union College.

The greatest passion of Wise's public life was Zionism. He joined with Richard Gottheil, Harry Friedenwald, and others in 1897 to found the Federation of American Zionists, of which he became honorary secretary. The following year, he attended the Second World Zionist Congress in Basel. Wise made his first trip to Palestine in 1913. The next year, after the outbreak of World War I, he joined with Louis D. Brandeis to found the Provisional Executive Committee for Central Zionist Affairs, which led the fight for Zionism in America, and especially within the American Jewish community. In 1918 Wise was elected president of the newly formed Zionist Organization of America. The following year, he sailed to France as delegate of the American Jewish Congress to lobby for the Jewish cause at the Paris peace conference. In 1921 the Brandeis group of the Zionist Organization of America was defeated in an internal power struggle, but Wise continued his Zionist activities. He was named honorary vice president of the Palestine Development Council that year, and in 1925 he appeared at the Fourteenth Zionist Congress to fight Chaim Weizmann's plans for extending the Jewish Agency for Palestine to include non-Zionists. The same year, he was elected president of the permanent American Jewish Congress, a post he held until his death.

With Hitler's rise to power in 1933, Wise mobilized both Jews and non-Jews to protest against Hitler's anti-Semitic policies. In 1939, as head of the American delegation, Wise attended the Round Table Conference of Jews and Arabs in London (St. James Conference). Having learned in 1942 from the office of the World Jewish Congress in Geneva that Hitler was conducting an all-out campaign to exterminate European Jews, Wise continually railed against the Allied governments, demanding that something be done to save the victims of mass murder. Wise's cochairmanship of the Zionist Emergency Council with Abba Hillel Silver, 1943–46, was marked by constant turmoil. Wise came to the

Twenty-second Zionist Congress in 1946, the first postwar meeting, no longer the acknowledged leader of American Zionists.

WISE, THOMAS ALFRED (*b. Faversham, England, 1865; d. New York, N.Y., 1928*), actor, dramatist. Known as Tom Wise. Came to America as a child. A highly competent character actor, he specialized in farce-comedy.

WISLIZENUS, FREDERICK ADOLPH (*b. Königsee, Germany, 1810; d. St. Louis, Mo., 1889*), physician, traveler, author. Immigrated to America, 1835; began practice in rural Illinois. Accompanied a fur-trading party to the Far West, 1839, journeying to the rendezvous on Green River and to Fort Hall, and returning by way of Laramie plains, the Arkansas River, and the Santa Fe Trail to St. Louis. Published an account of the journey as *Ein Ausflug nach den Felsen-Gebirgen* (1840), which was afterward issued in translation. After further practice of medicine in St. Louis in partnership with Dr. George Engelmann, he joined a trading caravan for Santa Fe and Chihuahua in 1846 and made close observations of the fauna, flora, and geology of that region. Joining Alexander W. Doniphan's regiment in March 1847 in Mexico, he returned by way of the Rio Grande and the Mississippi to his home. His account of this adventure appeared in 1848 in *Senate Miscellaneous Document 26, 30 Cong., 1 Sess.*, and was praised for its scientific observations by Alexander von Humboldt.

WISLOCKI, GEORGE BERNAYS (*b. San Jose, Calif., 1892; d. Milton, Mass., 1956*), anatomist. Studied at Washington University (B.A., 1912), Johns Hopkins University Medical School (M.D., 1916). Taught at Johns Hopkins, 1920–31, Harvard University, 1931–56. An influential experimenter in the fields of placentology and histochemistry, Wislocki published numerous monograms and papers. Member of the National Academy of Sciences and the American Academy of Arts and Sciences.

WISNER, HENRY (*b. Goshen, N.Y., 1720; d. 1790*), farmer, New York legislator, powder manufacturer. Represented Orange Co. in New York Colonial Assembly, 1759–69, and in the first Continental Congress, 1774. A member of the New York Provincial Congress, 1775–77, he served on the committee which drafted the first state constitution and was appointed as a New York delegate to the second Continental Congress, May 1775–May 1777. He served in the state senate, 1777–82. He operated powder mills in Ulster and Orange counties during the Revolution and expedited the laying of chains across the Hudson River to prevent British passage upstream.

WISSLER, CLARK (*b. Wayne County, Ind., 1870; d. New York, N.Y., 1947*), anthropologist. Christened Clarkson Davis Wissler. Graduated Indiana University, 1897; M.A., 1899; Ph.D., Columbia University, 1901. Trained in psychology, he shifted his interest to anthropology through influence of Franz Boas, under whom he served as assistant in ethnology at American Museum of Natural History, 1902–05; he was also assistant and then lecturer in anthropology at Columbia, 1903–09. Succeeding Boas as head of anthropological work at the American Museum in 1905, he remained in charge until his retirement, 1942; in 1931, he became professor of anthropology at Yale. Among his books were *The American Indian* (1917, and later editions); *Man and Culture* (1923), which was important in disseminating anthropological thinking about culture to the other social sciences; and *The Relation of Nature to Man in Aboriginal America* (1926).

WISTAR, CASPAR (*b. Wald-Hilsbach, near Heidelberg, Baden, 1696; d. 1752*), glass manufacturer. Immigrated to Philadelphia, Pa., 1717, where he engaged in brass-button making. He located a factory for manufacture of window and bottle glass in Salem Co., West Jersey, which began work in July 1740. Staffed by Belgian and other foreign glassblowers working on shares, it was one of the earliest successful cooperative ventures in North America and exerted a lasting influence on American glassmaking by providing a technique and tradition of good workmanship. After the Revolution and the failure of the Wistar works, the workmen established glass industries both locally and in New York State and the Middle West.

WISTAR, CASPAR (*b. Philadelphia, Pa., 1761; d. 1818*), physician. Grandson of Caspar Wistar (1696–1752). Studied medicine under John Redman; B.M., University of Pennsylvania, 1782; M.D., Edinburgh University, 1786. Practiced thereafter in Philadelphia; succeeded Benjamin Rush as professor of chemistry in the medical school of the College of Philadelphia (present University of Pennsylvania, 1789; taught chiefly anatomy at University of Pennsylvania *post* 1792. Author of *System of Anatomy* (1811), the first American textbook on that subject, he was also extremely active in the work of the American Philosophical Society (president, 1815–18). The weekly open house which he kept for members of the society and visiting scientists became a tradition which was long continued as the "Wistar Parties." Thomas Nuttall named the wistaria, or wisteria, for him in 1818.

WISTER, OWEN (*b. Germantown, Pa., 1860; d. North Kingstown, R.I., 1938*), author. Grandson of Fanny Kemble. Reared in a markedly intellectual household, Wister graduated from Harvard, 1882, and at first looked forward to a musical career. While a student at Harvard Law School, 1885–88, he spent the summer vacations in the West, and after admission to the Philadelphia bar, 1889, set himself to report the West faithfully in fiction. After publishing a number of short stories, he brought out *The Virginian* (1902), a novel which became the model and high-water mark in cowboy fiction. Realistic in surface details, it is less notable as realism than as a triumphant definition of the cowboy as a folk hero, and was an instant success. Wister was author of a number of other books of no particular importance, including biographies, satires, and farces, and several works on World War I and the tensions which followed it. In domestic politics, Wister was a decided, and even angry, conservative.

WISTER, SARAH (*b. Philadelphia, Pa., 1761; d. Germantown, Pa., 1804*), diarist. Author of a lively journal of everyday events and experiences in the period from Sept. 25, 1777 to June 20, 1778, which illustrates social conditions in and about Philadelphia while the British were occupying that city.

WITHERS, FREDERICK CLARKE (*b. Shepton Mallet, Somersetshire, England, 1828; d. Yonkers, N.Y., 1901*), architect. Trained in London, England, he immigrated to America, 1853, and became in time a partner of Calvert Vaux and F. L. Olmsted, working with them on New York City's Central Park. He practiced alone *post* 1871. In high repute during his lifetime, he worked in a style about halfway between the Gothic revival style of the elder Richard Upjohn and the developed Victorian Gothic of such men as Russell Sturgis. He was the architect of a number of churches and did a considerable amount of work for the City of New York, for which he designed, among other buildings, the Jefferson Market Police Court in Greenwich Village.

WITHERSPOON, ALEXANDER MACLAREN (*b. Bowling Green, Ky., 1894; d. Hampden, Conn., 1964*), educator. Attended Ogden College and Yale (Ph.D., 1923). Taught at Yale for almost forty years. His widely used texts were *A Book of Seventeenth Century Prose* (1929), *The College Survey of English Literature* (1951), and *Seventeenth-Century Prose and Poetry* (1963). On board of editors of *The Complete Prose Works of John Milton* (1943–64).

WITHERSPOON, HERBERT (*b. Buffalo, N.Y., 1873; d. New York, N.Y., 1935*), bass singer, opera manager. Graduated Yale, 1895; studied singing in London, Paris, and Berlin. Made operatic debut with the Castle Square Opera Co.; starred as basso at Metropolitan Opera, New York, 1908–16; devoted himself thereafter to concerts and teaching. Appointed general manager of the Metropolitan Opera, 1935, but died before season began.

WITHERSPOON, JOHN (*b. Yester, near Edinburgh, Scotland, 1723; d. near Princeton, N.J., 1794*), Presbyterian clergyman, educator, statesman. M.A., University of Edinburgh, 1739; D.D., 1743. Notable during his ministry in Scotland as a champion of the so-called Popular party, as a conservative in theology and morals, and as a defender of the traditional rights of the people to choose their own ministers, Witherspoon immigrated to America in 1768 to become president of the College of New Jersey (Princeton). The choice of the New Side school, he held views that were not obnoxious to the Old Side, and his leadership soon healed the factional schism that had existed among the Presbyterians. Thanks to his efforts in great part, the Presbyterian church grew rapidly and was strongly entrenched in the middle colonies and on the frontiers by 1776. He also gave the College of New Jersey a new lease on life, increasing the endowment, the faculty, and the student body up to the time of the Revolution. He introduced into the curriculum the study of philosophy, French, history, and oratory, and insisted upon mastery of the English language. To his mind, an education should fit a man for public usefulness, and he placed a comparatively low value upon mere scholarship. He decried the philosophy of Berkeley and stood foursquare upon empiricism and "common sense."

Witherspoon engaged actively in the controversy with England, *ca.* 1774, making common cause with his neighbors. As a member of various Revolutionary committees and a delegate to provincial conventions, he helped bring New Jersey into line with the other colonies. Elected to the Continental Congress on June 22, 1776, he boldly upheld and signed the Declaration of Independence, stating that the country was in his judgment "not only ripe for the measure but in danger of rotting for the want of it." Widely influential in Great Britain as well as in America through his writings, he explained the controversy with the mother country in a number of terse and telling written arguments, showing a remarkably clear comprehension of its precise nature. Serving in Congress with a few intermissions from June 1776 until November 1782, he was a useful member of more than a hundred committees; of these, the most important were the Board of War and the Committee on Secret Correspondence (foreign affairs). He was active in the debates on the Articles of Confederation, assisted in organizing the executive departments, and played a foremost part in drawing up the instructions of the American peace commissioners. He opposed the floods of paper money which were issued and the issue of bonds without provision for amortization. His patience, courage, and executive abilities give him high rank among the leaders of the American Revolution.

He spent 1782–94 in endeavoring to rebuild the college at Princeton; however, during his lifetime the institution never fully recovered from the effects of the Revolution. He also served in the New Jersey legislature and was a member of the New Jersey convention which ratified the U.S. Constitution. A leader also in the organization of the Presbyterian church along national lines, he was largely the author of the catechisms, the confessions of faith, the directory of worship, and the form of government and discipline adopted by it. In 1781 in an article on language in the *Pennsylvania Journal*, he coined the term "Americanism."

WITHERSPOON, JOHN ALEXANDER (*b. Columbia, Tenn., 1864; d. 1929*), physician, educator. M.D., University of Pennsylvania, 1887. Taught physiology and medicine at University of

Tennessee, *post* 1889. Became professor of medicine and clinical medicine at Vanderbilt University, 1895, serving until his death and laboring to raise standards of medical education.

WITMARK, ISIDORE (*b. New York, N.Y., 1869; d. New York, 1941*), music publisher, composer. Founded, with his brothers Julius and Jay, the firm of M. Witmark & Sons, 1886, publishers and printers of popular music. The firm held a commanding position in the industry and flourished up until the 1920's, when the advent of radio, the decline of vaudeville, and other factors depressed the market for sheet music. In 1928, the firm was sold to the Warner Brothers film studio.

WITTE, EDWIN EMIL (*b. Watertown, Wis., 1887: d. Madison, Wis., 1960*), labor economist. Studied at the University of Wisconsin (Ph.D., 1927); taught there (1920–57), twice chairman of the economics department (1936–41; 1946–53). Published *The Government in Labor Disputes* (1932). Knowledge of the application of economics to government legislation won him President Franklin D. Roosevelt's appointment to head a cabinet-level Committee on Economic Security that formulated the Social Security Act of 1935. President of the American Economic Association in 1956.

WITTHAUS, RUDOLPH AUGUST (*b. New York, N.Y., 1846; d. 1915*), chemist, toxicologist. A.B., Columbia, 1867; studied at the Sorbonne and Collège de France, 1867–69; M.D., University of the City of New York, 1875. Taught at University of the City of New York and at universities of Vermont and Buffalo; professor of chemistry and physics at Cornell University *post* 1898, retiring emeritus in 1911. Won worldwide eminence in legal medicine and as expert witness at murder trials; wrote a number of important books. His greatest achievement was as editor, with T. C. Becker, of *Medical Jurisprudence, Forensic Medicine and Toxicology* (1894–96).

WOERNER, JOHN GABRIEL (*b. Möhringen, Germany, 1826; d. St. Louis, Mo., 1900*), Missouri legislator, journalist and jurist. St. Louis, Mo., probate judge, 1870–94. Widely known as an authority on probate judicature, he was author of, among other works, *Treatise on the American Law of Administration* (1889) and *A Treatise on the American Law of Guardianship* (1897).

WOFFORD, WILLIAM TATUM (*b. Habersham Co., Ga., 1823; d. near Cass Station, Ga., 1884*), planter, Georgia legislator, Confederate brigadier general, lawyer.

WOLCOTT, EDWARD OLIVER (*b. Longmeadow, Mass., 1848; d. Monte Carlo, Monaco, 1905*), lawyer, politician. Practiced in Colorado *post ca.* 1872; prospered as a railroad lawyer; was a conservative leader of the state Republican party. U.S. senator from Colorado, 1889–1901. Advocated free coinage of silver; opposed federal election bill of 1890 and President Cleveland's Venezuelan message.

WOLCOTT, OLIVER (*b. Windsor, Conn., 1726; d. 1797*), lawyer, Connecticut public official. Son of Roger Wolcott; father of Oliver Wolcott (1760–1833). Graduated Yale, 1747. Removed to Litchfield, Conn., 1751, serving as sheriff there for 20 years. Deputy for Litchfield, 1764, 1767, 1768, and 1770; Connecticut assistant, 1771–86. Judge, Litchfield probate court, 1772–81; judge, county courts in and for Litchfield, 1774–78. A commissioner of Indian affairs for the northern department, he helped settle the Wyoming Valley and New York–Vermont boundary questions. Delegate to the Continental Congress, 1775–83 (with exception of 1779), he signed the Declaration of Independence in October 1776; he was noted in Congress as a man of integrity who spoke his mind but was lacking in political knowledge. As brigadier general, he commanded militia sent to reinforce General Israel Putnam on the Hudson River, 1776; as major general, 1779, he defended Connecticut's seacoast against Tryon's raids. Lieutenant governor of Connecticut, 1787. Helped conclude 1789 treaty to which the Wyandotte surrendered title to the Western Reserve. Conservative Federalist governor of Connecticut, 1796–97.

WOLCOTT, OLIVER (*b. Litchfield, Conn., 1760; d. New York, N.Y., 1833*), lawyer, Connecticut public official, cabinet officer. Son of Oliver Wolcott (1726–97). Graduated Yale, 1778; studied law under Tapping Reeve. Notably successful in Connecticut as reorganizer of the state's financial affairs after the Revolution, he was appointed auditor of the U.S. treasury, 1789. In this capacity he labored over the routine operations of the department to such good effect that Alexander Hamilton recommended him for appointment as comptroller of the treasury, June 1791. Unwavering in his loyalty to Hamilton, who was his close friend also, he succeeded Hamilton as secretary of the treasury, February 1795. Mounting expenditures by the federal government, the spirit of speculation in American commerce, and increasing demoralization of the European money market created grave problems for the treasury; moreover, the Democratic-Republican majority in Congress, under the leadership of Albert Gallatin, were trying to take the initiative in financial matters away from the secretary. Wolcott did not enjoy the quasi-independence in allotting government funds which Hamilton had so cavalierly employed. Although given the confidence of President John Adams, 1797–1800, Wolcott remained subservient to Hamilton's directions and cooperated with Timothy Pickering and James McHenry in intrigues against the Adams administration.

Resigning the secretaryship at the end of the year 1800, he returned to Connecticut a poor man, despite charges by his political enemies that he was guilty of all manner of financial crimes. Removing to New York City *ca.* 1803, he engaged in a number of short-lived business activities and was president of the Bank of America, 1812–14. Settling in Litchfield, Conn., 1815, he occupied himself as a gentleman farmer and promoter of manufacturing in Connecticut. Having become a Democratic-Republican in politics, he was elected governor of Connecticut, 1817, and brought about a political revolution in that state. As governor he succeeded in overthrowing Federalist control of the aristocratic state council; after reelection in April 1818, he presided over a constitutional convention at which a new constitution (which he was influential in drafting) was adopted. The new constitution separated church and state, guaranteed full freedom of conscience, separated the powers of government, and established a more influential executive and an independent judiciary. Able and popular, Wolcott was reelected governor year after year until 1827. During this time he made expert revisions in the tax laws, but failed in efforts to promote state aid for agriculture and industry and other liberal measures.

WOLCOTT, ROGER (*b. Windsor, Conn., 1679; d. 1767*), farmer, businessman, lawyer, Connecticut public official. Father of Oliver Wolcott (1726–97). Assistant, Connecticut colony, 1714–41, with exception of 1718 and 1719; deputy governor of Connecticut, 1741–50; governor, 1750–54. Became judge of the Hartford Co. court, 1721, and of the superior court, 1732; became chief justice of the latter, 1741. As major general, 1745, he was second in command on the expedition which took Louisburg. Author of, among other books, *Poetical Meditations* (1725), the first volume of verse published in Connecticut.

WOLF, GEORGE (*b. Northampton Co., Pa., 1777; d. 1840*), lawyer, Pennsylvania legislator. Began practice in Easton, Pa. As congressman, Democrat, from Pennsylvania, December

1824–29, he supported the protective tariff and other measures to aid American industry. Elected governor of Pennsylvania in 1829, he served six years; he began a revision of the state statute law, reestablished state credit, and secured passage of the free public school act, 1834. Wolf opposed President Jackson on the second Bank of the United States and fought for renewal of the bank charter. He served as comptroller of the U.S. treasury, 1836–38, and as collector of customs, port of Philadelphia, thereafter.

WOLF, HENRY (*b. Eckwersheim, Alsace, 1852; d. New York, N.Y., 1916*), wood engraver. Immigrated to America, 1871; settled in New York, 1873. Became preeminent in reproduction of paintings by contemporary American artists.

WOLF, INNOCENT WILLIAM (*b. Schmidheim, Rhenish Prussia, 1843; d. 1922*), Roman Catholic clergyman, Benedictine. Immigrated to Brighton, Wis., 1851. Ordained priest, 1866, after studies at St. Vincent Abbey, Latrobe, Pa. Returning to St. Vincent, 1870, after further study in Rome, he taught theology and was successively master of novices, treasurer of the abbey, and prior of the monastery. Elected first abbot of St. Benedict's, Atchison, Kans., 1876, he served actively until 1921.

WOLF, SIMON (*b. Bavaria, 1836; d. Washington, D.C., 1923*), lawyer, philanthropist. Immigrated to America, 1848. Graduated Ohio Law College, Cleveland, Ohio, 1861. Practiced in Washington *post* 1862. Appointed recorder, District of Columbia, 1869; served as civil judge, 1878–81. Won reputation as vigorous champion of civic and religious rights of eastern European Jews. Founder and lifelong president, Hebrew Orphans' Home, Atlanta, Ga.

WOLFE, CATHARINE LORILLARD (*b. New York, N.Y., 1828; d. New York, 1887*), philanthropist, art patron. Daughter of John D. Wolfe. A munificent benefactor of the Protestant Episcopal church; bequeathed her collection of 19th-century European paintings and an endowment to the Metropolitan Museum of Art, New York City.

WOLFE, HARRY KIRKE (*b. Bloomington, Ill., 1858; d. 1918*), psychologist, educator. Graduated University of Nebraska, 1880; Ph.D., Leipzig, 1886; studied under Wilhelm Wundt. Professor and head of philosophy and psychology department, University of Nebraska, 1891–97; professor of educational psychology, 1906–09; professor of philosophy and psychology again, 1909–18. Served in secondary school and other educational work, 1897–1905.

WOLFE, JOHN DAVID (*b. New York, N.Y., 1792; d. New York, 1872*), hardware merchant, philanthropist. Father of Catharine L. Wolfe. Benefactor of the Protestant Episcopal church, 1841–72, he helped support western dioceses and schools and took an important part in the promotion and support of New York charitable institutions.

WOLFE, THOMAS CLAYTON (*b. Asheville, N.C., 1900; d. Baltimore, Md., 1938*), novelist. The character of Eugene Gant in Wolfe's first novel, *Look Homeward, Angel* (1929), offers a recognizable account of his creator's life up to the age of 20. Product of an unsettled household, Wolfe was directed to literature and encouraged throughout his career by one of his early schoolteachers. While at the University of North Carolina, from which he graduated in 1920, he was encouraged to write by Edwin Greenlaw and others and wrote several plays (*The Return of Buck Gavin*, published 1924; *The Third Night*, published 1938), which were produced by the Carolina Playmakers. A student of playwriting in the famous "47 Workshop" under George P. Baker at Harvard, he received an M.A. in English, 1922. Resolving to dedicate himself to a truthful presentation of life in all its complexity, he gave up writing about Carolina mountaineers and attempted a more comprehensive picture of life in his play *Welcome to Our City* (produced 1923 at Harvard), for which he was unable to achieve professional production. While teaching intermittently at New York University until 1930, he traveled in England, France, and Italy, and was given love, understanding, and financial help by Mrs. Aline Bernstein, a stage designer who became an important influence in his life. After another unsuccessful attempt at the drama (a Civil War play, *Mannerhouse*, published 1948), he turned to prose narrative and began to write an autobiographical novel in a new, energetic, metaphorical style.

After 20 months' labor, he produced a huge manuscript, powerful in cumulative effect, but weakened by digressions and excessive detail. In association with Maxwell Perkins, editor at Charles Scribner's Sons, Wolfe reduced his work to a publishable volume, which appeared in October 1929 as *Look Homeward, Angel* and was enthusiastically reviewed. The author, elated by the praise and burdened by a consciousness of artistic responsibility, next attempted a book which would characterize the restlessness of the modern American and render a sense of the variety and vastness of the American continent. His ideas multiplied until he had in hand a project for a series of novels whose main narrative thread would be his own experiences. Overwhelmed by the bulk of his scheme as his material developed in length and complexity, he was once again assisted by Perkins to reduce his manuscript to order. Perkins divided the work into two separate books and set Wolfe to writing fillers for the narrative gaps in the first of these. Although Wolfe was reluctant to permit issue of the work, it was published in March 1935 as *Of Time and the River*. Parts were magnificent, but as a whole it was uneven and anthology-like in its variety; thousands of sensitive impressions of the whole 20th-century scene served as backdrop to the story of youth's insatiable hunger for life. The critics now began to compare Wolfe to Whitman and Melville. A man of enormous appetites, egoistic as a child, he was one moment elated and the next despondent; now full of goodwill and now overcome with suspicion or anger. After publication of a collection of short stories, *From Death to Morning*, he decided to set aside his six-volume series temporarily while he wrote a different kind of book—a story about an innocent, gullible man discovering the harsh truths of life through disillusionment and trial. As he worked out the narrative, the original grandiose plan was scrapped in favor of a long chronicle about a new hero, George Webber. At this point, he broke off with Maxwell Perkins, in part to show his independence and in part because of a dispute over a libel suit which Wolfe had wanted to fight in court. He did not live to see his new work completed. Out of the vast manuscript which he left behind after his death, three books were fashioned: *The Web and the Rock* (1939), *You Can't Go Home Again* (1940), and *The Hills Beyond* (1941).

Thomas Wolfe's books have maintained favor largely because of the richness of his work. As a descriptive writer, he evokes a poetic response with his rhythmical and lyric passages; as a writer of narrative, he achieves at his best the brooding depths of Dostoevski and the vivid portraiture of Dickens. His work is tempered with broad humor which becomes predominantly satirical in his later work. Although his minor figures tend to caricature, his great characterizations display a full range of the strengths and weaknesses of humankind.

WOLFF, KURT AUGUST PAUL (*b. Bonn, Germany, 1887; d. Ludwigsburg, Germany, 1963*), publisher. Established Pantheon Books in 1942, first publishing Charles Péguy's *Basic Verities* (1943); his policy was to publish "books of fine quality which although not designed for a mass audience would nevertheless appeal to a large number of people." During the 1950's several Pantheon books became best-sellers, including Anne Morrow Lindbergh's *Gift from the Sea*, Joy Adamnson's *Born Free*, and

Boris Pasternak's *Dr. Zhivago*. After a dispute with associates he resigned in 1960; in 1961 he and his wife arranged with Harcourt, Brace and World to publish Helen and Kurt Wolff Books.

WOLFSKILL, WILLIAM (*b. near Richmond, Ky., 1798; d. near Los Angeles, Calif., 1866*), trapper, California pioneer. After extensive experience as a trapper along the Rio Grande and the Gila, he led a trapping party from Taos, September 1830, which opened a new route to California, approximating what became known as the western part of the Spanish Trail. Settling near Los Angeles, he acquired land and began to develop it as a vineyard in 1838. Becoming wealthy and influential as a rancher and farmer, he introduced the culture of the persimmon and the Italian chestnut and was the first in the area to ship oranges commercially.

WOLFSOHN, CARL (*b. Alzey, Germany, 1834; d. Deal Beach, N.J., 1907*), pianist, teacher, conductor. Came to America, 1854, settling in Philadelphia, Pa. Associated with Theodore Thomas in chamber music recitals *post* 1856. Presented notable recitals of all Beethoven piano sonatas in Philadelphia and in Steinway Hall, New York City, 1863–64. Founded Beethoven Society, 1869; conducted a similar society in Chicago, Ill., 1873–84. Wolfsohn was one of the earliest in America to espouse the cause of Richard Wagner's music.

WOLFSON, ERWIN SERVICE (*b. Cincinnati, Ohio, 1902; d. Purchase, N.Y., 1962*), investment builder and contractor who through the establishment of the Diesel Construction Company and Wolfson Management Corporation became New York City's leading builder by 1960. From 1946 to 1962 he and his firms were associated either as principal investor or general contractor in the construction of over sixty major edifices, including projects for RKO Pictures, NBC studios, and Bankers Trust. The Pan Am Building was the climax of his career (completed in 1963).

WOLHEIM, LOUIS ROBERT (*b. New York, N.Y., 1881; d. Los Angeles, Calif., 1931*), mechanical engineer, mathematician, stage and screen actor. Graduated College of the City of New York, 1903; M.E., Cornell University, 1906. After winning great applause for his performance with the Provincetown Players in Eugene O'Neill's *The Hairy Ape*, 1922–24, Wolheim attained the high point of his career as Captain Flagg in *What Price Glory?* Thereafter, he was engaged principally in motion-picture work as the best delineator of hard-boiled parts.

WOLL, MATTHEW (*b. Luxembourg, 1880; d. 1956*), labor leader. Studied at Lake Forest College of Law (LL.B., 1904). Elected president of the International Photo-Engravers Union of North America in 1906; became eighth vice president and a member of the Executive Council of the American Federation of Labor in 1919. Woll's most outstanding contribution to the labor movement began when he was appointed president of the Free Trade Union Committee in 1944. In Germany Woll worked effectively to prevent infiltration by communists of the labor unions by resisting the dismantling of German industry, by defending the code termination of the German workers, and by calling on United States Government officials to restore a democratic Germany to the family of nations. Decorated by Chancellor Konrad Adenauer in 1953 for his efforts.

WOLLE, JOHN FREDERICK (*b. Bethlehem, Pa., 1863; d. Bethlehem, 1933*), musician. Organist of Moravian Church, Bethlehem, Pa., 1885–1905; of Lehigh University, 1887–1905. Chiefly remembered as founder, 1898, and conductor, Bethlehem Bach Choir; conducted Bach festivals, Lehigh University, 1912–32. Held chair of music, University of California, 1905–11.

WOLMAN, LEO (*b. Baltimore, Md., 1890; d. New York, N.Y., 1961*), economist. Attended Johns Hopkins (Ph.D., 1916). Taught at Hobart, the University of Michigan, Johns Hopkins, the New School for Social Research, and Columbia. Chief of the production statistic section of the War Industries Board (1918) and attached to the Versailles peace mission, his responsibility to prepare memos on the economies of dependent countries. Associated with the Amalgamated Clothing Workers of America, 1920–33. During the New Deal he was chairman of the Labor Advisory Board and a member of the National Labor Board. In 1937 he proposed amendments to the Wagner Act that became part of the Taft-Hartley Act.

WONG, ANNA MAY (*b. Los Angeles, Calif., 1907; d. Santa Monica, Calif., 1961*), actress who came to national attention in the Douglas Fairbanks film *The Thief of Baghdad* (1924). During the 1920's and 1930's, the accepted rule in Hollywood was that ethnic minorities could not rise above the level of menials or stock characters of fun or menace, but Wong was in great demand for films about China or the Orient, appearing in *Mr. Wu* (1927), *Across to Singapore* (1928), *Daughter of the Dragon* (1931), and *Shanghai Express* (1932), her most memorable American performance. In England she appeared in her first stage play, *The Circle of Chalk* (1929), playing opposite Lawrence Olivier, and in such films as *A Study in Scarlet* (1933), a Sherlock Holmes film.

WOOD, ABRAHAM (*fl. 1638–80*), soldier, explorer, Virginia landowner and official. Member of the Virginia Council, 1658–*ca.* 1680. Maintained a garrison at Fort Henry (Petersburg) *post* 1646; sent out expedition, 1671, which achieved the first recorded passage of the Appalachian Mountains; sent out party, under James Needham, which traced trail to present Tennessee in 1673 and opened trade with the Cherokee.

WOOD, CASEY ALBERT (*b. Wellington, Ontario, Canada, 1856; d. La Jolla, Calif., 1942*), ophthalmologist. Graduated as Master of Surgery and M.D., 1877, from the medical school of the University of Bishop's College, Montreal. After practicing general medicine in Montreal, in 1886 he began training in diseases of the eye at New York Eye and Ear Infirmary and at Post-Graduate Medical School; he studied also at eye clinics in Berlin, Vienna, Paris, and London. Settling in Chicago, Ill., 1890, he served on the staffs of several hospitals and was professor of clinical ophthalmology at Chicago Post-Graduate, University of Illinois, and Northwestern University. After World War I service, he removed to Palo Alto, Calif., and devoted himself to his avocations, which included research in the mechanism of sight in birds and the assembly of source materials on the history of ophthalmology. He was editor, translator, or author of a number of books on his specialties and a founding member of the American College of Surgeons.

WOOD, CHARLES ERSKINE SCOTT (*b. Erie, Pa., 1852; d. near Los Gatos, Calif., 1944*), army officer, lawyer, author. Graduated West Point, 1874; assigned as second lieutenant to 21st Infantry, he served principally in the Northwest and was aide to General O. O. Howard. After taking the degrees of Ph.B., 1882, and LL.B., 1883, at Columbia University, he resigned from the army and practiced law in Portland, Oreg. Successful in maritime and corporation practice, he also became a crusader for a variety of reform causes and an anarchist. Inclined to literature from his youth, he devoted himself to writing subsequent to his retirement from practice, *ca.* 1918. Of his published works, the best known are *The Poet in the Desert* (1915, with later versions in 1918 and 1929) and *Heavenly Discourse* (1927).

WOOD, CRAIG RALPH (*b. Lake Placid, N.Y., ca. 1901; d. Palm Springs, Fla., 1968*), professional golfer. Joined the profes-

sional circuit in the late 1920's. He was a top money winner and member of the U.S. Ryder Cup team during the 1930's, but he failed to win major championships. In 1940 he won the Metropolitan Open with the score of 264, then the world record for a four-round tournament. He won the Masters and U.S. National championships in 1941 and was captain of the U.S. Ryder Cup team in 1942.

WOOD, DAVID DUFFLE (*b. Pittsburgh, Pa., 1838; d. Philadelphia, Pa., 1910*), organist. Blind from childhood and mainly self-taught in music, Wood was an instructor of music at the Pennsylvania Institution for the Instruction of the Blind, Philadelphia, *post* 1862, and principal instructor from 1887 until his death. Organist of St. Stephen's Church, Philadelphia, 1864–1910, he was also choirmaster *post* 1870. He was instructor of organ at the Philadelphia Musical Academy for thirty years. Author of *A Dictionary of Musical Terms, for the Use of the Blind* (1869). A notable interpreter of Bach.

WOOD, EDITH ELMER (*b. Portsmouth, N.H., 1871; d. Greystone Park, N.J., 1945*), housing reformer. B.L., Smith College, 1890. Married Albert N. Wood, a career naval officer, 1893. Convinced by her work in the control and cure of tuberculosis that the disease was an effect of slum conditions, she devoted her life to securing federal support for proper housing. She was vice president of the National Public Housing Conference, which mobilized support for the Wagner-Steagall Act, 1937, and served as consultant to the U.S. Housing Authority, which was set up under that act.

WOOD, EDWARD STICKNEY (*b. Cambridge, Mass., 1846; d. Pocasset, Mass., 1905*), physician, chemist. M.D., Harvard Medical School, 1871; professor of chemistry there from 1876 until his death. Chemist, Massachusetts General Hospital, Boston, Mass. A legal expert in chemistry, he was well known in his time as an expert witness in many trials.

WOOD, FERNANDO (*b. Philadelphia, Pa., 1812; d. Hot Springs, Ark., 1881*), businessman, politician. Entering politics in New York City, 1834, he was active in Tammany Hall and served as a member of Congress, 1841–43. Prospering as a ship chandler and merchant during the California gold rush, he invested his large profits in New York and San Francisco real estate. Meanwhile, he had become a leader of Tammany Hall. Elected mayor of New York City, 1854, and reelected, 1856, he was influential in creating Central Park, but permitted graft to run riot in the city government. During his term of office the city was plagued by the existence of two separate police forces, one under state control, the other under the mayor; consequent confusion over jurisdiction assisted the growth of crime and corruption. Ousted by fellow leaders from Tammany Hall, Wood organized his personal following as the so-called Mozart Hall and through it secured his third election as mayor in 1859. He appeared at the Democratic convention of 1860 at the head of a contesting New York delegation with pro-Southern leanings. Believing that the Union was about to be dissolved, he proposed in January 1861 that New York should become a free city. Defeated for reelection, he denounced the Civil War and advocated peace by conciliation; early in 1863 he joined with C. L. Vallandigham in organizing the Peace Democrats. A New York congressman, 1863–65 and 1867–81, he reflected in his views the dominant banking and mercantile interests of New York, insisting, in opposition to his own Democratic party, upon a sound currency and a tariff for revenue only. He was majority floor leader *post* 1877 and chairman of the Ways and Means Committee. A man of engaging manners, Wood had an uncanny ability to estimate the course of public opinion and a genius for political organization.

WOOD, FREDERICK HILL (*b. Lebanon, Maine, 1877; d. New York, N.Y., 1943*), lawyer. A.B., University of Kansas, 1897; LL.B., 1899. After successful practice as a railroad lawyer in the Midwest, he moved to New York City in 1913 as general attorney of the Southern Pacific Railway. In 1924, he joined the firm of Cravath, Henderson and de Gersdorff (*post* 1928, Cravath, de Gersdorff, Swaine, and Wood). A faithful servant of his corporate clients, he became known as one of the most successful anti–New Deal lawyers in the nation. Among other cases in which he challenged the constitutionality of federal measures was the landmark *Schechter Poultry Corporation* v. *United States*, overturning the National Industrial Recovery Act.

WOOD, GEORGE (*b. Chesterfield, N.J., 1789; d. 1860*), lawyer, regarded by contemporaries as the leader of the New Jersey and New York bar. Graduated College of New Jersey (Princeton), 1808. Studied law under Richard Stockton (1764–1828); began practice at New Brunswick, N.J., 1812. Wood appeared frequently before the U.S. Supreme Court and is of particular importance for his influence in forming the New Jersey law on charitable devises (*e.g.*, *Hendrickson* v. *Shotwell*). He removed to New York City, 1831. In *Martin* v. *Waddell*, he expounded the law concerning the right of the sovereign to underwater lands. He was a master of clear and comprehensive statement.

WOOD, GEORGE BACON (*b. Greenwich, N.J., 1797; d. Philadelphia, Pa., 1879*), physician. Uncle of Horatio C. Wood. M.D., University of Pennsylvania, 1818. Professor of chemistry, Philadelphia College of Pharmacy, 1822–35; also professor of materia medica, 1831–35. Wood then became professor of materia medica and pharmacy at University of Pennsylvania; from 1850 to 1860, he served there as professor of the theory and practice of medicine. Attending physician, Pennsylvania Hospital, 1835–59; president, College of Physicians of Philadelphia, 1848 until his death; president, American Philosophical Society, 1859–79. Chairman, National Committee for Revision of U.S. Pharmacopeia, 1850–60. Author of, among other works, *The Dispensatory of the United States* (1833, with Franklin Bache) and *Treatise on the Practice of Medicine* (1847).

WOOD, GRANT (*b. near Anamosa, Iowa, 1892; d. Iowa City, Iowa, 1942*), painter. Influenced in some degree by the style and techniques of the late medieval primitive painters of Germany and Flanders, he produced a body of work expressive of the stern and intense character of his native state. Achieving national prominence, he was a principal figure in the regionalism movement in the arts which flourished during the 1930's. *Post* 1934, he was associate professor of art at the University of Iowa, where he conducted what was in essence a studio class in the European tradition of teaching. Among his best known paintings are: *Woman with Plants* (1929); *American Gothic* (1930); and *Daughters of Revolution* (1932).

WOOD, HENRY ALEXANDER WISE (*b. New York, N.Y., 1866; d. 1939*), inventor, manufacturer. Son of Fernando Wood. Devised and made a series of printing machinery improvements which brought about great changes in the printing of newspapers. Among these were the Autoplate (final patent, 1903), whereby an entire newspaper page was cast in metal, and high-speed press-feeding devices. An early advocate of aviation, he also engaged in propaganda against American entry into the League of Nations and for limitation of immigration.

WOOD, HORATIO CHARLES (*b. Philadelphia, Pa., 1841; d. Philadelphia, 1920*), physician. Nephew of George B. Wood. M.D., University of Pennsylvania, 1862. Professor of botany, University of Pennsylvania, 1866–76; clinical professor of nervous diseases, 1876–1901; professor of materia medica, pharmacy, and general therapeutics, 1876–1906. Worked also as an entomologist. Associated with Philadelphia Hospital (Blockley), 1870–88. Author of approximately 300 papers and 6 books on scientific subjects, including *A Treatise on Therapeutics* (1874) and revisions of his uncle's *Dispensatory of the United States*; edited, among other medical journals, *Therapeutic Gazette*, 1884–1900.

WOOD, JAMES (*b. Greenfield, N.Y., 1799; d. Hightstown, N.J., 1867*), Presbyterian clergyman, educator. Strong adherent of "old school" party. Professor, New Albany (Ind.) Theological Seminary, 1840–51; president, Hanover (Ind.) College, 1859–66.

WOOD, JAMES B. (*b. Mount Kisco, N.Y., 1839; d. Mount Kisco, 1925*), Quaker leader, farmer, horticulturist. Served as presiding clerk of the New York Yearly Meeting of Friends, 1885–1925, and as clerk of Five Years Meeting, 1907; helped found *American Friend*; wrote on Quaker doctrines and ideals; was a manager of Haverford College and a trustee of Bryn Mawr.

WOOD, JAMES FREDERICK (*b. Philadelphia, Pa., 1813; d. 1883*), Roman Catholic clergyman. A convert to Catholicism in Cincinnati, Ohio, 1836, Wood studied in Rome at the Irish College and at the Propaganda. After ordination in Rome, 1844, he served in Cincinnati. Appointed titular bishop of Antigonia and coadjutor to Bishop J. N. Neumann of Philadelphia, he was consecrated, 1857, and succeeded to full authority in 1860. Became first archbishop of Philadelphia, 1875. An able and somewhat rigorous administrator of his diocese.

WOOD, JAMES J. (*b. Kinsale, Ireland, 1856; d. Asheville, N.C., 1928*), engineer, inventor. Came to America as a boy; was raised in Connecticut. Patented an arc-light dynamo, 1880, which was the first of some 240 electrical and other patents which he took out. These included a floodlighting system which was first used successfully to light the Statue of Liberty, 1885; an internal combustion engine which was installed in the first Holland submarine; and the machines for constructing the main cables on the original Brooklyn Bridge. His later inventions were mainly in the field of alternating-current generators, motors, transformers, and other devices. Becoming a consulting engineer *ca.* 1885, he was chief engineer of the General Electric Co. and later consultant of its Fort Wayne, Ind., works.

WOOD, JAMES RUSHMORE (*b. Mamaroneck, N.Y., 1813; d. New York, N.Y., 1882*), surgeon. Graduated Vermont Academy of Medicine, Castleton, Vt., 1834. Practiced in New York City *post* 1837. A cofounder of Bellevue Hospital, 1847, Wood was a moving spirit in that institution until his death and won fame as a brilliant and successful radical operator. He introduced at Bellevue the first city hospital ambulance service, 1869, and established there the first training school for nurses in the United States, 1873. An organizer of Bellevue Hospital Medical College, 1856, he served it as professor of operative surgery and surgical pathology. Famous for his skill in nerve and bone surgery, he was among the first to cure aneurism by pressure. His collection of postmortem material grew into the Wood Museum, one of the richest collections of pathological specimens in the world.

WOOD, JETHRO (*b. Dartmouth, Mass., or White Creek, N.Y., 1774; d. Cayuga Co., N.Y., 1834*), inventor of plow improvements. Patented a cast-iron plow, 1819, whose design and principles of construction were copied widely throughout the North. The peculiar virtue of the Wood plow lay in the shaping of the moldboard and a combination of good balance, strength, light draft, interchangeability of parts, and cheapness of manufacture.

WOOD, JOHN (*b. Scotland, ca. 1775; d. Richmond, Va., 1822*), political pamphleteer, surveyor and mapmaker. Immigrated to America *ca.* 1800. Served as tutor to Theodosia Burr; worked as a writer in Aaron Burr's interest; was author of, among other political tracts, *The History of the Administration of John Adams* (1802). Associated with the publication of the Frankfort, Ky., *Western World*, 1806; published *A Full Statement of the Trial and Acquittal of Aaron Burr* at Alexandria, Va., 1807. Recommended to the governor of Virginia by Thomas Jefferson, Wood was appointed by the state in 1819 to survey and map each Virginia county, and to execute a general map of the state. By the time of his death, he had supplied all but six of the county charts and had completed, it was believed, a fifth of the general map.

WOOD, JOHN STEPHENS (*b. near Ball Ground, Ga., 1885; d. Marietta, Ga., 1968*), U.S. congressman. Studied at North Georgia Agricultural College and Mercer University (LL.B., 1910) and practiced law in Jasper and Canton. He was Canton city attorney (1915–16), a member of the Georgia House of Representatives (1916–18), solicitor general of the Blue Ridge judicial circuit (1921–26), and superior court judge (1926–31). A Democrat, he served in the U.S. House of Representatives (1933–35, 1945–53). As chairman of the House Un-American Activities Committee, Wood helped broaden the scope of its investigations by probing radio news commentators. He also contributed to the formulation of the Internal Security (McCarran) Act of 1950. Wood was also a member of the House Education and Labor and, briefly, Foreign Affairs committees.

WOOD, JOHN TAYLOR (*b. Fort Snelling, present Minn., 1830; d. Halifax, Nova Scotia, Canada, 1904*), naval officer. Grandson of Zachary Taylor. Graduated Annapolis, 1853. Resigning from the U.S. Navy, 1861, he was commissioned lieutenant in the Confederate navy and served aboard the *Virginia* (*Merrimack*). Appointed naval aide to President Jefferson Davis, 1863, he distinguished himself by a series of boat expeditions in the Chesapeake and lower Potomac, raiding and destroying Union vessels. In August 1864 he commanded the steam sloop *Tallahassee* on a raiding expedition from Wilmington, N.C., to Halifax, Nova Scotia, and back, capturing or destroying more than 60 vessels. Promoted captain, February 1865, he accompanied Davis in the retreat from Richmond, but managed to escape through Florida to Cuba. After the war he engaged in the shipping and marine insurance business in Halifax.

WOOD, JOSEPH (*b. Clarkstown, N.Y., ca. 1778; d. Washington, D.C., ca. 1832*), miniaturist, portrait painter. In partnership with John W. Jarvis as maker of *eglomisé* silhouettes, 1804–09; received instruction in miniature painting from Edward G. Malbone. Maintained New York studio until 1812 or 1813; removing to Philadelphia, he exhibited regularly at the Pennsylvania Academy of the Fine Arts until 1817. By 1827, he was established in Washington, D.C.

WOOD, LEONARD (*b. Winchester, N.H., 1860; d. 1927*), soldier, military surgeon. M.D., Harvard Medical School, 1884. Appointed a contract surgeon in the U.S. Army Medical Corps, he won commendation for service during campaigns against the Apache of Geronimo and was regularly commissioned in 1886. After routine duty in California and the East, he was transferred to Washington, D.C., 1895, where he became physician to President and Mrs. McKinley. A friend of Theodore Roosevelt, he joined with him in organizing the Rough Riders. Wood took command of the unit as colonel and led in the first engagement at Las Guasimas, Cuba, June 1898. He became military governor of Santiago after its surrender. Successful in cleaning up and restoring the city, he was then given charge of the entire province; in December 1899 he was appointed military governor of all Cuba,

serving until 1902. A physical giant, extraordinarily energetic and ambitious, Wood was a strong nationalist and no respecter of persons. During his term in Cuba he stabilized the affairs of that island, establishing educational, police, and physical systems and modernizing the administration of justice. He also superintended great advances in sanitation.

As governor of the Moro Province of the Philippines, 1903–06, he pacified the province and brought about a relatively high degree of prosperity there, although criticized for ruthlessness in stamping out local institutions. In August 1903 he had been promoted major general in the regular army. After command of the Philippine Division, 1906–08, he returned home. Chief of staff of the U.S. Army, 1910–14, he supervised the new organization of the War Department, which had been necessitated by the creation of the General Staff in 1903; after an epic contest with conservative bureau heads, Wood was partially successful in organizing the regular army into a coherent force. *Post* 1914 he engaged in development of the civilian training-camp movement and the "preparedness" movement; these activities frequently brought him into conflict with the administration of President Wilson. Although senior officer of the army when the United States entered World War I, Wood was passed over for command either abroad or at home. Following the war he openly sought the Republican nomination for the presidency; he came to the Republican convention at Chicago, 1920, with the largest single following of delegates, but failed of the nomination. Appointed a member of a special mission to the Philippines, 1921, he soon became governor general of the Philippines, serving until 1927 when he returned to the United States for a surgical operation which proved fatal.

WOOD, MARY ELIZABETH (*b. near Batavia, N.Y., 1861; d. Wuchang, China, 1931*), librarian. Served at Boone College, Wuchang, China, *post* 1904; oversaw erection of Boone Library building, 1910, and founding of Boone Library School, 1920. Promoted China-wide library movement *post* 1923; helped obtain U.S. congressional appropriation for Chinese educational-cultural activities.

WOOD, REUBEN (*b. Middletown, Vt., ca. 1792; d. 1864*), jurist. Ohio legislator. Removed to Cleveland, Ohio, 1818. President judge, 3rd common pleas circuit of Ohio, January 1830–February 1833; justice, Ohio Supreme Court, 1833–47. Democratic governor of Ohio, 1850–53. Acting U.S. minister to Chile, 1853–55.

WOOD, ROBERT ELKINGTON (*b. Kansas City, Mo., 1879; d. Lake Forest, Ill., 1969*), army officer and merchant. Graduated from West Point (1900) and served in Panama (1905–15), where he was involved in the construction of the Panama Canal. During World War I he was responsible for all supply services for the American Expeditionary Force. In 1919 he became vice president for merchandising of Montgomery Ward and Company, and in 1924 he joined Sears, Roebuck, and Company. Wood began adding retail stores to the company's mail-order system, and by the time he became president and chief executive in 1928, he had created a nationwide chain of retail stores. When he retired as chairman of the board in 1954, Sears had become the world's largest general merchandise distributor.

WOOD, SAMUEL (*b. Oyster Bay, N.Y., 1760; d. 1844*), bookseller and publisher, philanthropist. Began business in New York City, 1804; organized publishing firm of Samuel Wood & Sons, 1815, later the largest American medical-book publishers. Produced a long series of children's books (earliest imprint, 1806).

WOOD, SARAH SAYWARD BARRELL KEATING (*b. York, Maine, 1759; d. Kennebunk, Maine, 1855*), novelist. Maine's first fiction writer, she was author of, among other books, *Julia and the Illuminated Baron*, a Gothic romance (1800), and *Tales of the Night* (1827).

WOOD, THOMAS (*b. Smithfield, Ohio, 1813; d. 1880*), surgeon. M.D., University of Pennsylvania, 1839. Practiced in Cincinnati, Ohio, *post ca.* 1845. Taught anatomy and physiology at Ohio College of Dental Surgery and at Medical College of Ohio. A daring and successful operator, he was particularly skillful in treating women's diseases.

WOOD, THOMAS BOND (*b. Lafayette, Ind., 1844; d. Tacoma, Wash., 1922*), Methodist clergyman. Active as a missionary, mission executive, and educator in Latin America, 1870–1913.

WOOD, THOMAS JOHN (*b. Mundfordville, Ky., 1823; d. 1906*), soldier. Graduated West Point, 1845. Commissioned in the engineers, he distinguished himself as staff officer under General Zachary Taylor at the Mexican War battles of Palo Alto and Buena Vista. Transferring to the cavalry, he rose to colonel, 1861, after almost continuous frontier service in the West. As brigadier general of Union volunteers, he commanded a division after the spring of 1862 and was outstanding in the battle of Stone's River. At Chickamauga, September 1863, the removal of his division from line permitted the Confederate breakthrough and occasioned a bitter controversy between Wood and General W. S. Rosecrans. Wood's division was highly effective at Missionary Ridge and in the Atlanta campaign. He commanded the IV Corps in the pursuit of General John Hood's broken Confederate army after the battle of Nashville, 1864. Several times badly wounded, he retired for disability as major general, U.S. Army, 1868.

WOOD, WALTER ABBOTT (*b. Mason, N.H., 1815; d. Hoosick Falls, N.Y., 1892*), manufacturer and inventor of agricultural implements. Produced the Wood mowers, reapers, and binders at Hoosick Falls *post ca.* 1852; made numerous improvements on mowers and reapers built originally under the John H. Manny patents.

WOOD, WILLIAM (*fl. 1629–35*), author. Immigrating from England to Massachusetts, 1629, Wood probably settled in Lynn; very little is known of his life. He left the colony on Aug. 15, 1633, and on July 7, 1634, his book *New Englands Prospect* was entered in the Stationers' Register in London. The book is an account of New England as the author observed it from 1629 to 1633; the first part is a description of the country and its settlements; the second, a number of observations on the Indians. It is clearly the work of a man with some literary training and is unusual among books of its type for vigor of style and relatively polished form.

WOOD, WILLIAM BURKE (*b. Montreal, Canada, 1779; d. 1861*), actor, theatrical manager. Made American debut with the company of Thomas Wignell at Annapolis, Md., 1798. Celebrated as a player in genteel comedy, Wood was identified principally with the Philadelphia theaters in association with William Warren. He was author of *Personal Recollections of the Stage* (1855).

WOOD, WILLIAM ROBERT (*b. Oxford, Ind., 1861; d. New York, N.Y., 1933*), lawyer, Indiana legislator. Congressman, Republican, from Indiana, 1915–33, he was first famous as one of the most active Republican critics of the administration of President Woodrow Wilson; he was later a most influential figure as chairman of the House Appropriations Committee. His political philosophy reflected a rural background and included a marked suspicion of the "money power." Economy and retrenchment were his watchwords, and his success was owing to hard work and conscientious application to his duties rather than to any intellectual brilliance.

WOODBERRY, GEORGE EDWARD (*b. Beverly, Mass., 1855; d. Beverly, 1930*), poet, critic, educator. Graduated Harvard, 1877; was influenced there by Henry Adams and Charles E. Norton. Taught English at University of Nebraska, 1877–78 and 1880–82; engaged in writing for *Atlantic Monthly* and *Nation* and other periodicals. As professor of literature (later of comparative literature), Columbia University, 1891–1904, Woodberry was brilliant as a teacher; he also built up a graduate department which transformed the methods of higher instruction in literature and left a deep mark on university teaching in this field throughout the country. After resigning his chair in 1904, he traveled widely, spending part of his time as a sort of itinerant teacher. A prolific writer, he was author of a number of books, including important biographies of Edgar Allan Poe, Nathaniel Hawthorne, and Ralph Waldo Emerson. *The Torch* (1905) contains probably the fullest expression of his philosophy of literature; his poems (he thought of himself essentially as a poet) were issued in a number of small volumes, from which a selection was made by three of his former students in 1933. A lonely and somewhat enigmatic figure, he displayed in his best critical work a subtle intuition of the emotional experience that produced the work of literature with which he was dealing and a deep sense of its relation to the spiritual background of Western man.

WOODBRIDGE, FREDERICK JAMES EUGENE (*b. Windsor, Ontario, Canada, 1867; d. New York, N.Y., 1940*), educator, philosopher. Raised in Michigan. Graduated Amherst, 1889; Union Theological Seminary, New York, 1892. After further study in Berlin, he built up an outstanding philosophy department at the University of Minnesota, 1894–1902; *post* 1902 he was professor of philosophy at Columbia University. A cofounder and for many years editor of the *Journal of Philosophy*, he served also as dean of the graduate faculties of Columbia, 1912–29. A leader of the American "realist" movement, he described his own form of this philosophy as "naive realism" and identified it with the core of Aristotle's metaphysics. He made the *Journal of Philosophy* the chief medium for the attacks of the new pragmatism, realism, and naturalism on the then-dominant school of philosophical idealism.

WOODBRIDGE, JOHN (*b. Stanton, Wiltshire, England, 1613; d. 1695*), colonial magistrate, clergyman. Nephew of Thomas Parker; brother-in-law of Simon Bradstreet. Immigrated to New England, 1634. Public official in Newbury, Mass., 1636–41 (excepting 1639), 1677–79, 1681, 1683–84, and 1690. Helped settle Andover, Mass.; was first pastor of the church at Andover, 1645–47. Removed to England, 1648, returning to Massachusetts, 1663. Assistant minister at Newbury, 1663–70. Conducted a bank of deposit and issue with land and commodities as collateral *post ca.* 1671. Author of *Severals Relating to the Fund* . . . (1681/2), the oldest American tract on currency and banking extant.

WOODBRIDGE, SAMUEL MERRILL (*b. Greenfield, Mass., 1819; d. New Brunswick, N.J., 1905*), Reformed clergyman. Graduated New Brunswick (N.J.) Theological Seminary, 1841. Held New York and New Jersey pastorates, 1841–5. Professor of ecclesiastical history and church government at New Brunswick Seminary, 1857–1901; dean, 1883–88; president of the faculty, 1888–1901. Was also professor of metaphysics and mental philosophy, Rutgers College, 1857–64.

WOODBRIDGE, WILLIAM (*b. Norwich, Conn., 1780; d. Detroit, Mich., 1861*), lawyer, Ohio and Michigan legislator. Friend of Lewis Cass; son-in-law of John Trumbull, the poet. Secretary of Michigan Territory, 1814–24; appointed collector of customs at Detroit, 1814. Chosen Michigan's first territorial delegate, 1819; served as territorial judge, 1828–32. Elected

Whig governor of Michigan, 1839, he served 14 months, implementing complete program of state rehabilitation. U.S. senator, Whig, from Michigan, 1841–47, he was chairman of the Committee on Public Lands and sponsored measures for internal improvements.

WOODBRIDGE, WILLIAM CHANNING (*b. Medford, Mass., 1794; d. Boston, Mass., 1845*), educator, Congregational clergyman. Graduated Yale, 1811. Edited *American Annals of Education and Instruction* 1831–37; was a pioneer in advocating teaching of physiology and music in common schools and an early American expounder of the Pestalozzian system. Author of *Rudiments of Geography . . . by Comparison and Classification* (1821) and *Universal Geography, Ancient and Modern* (1824), both of which revolutionized presentation of geographical facts in American schools.

WOODBURY, CHARLES JEPTHA HILL (*b. Lynn, Mass., 1851; d. 1916*), industrial engineer, authority on fire prevention. C.E., Massachusetts Institute of Technology, 1873. Became engineer, 1878, and later vice president, Boston Manufacturers Mutual Fire Insurance Co.; assistant engineer, American Telephone & Telegraph Co., 1894–1907; secretary, National Association of Cotton Manufacturers, 1894–1916. Received honors for work on mill construction and formulation of insurance rules for electric lighting.

WOODBURY, DANIEL PHINEAS (*b. New London, N.H., 1812; d. Key West, Fla., 1864*), Union soldier, engineer. Graduated West Point, 1836. Engaged in building Fort Kearny on Missouri River and Fort Laramie, Wyo., 1847–50; supervised construction of Fort Jefferson in the Tortugas and Fort Taylor at Key West. Commissioned brigadier general of volunteers, 1862; commanded engineer brigade, Army of Potomac, in the Peninsular Campaign, constructing siege works, roads, and bridges. Died of yellow fever while commanding Key West district.

WOODBURY, HELEN LAURA SUMNER (*b. Sheboygan, Wis., 1876; d. New York, N.Y., 1933*), social economist. A.B., Wellesley, 1898; Ph.D., Wisconsin, 1908. Appointed industrial expert, U.S. Children's Bureau, 1913, and assistant chief, 1915; studied child labor laws and employment certificate systems. Author of original works on citizenship and the history of women in American industry, and, among others, *Labor Problems* (1905), with Thomas S. Adams. She was one of the first in the American academic world to study and analyze labor problems and did pioneering work in the technique of social legislation administration.

WOODBURY, ISAAC BAKER (*b. Beverly, Mass., 1819; d. Charleston, S.C., 1858*), composer. Editor, *American Monthly Musical Review*. Compiled and edited, among other music books, *Boston Musical Education Society's Collection* (1842) and *Choral* (1845), both with Benjamin F. Baker; *Dulcimer* (1850); *Lute of Zion* (1853); *Cythara* (1854); and *Harp of the South* (1853). Many of his compositions were published, including a popular song, "The Indian's Lament" (1846).

WOODBURY, LEVI (*b. Francestown, N.H., 1789; d. Portsmouth, N.H., 1851*), statesman, jurist, U.S. Supreme Court justice. Studied law with Jeremiah Smith (1759–1842), as well as in Litchfield (Conn.) Law School and in Boston; admitted to the bar, 1812. Associate justice, New Hampshire Superior Court, 1817–23. Elected governor of New Hampshire, 1823, by "Young America" Democrats and Federalists, he served until 1824. Congressman from New Hampshire, 1825, he was chosen Speaker of the House. As U.S. senator, 1825–31 and 1841–45, he supported Democratic measures, served on Commerce, Navy, and Agriculture committees, and was an isolationist and supporter of a mildly

protective tariff. As U.S. secretary of the navy, May 1831–June 1834, he reformed rules of conduct and procedure. Appointed U.S. secretary of the treasury, June 1834, he opposed the rechartering of the Bank of the United States and strongly supported President Jackson's bank policy. He favored the independent treasury and warned the country against inflation in 1836. He attempted to popularize use of hard money and urged Congress to use the unprecedented treasury surplus for public works, 1835–36, and for purchase of sound state bonds. He opposed division of the surplus among the states. In the panic of 1837 he perfected a defense against depreciated paper money by which public holders of federal obligations suffered no loss. He was associate justice of the U.S. Supreme Court in 1846–51. He was considered as a Democrat presidential nominee in 1848. Conservative in politics, Woodbury was a party man and a strict constructionist; his personal morals were puritan.

WOODFORD, STEWART LYNDON (*b. New York, N.Y., 1835. d. New York, 1913*), lawyer, Union soldier, diplomat. Admitted to the bar, 1857; practiced in New York City, Republican lieutenant governor of New York, 1867–69; congressman, March 1873–July 1874. Federal district attorney, southern district of New York, 1877–83. As U.S. minister to Spain, 1897–98, he worked with skill but without success to prevent war.

WOODFORD, WILLIAM (*b. Caroline Co., Va., 1734; d. New York, N.Y., 1780*), Revolutionary patriot and soldier. Appointed colonel, 3rd Virginia Regiment, 1775, he defended Hampton and was victorious at Great Bridge. Made colonel, 2nd Virginia Regiment, 1776; promoted brigadier general, 1777. Fought at Brandywine, Germantown, and Monmouth; wintered at Valley Forge. Captured defending Charleston, S.C., 1780, he died as a prisoner of war.

WOODHOUSE, JAMES (*b. Philadelphia, Pa., 1770; d. 1809*), physician, chemist. Graduated present University of Pennsylvania, 1787; M.D., 1792. Studied also with Benjamin Rush. Founded the Chemical Society of Philadelphia, 1792, one of the earliest such societies in the world, and served it as senior president for many years. Becoming professor of chemistry in the University of Pennsylvania, 1795, Woodhouse entered upon a career of research. Among other accomplishments, he gave the most convincing arguments against the doctrine of phlogiston; liberated metallic potassium by original methods; confirmed the anesthetic properties of nitrous oxide gas, 1806; engaged in profound studies of the chemistry and production of white starch; demonstrated the superiority of anthracite over bituminous coal for industrial purposes. Woodhouse was a pioneer in plant chemistry, in the development of chemical analysis, in the elaboration of many industrial processes, and in the use of laboratory methods of instruction in chemistry. Among others who frequented his laboratory were Joseph Priestly, Robert Hare, and the elder Benjamin Silliman.

WOODHULL, ALFRED ALEXANDER (*b. Princeton, N.J., 1837; d. Princeton, 1921*), military surgeon, sanitation expert. Graduated medical department, University of Pennsylvania, 1859. Served in Union army medical corps; was medical inspector, Army of the James, 1864–65. Brevetted lieutenant colonel, 1865, he remained in the army until retirement in 1901. He advanced to brigadier general on the retired list, 1904. Author of, among other writings, the "Surgical Section" of the *Catalogue of the United States Army Medical Museum* (1866) and *Notes on Military Hygiene for Officers of the Line* (1898–1909).

WOODHULL, NATHANIEL (*b. Mastic, N.Y., 1722; d. 1776*), farmer, soldier. Brother-in-law of William Floyd. Active as a New York assemblyman in protesting crown interference in colonial affairs; served as president of the New York Provincial Congress, 1775. Appointed brigadier general of militia, October, 1775, he was wounded at his headquarters at Jamaica, N.Y., after the battle of Long Island, dying subsequently of ill treatment.

WOODHULL, VICTORIA CLAFLIN (*b. Homer, Ohio, 1838; d. 1927*), adventuress, feminist. Began giving spiritualistic exhibitions with her sister, Tennessee Celeste Claflin (1846–1923), *ca.* 1853; traveled for a time with her family in a medicine and fortune-telling show; worked with her sister as a clairvoyant in Cincinnati, Chicago, and elsewhere in the Midwest. The sisters removed to New York City, 1868, where they won the interest of Cornelius Vanderbilt and made considerable profits in the stock market through his advice. In 1870 they began *Woodhull and Claflin's Weekly*, advocating equal rights for women and free love. Nominated for the presidency by the Equal Rights party in 1872, Victoria went to the polls and made a futile attempt to vote. The Claflin sisters precipitated the greatest sensation of the time by publishing in their *Weekly* on Nov. 2, 1872, the story of the alleged intimacy of Henry Ward Beecher with the wife of Theodore Tilton. Resident in England *post* 1877, both sisters married into respectable English society and became noted for charitable works.

WOODIN, WILLIAM HARTMAN (*b. Berwick, Pa., 1868; d. New York, N.Y., 1934*), industrialist. President of the American Car & Foundry Co. and for many years chairman of the board of the American Locomotive Co., Woodin was a close friend of Franklin D. Roosevelt and supported him for the presidency in 1932. After the election he became one of the inner circle of Roosevelt advisers and was named U.S. secretary of the treasury early in 1933. Woodin addressed himself with great energy and devotion to the task of restoring financial confidence and to carrying out the president's financial and monetary policies; he supervised promulgation of new banking regulations and undertook to stop hoarding of gold. His health failing, he resigned in December 1933.

WOODRING, HARRY HINES (*b. Elk City, Kans., 1887; d. Topeka, Kans., 1967*), governor of Kansas and secretary of war. Worked in banking until 1929. He was Democratic governor of Kansas (1931–33). Following his defeat for reelection in 1933, President Roosevelt named him assistant secretary of war. In 1936 he was given a recess appointment as secretary of war, and the following year the assignment was made permanent. Woodring came into conflict with Roosevelt due to his opposition to providing military equipment to Britain and France. In 1940 Roosevelt asked for, and received, his resignation. Woodring ran unsuccessfully for governor in 1946 and 1956.

WOODROW, JAMES (*b. Carlisle, England, 1828; d. 1907*), Presbyterian clergyman, educator. Uncle of Woodrow Wilson. Came to America as a boy. Graduated Jefferson College, Pennsylvania, 1849; Ph.D., Heidelberg, 1856. Professor of natural science, Oglethorpe University, Georgia, 1856–61. Became professor of science, University of South Carolina, 1869; served as president, 1891–97. Published the *Southern Presbyterian*, 1865–93. His address, *Evolution* (1884), denying any essential conflict between the Bible and science, brought him nationwide attention and aroused a southern church controversy which lasted until 1888. Woodrow's speech in defense of his views before the Synod of South Carolina, 1884, is one of the most enlightened expositions in Southern ecclesiastical history, but he was removed from his chair at the seminary.

WOODRUFF, CHARLES EDWARD (*b. Philadelphia, Pa., 1860; d. New Rochelle, N.Y., 1915*), ethnologist, army surgeon. M.D., Jefferson Medical College, 1886. During Spanish-Ameri-can War, served as brigade surgeon under Major General Wesley Merritt in Philippine Islands. Brigade surgeon, 4th Brigade, during Philippine Insurrection, 1902. Author of, among other writings, *The Expansion of Races* (1909) and *Medical Ethnology* (1915).

WOODRUFF, LORANDE LOSS (*b. New York, N.Y., 1879; d. New Haven, Conn., 1947*), biologist. Attended College of the City of New York. B.A., Columbia University, 1901; M.A., 1902; Ph.D., 1905. Taught at Williams College, 1903–07. Instructor at Yale University, 1907–09; assistant professor, 1909–15; associate professor, 1915–22; professor of protozoology, 1922–47. Appointed director of the Osborn Zoological Laboratory at Yale and chairman of the Department of Zoology, 1938, he continued to serve in these positions for the rest of his life. His research publications were numerous; he dealt in particular with the life history and physiology of the ciliated protozoa (mainly with *Paramecium*) and with the history of biology. He was author of, among other books, *Foundations of Biology* (1922).

WOODRUFF, THEODORE TUTTLE (*b. near Watertown, N.Y., 1811; d. Gloucester, N.J., 1892*), inventor. Patented railway-car seat and couch, 1856, and improvements, 1859 and 1860; began manufacture of sleeping cars in Philadelphia, Pa., 1858. Patented a process and apparatus for indigo manufacture, 1872, and a coffee-hulling machine. Later patents include a steam plow.

WOODRUFF, TIMOTHY LESTER (*b. New Haven, Conn., 1858; d. 1913*), merchant, New York politician. Removed to Brooklyn, N.Y., 1881. Republican lieutenant governor of New York, 1897–1903; strengthened Kings County organization of Republican party.

WOODRUFF, WILFORD (*b. Farmington, now Avon, Conn., 1807; d. San Francisco, Calif., 1898*), Mormon leader. Converted to Mormonism at Richland, N.Y., 1833. Removed to Kirtland, Ohio, 1834, and was sent by Joseph Smith to aid distressed Mormons in Missouri. Ordained apostle by Brigham Young, 1839. A member of the first company to enter Great Salt Lake Valley, 1847. Became president of the quorum of the Twelve Apostles, 1880; succeeded to presidency, Utah branch, Mormon church, 1889. One of Mormon's most effective proselyters, his missionary travels covered England, Scotland, Wales, and 23 states and 5 territories of the Union. In 1875 he became Mormon's official historian and recorder; as president, he issued the famous "Manifesto," 1890, in which plural marriage was officially abandoned.

WOODRUFF, WILLIAM EDWARD (*b. Fireplace, N.Y., 1795; d. Little Rock, Ark., 1885*), newspaper publisher. Founder-editor, *Arkansas Gazette*, 1819–38 and 1841–43; established *Arkansas Democrat*, 1846.

WOODS, ALVA (*b. Shoreham, Vt., 1794; d. Providence, R.I., 1887*), Baptist clergyman, educator. Graduated Harvard, 1817; ordained, 1821. President of Transylvania University, Kentucky, 1828–31; of the University of Alabama, 1831–37.

WOODS, CHARLES ROBERT (*b. Newark, Ohio, 1827; d. Ohio, 1885*), soldier. Brother of William B. Woods. Graduated West Point, 1852. Commanded army force aboard *Star of the West* in attempt to relieve Fort Sumter, 1861; appointed colonel, 76th Ohio Infantry, 1861. For gallant service in Vicksburg campaign, was appointed brigadier general of volunteers, 1863. Led assault on Lookout Mountain; played prominent part at Resaca and Atlanta, 1864; brevetted major general of volunteers in 1865. He served in the West as regular colonel in infantry, 1866–74.

WOODS, JAMES HAUGHTON (*b. Boston, Mass., 1864; d. Tokyo, Japan, 1935*), educator, student of Indian philosophy. Graduated Harvard, 1887; Ph.D., Strassburg, 1896; studied also at Episcopal Theological School in Cambridge, Mass., and at Oxford, Harvard, and the University of Berlin. Taught several subjects intermittently at Harvard. Made special Oriental studies at Kiel, and traveled and studied in India until 1903 when he became a member of the Harvard Department of Philosophy and instructor in the philosophical systems of India. He was professor of philosophy at Harvard, 1913–34, continuing, however, his travels and further studies in Oriental subjects. He was editor and author of texts and translations in his special field.

WOODS, LEONARD (*b. Princeton, Mass., 1774; d. Andover, Mass., 1854*), Congregational clergyman. Father of Leonard Woods (1807–78). Ordained pastor of church at Newbury (now West Newbury), Mass., 1798. A moderate Calvinist, he mediated successfully between the Hopkinsians and the Old Calvinists. He was the first professor of theology at Andover Theological Seminary, 1808–46.

WOODS, LEONARD (*b. Newbury, Mass., 1807; d. Boston, Mass., 1878*), clergyman, educator. Son of Leonard Woods (1774–1854). Graduated Union, 1827; Andover Theological Seminary, 1830. Ordained by Third Presbytery of New York, 1833; was editor, *Literary and Theological Review*, New York City, 1833–36. Called to chair of biblical literature, Bangor (Maine) Theological Seminary, 1836. As president of Bowdoin College, 1839–66, he inspired affection and respect. He was an excellent teacher, was largely responsible for erection of King Chapel, and helped win for the college the reversionary interest in the James Bowdoin estate.

WOODS, ROBERT ARCHEY (*b. Pittsburgh, Pa., 1865; d. 1925*), sociologist, reformer. Graduated Amherst, 1886; studied at Andover Theological Seminary; worked at Toynbee Hall, London, England. Head of Andover House (South End House) settlement, Boston, Mass., *post* 1891. Woods's outstanding contribution to sociology and social work is the concept that the neighborhood or village is the primary community unit and that towns, metropolitan areas, the nation itself, are "federations" of neighborhoods. He organized Boston settlements into a federation, and initiated organization of the National Federation of Settlements, 1911. Author of *English Social Movements* (1891), *The City Wilderness* (1898), the first thoroughgoing study of a depressed area in an American city; *Americans in Process* (1902); and *Neighborhood in Nation-Building* (1923). Coauthor with Albert J. Kennedy of, among others, *The Settlement Horizon* (1922), an authoritative text on the history of American settlements.

WOODS, WILLIAM ALLEN (*b. near Farmington, Tenn., 1837; d. Indianapolis, Ind., 1901*), jurist. Raised in Iowa; admitted to Indiana bar, 1861. Judge, 34th judicial circuit of Indiana, 1873–80; Indiana Supreme Court, 1880–82; U.S. district judge for Indiana, 1882–92; judge of 7th U.S. circuit court *post* 1892. His most widely known case was *United States v. Debs*, in which he sentenced the Socialist Eugene V. Debs to prison for violation of an antistrike injunction.

WOODS, WILLIAM BURNHAM (*b. Newark, Ohio, 1824; d. Washington, D.C., 1887*), Ohio Democratic legislator, Union brigadier general, jurist, U.S. Supreme Court justice. Brother of Charles R. Woods. Removed to Alabama, 1866, where he was active in Reconstruction as a Republican. Appointed judge of the U.S. circuit court, 5th circuit, 1869, he removed to Atlanta, Ga. Appointed associate justice of the U.S. Supreme Court, 1880, Woods wrote the opinion in *U.S. v. Harris*, determining that

protection of black civil rights was not to be found in federal statutes or by federal court indictments. He also wrote the opinion in *Presser v. Illinois* and in many patent and equity cases.

WOODSON, CARTER GODWIN (*b. New Canton, Va., 1875; Washington, D.C., 1950*), historian. Child of former slaves, he was largely self-taught until, after working several years in West Virginia coal mines, he attended high school in Huntington. He received the B.Litt., Berea College, 1903. His graduate studies were made (again in periods between various employments) at University of Chicago (B.A. and M.A., 1908) and at Harvard (Ph.D., 1912). From 1909 until 1918, he taught a variety of subjects at the M St. (Dunbar) High School in Washington, D.C. In 1915, he organized the Association for the Study of Negro Life and History, which he headed until his death; he was also editor *post* 1916 of the association's quarterly, *Journal of Negro History*, and, *post* 1937, of the *Negro History Bulletin*. In 1921, he founded Associated Publishers, a firm for the publication of books by and about blacks. His last academic employment was as dean of West Virginia State College, 1920–22; thereafter, he gave his full time to the study and dissemination of black history and the encouragement of black historians. He was author of, among other works, *The Education of the Negro Prior to 1861* (1915); *A Century of Negro Migration* (1918); *The Negro Wage Earner* (1930, with Lorenzo Greene); and a widely used textbook, *The Negro in Our History* (1922, and later editions).

WOODWARD, AUGUSTUS BREVOORT (*b. New York, N.Y., 1774; d. Tallahassee, Fla., 1827*), jurist, political philosopher. Graduated Columbia, 1793. Active in incorporation of city of Washington, 1801–02; was member of its first council. A judge of Michigan Territory, 1805–24, Woodward was the dominant figure in the Michigan court and legislature. He prepared a plan for rebuilding the city of Detroit and compiled *The Laws of Michigan* (1806), known as "The Woodward Code." His *A System of Universal Science* (1816) contained the idea (expanded in 1817 in a legislative act written by him) of the "Catholepistemiad, or University, of Michigania" (University of Michigan). In 1824 he was appointed to a Florida federal court, where he served until his death. He was a friend and admirer of Thomas Jefferson. Author of, among other works, *Considerations on the Executive Governments of the United States of America* (1809).

WOODWARD, CALVIN MILTON (*b. near Fitchburg, Mass., 1837; d. St. Louis, Mo., 1914*), educator. Graduated Harvard, 1860. Taught geometry at Washington University, St. Louis, Mo.; was dean of its polytechnic school, 1870–96 and 1901–10, and Thayer professor of mathematics and applied mechanics. He accomplished his most important work, however, as originator and director of the St. Louis Manual Training School (opened 1880), which served as model for similar schools in other cities. Author of, among other works, *Manual Training in Education* (1890).

WOODWARD, HENRY (*b. possibly Barbados, British West Indies, ca. 1646; d. ca. 1686*), surgeon, first English settler in South Carolina and a pioneer of English expansion in the lower South. Joined Carolina settlement near Cape Fear, 1664; explored Port Royal, 1666. Acquired important information concerning Indians on northern Florida border and Spaniards in Florida, while a prisoner at St. Augustine. Interpreter and Indian agent with Carolina fleet of 1669–70. On mission to open the interior Indian trade for the earl of Shaftesbury, 1674, he effected an alliance with the Westo on the Savannah River. Later he pressed the Carolina trading frontier westward to the towns of the Lower Creek on middle Chattahoochee. By 1686 Woodward had laid a firm foundation for English alliance with the Lower Creek.

WOODWARD, JOSEPH JANVIER (*b. Philadelphia, Pa., 1833; d. Wawa, Pa., 1884*), army medical officer. M.D., University of Pennsylvania, 1853. Practiced in Philadelphia, Surgeon with Army of the Potomac, 1861–62; then assigned to surgeon general's office, Washington, D.C. Prepared medical section of the *Medical and Surgical History of the War of the Rebellion* (1870–88). He was among first to apply photomicrography to use in pathology and was instrumental in improving the photomicrographic camera. Attended President James A. Garfield between his shooting and death, 1881.

WOODWARD, ROBERT SIMPSON (*b. Rochester, Mich., 1849; d. Washington, D.C., 1924*), engineer, mathematical physicist. C.E., University of Michigan, 1872. Chief geographer, U.S. Geological Survey *post* 1884. Wrote important papers of a geophysical nature on deformations of the earth's surface and on secular cooling of the earth. Put field methods for topographic mapping and primary and secondary triangulation on practical engineering basis. Developed iced-bar apparatus for measuring baselines and for calibrating steel tapes and was first to prove baselines could be measured with sufficient accuracy by means of long steel tapes. Appointed professor of mechanics and mathematical physics, Columbia University, 1893, he shortly thereafter became dean of its College of Pure Science. President, Carnegie Institution of Washington, 1904–20. He was an editor of *Science*, 1884–1924.

WOODWARD, SAMUEL BAYARD (*b. Torrington, Conn., 1787; d. Northampton, Mass., 1850*), mental disease expert. Instrumental in founding Connecticut Retreat for the Insane, Hartford, 1824. Served as superintendent, Massachusetts State Lunatic Asylum, Worcester, 1832–46. Founder and first president, Association of Medical Superintendents of American Institutions for the Insane (American Psychiatric Association).

WOODWARD, WILLIAM (*b. New York, N.Y., 1876; d. New York, 1953*), banker and horseman. Graduated from Harvard Law School, 1901. Joined the Hanover Bank in New York in 1903; vice president, 1904; president, 1910. When the Hanover became the Central Hanover Bank and Trust Company in 1929, Woodward served as chairman of the board until 1933. Owner of the Belair stud farm in Maryland, he bred ninety-two winners of major American stakes races, including two winners of the "Triple Crown," Gallant Fox (1930), Omaha (1935), and the famed Nashua. Active also in British racing, he was a prominent figure in the racing world.

WOODWORTH, JAY BACKUS (*b. Newfield, N.Y., 1865; d. Cambridge, Mass., 1925*), geologist. Studied under Nathaniel S. Shaler at Lawrence Scientific School. B.A., Harvard, 1894, where he served as associate professor of geology, 1912 until his death. He was also assistant geologist, U.S. Geological Survey. Woodworth was a pioneer of seismological studies in relation to geology. He was founder and director of the Harvard seismological station, one of the first in America, 1908–25.

WOODWORTH, SAMUEL (*b. Scituate, Mass., 1784; d. 1842*), printer, journalist, poet. Apprenticed to Benjamin Russell in Boston, Mass., 1800–06. After brief residences in New Haven, Conn., and Baltimore, Md., he settled in New York City, 1809. Engaged throughout his life in a great number of journalistic and literary pursuits, he is remembered principally as the author of "The Bucket" ("The Old Oaken Bucket"). A frequent contributor of poetry to the periodical press over the signature "Selim," he was author of three satires—*New-Haven* (1809), *Beasts at Law* (1811), and *Quarter-Day* (1812)—and of a number of plays, which included the long-popular *The Forest Rose* (1825).

WOOL, JOHN ELLIS (*b. Newburgh, N.Y., 1784; d. Troy, N.Y., 1869*), soldier. Raising a company of volunteers in Troy, N.Y., at the outbreak of the War of 1812, he served in the northern campaigns with gallantry and received the brevet of lieutenant colonel, September 1814, for his conduct at the battle of Plattsburgh, N.Y. Promoted colonel and inspector general of the army, April 1816, he remained in this grade until 1841 when he was promoted brigadier general. After mustering in about 12,000 volunteers at Cincinnati, Ohio, 1846, for service in the war with Mexico, he went to San Antonio, Tex., in August to lead a new command on a march through Chihuahua. Starting thence with a spiritless force of some 1,400 men in September, he crossed 900 miles of hostile country and arrived in Saltillo on Dec. 22. His efficiency and speed of movement were largely responsible for the American victory of Buena Vista; he selected the position and held the Mexicans while General Zachary Taylor went back to Saltillo. He later commanded the Eastern Military Division and the Department of the Pacific. At the opening of the Civil War he saved Fortress Monroe by timely reinforcements. Promoted major general, 1862, he commanded the Middle Department and the Department of the East until his retirement, 1863.

WOOLEY, EDGAR MONTILLION ("MONTY") (*b. New York, N.Y., 1888; d. Saratoga Springs, N.Y., 1963*), director and actor. Graduated Yale (1911) and became drama coach there (1914–17) and assistant professor of drama (1919). His first Broadway success was directing Cole Porter's *Fifty Million Frenchmen* (1920). In the mid-1930's he played numerous bit parts in films, including *Night and Day* (1946). His main claim to fame resulted from his role in the play (1939) and film (1942) of *The Man Who Came to Dinner*. Received an Oscar nomination for best actor for *The Pied Piper* (1942) and for best supporting actor for *Since You Went Away* (1944).

WOOLF, BENJAMIN EDWARD (*b. London, England, 1836; d. Boston, Mass., 1901*), musician, composer, music critic. Came to America as a child. Joined editorial staff of the *Saturday Evening Gazette*, Boston, Mass., 1871; became publisher and editor, 1892. As music critic of the *Boston Herald*, he was noted for the clarity and severity of his reviews. Author of once-popular plays and light operas, including *Pounce & Co., or Capital vs. Labor* (1882).

WOOLLCOTT, ALEXANDER HUMPHREYS (*b. near Red Bank, N.J., 1887; d. New York, N.Y., 1943*), author, dramatic critic, radio commentator. Ph.B., Hamilton College, 1909. A talented reporter on the *New York Times*, he was made the paper's dramatic critic, 1914; his column, "Second Thoughts on First Nights," was soon popular, and a dispute with the Shubert brothers made him a celebrity. Enlisting in the U.S. Army, 1917, he served in France as a hospital orderly; later, transferred to Paris, he wrote for the service newspaper, *Stars and Stripes*. He resumed his place on the *Times* in the summer of 1919, moved to the *New York Herald*, 1922, and, after a brief period with the New York *Sun*, was critic for the New York *World*, 1925–28. In the 1920's he was one of the wits who made up the famous "Roundtable" at New York's Algonquin Hotel. He turned then to free-lance writing for leading magazines, and in September 1929 made his debut as a radio commentator; *post* 1937, he became known from coast to coast as "The Town Crier." Playing a role obviously modeled on himself, he toured in the Pacific Coast company of *The Man Who Came to Dinner* (1939), by George S. Kaufman and Moss Hart. Despite failing health *post* 1940, he remained active, especially in support of the Allied cause in World War II. Arbitrary, subjective, and given to romantic sentimentality as a critic, he was a gifted maker of phrases who made and broke reputations. His calculated poses and passion for celebrity obscured his native qualities of generosity, patriotism, loyalty, and industry.

WOOLLEY, CELIA PARKER (*b. Toledo, Ohio, 1848; d. Chicago, Ill., 1918*), settlement worker, author. Ordained into the Unitarian fellowship, 1894; held Illinois pastorates. Established and lived in Frederick Douglass Center, a black settlement on Chicago's South Side, 1904–18. Associated with *Unity*, a Chicago religious weekly, *post* 1884. Active in Chicago's cultural and social service circles.

WOOLLEY, JOHN GRANVILLE (*b. Collinsville, Ohio, 1850; d. Spain, 1922*), prohibitionist, lawyer. Active in prohibition movement *post* 1888 as lecturer and editor; Prohibition party presidential candidate, 1900.

WOOLLEY, MARY EMMA (*b. South Norwalk, Conn., 1863; d. West Port, N.Y., 1947*), educator, advocate of woman's rights and world peace. Graduated Wheaton Seminary, 1884. B.A., Brown University, 1894; M.A., 1895. Taught biblical history and literature at Wellesley College, 1895–1900. President of Mount Holyoke College, 1901–37.

WOOLMAN, COLLETT EVERMAN (*b. Bloomington, Ind., 1889; d. Houston, Tex., 1966*), airline executive. Studied at the University of Illinois (B.S., 1912), then worked for the Louisiana State Extension Service. In 1925 he joined the Huff Daland aircraft manufacturing company to sell its crop-dusting services to planters. In 1928 he purchased Huff Daland's dusting operation and founded an independent dusting company, Delta Air Service. The parent company of Delta Air Lines, this firm added passenger service in 1929. Woolman moved Delta's headquarters to Atlanta in 1941, acquired some Douglas DC-3 airplanes, and began a long series of new route acquisitions. Delta pioneered in the operation of such jet aircraft as the DC-8 in 1959 and the DC-9 in 1964.

WOOLMAN, JOHN (*b. Rancocas, West Jersey, 1720; d. York, England, 1772*), tailor, teacher, Quaker leader. Called to the Quaker ministry *ca.* 1743, he embarked on a 30-year series of journeys from North Carolina to New Hampshire and from the northern frontier of Pennsylvania to Yorkshire, England. His ministry was concerned principally with the abolition of slavery; he visited especially the slave-trade centers such as Perth Amboy and Newport. Woolman's writings include his celebrated *Journal* (1774), which won the praise of Charles Lamb, W. E. Channing, and others, and an essay, *Some Considerations on the Keeping of Negroes* (1754).

WOOLSEY, JOHN MUNRO (*b. Aiken, S.C., 1877; d. New York, N.Y., 1945*), jurist. Grandnephew of Theodore Dwight Woolsey. Graduated Yale, 1898. LL.B., Columbia Law School, 1901. Practiced principally admiralty law in New York City until 1929; U.S. district court judge, Southern District of New York, 1929–43. Respected in his profession for his grasp of detail and economy of expression when ruling, he became known to the general public for his decisions permitting the importation of books by Marie C. Stopes, 1931, and the publication and free circulation of James Joyce's *Ulysses*, 1933.

WOOLSEY, MELANCTHON TAYLOR (*b. New York State, 1780; d. Utica, N.Y., 1838*), naval officer. Nephew of John H. Livingston. Entered navy as midshipman, 1800. Served on Great Lakes, 1808–25. In War of 1812 commanded at Sacketts Harbor, and was second in command under Isaac Chauncey. In charge of Pensacola navy yard, 1826–30; commanded Brazil Squadron as commodore, 1832–34.

WOOLSEY, SARAH CHAUNCY (*b. Cleveland, Ohio, 1835; d. 1905*), author. Niece of Theodore D. Woolsey. Wrote under pseudonym "Susan Coolidge." Chiefly remembered as a popular writer of stories for young people; among these are *What Katy Did* (1872), *A Little Country Girl* (1885), and *An Old Convent School in Paris and Other Papers* (1895). Edited, among others, *The Diary and Letters of Frances Burney* (1880) and *Letters of Jane Austen* (1892).

WOOLSEY, THEODORE DWIGHT (*b. New York, N.Y., 1801; d. 1889*), educator, political scientist. Father of Theodore S. Woolsey. Connected by blood with the Dwight and Edwards families (nephew of Theodore Dwight, 1764–1846), he graduated from Yale in 1820. After making theological studies at both Princeton and Yale, he went abroad for further study at Paris, Leipzig, Bonn, and Berlin. Accepting the chair of Greek language and literature at Yale, 1831, he was notably successful as a teacher and as a writer of superior textbooks in his field. Called to the presidency of Yale, 1846, he served until 1871; during his time Yale made greater progress than in any similar period theretofore. Subsequent to his acceptance of the presidency, he had given up teaching Greek and begun giving instruction in history, political science, and international law. He became a recognized authority in the last two subjects both at home and abroad, and was the author of, among other works, the celebrated *Introduction to the Study of International Law* (1860 and many subsequent editions) and *Political Science* (1878). A scholar of extensive and accurate knowledge, he was also a clear-visioned and effective administrator; his dignity and reserve, however, tended to keep people at a distance.

WOOLSEY, THEODORE SALISBURY (*b. New Haven, Conn., 1852; d. New Haven, 1929*), educator. Son of Theodore D. Woolsey. Graduated Yale, 1872; LL.B., Yale Law School, 1876. Professor of international law, Yale Law School, 1878–1911, except for 1886–90. Author of, among other writings, *America's Foreign Policy* (1898).

WOOLSON, ABBA LOUISA GOOLD (*b. Windham, Maine, 1838; d. Maine, 1921*), writer. Held several teaching positions, including professorship of belles lettres at Mount Auburn Ladies' Institute, Cincinnati, Ohio. Lectured on English literature. Author of, among other books, *Woman in American Society* (1873), with a foreword by her personal friend John G. Whittier.

WOOLSON, CONSTANCE FENIMORE (*b. Claremont, N.H., 1840; d. Venice, Italy, 1894*), author. Grandniece of James Fenimore Cooper. Raised in Cleveland, Ohio. During trips as a young girl through Ohio, Wisconsin, and Mackinac Island, she acquired a thorough knowledge of the lake region. She later traveled widely on the Atlantic seaboard and lived in the Carolinas and Florida, 1873–79. She resided in Europe *post* 1879. Author of, among other regional works, *Castle Nowhere: Lake Country Sketches* (1875); *Rodman the Keeper: Southern Sketches* (1880); *East Angels* (1886); *Jupiter Lights* (1889); and *Horace Chase* (1894). *For the Major* (1883), in many respects her best novel, is a comparatively unlocalized account of village life in the eastern Appalachians. Her collections of European stories, *The Front Yard* (1895) and *Dorothy* (1896), are accounts of Americans projected against the background of an older civilization, in the manner of her friend and critic Henry James.

WOOLWORTH, FRANK WINFIELD (*b. Rodman, N.Y., 1852; d. 1919*), merchant. After a succession of business failures, he opened a prosperous store in Lancaster, Pa., 1879, featuring an array of goods at the fixed prices of five and ten cents. Establishing other stores and absorbing chains of stores run by competitors, he built up the F. W. Woolworth Co. He strove constantly to add articles to his line and to offer at his low price goods which had never been sold at such a figure before; this policy was a principal factor in his success.

WOOSTER, CHARLES WHITING (*b. New Haven, Conn., 1780; d. San Francisco, Calif., 1848*), merchant mariner, War of 1812 privateer, Chilean navy commander in chief, 1822–35. Grandson of David Wooster.

WOOSTER, DAVID (*b. present Huntington, Conn., 1711; d. Connecticut, 1777*), merchant, Revolutionary brigadier general. A practical soldier in the colonial wars *post* 1745, he was appointed a major general of six regiments and colonel of the 1st Regiment by the Connecticut Assembly in 1775. He was made a Continental brigadier general, June 1775. As ranking officer in Canada after General Richard Montgomery's death, he was unsuccessful and was superseded by General John Thomas. Reappointed major general of Connecticut militia in the fall of 1776, he was mortally wounded in the defense of Ridgefield, Conn., during Tryon's raid on Danbury, April 1777.

WOOTASSITE. *See* OUTACITY.

WOOTTON, RICHENS LACY (*b. Mecklenburg Co., Va., 1816; d. near Trinidad, Colo., 1893*), trapper, pioneer settler. Raised in Kentucky. Traded and trapped in almost every section of the western fur country, 1836–40; ranched and traded on site of present Pueblo, Colo. *post* 1841. Helped suppress Taos insurrection and participated in battle of Sacramento, 1847. Served as scout with Col. A. W. Doniphan on Chihuahua expedition and with other army expeditions; engaged in freighting. Perhaps best known for building in 1865 a 27-mile road over the roughest portion of the Santa Fe Trail mountain division from Trinidad, Colo., across Raton Pass and down to the Canadian River.

WORCESTER, EDWIN DEAN (*b. Albany, N.Y., 1828; d. New York, N.Y., 1904*), railroad official. Employed by Erastus Corning as chief accountant of the newly consolidated New York Central, 1853, Worcester was associated with that road and its subsequent expansion under the Vanderbilts until his death.

WORCESTER, ELWOOD (*b. Massillon, Ohio, 1862; d. Kennebunkport, Maine, 1940*), Episcopal clergyman. Graduated Columbia, 1886; General Theological Seminary, New York, 1887; Ph.D., Leipzig, 1889. After teaching at Lehigh University and a pastorate in Philadelphia, Pa., he was called to Emmanuel Church, Boston, Mass., 1904, where with the cooperation of physicians he pioneered in the Christian application of psychotherapy, developing what became known as the Emmanuel Movement.

WORCESTER, JOSEPH EMERSON (*b. Bedford, N.H., 1784; d. Cambridge, Mass., 1865*), lexicographer, geographer, historian. Nephew of Noah and Samuel Worcester. Graduated Yale, 1811. From 1817 to 1826, he published geographical gazetteers and works on geography and history used extensively as textbooks. Compiler of, among other dictionaries, the *Comprehensive Pronouncing and Explanatory Dictionary of the English Language* (1830, 1847, 1849; issued in 1855 as *A Pronouncing, Explanatory, and Synonymous Dictionary of the English Language*), containing his linguistic contribution of the "compromise vowel." This work evoked Noah Webster's charge of plagiarism, which Worcester refuted, and initiated the "War of the Dictionaries." In 1831 he assumed an 11-year editorship of *The American Almanac and Repository of Useful Knowledge*. His illustrated quarto *A Dictionary of the English Language* (1860) was the most elaborate and important of all his works. A conservative in lexicography, Worcester held closely to British usage.

WORCESTER, NOAH (*b. Hollis, N.H., 1758; d. Brighton, Mass., 1837*), Congregational and Unitarian clergyman. Brother of Samuel Worcester. Minister of the church at Thornton, N.H., 1787–1810. Editor, *Christian Disciple* (later *Christian Examiner*), 1813–18. His most important contribution was in the promotion of peace; he established and conducted *The Friend of Peace*, 1819–28, and wrote, among other works, *A Solemn Review of the Custom of War* (1814).

WORCESTER, SAMUEL (*b. Hollis, N.H., 1770; d. Brainerd, Tenn., 1821*), Congregational clergyman. Brother of Noah Worcester. Graduated Dartmouth, 1795. Pastor at Fitchburg, Mass., 1797–1802. An inflexible Hopkinsian Calvinist, he was dismissed from his pastorate and became pastor of Tabernacle Church, Salem, Mass., 1803. Involved in famous controversy with William Ellery Channing (1780–1842), 1815. Was a founder, 1810, and corresponding secretary of the American Board of Commissioners for Foreign Missions.

WORCESTER, SAMUEL AUSTIN (*b. Worcester, Mass., 1798; d. present Oklahoma, 1859*), Congregational clergyman. Nephew of Noah and Samuel Worcester, and of Samuel Austin. Graduated Andover Theological Seminary, 1823. Missionary to the Cherokee *post* 1825 in Tennessee and at New Echota, Ga.; translated portions of the Bible into Cherokee; and helped found the *Cherokee Phoenix*. Imprisoned by Georgia, 1831–33, for refusal to quit his mission. Began establishment of important Cherokee Park Hill Mission in Indian Territory, 1835; set up first printing press there. Urged adoption by Cherokee of written language invented by Sequoyah.

WORDEN, JOHN LORIMER (*b. Westchester Co., N.Y., 1818; d. Washington, D.C., 1897*), naval officer. Appointed midshipman, 1834. Commanded original *Monitor* in battle with CSS *Merrimack*, March 9, 1862, gaining national renown and promotion to captain, 1863. Commanded monitor *Montauk*, South Atlantic Blockading Squadron, October 1862–April 1863. Made rear admiral, 1872. Superintendent, U.S. Naval Academy, 1869–74, he commanded European Squadron, 1875–77. Retired, 1886.

WORK, HENRY CLAY (*b. Middletown, Conn., 1832, d. Hartford, Conn., 1884*), printer, songwriter. Wrote famous temperance song "Come Home, Father" in 1864; was author, among other Civil War songs, of "Kingdom Coming" (1861), "Babylon Is Fallen!" (1863), "Wake Nicodemus" (1864), and "Marching Through Georgia" (1865). Later, among many other successes, he composed "Grandfather's Clock."

WORK, HUBERT (*b. Marion Center, Pa., 1860; d. Denver, Colo., 1942*), physician, cabinet officer. M.D., University of Pennsylvania, 1885. Practiced in Greeley, Fort Morgan, and Pueblo, Colo. Active in Republican politics, and a member of the party's national committee, 1913–19, he was appointed first assistant postmaster general, 1921. In March 1922, he became postmaster general and instituted more-efficient management methods. Inheriting a department under attack as both corrupt and inefficient, when he took over as U.S. secretary of the interior in March 1923, he centralized its activities, brought in new employees from the business world, and served notice that he was fully in support of the conservation of all natural resources. He reorganized the Reclamation Service and made improvements in the Bureau of Indian Affairs, stressing benefits for the Indians and requesting a broad resurvey of federal Indian policy. He left the Interior Department in July 1928 to direct the successful presidential campaign of Herbert Hoover.

WORK, MILTON COOPER (*b. Philadelphia, Pa., 1864; d. 1934*), lawyer, auction and contract bridge expert. Abandoned

Philadelphia law practice, 1917, for bridge lectures and demonstrations; associated with Wilbur C. Whitehead in radio bridge games, 1925–30, and as an editor, *Auction Bridge Magazine*. Developed "artificial two-club game-demand" bid. Author of *Auction Developments* (1913) and other books.

WORKMAN, FANNY BULLOCK (*b. Worcester, Mass., 1859; d. Cannes, France, 1925*), explorer. On expedition to the Himalayas and Karakoram (or Mustagh) Range, she achieved the women's world mountaineering record, 1906. Her books of geographical value include *Algerian Memories* (1895), *Sketches Awheel in Modern Iberia* (1897), *Peaks and Glaciers of Nun Kun* (1909), and *The Call of the Snowy Hispar* (1910).

WORMELEY, KATHARINE PRESCOTT (*b. Ipswich, England, 1830; d. Jackson, N.H., 1908*), author, translator, philanthropist. Sister of Mary E. W. Latimer. Came to America *ca.* 1848. Best known for translations of noted French writers, particularly *The Works of Balzac* (1899–); among her other translations are *Letters of Mlle. de Lespinasse* (1901) and Sainte-Beuve's *Portraits of the Eighteenth Century* (1905). Author of *The Other Side of War* (1889) and *Memoir of Honoré de Balzac* (1892).

WORMELEY, MARY ELIZABETH. *See* LATIMER, MARY ELIZABETH WORMELEY.

WORMLEY, JAMES (*b. Washington, D.C., 1819; d. Boston, Mass., 1884*), hotel keeper. Of free black parentage. Steward for the Metropolitan Club, Washington, D.C., *post ca.* 1853; established Wormley's hotel and catering service in Washington *ca.* 1860; won national reputation for cuisine.

WORMLEY, THEODORE GEORGE (*b. Wormleysburg, Pa., 1826; d. 1897*), physician, toxicologist. M.D., Philadelphia College of Medicine, 1849. Professor of toxicology at Capitol University, Columbus, Ohio, 1852–63; at Starling Medical College, Columbus, 1852–77. Held chair of chemistry and toxicology, medical department, University of Pennsylvania *post* 1877. Author of *The Micro-chemistry of Poisons* (1867).

WORTH, JONATHAN (*b. Guilford Co., N.C., 1802; d. Raleigh, N.C., 1869*), lawyer, businessman, North Carolina official and legislator. Studied law under Archibald D. Murphey; began practice at Asheboro, N.C., 1824. In the North Carolina legislature, 1831, he protested nullification, but opposed the Jackson administration later and became a Whig; he opposed the secession movement in the legislature, 1860. Elected state treasurer, 1862, he served until 1865. As governor of North Carolina, 1865–68, he displayed tact and sound judgment. He supported President Johnson and ratification of the new state constitution submitted in 1866; he opposed ratification of the 14th Amendment.

WORTH, WILLIAM JENKINS (*b. Hudson, N.Y., 1794; d. Tex., 1849*), soldier. Commissioned first lieutenant, 23rd Infantry, March 1813, he became aide-de-camp to General Winfield Scott and was commended for bravery at the battles of Chippewa and Lundy's Lane. Remaining in the army after the War of 1812, he served in the artillery and in the Ordnance Department; he was commandant of cadets at West Point, 1820–28. As colonel of the 8th Infantry, he commanded in Florida against the Seminole, 1838, defeating them at the battle of Palaklaklaha. Ordered to join General Zachary Taylor in the Army of Occupation prior to the war with Mexico, he took part in a controversy over rank with General David E. Twiggs. A great part of the credit for victory at Monterey belongs to his successful storming of the heights. Receiving the brevet of major general, he joined General Winfield Scott's army and took part in all the engagements from Veracruz to Mexico City. Narrow and self-centered, he damaged his reputa-

tion subsequent to the victory by engaging in intrigues against General Scott who had been his benefactor.

WORTHEN, AMOS HENRY (*b. Bradford, Vt., 1813; d. 1888*), businessman, geologist. Appointed Illinois state geologist, 1858; published seven volumes of *Geological Survey of Illinois* (1866–90). Worthen was a pioneer in classification of the Lower Carboniferous strata.

WORTHEN, WILLIAM EZRA (*b. Amesbury, Mass., 1819; d. 1897*), civil engineer. Graduated Harvard, 1838. Assisted in water supply and hydraulic work in offices of the younger Loammi Baldwin and James B. Francis. Employed by George W. Whistler on Albany & West Stockbridge Railroad. Settled in New York, 1849, engaging in building and mill construction. Worthen was an expert on pumping machinery and drainage; he held many important consultative posts.

WORTHINGTON, HENRY ROSSITER (*b. New York, N.Y., 1817; d. 1880*), hydraulic engineer, inventor. Patented improvements in canal-boat navigation and pumping engines. First proposer and constructor of the direct steam pump, he perfected an ingenious, widely used duplex steam feed pump, 1859, and built the first waterworks engine of this kind, 1860. He also developed a pumping engine that needed no flywheel to carry the piston past the dead point at the end of a stroke.

WORTHINGTON, JOHN (*b. Springfield, Mass., 1719; d. 1800*), lawyer, politician. Father-in-law of Jonathan Bliss and Fisher Ames. For many years king's attorney in western Massachusetts, he was a noted land speculator and was responsible for settlement of Worthington, Mass., 1768. Political dictator of Springfield, Mass., he was its representative in the Massachusetts General Court almost continuously, 1747–74; his conservatism then ended his influence in colony affairs.

WORTHINGTON, THOMAS (*b. near Charleston, Va., now W.Va., 1773; d. New York, N.Y., 1827*), surveyor, Ohio legislator. Brother-in-law of Edward Tiffin. A leader of the "Chillicothe Junto," which secured Ohio's statehood and the triumph of Jeffersonianism there. U.S. senator from Ohio, 1803–07 and 1811–14, he was influential in matters concerning public lands and the Indian frontier. As governor of Ohio, 1814–18, he suggested social reforms and was responsible for founding the state library.

WOVOKA (*b. near Walker Lake, Nev. ca. 1856; d. 1932*), Indian mystic. A Paiute, he founded the Ghost Dance religion, which swept the Indian country and became important to the white man's political economy during the Messiah agitation of 1890.

WOYTINSKY, WLADIMIR SAVELIEVICH (*b. St. Petersburg, Russia, 1885; d. Washington D.C., 1960*), statistician, economist, public official. Studied at the University of St. Petersburg (1904–08). In 1917 he and his wife Emma fled to Tiflis, Georgia, because of conflicts with the Bolshevik regime. Moved to Berlin, Germany, in 1922, where Woytinsky wrote *Die Welt in Zahlen* (1924–28), a seven-volume set of statistics on the world. As a statistician for German labor unions, he was forced to flee with the rise of Hitler. Immigrated in 1935 to the United States, where he worked for the Central Statistical Board in Washington; also researched for the Social Security Board. His idea of a pay-as-you-go basis for social security was adopted by the government. From 1947 the Woytinskys did research for the Twentieth Century Fund in New York City.

WRAGG, WILLIAM (*b. probably Charlestown, S.C., 1714; d. off coast of the Netherlands, 1777*), lawyer, planter, South Carolina public official. Father-in-law of John Mathews and William L. Smith. Inheritor of the Wragg barony, he was a Loyalist leader; as a member of the South Carolina Assembly, 1763–68; he alone voted against approving action of Stamp Act Congress, 1766. He was a nonsubscriber to the nonimportation agreement, 1769. Banished from the colony, 1777.

WRATHER, WILLIAM EMBRY (*b. Meade County, Ky., 1883; d. Washington, D.C., 1963*), petroleum geologist and federal official. Attended University of Chicago (Ph.D., 1908). Worked for Gulf Oil until 1916, when he became an independent consultant, entering into a partnership with Michael Benedum, a wildcatter, that led to the discovery of the Desdemona field (1918) and the Nigger Creek field (1926). His consulting work was largely the valuation of oil properties for the Internal Revenue Service and investors. He supported the running of each field as a unit to maximize its producing life, contrary to the wasteful practice of the time. Founder (1916) and president (1922–23) of the American Association of Petroleum Geologists and president of the Society of Economic Geologists (1934) and American Institute of Mining and Metallurgical Engineers (1948). Director of the U.S. Geological Survey (1943–56).

WRAXALL, PETER (*b. probably Bristol, England, date unknown; d. New York, N.Y., 1759*), soldier. Came to New York *ante* 1746. Secretary for Indian affairs, New York province, *post* 1752; aide to Sir William Johnson. Author of an outstanding survey of the Indian question, 1755–56 (published in E. B. O'Callaghan, *Documents Relative . . . State of New York*, Vol. 7, 1856).

WRIGHT, BENJAMIN (*b. Wethersfield, Conn., 1770; d. New York, N.Y., 1842*), surveyor, engineer, New York legislator. Senior engineer of the Erie Canal, Wright was in charge of construction of the canal's middle section *post* 1816, and later of its eastern division as well. An able executive, he gathered around him such associates as Canvass White, John B. Jervis, and Nathan S. Roberts. Resigning as the Erie's chief engineer, 1827, Wright was chief engineer of the Chesapeake & Ohio Canal, 1828–31, and of the St. Lawrence Canal, 1833. He was consulting engineer on a number of other canal and railroad projects.

WRIGHT, CARROLL DAVIDSON (*b. Dunbarton, N.H., 1840; d. Worcester, Mass., 1909*), statistician, social economist, public official, Massachusetts legislator. Chief, Massachusetts Bureau of Statistics of Labor, 1873–88. Organized National Convention of Chiefs and Commissioners of Bureaus of Statistics of Labor, 1883; served as president for practically 20 years. First commissioner, U.S. Bureau of Labor, 1885–1905. Chairman, Pullman strike commission, 1894; recorder, anthracite strike commission, 1902. He was also honorary professor of social economics, Catholic University, Washington, D.C., 1895–1904; professor of statistics and social economics, Columbian (later George Washington) University, *post* 1900. Wright was president of the American Statistical Association from 1897 until his death. In 1902 he was chosen first president of Clark College, Worcester, Mass. Author of, among other publications, *The Relation of Political Economy to the Labor Question* (1882) and *The Industrial Evolution of the United States* (1895).

WRIGHT, CHARLES (*b. Wethersfield, Conn., 1811; d. Wethersfield, 1885*), surveyor, teacher, botanical explorer. Graduated Yale, 1835. Initiated important correspondence with Asa Gray of Harvard, 1844, to whom he supplied specimens from the Southwest. Explored and collected in eastern Texas, 1837–45; from San Antonio to El Paso, 1849; in New Mexico and Arizona, 1851–52; and in Cuba, 1856–67. Discovered many new species, described in Gray's "*Plantae Wrightianae*," and in *Botany of the*

Mexican Boundary Survey (1859) and in other works. As botanist, North Pacific Exploring and Surveying Expedition, 1853–56, he made notable collections in China and Japan.

WRIGHT, CHARLES BARSTOW (*b. Wysox, Pa., 1822; d. Philadelphia, Pa., 1898*), financier. Prospered in real estate transactions in neighborhood of Chicago, Ill., 1843–46, and in Philadelphia banking thereafter. Entered directorship, Northern Pacific Railroad, 1870, and was a principal factor in its completion and eventual success. He served as its president, 1874–79.

WRIGHT, CHAUNCEY (*b. Northampton, Mass., 1830; d. 1875*), mathematician, philosopher. Graduated Harvard, 1852. Recording secretary, American Academy of Arts and Sciences, 1863–70. Began publication of a notable series of philosophical essays in the *North American Review*, 1864. Commended by Darwin for essays on arrangements of leaves in plants and genesis of species. A thoroughgoing naturalist, Wright dealt in his most valuable article, "Evolution of Self-Consciousness," with an instrumentalist conception of mental activities which anticipated later trends in thought. He was among the first to introduce methods of British empiricism to America.

WRIGHT, ELIZUR (*b. South Canaan, Conn., 1804; d. 1885*), reformer, actuary. Raised in Tallmadge, Ohio. Graduated Yale, 1826. While a professor at the Western Reserve College, he was enlisted in the antislavery cause by Theodore Weld and served *post* 1833 as secretary of the American Anti-Slavery Society. Resigning in 1839, he became editor of the *Massachusetts Abolitionist*, organ of the conservative opponents of William L. Garrison, but was soon dropped. Unsuccessful in several further attempts as editor of reforming journals, he became widely known as a critic of the financial methods of life insurance companies. Tables published by him enabled life insurance companies for the first time to formulate reserve policies which would render them stable, Wright then lobbied, 1853–58, in the Massachusetts legislature for a law to force all companies doing business in that state to maintain adequate reserves; subsequent to its passage, he was appointed state commissioner of insurance to oversee the new law's enforcement. His efforts at that time and subsequently probably had more to do with the development of sound standards for life insurance than those of any other man in the history of the industry. Ousted from his office in 1866, he became an actuary for several companies, but continued his lobbying for sound insurance legislation and was active in other reform movements.

WRIGHT, FIELDING LEWIS (*b. Rolling Fork, Miss., 1895; d. Rolling Fork, Miss., 1956*), politician and lawyer. Studied at the University of Alabama (LL.B.). Served in the Mississippi State Senate and legislature in 1928; elected lieutenant governor in 1943; became acting governor when Governor Thomas Bailey died in 1946; and won election to a full term in 1947. In the 1948 presidential campaign, he and J. Strom Thurmond formed the Dixiecrat party in opposition to the Truman Administration's civil rights platform. Wright ran for vice president, Thurmond for president; the Dixiecrats captured only thirty-nine electoral votes. Wright was defeated in a bid for the governorship in 1955.

WRIGHT, FRANCES (*b. Dundee, Scotland, 1795; d. 1852*), reformer, freethinker. Heiress to a large fortune, she early showed herself a difficult and rebellious child. At the age of 18 she wrote a work which contained in essence the materialistic philosophy that she followed throughout life, *A Few Days in Athens* (1822). Immigrating to New York City, 1818, she made a tour of the northern and eastern states; on her return to England in 1820 she composed her *Views of Society and Manners in America* (1821) which expressed an appreciation of America unusual at that time among Europeans. Returning to the United States, 1824, in company with the Marquis de Lafayette, she visited Thomas Jefferson and James Madison and won their approval for a plan of emancipation for black slaves which she had devised. Investing a large amount of her money in a tract in western Tennessee which she called Nashoba, she attempted to give a practical demonstration of her emancipation theory. Socialist associates within the colony, however, introduced the idea of free love, a point of view which public opinion attached wrongfully to Fanny Wright herself. Coeditor with Robert D. Owen of the *New Harmony Gazette*, she further shocked public sensibilities by appearing as a lecturer in public, attacking religion, the existing system of education, the subjugation of women, and the current state of marriage. In 1829 she settled in New York City, where she published the *Free Enquirer*, also in association with Robert D. Owen. After traveling abroad *ca.* 1830–35, she returned to the United States and continued her writing and lecturing, taking up such causes as birth control and the more equal distribution of property. During her last years, she gave a great deal of time to propaganda for the abolition of the banking system. Frances Wright's fearlessness and initiative contributed to the emancipation of women, although her influence was exerted more by her example than by her doctrines.

WRIGHT, FRANK LLOYD (*b. Richland Center, Wis., 1867; d. Phoenix, Ariz., 1959*), architect. Studied at the University of Wisconsin. Acknowledged widely as one of history's most original, influential, and prolific architects, Wright was never formally trained in his art. From 1888 to 1893 worked as chief assistant to Louis H. Sullivan, the prominent, Chicago-based architect. Wright then became the leader of a group of local architects known as the Prairie School. It was during this period that he developed the principles that were to rule his work. The essence of these he called organic architecture, a concept of linking people to their surroundings, both natural and man-made, that, he felt, would lead to a democratic organic society. To achieve this, building materials should be used deliberately to show their character and methods of handling. Wright emphasized what he called plasticity, the potential of surfaces of materials—their textures and coloring used as ornamentation—which then are manipulated to mold space, not confine it. Such space was to flow in a continuous, organized way, and became the chief instrument of Wright's art. Of the over 1,000 works designed by Wright, some 400 were constructed.

WRIGHT, GEORGE (*b. New York, N.Y., 1847; d. Boston, Mass., 1937*), professional baseball player, sportsman, merchant. Brother of Henry Wright (1835–95). While shortstop of the Cincinnati Red Stockings, baseball's first professional team, 1869–71, he became the game's first home-run king, making 59 home runs in 52 games in 1869. He later played with Boston of the National League and with Providence. In 1871 he opened a Boston sporting goods store which became Wright & Ditson; he introduced the game of golf in Boston, 1890.

WRIGHT, GEORGE FREDERICK (*b. Whitehall, N.Y., 1838; d. 1921*), geologist, Congregational clergyman. Graduated Oberlin, 1859; Oberlin Theological Seminary, 1862. Held Vermont and Massachusetts pastorates, 1862–81. Presented theory of glacial origin of New England gravel ridges, 1875 and 1876. An expert in glacial geology, he made the first scientific study of Muir Glacier, Alaska, 1886. Professor New Testament language and literature at Oberlin, 1881–92; held chair of harmony of science and religion there, 1892–1907. Editor, *Bibliotheca Sacra*, 1883–1921. Author of, among other works, *The Ice Age in North America* (1889).

WRIGHT, GEORGE GROVER (*b. Bloomington, Ind., 1820; d. 1896*), jurist. Brother of Joseph A. Wright. Chief justice, Iowa

Supreme Court, 1855–70. Rigorous in basing decisions on principles, he was a dominant influence on the new state's jurisprudence and formulated Iowa interpretations of domestic relations, libel, contracts, and procedure. As U.S. senator from Iowa, 1871–77, he favored "soft" money and opposed the liquor traffic.

WRIGHT, HAMILTON KEMP (*b. Cleveland, Ohio, 1867; d. Washington, D.C., 1917*), medical scientist. Graduated in medicine, McGill University, Canada, 1895. Worked in neuropathology at Cambridge University; studied at Heidelberg and other continental universities, 1897–98. Established and directed Kuala Lumpur beriberi research laboratory, Straits Settlements, 1899–1903; materially advanced knowledge of beriberi and concluded food was an agent in its transmission. Engaged in research at Johns Hopkins and at various places in the United States and Europe, 1903–08. Appointed to International Opium Commission, 1908; chairman of American delegation, International Opium Conferences, The Hague, 1911 and 1913; was instrumental in preparation of the Harrison Narcotic Law and other federal legislation for drug control.

WRIGHT, HAROLD BELL (*b. near Rome, N.Y., 1872; d. La Jolla, Calif., 1944*), novelist. A minister of the Christian Church (Disciples), 1897–1908, he devoted full time thereafter to writing novels in the hope that he might thereby impress a wider public with his message of simple living according to Christian principles. The 19 books which he published during his lifetime sold more than 10 million copies, although they won no praise from literary critics. Among them were *That Printer of Udell's* (1903); *The Shepherd of the Hills* (1907); *The Calling of Dan Matthews* (1909); and *The Winning of Barbara Worth* (1911).

WRIGHT, HENDRICK BRADLEY (*b. Plymouth, Pa., 1808; d. 1881*), lawyer, Pennsylvania legislator. Chairman, Democratic National Convention, Baltimore, Md., 1844. Congressman, Democrat, from Pennsylvania, 1853–55, 1861–63, and 1877–81. Nominated by the Democrats in 1876 and 1878, his election was due largely to labor and Greenback support. His career was a triumph of demagoguery.

WRIGHT, HENRY (*b. Sheffield, England, 1835; d. Atlantic City, N.J., 1895*), professional baseball player. Came to America as an infant. Brother of George Wright. Organizer, manager, captain, and center fielder of the Cincinnati Red Stockings, first full professional baseball team, 1869–71. Managed National League teams of Boston, 1876–81; Philadelphia, 1884–93; and others.

WRIGHT, HENRY (*b. Lawrence, Kans., 1878; d. Newton, N.J., 1936*), architect, landscape designer, community planner. Raised in Kansas City, Mo. Graduated University of Pennsylvania, 1901. Associated for a number of years with George E. Kessler, a pupil of Frederick L. Olmsted, Wright entered practice for himself in 1909. Carrying on the Olmsted tradition, he designed a number of subdivisions in the St. Louis, Ohio, area showing characteristic sensitivity to community needs and the integration of all necessary private and civic facilities into an orderly pattern. He was coplanner for the New York City Housing Corporation in creating Sunnyside Gardens in Queens County *post* 1923. He introduced even more radical innovations in the design of Radburn, N.J., 1928–29, among them a park at the core of each superblock, forming a broad river of green flowing through the community. Probably the finest example of his art as site planner was the second part of Chatham Village, Pittsburgh, Pa. He was author of a classic document, *A Plan for the State of New York* (1926), the first report of its kind in the United States. *Post* 1923 he persistently attacked the sterile character of zoning, with its tendency toward segregation and architectural monotony.

WRIGHT, HORATIO GOUVERNEUR (*b. Clinton, Conn.,
1820; d. Washington, D.C., 1899*), soldier, engineer. Graduated
West Point, 1841. Chief engineer at Bull Run of General S. P.
Heintzelman's division and later of the Port Royal expedition.
Promoted brigadier general of volunteers, September 1861; led
successful campaign in Florida, February 1862; appointed to
command Department of the Ohio, August 1862. Heading the 1st
Division of General John Sedgwick's VI Corps after May 1863, he
played an important part in the Mine Run campaign. Commissioned major general of volunteers, 1864, he took over the command of the VI Corps at Spotsylvania, fought the Wilderness
campaign, and repelled Confederate General Jubal Early's raid on
Washington, D.C., July 12, 1864. On Oct. 19, he commanded at
Cedar Creek until General P. H. Sheridan's arrival on the field.
Wright commanded the Department of Texas, 1865–66. *Post*
1866 he was engaged in important engineering projects, which
included the Sutro Tunnel, Nevada, and the completion of the
Washington Monument. Promoted through the grades to brigadier general, regular army, and chief of engineers, 1879, he
retired, 1884.

WRIGHT, JAMES LENDREW (*b. Co. Tyrone, Ireland, 1816; d.
Germantown, Pa., 1893*), tailor, labor leader. Came to America
as a boy. In 1862, with Uriah S. Stephens, organized the Garment
Cutters' Association and served as its president. Wright was also
treasurer and cofounder, 1863, of the Philadelphia Trades' Assembly. He was a founder, 1869, of the Noble Order of the Knights of
Labor, whose name he devised and of which he was a leading
functionary for over two decades.

WRIGHT, JOHN HENRY (*b. Urmia, Persia, 1852; d. Cambridge, Mass., 1908*), Hellenist. A.B., Dartmouth, 1873. Taught
at Ohio State, Dartmouth, and Johns Hopkins. Professor of Greek
at Harvard *post* 1887; dean, Harvard Graduate School *post* 1895.
Editor in chief, *American Journal of Archaeology*, 1897–1906;
coeditor, *Classical Review*, 1889–1906. Author of, among other
works, *Herondaea* (1893) and *The Origin of Plato's Cave* (1906).

WRIGHT, JOHN STEPHEN (*b. Sheffield, Mass., 1815; d. Philadelphia, Pa., 1874*), promoter, journalist. Settled in Chicago,
Ill., 1832, where he was successful as a real estate operator,
1834–36 and 1846–57. While owner and manager of the *Prairie
Farmer*, 1843–57, he promoted western industry and the advantages of Illinois and Chicago in his own paper and in articles for
eastern journals. In 1848 he lobbied for a Chicago–Gulf of
Mexico railroad. A leader in Illinois education, he built Chicago's
first public school building at his own expense, 1835.

WRIGHT, JONATHAN JASPER (*b. Luzerne Co., Pa., 1840; d.
Charleston, S.C., 1885*), educator, South Carolina legislator,
jurist. Attended Lancasterian University, Ithaca, N.Y.; was first
black admitted to the Pennsylvania bar, 1866. Associate justice of
the South Carolina Supreme Court, 1870–77, he was a center of
controversy in the South Carolina gubernatorial contest between
D. H. Chamberlain and Wade Hampton, 1876.

WRIGHT, JOSEPH (*b. Bordentown, N.J., 1756; d. Philadelphia, Pa., 1793*), portrait painter, die-sinker. Son of Patience L.
Wright, who taught him clay- and wax-modeling. Resident in
London, England, *ca.* 1772–82, he studied painting with John
Trumbull (1756–1843) and Benjamin West. By 1780 he was
exhibiting at the Royal Academy, London. Returning to America,
1783, he worked in New York and Philadelphia, executing,
among other works, portraits of George Washington, 1783, 1784,
and an etching from a sketch in 1790. Appointed first draftsman
and die-sinker, U.S. Mint, 1792, he probably designed the first
U.S. coins and medals.

WRIGHT, JOSEPH ALBERT (*b. Washington, Pa., 1810; d.
Berlin, Germany, 1867*), lawyer, Indiana legislator. Brother of
George G. Wright. Congressman, Democrat, from Indiana,
1843–45; governor of Indiana, December 1849–January 1857;
U.S. senator, February 1862–January 1863. U.S. minister to
Prussia, 1857–61, and from 1865 until his death. Wright, as
governor, directed most of his efforts to raising the standard of
living and the educational level of Indiana farmers.

WRIGHT, JOSEPH JEFFERSON BURR (*b. Wilkes-Barre, Pa.,
1801; d. Carlisle, Pa., 1878*), army medical officer. Appointed
assistant surgeon, U.S. Army, 1833. In a long and varied career of
field and staff duty, he was outstanding during the Mexican War.
He retired as colonel, 1876.

WRIGHT, LUKE EDWARD (*b. Giles Co., Tenn., 1846; d.
1922*), Confederate soldier, Tennessee lawyer. Became vice-governor of the Philippines in 1901, governor in 1904, and
governor general in 1905; a strong, competent executive. First
U.S. ambassador to Japan, 1906, U.S. secretary of war, 1908–09,
he was not retained in office by President W. H. Taft, a circumstance which is said to have contributed to the split between Taft
and Theodore Roosevelt.

WRIGHT, MARCUS JOSEPH (*b. Purdy, Tenn., 1831; d. Washington, D.C., 1922*), lawyer, Confederate brigadier general. U.S.
government agent for collection of Confederate archives,
1878–1917. Author of, among other works, *Tennessee in the War,
1861–1865* (1908) and *General Officers of the Confederate Army*
(1911).

WRIGHT, ORVILLE (*b. Dayton, Ohio, 1871; d. Dayton,
1948*), inventor, pioneer in aviation. Brother of Wilbur Wright. It
is impossible to consider the career of Orville Wright apart from
that of his brother Wilbur, four years his senior. The gift by their
father when they were children of a rubber-band-driven toy
hélicoptère had stirred their curiosity about the dynamics of flight,
but their mature attention was turned to the subject by the gliding
successes of the German engineer Otto Lilienthal. They began
with the problem of control in the air. Their control system was
successfully tested in a small kite-glider in July 1899, and they
decided to build a man-carrying glider the next year. As their test
grounds they chose the sand dunes and beaches near Kitty Hawk,
N.C., where they made thousands of experimental flights with a
series of gliders. In 1901 they built a wind tunnel in order to verify
and refine the ideas gained in practical gliding. From these data
they build a vastly more efficient glider in 1902. The culmination
of four and a half years of intensive thought and labor was attained
on Dec. 17, 1903, at Kitty Hawk, when Orville made the powered
flight of 120 feet.

Orville survived his brother almost 36 years. Until he sold the
Wright Co. in 1915, he personally flew and tested improvements
on all Wright planes. His last flight as pilot was made in 1918.
From 1915 on, he spent much time in his Dayton laboratory. In
World War I he was commissioned a major in the U.S. Army and
did much work on aircraft design and development. He was
director and engineer of the Dayton-Wright Co., connected with
U.S. adoption of the British DH-4. For many years he served on
the National Advisory Committee for Aeronautics.

WRIGHT, PATIENCE LOVELL (*b. Bordentown, N.J., 1725; d.
London, England, 1786*), modeler in wax, Revolutionary spy.
Mother of Joseph Wright. Well known in the colonies as a sculptor
of wax portraits, she removed to London, *ca.* 1772, where she
exhibited historical groups, busts, and life-size figures of contemporary notables and enjoyed success until her death. She sent
information of English military plans to Benjamin Franklin at
Passy.

Wright, Philip Green (*b. Boston, Mass., 1861; d. 1934*), teacher, economist, poet. Grandson of Elizur Wright and Beriah Green. Graduated Tufts College, 1884; M.A., Harvard, 1887. Taught mathematics and other subjects, Lombard College, Illinois, 1892–1912; instructed in economics at Williams, 1912–13, and Harvard, 1913–17. On staff of Institute of Economics (later part of Brookings Institution), 1922–31. Author of, among others, important volumes on commercial policy and the tariff, and poems on labor.

Wright, Richard Nathaniel (*b. Roxie, Miss., 1908; d. Paris, France, 1960*), novelist. The son of a sharecropper, Wright received only a ninth grade education. Moved to Chicago in 1927, where he joined the John Reed Club and the Communist Party in 1932. After publishing poems in various magazines, including *Partisan Review*, Wright joined the Federal Writers' Project in 1935 and wrote his first novel, *Lawd Today* (not published until 1963). Moved to New York (1937) and helped edit the magazine *New Challenge* and was Harlem editor of the *Daily Worker*. Published *Uncle Tom's Children* (1938); *Native Son* (1940), which brought him an international reputation; and *Black Boy* (1945). In 1945 Wright traveled to Europe and became involved with the existentialist movement. Settled in France two years later. His final works include *Black Power* (1954), *White Man, Listen!* (1957), and the first novel in an unfinished trilogy, *The Long Dream* (1958). His excellent analysis of modern society and championship of Third World liberation ranks him in importance with Ralph Ellison and James Baldwin.

Wright, Richard Robert (*b. near Dalton, Ga., 1853; d. Philadelphia, Pa., 1947*), educator, banker. Graduated Atlanta University, 1876. While principal of the elementary school in Cuthbert, Ga., where he had been a slave as a child, he organized farmers' cooperatives for the local black community; in 1878, he called a convention of black teachers and organized the Georgia State Teachers' Association, serving as its first president. In 1880, he established and headed the state's first public high school for blacks in Augusta. From 1891 to 1921, he was president of the State Industrial College in Savannah. Along with his academic duties, he was active in Republican politics up to about 1900 and in commercial dealings (especially Savannah real estate) until his retirement from the college. Removing to Philadelphia, Pa., he opened the Citizens and Southern Banking Co. (chartered in 1926 as the Citizens and Southern Bank and Trust Co.), which, at the time of his death, was regarded as a model of sound and prudent management.

Wright, Robert (*b. Queen Annes Co., Md., 1752; d. Queen Annes Co., 1826*), lawyer, Revolutionary soldier, Maryland legislator. U.S. senator, Democratic-Republican, from Maryland, 1801–06; governor of Maryland, 1806–09. Congressman, 1810–17 and 1821–23, he was a member of the Judiciary Committee, 1815–17, and of the Foreign Affairs Committee, 1821–23. Judge of the lower Eastern Shore district court *post* 1823. A consistent supporter of administration policies.

Wright, Robert William (*b. Ludlow, Vt., 1816; d. Cleveland, Ohio, 1885*), editor, satirist, lawyer. Wright was editor of Democratic newspapers in Waterbury, Hartford, and New Haven, Conn.; New York City; and Richmond, Va., 1856–77. Author of, among other works, political verse satires, satires on local clerical squabbles, and *Life, Its True Genesis* (1880), an anti-Darwinian study.

Wright, Silas (*b. Amherst, Mass., 1795; d. Canton, N.Y., 1847*), lawyer, New York official, statesman. Graduated Middlebury College, 1815. Admitted to the bar, 1819, he began practice in Canton, N.Y. Throughout his life a nationalist and a Democrat, he served in the New York State Senate, 1824–27, and soon became a member of the directing group of New York Democrats known as the Albany Regency. A lifelong defender of popular rights, he yet held that the people needed the leadership of bosses and an honest use of the spoils system to obtain that strong party unity in which lay their hope in a battle against special privilege. As congressman from New York, 1827–29, he helped frame the Tariff of Abominations of 1828 and took a leading part in defending it; as comptroller of New York, 1829–33, he continued to oppose extension of the state canal system, except when expected revenues promised to reimburse the state. While U.S. senator from New York, 1833–44, he served on a number of important committees and came to hold high rank in the Senate for solid judgment and unselfish service. He was recognized as manager of his friend Martin Van Buren's political interests and employed on behalf of Van Buren his uncannily accurate sense of public opinion. Following Van Buren's election to the presidency, Wright served as chairman of the Senate Finance Committee, 1836–41. He opposed all measures for rechartering the Bank of the United States and opposed distribution of the federal surplus among the states. In the panic of 1837 he urged a complete divorce of federal finance from the banks and much stricter regulation of banking by the states; he also introduced the administration's relief bills and headed the fight for an independent U.S. treasury until victory in 1840. After the accession of President John Tyler, Wright urged a tax-and-pay policy, continuing to oppose distribution of public-land sales income and any increase in the tariff. In 1844 he campaigned for the nomination of Van Buren for the presidency, declining to be a candidate himself. As governor of New York, 1845–47, he acted with evenhanded justice to all, thereby alienating all elements of the community; his suppression of violence during the antirent disturbances caused bitter popular feeling and his tax on rent income alienated the landlords. Renominated in 1846, he failed of reelection, but had the satisfaction of seeing many reforms which he had advocated incorporated in the new state constitution of 1846. Honesty, simplicity, and disinterestedness were his outstanding characteristics.

Wright, Theodore Lyman (*b. Beloit, Wis., 1858; d. 1926*), teacher. Graduated Beloit College, 1880; M.A., Harvard, 1884; also attended American School of Classical Studies, Athens, 1887. Taught Greek literature and art at Beloit College *post* 1892; produced a series of the Greek dramas in English.

Wright, Theodore Paul (*b. Galesburg, Ill., 1895; d. Ithaca, N.Y., 1970*), aeronautical engineer and administrator. Studied at Lombard College (B.S., 1915) and the Massachusetts Institute of Technology (B.S., 1918). While in the navy (1917–21), he worked as a naval aircraft inspector. In 1921 he joined the Curtiss Aeroplane and Motor Company as an engineer; he became chief engineer of the airplane division in 1925. With the formation of the Curtiss-Wright Corporation in 1928, he rose to become vice president and director of engineering in 1937. Wright supervised the design and production of numerous military and commercial aircraft, including the Hawk, Helldiver, Condor, C-46, and Tanager. He joined the National Defense Advisory Commission (1940), became assistant chief of the aircraft section in the Office of Production Management (1941), and served as chairman of the Joint Aircraft Committee, director of the Aircraft Resources Control Office, and member of the Aircraft Production Board of the War Production Board. He was administrator of the Civil Aeronautics Administration (1944–48). In 1948 Wright became vice president for research of Cornell University and president of the Cornell Aeronautical Laboratory. In 1950 he became chairman of the Cornell-Guggenheim Aviation Safety Center. He retired in 1960.

WRIGHT, WILBUR (b. Millville, near New Castle, Ind., 1867; d. 1912), aviation pioneer. Wilbur and his brother Orville (born at Dayton, Ohio, 1871) were inseparable partners throughout their lives. As youths, they earned pocket money by selling homemade mechanical toys, later issuing the weekly *West Side News* in Dayton, of which Wilbur was editor. He also wrote on occasion for the *Religious Telescope*, of which his father was editor. Wilbur was the more scholarly and exact-minded of the brothers; Orville was quicker with suggestions, but was inclined to dream. They formed the Wright Cycle Co. *ca.* 1892 and built the "Van Cleve" bicycle, which soon achieved a reputation.

They began thinking about the possibility of flight in 1896, stimulated by the work and writings of Otto Lilienthal, Octave Chanute, S. P. Langley, and other experimenters and theorists. Planning to work on a captive man-carrying glider, they first experimented with kites; in 1899 Wilbur Wright built a model biplane with a wingspread of five feet, which he flew as a kite. From this and other experiments, considerable study of theory, and advice from Chanute, they produced their first glider. Air resistance was reduced by placing the operator in a horizontal position; a front surface gave longitudinal stability and control; lateral balance was obtained by warping the wing extremities to decrease lift on either side, thus supplying a rolling moment at the will of the pilot. Vertical steering was not provided for in the first glider, but the Wrights understood its functions and provided it in their second machine, 1902.

With the advice of the U.S. Weather Bureau, the brothers selected for trial of their glider a strip of sand called Kill Devil Hill, near Kitty Hawk, N.C., and set up camp there in September 1900. Failing in efforts to fly the glider as a kite, they turned to free gliding and were soon operating safely under perfect control in winds of 27 miles per hour, making glides of more than 300 feet. They kept careful tabulation of their findings and concluded that a vertical steering rudder was essential; that the warping of the wing extremities could be relied on for lateral control; that the movement of the center of pressure on a curved wing produced instability; and that calculations based on existing data were in error. It was plain that they would have to find their own correct basic data.

They returned to Dayton, where Orville devised a wind tunnel for further lengthy experiments, testing over 200 wing and biplane combinations to determine accurate values for lift, drag, and center of pressure. In 1902 at Kitty Hawk, they made nearly 1,000 glides in a new glider based on their latest data, and confirmed the accuracy of their findings. They then built a powered machine weighing 750 pounds fully loaded, capable of a 31 mile speed, and with a four-cylinder, twelve horsepower motor they had made. In this new machine on Dec. 17, 1903, Orville made the first powered flight, which lasted only 12 seconds. Several hours later Wilbur made a flight of 51 seconds, but the machine, forced down by a sudden gust, was so damaged that further flights were impossible.

Despite this serious loss, the Wright brothers built a stronger machine, and on Oct. 5, 1905, at Huffman Field, Dayton, during a 24-mile circuit flight, they solved the equilibrium problem in turning.

Thereafter, despite lack of public encouragement, they abandoned other interests and devoted themselves to constructing a practicable machine. They obtained a patent for a flying machine in 1906. Only after successful negotiations had been conducted with foreign interests did the American government awake to the value of the new device. In late 1907 General James Allen, chief U.S. Army signal officer, opened bids for a "gasless flying machine" to carry two men weighing 350 pounds, with sufficient fuel for 125 miles. The Wrights offered to build a biplane and instruct two operators for $25,000; other bids were accepted, but the Wrights alone completed the contract. Meanwhile, they made highly publicized successful trial flights at Kitty Hawk. Orville, demonstrating the contract plane at Fort Myer, Va. (Sept. 9, 1908), made 57 complete circles at 120-feet altitude, remaining aloft 62 minutes, thus establishing several records simultaneously. On Sept. 17 occurred the most serious accident in the brothers' career, which had been singularly free of them. A stray wire tangled with a propeller blade, and the machine crashed. Orville suffered a fractured thigh and two ribs, and his passenger, Lt. Thomas E. Selfridge, was killed. Fully recovered, Orville completed the official tests eight months later. Meanwhile, in France, Wilbur had been flying at the Hunandrières race course so successfully that he concluded satisfactory arrangements with a French syndicate to manufacture his machine in France. During the 1909 Hudson-Fulton celebration at New York, he made demonstration flights from Governor's Island, around the Statue of Liberty, and up to Grant's Tomb. This led to formation of the American Wright Co., and subsequent negotiations were concluded providing for manufacture of airplanes in England, Germany, Italy, and America.

WRIGHT, WILLARD HUNTINGTON (b. Charlottesville, Va., 1888; d. New York, N.Y., 1939), art critic, detective-story writer under pseudonym "S. S. Van Dine." Creator of the fictional detective Philo Vance, whose ostentatiously displayed erudition lent contemporary interest to such books as *The Benson Murder Case* (1926), *The Canary Murder Case* (1927), *The Greene Murder Case* (1928), and others.

WRIGHT, WILLIAM (b. near Nyack, N.Y., 1794; d. Newark, N.J., 1866), manufacturer. Cofounder of the saddlery firm of Smith & Wright, Newark, N.J. Mayor of Newark, 1840–43. Congressman, Whig, from New Jersey, 1843–47; U.S. senator, Democrat, 1853–59 and *post* 1863. Chairman, Senate Committee on Manufactures.

WRIGHT, WILLIAM (b. Ohio, 1829; d. West Lafayette, Iowa, 1898), journalist, better known under pseudonym "Dan De Quille." Began journalistic career in Iowa; prospected in California and Nevada, 1857–61. Becoming city editor of the Virginia City, Nev. *Daily Territorial Enterprise*, 1861, he held this post for practically the remainder of his life and lived to see the city dwindle into a ghost town and his newspaper cease publication. Mark Twain, his associate on the newspaper in 1862, was his lifelong friend and encouraged Wright to publish his *History of the Big Bonanza* (1877). Late in life, sick and without occupation, he was befriended and helped by John W. Mackay.

WRIGLEY, WILLIAM (b. Philadelphia, Pa., 1861; d. Phoenix, Ariz., 1932), chewing gum manufacturer. A gifted salesman and organizer, Wrigley developed a multimillion-dollar chewing gum business out of a small concern for the manufacture of soap which he started in Chicago, Ill., 1891. After becoming wealthy, he bought a controlling interest in the Chicago National League baseball club and other clubs and was the developer of Santa Catalina Island, off the California coast.

WROSETASATOW. See OUTACITY.

WU P'AN-CHAO. See NG, POON CHEW.

WURTZ, HENRY (b. Easton, Pa., ca. 1828; d. Brooklyn, N.Y., 1910), chemist, editor. After graduation from College of New Jersey (Princeton), 1848, Wurtz studied chemistry at Lawrence Scientific School, Harvard, and conducted mineral analyses in New York laboratory of Dr. Oliver W. Gibbs. State chemist and geologist, New Jersey geological survey, 1854–56. Conducted research on sodium amalgams for extracting precious metals from their ores, securing patent, 1865. Edited *American Gas Light Journal*, 1868–71. Devised new method of manufacturing fuel gas by alternating action of air and steam upon cheap coal, 1869; took out a number of patents relating to distillation of paraffin hydrocarbons and other chemical products.

WYANT, ALEXANDER HELWIG (*b. Evans Creek, Ohio, 1836; d. New York, N.Y., 1892*), landscape painter. Wyant was an outstanding master of American landscape painting during the latter half of the 19th century. Encouraged by George Inness, 1857, and with the assistance of the elder Nicholas Longworth, he studied in New York and briefly in Germany. He was elected member of the National Academy, 1869, for his *The Upper Susquehanna.* Wyant's early painting is characterized by a photographic fidelity to nature; his middle period is dominated by the environment of the mountains of New York State. His pictures have a thematic conception, an organized unity, and a universal appeal. Mood is transcendent; composition is simple. The rhythmic action is rendered by movement of light and dark sequences related to a fixed point of focal concentration. As a pure naturalist he is unsurpassed; as a poetic tonalist he was master of aerial perspective and atmospheric envelopment. Among his paintings are *The Mohawk Valley* (1866), *An Old Clearing* (1881), *Passing Clouds*, and *Landscape in the Adirondacks.*

WYATT, FRANCIS (*b. Kent, England, 1588; d. Kent, 1644*), baronet. A connection by marriage of Sir Edwin Sandys who gained control of the London Co. in 1619, Wyatt had invested in the company and was designated governor of Virginia, arriving there in October 1621. Forced by the weakness of the London Co. to abandon the prospect of building Virginia into a prosperous community which would serve the ends of mercantilist policy, he rallied the planters and settlers to demand preservation of their liberties after the dissolution of the company in 1624. Continuing in office as the first royal governor of Virginia, he summoned the famous "Convention Assembly" of 1625, which pressed petitions on the home government for the continuation of the liberty of general assembly in the colony. He gave up the governorship in 1626, but succeeded Sir John Harvey as governor again in 1639. On his return to Virginia he was able to announce that the liberty of general assembly, so long desired, had been confirmed by the royal authority. He was replaced by Sir William Berkeley in 1641.

WYCKOFF, JOHN HENRY (*b. Tindivanam, East Madras, India, 1881; d. New York, N.Y., 1937*), physician, medical educator. M.D., Bellevue Hospital Medical College, 1907. After service in the cardiac clinic at Bellevue and military service in World War I, he returned to the clinic *ca.* 1919. In 1927 he was appointed director of the division of Bellevue under supervision of New York College with title of associate professor of medicine. In 1932 he became dean of the University of Medicine and professor. A pioneer in the use of digitalis in the United States, he helped to develop the practice of multiple diagnosis (anatomical, pathological, clinical, etc.) in treating cases of heart disease. He played a leading role in formation of the New York Heart Association.

WYCKOFF, WALTER AUGUSTUS (*b. Mainpuri, India, 1865; d. 1908*), author, sociologist. B.A., College of New Jersey (Princeton), 1888. Assistant professor of political economy at Princeton *post* 1898. Author of *The Workers: An Experiment in Reality—The East* (1897) and a second part, *The West* (1898).

WYETH, JOHN (*b. Cambridge, Mass., 1770; d. Philadelphia, Pa., 1858*), editor, publisher. Cofounder and editor, *Oracle of Dauphin County & Harrisburg* (Pa.) *Advertiser*, 1792–1827, during which time he established a bookstore and general publishing house. Served as first postmaster of Harrisburg, 1793–98, and was active in Harrisburg public affairs.

WYETH, JOHN ALLAN (*b. Marshall Co., Ala., 1845; d. 1922*), surgeon, medical educator. Graduated medical depart-

ment, University of Louisville, 1869; M.D., Bellevue Medical School, 1873. Instrumental in organizing New York Polyclinic Hospital and Medical School, 1881, serving as surgeon in chief and subsequently as president until his death. Devised new surgical procedures, including ligation of the external carotid artery and "Wyeth's operation." Author of A *Textbook on Surgery* (1887).

WYETH, NATHANIEL JARVIS (*b. Cambridge, Mass., 1802; d. 1856*), trader, explorer. Nephew of John Wyeth. Successful with Frederic Tudor in building an important trade in ice to the West Indies, Wyeth is remembered particularly for his attempt to plant an American commercial and agricultural colony in Oregon. Inspired by Hall J. Kelley, Wyeth made his first overland journey to Oregon, 1832–33; nothing concrete resulted from it. Organizing a company for salmon-packing on the lower Columbia and for fur-trading, Wyeth and a party traveled overland again to Oregon in 1834. He was accompanied by Thomas Nuttall and John K. Townsend, the latter of whom published a *Narrative of a Journey Across the Rocky Mountains to the Columbia River* (1839), descriptive of the trip. Wyeth built a small fort named Fort William at the mouth of the Willamette; in present Idaho he built Fort Hall, which became a famous station on the Oregon and California trail. Failing to make progress against the competition of the Hudson's Bay Co., Wyeth returned to the ice business. Although unsuccessful in his primary aim, he succeeded in familiarizing important sections of the eastern population with the facts about Oregon.

WYETH, NEWELL CONVERS (*b. Needham, Mass., 1882; d. near Chadds Ford, Pa., 1945*), painter and illustrator. After studying art at the Mechanic Art High School in Boston, he continued his education at the Massachusetts Normal Art School and the Eric Pape School of Art in Boston, and studied with Charles W. Reed. In 1902 Wyeth went to Wilmington, Del., to join the small art school conducted by the famous illustrator Howard Pyle. Winters were spent in the Wilmington studio, summers at nearby Chadds Ford, Pa., in the Brandywine Valley.

In 1904 Wyeth took his small savings and journeyed to a Colorado ranch, where he sketched cowboys, cattle, and the new landscape. When his money was stolen, he got a job as a government mail rider and traveled south to New Mexico. Soon he began to receive commissions from publishing houses for book illustrations, the first of which were published in 1906. Of Wyeth's five children, three became artists; Henriette Zirngiebel (born in 1907), Carolyn Brenneman (1909), and Andrew (1917). Both the coast and the people of Maine became subjects for Wyeth's imagination. The death of a fisherman friend inspired his famous *Island Funeral* and his illustrations for Kenneth Roberts' *Trending into Maine* (1938) were based on a rich store of experience. Of his book illustrations, his work for children reached the widest audience. Beginning in 1911 with Robert Louis Stevenson's *Treasure Island*, he illustrated 18 volumes in Scribner's Illustrated Classics series.

After accepting an initial invitation to paint a mural for a hotel in Utica, N.Y., he went on to paint many others in various parts of the United States. Only during the last two decades of his life did Wyeth find the time to turn to easel painting of his own. His several hundred still lifes, portraits, studies, and landscapes were not well known until after his death. From his son-in-law Peter Hurd he learned to work in egg tempera, and he spent increasing amounts of time with this medium. Wyeth was a member of the National Academy of Design and the Society of Illustrators. He received the gold medal at the Panama-Pacific Exposition in San Francisco, 1915, and the W. A. Clarke Prize of the Corcoran Gallery in Washington, D.C., 1932.

WYLIE, ANDREW (*b. Washington, Pa., 1789; d. 1851*), educator, Episcopal clergyman, author. Graduated Jefferson College, Pennsylvania, 1810. President, Washington College, 1816–28. First president, Indiana College (later University), 1828 until his death. Introduced "specialization by rotation," or study and mastery of one subject at a time. Also served at Indiana as professor of moral and mental philosophy, political economy, and polite literature.

WYLIE, ELINOR MORTON HOYT (*b. Somerville, N.J., 1885; d. New York, N.Y., 1928*), poet, novelist. Great-granddaughter of Morton McMichael; granddaughter of Henry M. Hoyt. A lyric poet of distinction and a writer of novels outstanding for their mannered style and high comic conception, Wylie was remarkable throughout her life for an obsession with the memory and personality of the English poet Percy B. Shelley. Her volumes of poetry included *Incidental Numbers* (1912); *Nets to Catch the Wind* (1921); *Black Armour* (1923); and *Angels and Earthly Creatures* (1929). Her novels included *Jennifer Lorn* (1923); *The Venetian Glass Nephew* (1925); *The Orphan Angel* (1926), a fantasy about Shelley; and *Mr. Hodge and Mr. Hazard* (1928).

WYLIE, ROBERT (*b. Douglas, Isle of Man, England, 1839; d. Pont-Aven, France, 1877*), landscape and genre painter. Came to America as a child. Studied at the Pennsylvania Academy, Philadelphia; resided in France *post ca.* 1864, where he was a pupil in Paris of J. L. Gérôme, Thomas Couture, and others. Among the first American artists to discover Brittany and Breton life as subjects, he was largely responsible for the popularity of that region among French artists as well as fellow Americans. An excellent draftsman and a sober colorist, he produced comparatively few works.

WYLIE, SAMUEL BROWN (*b. Moylarg, Ireland, 1773; d. 1852*), educator, Reformed Presbyterian clergyman. M.A., University of Glasgow, 1797. Immigrated to Philadelphia, Pa., 1797. Presumably the first Covenanter to receive American ordination, 1800, he was pastor and cofounder of the Philadelphia congregation, which he served *post* 1803. Professor of Latin and Greek, University of Pennsylvania, 1828–45; vice-provost, 1836–45.

WYLLYS, GEORGE (*b. Hartford, Conn., 1710; d. Hartford, 1796*), Connecticut official. Secretary, colony of Connecticut, pro tempore 1730–34, and in full tenure from 1734 until death. Town clerk of Hartford *post* 1732.

WYMAN, HORACE (*b. Woburn, Mass., 1827; d. Princeton, Mass., 1915*), machinist, inventor. Superintendent of George Crompton's loom works *post ca.* 1861; vice president and consulting engineer, Crompton & Knowles Loom Works, Worcester, Mass., from 1897 until his death. Took out over 200 patents for improvement in process and mechanism of looms and other textile machinery. Among his inventions are a loom-box operating mechanism, 1871; a pile-fabric loom, 1872; processes for fabric weaving in different sizes and colors; the first American "dobby" loom, 1879; and the weft replenishing loom with drop shuttle boxes, 1901.

WYMAN, JEFFRIES (*b. Chelmsford, Mass., 1814; d. Bethlehem, N.H., 1874*), anatomist, ethnologist. Brother of Morrill Wyman. Graduated Harvard, 1833; M.D., 1837. Made curator and lecturer, Lowell Institute, 1840. Became professor of anatomy and physiology, Hampden-Sydney College medical school, Richmond, Va., 1843. Appointed Hersey professor of anatomy, Harvard, 1847. Built up anatomical museum at Harvard, nucleus of present Peabody Museum. Made collecting expeditions to Florida, 1851–52; Surinam, 1856; and South America, 1858. Became curator of department and museum of archaeology and ethnology at Harvard, 1866. President, Boston Society of Natural History, 1856–70. Wyman's most important papers deal with the structure of the gorilla. His monograph on the nervous system of the frog (published by the Smithsonian Institution in 1852–53) and papers on the anatomy of the blind fish of Mammoth Cave (published in the *American Journal of Science* between 1843 and 1854) are also noteworthy. He was considered the leading American anatomist of his time.

WYMAN, MORRILL (*b. Chelmsford, Mass., 1812; d. 1903*), physician. Brother of Jeffries Wyman. Graduated Harvard, 1833; Harvard Medical School, 1837. Practiced for more than 60 years in Cambridge, Mass. Wyman's most effective service to American medical science occurred in 1850. In association with H. I. Bowditch, he improved the operation of thoracentesis, or surgical drainage of the pleural cavity, by substituting a small hollow needle for the large cannula formerly used. This was a landmark in pleurisy treatment. Author of *A Practical Treatise on Ventilation* (1846); a report on ventilators and chimneys (*Proceedings*, American Academy of Arts and Sciences, 1848); and *Autumnal Catarrh: Hay Fever* (1872, with additions, 1876). Adjunct Hersey professor of theory and practice of medicine, Harvard Medical School, 1853–56. Founded Cambridge Hospital, 1886; served for many years as consulting physician, Massachusetts General Hospital.

WYMAN, ROBERT HARRIS (*b. Portsmouth, N.H., 1822; d. 1882*), naval officer. Appointed midshipman, 1837. Served with credit in Mexican War. During Civil War, served in blockade duty in the Atlantic and commanded the Potomac Flotilla early in 1862. Headed Hydrographic Office at Washington, D.C., 1871–79, and was author of a number of useful publications on navigation. Commissioned rear admiral, 1878, he commanded the North Atlantic Squadron; he died as chairman of the Lighthouse Board.

WYMAN, SETH (*b. Goffstown, N.H., 1784; d. Goffstown, 1843*), burglar. Author of a popular *Life and Adventures* (1843).

WYNN, ED (*b. Isaiah Edwin Leopold, Philadelphia, Pa., 1886; d. Beverly Hills, Calif., 1966*), comedian and actor. Left school at fifteen to join the Thurber-Nasher Repertoire Company. In 1902 he formed a comedy act with Jack Lewis called the "Rah! Rah! Boys." Wynn then went on to become a headliner in Vaudeville. He performed in the 1914 and 1915 *Ziegfeld Follies*, then wrote and produced *Ed Wynn's Carnival* (1920), *The Perfect Fool* (1921), *The Grab Bag* (1924), and *Laugh Parade* (1931). He also appeared in *Manhattan Mary* (1927) and *Simple Simon* (1930). Wynn appeared on radio as the Texaco Fire Chief (1932–35) and returned to Broadway in 1940 in *Boys and Girls Together*. He worked in television, and, prodded by his son, Keenan, took a role in the movie *The Great Man* (1956). Shortly thereafter, he appeared with his son in the television drama *Requiem for a Heavyweight*. His other movies include *Marjorie Morningstar* (1958), *The Diary of Anne Frank* (1959), and *Mary Poppins* (1964).

WYTHE, GEORGE (*b. Back River, Elizabeth City Co., Va., 1726; d. Richmond, Va., 1806*), statesman, professor of law, jurist. Received little formal education, briefly attending College of William and Mary. Admitted to the bar, 1746, he began practice in Spotsylvania Co. Briefly attorney general of Virginia, 1754, while Peyton Randolph was in England, Wythe removed he residence to Williamsburg, Va., 1755. His career really began in 1758 when he became the intimate friend and associate of Governor Francis Fauquier. A member of the House of Burgesses, 1754–55 and 1758–68, he served as clerk of the House, 1769–75. On the announcement of the stamp tax, Wythe maintained the concept (later expounded by Richard Bland) that

England and Virginia were coordinate nations united by the crown alone. Wythe drafted the Virginia Resolutions of Remonstrance, which were modified before their adoption by his colleagues in the House. On the approach of the Revolution he wisely recommended the raising of a regular army instead of the use of militia and himself volunteered for service. Sent to the Continental Congress in 1775, he served until the close of 1776. He supported Richard H. Lee's resolution for independence and signed the Declaration. He was probably the designer of the seal of Virginia, adopted 1776. Assigned with Thomas Jefferson and Edmund Pendleton to the task of revising the Virginia laws, he covered the period from the revolution in England, 1688, to American independence; the revision was thorough and intelligent and the various bills embodying it were passed over a period of years subsequent to its submission in 1779. Speaker of the House of Delegates, 1777, he became one of the three judges of the Virginia High Court of Chancery, 1778, and henceforth was known as Chancellor Wythe.

On accepting the chair of law at the College of William and Mary, 1779 (the first chair of law in an American college), Wythe began that part of his career which perhaps constitutes his greatest service, for he literally charted the way in American jurisprudence and was teacher of, among others later famous, John Marshall. He was a delegate to the Virginia convention which ratified the U.S. Constitution, 1788, but engaged little in debate; in offering the resolution for ratification he emphasized the derivative character of federal power. On reorganization of the state judicial system in 1788, he became sole chancellor, holding this office until 1801, after which he continued to preside over the Richmond district. He resigned his professorship in 1790 and, removing to Richmond, formed a small law school of his own. Among his students was Henry Clay.

As chancellor and ex officio member of the supreme court of appeals, he delivered a significant opinion in the case of *Commonwealth v. Caton*, 1782. An obiter dictum which he made in his concurring opinion was clearly one of the earliest enunciations of the doctrine of judicial review, America's unique contribution to juridical theory; at the time, it was the most complete such statement which had been made. Superbly ethical as an attorney, Wythe refused unjust causes and abandoned any case regarding which he felt he had been misled. Probably the best classical scholar in Virginia, he was widely read in Roman and English law. Opposed to slavery, he emancipated his servants by his will.

Wythe died after drinking coffee poisoned by his grandnephew and heir.

X

XÁNTUS, JÁNOS (b. Csokonya, Somogy Co., Hungary, 1825; d. Hungary, 1894), ornithologist, author. Immigrated to America, 1851; was employed by the Pacific Railroad and U.S. Coast surveys. Made valuable bird collections in California for the Smithsonian Institution, uncovering many new species. His descriptions and catalogues of new species appear in *Proceedings of the Academy of Natural Sciences of Philadelphia* (Vols X–XII, 1859–61). Appointed U.S. consul at Manzanillo, Mexico, he led a scientific research party into the Sierra Madre. Returned to Hungary, 1864; published accounts of his travels.

Y

YALE, CAROLINE ARDELIA (b. Charlotte, Vt., 1848; d. 1933), educator. Joined staff of Clarke Institution for Deaf Mutes, 1870; became principal, 1886, emeritus, 1922. Pioneer in use of oral method; established, 1889, and directed normal classes for teacher-training of the deaf. Author of *Years of Building* (1931).

YALE, ELIHU (b. Boston, Mass., 1649; d. London, England, 1721), official of the East India Co., philanthropist. After an application made by Cotton Mather for aid to the struggling Collegiate School at Saybrook, Conn., in January 1718, Yale made a gift of various goods to the institution which sold for £562 12s., the largest private contribution made to the college for over a century. At the September commencement, the new building at New Haven and the college were given Yale's name in appreciation.

YALE, LINUS (b. Salisbury, N.Y., 1821; d. New York, N.Y., 1868), inventor, manufacturer. Invented the "Yale Infallible Bank Lock" ca. 1851; to change the combination, the key's component parts could be separated and reassembled. His "Yale Magic Bank Lock" was an improvement on the first, and was followed by the "Yale Double Treasury Bank Lock," the most notable bank lock operated by keys. About 1862 he began to market the "Monitor Bank Lock," the first dial or combination bank lock, and in 1863 the "Yale Double Dial Bank Lock," whose principles of construction are in general use in America. Between 1860 and 1865 he improved small key locks by devising the "Cylinder Lock," based on the pin-tumbler mechanism of the Egyptians; he obtained patents, 1861 and 1865. Partner with J. H. Towne and H. R. Towne in the Yale Lock Manufacturing Co. (established 1868).

YANCEY, JAMES EDWARD ("JIMMY") (b. 1894[?]; d. Chicago, Ill., 1951), jazz musician. Originator of the boogie-woogie piano style, Yancey played professionally until 1925 when he became grounds keeper for the Chicago White Sox baseball club. After World War II there was a revival of his music and he appeared in Chicago clubs and in concert at Carnegie Hall in New York in 1948. His first recordings were made in Chicago in 1939 and 1940: "The Fives" and two vocals, "Death Letter Blues" and "Cryin' in My Sleep."

YANCEY, WILLIAM LOWNDES (b. Warren Co., Ga., 1814; d. Montgomery, Ala., 1863), lawyer, Alabama legislator, secessionist. Stepson of Nathan S. S. Beman. Attended Williams College, 1830–33; studied in law office of Benjamin F. Perry at Greenville, S.C. An active Unionist as editor of a Greenville newspaper during the nullification controversy, Yancey removed to Alabama in the winter of 1836–37, where he attempted farming, edited a newspaper at Wetumpka, and practiced law with great success. As a legislator, 1841–44, he was noted as a supporter of representation on the basis of white population only, of a free public school system, and of a nonpolitical state banking system. Elected to Congress in 1844, he served until his resignation on Sept. 1, 1846.

Yancey now resumed the practice of law and began a career of unofficial political action on behalf of Southern independence which transcended party lines. Operating on a narrow but well-defined body of principles, he refused any compromise for the sake of party continuity or for any other reason; contemporary politicians considered him everything from an unwelcome pest to an insufferable firebrand. His body of principles is to be found in the Alabama Platform, written by him, 1848, in answer to the Wilmot Proviso. In brief, the platform demanded a constitution designed to curb the will of the majority and preserve to the states all powers not expressly granted to the federal government, equal rights of citizens and states in the territories, and action by Congress to protect property rights in the territories so long as they remained in territorial status. He presented this simple statement of abstractions to the people of the South on every occasion with an oratorical excellence seldom equaled. After the rejection of his platform by the Democrats in their convention at Baltimore, 1848, he appealed to the people from the decision and in the course of the next 12 years made his platform the Southern creed. In order to arouse the South to the need of a union of all Southern men in a sectional party, he was active in promoting Southern rights associations which would work for the nomination of public office of states' rights men within each party. In 1858 he sought to perfect the system by organizing the League of United Southerners. He traveled widely, delivering hundreds of addresses in support of his views. Dominant in the Democratic party in Alabama as the presidential campaign of 1860 approached, he recommended that if the demands of the South were rejected at the Charleston convention, a "Constitutional Democratic party" should be organized and candidates presented to the people. He furthermore stated that if a Republican president should be elected, then secession should be carried through before his inauguration.

At the Alabama Democratic convention in Montgomery on Jan. 11, 1860, Yancey prepared the Alabama platform of principles—a restatement of the platform of 1848 in line with all that had transpired meantime. The platform also instructed the Alabama delegation to the Charleston convention to present this platform for adoption and to withdraw if it were rejected. At the Charleston convention Yancey delivered the greatest speech of his career in defense of his platform; after its qualified rejection, a majority of the Southern delegates withdrew. When the adjourned convention met later at Baltimore, Md., the supporters of Stephen A. Douglas refused to seat the Yancey delegation from Alabama. Subsequent to this, under Yancey's guidance, the Constitutional Democratic party was organized and nominated John Breckinridge for the presidency. Following the election of Abraham Lincoln, Yancey dominated the proceedings of the Alabama convention and wrote the Ordinance of Secession. A Confederate commissioner in France and England, 1861–62, he served briefly in the Confederate Senate after his return; during this time he fought against the increase of centralized power in the Confederacy just as fiercely as he had fought it in the Union.

YANDELL, DAVID WENDELL (*b. near Murfreesboro, Tenn., 1826; d. Louisville, Ky., 1898*), physician. Son of Lunsford P. Yandell. Graduated University of Louisville, 1846. Practiced in Louisville; founded the Stokes Dispensary and pioneered in medical education by establishing classes in clinical medicine; was appointed to the chair of clinical medicine at the University of Louisville. During the Civil War he served as medical director, Confederate Department of the West. Professor of clinical surgery, University of Louisville, *post* 1869. Cofounder of *The American Practitioner and News*, which he edited from 1870 until shortly before his death.

YANDELL, LUNSFORD PITTS (*b. near Hartsville, Tenn., 1805; d. Louisville, Ky., 1878*), paleontologist, physician. Father of David W. Yandell. Graduated University of Maryland, 1825. Professor of chemistry and pharmacy, Transylvania University, 1831–37. Held chairs of chemistry and materia medica, and, *post* 1849, physiology, in the medical department, University of Louisville; taught there from 1837 until 1859. Editor of medical journals, and coeditor of *Western Journal of Medicine and Surgery* 1840–55. Made extensive geological and paleontological explorations in the vicinity of Louisville; studied the Ohio falls coral reefs, the Beargrass Creek fossiliferous beds, and Kentucky and Indiana quarries. Discovered and collected numerous fossils. Author of *Contributions to the Geology of Kentucky* (1847), with B. F. Shumard and of many contributions to scientific journals.

YATES, ABRAHAM (*b. Albany, N.Y., 1724; d. 1796*), Revolutionary patriot, public official, Antifederalist pamphleteer. Also known as Abraham Yates, Jr. Chairman, Albany Committee of Correspondence, 1774–76. Headed committee of the convention which drafted New York State's first constitution, 1776–77, and of the committee for putting the new government into operation. State senator, 1777–90. His printed letters and pamphlets are perhaps the ablest exposition of the views of agrarian democrats and of followers of Governor George Clinton. Played role of Antifederalist in Continental Congress, 1787–88. Mayor of Albany from 1790 until his death.

YATES, HERBERT JOHN (*b. Brooklyn, N.Y., 1880; d. Sherman Oaks, Calif., 1966*), motion-picture executive. Cofounded Republic Film Laboratories in 1917. In 1922 he established, and became chairman of, Consolidated Film Industries, which developed into one of the nation's largest producers and developers of motion-picture film. During the 1930's Yates gradually shifted his main interest from film lab services to moviemaking. In 1935 he established Republic Productions in North Hollywood, Calif. Under his leadership Republic quickly became a major producer of movie serials and B-films; among its stars were John Wayne, Gene Autry, and Roy Rogers. Yates sold out his interests in Republic and resigned its chairmanship in 1959.

YATES, JOHN VAN NESS (*b. Albany, N.Y., 1779; d. Albany, 1839*), lawyer, New York official. Son of Robert Yates. Editor of William Smith's *History of New York* (1814) and author of legal works. Democratic-Republican in politics and a partisan of the Clintons, he was New York secretary of state, 1818–26. He was regarded as erratic in character.

YATES, MATTHEW TYSON (*b. Wake Co., N.C., 1819; d. Shanghai, China, 1888*), missionary. Graduated Wake Forest College, 1846. Pioneer Southern Baptist missionary in Shanghai, China, 1847–88.

YATES, RICHARD (*b. Warsaw, Ky., 1815; d. St. Louis, Mo., 1873*), lawyer, Illinois legislator. Congressman, Whig, from Illinois, 1851–55. Opposed to slavery, he then joined the Republican party. As governor of Illinois, 1861–65, he was highly effective in war administration. He gave General U. S. Grant his first Civil War commission and assignments. In 1863, he prorogued the largely Democratic state assembly for passing a resolution urging an armistice and national peace convention. As U.S. senator, 1865–71, Yates was a party regular, favoring vindictive measures against the South, voting for Johnson's impeachment, and supporting the prevailing Radical Republican program.

YATES, ROBERT (*b. Schenectady, N.Y., 1738; d. 1801*), Revolutionary patriot, jurist. Father of John Van N. Yates. Studied law with William Livingston; admitted to the bar at Albany, N.Y., 1760. A radical Whig in the period before the Revolution, he was a member of the Albany Committee of Safety and represented Albany Co. in the four New York provincial congresses. Among other important committee work, he served on the committee which drafted the first New York State constitution. Appointed a justice of the state supreme court, 1777, he was advanced to chief justice in 1790 and resigned the office in 1798. A leader of the Antifederalists, he was a supporter of Governor George Clinton. A delegate from New York to the Federal Convention, 1787, with John Lansing and Alexander Hamilton, he refused further attendance after July 5 on the ground that the Convention was exceeding its powers in attempting to write a new instrument of government. He wrote several series of letters attacking the U.S. Constitution, 1787–88, and voted against ratification of it at the Poughkeepsie, N.Y., convention.

YEADON, RICHARD (*b. Charleston, S.C., 1802; d. 1870*), lawyer, editor, South Carolina legislator. Editor of the Unionist *Charleston Daily Courier*, 1832–44. An ardent Whig and antisecessionist up to the Civil War, he supported President Jefferson Davis against opposition of R. B. Rhett. He was a benefactor of the College of Charleston and originated the ordinance establishing Charleston High School.

YEAGER, JOSEPH (*b. possibly Philadelphia, Pa. ca. 1792; d. Philadelphia, 1859*), engraver, publisher. Active in Philadelphia, 1809–45, as line engraver and as portrait etcher; published toy books for children. Became president of Harrisburg and Lancaster Railroad Co., 1848.

YEAMAN, WILLIAM POPE (*b. Hardin Co., Ky., 1832; d. 1904*), Baptist clergyman. Held various pastorates, notably in St. Louis, Mo., 1870–*ca.* 1879. Secretary, Board of State Missions, General Association of Missouri Baptists, 1884–86. Moderator, General Association of Missouri Baptists, 1877–97; also corresponding secretary. Vice president, Southern Baptist Convention, 1880.

YEAMANS, SIR JOHN (*b. probably Bristol, England, 1610/1; d. 1674*), colonial official. Commissioned governor of Carolina under the proprietors, January 1665, he sailed with the first settlers to the Cape Fear River late in that year, but soon returned to Barbados. After the abandonment of the first settlement, 1667, Yeamans still held the title of governor, but made little effort to serve actively during the second settlement under Joseph West. In 1671 he settled in Carolina and introduced the first slaves there; his claim to be governor was confirmed in 1672 and he then laid out the site of Charles Town on the Ashley River. Unpopular with both people and proprietors, he was discharged by the proprietors, 1674, but word of the change had not yet reached Carolina when Yeamans died.

YEARDLEY, SIR GEORGE (*b. London, England, ca. 1587; d. 1627*), Virginia colonial official. Sailing for Virginia, 1609, he served there several years in a military capacity. Acting governor of Virginia, 1616–17, he was commissioned governor in England and knighted, 1618. He returned to the colony with instructions, important in the history of English colonization, to abolish martial law, to summon the first English colonial representative assembly (over which he presided in 1619), and to amend land tenure terms. Plans to admit numbers of new settlers and establish private plantations ("hundreds") proved failures, primarily because of conditions in the London Co. Retiring, 1621, he was active thereafter as governor and captain of Southampton Hundred plantation and in the colony's affairs. Following dissolution of the London Co., Yeardley went to England in 1625 with important petitions from the "convention" assembly, presenting the needs of the settlers and asking for continuation of their general assembly. Although he failed to secure a definite commitment from the Privy Council on the latter point, the favorable impression he made led to his commission again as governor, 1626. He served until his death.

YEATES, JASPER (*b. Philadelphia, Pa., 1745; d. Lancaster, Pa., 1817*), lawyer, jurist. Studied law under Edward Shippen, 1728–1806. Admitted to the bar, 1765, he practiced successfully in Lancaster, Pa. Active in local politics, Yeates was a moderate Whig and chairman of the Lancaster Co. Committee of Correspondence, 1775. He opposed the Pennsylvania Constitution of 1776; later he was instrumental in ratification of the Federal Constitution at the Pennsylvania convention. Associate justice, Pennsylvania Supreme Court, from 1791 until his death.

YEATMAN, JAMES ERWIN (*b. near Wartrace, Tenn., 1818; d. St. Louis, Mo., 1901*), banker, civic leader, philanthropist. A founder, 1850, and president of the Merchants' National Bank, St. Louis, 1860–95. His most important work was as president of the Western Sanitary Commission, created at St. Louis in 1861. Cooperating with Dorothea Dix, Yeatman organized hospitals, recruited nurses, established homes, and outfitted probably the first railroad hospital cars. He was a generous benefactor of Washington University.

YELL, ARCHIBALD (*b. North Carolina, 1797; d. Buena Vista, Mexico, 1847*), lawyer, soldier. Served under Andrew Jackson in the War of 1812 and against the Seminole in Florida; became a protégé of Jackson. Removed to Little Rock, Ark., *ca.* 1831; appointed Arkansas territorial judge, 1835. First congressman from Arkansas, 1836–39 and 1845–47, he supported the annexation of Texas and Polk's Oregon policy. As governor of Arkansas, 1840–44, he demanded strong measures for control of the state bank and the real estate bank, recommended a board of internal improvements, and urged agricultural schools based on liberal government donations. As colonel of the 1st Arkansas Volunteer Cavalry he was killed at the battle of Buena Vista while leading a charge of his troops.

YELLIN, SAMUEL (*b. Mogilev-Podolski, Russia, 1885; d. New York, N.Y., 1940*), decorative metal designer and craftsman. Apprenticed in Europe, he came to America as a young man, settled in Philadelphia, Pa., and was soon made an instructor in wrought-iron work at the Pennsylvania Museum School of Industrial Art. He became an initiator and a leader of the revival of decorative metalwork in the United States during the 1920's and 1930's. Among his more important works are the hand-wrought fixtures at Valley Forge, Pa., Memorial Chapel; the gates of the Harkness Memorial Quadrangle at Yale; decorations at the Hall of Fame, New York City, at the National Cathedral, Washington, D.C., and at the Bok carillon near Lake Wales, Fla. His largest single commission was a pair of gates for the Packard Building, Philadelphia.

YELLOWLEY, EDWARD CLEMENTS (*b. near Ridgeland, Miss., 1873; d. Chicago, Ill., 1962*), federal Prohibition administrator. Joined the Internal Revenue Bureau in 1899. In 1921, after the adoption of the Eighteenth Amendment, Internal Revenue

organized a nationwide enforcement unit, and Yellowley was placed in charge of special agents. After success in New York City, he was put in charge of the Chicago office (1925–30), but was stymied by the power of mobster Al Capone. Left Prohibition enforcement in 1930. In 1934 he designed a system for collection of federal liquor taxes that was a model for the rest of the country.

YEOMANS, JOHN WILLIAM (*b. Hinsdale, Mass., 1800; d. Danville, Pa., 1863*), Congregational and Presbyterian clergyman, educator. Graduated Williams, 1824. Attended Andover Theological Seminary, 1824–26; ordained, 1828. President, Lafayette College, Easton, Pa., 1841–44. Among other pastorates, he served at Mahoning Presbyterian Church, Danville, Pa., from 1845 until shortly before his death. Chosen moderator, General Assembly, Old School Presbyterian Church, 1860.

YERGER, WILLIAM (*b. Lebanon, Tenn., 1816; d. 1872*), lawyer. Graduated University of Nashville, 1833. Removed to Jackson, Miss., 1837, where he achieved outstandingly successful law practice. Associate justice, Mississippi Supreme Court, 1851–53. A staunch Whig, he actively opposed secession. Although he remained a Unionist in sympathy, he was a member and, for a time, a president of the state senate during the Civil War. Able member of the Mississippi constitutional convention, 1865.

YERKES, CHARLES TYSON (*b. Philadelphia, Pa., 1837; d. 1905*), financier, traction magnate. Established Philadelphia banking house, 1862; gained reputation as brilliant dealer in municipal securities, 1866. Helped organize Continental Passenger Railway Co., 1875, and was its largest stockholder until 1880. Removed to Chicago, Ill., 1882. In 1886 he was in majority control of all major North Chicago and West Division streetcar companies. Because of devious financial methods, his street-railway enterprises were called the "Chicago traction tangle." Yerkes was a master of bribery and legislative manipulation. In 1899 he sold his holdings to P. A. B. Widener and W. L. Elkins for approximately $20 million. His unsuccessful attempt to extend his franchises, 1897–99, was largely responsible for introduction of bills for municipal ownership and control of street railways into the state legislature by 1901. He presented Yerkes Observatory at Lake Geneva, Wis., to the University of Chicago, 1892.

YERKES, ROBERT MEARNS (*b. Breadysville, Pa., 1876; d. New Haven, Conn., 1956*), animal psychologist. Studied at Ursinus College and at Harvard University (Ph.D., 1902). Taught at Harvard from 1902 to 1917. Owned and edited, with John R. Watson, the *Journal of Animal Behavior* (1911–19). Commander of the Psychological Corps of the Office of the Army Surgeon General, and chairman of the Research Information Service of the National Research Council in Washington, 1919–24. An early exponent of mental tests, Yerkes became involved in the controversies over army test results and immigration restrictions. From 1924 to 1941 he taught at Yale University, founding the Yale Laboratories of Primate Biology in Florida in 1929, director until 1941. After his retirement, the laboratories were administered by Harvard and Yale and renamed the Yerkes Laboratory of Primate Biology. Books include *The Great Apes* (1929).

YOAKUM, BENJAMIN FRANKLIN (*b. near Tehuacana, Tex., 1859; d. 1929*), promoter, railroad executive. Dominant figure in the St. Louis & San Francisco and Rock Island roads, 1903–13; held responsible for their failure because of extravagant profits by "insiders" during construction.

YOAKUM, HENDERSON (*b. Powell's Valley, Tenn., 1810; d. Houston, Tex., 1856*), lawyer, Tennessee legislator, historian. Graduated West Point, 1832. Removed from Tennessee to Huntsville, Tex., 1845. Principally remembered as author of

History of Texas (1855), for many years the standard history of the state.

YOHN, FREDERICK COFFAY (*b. Indianapolis, Ind., 1875; d. Norwalk, Conn., 1933*), illustrator, painter. Studied at Art Students League, N.Y., under Henry S. Mowbray. Yohn was a specialist in battle scenes and painted numerous historical subjects. During World War I he painted *America's Answer*, the second official war poster picture.

YON, PIETRO ALESSANDRO (*b. Settimo Vittone, Italy, 1886; d. Huntington, N.Y., 1943*), organist, composer. Studied at conservatories of Milan and Turin; graduated Liceo di S. Cecilia, Rome, 1905. Immigrated to New York City, 1907. Organist and choir director, Church of St. Francis Xavier; and at St. Patrick's Cathedral, New York City, 1927–43. A virtuoso player, he was also a dedicated musician and teacher. His long list of compositions includes oratorios, masses, motets, chamber music, and songs.

YORK, ALVIN CULLUM (*b. Pall Mall, Tenn., 1887; d. Nashville, Tenn., 1964*), soldier. A member of a fundamentalist church, York led a relatively uneventful life until he was inducted into the Army in 1917. Already a crackerjack rifleman, York became a fine soldier, but his religious convictions made him balk at killing others. Eventually satisfied that the Bible permitted killing under certain circumstances, York accompanied his division to France in 1918. During the Meuse-Argonne offensive, he proved himself such a marksman that he killed seventeen Germans with as many shots; then, having run out of bullets, he killed another eight with his pistol. Believing York to be at the head of hundreds, ninety more Germans surrendered. When York and his seven surviving buddies returned to camp, they delivered a total of 132 prisoners to battalion headquarters, and York, "the greatest civilian soldier of the war," became the most renowned doughboy of World War I. He was promoted to sergeant and received the Congressional Medal of Honor and France's Croix de Guerre, among other honors. After the war he helped found the American Legion. He was the subject of *Sergeant York*, a 1941 film with Gary Cooper.

YORKE, PETER CHRISTOPHER (*b. Galway, Ireland, 1864; d. 1925*), Roman Catholic clergyman. Ordained in Baltimore, Md., 1887. S.T.B., Catholic University, Washington, D.C., 1890; S.T.L., 1891. Chancellor of the San Francisco diocese *post* 1894; editor of the *Monitor*. Permanent rector, St. Anthony's Church, Oakland, Calif., 1903–13; rector, St. Peter's Church, San Francisco, 1913–25. Best known as a hard-hitting controversialist, he fought successful campaigns against bigotry on the West Coast. He was an active laborite and ardent Irish nationalist.

YOST, CASPER SALATHIEL (*b. Sedalia, Mo., 1864; d. St. Louis, Mo., 1941*), journalist. Associated *post* 1889 with the *St. Louis Globe-Democrat*, he became editor of the editorial page in 1915. A conservative Republican and deeply religious, he was a pioneer in concern for professional standards among newspapermen. He led in the founding of the American Society of Newspaper Editors and served as its first president, 1922–26. He was author of a number of books, among them *The Principles of Journalism* (1924).

YOST, FIELDING HARRIS (*b. Fairview, W.Va., 1871; d. Ann Arbor, Mich., 1946*), football coach, athletic director. Attended Ohio Normal University (later Ohio Northern). LL.B., West Virginia University, 1897. Football coach at Ohio Wesleyan and at universities of Nebraska, Kansas, and Stanford, 1897–1900, at each of which he led the team to a conference championship. As head coach at University of Michigan, 1901–23 and 1925–27, he produced teams which had eight undefeated seasons and were

eight times champions of the "Big Ten." His success was based less on gridiron theory than on skill in player recruitment and in management. His insistence on swift execution of plays on the practice field won him the nickname "Hurry-up." From 1921 through 1941, he was athletic director at Michigan.

YOU, DOMINIQUE (*b. Port-au-Prince, Haiti, or St.-Jean-d'Angély, France, ca. 1772; d. New Orleans, La., 1830*), buccaneer. Associated with Jean Laffite's smugglers at Barataria, La., *post* 1810; held command in Andrew Jackson's artillery defending New Orleans against the British, 1814–15. A legendary figure in Louisiana.

YOUMANS, EDWARD LIVINGSTON (*b. Coeymans, N.Y., 1821; d. 1887*), writer, editor. Brother of William J. Youmans. A popular lecturer on science, 1851–68, Youmans was the chief promoter in America of Herbert Spencer's publications. He was author of, among other works, *A Class-Book of Chemistry* (1851), a standard text; and *Chemical Atlas; or the Chemistry of Familiar Objects* (1854). He edited *The Culture Demanded by Modern Life* (1867), and began the International Scientific Series, 1871. He founded and edited *Popular Science Monthly* (later *Scientific Monthly*), 1872 and after.

YOUMANS, VINCENT MILLIE (*b. New York, N.Y., 1898; d. Denver, Colo., 1946*), composer, theatrical producer. Intended by his parents to study engineering at Yale, he enlisted in the U.S. Navy at the declaration of war in 1917. Assigned to an entertainment unit at Great Lakes Training Station, Youmans was fortunate enough to spend his service years composing musical shows; one joyous song that attracted the navy bandmaster's attention survived to become "Hallelujah!" in *Hit the Deck* (1927). Upon leaving the service, he went to work for the Harms Music Co. in New York as a "song-plugger."

In 1920 Youmans published his first song and made his first stage contributions for *Two Little Girls in Blue* (1921). The year 1923 saw two Youmans shows; the short-lived *Mary Jane McKane*, and *Wildflower*. Only three years after Youmans' first produced show, he composed the music for *No, No, Nanette*, a fluffball farce that captured the gaiety of the 1920's. *No, No, Nanette* opened in London in March 1925 and in New York that same September. Although *Wildflower* ran longer on Broadway, within months 17 companies were performing *Nanette* around the world.

Oh, Please! (1926) contained one song that has remained popular, "I Know That You Know." As a result, he became his own producer to present *Hit the Deck* (1927), one of Youmans' best scores; it held two hit songs, the jubilant "Hallelujah!" and the sophisticated rhythm ballad "Sometimes I'm Happy." Youmans composed several songs for Florenz Ziegfeld's *Smiles* (1930), although his best effort, "Time on My Hands," was dropped from the show. Youmans himself produced *Through the Years* (1932), a failure whose title song was reputedly the composer's favorite. *Take a Chance* (1932) was his last Broadway contribution, with five Youmans songs supplementing the basic score. The young Ethel Merman shone brightly in the latter show, and the song "Rise 'n' Shine" joined the earlier "Hallelujah!," "Great Day!," and "Drums in My Heart." His final work of any substance was the film score for *Flying Down to Rio* (1933).

YOUMANS, WILLIAM JAY (*b. Milton, N.Y., 1838; d. 1901*), scientific writer, editor. Brother of Edward L. Youmans. Graduated in medicine, University of the City of New York (New York University), 1865. Prepared for publication *The Elements of Physiology and Hygiene* (1868), by Thomas Huxley. Actively associated with *Popular Science Monthly* from 1872, he was sole editor, 1887–1900. Author of *Pioneers of Science in America*

(1896); contributed to *Appleton's Annual Cyclopaedia,* 1880–1900.

YOUNG, AARON (*b. Wiscasset, Maine, 1819; d. Belmont, Mass., 1898*), physician, pharmacist, botanist. Studied under Parker Cleaveland at Bowdoin. State botanist of Maine, 1847–49; wrote survey of Mount Katahdin; was a pioneer in afforestation. He served as U.S. consul to Rio Grande do Sul, Brazil, 1863–73.

YOUNG, ALEXANDER (*b. Boston, Mass., 1800; d. Boston, 1854*), Unitarian clergyman, antiquarian. Graduated Harvard, 1820; Harvard Divinity School, 1824. Pastor at New South Church, Boston. Published *Chronicles of the Pilgrim Fathers of the Colony of Plymouth from 1602 to 1625* (1841) and *Chronicles of the First Planters of the Colony of Massachusetts Bay from 1623 to 1636* (1846).

YOUNG, ALFRED (*b. Bristol, England, 1831; d. New York, N.Y., 1900*), Roman Catholic clergyman, musician. Came to America as an infant. Graduated College of New Jersey (Princeton), 1848; M.D., present New York University, 1852. A convert to Catholicism, 1850, he studied theology at St. Sulpice, Paris; he was ordained in Newark, N.J., 1856. Joined Society of St. Paul, 1862. A leader in laymen's retreats and missions for non-Catholics. Founded Paulist Choir, 1873. Promoted Gregorian chant and composed hymnals.

YOUNG, ALLYN ABBOTT (*b. Kenton, Ohio, 1876; d. London, England, 1929*), economist. Ph.D., University of Wisconsin, 1902. Taught at numerous institutions including Stanford, Cornell, Harvard, and the London School of Economics, 1927. Author of *Economic Problems New and Old* (1927).

YOUNG, AMMI BURNHAM (*b. Lebanon, N.H., 1798; d. Washington, D.C., 1874*), architect. Began his career as a builder; was a pupil and assistant of Alexander Parris in Boston, Mass. Architect of Thornton and Wentworth halls at Dartmouth College, 1828–29, he designed Reed Hall there, 1839. He was also architect for the State Capitol at Montpelier, Vt., 1833–36 (later destroyed). Removing to Boston *ca.* 1837, he was busy for about ten years with the construction of the Boston Customs House and did other work in that city and elsewhere. Its powerful design won high praise, and Young was appointed to succeed Robert Mills as architect of federal buildings *ca.* 1850. He continued in federal service until 1862. During his years as architect for the Treasury Department, Young designed a great number of customhouses, federal courthouses, post offices, and marine hospitals, employing in the interest of speed and economy a fruitful standardization of types and rationalized construction method. His most important innovation was the wide use of iron in these buildings. His work for the government ranged from monumental classic edifices like the customhouse at Norfolk, Va., to the Appraiser's Stores at St. Louis, Mo., and San Francisco, Calif., to small classical-revival public buildings in minor eastern towns.

YOUNG, ART (*b. near Orangeville, Ill., 1866; d. New York, N.Y., 1943*), cartoonist, socialist. Raised in Monroe, Wis. Studied at Chicago Academy of Design, Art Students League in New York City, and Académie Julian in Paris; staff artist and cartoonist for newspapers in Chicago and Denver. Removed to New York City, where he made comic drawings for *Life, Puck,* and *Judge,* and editorial cartoons for the Hearst newspapers; through the influence of the muckrakers and of radical writers generally, he developed his earlier questionings of capitalism into a full commitment to socialism. He was a contributor to *The Masses* from its first number (January 1911) and to the *Liberator;* he was also Washington correspondent, 1912–17, for *Metropolitan* magazine. From 1919 to 1921, he published his own weekly of art and comment, *Good Morning.* Possessed of a clear, uncluttered style, richly expressive and stripped of nonessentials, he was able to satirize society without becoming either sour or cantankerous; his love of humanity more than balanced his scorn for its follies and failures.

YOUNG, BRIGHAM (*b. Whitingham, Vt., 1801; d. Utah, 1877*), colonizer of Utah, second president of the Mormon church. Young's family belonged to the same class of restless frontier drifters from which Joseph Smith (1805–44) came; as a youth in western New York he resided in several places in the neighborhood of Smith's wanderings. A competent farmer as well as a journeyman house painter, he settled with his first wife in Mendon, N.Y., 1829. A Methodist from the age of 22, Young first read *The Book of Mormon* within a few weeks of its publication; after two years' study, he was baptized at Mendon, April 1832. His conversion to his new faith integrated all his vast energies, and the rest of his life was devoted to building up the Mormon church in highly practical ways.

In July 1833 he led a band of converts to Kirtland, Ohio, and soon thereafter traveled throughout the eastern United States as the most successful of the Mormon missionaries. He was chosen third of the newly organized Quorum of the Twelve Apostles in February 1835, and by 1838, when the Mormons were expelled from Missouri, he had become the senior member of the body. He directed the removal to Nauvoo, Ill., during Joseph Smith's imprisonment. After heading a most successful mission in England, 1839–41, he became the leading fiscal officer of the church at Nauvoo. Electioneering in behalf of Smith's campaign for the presidency of the United States, 1844, he was in Boston when he learned of the prophet's murder. Hurrying back to Nauvoo, he rallied the shaken church behind the authority of the Twelve Apostles, of whom he was the head.

Having taken command of a church already responsive to authoritarian control and shaped to cooperative effort, he began one of the most successful colonizing endeavors in U.S. history. Obviously the Mormons could not survive in the American social system. With assistance from abroad and from the U.S. government, Young undertook to remove the church to the western wilderness and completed his preparations for the exodus by 1847. On Dec. 5, 1847, he had himself elected president of the church at Winter Quarters, Nebr. Having determined on the valley of Great Salt Lake as the site of Zion, he supervised the migration with great success. He had hoped for a long period of isolation for the Mormon people, but the gold rush to California in 1849 soon upset his expectation and it was ended by the completion of the Union Pacific Railroad during the 1860's. Once in Deseret (the Mormon name for the colony, later changed to Utah by Congress), Young displayed brilliance and genius as a city planner and colonizer. He instituted systems of irrigation which were indispensable to agricultural success and dispatched groups of settlers to occupy fertile valleys throughout the intermountain country, each group supplied with its own quota of mechanics and specialists. Meanwhile, his missionaries were bringing a steady stream of immigrants to the settlements, and Young instituted public works to occupy them while places were being found for them in the agricultural system. The greatest number of converts came from the tenant farmers and the city unemployed of Europe and America.

If Brigham Young was soon nationally infamous as a despot, it was because nothing less than a united effort could preserve his group. Because the first essential was food and agricultural development, he forbade the opening of mines. High freight rates for transport from the East led him to develop home industries, which he supported with a curious blend of the Rochdale Plan and the joint-stock company. His policy, however, gave the church organization financial and industrial interests separate from the people and began a change from cooperation to corporate control which accelerated after Young's death. He met the threat of competition from gentile merchants by organizing Zion's Cooperative Mercantile Institution and similar concerns which kept Mormon money at home. Young's greatest achievement was his transformation of a loose hierarchy into a magnificent fiscal organization for social and economic management. He discountenanced prophecy and similar evangelical gifts, stating that the Kingdom must be built upon earth before it could aspire to any celestial inheritance.

His 20-year struggle with the federal government and occasional local terrorism were political expressions of a social and economic fact. Young was dictator of a society whose methods and ideals were radically different from those of the 19th-century American society which surrounded it. He managed to make the theocracy coextensive with the political state for some years, but after the organization of Utah Territory by Congress in 1850, he was forced to permit the exterior form of government to come increasingly into accord with the American system. Appointed the first governor of the territory, he refused to vacate his office when displaced. Although he yielded to the threat of a U.S. expeditionary force under General A. S. Johnston, 1857, his successors were mere figureheads and Young governed as effectively as before.

Brigham Young had no interest in systematic thought and was impatient of theory; he was perhaps the foremost social pragmatist of his time. His mind worked rapidly and could carry a myriad relevant details about every activity and personality of his church. Ruthless and domineering as a leader, he was in private life a genial, benevolent man who had strong family affections and loved dancing, singing, and the theater. He had a fanatical belief in salvation by labor and abhorred all forms of waste. The number of his wives is variously given from 19 to 27. He had 56 children.

YOUNG, CHARLES AUGUSTUS (*b. Hanover, N.H., 1834; d. Hanover, 1908*), astronomer. Grandson of Ebenezer Adams. Graduated Dartmouth, 1853. As professor of natural philosophy and astronomy at Dartmouth, 1866–77, Young engaged in pioneering studies in solar physics with a spectroscope of his own design. He was professor of astronomy at the College of New Jersey (Princeton), 1877–1905, and was author of *The Sun* (1881) and of several astronomy textbooks.

YOUNG, CLARK MONTGOMERY (*b. Hiram, Ohio, 1856; d. 1908*), educator. Ph.B., Hiram College, 1883. Became professor of history and political science. South Dakota University, 1892; was first dean of the college of arts and sciences from 1902 until his death. Active in South Dakota educational progress, he helped draft state school laws and conducted teachers institutes.

YOUNG, DAVID (*b. Pine Brook, N.J., 1781; d. 1852*), New Jersey almanac-maker, author. Self-educated. As "David Young, Philom," he published *Citizens' & Farmers' Almanac* (1814) and numerous others until his death. Author of *The Contrast* (1804), a religious poem in blank verse; *The Perusal* (1818), a cosmic, Miltonian poem; *Lectures on the Science of Astronomy* (1821); and *The Wonderful History of the Morristown Ghost* (1826).

YOUNG, DENTON TRUE ("CY") (*b. Gilmore, Ohio, 1867; d. Newcomerstown, Ohio, 1955*), baseball player. 1890–99 was pitcher for the Cleveland Spiders; 1900–09 he pitched for the American League team in Boston, playing in the first game of the modern World Series in 1903. Young achieved an unmatched record of 509 wins and 316 losses. One of baseball's greatest pitchers, he retired in 1912. Elected to the National Baseball Hall of Fame in 1937.

YOUNG, ELLA FLAGG (*b. Buffalo, N.Y., 1845; d. 1918*), educator. District superintendent, Chicago, Ill., schools, 1887–99. Ph.D., University of Chicago, 1900; professor of education at the university, 1899–1904. Principal, Chicago Normal School, 1905–09, and superintendent, Chicago public school system, 1909–15. She was the first woman president of the National Education Association, 1910.

YOUNG, EWING (*b. eastern Tennessee, date unknown; d. Oregon, 1841*), trapper, pioneer. Probably accompanied expedition under William Becknell which opened Santa Fe Trail, 1821; thereafter worked as a trapper out of Taos. In 1829 he led a party which included Kit Carson across the Mojave Desert into California. Returning to Taos, 1831, he joined with David Waldo and others in organizing two expeditions to California. Between 1832 and 1834, he journeyed over a great part of California and to the Colorado River at Yuma. In association with Hall J. Kelley, he went from Monterey, Calif., to Fort Vancouver, arriving in the fall of 1834 and settling on a farm on the Chehalem. At first shunned because of a false accusation of horse theft, he cleared himself by 1837 and was thereafter a leader in the young Oregon community. He was a man of intelligence, active and scrupulously honest.

YOUNG, GEORGE (*b. near South Boston, Va., 1870; d. New York, N.Y., 1935*), pullman porter, bookseller, bibliophile. Born of black parents who had been slaves, Young educated himself principally in night schools and by wide outside reading. In the course of many years' collecting, he built up an outstanding library of some 9,000 books by or about blacks which is now contained in the New York Public Library system. He was also a lifelong worker for the cultural advancement of blacks.

YOUNG, HUGH HAMPTON (*b. San Antonio, Tex., 1870; d. Baltimore, Md., 1945*), urologist. A.B. and A.M., University of Virginia, 1893; M.D., 1894. After graduate study at Johns Hopkins Hospital, he interned there and then became head of the genitourinary dispensary, 1897. From 1898 until 1942, he taught genitourinary diseases and surgery at Johns Hopkins Medical School (professor of urology *post* 1932); he also carried on a private practice in Baltimore. An eminent pioneer in the development of modern urology, he designed improved versions of the cystoscope and other instruments and invented a number of new instruments and novel surgical procedures. In 1903, he devised a radical operation for total removal of the cancerous prostate gland. Director *post* 1915 of the Brady Urological Institute at Johns Hopkins Hospital, he and associates developed mercurochrome there and pioneered in use of sulfa and other modern drugs for treatment of venereal disease. He was author of more than 350 technical papers and of *Young's Practice of Urology* (1926, with collaborators).

YOUNG, JESSE BOWMAN (*b. Berwick, Pa., 1844; d. Chicago, Ill., 1914*), Union soldier, Methodist clergyman, editor. A.B., Dickinson College, 1868. Held pastorates in Pennsylvania, Missouri, Ohio, and Florida; edited *Central Christian Advocate*, 1892–1900. Author of, among other works, *The Battle of Gettysburg* (1913).

YOUNG, JOHN (*b. Chelsea, Vt., 1802; d. New York, N.Y., 1852*), lawyer, New York legislator. Congressman, Whig, from New York, 1836–37 and 1841–43. As assemblyman from Livingston Co., 1845, he secured passage of the Whig measure calling a convention to revise the state constitution. As Whig and Antirent governor of New York, 1847–49, he alienated conservatives of his party by pardoning imprisoned Antirent rioters and by supporting the Mexican War.

YOUNG, JOHN CLARKE (*b. Greencastle, Pa., 1803; d. 1857*), Presbyterian clergyman, educator. Graduated Dickinson College, 1823; Princeton Theological Seminary, 1827. President, Centre College, Danville, Ky., 1830–57. Became pastor of Danville

Presbyterian Church, 1834; organized Second Presbyterian Church for students of the college, 1852. Became moderator of the General Assembly, 1853. An "old school" minister, distinguished for high principles and common sense.

Young, John Richardson (*b. Elizabethtown, Md., 1782; d. 1804*), physician. M.D., University of Pennsylvania, 1803. Author of *An Experimental Inquiry into the Principles of Nutrition and the Digestive Process* (1803), a brilliant anticipation of the work of William Beaumont.

Young, John Russell (*b. Co. Tyrone, Ireland, 1840; d. 1899*), journalist. Came to America as an infant. A reporter on the Philadelphia *Press*, he came to be a favorite of John W. Forney; as war correspondent, 1861, he became famous for an account of the Union defeat at first Bull Run. After serving as managing editor of Forney's newspapers, 1862–65, he became managing editor of the *New York Tribune*, 1866. In 1870 and 1871, he went abroad on confidential missions for the U.S. secretaries of the treasury and of state; in the course of this work, he witnessed the Paris Commune, of which he wrote a brilliant report. An editor of the *New York Herald* from 1872, he worked in London and Paris; in 1877, he accompanied U. S. Grant on a tour around the world. As U.S. minister to China, 1882–85, Young settled many outstanding claims and mediated in the dispute between France and China over Annam; he then resumed work on the *Herald*. He served as Librarian of Congress *post* 1897. Author of *Around the World with General Grant* (1879) and *Men and Memories* (1901).

Young, John Wesley (*b. Columbus, Ohio, 1879; d. Hanover, N.H., 1932*), mathematician, educator. Graduated Ohio State, 1899; Ph.D., Cornell University, 1904. Taught at Northwestern, Princeton, Illinois, and Kansas universities; at Dartmouth *post* 1911. Editor of the American Mathematical Society *Bulletin*, 1907–25; Coauthor of *Projective Geometry* (1910, 1918); author of *Lectures on Fundamental Concepts of Algebra and Geometry* (1911).

Young, Josue Maria (*b. Shapleigh, Maine, 1808; d. 1866*), Roman Catholic clergyman. A printer-journalist in Maine, Kentucky, and Ohio, he was a convert to Catholicism, 1828. After studies at Mount St. Mary's, Emmitsburg, Md., he was ordained in 1838 and worked in the diocese of Cincinnati, Ohio. Consecrated bishop of Erie, Pa., 1854, he served until his death.

Young, Karl (*b. Clinton, Iowa, 1879; d. New Haven, Conn., 1943*), medievalist, educator. A.B., University of Michigan, 1901. A.M., Harvard, 1902; Ph.D., 1907. Taught English at University of Wisconsin, 1909–23; professor of English (*post* 1938 Sterling professor) at Yale, 1923–43. Author of scholarly works on Chaucer's literary sources and of *The Drama of the Medieval Church* (1933), a definitive corpus of texts with accompanying exposition, interpretation, and evaluation.

Young, Lafayette (*b. near Eddyville, Iowa, 1848; d. Des Moines, Iowa, 1926*), Iowa journalist and legislator. Editor-publisher of the *Des Moines Capital*, 1890–1926. A correspondent in Cuba, 1898, he won the friendship of Theodore Roosevelt and placed Roosevelt's name in nomination for the vice-presidency at the Republican National Convention, 1900. U.S. senator, Republican, from Iowa, 1910–April, 1911.

Young, Mahonri Mackintosh (*b. Salt Lake City, Utah, 1877; d. Norwalk, Conn., 1957*), artist. Studied at the Art Students League in New York and at the Académie Julian in Paris. Remembered for his bronze sculptures and watercolors of the American West, of athletes, and of cowboys and Indians. Young, the grandson of Brigham Young, sculpted the famous Sea Gull

monument (1913) and *This Is the Place* sculpture (1947) in Utah. He helped organize the famed Armory Show of 1913. His works can be seen in the Metropolitan Museum of Art, the Whitney Museum of American Art in New York, the American Museum of Natural History, and the Brooklyn Museum, as well as many others across the country.

Young, Owen D. (*b. Van Hornersville, N.Y., 1874; d. St. Augustine, Fla., 1962*), lawyer, industrialist, political adviser, and diplomat. A lawyer experienced in the electrical industry, Young joined the General Electric Company (GE) as general counsel and vice president in 1913. There he became one of the first industrialists to recognize the importance of bettering industrial relations within the company and improving GE's image with the public. In 1919, he organized, and became chairman of, the board of the Radio Corporation of America (RCA). In the mid-1920's Young helped found the National Broadcasting Company. In 1922 he became chairman of the board of GE. In 1933 he resigned the chairmanship of RCA because of federal court order forcing him to choose between chairing GE or RCA. Young retired from GE in 1939, returning briefly as chairman during World War II (1942–44). He also enjoyed a career in international diplomacy beginning in the 1920's when he was chief architect of the Dawes Plan (1924) to reconstruct the German economy and reduce reparations payment. He was a close adviser to Franklin D. Roosevelt during the 1932 campaign, but later criticized the New Deal. In 1947 Young served on the Committee on Foreign Aid, which made recommendations on European relief and reconstruction under the Marshall Plan.

Young, Pierce Manning Butler (*b. Spartanburg, S.C., 1836; d. New York, N.Y., 1896*), Confederate soldier, diplomat. Raised in Georgia. Attended West Point, 1857–61, resigning to enter Confederate artillery. Served with great gallantry in the Virginia campaigns with the cavalry of Cobb's Legion; won commendation for his behavior at Gettysburg and Brandy Station. He was made brigadier general, 1863, and given command of Hampton's brigade. In 1864 he defended Augusta, Ga., against General W. T. Sherman, rising to major general in December. Congressman, Democrat, from Georgia, July 1868–March 1869 and December 1870–March 1875. U.S. consul general at St. Petersburg, Russia, 1885–87; U.S. minister to Guatemala and Honduras, 1893–96.

Young, Robert Ralph (*b. Canadian, Tex., 1897; d. Palm Beach, Fla., 1958*), railway executive. Studied briefly at the University of Virginia. After working for E. I. du Pont, 1916, and General Motors, 1922, assistant treasurer, 1928, Young made a fortune in the stock market crash of 1929. He thereafter sought to control railroads with the idea of a true coast-to-coast passenger service. Gained control of the Chesapeake and Ohio in the early 1930's and embarked on a long battle to win the New York Central, something he realized in 1954. But the government and other railroads never cooperated in allowing him to connect his transcontinental system. In one of his recurring bouts of depression, he committed suicide.

Young, Samuel Hall (*b. Butler, Pa., 1847; d. near Clarksburg, W.Va., 1927*), Presbyterian clergyman. Ordained in 1878 as a missionary to Alaska, he spent the greater part of his life in service there. He organized the first Protestant and first American church in Alaska at Fort Wrangell, 1879. With John Muir, he explored Glacier Bay and discovered the Muir Glacier. He was also organizer and secretary of the first territorial convention, 1881, and drafted a memorial to Congress asking for better government.

YOUNG, STARK (*b. Como, Miss., 1881; d. Fairfield, Conn., 1963*), drama critic, novelist, playwright. Attended the University of Mississippi (B.A., 1901) and Columbia (M.A., 1902). Faculty member of the University of Texas at Austin where he founded the Curtin Club (1909). In 1914 he founded and edited the *Texas* (later *Southwest*) *Review*, then was an English professor at Amherst College (1915–21). At Amherst he published numerous poems and articles while his play, *At the Shrine*, was published in *Theatre Arts Magazine*. Left his academic career to devote himself fully to the arts as a staff member of the *New Republic* (1922–47) and *Theatre Arts Magazine* (1922–48). His novel, *So Red the Rose*, one of the best-sellers of 1934, brought him widespread acclaim and became a motion picture in 1935.

YOUNG, THOMAS (*b. New Windsor, N.Y., 1731/2; d. Philadelphia, Pa., 1777*), Revolutionary patriot, physician. Began practice of medicine in Amenia, N.Y., 1753; removed to Boston, Mass., 1766, where he was second only to Samuel Adams in pre-Revolutionary activity. Resident in Newport, R.I., 1774–75, he then escaped possible capture by the British by removal to Philadelphia, where he was secretary of the Whig Society. He suggested the name Vermont for the new state proposed by delegates from the New Hampshire grants, 1777. He died while serving as surgeon in a Continental army hospital.

YOUNGER, MAUD (*b. San Francisco, Calif., 1870; d. Los Gatos, Calif., 1936*), woman suffragist, trade unionist. Washington lobby chairman of the Congressional Union for Woman Suffrage (later the National Woman's Party).

YOUNGER, THOMAS COLEMAN (*b. near Lee's Summit, Mo., 1844; d. near Lee's Summit, 1916*), desperado, better known as "Cole" Younger. After service as a Confederate guerrilla, he was active in the gang of bandits reputedly led by Jesse James. Captured with his brothers and others of the gang after their attempt to rob the bank at Northfield, Minn., September 1876, he was tried and sentenced to life imprisonment. Paroled in 1901, he was pardoned early in 1903.

YOUNGS, JOHN (*b. Southwold, England, 1623; d. 1698*), colonial soldier and official. Immigrated to Salem, Mass., 1637; was a settler of Southold, N.Y., *ca.* 1640. Appointed magistrate and a deputy from Southold to New Haven, 1660, he worked to establish the complete jurisdiction of Connecticut over the Long Island towns and became a member of the Connecticut council, 1664. He aided in the capture of New Amsterdam, 1664, but later led a protest against the newly imposed rule of the duke of York and restored Southold and neighboring towns to Connecticut after the Dutch recaptured New York in 1673. However, he accepted a share in the patent of Southold from the duke of York, 1676, and returned to New York allegiance. In 1681 he drafted a petition to the duke for a representative assembly (first held in New York, October 1683), while serving as the high sheriff of the county of Yorkshire. He was a member of the Governor's Council of New York *post* 1686.

YOUNT, GEORGE CONCEPCÍON (*b. Dowden Creek, N.C., 1794; d. Caymus Rancho, Calif., 1865*), farmer, trapper, California pioneer. Raised in Missouri. Removing to Santa Fe, 1825, he became a trapper and worked with Ewing Young and others; during 1829, he worked in the northern fur country around the source of the Yellowstone. Influenced by Jedediah S. Smith, he joined William Wolfskill's 1830 expedition to California, arriving in Los Angeles in February 1831. After a period of drifting up and down the coast, he became a Mexican citizen and was given a grant of land in the Napa Valley, 1836, on which he built a fort and began cultivation and improvement. Suffering heavy loss after the American conquest of California, he later recovered much of his property.

YULEE, DAVID LEVY (*b. St. Thomas, Danish West Indies, 1810; d. New York, N.Y., 1886*), lawyer, Florida politician, railroad promoter. Admitted to the Florida bar, 1836, he served as Florida territorial delegate to Congress *post* 1841, and as U.S. senator, Democrat, from Florida, 1845–51, and 1855–61. Originally a leader in the Southern rights movement, he later became much more conservative. One of the earliest railroad promoters in the South, he incorporated the Atlantic & Gulf Railroad, 1853, which he completed after difficulties in 1860; it connected Fernandina, Fla. with Cedar Keys. During the Civil War he devoted his energies to his plantation and to the running of his railroad, successfully preventing seizure of its material by the Confederate authorities for use in repair of other lines.

YUNG, WING (*b. Nam Ping, Pedro Island, near Macao, China, 1828; d. Hartford, Conn., 1912*), educator, Chinese official. Graduated Yale, 1854, the first Chinese alumnus of an American college. Initiated, and served as commissioner of, the Chinese Educational Commission, 1870–81, for placing young Chinese in U.S. educational institutions. Associated with reforming and "Westernizing" movements as a Chinese official, he fled his own country in 1899 and resided in the United States *post* 1902.

Z

ZACH, MAX WILHELM (*b. Lemberg, Austria, 1864; d. 1921*), orchestral conductor, composer. Violist, Boston Symphony Orchestra, 1886–1907; Adamowski String Quartette, 1890–1906. Conductor, St. Louis Symphony Orchestra, 1907–21. His most significant contribution to American music was his advocacy of works by American composers. He wrote marches and waltzes in the Viennese style.

ZACHARIAS, ELLIS MARK (*b. Jacksonville, Fla., 1890; d. West Springfield, NH., 1961*), naval officer. Began a lifelong study of Japanese language and culture at the U.S. Naval Academy, from which he was graduated in 1912. During his 1920 assignment to Tokyo as naval attaché, he became fluent in Japanese and met many of the men who later directed Japan's war effort during World War II. After serving both in combat and in naval intelligence during World War II, he played a key role in the preparation of psychological operations to induce Japan to surrender unconditionally. Zacharias was awarded a Legion of Merit for the part he took in the Japanese surrender. He retired as a rear admiral in 1946.

ZACHOS, JOHN CELIVERGOS (*b. Constantinople, Turkey, 1820; d. New York, N.Y., 1898*), educator, Union army surgeon, Unitarian clergyman, author, inventor. Brought to America by Samuel G. Howe, 1830. B.A., Kenyon, 1840; studied medicine at Miami University, Ohio, 1842–45. Associated for a number of years with Ohio educational institutions. Curator and teacher of literature and oratory, Cooper Union, New York City, *post* 1871. Patented machine for printing at high reporting speed, 1876. Author of, among other works, *A Sketch of the Life and Opinions of Mr. Peter Cooper* (1876) and *The Phonic Primer and Reader* (1864).

ZAHARIAS, MILDRED ("BABE") DIDRIKSON (*b. Port Arthur, Tex., 1914; d. Galveston, Tex., 1956*), athlete. One of the greatest women athletes of all time, Babe Zaharias broke 4 world records at the 1936 Olympics: in the javelin throw, the 80-meter hurdles (twice), and the high jump. It is as a golfer that she is most remembered. She became the first American woman to win the British Ladies' Amateur Open in 1947. She won 17 consecutive tournaments in 1946–47, and 82 between 1933 and 1953, making her the greatest woman golfer of all time. The Associated Press voted her "Woman of the Year" in 1936, 1945, 1947, 1950, and 1954.

ZAHM, JOHN AUGUSTINE (*b. New Lexington, Ohio, 1851; d. Munich, Germany, 1921*), Roman Catholic clergyman, educator. Graduated Notre Dame University, 1871; entered Congregation of the Holy Cross. Ordained, 1875, he taught at Notre Dame and held administrative posts in his order. Occupied chiefly as a writer *post* 1905, he was author of scientific and theological books, and authoritative texts on South America, sometimes under pseudonym "J. H. Mozans." He was a friend and traveling associate of Theodore Roosevelt.

ZAHNISER, HOWARD CLINTON (*b. Franklin, Pa., 1906; d. Hyattsville, Md., 1964*), conservationist, editor. Attended the Greenville College, Ill. (B.A., 1928) and did postgraduate work at American University and George Washington University in Washington, D.C. After a series of positions with the federal government as an editor, writer, and broadcaster, Zahniser became executive secretary (later executive director) of the Wilderness Society and editor of its magazine, *The Living Wilderness* (1945–64). In the 1950's he successfully led a movement to defeat construction of a dam at Dinosaur National Monument on the Colorado-Utah border. Was instrumental in creating a national wilderness preservation system. He was also an essayist and book editor for *Nature* magazine (1935–59).

ZAKRZEWSKA, MARIE ELIZABETH (*b. Berlin, Germany, 1829; d. 1902*), physician. Immigrated to America, 1853. Aided by Elizabeth Blackwell, she graduated M.D. from Cleveland Medical College, 1856. Founder, and virtual head, of the New England Hospital for Women and Children, 1862–99, she became the outstanding woman physician in New England.

ZAMORANO, AGUSTIN JUAN VICENTE (*b. St. Augustine, Fla., 1798; d. 1842*), military engineer, Mexican official. Executive secretary of California, 1825–36; also commandant of the *presidio* at Monterey, 1831–36. Chiefly remembered as California's first printer. Among his known imprints are letterheads, official broadsides or folders, and four books, including José Figueroa's *Manifesto a la Republica Mejicana* (1835). Military commander of Lower California, 1839–40, he was appointed adjutant inspector of California, 1842, but died soon after reaching San Diego.

ZANE, CHARLES SHUSTER (*b. Cape May Co., N.J., 1831; d. Salt Lake City, Utah, 1915*), jurist. Admitted to the Illinois bar, 1857. Law partner of W. H. Herndon and S. M. Cullom. Illinois circuit judge, 1873–84; chief justice of Utah Territory, 1884–88 and 1889–94. Enforced Edmunds Law against polygamy and related offenses with efficient sternness, yet won respect of the Mormons and protected their legal rights. First chief justice of the state of Utah, 1896–99.

ZANE, EBENEZER (*b. near Moorefield, Va., now W.Va., 1747; d. 1812*), pioneer, land speculator. Established Wheeling, Va., settlement, 1769. A colonel in Dunmore's War, he also played a prominent part in sieges of Fort Fincastle (Fort Henry), 1777 and 1782. He received, 1796, federal grants of land where Zanesville and Lancaster, Ohio, were later laid out, on condition that he blaze a road from Wheeling to Limestone, Ky., before 1797.

ZEILIN, JACOB (*b. Philadelphia, Pa., 1806; d. 1880*), U.S. Marine Corps officer. Attended West Point for several years *post* 1822; entered marines as second lieutenant, 1831. Served in California during Mexican War; also on M. C. Perry's expedition to Japan; was wounded at first Bull Run. First marine officer to attain rank of brigadier general, 1867, he was commandant of the corps, 1864–76.

ZEISBERGER, DAVID (*b. Zauchtenthal, Moravia, 1721; d. Goshen, Ohio, 1808*), Moravian missionary. Immigrating first to Savannah, Ga., he removed to Pennsylvania in 1739. A successful and devoted missionary to the Iroquois and the Delaware tribes, Zeisberger was involved from 1745 until his death in all the complicated politics of the frontier. Invaluable in conferences with the Indians because of his knowledge of their habits and languages, he gave his primary attention to making the Indians useful members of society. He lived about ten years among the Iroquois between 1745 and 1763. He then worked principally with the Delaware, following them as they were pushed westward by the tide of settlement and establishing a Christian Indian settlement in the Tuscarawas Valley, 1771. Here he erected the first church building and schoolhouse west of the Ohio River; within a few years three similar centers were erected nearby. After the ruin of these Indian settlements during the Revolution, Zeisberger helped establish settlements for Indian converts in what is now Michigan and also at New Salem, Ohio, and Fairfield, Canada.

ZEISLER, FANNIE BLOOMFIELD (*b. Bielitz, Austrian Silesia, 1863; d. 1927*), pianist, teacher. Wife of Sigmund Zeisler; sister of Maurice Bloomfield. Came to America as a child; was raised in Chicago, Ill. A pupil of Bernhard Ziehn and Carl Wolfsohn; studied also with Leschetizky in Vienna. Played with major European orchestras on continental tours, 1893–1912; noted for technique and poetic feeling.

ZEISLER, SIGMUND (*b. Bielitz, Austrian Silesia, 1860; d. Chicago, Ill., 1931*), lawyer. Husband of Fannie B. Zeisler. Immigrated to America, 1883. J.D., University of Vienna, 1883; LL.B., Northwestern University, 1884. Practiced law in Chicago, Ill., *post* 1884. Assistant corporation counsel of Chicago, 1893–94; master in chancery, Cook Co. circuit court, 1904–20.

ZELLERBACH, JAMES DAVID (*b. San Francisco, Calif., 1892; d. San Francisco, 1963.*), industrialist, diplomat. Entered the Zellerbach Corporation, founded by his grandfather, as a counterman after graduating from the University of California in 1913. In 1929 Zellerbach Corporation merged with the Crown Williamette Corporation to become Crown Zellerbach, the nation's leading manufacturer of paper and paper products. Zellerbach was its first president; he became chairman in 1938. As a labor expert, he served as vice chairman of the International Labor Organization (1945–48) and headed the Economic Cooperation Administration's mission to implement the Marshall Plan in Italy (1948). From 1956 to the end of the Eisenhower administration was U.S. ambassador to Italy.

ZENGER, JOHN PETER (*b. Germany, 1697; d. New York, N.Y., 1746*), printer, journalist. Immigrated to New York *ca.* 1710; was apprenticed in 1711 to William Bradford, the pioneer printer of the middle colonies. After a residence in Kent Co., Md., 1719–21, he returned to New York, forming a partnership with Bradford, 1725. He set up in business for himself, 1726, and printed a number of unimportant works in English and Dutch. He brought out Venema's *Arithmetica*, 1730, the first arithmetic text printed in the New York colony.

Backed by Lewis Morris, James Alexander, and William Smith (1697–1769) as editor of a journal which would oppose the administration of Governor William Cosby, Zenger brought an independent and truculent spirit to New York journalism. The first number of his *New-York Weekly Journal* appeared Nov. 5, 1733. Although its major articles were contributed by his backers, Zenger was legally responsible for them as publisher, and he was arrested in the fall of 1734 for alleged libelous statements in the

issues numbered 7, 47, 48, and 49 of the *Journal*. Confined for some ten months before trial, he continued to bring out his paper through the management of his wife. Brought to trial in April 1735 for criminal libel, he appeared to have very little chance. Alexander and Smith, who represented him, were disbarred when they questioned the validity of appointment of two of the judges. However, at the trial in August, Zenger was represented by Andrew Hamilton (d. 1741) of Philadelphia, who overrode the strict construction of criminal libel under common law and pleaded for the right of the jury to inquire into the truth or falsity of the libel. When his argument was cut off by the court, Hamilton appealed to the jury, which responded with a verdict of not guilty. This was the first major victory for the freedom of the press in the American colonies, and the account of the trial, published as *A Brief Narrative of the Case and Tryal of John Peter Zenger* (1736), aroused great interest both in America and in Great Britain. Appointed public printer for the colony of New York in 1737, Zenger was appointed to the same office for New Jersey the following year.

ZENTMAYER, JOSEPH (*b. Mannheim, Germany, 1826; d. Philadelphia, Pa., 1888*), inventor, manufacturer. Immigrated to America 1848. Established himself in Philadelphia, 1853, as a scientific instrument-maker. Made a number of improvements in the microscope; invented, 1865, and patented an improved photographic lens.

ZERRAHN, CARL (*b. Malchow, Germany, 1826; d. Milton, Mass., 1909*), musician, conductor. Came to the United States, 1848. Conductor, Boston, Mass., Handel and Haydn Society, 1854–96. Directed Harvard Musical Association, 1865–82. Active as conductor of Massachusetts orchestras and music festivals. Taught singing, harmony, and composition at the New England Conservatory of Music, Boston.

ZEUNER, CHARLES (*b. Eisleben, Saxony, 1795; d. probably Camden, N.J., 1857*), composer, organist. Immigrated to America *ante* 1830. Organist, Boston, Mass., Handel and Haydn Society, 1830–39. Author of, among other publications, *Church Music . . . Anthems, Motets, and Chants* (1831); *Organ Voluntaries* (1840); and an oratorio, *The Feast of Tabernacles* (*ca.* 1832), the first American work of its kind, presented by the Boston Academy of Music, 1837.

ZEVIN, ISRAEL JOSEPH (*b. Horki, Mohilev, Russia, 1872; d. 1926*), editor, writer. Best known under pseudonym "Tashrak." Immigrated to New York City, 1889. Associated with *Jewish Daily News* thereafter until his death as a chief contributor, and as editor in chief for a time *post* 1907. He wrote humorous stories depicting immigrant American Jews which were widely popular. Among his books were *Tashrak's beste Erzeilungen* (1910) and *Ale Agodos fun Talmud* (1922).

ZIEGEMEIER, HENRY JOSEPH (*b. Allegheny, Pa., 1869; d. probably Bremerton, Wash., 1930*), naval officer. Graduated Annapolis, 1890. After varied service at sea and staff duty, he was promoted captain, 1916, and commanded the battleship *Virginia*, 1917–19. He had charge of the organization and training of the Naval Reserve Force, 1919–21. Promoted rear admiral, 1922, he died as commandant of the 13th Naval District and the Puget Sound navy yard.

ZIEGFELD, FLORENZ (*b. Chicago, Ill., 1869; d. Hollywood, Calif., 1932*), theatrical producer. Entered show business as promoter of musical features for the Chicago World's Fair, 1893. Acted as manager for Sandow the Strong Man, and for Anna Held, displaying great gifts for publicity. Introduced the musical revue to the United States as *The Follies of 1907* and followed its success by similar shows produced for more than 20 years. The *Ziegfeld*

Follies became noted for lavish beauty of setting and for the attractiveness of its chorus types. Ziegfeld's "glorification of the American girl" was responsible for a change in feminine style of beauty. Despite the lavishness of his productions, he possessed an instinctive taste which held them within bounds. Among other successful shows which he produced were *Sally* (1920), *Show Boat* (1927), and *Bitter Sweet* (1929).

ZIEGLER, DAVID (*b.* Heidelberg, Germany, 1748; *d.* 1811), soldier, Ohio pioneer and civic official. Immigrated to Pennsylvania, 1774. Fought in Revolution from Boston siege to Yorktown. Held captain's commission in regular army, 1784–90; major, 1st Infantry, 1790–92. President, Cincinnati, Ohio, council, 1802–04. Appointed first marshal, Ohio district, 1803; Ohio adjutant general, 1807. Ziegler served as surveyor of the port of Cincinnati from 1807 until his death.

ZIEGLER, WILLIAM (*b.* Beaver Co., Pa., 1843; *d.* 1905), businessman. An organizer and official of the Royal Chemical Co., manufacturers of Royal Baking Powder. Patron of North Pole scientific expeditions, 1901 and 1903.

ZIEHN, BERNHARD (*b.* Erfurt, Germany, 1845; *d.* 1912), musical theorist, teacher. Immigrated to America, 1868; settled in Chicago, Ill. Ziehn developed the idea of symmetrical inversion of melodic phrases and solved the problem of the unfinished final fugue in J. S. Bach's *Art of the Fugue*. His greatest contribution to the history of music was his monographic demonstration of the spuriousness of the *St. Luke Passion*. He was author of, among other works, *Harmonie- und Modulationslehre* (1888), an epoch-making work on harmonic analysis; *Manual of Harmony* (1907); *Five- and Six-Point Harmonies* (1911); and *Canonical Studies: A New Technic in Composition* (1912).

ZIFF, WILLIAM BERNARD (*b.* Chicago, Ill., 1898; *d.* New York, N.Y., 1953), publisher, author, and editor. Studied at the Art Institute of Chicago before founding an advertising company; in 1923, he became head of a Chicago publishing company, E.C. Auld Co., which in 1933 became the Ziff-Davis Publishing Co. Beginning with *Ziff's Magazine* (later *America's Humor*), the company went on to publish *Flying*, *Popular Photography*, *Amazing Stories*, *Air Adventures*, and *Mammoth Detective*. Ziff's books include *The Rape of Palestine* (1938) and *The Coming Battle of Germany* (1942), a best-seller that argued that the use of air power, long an interest of Ziff's, was the only way to achieve victory over Nazi Germany.

ZILBOORG, GREGORY (*b.* Kiev, Russia, 1890; *d.* New York, N.Y., 1959), psychoanalyst and psychiatric historian. Studied at the Faculty of Medicine in St. Petersburg and at Columbia University's College of Physicians and Surgeons. Immigrated to the U.S. in 1919. Zilboorg practiced privately in New York from 1931 and was a charter member of the New York Psychoanalytic Institute (1931). Remembered as a historian of psychiatry, Zilboorg wrote many works in the field: *The Medical Man and the Witch During the Renaissance* (1935), *History of Medical Psychology* (1941), and *Mind, Medicine and Man* (1943). Zilboorg was critical of Freud's view on religion and deplored the lack of a clear synthesis of psychoanalysis, psychiatry, and medicine in the United States.

ZIMMERMAN, EUGENE (*b.* Vicksburg, Miss., 1845; *d.* 1914), Ohio capitalist, railroad official.

ZIMMERMAN, EUGENE (*b.* Basel, Switzerland, 1862; *d.* 1935), cartoonist. Came to America as a child. Encouraged by Joseph Keppler, he began his career on *Puck*; he served as political cartoonist and comic draftsman on the staff of *Judge*, 1885–1913. Limited in technique, he was a shrewd, humorous observer of human nature and belonged with F. B. Opper to the grotesque or "exaggerated distortion" phase of American graphic humor.

ZIMMERMAN, HENRY ("HEINIE") (*b.* Bronx, N.Y., 1896; *d.* New York, N.Y., 1960), baseball player. Played for the Chicago Cubs; in 1916 he was recognized as the best third baseman in the National League. That same year he was traded to the New York Giants where he was responsible for the infamous "bonehead" play in the fourth inning of the sixth and final game of the World Series between the Giants and the Chicago White Sox. Ever after known as "the man who chased Eddie Collins across the plate," Zimmerman perpetrated, according to the *New York Times*, "one of the stupidest plays that has ever been seen in a world's series." His career ended in 1919 when he was suspended for having thrown games.

ZINSSER, HANS (*b.* New York, N.Y., 1878; *d.* New York, 1940), physician, bacteriologist, author. Graduated Columbia, 1899; M.D., Columbia, 1903. Bacteriologist at Roosevelt Hospital, New York City, 1906–10; he also taught that subject at Columbia. After teaching bacteriology and immunology at Stanford University, 1910–13, he returned to Columbia as professor in the College of Physicians and Surgeons until 1923 when he became professor of bacteriology and immunology at Harvard University Medical School. Remaining at Harvard until his death, he engaged in research, particularly on typhus, for which he became widely known. He was author of a number of scientific papers and several important textbooks, but is principally remembered by the public for his *Rats, Lice and History* (1935) and his autobiography, *As I Remember Him* (1940). A leader in development of the science of immunology, he made important investigations into four broad subjects: (1) the nature of antigens and antibodies and the colloid chemical aspects of immunological reactions; (2) the early emphasis on "residue antigens," from the tubercle bacillus and other bacteria (nonprotein substances, particularly proteoses and polysaccharides); (3) studies of *Treponema pallidum*, the spirochete of syphilis; and (4) studies on typhus fever.

ZINZENDORF, NICOLAUS LUDWIG, COUNT VON (*b.* Dresden, Saxony, 1700; *d.* Herrnhut, Saxony, 1760), Moravian leader and bishop. His career as a whole belongs to German biography, but he played a personal part in American ecclesiastical affairs on a visit to Pennsylvania, December 1741–January 1743. Attempting to work with Henry Antes and others in an effort to unite all Pennsylvania German Protestants in a single association, Zinzendorf held a series of conferences during the first six months of 1742 at various places, but was so mercilessly attacked by Samuel Blair, J. P. Boehm, Gilbert Tennent, and others that he abandoned his plan. He later journeyed among the Indians in the interest of Moravian missions and helped establish Moravian congregations at Bethlehem (which owes its name to him), Nazareth, Philadelphia, Lancaster, and York, Pa., and at New York and on Staten Island.

ZNANIECKI, FLORIAN WITOLD (*b.* Swiatniki, Poland, 1882. *d.* Urbana, Ill., 1958), sociologist and philosopher. Studied at the Jagiellonian University of Krakow (Ph.D., 1910). In collaboration with American sociologist, W. I. Thomas, Znaniecki traveled to Chicago in 1914 to complete their book, *The Polish Peasant in Europe and America* (5 vols., 1919–1927), which was a landmark in sociology because of its use of personal documents and biograms.

Founded the first department of sociology in Poland at the University of Poznan in 1922. Was forced to flee Hitler in 1939. Taught at the University of Illinois from 1942 to 1950. Works include *Cultural Reality* (1919), *The Method of Sociology* (1934), and *Cultural Sciences, Their Origin and Development* (1952).

ZOGBAUM, RUFUS FAIRCHILD (*b. Charleston, S.C., 1849; d. New York, N.Y., 1925*), illustrator, noted for the vivid realism and the high spirit of his depictions of military actions and army and navy life. Studied at the University of Heidelberg, at the New York City Art Students League, 1878–79, and in Paris under L. J. F. Bonnat, 1880–82.

ZOLLARS, ELY VAUGHAN (*b. near Lower Salem, Ohio, 1847; d. Warren, Ohio, 1916*), educator, Disciples of Christ clergyman, author. Graduated Bethany, 1875. President of, among others, Hiram College, 1888–1902. Established Oklahoma Christian University (Phillips University), chartered 1907, serving it as president and president emeritus until his death.

ZOLLICOFFER, FELIX KIRK (*b. Maury Co., Tenn., 1812; d. near Mill Springs, Ky., 1862*), Tennessee journalist, politician and official, Confederate brigadier general. A vehement states' rights Whig, he edited a number of small newspapers and was notable as editor of the *Nashville Banner*, 1850–52. A power in state politics, he served as a congressman from Tennessee, 1853–59, working for peace and understanding between North and South. Commissioned Confederate brigadier general, 1861, he commanded in East Tennessee and was killed early in January 1862 while moving with his army into Kentucky.

ZOOK, GEORGE FREDERICK (*b. Fort Scott, Kan., 1885; d. Arlington, Va., 1951*), historian, government official, educator. Studied at the University of Kansas (B.A., 1906) and at Cornell University (Ph.D., 1913). Taught at Penn State, 1912–20. After World War I, chief of higher education in the U.S. Bureau of Education, serving until 1925. President of Akron University, 1925–29. In 1933 President Franklin D. Roosevelt appointed him commissioner of education, a post he held for one year. From 1934 on, he was director and president of the American Council on Education. Became the most prominent lobbyist for higher education; supported the growth of junior colleges and vocational training programs; sought federal aid to servicemen; encouraged exchange programs and was responsible in revamping the educational systems of Germany and Japan after the war. United States national commissioner for UNESCO from 1946 to 1951.

ZORACH, WILLIAM (*b. Euberick, Lithuania, 1889; d. Bath, Maine, 1960*), sculptor. Came to the United States in 1893. Studied painting and drawing at the National Academy of Design in New York City during the winters of 1908–10, and decided to continue his studies in Paris (1910–11). Exhibited at the 1913 Armory Show. Increasingly attracted to carving, he "realized that sculpture, not painting, would have to become my lifework..." In 1927 he began one of his best-known compositions, *Mother and Child*, later acquired by the Metropolitan Museum of Art. Taught at the Art Students League in New York City, 1929–60. Was the subject of a major retrospective exhibition at the Whitney Museum of American Art in 1959.

ZUBLY, JOHN JOACHIM (*b. St. Gall, Switzerland, 1724; d. Savannah, Ga., 1781*), Presbyterian clergyman, pamphleteer. Immigrated to South Carolina, 1744; removed to Georgia, 1760, to become pastor of the Independent Presbyterian Church at Savannah. A chief spokesman for dissenting groups against what they considered local oppressions, he was also an early champion of colonial rights against the British government. He was author of a number of pamphlets and articles on the difficulties with Great Britain, 1766–75. Chosen a delegate from Savannah to the Georgia provincial congress, he also represented Georgia in the second Continental Congress, 1775. Opposing a complete break with the mother country, he returned to Georgia, October 1775, where he was arrested as a Loyalist and later banished from the province. He returned to Savannah, 1779, after restoration of the royal authority and continued his pastoral work until his death.

ZUNSER, ELIAKUM (*b. Vilnius, Russia, 1836; d. 1913*), Yiddish poet. Immigrated to America, 1889; settled in New York City. Celebrated as author-composer of Yiddish folk songs.

ZUPPKE, ROBERT CARL (*b. Berlin, Germany, 1879; d. Champaign, Ill., 1957*), football coach. Immigrated to the United States, 1881. Studied at the University of Wisconsin (Ph.B., 1905). Legendary coach of the Illini of the University of Illinois from 1913 to 1941, Zuppke led his teams to 131 victories, 81 defeats, and 12 ties. Won the national championship in 1914, 1919, 1923, and 1927. As were many of his famous players, Red Grange among them, Zuppke was elected to the National Football Hall of Fame (1951).

OCCUPATIONS INDEX

ABOLITIONIST
Bailey, Gamaliel
Birney, James Gillespie
Bourne, George
Bowditch, Henry Ingersoll
Brown, John
Buffum, Arnold
Burleigh, Charles Calistus
Chace, Elizabeth Buffum
Child, Lydia Maria Francis
Christy, David
Clay, Cassius Marcellus
Coffin, Levi
Coles, Edward
Collins, John Anderson
Colman, Lucy Newhall
Cooper, Thomas
Cox, Hannah Peirce
Deitzler, George Washington
Douglass, Frederick
Edgerton, Sidney
Embree, Elihu
Fairbank, Calvin
Fee, John Gregg
Fessenden, Samuel
Follen, Charles
Follen, Eliza Lee Cabot
Foster, Abigail Kelley
Foster, Stephen Symonds
Garnet, Henry Highland
Garrett, Thomas
Gibbons, Abigail Hopper
Gibbons, James Sloan
Giddings, Joshua Reed
Grimké, Angelina Emily
Grimké, Sarah Moore
Grinnell, Josiah Bushnell
Hallowell, Richard Price
Haven, Gilbert
Hazard, Thomas
Holley, Myron
Hopper, Isaac Tatem
Jackson, James Caleb
Johnson, Oliver
Julian, George Washington
Leavitt, Joshua
Lee, Luther
LeMoyne, Francis Julius
Loring, Ellis Gray
Lovejoy, Elijah Parish
Lovejoy, Owen
Lundy, Benjamin
McKim, James Miller

Mercer, Margaret
Miller, Jonathan Peckham
Mott, James
Nelson, David
Osborn, Charles
Post, Issac
Realf, Richard
Sands, David
Scott, Orange
Stewart, Alvan
Stuart, Charles
Sumner, Charles
Sunderland, La Roy
Tappan, Arthur
Tappan, Benjamin
Tappan, Lewis
Taylor, John W.
Torrey, Charles Turner
Tubman, Harriet
Ward, Samuel Ringgold
Weld, Theodore Dwight
Whittier, John Greenleaf
Woolman, John
ACCOUNTANT (**See** also TAX EXPERT)
Lasser, Jacob Kay
Lybrand, William Mitchell
ACTOR (**See** also ENTERTAINER)
Adams, Edwin
Aiken, George L.
Aldrich, Louis
Aldridge, Ira Frederick
Arden, Edwin Hunter Pendleton
Arliss, George
Arnold, Edward
Bacon, Frank
Baker, Benjamin A.
Bangs, Frank C.
Bannister, Nathaniel Harrington
Barnabee, Henry Clay
Barrett, George Horton
Barrett, Lawrence
Barrymore, John
Barrymore, Lionel
Barrymore, Maurice
Barthelmess, Richard
Beery, Wallace Fitzgerald
Begley, Edward James ("Ed")
Belasco, David
Benchley, Robert Charles
Bennett, Richard
Bernard, John
Blake, William Rufus
Blinn, Holbrook

Blue, Gerald Montgomery
  ("Monte")
Bogart, Humphrey DeForest
Booth, Edwin Thomas
Booth, John Wilkes
Booth, Junius Brutus
Boucicault, Dion
Bradford, Joseph
Brougham, John
Browning, Tod
Burgess, Neil
Burke, Charles St. Thomas
Burns, Bob
Burton, William Evans
Bushman, Francis Xavier
Carson, Jack
Chaney, Lon
Chanfrau, Francis S.
Clarke, John Sleeper
Clift, Edward Montgomery
Cohan, George Michael
Colman, Ronald Charles
Conried, Heinrich
Conway, Frederick Bartlett
Cooper, Gary
Cooper, Thomas Abthorpe
Couldock, Charles Walter
Crane, William Henry
Craven, Frank
Daly, Peter Christopher Arnold
Davenport, Edward Loomis
Davidge, William Pleater
Dean, James Byron
De Angelis, Thomas Jefferson
DeMille, Cecil Blount
Digges, Dudley
Ditrichstein, Leo
Dockstader, Lew
Drake, Samuel
Drew, John, 1827–1862
Drew, John, 1853–1927
Eddy, Nelson
Edeson, Robert
Fairbanks, Douglas
Farnum, Charles Albert
Farnum, Dustin Lancy
Farnum, Franklyn
Faversham, William Alfred
Fay, Francis Anthony ("Frank")
Fennell, James
Ferguson, William Jason
Field, Joseph M.
Finn, Henry James William

Carter, Caroline Louise Dudley
Castle, Irene Foote
Cayvan, Georgia
Chanfrau, Henrietta Baker
Chatterton, Ruth
Claxton, Kate
Clifton, Josephine
Coghlan, Rose
Collier, Constance
Cowl, Jane
Crabtree, Lotta
Cushman, Charlotte Saunders
Cushman, Pauline
Cushman, Susan Webb
Dandridge, Dorothy Jean
Darwell, Jane
Davenport, Fanny Lily Gypsy
Davies, Marion Cecilia
Dean, Julia
De Wolfe, Elsie
Dickinson, Anna Elizabeth
Drake, Frances Ann Denny
Dresser, Louise Kerlin
Dressler, Marie
Duff, Mary Ann Dyke
Dumont, Margaret
Eagels, Jeanne
Elliott, Maxine
Eytinge, Rose
Fazenda, Louise Marie
Field, Mary Katherine Kemble
Fisher, Clara
Fiske, Minnie Maddern
Francis, Kay
Garland, Judy
George, Gladys
George, Grace
Gilbert, Anne Hartley
Gish, Dorothy
Hale, Louise Closser
Hall, Juanita Armethea
Harlow, Jean
Henie, Sonja
Herne, Chrystal Katharine
Heron, Matilda Agnes
Holliday, Judy
Hopper, Hedda
Hull, Josephine
Illington, Margaret
Irwin, May
Jananschek, Franziska Magdalena
   Romance
Kane, Helen
Keene, Laura
Kemble, Frances Anne
Lander, Jean Margaret Davenport
Lawrence, Gertrude
Leigh, Vivien
Logan, Olive
Lombard, Carole
Lord, Pauline
McCracken, Joan
McDaniel, Hattie
MacDonald, Jeanette Anna
Mansfield, Jayne
Marlowe, Julia

Menken, Adah Isaacs
Merry, Ann Brunton
Mitchell, Margaret Julia
Modjeska, Helena
Monroe, Marilyn
Morgan, Helen
Morris, Clara
Morris, Elizabeth
Mowatt, Anna Cora Ogden
Murray, Mae
Nazimova, Alla
Perry, Antoinette
Pitts, Zasu
Rehan, Ada
Robson, May
Rowson, Susanna Haswell
Russell, Annie
Shaw, Mary
Stevens, Emily
Strange, Michael
Sullavan, Margaret
Talmadge, Norma
Taylor, Laurette
Tucker, Sophie
Vincent, Mary Ann
Waller, Emma
Walsh, Blanche
Ward, Genevieve
Western, Lucille
Westley, Helen
White, Pearl
Wong, Anna May

ACTUARY (**See also** INSURANCE
   EXECUTIVE)
Fackler, David Parks
McCay, Charles Francis
McClintock, Emory
Wright, Elizur

ADMINISTRATOR (**See also** COLLEGE
   ADMINISTRATOR, PRISON
   ADMINISTRATOR)
Abernethy, George
Adams, Jasper
Cloud, Henry Roe
Coburn, Foster Dwight
Crafts, James Mason
Dinwiddie, Robert
Geddes, James Loraine
Goethals, George Washington
Goode, George Brown
Hatfield, Edwin Francis
Hawley, Gideon, 1785–1870
King, Clarence
Landis, James McCauley
Lynds, Elam
Magoon, Charles Edward
Mendenhall, Thomas Corwin
Nelson, Reuben
Perkins, George Henry
Pickering, Timothy
Pilsbury, Amos
Powell, John Wesley
Randall, Alexander Williams
Richmond, Mary Ellen
Runkle, John Daniel
Sargent, Winthrop, 1753–1820

Smith, Edgar Fahs
Smith, James Francis
Taylor, James Barnett
Thacher, Thomas Anthony
Tompkins, Sally Louisa
Valentine, Robert Grosvenor
Vaughan, Victor Clarence
Walcott, Charles Doolittle
Wilson, Peter
Woodward, Robert Simpson

ADVENTURER (**See also** COLONIZER,
   EXPLORER, FILIBUSTER, FUR
   TRADER, PRIVATEER, SPY,
   SWINDLER, Trader, Traveler)
Argall, Sir Samuel
Bartlett, Joseph
Bowles, William Augustus
Boyd, John Parker
Burgevine, Henry Andrea
Clarke, Elijah
Coode, John
Crowne, William
Gibson, Walter Murray
Graffenried, Christopher, Baron de
Harlan, Josiah
Hayes, William Henry ("Bully")
Henry, John, *fl.* 1807–1820
Judson, Edward Zane Carroll
Laffite, Jean
Long, James
MacDonald, Ranald
Morton, Thomas
Peñalosa Briceño, Diego Dioniso
   de
Revere, Joseph Warren
Scott, John
Smith, John, 1579/80–1631
Thrasher, John Sidney
Walker, William
Ward, Frederick Townsend
Wikoff, Henry
Wingfield, Edward Maria
Yeardley, Sir George

ADVENTURESS
Livingstone, Belle

ADVERTISING AGENT
Ayer, Francis Wayland
Post, Charles William
Rowell, George Presbury

ADVERTISING EXECUTIVE
Ayer, Francis Wayland
Barton, Bruce Fairchild
Block, Paul
Brophy, Thomas D'Arcy
Calkins, Earnest Elmo
Durstine, Roy Sarles
Emmett, Burton
Lasker, Albert Davis
Resor, Stanley Burnet
Watson, John Broadus

AERONAUT (**See also** AVIATOR,
   BALLOONIST)
Chanute, Octave
Durant, Charles Ferson
Herring, Augustus Moore
King, Samuel Archer

AMERICAN INDIAN RIGHTS ADVOCATE
Madigan, Laverne

AMERICAN RED CROSS OFFICIAL
Boardman, Mabel Thorp
Olds, Robert Edwin
Payne, John Barton

AMUSEMENT PARK CREATOR
Disney, Walter Elias ("Walt")

ANARCHIST
Berkman, Alexander
Goldman, Emma
Most, Johann Joseph
Parsons, Albert Richard
Tucker, Benjamin Ricketson
Warren, Josiah

ANATOMIST (See also PHYSICIAN)
Allen, Edgar
Allen, Harrison
Baker, Frank
Bensley, Robert Russell
Brödel, Max
Chovet, Abraham
Coghill, George Ellett
Davidge, John Beale
Dorsey, John Syng
Dwight, Thomas
Gerrish, Frederic Henry
Goddard, Paul Beck
Godman, John Davidson
Horner, William Edmonds
Huber, Gotthelf Carl
Jackson, Clarence Martin
McClellan, George, 1796–1847
McClellan, George, 1849–1913
McMurrich, James Playfair
Mall, Franklin Paine
March, Alden
Miller, William Snow
Nelson, Marjorie Maxine
Pancoast, Joseph
Pancoast, Seth
Papanicolaou, George Nicholas
Pattison, Granville Sharp
Ramsay, Alexander
Ranson, Stephen Walter
Robinson, Frederick Byron
Sabin, Florence Rena
Souchon, Edmond
Spitzka, Edward Anthony
Stockard, Charles Rupert
Todd, Thomas Wingate
Tuckerman, Frederick
Weed, Lewis Hill
Wislocki, George Bernays
Wyman, Jeffries

ANESTHESIOLOGIST (PHYSICIAN)
Colton, Gardner Quincy
Long, Crawford Williamson
Morton, William Thomas Green
Rovenstine, Emery Andrew
Wells, Horace

ANIMAL PSYCHOLOGIST
Yerkes, Robert Mearns

ANIMATOR
Disney, Walter Elias ("Walt")

ANTHOLOGIST
Bronson, Walter Cochrane
Griswold, Rufus Wilmot
Kennedy, William Sloane
Tappan, Eva March

ANTHROPOGEOGRAPHER (See also
ANTHROPOLOGIST)
Semple, Ellen Churchill

ANTHROPOLOGIST (See also
ETHNOLOGIST, FOLKLORIST)
Alexander, Hartley Burr
Bandelier, Adolph Francis
   Alphonse
Barrows, David Prescott
Benedict, Ruth Fulton
Boas, Franz
Brinton, Daniel Garrison
Chamberlain, Alexander Francis
Dixon, Roland Burrage
Dorsey, George Amos
Farabee, William Curtis
Farrand, Livingston
Fejos, Paul
Goldenweiser, Alexander
   Alexandrovich
Hooton, Earnest Albert
Hough, Walter
Hrdlička, Aleš
Hurston, Zora Neale
Kroeber, Alfred Louis
La Farge, Oliver Hazard Perry
Lewis, Oscar
Linton, Ralph
MacCurdy, George Grant
McGee, William John
McGuire, Joseph Deakins
Meigs, James Aitken
Nelson, Nels Christian
Parker, Arthur Caswell
Parsons, Elsie Worthington Clews
Powdermaker, Hortense
Radin, Paul
Redfield, Robert
Roheim, Geza
Sapir, Edward
Skinner, Alanson Buck
Spier, Leslie
Starr, Frederick
Sullivan, Louis Robert
Swanton, John Reed
Todd, Thomas Wingate
Warner, William Lloyd
Weidenreich, Franz
Wheelwright, Mary Cabot
Wissler, Clark

ANTIQUARIAN
Alden, Timothy
Appleton, William Sumner
Arthur, William
Bartlett, John Russell
Campbell, Charles
Chester, Joseph Lemuel
Davis, Andrew McFarland
Dexter, Franklin Bowditch
Drake, Samuel Gardner
Du Simitière, Pierre Eugène

Earle, Alice Morse
Endicott, Charles Moses
Farmer, John
Felt, Joseph Barlow
Folsom, George
Green, Samuel Abbott
Grim, David
Hazard, Samuel
Hoyt, Albert Harrison
Jordan, John Woolf
Livermore, George
McCabe, John Collins
Malcolm, James Peller
Mercer, Henry Chapman
Munsell, Joel
Nutting, Wallace
Robbins, Thomas
Sachse, Julius Friedrich
Sargent, Lucius Manlius
Savage, James
Shurtleff, Nathaniel Bradstreet
Smith, Buckingham
Stanard, William Glover
Stevens, Benjamin Franklin
Taylor, Richard Cowling
Van Schaack, Henry Cruger
Watson, John Fanning
Whitmore, William Henry
Young, Alexander

ANTIQUE DEALER
Rosenbach, Abraham Simon Wolf
Rosenbach, Philip Hyman
Sack, Israel

ANTISUFFRAGIST
Meyer, Annie Nathan

APIARIST
Langstroth, Lorenzo Lorraine
Root, Amos Ives

APOTHECARY (See also DRUGGIST,
PHARMACIST)
Craigie, Andrew
Jackson, David

ARACHNOLOGIST
Emerton, James Henry

ARBORICULTURIST (See also
AGRICULTURIST, BOTANIST,
FORESTER, HORTICULTURIST,
NURSERYMAN, Plant Breeder,
Pomologist, Silviculturist, Tree-
Care Expert, Tree Surgeon)
Sargent, Charles Sprague

ARCHABBOT (See also RELIGIOUS
LEADER)
Schnerr, Leander
Stehle, Aurelius Aloysius

ARCHBISHOP (See also RELIGIOUS
LEADER)
Alemany, José Sadoc
Blanc, Antoine
Blanchet, François Norbert
Blenk, James Hubert
Chapelle, Placide Louis
Corrigan, Michael Augustine
Dowling, Austin
Feehan, Patrick Augustine
Glennon, John Joseph

Hanna, Edward Joseph
Janssens, Francis
McNicholas, John Timothy
O'Connell, William Henry
Rummel, Joseph Francis
Stritch, Samuel Alphonsus

ARCHEOLOGIST (See also SCHOLAR)
Abbott, Charles Conrad
Badè, William Frederic
Barber, Edwin Atlee
Beauchamp, William Martin
Bliss, Frederick Jones
Bowditch, Charles Pickering
Breasted, James Henry
Brower, Jacob Vradenberg
Butler, Howard Crosby
Casanowicz, Immanuel Moses
Cesnola, Luigi Palma di
Clarke, Sir Caspar Purdon
Conant, Alban Jasper
Davis, Edwin Hamilton
Fisher, Clarence Stanley
Fowke, Gerard
Goodyear, William Henry
Gordon, George Byron
Hawes, Harriet Ann Boyd
Haynes, John Henry
Holmes, William Henry
Hoppin, Joseph Clark
Kelsey, Francis Willey
Kidder, Alfred Vincent
MacCurdy, George Grant
Mercer, Henry Chapman
Merriam, Augustus Chapman
Merrill, Selah
Middleton, John Izard
Morley, Sylvanus Griswold
Murray, Louise Shipman Welles
Nies, James Buchanan
Paine, John Alsop
Parker, Arthur Caswell
Paton, Lewis Bayles
Peet, Stephen Denison
Peters, John Punnett
Porter, Arthur Kingsley
Putnam, Frederic Ward
Rau, Charles
Richardson, Rufus Byam
Rostovtzeff, Michael Ivanovitch
Saville, Marshall Howard
Seyffarth, Gustavus
Shear, Theodore Leslie
Snyder, John Francis
Speiser, Ephraim Avigdor
Squier, Ephraim George
Sterrett, John Robert Sitlington
Stevenson, Sara Yorke
Tarbell, Frank Bigelow
Thompson, Edward Herbert
Upham, Warren
Vaillant, George Clapp
Van Deman, Esther Boise
Wheeler, James Rignall
Whitehouse, Frederic Cope
Whittemore, Thomas
Winchell, Newton Horace

Winslow, William Copley
ARCHITECT (See also NAVAL ARCHITECT)
Albro, Lewis Colt
Aldrich, Chester Holmes
Atterbury, Grosvenor
Atwood, Charles B.
Audsley, George Ashdown
Austin, Henry
Bacon, Henry
Banner, Peter
Barber, Donn
Behrendt, Walter Curt
Benjamin, Asher
Blodget, Samuel
Bluemner, Oscar Florians
Boring, William Alciphron
Boucher, Horace Edward
Bragdon, Claude Fayette
Browne, Herbert Wheildon Cotton
Brunner, Arnold William
Bulfinch, Charles
Burnham, Daniel Hudson
Cabot, Edward Clarke
Carrère, John Merven
Carter, Elias
Clarke, Sir Caspar Purdon
Cook, Walter
Coolidge, Charles Allerton
Cope, Walter
Corbett, Harvey Wiley
Cram, Ralph Adams
Cret, Paul Philippe
Culter, James Goold
Cummings, Charles Amos
Dakin, James Harrison
Davis, Alexander Jackson
Day, Frank Miles
Delano, William Adams
Downing, Andrew Jackson
Eidlitz, Cyrus Lazelle Warner
Eidlitz, Leopold
Elmslie, George Grant
Fenner, Burt Leslie
Flagg, Ernest
Ford, George Burdett
Gallier, James
Gilbert, Cass
Gilman, Arthur Delevan
Godefroy, Maximilian
Goodhue, Bertram Grosvenor
Graham, Ernest Robert
Granger, Alfred Hoyt
Greene, Charles Sumner
Greene, Henry Mather
Greenough, Henry
Gropius, Walter Adolf Georg
Hadfield, George
Haight, Charles Coolidge
Hallet, Étienne Sulpice
Hamlin, Alfred Dwight Foster
Hamlin, Talbot Faulkner
Hardenberg, Henry Janeway
Harrison, Peter
Hastings, Thomas
Haviland, John

Hawks, John
Higgins, Daniel Paul
Hoadley, David
Hoban, James
Holabird, William
Hood, Raymond Mathewson
Hooker, Philip
Hunt, Richard Morris
Jefferson, Thomas
Jenney, William Le Baron
Joy, Thomas
Kahn, Albert
Kearsley, John
Kimball, (Sidney) Fiske
Klauder, Charles Zeller
Kneass, Samuel Honeyman
La Farge, Christopher Grant
Lafever, Minard
Lamb, William Frederick
Latrobe, Benjamin Henry, 1764–1820
Le Brun, Napoléon Eugène Henry Charles
Lienau, Detlef
Longfellow, William Pitt Preble
Lowell, Guy
McArthur, John, 1823–1890
McComb, John
McIntire, Samuel
McKim, Charles Folley
Maginnis, Charles Donagh
Magonigle, Harold Van Buren
Mangin, Joseph François
Marshall, Henry Rutgers
Mauran, John Lawrence
Maybeck, Bernard Ralph
Mazzuchelli, Samuel Charles
Mead, William Rutherford
Medary, Milton Bennett
Mendelsohn, Erich (*or* Eric)
Mies van der Rohe, Ludwig
Mills, Robert, 1781–1855
Mizner, Addison
Morgan, Julia
Neutra, Richard Joseph
Parris, Alexander
Peabody, Robert Swain
Pelz, Paul Johannes
Perkins, Dwight Heald
Platt, Charles Adams
Polk, Willis, Jefferson
Pond, Allen Bartlit
Pond, Irving Kane
Pope, John Russell
Post, George Browne
Poulson, Niels
Price, Bruce
Ramée, Joseph Jacques
Renwick, James, 1818–1895
Richardson, Henry Hobson
Rogers, Isaiah
Rogers, James Gamble
Root, John Wellborn
Rotch, Arthur
Saarinen, Eero
Saarinen, Gottlieb Eliel

Schindler, Rudolph Michael
Shaw, Howard Van Doren
Sherman, Frank Dempster
Skidmore, Louis
Smith, Robert, 1722-1777
Starrett, William Aiken
Stewardson, John
Stewart, John George
Stokes, Isaac Newton Phelps
Strickland, William
Sturgis, Russell
Sullivan, Louis Henri
Thompson, Martin E.
Thornton, William
Tilton, Edward Lippincott
Town, Ithiel
Trumbauer, Horace
Tucker, Allen
Tuthill, William Burnet
Upjohn, Richard
Upjohn, Richard Michell
Urban, Joseph
Van Brunt, Henry
Van Osdel, John Mills
Walter, Thomas Ustick
Ware, William Robert
Warren, Herbert Langford
Warren, Russell
Wheelwright, Edmund March
White, Stanford
Wight, Peter Bonnett
Willard, Soloman
Wilson, Joseph Miller
Withers, Frederick Clarke
Wright, Frank Lloyd
Wright, Henry
Young, Ammi Burnham

ARCHIVIST (**See also** LIBRARIAN, SCHOLAR)
Connor, Robert Digges Wimberly
Fernow, Berthold
Force, Peter
Ford, Worthington Chauncey
Knight, Lucian Lamar
Leland, Waldo Gifford
Owen, Thomas McAdory

ARMOR EXPERT
Dean, Bashford

ARMY AIR CORPS OFFICER
Andrews, Frank Maxwell

ARMY MEDICAL OFFICER (**See also** PHYSICIAN, SOLDIER)
Hume, Edgar Erskine
Simmons, James Stevens

ARMY OFFICER (**See also** GENERAL, SOLDIER)
Ainsworth, Frederick Crayton
Ames, Adelbert
Arnold, Henry Harley
Bell, James Franklin
Black, William Murray
Brereton, Lewis Hyde
Buckner, Simon Bolivar
Bullard, Robert Lee
Casey, Thomas Lincoln
Chaffee, Adna Romanza

Craig, Malin
Crowder, Enoch Herbert
Crozier, William
Davis, Benjamin Oliver, Sr.
Drum, Hugh Aloysius
Eddy, Manton Sprague
Edwards, Clarence Ransom
Eichelberger, Robert Lawrence
Eisenhower, Dwight David
Ely, Hanson Edward
Fairchild, Muir Stephen
Foulois, Benjamin Delahauf
Glassford, Pelham Davis
Graves, William Sidney
Groves, Leslie Richard, Jr.
Guild, La Fayette
Harbord, James Guthrie
Hawley, Paul Ramsey
Heintzelman, Stuart
Hines, Frank Thomas
Hines, John Leonard ("Birdie")
Hodes, Henry Irving
Hodge, John Reed
Hodges, Courtney Hicks
Johnson, Hugh Samuel
Johnston, William Hartshorne
King, Edward Leonard
Krueger, Walter
Kuhn, Joseph Ernst
Lear, Ben
Lee, John Clifford Hodges
Liggett, Hunter
Lynch, John Roy
McAlexander, Ulysses Grant
MacArthur, Arthur
MacArthur, Douglas
McClure, Robert Alexis
McNair, Lesley James
MacNider, Hanford
Marshall, George Catlett, Jr.
Michler, Nathaniel
Mitchell, William
Morton, Charles Gould
Muir, Charles Henry
Neyland, Robert Reese, Jr.
Palmer, John McAuley
Patch, Alexander McCarrell
Patrick, Mason Mathews
Patton, George Smith
Pick, Lewis Andrew
Read, George Windle
Roosevelt, Kermit
Roosevelt, Theodore
Schroeder, Rudolph William
Scott, Hugh Lenox
Short, Walter Campbell
Smith, Walter Bedell
Snyder, Howard McCrum
Somervell, Brehon Burke
Stilwell, Joseph Warren
Sutherland, Richard Kerens
Vedder, Edward Bright
Wagener, John Andreas
Wainwright, Jonathan Mayhew
Walker, Walton Harris
Whitney, Courtney

Winship, Blanton
Wood, Charles Erskine Scott
Wood, Robert Elkington

ART COLLECTOR (**See also** COLLECTOR)
Arensberg, Walter Conrad
Bache, Jules Semon
Barnes, Albert Coombs
Berenson, Bernard
Cone, Claribel
Cone, Etta
Dale, Chester
Dale, Maud Murray Thompson
Emmett, Burton
Freer, Charles Lang
Gardner, Isabella Stewart
Gellatly, John
Goodyear, Anson Conger
Jarves, James Jackson
Johnson, John Graver
Johnston, John Taylor
Kress, Samuel Henry
Lasker, Albert Davis
Lehman, Adele Lewisohn
Lewisohn, Adolph
Mellon, Andrew William
Reisinger, Hugo
Rosenberg, Paul
Ross, Denman Waldo
Ryerson, Martin Antoine
Walker, Thomas Barlow
Walters, Henry
Walters, William Thompson
White, Alexander

ART CONNOISSEUR
Avery, Samuel Putnam
Berenson, Bernard
Cahill, Holger
Clarke, Sir Caspar Purdon
Frankfurter, Alfred Moritz
Hart, Charles Henry
Laffan, William Mackay
Lyon, Caleb

ART CRITIC
Berenson, Bernard
Cary, Elisabeth Luther
Coffin, William Anderson
Cook, Clarence Chatham
Cortissoz, Royal
Cox, Kenyon
Foster, Benjamin
Frankfurter, Alfred Moritz
Hartmann, Carl Sadakichi
Hitchcock, James Ripley Wellman
Keppel, Frederick
Perkins, Charles Callahan
Rosenfeld, Paul Leopold
Stein, Leo Daniel
Van Dyke, John Charles
Van Rensselaer, Mariana Griswold
Wallace, Horace Binney

ART DEALER
Avery, Samuel Putnam
Halpert, Edith Gregor
Rosenberg, Paul

Moore, Joseph Haines
Moulton, Forest Ray
Newcomb, Simon
Nicholson, Seth Barnes
Parkhurst, John Adelbert
Paul, Henry Martyn
Peirce, Benjamin
Perrine, Charles Dillon
Peters, Christian Henry Frederick
Pickering, Edward Charles
Porter, Jermain Gildersleeve
Pritchett, Henry Smith
Rees, John Krom
Rigge, William Francis
Ritchey, George Willis
Rittenhouse, David
Rogers, William Augustus
Russell, Henry Norris
Safford, Truman Henry
St. John, Charles Edward
Schaeberle, John Martin
Schlesinger, Frank
Searle, Arthur
Sestini, Benedict
Skinner, Aaron Nichols
Slipher, Vesto Melvin
Stockwell, John Nelson
Stone, Ormond
Struve, Otto
Swift, Lewis
Tuttle, Charles Wesley
Twining, Alexander Catlin
Upton, Winslow
Vaughan, Daniel
Walker, Sears Cook
Watson, James Craig
West, Benjamin
Whitney, Mary Watson
Winlock, Joseph
Winthrop, John
Young, Charles Augustus
Young, David

ASTRONOMICAL LENSMAKER
Brashear, John Alfred
Clark, Alvan
Clark, Alvan Graham

ASTRONOMICAL PHOTOGRAPHER (See also ASTRONOMER, PHOTOGRAPHER**)**
Draper, Henry

ASTROPHYSICIST (See also ASTRONOMER, PHYSICIST**)**
Mason, Max
Rutherfurd, Lewis Morris

ATHLETE (See also SPECIFIC SPORTS**)**
Blaikie, William
Clothier, William Jackson
McGrath, Matthew J.
Pilkington, James
Thorpe, James Francis
Zaharias, Mildred ("Babe") Didrikson

ATHLETIC COACH
Lapchick, Joseph Bohomiel

ATHLETIC TRAINER
Murphy, Michael Charles

ATTORNEY (See LAWYER**)**

ATTORNEY GENERAL (CONFEDERATE)
Benjamin, Judah Philip
Davis, George
Watts, Thomas Hill

ATTORNEY GENERAL (FEDERAL)
Beck, James Montgomery
Biddle, Francis Beverley
Black, Jeremiah Sullivan
Bonaparte, Charles Joseph
Brewster, Benjamin Harris
Cummings, Homer Stillé
Daugherty, Harry Micajah
Devens, Charles
Garland, Augustus Hill
Gilpin, Henry Dilworth
Gregory, Thomas Watt
Harmon, Judson
Hoar, Ebenezer Rockwood
Kennedy, Robert Francis
Lee, Charles, 1758–1815
Legaré, Hugh Swinton
McGranery, James Patrick
McGrath, James Howard
Miller, William Henry Harrison
Moody, William Henry
Murphy, Frank
Olney, Richard
Palmer, Alexander Mitchell
Perlman, Philip Benjamin
Pierrepont, Edwards
Randolph, Edmund, 1753–1813
Speed, James
Stanbery, Henry
Stanton, Edwin McMasters
Stockton, John Potter
Taft, Alphonso
Taney, Roger Brooke
Thacher, Thomas Day
Toucey, Isaac
Wickersham, George Woodward
Williams, George Henry
Wirt, William

ATTORNEY GENERAL (STATE)
Conner, James
Gilchrist, Robert
Johnston, Augustus
Martin, Luther
Pringle, John Julius
Robeson, George Maxwell
Trott, Nicholas
Updike, Daniel

AUTHOR (See also BIOGRAPHER, CRITIC, DIARIST, DRAMATIST, ESSAYIST, LITTERATEUR, Novelist, Poet, Writer**)**
Abbot, Willis John
Abbott, Austin
Abbott, Benjamin Vaughan
Abbott, Charles Conrad
Abbott, Edith
Abbott, Jacob
Abbott, Lyman
Acrelius, Israel
Adair, James
Adams, Andy

Adams, Frederick Upham
Adams, John Coleman
Adams, Samuel Hopkins
Ade, George
Adler, Polly
Akeley, Mary Leonore
Akers, Elizabeth Chase
Alcott, Amos Bronson
Alcott, Louisa May
Alden, Henry Mills
Alden, Isabella Macdonald
Alden, Joseph
Alexander, Archibald
Alexander, Edward Porter
Alexander, Joseph Addison
Alger, William Rounseville
Allen, Alexander Viets Griswold
Allen, Anthony Benezet
Allen, Ethan
Allen, George
Allen, Joel Asaph
Allen, Joseph Henry
Allen, William
Allen, Zachariah
Allston, Washington
Alsop, Charles
Altsheler, Joseph Alexander
Anderson, Sherwood
Anderson, Victor Vance
Andrews, Christopher Columbus
Andrews, Roy Chapman
Antin, Mary
Apes, William
Arthur, Timothy Shay
Artzybasheff, Boris
Ashhurst, John
Atkinson, George Wesley
Atwater, Caleb
Audsley, George Ashdown
Austin, Jane Goodwin
Austin, Mary
Austin, William
Azarias, Brother
Babbitt, Irving
Babcock, Maltbie Davenport
Babson, Roger Ward
Bacon, Alice Mabel
Bacon, Delia Salter
Bacon, Edwin Munroe
Badeau, Adam
Bagby, George William
Baird, Samuel John
Baker, Ray Stannard
Baker, William Mumford
Baldwin, Joseph
Baldwin, Joseph Glover
Baldwin, Loammi
Balestier, Charles Wolcott
Ballou, Hosea
Ballou, Maturin Murray
Bancroft, Aaron
Bancroft, Edward
Banvard, John
Banvard, Joseph
Barbour, Oliver Lorenzo
Bardeen, Charles William

Cook, Martha Elizabeth Duncan
  Walker
Cooke, George Willis
Cooke, Josiah Parsons
Cooke, Philip St. George
Copway, George
Cornwallis, Kinahan
Corson, Hiram
Cortambert, Louis Richard
Cory, Charles Barney
Cotton, John
Cowley, Charles
Cox, Jacob Dolson
Cox, Palmer
Cox, Rowland
Cox, Samuel Sullivan
Coxe, Arthur Cleveland
Cozzens, Frederick Swartwout
Crafts, William
Crane, Anne Moncure
Crane, Stephen
Crane, Thomas Frederick
Crapsey, Algernon Sidney
Crocker, Hannah Mather
Croly, Herbert David
Crosby, Ernest Howard
Crothers, Samuel McChord
Crouse, Russel McKinley
Crowninshield, Frederic
Cullum, George Washington
Cuming, Fortescue
Cummins, Maria Susanna
Currier, Charles Warren
Curry, Jabez Lamar Monroe
Curtis, Charles Pelham
Curtis, George Ticknor
Curtis, George William
Curwen, Samuel
Cushing, Luther Stearns
Cutler, Lizzie Petit
Cuyler, Theodore Ledyard
Dabney, Robert Lewis
Dabney, Virginius
Dagg, John Leadley
Dahlgren, Sarah Madeleine Vinton
Dall, Caroline Wells Healey
Daly, Charles Patrick
Dana, John Cotton
Dana, Richard Henry
Darby, John
Darling, Flora Adams
Davenport, John
Davidson, James Wood
Davies, Joseph Edward
Davies, Maria Thompson
Davis, Andrew McFarland
Davis, Mary Evelyn Moore
Davis, Noah Knowles
Davis, Oscar King
Davis, Richard Harding
Davis, Varina Anne Jefferson
Davis, Varina Howell
Davis, William Thomas
Day, Clarence Shepard
Dean, Sidney

Dearborn, Henry Alexander
  Scammell
De Costa, Benjamin Franklin
Deems, Charles Force
Deering, Nathaniel
De Fontaine, Felix Gregory
De Forest, John William
De Kay, James Ellsworth
Deland, Margaret
Delano, Amassa
De Leon, Thomas Cooper
Deléry, François Charles
Dellenbaugh, Frederick Samuel
Deming, Philander
De Peyster, John Watts
Detmold, Christian Edward
De Trobriand, Régis Denis de
  Keredern
Dewey, Orville
Diat, Louis Felix
Diaz, Abby Morton
Dibble, Roy Floyd
Didier, Eugene Lemoine
Dimitry, Charles Patton
Ditson, George Leighton
Dixon, Thomas
Dodd, Lee Wilson
Doddridge, Joseph
Dodge, Mary Abigail
Dodge, Mary Elizabeth Mapes
Dole, Nathan Haskell
Donnelly, Eleanor Cecilia
Dorchester, Daniel
Dorr, Julia Caroline Ripley
Dorsey, Anna Hanson McKenney
Dorsey, George Amos
Dorsey, Sarah Anne Ellis
Douglas, Amanda Minnie
Downey, June Etta
Downing, Charles
Drayton, John
Dromgoole, William Allen
Duganne, Augustine Joseph Hickey
Dummer, Jeremiah
Dunlop, James
Du Ponceau, Pierre Étienne
Durfee, Job
Durivage, Francis Alexander
Dwight, Benjamin Woodbridge
Dwight, Theodore, 1764–1846
Dwight, Theodore, 1796–1866
Dwight, Timothy
Dyer, Louis
Earle, Alice Morse
Eckstorm, Fannie Hardy
Eddy, Daniel Clarke
Edes, Robert Thaxter
Edwards, Charles
Egan, Maurice Francis
Elder, Susan Blanchard
Elder, William
Eliot, Charles
Ellet, Elizabeth Fries Lummis
Elliott, Benjamin
Elliott, Sarah Barnwell
Elliott, Walter Hackett Robert

Ellis, Edward Sylvester
Ellis, George Washington
Elson, Louis Charles
Embree, Edwin Rogers
Embury, Emma Catherine
Emerson, Edward Waldo
Emerson, Ellen Russell
Erskine, John
Evans, Augusta Jane
Evans, Warren Felt
Everett, David
Ewbank, Thomas
Ewing, Hugh Boyle
Eytinge, Rose
Fairchild, David Grandison
Farley, Harriet
Farnham, Eliza Woodson Burhans
Farnham, Thomas Jefferson
Farrar, Timothy
Farwell, Arthur
Faust, Frederick Shiller
Fawcett, Edgar
Fay, Edwin Whitefield
Fay, Theodore Sedgwick
Felton, Rebecca Latimer
Fernald, James Champlin
Fernow, Bernhard Eduard
Feuchtwanger, Lion
Field, Eugene
Field, Henry Martyn
Field, Mary Katherine Kemble
Field, Maunsell Bradhurst
Field, Richard Stockton
Field, Roswell Martin
Field, Thomas Warren
Fields, Annie Adams
Fields, James Thomas
Fillebrown, Thomas
Finck, Henry Theophilus
Finley, John Huston
Finley, Martha Farquharson
Finn, Francis James
Fisher, Dorothea Frances Canfield
Fisher, Sidney George
Fiske, Amos Kidder
Fitzgerald, Oscar Penn
Flagg, Edmund
Flagg, James Montgomery
Flagg, Thomas Wilson
Flanders, Henry
Flandrau, Charles Eugene
Flint, Timothy
Florence, William Jermyn
Floy, James
Follen, Eliza Lee Cabot
Follett, Mary Parker
Folsom, George
Forbes, Edwin
Forbes, Robert Bennett
Force, Manning Ferguson
Forman, Justus Miles
Fortier, Alcée
Fosdick, Charles Austin
Fosdick, Harry Emerson
Fosdick, William Whiteman
Foster, David Skaats

Foster, Hannah Webster
Foster, Roger Sherman Baldwin
Foulke, William Dudley
Fowle, Daniel
Fowler, Gene
Francis, Samuel Ward
Frank, Jerome
Frank, Lawrence Kelso
Franklin, Benjamin
Freeman, James Edwards
Freeman, Mary Eleanor Wilkins
Frémont, Jessie Benton
French, Alice
French, Lucy Virginia Smith
Frothingham, Arthur Lincoln
Frothingham, Octavius Brooks
Frothingham, Paul Revere
Fry, James Barnet
Fulton, John Farquhar
Gage, Frances Dana Barker
Gage, Matilda Joslyn
Gaillardet, Théodore Frédéric
Gale, Zona
Garden, Alexander
Gardener, Helen Hamilton
Garis, Howard Roger
Garretson, James
Garrett, Edmund Henry
Gass, Patrick
Gay, Sydney Howard
Gernsback, Hugo
Ghent, William James
Gholson, William Yates
Gibbes, Robert Wilson
Gibbons, Herbert Adams
Gibbons, James Sloan
Gibbs, Arthur Hamilton
Gibbs, (Oliver) Wolcott
Giesler-Anneke, Mathilde Franziska
Gildersleeve, Basil Lanneau
Giles, Chauncey
Gillett, Ezra Hall
Gillman, Henry
Gilman, Arthur
Gilman, Caroline Howard
Gilman, Daniel Coit
Gilman, Samuel
Gilmer, Francis Walker
Gilmer, George Rockingham
Gilmore, James Roberts
Gilpin, Henry Dilworth
Gitlow, Benjamin
Glaspell, Susan Keating
Glass, Montague Marsden
Godwin, Parke
Goode, George Brown
Goodrich, Alfred John
Goodrich, Charles Augustus
Goodrich, Frank Boott
Goodrich, Samuel Griswold
Goodyear, William Henry
Gordon, George Angier
Gordon, George Henry
Gordon, William
Gould, Edward Sherman
Gould, George Milbry

Goulding, Francis Robert
Graham, David
Graham, John Andrew
Gray, John Chipman
Graydon, Alexander
Greely, Adolphus Washington
Green, Asa
Green, Frances Harriet Whipple
Green, Joseph
Green, Samuel Abbott
Greene, George Washington
Greenleaf, Moses
Greenleaf, Simon
Greenough, Henry
Gregg, Josiah
Grew, Joseph Clark
Grey, Zane
Grierson, Francis
Griffis, William Elliot
Grimké, Archibald Henry
Griswold, Rufus Wilmot
Gross, Milt
Gross, Samuel David
Grund, Francis Joseph
Guild, Curtis, 1827–1911
Gulick, Luther Halsey, 1865–1918
Gunther, John
Gurowski, Adam
Habberton, John
Hackett, Frank Warren
Haines, Charles Glidden
Haldeman-Julius, Emanuel
Hale, Louise Closser
Hale, Lucretia Peabody
Hale, Sarah Josepha Buell
Hales, Edward Everett
Hall, Abraham Oakey
Hall, Arethusa
Hall, Baynard Rush
Hall, Florence Marion Howe
Hall, James, 1793–1868
Hall, James Norman
Halleck, Henry Wager
Hallock, Charles
Hamilton, Allan McLane
Hamilton, Edith
Hammett, Samuel Adams
Hammett, Samuel Dashiell
Hanaford, Phoebe Ann Coffin
Hanchett, Henry Granger
Hapgood, Hutchins
Hapgood, Isabel Florence
Harbaugh, Henry
Harland, Henry
Harper, Ida Husted
Harris, Benjamin
Harris, Joel Chandler
Harris, Joseph
Harrison, Constance Cary
Harrison, Gabriel
Hart, Charles Henry
Harte, Francis Brett
Hartmann, Carl Sadakichi
Hatcher, William Eldridge
Haupt, Herman
Haven, Emily Bradley Neal

Hawthorne, Julian
Hayes, John Lord
Hays, Arthur Garfield
Hazard, Thomas Robinson
Headley, Joel Tyler
Hearn, Lafcadio
Heath, James Ewell
Heilprin, Michael
Heinzen, Karl Peter
Helmuth, William Tod
Helper, Hinton Rowan
Hempel, Charles Julius
Henderson, Peter
Hendrick, Ellwood
Hennepin, Louis
Henningsen, Charles Frederick
Henry, Caleb Sprague
Hentz, Caroline Lee Whiting
Herbermann, Charles George
Herbert, Henry William
Herford, Oliver Brooke
Herrick, Sophia McIlvaine Bledsoe
Herron, George Davis
Higginson, Thomas Wentworth
Hildreth, Richard
Hilgard, Theodor Erasmus
Hill, Frederick Trevor
Hill, Grace Livingston
Hilliard, Henry Washington
Hillis, Newell Dwight
Hillquit, Morris
Hine, Charles De Lano
Hinsdale, Burke Aaron
Hinshaw, David Schull
Hirst, Barton Cooke
Hitchcock, Enos
Hitchcock, Ethan Allen,
 1798–1870
Hitchcock, James Ripley Wellman
Hittell, John Shertzer
Hittell, Theodore Henry
Hodges, George
Hofstadter, Richard
Hogue, Wilson Thomas
Hoisington, Henry Richard
Holcombe, William Henry
Holder, Joseph Bassett
Holland, Edwin Clifford
Holland, Josiah Gilbert
Holley, Alexander Lyman
Hollister, Gideon Hiram
Holmes, George Frederick
Holt, Henry
Hooker, Worthington
Hopkinson, Francis
Hosmer, Hezekiah Lord
Hosmer, James Kendall
Houdini, Harry
Hough, Emerson
House, Edward Howard
Howard, Blanche Willis
Howe, Edgar Watson
Howe, Julia Ward
Hoyt, Henry Martyn
Hubbard, Elbert
Hubbard, Wynant Davis

Hudson, Charles
Hudson, Thomson Jay
Hughes, Henry
Hughes, Rupert
Huneker, James Gibbons
Hunt, Isaac
Hunt, Theodore Whitefield
Hunter, William C.
Huntington, William Reed
Hunton, William Lee
Hurlbert, William Henry
Hurlbut, Jesse Lyman
Husmann, George
Hutchinson, Woods
Hutton, Laurence
Hyde, William De Witt
Ickes, Harold Le Clair
Ide, John Jay
Imlay, Gilbert
Ingersoll, Charles Jared
Ingersoll, Edward
Inglis, Alexander James
Ingraham, Edward Duffield
Ingraham, Joseph Holt
Ingraham, Prentiss
Inman, Henry
Irving, John Treat
Irving, Peter
Irving, Pierre Munro
Irving, Washington
Irwin, William Henry
Isham, Samuel
Jackson, Edward Payson
Jacobi, Mary Cerinna Putnam
James, Marquis
James, Thomas
James, Will Roderick
Jamison, Cecilia Viets Dakin
   Hamilton
Jamison, David Flavel
Janes, Lewis George
Janney, Russell Dixon
Janney, Samuel McPherson
Janvier, Catharine Ann
Janvier, Margaret Thomson
Janvier, Thomas Allibone
Jarves, James Jackson
Jay, John
Jay, William
Jefferson, Thomas
Jenkins, John Stilwell
Jenks, Tudor Storrs
Jewett, Sarah Orne
Johnson, Alexander Bryan
Johnson, Franklin
Johnson, Helen Louise Kendrick
Johnson, James Weldon
Johnson, Joseph
Johnson, Osa
Johnson, Richard W.
Johnson, Samuel
Johnson, Samuel William
Johnson, Virginia Wales
Johnston, Richard Malcolm
Johnston, William Andrew
Joline, Adrian Hoffman

Jones, Alexander
Jones, Amanda Theodosia
Jones, George
Jones, John Beauchamp
Jones, William Alfred
Jordan, William George
Josselyn, John
Joutel, Henri
Joynes, Edward Southey
Judah, Samuel Benjamin Helbert
Judd, Sylvester
Judson, Edward Zane Carroll
   ("Ned Buntline")
Judson, Emily Chubbuck
Kaempffert, Waldemar Bernhard
Kaye, Frederick Benjamin
Keating, John McLeod
Keating, John Marie
Keener, William Albert
Keller, Helen Adams
Kelley, Edith Summers
Kelley, James Douglas Jerrold
Kellogg, Elijah
Kelly, Aloysius Oliver Joseph
Kelly, Myra
Kemble, Frances Anne
Kennan, George
Kennedy, John Pendleton
Kent, Charles Foster
Kidder, Frederic
Kimball, Richard Burleigh
King, Alexander
King, Clarence
King, Edward Smith
King, Grace Elizabeth
King, Thomas Starr
Kinsey, Alfred Charles
Kirk, John Foster
Kirkland, Caroline Matilda
   Stansbury
Kirkland, Joseph
Kirkman, Marshall Monroe
Kirlin, Joseph Louis Jerome
Klingelsmith, Margaret Center
Knapp, Samuel Lorenzo
Knapp, William Ireland
Kneeland, Stillman Foster
Knight, Edward Henry
Knight, Henry Cogswell
Knox, George William
Knox, Thomas Wallace
Kobbé, Gustav
Koebler, Sylvester Rosa
Kohler, Max James
Krapp, George Philip
Krauth, Charles Porterfield
Krehbiel, Henry Edward
Kyne, Peter Bernard
La Borde, Maximilian
La Farge, John
La Farge, Oliver Hazard Perry
Lamb, Martha Joanna Reade Nash
Lambert, Louis Aloisius
Landon, Melville de Lancey
Landreth, David
Lane, Arthur Bliss

Langley, Samuel Pierpont
Lanman, Charles
Larcom, Lucy
Lardner, Ringgold Wilmer
Larned, Josephus Nelson
Larpenteur, Charles
Lathbury, Mary Artemisia
Lathrop, George Parsons
Latimer, Mary Elizabeth Wormeley
Lawson, James
Lawson, John
Lawson, Robert Ripley
Lawson, Thomas William
Lea, Homer
Leach, Daniel Dyer
Leavitt, Dudley
Lee, Eliza Buckminster
Lee, Hannah Farnham Sawyer
Lee, Henry, 1787–1837
Lee, James Melvin
Lee, James Wideman
Leeds, Daniel
Leeser, Isaac
Legler, Henry Eduard
Leigh, William Robinson
Leland, Charles Godfrey
Leonard, Sterling Andrus
Leonard, Zenas
Leslie, Charles Robert
Leslie, Eliza
Lester, Charles Edwards
Levy, Louis Edward
Lewis, Alfred Henry
Lewis, Estelle Anna Blanche
   Robinson
Lewis, Lawrence
Lewis, Orlando Faulkland
Liebling, Abbott Joseph
Liebman, Joshua Loth
Lincoln, John Larkin
Lincoln, Mary Johnson Bailey
Lindsey, William
Linn, William Alexander
Lippincott, Sara Jane Clarke
Littell, William
Little, Arthur Dehon
Livermore, Abiel Abbot
Livermore, Mary Ashton Rice
Lloyd, Henry Demarest
Lockwood, Ralph Ingersoll
Lodge, Henry Cabot
Loeb, Sophie Irene Simon
Logan, Olive
Lomax, Louis Emanuel
London, Jack
Long, John Luther
Longfellow, William Pitt Preble
Longstreet, Augustus Baldwin
Lord, Eleazar
Loring, Frederick Wadsworth
Lossing, Benson John
Lounsbury, Thomas Raynesford
Love, Robertus Donnell
Loveman, Amy
Lowell, James Russell
Lowell, Percival

Lowell, Robert Traill Spence
Lucas, Daniel Bedinger
Ludlow, Fitz Hugh
Ludlow, Noah Miller
Luhan, Mabel Dodge
Lummis, Charles Fletcher
Lunt, George
Lyman, Albert Josiah
Lyman, Theodore, 1792–1849
Lynch, James Daniel
Lynd, Robert Staughton
Lyon, Harris Merton
Lyttelton, William Henry
MacArthur, Robert Stuart
McCabe, William Gordon
McClure, Alexander Wilson
McClure, Samuel Sidney
McConnel, John Ludlum
McCrae, Thomas
McCullough, Ernest
MacDonald, Betty
McGarvey, John William
McGovern, John
McKenney, Thomas Loraine
Mackenzie, Alexander Slidell
Mackenzie, Robert Shelton
Maclay, Edgar Stanton
McLeod, Alexander
McPherson, Edward
McQuillen, John Hugh
MacVicar, Malcolm
Macy, John Albert
Malcolm, James Peller
Malcom, Howard
Mann, Mary Tyler Peabody
Mann, Newton
Mann, William Julius
Mansfield, Edward Deering
Marble, Albert Prescott
Marden, Orison Swett
Margalis, Max Leopold
Marshall, Henry Rutgers
Martin, Anne Henrietta
Martin, François-Xavier
Martin, Frederick Townsend
Martin, John Hill
Martin, Thomas Commerford
Martin, William Alexander Parsons
Martyn, Sarah Towne Smith
Mason, Daniel Gregory
Mather, Cotton
Mather, Frank Jewett, Jr.
Mather, Fred
Mather, Increase
Mather, Richard
Mather, Samuel
Mathews, Albert
Mathews, Cornelius
Mathews, William
Matthews, Franklin
Matthews, Joseph Brown
Maxwell, Elsa
Maxwell, Samuel
Mayer, Brantz
Mayes, Edward
Mayhew, Experience

Mayo, Sarah Carter Edgarton
Mayo, William Starbuck
Mead, Edwin Doak
Mears, John William
Mease, James
Mechem, Floyd Russell
Meehan, Thomas
Meek, Alexander Beaufort
Meigs, Arthur Vincent
Meigs, Charles Delucena
Meigs, John Forsyth
Mell, Patrick Hues
Mellen, Grenville
Melville, Herman
Mercier, Charles Alfred
Merrill, Stephen Mason
Metcalf, Henry Harrison
Micheaux, Oscar
Mielziner, Moses
Miller, Emily Clark Huntington
Miller, Harriet Mann
Miller, James Russell
Miller, Samuel
Millet, Francis Davis
Mills, Enos Abijah
Minor, Raleigh Colston
Mitchell, Donald Grant
Mitchell, John, d. 1768
Mitchell, Margaret Munnerlyn
Mitchell, Nahum
Moffett, Cleveland Langston
Möllhausen, Heinrich Baldwin
Mombert, Jacob Isidor
Montefiore, Joshua
Moore, Annie Aubertine
   Woodward
Moore, Frank
Moore, Jacob Bailey
Moore, John Trotwood
Moran, Benjamin
Morford, Henry
Morgan, James Morris
Morley, Christopher Darlington
Morley, Margaret Warner
Morris, Edward Joy
Morris, William Hopkins
Morse, Sidney Edwards
Morton, Charles Walter
Morton, Nathaniel
Mott, Frank Luther
Moulton, Richard Green
Mowatt, Anna Cora Ogden
Mowry, William Augustus
Mulford, Clarence Edward
Mulford, Elisha
Mullins, Edgar Young
Mumford, James Gregory
Murat, Achille
Murdock, James
Murray, David
Murray, Judith Sargent Stevens
Nadal, Ehrman Syme
Nash, Henry Sylvester
Nash, Simeon
Nason, Elias
Nathan, George Jean

Neal, John
Neely, Thomas Benjamin
Nelson, Henry Loomis
Neuberger, Richard Lewis
Nevin, Alfred
Nevin, Edwin Henry
Newcomb, Harvey
Newman, Samuel Phillips
Newton, Joseph Fort
Nichols, Charles Lemuel
Nichols, Mary Sargeant Neal Gove
Nichols, Thomas Low
Nicholson, Meredith
Niza, Marcos de
Nock, Albert Jay
Nordhoff, Charles
Nordhoff, Charles Bernard
Norris, Mary Harriott
Northen, William Jonathan
Norton, Charles Eliot
Nott, Henry Junius
Oberholtzer, Sara Louisa Vickers
O'Brien, Fitz-James
O'Brien, Frederick
O'Callaghan, Jeremiah
O'Connor, William Douglas
Ogg, Frederic Austin
Okey, John Waterman
O'Malley, Frank Ward
O'Neall, John Belton
O'Neill, Rose Cecil
O'Reilly, Henry
Orton, Helen Fuller
Osborn, Henry Stafford
Osgood, Howard
O'Shea, Michael Vincent
Otis, Arthur Sinton
Ott, Isaac
Ottley, Roi
Owen, Robert Dale
Oxnam, Garfield Bromley
Paine, Ralph Delahaye
Paine, Thomas
Paley, John
Pallen, Condé Benoist
Palmer, Horatio Richmond
Palmer, Joel
Palmer, John McAuley
Palmer, John Williamson
Parish, Elijah
Parker, Jane Marsh
Parker, William Harwar
Parton, James
Parton, Sara Payson Willis
Partridge, William Ordway
Paschal, George Washington
Pastorius, Francis Daniel
Patterson, Robert Mayne
Pattie, James Ohio
Pattison, James William
Patton, William
Paulding, James Kirke
Peabody, Andrew Preston
Peabody, Elizabeth Palmer
Pearson, Edmund Lester
Peattie, Donald Culross

Peck, George Washington
Peck, John Mason
Pedder, James
Peloubet, Francis Nathan
Penfield, Edward
Penfield, Frederic Courtland
Penniman, James Hosmer
Pennington, James W. C.
Pentecost, George Frederick
Percy, George
Percy, William Alexander
Perkins, Frederic Beecher
Perkins, James Handasyd
Perry, Bliss
Perry, Edward Baxter
Perry, Thomas Sergeant
Peterkin, Julia Mood
Peters, Absalom
Peters, Madison Clinton
Peterson, Charles Jacobs
Peyton, John Lewis
Phelan, James, 1856–1891
Phelps, Almira Hart Lincoln
Phelps, Charles Edward
Phillips, Willard
Phillips, William Addison
Phisterer, Frederick
Pickard, Samuel Thomas
Picket, Albert
Pidgin, Charles Felton
Pierce, Gilbert Ashville
Pierson, Arthur Tappan
Pierson, Hamilton Wilcox
Pike, Albert
Pike, James Shepherd
Pise, Charles Constantine
Pollard, Edward Alfred
Pollard, Joseph Percival
Pollock, Channing
Pond, Enoch
Pond, Frederick Eugene
Pool, Maria Louise
Poore, Benjamin Perley
Porter, Robert Percival
Post, Louis Freeland
Poston, Charles Debrill
Potter, Elisha Reynolds
Powel, John Hare
Powell, Edward Payson
Prang, Mary Amelia Dana Hicks
Pratt, Sereno Stansbury
Preble, George Henry
Prentiss, George Lewis
Prescott, George Bartlett
Preston, Harriet Waters
Preston, Margaret Junkin
Preston, Thomas Scott
Price, William Thompson
Prime, Edward Dorr Griffin
Prime, Samuel Irenaeus
Prime, William Cowper
Proctor, William
Pugh, Ellis
Pulte, Joseph Hippolyt
Putnam, George Haven
Putnam, Nina Wilcox

Putnam, Ruth
Pyle, Howard
Quick, John Herbert
Quincy, Edmund
Quincy, Josiah Phillips
Rains, George Washington
Ramsey, James Gettys McGready
Randall, Henry Stephens
Randolph, Sarah Nicholas
Randolph, Thomas Jefferson
Ravenel, Harriott Horry Rutledge
Rawle, Francis, 1846–1930
Raymond, George Lansing
Read, Opie Pope
Redfield, Isaac Fletcher
Redman, Ben Ray
Reed, Earl Howell
Reed, Myrtle
Reed, Richard Clark
Reed, William Bradford
Reid, Gilbert
Reiersen, Johan Reinert
Remington, Frederic
Rémy, Henri
Renwick, James, 1792–1863
Reuterdahl, Henry
Revere, Joseph Warren
Reynolds, Quentin James
Rhodes, Eugene Manlove
Rice, Alice Caldwell Hegan
Rice, Nathan Lewis
Richards, Laura Elizabeth Howe
Richards, Thomas Addison
Richardson, Charles Francis
Richardson, Robert
Richmond, Mary Ellen
Rickert, Martha Edith
Riddle, Albert Gallatin
Rideing, William Henry
Rideout, Henry Milner
Riis, Jacob August
Riley, Benjamin Franklin
Rivers, William James
Roberts, Elizabeth Madox
Roberts, Kenneth Lewis
Robertson, George
Robertson, John
Robertson, Morgan Andrew
Robinson, Charles Mulford
Robinson, Conway
Robinson, Henry Morton
Robinson, Rowland Evans
Robinson, Solon
Robinson, Stillman Williams
Robinson, Therese Albertine Louise
 Von Jakob
Robinson, William Callyhan
Rodenbough, Theophilus Francis
Roe, Edward Payson
Roe, Gilbert Ernstein
Rogers, Clara Kathleen Barnett
Rollins, Alice Marland Wellington
Rölvaag, Ole Edvart
Romans, Bernard
Rombro, Jacob
Roosevelt, Robert Barnwell

Root, Frank Albert
Rose, John Carter
Rosenberg, Abraham Hayyim
Rosenthal, Herman
Ross, Alexander
Rowland, Henry Cottrell
Rowlandson, Mary White
Royall, Anne Newport
Ruffner, Henry
Rugg, Harold Ordway
Ruhl, Arthur Brown
Russell, Charles Edward
Russell, Osborne
Rynning, Ole
Sachs, Hanns
Sachse, Julius Friedrich
Sadlier, Mary Anne Madden
Sadtler, Samuel Philip
Sage, Bernard Janin
Salter, William
Salter, William Mackintire
Sanborn, Franklin Benjamin
Sanborn, Katherine Abbott
Sanders, Elizabeth Elkins
Sanders, Frank Knight
Sanderson, John
Sands, Robert Charles
Sangster, Margaret Elizabeth
 Munson
Sarg, Tony
Sargent, Epes
Sargent, John Osborne
Sargent, Lucius Manlius
Sargent, Winthrop, 1825–1870
Saunders, Frederick
Saunders, Prince
Savage, Minot Judson
Sawyer, Lemuel
Schechter, Solomon
Schofield, William Henry
Schroeder, John Frederick
Schultze, Augustus
Schuyler, George Washington
Schuyler, Montgomery
Scidmore, Eliza Ruhamah
Scott, Leroy
Scott, Samuel Parsons
Scott, William Anderson
Scruggs, William Lindsay
Scudder, Horace Elisha
Sears, Edmund Hamilton
Seawell, Molly Elliot
Sedgwick, Catharine Maria
Sedgwick, Theodore, 1780–1839
Sedgwick, Theodore, 1811–1859
Seiss, Joseph Augustus
Selikovitsch, Goetzel
Semmes, Raphael
Seton, Grace Gallatin Thompson
Seton, William
Severance, Frank Hayward
Sewall, Jonathan
Seward, Theodore Frelinghuysen
Shaler, William
Sharp, Dallas Lore

Shecut, John Linnaeus Edward Whitridge
Shedd, William Greenough Thayer
Sheldon, Charles Monroe
Shelton, Frederick William
Sherwood, Katharine Margaret Brownlee
Sherwood, Mary Elizabeth Wilson
Shields, Charles Woodruff
Shields, George Oliver
Showerman, Grant
Shreve, Thomas Hopkins
Shuey, Edwin Longstreet
Sigourney, Lydia Howard Huntley
Sikes, William Wirt
Simpson, James Hervey
Simpson, Stephen
Singleton, Esther
Siringo, Charles A.
Skinner, John Stuart
Skinner, Thomas Harvey
Slafter, Edmund Farwell
Sloan, Harold Paul
Sloan, Richard Elihu
Slocum, Joshua
Slosson, Edwin Emery
Smedley, Agnes
Smith, Alexander
Smith, Arthur Henderson
Smith, Charles Alphonso
Smith, Edmund Munroe
Smith, Elias
Smith, Elihu Hubbard
Smith, Elizabeth Oakes Prince
Smith, Francis Hopkinson
Smith, Hannah Whitall
Smith, Henry Justin
Smith, James McCune
Smith, James 1737–1814
Smith, John, 1579–1631
Smith, John Augustine
Smith, John Cotton, 1826–1882
Smith, Margaret Bayard
Smith, Richard Penn
Smith, Samuel Harrison
Smith, William Andrew
Smith, William Russell
Smythe, Albert Henry
Smythe, Thomas
Snead, Thomas Lowndes
Snider, Denton Jaques
Snyder, John Francis
Sobolewski, J. Friedrich Eduard
Sokolsky, George Ephraim
Solger, Reinhold
Sounichsen, Albert
Spalding, Thomas
Spangler, Henry Wilson
Spencer, Cornelia Phillips
Spencer, Jesse Ames
Spivak, Charles David
Spofford, Harriet Elizabeth Prescott
Sprague, Achsa W.
Sprague, Oliver Mitchell Wentworth
Sprunt, James

Starr, Eliza Allen
Stauffer, David McNeely
Steele, Daniel
Steffens, Lincoln
Stein, Evaleen
Stein, Gertrude
Stein, Leo Daniel
Stephens, Ann Sophia
Stephens, Charles Asbury
Stephens, John Lloyd
Sterling, James
Stevens, George Washington
Stevens, John Austin, 1827–1910
Stimson, Alexander Lovett
Stimson, Frederic Jesup
Stitt, Edward Rhodes
Stoddard, Charles Warren
Stoddard, John Lawson
Stoddard, William Osborn
Stoever, Martin Luther
Stong, Phil(lip Duffield)
Storey, Moorfield
Story, Isaac
Stowe, Harriet Elizabeth Beecher
Straus, Oscar Solomon
Stromme, Peer Olsen
Strong, Josiah
Strother, David Hunter
Stuart, Charles Beebe
Stuart, Ruth McEnery
Sturgis, Russell
Sullivan, James William
Sullivan, William
Sunderland, Eliza Jane Read
Swensson, Carl Aaron
Swift, Lucius Burrie
Swinton, William
Tappan, Eli Todd
Tarbox, Increase Niles
Taylor, Bert Leston
Taylor, George Boardman
Taylor, James Wickes
Taylor, Joseph Deems
Temple, Oliver Perry
Tennent, John
Tenney, Edward Payson
Terhune, Albert Payson
Terhune, Mary Virginia Hawes
Thacher, John Boyd
Thacher, Samuel Cooper
Thatcher, Benjamin Bussey
Thayer, Thomas Baldwin
Thayer, William Makepeace
Thomas, John Jacobs
Thomas, Richard Henry
Thomes, William Henry
Thompson, Benjamin
Thompson, Daniel Pierce
Thompson, Edward William
Thompson, James Maurice
Thompson, Joseph Parrish
Thompson, Richard Wigginton
Thompson, Slason
Thorburn, Grant
Thorpe, Rose Alnora Hartwick
Thorpe, Thomas Bangs

Thrasher, John Sidney
Thurber, George
Ticknor, George
Tiernan, Frances Christine Fisher
Todd, John
Todd, Mabel Loomis
Todd, Sereno Edwards
Tolman, Herbert Cushing
Tomlinson, Everett Titsworth
Toner, Joseph Meredith
Topliff, Samuel
Torrey, Bradford
Tourgée, Albion Winegar
Towle, George Makepeace
Towne, Charles Hanson
Townsend, George Alfred
Townsend, Luther Tracy
Townsend, Mary Ashley
Townsend, Virginia Frances
Tracy, Joseph
Train, Arthur Cheney
Train, George Francis
Traubel, Horace L.
Trowbridge, John Townsend
Truman, Benjamin Cummings
Trumbull, Henry Clay
Tucker, George
Tucker, Gilbert Milligan
Tucker, Nathaniel Beverley, 1784–1851
Tuckerman, Bayard
Tudor, William
Turner, George Kibbe
Turner, Henry McNeal
Turner, William
Tyler, Samuel
Underwood, Francis Henry
Upham, Thomas Cogswell
Upton, Emory
Upton, George Putnam
Van Brunt, Henry
Vance, Louis Joseph
Van Der Kemp, Francis Adrian
Van Dyke, Henry
Van Rensselaer, Mariana Griswold
Van Schaack, Henry Cruger
Venable, William Henry
Verplanck, Gulian Crommelin
Verrill, Alpheus Hyatt
Very, Lydia Louisa Ann
Victor, Frances Fuller
Victor, Orville James
Villard, Oswald Garrison
Vincent, Frank
Vorse, Mary Heaton
Waddell, Alfred Moore
Waggaman, Mary Teresa McKee
Wakeley, Joseph Burton
Walden, Jacob Treadwell
Waldo, Samuel Putnam
Walker, Alexander
Wallace, John William
Wallace, Lewis
Wallis, Severn Teackle
Waln, Robert, 1794–1825
Walsh, Edmund Aloysius

BANDIT (See also BRIGAND,
    BUCCANEER, BURGLAR,
    DESPERADO, OUTLAW, PIRATE)
Dillinger, John
Plummer, Henry
BANDLEADER (See also CONDUCTOR,
    MUSICIAN)
Dorsey, Thomas Francis
    ("Tommy")
Elman, Harry ("Ziggy")
Gilmore, Patrick Sarsfield
Goldman, Edwin Franko
Gray, Glen
Handy, William Christopher
Henderson, Fletcher Hamilton
Jones, Lindley Armstrong ("Spike")
Lunceford, James Melvin
    ("Jimmie")
Miller, Glenn
Page, Oran Thaddeus ("Lips")
Pryor, Arthur W.
Sousa, John Philip
Teagarden, Weldon Leo ("Jack")
Weems, Ted
Whiteman, Paul Samuel ("Pops")
BANKER (See also CAPITALIST,
    FINANCIER)
Adams, Edward Dean
Appleton, Nathan
Armstrong, Samuel Turell
Bacon, Robert
Baker, George Fisher
Beatty, John
Belmont, August
Binga, Jesse
Bingham, William
Bishop, Charles Reed
Black, Eugene Robert
Bliss, George
Bradford, Gamaliel
Brinkerhoff, Roeliff
Brown, Alexander
Brown, Fayette
Brown, James
Brown, John A.
Cannon, James Graham
Catchings, Waddill
Cattell, Alexander Gilmore
Chaffee, Jerome Bonaparte
Chetlain, Augustus Louis
Clark, Horace Francis
Coe, George Simmons
Cooke, Henry David
Cooke, Jay
Corbett, Henry Winslow
Corcoran, William Wilson
Creighton, Edward
Cummings, Walter Joseph
Cutler, James Goold
Dale, Chester
Davis, Norman Hezekiah
Davison, George Willets
Davison, Henry Pomeroy
Dawes, Charles Gates
De Coppet, Edward J.
Dodge, Joseph Morrell

Drexel, Anthony Joseph
Drexel, Francis Martin
Drexel, Joseph William
Eells, Dan Parmelee
Ellis, John Washington
Elmore, Franklin Harper
Fahnestock, Harris Charles
Fenton, Reuben Eaton
Few, William
Fish, Stuyvesant
Flannery, John
Fletcher, Calvin
Forbes, William Cameron
Forgan, James Berwick
Forrestal, James Vincent
Fraley, Frederick
Fraser, Leon
Gage, Lyman Judson
Garrett, John Work
Gaston, Herbert Earle
Gates, Thomas Sovereign
Giannini, Amadeo Peter
Goldschmidt, Jakob
Grant, James Benton
Greene, Jerome Davis
Hall, James 1793–1868
Hammond, Bray
Hammond, Samuel
Harding, William Procter Gould
Hascall, Milo Smith
Heard, Dwight Bancroft
Hendrix, Joseph Clifford
Henrotin, Charles
Hepburn, Alonzo Barton
Herrick, Myron Timothy
Higginson, Henry Lee
Hunnewell, Horatio Hollis
Hutchinson, Charles Lawrence
Jeffrey, Joseph Andrew
Johnson, Alexander Bryan
Jones, Jesse Holman
Kahn, Otto Herman
Kelly, Eugene
Ladd, William Sargent
Laimbeer, Nathalie Schenck
Lamar, Gazaway Bugg
Lamont, Thomas William
Lee, Thomas
Leffingwell, Russell Cornell
Lehman, Arthur
Lehman, Herbert Henry
Lehman, Robert
Lewis, William David
Littlefield, George Washington
Livingstone, William
Loeb, James
Low, Frederick Ferdinand
Lucas, James H.
Ludlow, Daniel
McFadden, Louis Thomas
McGarrah, Gates White
Marcus, Bernard Kent
Mather, Samuel Holmes
Merriam, William Rush
Merrill, Charles Edward
Meyer, Eugene Isaac

Mills, Darius Ogden
Mitchell, Alexander
Morgan, James Dada
Morgan, John Pierpont
Morgan, Junius Spencer
Morrow, Dwight Whitney
Newberry, Walter Loomis
Peabody, George Foster
Perkins, George Clement
Perkins, George Walbridge
Perkins, James Handasyd
Powers, Daniel William
Price, Hiram
Prince, Frederick Henry
Ralston, William Chapman
Reynolds, George McClelland
Riggs, George Washington
Robb, James
Rollins, Frank West
Rosenberg, Henry
Sabin, Charles Hamilton
Salomon, Haym
Sayre, Stephen
Schneider, George
Seligman, Arthur
Seligman, Isaac Newton
Seligman, Jesse
Seney, George Ingraham
Shaw, Leslie Mortier
Smith, George
Smith, Samuel Harrison
Spaulding, Charles Clinton
Spaulding, Elbridge Gerry
Sprague, Charles
Sprague, Charles Ezra
Spreckels, Rudolph
Stanley, Harold
Stevens, John Austin, 1795–1874
Stewart, John Aikman
Stillman, James
Stokes, Anson Phelps
Stotesbury, Edward Townsend
Straus, Simon William
Strong, Benjamin
Taggart, Thomas
Tappen, Frederick Dobbs
Taylor, Moses
Thatcher, Mahlon Daniel
Thomas, George Clifford
Thompson, David P.
Thompson, John
Thompson, Josiah Van Kirk
Tome, Jacob
Traylor, Melvin Alvah
Vanderlip, Frank Arthur
Waldo, David
Warburg, Paul Moritz
Ward, Samuel, 1786–1839
Westcott, Edward Noyes
White, Stephen Van Culen
Whitney, George
Wiggin, Albert Henry
Williams, Samuel May
Willing, Thomas
Woodward, William
Wright, Richard Robert

Yeatman, James Erwin
BARITONE (See **SINGER**)
BASEBALL CLUB OWNER
Comiskey, Grace Elizabeth Reidy
Crosley, Powel, Jr.
BASEBALL COMMISSIONER
Landis, Kenesaw Mountain
BASEBALL EXECUTIVE
Barrow, Edward Grant
Griffith, Clark Calvin
Johnson, Byron Bancroft
Rickey, Wesley Branch
BASEBALL MANAGER
Collins, Edward Trowbridge
Dressen, Charles Walter
Griffith, Clark Calvin
McGraw, John Joseph
Mack, Connie
McKechnie, William Boyd
Rolfe, Robert Abial ("Red")
BASEBALL ORIGINATOR
Doubleday, Abner
BASEBALL PLAYER
Alexander, Grover Cleveland
Anson, Adrian Constantine
Baker, John Franklin
Bender, Charles Albert ("Chief")
Bridges, Thomas Jefferson Davis
("Tommy")
Cicotte, Edward Victor
Clarkson, John Gibson
Cobb, Tyrus Raymond ("Ty")
Cochrane, Gordon Stanley
("Mickey")
Collins, Edward Trowbridge
Crawford, Samuel Earl
Dressen, Charles Walter ("Chuck")
Duffy, Hugh
Foxx, James Emory
Gehrig, Henry Louis ("Lou")
Gibson, Joshua
Griffith, Clark Calvin
Heilmann, Harry
Hornsby, Rogers
Huggins, Miller James
Johnson, Walter Perry
Kelly, Michael J.
Klein, Charles Herbert ("Chuck")
Lajoie, Napoleon ("Larry")
McGraw, John Joseph
Maranville, Walter James Vincent
("Rabbit")
Martin, Johnny Leonard Roosevelt
("Pepper")
Mathewson, Christopher ("Christy")
O'Doul, Francis Joseph ("Lefty")
Ott, Melvin Thomas ("Mel")
Reach, Alfred James
Rolfe, Robert Abial ("Red")
Rommel, Edwin Americus
("Eddie")
Rowe, Lynwood Thomas
Rucker, George ("Nap")
Ruth, George Herman ("Babe")
Schalk, Raymond William
("Cracker")

Simmons (Szymanski), Aloysius
Harry
Speaker, Tris E.
Vance, Arthur Charles ("Dazzy")
Wagner, John Peter
Walsh, Edward Augustine
Waner, Paul Glee
Wright, George
Wright, Henry
Young, Denton True ("Cy")
Zimmerman, Henry ("Heinie")
BASEBALL UMPIRE
Connolly, Thomas H.
Klem, William J. (Bill)
BASKETBALL ORIGINATOR
Naismith, James
BASKETBALL PLAYER
Lapchick, Joseph Bohomiel
Stokes, Maurice
BEAUTY EXPERT
Arden, Elizabeth
Rubinstein, Helena
BELL FOUNDER (See **IRON FOUNDER**)
BIBLICAL SCHOLAR
Barton, George Aaron
Lake, Kirsopp
Moffatt, James
Montgomery, James Alan
Speiser, Ephraim Avigdor
Willett, Herbert Lockwood
BIBLIOGRAPHER (See also **SCHOLAR**)
Bartlett, John Russell
Bolton, Henry Carrington
Bowker, Richard Rogers
Cole, George Watson
Eames, Wilberforce
Evans, Charles
Field, Herbert Haviland
Finotti, Joseph Maria
Fletcher, Robert
Ford, Worthington Chauncey
Garrison, Fielding Hudson
Greene, Belle Da Costa
Griffin, Appleton Prentiss Clark
Griswold, William McCrillis
Harrisse, Henry
Jackson, William Alexander
Jewett, Charles Coffin
Leypoldt, Frederick
McMurtrie, Douglas Crawford
Moore, George Henry
Nelson, Charles Alexander
Rand, Benjamin
Rhees, William Jones
Rich, Obadiah
Sabin, Joseph
Sargent, George Henry
Trumbull, James Hammond
Vail, Robert William Glenroie
Weeks, Stephen Beauregard
Wilson, Halsey William
Winship, George Parker
BIBLIOPHILE (See also **BOOK**
COLLECTOR, COLLECTOR)
Adler, Elmer
Alden, Ebenezer

Andrews, William Loring
Ayer, Edward Everett
Barton, Thomas Pennant
Dowse, Thomas
Fisher, George Jackson
Ford, Gordon Lester
Fulton, John Farquhar
Gowans, William
Harris, Caleb Fiske
Hoe, Robert, 1839–1909
Hutton, Laurence
Jones, Herschel Vespasian
Mackenzie William
Nichols, Charles Lemuel
Penniman, James Hosmer
Pennypacker, Samuel Whitaker
Polock, Moses
Prince, Thomas
Sabin, Joseph
Thacher, John Boyd
Wood, Casey Albert
Young, George
BILLIARD PLAYER
Hoppe, William Frederick
("Willie")
BIOCHEMIST (See also **CHEMIST,**
PHYSICIAN, SCIENTIST)
Bergmann, Max
Chittenden, Russell Henry
Cohn, Edwin Joseph
Cori, Gerty Theresa Radnitz
Dakin, Henry Drysdale
Elvehjem, Conrad Arnold
Funk, Casimir
Gortner, Ross Aiken
Hart, Edwin Bret
Henderson, Lawrence Joseph
Herter, Christian Archibald
Hoagland, Charles Lee
Koch, Fred Conrad
Levene, Phoebus Aaron Theodore
Marriott, Williams McKim
Meyerhof, Otto
Osborne, Thomas Burr
Schmidt, Carl Louis August
Schoenheimer, Rudolf
Schweinitz, Emil Alexander de
Stern, Kurt Guenter
Sumner, James Batcheller
Vaughan, Victor Clarence
BIOGRAPHER (See also **AUTHOR,**
WRITER)
Allen, Hervey
Anthony, Katharine Susan
Atkinson, William Biddle
Beer, Thomas
Bernard, William Bayle
Bradford, Gamaliel
Brooks, Van Wyck
Bruce, William Cabell
Drake, Benjamin
Duyckinck, Evert Augustus
Duyckinck, George Long
Forester, Cecil Scott
Greenslet, Ferris

Hagedorn, Hermann Ludwig
  Gebhard
Hendrick, Burton Jesse
Hergesheimer, Joseph
Howe, Mark Antony De Wolfe
Johnson, Allen
Kennedy, William Sloane
Lewis, Lloyd Downs
Long, Armistead Lindsay
Morse, John Torrey
Nicolay, John George
Paine, Albert Bigelow
Parton, James
Pickard, Samuel Thomas
Pierce, Edward Lillie
Pringle, Henry Fowles
Proctor, Lucien Brock
Quinn, Arthur Hobson
Sandburg, Carl August
Shellabarger, Samuel
Sprague, William Buell
Thayer, Alexander Wheelock
Thayer, William Roscoe
Van Doren, Carl Clinton
BIOLOGIST (See also BOTANIST,
  SCIENTIST, ZOOLOGIST)
Carrel, Alexis
Chapman, Henry Cadwalader
Coghill, George Ellett
Conklin, Edwin Grant
Davenport, Charles Benedict
Harrison, Ross Granville
Jayne, Horace Fort
Jennings, Herbert Spencer
Lillie, Frank Rattray
Loeb, Leo
McClung, Clarence Erwin
McMurrich, James Playfair
Mayor, Alfred Goldsborough
Minot, Charles Sedgwick
Nelson, Julius
Noble, Gladwyn Kingsley
Pearl, Raymond
Pincus, Gregory Goodwin
  ("Goody")
Sedgwick, William Thompson
Stockard, Charles Rupert
Whitman, Charles Otis
Wilson, Edmund Beecher
Woodruff, Lorande Loss
BIOMETRICIAN (See also BIOLOGIST,
  PHYSICIAN, SCIENTIST,
  STATISTICIAN)
Harris, James Arthur
BIOPHYSICIST (See also BIOLOGIST,
  PHYSICIST, SCIENTIST)
Bovie, William T.
Hecht, Selig
BIRTH CONTROL ADVOCATE
Hepburn, Katharine Houghton
Sanger, Margaret Higgins
Stone, Abraham
BISHOP (See also RELIGIOUS LEADER)
African Methodist Episcopal
Allen, Richard
Brown, John Mifflin

Brown, Morris
Clinton, George Wylie
Gaines, Wesley John
Gregg, John Andrew
Holsey, Lucius Henry
Hood, James Walker
Loguen, Jermain Wesley
Payne, Daniel Alexander
Tanner, Benjamin Tucker
Turner, Henry McNeal
Walters, Alexander
Wayman, Alexander Walker
Anglican
Inglis, Charles
Episcopal
Atkinson, Thomas
Bass, Edward
Brooks, Phillips
Brownell, Thomas Church
Burgess, Alexander
Burgess, George
Burleson, Hugh Latimer
Capers, Ellison
Chase, Philander
Cheney, Charles Edward
Clark, Thomas March
Coleman, Leighton
Coxe, Arthur Cleveland
De Lancey, William Heathcote
Doane, George Washington
Doane, William Croswell
Fallows, Samuel
Grafton, Charles Chapman
Graves, Frederick Rogers
Greer, David Hummell
Griswold, Alexander Viets
Hale, Charles Reuben
Hall, Arthur Crawshay Alliston
Hare, William Hobart
Hobart, John Henry
Holly, James Theodore
Hopkins, John Henry
Howe, Mark Anthony De Wolfe
Huntington, Frederic Dan
Ives, Levi Silliman
Jarvis, Abraham
Johns, John
Kemp, James
Kemper, Jackson
Kerfoot, John Barrett
Kip, William Ingraham
Lay, Henry Champlin
Lee, Alfred
Leonard, William Andrew
Littlejohn, Abram Newkirk
McIlvaine, Charles Pettit
McLaren, William Edward
McVickar, William Neilson
Madison, James
Meade, William
Moore, Benjamin
Moore, Richard Channing
Murray, John Gardner
Nichols, William Ford
Odenheimer, William Henry
Onderdonk, Benjamin Tredwell

Onderdonk, Henry Ustick
Otey, James Hervey
Paddock, Benjamin Henry
Paddock, John Adams
Penick, Charles Clifton
Perry, William Stevens
Peterkin, George William
Polk, Leonidas
Potter, Alonzo
Potter, Henry Codman
Potter, Horatio
Provoost, Samuel
Quintard, Charles Todd
Randolph, Alfred Magill
Ravenscroft, John Stark
Satterlee, Henry Yates
Schereschewsky, Samuel Isaac
  Joseph
Scott, Thomas Fielding
Seabury, Samuel, 1729–1796
Seymour, George Franklin
Slattery, Charles Lewis
Smith, Robert, 1732–1801
Spalding, Franklin Spencer
Stevens, William Bacon
Talbot, Ethelbert
Thompson, Hugh Miller
Tucker, Henry St. George
Tuttle, Daniel Sylvester
Wainwright, Jonathan Mayhew,
  1792–1854
Whipple, Henry Benjamin
White, William
Whittingham, William Rollinson
Williams, Channing Moore
Williams, Charles David
Williams, John, 1817–1899
Wilmer, Joseph Père Bell
Wilmer, Richard Hooker
Evangelical
Esher, John Jacob
Seybert, John
German Baptist Brethren
Sower, Christopher, 1721–1784
Mennonite
Boehm, Martin
Methodist
Ames, Edward Raymond
Andrew, James Osgood
Andrews, Edward Gayer
Asbury, Francis
Baker, Osmon Cleander
Bascom, Henry Bidleman
Bashford, James Whitford
Bowman, Thomas
Capers, William
Coke, Thomas
Early, John
Emory, John
Fitzgerald, Oscar Penn
Foss, Cyrus David
Foster, Randolph Sinks
Fowler, Charles Henry
Galloway, Charles Betts
Goodsell, Daniel Ayres
Hamline, Leonidas Lent

Chamberlain, Charles Joseph
Chase, (Mary) Agnes Merrill
Clark, Henry James
Clayton, John
Clements, Frederic Edward
Colden, Jane
Collins, Frank Shipley
Coulter, John Merle
Cowles, Henry Chandler
Curtis, Moses Ashley
Cutler, Manasseh
Darlington, William
Dudley, William Russel
Duggar, Benjamin Minge
Durand, Élie Magloire
Eaton, Daniel Cady
Elliott, Stephen
Ellis, Job Bicknell
Engelmann, George
Fairchild, David Grandison
Farlow, William Gilson
Fernald, Merritt Lyndon
Goodale, George Lincoln
Gray, Asa
Greene, Edward Lee
Harris, James Arthur
Harshberger, John William
Hollick, Charles Arthur
Howell, Thomas Jefferson
James, Thomas Potts
Jeffrey, Edward Charles
Jepson, Willis Linn
Kauffman, Calvin Henry
Kellogg, Albert
Knowlton, Frank Hall
Kraemer, Henry
Kuhn, Adam
Lemmon, John Gill
Lindheimer, Ferdinand Jacob
Marshall, Humphry
Meehan, Thomas
Michaux, André
Michaux, François André
Michener, Ezra
Millspaugh, Charles Frederick
Mitchell, Elisha
Mitchell, John, d. 1768
Mohr, Charles Theodore
Mühlenberg, Gotthilf Henry Ernest
Nieuwland, Julius Arthur
Nuttall, Thomas
Paine, John Alsop
Pammel, Louis Hermann
Parry, Charles Christopher
Porcher, Francis Peyre
Porter, Thomas Conrad
Pound, (Nathan) Roscoe
Pursh, Frederick
Ravenel, Henry William
Riddell, John Leonard
Robinson, Benjamin Lincoln
Rose, Joseph Nelson
Rothrock, Joseph Trimble
Rydberg, Per Axel
Safford, William Edwin
Sartwell, Henry Parker

Schweinitz, Lewis David von
Setchell, William Albert
Shecut, John Linnaeus Edward
    Whitridge
Short, Charles Wilkins
Sinnott, Edmund Ware
Smith, Edwin Frink
Spalding, Volney Morgan
Sullivant, William Starling
Thaxter, Roland
Thurber, George
Torrey, John
Trelease, William
Tuckerman, Edward
Underwood, Lucien Marcus
Vasey, George
Walter, Thomas, ca. 1740–1789
Watson, Sereno
White, David
Wilson, Ernest Henry
Wright, Charles
BOXER (See also ATHLETE, PUGILIST)
Dundee, Johnny
Jeffries, James Jackson
Johnson, Jack
Langford, Samuel
Marciano, Rocky
Wills, Harry
BOY SCOUT LEADER
West, James Edward
BREEDER OF DOGS
Sloane, Isabel Cleves Dodge
BREEDER OF RACEHORSES (See also
    HORSEMAN)
Jones, Benjamin Allyn
Lorillard, Pierre
Madden, John Edward
White, Benjamin Franklin
BREWER
Busch, Adolphus
Jones, Frank
Ruppert, Jacob
Vassar, Matthew
Wacker, Charles Henry
BRIDGE BUILDER (See also ENGINEER,
    BRIDGE; ENGINEER, CIVIL)
Harrington, John Lyle
Lindenthal, Gustav
BRIDGE PLAYER (CONTRACT)
Culbertson, Ely
Culbertson, Josephine Murphy
Lenz, Sidney Samuel
Whitehead, Wilbur Cherrier
Work, Milton Cooper
BRIGAND (See also BANDIT,
    DESPERADO, OUTLAW)
Murrieta, Joaquin
BROADCAST AUDIENCE ANALYST
Hooper, Claude Ernest
BRONZE FOUNDER (See also IRON
    FOUNDER)
Mills, Clark

BRYOLOGIST (See also BOTANIST,
    BIOLOGIST)
BUCCANEER (See also BANDIT,
    BRIGAND, CRIMINAL,
    DESPERADO, OUTLAW, PIRATE)
You, Dominique
BUCK ROGERS ORIGINATOR
Dille, John Flint
BUILDER (See also CANAL BUILDER,
    RAILROAD BUILDER,
    SHIPBUILDER)
Allaire, James Peter
Hawks, John
Hoban, James
Hooker, Philip
Joy, Thomas
Macfarlane, Charles William
Parris, Alexander
Starrett, Paul
Starrett, William Aiken
Wolfson, Erwin Service
BUILDING CONTRACTOR (See also
    CONTRACTOR)
Kelly, John Brendan
BURGLAR (See also BANDIT, BRIGAND,
    BUCCANEER, CRIMINAL,
    DESPERADO, OUTLAW, PIRATE)
Wyman, Seth
BUSINESS FORECASTER
Babson, Roger Ward
BUSINESSMAN (See also
    BUSINESSWOMAN, CAPITALIST,
    ENTREPRENEUR EXECUTIVE,
    FACTOR, Industrialist,
    Manufacturer, Merchant)
Abernethy, George
Adams, Charles Francis
Aldrich, Nelson Wilmarth
Baldwin, Henry Porter
Batterson, James Goodwin
Bean, Leon Lenwood
Behn, Sosthenes
Bement, Clarence Sweet
Besse, Arthur Lyman
Bliss, Cornelius Newton
Borg, George William
Brady, Anthony Nicholas
Bruce, Edward Bright
Buchanan, William Insco
Buchtel, John Richards
Bucknell, William
Bunker, Arthur Hugh
Caldwell, Alexander
Camden, Johnson Newlon
Caroll, Howard
Chester, Colby Mitchell
Cobo, Albert Eugene
Coburn, Abner
Comer, Braxton Bragg
Cooke, Samuel
Cooper, Mark Anthony
Coxey, Jacob Sechler
Crane, Charles Richard
Dana, Napoleon Jackson Tecumseh
Dawes, Rufus Cutler
Dexter, Henry

Dow, Lorenzo
Early, Stephen Tyree
Eastman, Harvey Gridley
Edison, Charles
Emery, Henry Crosby
Farwell, Charles Benjamin
Forbes, John Murray
Franklin, William Buel
Goldfine, Bernard
Gorham, Nathaniel
Grady, Henry Francis
Hamlin, Charles
Hartford, George Huntington
Hartford, George Ludlum
Hartford, John Augustine
Haugen, Gilbert Nelson
Hiester, Daniel
Hogan, John
Holt, William Franklin
Hoyt, John Sherman
Huidekoper, Harm Jan
Keyes, Erasmus Darwin
Kimball, Dan Able
Knauth, Oswald Whitman
Kraft, James Lewis
Ladd, William Sargent
Lasater, Edward Cunningham
Lowell, Percival
McCormick, Richard Cunningham
MacNider, Hanford
Manigault, Peter
Matthews, Francis Patrick
Miller, David Hunter
Millikin, Eugene Donald
Mills, Cyrus Taggart
Mitchell, James Paul
Morton, Paul
Mosessohn, David Nehemiah
Murphy, Gerald Clery
Newberry, Truman Handy
Niles, Nathaniel, 1741–1828
O'Daniel, Wilbert Lee ("Pappy")
Olds, Irving Sands
Pate, Maurice
Peek, George Nelson
Petri, Angelo
Phelps, William Walter
Rand, James Henry
Reece, Brazilla Carroll
Rich, Robert
Richmond, Dean
Roosevelt, Theodore
Scammon, Jonathan Young
Schell, Augustus
Scott, Allen Cecil
Shuey, Edwin Longstreet
Sibley, Hiram
Smoot, Reed Owen
Snell, Bertrand Hollis
Sprunt, James
Strawn, Silas Hardy
Stuart, Elbridge Amos
Taussig, William
Thomas, John Parnell
Thomas, (John William) Elmer
Walker, Amasa

Whalen, Grover Aloysius
Wherry, Kenneth Spicer
BUSINESSWOMAN
Arden, Elizabeth
Gleason, Kate
Rubinstein, Helena
Walker, Sarah Breedlove
Willard, Mary Hatch
BYZANTINE SCHOLAR
Vasiliev, Alexander Alexandrovich

CABALIST (See also RELIGIOUS
    LEADER)
Pancoast, Seth
CABINETMAKER (See CARPENTER)
CABLE PROMOTER
Eastman, Arthur MacArthur
Field, Cyrus West
Scrymser, James Alexander
CALLIGRAPHER
Dwiggins, William Addison
CANAL BUILDER
Goethals, George Washington
Lacock, Abner
Moorhead, James Kennedy
CANAL PROMOTER
Shonts, Theodore Perry
Watson, Elkanah
CANNON MAKER (See also IRON
    FOUNDER)
Denning, William
CANTOR (See also SINGER)
Kaiser, Alois
Rosenblatt, Joseph
Stark, Edward Josef
CAPITALIST (See also FINANCIER)
Allerton, Samuel Waters
Ames, Frederick Lothrop
Ames, Oakes
Ames, Oliver
Archbold, John Dustin
Astor, John Jacob, 1763–1848
Astor, John Jacob, 1822–1890
Astor, John Jacob, 1864–1914
Astor, William Backhouse
Astor, William Waldorf
Ayer, James Cook
Baldwin, Henry Perrine
Barber, Amzi Lorenzo
Barnum, Zenus
Bennett, James Gordon
Berwind, Edward Julius
Blair, John Insley
Blow, Henry Taylor
Boies, Henry Martyn
Brainerd, Lawrence
Brown, Henry Cordis
Burt, John
Campbell, Robert
Collier, Barron Gift
Converse, Edmund Cogswell
Cook, James Merrill
Corbin, Austin
Cornell, Ezra
Crimmins, John Daniel
Crocker, Charles

Daly, Marcus
De Lamar, Joseph Raphael
Dennis, Graham Barclay
Dickson, Thomas
Dolan, Thomas
Donahue, Peter
Drew, Daniel
Du Pont, Thomas Coleman
Eells, Dan Parmelee
Elkins, William Lukens
Field, Cyrus West
Fisk, James
Fiske, John
Flagler, Henry Morrison
Flagler, John Haldane
Fleischmann, Charles Louis
Folger, Henry Clay
Freedman, Andrew
Frick, Henry Clay
Gerstle, Lewis
Gilbert, William Lewis
Glidden, Joseph Farwell
Grace, William Russell
Grant, John Thomas
Guggenheim, Daniel
Haggin, James Ben Ali
Halleck, Henry Wager
Hanna, Marcus Alonzo
Harrah, Charles Jefferson
Hauser, Samuel Thomas
Havemeyer, Henry Osborne
Havemeyer, William Frederick
Huntington, Collis Potter
Jesup, Morris Ketchum
Jones, Frank
Juilliard, Augustus D.
Keith, Minor Cooper
Kennedy, John Stewart
Knight, Edward Collings
Leach, Shepherd
Leary, John
Leiter, Joseph
Lewisohn, Adolph
Logan, Thomas Muldrup,
    1840–1914
Longyear, John Munroe
Lowry, Thomas
Lucas, James H.
Mackay, Clarence Hungerford
Mackay, John William
Macy, Valentine Everit
Markoe, Abraham
Marquand, Henry Gurdon
Mather, Samuel Livingston
Moffat, David Halliday
Moore, William Henry
O'Brien, William Shoney
Paine, Charles Jackson
Patten, James A.
Payne, Oliver Hazard
Phelan, James, 1824–1892
Pratt, Enoch
Ralston, William Chapman
Raymond, Benjamin Wright
Ream, Norman Bruce
Reed, Simeon Gannett

Roberts, Marshall Owen
Rogers, Henry Huttleston
Ryan, John Dennis
Ryerson, Martin Antoine
Scrymser, James Alexander
Severance, Louis Henry
Sheedy, Dennis
Simpson, Michael Hodge
Sloss, Louis
Smith, Francis Marion
Smith, Robert Alexander C.
Spreckels, Claus
Spreckels, John Diedrich
Squire, Watson Carvosso
Stewart, William Rhinelander
Stillman, James
Stokes, William Earl Dodge
Stone, Amasa
Stranahan, James Samuel Thomas
Taylor, Moses
Tevis, Lloyd
Thaw, William
Tobey, Edward Silas
Tod, David
Upton, George Bruce
Vanderbilt, George Washington
Vanderbilt, William Kissam
Vibbard, Chauncey
Waldo, Samuel
Walters, Henry
Waterhouse, Frank
Welch, Charles Clark
Winslow, Sidney Wilmot
Zimmerman, Eugene

CARDINAL
Brennan, Francis James
Cushing, Richard James
Glennon, John Joseph
Meyer, Albert Gregory
Ritter, Joseph Elmer
Spellman, Francis Joseph

CARDIOLOGIST (See also PHYSICIAN)
Libman, Emanuel

CARE EXECUTIVE DIRECTOR
French, Paul Comly

CARICATURIST (See CARTOONIST)

CARPENTER
Goddard, John
Gostelowe, Jonathan
Holden, Oliver
Luther, Seth
Phyfe, Duncan
Savery, William, 1721–1787

CARPETBAGGER (See also
   ADVENTURER, SPECULATOR)
Clarke, William Thomas
Tourgée, Albion Winegar

CARRIAGE BUILDER
Brewster, James

CARTOGRAPHER (See also MAPMAKER)
Farmer, John
Herrman, Augustine
Kino, Eusebio Francisco
Lindenkohl, Adolph
Ogden, Herbert Gouverneur
Pelham, Henry

Pound, Thomas
Romans, Bernard
Southack, Cyprian
Tanner, Henry Schenck
White, John

CARTOONIST (See also ARTIST,
   ILLUSTRATOR)
Arno, Peter
Bellew, Frank Henry Temple
Berryman, Clifford Kennedy
Briggs, Clare A.
Cesare, Oscar Edward
Charles, William
Clay, Edward Williams
Crosby, Percy Lee
Darling, Jay Norwood ("Ding")
Davenport, Homer Calvin
Dorgan, Thomas Aloysius
Duffy, Edmund
Fisher, Hammond Edward
Fisher, Henry Conroy ("Bud")
Fitzpatrick, Daniel Robert
Fox, Fontaine Talbot, Jr.
Gibson, Charles Dana
Gillam, Bernhard
Goldberg, Reuben Lucius ("Rube")
Gray, Harold Lincoln
Gross, Milt
Grosz, George
Hatlo, Jimmy
Held, John, Jr.
Herriman, George Joseph
Hubbard, Frank McKinney
Keppler, Joseph
Kirby, Rollin
McManus, George
Minor, Robert
Morgan, Matthew Somerville
Nast, Thomas
Newell, Peter Sheaf Hersey
Opper, Frederick Burr
Raymond, Alexander Gillespie
Rogers, William Allen
Smith, Robert Sidney
Szyk, Arthur
Thurber, James Grover
Volck, Adalbert John
Wales, James Albert
Webster, Harold Tucker
Willard, Frank Henry
Williams, Gaar Campbell
Young, Art
Zimmerman, Eugene

CATERER (See RESTAURATEUR)

CATTLEMAN (See also DAIRY
   HUSBANDMAN, RANCHER, STOCK
   BREEDER)
Chisum, John Simpson
Goodnight, Charles
Lasater, Edward Cunningham
Littlefield, George Washington
McCoy, Joseph Geating
Mackenzie, Murdo
Renick, Felix
Springer, Charles
Strawn, Jacob

CENSUS DIRECTOR
Kennedy, Joseph Camp Griffith
Merriam, William Rush

CHANCELLOR (STATE)
Harrington, Samuel Maxwell
Livingston, Robert R., 1746–1813
Saulsbury, Willard, 1820–1892
Walworth, Reuben Hyde

CHANDLER
Jackson, William, 1783–1855

CHAPLAIN (See also CLERGYMAN,
   RELIGIOUS LEADER)
Hunter, Andrew
Jones, David
Jones, George
Munro, Henry

CHEF
Diat, Louis Felix

CHEMIST (See also BIOCHEMIST,
   SCIENTIST)
Abel, John Jacob
Adkins, Homer Burton
Austen, Peter Townsend
Babcock, James Francis
Bache, Franklin
Bailey, Jacob Whitman
Bancroft, Wilder Dwight
Barker, George Frederick
Baskerville, Charles
Beck, Lewis Caleb
Benedict, Stanley Rossiter
Bolton, Henry Carrington
Boltwood, Bertram Borden
Booth, James Curtis
Boyé, Martin Hans
Browne, Charles Albert
Burnett, Joseph
Carothers, Wallace Hume
Chandler, Charles Frederick
Clarke, Frank Wigglesworth
Cooke, Josiah Parsons
Cope, Arthur Clay
Cottrell, Frederick Gardner
Crafts, James Mason
Cutbush, James
Dabney, Charles William
Dana, James Freeman
Dana, Samuel Luther
Day, David Talbot
Debye, Peter Joseph William
Doremus, Robert Ogden
Dorset, Marion
Dow, Herbert Henry
Draper, John William
Drown, Thomas Messinger
Dudley, Charles Benjamin
Duncan, Robert Kennedy
Du Pont, Francis Irénée
Ellis, Carleton
Folin, Otto Knut Olof
Franklin, Edward Curtis
Freas, Thomas Bruce
Fullam, Frank L.
Genth, Frederick Augustus
Gibbs, Oliver Wolcott
Goessmann, Charles Anthony

Gomberg, Moses
Gorham, John
Grasselli, Caesar Augustin
Green, Jacob
Griscom, John
Guthrie, Samuel
Hall, Charles Martin
Hare, Robert
Harkins, William Draper
Hart, Edward
Hayes, Augustus Allen
Hendrick, Ellwood
Herty, Charles Holmes
Hill, Henry Barker
Hillebrand, William Francis
Hooker, Samuel Cox
Horsford, Eben Norton
Hudson, Claude Silbert
Hunt, Thomas Sterry
Jackson, Charles Thomas
James, Charles
Jarves, Deming
Johnson, Treat Baldwin
Johnston, John
Jones, Harry Clary
Keating, William Hypolitus
Kedzie, Robert Clark
Kharasch, Morris Selig
Kinnicutt, Leonard Parker
Kirkwood, John Gamble
Koenig, George Augustus
Kohler, Elmer Peter
Ladd, Edwin Fremont
Lamb, Arthur Becket
Langley, John Williams
Langmuir, Irving
Latimer, Wendell Mitchell
Lea, Mathew Carey
Leffmann, Henry
Levy, Louis Edward
Lewis, Gilbert Newton
Loeb, Morris
Long, John Harper
Mabery, Charles Frederic
Maclean, John
McMurtrie, William
Mallet, John William
Mallinckrodt, Edward, Jr.
Matheson, William John
Matthews, Joseph Merritt
Merrill, Joshua
Metcalfe, Samuel Lytler
Michael, Arthur
Michaelis, Leonor
Midgley, Thomas
Mitchell, John Kearsley
Moore, Richard Bishop
Morfit, Campbell
Morley, Edward Williams
Mulliken, Samuel Parsons
Munroe, Charles Edward
Nef, John Ulric
Nichols, James Robinson
Nieuwland, Julius Arthur
Norris, James Flack
Norton, John Pitkin

Noyes, Arthur Amos
Noyes, William Albert
Ostromislensky, Iwan Iwanowich
Parr, Samuel Wilson
Peckham, Stephen Farnum
Pendleton, Edmund Monroe
Peter, Robert
Phillips, Francis Clifford
Piccard, Jean Felix
Porter, John Addison
Power, Frederick Belding
Prescott, Albert Benjamin
Pugh, Evan
Randall, Wyatt William
Reese, Charles Lee
Reid, David Boswell
Remsen, Ira
Rice, Charles
Richards, Ellen Henrietta Swallow
Richards, Theodore William
Rogers, James Blythe
Rogers, Robert Empie
Sadtler, Samuel Philip
Sanger, Charles Robert
Scovell, Melville Amasa
Seabury, George John
Shepard, James Henry
Sheppard, Samuel Edward
Silliman, Benjamin, 1816–1885
Slosson, Edwin Emery
Smith, Alexander
Smith, Edgar Fahs
Smith, John Lawrence
Squibb, Edward Robinson
Stern, Otto
Stieglitz, Julius
Stillman, Thomas Bliss
Stine, Charles Milton Altland
Stoddard, John Tappan
Storer, Francis Humphreys
Takamine, Jokichi
Talbot, Henry Paul
Taylor, William Chittenden
Teeple, John Edgar
Tilghman, Richard Albert
Tolman, Richard Chace
Torrey, John
Vaughan, Daniel
Warren, Cyrus Moors
Washburn, Edward Wight
Weber, Henry Adam
Weightman, William
Wetherill, Charles Mayer
White, Henry Clay
Whitmore, Frank Clifford
Whitney, Josiah Dwight
Whitney, Willis Rodney
Wiechmann, Ferdinand Gerhard
Wiley, Harvey Washington
Witthaus, Rudolph August
Wood, Edward Stickney
Woodhouse, James
Wurtz, Henry

CHESS PLAYER
Loyd, Samuel
Mackenzie, George Henry

Marshall, Frank James
Morphy, Paul Charles
Pillsbury, Harry Nelson
Rice, Isaac Leopold
Steinitz, William

CHIEF JUSTICE (STATE) (See also
    JUDGE, JURIST, LAWYER,
    SUPREME COURT JUSTICE)
De Lancey, James
Gaines, Reuben Reid
Horsmanden, Daniel
Livermore, Arthur
Lloyd, David
Lowe, Ralph Phillips
Lumpkin, Joseph Henry
Mellen, Prentiss
More, Nicholas
Morris, Lewis, 1671–1746
Morris, Robert Hunter
Morton, Marcus, 1819–1891
Nicholls, Francis Redding Tillon
Read, George
Rusk, Thomas Jefferson
Shippen, Edward, 1728–1806
Simpson, William Dunlap

CHINESE ART SPECIALIST
Ferguson, John Calvin

CHOIRMASTER (See also CONDUCTOR)
Dett, Robert Nathaniel
Tuckey, William

CHOREOGRAPHER
Bolm, Adolph Rudolphovitch
Fokine, Michel
Humphrey, Doris
Tamiris, Helen

CHRISTIAN SCIENCE LEADER (See also
    RELIGIOUS LEADER)
Eddy, Mary Morse Baker
Stetson, Augusta Emma Simmons

CHRONICLER (See also DIARIST,
    HISTORIAN)
Clyman, James
Johnson, Edward

CHURCH HISTORIAN (See also
    HISTORIAN)
Dubbs, Joseph Henry
Edwards, Morgan
Guilday, Peter Keenan
Jackson, Samuel Macauley
Moffatt, James
Perry, William Stevens
Schaff, Philip
Walker, Williston
Whitsitt, William Heth

CIRCUS CLOWN (See CLOWN)
CIRCUS PROPRIETOR (See SHOWMAN)
CITY PLANNER
Atterbury, Grosvenor
Bassett, Edward Murray
Bettman, Alfred
Brunner, Arnold William
Ford, George Burdett
Moore, Charles
Nolen, John
Robinson, Charles Mulford
Saarinen, Gottlieb Eliel

Frey, Joseph Samuel Christian
   Frederick
Fuller, Richard
Fulton, Justin Dewey
Furman, James Clement
Furman, Richard
Gale, Elbridge
Gambrell, James Bruton
Gano, John
Gano, Stephen
Garrard, James
Gilmore, Joseph Henry
Going, Jonathan
Goodspeed, Thomas Wakefield
Graves, James Robinson
Gregory, John Milton
Griffith, Benjamin
Hatcher, William Eldridge
Henderson, Charles Richmond
Holcombe, Henry
Holman, Jesse Lynch
Horr, George Edwin
Hovey, Alvah
Howell, Robert Boyté Crawford
Jeter, Jeremiah Bell
Johnson, Franklin
Johnson, William Bullein
Jones, David
Judson, Edward
King, Henry Melville
King, Martin Luther, Jr.
Lamb, Isaac Wixom
Lane, Tidence
Leland, John
Lightburn, Joseph Andrew Jackson
Lorimer, George Claude
Love, Emanuel King
Lowrey, Mark Perrin
MacArthur, Robert Stuart
McGlothlin, William Joseph
Macintosh, Douglas Clyde
Malcolm, Howard
Manly, Basil, 1798–1868
Manly, Basil, 1825–1892
Manning, James
Marshall, Daniel
Martin, Warren Homer
Massey, John Edward
Mell, Patrick Hues
Mercer, Jesse
Merrill, Daniel
Merrill, George Edmands
Morehouse, Henry Lyman
Morgan, Abel
Morgan, Thomas Jefferson
Moss, Lemuel
Moxom, Philip Stafford
Mullins, Edgar Young
Myles, John
Osgood, Howard
Payne, Christopher Harrison
Peck, John Mason
Pendleton, James Madison
Pentecost, George Frederick
Perry, Rufus Lewis
Potter, Charles Francis

Powell, Adam Clayton, Sr.
Rauschenbusch, Walter
Rhees, Morgan John
Rhees, Rush
Rice, Luther
Richmond, John Lambert
Riley, Benjamin Franklin
Riley, William Bell
Robins, Henry Ephraim
Robinson, Ezekiel Gilman
Ross, Martin
Ryland, Robert
Sanders, Billington McCarter
Sears, Barnas
Sharp, Daniel
Sherwood, Adiel
Smith, Hezekiah
Smith, John, *ca.* 1735–*ca.* 1824
Smith, Samuel Francis
Stanford, John
Staughton, William
Stearns, Shubal
Stillman, Samuel
Stow, Baron
Straton, John Roach
Taylor, George Boardman
Taylor, James Barnett
Taylor, James Monroe
Taylor, John
Thomas, Jesse Burgess
Tichenor, Isaac Taylor
Tomlinson, Everett Titsworth
Tucker, Henry Holcombe
Tupper, Henry Allen
Vedder, Henry Clay
Waller, John Lightfoot
Wayland, Francis, 1796–1865
Whitfield, Owen
Whitsitt, William Heth
Williams, George Washington
Williams, William R.
Willingham, Robert Josiah
Winchester, Elhanan
Winkler, Edwin Theodore
Woods, Alva
Yeaman, William Pope
Campbellite (**See** *Disciples of Christ*)
Catholic (**See** *Roman Catholic*)
Christian Connection
   Shaw, Elijah
   Smith, Elias
   Wellons, William Brock
Church of England (**See** *Anglican*)
Church of God
   Michaux, Lightfoot Solomon
Church of the New Jerusalem (**See**
Swedenborgian)
Congregational
   Abbott, Edward
   Abbott, Jacob
   Abbott, John Stevens Cabot
   Abbott, Lyman
   Adams, Nehemiah
   Alden, Timothy
   Allen, William
   Ament, William Scott

Andrew, Samuel
Atkinson, George Henry
Atkinson, Henry Avery
Atwater, Lyman Hotchkiss
Austin, David
Austin, Samuel
Backus, Azel
Bacon, Benjamin Wisner
Bacon, David
Bacon, John
Bacon, Leonard
Bacon, Leonard Woolsey
Bailey, Rufus William
Bancroft, Aaron
Barnard, John
Barrows, John Henry
Bartlett, Samuel Colcord
Barton, James Levi
Barton, William Eleazar
Beecher, Charles
Beecher, Edward
Beecher, Henry Ward
Beecher, Thomas Kinnicut
Behrends, Adolphus Julius
   Frederick
Belknap, Jeremy
Bissell, Edwin Cone
Blakeslee, Erastus
Bosworth, Edward Increase
Boynton, Charles Brandon
Bradford, Amory Howe
Brattle, William
Brown, Charles Reynolds
Bumstead, Horace
Burr, Enoch Fitch
Burton, Asa
Burton, Marion Le Roy
Burton, Nathaniel Judson
Bushnell, Horace
Byles, Mather
Calkins, Phineas Wolcott
Chapin, Aaron Lucius
Chapin, Calvin
Cheever, George Barrell
Child, Frank Samuel
Clap, Thomas
Clark, Francis Edward
Clark, Jonas
Clark, Joseph Sylvester
Cleveland, Aaron
Cobb, William Henry
Condon, Thomas
Cook, Russell S.
Cooper, Samuel, 1725–1783
Crane, Frank
Cravath, Erastus Milo
Cushman, Joshua
Cutler, Carroll
Cutler, Manasseh
Daggett, Naphtali
Dana, James
Davenport, James
Davis, Jerome Dean
Day, Henry Noble
Deane, Samuel
Dewey, Chester

Dexter, Henry Martyn
Dike, Samuel Warren
Diman, Jeremiah Lewis
Dole, Charles Fletcher
Douglas, Lloyd Cassel
Dunning, Albert Elijah
Durant, Henry
Dwight, Sereno Edwards
Dwight, Timothy, 1752–1817
Dwight, Timothy, 1828–1916
Eastman, William Reed
Edwards, Jonathan
Edwards, Justin
Eliot, Jared
Emerson, Joseph
Emmons, Nathanael
Everett, Robert
Fairbanks, Henry
Field, David Dudley
Fisher, George Park
Fowler, Orin
Gay, Ebenezer
Gladden, Washington
Goodrich, Charles Augustus
Goodrich, Chauncey Allen
Goodrich, Elizur
Gordon, George Angier
Gordon, William
Griffin, Edward Dorr
Griffis, William Elliot
Grinnell, Josiah Bushnell
Gulick, Sidney Lewis
Gunsaulus, Frank Wakeley
Hall, Sherman
Harris, George
Haven, Joseph
Hepworth, George Hughes
Herron, George Davis
Hiacoomes
Higginson, John
Hillis, Newell Dwight
Hitchcock, Edward, 1793–1864
Hitchcock, Enos
Hitchcock, Roswell Dwight
Hoisington, Henry Richard
Holmes, Abiel
Holt, Arthur Erastus
Hooker, Thomas
Hubbard, William
Hume, Robert Allen
Humphrey, Heman
Jefferson, Charles Edward
Jenks, William
Kellogg, Elijah
Kellogg, Martin
Kyle, James Henderson
Langdon, Samuel
Leavitt, Joshua
L'Halle, Constantin de
Lord, Nathan
Lovejoy, Owen Reed
Lyman, Albert Josiah
McCulloch, Oscar Carleton
McKeen, Joseph
McKenzie, Alexander
Magoun, George Frederic

Mahan, Asa
Marsh, John
Mather, Samuel
Mayhew, Thomas
Mead, Charles Marsh
Mears, David Otis
Merrill, Selah
Mills, Samuel John
Mitchell, Jonathan
Moore, Zephaniah Swift
Morril, David Lawrence
Morrison, Nathan Jackson
Morse, Jedidiah
Munger, Theodore Thornton
Murdock, James
Nash, Charles Sumner
Nason, Elias
Newcomb, Harvey
Newman, Samuel Phillips
Niles, Samuel
Noble, Frederick Alphonso
Norris, Edward
North, Simeon, 1802–1884
Nott, Samuel
Nutting, Wallace
Oakes, Urian
Palmer, Ray
Parish, Elijah
Parker, Edwin Pond
Parker, Samuel
Payson, Edward
Payson, Seth
Peet, Stephen Denison
Peloubet, Francis Nathan
Pennington, James W. C.
Peter, Hugh
Phelps, Austin
Phillips, George
Pierce, John Davis
Pierpont, James
Pierson, Abraham, 1645–1707
Pond, Enoch
Porter, Ebenezer
Porter, Noah
Post, Truman Marcellus
Proctor, Henry Hugh
Rankin, Jeremiah Eames
Rice, Edwin Wilbur
Richards, Charles Herbert
Robbins, Thomas
Rogers, John Almanza Rowley
Ross, Abel Hastings
Salter, William
Saltonstall, Gurdon
Sanders, Daniel Clarke
Sanford, Elias Benjamin
Schauffler, Henry Albert
Seccomb, John
Sheldon, Charles Monroe
Shepard, Thomas
Smyth, Egbert Coffin
Smyth, Newman
Sperry, Willard Learoyd
Sprague, William Buell
Spring, Leverett Wilson
Spring, Samuel

Stearns, William Augustus
Stiles, Ezra
Stoddard, Solomon
Storrs, Richard Salter, 1787–1873
Storrs, Richard Salter, 1821–1900
Strong, James Woodward
Strong, Josiah
Stuart, Moses
Sturtevant, Julian Monson
Tappan, Henry Philip
Tarbox, Increase Niles
Taylor, William Mackergo
Tenney, Edward Payson
Thacher, Peter
Thayer, Joseph Henry
Thayer, William Makepeace
Thompson, Joseph Parrish
Todd, John
Tracy, Joseph
Trumbull, Benjamin
Tucker, William Jewett
Tufts, John
Turner, Asa
Twichell, Joseph Hopkins
Tyler, Charles Mellen
Walker, Timothy, 1705–1782
Walter, Thomas, 1696–1725
Ward, Joseph
Ware, Henry, 1764–1845
Warren, Israel Perkins
Welles, Noah
Wheelock, Eleazar
Whiton, James Morris
Willard, Samuel, 1775–1859
Williams, Elisha
Williams, John, 1664–1729
Williston, Seth
Wines, Enoch Cobb
Wingate, Paine
Winship, Albert Edward
Winslow, Hubbard
Wise, John
Woods, Leonard, 1774–1854
Worcester, Noah
Worcester, Samuel
Wright, George Frederick
Yeomans, John William
Disciples of Christ
Adams, William Lysander
Ainslie, Peter
Allen, Thomas M.
Ames, Edward Scribner
Anderson, Henry Tompkins
Baxter, William
Campbell, Alexander
Creath, Jacob, 1777–1854
Creath, Jacob, 1799–1886
Errett, Isaac
Fanning, Tolbert
Franklin, Benjamin
Goodwin, Elijah
Goss, James Walker
Hayden, Amos Sutton
Hoshour, Samuel Klinefelter
Lard, Moses E.
Loos, Charles Louis

McGarvey, John William
McLean, Archibald
Milligan, Robert
Moore, William Thomas
Pendleton, William Kimbrough
Pinkerton, Lewis Letig
Power, Frederick Dunglison
Scott, Walter
Willett, Herbert Lockwood
Zollars, Ely Vaughn

Dutch Reformed
Berg, Joseph Frederic
Bethune, George Washington
Bourne, George
Chambers, Talbot Wilson
Corwin, Edward Tanjore
Drury, John Benjamin
Ferris, Isaac
Freeman, Bernardus
Frelinghuysen, Theodorus Jacobus
Goetschius, John Henry
Hardenbergh, Jacob Rutsen
Hartranft, Chester David
Livingston, John Henry
McClure, Alexander Wilson
Megapolensis, Johannes
Michaêlius, Jonas
Milledoler, Philip
Riddle, Matthew Brown
Seelye, Julius Hawley
Selijns, Henricus
Talmage, Thomas DeWitt
Taylor, Graham
Van Rensselaer, Nicholas

Episcopal (**See also** *Anglican*)
Abbott, Edward
Adams, Jasper
Allen, Alexander Viets Griswold
Allen, George
Andrews, John
Beardsley, Eben Edwards
Beasley, Frederick
Bell, Bernard Iddings
Bird, Frederic Mayer
Blake, John Lauris
Brady, Cyrus Townsend
Breck, James Lloyd
Briggs, Charles Augustus
Bristed, John
Chamberlain, Nathan Henry
Chapin, Alonzo Bowen
Coit, Henry Augustus
Coit, Thomas Winthrop
Cooper, Myles
Crapsey, Algernon Sidney
Croswell, Harry
Cummins, George David
Curtis, Moses Ashley
Cutler, Timothy
Dalcho, Frederick
De Costa, Benjamin Franklin
De Koven, James
Dix, Morgan
Doddridge, Joseph
Ewer, Ferdinand Cartwright
Flagg, Jared Bradley

Francis, Paul James
Gavin, Frank Stanton Burns
Goodwin, Hannibal Williston
Grant, Percy Stickney
Griswold, Alexander Viets
Hall, Charles Henry
Hare, George Emlen
Harris, William
Hawks, Francis Lister
Henry, Caleb Sprague
Hodges, George
Hoffman, Eugene Augustus
Houghton, George Hendric
Humes, Thomas William
Huntington, William Reed
Ingraham, Joseph Holt
Jarratt, Devereux
Jarvis, Abraham
Jones, Hugh
Kilbourne, James
King, William Benjamin Basil
Knight, Henry Cogswell
Langdon, William Chauncy
Leach, Daniel Dyer
Leaming, Jeremiah
Le Jau, Francis
Lord, William Wilberforce
Lowell, Robert Traill Spence
McCabe, John Collins
McCook, John James
MacSparran, James
McVickar, John
Mahan, Milo
Mansfield, Richard
Mombert, Jacob Isidor
Montgomery, James Alan
Moore, James, 1764–1814
Muhlenberg, William Augustus
Mulford, Elisha
Murphy, Edgar Gardner
Nash, Daniel
Nash, Henry Sylvester
Newton, Richard
Newton, Richard Heber
Newton, William Wilberforce
Nies, James Buchanan
Norton, John Nicholas
Norwood, Robert Winkworth
Oertel, Johannes Adam Simon
Ogden, Uzal
Packard, Joseph
Park, Roswell
Pendleton, William Nelson
Penick, Charles Clifton
Peterkin, George William
Peters, John Punnett
Pettigrew, Charles
Piggot, Robert
Pilmore, Joseph
Pinney, Norman
Pott, Francis Lister Hawks
Potter, Eliphalet Nott
Pynchon, Thomas Ruggles
Rainsford, William Stephen
Russell, James Solomon
Satterlee, Henry Yates

Savage, Thomas Staughton
Schroeder, John Frederick
Scott, Thomas Fielding
Seabury, Samuel, 1801–1872
Shelton, Frederick William
Shields, Charles Woodruff
Shoup, Francis Asbury
Slafter, Edmund Farwell
Slaughter, Philip
Smith, John Cotton, 1826–1882
Smith, William, 1754–1821
Sparrow, William
Spencer, Jesse Ames
Sterrett, James Macbride
Stokes, Anson Phelps
Stone, John Seely
Stuck, Hudson
Tolman, Herbert Cushing
Tomkins, Floyd Williams
Tucker, Henry St. George
Turner, Samuel Hulbeart
Tyng, Stephen Higginson
Tyson, Stuart Lawrence
Vesey, William
Vinton, Alexander Hamilton
Vinton, Francis
Walden, Jacob Treadwell
Ward, Henry Dana
Washburn, Edward Abiel
Weems, Mason Locke
Wharton, Charles Henry
Wharton, Francis
Wheaton, Nathaniel Sheldon
White, George
Wilmer, James Jones
Wilmer, William Holland
Wilson, Bird
Wilson, William Dexter
Winslow, William Copley
Worcester, Elwood

Evangelical Lutheran
Dinwiddie, Edwin Courtland

Friends (**See** *Quaker*)

German Reformed
Bausman, Benjamin
Boehm, John Philip
Bomberger, John Henry
Bucher, John Conrad
Dubbs, Joseph Henry
Good, James Isaac
Good, Jeremiah Haak
Gros, John Daniel
Harbaugh, Henry
Helffenstein, John Albert Conrad
Hendel, John William
Herman, Lebrecht Frederick
Mayer, Lewis
Miller, John Peter
Otterbein, Philip William
Rupp, William
Schlatter, Michael
Stahr, John Summers

Greek Orthodox
Callimachos, Panos Demetrios

Jewish
Adler, Samuel

Asher, Joseph Mayor
Berkowitz, Henry
Blaustein, David
Einhorn, David
Enelow, Hyman Gerson
Felsenthal, Bernhard
Gottheil, Gustav
Grossmann, Louis
Harris, Maurice Henry
Heller, Maximilian
Hirsch, Emil Gustav
Hirschensohn, Chaim
Isaacs, Samuel Myer
Jastrow, Marcus
Kagan, Henry Enoch
Kalisch, Isidor
Kohler, Kaufmann
Kohut, Alexander
Kohut, George Alexander
Krauskopf, Joseph
Leeser, Isaac
Levy, Joseph Leonard
Liebman, Joshua Loth
Lilienthal, Max
Magnes, Judah Leon
Mendes, Frederic De Sola
Mendes, Henry Pereira
Meyer, Martin Abraham
Mielziner, Moses
Morais, Sabato
Philipson, David
Raphall, Morris Jacob
Schindler, Solomon
Seixas, Gershom Mendes
Silver, Abba Hillel
Silverman, Joseph
Szold, Benjamin
Voorsanger, Jacob
Wise, Aaron
Wise, Isaac Mayer
Wise, Stephen Samuel
Latter-Day Saints (**See** *Mormon*)
Lutheran
Acrelius, Israel
Bachman, John
Baugher, Henry Louis
Berkenmeyer, Wilhelm Christoph
Bird, Frederic Mayer
Boltzius, Johann Martin
Campanius, John
Clausen, Claus Lauritz
Dahl, Theodor Halvorson
Deindörfer, Johannes
Demme, Charles Rudolph
Dietrichson, Johannes Wilhelm
   Christian
Douglas, Lloyd Cassel
Dylander, John
Eielsen, Elling
Esbjörn, Lars Paul
Falckner, Daniel
Falckner, Justus
Funk, Isaac Kauffman
Grabau, Johannes Andreas August
Greenwald, Emanuel
Grossmann, Georg Martin

Hartwig, Johann Christoph
Hasselquist, Tuve Nilsson
Hay, Charles Augustus
Hayme, Gjermund
Hazelius, Ernest Lewis
Helmuth, Justus Henry Christian
Henkel, Paul
Hoenecke, Gustav Adolf Felix
   Theodor
Hoffmann, Francis Arnold
Horn, Edward Traill
Hunton, William Lee
Jacobs, Michael
Kildahl, Johan Nathan
Kocherthal, Josua von
Koren, John
Koren, Ulrik Vihelm
Krauth, Charles Philip
Krauth, Charles Porterfield
Kunze, John Christopher
Kurtz, Benjamin
Larsen, Peter Laurentius
Lenker, John Nicholas
Lindberg, Conrad Emil
Lochman, John George
Loy, Matthias
Maier, Walter Arthur
Mann, William Julius
Mayer, Philip Frederick
Melsheimer, Friedrich Valentin
Moldehnke, Edward Frederick
Morris, John Gottlieb
Muhlenberg, Frederick Augustus
Muhlenberg, Frederick Augustus
   Conrad
Mühlenberg, Gotthilf Henry Ernest
Muhlenberg, Henry Augustus
   Philip
Mühlenberg, Henry Melchior
Muhlenberg, John Peter Gabriel
Norelius, Eric
Oftedal, Sven
Passavant, William Alfred
Preus, Christian Keyser
Richard, James William
Sadtler, John Philip Benjamin
Schaeffer, Charles Frederick
Schaeffer, Charles William
Schaeffer, David Frederick
Schaeffer, Frederick Christian
Schaeffer, Frederick David
Schmauk, Theodore Emanuel
Schmucker, Beale Melanchthon
Schmucker, John George
Schmucker, Samuel Simon
Schodde, George Henry
Seip, Theodore Lorenzo
Seiss, Joseph Augustus
Spaeth, Adolph
Sprecher, Samuel
Stöckhardt, Karl Georg
Stub, Hans Gerhard
Swensson, Carl Aaron
Walther, Carl Ferdinand Wilhelm
Wenner, George Unangst
Mennonite

Goerz, David
Kolb, Dielman
Krehbiel, Christian
Rittenhouse, William
Methodist
Alexander, Gross
Asbury, Francis
Atkinson, John
Bangs, Nathan
Beauchamp, William
Bewley, Anthony
Boehm, Henry
Brown, Ebenezer
Buckley, James Monroe
Buttz, Henry Anson
Cadman, Samuel Parkes
Cain, Richard Harvey
Candler, Warren Akin
Cannon, James
Cartwright, Peter
Collyer, Robert
Cooper, Ezekiel
Cramer, Michael John
Crane, Frank
Crane, Jonathan Townley
Crooks, George Richard
Cummings, Joseph
Day, James Roscoe
Dean, Sidney
Deems, Charles Force
Dickins, John
Dorchester, Daniel
Durbin, John Price
Eaton, Homer
Elliott, Charles
Embury, Philip
Evans, Warren Felt
Fairbank, Calvin
Finley, James Bradley
Fisk, Wilbur
Floy, James
Foss, Cyrus David
Gammon, Elijah Hedding
Garrettson, Freeborn
Green, Alexander Little Page
Hamline, Leonidas Lent
Harrell, John
Harrison, William Pope
Hibbard, Freeborn Garrettson
Hogan, John
Hogue, Wilson Thomas
Hopkins, Isaac Stiles
Huntington, William Edwards
Hurlbut, Jesse Lyman
Inskip, John Swanel
Jaquess, James Frazier
Kidder, Daniel Parish
Kynett, Alpha Jefferson
Lane, John
Larrabee, William Clark
Lee, Jesse
Lee, Luther
Lipscomb, Andrew Adgate
McAnally, David Rice
McCaine, Alexander
M'Clintock, John

McFarland, John Thomas
McFerrin, John Berry
Mattison, Hiram
Merrick, Frederick
Milburn, William Henry
Mitchell, Hinckley Gilbert Thomas
Mood, Francis Asbury
Mudge, Enoch
Mudge, James
Nast, William
Nelson, Reuben
O'Kelly James
Olin, Stephen
Palmore, William Beverly
Parkhurst, Charles
Peck, George
Peirce, Bradford Kinney
Ray, Charles Bennett
Reid, John Morrison
Revels, Hiram Rhoades
Ridgaway, Henry Bascom
Roberts, Benjamin Titus
Rowlands, William
Rust, Richard Sutton
Ruter, Martin
Shaw, Anna Howard
Shinn, Asa
Shipp, Albert Micajah
Sims, Charles N.
Sloan, Harold Paul
Smith, William Andrew
Snethen, Nicholas
Steele, Daniel
Stevens, Abel
Stockton, Thomas Hewlings
Strawbridge, Robert
Stuart, Charles Macaulay
Summers, Thomas Osmond
Swallow, Silas Comfort
Taylor, Marshall William
Terry, Milton Spenser
Tigert, John James
Tittle, Ernest Fremont
Townsend, Luther Tracy
Upham, Samuel Foster
Vail, Stephen Montfort
Van Meter, John Blackford
Wakeley, Joseph Burton
Warren, William Fairfield
Webb, Thomas
Whedon, Daniel Denison
Wiley, Ephraim Emerson
Williams, Robert
Winans, William
Wise, Daniel
Young, Jesse Bowman
Methodist Episcopal
  North, Frank Mason
  Wilson, Clarence True
Moravian (**See** *United Brethren*)
Mormon
  Cannon, George Quayle
  Clark, Joshua Reuben, Jr.
  Godbe, William Samuel
  Kimball, Heber Chase
  Lee, John Doyle

Pratt, Parley Parker
Rigdon, Sidney
Roberts, Brigham Henry
Sharp, John
Smith, Joseph, 1805–1844
Smith, Joseph, 1832–1914
Snow, Lorenzo
Strang, James Jesse
Taylor, John
Whitmer, David
Woodruff, Wilford
Young, Brigham
Nonconformist
  Chauncy, Charles 1592–1671/2
  Chauncy, Charles 1705–1787
  Eaton, Samuel
  Higginson, Francis
  Lothropp, John
  Ward, Nathaniel
Presbyterian
  Abbot, Gorham Dummer
  Adams, William
  Alexander, Archibald
  Alexander, Samuel Davies
  Alison, Francis
  Anderson, John Alexander
  Armstrong, George Dod
  Babcock, Maltbie Davenport
  Baird, Charles Washington
  Baird, Henry Martyn
  Baird, Robert
  Baird, Samuel John
  Baker, Daniel
  Baker, William Mumford
  Baldwin, Elihu Whittlesey
  Barnes, Albert
  Beard, Richard
  Beattie, Francis Robert
  Beatty, Charles Clinton
  Beecher, Lyman
  Beman, Nathan Sidney Smith
  Bishop, Robert Hamilton
  Blackburn, Gideon
  Blackburn, William Maxwell
  Blair, Samuel
  Blanchard, Jonathan
  Bourne, George
  Boynton, Charles Brandon
  Brainerd, Thomas
  Breckinridge, John, 1797–1841
  Breckinridge, Robert Jefferson
  Brown, Isaac Van Arsdale
  Brown, William Adams
  Brownlee, William Craig
  Bruce, Robert
  Burchard, Samuel Dickinson
  Burr, Aaron
  Burrell, David James
  Bush, George
  Caldwell, David
  Caldwell, James
  Cameron, Archibald
  Campbell, William Henry
  Carrick, Samuel
  Cattell, William Cassaday
  Chavis, John

Coffin, Henry Sloane
Colman, Benjamin
Converse, James Booth
Corrothers, James David
Cox, Samuel Hanson
Crosby, Howard
Curtis, Edward Lewis
Cuyler, Theodore Ledyard
Darling, Henry
Davidson, Robert
Doak, Samuel
Dod, Albert Baldwin
Dod, Thaddeus
Donnell, Robert
Duffield, George, 1732–1790
Duffield, George, 1794–1868
Duffield, Samuel Augustus
  Willoughby
Dwight, Benjamin Woodbridge
Ewing, John
Field, Henry Martyn
Finley, Robert
Finley, Samuel
Fisher, Daniel Webster
Foote, William Henry
Frey, Joseph Samuel Christian
  Frederick
Frissell, Hollis Burke
Gale, George Washington
Gally, Merritt
Garnet, Henry Highland
Gaut, John McReynolds
Gilbert, Eliphalet Wheeler
Gillett, Ezra Hall
Girardeau, John Lafayette
Goulding, Francis Robert
Green, Ashbel
Green, Jacob
Green, Lewis Warner
Gregory, Daniel Seelye
Hall, Baynard Rush
Hall, Charles Cuthbert
Hall, James, 1744–1826
Hall, John
Hatfield, Edwin Francis
Headley, Phineas Camp
Henry, Robert
Hewat, Alexander
Hickok, Laurens Perseus
Hoge, Moses
Hoge, Moses Drury
House, Samuel Reynolds
Howe, George
Hunter, Andrew
Jackson, Samuel Macauley
Jacobs, William Plumer
Junkin, George
Kellogg, Samuel Henry
Kirk, Edward Norris
Knox, Samuel
Lacy, Drury
Lindley, Daniel
Lindsley, John Berrien
Lindsley, Philip
Linn, John Blair
Lunn, George Richard

Lyon, James
McAfee, John Armstrong
McAuley, Thomas
McBride, F(rancis) Scott
McCalla, William Latta
McCook, Henry Christopher
McCormick, Samuel Black
MacCracken, Henry Mitchell
McDowell, John
McFarland, Samuel Gamble
McGready, James
McIlwaine, Richard
McLeod, Alexander
MacWhorter, Alexander
Makemie, Francis
Marquis, John Abner
Mason, John Mitchell
Mattoon, Stephen
Mears, David Otis
Mears, John William
Miller, James Russell
Miller, John
Miller, Samuel
Mitchell, Edwin Knox
Moorehead, William Gallogly
Morris, Edward Dafydd
Morrison, William McCutchan
Murray, James Ormsbee
Neill, Edward Duffield
Neill, William
Nelson, David
Nevin, Alfred
Nevin, Edwin Henry
Nisbet, Charles
Noble, Frederick Alphonso
Nott, Eliphalet
Osborn, Henry Stafford
Palmer, Benjamin Morgan
Parker, Joel
Parker, Thomas
Parkhurst, Charles Henry
Patillo, Henry
Patterson, Robert Mayne
Patton, Francis Landey
Patton, William
Peck, Thomas Ephraim
Peters, Absalom
Peters, Madison Clinton
Pierson, Arthur Tappan
Pierson, Hamilton Wilcox
Plumer, William Swan
Prentiss, George Lewis
Prime, Edward Dorr Griffin
Prime, Samuel Irenaeus
Purviance, David
Reed, Richard Clark
Reid, William Shields
Rice, David
Rice, John Holt
Rice, Nathan Lewis
Roberts, William Charles
Roberts, William Henry
Robinson, Charles Seymour
Robinson, Stuart
Rodgers, John, 1727-1811
Ruffner, Henry

Ruffner, William Henry
Sanders, Daniel Jackson
Sawyer, Leicester Ambrose
Scott, William Anderson
Simpson, Albert Benjamin
Skinner, Thomas Harvey
Smith, Asa Dodge
Smith, Benjamin Mosby
Smith, Henry Boynton
Smith, Henry Preserved
Smith, John Blair
Smith, Samuel Stanhope
Smyth, Thomas
Speer, Robert Elliott
Spencer, Elihu
Spring, Gardiner
Sproull, Thomas
Stelzle, Charles
Stryker, Melancthon Woolsey
Swing, David
Taylor, Archibald Alexander
    Edward
Tennent, Gilbert
Tennent, William, 1673-1745
Tennent, William, 1705-1777
Thacher, Peter
Thompson, William Oxley
Thornwell, James Henley
Van Dyke, Henry
Van Rensselaer, Cortlandt
Vincent, Marvin Richardson
Voris, John Ralph
Waddel, James
Waddel, John Newton
Waddel, Moses
Walker, James Barr
Warfield, Benjamin Breckinridge
Whitaker, Nathaniel
Whitworth, George Frederic
Wiley, David
Willey, Samuel Hopkins
Wilson, Joshua Lacy
Wilson, Samuel Ramsay
Wilson, Warren Hugh
Witherspoon, John
Wood, James
Woodrow, James
Woods, Leonard, 1807-1878
Yeomans, John William
Young, John Clarke
Zubly, John Joachim
Protestant Episcopal (**See** *Episcopal*)
Puritan
Bulkeley, Peter
Cotton, John
Holden, Oliver
Mather, Cotton
Mather, Increase
Mather, Richard
Mayhew, Jonathan
Morton, Charles
Norton, John
Parris, Samuel
Sherman, John, 1613-1685
Stone, Samuel
Taylor, Edward

Weld, Thomas
Whitfield, Henry
Wigglesworth, Michael
Williams, Roger
Wilson, John
Woodbridge, John
Quaker
Chalkley, Thomas
Coffin, Charles Fisher
Comstock, Elizabeth L.
Evans, Thomas
Grellet, Stephen
Hallowell, Benjamin
Hicks, Elias
Hoag, Joseph
Hubbs, Rebecca
Hunt, Nathan
Janney, Samuel McPherson
Jay, Allen
Jones, Sybil
Kelsey, Rayner Wickersham
Mott, Lucretia Coffin
Muste, Abraham Johannes
Owen, Griffith
Pemberton, John
Pugh, Ellis
Sands, David
Savery, William, 1750-1804
Scattergood, Thomas
Scott, Job
Updegraff, David Brainard
Waln, Nicholas
Wilbur, John
Reformed Church in America
Schenck, Ferdinand Schureman
Searle, John Preston
Thompson, John Bodine
Van Nest, Abraham Rynier
Woodbridge, Samuel Merrill
Roman Catholic
Alphonsa, Mother
Andreis, Andrew James Felix
    Bartholomew de
Andrews, Samuel James
Andrews, William Watson
Angela, Mother
Antoine, Père
Ayres, Anne
Barzyński, Vincent
Bayma, Joseph
Behrens, Henry
Benavides, Alonzo de
Burke, John Joseph
Campbell, Thomas Joseph
Carr, Thomas Matthew
Clarke, Mary Francis
Conaty, Thomas James
Cooper, John Montgomery
Coppens, Charles
Corcoran, James Andrew
Cosby, William
Curran, John Joseph
Currier, Charles Warren
Cushing, Richard James
Dabrowski, Joseph
Dietz, Peter Ernest

Sewall, Frank
Smyth, Julian Kennedy
Unaffiliated
Craig, Austin
Newton, Joseph Fort
Spencer, Anna Garlin
Unitarian
Abbot, Francis Ellingwood
Alger, William Rounseville
Allen, Joseph Henry
Ames, Charles Gordon
Barnard, Charles Francis
Barrows, Samuel June
Bartol, Cyrus Augustus
Batchelor, George
Bellows, Henry Whitney
Bentley, William
Bixby, James Thompson
Brazer, John
Brooks, Charles
Brooks, Charles Timothy
Buckminster, Joseph Stevens
Burnap, George Washington
Burton, Warren
Chadwick, John White
Channing, William Ellery
Channing, William Henry
Clarke, James Freeman
Colman, Henry
Conway, Moncure Daniel
Cooke, George Willis
Cranch, Christopher Pearse
Crothers, Samuel McChord
Cummings, Edward
Dewey, Orville
Ellis, George Edward
Emerson, William
Everett, Edward
Fenn, William Wallace
Follen, Charles
Francis, Convers
Freeman, James
Frothingham, Nathaniel Langdon
Frothingham, Octavius Brooks
Frothingham, Paul Revere
Furness, William Henry
Gannett, Ezra Stiles
Gannett, William Channing
Gilman, Samuel
Hale, Edward Everett
Harris, Thaddeus Mason
Hedge, Frederic Henry
Hill, Thomas
Holley, Horace
Holmes, John Haynes
Hosmer, Frederick Lucian
Huntington, Frederic Dan
Janson, Kristofer Nagel
Jones, Jenkin Lloyd
Judd, Sylvester
King, Thomas Starr
Leonard, Levi Washburn
Livermore, Abiel Abbot
Longfellow, Samuel
Lowe, Charles
MacCauley, Clay

Mann, Newton
May, Samuel Joseph
Mayo, Amory Dwight
Metcalf, Joel Hastings
Miles, Henry Adolphus
Noyes, George Rapall
Palfrey, John Gorham
Parker, Theodore
Peabody, Andrew Preston
Peabody, Francis Greenwood
Peabody, Oliver William Bourn
Peabody, William Bourn Oliver
Pierpont, John
Potter, William James
Powell, Edward Payson
Reed, David
Ripley, Ezra
Robbins, Chandler
Savage, Minot Judson
Sears, Edmund Hamilton
Slicer, Thomas Roberts
Stearns, Oliver
Stebbins, Horatio
Stebbins, Rufus Phineas
Tuckerman, Joseph
Upham, Charles Wentworth
Walker, James
Ware, Henry 1794–1843
Ware, John Fothergill Waterhouse
Ware, William
Weiss, John
Wendte, Charles William
West, Samuel
Wheelwright, John
Wiggin, James Henry
Willard, Samuel, 1775–1859
Woolley, Celia Parker
Young, Alexander
Zachos, John Celivergos
United Brethren
Beardshear, William Miller
Berger, Daniel
Clewell, John Henry
Flickinger, Daniel Kumler
Holland, William Jacob
Jungman, John George
Kephart, Isaiah Lafayette
Peter, John Frederick
Reichel, William Cornelius
Schultze, Augustus
Schweinitz, Lewis David von
Shuey, William John
Zinzendorf, Nicolaus Ludwig
United Evangelical
Poling, Daniel Alfred
Universalist
Adams, John Coleman
Ballou, Adin
Ballou, Hosea
Cobb, Sylvanus
Edwin, Hubbell Chapin
Ferguson, William Porter Frisbee
Fisher, Ebenezer
Hanaford, Phoebe Ann Coffin
Hudson, Charles
Kneeland, Abner

Miner, Alonzo Ames
Sawyer, Thomas Jefferson
Spear, Charles
Thayer, Thomas Baldwin
Whittemore, Thomas
CLIMATOLOGIST (See also
      METEOROLOGIST)
De Brahm, William Gerard
Logan, Thomas Muldrup,
      1808–1876
Ward, Robert De Courcy
CLOCKMAKER (See also
      MANUFACTURER, WATCH)
Camp, Hiram
Harland, Thomas
Jerome, Chauncey
Terry, Eli
Thomas, Seth
Willard, Simon
CLOWN
Adler, Felix
Rice, Dan
CLUB WOMAN
Choate, Anne Hyde Clarke
COAL MERCHANT
Clothier, William Jackson
COAL MINER
Haywood, Allan Shaw
COAL OPERATOR (See also
      INDUSTRIALIST)
Brown, William Hughey
Horton, Valentine Baxter
Pardee, Ario
Parrish, Charles
Scott, William Lawrence
Thompson, Josiah Van Kirk
COAST GUARD OFFICER (See also
      NAVAL OFFICER)
Smith, Edward Hanson
Waesche, Russell Randolph
COLLECTOR (See also ART
      COLLECTOR, BOOK COLLECTOR,
      NUMISMATIST)
Bement, Clarence Sweet (minerals)
Clarke, Thomas Benedict (art)
Cone, Claribel (art)
Cone, Etta (art)
Disbrow, William Stephen (misc.)
Draper, Lyman Copeland (frontier
      history)
Emmett, Burton (prints)
Ffoulke, Charles Mather (tapestries)
Fisher, George Jackson (anatomical
      illustrations)
Folger, Henry Clay
      (Shakespeareana)
Guggenheim, Solomon Robert (art)
Hawkins, Rush Christopher
      (incunabula)
Horner, Henry (Lincolniana)
Isham, Ralph Heyward
      (manuscripts)
Jacobs, Joseph, 1859–1929
      (Burnsiana)
Lewis, Edmund Darch (misc.)
Lomax, John Avery (folk songs)

Lowery, Woodbury (maps)
Meserve, Frederick Hill
   (Lincolniana)
Nutting, Wallace (antiques)
Pringle, Cyrus Guernsey (plants)
Riggs, William Henry (armor)
Rindge, Frederick Hastings (coins)
Scharf, John Thomas (Americana)
Sprague, William Buell
   (autographs)
Stauffer, David McNeely
   (autographic historical material)
Steinert, Morris (musical
   instruments)
Thomas, George Clifford
   (autographic historical material)
Vincent, Frank (antiquities)
Wilson, Ernest Henry (plants)

COLLEGE ADMINISTRATOR
Fulton, Robert Burwell
Geddes, James Lorraine
Keppel, Frederick Paul
Perkins, George Henry
Royster, James Finch
Small, Albion Woodbury

COLLEGE PRESIDENT
Adams, Charles Kendall
Adams, Jasper
Alden, Timothy
Alderman, Edwin Anderson
Allen, William Henry
Ames, Joseph Sweetman
Anderson, Galusha
Anderson, John Alexander
Anderson, Martin Brewer
Andrews, Elisha Benjamin
Andrews, Israel Ward
Andrews, Lorin
Angell, James Burrill
Angell, James Rowland
Atherton, George Washington
Atwood, Wallace Walter
Aydelotte, Frank
Ayres, Brown
Backus, Azel
Bailey, Rufus William
Baker, Hugh Potter
Baker, James Hutchins
Baldwin, Elihu Whittlesey
Ballou, Hosea
Barnard, Frederick Augustus Porter
Barrows, David Prescott
Barrows, John Henry
Bartlett, Samuel Colcord
Bascom, Henry Bidleman
Bascom, John
Bashford, James Whitford
Bass, William Capers
Battle, Kemp Plummer
Baugher, Henry Louis
Beardshear, William Miller
Beecher, Edward
Beman, Nathan Sidney Smith
Bennett, Henry Garland
Benton, Allen Richardson
Bethune, Mary McLeod

Blackburn, Gideon
Blackburn, William Maxwell
Blanchard, Jonathan
Bomberger, John Henry Augustus
Bowman, Isaiah
Bradley, John Edwin
Breckinridge, Robert Jefferson
Brown, Elmer Ellsworth
Brown, Francis
Brown, Samuel Gilman
Brownell, Thomas Church
Bryan, John Stewart
Burr, Aaron
Burton, Ernest DeWitt
Burton, Marion Le Roy
Butler, Nicholas Murray
Butterfield, Kenyon Leech
Cain, Richard Harvey
Caldwell, Joseph
Camm, John
Campbell, Prince Lucien
Campbell, William Henry
Candler, Warren Akin
Capen, Elmer Hewitt
Carnahan, James
Carrick, Samuel
Carter, Franklin
Caswell, Alexis
Cattell, William Cassaday
Chadbourne, Paul Ansel
Chandler, Julian Alvin Carroll
Chapin, Aaron Lucius
Chaplin, Jeremiah
Chase, Harry Woodburn
Chase, Thomas
Chauncey, Charles
Cheney, Oren Burbank
Clapp, Charles Horace
Clark, William Smith
Coffman, Lotus Delta
Compton, Karl Taylor
Cooper, Myles
Corby, William
Crafts, James Mason
Cravath, Erastus Milo
Craven, Braxton
Cummings, Joseph
Cutler, Carroll
Daggett, Naphtali
Darling, Henry
Davies, Samuel
Davis, Harvey Nathaniel
Davis, Henry
Day, Jeremiah
Dennett, Tyler (Wilbur)
Dickinson, Jonathan
Dunster, Henry
Durant, Henry
Dwight, Timothy, 1752–1817
Dwight, Timothy, 1828–1916
Dykstra, Clarence Addison
Eaton, Nathaniel
Eisenhower, Dwight D.
Eliot, Charles William
Estabrook, Joseph
Fairchild, George Thompson

Fairchild, James Harris
Farrand, Livingston
Faunce, William Herbert Perry
Ferris, Isaac
Few, Ignatius Alphonso
Fisher, Daniel Webster
Folwell, William Watts
Foster, William Trufant
Fox, Dixon Ryan
Fraley, Samuel
Frank, Glenn
Frelinghuysen, Theodore
Frieze, Henry Simmons
Furman, James Clement
Garfield, Harry Augustus
Garland, Landon Cabell
Gates, Caleb Frank
Gates, Thomas Sovereign
Gerhart, Emanuel Vogel
Gilbert, Eliphalet Wheeler
Gilman, Daniel Coit
Goodell, Henry Hill
Goodnow, Frank Johnson
Goodwin, Daniel Raynes
Goucher, John Franklin
Graham, Edward Kidder
Graves, Zuinglius Calvin
Green, Ashbel
Gregg, John Andrew
Gregory, John Milton
Griffin, Edward Dorr
Griswold, Alfred Whitney
Gummere, Samuel James
Hadley, Arthur Twining
Hadley, Herbert Spencer
Hardenbergh, Jacob Rutsen
Harris, William
Hasbrouck, Abraham Bruyn
Hibben, John Grier
Hickok, Laurens Perseus
Hill, David Jayne
Hill, Thomas
Hinman, George Wheeler
Hoar, Leonard
Holt, Hamilton Bowen
Horrocks, James
Howard, Ada Lydia
Humes, Thomas William
Humphrey, Heman
Huntington, William Edwards
Hutchins, Harry Burns
Hyer, Robert Stewart
James, Edmund Janes
Jessup, Walter Albert
Johns, John
Johnson, Samuel
Jordan, David Starr
Kephart, Ezekiel Boring
King, Charles
King, Stanley
Kirkland, James Hampton
Kirkland, John Thornton
Knapp, Bradford
Krauth, Charles Philip
Langdon, Samuel
Lathrop, John Hiram

Leverett, John, 1662–1724
Lipscomb, Andrew Adgate
Livermore, Abiel Abbot
Loos, Charles Louis
Lord, Nathan
Low, Seth
Lowell, Abbott Lawrence
McBryde, John McLaren
McCosh, James
McGlothlin, William Joseph
McIlwaine, Richard
McKeen, Joseph
Maclean, John
McNair, Fred Walter
McVey, Frank Lerond
Madison, James
Magill, Edward Hicks
Magnes, Judah Leon
Magoun, George Frederic
Mahan, Asa
Main, John Hanson Thomas
Manning, James
Marquis, John Abner
Marsh, James
Maxcy, Jonathan
Maxwell, William
Mayes, Edward
Mendenhall, Thomas Corwin
Merrill, George Edmands
Middleton, Nathaniel Russell
Miner, Alonzo Ames
Mitchell, Edward Cushing
Moore, Benjamin
Moore, Nathaniel Fish
Moore, Zephaniah Swift
Morgan, John Harcourt Alexander
Morrison, Nathan Jackson
Mortimer, Mary
Morton, Henry
Muhlenberg, Frederick Augustus
Neilson, William Allan
Nichols, Ernest Fox
Nisbet, Charles
Northrop, Cyrus
Nott, Eliphalet
Oakes, Urian
Parrish, Edward
Patrick, Mary Mills
Patton, Francis Landey
Payne, Bruce Ryburn
Payne, Daniel Alexander
Pearson, Raymond Allen
Pendleton, Ellen Fitz
Pendleton, William Kimbrough
Porter, Noah
Pott, Francis Lister Hawks
Potter, Eliphalet Nott
Preus, Christian Keyser
Pritchett, Henry Smith
Pugh, Evan
Purnell, William Henry
Pynchon, Thomas Ruggles
Quincy, Josiah, 1772–1864
Rankin, Jeremiah Eames
Raymond, John Howard
Reid, John Morrison

Reinhardt, Aurelia Isabel Henry
Rhees, Rush
Rhoades, James E.
Robinson, Ezekiel Gilman
Runkle, John Daniel
Sadtler, John Philip Benjamin
Sanford, Edmund Clark
Scarborough, William Saunders
Schurman, Jacob Gould
Scott, Austin
Scott, Walter Dill
Seelye, Laurenus Clark
Seip, Theodore Lorenzo
Sewall, Joseph Addison
Seymour, Charles
Shafer, Helen Almira
Sharpless, Isaac
Shepard, James Edward
Sims, Charles N.
Smart, James Henry
Smith, Asa Dodge
Smith, John Augustine
Smith, John Blair
Smith, Samuel Stanhope
Smith, William Andrew
Smith, William Waugh
Sparks, Edwin Erle
Stearns, William Augustus
Stewart, Alexander Peter
Stiles, Ezra
Stith, William
Stockbridge, Horace Edward
Strong, James Woodward
Stryker, Melancthon Woolsey
Stuart, John Leighton
Swain, David Lowry
Tappan, Henry Philip
Taylor, James Monroe
Thatcher, Roscoe Wilfred
Thomas, Martha Carey
Thompson, William Oxley
Thomson, Edward
Thornwell, James Henley
Thwing, Charles Franklin
Tigert, John James, IV
Tyler, Lyon Gardiner
Van Hise, Charles Richard
Venable, Francis Preston
Vincent, George Edgar
Waddel, Moses
Wait, Samuel
Walker, James
Warren, William Fairfield
Wayland, Francis, 1796–1865
Webb, Alexander Stewart
Wheeler, Benjamin Ide
Wheelock, Eleazar
Wheelock, John
White, Andrew Dickson
White, Henry Clay
Whitsitt, William Heth
Wilbur, Ray Lyman
Willard, Joseph
Willard, Samuel
Williams, Walter
Wilson, Woodrow

Woods, Alva
Woods, Leonard
Woolley, Mary Emma
Woolsey, Theodore Dwight
Wylie, Andrew

COLONIAL AGENT

Argall, Sir Samuel
Ashmun, Jehudi
Barnwell, John
Bollan, William
De Berdt, Dennys
Dummer, Jeremiah
Partridge, Richard
Randolph, Edward
Sebastian, Benjamin
Vassall, John
Weld, Thomas

COLONIAL LEADER

Bacon, Nathaniel
Byrd, William
Carter, Robert
Clarke, George
Dinwiddie, Robert
Gayoso de Lemos, Manuel
Habersham, James
Hathorne, William
Holloway, John
Jenifer, Daniel of St. Thomas
Kennedy, Archibald
Minuit, Peter
Moore, John, ca. 1659–1732
Newton, Thomas, 1660–1721
Nicholas, Robert Carter
Norris, Isaac, 1671–1735
Núñez Cabeza De Vaca, Alvar
Owen, Griffith
Pike, Robert
Randolph, William
Schuyler, Peter
Stuyvesant, Petrus
Van Cortlandt, Stephanus
Weare, Meshech
Wharton, Richard
Wingfield, Edward Maria
Wragg, William
Yeardley, Sir George
Youngs, John

COLONIST

Blackstone, William
Claiborne, William
Fenwick, George
Fenwick, John
Gardiner, Lion
Gookin, Daniel
Gorton, Samuel
Hack, George
Lane, Sir Ralph
Mason, George
Maverick, George
Oldham, John
Popham, George
Rolfe, John
Saltonstall, Richard
Sandys, George
Scholte, Hendrik Peter
Sedgwick, Robert

Van Curler, Arent
Van Der Donck, Adriaen
Weston, Thomas
Wilbur, Samuel
Willard, Simon

COLONIZER
Cameron, Robert Alexander
Coram, Thomas
Cutler, Manasseh
Dale, Sir Thomas
De Vries, David Pietersen
Durkee, John
Eaton, Theophilus
Finley, Robert
Gosnold, Bartholomew
Graffenried, Christopher, Baron de
Henderson, Richard
Hite, Jost
Krehbiel, Christian
Oñate, Juan de
Peerson, Cleng
Purry, Jean Pierre
Ribaut, Jean
St. Denis (Denys), Louis Juchereau de
Smith, Robert, 1722–1777
Turnbull, Andrew
Wingfield, Edward Maria
Young, Brigham

COLOR CINEMATOGRAPHER
Kalmus, Natalie Mabelle Dunfee

COMEDIAN (See also ACTOR, CLOWN, COMEDIENNE, ENTERTAINER, HUMORIST, WIT)
Allen, Fred
Barton, James Edward
Bruce, Lenny
Cantor, Eddie
Carson, Jack
Costello, Lou
Daniels, Frank Albert
Errol, Leon
Fields, Lewis Maurice
Fields, William Claude
Foy, Eddie
Hardy, Oliver Norvell
Hayes, Gabby
Holland, George
Howard, Willie
Johnson, Harold Ogden ("Chic")
Jones, Lindley Armstrong ("Spike")
Keaton, Joseph Francis, V ("Buster")
Langdon, Harry Philmore
Laurel, Stan
Marx, Adolf Arthur ("Harpo")
Marx, Leonard ("Chico")
Olsen, John Sigvard ("Ole")
Shean, Albert
Smith, Solomon Franklin
Turpin, Ben
Weber, Joseph Morris
Wynn, Ed

COMEDIENNE (See also ACTRESS, ENTERTAINER, HUMORIST)
Brice, Fanny

Fazenda, Louise Marie
COMIC ARTIST (See CARTOONIST)
COMMERCIAL COUNSELOR
Kuskov, Ivan Aleksandrovich
COMMISSIONER OF EDUCATION
Tigert, John James, IV
COMMUNIST (See also MARXIST THEORIST)
Cabet, Étienne
Dennis, Eugene
Eisler, Gerhart
Fischer, Ruth
Minor, Robert
COMMUNIST LEADER
Bloor, Ella Reeve
Foster, William Z.
Perry, Pettis
COMMUNITY BUILDER (See also CITY PLANNER, CIVIC LEADER)
Atkinson, George Henry
Kelley, Alfred
Wadsworth, James
COMMUNITY ORGANIZER
Collier, John
COMPILER (See also BIBLIOGRAPHER, SCHOLAR)
Adams, Hannah
Disturnell, John
Law, Andrew
Sears, Robert
Swan, Timothy
Tenney, Tabitha Gilman
Tufts, John
Valentine, David Thomas
COMPOSER (See also HYMNOLOGIST, MUSICIAN, SONGWRITER)
Allen, Nathan H.
Armstrong, Henry Worthington ("Harry")
Baker, Benjamin Franklin
Bartlett, Homer Newton
Beach, Amy Marcy Cheney
Beck, Johann Heinrich
Bird, Arthur
Blitzstein, Marc
Bloch, Ernest
Blodgett, Benjamin Colman
Bond, Carrie Jacobs
Bristow, George Frederick
Buck, Dudley
Burleigh, Henry Thacker
Burton, Frederick Russell
Cadman, Charles Wakefield
Carpenter, John Alden
Carr, Benjamin
Chadwick, George Whitefield
Coerne, Louis Adolphe
Cohan, George Michael
Coltrane, John William
Converse, Charles Crozat
Converse, Frederick Shepherd
Cook, Will Marion
Damrosch, Leopold
Damrosch, Walter Johannes
De Koven, Henry Louis Reginald
De Rose, Peter

Dett, Robert Nathaniel
Dresel, Otto
Duke, Vernon
Dunham, Henry Morton
Edwards, Julian
Eichberg, Julius
Elman, Harry ("Ziggy")
Emery, Stephen Albert
Engel, Carl
Fairchild, Blair
Fairlamb, James Remington
Farwell, Arthur
Fisher, William Arms
Foote, Arthur William
Foster, Stephen Collins
Fry, William Henry
Ganss, Henry George
Gershwin, George
Gilbert, Henry Franklin Belknap
Gilchrist, William Wallace
Gleason, Frederic Grant
Godowsky, Leopold
Goldbeck, Robert
Goldman, Edwin Franko
Goldmark, Rubin
Gottschalk, Louis Moreau
Grainger, George Percy
Griffes, Charles Tomlinson
Hadley, Henry Kimball
Hammerstein, Oscar
Harney, Benjamin Robertson
Hastings, Thomas
Hays, William Shakespeare
Heinrich, Antony Philip
Hemmeter, John Conrad
Henderson, Ray
Hewitt, James
Hoffman, Richard
Hofmann, Josef Casimir
Holyoke, Samuel
Humiston, William Henry
Ives, Charles Edward
Jackson, George K.
Johns, Clayton
Jones, Lindley Armstrong ("Spike")
Kaiser, Alois
Keller, Mathias
Kelley, Edgar Stillman
Kern, Jerome David
Klein, Bruno Oscar
Koemmenich, Louis
Korngold, Erich Wolfgang
Kreisler, Fritz
Kroeger, Ernest Richard
Landowska, Wanda Aleksandra
Lang, Benjamin Johnson
Law, Andrew
Ledbetter, Huddie ("Leadbelly")
Liebling, Emil
Liebling, Estelle
Loeffler, Charles Martin
Loesser, Frank
Lutkin, Peter Christian
MacDowell, Edward Alexander
Mannes, Leopold Damrosch
Maretzek, Max

Marzo, Eduardo
Mason, Daniel Gregory
Mason, William
Mitchell, Nahum
Mitropoulos, Dimitri
Morton, Ferdinand Joseph ("Jelly
    Roll")
Musin, Ovide
Nevin, Ethelbert Woodbridge
Nevin, George Balch
Newman, Alfred
Nunó, Jaime
Oehmler, Leo Carl Martin
Oliver, Joseph
Osgood, George Laurie
Paine, John Knowles
Palmer, Horatio Richmond
Parker, Charlie ("Bird")
Parker, Horatio William
Parker, James Cutler Dunn
Pease, Alfred Humphreys
Perabo, Johann Ernst
Phillips, Philip
Porter, Cole
Pratt, Silas Gamaliel
Pryor, Arthur W.
Rachmaninoff, Sergei Vasilyevich
Reinagle, Alexander
Riegger, Wallingford
Ritter, Frédéric Louis
Rogers, Clara Kathleen Barnett
Romberg, Sigmund
Root, Frederic Woodman
Root, George Frederick
Rosenblatt, Joseph
Runcie, Constance Faunt Le Roy
Rybner, Martin Cornelius
Sandler, Jacob Koppel
Schelling, Ernest Henry
Schillinger, Joseph
Schindler, Kurt
Schnabel, Artur
Schoenberg, Arnold
Scott, John Prindle
Selby, William
Shaw, Oliver
Sherwood, William Hall
Silvers, Louis
Sobolewski, J. Friedrich Eduard
Sousa, John Philip
Southard, Lucien H.
Speaks, Oley
Spicker, Max
Stanley, Albert Augustus
Stark, Edward Josef
Sternberg, Constantin Ivanovich,
    Edler von
Stewart, Humphrey John
Stoessel, Albert Frederic
Swan, Timothy
Taylor, Joseph Deems
Taylor, Raynor
Thayer, Whitney Eugene
Tilzer, Harry Von
Tobani, Theodore Moses
Trajetta, Philip

Tuckey, William
Van Der Stucken, Frank Valentin
Varèse, Edgard
Vogrich, Max Wilhelm Karl
Waller, Thomas Wright ("Fats")
Warren, Richard Henry
Warren, Samuel Prowse
Waxman, Franz
Webb, George James
Weems, Ted
Weidig, Adolf
Weill, Kurt
Weld, Arthur Cyril Gordon
White, Clarence Cameron
White, Joseph Malachy
Whiting, Arthur Battelle
Whiting, George Elbridge
Wight, Frederick Coit
Wilson, Mortimer
Witmark, Isidore
Wolle, John Frederick
Woodbury, Isaac Baker
Woolf, Benjamin Edward
Yon, Pietro Alessandro
Youmans, Vincent Millie
Zach, Max Wilhelm
Zeuner, Charles

**COMPTROLLER OF CURRENCY (See
    also BANKER, ECONOMIST,
    FINANCIER)**
Crissinger, Daniel Richard
Eckels, James Herron
Knox, John Jay
McCulloch, Hugh
Steele, John

CONCESSIONAIRE
Grace, William Russell
Tilyou, George Cornelius

**CONCHOLOGIST (See also BIOLOGIST,
    ZOOLOGIST)**
Gould, Augustus Addison
Say, Thomas
Tryon, George Washington

**CONDUCTOR (See also BANDLEADER,
    MUSICIAN)**
Barrère, Georges
Beck, Johann Heinrich
Bergman, Carl
Bodanzky, Artur
Damrosch, Leopold
Damrosch, Walter Johannes
Dannreuther, Gustav
Duchin, Edward Frank ("Eddy")
Gabrilowitsch, Ossip
Gericke, Wilhelm
Gilchrist, William Wallace
Gould, Nathaniel Duren
Hadley, Henry Kimball
Hertz, Alfred
Hill, Ureli Corelli
Koussevitzky, Serge Alexandrovich
Kroeger, Ernest Richard
Lang, Benjamin Johnson
Listemann, Bernhard
Lunceford, James Melvin
    ("Jimmie")

Lutkin, Peter Christian
Mannes, David
Mees, Arthur
Miller, Glenn
Mitropoulos, Dimitri
Mollenhauer, Emil
Monteux, Pierre Benjamin
Munch, Charles
Neuendorff, Adolph Heinrich
    Anton Magnus
Newman, Alfred
Nunó, Jaime
Oberhoffer, Emil Johann
Osgood, George Laurie
Palmer, Horatio Richmond
Pratt, Silas Gamaliel
Rachmaninoff, Sergei Vasilyevich
Reiner, Fritz
Rodzinski, Artur
Root, Frederic Woodman
Saslavsky, Alexander
Scheel, Fritz
Schelling, Ernest Henry
Schradieck, Henry
Seidl, Anton
Siloti, Alexander Ilyitch
Silvers, Louis
Sobolewski, J. Friedrich Eduard
Spicker, Max
Spiering, Theodore
Stanley, Albert Augustus
Stock, Frederick August
Stoessel, Albert Frederic
Szell, George
Thomas, Christian Friedrich
    Theodore
Timm, Henry Christian
Toscanini, Arturo
Van Der Stucken, Frank Valentin
Verbrugghen, Henri
Walter, Bruno
Waxman, Franz
Weidig, Adolf
White, George Leonard
Whiteman, Paul Samuel ("Pops")
Wilson, Mortimer
Woolle, John Frederick
Zach, Max Wilhelm
Zerralin, Carl

CONFEDERATE AGENT (See also SPY)
Bulloch, James Dunwody
Clay, Clement Claiborne
Helm, Charles John
Holcombe, James Philemon
Kenner, Duncan Farrar
Lamar, Gazaway Bugg
Peyton, John Lewis
Sanders, George Nicholas
Thompson, Jacob
Tucker, Nathaniel Beverley,
    1820–1890

**CONGRESSMAN (CONFEDERATE) (See
    also CONGRESSMAN)**
Bridgers, Robert Rufus
Shorter, John Gill
Smith, Robert Hardy

Staples, Waller Redd
CONGRESSMAN (CONTINENTAL) (See
   also CONGRESSMAN)
Burnet, William
Clay, Joseph
Deane, Silas
Goldsborough, Robert
Grayson, William
Griffin, Cyrus
Hanson, John
Henry, John, 1750–1798
Howell, David
Huntington, Samuel, 1731–1796
Johnson, Thomas
Jones, Allen
Langworthy, Edward
Low, Isaac
Lynch, Thomas, 1727–1776
McClurg, James
Marchant, Henry
Mathews, John
Mercer, James
Middleton, Henry
Mifflin, Thomas
Nash, Abner
Neilson, John
Pierce, William Leigh
Randolph, Peyton
Read, Jacob
Root, Jesse
Scudder, Nathaniel
Searle, James
Smith, Jonathan Bayard
Smith, Melancton, 1744–1798
Smith, Richard
Telfair, Edward
Tilghman, Matthew
Van Dyke, Nicholas, 1738–1789
Ward, Samuel, 1725–1776
Wisner, Henry
Zubly, John Joachim
CONGRESSMAN (See also
   CONGRESSMAN, CONFEDERATE;
   CONGRESSMAN, CONTINENTAL;
   CONGRESSWOMAN)
Aandahl, Fred George
Adams, Henry Cullen
Aiken, David Wyatt
Alexander, de Alva Stanwood
Allen, Elisha Hunt
Allen, Thomas
Allen, William
Allen, William Joshua
Allison, William Boyd
Anderson, John Alexander
Andrew, Abram Piatt
Andrews, Sherlock James
Appleton, John
Archer, William Segar
Arnold, Isaac Newton
Ashe, William Shepperd
Ashley, James Mitchell
Ashley, William Henry
Ashmun, George
Ayres, William Augustus
Babcock, Joseph Weeks

Bailey, Joseph Weldon
Baker, Jehu
Banks, Nathaniel Prentiss
Barbour, John Strode
Barden, Graham Arthur
Barkley, Alben William
Barksdale, William
Barrett, Frank Aloysius
Barringer, Daniel Moreau
Barrow, Washington
Bartholdt, Richard
Barton, Bruce Fairchild
Bates, James
Bayly, Thomas Henry
Beardsley, Samuel
Beck, James Montgomery
Bedinger, George Michael
Bell, Peter Hansborough
Bender, George Harrison
Berger, Victor Louis
Berrien, John Macpherson
Bissell, William Henry
Blair, Henry William
Bland, Richard Parks
Bliss, Philemon
Bloom, Sol
Blount, James Henderson
Blow, Henry Taylor
Bocock, Thomas Stanley
Boteler, Alexander Robinson
Botts, John Minor
Boutelle, Charles Addison
Boyd, Lynn
Bradley, William Czar
Bragg, Edward Stuyvesant
Branch, Lawrence O'Bryan
Brawley, William Hiram
Breckenridge, James
Breckinridge, William Campbell
   Preston
Brewer, Mark Spencer
Broadhead, James Overton
Brooks, Overton
Brooks, Preston Smith
Brown, Aaron Venable
Brown, Albert Gallatin
Brown, Clarence James
Brown, John Young
Burdick, Usher Lloyd
Burke, Aedanus
Burleson, Albert Sidney
Burlingame, Anson
Burton, Theodore Elijah
Butler, Benjamin Franklin
Butler, Ezra
Butler, William
Butler, William Orlando
Cabell, Samuel Jordan
Calvert, Charles Benedict
Cambreleng, Churchill Caldom
Campbell, James Hepburn
Campbell, John Wilson
Campbell, Lewis Davis
Campbell, William Bowen
Campbell, William W.
Candler, Allen Daniel

Cannon, Clarence
Cannon, Joseph Gurney
Cannon, Newton
Case, Francis Higbee
Chalmers, James Ronald
Chambers, John
Chandler, Joseph Ripley
Cheves, Langdon
Chittenden, Simeon Baldwin
Claiborne, John Francis
   Hamtramck
Claiborne, Nathaniel Herbert
Clark, James
Clay, Henry
Clay, Matthew
Clayton, Augustin Smith
Clayton, Henry De Lamar
Clements, Judson Claudius
Cleveland, Chauncey Fitch
Clopton, John
Cockran, William Bourke
Condit, John
Conger, Edwin Hurd
Conkling, Alfred
Connally, Thomas Terry ("Tom")
Conway, Martin Franklin
Cook, Philip
Cooper, (Leon) Jere
Copley, Ira Clifton
Covode, John
Cox, Edward Eugene
Cox, Samuel Sullivan
Crawford, Martin Jenkins
Creighton, William
Crisp, Charles Frederick
Crosser, Robert
Crowninshield, Jacob
Crump, Edward Hull
Cummings, Amos Jay
Curtis, Charles
Cushman, Joshua
Dalzell, John
Davis, Garret
Davis, Horace
Davis, John Wesley
Davis, John William
Dawes, Henry Laurens
Dawson, William Levi
Dayton, Jonathan
Dean, Sidney
Dearborn, Henry
Delano, Columbus
De Priest, Oscar Stanton
Desha, Joseph
Dickinson, Philemon
Dingley, Nelson
Dirksen, Everett McKinley
Dixon, James
Doughton, Robert Lee
Drayton, William
Dudley, Edward Bishop
Dunn, William McKee
Duval, William Pope
Duvall, Gabriel
Dworshak, Henry Clarence
Eaton, Charles Aubrey

Edgerton, Sidney
Edwards, Henry Waggaman
Ellsworth, William Wolcott
Engle, Clair William Walter
English, William Hayden
Eppes, John Wayles
Esch, John Jacob
Evans, Walter
Ewing, Thomas
Ferry, Orris Sanford
Fess, Simeon Davidson
Findlay, James
Findley, William
Fitzpatrick, Morgan Cassius
Fitzsimmons, Thomas
Florence, Thomas Birch
Floyd, William
Foot, Samuel Augustus
Fordney, Joseph Warren
Forney, William Henry
Forward, Walter
Foster, Abiel
Foster, Charles
Fowler, Orin
Frye, William Pierce
Galloway, Samuel
Garfield, James Abram
Garrett, Finis James
Gear, John Henry
Gillett, Frederick Huntington
Gilmer, George Rockingham
Gilmer, John Adams
Glynn, Martin Henry
Goldsborough, Charles
Goldsborough, Thomas Alan
Goodenow, John Milton
Green, James Stephens
Green, William Joseph, Jr.
Greenhalge, Frederic Thomas
Greenup, Christopher
Griswold, John Augustus
Groesbeck, William Slocum
Grosvenor, Charles Henry
Hahn, Georg Michael Decker
Hale, Robert Safford
Hamer, Thomas Lyon
Hamilton, William Thomas
Hampton, Wade, 1751–1835
Hancock, John, 1824–1893
Hanson, Alexander Contee,
  1786–1819
Hardin, Ben
Hardin, John J.
Harding, Abner Clark
Hardwick, Thomas William
Harlan, James
Harris, Wiley Pope
Harrison, Byron Patton
Harrison, Francis Burton
Hartley, Fred Allen, Jr.
Hartley, Thomas
Hasbrouck, Abraham Bruyn
Hastings, William Wirt
Hatch, William Henry
Haugen, Gilbert Nelson
Haugen, Nils Pederson

Havens, James Smith
Hawley, Willis Chatman
Heflin, James Thomas
Hemphill, Joseph
Henderson, Archibald
Hendricks, Thomas Andrews
Hendricks, William
Hendrix, Joseph Clifford
Hepburn, William Peters
Herbert, Hilary Abner
Herter, Christian Archibald
Hiester, Daniel
Hiester, Joseph
Hillhouse, James
Hilliard, Henry Washington
Hillyer, Junius
Hinds, Asher Crosby
Hitt, Robert Roberts
Hoar, Ebenezer Rockwood
Hoar, George Frisbie
Hoar, Samuel
Hobson, Richmond Pearson
Hoey, Clyde Roark
Hoffman, Clare Eugene
Hoffman, Ogden
Hogan, John
Holman, William Steele
Holmes, Isaac Edward
Hope, Clifford Ragsdale
Hopkinson, Joseph
Houghton, Alanson Bigelow
Houk, Leonidas Campbell
Howard, Benjamin
Howard, Jacob Merritt
Howard, Volney Erskine
Hubbard, David
Hughes, Dudley Mays
Hull, Cordell
Hunt, Carleton
Hunter, Whiteside Godfrey
Hurlbut, Stephen Augustus
Ingersoll, Charles Jared
Ingham, Samuel Delucenna
Iverson, Alfred
Jackson, James, 1819–1887
Jackson, John George
Jackson, William, 1783–1855
James, Ollie Murray
Jenkins, Albert Gallatin
Jensen, Benton Franklin ("Ben")
Johns, Kensey
Johnson, Cave
Johnson, James
Johnson, Magnus
Johnson, Robert Ward
Johnson, Tom Loftin
Jones, Frank
Jones, Jehu Glancy
Jones, John Winston
Jones, William
Judd, Norman Buel
Kahn, Julius
Keifer, Joseph Warren
Keitt, Lawrence Massillon
Kelley, William Darrah
Kelly, John

Kenna, John Edward
Kennedy, John Fitzgerald
Kennedy, Robert Patterson
Kent, Joseph
Key, Philip Barton
Kilbourne, James
King, Austin Augustus
King, John Alsop
King, Thomas Butler
King, William Rufus Devane
Kitchin, Claude
Kitchin, William Walton
Knickerbocker, Herman
Knott, James Proctor
Knutson, Harold
Lacey, John Fletcher
Lacock, Abner
La Guardia, Fiorello Henry
Lane, Henry Smith
Lanham, Frederick Garland
  ("Fritz")
Lattimore, William
Law, John
Lawrence, William, 1819–1899
Leavitt, Humphrey Howe
Lee, William Henry Fitzhugh
Leffler, Isaac
Leffler, Shepherd
Leib, Michael
Lemke, William Frederick
Lenroot, Irvine Luther
Letcher, John
Letcher, Robert Perkins
Lever, Asbury Francis
Levin, Lewis Charles
Lewis, Dixon Hall
Lewis, James Hamilton
Lewis, Joseph Horace
Ligon, Thomas Watkins
Lind, John
Lindbergh, Charles Augustus
Littauer, Lucius Nathan
Littleton, Martin Wiley
Livermore, Arthur
Livermore, Edward St. Loe
Livermore, Samuel, 1732–1803
Lloyd, Edward, 1779–1834
Locke, Matthew
Long, John Davis
Longfellow, Stephen
Loomis, Arphaxed
Loomis, Dwight
Lorimer, William
Lowndes, William
Lucas, John Baptiste Charles
Lucas, Scott Wike
Lundeen, Ernest
Lynch, John Roy
Lyon, Francis Strother
McArthur, Duncan
McCall, Samuel Walker
McClelland, Robert
McClernand, John Alexander
McClurg, Joseph Washington
McComas, Louis Emory
McCook, Anson George

McCrary, George Washington
McCreary, James Bennett
McFadden, Louis Thomas
McGranery, James Patrick
McKay, James Iver
McKean, Samuel
McKee, John
McKennan, Thomas McKean
    Thompson
McKim, Isaac
McKinley, John
McKinley, William Brown
McLane, Robert Milligan
Maclay, Samuel
McLean, John
McMillin, Benton
McNulty, Frank Joseph
McPherson, Edward
McPherson, Smith
McRae, Thomas Chipman
McReynolds, Samuel Davis
Madden, Martin Barnaby
Maginnis, Martin
Mallary, Rollin Carolas
Mann, James Robert
Marcantonio, Vito Anthony
Marland, Ernest Whitworth
Marshall, Thomas Alexander
Martin, Joseph William, Jr.
Marvin, Dudley
Mason, John Young
Mathews, George
Mattocks, John
Maverick, (Fontaine) Maury
Maxwell, Augustus Emmett
Maxwell, Samuel
May, Andrew Jackson
Maynard, Horace
Mercee, John Francis
Mercer, Charles Fenton
Mercier, Ulysses
Miles, William Porcher
Miller, John
Mills, Elijah Hunt
Mills, Roger Quarles
Miner, Charles
Mitchell, Alexander
Mitchell, George Edward
Mitchell, Nahum
Mitchill, Samuel Latham
Mondell, Frank Wheeler
Money, Hernando De Soto
Montague, Andrew Jackson
Moody, William Henry
Moore, Andrew
Moore, Ely
Moore, Gabriel
Moore, Thomas Patrick
Moorhead, James Kennedy
Morehead, Charles Slaughter
Morgan, George Washington
Morrill, Anson Peaslee
Morrill, Edmund Needham
Morrill, Justin Smith
Morris, Lewis Richard
Morrison, William Ralls

Morrissey, John
Morrow, Jeremiah
Morrow, William W.
Morse, Freeman Harlow
Murdock, Victor
Murray, William Henry David
Neely, Matthew Mansfield
Negley, James Scott
Nelson, Roger
Newberry, John Stoughton
Newell, William Augustus
Newlands, Francis Griffith
Newton, Thomas, 1768–1847
Niblack, William Ellis
Nicholas, John
Nicholas, Wilson Cary
Nicholson, Joseph Hopper
Niedringhaus, Frederick Gottlieb
Nisbet, Eugenius Aristides
Norris, George William
Norton, Elijah Hise
Nott, Abraham
Oates, William Calvin
O'Ferrall, Charles Triplett
Olmsted, Marlin Edgar
Orth, Godlove Stein
Pacheco, Romualdo
Packer, Asa
Page, John
Paine, Halbert Eleazer
Palmer, Alexander Mitchell
Palmer, Henry Wilbur
Parker, Isaac Charles
Pattison, John M.
Payne, Henry B.
Pearce, James Alfred
Pendleton, George Hunt
Pennington, William
Perkins, George Douglas
Perkins, James Breck
Phelan, James, 1856–1891
Phelps, Charles Edward
Phelps, John Smith
Phelps, William Walter
Philips, John Finis
Phillips, Thomas Wharton
Phillips, William Addison
Pickens, Francis Wilkinson
Pierce, Henry Lillie
Pinckney, Henry Laurens
Plaisted, Harris Merrill
Plumley, Frank
Poindexter, George
Poland, Luke Potter
Pollock, James
Pool, Joe Richard
Porter, Albert Gallatin
Porter, Peter Buell
Porter, Stephen Geyer
Potter, Elisha Reynolds
Potter, Robert
Pou, Edward William
Pratt, Zadock
Prentiss, Seargent Smith
Preston, William
Preston, William Ballard

Price, Hiram
Price, Sterling
Price, Thomas Lawson
Pryor, Roger Atkinson
Pujo, Arsène Paulin
Quigg, Lemuel Ely
Rainey, Joseph Hayne
Randall, Samuel Jackson
Randolph, Thomas Mann
Rankin, John Elliott
Rayner, Kenneth
Read, Nathan
Reagan, John Henninger
Reece, Brazilla Carroll
Reed, Daniel Alden
Rhea, John
Rice, Alexander Hamilton
Rice, Edmund
Rich, Robert
Riddle, Albert Gallatin
Rivers, Lucius Mendel
Roberts, Ellis Henry
Roberts, Jonathan
Roberts, William Randall
Robertson, Alice Mary
Robertson, George
Robertson, John
Robinson, Joseph Taylor
Rollins, James Sidney
Rousseau, Lovell Harrison
Rowan, John
Rusk, Jeremiah McClain
Sabath, Adolph J.
Sage, Russell
Saunders, Romulus Mitchell
Sawyer, Lemuel
Schenck, Robert Cumming
Seddon, James Alexander
Sergeant, John, 1779–1852
Sergeant, Jonathan Dickinson
Sevier, Ambrose Hundley
Seybert, Adam
Seymour, Thomas Hart
Shafroth, John Franklin
Shepard, William
Sheppard, John Morris
Sherwood, Isaac Ruth
Shouse, Jouett
Sibley, Joseph Crocker
Sickles, Daniel Edgar
Simms, William Elliott
Simpson, Jerry
Singleton, James Washington
Skinner, Harry
Slemp, Campbell Bascom
Smalls, Robert
Smith, Caleb Blood
Smith, Jeremiah, 1759–1842
Smith, Oliver Hampton
Smith, Truman
Smith, Walter Inglewood
Smith, William, 1797–1887
Smith, William Loughton
Smith, William Nathan Harrell
Smith, William Russell
Smyth, Alexander

Snell, Bertrand Hollis
Spaight, Richard Dobbs
Spalding, Thomas
Sparks, William Andrew Jackson
Spaulding, Elbridge Gerry
Speer, Emory
Spence, Brent
Spencer, Ambrose
Spencer, John Canfield
Sperry, Nehemiah Day
Springer, William McKendree
Stanley, Augustus Owsley
Stanly, Edward
Stanton, Frederick Perry
Stanton, Richard Henry
Starin, John Henry
Steagall, Henry Bascom
Steele, John
Stephens, Alexander Hamilton
Stephenson, Andrew
Stephenson, Isaac
Stevens, Thaddeus
Stevenson, Adlai Ewing
Stevenson, John White
Stewart, Andrew
Stigler, William Grady
Stockdale, Thomas Ringland
Stone, David
Stone, William Joel
Storer, Bellamy
Stuart, Alexander Hugh Holmes
Stuart, John Todd
Sullivan, George
Sulzer, William
Summers, George William
Sumners, Hatton, William
Sumter, Thomas
Sutherland, Joel Barlow
Swann, Thomas
Swanson, Claude Augustus
Sweeney, Martin Leonard
Taber, John
Tallmadge, Benjamin
Tawney, James Albertus
Taylor, Alfred Alexander
Thacher, George
Thayer, Eli
Thomas, David
Thomas, Francis
Thomas, John Parnell
Thomas, Philip Francis
Thompson, Jacob
Thompson, Thomas Larkin
Thompson, Waddy
Thompson, Wiley
Throop, Enos Thompson
Thurman, Allen Granberry
Tilson, John Quillin
Tinkham, George Holden
Tod, John
Toucey, Isaac
Towne, Charles Arnette
Towns, George Washington
    Bonaparte
Tracy, Uriah
Troup, George Michael

Trumbull, Jonathan, 1740–1809
Tuck, Amos
Tucker, Henry St. George,
    1853–1932
Tucker, John Randolph,
    1823–1897
Tyson, Job Roberts
Upham, Charles Wentworth
Van Cortlandt, Philip
Van Horn, Robert Thompson
Van Rensselaer, Solomon
Van Rensselaer, Stephen
Verplanck, Julian Crommelin
Vibbard, Chauncey
Vinson, Fred(erick) Moore
Vinton, Samuel Finley
Volstead, Andrew John
Vroom, Peter Dumont
Waddell, Alfred Moore
Wadsworth, James Wolcott, Jr.
Wadsworth, Jeremiah
Wadsworth, Peleg
Walker, Amasa
Walker, Gilbert Carlton
Wallace, David
Wallgren, Mon(rad) C(harles)
Walter, Francis Eugene
Ward, Marcus Lawrence
Warner, Adoniram Judson
Warner, Hiram
Warner, William
Washburn, Cadwallader Colden
Washburn, Charles Grenfill
Washburn, Israel
Washburn, William Drew
Washburne, Elihu Benjamin
Watson, James Eli
Watterson, Harvey Magee
Weaver, James Baird
Weeks, John Wingate
Welch, John
Weller, John B.
Wells, Erastus
Wentworth, John, 1815–1888
West, George
Wheeler, Joseph
White, Alexander
White, Stephen Van Culen
Whitehill, Robert
Whitman, Ezekiel
Wickliffe, Charles Anderson
Wilde, Richard Henry
Williams, David Rogerson
Willis, Albert Shelby
Wilmot, David
Wilson, James
Wilson, James Falconer
Wilson, William Bauchop
Wilson, William Lyne
Windom, William
Winn, Richard
Winthrop, Robert Charles
Wise, Henry Alexander
Wolf, George
Wood, Fernando
Wood, John Stephens

Wood, William Robert
Wright, Hendrick Bradley
Wright, Joseph Albert
Wright, Robert
Yates, Abraham
Yell, Archibald
Young, Pierce Manning Butler
Zollicoffer, Felix Kirk

CONGRESSWOMAN

Kahn, Florence Prag
Norton, Mary Teresa Hopkins
Rogers, Edith Nourse
Rohde, Ruth Bryan Owen
Simms, Ruth Hanna McCormick

CONSERVATIONIST (See also
ECOLOGIST)

Darling, Jay Norwood ("Ding")
Grinnell, George Bird
McAdams, Clark
McFarland, John Horace
Maxwell, George Hebard
Merriam, John Campbell
Olmsted, Frederick Law
Osborn, Henry Fairfield
Pack, Charles Lathrop
Pammel, Louis Hermann
Pearson, Thomas Gilbert
Pinchot, Gifford
Roosevelt, Robert Barnwell
Shields, George Oliver
Silcox, Ferdinand Augustus
Zahniser, Howard Clinton

CONSTITUTIONAL SCHOLAR

Warren, Charles

CONSUL (See also DIPLOMAT,
STATESMAN)

Andrews, Israel DeWolf
Cathcart, James Leander
De Forest, David Curtis
Foresti, Eleutario Felice
Gillman, Henry
Hale, Charles
Halsey, Thomas Lloyd
Heap, Samuel Davies
Helm, Charles John
Jarvis, William
Jones, William Patterson
King, Jonas
Lear, Tobias
McRae, Duncan Kirkland
Magoffin, James Wiley
Merrill, Selah
Morse, Freeman Harlow
Murphy, Dominic Ignatius
Murphy, William Walton
O'Brien, Richard
Offley, David
Ogden, Francis Barber
Osterhaus, Peter Joseph
Shaler, William
Stahel, Julius
Taylor, James Wickes
Thayer, Alexander Wheelock
Underwood, Francis Henry
Wood, Leonard

Miller, Willoughby Dayton
Morton, William Thomas Green
Owre, Alfred
Parsons, Thomas William
Riggs, John Mankey
Spooner, Shearjashub
Volck, Adalbert John
Wells, Horace
White, John de Haven

DEPARTMENT STORE EXECUTIVE
Straus, Percy Selden

DERMATOLOGIST (See also PHYSICIAN)
Duhring, Louis Adolphus
Jackson, George Thomas
Pusey, William Allen
Schamberg, Jay Frank
Wende, Ernest
Wende, Grover William
White, James Clarke
Wigglesworth, Edward

DESIGNER (CINEMATOGRAPHIC EQUIPMENT)
Howell, Albert Summers

DESIGNER (COSTUME)
Bernstein, Aline

DESIGNER (FASHION)
Adrian, Gilbert
Carnegie, Hattie
Kiam, Omar
McCardell, Claire
Orry-Kelly

DESIGNER (INTERIOR)
Herter, Christian

DESIGNER (SCENIC)
Bernstein, Aline

DESPERADO (See also BANDIT, BRIGAND, BUCCANEER, BURGLAR, CRIMINAL, OUTLAW, PIRATE)
Bass, Sam
Billy the Kid
Dalton, Robert
James, Jesse Woodson
Mason, Samuel
Slade, Joseph Alfred
Younger, Thomas Coleman

DETECTIVE
Burns, William John
Means, Gaston Bullock
Pinkerton, Allan
Ruditsky, Barney
Siringo, Charles A.

DIAMOND CUTTER (See also CRAFTSMAN)
Morse, Henry Dutton

DIARIST (See also CHRONICLER)
Breen, Patrick
Hone, Philip
Knight, Sarah Kemble
Laudonnière, René Goulaine de
Maclay, William
Marshall, Christopher
Sewall, Samuel
Smith, Richard
Wister, Sarah

DIESINKER (See also ENGRAVER)
Gobrecht, Christian
Kneass, William
Wright, Joseph

DIETICIAN (See also NUTRITIONIST, PHYSICIAN)
Nichols, Thomas Low

DIPLOMAT (See also CONSUL, STATESMAN)
Adams, Charles
Adams, Charles Francis
Adee, Alvey Augustus
Allen, Elisha Hunt
Allen, George Venable
Anderson, Richard Clough
Angel, Benjamin Franklin
Angell, James Burrill
Appleton, John
Armstrong, John
Avery, Benjamin Parke
Bacon, Robert
Badeau, Adam
Bagby, Arthur Pendleton
Baker, Jehu
Bancroft, Edgar Addison
Bancroft, George
Barrett, John
Barringer, Daniel Moreau
Barton, Thomas Pennant
Bayard, James Ach(e)ton
Bayard, Thomas Francis
Beaupré, Arthur Matthias
Belmont, August
Benjamin, Samuel Greene Wheeler
Bernstein, Herman
Biddle, Anthony Joseph Drexel, Jr.
Bidlack, Benjamin Alden
Bigelow, John
Bingham, Robert Worth
Birney, James
Bliss, Robert Woods
Bliss, Tasker Howard
Blount, James Henderson
Blow, Henry Taylor
Bogardus, Everardus
Boker, George Henry
Bonsal, Stephen
Borland, Solon
Boutell, Henry Sherman
Bowdoin, James
Bowen, Herbert Wolcott
Bowers, Claude Gernade
Bradish, Luther
Bradley, Charles William
Bristol, Mark Lambert
Broadhead, James Overton
Brown, James
Brown, John Porter
Buchanan, William Insco
Bullitt, William Christian
Burlingame, Anson
Calhoun, William James
Cambreleng, Churchill Caldom
Cameron, Simon
Campbell, George Washington
Campbell, Lewis Davis

Carmichael, William
Carr, Dabney Smith
Carter, Henry Alpheus Peirce
Cass, Lewis
Castle, William Richards, Jr.
Child, Richard Washburn
Choate, Joseph Hodges
Clark, Joshua Reuben, Jr.
Clay, Clement Claiborne
Conger, Edwin Hurd
Coolidge, Thomas Jefferson
Cooper, Henry Ernest
Cramer, Michael John
Crowder, Enoch Herbert
Dallas, George Mifflin
Dana, Francis
Daniel, John Moncure
Daniels, Josephus
D'Avezac, Auguste Geneviève Valentin
Davies, Joseph Edward
Davis, John Chandler Bancroft
Davis, John William
Davis, Norman Hezekiah
Dawson, Thomas Cleland
Dayton, William Lewis
Deane, Silas
Denby, Charles
Dickinson, Charles Monroe
Dodd, William Edward
Dodge, Augustus Caesar
Donelson, Andrew Jackson
Donovan, William Joseph
Draper, William Franklin
Dulles, Allen Welsh
Dulles, John Foster
Du Pont, Victor Marie
Eames, Charles
Eaton, William
Edge, Walter Evans
Egan, Maurice Francis
Egan, Patrick
Ellis, Powhatan
Ellsworth, Henry William
Erving, George William
Eustis, George
Eustis, James Biddle
Eustis, William
Everett, Alexander Hill
Fairchild, Lucius
Farman, Elbert Eli
Fay, Theodore Sedgwick
Fearn, John Walker
Ferguson, Thomas Barker
Flagg, Edmund
Fletcher, Henry Prather
Fogg, George Gilman
Foote, Lucius Harwood
Forbes, John Murray
Foster, John Watson
Foulk, George Clayton
Fox, Williams Carleton
Francis, Charles Spencer
Francis, John Morgan
Franklin, Benjamin
Gadsden, James

Gallatin, Abraham Alfonse Albert
Gauss, Clarence Edward
Genet, Edmond Charles
Gerard, James Watson
Gifford, Walter Sherman
Grady, Henry Francis
Graham, John
Gray, Isaac Pusey
Greathouse, Clarence Ridgeby
Green, Benjamin Edwards
Greene, Roger Sherman
Grew, Joseph Clark
Grieve, Miller
Griscom, Lloyd Carpenter
Gummere, Samuel René
Guthrie, George Wilkins
Halderman, John A.
Hale, Edward Joseph
Hale, John Parker
Hamilton, Maxwell McGaughey
Hardy, Arthur Sherburne
Harriman, Florence Jaffray Hurst
Harris, Townsend
Harvey, George Brinton McClellan
Hassaurek, Friedrich
Hay, Joh Milton
Hayes, Carlton Joseph Huntley
Herrick, Myron Timothy
Hibben, Paxton Pattison
Hicks, John, 1847–1917
Hill, David Jayne
Hise, Elijah
Hoffman, Wickham
Holcombe, Chester
Holmes, Julius Cecil
Hoover, Herbert Clark, Jr.
Hopkins, Harry Lloyd
Houghton, Alanson Bigelow
Hughes, Christopher
Hunt, William Henry
Hunter, William
Hurley, Patrick Jay
Ide, Henry Clay
Izard, Ralph
Jackson, Charles Douglas
Jackson, Henry Rootes
Jackson, John Brinckerhoff
Jackson, Mortimer Melville
Jardine, William Marion
Jay, John, 1745–1829
Jay, John, 1817–1894
Jefferson, Thomas
Johnson, Reverdy
Judd, Norman Buel
Kasson, John Adam
Kavanagh, Edward
Kilpatrick, Hugh Judson
King, Rufus
King, Thomas Butler
King, William Rufus Devane
Kinney, William Burnet
Kirk, Alan Goodrich
Lane, Arthur Bliss
Langston, John Mercer
Larkin, Thomas Oliver
Larrínaga, Tulio

Laurens, John
Lawrence, Abbott
Lee, Arthur
Lee, William
LeGendre, Charles William
Leishman, John G. A.
Lincoln, Robert Todd
Lind, John
Livingston, Robert R., 1746–1813
Long, Breckinridge
Lothrop, George Van Ness
Low, Frederick Ferdinand
McCartee, Divie Bethune
McCook, Edward Moody
McCormick, Robert Sanderson
McDonald, James Grover
McLane, Louis
McLane, Robert Milligan
McMillin, Benton
McNutt, Paul Vories
MacVeagh, Charles
MacVeagh, Isaac Wayne
Maney, George Earl
Mann, Ambrose Dudley
Marling, John Leake
Marsh, George Perkins
Marshall, Humphrey
Marshall, James Fowle Baldwin
Mason, James Murray
Mason, John Young
Maxcy, Virgil
Merry, William Lawrence
Messersmith, George Strausser
Meyer, George Von Lengerke
Miller, David Hunter
Moffat, Jay Pierrepont
Montgomery, George Washington
Moore, Thomas Patrick
Moran, Benjamin
Morgan, Edwin Vernon
Morgan, Philip Hicky
Morgenthau, Henry
Morris, Edward Joy
Morris, Gouverneur
Morris, Richard Valentine
Morrison, Delesseps Story
Morrow, Dwight Whitney
Morton, Levi Parsons
Motley, John Lothrop
Muhlenberg, Henry Augustus
  Philip
Muñoz-Rivera, Luis
Murray, William Vans
Nelson, Donald Marr
Nelson, Hugh
Nelson, Thomas Henry
Newel, Stanford
Nicholson, Meredith
Niles, Nathaniel, 1791–1869
Noyes, Edward Follansbee
O'Brien, Edward Charles
O'Brien, Thomas James
Offley, David
Osborn, Thomas Andrew
Osborn, Thomas Ogden

O'Shaughnessy, Nelson Jarvis
  Waterbury
Osten Sacken, Carl Robert
  Romanovich von der
O'Sullivan, John Louis
Pacheco, Romualdo
Page, Thomas Nelson
Page, Walter Hines
Palmer, Thomas Witherell
Parker, Peter
Partridge, James Rudolph
Patterson, Richard Cunningham,
  Jr.
Payne, John Howard
Peirce, Henry Augustus
Peixotto, Benjamin Franklin
Pendleton, George Hunt
Pendleton, John Strother
Penfield, Frederic Courtland
Phelps, Edward John
Phelps, William Walter
Phillips, William
Pickett, James Chamberlayne
Pierrepont, Edwards
Pinckney, Charles
Pinckney, Charles Cotesworth
Pinckney, Thomas
Pinkney, William
Poinsett, Joel Roberts
Polk, Frank Lyon
Porter, Horace
Preble, William Pitt
Preston, William
Pruyn, Robert Hewson
Putnam, James Osborne
Putnam, William LeBaron
Randolph, Sir John
Read, John Meredith, 1837–1896
Reed, William Bradford
Reid, Whitelaw
Reinsch, Paul Samuel
Rhind, Charles
Richards, William
Rives, William Cabell
Roberts, Edmund
Robinson, Christopher
Rockhill, William Woodville
Rodney, Caesar Augustus
Rohde, Ruth Bryan Owen
Root, Joseph Pomeroy
Rowe, Leo Stanton
Rublee, Horace
Rush, Richard
Russell, Charles Wells
Russell, Jonathan
Sanford, Henry Shelton
Saunders, Romulus Mitchell
Sayre, Stephen
Schenck, Robert Cumming
Schurman, Jacob Gould
Schurz, Carl
Schuyler, Eugene
Scruggs, William Lindsay
Sedgwick, Theodore, 1811–1859
Sewall, Harold Marsh
Seward, Frederick William

Patten, Simon Nelson
Perlman, Selig
Perry, Arthur Latham
Persons, Warren Milton
Pitkin, Timothy
Poor, Henry Varnum
Rae, John
Raguet, Condy
Remington, William Walter
Ripley, William Zebina
Robinson, Edward Van Dyke
Rogers, James Harvey
Schoenhof, Jacob
Schultz, Henry
Schumpeter, Joseph Alois
Schwab, John Christopher
Seager, Henry Rogers
Seligman, Edwin Robert Anderson
Shearman, Thomas Gaskell
Simons, Algie Martin
Simons, Henry Calvert
Slichter, Sumner Huber
Spahr, Charles Brazillai
Spillman, William Jasper
Stewart, Walter Winne
Sumner, William Graham
Taussig, Frank William
Taylor, Fred Manville
Thompson, Robert Ellis
Tucker, George
Vaughan, Benjamin
Veblen, Thorstein Bunde
Vethake, Henry
Viner, Jacob
Walker, Amasa
Walker, Francis Amasa
Webster, Pelatiah
Wells, David Ames
Weston, Nathan Austin
White, Horace
Wildman, Murray Shipley
Willis, Henry Parker
Wolman, Leo
Woodbury, Helen Laura Sumner
Woytinsky, Wladimir Savelievich
Wright, Philip Green
Young, Allyn Abbott
ECUMENICAL MOVEMENT LEADER
Brown, William Adams
ECUMENICAL PIONEER
Mott, John R.
EDITOR
Abbott, Lyman
Adams, Cyrus Cornelius
Adams, William Lysander
Aikens, Andrew Jackson
Alden, Henry Mills
Aldrich, Thomas Bailey
Allen, Frederick Lewis
Allen, Joseph Henry
Allen, Paul
Allen, Richard Lamb
Altsheler, Joseph Alexander
Ameringer, Oscar
Ames, Charles Gordon
Arthur, Timothy Shay

Atwood, David
Bagby, George William
Bangs, John Kendrick
Barron, Clarence Walker
Barrow, Washington
Barrows, Samuel June
Barsotti, Charles
Bartholdt, Richard
Bartlett, John
Bausman, Benjamin
Bayles, James Copper
Benét, William Rose
Benjamin, Park
Bennett, James Gordon
Bidwell, Walter Hilliard
Bigelow, John
Bird, Frederic Mayer
Bird, Robert Montgomery
Blackwell, Alice Stone
Blackwell, Henry Brown
Bledsoe, Albert Taylor
Bliss, Edwin Munsell
Bok, Edward William
Boner, John Henry
Booth, Mary Louise
Botts, Charles Tyler
Boudinot, Elias
Bowen, Henry Chandler
Bowker, Richard Rogers
Bowles, Samuel, 1797–1851
Bowles, Samuel, 1826–1878
Bowles, Samuel, 1851–1915
Brace, John Pierce
Bradwell, Myra
Brainerd, Erastus
Brainerd, Thomas
Brann, William Cowper
Brayman, Mason
Breckinridge, Desha
Breckinridge, William Campbell
    Preston
Brickell, Henry Herschel
Bright, Edward
Brisbane, Arthur
Bronson, Walter Cochrane
Brooks, James Gordon
Browne, Francis Fisher
Bryant, Louise Frances Stevens
Bryant, William Cullen
Buckingham, Joseph Tinker
Burlingame, Edward Livermore
Burr, Alfred Edmund
Burrage, Henry Sweetser
Butts, Isaac
Calverton, Victor Francis
Cameron, William Evelyn
Campbell, Charles
Campbell, Lewis Davis
Canby, Henry Seidel
Cardozo, Jacob Newton
Carruth, Fred Hayden
Carter, John
Carter, Robert
Cary, Edward
Chamberlain, Henry Richardson
Champlin, John Denison

Channing, Edward Tyrrell
Chase, Edna Woolman
Childs, Cephas Grier
Church, William Conant
Cist, Charles
Claiborne, John Francis
    Hamtramck
Clark, Charles Hopkins
Clark, Lewis Gaylord
Clark, Willis Gaylord
Clarke, Helen Archibald
Clarkson, Coker Fifield
Cobb, Frank Irving
Coffin, Robert Peter Tristram
Cohen, John Sanford
Colby, Frank Moore
Colver, William Byron
Cook, Martha Elizabeth Duncan
    Walker
Corcoran, James Andrew
Cornwallis, Kinahan
Costain, Thomas Bertram
Covici, Pascal ("Pat")
Croly, Herbert David
Crooks, George Richard
Croswell, Harry
Crowninshield, Francis Welch
Cunliffe-Owen, Philip Frederick
Dana, Charles Anderson
Dana, Edward Salisbury
Daniels, Josephus
Dart, Henry Paluché
Davenport, Russell Wheeler
Davis, Paulina Kellogg Wright
Davis, Watson
Dawson, Henry Barton
De Bow, James Dunwoody
    Brownson
Deering, Nathaniel
Dell, Floyd James
Dennie, Joseph
De Young, Michel Harry
Dingley, Nelson
Dodge, Mary Elizabeth Mapes
Dole, Nathan Haskell
Doyle, Alexander Patrick
Drake, Benjamin
Drury, John Benjamin
Du Bois, William Edward
    Burghardt
Dunbar, Charles Franklin
Dunning, Albert Elijah
Duyckinck, Evert Augustus
Duyckinck, George Long
Dwight, Henry Otis
Dwight, John Sullivan
Dwight, Theodore
Dymond, John
Edwards, Bela Bates
Elliot, Jonathan
Elliott, Charles
Ellmaker, (Emmett) Lee
Elwell, John Johnson
English, Thomas Dunn
Errett, Isaac
Evans, George Henry

Evans, Thomas
Everett, Alexander Hill
Fanning, Tolbert
Faran, James John
Farley, Harriet
Fauset, Jessie Redmon
Fenno, John
Fernald, James Champlin
Fernow, Berthold
Finley, John Huston
Fiske, Amos Kidder
Fiske, Daniel Willard
Fitzgerald, Thomas
Fitzpatrick, John Clement
Flagg, Azariah Cutting
Fleisher, Benjamin Wilfrid
Florence, Thomas Birch
Flower, Benjamin Orange
Floy, James
Fogg, George Gilman
Folsom, Charles
Ford, Daniel Sharp
Ford, Guy Stanton
Ford, Henry Jones
Forney, Matthias Nace
Foster, Charles James
Foster, Frank Pierce
Foster, John Watson
Foster, Lafayette Sabine
Francis, Charles Spencer
Francis, John Morgan
Frank, Glenn
Frazer, John Fries
Freneau, Philip Morin
Fuller, Andrew S.
Fuller, Joseph Vincent
Funk, Isaac Kauffman
Gaillard, Edwin Samuel
Gallagher, William Davis
Gambrell, James Bruton
Gernsback, Hugo
Gibbs, (Oliver) Wolcott
Gilder, Jeannette Leonard
Gilder, Richard Watson
Gildersleeve, Basil Lanneau
Giles, Chauncey
Gillis, James Martin
Gilpin, Henry Dilworth
Glass, Franklin Potts
Glynn, Martin Henry
Godkin, Edwin Lawrence
Godman, John Davison
Godwin, Parke
Goodhue, James Madison
Goodwin, Elijah
Gordon, Laura De Force
Gould, George Milbry
Graham, George Rex
Grasty, Charles Henry
Greeley, Horace
Green, Thomas
Greene, Nathaniel
Gregory, Daniel Seelye
Griffin, Solomon Bulkley
Griswold, Stanley
Grosvenor, Gilbert Hovey

Gunton, George
Habberton, John
Hackett, Francis
Hahn, Georg Michael Decker
Haines, Lynn
Haldeman-Julius, Emanuel
Hale, Edward Joseph
Hale, Sarah Josepha Buell
Hall, John Elihu
Hall, William Whitty
Hallett, Benjamin Franklin
Hanson, Alexander Contee,
    1786–1819
Hapgood, Norman
Harris, Chapin Aaron
Harris, Joseph
Hart, Edward
Hart, John Seely
Harvey, George Brinton McClellan
Hasbrouck, Lydia Sayer
Hasselquist, Tuve Nilsson
Haswell, Anthony
Haven, Emily Bradley Neal
Hawley, Joseph Roswell
Hayes, Max Sebastian
Hays, Isaac
Hazard, Ebenezer
Hazard, Samuel
Heaton, John Langdon
Helmer, Bessie Bradwell
Hepworth, George Hughes
Herbermann, Charles George
Herrick, Sophia McIlvaine Bledsoe
Hewett, Waterman Thomas
Hicks, John, 1847–1917
High, Stanley Hoflund
Hildreth, Richard
Hill, Isaac
Hinman, George Wheeler
Hinsdale, Burke Aaron
Hoard, William Dempster
Hobby, William Pettus
Hoffman, Charles Fenno
Holland, Josiah Gilbert
Holmes, Ezekiel
Holt, Hamilton Bowen
Hooker, Donald Russell
Hooper, Lucy Hamilton
Horr, George Edwin
Howard, Edgar
Howe, Mark Antony De Wolfe
Howell, Evan Park
Howell, James Bruen
Hubbard, Elbert
Hudson, Daniel Eldred
Hughes, Robert William
Hunt, Freeman
Hunt, William Gibbes
Huntington, Jedediah Vincent
Hunton, George Kenneth
Hunton, William Lee
Hurlbut, Jesse Lyman
Hutchinson, Paul
Hutton, Laurence
Inman, John
Jackson, Henry Rootes

Jackson, Joseph Henry
Jameson, John Franklin
Jarves, James Jackson
Jenkins, Howard Malcolm
Jenkins, John Stilwell
Jeter, Jeremiah Bell
Johnson, Allen
Johnson, John Albert
Johnson, Oliver
Johnson, Robert Underwood
Johnson, Willis Fletcher
Jones, Jenkins Lloyd
Jones, Thomas P.
Jordan, John Woolf
Jordan, William George
Joseffy, Rafael
Kaempffert, Waldemar Bernhard
Keating, John Marie
Kellogg, Paul Underwood
Kent, William
Kephart, Isaiah Lafayette
Kerney, James
Kettell, Samuel
Keyes, Frances Parkinson
King, Alexander
King, Charles
King, Horatio
King, Rufus
King of William, James
Kinsella, Thomas
Kirchoff, Charles William Henry
Kirk, John Foster
Kline, George
Knopf, Blanche Wolf
Kohlsaat, Herman Henry
Kreymborg, Alfred Francis
Kurtz, Benjamin
LaFarge, John
Lamb, Martha Joanna Reade Nash
Lamont, Hammond
Lane, Gertrude Battles
Lange, Louis
Lathrop, George Parsons
Lawson, James
Learned, Marion Dexter
Leavitt, Joshua
Lee, James Melvin
Lee, James Wideman
Leeser, Isaac
Levin, Lewis Charles
Lewis, Charlton Thomas
Lewis, Enoch
Lewisohn, Ludwig
Liggett, Walter William
Linn, William Alexander
Littell, Eliakim
Littledale, Clara Savage
Loos, Charles Louis
Lord, Chester Sanders
Lossing, Benson John
Loveman, Amy
Lovett, Robert Morss
Luce, Henry Robinson
Lummis, Charles Fletcher
Mabie, Hamilton Wright
McAdams, Clark

MacArthur, Robert Stuart
McCaw, James Brown
M'Clintock, John
McClure, Alexander Kelly
McClure, Alexander Wilson
McClure, Samuel Sidney
McCord, David James
McCullough, Ernest
McElroy, John
McKelway, St. Clair
McKinley, Albert Edward
Maclay, William Brown
McLeod, Alexander
McMichael, Morton
McPherson, Edward
McQuillen, John Hugh
Mansfield, Edward Deering
Marble, Manton Malone
Marsh, Charles Wesley
Martin, Franklin Henry
Martin, Thomas Commerford
Masson, Thomas Lansing
Mead, Edwin Doak
Medary, Samuel
Meigs, Josiah
Melcher, Frederic Gershom
Mencken, Henry Louis
Merrill, William Bradford
Metcalf, Henry Harrison
Mich, Daniel Danforth
Miller, Charles Ransom
Miller, David Hunter
Miller, Emily Clark Huntington
Miller, James Russell
Miller, John Henry
Miner, Charles
Minor, Benjamin Blake
Mitchell, Edward Page
Mitchell, Isaac
Mitchell, John Ames
Money, Hernando De Soto
Monroe, Harriet
Montgomery, William Bell
Moody, John
Moore, Frank
Moore, John Weeks
Morley, Christopher Darlington
Morris, Edmund
Morse, John Torrey
Morton, Charles Walter
Moses, Montrose Jonas
Mosessohn, David Nehemiah
Moss, Lemuel
Munn, Orson Desaix
Muñoz-Rivera, Luis
Nancrède, Paul Joseph Guérard de
Nast, William
Nathan, George Jean
Neal, John
Nelson, Henry Loomis
Nevin, Alfred
Newcomb, Harvey
Newell, William Wells
Newton, Robert Safford
Ng Poon Chew
Nichols, Clarina Irene Howard

Nichols, Thomas Low
Nicola, Lewis
Nieman, Lucius William
Niles, Hezekiah
Niles, John Milton
Nock, Albert Jay
North, Simon Newton Dexter
Northen, William Jonathan
Norton, Charles Eliot
Oakes, George Washington Ochs
O'Brien, Robert Lincoln
Ogg, Frederic Austin
Older, Fremont
O'Reilly, Henry
O'Reilly, John Boyle
Osborn, Norris Galpin
Otis, George Alexander
Oursler, (Charles) Fulton
Packard, Frederick Adolphus
Packer, William Fisher
Paley, John
Palfrey, John Gorham
Pallen, Condé Benoist
Palmore, William Beverly
Parkhurst, Charles
Passavant, William Alfred
Patterson, Robert Mayne
Patterson, Thomas MacDonald
Paul, Elliot Harold
Payne, John Howard
Peck, George
Peck, Harry Thurston
Pedder, James
Peirce, Bradford Kinney
Peloubet, Francis Nathan
Pendleton, William Kimbrough
Perché, Napoleon Joseph
Perkins, Frederic Beecher
Perkins, George Douglas
Perkins, Maxwell Evarts
Perry, Bliss
Peters, Absalom
Peterson, Charles Jacobs
Peterson, Henry
Phillips, John Sanburn
Pickard, Samuel Thomas
Pierson, Arthur Tappan
Pilcher, Lewis Stephen
Pinckney, Henry Laurens
Pinkerton, Lewis Letig
Pinkney, Edward Coote
Polk, Leonidas Lafayette
Pollak, Gustav
Pomeroy, Marcus Mills
Pond, George Edward
Poore, Benjamin Perley
Potter, William James
Powell, John Benjamin
Pratt, Eliza Anna Farman
Pratt, Sereno Stansbury
Presser, Theodore
Price, Thomas Frederick
Prime, Samuel Irenaeus
Pulitzer, Joseph, Jr.
Purple, Samuel Smith
Putnam, Eben

Quick, John Herbert
Raguet, Condy
Raymond, Henry Jarvis
Raymond, Rossiter Worthington
Redman, Ben Ray
Redpath, James
Reed, David
Reid, Gilbert
Reid, John Morrison
Reiersen, Johan Reinert
Reitzel, Robert
Rémy, Henri
Rhoades, James E.
Rice, Edwin Wilbur
Rideing, William Henry
Ripley, George
Robertson, James Alexander
Robinson, Charles Seymour
Robinson, Stuart
Rombro, Jacob
Ross, Charles Griffith
Ross, Harold Wallace
Rothwell, Richard Pennefather
Rowlands, William
Rublee, Horace
Rupp, William
Sanders, Daniel Jackson
Sanger, George Partridge
Sangster, Margaret Elizabeth
  Munson
Saunders, William Laurence
Sawyer, Thomas Jefferson
Saxton, Eugene Francis
Schem, Alexander Jacob
Schnauffer, Carl Heinrich
Schouler, William
Schultze, Augustus
Schuster, Max Lincoln
Schuyler, Robert Livingston
Schwimmer, Rosika
Scott, Harvey Whitefield
Screws, William Wallace
Scudder, Horace Elisha
Scull, John
Seymour, Horatio Winslow
Shattuck, George Brune
Shea, John Dawson Gilmary
Sherwood, Isaac Ruth
Shields, George Oliver
Shreve, Thomas Hopkins
Sigel, Franz
Silverman, Sime
Simpson, Stephen
Singerly, William Miskey
Singleton, Esther
Sloan, Harold Paul
Smalley, Eugene Virgil
Smith, Benjamin Eli
Smith, Charles Perrin
Smith, Edmund Munroe
Smith, Elias
Smith, Elihu Hubbard
Smith, John Augustine
Smith, John Cotton, 1826–1882
Smith, John Jay
Smith, Lillian Eugenia

Smith, Lloyd Pearsall
Smith, Samuel Francis
Smith, Uriah
Smyth, Albert Henry
Snow, Carmel White
Spahr, Charles Barzillai
Sparks, Jared
Spivak, Charles David
Spooner, Shearjashub
Sprague, Charles Arthur
Stanard, William Glover
Stanwood, Edward
Stauffer, David McNeely
Stedman, Edmund Clarence
Stephens, Ann Sophia
Stephens, Edwin William
Steuben, John
Stevens, Abel
Stoddard, Richard Henry
Stoddart, Joseph Marshall
Stone, David Marvin
Stone, Richard French
Storey, Wilbur Fisk
Stovall, Pleasant Alexander
Street, Joseph Montfort
Stuart, Charles Macaulay
Summers, Thomas Osmond
Swisshelm, Jane Grey Cannon
Talmage, Thomas De Witt
Taylor, Marshall William
Teall, Francis Augustus
Tenney, William Jewett
Thatcher, Benjamin Bussey
Thayer, Thomas Baldwin
Thayer, William Makepeace
Thomas, John Jacobs
Thomas, Robert Bailey
Thompson, John Reuben
Thompson, Joseph Parrish
Thompson, Thomas Larkin
Thompson, William Tappan
Thomson, Edward
Thomson, Edward William
Thrasher, John Sidney
Thurber, George
Thurston, Lorrin Andrews
Thwaites, Reuben Gold
Tigert, John James
Tilton, Theodore
Todd, Henry Alfred
Torrence, Frederick Ridgely
Towne, Charles Hanson
Tracy, Joseph
Trumbull, Henry Clay
Tucker, Gilbert Milligan
Turner, George Kibbe
Turner, Henry McNeal
Turner, Josiah
Tyler, Robert
Underwood, Benjamin Franklin
Updegraff, David Brainard
Vanderlip, Frank Arthur
Van Doren, Irita Bradford
Villard, Oswald Garrison
Vizetelly, Frank Horace
Vogrich, Max Wilhelm Karl

Walker, James Barr
Wallace, Henry
Waller, John Lightfoot
Walsh, Henry Collins
Walsh, Michael
Walsh, Thomas
Ward, Cyrenus Osborne
Ware, Ashur
Ware, John
Warner, Charles Dudley
Warren, Israel Perkins
Watson, Henry Clay
Watson, Henry Cood
Watterson, Harvey Magee
Watterson, Henry
Wellington, Arthur Mellen
Wentworth, John, 1815–1888
Wertenbaker, Charles Christian
Wharton, Francis
Whedon, Daniel Denison
Wheelock, Joseph Albert
Whelpley, Henry Milton
Whitaker, Charles Harris
Whitaker, Daniel Kimball
White, Charles Ignatius
White, William Allen
White, William Nathaniel
Whitney, Caspar
Whittelsey, Abigail Goodrich
Whittemore, Thomas
Wiggin, James Henry
Willcox, Louise Collier
Williams, Charles Richard
Williams, Jesse Lynch
Willis, Henry Parker
Willis, Nathaniel
Willis, Nathaniel Parker
Wilson, George Grafton
Wilson, James Grant
Wilson, James Southall
Winchester, Caleb Thomas
Winchevsky, Morris
Winkler, Edwin Theodore
Winship, Albert Edward
Wise, Daniel
Woodruff, Lorande Loss
Woodruff, William Edward
Worcester, Noah
Wright, John Stephen
Wright, Marcus Joseph
Wright, Robert William
Wurtz, Henry
Wyeth, John
Yeadon, Richard
Yost, Casper Salathiel
Youmans, Edward Livingston
Youmans, William Jay
Young, Jesse Bowman
Young, Lafayette
Zahniser, Howard Clinton
Zevin, Israel Joseph
Ziff, William Bernard
EDITOR (AGRICULTURAL) (See also
  AGRICULTURIST)
Aiken, David Wyatt
Brown, Simon

Coburn, Foster Dwight
Gaylord, Willis
Judd, Orange
Myrick, Herbert
Skinner, John Stuart
Stockbridge, Horace Edward
Wiley, David
EDITOR (ANARCHIST)
Goldman, Emma
EDITOR (MAGAZINE)
Brady, Mildred Alice Edie
Lorimer, George Horace
Patrick, Edwin Hill ("Ted")
Patterson, Alicia
Sedgwick, Ellery
Woodward, Robert Simpson
EDITOR (MEDICAL)
Jelliffe, Smith Ely
Simmons, George Henry
EDITOR (NEWSPAPER)
Abbott, Robert Sengstacke
Bingay, Malcolm Wallace
Bovard, Oliver Kirby
Brokenshire, Norman Ernest
Freeman, Douglas Southall
Gauvreau, Emile Henry
Goddard, Morrill
Howard, Joseph Kinsey
Howe, Edgar Watson
Howell, Clark
Johnson, Albert
Lait, Jacquin Leonard (Jack)
McClatchy, Charles Kenny
Ogden, Rollo
Patterson, Eleanor Medill
Pulitzer, Ralph
Reid, Ogden Mills
Shedd, Fred Fuller
Smith, Henry Justin
EDITOR (SCIENCE)
Blakeslee, Howard Walter
Cattell, James McKeen
Woodward, Robert Simpson
EDUCATOR (See also COLLEGE
  PRESIDENT, PROFESSOR,
  SCHOLAR, TEACHER)
Abbot, Benjamin
Abbot, Gorham Dummer
Abbott, Edith
Abbott, Jacob
Adams, Daniel
Adams, Ebenezer
Adams, John
Adler, Felix
Agassiz, Elizabeth Cabot Cary
Aggrey, James Emman Kwegyir
Aiken, Charles Augustus
Akeley, Mary Leonore
Alcott, Amos Bronson
Alcott, William Andrus
Alden, Joseph
Alderman, Edwin Anderson
Aldrich, Charles Anderson
Alexander, Archibald
Alexander, Joseph Addison
Alison, Francis

Allen, Alexander Viets Griswold
Allen, George
Allen, William
Allen, Young John
Allinson, Anne Crosby Emery
Allyn, Robert
Alvord, Henry Elijah
Ames, Herman Vandenburg
Ames, James Barr
Anderson, David Lawrence
Anderson, Victor Vance
Andrews, John
Andrews, Lorrin
Andrus, Ethel Percy
Angela, Mother
Anthon, Charles Edward
Apple, Thomas Gilmore
Appleton, Jesse
Armstrong, Samuel Chapman
Arnold, Thurman Wesley
Atkinson, George Henry
Atwater, Lyman Hotchkiss
Azarias, Brother
Backus, Truman Jay
Bagley, William Chandler
Bailey, Ebenezer
Bailey, Liberty Hyde
Baker, Daniel
Baldwin, Elihu Whittlesey
Baldwin, Joseph
Baldwin, Theron
Bancroft, Cecil Franklin Patch
Banister, Zilpah Polly Grant
Bapst, John
Barbour, Clarence Augustus
Bardeen, Charles William
Barnard, Henry
Barnes, Mary Downing Sheldon
Barnwell, Robert Woodward
Barrett, Janie Porter
Bateman, Newton
Bates, Arlo
Bates, Katharine Lee
Bates, Samuel Penniman
Baxter, William
Beadle, William Henry Harrison
Beals, Ralph Albert
Beard, Mary
Beard, Richard
Beatty, Willard Walcott
Beckwith, Clarence Augustine
Beecher, Catharine Esther
Beers, Henry Augustin
Bell, Alexander Graham
Bell, Alexander Melville
Bell, Bernard Iddings
Bell, Eric Temple
Bemis, Harold Edward
Benedict, Erastus Cornelius
Benson, Oscar Herman
Benton, Thomas Hart
Berry, Edward Wilber
Berry, Martha McChesney
Bestor, Arthur Eugene
Bickmore, Albert Smith
Bigelow, Harry Augustus

Bigelow, Melville Madison
Bingham, William
Binkley, Wilfred Ellsworth
Bishop, Nathan
Bishop, Robert Hamilton
Blalock, Alfred
Blaustein, David
Bliss, Daniel
Bliss, Gilbert Ames
Bliss, Howard Sweetser
Bode, Boyd Henry
Bond, Elizabeth Powell
Bonney, Charles Carroll
Bosworth, Edward Increase
Bourne, Edward Gaylord
Bowden, John
Bowman, Thomas
Boyce, James Petigru
Boyd, David French
Boyd, Thomas Duckett
Boyesen, Hjalmar Hjorth
Brace, John Pierce
Brackett, Anna Callender
Brackett, Jeffrey Richardson
Bradford, Edward Hickling
Bradley, Charles Henry
Brainard, Daniel
Brainerd, Ezra
Brattle, William
Breaux, Joseph Arsenne
Briggs, LeBaron Russell
Brigham, Mary Ann
Brightman, Edgar Sheffield
Bronson, Walter Cochrane
Brookings, Robert Somers
Brooks, Charles
Brough, Charles Hillman
Brown, Charles Rufus
Brown, Charlotte Hawkins
Brown, George
Brown, George Pliny
Brown, Samuel Robbins
Browne, William Hand
Bruce, Robert
Brumby, Richard Trapier
Bryant, Joseph Decatur
Bryant, Ralph Clement
Bryson, Lyman Lloyd
Buchanan, Joseph
Buchanan, Scott Milross
Buehler, Huber Gray
Bulkley, John Williams
Bumstead, Horace
Burk, Frederic Lister
Burleson, Rufus Clarence
Burnam, John Miller
Burr, William Hubert
Burroughs, John Curtis
Burrowes, Thomas Henry
Burt, Mary Elizabeth
Buttrick, Wallace
Buttz, Henry Anson
Cabell, James Lawrence
Cady, Sarah Louise Ensign
Caldwell, Otis William
Calhoun, William Barron

Calkins, Norman Allison
Camp, David Nelson
Canby, Henry Seidel
Canfield, James Hulme
Cannon, James
Capen, Samuel Paul
Carmichael, Oliver Cromwell
Carnap, Rudolf
Carpenter, George Rice
Carpenter, Stephen Haskins
Carter, James Gordon
Carver, George Washington
Chamberlain, Joshua Lawrence
Chamberlin, Edward Hastings
Chandler, Julian Alvin Carroll
Channing, Edward Tyrrell
Chase, Harry Woodburn
Chase, Irah
Chavis, John
Cheever, Ezekiel
Church, Alonzo
Church, Irving Porter
Clark, Felton Grandison
Claypole, Edward Waller
Clement, Rufus Early
Clewell, John Henry
Cloud, Henry Roe
Cobb, Lyman
Coe, George Albert
Coffin, Henry Sloane
Coffman, Lotus Delta
Colburn, Dana Pond
Coleman, Lyman
Colton, Elizabeth Avery
Colvin, Stephen Sheldon
Conklin, Edwin Grant
Conover, Obadiah Milton
Cook, George Hammell
Cook, John Williston
Cooley, Edwin Gilbert
Cooley, Mortimer Elwyn
Cooper, Thomas
Cooper, William John
Cooper-Poucher, Matilda S.
Coppée, Henry
Coppens, Charles
Cox, Samuel Hanson
Craig, Austin
Craighead, Edwin Boone
Crandall, Prudence
Crary, Isaac Edwin
Crooks, George Richard
Crunden, Frederick Morgan
Cubberley, Ellwood Patterson
Curry, Jabez Lamar Monroe
Curtis, Edwards Lewis
Dagg, John Leadley
Darby, John
Dawley, Almena
Day, Edmund Ezra
Day, Henry Noble
Day, James Roscoe
Day, Jeremiah
Dean, Amos
Denny, George Vernon, Jr.
Deutsch, Gotthard

Dewey, Chester
Dewey, John
Dickinson, John
Dickinson, John Woodbridge
Dickson, Leonard Eugene
Dillard, James Hardy
Diman, Jeremiah Lewis
Dimitry, Alexander
Dinwiddie, Albert Bledsoe
Doak, Samuel
Dod, Thaddeus
Dodge, Ebenezer
Donovan, James Britt
Dorchester, Daniel
Dove, David James
Downey, John
Draper, Andrew Sloan
Drinker, Cecil Kent
Drisler, Henry
Drown, Thomas Messinger
Dunham, Henry Morton
Dutton, Samuel Train
Dwight, Benjamin Woodbridge
Dwight, Francis
Dwight, Nathaniel
Dwight, Sereno Edwards
Dwight, Theodore, 1796–1866
Dwight, Theodore William
Dwight, Timothy
Dyer, Isadore
Dykstra, Clarence Addison
Earle, Edward Mead
Earle, Mortimer Lamson
Earle, Ralph
Eastman, Harvey Gridley
Eaton, Amos
Eaton, John
Edwards, Ninian Wirt
Eigenmann, Carl H.
Eliot, Charles William
Elman, Robert
Elvehjem, Conrad Arnold
Emerson, Benjamin Kendall
Emerson, George Barrell
Emerson, Joseph
Emerton, Ephraim
Erdman, Charles Rosenbury
Esbjörn, Lars Paul
Espy, James Pollard
Ewell, Benjamin Stoddert
Fairchild, Fred Rogers
Fairchild, George Thompson
Fairchild, James Harris
Fairfield, Edmund Burke
Fairlie, John Archibald
Fanning, Tolbert
Fay, Sidney Bradshaw
Ferguson, John Calvin
Ferris, Woodbridge Nathan
Fess, Simeon Davidson
Few, William Preston
Fillebrown, Thomas
Finley, John Huston
Finley, Robert
Finn, Francis James
Finney, Charles Grandison

Fisher, Ebenezer
Fisk, Wilbur
Fiske, George Converse
Fite, Warner
Fitzpatrick, Morgan Cassius
Fleming, Walter Lynwood
Fletcher, Robert
Flexner, Abraham
Follen, Charles
Ford, Guy Stanton
Fortier, Alcée
Foss, Cyrus David
Foster, George Burman
Fowle, William Bentley
Frame, Alice Seymour Browne
Francis, Convers
Frank, Philipp G.
Frazier, Edward Franklin
Frear, William
Friedlaender, Walter Ferdinand
Frissell, Hollis Burke
Fuertes, Estevan Antonio
Furman, Richard
Furst, Clyde Bowman
Gale, George Washington
Galloway, Samuel
Gambrell, James Bruton
Garland, Landon Cabell
Garnet, Henry Highland
Garnett, James Mercer
Garrett, William Robertson
Gasson, Thomas Ignatius
Gates, George Augustus
Gauss, Christian Frederick
Giddings, Franklin Henry
Giesler-Anneke, Mathilde Franziska
Gildersleeve, Virginia Crocheron
Gill, Laura Drake
Gillespie, William Mitchell
Gillett, Ezra Hall
Gilman, Arthur
Gilmer, Francis Walker
Going, Jonathan
Goldbeck, Robert
Goodale, George Lincoln
Goodell, Henry Hill
Goodnow, Isaac Tichenor
Goodrich, Annie Warburton
Goodrich, Chauncey Allen
Goodrich, Elizur
Goodspeed, Thomas Wakefield
Gordy, John Pancoast
Goss, James Walker
Gove, Aaron Estellus
Grady, Henry Francis
Graham, Evarts Ambrose
Gray, John Chipman
Gray, William Scott, Jr.
Green, Lewis Warner
Green, Samuel Bowdlear
Greene, Charles Ezra
Greene, George Washington
Greene, Samuel Stillman
Greener, Richard Theodore
Greenlaw, Edwin Almiron
Greenleaf, Benjamin

Gregg, Alan
Gregory, Charles Noble
Gregory, Daniel Seelye
Gregory, John Milton
Griffis, William Elliot
Grimké, Thomas Smith
Gros, John Daniel
Gross, Charles
Grossmann, Louis
Guérin, Anne-Thérèse
Guilford, Nathan
Gurney, Ephraim Whitman
Guthe, Karl Eugen
Haas, Francis Joseph
Haddock, Charles Brickett
Hale, Benjamin
Hall, Arethusa
Hall, Baynard Rush
Hall, Granville Stanley
Hall, Samuel Read
Hall, Willard
Hallowell, Benjamin
Hamlin, Cyrus
Hamlin, Talbot Faulkner
Hammond, William Gardiner
Hanus, Paul Henry
Hare, George Emlen
Harlow, Ralph Volney
Harper, William Rainey
Harpur, Robert
Harrell, John
Harrington, Charles
Harris, George
Harris, Samuel
Harris, William Torrey
Harrison, Charles Custis
Hart, Edward
Hart, John Seely
Hartranft, Chester David
Hasselquist, Tuve Nilsson
Haven, Erastus Otis
Hawkins, Dexter Arnold
Hawley, Gideon, 1785–1870
Hawley, Willis Chatman
Hayden, Amos Sutton
Haygood, Atticus Green
Heiss, Michael
Henck, John Benjamin
Henry, Caleb Sprague
Henry, Robert
Hewett, Waterman Thomas
Hibben, John Grier
Hill, Daniel Harvey
Hill, Frank Alpine
Hill, Henry Barker
Hill, John Henry
Hill, Patty Smith
Hill, Walter Barnard
Hills, Elijah Clarence
Himes, Charles Francis
Hinman, George Wheeler
Hinsdale, Burke Aaron
Hitchcock, Edward, 1793–1864
Hitchcock, Edward, 1828–1911
Hitchcock, Roswell Dwight
Hocking, William Ernest

Hoerr, Normand Louis
Hoffman, Eugene Augustus
Hoge, Moses
Hogue, Wilson Thomas
Holbrook, Alfred
Holcombe, James Philemon
Holland, William Jacob
Holley, Horace
Hollis, Ira Nelson
Holmes, Ezekiel
Holmes, George Frederick
Hope, John
Hopkins, Isaac Stiles
Hopkins, Mark
Horr, George Edwin
Hoshour, Samuel Klinefelter
Houston, David Franklin
Houston, Edwin James
Hovey, Alvah
Hovey, Charles Edward
Howard, Ada Lydia
Howe, George
Howe, Herbert Alonzo
Howland, Emily
Hoyt, John Wesley
Huber, Gotthelf Carl
Humphreys, Alexander Crombie
Hunt, Carleton
Hunt, Mary Hannah Hanchett
Hunt, Nathan
Hunter, Thomas
Huntington, Margaret Jane Evans
Hutchins, Harry Burns
Hyde, William DeWitt
Inglis, Alexander James
Irvine, William Mann
Irwin, Elisabeth Antoinette
Irwin, Robert Benjamin
Jackman, Wilbur Samuel
Jackson, Dugald Caleb
Jackson, Edward Payson
Jackson, Mercy Ruggles Bisbe
Jacobi, Mary Corinna Putnam
Jacobs, Michael
Jacobson, John Christian
Janes, Lewis George
Jaquess, James Frazier
Jardine, William Marion
Jay, Allen
Jeffrey, Edward Charles
Jesse, Richard Henry
Jessup, Walter Albert
Jewett, Milo Parker
Johnson, Charles Spurgeon
Johnson, David Bancroft
Johnson, Edward Austin
Johnson, Ellen Cheney
Johnson, Franklin
Johnson, George
Johnson, James Weldon
Johnson, Joseph French
Johnson, Wendell Andrew Leroy
Johnson, William Bullein
Johnston, Henry Phelps
Johnston, Richard Malcolm
Johnston, Robert Matteson

Johnston, William Preston
Johnstone, Edward Ransom
Jones, Richard Foster
Jones, William Patterson
Joynes, Edward Southey
Judson, Harry Pratt
Julia, Sister
Junkin, George
Kafer, John Christian
Keagy, John Miller
Keener, William Albert
Keep, Robert Porter
Kefauver, Grayson Neikirk
Kent, Charles Foster
Key, Valdimer Orlando, Jr.
Kidder, Daniel Parish
Kilpatrick, William Heard
Kimball, Dexter Simpson
King, Henry Churchill
Kingsbury, John
Kingsley, James Luce
Kinnicutt, Leonard Parker
Kirby-Smith, Edmund
Kirchwey, George Washington
Kirkland, James Hampton
Knox, George William
Knox, Samuel
Kohlmann, Anthony
Krapp, George Philip
Kraus, John
Kraus-Boelté, Maria
Krauth, Charles Porterfield
Krüsi, Johann Heinrich Hermann
La Borde, Maximilian
Lacy, Drury
Lacy, Ernest
Lamont, Hammond
Lane, James Henry
Langdon, Courtney
Lange, Alexis Frederick
Langley, John Williams
Langston, John Mercer
Larkin, John
Larrabee, William Clark
Larsen, Peter Laurentius
Latané, John Holladay
Lathrop, John Hiram
Latourette, Kenneth Scott
Law, Evander McIvor
Laws, Samuel Spahr
Lawson, Andrew Cowper
Leach, Daniel Dyer
Leathers, Waller Smith
Lee, George Washington Custis
Lee, Stephen Dill
Leipziger, Henry Marcus
Leland, George Adams
Leonard, Levi Washburn
Leonard, Robert Josselyn
Leonard, Sterling Andrus
Levermore, Charles Herbert
Lewis, Clarence Irving
Lewis, Enoch
Lewis, Exum Percival
Lewis, Oscar
Lewis, Samuel

Lieber, Francis
Lindeman, Eduard Christian
Lindsley, John Berrien
Lindsley, Philip
Lipman, Jacob Goodale
Listemann, Bernhard
Littlefield, George Washington
Livingston, John Henry
Locke, Alain Leroy
Locke, Bessie
Longcope, Warfield Theobald
Longstreet, Augustus Baldwin
Lord, Asa Dearborn
Lord, Chester Sanders
Loughridge, Robert McGill
Lovell, John Epy
Lovett, Robert Morss
Lowes, John Livingston
Lowrey, Mark Perrin
Luce, Henry Winters
Lutkin, Peter Christian
Lyon, David Gordon
Lyon, Mary
Maas, Anthony J.
McAfee, John Armstrong
MacAlister, James
McAnally, David Rice
McAndrew, William
McAuley, Thomas
McCaleb, Theodore Howard
McCartee, Divie Bethune
McCartney, Washington
McClellan, Henry Brainerd
McClenahan, Howard
M'Clintock, John
McCook, John James
McCormick, Samuel Black
MacCracken, Henry Mitchell
McDonald, James Grover
McDowell, John
McFarland, John Thomas
McFarland, Samuel Gamble
McGarvey, John William
McGuffey, William Holmes
McHale, Kathryn
McIver, Charles Duncan
Mackenzie, James Cameron
McKenzie, Robert Tait
MacLean, George Edwin
Maclean, John
McMurry, Frank Morton
MacVicar Malcolm
Mahan, Dennis Hart
Mahan, Milo
Main, John Hanson Thomas
Malcom, Howard
Manly, Basil, 1798–1868
Manly, Basil, 1825–1892
Mann, Horace
Mann, Mary Tyler Peabody
Mannes, Clara Damrosch
Mannes, David
Marble, Albert Prescott
Marks, Elias
Marshall, James Fowle Baldwin
Martin, Everett Dean

Martin, William Alexander Parsons
Mason, John Mitchell
Maxwell, William Henry
Mayo, Amory Dwight
Meany, Edmond Stephen
Mears, John William
Meigs, John
Meigs, Josiah
Meiklejohn, Alexander
Mell, Patrick Hues
Mendenhall, Thomas Corwin
Menetrey, Joseph
Mengarini, Gregory
Mercer, Margaret
Merrick, Frederick
Merrill, James Griswold
Messer, Asa
Mezes, Sidney Edward
Michel, Virgil George
Michie, Peter Smith
Middleton, Thomas Cooke
Milledoler, Philip
Miller, Emily Clark Huntington
Miller, Kelly
Miller, Leslie William
Miller, Samuel
Milligan, Robert
Millikan, Robert Andrews
Mills, Cyrus Taggart
Mills, Susan Lincoln Tolman
Miner, Myrtilla
Minor, Benjamin Blake
Minot, Charles Sedgwick
Mitchell, Albert Graeme
Mitchell, Lucy Sprague
Molyneux, Robert
Monis, Judah
Monroe, Paul
Montague, William Pepperell
Mood, Francis Asbury
Moody, William Vaughn
Moore, James, 1764–1814
Moore, Joseph Earle
Morgan, Thomas Jefferson
Morley, Margaret Warner
Morris, Edward Dafydd
Morris, George Sylvester
Morrison, John Irwin
Morse, Anson Daniel
Morton, Robert Russa
Mosher, Eliza Maria
Moss, Lemuel
Mott, Frank Luther
Mowry, William Augustus
Mullins, Edgar Young
Munro, William Bennett
Murfee, James Thomas
Murray, David
Muste, Abraham Johannes
Muzzey, David Saville
Nash, Charles Sumner
Nason, Henry Bradford
Neef, Francis Joseph Nicholas
Neill, Edward Duffield
Neill, William
Nelson, David

Nelson, Reuben
Nevin, Edwin Henry
Nevin, John Williamson
Newlon, Jesse Homer
Newman, Albert Henry
Nicholls, Rhoda Holmes
Niebuhr, Helmut Richard
Nobili, John
Norris, Mary Harriott
Norsworthy, Naomi
North, Edward
North, Simeon, 1802–1884
Northend, Charles
Northrop, Birdsey Grant
Norton, John Pitkin
Noss, Theodore Bland
Notestein, Wallace
Nott, Henry Junius
Notz, Frederick William Augustus
Noyes, Clara Dutton
Nutting, Mary Adelaide
O'Callahan, Joseph Timothy
Odell, George Clinton Densmore
Ogden, Robert Curtis
O'Gorman, Thomas
Olin, Stephen
Orcutt, Hiram
Orr, Gustavus John
Orton, Edward Francis Baxter
Orton, James
Osborn, Henry Fairfield
O'Shea, Michael Vincent
Overstreet, Harry Allen
Owen, Edward Thomas
Owre, Alfred
Pace, Edward Aloysius
Packard, Silas Sadler
Page, David Perkins
Page, Leigh
Palmer, Alice Elvira Freeman
Palmer, Walter Walker
Pardow, William O'Brien
Park, Roswell
Parker, Amasa Junius
Parker, Francis Wayland
Parker, Samuel Chester
Parrish, Celestia Susannah
Partridge, Alden
Patri, Angelo
Patterson, James Kennedy
Patterson, James Willis
Payne, Bruce Ryburn
Payne, William Harold
Peabody, Cecil Hobart
Peabody, Elizabeth Palmer
Peabody, Endicott
Peabody, Selim Hobart
Pearce, Richard Mills
Pearson, Eliphalet
Peers, Benjamin Orrs
Peirce, Cyrus
Peirce, James Mills
Pendleton, James Madison
Penniman, James Hosmer
Pepper, William
Perkins, George Henry

Perry, Ralph Barton
Perry, Rufus Lewis
Perry, Thomas Sergeant
Perry, Walter Scott
Perry, William Flake
Phelps, Almira Hart Lincoln
Phelps, William Franklin
Pickens, William
Pierce, George Foster
Pierce, John Davis
Pinney, Norman
Poor, John
Porter, Ebenezer
Porter, James Davis
Porter, Noah
Post, Truman Marcellus
Potamian, Brother
Powell, John Wesley
Powell, William Bramwell
Pratt, Richard Henry
Priestley, James
Priestley, Joseph
Prosser, Charles Smith
Proud, Robert
Puryear, Bennet
Putnam, Helen Cordelia
Quinby, Isaac Ferdinand
Quinn, Arthur Hobson
Rademacher, Hans
Rambaut, Mary Lucinda Bonney
Randall, Henry Stephens
Randall, Samuel Sidwell
Rauch, Frederick Augustus
Rautenstrauch, Walter
Raymond, George Lansing
Raymond, Miner
Read, Daniel, 1805–1878
Redfield, Robert
Regan, Agnes Gertrude
Reichel, Charles Gotthold
Reichel, William Cornelius
Reichenbach, Hans
Reid, David Boswell
Reid, Ira De Augustine
Reid, William Shields
Reilly, Marion
Reinsch, Paul Samuel
Remsen, Ira
Reuter, Dominic
Revel, Bernard
Revels, Hiram Rhoades
Rice, John Holt
Rice, Luther
Rice, Victor Moreau
Rice, William North
Richard, Gabriel
Richard, James William
Richards, Zalmon
Richardson, Tobias Gibson
Ricketts, Palmer Chamberlaine
Ridpath, John Clark
Riley, Benjamin Franklin
Roark, Rurio Nevel
Robb, William Lispenard
Roberts, William Charles
Robertson, Alice Mary

Robertson, William Schenck
Robins, Henry Ephraim
Robinson, Ezekiel Gilman
Robinson, George Canby
Robinson, Stillman Williams
Robinson, William Callyhan
Rogers, Henry Darwin
Rogers, Henry Wade
Rogers, James Blythe
Rogers, John Almanza Rowley
Rogers, Robert Empie
Rogers William Barton
Rohé, George Henry
Rölvaag, Ole Edvart
Ross, Denman Waldo
Rowson, Susanna Haswell
Ruffner, Henry
Ruffner, William Henry
Rugg, Harold Ordway
Russell, James Earl
Russell, James Solomon
Russell, William
Russwurm, John Brown
Rust, Richard Sutton
Ruter, Martin
Ryland, Robert
Saarinen, Gottlieb Eliel
Sachs, Julius
Safford, James Merrill
St. John, Charles Edward
Salisbury, Albert
Salisbury, Rollin D.
Salmon, Lucy Maynard
Sanborn, Edwin David
Sanders, Billington McCarter
Sanders, Charles Walton
Sanders, Daniel Clarke
Sanders, Daniel Jackson
Sartain, Emily
Sawyer, Thomas Jefferson
Scarborough, Lee Rutland
Schaeffer, Nathan Christ
Schlatter, Michael
Schmucker, Samuel Simon
Schodde, George Henry
Schultze, Augustus
Schuyler, Robert Livingston
Scopes, John Thomas
Scott, Austin
Scott, Emmett Jay
Scott, Walter Dill
Scott, William Anderson
Scovell, Melville Amasa
Sears, Barnas
Seelye, Julius Hawley
Shafer, Helen Almira
Shahan, Thomas Joseph
Shaler, Nathaniel Southgate
Sharp, Dallas Lore
Shaw, Edward Richard
Sheldon, Edward Austin
Sheldon, William Evarts
Shellabarger, Samuel
Sherman, Stuart Pratt
Sherwin, Thomas
Sherwood, Adiel

Shields, Thomas Edward
Shipp, Albert Micajah
Shipp, Scott
Shoup, Francis Asbury
Skinner, Charles Rufus
Skinner, Thomas Harvey
Slade, William
Sloane, William Milligan
Smart, James Henry
Smiley, Albert Keith
Smith, Alexander
Smith, Benjamin Mosby
Smith, Charles Alphonso
Smith, Charles Sprague
Smith, Courtney Craig
Smith, Daniel B.
Smith, David Eugene
Smith, Francis Henney
Smith, Harold Babbitt
Smith, Henry Louis
Smith, Judson
Smith, Lucy Harth
Smith, Richard Somers
Smith, William, 1727–1803
Smith, William Waugh
Smyth, Albert Henry
Smyth, John Henry
Snider, Denton Jaques
Snow, Francis Huntington
Snyder, Edwin Reagan
Soldan, Frank Louis
Son of Many Beads
Sorin, Edward Frederick
Soulé, George
Spaeth, John Duncan
Spalding, John Lancaster
Spangler, Henry Wilson
Sparrow, William
Spencer, Anna Garlin
Spencer, Jesse Ames
Sperry, Willard Learoyd
Sprague, Homer Baxter
Sprecher, Samuel
Stahr, John Summers
Stang, William
Stanley, Albert Augustus
Staughton, William
Stearns, Eben Sperry
Steele, Joel Dorman
Stengel, Alfred
Stephens, Henry Morse
Sterling, John Whalen
Stetson, William Wallace
Stevens, George Barker
Stevens, George Washington
Stillé, Charles Janeway
Stillman, Thomas Bliss
Stockbridge, Levi
Stoddard, John Fair
Stoek, Harry Harkness
Stoever, Martin Luther
Stokes, Anson Phelps
Stone, James Kent
Stone, John Seely
Stowe, Calvin Ellis
Strong, Richard Pearson

Stuart, Charles Macaulay
Sturtevant, Julian Monson
Summerall, Charles Pelot
Sumner, William Graham
Sunderland, Eliza Jane Read
Sutton, William Seneca
Suzzallo, Henry
Sverdrup, Georg
Swensson, Carl Aaron
Swett, John
Talbot, Arthur Newell
Tappan, Eli Todd
Taylor, Archibald Alexander
  Edward
Taylor, Nathaniel William
Taylor, Samuel Harvey
Tenney, Charles Daniel
Tenney, Edward Payson
Terrell, Mary Eliza Church
Terry, Milton Spenser
Thayer, Eli
Thayer, Gideon French
Thayer, Sylvanus
Thébaud, Augustus J.
Thoburn, Isabella
Thomas, Elbert Duncan
Thomas, Joseph
Thomas, Martha Carey
Thompson, Benjamin
Thompson, Charles Oliver
Thompson, Hugh Smith
Thompson, John Bodine
Thompson, Robert Ellis
Thompson, Samuel Rankin
Thurston, Robert Henry
Tichenor, Isaac Taylor
Ticknor, Elisha
Ticknor, George
Tomlinson, Everett Titsworth
Tompkins, Arnold
Toulmin, Harry
Townsend, Luther Tracy
Trowbridge, John
Trowbridge, William Petit
Trueblood, Benjamin Franklin
Tucker, William Jewett
Turner, Asa
Turner, Jonathan Baldwin
Turner, Samuel Hulbeart
Turner, William
Tutwiler, Henry
Tutwiler, Julia Strudwick
Tyler, Bennet
Tyler, Moses Coit
Vail, Stephen Montfort
Valentine, Milton
Van Lennep, Henry John
Van Meter, John Blackford
Van Quickenborne, Charles Felix
Varela y Morales, Félix Francisco
  José María de la Concepción
Vawtor, Charles Erastus
Venable, Charles Scott
Verbeck, William
Verhaegen, Peter Joseph
Vincent, George Edgar

James, Charles Tillinghast
Jervis, John Bloomfield
Jones, William Richard
Judah, Theodore Dehone
Kafer, John Christian
Kármán, Theodore (Todor) Von
Kerr, Walter Craig
Lamme, Benjamin Garver
La Tour, Le Blond de
Latrobe, Benjamin Henry,
  1764–1820
Lefferts, Marshall
L'Enfant, Pierre Charles
Léry, Joseph Gaspard Chaussegros
  de
Lewis, William Gaston
Long, Stephen Harriman
Lucas, Anthony Francis
Ludlow, William
Lundie, John
McCallum, Daniel Craig
Macfarlane, Charles William
Mangin, Joseph François
Marshall, William Louis
Mason, Arthur John
Maxim, Hiram Stevens
Meigs, Montgomery Cunningham
Merrill, William Emery
Miller, Ezra
Millington, John
Mills, Robert, 1781–1855
Mitchell, Henry
Mordecai, Alfred
Morell, George Webb
Morgan, Charles Hill
Morris, Thomas Armstrong
Morton, James St. Clair
Murray, Thomas Edward
Newton, John
Ockerson, John Augustus
Ogden, Francis Barber
Packard, James Ward
Painter, William
Palfrey, John Carver
Pardee, Ario
Parker, Ely Samuel
Parsons, William Barclay
Patterson, Richard Cunningham,
  Jr.
Pauger, Adrien de
Paul, Henry Martyn
Pearson, Fred Stark
Peters, Edward Dyer
Poe, Orlando Metcalfe
Reid, David Boswell
Renwick, Henry Brevoort
Renwick, James, 1792–1863
Reynolds, Edwin
Rice, Richard Henry
Ricketts, Palmer Chamberlaine
Roberts, Benjamin Stone
Robinson, Stillman Williams
Robinson, William
Roebling, John Augustus
Roosevelt, Nicholas J.
Rosser, Thomas Lafayette

Rousseau, Harry Harwood
Ryan, Walter D'Arcy
St. John, Isaac Munroe
Sargent, Frederick
Saunders, William Lawrence
Sawyer, Walter Howard
Scovel, Henry Sylvester
Sellers, Coleman
Sidell, William Henry
Simpson, James Hervey
Smith, Francis Hopkinson
Smith, William Farrar
Spangler, Henry Wilson
Sperry, Elmer Ambrose
Starrett, William Aiken
Stevens, Edwin Augustus
Stevens, John
Stevens, Robert Livingston
Storrow, Charles Storer
Strickland, William
Strong, Harriet Williams Russel
Stuart, Charles Beebe
Swift, Joseph Gardner
Swift, William Henry
Talcott, Andrew
Thompson, Charles Oliver
Thurston, Robert Henry
Tompkins, Daniel Augustus
Totten, George Muirson
Totten, Joseph Gilbert
Tower, Zealous Bates
Towne, Henry Robinson
Towne, John Henry
Trautwine, John Cresson
Trimble, Isaac Ridgeway
Troland, Leonard Thompson
Trowbridge, William Petit
Turnbull, William
Turner, Walter Victor
Twining, Alexander Catlin
Viele, Egbert Ludovicus
Vose, George Leonard
Ward, George Gray
Warren, Gouverneur Kemble
Warren, Russell
Watkins, John Elfreth
Watson, William
Webb, John Burkitt
Webster, Joseph Dana
Weitzel, Godfrey
Wellman, Samuel Thomas
Wheeler, William
Whistler, George Washington
White, Canvass
Wilcox, Stephen
Wilson, James Harrison
Winans, Thomas De Kay
Wood, James J.
Woodbury, Daniel Phineas
Woodward, Robert Simpson
Worthington, Henry Rossiter
Wright, Horatio Gouverneur
ENGINEER (AERONAUTICAL)
Acosta, Bertram Blanchard ("Bert")
Durand, William Frederick
Lawrance, Charles Lanier

Lewis, George William
Millikan, Clark Blanchard
Piccard, Jean Felix
Warner, Edward Pearson
Wright, Theodore Paul
ENGINEER (ARMY)
Casey, Thomas Lincoln
Robert, Henry Martyn
Sibert, William Luther
ENGINEER (AUTOMOTIVE)
Coffin, Howard Earle
ENGINEER (BRIDGE)
Cooper, Theodore
Cox, Lemuel
Hovey, Otis Ellis
Mason, Claibourne Rice
Modjeski, Ralph
Moisseiff, Leon Solomon
Morison, George Shattuck
Murphy, John. W.
Roebling, John Augustus
Smith, Charles Shaler
Steinman, David Barnard
Strauss, Joseph Baermann
Wernwag, Lewis
ENGINEER (CHEMICAL)
Frary, Francis Cowles
Howard, Henry
Landis, Walter Savage
Little, Arthur Dehon
Morehead, John Motley
Whorf, Benjamin Lee
ENGINEER (CIVIL)
Alden, John Ferris
Allen, Horatio
Ammann, Othmar Hermann
Baldwin, Loammi, 1740–1807
Baldwin, Loammi, 1780–1838
Bates, Onward
Billings, Asa White Kenney
Bogue, Virgil Gay
Boller, Alfred Pancoast
Borden, Simeon
Brown, William Henry
Bryant, Gridley
Buck, Leffert Lefferts
Buckhout, Isaac Craig
Bush, Lincoln
Cambpell, Allen
Carll, John Franklin
Cassatt, Alexander Johnston
Chanute, Octave
Childe, John
Church, George Earl
Cohen, Mendes
Cone, Russell Glenn
Cooley, Lyman Edgar
Cooper, Theodore
Corthell, Elmer Lawrence
Crowe, Francis Trenholm
Davies, John Vipond
Detmold, Christian Edward
Devereux, John Henry
Dodge, Grenville Mellon
Duane, James Chatham
Dubois, Augustus Jay

Ellet, Charles
Ellsworth, Lincoln
Evans, Anthony Walton Whyte
Felton, Samuel Morse
Ferris, George Washington Gale
Freeman, John Ripley
Freeman, Thomas
Fulton, Robert
Geddes, James
Gillespie, William Mitchell
Goldmark, Henry
Graff, Frederic
Graham, Charles Kinnaird
Greene, Charles Ezra
Greene, George Sears, 1801–1899
Greene, George Sears, 1837–1922
Harrington, John Lyle
Harrod, Benjamin Morgan
Haupt, Herman
Hayford, John Fillmore
Hill, Louis Clarence
Hoadley, John Chipman
Holland, Clifford Milburn
Hooker, Elon Huntington
Hovey, Otis Ellis
Hughes, Hector James
Johnson, Edwin Ferry
Johnson, John Butler
Katte, Walter
Knappen, Theodore Temple
Kneass, Samuel Honeyman
Kneass, Strickland
Knight, Jonathan
Koyl, Charles Herschel
Latrobe, Benjamin Henry,
    1806–1878
Latrobe, Charles Hazlehurst
Laurie, James
Lindenthal, Gustav
Lovell, Mansfield
McAlpine, William Jarvis
McConnell, Ira Welch
McCullough, Ernest
McMath, Robert Emmet
McNeill, William Gibbs
Menocal, Aniceto Garcia
Milner, John Turner
Moran, Daniel Edward
Nettleton, Edwin S.
Newell, Frederick Haynes
Noble, Alfred
Norcross, Orlando Whitney
Parker, Theodore Bissell
Peters, Richard, 1810–1889
Pick, Lewis Andrew
Pratt, Thomas Willis
Rafter, George W.
Randolph, Isham
Rea, Samuel
Ridgway, Robert
Roberdeau, Isaac
Roberts, Nathan S.
Roberts, Solomon White
Roberts, William Milnor
Robinson, Albert Alonzo
Robinson, Moncure

Roebling, Washington Augustus
Romans, Bernard
Rugg, Harold Ordway
Savage, John Lucian ("Jack")
Sayre, Robert Heysham
Schneider, Herman
Serrell, Edward Wellman
Silver, Thomas
Smillie, Ralph
Smith, Gustavus Woodson
Smith, Jonas Waldo
Smith, Jonas Waldo
Smith, William Sooy
Snow, Jessie Baker
Sooysmith, Charles
Staley, Cady
Stauffer, David McNeely
Stearns, Frederic Pike
Stevens, John Frank
Strobel, Charles Louis
Stuart, Francis Lee
Swain, George Fillmore
Talbot, Arthur Newell
Tatham, William
Thacher, Edwin
Waddell, John Alexander Low
Waite, Henry Matson
Walker, Reuben Lindsay
Wallace, John Findley
Wegmann, Edward
Welch, Ashbel
Wellington, Arthur Mellen
Westergaard, Harald Malcolm
Weston, William
Whipple, Squire
Williams, Frank Martin
Williams, Jesse Lynch
Wilson, Joseph Miller
Wilson, William Hasell
Worthen, William Ezra
Wright, Benjamin
ENGINEER (COMMUNICATIONS)
Colpitts, Edwin Henry
Hoover, Herbert Clark, Jr.
ENGINEER (ELECTRICAL)
Anthony, William Arnold
Armstrong, Edwin Howard
Baker, Walter Ransom Gail
Behrend, Bernard Arthur
Billings, Asa White Kenney
Cable, Frank Taylor
Carson, John Renshaw
Carty, John Joseph
Conrad, Frank
Crocker, Francis Bacon
Daft, Leo
Delaney, Patrick Bernard
Dumont, Allen Balcom
Emmet, William Le Roy
Faccioli, Giuseppe
Field, Stephen Dudley
Fortescue, Charles LeGeyt
Gotshall, William Charles
Griffin, Eugene
Hammer, William Joseph
Harper, John Lyell

Heineman, Daniel Webster
    ("Dannie")
Hering, Carl
Hill, Ernest Rowland
Hogan, John Vincent Lawless
Houston, Edwin James
Jackson, Dugald Caleb
Jansky, Karl Guthe
Kennelly, Arthur Edwin
Kettering, Charles Franklin
Leonard, Harry Ward
Loomis, Mahlon
Moorhead, James Kennedy
O'Reilly, Henry
Peek, Frank William
Perrine, Frederic Anten Combs
Potter, William Bancroft
Prescott, George Bartlett
Priest, Edward Dwight
Rice, Edwin Wilbur
Robb, William Lispenard
Rogers, Henry J.
Rosenberg, Julius
Ross, James Delmage McKenzie
Ryan, Harris Joseph
Sargent, Frederick
Short, Sidney Howe
Smith, Harold Babbitt
Sprague, Frank Julian
Squier, George Owen
Stanley, William
Steinmetz, Charles Proteus
Stone, Charles Augustus
Stott, Henry Gordon
Swope, Gerard
Tesla, Nikola
Van Depoele, Charles Joseph
Weaver, William Dixon
Webster, Edwin Sibley
Weston, Edward
ENGINEER (HIGHWAY)
Merrill, Frank Dow
ENGINEER (HYDRAULIC)
Davis, Arthur Powell
Fanning, John Thomas
Fitzgerald, Desmond
Francis, James Bicheno
Frizell, Joseph Palmer
Hazen, Allen
Henny, David Christiaan
Herschel, Clemens
Hill, Louis Clarence
Knappen, Theodore Temple
Matthes, Gerard Hendrik
Mills, Hiram Francis
O'Shaughnessy, Michael Maurice
Schuyler, James Dix
Shedd, Joel Herbert
Weymouth, Frank Elwin
ENGINEER (HYDROELECTRIC)
Cooper, Hugh Lincoln
ENGINEER (INDUSTRIAL)
Gunn, James Newton
Hine, Charles De Lano
Porter, Holbrook Fitz-John
Rautenstrauch, Walter

Birch, William Russell
Buell, Abel
Burgis, William
Casilear, John William
Charles, William
Cheney, John
Cheney, Seth Wells
Childs, Cephas Grier
Clay, Edward Williams
Closson, William Baxter
Cushman, George Hewitt
Danforth, Moseley Isaac
Dawkins, Henry
Dewing, Francis
Doolittle, Amos
Dummer, Jeremiah
Durand, Asher Brown
Durand, Cyrus
Eckstein, John
Edwin, David
Field, Robert
Folwell, Samuel
Foster, John
Fox, Gilbert
French, Edwin Davis
Girsch, Frederick
Gobrecht, Christian
Goodman, Charles
Hall, Henry Bryan
Hamlin, William
Havell, Robert
Hill, John
Hollyer, Samuel
Hooker, William
Hurd, Nathaniel
Jocelyn, Nathaniel
Johnston, David Claypoole
Johnston, Thomas
Jones, Alfred
Kearny, Francis
Keith, William
Kensett, John Frederick
Kingsley, Elbridge
Kneass, William
Lawson, Alexander
Leney, William Satchwell
Le Roux, Charles
Longacre, James Barton
Malcolm, James Peller
Maverick, Peter
Norman, John
Ormsby, Waterman Lilly
Otis, Bass
Pease, Joseph Ives
Pelham, Henry
Pelham, Peter
Piggot, Robert
Prud'homme, John Francis Eugene
Ritchie, Alexander Hay
Rollinson, William
Rosenthal, Max
Saint-Mémin, Charles Balthazar
    Julien Fevret de
Sartain, Emily
Sartain, John
Sartain, Samuel

Savage, Edward
Schoff, Stephen Alonzo
Shirlaw, Walter
Smillie, James
Smillie, James David
Smith, John Rubens
Strickland, William
Tanner, Benjamin
Tiebout, Cornelius
Yeager, Joseph
ENGRAVER (WOOD) (See also ARTIST)
Adams, Joseph Alexander
Anthony, Andrew Varick Stout
Bowen, Abel
Cole, Timothy
Drake, Alexander Wilson
Heinemann, Ernst
Juengling, Frederick
Kruell, Gustav
Leslie, Frank
Linton, William James
Lossing, Benson John
Wolf, Henry
ENTERTAINER (See also ACTOR,
    ACTRESS, CLOWN, COMEDIAN,
    COMEDIENNE, HUMORIST, WIT)
Allen, Gracie
Clark, Bobby
Gray, Gilda
Hopper, Edna Wallace
Janis, Elsie
Lee, Gypsy Rose
Mansfield, Jayne
Maxwell, Elsa
Nesbit, Evelyn Florence
Palmer, William Henry
Rooney, Pat
Waller, Thomas Wright ("Fats")
ENTOMOLOGIST (See also ZOOLOGIST)
Ashmead, William Harris
Burgess, Edward
Comstock, John Henry
Coquillett, Daniel William
Cresson, Ezra Townsend
Dyar, Harrison Gray
Edwards, William Henry
Fernald, Charles Henry
Fitch, Asa
Forbes, Stephen Alfred
Glover, Townend
Grote, Augustus Radcliffe
Hagen, Hermann August
Harris, Thaddeus William
Horn, George Henry
Howard, Leland Ossian
Hubbard, Henry Guernsey
Hunter, Walter David
Kinsey, Alfred Charles
Knab, Frederick
LeConte, John Lawrence
Lintner, Joseph Albert
Lutz, Frank Eugene
Melsheimer, Friedrich Valentin
Morgan, John Harcourt Alexander
Osten Sacken, Carl Robert
    Romanovich von der

Packard, Alpheus Spring
Peckham, George Williams
Riley, Charles Valentine
Sanderson, Ezra Dwight
Say, Thomas
Schwarz, Eugene Amandus
Scudder, Samuel Hubbard
Smith, John Bernhard
Taylor, Charlotte De Bernier
Thomas, Cyrus
Uhler, Philip Reese
Walsh, Benjamin Dann
Wheeler, William Morton
Williston, Samuel Wendell
ENTREPRENEUR (See also
    BUSINESSMAN, CAPITALIST,
    INDUSTRIALIST, MANUFACTURER,
    MERCHANT)
Farquhar, Percival
Kennedy, Joseph Patrick
Pincus, Gregory Goodwin
    ("Goody")
EPIDEMIOLOGIST (See also PHYSICIAN)
Carter, Henry Rose
Chapin, Charles Value
Doull, James Angus
Frost, Wade Hampton
Rosenau, Milton Joseph
Sedgwick, William Thompson
Sternberg, George Miller
ESSAYIST (See also AUTHOR, WRITER)
Agee, James Rufus
Appleton, Thomas Gold
Bourne, Randolph Silliman
Calvert, George Henry
Crèvecoeur, Michel-Guillaume
    Jean de
Crothers, Samuel McChord
Dana, Richard Henry
Dennie, Joseph
Douglas, Lloyd Cassel
Downey, John
Emerson, Ralph Waldo
Gregory, Eliot
Guiney, Louise Imogen
Hall, Sarah Ewing
Holley, Marietta
Holmes, Oliver Wendell
Kinney, Elizabeth Clementine
    Dodge Stedman
Lazarus, Emma
McKinley, Carlyle
Saltus, Edgar Evertson
Sperry, Willard Learoyd
Story, William Wetmore
Thoreau, Henry David
Tuckerman, Henry Theodore
Warner, Charles Dudley
Willcox, Louise Collier
Winchevsky, Morris
Winter, William
ETCHER (See also ARTIST, ENGRAVER)
Bacher, Otto Henry
Bellows, Albert Fitch
Benson, Frank Weston
Charles, William

Champlain, Samuel de (Canada)

Clark, Francis Edward (Young People's Society of Christian Endeavor)

Coit, Stanton (America's first social settlement)

Connelly, Cornelia (Society of the Holy Child Jesus)

Conover, Harry Sayles (Harry Conover Modeling Agency)

Considérant, Victor Prosper (utopian community in Texas)

Cook, George Cram (Provincetown Players)

Cooke, Samuel (Penn Fruit Company)

Cooper, Sarah Brown Ingersoll (kindergartens)

Cornell, Ezra (Cornell University)

Coulter, Ernest Kent (Big Brother Movement)

Crittenton, Charles Nelson (Florence Crittenton Missions)

Cummins, George David (Reformed Episcopal Church)

Cunningham, Ann Pamela (Mount Vernon Ladies' Association of the Union)

Dabrowski, Joseph (S.S. Cyril and Methodius Seminary)

Darling, Flora Adams (patriotic organizations)

Davenport, George (Davenport, Iowa)

Davidge, John Beale (Univ. of Maryland)

Dempster, John (Methodist theological seminaries)

Dodge, David Low (New York Peace Society)

Dole, James Drummond (Hawaiian Pineapple Company)

Donahue, Peter (Union Iron Workers)

Dooley, Thomas Anthony, III (Medical International Corporation Organization, MEDICO)

Dorrell, William (Dorrellites)

Dowie, John Alexander (Christian Catholic Apostolic Church in Zion)

Drexel, Katharine Mary (Sisters of the Blessed Sacrament for Indians and Colored People)

Dufour, John James (Swiss vineyards in America)

Easley, Ralph Montgomery (National Civic Federation)

Eddy, Mary Morse Baker (Christian Science)

Eggleston, Thomas (School of Mines, Columbia Univ.)

Eielsen, Elling (Norwegian Evangelical Church of North America)

Eliot, William Greenleaf (Washington University of St. Louis)

Estaugh, Elizabeth Haddon (Haddonfield home for travelling ministers)

Eustis, Dorothy Leib Harrison Wood (The Seeing Eye)

Evans, John (Northwestern University, Colorado Seminary)

Ewing, Finis (Cumberland Presbyterian Church)

Fee, John Gregg (Berea College)

Few, Ignatius Alphonso (Emory College)

Fillmore, Charles (Unity School of Christianity)

Flanagan, Edward Joseph (Boys Town)

Foster, Thomas Jefferson (International Correspondence Schools)

Francis, Paul James (Society of the Atonement)

George, William Reuben (George Junior Republic)

Goodall, Harvey L. (livestock market paper)

Guérin, Anne-Thérèse (Mother Theodore) (Sisters of Providence of Saint Mary-of-the-Woods)

Hallett, Benjamin (Seamen's Bethels)

Harris, John (Harrisburg, Pa.)

Harris, Paul Percy (Rotary International)

Harvard, John (Harvard College)

Haynes, George Edmund (Urban League)

Hecker, Isaac Thomas (Paulists)

Herr, John (Reformed Mennonites)

Higginson, Henry Lee (Boston Symphony Orchestra)

Hodur, Francis (Polish National Catholic Church in America)

Holmes, Joseph Austin (U. S. Bureau of Mines)

Houghton, George Hendric (Church of the Transfiguration, N.Y.C.)

Hubbard, Gardiner Greene (National Geographic Society)

Huidekoper, Harm Jan (Meadville Theological School)

Huntington, Henry Edwards (Hungington Library and Art Gallery)

Hyde, Henry Baldwin (Equitable Life Assurance Society of the U.S.)

Jackson, Patrick Tracy (cotton factories at Lowell, Mass.)

Jansky, Karl Guthe (science of radio astronomy)

Jenckes, Joseph (Pawtucket, R.I.)

Johnson, Elijah (Liberia)

Jones, Robert Reynolds ("Bob") (Bob Jones University)

Joubert de la Muraille, James Hector Marie Nicholas (Oblate Sisters of Providence)

Juneau, Solomon Laurent (Milwaukee, Wis.)

Kalmus, Herbert Thomas (Technicolor Incorporated)

Keeley, Oliver Hudson (Grange)

Keith, George ("Christian Quakers")

Keith, Minor Cooper (American Fruit Company)

Keppler, Joseph (*Puck*)

King, John (eclectic school of medicine)

King, Richard (ranch)

Kneisel, Franz (Kneisel Quartet)

Knight, Jonathan (American Medical Association, Yale Medical School)

Kroger, Bernhard Henry (Kroger grocery store chain)

Kuskov, Ivan Aleksandrovich (Russian settlement in California)

Laclede, Pierre (St. Louis, Mo.)

Lambeau, Earl Louis ("Curly") (Green Bay Packers football team)

Lane, John (Vicksburg, Miss.)

Lee, Ann (Shakers in America)

Lewis, Samuel (free public school system of Ohio)

Liggett, Louis Kroh (United Drug Company)

Lindley, Jacob (Ohio University)

Lippard, George (Brotherhood of the Union)

Lorimier, Pierre Louis (Cape Girardeau, Mo.)

Lovejoy, Asa Lawrence (Portland, Oreg.)

Low, Juliette Gordon (Girl Scouts of America)

Lowell, John, 1799–1836 (Lowell Institute)

Lyon, David Willard (YMCA in China)

McClellan, George, 1796–1847 (Jefferson Medical College)

Maclay, Robert Samuel (colleges)

McPherson, Aimee Semple (International Church of the Foursquare Gospel)

Mannes, David (Mannes College of Music)

Marquis, Albert Nelson (*Who's Who in America*)

Maslow, Abraham H. (humanistic psychology)

Maurin, Peter Aristide (Catholic Worker Movement)

Meeker, Nathan Cook (Union Colony of Colorado)

Menninger, Charles Frederick (Menninger Clinic)

Meyer, Annie Nathan (Barnard College)

Mooney, William (New York Society of Tammany)

Morgan, John (University of Penn. Medical School)

Muller, Hermann Joseph (radiation genetics)

Murray, John, 1741–1815 (Universalism in America)

Myer, Albert James (Weather Bureau)

Nast, William (first German Methodist church in the U.S.)

Newbrough, John Ballou (Shalam religious community)

Newcomer, Christian (Church of the United Brethren in Christ)

Noble, Samuel (Anniston, Ala.)

Noyes, John Humphrey (Oneida Community)

Oglethorpe, James Edward (colony of Georgia)

Osgood, Jacob (Osgoodites)

Otterbein, Philip William (Church of the United Brethren in Christ)

Painter, Gamaliel (Middlebury College)

Palmer, Daniel David (chiropractic)

Parmly, Eleazer (dentistry, as an organized profession)

Pastorius, Francis Daniel (Germantown, Pa.)

Peirce, Charles Sanders (pragmatism)

Penn, William (Pennsylvania)

Peralta, Pedro de (Santa Fe, N.Mex.)

Phelps, Guy Rowland (Connecticut Mutual Life Insurance Company)

Phillips, Frank (Phillips Petroleum Company)

Phillips, John (Phillips Exeter Academy)

Phillips, Lena Madesin (International Federation of Business and Professional Women, National Federation of Business and Professional Women's Clubs)

Phillips, Samuel (Phillips Academy, Andover)

Pierpont, James (Yale College)

Plant, Henry Bradley (Plant system of railroads)

Porter, James Madison (Lafayette College)

Porter, Rufus (*Scientific American*)

Portolá, Gaspar de (San Diego and Monterey, Cal.)

Purnell, Benjamin (House of David)

Purviance, David (Christian denomination)

Putnam, Gideon (Saratoga Springs, N.Y.)

Quimby, Phineas Parkhurst (mental healing)

Radcliff, Jacob (Jersey City, N.J.)

Randall, Benjamin (Free-Will Baptists)

Rapp, George (Harmony Society)

Rathbone, Justus Henry (Order of Knights of Pythias)

Rezanov, Nikolai Petrovich (Russian-American Company)

Rice, John Andrew (Black Mountain College)

Rice, William Marsh (William Marsh Rice Institute)

Robinson-Smith, Gertrude (Berkshire Symphony Festival, Inc., Tanglewood)

Rochester, Nathaniel (Rochester, N.Y.)

Rogers, John, 1648–1721 (Rogerenes)

Rogers, Mary Josephine (Maryknoll Sisters)

Ross, Harold Wallace (*New Yorker*)

Rowell, George Presbury (*Printer's Ink*)

Russell, Mother Mary Baptist (Sisters of Mercy in California)

Russell, William Hepburn (Pony Express)

Sanford, Henry Shelton (Sanford, Fla.)

Scherman, Harry (Book-of-the-Month Club)

Schneider, Herman (cooperative system of education)

Schrieck, Sister Louise Van der (Sisters of Notre Dame de Namur)

Seton, Elizabeth Ann Bayley (American Society of Charity)

Severance, Caroline Maria Seymour (women's clubs)

Shaw, Henry (Missouri Botanical Garden)

Shelekhov, Grigori Ivanovich (first Russian colony in America)

Shinn, Asa (Methodist Protestant Church)

Shipherd, John Jay (Oberlin College)

Simmons, William Joseph (Ku Klux Klan)

Simpson, Albert Benjamin (Christian and Missionary Alliance)

Slater, Samuel (American cotton industry)

Smith, Sophia (Smith College)

Snethen, Nicholas (Methodist Protestant Church)

Sorin, Edward Frederick (University of Notre Dame)

Spalding, Catherine (Sisters of Charity of Nazareth)

Spring, Samuel (American Board of Commissioners for Foreign Missions)

Spring, Samuel (Andover Theological Seminary)

Stephenson, Benjamin Franklin (Grand Army of the Republic)

Stewart, Philo Penfield (Oberlin College)

Still, Andrew Taylor (osteopathy)

Taylor, Joseph Wright (Bryn Mawr College)

Teresa, Mother (Visitation Order in U.S.)

Teusler, Rudolf Bolling (St. Luke's Hospital, Tokyo)

Thomas, Isaiah (American Antiquarian Society)

Thomas, Robert Bailey (*Farmer's Almanack*)

Tonty, Henry de (Mississippi Valley settlements)

Tourjée, Eben (New England Conservatory of Music)

Townley, Arthur Charles (Nonpartisan League)

Townsend, Francis Everett (Old Age Revolving Pension Plan)

Tufts, Charles (Tufts College)

Upchurch, John Jordan (Ancient Order of United Workmen)

Valentine, Robert Grosvenor (industrial counseling)

Van Raalte, Albertus Christiaan (Dutch settlement in Holland, Mich.)

Varick, James (African Methodist Episcopal Zion Church)

Vassar, Matthew (Vassar College)

Vattemare, Nicholas Marie Alexandre (system of international exchanges)

Vincennes, François Marie Bissot, Sieur de (Vincennes Ind.)

Wade, Jeptha Homer (American commercial telegraph system)

Walgreen, Charles Rudolph (Walgreen drugstore chain)

Wertheimer, Max (Gestalt movement)

Wetherill, Samuel (Free Quakers)

White, Alma Bridwell (Pillar of Fire Church)

White, Thomas Willis (*Southern Literary Messenger*)

FRATERNAL ORDER LEADER
Davis, James John
Wilson, J(ames) Finley

FREEMASON
Morgan, William
Pike, Albert

FREE-SOILER
Stearns, George Luther

Macdonald, Charles Blair
Ouimet, Francis Desales
Smith, Horton
Travers, Jerome Dunstan
Travis, Walter John
Wood, Craig Ralph
GOVERNMENT OFFICIAL (See also
    PUBLIC OFFICIAL)
Ames, Joseph Sweetman
Arnold, Thurman Wesley
Ballantine, Arthur Atwood
Bennett, Henry Garland
Bethune, Mary McLeod
Biffle, Leslie L.
Breckinridge, Henry Skillman
Bundy, Harvey Hollister
Bunker, Arthur Hugh
Clayton, William Lockhart
Coolidge, Thomas Jefferson
Cooper, William John
Creel, George
Dennett, Tyler (Wilbur)
Dodge, Joseph Morrell
Dorn, Harold Fred
Early, Stephen Tyree
Flint, Weston
Fly, James Lawrence
Gaston, Herbert Earle
Haas, Francis Joseph
Hannegan, Robert Emmet
Herrick, Robert Welch
Hines, Frank Thomas
Hopkins, Harry Lloyd
Hunt, Gaillard
Johnson, Hugh Samuel
Kennedy, Joseph Patrick
Knudsen, William S.
Krug, Julius Albert
Leffingwell, Russell Cornell
Legge, Alexander
McEntee, James Joseph
Manly, Basil Maxwell
Merriam, Charles Edward, Jr.
Meyer, Eugene Isaac
Mitchell, William DeWitt
Nelson, Donald Marr
Niles, David K.
Pasvolsky, Leo
Payne, Christopher Harrison
Pelham, Robert A.
Pickens, William
Post, Louis Freeland
Powderly, Terence Vincent
Richberg, Donald Randall
Russell, Charles Wells
Sargent, Frank Pierce
Sherwood, Robert Emmet
Talbott, Harold Elstner
Vance, Harold Sines
Vanderlip, Frank Arthur
Wadsworth, Eliot
Warburg, James Paul
Warner, Edward Pearson
Waterman, Alan Tower
Waymack, William Wesley
Wharton, Francis

Zook, George Frederick
GOVERNOR (ACTING)
Argall, Sir Samuel (Va.)
Blair, John (Va.)
Danforth, Thomas (Mass.)
Evans, John (Pa.)
Hamilton, Andrew, d.1703 (Pa.)
Hamilton, Andrew Jackson (Tex.)
Hamilton, James, 1710–1783 (Pa.)
Lloyd, Thomas (Pa.)
Nelson, William, 1711–1722 (Va.)
Paddock, Algernon Sidney (Nebr.)
Parsons, Lewis Eliphalet (Ala.)
St. Ange de Bellerive, Louis (La.)
Sharkey, William Lewis (Miss.)
Shippen, Edward, 1639–1712 (Pa.)
Stanton, Frederick Perry (Kans.)
Stoddard, Amos (La.)
GOVERNOR (COLONIAL)
Andros, Sir Edmund
Archdale, John
Basse, Jeremiah
Belcher, Jonathan
Bellingham, Richard
Berkeley, Sir William
Bernard, Sir Francis
Botetourt, Norborne Berkeley,
    Baron de
Burnet, William
Burrington, George
Calvert, Leonard
Campbell, Lord William
Clarke, Walter
Clinton, George
Coote, Richard
Copley, Lionel
Cosby, William
Cranston, John
Cranston, Samuel
Cubero, Pedro Rodriguez
Culpeper, Thomas, Lord
Dobbs, Arthur
Dongan, Thomas
Dudley, Joseph
Dudley, Thomas
Dunmore, John Murray, Earl of
Eden, Robert
Ellis, Henry
Fendall, Josias
Fitch, Thomas
Fletcher, Benjamin
Franklin, William
Gage, Thomas
Gates, Sir Thomas
Gooch, Sir William
Greene, William
Hamilton, Andrew, d. 1703
Harvey, Sir John
Hopkins, Stephen
Hunter, Robert
Hutchinson, Thomas
Hyde, Edward
Johnson, Robert
Johnson, Sir Nathaniel
Johnston, Gabriel
Keith, Sir William

Kieft, Willem
Law, Jonathan
Leete, William
Leverett, John, 1616–1679
Lovelace, Francis
Ludwell, Philip
Lyttelton, William Henry
Markham, William
Martin, Josiah
Mayhew, Thomas
Middleton, Arthur
Miró, Esteban Rodríguez
Moore, James, d. 1706
Moore, Sir Henry
Nicholson, Francis
Nicolls, Richard
Ogle, Samuel
Phips, Sir William
Pierpont, Francis Harrison
Pott, John
Pownall, Thomas
Printz, Johan Björnsson
Reynolds, John
Rising, Johan Classon
Russwurm, John Brown
Saltonstall, Gurdon
Sharpe, Horatio
Shirley, William
Shute, Samuel
Stone, William
Talcott, Joseph
Thomas, George
Treat, Robert
Trumbull, Jonathan, 1710–1785
Tryon, William
Ulloa, Antonio de
Vane, Sir Henry
Van Twiller, Wouter
Villeré, Jacques Philippe
Ward, Richard
Ward, Samuel, 1725–1776
Wentworth, Benning
Wentworth, John, 1737 N.S.–1820
West, Joseph
Winslow, Josiah
Winthrop, John, 1587/88
    O.S.–1649
Winthrop, John, 1605/06
    O.S.–1676
Winthrop, John, 1638–1707
Wolcott, Oliver, 1726–1797
Wolcott, Roger
Wyatt, Sir Francis
Yeamans, Sir John
Yeardley, Sir George
GOVERNOR (GENERAL)
Alvarado, Juan Bautista (Mexican
    California)
Brown, William (Bermuda)
Coddington, William (Aquidneck)
Colton, George Radcliffe (Puerto
    Rico)
Corondo, Francisco Vázquez
    (Nueva Galicia)
Hasket, Elias (Bahamas)
Minuit, Peter (New Sweden)

Vandreuli-Cavagnal, Pierre de Riguad, Marquis de (Canada)
Wright, Luke Edward (Philippines)

GOVERNOR (STATE)

Aandahl, Fred George (N.Dak.)
Abbett, Leon (N.J.)
Adams, Alva (Colo.)
Adams, James Hopkins (S.C.)
Alcorn, James Lusk (Miss.)
Alger, Russell Alexander (Mich.)
Allen, Henry Justin (Kans.)
Allen, Henry Watkins (La.)
Allen, Philip (R.I.)
Allen, William (Ohio)
Allston, Robert Francis Withers (S.C.)
Altgeld, John Peter (Ill.)
Ames, Adelbert (Miss.)
Ames, Oliver (Mass.)
Ammons, Elias Milton (Colo.)
Andrew, John Albion (Mass.)
Anthony, George Tobey (Kans.)
Ashe, Samuel (N.C.)
Atkinson, William Yates (Ga.)
Aycock, Charles Brantley (N.C.)
Bagby, Arthur Pendleton (Ala.)
Baldwin, Henry Porter (Mich.)
Baldwin, Roger Sherman (Conn.)
Baldwin, Simeon Eben (Conn.)
Banks, Nathaniel Prentiss (Mass.)
Barrett, Frank Aloysius (Wyo.)
Barry, John Stewart (Mich.)
Barstow, William Augustus (Wis.)
Bartlett, Josiah (N.H.)
Bartley, Mordecai (Ohio)
Bashford, Coles (Wis.)
Bate, William Brimage (Tenn.)
Bates, Frederick (Mo.)
Beaver, James Addams (Pa.)
Bell, Peter Hansborough (Tex.)
Bell, Samuel (N.H.)
Bennett, Caleb Prew (Del.)
Berry, James Henderson (Ark.)
Berry, Nathaniel Springer (N.H.)
Bibb, William Wyatt (Ala.)
Bickett, Thomas Walter (N.C.)
Bienville, Jean Baptiste Le Moyne, Sieur de (La.)
Bigler, John (Calif.)
Bigler, William (Pa.)
Bilbo, Theodore Gilmore (Miss.)
Bissell, William Henry (Ill.)
Black, Frank Swett (N.Y.)
Blackburn, Luke Pryor (Ky.)
Blaine, John James (Wis.)
Blair, Austin (Mich.)
Blanchard, Newton Crain (La.)
Blasdel, Henry Goode (Nev.)
Blease, Coleman Livingston (S.C.)
Bliss, Aaron Thomas (Mich.)
Blount, Willie (Tenn.)
Bloxham, William Dunnington (Fla.)
Boggs, Lillburn W. (Mo.)
Boies, Horace (Iowa)
Bond, Shadrach (Ill.)

Bonham, Milledge Lake (S.C.)
Booth, Newton (Calif.)
Boreman, Arthur Ingram (W.Va.)
Bouck, William C. (N.Y.)
Bowdoin, James (Mass.)
Bowie, Oden (Md.)
Bowie, Robert (Md.)
Bradford, Augustus Williamson (Md.)
Bradly, William O'Connell (Ky.)
Bramlette, Thomas E. (Ky.)
Branch, John (N.C.)
Brandon, Gerard Chittocque (Miss.)
Brewster, Ralph Owen (Maine)
Bridges, (Henry) Styles (N.H.)
Brough, John (Ohio)
Broward, Napoleon Bonaparte (Fla.)
Brown, Aaron Venable (Tenn.)
Brown, Albert Gallatin (Miss.)
Brown, Benjamin Gratz (Mo.)
Brown, John Calvin (Tenn.)
Brown, John Young (Ky.)
Brownlow, William Gannaway (Tenn.)
Bryan, Charles Wayland (Nebr.)
Buckingham, William Alfred (Conn.)
Bulkeley, Morgan Gardner (Conn.)
Bull, William (S.C.)
Bullock, Rufus Brown (Ga.)
Burke, Thomas (N.C.)
Burton, Hutchins Gordon (N.C.)
Burton, William (Del.)
Bushnell, Asa Smith (Ohio)
Butler, Benjamin Franklin (Mass.)
Butler, Ezra (Vt.)
Butler, Pierce Mason (S.C.)
Byrd, Harry Flood (Va.)
Cabell, William H. (Va.)
Cadillac, Antoine de la Mothe (La.)
Call, Richard Keith (Fla.)
Cameron, William Evelyn (Va.)
Campbell, William Bowen (Tenn.)
Candler, Allen Daniel (Ga.)
Cannon, Newton (Tenn.)
Cannon, William (Del.)
Capper, Arthur (Kans.)
Carney, Thomas (Kans.)
Carondelet, Francisco Luis Hector, Baron de (La.)
Carpenter, Cyrus Clay (Iowa)
Carr, Elias (N.C.)
Carroll, John Lee (Md.)
Carroll, William (Tenn.)
Carteret, Philip (N.J.)
Chamberlain, Daniel Henry (S.C.)
Chamberlain, George Earle (Oreg.)
Chamberlain, Joshua Lawrence (Maine)
Chambers, John (Iowa)
Chapman, Reuben (Ala.)
Cheney, Person Colby (N.H.)
Chittenden, Martin (Vt.)

Chittenden, Thomas (Vt.)
Churchill, Thomas James (Ark.)
Claflin, William (Mass.)
Claiborne, William Charles Coles (La.)
Clark, Charles (Miss.)
Clark, James (Ky.)
Clark, John (Ga.)
Clark, Myron Holley (N.Y.)
Clarke, James Paul (Ark.)
Clay, Clement Comer (Ala.)
Clayton, Joshua (Del.)
Clayton, Powell (Ark.)
Clement, Frank Goad (Tenn.)
Cleveland, Chauncey Fitch (Conn.)
Cleveland, Stephen Grover (N.Y.)
Coburn, Abner (Maine)
Coke, Richard (Tex.)
Coles, Edward (Ill.)
Collier, Henry Watkins (Ala.)
Comer, Braxton Bragg (Ala.)
Conway, James Sevier (Ark.)
Cornbury, Edward Hyde (N.Y. and N.J.)
Cornell, Alonzo B. (N.Y.)
Corwin, Thomas (Ohio)
Cox, Jacob Dolson (Ohio)
Crane, Winthrop Murray (Mass.)
Crawford, George Walker (Ga.)
Crawford, Samuel Johnson (Kans.)
Crittenden, Thomas Theodore (Mo.)
Cross, Wilbur Lucius (Conn.)
Crounse, Lorenzo (Nebr.)
Curtin, Andrew Gregg (Pa.)
Davie, William Richardson (N.C.)
Davis, Cushman Kellogg (Minn.)
Davis, Edmund Jackson (Tex.)
Davis, Jeff (Ark.)
De La Warr, Thomas West, Baron (Va.)
Dennison, William (Ohio)
Derbigny, Pierre Auguste Charles Bourguignon (La.)
Dern, George Henry (Utah)
Desha, Joseph (Ky.)
Dickerson, Mahlon (N.J.)
Dingley, Nelson (Maine)
Dix, John Adams (N.Y.)
Douglas, William Lewis (Mass.)
Drake, Francis Marion (Iowa)
Drayton, John (S.C.)
Dudley, Edward Bishop (N.C.)
Duff, James Henderson (Pa.)
Duncan, Joseph (Ill.)
Dunlap, Robert Pinckney (Maine)
Duval, William Pope (Fla.)
Easton, John (R.I.)
Easton, Nicholas (R.I.)
Eden, Charles (N.C.)
Edge, Walter Evans (N.J.)
Edison, Charles (N.J.)
Edwards, Henry Waggaman (Conn.)
Edwards, Ninian (Ill.)

Spaight, Richard Dobbs (N.C.)
Sprague, Charles Arthur (Oreg.)
Sprague, William, 1830–1915
 (R.I.)
Sproul, William Cameron (Pa.)
Stanford, Leland (Calif.)
Sterling, Ross Shaw (Tex.)
Stevenson, Adlai Ewing, II (Ill.)
Stevenson, John White (Ky.)
Stewart, Robert Marcellus (Mo.)
Stokes, Montfort (N.C.)
Stone, John Marshall (Miss.)
Stone, William Joel (Mo.)
Stoneman, George (Calif.)
Stubbs, Walter Roscoe (Kans.)
Sulzer, William (N.Y.)
Sumner, Increase (Mass.)
Swain, David Lowry (N.C.)
Swann, Thomas (Md.)
Swanson, Claude Augustus (Va.)
Talmadge, Eugene (Ga.)
Taylor, Alfred Alexander (Tenn.)
Taylor, Robert Love (Tenn.)
Tazewell, Littleton Waller (Va.)
Telfair, Edward (Ga.)
Thomas, Francis (Md.)
Thomas, Philip Francis (Md.)
Thompson, Hugh Smith (S.C.)
Throop, Enos Thompson (N.Y.)
Thye, Edward John (Minn.)
Tiffin, Edward (Ohio)
Tilden, Samuel Jones (N.Y.)
Tillman, Benjamin Ryan (S.C.)
Tobey, Charles William (N.H.)
Tobin, Maurice Joseph (Mass.)
Tod, David (Ohio)
Tompkins, Daniel D. (N.Y.)
Toole, Joseph Kemp (Mont.)
Toucey, Isaac (Conn.)
Towns, George Washington
 Bonaparte (Ga.)
Trimble, Allen (Ohio)
Trumbull, Jonathan, 1740–1809
 (Conn.)
Turney, Peter (Tenn.)
Tyler, John, 1747–1813 (Va.)
Vance, Zebulon Baird (N.C.)
Vardaman, James Kimble (Miss.)
Veazey, Thomas Ward (Md.)
Vroom, Peter Dumont (N.J.)
Walker, David Shelby (Fla.)
Walker, Gilbert Carlton (Va.)
Wallace, David (Ind.)
Wallace, Lurleen Burns (Ala.)
Waller, Thomas Macdonald
 (Conn.)
Wallgren, Mon(rad) C(harles)
 (Wash.)
Walsh, David Ignatius (Mass.)
Wanton, Joseph (R.I.)
Ward, Marcus Lawrence (N.J.)
Warmoth, Henry Clay (La.)
Warner, Fred Maltby (Mich.)
Washburn, Cadwallader Colden
 (Wis.)
Washburn, Emory (Mass.)

Washburn, Israel (Maine)
Watts, Thomas Hill (Ala.)
Weller, John B. (Calif.)
Wells, James Madison (La.)
West, Francis (Va.)
West, Oswald (Oreg.)
Whitcomb, James (Ind.)
White, John (Va.)
Whitman, Charles Seymour (N.Y.)
Wickliffe, Robert Charles (La.)
Williams, David Rogerson (S.C.)
Williams, James Douglas (Ind.)
Williamson, Isaac Halsted (N.J.)
Williamson, William Durkee
 (Maine)
Willson, Augustus Everett (Ky.)
Wiltz, Louis Alfred (La.)
Winant, John Gilbert (N.H.)
Winder, Levin (Md.)
Winston, John Anthony (Ala.)
Wise, Henry Alexander (Va.)
Wolcott, Oliver, 1760–1833
 (Conn.)
Wolf, George (Pa.)
Wood, Reuben (Ohio)
Woodbridge, William (Mich.)
Woodring, Harry Hines (Kans.)
Worth, Jonathan (N.C.)
Worthington, Thomas (Ohio)
Wright, Fielding Lewis (Miss.)
Wright, Joseph Albert (Ind.)
Wright, Robert (Md.)
Wright, Silas (N.Y.)
Yates, Richard (Ill.)
Yell, Archibald (Ark.)

GOVERNOR (TERRITORIAL)
Blount, William (Tenn.)
Brady, John Green (Alaska)
Clark, William (Mo.)
Cotton, George Radcliff (P.R.)
Connelly, Henry (N.Mex.)
Cumming, Alfred (Utah)
Curry, George Law (Oreg.)
Davis, Dwight Filley (Philippines)
De Vargas Zapata y Lujan Ponce
 De Leon, Diego (N.Mex.)
Dodge, Henry (Wis.)
Dole, Sanford Ballard (Hawaii)
Edgerton, Sidney (Mont.)
Farrington, Wallace Rider (Hawaii)
Forbes, William Cameron
 (Philippines)
Gaines, John Pollard (Oreg.)
Geary, John White (Kans.)
Gilpin, William (Colo.)
Gorman, Willis Arnold (Minn.)
Hammond, Samuel (Mo.)
Hauser, Samuel Thomas (Mont.)
Howard, Benjamin (La.)
Hoyt, John Wesley (Wyo.)
Izard, George (Ark.)
Lane, Joseph (Oreg.)
Lewis, Meriwether (La.)
Lyon, Caleb (Idaho)
McCook, Edward Moody (Colo.)
Magoon, Charles Edward (C.Z.)

Mathews, George (Miss.)
Mitchell, Robert Byington
 (N.Mex.)
Murphy, Frank (Philippines)
Nye, James Warren (Nev.)
Peñalosa Briceñ, Deigo Dionisio
 (N.Mex.)
Pierce, Gilbert Ashville (Dakota)
Piñero Jiménez, Jesús Toribio
 (P.R.)
Portolá, Gaspar de (Upper Calif.)
Posey, Thomas (Indian Terr.)
Potts, Benjamin Franklin (Mont.)
Prince, Le Baron Bradford
 (N.Mex.)
Reeder, Andrew Horatio (Kans.)
St. Clair, Arthur (Northwest)
Sargent, Winthrop, 1753–1820
 (Miss.)
Saunders, Alvin (Nebr.)
Shepherd, Alexander Robey (D.C.)
Shepley, George Foster (La.)
Sloan, Richard Elihu (Ariz.)
Squire, Watson Carvosso (Wash.)
Stevens, Isaac Ingalls (Wash.)
Walker, Robert John (Kans.)
Winship, Blanton (P.R.)

GRAMMARIAN
Brown, Goold
Murray, Lindley
Scott, Fred Newton

GRANGE (See also AGRICULTURIST)
Adams, Dudley W.
Ellis, Seth Hockett
Mayo, Mary Anne Bryant

GRAPHIC ARTIST
Archipenko, Alexander
Marsh, Reginald

GUERRILLA CHIEFTAIN
Quantrill, William Clarke
Sumter, Thomas

GUIDE (See also SCOUT)
Baker, James
Bottineau, Pierre
Carson, Christopher ("Kit")
Fitzpatrick, Thomas
Provost, Etienne
Reynolds, Charles Alexander
Rose, Edward
Walker, Joseph Reddeford
Williams, William Sherley

GUITARIST
Hendrix, Jimi
White, Josh
Williams, (Hiram) Hank

GUNSMITH (See also ORDNANCE EXPERT)
Henry, William
Lawrence, Richard Smith
Pomeroy, Seth
Whittemore, Amos

GYNECOLOGIST (See also PHYSICIAN)
Byford, William Heath
Cullen, Thomas Stephen
Dickinson, Robert Latou
Engelmann, George Julius

Gilliam, David Tod
Graves, William Phillips
Howard, William Travis
Jackson, Abraham Reeves
Kelly, Howard Atwood
Marcy, Henry Orlando
Parry, John Stubbs
Parvin, Theophilus
Polak, John Osborn
Rubin, Isidor Clinton
Sims, James Marion
Skene, Alexander Johnston
    Chalmers
Smith, Albert Holmes
Storer, Horatio Robinson
Taussig, Frederick Joseph
Thomas, Theodore Gaillard
Van de Warker, Edward Ely
Wilson, Henry Parke Custis

HARNESS MAKER (See
    MANUFACTURER, HARNESS
    MAKER)
HARNESS RACER
    White, Benjamin Franklin
HARPSICHORDIST
    Landowska, Wanda Aleksandra
HATTER (See MANUFACTURER,
    HATTER)
HEALTH CARE ADMINISTRATOR
    Fitzgerald, Alice Louise Florence
HEALTH PROPAGANDIST
    Kellogg, John Harvey
HEBRAIST (See also SEMITIST,
    SCHOLAR)
    Davidson, Israel
    Harper, William Rainey
    Revel, Bernard
    Schechter, Solomon
    Sewall, Stephen
HELLENIST (See also CLASSICIST,
    SCHOLAR)
    Callimachos, Panos Demetrios
    Goodwin, William Watson
    Smyth, Herbert Weir
    White, John William
    Wright, John Henry
HEROINE
    Bailey, Anna Warner
    Corbin, Margaret
    McCauley, Mary Ludwig Hays
HERPETOLOGIST (See also ZOOLOGIST)
    Barbour, Thomas
    Ditmars, Raymond Lee
HISPANIST
    Crawford, James Pyle Wickersham
HISTOLOGIST (See also ANATOMIST,
    PHYSICIAN)
    Hoerr, Normand Louis
HISTORIAN (See also CHRONICLER,
    CHURCH HISTORIAN, LITERARY
    HISTORIAN, MEDICAL
    HISTORIAN, MEDIEVALIST)
    Abbott, John Stevens Cabot
    Abel-Henderson, Annie Heloise
    Absalom, Harris Chappell

Adams, Brooks
Adams, Charles Francis
Adams, Charles Kendall
Adams, Ephraim Douglass
Adams, George Burton
Adams, Henry Brooks
Adams, James Truslow
Adams, Randolph Greenfield
Alexander, de Alva Stanwood
Alexander, William Dewitt
Allen, Frederick Lewis
Alvord, Clarence Walworth
Ames, Herman Vandenburg
Andrews, Charles McLean
Arnold, Isaac Newton
Arnold, Samuel Greene
Asbury, Herbert
Atkinson, John
Backus, Isaac
Baird, Charles Washington
Baird, Henry Martyn
Baker, Carl Lotus
Baker, Frank
Bancroft, Frederic
Bancroft, George
Bancroft, Hubert Howe
Bandelier, Adolph Francis
    Alphonse
Banks, Charles Edward
Barber, John Warner
Bassett, John Spencer
Bayley, James Roosevelt
Beard, Charles Austin
Beard, Mary Ritter
Beauchamp, William Martin
Beer, George Louis
Benedict, David
Berenson, Bernard
Beveridge, Albert Jeremiah
Beverley, Robert
Binkley, Robert Cedric
Bolton, Herbert Eugene
Botsford, George Willis
Bourne, Edward Gaylord
Bouton, Nathaniel
Bowers, Claude Gernade
Boyd, William Kenneth
Bozman, John Leeds
Breasted, James Henry
Brinton, Clarence Crane
Brodhead, John Romeyn
Bronson, Henry
Brown, Alexander
Brown, William Wells
Bruce, Philip Alexander
Buley, Roscoe Carlyle
Burr, George Lincoln
Burrage, Henry Sweetser
Burton, Clarence Monroe
Cabell, James Branch
Cajori, Florian
Callender, Guy Stevens
Campbell, Charles
Campbell, William W.
Carson, Hampton Lawrence
Case, Shirley Jackson

Cathcart, William
Chamberlain, Mellen
Channing, Edward
Charlevoix, Pierre François Xavier
    de
Cheyney, Edward Potts
Chittenden, Hiram Martin
Cist, Henry Martyn
Claiborne, John Francis
    Hamtramck
Clark, Arthur Hamilton
Colcord, Lincoln Ross
Connor, Robert Digges Wimberly
Cooke, John Esten
Coolidge, Archibald Cary
Corwin, Edward Samuel
Corwin, Edwin Tanjore
Crawford, Francis Marion
Cross, Arthur Lyon
Dart, Henry Paluché
Dawson, Henry Barton
Deane, Charles
Del Mar, Alexander
Dennett, Tyler (Wilbur)
Dennis, Alfred Lewis Pinneo
Dennis, James Shepard
DeVoto, Bernard Augustine
Dexter, Franklin Bowditch
Dodd, William Edward
Dodge, Theodore Ayrault
Dos Passos, John Roderigo
Drake, Francis Samuel
Drake, Samuel Adams
Drake, Samuel Gardner
Draper, John William
Draper, Lyman Copeland
Du Bois, William Edward
    Burghardt
Dunlap, William
Dunning, William Archibald
Dupratz, Antoine Simon Le Page
Durrett, Reuben Thomas
Eggleston, Edward
Egle, William Henry
Eliot, Samuel
Elliott, Charles
Ellis, George Edward
Emerton, Ephraim
Engelhardt, Zephyrin
English, William Hayden
Evans, Clement Anselm
Fall, Bernard B.
Farrand, Max
Fay, Sidney Bradshaw
Fernow, Berthold
Field, David Dudley
Filson, John
Finney, Charles Grandison
Fish, Carl Russell
Fisher, George Park
Fisher, Sydney George
Fiske, John
Fleming, Walter Lynwood
Folwell, William Watts
Forbes, Esther
Force, Peter

Ford, Henry Jones
Ford, Paul Leicester
Fortier, Alcée
Fox, Dixon Ryan
Francis, Joshua Francis
Francke, Kuno
Frank, Tenney
Freeman, Douglas Southall
Frothingham, Richard
Fulton, John Farquhar
Garrett, William Robertson
Garrison, Fielding Hudson
Gavin, Frank Stanton Burns
Gay, Edwin Francis
Gayarré, Charles Étienne Arthur
Goddard, Calvin Hooker
Golder, Frank Alfred
Good, James Isaac
Gordy, John Pancoast
Gräbner, August Lawrence
Greene, Francis Vinton
Greenhow, Robert
Griffin, Martin Ignatius Joseph
Grigsby, Hugh Blair
Gross, Charles
Hall, Hiland
Hamilton, Alexander, 1712–1756
Hammond, Bray
Hammond, Jabez Delano
Hansen, Marcus Lee
Haring, Clarence
Harlow, Ralph Volney
Harrisse, Henry
Hart, Albert Bushnell
Haskins, Charles Homer
Hawks, Francis Lister
Hay, John Milton
Hayes, Carlton Joseph Huntley
Haynes, Williams
Haywood, John
Hendrick, Burton Jesse
Henry, William Wirt
Hewat, Alexander
Hildreth, Samuel Prescott
Hill, Frederick Trevor
Hoffman, David
Hofstadter, Richard
Holbrook, Stewart Hall
Holmes, Abiel
Holst, Hermann Eduard von
Howard, Joseph Kinsey
Howe, George
Howe, Henry
Howe, Mark De Wolfe
Hubbard, William
Hulbert, Archer Butler
Hunt, Gaillard
Ireland, Joseph Norton
Jacobs, Joseph, 1854–1916
Jameson, John Franklin
Jenkins, Howard Malcolm
Jewett, Clarence Frederick
Johnson, Allen
Johnston, Alexander
Johnston, Henry Phelps
Johnston, Robert Matteson

Jones, Charles Colcock
Jones, Hugh
Kapp, Friedrich
Kelsey, Rayner Wickersham
Knight, Lucian Lamar
Knox, Dudley Wright
Kobbé, Gustav
Körner, Gustav Philip
Krehbiel, Henry Edward
Kuykendall, Ralph Simpson
Lacy, William Albert
Lambing, Andrew Arnold
Larson, Laurence Marcellus
Latané, John Holladay
Latourette, Kenneth Scott
Lea, Henry Charles
Learned, Marion Dexter
Lee, Jesse
Leland, Waldo Gifford
Lenker, John Nicholas
Levering, Joseph Mortimer
Libby, Orin Grant
Lingelbach, Anna Lane
Logan, Deborah Norris
Lovejoy, Arthur Oncken
Lowell, Edward Jackson
Lowery, Woodbury
McAfee, Robert Breckinridge
McCrady, Edward
McElroy, Robert McNutt
McGiffert, Arthur Cushman
McKinley, Albert Edward
McLaughlin, Andrew Cunningham
McMahon, John Van Lear
McMaster, John Bach
MacNair, Harley Farnsworth
Mahan, Alfred Thayer
Marquand, Allan
Marsh, Frank Burr
Marshall, Humphrey
Mattingly, Garrett
Meigs, William Montgomery
Merrill, Elmer Truesdell
Miles, Henry Adolphus
Miller, David Hunter
Miller, William Snow
Milton, George Fort
Minot, George Richards
Mitchell, Lucy Myers Wright
Moffat, James Clement
Monette, John Wesley
Moon, Parker Thomas
Moore, George Foot
Moore, George Henry
Moreau De Saint-Méry, Médéric-
    Louis-Elie
Morse, Anson Daniel
Moses, Bernard
Motley, John Lothrop
Munro, Dana Carleton
Murray, Louise Shipman Welles
Muzzey, David Saville
Myers, Gustavus
Neill, Edward Duffield
Nelson, William, 1847–1914
Newman, Albert Henry

Niles, Samuel
Notestein, Wallace
Oberholtzer, Ellis Paxson
O'Callaghan, Edmund Bailey
Odell, George Clinton Densmore
Oliver, Fitch Edward
Olmstead, Albert Ten Eyck
Onderdonk, Henry
Osgood, Herbert Levi
Owen, Thomas McAdory
Owsley, Frank Lawrence
Palfrey, John Gorham
Palón, Francisco
Parkman, Francis
Parrington, Vernon Louis
Penhallow, Samuel
Pennypacker, Samuel Whitaker
Perkins, James Breck
Phillips, Ulrich Bonnell
Pickett, Albert James
Pitkin, Timothy
Poole, William Frederick
Prescott, William Hickling
Proud, Robert
Putnam, Eben
Quincy, Josiah Phillips
Quinn, Arthur Hobson
Ramsay, David
Rand, Edward Kennard
Randall, James Garfield
Rattermann, Heinrich Armin
Read, Conyers
Reeves, Arthur Middleton
Reichel, William Cornelius
Rhodes, James Ford
Ricketson, Daniel
Ridpath, John Clark
Rister, Carl Coke
Rives, George Lockhart
Robertson, James Alexander
Robertson, William Spence
Robinson, James Harvey
Ropes, John Codman
Rostovtzeff, Michael Ivanovitch
Rourke, Constance Mayfield
Rupp, Israel Daniel
Sabine, Lorenzo
Salmon, Lucy Maynard
Salter, William
Sandoz, Mari
Sarton, George Alfred Léon
Saunders, William Laurence
Scharf, John Thomas
Schlesinger, Arthur Meier
Schmidt, Nathaniel
Schouler, James
Schouler, William
Schuyler, Robert Livingston
Schweinitz, Edmund Alexander de
Seidensticker, Oswald
Severance, Frank Hayward
Seymour, Charles
Shannon, Fred Albert
Shea, John Dawson Gilmary
Shepherd, William Robert
Shotwell, James Thomson

Simonds, Frank Herbert
Slaughter, Philip
Sloane, William Milligan
Smith, David Eugene
Smith, Henry Augustus Middleton
Smith, Justin Harvey
Smith, Preserved
Smith, William, 1728–1793
Sonneck, Oscar George Theodore
Spargo, John
Sparks, Edwin Erle
Sparks, Jared
Spring, Leverett Wilson
Stanard, Mary Mann Page Newton
Stanwood, Edward
Staples, William Read
Steiner, Bernard Christian
Stephens, Henry Morse
Stephenson, Nathaniel Wright
Stevens, Abel
Stevens, William Bacon
Stiles, Henry Reed
Stillé, Charles Janeway
Stith, William
Stone, William Leete, 1792–1844
Stone, William Leete, 1835–1908
Strachey, William
Stuart, Isaac William
Swank, James Moore
Switzler, William Franklin
Sydnor, Charles Sackett
Tansill, Charles Callan
Taylor, Henry Osborn
Teggart, Frederick John
Thacher, James
Thayer, William Roscoe
Thomas, Isaiah
Thompson, Zadock
Thornton, John Wingate
Trent, William Peterfield
Trescot, William Henry
Trumbull, Benjamin
Trumbull, James Hammond
Turner, Edward Raymond
Turner, Frederick Jackson
Tuttle, Charles Wesley
Tuttle, Herbert
Tyler, Lyon Gardiner
Tyler, Moses Coit
Tyler, Royall
Tyson, Job Roberts
Upham, Charles Wentworth
Upham, Warren
Vail, Robert William Glenroie
Van Dyke, Paul
Van Loon, Hendrik Willem
Van Tyne, Claude Halstead
Vedder, Henry Clay
Victor, Frances Fuller
Vignaud, Henry
Warren, Charles
Warren, Herbert Langford
Warren, Mercy Otis
Washburne, Elihu Benjamin
Webb, Walter Prescott
Weeden, William Babcock

Weeks, Stephen Beauregard
Wergeland, Agnes Mathilde
Wertenbaker, Thomas Jefferson
West, Allen Brown
Westcott, Thompson
Westermann, William Linn
Wheaton, Henry
Wheeler, John Hill
White, Andrew Dickson
White, Leonard Dupee
Whitehead, William Adee
Wickes, Stephen
Wiener, Leo
Willard, James Field
Willard, Joseph
Williamson, William Durkee
Willis, William
Winsor, Justin
Woodson, Carter Godwin
Worcester, Joseph Emerson
Yoakum, Henderson
Zook, George Frederick

HOME ECONOMIST (See also
        ECONOMIST)
Bevier, Isabel
Marlatt, Abby Lillian
Norton, Mary Alice Peloubet
Richards, Ellen Henrietta Swallow
Richardson, Anna Euretta
Van Rensselaer, Martha

HOMEOPATHIST (See also PHYSICAN)
Hering, Constantine
Neidhard, Charles
Thomas, Amos Russell

HORSE BREEDER (See also
        HORSEMAN)
Jacobs, Hirsch

HORSEMAN (See also HORSE
        BREEDER, RACEHORSE OWNER)
Breckinridge, Desha
Ten Broeck, Richard
Woodward, William

HORSE TAMER (See also COWBOY,
        HORSEMAN)
Rarey, John Solomon

HORSE TRAINER
Fitzsimmons, James Edward
        ("Sunny Jim")
Hirsch, Maximilian Justice
Jacobs, Hirsch
Jones, Benjamin Allyn
Sande, Earl
White, Benjamin Franklin

HORTICULTURIST (See also
        AGRICULTURIST)
Adams, Dudley W.
Bailey, Liberty Hyde
Barry, Patrick
Budd, Joseph Lancaster
Bull, Ephraim Wales
Burrill, Thomas Jonathan
Campbell, George Washington
Cook, Zebedee
Downing, Andrew Jackson
Downing, Charles
Fuller, Andrew S.

Gale, Elbridge
Garey, Thomas Andrew
Goff, Emmet Stull
Goodrich, Chauncey
Green, Samuel Bowdlear
Hansen, George
Hansen, Niels Ebbesen
Haraszthy De Mokcsa, Agoston
Hart, Edmund Hall
Henderson, Peter
Hilgard, Theodor Erasmus
Hovey, Charles Mason
Hunnewell, Horatio Hollis
Hunt, Benjamin Weeks
Lippincott, James Starr
Logan, James Harvey
Longworth, Nicholas, 1782–1863
McFarland, John Horace
McLaren, John
McMahon, Bernard
Mazzei, Philip
Meehan, Thomas
Miller, Samuel
Munson, Thomas Volney
Nehrling, Henry
Parmentier, Andrew
Parsons, Samuel Bowne
Periam, Jonathan
Powell, George Harold
Pursh, Frederick
Pyle, Robert
Roeding, George Christian
Rogers, Edward Staniford
Sargent, Henry Winthrop
Saunders, William
Strong, Harriet Williams Russell
Thurber, George
Van Fleet, Walter
Warder, John Aston
White, Wiliam Nathaniel
Wickson, Edward James

HOSPITAL ADMINISTRATOR
Goldwater, Sigismund Schulz
McFarland, George Bradley
White, William Alanson

HOSTESS (See also SOCIALITE)
Botta, Anne Charlotte Lynch
Carnegie, Mary Crowninshield
        Endicott Chamberlain
De Wolfe, Elsie
Madison, Dolly Payne
Maxwell, Elsa
Meredith, Edna C. Elliott
Schuyler, Margarita
Sprague, Kate Chase

HOTELMAN
Barnum, Zenus
Boldt, George C.
Drake, John Burroughs
Fraunces, Samuel
Grim, David
Niblo, William
Statler, Ellsworth Milton
Stetson, Charles Augustus
Stokes, William Earl Dodge
Taggart, Thomas

Berliner, Emile
Bettendorf, William Peter
Bigelow, Erastus Brigham
Blair, William Richards
Blake, Eli Whitney
Blake, Francis
Blake, Lyman Reed
Blanchard, Thomas
Bogardus, James
Bonard, Louis
Bonwill, William Gibson Arlington
Bonzano, Adolphus
Borden, Gail
Borg, George William
Bovie, William T.
Boyden, Seth
Boyden, Uriah Atherton
Brooks, Byron Alden
Brown, Alexander Ephraim
Brown, Fayette
Brown, James Salisbury
Brown, Joseph Rogers
Brown, Sylvanus
Browning, John Moses
Brunton, David William
Brush, Charles Francis
Bryant, Gridley
Buchanan, Joseph
Buckland, Cyrus
Bullock, William A.
Burden, Henry
Burgess, W(illiam) Starling
Burroughs, William Seward
Burrowes, Edward Thomas
Burson, William Worth
Burt, John
Burt, William Austin
Bushnell, David
Butterick, Ebenezer
Campbell, Andrew
Carlson, Chester Floyd
Carothers, Wallace Hume
Channing, William Francis
Christie, John Walter
Cist, Jacob
Cluett, Sanford Lockwood
Clymer, George E.
Coates, George Henry
Colburn, Irving Wightman
Colles, Christopher
Colt, Samuel
Conant, Hezekiah
Converse, Edmund Cogswell
Cooper, Peter
Corliss, George Henry
Cottrell, Calvert Byron
Cottrell, Frederick Gardner
Cowen, Joshua Lionel
Craven, John Joseph
Crompton, George
Crompton, William
Crowell, Luther Childs
Crozier, William
Curtiss, Glenn Hammond
Cutler, James Goold
Cutting, James Ambrose

Daft, Leo
Dahlgren, John Adolphus Bernard
Dalzell, Robert M.
Dancel, Christian
Danforth, Charles
Daniels, Fred Harris
Davenport, Thomas
Davis, Phineas
Davis, William Augustine
Davison, Gregory Caldwell
De Forest, Lee
Delany, Patrick Bernard
Dickson, Earle Ensign
Dixon, Joseph
Dod, Daniel
Doremus, Robert Ogden
Dow, Lorenzo
Draper, Ira
Dripps, Isaac L.
Dunbar, Robert
Du Pont, Francis Irénée
Durand, Cyrus
Durfee, William Franklin
Durfee, Zoheth Sherman
Durham, Caleb Wheeler
Duryea, Charles Edgar
Duryea, James Frank
Dymond, John
Eads, James Buchanan
Earle, Pliny
Eastman, George
Edgar, Charles
Edison, Thomas Alva
Edwards, Oliver
Edwards, William
Eickemeyer, Rudolf
Ellis, Carleton
Emerson, James Ezekiel
Emerson, Ralph
Emery, Albert Hamilton
Ericsson, John
Esterly, George
Evans, Oliver
Eve, Joseph
Ewbank, Thomas
Fairbanks, Henry
Fairbanks, Thaddeus
Farmer, Moses Gerrish
Ferris, George Washington Gale
Fessenden, Reginald Aubrey
Fessenden, Thomas Green
Field, Stephen Dudley
Fisher, Clark
Fitch, John
Flad, Henry
Ford, Hannibal Choate
Ford, John Baptiste
Forney, Matthias Vace
Fortescue, Charles LeGeyt
Francis, Joseph
Franklin, Benjamin
Frash, Herman
French, Aaron
Fuller, Levi Knight
Fuller, Robert Mason
Fulton, Robert

Furlow, Floyd Charles
Gally, Merritt
Gaskill, Harvey Freeman
Gatling, Richard Jordan
Gayley, James
Gernsback, Hugo
Gibbs, James Ethan Allen
Gilbert, Alfred Carlton
Gilbert, Rufus Henry
Gillette, King Camp
Glidden, Joseph Farwell
Goddard, Calvin Luther
Goddu, Louis
Godfrey, Thomas
Good, John
Goodwin, Hannibal Williston
Goodyear, Charles
Gordon, George Phineas
Grant, George Barnard
Gray, Elisha
Grinnell, Frederick
Haish, Jacob
Hall, Thomas
Hall, Thomas Seavey
Hallidie, Andrew Smith
Hamlin, Emmons
Hammerstein, Oscar
Hammond, James Bartlett
Harvey, Hayward Augustus
Haupt, Herman
Hayden, Hiram Washington
Hayden, Joseph Shepard
Hayward, Nathaniel Manley
Herdic, Peter
Herreshoff, James Brown
Hewitt, Peter Cooper
Heywood, Levi
Hoe, Richard March
Hogan, John Vincent Lawless
Holland, John Philip
Hollerith, Herman
Hotchkiss, Benjamin Berkeley
Houdry, Eugene Jules
House, Henry Alonzo
House, Royal Earl
Howe, Elias
Howe, Frederick Webster
Howe, John Ireland
Howe, William
Howell, Albert Summers
Howell, John Adams
Howey, Walter Crawford
Hoxie, William Dixie
Hubbard, Henry Griswold
Hubert, Conrad
Hudson, William Smith
Hughes, David Edward
Hughes, Howard Robard
Hussey, Obed
Hyatt, John Wesley
Ingersoll, Simon
Ives, Frederic Eugene
Janney, Eli Hamilton
Jarves, Deming
Jenkins, Nathaniel
Jenks, Joseph

Jenney, William Le Baron
Jerome, Chauncey
Johnson, Eldridge Reeves
Johnson, Tom Loftin
Johnston, Samuel
Jones, Amanda Theodosia
Jones, Evan William
Jones, Samuel Milton
Judson, Egbert Putnam
Kalmus, Herbert Thomas
Kalmus, Natalie Mabelle Dunfee
Keely, John Ernst Worrell
Keen, Morris Longstreth
Kelly, William
Kent, Arthur Atwater
Kettering, Charles Franklin
Kingsford, Thomas
Knight, Edward Collings
Knowles, Lucius James
Knox, Thomas Wallace
Kraft, James Lewis
Kruesi, John
Lake, Simon
Lamb, Isaac Wixom
Lamme, Benjamin Garver
Lanston, Tolbert
Larned, Joseph Gay Eaton
Latrobe, John Hazlehurst Boneval
Latta, Alexander Bonner
Lawrence, Richard Smith
Lay, John Louis
Leavitt, Frank McDowell
Leffel, James
Leonard, Harry Ward
Levy, Louis Edward
Levy, Max
Lewis, Isaac Newton
Leyner, John George
Lloyd, Marshall Burns
Locke, John
Lockheed, Malcolm
Longstreet, William
Lowe, Thaddeus Sobieski
    Coulincourt
Lucas, Jonathan, 1775–1832
Lundie, John
Lyall, James
McCarroll, James
McCormick, Cyrus Hall
McCormick, Robert
McCormick, Stephen
McCoy, Elijah
McDougall, Alexander
McKay, Gordon
McTammany, John
Manly, Charles Matthews
Mannes, Leopold Damrosch
Marks, Amasa Abraham
Marsh, Charles Wesley
Marsh, Sylvester
Marsh, William Wallace
Mason, Arthur John
Mason, William
Mast, Phineas Price
Masury, John Wesley
Matthews, John

Matzeliger, Jan Ernst
Maxim, Hiram Percy
Maxim, Hiram Stevens
Maxim, Hudson
Maynard, Edward
Melville, David
Mendelsohn, Samuel
Mercer, Henry Chapman
Mergenthaler, Ottmar
Merritt, Israel John
Midgley, Thomas
Miller, Ezra
Miller, Lewis
Mills, Anson
Moody, Paul
Morehead, John Motley
Morey, Samuel
Morgan, Charles Hill
Morse, Samuel Finley Breese
Morse, Sidney Edwards
Mowbray, George Mordey
Munger, Robert Sylvester
Murray, Thomas Edward
Nesmith, John
Nessler, Karl Ludwig
Newcomb, Charles Leonard
Newton, Henry Jotham
Nicholson, William Thomas
Niles, Nathaniel, 1741–1828
Norden, Carl Lukas
Nott, Eliphalet
Noyes, La Verne
Olds, Ransom Eli
Oliver, James
Oliver, Paul Ambrose
Orr, Hugh
Otis, Charles Rollin
Otis, Elisha Graves
Owens, Michael Joseph
Packard, James Ward
Painter, William
Parr, Samuel Wilson
Parrott, Robert Parker
Patterson, Rufus Lenoir
Perkins, Jacob
Perry, Stuart
Pidgin, Charles Felton
Pitts, Hiram Avery
Pope, Franklin Leonard
Porter, Rufus
Potter, William Bancroft
Pratt, Francis Ashbury
Pratt, John
Pratt, Thomas Willis
Prince, Frederick Henry
Pullman, George Mortimer
Rains, George Washington
Ramsay, Erskine
Rand, James Henry
Read, Nathan
Rees, James
Reese, Abram
Reese, Isaac
Reese, Jacob
Renwick, Edward Sabine
Reynolds, Edwin

Reynolds, Samuel Godfrey
Rice, Richard Henry
Riddell, John Leonard
Roberts, Benjamin Stone
Robinson, Stillman Williams
Robinson, William
Rodman, Thomas Jackson
Rogers, Henry J.
Rogers, James Harris
Rogers, John Raphael
Rogers, Thomas
Roosevelt, Hilborne Lewis
Roosevelt, Nicholas J.
Root, Elisha King
Rowland, Thomas Fitch
Rumsey, James
Rust, John Daniel
Sargent, James
Saunders, William Lawrence
Sawyer, Sylvanus
Saxton, Joseph
Schieren, Charles Adolph
Schneller, George Otto
See, Horace
Seiberling, Frank Augustus
Selden, George Baldwin
Sellers, Coleman
Sellers, William
Sergeant, Henry Clark
Sessions, Henry Howard
Shaw, Thomas
Sholes, Christopher Latham
Short, Sidney Howe
Sickles, Frederick Ellsworth
Silver, Thomas
Simpson, Michael Hodge
Sims, Winfield Scott
Singer, Isaac Merrit
Skinner, Halcyon
Slocum, Samuel
Smith, Horace
Spencer, Christopher Miner
Sperry, Elmer Ambrose
Sprague, Frank Julian
Stanley, Francis Edgar
Stanley, William
Starrett, Laroy S.
Stearns, Frank Ballou
Stetefeldt, Carl August
Stevens, Edwin Augustus
Stevens, John
Stevens, Robert Livingston
Stewart, Philo Penfield
Stoddard, Joshua C.
Stoddard, William Osborn
Sturtevant, Benjamin Franklin
Tagliabue, Giuseppe
Taylor, Frederick Winslow
Terry, Eli
Tesla, Nikola
Thomson, Elihu
Thomson, John
Thornton, William
Thorp, John
Thurber, Charles
Timby, Theodore Ruggles

Pritchard, Jeter Connelly
Randall, Samuel
Raulston, John Tate
Redfield, Isaac Fletcher
Rellstab, John
Richardson, William Merchant
Ross, Erskine Mayo
Ruggles, Timothy
Sanborn, Walter Henry
Sharswood, George
Shepley, George Foster
Sloan, Richard Elihu
Smith, William Nathan Harrell
Taft, Alphonso
Taylor, Creed
Tazewell, Henry
Thacher, Thomas Day
Thomas, Jesse Burgess
Toulmin, Harry
Tyler, John, 1747–1813
Van Devanter, Willis
Wales, Leonard Eugene
Waring, Julius Waties

JURIST (See also CHIEF JUSTICE
       [STATE], JUDGE, LAWYER,
       MAGISTRATE, SUPREME COURT
       JUSTICE)
Adams, Andrew
Aldrich, Edgar
Allen, Charles
Allen, Florence Ellinwood
Allen, John James
Allen, William
Allen, William Joshua
Alvey, Richard Henry
Ames, Samuel
Amidon, Charles Fremont
Anderson, Joseph
Andrews, Charles
Andrews, Charles Bartlett
Andrews, George Pierce
Archer, Stevenson
Ashe, Samuel
Atkinson, George Wesley
Auchmuty, Robert, d. 1750
Auchmuty, Robert, d. Nov. 1788
Axtell, Samuel Beach
Badger, George Edmund
Baldwin, Joseph Glover
Baldwin, Simeon
Baldwin, Simeon Eben
Barbour, Philip Pendleton
Bassett, Richard
Bates, Daniel Moore
Battle, Burrell Bunn
Battle, William Horn
Batts, Robert Lynn
Baxter, Elisha
Bayard, Samuel
Baylor, Robert Emmet Bledsoe
Bayly, Thomas Henry
Beasley, Mercer
Beatty, William Henry
Bennett, Edmund Hatch
Bennett, Nathaniel
Benning, Henry Lewis

Bermudez, Edouard Edmond
Betts, Samuel Rossiter
Biddle, Horace P.
Biggs, Asa
Bishop, Robert Roberts
Blair, John
Blatchford, Samuel
Bleckley, Logan Edwin
Bliss, Jonathan
Bliss, Philemon
Blount, Willie
Blowers, Sampson Salter
Boise, Reuben Patrick
Bond, Hugh Lennox
Bourne, Benjamin
Brackenridge, Hugh Henry
Bradbury, Theophilus
Bradford, Edward Green
Bradford, William
Bradley, Stephen Row
Brannon, Henry
Brearly, David
Breaux, Joseph Arsenne
Breese, Sidney
Brennan, Francis James
Brewer, David Josiah
Brewster, Frederick Carroll
Brickell, Robert Coman
Brinkerhoff, Jacob
Brooke, Francis Taliaferro
Brown, Addison
Brown, Henry Billings
Bruce, Andrew Alexander
Bryan, George
Buchanan, John
Bullard, Henry Adams
Burke, Aedanus
Butler, Thomas Belden
Bynum, William Preston
Cadwalader, John
Cady, Daniel
Caldwell, Henry Clay
Campbell, James Valentine
Campbell, John Wilson
Campbell, Josiah A. Patterson
Campbell, William W.
Cardozo, Benjamin Nathan
Carleton, Henry
Carr, Dabney
Carrington, Paul
Case, William Scoville
Casey, Joseph
Cassoday, John Bolivar
Caton, John Dean
Catron, John
Chambers, Ezekiel Forman
Champlin, John Wayne
Charlton, Thomas Usher Pulaski
Chew, Benjamin
Chilton, William Paris
Chipman, Nathaniel
Clark, Daniel
Clark, Greenleaf
Clark, Walter
Clay, Joseph
Clayton, Thomas

Clifford, Nathan
Clopton, David
Cobb, Andrew Jackson
Cofer, Martin Hardin
Coffey, James Vincent
Cole, Chester Cicero
Collens, Thomas Wharton
Collier, Henry Watkins
Colt, Le Baron Bradford
Comstock, George Franklin
Conrad, Robert Taylor
Cooley, Thomas McIntyre
Cooper, William
Cranch, William
Cross, Edward
Crounse, Lorenzo
Crump, William Wood
Curtis, Benjamin Robbins
Cushing, Luther Stearns
Cushing, William
Daly, Charles Patrick
Dana, Francis
Daniel, Peter Vivian
Dargan, Edmund Strother
Davis, David
Davis, John
Davis, Noah
Day, James Gamble
Day, Luther
Deady, Matthew Paul
Deemer, Horace Emerson
Devaney, John Patrick
Devens, Charles
Dick, Robert Paine
Dickerson, Philemon
Dickey, Theophilus Lyle
Dickinson, John
Dill, James Brooks
Dillon, John Forrest
Dixon, Luther Swift
Doe, Charles
Doggett, David
Drake, Charles Daniel
Drayton, John
Drayton, William
Duane, James
Dudley, Paul
Duer, John
Dunn, Charles
Durell, Edward Henry
Durfee, Job
Durfee, Thomas
Dutton, Henry
Dyer, Eliphalet
Edmonds, John Worth
Edwards, Pierpont
Elliott, Charles Burke
Ellis, Powhatan
Elmer, Jonathan
Elmer, Lucius Quintus
       Cincinnatus
Emery, Lucilius Alonzo
Emott, James, 1771–1850
Emott, James, 1823–1884
Endicott, William Crowninshield
Erskine, John

Eustis, George
Evans, Walter
Ewing, Charles
Farman, Elbert Eli
Farrar, Timothy
Fenner, Charles Erasmus
Field, Fred Tarbell
Field, Richard Stockton
Field, Walbridge Abner
Finch, Francis Miles
Fisher, George Purnell
Flandrau, Charles Eugene
Fleming, Aretas Brooks
Fletcher, Richard
Fletcher, William Asa
Folger, Charles James
Force, Manning Ferguson
Gaston, William
Gaynor, William Jay
George, James Zachariah
Gholson, Samuel Jameson
Gholson, Thomas Saunders
Gholson, William Yates
Gibson, John Bannister
Gilpin, Edward Woodward
Goddard, Luther Marcellus
Goff, John William
Goldthwaite, George
Goldthwaite, Henry Barnes
Goodenow, John Milton
Gould, James
Gould, Robert Simonton
Grant, Claudius Buchanan
Gray, George
Gray, Horace
Green, Henry Woodhull
Greene, Albert Gorton
Gresham, Walter Quintin
Griffin, Cyrus
Grimké, John Faucheraud
Griswold, Matthew
Groesbeck, William Slocum
Grosscup, Peter Stenger
Grundy, Felix
Gummere, William Stryker
Haines, Daniel
Hall, Hiland
Hall, James, 1793–1868
Hall, Nathan Kelsey
Hall, Willard
Hallett, Moses
Hamilton, Walton Hale
Handy, Alexander Hamilton
Hanson, Alexander Contee,
    1749–1806
Hare, John Innes Clark
Harlan, John Marshall
Harmon, Judson
Harrington, Samuel Maxwell
Harris, Ira
Harris, William Littleton
Haselton, Seneca
Hastings, Serranus Clinton
Hay, George
Haywood, John
Hemphill, John

Henderson, Leonard
Heyward, Thomas
Hill, Robert Andrews
Hinman, Joel
Hitchcock, Peter
Hoadly, George
Hoar, Ebenezer Rockwood
Hoffman, David Murray
Hopkinson, Joseph
Hornblower, Joseph Coerten
Hornblower, William Butler
Hough, Charles Merrill
Hovey, Alvin Peterson
Howard, Timothy Edward
Howe, Samuel
Howe, William Wirt
Howell, David
Howry, Charles Bowen
Hughes, Robert William
Humphreys, West Hughes
Hunt, William Henry
Hutson, Richard
Iredell, James
Iverson, Alfred
Jackson, Howell Edmunds
Jackson, James, 1819–1887
Jackson, John George
Jackson, Mortimer Melville
Jackson, Robert Houghwout
Jameson, John Alexander
Jenckes, Thomas Allen
Jenkins, Charles Jones
Johns, Kensey, 1759–1848
Johns, Kensey, 1791–1857
Johnson, Alexander Smith
Johnson, Herschel Vespasian
Johnson, William
Johnson, William Samuel
Johnston, Job
Johnston, Peter
Jones, Joseph
Jones, Leonard Augustus
Jones, Samuel
Jones, Thomas
Jones, Thomas Goode
Kalisch, Samuel
Kane, John Kintzing
Keith, James
Kent, Edward
Kent, James
Kenyon, William Squire
Kephart, John William
Kershaw, Joseph Brevard
Kilty, William
Kinkead, Edgar Benton
Kinne, La Vega George
Kinsey, John
Kirkpatrick, Andrew
Knapp, Martin Augustine
Knowlton, Marcus Perrin
Körner, Gustav Philip
Lamar, Joseph Rucker
Lander, Edward
Landis, Kenesaw Mountain
Lansing, John
Larrazolo, Octaviano Ambrosio

Law, Richard
Lawrence, William, 1819–1899
Leavitt, Humphrey Howe
Lee, Charles, 1758–1815
Lee, Thomas
Lee, William Little
Lehman, Irving
Lewis, Ellis
Lewis, Joseph Horace
Lewis, Morgan
Lindley, Curtis Holbrook
Lindsay, William
Lipscomb, Abner Smith
Livermore, Samuel, 1732–1803
Livingston, Henry Brockholst
Livingston, Robert R., 1718–1775
Lockwood, Samuel Drake
Logan, James Harvey
Logan, Stephen Trigg
Lomax, John Tayloe
Longstreet, Augustus Baldwin
Loomis, Dwight
Lord, Otis Phillips
Lord, William Paine
Lowell, John, 1743–1802
Lowell, John, 1824–1897
Lucas, Daniel Bedinger
Lucas, John Baptiste Charles
Ludeling, John Theodore
Ludlow, George Duncan
Lurton, Horace Harmon
Lynde, Benjamin
Lyon, William Penn
Lyons, Peter
McAllister, Matthew Hall
McCaleb, Theodore Howard
McCarran, Patrick Anthony
McCay, Henry Kent
McComas, Louis Emory
McCrary, George Washington
McDonald, Charles James
McEnery, Samuel Douglas
McFarland, Thomas Bard
McGowan, Samuel
Mack, Julian William
McKean, Joseph Borden
McKenna, Joseph
McKinstry, Elisha Williams
McLean, John
McMaster, Guy Humphreys
Magie, William Jay
Magrath, Andrew Gordon
Malone, Walter
Manning, Thomas Courtland
Marchant, Henry
Marshall, Thomas Alexander
Martin, François-Xavier
Mason, Charles
Mason, John Young
Matthews, Stanley
Maxwell, Augustus Emmett
Maxwell, Samuel
Mercur, Ulysses
Merrick, Edwin Thomas
Merrick, Pliny
Merrimon, Augustus Summerfield

Metcalf, Theron
Miller, Oliver
Mills, Benjamin
Minot, George Richards
Mitchell, James Tyndale
Mitchell, Nahum
Mitchell, Stephen Mix
Mitchell, William, 1801–1886
Moncure, Richard Cassius Lee
Moody, William Henry
Moore, John Bassett
Moore, Maurice
Moore, William, 1699–1783
Moore, William, 1735–1793
Moreau-Lislet, Louis Casimir
    Elisabeth
Morgan, Philip Hicky
Morris, Richard
Morrow, William W.
Morton, Marcus, 1784–1864
Murphey, Archibald De Bow
Napton, William Barclay
Nash, Frederick
Nelson, Hugh
Nelson, Rensselaer Russell
Nelson, Roger
Nelson, Samuel
Nicholas, Philip Norborne
Nicholson, Alfred Osborne Pope
Nicholson, Joseph Hopper
Nicolls, Matthias
Nixon, John Thompson
Norton, Elijah Hise
Nott, Abraham
Nott, Charles Cooper
Noyes, Walter Chadwick
Oakley, Thomas Jackson
O'Brien, Morgan Joseph
Oldham, Williamson Simpson
Oliver, Andrew
O'Neall, John Belton
Orton, Harlow South
Otis, Charles Eugene
Otto, William Tod
Overton, John
Owsley, William
Paca, William
Paine, Elijah
Paine, Robert Treat
Pardee, Don Albert
Parke, Benjamin
Parker, Alton Brooks
Parker, Amasa Junius
Parker, Edwin Brewington
Parker, Isaac
Parker, Joel, 1795–1875
Parker, Joel, 1816–1888
Parker, John Johnston
Parker, Richard Elliot
Parsons, Theophilus
Paschal, George Washington
Paterson, William
Pearson, Richmond Mumford
Pease, Calvin
Peck, James Hawkins
Pendleton, Edmund

Penfield, William Lawrence
Pennington, William Sandford
Perley, Ira
Pettit, Thomas McKean
Phelps, Charles Edward
Philips, John Finis
Pitkin, William, 1725–1789
Plumley, Frank
Poland, Luke Potter
Porter, Alexander
Porter, James Madison
Potter, Elisha Reynolds
Potter, Platt
Potts, Richard
Pound, Cuthbert Winfred
Pound, (Nathan) Roscoe
Preble, William Pitt
Prentice, Samuel Oscar
Prentiss, Samuel
Prince, Le Baron Bradford
Provosty, Olivier Otis
Pryor, Roger Atkinson
Putnam, William Le Baron
Raney, George Pettus
Ranney, Rufus Percival
Read, Edwin Godwin
Read, John Meredith, 1797–1874
Reeve, Tapping
Requier, Augustus Julian
Richards, John Kelvey
Richardson, William Adams
Ridgely, Nicholas
Roane, Spencer
Roberts, Oran Milo
Robertson, George
Robertson, John
Robinson, John Mitchell
Robinson, Moses
Rodney, Thomas
Rogers, Henry Wade
Root, Jesse
Rose, John Carter
Rose, Uriah Milton
Ross, George
Rowan, John
Ruffin, Thomas
Rugg, Arthur Prentice
Rumsey, William
Rutledge, John
Ryan, Edward George
Sanford, Edward Terry
Sanford, Nathan
Sawyer, Lorenzo
Scott, William
Seabury, Samuel
Sebastian, Benjamin
Sedgwick, Theodore, 1746–1813
Seevers, William Henry
Sergeant, Thomas
Settle, Thomas
Shauck, John Allen
Shaw, Lemuel
Sheldon, Henry Newton
Shepard, Seth
Shepley, Ether
Sherwood, Thomas Adiel

Shields, George Howell
Shields, John Knight
Shiras, George
Shiras, Oliver Perry
Shorter, John Gill
Simmons, Thomas Jefferson
Simonton, Charles Henry
Smith, Erasmus Darwin
Smith, Henry Augustus Middleton
Smith, James Francis
Smith, Jeremiah, 1759–1842
Smith, Jeremiah, 1837–1921
Smith, Nathan, 1770–1835
Smith, Nathaniel
Smith, Walter Inglewood
Smith, William, 1697–1769
Smith, William, 1728–1793
Soulé, Pierre
Southard, Samuel Lewis
Spear, William Thomas
Speer, Emory
Spencer, Ambrose
Sprague, Peleg
Stacy, Walter Parker
Stanton, Richard Henry
Staples, Waller Redd
Stayton, John William
Stephens, Linton
Stiness, John Henry
Stockbridge, Henry
Stone, George Washington
Stone, John Wesley
Stone, Wilbur Fisk
Story, Joseph
Stuart, Archibald
Sulzberger, Mayer
Sumner, Increase
Swan, Joseph Rockwell
Swayne, Noah Haynes
Swift, Zephaniah
Tait, Charles
Tappan, Benjamin
Taylor, John Louis
Ten Broeck, Abraham
Terry, David Smith
Thacher, George
Thayer, Amos Madden
Thompson, Seymour Dwight
Thompson, Smith
Throop, Enos Thompson
Throop, Montgomery Hunt
Tichenor, Isaac
Tilghman, William
Tod, George
Toulmin, Harry Theophilus
Treat, Samuel
Treat, Samuel Hubbel
Tree, Lambert
Trimble, Robert
Tripp, Bartlett
Trott, Nicholas
Troup, Robert
Trowbridge, Edmund
Trumbull, John, 1750–1831
Trumbull, Lyman

Breckinridge, Henry Skillman
Breckinridge, John
Breckinridge, Robert Jefferson
Breckinridge, William Campbell
    Preston
Brennan, Francis James
Brewster, Frederick Carroll
Brewster, Ralph Owen
Briggs, George Nixon
Brightly, Frederick Charles
Brinkerhoff, Roeliff
Bristow, Benjamin Helm
Brown, David Paul
Brown, George William
Brown, Joseph Emerson
Brown, Neill Smith
Brown, Walter Folger
Browning, Orville Hickman
Bruce, Edward Bright
Buck, Daniel
Buckland, Ralph Pomeroy
Buckner, Emory Roy
Bundy, Harvey Hollister
Burdick, Usher Lloyd
Burke, Stevenson
Burke, Thomas
Burlingham, Charles Culp
Burnet, Jacob
Burnett, Henry Lawrence
Burr, Aaron
Burrall, William Porter
Burrell, Alexander Mansfield
Burrill, James
Burton, Clarence Monroe
Butler, Andrew Pickens
Butler, Benjamin Franklin
Butler, Charles
Butler, Pierce
Butler, William Allen
Butler, William Orlando
Butterworth, Benjamin
Byran, Thomas Barbour
Cabell, William Lewis
Cahn, Edmond Nathaniel
Caines, George
Calhoun, Patrick
Calhoun, William Barron
Camp, John Lafayette
Campbell, John Archibald
Cardozo, Benjamin Nathan
Carlile, John Snyder
Carlisle, James Mandeville
Carlson, Chester Floyd
Carpenter, Matthew Hale
Carrington, Henry Beebee
Carson, Hampton Lawrence
Carter, James Coolidge
Case, Leonard
Case, William Scoville
Chalmers, James Ronald
Chamberlain, George Earle
Chamberlain, Joseph Perkins
Chambers, George
Chandler, Peleg Whitman
Chavez, Dennis
Chester, Colby Mitchell

Chestnut, James
Chipman, Daniel
Choate, Joseph Hodges
Choate, Rufus
Christiancy, Isaac Peckham
Clagett, Wyseman
Clark, Abraham
Clark, Horace Francis
Clark, Joshua Reuben, Jr.
Clarke, John Hessin
Clay, Clement Claiborne
Clay, Joseph
Clayton, Augustin Smith
Clayton, John Middleton
Cleveland, Chauncey Fitch
Clifford, John Henry
Cline, Genevieve Rose
Clough, William Pitt
Cobb, Jonathan Holmes
Cobb, Thomas Reade Rootes
Cochran, William Bourke
Cogdell, John Stevens
Cohen, Felix Solomon
Colby, Bainbridge
Colden, Cadwallader David
Colquitt, Walter Terry
Conboy, Martin
Connally, Thomas Terry ("Tom")
Conner, James
Conover, Obadiah Milton
Conrad, Charles Magill
Conrad, Holmes
Converse, Charles Crozat
Cook, Philip
Cooke, John Rogers
Cooper, Henry Ernest
Cooper, James
Cornwallis, Kinahan
Costigan, Edward Prentiss
Cotton, Joseph Potter
Coudert, Frederic René
Cowen, John Kissig
Cowles, Charles
Cox, Edward Eugene
Cox, Rowland
Crafts, William
Crane, Frederick Evan
Cravath, Paul Drennan
Creighton, William
Crittenden, John Jordan
Crittenden, Thomas Leonidas
Cromwell, William Nelson
Crowder, Enoch Herbert
Culberson, Charles Allen
Culberson, David Browning
Cullom, Shelby Moore
Cummins, Albert Baird
Curran, Thomas Jerome
Curtis, Charles Pelham
Curtis, George Ticknor
Curtis, Samuel Ryan
Cuyler, Theodore
Daggett, David
Dallas, Alexander James
Dana, Richard
Dana, Richard Henry

Dana, Samuel Whittelsey
Dane, Nathan
Darrow, Clarence Seward
Dart, Henry Paluché
Daugherty, Harry Micajah
Daveis, Charles Stewart
Daveiss, Joseph Hamilton
D'Avezac, Auguste Geneviève
    Valentin
Davies, Joseph Edward
Davis, Cushman Kellogg
Davis, Garret
Davis, George
Davis, John
Davis, John William
Davis, Reuben
Davis, William Thomas
Davison, George Willets
Dayton, William Lewis
Dean, Amos
Dean, Gordon Evans
De Forest, Robert Weeks
Delmas, Delphin Michael
Deming, Henry Champion
Deming, Philander
Denby, Charles
Denver, James William
Depew, Chauncey Mitchell
Derby, Elias Hasket
De Saussure, Henry William
Devaney, John Patrick
Dexter, Franklin
Dexter, Samuel
Dexter, Wirt
Dickerson, Edward Nicoll
Dickinson, Daniel Stevens
Dickinson, Donald McDonald
Dickinson, Jacob McGavack
Dillingham, William Paul
Diven, Alexander Samuel
Dodd, Samuel Calvin Tate
Doddridge, Philip
Donelson, Andrew Jackson
Donnelly, Charles Francis
Donovan, James Britt
Donovan, William Joseph
Doolittle, James Rood
Dorsheimer, William Edward
Dos Passos, John Randolph
Douglas, Henry Kyd
Dow, Neal
Doyle, John Thomas
Drake, Benjamin
Drake, Charles Daniel
Drayton, William
Dropsie, Moses Aaron
Duane, William John
Duff, James Henderson
Dulany, Daniel, 1685–1753
Dulany, Daniel, 1722–1797
Dulles, Allen Welsh
Dulles, John Foster
Dunlop, James
Dunn, Charles
Du Ponceau, Pierre Étienne
Durant, Henry Fowle

Durant, Thomas Jefferson
Durrett, Reuben Thomas
Duval, William Pope
Dwight, Francis
Dwight, Theodore
Dwight, Theodore William
Eames, Charles
Earle, Thomas
Eaton, Dorman Bridgman
Eaton, John Henry
Echols, John
Eckels, James Herron
Edmunds, George Franklin
Edwards, Charles
Edwards, Henry Waggaman
Edwards, Pierpont
Elder, Samuel James
Elliott, Benjamin
Elliott, Charles Burke
Ellis, George Washington
Ellsworth, Henry William
Ellsworth, William Wolcott
Elwell, John Johnson
Emmet, Thomas Addis
Evans, George
Evans, Hugh Davey
Evans, Lawrence Boyd
Evarts, Jeremiah
Evarts, William Maxwell
Everett, David
Ewing, Thomas
Fairfield, John
Fall, Albert Bacon
Farnham, Thomas Jefferson
Farrar, Edgar Howard
Fearn, John Walker
Featherston, Winfield Scott
Felch, Alpheus
Ferry, Elisha Peyre
Fessenden, Francis
Fessenden, James Deering
Fessenden, Samuel
Fessenden, William Pitt
Field, David Dudley
Field, Maunsell Bradhurst
Fisher, George Purnell
Fisher, Sidney George
Fisher, Sydney George
Fisher, Walter Lowrie
Fisk, James
Fiske, Haley
Fitch, Samuel
Fitch, Thomas
Fitzhugh, George
Fitzhugh, William
Flanders, Henry
Fletcher, Calvin
Fletcher, Thomas Clement
Flexner, Bernard
Fly, James Lawrence
Fogg, George Gilman
Folger, Henry Clay
Folger, Walter
Folk, Joseph Wingate
Foot, Solomon
Foote, Lucius Harwood

Forbes, John Murray
Ford, Gordon Lester
Forney, William Henry
Foster, John Watson
Foster, Judith Ellen Horton
Foster, Murphy James
Foster, Roger Sherman Baldwin
Foulke, William Dudley
Freeman, Nathaniel
Frelinghuysen, Frederick
Frelinghuysen, Theodore
Freund, Ernst
Fry, Birkett Davenport
Gaines, John Pollard
Gaither, Horace Rowan, Jr.
Gamble, Hamilton Rowan
Gansevoort, Leonard
Gardiner, John
Garfield, Harry Augustus
Garfield, James Rudolph
Garrison, Lindley Miller
Gartrell, Lucius Jeremiah
Gary, Elbert Henry
Gaut, John McReynolds
Gerard, James Watson
Gerry, Elbridge Thomas
Geyer, Henry Sheffie
Gibbes, William Hasell
Gibbons, Thomas
Gibbons, William
Gibson, Randall Lee
Gilbert, Seymour Parker
Gilchrist, Robert
Gilmer, Francis Walker
Gilpin, Henry Dilworth
Glover, Samuel Taylor
Goldman, Mayer C.
Goldsborough, Robert
Goldsborough, Thomas Alan
Goode, John
Goodhue, James Madison
Goodman, Charles
Goodrich, Chauncey
Goodrich, Elizur
Goodwin, John Noble
Gordon, George Washington
Gordon, Laura De Force
Gordon, William Fitzhugh
Gordon, William Washington
Gorman, Willis Arnold
Goudy, William Charles
Gowen, Franklin Benjamin
Graham, David
Graham, John Andrew
Graham, William Alexander
Granger, Gideon
Grant, Madison
Gray, John Chipman
Greathouse, Clarence Ridgeby
Green, Andrew Haswell
Green, Benjamin Edwards
Green, William
Greenbaum, Edward Samuel
Greener, Richard Theodore
Greenleaf, Simon
Greenup, Christopher

Gregory, Charles Noble
Gregory, Thomas Watt
Gridley, Jeremiah
Griffith, William
Griggs, John William
Grimes, James Wilson
Grimké, Archibald Henry
Griscom, Lloyd Carpenter
Griswold, Roger
Grosvenor, Edwin Prescott
Grover, La Fayette
Grundy, Felix
Gummere, Samuel René
Guthrie, George Wilkins
Guthrie, William Dameron
Hackett, Frank Warren
Hager, John Sharpenstein
Haggin, James Ben Ali
Haight, Henry Huntly
Haines, Charles Glidden
Hale, Eugene
Hale, John Parker
Hale, Robert Safford
Hall, Abraham Oakey
Hall, John Elihu
Hall, Willard Preble
Halleck, Henry Wager
Hamilton, Andrew, d. 1741
Hamilton, James, 1710–1783
Hamilton, James Alexander
Hamilton, Peter
Hamlin, Charles
Hamlin, Charles Sumner
Hammond, Charles
Hammond, Nathaniel Job
Hammond, William Gardiner
Hancock, John, 1824–1893
Hardin, Ben
Hardin, Martin D.
Harding, George
Hardy, William Harris
Harlan, James
Harris, John Woods
Harris, Nathaniel Harrison
Harris, Wiley Pope
Harrison, Fairfax
Hart, Charles Henry
Hartley, Thomas
Hasbrouck, Abraham Bruyn
Hascall, Milo Smith
Haskell, Ella Louise Knowles
Havens, James Smith
Hawkins, Dexter Arnold
Hawley, Gideon, 1785–1870
Hawley, James Henry
Hawley, Joseph
Hayes, John Lord
Hayne, Robert Young
Hays, Arthur Garfield
Hays, Harry Thompson
Hays, Will H.
Hazelton, George Cochrane
Helmer, Bessie Bradwell
Hemphill, Joseph
Henderson, Archibald
Henderson, John

McClure, Alexander Kelly
McCord, David James
McCrady, Edward
McCreery, James Work
McCullough, John Griffith
McCumber, Porter James
McDaniel, Henry Dickerson
McDonald, Joseph Ewing
McDowell, John
Mack, Julian William
McKinstry, Alexander
McLane, Robert Milligan
Maclay, William
Maclay, William Brown
McLean, Angus Wilton
McMahon, Brien
McMahon, John Van Lear
McNutt, Paul Vories
McRae, Duncan Kirkland
McRae, Thomas Chipman
MacVeagh, Charles
MacVeagh, Isaac Wayne
Magoffin, Beriah
Magoon, Charles Edward
Malone, Dudley Field
Manderson, Charles Frederick
Maney, George Earl
Mann, James Robert
Marcy, William Learned
Marquett, Turner Mastin
Marsh, George Perkins
Marshall, Louis
Martin, John Hill
Martindale, John Henry
Mason, Jeremiah
Mather, Samuel Holmes
Matthews, Francis Patrick
Maxcy, Virgil
Maxwell, George Hebard
Maxwell, Hugh
Maxwell, William
Mayer, Brantz
Mazureau, Étienne
Meagher, Thomas Francis
Mechem, Floyd Russell
Meigs, Josiah
Meigs, Return Jonathan
Meigs, William Montgomery
Meredith, William Morris
Miller, Nathan Lewis
Millikin, Eugene Donald
Mills, Elijah Hunt
Mills, Ogden Livingston
Minor, Benjamin Blake
Mitchel, John Purroy
Mitchell, John Hipple
Mitchell, William DeWitt
Money, Hernando De Soto
Monsky, Henry
Montague, Gilbert Holland
Montefiore, Joshua
Moore, Bartholomew Figures
Moore, John Bassett
Morawetz, Victor
Morell, George Webb
Morgan, George Washington

Morgenthau, Henry
Morris, Luzon Burritt
Morrow, Dwight Whitney
Morrow, Edwin Porch
Morton, Ferdinand Quintin
Moseley, Edward Augustus
Mosessohn, David Nehemiah
Murphy, Henry Cruse
Murray, Joseph
Murray, William Henry David
Mussey, Ellen Spencer
Nelson, Thomas Henry
Nelson, William, 1847–1914
Nesmith, James Willis
Neumann, Franz Leopold
Newberry, John Stoughton
Newel, Stanford
Nicoll, De Lancey
Nicolls, William
Noah, Mordecai Manuel
Noble, John Willock
Noyes, William Curtis
O'Brien, Morgan Joseph
O'Brien, Thomas James
O'Conor, Charles
O'Donnell, Thomas Jefferson
O'Dwyer, William
Ogden, Aaron
Ogden, David
Ogden, David Bayard
Ogden, Thomas Ludlow
Olds, Irving Sands
Olds, Robert Edwin
Oliver, George Tener
Olmsted, Marlin Edgar
Olney, Richard
Ordronaux, John
Orr, Jehu Amaziah
Orton, Harlow South
Osborn, Thomas Andrew
Osborn, Thomas Ogden
Osborne, James Walker
Owen, Thomas McAdory
Paine, Halbert Eleazer
Paine, Henry Warren
Palmer, Alexander Mitchell
Palmer, Henry Wilbur
Palmer, William Adams
Park, Trenor William
Parker, Amasa Junius
Parker, John Cortlandt
Parkinson, Thomas Ignatius
Parsons, John Edward
Parsons, Lewis Baldwin
Parvin, Theodore Sutton
Pastorius, Francis Daniel
Patterson, Robert Porter
Patterson, Thomas MacDonald
Pattison, Robert Emory
Patton, John Mercer
Payne, Christopher Harrison
Payne, John Barton
Peabody, Oliver William Bourn
Peck, George Record
Peckham, Wheeler Hazard
Pennypacker, Samuel Whitaker

Penrose, Boies
Penrose, Charles Bingham
Pepper, George Wharton
Perkins, James Breck
Perkins, Thomas Nelson
Perley, Ira
Perlman, Philip Benjamin
Peters, John Andrew
Peters, Richard, 1744–1828
Petigru, James Louis
Pettigrew, James Johnston
Phelps, Edward John
Phelps, William Walter
Phillips, Willard
Pickering, John
Pierce, Edward Lillie
Pierrepont, Edwards
Piexotto, Benjamin Franklin
Pike, Albert
Pinchot, Amos Richards Eno
Pinkney, William
Pitkin, Frederick Walker
Pitkin, William, 1635–1694
Plumb, Glenn Edward
Polk, Frank Lyon
Pollak, Walter Heilprin
Pomerene, Atlee
Pool, Joe Richard
Poor, John Alfred
Pope, James Pinckney
Post, Melville Davisson
Powell, Thomas Reed
Pressman, Lee
Price, Eli Kirk
Prouty, Charles Azro
Pruyn, John Van Schaick Lansing
Pruyn, Robert Hewson
Pujo, Arsène Paulin
Purnell, William Henry
Putnam, (George) Herbert
Putnam, James Osborne
Quick, John Herbert
Quincy, Josiah, 1744–1775
Quitman, John Anthony
Radcliff, Jacob
Radin, Max
Raines, John
Ralston, Samuel Moffett
Randall, Alexander Williams
Randolph, Edmund, 1819–1861
Randolph, George Wythe
Rankine, William Birch
Raulston, John Tate
Rawle, Francis, 1846–1930
Rawle, William
Rawle, William Henry
Raymond, Daniel
Rayner, Isidor
Read, Charles
Read, George
Read, John, 1679/80–1749
Read, John, 1769–1854
Rector, Henry Massey
Redfield, Amasa Angell
Reed, David Aiken
Reed, James Hay

Reed, Joseph
Reed, Thomas Brackett
Reed, William Bradford
Rellstab, John
Rice, Isaac Leopold
Richberg, Donald Randall
Riddle, Albert Gallatin
Ritchie, Albert Cabell
Rives, George Lockhart
Roane, John Selden
Roberts, Oran Milo
Robertson, William Joseph
Robinson, Christopher
Robinson, Conway
Robinson, Henry Cornelius
Rodney, Caesar Augustus
Roe, Gilbert Ernstein
Rogers, John Ignatius
Root, Elihu
Root, Erastus
Rorer, David
Roselius, Christian
Ross, James
Rublee, George
Ruggles, Samuel Bulkley
Rush, Richard
Russell, Charles Wells
Rutherford, Joseph Franklin
Rutledge, Wiley Blount
Sackett, Henry Woodward
Sage, Bernard Janin
Sampson, William
Sanders, Wilbur Fisk
Sanger, George Partridge
Sargent, John Osborne
Sayles, John
Scammon, Jonathan Young
Schell, Augustus
Schoeppel, Andrew Frank
Schouler, James
Scott, Gustavus
Scott, James Brown
Scott, John Morin
Scott, Samuel Parsons
Seabury, Samuel
Sedgwick, Arthur George
Sedgwick, Theodore, 1780–1839
Sedgwick, Theodore, 1811–1859
Semmes, Thomas Jenkins
Sergeant, John, 1779–1852
Sergeant, Jonathan Dickinson
Sewall, Jonathan
Sewall, Jonathan Mitchell
Shannon, Wilson
Shearman, Thomas Gaskell
Shepard, Edward Morse
Shipman, Andrew Jackson
Shuster, W(illiam) Morgan
Simms, William Elliott
Smith, Buckingham
Smith, Caleb Blood
Smith, Chauncey
Smith, Israel
Smith, James Francis
Smith, Jeremiah
Smith, Junius

Smith, Melancton, 1744–1798
Smith, Oliver Hampton
Smith, Richard
Smith, Richard Penn
Smith, Robert Hardy
Smith, Roswell
Smith, Truman
Smith, William, 1762–1840
Smith, William Russell
Smyth, John Henry
Snowden, James Ross
Soley, James Russell
Southmayd, Charles Ferdinand
Sparks, William Andrew Jackson
Speed, James
Spencer, John Canfield
Spooner, Lysander
Springer, Charles
Springer, Frank
Springer, William McKendree
Stallo, Johann Bernhard
Stanbery, Henry
Stanchfield, John Barry
Stanley, Augustus Owsley
Stanton, Henry Brewster
Starr, Merritt
Stearns, Asahel
Steinhardt, Laurence Adolph
Sterling, John William
Sterne, Simon
Stetson, Francis Lynde
Steuer, Max David
Stevens, Hiram Fairchild
Stevens, Thaddeus
Stewart, Alvan
Stewart, William Morris
Stickney, Alpheus Beede
Stillman, Thomas Edgar
Stilwell, Silas Moore
Stimson, Frederic Jesup
Stockbridge, Henry Smith
Stockton, Richard, 1730–1781
Stockton, Richard, 1764–1828
Stoddard, Amos
Stone, John Wesley
Storey, Moorfield
Storrow, James Jackson
Stoughton, Edwin Wallace
Straus, Oscar Solomon
Strawn, Silas Hardy
Street, Alfred Billings
Strong, Caleb
Strong, Moses McCure
Stryker, Lloyd Paul
Stuart, John Todd
Sullivan, George
Sullivan, William
Sumners, Hatton William
Swayne, Wager
Sweeney, Martin Leonard
Swift, John Franklin
Swift, Lucius Burrie
Taber, John
Taft, Charles Phelps
Taft, Henry Waters
Taft, Robert Alphonso

Tallmadge, James
Taylor, Hannis
Tazewell, Henry
Tazewell, Littleton Waller
Teller, Henry Moore
Temple, Oliver Perry
Tench, Francis
Terrell, Edwin Holland
Thatcher, Benjamin Bussey
Thayer, John Milton
Thomas, Charles Spalding
Thomas, William Widgery
Thompson, Daniel Pierce
Thompson, Richard Wigginton
Thompson, Robert Means
Thurston, Lorrin Andrews
Tichenor, Isaac
Tilden, Samuel Jones
Tilghman, Edward
Tilson, John Quillin
Todd, Charles Stewart
Toole, Edwin Warren
Towne, Charles Arnette
Tracy, Benjamin Franklin
Train, Arthur Cheney
Tremain, Henry Edwin
Trude, Alfred Samuel
Tucker, Henry St. George,
   1853–1932
Tucker, John Randolph,
   1823–1897
Turner, George
Tuttle, Charles Wesley
Tweed, Harrison
Tydings, Millard Evelyn
Tyler, Robert
Tyler, Samuel
Tyson, Job Roberts
Underwood, Francis Henry
Untermyer, Samuel
Usher, John Palmer
Van Buren, John
Vandenhoff, George
Vanderbilt, Arthur T.
Van Der Donck, Adriaen
Van Devanter, Willis
Van Dyke, Nicholas, 1770–1826
Van Schaack, Peter
Van Vechten, Abraham
Van Winkle, Peter Godwin
Van Wyck, Charles Henry
Varnum, James Mitchell
Vaux, Richard
Vilas, William Freeman
Vinton, Samuel Finley
Vroom, Peter Dumont
Wait, William
Walker, Frank Comerford
Wallace, Lewis
Waller, Thomas Macdonald
Wallis, Severn Teackle
Waln, Nicholas
Walsh, Francis Patrick
Walter, Francis Eugene
Ward, John Elliott
Waring, Julius Waties

Leffler, Shepherd
L'Hommedieu, Ezra
Lord, Otis Phillips
Low, Nicholas
Lowell, John, 1743–1802
Lyon, William Penn
McClure, Alexander Kelly
McCreery, James Work
Maclay, William Brown
Marshall, Thomas
Mason, Thomson
Maxcy, Virgil
Maxwell, David Hervey
Maxwell, George Troup
Memminger, Christopher Gustavus
Mills, Benjamin
Morris, Edward Joy
Munford, William
Nesmith, James Willis
Nisbet, Eugenius Aristides
Northen, William Jonathan
Orr, Jehu Amaziah
Osgood, Samuel
Parker, James
Pendleton, John Strother
Pitney, Mahlon
Pruyn, Robert Hewson
Purviance, David
Raines, John
Raney, George Pettus
Ridgely, Nicholas
Robinson, Henry Cornelius
Rodman, Isaac Peace
Rollins, Edward Henry
Sanford, Nathan
Sedgwick, Theodore, 1746–1813
Seevers, William Henry
Silver, Gray
Spalding, Thomas
Stephens, Linton
Strong, Moses McCure
Stuart, Archibald
Van Wyck, Charles Henry
White, James
Wingate, Paine
Wofford, William Tatum

LETTERING ARTIST
Goudy, Frederic William

LEXICOGRAPHER (See also
   PHILOLOGIST)
Allibone, Samuel Austin
Foster, Frank Pierce
Funk, Wilfred John
Goodrich, Chauncey Allen
Jastrow, Marcus
Kohut, Alexander
McFarland, George Bradley
March, Francis Andrew
Sheldon, Edward Stevens
Thomas, Joseph
Vizetelly, Frank Horace
Webster, Noah
Wheeler, William Adolphus
Worcester, Joseph Emerson

LIBRARIAN
Adams, Randolph Greenfield

Allibone, Samuel Austin
Anderson, Edwin Hatfield
Beals, Ralph Albert
Beer, William
Billings, John Shaw
Binkley, Robert Cedric
Bjerregaard, Carl Henrik Andreas
Bostwick, Arthur Elmore
Brett, William Howard
Burr, George Lincoln
Canfield, James Hulme
Chadwick, James Read
Cheney, John Vance
Cobb, William Henry
Cogswell, Joseph Green
Cole, George Watson
Crunden, Frederick Morgan
Cutter, Charles Ammi
Dana, John Cotton
Davis, Raymond Cazallis
Dewey, Melvil
Draper, Lyman Copeland
Durrie, Daniel Steele
Eames, Wilberforce
Eastman, William Reed
Edmonds, John
Evans, Charles
Fairchild, Mary Salome Cutler
Farrand, Max
Fiske, Daniel Willard
Flexner, Jennie Maas
Flint, Weston
Folsom, Charles
Foss, Sam Walter
Galbreath, Charles Burleigh
Green, Samuel Abbott
Green, Samuel Swett
Greene, Belle Da Costa
Griffin, Appleton Prentiss Clark
Guild, Reuben Aldridge
Hamlin, Talbot Faulkner
Hanson, James Christian Meinich
Harris, Thaddeus William
Herrick, Edward Claudius
Holden, Edward Singleton
Homes, Henry Augustus
Hosmer, James Kendall
Isom, Mary Frances
Jackson, William Alexander
Jewett, Charles Coffin
Jordan, John Woolf
Klingelsmith, Margaret Center
Lamoureux, Andrew Jackson
Larned, Josephus Nelson
Legler, Henry Eduard
Lydenberg, Harry Miller
Martel, Charles
Moore, Anne Carroll
Moore, George Henry
Moore, Nathaniel Fish
Nelson, Charles Alexander
Parvin, Theodore Sutton
Pearson, Edmund Lester
Peckham, George Williams
Perkins, Frederic Beecher
Plummer, Mary Wright

Poole, Fitch
Poole, William Frederick
Putnam, (George) Herbert
Robertson, James Alexander
Rosenthal, Herman
Saunders, Frederick
Schwab, John Christopher
Sharp, Katharine Lucinda
Shaw, William Smith
Sibley, John Langdon
Skinner, Charles Rufus
Smith, John J.
Smith, Lloyd Pearsall
Sonneck, Oscar George Theodore
Spofford, Ainsworth Rand
Steiner, Bernard Christian
Steiner, Lewis Henry
Street, Alfred Billings
Thwaites, Reuben Gold
Uhler, Philip Reese
Utley, George Burwell
Vail, Robert William Glenroie
Van Dyke, John Charles
Van Name, Addison
Vinton, Frederic
Ward, James Warner
Watterston, George
Whitney, James Lyman
Williams, John Fletcher
Winship, George Parker
Winsor, Justin
Winthrop, James
Wood, Mary Elizabeth

LIBRARY PROMOTER
Bowker, Richard Rogers

LIBRETTIST
Da Ponte, Lorenzo
Hammerstein, Oscar, II
Smith, Harry Bache

LIEUTENANT GOVERNOR
Bull, William (S.C.)
Bullitt, Alexander Scott (Ky.)
Carlisle, John Griffin (Ky.)
Colden, Cadwallader (N.Y.)
De Lancey, James (N.Y.)
Eastman, Enoch Worthen (Iowa)
Gray, William (Mass.)
Gue, Benjamin F. (Iowa)
Hamilton, James, 1710–1783 (Pa.)
Hoffmann, Francis Arnold (Ill.)
Leisler, Jacob (N.Y.)
McKinstry, Alexander (Ala.)
Moultrie, John (East Fla.)
Oliver, Andrew (Mass.)
Penn, John (Pa.)
Penn, Richard (Pa.)
Phillips, William (Mass.)
Spotswood, Alexander (Va.)
Van Cortlandt, Pierre (N.Y.)
Woodruff, Timothy Lester (N.Y.)

LIGHTHOUSE BUILDER
Lewis, Winslow

LIMNOLOGIST (See also BIOLOGIST,
   HYDROGRAPHER, HYDROLOGIST)
Birge, Edward Asahel
Juday, Chancey

LINGUIST (**See also** INTERPRETER)
André, Louis
Avery, John
Bloomfield, Leonard
Bouvet, Marie Marguerite
Burritt, Elihu
Curtin, Jeremiah
Gatschet, Albert Samuel
Greenhow, Robert
McFarland, George Bradley
Radin, Paul
Riggs, Elias
Sapir, Edward
Speiser, Ephraim Avigdor
Verwyst, Chrysostom Adrian
Whitney, William Dwight
Whorf, Benjamin Lee

LITERARY CRITIC (**See also** CRITIC,
     SCHOLAR)
Arvin, Newton
Blackmur, Richard Palmer
Burton, Richard Eugene
Canby, Henry Seidel
Cuppy, William Jacob ("Will")
Goldman, Emma
Hackett, Francis
Hazeltine, Mayo Williamson
Jackson, Joseph Henry
Lewisohn, Ludwig
Lowes, John Livingston
Macy, John Albert
Matthiessen, Francis Otto
More, Paul Elmer
Payne, William Morton
Peck, Harry Thurston
Phelps, William Lyon
Pollard, Joseph Percival
Ripley, George
Rosenfeld, Paul Leopold
Sherman, Stuart Pratt
Spingarn, Joel Elias
Van Doren, Carl Clinton
Wallace, Horace Binney

LITERARY HISTORIAN (**See also**
     HISTORIAN)
Brooks, Van Wyck
Lancaster, Henry Carrington

LITHOGRAPHER (**See also** ARTIST,
     ENGRAVER, ENGRAVER WOOD)
Alexander, Francis
Bellows, George Wesley
Bien, Julius
Haskell, Ernest
Hoen, August
Imbert, Antoine
Ives, James Merritt
Johnston, David Claypoole
Newsam, Albert
Otis, Bass
Pendleton, John B.
Prang, Louis
Rosenthal, Max
Rowse, Samuel Worcester

LITHOTOMIST (**See also** PHYSICIAN)
Spencer, Pitman Clemens

LITTERATEUR (**See also** AUTHOR,
     WRITER)
Biddle, Nicholas
Eliot, Samuel Atkins
Evans, Edward Payson
Hassard, John Rose Greene
Hillard, George Stillman
Lowell, James Russell
Matthews, James Brander
Norton, Andrews
Page, Thomas Nelson
Palmer, George Herbert
Peabody, Oliver William Bourn
Rae, John
Rattermann, Heinrich Armin
Reed, Henry Hope
Ricord, Frederick William
Simms, William Gilmore
Taylor, Bayard
Walsh, Robert
Wendell, Barrett
White, Richard Grant

LOBBYIST (**See also** POLITICIAN)
Tanner, James
Ward, Samuel, 1814–1884

LOCK EXPERT (**See** MANUFACTURER)

LOCOMOTIVE BUILDER (**See**
     MANUFACTURER)

LOGICIAN (**See also** MATHEMATICIAN,
     PHILOSOPHER, SCHOLAR)
Ladd-Franklin, Christine
Peirce, Charles Sanders
Reichenbach, Hans

LOYALIST (**See also** PATRIOT)
Allen, Andrew
Atherton, Joshua
Auchmuty, Robert
Auchmuty, Samuel
Bailey, Jacob
Barclay, Thomas
Bates, Walter
Boucher, Jonathan
Browne, William
Butler, John
Butler, Walter N.
Chandler, Thomas Bradbury
Chipman, Ward
Clarke, Richard
Coffin, John
Colden, Cadwallader
Connolly, John
Coombe, Thomas
Cooper, Myles
Curwen, Samuel
De Lancy, James
Duché, Jacob
Eddis, William
Fanning, David
Fanning, Edmund
Fitch, Samuel
Fleming, John
Galloway, Joseph
Graham, John
Green, Francis
Hewat, Alexander
Inglis, Charles

Johnson, Guy
Johnson, Sir John
Jones, Thomas
Leonard, Daniel
Leonard, George
Loring, Joshua, 1716–1781
Loring, Joshua, 1744–1789
Low, Isaac
Ludlow, Gabriel George
Morris, Roger
Moultrie, John
Munro, Henry
Odell, Jonathan
Ogden, David
Oliver, Peter
Peters, Samuel Andrew
Randolph, John, 1727 or
     1728–1784
Robinson, Beverley
Ruggles, Timothy
Sewall, Jonathan
Smith, William, 1728–1793
Sower, Christopher, 1754–1799
Stansbury, Joseph
Wentworth, John, 1737 N.S.–1820
White, Henry
Williams, Israel
Wragg, William

LUMBERMAN (**See also**
     MANUFACTURER)
Ayer, Edward Everett
Bell, Frederic Somers
Blodgett, John Wood
Donovan, John Joseph
Edgar, Charles
Fleming, Arthur Henry
Fordney, Joseph Warren
Griggs, Everett Gallup
Hackley, Charles Henry
Herdic, Peter
Jones, Jesse Holman
Sawyer, Philetus
Stephenson, Isaac
Sullivan, William Henry
Walker, Thomas Barlow
Weyerhaeuser, Frederick Edward

LYRICIST (**See also** BALLADIST,
     COMPOSER, SONGWRITER)
Adams, Frank Ramsay
Cohan, George Michael
De Sylva, George Gard ("Buddy")
Hammerstein, Oscar, II
Hart, Lorenz Milton
Kahn, Gustav Gerson
Loesser, Frank
Porter, Cole
White, George
White, Joseph Malachy

MACHINE DESIGNER
De Leeuw, Adolph Lodewyk
Norton, Charles Hotchkiss

MADAM
Adler, Polly
Everleigh, Ada
Everleigh, Minna

McArthur, John, 1826–1906
McCormick, Cyrus Hall
McCormick, Leander James
McCormick, Stephen
Mapes, Charles Victor
Marks, Amasa Abraham
Marsh, Charles Wesley
Marsh, William Wallace
Marshall, Benjamin
Mason, William
Mast, Phineas Price
Masury, John Wesley
Matthews, John
Matthiessen, Frederick William
Merrick, Samuel Vaughan
Miller, Lewis
Munger, Robert Sylvester
Murphy, Franklin
Nelson, Nelson Olsen
Nesmith, John
Newberry, John Stoughton
Newton, Henry Jotham
Nicholson, William Thomas
Niedringhaus, Frederick Gottlieb
Noyes, La Verne
O'Hara, James
Oliver, James
Oliver, Paul Ambrose
Otis, Charles Rollin
Otis, Elisha Graves
Packard, James Ward
Paine, Charles
Paine, Elijah
Palmer, Joseph
Parrott, Robert Parker
Phipps, Henry
Pingree, Hazen Stuart
Pitcairn, John
Pitkin, William, 1725–1789
Post, George Adams
Pratt, Zadock
Rand, Edward Sprague
Redfield, William Cox
Reese, Abram
Remington, Eliphalet
Remington, Philo
Rice, Alexander Hamilton
Richardson, Edmund
Roebling, John Augustus
Rowland, Thomas Fitch
Schieren, Charles Adolph
Schneller, George Otto
Scullin, John
Seed, Miles Ainscough
Seiberling, Frank Augustus
Simpson, Michael Hodge
Slater, John Fox
Slocum, Samuel
Smith, Horace
Smith, James Youngs
Spencer, Christopher Miner
Sproul, William Cameron
Stanley, Francis Edgar
Starrett, Laroy S.
Stearns, Frank Ballou
Sturtevant, Benjamin Franklin

Sweet, John Edson
Thomson, John
Thurber, Charles
Timken, Henry
Tompkins, Daniel Augustus
Towne, Henry Robinson
Tucker, Stephen Davis
Vought, Chance Milton
Wallace, William
Waller, Frederic
Waln, Robert, 1765–1836
Warner, Worcester Reed
Warren, Cyrus Moors
Washburn, Charles Grenfill
Washburn, Ichabod
Washburn, Nathan
Waterman, Lewis Edson
Weeden, William Babcock
Weightman, William
Wesson, Daniel Baird
Westinghouse, George
Wetherill, Samuel
Wharton, Joseph
Wheeler, Nathaniel
White, Samuel Stockton
Whitney, Asa
Wilkinson, David
Williams, David Rogerson
Wilson, George Francis
Winchester, Oliver Fisher
Winslow, Sidney Wilmot
Woodruff, Theodore Tuttle
Wright, John Stephen
Wright, William
Yale, Linus
Ziegler, William

MANUFACTURER (SPECIFIC)

Adding Machines
  Burroughs, William Seward
Agricultural Equipment
  Legge, Alexander
Agricultural Machinery
  Wood, Walter Abbott
Aircraft
  Martin, Glenn Luther ("Cy")
Airplanes
  Bellanca, Giuseppe Mario
  Burgess, W(illiam) Starling
  Lockheed, Allan Haines
  Lockheed, Malcolm
  Piper, William Thomas
Automobiles
  Chapin, Roy Dikeman
  Chrysler, Walter Percy
  Couzens, James
  Durant, William Crapo
  Duryea, Charles Edgar
  Duryea, James Frank
  Fisher, Frederic John
  Ford, Edsel Bryant
  Ford, Henry
  Hupp, Louis Gorham
  Knudsen, William S.
  Nash, Charles Williams
  Olds, Ransom Eli
  Pope, Albert Augustus

  Stutz, Harry Clayton
  Wills, Childe Harold
  Winton, Alexander
Automobile Bodies
  Fisher, Alfred J.
  Fisher, Charles T.
Baby Food
  Gerber, (Daniel) Frank
  Gerber, Daniel (Frank)
Brass
  Coe, Israel
  Hayden, Hiram Washington
  Holmes, Israel
Bricks
  Reese, Isaac
Business Machines
  Watson, Thomas John
Candy
  Gunther, Charles Frederick
Cash Registers
  Patterson, John Henry
Cereal
  Kellogg, John Harvey
  Kellogg, Will Keith
Chemicals
  Dow, Herbert Henry
  Mallinckrodt, Edward
  Merck, George Wilhelm
  Pfister, Alfred
Chewing Gum
  Wrigley, William
Chocolate
  Hershey, Milton Snavely
Cigarettes
  Hill, George Washington
Cocoa
  Pierce, Henry Lillie
Collars (Detachable)
  Brown, Ebenezer
Conveying Equipment
  Piez, Charles
Cosmetics
  Arden, Elizabeth
  Rubinstein, Helena
Cotton
  Fry, Birkett Davenport
  Gray, George Alexander
  Gregg, William
  Hammett, Henry Pinckney
  Holt, Edwin Michael
  Lowell, Francis Cabot
  Oliver, Henry Kamble
  Sprague, William, 1773–1836
  Weaver, Philip
Cotton Machinery
  Earle, Pliny
Drugs
  Lloyd, John Uri
Explosives
  Du Pont, Irénée
  Everendon, Walter
  Judson, Egbert Putnam
Farm Machinery
  McCormick, Cyrus Hall
Firearms
  Eastman, Arthur MacArthur

Hoffman, John Thompson (New York)
Hylan, John Francis (New York City)
Johnson, Tom Loftin (Cleveland)
Kelly, Edward Joseph (Chicago)
La Guardia, Fiorello Henry (New York)
Lawrence, David Leo (Pittsburgh)
Lunn, George Richard (Schenectady)
Lyman, Theodore, 1792–1849 (Boston)
McMichael, Morton (Philadelphia)
Maverick, (Fontaine) Maury (San Antonio)
Mitchel, John Purroy (New York)
Murphy, Frank (Detroit)
Norris, Isaac, 1671–1735 (Philadelphia)
O'Dwyer, William (New York)
Phelan, James Duval (San Francisco)
Pierce, Henry Lillie (Boston)
Pinckney, Henry Laurens (Charleston)
Pingree, Hazen Stuart (Detroit)
Radcliff, Jacob (New York)
Seidel, George Lukas Emil (Milwaukee)
Shippen, Edward, 1639–1712 (Philadelphia)
Shurtleff, Nathaniel Bradstreet (Boston)
Strong, William Lafayette (New York)
Swann, Thomas (Baltimore)
Thompson, William Hale (Chicago)
Tobin, Maurice Joseph (Boston)
Walker, James John (New York)
Wentworth, John, 1815–1888 (Chicago)
Westervelt, Jacob Aaron (New York)
Wharton, Robert (Philadelphia)
Whitlock, Brand (Toledo)
Wood, Fernando (New York)

MEAT PACKER (See also INDUSTRIALIST, MANUFACTURER)
Armour, Philip Danforth
Cudahy, Michael
Dold, Jacob
Eastman, Timothy Corser
Hammond, George Henry
Hormel, Jay Catherwood
Hubbard, Gurdon Saltonstall
Hutchinson, Benjamin Peters
Mayer, Oscar Gottfried
Morris, Nelson
Swift, Gustavus Franklin
Swift, Louis Franklin
Wilson, Samuel

MECHANIC
Allaire, James Peter
Ames, James Tyler

Borden, Simeon
Cox, Lemuel
Emerson, James Ezekiel
Knight, Edward Henry
Kruesi, John
Peale, Titian Ramsay
Root, Elisha King
Winans, Ross

MEDALIST (See also CRAFTSMAN, GOLDSMITH, JEWELER, SILVERSMITH)
Brenner, Victor David

MEDICAL ADMINISTRATOR
Weed, Lewis Hill

MEDICAL CHARLATAN
Brinkley, John Richard

MEDICAL EDUCATOR (See also EDUCATOR)
Cabot, Hugh
Edsall, David Linn
Vaughan, Victor Clarence
Wilson, Louis Blanchard

MEDICAL HISTORIAN (See also HISTORIAN, PHYSICIAN)
Alden, Ebenezer
Buck, Albert Henry
Handerson, Henry Ebenezer
Sigerist, Henry Ernest
Williams, Stephen West

MEDICAL ILLUSTRATOR (See also ILLUSTRATOR)
Brödel, Max

MEDICAL INSTRUMENT MAKER
Schwidetzky, Oscar Otto Rudolf

MEDICAL REFORMER
Cabot, Hugh

MEDICAL RESEARCH WORKER (See also PHYSICIAN)
Agramonte y Simoni, Aristides
Ashford, Bailey Kelly
Goldberger, Joseph
Rous, Francis Peyton
Sawyer, Wilbur Augustus
Trask, James Dowling
Weil, Richard

MEDICAL SCIENTIST (See also BACTERIOLOGIST, PATHOLOGIST)
Smith, Theobald

MEDICAL STATISTICIAN (See also STATISTICIAN)
Dorn, Harold Fred

MEDIEVALIST (See also HISTORIAN)
Beeson, Charles Henry
Rand, Edward Kennard
Stephenson, Carl
Tatlock, John Strong Perry
Thorndike, Lynn
Young, Karl

MEDIUM (See SPIRITUALIST)

MENTAL HYGIENIST (See also PHYSICIAN)
Burnham, William Henry
Salmon, Thomas William

MERCANTILE AGENT (See also MERCHANT)
Dun, Robert Graham

MERCENARY
Boyd, John Parker
Burgevine, Henry Andrea

MERCHANT (See also BUSINESSMAN, EXECUTIVE, FACTOR, MERCANTILE AGENT)
Abernethy, George
Allen, William
Altman, Benjamin
Amory, Thomas
Appleton, Samuel
Arbuckle, John
Archer, Samuel
Aspinwall, William Henry
Austin, Jonathan Loring
Austin, Moses
Bache, Richard
Bache, Theophylact
Bain, George Luke Scobie
Baker, Lorenzo Dow
Bamberger, Louis
Barker, Jacob
Barker, James William
Bartlet, William
Bayard, John Bubenheim
Bayard, William
Belcher, Jonathan
Bell, Isaac
Benner, Philip
Bertram, John
Biddle, Clement
Bliss, Cornelius Newton
Bliss, George
Blodget, Samuel
Blount, Thomas
Boorman, James
Borie, Adolph Edward
Bowdoin, James, 1726–1790
Bowdoin, James, 1752–1811
Bowen, Henry Chandler
Brattle, Thomas
Brewer, Charles
Bromfield, John
Brooks, Peter Chardon
Brown, John
Brown, Moses
Brown, Nicholas
Brown, Nicolas
Brown, Obadiah
Buchanan, Thomas
Byrd, William
Cabot, George
Calef, Robert
Capen, Samuel Billings
Carter, Henry Alpheus Peirce
Cerré, Jean Gabriel
Chalkley, Thomas
Chittenden, Simeon Baldwin
Chouteau, Pierre
Claflin, Horace Brigham
Claflin, John
Clapp, Asa
Clark, Daniel
Clarke, Richard
Clay, Joseph
Cleveland, Richard Jeffry

Coates, Samuel
Colby, Gardner
Coleman, William Tell
Colman, John
Cone, Moses Herman
Cook, Isaac
Coolidge, Thomas Jefferson
Cope, Thomas Pym
Coram, Thomas
Corbett, Henry Winslow
Corson, Robert Rodgers
Cozzens, Frederick Swar
Cress, Elliott
Crocker, Charles
Crowninshield, Benjamin Williams
Crowninshield, George
Crowninshield, Jacob
Cruger, Henry
Cupples, Samuel
Cushing, John Perkins
Cushing, Thomas
Deane, Charles
Deas, Zachariah Cantey
De Forest, David Curtis
Delafield, John
De Peyster, Abraham
Derby, Elias Hasket, 1739–1799
Derby, Elias Hasket, 1766–1826
Derby, Richard
De Vries, David Pietersen
Dexter, Samuel
Dexter, Timothy
Dibrell, George Gibbs
Dodge, David Low
Dodge, William Earl
Duer, William
Dunwoody, William Hood
Duryée, Abram
Dwight, Edmund
Eaton, Theophilus
Espejo, Antonio de
Faneuil, Peter
Fell, John
Field, Cyrus West
Field, Marshall
Filene, Edward Albert
Finlay, Hugh
Fish, Preserved
Forbes, John
Forbes, Robert Bennet
Foster, Charles
Fraley, Frederick
Francis, David Rowland
Gadsden, Christopher
Gaines, George Strother
Gardner, Caleb
Garrett, Robert
Genin, John Nicholas
Gillon, Alexander
Gimbel, Bernard Feustman
Girard, Stephen
Glenn, Hugh
Godfrey, Benjamin
Goodhue, Benjamin
Goodwin, Ichabod
Gorham, Jabez

Gould, Benjamin Apthorp
Grace, William Russell
Gratz, Barnard
Gratz, Michael
Gray, William
Green, John Cleve
Green, Joseph
Grim, David
Grinnell, Henry
Grinnell, Joseph
Grinnell, Moses Hicks
Habersham, Alexander Wylly
Habersham, James
Hack, George
Hallowell, Richard Price
Hancock, John, 1736–1793
Hancock, Thomas
Hand, Daniel
Harris, Caleb Fiske
Harris, Townsend
Harrison, James
Haven, Henry Philemon
Hazard, Augustus George
Heard, Augustine
Heathcote, Caleb
Henchman, Daniel
Henderson, Peter
Herrman, Augustine
Hiester, Joseph
Higginson, Nathaniel
Higginson, Stephen
Higinbotham, Harlow Niles
Hill, Richard
Hillegas, Michael
Hogg, George
Hooper, Samuel
Hopkins, Johns
Howland, Gardiner Greene
Hubbard, Gurdon Saltonstall
Hull, John
Hunnewell, James
Hunter, William C.
Huntington, Jabez
Hutchinson, Charles Lawrence
Ingersoll, Robert Hawley
Inman, John Hamilton
Inman, Samuel Martin
Irving, William
James, Daniel Willis
Jarvis, William
Jones, George Wallace
Jordon, Eben Dyer
Juilliard, Augustus D.
Jumel, Stephen
Kemp, Robert H.
Kilby, Christopher
King, Charles
King, Charles William
Kirstein, Louis Edward
Kresge, Sebastian Spering
Kress, Samuel Henry
Ladd, William Sargent
Lamar, Gazaway Bugg
Lampson, Sir Curtis Miranda
Landreth, David
Langdon, John

Langdon, Woodbury
Larkin, Thomas Oliver
Laurens, Henry
Lawrence, Abbott
Lawrence, Amos
Lawrence, Amos Adams
Lawrence, William, 1783–1848
Leaming, Thomas
Lee, Henry, 1782–1867
Lee, William
Leiper, Thomas
Leiter, Levi Zeigler
Lewis, Francis
Lewis, William David
Livingston, Peter Van Brugh
Livingston, Philip
Lopez, Aaron
Lord, David Nevins
Lorillard, Pierre
Loudon, Samuel
Loveland, William Austin
    Hamilton
Low, Abiel Abbot
Low, Isaac
Low, Nicholas
Low, Seth
Ludlow, Daniel
Lumbrozo, Jacob
Macalester, Charles, 1765–1832
McClintock, Oliver
McDonogh, John
Mackenzie, Kenneth
McKim, Isaac
Macy, Josiah
Malcolm, Daniel
Manigault, Gabriel
Manigault, Pierre
Marshall, Benjamin
Marshall, James Fowle Baldwin
Mather, Samuel
May, Morton Jay
Mazzei, Philip
Meade, George
Meade, Richard Worsam
Melish, John
Menard, Pierre
Merry, William Lawrence
Mifflin, Thomas
Mills, Darius Ogden
Mills, Robert, 1809–1888
Minturn, Robert Bowne
Moore, William, 1735–1793
Mordecai, Moses Cohen
Morgan, Edwin Barber
Morgan, James Dada
Morris, Anthony, 1766–1860
Morris, Cadwalader
Morrison, William
Murray, John, 1737–1808
Murray, Robert
Nash, Arthur
Nelson, Thomas
Nelson, William, 1711–1772
Nesbitt, John Maxwell
Nesmith, John
Newberry, Oliver

Newberry, Walter Loomis
Nicola, Lewis
Nixon, John, 1733–1808
Norris, Isaac, 1671–1735
Norris, Isaac, 1701–1766
O'Brien, Edward Charles
Ochs, Julius
O'Fallon, John
Offley, David
Ogden, Robert Curtis
Olyphant, David Washington
   Cincinnatus
Olyphant, Robert Morrison
Opdyke, George
Orr, Alexander Ector
Orthwein, Charles F.
Outerbridge, Eugenius Harvey
Palmer, Potter
Partridge, Richard
Patten, James A.
Patterson, Morris
Patterson, William
Peabody, George
Peabody, Joseph
Peirce, Henry Augustus
Pemberton, Israel
Pemberton, James
Penhallow, Samuel
Penington, Edward
Pepperrell, Sir William
Perkins, Thomas Handasyd
Pettit, Charles
Phelan, James, 1824–1892
Phelps, Anson Greene
Phelps, Oliver
Phillips, William
Phinizy, Ferdinand
Pintard, John
Pintard, Lewis
Pinto, Isaac
Pratt, Charles
Pratte, Bernard
Price, Theodore Hazeltine
Purdue, John
Rand, Edward Sprague
Randall, Robert Richard
Randolph, William
Rawle, Francis, 1662–1726/27
Raymond, Benjamin Wright
Redwood, Abraham
Reed, Luman
Reed, Simeon Gannett
Reisinger, Hugo
Rhind, Charles
Rice, William Marsh
Rich, Isaac
Roberdeau, Daniel
Robert, Christopher Rhinelander
Roberts, Edmund
Robinson, Edward Mott
Rochester, Nathaniel
Roddey, Philip Dale
Ropes, Joseph
Rosenberg, Henry
Rosenwald, Julius
Rotch, William

Russell, Joseph
Sage, Henry Williams
St. Vrain, Ceran de Hault de
   Lassus de
Salomon, Haym
Sands, Comfort
Saunders, Clarence
Sayre, Stephen
Searle, James
Sears, Richard Warren
Seligman, Arthur
Servoss, Thomas Lowery
Sewall, Samuel
Shaw, Nathaniel
Shedd, John Graves
Sheedy, Dennis
Sheffield, Joseph Earl
Shelekhov, Grigorii Ivanovich
Silsbee, Nathaniel
Sleeper, Jacob
Smith, John, 1735–1824
Smith, Jonathan Bayard
Smith, Junius
Smith, Melancton, 1744–1798
Spalding, Albert Goodwill
Spreckels, John Diedrich
Stearns, Frank Waterman
Steenwyck, Cornelis
Stewart, Alexander Turney
Stokes, Anson Phelps
Straus, Isidor
Straus, Jesse Isidor
Strong, William Lafayette
Sturgis, William
Sublette, William Lewis
Sulzberger, Cyrus Lindauer
Swartwout, Samuel
Tappan, Lewis
Taylor, Joseph Wright
Telfair, Edward
Thatcher, Mahlon Daniel
Thompson, Jeremiah
Thorndike, Israel
Ticknor, Elisha
Tileston, Thomas
Tobey, Edward Silas
Tome, Jacob
Tracy, Nathaniel
Train, Enoch
Train, George Francis
Tulane, Paul
Tyndale, Hector
Upton, George Bruce
Van Cortlandt, Oloff Stevenszen
Van Cortlandt, Stephanus
Van Dam, Rip
Vassar, Matthew
Vaughan, Charles
Vernon, William
Vigo, Joseph Maria Francesco
Wagner, William
Waldo, Samuel
Waln, Robert, 1765–1836
Walters, William Thompson
Wanamaker, John
Wanamaker, Lewis Rodman

Ward, Aaron Montgomery
Ward, Samuel, 1756–1832
Ward, Thomas Wren
Watson, Elkanah
Weston, Thomas
Wharton, Richard
Wharton, Robert
Wharton, Samuel
Wharton, Thomas
White, Alexander
Whitney, Asa
Wilbur, Samuel
Wilder, Marshall Pinckney
Williams, Jonathan
Wolfe, John David
Wood, Robert Elkington
Woodruff, Timothy Lester
Woolworth, Frank Winfield

MESSENGER (See also TRANSPORTER)
Bailey, Ann

METAL DESIGNER
Yellin, Samuel

METALLOGRAPHER
Sauveur, Albert

METALLURGIST (See also CHEMIST,
   GEOLOGIST, MINERALOGIST)
Arents, Albert
Argall, Philip
Balback, Edward
Becket, Frederick Mark
Campbell, William
Church, John Adams
Daggett, Ellsworth
Daniels, Fred Harris
De Forest, Alfred Victor
Douglas, James
Eilers, Frederic Anton
Gayley, James
Gillett, Horace Wadsworth
Goetz, George Washington
Grant, James Benton
Hill, Nathaniel Peter
Hofman, Heinrich Oscar
Holley, Alexander Lyman
Howe, Henry Marion
Hunt, Alfred Ephraim
Hunt, Robert Woolston
Jackling, Daniel Cowan
Johnston, John
Mathews, John Alexander
Mathewson, Edward Payson
Matthiessen, Frederick William
Metcalf, William
Moldenke, Richard George Gottlob
Outerbridge, Alexander Ewing
Overman, Frederick
Pearce, Richard
Pearse, John Barnard Swett
Raht, August Wilhelm
Reese, Jacob
Richards, Joseph William
Sauveur, Albert
Spilsbury, Edmund Gybbon
Stanley, Robert Crooks
Stetefeldt, Carl August
Wahl, William Henry

Wills, Childe Harold

METAPHYSICIAN (See also
    PHILOSOPHER, RELIGIOUS
    LEADER)
Coomaraswamy, Ananda Kentish
Upham, Thomas Cogswell

METEOROLOGIST (See also
    CLIMATOLOGIST)
Abbe, Cleveland
Bentley, Wilson Alwyn
Bigelow, Frank Hagar
Coffin, James Henry
De Brahm, William Gerard
Engelmann, George
Espy, James Pollard
Ferrel, William
Gregg, Willis Ray
Harrington, Mark Walrod
Hayden, Edward Everett
Hazen, Henry Allen
Humphreys, Wiliam Jackson
Lippincott, James Starr
Lowe, Thaddeus Sobieski
    Coulincourt
McAdie, Alexander George
Marvin, Charles Frederick
Odenbach, Frederick Louis
Redfield, William C.
Rotch, Abbott Lawrence
Upton, Winslow

MICROBIOLOGIST
Gifford, Sanford Robinson
Henrici, Arthur Trautwein
Kelser, Raymond Alexander
Novy, Frederick George

MICROPALEONTOLOGIST (See also
    PALEONTOLOGIST)
Cushman, Joseph Augustine

MICROSCOPIST (See also PHYSICIAN)
Ward, Richard Halsted

MIDGET
Stratton, Charles Sherwood

MILITARY ENGINEER (See ENGINEER,
    MILITARY

MILLER (See MANUFACTURER)

MILLWRIGHT (See also ENGINEER)
Brown, Sylvanus
Coney, Jabez
Dalzell, Robert M.
Lucas, Jonathan, 1754–1821
Lucas, Jonathan, 1775–1832

MINE OPERATOR (See also MINE
    OWNER, MINER)
Dern, George Henry
Harvey, William Hope
Mondell, Frank Wheeler
Penrose, Spencer

MINE OWNER (See also MINER)
Guggenheim, Solomon Robert
Heckscher, August
Scott, Walter Edward

MINER (See also INDUSTRIALIST,
    METALLURGIST, MINE
    OPERATOR, MINE OWNER,
    PROSPECTOR)
Agassiz, Alexander

Andrews, Chauncey Hummason
Austin, Moses
Bowen, Thomas Meade
Cist, Jacob
Daly, Marcus
Fleming, Aretas Brooks
Godbe, William Samuel
Goold, William A.
Greene, William Cornell
Hauser, Samuel Thomas
Hearst, George
Henry, Andrew
Hussey, Curtis Grubb
Hutton, Levi William
Imboden, John Daniel
Jones, George Wallace
Mackay, John William
McKnight, Robert
Meeker, Moses
Newhouse, Samuel
Nicholson, Samuel Danford
O'Brien, William Shoney
Reed, John, 1757–1845
Ryan, John Dennis
Tabor, Horace Austin Warner
Thompson, William Boyce
Welch, Charles Clark

MINERALOGIST (See also GEOLOGIST)
Bruce, Archibald
Brush, George Jarvis
Dana, Edward Salisbury
Eggleston, Thomas
Koenig, George Augustus
Seybert, Henry
Shepard, Charles Upham
Smith, John Lawrence
Williams, George Huntington

MINIATURIST (See PAINTER)

MINING ENGINEER (See ENGINEER
    MINING

MINING PROMOTER (See MINER)

MINSTREL (See also BALLADIST,
    FOLKLORIST, SINGER)
Christy, Edwin P.
Dockstader, Lew
Heath, Thomas Kurton
McIntyre, James
Rice, Thomas Dartmouth

MISSIONARY (See also CLERGYMAN,
    RELIGIOUS LEADER)
Abeel, David
Agnew, Eliza
Alemany, José Sadoc
Allen, David Oliver
Allen, Young John
Allonez, Claude Jean
Altham, John
Anderson, David Lawrence
André, Louis
Andrews, Lorrin
Apes, William
Appenzeller, Henry Gerhard
Ashmore, William
Bacon, David
Badger, Joseph
Badin, Stephen Theodore

Bailey, Jacob
Baldwin, Theron
Bapst, John
Baraga, Frederic
Barton, James Levi
Bashford, James Whitford
Bassett, James
Beach, Harlan Page
Belcourt, George Antoine
Benjamin, Nathan
Biard, Pierre
Bickel, Luke Washington
Bingham, Hiram, 1789–1869
Bingham, Hiram, 1831–1908
Blackburn, Gideon
Blanchet, François Norbert
Bliss, Daniel
Bliss, Edwin Elisha
Bliss, Edwin Munsell
Bliss, Howard Sweetser
Bowen, George
Brainerd, David
Brainerd, John
Bridgman, Elijah Coleman
Brondel, John Baptist
Brown, Samuel Robbins
Buck, Philo Melvin
Butler, John Wesley
Butler, William
Byington, Cyrus
Cammerhoff, John Christopher
    Frederick
Campanius, John
Cary, Lott
Cataldo, Joseph Maria
Chamberlain, Jacob
Chandler, John Scudder
Clough, John Everett
Coan, Titus
Copley, Thomas
Copway, George
Cort, Edwin Charles
Crespi, Juan
Cushing, Josiah Nelson
Dablon, Claude
Daeger, Albert Thomas
David, John Baptist Mary
Davis, Jerome Dean
Day, David Alexander
Dearing, John Lincoln
De Forest, John Kinne Hyde
Dennis, James Shepard
De Smet, Pierre-Jean
Doty, Elihu
Dougherty, Raymond Philip
Doyle, Alexander Patrick
Druillettes, Gabriel
Dwight, Harrison Gray Otis
Dwight, Henry Otis
Eliot, John
Elliott, Walter Hackett Robert
Engelhardt, Zephyrin
Ewing, James Caruthers Rhea
Farmer, Ferdinand
Ferguson, John Calvin
Filton, James

Fiske, Fidelia
Fleming, John
Fletcher, James Cooley
Flint, Timothy
Fout, Pedro
Frame, Alice Seymour Browne
Gallitzin, Demetrius Augustine
Garcés, Francisco Tomás
    Hermenegildo
Garry, Spokane
Gates, Caleb Frank
Gibault, Pierre
Going, Jonathan
Good, Adolphus Clemens
Goodell, William
Goodrich, Chauncey
Gordon, Andrew
Goupil, René
Graessl, Lawrence
Grant, Asahel
Graves, Rosewell Hobart
Greaton, Joseph
Greene, Daniel Crosby
Grube, Bernhard Adam
Guignas, Michel
Gulick, John Thomas
Gulick, Luther Halsey, 1828–1891
Gulick, Sidney Lewis
Hall, Sherman
Hamlin, Cyrus
Happer, Andrew Patton
Harding, Robert
Harpster, John Henry
Hart, Virgil Chittenden
Hawley, Gideon, 1727–1807
Haygood, Laura Askew
Heckewelder, John Gottlieb
    Ernestus
Heiss, Michael
Helbron, Peter
Hepburn, James Curtis
Heyer, John Christian Frederick
Hill, John Henry
Hoecken, Christian
Hoisington, Henry Richard
Holcombe, Chester
Homes, Henry Augustus
Hoover, James Matthews
Hume, Robert Allen
Ingalls, Marilla Baker
Innokentii
Jackson, Sheldon
Jacoby, Ludwig Sigmund
Jessup, Henry Harris
Jogues, Isaac
Jones, George Heber
Jones, John Peter
Jones, John Taylor
Judge, Thomas Augustine
Judson, Adoniram
Judson, Ann Hasseltine
Judson, Emily Chubbuck
Judson, Sarah Hall Boardman
Keith, George
Kellogg, Samuel Henry
King, Jonas

Kino, Eusebio Francisco
Kirkland, Samuel
Kohlmann, Anthony
Lambuth, James William
Lambuth, Walter Russell
Lane, Horace M.
Lansing, Gulian
Lee, Jason
Lefevere, Peter Paul
Lemke, Peter Henry
Lindley, Daniel
Loewenthal, Isidor
Loughridge, Robert McGill
Lowrie, James Walter
Lowrie, Walter
Lowry, Hiram Harrison
Luce, Henry Winters
McCartee, Divie Bethune
MacCauley, Clay
McCord, James Bennett
McCoy, Isaac
McElroy, John
McFarland, Samuel Gamble
McGilvary, Daniel
McKay, David Oman
McKean, James William
McKenna, Charles Hyacinth
Maclay, Robert Samuel
MacSparran, James
Mansell, William Albert
Marquette, Jacques
Martin, William Alexander Parsons
Marty, Martin
Mason, Francis
Mateer, Calvin Wilson
Mayhew, Experience
Mayhew, Thomas, 1593–1682
Mayhew, Thomas, 1621–1657
Mazzuchelli, Samuel Charles
Meeker, Jotham
Meerschaert, Théophile
Membré, Zenobius
Ménard, René
Menetrey, Joseph
Mengarini, Gregory
Mills, Cyrus Taggart
Mills, Susan Lincoln Tolman
Morrison, William McCutchan
Mott, John R.
Mudge, James
Murrow, Joseph Samuel
Nash, Daniel
Nassau, Robert Hamill
Nevins, John Livingston
Niza, Marcos de
O'Brien, Matthew Anthony
Occom, Samson
Padilla, Juan de
Palladino, Lawrence Benedict
Palóu, Francisco
Parker, Alvin Pierson
Parker, Edwin Wallace
Parker, Peter
Parker, Samuel
Perkins, Justin
Perry, Rufus Lewis

Pierre, Joseph Marie Chaumonot
Pierson, Arthur Tappan
Pierz, Franz
Pond, Samuel William
Poor, Daniel
Post, Christian Frederick
Post, George Edward
Pott, Francis Lister Hawks
Price, Thomas Frederick
Pye, Watts Orson
Raffeimer, John Stephen
Râle, Sébastien
Ravalli, Antonio
Ravoux, Augustin
Rawlinson, Frank Joseph
Reed, Mary
Reid, Gilbert
Reid, John Morrison
Rice, Luther
Richard, Gabriel
Richards, William
Riggs, Elias
Riggs, Stephen Return
Roberts, Issachar Jacob
Robot, Isidore
Ruter, Martin
Ryan, Arthur Clayton
Saenderl, Simon
Savage, Thomas Staughton
Schauffler, Henry Albert
Schauffler, William Gottlieb
Schereschewsky, Samuel Isaac
    Joseph
Schneider, Benjamin
Schneider, Theodore
Scudder, John
Seagrave, Gordon Stifler
Seghers, Charles Jean
Sergeant, John, 1710–1749
Serra, Junípero
Shedd, William Ambrose
Sheffield, Devello Zelotes
Shelton, Albert Leroy
Shepard, Fred Douglas
Shipherd, John Jay
Shuck, Jehu Lewis
Smith, Arthur Henderson
Smith, Azariah
Smith, Eli
Smith, Judson
Spaulding, Levi
Speer, William
Stewart, Philo Penfield
Stewart, Robert
Stoddard, David Tappan
Stone, Ellen Maria
Stuart, John Leighton
Swain, Clara A.
Talbot, John
Talcott, Eliza
Talmage, John Van Nest
Taylor, George Boardman
Taylor, William
Tenney, Charles Daniel
Thayer, John
Thoburn, Isabella

Thomson, William McClure
Tichenor, Isaac Taylor
Tou, Erik Hansen
Trumbull, Henry Clay
Tupper, Henry Allen
Turner, Fennell Parrish
Unangst, Erias
Underwood, Horace Grant
Van Allen, Frank
Van Dyck, Cornelius Van Alen
Van Lennep, Henry John
Van Quickenborne, Charles Felix
Verbeck, Guido Herman Fridolin
Verwyst, Chrysostom Adrian
Walworth, Clarence Augustus
Wanless, William James
Washburn, George
Watson, Andrew
Watson, Charles Roger
West, Henry Sergeant
Wharton, Greene Lawrence
Wherry, Elwood Morris
White, Andrew
Whitman, Marcus
Williams, Channing Moore
Williams, Edward Thomas
Williams, Eleazar
Williams, John Elias
Williams, Samuel Wells
Willingham, Robert Josiah
Williston, Seth
Wilson, John Leighton
Wilson, Samuel Graham
Winslow, Miron
Wood, Thomas Bond
Worcester, Samuel Austin
Yates, Matthew Tyson
Young, Samuel Hall
Zeisberger, David

MODELER (See also ARTIST,
     CRAFTSMAN, SCULPTOR)
Wright, Patience Lovell

MONOLOGUIST
Draper, Ruth

MORALIST
Fisher, Dorothea Frances Canfield

MOTION PICTURE CAMERAMAN
Bitzer, George William

MOTION PICTURE DIRECTOR (See also
     DIRECTOR, FILMMAKER)
Borzage, Frank
Browning, Tod
Curtiz, Michael
Del Ruth, Roy
Fejos, Paul
Sennett, Mack
Sturges, Preston
Von Stroheim, Erich

MOTION PICTURE DISTRIBUTOR
Laemmle, Carl

MOTION PICTURE EXECUTIVE
Johnston, Eric Allen
Mayer, Louis Burt
Warner, Harry Morris

MOTION PICTURE PIONEER
Blackton, James Stuart

Lasky, Jesse Louis
MOTION PICTURE PRODUCER
Borzage, Frank
Fox, William
Selznick, David O.
Sennett, Mack
Sturges, Preston
Todd, Mike
Waller, Frederic
Yates, Herbert John

MOTORIST (See also TRANSPORTER)
Glidden, Charles Jasper

MUCKRAKER (See AUTHOR,
     JOURNALIST, WRITER)

MURALIST (See also ARTIST, PAINTER)
Christy, Howard Chandler
Lebrun, Federico ("Rico")
Meière, Marie Hildreth
Sterne, Maurice

MURDERESS (ALLEGED)
Borden, Lizzie Andrew

MUSEUM DIRECTOR (See also
     CURATOR)
Barbour, Thomas
Cesnola, Luigi Palma di
Clarke, Sir Caspar Purdon
Dana, John Cotton
D'Harnoncourt, René
Force, Juliana Rieser
French, William Merchant
     Richardson
Harshe, Robert Bartholow
Heye, George Gustav
Ives, Halsey Cooley
Johnston, John Taylor
Lodge, John Ellerton
Lucas, Frederic Augustus
Mather, Frank Jewett, Jr.
Miller, Gerrit Smith, Jr.
Morse, Edward Sylvester
Osborn, Henry Fairfield
Parker, Arthur Caswell
Putnam, Frederic Ward
Rathbun, Richard
Robinson, Edward, 1858–1931
Rorimer, James Joseph
Spargo, John
Stevens, George Washington
Taylor, Francis Henry
Vaillant, George Clapp
Winlock, Herbert Eustis

MUSEUM FOUNDER
Guggenheim, Solomon Robert

MUSICAL SATIRIST
Templeton, Alec Andrew

MUSIC ARRANGER
Henderson, Fletcher Hamilton

MUSIC CRITIC (See also CRITIC)
Aldrich, Richard
Apthorp, William Foster
Chotzinoff, Samuel
Downes, (Edwin) Olin
Dwight, John Sullivan
Elson, Louis Charles
Finck, Henry Theophilus
Fry, William Henry

Gilman, Lawrence
Gleason, Frederic Grant
Hale, Philip
Henderson, William James
Krehbiel, Henry Edward
Parker, Henry Taylor
Peck, George Washington
Rosenfeld, Paul Leopold
Singleton, Esther
Taylor, Joseph Deems
Thompson, Oscar Lee
Upton, George Putnam
Van Vechten, Carl
Watson, Henry Cood
Woolf, Benjamin Edward

MUSIC EDUCATOR (See also
     EDUCATOR)
Bauer, Harold Victor
Damrosch, Frank Heino
Farwell, Arthur
Goldmark, Rubin
Mannes, Leopold Damrosch
White, Clarence Cameron

MUSICIAN (See also SPECIFIC
     INSTRUMENTS)
Adgate, Andrew
Allen, Nathan H.
Baker, Benjamin Franklin
Bechet, Sidney
Brown, Gertrude Foster
Clarke, Helen Archibald
Coltrane, John William
Cook, Will Marion
Duchin, Edward Frank ("Eddy")
Elman, Harry ("Ziggy")
Elman, Mischa
Erskine, John
Fillmore, John Comfort
Flagg, Josiah
Gericke, Wilhelm
Gleason, Frederic Grant
Graupner, Johann Christian
     Gottlieb
Grierson, Francis
Hale, Philip
Herbert, Victor
Hewitt, John Hill
Holden, Oliver
Holly, Charles Hardin ("Buddy")
Holmes, Daniel Henry
Hopkinson, Francis
Horst, Louis
House, Edward Howard
Humiston, William Henry
Huneker, James Gibbons
Koemmenich, Louis
Kroeger, Ernest Richard
Lanier, Sidney
Mason, Frank Stuart
Mathews, William Smythe Babcock
Merz, Karl
Moore, Annie Aubertine
     Woodward
Neuendorff, Adolph Heinrich
     Anton Magnus
Oberhoffer, Emil Johann

Oehmler, Leo Carl Martin
Oliver, Henry Kemble
Parsons, Albert Ross
Pearce, Stephen Austen
Peter, John Frederick
Peters, William Cumming
Pryor, Arthur W.
Read, Daniel, 1757–1836
Reinagle, Alexander
Russell, Charles Ellsworth ("Pee
  Wee")
Scheve, Edward Benjamin
Schindler, Kurt
Seidl, Anton
Selby, William
Seward, Theodore Frelinghuysen
Shaw, Oliver
Sonneck, Oscar George Theodore
Southard, Lucien H.
Spicker, Max
Taylor, Raynor
Thomas, Christian Friedrich
  Theodore
Timm, Henry Christian
Tourjée, Eben
Trajetta, Philip
Ward, Thomas
Webb, George James
Weber, Max
Weld, Arthur Cyril Gordon
Wight, Frederick Coit
Wolfsohn, Carl
Yancey, James Edward ("Jimmy")
Young, Alfred
Zerralin, Carl
Ziehn, Bernhard

MUSICOLOGIST
Engel, Carl
Landowska, Wanda Aleksandra
Pratt, Waldo Selden
Spaeth, Sigmund

MUSIC PATRON (See also
  PHILANTHROPIST)
Coolidge, Elizabeth Penn Sprague
De Coppet, Edward J.
Frieze, Henry Simmons
Jordan, Eben Dyer
Juilliard, Augustus D.
Nichols, George Ward
Robinson-Smith, Gertrude
Scherman, Harry
Sloan, George Arthur
Stoeckel, Carl
Thurber, Jeannette Meyer
Webb, Thomas Smith

MUSIC PUBLISHER (See also EDITOR,
  PUBLISHER)
Bloom, Sol
Ditson, Oliver
Dreyfus, Max
Fisher, William Arms
Handy, William Christopher
Harris, Charles Kassell
Peters, William Cumming
Presser, Theodore
Schirmer, Gustav

Schirmer, Rudolph Edward
Schmidt, Arthur Paul
Stern, Joseph William
Witmark, Isidore
MUSIC THEORIST
Goetschius, Percy
Schillinger, Joseph
MYCOLOGIST (See also BOTANIST)
Ellis, Job Bicknell
Peck, Charles Horton
Schweinitz, Lewis David von
Whetzel, Herbert Hice
MYSTIC (See also RELIGIOUS LEADER)
Alcott, Amos Bronson
Blood, Benjamin Paul
Harris, Thomas Lake
Kelpius, Johann
Very, Jones

**NATIONAL FOOTBALL LEAGUE
  COMMISSIONER**
Bell, De Benneville ("Bert")
**NATIONAL LABOR RELATIONS BOARD
  CHAIRMAN**
Leedom, Boyd Stewart
NATURALIST (See also BIOLOGIST,
  BOTANIST, ECOLOGIST,
  ZOOLOGIST)
Abbott, Charles Conrad
Adams, Charles Baker
Agassiz, Jean Louis Rodolphe
Akeley, Carl Ethan
Allen, Glover Morrill
Bachman, John
Barbour, Thomas
Barton, Benjamin Smith
Bartram, William
Beebe, (Charles) William
Bland, Thomas
Boll, Jacob
Buckley, Samuel Botsford
Catesby, Mark
Cist, Jacob
Cockerell, Theodore Dru Alison
Cooper, James Graham
Dall, William Healey
De Brahm, William Gerard
De Kay, James Ellsworth
Doubleday, Neltje de Graff
Du Simitière, Pierre Eugène
Emerton, James Henry
Flagg, Thomas Wilson
Forbes, Stephen Alfred
Garden, Alexander
Gibson, William Hamilton
Godman, John Davidson
Good, Adolphus Clemens
Goode, George Brown
Grant, Madison
Green, Jacob
Grinnell, George Bird
Grosvenor, Gilbert Hovey
Gulick, John Thomas
Harlan, Richard
Harshberger, John William
Henshall, James Alexander

Henshaw, Henry Wetherbee
Hildreth, Samuel Prescott
Holder, Charles Frederick
Holder, Joseph Bassett
Holland, William Jacob
Hornaday, William Temple
Horsfield, Thomas
Hubbard, Wynant Davis
James, Edwin
Jordan, David Starr
Kennicott, Robert
Kirtland, Jared Potter
Kunze, Richard Ernest
Leidy, Joseph
Lesueur, Charles Alexandre
Lincecum, Gideon
Lucas, Frederick Augustus
McCook, Henry Christopher
Maynard, Charles Johnson
Mearns, Edgar Alexander
Merriam, Clinton Hart
Miles, Manly
Miller, Harriet Mann
Mills, Enos Abijah
Morton, Samuel George
Muir, John
Nelson, Edward William
Osborn, Henry Fairfield
Pavy, Octave
Peale, Charles Willson
Peale, Titian Ramsay
Peck, William Dandridge
Pickering, Charles
Pitcher, Zina
Putnam, Frederic Ward
Rafinesque, Constantine Samuel
Ravenel, Edmund
Ritter, William Emerson
Romans, Bernard
Samuels, Edward Augustus
Saugrain de Vigni, Antoine
  François
Savage, Thomas Staughton
Seton, Ernest Thompson
Sharp, Dallas Lore
Snow, Francis Huntington
Stearns, Robert Edwards Carter
Stimpson, William
Stone, Witmer
Storer, David Humphreys
Thompson, Zadock
Tuckerman, Frederick
Verrill, Alpheus Hyatt
Ward, Henry Augustus
Webber, Charles Wilkins
White, Charles Abiathar
NAVAL ARCHITECT (See also
  ARCHITECT)
Babcock, Washington Irving
Burgess, W(illiam) Starling
Eckford, Henry
Fairburn, William Armstrong
Forman, Cheesman
Griffiths, John Willis
Herreshoff, Nathanael Greene
Hovgaard, William

Humphreys, Joshua
Isherwood, Benjamin Franklin
Lenthall, John
McKay, Donald
Newton, Isaac, 1794–1858
Porter, John Luke
See, Horace
Steers, George
Stevens, Robert Livingston
Ward, Charles Alfred
Wilson, Theodore Delavan

NAVAL AVIATOR
Towers, John Henry

NAVAL CONSTRUCTOR
Taylor, David Watson

NAVAL ENGINEER (See ENGINEER,
   NAVAL)

NAVAL OFFICER
Abbot, Joel
Alden, James
Allen, William Henry
Almy, John Jay
Ammen, Daniel
Astor, William Vincent
Aylwin, John Cushing
Badger, Charles Johnston
Badger, Oscar Charles
Bailey, Frank Harvey
Bailey, Theodorus
Bainbridge, William
Balch, George Beall
Barbey, Daniel Edward
Barker, Albert Smith
Barney, Joshua
Barron, James
Barron, Samuel
Barry, John
Beary, Donald Bradford
Beaumont, John Colt
Belknap, George Eugene
Bell, Henry Haywood
Benson, William Shepherd
Bent, Silas
Biddle, James
Biddle, Nicholas
Blake, Homer Crane
Blakely, Johnston
Blandy, William Henry Purnell
Bloch, Claude Charles
Blue, Victor
Boggs, Charles Stuart
Bourne, Nehemiah
Boutelle, Charles Addison
Breese, Kidder Randolph
Bristol, Mark Lambert
Brooke, John Mercer
Brownson, Willard Herbert
Buchanan, Franklin
Bullard, William Hannum Grubb
Bulloch, James Dunwody
Burrows, William
Caldwell, Charles Henry Bromedge
Capps, Washington Lee
Carter, Samuel Powhatan
Chadwick, French Ensor
Chaffee, Roger Bruce

Champlin, Stephen
Chauncey, Isaac
Chester, Colby Mitchell
Clark, Charles Edgar
Coffin, Sir Isaac
Collins, Napoleon
Colvocoresses, George Musalas
Cone, Hutchinson Ingham
Conner, David
Conyngham, Gustavus
Coontz, Robert Edward
Crane, William Montgomery
Craven, Thomas Tingey
Craven, Tunis Augustus
   MacDonough
Crosby, Peirce
Cushing, William Baker
Dahlgren, John Adolphus Bernard
Dale, Richard
Dale, Sir Thomas
Davis, Charles Henry, 1807–1877
Davis, Charles Henry, 1845–1921
Davis, John Lee
Davison, Gregory Caldwell
Decatur, Stephen
Decatur, Stephen (son of Stephen)
De Haven, Edwin Jesse
Delano, Amassa
Dewey, George
Dornin, Thomas Aloysius
Downes, John
Drayton, Percival
Du Pont, Samuel Francis
Dyer, Nehemiah Mayo
Earle, Ralph
Eberle, Edward Walter
Edwards, Richard Stanislaus
Elliott, Jesse Duncan
Emmons, George Foster
Evans, Robley Dunglison
Fairfax, Donald McNeill
Fanning, Nathaniel
Farragut, David Glasgow
Farragut, George
Fiske, Bradley Allen
Fiske, John
Foote, Andrew Hull
Forrest, French
Foulk, George Clayton
Frost, Holloway Halstead
Gherardi, Bancroft
Gillon, Alexander
Gleaves, Albert
Glynn, James
Goldsborough, Louis Malesherbes
Gorringe, Henry Honeychurch
Grant, Albert Weston
Greene, Samuel Dana
Greer, James Augustin
Gridley, Charles Vernon
Griffin, Robert Stanislaus
Grinnell, Henry Walton
Habersham, Alexander Wylly
Halsey, William Frederick ("Bull"),
   Jr.
Haraden, Jonathan

Harding, Seth
Hayden, Edward Everett
Hazelwood, John
Henley, Robert
Herndon, William Lewis
Hichborn, Philip
Hinman, Elisha
Hobson, Richmond Pearson
Hollins, George Nichols
Hopkins, Esek
Hopkins, John Burroughs
Howell, John Adams
Hudde, Andries
Hughes, Charles Frederick
Hull, Isaac
Ingersoll, Royal Rodney
Ingraham, Duncan Nathaniel
Ingram, Jonas Howard
Jeffers, William Nicholson
Jenkins, Thornton Alexander
Jewett, David
Jones, Catesby Ap Roger
Jones, Hilary Pollard
Jones, Jacob
Jones, John Paul
Jones, Thomas Ap Catesby
Jouett, James Edward
Joy, Charles Turner
Kane, Elisha Kent
Kearney, Lawrence
Kelley, James Douglas Jerrold
Kempff, Louis
Kimball, William Wirt
Kimmel, Husband Edward
King, Ernest Joseph
Kirk, Alan Goodrich
Knight, Austin Melvin
Knox, Dudley Wright
Lamberton, Benjamin Peffer
Landais, Pierre
Lanman, Joseph
Lardner, James Lawrence
La Ronde, Louis Denis, Sieur de
Lawrence, James
Leahy, William Daniel
Lee, Samuel Phillips
Lee, Willis Augustus
Little, George
Livingston, John William
Loring, Charles Harding
Loring, Joshua, 1716–1781
Luce, Stephen Bleecker
Lull, Edward Phelps
Lynch, William Francis
McArthur, William Pope
McCall, Edward Rutledge
McCalla, Bowman Hendry
McCann, William Penn
McCauley, Charles Stewart
McCauley, Edward Yorke
McCormick, Lynde Dupuy
Macdonough, Thomas
McDougal, David Stockton
McGiffin, Philo Norton
McKean, William Wister
Mackenzie, Alexander Slidell

NAVIGATOR (See also MARINER,
    STEAMBOAT OPERATOR)
    Allefonsce, Jean
    Amadas, Philip
    Ayala, Juan Manuel de
    De Brahm, William Gerard
    Gosnold, Bartholomew
    Gray, Robert
    Hudson, Henry
    Ingraham, Joseph
    Kendrick, John
    Waymouth, George
NAVY SURGEON GENERAL
    McIntire, Ross
NAZI PARTY (AMERICAN) LEADER
    Rockwell, George Lincoln
NEMATOLOGIST (See also ANATOMIST)
    Cobb, Nathan Augustus
NEUROANATOMIST (See also
    ANATOMIST)
    Hoerr, Normand Louis
NEUROBIOLOGIST
    Loewi, Otto
NEUROLOGIST (See also PHYSICIAN)
    Coriat, Isador Henry
    Dana, Charles Loomis
    Donaldson, Henry Herbert
    Hammond, William Alexander
    Jelliffe, Smith Ely
    Kennedy, Robert Foster
    Knapp, Philip Coombs
    McCarthy, Daniel Joseph
    Mills, Charles Karsner
    Mitchell, Silas Weir
    Morton, William James
    Patrick, Hugh Talbot
    Potts, Charles Sower
    Putnam, James Jackson
    Ranson, Stephen Walter
    Sachs, Bernard
    Seguin, Edward Constant
    Spitzka, Edward Charles
    Starr, Moses Allen
    Tilney, Frederick
    Timme, Walter
    Weisenburg, Theodore Herman
NEUROPATHOLOGIST (See also
    PATHOLOGIST)
    Barrett, Albert Moore
    Southard, Elmer Ernest
NEUROPHARMACOLOGIST (See also
    PHARMACOLOGIST)
    Loewi, Otto
NEUROPHYSIOLOGIST (See also
    PHYSIOLOGIST)
    Fulton, John Farquhar
NEUROPSYCHIATRIST (See also
    PSYCHIATRIST)
    Myerson, Abraham
NEUROSURGEON (See also SURGEON)
    Craig, Winchell McKendree
NEWSAGENT (See also PUBLICIST)
    Topliff, Samuel
    Tousey, Sinclair
NEWS COMMENTATOR
    Swing, Raymond Edwards (Gram)

NEWSPAPER COLUMNIST
    Berger, Meyer
    Broun, Heywood Campbell
    Clapper, Raymond Lewis
    Crouse, Russel McKinley
    Gilmer, Elizabeth Meriwether
        ("Dorothy Dix")
    Guest, Edgar Albert
    Hopper, Hedda
    Kilgallen, Dorothy Mae
    Lewis, Fulton, Jr.
    McIntyre, Oscar Odd
    Morehouse, Ward
    Patri, Angelo
    Pyle, Ernest Taylor
    Stevens, Ashton
NEWSPAPER CORRESPONDENT (See
    also FOREIGN CORRESPONDENT,
    JOURNALIST, NEWSPAPER
    REPORTER)
    Andrews, Bert
    Ross, Charles Griffith
    Stark, Louis
NEWSPAPER EXECUTIVE
    Carvalho, Solomon Solis
    Dryfoos, Orvil E.
    Grant, Harry Johnston
    Howard, Roy Wilson
    Laffan, William Mackay
NEWSPAPERMAN (See also
    JOURNALIST)
    Asbury, Herbert
    Cobb, Irvin Shrewsbury
    Early, Stephen Tyree
    Farrington, Wallace Rider
    Hapgood, Hutchins
    Mankiewicz, Herman Jacob
    Neuberger, Richard Lewis
    Wilson, J(ames) Finley
NEWSPAPER OWNER
    Bingham, Robert Worth
    Chandler, Harry
    Farrington, Joseph Rider
    Grasty, Charles Henry
    Knutson, Harold
    Lea, Luke
    Livingstone, William
    McCormick, Robert Rutherford
    Nicholson, Eliza Jane Poitevent
        Holbrook
    Patterson, Alicia
    Pulitzer, Joseph, Jr.
    Scripps, William Edmund
NEWSPAPER PUBLISHER (See also
    PUBLISHER)
    Abbott, Robert Sengstacke
    Annenberg, Moses Louis
    Block, Paul
    Bryan, John Stewart
    Copley, Ira Clifton
    Cowles, Gardner
    Cox, James Middleton
    Dealey, George Bannerman
    Fitzgerald, John Francis
    Fleisher, Benjamin Wilfrid
    Glass, Carter

McClatchy, Charles Kenny
McLean, Edward Beale
Murphy, Frederick E.
Noyes, Frank Brett
Patterson, Eleanor Medill
Patterson, Joseph Medill
Pulitzer, Ralph
Reid, Ogden Mills
Scripps, Robert Paine
Sulzberger, Arthur Hays
NEWSPAPER REPORTER (See also
    FOREIGN CORRESPONDENT,
    JOURNALIST, NEWSPAPER
    CORRESPONDENT)
    Berger, Meyer
    Kilgallen, Dorothy Mae
    Manning, Marie
    Powell, John Benjamin
    Stark, Louis
NEWSPAPER SYNDICATOR
    Dille, John Flint
NIGHTCLUB OWNER
    Billingsley, John Sherman
    Livingstone, Belle
    Rose, Billy
NOVELIST (See also AUTHOR,
    WRITER)
    Abbott, Eleanor Hallowell
    Adamic, Louis
    Adams, Frank Ramsay
    Agee, James Rufus
    Aldrich, Bess Genevra Streeter
    Allen, Hervey
    Allen, James Lane
    Arlen, Michael
    Atherton, Gertrude Franklin (Horn)
    Bacheller, Irving
    Bailey, (Irene) Temple
    Baker, Dorothy Dodds
    Basso, (Joseph) Hamilton
    Baum, Hedwig ("Vicki")
    Beach, Rex
    Beer, Thomas
    Benét, Stephen Vincent
    Bennett, Emerson
    Biggers, Earl Derr
    Bird, Robert Montgomery
    Boyd, James
    Boyd, Thomas Alexander
    Bradford, Roark Whitney Wickliffe
    Brown, Charles Brockden
    Buntline, Ned (See Judson, Edward
        Zane Carroll)
    Burgess, Frank Gelett
    Cabell, James Branch
    Cahan, Abraham
    Campbell, William Edward March
    Catherwood, Mary Hartwell
    Chambers, Robert William
    Chatterton, Ruth
    Churchill, Winston
    Cleghorn, Sarah Norcliffe
    Clemens, Jeremiah
    Clemens, Samuel Langhorne
    Cobb, Sylvanus
    Cohen, Octavus Roy

ORGANIZATION EXECUTIVE
Breckinridge, Aida de Acosta
ORGANIZED CRIME LEADER (**See also**
CRIMINAL, GANGSTER)
Luchese, Thomas
Luciano, Charles ("Lucky")
Profaci, Joseph
ORGANIZER (**See** PROMOTER)
ORIENTALIST (**See also** SCHOLAR,
SINOLOGUE)
Adler, Cyrus
Barton, George Aaron
Bigelow, William Sturgis
Bloomfield, Maurice
Brown, John Porter
Casanowicz, Immanuel Moses
Chiera, Edward
Clay, Albert Tobias
Davis, Charles Henry Stanley
Gibbs, Josiah Willard
Hall, Isaac Hollister
Hodgson, William Brown
Hopkins, Edward Washburn
Hyvernat, Henri
Jackson, Abraham Valentine
Williams
Lanman, Charles Rockwell
Lewis, Tayler
Lyon, David Gordon
Moore, George Foot
Müller, Wilhelm Max
Newbold, William Romaine
Nordheimer, Isaac
Olmstead, Albert Ten Eyck
Orne, John
Rockhill, William Woodville
Rogers, Robert William
Salisbury, Edward Elbridge
Schmidt, Nathaniel
Smith, Eli
Toy, Crawford Howell
Ward, William Hayes
Warren, Henry Clarke
ORNITHOLOGIST (**See also**
NATURALIST, ZOOLOGIST)
Allen, Arthur Augustus
Audubon, John James
Bailey, Florence Augusta Merriam
Brewer, Thomas Mayo
Brewster, William
Cassin, John
Chapin, James Paul
Chapman, Frank Michler
Cory, Charles Barney
Coues, Elliott
Eckstorm, Fannie Hardy
Eklund, Carl Robert
Forbush, Edward Howe
Griscom, Ludlow
Henshaw, Henry Wetherbee
Jones, Lynds
Lawrence, George Newbold
Nehrling, Henry
Nuttall, Thomas
Nutting, Charles Cleveland
Ober, Frederick Albion

Oberholser, Harry Church
Pearson, Thomas Gilbert
Richmond, Charles Wallace
Ridgway, Robert
Samuels, Edward Augustus
Sennett, George Burritt
Todd, Walter Edmond Clyde
Torrey, Bradford
Townsend, John Kirk
Wayne, Arthur Trezevant
Wilson, Alexander
Wood, Casey Albert
Xántus, János
OTOLOGIST (**See also** PHYSICIAN)
Buck, Albert Henry
Burnett, Charles Henry
Gruening, Emil
Leland, George Adams
Randall, Burton Alexander
OUTLAW (**See also** BANDIT,
JAYHAWKER, VIGILANTE)
Laffite, Jean
Murrell, John A.
OYSTER CULTURIST
Nelson, Julius
Oemler, Arminius

PAINTER (**See also** ARTIST,
ILLUSTRATOR, MURALIST)
Abbey, Edwin Austin
Agate, Alfred T.
Agate, Frederick Styles
Alexander, Francis
Alexander, John White
Ames, Ezra
Ames, Joseph Alexander
Anshutz, Thomas Pollock
Archipenko, Alexander
Armstrong, David Maitland
Badger, Joseph
Baker, George Augustus
Banvard, John
Beaux, Cecilia
Beckwith, James Carroll
Bellows, Albert Fitch
Bellows, George Wesley
Benbridge, Henry
Benjamin, Samuel Greene Wheeler
Benson, Eugene
Benson, Frank Weston
Bierstadt, Albert
Bingham, George Caleb
Birch, Thomas
Birch, William Russell
Blackburn, Joseph
Blakelock, Ralph Albert
Blashfield, Edwin Howland
Bluemner, Oscar Florians
Blum, Robert Frederick
Bohm, Max
Borglum, John Gutzon de la
Mothe
Borie, Adolphe
Bouché, René Robert
Bounetheau, Henry Brintnell
Bradford, William

Breck, George William
Brevoort, James Renwick
Bridgman, Frederick Arthur
Bristol, John Bunyan
Brown, John Appleton
Brown, John George
Brown, Mather
Bruce, Edward Bright
Brumidi, Constantino
Brush, George de Forest
Bunce, William Gedney
Burchfield, Charles Ephraim
Carpenter, Francis Bicknell
Casilear, John William
Champney, Benjamin
Champney, James Wells
Chapman, John Gadsby
Church, Frederick Edwin
Church, Frederick Stuart
Clarke, Thomas Shields
Closson, William Baxter
Coffin, William Anderson
Cogdell, John Stevens
Cole, Joseph Foxcroft
Coleman, Charles Caryl
Colman, Samuel
Copley, John Singleton
Cornoyer, Paul
Cox, Kenyon
Cranch, Christopher Pearse
Cropsey, Jaspar Francis
Crowninshield, Frederic
Cummings, Thomas Seir
Curry, John Steuart
Cushman, George Hewitt
Danforth, Moseley Isaac
Davies, Arthur Bowen
Daviess, Maria Thompson
Dearth, Henry Golden
De Camp, Joseph Rodefer
Dewing, Maria Richards Oakey
Dewing, Thomas Wilmer
Dickinson, Anson
Dickinson, Preston
Dielman, Frederick
Diller, Burgoyne
Doughty, Thomas
Dove, Arthur Garfield
Dummer, Jeremiah
Dunlap, William
Durand, Asher Brown
Duveneck, Frank
Eakins, Thomas
Earle, James
Earle, Ralph
Eaton, Joseph Oriel
Eaton, Wyatt
Eckstein, John
Edmonds, Francis William
Ehninger, John Whetten
Eichholtz, Jacob
Eilshemius, Louis Michel
Elliott, Charles Loring
Elliott, John
Ennecking, John Joseph
Farrer, Henry

Rosenthal, Toby Edward
Rossiter, Thomas Prichard
Rothko, Mark
Rowse, Samuel Worcester
Ryder, Albert Pinkham
Sandham, Henry
Sargent, Henry
Sargent, John Singer
Sartain, Emily
Sartain, William
Savage, Edward
Schussele, Christian
Sellstedt, Lars Gustaf
Shahn, Benjamin ("Ben")
Sharples, James
Shattuck, Aaron Draper
Shinn, Everett
Shirlaw, Walter
Shurtleff, Roswell Morse
Simmons, Edward
Sloan, John French
Smedley, William Thomas
Smillie, George Henry
Smith, Archibald Cary
Smith, John Rowson
Smith, John Rubens
Smith, Russell
Smith, Xanthus Russell
Spencer, Robert
Stanley, John Mix
Stella, Joseph
Sterne, Maurice
Stetson, Charles Walter
Stone, William Oliver
Story, Julian Russell
Stuart, Gilbert
Sully, Thomas
Sylvester, Frederick Oakes
Symons, George Gardner
Szyk, Arthur
Tait, Arthur Fitzwilliam
Tanner, Henry Ossawa
Tarbell, Edmund Charles
Taylor, Frank Walter
Tchelitchew, Pavel
Thayer, Abbott Handerson
Theus, Jeremiah
Thompson, Alfred Wordsworth
Thompson, Cephas Giovanni
Thompson, Jerome B.
Thulstrup, Bror Thure
Tilton, John Rollin
Tomlin, Bradley Walker
Trott, Benjamin
Troye, Edward
Trumbull, John 1756–1843
Tryon, Dwight William
Tucker, Allen
Turner, Charles Yardley
Turner, Ross Sterling
Twachtman, John Henry
Vanderlyn, John
Vedder, Elihu
Vinton, Frederic Porter
Vonnoh, Robert William
Waldo, Samuel Lovett

Walker, Henry Oliver
Waugh, Frederick Judd
Weeks, Edwin Lord
Weir, Julian Alden
Weir, Robert Walter
Wentworth, Cecile de
West, Benjamin
West, William Edward
Whistler, James Abbott McNeill
Whitteredge, Worthington
Wiggins, Carleton
Wilmarth, Lemuel Everett
Wilson, Robert Burns
Wimar, Carl
Wood, Grant
Wood, Joseph
Wright, Joseph
Wyant, Alexander Helwig
Wyeth, Newell Convers
Wylie, Robert
Yohn, Frederick Coffay
Young, Mahonri Mackintosh

PALEOBOTANIST (See also BOTANIST,
   GEOLOGIST)
Berry, Edward Wilber
Lesquereux, Leo

PALEOGRAPHER
Beeson, Charles Henry

PALEONTOLOGIST (See also
   GEOLOGIST)
Beecher, Charles Emerson
Clarke, John Mason
Cope, Edward Drinker
Gabb, William More
Gidley, James Williams
Grabau, Amadeus William
Granger, Walter
Hall, James, 1811–1898
Hay, Oliver Perry
Heilprin, Angelo
Hyatt, Alpheus
Knowlton, Frank Hall
Marsh, Othniel Charles
Matthew, William Diller
Meek, Fielding Bradford
Merriam, John Campbell
Newberry, John Strong
Osborn, Henry Fairfield
Patten, William
Schuchert, Charles
Scott, William Berryman
Smith, James Perrin
Springer, Frank
Ulrich, Edward Oscar
Vaughan, Thomas Wayland
Wachsmuth, Charles
Walcott, Charles Doolittle
White, Charles Abiathar
Whitfield, Robert Parr
Wieland, George Reber
Williams, Henry Shaler
Williston, Samuel Wendell
Yandell, Lunsford Pitts

PAMPHLETEER (See also PUBLICIST)
Dove, David James
Heywood, Ezra Hervey

King, Dan
Paine, Thomas
Penington, Edward
Pickering, Timothy
Smith, William Loughton
Wood, John
Yates, Abraham
Zubly, John Joachim

PAPYROLOGIST
Westermann, William Linn

PARACHUTE DESIGNER
Scott, Allen Cecil

PARASITOLOGIST (See also
   ZOOLOGIST)
Noguchi, Hideyo
Ward, Henry Baldwin

PARLIAMENTARIAN
Dalzell, John
Hinds, Asher Crosby
Reed, Thomas Brackett
Robert, Henry Martyn

PASSPORT DIVISION CHIEF
Shipley, Ruth Bielaski

PATENT COMMISSIONER
Ellsworth, Henry Leavitt
Leggett, Mortimer Dormer
Paine, Halbert Eleazer

PATENT EXPERT
Benjamin, George Hillard
Hall, Thomas
Knight, Edward Henry
Langner, Lawrence
Renwick, Edward Sabine
Renwick, Henry Brevoort
Selden, George Baldwin

PATENT LAWYER
Davis, William Hammatt

"PATENT MEDICINE KING"
Dyott, Thomas W.

PATHOLOGIST (See also PHYSICIAN)
Biggs, Herman Michael
Bloodgood, Joseph Colt
Carroll, James
Councilman, William Thomas
Darling, Samuel Taylor
Delafield, Francis
Ewing, James
Fenger, Christian
Fitz, Reginald Heber
Flexner, Simon
Gardner, Leroy Upson
Hess, Alfred Fabian
Landsteiner, Karl
Libman, Emanuel
Loeb, Leo
MacCallum, William George
Mallory, Frank Burr
Moore, Veranus Alva
Murphy, James Bumgardner
Ohlmacher, Albert Philip
Pearce, Richard Mills
Prudden, Theophil Mitchell
Ricketts, Howard Taylor
Stengel, Alfred
Welch, William Henry
Wells, Harry Gideon

Camp, Hiram
Candler, Asa Griggs
Carnegie, Andrew
Case, Leonard
Childs, George William
Clark, Jonas Gilman
Clarkson, Matthew
Clinton, De Witt
Coates, Samuel
Coburn, Abner
Cochran, Alexander Smith
Coffin, Lorenzo S.
Coker, David Robert
Coker, James Lide
Colby, Gardner
Colgate, James Boorman
Combs, Moses Newell
Comstock, Elizabeth L.
Converse, Edmund Cogswell
Cooper, Peter
Cooper, Sarah Brown Ingersoll
Cope, Thomas Pym
Corcoran, William Wilson
Crane, Charles Richard
Creighton, Edward
Creighton, John Andrew
Crerar, John
Cresson, Elliott
Crozer, John Price
Cullen, Hugh Roy
Cupples, Samuel
Cushing, John Perkins
Cutting, Robert Fulton
Davis, Arthur Vining
De Forest, Robert Weeks
De Pauw, Washington Charles
Dodge, Grace Hoadley
Drake, Francis Marion
Dreier, Mary Elisabeth
Drexel, Anthony Joseph
Drexel, Joseph William
Duke, Benjamin Newton
Durant, Henry Fowle
Dwight, Edmund
Dyer, Isadore
Eastman, George
Eliot, Samuel
Eustis, Dorothy Leib Harrison
   Wood
Evans, Thomas Wiltberger
Evarts, Jeremiah
Fahnestock, Harris Charles
Falk, Maurice
Farmer, Hannah Tobey Shapleigh
Farnam, Henry
Farnam, Henry Walcott
Farnham, Eliza Woodson Burhans
Fels, Samuel Simeon
Field, Benjamin Hazard
Field, Marshall, III
Fleming, Arthur Henry
Flexner, Bernard
Flower, Lucy Louisa Coues
Folger, Henry Clay
Ford, Daniel Sharp
Franklin Benjamin

Gammon, Elijah Hedding
Gardiner, Robert Hallowell
George, William Reuben
Gerard, James Watson
Gerry, Elbridge Thomas
Gibbons, Abigail Hopper
Gilbert, Linda
Ginn, Edwin
Ginter, Lewis
Girard, Stephen
Gleason, Kate
Godfrey, Benjamin
Goucher, John Franklin
Graff, Everett Dwight
Graham, Isabella Marshall
Grasselli, Caesar Augustin
Gratz, Rebecca
Gray, Francis Calley
Green, Francis
Green, John Cleve
Griffith, Goldsborough Sappington
Grinnell, Henry
Griscom, John
Guggenheim, Daniel
Guggenheim, Simon
Gurley, Ralph Randolph
Hackley, Charles Henry
Hand, Daniel
Hardin, Charles Henry
Harkness, Edward Stephen
Hart, Abraham
Haughery, Margaret Gaffney
Hayden, Charles
Hearst, Phoebe Apperson
Heckscher, August
Heilprin, Michael
Hemenway, Mary Porter Tileston
Hepburn, Alonzo Barton
Hershey, Milton Snavely
Hewitt, Abram Stevens
Heye, George Gustav
Higinbotham, Harlow Niles
Hopkins, Johns
Horlick, William
Hoyt, John Sherman
Hutton, Levi William
Inman, Samuel Martin
Irene, Sister
Jackson, Helen Maria Fiske Hunt
Jackson, Samuel Macauley
Jacobs, Joseph, 1859–1929
James, Arthur Curtiss
James, Daniel Willis
Janney, Oliver Edward
Jeanes, Anna T.
Jesup, Morris Ketchum
Kelly, Eugene
Kennedy, John Stewart
Knapp, Joseph Palmer
Kresge, Sebastian Spering
Kress, Samuel Henry
Ladd, Kate Macy
Lafon, Thomy
Lamont, Thomas William
Lasker, Albert Davis
Lawrence, Abbott

Lawrence, Amos
Lawrence, Amos Adams
Lawrence, William, 1783–1848
Lehman, Adele Lewisohn
Lenox, James
Letchworth, William Pryor
Lewisohn, Adolph
Lewisohn, Sam Adolph
Libbey, Edward Drummond
Lick, James
Littauer, Lucius Nathan
Loeb, James
Lowell, Josephine Shaw
Ludwick, Christopher
Lunt, Orrington
Lyman, Theodore, 1792–1849
McCormick, Cyrus Hall
McCormick, Leander James
McDonogh, John
Mackay, Clarence Hungerford
McKinley, William Brown
McLean, William Lippard
Maclure, William
Macy, Valentine Everit
Magee, Christopher Lyman
Mallinckrodt, Edward
Mallinckrodt, Edward, Jr.
Maloney, Martin
Marquand Henry Gurdon
Martin, Frederick Townsend
Mather, Samuel
Matheson, William John
Matthiessen, Frederick William
Mercer, Jesse
Meyer, Agnes Elizabeth Ernst
Miller, Lewis
Mills, Darius Ogden
Morehead, John Motley
Morgan, Edwin Barber
Newberry, Walter Loomis
Newcomb, Josephine Louise Le
   Monnier
Newman, Henry
O'Fallon, John
Oglethorpe, James Edward
Olyphant, David Washington
   Cincinnatus
Osborn, William Henry
Ottendorfer, Anna Behr Uhl
Ottendorfer, Oswald
Packer, Asa
Paine, Robert Treat
Pardee, Ario
Parrish, Anne
Passavant, William Alfred
Patten, James A.
Patterson, Morris
Peabody, George
Peabody, George Foster
Pearsons, Daniel Kimball
Pellew, Henry Edward
Pemberton, Israel
Pemberton, James
Penrose, Spencer
Pepper, George Seckel
Pepper, William

Bode, Boyd Henry
Bowen, Francis
Bowne, Borden Parker
Bridgman, Percy Williams
Brightman, Edgar Sheffield
Brokmeyer, Henry C.
Buchanan, Joseph
Buchanan, Scott Milross
Calhoun, John Caldwell
Calkins, Mary Whiton
Carnap, Rudolf
Carus, Paul
Cohen, Morris Raphael
Creighton, James Edwin
Davidson, Thomas
Dewey, John
Edwards, Jonathan
Fiske, John
Fite, Warner
Frank, Philipp G.
Fullerton, George Stuart
Gardiner, Harry Norman
Gordy, John Pancoast
Grimes, James Stanley
Gros, John Daniel
Hall, Granville Stanley
Hamilton, Edward John
Harris, William Torrey
Hedge, Levi
Hibben, John Grier
Hickok, Laurens Perseus
Hocking, William Ernest
Howison, George Holmes
Hyslop, James Hervey
James, William
Jones, Rufus Matthew
Kroeger, Adolph Ernst
Ladd, George Trumbull
Laguna, Theodore de Leo de
Lewis, Clarence Irving
Lloyd, Alfred Henry
Locke, Alain Leroy
Longfellow, Samuel
Lovejoy, Arthur Oncken
Lyman, Eugene William
Macy, Jesse
Marsh, James
Mead, George Herbert
Michel, Virgil George
Montague, William Pepperell
Montgomery, Edmund Duncan
Moore, Addison Webster
More, Paul Elmer
Morris, George Sylvester
Mulford, Prentice
Neumark, David
Newbold, William Romaine
Overstreet, Harry Allen
Pace, Edward Aloysius
Palmer, George Herbert
Peirce, Charles Sanders
Perry, Ralph Barton
Powell, John Wesley
Prall, David Wight
Pratt, James Bissett
Radin, Max

Rauch, Frederick Augustus
Reichenbach, Hans
Riley, Isaac Woodbridge
Royce, Josiah
Salter, William Mackintire
Santayana, George
Saugrain de Vigni, Antoine
     François
Schurman, Jacob Gould
Seth, James
Smith, Thomas Vernor
Spaulding, Edward Gleason
Sterrett, James Macbride
Strong, Charles Augustus
Swenson, David Ferdinand
Tappan, Henry Philip
Thilly, Frank
Tillich, Paul
Tufts, James Hayden
Wenley, Robert Mark
Whitehead, Alfred North
Wilder, Alexander
Woodbridge, Frederick James
     Eugene
Woodward, Augustus Brevoort
Wright, Chauncey
Znaniecki, Florian Witold

PHONETIC SPELLING PIONEER
Masquerier, Lewis

PHONOGRAPHER
Pitman, Benn

**PHOTOENGRAVER (See also
     ENGRAVER)**
Levy, Max
Moss, John Calvin

PHOTOGRAPHER
Austen, (Elizabeth) Alice
Bachrach, Louis Fabian
Brady, Mathew B.
Carbutt, John
Curtis, Edward Sheriff
Genthe, Arnold
Goddard, Paul Beck
Hare, James H.
Hine, Lewis Wickes
Hubbard, Bernard Rosecrans
Jackson, William Henry
Johnston, Frances Benjamin
Lange, Dorothea
Muybridge, Eadweard
Plumbe, John
Sheeler, Charles R., Jr.
Stieglitz, Alfred
Van Vechten, Carl
Weston, Edward Henry

PHOTOGRAPHIC SCIENTIST
Mees, Charles Edward Kenneth

PHOTOJOURNALIST
Chapelle, Dickey

PHRENOLOGIST
Fowler, Orson Squire
Sizer, Nelson
Wells, Samuel Roberts

PHYLOBIOLOGIST
Burrow, Trigant

PHYSICAL CULTURIST
Macfadden, Bernarr

**PHYSICAL EDUCATION LEADER (See
     also PHYSICIAN)**
Alcott, William Andrus
Berenson, Senda
Blaikie, William
Gulick, Luther Halsey, 1865–1918
Kiphuth, Robert John Herman
Lewis, Dioclesian
Naismith, James
Sargent, Dudley Allen

PHYSICAL TRAINER
Muldoon, William

**PHYSICIAN (See also ALIENIST,
     ANESTHESIOLOGIST, ANATOMIST,
     APOTHECARY, BACTERIOLOGIST,
     Biochemist, Biometrician,
     Dentist, Dermatologist,
     Dietician, Druggist, Electro-
     Therapist, Embryologist,
     Epidemiologist, Gynecologist,
     Homeopathist, Hydrotherapist,
     Hygienist, Immunologist,
     Laryngologist, Lithotomist,
     Medical Historian, Medical
     Research Worker, Mental
     Hygienist, Microscopist,
     Neurologist, Neuropathologist,
     Nurse, Obstetrician, Oculist,
     Ophthalmologist, Optician,
     Otologist, Pathologist,
     Pediatrician, Pharmacist,
     Pharmacologist, Physical
     Education Leader, Physiologist,
     Psychiatrist, Phychoanalyst,
     Psychopathologist, Public Health
     Official, Radiographer,
     Rhinologist, Roentgenologist,
     Sanitarian, Surgeon,
     Toxicologist, Urologist,
     Vaccinator, Veterinarian)**
Abbott, Samuel Warren
Abrams, Albert
Adams, Daniel
Adams, William Lysander
Allen, Harrison
Allen, Nathan
Allen, Timothy Field
Allison, Richard
Alter, David
Ames, Nathaniel
Anderson, Victor Vance
Appleton, Nathaniel Walker
Arnold, Richard Dennis
Aspinwall, William
Ayer, James Cook
Bache, Franklin
Baetjer, Frederick Henry
Baker, Sara Josephine
Baldwin, Edward Robinson
Baldwin, William
Bard, John
Bard, Samuel
Barker, Benjamin Fordyce
Barker, Jeremiah

Bartholow, Roberts
Bartlett, Elisha
Bartlett, John Sherren
Bartlett, Josiah
Barton, Benjamin Smith
Baruch, Simon
Batchelder, John Putnam
Bates, James
Battey, Robert
Baxley, Henry Willis
Bayley, Richard
Beach, Wooster
Beard, George Miller
Beck, John Brodhead
Beck, Lewis Caleb
Beck, Theodric Romeyn
Bell, Luther Vose
Bennet, Sanford Fillmore
Bigelow, Jacob
Bigelow, William Sturgis
Biggs, Hermann Michael
Billings, Frank
Bird, Robert Montgomery
Blackburn, Luke Pryor
Blackwell, Elizabeth
Blake, Francis Gilman
Blalock, Nelson Gales
Blunt, James Gillpatrick
Bohune, Lawrence
Bond, Thomas
Bowditch, Henry Ingersoll
Boylston, Zabdiel
Bozeman, Nathan
Bridges, Robert
Brigham, Amariah
Brill, Nathan Edwin
Brincklé, William Draper
Brockett, Linus Pierpont
Bronson, Henry
Brown, George
Brown, Lawrason
Brown, Percy
Brown, Samuel
Brown, William
Bruce, Archibald
Brühl, Gustav
Buchanan, Joseph Rodes
Buckler, Thomas Hepburn
Bulkley, Lucius Duncan
Bullitt, Henry Massie
Burnett, Swan Moses
Burrage, Walter Lincoln
Burton, William
Bushnell, George Ensign
Byrne, John
Cabell, James Lawrence
Cabot, Richard Clarke
Cadwalader, Thomas
Caldwell, Charles
Campbell, Henry Fraser
Carson, Joseph
Carson, Simeon Lewis
Chadwick, James Read
Channing, Walter
Chapman, Alvan Wentworth
Chapman, Henry Cadwalader

Chapman, Nathaniel
Child, Robert
Christian, Henry Asbury
Church, Benjamin
Clayton, Joshua
Cochran, John
Cohen, Jacob da Silva Solis
Cohn, Alfred Einstein
Coit, Henry Leber
Cook, Frederick Albert
Cooke, Elisha
Cooke, John Esten
Cooke, Robert Anderson
Copeland, Royal Samuel
Craik, James
Cranston, John
Craven, John Joseph
Crawford, John
Crawford, John Martin
Crumbine, Samuel Jay
Cullis, Charles
Cushny, Arthur Robertson
Cutler, Ephraim
Da Costa, Jacob Mendez
Dalcho, Frederick
Darling, Samuel Taylor
Davis, Charles Henry Stanley
Davis, Edwin Hamilton
Davis, Nathan Smith
Delafield, Francis
Deléry, François Charles
Dercum, Francis Xavier
De Rosset, Moses John
Dewees, William Potts
Dick, Elisha Cullen
Dickson, Samuel Henry
Disbrow, William Stephen
Doddridge, Joseph
Dooley, Thomas Anthony, III
Dorsch, Eduard
Doughty, William Henry
Douglass, William
Drake, Daniel
Dwight, Nathaniel
Dyer, Isadore
Earle, Pliny
Eberle, John
Edder, William
Edes, Robert Thaxter
Edsall, David Linn
Eliot, Charles
Ellis, Calvin
Elmer, Ebenezer
Elmer, Jonathan
Elwell, John Johnson
Elwyn, Alfred Langdon
Emerson, Gouverneur
Emmet, Thomas Addis
Emmons, Ebenezer
Engelmann, George
Evans, George Alfred
Evans, John
Ewell, James
Ewell, Thomas
Faget, Jean Charles
Favill, Henry Baird

Fay, Jonas
Fayssoux, Peter
Finlay, Carlos Juan
Fisher, George Jackson
Fisher, John Dix
Fletcher, William Baldwin
Flick, Lawrence Francis
Flint, Austin, 1812–1886
Flint, Austin, 1836–1915
Foote, John Ambrose
Fordyce, John Addison
Forwood, William Henry
Foster, Frank Pierce
Foster, John Pierrepont Codrington
Francis, John Wakefield
Francis, Samuel Ward
Freeman, Nathaniel
Friedenwald, Aaron
Fuller, Robert Mason
Fussell, Bartholomew
Gale, Benjamin
Gallinger, Jacob Harold
Gallup, Joseph Adams
Garcelon, Alonzo
Garden, Alexander
Gardiner, Silvester
Garnett, Alexander Yelverton
   Peyton
Garvin, Lucius Fayette Clark
Gerhard, William Wood
Gibbes, Robert Wilson
Gibbons, William
Gilbert, Rufus Henry
Girard, Charles Frédéric
Goddard, Paul Beck
Goforth, William
Goldsmith, Middleton
Goldstein, Max Aaron
Goodrich, Benjamin Franklin
Gorham, John
Gorrie, John
Gould, Augustus Addison
Gould, George Milbry
Gradle, Henry
Grant, Asahel
Gray, John Purdue
Green, Asa
Green, Horace
Green, Norvin
Green, Samuel Abbott
Greenhow, Robert
Guernsey, Egbert
Guild, La Fayette
Guiteras, Juan
Guthrie, Samuel
Hack, George
Hale, Edwin Moses
Hale, Enoch
Hall, William Whitty
Hamilton, Alexander, 1712–1756
Hamilton, Alice
Hamilton, Allan McLane
Hand, Edward
Harlan, Richard
Harrington, Thomas Francis
Hartshorne, Henry

Haviland, Clarence Floyd
Hawley, Paul Ramsey
Hayes, Isaac Israel
Hays, Isaac
Hempel, Charles Julius
Hench, Philip Showalter
Henderson, Thomas
Henry, Morris Henry
Henshall, James Alexander
Hering, Constantine
Herter, Christian Archibald
Hewes, Robert
Hildreth, Samuel Prescott
Hoagland, Charles Lee
Hoff, John Van Rensselaer
Holcombe, William Henry
Holder, Joseph Bassett
Holten, Samuel
Holyoke, Edward Augustus
Hooker, Worthington
Hoover, Charles Franklin
Hopkins, Lemuel
Horn, George Henry
Horsfield, Thomas
Hosack, David
Hough, Franklin Benjamin
House, Samuel Reynolds
Hubbard, John
Huger, Francis Kinloch
Hunt, Harriot Kezia
Huntington, Elisha
Husk, Charles Ellsworth
Huston, Charles
Hutchinson, James
Hutchinson, Woods
Hyde, James Nevins
Ingals, Ephraim Fletcher
Ives, Eli
Jackson, Abraham Reeves
Jackson, Chevalier
Jackson, David
Jackson, Hall
Jackson, James, 1777–1867
Jackson, James Caleb
Jackson, John Davies
Jackson, Mercy Ruggles Bisbe
Jackson, Samuel
Jacobi, Abraham
Jacobi, Mary Corinna Putnam
James, Edwin
James, Thomas Chalkley
Jameson, Horatio Gates
Janeway, Edward Gamaliel
Janeway, Theodore Caldwell
Janney, Oliver Edward
Jarvis, Edward
Jarvis, Wiliam Chapman
Jay, Sir James
Jeffries, John
Johnson, Joseph
Jones, Alexander
Jones, Calvin
Jones, Joseph
Jones, William Palmer
Kane, Elisha Kent
Keagy, John Miller

Kearsley, John
Keating, John Marie
Kedzie, Robert Clark
Keeley, Leslie E.
Kellogg, Albert
Kelly, Aloysius Oliver Joseph
Kempster, Walter
Kerr, John Glasgow
Keyt, Alonzo Thrasher
King, Albert Freeman Africanus
King, Dan
King, John
King, Samuel Ward
Kirkbride, Thomas Story
Kirkland, Jared Potter
Kneeland, Samuel
Knight, Frederick Irving
Knight, Jonathan
Knowlton, Charles
Kober, George Martin
Kolle, Frederick Strange
Krause, Allen Kramer
Kuhn, Adam
Kunze, Richard Ernest
La Borde, Maximilian
Ladd, Joseph Brown
Landis, Henry Robert Murray
Lane, William Carr
Lapham, William Berry
La Roche, René
Lattimore, William
Lawson, Leonidas Merion
Lazear, Jesse William
Leathers, Waller Smith
Le Conte, John Lawrence
Lee, Charles Alfred
Leib, Michael
Leland, George Adams
Le Moyne, Francis Julius
Leonard, Charles Lester
Letterman, Jonathan
Lincecum, Gideon
Lincoln, Rufus Pratt
Linde, Christian
Lindsley, John Berrien
Lining, John
Linn, Lewis Fields
Littell, Squier
Lloyd, Thomas
Locke, John
Logan, Cornelius Ambrose
Logan, George
Long, Perrin Hamilton
Longcope, Warfield, Theobald
Loring, George Bailey
Lozier, Clemence Sophia Harned
Lumbrozo, Jacob
Lydston, George Frank
Lynch, Robert Clyde
Lyster, Henry Francis Le Hunte
McCaw, James Brown
McClellan, George, 1849–1913
McClurg, James
McCormack, Joseph Nathaniel
McCrae, Thomas
McCreery, Charles

McDowell, Ephraim
McFarland, George Bradley
McIntire, Ross
Mackenzie, John Noland
McKenzie, Robert Tait
MacNeven, William James
Magruder, George Lloyd
Mahoney, John Friend
Manson, Otis Frederick
Marks, Elias
Marshall, Clara
Marshall, Louis
Massey, George Betton
Matas, Rudolph
Maxwell, David Hervey
Maxwell, George Troup
Mayo, William Starbuck
Mayo, William Worrell
Mazzei, Philip
Mease, James
Meeker, Moses
Meigs, Arthur Vincent
Meigs, Charles Delucena
Meigs, James Aitken
Meigs, John Forsyth
Meltzer, Samuel James
Menninger, Charles Frederick
Mergler, Marie Josepha
Metcalfe, Samuel Lytler
Mettauer, John Peter
Michel, William Middleton
Michener, Ezra
Middleton, Peter
Miles, Manly
Miller, Edward
Miller, Henry
Miller, James Alexander
Minot, George Richards
Mitchell, George Edward
Mitchell, John, d. 1768
Mitchell, John Kearsley
Mitchell, Silas Weir
Mitchell, Thomas Duché
Mitchill, Samuel Latham
Monette, John Wesley
Moore, Joseph Earle
Morgan, John
Morril, David Lawrence
Morris, Caspar
Morrow, Prince Albert
Morrow, Thomas Vaughan
Morton, Samuel George
Morwitz, Edward
Mosher, Eliza Maria
Moultrie, John
Mundé, Paul Fortunatus
Neal, Josephine Bicknell
Neidhard, Charles
Newton, Robert Safford
Nichols, Charles Henry
Nichols, Charles Lemuel
Nichols, Mary Sargeant Neal Gove
Noeggerath, Emil Oscar Jacob
  Bruno
North, Elisha
Nott, Josiah Clark

Krez, Konrad
Lacy, Ernest
Ladd, Joseph Brown
La Farge, Christopher Grant
Lander, Frederick West
Lanier, Sidney
Lathrop, John
Latil, Alexandre
Lazarus, Emma
Leonard, William Ellery
Lindsay, Nicholas Vachel
Linn, John Blair
Linton, William James
Lodge, George Cabot
Longfellow, Henry Wadsworth
Longfellow, Samuel
Lord, William Wilberforce
Lowell, Amy
Lucas, Daniel Bedinger
Lytle, William Haines
McCarroll, James
McHenry, James
McKay, Claude
MacKaye, Percy Wallace
MacKellar, Thomas
McKinley, Carlyle
McLellan, Isaac
McMaster, Guy Humphreys
Macy, John
Malone, Walter
Markham, Edwin
Markoe, Peter
Marquis, Donald Robert Perry
Martin, Edward Sandford
Masters, Edgar Lee
Menken, Adah Isaacs
Merrill, Stuart FitzRandolph
Mifflin, Lloyd
Miles, George Henry
Millay, Edna St. Vincent
Miller, Cincinnatus Hiner
Mitchell, Langdon Elwyn
Mitchell, Silas Weir
Möise, Penina
Monroe, Harriet
Moody, William Vaughn
Moore, (Austin) Merrill
Morris, George Pope
Morton, Sarah Wentworth Apthorp
Munford, William
Muñoz-Rivera, Luis
Nack, James M.
Newell, Robert Henry
Nicholson, Eliza Jane Poitevent
   Holbrook
Nies, Konrad
Niles, Nathaniel
Oakes, Urian
Oppenheim, James
O'Reilly, John Boyle
Osborn, Laughton
Osborn, Selleck
Osgood, Frances Sargent Locke
Paine, Robert Treat
Parke, John
Parker, Dorothy Rothschild

Parsons, Thomas William
Peabody, Josephine Preston
Percival, James Gates
Perry, Nora
Peterson, Henry
Piatt, John James
Piatt, Sarah Morgan Bryan
Pierpont, John
Pinkney, Edward Coote
Plath, Sylvia
Plummer, Jonathan
Plummer, Mary Wright
Poe, Edgar Allan
Posey, Alexander Lawrence
Powell, Thomas
Poydras, Julien de Lelande
Preston, Margaret Junkin
Randall, James Ryder
Rankin, Jeremiah Eames
Read, Thomas Buchanan
Realf, Richard
Reed, John, 1887–1920
Reese, Lizette Woodworth
Reitzel, Robert
Requier, Augustus Julian
Ricketson, Daniel
Riley, James Whitcomb
Rittenhouse, Jessie Belle
Robinson, Edwin Arlington
Roche, James Jeffrey
Roethke, Theodore Huebner
Rose, Aquila
Rosenfeld, Morris
Rouquette, Adrien Emmanuel
Rouquette, François Dominique
Russell, Irwin
Ryan, Abram Joseph
Saltus, Edgar Evertson
Sandburg, Carl August
Sandys, George
Santayana, George
Sargent, Epes
Savage, Philip Henry
Saxe, John Godfrey
Schnauffer, Carl Heinrich
Scollard, Clinton
Searing, Laura Catherine Redden
Seeger, Alan
Service, Robert William
Sewall, Jonathan Mitchell
Shaw, John, 1778–1809
Sherman, Frank Dempster
Shillaber, Benjamin Penhallow
Sill, Edward Rowland
Smith, Samuel Francis
Snow, Eliza Roxey
Spingarn, Joel Elias
Sprague, Charles
Stanton, Frank Lebby
Stedman, Edmund Clarence
Steendam, Jacob
Stein, Evaleen
Sterling, George
Stevens, Wallace
Stoddard, Elizabeth Drew Barstow
Stoddard, Richard Henry

Story, Isaac
Story, William Wetmore
Strange, Michael
Street, Alfred Billings
Sylvester, Frederick Oakes
Tabb, John Banister
Taggard, Genevieve
Taylor, Benjamin Franklin
Taylor, Edward
Teasdale, Sara
Testut, Charles
Thaxter, Celia Laighton
Thierry, Camille
Thomas, Edith Matilda
Thompson, James Maurice
Thompson, John Reuben
Thomson, Edward William
Thoreau, Henry David
Thorpe, Rose Alnora Hartwick
Ticknor, Francis Orray
Timrod, Henry
Torrence, Frederick Ridgely
Townsend, Mary Ashley
Trumbull, John, 1750–1831
Tuckerman, Frederick Goddard
Tuckerman, Henry Theodore
Turell, Jane
Van Dyke, Henry
Villagrá, Gasper Pérez de
Wallace, William Ross
Walsh, Thomas
Ward, Thomas
Warfield, Catherine Ann Ware
Warren, Mercy Otis
Wheatley, Phillis
Whitman, Albery Allson
Whitman, Sarah Ellen Power
Whitman, Walt
Whitney, Anne
Whittier, John Greenleaf
Wilcox, Ella Wheeler
Wilde, Richard Henry
Williams, Catharine Read Arnold
Williams, William Carlos
Willis, Nathaniel Parker
Wilson, Robert Burns
Wilson, William
Winchevsky, Morris
Winter, William
Woodberry, George Edward
Woodworth, Samuel
Wright, Philip Green
Wylie, Elinor Morton Hoyt
Young, David
Zunser, Eliakum
POLICE CONSULTANT
Smith, Bruce
POLICE EXECUTIVE
Byrnes, Thomas F.
Curtis, Edwin Upton
POLICE OFFICER
Glassford, Pelham Davis
McGrath, Matthew J.
Ruditsky, Barney

De Lancey, James, 1703–1760
De Lancey, James, 1732–1800
De Lancey, Oliver
Deming, Henry Champion
Devaney, John Patrick
Dibrell, George Gibbs
Dickinson, Daniel Stevens
Doddridge, Philip
Dodge, Grenville Mellon
Donelson, Andrew Jackson
Donnelly, Ignatius
Dorr, Thomas Wilson
Dorsheimer, William Edward
Doty, James Duane
Douglas, Stephen Arnold
Draper, Andrew Sloan
Draper, Eben Sumner
Duane, William
Dudley, Charles Edward
Duncan, Joseph
Durant, Thomas Jefferson
Early, Peter
Eastman, Charles Gamage
Eastman, Enoch Worthen
Eastman, Harvey Gridley
Eaton, John Henry
Edgerton, Alfred Peck
Edwards, Pierpont
Egan, Patrick
Elliot, James
Ellis, Seth Hockett
English, Thomas Dunn
Evans, George
Evans, Henry Clay
Fairfield, John
Faran, James John
Farnsworth, John Franklin
Farwell, Charles Benjamin
Fay, Jonas
Felton, William Harrell
Fessenden, William Pitt
Fisk, James
Fitzgerald, John Francis
Flagg, Azariah Cutting
Flanagan, Webster
Flynn, Edward Joseph
Folsom, Nathaniel
Foot, Solomon
Frazier, Lynn Joseph
Frémont, John Charles
Gallinger, Jacob Harold
Gansevoort, Leonard
Gartrell, Lucius Jeremiah
Gary, James Albert
Gibbons, Thomas
Gibson, Walter Murray
Gillet, Ransom Hooker
Gilman, John Taylor
Gilman, Nicholas
Gitlow, Benjamin
Goodloe, William Cassius
Goodrich, Elizur
Goodwin, Ichabod
Goodwin, John Noble
Gordon, George Washington
Granger, Francis

Granger, Gideon
Greeley, Horace
Green, Duff
Greene, Nathaniel
Gregg, Andrew
Gregg, Maxcy
Griswold, Roger
Griswold, Stanley
Grover, La Fayette
Grow, Galusha Aaron
Grund, Francis Joseph
Grundy, Felix
Gwin, William McKendree
Hague, Frank
Haines, Charles Glidden
Hale, Charles
Hale, Eugene
Hale, John Parker
Hall, Abraham, Oakey
Hallett, Benjamin Franklin
Hamilton, James Alexander
Hammond, Jabez Delano
Hancock, John, 1736–1793
Hanna, Marcus Alonzo
Hannegan, Robert Emmet
Hanson, Ole
Harper, Robert Goodloe
Harris, Isham Green
Harris, Townsend
Harrison, Carter Henry, Jr.
Harrison, George Paul
Hartranft, John Frederick
Haskell, Dudley Chase
Haskell, Ella Louise Knowles
Hassaurek, Friedrich
Hays, Will H.
Hazard, Jonathan J.
Heath, Perry Sanford
Heney, Francis Joseph
Henshaw, David
Higgins, Frank Wayland
Hill, David Bennett
Hill, Isaac
Hines, James J.
Hitchcock, Phineas Warrener
Hoan, Daniel Webster
Hoey, Clyde Roark
Hoffman, John Thompson
Holcomb, Silas Alexander
Howard, Benjamin Chew
Howard, Edgar
Howard, William Alanson
Howell, Clark
Hoyt, Henry Martyn
Hubbard, David
Hughes, James
Hunter, Whiteside Godfrey
Husting, Paul Oscar
Imlay, Gilbert
Irving, William
Jackson, Robert R.
Jardine, William Marion
Johnson, Albert
Johnson, Bradley Tyler
Johnson, Edward Austin
Kelly, Edward Joseph

Kelly, John
Kelly, John Brendan
Kennedy, John Doby
Kerens, Richard C.
Kerman, Francis
Keyes, Elisha Williams
King, Preston
Kinsella, Thomas
Kinsey, John
Knott, Aloysius Leo
Knox, Frank
Lane, James Henry
Langdon, John
Lasker, Albert Davis
Lewis, William Berkeley
Lexow, Clarence
Lincoln, Enoch
Lincoln, Levi, 1749–1820
Lincoln, Levi, 1782–1868
Lloyd, David
Logan, Cornelius Ambrose
Lorimer, William
Loring, George Bailey
Loucks, Henry Langford
Lovell, James
Lunn, George Richard
Lyon, Caleb
Lyon, Matthew
McAfee, Robert Breckinridge
McCarren, Patrick Henry
McClellan, George Brinton
McCormick, Richard Cunningham
McCumber, Porter James
McDonald, Joseph Ewing
McDowell, Joseph
McLaughlin, Hugh
McLevy, Jasper
McMahon, Brien
McManes, James
McNutt, Paul Vories
Magee, Christopher Lyman
Maginnis, Martin
Manigault, Peter
Manley, Joseph Homan
Marcantonio, Vito Anthony
Massey, John Edward
Mather, Increase
Meagher, Thomas Francis
Merriam, William Rush
Mills, Ogden Livingston
Minor, Robert
Moore, Andrew
Moreau-Lislet, Louis Casimir
  Elisabeth
Morrissey, John
Morton, Ferdinand Quintin
Moses, George Higgins
Muhlenberg, Frederick Augustus
  Conrad
Muhlenberg, Henry Augustus
  Philip
Muhlenberg, John Peter Gabriel
Muñoz-Rivera, Luis
Murphy, Charles Francis
Murphy, Henry Cruse
Nairne, Thomas

Nelson, Hugh
New, Harry Stewart
Nicholas, George
Nicholas, Philip Norborne
Nicolls, William
Niles, David K.
Niles, Nathaniel
Norris, Isaac, 1701–1766
O'Dwyer, William
O'Fallon, James
Orth, Godlove Stein
Osgood, Samuel
Otis, James
Overton, John
Packer, William Fisher
Palmer, William Adams
Parker, John Milliken
Parker, Josiah
Partridge, James Rudolph
Patterson, James Willis
Payne, Sereno Elisha
Pelham, Robert A.
Penrose, Boies
Penrose, Charles Bingham
Perez, Leander Henry
Petigru, James Louis
Pew, Joseph Newton, Jr.
Pickering, Timothy
Pinchback, Pinckney Benton
　　Stewart
Platt, Thomas Collier
Pleasants, John Hampden
Pomeroy, Marcus Mills
Porter, James Madison
Pringle, John Julius
Pusey, Caleb
Quay, Matthew Stanley
Quick, John Herbert
Quincy, Josiah, 1772–1864
Ramsay, Nathaniel
Randall, Alexander Williams
Randolph, John, 1728–1784
Ranney, Rufus Percival
Raum, Green Berry
Raymond, Henry Jarvis
Requa, Mark Lawrence
Richmond, Dean
Ritchie, Thomas
Rives, William Cabell
Roberts, William Randall
Robertson, William Henry
Robins, Raymond
Robinson, William Erigena
Rollins, Edward Henry
Rollins, Frank West
Root, Erastus
Rosewater, Edward
Rosewater, Victor
Rowell, Chester Harvey
Ruef, Abraham
Russell, William Henry
Schell, Augustus
Schoeppel, Andrew Frank
Seidel, George Lukas Emil
Settle, Thomas
Sewell, William Joyce

Shannon, Wilson
Shields, George Howell
Shippen, Edward, 1639–1712
Sibley, John
Simmons, Roscoe Conkling Murray
Simons, Algie Martin
Skinner, Charles Rufus
Slidell, John
Smith, Buckingham
Smith, Charles Perrin
Smith, Frank Leslie
Smith, Israel
Smith, James, 1851–1927
Smith, Nathan, 1770–1835
Smith, Thomas Vernor
Springer, Charles
Steedman, James Blair
Stevens, Thaddeus
Stevenson, Adlai Ewing, II
Stockton, Richard
Sullivan, Timothy Daniel
Swartwout, Samuel
Sweeny, Peter Barr
Swensson, Carl Aaron
Switzler, William Franklin
Taggart, Thomas
Terry, David Smith
Thayer, John Milton
Thomas, David
Thomas, Elbert Duncan
Thomas, (John William) Elmer
Thomas, William Widgery
Thompson, Richard Wigginton
Tichenor, Isaac
Tipton, John
Tumulty, Joseph Patrick
Tweed, William Marcy
Tyler, Robert
Upshaw, William David
Vallandigham, Clement Laird
Van Buren, John
Van Dam, Rip
Van Ness, William Peter
Vare, William Scott
Wagner, Robert Ferdinand
Walcott, Edward Oliver
Waldo, Samuel
Walker, Frank Comerford
Wallace, Hugh Campbell
Waln, Robert, 1765–1836
Walsh, Michael
Ward, John Elliott
Warren, James
Watson, Thomas Edward
Weed, Thurlow
West, Roy Owen
White, Edward Douglass
Williams, Elisha
Wilson, J(ames) Finley
Wise, John Sergeant

POLO PLAYER
Rumsey, Charles Cary

POMOLOGIST (See also
　　AGRICULTURIST)
Brincklé, William Draper
Coxe, William

Downing, Charles
Gideon, Peter Miller
Lyon, Theodatus Timothy
Manning, Robert
Thomas, John Jacobs

PORTRAITIST
Bachrach, Louis Fabian
Christy, Howard Chandler

POSTAL PIONEER
Bates, Barnabas
Chorpenning, George
Davis, William Augustine
Holt, John
Majors, Alexander

POSTMASTER GENERAL
　　(CONFEDERATE)
Reagan, John Henninger

POSTMASTER GENERAL (See also
　　POSTAL PIONEER)
Brown, Walter Folger
Burleson, Albert Sidney
Campbell, James
Collamer, Jacob
Cortelyou, George Bruce
Creswell, John Angel James
Dickinson, Donald McDonald
Donaldson, Jesse Monroe
Gary, James Albert
Habersham, Joseph
Hatton, Frank
Hazard, Ebenezer
Hitchcock, Frank Harris
Holt, Joseph
Howe, Timothy Otis
James, Thomas Lemuel
Jewell, Marshall
Johnson, Cave
Kendall, Amos
King, Horatio
McLean, John
Meigs, Return Jonathan
Meyer, George von Lengerke
Niles, John Milton
Payne, Henry Clay
Randall, Alexander Williams
Smith, Charles Emory
Vilas, William Freeman
Walker, Frank Comerford
Wickliffe, Charles Anderson
Wilson, William Lyne

POTTER (See also CRAFTSMAN)
Low, John Gardner
Rellstab, John

POWDER MAKER (See also
　　MANUFACTURER, *Explosives*)
Keppel, Frederick

PRESIDENT, COLLEGE (See COLLEGE
　　PRESIDENT)

PRESIDENT (COMMONWEALTH OF THE
　　PHILIPPINES)
Quezon, Manuel Luis

PRESIDENT (CONFEDERATE STATES)
Davis, Jefferson

PRESIDENTIAL ADVISER
House, Edward Mandell
Howe, Louis McHenry

Mason, Daniel Gregory
Matthews, James Brander
Mead, George Herbert
Mendenhall, Thomas Corwin
Meyer, Adolf
Miller, George Abram
Mitchell, Edwin Knox
Mitchell, Langdon Elwyn
Moore, Eliakim Hastings
Moore, Nathaniel Fish
Morse, Harmon Northrop
Moulton, Richard Green
Muller, Hermann Joseph
Naismith, James
Neilson, William Allan
Noyes, George Rapall
Ogg, Frederic Austin
Oldfather, William Abbott
Osgood, William Fogg
Owsley, Frank Lawrence
Packard, Alpheus Spring
Panofsky, Erwin
Parker, George Howard
Parsons, Theophilus
Parvin, Theodore Sutton
Peabody, Andrew Preston
Peabody, Francis Greenwood
Perrin, Bernadotte
Perry, Bliss
Phelps, Austin
Phelps, William Lyon
Phillips, Ulrich Bonnell
Pirsson, Louis Valentine
Pond, Enoch
Pound, (Nathan) Roscoe
Prime, William Cowper
Putnam, Frederic Ward
Quine, William Edward
Rand, Edward Kennard
Randall, James Garfield
Rauschenbusch, Walter
Ravenel, Edmund
Read, Conyers
Reed, Richard Clark
Richardson, Robert
Rister, Carl Coke
Ritter, Frédéric Louis
Robertson, William Spence
Robinson, Edward, 1794–1863
Rostovtzeff, Michael Ivanovitch
Rupp, William
Russell, James Earl
Rutledge, Wiley Blount
Sampson, Martin Wright
Schelling, Felix Emanuel
Schevill, Rudolph
Schinz, Albert
Schlesinger, Arthur Meier
Schmidt, Nathaniel
Scott, Walter Dill
Scudder, (Julia) Vida Dutton
Searle, John Preston
Shannon, Fred Albert
Sherman, Henry Clapp
Shields, Charles Woodruff
Silliman, Benjamin, 1779–1864

Smith, Charles Forster
Smith, David Eugene
Smith, Edgar Fahs
Smith, Edmund Munroe
Smith, Henry Louis
Smith, Horatio Elwin
Smith, Nathan, 1762–1829
Smyth, Egbert Coffin
Smyth, Herbert Weir
Smyth, William
Sprague, Oliver Mitchell
    Wentworth
Spring, Leverett Wilson
Stephenson, Carl
Sumner, James Batcheller
Tansill, Charles Callan
Tatlock, John Strong Perry
Thacher, Thomas Anthony
Thayer, Ezra Ripley
Thayer, James Bradley
Thorndike, Lynn
Thurstone, Louis Leon
Tiedeman, Christopher Gustavus
Tigert, John James, IV
Timberlake, Gideon
Towler, John
Treadwell, Daniel
Trent, William Peterfield
Tucker, Nathaniel Beverley,
    1784–1851
Tuttle, Herbert
Tyler, Charles Mellen
Tyler, William Seymour
Van Amringe, John Howard
Vasiliev, Alexander Alexandrovich
Venable, Francis Preston
Vincent, Marvin Richardson
Ward, Robert De Courcy
Ware, Henry, 1764–1845
Warner, Langdon
Webb, John Burkitt
Webster, John White
Weed, Lewis Hill
Weiss, Soma
Wertenbaker, Thomas Jefferson
West, Allen Brown
West, Andrew Fleming
Weyl, Hermann
Wheeler, Arthur Leslie
Willard, James Field
Williams, Edward Thomas
Willis, Henry Parker
Wilson, Bird
Wilson, George Grafton
Wilson, Peter
Woodbridge, Samuel Merrill
Woods, James Haughton
Woods, Leonard
Young, Karl

PROHIBITION ADMINISTRATOR
Yellowley, Edward Clements

PROHIBITIONIST (See also REFORMER,
    TEMPERANCE REFORMER)
Carmack, Edward Ward
Fisk, Clinton Bowen
Poling, Daniel Alfred

St. John, John Pierce
Wheeler, Wayne Bidwell
Wilson, Clarence True
Woolley, John Granville

PROMOTER (See also LAND
    PROMOTER, LECTURE
    PROMOTER, PRODUCER,
    SHOWMAN)
Addicks, John Edward O'Sullivan
Agnew, Cornelius Rea
Andrews, Israel DeWolf
Brady, Anthony Nicholas
Brown, Charlotte Emerson
Collier, Barron Gift
Durant, Henry
Fanning, Edmund
Flagler, Henry Morrison
Gates, John Warne
    ("Bet–You–a–Million")
Goerz, David
Goldschmidt, Jakob
Green, Benjamin Edwards
Harrah, Charles Jefferson
Harvey, William Hope
Hatch, Rufus
Holladay, Ben
Holliday, Cyrus Kurtz
Hopkins, Edward Augustus
Hotchkiss, Horace Leslie
Hubbard, Gardiner Greene
Kearns, Jack
Law, Sallie Chapman Gordon
Lawrance, Uriah Marion
Moore, William Henry
Morgan, Anne
Morse, Charles Wyman
Patterson, John Henry
Penrose, Spencer
Perkins, Charles Callahan
Rankine, William Birch
Reed, James Hay
Rickard, George Lewis
Ryan, Thomas Fortune
Sanders, George Nicholas
Seiberling, Frank Augustus
Sheedy, Dennis
Sibley, Hiram
Smart, David Archibald
Smith, Junius
Smith, Robert Alexander C.
Thompson, Benjamin
Train, George Francis
Whalen, Grover Aloysius
Wharton, Richard
Wright, John Stephen

PROPAGANDIST (See also AGITATOR,
    REFORMER)
Bergh, Henry
Goldman, Emma
Kelley, Hall Jackson
Lovejoy, Owen Reed
Pomeroy, Marcus Mills
Viereck, George Sylvester

PROSPECTOR (See also MINER)
Broderick, David Colbreth
Fair, James Graham

Goold, William A.
La Ronde, Louis Denis, Sieur de
Marshall, James Wilson
Merritt, Leonidas
Osborn, Chase Salmon
Scott, Walter Edward

PROTESTANT SPOKESMAN
Lyman, Eugene William

PSYCHIATRIC HISTORIAN (See also
    HISTORIAN, PSYCHIATRIST)
Zilboorg, Gregory

PSYCHIATRIST (See also
    PSYCHOANALYST,
    PSYCHOLOGIST, PHYSICIAN)
Anderson, Victor Vance
Babcock, James Woods
Barrett, Albert Moore
Briggs, Lloyd Vernon
Brush, Edward Nathaniel
Burrow, Trigant
Campbell, Charles Macfie
Clevenger, Shobal Vail
Dewey, Richard Smith
Earle, Pliny
Fisher, Theodore Willis
Fromm-Reichmann, Frieda
Gregory, Menas Sarkas
    Boulgourjian
Haviland, Clarence Floyd
Hinkle, Beatrice Moses
Hoch, August
Jones, William Parker
Kempster, Walter
Kerlin, Isaac Newton
Kirby, George Hughes
Little, Charles Sherman
Menninger, William Claire
Meyer, Adolf
Moore, (Austin) Merrill
Nichols, Charles Henry
Ray, Isaac
Rohé, George Henry
Sakel, Manfred Joshua
Salmon, Thomas William
Seguin, Edouard
Southard, Elmer Ernest
Spitzka, Edward Charles
White, William Alanson

PSYCHOANALYST (See also ALIENIST,
    PHYSICIAN, PSYCHIATRIST,
    PSYCHOLOGIST)
Alexander, Franz Gabriel
Brill, Abraham Arden
Brunswick, Ruth Mack
Coriat, Isador Henry
Dunbar, (Helen) Flanders
Fenichel, Otto
Fromm-Reichmann, Frieda
Hinkle, Beatrice Moses
Horney, Karen Danielssen
Jelliffe, Smith Ely
Oberndorf, Clarence Paul
Rapaport, David
Reik, Theodor
Roheim, Geza
Sachs, Hanns

Zilboorg, Gregory

PSYCHOLOGIST (See also ALIENIST,
    EDUCATOR, PHYSICIAN,
    PSYCHIATRIST, PSYCHOANALYST,
    Psychopathologist, Professor,
    Scholar)
Allport, Gordon Willard
Angell, James Rowland
Baldwin, James Mark
Bingham, Walter Van Dyke
Boisen, Anton Theophilus
Boring, Edwin Garrigues
Burnham, William Henry
Cattell, James McKeen
Dodge, Raymond
Downey, June Etta
Farrand, Livingston
Franz, Shepherd Ivory
Fryer, Douglas Henry
Gesell, Arnold Lucius
Goddard, Henry Herbert
Guthrie, Edwin Ray, Jr.
Haggerty, Melvin Everett
Hall, Granville, Stanley
Hollingworth, Leta Stetter
Holt, Edwin Bissell
Hull, Clark Leonard
Hyslop, James Hervey
James, William
Jastrow, Joseph
Johnson, Wendell Andrew Leroy
Judd, Charles Hubbard
Kagan, Henry Enoch
Koffka, Kurt
Köhler, Wolfgang
Ladd, George Trumbull
Ladd-Franklin, Christine
Lashley, Karl Spencer
Lewin, Kurt
McDougall, William
McHale, Kathryn
Marshall, Henry Rutgers
Maslow, Abraham H.
Münsterberg, Hugo
Newbold, William Romaine
Norsworthy, Naomi
Otis, Arthur Sinton
Pace, Edward Aloysius
Prince, Morton
Robinson, Edward Stevens
Rush, James
Sandford, Edmund Clark
Scott, Colin Alexander
Scott, Walter Dill
Seashore, Carl Emil
Smith, Theodate Louise
Starbuck, Edwin Diller
Strong, Charles Augustus
Terman, Lewis Madison
Thorndike, Edward Lee
Thurstone, Louis Leon
Titchener, Edward Bradford
Tolman, Edward Chace
Troland, Leonard Thompson
Warren, Howard Crosby
Washburn, Margaret Floy

Watson, John Broadus
Wertheimer, Max
Wolfe, Harry Kirke

PSYCHOPATHOLOGIST (See also
    ALIENIST, PHYSICIAN,
    PSYCHIATRIST, PSYCHOANALYST,
    PSYCHOLOGIST)
Sidis, Boris

PSYCHOSOMATIC MOVEMENT LEADER
Dunbar, (Helen) Flanders

PUBLIC ADMINISTRATOR
Abbott, Grace
Eastman, Joseph Bartlett
Hoover, Herbert Clark

PUBLIC ADVISER
Baruch, Bernard Mannes

PUBLIC AFFAIRS BROADCASTER
Murrow, Edward (Egbert) Roscoe

PUBLIC DEFENDER ADVOCATE
Goldman, Mayer C.

PUBLIC HEALTH ADMINISTRATOR
Baker, Sara Josephine

PUBLIC HEALTH EXPERT
Winslow, Charles-Edward Amory

PUBLIC HEALTH LEADER
Abbott, Samuel Warren
Beard, Mary
Emerson, Haven
Mahoney, John Friend
Price, George Moses
Ravenel, Mazyck Porcher
Rosenau, Milton Joseph
Smith, Stephen
Stiles, Charles Wardell
Strong, Richard Pearson
Walcott, Henry Pickering

PUBLIC HEALTH OFFICIAL (See also
    PHYSICIAN)
Banks, Charles Edward
Chapin, Charles Value
Copeland, Royal Samuel
Crumbine, Samuel Jay
Goldwater, Sigismund Schulz
Gunn, Selskar Michael
Park, William Hallock
Rose, Wickliffe
Sawyer, Wilbur Augustus
Snow, William Freeman
Wende, Ernest

PUBLICIST (See also EDITOR,
    NEWSAGENT, PAMPHLETEER)
Alford, Leon Pratt
Ames, Fisher
Applegate, Jesse
Balch, Thomas Willing
Barker, Wharton
Barrett, John
Bates, George Handy
Beck, James Montgomery
Beer, George Louis
Bement, Caleb N.
Bemis, George
Birkbeck, Morris
Bradford, Gamaliel
Carnegie, Andrew
Clark, Willis Gaylord

Bradford, Thomas
Bradford, William
Breckinridge, Desha
Brett, George Platt
Brewster, Osmyn
Bridgman, Herbert Lawrence
Brown, James
Bunce, Oliver Bell
Butler, Burridge Davenal
Butler, Simeon
Cameron, Andrew Carr
Capper, Arthur
Carey, Henry Charles
Carey, Mathew
Charless, Joseph
Childs, Aphas Grier
Childs, George William
Cist, Charles
Clarke, Robert
Collier, Peter Fenelon
Cook, Robert Johnson
Covici, Pascal ("Pat")
Crocker, Uriel
Currier, Nathaniel
Curtis, Cyrus Hermann
  Kotzschmar
Day, George Parmly
Delavan, Edward Cornelius
De Young, Michel Harry
Dodd, Frank Howard
Doran, George Henry
Doubleday, Frank Nelson
Doubleday, Nelson
Draper, Margaret Green
Dworshak, Henry Clarence
Ellmaker, (Emmett) Lee
Estes, Dana
Everett, Robert
Field, Marshall, III
Field, Marshall, IV
Fields, James Thomas
Fitzgerald, Thomas
Ford, Daniel Sharp
Francis, Charles Stephen
Funk, Isaac Kauffman
Funk, Wilfred John
Gannett, Frank Ernest
Gernsback, Hugo
Ginn, Edwin
Glass, Franklin Potts
Godey, Louis Antoine
Gonzales, Ambrose Elliott
Goodrich, Samuel Griswold
Gowans, William
Graham, George Rex
Graham, Philip Leslie
Grasty, Charles Henry
Greenslet, Ferris
Griscom, Lloyd Carpenter
Grosset, Alexander
Guinzburg, Harold Kleinert
Gunter, Archibald Clavering
Haldeman-Julius, Emanuel
Harcourt, Alfred
Harding, Jesper
Harding, William White

Harper, Fletcher
Harper, James
Harris, Benjamin
Harris, Julian La Rose
Hart, Abraham
Haynes, Williams
Heard, Dwight Bancroft
Hearst, William Randolph
Helmer, Bessie Bradwell
Hill, David Jayne
Hitchcock, Gilbert Monell
Hobby, William Pettus
Holt, Henry
Houghton, Henry Oscar
Huebsch, Benjamin W.
Humphreys, James
Hunt, Freeman
Jackson, Charles Samuel
Jewett, John Punchard
Jones, George
Judd, Orange
Kenedy, Patrick John
Kiplinger, Willard Monroe
Kline, George
Klopch, Louis
Knapp, Joseph Palmer
Kneeland, Samuel
Knopf, Blanche Wolf
Kohlberg, Alfred
Kollock, Shepard
Lange, Louis
Langlie, Arthur Bernard
Lea, Henry Charles
Lea, Isaac
Leslie, Frank
Leslie, Miriam Florence Folline
Leypoldt, Frederick
Lippincott, Joshua Ballinger
Littell, Eliakim
Little, Charles Coffin
Liveright, Horace Brisbin
Longley, Alcander
Lothrop, Daniel
Loudon, Samuel
Luce, Henry Robinson
McClurg, Alexander Caldwell
McCook, Anson George
McElrath, Thomas
Macfadden, Bernarr
McGraw, James Herbert
McIntyre, Alfred Robert
McLean, William Lippard
Macrae, John
McRae, Milton Alexander
Marble, Manton Malone
Marquis, Albert Nelson
Mattson, Hans
Maxwell, William
Melcher, Frederic Gershom
Meredith, Edna C. Elliott
Meredith, Edwin Thomas
Merriam, Charles
Miller, John Henry
Mitchell, Samuel Augustus
Moody, John

Moreau de Saint-Méry, Médéric-
  Louis-Élie
Morwitz, Edward
Mosher, Thomas Bird
Munn, Orson Desaix
Munro, George
Munsey, Frank Andrew
Murphy, John
Myrick, Herbert
Nieman, Lucius William
Norman, John
Norton, William Warder
Oliver, George Tener
Parks, William
Patterson, Alicia
Peterson, Charles Jacobs
Pittock, Henry Lewis
Plimpton, George Arthur
Polock, Moses
Pomeroy, Marcus Mills
Poulson, Zachariah
Prang, Louis
Pulitzer, Joseph, Jr.
Putnam, Eben
Putnam, George Haven
Putnam, George Palmer
Redfield, Justus Starr
Revell, Fleming Hewitt
Rice, Edwin Wilbur
Ridder, Herman
Rinehart, Stanley Marshall, Jr.
Root, Frank Albert
Rossiter, William Sidney
Rowell, George Presbury
Rudge, William Edwin
Ruffin, Edmund
Sadlier, Denis
Sartain, John
Saxton, Eugene Francis
Scherman, Harry
Schuster, Max Lincoln
Scribner, Charles, 1821–1871
Scribner, Charles, 1854–1930
Scribner, Charles, 1890–1952
Scripps, Edward Wyllis
Scripps, James Edmund
Sears, Robert
Shuster, W(illiam) Morgan
Silverman, Sime
Simon, Richard Leo
Singerly, William Miskey
Smith, Lloyd Pearsall
Smith, Ormond Gerald
Smith, Roswell
Sower, Christopher, 1693–1758
Sower, Christopher, 1721–1784
Sower, Christopher, 1754–1799
Stahlman, Edward Bushrod
Stephens, Edwin William
Stoddart, Joseph Marshall
Stokes, Frederick Abbot
Stone, David Marvin
Strong, Walter Ansel
Taft, Charles Phelps
Tammen, Harry Heye
Thomas, Robert Bailey

Jeffrey, Edward Turner
Jewett, Hugh Judge
Johnston, John Taylor
Jones, Frank
King, John Pendleton
Kirkman, Marshall Monroe
Kneass, Strickland
Lord, Eleazar
Loree, Leonor Fresnel
Lovett, Robert Scott
Lucas, James H.
McCullough, John Griffith
McKennan, Thomas McKean
   Thompson
Mahone, William
Markham, Charles Henry
Mellen, Charles Sanger
Merrick, Samuel Vaughan
Messler, Thomas Doremus
Minty, Robert Horatio George
Negley, James Scott
Newman, William H.
Oakes, Thomas Fletcher
Ogden, William Butler
Olyphant, Robert Morrison
Osborn, William Henry
Palmer, William Jackson
Parsons, Lewis Baldwin
Payne, Henry Clay
Pearson, Edward Jones
Perham, Josiah
Perkins, Charles Elliott
Peters, Richard, 1810–1889
Plumbe, John
Poor, John Alfred
Porter, Horace
Preble, William Pitt
Randolph, Epes
Rea, Samuel
Rice, Edmund
Ripley, Edward Payson
Robb, James
Roberts, George Brooke
Sayre, Robert Heysham
Scott, Thomas Alexander
Scott, William Lawrence
Sewell, William Joyce
Shonts, Theodore Perry
Sloan, Samuel
Smith, Alfred Holland
Smith, John Gregory
Smith, Milton Hannibal
Spencer, Samuel
Sproule, William
Stahlman, Edward Bushrod
Stephens, John Lloyd
Stevens, John Frank
Stewart, Robert Marcellus
Strong, William Barstow
Thomas, John Wilson
Thompson, Arthur Webster
Thomson, Frank
Thomson, John Edgar
Thornton, Henry Worth
Underwood, Frederick Douglas
Vanderbilt, William Henry

Van Horne, William Cornelius
Van Sweringen, Mantis James
Vibbard, Chauncey
Wallace, John Findley
Walters, William Thompson
Willard, Daniel
Worcester, Edwin Dean
Wright, Charles Barston
Yeager, Joseph
Yoakum, Benjamin Franklin
Young, Robert Ralph
Zimmerman, Eugene

RAILROAD EXPERT
Adams, Charles Francis
Allen, William Frederick
Reagan, John Henninger

RAILROAD OWNER
James, Arthur Curtiss
Morgan, Charles
Starin, John Henry

RAILROAD PROMOTER (See also
   PROMOTER)
Ames, Oliver
Andrews, Alexander Boyd
Brewster, James
Brown, George
Burke, Stevenson
Chapin, Chester William
Corbett, Henry Winslow
Diven, Alexander Samuel
Guthrie, James
Hardy, William Harris
Jackson, William, 1783–1855
Law, George
Le Duc, William Gates
Loveland, William Austin
   Hamilton
Paine, Charles
Rice, Edmund
Thomas, Philip Evan
Vanderbilt, Cornelius, 1794–1877
Villard, Henry
Whitney, Asa
Yulee, David Levy

RANCHER (See also COWBOY,
   CATTLEMAN, RANGER, STOCK
   BREEDER)
Ammons, Elias Milton
Haggin, James Ben Ali
Jardine, William Marion
Kendrick, John Benjamin
Maxwell, Lucien Bonaparte

RANGER (See also RANCHER)
McNeill, John Hanson
Mosby, John Singleton
Rogers, Robert
Wallace, William Alexander
   Anderson

RARE BOOK DEALER (See also
   BIBLIOPHILE)
Rosenbach, Abraham Simon Wolf
Rosenbach, Philip Hyman

READER (See also LECTURER,
   RACONTEUR)
Kemble, Frances Anne
Riddle, George Peabody

READING DEVELOPMENT EXPERT
Gray, William Scott, Jr.
REAL-ESTATE DEVELOPER
Chandler, Harry
REAL-ESTATE OPERATOR (See also
   LAND AGENT)
Binga, Jesse
Bloom, Sol
Bowes, Edward J.
Hanson, Ole
Heckscher, August
Marling, Alfred Erskine
Morgenthau, Henry
Palmer, Potter
Savage, Henry Wilson
Wright, John Stephen
REALTOR
De Priest, Oscar Stanton
REBEL (See also AGITATOR,
   INSURGENT, RADICAL,
   REVOLUTIONIST)
Ingle, Richard
Vesey, Denmark
REFORMER (See also AGITATOR,
   FEMINIST, HUMANITARIAN,
   PEACE ADVOCATE, POLITICAL
   REFORMER, Prison Reformer,
   Prohibitionist, Propagandist,
   Social Reformer, Temperance
   Reformer)
Allen, Zachariah
Andrews, Stephen Pearl
Angell, George Thorndike
Anthony, Susan Brownell
Appleton, James
Ballou, Adin
Barrows, Samuel June
Beecher, Catharine Esther
Bishop, Robert Hamilton
Blackwell, Antoinette Louisa Brown
Blake, Lillie Devereux
Bloomer, Amelia Jenks
Boissevain, Inez Milholland
Bolton, Sarah Knowles
Bonney, Charles Carroll
Bright Eyes
Brooks, John Graham
Brown, William Wells
Bruce, William Cabell
Burleigh, George Shepard
Burleigh, William Henry
Burritt, Elihu
Cabet, Étienne
Cannon, Ida Maud
Chapman, Maria Weston
Cheever, George Barrell
Cheney, Ednah Dow Littlehale
Cleghorn, Sarah Norcliffe
Collier, John
Colver, Nathaniel
Comstock, Anthony
Coxey, Jacob Sechler
Crandall, Prudence
Dall, Caroline Wells Healey
Delavan, Edward Cornelius
Dewey, Melvil

Dike, Samuel Warren
Dinwiddie, Edwin Courtland
Donnelly, Ignatius
Dorr, Thomas Wilson
Easley, Ralph Montgomery
Eastman, Joseph Bartlett
Eddy, Thomas
Ely, Richard Theodore
Evans, Frederick William
Evans, George Henry
Farnam, Henry Walcott
Ferguson, William Porter Frisbee
Field, David Dudley
Filene, Edward Albert
Flower, Benjamin Orange
Fussell, Bartholomew
Gage, Frances Dana Barker
Gales, Joseph
Garrison, William Lloyd
George, Henry
Giesler-Anneke, Mathilde Franziska
Goodell, William
Gould, Elgin Ralston Lovell
Graham, Sylvester
Green, Beriah
Green, Frances Harriet Whipple
Griffing, Josephine Sophie White
Grimké, Thomas Smith
Hall, Bolton
Hapgood, Norman
Harriman, Florence Jaffray Hurst
Hastings, Samuel Dexter
Hepburn, William Peters
Higginson, Thomas Wentworth
Himes, Joshua Vaughan
Holbrook, Josiah
Hooker, Isabella Beecher
Howe, Frederic Clemson
Howe, Julia Ward
Howland, Emily
Hunt, Harriot Kezia
Ivins, William Mills
Jay, William
Johnson, Magnus
Jones, Samuel Milton
Kellor, Frances (Alice)
Kynett, Alpha Jefferson
Lay, Benjamin
Leavitt, Joshua
Lewelling, Lorenzo Dow
Livermore, Mary Ashton Rice
Loomis, Arphaxed
Lowell, Josephine Shaw
Luther, Seth
McCann, Alfred Watterson
Marsh, John
Masquerier, Lewis
Matthews, Joseph Brown
Matthews, Nathan
Mattison, Hiram
May, Samuel Joseph
Mead, Edwin Doak
Mifflin, Warner
Moss, Frank
Mott, James
Mott, Lucretia Coffin

Murphey, Archibald de Bow
Myers, Gustavus
Nichols, Clarina Irene Howard
Nichols, Mary Sargeant Neal Gove
Noyes, John Humphrey
Opdyke, George
O'Sullivan, Mary Kenney
Parkhurst, Charles Henry
Pennypacker, Elijah Funk
Philips, Martin Wilson
Phillips, Wendell
Pierpont, John
Pillsbury, Parker
Polk, Frank Lyon
Post, Louis Freeland
Poznanski, Gustavus
Price, Eli Kirk
Quincy, Edmund
Quincy, Josiah, 1772–1864
Rambaut, Mary Lucinda Bonney
Rantoul, Robert, 1778–1858
Rantoul, Robert, 1805–1852
Riis, Jacob August
Ripley, George
Rose, Ernestine Louise Siismondi
	Potowski
Rose, John Carter
Russell, Charles Edward
Sanders, Elizabeth Elkins
Saunders, Prince
Scott, Colin Alexander
Scott, Walter
Seidel, George Lukas Emil
Shaw, Albert
Shaw, Anna Howard
Sherwood, Katharine Margaret
	Brownlee
Sims, William Sowden
Smith, Elizabeth Oakes Prince
Smith, Fred Burton
Smith, Gerrit
Smith, Hannah Whitall
Spargo, John
Spencer, Anna Garlin
Spingarn, Joel Elias
Spreckels, Rudolph
Stanton, Elizabeth Cady
Stanton, Henry Brewster
Steffens, Lincoln
Sterne, Simon
Still, William
Stone, Lucy
Straton, John Roach
Sunderland, Eliza Jane Read
Swallow, Silas Comfort
Swisshelm, Jane Grey Cannon
Sylvis, William H.
Thomas, Norman Mattoon
Tutwiler, Julia Strudwick
Villard, Helen Frances Garrison
Villard, Oswald Garrison
Ward, Henry Dana
Warren, Josiah
Weber, Henry Adam
Whipple, Henry Benjamin
White, Alfred Tredway

Wiley, Harvey Washington
Willard, Frances Elizabeth
	Caroline
Woodhull, Victoria Claflin
Woods, Robert Archey
Wright, Elizur
Wright, Frances

REGICIDE
Dixwell, John
Goffe, William
Whalley, Edward

REGIONAL PLANNER
Behrendt, Walter Curt

RELIEF ORGANIZER
Morgan, Anne

RELIGIOUS ACTIVIST
Robins, Raymond

RELIGIOUS LEADER (See also
	ARCHABBOT, ARCHBISHOP,
	BISHOP, CABALIST, CHAPLAIN,
	CHRISTIAN Science Leader,
	Clergyman, Evangelist, Indian
	Prophet, Metaphysician,
	Missionary, Mystic, Revivalist,
	Spiritualist, Theologian,
	Theosophist, Transcendentalist
Abbott, Benjamin
Adler, Cyrus
Adler, Felix
Albright, Jacob
Antes, Henry
Backus, Isaac
Bowne, John
Coe, George Albert
Coffin, Henry Sloane
Cox, Henry Hamilton
Dittemore, John Valentine
Divine, Father
Drexel, Katharine Mary
Eddy, Mary Morse Baker
Haven, Henry Philemon
Hodur, Francis
Hutchinson, Anne
Ivins, Anthony Woodward
Jones, Abner
McKay, David Oman
Metz, Christian
Middleton, Arthur
Mills, Benjamin Fay
Morris, Anthony, 1654–1721
Norris, Isaac, 1701–1766
Osgood, Jacob
Poznanski, Gustavus
Pratt, Orson
Rapp, George
Russell, Charles Taze
Rutherford, Joseph Franklin
Sharpless, Isaac
Skaniadariio
Smith, George Albert
Smith, Uriah
Thomas, Richard Henry
Tobias, Channing Heggie
Wilkinson, Jemima
Wood, James
Woolman, John

REMONSTRANT
Child, Robert

RESETTLEMENT EXPERT
Rosen, Joseph A.

RESTAURANT CRITIC
Hines, Duncan

RESTAURATEUR
Delmonico, Lorenzo
Kohlsaat, Herman Henry
Sardi, Melchiorre Pio Vencenzo
("Vincent")
Sherry, Louis
Stevens, Frank Mozley

REVIVALIST (See also EVANGELIST,
RELIGIOUS LEADER)
Alline, Henry
Finney, Charles Grandison
Kirk, Edward Norris
Wormley, James

REVOLUTIONARY HEROINE (See
HEROINE)

REVOLUTIONARY LEADER (See also
PATRIOT, REVOLUTIONARY
PATRIOT, SOLDIER, STATESMAN)
Benson, Egbert
Carroll, Charles
Chase, Samuel
Drayton, William Henry
Gadsden, Christopher
Hanson, John
Hindman, William
Hobart, John Sloss
Houston, William Churchill
Houstoun, John
Huger, Isaac
Huger, John
Johnston, Samuel
Jones, Willie
Person, Thomas
Scott, John Morin
Sears, Isaac
Tilghman, Matthew

REVOLUTIONARY PATRIOT (See also
PATRIOT, REVOLUTIONARY
LEADER, SOLDIER)
Alexander, Abraham
Arnold, Benedict
Arnold, Jonathan
Banister, John
Bartlett, Josiah
Cabell, William
Frelinghuysen, Frederick
Habersham, Joseph
Harvie, John
Howell, Richard
Howley, Richard
Izard, Ralph
Jones, Noble Wymberley
Jouett, John
Lamb, John
Leaming, Thomas
Lewis, Andrew
Lewis, Fielding
Livingston, Robert R., 1718–1775
Marshall, Christopher
Mason, Thomson

Matlock, Timothy
Mercer, James
Milledge, John
Moore, Maurice
Moore, William, 1735–1793
Nicholas, Robert Carter
Nixon, John, 1733–1808
Page, John
Parsons, Samuel Holden
Peabody, Nathaniel
Pendleton, Edmund
Peters, Richard, 1744–1828
Pettit, Charles
Roberdeau, Daniel
Sands, Comfort
Smith, Robert, 1732–1801
Thornton, Matthew
Tyler, John, 1747–1813
Warren, Joseph
Weare, Meshech
Whipple, William
Yates, Abraham
Yates, Robert
Young, Thomas

REVOLUTIONIST (See also AGITATOR,
INSURGENT, RADICAL)
Hecker, Friedrich Karl Franz
Heinzen, Karl Peter
Lee, Francis Lightfoot
Rapp, Wilhelm
Reed, John, 1887–1920
Sanders, George Nicholas
Wharton, William H.

RHEUMATOLOGIST (See also
PHYSICIAN)
Hench, Philip Showalter

RHINOLOGIST (See also PHYSICIAN)
Jarvis, William Chapman

ROAD BUILDER
Mears, Otto
Mullan, John

ROCKET PIONEER
Goddard, Robert Hutchings

ROCKET SCIENTIST
Ley, Willy

ROENTGENOLOGIST (See also
PHYSICIAN, RADIOGRAPHER,
RADIOLOGIST)
Baetjer, Frederick Henry
Brown, Percy
Caldwell, Eugene Wilson
Williams, Francis Henry

ROWING CHAMPION (See also
OARSMAN)
Kelly, John Brendan

ROWING COACH (See also ATHLETE,
OARSMAN)
Cook, Robert Johnson
Courtney, Charles Edward

SAILMAKER
Forten, James

SAILOR (See MARINER)

SALVAGE EXPERT
Merritt, Israel John

SALVATION ARMY GENERAL
Booth, Evangeline Cory

SANITARIAN (See also ENGINEER,
SANITARY)
Carter, Henry Rose
Freeman, Allen Weir
Gorgas, William Crawford
Harrington, Charles
Harris, Elisha
Jones, Joseph
Jordan, Edwin Oakes
Kedzie, Robert Clark
Logan, Thomas Muldrup,
1808–1876
McCormack, Joseph Nathaniel
Magruder, George Lloyd
Richards, Ellen Henrietta Swallow
Souchon, Edmond

SATIRIST (See also HUMORIST, WIT)
Alsop, Richard
Hopkins, Lemuel
Locke, David Ross
Smith, Seba
Snelling, William Joseph
Wright, Robert William

SAXOPHONIST
Gray, Glen

SCENARIST
Beach, Rex

SCHOLAR (See also ARCHAEOLOGIST,
ASSYRIOLOGIST, CLASSICIST,
EGYPTOLOGIST, GENEALOGIST,
Grammarian, Hebraist,
Hellenist, Logician, Orientalist,
Philologist, Philosopher,
Semitist, Sinologue)
Abbot, Ezra
Abbott, Frank Frost
Adams, Jasper
Allen, Frederic de Forest
Allen, William Francis
Anderson, Henry Tompkins
Anthon, Charles
Baylies, Francis
Beck, Charles
Beeson, Charles Henry
Bennett, Charles Edwin
Biddle, Nicholas
Bliss, Tasker Howard
Botta, Vincenzo
Carter, Jesse Benedict
Chase, Thomas
Clinton, DeWitt
Coe, George Albert
Cook, Albert Stanburrough
Crane, Thomas Frederick
Cross, Wilbur Lucius
Curme, George Oliver
Currier, Charles Warren
Curtin, Jeremiah
Dargan, Edwin Preston
Davidson, Thomas
Dennison, Walter
D'Ooge, Martin Luther
Dowling, Noel Thomas
Dunbar, (Helen) Flanders

Dyer, Louis
Edgren, August Hjalmar
Eliot, Samuel
Fay, Edwin Whitefield
Felton, Cornelius Conway
Fenollosa, Ernest Francisco
Fletcher, Robert
Frothingham, Arthur Lincoln
Furness, Horace Howard,
   1833–1912
Furness, Horace Howard,
   1865–1930
Grandgent, Charles Hall
Green, William Henry
Griswold, Alfred Whitney
Gruening, Emil
Hale, William Gardner
Harkness, Albert
Haven, Joseph
Heilprin, Michael
Hirsch, Emil Gustav
Hohfeld, Wesley Newcomb
Holmes, George Frederick
Hudson, Henry Norman
Humphreys, Milton Wylie
Humphries, George Rolfe
Isaacs, Abram Samuel
Jastrow, Morris
Kaye, Frederick Benjamin
Kendrick, Asahel Clark
Knapp, William Ireland
Kohut, George Alexander
Lewis, William Draper
Lincoln, John Larkin
Logan, James, 1674–1751
MacLean, George Edwin
Malter, Henry
Margolis, Max Leopold
Marsh, George Perkins
Mather, Cotton
Matthiessen, Francis Otto
Merrill, Elmer Truesdell
Miller, Perry Gilbert Eddy
Mills, Lawrence Heyworth
Mitchell, Hinckley Gilbert Thomas
Monis, Judah
Moore, Clement Clarke
Murphy, Henry Cruse
Newell, William Wells
O'Brien, Justin
Perrin, Bernadotte
Perry, Thomas Sergeant
Pinto, Isaac
Platner, Samuel Ball
Prince, Thomas
Richardson, Rufus Byam
Rorimer, James Joseph
Schinz, Albert
Schofield, William Henry
Schuyler, Eugene
Scott, Samuel Parsons
Shipman, Andrew Jackson
Soldan, Frank Louis
Solger, Reinhold
Sprecher, Samuel
Stiles, Ezra

Sulzberger, Mayer
Tait, Charles
Taylor, Hannis
Thomas, Calvin
Thorndike, Ashley Horace
Tolman, Herbert Cushing
Torrey, Charles Cutler
Trent, William Peterfield
Updike, Daniel Berkeley
Van der Kemp, Francis Adrian
Van Dyck, Cornelius van Alen
Viel, François Étienne Bernard
   Alexandre
Wallace, Charles William
Wallace, John William
Warren, Minton
Wiener, Leo
Wigmore, John Henry
Wilde, Richard Henry
Woolsey, Theodore Dwight

SCHOLAR (BIBLICAL)
Cone, Orello
Gregory, Caspar René
Hackett, Horatio Balch
Kent, Charles Foster
Mead, Charles Marsh
Mitchell, Edward Cushing
Moorehead, William Gallogly
Morgan, Abel
Norton, Andrews
Packard, Joseph
Paton, Lewis Boyles
Riddle, Matthew Brown
Ropes, James Hardy
Rosenberg, Abraham Hayyim
Sanders, Frank Knight
Sawyer, Leicester Ambrose
Smith, Henry Preserved
Smith, John Merlin Powis
Stevens, William Arnold
Strong, James
Stuart, Moses
Thayer, Joseph Henry

SCHOLAR (LAW)
Cook, Walter Wheeler

SCHOOL BUILDING SPECIALIST
Barrows, Alice Prentice

SCHOOLMASTER (See also EDUCATOR,
   TEACHER)
Coit, Henry Augustus
Dock, Christopher
Gould, Benjamin Apthorp
Gummere, John
Gunn, Frederick William
Keith, George
Ladd, Catherine
Lovell, James
Lovell, John
McCabe, William Gordon
Mazzuchelli, Samuel Charles
Morton, Charles
Nason, Elias
Peter, John Frederick
Pormort, Philemon
Truteau, Jean Baptiste
Williams, Nathanael

SCIENCE ADMINISTRATOR
Merriam, John Campbell
Ritter, William Emerson

SCIENCE HISTORIAN (See also
   HISTORIAN)
Thorndike, Lynn

SCIENTIFIC MANAGEMENT
   CONSULTANT
Cooke, Morris Llewellyn

SCIENTIST (See also SPECIFIC
   SCIENCES)
Agassiz, Jean Louis Rodolphe
Alexander, John Henry
Alexander, William Dewitt
Allen, Zachariah
Arnold, Harold DeForest
Birdseye, Clarence
Brashear, John Alfred
Brewer, William Henry
Brooke, John Mercer
Caswell, Alexis
Clark, William Smith
Cleaveland, Parker
Cooper, Thomas
Dewey, Chester
Drake, Daniel
Dunbar, William
Durant, Charles Ferson
Eaton, Amos
Emerson, Rollins Adams
Eve, Joseph
Ferguson, Thomas Barker
Ferree, Clarence Errol
Folger, Walter
Franklin, Benjamin
Frazer, John Fries
Frazer, Persifor
Gibbes, Robert Wilson
Gillman, Henry
Greely, Adolphus Washington
Greenhow, Robert
Haldeman, Samuel Steman
Hallock, Charles
Hayes, John Lord
Herrick, Edward Claudius
Hewitt, Peter Cooper
Hill, Thomas
Himes, Charles Francis
Humphreys, Andrew Atkinson
Hyer, Robert Stewart
Jefferson, Thomas
Jeffries, John
Lapham, Increase Allen
LeConte, John
Lee, Charles Alfred
Locke, John
Measc, James
Mell, Patrick Hues
Michaelis, Leonor
Minot, George Richards
Mitchill, Samuel Latham
Morton, Henry
Oliver, Andrew
Olmsted, Denison
Palmer, Walter Walker
Peirce, Charles Sanders

Pliny, Earle Chase
Potamian, Brother
Priestley, Joseph
Rhoads, Cornelius Packard
Saugrain de Vigni, Antoine
   François
Schöpf, Johann David
Seybert, Adam
Sheppard, Samuel Edward
Simpson, Charles Torrey
Spillman, William Jasper
Squier, George Owen
Stallo, Johann Bernhard
Thompson, Samuel Rankin
Thomson, Elihu
Totten, Joseph Gilbert
Trowbridge, William Petit
Van Depoele, Charles Joseph
Wailes, Benjamin Leonard
   Covington
Westergaard, Harald Malcolm
Wilder, Russell Morse
Williamson, Hugh
Wright, Hamilton Kemp

SCOUT (**See** also GUIDE,
   FRONTIERSMAN, PIONEER)
Bailey, Ann
Bridger, James
Burnham, Frederick Russell
Cody, William Frederick
Dixon, William
Grouard, Frank
Hamilton, William Thomas
Hickok, James Butler
Horn, Tom
Kelly, Luther Sage
McClellan, Robert
Navarre, Pierre
North, Frank Joshua
Reynolds, Charles Alexander
Sieber, Al
Stilwell, Simpson Everett
Stringfellow, Franklin

SCREENWRITER (**See** AUTHOR,
   DRAMATIST, WRITER)

SCULPTOR (**See** also ARTIST,
   MODELER)
Adams, Herbert Samuel
Akers, Benjamin Paul
Amateis, Louis
Archipenko, Alexander
Augur, Hezekiah
Bailly, Joseph Alexis
Ball, Thomas
Barnard, George Grey
Bartholomew, Edward Sheffield
Bartlett, Paul Wayland
Bissell, George Edwin
Bitter, Karl Theodore Francis
Borglum, John Gutzon de la
   Mothe
Borglum, Solon Hannibal
Boyle, John J.
Brackett, Edward Augustus
Brenner, Victor David
Brooks, Richard Edwin

Browere, John Henri Isaac
Brown, Henry Kirke
Bush-Brown, Henry Kirke
Calder, Alexander Stirling
Calverley, Charles
Clarke, Thomas Shields
Clevenger, Shobal Vail
Cogdell, John Stevens
Connelly, Pierce Francis
Crawford, Thomas
Dallin, Cyrus Edwin
Davidson, Jo
Dexter, Henry
Diller, Burgoyne
Donoghue, John
Doyle, Alexander
Duveneck, Frank
Eakins, Thomas
Eckstein, John
Edmondson, William
Elwell, Frank Edwin
Epstein, Jacob
Ezekiel, Moses Jacob
Flannagan, John Bernard
Fraser, James Earle
Frazee, John
French, Daniel Chester
Garlick, Theodatus
Goldberg, Reuben Lucius ("Rube")
Gould, Thomas Ridgeway
Grafly, Charles
Greenough, Horatio
Greenough, Richard Saltonstall
Hart, Joel Tanner
Hartley, Jonathan Scott
Haseltine, James Henry
Hosmer, Harriet Goodhue
Hoxie, Vinnie Ream
Hughes, Robert Ball
Ives, Chauncey Bradley
Jackson, John Adams
Kemeys, Edward
Kingsley, Norman William
Lachaise, Gaston
Launitz, Robert Eberhard Schmidt
   von der
Lebrun, Federico ("Rico")
Lukeman, Henry Augustus
MacDonald, James Wilson
   Alexander
McKenzie, Robert Tait
MacMonnies, Frederick William
MacNeil, Hermon Atkins
Magonigle, Harold Van Buren
Manship, Paul Howard
Martiny, Philip
Mead, Larkin Goldsmith
Mears, Helen Farnsworth
Meštrović, Ivan
Mills, Clark
Milmore, Martin
Mozier, Joseph
Mulligan, Charles J.
Nadelman, Elie
Newman, Barnett
Ney, Elisabet

Niehaus, Charles Henry
O'Donovan, William Rudolf
Palmer, Erastus Dow
Partridge, William Ordway
Perkins, Marion
Potter, Edward Clark
Potter, Louis McClellan
Powers, Hiram
Pratt, Bela Lyon
Putnam, Arthur
Quinn, Edmond Thomas
Remington, Frederic
Rimmer, William
Rinehart, William Henry
Roberts, Howard
Rogers, John, 1829–1904
Rogers, Randolph
Ruckstull, Frederick Wellington
Rumsey, Charles Cary
Rush, William
Saint-Gaudens, Augustus
Shrady, Henry Merwin
Simmons, Franklin
Smith, David Roland
Sterne, Maurice
Stone, Horatio
Story, William Wetmore
Taft, Lorado Zadoc
Thompson, Launt
Valentin, Edward Virginius
Volk, Leonard Wells
Ward, John Quincy Adams
Warner, Olin Levi
Whitney, Gertrude Vanderbilt
Whitney, Anne
Willard, Solomon
Young, Mahonri Mackintosh
Zorach, William

SEA CAPTAIN (**See** also MARINER,
   WHALING CAPTAIN)
Baker, Lorenzo Dow
Bertram, John
Boyle, Thomas
Brewer, Charles
Chever, James W.
Cobb, Elijah
Codman, John
Coggeshell, George
Creesy, Josiah Perkins
Crowninshield, George
Crowninshield, Jacob
Endicott, Charles Moses
Fanning, Edmund
Forbes, Robert Bennet
Godfrey, Benjamin
Harvey, Sir John
Heard, Augustine
Hunnewell, James
Malcolm, Daniel
Marshall, Charles Henry
Merry, William Lawrence
Morrell, Benjamin
Olmsted, Gideon
Palmer, Nathaniel Brown
Reid, Samuel Chester
Rogers, William Crowninshield

Shaler, William
Tompkins, Sally Louisa
Waterman, Robert H.
SECESSIONIST
Edwards, Weldon Nathaniel
Yancey, William Lowndes
SECRETARY
Thompson, Malvina Cynthia
SECRETARY OF AGRICULTURE (See also
  AGRICULTURIST)
Colman, Norman Jay
Houston, David Franklin
Hyde, Arthur Mastick
Jardine, William Marion
Meredith, Edwin Thomas
Morton, Julius Sterling
Rusk, Jeremiah McClain
Wallace, Henry Agard
Wallace, Henry Cantwell
Wickard, Claude Raymond
Wilson, James
SECRETARY OF ARMY
Brucker, Wilber Marion
SECRETARY OF COMMERCE
Chapin, Roy Dikeman
Redfield, William Cox
Roper, Daniel Calhoun
Wallace, Henry Agard
SECRETARY OF DEFENSE (See also
  SECRETARY OF WAR)
Forrestal, James Vincent
Johnson, Louis Arthur
Wilson, Charles Erwin
SECRETARY OF LABOR
Davis, James John
Mitchell, James Paul
Perkins, Frances
Schwellenbach, Lewis Baxter
Tobin, Maurice Joseph
Wilson, William Bauchop
SECRETARY OF NAVY
Badger, George Edmund
Chandler, William Eaton
Daniels, Josephus
Denby, Edwin
Dickerson, Mahlon
Dobbin, James Cochran
Edison, Charles
Forrestal, James Vincent
Hamilton, Paul
Henshaw, David
Herbert, Hilary Abner
Hunt, William Henry
Jones, William, 1760–1831
Kimball, Dan Able
Knox, Frank
Long, John Davis
Meyer, George von Lengerke
Morton, Paul
Preston, William Ballard
Robeson, George Maxwell
Smith, Robert, 1757–1842
Southard, Samuel Lewis
Stoddert, Benjamin
Swanson, Claude Augustus
Tracy, Benjamin Franklin

Upshur, Abel Parker
Welles, Gideon
Whitney, William Collins
Wilbur, Curtis Dwight
SECRETARY OF NAVY (CONFEDERATE)
Mallory, Stephen Russell
SECRETARY OF STATE
Adams, John Quincy
Bacon, Robert
Bayard, Thomas Francis
Black, Jeremiah Sullivan
Blaine, James Gillespie
Bryan, William Jennings
Buchanan, James
Calhoun, John Caldwell
Cass, Lewis
Clay, Henry
Clayton, John Middleton
Colby, Bainbridge
Day, William Rufus
Dulles, John Foster
Evarts, William Maxwell
Everett, Edward
Fish, Hamilton
Forsyth, John
Foster, John Watson
Frelinghuysen, Frederick Theodore
Gresham, Walter Quintin
Hay, John Milton
Herter, Christian Archibald
Hughes, Charles Evans
Hull, Cordell
Jay, John
Jefferson, Thomas
Kellogg, Frank Billings
Knox, Philander Chase
Lansing, Robert
Legaré, Hugh Swinton
Livingston, Edward
McLane, Louis
Madison, James
Marcy, William Learned
Marshall, John
Monroe, James
Olney, Richard
Pickering, Timothy
Randolph, Edmund, 1753–1813
Root, Elihu
Seward, William Henry
Sherman, John
Smith, Robert, 1757–1842
Stettinius, Edward Reilly
Stimson, Henry Lewis
Upshur, Abel Parker
Van Buren, Martin
Washburne, Elihu Benjamin
Webster, Daniel
SECRETARY OF STATE (CONFEDERATE)
Benjamin, Judah Philip
Hunter, Robert Mercer Taliaferro
SECRETARY OF THE INTERIOR
Ballinger, Richard Achilles
Bliss, Cornelius Newton
Browning, Orville Hickman
Chandler, Zachariah
Cox, Jacob Dolson

Delano, Columbus
Ewing, Thomas
Fall, Albert Bacon
Fisher, Walter Lowrie
Francis, David Rowland
Garfield, James Rudolph
Harlan, James
Hitchcock, Ethan Allen,
  1835–1909
Ickes, Harold Le Clair
Kirkwood, Samuel Jordan
Lamar, Lucius Quintus Cincinatus
Lane, Franklin Knight
McClelland, Robert
McKay, (James) Douglas
McKennan, Thomas McKean
  Thompson
Noble, John Willock
Payne, John Barton
Schurz, Carl
Smith, Caleb Blood
Smith, Hoke
Stuart, Alexander Hugh Holmes
Teller, Henry Moore
Thompson, Jacob
Usher, John Palmer
Vilas, William Freeman
West, Roy Owen
Wilbur, Ray Lyman
Work, Hubert
SECRETARY OF TREASURY
Campbell, George Washington
Carlisle, John Griffin
Chase, Salmon Portland
Corwin, Thomas
Dallas, Alexander James
Dix, John Adams
Ewing, Thomas
Fairchild, Charles Stebbins
Folger, Charles James
Forward, Walter
Gage, Lyman Judson
Gallatin, Abraham Alfonse Albert
Glass, Carter
Guthrie, James
Hamilton, Alexander
Humphrey, George Magoffin
Ingham, Samuel Delucenna
McAdoo, William Gibbs
McCulloch, Hugh
MacVeagh, Franklin
Manning, Daniel
Mellon, Andrew William
Meredith, William Morris
Mills, Ogden Livingston
Morgenthau, Henry, Jr.
Morrill, Lot Myrick
Richardson, William Adams
Shaw, Leslie Mortier
Spencer, John Canfield
Taney, Roger Brooke
Thomas, Philip Francis
Vinson, Fred(erick) Moore
Walker, Robert John
Wolcott, Oliver
Woodbury, Levi

Woodin, William Hartman
SECRETARY OF TREASURY
　　(**CONFEDERATE**)
Trenholm, George Alfred
SECRETARY OF WAR (See also
　　SECRETARY OF DEFENSE)
Alger, Russell Alexander
Baker, Newton Diehl
Belknap, William Worth
Calhoun, John Caldwell
Cameron, James Donald
Cameron, Simon
Crawford, William Harris
Davis, Dwight Filley
Dearborn, Henry
Dern, George Henry
Dickinson, Jacob McGavack
Elkins, Stephen Benton
Endicott, William Crowninshield
Floyd, John Buchanan
Garrison, Lindley Miller
Holt, Joseph
Knox, Henry
Lamont, Daniel Scott
Lincoln, Robert Todd
McHenry, James
Patterson, Robert Porter
Porter, Peter Buell
Proctor, Redfield
Ramsey, Alexander
Spencer, John Canfield
Stanton, Edwin McMasters
Stimson, Henry Lewis
Taft, Alphonso
Weeks, John Wingate
Wilkins, William
Woodring, Harry Hines
Wright, Luke Edward
SECRETARY OF WAR (**CONFEDERATE**)
Benjamin, Judah Philip
SECURITIES EXPERT
Stanley, Harold
SEEDSMAN (See also AGRICULTURIST)
Thorburn, Grant
Vick, James
SEGREGATIONIST LEADER
Perez, Leander Henry
SEISMOLOGIST
Tondorf, Francis Anthony
SEMITIST (See also SCHOLAR)
Friedlaender, Israel
Gottheil, Richard James Horatio
Meyer, Martin Abraham
Torrey, Charles Cutler
SENATOR
Alcorn, James Lusk
Allen, Philip
Allen, William Vincent
Anderson, Joseph
Ashurst, Henry Fountain
Atchison, David Rice
Austin, Warren Robinson
Bacon, Augustus Octavius
Badger, George Edwin
Bagby, Arthur Pendleton
Bailey, Joseph Weldon

Bailey, Josiah William
Baker, Edward Dickinson
Baldwin, Henry Porter
Baldwin, Roger Sherman
Bankhead, John Hollis
Barkley, Alben William
Barrett, Frank Aloysius
Bartlett, Edward Lewis ("Bob")
Barton, David
Bayard, James Asheton
Bayard, Richard Henry
Bender, George Harrison
Berry, George Leonard
Berry, James Henderson
Beveridge, Albert Jeremiah
Bibb, George Mortimer
Bigler, William
Bilbo, Theodore Gilmore
Bingham, Hiram
Blackburn, Joseph Clay Styles
Blaine, John James
Blease, Coleman Livingston
Blount, William
Bogy, Lewis Vital
Booth, Newton
Borah, William Edgar
Boreman, Arthur Ingram
Borland, Solon
Bourne, Jonathan
Bradbury, James Ware
Bradley, Stephen Row
Bradley, William O'Connell
Brainerd, Lawrence
Brewster, Ralph Owen
Brice, Calvin Stewart
Bridges, (Henry) Styles
Bristow, Joseph Little
Brookhart, Smith Wildman
Brown, Bedford
Brown, Benjamin Gratz
Brown, James
Brown, John
Bruce, Blanche K.
Bruce, William Cabell
Buckalew, Charles Rollin
Buckingham, William Alfred
Bulkeley, Morgan Gardner
Burnet, Jacob
Burr, Aaron
Burrows, Julius Caesar
Burton, Theodore Elijah
Butler, Marion
Butler, Matthew Calbraith
Butler, Pierce
Butler, William Pickens
Byrd, Harry Flood
Cabat, George
Caffery, Donelson
Camden, Johnson Newlon
Cameron, James Donald
Cameron, Simon
Campbell, George Washington
Capper, Arthur
Caraway, Hattie Ophelia Wyatt
Caraway, Thaddeus Horatius
Carlile, John Snyder

Carlisle, John Griffin
Carpenter, Matthew Hale
Carter, Thomas Henry
Case, Francis Higbee
Chamberlain, George Earle
Chandler, John
Chandler, William Eaton
Chandler, Zachariah
Chavez, Dennis
Chesnut, James
Christiancy, Isaac Peckham
Clark, Bennett Champ
Clark, William Andrews
Clarke, James Paul
Clay, Clement Claiborne
Clay, Clement Comer
Clay, Henry
Clemens, Jeremiah
Cobb, Howell
Cockrell, Francis Marion
Cohen, John Sanford
Coke, Richard
Collamer, Jacob
Colt, Le Baron Bradford
Conkling, Roscoe
Connally, Thomas Terry ("Tom")
Cooper, James
Copeland, Royal Samuel
Cordon, Guy
Corwin, Thomas
Costigan, Edward Prentiss
Couzens, James
Crane, Winthrop Murray
Crawford, William Harris
Curtis, Charles
Cutting, Bronson Murray
Daniel, John Warwick
Davis, Cushman Kellogg
Davis, Garret
Davis, Henry Gassaway
Davis, James John
Davis, Jeff
Dawes, Henry Laurens
Dawson, William Crosby
Depew, Chauncey Mitchell
De Wolf, James
Dickerson, Mahlon
Dirksen, Everett McKinley
Dodge, Augustus Caesar
Dodge, Henry
Dolph, Joseph Norton
Dorsey, Stephen Wallace
Douglas, Stephen Arnold
Downey, Sheridan
Drake, Charles Daniel
Dryden, John Fairfield
Duff, James Henderson
Du Pont, Henry Algernon
Dworshak, Henry Clarence
Edge, Walter Evans
Edmunds, George Franklin
Edwards, John
Edwards, Ninian
Elkins, Stephen Benton
Ellis, Powhatan
Elmore, Franklin Harper

Engle, Clair William Walter
Eppes, John Wayles
Ewing, Thomas
Fairbanks, Charles Warren
Fall, Albert Bacon
Felch, Alpheus
Felton, Rebecca Latimer
Fenton, Reuben Eaton
Ferris, Woodbridge Nathan
Ferry, Orris Sanford
Ferry, Thomas White
Fess, Simeon Davidson
Field, Richard Stockton
Fitzpatrick, Benjamin
Flanders, Ralph Edward
Fletcher, Duncan Upshaw
Foot, Samuel Augustus
Foote, Henry Stuart
Foraker, Joseph Benson
Foster, Ephraim Hubbard
Foster, Lafayette Sabine
Foster, Theodore
Fowler, Joseph Smith
Francis, John Brown
Franklin, Jesse
Frazier, Lynn Joseph
Frelinghuysen, Frederick
Frelinghuysen, Theodore
Frye, William Pierce
Gaillard, John
Gear, John Henry
George, James Zachariah
George, Walter Franklin
Geyer, Henry Sheffie
Gibson, Paris
Gillett, Frederick Huntington
Glass, Carter
Goldthwaite, George
Goodhue, Benjamin
Goodrich, Chauncey
Gordon, James
Gore, Thomas Pryor
Gorman, Arthur Pue
Grayson, William
Green, James Stephens
Green, Theodore Francis
Grimes, James Wilson
Grundy, Joseph Ridgway
Guffey, Joseph F.
Guggenheim, Simon
Hager, John Sharpenstein
Hale, Frederick
Hamilton, William Thomas
Hamlin, Hannibal
Hammond, James Henry
Hampton, Wade, 1818–1902
Hanna, Marcus Alonzo
Hannegan, Edward Allen
Hanson, Alexander Contee,
  1786–1819
Hardin, Martin D.
Hardwick, Thomas William
Harlan, James
Harris, William Alexander
Harrison, Byron Patton
Hastings, Daniel Oren

Hatch, Carl A.
Hawkins, Benjamin
Hawley, Joseph Roswell
Hayne, Robert Young
Hearst, George
Heflin, James Thomas
Henderson, John
Henderson, John Brooks
Hendricks, Thomas Andrews
Henry, John, 1750–1798
Hill, Joshua
Hill, Nathaniel Peter
Hindman, William
Hoar, George Frisbie
Holmes, John
Hopkins, Samuel, 1753–1819
Houston, George Smith
Howard, Jacob Merritt
Howe, Timothy Otis
Hull, Cordell
Hunt, Lester Callaway
Hunter, William
Hunton, Eppa
Ingalls, John James
Iverson, Alfred
Ives, Irving McNeil
Izard, Ralph
Jackson, Howell Edmunds
Jackson, James, 1757–1806
James, Charles Tillinghast
James, Ollie Murray
Johnson, Edwin Carl
Johnson, Hiram Warren
Johnson, Magnus
Johnston, Joseph Forney
Johnston, Olin DeWitt Talmadge
Jones, James Chamberlayne
Jones, James Kimbrough
Jones, John Percival
Jones, Wesley Livsey
Kefauver, (Carey) Estes
Kellogg, Frank Billings
Kellogg, William Pitt
Kendrick, John Benjamin
Kenna, John Edward
Kennedy, John Fitzgerald
Kennedy, Robert Francis
Kent, Joseph
Kenyon, William Squire
Kerr, Robert Samuel
Key, David McKendree
Kilgore, Harley Martin
King, John Pendleton
Kirkwood, Samuel Jordan
Knox, Philander Chase
Kyle, James Henderson
Lacock, Abner
Lad, Edwin Fremont
La Follette, Robert Marion
La Follette, Robert Marion, Jr.
Lamar, Lucius Quintus
  Cincinnatus
Lane, Henry Smith
Langer, William
Larrazolo, Octaviano Ambrosio
Latham, Milton Slocum

Laurence, John
Lea, Luke
Lehman, Herbert Henry
Leib, Michael
Lenroot, Irvine Luther
Lewis, Dixon Hall
Lewis, John Francis
Lindsay, William
Linn, Lewis Fields
Livermore, Samuel, 1732–1803
Lodge, Henry Cabot
Logan, George
Logan, John Alexander
Long, Huey Pierce
Lorimer, William
Lowrie, Walter
Lucas, Scott Wike
Lundeen, Ernest
McCarran, Patrick Anthony
McCarthy, Joseph Raymond
McComas, Louis Emory
McCormick, Joseph Medill
McCreary, James Bennett
McDill, James Wilson
McDuffie, George
McEnery, Samuel Douglas
McGrath, James Howard
McKean, Samuel
McKellar, Kenneth Douglas
McKinley, John
McKinley, William Brown
McLauren, Anselm Joseph
Maclay, Samuel
Maclay, William
McMillan, James
McNary, Charles Linza
Macon, Nathaniel
Manderson, Charles Frederick
Mangum, Willie Person
Marshall, Humphrey
Martin, Alexander
Martin, Thomas Staples
Mason, James Murray
Mason, Jonathan
Mason, Stevens Thomson
Mason, William Ernest
Maxey, Samuel Bell
Maybank, Burnet Rhett
Mead, James Michael
Meigs, Return Jonathan
Mellen, Prentiss
Metcalfe, Thomas
Milledge, John
Miller, John Franklin
Miller, Stephen Decatur
Miller, Warner
Mills, Roger Quarles
Minton, Sherman
Mitchell, John Hipple
Mitchell, Samuel Latham
Money, Hernando De Soto
Moody, (Arthur Edson) Blair
Moore, Andrew
Moore, Gabriel
Morehead, James Turner
Morgan, Edwin Denison

Morgan, John Tyler
Morril, David Lawrence
Morrill, Justin Smith
Morrill, Lot Myrick
Morris, Thomas
Morrow, Jeremiah
Morton, Oliver Perry
Mouton, Alexander
Murray, James Edward
Neely, Matthew Mansfield
Nelson, Knute
Neuberger, Richard Lewis
Newberry, Truman Handy
Newlands, Francis Griffith
Nicholas, Wilson Cary
Nicholson, Alfred Osborne Pope
Nicholson, Samuel Danford
Niles, John Milton
Noble, James
Norbeck, Peter
Norris, George William
Nugent, John Frost
Nye, James Warren
O'Daniel, Wilbert Lee ("Pappy")
Ogden, Aaron
Oglesby, Richard James
Oliver, George Tener
O'Mahoney, Joseph Christopher
Overman, Lee Slater
Owen, Robert Latham
Paddock, Algernon Sidney
Palmer, John McAuley
Palmer, Thomas Witherell
Parris, Albion Keith
Pasco, Samuel
Patterson, Thomas MacDonald
Payne, Henry B.
Pearce, James Alfred
Peffer, William Alfred
Pendleton, George Hunt
Penrose, Boies
Pepper, George Wharton
Perkins, George Clement
Pettigrew, Richard Franklin
Pettus, Edmund Winston
Phelan, James Duval
Phipps, Lawrence Cowle
Pierce, Gilbert Ashville
Pinckney, Charles
Pittman, Key
Platt, Orville Hitchcock
Plumb, Preston B.
Plumer, William
Poindexter, George
Poindexter, Miles
Poland, Luke Potter
Polk, Trusten
Pomerene, Atlee
Pomeroy, Samuel Clarke
Pool, John
Pope, James Pinckney
Porter, Alexander
Potts, Richard
Prentiss, Samuel
Preston, William Campbell
Pritchard, Jeter Connelly

Pugh, George Ellis
Ralston, Samuel Moffett
Ramsey, Alexander
Randolph, Theodore Fitz
Ransom, Matt Whitaker
Rayner, Isidor
Read, George
Read, Jacob
Reagan, John Henninger
Reed, David Aiken
Reed, James Alexander
Revels, Hiram Rhoades
Reynolds, Robert Rice
Rice, Henry Mower
Roberts, Jonathan
Robinson, Joseph Taylor
Ross, Edmund Gibson
Ross, James
Rowan, John
Rusk, Thomas Jefferson
Sanders, Wilbur Fisk
Sargent, Aaron Augustus
Saulsbury, Eli
Saulsbury, Willard, 1820–1892
Saulsbury, Willard, 1861–1927
Saunders, Alvin
Sawyer, Philetus
Schall, Thomas David
Schurz, Carl
Schwellenbach, Lewis Baxter
Scott, W(illiam) Kerr
Sevier, Ambrose Hundley
Shafroth, John Franklin
Shepley, Ether
Sheppard, John Morris
Shields, James
Shields, John Knight
Shipstead, Henrik
Simmons, Furnifold McLendel
Smith, Ellison DuRant
Smith, Hoke
Smith, James, 1851–1927
Smith, John, 1735–1824
Smith, Nathan, 1770–1835
Smith, Oliver Hampton
Smith, William, 1762–1840
Smoot, Reed Owen
Southard, Samuel Lewis
Spooner, John Coit
Sprague, William, 1830–1915
Squire, Watson Carvosso
Stanford, Leland
Stanley, Augustus Owsley
Stephenson, Isaac
Stevenson, John White
Stewart, William Morris
Stockton, John Potter
Stokes, Montfort
Stone, David
Stone, William Joel
Sumner, Charles
Sumter, Thomas
Sutherland, George
Swanson, Claude Augustus
Taft, Robert Alphonso
Tait, Charles

Tappan, Benjamin
Tazewell, Littleton Waller
Taylor, Robert Love
Tazewell, Henry
Teller, Henry Moore
Thomas, Charles Spalding
Thomas, Elbert Duncan
Thomas, Jesse Burgess
Thurman, Allen Granberry
Thye, Edward John
Tillman, Benjamin Ryan
Tipton, John
Tobey, Charles William
Toombs, Robert Augustus
Toucey, Isaac
Tracy, Uriah
Troup, George Michael
Trumbull, Jonathan, 1740–1809
Trumbull, Lyman
Turner, George
Tydings, Millard Evelyn
Tyson, Lawrence Davis
Underwood, Joseph Rogers
Underwood, Oscar Wilder
Vance, Zebulon Baird
Vandenberg, Arthur Hendrick
Van Dyke, Nicholas, 1770–1826
Van Winkle, Peter Godwin
Vardaman, James Kimble
Varnum, Joseph Bradley
Vest, George Graham
Vilas, William Freeman
Voorhees, Daniel Wolsey
Wade, Benjamin Franklin
Wadsworth, James Wolcott, Jr.
Wagner, Robert Ferdinand
Walker, Robert John
Wallgren, Mon(rad) C(harles)
Walsh, David Ignatius
Walsh, Thomas James
Walthall, Edward Cary
Walton, George
Warner, William
Warren, Francis Emroy
Washburn, William Drew
Watson, James Eli
Webb, William Robert
Weeks, John Wingate
Welker, Herman
Weller, John B.
Wherry, Kenneth Spicer
Whitcomb, James
White, Albert Smith
White, Hugh Lawson
White, Samuel
White, Stephen Mallary
Whyte, William Pinkney
Wigfall, Louis Frezevant
Wiley, Alexander
Wilkins, William
Willey, Waitman Thomas
Williams, George Henry
Williams, John
Williams, John Sharp
Williams, Reuel
Wilson, Henry

Collins, John Anderson
Crosby, Ernest Howard
Darrow, Clarence Seward
Dennison, Henry Sturgis
Dietz, Peter Ernest
Dock, Lavinia Lloyd
Dreier, Mary Elisabeth
Fuller, Sarah Margaret
Gillette, King Camp
Gilman, Charlotte Perkins Stetson
Hamilton, Alice
Hazard, Thomas Robinson
Holmes, John Haynes
Jemison, Alice Mae Lee
Jones, Rufus Matthew
Kellogg, Paul Underwood
Lindsey, Benjamin Barr
Longley, Alcander
McBride, F(rancis) Scott
McClure, Samuel Sidney
Mussey, Ellen Spencer
Nathan, Maud
O'Hare, Kate (Richards)
    Cunningham
Owen, Robert Dale
Oxnam, Garfield Bromley
Peck, Lillie
Pinchot, Cornelia Elizabeth Bryce
Poling, Daniel Alfred
Regan, Agnes Gertrude
Robins, Margaret Dreier
Robins, Raymond
Roosevelt, (Anna) Eleanor
Ryan, John Augustine
Simkhovitch, Mary Melinda
    Kingsbury
Strong, Josiah
Swinton, John
Taylor, Graham
Tibbles, Thomas Henry
Tiffany, Katrina Brandes Ely
Voris, John Ralph
SOCIAL RESEARCHER
Bryant, Louise Frances Stevens
SOCIAL SCIENTIST (See also SPECIFIC
    SOCIAL SCIENCES)
Frank, Lawrence Kelso
Kracauer, Siegfried
Mayo, George Elton
Merriam, Charles Edward, Jr.
Mitchell, Wesley Clair
Sullivan, Harry Stack
Sumner, William Graham
SOCIAL WELFARE LEADER
Brackett, Jeffrey Richardson
Mack, Julian William
Swift, Linton Bishop
SOCIAL WORKER (See also
    SETTLEMENT WORKER)
Abbott, Edith
Abbott, Grace
Adie, David Craig
Antin, Mary
Balch, Emily Greene
Barrett, Janie Porter
Billikopf, Jacob

Binford, Jessie Florence
Blaustein, David
Bloomfield, Meyer
Bowen, Louise De Koven
Brace, Charles Loring
Breckenridge, Sophonisba Preston
Cabot, Richard Clarke
Cannon, Ida Maud
Carr, Charlotte Elizabeth
Coyle, Grace Longwell
Cratty, Mabel
Devine, Edward Thomas
Dinwiddie, Courtenay
Dodge, Grace Hoadley
Doremus, Sarah Platt Haines
Dyott, Thomas W.
Elliott, John Lovejoy
Hart, Hastings Hornell
Hersey, Evelyn Weeks
Hopkins, Harry Lloyd
Hunter, Robert
Johnson, Alexander
Kelley, Florence
Kober, George Martin
Lathrop, Alice Louise Higgins
Lathrop, Julia Clifford
Lee, Joseph
Lee, Porter Raymond
Lewis, Orlando Faulkland
Loeb, Sophie Irene Simon
Lovejoy, Owen Reed
McDowell, Mary Eliza
McHugh, Rose John
Mason, Lucy Randolph
Park, Maud Wood
Peirce, Bradford Kinney
Perkins, James Handasyd
Perry, Clarence Arthur
Potter, Ellen Culver
Richmond, Mary Ellen
Robertson, Alice Mary
Rubinow, Isaac Max
Schuyler, Louisa Lee
Shuey, Edwin Longstreet
Thurber, Christopher Carson
Veiller, Lawrence Turnure
West, James Edward
Willard, Mary Hatch
Williams, Aubrey Willis
SOCIAL WORK LEADER
Glenn, John Mark
SOCIOLOGIST
Bentley, Arthur Fisher
Brooks, John Graham
Butterfield, Kenyon Leech
Cayton, Horace Roscoe
Davis, Katharine Bement
Dawley, Almena
Dike, Samuel Warren
Du Bois, William Edward
    Burghardt
Ellis, George Washington
Fitzhugh, George
Frazier, Edward Franklin
Galpin, Charles Josiah
Giddings, Franklin Henry

Hayes, Edward Carey
Haynes, George Edmund
Henderson, Charles Richmond
Johnson, Charles Spurgeon
Kellor, Frances (Alice)
Kelly, Edmond
Kerby, William Joseph
Lynd, Robert Staughton
MacIver, Robert Morrison
Mills, Charles Wright
Morrow, Prince Albert
Odum, Howard Washington
Ogburn, William Fielding
Park, Robert Ezra
Parsons, Elsie Worthington Clews
Reid, Ira De Augustine
Ross, Edward Alsworth
Sanderson, Ezra Dwight
Small, Albion Woodbury
Stouffer, Samuel Andrew
Stuckenberg, John Henry
    Wilbrandt
Sutherland, Edwin Hardin
Teggart, Frederick John
Thomas, William Isaac
Vincent, George Edgar
Waller, Willard Walter
Warbasse, James Peter
Ward, Lester Frank
Warner, Amos Griswold
Wilson, Warren Hugh
Wing, John Joseph
Woods, Robert Archey
Wyckoff, Walter Augustus
Znaniecki, Florian Witold
SOIL CHEMIST (See also CHEMIST)
Hoagland, Dennis Robert
SOIL CONSERVATIONIST
Bennett, Hugh Hammond
SOIL EXPERT (See also
    AGRICULTURIST)
Hilgard, Eugene Woldemar
Marbut, Curtis Fletcher
SOIL SCIENTIST (See also
    AGRICULTURIST)
Lipman, Jacob Goodale
SOLDIER OF FORTUNE (See also
    ADVENTURER)
Burnham, Frederick Russell
Lee, Charles, 1731–1782
Littlepage, Lewis
Picton, Thomas
SOLDIER (See also ARMY OFFICER,
    GENERAL, INDIAN CHIEF,
    JAYHAWKER)
Adair, John
Adams, Charles
Adams, Daniel Weissiger
Adams, John
Adams, William Wirt
Agnus, Felix
Alden, Ichabod
Alexander, Barton Stone
Alexander, Edward Porter
Alexander, William
Alger, Russell Alexander

Grant, Frederick Dent
Grant, Lewis Addison
Gray, Isaac Pusey
Grayson, William
Greaton, John
Greely, Adolphus Washington
Greene, Christopher
Greene, Francis Vinton
Greene, George Sears
Gregg, David McMurtrie
Gregg, Maxcy
Gresham, Walter Quintin
Gridley, Richard
Grierson, Benjamin Henry
Griffin, Charles
Griffin, Eugene
Griffin, Simon Goodell
Grose, William
Grosvenor, Charles Henry
Grover, Cuvier
Guild, Curtis, 1860–1915
Haan, William George
Hagood, Johnson
Halderman, John A.
Hall, Willard Preble
Halleck, Henry Wager
Hamblin, Joseph Eldridge
Hamer, Thomas Lyon
Hamilton, Charles Smith
Hamilton, Schuyler
Hamlin, Charles
Hammond, Samuel
Hampton, Wade, 1751–1835
Hampton, Wade, 1818–1902
Hamtramck, John Francis
Hancock, Winfield Scott
Hand, Edward
Hardee, William Joseph
Hardie, James Allen
Hardin, John
Hardin, John J.
Hardin, Martin D.
Harding, Abner Clark
Harlan, Josiah
Harmar, Josiah
Harney, William Selby
Harriman, Walter
Harris, Nathaniel Harrison
Harrison, George Paul
Harrod, James
Hartley, Thomas
Hartranft, John Frederick
Hartsuff, George Lucas
Hascall, Milo Smith
Hatch, Edward
Hatch, John Porter
Hawkins, Rush Christopher
Hawley, Joseph Roswell
Hayne, Isaac
Hays, Alexander
Hays, Harry Thompson
Hays, John Coffee
Hazen, Moses
Hazen, William Babcock
Heath, William
Hébert, Louis

Hébert, Paul Octave
Hecker, Friedrich Karl Franz
Heintzelman, Samuel Peter
Henderson, David Bremner
Henderson, Thomas
Henningsen, Charles Frederick
Herbert, Hilary Abner
Herkimer, Nicholas
Heth, Henry
Heyward, Thomas
Hibben, Paxton Pattison
Hickenlooper, Andrew
Hickok, James Butler
Hiester, Joseph
Higginson, Henry Lee
Higginson, Thomas Wentworth
Hill, Ambrose Powell
Hill, Daniel Harvey
Hill, James
Hill, William
Hindman, Thomas Carmichael
Hitchcock, Ethan Allen,
　1798–1870
Hitchcock, Henry
Hobson, Edward Henry
Hodes, Henry Irving
Hodges, Courtney Hicks
Hoffman, Wickham
Hogun, James
Hoke, Robert Frederick
Holmes, Julius Cecil
Holmes, Theophilus Hunter
Hood, John Bell
Hooker, Joseph
Hopkins, Samuel, 1753–1819
Hough, Warwick
Houston, Samuel
Hovey, Alvin Peterson
Hovey, Charles Edward
Howard, Benjamin
Howard, John Eager
Howard, Oliver Otis
Howe, Albion Parris
Howe, Robert
Howe, William Wirt
Howze, Robert Lee
Hubbard, Lucius Frederick
Hubbard, Richard Bennett
Hubbard, Thomas Hamlin
Huger, Benjamin
Huger, Francis Kinloch
Hughes, George Wurtz
Hull, William
Humbert, Jean Joseph Amable
Humphreys, Andrew Atkinson
Humphreys, Benjamin Grubb
Humphreys, David
Hunt, Henry Jackson
Hunter, David
Huntington, Jedediah
Hunton, Eppa
Hurlbut, Stephen Augustus
Huse, Caleb
Hyrne, Edmund Massingberd
Imboden, John Daniel
Ingraham, Prentiss

Inman, George
Inman, Henry
Ireland, John, 1827–1896
Irvine, James
Irvine, William
Irwin, George Le Roy
Ives, Joseph Christmas
Izard, George
Jackson, Henry Rootes
Jackson, Thomas Jonathan
Jackson, William, 1759–1828
Jacob, Richard Taylor
Jadwin, Edgar
Jaquess, James Frazier
Jasper, William
Jenkins, Albert Gallatin
Jenkins, John
Jenkins, Micah
Jennings, John
Jesup, Thomas Sidney
Johnson, Bradley Tyler
Johnson, Bushrod Rust
Johnson, Edward
Johnson, James
Johnson, Richard W.
Johnston, Albert Sidney
Johnston, Joseph Eggleston
Johnston, Peter
Johnston, William Preston
Johnston, Zachariah
Jones, Allen
Jones, David Rumph
Jones, John B.
Jones, William
Jordan, Thomas
Kane, Thomas Leiper
Kautz, August Valentine
Kearney, Philip
Kearney, Stephen Watts
Keifer, Joseph Warren
Keitt, Lawrence Massillon
Kelton, John Cunningham
Kemper, James Lawson
Kennedy, John Doby
Kennedy, Robert Patterson
Kershaw, Joseph Brevard
Key, David McKendree
Keyes, Erasmus Darwin
Kilmer, Alfred Joyce
Kilpatrick, Hugh Judson
Kimball, Nathan
King, Rufus
Kirby-Smith, Edmund
Knowlton, Thomas
Kościuszko, Tadeusz Andrzej
　Bonawentura
Lacey, John
Lacey, John Fletcher
Lafayette, Marie Joseph Paul Yves
　Roch Gilbert du Motier, Marquis
　de
Lamb, John
Lander, Frederick West
Lane, James Henry, 1814–1866
Lane, James Henry, 1833–1907
Lane, Joseph

Lane, Walter Paye
Larrabee, Charles Hathaway
Laurance, John
Laurens, John
Law, Evander McIvor
Lawton, Alexander Robert
Lawton, Henry Ware
Lea, Homer
Leaming, Thomas
Learned, Ebenezer
Leavenworth, Henry
Le Duc, William Gates
Ledyard, William
Lee, Fitzhugh
Lee, George Washington Custis
Lee, Henry ("Light-Horse Harry"),
   1756–1818
Lee, Henry, 1787–1837
Lee, Robert Edward
Lee, Stephen Dill
Lee, William Henry Fitzhugh
Le Gendre, Charles William
Leggett, Mortimer Dormer
L'Enfant, Pierre Charles
Lewis, Andrew
Lewis, Isaac Newton
Lewis, Joseph Horace
Lewis, Morgan
Lewis, William Gaston
Liggett, Hunter
Lightburn, Joseph Andrew Jackson
Lincoln, Benjamin
Livingston, James
Locke, Matthew
Lockwood, James Booth
Logan, John Alexander
Lomax, Lunsford Lindsay
Longstreet, James
Lorimier, Pierre Louis
Loring, William Wing
Lovell, Mansfield
Lowrey, Mark Perrin
Lowry, Robert
Lubbock, Francis Richard
Ludlow, William
Lynch, Charles
Lynch, James Daniel
Lyon, Matthew
Lyon, Nathaniel
Lytle, William Haines
McArthur, John, 1826–1906
McCausland, John
McCawley, Charles Grymes
McCay, Henry Kent
McClellan, George Brinton
McClellan, Henry Brainerd
McClernand, John Alexander
McClintock, James Harvey
McClure, George
McClurg, Alexander Caldwell
McClurg, James
McCook, Alexander McDowell
McCook, Anson George
McCook, Edward Moody
McCrady, Edward
McCulloch, Ben

McCullough, Ernest
McDaniel, Henry Dickerson
McDougall, Alexander
McDowell, Charles
McDowell, Irvin
McDowell, Joseph
McElroy, John
McGowan, Samuel
McHenry, James
McIntosh, John Baillie
McIntosh, Lachlan
Mackenzie, Ronald Slidell
McKinstry, Alexander
McLane, Allan
McLaws, Lafayette
McLeod, Hugh
McMillan, James Winning
Macomb, Alexander
Macon, Nathaniel
McPherson, James Birdseye
McRae, Duncan Kirkland
Maginnis, Martin
Magruder, John Bankhead
Mahan, Dennis Hart
Mahone, William
Mallery, Garrick
Manderson, Charles Frederick
Maney, George Earl
Mappa, Adam Gerard
March, Peyton Conway
Marcy, Randolph Barnes
Marmaduke, John Sappington
Marshall, George Catlett, Jr.
Marshall, Humphrey
Marshall, Thomas
Marshall, William Louis
Marshall, William Rainey
Martin, Alexander
Martin, James Green
Martin, John Alexander
Martin, William Thompson
Martindale, John Henry
Mason, John
Mason, Richard Barnes
Matthews, George
Maury, Dabney Herndon
Maus, Marion Perry
Maxwell, William
Meade, George Gordon
Meade, Richard Kidder
Meade, Robert Leamy
Meagher, Thomas Francis
Meigs, Montgomery Cunningham
Meigs, Return Jonathan
Menoher, Charles Thomas
Mercer, Hugh
Mercer, John Francis
Merriam, Henry Clay
Merrill, Frank Dow
Merrill, William Emery
Merritt, Wesley
Meserve, Nathaniel
Michie, Peter Smith
Miles, Nelson Appleton
Mills, Anson
Milroy, Robert Huston

Minty, Robert Horatio George
Mitchel, Ormsby MacKnight
Mitchell, David Dawson
Mitchell, George Edward
Mitchell, Nathaniel
Mitchell, Robert Byington
Montefiore, Joshua
Montgomery, James
Montgomery, Richard
Moore, Alfred
Moore, James, 1737–1777
Mordecai, Alfred
Morell, George Webb
Morgan, Daniel
Morgan, George Washington
Morgan, James Dada
Morgan, James Morris
Morgan, John Hunt
Morgan, Thomas Jefferson
Morris, Roger
Morris, William Hopkins
Morton, James St. Clair
Mott, Gershom
Mower, Joseph Anthony
Moylan, Stephen
Muhlenberg, John Peter Gabriel
Mulholland, St. Clair Augustin
Munford, Robert
Myer, Albert James
Myers, Abraham Charles
Nancrède, Paul Joseph Guérard de
Narváez, Pánfilo de
Nash, Francis
Negley, James Scott
Neill, Thomas Hewson
Neilson, John
Nelson, Roger
Nelson, Thomas
Nelson, William, 1824–1862
Nesmith, James Willis
Nettleton, Alvred Bayard
Neville, John
Neville, Wendell Cushing
Newton, John
Nicholson, William Jones
Nicola, Lewis
Nixon, John, 1727–1815
Noailles, Louis Marie, Vicomte de
Noble, John Willock
North, William
Northen, William Jonathan
Northrop, Lucius Bellringer
Noyan, Gilles-Augustin Payen de
Noyen, Pierre-Jacques Payen de
Oates, William Calvin
O'Fallon, James
O'Fallon, John
Ogden, Aaron
Oglethorpe, James Edward
O'Hara, James
O'Hara, Theodore
Oliver, Paul Ambrose
O'Neal, Edward Asbury
O'Neill, John
Ord, Edward Otho Cresap
O'Reilly, Alexander

Osborn, Thomas Ogden
Osceola
Osgood, Samuel
Osterhaus, Peter Joseph
Otis, Elwell Stephen
Otis, Harrison Gray
Page, Richard Lucian
Paine, Charles Jackson
Paine, Halbert Eleazer
Painter, Gamaliel
Palfrey, John Carver
Palmer, Innis Newton
Palmer, John McAuley
Palmer, Joseph
Palmer, William Jackson
Pardee, Don Albert
Parke, Benjamin
Parke, John
Parke, John Grubb
Parker, Ely Samuel
Parker, John
Parker, Josiah
Parker, Richard Elliot
Parsons, Lewis Baldwin
Parsons, Samuel Holden
Paterson, John
Patrick, Marsena Rudolph
Patterson, Robert
Peck, John James
Pelham, John
Pemberton, John Clifford
Peñalosa Briceño, Diego Dionisio
Pender, William Dorsey
Pendleton, William Nelson
Pennypacker, Galusha
Pepperrell, Sir William
Perry, Edward Aylesworth
Pettigrew, James Johnston
Pettus, Edmund Winston
Phelps, Charles Edward
Philips, John Finis
Phillips, William Addison
Phisterer, Frederick
Pickens, Andrew
Pickering, Timothy
Pickett, George Edward
Pierce, William Leigh
Pike, Albert
Pike, Zebulon Montgomery
Pillow, Gideon Johnson
Pinckney, Charles Cotesworth
Pinckney, Thomas
Pitcairn, John
Plaisted, Harris Merrill
Pleasonton, Alfred
Plumb, Preston B.
Poe, Orlando Metcalfe
Polk, Lucius Eugene
Polk, Thomas
Polk, William
Pomeroy, Seth
Pond, Peter
Poor, Enoch
Pope, John
Porter, Andrew
Porter, Fitz-John

Porter, Horace
Posey, Thomas
Potter, James
Potter, Robert Brown
Potts, Benjamin Franklin
Powel, John Hare
Pratt, Richard Henry
Prentiss, Benjamin Mayberry
Prescott, Oliver
Prescott, William
Preston, John Smith
Preston, William
Price, Sterling
Pryor, Nathaniel
Pryor, Roger Atkinson
Pulaski, Casimir
Putnam, Eben
Putnam, George Haven
Putnam, Israel
Putnam, Rufus
Quesnay, Alexandre-Marie
Quimby, Isaac Ferdinand
Quitman, John Anthony
Rains, Gabriel James
Rains, George Washington
Ramsay, George Douglas
Ramsay, Nathaniel
Ramseur, Stephen Dodson
Ransom, Matt Whitaker
Ransom, Thomas Edward
  Greenfield
Raum, Green Berry
Rawlins, John Aaron
Read, Jacob
Reed, James, 1772–1807
Reed, John, 1757–1845
Reed, Joseph
Reno, Jesse Lee
Revere, Joseph Warren
Reynolds, Alexander Welch
Reynolds, John Fulton
Reynolds, Joseph Jones
Richardson, Israel Bush
Richardson, Wilds Preston
Ricketts, James Brewerton
Riley, Bennet
Ripley, Edward Hastings
Ripley, Eleazar Wheelock
Ripley, James Wolfe
Ripley, Roswell Sabine
Roane, John Selden
Roberts, Benjamin Stone
Roberts, Oran Milo
Robertson, Jerome Bonaparte
Robinson, John Cleveland
Robinson, Moses
Rochambeau, Jean Baptiste
  Donatien Vimeur, Comte de
Rockwell, Kiffin Yates
Roddey, Philip Dale
Rodenbough, Theophilus Francis
Rodes, Robert Emmett
Rodman, Isaac Peace
Rodman, Thomas Jackson
Rodney, Thomas
Romans, Bernard

Rosecrans, William Starke
Ross, Lawrence Sullivan
Rosser, Thomas Lafayette
Rousseau, Lovell Harrison
Ruger, Thomas Howard
Ruggles, Timothy
Rusk, Thomas Jefferson
Russell, David Allen
Rutgers, Henry
St. Ange Bellerive, Louis de
St. Clair, Arthur
St. Denis (Denys), Louis Juchereau
  de
St. Lusson, Simon François
  Daumont, Sieur de
St. Vrain, Ceran de Hault de
  Lassus de
Sargent, Henry
Sargent, Winthrop, 1753–1820
Scammell, Alexander
Scharf, John Thomas
Schenck, Robert Cumming
Schnauffer, Carl Heinrich
Schofield, John McAllister
Schriver, Edmund
Schurz, Carl
Schuyler, Peter
Schuyler, Philip John
Scott, Charles
Scott, Robert Kingston
Scott, Winfield
Scudder, Nathaniel
Sedgwick, John
Sedgwick, Robert
Seeger, Alan
Sevier, John
Sewell, William Joyce
Seymour, Truman
Shafter, William Rufus
Shaw, Samuel
Shays, Daniel
Shelby, Evan
Shelby, Isaac
Shelby, Joseph Orville
Shepard, William
Shepley, George Foster
Sheridan, Philip Henry
Sherman, Thomas West
Sherman, William Tecumseh
Sherwood, Isaac Ruth
Shields, James
Shipp, Scott
Shoup, Francis Asbury
Sickles, Daniel Edgar
Sidell, William Henry
Sigel, Franz
Simmons, Thomas Jefferson
Simms, William Elliott
Simonton, Charles Henry
Simpson, James Hervey
Smallwood, William
Smith, Andrew Jackson
Smith, Charles Ferguson
Smith, Charles Henry, 1827–1902
Smith, Daniel
Smith, Francis Henney

Bragg, Thomas
Braxton, Carter
Brearly, David
Breckenridge, John
Breckinridge, John Cabell
Brentano, Lorenz
Briggs, George Nixon
Bristow, Benjamin Helm
Brown, Joseph Emerson
Cary, Archibald
Cass, Lewis
Chase, Salmon Portland
Choate, Rufus
Clarke, John
Clayton, John Middleton
Clinton, De Witt
Clinton, George
Colquitt, Alfred Holt
Colquitt, Walter Terry
Conrad, Charles Magill
Cooke, Elisha
Crittenden, John Jordan
Culberson, Charles Allen
Culberson, David Browning
Cullom, Shelby Moore
Cummings, Albert Baird
Curry, Jabez Lamar Monroe
Cushing, Caleb
Dana, Samuel Whittelsey
Dane, Nathan
Davis, Henry Winter
Davis, John
Dawson, John
Dickinson, John
Dillingham, William Paul
Dolliver, Jonathan Prentiss
Doniphan, Alexander William
Doolittle, James Rood
Dow, Henry
Eaton, Charles Aubrey
Eliot, Samuel Atkins
Ellsworth, Oliver
Emerson, Haven
Eustis, George
Eustis, James Biddle
Evarts, William Maxwell
Everett, Edward
Fersen, Hans Axel
Few, William
Fish, Hamilton
Fleming, William
Forsyth, John
Franklin, Benjamin
Frelinghuysen, Frederick Theodore
Galloway, Joseph
Garnett, Muscoe Russell Hunter
Gerry, Elbridge
Gholson, Thomas Saunders
Gibson, Randall Lee
Giles, William Branch
Gillette, Francis
Gilmer, Thomas Walker
Goode, John
Gordon, John Brown
Gordon, William Fitzhugh
Gorham, Nathaniel

Graham, William Alexander
Gresham, Walter Quintin
Griffin, Cyrus
Griggs, John William
Hall, Lyman
Hamilton, Alexander, 1757–1804
Hardy, Samuel
Harnett, Cornelius
Harpur, Robert
Harrison, Benjamin, 1726–1791
Harvie, John
Heathcote, Caleb
Henry, Patrick
Hewitt, Abram Stevens
Hill, Benjamin Harvey
Hindman, Thomas Carmichael
Hopkinson, Francis
Hosmer, Titus
Houston, Samuel
Humphreys, David
Hunter, Robert Mercer Taliaferro
Ide, Henry Clay
Iredell, James
Jay, John
Jefferson, Thomas
Jenifer, Daniel of St. Thomas
Johnson, William Samuel
Johnston, Josiah Stoddard
Johnston, Zachariah
Jones, Joseph
Judd, Gerrit Parmele
Kennedy, John Pendleton
Kern, John Worth
Körner, Gustav Philip
Lafayette, Marie Joseph Paul Yves Roch Gilbert du Motier Marquis de
Lamar, Lucius Quintus Cincinnatus
Laurens, Henry
Lawrence, Abbott
Lee, Francis Lightfoot
Lee, Henry, 1756–1818
Lee, Richard
Lee, Richard Bland
Lee, Richard Henry
Leigh, Benjamin Watkins
Livingston, Edward
Livingston, Robert R., 1746–1813
Logan, James, 1674–1751
Lovejoy, Owen
Lumpkin, Wilson
McKean, Thomas
Marcy, William Learned
Marshall, George Catlett, Jr.
Mason, George
Menard, Pierre
Mitchell, Stephen Mix
Morris, Gouverneur
Morris, Lewis Richard
Nelson, John
Osborn, Thomas Andrew
Otis, Harrison Gray
Parker, Joel
Parker, Richard Elliot
Pattison, Robert Emory

Patton, John Mercer
Pinckney, Charles Cotesworth
Pinkney, William
Pitkin, Timothy
Poinsett, Joel Roberts
Porter, David Rittenhouse
Powel, John Hare
Randolph, John, 1773–1833
Reed, Joseph
Rhett, Robert Barnwell
Richardson, James Daniel
Roberts, Oran Milo
Robinson, Moses
Rodney, Caesar
Rodney, Caesar Augustus
Rublee, George
Rush, Richard
Rutledge, John
Schuyler, Philip John
Seward, William Henry
Sherman, John, 1823–1900
Sherman, Roger
Silsbee, Nathaniel
Slade, William
Smith, Meriwether
Smith, Samuel
Strong, Caleb
Sullivan, James
Sullivan, John
Tallmadge, James
Vane, Sir Henry
Watterson, Henry
Webster, Daniel
Williamson, Hugh

STATES RIGHTS ADVOCATE (**See also** AGITATOR, REFORMER)
Paine, Byron
Quitman, John Anthony

STATISTICIAN (**See also** INSURANCE EXPERT)
Abbott, Samuel Warren
Adams, Henry Carter
Ayres, Leonard Porter
Babson, Roger Ward
Day, David Talbot
De Bow, James Dunwoody Brownson
Dennis, James Shepard
Dodge, Jacob Richards
Dorchester, Daniel
Falkner, Roland Post
Hill, Joseph Adna
Hittell, John Shertzer
Hoffman, Frederick Ludwig
Hourwich, Isaac Aaronovich
Jarvis, Edward
Kennedy, Joseph Camp Griffith
Koren, John
McPherson, Logan Grant
Mayo-Smith, Richmond
North, Simon Newton Dexter
Ogburn, William Fielding
Pearl, Raymond
Persons, Warren Milton
Pidgin, Charles Felton
Rossiter, William Sidney

Rubinow, Isaac Max
Schem, Alexander Jacob
Shattuck, Lemuel
Stouffer, Samuel Andrew
Swank, James Moore
Sydenstricker, Edgar
Walker, Francis Amasa
Weeks, Joseph Dame
Wilbur, Cressy Livingston
Woytinsky, Wladimir Savelievich
Wright, Carroll Davidson

STEAMBOAT BUILDER
Rees, James

STEAMBOAT CAPTAIN (See also SHIP CAPTAIN)
Bixby, Horace Ezra
Ford, John Baptiste
King, Richard
Marsh, Grant Prince
Rogers, Moses
Sellers, Isaiah
Shreve, Henry Miller
Vandergrift, Jacob Jay

STEAMBOAT OPERATOR
Gibbons, Thomas
La Barge, Joseph
Ogden, Aaron
Reed, Simeon Gannett

STEAMSHIP OWNER (See also SHIPOWNER)
Grace, William Russell
Hallett, Benjamin
Newton, Isaac, 1794–1858
Ralston, William Chapman

STEEL COMPANY EXECUTIVE
Farrell, James Augustine
Graff, Everett Dwight

STOCK BREEDER (See also CATTLEMAN)
Allen, Lewis Falley
Buford, Abraham
Hammond, Edwin
Harris, William Alexander
Jackson, William Hicks
McNeill, John Hanson
Matthews, Claude
Morris, Nelson
Sheedy, Dennis

STOCKBROKER (See also BANKER, CAPITALIST, FINANCIER)
Colgate, James Boorman
Cuppia, Jerome Chester
Du Pont, Francis Irénée
Hendrick, Ellwood
Hutton, Edward Francis
Lawson, Thomas William
Merrill, Charles Edward
Ouimet, Francis Desales
Riis, Mary Phillips

STONEMASON
Edmondson, William

STREET RAILWAY BUILDER
Stephenson, John
Wells, Erastus

STREET RAILWAY OPERATOR
Johnson, Tom Loftin

Mitten, Thomas Eugene
Scullin, John

SUBMARINE PIONEER
Lake, Simon

SUFFRAGIST (See also FEMINIST)
Belmont, Alva Ertskin Smith Vanderbilt
Blackwell, Alice Stone
Brown, Gertrude Foster
Catt, Carrie Clinton Lane Chapman
Flynn, Elizabeth Gurley
Hooper, Jessie Annette Jack
Stevens, Doris
Wells, Harriet Sheldon
Whitney, Charlotte Anita
Younger, Maud

SUGAR PLANTER (See also AGRICULTURIST, FARMER, PLANTER)
Behan, William James
Boré, Jean Étienne

SUGAR REFINER
Havemeyer, Henry Osborne
Havemeyer, William Frederick
Stuart, Robert Leighton

SUGAR TECHNOLOGIST
Hooker, Samuel Cox

SUPERINTENDENT OF INDIAN AFFAIRS
Johnson, Guy
Johnson, Sir John
Johnson, Sir William
Mitchell, David Dawson
Pilcher, Joshua
Stuart, John

SUPREME COURT CHIEF JUSTICE
Chase, Salmon Portland
Ellsworth, Oliver
Fuller, Melville Weston
Hughes, Charles Evans
Jay, John
Marshall, John
Stone, Harlan Fiske
Taft, William Howard
Taney, Roger Brooke
Vinson, Fred(erick) Moore
Waite, Morrison Remick
White, Edward Douglass

SUPREME COURT JUSTICE
Baldwin, Henry
Barbour, Philip Pendleton
Blair, John
Blatchford, Samuel
Bradley, Joseph P.
Brandeis, Louis Dembitz
Brewer, David Josiah
Brown, Henry Billings
Burton, Harold Hitz
Butler, Pierce
Campbell, John Archibald
Cardozo, Benjamin Nathan
Catron, John
Chase, Samuel
Clarke, John Hessin
Clifford, Nathan
Curtis, Benjamin Robbins

Cushing, William
Daniel, Peter Vivian
Davis, David
Day, William Rufus
Duvall, Gabriel
Field, Stephen Johnson
Frankfurter, Felix
Gray, Horace
Grier, Robert Cooper
Harlan, John Marshall
Holmes, Oliver Wendell
Hughes, Charles Evans
Hunt, Ward
Iredell, James
Jackson, Howell Edmunds
Jackson, Robert Houghwout
Johnson, Thomas
Johnson, William
Lamar, Lucius Quintus Cincinnatus
Livingston, Henry Brockholst
Lurton, Horace Harmon
McKenna, Joseph
McKinley, John
McLean, John
McReynolds, James Clark
Matthews, Stanley
Miller, Samuel Freeman
Minton, Sherman
Moody, William Henry
Moore, Alfred
Murphy, Frank
Nelson, Samuel
Peckham, Rufus Wheeler
Pitney, Mahlon
Roberts, Owen Josephus
Rutledge, John
Rutledge, Wiley Blount
Sanford, Edward Terry
Shiras, George
Stone, Harlan Fiske
Story, Joseph
Strong, William
Sutherland, George
Swayne, Noah Haynes
Thompson, Smith
Todd, Thomas
Trimble, Robert
Van Devanter, Willis
Washington, Bushrod
Wayne, James Moore
White, Edward Douglass
Wilson, James
Woodbury, Levi
Woods, William Burnham

SURGEON (See also PHYSICIAN)
Agnew, David Hayes
Allison, Nathaniel
Ambler, James Markham Marshall
Ashhurst, John
Atlee, John Light
Atlee, Washington Lemuel
Baer, William Stevenson
Barnes, Joseph K.
Barton, John Rhea
Barton, William Paul Crillon

Batchelder, John Putnam
Battey, Robert
Baxley, Henry Willis
Beaumont, William
Beck, Carl
Bernays, Augustus Charles
Bevan, Arthur Dean
Bigelow, Henry Jacob
Billings, John Shaw
Blackburn, Luke Pryor
Blalock, Alfred
Bloodgood, Joseph Colt
Bradford, Edward Hickling
Brainard, Daniel
Brinton, John Hill
Brophy, Truman William
Brown, Frederic Tilden
Bryant, Joseph Decatur
Buck, Gurdon
Bull, William Tillinghast
Bumstead, Freeman Josiah
Burnet, William
Cabot, Arthur Tracy
Cabot, Hugh
Carnochan, John Murray
Carrel, Alexis
Carson, Simeon Lewis
Chisolm, John Julian
Chovet, Abraham
Condit, John
Cooper, Elias Samuel
Crile, George Washington
Cushing, Harvey Williams
Cutler, Elliott Carr
Da Costa, John Chalmers
Dandy, Walter Edward
Davidge, John Beale
Davis, Henry Gassett
Davis, John Staige
Deaver, John Blair
Delafield, Edward
Dennis, Frederic Shepard
Dorsey, John Syng
Dowell, Greensville
Downer, Eliphalet
Drew, Charles Richard
Dudley, Benjamin Winslow
Edebohls, George Michael
Elman, Robert
Elsberg, Charles Albert
Eve, Paul Fitzsimons
Fayssoux, Peter
Fenger, Christian
Ferguson, Alexander High
Finney, John Miller Turpin
Floyd, John
Fowler, George Ryerson
Fowler, Russell Story
Frazier, Charles Harrison
Gaillard, Edwin Samuel
Garlick, Theodatus
Garretson, James
Gaston, James McFadden
Gerrish, Frederic Henry
Gerster, Arpad Geyza Charles
Gibson, William

Gihon, Albert Leary
Gilliam, David Tod
Goldsmith, Middleton
Gorgas, William Crawford
Graham, Evarts Ambrose
Gross, Samuel David
Gross, Samuel Weissell
Halsted, William Stewart
Hamilton, Frank Hastings
Hammond, William Alexander
Hartley, Frank
Hays, John Coffee
Hayward, George
Heap, Samuel Davies
Helmuth, William Tod
Henrotin, Fernand
Hodgen, John Thompson
Holmes, Bayard Taylor
Hosack, Alexander Eddy
Howe, Andrew Jackson
Hullihen, Simon P.
Jackson, Edward
Jackson, Hall
Jameson, Horatio Gates
Jeffries, Benjamin Joy
Johnston, George Ben
Jones, John
Judd, Edward Starr
Judson, Adoniram Brown
Kean, Jefferson Randolph
Keen, William Williams
Kellogg, John Harvey
Kelly, Howard Atwood
Keyes, Edward Lawrence
Kilty, William
Kimball, Gilman
Kinloch, Robert Alexander
Kirk, Norman Thomas
Kolle, Frederick Strange
Lahey, Frank Howard
Lane, Levi Cooper
Lawson, Thomas
Lefferts, George Morewood
Lewis, Dean De Witt
Lincoln, Rufus Pratt
Lloyd, James
Lockrey, Sarah Hunt
Long, Crawford Williamson
Lovell, Joseph
Lovett, Robert Williamson
Lower, William Edgar
McBurney, Charles
McClellan, George, 1796–1847
McCosh, Andrew James
McDowell, Ephraim
McGuire, Hunter Holmes
Mann, James
March, Alden
Marcy, Henry Orlando
Martin, Franklin Henry
Martin, Henry Austin
Mastin, Claudius Henry
Matas, Rudolph
Maury, Francis Fontaine
Maynard, Edward
Mayo, Charles Horace

Mayo, William James
Mayo, William Worrell
Mearns, Edgar Alexander
Merrill, James Cushing
Mettauer, John Peter
Mixter, Samuel Jason
Moore, Edward Mott
Moore, James Edward
Moore, Samuel Preston
Mott, Valentine
Mumford, James Gregory
Murphy, John Benjamin
Mussey, Reuben Dimond
Nancrède, Charles Beylard Guérard
   de
Neill, John
Norris, George Washington
Ochsner, Albert John
O'Reilly, Robert Maitland
Otto, Bodo
Owen, Griffith
Packard, John Hooker
Palmer, James Croxall
Pancoast, Joseph
Park, Roswell
Parker, Willard
Parsons, Usher
Peck, Charles Howard
Physick, Philip Syng
Pilcher, Lewis Stephen
Pilcher, Paul Monroe
Pinkney, Ninian
Post, Wright
Prevost, François Marie
Price, Joseph
Randolph, Jacob
Ransohoff, Joseph
Reid, Mont Rogers
Reid, William Wharry
Richardson, Maurice Howe
Richardson, Tobias Gibson
Robinson, Frederick Byron
Rogers, Stephen
Satterlee, Richard Sherwood
Sayre, Lewis Albert
Sayre, Reginald Hall
Senn, Nicholas
Shrady, George Frederick
Smith, Ashbel
Smith, Nathan, 1762–1829
Smith, Nathan Ryno
Smith, Stephen
Souchon, Edmond
Spalding, Lyman
Spencer, Pitman Clemens
Sternberg, George Miller
Stevens, Alexander Hodgdon
Stimson, Lewis Atterbury
Stitt, Edward Rhodes
Stone, Warren
Taylor, Charles Fayette
Teusler, Rudolf Bolling
Thorek, Max
Tiffany, Louis McLane
Tilton, James
Toland, Hugh Huger

Twitchell, Amos
Van Buren, William Holme
Vance, Ap Morgan
Vander Veer, Albert
Van Hook, Weller
Van Lennep, William Bird
Walter, Albert G.
Warbasse, James Peter
Warren, John
Warren, John Collins, 1778–1856
Warren, John Collins, 1842–1927
Weir, Robert Fulton
White, James William
Whitman, Royal
Willard, De Forest
Williams, Daniel Hale
Wilson, Henry Parke Custis
Wood, James Rushmore
Wood, Thomas
Woodhull, Alfred Alexander
Woodward, Henry
Wyeth, John Allan

SURVEYOR (**See also** GEODESIST,
　　HYDROGRAPHER)
Applegate, Jesse
Borden, Gail
Burt, William Austin
Clark, Abraham
De Brahm, William Gerard
De Witt, Simeon
Ellicott, Andrew
Fry, Joshua
Holme, Thomas
Hooker, Philip
Hudde, Andries
Hulbert, Edwin James
Jenkins, John, 1728–1785
Jenkins, John, 1751 o.s.–1827
Kilbourne, James
Leeds, Daniel
Marshall, Thomas
Mayo, William
Penington, Edward
Porter, Andrew
Strong, Moses McCure

SWIMMING COACH
Kiphuth, Robert John Herman
SWINDLER (**See also** CRIMINAL)
Means, Gaston Bullock
Musica, Philip Mariano Fausto
Scott, John
SYPHILOLOGIST (**See also** PHYSICIAN)
Pusey, William Allen

TANK (**MILITARY**) **DESIGNER**
Christie, John Walter
TANNER
Cummings, John
Easton, Nicholas
Edwards, William
TARIFF EXPERT
O'Brien, Robert Lincoln
TAVERN KEEPER (**See** HOTELMAN)
TAX COMMISSIONER
Haugen, Nils Pederson

TAX EXPERT (**See also** ACCOUNTANT)
Lasser, Jacob Kay
Purdy, Lawson
TAXIDERMIST
Akeley, Carl Ethan
Maynard, Charles Johnson
TAXONOMIST (**See also** BOTANIST,
　　ZOOLOGIST)
Gill, Theodore Nicholas
Merrill, Elmer Drew
TEACHER (**See also** EDUCATOR,
　　PROFESSOR, SCHOLAR)
General
Agnew, David Hayes
Allen, Hervey
Archer, John
Arvin, Newton
Bache, Franklin
Bacon, Alice Mabel
Baermann, Carl
Bailey, Florence Augusta Merriam
Baker, Benjamin Franklin
Barrows, Alice Prentice
Bartlett, Elisha
Barton, William Paul Crillon
Beal, William James
Beck, Johann Heinrich
Blackmur, Richard Palmer
Blodgett, Benjamin Colman
Bradbury, William Batchelder
Brooks, Byron Alden
Brown, Solyman
Bumstead, Harry Andrews
Cobb, Andrew Jackson
Coerne, Louis Adolphe
Coffin, Robert Peter Tristram
Cogswell, Joseph Green
Cole, Chester Cicero
Cooke, Josiah Parsons
Corson, Hiram
Crafts, James Mason
Crane, Thomas Frederick
Dabney, Robert Lewis
Dabney, Virginius
Dannreuther, Gustav
Davis, Noah Knowles
Delano, Jane Arminda
Dennison, Walter
Douglass, David Bates
Doyle, Sarah Elizabeth
Duchesne, Rose Philippine
Dunglison, Robley
Dunning, William Archibald
Durant, Henry
Duveneck, Frank
Eakins, Thomas
Edman, Irwin
Eichbery, Julius
Elson, Louis Charles
Emery, Henry Crosby
Emery, Stephen Albert
Emmons, Ebenezer
Erskine, John
Estabrook, Joseph
Eustis, Henry Lawrence
Everett, Edward

Eytinge, Rose
Fauset, Jessie Redmon
Fay, Edwin Whitefield
Fernald, Charles Henry
Fernow, Bernhard Eduard
Flint, Austin
Folsom, Charles
Francke, Kuno
Frazer, John Fries
Frothingham, Arthur Lincoln
Fulton, Robert Burwell
Gallaudet, Edward Miner
Garman, Charles Edward
Garry, Spokane
Gaston, James McFadden
Gibbs, Josiah Willard
Goessmann, Charles Anthony
Goodrich, Alfred John
Gorgas, Josiah
Gould, Nathaniel Duren
Gould, Robert Simonton
Green, Jacob
Griffes, Charles Tomlinson
Griscom, John
Gross, Samuel David
Gross, Samuel Weissell
Gruening, Emil
Hale, Philip Leslie
Hamilton, Edith
Hamlin, Alfred Dwight Foster
Hanchett, Henry Granger
Harrison, Gessner
Harshberger, John William
Haven, Joseph
Henri, Robert
Herbermann, Charles George
Hodge, Archibald Alexander
Hoffman, David
Hoffman, Richard
Holmes, Nathaniel
Holmes, Oliver Wendell
Holyoke, Samuel
Hoppin, James Mason
Houston, William Churchill
Howard, George Elliott
Humphreys, Milton Wylie
Hyde, Charles Cheney
Inglis, Alexander James
Ives, Halsey Cooley
Jackson, George K.
James, Thomas Chalkley
Jameson, Horatio Gates
Jarrell, Randall
Jarvis, Charles H.
Jenks, Jeremiah Whipple
Johnson, Allen
Johnson, Henry
Jordan, David Starr
Joseffy, Rafael
Kay, Edgar Boyd
Kearsley, John
Kelly, Aloysius Oliver Joseph
Kinnersley, Ebenezer
Kirkwood, Daniel
Klein, Bruno Oscar
Klein, Joseph Frederic

Knapp, Seaman Asabel
Knapp, William Ireland
Kneisel, Franz
Knight, Sarah Kemble
Larcom, Lucy
Law, Andrew
Leavenworth, Francis Preserved
Leavitt, Dudley
LeConte, John
Lee, James Melvin
Le Jan, Francis
Lewisohn, Ludwig
Liebling, Emil
Lincoln, John Larkin
Lincoln, Mary Johnson Bailey
Lockwood, Belva Ann Bennett
Locy, William Albert
Lomax, John Taylor
Longfellow, Samuel
Lowell, James Russell
McCaw, James Brown
McClain, Emlin
MacDonald, Ronald
Magill, Edward Hicks
Malin, Patrick Murphy
Malter, Henry
Mansfield, Jared
Margolis, Max Leopold
Marshall, Louis
Marzo, Eduardo
Mason, Lowell
Mason, Luther Whiting
Mason, William
Mathews, William
Mathews, William Smythe Babcock
Mechem, Floyd Russell
Mees, Arthur
Meigs, James Aitken
Mell, Patrick Hues
Mielziner, Moses
Miles, George Henry
Miller, Kenneth Hayes
Millington, John
Minor, John Barbee
Minor, Raleigh Colston
Mitchell, Maria
Montgomery, Thomas Harrison
Moore, Charles Herbert
Mortimer, Mary
Muhlenberg, Frederick Augustus
Mulford, Elisha
Nancrède, Paul Joseph Guérard de
Nash, Henry Sylvester
Nelson, Henry Loomis
Newman, Samuel Phillips
Nichols, Ernest Fox
Niemeyer, John Henry
Northen, William Jonathan
Norton, Charles Eliot
Ogilvie, James
Oliver, Henry Kemble
Olmsted, Denison
Onderdonk, Henry
Osgood, George Laurie
Osgood, Howard
Packard, Alpheus Spring

Paine, John Knowles
Palmer, Alonzo Benjamin
Palmer, George Herbert
Parker, James Cutler Dunn
Parker, Richard Green
Parr, Samuel Wilson
Parrington, Vernon Louis
Parrish, Edward
Parrish, Joseph
Parsons, Albert Ross
Paul, Henry Martyn
Payne, William Morton
Peck, Thomas Ephraim
Peck, Tracy
Peckham, George Williams
Pennington, James W. C.
Pepper, William
Perabo, Johann Ernst
Pickett, Albert
Pike, Nicolas
Pitkin, Walter Boughton
Platner, Samuel Ball
Plummer, Mary Wright
Pomeroy, John Norton
Porter, Andrew
Porter, Sarah
Powell, Alma Webster
Powell, Edward Payson
Prang, Mary Amelia Dana Hicks
Prentiss, George Lewis
Price, William Thompson
Proctor, William
Pyle, Howard
Randolph, Sarah Nicholas
Reeve, Tapping
Renwick, James, 1792–1863
Rice, Fenelon Bird
Rice, Nathan Lewis
Richards, Joseph William
Richards, Thomas Addison
Richardson, Charles Francis
Riddle, Matthew Brown
Rivers, William James
Roethke, Theodore Huebner
Rolfe, William James
Root, Frederic Woodman
Root, George Frederick
Royce, Josiah
Rybner, Martin Cornelius
Sadtler, Samuel Philip
Safford, Truman Henry
Salisbury, Edward Elbridge
Sanborn, Katherine Abbott
Sanderson, John
Schofield, Henry
Schradieck, Henry
Schussele, Christian
Sedgwick, William Thompson
Sherwood, William Hall
Shippen, William
Short, Charles Wilkins
Sill, Edward Rowland
Small, Albion Woodbury
Smith, James Perrin
Smith, Jeremiah, 1837–1921
Smith, John Augustine

Smith, Lucy Harth
Smith, Nathan Ryno
Soley, James Russell
Southard, Elmer Ernest
Spiering, Theodore
Sprague, Charles Ezra
Sproull, Thomas
Stanford, John
Steele, Daniel
Steiner, Bernard Christian
Sternberg, Constantin Ivanovich,
   Edler von
Stoddard, John Tappan
Suzzallo, Henry
Tapper, Bertha Feiring
Tarr, Ralph Stockman
Taylor, Creed
Thayer, Amos Madden
Thomas, Amos Russell
Thurber, Charles
Thursby, Emma Cecilia
Tomlins, William Lawrence
Toumey, James William
Toy, Crawford Howell
Treat, Samuel
Tucker, John Randolph,
   1823–1897
Turner, Ross Sterling
Tyson, James
Upham, Thomas Cogswell
Van Dyke, Henry
Venable, William Henry
Vethake, Henry
Waddel, Moses
Walker, Timothy, 1802–1856
Warren, Minton
Washburn, Emory
Weidig, Adolf
Weir, John Ferguson
Weir, Robert Walter
Wendell, Barrett
Wentworth, George Albert
Wharton, Francis
Whedon, Daniel Denison
Whelpley, Henry Milton
Whitcomb, Selden Lincoln
White, George
White, Henry Clay
Whitney, Mary Watson
Wiley, Harvey Washington
Williams, Frederick Wells
Williams, George Huntington
Wilmarth, Lemuel Everett
Winchell, Alexander
Winchester, Caleb Thomas
Winship, Albert Edward
Winslow, Hubbard
Wood, Horatio Charles
Woodberry, George Edward
Woolson, Abba Louisa Goold
Wright, Philip Green
Wright, Theodore Lyman
Young, David
Zehn, Bernhard
Of American Literature
   Miller, Perry Gilbert Eddy

VENTRILOQUIST (See also
 ENTERTAINER)
 Vattemare, Nicholas Marie
  Alexandre

VETERINARIAN (See also PHYSICIAN)
 Bemis, Harold Edward
 Kelser, Raymond Alexander
 Moore, Veranus Alva
 Pearson, Leonard
 Salmon, Daniel Elmer

VICE PRESIDENT OF CONFEDERACY
 Stephens, Alexander Hamilton

VICE PRESIDENT OF UNITED STATES
 Adams, John
 Arthur, Chester Alan
 Barkley, Alben William
 Breckinridge, John Cabell
 Burr, Aaron
 Calhoun, John Caldwell
 Clinton, George
 Colfax, Schuyler
 Coolidge, Calvin
 Curtis, Charles
 Dallas, George Mifflin
 Dawes, Charles Gates
 Fairbanks, Charles Warren
 Fillmore, Millard
 Garner, John Nance
 Gerry, Elbridge
 Hamlin, Hannibal
 Hendricks, Thomas Andrews
 Hobart, Garret Augustus
 Jefferson, Thomas
 Johnson, Andrew
 Johnson, Richard Mentor
 King, William Rufus Devane
 Marshall, Thomas Riley
 Morton, Levi Parsons
 Roosevelt, Theodore
 Sherman, James Schoolcraft
 Stevenson, Adlai Ewing
 Tompkins, Daniel D.
 Tyler, John
 Van Buren, Martin
 Wallace, Henry Agard
 Wheeler, William Almon
 Wilson, Henry

VIGILANTE (See also JAYHAWKER,
  OUTLAW)
 Langford, Nathaniel Pitt

VINTNER
 Petri, Angelo

VIOLINIST
 Beck, Johann Heinrich
 Bristow, George Frederick
 Damrosch, Leopold
 Dannreuther, Gustav
 Eichberg, Julius
 Elman, Mischa
 Hill, Ureli Corelli
 Kneisel, Franz
 Kreisler, Fritz
 Listemann, Bernhard
 Loeffler, Charles Martin
 Mannes, David
 Mollenhauer, Emil

Musin, Ovide
 Powell, Maud
 Saslavsky, Alexander
 Scheel, Fritz
 Schradieck, Henry
 Spalding, Albert
 Spiering, Theodore
 Stoessel, Albert Frederic
 Urso, Camilla
 Verbrugghen, Henri
 White, Clarence Cameron

VIROLOGIST
 Rivers, Thomas Milton

VITICULTURIST (See also
  AGRICULTURIST)
 Adlum, John
 Dufour, John James
 Husmann, George
 Munson, Thomas Volney

VOCATIONAL GUIDANCE PIONEER
 Hatcher, Orie Latham

VOLCANOLOGIST
 Jaggar, Thomas Augustus, Jr.

WALKER (See also ATHLETE)
 O'Leary, Daniel
 Weston, Edward Payson

WAR CORRESPONDENT (See also
  FOREIGN CORRESPONDENT,
  JOURNALIST, NEWSPAPER
  CORRESPONDENT, NEWSPAPER
  Reporter, Photojournalist)
 Chapelle, Dickey
 Comfort, Will Levington
 Fall, Bernard B.
 Gibbons, Floyd
 Hare, James H.
 Higgins, Marguerite
 Pyle, Ernest Taylor
 Reynolds, Quentin James
 Whitney, Caspar

WAR HERO (See also SOLDIER)
 York, Alvin Cullum

WELFARE ADMINISTRATOR
 Hodson, William

WELFARE PLANNER
 Dennison, Henry Sturgis

WELFARE WORKER (See also SOCIAL
  WORKER)
 Billikopf, Jacob
 Folks, Homer
 Moskowitz, Belle Lindner Israels

WHALING CAPTAIN (SEE ALSO SEA
  CAPTAIN)
 Tyson, George Emory

WILD ANIMAL TRAINER
 Beatty, Clyde Raymond

WILDLIFE CONSERVATIONIST
 Hornaday, William Temple

WIT (See also COMEDIAN,
  COMEDIENNE, HUMORIST,
  SATIRIST)
 Depew, Chauncey Mitchell
 Herford, Oliver Brooke
 Hughes, Christopher

WITCHCRAFT VICTIM
 Hibbins, Ann

WOMEN'S FOREIGN MISSIONS LEADER
 Peabody, Lucy Whitehead

WOOD CARVER (See also CRAFTSMAN)
 Kirchmayer, John
 McIntire, Samuel
 Morse, Freeman Harlow

WRESTLER
 Leavitt, Frank Simmons ("Man
  Mountain Dean")
 Lewis, Ed ("Strangler")
 Muldoon, William

WRITER (Note: The following are
  classified under writers because
  the specific field in which they
  wrote was so designated at head
  of the article. For complete list
  of writers see, in addition,
  AUTHOR, BIOGRAPHER, DIARIST,
  DRAMATIST, ESSAYIST,
  HISTORIAN, JOURNALIST,
  LITERATEUR)
 Abbott, Eleanor Hallowell (short
  story)
 Adamic, Louis
 Adams, Abigail (letter)
 Adams, Cyrus Cornelius
  (geographical)
 Adams, Frank Ramsay (screen)
 Adams, Hannah (history)
 Adams, William Taylor (juvenile)
 Affleck, Thomas (agricultural)
 Agee, James Rufus (screen)
 Akins, Zoë (screen)
 Aldrich, Bess Genevra Streeter
  (short story)
 Aldrich, Thomas Bailey (story)
 Alger, Horatio (juvenile)
 Allen, James Lane (short story)
 Allen, Lewis Falley (agricultural)
 Allinson, Anne Crosby Emery
 Ames, James Barr (legal)
 Ammen, Daniel (naval)
 Angell, Joseph Kinnicutt (legal)
 Anthony, Katharine Susan
 Arlen, Michael (short story)
 Armstrong, George Dod
  (controversial)
 Bailey, Florence Augusta Merriam
 Bailey, (Irene) Temple (short story)
 Baird, Henry Carey (economics)
 Bard, Samuel (midwifery)
 Barrett, Benjamin Fiske (religious)
 Beatty, Adam (agricultural)
 Beer, Thomas (short story)
 Bemelmans, Ludwig
 Benchley, Robert Charles
 Benét, Stephen Vincent (short
  story)
 Bennett, Edmund Hatch (legal)
 Bigelow, Melville Madison (legal)
 Bingham, Caleb (textbook)
 Blair, Emily Newell
 Blakeslee, Howard Walter (science)

Blatch, Harriot Eaton Stanton
(woman suffrage, peace)
Bogan, Louise Marie (short story)
Bolles, Frank (nature)
Bouvier, John (legal)
Bradford, Roark Whitney Wickliffe
(short story)
Brickell, Henry Herschel
Brisbane, Arthur
Brown, John Mason, Jr.
Browne, Daniel Jay (agricultural)
Browne, Irving (legal)
Browning, Tod
Burdick, Eugene Leonard
Burdick, Francis Marion (legal)
Burgess, Thornton Waldo (juvenile)
Cabell, James Branch (essayist)
Callender, James Thomson
(political)
Calverton, Victor Francis
Campbell, William Edward March
(short story)
Carrington, Elaine Stern
(magazine, radio script)
Carson, Rachel Louise (nature)
Catchings, Waddill
Cayton, Horace Roscoe
Chambers, Whittaker
Chapman, John Jay (essayist)
Checkley, John (controversial)
Clarke, Rebecca Sophia (juvenile)
Cocke, Philip St. George
(agricultural)
Cohen, Octavus Roy (screen)
Cohn, Alfred A. (magazine, screen)
Colburn, Dana Pond (textbook)
Coleman, Lyman (teligious)
Colman, Henry (agricultural)
Cooke, Philip Pendleton (story)
Cooke, Rose Terry (story)
Cullen, Countée Porter (essayist)
Da Ponte, Lorenzo (librettist)
Davenport, Russell Wheeler
Davis, Elmer Holmes (magazine)
Davis, Watson (science)
Deane, Samuel (agricultural)
Dercum, Francis Xavier (medical)
Dickson, David (agricultural)
Dobie, J(ames) Frank
Drinkwater, Jennie Maria (juvenile)
Dunglison, Robley (medical)
Eastman, Max Forrester
Edman, Irwin (philosophy)
Elliott, Charles Burke (legal)
Epstein, Philip G. (screen)
Faulkner (Falkner), William
Cuthbert (short story)
Fauset, Jessie Redmon
Ferguson, Elizabeth Graeme (letter)
Fischer, Louis
Fischer, Ruth
Flandrau, Charles Macomb
(essayist)
Fletcher, Alice Cunningham
(Indian music)
Fletcher, Horace (nutrition)

Frank, Waldo David
Gág, Wanda (Hazel) (juvenile)
Gale, Benjamin (political)
Gardner, Erle Stanley (detective
fiction)
Gaylord, Willis (agricultural)
Genung, John Franklin (religious)
Gilman, Charlotte Perkins Stetson
Gold, Michael
Goldbeck, Robert (music)
Gonzales, Ambrose Elliott (Negro
dialect story)
Gouge, William M. (financial)
Greene, Samuel Stillman (textbook)
Greenleaf, Benjamin (mathematical
textbook)
Guest, Edgar Albert (popular verse)
Gulick, John Thomas (evolution)
Hall, Bolton
Hammett, Samuel Dashiell
(detective fiction)
Hawes, Charles Boardman
(adventure)
Hazard, Rowland Gibson
(philosophy)
Headley, Phineas Camp (biography)
Heard, Franklin Fiske (legal)
Heaton, John Langdon (editorial)
Hecht, Ben (screen)
Held, John, Jr.
Hemingway, Ernest Miller (short
story)
Hening, William Waller (legal)
Henshall, James Alexander
(angling)
Herbert, Frederick Hugh (screen)
Hergesheimer, Joseph (short story)
High, Stanley Hoflund (magazine)
Hilliard, Francis (legal)
Hindus, Maurice Gerschon
Hobart, Alice Nourse Tisdale
Hoffman, Frederick Ludwig
Hoffmann, Francis Arnold
(agricultural)
Horner, William Edmonds
(medical)
Huebner, Solomon Stephen
Hunter, Robert
Hutchinson, Paul (religious
subjects)
Huxley, Aldous Leonard
Jackson, Charles Reginald (short
story)
Jackson, Joseph Henry
Jackson, Shirley Hardie (short story)
James, George Wharton
(Southwest)
James, Henry, 1811–1882
(religious)
Jarrell, Randall (essayist)
Jenks, George Charles (dime novel)
Johnson, Joseph French (financial)
Johnson, Owen McMahon (short
story)
Johnston, Annie Fellows (juvenile)
Jones, Leonard Augustus (legal)

Judson, Frederick Newton (legal)
Kaufman, George S. (screen)
Kellogg, Edward (commercial
reform)
Kent, James (legal)
Kerouac, Jack (essayist)
Kerr, Sophie (short story)
Keyes, Frances Parkinson
Klippart, John Hancock
(agricultural)
Kracauer, Siegfried
Krutch, Joseph Wood
Lahontan, Louis-Armand de Lom
D'Arce, Baron de (travel)
Laimbeer, Nathalie Schenck
(financial)
Lait, Jacquin Leonard (Jack)
(newspaper)
Langdell, Christopher Columbus
(legal)
Lathrop, Harriett Mulford Stone
(juvenile)
Lawrence, William Beach (legal)
Lease, Mary Elizabeth Clyens
Lee, Gypsy Rose
Ley, Willy
Liggett, Walter William
Linton, Ralph (popular)
Livermore, Samuel, 1786–1833
(legal)
Long, Joseph Ragland (legal)
Lowell, John, 1769–1840 (political)
McClintock, James Harvey
(historical)
McCord, Louisa Susanna Cheves
(Antebellum South)
McCullers, Carson (short story)
MacDowell, Katherine Sherwood
Bonner (short story)
McFee, William (essayist, novelist)
MacKaye, Percy Wallace (essayist)
Mackey, Albert Gallatin (Masonic)
McNulty, John Augustine (short
story)
Magruder, Julia (short story)
Mankiewicz, Herman Jacob
(screen)
Martin, Edward Sandford (essayist)
Mathews, William Smythe Babcock
(music)
Merton, Thomas (religious)
Metalious, Grace
Meyer, Agnes Elizabeth Ernst
Meyer, Annie Nathan
Millay, Edna St. Vincent (poetry)
Millington, John (scientific)
Millis, Walter
Minor, John Barbee (legal)
Montgomery, David Henry
(textbook)
Moore, Charles Herbert (fine arts)
Moore, John Weeks (music)
Morley, Christopher Darlington
(essayist)
Morris, Edmund (agricultural)

Morris, Robert, 1818–1888
  (Masonic)
Morton, James St, Clair
  (engineering)
Moulton, Ellen Louise Chandler
  (juvenile)
Mulford, Clarence Edward
  (magazine)
Murfree, Mary Noailles (short story)
Musmanno, Michael Angelo
Nichols, Dudley (screen)
Nitchie, Edward Bartlett (lip-
  reading)
O'Connor, Mary Flannery (short
  story)
Odets, Clifford (screen)
O'Hara, John Henry (short story)
Olney, Jesse (textbook)
Oursler, (Charles) Fulton
Paine, Albert Bigelow (light fiction)
Palmer, Alonzo Benjamin (medical)
Parker, Dorothy Rothschild (short
  story)
Parker, Henry Taylor (essayist)
Parker, Richard Green (textbook)
Peabody, Francis Greenwood
  (religious thought)
Pearson, Edmund Lester (crime
  stories)
Peary, Josephine Diebitsch
Peattie, Donald Culross (magazine)
Periam, Jonathan (agricultural)
Perkins, Samuel Elliott (legal)
Perry, Nora (juvenile)
Peterkin, Julia Mood (short story)
Peters, John Charles (medical)
Philips, Martin Wilson
  (agricultural)
Phillips, Thomas Wharton
  (religious)
Pitkin, Walter Boughton
Poe, Edgar Allan (short story)
Pomeroy, John Norton (legal)
Porter, Gene Stratton (nature)
Porter, William Sydney (short story)
Post, Augustus
Post, Melville Davisson (short story)
Powell, John Benjamin
Pratt, Eliza Anna Farman (juvenile)
Prentiss, Elizabeth Payson,
  (juvenile)
Priestley, Joseph (religious)
Prince, William Robert
  (agricultural)
Proctor, Lucien Brock (legal)
Pusey, Caleb (Quaker controversial)
Quinan, John Russell (medical)
Ralph, James (political)
Rauschenbusch, Walter (religious)
Ravenel, Henry William
  (agricultural)
Rawle, William Henry (legal)
Redfield, Amasa Angell (legal)
Reed, Elizabeth Armstrong
  (Oriental literature)
Reed, Sampson (Swedenborgian)

Reeve, Tapping, (legal)
Reid, Thomas Mayne, (juvenile)
Reik, Theodor (psychology)
Repplier, Agnes
Richter, Conrad Michael
Rinehart, Mary Roberts (mystery
  story)
Ritter, Frédéric Louis (music)
Roane, Spencer (political)
Rohlfs, Anna Katharine Green
  (detective stories)
Rombauer, Irma Louise (cookbook)
Rorer, David
Rossen, Robert (screen)
Rumsey, William (legal)
Runyon, Damon (short story)
Sayles, John (legal)
Schofield, Henry (legal)
Schwartz, Delmore David (poetry)
Schwimmer, Rosika
Scudder, (Julia) Vida Dutton
Sergeant, Thomas (legal)
Seton, Ernest Thompson (nature)
Sherwood, Robert Emmet
  (dramatist)
Smith, George Henry (juvenile)
Smith, Lillian Eugenia
Smith, Lloyd Logan Pearsall
  (essayist)
Soley, James Russell (naval)
Spooner, Lysander (political)
Sprague, Charles Ezra
  (accountancy)
Stallings, Laurence Tucker
Stanton, Richard Henry (legal)
Stark, Louis (editorial)
Steele, Joel Dorman (textbook)
Steele, Wilbur Daniel
Steinbeck, John Ernst, Jr.
Stilwell, Silas Moore (financial)
Stockton, Frank Richard (story)
Stoddard, John Fair (textbook)
Stratemeyer, Edward (juvenile)
Stribling, Thomas Sigismund (short
  story)
Strunsky, Simeon (essayist)
Swan, Joseph Rockwell (legal)
Talbot, Francis Xavier
Tappan, Eva March (juvenile)
Tarbell, Ida Minerva
Taylor, Charles Alonzo
Taylor, John (political)
Terhune, Mary Virginia Hawes
  (household management)
Thomson, John (political)
Thurber, James Grover (humor)
Tiedeman, Christopher Gustavus
  (legal)
Toklas, Alice Babette
Towler, John (photography)
Tyler, Ransom Hubert (legal)
Upshaw, William David
Viereck, George Sylvester
  (magazine, newspaper)
Wahl, William Henry (science)
Wait, William (legal)

Walker, James Barr (religious)
Walker, Timothy, 1802–1856
  (legal)
Wallace, Henry (agricultural)
Ward, Charles Henshaw
Warner, Anna Bartlett (juvenile)
Warner, Anne Richmond (fiction)
Watson, Henry Clay (editorial,
  historical, juvenile)
Watson, James Madison (textbook)
Wentworth, George Albert
  (mathematics textbooks)
Will, Allen Sinclair (biography)
Willard, Josiah Flint (vagrancy,
  criminology)
Williams, Ben Ames (short story)
Williams, Catharine Read Arnold
  (biography)
Wood, Sarah Sayward Barrell
  Keating (fiction)
Wright, Willard Huntington
  (detective fiction)
Youmans, William Jay (scientific)
Zevin, Israel Joseph (story)

YACHT DESIGNER (See also
   SHIPBUILDER)
Burgess, Edward
Herreshoff, John Brown
Lawley, George Frederick
Smith, Archibald Cary
Steers, George

YACHTSMAN (See also ATHLETE)
Adams, Charles Francis
Barr, Charles
Crowninshield, George
Paine, Charles Jackson

YMCA OFFICIAL
Mott, John R.
Tobias, Channing Heggie

YOUTH LEADER
Beard, Daniel Carter
Smith, George Albert

YWCA OFFICIAL
Cushman, Vera Charlotte Scott
Speer, Emma Bailey

ZIONIST LEADER
Flexner, Bernard
Haas, Jacob Judah Aaron de
Lewisohn, Ludwig
Masliansky, Zvi Hirsch
Rosenblatt, Bernard Abraham
Silver, Abba Hillel
Szold, Henrietta
Wise, Stephen Samuel

ZONING EXPERT
Purdy, Lawson

ZOOLOGIST (See also APIARIST,
   ARACHNOLOGIST,
   CONCHOLOGIST,
   ENTOMOLOGIST,
   HERPETOLOGIST,
   ICHTHYOLOGIST,
   MALACOLOGIST, MAMMALOGIST,
   MARINE ALGAE AUTHORITY,

MARINE BIOLOGIST,
MICROBIOLOGIST, NATURALIST,
ORNITHOLOGIST,
PARASITOLOGIST,
PISCICULTURIST, TAXONOMIST,
VIROLOGIST)
Agassiz, Alexander
Agassiz, Jean Louis Rodolphe
Allen, Joel Asaph
Andrews, Roy Chapman
Anthony, John Gould
Baird, Spencer Fullerton
Binney, Amos
Brooks, William Keith
Calkins, Gary Nathan
Child, Charles Manning
Clark, Henry James
Cope, Edward Drinker

Dana, James Dwight
Dean, Bashford
Eigenmann, Carl H.
Elliot, Daniel Giraud
Field, Herbert Haviland
Garmon, Samuel
Gilbert, Charles Henry
Gill, Theodore Nicholas
Girard, Charles Frédéric
Holbrook, John Edwards
Hyatt, Alpheus
Just, Ernest Everett
Kinsey, Alfred Charles
Kneeland, Samuel
Kofoid, Charles Atwood
Locy, William Albert
Lyman, Theodore, 1833–1897
Montgomery, Thomas Harrison

Morgan, Thomas Hunt
Morse, Edward Sylvester
Nutting, Charles Cleveland
Orton, James
Parker, George Howard
Patten, William
Pourtalès, Louis François de
Rathbun, Richard
Stejneger, Leonhard Hess
Stiles, Charles Wardell
Sumner, Francis Bertody
True, Frederick William
Verrill, Addison Emery
Ward, Henry Baldwin
Wheeler, William Morton
Wilder, Harris Hawthorne